2022
Harris
Michigan
Industrial Directory

Published February 2022 next update February 2023

WARNING: Purchasers and users of this directory may not use this directory to compile mailing lists, other marketing aids and other types of data, which are sold or otherwise provided to third parties. Such use is wrongful, illegal and a violation of the federal copyright laws.

CAUTION: Because of the many thousands of establishment listings contained in this directory and the possibilities of both human and mechanical error in processing this information, Harris InfoSource cannot assume liability for the correctness of the listings or information on which they are based. Hence, no information contained in this work should be relied upon in any instance where there is a possibility of any loss or damage as a consequence of any error or omission in this volume.

Publisher
Mergent Inc.
444 Madison Ave
New York, NY 10022

©Mergent Inc All Rights Reserved
2022 Mergent Business Press
ISSN 1080-2614
ISBN 978-1-64972-666-7

TABLE OF CONTENTS

Summary of Contents & Explanatory Notes 4
User's Guide to Listings 6

Geographic Section
County/City Cross-Reference Index 9
Firms Listed by Location 13

Standard Industrial Classification (SIC) Section
SIC Alphabetical Index 719
SIC Numerical Index 721
Firms Listed by SIC 725

Alphabetic Section
Firms Listed by Firm Name 915

Product Section
Product Index 1157
Firms Listed by Product Category 1179

SUMMARY OF CONTENTS

Number of Companies	19,101
Number of Decision Makers	40,378
Minimum Number of Employees	3

EXPLANATORY NOTES

How to Cross-Reference in This Directory

Sequential Entry Numbers. Each establishment in the Geographic Section is numbered sequentially (G-0000). The number assigned to each establishment is referred to as its "entry number." To make cross-referencing easier, each listing in the Geographic, SIC, Alphabetic and Product Sections includes the establishment's entry number. To facilitate locating an entry in the Geographic Section, the entry numbers for the first listing on the left page and the last listing on the right page are printed at the top of the page next to the city name.

Source Suggestions Welcome

Although all known sources were used to compile this directory, it is possible that companies were inadvertently omitted. Your assistance in calling attention to such omissions would be greatly appreciated. A special form on the facing page will help you in the reporting process.

Analysis

Every effort has been made to contact all firms to verify their information. The one exception to this rule is the annual sales figure, which is considered by many companies to be confidential information. Therefore, estimated sales have been calculated by multiplying the nationwide average sales per employee for the firm's major SIC/NAICS code by the firm's number of employees. Nationwide averages for sales per employee by SIC/NAICS codes are provided by the U.S. Department of Commerce and are updated annually. All sales—sales (est)—have been estimated by this method. The exceptions are parent companies (PA), division headquarters (DH) and headquarter locations (HQ) which may include an actual corporate sales figure—sales (corporate-wide) if available.

Types of Companies

Descriptive and statistical data are included for companies in the entire state. These comprise manufacturers, machine shops, fabricators, assemblers and printers. Also identified are corporate offices in the state.

Employment Data

The employment figure shown in the Geographic Section includes male and female employees and embraces all levels of the company: administrative, clerical, sales and maintenance. This figure is for the facility listed and does not include other plants or offices. It should be recognized that these figures represent an approximate year-round average. These employment figures are broken into codes A through G and used in the Product and SIC Sections to further help you in qualifying a company. Be sure to check the footnotes on the bottom of pages for the code breakdowns.

Standard Industrial Classification (SIC)

The Standard Industrial Classification (SIC) system used in this directory was developed by the federal government for use in classifying establishments by the type of activity they are engaged in. The SIC classifications used in this directory are from the 1987 edition published by the U.S. Government's Office of Management and Budget. The SIC system separates all activities into broad industrial divisions (e.g., manufacturing, mining, retail trade). It further subdivides each division. The range of manufacturing industry classes extends from two-digit codes (major industry group) to four-digit codes (product).

For example:

Industry Breakdown	Code	Industry, Product, etc.
*Major industry group	20	Food and kindred products
Industry group	203	Canned and frozen foods
*Industry	2033	Fruits and vegetables, etc.

*Classifications used in this directory

Only two-digit and four-digit codes are used in this directory.

Arrangement

1. The **Geographic Section** contains complete in-depth corporate data. This section is sorted by cities listed in alphabetical order and companies listed alphabetically within each city. A County/City Index for referencing cities within counties precedes this section.

> IMPORTANT NOTICE: It is a violation of both federal and state law to transmit an unsolicited advertisement to a facsimile machine. Any user of this product that violates such laws may be subject to civil and criminal penalties, which may exceed $500 for each transmission of an unsolicited facsimile. Harris InfoSource provides fax numbers for lawful purposes only and expressly forbids the use of these numbers in any unlawful manner.

2. The **Standard Industrial Classification (SIC) Section** lists companies under approximately 500 four-digit SIC codes. An alphabetical and a numerical index precedes this section. A company can be listed under several codes. The codes are in numerical order with companies listed alphabetically under each code.

3. The **Alphabetic Section** lists all companies with their full physical or mailing addresses and telephone number.

4. The **Product Section** lists companies under unique Harris categories. An index preceding this section lists all product categories in alphabetical order. Companies can be listed under several categories.

USER'S GUIDE TO LISTINGS

GEOGRAPHIC SECTION

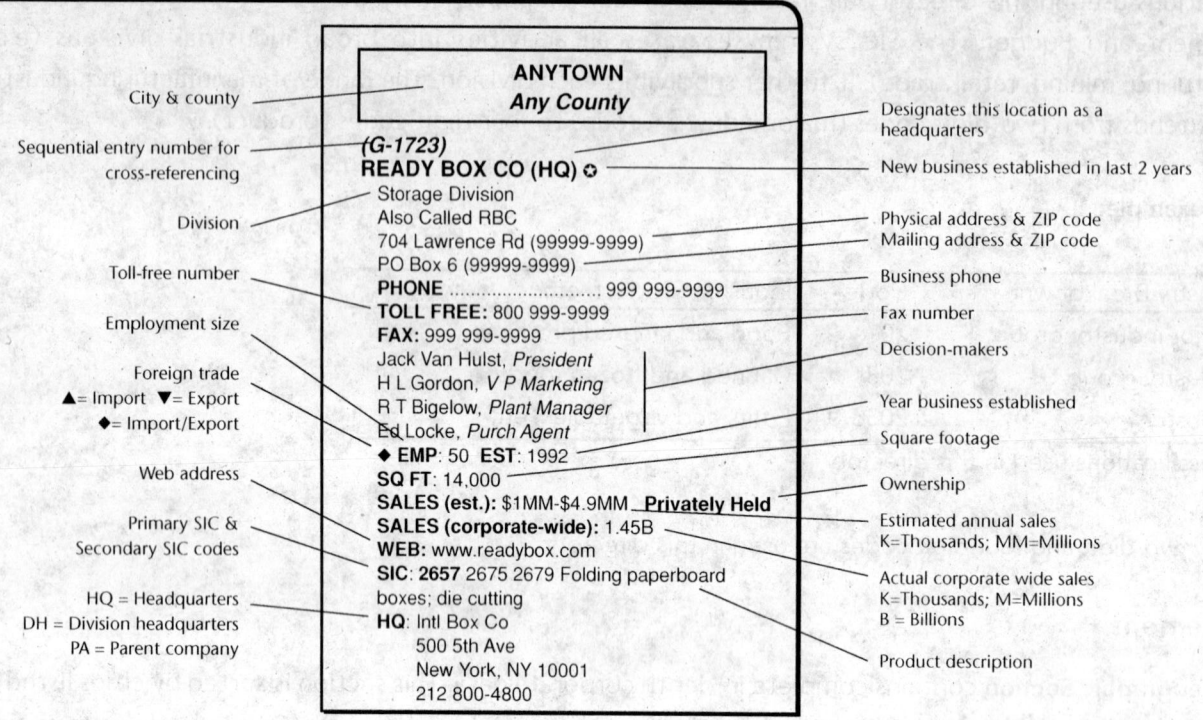

SIC SECTION

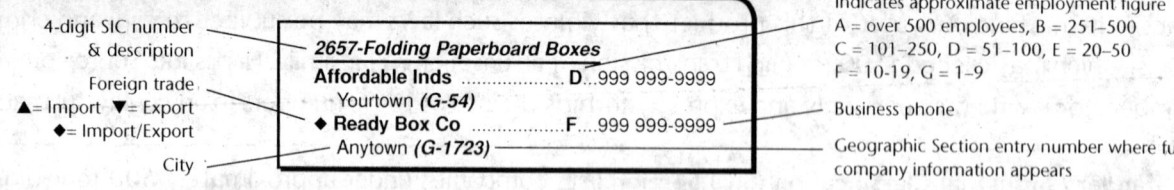

ALPHABETIC SECTION

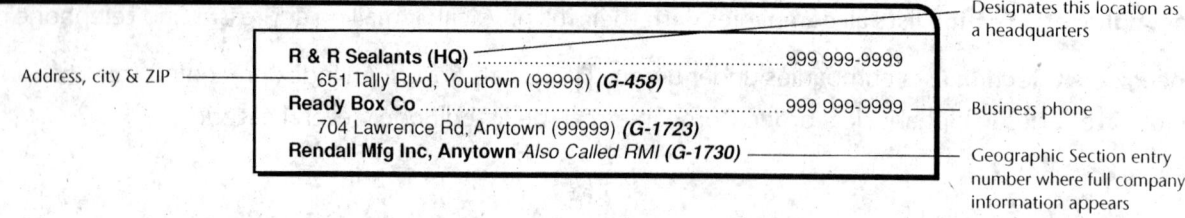

PRODUCT SECTION

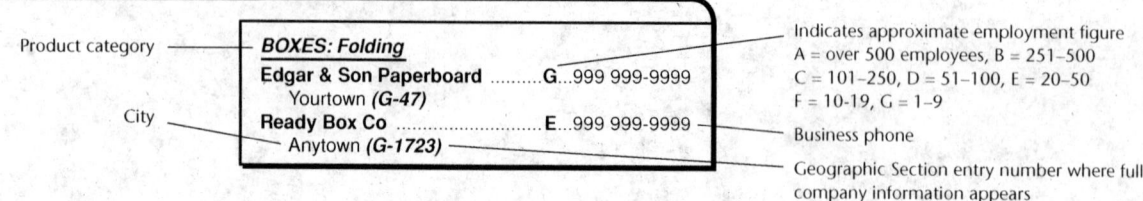

GEOGRAPHIC SECTION
Companies sorted by city in alphabetical order
In-depth company data listed

STANDARD INDUSTRIAL CLASSIFICATIONS
Alphabetical index of classifcation descriptions
Numerical index of classifcation descriptions
Companies sorted by SIC product groupings

ALPHABETIC SECTION
Company listings in alphabetical order

PRODUCT INDEX
Product categories listed in alphabetical order

PRODUCT SECTION
Companies sorted by product and manufacturing service classifications

Michigan
County Map

COUNTY/CITY CROSS-REFERENCE INDEX

Alcona
City	Entry #
Curran	(G-3749)
Glennie	(G-6212)
Greenbush	(G-7472)
Harrisville	(G-7740)
Lincoln	(G-10033)
Spruce	(G-15885)

Alger
City	Entry #
Chatham	(G-2778)
Eben Junction	(G-4978)
Munising	(G-11752)
Trenary	(G-16883)
Wetmore	(G-18435)

Allegan
City	Entry #
Allegan	(G-144)
Burnips	(G-2210)
Dorr	(G-4767)
Douglas	(G-4772)
Fennville	(G-5433)
Hamilton	(G-7594)
Hopkins	(G-8366)
Martin	(G-11079)
Moline	(G-11518)
Otsego	(G-12784)
Plainwell	(G-13069)
Saugatuck	(G-15083)
Shelbyville	(G-15374)
Wayland	(G-18186)

Alpena
City	Entry #
Alpena	(G-273)
Hubbard Lake	(G-8546)
Lachine	(G-9531)
Ossineke	(G-12778)

Antrim
City	Entry #
Alba	(G-113)
Alden	(G-136)
Bellaire	(G-1468)
Central Lake	(G-2691)
Eastport	(G-4949)
Elk Rapids	(G-5021)
Ellsworth	(G-5035)
Kewadin	(G-9486)
Mancelona	(G-10865)

Arenac
City	Entry #
Alger	(G-137)
Au Gres	(G-754)
Omer	(G-12696)
Standish	(G-15886)
Sterling	(G-15913)
Turner	(G-17462)

Baraga
City	Entry #
Baraga	(G-1133)
Covington	(G-3727)
Keweenaw Bay	(G-9490)
Lanse	(G-9656)
Watton	(G-18185)

Barry
City	Entry #
Delton	(G-3961)
Dowling	(G-4799)
Freeport	(G-6032)
Hastings	(G-7780)
Hickory Corners	(G-7875)
Middleville	(G-11301)
Nashville	(G-11954)

Bay
City	Entry #
Auburn	(G-762)
Bay City	(G-1313)
Essexville	(G-5108)
Kawkawlin	(G-9413)
Linwood	(G-10073)
Munger	(G-11751)
Pinconning	(G-13059)

Benzie
City	Entry #
Benzonia	(G-1612)
Beulah	(G-1652)
Frankfort	(G-5875)
Honor	(G-8359)
Lake Ann	(G-9540)
Thompsonville	(G-16553)

Berrien
City	Entry #
Baroda	(G-1158)
Benton Harbor	(G-1524)
Berrien Center	(G-1635)
Berrien Springs	(G-1636)
Bridgman	(G-1920)
Buchanan	(G-2189)
Coloma	(G-3474)
Eau Claire	(G-4976)
Galien	(G-6087)
Lakeside	(G-9639)
New Buffalo	(G-12022)
New Troy	(G-12075)
Niles	(G-12108)
Riverside	(G-13864)
Saint Joseph	(G-14921)
Sawyer	(G-15106)
Sodus	(G-15392)
Stevensville	(G-16237)
Three Oaks	(G-16554)
Union Pier	(G-17499)
Watervliet	(G-18179)

Branch
City	Entry #
Bronson	(G-2110)
Coldwater	(G-3417)
Montgomery	(G-11604)
Quincy	(G-13661)
Sherwood	(G-15387)
Union City	(G-17490)

Calhoun
City	Entry #
Albion	(G-114)
Athens	(G-743)
Battle Creek	(G-1175)
Burlington	(G-2209)
Ceresco	(G-2702)
East Leroy	(G-4915)
Homer	(G-8344)
Marshall	(G-11052)
Springfield	(G-15859)
Tekonsha	(G-16522)

Cass
City	Entry #
Cassopolis	(G-2625)
Dowagiac	(G-4775)
Edwardsburg	(G-4998)
Jones	(G-9083)
Marcellus	(G-10946)
Union	(G-17486)

Charlevoix
City	Entry #
Boyne City	(G-1882)
Boyne Falls	(G-1907)
Charlevoix	(G-2707)
East Jordan	(G-4860)

Cheboygan
City	Entry #
Afton	(G-106)
Cheboygan	(G-2779)
Indian River	(G-8652)
Mackinaw City	(G-10568)
Wolverine	(G-18795)

Chippewa
City	Entry #
Barbeau	(G-1152)
Brimley	(G-2100)
De Tour Village	(G-3802)
Drummond Island	(G-4800)
Kincheloe	(G-9501)
Kinross	(G-9527)
Paradise	(G-12931)
Pickford	(G-13030)
Rudyard	(G-14594)
Sault Sainte Marie	(G-15086)

Clare
City	Entry #
Clare	(G-2971)
Farwell	(G-5420)
Harrison	(G-7675)

Clinton
City	Entry #
Bath	(G-1174)
Dewitt	(G-4705)
Eagle	(G-4851)
Fowler	(G-5829)
Lansing	(G-9670)
Maple Rapids	(G-10945)
Ovid	(G-12813)
Saint Johns	(G-14897)
Westphalia	(G-18434)

Crawford
City	Entry #
Frederic	(G-6014)
Grayling	(G-7454)

Delta
City	Entry #
Bark River	(G-1153)
Cornell	(G-3701)
Escanaba	(G-5056)
Gladstone	(G-6173)
Rapid River	(G-13682)
Rock	(G-14150)

Dickinson
City	Entry #
Channing	(G-2705)
Felch	(G-5431)
Iron Mountain	(G-8717)
Kingsford	(G-9506)
Norway	(G-12353)
Quinnesec	(G-13676)
Sagola	(G-14798)
Vulcan	(G-17616)

Eaton
City	Entry #
Bellevue	(G-1497)
Charlotte	(G-2737)
Dimondale	(G-4763)
Eaton Rapids	(G-4950)
Grand Ledge	(G-6384)
Lansing	(G-9751)
Mulliken	(G-11748)
Olivet	(G-12693)
Potterville	(G-13645)
Sunfield	(G-16333)
Vermontville	(G-17587)

Emmet
City	Entry #
Alanson	(G-111)
Harbor Springs	(G-7639)
Levering	(G-10016)
Pellston	(G-12967)
Petoskey	(G-12987)

Genesee
City	Entry #
Burton	(G-2224)
Clio	(G-3394)
Davison	(G-3774)
Fenton	(G-5445)
Flint	(G-5632)
Flushing	(G-5800)
Genesee	(G-6168)
Goodrich	(G-6221)
Grand Blanc	(G-6231)
Lennon	(G-9992)
Linden	(G-10059)
Montrose	(G-11605)
Mount Morris	(G-11665)
Otisville	(G-12781)
Swartz Creek	(G-16348)

Gladwin
City	Entry #
Beaverton	(G-1423)
Gladwin	(G-6188)
Rhodes	(G-13822)

Gogebic
City	Entry #
Bessemer	(G-1647)
Ironwood	(G-8758)
Wakefield	(G-17618)
Watersmeet	(G-18178)

Grand Traverse
City	Entry #
Acme	(G-1)
Grawn	(G-7448)
Interlochen	(G-8678)
Kingsley	(G-9520)
Traverse City	(G-16594)
Williamsburg	(G-18551)

Gratiot
City	Entry #
Alma	(G-233)
Ashley	(G-741)
Breckenridge	(G-1911)
Elwell	(G-5041)
Ithaca	(G-8784)
Middleton	(G-11298)
North Star	(G-12185)
Perrinton	(G-12976)
Riverdale	(G-13863)
Saint Louis	(G-14983)
Sumner	(G-16331)
Wheeler	(G-18436)

Hillsdale
City	Entry #
Camden	(G-2419)
Hillsdale	(G-7919)
Jerome	(G-9078)
Jonesville	(G-9085)
Litchfield	(G-10076)
North Adams	(G-12176)
Osseo	(G-12775)
Pittsford	(G-13067)
Reading	(G-13704)

Houghton
City	Entry #
Atlantic Mine	(G-749)
Calumet	(G-2408)
Chassell	(G-2776)
Dollar Bay	(G-4766)
Hancock	(G-7614)
Houghton	(G-8379)
Lake Linden	(G-9566)
Laurium	(G-9979)
Pelkie	(G-12964)
South Range	(G-15461)
Toivola	(G-16592)

Huron
City	Entry #
Bad Axe	(G-1095)
Bay Port	(G-1413)
Caseville	(G-2603)
Elkton	(G-5031)
Filion	(G-5612)
Harbor Beach	(G-7628)
Pigeon	(G-13034)
Port Austin	(G-13428)
Port Hope	(G-13429)
Ruth	(G-14597)
Sebewaing	(G-15139)
Ubly	(G-17475)

Ingham
City	Entry #
Dansville	(G-3755)
East Lansing	(G-4884)
Haslett	(G-7775)
Holt	(G-8303)
Lansing	(G-9797)
Leslie	(G-10013)
Mason	(G-11115)
Okemos	(G-12655)
Stockbridge	(G-16272)
Webberville	(G-18241)
Williamston	(G-18568)

Ionia
City	Entry #
Belding	(G-1434)
Clarksville	(G-3077)
Ionia	(G-8687)
Lake Odessa	(G-9571)
Lyons	(G-10564)
Orleans	(G-12740)
Pewamo	(G-13027)
Portland	(G-13637)
Saranac	(G-15075)

Iosco
City	Entry #
East Tawas	(G-4916)
Hale	(G-7588)
National City	(G-11959)
Oscoda	(G-12753)
Tawas City	(G-16364)
Whittemore	(G-18550)

Iron
City	Entry #
Amasa	(G-338)
Caspian	(G-2608)
Crystal Falls	(G-3741)
Iron River	(G-8739)

Charlevoix (additional)
City	Entry #
Vandalia	(G-17565)

COUNTY/CITY CROSS-REFERENCE

Isabella
- Blanchard (G-1759)
- Mount Pleasant (G-11678)
- Rosebush (G-14366)
- Shepherd (G-15376)
- Weidman (G-18249)
- Winn (G-18589)

Jackson
- Brooklyn (G-2122)
- Clarklake (G-3003)
- Concord (G-3654)
- Grass Lake (G-7434)
- Hanover (G-7624)
- Horton (G-8372)
- Jackson (G-8797)
- Michigan Center (G-11290)
- Munith (G-11757)
- Napoleon (G-11953)
- Parma (G-12936)
- Pleasant Lake (G-13103)
- Rives Junction (G-13885)
- Spring Arbor (G-15789)
- Springport (G-15879)

Kalamazoo
- Augusta (G-1091)
- Climax (G-3134)
- Fulton (G-6072)
- Galesburg (G-6073)
- Kalamazoo (G-9105)
- Portage (G-13543)
- Richland (G-13824)
- Schoolcraft (G-15112)
- Scotts (G-15130)
- Vicksburg (G-17597)

Kalkaska
- Fife Lake (G-5605)
- Kalkaska (G-9381)
- Rapid City (G-13681)
- South Boardman (G-15395)

Kent
- Ada (G-3)
- Alto (G-329)
- Belmont (G-1499)
- Byron Center (G-2257)
- Caledonia (G-2365)
- Cedar Springs (G-2641)
- Comstock Park (G-3584)
- Gowen (G-6229)
- Grand Rapids (G-6402)
- Grandville (G-7360)
- Kent City (G-9425)
- Kentwood (G-9441)
- Lowell (G-10493)
- Rockford (G-14151)
- Sand Lake (G-15048)
- Sparta (G-15760)
- Walker (G-17631)
- Wyoming (G-18846)

Keweenaw
- Ahmeek (G-109)
- Eagle Harbor (G-4853)
- Mohawk (G-11517)

Lake
- Baldwin (G-1121)
- Chase (G-2775)
- Irons (G-8757)
- Luther (G-10563)

Lapeer
- Almont (G-255)
- Attica (G-752)
- Clifford (G-3130)
- Columbiaville (G-3494)
- Dryden (G-4804)
- Imlay City (G-8626)
- Lapeer (G-9910)
- Lum (G-10559)
- Metamora (G-11276)
- North Branch (G-12177)

Leelanau
- Cedar (G-2636)
- Empire (G-5042)
- Glen Arbor (G-6209)
- Lake Leelanau (G-9557)
- Maple City (G-10940)
- Northport (G-12187)
- Suttons Bay (G-16338)

Lenawee
- Addison (G-43)
- Adrian (G-46)
- Blissfield (G-1760)
- Cement City (G-2675)
- Clayton (G-3129)
- Clinton (G-3136)
- Deerfield (G-3957)
- Hudson (G-8547)
- Manitou Beach (G-10925)
- Morenci (G-11611)
- Onsted (G-12704)
- Riga (G-13848)
- Tecumseh (G-16491)
- Tipton (G-16591)
- Weston (G-18433)

Livingston
- Brighton (G-1935)
- Fowlerville (G-5832)
- Gregory (G-7513)
- Hamburg (G-7591)
- Hartland (G-7767)
- Howell (G-8421)
- Pinckney (G-13043)

Luce
- Mc Millan (G-11188)
- Newberry (G-12092)

Mackinac
- Cedarville (G-2668)
- Curtis (G-3750)
- Engadine (G-5043)
- Gould City (G-6228)
- Hessel (G-7873)
- Mackinac Island (G-10567)
- Moran (G-11609)
- Naubinway (G-11961)
- Saint Ignace (G-14894)

Macomb
- Armada (G-729)
- Bruce Twp (G-2162)
- Center Line (G-2677)
- Chesterfield (G-2832)
- Clinton Township (G-3143)
- Eastpointe (G-4926)
- Fraser (G-5886)
- Harrison Township (G-7683)
- Harrison Twp (G-7737)
- Lenox (G-9997)
- Macomb (G-10570)
- Mount Clemens (G-11626)
- New Baltimore (G-11977)
- New Haven (G-12029)
- Ray (G-13697)
- Richmond (G-13831)
- Romeo (G-14219)
- Roseville (G-14368)
- Saint Clair Shores (G-14846)
- Selfridge Angb (G-15147)
- Shelby Township (G-15161)
- Sterling Heights (G-15915)
- Sterling Hts (G-16235)
- Utica (G-17501)
- Warren (G-17677)
- Washington (G-18078)
- Washington Township (G-18096)

Manistee
- Bear Lake (G-1416)
- Copemish (G-3698)
- Filer City (G-5610)
- Kaleva (G-9376)
- Manistee (G-10893)
- Onekama (G-12703)
- Wellston (G-18258)

Marquette
- Arnold (G-740)
- Champion (G-2704)
- Gwinn (G-7580)
- Ishpeming (G-8774)
- Marquette (G-11003)
- Negaunee (G-11962)
- Palmer (G-12930)
- Republic (G-13819)

Mason
- Custer (G-3752)
- Fountain (G-5826)
- Ludington (G-10524)
- Scottville (G-15135)

Mecosta
- Barryton (G-1172)
- Big Rapids (G-1669)
- Mecosta (G-11190)
- Morley (G-11619)
- Paris (G-12932)
- Remus (G-13812)
- Rodney (G-14206)
- Stanwood (G-15902)

Menominee
- Carney (G-2563)
- Daggett (G-3753)
- Hermansville (G-7860)
- Ingalls (G-8657)
- Menominee (G-11224)
- Powers (G-13648)
- Spalding (G-15759)
- Stephenson (G-15906)
- Wallace (G-17659)

Midland
- Coleman (G-3462)
- Hope (G-8361)
- Midland (G-11317)
- Sanford (G-15072)

Missaukee
- Falmouth (G-5131)
- Lake City (G-9544)

Mc Bain (G-11176)
Merritt (G-11266)

Monroe
- Carleton (G-2549)
- Dundee (G-4809)
- Erie (G-5044)
- Ida (G-8624)
- La Salle (G-9528)
- Lambertville (G-9650)
- Luna Pier (G-10560)
- Maybee (G-11170)
- Milan (G-11429)
- Monroe (G-11520)
- Newport (G-12102)
- Ottawa Lake (G-12803)
- Petersburg (G-12983)
- South Rockwood (G-15463)
- Temperance (G-16525)

Montcalm
- Carson City (G-2591)
- Coral (G-3699)
- Crystal (G-3739)
- Edmore (G-4990)
- Fenwick (G-5516)
- Greenville (G-7474)
- Howard City (G-8408)
- Lakeview (G-9640)
- Pierson (G-13033)
- Sheridan (G-15380)
- Six Lakes (G-15388)
- Stanton (G-15898)
- Vestaburg (G-17593)

Montmorency
- Atlanta (G-744)
- Hillman (G-7911)
- Lewiston (G-10017)

Muskegon
- Bailey (G-1118)
- Casnovia (G-2606)
- Fruitport (G-6058)
- Holton (G-8337)
- Montague (G-11594)
- Muskegon (G-11758)
- Norton Shores (G-12273)
- Ravenna (G-13688)
- Twin Lake (G-17467)
- Whitehall (G-18488)

Newaygo
- Bitely (G-1758)
- Brohman (G-2109)
- Fremont (G-6037)
- Grant (G-7425)
- Newaygo (G-12077)
- White Cloud (G-18437)

Oakland
- Auburn Hills (G-772)
- Berkley (G-1617)
- Beverly Hills (G-1660)
- Bingham Farms (G-1691)
- Birmingham (G-1717)
- Bloomfield (G-1780)
- Bloomfield Hills (G-1787)
- Clarkston (G-3011)
- Clawson (G-3083)
- Commerce Township (G-3505)
- Davisburg (G-3756)
- Detroit (G-3968)
- Farmington (G-5134)
- Farmington Hills (G-5156)
- Ferndale (G-5517)
- Franklin (G-5882)
- Hazel Park (G-7817)
- Highland (G-7877)
- Holly (G-8260)
- Huntington Woods (G-8620)
- Keego Harbor (G-9421)
- Lake Angelus (G-9539)
- Lake Orion (G-9581)
- Lakeville (G-9647)
- Lathrup Village (G-9973)
- Leonard (G-10001)
- Madison Heights (G-10654)
- Milford (G-11452)
- New Hudson (G-12041)
- Novi (G-12358)
- Oak Park (G-12591)
- Oakland (G-12652)
- Oakland Twp (G-12653)
- Orchard Lake (G-12715)
- Orion (G-12722)
- Ortonville (G-12741)
- Oxford (G-12870)
- Pleasant Ridge (G-13105)
- Pontiac (G-13343)
- Rochester (G-13889)
- Rochester Hills (G-13938)
- Royal Oak (G-14500)
- South Lyon (G-15427)
- Southfield (G-15467)
- Sylvan Lake (G-16359)
- Troy (G-16898)
- Walled Lake (G-17662)
- Waterford (G-18098)
- West Bloomfield (G-18261)
- White Lake (G-18448)
- Wixom (G-18591)
- Wolverine Lake (G-18796)

Oceana
- Hart (G-7750)
- Hesperia (G-7870)
- Mears (G-11189)
- New ERA (G-12026)
- Pentwater (G-12970)
- Rothbury (G-14498)
- Shelby (G-15148)
- Walkerville (G-17658)

Ogemaw
- Lupton (G-10561)
- Prescott (G-13651)
- Rose City (G-14358)
- South Branch (G-15396)
- West Branch (G-18324)

Ontonagon
- Kenton (G-9439)
- Mass City (G-11161)
- Ontonagon (G-12709)
- Trout Creek (G-16897)
- White Pine (G-18487)

Osceola
- Evart (G-5118)
- Hersey (G-7866)
- Leroy (G-10004)
- Marion (G-10971)
- Reed City (G-13788)
- Sears (G-15137)

COUNTY/CITY CROSS-REFERENCE

	ENTRY #		ENTRY #		ENTRY #		ENTRY #		ENTRY #
Tustin	(G-17465)	**Saginaw**		**St. Clair**		Cass City	(G-2610)	Detroit	(G-3969)
Oscoda		Birch Run	(G-1706)	Algonac	(G-141)	Deford	(G-3960)	Ecorse	(G-4979)
Comins	(G-3503)	Bridgeport	(G-1914)	Allenton	(G-230)	Fostoria	(G-5825)	Flat Rock	(G-5613)
Fairview	(G-5129)	Burt	(G-2215)	Anchorville	(G-339)	Kingston	(G-9526)	Garden City	(G-6091)
Mio	(G-11507)	Carrollton	(G-2587)	Brockway	(G-2106)	Mayville	(G-11174)	Gibraltar	(G-6170)
Otsego		Chesaning	(G-2827)	Burtchville	(G-2218)	Millington	(G-11498)	Grosse Ile	(G-7516)
Elmira	(G-5038)	Frankenmuth	(G-5859)	Capac	(G-2546)	Reese	(G-13805)	Grosse Pointe	(G-7527)
Gaylord	(G-6116)	Freeland	(G-6017)	Casco	(G-2597)	Vassar	(G-17576)	Grosse Pointe Farms	(G-7534)
Johannesburg	(G-9080)	Hemlock	(G-7849)	China	(G-2968)	**Van Buren**		Grosse Pointe Park	(G-7543)
Vanderbilt	(G-17568)	Merrill	(G-11263)	Clay	(G-3113)	Bangor	(G-1128)	Grosse Pointe Shores	
Ottawa		Oakley	(G-12654)	Clyde	(G-3412)	Bloomingdale	(G-1876)	(G-7561)	
Allendale	(G-212)	Saginaw	(G-14599)	Columbus	(G-3496)	Covert	(G-3725)	Grosse Pointe Woods	
Conklin	(G-3659)	Saint Charles	(G-14800)	Cottrellville	(G-3720)	Decatur	(G-3945)	(G-7564)	
Coopersville	(G-3678)	**Sanilac**		East China	(G-4854)	Gobles	(G-6216)	Hamtramck	(G-7610)
Ferrysburg	(G-5600)	Applegate	(G-727)	Fort Gratiot	(G-5818)	Grand Junction	(G-6383)	Harper Woods	(G-7662)
Grand Haven	(G-6270)	Argyle	(G-728)	Greenwood	(G-7512)	Hartford	(G-7761)	Highland Park	(G-7902)
Holland	(G-7951)	Brown City	(G-2133)	Harsens Island	(G-7748)	Lawrence	(G-9980)	Inkster	(G-8659)
Hudsonville	(G-8564)	Carsonville	(G-2596)	Ira	(G-8695)	Lawton	(G-9987)	Lincoln Park	(G-10042)
Jenison	(G-9042)	Croswell	(G-3729)	Kenockee	(G-9423)	Mattawan	(G-11162)	Livonia	(G-10088)
Macatawa	(G-10566)	Deckerville	(G-3953)	Kimball	(G-9491)	Paw Paw	(G-12941)	Melvindale	(G-11196)
Marne	(G-10988)	Lexington	(G-10027)	Marine City	(G-10954)	South Haven	(G-15398)	New Boston	(G-11998)
Norton Shores	(G-12344)	Marlette	(G-10977)	Marysville	(G-11081)	**Washtenaw**		Northville	(G-12194)
Nunica	(G-12575)	Melvin	(G-11195)	Memphis	(G-11212)	Ann Arbor	(G-340)	Plymouth	(G-13108)
Spring Lake	(G-15799)	Minden City	(G-11506)	North Street	(G-12186)	Chelsea	(G-2801)	Redford	(G-13708)
West Olive	(G-18347)	Peck	(G-12960)	Port Huron	(G-13430)	Dexter	(G-4719)	River Rouge	(G-13852)
Zeeland	(G-18988)	Sandusky	(G-15054)	Riley	(G-13849)	Manchester	(G-10880)	Riverview	(G-13867)
Presque Isle		Snover	(G-15389)	Saint Clair	(G-14813)	Saline	(G-14997)	Rockwood	(G-14198)
Hawks	(G-7814)	**Schoolcraft**		Wales	(G-17626)	Superior Township	(G-16336)	Romulus	(G-14242)
Millersburg	(G-11497)	Germfask	(G-6169)	Yale	(G-18919)	Whitmore Lake	(G-18515)	Southgate	(G-15747)
Onaway	(G-12697)	Gulliver	(G-7578)	**St. Joseph**		Willis	(G-18587)	Taylor	(G-16374)
Posen	(G-13643)	Manistique	(G-10916)	Burr Oak	(G-2211)	Ypsilanti	(G-18922)	Trenton	(G-16886)
Presque Isle	(G-13653)	**Shiawassee**		Centreville	(G-2696)	**Wayne**		Van Buren Twp	(G-17505)
Rogers City	(G-14208)	Bancroft	(G-1126)	Colon	(G-3486)	Allen Park	(G-187)	Wayne	(G-18211)
Roscommon		Byron	(G-2252)	Constantine	(G-3663)	Belleville	(G-1478)	Westland	(G-18351)
Higgins Lake	(G-7876)	Corunna	(G-3704)	Mendon	(G-11215)	Brownstown	(G-2143)	Woodhaven	(G-18798)
Houghton Lake	(G-8394)	Durand	(G-4838)	Sturgis	(G-16279)	Brownstown Township		Wyandotte	(G-18805)
Prudenville	(G-13655)	Henderson	(G-7859)	Three Rivers	(G-16562)	(G-2152)		**Wexford**	
Roscommon	(G-14346)	Laingsburg	(G-9536)	White Pigeon	(G-18472)	Brownstown Twp	(G-2153)	Boon	(G-1881)
Saint Helen	(G-14893)	Morrice	(G-11625)	**Tuscola**		Canton	(G-2425)	Buckley	(G-2204)
		Owosso	(G-12818)	Akron	(G-110)	Dearborn	(G-3803)	Cadillac	(G-2305)
		Perry	(G-12977)	Caro	(G-2565)	Dearborn Heights	(G-3918)	Manton	(G-10929)
								Mesick	(G-11269)

GEOGRAPHIC SECTION

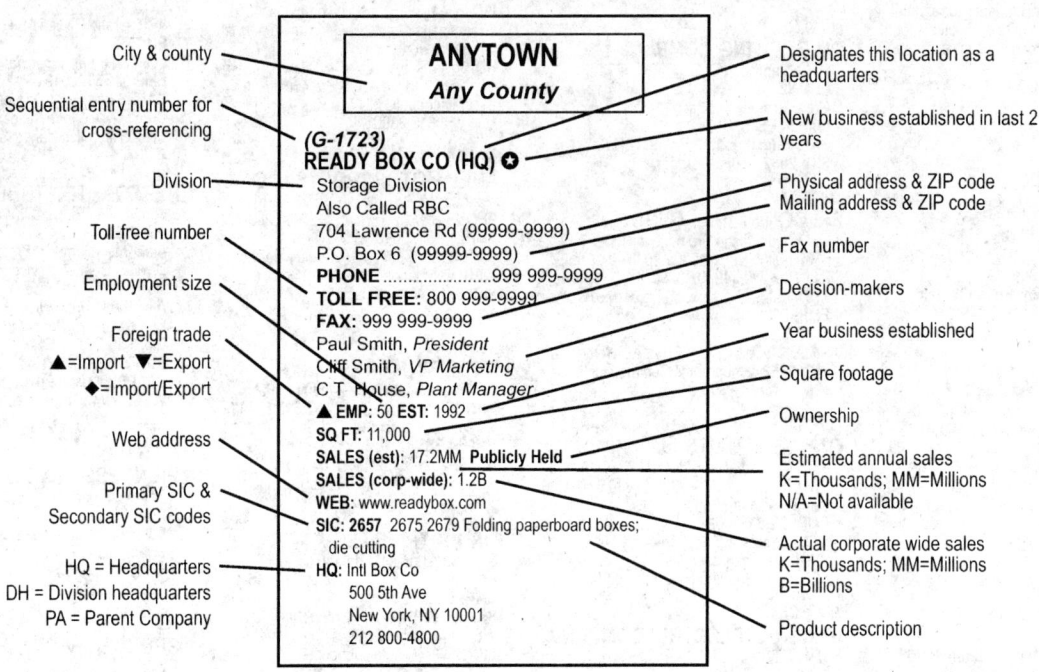

See footnotes for symbols and codes identification.
- This section is in alphabetical order by city.
- Companies are sorted alphabetically under their respective cities.
- To locate cities within a county refer to the County/City Cross Reference Index.

IMPORTANT NOTICE: It is a violation of both federal and state law to transmit an unsolicited advertisement to a facsimile machine. Any user of this product that violates such laws may be subject to civil and criminal penalties which may exceed $500 for each transmission of an unsolicited facsimile. Harris InfoSource provides fax numbers for lawful purposes only and expressly forbids the use of these numbers in any unlawful manner.

Acme
Grand Traverse County

(G-1)
ACME TOOL & DIE CO
5181 S Lautner Rd (49610)
P.O. Box 208 (49610-0208)
PHONE.................................231 938-1260
Lewis C Griffith, *Owner*
EMP: 4 **EST:** 1964
SALES (est): 160K Privately Held
SIC: 3469 3585 3312 3544 Stamping metal for the trade; ice making machinery; tool & die steel; special dies, tools, jigs & fixtures; sheet metalwork

(G-2)
ADVANCED INC
5474 Em 72 (49610)
P.O. Box 157 (49610-0157)
PHONE.................................231 938-2233
Christopher Stoppel, *President*
Lois Stoppel, *Vice Pres*
EMP: 6 **EST:** 1986
SQ FT: 3,000
SALES (est): 521K Privately Held
WEB: www.advanceddawnings.net
SIC: 5999 2394 Awnings; canvas & related products

Ada
Kent County

(G-3)
ACCESS BUSINESS GROUP LLC (DH)
7575 Fulton St E (49355-0001)
P.O. Box 513 (49301-0513)
PHONE.................................616 787-6000
Allen Senninger, *Superintendent*
Steve Van Andel, *Chairman*
Jamie Francis, *Business Mgr*
Rob Hunter, *Vice Pres*
Michael Pelc, *Project Mgr*
▲ **EMP:** 1957 **EST:** 2000
SQ FT: 3,200,000
SALES (est): 666.8MM Privately Held
WEB: www.accessbusinessgroup.com
SIC: 2842 5122 2833 5136 Specialty cleaning, polishes & sanitation goods; drugs, proprietaries & sundries; toiletries; cosmetics, perfumes & hair products; vitamins, natural or synthetic: bulk, uncompounded; men's & boys' clothing; women's & children's clothing; detergents & soaps, except specialty cleaning
HQ: Alticor Inc.
7575 Fulton St E
Ada MI 49355
616 787-1000

(G-4)
ADA GAGE INC
9450 Grand River Dr Se (49301-9246)
PHONE.................................616 676-3338
David Theule Jr, *President*
Kim Tubergen, *Opers Dir*
EMP: 6 **EST:** 1995
SALES (est): 457.5K Privately Held
WEB: www.adaage.com
SIC: 3544 Special dies & tools

(G-5)
ALTICOR GLOBAL HOLDINGS INC (PA)
7575 Fulton St E (49301)
PHONE.................................616 787-1000
Stephen Van Andel, *Ch of Bd*
Doug Devos, *President*
Joseph Heindlmeyer, *Principal*
Alvin Koop, *COO*
Barb Alviar, *Vice Pres*
EMP: 10 **EST:** 2004
SQ FT: 3,200,000
SALES (est): 2.3B Privately Held
WEB: www.amway.com
SIC: 5963 2833 5136 5137 Direct selling establishments; vitamins, natural or synthetic: bulk, uncompounded; men's & boys' clothing; women's & children's clothing; furniture; detergents & soaps, except specialty cleaning

(G-6)
ALTICOR INC (DH)
Also Called: Amway
7575 Fulton St E (49355-0001)
PHONE.................................616 787-1000
Doug Devos, *President*
Richard M Devos Sr, *President*
Steve Van Andel, *Chairman*
Brad Rick, *COO*
Sherry Gunderson-Schip, *Counsel*
◆ **EMP:** 4203 **EST:** 1949
SQ FT: 3,200,000

SALES (est): 2.3B Privately Held
WEB: www.amway.com
SIC: 5963 2833 5136 5137 Direct selling establishments; food services, direct sales; beverage services, direct sales; vitamins, natural or synthetic: bulk, uncompounded; men's & boys' clothing; women's & children's clothing; furniture; detergents & soaps, except specialty cleaning

(G-7)
AMWAY INTERNATIONAL DEV INC (DH)
7575 Fulton St E (49301)
PHONE.................................616 787-6000
Lynn J Lyall, *Principal*
Bill Roth, *Treasurer*
EMP: 569 **EST:** 1989
SALES (est): 2.4MM Privately Held
WEB: www.amway.com
SIC: 2844 2841 Toilet preparations; soap & other detergents
HQ: Amway International Inc.
7575 Fulton St E
Ada MI 49355
616 787-1000

(G-8)
AMWAY INTERNATIONAL INC (DH)
7575 Fulton St E (49355-0001)
PHONE.................................616 787-1000
Stephen Van Andel, *Ch of Bd*
Douglas Devos, *President*
Candace Matthews, *President*
George D Calvert, *Vice Pres*
Edward Van Dam, *Vice Pres*
◆ **EMP:** 27 **EST:** 1978
SQ FT: 2,800,000

Ada - Kent County (G-9)

SALES (est): 390.7MM **Privately Held**
WEB: www.amway.com
SIC: 5963 5122 5099 5199 Direct selling establishments; toiletries; child restraint seats, automotive; gifts & novelties; food preparations; canned specialties
HQ: Alticor, Inc.
7575 Fulton St E
Ada MI 49355
616 787-1000

(G-9)
ARCTUITION LLC
8011 Thornapple Clb Dr Se (49301-9415)
PHONE 616 635-9959
Pei Zhan, *CEO*
Charles Nivison,
EMP: 6 **EST:** 2015
SALES (est): 547.2K **Privately Held**
WEB: www.arcsite.com
SIC: 7372 Application computer software

(G-10)
BAKER BOOK HOUSE COMPANY (PA)
Also Called: Baker Publishing Group
6030 Fulton St E (49301-9156)
P.O. Box 6287, Grand Rapids (49516-6287)
PHONE 616 676-9185
Dwight Baker, *CEO*
Kristin Adkinson, *Editor*
Bryan Dyer, *Editor*
Rebekah Guzman, *Editor*
Amanda Hall, *Editor*
◆ **EMP:** 148 **EST:** 1939
SQ FT: 90,000
SALES (est): 35.8MM **Privately Held**
WEB: www.bakerbookhouse.com
SIC: 2731 5942 Books: publishing only; book stores; books, religious

(G-11)
BETHANY HOUSE PUBLISHERS
6030 Fulton St E (49301-9106)
PHONE 616 676-9185
Jessica Barnes, *Editor*
Teri Underwood, *Author*
EMP: 6 **EST:** 2019
SALES (est): 141K **Privately Held**
SIC: 2741 Miscellaneous publishing

(G-12)
BPG INTERNATIONAL FIN CO LLC (PA)
Also Called: Burke Porter Group
4760 Fulton St E Ste 201 (49301-9097)
P.O. Box 67, Deerton (49822-0067)
PHONE 616 855-1480
Daniel Webber, *CFO*
Bert Vermeersch, *Finance*
Lindsey Gort, *Manager*
Jon Eldersveld, *Director*
EMP: 1 **EST:** 2016
SALES (est): 32.7MM **Privately Held**
WEB: www.burkeportergroup.com
SIC: 3552 8711 7363 Opening machinery & equipment; engineering services; engineering help service

(G-13)
BRAMBLES WOODWORK LLC
6344 Dunbarton St Se (49301-7848)
PHONE 616 446-9118
Jarrod Napierkowski, *Principal*
EMP: 5 **EST:** 2019
SALES (est): 99.5K **Privately Held**
WEB: www.brambleswoodwork.com
SIC: 2431 Millwork

(G-14)
CD TOOL & GAGE
6490 Fulton St E (49301-9006)
PHONE 616 682-1111
Terry L Bush, *Owner*
EMP: 15 **EST:** 2001
SALES (est): 1.7MM **Privately Held**
WEB: www.cdgage.com
SIC: 3559 Automotive related machinery

(G-15)
DAILY DE-LISH
1235 Thrnpple River Dr Se (49301-7574)
PHONE 616 450-9562
Molly Dawson, *Principal*
EMP: 4 **EST:** 2010

SALES (est): 80K **Privately Held**
SIC: 2711 Newspapers, publishing & printing

(G-16)
DG BREWING COMPANY LLC
5530 Clemwood Ct Se (49301-7747)
PHONE 616 427-3242
Greg Custer, *Principal*
EMP: 4 **EST:** 2015
SALES (est): 62.5K **Privately Held**
SIC: 2082 Malt beverages

(G-17)
FALCON PRINTING INC
Also Called: Falcon Promotional Tools
6360 Fulton St E (49301-9038)
P.O. Box 280 (49301-0280)
PHONE 616 676-3737
EMP: 20
SQ FT: 23,000
SALES (est): 3.7MM **Privately Held**
SIC: 2752 Lithographic Commercial Printing

(G-18)
GARNEAU BAITS LLC
9575 Conservation St Ne (49301-9752)
PHONE 616 676-0186
James Willman, *Principal*
EMP: 5 **EST:** 2008
SALES (est): 125.6K **Privately Held**
WEB: www.garneaubaits.com
SIC: 3949 Sporting & athletic goods

(G-19)
GENERAL ELECTRIC COMPANY
7575 Fulton St E 74-1a (49355-0001)
P.O. Box 767 (49301-0767)
PHONE 616 676-0870
Michael Mazowita, *Partner*
Buck Surratt, *Manager*
EMP: 10
SALES (corp-wide): 79.6B **Publicly Held**
WEB: www.ge.com
SIC: 3569 Assembly machines, non-metalworking
PA: General Electric Company
5 Necco St
Boston MA 02210
617 443-3000

(G-20)
GRAVELLE WOODS
7000 4 Mile Rd Ne (49301-9626)
PHONE 616 617-7712
Gregory Gravelle, *Principal*
EMP: 5 **EST:** 2012
SALES (est): 98.9K **Privately Held**
WEB: www.gravellewoods.com
SIC: 2431 Millwork

(G-21)
GUDHO USA INC
138 Deer Run Dr Ne (49301-9541)
PHONE 616 682-7814
Karin Deutschler, *President*
EMP: 5 **EST:** 2005
SALES (est): 77.8K **Privately Held**
SIC: 3553 Woodworking machinery

(G-22)
HONEY CREEK WOODWORKS
8321 Conservation St Ne (49301-9705)
PHONE 616 706-2539
Drew Nelson, *Principal*
EMP: 6 **EST:** 2018
SALES (est): 54.1K **Privately Held**
WEB: www.honeycreekwoodworks.com
SIC: 2431 Millwork

(G-23)
HUBBLE ENTERPRISES INC
7807 Ashwood Dr Se (49301-8542)
PHONE 616 676-4485
Julie Hubble, *President*
EMP: 6 **EST:** 2001
SALES (est): 103.6K **Privately Held**
WEB: www.hubbleenterprisesinc.com
SIC: 3089 Plastics products

(G-24)
JOSTENS INC
4670 Fulton St E Ste 202 (49301-8409)
PHONE 734 308-3879
EMP: 6

SALES (corp-wide): 691.1MM **Privately Held**
WEB: www.jostens.com
SIC: 5944 3915 Jewelry, precious stones & precious metals; jewelers' materials & lapidary work
HQ: Jostens, Inc.
7760 France Ave S Ste 400
Minneapolis MN 55435
952 830-3300

(G-25)
LABEL MOTORSPORTS LLC
4920 Fulton St E Ste 3 (49301-9275)
PHONE 616 288-7710
EMP: 4 **EST:** 2018
SALES (est): 137.1K **Privately Held**
WEB: www.labelmotorsports.com
SIC: 3714 Motor vehicle parts & accessories

(G-26)
LITTLE BIRD PRESS LLC
8550 Vergennes St Se (49301-8909)
PHONE 616 676-9052
Karen Stacy, *Agent*
EMP: 4 **EST:** 2018
SALES (est): 96.2K **Privately Held**
SIC: 2741 Miscellaneous publishing

(G-27)
M INDUSTRIES LLC
6060 Sagebrook Dr Ne (49301-9663)
PHONE 616 745-4279
EMP: 8 **EST:** 2011
SALES (est): 114.4K **Privately Held**
WEB: www.mindustries.com
SIC: 3999 Manufacturing industries

(G-28)
M-INDUSTRIES LLC
6352 Fulton St E (49301-9038)
PHONE 616 682-4642
Karlis Mateus, *CEO*
Greg Bode, *Engineer*
Jack McNally, *Marketing Staff*
EMP: 25 **EST:** 2011
SALES (est): 2.6MM
SALES (corp-wide): 996.3MM **Privately Held**
WEB: www.mindustries.com
SIC: 2631 Container, packaging & boxboard
HQ: Tri-Seal Llc
460 E Swedesford Rd # 3000
Wayne PA 19087
330 821-1166

(G-29)
MERCHANDISING PRODUCTIONS
7575 Fulton St E (49356-0001)
PHONE 616 676-6000
Jay Van Andel, *Ch of Bd*
Richard De Vos, *President*
Lawrence M Call, *Treasurer*
EMP: 52 **EST:** 1983
SALES (est): 3.2MM **Privately Held**
WEB: www.amway.com
SIC: 2844 Cosmetic preparations
HQ: Alticor, Inc.
7575 Fulton St E
Ada MI 49355
616 787-1000

(G-30)
MICHIGAN MED INNOVATIONS LLC
481 Pettis Ave Se (49301-9540)
PHONE 616 682-4848
Robert C Shaver, *Mng Member*
EMP: 5 **EST:** 2008
SALES (est): 188.1K **Privately Held**
SIC: 3841 Diagnostic apparatus, medical

(G-31)
NOBLE FILMS CORPORATION
967 Spaulding Ave Se B1 (49301-3703)
PHONE 616 977-3770
Christine Nicoletti, *President*
▲ **EMP:** 9 **EST:** 2006
SALES (est): 806.2K **Privately Held**
WEB: www.noblefilmscorp.com
SIC: 2671 Packaging paper & plastics film, coated & laminated

(G-32)
ONE TREE RESEARCH GROUP LLC
8510 Grand River Dr Se (49301-9347)
PHONE 616 466-4880
Leah Sherman, *Principal*
EMP: 4 **EST:** 2019
SALES (est): 73K **Privately Held**
WEB: www.onetreeresearchgroup.com
SIC: 2741 Miscellaneous publishing

(G-33)
PERFORATED TUBES INC
4850 Fulton St E (49301-9062)
PHONE 616 942-4550
Alan C Doezema Jr, *President*
David B Doezema, *Vice Pres*
David Doezema, *Vice Pres*
Amy Rank, *Production*
Bruce Daniels, *Purch Mgr*
EMP: 30 **EST:** 1954
SQ FT: 36,000
SALES: 9.3MM **Privately Held**
WEB: www.perftubes.com
SIC: 3317 Tubes, seamless steel

(G-34)
PRINCESSA DESIGNS INC
743 W Woodmeade Ct Se (49301-2384)
PHONE 616 285 6868
Bonnie Moore, *Administration*
EMP: 5 **EST:** 2014
SALES (est): 92K **Privately Held**
SIC: 3993 Signs & advertising specialties

(G-35)
SPENCER FARMS AND TIMBER LLC
2585 Shadlow Trl Se (49301-9315)
PHONE 810 459-4487
Todd Spencer,
EMP: 5 **EST:** 2017
SALES (est): 81.7K **Privately Held**
WEB: www.spencer-farms-and-timber-llc.business.site
SIC: 2411 Timber, cut at logging camp

(G-36)
TIMES AND TITLES
396 Pettis Ave Se Ste 200 (49301-8715)
PHONE 616 828-5640
EMP: 4 **EST:** 2017
SALES (est): 86.3K **Privately Held**
SIC: 2711 Newspapers, publishing & printing

(G-37)
TIP TOP GRAVEL CO INC
9741 Fulton St E (49301-8915)
PHONE 616 897-8342
John Mathews, *President*
June Mathews, *Vice Pres*
EMP: 7 **EST:** 1966
SQ FT: 500
SALES (est): 1.9MM **Privately Held**
WEB: www.tiptopgravel.com
SIC: 1442 1794 Gravel mining; excavation work

(G-38)
TITANIUM OPERATIONS LLC
5199 Mountain Ridge Dr Ne (49301-9557)
PHONE 616 717-0218
Jacob Lueder, *Principal*
EMP: 7 **EST:** 2011
SALES (est): 263K **Privately Held**
SIC: 3356 Titanium

(G-39)
ULTIMATE SOFTWARE GROUP INC
5990 Fulton St E Ste E (49301-8432)
PHONE 616 682-9639
Rhonda Schuiteman, *Branch Mgr*
EMP: 4
SALES (corp-wide): 1.1B **Privately Held**
WEB: www.ultimatesoftware.com
SIC: 7372 Business oriented computer software
HQ: Ukg Inc.
900 Chelmsford St Ste 212
Lowell MA 01851

▲ = Import ▼ = Export
◆ = Import/Export

GEOGRAPHIC SECTION

Adrian - Lenawee County (G-66)

(G-40)
WALTZ-HOLST BLOW PIPE COMPANY
230 Alta Dale Ave Se (49301-9113)
PHONE.................................616 676-8119
Karl Paganelli, *President*
Jim Holst, *Vice Pres*
Matt Paganelli, *Vice Pres*
James Holst, *CFO*
James D Holst, *Treasurer*
EMP: 40 **EST:** 1933
SQ FT: 33,500
SALES: 16.1MM **Privately Held**
WEB: www.waltzholst.com
SIC: 3444 3564 1796 3443 Sheet metalwork; air cleaning systems; installing building equipment; fabricated plate work (boiler shop)

(G-41)
WEST MICHIGAN PRINTING INC
Also Called: Grand Rapids Legal News
513 Pine Land Dr Se (49301-9119)
PHONE.................................616 676-2190
EMP: 5 **EST:** 1935
SQ FT: 13,500
SALES (est): 410K **Privately Held**
SIC: 2752 2721 Lithographic Commercial Printing Periodicals-Publishing/Printing

(G-42)
WMC SALES LLC
4455 Tiffany Ave Ne (49301-8216)
PHONE.................................616 813-7237
Mark Putnam, *President*
EMP: 8 **EST:** 2005
SALES (est): 197.1K **Privately Held**
SIC: 3531 Cranes

Addison
Lenawee County

(G-43)
DARBY READY MIX CONCRETE CO
Also Called: Darbyreadymix.com
U.S 12 & Herold Hwy (49220)
PHONE.................................517 547-7004
Randy Darby, *President*
Mike Comstock, *Vice Pres*
EMP: 22 **EST:** 1964
SQ FT: 2,500
SALES (est): 2.9MM **Privately Held**
WEB: www.darbyreadymix.com
SIC: 3273 3272 Ready-mixed concrete; concrete products

(G-44)
ROUND LAKE SAND & GRAVEL INC
8707 Round Lake Hwy (49220-9736)
P.O. Box 90, West Millgrove OH (43467-0090)
PHONE.................................517 467-4458
Tim Cottrill, *Opers-Prdtn-Mfg*
EMP: 7
SQ FT: 500
SALES (corp-wide): 2.2MM **Privately Held**
WEB: www.gerkencompanies.com
SIC: 1442 Common sand mining; gravel mining
PA: Round Lake Sand & Gravel, Inc.
6126 S Main St
West Millgrove OH
419 288-2790

(G-45)
SEAGATE PLASTICS COMPANY
320 S Steer St (49220-9632)
PHONE.................................517 547-8123
Eric Harbaugh, *Branch Mgr*
Corey McCree, *Receptionist*
EMP: 8
SQ FT: 8,500
SALES (corp-wide): 9.4MM **Privately Held**
WEB: www.seagateplastics.com
SIC: 3089 Injection molding of plastics; plastic processing
PA: Seagate Plastics Company
1110 Disher Dr
Waterville OH 43566
419 878-5010

Adrian
Lenawee County

(G-46)
5 LAKES PRINTING AND SIGN LLC
358 Mulzer Ave (49221-3953)
PHONE.................................517 265-3202
Robert O'Leary, *Principal*
EMP: 4 **EST:** 2016
SALES (est): 65.2K **Privately Held**
SIC: 3993 Signs & advertising specialties

(G-47)
ACE DRILL CORPORATION
2600 E Maumee St (49221-3533)
P.O. Box 160 (49221-0160)
PHONE.................................517 265-5184
Alfred J Brown, *CEO*
Joan Brown, *Corp Secy*
Alfred J Brown III, *Vice Pres*
EMP: 6 **EST:** 1933
SQ FT: 50,000
SALES (est): 1.3MM **Privately Held**
WEB: www.acedrill.com
SIC: 5051 3545 3546 Steel; drills (machine tool accessories); reamers, machine tool; drills & drilling tools

(G-48)
ADRIAN LVA BIOFUEL LLC
Also Called: W2fuel Adrian
1571 W Beecher Rd (49221-8754)
PHONE.................................517 920-4863
Paul Orentas,
EMP: 6 **EST:** 2011
SALES (est): 611.4K **Privately Held**
WEB: www.nextdiesel.net
SIC: 2869 Fuels

(G-49)
ADRIAN PRECISION MACHINING LLC
605 Industrial Dr (49221-8767)
PHONE.................................517 263-4564
Jason Fisher,
EMP: 12 **EST:** 2011
SQ FT: 800
SALES (est): 1.8MM **Privately Held**
WEB: www.adrianprecision.com
SIC: 3544 Special dies & tools

(G-50)
ADRIAN STEEL COMPANY (PA)
Also Called: Distyll Graphics
906 James St (49221-3996)
PHONE.................................517 265-6194
Harley J Westfall, *Ch of Bd*
David E Pilmore, *President*
Bob Southward, *General Mgr*
Dale Leveque, *Maint Spvr*
Barry Barnhart, *Production*
▼ **EMP:** 375 **EST:** 1953
SQ FT: 165,000
SALES (est): 120.1MM **Privately Held**
WEB: www.adriansteel.com
SIC: 3496 3469 Shelving, made from purchased wire; boxes: tool, lunch, mail, etc.: stamped metal

(G-51)
ADRIAN TEAM LLC
795 Richlyn Dr (49221-9297)
PHONE.................................517 264-6148
J P McDevitt, *Principal*
EMP: 10 **EST:** 2006
SALES (est): 143.4K **Privately Held**
WEB: www.adrian.edu
SIC: 2711 Newspapers

(G-52)
ADRIAN TOOL CORPORATION
1441 Enterprise Ave (49221-8789)
PHONE.................................517 263-6530
G Steven Pickle, *President*
Tim Czamiak, *Sales Associate*
EMP: 23 **EST:** 1969
SQ FT: 20,000
SALES (est): 3.9MM **Privately Held**
WEB: www.adriantool.com
SIC: 3441 3544 Fabricated structural metal; special dies, tools, jigs & fixtures

(G-53)
ANDERSON DEVELOPMENT COMPANY
Also Called: ADC
1415 E Michigan St (49221-3499)
PHONE.................................517 263-2121
Mark Kramer, *President*
Joseph Greulich, *President*
Naoya Sakamoto, *Exec VP*
Chris Goeloe, *Vice Pres*
Steve Vanausdale, *Purchasing*
◆ **EMP:** 115 **EST:** 1965
SQ FT: 183,000
SALES (est): 43MM **Privately Held**
WEB: www.andersondevelopment.com
SIC: 2821 Plastics materials & resins
HQ: Mitsui Chemicals America, Inc.
800 Westchester Ave N607
Rye Brook NY 10573

(G-54)
BRAZEWAY LLC (PA)
2711 E Maumee St (49221-3586)
PHONE.................................517 265-2121
Stephen L Hickman, *Ch of Bd*
Stephanie Hickman Boyse, *President*
Michael Adams, *Vice Pres*
John P Benzing, *Vice Pres*
Emory M Schmidt, *Vice Pres*
◆ **EMP:** 100 **EST:** 1946
SQ FT: 102,000
SALES (est): 195.1MM **Privately Held**
WEB: www.brazeway.com
SIC: 3354 3353 Tube, extruded or drawn, aluminum; aluminum sheet, plate & foil

(G-55)
C & J PALLETS INC
2368 E Us Highway 223 (49221-9251)
PHONE.................................517 263-7415
Edd Keck, *President*
Nancy Keck, *Vice Pres*
EMP: 6
SQ FT: 3,000
SALES (est): 481.1K **Privately Held**
SIC: 2448 Pallets, wood

(G-56)
CARTER INDUSTRIES INC
906 James St (49221-3914)
PHONE.................................510 324-6700
David Pilmore, *President*
Joseph E Emens, *CFO*
Harley Westfall, *Treasurer*
EMP: 71 **EST:** 1961
SQ FT: 62,000
SALES (est): 2.4MM
SALES (corp-wide): 120.1MM **Privately Held**
WEB: www.adriansteel.com
SIC: 3713 5531 5013 3714 Truck & bus bodies; truck equipment & parts; motor vehicle supplies & new parts; motor vehicle parts & accessories
PA: Adrian Steel Company
906 James St
Adrian MI 49221
517 265-6194

(G-57)
CREEK PLASTICS LLC
638 W Maumee St (49221-2030)
PHONE.................................517 423-1003
Jason Derby, *President*
Eric Harbaugh, *Vice Pres*
Frank Willett, *Treasurer*
McKenzie Rowe, *Sales Staff*
Scott Kolanek, *Admin Sec*
EMP: 10 **EST:** 2011
SALES (est): 2.3MM **Privately Held**
WEB: www.creekplastics.com
SIC: 3084 Plastics pipe

(G-58)
DAIRY FARMERS AMERICA INC
1336 E Maumee St (49221-3444)
PHONE.................................517 265-5045
Dan Hofbauer, *Prdtn Mgr*
Mark Keller, *Branch Mgr*
EMP: 87
SQ FT: 15,000
SALES (corp-wide): 17.8B **Privately Held**
WEB: www.dfamilk.com
SIC: 2023 2026 Dry, condensed, evaporated dairy products; fluid milk
PA: Dairy Farmers Of America, Inc.
1405 N 98th St
Kansas City KS 66111
816 801-6455

(G-59)
DEPIERRE INDUSTRIES INC
Also Called: Aget Manufacturing Company
1408 E Church St (49221-3437)
PHONE.................................517 263-5781
Robert Depierre, *President*
Timothy Kirkendall, *CFO*
EMP: 25 **EST:** 2016
SQ FT: 45,000
SALES (est): 5MM **Privately Held**
WEB: www.agetmfg.com
SIC: 3564 Purification & dust collection equipment

(G-60)
DH CUSTOM FABRICATION
1209 E Beecher St (49221-4019)
PHONE.................................517 264-8045
EMP: 5 **EST:** 2017
SALES (est): 222.7K **Privately Held**
SIC: 7692 Welding repair

(G-61)
DH CUSTOM FABRICATION
2314 Treat St (49221-4008)
PHONE.................................517 366-9067
EMP: 6 **EST:** 2019
SALES (est): 276K **Privately Held**
SIC: 7692 Welding repair

(G-62)
DIEHL INC
1336 E Maumee St (49221-3444)
PHONE.................................517 265-5045
Peter Diehl, *President*
EMP: 4 **EST:** 1899
SALES (est): 95.9K **Privately Held**
SIC: 2099 Food preparations

(G-63)
EAGLE PRESS REPAIRS & SER
2025 E Gier Rd (49221-9667)
PHONE.................................419 539-7206
Chuck Collins, *President*
EMP: 9 **EST:** 1999
SALES (est): 995.7K **Privately Held**
WEB: www.eaglepressrepairs.com
SIC: 3555 Printing presses

(G-64)
ERVIN INDUSTRIES INC
Ervin Amasteel Div Ervin Inds
915 Tabor St (49221-3995)
PHONE.................................517 265-6118
Dinius Mark, *Prdtn Mgr*
James C Lemon, *Opers-Prdtn-Mfg*
Nancy Hindman, *Buyer*
James Jazwinski, *Engineer*
Sheri Weasel, *Credit Staff*
EMP: 100
SALES (corp-wide): 200MM **Privately Held**
WEB: www.ervinindustries.com
SIC: 3291 Steel shot abrasive
PA: Ervin Industries, Inc.
3893 Research Park Dr
Ann Arbor MI 48108
734 769-4600

(G-65)
EVERGREEN GREASE SERVICE INC
1445 Enterprise Ave (49221-8789)
PHONE.................................517 264-9913
Neil T Liston, *President*
Diana Liston, *Admin Sec*
EMP: 5 **EST:** 1996
SALES (est): 645.7K **Privately Held**
WEB: www.evergreengrease.com
SIC: 2077 Animal & marine fats & oils

(G-66)
FISHES & LOAVES FOOD PANTRY
410 E Maumee St (49221-3047)
PHONE.................................517 759-4421

Adrian - Lenawee County (G-67)   GEOGRAPHIC SECTION

EMP: 4 EST: 2016
SALES (est): 62.3K **Privately Held**
WEB: www.neighborsofhope.com
SIC: 2048 Fish food

(G-67)
FLURESH LLC
1751 W Beecher Rd (49221-8773)
PHONE..................................616 600-0420
EMP: 23
SALES (corp-wide): 9.6MM **Privately Held**
WEB: www.fluresh.com
SIC: 3999
PA: Fluresh Llc
   1213 Phillips Ave Sw
   Grand Rapids MI 49507
   616 600-0420

(G-68)
FLYING OTTER WINERY LLC
3402 Chase Rd (49221-8305)
PHONE..................................517 424-7107
EMP: 4
SALES (est): 1K **Privately Held**
SIC: 2084 Wines, Brandy, And Brandy Spirits, Nsk

(G-69)
GATEHOUSE MEDIA LLC
Also Called: Daily Telegram, The
133 N Winter St (49221-2042)
P.O. Box 647 (49221-0647)
PHONE..................................517 265-5111
Paul Heidbrder, *Manager*
EMP: 25
SALES (corp-wide): 3.4B **Publicly Held**
WEB: www.gannett.com
SIC: 2711 Newspapers, publishing & printing; newspapers: publishing only, not printed on site
HQ: Gatehouse Media, Llc
   175 Sullys Trl Fl 3
   Pittsford NY 14534
   585 598-0030

(G-70)
GENSTONE LLC
1273 Evergreen Trl (49221-8455)
PHONE..................................517 902-4730
Genene Gray, *CEO*
EMP: 5 EST: 2017
SALES (est): 203.4K **Privately Held**
WEB: www.genstonellc.com
SIC: 3999 1541 2499 7299 Manufacturing industries; food products manufacturing or packing plant construction; food handling & processing products, wood; consumer purchasing services; housing programs; medical & hospital uniforms, men's

(G-71)
GMC (GENERAL MOTORS)
1450 E Beecher St (49221-3562)
PHONE..................................517 265-4222
Mary Gray, *Principal*
EMP: 6 EST: 2017
SALES (est): 118.9K **Privately Held**
SIC: 3714 Motor vehicle parts & accessories

(G-72)
H E LYONS INC
10125 W Us Highway 223 (49221-9481)
PHONE..................................517 467-2232
Harold Lyons, *President*
EMP: 10 EST: 2011
SALES (est): 350K **Privately Held**
SIC: 2599 Bar, restaurant & cafeteria furniture

(G-73)
II ADRIAN LLC W2FUEL
Also Called: W2fuel Adrian II
1571 W Beecher Rd (49221-8754)
PHONE..................................517 920-4863
Graham Towerton, *CEO*
EMP: 5 EST: 2012
SALES (est): 176.4K **Privately Held**
SIC: 2869 Fuels

(G-74)
INTEVA PRODUCTS LLC
Also Called: Inteva Adrian
1450 E Beecher St (49221-3562)
PHONE..................................517 266-8030
Ronald Stanford, *Plant Mgr*
Scott Baumgartner, *Engineer*
Clive Smith, *Branch Mgr*
Stewart Witte, *Info Tech Mgr*
Joe Moorton, *Administration*
EMP: 300
SALES (corp-wide): 3.2B **Privately Held**
WEB: www.intevaproducts.com
SIC: 3089 Injection molding of plastics
HQ: Inteva Products, Llc
   1401 Crooks Rd
   Troy MI 48084

(G-75)
J & M PRODUCTS AND SERVICE LLC
615 N Scott St (49221-1338)
PHONE..................................517 263-3082
Marcia Mikuski, *Owner*
Jack Mikuski, *Owner*
EMP: 6 EST: 1999
SALES (est): 403.5K **Privately Held**
SIC: 3648 Lighting equipment

(G-76)
JACK WEAVER CORP
343 Lawrence Ave (49221-3340)
PHONE..................................517 263-6500
Alfred J Brown, *President*
Terry L Tornow, *Vice Pres*
William Brown, *Admin Sec*
EMP: 9
SQ FT: 30,000
SALES (est): 1.7MM **Privately Held**
WEB: www.meyersboats.com
SIC: 3569 Jacks, hydraulic

(G-77)
JELAGA INC
371 Miles Dr (49221-4025)
PHONE..................................517 263-5190
EMP: 4 EST: 2019
SALES (est): 213.5K **Privately Held**
SIC: 3089 Injection molding of plastics

(G-78)
KING TOOL & DIE INC
971 Division St (49221-4097)
PHONE..................................517 265-2741
Larry King, *President*
Kevin King, *Treasurer*
David L King, *Shareholder*
▲ EMP: 27 EST: 1965
SQ FT: 31,000
SALES (est): 1.8MM **Privately Held**
WEB: www.kingmachines.com
SIC: 3599 Machine shop, jobbing & repair

(G-79)
LESSO KITCHEN AND BATH
2075 W Beecher Rd (49221-8747)
PHONE..................................517 662-3230
EMP: 7 EST: 2017
SALES (est): 256.3K **Privately Held**
WEB: www.lessokitchenandbath.com
SIC: 2434 Wood kitchen cabinets

(G-80)
MACHINED SOLUTIONS
360 Mulzer Ave (49221-3953)
PHONE..................................517 759-4075
Isaac Snead, *Principal*
EMP: 4 EST: 2015
SALES (est): 172.4K **Privately Held**
WEB: www.machinedsolutions.com
SIC: 3599 Machine shop, jobbing & repair

(G-81)
MADISON STREET HOLDINGS LLC
Also Called: Aget Manufacturing Company
1408 E Church St (49221-3437)
P.O. Box 248 (49221-0248)
PHONE..................................517 252-2031
Lauren Cato, *CEO*
John Mitchem, *COO*
Timothy Kirkendall, *Vice Pres*
Mark Gibbs, *Mfg Mgr*
Steph Hoagland, *Traffic Mgr*
EMP: 25 EST: 1938

SQ FT: 45,000
SALES (est): 4.3MM **Privately Held**
WEB: www.agetmfg.com
SIC: 3564 5084 Dust or fume collecting equipment, industrial; precipitators, electrostatic; purification & dust collection equipment; industrial machinery & equipment

(G-82)
MASCO CABINETRY LLC
5353 W Us Highway 223 (49221-8901)
PHONE..................................517 263-0771
Jill Isham, *Buyer*
Sana El, *Accounting Mgr*
Alyssa Corbin, *Sales Staff*
Rebecca Baigrie, *Marketing Staff*
Karen Strauss, *Branch Mgr*
EMP: 110
SALES (corp-wide): 1.6B **Privately Held**
SIC: 2434 Vanities, bathroom: wood
PA: Cabinetworks Group Michigan, Llc
   4600 Arrowhead Dr
   Ann Arbor MI 48105
   734 205-4600

(G-83)
MERILLAT INDUSTRIES LLC
5353 W Us Highway 223 (49221-8901)
P.O. Box 1946 (49221-7946)
PHONE..................................517 263-0269
Jeff Anderson, *Sales Staff*
EMP: 16 EST: 2016
SALES (est): 560.8K **Privately Held**
WEB: www.merillat.com
SIC: 2434 Wood kitchen cabinets

(G-84)
MERILLAT LP (HQ)
5353 W Us Highway 223 (49221-8901)
P.O. Box 1946 (49221-7946)
PHONE..................................517 263-0771
Eugene A Gargaro Jr, *Partner*
Warren J Potter, *Partner*
Clay Kiefaber, *General Ptnr*
John Finn, *Manager*
▲ EMP: 110 EST: 1989
SQ FT: 63,000
SALES (est): 93.5MM
SALES (corp-wide): 1.6B **Privately Held**
WEB: www.adrianbulldogs.com
SIC: 2434 Wood kitchen cabinets
PA: Cabinetworks Group Michigan, Llc
   4600 Arrowhead Dr
   Ann Arbor MI 48105
   734 205-4600

(G-85)
MEYERS BOAT COMPANY INC
343 Lawrence Ave (49221-3340)
PHONE..................................517 265-9821
Alfred James Brown, *President*
Joshua Hoff, *General Mgr*
William Brown, *Vice Pres*
Bill Brown, *QC Mgr*
EMP: 22 EST: 1991
SQ FT: 2,000
SALES (est): 1MM **Privately Held**
WEB: www.meyersboat.com
SIC: 3089 3732 Boats, nonrigid: plastic; boat building & repairing

(G-86)
OLIVER OF ADRIAN INC
1111 E Beecher St (49221-4017)
P.O. Box 189 (49221-0189)
PHONE..................................517 263-2132
Neal E Garrison Jr, *President*
Dale E Thielan, *Vice Pres*
Michael Borton, *Treasurer*
EMP: 9 EST: 1913
SQ FT: 50,000
SALES (est): 891K **Privately Held**
WEB: www.oliverofadrian.com
SIC: 3541 5084 Machine tools, metal cutting type; industrial machinery & equipment

(G-87)
PLANEWAVE INSTRUMENTS INC
1375 N Main St Ste 1 (49221-1774)
PHONE..................................310 639-1662
Richard Hedrick, *President*
Joseph Haberman, *Vice Pres*
Shelby Stubbe, *Engineer*

David Rowe, *Officer*
Jason Fourier, *Admin Sec*
EMP: 70 EST: 2006
SALES (est): 4MM **Privately Held**
WEB: www.pw-ecommerce.com
SIC: 3827 Optical instruments & lenses

(G-88)
PLASTIC OMNIUM AUTO INRGY USA
1549 W Beecher Rd (49221-8754)
PHONE..................................517 265-1100
Daniel Forche, *Buyer*
Ross Johnson, *Director*
Vincent Torres, *Technician*
EMP: 242
SALES (corp-wide): 1.8MM **Privately Held**
WEB: www.plasticomnium.com
SIC: 3089 3714 Blow molded finished plastic products; motor vehicle parts & accessories
HQ: Plastic Omnium Auto Inergy (Usa) Llc
   2710 Bellingham Dr
   Troy MI 48083
   248 743-5700

(G-89)
PRIMORE INC (PA)
Also Called: Sedco Division Primore, Inc.
2300 W Beecher Rd (49221-9769)
P.O. Box 605 (49221-0605)
PHONE..................................517 263-2220
Robert E Price, *President*
Richard Hutt, *Vice Pres*
Mark Roberts, *Purchasing*
EMP: 14 EST: 1946
SQ FT: 9,500
SALES (est): 8.3MM **Privately Held**
WEB: www.sedco-prv.com
SIC: 3491 3563 Valves, automatic control; air & gas compressors

(G-90)
QUICKPRINT OF ADRIAN INC
Also Called: Quick Print
142 N Main St (49221-2745)
PHONE..................................517 263-2290
Dennis Swartzlander, *President*
Duane Swartzlander, *Corp Secy*
Gary Swartzlander, *Vice Pres*
EMP: 10 EST: 1972
SQ FT: 7,000
SALES (est): 877.2K **Privately Held**
SIC: 2752 7334 Commercial printing, offset; photocopying & duplicating services

(G-91)
ROBOGISTICS LLC
100 Industrial Dr (49221-9767)
PHONE..................................409 234-1033
Kerry Powell, *Branch Mgr*
EMP: 18
SQ FT: 1,200
SALES (corp-wide): 5.8MM **Privately Held**
WEB: www.txrobogistics.com
SIC: 3646 Commercial indusl & institutional electric lighting fixtures
PA: Robogistics Llc
   363 N Sam Houston Pkwy E # 1100
   Houston TX 77060
   409 234-1033

(G-92)
ROTO-PLASTICS CORPORATION
Also Called: Tuff Body Padding Company
1001 Division St (49221-4023)
P.O. Box 779 (49221-0779)
PHONE..................................517 263-8981
David Mulligan, *President*
Clyne W Durst Jr, *Corp Secy*
Joe Cabello, *Vice Pres*
Jason Rule, *Maintence Staff*
EMP: 55
SQ FT: 62,000
SALES (est): 7.9MM **Privately Held**
WEB: www.rotoplastics.com
SIC: 3089 Injection molding of plastics

(G-93)
SCHAFERS ELEVATOR CO
4105 Country Club Rd (49221-9216)
PHONE..................................517 263-7202
Keith Schafer, *Partner*
Ralph Schafer, *Corp Secy*

GEOGRAPHIC SECTION
Albion - Calhoun County (G-117)

Alan Schafer, *Vice Pres*
EMP: 4 EST: 1977
SQ FT: 19,000
SALES (est): 449.6K Privately Held
SIC: 3534 5153 Elevators & equipment; grains

(G-94)
SCIENTEMP CORP
3565 S Adrian Hwy (49221-9293)
PHONE 517 263-6020
Howard J Tenniswood, *President*
Steven Tenniswood, *Vice Pres*
EMP: 20 EST: 1968
SQ FT: 10,000
SALES (est): 3.9MM Privately Held
WEB: www.scientemp.com
SIC: 3585 5064 3632 Refrigeration & heating equipment; electrical appliances, television & radio; household refrigerators & freezers

(G-95)
SEDCO INC
2304 W Beecher Rd (49221-9769)
P.O. Box 624 (49221-0624)
PHONE 517 263-2220
Robert E Price, *President*
Larry Ansthuetz, *President*
Bob Curley, *Vice Pres*
Bob Curly, *Vice Pres*
Richard D Hutt, *Vice Pres*
▼ EMP: 36 EST: 1956
SQ FT: 25,000
SALES (est): 6.5MM
SALES (corp-wide): 8.3MM Privately Held
WEB: www.sedco-prv.com
SIC: 3491 Industrial valves
PA: Primore, Inc.
2300 W Beecher Rd
Adrian MI 49221
517 263-2220

(G-96)
SERVICE TECTONICS INC
2827 Treat St (49221-4499)
PHONE 517 263-0758
Stephen J Dalton, *President*
Jon Dalton, *Vice Pres*
Shirly Dalton, *Treasurer*
▲ EMP: 27 EST: 1964
SQ FT: 15,000
SALES (est): 4MM Privately Held
WEB: www.padprinting.net
SIC: 3569 Assembly machines, non-metalworking

(G-97)
SPOTTED COW
1336 N Main St (49221-1773)
PHONE 517 265-6188
Don Barron, *Principal*
EMP: 6 EST: 2008
SALES (est): 228.2K Privately Held
WEB: www.spottedcowlenawee.com
SIC: 3556 Ice cream manufacturing machinery

(G-98)
TEXWOOD INDUSTRIES
5353 W Us Highway 223 (49221-8901)
PHONE 517 266-4739
EMP: 5 EST: 2019
SALES (est): 64.2K Privately Held
SIC: 3999 Manufacturing industries

(G-99)
TOMS WORLD OF WOOD
105 Sand Creek Hwy (49221-9130)
PHONE 517 264-2836
EMP: 4
SQ FT: 2,560
SALES: 150K Privately Held
SIC: 2499 5945 5251 Custom Woodworking Ret Arts & Crafts & Woodworking Tools

(G-100)
VENCHURS INC
Also Called: Venchurs Packaging
800 Liberty St (49221-3955)
PHONE 517 263-8937
▲ EMP: 175
SQ FT: 200,000
SALES (est): 2.2MM Privately Held
WEB: www.venchurs.com
SIC: 2671 Paper; Coated And Laminated Packaging,Nsk

(G-101)
W2FUEL LLC (PA)
Also Called: W2fuel Keokuk I
1571 W Beecher Rd (49221-8754)
PHONE 517 920-4868
Graham Towerton, *CEO*
Roy Strom, *CFO*
Adam Gibson, *Manager*
Nicole Megale, *Administration*
EMP: 38 EST: 2011
SALES (est): 7.6MM Privately Held
WEB: www.w2fuel.com
SIC: 2911 Diesel fuels

(G-102)
WACKER BIOCHEM CORPORATION
3301 Sutton Rd (49221-9335)
PHONE 517 264-8500
Ingo Kavor, *President*
Archie Dowdy, *Supervisor*
▲ EMP: 120 EST: 1997
SALES (est): 11.9MM
SALES (corp-wide): 5.5B Privately Held
WEB: www.wackerrelay4life.com
SIC: 2899 Chemical preparations
HQ: Wacker Chemical Corporation
3301 Sutton Rd
Adrian MI 49221
517 264-8500

(G-103)
WACKER CHEMICAL CORPORATION (DH)
3301 Sutton Rd (49221-9335)
PHONE 517 264-8500
David Wilhoit, *President*
Jochen Ebenhoch, *Managing Dir*
Zsolt Ligethy, *Managing Dir*
Laurent Morineaux, *Managing Dir*
Gregory Brabec, *Counsel*
◆ EMP: 525 EST: 1974
SQ FT: 1,000,000
SALES (est): 1.9B
SALES (corp-wide): 5.5B Privately Held
WEB: www.wackerrelay4life.com
SIC: 2869 5169 Silicones; industrial chemicals
HQ: Wacker Chemie Ag
Hanns-Seidel-Platz 4
Munchen BY 81737
896 279-0

(G-104)
WHOLESALE PROC SYSTEMS LLC
4315 N Adrian Hwy (49221-8314)
P.O. Box 314, Brooklyn (49230-0314)
PHONE 833 755-6696
Thomas Troyer, *CEO*
EMP: 5 EST: 2018
SALES (est): 259.2K Privately Held
WEB: www.wholesaleprocessingsystems.com
SIC: 7389 6141 3578 8742 Credit card service; industrial loan banks & companies, not a deposit bank; point-of-sale devices; marketing consulting services; advisory services, insurance

(G-105)
WORKFORCE PAYHUB INC
104 E Maumee St (49221-2704)
PHONE 517 759-4026
Eric Jones, *President*
EMP: 7 EST: 2011
SQ FT: 4,400
SALES (est): 395.3K Privately Held
WEB: www.workforcepayhub.com
SIC: 8721 7372 Payroll accounting service; business oriented computer software

Afton
Cheboygan County

(G-106)
ARROWHEAD INDUSTRIES INC
1715 E M 68 Hwy (49705-9715)
PHONE 231 238-9366
Thomas J Redman, *President*
EMP: 10 EST: 2007 Privately Held
SIC: 3499 Fabricated metal products

(G-107)
ROMAN ENGINEERING
1715 E M 68 Hwy (49705-9715)
PHONE 231 238-7644
Thomas Radman, *President*
Robert Radman, *Chairman*
EMP: 23 EST: 1970
SALES (est): 448.7K Privately Held
WEB: www.tubefab.org
SIC: 5014 3498 3317 8711 Tires & tubes; fabricated pipe & fittings; steel pipe & tubes; engineering services

(G-108)
TUBE FAB/ROMAN ENGRG CO INC
1715 Michigan 68 Afton (49705)
PHONE 231 238-9366
Thomas J Redman, *President*
Robert J Redman, *Chairman*
Cynthia A Redman, *Corp Secy*
Karen Work, *Project Mgr*
Matt Morton, *Engineer*
EMP: 136 EST: 1970
SQ FT: 190,000
SALES (est): 18.9MM Privately Held
WEB: www.tubefab.org
SIC: 3441 Fabricated structural metal

Ahmeek
Keweenaw County

(G-109)
NEUVOKAS CORPORATION
32066 Rd (49901)
P.O. Box 220 (49901-0220)
PHONE 906 934-2661
Erik Kiilunen, *CEO*
Ken Keranen, *COO*
Matt Kero, *Vice Pres*
Matt P Kero, *Vice Pres*
Steve Eskola, *Sales Staff*
EMP: 5 EST: 2013
SALES (est): 1.4MM Privately Held
WEB: www.neuvokascorp.com
SIC: 3299 Mica products

Akron
Tuscola County

(G-110)
OREOS WLDG & FABRICATION LLC
2681 Ringle Rd (48701-9602)
PHONE 989 529-0815
Carey Butterfield, *Principal*
EMP: 4 EST: 2017
SALES (est): 51.2K Privately Held
WEB: www.oreowelding.com
SIC: 7692 Welding repair

Alanson
Emmet County

(G-111)
HALE MANUFACTURING INC
6235 Cupp Rd (49706-9512)
PHONE 231 529-6271
Wayne Hunter, *President*
EMP: 9 EST: 1963
SQ FT: 5,000 Privately Held
WEB: www.haleman.com
SIC: 3825 Electrical power measuring equipment

(G-112)
UP NORTH SIGN LLC
7726 Lake St (49706-9273)
PHONE 231 838-6328
Laura Elyea, *Principal*
EMP: 4 EST: 2017
SALES (est): 56.5K Privately Held
SIC: 3993 Signs & advertising specialties

Alba
Antrim County

(G-113)
C & R TOOL DIE
4643 Alba Hwy (49611)
P.O. Box 148 (49611-0148)
PHONE 231 584-3588
Calvin Hoogerhyde, *Owner*
EMP: 4 EST: 1990
SQ FT: 4,000
SALES (est): 100K Privately Held
SIC: 3544 7692 Special dies & tools; welding repair

Albion
Calhoun County

(G-114)
ALBION INDUSTRIES LLC (PA)
800 N Clark St (49224-1455)
PHONE 800 835-8911
Terri Rush, *Buyer*
Mary Sus, *Purchasing*
Christopher Longrey, *Engineer*
Dennis Byrd, *Treasurer*
Rex Buckner, *Regl Sales Mgr*
▲ EMP: 158 EST: 1947
SQ FT: 70,000
SALES (est): 23.9MM Privately Held
WEB: www.albioncasters.com
SIC: 3429 5084 Manufactured hardware (general); materials handling machinery

(G-115)
ALBION MACHINE AND TOOL LLC
1001 Industrial Blvd (49224-8551)
PHONE 517 629-8838
William Dobbins, *Manager*
EMP: 14 EST: 2014
SALES (est): 600.3K Privately Held
WEB: www.albionmachine.com
SIC: 3544 Special dies, tools, jigs & fixtures

(G-116)
AMCOL INTERNATIONAL CORP
807 Austin Ave (49224-1000)
P.O. Box 35 (49224-0035)
PHONE 517 629-6808
George Johnson, *Branch Mgr*
EMP: 4 Publicly Held
WEB: www.mineralstech.com
SIC: 2869 Industrial organic chemicals
HQ: Amcol International Corp
2870 Forbs Ave
Hoffman Estates IL 60192
847 851-1500

(G-117)
AVIENT COLORANTS USA LLC
Masterbatch Division
926 Elliott St (49224-9506)
PHONE 517 629-9101
Dinesh Pandya, *Opers-Prdtn-Mfg*
Jerry Willis, *QC Mgr*
Denise Richardson, *Manager*
Tina Delaney, *CTO*
Carissa Dane, *Analyst*
EMP: 229
SQ FT: 52,000 Publicly Held
SIC: 2869 Industrial organic chemicals
HQ: Avient Colorants Usa Llc
85 Industrial Dr
Holden MA 01520
508 829-6321

Albion - Calhoun County

(G-118)
CALHOUN COMMUNICATIONS INC (PA)
Also Called: Albion Recorder
125 E Cass St (49224-1726)
PHONE................................517 629-0041
Richard Milliman II, *President*
Teresa Fitzwater, *Publisher*
EMP: 15 EST: 1904
SQ FT: 30,000
SALES (est): 1MM **Privately Held**
WEB: www.albionrecorder.com
SIC: 2711 Commercial printing & newspaper publishing combined

(G-119)
CARR BROTHERS AND SONS INC
14555 Elm Row Rd (49224-9646)
PHONE................................517 629-3549
Michelle Moulton, *Manager*
EMP: 33
SALES (corp-wide): 10.4MM **Privately Held**
WEB: www.carrbrothersandsons.com
SIC: 1442 1794 Gravel mining; excavation work
PA: Carr Brothers And Sons, Inc.
   13613 E Erie Rd
   Albion MI 49224
   517 531-3358

(G-120)
CARR BROTHERS AND SONS INC (PA)
13613 E Erie Rd (49224-9620)
PHONE................................517 531-3358
John R Carr Jr, *Vice Pres*
William B Carr III, *Treasurer*
EMP: 10
SQ FT: 5,000
SALES (est): 10.4MM **Privately Held**
WEB: www.carrbrothersandsons.com
SIC: 1442 1794 Gravel mining; excavation work

(G-121)
CASTER CONCEPTS INC
Also Called: Machine Center, The
214 E Michigan Ave (49224-1738)
PHONE................................517 629-2456
Charles James, *Branch Mgr*
EMP: 4 **Privately Held**
WEB: www.casterconcepts.com
SIC: 3429 Manufactured hardware (general)
PA: Caster Concepts, Inc.
   16000 E Michigan Ave
   Albion MI 49224

(G-122)
CASTER CONCEPTS INC (PA)
16000 E Michigan Ave (49224-9193)
PHONE................................888 781-1470
William Dobbins, *President*
Andrew R Dobbins, *Vice Pres*
Jack Turner, *Vice Pres*
Alex Harden, *Research*
Elmer Lee, *Engineer*
◆ EMP: 37 EST: 1988
SQ FT: 48,000
SALES (est): 14.3MM **Privately Held**
WEB: www.casterconcepts.com
SIC: 3562 5072 Casters; casters & glides

(G-123)
CHALLENGER COMMUNICATIONS LLC
704 N Clark St (49224-1481)
PHONE................................517 680-0375
Jill Sorgi, *Sales Staff*
Jill Reschke, *Marketing Staff*
Eugene Sorgi,
Gene Sorgi,
EMP: 14 EST: 2011
SALES (est): 3MM **Privately Held**
WEB: www.challengercommunications.com
SIC: 4899 3699 Communication services; electrical equipment & supplies

(G-124)
DECKER MANUFACTURING CORP (PA)
703 N Clark St (49224-1456)
PHONE................................517 629-3955
Steve Konkle, *President*
Bernard L Konkle, *Chairman*
Henry R Konkle, *Chairman*
Bernard L Konkle II, *COO*
John C Hagy, *Exec VP*
▲ EMP: 93 EST: 1927
SQ FT: 130,000
SALES (est): 21.1MM **Privately Held**
WEB: www.deckernut.com
SIC: 3452 3432 Bolts, nuts, rivets & washers; plumbing fixture fittings & trim

(G-125)
ERNIE ROMANCO
Also Called: Co2 Central
661 N Concord Rd (49224-9647)
PHONE................................517 531-3686
Ernest Romanco, *Owner*
EMP: 5 EST: 1984
SQ FT: 10,000
SALES (est): 108.8K **Privately Held**
WEB: www.co2central.com
SIC: 8748 2899 8711 7381 Business consulting; fire extinguisher charges; engineering services; detective & armored car services

(G-126)
GREAT LAKES WATERJET LASER LLC
1101 Industrial Blvd (49224-9515)
PHONE................................517 629-9900
Kathleen N Johnson, *Mng Member*
Howard Johnson,
EMP: 6 EST: 2010
SQ FT: 12,000
SALES (est): 180K **Privately Held**
WEB: www.greatlakeswaterjetandlaser.com
SIC: 3541 Machine tool replacement & repair parts, metal cutting types

(G-127)
GUARDIAN INDUSTRIES LLC
1000 E North St (49224-1440)
PHONE................................517 629-9464
Duane Faulkner, *Branch Mgr*
EMP: 10
SALES (corp-wide): 36.9B **Privately Held**
WEB: www.guardian.com
SIC: 3211 Flat glass
HQ: Guardian Industries, Llc
   2300 Harmon Rd
   Auburn Hills MI 48326
   248 340-1800

(G-128)
KNAUF INSULATION INC
Also Called: Guardian Fiberglass
1000 E North St (49224-1440)
PHONE................................517 630-2000
Tom Campion, *Manager*
EMP: 103
SALES (corp-wide): 10.7B **Privately Held**
WEB: www.knaufnorthamerica.com
SIC: 3296 1742 Fiberglass insulation; insulation, buildings
HQ: Knauf Insulation, Inc.
   1 Knauf Dr
   Shelbyville IN 46176
   317 398-4434

(G-129)
PATRIOT SOLAR GROUP LLC
708 Valhalla Dr (49224-9402)
PHONE................................517 629-9292
Josh Mathie, *Sales Staff*
Jeffrey Mathie, *Mng Member*
▲ EMP: 27 EST: 2009
SALES (est): 12MM **Privately Held**
WEB: www.patriotsolargroup.com
SIC: 3674 4911 Solar cells;

(G-130)
PREMIER CORRUGATED INC
916 Burstein Dr (49224-4011)
PHONE................................517 629-5700
Jack Schwarz, *President*
EMP: 180 EST: 1986
SALES (est): 8.3MM
SALES (corp-wide): 36.9B **Privately Held**
SIC: 2653 Boxes, corrugated: made from purchased materials
HQ: Georgia-Pacific Corrugated Iii Llc
   5645 W 82nd St
   Indianapolis IN 46278

(G-131)
SHAFER BROS INC
29150 C Dr N (49224-9410)
PHONE................................517 629-4800
Gerald C Shafer, *President*
Ester W Shafer, *Admin Sec*
EMP: 17 EST: 1994
SALES (est): 612.4K **Privately Held**
WEB: www.shaferbros.com
SIC: 3273 Ready-mixed concrete

(G-132)
SHAFER REDI-MIX INC (PA)
Also Called: Shafer Brothers
29150 C Dr N (49224-9410)
P.O. Box 178 (49224-0178)
PHONE................................517 629-4800
Gerald C Shafer, *President*
Doug Shafer, *Vice Pres*
Shawn Patrick, *Manager*
Judd Snider, *Manager*
EMP: 10 EST: 1982
SQ FT: 2,000
SALES (est): 12.5MM **Privately Held**
WEB: www.shaferbros.com
SIC: 3273 Ready-mixed concrete

(G-133)
SINCLAIR DESIGNS & ENGRG LLC
1104 Industrial Blvd (49224-9515)
PHONE................................877 517-0311
Kevin Sinclair, *CEO*
EMP: 24 EST: 2007
SQ FT: 2,500
SALES (est): 3.3MM **Privately Held**
WEB: www.sinclair-designs.com
SIC: 3663 3469 1711 Satellites, communications; stamping metal for the trade; solar energy contractor

(G-134)
SPINDLE GRINDING SERVICE INC
826 Jupiter Dr (49224-9172)
P.O. Box 128 (49224-0128)
PHONE................................517 629-9334
Sally Ammerman, *President*
EMP: 6 EST: 1982
SALES (est): 500K **Privately Held**
WEB: www.spindlegrinding.com
SIC: 3599 Machine shop, jobbing & repair

(G-135)
WORLD CORRUGATED CONTAINER INC
930 Elliott St (49224-9506)
P.O. Box 840 (49224-0840)
PHONE................................517 629-9400
Connie Reuther, *Ch of Bd*
Charles Reuther, *President*
EMP: 16 EST: 1991
SQ FT: 106,000
SALES (est): 737K **Privately Held**
WEB: www.baycorr.com
SIC: 2653 Boxes, corrugated: made from purchased materials

Alden
Antrim County

(G-136)
TRI COUNTY SAND AND STONE INC
Also Called: Tri County Sand & Stone Shop
5318 Bebb Rd (49612)
P.O. Box 268 (49612-0268)
PHONE................................231 331-6549
Larry McCulloch, *President*
Joann McCulloch, *Corp Secy*
Greg McCulloch, *Vice Pres*
Rick McCulloch, *Vice Pres*
EMP: 4 EST: 1966
SALES (est): 537.9K **Privately Held**
SIC: 1442 Common sand mining; gravel mining

Alger
Arenac County

(G-137)
DOWD BROTHERS FORESTRY
Also Called: Dowd Brothers Forest Products
2718 School Rd (48610-9652)
PHONE................................989 345-7459
EMP: 4 EST: 1984
SALES: 150K **Privately Held**
SIC: 2421 Sawmill/Planing Mill

(G-138)
LAHTI FABRICATION INC
2574 School Rd (48610-9651)
PHONE................................989 343-0420
Goerge O Lahti, *President*
George O Lahti, *President*
Joel Heaton, *Info Tech Mgr*
EMP: 36 EST: 1997
SALES (est): 5MM **Privately Held**
WEB: www.lahtifab.com
SIC: 3444 Sheet metal specialties, not stamped

(G-139)
T&K MACHINE
1486 N M 76 (48610-9744)
PHONE................................989 836-0811
Thomas Spencer, *Owner*
EMP: 5 EST: 2005
SALES (est): 249.5K **Privately Held**
WEB: www.tk-machine.com
SIC: 3599 Machine shop, jobbing & repair

(G-140)
ZK ENTERPRISES INC (PA)
Also Called: PSI Satellite
2382 M 33 (48610-9439)
PHONE................................989 728-4439
Rick Kalosis, *President*
Gerard Zajechowski, *Corp Secy*
EMP: 4 EST: 1983
SQ FT: 6,250
SALES (est): 450K **Privately Held**
SIC: 3993 Electric signs

Algonac
St. Clair County

(G-141)
FANNON PRODUCTS LLC (PA)
5318 Pointe Tremble Rd (48001-4367)
PHONE................................810 794-2000
David P Fannon, *Managing Prtnr*
Keith Fannon, *Sales Engr*
David Fannon, *Technology*
▲ EMP: 15 EST: 1993
SQ FT: 800
SALES (est): 1.5MM **Privately Held**
WEB: www.fannoninfrared.com
SIC: 3823 Industrial instrmnts msrmnt display/control process variable

(G-142)
FORMULA ONE TOOL & ENGINEERING
6052 Pointe Tremble Rd (48001-4296)
PHONE................................810 794-3617
Carl W Reams, *President*
EMP: 6 EST: 1989
SQ FT: 2,800
SALES (est): 250K **Privately Held**
SIC: 3545 Machine tool accessories

(G-143)
SIGN WITH SALLY C LLC
10051 Saint John Dr (48001-4238)
PHONE................................586 612-5100
Sally Constance, *Principal*
EMP: 4 EST: 2017
SALES (est): 64.8K **Privately Held**
SIC: 3993 Signs & advertising specialties

▲ = Import ▼ = Export
◆ = Import/Export

Allegan
Allegan County

(G-144)
AGGREGATE AND DEVELOPING LLC
1108 Lincoln Rd (49010-9075)
PHONE..................................269 217-5492
Bill W Smith,
EMP: 5 EST: 2005
SALES (est): 691.9K Privately Held
SIC: 1422 Crushed & broken limestone

(G-145)
ALL-FAB CORPORATION
1235 Lincoln Rd Unit 1235 # 1235 (49010-9706)
PHONE..................................269 673-6572
Jim Plesnicar, *President*
Joe Plesnicar, *Vice Pres*
▲ EMP: 8 EST: 1990
SQ FT: 12,000
SALES (est): 1.5MM Privately Held
WEB: www.allfabcorp.com
SIC: 5084 1799 3548 Machine tools & accessories; welding on site; welding apparatus

(G-146)
ALLEGAN TUBULAR PRODUCTS INC
1276 Lincoln Rd (49010-9172)
P.O. Box 217 (49010-0217)
PHONE..................................269 673-6636
Bernard Sosnowski, *President*
Ed Sosnowski, *Principal*
Ja Dalm, *Vice Pres*
J Verdonk, *Treasurer*
Kris Foerch, *Supervisor*
EMP: 65
SQ FT: 45,000
SALES (est): 12.8MM Privately Held
WEB: www.allegantube.com
SIC: 3498 3714 3567 Tube fabricating (contract bending & shaping); motor vehicle parts & accessories; industrial furnaces & ovens

(G-147)
ALLEGAN VOCAL STUDIO
1871 23rd St (49010-9534)
PHONE..................................719 209-8957
Rachael McKinnon, *Principal*
EMP: 4 EST: 2019
SALES (est): 65.6K Privately Held
WEB: www.wilcoxnewspapers.com
SIC: 2711 Newspapers, publishing & printing

(G-148)
ALLEN PARTNERS LLC
611 N Eastern Ave (49010-9593)
PHONE..................................269 673-4010
Mark Allen,
EMP: 10 EST: 2015
SALES (est): 1.6MM Privately Held
WEB: www.allenpartnersfab.com
SIC: 3441 Fabricated structural metal

(G-149)
B & G CUSTOM WORKS INC
Also Called: Advanced Conveyor Systems
2830 113th Ave (49010-9096)
PHONE..................................269 686-9420
Jennifer Edson, *President*
John Hare, *Admin Sec*
EMP: 17 EST: 1978
SQ FT: 70,000
SALES (est): 1.2MM Privately Held
WEB: www.bgcustomworks.com
SIC: 7692 3441 Welding repair; fabricated structural metal

(G-150)
B AND L METAL FINISHING LLC
755 Airway Dr (49010-8507)
P.O. Box 176 (49010-0176)
PHONE..................................269 767-2225
Kim Collins, *Principal*
EMP: 5 EST: 2017
SALES (est): 155.4K Privately Held
SIC: 3471 Plating & polishing

(G-151)
CHRISTIAN OIL COMPANY
2589 30th St (49010-9268)
PHONE..................................269 673-2218
Aaron Hartman, *President*
Pamela Hartman, *Admin Sec*
EMP: 10 EST: 1946
SQ FT: 10,000
SALES (est): 2.2MM Privately Held
WEB: www.christianoil.com
SIC: 1311 Crude petroleum production; natural gas production

(G-152)
CYRUS FOREST PRODUCTS
4234 127th Ave (49010-9434)
PHONE..................................269 751-6535
Fax: 269 751-6535
EMP: 6
SALES (est): 130K Privately Held
SIC: 2421 Sawmill/Planing Mill

(G-153)
D & J PRECISION MACHINE SVCS
611 N Eastern Ave (49010-9593)
PHONE..................................269 673-4010
Darrel Shank, *President*
James Smith, *Vice Pres*
EMP: 5 EST: 1988
SQ FT: 6,000
SALES (est): 488K Privately Held
WEB: www.djmach.com
SIC: 3599 7692 Machine shop, jobbing & repair; welding repair

(G-154)
DDR HEATING INC (PA)
Also Called: Electro-Heat
700 Grand St (49010-8012)
P.O. Box 190 (49010-0190)
PHONE..................................269 673-2145
Randy Hunziker, *President*
Anita Sponseller, *Purchasing*
David Blair, *Treasurer*
Fred Wilkes, *Marketing Staff*
Diana McDaniel, *Office Mgr*
▲ EMP: 25 EST: 2011
SQ FT: 44,000
SALES (est): 4.1MM Privately Held
WEB: www.ddrheating.com
SIC: 3567 Heating units & devices, industrial: electric

(G-155)
DIGITAL IMAGING GROUP INC
Also Called: Jh Packaging
504 Eastern Ave (49010-9070)
PHONE..................................269 686-8744
Tim Shultz, *President*
Herb Dekoff, *Technical Mgr*
Heidi Schrott, *Manager*
Jeff Wille, *Info Tech Dir*
EMP: 82 EST: 1990
SALES (est): 5.8MM
SALES (corp-wide): 17.5B Publicly Held
SIC: 2752 2759 Business form & card printing, lithographic; commercial printing
HQ: Mps Holdco, Inc.
5800 W Grand River Ave
Lansing MI 48906

(G-156)
E H INC
2870 116th Ave (49010-9004)
PHONE..................................269 673-6456
David Wade, *Ch of Bd*
▲ EMP: 10 EST: 1958
SQ FT: 25,000
SALES (est): 469.2K Privately Held
SIC: 3567 3634 Heating units & devices, industrial: electric; electric housewares & fans

(G-157)
FABRICTED CMPNNTS ASSMBLIES IN
Also Called: F C & A
603 N Eastern Ave (49010-9593)
PHONE..................................269 673-7100
Brian Hicks, *President*
Chris Hicks, *Vice Pres*
Lisa Hizer, *Manager*
EMP: 10 EST: 2003
SQ FT: 12,000
SALES (est): 3.2MM Privately Held
WEB: www.fcanda.com
SIC: 3441 Fabricated structural metal

(G-158)
FINISH LINE FABRICATING LLC
779 38th St (49010-9131)
PHONE..................................269 686-8400
Tim Curry, *Mng Member*
Judy Curry, *Mng Member*
EMP: 5 EST: 1996
SALES (est): 824.9K Privately Held
WEB: www.finishlinefab.com
SIC: 3711 Automobile assembly, including specialty automobiles

(G-159)
FRONTIER TECHNOLOGY INC
2489 118th Ave (49010-9552)
PHONE..................................269 673-9464
Sandra Anderson, *President*
▲ EMP: 10 EST: 1989
SQ FT: 14,000
SALES (est): 943.1K Privately Held
SIC: 3556 3559 Food products machinery; chemical machinery & equipment

(G-160)
HANSE ENVIRONMENTAL INC (PA)
235 Hubbard St (49010-1320)
PHONE..................................269 673-8638
John K Hanse, *President*
John C Hanse, *Corp Secy*
Peter Hanse, *Vice Pres*
John Hanse, *Sales Staff*
▲ EMP: 9 EST: 1991
SQ FT: 5,000
SALES (est): 1.1MM Privately Held
WEB: www.hanseenv.com
SIC: 3829 Measuring & controlling devices

(G-161)
INDEPENDENT TOOL AND MFG CO
661 44th St (49010-9382)
PHONE..................................269 521-4811
James Muenzer, *President*
Linda Muenzer, *Corp Secy*
EMP: 23 EST: 1971
SQ FT: 60,000
SALES (est): 3.4MM Privately Held
WEB: www.independenttool.net
SIC: 3469 3544 Stamping metal for the trade; special dies, tools, jigs & fixtures

(G-162)
KAECHELE PUBLICATIONS INC
Also Called: Allegan News & Gazette
241 Hubbard St (49010-1320)
P.O. Box 189 (49010-0189)
PHONE..................................269 673-5534
Cheryl Kaechele, *President*
Scott Sullivan, *Editor*
Walter Kaechele, *Vice Pres*
EMP: 18 EST: 1982
SALES (est): 1.2MM Privately Held
WEB: www.wilcoxnewspapers.com
SIC: 2711 Newspapers, publishing & printing

(G-163)
KEY GAS COMPONENTS INC
Also Called: Crescent Div Key Gas Cmponents
1303 Lincoln Rd (49010-9701)
PHONE..................................269 673-2151
Greg Huyck, *Engineer*
Michelle Cline, *Office Mgr*
Margaret Williams, *Office Mgr*
Lloyd Esterline, *Branch Mgr*
James Dewitt, *Podiatrist*
EMP: 46
SALES (corp-wide): 12.1MM Privately Held
WEB: www.keygas.com
SIC: 3491 3498 3432 3564 Gas valves & parts, industrial; manifolds, pipe: fabricated from purchased pipe; plumbing fixture fittings & trim; blowers & fans; valves & pipe fittings
PA: Key Gas Components, Inc.
160 Clay St
Marion NC 28752
828 655-1700

(G-164)
L PERRIGO COMPANY (DH)
515 Eastern Ave (49010-9070)
PHONE..................................269 673-8451
Joseph Papa, *CEO*
David Gibbons, *Ch of Bd*
Arthur J Shannon, *Principal*
Ron Janish, *Exec VP*
Richard Hansen, *Vice Pres*
◆ EMP: 4944 EST: 1887
SALES (est): 1.7B Privately Held
WEB: www.perrigo.com
SIC: 2834 Pharmaceutical preparations
HQ: Perrigo Company
515 Eastern Ave
Allegan MI 49010
269 673-8451

(G-165)
L PERRIGO COMPANY
300 Water St (49010-1308)
PHONE..................................269 673-7962
Richard Stec, *Managing Dir*
Jamie Scott, *Editor*
Kristine Smith, *Business Mgr*
Vincent Egolf, *Counsel*
James E Dillard, *Exec VP*
EMP: 5 Privately Held
WEB: www.perrigo.com
SIC: 2834 Adrenal pharmaceutical preparations
HQ: L. Perrigo Company
515 Eastern Ave
Allegan MI 49010
269 673-8451

(G-166)
L PERRIGO COMPANY
809 Airway Dr (49010-8516)
PHONE..................................269 673-7962
EMP: 4 Privately Held
WEB: www.perrigo.com
SIC: 2834 Pharmaceutical preparations
HQ: L. Perrigo Company
515 Eastern Ave
Allegan MI 49010
269 673-8451

(G-167)
L PERRIGO COMPANY
500 Eastern Ave (49010-9070)
PHONE..................................269 673-1608
Diane Morgan, *Project Mgr*
Susan Dalton-Akers, *Opers Staff*
Guillermo Diaz, *Opers Staff*
Harliss Fortin, *Mfg Staff*
Ryan Kastamo, *Engineer*
EMP: 4 Privately Held
WEB: www.perrigo.com
SIC: 2834 Pharmaceutical preparations
HQ: L. Perrigo Company
515 Eastern Ave
Allegan MI 49010
269 673-8451

(G-168)
LAKESIDE MECHANICAL CONTRS
1741 Forest Cove Trl (49010-8407)
P.O. Box 610, Douglas (49406-0610)
PHONE..................................616 786-0211
Bruce Visser, *President*
Tara Kolkema, *General Mgr*
EMP: 36 EST: 1986
SQ FT: 4,800
SALES (est): 511.7K Privately Held
WEB: www.lakesidemechanical.com
SIC: 7692 1799 Welding repair; welding on site

(G-169)
LANE SOFT WATER
132 Grand St (49010-1196)
PHONE..................................269 673-3272
Terry W Johnson, *Partner*
Pamela Johnson, *Partner*
EMP: 6 EST: 1959
SALES (est): 500K Privately Held
SIC: 3589 7389 Water filters & softeners, household type; water softener service

Allegan - Allegan County (G-170)

(G-170)
MATERIAL TRANSFER AND STOR INC
1214 Lincoln Rd (49010-9077)
P.O. Box 218 (49010-0218)
PHONE.................................269 673-2125
Scott Nyhof, *President*
Brenda Nyhof, *Corp Secy*
Tom Hofman, *Vice Pres*
Abby Vandenberg, *Purchasing*
EMP: 25 **EST:** 1989
SQ FT: 250,000
SALES (est): 5.5MM **Privately Held**
WEB: www.materialtransfer.com
SIC: 3535 Conveyors & conveying equipment

(G-171)
NASH CAR TRAILER CORPORATION
1305 Lincoln Rd (49010-9169)
P.O. Box 44 (49010-0044)
PHONE.................................269 673-5776
Monty Sailer, *President*
Daven Hansen, *Vice Pres*
Kris Nash, *Treasurer*
EMP: 7 **EST:** 2005
SALES (est): 158K **Privately Held**
SIC: 3799 Trailers & trailer equipment

(G-172)
P J PRINTING
633 114th Ave Ste 5 (49010-9061)
P.O. Box 278 (49010-0278)
PHONE.................................269 673-3372
Douglas Ernst, *President*
EMP: 5 **EST:** 1975
SALES (est): 428.3K **Privately Held**
WEB: www.pjprinting.org
SIC: 2752 Commercial printing, offset

(G-173)
PBM NUTRITIONALS LLC
515 Eastern Ave (49010-9070)
PHONE.................................269 673-8451
Joseph C Papa, *Ch of Bd*
Judy L Brown, *Vice Pres*
John T Hendrickson, *Vice Pres*
Art Shannon, *Vice Pres*
Thelma Edwards, *Buyer*
EMP: 21 **EST:** 2015
SALES (est): 7.7MM **Privately Held**
WEB: www.perrigo.com
SIC: 2834 Pharmaceutical preparations
HQ: Perrigo Company
515 Eastern Ave
Allegan MI 49010
269 673-8451

(G-174)
PERRIGO CHINA BUS TRUSTEE LLC
515 Eastern Ave (49010-9070)
PHONE.................................269 673-8451
EMP: 33 **EST:** 2005
SALES (est): 1.3MM **Privately Held**
WEB: www.perrigo.com
SIC: 2834 Analgesics
HQ: Perrigo Company
515 Eastern Ave
Allegan MI 49010
269 673-8451

(G-175)
PERRIGO COMPANY
Also Called: Perrigo Logistics Center
900 Industrial Dr (49010-8544)
PHONE.................................269 686-1973
David Stahl, *Opers Spvr*
Scott Schroeder, *Engineer*
Gary Tenney, *Credit Mgr*
Kara Goodnature, *Marketing Staff*
Nathan Hoffman, *Branch Mgr*
EMP: 4 **Privately Held**
WEB: www.perrigo.com
SIC: 2834 Pharmaceutical preparations
HQ: Perrigo Company
515 Eastern Ave
Allegan MI 49010
269 673-8451

(G-176)
PERRIGO COMPANY (HQ)
515 Eastern Ave (49010-9070)
PHONE.................................269 673-8451
Murray S Kessler, *President*
Svend Andersen, *President*
Douglas S Boothe, *President*
Rich Sorota, *President*
Heather Wesler, *Editor*
◆ **EMP:** 4400 **EST:** 1987
SALES (est): 2.5B **Privately Held**
WEB: www.perrigo.com
SIC: 2834 Analgesics

(G-177)
PERRIGO COMPANY
515 Eastern Ave (49010-9070)
PHONE.................................269 673-7962
EMP: 12 **Privately Held**
SIC: 2834 Mfg Pharmaceutical Preparations
HQ: Perrigo Company
515 Eastern Ave
Allegan MI 49010
269 673-8451

(G-178)
PERRIGO NEW YORK INC
515 Eastern Ave (49010-9070)
PHONE.................................269 673-8451
EMP: 15 **Privately Held**
WEB: www.perrigo.com
SIC: 2834 Pharmaceutical preparations
HQ: Perrigo New York, Inc.
1700 Bathgate Ave
Bronx NY 10457
718 960-9900

(G-179)
PMI BRANDED PHARMACEUTICALS
Also Called: Perrigo Brnded Phrmcticals Inc
515 Eastern Ave (49010-9070)
PHONE.................................269 673-8451
Murray S Kessler, *President*
EMP: 10 **EST:** 2019
SALES (est): 3.9MM **Privately Held**
WEB: www.perrigo.com
SIC: 2834 Pharmaceutical preparations
HQ: Perrigo Company
515 Eastern Ave
Allegan MI 49010
269 673-8451

(G-180)
RAPA ELECTRIC INC
1173 Lincoln Rd (49010-9077)
PHONE.................................269 673-3157
Ronnie E Rapa, *President*
Dominik Bergner, *VP Opers*
William Wall, *Purch Mgr*
Misty Jackson, *Buyer*
Steve Wilcox, *Engineer*
EMP: 25 **EST:** 1966
SQ FT: 15,000
SALES (est): 6MM **Privately Held**
WEB: www.rapaelectric.com
SIC: 5063 7694 Motors, electric; electric motor repair

(G-181)
RIVER VALLEY MACHINE INC
600 N Eastern Ave (49010-9592)
PHONE.................................269 673-8070
Lyle Kollar, *President*
Gale Kollar, *Admin Sec*
EMP: 10 **EST:** 1981
SALES (est): 397.6K **Privately Held**
SIC: 3312 3498 3494 3433 Tubes, steel & iron; fabricated pipe & fittings; valves & pipe fittings; heating equipment, except electric; manufactured hardware (general)

(G-182)
SOUTHWEST GRAVEL INC
Also Called: R Smith and Sons
3641 108th Ave (49010-8111)
PHONE.................................269 673-4665
Roger A Smith, *President*
EMP: 6 **EST:** 1992
SALES (est): 866.9K **Privately Held**
WEB: www.rsmithandsons.com
SIC: 1442 Construction sand mining; gravel mining

(G-183)
STUDTMANS STUFF (PA)
422 N Cedar St (49010-1206)
PHONE.................................269 673-3126
EMP: 4

SALES: 40K **Privately Held**
SIC: 3999 5999 Mfg Misc Products Ret Misc Merchandise

(G-184)
WAANDERS CONCRETE CO
3169 Babylon Rd (49010-9205)
PHONE.................................269 673-6352
Mark Waanders, *President*
Chuck Waanders, *Vice Pres*
Irene Waanders, *Treasurer*
EMP: 17 **EST:** 1935
SALES (est): 3.2MM **Privately Held**
WEB: www.waandersconcrete.com
SIC: 3273 3271 1442 1422 Ready-mixed concrete; concrete block & brick; construction sand & gravel; crushed & broken limestone

(G-185)
WEST MICHIGAN MEDICAL
595 Jenner Dr (49010-1516)
PHONE.................................269 673-2141
Debbie Sloan, *Editor*
Bill Carlson, *Manager*
EMP: 5 **EST:** 2015
SALES (est): 107.3K **Privately Held**
SIC: 2711 Newspapers

(G-186)
WEST MICHIGAN METALS LLC
1168 33rd St (49010-8302)
PHONE.................................269 978-7021
Gerard H Bierling,
EMP: 5 **EST:** 2007
SALES (est): 626K **Privately Held**
SIC: 1751 1791 3441 Lightweight steel framing (metal stud) installation; building front installation metal; fabricated structural metal

Allen Park
Wayne County

(G-187)
AEES POWER SYSTEMS LTD PARTNR (DH)
Also Called: Engineered Plastic Components
999 Republic Dr (48101-3668)
PHONE.................................248 489-4900
Brian Schubert, *President*
James Waling, *Sales Staff*
Frank Sovis, *Mng Member*
Walter E Frankiewicz,
▲ **EMP:** 80 **EST:** 2002
SALES (est): 465MM **Privately Held**
WEB: www.aeesinc.com
SIC: 3694 Harness wiring sets, internal combustion engines

(G-188)
ALLEGRA MARKETING PRINT MAIL
17140 Ecorse Rd (48101-2454)
PHONE.................................313 382-8033
EMP: 5 **EST:** 2019
SALES (est): 110.2K **Privately Held**
WEB: www.allegramarketingprint.com
SIC: 2752 Commercial printing, offset

(G-189)
ALLEGRA MARKETING PRINT MAIL
7307 Allen Rd (48101-1920)
PHONE.................................313 429-0916
EMP: 5 **EST:** 2019
SALES (est): 82.4K **Privately Held**
WEB: www.allegramarketingprint.com
SIC: 2752 Commercial printing, offset

(G-190)
ARGO AI LLC
17000 Federal Dr (48101-3645)
PHONE.................................313 908-2447
Ryan Skaff, *Engineer*
Dave Newman, *Software Engr*
Tintin Yu, *Software Engr*
Sonal Onkar, *Technical Staff*
Ghassan Atmeh, *Sr Software Eng*
EMP: 7

SALES (corp-wide): 26.6MM **Privately Held**
WEB: www.argo.ai
SIC: 3714 Motor vehicle parts & accessories
PA: Argo Ai, Llc
2545 Railroad St Ste 400
Pittsburgh PA 15222
412 525-3483

(G-191)
CULTIVATION STATION INC
6540 Allen Rd (48101-2002)
PHONE.................................313 383-1766
Jeffrey Shahady, *Branch Mgr*
EMP: 5
SALES (corp-wide): 1.4MM **Privately Held**
WEB: www.cultivationstation.com
SIC: 3999 Hydroponic equipment
PA: The Cultivation Station Inc
19690 E 9 Mile Rd
Saint Clair Shores MI 48080
586 775-9485

(G-192)
DIAS HOLDING INC
16630 Southfield Rd (48101-2555)
PHONE.................................313 928-1254
Hung L Huang, *Ch of Bd*
Wang B C Huang, *CFO*
EMP: 13 **EST:** 1999
SALES (est): 296.7K **Privately Held**
WEB: www.diasholding.wordpress.com
SIC: 3462 3452 Automotive & internal combustion engine forgings; automotive forgings, ferrous: crankshaft, engine, axle, etc.; machinery forgings, ferrous; railroad wheels, axles, frogs or other equipment: forged; cotter pins, metal; dowel pins, metal; screw eyes & hooks; spring washers, metal

(G-193)
DOWNRIVER CREATIVE WOODWORKING
4631 Parkside Blvd (48101-3205)
PHONE.................................313 274-4090
Stephen Nikodemski, *Principal*
Scott Berels, *Technical Staff*
EMP: 4 **EST:** 2010
SALES (est): 303.5K **Privately Held**
SIC: 2431 Millwork

(G-194)
FORD MOTOR COMPANY
1555 Fairlane Dr Ste 100 (48101-3629)
PHONE.................................313 594-4090
Jennifer Balthis, *Opers Mgr*
Karen Fisher, *Opers Staff*
Suzie Furton, *Manager*
Michael Gagnon, *Network Enginr*
EMP: 14
SALES (corp-wide): 127.1B **Publicly Held**
WEB: www.ford.com
SIC: 5511 3714 Automobiles, new & used; motor vehicle parts & accessories
PA: Ford Motor Company
1 American Rd
Dearborn MI 48126
313 322-3000

(G-195)
GATY
8989 Fox Ave (48101-1501)
PHONE.................................313 381-2853
James Gaty, *Principal*
EMP: 5 **EST:** 2010
SALES (est): 65.8K **Privately Held**
SIC: 2741 Miscellaneous publishing

(G-196)
HUMMUS & CO
23117 Outer Dr (48101-3100)
PHONE.................................313 769-5557
EMP: 4 **EST:** 2018
SALES (est): 33.3K **Privately Held**
SIC: 2731 Book publishing

(G-197)
JOBS INC
14829 Philomene Blvd (48101-2123)
PHONE.................................810 714-0522
Marco Livelli, *President*
▲ **EMP:** 3 **EST:** 1984

GEOGRAPHIC SECTION

Allendale - Ottawa County (G-223)

SALES (est): 1.5MM **Privately Held**
WEB: www.jobs.it
SIC: 3599 Custom machinery
HQ: Jobs Automazione Spa
Via Emilia Parmense 164
Piacenza PC 29122

(G-198)
LISA BAIN
9636 Chatham Ave (48101-1361)
PHONE..................................313 389-9661
Lisa Bain, *Principal*
EMP: 5 EST: 2005
SALES (est): 78.1K **Privately Held**
SIC: 2674 Cement bags: made from purchased materials

(G-199)
M J DAY MACHINE TOOL COMPANY
19231 Van Born Rd (48101-2814)
PHONE..................................313 730-1200
Mitchell Day, *President*
Mitch Day, *Principal*
EMP: 6 EST: 1979
SALES (est): 598.1K **Privately Held**
SIC: 3449 Miscellaneous metalwork

(G-200)
MARTEL TOOL CORPORATION
5831 Pelham Rd (48101-2899)
PHONE..................................313 278-2420
Steven Martel, *CEO*
David Martel, *President*
Don Hass, *Principal*
Denise Clark, *Corp Secy*
Joseph Slifka, *Vice Pres*
EMP: 11
SQ FT: 10,000
SALES (est): 1.5MM **Privately Held**
WEB: www.marteltool.com
SIC: 3823 3829 3545 Industrial instrmnts msrmnt display/control process variable; measuring & controlling devices; gauges (machine tool accessories)

(G-201)
ONESIAN ENTERPRISES INC
10520 Balfour Ave (48101-1143)
PHONE..................................313 382-5875
Charles Onesian, *President*
EMP: 10 EST: 1997
SALES (est): 200.1K **Privately Held**
SIC: 2711 Newspapers

(G-202)
PERMACOAT INC
14868 Champaign Rd (48101-1619)
PHONE..................................313 388-7798
Robert Lahousse, *CEO*
Shane La Housse, *President*
EMP: 8 EST: 2002
SQ FT: 2,000
SALES (est): 105.1K **Privately Held**
SIC: 3479 Aluminum coating of metal products

(G-203)
RIVIERA INDUSTRIES INC
Also Called: Major Products
16038 Southfield Rd (48101-2563)
PHONE..................................313 381-5500
Donald Riviera, *President*
EMP: 7 EST: 1993
SQ FT: 4,000 **Privately Held**
WEB: www.rivieratech.com
SIC: 3545 Boring machine attachments (machine tool accessories)

(G-204)
ROSE NAIL
3565 Fairlane Dr (48101-2876)
PHONE..................................313 271-8804
Nghien Hoang, *Owner*
EMP: 6 EST: 2007
SALES (est): 128.9K **Privately Held**
SIC: 2844 Manicure preparations

(G-205)
ROUSH ENTERPRISES INC
16630 Southfield Rd (48101-2555)
PHONE..................................313 294-8200
Patrick German, *Project Mgr*
Patrick Marke, *Opers Mgr*
John Gerke, *Mfg Staff*
Andrew Backy, *Buyer*

Tony Labedz, *Buyer*
EMP: 646 **Privately Held**
WEB: www.roush.com
SIC: 3714 3711 Motor vehicle parts & accessories; motor vehicles & car bodies
PA: Roush Enterprises, Inc.
34300 W 9 Mile Rd
Farmington MI 48335

(G-206)
SIEMENS INDUSTRY SOFTWARE INC
1555 Fairlane Dr Ste 300 (48101-2869)
PHONE..................................313 317-6100
Barbara Havard, *Manager*
EMP: 4
SALES (corp-wide): 67.4B **Privately Held**
WEB: www.siemens.com
SIC: 7372 Business oriented computer software
HQ: Siemens Industry Software Inc.
5800 Granite Pkwy Ste 600
Plano TX 75024
972 987-3000

(G-207)
STEEL MILL COMPONENTS INC (PA)
17000 Ecorse Rd (48101-2452)
PHONE..................................313 386-0893
Andrew B Pellegrino, *CEO*
Chris Klompstra, *CFO*
EMP: 4 EST: 2008
SQ FT: 40,000
SALES (est): 3.6MM **Privately Held**
WEB: www.steelmillcomponents.com
SIC: 3441 Building components, structural steel

(G-208)
TERADYNE INC
Also Called: Teradyne Diagnostic Solutions
1800 Fairlane Dr Ste 200 (48101-2777)
PHONE..................................313 425-3900
EMP: 5
SALES (corp-wide): 3.1B **Publicly Held**
WEB: www.teradyne.com
SIC: 3825 3643 3829 3678 Semiconductor test equipment; connectors & terminals for electrical devices; measuring & controlling devices; electronic connectors; semiconductors & related devices
PA: Teradyne, Inc.
600 Riverpark Dr
North Reading MA 01864
978 370-2700

(G-209)
VENTCON INC
500 Enterprise Dr (48101-3091)
PHONE..................................313 336-4000
Sammy Speen, *Vice Ch Bd*
Dennis Berger, *Vice Ch Bd*
Todd W Hill, *President*
Ray Sliwinski, *Exec VP*
Dennis T Monaghan, *Vice Pres*
EMP: 120 EST: 1970
SQ FT: 32,000
SALES (est): 24.4MM **Privately Held**
WEB: www.ventcon.com
SIC: 3444 Sheet metalwork

(G-210)
WHIPPLE PRINTING INC
17140 Ecorse Rd (48101-1982)
PHONE..................................313 382-8033
Joe Hirsch, *President*
EMP: 4 EST: 1967
SALES (est): 367K **Privately Held**
SIC: 2759 2752 Letterpress printing; commercial printing, offset

(G-211)
ZELEDYNE GLASS CORP
17333 Federal Dr Ste 230 (48101-3647)
PHONE..................................615 350-7500
Jeff Kaiser, *Principal*
EMP: 9 EST: 2018
SALES (est): 448.6K **Privately Held**
SIC: 3465 Automotive stampings

Allendale
Ottawa County

(G-212)
ALLEGRA PRINT IMAGING
5985 Farmview Dr (49401-9001)
PHONE..................................616 446-6269
EMP: 4 EST: 2018
SALES (est): 83.9K **Privately Held**
WEB: www.allegramarketingprint.com
SIC: 2752 Commercial printing, offset

(G-213)
ALUWAX DENTAL PRODUCTS CO INC
5260 Edgewater Dr (49401-8401)
P.O. Box 87 (49401-0087)
PHONE..................................616 895-4385
Patrick Gemmen, *President*
EMP: 5 EST: 1935
SQ FT: 2,190
SALES (est): 681.7K **Privately Held**
WEB: www.aluwaxdental.com
SIC: 3843 Impression material, dental; wax, dental

(G-214)
ANTARA SYSTEMS LLC
Also Called: Jimdi Plastics
5375 Edgeway Dr (49401-8476)
PHONE..................................616 895-7766
Dave Gerdeman, *VP Sls/Mktg*
Jay Dewitt, *CFO*
Reed Lawrie, *Mng Member*
EMP: 70 EST: 2018
SALES (est): 5MM **Privately Held**
SIC: 3089 Injection molding of plastics

(G-215)
BLIND BULL LLC
7420 Watermark Dr (49401-8627)
PHONE..................................616 516-4881
Neal Deridder, *Principal*
EMP: 5 EST: 2016
SALES (est): 82.3K **Privately Held**
SIC: 2591 Window blinds

(G-216)
CANVAS TOWNHOMES ALLENDALE
10295 48th Ave (49401-7335)
PHONE..................................616 499-2680
EMP: 4 EST: 2019
SALES (est): 46.5K **Privately Held**
WEB: www.canvasallendale.com
SIC: 2211 Canvas

(G-217)
CONSTRUCTIVE SHEET METAL INC
Also Called: C S M
11670 46th Ave (49401-8834)
PHONE..................................616 245-5306
Terry Lantz, *President*
Carl Vrooman, *Project Mgr*
Tab Jonge, *Sales Executive*
John Luscomb, *Supervisor*
EMP: 34 EST: 1958
SQ FT: 36,000
SALES (est): 4.1MM **Privately Held**
WEB: www.csm-gr.com
SIC: 3444 1796 3564 3535 Ducts, sheet metal; installing building equipment; blowers & fans; conveyors & conveying equipment; miscellaneous fabricated wire products; fabricated plate work (boiler shop)

(G-218)
FRANDALE SUB SHOP
11250 Kistler Dr Unit 5 (49401-8070)
PHONE..................................616 446-6311
Sonya Bolks, *President*
EMP: 10 EST: 1976
SALES (est): 495.9K **Privately Held**
SIC: 2099 2038 Sandwiches, assembled & packaged: for wholesale market; pizza, frozen

(G-219)
GRAND VALLEY STATE UNIVERSITY
Also Called: University Communications
1 Campus Dr (49401-9403)
PHONE..................................847 744-0508
Lynn M Blue, *Vice Pres*
Janet Vail, *Research*
David Good, *Marketing Staff*
Sally Langa, *Manager*
Tim Selgo, *Director*
EMP: 7
SALES (corp-wide): 381.1MM **Privately Held**
WEB: www.gvsu.edu
SIC: 2741 8221 Newsletter publishing; university
PA: Grand Valley State University
1 Campus Dr
Allendale MI 49401
616 331-5000

(G-220)
GREAT LAKES LASER DYNAMICS INC
Also Called: Laser-Dynamics
4881 Allen Park Dr (49401-8625)
PHONE..................................616 892-7070
William Herberg, *President*
Ken Koster, *Vice Pres*
Paula Mayers, *Purch Agent*
Derek Gorter, *Engineer*
Billie Austin, *Manager*
EMP: 60 EST: 1999
SQ FT: 48,000
SALES (est): 15.4MM **Privately Held**
WEB: www.laserdynamics.com
SIC: 3443 3499 Fabricated plate work (boiler shop); machine bases, metal; metal household articles

(G-221)
JIMDI RECEIVABLES INC
5375 Edgeway Dr (49401-8476)
PHONE..................................616 895-7766
Richard Schrotenboer, *President*
David L Gerdeman, *Vice Pres*
Ken Koetsier, *Engineer*
Jay Dewitt, *CFO*
Mike McDaniel, *Info Tech Dir*
▲ EMP: 30 EST: 1997
SQ FT: 25,000
SALES (est): 5.3MM **Privately Held**
WEB: www.jimdiplastics.com
SIC: 3544 3089 Special dies, tools, jigs & fixtures; injection molding of plastics

(G-222)
LAW ENFORCEMENT SUPPLY INC
10920 64th Ave (49401-8065)
P.O. Box 85 (49401-0085)
PHONE..................................616 895-7875
Gerald Carter Sr, *President*
Michael Steel, *District Mgr*
Rod Bosker, *Vice Pres*
Sheryle Boscar, *Treasurer*
Jose Ferrando, *Manager*
EMP: 4 EST: 1973
SQ FT: 2,184
SALES (est): 534.5K **Privately Held**
WEB: www.porta-clip.com
SIC: 3496 Clips & fasteners, made from purchased wire

(G-223)
LEPRINO FOODS COMPANY
4700 Rich St (49401-9237)
PHONE..................................616 895-5800
Steven Burchett, *Safety Dir*
Nick Opper, *Branch Mgr*
Jennifer Schafer, *Supervisor*
Kenitha Severn, *Supervisor*
EMP: 253
SALES (corp-wide): 1.9B **Privately Held**
WEB: www.leprinofoods.com
SIC: 2022 Natural cheese
PA: Leprino Foods Company
1830 W 38th Ave
Denver CO 80211
303 480-2600

Allendale - Ottawa County (G-224)

(G-224)
M2 SCIENTIFICS LLC
4850 Allen Park Dr Ste 2 (49401-8615)
PHONE..................................616 379-9080
Jonathan Mosher, *CEO*
Joshua Mosher, *General Mgr*
EMP: 17 **EST:** 2012
SALES (est): 1MM **Privately Held**
WEB: www.m2sci.com
SIC: 3821 3231 3596 7389 Centrifuges, laboratory; laboratory glassware; scales & balances, except laboratory; business services

(G-225)
METTEK LLC
11480 53rd Ave Ste B (49401-8502)
PHONE..................................616 895-2033
Dave Munkres, *Cust Mgr*
Mark Ensink, *Sales Staff*
Doug Ensink,
Sandy Ensink,
Tracy Ensink,
EMP: 4 **EST:** 2006
SQ FT: 8,300
SALES (est): 358.1K **Privately Held**
WEB: www.mettekllc.com
SIC: 2759 Screen printing

(G-226)
MORREN MOLD & MACHINE INC
10345 60th Ave (49401-8355)
PHONE..................................616 892-7474
David Morren, *President*
Sandra Morren, *Vice Pres*
EMP: 7 **EST:** 1995
SQ FT: 12,500
SALES (est): 500K **Privately Held**
SIC: 3089 3599 Injection molding of plastics; machine & other job shop work

(G-227)
MUG SHOTS BURGERS AND BREWS
4633 Lake Michigan Dr (49401-9529)
PHONE..................................616 895-2337
Michael Sirotko, *Principal*
EMP: 5 **EST:** 2015
SALES (est): 231.1K **Privately Held**
WEB: www.mugshotsburgersandbrews.com
SIC: 2082 Malt beverages

(G-228)
SKYLINE WINDOW CLEANING INC
Also Called: Skyline Fall Protection
8528 Lake Michigan Dr (49401-7533)
PHONE..................................616 895-4143
Rick Ensing, *President*
Matthew Ensing, *Vice Pres*
Joel Buck, *Opers Mgr*
EMP: 23 **EST:** 2007
SQ FT: 2,600
SALES (est): 2.9MM **Privately Held**
WEB: www.skylinefp.com
SIC: 3842 5999 Personal safety equipment; safety supplies & equipment

(G-229)
WEST SHORE SERVICES INC (PA)
6620 Lake Michigan Dr (49401-9257)
P.O. Box 188 (49401-0188)
PHONE..................................616 895-4347
Jeff Dupilka, *President*
Dan Stollings, *Project Mgr*
Luke Miller, *Opers Staff*
Ken Council, *Human Res Dir*
Larry Jones, *Sales Staff*
EMP: 24 **EST:** 1972
SQ FT: 13,100
SALES (est): 4.5MM **Privately Held**
WEB: www.westshoreservices.com
SIC: 3669 1799 2521 Sirens, electric: vehicle, marine, industrial & air raid; building mover, including houses; wood office furniture

Allenton
St. Clair County

(G-230)
LEHMAN PUBLISHINGCOM
15997 Hough Rd (48002-3508)
PHONE..................................810 395-4535
Dana Lehman, *Principal*
EMP: 4 **EST:** 2017
SALES (est): 37.5K **Privately Held**
WEB: www.lehmanpublishing.com
SIC: 2741 Miscellaneous publishing

(G-231)
MCCALLUM FABRICATING LLC
13927 Hough Rd (48002-3913)
PHONE..................................586 784-5555
Donald Mc Callum, *Owner*
EMP: 10 **EST:** 1948
SQ FT: 7,200
SALES (est): 492.5K **Privately Held**
SIC: 3914 Stainless steel ware

(G-232)
TIDE RINGS LLC
14150 Hough Rd (48002-3809)
PHONE..................................586 206-3142
Kevin M Lutz, *Principal*
EMP: 4 **EST:** 2009
SALES (est): 250K **Privately Held**
WEB: www.tidering.com
SIC: 3999 Manufacturing industries

Alma
Gratiot County

(G-233)
ADW INDUSTRIES INC
130 Woodworth Ave (48801-2441)
P.O. Box 878 (48801-0878)
PHONE..................................989 466-4742
Thomas C Adle, *President*
EMP: 25 **EST:** 1982
SQ FT: 10,000
SALES (est): 3.8MM **Privately Held**
WEB: www.hiumc.org
SIC: 3535 3714 3441 Conveyors & conveying equipment; motor vehicle parts & accessories; fabricated structural metal

(G-234)
ALMA CONCRETE PRODUCTS COMPANY (PA)
1277 Bridge Rd (48801-9700)
P.O. Box 389, Mount Pleasant (48804-0389)
PHONE..................................989 463-5476
Ralph J Fisher Jr, *President*
James O Fisher, *Corp Secy*
Arthur J Fisher, *Vice Pres*
EMP: 3 **EST:** 1959
SALES (est): 1.2MM **Privately Held**
WEB: www.central-concrete.net
SIC: 3273 Ready-mixed concrete

(G-235)
ALMA CONTAINER CORPORATION
1000 Charles Ave (48801-9603)
P.O. Box 98 (48801-0098)
PHONE..................................989 463-2106
Michael D Maybank, *President*
Michael Maybank, *Vice Pres*
Don Weaver, *Site Mgr*
Susan Maybank, *Treasurer*
Kathy Legene, *Admin Sec*
EMP: 28 **EST:** 1962
SQ FT: 52,000
SALES (est): 5MM **Privately Held**
WEB: www.almacontainer.com
SIC: 2653 Boxes, corrugated: made from purchased materials

(G-236)
ALMA PRODUCTS COMPANY
150 N Court Ave (48801-1910)
PHONE..................................989 463-1151
Bill Carroll, *Site Mgr*
Jason Alderson, *Engineer*
Brad Broucher, *Manager*
Dennis Snyder, *Manager*
EMP: 4 **Privately Held**
WEB: www.almaproducts.com
SIC: 3566 Torque converters, except automotive
HQ: Alma Products I Llc
  2000 Michigan Ave
  Alma MI 48801
  989 463-1151

(G-237)
ALMA PRODUCTS I LLC (DH)
2000 Michigan Ave (48801-9796)
PHONE..................................989 463-1151
Alan Galtan, *CEO*
Thomas H Quinn, *Ch of Bd*
Michael Flint, *President*
William Schader, *Engineer*
Andy Gasser, *CFO*
◆ **EMP:** 178 **EST:** 1999
SQ FT: 180,000
SALES (est): 25.7MM **Privately Held**
WEB: www.almaproducts.com
SIC: 3714 Motor vehicle parts & accessories

(G-238)
ALUDYNE NORTH AMERICA LLC
250 Adams St (48801-2517)
PHONE..................................989 463-6166
Dustin McDonald, *Branch Mgr*
EMP: 330
SALES (corp-wide): 1.5B **Privately Held**
SIC: 3363 3714 Aluminum die-castings; motor vehicle parts & accessories
HQ: Aludyne North America Llc
  300 Galleria Ofcntr Ste 5
  Southfield MI 48034
  248 728-8700

(G-239)
AVALON & TAHOE MFG INC
903 Michigan Ave (48801-1933)
P.O. Box 698 (48801-0698)
PHONE..................................989 463-2112
Jim Wolf, *President*
Gregg Knight, *Exec VP*
Brian Richards, *Vice Pres*
Kelly Trevino, *Purch Agent*
Duane Dinninger, *Engineer*
▼ **EMP:** 130 **EST:** 1981
SQ FT: 150,000
SALES (est): 23.3MM **Privately Held**
WEB: www.avalonpontoons.com
SIC: 3732 Pontoons, except aircraft & inflatable

(G-240)
ETX INC (DH)
Also Called: Alma Products Company
2000 Michigan Ave (48801-9703)
PHONE..................................989 463-1151
Alan Gatlin, *President*
Lorie Sparks, *Cust Mgr*
Linda Gray, *Manager*
EMP: 2128 **EST:** 2006
SALES (est): 154.9MM **Privately Held**
WEB: www.transtar1.com
SIC: 3714 Motor vehicle parts & accessories
HQ: Transtar Industries Llc
  7350 Young Dr
  Cleveland OH 44146
  440 232-5100

(G-241)
ETX HOLDINGS INC (DH)
2000 Michigan Ave (48801-9703)
PHONE..................................989 463-1151
Thomas H Quinn, *Ch of Bd*
Alan Gatlin, *President*
Andy Gasser, *CFO*
▼ **EMP:** 3 **EST:** 2006
SALES (est): 183.5MM **Privately Held**
WEB: www.transtar1.com
SIC: 3585 3621 3714 5013 Compressors for refrigeration & air conditioning equipment; motors & generators; motor vehicle parts & accessories; automotive supplies & parts; fittings for pipe, plastic
HQ: Transtar Industries Llc
  7350 Young Dr
  Cleveland OH 44146
  440 232-5100

(G-242)
INTEGRITY SLTONS FELD SVCS INC
Also Called: Is Field Services
401 Republic Ave (48801-2046)
PHONE..................................517 481-4724
Joshua Brewer, *President*
Josh Brewer, *President*
EMP: 49 **EST:** 2013
SALES (est): 6.8MM **Privately Held**
WEB: www.isfieldservices.com
SIC: 1389 7389 Servicing oil & gas wells;

(G-243)
INTERNTNAL AUTO CMPNNTS GROUP
1965 Williams Rd (48801-2086)
PHONE..................................989 620-7649
Brian Tenny, *COO*
Jackie Kuzmanovski, *Accounts Mgr*
Susan Gardner, *Manager*
Tammy Wright, *Manager*
David Dickey, *Technology*
EMP: 115 **Privately Held**
WEB: www.iacgroup.com
SIC: 3714 Motor vehicle parts & accessories
HQ: International Automotive Components Group North America, Inc.
  27777 Franklin Rd # 2000
  Southfield MI 48034

(G-244)
KIDS WORLD NEWS TOO
555 E Downie St (48801-1919)
PHONE..................................517 202-1808
William Miniard, *Principal*
EMP: 5 **EST:** 2007
SALES (est): 180.3K **Privately Held**
SIC: 2711 Newspapers, publishing & printing

(G-245)
MERRILL INSTITUTE INC
520 Republic Ave (48801-2049)
PHONE..................................989 462-0330
Jacob Bebow, *IT/INT Sup*
Mark Johnston, *Director*
Teri Webster, *Education*
EMP: 6 **EST:** 2012
SALES (est): 575.2K **Privately Held**
WEB: www.merrillinstitute.com
SIC: 3441 Fabricated structural metal

(G-246)
MERRILL TECHNOLOGIES GROUP INC
Also Called: Merrill Fabricators
520 Republic Ave (48801-2049)
PHONE..................................989 462-0330
Robert Yackel, *CEO*
EMP: 123
SALES (corp-wide): 191.1MM **Privately Held**
WEB: www.merrilltg.com
SIC: 3533 3443 3446 Oil & gas field machinery; tanks, standard or custom fabricated: metal plate; architectural metalwork
PA: Merrill Technologies Group, Inc.
  400 Florence St
  Saginaw MI 48602
  989 791-6676

(G-247)
MICHIGAN PAVING AND MTLS CO
1950 Williams Rd (48801-2085)
PHONE..................................989 463-1323
James Monroe, *Division Mgr*
EMP: 14
SALES (corp-wide): 27.5B **Privately Held**
WEB: www.michiganpaving.com
SIC: 1771 2951 Blacktop (asphalt) work; asphalt paving mixtures & blocks
HQ: Michigan Paving And Materials Company
  2575 S Haggerty Rd # 100
  Canton MI 48188
  734 397-2050

GEOGRAPHIC SECTION

Alpena - Alpena County (G-275)

(G-248)
MORNING STAR PUBLISHING CO
Also Called: Alma Reminder
311 E Superior St Ste A (48801-1832)
PHONE.................................989 463-6071
Tamaera Fischer, *General Mgr*
EMP: 10
SALES (corp-wide): 274.1MM **Privately Held**
WEB: www.themorningsun.com
SIC: 2711 2741 Newspapers, publishing & printing; miscellaneous publishing
HQ: Morning Star Publishing Company
    311 E Superior St Ste A
    Alma MI 48801
    989 779-6000

(G-249)
MORNING STAR PUBLISHING CO (DH)
311 E Superior St Ste A (48801-1832)
PHONE.................................989 779-6000
Bill McHugh, *President*
EMP: 150 **EST:** 2002
SQ FT: 60,000
SALES (est): 27MM
SALES (corp-wide): 274.1MM **Privately Held**
WEB: www.themorningsun.com
SIC: 2711 Newspapers, publishing & printing
HQ: 21st Century Newspapers, Inc.
    6250 Metropolitan Pkwy
    Sterling Heights MI 48312
    586 469-4510

(G-250)
MORNING STAR PUBLISHING CO
Also Called: St Johns Reminder
311 E Superior St Ste A (48801-1832)
P.O. Box 473, Saint Johns (48879-0473)
PHONE.................................989 779-6000
Bonnie Fyvie, *Manager*
EMP: 5
SALES (corp-wide): 274.1MM **Privately Held**
WEB: www.themorningsun.com
SIC: 2711 7313 2741 Newspapers, publishing & printing; newspaper advertising representative; shopping news: publishing & printing
HQ: Morning Star Publishing Company
    311 E Superior St Ste A
    Alma MI 48801
    989 779-6000

(G-251)
OERLIKON BLZERS CATING USA INC
7800 N Alger Rd (48801-9321)
PHONE.................................989 463-6268
Robert Smith, *Principal*
EMP: 8
SALES (corp-wide): 2.4B **Privately Held**
WEB: www.oerlikon.com
SIC: 3479 Coating of metals & formed products
HQ: Oerlikon Balzers Coating Usa Inc.
    1700 E Golf Rd Ste 200
    Schaumburg IL 60173
    847 619-5541

(G-252)
PERISCOPE PLAYSCHOOL
3676 N Bagley Rd (48801-9735)
PHONE.................................989 875-4409
Emily Fisher, *Owner*
EMP: 4 **EST:** 2017
SALES (est): 61.7K **Privately Held**
SIC: 3827 Periscopes

(G-253)
PRODUCTION MACHINING OF ALMA
6595 N Jerome Rd (48801-9706)
PHONE.................................989 463-1495
Raymond Cull, *President*
Dennis Cull, *Vice Pres*
Cull Raymond Jr, *Manager*
William Bell, *Admin Sec*
▲ **EMP:** 22 **EST:** 1986
SQ FT: 33,000
SALES (est): 1.4MM **Privately Held**
WEB: www.productionmachining.net
SIC: 3599 Machine shop, jobbing & repair

(G-254)
REBEATS (PA)
219 Prospect Ave (48801-2262)
P.O. Box 6 (48801-0006)
PHONE.................................989 463-4757
George Robert Cook, *Owner*
EMP: 11 **EST:** 1972
SQ FT: 2,000
SALES (est): 1.1MM **Privately Held**
WEB: www.rebeats.com
SIC: 3931 5736 5731 Drums, parts & accessories (musical instruments); drums & related percussion instruments; high fidelity stereo equipment

Almont
Lapeer County

(G-255)
AFGCO SAND & GRAVEL CO INC
5171 Sandhill Rd (48003-9735)
PHONE.................................810 798-3293
Ken Measel, *President*
EMP: 5
SQ FT: 2,500
SALES (est): 423.7K **Privately Held**
SIC: 1442 Construction sand & gravel

(G-256)
ASSOCIATED BROACH CORPORATION
7481 Research Dr (48003-8513)
PHONE.................................810 798-9112
Fax: 810 798-2270
EMP: 24
SQ FT: 10,000
SALES (est): 1.6MM **Privately Held**
SIC: 3545 Mfg Broaches

(G-257)
CONCORDANT PUBLISHING CONCERN
6800 Hough Rd (48003-9710)
P.O. Box 449 (48003-0449)
PHONE.................................810 798-3563
James Coram, *President*
EMP: 7 **EST:** 2012
SALES (est): 347.7K **Privately Held**
WEB: www.concordant.org
SIC: 2741 Miscellaneous publishing

(G-258)
D & D FABRICATIONS INC
8005 Tiffany Dr (48003-8642)
PHONE.................................810 798-2491
Allan Lagrou, *President*
Karen S Lagrou, *Co-Owner*
EMP: 4 **EST:** 1973
SALES (est): 444.9K **Privately Held**
WEB: www.aluminumv8.com
SIC: 5015 3449 Automotive parts & supplies, used; bars, concrete reinforcing: fabricated steel

(G-259)
ELMONT DISTRICT LIBRARY
Also Called: Henry Stephens Memorial Lib
213 W Saint Clair St (48003-8476)
P.O. Box 517 (48003-0517)
PHONE.................................810 798-3100
Maybelle Smith, *Chairman*
Kay Hurd, *Director*
EMP: 8 **EST:** 1919
SALES (est): 439K **Privately Held**
WEB: www.adlmi.org
SIC: 8231 2731 Public library; book publishing

(G-260)
GEAR MASTER INC
7481 Research Dr (48003-8513)
PHONE.................................810 798-9254
Gerald Stroud, *President*
Terry Roach, *Sales Mgr*
Bill Abke, *Manager*
EMP: 10 **EST:** 1997
SQ FT: 2,400
SALES (est): 1.2MM **Privately Held**
WEB: www.gearmaster.us
SIC: 7389 3728 Grinding, precision: commercial or industrial; gears, aircraft power transmission

(G-261)
GRABILL WINDOWS & DOORS LLC
7463 Research Dr (48003-8513)
PHONE.................................810 798-2817
Ray Bisbee, *President*
Frank Kosciolek, *General Mgr*
EMP: 40 **EST:** 2015
SALES (est): 4.7MM
SALES (corp-wide): 2B **Privately Held**
WEB: www.grabillwindow.com
SIC: 2431 3442 Doors & door parts & trim, wood; windows & window parts & trim, wood; screen & storm doors & windows; metal doors
PA: Pella Corporation
    102 Main St
    Pella IA 50219
    641 621-1000

(G-262)
INTER-POWER CORPORATION (PA)
Also Called: Tarifa
3578 Van Dyke Rd (48003-8045)
PHONE.................................810 798-9201
Gary Gariglio, *President*
Dan Maran, *Engineer*
Mike Alcantara, *Sales Staff*
▲ **EMP:** 27 **EST:** 1995
SQ FT: 60,000
SALES (est): 12MM **Privately Held**
WEB: www.interpowereurope.com
SIC: 3567 Induction heating equipment

(G-263)
KEN MEASEL SUPPLY INC
6343 Hayfield Ln (48003-9706)
PHONE.................................810 798-3293
Ken Measel, *President*
EMP: 5 **EST:** 1956
SALES (est): 865.3K **Privately Held**
SIC: 1442 Sand mining

(G-264)
MARJEANNES CREATIONS
7346 Hollow Corners Rd (48003-8011)
PHONE.................................810 798-7278
Marjeanne Showalter, *Owner*
EMP: 6 **EST:** 2011
SALES (est): 159.2K **Privately Held**
WEB: www.marjeannescreations.com
SIC: 2841 Textile soap

(G-265)
MERC-O-TRONIC INSTRUMENTS CORP
215 Branch St (48003-1004)
P.O. Box 454 (48003-0454)
PHONE.................................586 894-9529
Arthur W Schafer Jr, *President*
Dane A Schafer, *Treasurer*
EMP: 12 **EST:** 1955
SQ FT: 5,000
SALES (est): 544.6K **Privately Held**
SIC: 3825 Instruments to measure electricity

(G-266)
MIG MOLDING LLC
3778 Van Dyke Rd (48003-8043)
PHONE.................................810 660-8435
EMP: 6 **EST:** 2014
SALES (est): 259.2K **Privately Held**
SIC: 3089 Molding primary plastic

(G-267)
SPRING DYNAMICS INC
7378 Research Dr (48003-8512)
PHONE.................................810 798-2622
Thomas Boles, *President*
John Redner, *Opers Mgr*
Eric Roskey, *Engineer*
Connie Hosner, *Sales Staff*
Jeff Bristol, *Manager*
▲ **EMP:** 45 **EST:** 1985
SQ FT: 33,000
SALES (est): 8.9MM **Privately Held**
WEB: www.springdynamics.com
SIC: 3495 Wire springs

(G-268)
SUMMERS ROAD GRAVEL & DEV LLC
Also Called: Summers Rd Gravel
3620 Van Dyke Rd (48003-8041)
PHONE.................................810 798-8533
EMP: 9 **EST:** 2001
SALES (est): 841.5K **Privately Held**
SIC: 1442 Construction sand & gravel

(G-269)
TRIMS UNLIMITED LLC
3863 Van Dyke Rd (48003-8049)
PHONE.................................810 724-3500
George Mansour, *Partner*
William Welch,
EMP: 45 **EST:** 1980
SALES (est): 5.2MM **Privately Held**
WEB: www.trimsllc.com
SIC: 2396 2329 2389 Automotive trimmings, fabric; field jackets, military; hospital gowns

(G-270)
VEHICLE RESEARCH AND DEV
3863 Van Dyke Rd (48003-8049)
PHONE.................................586 504-1163
Larry R Bruzzese, *President*
Laura Winans, *Bookkeeper*
EMP: 9 **EST:** 1987
SQ FT: 33,000
SALES (est): 1MM **Privately Held**
WEB: www.vrdtest.com
SIC: 8731 3714 Commercial physical research; motor vehicle parts & accessories

(G-271)
VICTORA USA INC
3776 Van Dyke Rd (48003-8047)
PHONE.................................810 798-0253
James T Ligon, *COO*
Deepak Kumar, *Vice Pres*
▲ **EMP:** 7 **EST:** 2013
SALES (est): 2.6MM **Privately Held**
WEB: www.victorausa.com
SIC: 3714 Camshafts, motor vehicle
PA: Victora Auto Private Limited
    Scf-24, Huda Market Sector-11 D
    Faridabad HR 121 0

(G-272)
WEATHER PANE INC
6209 Bordman Rd (48003-9704)
PHONE.................................810 798-8695
Richard Keller, *President*
Barbara Keller, *Corp Secy*
EMP: 5 **EST:** 1983
SQ FT: 8,000
SALES (est): 478.3K **Privately Held**
SIC: 3089 Windows, plastic

Alpena
Alpena County

(G-273)
ACADIAN WOODWORKING LLC
4357 M 32 W (49707-8133)
PHONE.................................989 356-0229
EMP: 4 **EST:** 2019
SALES (est): 78.7K **Privately Held**
SIC: 2431 Millwork

(G-274)
ADMIRAL
2520 Us Highway 23 S (49707-4618)
PHONE.................................989 356-6419
G Kendzirorski, *Manager*
Gary Kendzirorski, *Manager*
EMP: 6 **EST:** 2011
SALES (est): 439.4K **Privately Held**
SIC: 5541 5411 3589 Filling stations, gasoline; convenience stores; car washing machinery

(G-275)
ALPENA AGGREGATE INC
7590 Weiss Rd (49707-8963)
PHONE.................................989 595-2511
Earl R Dubey, *President*

Alpena - Alpena County (G-276)

EMP: 26 EST: 1930
SQ FT: 300,000
SALES (est): 3MM Privately Held
WEB: www.alpena.mi.us
SIC: 1442 Common sand mining; gravel mining

(G-276)
ALPENA BIOREFINERY
412 Ford Ave (49707-2346)
PHONE....................989 340-1190
Mark Szczepanik, *Administration*
EMP: 11 EST: 2012
SALES (est): 167.3K Privately Held
WEB: www.americanprocess.com
SIC: 2493 Reconstituted wood products

(G-277)
ALPENA ELECTRIC MOTOR SERVICE
1581 M 32 W (49707-8193)
P.O. Box 565 (49707-0565)
PHONE....................989 354-8780
James E Vivian II, *President*
Judith K Vivian, *Admin Sec*
EMP: 6 EST: 1960
SQ FT: 15,000
SALES (est): 640.4K Privately Held
WEB: www.alpena.com
SIC: 7694 5063 Rebuilding motors, except automotive; rewinding services; motors, electric

(G-278)
AMOS MFG INC
3490 Us Highway 23 N (49707-6910)
P.O. Box 177 (49707-0177)
PHONE....................989 358-7187
Debra J Winter, *President*
Jeff Beaudoin, *Opers Staff*
Gregg Schefferly, *Manager*
EMP: 17 EST: 2001
SALES (est): 1.5MM Privately Held
WEB: www.amos-mfg.com
SIC: 3589 Shredders, industrial & commercial

(G-279)
ATLANTIS TECH CORP
706 Island View Dr (49707-1325)
P.O. Box 205 (49707-0205)
PHONE....................989 356-6954
Paul Diamond, *Principal*
EMP: 8 EST: 2007
SALES (est): 211.3K Privately Held
WEB: www.atlantisconveyor.com
SIC: 3312 Stainless steel

(G-280)
AUNT MILLIES BAKERIES
3450 Us Highway 23 S (49707-4840)
PHONE....................989 356-6688
Fax: 989 354-3212
EMP: 7
SALES (est): 411.5K Privately Held
SIC: 2051 Mfg Bread/Related Products

(G-281)
BAKER ENTERPRISES INC (HQ)
801 Johnson St (49707-1870)
PHONE....................989 354-2189
Gary Stevens, *President*
EMP: 30 EST: 1929
SQ FT: 45,000
SALES (est): 17.4MM
SALES (corp-wide): 213.4MM Privately Held
WEB: www.besser.com
SIC: 3564 3443 3537 3441 Dust or fume collecting equipment, industrial; fabricated plate work (boiler shop); industrial trucks & tractors; fabricated structural metal
PA: Besser Company
    801 Johnson St
    Alpena MI 49707
    989 354-4111

(G-282)
BAY MANUFACTURING CORPORATION
3750 Us Highway 23 N (49707-7949)
P.O. Box 205 (49707-0205)
PHONE....................989 358-7198
Gregory Winter, *President*
Debra Winter, *Treasurer*
EMP: 13 EST: 1988
SALES (est): 718.5K Privately Held
SIC: 3469 3535 Machine parts, stamped or pressed metal; conveyors & conveying equipment

(G-283)
BCUBED MANUFACTURING LLC
666 Mckinley Ave (49707-2600)
PHONE....................989 356-2294
Douglas A Kowalski, *Principal*
EMP: 9 EST: 2018
SALES (est): 726.7K Privately Held
WEB: www.bcubedmanufacturing.com
SIC: 3999 Manufacturing industries

(G-284)
BESSER COMPANY (PA)
801 Johnson St (49707-1897)
PHONE....................989 354-4111
Kevin L Curtis, *CEO*
Brian Christle, *Opers Mgr*
Todd Shinew, *Engineer*
Juli S Musch, *CFO*
Donna Pollard, *Credit Staff*
◆ EMP: 350 EST: 1897
SQ FT: 500,000
SALES (est): 213.4MM Privately Held
WEB: www.besser.com
SIC: 3531 3559 3564 3443 Concrete plants; concrete products machinery; dust or fume collecting equipment, industrial; fabricated plate work (boiler shop)

(G-285)
BROTHERS IN ARMS MFG LLC
509 Lockwood St (49707-2547)
PHONE....................989 464-9615
Michael Richards, *Principal*
EMP: 4 EST: 2020
SALES (est): 116.1K Privately Held
SIC: 3999 Manufacturing industries

(G-286)
CHEBOYGAN CEMENT PRODUCTS INC
Also Called: Gildner's Concrete Products
400 Commerce Dr (49707-1952)
PHONE....................989 356-5156
Alex Ptasnik, *Sales Staff*
Greg Gildner, *Branch Mgr*
EMP: 4
SALES (corp-wide): 8.7MM Privately Held
WEB: www.cheboygancement.com
SIC: 3273 Ready-mixed concrete
PA: Cheboygan Cement Products Inc
    702 Lafayette Ave
    Cheboygan MI 49721
    231 627-5631

(G-287)
CLAY & GRAHAM INC
Also Called: Thunder Bay Concrete Products
4770 Werth Rd (49707-9551)
PHONE....................989 354-5292
Norma Clay, *President*
EMP: 8 EST: 1947
SQ FT: 5,000
SALES (est): 619K Privately Held
SIC: 3271 5211 Blocks, concrete or cinder: standard; masonry materials & supplies

(G-288)
CORR-FAC CORPORATION
Also Called: Rack Engineering Division
4040 Us Highway 23 N (49707-7944)
P.O. Box 205 (49707-0205)
PHONE....................989 358-7050
Gregory C Winter, *President*
Debra J Winter, *Corp Secy*
EMP: 4 EST: 1993
SALES (est): 420.1K Privately Held
WEB: www.rack-eng.com
SIC: 3559 5084 Foundry machinery & equipment; conveyor systems

(G-289)
CSI SERVICE PARTS CORP
Also Called: Conveyor Systems
1995 Hamilton Rd (49707-7820)
P.O. Box 33 (49707-0033)
PHONE....................989 358-7199
Gregory C Winter, *President*
Debra J Winter, *Admin Sec*
EMP: 4 EST: 1986
SALES (est): 502.1K Privately Held
SIC: 3535 Conveyors & conveying equipment

(G-290)
DECORATIVE PANELS INTL INC
416 Ford Ave (49707-2346)
PHONE....................989 354-2121
Len Werda, *Plant Mgr*
Lloyd Springer, *Manager*
Stephen Nofzinger, *Senior Mgr*
EMP: 50 Privately Held
WEB: www.decpanels.com
SIC: 2421 Building & structural materials, wood
HQ: Decorative Panels International, Inc.
    2900 Hill Ave
    Toledo OH 43607
    419 535-5921

(G-291)
EAGLE ENGINEERING & SUPPLY CO
101 N Industrial Hwy (49707-8167)
PHONE....................989 356-4526
Curtis Eagle, *President*
Curtis D Eagle, *President*
Joan Eagle, *Corp Secy*
Bradley Eagle, *Vice Pres*
EMP: 20 EST: 1970
SQ FT: 15,000
SALES (est): 1.9MM Privately Held
WEB: www.eaglecompanies.com
SIC: 3535 3441 3564 3613 Conveyors & conveying equipment; building components, structural steel; air cleaning systems; control panels, electric; industrial controls: push button, selector switches, pilot

(G-292)
ENDURA-VEYOR INC
3490 Us Highway 23 N (49707-6910)
P.O. Box 205 (49707-0205)
PHONE....................989 358-7060
Gregory C Winter, *Principal*
▼ EMP: 25 EST: 2001
SALES (est): 3.5MM Privately Held
WEB: www.endura-veyor.com
SIC: 3535 Conveyors & conveying equipment

(G-293)
FALCON CONSULTING SERVICES LLC
112 1/2 W Chisholm St A (49707-2446)
PHONE....................989 262-9325
Lori Fields,
EMP: 4 EST: 2017
SALES (est): 160.3K Privately Held
SIC: 3599 7371 8742 Machine & other job shop work; custom computer programming services; materials mgmt. (purchasing, handling, inventory) consultant

(G-294)
FIBER-CHAR CORPORATION
3336 Piper Rd (49707-4751)
P.O. Box 307 (49707-0307)
PHONE....................989 356-5501
Dennis A Schultz, *President*
Patricia Schultz, *Corp Secy*
Adam Zeeman, *Sales Associate*
▼ EMP: 20 EST: 1978
SQ FT: 30,000
SALES (est): 3.7MM Privately Held
WEB: www.fiberchar.com
SIC: 2431 Moldings, wood: unfinished & prefinished; trim, wood

(G-295)
FRAMON MFG CO INC (PA)
1201 W Chisholm St (49707-1619)
PHONE....................989 354-5623
Frank Michael Aguis, *President*
Ann McConnell, *Principal*
Ann Aguis, *Corp Secy*
Phil Aguis, *Vice Pres*
EMP: 6 EST: 1972
SQ FT: 2,000
SALES (est): 763.7K Privately Held
WEB: www.framon.com
SIC: 3541 Machine tools, metal cutting type

(G-296)
GARANTS OFFICE SUPS & PRTG INC
117 W Washington Ave (49707-2757)
PHONE....................989 356-3930
Ronald Garant, *President*
Darlene Garant, *Admin Sec*
EMP: 5 EST: 1984
SALES (est): 287.2K Privately Held
WEB: www.garantsofficesupplies.com
SIC: 5943 2752 5712 Office forms & supplies; commercial printing, offset; office furniture

(G-297)
HISTORIC DENVER INC
416 Ford Ave (49707-2346)
PHONE....................989 354-2121
Kelly Kania, *Purch Agent*
Scott Ickes, *Senior Mgr*
EMP: 6 EST: 2015
SALES (est): 110.7K Privately Held
WEB: www.historicdenver.org
SIC: 3444 Sheet metalwork

(G-298)
L & S TRANSIT MIX CONCRETE CO
500 Tuttle St (49707-2733)
PHONE....................989 354-5363
Gerold Lancaster, *President*
Tim Lancaster, *Vice Pres*
Evelyn Lancaster, *Treasurer*
▲ EMP: 31 EST: 1950
SALES (est): 2.2MM Privately Held
SIC: 3273 5211 Ready-mixed concrete; masonry materials & supplies

(G-299)
LAFARGE NORTH AMERICA INC
1435 Ford Ave (49707-2100)
P.O. Box 396 (49707-0396)
PHONE....................989 354-4171
Paul Rogers, *Plant Mgr*
George Kistler, *Enginr/R&D Mgr*
Randy Hartman, *Maintence Staff*
Klay Wagner, *Maintence Staff*
EMP: 8
SALES (corp-wide): 25.3B Privately Held
WEB: www.lafarge-na.com
SIC: 3241 5032 Portland cement; cement
HQ: Lafarge North America Inc.
    8700 W Bryn Mawr Ave # 30
    Chicago IL 60631
    773 372-1000

(G-300)
MADISON MACHINE COMPANY
801 Johnson St (49707-1870)
PHONE....................517 265-8532
Gregory M Betz, *President*
Gail Betz, *Corp Secy*
EMP: 8 EST: 1951
SALES (est): 787.9K Privately Held
WEB: www.madisonmachineco.com
SIC: 3599 Machine shop, jobbing & repair

(G-301)
MANIGG ENTERPRISES INC (PA)
1010 Us Highway 23 N (49707-1250)
P.O. Box 678 (49707-0678)
PHONE....................989 356-4986
Roger Glawe, *President*
Jeff Weiland, *Corp Secy*
Gary Glawe, *Vice Pres*
EMP: 17 EST: 1978
SQ FT: 2,500
SALES (est): 9.4MM Privately Held
SIC: 1794 2411 1411 4213 Excavation work; wood chips, produced in the field; limestone, dimension-quarrying; trucking, except local

(G-302)
MICHIGAN EAST SIDE SALES LLC
4220 Us Highway 23 S (49707-5140)
PHONE....................989 354-6867
Robert Papin, *Mng Member*
EMP: 3 EST: 1998

▲ = Import ▼ = Export
◆ = Import/Export

GEOGRAPHIC SECTION

Alto - Kent County (G-330)

SALES (est): 1.5MM **Privately Held**
WEB: www.michiganeastsidesales.com
SIC: **5012** 3792 6531 5511 Recreational vehicles, motor homes & trailers; house trailers, except as permanent dwellings; real estate leasing & rentals; new & used car dealers

(G-303)
MID-WEST INNOVATORS INC
Also Called: Mid-West Mfg.
3810 Us Highway 23 N (49707-7925)
P.O. Box 115 (49707-0115)
PHONE..................989 358-7147
Gregory C Winter, *President*
Deborah J Winter, *Treasurer*
EMP: 20 **EST:** 2004
SALES (est): 1.1MM **Privately Held**
WEB: www.mid-westinnovators.com
SIC: **3599** Machine shop, jobbing & repair

(G-304)
MODEL PRINTING SERVICE INC
Also Called: Allegra Alpena
829 W Chisholm St (49707-1717)
PHONE..................989 356-0834
Edward Klimczak, *President*
Glen Klimczak, *Prdtn Mgr*
Lori Ann Klimzzak, *Bookkeeper*
Mary Killion,
EMP: 12 **EST:** 1963
SQ FT: 4,500
SALES (est): 2.1MM **Privately Held**
WEB: www.modelprintingservice.com
SIC: **2752** Commercial printing, offset

(G-305)
NOVA-TRON CONTROLS CORP
111 S Second Ave (49707-2813)
P.O. Box 103 (49707-0103)
PHONE..................989 358-6126
EMP: 13 **EST:** 2004
SALES (est): 2.9MM **Privately Held**
WEB: www.nova-tron.com
SIC: **3679** Electronic circuits

(G-306)
OMNI METALCRAFT CORP (PA)
4040 Us Highway 23 N (49707-7923)
P.O. Box 352 (49707-0352)
PHONE..................989 354-4075
Ronald W Winter, *Chairman*
Gregory C Winter, *COO*
Paul L Diamond, *Vice Pres*
William C Kaschner, *Vice Pres*
Debra J Winter, *CFO*
▲ EMP: 32 **EST:** 1976
SQ FT: 7,200
SALES (est): 9.6MM **Privately Held**
WEB: www.omni.com
SIC: **3535** 5084 Conveyors & conveying equipment; industrial machinery & equipment

(G-307)
OVERHEAD DOOR COMPANY ALPENA
Also Called: Thermo-Shield Window Mfg
2550 Us Highway 23 S (49707-4618)
PHONE..................989 354-8316
John G Adams, *President*
Norma Adams, *Corp Secy*
Steven Adams, *Vice Pres*
EMP: 5 **EST:** 1965
SQ FT: 8,600
SALES (est): 630.2K **Privately Held**
WEB: www.overheaddooralpena.com
SIC: **5211** 1521 3089 Garage doors, sale & installation; doors, wood or metal, except storm; doors, storm; wood or metal; general remodeling, single-family houses; windows, plastic

(G-308)
PANEL PROCESSING NEW JERSEY
1030 Devere Dr (49707-8163)
PHONE..................856 317-1998
Gene Gold, *Owner*
EMP: 7 **EST:** 2018
SALES (est): 316.8K **Privately Held**
WEB: www.panel.com
SIC: **2499** Wood products

(G-309)
PANEL PROCESSING OREGON INC (HQ)
Also Called: Thermo Pressed Laminates
1030 Devere Dr (49707-8163)
PHONE..................989 356-9007
Charles T Smith, *President*
Chris Boyk, *Chief Engr*
EMP: 77 **EST:** 1971
SALES (est): 13.8MM
SALES (corp-wide): 91.6MM **Privately Held**
WEB: www.panel.com
SIC: **2541** 3442 Store fixtures, wood; metal doors, sash & trim
PA: Panel Processing, Inc.
1030 Devere Dr
Alpena MI 49707
800 433-7142

(G-310)
PANEL PROCESSING TEXAS INC
1030 Devere Dr (49707-8163)
PHONE..................903 586-2423
Eric Smith, *President*
Angie Belcher, *Accounts Mgr*
Johnny Gardner, *Maintence Staff*
EMP: 40 **EST:** 1975
SALES (est): 8.8MM
SALES (corp-wide): 91.6MM **Privately Held**
WEB: www.panel.com
SIC: **2541** Store fixtures, wood; display fixtures, wood
PA: Panel Processing, Inc.
1030 Devere Dr
Alpena MI 49707
800 433-7142

(G-311)
PCI PROCAL INC
3810 Us Highway 23 N (49707-7925)
P.O. Box 115 (49707-0115)
PHONE..................989 358-7070
Maureen Bolda, *Principal*
Nancy Pomish, *Human Res Dir*
EMP: 14 **EST:** 2001
SALES (est): 1MM **Privately Held**
WEB: www.pcimfg.com
SIC: **3571** 3714 3568 3537 Electronic computers; motor vehicle parts & accessories; power transmission equipment; industrial trucks & tractors; conveyors & conveying equipment

(G-312)
PRO-BUILT MFG
820 Long Lake Ave (49707-1855)
P.O. Box 115 (49707-0115)
PHONE..................989 354-1321
EMP: 9 **EST:** 2010
SALES (est): 156.4K **Privately Held**
WEB: www.pcimfg.com
SIC: **3999** Manufacturing industries

(G-313)
PUNCHING CONCEPTS INC
Also Called: Procal
3810 Us Highway 23 N (49707-7925)
P.O. Box 115 (49707-0115)
PHONE..................989 358-7070
Gregory C Winter, *President*
Debra J Winter, *Corp Secy*
EMP: 15 **EST:** 1987
SALES (est): 2.5MM **Privately Held**
WEB: www.pcimfg.com
SIC: **3469** Metal stampings

(G-314)
QSR OUTDOOR PRODUCTS INC
600 W Campbell St (49707-3004)
PHONE..................989 354-0777
EMP: 9 **EST:** 2012
SALES (est): 780.8K **Privately Held**
WEB: www.qsroutdoors.com
SIC: **3949** Sporting & athletic goods

(G-315)
RAND L INDUSTRIES INC
2046 Partridge St (49707-8990)
PHONE..................989 657-5175
Randy Benoit, *Principal*
EMP: 6 **EST:** 2009

SALES (est): 192.1K **Privately Held**
SIC: **3131** Rands

(G-316)
RECON FISHING SYSTEMS INC
1504 S Second Ave (49707-3606)
PHONE..................989 358-2923
Carl Hatala, *President*
EMP: 4 **EST:** 2020
SALES (est): 54.6K **Privately Held**
SIC: **3732** 5551 Kayaks, building & repairing; kayaks

(G-317)
SMIGELSKI PROPERTIES LLC
712 N Second Ave (49707-2230)
PHONE..................989 255-6252
Andrew Smigelski,
EMP: 5 **EST:** 2010
SALES (est): 275.5K **Privately Held**
WEB: www.smigelskicottage.com
SIC: **2013** Prepared beef products from purchased beef

(G-318)
SPEEDY BLAZE INC ✪
Also Called: Innovative Firewood Products
307 S Third Ave (49707-2567)
PHONE..................989 340-2028
Sherman Hubbard, *CEO*
EMP: 5 **EST:** 2021
SALES (est): 850K **Privately Held**
WEB: www.info.speedyblaze.com
SIC: **2421** 2411 5099 Wood chips, produced at mill; wooden logs; firewood

(G-319)
STANDARD PROVISION LLC
1505 Greenhaven Ln (49707-4257)
PHONE..................989 354-4975
Vicki Shooks, *Principal*
EMP: 6 **EST:** 2005
SALES (est): 442.2K **Privately Held**
SIC: **2011** Meat packing plants

(G-320)
STEEL CRAFT INC
1086 Hamilton Rd (49707-7719)
P.O. Box 205 (49707-0205)
PHONE..................989 358-7196
Gregory Winter, *President*
Debra Winter, *Corp Secy*
EMP: 9 **EST:** 1985
SQ FT: 20,000
SALES (est): 891.2K **Privately Held**
SIC: **3535** 3441 Conveyors & conveying equipment; fabricated structural metal

(G-321)
STEVENS CUSTOM FABRICATION
928 Lockwood St (49707-1744)
PHONE..................989 340-1184
Scott Stevens, *Owner*
EMP: 5 **EST:** 2008
SALES (est): 158.2K **Privately Held**
WEB: www.stevenscustomfabrication.com
SIC: **3441** 3599 Fabricated structural metal; machine shop, jobbing & repair

(G-322)
STEVENS CUSTOM FABRICATION
615 W Campbell St (49707-3003)
PHONE..................989 340-1184
Scott Stevens,
Todd Briton,
Will Rensberry,
Ann Sherman,
Trent Sherman,
EMP: 5 **EST:** 2013 **Privately Held**
WEB: www.stevenscustomfabrication.com
SIC: **3441** Fabricated structural metal

(G-323)
STONEY ACRES WINERY
4268 Truckey Rd (49707-9701)
PHONE..................989 356-1041
Jim Grochowski, *Partner*
Helen Grochowski, *Partner*
EMP: 5 **EST:** 2000
SALES (est): 234.1K **Privately Held**
WEB: www.stoneyacreswinery.net
SIC: **2084** Wines

(G-324)
SUPERIOR FABRICATING INC
320 N Eleventh Ave (49707-1716)
P.O. Box 501 (49707-0501)
PHONE..................989 354-8877
Robert Westenbarger, *President*
Diedre Westenbarger, *Treasurer*
EMP: 10 **EST:** 1975
SQ FT: 6,000
SALES (est): 744.6K **Privately Held**
SIC: **3441** Fabricated structural metal

(G-325)
TERRA CALORIC LLC
3336 Piper Rd (49707-4733)
PHONE..................989 356-2113
Dennis A Schultz, *Mng Member*
EMP: 19 **EST:** 2006
SALES (est): 1.3MM **Privately Held**
WEB: www.wellconnectgeo.com
SIC: **3585** Heating & air conditioning combination units

(G-326)
THUNDER BAY WINERY
109 N Second Ave Ste 101 (49707-2850)
PHONE..................989 358-9463
Janis Sahr, *Principal*
EMP: 6 **EST:** 2019
SALES (est): 274.2K **Privately Held**
WEB: www.thunderbaywinery.com
SIC: **2084** Wines

(G-327)
W G BENJEY INC (PA)
2293 Werth Rd (49707-4652)
PHONE..................989 356-0016
Michael Ableidinger, *President*
Wayne Bates, *Foreman/Supr*
EMP: 15 **EST:** 1960
SQ FT: 4,000
SALES (est): 5.1MM **Privately Held**
WEB: www.benjey.com
SIC: **3559** 8711 Automotive related machinery; consulting engineer

(G-328)
W G BENJEY INC
Also Called: W G Benjey North
108 E Herman St (49707-2140)
PHONE..................989 356-0027
Wayne Bates, *Manager*
EMP: 5
SALES (corp-wide): 5.1MM **Privately Held**
WEB: www.benjey.com
SIC: **3452** 5084 Screws, metal; conveyor systems
PA: W. G. Benjey, Inc.
2293 Werth Rd
Alpena MI 49707
989 356-0016

Alto
Kent County

(G-329)
BV TECHNOLOGY LLC
7855 Sandy Hollow Dr Se (49302-9796)
PHONE..................616 558-1746
Robert Briody, *CEO*
Richard Anthony Marquis, *Principal*
Bobby Neal Wilmoth Jr, *Principal*
Yen-Oahn Thi Vo, *Manager*
EMP: 4 **EST:** 2014
SALES (est): 165.5K **Privately Held**
SIC: **2899** 7389 Rifle bore cleaning compounds; business services

(G-330)
CALEDONIA CMNTY SAWMILL LLC
8298 96th St Se (49302-9598)
PHONE..................616 891-8561
Matthew Brown, *Principal*
EMP: 7 **EST:** 2007
SALES (est): 180.5K **Privately Held**
SIC: **2421** Sawmills & planing mills, general

Alto - Kent County (G-331)

(G-331)
CONCORD EDITORIAL & DESIGN LLC
5583 Bancroft Ave Se (49302-9251)
PHONE.....................616 868-0148
EMP: 6 **EST:** 1991
SALES (est): 34.4K **Privately Held**
WEB: www.concordeditorial.com
SIC: 2731 Book publishing

(G-332)
FIREWATER LIGHTING LLC
7929 Fitzsimmons Ct Se (49302-9725)
PHONE.....................616 570-0088
EMP: 8 **EST:** 2012
SALES (est): 151.8K **Privately Held**
SIC: 3648 Lighting equipment

(G-333)
GOOD LIFE NATURALS LLC
6555 Alden Nash Ave Se (49302-8960)
PHONE.....................616 207-9230
Holly Valencia,
EMP: 4 **EST:** 2017
SALES (est): 68.6K **Privately Held**
WEB: www.goodlifenaturals.com
SIC: 2099 Food preparations

(G-334)
JANDYS HOME
6330 Snow Ave Se (49302-9750)
PHONE.....................616 446-7013
Amy Pietras, *Owner*
EMP: 7 **EST:** 2009
SALES (est): 250K **Privately Held**
WEB: www.jandyshome.org
SIC: 3999 Pet supplies

(G-335)
LYNCS METAL FABRICATION
12490 64th St Se (49302-9667)
PHONE.....................616 813-2071
Joe Lynch, *Principal*
EMP: 6 **EST:** 2016
SALES (est): 281.4K **Privately Held**
SIC: 3499 Fabricated metal products

(G-336)
MAGNA MIRRORS NORTH AMER LLC (HQ)
Also Called: Lowell Engineering
6151 Bancroft Ave Se (49302-9313)
P.O. Box 96 (49302-0096)
PHONE.....................616 868-6122
Rhonda McNally, *Vice Pres*
Anirudh Hegde, *Engineer*
Matthew Travis, *Engineer*
Dan Pletcher, *Program Mgr*
Hussam Azar, *Manager*
◆ **EMP:** 650 **EST:** 1954
SQ FT: 172,000
SALES (est): 309.5MM
SALES (corp-wide): 32.6B **Privately Held**
WEB: www.magna.com
SIC: 3231 3442 Mirrors, truck & automobile: made from purchased glass; metal doors, sash & trim
PA: Magna International Inc
  337 Magna Dr
  Aurora ON L4G 7
  905 726-2462

(G-337)
MSSB LLC
Also Called: Glide Bearings & Seal Systems
6090 Alden Nash Ave Se (49302-9802)
PHONE.....................616 868-9730
Tim Creighton, *Opers Staff*
EMP: 5 **EST:** 2016
SALES (est): 525.4K **Privately Held**
WEB: www.glidebearings.com
SIC: 3366 Bushings & bearings

Amasa
Iron County

(G-338)
CONNOR SPORTS FLOORING LLC
251 Industrial Park Rd (49903)
P.O. Box 246 (49903-0246)
PHONE.....................906 822-7311
Conred Stromberg, *Manager*

David Grandt, *Director*
EMP: 10
SALES (corp-wide): 637.5MM **Privately Held**
WEB: www.connorsports.com
SIC: 2426 Flooring, hardwood
HQ: Connor Sports Flooring, Llc
  595 Supreme Dr
  Bensenville IL 60106

Anchorville
St. Clair County

(G-339)
INSTASET PLASTICS COMPANY LLC
10101 Marine City Hwy (48004)
PHONE.....................586 725-0229
Christopher Goetz, *Mng Member*
Jennifer Emig, *Manager*
Tammy Green, *Manager*
Peggy Lang, *Executive*
▲ **EMP:** 218 **EST:** 2015
SALES (est): 9.3MM **Privately Held**
WEB: www.instaset.net
SIC: 3089 Injection molded finished plastic products; thermoformed finished plastic products
PA: Wgs Global Services, L.C.
  6350 Taylor Dr
  Flint MI 48507

Ann Arbor
Washtenaw County

(G-340)
123GO LLC
455 E Eisenhower Pkwy (48108-3356)
PHONE.....................734 773-0049
Dominic REA, *CEO*
Walter Dougoveto,
EMP: 4 **EST:** 2018
SALES (est): 903.2K **Privately Held**
WEB: www.123go.io
SIC: 5045 7372 7371 Computer software; application computer software; business oriented computer software; software programming applications

(G-341)
A&D TECHNOLOGY INC
4622 Runway Blvd (48108-9555)
PHONE.....................734 973-1111
Teru Moriya, *CEO*
Yoichiro Eddie Koyama, *President*
Tony Iannelli, *Senior Buyer*
Kyle Melzer, *Engineer*
Mark Menge, *Engineer*
▲ **EMP:** 90
SQ FT: 61,000
SALES (est): 15.6MM **Privately Held**
WEB: www.aanddtech.com
SIC: 3823 3825 3829 Industrial instrmnts msrmnt display/control process variable; instruments to measure electricity; measuring & controlling devices
PA: A&D Company, Limited
  1-243, Asahi
  Kitamoto STM 364-0

(G-342)
A-1 SCREENPRINTING LLC (PA)
Also Called: Underground Printing
260 Metty Dr Ste G (48103-9154)
PHONE.....................734 665-2692
Ryan Greg, *Managing Dir*
Anthony Kuszak, *Store Mgr*
Evan Mitchell, *Store Mgr*
Danny Szopo, *Store Mgr*
Annie Dunsky, *Opers Staff*
EMP: 53 **EST:** 1990
SQ FT: 33,000
SALES (est): 16.6MM **Privately Held**
WEB: www.undergroundshirts.com
SIC: 2759 Screen printing

(G-343)
A2 MOTUS LLC
3575 Stanton Ct (48105-3032)
PHONE.....................734 780-7334
Mark Moldwin, *CEO*
Perry Samson, *Co-Owner*

Lauro Ojeda, *Chief Engr*
Arie Sheinker, *Development*
EMP: 4 **EST:** 2015
SALES (est): 206.2K **Privately Held**
SIC: 3812 Search & navigation equipment

(G-344)
AAPHARMASYN LLC
3915 Res Pk Dr Ste A1 (48108)
PHONE.....................734 213-2123
Ruslan Pryadun, *Mng Member*
Lisa Durham, *Admin Sec*
Samantha Danziger, *Teacher*
Gary L Bolton,
Xue Min Cheng,
EMP: 10 **EST:** 2007
SQ FT: 4,000
SALES (est): 3.2MM **Privately Held**
WEB: www.aapharmasyn.com
SIC: 2869 2899 2833 Industrial organic chemicals; chemical preparations; medicinals & botanicals
PA: Aprc Corporation
  3915 Res Pk Dr Ste 1a
  Ann Arbor MI 48108
  734 213-2123

(G-345)
ABRACADABRA JEWELRY
Also Called: Gem Gallery
205 E Liberty St (48104-2120)
PHONE.....................734 994-4848
Katherine Lesse, *Owner*
EMP: 8 **EST:** 1973
SQ FT: 2,000 **Privately Held**
WEB: www.abragem.com
SIC: 3911 5944 7631 Jewelry apparel; jewelry, precious stones & precious metals; jewelry repair services

(G-346)
ACCURI CYTOMETERS INC
173 Parkland Plz (48103-6299)
P.O. Box 1388 (48106-1388)
PHONE.....................734 994-8000
Jeffrey S Williams, *CEO*
Collin Rich, *Vice Pres*
Steven Calef, *Treasurer*
EMP: 50 **EST:** 2007
SALES (est): 13.5MM
SALES (corp-wide): 17.1B **Publicly Held**
WEB: www.bd.com
SIC: 3821 Laboratory apparatus, except heating & measuring
PA: Becton, Dickinson And Company
  1 Becton Dr
  Franklin Lakes NJ 07417
  201 847-6800

(G-347)
ACOUSYS BIODEVICES INC
1777 Highland Dr Ste B (48108-2285)
PHONE.....................573 823-3849
John A Viator, *President*
EMP: 4
SALES (est): 206.6K **Privately Held**
SIC: 3841 Surgical & medical instruments

(G-348)
ACTION OUTDOOR SERVICES LLC
2543 Andrew Thomas Trl (48103-8323)
PHONE.....................719 596-5341
EMP: 4 **EST:** 2018
SALES (est): 54.1K **Privately Held**
SIC: 2431 Millwork

(G-349)
ADADAPTED INC
330 E Liberty St (48104-2274)
PHONE.....................313 744-3383
Adam Fine, *Vice Pres*
Erin Amundson, *Accounts Exec*
Jessie Stachowiak, *Marketing Staff*
Jamie Kowalski, *Manager*
EMP: 14 **EST:** 2018
SALES (est): 2.8MM **Privately Held**
WEB: www.adadapted.com
SIC: 7372 Prepackaged software

(G-350)
ADAMS STREET PUBLISHING
3003 Washtenaw Ave Ste 3 (48104-5107)
PHONE.....................734 668-4044
EMP: 8 **EST:** 2019

SALES (est): 141.3K **Privately Held**
SIC: 2741 Miscellaneous publishing

(G-351)
ADANA VOLTAICS LLC
5776 Cedar Ridge Dr (48103-9098)
PHONE.....................734 622-0193
Ibrahim Oraiqat, *President*
Cagliyan Kurdak, *Manager*
EMP: 6
SALES (est): 361.8K **Privately Held**
SIC: 3691 Batteries, rechargeable

(G-352)
ADCAA LLC
Also Called: Apex Dental Milling
3110 W Liberty Rd Ste B (48103-8000)
PHONE.....................734 623-4236
Dave Molnar, *Accounts Mgr*
Jackie Farah, *Technical Staff*
John Farah,
John Powers,
EMP: 7 **EST:** 2007
SQ FT: 3,000
SALES (est): 640K **Privately Held**
WEB: www.apexdentalmilling.com
SIC: 3466 Crowns & closures

(G-353)
ADD-SAVVY DIGITAL SIGNAGE
2723 S State St (48104-6188)
PHONE.....................844 233-7288
Justin Fishman, *Mng Member*
EMP: 15 **EST:** 2017
SALES (est): 700.6K **Privately Held**
WEB: www.add-savvy.com
SIC: 3993 Signs & advertising specialties

(G-354)
ADVANCE PRINT & GRAPHICS INC
Also Called: Advance Specialties
4553 Concourse Dr (48108-9631)
PHONE.....................734 663-6816
Gary Hambell, *President*
Sheila Worton, *Business Mgr*
Bill Christie, *Vice Pres*
Ed Warzyniec, *Graphic Designe*
EMP: 20 **EST:** 1987
SQ FT: 12,000
SALES (est): 2.4MM **Privately Held**
WEB: www.advprint.net
SIC: 2752 Commercial printing, offset

(G-355)
ADVANCED PHOTONIX INC (PA)
2925 Boardwalk St (48104-6765)
PHONE.....................734 864-5647
Rick Madden, *Sales Mgr*
Dominic Schneider, *Manager*
Richard D Kurtz, *Administration*
EMP: 49 **EST:** 2016
SALES (est): 1.5MM **Privately Held**
WEB: www.advancedphotonix.com
SIC: 3674 Semiconductors & related devices

(G-356)
ADVANTAGE TRUCK ACC INC
5400 S State Rd (48108-9754)
PHONE.....................800 773-3110
William Reminder, *President*
Kelly Kneifl, *COO*
Jim Bresingham, *CFO*
Maria Zwas, *Admin Sec*
▼ **EMP:** 1 **EST:** 2002
SQ FT: 50,000
SALES (est): 7.5MM
SALES (corp-wide): 623.9MM **Privately Held**
WEB: www.truck-hero.com
SIC: 3714 Motor vehicle parts & accessories
HQ: Tectum Holdings, Inc.
  5400 Data Ct
  Ann Arbor MI 48108
  734 677-0444

(G-357)
AFFINIA GROUP INC
1101 Technology Dr (48108-8921)
P.O. Box 1967, Gastonia NC (28053-1967)
PHONE.....................734 827-5400
Terry McCormack, *CEO*
EMP: 43 **EST:** 2016

GEOGRAPHIC SECTION   Ann Arbor - Washtenaw County (G-384)

SALES (est): 698.8K Privately Held
SIC: 3714 Motor vehicle parts & accessories

(G-358)
AK REWARDS LLC
Also Called: Stridepost
2723 S State St Ste 150 (48104-6188)
PHONE....................................734 272-7078
EMP: 6
SALES (est): 215K Privately Held
SIC: 7372 Prepackaged Software Services

(G-359)
AKORN INC
Also Called: Akorn Consumer Health
2929 Plymouth Rd (48105-3206)
PHONE....................................800 579-8327
EMP: 38
SALES (corp-wide): 682.4MM Privately Held
SIC: 2834 Pharmaceutical Preparations
PA: Akorn, Inc.
   1925 W Field Ct Ste 300
   Lake Forest IL 60045
   847 279-6100

(G-360)
ALF ENTERPRISES INC
Also Called: Alf Studios
1342 N Main St Ste 11a (48104-1008)
PHONE....................................734 665-2012
Gregg Alf, President
EMP: 4 EST: 1976
SQ FT: 2,700
SALES (est): 332.6K Privately Held
WEB: www.alfstudios.com
SIC: 3931 5736 Violins & parts; string instruments

(G-361)
ALPHACORE PHARMA LLC
2425 Meadowridge Ct (48105-9661)
PHONE....................................734 330-0265
Michael Auerbach, CEO
Bruce Auerbach, President
Reynold Homan, Vice Pres
Bryan Krause, Security Dir
EMP: 5 EST: 2007
SALES (est): 584.4K
SALES (corp-wide): 26.6B Privately Held
WEB: www.astrazeneca.com
SIC: 2834 Pharmaceutical preparations
HQ: Medimmune, Llc
   1 Medimmune Way
   Gaithersburg MD 20878
   301 398-0000

(G-362)
ALUMABRIDGE LLC
2723 S State St Ste 150 (48104-6188)
PHONE....................................855 373-7500
Gregory Osberg, Mng Member
EMP: 11 EST: 2013
SALES (est): 645.6K Privately Held
WEB: www.alumabridge.com
SIC: 3441 Fabricated structural metal for bridges

(G-363)
AMCOR PHRM PACKG USA LLC
Also Called: Amcor Rigid Plastics
935 Technology Dr Ste 100 (48108-8964)
PHONE....................................734 428-9741
Micheal S Schmitt, President
Jim Iverson, Exec VP
Robert Collins, Vice Pres
Gary Hoeppner, Vice Pres
Bala Lakshmanan, Vice Pres
EMP: 108
SALES (corp-wide): 12.4B Privately Held
SIC: 3221 Cosmetic jars, glass
HQ: Amcor Pharmaceutical Packaging Usa, Llc
   625 Sharp St N
   Millville NJ 08332
   856 327-1540

(G-364)
AMERICAN MATHEMATICAL SOCIETY
Mathematical Reviews
416 4th St (48103-4816)
P.O. Box 8604 (48107-8604)
PHONE....................................734 996-5250
Jane Kister, Principal

Jill M Connolly, Human Resources
Scott Turner, Corp Comm Staff
Nicola Poser, Marketing Staff
Louise Jakobson, Officer
EMP: 12
SALES (corp-wide): 35MM Privately Held
WEB: www.ams.org
SIC: 2741 Miscellaneous publishing
PA: American Mathematical Society Inc
   201 Charles St
   Providence RI 02904
   401 455-4000

(G-365)
AMONG FRIENDS LLC
Also Called: Among Friends Baking Mixes
191 Orchard Hills Ct (48104-1826)
PHONE....................................734 997-9720
EMP: 11
SALES (est): 1.3MM Privately Held
SIC: 2052 2099 Mfg Cookies/Crackers Mfg Food Preparations

(G-366)
ANA FUEL INC
2759 Seminole Rd (48108-1324)
PHONE....................................810 422-5659
EMP: 4
SALES (est): 338.4K Privately Held
SIC: 2869 Mfg Industrial Organic Chemicals

(G-367)
ANN ARBOR CHRONICLE
330 Mulholland Ave (48103-4357)
PHONE....................................734 645-2633
Mary Morgan, Principal
EMP: 4 EST: 2011
SALES (est): 60.3K Privately Held
WEB: www.annarborchronicle.com
SIC: 2711 Newspapers, publishing & printing

(G-368)
ANN ARBOR OBSERVER COMPANY
2390 Winewood Ave (48103-1400)
PHONE....................................734 769-3175
Patricia M Garcia, Partner
John Hilton, Partner
EMP: 24 EST: 1976
SQ FT: 5,000
SALES (est): 1.7MM Privately Held
WEB: www.annarborobserver.com
SIC: 2721 2711 Magazines: publishing only, not printed on site; newspapers

(G-369)
ANN ARBOR OFFSET
5690 Hines Dr (48108-7940)
PHONE....................................734 926-4500
EMP: 5 EST: 2018
SALES (est): 62.9K Privately Held
SIC: 2711 Newspapers

(G-370)
ANN ARBOR STAINLESS
1123 Pontiac Trl (48105-1716)
PHONE....................................734 741-9499
EMP: 4 EST: 2019
SALES (est): 80K Privately Held
SIC: 3312 Blast furnaces & steel mills

(G-371)
ANSYS INC
2805 S Industrial Hwy # 100 (48104-6791)
PHONE....................................248 613-2677
Bil Cody, Principal
Ibrahim Yavuz, Engineer
Xiaoyi Zhao, Engineer
John Wilson, Sales Staff
EMP: 6
SALES (corp-wide): 1.6B Publicly Held
WEB: www.ansys.com
SIC: 7372 Prepackaged software
PA: Ansys, Inc.
   2600 Ansys Dr
   Canonsburg PA 15317
   724 746-3304

(G-372)
API / INMET INC
300 Dino Dr (48103-9502)
PHONE....................................734 426-5553
Jill Kale, President

Jon Carlson, Corp Secy
Paul Kovacich, Engineer
Eric Gettel, Accounting Mgr
Lynn McLean, Cust Mgr
EMP: 104 EST: 1994
SQ FT: 25,000
SALES (est): 23.4MM Privately Held
WEB: www.apitech.com
SIC: 3674 Semiconductors & related devices
PA: Api Technologies Corp.
   400 Nickerson Rd Ste 1
   Marlborough MA 01752

(G-373)
ARBOR ASSAYS INC
1514 Eisenhower Pl (48108-3284)
PHONE....................................734 677-1774
Bobbi O'Hara, CEO
Barbara Scheuer, CEO
Russell Hart, Principal
Heather Jackson, Business Mgr
Mindy Arden, Mfg Mgr
EMP: 15 EST: 2017
SALES (est): 2.4MM Privately Held
SIC: 2836 Veterinary biological products

(G-374)
ARBOR INTERNATIONAL INC
143 Enterprise Dr (48103-9561)
PHONE....................................734 761-5200
George Yoanides, President
Evelyn Yoanides, Treasurer
EMP: 4 EST: 1963
SQ FT: 8,000
SALES (est): 395.7K Privately Held
WEB: www.journeysinternational.com
SIC: 3569 Jacks, hydraulic

(G-375)
ARBOR KITCHEN LLC
124 W Summit St Ste B (48105-3208)
PHONE....................................248 921-4602
EMP: 4 EST: 2018
SALES (est): 224.4K Privately Held
SIC: 3999 5812 ; eating places

(G-376)
ARBOR SPRINGS WATER COMPANY (PA)
1440 Plymouth Rd (48105-1702)
PHONE....................................734 668-8270
William J Davis Jr, President
Judith Davis, Treasurer
Spencer Davis, Sales Executive
EMP: 20 EST: 1926
SQ FT: 22,500
SALES (est): 1.8MM Privately Held
WEB: www.arborspringswater.com
SIC: 5499 2086 Water: distilled mineral or spring; pasteurized & mineral waters, bottled & canned

(G-377)
ARBORMETRIX INC
339 E Liberty St Ste 210 (48104-2258)
PHONE....................................734 661-7944
Brett Furst, CEO
Christian Birkmeyer, COO
Shannon Eubank, Vice Pres
Lukasz Paszek, Vice Pres
Elise Kofke, Opers Staff
EMP: 104 EST: 2011
SQ FT: 3,500
SALES (est): 14.6MM Privately Held
WEB: www.arbormetrix.com
SIC: 7372 Application computer software

(G-378)
ARBORTEXT INC (HQ)
3767 Ranchero Dr Ste 100 (48108-2770)
PHONE....................................734 997-0200
Jim Heppleman, President
Jim Haggarty, Vice Pres
Jim Sterken, Vice Pres
EMP: 109 EST: 1982
SQ FT: 40,000
SALES (est): 54.8MM
SALES (corp-wide): 1.4B Publicly Held
WEB: www.ptc.com
SIC: 7372 7371 7379 Prepackaged software; computer software development; computer related consulting services

PA: Ptc Inc.
   121 Seaport Blvd
   Boston MA 02210
   781 370-5000

(G-379)
ARNETS INC (PA)
Also Called: Arnet's Memorials
5060 Jackson Rd Ste H (48103-1894)
PHONE....................................734 665-3650
Martha Moomey, Treasurer
Stephen T Arnet, Shareholder
Jimmey Moomey, Admin Sec
▲ EMP: 11 EST: 1904
SQ FT: 8,000
SALES (est): 958.5K Privately Held
WEB: www.arnetsmonuments.com
SIC: 5999 7261 3272 3993 Monuments, finished to custom order; crematory; grave markers, concrete; monuments, concrete; signs, not made in custom sign painting shops

(G-380)
AROTECH CORPORATION (PA)
1229 Oak Valley Dr (48108-9675)
PHONE....................................800 281-0356
Jon B Kutler, Ch of Bd
Dean M Krutty, President
Yaakov Har-Oz, Vice Pres
Kelli L Kellar, CFO
Obey Al, Manager
EMP: 73 EST: 1990
SQ FT: 17,300
SALES: 96.6MM Privately Held
WEB: www.arotech.com
SIC: 3691 3694 Batteries, rechargeable; battery charging alternators & generators

(G-381)
ASCOTT CORPORATION
1202 N Main St (48104-1091)
PHONE....................................734 663-2023
Andrew S Crawford, President
EMP: 5 EST: 1974
SQ FT: 6,800
SALES (est): 486.8K Privately Held
SIC: 2396 Screen printing on fabric articles

(G-382)
ASHINE DIAMOND TOOLS
4872 S Ridgeside Cir (48105-9403)
PHONE....................................734 668-9067
WEI LI, Principal
EMP: 7 EST: 2005
SALES (est): 150.4K Privately Held
SIC: 3545 Machine tool accessories

(G-383)
ASSAY DESIGNS INC
5777 Hines Dr (48108-7901)
P.O. Box 3909 (48106-3909)
PHONE....................................734 214-0923
Daniel Calvo, President
Eitan Akirav, Vice Pres
EMP: 37 EST: 1991
SQ FT: 14,000
SALES (est): 9.7MM
SALES (corp-wide): 117.7MM Publicly Held
WEB: www.enzo.com
SIC: 3829 2819 Medical diagnostic systems, nuclear; industrial inorganic chemicals
PA: Enzo Biochem, Inc.
   527 Madison Ave Rm 901
   New York NY 10022
   212 583-0100

(G-384)
ASSOCIATED METALS INC
Also Called: National Discount X-Ray Supply
6235 Jackson Rd Ste B (48103-9933)
PHONE....................................734 369-3851
Kenneth W Fil, CEO
EMP: 5 EST: 1986
SQ FT: 6,000
SALES (est): 471.5K Privately Held
SIC: 3412 5047 5085 5113 Metal barrels, drums & pails; X-ray film & supplies; commercial containers; industrial & personal service paper

Ann Arbor - Washtenaw County (G-385)

(G-385)
ATTEROCOR INC
301 N Main St Ste 100 (48104-1296)
PHONE 734 845-9300
Julia C Owens, *CEO*
Keri Mattox, *Principal*
Jeffery M Brinza, *Senior VP*
Pharis Mohideen, *Officer*
EMP: 6 **EST:** 2012
SALES (est): 800.3K **Privately Held**
WEB: www.millendo.com
SIC: 2834 Adrenal pharmaceutical preparations

(G-386)
AVABELLA PRESS
4299 Katie Jo Ct (48103-9038)
PHONE 734 662-0048
James Obrecht, *Principal*
EMP: 5 **EST:** 2009
SALES (est): 133.2K **Privately Held**
SIC: 2741 Miscellaneous publishing

(G-387)
AVEN INC
Also Called: Aven Tools
4330 Varsity Dr (48108-2241)
PHONE 734 973-0099
Mike Shahpurwala, *President*
Bakir Kanpurwala, *CFO*
George Fielder, *Sales Mgr*
Katelyn Myers, *Cust Mgr*
Mark Kanpurwala, *Director*
▲ **EMP:** 10 **EST:** 1983
SQ FT: 12,000
SALES (est): 1.7MM **Privately Held**
WEB: www.aventools.com
SIC: 3423 Hand & edge tools

(G-388)
AVFLIGHT CORPORATION (HQ)
47 W Ellsworth Rd (48108-2206)
P.O. Box 1387 (48106-1387)
PHONE 734 663-6466
Mark Cloete, *Controller*
Carl Muhs, *Manager*
EMP: 1 **EST:** 2000
SALES (est): 87.7MM
SALES (corp-wide): 378.7MM **Privately Held**
WEB: www.avflight.com
SIC: 2911 Jet fuels
PA: Crs Acquisition Corporation
   47 W Ellsworth Rd
   Ann Arbor MI
   734 663-6466

(G-389)
AVISSA SKIN+BODY
1715 Plymouth Rd (48105-1800)
PHONE 734 316-5556
EMP: 9 **EST:** 2017
SALES (est): 647.1K **Privately Held**
WEB: www.avissaskin.com
SIC: 8062 8049 7231 2844 General medical & surgical hospitals; offices of health practitioner; beauty shops; toilet preparations

(G-390)
AVOMEEN LLC
Also Called: Avomeen Analytical Services
4840 Venture Dr (48108-9559)
PHONE 734 222-1090
Mark Harvill, *CEO*
Andrew C Kolbert, *President*
Luke Miller, *Senior VP*
Ying Long, *Project Dir*
Alan Gradolph, *Project Mgr*
EMP: 82 **EST:** 2010
SQ FT: 25,000
SALES (est): 11.2MM
SALES (corp-wide): 782.6MM **Privately Held**
WEB: www.avomeen.com
SIC: 8734 2834 Testing laboratories; pharmaceutical preparations
HQ: Element Materials Technology Limited
   3rd Floor
   London WC2E
   808 234-1667

(G-391)
AXIOBIONICS
6111 Jackson Rd Ste 200 (48103-9167)
PHONE 734 327-2946
Philip Muccio, *General Mgr*
Philip E Muccio, *Principal*
Richard Barnes, *CIO*
EMP: 4 **EST:** 2010
SALES (est): 452.1K **Privately Held**
WEB: www.axiobionics.com
SIC: 3842 Prosthetic appliances

(G-392)
AZOTH LLC
1099 Highland Dr Ste F (48108-5002)
PHONE 734 669-3797
Manoj Sachdeva, *Mng Member*
Scott Burk,
Cody Cochran,
Jay Mullick,
EMP: 10 **EST:** 2018
SALES (est): 500K
SALES (corp-wide): 111.1MM **Privately Held**
WEB: www.azoth3d.com
SIC: 2759 Commercial printing
PA: Production Services Management, Inc.
   1255 Beach Ct
   Saline MI 48176
   734 677-0454

(G-393)
AZURE TRAINING SYSTEMS JV LLC ✪
1229 Oak Valley Dr (48108-9675)
PHONE 734 761-5836
Kurt Flosky, *Mng Member*
EMP: 5 **EST:** 2021
SALES (est): 88.3K **Privately Held**
SIC: 3699 Flight simulators (training aids), electronic

(G-394)
B & B HEARTWOODS INC
5444 Whitmore Lake Rd (48105-9635)
PHONE 734 332-9525
William J Geschwender, *President*
Bonnie J Geschwender, *Vice Pres*
EMP: 4 **EST:** 1985
SQ FT: 3,000
SALES (est): 320.8K **Privately Held**
WEB: www.bandbheartwoods.com
SIC: 2426 5211 Hardwood dimension & flooring mills; lumber products

(G-395)
BANGGAMEUS
2590 Cook Creek Dr (48103-8971)
PHONE 734 904-1916
Chris Lin,
EMP: 8 **EST:** 2010
SALES (est): 317.3K **Privately Held**
SIC: 2731 Book publishing

(G-396)
BEAD GALLERY
311 E Liberty St (48104-2276)
PHONE 734 663-6800
Julie Van Dyke, *Owner*
EMP: 10 **EST:** 1986
SQ FT: 1,200
SALES (est): 611.8K **Privately Held**
WEB: www.beadgalleryannarbor.com
SIC: 5944 3961 Jewelry stores; jewelry apparel, non-precious metals; costume jewelry, ex. precious metal & semi-precious stones

(G-397)
BEANS BEST LLC
1240 Jewett St (48104-6224)
PHONE 734 707-7378
Julian Carpenter, *Administration*
EMP: 9 **EST:** 2011
SALES (est): 316.9K **Privately Held**
WEB: www.beansbestllc.com
SIC: 3231 3432 3291 Reflector glass beads, for highway signs or reflectors; faucets & spigots, metal & plastic; steel shot abrasive

(G-398)
BEAU SATCHELLE LLC
4860 Washtenaw Ave Ste I (48108-3401)
PHONE 313 374-8462
April J Bayles,
EMP: 4 **EST:** 2015
SALES (est): 15K **Privately Held**
SIC: 3111 Handbag leather

(G-399)
BENCHMARK COATING SYSTEMS LLC
2075 W Stadium Blvd (48106-7700)
PHONE 517 782-4061
Terry Kelly, *Principal*
EMP: 6 **EST:** 2008
SALES (est): 112.1K **Privately Held**
SIC: 2851 Paints & paint additives

(G-400)
BESSENBERG BINDERY CORPORATION
215 N 5th Ave (48104-1407)
P.O. Box 7970 (48107-7970)
PHONE 734 996-9696
Fax: 734 996-1445
EMP: 4
SQ FT: 3,000
SALES (est): 250K **Privately Held**
SIC: 2789 Book Binding & Restoration Services

(G-401)
BIOFLEX INC
6111 Jackson Rd Ste 200 (48103-9167)
PHONE 734 327-2946
Philip Muccio, *President*
EMP: 5 **EST:** 1988
SALES (est): 448K **Privately Held**
WEB: www.bioflexlaser.com
SIC: 2389 Apparel for handicapped

(G-402)
BOARD FOR STUDENT PUBLICATIONS
420 Maynard St (48109-1327)
PHONE 734 418-4115
Mark Bealafeld, *General Mgr*
Derek Wolfe, *Manager*
EMP: 78 **EST:** 1890
SALES (est): 1.2MM **Privately Held**
SIC: 2711 Newspapers, publishing & printing

(G-403)
BOROPHARM INC
2800 Plymouth Rd Bldg 40 (48109-2800)
PHONE 517 455-7847
Andrew Cipa, *Business Mgr*
Paul Herritson, *Vice Pres*
EMP: 20
SALES (corp-wide): 12MM **Privately Held**
WEB: www.boropharm.com
SIC: 2869 Laboratory chemicals, organic
PA: Boropharm, Inc.
   39555 Orchard Hill Pl # 600
   Novi MI 48375
   248 348-5776

(G-404)
BORRIES MKG SYSTEMS PARTNR
3744 Plaza Dr Ste 1c (48108-1665)
PHONE 734 761-9549
Lothar Von Arnin, *Partner*
Donald Hubchik, *General Mgr*
L Von Arnin, *Ltd Ptnr*
Holger Markgraf, *Marketing Staff*
Klaus Kihr, *Manager*
EMP: 5 **EST:** 1988
SQ FT: 3,200
SALES (est): 1.2MM
SALES (corp-wide): 177.9K **Privately Held**
WEB: www.borries.com
SIC: 3953 Marking devices
HQ: Borries Markier-Systeme Gmbh
   Siemensstr. 3
   Pliezhausen 72124
   712 797-970

(G-405)
BPI HOLDINGS INTERNATIONAL INC
1101 Technology Dr (48108-8921)
PHONE 815 363-9000
EMP: 7
SALES (corp-wide): 3.3B **Privately Held**
WEB: www.brakepartsinc.com
SIC: 3714 Motor vehicle brake systems & parts
HQ: Bpi Holdings International, Inc.
   4400 Prime Pkwy
   Mchenry IL 60050
   815 363-9000

(G-406)
BRIO DEVICE LLC
2104 Georgetown Blvd (48105-1535)
PHONE 734 945-5728
Laura L Walz,
Hannah Hensel,
Laura McCormick,
Douglas Mullen,
Sabina Siddiqui,
EMP: 4 **EST:** 2011
SALES (est): 279.7K **Privately Held**
WEB: www.briodevice.com
SIC: 3841 Surgical & medical instruments

(G-407)
BS BARS
4175 Whitmore Lake Rd (48105-9634)
PHONE 734 358-3832
EMP: 6 **EST:** 2012
SALES (est): 126.1K **Privately Held**
SIC: 2064 Candy & other confectionery products

(G-408)
BUDGET EUROPE TRAVEL SERVICE
2557 Meade Ct (48105-1304)
PHONE 734 668-0529
Robert L Brown, *President*
Linda Pogreba, *Vice Pres*
EMP: 5 **EST:** 1978
SALES (est): 880K **Privately Held**
WEB: www.budgeteuropetravel.com
SIC: 4724 4725 2711 Tourist agency arranging transport, lodging & car rental; tour operators; newspapers; publishing only, not printed on site

(G-409)
BULLDOG FABRICATING CORP
50 Enterprise Dr (48103-9503)
P.O. Box 106, Dexter (48130-0106)
PHONE 734 761-3111
Steven C Kern, *President*
EMP: 5 **EST:** 1990
SQ FT: 10,000
SALES (est): 1.2MM **Privately Held**
WEB: www.bulldogfab.com
SIC: 5085 3569 Filters, industrial; filter elements, fluid, hydraulic line

(G-410)
BURLWOODBOX
3735 N Territorial Rd E (48105-9320)
PHONE 734 662-7274
Deborah Keese, *Principal*
EMP: 4 **EST:** 2011
SALES (est): 109K **Privately Held**
WEB: www.burlwoodbox.com
SIC: 2499 Decorative wood & woodwork

(G-411)
BUYERS DEVELOPMENT GROUP LLC (PA)
Also Called: Grow Show, The
4095 Stone School Rd (48108-9723)
PHONE 734 677-0009
Cayman Hartigan,
EMP: 11 **EST:** 2009
SQ FT: 4,800
SALES (est): 1.2MM **Privately Held**
WEB: www.thegrowshow.org
SIC: 3524 Lawn & garden equipment

(G-412)
C3 INDUSTRIES INC
2082 S State St (48104-4608)
PHONE 248 255-1283
Vishal Rungta, *President*
EMP: 7 **EST:** 2020
SALES (est): 1MM **Privately Held**
SIC: 2833 Medicinals & botanicals

(G-413)
CABINETWORKS GROUP MICH LLC (PA)
Also Called: Denova
4600 Arrowhead Dr (48105-2773)
PHONE 734 205-4600
Christian Cook, *CEO*

GEOGRAPHIC SECTION

Ann Arbor - Washtenaw County (G-440)

Mark Trexler, *COO*
Michael Gulbernat, *Vice Pres*
Christopher Harley, *Vice Pres*
Jessica Joffe, *Vice Pres*
◆ **EMP:** 360 **EST:** 2000
SQ FT: 150,000
SALES (est): 1.6B **Privately Held**
WEB: www.acpicorp.com
SIC: 2434 Wood kitchen cabinets

(G-414)
CARDINAL ECONOMIC SAND FINANCE
315 2nd St Apt 504 (48103-4991)
PHONE.................................734 926-6989
Jason Hall, *Principal*
Brendan Cupchak, *Research Analys*
EMP: 5 **EST:** 2016
SALES (est): 66K **Privately Held**
WEB:
www.cardinaleconomicsandfinance.com
SIC: 1442 Construction sand & gravel

(G-415)
CASTLE REMEDIES INC
2345 S Huron Pkwy Ste 1 (48104-5124)
PHONE.................................734 973-8990
Edward Linkner MD, *President*
Marian Smith, *General Mgr*
Aarti Batavia, *Nutritionist*
Mary Tillinghaft, *Manager*
Cindy Klement, *Consultant*
EMP: 13 **EST:** 1983
SALES (est): 1.5MM **Privately Held**
WEB: www.castleremedies.com
SIC: 2023 Dietary supplements, dairy & non-dairy based

(G-416)
CATYLIST INC
Also Called: Brother Industrial Equipment
2360 E Stadium Blvd # 16 (48104-4887)
P.O. Box 8151, Port Saint Lucie FL (34985-8151)
PHONE.................................734 973-3185
Christopher Treppler, *President*
EMP: 1 **EST:** 2012
SALES (est): 1.1MM
SALES (corp-wide): 5.3B **Publicly Held**
WEB: www.catylist.com
SIC: 6531 7372 Real estate listing services; application computer software
PA: Moody's Corporation
250 Greenwich St
New York NY 10007
212 553-0300

(G-417)
CAYMAN CHEMICAL COMPANY INC (PA)
1180 E Ellsworth Rd (48108-2419)
PHONE.................................734 971-3335
Kirk M Maxey, *President*
Gregory W Endres, *Vice Pres*
Jeffrey K Johnson, *Vice Pres*
Craig Maxey, *Vice Pres*
Barbara J Rice, *Vice Pres*
EMP: 92 **EST:** 1980
SQ FT: 80,000
SALES (est): 62.1MM **Privately Held**
WEB: www.caymanchem.com
SIC: 2834 2899 Pharmaceutical preparations; chemical preparations

(G-418)
CBM LLC
Also Called: Sleeping Bear Press
2395 S Huron Pkwy Ste 200 (48104-5170)
PHONE.................................800 487-2323
Heather Hughes, *Publisher*
Amy Patrick, *Marketing Staff*
Ben Mondloch, *Branch Mgr*
EMP: 6 **Privately Held**
WEB: www.cherrylakepublishing.com
SIC: 2741 Miscellaneous publishing
PA: Cbm, Llc
1750 Northway Dr Ste 101
North Mankato MN 56003

(G-419)
CELSEE INC
100 Phoenix Dr Ste 321 (48108-2600)
PHONE.................................866 748-1448
Kalyan Handique, *CEO*
Lisa Sherman, *Vice Pres*
EMP: 54 **EST:** 2010
SALES (est): 8.1MM
SALES (corp-wide): 2.5B **Publicly Held**
WEB: www.info.bio-rad.com
SIC: 3826 Environmental testing equipment
PA: Bio-Rad Laboratories, Inc.
1000 Alfred Nobel Dr
Hercules CA 94547
510 724-7000

(G-420)
CENTRUM FORCE FABRICATION LLC
3425 Stone School Rd (48108-2305)
PHONE.................................517 857-4774
Thomas B Monahan,
Greg Turcotte,
EMP: 4 **EST:** 2011
SALES (est): 464.7K **Privately Held**
WEB: www.centrumforce.com
SIC: 3569 Centrifuges, industrial

(G-421)
CHAOSIUM INC
3450 Wooddale Ct (48104-4274)
PHONE.................................734 972-9551
Charlie Krank, *President*
Dustin Wright, *Publisher*
EMP: 5 **EST:** 1975
SQ FT: 1,800
SALES (est): 638.5K **Privately Held**
WEB: www.chaosium.com
SIC: 2731 Books: publishing only

(G-422)
CHEAP ELECTRIC CONTRACTORS CO
2424 E Stadium Blvd (48104-4813)
PHONE.................................734 205-9591
EMP: 4 **EST:** 2016
SALES (est): 93.7K **Privately Held**
SIC: 5082 3699 General construction machinery & equipment; electrical equipment & supplies

(G-423)
CHEAP ELECTRIC CONTRACTORS CO
3205 Boardwalk St (48108-1773)
PHONE.................................734 205-9596
EMP: 4 **EST:** 2016
SALES (est): 126K **Privately Held**
SIC: 5082 3699 General construction machinery & equipment; electrical equipment & supplies

(G-424)
CHOUTEAU FUELS COMPANY LLC
414 S Main St Ste 600 (48104-2398)
PHONE.................................734 302-4800
EMP: 5 **EST:** 2011
SALES (est): 1.4MM **Privately Held**
WEB: www.dtepowerandindustrial.com
SIC: 2869 Fuels

(G-425)
CLARIOS LLC
Also Called: Johnson Controls
1935 S Industrial Hwy (48104-4613)
PHONE.................................734 995-3016
Cara Luff, *Manager*
EMP: 6
SALES (corp-wide): 47.9B **Publicly Held**
WEB: www.clarios.com
SIC: 3691 Lead acid batteries (storage batteries)
HQ: Clarios, Llc
5757 N Green Bay Ave
Milwaukee WI 53209

(G-426)
CLEAR ESTIMATES INC
1509 Granger Ave (48104-4426)
PHONE.................................734 368-9951
Nolan Orfield, *CEO*
EMP: 10 **EST:** 2014
SALES (est): 299.3K **Privately Held**
WEB: www.clearestimates.com
SIC: 7372 Business oriented computer software

(G-427)
CLEAR IMAGE DEVICES LLC
3930 N Michael Rd (48103-9344)
PHONE.................................734 645-6459
John L Stinson, *President*
Jennie Stinson, *Director*
EMP: 6 **EST:** 2005
SALES (est): 519.9K **Privately Held**
WEB: www.clearimagedevices.com
SIC: 3841 Surgical & medical instruments

(G-428)
CLIFF KEEN WRESTLING PDTS INC
Also Called: Cliff Keen Athletic
4480 Varsity Dr Ste B (48108-5007)
P.O. Box 1447 (48106-1447)
PHONE.................................734 975-8800
James C Keen, *President*
Mark Churella Sr, *Corp Secy*
Barry Bellaire, *Vice Pres*
Ryan Churella, *Vice Pres*
Chad Clark, *Vice Pres*
▲ **EMP:** 45 **EST:** 1958
SQ FT: 25,000
SALES (est): 6.9MM **Privately Held**
WEB: www.cliffkeen.com
SIC: 2329 2339 Men's & boys' athletic uniforms; men's & boys' sportswear & athletic clothing; women's & misses' athletic clothing & sportswear

(G-429)
COBALT FRICTION TECH LLC
330 Meadow Creek Dr (48105-3052)
PHONE.................................734 930-6902
WEI-Ku Lin, *Principal*
EMP: 5 **EST:** 2015
SALES (est): 105.7K **Privately Held**
WEB: www.cobaltfriction.com
SIC: 3599 Industrial machinery

(G-430)
COBALT FRICTION TECHNOLOGIES
4595 Platt Rd (48108-9726)
PHONE.................................734 274-3030
Ernest G Bocchino, *President*
Headley G Lee, *Vice Pres*
Cleve A Bispott, *Admin Sec*
EMP: 12 **EST:** 2002
SALES (est): 943.7K **Privately Held**
WEB: www.cobaltfriction.com
SIC: 3292 Asbestos friction materials

(G-431)
COBHAM MCRLCTRNIC SLUTIONS INC (DH)
310 Dino Dr (48103-9502)
PHONE.................................734 426-1230
Jill Kale, *CEO*
Jon E Carlson, *CFO*
EMP: 9 **EST:** 1994
SQ FT: 4,000
SALES (est): 67.6MM
SALES (corp-wide): 177.9K **Privately Held**
WEB: www.cobham.com
SIC: 3679 3825 Microwave components; microwave test equipment

(G-432)
COHDA WIRELESS AMERICA LLC
3135 S State St Ste 102 (48108-1653)
PHONE.................................248 513-2105
Ulrich Stauss, *Program Mgr*
Patrick Brunett,
Jane Cooke,
EMP: 1 **EST:** 2013
SQ FT: 16,800
SALES (est): 1MM **Privately Held**
WEB: www.cohdawireless.com
SIC: 3663 Carrier equipment, radio communications
PA: Cohda Wireless Pty Ltd
27 Greenhill Rd
Wayville SA 5034

(G-433)
COLOR EXPRESS PRINTING INC
625 State Cir Ste 1 (48108-3342)
PHONE.................................734 213-4980
Dan Payeur, *President*
Susan Payeur, *Vice Pres*
EMP: 8 **EST:** 1995
SQ FT: 12,000 **Privately Held**
SIC: 2752 Commercial printing, offset

(G-434)
COMPUTER SCIENCES CORP
1947 S Industrial Hwy (48104-4613)
PHONE.................................734 761-8513
EMP: 9 **EST:** 2015
SALES (est): 68.8K **Privately Held**
WEB: www.dxc.com
SIC: 7372 Prepackaged software

(G-435)
CONSIDER MAGAZINE
1429 Hill St (48104-3105)
PHONE.................................734 769-0500
EMP: 4 **EST:** 2019
SALES (est): 73.1K **Privately Held**
WEB: www.consideronline.org
SIC: 2721 Magazines: publishing only, not printed on site

(G-436)
CONTROL GAGING INC
847 Avis Dr (48108-9615)
PHONE.................................734 668-6750
David Hayes, *President*
Jody Scott, *Vice Pres*
▲ **EMP:** 32 **EST:** 1972
SQ FT: 24,000
SALES (est): 6.4MM
SALES (corp-wide): 988.5K **Privately Held**
WEB: www.marposs.com
SIC: 3545 Precision measuring tools
HQ: Marposs Spa
Via Saliceto 13
Bentivoglio BO 40010
051 899-111

(G-437)
COPYTWO INC
Also Called: Dollar Bill Copying
611 Church St (48104-3028)
PHONE.................................734 665-9200
Michael J Leonard, *Principal*
EMP: 23 **EST:** 1991
SALES (est): 3.2MM **Privately Held**
WEB: www.dollarbillcopying.com
SIC: 2752 Commercial printing, offset

(G-438)
COVALENT MEDICAL INC
4750 S State Rd (48108-9719)
PHONE.................................734 604-0688
Bruno Lowinger, *President*
Johan Lowinger, *General Mgr*
EMP: 4 **EST:** 2002
SQ FT: 4,000
SALES (est): 345.5K **Privately Held**
WEB: www.covamed.com
SIC: 2891 Adhesives; glue

(G-439)
CREATIVE ENGINEERING INC
Also Called: Creative Health Products
7621 E Joy Rd (48105-9682)
PHONE.................................734 996-5900
Marlene Donoghue, *President*
Wallace Donoghue, *CFO*
Robin Mack, *Manager*
Wally Donoghue, *Technology*
EMP: 8 **EST:** 1976
SALES (est): 1.6MM **Privately Held**
WEB: www.chponline.com
SIC: 5047 5999 3829 Hospital equipment & furniture; alarm & safety equipment stores; aircraft & motor vehicle measurement equipment

(G-440)
CUSHING-MALLOY INC
Also Called: CM Book
1350 N Main St (48104-1045)
P.O. Box 8632 (48107-8632)
PHONE.................................734 663-8554
Tom Cushing, *Ch of Bd*
Connie Cushing, *President*
Thomas Weber, *President*
Laurie Jean, *Office Mgr*
EMP: 30 **EST:** 1948
SQ FT: 40,000

Ann Arbor - Washtenaw County (G-441)

SALES (est): 3.9MM **Privately Held**
WEB: www.cushing-malloy.com
SIC: **2752** 2789 2732 Commercial printing, offset; bookbinding & related work; book printing

(G-441)
D & C INVESTMENT GROUP INC (PA)
Also Called: Nematron
5840 Interface Dr (48103-9176)
PHONE..................................734 994-0591
Gregory Chandler, *President*
EMP: 14 EST: 2004
SQ FT: 51,000
SALES (est): 3.3MM **Privately Held**
SIC: **3823** Computer interface equipment for industrial process control

(G-442)
DAILY GARDENER LLC
5211 Pontiac Trl (48105-9493)
PHONE..................................734 754-6527
Doris Hill, *Principal*
EMP: 6 EST: 2016
SALES (est): 85.7K **Privately Held**
WEB: www.thedailygardener.com
SIC: **2711** Newspapers, publishing & printing

(G-443)
DANMAR PRODUCTS INC (PA)
221 Jackson Industrial Dr (48103-9104)
PHONE..................................734 761-1990
Hidie Bowman, *CEO*
Roger Bowman, *President*
Steve Richards, *General Mgr*
Amy Bowman, *COO*
Cody Bowman, *Vice Pres*
EMP: 22 EST: 1967
SQ FT: 9,000
SALES (est): 4.1MM **Privately Held**
WEB: www.danmarproducts.com
SIC: **3842** Surgical appliances & supplies

(G-444)
DATAMARTZ LLC
2232 S Main St (48103-6938)
PHONE..................................248 202-1559
Jordan Martz, *Principal*
EMP: 9 EST: 2013
SALES (est): 785.9K **Privately Held**
WEB: www.datamartz.com
SIC: **2741** Miscellaneous publishing

(G-445)
DEGRASYN BIOSCIENCES LLC
4476 Boulder Pond Dr (48108-8601)
PHONE..................................713 582-3395
Nicholas Donato,
EMP: 5
SALES (est): 260.3K **Privately Held**
SIC: **2833** Medicinal chemicals

(G-446)
DELMAS TYPESETTING
461 Hilldale Dr (48105-1120)
PHONE..................................734 662-8899
William Kalvin, *President*
EMP: 8 EST: 1979 **Privately Held**
WEB: www.delmastype.com
SIC: **2791** Typesetting

(G-447)
DENTAL CONSULTANTS INC
3100 W Liberty Rd (48103-8724)
PHONE..................................734 663-6777
John W Farah, *President*
Sabiha Bunek, *Chief*
John M Powers, *Treasurer*
Chris Voigtman, *Sales Staff*
Jim Dombrowski, *Creative Dir*
EMP: 19 EST: 1983
SQ FT: 1,000
SALES (est): 2.1MM **Privately Held**
WEB: www.dentaladvisor.com
SIC: **2721** Trade journals: publishing only, not printed on site

(G-448)
DESIGN & TEST TECHNOLOGY INC (PA)
3744 Plaza Dr Ste 2 (48108-1651)
P.O. Box 1526 (48106-1526)
PHONE..................................734 665-4316
Michael Murphy, *President*
Nancy Murphy, *Vice Pres*
EMP: 9 EST: 1982
SQ FT: 6,000
SALES (est): 1.3MM **Privately Held**
WEB: www.designtest.com
SIC: **3825** 7373 Test equipment for electronic & electric measurement; computer systems analysis & design

(G-449)
DETROIT FUDGE COMPANY INC
2251 W Liberty St (48103-4405)
PHONE..................................734 369-8573
EMP: 5 EST: 2018
SALES (est): 463.4K **Privately Held**
WEB: www.detroitediblecompany.com
SIC: **2064** Fudge (candy)

(G-450)
DETROIT LEGAL NEWS PUBG LLC
Also Called: Washtenaw Legal News
2301 Platt Rd Ste 300 (48104-5149)
P.O. Box 1367 (48106-1367)
PHONE..................................734 477-0201
Brad Thompson, *President*
Melanie Deeds, *Manager*
Bradley L Thompson II,
EMP: 15 EST: 1998
SALES (est): 642.7K **Privately Held**
SIC: **2711** Newspapers, publishing & printing

(G-451)
DIAMOND ELECTRIC
455 E Eisenhower Pkwy # 200 (48108-3323)
PHONE..................................734 995-5525
EMP: 4
SALES (est): 133.8K **Privately Held**
SIC: **4911** 3699 Electric Services Mfg Electrical Equipment/Supplies

(G-452)
DIAMOND POWER SPECIALTY CO
1779 Oakview Dr (48108-8521)
PHONE..................................734 429-8527
Jim Schorr, *Manager*
EMP: 5 EST: 2017
SALES (est): 153.9K **Privately Held**
SIC: **3511** Turbines & turbine generator sets

(G-453)
DLR LOGISTICS INC
2735 S Wagner Rd Unit 6a (48103-8728)
PHONE..................................248 499-2368
John McCormick, *CEO*
EMP: 4 EST: 2020
SALES (est): 265K **Privately Held**
SIC: **3537** Trucks: freight, baggage, etc.: industrial, except mining

(G-454)
DOCNETWORK INC
5430 Data Ct Ste 250 (48108-8967)
PHONE..................................734 619-8300
Michael Ambrose, *CEO*
Jeff Beckett, *Engineer*
Rori Ladhoff, *Accounts Mgr*
Adam Lane, *Accounts Mgr*
Gabriel Ribeiro, *Sales Staff*
EMP: 35 EST: 2009
SALES (est): 2.8MM **Privately Held**
WEB: www.docnetwork.org
SIC: **7372** Prepackaged software

(G-455)
DOG MIGHT LLC
303 Metty Dr (48103-8330)
PHONE..................................734 679-0646
EMP: 17 EST: 2013
SALES (est): 1.7MM **Privately Held**
WEB: www.dogmight.com
SIC: **5199** 5945 3944 Wood carvings; toys & games; board games, puzzles & models, except electronic

(G-456)
DOMINOS PIZZA LLC (HQ)
30 Frank Lloyd Wright Dr (48105-9757)
P.O. Box 997 (48106-0997)
PHONE..................................734 930-3030
Stan Gage, *Vice Pres*
Archie Vincent, *Site Mgr*
Biily Moore, *Branch Mgr*
David A Brandon, *Mng Member*
Hank Benedetto, *Manager*
▲ EMP: 150 EST: 1960
SQ FT: 320,000
SALES (est): 2B
SALES (corp-wide): 4.1B **Publicly Held**
WEB: www.dominos.com
SIC: **5812** 6794 5046 5149 Pizzeria, chain; franchises, selling or licensing; restaurant equipment & supplies; pizza supplies; management services; prepared flour mixes & doughs
PA: Domino's Pizza, Inc.
30 Frank Lloyd Wright Dr
Ann Arbor MI 48105
734 930-3030

(G-457)
DON THEYKEN
1319 Algonac St (48103-5302)
PHONE..................................734 996-8359
Don Theyken, *Chairman*
EMP: 4 EST: 2016
SALES (est): 85.9K **Privately Held**
WEB: www.theyken.net
SIC: **3572** Computer storage devices

(G-458)
DREW TECHNOLOGIES INC (HQ)
3915 Res Pk Dr Ste A10 (48108)
PHONE..................................734 222-5228
▲ EMP: 9
SQ FT: 4,500
SALES (est): 2.7MM **Privately Held**
SIC: **3559** Manufactures Misc Industry Machinery

(G-459)
DTE ENERGY RESOURCES INC (HQ)
414 S Main St Ste 600 (48104-2398)
PHONE..................................734 302-4800
Lillian Bauder, *Vice Pres*
Steven Dugan, *Manager*
▼ EMP: 100 EST: 1994
SALES (est): 839.6MM **Publicly Held**
WEB: www.dtepowerandindustrial.com
SIC: **4911** 1389 Electric services; gas field services

(G-460)
DUO SECURITY INC
130 S 1st St Ste 100 (48104-1343)
PHONE..................................866 768-4247
Lakshmi Akella, *Opers Staff*
Ron Martin, *Engineer*
Stevie Straka, *Engineer*
Nicholas Kogelman, *Cust Mgr*
Jack Flynn, *Accounts Exec*
EMP: 75
SALES (corp-wide): 49.8B **Publicly Held**
WEB: www.duo.com
SIC: **7372** Prepackaged software
HQ: Duo Security Llc
123 N Ashley St Ste 200
Ann Arbor MI 48104

(G-461)
DUO SECURITY LLC (HQ)
123 N Ashley St Ste 200 (48104-1316)
PHONE..................................734 330-2673
Douglas Song, *CEO*
William Welch, *President*
Trevor Darr, *Partner*
Alexander Glass, *Partner*
Derek Hart, *Partner*
EMP: 200 EST: 2010
SALES (est): 76.2MM
SALES (corp-wide): 49.8B **Publicly Held**
WEB: www.duo.com
SIC: **7372** Prepackaged software
PA: Cisco Systems, Inc.
170 W Tasman Dr
San Jose CA 95134
408 526-4000

(G-462)
DYNICS INC
620 Technology Dr (48108-8937)
PHONE..................................734 677-6100
Edward Gatt, *President*
Chet Biegalski, *Prdtn Mgr*
Kimberly Dornes, *Purch Agent*
Kimberly Herrst, *Purch Agent*
Brandon Mirto, *Electrical Engi*
EMP: 75
SQ FT: 18,000
SALES (est): 17.7MM **Privately Held**
WEB: www.dynics.com
SIC: **3575** 5734 Computer terminals, monitors & components; software, business & non-game

(G-463)
EATON CORPORATION
4743 Venture Dr (48108-9560)
PHONE..................................517 787-8121
Becca Gorman, *Principal*
Bill Lopez, *Principal*
John Perkin, *Engineer*
Rex Robb, *Manager*
EMP: 4 **Privately Held**
WEB: www.eatonelectrical.com
SIC: **8711** 3812 Engineering services; search & navigation equipment
HQ: Eaton Corporation
1000 Eaton Blvd
Cleveland OH 44122
440 523-5000

(G-464)
EATON INDUSTRIES INC (PA)
254 S Wagner Rd (48103-1940)
P.O. Box 669, Manchester (48158-0669)
PHONE..................................734 428-0000
EMP: 8
SALES (est): 2.9MM **Privately Held**
SIC: **3845** Electromedical Equipment

(G-465)
ECO SIGN SOLUTIONS LLC
37 Enterprise Dr (48103-9503)
PHONE..................................734 276-8585
Dave Small, *Owner*
EMP: 7 EST: 2012
SALES (est): 421.6K **Privately Held**
WEB: www.ecosignsolutions.net
SIC: **3993** Electric signs

(G-466)
ECOVIA RENEWABLES INC
600 Suth Wagner Rd Ste 15 (48103)
PHONE..................................248 953-0594
Constance Bahr, *Research*
Ian Graves, *Research*
Chao Peng, *Research*
Samuel Kohley, *Manager*
Jeremy Minty,
EMP: 3 EST: 2014
SALES (est): 2MM **Privately Held**
WEB: www.ecoviarenewables.com
SIC: **2869** 7389 Industrial organic chemicals;

(G-467)
EDWARD AND COLE INC
Also Called: Dotmine Day Planners
5540 Tanglewood Dr (48105-9549)
PHONE..................................734 996-9074
EMP: 4
SALES (est): 471.1K **Privately Held**
SIC: **2678** Mfg Stationery Products

(G-468)
EES COKE BATTERY LLC
414 S Main St Ste 600 (48104-2398)
PHONE..................................313 235-4000
David Ruud, *President*
EMP: 13 EST: 2000
SALES (est): 17MM **Publicly Held**
WEB: www.dtepowerandindustrial.com
SIC: **2911** Petroleum refining; gases & liquefied petroleum gases; coke, petroleum
HQ: Dte Energy Resources, Inc.
414 S Main St Ste 600
Ann Arbor MI 48104

(G-469)
ELECTRIC CONTRACTORS COMPANY
1501 Briarwood Cir (48108-1662)
PHONE..................................734 205-9594
EMP: 4 EST: 2016
SALES (est): 88.7K **Privately Held**
SIC: **5082** 3699 General construction machinery & equipment; electrical equipment & supplies

GEOGRAPHIC SECTION
Ann Arbor - Washtenaw County (G-496)

(G-470)
ELECTRIC EYE CAFE
811 N Main St (48104-1032)
PHONE..................................734 369-6904
Rachel Pell, *Principal*
EMP: 6 EST: 2017
SALES (est): 108.8K **Privately Held**
SIC: **5812** 3699 Cafe; electrical equipment & supplies

(G-471)
ELMO MANUFACTURING CO INC
98 Valhalla Dr 950 (48103-5847)
P.O. Box 1312 (48106-1312)
PHONE..................................734 995-5966
Ellen Pesko, *President*
Robert Pesko, *Vice Pres*
EMP: 6 EST: 1993
SQ FT: 1,000
SALES (est): 623.2K **Privately Held**
WEB: www.elmomfg.com
SIC: **3546** Saws & sawing equipment

(G-472)
EMAG TECHNOLOGIES INC
775 Technology Dr Ste 300 (48108-8948)
PHONE..................................734 996-3624
Kazem F Sabet, *President*
EMP: 10 EST: 1994
SQ FT: 8,000
SALES (est): 1.8MM **Privately Held**
WEB: www.emagtech.com
SIC: **8732** 3663 Business research service; radio & TV communications equipment

(G-473)
EMPOWER FINANCIALS INC
4343 Concourse Dr Ste 140 (48108-8672)
PHONE..................................734 747-9393
Robert Murray, *President*
Kathy Holbel, *Controller*
EMP: 8 EST: 1983
SQ FT: 1,800
SALES (est): 138.2K **Privately Held**
WEB: www.empowerfin.com
SIC: **7371** 7372 Computer software development; prepackaged software

(G-474)
ENDRA LIFE SCIENCES INC
3600 Green Ct Ste 350 (48105-2440)
PHONE..................................734 335-0468
Francois Michelon, *Ch of Bd*
Renaud Maloberti, *Ch Credit Ofcr*
Michael Thornton, *CTO*
Irina Pestrikova, *Surgery Dir*
EMP: 18 EST: 2007
SQ FT: 7,200 **Privately Held**
WEB: www.endrainc.com
SIC: **3845** Ultrasonic scanning devices, medical

(G-475)
ENSIGN PUBLISHING HOUSE
2830 Pebble Creek Dr (48108-1728)
PHONE..................................734 369-3983
Elaine Stienon, *Principal*
EMP: 4 EST: 2018
SALES (est): 59.2K **Privately Held**
WEB: www.ensignpublishing.com
SIC: **2741** Miscellaneous publishing

(G-476)
EOTECH INC
1201 E Ellsworth Rd (48108-2420)
PHONE..................................734 741-8868
Rick Berger, *President*
King Charles, *Technical Staff*
Gentile Joseph, *Director*
EMP: 24 EST: 2008
SALES (est): 3.2MM **Privately Held**
WEB: www.eotechinc.com
SIC: **3827** Optical instruments & lenses

(G-477)
EOTECH LLC
1201 E Ellsworth Rd (48108-2420)
PHONE..................................248 971-4027
Matthew Van Haaren, *Mng Member*
EMP: 114 EST: 2020
SALES (est): 11.7MM
SALES (corp-wide): 17.4MM **Privately Held**
WEB: www.eotechinc.com
SIC: **3812** Defense systems & equipment

PA: Project Echo, Llc
1332 Anderson Rd
Clawson MI 48017
248 971-4027

(G-478)
ERVIN INDUSTRIES INC (PA)
Also Called: Ervin Amasteel
3893 Research Park Dr (48108-2267)
P.O. Box 1168 (48106-1168)
PHONE..................................734 769-4600
John E Pearson, *President*
James Trent Pearson, *Exec VP*
Becky Gutherie, *Vice Pres*
Bill Rhodaberger, *Vice Pres*
Kenneth R Prior, *VP Mfg*
◆ EMP: 50 EST: 1920
SQ FT: 40,000
SALES (est): 200MM **Privately Held**
WEB: www.ervinindustries.com
SIC: **3291** 6159 Steel shot abrasive; machinery & equipment finance leasing

(G-479)
ESPERION THERAPEUTICS INC
3891 Ranchero Dr Ste 150 (48108-2837)
PHONE..................................734 887-3903
Sheldon Koenig, *President*
Naredra Lalwani, *COO*
Narendra D Lalwani, *COO*
Matthew Daly, *Counsel*
Marianne Andreach, *Vice Pres*
EMP: 57 EST: 2008
SQ FT: 7,900
SALES (est): 227.5MM **Privately Held**
WEB: www.esperion.com
SIC: **2834** Pharmaceutical preparations

(G-480)
ESSEN INSTRUMENTS INC (HQ)
Also Called: Essen Bioscience
300 W Morgan Rd (48108-9108)
PHONE..................................734 769-1600
Brett Williams, *CEO*
Jim Ryder, *Vice Pres*
Eric Lucas, *Mfg Staff*
Marcel Howard, *Buyer*
Krys Jackson, *Purchasing*
EMP: 74 EST: 1999
SQ FT: 25,000
SALES (est): 33.5MM
SALES (corp-wide): 2.7B **Privately Held**
WEB: www.essen-instruments.com
SIC: **3826** Analytical instruments
PA: Sartorius Ag
Otto-Brenner-Str. 20
Gottingen NI 37079
551 308-0

(G-481)
EXPRESSIGN DESIGN
2239 W Liberty St (48103-4405)
PHONE..................................734 747-7444
Jim Fisher, *Owner*
EMP: 4 EST: 1990 **Privately Held**
WEB: www.annarborsigns.com
SIC: **3993** Signs, not made in custom sign painting shops

(G-482)
EXTANG CORPORATION
5400 S State Rd (48108-9754)
PHONE..................................734 677-0444
William Reminder, *President*
Kelly Kneifl, *COO*
James Bresingham, *CFO*
Maria Zwas, *Admin Sec*
▲ EMP: 100 EST: 1982
SQ FT: 56,900
SALES (est): 24.3MM
SALES (corp-wide): 623.9MM **Privately Held**
WEB: www.extang.com
SIC: **3714** Motor vehicle parts & accessories
HQ: Tectum Holdings, Inc.
5400 Data Ct
Ann Arbor MI 48108
734 677-0444

(G-483)
EYRY OF EAGLE PUBLISH
625 Liberty Pointe Dr (48103-2097)
PHONE..................................734 623-0337
EMP: 5 EST: 2017

SALES (est): 90.5K **Privately Held**
WEB: www.eyryoftheeagle.com
SIC: **2741** Miscellaneous publishing

(G-484)
FAAC INCORPORATED
1195 Oak Valley Dr (48108-9674)
PHONE..................................734 761-5836
EMP: 8 **Privately Held**
WEB: www.faac.com
SIC: **3699** Electrical equipment & supplies
HQ: Faac Incorporated
1229 Oak Valley Dr
Ann Arbor MI 48108
734 761-5836

(G-485)
FAAC INCORPORATED (HQ)
Also Called: Milo Range Training Systems
1229 Oak Valley Dr (48108-9675)
PHONE..................................734 761-5836
Kurt A Flosky, *President*
Rob McCue, *General Mgr*
John Dibbs, *Principal*
Deborah Fuller, *COO*
Christopher J Caruana, *Exec VP*
EMP: 103 EST: 1963
SQ FT: 20,000
SALES (est): 46.2MM **Privately Held**
WEB: www.faac.com
SIC: **8711** 7372 Engineering services; business oriented computer software

(G-486)
FALCON GLOBAL LLC
1630 Timber Trl (48103-2388)
PHONE..................................734 302-3025
Habib Fakhouri, *Agent*
EMP: 15 EST: 2018
SALES (est): 404.5K
SALES (corp-wide): 141.8MM **Publicly Held**
WEB: www.seacormarine.com
SIC: **3546** Power-driven handtools
PA: Seacor Marine Holdings Inc.
12121 Wickchester Ln # 500
Houston TX 77079
346 980-1700

(G-487)
FEDEX OFFICE & PRINT SVCS INC
505 E Liberty St Ste 400 (48104-2465)
PHONE..................................734 761-4539
EMP: 10
SALES (corp-wide): 83.9B **Publicly Held**
SIC: **7334** 2791 2789 7338 Photocopying & duplicating services; typesetting; bookbinding & related work; secretarial & court reporting
HQ: Fedex Office And Print Services, Inc.
7900 Legacy Dr
Plano TX 75024
800 463-3339

(G-488)
FENDT BUILDERS SUPPLY INC
3285 W Liberty Rd (48103-9795)
PHONE..................................734 663-4277
Alan Fendt, *Owner*
Bill Killen, *Sales Staff*
EMP: 15
SALES (corp-wide): 8MM **Privately Held**
WEB: www.fendtproducts.com
SIC: **3271** 5211 Blocks, concrete or cinder: standard; lumber & other building materials
PA: Fendt Builders Supply Inc
22005 Gill Rd
Farmington Hills MI 48335
248 474-3211

(G-489)
FISHER SCIENTIFIC INTL LLC
110 Miller Ave Ste 200 (48104-1305)
PHONE..................................734 622-0413
Ariana Gleisberg, *QC Mgr*
Charles Smith, *Engineer*
Janice Tain, *Branch Mgr*
EMP: 5
SALES (corp-wide): 32.2B **Publicly Held**
WEB: www.thermofisher.com
SIC: **3826** Analytical instruments
HQ: Fisher Scientific International Llc
81 Wyman St
Waltham MA 02451

(G-490)
FLASHPLAYS LIVE LLC
412 Hamilton Pl (48104-2308)
PHONE..................................978 888-3935
Parth Valecha, *CEO*
EMP: 5
SALES (est): 117.2K **Privately Held**
SIC: **7372** 7389 Application computer software; business services

(G-491)
FLOW EZY FILTERS INC
147 Enterprise Dr (48103-9282)
P.O. Box 1749 (48106-1749)
PHONE..................................734 665-8777
Theodore Fosdick, *President*
Tony Day, *Purch Mgr*
Dale Fosdick, *Treasurer*
Don Krause, *Office Mgr*
Bill Crowell, *Manager*
EMP: 18 EST: 1967
SALES (est): 4.1MM **Privately Held**
WEB: www.flowezyfilters.com
SIC: **3569** 5084 Filters, general line: industrial; industrial machinery & equipment

(G-492)
FORESEE SESSION REPLAY INC
2500 Green Rd Ste 400 (48105-1573)
PHONE..................................800 621-2850
Bill Ruckelshaus, *President*
Jay Sinder, *Treasurer*
Eugene Davis, *Director*
Caleb Chill, *Admin Sec*
EMP: 4 EST: 2008
SALES (est): 847K **Publicly Held**
WEB: www.foresee.com
SIC: **7372** Prepackaged software
HQ: Foresee Results, Inc.
2500 Green Rd Ste 400
Ann Arbor MI 48105
734 205-2600

(G-493)
FOURTH AVE BIRKENSTOCK
209 N 4th Ave (48104-1403)
PHONE..................................734 663-1644
Paul Tinkerhess, *Owner*
EMP: 7 EST: 1985
SALES (est): 532.9K **Privately Held**
WEB: www.annarborbirkenstock.com
SIC: **5661** 3944 Shoes, custom; games, toys & children's vehicles

(G-494)
GAN SYSTEMS CORP
2723 S State St Ste 150 (48104-6188)
PHONE..................................248 609-7643
Larry Spaziani, *Vice Pres*
Paul Wiener, *Vice Pres*
Charles Bailley, *Sales Staff*
EMP: 9 EST: 2015
SALES (est): 1MM **Privately Held**
WEB: www.gansystems.com
SIC: **3674** Semiconductors & related devices

(G-495)
GB SPORTZ
5277 Jackson Rd (48103-1869)
PHONE..................................734 604-8919
Geoff Blow, *Principal*
EMP: 5 EST: 2008
SALES (est): 77.8K **Privately Held**
WEB: www.gbsportservices.blogspot.com
SIC: **3949** Sporting & athletic goods

(G-496)
GELMAN SCIENCES INC
Also Called: Pall Life Sciences
674 S Wagner Rd (48103-9793)
PHONE..................................734 665-0651
Eric Krasnoff, *Ch of Bd*
Don Stevens, *COO*
Lisa McDermott, *CFO*
▲ EMP: 136 EST: 1980
SQ FT: 180,000

Ann Arbor - Washtenaw County (G-497)   GEOGRAPHIC SECTION

SALES (est): 42.8MM
SALES (corp-wide): 22.2B **Publicly Held**
WEB: www.pall.com
SIC: **3821** 3569 3564 3841 Laboratory apparatus, except heating & measuring; filters, general line: industrial; air purification equipment; surgical instruments & apparatus; electromedical apparatus; insect lamps, electric
HQ: Pall Corporation
25 Harbor Park Dr
Port Washington NY 11050
516 484-5400

(G-497)
GENE CODES FORENSICS INC
525 Avis Dr Ste 8 (48108-9616)
PHONE.................................734 769-7249
Howard Cash, *CEO*
Natalie Kerns, *Accountant*
EMP: 5
SALES (est): 144.4K **Privately Held**
WEB: www.genecodes.com
SIC: **7372** Application computer software

(G-498)
GENERAL SCIENTIFIC CORPORATION
77 Enterprise Dr (48103-9503)
PHONE.................................734 996-9200
Byung Jin Chang, *President*
Aura Gannon, *COO*
Sharon Chang, *Vice Pres*
Henry Gretzinger, *Vice Pres*
Byung Chang, *Plant Mgr*
▲ EMP: 45
SQ FT: 21,600
SALES (est): 9.4MM **Privately Held**
WEB: www.surgitel.com
SIC: **3827** 3851 3229 Lenses, optical: all types except ophthalmic; lupes magnifying instruments, optical; ophthalmic goods; pressed & blown glass

(G-499)
GENOMIC DIAGNOSTICS NA INC
2890 Carptr Rd Ste 2000 (48108)
PHONE.................................734 730-8399
Srinivasa Maddineni, *Principal*
EMP: 5 EST: 2020
SALES (est): 2MM **Privately Held**
SIC: **5047** 2819 Diagnostic equipment, medical; chemicals, reagent grade: refined from technical grade

(G-500)
GFG INSTRUMENTATION INC
Also Called: Gfg Dynamation
1194 Oak Valley Dr Ste 20 (48108-8942)
PHONE.................................734 769-0573
Robert Henderson, *President*
Michael Fleck, *Purch Mgr*
Jeff Allsworth, *Engineer*
Francis Johnson, *Regl Sales Mgr*
EMP: 25 EST: 1969
SQ FT: 13,000
SALES (est): 5.1MM **Privately Held**
SIC: **3829** Gas detectors

(G-501)
GLOBAL GREEN CORPORATION
5068 Plymouth Rd Ste 3 (48105-9520)
PHONE.................................734 560-1743
Doug Benit, *President*
David Sudia, *Sales Staff*
EMP: 10 EST: 2014
SALES (est): 1MM **Privately Held**
WEB: www.globalgreenled.com
SIC: **5063** 1731 3646 3648 Lighting fixtures, commercial & industrial; energy management controls; lighting contractor; commercial indusl & institutional electric lighting fixtures; lighting equipment

(G-502)
GMI PACKAGING CO (PA)
1371 Centennial Ln (48103)
PHONE.................................734 972-7389
Joyce Mueller, *President*
EMP: 10 EST: 2013 **Privately Held**
WEB: www.gmipackaging.com
SIC: **3535** Unit handling conveying systems

(G-503)
GPBC INC
Also Called: Grizzly Peak Brewing Company
120 W Washington St Ste 1 (48104-1356)
PHONE.................................734 741-7325
Jon Carlson, *President*
Bery Haven, *President*
Scott Keller, *Manager*
EMP: 11 EST: 1994
SQ FT: 6,000
SALES (est): 744.4K **Privately Held**
WEB: www.grizzlypeak.net
SIC: **2082** 5813 5812 Beer (alcoholic beverage); tavern (drinking places); eating places

(G-504)
GRAFAKTRI INC
1200 N Main St (48104-1041)
PHONE.................................734 665-0717
W A P John, *President*
Waldemar John, *President*
Julie Ritter, *Vice Pres*
EMP: 7 EST: 1980
SQ FT: 10,000
SALES (est): 996.5K **Privately Held**
WEB: www.grafaktri.com
SIC: **3993** 2759 Displays & cutouts, window & lobby; screen printing; posters, including billboards: printing

(G-505)
GRAPHO LLC
2410 Foxway Dr (48105-9667)
PHONE.................................734 223-2144
Brian D Ross, *Principal*
EMP: 5 EST: 2015
SALES (est): 59.3K **Privately Held**
SIC: **2741** Miscellaneous publishing

(G-506)
GRAVIKOR INC
401 W Morgan Rd (48108-9109)
PHONE.................................734 302-3200
Andrew Taylor, *President*
James Richter, *Principal*
EMP: 5 EST: 2006
SQ FT: 500
SALES (est): 385.9K **Privately Held**
SIC: **3829** Medical diagnostic systems, nuclear

(G-507)
GREAT LAKES SPT PUBLICATIONS
3588 Plymouth Rd (48105-2603)
PHONE.................................734 507-0241
Art McCafferty, *CEO*
Jennie McCafferty, *Editor*
EMP: 5 EST: 1979
SALES (est): 300K **Privately Held**
SIC: **2741** Miscellaneous publishing

(G-508)
GUDEL INC
4881 Runway Blvd (48108-9558)
PHONE.................................734 214-0000
Stefan Nilsson, *CEO*
Joe Campbell, *Vice Pres*
Mark Covel, *Mfg Staff*
John Owen, *Purchasing*
Austin Joyce, *Engineer*
▲ EMP: 78 EST: 1995
SQ FT: 7,000
SALES (est): 29.6MM
SALES (corp-wide): 195.7MM **Privately Held**
WEB: www.gudel.com
SIC: **3535** Conveyors & conveying equipment
HQ: Gudel Group Ag
C/O Gudel Ag
Langenthal BE 4900
629 169-191

(G-509)
HARLOW SHEET METAL LLC
5140 Park Rd (48103-9549)
PHONE.................................734 996-1509
EMP: 4
SALES (est): 374.5K **Privately Held**
SIC: **3446** Mfg Architectural Metalwork

(G-510)
HEALTHCARE DRBLE MED EQPMNTS L
Also Called: Healthcare Medical Supply
2911 Carpenter Rd (48108-1163)
PHONE.................................734 975-6668
Ashfaq Kadwani, *CEO*
Joseph Wucker, *Materials Mgr*
Aisha Ashfaq, *Treasurer*
Kristen Kiester, *Human Res Mgr*
Shahzeb Ashfaq, *Sales Mgr*
EMP: 8 EST: 2005
SQ FT: 2,500
SALES (est): 252K **Privately Held**
WEB: www.healthcaredme.com
SIC: **5047** 5049 3841 3845 Medical equipment & supplies; laboratory equipment, except medical or dental; surgical & medical instruments; respiratory analysis equipment, electromedical

(G-511)
HEARING HEALTH SCIENCE INC
Also Called: Hhsi
2723 S State St Ste 150 (48104-6188)
PHONE.................................734 476-9490
Barry S Seifer, *CEO*
EMP: 7 EST: 2011
SALES (est): 765K **Privately Held**
WEB: www.soundbites.com
SIC: **2833** Medicinals & botanicals

(G-512)
HEART SYNC INC
4401 Varsity Dr Ste D (48108-5003)
PHONE.................................734 213-5530
Stuart Shulman, *President*
Megan Kerns, *Opers Staff*
EMP: 14 EST: 2007
SALES (est): 2.2MM **Privately Held**
SIC: **3845** Electromedical apparatus

(G-513)
HERALD NEWSPAPERS COMPANY INC
Also Called: Ann Arbor News, The
704 Airport Blvd Ste 6 (48108-3607)
PHONE.................................734 926-4510
Karl Metzgeer, *Branch Mgr*
EMP: 6
SALES (corp-wide): 2.8B **Privately Held**
WEB: www.advancemediany.com
SIC: **2711** Newspapers, publishing & printing
HQ: The Herald Newspapers Company Inc
220 S Warren St
Syracuse NY 13202
315 470-0011

(G-514)
HERALD PUBLISHING COMPANY LLC
111 N Ashley St Ste 100 (48104-1307)
PHONE.................................734 623-2500
Christy Keizer, *Branch Mgr*
EMP: 20
SALES (corp-wide): 2.8B **Privately Held**
SIC: **2711** Newspapers, publishing & printing
HQ: The Herald Publishing Company Llc
3102 Walker Ridge Dr Nw
Walker MI 49544
616 222-5400

(G-515)
HIGH-PO-CHLOR INC
Also Called: Hypo-Systems
1181 Freesia Ct (48105-1972)
PHONE.................................734 942-1500
Michael Kenney, *President*
John Martin, *Vice Pres*
Marilee Slicker, *Vice Pres*
EMP: 6 EST: 1981
SQ FT: 1,800
SALES (est): 521.6K **Privately Held**
SIC: **2842** 2819 Bleaches, household: dry or liquid; industrial inorganic chemicals

(G-516)
HIGHLANDER GRAPHICS LLC
75 April Dr (48103-1901)
PHONE.................................734 449-9733
Brent Wall, *President*
Justin McLean, *General Mgr*
EMP: 4 EST: 2013
SQ FT: 4,000
SALES (est): 243.2K **Privately Held**
SIC: **3993** Signs & advertising specialties

(G-517)
HINES INDUSTRIES INC (PA)
240 Metty Dr Ste A (48103-9498)
PHONE.................................734 769-2300
Dawn Hines, *CEO*
Rick Rodriguez, *Project Mgr*
Doug Case, *Electrical Engi*
Jon Black, *Accounts Mgr*
Robin Mifsud, *Sales Engr*
◆ EMP: 39 EST: 1979
SQ FT: 40,000
SALES (est): 5MM **Privately Held**
WEB: www.hinesindustries.com
SIC: **3829** 3823 Measuring & controlling devices; industrial instrmnts msrmnt display/control process variable

(G-518)
HORIBA INSTRUMENTS INC
Automotive Systems Div
5900 Hines Dr (48108-7941)
PHONE.................................734 213-6555
Ken Mitera, *Branch Mgr*
EMP: 85
SQ FT: 1,000 **Privately Held**
WEB: www.horiba.com
SIC: **3823** 3826 3829 3511 Industrial instrmnts msrmnt display/control process variable; analytical instruments; measuring & controlling devices; turbines & turbine generator sets; instruments to measure electricity
HQ: Horiba Instruments Incorporated
9755 Research Dr
Irvine CA 92618
949 250-4811

(G-519)
HOSFORD & CO INC
1204 N Main St (48104-1041)
PHONE.................................734 769-5660
Jonathan Hosford, *President*
EMP: 5 EST: 1977
SQ FT: 11,000
SALES (est): 437.1K **Privately Held**
WEB: www.hosfordco.com
SIC: **3599** Machine shop, jobbing & repair

(G-520)
HYGRATEK LLC
333 Jackson Plz (48103-1922)
PHONE.................................847 962-6180
Anish Tuteja, *Principal*
Michael Gurin, *Manager*
EMP: 5 EST: 2013
SQ FT: 935
SALES (est): 287.9K **Privately Held**
WEB: www.hygratek.com
SIC: **2851** 8731 3559 Lacquers, varnishes, enamels & other coatings; commercial physical research; sewage & water treatment equipment

(G-521)
I-DRINK PRODUCTS INC
727 W Ellsworth Rd Ste 15 (48108-3446)
PHONE.................................734 531-6324
Douglas Wang, *CEO*
EMP: 5
SALES (corp-wide): 922.7K **Privately Held**
WEB: www.idrinkproducts.com
SIC: **3089** Plastic kitchenware, tableware & houseware
PA: I-Drink Products Inc
727 W Ellsworth Rd Ste 15
Ann Arbor MI 48108
734 531-6324

(G-522)
IDEATION INC
Also Called: All Things Made In America
3389 Breckland Ct (48108-9311)
PHONE.................................734 761-4360
Thomas Ungrodt, *President*
Chris Gallup, *CFO*
Virginia Lum, *Treasurer*
EMP: 50 EST: 1968
SQ FT: 18,000

▲ = Import ▼=Export
◆ =Import/Export

GEOGRAPHIC SECTION
Ann Arbor - Washtenaw County (G-549)

SALES (est): 5.3MM **Privately Held**
WEB: www.ideationgifts.com
SIC: **2741** Catalogs: publishing only, not printed on site

(G-523)
IMAGEMASTER LLC (PA)
Also Called: Imagemaster Printing
1182 Oak Valley Dr (48108-9624)
PHONE..................................734 821-2500
Daniel Rodriguez, *Vice Pres*
Jennifer Braun, *Production*
Leza Hoover, *Production*
Albert M Rodriguez, *Mng Member*
Lee McClelland, *Mng Member*
▲ EMP: 25 EST: 1988
SQ FT: 20,000
SALES (est): 6.1MM **Privately Held**
WEB: www.imagemaster.com
SIC: **2759** Business forms: printing

(G-524)
IMC DATAWORKS LLC
525 Avis Dr Ste 14 (48108-9787)
PHONE..................................248 356-4311
Ralf Winkelmann, *President*
Romy Michiels, *Manager*
Alex Zaciewski, *Technician*
EMP: 15 EST: 2014
SALES (est): 1.4MM **Privately Held**
WEB: www.imcdataworks.com
SIC: **3823** Industrial process measurement equipment

(G-525)
IMRA AMERICA INC (HQ)
1044 Woodridge Ave (48105-9774)
PHONE..................................734 669-7377
Takashi Omitsu, *President*
Mieko Horie, *President*
Bing Liu, *Technical Mgr*
Steven Schoeff, *Technical Staff*
Makoto Yoshida, *Admin Sec*
▲ EMP: 45 EST: 1990
SQ FT: 30,000
SALES (est): 25.4MM **Privately Held**
WEB: www.imra.com
SIC: **8732** **3699** Research services, except laboratory; laser systems & equipment

(G-526)
IN KNOW INC
723 W Madison St Apt 9 (48103-4873)
PHONE..................................734 827-9711
Danny Aronson, *Principal*
EMP: 6 EST: 2004
SALES (est): 137.1K **Privately Held**
WEB: www.shop.intheknowmedia.com
SIC: **2741** Miscellaneous publishing

(G-527)
INGHAM TOOL LLC
6155 Jackson Rd Ste B (48103-9170)
PHONE..................................734 929-2390
Jeff Cheesman, *Mng Member*
EMP: 5 EST: 2013
SALES (est): 750K **Privately Held**
WEB: www.inghamtool.com
SIC: **3599** Machine shop, jobbing & repair

(G-528)
INMATECH INC
1600 Huron Pkwy (48109-5001)
PHONE..................................734 717-8247
Levi Thompson, *Principal*
EMP: 18 EST: 2007
SALES (est): 860.6K **Privately Held**
WEB: www.inmatech-inc.com
SIC: **3629** Capacitors, fixed or variable

(G-529)
INORA TECHNOLOGIES INC (PA)
Also Called: Metronom US
525 Avis Dr Ste 11 (48108-9808)
PHONE..................................734 302-7488
Ingobert Schmadel, *President*
Thomas Gendera, *Senior Engr*
Jeffrey Armatis, *Design Engr*
Mary Jane Hourani, *Controller*
Mary Hourani, *Controller*
EMP: 9 EST: 2001

SALES (est): 2.1MM **Privately Held**
WEB: www.inora.com
SIC: **8748** **7372** **3829** **5049** Systems analysis & engineering consulting services; application computer software; aircraft & motor vehicle measurement equipment; scientific & engineering equipment & supplies

(G-530)
INTEGRATED SENSING SYSTEMS
1240 Severn Ct (48105-2863)
P.O. Box 130738 (48113-0738)
PHONE..................................734 604-4301
EMP: 4 EST: 2017
SALES (est): 90.7K **Privately Held**
WEB: www.mems-iss.com
SIC: **2834** Pharmaceutical preparations

(G-531)
INTERPLAI INC (PA)
330 E Liberty St (48104-2274)
PHONE..................................734 274-4628
Mark A Crawford Jr, *CEO*
Mark Crawford, *Principal*
EMP: 9 EST: 2020
SALES (est): 1MM **Privately Held**
SIC: **7372** Business oriented computer software

(G-532)
IX INNOVATIONS LLC
4488 Jackson Rd Ste 6 (48103-1812)
PHONE..................................
EMP: 4 EST: 2010
SALES: 20K **Privately Held**
SIC: **3825** Mfg Electrical Measuring Instruments

(G-533)
JDA SOFTWARE GROUP INC
900 Victors Way Ste 360 (48108-2832)
PHONE..................................734 741-4205
Fax: 734 887-4555
EMP: 8
SALES (corp-wide): 1.3B **Privately Held**
SIC: **7372** Prepackaged Software Services
HQ: Jda Software Group, Inc.
14400 N 87th St
Scottsdale AZ 85254

(G-534)
JODON ENGINEERING ASSOC INC
62 Enterprise Dr (48103-9562)
PHONE..................................734 761-4044
Michael Gillespie, *President*
Mark Haddox, *Vice Pres*
Bruce Gray, *Purch Agent*
Michael Klinske, *Sales Mgr*
Reuben Bjorkman, *Info Tech Mgr*
EMP: 12 EST: 1962
SQ FT: 15,000
SALES (est): 1.5MM **Privately Held**
WEB: www.jodon.com
SIC: **3826** **3841** **3825** Laser scientific & engineering instruments; analytical optical instruments; ophthalmic lasers; microwave test equipment; test equipment for electronic & electrical circuits

(G-535)
JOHN ALLEN ENTERPRISES
4281 Climbing Way (48103-9402)
PHONE..................................734 426-2507
John Towsley, *Principal*
▲ EMP: 6 EST: 2005
SALES (est): 85.9K **Privately Held**
SIC: **3089** Plastics products

(G-536)
K & S PRINTING CENTERS INC
Also Called: Qps Printing
4860 Greenway Ct (48103-9414)
PHONE..................................734 482-1680
Sherry Cradick, *President*
Kim Cradick, *Vice Pres*
EMP: 5 EST: 1977
SQ FT: 1,800
SALES (est): 287.4K **Privately Held**
SIC: **2752** **7334** Commercial printing, offset; photocopying & duplicating services

(G-537)
KAISER OPTICAL SYSTEMS INC (DH)
371 Parkland Plz (48103-6202)
PHONE..................................734 665-8083
Tim Harrison, *President*
Harry Owen, *Vice Pres*
Joe Slater, *Vice Pres*
Todd Mead, *CFO*
Ian Lewis, *Marketing Staff*
▲ EMP: 74 EST: 1979
SQ FT: 31,000
SALES (est): 23.8MM
SALES (corp-wide): 371.8MM **Privately Held**
WEB: www.kosi.com
SIC: **3827** Optical test & inspection equipment
HQ: Endress+Hauser (Deutschland)
Gmbh+Co. Kg
Colmarer Str. 6
Weil Am Rhein 79576
762 197-501

(G-538)
KAYDON CORPORATION (DH)
2723 S State St Ste 300 (48104-6188)
PHONE..................................734 747-7025
Timothy J Heasley, *President*
Les Miller, *President*
Peter C Dechants, *Senior VP*
Debra K Crane, *Vice Pres*
Laura Kowalchik, *Vice Pres*
◆ EMP: 317 EST: 1983
SALES (est): 441.4MM
SALES (corp-wide): 8.6B **Privately Held**
WEB: www.skf.com
SIC: **3562** **3569** **3592** **3053** Ball & roller bearings; ball bearings & parts; roller bearings & parts; filters, general line: industrial; pistons & piston rings; gaskets & sealing devices; sliprings, for motors or generators; electronic circuits

(G-539)
KINGS TIME PRINTING PRESS LLC
4245 Hawthorn Pl (48103-9454)
PHONE..................................734 426-8169
EMP: 5 EST: 2014
SALES (est): 59K **Privately Held**
WEB: www.kingstimeprinting.com
SIC: **2752** Commercial printing, offset

(G-540)
KOLOSSOS PRINTING INC (PA)
2055 W Stadium Blvd (48103-4570)
PHONE..................................734 994-5400
Nicholas Arhangelos, *President*
Kathleen Arhangelos, *Treasurer*
EMP: 18
SQ FT: 7,500
SALES (est): 3.3MM **Privately Held**
WEB: www.kolossosprinting.com
SIC: **2752** **7334** **7389** **4215** Commercial printing, offset; photocopying & duplicating services; sign painting & lettering shop; courier services, except by air; mailing services

(G-541)
KOLOSSOS PRINTING INC
301 E Liberty St (48104-2262)
PHONE..................................734 741-1600
Tony Arghenglos, *Branch Mgr*
EMP: 9
SALES (corp-wide): 3.3MM **Privately Held**
WEB: www.kolossosprinting.com
SIC: **2621** **4731** Wrapping & packaging papers; freight transportation arrangement
PA: Kolossos Printing Inc
2055 W Stadium Blvd
Ann Arbor MI 48103
734 994-5400

(G-542)
KORE GROUP INC (PA)
Also Called: Fastsigns
3500 Washtenaw Ave (48104-5244)
PHONE..................................734 677-1500
Roger Cunningham, *President*
Kevin Miller, *Vice Pres*
Mike Myers, *Sales Staff*

EMP: 8 EST: 1992
SQ FT: 1,800
SALES (est): 900K **Privately Held**
WEB: www.fastsigns.com
SIC: **3993** Signs & advertising specialties

(G-543)
KRAFT MAID CABINETRY
4600 Arrowhead Dr (48105-2773)
PHONE..................................734 205-4600
EMP: 7 EST: 2017
SALES (est): 176K **Privately Held**
WEB: www.kraftmaid.com
SIC: **2434** Wood kitchen cabinets

(G-544)
KRAIG BIOCRAFT LABS INC
2723 S State St Ste 150 (48104-6188)
PHONE..................................734 619-8066
Kim Thompson, *President*
Jonathan R Rice, *COO*
EMP: 9 EST: 2006 **Privately Held**
WEB: www.kraiglabs.com
SIC: **2823** Cellulosic manmade fibers

(G-545)
KUMANU INC
535 W William St Ste 4n (48103-4978)
PHONE..................................734 822-6673
Victor Strecher, *CEO*
David Gregorka, *COO*
Maureen Metzger, *Research*
Cheryl Brown, *Controller*
Haitham Maaieh, *Software Engr*
EMP: 36 EST: 2015
SQ FT: 5,000
SALES (est): 1.3MM **Privately Held**
WEB: www.kumanu.com
SIC: **7372** Application computer software

(G-546)
L3 TECHNOLOGIES INC
1201 E Ellsworth Rd (48108-2420)
PHONE..................................734 741-8868
Melissa Vasilevski, *General Mgr*
Edward Schoppman, *Principal*
Barney Glenn, *VP Bus Dvlpt*
Mark Cockman, *Sales Staff*
EMP: 6
SALES (corp-wide): 18.1B **Publicly Held**
WEB: www.l3harris.com
SIC: **3663** Telemetering equipment, electronic
HQ: L3 Technologies, Inc.
600 3rd Ave Fl 34
New York NY 10016
321 727-9100

(G-547)
LAKESIDE SOFTWARE LLC
201 S Main St Ste 200 (48104-2153)
PHONE..................................248 686-1700
Sharon Branchen, *Sales Staff*
Michael Schumacher, *Branch Mgr*
EMP: 4
SALES (corp-wide): 12.2MM **Privately Held**
WEB: www.lakesidesoftware.com
SIC: **7372** Prepackaged software
PA: Lakeside Software, Llc
2 Oliver St Ste 700
Boston MA 02109
248 686-1700

(G-548)
LAMBERT INDUSTRIES INC
69 Enterprise Dr (48103-9503)
PHONE..................................734 668-6864
Robert Lambert, *President*
Rose Lambert, *Vice Pres*
EMP: 10 EST: 1983
SQ FT: 6,500
SALES (est): 1.8MM **Privately Held**
WEB: www.lambertindinc.com
SIC: **3599** **3544** Machine shop, jobbing & repair; special dies & tools

(G-549)
LAUREN ZINN
918 Bath St (48103-3718)
PHONE..................................734 996-3524
Lauren Zinn, *President*
EMP: 4 EST: 2018
SALES (est): 94.2K **Privately Held**
SIC: **3052** Rubber & plastics hose & beltings

Ann Arbor - Washtenaw County (G-550)

GEOGRAPHIC SECTION

(G-550)
LIQUID MANUFACTURING LLC
305 Westwood Ave (48103-3550)
PHONE 810 220-2802
Peter W Paisley, *CEO*
▲ EMP: 40 EST: 1995
SQ FT: 78,000
SALES (est): 1.8MM Privately Held
SIC: 2085 2086 Rum (alcoholic beverage); vodka (alcoholic beverage); gin (alcoholic beverage); bottled & canned soft drinks

(G-551)
LITERATI LLC
Also Called: Literari Bookstore
124 E Washington St (48104-1905)
PHONE 909 921-5242
Hilary Lowe, *Mng Member*
Kelsey O'rourke, *Manager*
EMP: 16 EST: 2012
SALES (est): 4.3MM Privately Held
WEB: www.literatibookstore.com
SIC: 2731 Book publishing

(G-552)
LIVER TRANSPLANT/UNIV OF MICH
1500 E Medical Center Dr (48109-5000)
PHONE 734 936-7670
Jeffery Punch, *Director*
Robert J Merion, *Director*
EMP: 6 EST: 1980
SALES (est): 728.9K Privately Held
WEB: www.uofmhealth.org
SIC: 3523 7363 8093 Transplanters; medical help service; specialty outpatient clinics

(G-553)
LNA SOLUTIONS INC
3924a Varsity Dr Ste A (48108-2226)
PHONE 734 677-2305
Terence Doran, *CEO*
Luke Kurrle, *Sales Mgr*
Joseph Komaromi, *Sales Engr*
Terry Doran, *Manager*
Ed Stollenwerck, *Manager*
▲ EMP: 10 EST: 1995
SALES (est): 1.2MM
SALES (corp-wide): 626.8K Privately Held
WEB: www.lnasolutions.com
SIC: 3441 Building components, structural steel
HQ: Kee Safety, Inc.
100 Stradtman St Ste 8
Buffalo NY 14206
716 896-4949

(G-554)
LOGIC QUANTUM LLC
2929 Plymouth Rd Ste 207 (48105-3206)
PHONE 734 930-0009
EMP: 12 EST: 2011
SALES (est): 355.3K Privately Held
WEB: www.logicsolutions.com
SIC: 3652 Pre-recorded records & tapes

(G-555)
LOGICAL DIGITAL AUDIO VIDEO
Also Called: Silver Tortoise Sound Lab
4602 Central Blvd (48108-1346)
PHONE 734 572-0022
Jonas D Berzanskis, *Owner*
EMP: 4 EST: 1979
SQ FT: 1,000
SALES (est): 202.9K Privately Held
SIC: 3651 Household audio & video equipment

(G-556)
LTEK INDUSTRIES INC
Also Called: ASAP Source
2298 S Industrial Hwy (48104-6124)
PHONE 734 747-6105
Edsel Roberts, *President*
Deborah Roberts, *Vice Pres*
EMP: 6 EST: 1991
SQ FT: 14,000
SALES (est): 848.1K Privately Held
WEB: www.ltekindustries.com
SIC: 3599 5085 Machine shop, jobbing & repair; industrial supplies

(G-557)
LUNA OPTOELETRONICS
2925 Boardwalk St (48104-6765)
PHONE 734 864-5611
EMP: 5 EST: 2017
SALES (est): 262K Privately Held
WEB: www.lunainc.com
SIC: 3674 Semiconductors & related devices

(G-558)
M & M TYPEWRITER SERVICE INC
Also Called: Michigan Printer Service
251 Collingwood St (48103-3873)
PHONE 734 995-4033
John Mulcare, *President*
Claudia Nbee, *Treasurer*
Arlene Mulcare, *Admin Sec*
EMP: 5 EST: 1971
SQ FT: 4,710
SALES (est): 200K Privately Held
SIC: 3555 5087 7359 Copy holders, printers'; service establishment equipment; business machine & electronic equipment rental services

(G-559)
M4 CIC LLC
719 W Ellsworth Rd Ste 1a (48108-1663)
PHONE 734 436-8507
EMP: 8 EST: 2015
SALES (est): 321.5K Privately Held
SIC: 2082 Malt beverages

(G-560)
MACB WOODWORKING LLC
3036 Dhu Varren Ct (48105-9654)
PHONE 734 645-8990
EMP: 4 EST: 2018
SALES (est): 78.5K Privately Held
SIC: 2431 Millwork

(G-561)
MACOM TECHNOLOGY SOLUTIONS INC
2925 Boardwalk St (48104-6765)
PHONE 734 864-5664
Bruce Prater, *Administration*
EMP: 7 Publicly Held
WEB: www.macom.com
SIC: 3674 Semiconductors & related devices
HQ: Macom Technology Solutions Inc.
100 Chelmsford St
Lowell MA 01851

(G-562)
MAGNETIC MICHIGAN
101 N Main St (48104-5507)
PHONE 734 922-7068
Drew Stirton, *Branch Mgr*
EMP: 72
SALES (corp-wide): 17.9MM Privately Held
SIC: 7372 Prepackaged software
PA: Magnetic Michigan
167 2nd Ave
San Mateo CA 94401
650 544-2400

(G-563)
MAHINDRA TRACTOR ASSEMBLY INC
Also Called: Mahindra Genze
1901 E Ellsworth Rd (48108-2804)
PHONE 734 274-2239
Vish Palekar, *CEO*
EMP: 25 Privately Held
SIC: 3523 Tractors, farm
HQ: Mahindra Tractor Assembly, Inc.
275 Rex Blvd
Auburn Hills MI 48326
650 779-5180

(G-564)
MAHLE BEHR USA INC
1350 Eisenhower Pl (48108-3282)
PHONE 336 768-3429
Neto Pedro, *Project Mgr*
Alan Booth, *Manager*
EMP: 8
SALES (corp-wide): 504.6K Privately Held
WEB: www.us.mahle.com
SIC: 3714 Motor vehicle parts & accessories
HQ: Mahle Behr Usa Inc.
2700 Daley Dr
Troy MI 48083
248 743-3700

(G-565)
MAKER WORKS
3765 Plaza Dr (48108-1655)
PHONE 734 222-4911
Josh Williams, *Manager*
EMP: 6 EST: 2016
SALES (est): 539.6K Privately Held
WEB: www.maker-works.com
SIC: 3299 Art goods: plaster of paris, papier mache & scagliola

(G-566)
MARC SCHRREIBER & COMPANY LLC
1389 King George Blvd (48104-6958)
PHONE 734 222-9930
Marc Margolis,
EMP: 5 EST: 2003
SALES (est): 91.1K Privately Held
SIC: 7372 Prepackaged software

(G-567)
MAY MOBILITY INC
650 Avis Dr Ste 100 (48108-9623)
PHONE 312 869-2711
Edwin Olson, *CEO*
Alisyn Malek, *COO*
Brett McMillan, *Vice Pres*
Andres Tamez, *Engineer*
Steve Vozar, *Treasurer*
EMP: 10 EST: 2017
SALES (est): 2.4MM Privately Held
WEB: www.maymobility.com
SIC: 4119 3711 Local passenger transportation; motor vehicles & car bodies

(G-568)
MEDIMAGE INC
331 Metty Dr Ste 1 (48103-9156)
PHONE 734 665-5400
Robert A Helton, *CEO*
Patricia Van Riper, *Corp Secy*
Tod Henderstein, *Sales Mgr*
EMP: 8 EST: 1985
SQ FT: 2,000
SALES (est): 1.1MM Privately Held
WEB: www.medimage.com
SIC: 7372 7379 Prepackaged software; computer related maintenance services

(G-569)
MENDENHALL ASSOCIATES INC
Also Called: Orthopedic Network News
1500 Cedar Bend Dr (48105-2305)
PHONE 734 741-4710
Stanley T Mendenhall, *President*
EMP: 6 EST: 1990
SQ FT: 300
SALES (est): 565.9K
SALES (corp-wide): 1.4MM Privately Held
WEB: www.orthopedicnetworknews.com
SIC: 2731 7371 8742 Book publishing; computer software development; management consulting services
PA: Curvo Labs, Inc.
58 Adams Ave
Evansville IN 47713
619 316-1202

(G-570)
METEOR WEB MARKETING INC
Also Called: Us-Bingo.com
3438 E Ellsworth Rd Ste A (48108-2056)
PHONE 734 822-4999
Catherine Storie, *CEO*
Randy Storie, *Vice Pres*
Jermain Henley, *Warehouse Mgr*
EMP: 15 EST: 2002
SQ FT: 55,000
SALES (est): 2.8MM Privately Held
WEB: www.us-ticket.com
SIC: 2759 3944 5961 Tickets: printing; bingo boards (games);

(G-571)
MI CLASSICAL PRESS
2377 Timbercrest Ct (48105-9269)
PHONE 734 747-6337
Ellen Bauerle, *Principal*
EMP: 6 EST: 2007
SALES (est): 126.2K Privately Held
WEB: www.press.umich.edu
SIC: 2741 Miscellaneous publishing

(G-572)
MICHIGAN PEACEWORKS
911 N University Ave (48109-1265)
PHONE 734 262-4283
Robert Yecke, *CEO*
Jennifer Barber, *Research*
Kenneth M Langa, *Research*
Ryan Nunn, *Research*
Erik Lundberg, *Ch Invest Ofcr*
EMP: 13 EST: 2018
SALES (est): 1.9MM Privately Held
SIC: 2711 Newspapers, publishing & printing

(G-573)
MICHIGAN PEACEWORKS
1009 Greene St (48109-1432)
PHONE 734 232-3079
Eric Smith, *Project Mgr*
Scott Currington, *Opers Staff*
David Nelson, *Opers Staff*
Rong Wu, *Research*
Erik Lundberg, *Ch Invest Ofcr*
EMP: 7 EST: 2019
SALES (est): 163.5K Privately Held
SIC: 2711 Newspapers, publishing & printing

(G-574)
MICHIGAN PEACEWORKS
412 Maynard St (48109-1399)
PHONE 734 764-1717
Dennis Bernstein, *Managing Dir*
George Fulton, *Managing Dir*
Kimberly Myers, *Business Mgr*
Shaun Clarke, *Research*
Frank Marsik, *Research*
EMP: 8 EST: 2019
SALES (est): 422.2K Privately Held
SIC: 2711 Newspapers, publishing & printing

(G-575)
MICHIGAN SIGNS INC
5527 Gallery Park Dr (48109-5055)
P.O. Box 1162 (48106-1162)
PHONE 734 662-1503
Linda Braun, *President*
Harold Braun, *Vice Pres*
EMP: 7 EST: 1922
SQ FT: 7,500
SALES (est): 363.8K Privately Held
WEB: www.michigansigns.net
SIC: 3993 1799 Electric signs; sign installation & maintenance

(G-576)
MICHIGANENSIAN
420 Maynard St (48109-1327)
PHONE 734 418-4115
EMP: 8 EST: 2018
SALES (est): 87.9K Privately Held
WEB: www.michiganyearbook.com
SIC: 2741 Miscellaneous publishing

(G-577)
MID-TECH INC
175 Dino Dr (48103-9502)
PHONE 734 426-4327
Gerry Jedele, *President*
EMP: 9 EST: 1985
SQ FT: 7,200
SALES (est): 1MM Privately Held
WEB: www.mid-techinc.com
SIC: 3469 3599 3732 3544 Stamping metal for the trade; machine shop, jobbing & repair; boat building & repairing; special dies & tools

(G-578)
MILLENDO TRANSACTIONSUB INC
301 N Main St Ste 100 (48104-1296)
PHONE 734 845-9300
Julia C Owens, *President*

GEOGRAPHIC SECTION
Ann Arbor - Washtenaw County (G-606)

Jennifer Minai, *Vice Pres*
Andrew G Spencer, *Vice Pres*
Louis Arcudi III, *CFO*
Malachi Alston, *General Counsel*
EMP: 8 **EST:** 2012
SALES (est): 2.6MM **Publicly Held**
WEB: www.millendo.com
SIC: 2834 8731 Pharmaceutical preparations; medical research, commercial
PA: Tempest Therapeutics, Inc.
7000 Shoreline Ct Ste 275
South San Francisco CA 94080
415 798-8589

(G-579)
MISSION PATHWAYS LLC
3445 W Delhi Rd (48103-9411)
PHONE 734 260-9411
William Pressprich, *Principal*
EMP: 6 **EST:** 2018
SALES (est): 94.4K **Privately Held**
SIC: 7372 Prepackaged software

(G-580)
MLIVE MEDIA GROUP
111 N Ashley St Ste 100 (48104-1307)
PHONE 212 286-2860
Christy Keizer, *Principal*
Zhaohui Fan, *Manager*
Colleen Huff, *Director*
EMP: 8 **EST:** 2017
SALES (est): 62.9K **Privately Held**
WEB: www.mlivemediagroup.com
SIC: 2711 Newspapers

(G-581)
MOEHRLE INC
4305 Pontiac Trl (48105-9626)
PHONE 734 761-2000
EMP: 15 **EST:** 1945
SQ FT: 22,000
SALES (est): 2.5MM **Privately Held**
SIC: 3545 Mfg Machine Tool Accessories

(G-582)
MONROE FUEL COMPANY LLC
414 S Main St Ste 600 (48104-2398)
PHONE 734 302-4824
Dave Ruud, *President*
EMP: 5 **EST:** 2013
SALES (est): 767.4K **Privately Held**
SIC: 2869 Fuels

(G-583)
MONTRONIX INC
3820 Packard St Ste 110 (48108-5016)
PHONE 734 213-6500
Jeurg Vonwil, *President*
Sudhir Agarwal, *General Mgr*
Dennis Turner, *Engineer*
Patricia Son, *Controller*
EMP: 9 **EST:** 2001
SALES (est): 817.2K **Privately Held**
WEB: www.montronix.com
SIC: 3829 5084 3699 Measuring & controlling devices; industrial machinery & equipment; electrical equipment & supplies

(G-584)
MOTAWI TILEWORKS INC
170 Enterprise Dr (48103-9158)
PHONE 734 213-0017
Nawal Motawi, *President*
Karen Kromrei, *General Mgr*
Anastassia Fulmer, *Sales Staff*
EMP: 33 **EST:** 1992
SQ FT: 12,000
SALES (est): 3.8MM **Privately Held**
WEB: www.motawi.com
SIC: 3253 5032 Ceramic wall & floor tile; brick, stone & related material

(G-585)
MOVELLUS CIRCUITS INC (PA)
206 E Huron St (48104-1922)
PHONE 877 321-7667
Muhammad Faisal, *CEO*
Julie Ledford, *Office Mgr*
EMP: 7 **EST:** 2014
SALES (est): 1MM **Privately Held**
WEB: www.movellus.com
SIC: 3679 Electronic circuits

(G-586)
MSCSOFTWARE CORPORATION
201 Depot St Ste 100 (48104-1019)
PHONE 734 994-3800
Stephanie Du, *General Mgr*
Leo Kilfoy, *General Mgr*
Michi Egawa, *Business Mgr*
John Ellison, *Business Mgr*
Raj Behera, *Vice Pres*
EMP: 4
SALES (corp-wide): 4.5B **Privately Held**
WEB: www.mscsoftware.com
SIC: 7372 Business oriented computer software
HQ: Msc.Software Corporation
5161 California Ave # 200
Irvine CA 92617
714 540-8900

(G-587)
NAGEL PRECISION INC
288 Dino Dr (48103-9502)
PHONE 734 426-5650
Peter Nagel, *President*
Rolf Bochsler, *Vice Pres*
Jeff Kaiser, *Vice Pres*
Willi Koch, *Vice Pres*
Wolf Nagel, *Vice Pres*
◆ **EMP:** 130 **EST:** 1987
SQ FT: 42,260
SALES (est): 33.9MM **Privately Held**
WEB: www.nagelusa.com
SIC: 3541 3545 Honing & lapping machines; honing heads

(G-588)
NANOCEROX INC (PA)
712 State Cir (48108-1648)
PHONE 734 741-9522
Gregory Quarles, *President*
Todd Stefanik, *Vice Pres*
Merlyn Charboneau, *Engineer*
Kim Kochan, *Technology*
EMP: 8 **EST:** 1996
SQ FT: 11,900
SALES (est): 3.5MM **Privately Held**
WEB: www.nanocerox.com
SIC: 2819 Industrial inorganic chemicals

(G-589)
NANOSYSTEMS INC
3588 Plymouth Rd (48105-2603)
PHONE 734 274-0020
John Nanos, *President*
▲ **EMP:** 19 **EST:** 2002
SALES (est): 2.8MM **Privately Held**
SIC: 3086 2211 Padding, foamed plastic; bandages, gauzes & surgical fabrics, cotton

(G-590)
NATIONAL ADVNCED MBLITY CNSRTI
455 E Eisenhower Pkwy # 27 (48108-3356)
PHONE 734 205-5920
Rick Jarman, *Ch of Bd*
Christopher Rohe, *President*
Alissa Roath, *Principal*
Cindi Bousley, *Manager*
EMP: 2 **EST:** 2009
SALES (est): 131.4MM **Privately Held**
WEB: www.namconsortium.org
SIC: 5084 3549 7389 Robots, industrial; assembly machines, including robotic; automobile recovery service

(G-591)
NATURAL THERAPEUTICS LLC
401 W Morgan Rd (48108-9109)
PHONE 734 604-7313
James Richter,
EMP: 5 **EST:** 2003
SALES (est): 501.6K **Privately Held**
WEB: www.fungalnailrelief.com
SIC: 2834 5122 Pharmaceutical preparations; pharmaceuticals

(G-592)
NAVITAS ADVNCED SLTONS GROUP L (DH)
4880 Venture Dr (48108-9559)
PHONE 734 913-8176
Nancie Elshefai, *CEO*
Denise Roark, *Technician*
Alan Elshafei,
Thomas Golab,
EMP: 1 **EST:** 2013
SALES (est): 5.5MM
SALES (corp-wide): 2.8B **Privately Held**
WEB: www.navitassys.com
SIC: 3691 Storage batteries
HQ: Navitas Systems, Llc
2200 Cabot Dr Ste 105
Lisle IL 60532
630 755-7920

(G-593)
NEL GROUP INC (PA)
655 Fairfield Ct (48108-8958)
PHONE 734 730-9164
Daryl Kipke, *CEO*
EMP: 2 **EST:** 1993
SALES (est): 4.8MM **Privately Held**
SIC: 3841 Surgical instruments & apparatus

(G-594)
NIPGUARDS LLC
Also Called: Runguards
2232 S Main St Ste 361 (48103-6938)
PHONE 734 544-4490
Andrew C Hopper, *President*
EMP: 4 **EST:** 1998
SALES (est): 304.7K **Privately Held**
WEB: www.runguards.com
SIC: 5091 3949 Athletic goods; sporting & athletic goods

(G-595)
NSK AMERICAS INC (HQ)
4200 Goss Rd (48105-2799)
P.O. Box 134007 (48113-4007)
PHONE 734 913-7500
Brian Lindsay, *President*
Evelyne Gerniers, *Vice Pres*
Tony Wilson, *Vice Pres*
Jeremy Peters, *Plant Mgr*
Carrie Almquist, *Engineer*
▲ **EMP:** 214
SALES (est): 781MM **Privately Held**
WEB: www.nskamericas.com
SIC: 3714 5013 5085 Steering mechanisms, motor vehicle; automotive supplies & parts; industrial supplies

(G-596)
NSK STEERING SYSTEMS AMER INC (DH)
Also Called: Nssa Hq
4200 Goss Rd (48105-2799)
P.O. Box 134007 (48113-4007)
PHONE 734 913-7500
Michael Rivenburgh, *President*
Tsutomu Komori, *Exec VP*
Masahide Matsubara, *Exec VP*
Naoki Mitsue, *Exec VP*
Toshihiro Uchiyama, *Exec VP*
▲ **EMP:** 109 **EST:** 1988
SQ FT: 175,000
SALES (est): 89.4MM **Privately Held**
WEB: www.nskamericas.com
SIC: 3714 Steering mechanisms, motor vehicle

(G-597)
NUSTEP LLC
5111 Venture Dr Ste 1 (48108-5928)
PHONE 734 769-3939
Steven Sarns, *Principal*
Richard Sarns, *Principal*
Alejandro Capetillo, *Vice Pres*
Dwayne Hyzak, *Vice Pres*
Roger Fettes, *Engineer*
▲ **EMP:** 100 **EST:** 1987
SQ FT: 68,000
SALES (est): 18.7MM **Privately Held**
WEB: www.nustep.com
SIC: 3949 Exercise equipment

(G-598)
OCTET INDUSTRIES LLC
3471 Richmond Ct (48105-1521)
PHONE 225 302-0541
Richard Hazey, *Principal*
EMP: 4 **EST:** 2012
SALES (est): 60.3K **Privately Held**
SIC: 3999 Manufacturing industries

(G-599)
OG TECHNOLOGIES INC
4480 Varsity Dr Ste G (48108-5007)
PHONE 734 973-7500
Tzyy-Shuh Chang, *President*
Terence C Liddy, *Chairman*
Hongbin Jia, *Engineer*
◆ **EMP:** 15 **EST:** 1997
SQ FT: 5,400
SALES (est): 5.9MM **Privately Held**
WEB: www.ogtechnologies.com
SIC: 3829 Measuring & controlling devices

(G-600)
OLD XEMBEDDED LLC
3915 Res Pk Dr Ste A8 (48108)
PHONE 734 975-0577
Scott Kania, *Manager*
EMP: 9 **EST:** 2002
SALES (est): 983.8K
SALES (corp-wide): 12.5MM **Privately Held**
WEB: www.acromag.com
SIC: 3443 Process vessels, industrial: metal plate
PA: Acromag, Incorporated
30765 S Wixom Rd
Wixom MI 48393
248 624-1541

(G-601)
OPTEOS INC
775 Technology Dr Ste 200 (48108-8948)
PHONE 734 929-3333
Kyoung Yang, *President*
EMP: 5 **EST:** 2012
SALES (est): 599K **Privately Held**
WEB: www.emagtech.com
SIC: 3825 Test equipment for electronic & electric measurement

(G-602)
OPTONOMY INC
Also Called: Optilogic
303 Detroit St Ste 1 (48104-1128)
PHONE 734 604-6472
Donald Hicks, *CEO*
Craig Wigley, *COO*
John Ames, *Vice Pres*
Mike Lloyd, *Director*
EMP: 25 **EST:** 2019
SALES (est): 1.2MM **Privately Held**
SIC: 7372 Prepackaged software

(G-603)
OVASCIENCE INC
301 N Main St Ste 100 (48104-1296)
PHONE 617 351-2590
EMP: 5 **EST:** 2019
SALES (est): 107.9K **Privately Held**
SIC: 2835 In vitro & in vivo diagnostic substances

(G-604)
PACIFIC INDUSTRIAL DEV CORP (PA)
Also Called: Pidc
4788 Runway Blvd (48108-9557)
PHONE 734 930-9292
WEI Wu, *CEO*
Gang Wu, *General Mgr*
Bill Germond, *Vice Pres*
Jeffery Lachapelle, *Vice Pres*
Thomas Queenan, *Vice Pres*
▲ **EMP:** 80 **EST:** 1992
SQ FT: 150,000
SALES (est): 100MM **Privately Held**
WEB: www.pidc.com
SIC: 2819 Industrial inorganic chemicals

(G-605)
PAGEKICKER CORPORATION
1521 Martha Ave (48103-5333)
PHONE 734 646-6277
EMP: 4
SALES (est): 174.3K **Privately Held**
WEB: www.pagekicker.com
SIC: 2731 Book publishing

(G-606)
PASSIVEBOLT INC
2723 S State St Unit 1 (48104-6188)
PHONE 734 972-0306
Sheena Monnin, *Marketing Staff*
EMP: 10 **EST:** 2018

Ann Arbor - Washtenaw County (G-607)

SALES (est): 1.7MM **Privately Held**
WEB: www.passivebolt.com
SIC: 3699 Security control equipment & systems

(G-607)
PERFECTION SPRINKLER COMPANY
Also Called: Sure-Flo Fittings
2077 S State St (48104-4607)
P.O. Box 1363 (48106-1363)
PHONE 734 761-5110
Thomas R Wilkins, *President*
Charles Wilkins, *Admin Sec*
EMP: 8 **EST:** 1933
SQ FT: 9,500
SALES (est): 1.6MM **Privately Held**
WEB: www.sure-flo.com
SIC: 3494 Pipe fittings; line strainers, for use in piping systems

(G-608)
PERFORM3-D LLC
411 Huronview Blvd # 200 (48103-2973)
PHONE 734 604-4100
Timothy Lock,
EMP: 6 **EST:** 2013
SALES (est): 342.2K **Privately Held**
WEB: www.perform3-d.com
SIC: 3827 Optical instruments & apparatus

(G-609)
PHENOMICS HEALTH INC
1600 Huron Pkwy Fl 2 (48109-5001)
PHONE 410 336-2404
James Burns, *CEO*
EMP: 25 **EST:** 2018
SALES (est): 1.5MM **Privately Held**
WEB: www.phenomicshealth.com
SIC: 2834 Pharmaceutical preparations

(G-610)
PHILLIPS SERVICE INDS INC (PA)
Also Called: PSI
1800 Landsdowne Rd (48105-1055)
P.O. Box 701280, Plymouth (48170-0962)
PHONE 734 853-5000
W Scott Phillips, *President*
William T Phillips, *Chairman*
Robert Phillips, *Vice Pres*
David Wallace, *Mfg Staff*
Lawrence Perlin, *CFO*
EMP: 12 **EST:** 1984
SQ FT: 170,000
SALES (est): 54.3MM **Privately Held**
WEB: www.psi-online.com
SIC: 7699 7694 7629 3452 Pumps & pumping equipment repair; valve repair, industrial; electric motor repair; circuit board repair; bolts, nuts, rivets & washers

(G-611)
PINSTRIPE PUBLISHING LLC
3629 Greenook Blvd (48103-9089)
PHONE 734 276-0554
EMP: 4 **EST:** 2014
SALES (est): 69.7K **Privately Held**
SIC: 2741 Miscellaneous publishing

(G-612)
PITTSFIELD PRODUCTS INC (PA)
Also Called: Pittsfield of Indiana
5741 Jackson Rd (48103-9199)
P.O. Box 1027 (48106-1027)
PHONE 734 665-3771
Theodore Fosdick, *President*
▲ **EMP:** 45 **EST:** 1945
SQ FT: 15,000
SALES (est): 19.8MM **Privately Held**
WEB: www.pittsfieldproducts.com
SIC: 3569 3564 3496 3494 Filters, general line: industrial; blowers & fans; miscellaneous fabricated wire products; valves & pipe fittings

(G-613)
POLK GAS PRODUCER LLC
414 S Main St Ste 600 (48104-2398)
PHONE 734 913-2970
Mark Cousino, *Manager*
EMP: 4 **EST:** 2001

SALES (est): 374.1K **Privately Held**
SIC: 3569 Gas producers, generators & other gas related equipment

(G-614)
POLYTORX LLC (DH)
Also Called: Helix Steel
2300 Washtenaw Ave # 200 (48104-4500)
PHONE 734 322-2114
Chris Doran, *CEO*
Luke Pinkerton, *President*
Justin Idalski, *Design Engr*
Kate Hanke, *Office Mgr*
◆ **EMP:** 3 **EST:** 2002
SQ FT: 1,000
SALES (est): 2.4MM **Privately Held**
SIC: 3496 Concrete reinforcing mesh & wire

(G-615)
POSSIBILITIES FOR CHANGE LLC
674 S Wagner Rd (48103-9002)
P.O. Box 331, Brighton (48116-0331)
PHONE 810 333-1347
Jennifer Salerno, *CEO*
EMP: 4
SALES (est): 728.4K **Privately Held**
WEB: www.possibilitiesforchange.org
SIC: 7372 Educational computer software

(G-616)
POWER RANK INC
2390 Adare Rd (48104-4020)
PHONE 650 387-2336
Edward H Feng, *CEO*
EMP: 7 **EST:** 2014
SALES (est): 115.9K **Privately Held**
WEB: www.thepowerrank.com
SIC: 7372 Application computer software

(G-617)
POWER SPORTS ANN ARBOR LLC
Also Called: Nicholson's
4405 Jackson Rd (48103-1833)
PHONE 734 585-3300
Mary Gulliver, *Principal*
Charles Stephenson,
EMP: 9 **EST:** 2006
SALES (est): 490.1K **Privately Held**
SIC: 3799 All terrain vehicles (ATV); snowmobiles

(G-618)
PRAKKEN PUBLICATIONS INC
2851 Boardwalk St (48104-6715)
P.O. Box 8623 (48107-8623)
PHONE 734 975-2800
Turalee Barlow, *President*
Susanne Peckham, *Manager*
EMP: 14 **EST:** 1934
SQ FT: 6,500
SALES (est): 826.9K **Privately Held**
WEB: www.techdirections.com
SIC: 2721 2731 Magazines: publishing only, not printed on site; books: publishing only

(G-619)
PRECISE METAL COMPONENTS INC
91 Enterprise Dr Ste A (48103-9126)
PHONE 734 769-0790
James C Dickert, *President*
Andrea Stager, *Treasurer*
Gus Stager, *Admin Sec*
EMP: 6 **EST:** 1996
SQ FT: 5,000
SALES (est): 1.2MM **Privately Held**
WEB: www.precisemetalcomponents.com
SIC: 7389 3599 Grinding, precision: commercial or industrial; machine shop, jobbing & repair

(G-620)
PRECISION CONTROLS COMPANY
107 Enterprise Dr (48103-9564)
PHONE 734 663-3104
William Olzack, *President*
Lawrence Murphy, *Admin Sec*
▲ **EMP:** 15 **EST:** 1955
SQ FT: 6,000

SALES (est): 1.5MM **Privately Held**
WEB: www.precision-controls.com
SIC: 3625 Relays & industrial controls

(G-621)
PRECISION MANUFACTURING SVCS
3738 W Liberty Rd (48103-9014)
P.O. Box 1085 (48106-1085)
PHONE 734 995-3505
Borje Rosaen, *President*
Denver Lewis, *Corp Secy*
Tricia Rosaen, *Vice Pres*
EMP: 9 **EST:** 1979
SQ FT: 8,000
SALES (est): 660.2K **Privately Held**
SIC: 3599 Machine shop, jobbing & repair

(G-622)
PRECISION MEASUREMENT CO
885 Oakdale Rd (48105-1076)
P.O. Box 7676 (48107-7676)
PHONE 734 995-0041
Sam Clark, *President*
EMP: 10 **EST:** 1967
SALES (est): 264.4K **Privately Held**
WEB: www.pmctransducers.com
SIC: 3829 Pressure transducers

(G-623)
PREHAB TECHNOLOGIES LLC
Also Called: Prenovo
103 E Liberty St Ste 201 (48104-2136)
PHONE 734 368-9983
Lora Kerr, *CEO*
June Sullivan, *Partner*
Siobhan Norman, *General Mgr*
EMP: 9 **EST:** 2015
SQ FT: 700
SALES (est): 354.7K **Privately Held**
SIC: 7372 7371 Business oriented computer software; computer software development & applications

(G-624)
PRINT-TECH INC
6800 Jackson Rd (48103-9565)
PHONE 734 996-2345
James Ceely, *President*
Brad Steven, *Info Tech Mgr*
▲ **EMP:** 28 **EST:** 1985
SQ FT: 15,000
SALES (est): 4.2MM **Privately Held**
WEB: www.printtechinc.com
SIC: 2752 2791 2789 Commercial printing, offset; typesetting; bookbinding & related work

(G-625)
PRO-FACE AMERICA LLC (HQ)
Also Called: Proface America
1050 Highland Dr Ste D (48108-2262)
PHONE 734 477-0600
Peter Klein, *Vice Pres*
Art Erickson, *Materials Mgr*
Jeff Scallion, *Sales Staff*
John Yates, *Sales Staff*
Jeff Roberts, *Office Mgr*
▲ **EMP:** 48 **EST:** 1968
SQ FT: 108,000
SALES (est): 9.7MM
SALES (corp-wide): 177.9K **Privately Held**
WEB: www.profaceamerica.com
SIC: 3571 3575 3577 Minicomputers; computer terminals; computer peripheral equipment
PA: Schneider Electric Se
35 Rue Joseph Monier
Rueil Malmaison
146 046-982

(G-626)
PROQUEST OUTDOOR SOLUTIONS INC
789 E Eisenhower Pkwy (48108-3218)
PHONE 734 761-4700
Sandra Parr, *Publisher*
Bruce Rhoads, *Senior VP*
Simon Beale, *Vice Pres*
John Campbell, *Vice Pres*
Christopher Cowan, *Vice Pres*
EMP: 23

SALES (est): 560.7K
SALES (corp-wide): 769.1MM **Privately Held**
WEB: www.voyagersopris.com
SIC: 2741 Miscellaneous publishing
HQ: Voyager Learning Company
17855 Dallas Pkwy Ste 400
Dallas TX 75287
214 932-9500

(G-627)
PSI LABS
3970 Varsity Dr (48108-2226)
PHONE 734 369-6273
EMP: 13 **EST:** 2015
SALES (est): 2.9MM **Privately Held**
WEB: www.psilabs.org
SIC: 3999 8734 ; testing laboratories

(G-628)
Q-PHOTONICS LLC
3830 Packard St Ste 170 (48108-2272)
PHONE 734 477-0133
George Loutts, *CEO*
Run Liu, *Engineer*
Anna Berg, *Accountant*
WEI Yang, *Sales Engr*
◆ **EMP:** 4 **EST:** 2000
SQ FT: 1,200
SALES (est): 650.3K **Privately Held**
WEB: www.qphotonics.com
SIC: 3826 Laser scientific & engineering instruments

(G-629)
QUAD CITY INNOVATIONS LLC
Also Called: Q C I
600 S Wagner Rd (48103-9002)
PHONE 513 200-6980
Ronald Jona, *Mng Member*
EMP: 5 **EST:** 2009
SALES (est): 1.3MM **Privately Held**
SIC: 3699 Electrical equipment & supplies

(G-630)
QUALITY FILTERS INC
7215 Jackson Rd Ste 3 (48103-9536)
P.O. Box 129, Dexter (48130-0129)
PHONE 734 668-0211
George Spottswood, *CEO*
David M Husak, *President*
EMP: 13 **EST:** 1979
SQ FT: 20,000
SALES (est): 1.5MM **Privately Held**
WEB: www.qualityfiltersinc.com
SIC: 3569 3564 3496 3494 Filters, general line: industrial; filter elements, fluid, hydraulic line; blowers & fans; miscellaneous fabricated wire products; valves & pipe fittings

(G-631)
RANIS GRANOLA
Also Called: Rani Nutra Foods
3604 Platt Rd (48108-2016)
PHONE 734 223-2995
Rani Boovich, *President*
EMP: 6 **EST:** 2011
SALES (est): 67.8K **Privately Held**
SIC: 2064 Chocolate candy, except solid chocolate

(G-632)
RDI SWITCHING TECHNOLOGIES
1130 Elmwood Dr (48104-4234)
PHONE 951 699-8919
EMP: 5 **EST:** 2015
SALES (est): 241K **Privately Held**
SIC: 3679 Electronic switches

(G-633)
REBO LIGHTING & ELEC LLC
3990 Research Park Dr (48108-2220)
PHONE 734 213-4159
Yu Zhang, *Mng Member*
EMP: 17 **EST:** 2017
SQ FT: 100,000
SALES (est): 4.7MM **Privately Held**
SIC: 3647 Automotive lighting fixtures
HQ: Chongqing Boao Industry (Group) Co., Ltd.
No.2, Huixing Road, Beibu New Area
Chongqing 40112

▲ = Import ▼=Export
◆ =Import/Export

(G-634)
RED HAT INC
315 W Huron St (48103-4262)
PHONE..................................978 392-2459
Pavan Reddy, *Analyst*
EMP: 4
SALES (corp-wide): 73.6B **Publicly Held**
WEB: www.redhat.com
SIC: 7372 Operating systems computer software
HQ: Red Hat, Inc.
100 E Davie St
Raleigh NC 27601

(G-635)
RED TIN BOAT
4081 Thornoaks Dr (48104-4253)
PHONE..................................734 239-3796
Middy Matthews, *Principal*
EMP: 7 EST: 2010
SALES (est): 132.5K **Privately Held**
SIC: 3356 Tin

(G-636)
REGENER-EYES LLC
330 E Liberty St Ll (48104-2274)
PHONE..................................248 207-4641
Ranjit Kommineni, *CEO*
Ann Arbor,
EMP: 4
SALES (est): 160.9K **Privately Held**
WEB: www.regenereyes.com
SIC: 3674 Solid state electronic devices

(G-637)
REGENTS OF THE UNIVERSITY MICH
Also Called: University Michigan Software
3003 S State St Spc 1272 (48109-1272)
PHONE..................................734 936-0435
Kenneth Nisbet, *Director*
EMP: 34
SALES (corp-wide): 7.9B **Privately Held**
WEB: www.umich.edu
SIC: 7372 8221 Prepackaged software; university
PA: Regents Of The University Of Michigan
503 Thompson St
Ann Arbor MI 48109
734 764-1817

(G-638)
REGENTS OF THE UNIVERSITY MICH
Also Called: Orthotics & Prosthetics Center
2850 S Industrial Hwy # 400 (48104-6796)
PHONE..................................734 973-2400
Anita Limberman-Lampear, *Director*
Kristine Miller, *Associate*
EMP: 26
SALES (corp-wide): 7.9B **Privately Held**
WEB: www.umich.edu
SIC: 3842 8221 Surgical appliances & supplies; university
PA: Regents Of The University Of Michigan
503 Thompson St
Ann Arbor MI 48109
734 764-1817

(G-639)
RETROSENSE THERAPEUTICS LLC
330 E Liberty St Ll (48104-2274)
PHONE..................................734 369-9333
Sean Ainsworth, *CEO*
Steven Bramer, *Officer*
Peter Francis, *Officer*
CAM Gallagher, *Officer*
EMP: 4 EST: 2014
SALES (est): 1.2MM
SALES (corp-wide): 45.8B **Publicly Held**
WEB: www.retro-sense.com
SIC: 2835 8731 In vitro & in vivo diagnostic substances; biotechnical research, commercial
HQ: Allergan Holdings Unlimited Company
Clonshaugh Business & Technology Park
Dublin

(G-640)
REUTTER LLC (DH)
2723 S State St Ste 150 (48104-6188)
PHONE..................................248 466-0652
Frank Horlacher, *CEO*
Olivia Kaho, *Accounts Mgr*
Johannes Wienands, *Director*
◆ EMP: 4 EST: 2010
SQ FT: 3,000
SALES (est): 5MM
SALES (corp-wide): 177.9K **Privately Held**
WEB: www.reutter-group.com
SIC: 3089 3795 Closures, plastic; tanks & tank components
HQ: Reutter Gmbh
Hans-Paul-Kaysser-Str. 10
Leutenbach 71397
719 595-9870

(G-641)
RIPPLE SCIENCE CORPORATION
303 Detroit St Ste 100 (48104-1128)
PHONE..................................919 451-0241
Peter Falzon, *President*
Anthony Nitsos, *Finance*
Jacob Bonenberger, *Admin Sec*
EMP: 5 EST: 2016
SALES (est): 444.4K **Privately Held**
WEB: www.ripplescience.com
SIC: 7372 Application computer software

(G-642)
ROBBIE DEAN PRESS LLC
2910 E Eisenhower Pkwy (48108-3222)
PHONE..................................734 973-9511
Dr Fairy C Hayes-Scott, *Mng Member*
Donald Cardinal, *Assoc Prof*
▲ EMP: 5 EST: 1991
SALES (est): 233.5K **Privately Held**
WEB: www.robbiedeanpress.com
SIC: 2731 Books: publishing only

(G-643)
ROBERT BOSCH LLC
3021 Miller Rd (48103-2122)
PHONE..................................734 302-2000
EMP: 4
SALES (est): 271.3K **Privately Held**
SIC: 3565 Mfg Packaging Machinery

(G-644)
ROSEDALE PRODUCTS INC (PA)
3730 W Liberty Rd (48103-9763)
P.O. Box 1085 (48106-1085)
PHONE..................................734 665-8201
Nils N Rosaen, *President*
Denver Lewis, *Vice Pres*
Jill Wonsey, *Sales Staff*
Jeff Folks, *MIS Mgr*
Mark Lunde, *Technical Staff*
◆ EMP: 62
SQ FT: 35,000
SALES (est): 13.7MM **Privately Held**
WEB: www.rosedaleproducts.com
SIC: 3569 3564 3494 Filters, general line: industrial; blowers & fans; valves & pipe fittings

(G-645)
RSR SALES INC
Also Called: RSR Industries
232 Haeussler Ct (48103-6203)
P.O. Box 2741 (48106-2741)
PHONE..................................734 668-8166
Richard Cohen, *President*
▲ EMP: 20 EST: 1982
SQ FT: 6,000
SALES (est): 6.7MM **Privately Held**
SIC: 5072 3429 Hardware; manufactured hardware (general)

(G-646)
S-3 ENGINEERING INC
95 Enterprise Dr (48103-9503)
PHONE..................................734 996-2303
Andrea Stager, *President*
Augustus P Stager III, *Vice Pres*
EMP: 10 EST: 1973
SQ FT: 10,000
SALES (est): 941K **Privately Held**
WEB: www.s-three.com
SIC: 3599 Machine shop, jobbing & repair

(G-647)
SAAGARA LLC
709 W Ellsworth Rd # 200 (48108-3371)
PHONE..................................734 658-4693
Nagabhushanam Peddi, *CEO*
EMP: 10 EST: 2008
SALES (est): 720.1K **Privately Held**
WEB: www.saagara.com
SIC: 7372 Application computer software

(G-648)
SENSIGMA LLC
3660 Plaza Dr (48108-1685)
PHONE..................................734 998-8328
Aparajita Mazumber, *Vice Pres*
Jyoti Mazumder, *Officer*
EMP: 6 EST: 2011
SALES (est): 606.5K **Privately Held**
WEB: www.sensigmallc.com
SIC: 3699 8731 Electrical equipment & supplies; electronic research

(G-649)
SGM TRANSFORMER LLC
210 Little Lake Dr Ste 9 (48103-6218)
PHONE..................................734 922-2400
Sunita Patel, *Principal*
EMP: 4 EST: 2016
SALES (est): 105K **Privately Held**
WEB: www.sgmtransformer.com
SIC: 3612 Transformers, except electric

(G-650)
SHAREDBOOK INC
Also Called: Academicpub Xanedu
4750 Venture Dr Ste 400 (48108-9505)
PHONE..................................734 302-6500
Jason Plackowski, *CFO*
EMP: 20 EST: 2003
SALES (est): 1.3MM **Privately Held**
WEB: www.sharedbook.com
SIC: 2741 Miscellaneous publishing

(G-651)
SHUTTERBOOTH
4972 S Ridgeside Cir (48105-9447)
PHONE..................................734 680-6067
Michael Robins, *Principal*
EMP: 6 EST: 2016
SALES (est): 142.3K **Privately Held**
WEB: www.shutterbooth.com
SIC: 3442 Shutters, door or window: metal

(G-652)
SIEMENS INDUSTRY SOFTWARE INC
2600 Green Rd Ste 100 (48105-4632)
PHONE..................................734 994-7300
Dave Wilkins, *Mfg Staff*
Trevor Bengtsson, *Engineer*
Matt Gray, *VP Accounting*
Monique Morgan, *Marketing Mgr*
Rachel Gordon, *Business Anlyst*
EMP: 4
SALES (corp-wide): 67.4B **Privately Held**
WEB: www.siemens.com
SIC: 7372 Business oriented computer software
HQ: Siemens Industry Software Inc.
5800 Granite Pkwy Ste 600
Plano TX 75024
972 987-3000

(G-653)
SIGNAL 7 WINES LLC
1425 Pontiac Trl (48105-1766)
PHONE..................................616 581-8900
Rob Vanrenterghem, *Mng Member*
EMP: 10 EST: 2020
SALES (est): 508.3K **Privately Held**
SIC: 2084 Wines

(G-654)
SIZZL LLC
721 S Forest Ave Apt 309 (48104-3157)
PHONE..................................201 454-1938
Atharva Talpade, *Mng Member*
Bhavisk Gummadi,
Ryan Helmlinger,
EMP: 10 EST: 2018
SALES (est): 12K **Privately Held**
WEB: www.sizzl.org
SIC: 7372 7389 Application computer software;

(G-655)
SKYSYNC INC
Also Called: Portal Architects
30 Parkland Plz Ste B (48103-6201)
PHONE..................................734 822-6858
Mark Brazeau, *CEO*
Matthew Hastings, *Business Mgr*
Garth Jackson, *Corp Secy*
Nicky Borcea, *Vice Pres*
Lindsey Byers, *Vice Pres*
EMP: 50 EST: 2012
SQ FT: 3,156
SALES (est): 4.8MM **Privately Held**
WEB: www.skysync.com
SIC: 7372 Prepackaged software

(G-656)
SMART USA INC
777 E Eisenhower Pkwy # 10 (48108-3273)
PHONE..................................248 214-1022
EMP: 6 EST: 2019
SALES (est): 153.7K **Privately Held**
SIC: 2671 Thermoplastic coated paper for packaging

(G-657)
SNIFFER ROBOTICS LLC
330 E Liberty St Fl 4 (48104-2238)
PHONE..................................855 476-4333
Arthur Mohrm,
David Barron,
Bob Dentzman,
EMP: 4 EST: 2016
SALES (est): 555.6K **Privately Held**
WEB: www.snifferrobotics.com
SIC: 3812 Search & navigation equipment

(G-658)
SOLAR TONIC LLC (PA)
2232 S Main St Ste 364 (48103-6938)
PHONE..................................734 368-0215
Brian Tell, *Mng Member*
Harry Giles, *Mng Member*
EMP: 9 EST: 2011
SALES (est): 1MM **Privately Held**
WEB: www.solartonic.com
SIC: 3648 Street lighting fixtures

(G-659)
SOLIDICA INC
5840 Interface Dr Ste 200 (48103-9176)
P.O. Box 4248 (48106-4248)
PHONE..................................734 222-4680
Ken Johnson, *CEO*
John Ford, *COO*
EMP: 18 EST: 1999
SQ FT: 9,000
SALES (est): 1.7MM **Privately Held**
WEB: www.solidica.com
SIC: 3541 3822 Machine tools, metal cutting type; temperature sensors for motor windings

(G-660)
SOLOHILL ENGINEERING INC
4370 Varsity Dr Ste B (48108-2359)
PHONE..................................734 973-2956
Tim Solomon, *CEO*
David E Solomon, *Ch of Bd*
Mark Szczypka, *President*
Dr William J Hillegas, *Vice Pres*
Kris Conley, *CFO*
EMP: 30 EST: 1984
SQ FT: 24,000
SALES (est): 3.6MM **Privately Held**
WEB: www.solohill.com
SIC: 2833 Medicinal chemicals

(G-661)
SPES PUBLISHING CO LLC
3977 S Michael Rd (48103-9345)
PHONE..................................734 741-1241
Maurice Snyder, *Principal*
EMP: 7 EST: 2008
SALES (est): 104.5K **Privately Held**
WEB: www.spesdev.com
SIC: 2741 Miscellaneous publishing

(G-662)
SPOT DESIGN LLC
Also Called: Zero Hour Parts
275 Metty Dr (48103-9444)
PHONE..................................734 997-0866
Dan Schmidt, *Principal*
Jesse Sherwood, *Foreman/Supr*
Andrea Rickelmann, *Office Mgr*
EMP: 38 EST: 2001
SALES (est): 7.6MM **Privately Held**
WEB: www.zerohourparts.com
SIC: 3599 Machine shop, jobbing & repair

(PA)=Parent Co (HQ)=Headquarters (DH)=Div Headquarters
✪ = New Business established in last 2 years

Ann Arbor - Washtenaw County (G-663)

(G-663)
SSA CONSUMER BRANDS INC
455 E Eisenhower Pkwy # 30 (48103-3304)
PHONE................................734 430-0565
Prasad Duvvuri, *President*
EMP: 10
SALES (est): 300K **Privately Held**
SIC: 2099 Food preparations

(G-664)
STAMATOPOLOS & SONS
869 W Eisenhower Pkwy (48103-6641)
PHONE................................734 369-2995
EMP: 4 EST: 2016
SALES (est): 137.9K **Privately Held**
SIC: 2079 Olive oil

(G-665)
STEVES CUSTOM SIGNS INC
4676 Freedom Dr (48108-9104)
P.O. Box 799, Saline (48176-0799)
PHONE................................734 662-5964
Steve Jedele, *President*
EMP: 12 EST: 2005
SALES (est): 1.6MM **Privately Held**
WEB: www.unitedimagegroup.com
SIC: 3993 Electric signs

(G-666)
STM POWER INC (PA)
275 Metty Dr (48103-9444)
PHONE................................734 214-1448
Dorrance J Noonan Jr, *President*
Mark Abbo, *Vice Pres*
EMP: 36 EST: 1993
SQ FT: 19,000
SALES (est): 5MM **Privately Held**
WEB: www.stmpower.com
SIC: 3724 8731 Cooling systems, aircraft engine; industrial laboratory, except testing

(G-667)
STRATEGIC COMPUTER SOLUTIONS
Also Called: S C S
2625 Shefman Ter Ste 200 (48105-3441)
PHONE................................248 888-0666
Leeron Kopelman, *President*
Matthew Rindfleisch, *Vice Pres*
EMP: 4 EST: 1987
SQ FT: 1,550 **Privately Held**
WEB: www.stratcom.com
SIC: 7379 5045 7371 7372 Computer related consulting services; computer hardware requirements analysis; computers, peripherals & software; computer software systems analysis & design, custom; prepackaged software

(G-668)
SUNTECH INDUSTRIALS LLC
5137 Colonial Ct (48108-8651)
PHONE................................734 678-5922
Christina Luo, *Administration*
EMP: 4 EST: 2017
SALES (est): 134K **Privately Held**
WEB: www.suntechled.com
SIC: 3646 Commercial indusl & institutional electric lighting fixtures

(G-669)
SWIFT BIOSCIENCES INC
674 S Wagner Rd Ste 100 (48103-9002)
PHONE................................734 330-2568
David Olson, *President*
Jean-Marc Terral, *Vice Pres*
Diane Joynt, *Finance*
Allison Sotomayor, *Finance*
Ian Silber, *Sales Staff*
EMP: 4 EST: 2009
SALES (est): 2.9MM
SALES (corp-wide): 22.2B **Publicly Held**
WEB: www.swiftbiosci.com
SIC: 2835 In vitro & in vivo diagnostic substances
HQ: Integrated Dna Technologies, Inc.
1710 Commercial Park
Coralville IA 52241
800 328-2661

(G-670)
SYMOREX LTD
3728 Plaza Dr Ste 3 (48108-3625)
PHONE................................734 971-6000
Chris Erickson, *President*
Karl Neill, *General Mgr*
EMP: 18 EST: 1992
SQ FT: 6,000
SALES (est): 4MM **Privately Held**
WEB: www.symorex.com
SIC: 5085 3625 3536 3535 Industrial supplies; relays & industrial controls; hoists, cranes & monorails; conveyors & conveying equipment

(G-671)
TALL PAULS PICKLES LLC
4488 Jackson Rd (48103-1812)
PHONE................................734 476-2424
Paul Majewski, *Principal*
EMP: 4 EST: 2013
SALES (est): 159.8K **Privately Held**
WEB: www.tallpaulspickles.com
SIC: 2035 Pickled fruits & vegetables

(G-672)
TECAT PERFORMANCE SYSTEMS LLC
705 Technology Dr (48108-8909)
PHONE................................248 615-9862
Ron Rath, *CEO*
Douglas Baker, *Principal*
Joseph Byker, *Principal*
Don Keating, *VP Bus Dvlpt*
Brenda Duquette, *Administration*
EMP: 11 EST: 2016
SALES (est): 268.7K **Privately Held**
WEB: www.tecatperformance.com
SIC: 8711 3829 Engineering services; stress, strain & flaw detecting/measuring equipment

(G-673)
TECTUM HOLDINGS INC (DH)
5400 Data Ct (48108-8961)
PHONE................................734 677-0444
William Reminder, *President*
Kelly Kneifl, *COO*
Sean Marks, *Exec VP*
David Wells, *Exec VP*
Jim Bresingham, *CFO*
EMP: 100 EST: 2007
SALES (est): 377.5MM
SALES (corp-wide): 623.9MM **Privately Held**
WEB: www.truck-hero.com
SIC: 3713 5013 Truck bodies & parts; truck parts & accessories
HQ: Truck Hero, Inc.
5400 Data Ct Ste 100
Ann Arbor MI 48108
877 875-4376

(G-674)
TECTUM HOLDINGS INC
Also Called: Truck Hero Ann Arbor
4670 Runway Blvd (48108-9557)
PHONE................................734 926-2362
William Reminder, *CEO*
David Michaud, *Manager*
EMP: 100
SALES (corp-wide): 623.9MM **Privately Held**
WEB: www.truck-hero.com
SIC: 8748 3714 Test development & evaluation service; pickup truck bed liners
HQ: Tectum Holdings, Inc.
5400 Data Ct
Ann Arbor MI 48108
734 677-0444

(G-675)
TECUMSEH COMPRESSOR CO LLC
5683 Hines Dr (48108-7901)
PHONE................................662 566-2231
Doug Murdock, *President*
Michael Bauersfeld, *President*
William Prete, *Technical Staff*
EMP: 28 EST: 2002
SALES (est): 900.6K **Privately Held**
WEB: www.tecumseh.com
SIC: 3585 Compressors for refrigeration & air conditioning equipment

(G-676)
TECUMSEH COMPRESSOR COMPANY
1136 Oak Valley Dr (48108-9624)
PHONE................................734 585-9500
Michael Noelke, *Vice Pres*
Janice Stipp, *Treasurer*
Roger Jackson, *Admin Sec*
▲ EMP: 59 EST: 2002
SALES (est): 5.2MM **Publicly Held**
WEB: www.tecumseh.com
SIC: 3585 Compressors for refrigeration & air conditioning equipment
HQ: Tecumseh Products Company Llc
5683 Hines Dr
Ann Arbor MI 48108
734 585-9500

(G-677)
TECUMSEH PRODUCTS COMPANY LLC (DH)
5683 Hines Dr (48108-7901)
PHONE................................734 585-9500
Harold M Karp, *President*
Ronald E Pratt, *President*
Eric L Stolzenberg, *President*
Jerry L Mosingo, *Exec VP*
Ernani Nunes, *Senior VP*
◆ EMP: 1100 EST: 1930
SQ FT: 49,500
SALES (est): 1.2B **Publicly Held**
WEB: www.tecumseh.com
SIC: 3585 3679 Parts for heating, cooling & refrigerating equipment; compressors for refrigeration & air conditioning equipment; condensers, refrigeration; hermetic seals for electronic equipment
HQ: Tecumseh Products Holdings Llc
5683 Hines Dr
Ann Arbor MI 48108
734 585-9500

(G-678)
TECUMSEH PRODUCTS COMPANY LLC
Also Called: Applied Electronics Group
1136 Oak Valley Dr (48108-9624)
PHONE................................734 585-9500
Timothy Wright, *Vice Pres*
David Hammer, *Manager*
Jim Gladieux, *Technology*
Anita Carlton, *Director*
George Gatecliff, *Director*
EMP: 4 **Publicly Held**
WEB: www.tecumseh.com
SIC: 3585 Parts for heating, cooling & refrigerating equipment
HQ: Tecumseh Products Company Llc
5683 Hines Dr
Ann Arbor MI 48108
734 585-9500

(G-679)
TECUMSEH PRODUCTS COMPANY LLC
Also Called: Cool Products Division
5683 Hines Dr (48108-7901)
PHONE................................734 585-9500
Michael Forman, *Branch Mgr*
Don Lusk, *Analyst*
EMP: 6 **Publicly Held**
WEB: www.tecumseh.com
SIC: 3585 Parts for heating, cooling & refrigerating equipment
HQ: Tecumseh Products Company Llc
5683 Hines Dr
Ann Arbor MI 48108
734 585-9500

(G-680)
TECUMSEH PRODUCTS HOLDINGS LLC (HQ)
5683 Hines Dr (48108-7901)
PHONE................................734 585-9500
Gregory L Christopher, *CEO*
EMP: 115 EST: 2015
SALES (est): 2.3B **Publicly Held**
WEB: www.tecumseh.com
SIC: 3585 3679 6719 Parts for heating, cooling & refrigerating equipment; hermetic seals for electronic equipment; investment holding companies, except banks

(G-681)
TERAMETRIX LLC
2725 S Industrial Hwy # 100 (48104-6281)
PHONE................................540 769-8430
Ricahrd Kurtz, *CEO*
Scott Graeff, *President*
Robin Risser, *COO*
Heather Parry, *Buyer*
John Duquette, *Engineer*
EMP: 120 EST: 1992
SQ FT: 50,335
SALES (est): 7.9MM **Publicly Held**
SIC: 3674 3823 Semiconductors & related devices; industrial instrmnts msrmnt display/control process variable
HQ: Former Luna Subsidiary, Inc.
Camarillo CA 93012

(G-682)
TERRY BUTLER PRINTS LLC
2281 Manchester Rd (48104-4921)
PHONE................................734 255-8592
Terrence Butler, *Principal*
EMP: 5 EST: 2010
SALES (est): 131.4K **Privately Held**
SIC: 2752 Commercial printing, lithographic

(G-683)
TERUMO CRDVSCULAR SYSTEMS CORP (DH)
Also Called: T C V S
6200 Jackson Rd (48103-9586)
PHONE................................734 663-4145
Robert Deryke, *President*
Don Smith, *Plant Mgr*
Jessica McCumons, *Project Mgr*
Chris Hudson, *Senior Buyer*
Rotha Foster, *Buyer*
▲ EMP: 250 EST: 1999
SQ FT: 400,000
SALES (est): 221.5MM **Privately Held**
WEB: www.terumocv.com
SIC: 3845 3841 Electromedical equipment; surgical & medical instruments; needles, suture; catheters
HQ: Terumo Americas Holding, Inc.
265 Davidson Ave Ste 320
Somerset NJ 08873
732 302-4900

(G-684)
TERUMO HEART INCORPORATED
6190 Jackson Rd (48103-9140)
PHONE................................734 663-4145
William Pinon, *President*
Nora Abdulla, *QC Mgr*
Brent Couey, *QC Mgr*
Alexander Medvedev, *Research*
Tom Sahines, *Chief Engr*
▲ EMP: 31 EST: 2002
SALES (est): 3.3MM **Privately Held**
WEB: www.terumoheart.com
SIC: 3841 Surgical & medical instruments
HQ: Terumo Americas Holding, Inc.
265 Davidson Ave Ste 320
Somerset NJ 08873
732 302-4900

(G-685)
TGI DIRECT INC
Also Called: Grimbac Division
1225 Rosewood St (48104-6226)
PHONE................................810 239-5553
Loretta O'reilly, *Project Mgr*
Susan Skinner, *Controller*
Doughlas Bacon, *Manager*
Stephanie Geare, *Manager*
Jon Linfeld, *Manager*
EMP: 9
SQ FT: 9,600
SALES (corp-wide): 13.3MM **Privately Held**
WEB: www.tgidirect.com
SIC: 7331 2791 2759 2752 Mailing service; typesetting; commercial printing; commercial printing, lithographic
PA: Tgi Direct, Inc.
5365 Hill 23 Dr
Flint MI 48507
810 239-5553

▲ = Import ▼ = Export
◆ = Import/Export

GEOGRAPHIC SECTION

Ann Arbor - Washtenaw County (G-711)

(G-686)
THALNER ELECTRONIC LABS INC
Also Called: T E L
7235 Jackson Rd (48103-9550)
PHONE.....................734 761-4506
Timothy Boggs, *President*
Jeno Draganescu, *Project Mgr*
Tim Boggs, *Engineer*
Richard Schoenfeldt, *CFO*
EMP: 30 EST: 1965
SQ FT: 17,000
SALES (est): 14.7MM **Privately Held**
WEB: www.thalner.com
SIC: **1731** 3663 5099 Closed circuit television installation; television closed circuit equipment; video & audio equipment

(G-687)
THERMO FISHER SCIENTIFIC INC
2868 W Delhi Rd (48103-9011)
PHONE.....................734 662-4117
Kim Moug, *Sales Staff*
EMP: 5
SALES (corp-wide): 32.2B **Publicly Held**
WEB: www.thermofisher.com
SIC: **3826** Analytical instruments
PA: Thermo Fisher Scientific Inc.
168 3rd Ave
Waltham MA 02451
781 622-1000

(G-688)
THETFORD CORPORATION (DH)
7101 Jackson Rd (48103-9506)
P.O. Box 1285 (48106-1285)
PHONE.....................734 769-6000
Stephane Cordeille, *CEO*
Kevin Phillips, *President*
Rodney Curtis, *Vice Pres*
Barry Eckel, *Vice Pres*
Alissa Reyes, *Vice Pres*
◆ EMP: 217 EST: 1963
SQ FT: 89,000
SALES (est): 356.5MM
SALES (corp-wide): 754MM **Privately Held**
WEB: www.thetford.com
SIC: **3632** 3089 2842 2621 Refrigerators, mechanical & absorption: household; toilets, portable chemical: plastic; sanitation preparations; sanitary tissue paper; metal sanitary ware; chemical preparations
HQ: Dkm, Ltd.
2515 South Rd
Poughkeepsie NY 12601
212 661-4600

(G-689)
THOMAS-WARD SYSTEMS LLC
314 Pauline Blvd (48103-5565)
PHONE.....................734 929-0644
Alicia Frenette,
EMP: 4 EST: 2006
SALES (est): 420.5K **Privately Held**
WEB: www.thomaswardsystems.com
SIC: **3559** Automotive related machinery

(G-690)
THORATEC LLC
6190 Jackson Rd (48103-9140)
PHONE.....................734 827-7422
EMP: 155
SALES (corp-wide): 34.6B **Publicly Held**
SIC: **3845** 3841 Electromedical equipment; surgical & medical instruments
HQ: Thoratec Llc
6035 Stoneridge Dr
Pleasanton CA 94588
925 847-8600

(G-691)
TINILITE WORLD INC
2591 Carmel St (48104-6505)
PHONE.....................734 334-0839
Changming Fan, *President*
EMP: 6 EST: 1998
SALES (est): 404.9K **Privately Held**
SIC: **3674** Semiconductors & related devices

(G-692)
TISSUE SEAL LLC
Also Called: Medical Product Manufacturer
4401 Varsity Dr Ste D (48108-5003)
PHONE.....................734 213-5530
Stephen Shulman, *Mng Member*
Dale Hawkins, *Director*
EMP: 10 EST: 2007
SALES (est): 2.1MM **Privately Held**
WEB: www.tissueseal.com
SIC: **3069** Medical & laboratory rubber sundries & related products

(G-693)
TLS PRODUCTIONS INC
78 Jackson Plz (48103-1917)
PHONE.....................810 220-8577
William Ross, *President*
Kirt Bachiero, *Vice Pres*
Brad Hayes, *Vice Pres*
Phil Stroud, *Opers Mgr*
Drew Gansen, *Opers Staff*
EMP: 24 EST: 1996
SQ FT: 41,126
SALES (est): 6.2MM **Privately Held**
WEB: www.tlsproductionsinc.com
SIC: **1799** 3648 7922 Rigging, theatrical; stage lighting equipment; lighting, theatrical

(G-694)
TMC FURNITURE INC
119 E Ann St (48104-1414)
PHONE.....................734 622-0080
Blake Ratcliffe, *President*
Julie Moore, *Vice Pres*
Joy Johnsen, *Marketing Staff*
Christina Kirwin, *Administration*
EMP: 7
SALES (corp-wide): 3.3MM **Privately Held**
WEB: www.tmcfurniture.com
SIC: **2531** Public building & related furniture
PA: Tmc Furniture, Inc.
4525 Airwest Dr Se
Kentwood MI 49512
734 622-0080

(G-695)
TOMUKUN NOODLE BAR
505 E Liberty St Ste 200 (48104-2465)
PHONE.....................734 995-8668
EMP: 8 EST: 2010
SALES (est): 409.5K **Privately Held**
WEB: www.tomukun.com
SIC: **2098** Noodles (e.g. egg, plain & water), dry

(G-696)
TREE HOUSE SOFTWARE INC
1750 Fulmer St (48103-2455)
PHONE.....................503 208-6171
Brian Bawol, *President*
EMP: 5 EST: 2010
SALES (est): 87.7K **Privately Held**
SIC: **7372** Prepackaged software

(G-697)
TRENTON CORPORATION (PA)
7700 Jackson Rd (48103-9545)
PHONE.....................734 424-3600
Charles Kennedy, *President*
Chad Whitney, *Prdtn Mgr*
Milton Weidmayer, *Treasurer*
Jodi Rutledge, *Sales Mgr*
Paul Phillips, *Manager*
◆ EMP: 25 EST: 1949
SQ FT: 20,000
SALES (est): 16.2MM **Privately Held**
WEB: www.trentoncorp.com
SIC: **5169** 2891 Anti-corrosion products; mucilage

(G-698)
TRIMAS CORPORATION
315 E Eisenhower Pkwy (48108-3350)
PHONE.....................248 631-5451
EMP: 6
SALES (corp-wide): 769.9MM **Publicly Held**
WEB: www.trimascorp.com
SIC: **3799** Trailer hitches

PA: Trimas Corporation
38505 Woodward Ave # 200
Bloomfield Hills MI 48304
248 631-5450

(G-699)
TRUCK ACQUISITION INC (HQ)
5400 Data Ct (48108-8961)
PHONE.....................877 875-4376
William Reminder, *CEO*
EMP: 2 EST: 2017
SALES (est): 486.9MM
SALES (corp-wide): 623.9MM **Privately Held**
WEB: www.truck-hero.com
SIC: **3089** 3714 Automotive parts, plastic; pickup truck bed liners
PA: Truck Holdings Inc.
5400 Data Ct Ste 100
Ann Arbor MI 48108
877 875-4376

(G-700)
TRUCK HOLDINGS INC (PA)
5400 Data Ct Ste 100 (48108-8961)
PHONE.....................877 875-4376
William Reminder, *CEO*
Mark Hickey, *Exec VP*
Sid Millspaugh, *Vice Pres*
Tim Schaeffer, *Vice Pres*
Deb Truax, *Sales Staff*
EMP: 2 EST: 2017
SALES (est): 623.9MM **Privately Held**
WEB: www.truck-hero.com
SIC: **3714** 6719 Pickup truck bed liners; investment holding companies, except banks

(G-701)
TYLER TECHNOLOGIES INC
525 Avis Dr Ste 3 (48108-9616)
PHONE.....................734 677-0550
Marv McElzain, *Principal*
Michael Hitchcock, *Engineer*
Jenny Nielsen, *Manager*
EMP: 4
SALES (corp-wide): 1B **Publicly Held**
WEB: www.tylertech.com
SIC: **7371** 7372 Computer software development; prepackaged software
PA: Tyler Technologies, Inc.
5101 Tennyson Pkwy
Plano TX 75024
972 713-3700

(G-702)
UBE MACHINERY INC
Also Called: Ube Industries
5700 S State Rd (48108-9634)
PHONE.....................734 741-7000
Mitsuhiro Kawamura, *President*
Yasuhiro Inoue, *Principal*
Romica Vlad, *Engineer*
Josh Bordt, *Sales Staff*
Pat Berry, *Manager*
◆ EMP: 60 EST: 1992
SQ FT: 47,000
SALES (est): 17.9MM **Privately Held**
WEB: www.ubemachinery.com
SIC: **3559** 5084 3363 3354 Plastics working machinery; clay working & tempering machines; industrial machinery & equipment; plastic products machinery; aluminum die-castings; aluminum extruded products
HQ: Ube Machinery Corporation,Ltd.
1980, Azaokinoyama, Kogushi
Ube YMG 755-0

(G-703)
ULTRASEAL AMERICA INC
4343 Concourse Dr Ste 340 (48108-9422)
PHONE.....................734 222-9478
Michael Potts, *President*
Tom Dahl, *Sales Mgr*
EMP: 4 EST: 1999
SQ FT: 20,000
SALES (est): 1.7MM
SALES (corp-wide): 1.4B **Publicly Held**
WEB: www.ultraseal-impregnation.com
SIC: **3471** Electroplating of metals or formed products

HQ: Surface Technology (East Kilbride) Limited
Unit C
Coventry W MIDLANDS CV5 9
247 625-8444

(G-704)
UM ORTHOTICS PROS CNTR
2500 Green Rd Ste 100 (48105-1573)
PHONE.....................734 764-3100
EMP: 9 EST: 2015
SALES (est): 1.5MM **Privately Held**
SIC: **3842** Orthopedic appliances

(G-705)
UNDERGROUND SHIRTS
2248 S Main St (48103-5831)
PHONE.....................734 274-5494
Christopher Williams, *Sales Staff*
EMP: 7 EST: 2014
SALES (est): 121.1K **Privately Held**
WEB: www.undergroundshirts.com
SIC: **2759** Screen printing

(G-706)
UNIVERSITY PLASTICS INC
7150 Jackson Rd (48103-9552)
PHONE.....................734 668-8773
William C Trachet, *President*
Lydia Trachet, *Vice Pres*
EMP: 7 EST: 1975
SQ FT: 4,800
SALES (est): 700K **Privately Held**
WEB: www.thesmartclip.com
SIC: **3089** Injection molding of plastics

(G-707)
USA BRNGS SUP LLC DBA JSB GREA
210 Little Lake Dr (48103-6218)
PHONE.....................734 222-4177
Sunita Patel, *Mng Member*
▲ EMP: 4 EST: 2011
SALES (est): 439.7K **Privately Held**
WEB: www.jsbgreatbearings.com
SIC: **5085** 3562 Bearings; ball & roller bearings

(G-708)
VAN BOVEN INCORPORATED
Also Called: Van Boven Clothing
326 S State St (48104-2412)
P.O. Box 4600 (48106-4600)
PHONE.....................734 665-7228
James A Orr, *President*
Tom Haney, *General Mgr*
Susan A Orr, *Vice Pres*
EMP: 7 EST: 1921
SQ FT: 2,000
SALES (est): 836.3K **Privately Held**
WEB: www.vanboven.com
SIC: **5611** 2329 Suits, men's; clothing accessories: men's & boys'; men's & boys' sportswear & athletic clothing

(G-709)
VANROTH LLC
Also Called: Blue Lion Fitness
401 S Maple Rd (48103-3834)
PHONE.....................734 929-5268
Daniel Roth, *Mng Member*
Ryan Van Bergen,
EMP: 10 EST: 2015
SALES (est): 480K **Privately Held**
WEB: www.bluelionfitness.com
SIC: **7991** 7372 Physical fitness facilities; application computer software

(G-710)
VERSO SERVICES INC
4676 Freedom Dr (48108-9104)
P.O. Box 799, Saline (48176-0799)
PHONE.....................734 368-0989
Stephen Jedele, *President*
EMP: 7 EST: 2015
SALES (est): 102.8K **Privately Held**
WEB: www.versoservices.com
SIC: **2759** Letterpress & screen printing

(G-711)
VIPER TOOL COMPANY LLC
1310 Iroquois Pl (48104-4636)
PHONE.....................734 417-9974
Jeffrey Terrell, *Principal*
EMP: 6 EST: 2015

Ann Arbor - Washtenaw County (G-712)

GEOGRAPHIC SECTION

SALES (est): 84.1K **Privately Held**
WEB: www.vipertoolcompany.com
SIC: **3541** Machine tools, metal cutting type

(G-712)
WACKER CHEMICAL CORPORATION
Also Called: Silicones Rd Center
600 S Wagner Rd (48103-9002)
PHONE..................734 882-4055
David Wilhoit, *President*
Paul Mason, *CFO*
Terese Tomko, *Supervisor*
Mamun Monsoor, *CIO*
EMP: 4
SALES (corp-wide): 5.5B **Privately Held**
WEB: www.wackerrelay4life.com
SIC: **2869** Silicones
HQ: Wacker Chemical Corporation
3301 Sutton Rd
Adrian MI 49221
517 264-8500

(G-713)
WARMILU LLC
8186 Jackson Rd Ste C (48103-9802)
PHONE..................855 927-6458
Grace Hsia, *CEO*
Larrea Young, *COO*
Douglas Wolf, *Project Mgr*
Gerry Hanson, *Technical Staff*
EMP: 8 EST: 2012
SQ FT: 2,041
SALES (est): 47.5K **Privately Held**
WEB: www.warmilu.com
SIC: **3841** Surgical & medical instruments

(G-714)
WASHTENAW COMMUNICATIONS INC
1510 Saunders Cres (48103-2534)
PHONE..................734 662-7138
Kenneth L Aungst, *President*
EMP: 8 EST: 1979 **Privately Held**
WEB: www.welectronic.net
SIC: **5731** 7622 3663 Radios, two-way, citizens' band, weather, short-wave, etc.; radio repair & installation; radio broadcasting & communications equipment

(G-715)
WASHTENAW VOICE
4800 E Huron River Dr (48105-9481)
PHONE..................734 677-5405
EMP: 9 EST: 2015
SALES (est): 124.6K **Privately Held**
WEB: www.washtenawvoice.com
SIC: **2711** Newspapers, publishing & printing

(G-716)
WHITE LOTUS FARMS INC
7217 W Liberty Rd (48103-9381)
PHONE..................734 904-1379
Amy Blondin, *Info Tech Mgr*
EMP: 7 EST: 2013
SALES (est): 432.1K **Privately Held**
WEB: www.whitelotusfarms.com
SIC: **0214** 2051 0182 2022 Goat farm; buns, bread type: fresh or frozen; vegetable crops grown under cover; natural cheese

(G-717)
WORD BARON INC
315 E Eisenhower Pkwy # 2 (48108-3350)
PHONE..................248 471-4080
Cheryl E Baron, *President*
EMP: 10 EST: 1988
SQ FT: 9,600
SALES (est): 805.5K **Privately Held**
WEB: www.thewordbaroninc.com
SIC: **7336** 2752 Graphic arts & related design; poster & decal printing, lithographic

(G-718)
XORAN HOLDINGS LLC (PA)
5210 S State Rd (48108-7936)
PHONE..................734 418-5108
Jacqueline Vestevich,
EMP: 8 EST: 2015
SALES (est): 22.8MM **Privately Held**
WEB: www.xorantech.com
SIC: **3845** Ultrasonic scanning devices, medical

(G-719)
XORAN TECHNOLOGIES LLC
5210 S State Rd (48108-7936)
PHONE..................734 663-7194
Jodie Haberkorn, *Controller*
EMP: 60 EST: 2015
SALES (est): 22.8MM **Privately Held**
WEB: www.xorantech.com
SIC: **3845** Ultrasonic scanning devices, medical
PA: Xoran Holdings Llc
5210 S State Rd
Ann Arbor MI 48108
734 418-5108

(G-720)
XPO CNW INC (HQ)
2211 Old Earhart Rd (48105-2963)
PHONE..................734 757-1444
Douglas W Stotlar, *President*
Stephen K Krull, *Exec VP*
Kevin S Coel, *Senior VP*
Leslie P Lundberg, *Senior VP*
Gillian Graves, *Opers Spvr*
EMP: 120 EST: 1958
SALES (corp-wide): 16.2B **Publicly Held**
WEB: www.xpo.com
SIC: **4213** 4731 3715 Contract haulers; less-than-truckload (LTL) transport; trailer or container on flat car (TOFC/COFC); domestic freight forwarding; foreign freight forwarding; customhouse brokers; truck trailers
PA: Xpo Logistics, Inc.
5 American Ln
Greenwich CT 06831
844 742-5976

(G-721)
ZCC USA INC
3622 W Liberty Rd (48103-9049)
PHONE..................734 997-3811
Difei LI, *President*
Chuck Gonsalez, *Sales Engr*
Steve Ramirez, *Sales Staff*
▲ **EMP:** 16 EST: 2006
SALES (est): 5.1MM **Privately Held**
WEB: www.zccusa.com
SIC: **3545** Machine tool accessories
PA: Zhuzhou Cemented Carbide Cutting Tools Co., Ltd.
Huanghe South Rd., Hi-Tech Zone
Zhuzhou 41200

(G-722)
ZERO HOUR PRODUCTION LLC
275 Metty Dr (48103-9444)
PHONE..................616 498-3545
Daniel Schmidt,
EMP: 13 EST: 2017
SALES (est): 411.9K **Privately Held**
WEB: www.zerohourparts.com
SIC: **3999** Manufacturing industries

(G-723)
ZHUZHOU CMNTD CRBID WRKS USA
Also Called: Zccw
4651 Platt Rd (48108-9726)
PHONE..................734 302-0125
Wan Xin Yang, *President*
Drew Haddix, *Opers Staff*
Suki Xu, *Controller*
Dave Beasley, *Sales Staff*
Nataly Perez-Roman, *Marketing Staff*
▲ **EMP:** 2 EST: 2001
SQ FT: 2,000
SALES (est): 4.2MM **Privately Held**
WEB: www.zccamerica.com
SIC: **2819** Carbides
HQ: Zhuzhou Cemented Carbide Works Import & Export Company
Diamond Building, Diamond Road, Hetang District
Zhuzhou 41200

(G-724)
ZIEL OPTICS INC
7167 Jackson Rd (48103-9506)
PHONE..................734 994-9803
Eric Sieczka, *President*
Fred Collin, *Shareholder*
EMP: 7 EST: 2016
SALES (est): 636.1K **Privately Held**
SIC: **3674** Solid state electronic devices

(G-725)
ZINGERMANS BAKEHOUSE INC
3711 Plaza Dr Ste 5 (48108-1680)
PHONE..................734 761-2095
Frank Carollo, *President*
Amy Emberling, *Partner*
Paul Saginaw, *Corp Secy*
ARI Weinzweig, *Vice Pres*
Josh Pollock, *Project Mgr*
EMP: 60 EST: 1992
SQ FT: 6,400
SALES (est): 13.5MM **Privately Held**
WEB: www.zingermansbakehouse.com
SIC: **2051** Bread, all types (white, wheat, rye, etc): fresh or frozen; pastries, e.g. danish: except frozen

(G-726)
ZOMEDICA PHARMACEUTICALS INC (PA)
100 Phoenix Dr Ste 125 (48108-2600)
PHONE..................734 369-2555
Stephanie Morley, *President*
Ann Cotter, *CFO*
Bruk Herbst, *Ch Credit Ofcr*
EMP: 26 EST: 2015
SQ FT: 7,900 **Publicly Held**
WEB: www.zomedica.com
SIC: **2834** Veterinary pharmaceutical preparations

Applegate
Sanilac County

(G-727)
TROYS WELDING COMPANY
2572 Marlette Rd (48401-9652)
PHONE..................810 633-9388
EMP: 4 EST: 2014
SALES (est): 64.9K **Privately Held**
SIC: **7692** Welding repair

Argyle
Sanilac County

(G-728)
AVID INDUSTRIES INC
4887 Ubly Rd (48410-7702)
PHONE..................810 672-9100
William R Kroetsch, *President*
EMP: 4 EST: 1987 **Privately Held**
WEB: www.avidind.com
SIC: **3599** Machine shop, jobbing & repair

Armada
Macomb County

(G-729)
ARMADA GRAIN CO (PA)
73180 Fulton St (48005-4738)
P.O. Box 918 (48005-0918)
PHONE..................586 784-5911
Lance Hollweg, *Owner*
Robert Hollweg, *Vice Pres*
EMP: 21 EST: 1948
SQ FT: 40,000
SALES (est): 11.3MM **Privately Held**
WEB: www.armadagrain.com
SIC: **5153** 2048 Grains; feeds from meat & from meat & vegetable meals

(G-730)
ARMADA PRINTWEAR INC
Also Called: API Promotional Products
74135 Church St (48005-3334)
P.O. Box 518 (48005-0518)
PHONE..................586 784-5553
Richard Mills, *President*
Paulina Mills, *Admin Sec*
EMP: 6 EST: 1969
SQ FT: 9,000
SALES (est): 952.9K **Privately Held**
WEB: www.apicorporate.com
SIC: **2262** 5199 Screen printing: manmade fiber & silk broadwoven fabrics; advertising specialties

(G-731)
ARMADA RUBBER MANUFACTURING CO
24586 Armada Ridge Rd (48005-4827)
P.O. Box 579 (48005-0579)
PHONE..................586 784-9135
Lawrence Weymouth III, *President*
Lawrence Weymouth Jr, *President*
Dawn Weymouth, *Admin Sec*
EMP: 70
SQ FT: 53,000
SALES: 21.6MM **Privately Held**
WEB: www.armadarubber.com
SIC: **3069** 3713 3643 3061 Rubber hardware; truck & bus bodies; current-carrying wiring devices; mechanical rubber goods; gaskets, packing & sealing devices; synthetic rubber

(G-732)
BLAKES ORCHARD INC (PA)
Also Called: Blake's Orchard & Cider Mill
17985 Armada Center Rd (48005-2323)
PHONE..................586 784-5343
Peter Blake, *Owner*
Paul M Blake, *Treasurer*
Jake Sanders, *Sales Staff*
EMP: 3 EST: 1946
SQ FT: 19,400
SALES (est): 12.6MM **Privately Held**
WEB: www.blakesorchard.openfos.com
SIC: **0175** 2099 5148 0171 Apple orchard; cider, nonalcoholic; fruits; strawberry farm; canned fruits & specialties; vegetables & melons

(G-733)
DON YOHE ENTERPRISES INC
74054 Church St (48005-3447)
P.O. Box 250 (48005-0250)
PHONE..................586 784-5556
Dan Yohe, *President*
Jodi Hansen, *Corp Secy*
Brad Yohe, *Vice Pres*
EMP: 14 EST: 1967
SQ FT: 2,000
SALES (est): 1MM **Privately Held**
SIC: **1382** Oil & gas exploration services

(G-734)
EWELLIX USA LLC
69900 Powell Rd (48005-4030)
PHONE..................586 752-0060
Tarek Bugaighis, *President*
EMP: 117
SALES (corp-wide): 210.7MM **Privately Held**
SIC: **3562** Ball & roller bearings
HQ: Ewellix Usa Llc
3800 Sierra Cir Ste 310
Center Valley PA 18034
267 436-6000

(G-735)
EXPERIENCED CONCEPTS INC
15400 Chets Way St (48005-1160)
P.O. Box 556, Romeo (48065-0556)
PHONE..................586 752-4200
Robert Wood, *President*
Destinee Doutry, *Admin Mgr*
EMP: 15 EST: 1996
SQ FT: 18,000
SALES (est): 2.4MM **Privately Held**
WEB: www.expconcepts.com
SIC: **8711** 3544 3599 7539 Consulting engineer; jigs & fixtures; machine shop, jobbing & repair; air intake filters, internal combustion engine, except auto; machine shop, automotive; metalworking machinery

(G-736)
HENSHAW INC
70890 Powell Rd (48005-4037)
PHONE..................586 752-0700
Dave Clark, *CEO*
Craig Rick, *Engineer*
Greg Twaddle, *Engineer*
EMP: 70 EST: 1982
SQ FT: 42,000

GEOGRAPHIC SECTION

Auburn - Bay County (G-762)

SALES (est): 12.9MM **Privately Held**
WEB: www.henshawusa.com
SIC: 3823 3613 5084 3535 Industrial instrmnts msrmnt display/control process variable; switchgear & switchboard apparatus; materials handling machinery; conveyors & conveying equipment; machine bases, metal; industrial engineers

(G-737)
IAEC CORPORATION
21641 34 Mile Rd (48005-3102)
PHONE..............................586 354-5996
Chadwick Stayton, *CEO*
David White, *CTO*
▼ **EMP:** 8 **EST:** 2007
SQ FT: 2,800
SALES (est): 867.5K **Privately Held**
WEB: www.iaec.us
SIC: 3699 Electrical equipment & supplies

(G-738)
ORSCO INC
69900 Powell Rd (48005-4030)
PHONE..............................314 679-4200
Albert Adams, *Human Res Mgr*
Bob Borowski, *Manager*
Steve Clancy, *Manager*
▲ **EMP:** 5 **EST:** 1930
SQ FT: 18,000
SALES (est): 1.2MM
SALES (corp-wide): 8.6B **Privately Held**
WEB: www.lincoln.com
SIC: 3569 5085 Lubricating equipment; industrial supplies
HQ: Lincoln Industrial Corporation
5148 N Hanley Rd
Saint Louis MO 63134
314 679-4200

(G-739)
PATEREK MOLD & ENGINEERING
74081 Church St (48005-4710)
P.O. Box 519 (48005-0519)
PHONE..............................586 784-8030
John W Paterek, *President*
Annette Paterek, *Vice Pres*
EMP: 5 **EST:** 1985
SQ FT: 5,400
SALES (est): 500K **Privately Held**
SIC: 3544 Special dies & tools

Arnold
Marquette County

(G-740)
USHER LOGGING LLC
4423 Cty Rd 557 (49819)
P.O. Box 105 (49819-0105)
PHONE..............................906 238-4261
Terry Usher, *Bd of Directors*
EMP: 5 **EST:** 2011
SALES (est): 156.2K **Privately Held**
SIC: 2411 Logging

Ashley
Gratiot County

(G-741)
BELLINGER PACKING
1557 E Wilson Rd (48806-9745)
PHONE..............................989 838-2274
Mike Bellinger, *Owner*
EMP: 21 **EST:** 1952
SQ FT: 10,680
SALES (est): 532.4K **Privately Held**
WEB: www.bellingarspecialtymeats.com
SIC: 0751 5421 2011 Slaughtering: custom livestock services; meat markets, including freezer provisioners; meat packing plants

(G-742)
COG MARKETERS LTD
Also Called: Agro-Clture Liquid Fertilizers
302 W Sectionline Rd (48806-9354)
PHONE..............................434 455-3209
Bill Severns, *Supervisor*
EMP: 18

SALES (corp-wide): 37.7MM **Privately Held**
WEB: www.agroliquid.com
SIC: 2875 Fertilizers, mixing only
PA: Cog Marketers, Ltd.
3055 W M 21
Saint Johns MI 48879
989 227-3827

Athens
Calhoun County

(G-743)
TEACHOUT AND ASSOCIATES INC
Also Called: Rta Water Treatment
1887 M 66 (49011-9322)
P.O. Box 427 (49011-0427)
PHONE..............................269 729-4440
Rod Teachout, *President*
EMP: 6 **EST:** 1985
SQ FT: 5,600
SALES (est): 925.1K **Privately Held**
WEB: www.rtawatertreatment.com
SIC: 2899 Water treating compounds

Atlanta
Montmorency County

(G-744)
BRUNO WOJCIK
Also Called: Rogue Industrial Service
12270 E Shore (49709-9078)
PHONE..............................989 785-5555
EMP: 6
SQ FT: 2,400
SALES (est): 323.5K **Privately Held**
SIC: 1389 Oil & Gas Production Services

(G-745)
DENNY DAVIS
12090 Dennis St (49709-9018)
PHONE..............................989 785-3433
Denny Davis, *Principal*
EMP: 4 **EST:** 2005
SALES (est): 99.4K **Privately Held**
SIC: 2741 Miscellaneous publishing

(G-746)
MONTMORENCY PRESS INC
Also Called: Montmorency County Tribune
12625 State 33 N (49709)
P.O. Box 186 (49709-0186)
PHONE..............................989 785-4214
William Pinson, *President*
Michelle Pinson, *Admin Sec*
EMP: 8 **EST:** 1886
SQ FT: 5,000 **Privately Held**
WEB: www.montmorencytribune.com
SIC: 2711 Commercial printing & newspaper publishing combined

(G-747)
SMITH WELDING
9750 County Road 489 (49709-9024)
PHONE..............................989 306-0154
Mark Smith, *Principal*
EMP: 5 **EST:** 2008
SALES (est): 36.8K **Privately Held**
SIC: 7692 Welding repair

(G-748)
TRIAD INDUSTRIAL CORP
11656 Reimann Rd (49709-9535)
PHONE..............................989 358-7191
Hugo Benjamin, *Principal*
▲ **EMP:** 12 **EST:** 2002
SALES (est): 503.6K **Privately Held**
SIC: 3535 Conveyors & conveying equipment

Atlantic Mine
Houghton County

(G-749)
EVERBLADES INC
46104 State Highway M26 (49905-9160)
PHONE..............................906 483-0174
Benjamin Halonen, *President*

Josh Jenson, *Opers Staff*
EMP: 4 **EST:** 2016
SALES (est): 400K **Privately Held**
WEB: www.everblades.com
SIC: 3714 Windshield wiper systems, motor vehicle

(G-750)
LINDSAY NETTELL INC
47301 Janovosky Rd (49905-9015)
PHONE..............................906 482-3549
Lindsay Nettell, *President*
EMP: 8 **EST:** 2017
SALES (est): 254.1K **Privately Held**
SIC: 2411 Logging

(G-751)
NDSAY NETTELL LOGGING
47301 Janovosky Rd (49905-9015)
PHONE..............................906 482-3549
Lindsay Nettell, *Principal*
EMP: 6 **EST:** 2004
SALES (est): 469.6K **Privately Held**
SIC: 2411 Logging camps & contractors

Attica
Lapeer County

(G-752)
DJ CUSTOMS LLC
5238 Attica Rd (48412-9638)
PHONE..............................810 358-0236
Darion L Judd, *Principal*
EMP: 4 **EST:** 2016
SALES (est): 63.4K **Privately Held**
WEB: www.djcustomsigns.com
SIC: 3993 Signs & advertising specialties

(G-753)
INFINICOAT LLC
593 S Lake Pleasant Rd (48412-9675)
PHONE..............................810 721-9631
Roman Tucker, *Principal*
EMP: 6 **EST:** 2015
SALES (est): 81.4K **Privately Held**
SIC: 3599 Industrial machinery

Au Gres
Arenac County

(G-754)
AG HARVESTERS LLC
533 N Court St (48703-9204)
P.O. Box 647 (48703-0647)
PHONE..............................989 876-7161
Brandon Schnettler, *Principal*
Daniel Peterson, *Controller*
EMP: 6 **EST:** 2015
SQ FT: 43,000
SALES (est): 113.1K **Privately Held**
WEB: www.agharvesters.com
SIC: 3523 Planting, haying, harvesting & processing machinery

(G-755)
ATD ENGINEERING AND MCH LLC
533 N Court St (48703-9204)
P.O. Box 647 (48703-0647)
PHONE..............................989 876-7161
Daniel Minor, *Mng Member*
EMP: 35 **EST:** 2009
SQ FT: 43,000
SALES (est): 4.5MM **Privately Held**
WEB: www.atdemllc.com
SIC: 3599 Machine shop, jobbing & repair
PA: Cadillac Casting, Inc.
1500 4th Ave
Cadillac MI 49601

(G-756)
BESSINGER PICKLE CO INC
537 N Court St (48703-9204)
P.O. Box 396 (48703-0396)
PHONE..............................989 876-8008
Craig R Carruthers, *President*
Ladeema Carruthers, *Corp Secy*
Caroline Carruthers, *Vice Pres*
EMP: 4 **EST:** 1974
SQ FT: 28,940

SALES (est): 495.3K **Privately Held**
SIC: 2035 Pickled fruits & vegetables

(G-757)
BOPP-BUSCH MANUFACTURING CO (PA)
545 E Huron Rd (48703-9326)
P.O. Box 589 (48703-0589)
PHONE..............................989 876-7121
Robert Busch, *CEO*
William Busch, *President*
Micheal Busch, *Vice Pres*
Terrie Dittenber, *Purch Mgr*
Michael Busch, *VP Sales*
▲ **EMP:** 50 **EST:** 1948
SQ FT: 90,000
SALES (est): 15.6MM **Privately Held**
WEB: www.boppbusch.com
SIC: 3469 Stamping metal for the trade

(G-758)
BOPP-BUSCH MANUFACTURING CO
Also Called: Bopp-Busch Plant 2
205 N Mackinaw St (48703-9790)
P.O. Box 589 (48703-0589)
PHONE..............................989 876-7924
Doug Moulton, *Manager*
Joe Oswald, *Manager*
EMP: 36
SALES (corp-wide): 15.6MM **Privately Held**
WEB: www.boppbusch.com
SIC: 3471 7692 3496 3469 Finishing, metals or formed products; welding repair; miscellaneous fabricated wire products; metal stampings; automotive stampings
PA: Bopp-Busch Manufacturing Co.
545 E Huron Rd
Au Gres MI 48703
989 876-7121

(G-759)
INTERNATIONAL TEMPERATURE CTRL
2415 E Huron Rd (48703-9333)
P.O. Box 805 (48703-0805)
PHONE..............................989 876-8075
Louis Perrot, *President*
Vera Perrot, *Finance Mgr*
EMP: 8 **EST:** 1983
SQ FT: 6,500 **Privately Held**
WEB: www.itc-controls.com
SIC: 3823 Temperature instruments: industrial process type

(G-760)
MODERN CRAFT WINERY LLC
211 E Huron Rd (48703-5000)
P.O. Box 393 (48703-0393)
PHONE..............................989 876-4948
Tom Nixon, *Mng Member*
EMP: 7 **EST:** 2011
SALES (est): 671.5K **Privately Held**
WEB: www.moderncraftwine.com
SIC: 2084 Wines

(G-761)
MR E MACHINE LLC
2445 E Bay Ridge Dr (48703-9484)
PHONE..............................810 407-0319
Jack Esckelson, *Principal*
EMP: 4 **EST:** 2015
SALES (est): 80.8K **Privately Held**
SIC: 3599 Industrial machinery

Auburn
Bay County

(G-762)
A AND D DESIGN ELECTRONICS
301 W Midland Rd (48611-9360)
P.O. Box 311 (48611-0311)
PHONE..............................989 493-1884
Nicolas Jock, *Owner*
EMP: 4 **EST:** 1987
SALES (est): 209.1K **Privately Held**
WEB: www.shaynescounseling.com
SIC: 7389 3672 7539 Design services; printed circuit boards; trailer repair

Auburn - Bay County (G-763)

(G-763)
ANTIMICROBIAL SPECIALIST ASSOC
Also Called: Amsa
4714 Garfield Rd (48611-9434)
PHONE.....................989 662-0377
Attila Relenyi, *President*
Janice Shawl, *VP Opers*
Jerry Davis, *Prdtn Mgr*
Dick Smith, *Maint Spvr*
Anthony Haag, *Research*
▲ **EMP:** 12 **EST:** 1996
SQ FT: 4,000
SALES (est): 2.3MM **Privately Held**
WEB: www.amsainc.com
SIC: 2899 5084 Water treating compounds; pollution control equipment, water (environmental)

(G-764)
APPLIED GRAPHICS & FABRICATING
1994 W Midland Rd (48611-9514)
PHONE.....................989 662-3334
Stanley Baryla Sr, *President*
Frances Renneberg, *Admin Sec*
EMP: 13 **EST:** 1960
SALES (est): 726.9K **Privately Held**
WEB: www.appliedgraphicsmi.com
SIC: 2759 2396 Screen printing; screen printing on fabric articles

(G-765)
DOW SILICONES CORPORATION (DH)
Also Called: Dow Corning
2200 W Salzburg Rd (48611-9517)
P.O. Box 994, Midland (48686-0001)
PHONE.....................989 496-4000
Jim Fitterling, *CEO*
Howard Ungerleider, *President*
Steven Wood, *Business Mgr*
Torsten Kraef, *Senior VP*
John Sampson, *Senior VP*
◆ **EMP:** 900 **EST:** 1943
SQ FT: 50,000
SALES (est): 1.4B
SALES (corp-wide): 38.5B **Publicly Held**
WEB: www.dow.com
SIC: 2821 2869 Silicone resins; silicones
HQ: The Dow Chemical Company
2211 H H Dow Way
Midland MI 48642
989 636-1000

(G-766)
ITTNER BEAN & GRAIN INC (PA)
Also Called: Er Simons
301 Park Ave (48611-9447)
P.O. Box 4 (48611-0004)
PHONE.....................989 662-4461
Thomas Ittner, *President*
Jeanne Zielinski, *Treasurer*
Luella Ittner, *Admin Sec*
▲ **EMP:** 10 **EST:** 1968
SQ FT: 1,800
SALES (est): 7.2MM **Privately Held**
WEB: www.ittnerbg.com
SIC: 5153 5191 2041 Field beans; grains; fertilizers & agricultural chemicals; flour & other grain mill products

(G-767)
J & R TOOL INC
4575 Garfield Rd (48611-9504)
PHONE.....................989 662-0026
Robert Gray, *President*
Joseph Mapes, *Vice Pres*
EMP: 5 **EST:** 1997
SQ FT: 3,500 **Privately Held**
SIC: 3541 Lathes, metal cutting & polishing; milling machines

(G-768)
LASER CONNECTION LLC
947 W Midland Rd (48611-9406)
P.O. Box 46 (48611-0046)
PHONE.....................989 662-4022
Richard Mortellaro, *Sales Staff*
Mike Trapp, *Sales Staff*
Mike Assels, *Manager*
Stu Roy, *Technology*
Dan E Meeker, *Manager*
EMP: 24 **EST:** 1989
SQ FT: 7,000
SALES (est): 1.6MM **Privately Held**
WEB: www.laser-connection.com
SIC: 3861 Reproduction machines & equipment

(G-769)
MACHINERY PRTS SPECIALISTS LLC
4533d Garfield Rd (48611-9504)
P.O. Box 391 (48611-0391)
PHONE.....................989 662-7810
Steven D Clark,
EMP: 6 **EST:** 2010
SALES (est): 204.7K **Privately Held**
WEB: www.mapsllc-usa.com
SIC: 3714 Motor vehicle parts & accessories

(G-770)
MIKA TOOL & DIE INC
5127 Garfield Rd (48611-9555)
P.O. Box 116 (48611-0116)
PHONE.....................989 662-6979
Richard L Mapes, *President*
EMP: 9 **EST:** 1979
SQ FT: 4,859
SALES (est): 742K **Privately Held**
SIC: 3599 Machine shop, jobbing & repair

(G-771)
WINFORD ENGINEERING LLC
4561 Garfield Rd (48611-9504)
PHONE.....................989 671-9721
Ben Bright, *Mng Member*
John Bright, *Mng Member*
Philip Bright, *Mng Member*
EMP: 6 **EST:** 1999
SALES (est): 962.3K **Privately Held**
WEB: www.winford.com
SIC: 3678 3625 3629 7389 Electronic connectors; switches, electronic applications; power conversion units, a.c. to d.c.: static-electric;

Auburn Hills
Oakland County

(G-772)
ABA OF AMERICA INC (DH)
2430 E Walton Blvd (48326-1956)
PHONE.....................815 332-5170
Nils Bergstrom, *Ch of Bd*
Arne R Stegvik, *President*
Annette Gustafson-Guenther, *Admin Sec*
◆ **EMP:** 19 **EST:** 1978
SQ FT: 25,000
SALES (est): 7.3MM
SALES (corp-wide): 1.1B **Privately Held**
WEB: www.normaamericasds.com
SIC: 3429 Clamps & couplings, hose
HQ: Norma Sweden Ab
Visirgatan 1
Anderstorp 334 3
865 414-00

(G-773)
ACME MANUFACTURING COMPANY (PA)
4240 N Atlantic Blvd (48326-1578)
PHONE.....................248 393-7300
Glen Carlson III, *President*
Clark Merriman, *Chairman*
Diane Betti, *COO*
Floyd Fishleigh, *Vice Pres*
Jack Karagozian, *Vice Pres*
◆ **EMP:** 80 **EST:** 1910
SQ FT: 47,000
SALES (est): 14.2MM **Privately Held**
WEB: www.acmemfg.com
SIC: 3541 Grinding, polishing, buffing, lapping & honing machines; buffing & polishing machines; brushing machines (metalworking machinery); deburring machines

(G-774)
AEGIS WELDING SUPPLY
1080 Centre Rd (48326-2681)
PHONE.....................248 475-9860
Joan Cinquemani, *Administration*
EMP: 9 **EST:** 2016
SALES (est): 1.3MM **Privately Held**
WEB: www.aegisweldingsupply.com
SIC: 7692 Welding repair

(G-775)
AIR INTERNATIONAL (US) INC (DH)
Also Called: Air Intrntonal Thermal Systems
750 Standard Pkwy (48326-1448)
PHONE.....................248 391-7970
Jianguo Zhou, *CEO*
Yongming Zhang, *Chairman*
Michael Repetto, *Corp Secy*
Wayne Wright, *Engineer*
Duanhui Wan, *CFO*
▲ **EMP:** 59 **EST:** 1999
SQ FT: 57,000
SALES (est): 45.4MM **Privately Held**
WEB: www.ai-thermal.com
SIC: 3585 Air conditioning, motor vehicle

(G-776)
AIRBOSS FLEXIBLE PRODUCTS CO
2600 Auburn Ct (48326-3201)
PHONE.....................248 852-5500
Glenn Reid, *President*
Douglas L Reid, *Vice Pres*
Ronald J Dzierzawski, *Treasurer*
▲ **EMP:** 250 **EST:** 1946
SQ FT: 135,000
SALES (est): 49MM
SALES (corp-wide): 501.5MM **Privately Held**
WEB: www.airboss.com
SIC: 3069 3714 Rubber automotive products; motor vehicle parts & accessories
PA: Airboss Of America Corp
16441 Yonge St
Newmarket ON L3X 2
905 751-1188

(G-777)
ALLEGRO MICROSYSTEMS LLC
691 N Squirrel Rd Ste 107 (48326-2868)
PHONE.....................248 242-5044
Jason Boudreau, *Marketing Mgr*
Dan Jacques, *Marketing Staff*
Steve Anderson, *Branch Mgr*
EMP: 4 **Publicly Held**
WEB: www.allegromicro.com
SIC: 3674 Semiconductors & related devices
HQ: Allegro Microsystems, Llc
955 Perimeter Rd
Manchester NH 03103

(G-778)
ALLIED METALS CORP (PA)
2668 Lapeer Rd (48326-1925)
PHONE.....................248 680-2400
Gary L Wasserman, *CEO*
Mark Kroll, *President*
Mike Pivitt, *Opers Mgr*
Michael Pivitt, *Opers Staff*
Frank Kinney, *CFO*
◆ **EMP:** 24 **EST:** 1975
SALES (est): 9.9MM **Privately Held**
WEB: www.alliedmet.com
SIC: 5051 3325 3341 Iron or steel flat products; steel foundries; secondary non-ferrous metals

(G-779)
AM GENERAL LLC
1399 Pacific Dr (48326-1569)
PHONE.....................734 523-8098
Larry Payne, *Superintendent*
Stephanie Tucker, *Principal*
John Ross, *Counsel*
Daniel Dell'orto, *Exec VP*
Chris Vanslager, *Exec VP*
EMP: 275
SALES (corp-wide): 3.4B **Privately Held**
WEB: www.amgeneral.com
SIC: 8711 3713 Engineering services; truck & bus bodies
HQ: Am General Llc
105 N Niles Ave
South Bend IN 46617
574 237-6222

(G-780)
AME FOR AUTO DEALERS INC
1000 N Opdyke Rd Ste J (48326-2672)
PHONE.....................248 720-0245
David Easterbrook, *President*
Jerry Hall, *Vice Pres*
Bryan Talaga, *Vice Pres*
Bryan Douroujalian, *Project Mgr*
Ryan Kilgore, *Administration*
EMP: 5 **EST:** 2014
SALES (est): 1MM **Privately Held**
WEB: www.amecompanies.com
SIC: 2541 3531 3559 Cabinets, lockers & shelving; automobile wrecker hoists; wheel balancing equipment, automobile

(G-781)
AMERICAN AXLE & MFG INC
Also Called: AAM Qality Engrg Technical Ctr
1987 Taylor Rd (48326-1770)
PHONE.....................248 475-3475
Steve Fields, *Principal*
EMP: 7
SALES (corp-wide): 4.7B **Publicly Held**
WEB: www.aam.com
SIC: 3714 Motor vehicle parts & accessories
HQ: American Axle & Manufacturing, Inc.
1 Dauch Dr
Detroit MI 48211

(G-782)
AMERICAN AXLE & MFG INC
Also Called: Eng Advance Technology Dev Ctr
2007 Taylor Rd (48326-1772)
PHONE.....................248 276-2328
EMP: 18
SALES (corp-wide): 4.7B **Publicly Held**
WEB: www.aam.com
SIC: 3714 Motor vehicle parts & accessories
HQ: American Axle & Manufacturing, Inc.
1 Dauch Dr
Detroit MI 48211

(G-783)
AMK ENTERPRISE LLC
201 N Squirrel Rd (48326-4015)
PHONE.....................248 564-2549
EMP: 4 **EST:** 2019
SALES (est): 122.7K **Privately Held**
SIC: 2399 Fabricated textile products

(G-784)
ANALYTICAL PROCESS SYSTEMS INC
Also Called: A P S
1771 Harmon Rd Ste 100 (48326-1587)
PHONE.....................248 393-0700
Brian Kundinger, *President*
Terry Fazio, *Foreman/Supr*
John Leece, *CFO*
EMP: 25 **EST:** 1991
SQ FT: 17,000
SALES (est): 4.8MM **Privately Held**
WEB: www.kundinger.com
SIC: 5084 3829 Measuring & testing equipment, electrical; gas detectors; testing equipment: abrasion, shearing strength, etc.

(G-785)
ANDROID INDSTRS-SHREVEPORT LLC
2155 Executive Hills Dr (48326-2943)
PHONE.....................248 454-0500
David Donnay,
EMP: 49 **EST:** 2000
SQ FT: 160,000
SALES (est): 623.8K **Privately Held**
SIC: 3465 Body parts, automobile: stamped metal

(G-786)
ANDROID INDUSTRIES-WIXOM LLC (HQ)
4444 W Maple Dr (48326)
PHONE.....................248 732-0000
John Gregory, *CEO*
John Doroshewitz, *Managing Dir*
Kathryn Nichols, *Vice Pres*
Mark Graham, *Plant Mgr*
Gerard Stanaway, *Plant Mgr*
▲ **EMP:** 40 **EST:** 1999

SALES (est): 36.4MM
SALES (corp-wide): 474.4MM **Privately Held**
WEB: www.android-ind.com
SIC: 3714 Motor vehicle parts & accessories
PA: Android Industries, L.L.C.
2155 Executive Hills Dr
Auburn Hills MI 48326
248 454-0500

(G-787)
ANJUN AMERICA INC
2735 Paldan Dr (48326-1827)
PHONE..................................248 680-8825
Josh Park, *Manager*
▲ EMP: 9 EST: 2009
SALES (est): 349.8K **Privately Held**
WEB: www.anjunus.com
SIC: 3465 3714 Body parts, automobile: stamped metal; motor vehicle parts & accessories

(G-788)
ANROID INDUSTRIES INC
2155 Executive Hills Dr (48326-2943)
PHONE..................................248 732-0000
Kathryn Nicholas, *Vice Pres*
Wolfgang Imgartchen, *Vice Pres*
Keizo Kashimoto, *Vice Pres*
EMP: 85 EST: 2010
SALES (est): 2.6MM **Privately Held**
SIC: 3548 Welding apparatus

(G-789)
ANTOLIN INTERIORS USA INC (DH)
Also Called: Atreum
1700 Atlantic Blvd (48326-1504)
PHONE..................................248 373-1749
Pablo M Baroja, *President*
▲ EMP: 300 EST: 2001
SALES (est): 880.4MM
SALES (corp-wide): 2.6MM **Privately Held**
WEB: www.grupoantolin.com
SIC: 3714 Motor vehicle parts & accessories
HQ: Grupo Antolin North America, Inc.
1700 Atlantic Blvd
Auburn Hills MI 48326
248 373-1749

(G-790)
ANTOLIN SPRTNBURG ASSEMBLY LLC (DH)
1700 Atlantic Blvd (48326-1504)
PHONE..................................248 373-1749
Pablo Baroja,
Stacy Herkowitz,
EMP: 46 EST: 2017
SALES (est): 32.9MM
SALES (corp-wide): 2.6MM **Privately Held**
WEB: www.grupoantolin.com
SIC: 3714 Motor vehicle engines & parts
HQ: Grupo Antolin North America, Inc.
1700 Atlantic Blvd
Auburn Hills MI 48326
248 373-1749

(G-791)
APOLLO AMERICA INC
Also Called: Air Products and Controls
25 Corporate Dr (48326-2919)
PHONE..................................248 332-3900
Tyler Newsom, *President*
Jerry Black, *Vice Pres*
Andrew Frost, *Vice Pres*
Daniel Gundlach, *Vice Pres*
Louise Laing, *Vice Pres*
▲ EMP: 67 EST: 1982
SQ FT: 20,000
SALES (est): 17.9MM
SALES (corp-wide): 1.8B **Privately Held**
WEB: www.apollo-fire.co.uk
SIC: 3669 3625 3829 Smoke detectors; relays & industrial controls; measuring & controlling devices
HQ: Halma Holdings Inc.
11500 Northlake Dr # 306
Cincinnati OH 45249
513 772-5501

(G-792)
APOLLO MACHINING INC
70 S Squirrel Rd Ste W (48326-3281)
PHONE..................................248 961-3943
Paul Mispelon, *President*
EMP: 4 EST: 1988
SQ FT: 3,000 **Privately Held**
WEB: www.apollo-machining-inc.business.site
SIC: 3599 Machine shop, jobbing & repair

(G-793)
APPLIED & INTEGRATED MFG INC
Also Called: Aim
691 N Squirrel Rd 119 (48326-2846)
PHONE..................................248 370-8950
Jayanth Yale, *CEO*
EMP: 6 EST: 1995
SALES (est): 469.6K **Privately Held**
SIC: 3569 Robots, assembly line: industrial & commercial

(G-794)
APTIV CORPORATION
Also Called: Delphi
2611 Superior Ct (48326-4313)
PHONE..................................248 724-5900
Rodney O'Neal, *President*
Chris Zimmerman, *Manager*
EMP: 7
SALES (corp-wide): 14.3B **Privately Held**
WEB: www.aptiv.com
SIC: 3714 Motor vehicle parts & accessories
HQ: Aptiv Corporation
5820 Innovation Dr
Troy MI 48098

(G-795)
APTIV SERVICES US LLC
Also Called: Delphi Customer Tech Ctr Mich
3000 University Dr (48326-2496)
PHONE..................................810 459-8809
Chad Amoss, *Engineer*
Rodney O'Neal, *Branch Mgr*
Lisa McPhearson, *Analyst*
EMP: 7
SALES (corp-wide): 14.3B **Privately Held**
WEB: www.borgwarner.com
SIC: 3714 Motor vehicle parts & accessories
HQ: Aptiv Services Us, Llc
5725 Innovation Dr
Troy MI 48098

(G-796)
APTIV SERVICES US LLC
2611 Superior Ct (48326-4313)
PHONE..................................248 724-5900
EMP: 7
SALES (corp-wide): 14.3B **Privately Held**
SIC: 3714 Motor vehicle parts & accessories
HQ: Aptiv Services Us, Llc
5725 Innovation Dr
Troy MI 48098

(G-797)
ARROW AUTOMATION AND ENGRG INC ✪
4200 N Atlantic Blvd (48326-1578)
PHONE..................................248 660-1520
Robert Eickholt, *CEO*
Richard Womack, *Principal*
EMP: 12 EST: 2021
SALES (est): 1MM **Privately Held**
SIC: 3569 8742 Liquid automation machinery & equipment; automation & robotics consultant

(G-798)
ART LASER INC
Also Called: Laser Dynamics
4141 N Atlantic Blvd (48326-1570)
PHONE..................................248 391-6600
Donald H Bailey, *President*
Ralph Weil, *General Mgr*
Jeanette Cooley, *Treasurer*
Tim Fletcher, *Accounts Mgr*
Paul Williams, *Info Tech Mgr*
EMP: 37 EST: 1984
SQ FT: 70,000

SALES (est): 3.1MM **Privately Held**
WEB: www.laserdco.com
SIC: 3545 3599 Machine tool accessories; machine & other job shop work

(G-799)
ATLAS COPCO IAS LLC
3301 Cross Creek Pkwy (48326-2839)
PHONE..................................248 377-9722
Anders Hoperg, *Mng Member*
▲ EMP: 86 EST: 1986
SALES (est): 14.6MM
SALES (corp-wide): 11.5B **Privately Held**
WEB: www.atlascopco.com
SIC: 3563 Air & gas compressors
HQ: Atlas Copco North America Llc
6 Century Dr Ste 310
Parsippany NJ 07054

(G-800)
AUBURN HILLS MANUFACTURING INC
1987 Taylor Rd (48326-1770)
PHONE..................................313 758-2000
Norman Willemse, *President*
EMP: 175 EST: 2008
SQ FT: 76,000
SALES (est): 91MM
SALES (corp-wide): 4.7B **Publicly Held**
WEB: www.acmemfg.com
SIC: 3568 Pulleys, power transmission
HQ: American Axle & Manufacturing, Inc.
1 Dauch Dr
Detroit MI 48211

(G-801)
AUTOLIV ASP INC
2601 Cambridge Ct (48326-2569)
PHONE..................................248 475-9000
EMP: 239
SALES (corp-wide): 7.4B **Publicly Held**
SIC: 3714 3563 Motor vehicle parts & accessories; tire inflators, hand or compressor operated
HQ: Autoliv Asp, Inc.
3350 Airport Rd
Ogden UT 84405

(G-802)
AUTOLIV ASP INC
Also Called: Autoliv N Amer Technical Cntr
1320 Pacific Dr (48326-1569)
PHONE..................................248 475-9000
Dave Braegger, *Branch Mgr*
EMP: 239
SALES (corp-wide): 7.4B **Publicly Held**
SIC: 3714 Motor vehicle parts & accessories
HQ: Autoliv Asp, Inc.
3350 Airport Rd
Ogden UT 84405

(G-803)
AUTOLIV HOLDING INC (HQ)
Also Called: Autoliv Americas
1320 Pacific Dr (48326-1569)
PHONE..................................248 475-9000
Jan Carlson, *CEO*
Stuart Eustace, *Managing Dir*
Brad Kruse, *Business Mgr*
Raj Valera, *Business Mgr*
Peggy Pang, *Vice Pres*
EMP: 439 EST: 1997
SALES (est): 107.9MM
SALES (corp-wide): 7.4B **Publicly Held**
WEB: www.autoliv.com
SIC: 3714 Motor vehicle parts & accessories
PA: Autoliv, Inc.
3350 Airport Rd
Ogden UT 84405
801 629-9800

(G-804)
AUTOMATED SYSTEMS INC
2400 Commercial Dr (48326-2410)
PHONE..................................248 373-5600
Bruce Claycomb, *President*
Robert Yarmak, *Vice Pres*
◆ EMP: 39 EST: 1974
SQ FT: 32,000
SALES (est): 3.6MM **Privately Held**
WEB: www.automatedsystemsinc.org
SIC: 3535 3534 Conveyors & conveying equipment; elevators & moving stairways

(G-805)
AUTOMATIONSUPPLY365 LLC
1532 N Opdyke Rd Ste 800 (48326-2686)
PHONE..................................248 912-7354
Vince Barbisan, *President*
EMP: 6 EST: 2019
SALES (est): 555K **Privately Held**
WEB: www.automationsupply365.com
SIC: 3561 3586 5084 Pumps & pumping equipment; measuring & dispensing pumps; pumps & pumping equipment

(G-806)
AUTOMBILI LAMBORGHINI AMER LLC
Also Called: Volkswagen Group
3800 Hamlin Rd (48326-2829)
PHONE..................................866 681-6276
EMP: 12
SALES (corp-wide): 263.5B **Privately Held**
WEB: www.lamborghini.com
SIC: 3465 Body parts, automobile: stamped metal
HQ: Automobili Lamborghini America Llc
2200 Woodland Pointe Ave
Herndon VA 20171
866 681-6276

(G-807)
AUTOMOTIVE EXTERIORS LLC (DH)
2800 High Meadow Cir (48326-2772)
PHONE..................................248 458-0702
Marc Cornet, *President*
EMP: 1 EST: 2015
SALES (est): 62.7MM
SALES (corp-wide): 1.8MM **Privately Held**
SIC: 3714 Motor vehicle parts & accessories

(G-808)
AUTOTECH ENGRG R&D USA INC
Also Called: Industrial Processing
1600 Harmon Rd (48326-1546)
PHONE..................................248 743-3400
EMP: 1 EST: 2017
SALES (est): 5.7MM
SALES (corp-wide): 400.4MM **Privately Held**
WEB: www.gestamp.com
SIC: 3714 Motor vehicle parts & accessories
HQ: Gestamp North America, Inc.
2701 Troy Center Dr # 150
Troy MI 48084

(G-809)
BAE INDUSTRIES INC
1426 Pacific Dr (48326-1571)
PHONE..................................248 475-9600
Jesse Lopez, *President*
Mark Doetsch, *Vice Pres*
Bill Hoepner, *Maint Spvr*
David Conte, *Buyer*
Mark Gleason, *Engineer*
EMP: 225 **Privately Held**
WEB: www.baeind.com
SIC: 3465 3469 Body parts, automobile: stamped metal; metal stampings
HQ: Bae Industries, Inc.
26020 Sherwood Ave
Warren MI 48091
586 754-3000

(G-810)
BENTELER AUTOMOTIVE CORP
Also Called: Benteler Steel & Tube
2650 N Opdyke Rd Ste B (48326-1954)
PHONE..................................616 247-3936
Lawrence A Abbott, *President*
Mike Cornell, *Branch Mgr*
Chad Priest, *Manager*
EMP: 400
SQ FT: 135,000
SALES (corp-wide): 7.5B **Privately Held**
WEB: www.benteler.com
SIC: 3465 3544 3469 3444 Automotive stampings; special dies, tools, jigs & fixtures; metal stampings; sheet metalwork; steel pipe & tubes; blast furnaces & steel mills

Auburn Hills - Oakland County (G-811)   GEOGRAPHIC SECTION

HQ: Benteler Automotive Corporation
2650 N Opdyke Rd Ste B
Auburn Hills MI 48326
248 364-7190

(G-811)
BENTELER AUTOMOTIVE CORP (DH)
2650 N Opdyke Rd Ste B (48326-1954)
PHONE................................248 364-7190
Joachim Perske, *President*
Bob Heath, *Managing Dir*
Udo Klasfauseweh, *Managing Dir*
Senthilkumar Sivasamy, *Managing Dir*
Tobias Stork, *Managing Dir*
◆ EMP: 200 EST: 1980
SALES (est): 783.7MM
SALES (corp-wide): 7.5B **Privately Held**
WEB: www.benteler.com
SIC: 3714 3465 3999 Manifolds, motor vehicle; automotive stampings; atomizers, toiletry
HQ: Benteler Business Services Gmbh
Residenzstr. 1
Paderborn NW 33310
525 481-0

(G-812)
BGM ELECTRONIC SERVICES LLC
815 N Opdyke Rd Ste 200 (48326-2649)
PHONE................................586 997-7090
Terry Bishop, *President*
Joe Adams, *Engineer*
EMP: 7 EST: 2018
SALES (est): 1.5MM **Privately Held**
WEB: www.bgm-es.com
SIC: 3714 Motor vehicle electrical equipment

(G-813)
BONSAL AMERICAN INC
Also Called: Surface Coatings Company
2280 Auburn Rd (48326-3102)
PHONE................................248 338-0335
Lee Lowis, *Branch Mgr*
EMP: 10
SALES (corp-wide): 27.5B **Privately Held**
SIC: 3272 Concrete products
HQ: Bonsal American, Inc.
625 Griffith Rd Ste 100
Charlotte NC 28217
704 525-1621

(G-814)
BORGWARNER ARDEN LLC
3850 Hamlin Rd (48326-2872)
PHONE................................248 754-9200
EMP: 40 EST: 2018
SALES (est): 15.6MM
SALES (corp-wide): 10.1B **Publicly Held**
WEB: www.borgwarner.com
SIC: 3714 Motor vehicle parts & accessories
PA: Borgwarner Inc.
3850 Hamlin Rd
Auburn Hills MI 48326
248 754-9200

(G-815)
BORGWARNER GLOBAL HOLDING LLC (DH)
3850 Hamlin Rd (48326-2872)
PHONE................................248 754-9200
Frederic B Lissalde, *President*
EMP: 2252 EST: 2019
SALES (est): 15.6MM
SALES (corp-wide): 10.1B **Publicly Held**
WEB: www.borgwarner.com
SIC: 3714 Motor vehicle parts & accessories
HQ: Borgwarner Us Holding Llc
3850 Hamlin Rd
Auburn Hills MI 48326
248 754-9200

(G-816)
BORGWARNER INC
3800 Automation Ave # 100 (48326-1781)
PHONE................................248 371-0040
Tonit Calaway, *Exec VP*
Angeles Fabian, *Vice Pres*
David Kaitschuck, *Vice Pres*
Demetrios Samohin, *Vice Pres*
Jon Alumbaugh, *Project Mgr*

EMP: 5
SALES (corp-wide): 10.1B **Publicly Held**
WEB: www.borgwarner.com
SIC: 3714 Motor vehicle parts & accessories
PA: Borgwarner Inc.
3850 Hamlin Rd
Auburn Hills MI 48326
248 754-9200

(G-817)
BORGWARNER INC (PA)
3850 Hamlin Rd (48326-2872)
PHONE................................248 754-9200
Alexis P Michas, *Ch of Bd*
Frederic B Lissalde, *President*
Peggy Muensterman, *Counsel*
Stefan Demmerle, *Vice Pres*
Rob Deni, *Vice Pres*
EMP: 11692 EST: 1987
SALES (corp-wide): 10.1B **Publicly Held**
WEB: www.borgwarner.com
SIC: 3714 Motor vehicle parts & accessories; transmissions, motor vehicle

(G-818)
BORGWARNER INC
Borgwarner Drivetrain Systems
3800 Automation Ave (48326-1781)
PHONE................................248 754-9600
Steve Roskowski, *Principal*
Peggy Muensterman, *Counsel*
Felecia Pryor, *Exec VP*
Yvonne Everhart, *Vice Pres*
Anthony Hensel, *Vice Pres*
EMP: 30
SALES (corp-wide): 10.1B **Publicly Held**
WEB: www.borgwarner.com
SIC: 3714 Motor vehicle parts & accessories
PA: Borgwarner Inc.
3850 Hamlin Rd
Auburn Hills MI 48326
248 754-9200

(G-819)
BORGWARNER INC
Borgwarner Drivetrain Systems
3850 Hamlin Rd (48326-2872)
PHONE................................248 754-9200
EMP: 7
SALES (corp-wide): 10.1B **Publicly Held**
WEB: www.borgwarner.com
SIC: 3714 Motor vehicle parts & accessories
PA: Borgwarner Inc.
3850 Hamlin Rd
Auburn Hills MI 48326
248 754-9200

(G-820)
BORGWARNER INTL SVCS LLC
Also Called: Delphi Pwertrain Intl Svcs LLC
3000 University Dr (48326-2496)
PHONE................................248 813-2000
Rodney O'Neal, *President*
EMP: 17 EST: 2017
SALES (est): 6.3MM
SALES (corp-wide): 10.1B **Publicly Held**
WEB: www.borgwarner.com
SIC: 3714 Motor vehicle parts & accessories
HQ: Borgwarner Technologies Limited
13 Castle Street St Helier
Jersey JE1 1
163 423-4422

(G-821)
BORGWARNER INV HOLDG INC (HQ)
3850 Hamlin Rd (48326-2872)
PHONE................................248 754-9200
James R Verrier, *CEO*
Jan Carlson, *President*
EMP: 20 EST: 2001
SALES (est): 120.1MM
SALES (corp-wide): 10.1B **Publicly Held**
WEB: www.borgwarner.com
SIC: 3714 Motor vehicle parts & accessories
PA: Borgwarner Inc.
3850 Hamlin Rd
Auburn Hills MI 48326
248 754-9200

(G-822)
BORGWARNER JERSEY HOLDINGS LLC (DH)
3850 Hamlin Rd (48326-2872)
PHONE................................248 754-9200
Frederic Lissalde, *President*
EMP: 0 EST: 2020
SALES (est): 67.7MM
SALES (corp-wide): 10.1B **Publicly Held**
WEB: www.borgwarner.com
SIC: 3714 Motor vehicle parts & accessories
HQ: Borgwarner Investment Holding Inc.
3850 Hamlin Rd
Auburn Hills MI 48326
248 754-9200

(G-823)
BORGWARNER PDS (USA) INC (HQ)
3850 Hamlin Rd (48326-2872)
PHONE................................248 754-9600
James R Verrier, *President*
Steve G Carlson, *Vice Pres*
Ronald T Hundzinski, *CFO*
Thomas J McGill, *Treasurer*
Dave Williamson, *Supervisor*
▲ EMP: 400 EST: 1994
SQ FT: 80,000
SALES (est): 324.3MM
SALES (corp-wide): 10.1B **Publicly Held**
WEB: www.borgwarner.com
SIC: 3714 Motor vehicle parts & accessories
PA: Borgwarner Inc.
3850 Hamlin Rd
Auburn Hills MI 48326
248 754-9200

(G-824)
BORGWARNER TECH SVCS LLC
3000 University Dr (48326-2496)
PHONE................................248 754-9200
Kevin Clark, *Mng Member*
EMP: 23 EST: 2017
SALES (est): 60.8MM
SALES (corp-wide): 10.1B **Publicly Held**
WEB: www.borgwarner.com
SIC: 3714 Motor vehicle parts & accessories
HQ: Borgwarner Luxembourg Operations Sarl
Avenue De Luxembourg 1
Bascharage
501 851-10

(G-825)
BORGWARNER TRANSM PDTS LLC
3850 Hamlin Rd (48326-2872)
PHONE................................248 754-9200
Frederic B Lissalde, *President*
EMP: 57 EST: 2019
SALES (est): 14MM
SALES (corp-wide): 10.1B **Publicly Held**
WEB: www.borgwarner.com
SIC: 3714 Motor vehicle parts & accessories
PA: Borgwarner Inc.
3850 Hamlin Rd
Auburn Hills MI 48326
248 754-9200

(G-826)
BORGWARNER TRANSM SYSTEMS LLC (HQ)
3850 Hamlin Rd (48326-2872)
PHONE................................248 754-9200
John G Sanderson, *President*
Mark Cybulski, *Vice Pres*
Michelle Collins, *Marketing Staff*
Bob Welding, *Mng Member*
▲ EMP: 470 EST: 1995
SALES (est): 474.5MM
SALES (corp-wide): 10.1B **Publicly Held**
WEB: www.ts.aftermarket.borgwarner.com
SIC: 3714 Transmissions, motor vehicle
PA: Borgwarner Inc.
3850 Hamlin Rd
Auburn Hills MI 48326
248 754-9200

(G-827)
BORGWARNER US HOLDING LLC (DH)
3850 Hamlin Rd (48326-2872)
PHONE................................248 754-9200
Craig Aaron, *Mng Member*
EMP: 1 EST: 2019
SALES (est): 25.2MM
SALES (corp-wide): 10.1B **Publicly Held**
WEB: www.borgwarner.com
SIC: 3714 Motor vehicle parts & accessories
HQ: Borgwarner Investment Holding Inc.
3850 Hamlin Rd
Auburn Hills MI 48326
248 754-9200

(G-828)
BORGWARNER USA CORPORATION
Also Called: Delphi Powertrain Corporation
3000 University Dr (48326-2496)
PHONE................................248 813-2000
EMP: 31 EST: 2017
SALES (est): 9MM
SALES (corp-wide): 10.1B **Publicly Held**
WEB: www.borgwarner.com
SIC: 3714 Motor vehicle parts & accessories
HQ: Borgwarner Technologies Limited
13 Castle Street St Helier
Jersey JE1 1
163 423-4422

(G-829)
BORGWRNER EMSSIONS SYSTEMS LLC (HQ)
3850 Hamlin Rd (48326-2872)
PHONE................................248 754-9200
Joseph F Fadool, *President*
▲ EMP: 106 EST: 1987
SALES (est): 119.8MM
SALES (corp-wide): 10.1B **Publicly Held**
WEB: www.borgwarner.com
SIC: 3714 Motor vehicle parts & accessories
PA: Borgwarner Inc.
3850 Hamlin Rd
Auburn Hills MI 48326
248 754-9200

(G-830)
BORGWRNER EMSSONS SYSTEMS MICH (HQ)
Also Called: Borgwrner Trbo Emssion Systems
3800 Automation Ave # 200 (48326-1781)
PHONE................................248 754-9600
Roger J Wood, *President*
▲ EMP: 106 EST: 1996
SQ FT: 176,000
SALES (est): 308.2MM
SALES (corp-wide): 10.1B **Publicly Held**
WEB: www.borgwarner.com
SIC: 3714 Transmissions, motor vehicle
PA: Borgwarner Inc.
3850 Hamlin Rd
Auburn Hills MI 48326
248 754-9200

(G-831)
BORGWRNER PRPLSION SYSTEMS LLC (DH)
3000 University Dr (48326-2496)
PHONE................................248 707-5224
Kevin Clark, *President*
EMP: 1 EST: 2017
SALES (est): 220.8MM
SALES (corp-wide): 10.1B **Publicly Held**
WEB: www.borgwarner.com
SIC: 3714 Motor vehicle parts & accessories
HQ: Borgwarner Technologies Limited
13 Castle Street St Helier
Jersey JE1 1
163 423-4422

(G-832)
BORGWRNER PRPLSION SYSTEMS LLC
Also Called: Ctcm Auburn Hills
3000 University Dr (48326-2496)
PHONE................................248 813-2000
Kevin P Clark, *President*

▲ = Import ▼ = Export
◆ = Import/Export

GEOGRAPHIC SECTION

Auburn Hills - Oakland County (G-855)

EMP: 209
SALES (corp-wide): 10.1B **Publicly Held**
WEB: www.borgwarner.com
SIC: **3714** Motor vehicle parts & accessories
HQ: Borgwarner Propulsion Systems Llc
3000 University Dr
Auburn Hills MI 48326
248 707-5224

(G-833)
BRC RUBBER & PLASTICS INC
Also Called: BRC Automotive Engrg & Sls Off
1091 Centre Rd Ste 210 (48326-2671)
PHONE.................................248 745-9200
Charles V Chaffee, *CEO*
Paul Parsons, *Draft/Design*
EMP: 6
SALES (corp-wide): 95.9MM **Privately Held**
WEB: www.brcrp.com
SIC: **3061** Mechanical rubber goods
PA: Brc Rubber & Plastics, Inc.
589 S Main St
Churubusco IN 46723
260 693-2171

(G-834)
BROSE HARMON ROAD
1650 Harmon Rd (48326-1546)
PHONE.................................248 339-4702
EMP: 12 EST: 2018
SALES (est): 257K **Privately Held**
WEB: www.brose.com
SIC: **3714** Motor vehicle parts & accessories

(G-835)
BROSE NEW BOSTON INC
1107 Centre Rd (48326-2603)
PHONE.................................248 340-1100
Jan Kowal, *Branch Mgr*
EMP: 7
SALES (corp-wide): 1.4B **Privately Held**
WEB: www.brose.com
SIC: **3714** Motor vehicle parts & accessories
HQ: Brose New Boston, Inc.
23400 Bell Rd
New Boston MI 48164

(G-836)
BROSE NEW BOSTON INC
3933 Automation Ave (48326-1788)
PHONE.................................248 339-4000
Werner Appelmann, *President*
Surinder Chauhan, *General Mgr*
Thomas Spangler, *Exec VP*
Christoph Diehl, *Senior VP*
Tom Vanderlaan, *Senior VP*
EMP: 7
SALES (corp-wide): 1.4B **Privately Held**
WEB: www.brose.com
SIC: **3714** Motor vehicle parts & accessories
HQ: Brose New Boston, Inc.
23400 Bell Rd
New Boston MI 48164

(G-837)
BROSE NORTH AMERICA INC (HQ)
3933 Automation Ave (48326-1788)
PHONE.................................248 339-4000
Jrgen Otto, *CEO*
Wilm Uhlenbecker, *President*
Erik Penhollow, *Business Mgr*
Scott Conrad, *Vice Pres*
James Hopson, *Purch Agent*
▲ EMP: 250 EST: 1977
SALES (est): 1.8B
SALES (corp-wide): 1.4B **Privately Held**
WEB: www.brose.com
SIC: **3714** Motor vehicle parts & accessories
PA: Brose Fahrzeugteile Se & Co.Kg,
Coburg
Max-Brose-Str. 1
Coburg BY 96450
956 121-0

(G-838)
BWA RECEIVABLES CORPORATION
3850 Hamlin Rd (48326-2872)
PHONE.................................248 754-9200
James Verrier, *Principal*
EMP: 2 EST: 2010
SALES: 1MM
SALES (corp-wide): 10.1B **Publicly Held**
WEB: www.borgwarner.com
SIC: **3714** Motor vehicle parts & accessories
PA: Borgwarner Inc.
3850 Hamlin Rd
Auburn Hills MI 48326
248 754-9200

(G-839)
CAPSONIC AUTOMOTIVE INC
3121 University Dr # 120 (48326-2385)
PHONE.................................248 754-1100
Seth Gutkowski, *President*
Thomas Bradley, *General Mgr*
Dennis Breen, *Vice Pres*
Sabino Alvarez, *QC Mgr*
Isidro Botello, *QC Mgr*
EMP: 4 **Privately Held**
WEB: www.capsonic.com
SIC: **3089** 8748 8711 Automotive parts, plastic; testing services; engineering services
PA: Capsonic Automotive, Inc.
495 Renner Dr
Elgin IL 60123

(G-840)
CARDELL CORPORATION
Also Called: Cardell Automotive
2025 Taylor Rd (48326-1772)
PHONE.................................248 371-9700
Pete Krehbiel, *President*
David Prym, *President*
Louis Hecht, *Admin Sec*
EMP: 56 EST: 1979
SQ FT: 86,000
SALES (est): 1.8MM
SALES (corp-wide): 36.9B **Publicly Held**
WEB: www.molex.com
SIC: **3678** 3679 3643 3357 Electronic connectors; electronic switches; electronic circuits; connectors & terminals for electrical devices; communication wire; fiber optic cable (insulated)
HQ: Molex, Llc
2222 Wellington Ct
Lisle IL 60532
630 969-4550

(G-841)
CELANESE AMERICAS LLC
Also Called: Hoechst Celanese
1195 Centre Rd (48326-2603)
PHONE.................................248 377-2700
David Vranesich, *Principal*
EMP: 4
SALES (corp-wide): 5.6B **Publicly Held**
SIC: **2821** Plastics materials & resins
HQ: Celanese Americas Llc
222 Colinas Blvd W # 900
Irving TX 75039
972 443-4000

(G-842)
CHAMPION PLASTICS INC
1892 Taylor Rd (48326-1584)
PHONE.................................248 373-8995
Michael McDermott, *President*
Mathew McDermott, *Vice Pres*
Howard Wolf, *Executive*
EMP: 21 EST: 1981
SQ FT: 25,000
SALES (est): 4.2MM **Privately Held**
WEB: www.championplastics.net
SIC: **3089** 5162 Injection molding of plastics; plastics products

(G-843)
CI LIGHTING LLC
2083 Pontiac Rd (48326-2485)
PHONE.................................248 997-4415
Donald Bernier Jr, *Mng Member*
EMP: 6 EST: 2010
SQ FT: 6,000
SALES (est): 2MM **Privately Held**
WEB: www.made-usa.net
SIC: **3672** 3648 Printed circuit boards; lighting equipment

(G-844)
CLINTON RIVER MEDICAL PDTS LLC
1025 Doris Rd (48326-2614)
PHONE.................................248 289-1825
Tom Gitter, *CEO*
EMP: 6 EST: 2011
SALES (est): 311.2K **Privately Held**
WEB: www.clintonrivermedical.com
SIC: **3842** Wheelchairs

(G-845)
CODE SYSTEMS INC
2365 Pontiac Rd Frnt (48326-2484)
PHONE.................................248 307-3884
Peter J Stouffer, *President*
Kathleen Anderson, *Vice Pres*
Joseph Santavicca, *Vice Pres*
Michael Schroeder, *Vice Pres*
Joseph Dentamaro, *VP Sales*
EMP: 20 EST: 1979
SALES (est): 2.7MM
SALES (corp-wide): 563.6MM **Publicly Held**
WEB: www.voxxintl.com
SIC: **3679** Electronic circuits
PA: Voxx International Corporation
2351 J Lawson Blvd
Orlando FL 32824
800 645-7750

(G-846)
CONCORDE INC
4200 N Atlantic Blvd (48326-1578)
PHONE.................................248 391-8177
EMP: 10
SALES (est): 1.2MM **Privately Held**
SIC: **3714** 2674 Mfg Motor Vehicle Parts/Accessories Mfg Bags-Uncoated Paper

(G-847)
CONTINENTAL AUTO SYSTEMS INC
Emitec
2400 Executive Hills Dr (48326-2980)
PHONE.................................248 253-2969
Julie A Anderson, *Vice Pres*
Scott Brooks, *Vice Pres*
Chris Rinehart, *Project Mgr*
Bree Vanerp, *Purch Agent*
Farzad Omaraie, *Engineer*
EMP: 464
SQ FT: 164,422
SALES (corp-wide): 44.6B **Privately Held**
WEB: www.continental-automotive.com
SIC: **3694** Engine electrical equipment
HQ: Continental Automotive Systems, Inc.
1 Continental Dr
Auburn Hills MI 48326

(G-848)
CONTINENTAL AUTO SYSTEMS INC
Also Called: VDO Automotive
2400 Executive Hills Dr (48326-2980)
PHONE.................................248 874-2597
Wolfgang Burkhardt, *Manager*
EMP: 6
SALES (corp-wide): 44.6B **Privately Held**
WEB: www.continental-automotive.com
SIC: **3694** Automotive electrical equipment
HQ: Continental Automotive Systems, Inc.
1 Continental Dr
Auburn Hills MI 48326

(G-849)
CONTINENTAL AUTO SYSTEMS INC
2400 Executive Hills Dr (48326-2980)
PHONE.................................248 874-1801
Ralf Cramer, *Director*
EMP: 7
SALES (corp-wide): 44.6B **Privately Held**
WEB: www.continental-automotive.com
SIC: **3714** Fuel systems & parts, motor vehicle
HQ: Continental Automotive Systems, Inc.
1 Continental Dr
Auburn Hills MI 48326

(G-850)
COOPER-STANDARD AUTOMOTIVE INC
2545 N Opdyke Rd Ste 102 (48326-1970)
P.O. Box 615, Grand Blanc (48480-0615)
PHONE.................................248 630-7262
Matt Lang, *Accounts Mgr*
Mike Federle, *Branch Mgr*
EMP: 8
SQ FT: 2,600
SALES (corp-wide): 2.3B **Publicly Held**
WEB: www.cooperstandard.com
SIC: **3465** Body parts, automobile: stamped metal
HQ: Cooper-Standard Automotive Inc.
40300 Traditions Dr
Northville MI 48168
248 596-5900

(G-851)
COVESTRO LLC
2401 E Walton Blvd (48326-1957)
PHONE.................................248 475-7700
Samuel Stewart, *Branch Mgr*
EMP: 358
SQ FT: 30,000
SALES (corp-wide): 12.6B **Privately Held**
WEB: www.covestro.us
SIC: **2822** 2821 Synthetic rubber; plastics materials & resins
HQ: Covestro Llc
1 Covestro Cir
Pittsburgh PA 15205
412 413-2000

(G-852)
CSM PRODUCTS INC
1920 Opdyke Ct Ste 200 (48326-2479)
PHONE.................................248 836-4995
Paul Vanophem, *President*
Michael Fairbanks, *Manager*
EMP: 11 EST: 2006
SALES (est): 2.9MM
SALES (corp-wide): 775.7K **Privately Held**
WEB: www.csm.de
SIC: **3825** Instruments to measure electricity
HQ: Csm Computer-Systeme-Messtechnik Gmbh
Raiffeisenstr. 36
Filderstadt BW 70794
711 779-640

(G-853)
CSP HOLDING CORP (DH)
255 Rex Blvd (48326-2954)
PHONE.................................248 237-7800
EMP: 100 EST: 1998
SALES (est): 532.8MM **Privately Held**
WEB: www.teijinautomotive.com
SIC: **3089** Injection molding of plastics
HQ: Teijin Automotive Technologies Na Holdings Corp.
255 Rex Blvd
Auburn Hills MI 48326
248 237-7800

(G-854)
CSP HOLDING CORP
1200 Harmon Rd (48326-1550)
PHONE.................................248 724-4410
EMP: 4 **Privately Held**
WEB: www.teijinautomotive.com
SIC: **3089** Injection molding of plastics
HQ: Csp Holding Corp.
255 Rex Blvd
Auburn Hills MI 48326
248 237-7800

(G-855)
CUSTOM SERVICE & DESIGN INC (PA)
1259 Doris Rd Ste B (48326-2618)
P.O. Box 214923 (48321-4923)
PHONE.................................248 340-9005
Donald Saville, *President*
John Frosheiser, *Sales Mgr*
Megan Foster, *Admin Asst*
EMP: 16 EST: 1993
SALES (est): 3.2MM **Privately Held**
WEB: www.customserviceanddesign.com
SIC: **3564** 3589 Purification & dust collection equipment; commercial cleaning equipment

Auburn Hills - Oakland County

(G-856)
CZ INDUSTRIES INC
1929-1939 N Opdyke Rd Ste (48326)
PHONE................................248 475-4415
Petr Skrna
EMP: 4 **EST:** 2006
SQ FT: 5,600
SALES (est): 558.4K **Privately Held**
WEB: www.czind.com
SIC: 3545 Machine tool accessories

(G-857)
DANA DRIVESHAFT MFG LLC
Dana Driveshaft Products
4440 N Atlantic Blvd (48326-1580)
PHONE................................248 623-2185
Gregory Wojtalik, *Senior Engr*
Jeff Periat, *Manager*
EMP: 230 **Publicly Held**
WEB: www.dana.com
SIC: 3714 Motor vehicle parts & accessories
HQ: Dana Driveshaft Manufacturing, Llc
6515 Maumee Western Rd
Maumee OH 43537

(G-858)
DASSAULT SYSTMES AMERICAS CORP
900 N Squirrel Rd Ste 100 (48326-2789)
PHONE................................248 267-9696
Phil Borchard, *Vice Pres*
Patrick Michel, *Vice Pres*
Srini Lingampalli, *Opers Staff*
Nenad Apostolovic, *Research*
Brian Perles, *Research*
EMP: 195
SALES (corp-wide): 2B **Privately Held**
WEB: www.cadam.com
SIC: 7372 Application computer software
HQ: Dassault Systemes Americas Corp.
175 Wyman St
Waltham MA 02451
781 810-3000

(G-859)
DATA REPRODUCTIONS CORPORATION
4545 Glenmeade Ln (48326-1767)
PHONE................................248 371-3700
Dennis M Kavanagh, *President*
Kimberly Kavanagh, *Sales Mgr*
Bonnie Kahler, *Cust Mgr*
Gabriella Marino, *Manager*
Gail Fritz, *Admin Mgr*
▼ **EMP:** 55 **EST:** 1967
SQ FT: 100,000
SALES (est): 19.9MM **Privately Held**
WEB: www.datarepro.com
SIC: 2752 Commercial printing, offset

(G-860)
DE-STA-CO CYLINDERS INC
15 Corporate Dr (48326-2919)
P.O. Box 2800, Troy (48007-2800)
PHONE................................248 836-6700
Patric Carol, *President*
Tom Stimac, *Sales Dir*
▲ **EMP:** 400 **EST:** 1980
SALES (est): 199.5MM
SALES (corp-wide): 6.6B **Publicly Held**
WEB: www.destaco.com
SIC: 3593 3495 Fluid power cylinders, hydraulic or pneumatic; precision springs
HQ: Dover Engineered Systems, Inc.
3005 Highland Pkwy # 200
Downers Grove IL 60515
630 541-1540

(G-861)
DEFENSE COMPONENT DETROIT LLC
Also Called: Peacekeeper Cnc
1597 Atlantic Blvd (48326-1501)
PHONE................................248 393-2300
Jason Charest, *Plant Mgr*
Lara Webb, *QC Mgr*
Debra Woodward, *Office Mgr*
Jason Nihranz, *Manager*
Jim Carlton
EMP: 37 **EST:** 2009
SQ FT: 3,000
SALES: 666.9K **Privately Held**
WEB: www.defensecomponents1.com
SIC: 3599 Machine & other job shop work

(G-862)
DELUXE FRAME COMPANY INC
2275 N Opdyke Rd Ste D (48326-2469)
PHONE................................248 373-8811
Paul Meloche, *President*
Colleen Carter, *Corp Secy*
Tom Stevenson, *Vice Pres*
EMP: 20 **EST:** 1981
SALES (est): 2.8MM **Privately Held**
WEB: www.deluxeframe.com
SIC: 3089 Plastic hardware & building products

(G-863)
DETROIT WLBERT CRMTION SVCS LL
70 S Squirrel Rd (48326-3279)
PHONE................................248 853-0559
Chris Gordon, *Manager*
EMP: 6 **EST:** 2012
SALES (est): 363.8K **Privately Held**
WEB: www.detroitwilbert.com
SIC: 3272 Burial vaults, concrete or pre-cast terrazzo

(G-864)
DM3D TECHNOLOGY LLC
2350 Pontiac Rd (48326-2461)
PHONE................................248 409-7900
Roger D Parsons, *CEO*
Dr Bhaskar Dutta, *COO*
Johns M George, *CFO*
Johns George,
EMP: 12 **EST:** 2012
SQ FT: 37,000
SALES (est): 1.7MM **Privately Held**
WEB: www.dm3dtech.com
SIC: 3699 Electrical equipment & supplies

(G-865)
DOVER ENERGY INC
Also Called: Destaco Industries
15 Corporate Dr (48326-2919)
PHONE................................248 836-6750
Rob Weber, *General Mgr*
Cynthia Wells, *Vice Pres*
Heather Jones, *Buyer*
Chris Hineline, *QC Mgr*
Ken Baker, *Engineer*
EMP: 132
SALES (corp-wide): 6.6B **Publicly Held**
WEB: www.destaco.com
SIC: 3494 3495 Valves & pipe fittings; wire springs
HQ: Dover Energy, Inc.
691 N Squirrel Rd Ste 250
Auburn Hills MI 48326
248 836-6700

(G-866)
DOVER ENERGY INC (HQ)
Also Called: De-Sta-Co
691 N Squirrel Rd Ste 250 (48326-2871)
PHONE................................248 836-6700
Byron Paul, *President*
Bill Crusey, *Vice Pres*
Jason Foster, *Plant Mgr*
Jim Geary, *Project Mgr*
Chris Tomaselli, *Foreman/Supr*
▲ **EMP:** 111 **EST:** 1985
SQ FT: 50,000
SALES (est): 169.7MM
SALES (corp-wide): 6.6B **Publicly Held**
WEB: www.destaco.com
SIC: 3429 Clamps, metal
PA: Dover Corporation
3005 Highland Pkwy # 200
Downers Grove IL 60515
630 541-1540

(G-867)
DS AUTOMOTION LLC
691 N Squirrel Rd 119 (48326-2846)
PHONE................................248 370-8950
Jay Yale, *CEO*
EMP: 5 **EST:** 2016
SALES (est): 250K **Privately Held**
WEB: www.ds-automotion.com
SIC: 3799 Recreational vehicles

(G-868)
DURA OPERATING LLC (PA)
Also Called: Dura Automotive Systems
1780 Pond Run (48326-2752)
PHONE................................248 299-7500
Lyn Tilton, *CEO*
Tyrone Michael Jordan, *President*
David Pettyes, *Exec VP*
Sanjay Singh, *Exec VP*
Greg Wyatt, *Purchasing*
◆ **EMP:** 160 **EST:** 1990
SQ FT: 64,150
SALES (est): 540.6MM **Privately Held**
WEB: www.duraauto.com
SIC: 3429 3714 Motor vehicle hardware; motor vehicle electrical equipment

(G-869)
DUS OPERATING INC (DH)
Also Called: Dura Automotive Systems
1780 Pond Run (48326-2752)
PHONE................................248 299-7500
Kimberly Rodriguez, *CEO*
Michael Beckett, *COO*
Stephen Johnston, *CFO*
Sean McGuire, *Ch Credit Ofcr*
Sanjay Singh, *CTO*
EMP: 336 **EST:** 2020
SALES (est): 225.7MM
SALES (corp-wide): 847.6MM **Privately Held**
SIC: 3711 Automobile assembly, including specialty automobiles

(G-870)
DYNAMIC CORPORATION
Also Called: Dynamic Prototype Operations
2193 Executive Hills Dr (48326-2943)
PHONE................................248 338-1100
Ray Atwood, *Manager*
EMP: 32
SALES (corp-wide): 6MM **Privately Held**
WEB: www.dynamicinc.com
SIC: 3711 Cars, electric, assembly of
PA: Dynamic Corporation
2565 Van Ommen Dr
Holland MI 49424
616 399-2200

(G-871)
DYNAMIC ROBOTIC SOLUTIONS INC
Also Called: Shape Process Automation
1255 Harmon Rd (48326-1539)
PHONE................................248 829-2800
Bruce Potts, *President*
Sargon Haddad, *Vice Pres*
Bob Offer, *Vice Pres*
Robert J Offer, *Vice Pres*
Julie Danos, *Project Mgr*
▲ **EMP:** 120 **EST:** 1985
SQ FT: 93,000
SALES (est): 24.7MM
SALES (corp-wide): 593.9MM **Privately Held**
WEB: www.kmtrobotic.com
SIC: 3541 Robots for drilling, cutting, grinding, polishing, etc.
HQ: Shape Technologies Group, Inc.
23500 64th Ave S
Kent WA 98032
253 246-3200

(G-872)
E I DU PONT DE NEMOURS & CO
Also Called: Dupont Performance Materials
1250 Harmon Rd (48326-1550)
PHONE................................302 999-6566
Janet M Sawgle, *Branch Mgr*
EMP: 4
SALES (corp-wide): 14.2B **Publicly Held**
WEB: www.dupont.com
SIC: 2821 Plastics materials & resins
HQ: E. I. Du Pont De Nemours And Company
974 Centre Rd Bldg 735
Wilmington DE 19805
302 485-3000

(G-873)
E-PROCUREMENT SERVICES LLC
691 N Squirrel Rd Ste 220 (48326-2835)
PHONE................................248 630-7200
David Saroli, *CEO*
Mark Saroli, *Senior VP*
Nathan Kalso, *Manager*
Lisa Doane, *Supervisor*
EMP: 54 **EST:** 2010
SALES (est): 4.8MM **Privately Held**
SIC: 7372 Business oriented computer software

(G-874)
ECOLOGY COATINGS
2701 Cmbridge Ct Ste 100 (48326)
PHONE................................248 370-9900
EMP: 4 **EST:** 2017
SALES (est): 58.4K **Privately Held**
SIC: 3479 Galvanizing of iron, steel or end-formed products

(G-875)
EDW C LEVY CO
Clawson Concrete Division
2470 Auburn Rd (48326-3104)
PHONE................................248 334-4302
EMP: 15
SALES (corp-wide): 376.1MM **Privately Held**
SIC: 3273 Mfg Ready-Mix Concrete
PA: Edw. C. Levy Co.
9300 Dix
Dearborn MI 48120
313 429-2200

(G-876)
ELDEC LLC
3355 Bald Mountain Rd # 30 (48326-4312)
PHONE................................248 364-4750
Jochen Arnold, *President*
Rick Bovensiep, *Engineer*
EMP: 16 **EST:** 1998
SQ FT: 30,000
SALES (est): 4.9MM
SALES (corp-wide): 601.3MM **Privately Held**
WEB: www.eldec.net
SIC: 3567 Induction heating equipment
HQ: Emag Systems Gmbh
Austr. 24
Salach BW 73084
716 217-0

(G-877)
ELECTROHEAT TECHNOLOGIES LLC
691 N Squirrel Rd Ste 247 (48326-2871)
PHONE................................810 798-2400
EMP: 28
SQ FT: 20,000
SALES (est): 4MM **Privately Held**
SIC: 3567 Mfg Industrial Furnaces/Ovens

(G-878)
ELLIOTT TAPE INC (PA)
Also Called: Elliott Group International
1882 Pond Run (48326-2768)
PHONE................................248 475-2000
R Hugh Elliott, *President*
Charles Tafel, *Vice Pres*
Michael Cords, *Project Mgr*
Christopher Richardson, *Project Mgr*
Benjamin Dyson, *Opers Staff*
▲ **EMP:** 26 **EST:** 1974
SQ FT: 28,000
SALES (est): 17.2MM **Privately Held**
WEB: www.egitape.com
SIC: 5113 2672 5013 Pressure sensitive tape; tape, pressure sensitive: made from purchased materials; motor vehicle supplies & new parts

(G-879)
EMABOND SOLUTIONS LLC
1797 Atlantic Blvd (48326-1505)
PHONE................................248 481-8048
EMP: 12 **EST:** 2019
SALES (est): 5.7MM **Privately Held**
WEB: www.emabond.com
SIC: 3089 Injection molding of plastics

(G-880)
EMSSONS FAURECIA CTRL SYSTEMS
2800 High Meadow Cir (48326-2772)
PHONE................................248 724-5100
Yann Delabriere, *CEO*
Michael Morrow, *Engineer*
▲ **EMP:** 1 **EST:** 1988
SALES (est): 4MM
SALES (corp-wide): 41.2MM **Privately Held**
WEB: www.faurecia.com
SIC: 3714 Motor vehicle parts & accessories

▲ = Import ▼ = Export
◆ = Import/Export

GEOGRAPHIC SECTION
Auburn Hills - Oakland County (G-901)

HQ: Faurecia Usa Holdings, Inc.
2800 High Meadow Cir
Auburn Hills MI 48326
248 724-5100

(G-881)
ESYS AUTOMATION LLC (DH)
1000 Brown Rd (48326-1506)
PHONE..................248 484-9927
Michael Lashbrook, CEO
Todd Thelen, General Mgr
Kevin Whaley, General Mgr
Kevin Gaines, Vice Pres
Geoff Boufford, Project Mgr
EMP: 209 **EST:** 1999
SALES (est): 66.4MM **Privately Held**
WEB: www.jrautomation.com
SIC: 3549 3599 8711 8742 Assembly machines, including robotic; custom machinery; engineering services; automation & robotics consultant; robotic conveyors
HQ: J.R. Automation Technologies, Llc
13365 Tyler St
Holland MI 49424
616 399-2168

(G-882)
EVOSYS NORTH AMERICA CORP
1091 Centre Rd Ste 140 (48326-2670)
PHONE..................248 973-1703
EMP: 13 **EST:** 2020
SALES (est): 2.1MM
SALES (corp-wide): 9.1MM **Privately Held**
WEB: www.evosys-laser.com
SIC: 3841 Surgical & medical instruments
PA: Evosys Laser Gmbh
Felix-Klein-Str. 75
Erlangen BY 91058
913 181-4970

(G-883)
EXCEL CIRCUITS LLC
2601 Lapeer Rd (48326-1926)
PHONE..................248 373-0700
Tod Goslin, Controller
EMP: 10 **EST:** 2016
SALES (est): 1.6MM **Privately Held**
WEB: www.excelcircuits.com
SIC: 3672 Printed circuit boards

(G-884)
EXIDE TECHNOLOGIES LLC
2750 Auburn Rd (48326-3114)
P.O. Box 214410 (48321-4410)
PHONE..................248 853-5000
Carl Sickles, Manager
EMP: 6
SALES (corp-wide): 2B **Privately Held**
WEB: www.exide.com
SIC: 3691 3629 Storage batteries; battery chargers, rectifying or nonrotating
PA: Exide Technologies, Llc
13000 Drfeld Pkwy Bldg 20
Milton GA 30004
678 566-9000

(G-885)
F & S DIVERSIFIED PRODUCTS INC
Also Called: Lgi International
4260 Giddings Rd (48326-1529)
PHONE..................248 409-0960
Henry Fair, President
EMP: 16 **EST:** 2001
SALES (est): 332K **Privately Held**
SIC: 3465 Body parts, automobile: stamped metal

(G-886)
FATA AUTOMATION INC (PA)
2333 E Walton Blvd (48326-1955)
PHONE..................248 724-7660
Martin Wright, President
Ron Benish, Vice Pres
Ronald Benish, Vice Pres
Robert Smolinski, Vice Pres
Bob Smolinski, VP Opers
◆ **EMP:** 84 **EST:** 1989
SQ FT: 46,800
SALES (est): 25.1MM **Privately Held**
WEB: www.fatainc.com
SIC: 3535 Conveyors & conveying equipment

(G-887)
FAURECIA EMSSONS CTRL TECH USA (DH)
Also Called: Emcon Technologies
2800 High Meadow Cir (48326-2772)
P.O. Box 214588 (48321-4588)
PHONE..................248 724-5100
David Degraaf, President
Rob Steele, Business Mgr
Thomas Adam, Vice Pres
David Laudenslayer, Vice Pres
Bruno Rias, Vice Pres
◆ **EMP:** 174 **EST:** 2007
SALES (est): 1.8B
SALES (corp-wide): 41.2MM **Privately Held**
WEB: www.faurecia.com
SIC: 3714 Exhaust systems & parts, motor vehicle; filters: oil, fuel & air, motor vehicle
HQ: Faurecia Usa Holdings, Inc.
2800 High Meadow Cir
Auburn Hills MI 48326
248 724-5100

(G-888)
FAURECIA EXHAUST SYSTEMS LLC
2500 Executive Hills Dr (48326-2983)
P.O. Box 214829 (48321-4829)
PHONE..................248 409-3500
EMP: 37 **EST:** 2017
SALES (est): 6.2MM **Privately Held**
SIC: 3714 Motor vehicle parts & accessories

(G-889)
FAURECIA INTERIOR SYSTEMS INC (DH)
Also Called: Faurecia North America
2800 High Meadow Cir (48326-2772)
P.O. Box 214587 (48321-4587)
PHONE..................248 724-5100
Donald Hampton, President
Nick Miller, General Mgr
Aracely Lason, Buyer
Eric Di Nisi, Engineer
Christian Scheffler, Project Engr
▲ **EMP:** 320 **EST:** 1997
SALES (est): 833.2MM
SALES (corp-wide): 41.2MM **Privately Held**
WEB: www.faurecia.com
SIC: 3999 5013 Atomizers, toiletry; automotive supplies & parts
HQ: Faurecia Usa Holdings, Inc.
2800 High Meadow Cir
Auburn Hills MI 48326
248 724-5100

(G-890)
FAURECIA NORTH AMERICA INC
2800 High Meadow Cir (48326-2772)
PHONE..................248 288-1000
Mark Stdham, President
Jean-Michel Renaudie, Exec VP
Jean-Pierre Sounillac, Exec VP
Hagen Wiesner, Exec VP
Michel Favre, CFO
EMP: 16 **EST:** 2014
SALES (est): 797K
SALES (corp-wide): 41.2MM **Privately Held**
WEB: www.faurecia-us.com
SIC: 2399 5013 5012 Automotive covers, except seat & tire covers; automotive supplies & parts; automotive brokers
HQ: Faurecia Usa Holdings, Inc.
2800 High Meadow Cir
Auburn Hills MI 48326
248 724-5100

(G-891)
FAURECIA USA HOLDINGS INC (HQ)
2800 High Meadow Cir (48326-2772)
P.O. Box 214710 (48321-4710)
PHONE..................248 724-5100
Mark Stidham, President
Eduard Hamidullin, Plant Mgr
Corey Ruzzin, Mfg Staff
Samantha Mouchet, Production
Claudia Lares, Buyer
▲ **EMP:** 4 **EST:** 1999
SALES (est): 2.9B
SALES (corp-wide): 41.2MM **Privately Held**
WEB: www.faurecia.com
SIC: 3714 Mufflers (exhaust), motor vehicle
PA: Faurecia
23 27
Nanterre 92000
172 367-000

(G-892)
FCA INTRNTIONAL OPERATIONS LLC
1000 Chrysler Dr (48326-2766)
PHONE..................800 334-9200
Sergio Marchionne, CEO
Michael Manley, President
Alfredo Altavilla, Senior VP
Holly E Leese, Senior VP
Giorgio Fossati, Vice Pres
◆ **EMP:** 20 **EST:** 2009
SALES (est): 24.4MM
SALES (corp-wide): 102.5B **Privately Held**
WEB: www.chrysler.com
SIC: 5012 3714 Automobiles & other motor vehicles; motor vehicle engines & parts
PA: Stellantis N.V.
Taurusavenue 1
Hoofddorp
203 421-707

(G-893)
FCA NORTH AMERICA HOLDINGS LLC (DH)
1000 Chrysler Dr (48326-2766)
PHONE..................248 512-2950
Tama Carter, Chief
Richard Grady, Area Mgr
Mark Wittholz, Area Mgr
Devon Frazier, Production
Jake Vermiglio, Production
EMP: 77816 **EST:** 2009
SALES (est): 768.5MM
SALES (corp-wide): 102.5B **Privately Held**
WEB: www.stellantis.com
SIC: 3714 3711 Motor vehicle parts & accessories; automobile assembly, including specialty automobiles
HQ: Stellantis Nv
Via Plava 80
Torino TO 10135
011 005-6318

(G-894)
FCA US LLC
Also Called: Chrysler Twinsburg Stamping
1000 Chrysler Dr (48326-2766)
PHONE..................248 512-2950
Davide Mele, COO
Michael Novak, Vice Pres
Jason Russ, Vice Pres
Thomas Hoover, Production
Brian Hacker, Purchasing
EMP: 1850
SALES (corp-wide): 102.5B **Privately Held**
WEB: www.chrysler.com
SIC: 3465 Automotive stampings
HQ: Fca Us Llc
1000 Chrysler Dr
Auburn Hills MI 48326

(G-895)
FCA US LLC (HQ)
Also Called: Fiat Chrysler Automobiles
1000 Chrysler Dr (48326-2766)
P.O. Box 218004 (48321-8004)
PHONE..................248 576-5741
Michael Manley, CEO
Eric Quarles, General Mgr
Michael Miller, Chief
Jon Sundstrom, Area Mgr
Marjorie Loeb, Senior VP
◆ **EMP:** 77817 **EST:** 2009
SALES (est): 947.7MM
SALES (corp-wide): 102.5B **Privately Held**
WEB: www.chrysler.com
SIC: 5511 3711 Automobiles, new & used; automobile assembly, including specialty automobiles
PA: Stellantis N.V.
Taurusavenue 1
Hoofddorp
203 421-707

(G-896)
FEED - LEASE CORP
2750 Paldan Dr (48326-1826)
PHONE..................248 377-0000
John Stretten, President
Martha J Stretten, Corp Secy
Bill Konieczny, Engineer
Brian Thompson, CFO
Richard Balser, Sales Staff
▲ **EMP:** 25 **EST:** 1969
SQ FT: 12,000
SALES (est): 4.1MM **Privately Held**
WEB: www.universalfeedandmachine.com
SIC: 3621 3547 3545 3542 Motors & generators; rolling mill machinery; machine tool accessories; machine tools, metal forming type; coiling machinery

(G-897)
FEV TEST SYSTEMS INC
4554 Glenmeade Ln (48326-1766)
PHONE..................248 373-6000
Manfed Schaffrath, President
Ragnar Bergethon, Corp Secy
EMP: 5 **EST:** 2003
SALES (est): 1.7MM
SALES (corp-wide): 723.6MM **Privately Held**
WEB: www.fev.com
SIC: 3519 8711 Internal combustion engines; engineering services
HQ: Fev Europe Gmbh
Neuenhofstr. 181
Aachen NW 52078
241 568-90

(G-898)
FIREFISH TOPCO LLC (PA)
1780 Pond Run (48326-2752)
PHONE..................248 299-7500
John Stewart, Chairman
Martin Sjoquist, Vice Pres
Carl Beckwith, Mng Member
Scott Duncan, Director
Lauren Mulholland, Director
EMP: 85 **EST:** 2020
SALES (est): 847.6MM **Privately Held**
SIC: 3714 Motor vehicle parts & accessories

(G-899)
FISCHER AMERICA INC
Also Called: Fischer Automotive Systems
1084 Doris Rd (48326-2613)
PHONE..................248 276-1940
Klaus Fischer, Owner
Robert Anderson, Vice Pres
Peter Biske, Vice Pres
Jon Anderson, Maint Spvr
Carol Gutowski, Purchasing
◆ **EMP:** 136 **EST:** 1986
SQ FT: 60,773
SALES (est): 42.7MM
SALES (corp-wide): 409.2MM **Privately Held**
WEB: www.fischer-automotive.com
SIC: 3089 Automotive parts, plastic
HQ: Fischer Automotive Systems Gmbh & Co. Kg
Industriestr. 103
Horb Am Neckar BW 72160
744 312-5500

(G-900)
FIVE STAR MANUFACTURING INC
2430 E Walton Blvd (48326-1956)
PHONE..................815 723-2245
Mike McMorran, President
EMP: 14 **EST:** 1987
SQ FT: 11,000
SALES (est): 444.2K **Privately Held**
WEB: www.normaamericasds.com
SIC: 3429 Clamps, metal

(G-901)
FLAMBEAU INC (PA)
2701 Cambridge Ct Ste 515 (48326-2514)
PHONE..................248 364-3357
Patricia Adams, Principal
EMP: 9 **EST:** 1998

Auburn Hills - Oakland County (G-902)

SALES (est): 1.2MM **Privately Held**
WEB: www.flambeau.com
SIC: **3429** 3272 5199 Manufactured hardware (general); tanks, concrete; packaging materials

(G-902)
FLOTRONICS AUTOMATION INC
2704 Paldan Dr (48326-1826)
PHONE.............................248 625-8890
Stephen Schmaltz, *President*
Natalie Schmaltz, *Corp Secy*
EMP: **31** EST: 2017
SALES (est): 4.1MM **Privately Held**
WEB: www.flotronicsautomation.com
SIC: **3354** Aluminum extruded products

(G-903)
FLUID HUTCHINSON MANAGEMENT (DH)
Also Called: Hutchinson Fts, Inc.
3201 Cross Creek Pkwy (48326-2765)
PHONE.............................248 679-1327
Paul H Campbell, *CEO*
Sean Canty, *Vice Pres*
Walter Molitor, *Plant Mgr*
Michael Hayes, *Engineer*
Jim Horn, *Manager*
▲ EMP: **90** EST: 1947
SALES (est): 261.9MM
SALES (corp-wide): 4.6B **Publicly Held**
WEB: www.hutchinsonna.com
SIC: **3714** 3061 3567 3492 Air conditioner parts, motor vehtcle; mechanical rubber goods; industrial furnaces & ovens; fluid power valves & hose fittings; fabricated plate work (boiler shop); manufactured hardware (general)
HQ: Hutchinson Corporation
 460 Fuller Ave Ne
 Grand Rapids MI 49503
 616 459-4541

(G-904)
FLUXTROL INC
1388 Atlantic Blvd (48326-1572)
PHONE.............................248 393-2000
Raoul Montgomery Jr, *President*
Riccardo Ruffini, *President*
Christopher Yakey, *Engineer*
Michael Young, *Design Engr*
Ricardo Diaz, *Regl Sales Mgr*
EMP: **9** EST: 1984
SQ FT: 8,000
SALES (est): 1.7MM **Privately Held**
WEB: www.fluxtrol.com
SIC: **3499** Magnetic shields, metal

(G-905)
FTE AUTOMOTIVE NORTH AMER INC
4100 N Atlantic Blvd (48326-1570)
PHONE.............................248 340-1262
Wolfgang Bruens, *President*
Klas Gockler, *Vice Pres*
Michael Klasen, *Vice Pres*
Mark Wilhelms, *Vice Pres*
◆ EMP: **40** EST: 2004
SALES (est): 10.5MM
SALES (corp-wide): 177.9K **Privately Held**
WEB: www.fte-automotive.com
SIC: **3714** Motor vehicle transmissions, drive assemblies & parts
PA: Valeo
 43 Rue Bayen
 Paris
 140 687-476

(G-906)
GEM ASSET ACQUISITION LLC
Also Called: Gemseal Pvement Pdts - Detroit
2280 Auburn Rd (48326-3102)
PHONE.............................248 338-0335
EMP: **15**
SALES (corp-wide): 19.3MM **Privately Held**
SIC: **2951** Asphalt paving mixtures & blocks
PA: Gem Asset Acquisition Llc
 1855 Lindbergh St Ste 500
 Charlotte NC 28208
 704 225-3321

(G-907)
GEMO HOPKINS USA INC
2900 Auburn Ct (48326-3204)
PHONE.............................734 330-1271
Richard Conlin, *General Mgr*
EMP: **9** EST: 2014
SQ FT: 10,000
SALES (est): 2.5MM
SALES (corp-wide): 53.6MM **Privately Held**
WEB: www.gemo.de
SIC: **3357** 5015 Automotive wire & cable, except ignition sets: nonferrous; automotive accessories, used
PA: Gemo Gmbh & Co. Kg
 Saalestr. 21
 Krefeld NW 47800
 215 144-160

(G-908)
GENERAL MOTORS LLC
3000 University Dr Fl 2 (48326-2496)
PHONE.............................313 408-3987
Rebekah Brown, *Engineer*
Oscar Tache, *Engineer*
Bill Chung, *CFO*
EMP: **7** **Publicly Held**
WEB: www.gm.com
SIC: **3711** 3714 Motor vehicles & car bodies; motor vehicle parts & accessories
HQ: General Motors Llc
 300 Renaissance Ctr L1
 Detroit MI 48243

(G-909)
GEOFABRICA INC
2900 Auburn Ct (48326-3204)
PHONE.............................810 728-2468
George Caravias, *CEO*
Eric Altman, *Treasurer*
EMP: **12** EST: 2019
SALES (est): 1.1MM **Privately Held**
WEB: www.geofabrica.com
SIC: **3569** General industrial machinery

(G-910)
GEORGE P JOHNSON COMPANY (HQ)
Also Called: Intaglio Associates In Design
3600 Giddings Rd (48326-1515)
PHONE.............................248 475-2500
Chris Meyer, *CEO*
Denise Wong, *President*
Tiffany Fong, *Partner*
Sheila Martin, *Partner*
Brittney Nonn, *Partner*
▲ EMP: **100** EST: 1914
SQ FT: 435,000
SALES (est): 197.2MM
SALES (corp-wide): 280MM **Privately Held**
WEB: www.gpj.com
SIC: **3993** 7389 Signs & advertising specialties; advertising, promotional & trade show services
PA: Project Worldwide, Inc.
 3600 Giddings Rd
 Auburn Hills MI 48326
 248 475-8863

(G-911)
GKN DRIVELINE NORTH AMER INC (DH)
Also Called: GKN Automotive
2200 N Opdyke Rd (48326-2389)
PHONE.............................248 296-7000
Peter Molgg, *CEO*
Ramon Kuczera, *Senior VP*
Daniel Market, *Engineer*
Mike Kirk, *Sales Staff*
◆ EMP: **400** EST: 1977
SQ FT: 113,000
SALES (est): 503.3MM
SALES (corp-wide): 11.6B **Privately Held**
SIC: **3714** 5013 Universal joints, motor vehicle; drive shafts, motor vehicle; automotive engines & engine parts
HQ: Gkn America Corp.
 1180 Peachtree St Ne # 2450
 Atlanta GA 30309
 630 972-9300

(G-912)
GKN NORTH AMERICA INC
2200 N Opdyke Rd (48326-2389)
PHONE.............................248 296-7200
Robert Willig, *President*
Tejas Chhaya, *Associate Dir*
EMP: **151** EST: 1981
SQ FT: 110,000
SALES (est): 17.3MM
SALES (corp-wide): 11.6B **Privately Held**
WEB: www.gkn.com
SIC: **3714** 5013 7359 Motor vehicle transmissions, drive assemblies & parts; motor vehicle supplies & new parts; equipment rental & leasing
HQ: Gkn Holdings Limited
 Ipsley House
 Redditch WORCS B98 0

(G-913)
GKN NORTH AMERICA SERVICES INC
3300 University Dr (48326-2362)
PHONE.............................248 377-1200
Pat Barky, *Manager*
EMP: **7**
SALES (corp-wide): 11.6B **Privately Held**
SIC: **3714** Motor vehicle transmissions, drive assemblies & parts
HQ: Gkn North America Services, Inc.
 1180 Peachtree St Ne # 2450
 Atlanta GA 30309

(G-914)
GKN SINTER METALS LLC (DH)
Also Called: GKN Powder Metallurgy
1670 Opdyke Ct (48326)
PHONE.............................248 883-4500
Rich McCorry, *President*
Peter M Lgg, *Senior VP*
Mark Gleason, *Engineer*
Shannon Trent, *Engineer*
Darren Heartwell, *Accounts Mgr*
◆ EMP: **3** EST: 1991
SQ FT: 100,000
SALES (est): 494.2MM
SALES (corp-wide): 11.6B **Privately Held**
WEB: www.gknpm.com
SIC: **3714** 3568 3369 3366 Motor vehicle engines & parts; motor vehicle transmissions, drive assemblies & parts; gears, motor vehicle; bearings, motor vehicle; power transmission equipment; sprockets (power transmission equipment); bearings, plain; nonferrous foundries; copper foundries
HQ: Gkn Limited
 2nd Floor, One Central Boulevard
 Solihull W MIDLANDS B90 8
 121 210-9800

(G-915)
GLOBAL AUTOMOTIVE SYSTEMS LLC (PA)
Also Called: Dura Automotive - Global Fwdg
1780 Pond Run (48326-2752)
PHONE.............................248 299-7500
Lynn Tilton, *CEO*
Martin Becker, *COO*
Franois Stouvenot, *Exec VP*
Nizar Trigui, *Exec VP*
Rick Kelly, *Vice Pres*
EMP: **38** EST: 2005
SQ FT: 15,000
SALES (corp-wide): 708MM **Privately Held**
WEB: www.duraauto.com
SIC: **3714** Motor vehicle parts & accessories

(G-916)
GOLDE AUBURN HILLS LLC (DH)
4000 Pinnacle Ct (48326-1754)
PHONE.............................248 606-1912
Robert Magruder, *Mng Member*
EMP: **58** EST: 2018
SQ FT: 122,000
SALES (est): 14.4MM
SALES (corp-wide): 146.6MM **Privately Held**
WEB: www.cieautomotive.com
SIC: **3531** Roofing equipment

HQ: C.I.E. Automotive Usa, Inc.
 15030 23 Mile Rd
 Shelby Township MI 48315
 734 793-5320

(G-917)
GROUPER WILD LLC (DH) ✪
Also Called: Shiloh Inds Hot Stamping LLC
1780 Pond Run (48326-2752)
PHONE.............................248 299-7500
Carl Beckwith, *Mng Member*
EMP: **0** EST: 2021
SALES (est): 33.8MM
SALES (corp-wide): 1.6B **Privately Held**
SIC: **3465** Automotive stampings
HQ: Grouper Holdings, Llc
 1501 Oxford Rd
 Charlottesville VA 22903
 434 202-0554

(G-918)
GRUPO ANTOLIN NORTH AMER INC (DH)
1700 Atlantic Blvd (48326-1504)
PHONE.............................248 373-1749
Jesus Pascual Santos, *CEO*
Pablo Munoz Baroja, *President*
Ernesto Antolin Arribas, *President*
Mark Kubat, *Vice Pres*
Mara Helena Antoln Raybaud, *Vice Pres*
▲ EMP: **200** EST: 1993
SQ FT: 38,700
SALES (est): 1.1B
SALES (corp-wide): 2.6MM **Privately Held**
WEB: www.grupoantolin.com
SIC: **3714** Motor vehicle engines & parts
HQ: Grupo Antolin Holdco Sa
 Carretera Madrid-Irun (Burgos) (Km 244.8)
 Burgos 09007
 947 477-700

(G-919)
GUARDIAN FABRICATION LLC (HQ)
2300 Harmon Rd (48326-1714)
PHONE.............................248 340-1800
Richard Zoulek, *President*
Eric Woodward, *Treasurer*
Thomas Pastore, *Admin Sec*
EMP: **100** EST: 2015
SALES (est): 107.3MM
SALES (corp-wide): 36.9B **Privately Held**
WEB: www.kochind.com
SIC: **3211** 3231 Plate glass, polished & rough; tempered glass; insulating glass, sealed units; products of purchased glass; mirrored glass
PA: Koch Industries, Inc.
 4111 E 37th St N
 Wichita KS 67220
 316 828-5500

(G-920)
GUARDIAN FABRICATION INC
2300 Harmon Rd (48326-1714)
PHONE.............................248 340-1800
William Davidson, *President*
EMP: **200** EST: 1987
SALES (est): 5.6MM
SALES (corp-wide): 36.9B **Privately Held**
WEB: www.guardian.com
SIC: **3211** Flat glass
HQ: Guardian Industries, Llc
 2300 Harmon Rd
 Auburn Hills MI 48326
 248 340-1800

(G-921)
GUARDIAN GLASS LLC
2300 Harmon Rd (48326-1714)
PHONE.............................248 340-1800
EMP: **55** EST: 2017
SALES (est): 4.8MM
SALES (corp-wide): 36.9B **Privately Held**
WEB: www.guardianglass.com
SIC: **3211** Flat glass
HQ: Guardian Industries, Llc
 2300 Harmon Rd
 Auburn Hills MI 48326
 248 340-1800

GEOGRAPHIC SECTION
Auburn Hills - Oakland County (G-943)

(G-922)
GUARDIAN INDUSTRIES LLC (HQ)
2300 Harmon Rd (48326-1714)
PHONE................................248 340-1800
Ron Vaupel, *President*
Jerry Ray, *Partner*
Lance Altizer, *Vice Pres*
Kent Graham, *Project Mgr*
Thomas Haid, *Prdtn Mgr*
◆ **EMP:** 260 **EST:** 1968
SQ FT: 120,000
SALES (est): 1.5B
SALES (corp-wide): 36.9B **Privately Held**
WEB: www.guardian.com
SIC: 3211 Flat glass
PA: Koch Industries, Inc.
    4111 E 37th St N
    Wichita KS 67220
    316 828-5500

(G-923)
HAOSEN AUTOMATION N AMER INC
691 N Squirrel Rd Ste 288 (48326-2846)
PHONE................................248 556-6398
Yan Feng, *President*
EMP: 5 **EST:** 2016
SALES (est): 466.7K **Privately Held**
WEB: www.haosenusa.com
SIC: 3569 Assembly machines, non-metal-working; liquid automation machinery & equipment

(G-924)
HENNIGES AUTO HOLDINGS INC (DH)
Also Called: Hennigs Automobiles
2750 High Meadow Cir (48326-2796)
PHONE................................248 340-4100
Larry Williams, *President*
Charlie Tan, *Vice Pres*
Lawrence Williams, *Vice Pres*
Chris Eckhardt, *Plant Mgr*
Jim Eichelberger, *Plant Mgr*
EMP: 263 **EST:** 2007
SQ FT: 50,000
SALES (est): 867.6MM **Privately Held**
WEB: www.hennigesautomotive.com
SIC: 3069 2891 3714 Rubber automotive products; adhesives & sealants; motor vehicle electrical equipment

(G-925)
HENNIGES AUTO SLING SYSTEMS N (DH)
Also Called: Metzeler Auto Profile Systems
2750 High Meadow Cir (48326-2796)
PHONE................................248 340-4100
Rob Depierre, *CEO*
Lorenze Williams, *President*
◆ **EMP:** 160 **EST:** 2004
SQ FT: 60,000
SALES (est): 193.6MM **Privately Held**
WEB: www.hennigesautomotive.com
SIC: 3053 2891 3714 Gaskets, packing & sealing devices; adhesives & sealants; motor vehicle parts & accessories

(G-926)
HENNIGES AUTOMOTIVE N AMER INC (DH)
Also Called: Automotive Operations
2750 High Meadow Cir (48326-2796)
PHONE................................248 340-4100
Larry Williams, *President*
▲ **EMP:** 200 **EST:** 1973
SQ FT: 21,000
SALES (est): 154.7MM **Privately Held**
WEB: www.hennigesautomotive.com
SIC: 5013 3053 Automotive supplies & parts; automotive trim; gaskets, packing & sealing devices

(G-927)
HIROTEC AMERICA INC (DH)
3000 High Meadow Cir (48326-2837)
PHONE................................248 836-5100
Katsutoshi Uno, *CEO*
Jim Toeniskoetter, *President*
Paul Demarco, *Exec VP*
Scott Abbate, *Vice Pres*
Sharon Beetham, *Vice Pres*
◆ **EMP:** 300 **EST:** 1988
SQ FT: 215,000
SALES (est): 102.6MM **Privately Held**
WEB: www.hirotecamerica.com
SIC: 3569 Assembly machines, non-metal-working

(G-928)
HIRSCHMANN CAR COMM INC
Also Called: Hirschmann Electronics
1183 Centre Rd (48326-2603)
PHONE................................248 373-7150
Oliver Neil, *President*
James White, *Warehouse Mgr*
Ioan Stan, *Design Engr*
Bjoern Heimberger, *CFO*
Suresh Sainath, *Portfolio Mgr*
▲ **EMP:** 10 **EST:** 2005
SQ FT: 7,050
SALES (est): 6.8MM
SALES (corp-wide): 12.1B **Privately Held**
WEB: www.te.com
SIC: 3679 Electronic circuits
HQ: Hirschmann Car Communication Gmbh
    Stuttgarter Str. 45-51
    Neckartenzlingen BW 72654
    712 714-0

(G-929)
HUNTSMAN CORPORATION
2190 Exec Dr Blvd (48326)
PHONE................................248 322-8682
Pete Panourgias, *Safety Mgr*
Randy Wellman, *Sales Mgr*
Steve Wilaniskis, *Accounts Mgr*
Jon M Huntsman, *Branch Mgr*
Marguerite Johnson, *Manager*
EMP: 4
SALES (corp-wide): 6B **Publicly Held**
WEB: www.huntsman.com
SIC: 2821 Polystyrene resins
PA: Huntsman Corporation
    10003 Woodloch Forest Dr # 260
    The Woodlands TX 77380
    281 719-6000

(G-930)
HUNTSMAN-COOPER LLC
Also Called: Huntsman Polyurethanes
2190 Executive Hills Dr (48326-2947)
PHONE................................248 322-7300
Michael Anderson, *Business Mgr*
Peter De Vries, *Plant Mgr*
Ron Berendt, *Purch Agent*
Todd Bates, *Engineer*
Susan Hanrahan, *Human Res Mgr*
EMP: 38
SALES (corp-wide): 6B **Publicly Held**
SIC: 2821 Plastics materials & resins
HQ: Huntsman-Cooper, L.L.C.
    500 S Huntsman Way
    Salt Lake City UT 84108
    801 584-5700

(G-931)
HUTCHINSON SEAL CORPORATION
Also Called: Hutchinson Seal De Mexico
3201 Cross Creek Pkwy (48326-2765)
PHONE................................248 375-4190
Cedric Duclos, *Principal*
Toni Webster, *Office Mgr*
Gene Harning, *Executive*
EMP: 34
SALES (corp-wide): 4.6B **Publicly Held**
WEB: www.hutchinsonsealing-purchasing.com
SIC: 3069 Jar rings, rubber
HQ: Hutchinson Seal Corporation
    11634 Patton Rd
    Downey CA 90241

(G-932)
HUTCHINSON SEALING SYSTEMS INC (DH)
Also Called: Hutchinson SNC
3201 Cross Creek Pkwy (48326-2765)
PHONE................................248 375-3720
Robert C Hanson, *President*
Nancy Clark, *Purch Dir*
Jeanine Goven, *Senior Buyer*
John Attard, *Treasurer*
Bob Hanson, *VP Sales*
▲ **EMP:** 76 **EST:** 1999
SALES (est): 191MM
SALES (corp-wide): 4.6B **Publicly Held**
WEB: www.hutchinsonsealing-purchasing.com
SIC: 3069 Rubber automotive products
HQ: Hutchinson Corporation
    460 Fuller Ave Ne
    Grand Rapids MI 49503
    616 459-4541

(G-933)
IBC PRECISION INC
2715 Paldan Dr (48326-1827)
PHONE................................248 373-8202
Berry Buschmann, *President*
EMP: 7 **EST:** 1990
SQ FT: 8,800 **Privately Held**
WEB: www.ibcprecision.com
SIC: 3599 3365 Machine shop, jobbing & repair; aluminum foundries

(G-934)
INALFA HOLDING INC
1370 Pacific Dr (48326-1569)
PHONE................................248 371-3060
Frederick L M Welschen, *President*
Mary S Drexler, *Corp Secy*
▲ **EMP:** 15 **EST:** 1997
SALES (est): 1.2MM **Privately Held**
WEB: www.inalfa.com
SIC: 3714 Sun roofs, motor vehicle; products of purchased glass

(G-935)
INALFA ROOF SYSTEMS INC (DH)
Also Called: Inalfa-Hollandia
1370 Pacific Dr (48326-1569)
PHONE................................248 371-3060
Ton Hougen, *President*
Marek Kolarik, *General Mgr*
Michael Ellis, *Regional Mgr*
Michael Smith, *Exec VP*
Mike Smith, *Exec VP*
◆ **EMP:** 409 **EST:** 1984
SQ FT: 125,000
SALES (est): 350.3MM **Privately Held**
WEB: www.inalfa.com
SIC: 3714 Sun roofs, motor vehicle
HQ: Inalfa Roof Systems Group B.V.
    De Amfoor 2
    Oostrum Lb 5807
    478 555-444

(G-936)
INCOE CORPORATION (PA)
2850 High Meadow Cir (48326-2772)
P.O. Box 485, Troy (48099-0485)
PHONE................................248 616-0220
Eric J Seres Jr, *CEO*
Kurt Curtis, *General Mgr*
Courtney Seres, *Vice Pres*
Laura Lettieri, *Purch Agent*
Karla Beard, *Buyer*
EMP: 110 **EST:** 1958
SALES (est): 50.1MM **Privately Held**
WEB: www.incoe.com
SIC: 3544 3823 3499 3625 Dies, plastics forming; temperature instruments: industrial process type; nozzles, spray: aerosol, paint or insecticide; relays & industrial controls; plumbing fixture fittings & trim; manufactured hardware (general)

(G-937)
INCOE INTERNATIONAL INC (HQ)
2850 High Meadow Cir (48326-2772)
PHONE................................248 616-0220
Alex Seres, *Principal*
EMP: 254 **EST:** 1972
SALES (est): 293.4K
SALES (corp-wide): 50.1MM **Privately Held**
WEB: www.incoe.com
SIC: 3544 Dies, plastics forming
PA: Incoe Corporation
    2850 High Meadow Cir
    Auburn Hills MI 48326
    248 616-0220

(G-938)
INDUSTRIAL EXPRMENTAL TECH LLC
Also Called: I E T
3199 Lapeer Rd (48326-1937)
PHONE................................248 371-8000
Todd Hartzell, *General Mgr*
Christopher Karchon, *General Mgr*
Jeff Pickens, *Purchasing*
Karl Snitchler, *QC Mgr*
Dorton Mark, *Engineer*
EMP: 39 **EST:** 1999
SQ FT: 13,000
SALES (est): 7.2MM **Privately Held**
WEB: www.ietintl.com
SIC: 3599 Machine shop, jobbing & repair

(G-939)
INDUSTRIAL MODEL INC
Also Called: IMI
2170 Pontiac Rd (48326-2455)
PHONE................................586 254-0450
Peter H Koppi, *President*
Christian Koppi, *Vice Pres*
Agnes Koppi, *Treasurer*
EMP: 6 **EST:** 1988
SALES (est): 684.5K **Privately Held**
WEB: www.imi88.com
SIC: 3565 3543 Vacuum packaging machinery; industrial patterns

(G-940)
IQ MANUFACTURING LLC
1180 Centre Rd (48326-2602)
PHONE................................586 634-7185
Kelly Vaught, *CEO*
Michael Henderson, *Manager*
Chris Braniecki, *Director*
EMP: 5 **EST:** 2015
SALES (est): 551.7K **Privately Held**
WEB: www.iqmanufacturing.com
SIC: 3544 3599 Industrial molds; forms (molds), for foundry & plastics working machinery; dies & die holders for metal cutting, forming, die casting; crankshafts & camshafts, machining; electrical discharge machining (EDM)

(G-941)
JABIL CIRCUIT MICHIGAN INC
3800 Giddings Rd (48326-1519)
PHONE................................248 292-6000
Stefano Schiavoni, *Vice Pres*
Joe Stodola, *Vice Pres*
Cathleen Stief, *Buyer*
EMP: 105 **EST:** 1995
SALES (est): 4.1MM
SALES (corp-wide): 29.2B **Publicly Held**
WEB: www.jabil.com
SIC: 3672 Printed circuit boards
PA: Jabil Inc.
    10560 Dr Mrtn Lther King
    Saint Petersburg FL 33716
    727 577-9749

(G-942)
JABIL INC
3800 Giddings Rd (48326-1519)
PHONE................................248 292-6000
Marc Leaman, *Principal*
Andrew Priestley, *Vice Pres*
Steve Schultz, *Opers Staff*
Ian Hernandez, *Production*
Nicholas Devonce, *Buyer*
EMP: 502
SQ FT: 173,976
SALES (corp-wide): 29.2B **Publicly Held**
WEB: www.jabil.com
SIC: 3672 Printed circuit boards
PA: Jabil Inc.
    10560 Dr Mrtn Lther King
    Saint Petersburg FL 33716
    727 577-9749

(G-943)
JAMCO MANUFACTURING INC
2960 Auburn Ct (48326-3204)
PHONE................................248 852-1988
Jon D Wolfenberg, *President*
EMP: 8 **EST:** 1983
SQ FT: 17,400
SALES (est): 1.4MM **Privately Held**
WEB: www.jamcomanufacturing.com
SIC: 3451 3594 Screw machine products; motors, pneumatic; motors: hydraulic, fluid power or air

Auburn Hills - Oakland County (G-944)

(G-944)
JO-DAN INTERNATIONAL INC (PA)
Also Called: Jdi Technologies
2704 Paldan Dr (48326-1826)
PHONE.................................248 340-0300
Henry Milan, *President*
Christine Milan, *Corp Secy*
▲ **EMP:** 15 **EST:** 1984
SQ FT: 32,000
SALES (est): 3.3MM *Privately Held*
WEB: www.winlongusa.com
SIC: 5045 3577 5065 Computers, peripherals & software; computer peripheral equipment; input/output equipment, computer; electronic parts & equipment

(G-945)
JOHNSON CONTROLS INC
2875 High Meadow Cir (48326-2773)
PHONE.................................248 276-6000
Joshua Fricke, *Project Mgr*
Ray Cloutire, *Branch Mgr*
EMP: 65
SQ FT: 18,800 *Publicly Held*
WEB: www.johnsoncontrols.com
SIC: 3822 5084 Building services monitoring controls, automatic; industrial machinery & equipment
HQ: Johnson Controls, Inc.
5757 N Green Bay Ave
Glendale WI 53209
800 382-2804

(G-946)
JOYSON SFETY SYSTEMS ACQSTION
Also Called: Restraint Systems Division
2500 Innovation Dr (48326-2611)
PHONE.................................248 373-8040
Timothy Healy, *President*
Gary Vitale, *Facilities Mgr*
Jacquelyn Johnson, *Purchasing*
Jason Lisseman, *Engrg Dir*
Ron Martindale, *Technical Mgr*
EMP: 400
SALES (corp-wide): 7.2B *Privately Held*
WEB: www.joysonsafety.com
SIC: 3714 Motor vehicle parts & accessories
HQ: Joyson Safety Systems Acquisition Llc
2025 Harmon Rd
Auburn Hills MI 48326
248 373-8040

(G-947)
JOYSON SFETY SYSTEMS ACQSTION (HQ)
2025 Harmon Rd (48326-1776)
PHONE.................................248 373-8040
Guido Durrer, *President*
Claus Rudolf, *COO*
Jeff Healy, *Vice Pres*
Jon Hurford, *Vice Pres*
Michael Wild, *Vice Pres*
◆ **EMP:** 2151 **EST:** 2017
SALES (est): 6.8B
SALES (corp-wide): 7.2B *Privately Held*
WEB: www.joysonsafety.com
SIC: 3714 Motor vehicle parts & accessories
PA: Ningbo Joyson Electronic Corp.
No.99, Qingyi Road, High-Tech Zone
Ningbo 31500
574 879-0700

(G-948)
KATCON GLOBAL USA INC (HQ)
Also Called: Katcon USA
2965 Lapeer Rd (48326-1933)
PHONE.................................248 239-1362
Carlos Turner, *President*
Jose De Nigris, *Exec VP*
Vanessa Georges, *Engineer*
Sebastian Jarosinski, *Engineer*
Bob Houtschilt, *VP Bus Dvlpt*
EMP: 64 **EST:** 2019
SALES (est): 11.7MM *Privately Held*
WEB: www.katcon.com
SIC: 3714 Motor vehicle parts & accessories

(G-949)
KATHREIN AUTOMOTIVE N AMER INC
Also Called: Kathrein Automotive USA
1760 Opdyke Ct (48326-2474)
PHONE.................................248 230-2951
EMP: 12
SALES (est): 997.6K
SALES (corp-wide): 44.6B *Privately Held*
SIC: 3694 Engine Electrical Equipment, Nsk
HQ: Continental Advanced Antenna Gmbh
Romerring 1
Hildesheim 31137
512 199-8140

(G-950)
KEEN POINT INTERNATIONAL INC
1377 Atlantic Blvd (48326-1573)
PHONE.................................248 340-8732
▲ **EMP:** 25
SQ FT: 5,000
SALES (est): 2.3MM *Privately Held*
SIC: 3471 Plating/Polishing Service

(G-951)
KEY SAFETY SYSTEMS INC (DH)
Also Called: K S S
2025 Harmon Rd (48326-1776)
P.O. Box 428, Sterling Heights (48311-0428)
PHONE.................................248 373-8040
Jennifer Duke, *President*
Yuxin Tang, *President*
Andrea Victory, *President*
Wang Jianfeng, *Chairman*
Lawrence Buonomo, *Counsel*
▲ **EMP:** 200 **EST:** 1986
SALES (est): 1.6B
SALES (corp-wide): 7.2B *Privately Held*
WEB: www.joysonsafety.com
SIC: 2399 3714 Seat belts, automobile & aircraft; motor vehicle steering systems & parts
HQ: Joyson Safety Systems Acquisition Llc
2025 Harmon Rd
Auburn Hills MI 48326
248 373-8040

(G-952)
KEY SAFETY SYSTEMS INC
2025 Harmon Rd (48326-1776)
PHONE.................................586 726-3905
EMP: 11 **EST:** 2019
SALES (est): 325.3K *Privately Held*
WEB: www.joysonsafety.com
SIC: 2399 Seat belts, automobile & aircraft

(G-953)
KEY SFETY RSTRAINT SYSTEMS INC (DH)
Also Called: K S S
2025 Harmon Rd (48326-1776)
PHONE.................................586 726-3800
Manuel Cepeda, *Superintendent*
Joe Perkins, *Principal*
Jason Bustin, *Purchasing*
Ron Baughn, *QC Mgr*
Florin Dediu, *Controller*
◆ **EMP:** 600 **EST:** 1997
SALES (est): 219.6MM
SALES (corp-wide): 7.2B *Privately Held*
WEB: www.joysonsafety.com
SIC: 3714 2399 Motor vehicle parts & accessories, motor vehicle; seat belts, automobile & aircraft
HQ: Joyson Safety Systems Acquisition Llc
2025 Harmon Rd
Auburn Hills MI 48326
248 373-8040

(G-954)
KNIGHT INDUSTRIES INC
Also Called: Knight Global
2705 Commerce Pkwy (48326-1789)
PHONE.................................248 377-4950
EMP: 6 **EST:** 2014
SALES (est): 372K *Privately Held*
WEB: www.knightglobal.com
SIC: 3559 Sewing machines & hat & zipper making machinery

(G-955)
L & R LIMITED LLC ✪
1801 N Opdyke Rd (48326-2661)
PHONE.................................910 308-7278
Steven Curry, *Mng Member*
Leslee Risi,
Thomas Risi,
EMP: 5 **EST:** 2021
SALES (est): 299K *Privately Held*
SIC: 2299 Broadwoven fabrics: linen, jute, hemp & ramie

(G-956)
LDM TECHNOLOGIES INC
2500 Executive Hills Dr (48326-2983)
PHONE.................................248 858-2800
Julie Brown, *President*
Brad Frederick, *CFO*
Leslie Burns, *Controller*
EMP: 3199 **EST:** 1985
SQ FT: 110,000
SALES (est): 41.7MM *Privately Held*
SIC: 3089 3714 Injection molded finished plastic products; motor vehicle parts & accessories

(G-957)
LECREUSET
4000 Baldwin Rd (48326-1221)
PHONE.................................248 209-7025
EMP: 4 **EST:** 2016
SALES (est): 125.6K *Privately Held*
WEB: www.lecreuset.com
SIC: 5719 5023 3469 Miscellaneous home furnishings; kitchen tools & utensils; appliance parts, porcelain enameled

(G-958)
LJ/HAH HOLDINGS CORPORATION (DH)
2750 High Meadow Cir (48326-2796)
PHONE.................................248 340-4100
Larry Williams, *CEO*
EMP: 113 **EST:** 2010
SALES (est): 867.6MM *Privately Held*
SIC: 2891 3714 Adhesives & sealants; motor vehicle parts & accessories
HQ: Xileh Holding Inc.
2750 High Meadow Cir
Auburn Hills MI 48326
248 340-4100

(G-959)
LOUCA MOLD ARSPC MACHINING INC (PA)
Also Called: Louca Mold & Arospc Machining
1925 Taylor Rd (48326-1770)
PHONE.................................248 391-1616
Kyriacos P Louca, *President*
Randal Bellestri, *President*
Jeff Hutton, *Exec VP*
Kim Bellestri, *Vice Pres*
Brandon Bogusz, *Maint Spvr*
▲ **EMP:** 48 **EST:** 1968
SQ FT: 225,000
SALES (est): 42.2MM *Privately Held*
WEB: www.legacy-ind.com
SIC: 3544 Industrial molds

(G-960)
LUCERNE FORGING INC ✪
40 Corporate Dr (48326-2918)
PHONE.................................248 674-7210
Mary Buchzeiger, *President*
EMP: 9 **EST:** 2021
SALES (est): 438.7K *Privately Held*
SIC: 3462 Iron & steel forgings

(G-961)
LXR BIOTECH LLC (PA)
4225 N Atlantic Blvd (48326-1578)
PHONE.................................248 860-4246
Andrew Krause, *CEO*
Debbie Lucas, *Opers Mgr*
Mark Hervey, *Traffic Mgr*
Gary Krause, *Manager*
John Vanophem, *General Counsel*
EMP: 24 **EST:** 2011
SQ FT: 35,000
SALES (est): 5MM *Privately Held*
WEB: www.lxrbiotech.com
SIC: 2834 Vitamin, nutrient & hematinic preparations for human use

(G-962)
MAGNA ELECTRONICS INC (DH)
2050 Auburn Rd (48326-3100)
PHONE.................................248 729-2643
Carlos Mazzorine, *President*
Paul Bender, *Senior Buyer*
Frank Budzyn, *Engineer*
Jon Conger, *Engineer*
Veronica Luokkala, *Engineer*
▲ **EMP:** 250 **EST:** 1996
SQ FT: 35,000
SALES (est): 152.1MM
SALES (corp-wide): 32.6B *Privately Held*
WEB: www.magna.com
SIC: 3672 3679 Printed circuit boards; electronic circuits
HQ: Magna Mirrors Of America, Inc.
5085 Kraft Ave Se
Grand Rapids MI 49512
616 786-7000

(G-963)
MAGNA ELECTRONICS INC
Magna Elec Technical Ctr
2050 Auburn Rd (48326-3100)
PHONE.................................248 606-0606
John Lou, *Engineer*
Frank Budzyn, *Engineer*
Bruce Klein, *Engineer*
Houa Yang, *Engineer*
Steve Rosenkranz, *Finance Mgr*
EMP: 21
SALES (corp-wide): 32.6B *Privately Held*
WEB: www.magna.com
SIC: 3679 Electronic circuits
HQ: Magna Electronics Inc.
2050 Auburn Rd
Auburn Hills MI 48326

(G-964)
MAGNA SEATING AMERICA INC
Also Called: Magna Seating Auburn Hills
3800 Lapeer Rd (48326-1734)
PHONE.................................248 243-7158
Mike Pando, *General Mgr*
Bruce Anderson, *Engineer*
Michael Gustafson, *Engineer*
Karl Pierre, *Senior Engr*
Stacey Simeone, *Accounts Mgr*
EMP: 100
SALES (corp-wide): 32.6B *Privately Held*
WEB: www.magna.com
SIC: 3714 Motor vehicle parts & accessories
HQ: Magna Seating Of America, Inc.
30020 Cabot Dr
Novi MI 48377

(G-965)
MAHINDRA N AMRCN TCHNCAL CTR I (HQ)
Also Called: Mahindra Automotive N Amer Mfg
275 Rex Blvd (48326-2954)
PHONE.................................248 268-6600
Richard Haas, *President*
Sameer Deo, *General Mgr*
Narayan Shankar, *Exec VP*
Edwin Huang, *Purch Mgr*
Anand Bidre, *Research*
EMP: 130 **EST:** 2013
SQ FT: 31,000
SALES: 47.3MM
SALES (corp-wide): 46.7MM *Privately Held*
WEB: www.mahindra.com
SIC: 3711 3713 8711 Automobile assembly, including specialty automobiles; specialty motor vehicle bodies; mechanical engineering
PA: Mahindra Automotive North America Inc.
275 Rex Blvd
Auburn Hills MI 48326
248 268-6600

(G-966)
MAHINDRA TRACTOR ASSEMBLY INC (DH)
Also Called: Mahindra Genze
275 Rex Blvd (48326-2954)
PHONE.................................650 779-5180
Vish Palekar, *CEO*
Deven Kataria, *COO*
Sean Lanoie, *Opers Staff*
Sangeeta Laud, *Treasurer*

Holly Brinkman, *Manager*
▲ **EMP:** 30 **EST:** 2013
SALES (est): 11.2MM **Privately Held**
WEB: www.mahindrausa.com
SIC: 3751 Motor scooters & parts

(G-967)
MANRISA
2965 Lapeer Rd (48326-1933)
PHONE 248 364-4415
Jesse Lopez, *Principal*
EMP: 6 **EST:** 2009
SALES (est): 83.2K **Privately Held**
SIC: 3564 Blowers & fans

(G-968)
MARTINREA JONESVILLE LLC
Also Called: Martinrea Featherstone
2325 Featherstone Rd (48326-2808)
PHONE 248 630-7730
EMP: 6
SALES (corp-wide): 2.8B **Privately Held**
SIC: 3465 Mfg Automotive Stampings
HQ: Martinrea Jonesville Llc
260 Gaige St
Jonesville MI 49250

(G-969)
MARTINREA METAL INDUSTRIES INC (HQ)
2100 N Opdyke Rd (48326-2433)
PHONE 248 392-9700
Pat D Eramo, *President*
Robert Fairchild, *Exec VP*
Larry Paine, *Vice Pres*
Stuart Fraser, *VP Opers*
Marlene Crabtree, *Materials Mgr*
EMP: 75 **EST:** 2006
SQ FT: 55,000
SALES (est): 112.6MM
SALES (corp-wide): 2.5B **Privately Held**
WEB: www.martinrea.com
SIC: 3714 Motor vehicle parts & accessories
PA: Martinrea International Inc
3210 Langstaff Rd
Vaughan ON
416 749-0314

(G-970)
MATRIX MTLCRAFT LLP A LTD PRTN (PA)
68 S Squirrel Rd (48326-3282)
PHONE 248 724-1800
Anthony Carmen, *Partner*
Nicholas A Salvatore, *Partner*
EMP: 8 **EST:** 2016
SALES (est): 5MM **Privately Held**
WEB: www.tecinternational.com
SIC: 7389 1799 3479 7699 Metal cutting services; welding on site; coating of metals & formed products; industrial equipment services

(G-971)
MAYCO INTERNATIONAL LLC
Also Called: Njt Enterprises LLC
1020 Doris Rd (48326-2613)
P.O. Box 180149, Utica (48318-0149)
PHONE 586 803-6000
Allen L Grajek, *CFO*
EMP: 30 **Privately Held**
WEB: www.maycointernational.com
SIC: 3089 Injection molding of plastics
PA: Mayco International Llc
42400 Merrill Rd
Sterling Heights MI 48314

(G-972)
MELLO MEATS INC (PA)
Also Called: Kubisch Sausage
270 Rex Blvd (48326-3105)
PHONE 800 852-5019
Micheal Delly, *CEO*
EMP: 10 **EST:** 1936
SQ FT: 12,000
SALES (est): 2.1MM **Privately Held**
WEB: www.kubischsausage.com
SIC: 2013 Sausages from purchased meat; smoked meats from purchased meat

(G-973)
MONTAPLAST NORTH AMERICA INC
1849 Pond Run (48326-2769)
PHONE 248 353-5553
Mike Reed, *Opers Staff*
Paul Schappert, *Mfg Staff*
Scott Cherry, *Buyer*
Carl Scherfner, *Buyer*
Gary Sharp, *Technical Mgr*
EMP: 24
SALES (corp-wide): 1.3B **Privately Held**
SIC: 3089 3714 Plastic processing; motor vehicle parts & accessories
HQ: Montaplast Of North America, Inc.
2011 Hoover Blvd
Frankfort KY 40601

(G-974)
MORGAN MACHINING LLC
2760 Auburn Rd (48326-3114)
PHONE 248 293-3277
Patricia Mobley,
EMP: 13 **EST:** 2005
SALES (est): 1MM **Privately Held**
WEB: www.morganmachining.com
SIC: 3599 Machine shop, jobbing & repair

(G-975)
MORRELL INCORPORATED (PA)
3333 Bald Mountain Rd (48326-1808)
PHONE 248 373-1600
Steven L Tallman, *President*
James E Cook, *Vice Pres*
Russ Martin, *Vice Pres*
Douglas Boddy, *Engineer*
Robert Pitzer, *Engineer*
◆ **EMP:** 100
SQ FT: 70,000
SALES (est): 96.6MM **Privately Held**
WEB: www.morrell-group.com
SIC: 5084 5065 3621 3643 Hydraulic systems equipment & supplies; electronic parts; motors & generators; power line cable; metal finishing equipment for plating, etc.; nonferrous wiredrawing & insulating

(G-976)
MUBEA INC
1701 Harmon Rd (48326-1549)
PHONE 248 393-9600
Thomas Muhr, *President*
Ronnie Towe, *Maint Spvr*
David Johns, *QC Mgr*
Troy Abbott, *Sales Staff*
Angel Marinos, *Marketing Staff*
EMP: 5
SALES (corp-wide): 2.5B **Privately Held**
WEB: www.mubea-discsprings.com
SIC: 3089 Automotive parts, plastic
HQ: Mubea, Inc.
6800 Industrial Rd
Florence KY 41042
859 746-5300

(G-977)
MULTI PRECISION INTL LLC
2635 Paldan Dr (48326-1825)
PHONE 248 373-3330
EMP: 9 **EST:** 2019
SALES (est): 255.2K **Privately Held**
WEB: www.multi-precision.com
SIC: 3544 Special dies & tools

(G-978)
MULTI-PRECISION DETAIL INC
Also Called: M P D
2635 Paldan Dr (48326-1825)
PHONE 248 373-3330
Jeffrey Dean, *CEO*
Michael Dean, *President*
Jerry Tate, *QC Dir*
Richard Barnes, *Director*
Kevin McClellan, *Director*
EMP: 25 **EST:** 1968
SQ FT: 18,000
SALES (est): 4.4MM **Privately Held**
WEB: www.multi-precision.com
SIC: 3544 Special dies & tools

(G-979)
NATIONAL ORDANACE AUTO MFG LLC
2900 Auburn Ct (48326-3204)
PHONE 248 853-8822
Christopher Boes, *Mng Member*
Chris Boes,
EMP: 6 **EST:** 2011
SALES (est): 501.7K **Privately Held**
WEB: www.noamllc.com
SIC: 3441 Fabricated structural metal

(G-980)
NATIONAL ORDNANCE AUTO MFG LLC
2900 Auburn Ct (48326-3204)
PHONE 248 853-8822
Chris Boes, *Mng Member*
EMP: 7 **EST:** 1979
SQ FT: 12,000
SALES (est): 974.6K **Privately Held**
WEB: www.noamllc.com
SIC: 3444 3499 3714 Sheet metalwork; aerosol valves, metal; motor vehicle parts & accessories

(G-981)
NEW PIONEER CERAMICS LLC
3097 Lincolnview St (48326-3240)
PHONE 248 200-9893
Jeffrey Campbell, *Principal*
EMP: 4 **EST:** 2015
SALES (est): 55.6K **Privately Held**
SIC: 3269 Pottery products

(G-982)
NEXTEER AUTOMOTIVE CORPORATION (DH)
1272 Doris Rd (48326-2617)
PHONE 248 340-8200
Michael Richardson, *President*
Mike Kettler, *Opers Mgr*
Eric Hunter, *Maint Spvr*
Gary Weiss, *Mfg Staff*
Saad Jamoua, *Engrg Dir*
◆ **EMP:** 3500 **EST:** 2008
SALES (est): 870.2MM **Privately Held**
WEB: www.nexteer.com
SIC: 3714 Motor vehicle parts & accessories

(G-983)
NIDEC MOTORS & ACTUATORS (USA)
1800 Opdyke Ct (48326-2475)
PHONE 248 340-9977
Robert Hans-Kalb, *Branch Mgr*
EMP: 5 **Privately Held**
WEB: www.nidec-ma.de
SIC: 3621 Motors & generators
HQ: Nidec Motors & Actuators
133 B Rue De L Universite
Paris
153 579-236

(G-984)
NORMA MICHIGAN INC (HQ)
Also Called: Norma Americas
2430 E Walton Blvd (48326-1956)
PHONE 248 373-4300
Werner Deggim, *CEO*
Timothy Jones, *President*
John Stephenson, *COO*
Mark Behe, *Vice Pres*
Clawson Cannon, *Vice Pres*
▲ **EMP:** 164 **EST:** 1974
SQ FT: 4,000
SALES (est): 101.2MM
SALES (corp-wide): 1.1B **Privately Held**
WEB: www.normagroup.com
SIC: 3498 3714 3713 3429 Couplings, pipe: fabricated from purchased pipe; motor vehicle parts & accessories; truck & bus bodies; manufactured hardware (general)
PA: Norma Group Se
Edisonstr. 4
Maintal HE 63477
618 140-30

(G-985)
NORTH AMERICAN ASSEMBLY LLC
4325 Giddings Rd (48326-1532)
PHONE 248 335-6702
Thomas Papke, *Engineer*
Tom Schaenzer, *Sales Staff*
EMP: 50 **EST:** 1999
SQ FT: 54,000
SALES (est): 8MM **Privately Held**
WEB: www.naassembly.com
SIC: 3089 Automotive parts, plastic

(G-986)
NORTH AMERICAN MOLD LLC (PA)
4345 Giddings Rd (48326-1532)
PHONE 248 335-6702
Denise Schaenzer, *CEO*
Thomas Schaenzer,
EMP: 25 **EST:** 2017
SQ FT: 14,000
SALES (est): 500K **Privately Held**
WEB: www.naassembly.com
SIC: 3089 Automotive parts, plastic

(G-987)
NORTHERN SIGN CO
2181 E Walton Blvd # 100 (48326-1972)
PHONE 248 333-7733
EMP: 7 **EST:** 2020
SALES (est): 776.5K **Privately Held**
WEB: www.northernsign.com
SIC: 3993 Signs & advertising specialties

(G-988)
NOVACEUTICALS LLC
3201 University Dr # 250 (48326-2394)
PHONE 248 309-3402
Dawn Hanna,
EMP: 4
SQ FT: 1,000
SALES (est): 274.2K **Privately Held**
SIC: 3295 Minerals, ground or otherwise treated

(G-989)
OLD DURA INC (PA)
1780 Pond Run (48326-2752)
PHONE 248 299-7500
Lynn Tilton, *CEO*
Martin Becker, *Exec VP*
Mario Buttino, *Exec VP*
Jim Gregory, *Exec VP*
Francois Stouvenot, *Exec VP*
▲ **EMP:** 1 **EST:** 1994
SALES (est): 3MM **Privately Held**
WEB: www.duraauto.com
SIC: 3714 Motor vehicle brake systems & parts

(G-990)
ORION TEST SYSTEMS INC
Also Called: Orion Test Systems & Engrg
4260 Giddings Rd (48326-1529)
PHONE 248 373-9097
Robert Pilat, *President*
Anthony Zainea, *Manager*
Kurt Zdanio, *IT/INT Sup*
▲ **EMP:** 51 **EST:** 2004
SQ FT: 30,000
SALES (est): 6.7MM **Privately Held**
WEB: www.orionmeas.com
SIC: 3825 3861 Digital test equipment, electronic & electrical circuits; photo reconnaissance systems

(G-991)
OXUS AMERICA INC
2046 Brown Rd (48326-1702)
PHONE 248 475-0925
Gary Abusamra, *CEO*
Ryan Lenarcic, *QC Mgr*
Andy Voto, *Chief Engr*
Bud Thompson, *Project Engr*
Tim Hatt, *Marketing Staff*
▲ **EMP:** 80 **EST:** 2010
SQ FT: 13,612
SALES (est): 8MM **Privately Held**
WEB: www.oxusamerica.com
SIC: 3841 Surgical & medical instruments

Auburn Hills - Oakland County (G-992)

(G-992)
PALO ALTO MANUFACTURING LLC
2700 Auburn Ct (48326-3202)
PHONE..................248 266-3669
Sue Kwon, *Marketing Staff*
Donald Tinsley,
EMP: 4
SALES (est): 161.9K Privately Held
SIC: 3999 Manufacturing industries

(G-993)
PARAVIS INDUSTRIES INC
Also Called: CNC MACHINING
1597 Atlantic Blvd (48326-1501)
PHONE..................248 393-2300
Glenn M Charest, *President*
Robert Allor, *Senior Mgr*
EMP: 40 EST: 1979
SQ FT: 27,000
SALES: 4.9MM Privately Held
SIC: 3599 3544 Machine shop, jobbing & repair; special dies, tools, jigs & fixtures; special dies & tools

(G-994)
PCM US STEERING HOLDING LLC
1272 Doris Rd (48326-2617)
PHONE..................313 556-5000
EMP: 36 EST: 2009
SALES (est): 8.1MM Privately Held
WEB: www.nexteer.com
SIC: 3711 3714 Motor vehicles & car bodies; motor vehicle parts & accessories
HQ: Nexteer Automotive Group Limited
  C/O Maples Corporate Services Limited
  George Town GR CAYMAN

(G-995)
PENINSULA PLASTICS COMPANY INC (PA)
2800 Auburn Ct (48326-3203)
PHONE..................248 852-3731
Ryan Victory, *President*
Richard Jositas, *Chairman*
Mitchell Kelps, *Chief*
Duane O'brien, *Mfg Staff*
Jessica Davis, *Production*
EMP: 83 EST: 1980
SQ FT: 40,000
SALES (est): 15MM Privately Held
WEB: www.peninsulaplastics.com
SIC: 3089 Trays, plastic; plastic containers, except foam

(G-996)
PIERBURG PUMP TECH US LLC
975 S Opdyke Rd Ste 100 (48326-3437)
PHONE..................864 688-1322
Rene Gansauga, *Mng Member*
Stefano Fiorini, *Senior Mgr*
EMP: 87
SALES (corp-wide): 6.9B Privately Held
SIC: 3089 Automotive parts, plastic
HQ: Pierburg Pump Technology Us, Llc
  5 Southchase Ct
  Fountain Inn SC 29644

(G-997)
PIERBURG US LLC
975 S Opdyke Rd Ste 100 (48326-3437)
PHONE..................864 688-1322
Brandon Woltz, *Engineer*
Rene Gansauga, *Mng Member*
EMP: 121
SALES (corp-wide): 6.9B Privately Held
WEB: www.rheinmetall-automotive.com
SIC: 3714 Motor vehicle engines & parts
HQ: Pierburg Us, Llc
  5 Southchase Ct
  Fountain Inn SC 29644

(G-998)
PLASTIC ENGRG TCHNCAL SVCS INC
Also Called: P E T S
4141 Luella Ln (48326-1576)
PHONE..................248 373-0800
Patrick A Tooman, *President*
▲ EMP: 24 EST: 1984
SQ FT: 42,000
SALES (est): 3.5MM Privately Held
WEB: www.petsgroupintl.com
SIC: 3544 Industrial molds

(G-999)
PLASTICS PLUS INC (PA)
4237 N Atlantic Blvd (48326-1578)
PHONE..................800 975-8694
Roger Ziemba, *President*
Thomas Paul, *Opers Mgr*
Tom Paul, *Opers Mgr*
Linda McCormick, *Regl Sales Mgr*
Bill Palasieski, *Sales Staff*
▲ EMP: 21 EST: 1990
SALES (est): 9.9MM Privately Held
WEB: www.plasplus.com
SIC: 2821 Plastics materials & resins

(G-1000)
PONCRAFT DOOR CO INC
2005 Pontiac Rd (48326-2481)
PHONE..................248 373-6060
Kevin French, *President*
Dave Hughes, *General Mgr*
EMP: 15 EST: 1965
SQ FT: 30,000
SALES (est): 1.6MM Privately Held
WEB: www.poncraft.com
SIC: 3089 Doors, folding: plastic or plastic coated fabric

(G-1001)
PR39 INDUSTRIES LLC
2005 Pontiac Rd (48326-2481)
PHONE..................248 481-8512
Brandon Whitney, *Principal*
EMP: 9 EST: 2015
SALES (est): 782.3K Privately Held
WEB: www.pr39industries.com
SIC: 3563 Air & gas compressors

(G-1002)
PRECISION BORING AND MACHINE
2238 E Walton Blvd (48326-1952)
PHONE..................248 371-9140
Robert Fuller, *President*
Lisa Fuller, *Vice Pres*
EMP: 7 EST: 1993
SQ FT: 10,000
SALES (est): 818.3K Privately Held
WEB: www.limonfna.com
SIC: 3599 Machine shop, jobbing & repair

(G-1003)
PRECISION MASTERS INC
Also Called: Maple Mold Technologies
2441 N Opdyke Rd (48326-2442)
PHONE..................248 648-8071
Jeff Mansour, *Accounts Mgr*
Doug Bachan, *Branch Mgr*
Eric Niss, *Manager*
Mark Muniz, *Supervisor*
EMP: 21
SALES (corp-wide): 12.3MM Privately Held
WEB: www.maplemoldtechnologies.com
SIC: 3089 Injection molding of plastics
PA: Precision Masters Inc.
  1985 Northfield Dr
  Rochester Hills MI 48309
  248 853-0308

(G-1004)
PRESS PLAY LLC
2123 Willot Rd (48326-2669)
PHONE..................248 802-3837
Eric Mendieta, *Principal*
EMP: 9 EST: 2010
SALES (est): 413.2K Privately Held
SIC: 2741 Miscellaneous publishing

(G-1005)
PROTEAN ELECTRIC INC
1700 Harmon Rd Ste 3 (48326-1588)
PHONE..................248 504-4940
EMP: 90 EST: 2010
SALES (est): 10.3MM Privately Held
SIC: 3694 Mfg In-Wheel Electric Drive System For Automobiles & Other Vehicles
PA: Protean Holdings Corp
  1700 Harmon Rd Ste 3
  Auburn Hills MI 48326

(G-1006)
PROTEAN HOLDINGS CORP (PA)
1700 Harmon Rd Ste 3 (48326-1588)
PHONE..................248 504-4940
EMP: 4
SALES (est): 10.3MM Privately Held
SIC: 3694 Mfg In-Wheel Electric Drive System For Automobiles & Other Vehicles

(G-1007)
PROVISIONS PRINT LLC
196 Oakmont (48326-3359)
PHONE..................248 214-1766
Robert Ruple, *Principal*
Gil Martinez, *Purchasing*
EMP: 5 EST: 2016
SALES (est): 101.5K Privately Held
SIC: 2752 Commercial printing, lithographic

(G-1008)
PUNATI CHEMICAL CORP
1160 N Opdyke Rd (48326-2645)
PHONE..................248 276-0101
Bernard Shandler, *President*
Jeffrey J Shandler, *President*
Zach Shandler, *Business Mgr*
▼ EMP: 58 EST: 1978
SQ FT: 36,000
SALES (est): 3.9MM Privately Held
WEB: www.punati.com
SIC: 2842 Industrial plant disinfectants or deodorants

(G-1009)
QUANTUM DIGITAL GROUP LLC
1681 Harmon Rd (48326-1547)
PHONE..................888 408-3199
Lee Skandalaris, *Principal*
EMP: 4 EST: 2013
SALES (est): 236.6K Privately Held
WEB: www.qdvllc.com
SIC: 3651 Household audio & video equipment

(G-1010)
QUANTUM MANUFACTURING
2990 Lapeer Rd (48326-1932)
PHONE..................248 690-9410
EMP: 9 EST: 2019
SALES (est): 607.7K Privately Held
WEB: www.quantum-manufacturing.com
SIC: 3572 Computer storage devices

(G-1011)
R G RAY CORPORATION
2430 E Walton Blvd (48326-1956)
PHONE..................248 373-4300
Daniel J Mitrano, *President*
Tim Jones, *Vice Pres*
Durg Kumar, *Admin Sec*
▲ EMP: 92 EST: 1972
SQ FT: 125,000
SALES (est): 5.5MM
SALES (corp-wide): 1.1B Privately Held
WEB: www.normaamericasds.com
SIC: 3429 Clamps, metal
HQ: Norma Group Holding Gmbh
  Edisonstr. 4
  Maintal HE 63477
  618 140-30

(G-1012)
RALCO INDUSTRIES INC (PA)
1025 Doris Rd (48326-2614)
PHONE..................248 853-3200
Tom Gitter, *CEO*
Jim Piper, *President*
Dietrich Mackel, *Purchasing*
Paul C Delong, *CFO*
Stacey Lazor, *Human Res Mgr*
EMP: 88 EST: 1970
SALES (est): 19.6MM Privately Held
WEB: www.ralcoind.com
SIC: 3714 3544 Motor vehicle parts & accessories; special dies & tools

(G-1013)
RALCO INDUSTRIES INC
1025 Doris Rd (48326-2614)
PHONE..................248 853-3200
EMP: 20
SALES (corp-wide): 30.7MM Privately Held
SIC: 3714 3544 Motor Vehicle Parts And Accessories

PA: Ralco Industries, Inc.
  2720 Auburn Ct
  Auburn Hills MI 48326
  248 853-3200

(G-1014)
RALCO INDUSTRIES INC
2860 Auburn Ct (48326-3203)
PHONE..................248 853-3200
Tom Gitter, *Branch Mgr*
EMP: 12
SALES (corp-wide): 19.6MM Privately Held
WEB: www.ralcoind.com
SIC: 3465 Automotive stampings
PA: Ralco Industries, Inc.
  1025 Doris Rd
  Auburn Hills MI 48326
  248 853-3200

(G-1015)
RAYCE AMERICAS INC
2600 Auburn Rd Ste 120 (48326-3188)
PHONE..................248 537-3159
Hans-Juergen Lesser, *CEO*
EMP: 25 EST: 2009
SALES (est): 946.4K Privately Held
SALES (corp-wide): 177.9K Privately Held
WEB: www.araymond.com
SIC: 3399 Metal fasteners
PA: A Raymond Et Compagnie
  113 Cours Berriat
  Grenoble
  476 210-233

(G-1016)
RE-SOL LLC
1771 Harmon Rd Ste 150 (48326-1587)
PHONE..................248 270-7777
John Vaughn, *VP Opers*
Peter Kaub, *Mng Member*
EMP: 11 EST: 2003
SALES (est): 2.6MM Privately Held
WEB: www.re-sol.com
SIC: 3824 Fluid meters & counting devices

(G-1017)
REESE INSPECTION SERVICES LLC
3321 Lapeer Rd W (48326-1725)
PHONE..................248 481-3598
Jonathan Reese,
EMP: 15 EST: 2013
SALES (est): 540.6K Privately Held
WEB: www.reeseinspection.com
SIC: 8734 8744 3569 Product certification, safety or performance; facilities support services; robots, assembly line: industrial & commercial

(G-1018)
REPLY INC (DH)
691 N Squirrel Rd Ste 202 (48326-2871)
PHONE..................248 686-2481
Gianluca Di Stefano, *President*
Naaznin Tootla, *Consultant*
EMP: 152 EST: 2012
SALES (est): 50MM Privately Held
WEB: www.reply.com
SIC: 8748 7373 3571 Business consulting; computer integrated systems design; computers, digital, analog or hybrid
HQ: Logistics Reply Srl
  Via Castellanza 11
  Milano MI 20151
  025 357-61

(G-1019)
RIDER REPORT MAGAZINE
3906 Baldwin Rd (48321-7700)
PHONE..................248 854-8460
Mark Edward, *Owner*
EMP: 4 EST: 2012
SALES (est): 193.5K Privately Held
SIC: 2721 Magazines: publishing only, not printed on site

(G-1020)
RIGAKU INNOVATIVE TECH INC
1900 Taylor Rd (48326-1740)
PHONE..................248 232-6400
John McGill, *President*
Nick Grupido, *Vice Pres*
Licai Jiang, *Vice Pres*
Scott Bendle, *Opers Staff*

GEOGRAPHIC SECTION

Auburn Hills - Oakland County (G-1045)

Robin Markham, *Opers Staff*
EMP: 200 **EST:** 1985
SQ FT: 57,000
SALES (est): 24.6MM **Privately Held**
WEB: www.rigakuoptics.com
SIC: 3826 Analytical instruments
HQ: Rigaku Americas Corporation
  9009 New Trails Dr
  The Woodlands TX 77381
  281 362-2300

(G-1021)
RITE MARK STAMP COMPANY
Also Called: Clean Cut Divison
4141 N Atlantic Blvd (48326-1570)
PHONE 248 391-7600
Donald H Bailey, *President*
EMP: 14 **EST:** 1965
SQ FT: 70,000
SALES (est): 195.7K **Privately Held**
WEB: www.steelstamp.com
SIC: 3953 3599 Marking devices; machine shop, jobbing & repair

(G-1022)
ROBERT CARMICHAEL
1000 Chrysler Dr (48326-2766)
PHONE 248 576-5741
Robert Carmichael, *Principal*
EMP: 7 **EST:** 2007
SALES (est): 318.5K **Privately Held**
SIC: 3711 Motor vehicles & car bodies

(G-1023)
RTR ALPHA INC
Also Called: Allegra Marketing Print Signs
2285 N Opdyke Rd Ste G (48326-2468)
PHONE 248 377-4060
Michael Wysocki, *President*
EMP: 10 **EST:** 2010
SALES (est): 330K **Privately Held**
WEB: www.allegramarketingprint.com
SIC: 8742 7311 2752 Marketing consulting services; advertising agencies; commercial printing, offset

(G-1024)
RUBBER & PLASTICS CO (PA)
3650 Lapeer Rd (48326-1730)
PHONE 248 370-0700
Lawrence V Harding, *President*
M E Harding, *Vice Pres*
EMP: 13 **EST:** 1951
SQ FT: 15,000
SALES (est): 2.6MM **Privately Held**
WEB: www.rubberandplastics.com
SIC: 2821 Plastics materials & resins

(G-1025)
SAMSUNG SDI AMERICA INC (HQ)
4121 N Atlantic Blvd (48326-1570)
PHONE 408 544-4470
Kikwon Yoon, *CEO*
Young Joon Gil, *President*
Duck Yun Kim, *President*
Chang Baek, *General Mgr*
Jeong Hwan Seo, *Principal*
▼ **EMP:** 14 **EST:** 1988
SALES (est): 32.7MM **Privately Held**
WEB: www.samsungsdi.com
SIC: 3577 5045 Computer peripheral equipment; computer peripheral equipment

(G-1026)
SANHUA AUTOMOTIVE USA INC (DH)
3729 Auburn Rd (48326-3324)
PHONE 248 244-8870
Tiger Lu, *President*
Joanna Vhanz, *Principal*
▲ **EMP:** 4 **EST:** 2011
SALES (est): 1.6MM **Privately Held**
WEB: www.sanhuaautomotive.com
SIC: 3714 Motor vehicle parts & accessories

(G-1027)
SANIONES LLC
2660 Auburn Rd Ste 700 (48326-3186)
PHONE 833 726-4111
Yousif Khamis, *Mng Member*
EMP: 5 **EST:** 2020

SALES (est): 229.7K **Privately Held**
SIC: 2842 Sanitation preparations, disinfectants & deodorants

(G-1028)
SAUTER NORTH AMERICA INC
1116 Centre Rd (48326-2602)
PHONE 734 207-0900
Thomas E Gross, *CEO*
Markus Feder, *Senior Mgr*
Steffen Schlotterbeck, *Technician*
Anatoli Schotter, *Technician*
EMP: 1 **EST:** 2015
SQ FT: 75,000
SALES (est): 1.9MM
SALES (corp-wide): 889.5K **Privately Held**
WEB: www.sautertools.com
SIC: 3541 Drilling machine tools (metal cutting)
HQ: Sauter Feinmechanik Gmbh
  Carl-Zeiss-Str. 7
  Metzingen BW 72555
  712 392-60

(G-1029)
SBS CORP
2700 Auburn Ct (48326-3202)
PHONE 248 844-8200
Jeff Smith, *President*
EMP: 7 **EST:** 2020
SALES (est): 299.2K **Privately Held**
SIC: 3443 Fabricated plate work (boiler shop)

(G-1030)
SC THREAD CUTTING TOOLS INC
Also Called: SC Tools
1920 Opdyke Ct Ste 200 (48326-2479)
PHONE 248 365-4044
Lermit Diaz, *President*
EMP: 4 **EST:** 1997
SQ FT: 1,100
SALES (est): 1.2MM **Privately Held**
WEB: www.sctools.online
SIC: 3545 Cutting tools for machine tools

(G-1031)
SHANNON PRECISION FASTENER LLC
Purks Rd Mfg Plant
4425 Purks Rd (48326-1749)
PHONE 248 589-9670
Ed Lumm, *CEO*
EMP: 60
SALES (corp-wide): 125MM **Privately Held**
WEB: www.shannonpf.com
SIC: 3452 Bolts, nuts, rivets & washers
PA: Shannon Precision Fastener, Llc
  31600 Stephenson Hwy
  Madison Heights MI 48071
  248 589-9670

(G-1032)
SHIELD MATERIAL HANDLING INC
4280 N Atlantic Blvd (48326-1578)
PHONE 248 418-0986
John Grancaric, *CEO*
Sul Lee, *Ch of Bd*
Ben An, *CFO*
EMP: 67 **EST:** 2011
SALES (est): 5MM **Privately Held**
WEB: www.smhlogistics.com
SIC: 3669 4231 2542 Transportation signaling devices; trucking terminal facilities; racks, merchandise display or storage: except wood

(G-1033)
SHURE STAR LLC
2498 Commercial Dr (48326-2410)
PHONE 248 365-4382
Mark Vandellen, *Mng Member*
Bruce R Bacon,
EMP: 25 **EST:** 2011
SALES (est): 2.7MM **Privately Held**
WEB: www.shurestar.com
SIC: 3442 Window & door frames

(G-1034)
SL AMERICA CORPORATION
4375 Giddings Rd (48326-1532)
PHONE 586 731-8511
Mike Stringfield, *Mfg Mgr*
Billy Frank, *Buyer*
Kevin Jones, *Buyer*
Lalit Jain, *Engineer*
Donghun Kim, *Engineer*
EMP: 57 **Privately Held**
WEB: www.sl-america.com
SIC: 3714 Motor vehicle parts & accessories
HQ: Sl America Corporation
  312 Frank L Diggs Dr
  Clinton TN 37716

(G-1035)
SOLARONICS INC
3720 Lapeer Rd (48326-1732)
P.O. Box 80217, Rochester (48308-0217)
PHONE 248 651-5333
Richard F Rush Jr, *CEO*
Richard F Rush III, *COO*
Robert C Rush, *Vice Pres*
Jim Herr, *Project Mgr*
Robert O'Leary III, *CFO*
▲ **EMP:** 35 **EST:** 1962
SQ FT: 50,000
SALES (est): 5.6MM **Privately Held**
WEB: www.solaronicsusa.com
SIC: 3567 3589 3433 Radiant heating systems, industrial process; cooking equipment, commercial; heating equipment, except electric

(G-1036)
ST ONGE MASONRY LLC
4200 N Squirrel Rd (48326-1832)
PHONE 248 709-8161
Daniel St Onge,
EMP: 6 **EST:** 2014
SALES (est): 132.6K **Privately Held**
WEB: www.stongemasonrymi.com
SIC: 1741 3259 Masonry & other stonework; clay chimney products

(G-1037)
STACKPOLE PWRTRN INTL USA LLC
Also Called: Stackpole International
3201 University Dr # 350 (48326-2394)
PHONE 248 481-4600
Peter Ballantyne, *CEO*
Stuart Holtshouser, *Vice Pres*
Robert Mooy, *Vice Pres*
Kelly Dickinson, *Manager*
Vincent Williams, *Manager*
EMP: 6 **EST:** 2013
SALES (est): 905.5K **Privately Held**
WEB: www.stackpole.com
SIC: 3714 Motor vehicle parts & accessories

(G-1038)
STEGNER CONTROLS LLC
3333 Bald Mountain Rd (48326-1808)
PHONE 248 904-0400
EMP: 28 **EST:** 2002
SALES (est): 2.6MM **Privately Held**
WEB: www.morrell-group.com
SIC: 3625 Control equipment, electric

(G-1039)
STRATTEC POWER ACCESS LLC (HQ)
2998 Dutton Rd (48326-1864)
PHONE 248 649-9742
Richard Messina, *Mng Member*
Tom Scaife, *Mng Member*
Rainer Goelz,
Patrick J Hansen,
Harold M Stratton II,
▲ **EMP:** 34 **EST:** 2008
SALES (est): 10.2MM **Publicly Held**
WEB: www.strattec.com
SIC: 2396 Automotive & apparel trimmings

(G-1040)
STRATTEC SECURITY CORPORATION
2998 Dutton Rd (48326-1864)
PHONE 248 649-9742
Dennis Kazmierski, *Manager*
Kevin Habel, *Analyst*

EMP: 5 **Publicly Held**
WEB: www.strattec.com
SIC: 3429 3714 Locks or lock sets; keys & key blanks; motor vehicle parts & accessories
PA: Strattec Security Corporation
  3333 W Good Hope Rd
  Milwaukee WI 53209

(G-1041)
SUMMIT INDUSTRIAL SERVICES LLC
107 S Vista (48326-1447)
PHONE 248 762-0982
Jeff Benacquisto, *Principal*
EMP: 20 **EST:** 2017
SALES (est): 5.9MM **Privately Held**
WEB: www.summit.us
SIC: 2813 Industrial gases

(G-1042)
SURE SOLUTIONS CORPORATION
40 Corporate Dr (48326-2918)
PHONE 248 674-7210
Mary Buchzeiger, *CEO*
▲ **EMP:** 1 **EST:** 2011
SQ FT: 3,500
SALES (est): 14.8MM **Privately Held**
SIC: 3559 Automotive related machinery

(G-1043)
TAJCO NORTH AMERICA INC
2851 High Meadow Cir # 19 (48326-2792)
PHONE 248 418-7550
Rolf Ebbesen, *CEO*
Jakob Bonde Jessen, *COO*
Kenneth Bergstrom Andersen, *CFO*
Steve Widdett, *Ch Credit Ofcr*
Henri Kirchof, *CTO*
▲ **EMP:** 7 **EST:** 2009
SALES (est): 3.4MM
SALES (corp-wide): 108.7MM **Privately Held**
WEB: www.tajco-group.com
SIC: 3465 Body parts, automobile: stamped metal
HQ: Tajco A/S
  Jens Ravns Vej 11a
  Vejle 7100
  753 214-11

(G-1044)
TAKATA AMERICAS (DH)
Also Called: Tk Holdings
2500 Takata Dr Ste 300 (48326-2636)
PHONE 336 547-1600
Jonathan Halas, *Partner*
Dan Rose, *Technology*
Kirk Morris, *Officer*
EMP: 16832 **EST:** 2003
SQ FT: 600
SALES (est): 185.5MM
SALES (corp-wide): 7.2B **Privately Held**
WEB: www.joysonsafety.com
SIC: 2296 2221 2399 2396 Cord for reinforcing rubber tires; fabric for reinforcing rubber tires; passementeries, man-made fiber; seat belts, automobile & aircraft; seat covers, automobile; automotive trimmings, fabric; motor vehicle parts & accessories
HQ: Joyson Safety Systems Acquisition Llc
  2025 Harmon Rd
  Auburn Hills MI 48326
  248 373-8040

(G-1045)
TALL CITY LLC
3386 Countryside Cir (48326-2218)
PHONE 248 854-0713
Dennis Kruse, *Vice Pres*
Angela Staples, *Vice Pres*
Gary Womack, *VP Opers*
Craig Hanagan, *Opers Staff*
Marlu Hiller, *Controller*
EMP: 7 **EST:** 2008
SALES (est): 561K **Privately Held**
WEB: www.tallcityexploration.com
SIC: 2339 Women's & misses' outerwear

Auburn Hills - Oakland County (G-1046)

(G-1046)
TECTONICS INDUSTRIES LLC (PA)
1681 Harmon Rd (48326-1547)
PHONE..................248 597-1600
Lee Skandalaris, *Principal*
EMP: 27 EST: 2013
SALES (est): 6.9MM Privately Held
WEB: www.tectonics.com
SIC: 2759 Commercial printing

(G-1047)
TEIJIN ADVAN COMPO AMERI INC
1200 Harmon Rd (48326-1550)
PHONE..................248 365-6600
Jun Suzuki, *Principal*
Kazuhiro Yamamoto, *Exec VP*
Osamu Nishikawa, *Senior VP*
Noriaki Endo, *Auditor*
Masaru Onishi, *Director*
▲ EMP: 8 EST: 2011
SQ FT: 47,460
SALES (est): 3.2MM Privately Held
WEB: www.teijin.com
SIC: 3089 Plastic processing
HQ: Teijin Holdings Usa Inc.
600 Lexington Ave Fl 27
New York NY 10022
212 308-8744

(G-1048)
TEIJIN AUTO TECH NA HLDNGS COR (HQ)
Also Called: Continntal Strl Plas Hldngs Co
255 Rex Blvd (48326-2954)
PHONE..................248 237-7800
Steve Rooney, *President*
Eric Haiss, *Exec VP*
Frank Silvagi, *Vice Pres*
Mike Siwajek, *Vice Pres*
Dana Pebbles, *Engineer*
EMP: 150 EST: 2005
SALES (est): 795.3MM Privately Held
WEB: www.teijinautomotive.com
SIC: 3089 Injection molding of plastics

(G-1049)
TEIJIN AUTOMOTIVE TECH INC (DH)
255 Rex Blvd (48326-2954)
PHONE..................248 237-7800
Steve Rooney, *CEO*
Julie Benton, *Vice Pres*
Mike Siwajek, *Vice Pres*
Steven Wisniewski, *Vice Pres*
Patty McFadden, *Materials Mgr*
▲ EMP: 150 EST: 1998
SALES (est): 511.6MM Privately Held
WEB: www.teijinautomotive.com
SIC: 3089 Injection molding of plastics
HQ: Csp Holding Corp.
255 Rex Blvd
Auburn Hills MI 48326
248 237-7800

(G-1050)
TELESPECTOR CORPORATION
1460 N Opdyke Rd (48326-2651)
PHONE..................248 373-5400
David Piccirilli, *President*
Daniel Piccirilli, *Vice Pres*
David M Piccirilli, *Vice Pres*
Theodora Zurbrick, *Purchasing*
EMP: 22 EST: 1982
SQ FT: 6,500
SALES (est): 1.6MM Privately Held
WEB: www.telespector.com
SIC: 3589 Water treatment equipment, industrial

(G-1051)
THE POM GROUP INC
Also Called: Precision Optical Mfg
2350 Pontiac Rd (48326-2461)
PHONE..................248 409-7900
Jyothi Mazumder, *President*
EMP: 27 EST: 2000
SQ FT: 30,000
SALES (est): 3.2MM Privately Held
SIC: 3312 Tool & die steel & alloys

(G-1052)
THYSSENKRUPP SYSTEM ENGRG (DH)
901 Doris Rd (48326-2716)
P.O. Box 2440, Carol Stream IL (60132-2440)
PHONE..................248 340-8000
Daniel Stiers, *President*
Seloom Jim, *Project Mgr*
Kevin McBain, *Project Mgr*
Pascal Knecht, *Site Mgr*
Theresa Chapo, *Buyer*
◆ EMP: 150 EST: 2002
SQ FT: 165,000
SALES (est): 47.6MM
SALES (corp-wide): 34B Privately Held
WEB: www.thyssenkrupp-system-engineering.com
SIC: 7699 3548 3541 3569 Industrial machinery & equipment repair; welding apparatus; machine tools, metal cutting type; tapping machines; drilling machine tools (metal cutting); milling machines; robots, assembly line: industrial & commercial
HQ: Thyssenkrupp North America, Llc
111 W Jackson Blvd # 2400
Chicago IL 60604
312 525-2800

(G-1053)
TI FLUID SYSTEMS
Also Called: Millennium Machining & Asm
1700 Harmon Rd Ste 2 (48326-1588)
PHONE..................248 393-4525
Gus Ploss, *Manager*
EMP: 6
SALES (corp-wide): 3.3B Privately Held
WEB: www.tifluidsystems.com
SIC: 3714 Motor vehicle parts & accessories
HQ: Ti Fluid Systems L.L.C.
2020 Taylor Rd
Auburn Hills MI 48326
248 494-5000

(G-1054)
TI FLUID SYSTEMS LLC (DH)
2020 Taylor Rd (48326-1771)
PHONE..................248 494-5000
Melissa Stefanic, *Counsel*
Jeff White, *Opers Mgr*
Keith Reeves, *Maint Spvr*
Rich Lepley, *Production*
Debra Geier, *Purch Agent*
▼ EMP: 2446 EST: 2001
SALES (est): 281.3MM
SALES (corp-wide): 3.3B Privately Held
WEB: www.tifluidsystems.com
SIC: 3317 3312 3599 3052 Tubes, seamless steel; tubing, mechanical or hypodermic sizes: cold drawn stainless; tubes, steel & iron; amusement park equipment; plastic hose; filters: oil, fuel & air, motor vehicle; fuel systems & parts, motor vehicle; air conditioning equipment, complete

(G-1055)
TI GROUP AUTO SYSTEMS LLC (HQ)
2020 Taylor Rd (48326-1771)
PHONE..................248 296-8000
William Kozyra, *CEO*
Bill Laule, *President*
Kwang-Joon Jeong, *Business Mgr*
Hans Dieltjens, *Exec VP*
David Murrell, *Exec VP*
◆ EMP: 300 EST: 1922
SALES (est): 1B
SALES (corp-wide): 3.3B Privately Held
WEB: www.tifluidsystems.com
SIC: 3317 3312 3599 3052 Tubes, seamless steel; tubing, mechanical or hypodermic sizes: cold drawn stainless; tubes, steel & iron; hose, flexible metallic; plastic hose; fuel systems & parts, motor vehicle; filters: oil, fuel & air, motor vehicle; refrigeration & heating equipment
PA: Ti Fluid Systems Plc
4650 Kingsgate Cascade Way
Oxford OXON
186 587-1820

(G-1056)
TI GROUP AUTO SYSTEMS LLC
Also Called: Bundy Tubing Division
2020 Taylor Rd (48326-1771)
PHONE..................859 235-5420
Steve Foote, *Manager*
Mark Hill, *Manager*
EMP: 8
SALES (corp-wide): 3.3B Privately Held
WEB: www.tifluidsystems.com
SIC: 3317 3714 3498 Steel pipe & tubes; motor vehicle parts & accessories; fabricated pipe & fittings
HQ: Ti Group Automotive Systems, Llc
2020 Taylor Rd
Auburn Hills MI 48326
248 296-8000

(G-1057)
TI GROUP AUTO SYSTEMS LLC
1227 Centre Rd (48326-2605)
PHONE..................248 475-4663
Mohamad Aoun, *Engineer*
Jim Allen, *Branch Mgr*
Dan Mingledorff, *Info Tech Mgr*
EMP: 8
SALES (corp-wide): 3.3B Privately Held
WEB: www.tifluidsystems.com
SIC: 3317 3714 Tubes, seamless steel; motor vehicle parts & accessories
HQ: Ti Group Automotive Systems, Llc
2020 Taylor Rd
Auburn Hills MI 48326
248 296-8000

(G-1058)
TICONA POLYMERS INC
2600 N Opdyke Rd (48326-1940)
PHONE..................248 377-6868
Gayle Hinds, *Branch Mgr*
EMP: 35
SALES (corp-wide): 5.6B Publicly Held
SIC: 2821 Plastics materials & resins
HQ: Ticona Polymers, Inc.
222 Las Colinas Blvd W 900n
Irving TX 75039
859 525-4740

(G-1059)
TK MEXICO INC
2500 Innovation Dr (48326-2611)
PHONE..................248 373-8040
Ken Bowling, *Admin Sec*
EMP: 101 EST: 2004
SALES (est): 1.8MM
SALES (corp-wide): 7.2B Privately Held
WEB: www.joysonsafety.com
SIC: 2399 Seat covers, automobile
HQ: Joyson Safety Systems Acquisition Llc
2025 Harmon Rd
Auburn Hills MI 48326
248 373-8040

(G-1060)
TOOL HOUSE INC
1080 Centre Rd Ste C (48326-2681)
PHONE..................248 481-7092
Gregory Korn, *Regl Sales Mgr*
EMP: 7 EST: 2017
SALES (est): 93K Privately Held
WEB: www.toolhse.com
SIC: 3599 Machine shop, jobbing & repair

(G-1061)
TOTAL REPAIR EXPRESS MI LLC
2990 Lapeer Rd (48326-1932)
PHONE..................248 690-9410
Kirt Bennett,
EMP: 15 EST: 2011
SALES (est): 528.4K Privately Held
SIC: 3999 Manufacturing industries

(G-1062)
TRACE ZERO INC
2740 Auburn Ct (48326-3294)
PHONE..................248 289-1277
McGregor Neville, *President*
▲ EMP: 10 EST: 2009
SALES (est): 3MM Privately Held
WEB: www.trace-zero.com
SIC: 2899 Acids

(G-1063)
TRANSGLOBAL DESIGN & MFG LLC (PA)
1020 Doris Rd (48326-2613)
PHONE..................734 525-2651
Doug Nichol, *Vice Pres*
Tim Bradley, *Manager*
EMP: 75 EST: 2006
SQ FT: 67,000
SALES (est): 17.8MM Privately Held
WEB: www.transglobalco.com
SIC: 3711 Motor vehicles & car bodies

(G-1064)
TRANSIGN LLC
281 Collier Rd (48326-1405)
P.O. Box 300005, Drayton Plains (48330-0005)
PHONE..................248 623-6400
Martin Hilber, *CEO*
Jamie Lipka, *President*
Jill Youngblood,
EMP: 11 EST: 2011
SALES (est): 3.3MM Privately Held
WEB: www.transignllc.com
SIC: 3993 Electric signs

(G-1065)
TRINSEO LLC
691 N Squirrel Rd (48326-2846)
PHONE..................248 340-0109
EMP: 4 Publicly Held
WEB: www.trinseo.com
SIC: 2821 Plastics materials & resins
HQ: Trinseo Llc
1000 Chesterbrook Blvd # 300
Berwyn PA 19312

(G-1066)
TSM CORPORATION
1175 N Opdyke Rd (48326-2685)
PHONE..................248 276-4700
Thomas A Prior, *President*
Darin Hunt, *Production*
Dave Sutherland, *Manager*
Karalee Tabron, *Manager*
Hauschild Kristina, *Analyst*
▲ EMP: 60
SQ FT: 85,000
SALES (est): 19.4MM Privately Held
WEB: www.tsmcorp.com
SIC: 3599 Machine shop, jobbing & repair

(G-1067)
U S FARATHANE PORT HURON LLC
2700 High Meadow Cir (48326-2796)
PHONE..................248 754-7000
Andrew Greenlee, *Principal*
EMP: 19 EST: 2013
SALES (est): 1.1MM Privately Held
WEB: www.usfarathane.com
SIC: 3089 Plastics products

(G-1068)
UNIQUE FABRICATING INC (PA)
800 Standard Pkwy (48326-1415)
PHONE..................248 853-2333
Richard L Baum Jr, *Ch of Bd*
Byrd Douglas Cain III, *President*
Brian P Loftus, *CFO*
EMP: 561 EST: 1975
SQ FT: 150,000
SALES (est): 120.2MM Publicly Held
WEB: www.uniquefab.com
SIC: 3714 3053 3086 3296 Motor vehicle parts & accessories; gaskets, all materials; plastics foam products; mineral wool; packaging paper & plastics film, coated & laminated

(G-1069)
UNIQUE FABRICATING NA INC (HQ)
800 Standard Pkwy (48326-1415)
PHONE..................248 853-2333
Richard L Baum Jr, *Ch of Bd*
Thomas Tekiele, *CFO*
Douglas Stahl, *Manager*
▲ EMP: 320 EST: 1975
SQ FT: 150,000

SALES: 175.2MM
SALES (corp-wide): 120.2MM Publicly Held
WEB: www.uniquefab.com
SIC: 3053 3086 3296 2671 Gaskets, all materials; plastics foam products; mineral wool; packaging paper & plastics film, coated & laminated
PA: Unique Fabricating, Inc.
　800 Standard Pkwy
　Auburn Hills MI 48326
　248 853-2333

(G-1070)
UNIQUE-CHARDAN INC
800 Standard Pkwy (48326-1415)
PHONE.................................419 636-6900
Thomas Tekiele, *CFO*
EMP: 74 EST: 1997
SALES (est): 4.8MM
SALES (corp-wide): 120.2MM Publicly Held
WEB: www.uniquefab.com
SIC: 3086 3714 3089 3944 Plastics foam products; motor vehicle parts & accessories; injection molded finished plastic products; games, toys & children's vehicles; sporting & athletic goods
HQ: Unique Fabricating Na, Inc.
　800 Standard Pkwy
　Auburn Hills MI 48326
　248 853-2333

(G-1071)
UNIQUE-INTASCO USA INC
800 Standard Pkwy (48326-1415)
PHONE.................................810 982-3360
EMP: 9
SALES (est): 2.2MM
SALES (corp-wide): 175.2MM Publicly Held
SIC: 2752 3555 Lithographic Commercial Printing Manufacturing Printing Trades Machinery
HQ: Unique Fabricating Na, Inc.
　800 Standard Pkwy
　Auburn Hills MI 48326
　248 853-2333

(G-1072)
US FARATHANE LLC
2700 High Meadow Cir (48326-2796)
PHONE.................................248 754-7000
Tony Drumm, *General Mgr*
Eric Hoga, *Engineer*
Jeff Page, *Engineer*
Bart Bernocco, *Finance Mgr*
Andrew Greenlee, *Mng Member*
EMP: 250 EST: 2013
SALES (est): 99.6MM
SALES (corp-wide): 549.4MM Privately Held
WEB: www.usfarathane.com
SIC: 3089 Battery cases, plastic or plastic combination
PA: U.S. Farathane Holdings Corp.
　2700 High Meadow Cir
　Auburn Hills MI 48326
　248 754-7000

(G-1073)
US FARATHANE HOLDINGS CORP (PA)
Also Called: U.S. Frthane Corp Extrsion Gro
2700 High Meadow Cir (48326-2796)
PHONE.................................248 754-7000
Andy Greenlee, *President*
Phil Romzek, *President*
Carl Ammerman, *General Mgr*
Tony Drumm, *General Mgr*
David Howard, *General Mgr*
◆ EMP: 480 EST: 1981
SQ FT: 68,000
SALES (est): 549.4MM Privately Held
WEB: www.usfarathane.com
SIC: 3089 Injection molding of plastics; thermoformed finished plastic products; casting of plastic

(G-1074)
US FARATHANE HOLDINGS CORP
1350 Harmon Rd (48326-1540)
PHONE.................................780 246-1034
Andy Greenlee, *President*
EMP: 115

SALES (corp-wide): 549.4MM Privately Held
WEB: www.usfarathane.com
SIC: 3089 Automotive parts, plastic
PA: U.S. Farathane Holdings Corp.
　2700 High Meadow Cir
　Auburn Hills MI 48326
　248 754-7000

(G-1075)
USF DELTA TOOLING LLC (HQ)
Also Called: Delta Technologies, LLC
1350 Harmon Rd (48326-1540)
PHONE.................................248 391-6800
Peter Mozer, *CEO*
Rudolf W Mozer, *Chairman*
Tibor Toreki, *COO*
Dennis Carroll, *Plant Mgr*
John Nagy, *Engineer*
◆ EMP: 150 EST: 1953
SQ FT: 170,000
SALES (est): 26.1MM
SALES (corp-wide): 549.4MM Privately Held
WEB: www.deltatechgroup.com
SIC: 3544 3999 Industrial molds; jigs & fixtures; models, general, except toy
PA: U.S. Farathane Holdings Corp.
　2700 High Meadow Cir
　Auburn Hills MI 48326
　248 754-7000

(G-1076)
USF WESTLAND LLC
2700 High Meadow Cir (48326-2796)
PHONE.................................248 754-7000
EMP: 13 EST: 2016
SALES (est): 751.8K Privately Held
WEB: www.usfarathane.com
SIC: 3089 Injection molding of plastics

(G-1077)
VALEO NORTH AMERICA INC
Also Called: Valeo Inc Eng Coolg Auto Div
4100 N Atlantic Blvd (48326-1570)
PHONE.................................248 209-8253
Steven Ojeda, *Partner*
Thomas Hartleb, *General Mgr*
Dave Cure, *Business Mgr*
Bruno Guillemet, *Exec VP*
Michael Mlecsko, *Project Mgr*
EMP: 150
SQ FT: 119,000
SALES (corp-wide): 177.9K Privately Held
WEB: www.valeo.com
SIC: 3714 Motor vehicle parts & accessories
HQ: Valeo North America, Inc.
　150 Stephenson Hwy
　Troy MI 48083

(G-1078)
VALEO RADAR SYSTEMS INC
3000 University Dr (48326-2356)
PHONE.................................248 340-3126
EMP: 21
SALES (est): 3.4MM Privately Held
SIC: 3812 Mfg Search/Navigation Equipment

(G-1079)
VISIONEERING INC (PA)
2055 Taylor Rd (48326-1772)
PHONE.................................248 622-5600
Brad Hallett, *CEO*
John Thoel, *General Mgr*
Tim Bellestri, *Vice Pres*
Tony Robinson, *Vice Pres*
Chris Scandalis, *Mfg Staff*
▲ EMP: 283 EST: 1953
SQ FT: 183,000
SALES (est): 60.6MM Privately Held
WEB: www.vistool.com
SIC: 3544 Jigs & fixtures; industrial molds

(G-1080)
VITESCO TECHNOLOGIES USA LLC (DH)
2400 Executive Hills Dr (48326-2980)
PHONE.................................248 209-4000
Javier Mayo, *Engineer*
Scott Nelson, *Sales Mgr*
David Sharpe, *Sales Mgr*
Andreas Wolf, *Mng Member*
EMP: 433 EST: 2018

SALES (est): 667.4MM
SALES (corp-wide): 8.8B Privately Held
WEB: www.continental.com
SIC: 3714 Motor vehicle parts & accessories
HQ: Vitesco Technologies Holding Netherlands B.V.
　Bassin 100 -106
　Maastricht
　433 299-970

(G-1081)
VIVA ZEN SALES LLC
1139 Centre Rd (48326-2603)
PHONE.................................248 481-3605
EMP: 4 EST: 2015
SALES (est): 47.2K Privately Held
WEB: www.vivazen.com
SIC: 2833 Medicinals & botanicals

(G-1082)
VOLKSWAGEN GROUP AMERICA INC
Also Called: Volkswagen Auto Securitization
3800 Hamlin Rd (48326-2829)
PHONE.................................248 754-5000
Eric Nawrocki, *Marketing Staff*
Gerhard Riechel, *Branch Mgr*
Leslie Gulyas, *Manager*
Jean Sailland, *Manager*
Steve Webber, *Instructor*
EMP: 13
SALES (corp-wide): 263.5B Privately Held
WEB: www.vw.com
SIC: 3699 Security devices
HQ: Volkswagen Group Of America, Inc.
　2200 Woodland Pointe Ave
　Herndon VA 20171
　248 754-5000

(G-1083)
WABCO AIR COMPRSR HOLDINGS INC
1220 Pacific Dr (48326-1589)
PHONE.................................248 260-9032
EMP: 14 EST: 2019
SALES (est): 1.6MM
SALES (corp-wide): 216.2K Privately Held
WEB: www.wabco-auto.com
SIC: 3714 Motor vehicle parts & accessories
HQ: Wabco Holdings Inc.
　1220 Pacific Dr
　Auburn Hills MI 48326

(G-1084)
WABCO EXPATS INC
1220 Pacific Dr (48326-1589)
PHONE.................................248 260-9032
EMP: 35 EST: 2007
SALES (est): 1.5MM
SALES (corp-wide): 216.2K Privately Held
WEB: www.wabco-auto.com
SIC: 3714 Motor vehicle brake systems & parts
HQ: Wabco Holdings Inc.
　1220 Pacific Dr
　Auburn Hills MI 48326

(G-1085)
WABCO GROUP INTERNATIONAL INC
1220 Pacific Dr (48326-1589)
PHONE.................................248 260-9025
EMP: 8 EST: 2007
SALES (est): 74.4K Privately Held
SIC: 2899 Water treating compounds

(G-1086)
WABCO HOLDINGS INC (DH)
1220 Pacific Dr (48326-1589)
PHONE.................................248 260-9032
Jon Morrison, *CEO*
Gautham Appaya, *Vice Pres*
P Kaniappan, *Vice Pres*
Julio Mulato, *Opers Dir*
Joanna Swierad, *Prdtn Dir*
▲ EMP: 2635 EST: 1869

SALES (est): 3.4B
SALES (corp-wide): 216.2K Privately Held
WEB: www.wabco-auto.com
SIC: 3714 Motor vehicle brake systems & parts; motor vehicle steering systems & parts; motor vehicle transmissions, drive assemblies & parts
HQ: Zf Friedrichshafen Ag
　Lowentaler Str. 20
　Friedrichshafen BW 88046
　754 177-0

(G-1087)
WASHINGTON PENN PLASTIC CO INC
Also Called: Automotive Div
3256 University Dr Ste 15 (48326-2393)
PHONE.................................248 276-2275
Scola Dave, *Engineer*
Bruce Graves, *Manager*
EMP: 8
SALES (corp-wide): 541.4MM Privately Held
WEB: www.washingtonpenn.com
SIC: 2821 Plastics materials & resins
HQ: Washington Penn Plastic Co., Inc.
　450 Racetrack Rd
　Washington PA 15301
　724 228-1260

(G-1088)
WEBASTO ROOF SYSTEMS INC (HQ)
Also Called: Webasto Roofing
2500 Executive Hills Dr (48326-2983)
PHONE.................................248 997-5100
Andre Schoenekaes, *President*
Kozo Takenouchi, *Engineer*
Rommel Diones, *Senior Engr*
Philipp Schramm, *CFO*
Linda Tubbs, *Controller*
▲ EMP: 260 EST: 1974
SQ FT: 94,000
SALES (est): 519.6MM
SALES (corp-wide): 3.9B Privately Held
WEB: www.webasto-comfort.com
SIC: 3714 3441 Sun roofs, motor vehicle; fabricated structural metal
PA: Webasto Se
　Kraillinger Str. 5
　Stockdorf BY 82131
　898 579-40

(G-1089)
WEBER AUTOMOTIVE CORPORATION
1750 Summit Dr (48326-1780)
PHONE.................................248 393-5520
Dieter Albers, *COO*
Chip Quarrier, *Vice Pres*
Jeremy Kjorli, *Opers Staff*
Anke Winkler, *Finance Mgr*
Diane Dawes, *Finance Asst*
▲ EMP: 226 EST: 1996
SQ FT: 250,000
SALES (est): 58MM
SALES (corp-wide): 711.6K Privately Held
WEB: www.a-weber.com
SIC: 3714 Motor vehicle engines & parts
HQ: Wa Abwicklungs Gmbh
　Otto-Lilienthal-Str. 5
　Markdorf BW 88677
　754 496-30

(G-1090)
XILEH HOLDING INC (DH)
2750 High Meadow Cir (48326-2796)
PHONE.................................248 340-4100
Ping Liu, *CEO*
EMP: 0 EST: 2015
SALES (est): 867.6MM Privately Held
WEB: www.intl-bj.avic.com
SIC: 6719 2891 3714 Investment holding companies, except banks; adhesives & sealants; motor vehicle parts & accessories
HQ: Avic International Beijing Company Limited
　Floor 15,Building L1, Avic Intl Beijing Plaza, No. 13 Ronghuanan
　Beijing 10017
　108 709-1032

Augusta
Kalamazoo County

(G-1091)
BLUEFIRE INDUSTRIES LLC
16757 Fort Custer Dr (49012-9621)
PHONE..................................269 235-9779
Jesse Bright, *Principal*
EMP: 4 **EST:** 2016
SALES (est): 59.6K **Privately Held**
SIC: 3999 Manufacturing industries

(G-1092)
KNAPPEN MILLING COMPANY
110 S Water St (49012-9781)
P.O. Box 245 (49012-0245)
PHONE..................................269 731-4141
Emily Likens, *President*
Bob Likens, *Senior VP*
Charles Knappen, *Vice Pres*
Charles B Knappen, *Vice Pres*
John Shouse, *Vice Pres*
EMP: 37 **EST:** 1929
SQ FT: 3,000
SALES (est): 9.3MM **Privately Held**
WEB: www.knappenmilling.com
SIC: 2041 Flour; bran & middlings (except rice)

(G-1093)
SMITH METAL LLC
211 S Webster St (49012-9780)
PHONE..................................269 731-5211
David Sutton,
EMP: 8 **EST:** 2019
SALES (est): 617.8K **Privately Held**
WEB: www.smith-metal.com
SIC: 3599 Machine shop, jobbing & repair

(G-1094)
SMITH METAL TURNING INC
Also Called: Smith Metal Turning Service
211 S Webster St (49012-9780)
P.O. Box 218 (49012-0218)
PHONE..................................269 731-5211
Robert Smith, *President*
Patricia Smith, *Treasurer*
EMP: 6 **EST:** 1969
SQ FT: 4,500
SALES (est): 457.1K **Privately Held**
WEB: www.smithmetalturning.com
SIC: 3599 Machine shop, jobbing & repair

Bad Axe
Huron County

(G-1095)
AMERICAN TCHNCAL FBRCATORS LLC
414 E Soper Rd (48413-9500)
PHONE..................................989 269-6262
Bruce Grubba, *Accounts Mgr*
Bryan Barwig, *Mng Member*
EMP: 25 **EST:** 2005
SQ FT: 66,000
SALES (est): 2.7MM **Privately Held**
WEB: www.amtechfab.com
SIC: 3444 Sheet metalwork

(G-1096)
AXLY PRODUCTION MACHINING INC
Also Called: Axly-Briney Sales
700 E Soper Rd (48413-9497)
PHONE..................................989 269-2444
William Roberts, *President*
David Hyzer, *Vice Pres*
Clark Shuart Sr, *Treasurer*
Frank Peplinski, *Admin Sec*
EMP: 1 **EST:** 1980
SQ FT: 52,500
SALES (est): 2.1MM **Privately Held**
WEB: www.geminigroup.net
SIC: 3541 3325 3366 Machine tools, metal cutting type; bushings, cast steel: except investment; copper foundries
PA: Gemini Group, Inc.
175 Thompson Rd Ste A
Bad Axe MI 48413

(G-1097)
AXLY PRODUCTION MACHINING
727 Skinner St (48413-9489)
PHONE..................................989 269-9553
EMP: 10 **EST:** 2016
SALES (est): 250.7K **Privately Held**
WEB: www.geminigroup.net
SIC: 3544 Special dies, tools, jigs & fixtures

(G-1098)
BEAUMONT ENTERPRISE
211 N Heisterman St (48413-1239)
PHONE..................................989 269-6464
Robin Boyle, *Editor*
EMP: 6 **EST:** 2016
SALES (est): 62.9K **Privately Held**
SIC: 2711 Newspapers

(G-1099)
CLEMCO PRINTING INC
116 Scott St (48413-1212)
PHONE..................................989 269-8364
Terri Tschirhart, *President*
Gerald Tschirhart, *Corp Secy*
EMP: 6 **EST:** 1973
SQ FT: 1,500
SALES (est): 450.6K **Privately Held**
WEB: www.clemcoprinting.com
SIC: 2752 2759 Commercial printing, offset; letterpress printing

(G-1100)
ENTERPRISE TOOL AND GEAR INC (PA)
635 Liberty St (48413-9532)
PHONE..................................989 269-9797
Joel Dean, *President*
Neal Rogers, *Admin Sec*
EMP: 12 **EST:** 1986
SQ FT: 60,000
SALES (est): 11.1MM **Privately Held**
WEB: www.huron-tool.com
SIC: 3544 3545 3462 3366 Jigs & fixtures; machine tool accessories; iron & steel forgings; copper foundries

(G-1101)
GAINORS MEAT PACKING INC
317 N Port Crescent St (48413-1221)
PHONE..................................989 269-8161
EMP: 8 **EST:** 1946
SQ FT: 2,000
SALES (est): 470K **Privately Held**
SIC: 2011 Beat Packing Plant

(G-1102)
GEMINI GROUP INC (PA)
175 Thompson Rd Ste A (48413-8274)
P.O. Box 100 (48413-0100)
PHONE..................................989 269-6272
Kevin Nelson, *CEO*
Lynette Drake, *President*
Veronica Peterson, *Superintendent*
Joe Copes, *Plant Mgr*
Dennis Engelhart, *Plant Mgr*
EMP: 12 **EST:** 1996
SQ FT: 16,000
SALES (est): 450.2MM **Privately Held**
WEB: www.geminigroup.net
SIC: 8741 3089 Management services; extruded finished plastic products

(G-1103)
GEMINI GROUP ME & T
727 Skinner St (48413-9489)
PHONE..................................989 553-5685
EMP: 9 **EST:** 2018
SALES (est): 105K **Privately Held**
WEB: www.geminigroup.net
SIC: 3089 Injection molding of plastics

(G-1104)
GEMINI GROUP SERVICES INC
175 Thompson Rd Ste A (48413-8274)
P.O. Box 100 (48413-0100)
PHONE..................................248 435-7271
Lynette Drake, *President*
EMP: 11 **EST:** 2016
SALES (est): 284.3K **Privately Held**
WEB: www.geminigroup.net
SIC: 3089 Injection molding of plastics

(G-1105)
GEMINI PRECISION MACHINING INC (HQ)
Also Called: Axly Production Machining
700 E Soper Rd (48413-9497)
PHONE..................................989 269-9702
Lynette Drake, *President*
David Hyzer, *Vice Pres*
Kalvin Keilitz, *Engineer*
Frank Peplinski, *Treasurer*
Jennifer Sosnoski, *Personnel*
EMP: 124 **EST:** 1947
SALES (est): 28.3MM **Privately Held**
WEB: www.geminigroup.net
SIC: 3544 Special dies, tools, jigs & fixtures

(G-1106)
GLOBAL LIFT CORP
1330 Pigeon Rd (48413-8617)
PHONE..................................989 269-5900
Lee Steinman, *President*
Joshua Steinman, *Vice Pres*
EMP: 17 **EST:** 2011
SALES (est): 3MM **Privately Held**
WEB: www.global-poolproducts.com
SIC: 3449 Bars, concrete reinforcing: fabricated steel

(G-1107)
HURON PUBLISHING COMPANY INC (HQ)
Also Called: Huron Daily Tribune, The
211 N Heisterman St (48413-1239)
PHONE..................................989 269-6461
Jan Stoeckle, *Publisher*
Jerry Gibbard, *Prdtn Mgr*
Gail Soper, *Financial Exec*
Rebecca Watson, *Adv Dir*
Vicki Yaroch, *Advt Staff*
EMP: 58 **EST:** 1876
SQ FT: 5,000
SALES (est): 9.5MM
SALES (corp-wide): 4.2B **Privately Held**
WEB: www.michigansthumb.com
SIC: 2711 2752 Newspapers: publishing only, not printed on site; commercial printing, lithographic
PA: The Hearst Corporation
300 W 57th St Fl 42
New York NY 10019
212 649-2000

(G-1108)
HURON TOOL & ENGINEERING CO (HQ)
635 Liberty St (48413-9532)
PHONE..................................989 269-9927
Neil Rogers, *President*
Aaron Darbee, *Opers Mgr*
Rod Mausolf, *Engineer*
▲ **EMP:** 50 **EST:** 1972
SQ FT: 36,000
SALES (est): 11.1MM **Privately Held**
WEB: www.huron-tool.com
SIC: 3541 3544 3545 3452 Machine tool replacement & repair parts, metal cutting types; special dies, tools, jigs & fixtures; machine tool accessories; bolts, nuts, rivets & washers; copper foundries
PA: Enterprise Tool And Gear Inc
635 Liberty St
Bad Axe MI 48413
989 269-9797

(G-1109)
MINUTEMAN METAL WORKS INC
1600 Patterson St (48413-9479)
PHONE..................................989 269-8342
Gene Brade, *President*
EMP: 4 **EST:** 1987
SQ FT: 6,500
SALES (est): 500K **Privately Held**
WEB: www.performancetrends.com
SIC: 3441 Fabricated structural metal

(G-1110)
SIERRA PLASTICS INC
175 Thompson Rd Ste A (48413-8274)
P.O. Box 100 (48413-0100)
PHONE..................................989 269-6272
David Hyzer, *President*
EMP: 1 **EST:** 1998

SALES (est): 2.6MM **Privately Held**
WEB: www.geminigroup.net
SIC: 3089 Injection molding of plastics
PA: Gemini Group, Inc.
175 Thompson Rd Ste A
Bad Axe MI 48413

(G-1111)
SRW INC (PA)
175 Thompson Rd Ste A (48413-8274)
P.O. Box 100 (48413-0100)
PHONE..................................989 269-8528
David Hyzer, *President*
William F Roberts, *Vice Pres*
Frank M Peplinski, *Treasurer*
Clark K Shaurt, *Admin Sec*
EMP: 10 **EST:** 1987
SALES (est): 2.1MM **Privately Held**
SIC: 1381 1389 Drilling oil & gas wells; oil field services

(G-1112)
TALCO INDUSTRIES
705 E Woodworth St (48413-1548)
PHONE..................................989 269-6260
Eric Cook, *Owner*
EMP: 4 **EST:** 1996
SQ FT: 14,000
SALES (est): 359.9K **Privately Held**
SIC: 3089 Injection molding of plastics

(G-1113)
THUMB BLANKET
55 Westland Dr (48413-7741)
PHONE..................................989 269-9918
Jack Guza, *General Mgr*
EMP: 6 **EST:** 1980
SALES (est): 503K
SALES (corp-wide): 274.1MM **Privately Held**
WEB: www.huroncountyview.mihomepaper.com
SIC: 2741 Shopping news: publishing only, not printed on site
HQ: 21st Century Newspapers, Inc.
6250 Metropolitan Pkwy
Sterling Heights MI 48312
586 469-4510

(G-1114)
THUMB PLASTICS INC
400 Liberty St (48413-9490)
PHONE..................................989 269-9791
William Roberts, *CEO*
David Hyzer, *CFO*
Clark Shuart Sr, *Treasurer*
Frank Peplinski, *Admin Sec*
EMP: 293 **EST:** 1977
SQ FT: 27,000
SALES (est): 25.9MM **Privately Held**
WEB: www.geminigroup.net
SIC: 3089 Injection molding of plastics
HQ: Pepro Enterprises, Inc.
4385 Garfield St
Ubly MI 48475
989 658-3200

(G-1115)
THUMB TOOL & ENGINEERING CO
354 Liberty St (48413-9302)
PHONE..................................989 269-9731
Jack Rochefort, *President*
Lynette Drake, *Principal*
Clark K Shuart, *Corp Secy*
Gerald Rochefort, *Assistant VP*
Jeffrey Rochefort, *Assistant VP*
▲ **EMP:** 250 **EST:** 1967
SQ FT: 93,000
SALES (est): 48.8MM **Privately Held**
WEB: www.geminigroup.net
SIC: 3544 Special dies & tools; jigs & fixtures
PA: Gemini Group, Inc.
175 Thompson Rd Ste A
Bad Axe MI 48413

(G-1116)
VALLEY GEAR AND MACHINE INC
514 Chickory St (48413-1550)
PHONE..................................989 269-8177
Richard Booms, *President*
Ryan Booms, *Vice Pres*
EMP: 10 **EST:** 1989
SQ FT: 4,800

SALES (est): 1.9MM **Privately Held**
WEB: www.valley-gear.com
SIC: 3566 3559 Speed changers, drives & gears; plastics working machinery

(G-1117)
VINE-N-BERRY WINES
3475 Stein Rd (48413-9647)
PHONE.................................989 551-1616
EMP: 5 **EST:** 2014
SALES (est): 62.7K **Privately Held**
WEB: www.vinenberry.com
SIC: 2084 Wines

Bailey
Muskegon County

(G-1118)
BECMAR CORP
585 Canada Rd (49303-9731)
PHONE.................................616 675-7479
Arthur Proctor, *President*
Susan Proctor, *Vice Pres*
EMP: 7
SQ FT: 18,500
SALES (est): 580K **Privately Held**
SIC: 3552 Printing machinery, textile

(G-1119)
GUERNE PRECISION MACHINING
13761 Bailey Rd (49303-9706)
PHONE.................................231 834-7417
Wayne Guerne, *President*
EMP: 5 **EST:** 1974
SQ FT: 2,400
SALES (est): 433.7K **Privately Held**
WEB: www.guernes.com
SIC: 3599 Machine shop, jobbing & repair

(G-1120)
MCNEES MANUFACTURING INC
750 Canada Rd (49303-9732)
PHONE.................................616 675-7480
Richard McNees, *President*
EMP: 21 **EST:** 1991
SALES (est): 655.3K **Privately Held**
WEB: www.mcneesmfg.com
SIC: 3451 Screw machine products

Baldwin
Lake County

(G-1121)
AUSTIN TUBE PRODUCTS INC
5629 S Forman Rd (49304-8046)
P.O. Box 1120 (49304-1120)
PHONE.................................231 745-2741
Joe Day, *President*
Derrielene Day, *Admin Sec*
EMP: 18 **EST:** 1971
SQ FT: 15,000
SALES (est): 1MM **Privately Held**
SIC: 3492 3498 3444 3441 Hose & tube fittings & assemblies, hydraulic/pneumatic; fabricated pipe & fittings; sheet metalwork; fabricated structural metal; aluminum extruded products; steel pipe & tubes

(G-1122)
JEROME MILLER LUMBER CO (PA)
7027 S James Rd (49304-7135)
PHONE.................................231 745-3694
Jerome Miller, *Owner*
Toni Miller, *Co-Owner*
Shelly Miller, *Manager*
EMP: 8 **EST:** 1960
SALES (est): 990K **Privately Held**
SIC: 2421 Sawmills & planing mills, general

(G-1123)
JEROME MILLER LUMBER CO
Baldwin Rd (49304)
P.O. Box 60 (49304-0060)
PHONE.................................231 745-3694
Jerome Miller, *Owner*
EMP: 9

SALES (corp-wide): 990K **Privately Held**
SIC: 2421 2411 Sawmills & planing mills, general; logging
PA: Jerome Miller Lumber Co
   7027 S James Rd
   Baldwin MI 49304
   231 745-3694

(G-1124)
PEACOCK INDUSTRIES INC
254 S M 37 (49304-8260)
PHONE.................................231 745-4609
Kit L Bull, *President*
Toni Battle, *Agent*
Kit B Bull, *Director*
EMP: 23 **EST:** 1976
SQ FT: 20,000
SALES (est): 3.1MM **Privately Held**
WEB: www.peacockinds.com
SIC: 7692 Welding repair

(G-1125)
WHEELERS WOLF LAKE SAWMILL
195 N M 37 # 137 (49304-7896)
PHONE.................................231 745-7078
Patricia Wheeler, *President*
Rodney L Wheeler, *Admin Sec*
EMP: 8 **EST:** 2001
SALES (est): 860.3K **Privately Held**
SIC: 2421 Sawmills & planing mills, general

Bancroft
Shiawassee County

(G-1126)
CEREPHEX CORPORATION
3001 Miller Rd (48414-9308)
PHONE.................................517 719-0414
EMP: 5
SALES (est): 367.8K **Privately Held**
SIC: 3845 Electromedical Equipment

(G-1127)
CHARTER COMMUNICATION
2877 Miller Rd (48414-9748)
PHONE.................................989 634-1093
EMP: 4 **EST:** 2014
SALES (est): 117.5K **Privately Held**
SIC: 3651 Household audio & video equipment

Bangor
Van Buren County

(G-1128)
BANGOR PLASTICS INC
809 Washington St (49013-1155)
P.O. Box 99 (49013-0099)
PHONE.................................269 427-7971
Glenn F Wokeck, *President*
EMP: 20
SQ FT: 29,000
SALES (est): 3.6MM **Privately Held**
WEB: www.bangorplastics.net
SIC: 3089 3083 Injection molding of plastics; laminated plastics plate & sheet

(G-1129)
LINK TECH INC
59648 M 43 (49013-9617)
PHONE.................................269 427-8297
Bruce Linker, *CEO*
Randy Perkinson, *President*
Linda Irwin, *Office Mgr*
◆ **EMP:** 5 **EST:** 1991
SALES (est): 664.6K **Privately Held**
WEB: www.linktech-inc.com
SIC: 3081 8742 Packing materials, plastic sheet; productivity improvement consultant

(G-1130)
MARRONE MICHIGAN MANUFACTORING
700 Industrial Park Rd (49013-1266)
PHONE.................................269 427-0300
Jake Wahmoff, *Chairman*
EMP: 8 **EST:** 2013

SALES (est): 310.3K **Privately Held**
SIC: 3999 Manufacturing industries

(G-1131)
REMINDER SHOPPING GUIDE INC
416 Railroad St (49013-1366)
P.O. Box 218 (49013-0218)
PHONE.................................269 427-7474
Kim Montoy, *Director*
EMP: 7 **EST:** 1950
SALES (est): 459K **Privately Held**
WEB: www.vanburenreminder.com
SIC: 2711 Newspapers, publishing & printing

(G-1132)
WINDSHADOW FARM & DAIRY LLC
24681 County Road 681 (49013-9456)
P.O. Box 249 (49013-0249)
PHONE.................................269 599-0467
Ronald Klein,
EMP: 6
SALES (est): 381.4K **Privately Held**
SIC: 2022 Natural cheese

Baraga
Baraga County

(G-1133)
ALL-WOOD INC
101 Us Highway 41 S (49908-9789)
P.O. Box 489 (49908-0489)
PHONE.................................906 353-6642
Marie A Jacobson, *President*
EMP: 4 **EST:** 1965
SQ FT: 9,500
SALES (est): 338.9K **Privately Held**
SIC: 2421 Lumber: rough, sawed or planed

(G-1134)
BARAGA COUNTY CONCRETE COMPANY
468 N Superior Ave (49908-9602)
PHONE.................................906 353-6595
Arthur D Barrett, *President*
EMP: 5 **EST:** 1972
SALES (est): 479.8K **Privately Held**
WEB: www.baragacounty.org
SIC: 3273 Ready-mixed concrete

(G-1135)
BESSE FOREST PRODUCTS INC
Also Called: Baraga Lumber Division
16522 Westland Dr (49908-9211)
PHONE.................................906 353-7193
Don Rosenberger, *Manager*
EMP: 10 **Privately Held**
WEB: www.bessegroup.com
SIC: 5099 5031 2426 2421 Logs, hewn ties, posts & poles; lumber, plywood & millwork; veneer; hardwood dimension & flooring mills; sawmills & planing mills, general
PA: Forest Besse Products Inc
   933 N 8th St
   Gladstone MI 49837

(G-1136)
CCI ARNHEIM INC
14935 Arnheim (49908)
P.O. Box 861 (49908-0861)
PHONE.................................906 353-6330
David Mattson, *President*
EMP: 4 **EST:** 2009
SALES (est): 251.3K **Privately Held**
WEB: www.cciarnheim.com
SIC: 2451 Mobile buildings: for commercial use

(G-1137)
DAVID NEWMAN LOGGING
14673 Bellaire Rd (49908-9107)
PHONE.................................906 201-1125
David Newman, *Principal*
EMP: 4 **EST:** 2014
SALES (est): 100.6K **Privately Held**
SIC: 2411 Logging

(G-1138)
DESROCHERS BROTHERS INC
107 3rd St (49908)
P.O. Box 524 (49908-0524)
PHONE.................................906 353-6346
EMP: 15
SQ FT: 20,000
SALES (est): 1.9MM **Privately Held**
SIC: 3599 Fabrication And Machining

(G-1139)
DWAYNE THOMLEYS REDNECK
16172 Bellaire Rd (49908-9094)
PHONE.................................906 353-7376
Dwayne Thomley, *Principal*
EMP: 4 **EST:** 2016
SALES (est): 27.2K **Privately Held**
SIC: 7692 Welding repair

(G-1140)
HOMESTEAD GRAPHICS DESIGN INC
516 S Superior Ave (49908-9698)
P.O. Box 579 (49908-0579)
PHONE.................................906 353-6741
Joseph Kayramo, *President*
EMP: 7 **EST:** 1989
SQ FT: 6,000
SALES (est): 714.3K **Privately Held**
WEB: www.hgdesigns.net
SIC: 2759 2752 Screen printing; commercial printing, lithographic

(G-1141)
KEWEENAW BAY INDIAN COMMUNITY
Also Called: American Made Tubcraft Plus
16429 Bear Town Rd (49908-9210)
PHONE.................................906 524-5757
Richard Shalifoe, *President*
Susan Lafernier, *Chairman*
Amy St Arnold, *Treasurer*
EMP: 10 **EST:** 1972
SQ FT: 13,800
SALES (est): 911.4K **Privately Held**
WEB: www.kbic-nsn.gov
SIC: 3229 Glass fiber products

(G-1142)
KOSKI WELDING INC
13529 Old 41 Rd (49908-9022)
PHONE.................................906 353-7588
EMP: 7
SQ FT: 4,800
SALES: 500K **Privately Held**
SIC: 3599 7692 Machine Shop

(G-1143)
LASER NORTH INC
455 N Superior Ave (49908-9602)
P.O. Box 845 (49908-0845)
PHONE.................................906 353-6090
Mark Niemela, *Owner*
EMP: 7 **EST:** 1978
SALES (est): 928.7K **Privately Held**
WEB: www.lasernorthinc.com
SIC: 7389 7373 3448 Metal cutting services; computer-aided design (CAD) systems service; prefabricated metal components

(G-1144)
LASER NORTH INC (PA)
Also Called: Northern Tool & Engineering
442 N Superior Ave (49908-9602)
P.O. Box 845 (49908-0845)
PHONE.................................906 353-6090
Leo L Niemela, *President*
Mark Niemela, *General Mgr*
Darrel Coponen, *Vice Pres*
Carol Ketola, *Vice Pres*
EMP: 4 **EST:** 1974
SQ FT: 7,500
SALES (est): 1.3MM **Privately Held**
WEB: www.lasernorthinc.com
SIC: 3444 3443 Sheet metalwork; fabricated plate work (boiler shop)

(G-1145)
MASSIE MFG INC
445 N Superior Ave (49908-9602)
P.O. Box 339 (49908-0339)
PHONE.................................906 353-6381
Peter M Massie, *President*
Michael Hirzel, *General Mgr*

Baraga - Baraga County (G-1146)

David Massie, *Vice Pres*
Rick Knisely, *Production*
Siena Tober, *Admin Sec*
EMP: 20 **EST:** 1955
SALES (est): 2.1MM **Privately Held**
WEB: www.massiemfg.com
SIC: 3443 Fabricated plate work (boiler shop)

(G-1146)
PENINSULA POWDER COATING INC
128 Hemlock St (49908-9675)
P.O. Box 609 (49908-0609)
PHONE..................906 353-7234
Brian Baccus, *President*
Bill Kunick, *Opers Staff*
EMP: 24 **EST:** 2003
SQ FT: 5,000
SALES (est): 3MM **Privately Held**
WEB: www.peninsulapowdercoating.com
SIC: 3479 Coating of metals & formed products

(G-1147)
PETTIBONE/TRAVERSE LIFT LLC (DH)
Also Called: Pettibone Parts and Mch Svc
1100 S Superior Ave (49908-9629)
P.O. Box 368 (49908-0368)
PHONE..................906 353-4800
Scott Raffaelli, *Vice Pres*
John Westman, *Project Engr*
Steven Andrews, *Mng Member*
Bob Mayo, *Manager*
▲ **EMP:** 28 **EST:** 1946
SQ FT: 50,000
SALES (est): 22.5MM
SALES (corp-wide): 1.2B **Privately Held**
WEB: www.gopettibone.com
SIC: 3537 5084 Industrial trucks & tractors; materials handling machinery
HQ: Pettibone L.L.C.
27501 Bella Vista Pkwy
Warrenville IL 60555
630 353-5000

(G-1148)
SELKEY FABRICATORS LLC
13170 Lindblom Rd (49908-9150)
PHONE..................906 353-7104
Nicholas Lindemann, *General Mgr*
Nick Lindemann, *General Mgr*
EMP: 12 **EST:** 2015
SQ FT: 35,000
SALES (est): 1MM **Privately Held**
WEB: www.selkeyfab.com
SIC: 2899 Fluxes: brazing, soldering, galvanizing & welding

(G-1149)
USIMAKI LOGGING INC
12347 Arvidson Rd (49908-9131)
PHONE..................920 869-4183
Ryan Usimaki, *Administration*
EMP: 4 **EST:** 2017
SALES (est): 92.7K **Privately Held**
SIC: 2411 Logging camps & contractors

(G-1150)
VAN STRATEN BROTHERS INC
14908 Us Highway 41 (49908-9014)
PHONE..................906 353-6490
Peter Van Straten, *President*
George Van Straten, *Vice Pres*
EMP: 25 **EST:** 1950
SQ FT: 12,000
SALES (est): 1MM **Privately Held**
WEB: www.vanstratenbros.com
SIC: 7692 Welding repair

(G-1151)
XTREME MFG
125 Main St (49908-9671)
PHONE..................906 353-8005
Scott Nicklads, *Principal*
EMP: 6 **EST:** 2006
SALES (est): 17.8K **Privately Held**
SIC: 3999 Manufacturing industries

Barbeau
Chippewa County

(G-1152)
LUDHAVEN SUGARVUSH
8726 E Sawmill Point Rd (49710-9706)
PHONE..................906 647-2400
Fredrick Ludwig, *Owner*
EMP: 4 **EST:** 2001
SALES (est): 95.7K **Privately Held**
SIC: 2099 Maple syrup

Bark River
Delta County

(G-1153)
BARK RIVER CONCRETE PDTS CO (PA)
1397 Us Highway 2 41 (49807-8908)
P.O. Box 67 (49807-0067)
PHONE..................906 466-9940
Donald T Vanenkevort, *President*
James Vanenkevort, *Vice Pres*
Paul Vanenkevort, *Treasurer*
David Vanenkevort, *Admin Sec*
EMP: 6 **EST:** 1946
SQ FT: 20,000
SALES (est): 1.4MM **Privately Held**
WEB: www.upconcrete.com
SIC: 3271 Blocks, concrete or cinder: standard

(G-1154)
FOR THE LOVE OF CUPCAKES
5835 F Rd (49807-9575)
PHONE..................906 399-3004
Kelli Vanginhoven, *Principal*
EMP: 4 **EST:** 2014
SALES (est): 64.1K **Privately Held**
SIC: 2051 Bread, cake & related products

(G-1155)
LUCAS LOGGING
W1564 State Highway M69 (49807)
PHONE..................906 246-3629
Wayne Lucas, *Owner*
EMP: 8 **EST:** 2001
SALES (est): 147.8K **Privately Held**
SIC: 2411 Logging camps & contractors

(G-1156)
MESSERSMITH MANUFACTURING INC
2612 F Rd (49807-9718)
PHONE..................906 466-9010
Gailyn Messersmith, *President*
Valerie Messersmith, *Corp Secy*
EMP: 7 **EST:** 1980
SQ FT: 10,700
SALES (est): 1MM **Privately Held**
WEB: www.burnchips.com
SIC: 3433 Stokers, mechanical: domestic or industrial

(G-1157)
S & S MOWING INC
1460 15.5 Rd (49807-9529)
PHONE..................906 466-9009
Shelly Lippens, *President*
Gregory Knauf, *Vice Pres*
Scott Lippens, *Treasurer*
EMP: 4 **EST:** 2013
SALES (est): 316.1K **Privately Held**
SIC: 3523 Grounds mowing equipment

Baroda
Berrien County

(G-1158)
ACRA TRAINING CENTER
9202 Cleveland Ave (49101-9735)
PHONE..................269 326-7088
Jerry Klinke, *President*
EMP: 4 **EST:** 2017
SALES (est): 80K **Privately Held**
SIC: 2741 Miscellaneous publishing

(G-1159)
DABLON VINEYARDS LLC
111 W Shawnee Rd (49101-9774)
PHONE..................269 422-2846
EMP: 12 **EST:** 2009
SALES (est): 506.3K **Privately Held**
WEB: www.dablon.com
SIC: 2084 Wines

(G-1160)
EDWARDS MACHINERY AND REPA
2064 W Snow Rd (49101-9791)
PHONE..................616 422-2584
Robert Edwards, *Principal*
EMP: 4 **EST:** 2008
SALES (est): 75.5K **Privately Held**
SIC: 3569 General industrial machinery

(G-1161)
FARMHOUSE WOODWORKING LLC
8540 Ruggles Rd (49101-8730)
PHONE..................269 350-0582
Jake Pschigoda, *Principal*
EMP: 4 **EST:** 2017
SALES (est): 54.1K **Privately Held**
SIC: 2431 Millwork

(G-1162)
GAST CABINET CO
8836 Stvnsvlle Broda Rd L (49101-9349)
PHONE..................269 422-1587
Robert R Gast, *Owner*
EMP: 4 **EST:** 1967
SALES (est): 106.8K **Privately Held**
SIC: 1751 5947 2541 2434 Cabinet & finish carpentry; gift shop; wood partitions & fixtures; vanities, bathroom: wood

(G-1163)
LAKE MICHIGAN VINTNERS LLC
8972 First St (49101-8921)
PHONE..................269 326-7195
EMP: 7 **EST:** 2017
SALES (est): 125.8K **Privately Held**
WEB: www.lakemichiganvintners.com
SIC: 2084 Wines

(G-1164)
LAKESHORE DIE CAST INC
8829 Stvnsville Baroda Rd (49101-9301)
P.O. Box 96 (49101-0096)
PHONE..................269 422-1523
Fred Schaller, *President*
Adam Schaller, *Vice Pres*
EMP: 18 **EST:** 1959
SQ FT: 42,000
SALES (est): 2.1MM **Privately Held**
WEB: www.lakeshorediecast.com
SIC: 3364 3363 Zinc & zinc-base alloy die-castings; aluminum die-castings

(G-1165)
MIDWEST DIE CORP
9220 First St (49101-8923)
P.O. Box 132 (49101-0132)
PHONE..................269 422-2171
Rodney Nitz, *President*
Richard Nitz, *Vice Pres*
EMP: 23 **EST:** 1982
SQ FT: 9,000
SALES (est): 1.5MM **Privately Held**
WEB: www.midwestdiecorp.net
SIC: 3544 Dies & die holders for metal cutting, forming, die casting

(G-1166)
MORAINE VINEYARDS LLC
111 E Shawnee Rd (49101-8708)
PHONE..................269 422-1309
Rudy Shafer, *Principal*
EMP: 6 **EST:** 2012
SALES (est): 94.6K **Privately Held**
WEB: www.dablon.com
SIC: 2084 Wines

(G-1167)
ORONOKO IRON WORKS INC
9243 First St (49101-8923)
P.O. Box 313 (49101-0313)
PHONE..................269 326-7045
Rusty Riley, *President*
EMP: 6 **EST:** 2014
SQ FT: 10,000
SALES (est): 784.4K **Privately Held**
WEB: www.oronokoiron.com
SIC: 3499 Aerosol valves, metal

(G-1168)
Q M E INC
Also Called: Quality Mold and Engineering
9070 First St (49101-8924)
P.O. Box 285 (49101-0285)
PHONE..................269 422-2137
James T Florian, *President*
Patricia Florian, *Admin Sec*
▼ **EMP:** 23 **EST:** 1979
SQ FT: 30,000
SALES (est): 1.8MM **Privately Held**
WEB: www.quality-molds.com
SIC: 3544 Special dies & tools

(G-1169)
R C M S INC
Also Called: Heart of The Vnyrd Wnry/Bd/Brk
10981 Hills Rd (49101-8742)
PHONE..................269 422-1617
Richard C Moersch, *President*
Sherry Moersch, *Vice Pres*
EMP: 6 **EST:** 1988
SALES (est): 857.3K **Privately Held**
SIC: 5149 7011 2084 Wine makers' equipment & supplies; bed & breakfast inn; wines, brandy & brandy spirits

(G-1170)
SELECT TOOL AND DIE INC
9170 First St (49101-8927)
P.O. Box 247 (49101-0247)
PHONE..................269 422-2812
Michael J Conrad, *President*
Jamie Conrad, *Corp Secy*
EMP: 8 **EST:** 1995
SQ FT: 5,000
SALES (est): 1MM **Privately Held**
WEB: www.select-tool.com
SIC: 3544 Industrial molds; forms (molds), for foundry & plastics working machinery

(G-1171)
TIGMASTER CO
9283 First St (49101-8923)
P.O. Box 183 (49101-0183)
PHONE..................800 824-4830
Terry Schmaltz, *President*
Jeff Sukupchak, *President*
EMP: 40 **EST:** 1980
SQ FT: 31,000
SALES (est): 5.6MM **Privately Held**
WEB: www.tigmaster.com
SIC: 3444 3496 7692 Sheet metalwork; miscellaneous fabricated wire products; welding repair

Barryton
Mecosta County

(G-1172)
DANA & SEAN ROBERDS
53 E Marion Ave (49305-5115)
PHONE..................989 382-7564
Sean Roberds, *Principal*
EMP: 4 **EST:** 2007
SALES (est): 56.7K **Privately Held**
SIC: 3993 5099 Signs & advertising specialties; signs, except electric

(G-1173)
PRECISION WLDG & MCH REPR LLC
5301 S Birch Dr (49305-8500)
PHONE..................989 309-0699
EMP: 4 **EST:** 2016
SALES (est): 43.2K **Privately Held**
SIC: 7692 Welding repair

Bath
Clinton County

(G-1174)
WEBBER WOODWORKS LLC
5544 Timothy Ln (48808-9790)
PHONE..................517 896-8636
Kevin Webber, *Principal*
EMP: 5 **EST:** 2014

GEOGRAPHIC SECTION

Battle Creek - Calhoun County (G-1200)

SALES (est): 63.1K Privately Held
SIC: 2431 Millwork

Battle Creek
Calhoun County

(G-1175)
A C FOUNDRY INCORPORATED
Also Called: Melling Pattern and Prototype
202 Mcgrath Pl (49014-5859)
PHONE...................................269 963-4131
David Neunen, *General Mgr*
EMP: 10
SALES (corp-wide): 5.9MM Privately Held
WEB: www.mellingcastings.com
SIC: 3365 3369 Aluminum & aluminum-based alloy castings; nonferrous foundries
PA: A C Foundry, Incorporated
  1146 Raymond Rd N
  Battle Creek MI 49014
  269 963-8539

(G-1176)
ABRASIVE MATERIALS LLC
7253 Tower Rd (49014-7529)
PHONE...................................517 437-4796
Robert Hancock, *Natl Sales Mgr*
Christi Olmstead, *Info Tech Mgr*
Mike Trotta,
Ken Clark,
▲ **EMP:** 7 **EST:** 2003
SALES (est): 952.9K Privately Held
WEB: www.abrasivematerials.com
SIC: 3291 Abrasive products

(G-1177)
ADIENT US LLC
76 Armstrong Rd (49037-7315)
PHONE...................................269 968-3000
Todd Callis, *Controller*
Steve Johnson, *Manager*
EMP: 300 Privately Held
WEB: www.adient.com
SIC: 3714 Motor vehicle parts & accessories
HQ: Adient Us Llc
  49200 Halyard Dr
  Plymouth MI 48170
  734 254-5000

(G-1178)
ADLIB GRAFIX & APPAREL
10 Van Armon Ave (49017-5448)
PHONE...................................269 964-2810
Theodore Lawrence, *Partner*
Lisa Lawrence, *Partner*
EMP: 5 **EST:** 1990
SALES (est): 280K Privately Held
SIC: 7389 2759 2395 Textile & apparel services; screen printing; embroidery products, except schiffli machine

(G-1179)
ADVANCED SPECIAL TOOLS INC
320 Clark Rd (49037-7303)
PHONE...................................269 962-9697
Shigeyuki Fujiwara, *President*
Haruyasu Iida, *Vice Pres*
Stephanie Garcia, *Human Res Mgr*
Dan Busick, *Manager*
Marty Hawthorne, *Manager*
▲ **EMP:** 110
SQ FT: 20,500
SALES (est): 15.9MM Privately Held
WEB: www.advancedspecialtools.com
SIC: 3544 7692 3089 Forms (molds), for foundry & plastics working machinery; welding repair; molding primary plastic
PA: Katayama Corp.
  1-30, Himegaoka
  Kani GIF 509-0

(G-1180)
ADVANTAGE SINTERED METALS INC
5701 W Dickman Rd Ste A (49037-7310)
PHONE...................................269 964-1212
Jet Perelli, *President*
Dale Sinclair, *General Mgr*
Jason McDaniel, *Engineer*
Catherine Miller, *Controller*
Dan Walsh, *Sales Mgr*
▲ **EMP:** 101 **EST:** 1990
SALES (est): 20.8MM Privately Held
WEB: www.advantagesintered.com
SIC: 3399 Powder, metal

(G-1181)
ADVENTURES MONI AND KOKO LLC
188 Roosevelt Ave W (49037-2447)
PHONE...................................269 589-2154
Nicole Y Brown,
EMP: 4 **EST:** 2020
SALES (est): 25K Privately Held
SIC: 3999 Hair & hair-based products

(G-1182)
AKERS WOOD PRODUCTS INC (PA)
1124 River Rd W (49037-6101)
PHONE...................................269 962-3802
Toll Free:..................................888 -
Jerry Akers, *President*
Lydia Akers, *Corp Secy*
John Akers, *Vice Pres*
EMP: 6 **EST:** 1963
SQ FT: 6,000 Privately Held
WEB: www.ceoshelterinsurance.com
SIC: 2448 Pallets, wood

(G-1183)
ALLEGRA MARKETING PRINT MAIL
1514 Columbia Ave W (49015-2838)
PHONE...................................269 213-8840
EMP: 6 **EST:** 2018
SALES (est): 279.3K Privately Held
WEB: www.allegramarketingprint.com
SIC: 2752 Commercial printing, offset

(G-1184)
ALLEN PATTERN OF MICHIGAN
202 Mcgrath Pl (49014-5859)
PHONE...................................269 963-4131
Gregory G Allen, *President*
David L Habenicht, *Vice Pres*
EMP: 13 **EST:** 1979
SQ FT: 23,500
SALES (est): 661.9K Privately Held
SIC: 3543 3599 3993 2542 Industrial patterns; machine shop, jobbing & repair; signs & advertising specialties; partitions & fixtures, except wood

(G-1185)
ARCHER-DANIELS-MIDLAND COMPANY
Also Called: ADM
436 Porter St Unit F2 (49014-6806)
PHONE...................................269 968-2900
Bill Carr, *Branch Mgr*
EMP: 4
SALES (corp-wide): 64.3B Publicly Held
WEB: www.adm.com
SIC: 2041 Flour & other grain mill products
PA: Archer-Daniels-Midland Company
  77 W Wacker Dr Ste 4600
  Chicago IL 60601
  312 634-8100

(G-1186)
ASPIDISTRA NATURALS INC
191 N Eastway Dr (49015-3911)
PHONE...................................269 317-0996
Lori Olsen,
EMP: 5 **EST:** 2017
SALES (est): 176.5K Privately Held
WEB: www.aspidistranaturals.com
SIC: 3999 Manufacturing industries

(G-1187)
AUSTIN QUALITY SALES COMPANY
Also Called: Kellogg Co
1 Kellogg Sq (49017-3534)
PHONE...................................269 961-2000
EMP: 21 **EST:** 2014
SALES (est): 3.7MM
SALES (corp-wide): 13.7B Publicly Held
WEB: www.kelloggcompany.com
SIC: 2043 Cereal breakfast foods
PA: Kellogg Company
  1 Kellogg Sq
  Battle Creek MI 49017
  269 961-2000

(G-1188)
B & M IMAGING INC
Also Called: Allegra Battle Creek
1514 Columbia Ave W (49015-2838)
PHONE...................................269 968-2403
Eric Bird, *President*
EMP: 6 **EST:** 1981
SQ FT: 5,400
SALES (est): 1.5MM Privately Held
SIC: 2752 Commercial printing, offset

(G-1189)
BAHAMA SOUVENIRS INC (PA)
20260 North Ave (49017-9700)
PHONE...................................269 964-8275
Larry G Poley, *President*
Diane Polsey, *Vice Pres*
EMP: 7 **EST:** 1982
SALES (est): 643.2K Privately Held
SIC: 6513 5099 5094 2353 Apartment building operators; souvenirs; jewelry; hats & caps

(G-1190)
BARKER MANUFACTURING CO (PA)
Also Called: Braund Manufacturing Co
1125 Watkins Rd (49015-8605)
P.O. Box 460 (49016-0460)
PHONE...................................269 965-2371
Norma Barker, *President*
Jack Budrow, *Vice Pres*
Sue Stansberry, *Purch Mgr*
Tom Hancock, *CFO*
Tina Greene, *Admin Sec*
EMP: 27 **EST:** 1953
SQ FT: 7,500
SALES (est): 9.5MM Privately Held
WEB: www.barkermfg.com
SIC: 3714 Motor vehicle parts & accessories

(G-1191)
BARKER MANUFACTURING CO
781 Watkins Rd (49015-8695)
P.O. Box 460 (49016-0460)
PHONE...................................269 965-2371
Tom Hancock, *Accounting Mgr*
Mike Walters, *Branch Mgr*
EMP: 15
SALES (corp-wide): 9.5MM Privately Held
WEB: www.barkermfg.com
SIC: 3714 Motor vehicle parts & accessories
PA: Barker Manufacturing Co.
  1125 Watkins Rd
  Battle Creek MI 49015
  269 965-2371

(G-1192)
BATTLE CREEK FLYERS LLC
36 Hiawatha Dr (49015-3525)
PHONE...................................269 579-2914
Daniel Garcia, *Administration*
EMP: 7 **EST:** 2011
SALES (est): 138.8K Privately Held
SIC: 2752 Commercial printing, offset

(G-1193)
BEAR NAKED INC
1 Kellogg Sq (49017-3534)
PHONE...................................203 662-1136
Gary Pilnick, *President*
Richard Schell, *Treasurer*
Todd Haigh, *Admin Sec*
EMP: 17 **EST:** 2010
SALES (est): 567.1K
SALES (corp-wide): 13.7B Publicly Held
WEB: www.kelloggcompany.com
SIC: 2052 Pretzels
PA: Kellogg Company
  1 Kellogg Sq
  Battle Creek MI 49017
  269 961-2000

(G-1194)
BIG GREEN TOMATO LLC
478 Main St (49014-5136)
P.O. Box 770 (49016-0770)
PHONE...................................269 282-1593
Darren Lampert, *CEO*
EMP: 1 **EST:** 2011
SALES (est): 2.2MM
SALES (corp-wide): 193.3MM Publicly Held
WEB: www.growgeneration.com
SIC: 3524 Lawn & garden equipment
PA: Growgeneration Corp.
  930 W 7th Ave Ste A
  Denver CO 80204
  800 935-8420

(G-1195)
BIG MIKES WELDING
169 Van Buren St E (49017-3930)
PHONE...................................269 420-8017
Brant Miller, *Principal*
EMP: 4 **EST:** 2018
SALES (est): 25K Privately Held
SIC: 7692 Welding repair

(G-1196)
BLEISTAHL N AMER LTD PARTNR
190 Clark Rd (49037-7393)
PHONE...................................269 719-8585
Thomas Glas, *President*
Solomon Gaddam, *Engineer*
Michelle Henderson, *Human Res Mgr*
EMP: 35 **EST:** 2013
SALES (est): 68.6K
SALES (corp-wide): 170.4MM Privately Held
WEB: www.bleistahl.de
SIC: 3714 Cylinder heads, motor vehicle
HQ: Bleistahl Ltd.
  43311 Joy Rd Pmb 427
  Canton MI 48187
  248 202-1277

(G-1197)
BRAKE ROLLER CO INC
Also Called: BRC
1125 Watkins Rd (49015-8605)
P.O. Box 460 (49016-0460)
PHONE...................................269 965-2371
Jack Budrow, *President*
Norma Barker, *Vice Pres*
Jerry Beard, *Manager*
EMP: 13 **EST:** 1974
SQ FT: 7,500
SALES (est): 290.5K Privately Held
WEB: www.brakeroller.com
SIC: 3542 3312 Brakes, metal forming; blast furnaces & steel mills

(G-1198)
BROTHERS MEAD 3 LLC
19915 Capital Ave Ne # 208 (49017-8124)
PHONE...................................269 883-6241
Todd Blandford, *Project Mgr*
Austin Mead,
EMP: 6 **EST:** 2013
SALES (est): 884.2K Privately Held
WEB: www.brothersmead3.com
SIC: 3825 Test equipment for electronic & electrical circuits

(G-1199)
BRUTSCHE CONCRETE PRODUCTS CO (PA)
15150 6 1/2 Mile Rd (49014-9502)
P.O. Box 1031 (49016-1031)
PHONE...................................269 963-1554
Timothy J Brutsche, *President*
Katherine L Brutsche, *Vice Pres*
EMP: 15 **EST:** 1910
SQ FT: 40,000
SALES (est): 2.6MM Privately Held
WEB: www.brutscheconcrete.com
SIC: 3272 Burial vaults, concrete or precast terrazzo; building materials, except block or brick; concrete

(G-1200)
BRYDGES GROUP LLC
Also Called: Alt House Malts
4950 W Dickman Rd Ste C (49037-7362)
PHONE...................................734 649-6635
Michael Cooper, *CEO*
Vincent Coonce, *COO*
EMP: 6 **EST:**
SALES (est): 303.4K Privately Held
WEB: www.brydgesgroup.com
SIC: 2083 Malt

Battle Creek - Calhoun County (G-1201) GEOGRAPHIC SECTION

(G-1201)
BURR ENGINEERING & DEV CO (PA)
1125 Watkins Rd (49015-8605)
P.O. Box 460 (49016-0460)
PHONE..................................269 966-3122
Dan Budrow, *President*
Jack Budrow, *President*
Norma Barker, *Vice Pres*
Candy Fugate, *QC Mgr*
Martha Mc Millan, *Admin Sec*
EMP: 3 **EST:** 1960
SALES (est): 2.6MM **Privately Held**
WEB: www.burractuators.com
SIC: 3625 3714 Actuators, industrial; motor vehicle parts & accessories

(G-1202)
CA PICARD INC
305 Hill Brady Rd (49037-7389)
PHONE..................................269 962-2231
Carl August Picard, *Owner*
Peg Lieberman, *Partner*
Paul Diaz, *Sales Staff*
Jeanette Brown, *CTO*
EMP: 1 **EST:** 2017
SALES (est): 1.3MM **Privately Held**
WEB: www.capicard.de
SIC: 3443 Fabricated plate work (boiler shop)

(G-1203)
CA PICARD SURFACE ENGRG INC
305 Hill Brady Rd (49037-7360)
PHONE..................................440 366-5400
Mark Sink, *President*
▲ **EMP:** 23 **EST:** 1996
SALES (est): 2.1MM
SALES (corp-wide): 62.5MM **Privately Held**
WEB: www.capicard.de
SIC: 3469 5051 Machine parts, stamped or pressed metal; foundry products
HQ: Carl Aug. Picard Gmbh
   Haster Aue 9
   Remscheid NW 42857
   219 189-30

(G-1204)
CALHOUN COUNTY MED CARE FCILTY
1150 Michigan Ave E (49014-6113)
PHONE..................................269 962-5458
Dayle Kidney, *Chf Purch Ofc*
Donna Mahoney, *CFO*
John Castle, *Controller*
Ronald Rose, *Supervisor*
Vincent Jones, *Food Svc Dir*
EMP: 20 **EST:** 2010
SALES (est): 15.8MM **Privately Held**
WEB: www.ccmcf.com
SIC: 3829 Measuring & controlling devices

(G-1205)
CARIBBEAN ADVENTURE LLC
Also Called: Freshwater Communications
5420 Beckley Rd Ste 244 (49015-5719)
PHONE..................................269 441-5675
EMP: 10
SALES (est): 680K **Privately Held**
SIC: 2721 Periodicals-Publishing/Printing

(G-1206)
CELLO-FOIL PRODUCTS INC (PA)
155 Brook St (49037-3031)
PHONE..................................229 435-4777
Kenneth M Lesiow, *Ch of Bd*
Carol Rhodes, *Vice Pres*
John E Thomas, *CFO*
Cynthia Bauman, *Admin Sec*
EMP: 200 **EST:** 1949
SQ FT: 140,000
SALES (est): 23.4MM **Privately Held**
SIC: 2671 Packaging paper & plastics film, coated & laminated

(G-1207)
CENTRAL MICHIGAN CREMATORY
151506 One Half Mile Rd (49014)
P.O. Box 1031 (49016-1031)
PHONE..................................269 963-1554
Timothy Brutsche, *President*
Katherine L Brutsche, *Vice Pres*
EMP: 17 **EST:** 1982
SALES (est): 481.5K **Privately Held**
WEB: www.brutscheconcrete.com
SIC: 3272 Burial vaults, concrete or precast terrazzo

(G-1208)
CFF INC
570 Limewood Dr Apt E (49017-4567)
PHONE..................................517 242-6903
Chris Neagle, *Agent*
EMP: 4 **EST:** 2018
SALES (est): 178.9K **Privately Held**
SIC: 3084 Plastics pipe

(G-1209)
CLASSIC GLASS BATTLE CREEK INC
21472 Bedford Rd N (49017-8035)
PHONE..................................269 968-2791
Sharon Van Nortwick, *President*
Ronald Voelker, *Vice Pres*
Phillip A Voelker, *Admin Sec*
EMP: 11 **EST:** 1986
SQ FT: 9,000
SALES (est): 295.9K **Privately Held**
WEB: www.battlecreekglass.com
SIC: 3231 Insulating glass: made from purchased glass

(G-1210)
CLYDE UNION (HOLDINGS) INC
4600 W Dickman Rd (49037-7325)
PHONE..................................269 966-4600
Edward Behrndt, *Superintendent*
EMP: 321 **EST:** 1997
SALES (est): 43.3MM
SALES (corp-wide): 1.3B **Publicly Held**
WEB: www.spxflow.com
SIC: 3561 5084 Industrial pumps & parts; pumps & pumping equipment
PA: Spx Flow, Inc.
   13320 Balntyn Corp Pl
   Charlotte NC 28277
   704 752-4400

(G-1211)
CONSUMERS CONCRETE CORPORATION
1020 Raymond Rd N (49014-5936)
PHONE..................................269 965-2321
Jeff Gelbaugh, *Manager*
EMP: 6
SALES (corp-wide): 42.6MM **Privately Held**
WEB: www.consumersconcrete.com
SIC: 3273 Ready-mixed concrete
PA: Consumers Concrete Corporation
   3506 Lovers Ln
   Kalamazoo MI 49001
   269 342-0136

(G-1212)
COVERIS
155 Brook St (49037-3031)
PHONE..................................269 964-1130
Berry Fulpomer, *General Mgr*
EMP: 114 **EST:** 2014
SALES (est): 6.7MM
SALES (corp-wide): 1.9B **Privately Held**
WEB: www.coveris.com
SIC: 2673 2631 Bags: plastic, laminated & coated; paperboard mills
HQ: Transcontinental Holding Corp.
   8600 W Bryn Mawr Ave
   Chicago IL 60631

(G-1213)
CSE MORSE INC
Also Called: Honeywell Authorized Dealer
17 Race Ct (49017-4181)
P.O. Box 669 (49016-0669)
PHONE..................................269 962-5548
Bruce A Boyer, *President*
Stan N Zygadlo, *Treasurer*
Nicholas Zygadlo, *Admin Sec*
EMP: 65 **EST:** 2001
SQ FT: 25,000
SALES (est): 9.1MM **Privately Held**
WEB: www.csemorse.com
SIC: 3444 Sheet metal specialties, not stamped

(G-1214)
DAVID BROWN UNION PUMPS CO PAY
4600 W Dickman Rd (49037-7325)
PHONE..................................269 966-4702
Abraham Phothirath, *Principal*
EMP: 8 **EST:** 2012
SALES (est): 290.9K **Privately Held**
WEB: www.122981-us.all.biz
SIC: 3561 Pumps & pumping equipment

(G-1215)
DENSO AIR SYSTEMS MICHIGAN INC (DH)
300 Fritz Keiper Blvd (49037-5607)
PHONE..................................269 962-9676
Katsuaki Kawai, *Vice Pres*
Cindy Collins, *Production*
Charlie Mack, *Production*
Mike Reniger, *Production*
Gabriela Sanchez, *Buyer*
▲ **EMP:** 311 **EST:** 1986
SQ FT: 167,000
SALES (est): 58.2MM **Privately Held**
WEB: www.densocorp-na-asmi.com
SIC: 3714 3498 Air conditioner parts, motor vehicle; fabricated pipe & fittings

(G-1216)
DENSO MANUFACTURING MICH INC (DH)
Also Called: Dmmi
1 Denso Rd (49037-7313)
PHONE..................................269 965-3322
Hikaru Howard Sugi, *CEO*
Kazutaka Nimura, *Vice Pres*
Kazumasa Kimura, *COO*
Atsuhiko Art Shimmura, *Exec VP*
Ken Iguchi, *Vice Pres*
◆ **EMP:** 2463 **EST:** 1984
SQ FT: 838,000
SALES (est): 533.2MM **Privately Held**
WEB: www.densotac.com
SIC: 3714 Air conditioner parts, motor vehicle; heaters, motor vehicle; thermostats, motor vehicle
HQ: Denso International America, Inc.
   24777 Denso Dr
   Southfield MI 48033
   248 350-7500

(G-1217)
DENSO MANUFACTURING NC INC
500 Fritz Keiper Blvd (49037-7306)
PHONE..................................269 441-2040
Masanori Iyama, *President*
Chad De Shane, *Engineer*
Brian Fellabaum, *Engineer*
EMP: 700 **Privately Held**
SIC: 3621 3089 Motors, electric; plastic & fiberglass tanks
HQ: Denso Manufacturing North Carolina, Inc.
   470 Crawford Rd
   Statesville NC 28625

(G-1218)
DENSO SALES MICHIGAN INC
1 Denso Rd (49037-7313)
PHONE..................................269 965-3322
James O'Dowd, *Principal*
John Hahn, *Plant Engr Mgr*
Luke Boulter, *Engineer*
Kurt Burdick, *Engineer*
Said Musi, *Engineer*
▼ **EMP:** 46 **EST:** 2007
SALES (est): 1MM **Privately Held**
WEB: www.densocorp-na-asmi.com
SIC: 3714 Motor vehicle parts & accessories

(G-1219)
DIEOMATIC INCORPORATED
Also Called: Cosma Casting Michigan
10 Clark Rd (49037-7302)
PHONE..................................269 966-4900
Steve Flannery, *General Mgr*
EMP: 12
SALES (corp-wide): 32.6B **Privately Held**
SIC: 3714 Motor vehicle parts & accessories
HQ: Dieomatic Incorporated
   750 Twer Dr Mail Code 700
   Troy MI 48098

(G-1220)
DOUGLAS MILTON LAMP CO
208 Kensington Cir (49015-9500)
PHONE..................................888 738-3332
Michael Delmont, *Principal*
EMP: 6 **EST:** 2012
SALES (est): 319.5K **Privately Held**
WEB: www.lamps.miltondouglas.com
SIC: 5063 3646 3645 Lighting fixtures; commercial indusl & institutional electric lighting fixtures; residential lighting fixtures

(G-1221)
DRAKE PUBLISHING
664 Minges Rd E (49015-4759)
PHONE..................................269 963-4810
Ryan Drake Wellever, *Principal*
EMP: 4 **EST:** 2016
SALES (est): 61.8K **Privately Held**
SIC: 2741 Miscellaneous publishing

(G-1222)
DUNN BEVERAGE INTL LLC
95 Minges Rd N (49015-7909)
PHONE..................................269 420-1547
Sara Durkee, *Manager*
EMP: 5 **EST:** 2010
SALES (est): 93.1K **Privately Held**
SIC: 2084 Wines

(G-1223)
ENVIRON MANUFACTURING INC
972 Graham Lake Ter (49014-8309)
PHONE..................................616 644-6846
James Trent, *CEO*
EMP: 7 **EST:** 2018
SALES (est): 339.6K **Privately Held**
SIC: 3559 Electronic component making machinery

(G-1224)
EPI PRINTERS INC (PA)
Also Called: Epi Marketing Services
5404 Wayne Rd (49037-7300)
P.O. Box 1025 (49016-1025)
PHONE..................................800 562-9733
William Guzy, *President*
Dennis Bridges, *General Mgr*
Keith Martin, *Principal*
Jason Carte, *Business Mgr*
Dennis Briggs, *Vice Pres*
◆ **EMP:** 40
SQ FT: 30,000
SALES (est): 160.6MM **Privately Held**
WEB: www.epiinc.com
SIC: 2752 Commercial printing, offset

(G-1225)
EPI PRINTERS INC
61 Clark Rd (49037-7364)
P.O. Box 1025 (49016-1025)
PHONE..................................269 968-2221
Jeff Adams, *Manager*
EMP: 55
SALES (corp-wide): 160.6MM **Privately Held**
WEB: www.epiinc.com
SIC: 2752 7389 Commercial printing, offset; coupon redemption service
PA: Epi Printers, Inc.
   5404 Wayne Rd
   Battle Creek MI 49037
   800 562-9733

(G-1226)
EPI PRINTERS INC
Also Called: Epi Market
5350 W Dickman Rd (49037-7312)
P.O. Box 1025 (49016-1025)
PHONE..................................269 968-2221
William Guzy, *President*
Rich Fitch, *CIO*
EMP: 55
SALES (corp-wide): 160.6MM **Privately Held**
WEB: www.epiinc.com
SIC: 2752 Commercial printing, offset
PA: Epi Printers, Inc.
   5404 Wayne Rd
   Battle Creek MI 49037
   800 562-9733

▲ = Import ▼ = Export
◆ = Import/Export

GEOGRAPHIC SECTION
Battle Creek - Calhoun County (G-1250)

(G-1227)
EPI PRINTERS INC
Also Called: Arm Fulfillment
4956 Wayne Rd (49037-7332)
P.O. Box 1025 (49016-1025)
PHONE.................................269 964-4600
Dennis Briggs, *General Mgr*
Brian Blum, *Business Mgr*
Jenny Cormack, *Business Mgr*
Michael Medved, *Exec VP*
Rich Fitch, *Vice Pres*
EMP: 73
SALES (corp-wide): 160.6MM **Privately Held**
WEB: www.epiinc.com
SIC: 7389 2752 Coupon redemption service; commercial printing, lithographic
PA: Epi Printers, Inc.
   5404 Wayne Rd
   Battle Creek MI 49037
   800 562-9733

(G-1228)
EPI PRINTERS INC
Also Called: Epi Marketing Services
65 Clark Rd (49037-7364)
PHONE.................................269 964-6744
Duane Lantis, *Branch Mgr*
EMP: 55
SALES (corp-wide): 160.6MM **Privately Held**
WEB: www.epiinc.com
SIC: 2752 Commercial printing, offset
PA: Epi Printers, Inc.
   5404 Wayne Rd
   Battle Creek MI 49037
   800 562-9733

(G-1229)
FAST CASH
641 Capital Ave Sw (49015-5002)
PHONE.................................269 966-0079
Don Quada, *Manager*
EMP: 4 **EST:** 2001
SALES (est): 196.4K **Privately Held**
SIC: 3651 Audio electronic systems

(G-1230)
FERREES TOOLS INC
1477 Michigan Ave E (49014-7974)
PHONE.................................269 965-0511
Clifford M Ferree, *President*
Katherine Neeley, *Vice Pres*
EMP: 28 **EST:** 1946
SQ FT: 3,600
SALES (est): 3.2MM **Privately Held**
WEB: www.ferreestoolsinc.com
SIC: 3931 3423 Musical instruments; hand & edge tools

(G-1231)
FIVE-WAY SWITCH MUSIC
9478 Huntington Rd (49017-9731)
PHONE.................................269 425-2843
Matt Kirkland, *Principal*
EMP: 5 **EST:** 2016
SALES (est): 103.3K **Privately Held**
WEB: www.fivewayswitchmusic.word-press.com
SIC: 3679 Electronic switches

(G-1232)
FLEX-N-GATE BATTLE CREEK LLC
10250 F Dr N (49014-8237)
PHONE.................................269 962-2982
Eddie Charfauros, *QC Mgr*
Nancy Davis, *Human Resources*
Shahid Khan, *Mng Member*
William Goldstein,
▲ **EMP:** 185 **EST:** 2000
SALES (est): 58.4MM
SALES (corp-wide): 1.5B **Privately Held**
WEB: www.flex-n-gate.com
SIC: 3714 Motor vehicle parts & accessories
PA: Flex-N-Gate Llc
   1306 E University Ave
   Urbana IL 61802
   217 384-6600

(G-1233)
FRANKLIN IRON & METAL CO INC (PA)
Also Called: Franklin Plastics
120 South Ave (49014-4136)
P.O. Box 664 (49016-0664)
PHONE.................................269 968-6111
Susan Franklin Behnke, *President*
Travis Mumy, *Vice Pres*
David S Behnke, *Project Mgr*
Scott Brown, *Sales Staff*
EMP: 15 **EST:** 1900
SQ FT: 15,000
SALES (est): 11.5MM **Privately Held**
WEB: www.franklin-scrap.com
SIC: 5093 3341 Ferrous metal scrap & waste; secondary nonferrous metals

(G-1234)
GEISLINGER CORPORATION
200 Geislinger Dr (49037-5622)
PHONE.................................269 441-7000
Michael Krenn, *President*
Nelson Multer, *Technology*
Sabine Mosdorser, *Admin Sec*
▲ **EMP:** 14 **EST:** 2000
SQ FT: 40,000
SALES (est): 6.9MM
SALES (corp-wide): 17.3MM **Privately Held**
WEB: www.geislinger.com
SIC: 3568 3519 Power transmission equipment; internal combustion engines
PA: Ellergon Antriebstechnik Gmbh
   Hallwanger LandesstraBe 3
   Hallwang 5300
   662 669-990

(G-1235)
GRAPHIX 2 GO INC
7200 Tower Rd (49014-7529)
PHONE.................................269 969-7321
Denise Jones, *President*
Kim Harrington, *Vice Pres*
Jolene Nagy, *Opers Mgr*
Amy Howard, *Sales Mgr*
Lowell Schirado, *Sales Staff*
EMP: 8 **EST:** 1992
SQ FT: 5,000
SALES (est): 1.2MM **Privately Held**
WEB: www.graphix2goinc.com
SIC: 7389 2759 Advertising, promotional & trade show services; commercial printing; promotional printing; advertising literature: printing

(G-1236)
HDN F&A INC
Also Called: F & A Fabricating
104 Arbor St (49015-3026)
P.O. Box 102 (49016-0102)
PHONE.................................269 965-3268
Hiep D Nguyen, *President*
EMP: 54 **EST:** 1956
SQ FT: 24,000
SALES (est): 6.3MM **Privately Held**
SIC: 3444 Sheet metal specialties, not stamped

(G-1237)
HI-LEX AMERICA INCORPORATED (DH)
5200 Wayne Rd (49037-7392)
PHONE.................................269 968-0781
Katsuaki Shima, *Ch of Bd*
Tom Strictland, *President*
Felicia Smith, *Administration*
Shane Addington, *Associate*
▲ **EMP:** 323 **EST:** 1975
SQ FT: 175,000
SALES (est): 114.8MM **Privately Held**
WEB: www.hi-lex.com
SIC: 3496 3357 Cable, uninsulated wire: made from purchased wire; nonferrous wiredrawing & insulating
HQ: Tsk Of America, Inc.
   152 Simpson Dr
   Litchfield MI 49252
   517 542-2955

(G-1238)
HOTSET CORP
1045 Harts Lake Rd (49037-7357)
P.O. Box 2404 (49016-2404)
PHONE.................................269 964-0271

Rick Mell, *Principal*
Bernward Seeberg, *Project Engr*
Andreas Filler, *Manager*
EMP: 9 **EST:** 2016
SALES (est): 511.5K **Privately Held**
WEB: www.nexthermal.com
SIC: 3567 Heating units & devices, industrial: electric

(G-1239)
IF AND OR BUT PUBLISHING
33 Broad St N (49017-4703)
PHONE.................................269 274-6102
Michael Delaware, *Principal*
EMP: 4 **EST:** 2015
SALES (est): 69.8K **Privately Held**
WEB: www.ifandorbutpublishing.com
SIC: 2741 Miscellaneous publishing

(G-1240)
II STANLEY CO INC (DH)
1500 Hill Brady Rd (49037-7320)
PHONE.................................269 660-7777
Seiichi Fujii, *President*
James Huberty, *Exec VP*
Mike Isham, *Exec VP*
Shinishiro Kojima, *Exec VP*
Shoji Ichikawa, *Treasurer*
▲ **EMP:** 747 **EST:** 1985
SQ FT: 360,000
SALES (est): 102MM **Privately Held**
WEB: www.iistanley.com
SIC: 3647 Automotive lighting fixtures
HQ: Stanley Electric Us Co Inc
   420 E High St
   London OH 43140
   740 852-5200

(G-1241)
INSULATION WHOLESALE SUPPLY
Also Called: Wheeler Insulation
11280 Michigan Ave E (49014-8904)
PHONE.................................269 968-9746
Janet Wakenight, *Ch of Bd*
Ramar Wakenight, *President*
Loren Mills, *Vice Pres*
Richard Wakenight, *Treasurer*
Franklin Hill, *Admin Sec*
EMP: 6 **EST:** 1976
SQ FT: 9,000
SALES (est): 746.1K **Privately Held**
SIC: 5211 3699 1742 Insulation material, building; electrical equipment & supplies; insulation, buildings

(G-1242)
J J STEEL INC
2000 Ottawa Trl (49037-8282)
PHONE.................................269 964-0474
Gert Jensen, *President*
▲ **EMP:** 29 **EST:** 1990
SQ FT: 13,000
SALES (est): 7.3MM **Privately Held**
WEB: www.jjsteel.net
SIC: 3556 Dairy & milk machinery

(G-1243)
J-AD GRAPHICS INC
Battle Creek Shopper News
1001 Columbia Ave E (49014-4401)
P.O. Box 163 (49016-0163)
PHONE.................................269 965-3955
Fred Jacobs, *Publisher*
Donna Hazel, *General Mgr*
Shelly Sulser, *Editor*
EMP: 18
SALES (corp-wide): 15.1MM **Privately Held**
WEB: www.hastingsprintshop.com
SIC: 2741 2711 2789 2752 Shopping news: publishing & printing; newspapers, publishing & printing; bookbinding & related work; commercial printing, lithographic
PA: J-Ad Graphics, Inc.
   1351 N M 43 Hwy
   Hastings MI 49058
   800 870-7085

(G-1244)
JANESVILLE LLC
2500 Logistics Dr (49037-7388)
PHONE.................................269 964-5400
Dave Bradley, *Program Mgr*
Scott Eaton, *Director*

EMP: 4
SALES (corp-wide): 316MM **Privately Held**
WEB: www.janesvillesolutions.com
SIC: 2282 Manmade & synthetic fiber yarns: twisting, winding, etc.
HQ: Janesville, Llc
   29200 Northwestern Hwy # 400
   Southfield MI 48034
   248 948-1811

(G-1245)
JETCO SIGNS
302 Capital Ave Sw (49037-8680)
PHONE.................................269 420-0202
Tim Conlogue, *Principal*
EMP: 7 **EST:** 2008
SALES (est): 264.7K **Privately Held**
WEB: www.jetcosigns.com
SIC: 3993 Signs & advertising specialties

(G-1246)
JETECH INC
555 Industrial Park Dr (49037-7446)
PHONE.................................269 965-6311
Bin Qi, *CEO*
Jacob Harmon, *COO*
Donald Creager, *Opers Mgr*
Bill Holladay, *VP Bus Dvlpt*
John Vanoostendorp, *CFO*
◆ **EMP:** 31 **EST:** 1988
SQ FT: 1,600
SALES (est): 7.8MM **Privately Held**
WEB: www.jetech.com
SIC: 3561 5084 3599 7359 Industrial pumps & parts; industrial machinery & equipment; machine shop, jobbing & repair; equipment rental & leasing

(G-1247)
JOSEPH SCOTT FALBE
459 Orchard Ln (49015-3107)
PHONE.................................269 282-1597
Joseph Falbe, *Principal*
EMP: 5 **EST:** 2009
SALES (est): 114.9K **Privately Held**
SIC: 2741 Miscellaneous publishing

(G-1248)
K & L SHEET METAL LLC
131 Grand Trunk Ave Ste C (49037-8423)
PHONE.................................269 965-0027
Kurt Hansen, *Mng Member*
EMP: 8 **EST:** 2007
SALES (est): 736.8K **Privately Held**
WEB: www.klsheetmetal.com
SIC: 3441 5051 Fabricated structural metal; steel

(G-1249)
K-TWO INC
1 Kellogg Sq (49017-3534)
P.O. Box 3599 (49016-3599)
PHONE.................................269 961-2000
Carlo Guthierrez, *President*
◆ **EMP:** 90 **EST:** 2000
SALES (est): 4.4MM
SALES (corp-wide): 13.7B **Publicly Held**
WEB: www.kelloggcompany.com
SIC: 2043 Cereal breakfast foods
PA: Kellogg Company
   1 Kellogg Sq
   Battle Creek MI 49017
   269 961-2000

(G-1250)
KEEBLER COMPANY (HQ)
1 Kellogg Sq (49017-3534)
PHONE.................................269 961-2000
David McKay, *President*
Oli Morton, *Managing Dir*
David A Fedko, *Purchasing*
Janet Di Iorio, *Manager*
Susan Bell, *Director*
◆ **EMP:** 500 **EST:** 1927
SQ FT: 115,000
SALES (est): 1.8B
SALES (corp-wide): 13.7B **Publicly Held**
WEB: www.keebler.com
SIC: 2052 2051 Cookies; crackers, dry; cones, ice cream; pretzels; bread, cake & related products
PA: Kellogg Company
   1 Kellogg Sq
   Battle Creek MI 49017
   269 961-2000

Battle Creek - Calhoun County (G-1251)

GEOGRAPHIC SECTION

(G-1251)
KELLOGG (THAILAND) LIMITED
1 Kellogg Sq (49017-3534)
PHONE..................................269 969-8937
James M Jenness, *CEO*
EMP: 23 **EST:** 2000
SALES (est): 3.1MM
SALES (corp-wide): 13.7B **Publicly Held**
WEB: www.kellogg.edu
SIC: 2043 Cereal breakfast foods
PA: Kellogg Company
1 Kellogg Sq
Battle Creek MI 49017
269 961-2000

(G-1252)
KELLOGG ASIA MARKETING INC (HQ)
1 Kellogg Sq (49017-3534)
PHONE..................................269 961-2000
A D David Mackay, *President*
EMP: 1 **EST:** 1995
SALES (est): 1.7MM
SALES (corp-wide): 13.7B **Publicly Held**
WEB: www.kelloggcompany.com
SIC: 2043 Cereal breakfast foods
PA: Kellogg Company
1 Kellogg Sq
Battle Creek MI 49017
269 961-2000

(G-1253)
KELLOGG CHILE INC
1 Kellogg Sq (49017-3534)
PHONE..................................269 961-2000
EMP: 80 **EST:** 2000
SALES (est): 5.3MM
SALES (corp-wide): 13.7B **Publicly Held**
WEB: www.kelloggcompany.com
SIC: 2043 Cereal breakfast foods
PA: Kellogg Company
1 Kellogg Sq
Battle Creek MI 49017
269 961-2000

(G-1254)
KELLOGG COMPANY
Also Called: W.K. Kellogg Institute
2 Hamblin Ave E (49017-3560)
PHONE..................................269 961-2000
Fred Linabury, *Technical Mgr*
Viswas Ghorpade, *Engineer*
Eric Lewandowski, *Engineer*
Dave Maroukis, *Engineer*
Bruce Broughton, *Engng Exec*
EMP: 385
SALES (corp-wide): 13.7B **Publicly Held**
WEB: www.kelloggcompany.com
SIC: 2043 8733 Cereal breakfast foods; research institute
PA: Kellogg Company
1 Kellogg Sq
Battle Creek MI 49017
269 961-2000

(G-1255)
KELLOGG COMPANY (PA)
1 Kellogg Sq (49017-3534)
P.O. Box 3599 (49016-3599)
PHONE..................................269 961-2000
Gary Pilnick, *Vice Chairman*
Alistair D Hirst, *Senior VP*
Melissa A Howell, *Senior VP*
Nelson Almeida, *Vice Pres*
Margaret Bath, *Vice Pres*
◆ **EMP:** 600 **EST:** 1906
SALES (est): 13.7B **Publicly Held**
WEB: www.kelloggcompany.com
SIC: 2041 2052 2051 2038 Flour & other grain mill products; cookies; crackers, dry; pastries, e.g. danish: except frozen; waffles, frozen; corn flakes: prepared as cereal breakfast food

(G-1256)
KELLOGG COMPANY
70 Michigan Ave W Ste 750 (49017-3666)
PHONE..................................269 964-8525
Yuvraj Arora, *Vice Pres*
Kevin Shelton, *Opers Staff*
Jason Strongin, *Manager*
Jennifer Wells, *Senior Mgr*
Gary Dale, *Director*
EMP: 4
SALES (corp-wide): 13.7B **Publicly Held**
WEB: www.kelloggcompany.com
SIC: 2043 Cereal breakfast foods
PA: Kellogg Company
1 Kellogg Sq
Battle Creek MI 49017
269 961-2000

(G-1257)
KELLOGG COMPANY
235 Porter St (49014-6210)
PHONE..................................269 969-8107
EMP: 6
SALES (corp-wide): 12.9B **Publicly Held**
SIC: 2043 Mfg Cereal Breakfast Food
PA: Kellogg Company
1 Kellogg Sq
Battle Creek MI 49017
269 961-2000

(G-1258)
KELLOGG COMPANY
2 E Hammond Ave (49014)
P.O. Box 1988 (49016-1988)
PHONE..................................269 961-2000
EMP: 4
SALES (corp-wide): 13.7B **Publicly Held**
WEB: www.kelloggcompany.com
SIC: 8733 2043 Noncommercial research organizations; cereal breakfast foods
PA: Kellogg Company
1 Kellogg Sq
Battle Creek MI 49017
269 961-2000

(G-1259)
KELLOGG COMPANY
Financial Service Ctr (49014)
PHONE..................................269 961-6693
Philip Fishman, *Analyst*
EMP: 4
SALES (corp-wide): 13.7B **Publicly Held**
WEB: www.kelloggcompany.com
SIC: 2043 Corn flakes: prepared as cereal breakfast food
PA: Kellogg Company
1 Kellogg Sq
Battle Creek MI 49017
269 961-2000

(G-1260)
KELLOGG NORTH AMERICA COMPANY (DH)
1 Kellogg Sq (49017-3534)
P.O. Box 3599 (49016-3599)
PHONE..................................269 961-2000
David McKay, *President*
EMP: 200 **EST:** 1997
SALES (est): 18.5MM
SALES (corp-wide): 13.7B **Publicly Held**
WEB: www.keebler.com
SIC: 2052 Cookies
HQ: Keebler Company
1 Kellogg Sq
Battle Creek MI 49017
269 961-2000

(G-1261)
KELLOGG USA INC (HQ)
1 Kellogg Sq (49017-3534)
P.O. Box 3599 (49016-3599)
PHONE..................................269 961-2000
David Pfanzelter, *Principal*
▼ **EMP:** 200 **EST:** 1906
SALES (est): 840.9MM
SALES (corp-wide): 13.7B **Publicly Held**
WEB: www.kelloggcompany.com
SIC: 2043 Cereal breakfast foods
PA: Kellogg Company
1 Kellogg Sq
Battle Creek MI 49017
269 961-2000

(G-1262)
KELLOGG USA INC
425 Porter St (49014-6800)
PHONE..................................269 961-2000
Linda Pell, *Owner*
Jodi Rogers, *Corp Comm Staff*
Chris Deyoung, *Manager*
EMP: 1041
SALES (corp-wide): 13.7B **Publicly Held**
SIC: 2043 Cereal breakfast foods
HQ: Kellogg Usa Inc.
1 Kellogg Sq
Battle Creek MI 49017

(G-1263)
KMI CLEANING SOLUTIONS INC
Also Called: K M I
157 Beadle Lake Rd (49014-4504)
P.O. Box 2535 (49016-2535)
PHONE..................................269 964-2557
Russel Bloch, *President*
David Lafler, *Vice Pres*
Zach Lafler, *Sales Staff*
EMP: 10 **EST:** 1980
SQ FT: 4,600
SALES (est): 5.3MM **Privately Held**
WEB: www.kmicleaningsolutions.com
SIC: 5084 5169 2842 Cleaning equipment, high pressure, sand or steam; detergents & soaps, except specialty cleaning; specialty cleaning, polishes & sanitation goods

(G-1264)
KNOEDLER MANUFACTURERS INC
7185 Tower Rd (49014-8522)
PHONE..................................269 969-7722
Wilhelm Sturhan, *President*
▲ **EMP:** 10 **EST:** 1946
SALES (est): 1.7MM **Privately Held**
WEB: www.knoedler.com
SIC: 3714 2531 Motor vehicle parts & accessories; public building & related furniture

(G-1265)
KOYO CORP
300 Fritz Keiper Blvd (49037-5607)
PHONE..................................269 962-9676
Jon McVeigh, *Supervisor*
EMP: 7 **EST:** 2015
SALES (est): 160K **Privately Held**
WEB: www.koyocorporation.com
SIC: 3559 Special industry machinery

(G-1266)
KRUMB SNATCHER COOKIE CO LLC
Also Called: Krumb Satcher Cookies
92 Review Ave (49037-2406)
PHONE..................................313 408-6802
Daryll Gray, *CEO*
EMP: 5 **EST:** 2005
SALES (est): 62.3K **Privately Held**
SIC: 2052 Cookies & crackers

(G-1267)
LAWSON PRINTERS INC
685 Columbia Ave W (49015-3070)
PHONE..................................269 965-0525
Betty Rankin, *President*
Dennis Rankin, *Vice Pres*
EMP: 30 **EST:** 1932
SQ FT: 18,100
SALES (est): 4.8MM **Privately Held**
WEB: www.lawsonprinters.com
SIC: 2752 2759 2672 Commercial printing, offset; commercial printing; coated & laminated paper

(G-1268)
LIBERTY EMBROIDERY
257 Wagon Wheel Ln (49017-9452)
PHONE..................................269 419-0327
Amanda Harris, *Principal*
EMP: 4 **EST:** 2018
SALES (est): 31.2K **Privately Held**
SIC: 2395 Embroidery & art needlework

(G-1269)
LOTTE USA INCORPORATED
Also Called: Lotte U S A
5243 Wayne Rd (49037-7323)
P.O. Box 516, Augusta (49012-0516)
PHONE..................................269 963-6664
Takeo Shigemitsu, *President*
Hiroyuki Shigemitsu, *Vice Pres*
Cathy Morgan, *Sales Staff*
◆ **EMP:** 11 **EST:** 1978
SQ FT: 93,000
SALES (est): 4.5MM **Privately Held**
WEB: www.koalasmarch-usa.com
SIC: 2064 2052 2067 Candy & other confectionery products; cookies; chewing gum base
PA: Lotte Holdings Co., Ltd.
3-20-1, Nishishinjuku
Shinjuku-Ku TKY 160-0

(G-1270)
LS PRECISION TOOL & DIE INC
140 Jacaranda Dr (49015-8663)
PHONE..................................269 963-9910
Gerhard Loewe, *President*
Volker Schwarz, *Vice Pres*
Terri Loewe, *Admin Sec*
EMP: 7 **EST:** 1997
SQ FT: 6,000
SALES (est): 848.9K **Privately Held**
SIC: 3544 Special dies & tools

(G-1271)
MANNETRON
Also Called: Mannetron Animatronics
74 Leonard Wood Rd (49037-7309)
PHONE..................................269 962-3475
Michael Clark, *Owner*
Moran Jungen, *Production*
Peter Jungen, *Design Engr*
Gino Guarniere, *Marketing Staff*
Lanell Nystrom, *Asst Office Mgr*
EMP: 15 **EST:** 1989
SQ FT: 100,000
SALES (est): 2.9MM **Privately Held**
WEB: www.mannetron.com
SIC: 3999 5099 Puppets & marionettes; robots, service or novelty

(G-1272)
MARLEY PRECISION INC (HQ)
455 Fritz Keiper Blvd (49037-7305)
PHONE..................................269 963-7374
Hiro Kitagawa, *President*
Beth Brown, *Vice Pres*
Patty Lees, *Production*
EMP: 4 **EST:** 1995
SQ FT: 14,000
SALES (est): 2.5MM **Privately Held**
WEB: www.marueikogyo.jp
SIC: 3714 Motor vehicle parts & accessories

(G-1273)
METZGER SAWMILL
3100 W Halbert Rd (49017-8078)
PHONE..................................269 963-3022
Ronald Metzger, *Owner*
Gayla Metzger, *Co-Owner*
EMP: 4 **EST:** 1976
SALES (est): 360K **Privately Held**
SIC: 2448 Pallets, wood; skids, wood

(G-1274)
MICHIGAN CARTON PAPER BOY
79 Fountain St E (49017-4130)
PHONE..................................269 963-4004
David Scheible, *Principal*
EMP: 7 **EST:** 2008
SALES (est): 103.5K **Privately Held**
SIC: 2657 Folding paperboard boxes

(G-1275)
MODERN MACHINING INC
415 Upton Ave (49037-8382)
PHONE..................................269 964-4415
Patrick Ballinger, *President*
EMP: 4 **EST:** 1994
SQ FT: 5,000
SALES (est): 304.7K **Privately Held**
SIC: 3599 Machine shop, jobbing & repair

(G-1276)
MUSASHI AUTO PARTS MICH INC
Also Called: Technical Auto Parts
195 Brydges Dr (49037-7340)
PHONE..................................269 965-0057
Mr Takayuki Miyata, *President*
Steve Peine, *Prdtn Mgr*
Saeed Malik, *Engineer*
Brice Schoemer, *Engineer*
▲ **EMP:** 330
SQ FT: 97,000
SALES (est): 78.3MM **Privately Held**
WEB: www.musashi.co.jp
SIC: 3714 Motor vehicle transmissions, drive assemblies & parts
PA: Musashi Seimitsu Industry Co., Ltd.
39-5, Daizen, Uetacho
Toyohashi AIC 441-8

▲ = Import ▼ = Export
◆ = Import/Export

GEOGRAPHIC SECTION
Battle Creek - Calhoun County (G-1303)

(G-1277)
NATIONAL SIGN & SIGNAL CO
301 Armstrong Rd (49037-7374)
PHONE..................269 963-2817
Ronald E Scherer, *CEO*
John Cairns, *President*
David B Thompson, *Corp Secy*
Ken Baxter, *Purchasing*
EMP: 32 **EST:** 1946
SQ FT: 28,000
SALES (est): 4.4MM Privately Held
WEB: www.nationalssc.com
SIC: 3669 3993 Traffic signals, electric; signs, not made in custom sign painting shops

(G-1278)
NEW MOON NOODLE INCORPORATED
Also Called: Kowloon Noodle Company
909 Stanley Dr (49037-7370)
PHONE..................269 962-8820
Lee Lum, *President*
Lillian Lum, *Corp Secy*
EMP: 15 **EST:** 1983
SQ FT: 20,000
SALES (est): 3.2MM Privately Held
WEB: www.newmoonnoodle.com
SIC: 5149 2099 0182 Groceries & related products; noodles, fried (Chinese); bean sprouts grown under cover

(G-1279)
NEXTHERMAL CORPORATION
1045 Harts Lake Rd (49037-7357)
P.O. Box 2404 (49016-2404)
PHONE..................269 964-0271
Srekumar Bandyopadhyay, *President*
Ken Sunden, *Vice Pres*
Doug Green, *Safety Dir*
Phil Grant, *Production*
Kim Kopf, *Engineer*
▲ **EMP:** 95 **EST:** 1985
SQ FT: 25,000
SALES (est): 24.7MM Privately Held
WEB: www.nexthermal.com
SIC: 3567 Heating units & devices, industrial: electric
PA: Nexthermal Manufacturing India Private Limited
No 3b
Bengaluru KA 56007

(G-1280)
PALMER ENVELOPE CO
309 Fritz Keiper Blvd (49037-7305)
P.O. Box 428 (49016-0428)
PHONE..................269 965-1336
Charles A Stevenson, *President*
Shirley Stevenson, *Corp Secy*
EMP: 17 **EST:** 1939
SQ FT: 30,000
SALES (est): 263.9K Privately Held
WEB: www.printlinkonline.com
SIC: 2752 Commercial printing, offset

(G-1281)
POST FOODS LLC
275 Cliff St (49014-6354)
PHONE..................269 966-1000
Kevin Hunt, *CEO*
Don Holtan, *Plant Mgr*
Caitlin Clancy, *Project Mgr*
Phil Noakes, *Plant Engr*
Heather Ivey, *Project Engr*
EMP: 284 **EST:** 2007
SALES (est): 39.5MM Publicly Held
WEB: www.postconsumerbrands.com
SIC: 2043 Cereal breakfast foods
PA: Post Holdings, Inc.
2503 S Hanley Rd
Saint Louis MO 63144

(G-1282)
PRINGLES MANUFACTURING COMPANY
1 Kellogg Sq (49017-3534)
PHONE..................731 421-3148
EMP: 16 **EST:** 2015
SALES: 1MM
SALES (corp-wide): 13.7B Publicly Held
WEB: www.kelloggcompany.com
SIC: 3999 Manufacturing industries

PA: Kellogg Company
1 Kellogg Sq
Battle Creek MI 49017
269 961-2000

(G-1283)
PRINTLINK SHRT RUN BUS FRMS IN
309 Fritz Keiper Blvd (49037-7305)
PHONE..................269 965-1336
Paul E Punnett, *President*
Debra Punnett, *Vice Pres*
▲ **EMP:** 10 **EST:** 1994
SQ FT: 7,500
SALES (est): 1.2MM Privately Held
WEB: www.printlinkonline.com
SIC: 2752 Commercial printing, offset

(G-1284)
PROGRESSIVE PRTG & GRAPHICS
148 Columbia Ave E (49015-3735)
PHONE..................269 965-8909
Daniel Egan, *Owner*
▼ **EMP:** 4 **EST:** 1980
SQ FT: 4,000
SALES (est): 249.7K Privately Held
WEB: www.bcppg.com
SIC: 2752 5621 2791 Commercial printing, offset; bridal shops; typesetting

(G-1285)
R B CHRISTIAN INC (PA)
525 24th St N (49037-7807)
PHONE..................269 963-9327
Richard Christian, *President*
EMP: 5 **EST:** 1952
SALES (est): 566.1K Privately Held
WEB: www.rbchristian.com
SIC: 3446 5211 Architectural metalwork; lumber & other building materials; concrete & cinder block

(G-1286)
RB CHRISTIAN IRONWORKS LLC
298 Hamblin Ave W (49037-8430)
PHONE..................269 963-2222
Aaron Green,
EMP: 7 **EST:** 2018
SALES (est): 389K Privately Held
SIC: 3317 Steel pipe & tubes

(G-1287)
RECONSERVE OF MICHIGAN INC
170 Angell St (49037-8273)
P.O. Box 1413 (49016-1413)
PHONE..................269 965-0427
Meyer Luskin, *CEO*
David Luskin, *COO*
Kevin Kowalchuk, *Manager*
EMP: 1 **EST:** 2013
SALES (est): 6.1MM
SALES (corp-wide): 297.6MM Privately Held
WEB: www.reconserve.com
SIC: 2048 Prepared feeds
HQ: Reconserve, Inc.
2811 Wilshire Blvd # 410
Santa Monica CA 90403
310 458-1574

(G-1288)
RECYCLING FLUID TECHNOLOGIES
4039 Columbia Ave W (49015-9606)
PHONE..................269 788-0488
Malcolm Hikok, *President*
Patricia Hikok, *Vice Pres*
EMP: 10 **EST:** 1992 Privately Held
SIC: 5169 2899 Chemicals & allied products; antifreeze compounds

(G-1289)
RIVERSIDE SCREW MCH PDTS INC
52 Edison St S (49014-5795)
P.O. Box 486 (49016-0486)
PHONE..................269 962-5449
Mitchell Smith, *President*
▲ **EMP:** 18 **EST:** 1939
SQ FT: 21,000

SALES (est): 2.3MM Privately Held
WEB: www.riversidescrewmachineproducts.com
SIC: 3451 Screw machine products

(G-1290)
ROSLER METAL FINISHING USA LLC (PA)
1551 Denso Rd (49037-7390)
PHONE..................269 441-3000
Heather Roe, *Production*
Troy Palmer, *Technical Mgr*
Aj Abbas, *Engineer*
Steven Lunger, *Accountant*
Bret Eldrige, *Regl Sales Mgr*
▲ **EMP:** 29 **EST:** 1999
SQ FT: 300,000
SALES (est): 12.3MM Privately Held
WEB: www.rosler.us
SIC: 2821 3559 Plastics materials & resins; ; metal finishing equipment for plating, etc.

(G-1291)
RX OPTICAL LABORATORIES INC
65 Columbia Ave E (49015-3705)
PHONE..................269 965-5106
Gena Durt, *Manager*
EMP: 4
SALES (corp-wide): 36.9MM Privately Held
WEB: www.rxoptical.com
SIC: 5995 3851 Opticians; ophthalmic goods
PA: Rx Optical Laboratories, Inc.
1825 S Park St
Kalamazoo MI 49001
269 342-5958

(G-1292)
SGK LLC
Also Called: Schawk
70 Michigan Ave W Ste 400 (49017-3620)
PHONE..................269 381-3820
Ainjon Cook, *General Mgr*
Dustin Moran, *Info Tech Mgr*
Mark Buursma, *Account Dir*
EMP: 6
SALES (corp-wide): 1.5B Publicly Held
WEB: www.sgkinc.com
SIC: 3555 2796 Printing trades machinery; platemaking services
HQ: Sgk, Llc
2 N Shore Ctr
Pittsburgh PA 15212
847 827-9494

(G-1293)
SHOULDICE INDUS MFRS CNTRS INC
182 Elm St (49014-4000)
PHONE..................269 962-5579
David R Vanmiddlesworth, *President*
John Reed, *Division Mgr*
David Middlesworth, *Vice Pres*
David J Shouldice, *Vice Pres*
Karen Kupres, *Controller*
EMP: 75 **EST:** 1919
SQ FT: 14,982
SALES (est): 20.5MM Privately Held
WEB: www.shouldicebrothers.com
SIC: 3444 1761 Sheet metal specialties, not stamped; sheet metalwork

(G-1294)
SIGNS & DESIGNS INC
17 32nd St N (49015-4918)
PHONE..................269 968-8909
Jerry Ure, *President*
EMP: 4 **EST:** 1989
SALES (est): 389.5K Privately Held
WEB: www.signsndesigns.com
SIC: 3993 Signs, not made in custom sign painting shops

(G-1295)
SILENT OBSERVER
Also Called: Battle Creek Chamber Commerce
20 Division St N (49014-4004)
PHONE..................269 966-3550
James Boss, *Vice Pres*
EMP: 11 **EST:** 1990

SALES (est): 184.2K Privately Held
WEB: www.battlecreekmi.gov
SIC: 2711 Newspapers, publishing & printing

(G-1296)
SNACKWERKS OF MICHIGAN LLC
Also Called: Jpg Resources Food Mfg
180 Goodale Ave E (49037-2728)
PHONE..................269 719-8282
Jeff Grogg, *Managing Dir*
Ramona Elwell, *Manager*
Amy Usiak, *Manager*
Margie Jusick, *Software Dev*
Jeffrey P Grogg,
EMP: 20 **EST:** 2016
SALES (est): 3.7MM Privately Held
WEB: www.snackwerks.com
SIC: 2043 Cereal breakfast foods

(G-1297)
SOLAR FLARE BAR
250 Wahwahtaysee Way (49015-4063)
PHONE..................269 830-0499
Mikayla Diesch, *Principal*
EMP: 4 **EST:** 2017
SALES (est): 86.9K Privately Held
SIC: 2899 Flares

(G-1298)
SPX FLOW US LLC
4600 W Dickman Rd (49037-7325)
PHONE..................269 966-4782
Tim Frisbie,
EMP: 13 **EST:** 2017
SALES (est): 825.5K Privately Held
SIC: 3561 Pumps & pumping equipment

(G-1299)
STAIR SPECIALIST INC
2257 Columbia Ave W (49015-8639)
PHONE..................269 420-0486
Ted Goff, *President*
EMP: 4 **EST:** 1950
SQ FT: 4,000
SALES (est): 424.1K Privately Held
WEB: www.stairspecialistinc.com
SIC: 2431 Staircases & stairs, wood

(G-1300)
STANLEY ELC HOLDG AMER INC (HQ)
1500 Hill Brady Rd (49037-7320)
PHONE..................269 660-7777
Greg Bond, *Principal*
▲ **EMP:** 100 **EST:** 2000
SALES (est): 56MM Privately Held
WEB: www.iistanley.com
SIC: 3647 3679 Motor vehicle lighting equipment; electronic circuits

(G-1301)
STEWART INDUSTRIES LLC
150 Mcquiston Dr (49037-7376)
PHONE..................269 660-9290
Joseph Stewart, *CEO*
Erick Stewart, *President*
Steve Bishop, *Vice Pres*
Edward Devito, *Vice Pres*
EMP: 60 **EST:** 2000
SQ FT: 60,000
SALES (est): 10.6MM Privately Held
WEB: www.stewartindustriesusa.com
SIC: 3714 Air conditioner parts, motor vehicle

(G-1302)
STUDIO ONE MIDWEST INC
74 Leonard Wood Rd (49037-7309)
PHONE..................269 962-3475
Michael D Clark, *President*
EMP: 10 **EST:** 1978
SQ FT: 20,000
SALES (est): 1MM Privately Held
WEB: www.mannetron.com
SIC: 3999 3842 Figures, wax; models, anatomical

(G-1303)
SWEETWATERS DONUT MILL
2807 Capital Ave Sw (49015-4105)
PHONE..................269 979-1944
Harold Hell, *Manager*
Linda Bradshaw, *Manager*

Battle Creek - Calhoun County (G-1304) — GEOGRAPHIC SECTION

EMP: 8 EST: 1986
SALES (est): 233.3K Privately Held
WEB: www.sweetwatersdonuts.com
SIC: 5461 2051 Doughnuts; doughnuts, except frozen

(G-1304)
SYSTEX PRODUCTS CORPORATION (DH)
Also Called: Pyper Products Corporation
300 Buckner Rd (49037-5602)
PHONE 269 964-8800
Tamotsu Inoue, *Ch of Bd*
Naohisa Miyashita, *President*
John Maurer, *Plant Mgr*
Makoto Saito, *Treasurer*
Bernice Martin, *Human Res Mgr*
▲ EMP: 188 EST: 1992
SQ FT: 106,000
SALES (est): 46.1MM Privately Held
WEB: www.shimizu-industry.co.jp
SIC: 3089 Injection molded finished plastic products

(G-1305)
TODA AMERICA INCORPORATED
4750 W Dickman Rd (49037-7391)
PHONE 269 962-0353
Jun Nakano, *President*
Hiroyasu Watanabe, *Technical Mgr*
◆ EMP: 5 EST: 1996
SQ FT: 3,000
SALES (est): 3.1MM Privately Held
WEB: www.todakogyo.co.jp
SIC: 2899 Magnetic inspection oil or powder
PA: Toda Kogyo Corp.
  1-23, Kyobashicho, Minami-Ku
  Hiroshima HIR 732-0

(G-1306)
TRAM INC
100 Hill Brady Rd (49037-7301)
PHONE 269 966-0100
EMP: 7 Privately Held
WEB: www.tokai-rika-usa.com
SIC: 3714 3643 Motor vehicle electrical equipment; current-carrying wiring devices
HQ: Tram, Inc.
  47200 Port St
  Plymouth MI 48170
  734 254-8500

(G-1307)
TRMI INC
Also Called: Tokai Rika Group
100 Hill Brady Rd (49037-7301)
PHONE 269 966-0800
Ken Noguchi, *President*
Keith Eyre, *Engineer*
Neisha Loew, *Human Res Mgr*
Peter Vanniekerk, *Manager*
Theresa Dorsey, *Technical Staff*
▲ EMP: 550 EST: 1997
SQ FT: 205,000
SALES (est): 83MM Privately Held
WEB: www.tokai-rika-usa.com
SIC: 3714 3643 Motor vehicle electrical equipment; electric switches
HQ: Tram, Inc.
  47200 Port St
  Plymouth MI 48170
  734 254-8500

(G-1308)
UPSTON ASSOCIATES INC
5 Minges Ln (49015-7921)
PHONE 269 349-2782
Dwight Upston, *President*
Deborah Upston, *Vice Pres*
EMP: 7 EST: 1983
SQ FT: 1,200
SALES (est): 653.7K Privately Held
SIC: 2721 Periodicals: publishing & printing

(G-1309)
W W THAYNE ADVERTISING CONS
Also Called: Thayne Art Mart
4642 Capital Ave Sw (49015-9305)
PHONE 269 979-1411
Richard F De Ruiter, *President*
Sherii Sherban, *Editor*
Shirley De Ruiter, *Vice Pres*
Cyd Deane, *Marketing Staff*
Christyn McCleary, *Manager*
EMP: 10 EST: 1971
SQ FT: 2,800
SALES (est): 1.3MM Privately Held
WEB: www.scenepub.com
SIC: 7311 2721 Advertising consultant; magazines: publishing only, not printed on site

(G-1310)
WALTERS PLUMBING COMPANY
Also Called: Walters Plumbing & Htg Sups
189 20th St N (49015-1799)
PHONE 269 962-6253
Mark Saunders, *President*
EMP: 17 EST: 1919
SQ FT: 15,000
SALES (est): 505.8K Privately Held
WEB: www.waltersplumbingandheating.com
SIC: 1711 1381 5074 Plumbing contractors; warm air heating & air conditioning contractor; drilling water intake wells; plumbing & hydronic heating supplies

(G-1311)
WESTROCK RKT LLC
177 Angell St (49037-8274)
PHONE 269 963-5511
Carl Bhedwar, *General Mgr*
Steven Martinez, *General Mgr*
Kurt Patz, *General Mgr*
Robert Vandermeer, *General Mgr*
Larry Goins, *Superintendent*
EMP: 5
SALES (corp-wide): 17.5B Publicly Held
WEB: www.westrock.com
SIC: 2653 Boxes, corrugated: made from purchased materials
HQ: Westrock Rkt, Llc
  1000 Abernathy Rd Ste 125
  Atlanta GA 30328
  770 448-2193

(G-1312)
WRKCO INC
Westrock Box On Demand
4075 Columbia Ave W (49015-9606)
PHONE 269 964-7181
Chris Hansen, *Principal*
EMP: 30
SQ FT: 145,000
SALES (corp-wide): 17.5B Publicly Held
SIC: 2653 2657 5113 Boxes, corrugated: made from purchased materials; folding paperboard boxes; corrugated & solid fiber boxes
HQ: Wrkco Inc.
  1000 Abernathy Rd Ste 12
  Atlanta GA 30328
  770 448-2193

Bay City
Bay County

(G-1313)
4-HEALTH INC
Also Called: Journals Unlimited
701 5th St (48706-5915)
P.O. Box 1882 (48706-0882)
PHONE 989 686-3377
Barbara Morina, *President*
John Morina, *Vice Pres*
Ryan Sonefeld, *Sales Mgr*
▲ EMP: 4 EST: 1991
SALES (est): 1.6MM Privately Held
WEB: www.journalsunlimited.com
SIC: 2741 Miscellaneous publishing

(G-1314)
A & B DISPLAY SYSTEMS INC
Also Called: Mill Town Woodworks
1111 S Henry St (48706-5061)
PHONE 989 893-6642
James Belanger, *President*
Gregory Lundquist, *Treasurer*
Laure Belanger, *Admin Sec*
EMP: 13 EST: 1987
SQ FT: 40,000
SALES (est): 1.3MM Privately Held
WEB: www.abdisplays.com
SIC: 3999 7319 5211 1751 Advertising display products; display advertising service; cabinets, kitchen; cabinet & finish carpentry; products of purchased glass; adhesives & sealants

(G-1315)
ACKERMAN BROTHERS INC
200 S Linn St (48706-4943)
PHONE 989 892-4122
Richard T Swantek Jr, *President*
Cynthia Auger, *Manager*
EMP: 6 EST: 1933
SQ FT: 5,000
SALES (est): 550K Privately Held
WEB: www.ackermanbrothers.com
SIC: 3444 7692 Sheet metalwork; welding repair

(G-1316)
ACRA CAST INC
1837 1st St (48708-6298)
PHONE 989 893-3961
Richard Singer IV, *President*
▼ EMP: 22 EST: 1966
SQ FT: 9,130
SALES (est): 5.3MM Privately Held
WEB: www.acracast.com
SIC: 3365 3369 3324 Aluminum foundries; castings, except die-castings, precision; steel investment foundries

(G-1317)
ADMIRAL
212 S Euclid Ave (48706-2910)
PHONE 989 684-8314
Debbie Debowski, *Manager*
EMP: 5 EST: 2018
SALES (est): 90.7K Privately Held
SIC: 2911 Petroleum refining

(G-1318)
ADVANCED TEX SCREEN PRINTING
Also Called: Advanced Tex Screenprinting
4177 3 Mile Rd (48706-9607)
PHONE 989 643-7288
Dennis V Barthel, *President*
Bill Coppens, *Opers Mgr*
Kendall Bader, *Sales Staff*
John Turner, *Sales Staff*
Julie A Barthel, *Admin Sec*
▼ EMP: 20 EST: 1989
SQ FT: 15,000
SALES (est): 2.8MM Privately Held
SIC: 2759 Screen printing

(G-1319)
AEROSPACE AMERICA INC
900 Harry S Truman Pkwy (48706-4114)
P.O. Box 189 (48707-0189)
PHONE 989 684-2121
Arthur P Dore, *Ch of Bd*
Mike Alley, *President*
Murray Sutherland, *President*
Lori Grew, *Manager*
EMP: 20 EST: 1962
SQ FT: 80,000
SALES (est): 3.7MM Privately Held
WEB: www.aerospaceamerica.com
SIC: 3589 3949 3714 3825 Asbestos removal equipment; hunting equipment; radiators & radiator shells & cores, motor vehicle; test equipment for electronic & electrical circuits; small arms

(G-1320)
ALRO STEEL CORPORATION
3125 N Water St (48708-5455)
PHONE 989 893-9553
Mark Oliver, *Division Mgr*
Robert Wendland, *Finance Mgr*
EMP: 4
SQ FT: 40,000
SALES (corp-wide): 1.9B Privately Held
WEB: www.alrosteel.com
SIC: 5051 3498 3446 Steel; tube fabricating (contract bending & shaping); open flooring & grating for construction
PA: Alro Steel Corporation
  3100 E High St
  Jackson MI 49203
  517 787-5500

(G-1321)
AMERICAN PWR CNNECTION SYSTEMS
2460 Midland Rd (48706-9469)
PHONE 989 686-6302
Paul Wujek, *CEO*
Marcy Wujek, *President*
▲ EMP: 10 EST: 1992
SQ FT: 8,000
SALES (est): 1MM Privately Held
WEB: www.american-power.com
SIC: 3643 Connectors & terminals for electrical devices

(G-1322)
ARNOLD & SAUTTER CO (PA)
408 N Euclid Ave (48706-2996)
P.O. Box 1121 (48706-0121)
PHONE 989 684-7557
James G Arnold, *President*
EMP: 15 EST: 1947
SQ FT: 5,800
SALES (est): 3.4MM Privately Held
WEB: www.arnoldandsautter.com
SIC: 1521 3442 3446 3444 General remodeling, single-family houses; shutters, door or window: metal; storm doors or windows, metal; bank fixtures, ornamental metal; sheet metalwork; glass & glazing work; carpentry work

(G-1323)
AURORA PRESERVED FLOWERS
7201 Westside Saginaw Rd # 5 (48706-8327)
PHONE 989 498-0290
Jane A Huegel, *Owner*
EMP: 7 EST: 1969
SALES (est): 238.2K Privately Held
WEB: www.aurorapreservedflowers.com
SIC: 3999 Flowers, artificial & preserved

(G-1324)
BALDAUF ENTERPRISES INC (PA)
Also Called: Kerkau Manufacturing Company
1321 S Valley Center Dr (48706-9798)
PHONE 989 686-0350
Harold E Baldauf, *President*
Laura Horney, *Vice Pres*
Fred H May Jr, *Vice Pres*
Bryan Schindler, *QC Mgr*
David Baldauf, *Treasurer*
▲ EMP: 82 EST: 1983
SQ FT: 200,000
SALES (est): 22.6MM Privately Held
WEB: www.kerkau.com
SIC: 3444 3498 Sheet metalwork; fabricated pipe & fittings

(G-1325)
BALDAUF ENTERPRISES INC
Also Called: Kerkau Manufacturing
910 Harry S Truman Pkwy (48706-4171)
PHONE 989 686-0350
Joseph Lumsden, *Accounts Mgr*
Harold E Baldauf, *Branch Mgr*
EMP: 18
SALES (corp-wide): 22.6MM Privately Held
WEB: www.kerkau.com
SIC: 3542 Machine tools, metal forming type
PA: Baldauf Enterprises, Inc.
  1321 S Valley Center Dr
  Bay City MI 48706
  989 686-0350

(G-1326)
BAY CARBON INC
800 Marquette St Ste 2 (48706-4098)
P.O. Box 205 (48707-0205)
PHONE 989 686-8090
William Clare, *President*
James Clare, *Vice Pres*
Michael Clare, *Vice Pres*
EMP: 34 EST: 1978
SQ FT: 10,000
SALES (est): 4.3MM Privately Held
WEB: www.baycarbon.com
SIC: 3624 3674 Carbon & graphite products; semiconductor circuit networks

▲ = Import ▼ = Export ◆ = Import/Export

GEOGRAPHIC SECTION
Bay City - Bay County (G-1355)

(G-1327)
BAY CAST TECHNOLOGIES INC
2611 Center Ave (48708-6396)
P.O. Box 126 (48707-0126)
PHONE..................989 892-9500
Scott S Holman, *President*
Jason J Holman, *Vice Pres*
Marty Gow, *Maint Spvr*
Cynthia Hildinger, *Treasurer*
Max D Holman, *Director*
▼ **EMP:** 29 **EST:** 1987
SQ FT: 300,000
SALES (est): 6.1MM **Privately Held**
WEB: www.baycast.com
SIC: 3599 Machine shop, jobbing & repair

(G-1328)
BAY CITY FIREWORKS FESTIVAL
3296 E Fisher Rd (48706-3226)
P.O. Box 873 (48707-0873)
PHONE..................989 892-2264
EMP: 7
SALES: 273.5K **Privately Held**
SIC: 2899 Mfg Chemical Preparations

(G-1329)
BAY MACHINING AND SALES INC
4421 Ace Commercial Ct (48706-1974)
PHONE..................989 316-1801
Ronald Seymour, *President*
Julie Seymour, *Vice Pres*
Mark Seymour, *Purchasing*
EMP: 12 **EST:** 2010
SQ FT: 3,000
SALES (est): 678.7K **Privately Held**
WEB: www.baymachsales.com
SIC: 3599 Machine shop, jobbing & repair

(G-1330)
BAY PLASTICS MACHINERY CO LLC
3494 N Euclid Ave (48706-1637)
PHONE..................989 671-9630
Anthony Forgash, *CEO*
Jason Forgash, *President*
Dick Fetter, *Vice Pres*
Jamie Chomas, *Engineer*
Paul Grubaugh, *Engineer*
EMP: 50
SQ FT: 20,000
SALES (est): 8MM **Privately Held**
WEB: www.bayplasticsmachinery.com
SIC: 5046 3549 Commercial equipment; cutting & slitting machinery

(G-1331)
BAY UNITED MOTORS INC
4353 Wilder Rd (48706-2297)
PHONE..................989 684-3972
Joseph P Noonan, *President*
Patti Noonan, *Vice Pres*
EMP: 13 **EST:** 1962
SQ FT: 11,000
SALES (est): 4.4MM **Privately Held**
WEB: www.bayunitedmotors.net
SIC: 5063 7694 Motors, electric; electric motor repair

(G-1332)
BEST BARRICADE SYSYTEM INC
314 State Park Dr (48706-1775)
PHONE..................989 778-1482
EMP: 4 **EST:** 2015
SALES (est): 73.4K **Privately Held**
SIC: 3499 Barricades, metal

(G-1333)
BEST HARVEST
4115 7 Mile Rd (48706-9425)
PHONE..................888 947-6226
Curt Drous, *Principal*
EMP: 4 **EST:** 2013
SALES (est): 101.9K **Privately Held**
WEB: www.bestharveststore.com
SIC: 3523 Farm machinery & equipment

(G-1334)
CAMBRON ENGINEERING INC
3800 Wilder Rd (48706-2196)
PHONE..................989 684-5890
Stephen D Sheppard, *President*
David A Ferrio, *Vice Pres*
Renee Riddle, *Plant Mgr*
Cathy Chappel, *Office Mgr*
Bob Field, *Manager*
EMP: 44 **EST:** 1972
SQ FT: 30,500
SALES (est): 7.9MM **Privately Held**
WEB: www.cambronengineering.com
SIC: 3544 Special dies & tools

(G-1335)
CAR QUEST MACHINE SHOP
3616 Wilder Rd (48706-2126)
PHONE..................989 686-3111
EMP: 6 **EST:** 2017
SALES (est): 70.8K **Privately Held**
WEB: www.carquest.com
SIC: 3599 Machine shop, jobbing & repair

(G-1336)
CARBONE OF AMERICA
900 Harrison St (48708-8299)
PHONE..................989 894-2911
Kirk Keihly, *Office Mgr*
EMP: 12 **EST:** 2010
SALES (est): 1MM **Privately Held**
WEB: www.mersen.us
SIC: 3624 Carbon & graphite products

(G-1337)
CHARBONEAU INC
4361 Oakridge Rd (48706-1821)
PHONE..................989 293-1773
K Charboneau, *Principal*
EMP: 4 **EST:** 2009
SALES (est): 81K **Privately Held**
SIC: 3999 Manufacturing industries

(G-1338)
CLAMPTECH LLC
106 S Walnut St Ste 1 (48706-4990)
PHONE..................989 832-8027
Stacy Pastein,
EMP: 7 **EST:** 2005 **Privately Held**
WEB: www.theropeclamp.com
SIC: 3429 Manufactured hardware (general)

(G-1339)
CLAREY CUSTOM FRMNG & ART LLC
437 River Rd (48706-1449)
PHONE..................989 415-4152
Michelle Clarey, *Principal*
EMP: 4 **EST:** 2017
SALES (est): 89.1K **Privately Held**
WEB: www.clareysframing.com
SIC: 2499 Picture frame molding, finished

(G-1340)
COMPUTER OPERATED MFG
1710 Lewis St (48706-1133)
PHONE..................989 686-1333
Doug Rechsteiner, *President*
Gary Rechsteiner, *Principal*
EMP: 25 **EST:** 1980
SQ FT: 20,000
SALES (est): 939.5K **Privately Held**
WEB: www.comcncmachining.com
SIC: 3599 3498 3494 3462 Machine shop, jobbing & repair; fabricated pipe & fittings; valves & pipe fittings; iron & steel forgings; nonferrous foundries

(G-1341)
CONSOLIDATED COMPUTING SVCS
2001 S Farragut St (48708-3807)
PHONE..................989 906-0467
EMP: 5 **EST:** 2014
SALES (est): 151.5K **Privately Held**
SIC: 7372 Prepackaged software

(G-1342)
DELTA CONTAINERS INC (PA)
Also Called: Flint Packaging Systems Div
1400 Eddy St (48706-6179)
P.O. Box 623 (48707-0623)
PHONE..................810 742-2730
Virginia R Landaal, *Ch of Bd*
Diane McDonald, *Principal*
Stephen Landaal, *Exec VP*
Daniel Burnham, *Plant Mgr*
Matt Harding, *Plant Mgr*
▲ **EMP:** 225 **EST:** 1962
SQ FT: 325,000
SALES (est): 48.2MM **Privately Held**
WEB: www.landaal.com
SIC: 2653 4783 2675 2671 Boxes, corrugated: made from purchased materials; containerization of goods for shipping; die-cut paper & board; packaging paper & plastics film, coated & laminated; wood pallets & skids

(G-1343)
DICE CORPORATION
1410 S Valley Center Dr (48706-9754)
PHONE..................989 891-2800
Clifford V Dice, *President*
Jerry Corrion, *Vice Pres*
Jen Balash, *Project Mgr*
Dean Martin, *Facilities Mgr*
Vicki Rivard, *Accounts Mgr*
EMP: 50 **EST:** 1985
SQ FT: 30,000
SALES (est): 8.7MM **Privately Held**
WEB: www.dicecorp.com
SIC: 3699 1731 5063 7382 Security control equipment & systems; fire detection & burglar alarm systems specialization; alarm systems; burglar alarm systems; fire alarm systems; security systems services

(G-1344)
DIE STAMPCO INC
1301 N Lincoln St (48708-6172)
PHONE..................989 893-7790
Clyde Hart, *President*
Robbin Hart, *Vice Pres*
Jason Hart, *Production*
EMP: 17 **EST:** 1991
SQ FT: 2,400
SALES (est): 2.1MM **Privately Held**
WEB: www.diestampco.com
SIC: 3449 3061 3089 Miscellaneous metalwork; mechanical rubber goods; molding primary plastic

(G-1345)
DINO S DUMPSTERS LLC
900 Harry S Truman Pkwy (48706-4171)
PHONE..................989 225-5635
Dennis Dore, *Principal*
EMP: 7 **EST:** 2010
SALES (est): 157.7K **Privately Held**
SIC: 3443 Dumpsters, garbage

(G-1346)
DOBSON INDUSTRIAL INC (PA)
Also Called: Dobson Heavy Haul Inc Division
3660 N Euclid Ave (48706-2026)
P.O. Box 1368 (48706-0368)
PHONE..................800 298-6063
Dale Bash, *Chairman*
Jim Dobson, *Shareholder*
▲ **EMP:** 32 **EST:** 1947
SQ FT: 39,000
SALES (est): 10.9MM **Privately Held**
WEB: www.dobsonindustrial.com
SIC: 1799 1791 3441 5031 Rigging & scaffolding; structural steel erection; fabricated structural metal; doors; materials handling machinery

(G-1347)
DOUG WIRT ENTERPRISES INC
Also Called: Wirt Stone Dock
400 Martin St (48706-4121)
PHONE..................989 684-5777
Doug Wirt, *Manager*
EMP: 6
SALES (corp-wide): 1.7MM **Privately Held**
SIC: 1411 4212 5083 5032 Limestone & marble dimension stone; dump truck haulage; landscaping equipment; limestone
PA: Wirt Doug Enterprises Inc
4700 Crow Island Rd
Saginaw MI 48601
989 753-6404

(G-1348)
DOW SILICONES CORPORATION
1 E Main St (48708-7495)
PHONE..................989 895-3397
Lacey Cameron, *Branch Mgr*
EMP: 4
SALES (corp-wide): 38.5B **Publicly Held**
SIC: 2869 Industrial organic chemicals
HQ: Dow Silicones Corporation
2200 W Salzburg Rd
Auburn MI 48611
989 496-4000

(G-1349)
E J M BALL SCREW LLC
209 Morton St (48706-5348)
PHONE..................989 893-7674
Ernest Machelski, *Mng Member*
Michael Machelski,
EMP: 13 **EST:** 2001
SQ FT: 12,000
SALES (est): 497.9K **Privately Held**
WEB: www.ejmballscrew.com
SIC: 3452 3593 Screws, metal; fluid power cylinders & actuators

(G-1350)
EMCOR INC
5154 Alliance Dr (48706-8709)
PHONE..................989 667-0652
John P O'Brien, *President*
John P O Brien, *President*
Lisa Haight, *Vice Pres*
Ann M O Brien, *Treasurer*
Maxine Mauricio, *General Counsel*
EMP: 18 **EST:** 1982
SQ FT: 18,000
SALES (est): 2.4MM **Privately Held**
WEB: www.emcorballscrew.com
SIC: 3541 3544 Machine tool replacement & repair parts, metal cutting types; special dies & tools

(G-1351)
EUCLID COATING SYSTEMS INC
3494 N Euclid Ave (48706-1637)
PHONE..................989 922-4789
Scott A Seymour, *President*
EMP: 16 **EST:** 2001
SQ FT: 2,000
SALES (est): 1.3MM **Privately Held**
WEB: www.euclidlabcoaters.com
SIC: 3554 3559 Coating & finishing machinery, paper; fiber optics strand coating machinery

(G-1352)
EUCLID INDUSTRIES INC (PA)
1655 Tech Dr (48706-9792)
PHONE..................989 686-8920
Ronald Beebe, *President*
Carmen Gueli, *Vice Pres*
Kelli Kinde, *CFO*
▲ **EMP:** 125 **EST:** 1978
SQ FT: 117,000
SALES (est): 27.4MM **Privately Held**
WEB: www.euclidindustries.com
SIC: 3599 7389 3714 2431 Machine shop, jobbing & repair; packaging & labeling services; motor vehicle parts & accessories; millwork

(G-1353)
EVERGREEN WINERY LLC
Also Called: Cadillac Winery
3835 Huszan Dr (48706-2221)
PHONE..................989 392-2044
Jean Charbonneau, *Co-Owner*
EMP: 5 **EST:** 2017
SALES (est): 231.8K **Privately Held**
SIC: 2084 Wine cellars, bonded: engaged in blending wines

(G-1354)
EXCELL MANUFACTURING INC
3258 Patterson Rd (48706-1847)
P.O. Box 1607 (48706-0607)
PHONE..................989 496-0473
Rebecca Cox, *President*
Scott Johnson, *Owner*
EMP: 6 **EST:** 2002
SQ FT: 3,000
SALES (est): 361.7K **Privately Held**
WEB: www.excellmfginc.com
SIC: 3599 Machine shop, jobbing & repair

(G-1355)
F P HORAK COMPANY (PA)
Also Called: Horak Company, The
1311 Straits Dr (48706-8708)
P.O. Box 925 (48707-0925)
PHONE..................989 892-6505
Frederick Horak, *Ch of Bd*
Marisa Horak Belotti, *President*

Bay City - Bay County (G-1356)

Timothy Dust, *President*
Darrin Demott, *COO*
Dan Smith, *Vice Pres*
EMP: 115 **EST:** 1967
SQ FT: 147,000
SALES (est): 45.4MM **Privately Held**
WEB: www.fphorak.com
SIC: 2752 2761 2791 2789 Commercial printing, offset; continuous forms, office & business; computer forms, manifold or continuous; typesetting; bookbinding & related work; commercial printing

(G-1356)
FABIANO BROS DEV - WSCNSIN LLC
1885 Bevanda Ct (48706-8720)
PHONE...................989 509-0200
Joseph Fabiano, *Principal*
EMP: 13 **EST:** 2012
SALES (est): 344.2K **Privately Held**
WEB: www.fabianobrothers.com
SIC: 2082 Beer (alcoholic beverage)

(G-1357)
FBE ASSOCIATES INC
513 N Madison Ave Ste 101 (48708-6460)
PHONE...................989 894-2785
Patrick Race, *President*
Tom Goodman, *Corp Secy*
EMP: 5 **EST:** 1999
SALES (est): 250K **Privately Held**
WEB: www.fbe-inc.com
SIC: 7372 Educational computer software

(G-1358)
FOGELSONGER VAULT CO INC
Also Called: Sunset Valley Creamatory
210 Ausable State Rd (48706-3682)
PHONE...................989 684-0262
Gary Fogelsonger, *President*
EMP: 4 **EST:** 1939
SQ FT: 10,000
SALES (est): 377.6K **Privately Held**
SIC: 3272 Burial vaults, concrete or precast terrazzo

(G-1359)
GENERAL MOTORS LLC
1001 Woodside Ave (48708-5470)
PHONE...................989 894-7210
Jill Cummings, *Research*
Shane Bremer, *Engineer*
Dennis Hawley, *Engineer*
John Wing, *Engineer*
Joe Mazzeo, *Branch Mgr*
EMP: 14 **Publicly Held**
WEB: www.gm.com
SIC: 5511 3714 3592 3561 Automobiles, new & used; motor vehicle parts & accessories; carburetors, pistons, rings, valves; pumps & pumping equipment; bolts, nuts, rivets & washers; fabricated structural metal
HQ: General Motors Llc
300 Renaissance Ctr L1
Detroit MI 48243

(G-1360)
GENERAL PARTS INC
Also Called: Carquest Auto Parts
3616 Wilder Rd (48706-2126)
PHONE...................989 686-3114
Terry Schlager, *Manager*
EMP: 6
SALES (corp-wide): 10.1B **Publicly Held**
WEB: www.carquest.com
SIC: 5013 5531 3599 7539 Automotive supplies & parts; automotive parts; machine shop, jobbing & repair; machine shop, automotive
HQ: General Parts, Inc.
2635 E Millbrook Rd Ste C
Raleigh NC 27604
919 573-3000

(G-1361)
GOUGEON HOLDING CO (PA)
100 Patterson Ave (48706-4136)
P.O. Box 908 (48707-0908)
PHONE...................989 684-7286
Robert H Monroe, *President*
Meade Gougeon, *Chairman*
Joanne R Gradowski, *Corp Secy*
Grant W Urband, *Vice Pres*
EMP: 3 **EST:** 1969
SQ FT: 27,000
SALES (est): 27.6MM **Privately Held**
WEB: www.gougeon.com
SIC: 2851 Epoxy coatings

(G-1362)
GRAPHITE ELECTRODES LTD
Also Called: Dresco Machining & Fabrication
1311 N Sherman St (48708-6070)
PHONE...................989 893-3635
Patrick Martin, *President*
Leann Reed, *Finance*
Michelle L Martin, *Director*
EMP: 22 **EST:** 1961
SQ FT: 22,000
SALES (est): 3.4MM **Privately Held**
WEB: www.drescomachining.com
SIC: 3599 3624 Machine shop, jobbing & repair; carbon & graphite products

(G-1363)
GREAT LAKES COCA-COLA DIST LLC
2500 Broadway St (48708-8402)
PHONE...................989 895-8537
Russ Marvin, *Manager*
EMP: 12
SQ FT: 40,000 **Privately Held**
WEB: www.coca-cola.com
SIC: 2086 Bottled & canned soft drinks
HQ: Great Lakes Coca-Cola Distribution, Llc
6250 N River Rd Ste 9000
Rosemont IL 60018
847 227-6500

(G-1364)
GW FISHING LURES INC
3476 Killarney Beach Rd (48706-1176)
PHONE...................989 684-6431
Gordon Wilson, *Owner*
EMP: 5 **EST:** 1994
SALES (est): 171.3K **Privately Held**
SIC: 3949 Lures, fishing: artificial

(G-1365)
HIGHLAND INDUSTRIAL INC
Also Called: Caseway Industrial Products
3487 Highland Dr (48706-2414)
PHONE...................989 391-9992
Willis Wells, *President*
Suzanne Wells, *Vice Pres*
EMP: 6 **EST:** 1981
SALES (est): 525.8K **Privately Held**
WEB: www.casewayproducts.com
SIC: 2891 Adhesives, plastic

(G-1366)
IDEAL TOOL INC
1707 Marquette St (48706-4170)
P.O. Box 8 (48707-0008)
PHONE...................989 893-8336
Jack Covieo, *President*
Robert Spegel, *Vice Pres*
Robbin Spegel, *Admin Sec*
EMP: 15 **EST:** 1988
SQ FT: 6,000
SALES (est): 776.1K **Privately Held**
WEB: www.idealtoolinc.com
SIC: 3599 3541 3549 Machine shop, jobbing & repair; machine tools, metal cutting type; assembly machines, including robotic

(G-1367)
INNOVATION UNLIMITED LLC
1409 4th St (48708-6133)
PHONE...................574 635-1064
Michael Westenburg, *Mng Member*
EMP: 8
SALES (est): 429.7K **Privately Held**
SIC: 5015 3571 Automotive supplies, used; electronic computers

(G-1368)
J M KUSCH INC
3530 Wheeler Rd (48706-1711)
P.O. Box 1337 (48706-0337)
PHONE...................989 684-8820
Carole S Kusch, *President*
Wendy L Kusch, *Vice Pres*
EMP: 24 **EST:** 1979
SALES (est): 2.2MM **Privately Held**
SIC: 3544 Special dies & tools

(G-1369)
JOHNSON MULTIMEDIA GROUP LLC
506 Salzburg Ave (48706-5323)
PHONE...................989 753-1151
Phillip Johnson, *Executive*
EMP: 5 **EST:** 2014
SALES (est): 40.1K **Privately Held**
WEB: www.obertogili.com
SIC: 2741 Miscellaneous publishing

(G-1370)
K-R METAL ENGINEERS CORP
815 S Henry St (48706-4989)
PHONE...................989 892-1901
Susan Leitelt, *President*
Mark H Beyer, *Corp Secy*
EMP: 8 **EST:** 1938
SQ FT: 12,200
SALES (est): 2.2MM **Privately Held**
WEB: www.krmetal.com
SIC: 3441 3444 Fabricated structural metal; sheet metalwork

(G-1371)
KILOBAR COMPACTING MICH LLC
3916 Traxler Ct Ste C (48706-9612)
PHONE...................989 460-1981
EMP: 5 **EST:** 2010
SALES (est): 246.2K **Privately Held**
WEB: www.kilobarcompacting.com
SIC: 2048 Kelp meal & pellets: prepared as animal feed

(G-1372)
KRZYSIAK FAMILY RESTAURANT
Also Called: Krzysiak's House
1605 Michigan Ave (48708-8454)
PHONE...................989 894-5531
Donald J Krzysiak, *President*
Lois Krzysiak, *Vice Pres*
EMP: 60 **EST:** 1965
SQ FT: 1,500
SALES (est): 3MM **Privately Held**
WEB: www.krzysiaks.com
SIC: 5812 2098 2013 Restaurant, family: independent; noodles (e.g. egg, plain & water), dry; sausages from purchased meat

(G-1373)
MCG PLASTICS INC
3661 N Euclid Ave (48706-2041)
PHONE...................989 667-4349
Mario C Garza, *President*
Annette Garza, *Admin Sec*
EMP: 21 **EST:** 1992
SQ FT: 10,000
SALES (est): 2MM **Privately Held**
WEB: www.mcgplastics.com
SIC: 3089 Injection molded finished plastic products; injection molding of plastics

(G-1374)
MERSEN
900 Harrison St (48708-8244)
PHONE...................989 894-2911
Sohail Qamar, *Principal*
Bryan Tyler, *Purch Agent*
Maryann Yhalski, *Human Res Mgr*
EMP: 36 **EST:** 2015
SALES (est): 7.7MM **Privately Held**
WEB: www.graphite-eng.com
SIC: 3624 Carbon & graphite products

(G-1375)
MERSEN USA GS CORP
Also Called: Mersen USA Bay City-MI LLC
900 Harrison St (48708-8244)
PHONE...................989 894-2911
Joseph Tracey, *Principal*
Michael Colony, *Manager*
EMP: 120 **EST:** 2014
SQ FT: 104,000
SALES (est): 25MM
SALES (corp-wide): 889.5K **Privately Held**
WEB: www.graphite-eng.com
SIC: 3624 Carbon & graphite products
HQ: Mersen Usa Ptt Corp.
400 Myrtle Ave
Boonton NJ 07005
973 334-0700

(G-1376)
METAL SALES MANUFACTURING CORP
5209 Mackinaw Rd (48706-9700)
PHONE...................989 686-5879
Chris Vanwormer, *Branch Mgr*
EMP: 10
SALES (corp-wide): 347.3MM **Privately Held**
WEB: www.metalsales.us.com
SIC: 3444 Roof deck, sheet metal; siding, sheet metal
HQ: Metal Sales Manufacturing Corporation
545 S 3rd St Ste 200
Louisville KY 40202
502 855-4300

(G-1377)
METRO-FABRICATING LLC
1650 Tech Dr (48706-9792)
PHONE...................989 667-8100
Amy Lyday, *President*
Amy Cunningham, *Purch Mgr*
Mark Seymour, *Purch Mgr*
Mark Curtis, *Purch Agent*
John Raths, *Engineer*
EMP: 75
SQ FT: 56,000
SALES (est): 6.6MM **Privately Held**
WEB: www.metrofab.com
SIC: 3444 3613 Laundry hampers, sheet metal; control panels, electric

(G-1378)
MICHIGAN SUGAR COMPANY
107 Mcgraw St (48708-8275)
PHONE...................989 686-0161
EMP: 165
SALES (corp-wide): 189.4MM **Privately Held**
WEB: www.michigansugar.com
SIC: 2063 Beet sugar
PA: Michigan Sugar Company
122 Uptown Dr Unit 300
Bay City MI 48708
989 686-0161

(G-1379)
MICHIGAN SUGAR COMPANY (PA)
Also Called: Michigan Sugar Beet Growers
122 Uptown Dr Unit 300 (48708-5627)
P.O. Box 673089, Detroit (48267-3089)
PHONE...................989 686-0161
Mark Flegenheimer, *President*
Richard Gerstenberger, *Chairman*
Charles Bauer, *Vice Pres*
Jerry Coleman, *Vice Pres*
Pedro L Figueroa, *Vice Pres*
▲ **EMP:** 65 **EST:** 1906
SALES (est): 189.4MM **Privately Held**
WEB: www.michigansugar.com
SIC: 2063 Beet sugar

(G-1380)
MODERN MACHINE CO
1111 S Water St (48708-7097)
PHONE...................989 895-8563
Gary Emede, *President*
Julia Emede, *Treasurer*
EMP: 49 **EST:** 1956
SQ FT: 19,000
SALES (est): 3.3MM **Privately Held**
WEB: www.modernmachine.biz
SIC: 3599 Machine shop, jobbing & repair

(G-1381)
MORIN BOATS
377 State Park Dr (48706-1339)
PHONE...................989 686-7353
Douglas Morin, *Manager*
EMP: 6 **EST:** 1983
SALES (est): 440.4K **Privately Held**
SIC: 3732 Boat building & repairing

(G-1382)
NEETZ PRINTING INC
700 S Euclid Ave (48706-3304)
PHONE...................989 684-4620
Rick Neetz, *President*
Larry Neetz II, *President*
Sharon Neetz, *Admin Sec*
EMP: 4 **EST:** 1941
SQ FT: 5,000

SALES (est): 401.5K **Privately Held**
WEB: www.neetzprintinginc.com
SIC: **2752** Commercial printing, offset

(G-1383)
NORTHERN CONCRETE PIPE INC (PA)
401 Kelton St (48706-5395)
PHONE...................989 892-3545
William Washabaugh Jr, *President*
Brian Garver, *Engineer*
Dan Pletzke, *CFO*
Patrick Tagget, *Controller*
Brian Harman, *Sales Staff*
EMP: 40
SQ FT: 1,600
SALES (est): 20.6MM **Privately Held**
WEB: www.ncp-inc.com
SIC: **3272** 3441 Pipe, concrete or lined with concrete; fabricated structural metal

(G-1384)
OAKLAND ORTHOPEDIC APPLS INC (PA)
515 Mulholland St (48708-7644)
PHONE...................989 893-7544
Richard L Smith, *President*
Vivian J Smith, *Vice Pres*
Jennifer Draves, *Info Tech Mgr*
EMP: 12 EST: 1972
SQ FT: 2,500
SALES (est): 4.7MM **Privately Held**
WEB: www.oaklandoandp.com
SIC: **3842** 5999 Braces, orthopedic; orthopedic & prosthesis applications

(G-1385)
OILS AND ELEMENTS LLC
1211 N Williams St (48706-3666)
PHONE...................989 450-4081
Shirley Polaski, *Principal*
EMP: 4 EST: 2018
SALES (est): 148.5K **Privately Held**
SIC: **2819** Industrial inorganic chemicals

(G-1386)
PERSONAL POWER PRESS INC
5225 3 Mile Rd (48706-9029)
PHONE...................989 239-8628
Thomas Haller, *Principal*
EMP: 5 EST: 2019
SALES (est): 123.1K **Privately Held**
WEB: www.personalpowerpress.com
SIC: **2741** Miscellaneous publishing

(G-1387)
PLY-FORMS INCORPORATED
4684 Fraser Rd (48706-9423)
P.O. Box 136, Auburn (48611-0136)
PHONE...................989 686-5681
Bob Williams, *President*
EMP: 28 EST: 1973
SQ FT: 30,000
SALES (est): 2.3MM **Privately Held**
WEB: www.plyformsinc.com
SIC: **2436** 2435 Softwood veneer & plywood; hardwood veneer & plywood

(G-1388)
PONDER INDUSTRIAL
3780 N Euclid Ave (48706-2027)
PHONE...................989 391-4575
Kate Young, *Office Mgr*
EMP: 5 EST: 2018
SALES (est): 257.4K **Privately Held**
WEB: www.ponderwaterjet.com
SIC: **3999** Manufacturing industries

(G-1389)
PONDER INDUSTRIAL INCORPORATED
287 S River Rd (48708-9601)
PHONE...................989 684-9841
Dale A Bash, *President*
Barb J Bash, *Corp Secy*
EMP: 41 EST: 1999
SQ FT: 30,000
SALES (est): 4.5MM **Privately Held**
WEB: www.ponderindustrial.com
SIC: **3441** Fabricated structural metal

(G-1390)
PYRAMID PAVING AND CONTG CO (PA)
Also Called: Pyramid Paving Co
600 N Jefferson St (48708-6456)
PHONE...................989 895-5861
Bruce Weiss, *President*
Kurt Kloha, *Vice Pres*
Randy Jagielo, *QC Mgr*
John Freed, *Treasurer*
EMP: 59 EST: 1982
SQ FT: 22,000
SALES (est): 10.1MM **Privately Held**
WEB: www.pyramidpaving.com
SIC: **1611** 2951 1771 Resurfacing contractor; asphalt paving mixtures & blocks; concrete work

(G-1391)
QUALITY TRANSPARENT BAG INC (PA)
110 Mcgraw St (48708-8276)
P.O. Box 486 (48707-0486)
PHONE...................989 893-3561
Stephen Kessler, *President*
EMP: 10
SQ FT: 56,000
SALES (est): 14.1MM **Privately Held**
WEB: www.qualitybag.com
SIC: **2673** 2671 3081 Plastic bags; made from purchased materials; plastic film, coated or laminated for packaging; unsupported plastics film & sheet

(G-1392)
QUANTUM COMPOSITES INC
1310 S Valley Center Dr (48706-9798)
PHONE...................989 922-3863
Terry Morgan, *CEO*
Bill Kennedy, *President*
Ganesh RAO, *President*
Darrell Potter, *Exec VP*
Libby Doerr, *Buyer*
▲ EMP: 14 EST: 1979
SQ FT: 50,000
SALES (est): 6.1MM
SALES (corp-wide): 28.1B **Privately Held**
WEB: www.premix.com
SIC: **2821** Molding compounds, plastics
HQ: Premix, Inc.
3365 E Center St
North Kingsville OH 44068
440 224-2181

(G-1393)
R & R READY-MIX INC
1601 W Youngs Ditch Rd (48708-9173)
PHONE...................989 892-9313
EMP: 4
SALES (corp-wide): 3.3MM **Privately Held**
SIC: **5211** 3273 Ret Lumber/Building Materials Mfg Ready-Mixed Concrete
PA: R & R Ready-Mix, Inc.
6050 Melbourne Rd
Saginaw MI 48604
989 753-3862

(G-1394)
RAP PRODUCTS INC
500 Germania St (48706-5049)
P.O. Box 459 (48707-0459)
PHONE...................989 893-5583
Kelly D McDonald, *President*
EMP: 5 EST: 1950
SQ FT: 120,000
SALES (est): 924.1K **Privately Held**
SIC: **2851** 2992 3412 2869 Paint removers; oils & greases, blending & compounding; barrels, shipping: metal; industrial organic chemicals; industrial inorganic chemicals

(G-1395)
RWC INC (PA)
2105 S Euclid Ave (48706-3409)
P.O. Box 920 (48707-0920)
PHONE...................989 684-4030
William Perlberg, *President*
Rebecca Wynn, *General Mgr*
Brian Tobin, *Vice Pres*
Edward Callaghan, *Project Mgr*
Tom Navarre, *Project Mgr*
EMP: 69 EST: 1945
SQ FT: 123,160
SALES (est): 14MM **Privately Held**
WEB: www.rwcinc.com
SIC: **3541** Machine tools, metal cutting type

(G-1396)
S C JOHNSON & SON INC
Also Called: S C Johnson Wax
4867 Wilder Rd (48706-1942)
PHONE...................989 667-0211
Paul Bilello, *Branch Mgr*
EMP: 6
SALES (corp-wide): 1.1B **Privately Held**
WEB: www.scjohnson.com
SIC: **2842** Floor waxes
PA: S. C. Johnson & Son, Inc.
1525 Howe St
Racine WI 53403
262 260-2000

(G-1397)
SANDLOT SPORTS (PA)
600 N Euclid Ave (48706-2950)
PHONE...................989 391-9684
Adam McCauley, *Owner*
Ryan Dost, *Co-Owner*
EMP: 4 EST: 2008
SALES (est): 1.3MM **Privately Held**
WEB: www.sandlotsports301.com
SIC: **2759** Screen printing

(G-1398)
SC JOHNSON & SON
4867 Wilder Rd (48706-1942)
PHONE...................989 667-0235
Toni Garcia, *Marketing Staff*
Todd Bero, *Manager*
EMP: 51 EST: 2016
SALES (est): 8.8MM **Privately Held**
WEB: www.scjohnson.com
SIC: **2842** Specialty cleaning, polishes & sanitation goods

(G-1399)
SERVAPURE COMPANY
Also Called: Serv-A-Pure
5215 Mackinaw Rd (48706-9700)
PHONE...................989 892-7745
Richard Herzeberger, *President*
Jonathon Herberger, *Vice Pres*
Adam Wuerfel, *Sales Mgr*
Sandy Herzberger, *Office Mgr*
EMP: 8 EST: 1956
SQ FT: 20,000
SALES (est): 1.5MM **Privately Held**
WEB: www.servapure.com
SIC: **3589** Water treatment equipment, industrial; water filters & softeners, household type; water purification equipment, household type

(G-1400)
SHADVIN INDUSTRIES LLC
401 Harvard St (48706-8926)
PHONE...................509 263-7128
Simon Kipkoech, *Director*
Vince Kirioba, *Director*
EMP: 5 EST: 2009
SALES (est): 72.1K **Privately Held**
SIC: **2851** 7371 Paints & allied products; software programming applications

(G-1401)
SHELTI INC
3020 N Water St (48708-5454)
PHONE...................989 893-1739
Randy Eigner, *President*
Dave Straw, *President*
Mark Robbins, *CIO*
▲ EMP: 18 EST: 2001
SALES (est): 1.5MM **Privately Held**
WEB: www.shelti.com
SIC: **3944** Games, toys & children's vehicles

(G-1402)
SMM PRINTING INC
1914 3rd St (48708-6215)
PHONE...................989 893-8788
Anthony H Lebron, *Principal*
EMP: 5 EST: 2019
SALES (est): 267.8K **Privately Held**
SIC: **2752** Commercial printing, lithographic

(G-1403)
SNYDER PLASTICS INC
1707 Lewis St (48706-1100)
PHONE...................989 684-8355
Jeffrey L Preston, *President*
Christina M Preston, *Admin Sec*
EMP: 20 EST: 1976
SQ FT: 8,400
SALES (est): 2.1MM **Privately Held**
WEB: www.snyderplastics.com
SIC: **3339** 3053 Silicon, pure; gaskets, packing & sealing devices

(G-1404)
SOLI-BOND INC (PA)
2377 2 Mile Rd (48706-8130)
PHONE...................989 684-9611
Dwight Hartley, *President*
Gary Draeger, *Vice Pres*
William Solan, *Vice Pres*
EMP: 5 EST: 1989
SQ FT: 5,000
SALES (est): 17.9MM **Privately Held**
WEB: www.soli-bond.com
SIC: **1389** Oil field services

(G-1405)
ST LAURENT BROTHERS INC
Also Called: Saint Laurent Brothers
1101 N Water St (48708-5625)
P.O. Box 117 (48707-0117)
PHONE...................989 893-7522
Keith Whitney, *President*
Steve Frye, *Vice Pres*
EMP: 20 EST: 1904
SQ FT: 35,000
SALES (est): 995.2K **Privately Held**
WEB: www.stlaurentbrothers.com
SIC: **2099** 5441 2068 Peanut butter; candy, nut & confectionery stores; salted & roasted nuts & seeds

(G-1406)
THERAPEUTIC HEALTH CHOICES LLC
903 N Euclid Ave (48706-2478)
PHONE...................989 459-2020
EMP: 5 EST: 2017
SALES (est): 293.2K **Privately Held**
WEB: www.thchoice.com
SIC: **8734** 3999 Product testing laboratory, safety or performance;

(G-1407)
TWM TECHNOLOGY LLC
Also Called: Rotational Levitation Levi
3490 E North Union Rd (48706-2533)
PHONE...................989 684-7050
Henry Johnson,
EMP: 10
SALES (est): 100K **Privately Held**
SIC: **3621** Motors & generators

(G-1408)
UNIT STEP COMPANY INC
3788 S Huron Rd (48706-2065)
PHONE...................989 684-9361
Robert Koehler, *President*
EMP: 4 EST: 1954
SQ FT: 5,600
SALES (est): 353.8K **Privately Held**
WEB: www.unitstep.tripod.com
SIC: **3272** Steps, prefabricated concrete

(G-1409)
UNIVERSAL PRINT
2758 E Fisher Rd (48706-3020)
PHONE...................989 525-5055
Andrew Budd, *Principal*
EMP: 7 EST: 2010
SALES (est): 133.6K **Privately Held**
SIC: **2752** Commercial printing, lithographic

(G-1410)
UNIVERSAL PRINTING COMPANY INC
1200 Woodside Ave (48708-5000)
PHONE...................989 671-9409
Steven Budd, *Vice Pres*
Mary Kate Budd, *Technical Staff*
Richard Budd,
EMP: 22 EST: 2013

Bay City - Bay County (G-1411)

SALES (est): 685.2K **Privately Held**
WEB: www.universalprintinginc.net
SIC: 2752 Commercial printing, offset

(G-1411)
WEST SYSTEM INC
102 Patterson Ave (48706-4136)
P.O. Box 665 (48707-0665)
PHONE.................................989 684-7286
Robert Monroe, *President*
EMP: 87 **EST:** 2004
SALES (est): 368.3K **Privately Held**
WEB: www.westsystem.com
SIC: 2851 2891 Epoxy coatings; epoxy adhesives
PA: Gougeon Holding Co.
    100 Patterson Ave
    Bay City MI 48706

(G-1412)
YORK ELECTRIC INC (PA)
Also Called: York Servo Motor Repair
611 Andre St (48706-4195)
PHONE.................................989 684-7460
Franklin K York, *CEO*
Kevin Krupp, *President*
Chris Cathcart, *COO*
Steve Jezowski, *Foreman/Supr*
Danielle Krupp, *Treasurer*
EMP: 67 **EST:** 1978
SQ FT: 80,000
SALES (est): 15.7MM **Privately Held**
WEB: www.yorkrepair.com
SIC: 7694 5063 Electric motor repair; motors, electric

Bay Port
Huron County

(G-1413)
BERKLEY INDUSTRIES INC (PA)
9938 Pigeon Rd (48720-9702)
P.O. Box 207 (48720-0207)
PHONE.................................989 656-2171
Steven Pyykkonen, *President*
Dennis Carter, *QC Mgr*
EMP: 26 **EST:** 1973
SALES (est): 2.3MM **Privately Held**
WEB: www.sandstube.com
SIC: 3498 3317 Tube fabricating (contract bending & shaping); steel pipe & tubes

(G-1414)
FALCON TRUCKING COMPANY
Also Called: Wallace Stone Plant
8785 Ribble Rd (48720-9739)
PHONE.................................989 656-2831
Ralph D Bronson, *Manager*
EMP: 25
SQ FT: 20,000
SALES (corp-wide): 18.1MM **Privately Held**
SIC: 1442 1422 Sand mining; crushed & broken limestone
PA: Falcon Trucking Company
    9300 Dix
    Dearborn MI 48120
    313 843-7200

(G-1415)
S & S TUBE INC
9938 Pigeon Rd (48720-9702)
P.O. Box 207 (48720-0207)
PHONE.................................989 656-7211
Tim Sears, *President*
Dennis Carter, *QC Mgr*
EMP: 23 **EST:** 1980
SQ FT: 21,000
SALES (est): 1.2MM **Privately Held**
SIC: 3714 3498 3317 Motor vehicle brake systems & parts; transmission housings or parts, motor vehicle; gas tanks, motor vehicle; fabricated pipe & fittings; steel pipe & tubes

Bear Lake
Manistee County

(G-1416)
BLARNEY CASTLE INC (PA)
Also Called: Blarney Castle Oil
12218 West St (49614-9453)
P.O. Box 246 (49614-0246)
PHONE.................................231 864-3111
Dennis E Mc Carthy, *President*
Dennis B Mc Carthy, *President*
EMP: 3 **EST:** 1941
SQ FT: 5,000
SALES (est): 10.1MM **Privately Held**
WEB: www.blarneycastleoil.com
SIC: 5541 1311 Filling stations, gasoline; crude petroleum production

(G-1417)
CORRECT COMPRESSION INC
11903 Chippewa Hwy (49614-9424)
PHONE.................................231 864-2101
Tony Merrill, *President*
Reilly Merrill, *Opers Mgr*
Wayne Geisert, *Parts Mgr*
Angela Eisenlohr, *Office Mgr*
Bethany Merrill, *Office Mgr*
EMP: 6 **EST:** 1996
SALES (est): 994.2K **Privately Held**
WEB: www.correctcompression.com
SIC: 3563 7699 Air & gas compressors including vacuum pumps; compressor repair

(G-1418)
LC MATERIALS LLC
17443 Pleasanton Hwy (49614-9634)
PHONE.................................231 946-5600
Robert Cherry, *Branch Mgr*
EMP: 204
SALES (corp-wide): 170.1MM **Privately Held**
WEB: www.lcredimix.com
SIC: 3273 Ready-mixed concrete
HQ: Lc Materials, Llc
    805 W 13th St
    Cadillac MI 49601
    231 946-5600

(G-1419)
MOM & ME EMBROIDERY
12412 Milarch Rd (49614-9756)
PHONE.................................231 590-0256
Loree Brown, *Owner*
EMP: 5 **EST:** 2016
SALES (est): 51.5K **Privately Held**
SIC: 2395 Embroidery & art needlework

(G-1420)
PIER PRESSURE CUSTOM BOATS
14051 Lakeside Ave (49614-9226)
PHONE.................................231 723-0124
Richard Chmura, *Principal*
EMP: 5 **EST:** 2005
SALES (est): 120K **Privately Held**
SIC: 3732 Boat building & repairing

(G-1421)
PIONEER PRESS PRINTING (PA)
12326 Virginia St (49614-5100)
PHONE.................................231 864-2404
Larry L Marek, *Owner*
EMP: 4
SQ FT: 1,000
SALES (est): 460.6K **Privately Held**
SIC: 2752 2759 7311 Commercial printing, offset; letterpress printing; advertising agencies

(G-1422)
R E CAP INC
8100 11 Mile Rd (49614-9741)
PHONE.................................231 864-3959
EMP: 8 **EST:** 2019
SALES (est): 112.2K **Privately Held**
WEB: www.recapinc.net
SIC: 7692 Welding repair

Beaverton
Gladwin County

(G-1423)
ADVANCE ENGINEERING COMPANY
3982 Terry Dianne St (48612-9126)
P.O. Box 564 (48612-0564)
PHONE.................................989 435-3641
Pete Vining, *Manager*
EMP: 48
SALES (corp-wide): 42.7MM **Privately Held**
SIC: 3089 3086 2671 Thermoformed finished plastic products; plastics foam products; packaging paper & plastics film, coated & laminated
PA: Advance Engineering Company
    7505 Baron Dr
    Canton MI 48187
    313 537-3500

(G-1424)
BROWN MCH GROUP INTRMDATE HLDN (DH)
330 N Ross St (48612-8165)
P.O. Box 434 (48612-0434)
PHONE.................................989 435-7741
Bryan Redman, *President*
Jim Block, *Vice Pres*
Brian Keeley, *Vice Pres*
Ron Lejman, *Vice Pres*
Tim Sperry, *Purch Mgr*
◆ **EMP:** 200 **EST:** 1998
SQ FT: 140,000
SALES (est): 50.2MM **Privately Held**
SIC: 3555 3559 Printing trades machinery; plastics working machinery
HQ: Thermoforming Technology Group Llc
    330 N Ross St
    Beaverton MI 48612
    989 435-7741

(G-1425)
HOWE RACING ENTERPRISES INC
3195 Lyle Rd (48612-8617)
PHONE.................................989 435-7080
Charles E Howe, *President*
Charles K Howe, *President*
Dina Howe, *Corp Secy*
Mark Koboldt, *Facilities Mgr*
Dan Myers, *Purchasing*
EMP: 36 **EST:** 1973
SQ FT: 6,570
SALES (est): 5.5MM **Privately Held**
WEB: www.howeracing.com
SIC: 5531 3714 Automotive parts; motor vehicle parts & accessories

(G-1426)
KILN KREATIONS
5366 M 18 (48612-9118)
PHONE.................................989 435-3296
Edda Yost, *Principal*
EMP: 4 **EST:** 2008
SALES (est): 208.5K **Privately Held**
SIC: 3559 Kilns

(G-1427)
KINNE PLASTICS INC
5381 Roehrs Rd Fl 435437 (48612-9111)
PHONE.................................989 435-4373
EMP: 5
SALES (est): 377.5K **Privately Held**
SIC: 3089 Mfg Plastic Products

(G-1428)
LANG TOOL COMPANY
2520 Glidden Rd (48612-9209)
PHONE.................................989 435-9864
William J Lang, *President*
Nancy Lang, *Mktg Dir*
▲ **EMP:** 4 **EST:** 1991
SQ FT: 12,000
SALES (est): 812.3K **Privately Held**
WEB: www.langtool.com
SIC: 3531 Backhoe mounted, hydraulically powered attachments

(G-1429)
LYLE INDUSTRIES
4144 Lyle Rd (48612-8603)
P.O. Box 434 (48612-0434)
PHONE.................................989 435-7717
Brian Redmond, *President*
Brian Crawford, *Vice Pres*
Sandra Schwartz, *Vice Pres*
▲ **EMP:** 114 **EST:** 1965
SQ FT: 80,000
SALES (est): 3.4MM **Privately Held**
WEB: www.tenexcm.com
SIC: 3559 Plastics working machinery
PA: Tenex Capital Management, L.P.
    60 E 42nd St Rm 5230
    New York NY 10165

(G-1430)
SAINT-GOBAIN PRFMCE PLAS CORP
3910 Terry Dianne St (48612-9126)
PHONE.................................989 435-9533
Todd Cunning, *Branch Mgr*
EMP: 4
SALES (corp-wide): 2.1B **Privately Held**
WEB: www.plastics.saint-gobain.com
SIC: 2821 Plastics materials & resins
HQ: Saint-Gobain Performance Plastics Corporation
    31500 Solon Rd
    Solon OH 44139
    440 836-6900

(G-1431)
SAINT-GOBAIN PRFMCE PLAS CORP
3910 Industrial Dr (48612)
PHONE.................................989 435-9533
Tod Kundinger, *Manager*
EMP: 5
SALES (corp-wide): 2.1B **Privately Held**
WEB: www.plastics.saint-gobain.com
SIC: 3089 2822 Synthetic resin finished products; synthetic rubber
HQ: Saint-Gobain Performance Plastics Corporation
    31500 Solon Rd
    Solon OH 44139
    440 836-6900

(G-1432)
THERMFRMER PARTS SUPPLIERS LLC
Also Called: Tps
3818 Terry Dianne St (48612-8652)
P.O. Box 485 (48612-0485)
PHONE.................................989 435-3800
John Beebe, *President*
Chuck Fanslow, *Vice Pres*
Brad Moore, *Vice Pres*
EMP: 5 **EST:** 1990
SQ FT: 3,520
SALES (est): 726.6K **Privately Held**
WEB: www.thermoformerparts.com
SIC: 3559 3599 Plastics working machinery; machine shop, jobbing & repair

(G-1433)
THERMOFORMING TECH GROUP LLC (HQ)
330 N Ross St (48612-8165)
PHONE.................................989 435-7741
Ron Lejman, *CEO*
Kay McCandless, *Vice Pres*
Bryan Redman, *Vice Pres*
EMP: 3 **EST:** 2013
SALES (est): 50.2MM **Privately Held**
WEB: www.tenexcm.com
SIC: 3555 3559 Printing trades machinery; plastics working machinery

Belding
Ionia County

(G-1434)
ACE TOOL & ENGINEERING INC
500 Reed St (48809-1532)
PHONE.................................616 361-4800
Eugene Pratt II, *President*
EMP: 7 **EST:** 2001
SQ FT: 4,000

GEOGRAPHIC SECTION — Belding - Ionia County

SALES (est): 450K **Privately Held**
WEB: www.acetoolengineering.com
SIC: 3599 Machine shop, jobbing & repair

(G-1435)
B & O SAWS INC
825 Reed St (48809-1576)
P.O. Box 26 (48809-0026)
PHONE..................................616 794-7297
Jason Kohn, *President*
John Kohn, *Vice Pres*
Ian Larsen, *Purchasing*
Bryce Vanderwilt, *Engineer*
Sam Gavitt, *Sales Engr*
EMP: 28 **EST:** 1995
SQ FT: 29,550
SALES (est): 6.9MM **Privately Held**
WEB: www.bosaws.com
SIC: 3541 Saws & sawing machines

(G-1436)
BAKER ROAD UPHOLSTERY INC
Also Called: Baker Rd Seating & Restoration
1122 S Bridge St (48809-9703)
PHONE..................................616 794-3027
EMP: 9
SQ FT: 30,000
SALES (est): 1.4MM **Privately Held**
SIC: 2531 Manufacture Auditorium Seating

(G-1437)
BELCO INDUSTRIES INC
Also Called: Paint Finishing Div
9138 W Belding Rd (48809-1768)
PHONE..................................616 794-0410
Charles Kitchel, *President*
Kieran Simon, *Engineer*
Andy Steinaway, *Sales Engr*
EMP: 40
SALES (corp-wide): 32.1MM **Privately Held**
WEB: www.belcoind.com
SIC: 3567 3563 3541 3535 Industrial furnaces & ovens; air & gas compressors; machine tools, metal cutting type; conveyors & conveying equipment; sheet metalwork
PA: Belco Industries, Inc.
 9138 W Belding Rd
 Belding MI 48809
 616 794-0410

(G-1438)
BELCO INDUSTRIES INC (PA)
9138 W Belding Rd (48809-1768)
PHONE..................................616 794-0410
Thomas F Kohn, *CEO*
Mike Kohn, *President*
Larry Mercer, *Purchasing*
Christopher Kohn, *Sales Engr*
Pete Edwards, *Sales Staff*
▲ **EMP:** 20 **EST:** 1959
SQ FT: 15,000
SALES (est): 32.1MM **Privately Held**
WEB: www.belcoind.com
SIC: 3567 5084 3541 3535 Paint baking & drying ovens; industrial machinery & equipment; machine tools, metal cutting type; conveyors & conveying equipment; sheet metalwork

(G-1439)
BELDING MCHY & EQP LSG CORP (HQ)
Also Called: Extruded Aluminum
7200 Industrial Dr (48809-9259)
PHONE..................................616 794-0300
D Lee Satterlee, *President*
Charlie Hall, *Corp Secy*
Todd Myers, *Vice Pres*
Rick Kloska, *Opers Staff*
Tony Caterino, *Buyer*
EMP: 151 **EST:** 1987
SQ FT: 180,000
SALES (est): 56.5MM **Privately Held**
WEB: www.extrudedaluminum.com
SIC: 3354 Aluminum extruded products
PA: Btmc Holdings, Inc.
 1114 S Bridge St
 Belding MI 48809
 616 794-0100

(G-1440)
BELDING TOOL ACQUISITION LLC (PA)
Also Called: Belding Tool and Machine
1114 S Bridge St (48809-9703)
P.O. Box 235 (48809-0235)
PHONE..................................586 816-4450
Jason Markham,
EMP: 14 **EST:** 2014
SQ FT: 11,000
SALES (est): 1.7MM **Privately Held**
WEB: www.beldingtool.com
SIC: 3544 Custom machinery; machine shop, jobbing & repair

(G-1441)
BTM NATIONAL HOLDINGS LLC
Also Called: Belding Tool and Machine
1114 S Bridge St (48809-9703)
PHONE..................................616 794-0100
Peter K Tur,
Jason Markham,
EMP: 15 **EST:** 2016
SALES (est): 1.7MM **Privately Held**
WEB: www.beldingtool.com
SIC: 3544 Special dies, tools, jigs & fixtures

(G-1442)
BTMC HOLDINGS INC (PA)
1114 S Bridge St (48809-9703)
P.O. Box 235 (48809-0235)
PHONE..................................616 794-0100
Michael J Petersen, *President*
Jason Markham, *President*
EMP: 8 **EST:** 1940
SQ FT: 10,000
SALES (est): 56.5MM **Privately Held**
SIC: 3544 Special dies & tools

(G-1443)
CLARK GRANCO INC
7298 Storey Rd (48809-9360)
PHONE..................................616 794-2600
Jeffrey Ferman, *President*
Kirk Krouse, *Foreman/Supr*
Lynn Austin, *Engineer*
Nathan Hawkins, *Electrical Engi*
Robert Frostic, *CFO*
▲ **EMP:** 65 **EST:** 1981
SQ FT: 60,000
SALES (est): 16.6MM **Privately Held**
WEB: www.grancoclark.com
SIC: 3542 3567 Extruding machines (machine tools), metal; industrial furnaces & ovens

(G-1444)
D & R FABRICATION INC
Also Called: Belding Tank Technologies
200 Gooding St (48809-1865)
P.O. Box 160 (48809-0160)
PHONE..................................616 794-1130
Daniel Blunt Jr, *CEO*
Daniel W Blunt Sr, *President*
Fayth Reeve, *Human Resources*
Greg Kirgis, *Sales Engr*
EMP: 65
SQ FT: 25,000
SALES (est): 20.7MM **Privately Held**
WEB: www.beldingtank.com
SIC: 2519 Fiberglass & plastic furniture

(G-1445)
DIGITAL FABRICATION INC
7251 Whites Bridge Rd (48809-9404)
PHONE..................................616 794-2848
Richard Hebert, *President*
Tom Hebert, *Vice Pres*
▲ **EMP:** 10 **EST:** 1998
SQ FT: 18,000
SALES (est): 1.3MM **Privately Held**
WEB: www.digitalfab.net
SIC: 3441 Fabricated structural metal

(G-1446)
DRIVEN DESIGNS INC
1135 S Bridge St (48809-9703)
PHONE..................................616 794-9977
Gordon Lanting, *President*
▲ **EMP:** 5 **EST:** 1996
SALES (est): 580K **Privately Held**
WEB: www.poolpatrol.com
SIC: 8711 3651 Designing: ship, boat, machine & product; electronic kits for home assembly: radio, TV, phonograph

(G-1447)
DS MOLD LLC
807 Edna St (48809-2431)
PHONE..................................616 794-1639
Douglas Stearins, *Owner*
Dave Huizenga, *Engineer*
John Davis, *Project Engr*
Mark Nordgren, *Project Engr*
Tim Thornhill, *Sales Staff*
EMP: 21 **EST:** 2002
SQ FT: 70,000
SALES (est): 1.8MM **Privately Held**
WEB: www.dsmold.net
SIC: 3544 Industrial molds

(G-1448)
EXTRUDED ALUMINUM CORPORATION
7200 Industrial Dr (48809-9259)
PHONE..................................616 794-0300
Charles Hall, *President*
EMP: 140 **EST:** 2001
SALES (est): 56.5MM **Privately Held**
WEB: www.extrudedaluminum.com
SIC: 3354 Aluminum extruded products
HQ: Belding Machinery & Equipment Leasing Corporation
 7200 Industrial Dr
 Belding MI 48809
 616 794-0300

(G-1449)
FINISHING TECHNOLOGIES INC
Also Called: Fintech
7125 Whites Bridge Rd (48809-9404)
PHONE..................................616 794-4001
Robert J Greenland, *President*
Tom Barnes, *Sales Staff*
Kelly Cox, *Sales Executive*
Donna Greenland, *Admin Sec*
▲ **EMP:** 17 **EST:** 1983
SQ FT: 16,000
SALES (est): 3.6MM **Privately Held**
WEB: www.fintechabrasives.com
SIC: 5085 3291 Abrasives; abrasive products

(G-1450)
GERREF INDUSTRIES INC
206 N York St (48809-1834)
PHONE..................................616 794-3110
Harold Rich, *President*
Mark Rich, *President*
James Jones, *Vice Pres*
Adam Udell, *Engineer*
Joanne Strobel, *Treasurer*
EMP: 25 **EST:** 1974
SQ FT: 24,500
SALES (est): 5.1MM **Privately Held**
WEB: www.gerref.com
SIC: 3567 3441 Industrial furnaces & ovens; fabricated structural metal

(G-1451)
HILLS CRATE MILL INC
3851 Hoyt Rd (48809-9508)
PHONE..................................616 761-3555
Burton Hill Jr, *President*
EMP: 8 **EST:** 1952
SQ FT: 5,600
SALES (est): 628.7K **Privately Held**
SIC: 2448 Pallets, wood; cargo containers, wood

(G-1452)
HUNT HOPPOUGH CUSTOM CRAFTED
Also Called: Thomas Construction
700 Reed St (48809-1578)
PHONE..................................616 794-3455
James J Hunt, *President*
Todd Hoppough, *Vice Pres*
Cathy Hoppough, *Treasurer*
Kelly Hunt, *Admin Sec*
EMP: 8 **EST:** 1989
SQ FT: 4,100
SALES (est): 220.1K **Privately Held**
SIC: 2452 Modular homes, prefabricated, wood

(G-1453)
INDUSTRIAL ENGINEERING SERVICE
Also Called: Industrial Engnrng Service
215 E High St (48809-1500)
P.O. Box 415 (48809-0415)
PHONE..................................616 794-1330
David M Laux, *President*
EMP: 10 **EST:** 1953
SQ FT: 20,000
SALES (est): 1.5MM **Privately Held**
WEB: www.indeng.com
SIC: 3469 3312 Stamping metal for the trade; tool & die steel & alloys

(G-1454)
JORDAN MANUFACTURING COMPANY
308 Reed St (48809-1528)
P.O. Box 130 (48809-0130)
PHONE..................................616 794-0900
Steven Johnson, *President*
Karlene Johnson, *Vice Pres*
EMP: 20 **EST:** 1949
SQ FT: 25,000
SALES (est): 2.7MM **Privately Held**
WEB: www.jordanmfg.com
SIC: 3469 3544 Stamping metal for the trade; special dies, tools, jigs & fixtures

(G-1455)
KASSOUNI MANUFACTURING INC
Also Called: Kmi
815 S Front St (48809-2235)
PHONE..................................616 794-0989
Van Kassouni, *President*
Tom O'Malley, *Vice Pres*
Bob Hams, *Sales Mgr*
Tom O Malley, *VP Mktg*
▲ **EMP:** 48 **EST:** 1986
SQ FT: 90,000
SALES (est): 9MM **Privately Held**
WEB: www.thegardentamer.com
SIC: 2834 2812 Chlorination tablets & kits (water purification); chlorine, compressed or liquefied

(G-1456)
LAKE DESIGN AND MFG CO
7280 Storey Rd (48809-9360)
PHONE..................................616 794-0290
Ernest Hallas, *President*
John Elliott, *Vice Pres*
EMP: 8 **EST:** 1977
SQ FT: 14,000
SALES (est): 1MM **Privately Held**
WEB: www.lakedesignmfg.com
SIC: 3544 Special dies & tools

(G-1457)
MIZKAN AMERICA INC
Also Called: Indian Summer
700 Kiddville St (48809-9594)
PHONE..................................616 794-0226
Marcia Ause, *Transportation*
Michelle Jones, *Manager*
EMP: 51 **Privately Held**
WEB: www.mizkan.com
SIC: 2099 2033 Cider, nonalcoholic; vinegar; fruit juices: fresh
HQ: Mizkan America, Inc.
 1661 Feehanville Dr 100a
 Mount Prospect IL 60056
 847 590-0059

(G-1458)
MIZKAN AMERICA INC
702 Kiddville St (48809-9594)
PHONE..................................616 794-3670
Michelle Jones, *Manager*
EMP: 51 **Privately Held**
WEB: www.mizkan.com
SIC: 2099 Food preparations
HQ: Mizkan America, Inc.
 1661 Feehanville Dr 100a
 Mount Prospect IL 60056
 847 590-0059

(G-1459)
MUELLER BRASS CO
Also Called: Mueller Brass Products
302 Ashfield St (48809-1524)
PHONE..................................616 794-1200
Joseph Napolitan, *President*

▲ EMP: 14 EST: 1930
SALES (est): 440.6K Privately Held
WEB: www.muellerindustries.com
SIC: 3399 Brads: aluminum, brass or other nonferrous metal or wire

(G-1460)
NELSON RAPIDS CO INC
11834 Old Belding Rd Ne (48809-9389)
PHONE 616 691-8041
Gerald J Duncan, President
EMP: 4 EST: 1953
SQ FT: 10,000
SALES (est): 183.3K Privately Held
SIC: 2298 Cordage: abaca, sisal, henequen, hemp, jute or other fiber

(G-1461)
POSTHASTE ELECTRONICS LLC
1135 S Bridge St (48809-9703)
PHONE 616 794-9977
Paul M Sneller, Principal
Paul Sneller, Principal
EMP: 9 EST: 2019
SALES (est): 813.3K Privately Held
WEB: www.posthastedesign.com
SIC: 3672 Printed circuit boards

(G-1462)
ROBROY ENCLOSURES INC
Also Called: Stahlin Enclosures
505 W Maple St (48809-1936)
PHONE 616 794-0700
Craig Mitchell, President
Cameron Delet, Marketing Staff
Jeff Seagle, Executive
EMP: 215 EST: 1905
SALES (est): 27MM
SALES (corp-wide): 126.4MM Privately Held
WEB: www.stahlin.com
SIC: 3229 Glass fiber products
PA: Robroy Industries, Inc.
10 River Rd
Verona PA 15147
412 828-2100

(G-1463)
WEALTHY STREET CORPORATION
Also Called: Spectrum E-Coat, Inc.
2236 Crawford St (48809)
PHONE 800 222-8116
EMP: 157 Privately Held
SIC: 3479 Coating of metals & formed products
PA: Wealthy Street Corporation
700 Wealthy St Ne
Grand Rapids MI 49504

(G-1464)
WEST MICH AUTO STL & ENGRG INC
Also Called: Hillside Finsihing
550 E Ellis Ave (48809-1522)
P.O. Box 218 (48809-0218)
PHONE 616 560-8198
Herman C Siegel Jr, President
Herman C Siegel III, Vice Pres
EMP: 25 EST: 1965
SQ FT: 18,000
SALES (est): 1.2MM Privately Held
SIC: 3469 1796 3499 3714 Machine parts, stamped or pressed metal; machinery installation; welding tips, heat resistant: metal; motor vehicle parts & accessories; blowers & fans

(G-1465)
WEST MICHIGAN FAB CORP
321 Root St 3ph (48809-1561)
P.O. Box 296 (48809-0296)
PHONE 616 794-3750
Tony Walcutt, President
John Schofield, Principal
EMP: 4 EST: 2005
SQ FT: 30,000
SALES (est): 1MM Privately Held
WEB: www.wmfabcorp.com
SIC: 3441 Fabricated structural metal

(G-1466)
WIESEN EDM INC
Also Called: Wiesen Powdercoating
8634 Storey Rd (48809-9427)
PHONE 616 208-0000
Jeff Wiesen, President
EMP: 20 EST: 1993
SALES (est): 1.6MM Privately Held
WEB: www.weisenpowdercoating.com
SIC: 2851 Coating, air curing

(G-1467)
WIESEN EDM INC
8630 Storey Rd (48809-9427)
PHONE 616 794-9870
Jeff Wiesen, President
Scott Gladding, General Mgr
Nikki Gribble, Office Admin
EMP: 20 EST: 1993
SQ FT: 11,580
SALES (est): 900K Privately Held
WEB: www.wiesen.com
SIC: 3312 Tool & die steel

Bellaire
Antrim County

(G-1468)
ANCHOR LAMINA AMERICA INC
Lamina Bronze Products
3650 S Derenzy Rd (49615-9699)
P.O. Box 250 (49615-0250)
PHONE 231 533-8646
Steve Osborn, Engineer
Maryann Schuckel, Human Res Dir
Joe Lerman, Branch Mgr
Zach Brown, Manager
Mindy Moyer, Manager
EMP: 115
SQ FT: 95,000 Privately Held
WEB: www.daytonlamina.com
SIC: 3366 3545 3546 3452 Copper foundries; machine tool accessories; power-driven handtools; bolts, nuts, rivets & washers; nonferrous rolling & drawing; copper rolling & drawing
HQ: Anchor Lamina America, Inc.
3650 S Derenzy Rd
Bellaire MI 49615
248 489-9122

(G-1469)
ANCHOR LAMINA AMERICA INC (DH)
Also Called: Anchor Die Supply
3650 S Derenzy Rd (49615-9699)
PHONE 248 489-9122
Micahel Purchase, President
Michael Purchase, President
Scott Jones, General Mgr
Sawato Hayashi, Chairman
Bill Mills, Vice Pres
▲ EMP: 21 EST: 1997
SALES (est): 48.9MM Privately Held
WEB: www.daytonlamina.com
SIC: 3544 3546 3443 3366 Die sets for metal stamping (presses); drills, portable, except rock: electric or pneumatic; fabricated plate work (boiler shop); copper foundries; nonferrous rolling & drawing
HQ: Dayton Lamina Corporation
500 Progress Rd
Dayton OH 45449
937 859-5111

(G-1470)
ANTRIM REVIEW
4470 S M 88 Hwy (49615-5111)
P.O. Box 313 (49615-0313)
PHONE 231 533-5651
Hugh Conklin, Manager
EMP: 8 EST: 2017
SALES (est): 69.2K Privately Held
WEB: www.antrimreview.net
SIC: 2711 Newspapers: publishing only, not printed on site

(G-1471)
BELLAIRE LOG HOMES INDUS HM
6633 Bellaire Hwy (49615-9610)
PHONE 231 533-6669
Jim Barnard, Principal

EMP: 6 EST: 2001
SALES (est): 123K Privately Held
SIC: 3398 Metal heat treating

(G-1472)
BP PACK INC
3007 Akins Ln (49615-9181)
PHONE 612 594-0839
Betsy Poupard, Principal
EMP: 8 EST: 2015
SALES (est): 222.6K Privately Held
SIC: 3565 Packaging machinery

(G-1473)
DAYTON LAMINA CORP
3650 S Derenzy Rd (49615-9699)
PHONE 231 533-8646
Sawato Hayashi, Chairman
Andrew Chandler, Buyer
EMP: 15 EST: 2017
SALES (est): 1MM Privately Held
WEB: www.daytonlamina.com
SIC: 3544 Special dies & tools

(G-1474)
DEEP WOOD PRESS
121 Cedar River Dr (49615)
P.O. Box 726, Mancelona (49659-0726)
PHONE 231 587-0506
Chad Pastotnik, Principal
EMP: 4 EST: 2008
SALES (est): 57.1K Privately Held
WEB: www.deepwoodpress.com
SIC: 2741 Miscellaneous publishing

(G-1475)
HELLO VINO
122 N Bridge St (49615-5105)
P.O. Box 514 (49615-0514)
PHONE 231 350-7138
EMP: 4 EST: 2017
SALES (est): 132.4K Privately Held
SIC: 2084 Wines

(G-1476)
KENYON TJ & ASSOCIATES INC
902 Green Acres St (49615-9418)
PHONE 231 544-1144
Tom J Kenyon, Owner
Ken Schiffer, Engineer
Chuck Bultman, Director
EMP: 7 EST: 1975
SALES (est): 119.3K Privately Held
SIC: 3999 Manufacturing industries

(G-1477)
LAKE HOUSE PUBLISHING LLC
6377 Cottage Rd (49615-8857)
PHONE 231 377-2017
Marsha Clark, Principal
EMP: 5 EST: 2008
SALES (est): 123.9K Privately Held
WEB: www.lakehousepublishing.net
SIC: 2741 Miscellaneous publishing

Belleville
Wayne County

(G-1478)
ACTION AD NEWSPAPERS INC
Also Called: View, The
45223 Wear Rd (48111-9685)
PHONE 734 740-6966
Sharron Russell, President
Clarence Russell, Treasurer
EMP: 5 EST: 1983
SQ FT: 800
SALES (est): 100K Privately Held
SIC: 2711 Newspapers: publishing only, not printed on site

(G-1479)
AJW INDUSTRIES INC
43590 Harris Rd (48111-8910)
PHONE 313 595-5554
EMP: 4 EST: 2018
SALES (est): 39.6K Privately Held
SIC: 3999 Manufacturing industries

(G-1480)
BELLEVILLE AREA INDEPENDENT
152 Main St Ste 9 (48111-3911)
PHONE 734 699-9020
Rosemarie Otzman, President
Rosemary Otzman, Principal
EMP: 4 EST: 1998
SALES (est): 253.6K Privately Held
WEB: www.bellevilleareaindependent.com
SIC: 2711 Newspapers: publishing only, not printed on site

(G-1481)
BLACKMORE CO INC
10800 Blackmore Ave (48111-2500)
PHONE 734 483-8661
Fred N Blackmore Jr, CEO
Scott Blackmore, President
David Leach, General Mgr
Steve Meadows, Plant Engr
Bruce Hudson, CFO
◆ EMP: 52 EST: 1966
SQ FT: 47,000
SALES (est): 25.4MM Privately Held
WEB: www.blackmoreco.com
SIC: 3089 Planters, plastic

(G-1482)
BREAKAWAY MEDIA MARKETING LLC
44004 Harris Rd (48111-8935)
PHONE 734 787-3382
Drew Priebe,
EMP: 4 EST: 2017
SALES (est): 37K Privately Held
SIC: 2741

(G-1483)
EMERGING ADVANCED PRODUCTS LLC
39555 Intrstate 94 S Svc (48111)
PHONE 734 942-1060
Ravinder Sandhu, Mng Member
EMP: 82 EST: 2020
SALES (est): 13.4MM
SALES (corp-wide): 34.4MM Privately Held
WEB: www.aapincorp.com
SIC: 3465 Automotive stampings
PA: Advanced Assembly Products, Inc.
1300 E 9 Mile Rd
Hazel Park MI 48030
248 543-2427

(G-1484)
GORDON WOODWORK LLC
13909 Rawsonville Rd (48111-9402)
PHONE 734 612-3586
William Gordon, Principal
EMP: 5 EST: 2017
SALES (est): 93.8K Privately Held
SIC: 2431 Millwork

(G-1485)
GREAT LAKES COCA-COLA DIST LLC
100 Coca Cola Dr (48111-1633)
PHONE 734 397-2700
EMP: 12 Privately Held
WEB: www.coca-cola.com
SIC: 2086 Bottled & canned soft drinks
HQ: Great Lakes Coca-Cola Distribution, Llc
6250 N River Rd Ste 9000
Rosemont IL 60018
847 227-6500

(G-1486)
JL DUMPSTERS LLC
24133 Elwell Rd (48111-9360)
PHONE 313 258-0767
Jamie Bass, Principal
EMP: 4 EST: 2017
SALES (est): 69.1K Privately Held
SIC: 3443 Dumpsters, garbage

(G-1487)
KELTROL ENTERPRISES INC
35 Main St Ste 102 (48111-3287)
PHONE 734 697-3011
Dr Carol Moynihan DDS, President
EMP: 4 EST: 1976
SQ FT: 1,800

GEOGRAPHIC SECTION

Belmont - Kent County (G-1515)

SALES (est): 470K **Privately Held**
WEB: www.keltrolinc.com
SIC: 3089 Plastic processing

(G-1488)
LG ENERGY SOLUTION MICH INC
10885 Textile Rd (48111-2315)
PHONE....................616 494-7100
EMP: 119 **Privately Held**
SIC: 3691 Storage batteries
HQ: Lg Energy Solution Michigan, Inc.
    1 Lg Way
    Holland MI 49423

(G-1489)
NEXT TOOL LLC
41200 Coca Cola Dr (48111-1640)
PHONE....................734 405-7079
Nicholas Baise,
EMP: 10 EST: 2014
SQ FT: 18,060
SALES (est): 983.2K **Privately Held**
WEB: www.nexttoolgroup.com
SIC: 3544 Special dies & tools

(G-1490)
REAM LOGISTICS DLVRY SVCS LLC
419 Nevada (48111-9049)
PHONE....................877 246-7857
Bobby Bell, *Mng Member*
EMP: 6 EST: 2015
SALES (est): 250K **Privately Held**
SIC: 3537 Trucks: freight, baggage, etc.: industrial, except mining

(G-1491)
SMW MFG INC
41200 Coca Cola Dr (48111-1640)
PHONE....................517 596-3300
EMP: 26
SALES (corp-wide): 2.4B **Privately Held**
WEB: www.smw-mfg.com
SIC: 3599 Custom machinery
HQ: Smw Mfg, Inc.
    8707 Samuel Barton Dr
    Van Buren Twp MI 48111
    517 596-3300

(G-1492)
VAN BUREN PUBLISHING LLC
557 Main St (48111-2649)
PHONE....................734 740-8668
Robert Thorne, *Principal*
EMP: 8 EST: 2010
SALES (est): 72.9K **Privately Held**
WEB: www.vanburenschools.net
SIC: 2741 Miscellaneous publishing

(G-1493)
VERY BEST STEEL LLC
Also Called: Van Buren Steel
327 Davis St (48111-2911)
P.O. Box 954 (48112-0954)
PHONE....................734 697-8609
Matthew Sorna, *Opers Mgr*
David Costa, *Mng Member*
EMP: 7
SQ FT: 35,000
SALES (est): 4.3MM **Privately Held**
WEB: www.vanburensteel.com
SIC: 5051 3441 Steel; building components, structural steel

(G-1494)
VIEW NEWSPAPER
Also Called: Heritage Newspaper
159 Main St (48111-2759)
PHONE....................734 697-8255
Fax: 734 697-4610
EMP: 4 EST: 1997
SALES (est): 170K **Privately Held**
SIC: 2711 Newspaper Publishing And Printing

(G-1495)
WELLINGTON-ALMONT LLC (HQ)
39555 S Intrstate 94 Svc (48111)
PHONE....................734 942-1060
Marvin Tyghem,
Purnima Mistry,
EMP: 100 EST: 2005
SQ FT: 150,000
SALES (est): 30MM
SALES (corp-wide): 97.6MM **Privately Held**
WEB: www.aapincorp.com
SIC: 3465 Body parts, automobile: stamped metal

(G-1496)
WOOD WONDERS
23405 Sherwood Rd (48111-9306)
PHONE....................313 461-2369
Craig Kosmowski, *Owner*
EMP: 7 EST: 2015
SALES (est): 160K **Privately Held**
SIC: 2499 Wood products

Bellevue
Eaton County

(G-1497)
CUSTOM CRAFTERS
7889 S Ionia Rd (49021-9470)
P.O. Box 97 (49021-0097)
PHONE....................269 763-9180
James Treat, *Owner*
Thomas Fiore, *VP Opers*
Paul Kelly, *VP Sls/Mktg*
EMP: 4 EST: 1986
SALES (est): 361K **Privately Held**
WEB: www.custom-crafters.com
SIC: 2541 2521 1751 Counter & sink tops; cabinets, lockers & shelving; wood office furniture; cabinet & finish carpentry

(G-1498)
F G CHENEY LIMESTONE CO
9400 Sand Rd (49021-9720)
PHONE....................269 763-9541
William T Cheney, *President*
William S Cheney, *President*
Ronald Vogt, *Corp Secy*
EMP: 4 EST: 1946
SQ FT: 4,200
SALES (est): 875.1K **Privately Held**
WEB: www.cheneylimestone.com
SIC: 1422 Crushed & broken limestone

Belmont
Kent County

(G-1499)
ALTERNATIVE ENGINEERING INC
5670 West River Dr Ne (49306-9739)
PHONE....................616 785-7200
D Robert Rodriguez, *President*
Sharon E Rodriguez, *Vice Pres*
Shaun Brigham, *Purchasing*
Mike Panik, *Engineer*
Kelly Knapp, *Administration*
EMP: 24 EST: 1994
SQ FT: 44,000 **Privately Held**
WEB: www.aeinc.com
SIC: 3535 Bulk handling conveyor systems

(G-1500)
AVASURE HOLDINGS INC (PA)
5801 Safety Dr Ne (49306-8832)
PHONE....................616 301-0129
Brad Playford, *CEO*
Thomas Fusee, *Regional Mgr*
Kyle Pett, *COO*
Stacey Overholt, *Vice Pres*
Kaitlin Mazer, *Project Mgr*
EMP: 50 EST: 2008
SQ FT: 4,000
SALES (est): 21.9MM **Privately Held**
WEB: www.avasure.com
SIC: 3842 Orthopedic appliances

(G-1501)
BELMONT ENGINEERED PLAS LLC
5801 Safety Dr Ne (49306-8832)
P.O. Box 52250, Knoxville TN (37950-2250)
PHONE....................616 785-6279
Stephen King, *President*
Jody Craig, *Vice Pres*
David Schmid, *Vice Pres*
Chris Yerger, *Vice Pres*
Josh Boersma, *Mfg Staff*
▲ EMP: 55 EST: 2013
SQ FT: 149,000
SALES (est): 9MM **Privately Held**
WEB: www.beplastics.com
SIC: 3089 Injection molding of plastics

(G-1502)
BELMONT PLASTICS SOLUTIONS LLC
8211 Graphic Dr Ne (49306-8934)
PHONE....................616 340-3147
Greg Mumford, *Vice Pres*
EMP: 16 EST: 2010
SALES (est): 3MM **Privately Held**
WEB: www.belmontplastics.com
SIC: 3089 Injection molding of plastics

(G-1503)
BOOKCOMP INC
6124 Belmont Ave Ne (49306-9609)
PHONE....................616 774-9700
Jon Dertien, *President*
Carol Bifulco, *Prdtn Mgr*
EMP: 13 EST: 1990
SALES (est): 522.2K **Privately Held**
WEB: www.bookcomp.com
SIC: 2791 Typesetting

(G-1504)
CARDS OF WOOD INC
7754 Pine Island Ct Ne (49306-9720)
PHONE....................616 887-8680
Tate Lenderink, *President*
Sally Ann Lenderink, *Corp Secy*
◆ EMP: 8 EST: 1966
SQ FT: 2,500
SALES (est): 879.6K **Privately Held**
WEB: www.cardsofwood.com
SIC: 2499 Decorative wood & woodwork

(G-1505)
DIGISCROLL PRESS
2320 Rolling Meadow Dr Ne (49306-9320)
PHONE....................214 846-1826
Brian Webster, *Principal*
EMP: 5 EST: 2017
SALES (est): 136.5K **Privately Held**
SIC: 2741 Miscellaneous publishing

(G-1506)
ELTEK INC
6688 Wildwood Creek Dr Ne (49306-9325)
PHONE....................616 363-6397
EMP: 6
SQ FT: 4,000
SALES: 1.1MM **Privately Held**
SIC: 3621 Mfg Electronic Controls

(G-1507)
GRAND RAPIDS GRAVEL COMPANY
3800 7 Mile Rd Ne (49306-9654)
P.O. Box 9160, Grand Rapids (49509-0160)
PHONE....................616 538-9000
Gary Myers, *Manager*
EMP: 27
SALES (corp-wide): 23.9MM **Privately Held**
WEB: www.grgravel.com
SIC: 3273 1442 Ready-mixed concrete; construction sand & gravel
PA: Grand Rapids Gravel Company
    2700 28th St Sw
    Grand Rapids MI 49519
    616 538-9000

(G-1508)
JANT GROUP LLC
Also Called: Retail Sign Systems
8111 Belmont Ave Ne (49306-8823)
PHONE....................616 863-6600
Patrick Szymczak, *Vice Pres*
Tyler Szymczak, *Sales Staff*
EMP: 9 EST: 2001
SALES (est): 1.8MM **Privately Held**
WEB: www.retailsignsystems.com
SIC: 3577 Graphic displays, except graphic terminals

(G-1509)
KB STAMPING INC
8110 Graphic Dr Ne (49306-9448)
PHONE....................616 866-5917
Gary Kurtz, *President*
Rick Kurtz, *Vice Pres*
EMP: 10 EST: 2001
SQ FT: 10,000
SALES (est): 1.4MM **Privately Held**
WEB: www.kbstamping.com
SIC: 3469 Patterns on metal

(G-1510)
LBV SALES LLC
5669 Rolling Highlands Dr (49306)
P.O. Box 591, North Olmsted OH (44070-0591)
PHONE....................616 874-9390
Michael Wavra, *Mng Member*
EMP: 7 EST: 2005
SQ FT: 2,000
SALES (est): 564.1K **Privately Held**
SIC: 2673 Plastic bags: made from purchased materials

(G-1511)
LENDERINK INC
Also Called: Lenderink Family Tree Farms
1267 House St Ne (49306-9203)
PHONE....................616 887-8257
Thomas A Lenderink, *President*
Tracey Devries, *Director*
Sallyanne Lenderink, *Director*
EMP: 10 EST: 1964
SQ FT: 7,000
SALES (est): 3MM **Privately Held**
WEB: www.lenderink.com
SIC: 8732 2891 2899 Research services, except laboratory; adhesives; fire retardant chemicals

(G-1512)
LOGOSPOT
8200 Graphic Dr Ne (49306-8934)
PHONE....................616 785-7170
Phil Roode, *Principal*
EMP: 7 EST: 2015
SALES (est): 249.4K **Privately Held**
WEB: www.logospot.com
SIC: 2752 2395 Commercial printing, offset; embroidery products, except schiffli machine

(G-1513)
MAHLE BEHR INDUSTY AMERICA LP
5858 Safety Dr Ne (49306-9788)
P.O. Box 2840, Farmington Hills (48333-2840)
PHONE....................616 647-3490
Micheal Goerg, *Partner*
Armin Hagenloch, *General Mgr*
Kate Lane, *Senior Buyer*
Wolfgang Bubeck, *Engineer*
Tim Hirschberg, *Engineer*
▲ EMP: 99 EST: 2000
SQ FT: 60,000
SALES (est): 22.3MM
SALES (corp-wide): 504.6K **Privately Held**
WEB: www.mahle.com
SIC: 3585 Refrigeration & heating equipment
HQ: Mahle Industrial Thermal Systems
    Gmbh & Co. Kg
    Enzstr. 25-33
    Kornwestheim BW 70806
    711 501-4210

(G-1514)
MEGAPIXEL IDEAS LLC
5880 Egypt Valley Ave Ne (49306-9120)
PHONE....................616 307-5220
EMP: 4 EST: 2016
SALES (est): 56K **Privately Held**
WEB: www.cityinnovationlabs.com
SIC: 3652 Pre-recorded records & tapes

(G-1515)
PARTRIDGE POINTE PRESS LLC
2470 Strawberry Frm St Ne (49306-8808)
PHONE....................248 321-0475
Thomas R Carney, *Principal*
EMP: 5 EST: 2016
SALES (est): 79K **Privately Held**
SIC: 2741 Miscellaneous publishing

Belmont - Kent County (G-1516)

(G-1516)
SCOTT PHILIP CUSTOM WDWKG LLC
5865 Egypt Valley Ave Ne (49306-9120)
PHONE 616 723-9074
Scott P Colby, *Administration*
EMP: 6 **EST:** 2017
SALES (est): 212.7K **Privately Held**
SIC: 2431 Millwork

(G-1517)
SSI ELECTRONICS INC
8080 Graphic Dr Ne (49306-9448)
PHONE 616 866-8880
Daniel Anderson, *President*
John B Miller, *Chairman*
Shirley Grice, *Corp Secy*
Scott Miller, *Vice Pres*
Lynette Krystoff, *Purchasing*
▲ **EMP:** 36 **EST:** 1983
SQ FT: 19,200
SALES (est): 6.7MM **Privately Held**
WEB: www.ssi-electronics.com
SIC: 3679 3643 3613 Electronic switches; current-carrying wiring devices; switchgear & switchboard apparatus

(G-1518)
STEEL CRAFT TECHNOLOGIES INC
8057 Graphic Dr Ne (49306-9448)
PHONE 616 866-4400
Drew Boersma, *President*
Dan Vander Horn, *Vice Pres*
Julie Rounds, *Sales Staff*
Mike Smith, *Sales Staff*
Russ Vantol, *Sales Staff*
EMP: 120 **EST:** 2005
SALES (est): 21.6MM **Privately Held**
WEB: www.steelcrafttech.com
SIC: 3545 Precision tools, machinists'

(G-1519)
TECHNICAL AIR PRODUCTS LLC
8069 Belmont Ave Ne (49306-8877)
PHONE 616 863-9115
Aaron Kozminski, *Design Engr*
Joseph Morgan, *Mng Member*
EMP: 14 **EST:** 1992
SQ FT: 22,800
SALES (est): 3MM **Privately Held**
WEB: www.technicalairproducts.com
SIC: 3564 Air cleaning systems

(G-1520)
TRADEMARK DIE & ENGINEERING
8060 Graphic Dr Ne Unit 1 (49306-9448)
PHONE 616 863-6660
Michael O'Keefe, *President*
Deb O'keefe, *Manager*
Cory Ingersoll, *Technology*
EMP: 30 **EST:** 1994
SQ FT: 21,000
SALES (est): 3.7MM **Privately Held**
WEB: www.tmde.net
SIC: 3544 Special dies & tools

(G-1521)
WILLIAMS FORM ENGINEERING CORP (PA)
8165 Graphic Dr Ne (49306-9448)
PHONE 616 866-0815
Ronald R Williams Sr, *Ch of Bd*
Ronald Townsend, *President*
Bruce Jensen, *Exec VP*
Charles Braun, *Vice Pres*
Jon Roelofs, *Vice Pres*
◆ **EMP:** 75 **EST:** 1937
SQ FT: 15,000
SALES (est): 70.6MM **Privately Held**
WEB: www.williamsform.com
SIC: 3559 3452 Concrete products machinery; bolts, nuts, rivets & washers

(G-1522)
WYNALDA INTERNATIONAL LLC
8221 Graphic Dr Ne (49306-8934)
PHONE 616 866-1561
Bob Wynalda Sr, *Principal*
EMP: 11 **EST:** 2016
SALES (est): 140.4K **Privately Held**
WEB: www.wynalda.com
SIC: 2431 2657 Commercial printing, lithographic; folding paperboard boxes

(G-1523)
WYNALDA LITHO INC (PA)
Also Called: Wynalda Packaging
8221 Graphic Dr Ne (49306-8934)
PHONE 616 866-1561
Robert M Wynalda Sr, *Ch of Bd*
Robert M Wynalda Jr, *President*
Steve Hulbert, *Exec VP*
Janet Davis, *Controller*
Connie Wynalda, *Admin Sec*
◆ **EMP:** 206 **EST:** 1971
SALES (est): 43.3MM **Privately Held**
WEB: www.wynalda.com
SIC: 2752 2657 Commercial printing, offset; folding paperboard boxes

Benton Harbor
Berrien County

(G-1524)
12 CORNERS VINEYARDS (PA)
1201 N Benton Center Rd (49022-9754)
PHONE 269 926-7597
Glen Greiffendorf, *Principal*
EMP: 9 **EST:** 2013
SALES (est): 1.2MM **Privately Held**
WEB: www.12corners.com
SIC: 2084 Wines

(G-1525)
ABC PRECISION MACHINING INC
2077 Yore Ave (49022-9674)
PHONE 269 926-6322
Al Kasewurm, *President*
Doris Kasewurm, *Corp Secy*
EMP: 4 **EST:** 1962
SQ FT: 5,600
SALES (est): 363.1K **Privately Held**
WEB: www.abcprecision.com
SIC: 3541 3714 Machine tool replacement & repair parts, metal cutting types; filters: oil, fuel & air, motor vehicle

(G-1526)
ACUBAR INC (PA)
Also Called: Kelm Acubar
1055 N Shore Dr (49022-3516)
PHONE 269 927-3000
EMP: 2
SQ FT: 4,800
SALES (est): 1.1MM **Privately Held**
SIC: 3599 Mfg Machine Shop

(G-1527)
ADVANCE PRODUCTS CORPORATION
2527 N M 63 (49022-2599)
PHONE 269 849-1000
David Kraklau, *President*
Zachary Boff, *Plant Mgr*
Missy Holden, *Manager*
Dorthy Kraklau, *Shareholder*
Joan Kraklau, *Admin Sec*
▲ **EMP:** 40 **EST:** 1948
SQ FT: 25,000
SALES (est): 4.1MM **Privately Held**
WEB: www.advanceproductscorp.com
SIC: 3545 3569 3542 3564 Machine tool attachments & accessories; lubrication machinery, automatic; die casting machines; blowers & fans

(G-1528)
ALUDYNE WEST MICHIGAN LLC
1320 Paw Paw Ave (49022-2728)
PHONE 248 728-8642
Andreas Weller, *CEO*
EMP: 48 **EST:** 2003
SALES (est): 16.4MM
SALES (corp-wide): 1.5B **Privately Held**
WEB: www.aludyne.com
SIC: 3714 Motor vehicle parts & accessories
HQ: Aludyne International, Inc
  300 Galleria Ofcntr Ste 5
  Southfield MI 48034

(G-1529)
ANBREN INC
Also Called: Spartan Industries
1025 Point O Woods Dr (49022-9356)
P.O. Box 476, Coloma (49038-0476)
PHONE 269 944-5066
Andrew Baldwin, *President*
Brenda Baldwin, *Corp Secy*
EMP: 7 **EST:** 1965
SQ FT: 10,000
SALES (est): 886.9K **Privately Held**
SIC: 2448 2441 Pallets, wood; cargo containers, wood; nailed wood boxes & shook

(G-1530)
ARNT ASPHALT SEALING INC (PA)
Also Called: Great Lakes Coating
1240 S Crystal Ave (49022-1808)
PHONE 269 927-1532
Stanley L Arnt, *CEO*
Eric Anderson, *President*
Garson Bisnett, *Principal*
Jeffery Michels, *Principal*
Phil Ameling, *Vice Pres*
EMP: 65 **EST:** 1970
SQ FT: 15,000
SALES (est): 9.8MM **Privately Held**
WEB: www.arntasphaltsealing.com
SIC: 1771 2952 Blacktop (asphalt) work; asphalt felts & coatings

(G-1531)
ART & IMAGE
582 E Napier Ave (49022-5816)
PHONE 800 566-4162
Scott Schonschack, *Owner*
EMP: 8 **EST:** 2014
SALES (est): 716.8K **Privately Held**
WEB: www.artandimage.com
SIC: 3993 Signs & advertising specialties

(G-1532)
BATSON PRINTING INC
195 Michigan St (49022-4598)
PHONE 269 926-6011
William Batson, *CEO*
Todd Batson, *Manager*
▲ **EMP:** 65 **EST:** 1969
SQ FT: 30,000
SALES (est): 9MM **Privately Held**
WEB: www.batsonprinting.com
SIC: 2752 Commercial printing, offset

(G-1533)
BATTERIES PLUS
2061 M 139 (49022-6161)
PHONE 269 925-7367
Adrian Ryk, *Principal*
EMP: 5 **EST:** 2011
SALES (est): 132.4K **Privately Held**
WEB: www.batteriesplus.com
SIC: 5531 5063 3691 Batteries, automotive & truck; batteries; storage batteries

(G-1534)
BENTON CHASSIX HARBOR
1320 Paw Paw Ave (49022-2728)
PHONE 248 728-8700
Flint Miller, *Opers Staff*
EMP: 9 **EST:** 2013
SALES (est): 593.8K **Privately Held**
WEB: www.aludyne.com
SIC: 3599 Machine shop, jobbing & repair

(G-1535)
BENTON HARBOR AWNING & TENT
Also Called: B H Awning & Tent
2275 M 139 (49022-6190)
PHONE 800 272-2187
Charles Dill, *President*
Marilyn Dill, *Vice Pres*
EMP: 40 **EST:** 1922
SQ FT: 16,000
SALES (est): 2.6MM **Privately Held**
WEB: www.bhawning.com
SIC: 2394 2391 Awnings, fabric: made from purchased materials; curtains & draperies

(G-1536)
BENTON HARBOR LLC
Also Called: Benton Harbor Heat Treating
800 S Fair Ave (49022-3821)
PHONE 269 925-6581
EMP: 37 **EST:** 2006
SALES (est): 7.4MM **Privately Held**
WEB: www.bluewaterthermal.com
SIC: 3398 Metal heat treating
HQ: Bwt Llc
  201 Brookfield Pkwy
  Greenville SC 29607

(G-1537)
BLUEWATER THERMAL SOLUTIONS
800 S Fair Ave (49022-3821)
PHONE 269 925-6581
EMP: 8 **EST:** 2019
SALES (est): 1.6MM **Privately Held**
WEB: www.bluewaterthermal.com
SIC: 3398 Metal heat treating

(G-1538)
BULK AG INNOVATIONS LLC
Also Called: West Michigan Tool & Die
1007 Nickerson Ave (49022-2405)
PHONE 269 925-0900
Victor Mowatt, *CEO*
▲ **EMP:** 14 **EST:** 2011
SALES (est): 1.3MM **Privately Held**
WEB: www.wmtd.com
SIC: 3549 Metalworking machinery

(G-1539)
CHAMPLAIN SPECIALTY METALS INC
2235 Dewey Ave (49022-9604)
PHONE 269 926-7241
Tess Robinson, *General Mgr*
EMP: 25 **EST:** 2017
SALES (est): 5.4MM
SALES (corp-wide): 590.4MM **Privately Held**
WEB: www.champmetals.com
SIC: 3312 Rails, steel or iron
PA: American Industrial Acquisition Corporation
  250 Park Ave Fl 7
  New York NY 10177
  212 572-4853

(G-1540)
COLONIAL MANUFACTURING LLC
Also Called: Empire Molded Plastics
1246 E Empire Ave (49022-3834)
PHONE 269 926-1000
Barry Moore, *Materials Mgr*
Mike Catalano, *Purchasing*
Samir Lopez, *Engineer*
Greg Blaszczyk, *Design Engr*
Josh Craft, *Accounts Mgr*
▲ **EMP:** 4 **EST:** 1989
SQ FT: 17,500
SALES (est): 1.9MM
SALES (corp-wide): 6.4MM **Privately Held**
WEB: www.colonialengineering.com
SIC: 3089 Injection molding of plastics
PA: Colonial Engineering, Inc.
  6400 Corporate Ave
  Portage MI 49002
  269 323-2495

(G-1541)
CONNECTION SERVICE COMPANY
1377 M 139 (49022-5741)
P.O. Box 8728 (49023-8728)
PHONE 269 926-2658
Susan Adent, *President*
Melissa Henry, *Purch Mgr*
Todd Adent, *Manager*
▲ **EMP:** 21 **EST:** 1986
SQ FT: 6,500
SALES (est): 5.1MM **Privately Held**
WEB: www.connectionserviceco.com
SIC: 5072 3452 7389 Bolts; bolts, metal; packaging & labeling services

Benton Harbor - Berrien County

(G-1542)
CONSUMERS CONCRETE CORPORATION
1800 Yore Ave (49022-9674)
PHONE..................269 925-3109
Bruce Lynch, *Manager*
EMP: 12
SALES (corp-wide): 42.6MM **Privately Held**
WEB: www.consumersconcrete.com
SIC: 3273 Ready-mixed concrete
PA: Consumers Concrete Corporation
3506 Lovers Ln
Kalamazoo MI 49001
269 342-0136

(G-1543)
COVIA SOLUTIONS INC
400 Riverview Dr Ste 302 (49022-5071)
PHONE..................800 255-7263
Pedro Ochoa, *Terminal Mgr*
Kody Upchurch, *Manager*
David Franek, *Network Enginr*
Gerald Clancey, *Officer*
EMP: 5
SALES (corp-wide): 417.6MM **Privately Held**
WEB: www.coviacorp.com
SIC: 1446 Foundry sand mining
PA: Covia Solutions Inc.
3 Summit Park Dr Ste 700
Independence OH 44131
404 214-3200

(G-1544)
DAWSON MANUFACTURING COMPANY (PA)
1042 N Crystal Ave (49022-9266)
PHONE..................269 925-0100
Bob Trivedi, *President*
Mike Burk, *General Mgr*
Kevin Fosnaugh, *Vice Pres*
Sue Morgan, *Purch Mgr*
Jeff Scheinker, *QC Mgr*
◆ **EMP:** 160 **EST:** 1960
SQ FT: 78,000
SALES (est): 32MM **Privately Held**
WEB: www.dawsonmfg.com
SIC: 3069 Molded rubber products

(G-1545)
DAWSON MANUFACTURING COMPANY
1042 N Crystal Ave (49022-9266)
P.O. Box 603 (49023-0603)
PHONE..................269 925-0100
Bob Trivedi, *Manager*
EMP: 123
SQ FT: 50,000 **Privately Held**
WEB: www.dawsonmfg.com
SIC: 3061 3714 2822 Mechanical rubber goods; motor vehicle parts & accessories; synthetic rubber
PA: Dawson Manufacturing Company
1042 N Crystal Ave
Benton Harbor MI 49022

(G-1546)
DGH ENTERPRISES INC (PA)
Also Called: K-O Products Company
1225 Milton St (49022-4029)
PHONE..................269 925-0657
Barbara J Herrold, *President*
Dennis G Herrold, *Admin Sec*
▼ **EMP:** 23 **EST:** 1938
SQ FT: 150,000
SALES (est): 3MM **Privately Held**
WEB: www.koproducts.com
SIC: 3469 3465 3714 3999 Stamping metal for the trade; automotive stampings; motor vehicle parts & accessories; custom pulverizing & grinding of plastic materials; hardware

(G-1547)
DGH ENTERPRISES INC
Also Called: Ko Products
1225 Milton St (49022-4029)
PHONE..................269 925-0657
Barbara Herrold, *President*
EMP: 5
SALES (corp-wide): 3MM **Privately Held**
WEB: www.koproducts.com
SIC: 3429 3469 Manufactured hardware (general); stamping metal for the trade

PA: Dgh Enterprises, Inc.
1225 Milton St
Benton Harbor MI 49022
269 925-0657

(G-1548)
ELECTRIC EQUIPMENT COMPANY
401 Klock Rd (49022-3648)
P.O. Box 32, Riverside (49084-0032)
PHONE..................269 925-3266
Donald P Boerma, *President*
Georgia Boerma, *Vice Pres*
EMP: 4 **EST:** 1955
SALES (est): 240.2K **Privately Held**
WEB: www.electric-equip.com
SIC: 7694 5063 Electric motor repair; motors, electric

(G-1549)
FORTRESS MANUFACTURING INC
2255 Pipestone Rd (49022-2425)
PHONE..................269 925-1336
Fred Huff, *President*
EMP: 14 **EST:** 1996
SQ FT: 8,000
SALES (est): 2MM **Privately Held**
WEB: www.fortressmanufacturinginc.com
SIC: 3444 3469 Sheet metal specialties, not stamped; metal stampings

(G-1550)
GAISHIN MANUFACTURING INC
240 Urbandale Ave (49022-1943)
PHONE..................269 934-9340
Mike Gaishin Sr, *President*
Andrew Gaishin, *Vice Pres*
Scott A Gourlay, *Vice Pres*
Jeff Park, *Maint Spvr*
Andy Gaishin, *Engineer*
EMP: 24 **EST:** 1989
SQ FT: 6,000
SALES (est): 5.7MM **Privately Held**
WEB: www.gaishinmanufacturing.com
SIC: 3599 Machine shop, jobbing & repair

(G-1551)
GAST MANUFACTURING INC (HQ)
2300 M 139 (49022-6114)
P.O. Box 97 (49023-0097)
PHONE..................269 926-6171
Eric Ashelman, *President*
Kimberly Fields, *Principal*
Frank J Notaro, *Principal*
Drew Covert, *Engineer*
Gaston Leoni, *Engineer*
◆ **EMP:** 320 **EST:** 1921
SQ FT: 196,000
SALES (est): 95.9MM
SALES (corp-wide): 2.3B **Publicly Held**
WEB: www.gastmfg.com
SIC: 3563 3594 3621 3566 Vacuum pumps, except laboratory; air & gas compressors including vacuum pumps; motors: hydraulic, fluid power or air; motors & generators; speed changers, drives & gears; pumps & pumping equipment
PA: Idex Corporation
3100 Sanders Rd Ste 301
Northbrook IL 60062
847 498-7070

(G-1552)
GAST MANUFACTURING INC
2550 Meadowbrook Rd (49022-9609)
P.O. Box 97 (49023-0097)
PHONE..................269 926-6171
EMP: 80
SALES (corp-wide): 2.4B **Publicly Held**
SIC: 3563 Air And Gas Compressors, Nsk
HQ: Gast Manufacturing, Inc.
2300 M 139
Benton Harbor MI 49022
269 926-6171

(G-1553)
HARBOR GREEN SOLUTIONS LLC
900 Davis Dr (49022-2767)
P.O. Box 8711, Grand Rapids (49518-8711)
PHONE..................269 352-0265
Anthony Reeves II,

Robert Taylor,
EMP: 5
SALES (est): 324.8K **Privately Held**
SIC: 3089 2821 5162 5093 Plastic processing; plastics materials & resins; plastics materials & basic shapes; plastics resins; plastics scrap

(G-1554)
HARBOR SCREW MACHINE PRODUCTS
430 Cass St (49022-4402)
PHONE..................269 925-5855
Jerry Tomaszewki, *President*
Ken Bates, *Vice Pres*
EMP: 4 **EST:** 1990
SQ FT: 5,400
SALES (est): 331.9K **Privately Held**
SIC: 3451 Screw machine products

(G-1555)
HIGH GRADE MATERIALS COMPANY
1915 Yore Ave (49022-9674)
PHONE..................269 926-6900
Matt Craig, *Manager*
Christopher Shebester, *Manager*
EMP: 9
SALES (corp-wide): 17.2MM **Privately Held**
WEB: www.highgradematerials.com
SIC: 3273 Ready-mixed concrete
PA: High Grade Materials Company
9266 Snows Lake Rd
Greenville MI 48838
616 754-5545

(G-1556)
HOVERTECHNICS LLC
1520 Townline Rd Bldg A (49022-9656)
P.O. Box 237, Eau Claire (49111-0237)
PHONE..................269 461-3934
Chris Fitzgerald, *Mng Member*
EMP: 7 **EST:** 1984
SQ FT: 25,000
SALES (est): 955.9K **Privately Held**
WEB: www.hovertechnics.com
SIC: 3713 Specialty motor vehicle bodies

(G-1557)
INNOVATIVE WOODWORKING
2227 Plaza Dr (49022-2215)
PHONE..................269 926-9663
Jim Strouse, *Partner*
Kenneth Wenger,
EMP: 8 **EST:** 1997 **Privately Held**
WEB: www.inwoodworking.com
SIC: 2431 Millwork

(G-1558)
J B DOUGH CO
5600 E Napier Ave (49022-8619)
P.O. Box 557, Saint Joseph (49085-0557)
PHONE..................269 944-4160
John Dwan, *Partner*
Beverlee Dwan, *Partner*
EMP: 6 **EST:** 1989
SALES (est): 318.7K **Privately Held**
WEB: www.jbdough.com
SIC: 2099 Food preparations

(G-1559)
JOHNNYAMP MOBILE WELDING SVCS
2706 Territorial Rd (49022-7758)
PHONE..................269 338-8013
Heidi Closson, *Principal*
EMP: 4 **EST:** 2016
SALES (est): 91.3K **Privately Held**
WEB: www.johnnyampweld.com
SIC: 7692 Welding repair

(G-1560)
JOMAR INC
Also Called: Harbor Packaging
1090 S Crystal Ave (49022-1632)
P.O. Box 156 (49023-0156)
PHONE..................269 925-2222
Joseph Mazzucco Jr, *President*
Marc Deising, *Vice Pres*
Loucetta Crosse, *Treasurer*
Patricia E Mazzucco, *Admin Sec*
EMP: 29 **EST:** 1987
SQ FT: 24,000

SALES (est): 5.1MM **Privately Held**
SIC: 2759 Commercial printing

(G-1561)
KELM ACUBAR LC (PA)
Also Called: Kelm Acubar Company
1055 N Shore Dr (49022-3516)
PHONE..................269 927-3000
Tim Kill, *Plant Mgr*
Melissa Saltzman, *Engineer*
Andrew Bodnar,
◆ **EMP:** 37 **EST:** 1963
SQ FT: 40,000
SALES (est): 4.6MM **Privately Held**
WEB: www.kelmacubar.com
SIC: 3599 Machine shop, jobbing & repair

(G-1562)
KELM ACUBAR LC
1055 N Shore Dr (49022-3516)
PHONE..................269 925-2007
Andrew Bodnar, *President*
EMP: 8
SALES (corp-wide): 4.6MM **Privately Held**
WEB: www.kelmacubar.com
SIC: 3599 Machine shop, jobbing & repair
PA: Kelm Acubar Lc
1055 N Shore Dr
Benton Harbor MI 49022
269 927-3000

(G-1563)
KISER INDUSTRIAL MFG CO
1860 Yore Ave (49022-9674)
PHONE..................269 934-9220
Brian Kiser, *President*
Pam Kiser, *Admin Sec*
EMP: 13 **EST:** 2007
SQ FT: 17,500
SALES (est): 1.4MM **Privately Held**
WEB: www.kiserindustrialmfg.net
SIC: 3599 Machine shop, jobbing & repair

(G-1564)
KOEHLER INDUSTRIES INC
1520 Townline Rd (49022-9656)
PHONE..................269 934-9670
Mike Koehler, *Owner*
EMP: 6 **EST:** 2007
SALES (est): 261.8K **Privately Held**
WEB: www.koehlerindustries.com
SIC: 3599 Machine shop, jobbing & repair

(G-1565)
LAZER GRAPHICS
1101 Pipestone Rd (49022-4018)
PHONE..................269 926-1066
Dennis Barker, *President*
Debbie Barker, *Vice Pres*
EMP: 17 **EST:** 1991
SQ FT: 15,000
SALES (est): 2.2MM **Privately Held**
WEB: www.lazergraphics.com
SIC: 5699 7336 2396 2395 Customized clothing & apparel; commercial art & graphic design; automotive & apparel trimmings; pleating & stitching

(G-1566)
M T S CHENAULT LLC
665 Pipestone St (49022-4151)
PHONE..................269 861-0053
William Macgoodwin, *CEO*
EMP: 5 **EST:** 2011
SALES (est): 268K **Privately Held**
SIC: 3672 Printed circuit boards

(G-1567)
MARTIN BROS MILL FNDRY SUP CO
Also Called: Meltex
289 Hinkley St (49022-3603)
P.O. Box 246 (49023-0246)
PHONE..................269 927-1355
Ilene Martin, *President*
Stephen Martin, *Admin Sec*
EMP: 9 **EST:** 1930
SQ FT: 6,000
SALES (est): 1MM **Privately Held**
SIC: 5093 3341 Ferrous metal scrap & waste; secondary nonferrous metals

Benton Harbor - Berrien County (G-1568)

GEOGRAPHIC SECTION

(G-1568)
MAX CASTING COMPANY INC
116 Paw Paw Ave (49022-4416)
P.O. Box 1326 (49023-1326)
PHONE.....................................269 925-8081
Richard T Graebel Jr, *President*
Jean Graebel, *Corp Secy*
EMP: 15 **EST:** 1979
SQ FT: 8,000
SALES (est): 646.3K **Privately Held**
WEB: www.maxcasting.net
SIC: 3365 Aluminum & aluminum-based alloy castings

(G-1569)
MAX2 LLC
1440 Territorial Rd (49022-1959)
P.O. Box 152, Coloma (49038-0152)
PHONE.....................................269 468-3452
David A Lagrow, *Mng Member*
EMP: 10 **EST:** 2015
SQ FT: 400
SALES (est): 654K **Privately Held**
SIC: 3541 3469 Milling machines; electrochemical milling machines; machine parts, stamped or pressed metal

(G-1570)
MAX3 LLC
360 Urbandale Ave (49022-1944)
PHONE.....................................269 925-2044
David Lagrow, *Mng Member*
EMP: 30 **EST:** 2017
SQ FT: 30,000
SALES (est): 3MM **Privately Held**
WEB: www.max3.us
SIC: 3544 3083 Special dies, tools, jigs & fixtures; thermoplastic laminates: rods, tubes, plates & sheet

(G-1571)
MAXIMUM MOLD INC
1440 Territorial Rd (49022-1959)
PHONE.....................................269 468-6291
Dave Lagrow, *Principal*
Charlie Kreitner, *Plant Mgr*
Nathan Mukavetz, *QC Mgr*
Todd Crumley, *Maintence Staff*
Carrie Schinck, *Assistant*
▲ **EMP:** 12 **EST:** 2010
SALES (est): 2.6MM **Privately Held**
WEB: www.maximummold.com
SIC: 5085 3599 Industrial supplies; machine shop, jobbing & repair

(G-1572)
MAYTAG CORPORATION (HQ)
Also Called: Maytag Appliances
2000 N M 63 (49022-2632)
PHONE.....................................269 923-5000
Jeff M Fettig, *Ch of Bd*
William L Beer, *President*
Thomas A Briatico, *President*
Arthur B Learmonth, *President*
David R McConnaughey, *President*
◆ **EMP:** 181 **EST:** 1893
SQ FT: 500,000
SALES (est): 819.4MM
SALES (corp-wide): 19.4B **Publicly Held**
WEB: www.maytag.com
SIC: 3631 3632 3639 3635 Gas ranges, domestic; electric ranges, domestic; household refrigerators & freezers; dishwashing machines, household; garbage disposal units, household; household vacuum cleaners; automatic vending machines; laundry dryers, household or coin-operated
PA: Whirlpool Corporation
2000 N M 63
Benton Harbor MI 49022
269 923-5000

(G-1573)
MIDWEST TIMER SERVICE INC
Also Called: MTS
4815 M63 N (49022)
P.O. Box 126 (49023-0126)
PHONE.....................................269 849-2800
James R Chapman Jr, *President*
Bruce Chapman, *Owner*
Keith A Chapman, *Admin Sec*
▲ **EMP:** 70 **EST:** 1954
SQ FT: 60,000
SALES (est): 10MM **Privately Held**
WEB: www.midwesttimer.com
SIC: 3823 Time cycle & program controllers, industrial process type

(G-1574)
MODINEER COATINGS DIVISION
2200 E Empire Ave (49022-1647)
PHONE.....................................269 925-0702
EMP: 11 **EST:** 2015
SALES (est): 696.5K **Privately Held**
WEB: www.modineer.com
SIC: 3479 Metal coating & allied service

(G-1575)
MONO CERAMICS INC
2235 Pipestone Rd (49022-2425)
PHONE.....................................269 925-0212
Mukesh Rawal, *President*
Peter Jackson, *Purch Mgr*
Ashok Kedia, *VP Finance*
▲ **EMP:** 45 **EST:** 1983
SQ FT: 20,000
SALES (est): 10.6MM
SALES (corp-wide): 2.2MM **Privately Held**
WEB: www.monoceramics.com
SIC: 3255 Castable refractories, clay
HQ: Monocon International Refractories Limited
Davy Road Denaby Industrial Estate
Doncaster DN12
170 986-4848

(G-1576)
MPC COMPANY INC
Also Called: Midwest Fruit Package Co.
1891 Territorial Rd (49022-8035)
PHONE.....................................269 927-3371
Sam Monde, *Owner*
Dennis Monte, *General Mgr*
EMP: 5
SALES (corp-wide): 37.9MM **Privately Held**
SIC: 2033 5148 5921 Fruits: packaged in cans, jars, etc.; fruits; liquor stores
PA: Mpc Company, Inc.
3752 Riverside Rd
Riverside MI 49084
269 849-1722

(G-1577)
NATIONAL ZINC PROCESSORS INC
1256 Milton St (49022-4030)
PHONE.....................................269 926-1161
Dennis Rook, *President*
Bruce Sokol, *Principal*
EMP: 18 **EST:** 2001
SQ FT: 100,000
SALES (est): 547K **Privately Held**
WEB: www.bentonmetalrecycling.com
SIC: 4953 3341 3643 3471 Recycling, waste materials; zinc smelting & refining (secondary); current-carrying wiring devices; plating & polishing; lead & zinc ores

(G-1578)
OVERSTREET PROPERTY MGT CO
Also Called: Overstreet Management
1852 Commonwealth Rd (49022-7010)
P.O. Box 8629 (49023-8629)
PHONE.....................................269 281-3880
Nicholas R Overstreet, *Property Mgr*
EMP: 5 **EST:** 2014
SALES (est): 216.1K **Privately Held**
SIC: 6519 7349 7299 0782 Real property lessors; building maintenance services; home improvement & renovation contractor agency; mowing services, lawn; grounds mowing equipment

(G-1579)
R W PATTERSON PRINTING CO
1550 Territorial Rd (49022-1937)
PHONE.....................................269 925-2177
Leroy Patterson, *President*
Jim Terris, *President*
Greg Patterson, *Treasurer*
EMP: 80 **EST:** 1948
SQ FT: 65,000
SALES (est): 8.3MM **Privately Held**
WEB: www.pattersonprinting.com
SIC: 2752 2789 2732 Commercial printing, offset; bookbinding & related work; book printing

(G-1580)
RAPID GRAPHICS INC
Also Called: Rapid Printing
2185 M 139 (49022-6109)
PHONE.....................................269 925-7087
James Rice, *President*
Jennifer Dumont, *Vice Pres*
Jeff Rice, *Vice Pres*
Judith Rice, *Admin Sec*
EMP: 8 **EST:** 1972
SQ FT: 4,000
SALES (est): 759.8K **Privately Held**
WEB: www.rapidprint1.com
SIC: 2752 Commercial printing, offset

(G-1581)
ROSTA USA CORP
797 Ferguson Dr (49022-6401)
PHONE.....................................269 841-5448
Jeremy Thiele, *President*
Ian Osborn, *Vice Pres*
Shane Boughn, *Regl Sales Mgr*
Monty Proffitt, *Sales Staff*
EMP: 12 **EST:** 2013
SQ FT: 10,000
SALES (est): 2MM **Privately Held**
WEB: www.rosta.com
SIC: 3061 8711 Mechanical rubber goods; engineering services

(G-1582)
SANDVIK INC
Also Called: Sanvik Mtls Tech Strip Pdts Di
2235 Dewey Ave (49022-9604)
PHONE.....................................269 926-7241
Peter Frosini, *General Mgr*
Michell Muhlbradt, *Sales Staff*
EMP: 83
SALES (corp-wide): 9.9B **Privately Held**
WEB: www.home.sandvik
SIC: 3312 5051 3444 3316 Plate, sheet & strip, except coated products; metals service centers & offices; sheet metalwork; cold finishing of steel shapes
HQ: Sandvik, Inc.
1483 Dogwood Way
Mebane NC 27302
201 794-5000

(G-1583)
SERENA HINES (PA) ⊙
Also Called: McCoy's Care Transportation
668 E High St (49022-4308)
PHONE.....................................269 252-0895
Serena Hines, *Owner*
EMP: 8 **EST:** 2021
SALES (est): 674.4K **Privately Held**
SIC: 3711 Motor vehicles & car bodies

(G-1584)
SHORELINE MOLD & ENGRG LLC
1530 Townline Rd (49022-9656)
PHONE.....................................269 926-2223
Bryan Fillwock, *Plant Mgr*
Pam Fillwock, *Mng Member*
EMP: 5 **EST:** 1995
SQ FT: 8,100
SALES (est): 747.8K **Privately Held**
WEB: www.shorelinemold.com
SIC: 3544 3089 Dies, plastics forming; molding primary plastic

(G-1585)
SIGN DIVISION
1923 Pipestone Rd (49022-2314)
PHONE.....................................269 548-8978
EMP: 4 **EST:** 2017
SALES (est): 85K **Privately Held**
SIC: 3993 Signs & advertising specialties

(G-1586)
SMITH MANUFACTURING CO INC
1636 Red Arrow Hwy (49022-1916)
PHONE.....................................269 925-8155
Scott Smith, *President*
Robin Smith, *Treasurer*
Theresa Smith, *Admin Sec*
EMP: 14 **EST:** 1984
SQ FT: 34,000
SALES (est): 1.8MM **Privately Held**
SIC: 2499 Decorative wood & woodwork

(G-1587)
SOUTH SHORE TOOL & DIE INC
2460 Meadowbrook Rd (49022-9605)
P.O. Box 235, Baroda (49101-0235)
PHONE.....................................269 925-9660
Larry Keene, *President*
Doug Medlin, *Vice Pres*
EMP: 42 **EST:** 1983
SQ FT: 24,000
SALES (est): 6.7MM **Privately Held**
WEB: www.sstd.net
SIC: 3599 Machine shop, jobbing & repair

(G-1588)
SPECIAL-LITE INC - BENTON
1394 E Empire Ave (49022-2018)
PHONE.....................................269 423-7068
EMP: 9 **EST:** 2019
SALES (est): 39.6K **Privately Held**
WEB: www.special-lite.com
SIC: 3999 Manufacturing industries

(G-1589)
STATE TOOL & MANUFACTURING CO (PA)
1650 E Empire Ave (49022-2024)
PHONE.....................................269 927-3153
Manroe Raschke, *President*
Mary Ann Raschke, *Vice Pres*
Doug Christy, *Marketing Mgr*
EMP: 80 **EST:** 1968
SQ FT: 25,000
SALES (est): 9.6MM **Privately Held**
WEB: www.statetool.com
SIC: 3643 Sockets, electric

(G-1590)
TECHNI SAND INC
400 Riverview Dr (49022-5071)
PHONE.....................................269 465-5833
Charles D Fowler, *CEO*
EMP: 6 **EST:** 2012
SALES (est): 134.9K **Privately Held**
SIC: 3295 Minerals, ground or treated

(G-1591)
TECHNICKEL INC
1200 S Crystal Ave (49022-1808)
P.O. Box 1264 (49023-1264)
PHONE.....................................269 926-8505
Dave Vogl, *CEO*
Cynthia Zuhl, *Vice Pres*
Louis Vogl, *Opers Staff*
EMP: 15 **EST:** 1983
SQ FT: 45,000
SALES (est): 2.3MM **Privately Held**
WEB: www.technickel.com
SIC: 3471 Electroplating of metals or formed products

(G-1592)
TECHNISAND INC
400 Riverview Dr Ste 300 (49022-5009)
P.O. Box 400, Bridgman (49106-0400)
PHONE.....................................269 465-5833
Lee Stachurski, *Branch Mgr*
EMP: 5
SALES (corp-wide): 417.6MM **Privately Held**
SIC: 1442 Sand mining
HQ: Technisand, Inc.
3 Summit Park Dr Ste 700
Independence OH 44131

(G-1593)
TOWER TAG & LABEL LLC
1300 E Empire Ave (49022-2018)
P.O. Box 592, South Haven (49090-0592)
PHONE.....................................269 927-1065
Thomas Miller,
▼ **EMP:** 10 **EST:** 1997
SQ FT: 60,000
SALES (est): 1.7MM **Privately Held**
WEB: www.towertag.com
SIC: 3089 Clothes hangers, plastic

(G-1594)
TRELLBORG SLING SLTIONS US INC
1042 N Crystal Ave (49022-9266)
PHONE.....................................269 639-4217

▲ = Import ▼ = Export
◆ = Import/Export

Conny Torstensson, *Vice Pres*
Gary Madewell, *VP Mfg*
Jan Pettersson, *Branch Mgr*
EMP: 5
SALES (corp-wide): 3.8B **Privately Held**
WEB: www.trelleborg.com
SIC: 3089 Plastic processing
HQ: Trelleborg Sealing Solutions Us, Inc.
2531 Bremer Rd
Fort Wayne IN 46803
260 749-9631

(G-1595)
UNIVERSAL INDUCTION INC
352 W Britain Ave (49022-5002)
P.O. Box 516, Saint Joseph (49085-0516)
PHONE.................................269 925-9890
Manuel A Jack, *President*
Manuel Jack, *Executive*
EMP: 9 **EST:** 1996
SQ FT: 20,000
SALES (est): 1.1MM **Privately Held**
WEB: www.universalinduction.com
SIC: 3398 Metal heat treating

(G-1596)
UNIVERSAL STAMPING INC
1570 Townline Rd (49022-9656)
PHONE.................................269 925-5300
Richard C Jackson, *President*
Janet Jackson, *Vice Pres*
Andrea Thornton, *Officer*
EMP: 25 **EST:** 1987
SQ FT: 26,000
SALES (est): 4.9MM **Privately Held**
WEB: www.universalstamping.com
SIC: 3469 Stamping metal for the trade

(G-1597)
US JACK COMPANY
1125 Industrial Ct (49022-1879)
P.O. Box 8826 (49023-8826)
PHONE.................................269 925-7777
Dennis Housewirth, *President*
EMP: 8 **EST:** 1988
SQ FT: 8,500
SALES (est): 3.1MM **Privately Held**
WEB: www.usjack.com
SIC: 3569 Jacks, hydraulic

(G-1598)
VENT-RITE VALVE CORP
Also Called: Skidmore
1875 Dewey Ave (49022-9608)
PHONE.................................269 925-8812
David P Van Houten, *Vice Pres*
Scott Sichmeller, *Vice Pres*
Dustin Wagaman, *Electrical Engi*
Lisa McKellips, *Sales Staff*
Brett King, *IT/INT Sup*
EMP: 40
SQ FT: 60,000
SALES (corp-wide): 12.5MM **Privately Held**
WEB: www.emersonswan.com
SIC: 3561 3443 Pumps, domestic: water or sump; fabricated plate work (boiler shop)
PA: Vent-Rite Valve Corp.
300 Pond St
Randolph MA 02368
781 986-2000

(G-1599)
VINEYARD 2121 LLC
2121 Kerlikowske Rd (49022-9218)
PHONE.................................269 429-0555
Deborah Pallas,
EMP: 10 **EST:** 2015
SQ FT: 3,700
SALES (est): 788.7K **Privately Held**
WEB: www.vineyard2121.com
SIC: 2084 Wine cellars, bonded: engaged in blending wines

(G-1600)
VOMELA SPECIALTY COMPANY
Also Called: Harbor Graphics
375 Urbandale Ave (49022-1942)
PHONE.................................269 927-6500
EMP: 35
SALES (corp-wide): 128.5MM **Privately Held**
SIC: 7336 2396 Commercial Art And Graphic Design

PA: Vomela Specialty Company
845 Minnehaha Ave E
Saint Paul MN 55106
651 228-2200

(G-1601)
W VBH
78 W Wall St (49022-4735)
PHONE.................................269 927-1527
Charles Kelly, *Owner*
EMP: 4 **EST:** 2010
SALES (est): 73.3K **Privately Held**
WEB: www.wvbh.biz
SIC: 2711 Newspapers, publishing & printing

(G-1602)
WEST MICHIGAN TOOL & DIE CO
Also Called: Ark Industrial
1007 Nickerson Ave (49022-2405)
PHONE.................................269 925-0900
Jerry W Jackson, *President*
Fred Layton, *General Mgr*
Laura Jackson, *Accounting Mgr*
EMP: 22 **EST:** 1977
SQ FT: 8,800
SALES (est): 2.4MM **Privately Held**
WEB: www.wmtd.com
SIC: 3544 Special dies & tools

(G-1603)
WHIRLPOOL CORPORATION (PA)
2000 N M 63 (49022-2692)
PHONE.................................269 923-5000
Marc R Bitzer, *Ch of Bd*
Joseph T Liotine, *President*
Rusty Zay, *General Mgr*
Kirk Goodwin, *Counsel*
Joao C Brega, *Exec VP*
▼ **EMP:** 2200 **EST:** 1898
SALES (est): 19.4B **Publicly Held**
WEB: www.whirlpoolcorp.com
SIC: 3633 3585 3632 3635 Household laundry equipment; air conditioning units, complete: domestic or industrial; refrigerators, mechanical & absorption: household; freezers, home & farm; household vacuum cleaners

(G-1604)
WHIRLPOOL CORPORATION
553 Benson Rd (49022-2664)
PHONE.................................800 541-6390
Bryan Hedge, *Partner*
Eddie Manuel, *Business Mgr*
Juan Puente, *Vice Pres*
Doug Burns, *Mfg Staff*
Suzanne Williams, *Buyer*
EMP: 4
SALES (corp-wide): 19.4B **Publicly Held**
WEB: www.kitchenaid.com
SIC: 3556 Cutting, chopping, grinding, mixing & similar machinery
PA: Whirlpool Corporation
2000 N M 63
Benton Harbor MI 49022
269 923-5000

(G-1605)
WHIRLPOOL CORPORATION
600 W Main St (49022-3618)
PHONE.................................269 923-5000
Joseph T Liotine, *Exec VP*
Kenneth Kimmerly, *Production*
Jeffrey Sankey, *Engineer*
Dennis Tuckowski, *Engineer*
Brian Sullivan, *Auditor*
EMP: 5
SALES (corp-wide): 19.4B **Publicly Held**
WEB: www.whirlpoolcorp.com
SIC: 3633 3585 3632 3635 Household laundry equipment; air conditioning units, complete: domestic or industrial; refrigerators, mechanical & absorption: household; freezers, home & farm; household vacuum cleaners
PA: Whirlpool Corporation
2000 N M 63
Benton Harbor MI 49022
269 923-5000

(G-1606)
WHIRLPOOL CORPORATION
1800 Paw Paw Ave (49022-2648)
PHONE.................................269 923-7400
Mike Loftus, *General Mgr*
James Kuhn, *Safety Dir*
Kyle Russell, *Engineer*
Sue Zavadcky, *Engineer*
Steven Tolliver, *Design Engr*
EMP: 5
SALES (corp-wide): 19.4B **Publicly Held**
WEB: www.whirlpoolcorp.com
SIC: 3633 3632 Household laundry equipment; household refrigerators & freezers
PA: Whirlpool Corporation
2000 N M 63
Benton Harbor MI 49022
269 923-5000

(G-1607)
WHIRLPOOL CORPORATION
750 Monte Rd (49022-2600)
P.O. Box 218, Saint Joseph (49085-0218)
PHONE.................................269 923-5000
Bartosz Bienkowski, *Project Mgr*
Christopher Carlson, *Engineer*
Martin Lewis, *Engineer*
Michael Rock, *Engineer*
Brian Weackler, *Engineer*
EMP: 5
SALES (corp-wide): 19.4B **Publicly Held**
WEB: www.whirlpoolcorp.com
SIC: 3633 Household laundry equipment
PA: Whirlpool Corporation
2000 N M 63
Benton Harbor MI 49022
269 923-5000

(G-1608)
WHIRLPOOL CORPORATION
151 Riverview Dr (49022-3619)
PHONE.................................269 923-6486
Jennifer Guerin, *Buyer*
Andre Rado, *Technical Mgr*
Brian Janke, *Engineer*
Bruce Hopkinson, *Project Engr*
Jeff Hurdle, *Sales Dir*
EMP: 5
SALES (corp-wide): 19.4B **Publicly Held**
WEB: www.whirlpoolcorp.com
SIC: 3633 7371 Household laundry equipment; computer software development & applications
PA: Whirlpool Corporation
2000 N M 63
Benton Harbor MI 49022
269 923-5000

(G-1609)
WHIRLPOOL CORPORATION
2000 N M 63 (49022-2692)
PHONE.................................269 923-5000
Tom Egan, *Vice Pres*
EMP: 4
SALES (corp-wide): 19.4B **Publicly Held**
WEB: www.whirlpoolcorp.com
SIC: 3585 3632 3639 3635 Air conditioning units, complete: domestic or industrial; refrigerators, mechanical & absorption: household; freezers, home & farm; dishwashing machines, household; garbage disposal units, household; trash compactors, household; household vacuum cleaners; gas ranges, domestic; electric ranges, domestic; microwave ovens, including portable: household; washing machines, household: including coin-operated
PA: Whirlpool Corporation
2000 N M 63
Benton Harbor MI 49022
269 923-5000

(G-1610)
WHIRLPOOL CORPORATION
150 Hilltop Rd Mldrop 75 7590 Maildrop (49022)
PHONE.................................269 923-3009
Kevin Steinke, *Principal*
Charles Stenchfield, *Vice Pres*
John Lanham, *Purch Mgr*
Daniel Cavalcanti, *Engineer*
Gabe Bernhard, *Senior Mgr*
EMP: 5

SALES (corp-wide): 19.4B **Publicly Held**
WEB: www.whirlpoolcorp.com
SIC: 3633 3585 3632 3639 Household laundry machines, including coin-operated; washing machines, household: including coin-operated; laundry dryers, household or coin-operated; air conditioning units, complete: domestic or industrial; freezers, home & farm; refrigerators, mechanical & absorption: household; dishwashing machines, household; garbage disposal units, household; trash compactors, household
PA: Whirlpool Corporation
2000 N M 63
Benton Harbor MI 49022
269 923-5000

(G-1611)
WORTHINGTON ARMSTRONG VENTURE
Also Called: Wave
745 Enterprise Way (49022-2773)
PHONE.................................269 934-6200
Ron Badger, *Manager*
EMP: 10 **Privately Held**
WEB: www.worthingtonarmstrongventure.com
SIC: 3446 8051 3449 3444 Architectural metalwork; skilled nursing care facilities; miscellaneous metalwork; sheet metalwork
PA: Worthington Armstrong Venture
101 Lindenwood Dr Ste 350
Malvern PA 19355

Benzonia
Benzie County

(G-1612)
BEE DAZZLED CANDLE WORKS
6289 River Rd (49616-9713)
PHONE.................................231 882-7765
Sharon Jones, *Owner*
EMP: 4 **EST:** 1980
SALES (est): 172.4K **Privately Held**
WEB: www.beedazzled.com
SIC: 3999 Candles

(G-1613)
CHERRY HUT PRODUCTS LLC (PA)
1046 Michigan Ave (49616-8661)
P.O. Box 333 (49616-0333)
PHONE.................................231 882-4431
Leonard L Case Jr,
EMP: 2
SQ FT: 2,400
SALES (est): 1.4MM **Privately Held**
WEB: www.cherryhut.com
SIC: 5812 2033 Eating places; jams, including imitation: packaged in cans, jars, etc.; jellies, edible, including imitation: in cans, jars, etc.

(G-1614)
GILLISONS VAR FABRICATION INC (PA)
3033 Benzie Hwy (49616-8616)
PHONE.................................231 882-5921
Ronald Gillison, *President*
Dianne Gillison, *Corp Secy*
Courtney Gillison, *Sales Staff*
◆ **EMP:** 26 **EST:** 1977
SQ FT: 5,760
SALES: 8.3MM **Privately Held**
WEB: www.gillisons.com
SIC: 5999 3523 3599 Farm machinery; farm machinery & equipment; machine shop, jobbing & repair

(G-1615)
GLEASON RACE CARS
8244 Love Rd (49616-9752)
PHONE.................................231 882-2336
Lorene Gleason, *Owner*
EMP: 4 **EST:** 2008
SALES (est): 77.3K **Privately Held**
SIC: 3711 Automobile assembly, including specialty automobiles

Benzonia - Benzie County (G-1616) GEOGRAPHIC SECTION

(G-1616)
PRESSCRAFT PAPERS INC
Also Called: Gwen Frostic Prints
5140 River Rd (49616-8703)
P.O. Box 300 (49616-0300)
PHONE.....................231 882-5505
Pamela Lorenz, *President*
EMP: 13 **EST:** 1933
SQ FT: 7,500
SALES (est): 577.2K **Privately Held**
WEB: www.gwenfrostic.com
SIC: 2752 2759 2678 Cards, lithographed; commercial printing; stationery products

Berkley
Oakland County

(G-1617)
A & E AGG INC
3500 11 Mile Rd Ste D (48072-1225)
PHONE.....................248 547-4711
Ben Fyke, *President*
EMP: 21 **EST:** 1986
SQ FT: 2,000
SALES (est): 6.1MM **Privately Held**
SIC: 1442 Construction sand & gravel

(G-1618)
ACME TUBE BENDING COMPANY
3180 W 11 Mile Rd (48072-1207)
P.O. Box 888, Royal Oak (48068-0888)
PHONE.....................248 545-8500
Chris Lyons, *President*
◆ **EMP:** 8 **EST:** 1953
SQ FT: 7,500 **Privately Held**
WEB: www.acmetubebending.com
SIC: 3498 Tube fabricating (contract bending & shaping)

(G-1619)
AMERICAN & EFIRD LLC
1919 Coolidge Hwy (48072-1543)
PHONE.....................248 399-1166
Rich Bowman, *Manager*
EMP: 7
SALES (corp-wide): 1.9B **Privately Held**
WEB: www.amefird.com
SIC: 2284 Thread from natural fibers
HQ: American & Efird Llc
22 American St
Mount Holly NC 28120
704 827-4211

(G-1620)
AMERICAN INFORMATION SERVICES (HQ)
Also Called: Smith Processor Products
3010 Coolidge Hwy (48072-1648)
PHONE.....................248 399-4848
Ronald J Meyer, *Vice Pres*
EMP: 15 **EST:** 1981
SQ FT: 8,400
SALES (est): 1.1MM
SALES (corp-wide): 1.6MM **Privately Held**
SIC: 8742 7389 3861 5044 Management consulting services; microfilm recording & developing service; microfilm equipment: cameras, projectors, readers, etc.; microfilm equipment; computer rental & leasing
PA: Emergency Info Data Inc
3010 Coolidge Hwy Ste 100
Berkley MI
248 399-4848

(G-1621)
AU ENTERPRISES INC
3916 11 Mile Rd (48072-1005)
PHONE.....................248 544-9700
Linus L Drogs III, *President*
Lynn Drogs, *CFO*
EMP: 14 **EST:** 1987
SQ FT: 2,400
SALES (est): 1.5MM **Privately Held**
WEB: www.auenterprises.com
SIC: 3911 Jewelry, precious metal

(G-1622)
BERKLEY FROSTY FREEZE INC
2415 Coolidge Hwy (48072-1571)
PHONE.....................248 336-2634
Emily Tong, *Manager*
EMP: 5 **EST:** 2010
SALES (est): 139.6K **Privately Held**
SIC: 2024 Ice cream, bulk

(G-1623)
C AND N PRESS WD ENHNCENTS LLC
2375 Bacon Ave (48072-1012)
PHONE.....................810 712-7771
Christine Pressotto, *Administration*
EMP: 4 **EST:** 2015
SALES (est): 41.3K **Privately Held**
SIC: 2741 Miscellaneous publishing

(G-1624)
COBBLESTONE CABINETS
3311 12 Mile Rd (48072-1394)
PHONE.....................248 398-3700
EMP: 6 **EST:** 2014
SALES (est): 136.7K **Privately Held**
WEB: www.cobblestonecabinet.com
SIC: 2434 Wood kitchen cabinets

(G-1625)
COPILOT PRINTING
3754 Tyler Ave (48072-1445)
PHONE.....................248 797-0150
Ryan Malerman, *Owner*
EMP: 5 **EST:** 2007
SALES (est): 208.3K **Privately Held**
WEB: www.copilotprinting.com
SIC: 2752 Commercial printing, offset

(G-1626)
FYKE WASHED SAND GRAVEL
3500 11 Mile Rd Ste D (48072-1225)
PHONE.....................248 547-4714
Barb Edwards, *Manager*
EMP: 7 **EST:** 2010
SALES (est): 239.4K **Privately Held**
WEB: www.fykegravel.com
SIC: 1442 Construction sand & gravel

(G-1627)
HUNT & NOYER LLC
Also Called: Hunt & Noyer Woodworks
14861 W Eleven Mile Rd (48072)
PHONE.....................517 914-6259
Kyle Huntoon, *Manager*
EMP: 4 **EST:** 2015
SALES (est): 196.8K **Privately Held**
WEB: www.huntandnoyer.com
SIC: 2431 2426 Millwork; carvings, furniture: wood

(G-1628)
INDUSTRIAL PACKAGING CORP (PA)
3060 11 Mile Rd (48072-1206)
PHONE.....................248 677-0084
John B Mager Sr, *CEO*
John Mager Jr, *President*
Sandra Donia, *Treasurer*
EMP: 10 **EST:** 1960
SQ FT: 15,000
SALES (est): 2.2MM **Privately Held**
WEB: www.indpkg.com
SIC: 2448 2653 Pallets, wood; boxes, corrugated: made from purchased materials

(G-1629)
JOY OF MOLDINGS LLC
1574 Eaton Rd (48072-2028)
PHONE.....................248 543-9754
Kenneth O'Brien, *Principal*
EMP: 4 **EST:** 2016
SALES (est): 75.6K **Privately Held**
WEB: www.thejoyofmoldings.com
SIC: 2499 Wood products

(G-1630)
MCCREA CONTROLS INC
2193 Oxford Rd (48072-1737)
PHONE.....................248 544-1366
Andrew Morse, *President*
EMP: 6 **EST:** 1995
SALES (est): 122.5K **Privately Held**
SIC: 3829 Measuring & controlling devices

(G-1631)
MGM INDUSTRIES INC
2192 Oakshire Ave (48072-1287)
PHONE.....................248 561-7558
Michael Meinzinger, *Principal*
EMP: 6 **EST:** 2014
SALES (est): 241.3K **Privately Held**
WEB: www.mgmindustries.com
SIC: 3999 Manufacturing industries

(G-1632)
MICHIGAN PLAQUES & AWARDS INC
Also Called: Michigan Graphics & Awards
3742 12 Mile Rd (48072-1114)
PHONE.....................248 398-6400
Michael Hood, *President*
R Michael Hood, *President*
Toni G Hood, *Corp Secy*
Toni Hood, *Admin Sec*
▲ **EMP:** 20 **EST:** 1978
SQ FT: 7,500
SALES (est): 1.1MM **Privately Held**
WEB: www.mgaawards.com
SIC: 3993 3914 Signs, not made in custom sign painting shops; name plates: except engraved, etched, etc.: metal; displays & cutouts, window & lobby; trophies

(G-1633)
NOISEMETERS INC
3233 Coolidge Hwy (48072-1633)
PHONE.....................248 840-6559
Andrew Snell, *President*
Louise Snell, *Vice Pres*
EMP: 5 **EST:** 2009
SALES (est): 520.7K **Privately Held**
WEB: www.noisesign.com
SIC: 3625 Noise control equipment

(G-1634)
PANTHER JAMES LLC
Also Called: Drought
2070 11 Mile Rd (48072-3047)
PHONE.....................248 850-7522
Caitlin James,
EMP: 12 **EST:** 2010
SALES (est): 531.6K **Privately Held**
SIC: 2033 5499 Vegetable juices: fresh; beverage stores

Berrien Center
Berrien County

(G-1635)
CHILD EVNGELISM FELLOWSHIP INC
7463 Elm St (49102-9745)
P.O. Box 64 (49102)
PHONE.....................269 461-6953
EMP: 41
SALES (corp-wide): 17.6MM **Privately Held**
SIC: 2752 Lithographic Commercial Printing
PA: Child Evangelism Fellowship Incorporated
17482 Highway M
Warrenton MO 63383
636 456-4321

Berrien Springs
Berrien County

(G-1636)
2STONE MFG LLC
109 N Main St (49103-1156)
PHONE.....................269 214-6560
William Gustavsen, *Principal*
EMP: 4 **EST:** 2010
SALES (est): 87.9K **Privately Held**
SIC: 3999 Manufacturing industries

(G-1637)
APPLE VALLEY NATURAL FOODS (PA)
9067 Us Highway 31 Ofc A (49103-1806)
PHONE.....................269 471-3234
Kevin Benfield, *President*
George Schmidt, *Manager*
EMP: 124 **EST:** 1905
SALES (est): 17.4MM **Privately Held**
WEB: www.avnf.com
SIC: 5499 5411 2051 Health foods; grocery stores; bread, cake & related products

(G-1638)
BERRIEN CUSTOM CABINET INC
Also Called: Berrien Custom Cab & Design
4231 E Snow Rd (49103-9223)
PHONE.....................269 473-3404
Bradley Osborn, *President*
EMP: 6 **EST:** 1996
SQ FT: 6,000
SALES (est): 300.5K **Privately Held**
WEB: www.berriencustomcabinet.com
SIC: 2434 Wood kitchen cabinets

(G-1639)
FAB-N-WELD SHEETMETAL
4445 E Shawnee Rd (49103-9769)
PHONE.....................269 471-7453
Michael F Huspen, *Owner*
EMP: 5 **EST:** 1992
SQ FT: 40,000
SALES (est): 593.9K **Privately Held**
WEB: www.fabnweld.net
SIC: 7692 Welding repair

(G-1640)
FAIRVIEW FARMS
Also Called: Radtke Farms
6735 S Scottdale Rd (49103-9707)
PHONE.....................269 449-0500
Yvonne Radtke, *President*
David Radtke, *Vice Pres*
EMP: 5 **EST:** 1940
SALES (est): 312.3K **Privately Held**
WEB: www.radtkefarms.com
SIC: 2033 0191 Jams, including imitation: packaged in cans, jars, etc.; jellies, edible, including imitation: in cans, jars, etc.; general farms, primarily crop

(G-1641)
FAULKNER FABRICATORS INC
10106 N Tudor Rd (49103-9634)
PHONE.....................269 473-3073
Thomas A Faulkner, *President*
Ann Christensen, *Corp Secy*
Ed Faulkner, *Vice Pres*
▲ **EMP:** 12 **EST:** 1960
SQ FT: 24,000
SALES (est): 2.3MM **Privately Held**
WEB: www.faulknerfab.com
SIC: 2499 Spools, wood; spools, reels & pulleys: wood

(G-1642)
LEMON CREEK FRUIT FARM
533 E Lemon Creek Rd (49103-9714)
PHONE.....................269 471-1321
Jeffrey Lemon, *Partner*
Tim Lemon, *Partner*
EMP: 16 **EST:** 1974
SALES (est): 673.8K **Privately Held**
WEB: www.lemoncreekwinery.com
SIC: 2084 Wines

(G-1643)
LEMON CREEK WINERY LTD (PA)
Also Called: Lemon Creek Farm
533 E Lemon Creek Rd (49103-9714)
PHONE.....................269 471-1321
Tim Lemon, *President*
Jeffrey Lemon, *Vice Pres*
EMP: 23 **EST:** 1984
SQ FT: 5,200
SALES (est): 1.4MM **Privately Held**
WEB: www.lemoncreekwinery.com
SIC: 2084 5921 Wines; wine

(G-1644)
LITHOTECH
Also Called: Anders University Lithotech
212 Harrigan Hall (49104-0001)
PHONE.....................269 471-6027
Rod Church, *Manager*
EMP: 6 **EST:** 1992
SALES (est): 214.9K **Privately Held**
WEB: www.aulithotech.org
SIC: 2759 Commercial printing

(G-1645)
MILTONS CABINET SHOP INC
10331 Us Highway 31 (49103-9528)
PHONE..................................269 473-2743
Milton Jenks, *President*
Michael Jenks, *Vice Pres*
EMP: 5 **EST:** 1967
SQ FT: 5,500
SALES (est): 481K **Privately Held**
WEB: www.miltonscabinetshop.net
SIC: 2434 Wood kitchen cabinets

(G-1646)
TAFCOR INC
9918 N Tudor Rd (49103-9681)
P.O. Box 222 (49103-0222)
PHONE..................................269 471-2351
Edward Faulkner, *President*
Sandy Wirick, *Office Mgr*
Karen Faulkner, *Shareholder*
Laura Faulkner, *Shareholder*
Laura N Faulkner, *Shareholder*
▼ **EMP:** 11
SQ FT: 55,000
SALES (est): 1.9MM **Privately Held**
WEB: www.tafcor.com
SIC: 2431 Moldings, wood: unfinished & prefinished

Bessemer
Gogebic County

(G-1647)
BREAD OF LIFE BAKERY & CAFE
105 N Sophie St (49911-1150)
PHONE..................................906 663-4005
Robert Samson, *Owner*
EMP: 10 **EST:** 1950
SQ FT: 3,750
SALES (est): 150K **Privately Held**
SIC: 2051 5812 Bread, all types (white, wheat, rye, etc): fresh or frozen; cafe

(G-1648)
DECOTIES INC
807 Spring St (49911-1638)
PHONE..................................906 285-1286
Oscar Buselli, *President*
EMP: 4 **EST:** 2016
SQ FT: 700
SALES (est): 203.5K **Privately Held**
SIC: 3965 Fasteners

(G-1649)
FOREST CORULLO PRODUCTS CORP
300 S Massie Ave (49911-1329)
PHONE..................................906 667-0275
Raymond J Corullo, *President*
EMP: 34 **EST:** 1978
SALES (est): 5.8MM **Privately Held**
SIC: 2421 2611 2436 2435 Sawmills & planing mills, general; pulp mills; softwood veneer & plywood; hardwood veneer & plywood

(G-1650)
STEIGERS TIMBER OPERATIONS
401 S Tamarack Ave (49911-1259)
P.O. Box 112 (49911-0112)
PHONE..................................906 667-0266
Patrick Steiger, *Owner*
EMP: 4 **EST:** 2008
SALES (est): 292.3K **Privately Held**
SIC: 2411 Logging camps & contractors

(G-1651)
WOODLAND PIXIE
404 S Mine St (49911-1019)
PHONE..................................503 330-8033
Melissa Swartz, *Principal*
EMP: 4 **EST:** 2018
SALES (est): 54.1K **Privately Held**
SIC: 2431 Millwork

Beulah
Benzie County

(G-1652)
AURIC ENTERPRISES INC
Also Called: Diack
7755 Narrow Gauge Rd (49617-9792)
PHONE..................................231 882-7251
Robert Brown, *President*
Melanie Cederholm, *General Mgr*
EMP: 4 **EST:** 1994
SALES (est): 470.5K **Privately Held**
WEB: www.thornsmithlabs.com
SIC: 3826 3829 3842 3825 Analytical instruments; measuring & controlling devices; surgical appliances & supplies; instruments to measure electricity; industrial instrmnts msrmnt display/control process variable

(G-1653)
COLES CUSTOM CON COATINGS LLC
367 Spring Valley St (49617-5113)
P.O. Box 616 (49617-0616)
PHONE..................................231 651-0709
Jerry Cole, *Principal*
EMP: 5 **EST:** 2016
SALES (est): 85.2K **Privately Held**
SIC: 3479 Metal coating & allied service

(G-1654)
CSB INDUSTRIES LLC
90 S Haze Rd (49617-9745)
PHONE..................................231 651-9484
Cory Brown, *Principal*
EMP: 6 **EST:** 2018
SALES (est): 209.8K **Privately Held**
SIC: 3999 Manufacturing industries

(G-1655)
LEROY WORDEN
Also Called: Worden Farms
1944 N Marshall Rd (49617-8542)
PHONE..................................231 325-3837
Leroy Worden, *Owner*
EMP: 4 **EST:** 1958
SALES (est): 137.4K **Privately Held**
SIC: 2087 Flavoring extracts & syrups

(G-1656)
NIPPA SAUNA STOVES LLC
8862 Us Highway 31 (49617-9729)
P.O. Box 1151, Frankfort (49635-1151)
PHONE..................................231 882-7707
Dean Michael,
EMP: 8 **EST:** 2006
SQ FT: 12,000
SALES (est): 250K **Privately Held**
WEB: www.nippa.com
SIC: 3634 Sauna heaters, electric

(G-1657)
SLEEPING BEAR APIARIES LTD
Also Called: Sleeping Bear Farms
971 S Pioneer Rd (49617-9778)
PHONE..................................231 882-4456
Kirk Jones, *President*
Dave Nesky, *Vice Pres*
Sharon Jones, *Treasurer*
Mike Williams, *Admin Sec*
EMP: 10 **EST:** 1991
SALES (est): 1.3MM **Privately Held**
WEB: www.sleepingbearfarms.com
SIC: 2099 5947 Honey, strained & bottled; gift, novelty & souvenir shop

(G-1658)
SPIN LO ANGLER
6450 Bixler Rd (49617-9226)
PHONE..................................231 882-6450
Allen Vanderplow, *Principal*
EMP: 4 **EST:** 2016
SALES (est): 57.5K **Privately Held**
SIC: 2711 Newspapers

(G-1659)
ST AMBROSE CELLARS
971 S Pioneer Rd (49617-9778)
PHONE..................................231 383-4262
EMP: 6 **EST:** 2014
SALES (est): 347.5K **Privately Held**
WEB: www.stambrose-mead-wine.com
SIC: 2084 Wines

Beverly Hills
Oakland County

(G-1660)
ALDRIDGE INDUSTRIES LLC
18811 Riverside Dr (48025-3062)
PHONE..................................248 379-5357
EMP: 4 **EST:** 2018
SALES (est): 110.4K **Privately Held**
SIC: 3999 Manufacturing industries

(G-1661)
ARC PRINT SOLUTIONS LLC
19625 Riverside Dr (48025-2959)
PHONE..................................248 917-7052
James Steven Chapman, *President*
Giri Gondi, *CIO*
▼ **EMP:** 10 **EST:** 2009
SALES (est): 1.2MM **Privately Held**
SIC: 2759 Commercial printing

(G-1662)
CLEARVIEW LIGHTING LLC
31572 Mayfair Ln (48025-4032)
PHONE..................................248 709-8707
Thomas Jordan, *Principal*
EMP: 5 **EST:** 2012
SALES (est): 222.4K **Privately Held**
WEB: www.clearviewlightingled.com
SIC: 3648 Lighting equipment

(G-1663)
DRIVE SYSTEM INTEGRATION INC
32600 Westlady Dr (48025-2747)
PHONE..................................248 568-7750
Dare Sommer, *President*
Paul Wire, *Vice Pres*
EMP: 4
SALES (est): 230K **Privately Held**
SIC: 3544 Special dies, tools, jigs & fixtures

(G-1664)
HALL WOOD CREATIONS
15766 Birwood Ave (48025-3332)
PHONE..................................248 645-0983
Charles Hall, *President*
EMP: 5 **EST:** 2001
SALES (est): 154.5K **Privately Held**
SIC: 2431 Millwork

(G-1665)
J & E APPLIANCE COMPANY INC
30170 Stellamar St (48025-4925)
PHONE..................................248 642-9191
Eric Kopsch, *President*
EMP: 5 **EST:** 1968
SALES (est): 403.2K **Privately Held**
SIC: 3639 Major kitchen appliances, except refrigerators & stoves

(G-1666)
METAL MATES INC (PA)
20135 Elwood St (48025-5015)
PHONE..................................248 646-9831
A Clarence Karbum, *President*
Curt A Karbum, *Vice Pres*
Keith M Karbum, *Vice Pres*
Catherine J Karbum, *Admin Sec*
EMP: 2 **EST:** 1978
SQ FT: 10,000
SALES (est): 1.1MM **Privately Held**
WEB: www.metalmates.net
SIC: 2869 Industrial organic chemicals

(G-1667)
MICROFORMS INC
Also Called: Safran Group, The
30706 Georgetown Dr (48025-4735)
PHONE..................................586 939-7900
James A Safran, *President*
Michael Murphy, *Purch Mgr*
Cory Ward, *Buyer*
Veronica Klein, *Sales Staff*
Angela Mingo, *Sales Staff*
EMP: 38 **EST:** 1985
SQ FT: 20,400
SALES (est): 1.2MM **Privately Held**
WEB: www.thesafrangroup.com
SIC: 2752 2796 2791 2782 Commercial printing, offset; platemaking services; typesetting; blankbooks & looseleaf binders; manifold business forms; commercial printing

(G-1668)
SAFRAN PRINTING COMPANY INC
30706 Georgetown Dr (48025-4735)
PHONE..................................586 939-7600
James Safran, *President*
Oliver Laurence, *COO*
Tracey Price, *Vice Pres*
Steve Meserve, *Engineer*
Rebecca Koehnke, *Human Res Dir*
EMP: 103 **EST:** 1982
SQ FT: 20,000
SALES (est): 2.2MM **Privately Held**
WEB: www.scan-the-man.com
SIC: 2754 7338 2796 2791 Commercial printing, gravure; secretarial & court reporting; platemaking services; typesetting; commercial printing; commercial printing, lithographic

Big Rapids
Mecosta County

(G-1669)
BIG RAPIDS PRODUCTS INC (PA)
Also Called: Big Rapids Tool & Engineering
1313 Maple St (49301-1654)
PHONE..................................231 796-3593
John Chaput, *CEO*
Aaron Thompson, *Vice Pres*
Todd Schroeder, *Prdtn Mgr*
Kent Brooks, *Engineer*
Larry Feuerstein, *Engineer*
EMP: 65 **EST:** 1975
SALES (est): 26.3MM **Privately Held**
WEB: www.brproducts.com
SIC: 3469 Stamping metal for the trade

(G-1670)
BOWMAN WELDING AND FABRICATION
23855 19 Mile Rd (49307-9713)
PHONE..................................231 580-6438
EMP: 4 **EST:** 2014
SALES (est): 28.2K **Privately Held**
SIC: 7692 Welding repair

(G-1671)
COOKS BLACKSMITH WELDING INC
402 Bjornson St (49307-1202)
PHONE..................................231 796-6819
Robert Cook, *President*
EMP: 7 **EST:** 1981
SALES (est): 973.7K **Privately Held**
WEB: www.cooksblacksmithwelding.com
SIC: 7699 7692 Blacksmith shop; welding repair

(G-1672)
ELITE SIGN COMPANY
125 Howard St (49307-1611)
P.O. Box 264, Chassell (49916-0264)
PHONE..................................906 481-7446
Daniel Gorczewicz, *Principal*
EMP: 9 **EST:** 2014
SALES (est): 274.5K **Privately Held**
WEB: www.elitesigncompany.com
SIC: 3993 Signs, not made in custom sign painting shops

(G-1673)
FEDERAL SCREW WORKS
Also Called: Boyne City Division
400 N Dekraft Ave (49307-1273)
PHONE..................................734 941-4211
William Harness, *President*
Carman Bean, *General Mgr*
Jeffrey Harness, *Vice Pres*
Aaron Zurschmiede, *Vice Pres*
Shane Deangelis, *Production*
EMP: 87

Big Rapids - Mecosta County (G-1674)

GEOGRAPHIC SECTION

SALES (corp-wide): 78.9MM Privately Held
WEB: www.federalscrewworks.com
SIC: **3451** 3592 3452 Screw machine products; carburetors, pistons, rings, valves; bolts, nuts, rivets & washers
PA: Federal Screw Works
   34846 Goddard Rd
   Romulus MI 48174
   734 941-4211

(G-1674)
FEDERAL SCREW WORKS
Big Rapids Division
400 N Dekraft Ave (49307-1273)
PHONE.................................231 796-7664
Carman Bean, *Branch Mgr*
EMP: 87
SALES (corp-wide): 78.9MM Privately Held
WEB: www.federalscrewworks.com
SIC: **3452** 3714 Bolts, metal; motor vehicle parts & accessories
PA: Federal Screw Works
   34846 Goddard Rd
   Romulus MI 48174
   734 941-4211

(G-1675)
HAMTECH INC
1916 Industrial Dr N (49307-9011)
PHONE.................................231 796-3917
David Hamelund, *President*
EMP: 4 EST: 1976
SALES (est): 365.1K Privately Held
WEB: www.hamtechinc.com
SIC: **3599** Machine shop, jobbing & repair

(G-1676)
HANCHETT MANUFACTURING INC
20000 19 Mile Rd (49307-9737)
PHONE.................................231 796-7678
Ralph Manting, *President*
Don Selfridge, *President*
Brian Sauntman, *Vice Pres*
Mark Renne, *Purch Mgr*
Ken Shefferly, *Controller*
EMP: 44 EST: 1900
SQ FT: 95,000
SALES (est): 3MM Privately Held
WEB: www.hanchett.com
SIC: **3545** 3596 3423 Shaping tools (machine tool accessories); scales & balances, except laboratory; hand & edge tools

(G-1677)
HELP-U-SELL RE BIG RAPIDS
412 S State St Ofc A (49307-1963)
PHONE.................................231 796-3966
Claira Shwabb, *Owner*
EMP: 10 EST: 1987
SALES (est): 441.5K Privately Held
WEB: www.helpusell.com
SIC: **6531** 2759 Real estate brokers & agents; advertising literature: printing

(G-1678)
JACK BATDORSS (PA)
Also Called: Pioneer Press
22405 18 Mile Rd (49307-9720)
PHONE.................................231 796-4831
Jack Batdorss, *Owner*
Aaron Dekuiper, *Manager*
Sandra Card, *Executive*
EMP: 40 EST: 1972
SALES (est): 3.8MM Privately Held
SIC: **2752** Commercial printing, offset

(G-1679)
KMK MACHINING
10842 Northland Dr (49307-9294)
PHONE.................................231 629-8068
Kevin G Wells, *Manager*
EMP: 18 EST: 2012
SALES (est): 502.3K Privately Held
WEB: www.kmkmachining.com
SIC: **3599** Machine shop, jobbing & repair

(G-1680)
KURT DUBOWSKI
14472 Mckinley Rd (49307-9537)
PHONE.................................231 796-0055
Kurt Dubowski, *Principal*
EMP: 5 EST: 2010

SALES (est): 68.2K Privately Held
SIC: **3089** Plastics products

(G-1681)
ORIGINAL FOOTWEAR COMPANY
1005 Baldwin St (49307-1119)
PHONE.................................231 796-5828
Elizabeth Mercendetti, *Regional Mgr*
Kenneth Beaulieu, *Vice Pres*
Kerry Brozyna, *Vice Pres*
John Burch, *Vice Pres*
Christopher Deschenes, *Vice Pres*
EMP: 400
SALES (corp-wide): 59.4MM Privately Held
WEB: www.originalfootwear.com
SIC: **3172** 3021 3143 Personal leather goods; rubber & plastics footwear; boots, dress or casual: men's
PA: The Original Footwear Company Inc
   5968 Commerce Blvd
   Morristown TN 37814
   423 254-8022

(G-1682)
ORIGINAL FOOTWEAR MFG BR INC
Also Called: Original Footwear Mfg
1005 Baldwin St (49307-1119)
PHONE.................................231 796-5828
Kevin D Cole, *President*
Neal Silverman, *Regional Mgr*
EMP: 11 EST: 2017
SALES (est): 590K Privately Held
SIC: **3143** 3144 Men's footwear, except athletic; women's footwear, except athletic

(G-1683)
PGI HOLDINGS INC (DH)
Also Called: Lake County Star
115 N Michigan Ave (49307-1401)
P.O. Box 913 (49307-0913)
PHONE.................................231 796-4831
Mark Aldam, *President*
John Norton, *General Mgr*
Tom McHugh, *CFO*
Judy Hale, *Advt Staff*
Paula Laws, *Consultant*
EMP: 25 EST: 1862
SQ FT: 20,000
SALES (est): 18.7MM
SALES (corp-wide): 4.2B Privately Held
WEB: www.theheraldreview.com
SIC: **2752** 2711 Commercial printing, lithographic; commercial printing & newspaper publishing combined
HQ: Hearst Communications, Inc.
   300 W 57th St
   New York NY 10019
   212 649-2000

(G-1684)
PGI HOLDINGS INC
Also Called: River Valley Shopper
115 N Michigan Ave (49307-1401)
PHONE.................................231 937-4740
John Batdorff III, *Manager*
EMP: 4
SALES (corp-wide): 4.2B Privately Held
WEB: www.theheraldreview.com
SIC: **2711** 2741 Commercial printing & newspaper publishing combined; shopping news: publishing only, not printed on site
HQ: Pgi Holdings, Inc.
   115 N Michigan Ave
   Big Rapids MI 49307
   231 796-4831

(G-1685)
PRIMO TOOL & MANUFACTURING
20070 19 Mile Rd (49307-9737)
PHONE.................................231 592-5262
David Grveles, *President*
Holly Grveles, *Vice Pres*
EMP: 5 EST: 1995
SQ FT: 5,000
SALES (est): 325K Privately Held
WEB: www.ptmc.biz
SIC: **3599** Machine shop, jobbing & repair

(G-1686)
RODNEY E HARTER
12880 190th Ave (49307-9060)
PHONE.................................231 796-6734
Rodney E Harter, *Principal*
EMP: 7 EST: 2005
SALES (est): 229.1K Privately Held
SIC: **2411** Logging

(G-1687)
SIMONDS INTERNATIONAL LLC
Also Called: Simonds Industries
120 E Pere Marquette St (49307-1159)
PHONE.................................231 527-2322
Susan Kifer, *Vice Pres*
Doug Morrison, *Project Mgr*
Dave Campbell, *Branch Mgr*
Kenneth Daughtry, *Manager*
David Rosing, *Manager*
EMP: 5
SALES (corp-wide): 206MM Privately Held
WEB: www.simondsint.com
SIC: **3423** Hand & edge tools
HQ: Simonds International L.L.C.
   135 Intervale Rd
   Fitchburg MA 01420
   978 424-0100

(G-1688)
SRM CONCRETE LLC
Also Called: Lc Materials
15151 Old Millpond Rd (49307-9502)
PHONE.................................231 796-8685
Phil Potvin, *Manager*
EMP: 8
SALES (corp-wide): 170.1MM Privately Held
WEB: www.lcredimix.com
SIC: **3273** Ready-mixed concrete
PA: Srm Concrete, Llc
   1136 2nd Ave N
   Nashville TN 37208
   615 355-1028

(G-1689)
WHITE CLOUD MANUFACTURING CO (PA)
123 N Dekraft Ave (49307-1280)
P.O. Box 1117 (49307-0307)
PHONE.................................231 796-8603
Jack Benedict, *President*
Jill Aye, *Vice Pres*
Tom Benedict, *Vice Pres*
EMP: 30 EST: 1965
SQ FT: 30,000
SALES (est): 2.8MM Privately Held
SIC: **3369** Nonferrous foundries

(G-1690)
WOODVILLE HEIGHTS ENTERPRISES
7147 6 Mile Rd (49307-9147)
PHONE.................................231 629-7750
Alice Gerst, *President*
EMP: 10
SALES (est): 532.4K Privately Held
SIC: **3599** Industrial machinery

Bingham Farms
Oakland County

(G-1691)
ARDEN COMPANIES LLC (HQ)
30400 Telg Rd Ste 200 (48025)
PHONE.................................248 415-8500
Robert S Sachs, *CEO*
Cecil Kearse, *President*
Tonia Hickman, *Vice Pres*
Karyn Kummer, *Vice Pres*
Benjamin Rapp, *Vice Pres*
▲ EMP: 50 EST: 1964
SQ FT: 15,000
SALES (est): 161.6MM
SALES (corp-wide): 2.7B Publicly Held
WEB: www.ardencompanies.com
SIC: **2392** Cushions & pillows
PA: Central Garden & Pet Company
   1340 Treat Blvd Ste 600
   Walnut Creek CA 94597
   925 948-4000

(G-1692)
AUTHENTIC 3D
30800 Telg Rd Ste 4775 (48025)
PHONE.................................248 469-8809
Jorey Chernett, *CEO*
Shandin Jones, *Vice Pres*
Tom Bambrick, *Opers Staff*
John David, *Engineer*
Alexander Kappaz, *Accounts Mgr*
EMP: 20 EST: 2014
SALES (est): 2.2MM Privately Held
WEB: www.authentic4d.com
SIC: **3826** Magnetic resonance imaging apparatus

(G-1693)
CHALDEAN NEWS LLC
30850 Telg Rd Ste 220 (48025)
PHONE.................................248 996-8360
Martin Manna, *Owner*
Lamya Kory, *Executive*
EMP: 7 EST: 2003
SALES (est): 138.1K Privately Held
WEB: www.chaldeannews.com
SIC: **2721** Magazines: publishing only, not printed on site

(G-1694)
CONFORM AUTOMOTIVE LLC (PA)
Also Called: Conform Group
32500 Telg Rd Ste 207 (48025)
PHONE.................................248 647-0400
Steven Phillips, *CEO*
William Vaughn, *Exec VP*
Gary M Stanis, *CFO*
John Mastin, *Admin Sec*
▲ EMP: 15 EST: 1996
SQ FT: 4,000
SALES (est): 121.9MM Privately Held
WEB: www.conformgroup.com
SIC: **3714** Motor vehicle parts & accessories

(G-1695)
DTI MOLDED PRODUCTS INC (HQ)
Also Called: Conform Automotive
32500 Telg Rd Ste 207 (48025)
PHONE.................................248 647-0400
EMP: 10
SQ FT: 4,500
SALES (est): 16.9MM Privately Held
SIC: **3465** 3069 Automotive Stampings, Nsk

(G-1696)
FORD GLOBAL TECHNOLOGIES LLC (HQ)
30600 Telg Rd Ste 2345 (48025)
PHONE.................................313 312-3000
Rebecca Burtless-Creps, *Asst Sec*
EMP: 518 EST: 2002
SALES (est): 36.2MM
SALES (corp-wide): 127.1B Publicly Held
WEB: www.ford.com
SIC: **3465** Body parts, automobile: stamped metal
PA: Ford Motor Company
   1 American Rd
   Dearborn MI 48126
   313 322-3000

(G-1697)
GISSING NORTH AMERICA LLC (DH)
32500 Telegraph Rd Ste 20 (48025-2461)
PHONE.................................248 647-0400
Jon Anderson, *CFO*
Claudio Calado,
Steven Phillips,
William Vaughn,
EMP: 100 EST: 2013
SALES (est): 61.9MM
SALES (corp-wide): 51.7MM Privately Held
SIC: **3442** 3714 Moldings & trim, except automobile: metal; motor vehicle parts & accessories

(G-1698)
GREY WOLFE PUBLISHING LLC
23565 Old Orchard Trl (48025-3442)
PHONE.................................248 914-4027

EMP: 4 EST: 2018
SALES (est): 106.3K Privately Held
WEB: www.oldgreywolfepublishing.word-press.com
SIC: 2741 Miscellaneous publishing

(G-1699)
HIGH FIVE SPIRITS LLC
Also Called: Gypsy Vodka
32960 Bingham Rd (48025-2436)
PHONE..................................248 217-6057
Adam Kazanolski,
EMP: 4 EST: 2013
SALES (est): 116.5K Privately Held
SIC: 2085 Vodka (alcoholic beverage)

(G-1700)
HORIZON DIE COMPANY
30100 Telegraph Rd # 236 (48025-4515)
PHONE..................................248 590-2966
Dan Foelske, Opers Mgr
Doug Jameson, Prdtn Mgr
Jim Vitacco, Mfg Mgr
David Holch, Manager
Marcus Westlund, Associate
EMP: 6 EST: 2016
SALES (est): 83.2K Privately Held
SIC: 3544 Special dies & tools

(G-1701)
INTRINSIC4D LLC (PA)
Also Called: Legal Art Works
30800 Telg Rd Ste 4775 (48025)
PHONE..................................248 469-8811
Jorey Chernett, CEO
Marjorie McKenzie, Vice Pres
EMP: 7 EST: 2011
SALES (est): 1.5MM Privately Held
WEB: www.intrinsic4d.com
SIC: 7372 8099 Application computer software; medical services organization

(G-1702)
KRAMS ENTERPRISES INC
Also Called: Arden-Benhar Mills
30400 Telg Rd Ste 200 (48025)
PHONE..................................248 415-8500
Bob Sachs, President
Robert S Sachs, President
Kenneth Sachs, Corp Secy
John F Connell, Exec VP
Ronald P Zemenak, Exec VP
▲ EMP: 887 EST: 1986
SQ FT: 5,500
SALES (est): 28.5MM Privately Held
SIC: 2392 Cushions & pillows

(G-1703)
STREMA SALES CORP
Also Called: Wayne Wire Cloths
31000 Telg Rd Ste 240 (48025)
PHONE..................................248 645-0626
Michael G Brown, President
Newell Confer, Manager
EMP: 4 EST: 1970
SALES (est): 307.7K Privately Held
SIC: 3496 Miscellaneous fabricated wire products

(G-1704)
SUPERALLOY NORTH AMERICA LLC
31000 Telg Rd Ste 280 (48025)
PHONE..................................810 252-1552
EMP: 4 EST: 2013
SALES (est): 98K Privately Held
WEB: www.ussuperalloys.com
SIC: 3462 3711 3312 Gears, forged steel; chassis, motor vehicle; wheels

(G-1705)
TRILLACORPE/BK LLC
Also Called: Trillacorpe Construction
30100 Telg Rd Ste 366 (48025)
PHONE..................................248 433-0585
Martin Sudz, Vice Pres
Larry Goss,
EMP: 8
SALES (est): 20MM Privately Held
WEB: www.trillacorpeconstruction.com
SIC: 1442 Construction sand & gravel

Birch Run
Saginaw County

(G-1706)
EAGLE GRAFIX
10525 S Block Rd (48415-9431)
PHONE..................................989 624-4638
Gail Freckmann, Executive Asst
EMP: 6 EST: 2003
SALES (est): 198.9K Privately Held
WEB: www.eaglegrafix.net
SIC: 2759 Commercial printing

(G-1707)
INFLATABLE INDUSTRIES
9510 Burt Rd (48415-9451)
PHONE..................................517 505-0700
EMP: 4 EST: 2018
SALES (est): 248.2K Privately Held
WEB: www.duxboats.com
SIC: 3999 Manufacturing industries

(G-1708)
KRISELER WELDING INC
11877 Maple Rd (48415-8207)
PHONE..................................989 624-9266
David Bowns, President
Barbara Bowns, Treasurer
EMP: 6 EST: 1946
SQ FT: 6,000 Privately Held
SIC: 3599 7692 3544 3471 Machine shop, jobbing & repair; welding repair; special dies, tools, jigs & fixtures; plating & polishing

(G-1709)
LIGHTING PRINTING
2511 Busch Rd (48415-8918)
PHONE..................................989 792-2793
EMP: 5 EST: 2017
SALES (est): 97.1K Privately Held
WEB: www.lightningsaginaw.com
SIC: 2752 Commercial printing, offset

(G-1710)
LUXOTTICA OF AMERICA INC
Also Called: Sunglass Hut 4711
8825 Market Place Dr # 340 (48415-8344)
PHONE..................................989 624-8958
Lori Dillon, Manager
EMP: 5
SALES (corp-wide): 1.7MM Privately Held
WEB: www.luxottica.com
SIC: 3231 Products of purchased glass
HQ: Luxottica Of America Inc.
    4000 Luxottica Pl
    Mason OH 45040

(G-1711)
MID-MICHIGAN SCREEN PRINTING
Also Called: Mmsp
11917 Conquest St (48415-9294)
P.O. Box 333 (48415-0333)
PHONE..................................989 624-9827
Floyd McClintock, Owner
Janet McClintock, Bookkeeper
EMP: 4 EST: 1979
SQ FT: 1,600
SALES (est): 407.8K Privately Held
WEB: www.midmichiganscreenprinting.imprintableapparel.com
SIC: 2752 Commercial printing, lithographic

(G-1712)
PVH CORP
8925 Market Place Dr # 450 (48415-8346)
PHONE..................................989 624-5575
EMP: 33
SALES (corp-wide): 8.2B Publicly Held
SIC: 2339 Mfg Clothing
PA: Pvh Corp.
    200 Madison Ave Bsmt 1
    New York NY 10016
    212 381-3500

(G-1713)
PVH CORP
Also Called: Van Heusen
12245 S Beyer Rd Ste A060 (48415-8318)
PHONE..................................989 624-5651
EMP: 5
SALES (corp-wide): 8.2B Publicly Held
SIC: 2321 Mfg Men's/Boy's Furnishings
PA: Pvh Corp.
    200 Madison Ave Bsmt 1
    New York NY 10016
    212 381-3500

(G-1714)
ROCKY MTN CHOCLAT FCTRY INC
8825 Market Place Dr # 425 (48415-8345)
PHONE..................................989 624-4784
Jerilynn Daenzer, Manager
EMP: 4
SALES (corp-wide): 23.4MM Publicly Held
WEB: www.rmcf.com
SIC: 5441 2066 Candy; chocolate
PA: Rocky Mountain Chocolate Factory, Inc.
    265 Turner Dr
    Durango CO 81303
    970 247-4943

(G-1715)
SKECHERS USA INC
Also Called: Skechers Factory Outlet 235
12240 S Beyer Rd (48415-9401)
PHONE..................................989 624-9336
Sarah Snyder, General Mgr
Dawn Hempton, Store Mgr
EMP: 10 Publicly Held
WEB: www.skechers.com
SIC: 5661 2252 Footwear, athletic; socks
PA: Skechers U.S.A., Inc.
    228 Manhattan Beach Blvd # 200
    Manhattan Beach CA 90266

(G-1716)
SPRING SAGINAW COMPANY
11008 Dixie Hwy (48415-9745)
P.O. Box 328 (48415-0328)
PHONE..................................989 624-9333
Fern Wheeler, President
EMP: 4 EST: 1971
SQ FT: 3,500
SALES (est): 414.1K Privately Held
WEB: www.saginaw-spring-co.business.site
SIC: 3495 Wire springs

Birmingham
Oakland County

(G-1717)
ALFA FINANCIAL SOFTWARE INC
Also Called: Chp Consulting
350 N Old Woodward Ave (48009-5342)
PHONE..................................855 680-7100
Richard Raistrick, Director
Simon Clark, Director
Kirsten Fleming, Admin Sec
EMP: 70 EST: 2005
SQ FT: 3,209
SALES (est): 10.1MM
SALES (corp-wide): 104.8MM Privately Held
WEB: www.alfasystems.com
SIC: 8748 7371 7372 Business consulting; software programming applications; prepackaged software
HQ: Alfa Financial Software Limited
    1 Fore Street Avenue
    London EC2Y
    207 588-1800

(G-1718)
ALPHA DATA BUSINESS FORMS INC
Also Called: Graywolf Printing
757 S Eton St Ste D (48009-6841)
PHONE..................................248 540-5930
Max Grayvold, President
Marc Grayvold, Vice Pres
EMP: 5 EST: 1982
SQ FT: 800
SALES (est): 876K Privately Held
SIC: 5112 2761 2759 2752 Business forms; manifold business forms; commercial printing; commercial printing, lithographic; coated & laminated paper; packaging paper & plastics film, coated & laminated

(G-1719)
CANTRICK KIP CO
774 Lakeside Dr (48009-1382)
PHONE..................................248 644-7622
George A Cantrick Jr, President
EMP: 4 EST: 1979
SALES (est): 299K Privately Held
WEB: www.kipcantrickcompany.com
SIC: 3086 Packaging & shipping materials, foamed plastic

(G-1720)
CHERRY GROWERS INC (PA)
401 S Old Woodward Ave # 340 (48009-6621)
PHONE..................................231 276-9241
Ed Send, Vice Ch Bd
Brian Mitchell, President
Dan Winowiecki, Finance Dir
John Gallaher Jr, Admin Sec
Eric Macleod, Asst Sec
◆ EMP: 125
SALES (est): 14.6MM Privately Held
WEB: www.cherrygrowers.net
SIC: 2037 2033 Fruits, quick frozen & cold pack (frozen); fruits: packaged in cans, jars, etc.

(G-1721)
COLE WAGNER CABINETRY
735 Forest Ave (48009-6429)
PHONE..................................248 642-5330
Ashley Gibaud, Office Mgr
EMP: 6 EST: 2010
SALES (est): 186.8K Privately Held
WEB: www.cwcabinetry.com
SIC: 2434 Wood kitchen cabinets

(G-1722)
CONCEPT TECHNOLOGY INC (PA)
144 Wimbleton Dr (48009-5633)
PHONE..................................248 765-0100
Thomas F Hornung, President
Susan A Hornung, Admin Sec
EMP: 11 EST: 1971
SQ FT: 2,000
SALES (est): 2.1MM Privately Held
SIC: 3825 Engine electrical test equipment

(G-1723)
CRUSE HARDWOOD LUMBER INC
2499 Cole St (48009-7084)
PHONE..................................517 688-4891
Robert H Cruse, President
Gladys Anne Cruse, Corp Secy
EMP: 7 EST: 1969
SALES (est): 835.2K Privately Held
SIC: 2421 Sawmills & planing mills, general

(G-1724)
DYNAMIC METALS GROUP LLC
260 E Brown St Ste 280 (48009-6231)
PHONE..................................586 790-5615
Paul P Newman,
Cheryl Newman,
EMP: 18 EST: 2005
SALES (est): 3.2MM Privately Held
SIC: 3465 3795 3544 Automotive stampings; specialized tank components, military; special dies, tools, jigs & fixtures

(G-1725)
E-CON LLC
Also Called: Econ Global Services
320 Martin St Ste 60 (48009-1486)
PHONE..................................248 766-9000
Djeamourty Ramkumar,
EMP: 9 EST: 1999
SQ FT: 2,000
SALES (est): 311.3K Privately Held
SIC: 7379 7371 7376 7363 Computer related consulting services; computer software development; computer facilities management; labor resource services; business oriented computer software

Birmingham - Oakland County (G-1726)

(G-1726)
EDGEMARC ENERGY HOLDINGS LLC (PA)
401 S Old Woodward Ave # 340 (48009-6621)
PHONE...................724 749-8466
Kevin Eshbaugh, *General Mgr*
Kirby Walker, *Engineer*
Alan Shepard, *CFO*
Matthew Cantrell, *Marketing Staff*
Alice Rump, *Office Mgr*
EMP: 21 **EST:** 2011
SALES (est): 116MM **Privately Held**
WEB: www.edgemarcenergy.com
SIC: 1381 Drilling oil & gas wells

(G-1727)
ERNST BENZ COMPANY LLC
177 S Old Woodward Ave (48009-6102)
PHONE...................248 203-2323
Boris Khankin, *Director*
Leobud Khankin, *Director*
Efim Khankin,
▼ **EMP:** 6 **EST:** 2005
SALES (est): 576.8K **Privately Held**
WEB: www.ernstbenz.com
SIC: 3873 Watches, clocks, watchcases & parts

(G-1728)
GACO SOURCING LLC
2254 Cole St (48009-7072)
PHONE...................248 633-2656
Stephanie Wineman, *CEO*
Lisa Norton, *General Mgr*
Erin McGregor, *Opers Mgr*
Ted Farah, *CFO*
Cindy Gibbs, *Accountant*
▲ **EMP:** 5 **EST:** 2011
SALES (est): 1.5MM **Privately Held**
WEB: www.gacosourcing.com
SIC: 3069 Balloons, advertising & toy: rubber

(G-1729)
HOG FORGING LLC
1629 Banbury St (48009-7160)
PHONE...................248 765-7180
John P Ulrich Jr, *Principal*
John Ulrich, *Principal*
James WEI, *Principal*
EMP: 4 **EST:** 2020
SALES (est): 145.3K **Privately Held**
SIC: 3462 Iron & steel forgings

(G-1730)
HORIZON INTL GROUP LLC
1411 Westboro (48009-5862)
PHONE...................734 341-9336
Heather Gardner, *CEO*
EMP: 7 **EST:** 2003
SQ FT: 39,000
SALES (est): 431K **Privately Held**
SIC: 8742 5013 3714 Management consulting services; automotive supplies & parts; motor vehicle parts & accessories

(G-1731)
HUMMUS GOODNESS LLC
295 Henley St (48009-5608)
PHONE...................248 229-9606
Hannah Awada,
EMP: 5 **EST:** 2019
SALES (est): 519K **Privately Held**
WEB: www.hummusgoodness.com
SIC: 2873 Plant foods, mixed: from plants making nitrog. fertilizers

(G-1732)
KMJ GLOBAL INC
1137 S Adams Rd (48009-7101)
PHONE...................240 594-5050
Kyungmi Jung, *President*
EMP: 7 **EST:** 2018
SALES (est): 380.6K **Privately Held**
SIC: 2052 Bakery products, dry

(G-1733)
M & M IRISH ENTERPRISES INC
Also Called: Batteries Plus
34164 Woodward Ave (48009-0920)
P.O. Box 2539 (48012-2539)
PHONE...................248 644-0666
Barry Murphy, *Vice Pres*
EMP: 7 **EST:** 2002
SQ FT: 1,650
SALES (est): 980K **Privately Held**
WEB: www.batteriesplus.com
SIC: 3691 5531 5063 Storage batteries; batteries, automotive & truck; light bulbs & related supplies

(G-1734)
MAD DOG SOFTWARE
34100 Woodward Ave (48009-0961)
PHONE...................248 940-2963
EMP: 4 **EST:** 2019
SALES (est): 144.6K **Privately Held**
SIC: 7372 Prepackaged software

(G-1735)
MAGNI GROUP INC (PA)
390 Park St Ste 300 (48009-3400)
PHONE...................248 647-4500
Tim Berry, *President*
David E Berry, *Chairman*
Jack Benson, *Vice Pres*
Doug Paul, *Vice Pres*
Kirk Weaver, *Vice Pres*
▲ **EMP:** 14 **EST:** 1986
SQ FT: 8,000
SALES (est): 72.9MM **Privately Held**
WEB: www.magnicoatings.com
SIC: 2899 3479 Rust resisting compounds; coating, rust preventive

(G-1736)
MARK ADLER HOMES
401 S Old Woodward Ave # 3 (48009-6611)
PHONE...................586 850-0630
Mark Adler, *Administration*
EMP: 5 **EST:** 2011
SALES (est): 256.3K **Privately Held**
WEB: www.markadlerhomes.com
SIC: 3448 Buildings, portable: prefabricated metal

(G-1737)
MILLS PHRM & APOTHECARY LLC
Also Called: Epicure By Mills, The
1740 W Maple Rd (48009-1545)
PHONE...................248 633-2872
Pierre Pourtos, *Mng Member*
EMP: 8 **EST:** 2009
SALES (est): 1.3MM **Privately Held**
WEB: www.millspharmacy.com
SIC: 2834 Pharmaceutical preparations

(G-1738)
MOUNT-N-REPAIR
Also Called: Mount-N-Repair Silver Jewelry
205 Pierce St Ste 101 (48009-6014)
PHONE...................248 647-8670
Joel Kaber, *Owner*
EMP: 4 **EST:** 1985
SALES (est): 251.6K **Privately Held**
WEB: www.mountnrepair.com
SIC: 3911 5944 Jewelry, precious metal; jewelry stores

(G-1739)
NEPTIX
915 E Maple Rd (48009-6410)
PHONE...................248 520-6181
EMP: 4 **EST:** 2019
SALES (est): 160.2K **Privately Held**
WEB: www.neptix.com
SIC: 2752 Commercial printing, lithographic

(G-1740)
NORTHERN TRADING GROUP LLC
284 W Maple Rd (48009-3336)
P.O. Box 131008, Ann Arbor (48113-1008)
PHONE...................248 885-8750
Sandy Graham, *Branch Mgr*
EMP: 8
SALES (corp-wide): 4.1MM **Privately Held**
WEB: www.backcountrynorth.com
SIC: 3949 Camping equipment & supplies
PA: Northern Trading Group, Llc
227 E Front St
Traverse City MI 49684
231 946-1339

(G-1741)
OLD WOODWARD CELLAR
912 S Old Woodward Ave # 2 (48009-6716)
PHONE...................248 792-5452
EMP: 4 **EST:** 2017
SALES (est): 107.4K **Privately Held**
WEB: www.oldwoodwardcellar.com
SIC: 2084 Wines

(G-1742)
ON BASE FOOD GROUP LLC
Also Called: Plantet Dogs
146 W Maple Rd (48009-3322)
PHONE...................248 672-7659
EMP: 4
SALES (est): 116.1K **Privately Held**
SIC: 2099 Food preparations

(G-1743)
PERMAWICK COMPANY INC (PA)
255 E Brown St Ste 100 (48009-6207)
PHONE...................248 433-3500
Martin L Abel, *President*
Robert Corden, *Principal*
Joseph M Lane, *Treasurer*
▲ **EMP:** 2 **EST:** 1956
SALES (est): 2.5MM **Privately Held**
WEB: www.permawick.com
SIC: 2992 3569 Lubricating oils; lubricating equipment

(G-1744)
PIONEER MEATS LLC
915 E Maple Rd (48009-6410)
PHONE...................248 862-1988
Robert S File, *President*
Bob Capoccia, *Controller*
Robert George,
EMP: 10 **EST:** 2003
SALES (est): 1MM **Privately Held**
WEB: www.pioneermeats.com
SIC: 2013 Cooked meats from purchased meat

(G-1745)
QUESTOR PARTNERS FUND II LP (PA)
101 Southfield Rd 2 (48009-1601)
PHONE...................248 593-1930
Jay Alix, *Managing Prtnr*
Robert Shields, *Partner*
Robert D Denious, *Director*
Wallace Reuckel, *Director*
Mary Ellen Sanko, *Administration*
◆ **EMP:** 3 **EST:** 1995
SALES (est): 34.5MM **Privately Held**
SIC: 8742 2099 Business consultant; ready-to-eat meals, salads & sandwiches

(G-1746)
R J S TOOL & GAGE CO
Also Called: R J S
1081 S Eton St (48009-7133)
PHONE...................248 642-8620
Deborah S Stamp, *President*
Richard J Stamp Jr, *President*
Richard Stamp III, *Vice Pres*
Brian Carlson, *Opers Mgr*
John Mittelstaedt, *Sales Mgr*
EMP: 25 **EST:** 1948
SQ FT: 6,000
SALES (est): 3.5MM **Privately Held**
WEB: www.rjstool.com
SIC: 3545 3423 Tools & accessories for machine tools; gauges (machine tool accessories); hand & edge tools

(G-1747)
ROCHESTER PETROLEUM INC
33477 Woodward Ave # 800 (48009-0948)
PHONE...................507 533-9156
Jerry Asmussen, *President*
EMP: 8 **EST:** 2017
SALES (est): 299.6K **Privately Held**
SIC: 3563 Air & gas compressors including vacuum pumps

(G-1748)
S & W HOLDINGS LTD (PA)
114 S Old Woodward Ave (48009-6107)
PHONE...................248 723-2870
Paul Steffanutti, *President*
EMP: 1 **EST:** 1994
SQ FT: 1,000
SALES (est): 10MM **Privately Held**
SIC: 3714 3554 Transmission housings or parts, motor vehicle; die cutting & stamping machinery, paper converting; coating & finishing machinery, paper

(G-1749)
SHWAYDER COMPANY
2335 E Lincoln St (48009-7124)
PHONE...................248 645-9511
Mark Shwayder, *President*
EMP: 5 **EST:** 1954
SQ FT: 15,000
SALES (est): 512.6K **Privately Held**
WEB: www.shwayderco.com
SIC: 3429 3545 Keys, locks & related hardware; machine tool accessories

(G-1750)
SMARTPAT PLC
1785 Bradford Rd (48009-7252)
PHONE...................248 854-2233
EMP: 4 **EST:** 2018
SALES (est): 96.2K **Privately Held**
WEB: www.smartpat.net
SIC: 3714 Motor vehicle parts & accessories

(G-1751)
T R S FIELDBUS SYSTEMS INC
666 Baldwin Ct (48009-3863)
P.O. Box 4210, Troy (48099-4210)
PHONE...................586 826-9696
Karl Sachs, *President*
Adelheid Seidensticker, *Vice Pres*
EMP: 4 **EST:** 1994 **Privately Held**
SIC: 3357 Fiber optic cable (insulated)

(G-1752)
TESSONICS CORP
2019 Hazel St (48009-6825)
PHONE...................248 885-8335
Roman Maev, *President*
Joe Udzbinac, *CFO*
EMP: 6 **EST:** 2003
SALES (est): 522.1K **Privately Held**
WEB: www.tessonics.com
SIC: 3829 Measuring & controlling devices

(G-1753)
TITAN GLOBAL OIL SERVICES INC
401 S Old Woodward Ave # 308 (48009-6625)
PHONE...................248 594-5983
Jeffrey Groen, *Principal*
Kelly M Hayes, *Principal*
Edward Shehab, *Principal*
Michelle Jonna, *Opers Staff*
EMP: 10 **EST:** 2003
SALES (est): 266.7K **Privately Held**
WEB: www.titanglobaloil.com
SIC: 3533 Oil & gas field machinery

(G-1754)
TOTLE INC
260 E Brown St Ste 200 (48009-6231)
PHONE...................248 645-1111
David Bleznak, *CEO*
Colleen Stabler, *Business Mgr*
EMP: 9 **EST:** 2017
SALES (est): 7.2MM **Privately Held**
WEB: www.totle.com
SIC: 7389 7372 Financial services; application computer software

(G-1755)
U S DISTRIBUTING INC
Also Called: Sundog Construction Heaters
2333 Cole St (48009-7031)
PHONE...................248 646-0550
William E Beattie Jr, *President*
Glenn Lett, *Sales Staff*
Jeff Lewis, *Sales Staff*
Bill Pearre, *Manager*
EMP: 28 **EST:** 1972
SQ FT: 10,000
SALES (est): 2.7MM **Privately Held**
WEB: www.usdistributing.com
SIC: 3433 3585 7359 Room heaters, gas; air conditioning units, complete: domestic or industrial; propane equipment rental

GEOGRAPHIC SECTION

Bloomfield - Oakland County (G-1781)

(G-1756)
WELLSENSE USA INC
123 W Brown St (48009-6018)
PHONE..................888 335-0995
Eitan Machover, *CEO*
▲ EMP: 4 EST: 2011
SALES (est): 465K **Privately Held**
WEB: www.wellsensevu.com
SIC: 3829 Measuring & controlling devices

(G-1757)
WOOLLY & CO LLC
Also Called: Woolly and Co
575 Stanley Blvd (48009-1401)
PHONE..................248 480-4354
Aviva Susser, *Mng Member*
▲ EMP: 6 EST: 2015
SALES (est): 412.3K **Privately Held**
WEB: www.woollyandco.com
SIC: 2281 5199 Crochet yarn, spun; embroidery yarn, spun; knitting yarn, spun; spinning yarn; yarns

Bitely
Newaygo County

(G-1758)
DARRELL A CURTICE
669 E Roosevelt Rd (49309-9677)
PHONE..................231 745-9890
Darrell Curtice, *Principal*
EMP: 6 EST: 2008
SALES (est): 141.9K **Privately Held**
SIC: 2411 Logging

Blanchard
Isabella County

(G-1759)
NOBLE FORESTRY INC
Also Called: Thomas Dale Noble & Noble
5012 Taylor Rd (49310-9718)
PHONE..................989 866-6495
Tom Nobel, *President*
EMP: 5 EST: 1995
SALES (est): 390K **Privately Held**
SIC: 2411 Logging

Blissfield
Lenawee County

(G-1760)
ADAPTIVE METAL WORKS LLC
Also Called: Metal Fabrication
8611 E Us Highway 223 (49228-9604)
PHONE..................419 386-9336
Bruce Swan, *Mng Member*
EMP: 6 EST: 2020
SALES (est): 318.1K **Privately Held**
SIC: 3446 Architectural metalwork

(G-1761)
BLISSFIELD MANUFACTURING CO (PA)
626 Depot St (49228-1358)
PHONE..................517 486-2121
Patrick Farver, *CEO*
Patrick D Farver, *COO*
Nancy Schiffer, *Exec VP*
Jon Baucher, *Vice Pres*
Pat Howard, *Vice Pres*
▲ EMP: 149 EST: 1946
SQ FT: 250,000
SALES (est): 27.7MM **Privately Held**
WEB: www.blissfield.com
SIC: 3498 3599 3629 3585 Fabricated pipe & fittings; tubing, flexible metallic; condensers, for motors or generators; refrigeration & heating equipment; air & gas compressors

(G-1762)
BMC GLOBAL LLC
Also Called: Blissfield
626 Depot St (49228-1358)
PHONE..................517 486-2121
Peter Kos, *CEO*
Greg Wales, *CFO*
EMP: 52 EST: 2016
SALES (est): 3.3MM **Privately Held**
SIC: 3443 Heat exchangers, condensers & components

(G-1763)
CRESCENT MANUFACTURING COMPANY
368 Sherman St (49228-1174)
PHONE..................517 486-2670
Frank Wojick, *Owner*
EMP: 9
SALES (corp-wide): 22.4MM **Privately Held**
WEB: www.crescentblades.com
SIC: 3999 Barber & beauty shop equipment
PA: Crescent Manufacturing Company
1310 Majestic Dr
Fremont OH 43420
419 332-6484

(G-1764)
FORCHE RD WELDING
10187 Forche Rd (49228-9576)
PHONE..................517 920-3473
Keith Ermakov, *Principal*
EMP: 4 EST: 2018
SALES (est): 47K **Privately Held**
SIC: 3949 Skateboards

(G-1765)
JB MACHINERY LLC
Also Called: Bay Machinery
11118 Thompson Hwy (49228-9723)
PHONE..................419 727-1772
Jason Baird, *Mng Member*
EMP: 7 EST: 2020
SALES (est): 299.4K **Privately Held**
SIC: 3531 Construction machinery

(G-1766)
K AND J ABSORBENT PRODUCTS LLC
10009 E Us Highway 223 (49228-9566)
P.O. Box 45 (49228-0045)
PHONE..................517 486-3110
Janet Street,
Ken Street,
EMP: 7 EST: 1986
SALES (est): 487.7K **Privately Held**
WEB: www.filtersandsocks.com
SIC: 2392 3569 Dust cloths: made from purchased materials; filters, general line: industrial

(G-1767)
L & W INC
Also Called: Plant 4
11505 E Us Highway 223 (49228-9527)
P.O. Box 59 (49228-0059)
PHONE..................517 486-6321
Don Cattell, *QC Mgr*
Kurt Schauman, *Sales Staff*
Clair Stewart, *Manager*
EMP: 7
SALES (corp-wide): 3.1B **Privately Held**
WEB: www.autokiniton.com
SIC: 3465 3469 Automotive stampings; stamping metal for the trade
HQ: L & W, Inc.
17757 Woodland Dr
New Boston MI 48164
734 397-6300

(G-1768)
M FORCHE FARMS INC
1080 S Piotter Hwy (49228-9541)
PHONE..................517 447-3488
Michael Forche, *President*
Darlene Forche, *Principal*
Kathleen Forche, *Principal*
Leo Forche, *Principal*
EMP: 8 EST: 1989
SALES (est): 361.6K **Privately Held**
SIC: 2033 0139 Tomato products: packaged in cans, jars, etc.; food crops

(G-1769)
MAXITROL COMPANY
Also Called: Blissfield Div
235 Sugar St (49228-1367)
PHONE..................517 486-2820
Ivin Riddle, *Vice Pres*
Shawn Andrews, *Plant Mgr*
Scott Slomski, *Plant Mgr*
Ted Groustra, *Safety Mgr*
Kyle Curtis, *Senior Buyer*
EMP: 5
SQ FT: 7,000
SALES (corp-wide): 57MM **Privately Held**
WEB: www.mertik.net
SIC: 3621 3823 3625 3494 Motors & generators; industrial instrmnts msrmnt display/control process variable; relays & industrial controls; valves & pipe fittings
PA: Maxitrol Company
23555 Telegraph Rd
Southfield MI 48033
248 356-1400

(G-1770)
MIDWEST PANEL SYSTEMS INC
Also Called: Great Lakes Insulspan
9012 E Us Highway 223 (49228-9665)
P.O. Box 38 (49228-0038)
PHONE..................517 486-4844
Frank B Baker, *President*
EMP: 14 EST: 1990
SQ FT: 32,000
SALES (est): 300.2K **Privately Held**
SIC: 2452 1521 2439 2435 Panels & sections, prefabricated, wood; single-family housing construction; structural wood members; hardwood veneer & plywood

(G-1771)
NORTON EQUIPMENT CORPORATION (PA)
203 E Adrian St (49228-1301)
P.O. Box 68 (49228-0068)
PHONE..................517 486-2113
Steven D Cantrell, *President*
H Dwayne Cantrell, *Chairman*
C Sue Cantrell, *Corp Secy*
Scott Cantrell, *Vice Pres*
EMP: 4 EST: 1935
SQ FT: 22,000
SALES (est): 2.6MM **Privately Held**
WEB: www.nortonequipmentcorp.us
SIC: 3356 Magnesium & magnesium alloy bars, sheets, shapes, etc.

(G-1772)
PEARSON PRECAST CONCRETE PDTS
7951 E Us Highway 223 (49228-9664)
PHONE..................517 486-4060
Jamie Pearson, *President*
Dawn Pearson, *Corp Secy*
EMP: 5 **Privately Held**
WEB: www.pearsonprecast.com
SIC: 3281 3272 Burial vaults, stone; concrete products

(G-1773)
PFB MANUFACTURING LLC
Also Called: Insulspan
9012 E Us Highway 223 (49228-9665)
P.O. Box 38 (49228-0038)
PHONE..................517 486-4844
Stephen Munn, *General Mgr*
Keith Nelson, *Manager*
Kym Hurst, *Admin Sec*
EMP: 5 EST: 2004
SALES (est): 4.7MM
SALES (corp-wide): 62.9MM **Privately Held**
WEB: www.insulspan.com
SIC: 2899 5085 Insulating compounds; plastic pallets
PA: Pfb America Corporation
711 E Broadway Ave
Meridian ID 83642
208 887-1020

(G-1774)
RESCAR INC
11440 Cemetery Rd (49228)
P.O. Box 12, Riga (49276-0012)
PHONE..................517 486-3130
EMP: 9 EST: 2008
SALES (est): 136.6K **Privately Held**
WEB: www.rescar.com
SIC: 3743 Railroad equipment

(G-1775)
RIVER RAISIN PUBLICATIONS
Also Called: Advance Publishing & Printing
121 Newspaper St (49228-1248)
PHONE..................517 486-2400
Marcia Loder, *President*
EMP: 9 EST: 1996
SALES (est): 927.4K **Privately Held**
WEB: www.blissfieldadvance.com
SIC: 2711 Newspapers, publishing & printing

(G-1776)
RIVERBEND TIMBER FRAMING INC
9012 E Us Highway 223 (49228-9665)
P.O. Box 26 (49228-0026)
PHONE..................517 486-3629
Frank B Baker, *CEO*
Andrew Gitersonke, *Sales Staff*
EMP: 45 EST: 1980
SQ FT: 14,500
SALES (est): 6.3MM
SALES (corp-wide): 31.5MM **Privately Held**
WEB: www.riverbendtf.com
SIC: 2452 1521 2439 2421 Log cabins, prefabricated, wood; single-family housing construction; structural wood members; sawmills & planing mills, general
PA: Plasti-Fab Ltd
300-2891 Sunridge Way Ne
Calgary AB T1Y 7
403 569-4300

(G-1777)
TEC-OPTION INC
334 Sherman St (49228-1174)
PHONE..................517 486-6055
Bryan W Domschot, *President*
Kirk Chwialkowski, *Engineer*
▲ EMP: 11 EST: 1996
SQ FT: 6,800
SALES (est): 2.6MM **Privately Held**
WEB: www.tec-option.com
SIC: 7692 3599 Welding repair; amusement park equipment

(G-1778)
THERMALFAB PRODUCTS INC
10005 E Us Highway 223 (49228-9528)
P.O. Box 157 (49228-0157)
PHONE..................517 486-2073
Bill Bernard, *President*
EMP: 13 EST: 1997
SALES (est): 1MM **Privately Held**
SIC: 3567 Industrial furnaces & ovens

(G-1779)
UCKELE HEALTH AND NUTRITION (PA)
Also Called: Uckele Health & Nutrition
5600 Silberhorn Hwy (49228-9529)
P.O. Box 160 (49228-0160)
PHONE..................800 248-0330
Mike Uckele, *CEO*
Kevin Isley, *Vice Pres*
Jack Grogan, *Maint Spvr*
Jennifer Dempsey, *Purch Mgr*
Chris Drage, *VP Bus Dvlpt*
◆ EMP: 150 EST: 1962
SQ FT: 14,000
SALES (est): 35.6MM **Privately Held**
WEB: www.uckele.com
SIC: 2834 Pharmaceutical preparations

Bloomfield
Oakland County

(G-1780)
AAA LANGUAGE SERVICES
Also Called: Iterotext
1573 S Telegraph Rd (48302-0048)
PHONE..................248 239-1138
EMP: 12 EST: 1973
SQ FT: 3,000
SALES: 1.5MM **Privately Held**
SIC: 7389 2791 Business Services Typesetting Services

(G-1781)
BEDNARSH MRRIS JWLY DESIGN MFG
Also Called: M B Jewelry Design & Mfg
6600 Telegraph Rd (48301-3012)
PHONE..................248 671-0087
Morris Bednarsh, *President*
Anthony Ferrari, *Vice Pres*
Christopher Schornack, *Vice Pres*

Bloomfield - Oakland County

Marcia Bednarsh, *Treasurer*
EMP: 11 **EST:** 1975
SQ FT: 2,100
SALES (est): 689.2K **Privately Held**
WEB: www.mbjewelrydesign.com
SIC: 5944 3911 Jewelry, precious stones & precious metals; jewelry apparel

(G-1782)
KAYAYAN HAYK JEWELRY MFG CO (PA)
Also Called: J.L. McHael Hayk Kyyan Jwelers
869 W Long Lake Rd (48302-2011)
PHONE 248 626-3060
Hayk Kayayan, *President*
Harriet Kayayan, *Corp Secy*
EMP: 20 **EST:** 1970
SQ FT: 5,400
SALES (est): 1MM **Privately Held**
SIC: 3911 7631 5944 Jewelry, precious metal; jewelry repair services; jewelry, precious stones & precious metals

(G-1783)
LIGHTWORKS MAGAZINE INC
6966 Holiday Dr (48301-3754)
P.O. Box 1202, Birmingham (48012-1202)
PHONE 248 626-8026
Charlton Burch, *Principal*
EMP: 5 **EST:** 2001
SALES (est): 141.3K **Privately Held**
WEB: www.lightworks-mag.tumblr.com
SIC: 2721 Periodicals

(G-1784)
REZOOP LLC
1270 Romney Rd (48304-1537)
PHONE 248 952-8070
Rohit Singla,
Roli Rani Agrawal,
EMP: 4
SQ FT: 2,000
SALES (est): 234.3K **Privately Held**
WEB: www.rezoop.com
SIC: 7372 Application computer software

(G-1785)
SPECIFICATIONS SERVICE COMPANY
Also Called: Specs Office Supply
5444 Saint Martins Ct (48302-2549)
PHONE 248 353-0244
Richard Apakarien, *Owner*
Aruther Apaskarien, *Vice Pres*
EMP: 5 **EST:** 1938
SQ FT: 7,000
SALES (est): 134.2K **Privately Held**
SIC: 5943 7334 2752 Office forms & supplies; photocopying & duplicating services; commercial printing, offset

(G-1786)
WARD-WILLISTON COMPANY (PA)
36700 Woodward Ave # 101 (48304-0929)
PHONE 248 594-6622
Thomas Cunnington, *CEO*
James Con, *President*
Mr Laurie Cunnington, *President*
Nathan Conway, *COO*
Mr Rodney Conway, *Vice Pres*
EMP: 57 **EST:** 1952
SALES (est): 156.7K **Privately Held**
WEB: www.wardwilliston.com
SIC: 1382 Oil & gas exploration services

Bloomfield Hills
Oakland County

(G-1787)
313 CERTIFIED LLC
Also Called: 313certified
6379 Muirfield Dr (48301-1571)
PHONE 248 915-8419
EMP: 4 **EST:** 2013
SALES (est): 238.8K **Privately Held**
SIC: 7372 Prepackaged Software Services

(G-1788)
A PLUS ASPHALT LLC
41000 Woodward Ave (48304-5130)
PHONE 888 754-1125
EMP: 28

SALES (est): 1.4MM **Privately Held**
SIC: 2951 Mfg Asphalt Mixtures/Blocks

(G-1789)
A1 NOISE CONTROL
4578 Walden Dr (48301-1149)
PHONE 248 538-7585
Dr Prakash Thawani, *Principal*
EMP: 6 **EST:** 2010
SALES (est): 97.8K **Privately Held**
SIC: 3625 Noise control equipment

(G-1790)
ACCESSIBLE INFORMATION LLC
124 N Berkshire Rd (48302-0402)
PHONE 248 338-4928
Daniel Mc Clure, *Principal*
EMP: 4 **EST:** 1998
SALES (est): 250.5K **Privately Held**
SIC: 7372 Prepackaged software

(G-1791)
ACME MILLS COMPANY
Also Called: Great Lakes Filter
33 Bloomfield Hills Pkwy (48304-2944)
PHONE 800 521-8585
David Terry, *Manager*
EMP: 5
SALES (corp-wide): 75.1MM **Privately Held**
WEB: www.acmemills.com
SIC: 3569 Filters
PA: Acme Mills Company
    33 Blmfeld Hlls Pkwy Ste
    Bloomfield Hills MI 48304
    248 203-2000

(G-1792)
ADJUSTABLE LOCKING TECH LLC
Also Called: Alt
6632 Telegraph Rd Ste 298 (48301-3012)
PHONE 248 443-9664
John K Scheer Sr, *CEO*
Bill Sbordon, *President*
EMP: 9 **EST:** 1997
SALES (est): 311.3K **Privately Held**
WEB: www.adjustablelockingtech.com
SIC: 3429 Locks or lock sets

(G-1793)
AFJ WOODHAVEN LLC
4036 Telegraph Rd Ste 201 (48302-2073)
PHONE 248 593-6200
Arkan Jonna,
EMP: 6 **EST:** 2004
SALES (est): 382.6K **Privately Held**
SIC: 2752 Advertising posters, lithographed

(G-1794)
AJM PACKAGING CORPORATION (PA)
Also Called: A J M
E-4111 Andover Rd (48302)
PHONE 248 901-0040
Robert Epstein, *President*
Johnathan Branson, *Vice Pres*
John Nilles, *Plant Mgr*
Gary Desjardins, *Prdtn Mgr*
Brett Sigurdson, *Purch Mgr*
▲ **EMP:** 60 **EST:** 1949
SQ FT: 12,000
SALES (est): 419.9MM **Privately Held**
WEB: www.ajmpack.com
SIC: 2656 2674 Plates, paper: made from purchased material; paper bags: made from purchased materials

(G-1795)
AL BO CO
4115 Franklin Rd (48302-1838)
PHONE 248 240-9155
Alan Bodrie, *Principal*
EMP: 5 **EST:** 2016
SALES (est): 152.7K **Privately Held**
WEB: www.alboco.us
SIC: 3993 Signs & advertising specialties

(G-1796)
AMERICAN CONTROLS INC
3485 Bradway Blvd (48301-2407)
PHONE 248 476-0663
Ted Warren, *General Mgr*

Bill Berg, *Manager*
Denise Brown, *Manager*
EMP: 7 **EST:** 1990
SALES (est): 380.7K **Privately Held**
WEB: www.american-controls.com
SIC: 3822 Auto controls regulating residntl & coml environmt & applncs

(G-1797)
AMYS BAKING COMPANY
6399 Muirfield Dr (48301-1571)
PHONE 313 530-9694
Amy Baker, *Principal*
EMP: 5 **EST:** 2011
SALES (est): 80.9K **Privately Held**
SIC: 2051 Bread, cake & related products

(G-1798)
ANN WILLIAMS GROUP LLC
784 Industrial Ct (48302-0380)
PHONE 248 977-5831
Darby Zahradnik, *Natl Sales Mgr*
Sheila Wright, *Mng Member*
Dan Wright, *Mng Member*
EMP: 8 **EST:** 2007
SALES (est): 2MM
SALES (corp-wide): 30.1MM **Privately Held**
WEB: www.annwilliamsgroup.com
SIC: 3944 Games, toys & children's vehicles
PA: Playmonster Llc
    1400 E Inman Pkwy
    Beloit WI 53511
    608 362-6896

(G-1799)
ARBOR PLASTIC TECHNOLOGIES LLC
40900 Woodward Ave # 275 (48304-5120)
PHONE 734 678-5765
Michael Mann, *Opers Staff*
J James Caton,
◆ **EMP:** 10 **EST:** 2007
SALES (est): 1MM **Privately Held**
WEB: www.arborplastic.com
SIC: 2821 Plastics materials & resins

(G-1800)
ARCH CUTTING TOOLS LLC (PA)
2600 S Telegraph Rd (48302-0953)
PHONE 734 266-6900
Eli Crotzer, *CEO*
EMP: 178 **EST:** 2013
SALES (est): 35.8MM **Privately Held**
WEB: www.archcuttingtools.com
SIC: 3399 3545 3699 3542 Metal fasteners; cutting tools for machine tools; laser systems & equipment; marking machines

(G-1801)
ARCH PRECISION COMPONENTS (DH)
2600 S Telg Rd Ste 180 (48302)
PHONE 866 935-5771
Elijah Crotzer, *CEO*
EMP: 75 **EST:** 2019
SALES (est): 414MM
SALES (corp-wide): 1.5B **Privately Held**
WEB: www.archglobalprecision.com
SIC: 3599 Machine shop, jobbing & repair
HQ: Arch Global Holdings, Llc
    2600 S Telg Rd Ste 180
    Bloomfield Hills MI 48302
    734 266-6900

(G-1802)
B4 SPORTS INC
Also Called: National Flag Football
2055 Franklin Rd (48302-0327)
PHONE 248 454-9700
Kathleen Forsyth, *Principal*
Angela Smith, *Opers Staff*
Catey Avila, *Manager*
James Dugan, *Manager*
Kimberly Liepshutz, *Manager*
EMP: 27 **EST:** 2014
SALES (est): 3.6MM **Privately Held**
WEB: www.nationalflagfootball.com
SIC: 3949 Balls: baseball, football, basketball, etc.

(G-1803)
BBCM INC
1015 Golf Dr (48302-0108)
PHONE 248 410-2528
William Massie, *President*
EMP: 4 **EST:** 2006
SALES (est): 178.7K **Privately Held**
SIC: 7389 3577 Design services; computer peripheral equipment

(G-1804)
BOB ALLISON ENTERPRISES
Also Called: Ask Your Neighbor
6560 Red Maple Ln (48301-3224)
PHONE 248 540-8467
Robert A Allasee, *President*
Margaret Allesee, *Admin Sec*
EMP: 5 **EST:** 1978
SALES (est): 395.5K **Privately Held**
SIC: 3663 7389 4832 2721 Radio & TV communications equipment; promoters of shows & exhibitions; radio broadcasting stations; periodicals

(G-1805)
BOEING COMPANY
6001 N Adams Rd Ste 105 (48304-1575)
PHONE 248 258-7191
Lewis Seno, *Manager*
EMP: 4
SALES (corp-wide): 58.1B **Publicly Held**
WEB: www.boeing.com
SIC: 3721 Aircraft
PA: The Boeing Company
    100 N Riverside Plz
    Chicago IL 60606
    312 544-2000

(G-1806)
BREDE INC
378 S Cranbrook Rd (48301-3417)
PHONE 313 273-1079
Michael Brede, *President*
EMP: 6 **EST:** 1923
SALES (est): 960.6K **Privately Held**
WEB: www.bredefoods.com
SIC: 2035 Horseradish, prepared

(G-1807)
BROTHER MIKE PUBG & MUS CO LLC
4886 Beacon Hill Dr (48301-3500)
PHONE 313 506-8866
Michael L McNeal, *Principal*
EMP: 5 **EST:** 2016
SALES (est): 89.5K **Privately Held**
SIC: 2741 Miscellaneous publishing

(G-1808)
COEUS LLC
1605 S Telegraph Rd (48302-0044)
PHONE 248 564-1958
Brian Slaght, *Principal*
EMP: 10 **EST:** 2017
SALES (est): 376.2K **Privately Held**
SIC: 7371 7372 Computer software development & applications; business oriented computer software

(G-1809)
COLEMAN BOWMAN & ASSOCIATES
Also Called: Coleman Specialty Products
3535 Wooddale Ct (48301-2460)
PHONE 248 642-8221
Gordon Coleman, *President*
Catherine Coleman, *Treasurer*
Richard Poling, *Admin Sec*
EMP: 6 **EST:** 1994
SQ FT: 1,500
SALES (est): 5MM **Privately Held**
SIC: 5085 3565 Industrial supplies; packaging machinery

(G-1810)
CONCORD INDUSTRIAL CORPORATION
36400 Woodward Ave # 110 (48304-0912)
P.O. Box 217, Birmingham (48012-0217)
PHONE 248 646-9225
EMP: 4
SQ FT: 1,000
SALES (est): 390K **Privately Held**
SIC: 3089 Mfg Plastic Products

▲ = Import ▼ = Export
◆ = Import/Export

GEOGRAPHIC SECTION — Bloomfield Hills - Oakland County (G-1840)

(G-1811)
DAILY OAKLAND PRESS (DH)
38500 Woodward Ave # 100 (48304-5048)
P.O. Box 436009, Pontiac (48343-6009)
PHONE..................................248 332-8181
Jerry Bammel, *President*
Greg Mazanec, *Publisher*
Steve Frye, *Editor*
Jeff Kuehn, *Editor*
Matt Mowery, *Editor*
EMP: 365 EST: 1844
SALES (est): 54.8MM
SALES (corp-wide): 274.1MM **Privately Held**
WEB: www.theoaklandpress.com
SIC: **2711** 2791 2752 Newspapers, publishing & printing; typesetting; commercial printing, lithographic
HQ: 21st Century Newspapers, Inc.
  6250 Metropolitan Pkwy
  Sterling Heights MI 48312
  586 469-4510

(G-1812)
DELOREAN AEROSPACE LLC
2779 Amberly Rd (48301-2658)
PHONE..................................248 752-2380
Paul Delorean,
EMP: 6 EST: 2016
SALES (est): 156.5K **Privately Held**
WEB: www.deloreanaerospace.com
SIC: **3721** Aircraft

(G-1813)
DELOREAN ASSOCIATES INC
Also Called: Home & Garden Concepts
2779 Amberly Rd (48301-2658)
PHONE..................................248 646-1930
Jack De Lorean, *President*
Jack Z De Lorean, *Agent*
EMP: 6 EST: 1992
SQ FT: 3,400
SALES (est): 530K **Privately Held**
SIC: **8711** 3631 Designing: ship, boat, machine & product; household cooking equipment

(G-1814)
DIMENSION MACHINE TECH LLC
18815 Kelly Ct (48304)
PHONE..................................586 649-4747
Steve Davis,
James Russell,
EMP: 11 EST: 2014
SQ FT: 10,000
SALES (est): 1MM **Privately Held**
SIC: **7699** 3451 3599 3535 Industrial machinery & equipment repair; screw machine products; machine shop, jobbing & repair; robotic conveyors

(G-1815)
DOLL FACE CHEF LLC
41000 Woodward Ave # 350 (48304-5130)
P.O. Box 811, Royal Oak (48068-0811)
PHONE..................................248 495-8280
EMP: 5
SALES (est): 229.5K **Privately Held**
SIC: **2051** Bread, Cake, And Related Products

(G-1816)
DUPEARL TECHNOLOGY LLC
120 Hadsell Dr (48302-0408)
PHONE..................................248 390-9609
Theresa Varickattu, *CEO*
James George, *Chairman*
John Vari, *Vice Pres*
EMP: 9 EST: 1999
SALES (est): 258.6K **Privately Held**
SIC: **3679** 5084 7371 3089 Harness assemblies for electronic use: wire or cable; industrial machinery & equipment; computer software systems analysis & design, custom; automotive parts, plastic; printed circuit boards

(G-1817)
DVINE COOKIES
4467 Stony River Dr (48301-3655)
PHONE..................................248 417-7850
Rebecca Abel, *CEO*
Rebecca R Abel, *Mng Member*
EMP: 20 EST: 2017
SALES (est): 1.3MM **Privately Held**
WEB: www.dvinecookies.com
SIC: **2052** Bakery products, dry

(G-1818)
ELITE BUS SVCS EXEC STFFING IN
Also Called: Alure International
2510 S Telg Rd Ste L280 (48302)
PHONE..................................734 956-4550
Caree J Eason, *CEO*
EMP: 6 EST: 2003
SQ FT: 1,800
SALES (est): 133.8K **Privately Held**
SIC: **4812** 5999 7389 2759 Cellular telephone services; mobile telephones & equipment; telephone services; commercial printing

(G-1819)
ERVINS GROUP LLC (PA)
550 Hulet Dr Ste 103 (48302-0322)
PHONE..................................248 203-2000
Karol Ervins, *President*
EMP: 23 EST: 1996
SQ FT: 30,000
SALES (est): 2MM **Privately Held**
WEB: www.ervinsgroup.com
SIC: **8742** 3714 3429 Management consulting services; motor vehicle parts & accessories; manufactured hardware (general)

(G-1820)
EUTECTIC ENGINEERING CO INC
817 Rock Spring Rd (48304-3141)
PHONE..................................313 892-2248
Charles E Baer, *President*
Michael Eberle, *Vice Pres*
Maryanne Pruss, *Plant Mgr*
Dennis Arwood, *QC Mgr*
Tanya Royall, *Accountant*
EMP: 45 EST: 1961
SQ FT: 50,000
SALES (est): 2.7MM **Privately Held**
SIC: **3341** 3324 Secondary nonferrous metals; steel investment foundries

(G-1821)
FI PUBLISHING
3883 Telegraph Rd (48302-1476)
PHONE..................................248 282-9905
Steve Case, *Principal*
EMP: 6 EST: 2007
SALES (est): 123.8K **Privately Held**
SIC: **2741** Miscellaneous publishing

(G-1822)
GLAXOSMITHKLINE LLC
721 Parkman Dr (48304-2449)
PHONE..................................248 561-3022
EMP: 4
SALES (corp-wide): 45.3B **Privately Held**
WEB: www.us.gsk.com
SIC: **2834** Pharmaceutical preparations
HQ: Glaxosmithkline Llc
  5 Crescent Dr
  Philadelphia PA 19102
  215 751-4000

(G-1823)
GLOBAL ELECTRONICS LIMITED
2075 Franklin Rd (48302-0303)
PHONE..................................248 353-0100
Michael M Bahn, *CEO*
Mary C Bahn, *President*
Robert Wiebe, *Vice Pres*
EMP: 18 EST: 1997
SALES (est): 1.4MM **Privately Held**
WEB: www.geltd.net
SIC: **3569** 3825 Robots, assembly line: industrial & commercial; instruments to measure electricity

(G-1824)
GREAT LAKES POT PIES LLC
460 Laurelwood Ct (48302-1151)
PHONE..................................248 266-1160
Johanna S Teitelbaum,
EMP: 8 EST: 2015
SALES (est): 106.2K **Privately Held**
WEB: www.greatlakespotpies.com
SIC: **2051** Pies, bakery: except frozen

(G-1825)
HAARTZ CORPORATION
40950 Woodward Ave # 150 (48304-5125)
PHONE..................................248 646-8200
Tim Jackson, *Manager*
Matt Lark, *Executive*
Keith Loebs, *Executive*
EMP: 6
SALES (corp-wide): 120.9MM **Privately Held**
WEB: www.haartz.com
SIC: **2295** 5131 Resin or plastic coated fabrics; piece goods & notions
PA: The Haartz Corporation
  87 Hayward Rd
  Acton MA 01720
  978 264-2600

(G-1826)
HAMBLIN COMPANY
40900 Woodward Ave # 111 (48304-5116)
PHONE..................................517 423-7491
Raymond J Hamblin, *President*
Madlyn C Hamblin, *Vice Pres*
EMP: 40 EST: 1974
SALES (est): 4MM **Privately Held**
WEB: www.hamblincompany.com
SIC: **2752** 2796 2789 2759 Commercial printing, offset; platemaking services; bookbinding & related work; commercial printing; die-cut paper & board

(G-1827)
HAROLD G SCHAEVITZ INDS LLC
Also Called: Sensor Connection, The
42690 Woodward Ave # 200 (48304-5062)
PHONE..................................248 636-1515
Harold Schaevitz, *President*
Neill Murphy,
EMP: 8 EST: 2006
SALES (est): 2.1MM **Privately Held**
WEB: www.thesensorconnection.com
SIC: **3699** 3625 Electrical equipment & supplies; positioning controls, electric

(G-1828)
HMS MFG CO
1863 Long Pointe Dr (48302-0740)
PHONE..................................248 740-7040
Hugh Sofy, *Branch Mgr*
EMP: 7
SALES (corp-wide): 33.8MM **Privately Held**
WEB: www.hmsmfg.com
SIC: **3089** Injection molded finished plastic products
PA: Hms Mfg. Co.
  1230 E Big Beaver Rd
  Troy MI 48083
  248 689-3232

(G-1829)
HOUSE OF HERO LLC
7335 Deep Run Apt 513 (48301-3831)
PHONE..................................248 260-8300
Keith Young,
EMP: 5 EST: 2019
SALES (est): 100K **Privately Held**
SIC: **2741** Miscellaneous publishing

(G-1830)
LIFETIME COMPANY
2275 Cameo Lake Ct (48302-1605)
PHONE..................................248 862-2578
EMP: 5 EST: 2018
SALES (est): 134.8K **Privately Held**
WEB: www.lifetime.life
SIC: **2431** Millwork

(G-1831)
LIGHT METAL FORMING CORP
4397 Stony River Dr (48301-3652)
PHONE..................................248 851-3984
EMP: 17
SALES (est): 1.7MM **Privately Held**
SIC: **3086** Mfg Plastic Foam Products

(G-1832)
LSD INVESTMENTS INC
2350 Franklin Rd Ste 115 (48302-0337)
PHONE..................................248 333-9085
Tim Gronau, *Sales Staff*
Chris Caswell, *Branch Mgr*
EMP: 4 **Privately Held**
WEB: www.windowanddoorcenter.com
SIC: **5211** 2431 1751 Doors, storm: wood or metal; doors & door parts & trim, wood; window & door (prefabricated) installation
PA: Lsd Investments, Inc.
  3605 S Huron Rd
  Bay City MI
  989 684-9811

(G-1833)
LUMA LASER AND MEDI SPA
1920 S Telegraph Rd (48302-0245)
PHONE..................................248 817-5499
EMP: 5 EST: 2014
SALES (est): 152.8K **Privately Held**
WEB: www.lumalasermedspa.com
SIC: **3842** 7231 8011 Cosmetic restorations; cosmetologist; plastic surgeon

(G-1834)
LYNN SHALER FINE PRINTS LLC
4621 Kensington Rd (48304-3229)
PHONE..................................248 644-5148
Arlene B Shaler, *Agent*
EMP: 4 EST: 2016
SALES (est): 70.5K **Privately Held**
SIC: **2752** Commercial printing, lithographic

(G-1835)
MAYNE-MC KENNEY INC
100 W Long Lake Rd # 220 (48304-2774)
PHONE..................................248 258-0300
Edward F Mayne Jr, *President*
Edward Gordon, *Vice Pres*
Jeff Gates, *Accounts Mgr*
Jack Wilson, *Accounts Mgr*
Grace Florek, *Admin Sec*
EMP: 33 EST: 1948
SQ FT: 5,150
SALES (est): 1.2MM **Privately Held**
SIC: **3714** Motor vehicle parts & accessories

(G-1836)
MEDICAL INFRMTICS SLUTIONS LLC
7285 Cathedral Dr (48301-3733)
PHONE..................................248 851-3124
Gerald W Brouhard, *President*
EMP: 4 EST: 1997
SALES (est): 484.8K **Privately Held**
SIC: **8742** 3825 Hospital & health services consultant; network analyzers

(G-1837)
MICROMET CORP
3790 Burning Tree Dr (48302-1533)
PHONE..................................231 885-1047
Fax: 231 761-7106
EMP: 5
SQ FT: 2,000
SALES (est): 470K **Privately Held**
SIC: **3812** Mfg Search/Navigation Equipment

(G-1838)
MICROX LABS INC
565 Foxhall Ct (48304-1815)
PHONE..................................248 318-3548
L Vishwanathan, *CEO*
EMP: 5 EST: 2019
SALES (est): 272.5K **Privately Held**
WEB: www.microxlabs.com
SIC: **2835** In vitro diagnostics

(G-1839)
MODERN MONOGRAM
805 S Pemberton Rd (48302-1444)
PHONE..................................248 792-6266
EMP: 4 EST: 2010
SALES (est): 71.7K **Privately Held**
SIC: **3552** Embroidery machines

(G-1840)
MOORE FLAME CUTTING CO
1022 Top View Rd (48304-3160)
PHONE..................................586 978-1090
Gary Nadlicki, *President*
M Kathryn Finkbeiner-Nadlicki, *Corp Secy*
EMP: 16 EST: 1994
SQ FT: 29,000
SALES (est): 1MM **Privately Held**
SIC: **3443** 3441 Plate work for the metalworking trade; fabricated structural metal

Bloomfield Hills - Oakland County (G-1841)

(G-1841)
MOTOR CITY HOME INC
4537 Wagon Wheel Dr (48301-1139)
PHONE..................................248 562-7296
Ron Rocz, *Principal*
EMP: 4 **EST:** 2014
SALES (est): 91.9K **Privately Held**
SIC: 3716 Motor homes

(G-1842)
N A VISSCHER-CARAVELLE INC
2525 S Telg Rd Ste 302 (48302)
PHONE..................................248 851-9800
Robert Meek, *President*
▲ **EMP:** 9 **EST:** 2001
SALES (est): 13MM
SALES (corp-wide): 183.7K **Privately Held**
WEB: www.visscher-caravelle.com
SIC: 2273 Mats & matting
HQ: Visscher Caravelle Holding B.V.
Sisalstraat 85
Genemuiden 8281
383 855-015

(G-1843)
NANOTEX LLC (DH)
Also Called: Nano-Tex
38500 Woodward Ave # 201 (48304-5047)
PHONE..................................248 855-6000
Lance Keziah,
EMP: 1 **EST:** 2013
SALES (est): 1MM
SALES (corp-wide): 8.1B **Publicly Held**
WEB: www.nanotex.com
SIC: 2299 2297 Fabrics: linen, jute, hemp, ramie; nonwoven fabrics

(G-1844)
NOVATION ANALYTICS LLC
300 E Long Lake Rd # 200 (48304-2376)
PHONE..................................313 910-3280
Peter Varma, *Associate Dir*
Gregory M Pannone,
Heidi A Schroeder,
Michael F Shields,
EMP: 9 **EST:** 2014 **Privately Held**
SIC: 7372 7389 Application computer software; brokers' services

(G-1845)
O2/SPECIALTY MFG HOLDINGS LLC (PA)
40900 Woodward Ave # 130 (48304-5115)
PHONE..................................248 554-4228
EMP: 5
SALES (est): 15.9MM **Privately Held**
SIC: 3494 Holding Company For Valve Manufacturing Business

(G-1846)
OVSHINSKY TECHNOLOGIES LLC
2550 S Telg Rd Ste 106 (48302)
PHONE..................................248 752-2344
Guy Wicker, *Partner*
EMP: 4 **EST:** 2013
SALES (est): 177.6K **Privately Held**
WEB: www.ovshinskyinnovation.com
SIC: 8731 3674 3559 Natural resource research; solar cells; semiconductor manufacturing machinery

(G-1847)
PARISH PUBLICATIONS
63 Barden Ct (48304-2703)
PHONE..................................248 613-2384
Richard Meurer, *Principal*
EMP: 4 **EST:** 2010
SALES (est): 58K **Privately Held**
SIC: 2741 Miscellaneous publishing

(G-1848)
PCS PHARMACEUTICALS LLC
Also Called: Pcs Pharmacy
41000 Woodward Ave # 350 (48304-5130)
PHONE..................................248 289-7054
Kamil Saba, *Principal*
EMP: 6 **EST:** 2016
SALES (est): 545.3K **Privately Held**
SIC: 2834 Drugs affecting neoplasms & endocrine systems

(G-1849)
PENSKE COMPANY LLC (HQ)
2555 S Telegraph Rd (48302-0974)
PHONE..................................248 648-2000
Roger S Penske, *Mng Member*
Cheryl Wilson, *Analyst*
◆ **EMP:** 1 **EST:** 2000
SALES (est): 189.4MM
SALES (corp-wide): 5.1B **Privately Held**
WEB: www.penske.com
SIC: 3647 Vehicular lighting equipment
PA: Penske Corporation
2555 S Telegraph Rd
Bloomfield Hills MI 48302
248 648-2000

(G-1850)
PENZO AMERICA INC
6335 Thorncrest Dr (48301-1710)
PHONE..................................248 723-0802
Penelope A Vincent, *President*
Gerardus B Norrdanus, *Vice Pres*
EMP: 4 **EST:** 1999
SALES (est): 247.2K **Privately Held**
WEB: www.penzo.com
SIC: 3269 5023 Art & ornamental ware, pottery; pottery

(G-1851)
PERFECT EXPRESSIONS
3643 W Maple Rd (48301-3376)
PHONE..................................248 640-1287
Brian Klayman, *Principal*
EMP: 4 **EST:** 2011
SALES (est): 315.2K **Privately Held**
WEB: www.perfecttradingco.com
SIC: 3949 Camping equipment & supplies

(G-1852)
PHYSICIANS COMPOUNDING PHRM
1900 S Telg Rd Ste 102 (48302)
PHONE..................................248 758-9100
Debbie Vinuya, *President*
Jerrin Raehtz, *Vice Pres*
EMP: 4 **EST:** 2004
SALES (est): 750K **Privately Held**
WEB: www.physicianscompoundingpharmacy.com
SIC: 2834 Druggists' preparations (pharmaceuticals)

(G-1853)
PROTEIN PROCUREMENT SVCS INC (PA)
1750 S Telg Rd Ste 310 (48302)
PHONE..................................248 738-7970
Keith Jahnke, *CEO*
Claudia Hershey, *President*
Galina Martin, *Manager*
EMP: 4 **EST:** 2007
SQ FT: 4,800
SALES (est): 43MM **Privately Held**
WEB: www.arkkfood.com
SIC: 2824 5147 Protein fibers; meats & meat products

(G-1854)
REKO INTERNATIONAL HOLDINGS (HQ)
6001 N Adams Rd Ste 251 (48304-1547)
PHONE..................................519 737-6974
Diane St John, *President*
EMP: 2 **EST:** 1995
SALES (est): 19.2MM
SALES (corp-wide): 31.7MM **Privately Held**
WEB: www.rekointl.com
SIC: 5084 3465 Industrial machinery & equipment; automotive stampings
PA: Reko International Group Inc
469 Silver Creek Industrial Dr
Windsor ON N8N 4
519 727-3287

(G-1855)
REVEAL PUBLISHING LLC
2749 Pendleton Dr (48304-1644)
PHONE..................................248 798-3440
EMP: 5 **EST:** 2018
SALES (est): 121.5K **Privately Held**
SIC: 2741 Miscellaneous publishing

(G-1856)
RGI BRANDS LLC (PA)
Also Called: Dragon Bleu USA
3950 Wabeek Lake Dr E (48301-1262)
PHONE..................................312 253-7400
Jared Rapp, *Mng Member*
▲ **EMP:** 10 **EST:** 2008
SQ FT: 14,000
SALES (est): 7MM **Privately Held**
SIC: 2085 5182 Bourbon whiskey; cocktails, alcoholic; premixed

(G-1857)
RIEKE-ARMINAK CORP
39400 Woodward Ave # 130 (48304-5150)
PHONE..................................248 631-5450
EMP: 44 **EST:** 2012
SALES (est): 2.2MM
SALES (corp-wide): 769.9MM **Publicly Held**
WEB: www.trimascorp.com
SIC: 3799 3714 Trailer hitches; motor vehicle parts & accessories
PA: Trimas Corporation
38505 Woodward Ave # 200
Bloomfield Hills MI 48304
248 631-5450

(G-1858)
ROCK INDUSTRIES INC (PA)
Also Called: Rock Construction
6125 Old Orchard Dr (48301-1472)
PHONE..................................248 338-2800
Robert Bruza, *President*
EMP: 35 **EST:** 1999
SALES (est): 5.9MM **Privately Held**
WEB: www.buildwithrock.com
SIC: 1389 1799 5085 8741 Construction, repair & dismantling services; coating, caulking & weather, water & fireproofing; industrial supplies; construction management; institutional building construction

(G-1859)
ROSE MOBILE COMPUTER REPR LLC
Also Called: Rose Computer Consulting
4881 Old Post Ct (48301-3554)
PHONE..................................248 653-0865
Adam Rosenman, *CEO*
EMP: 10 **EST:** 2012
SALES (est): 617.1K **Privately Held**
WEB: www.rosemobilecomputerrepair.com
SIC: 7378 7372 7379 Computer maintenance & repair; application computer software; computer related consulting services

(G-1860)
SAWTELLE INDUSTRIES LLC
1158 Ardmoor Dr (48301-2156)
PHONE..................................248 645-1869
Darris Sawtelle, *Principal*
EMP: 4 **EST:** 2017
SALES (est): 52.8K **Privately Held**
SIC: 3999 Manufacturing industries

(G-1861)
SCHMALTZ HSPTLITY WESTLAND LLC
6400 Telg Rd Ste 2000 (48301)
PHONE..................................734 728-6170
Zack Sklar, *Manager*
EMP: 5 **EST:** 2016
SALES (est): 117K **Privately Held**
SIC: 2599 Bar, restaurant & cafeteria furniture

(G-1862)
STELLAR FORGE PRODUCTS INC (PA)
6651 Timber Ridge Dr (48301-3063)
PHONE..................................313 535-7631
Diran D Arslanian, *President*
Anto Arslanian, *Vice Pres*
Bruce D Franz, *Admin Sec*
▲ **EMP:** 12 **EST:** 1988
SALES (est): 2MM **Privately Held**
WEB: www.stellarforgeproducts.com
SIC: 3544 Special dies & tools

(G-1863)
SUPERIOR POLYOLEFIN FILMS INC
465 Fox River Dr (48304-1009)
PHONE..................................248 334-8074
Frank Baker Jr, *Partner*
Francis E Baker Sr, *Partner*
EMP: 5 **EST:** 1995
SALES (est): 437.9K **Privately Held**
SIC: 2673 Plastic & pliofilm bags

(G-1864)
TEMPERFORM CORP
1975 Tuckaway Dr (48302-1779)
PHONE..................................248 851-9611
A Bartoletto, *Principal*
EMP: 10 **EST:** 2015
SALES (est): 249.3K **Privately Held**
WEB: www.temperform.com
SIC: 3325 Steel foundries

(G-1865)
TESLIR LLC
100 W Long Lake Rd # 102 (48304-2772)
PHONE..................................248 644-5500
Paul Nine,
Douglas Miller,
EMP: 5 **EST:** 2012
SALES (est): 328.9K **Privately Held**
SIC: 3812 3674 Infrared object detection equipment; infrared sensors, solid state

(G-1866)
TORENZO INC
6632 Telegraph Rd Ste 122 (48301-3012)
PHONE..................................313 732-7874
EMP: 10 **EST:** 2015
SQ FT: 600
SALES (est): 263.2K **Privately Held**
SIC: 7371 7372 7379 8748 Computer Programming Svc Prepackaged Software Svc Computer Related Svcs Business Consulting Svcs

(G-1867)
TOTAL TENNIS LLC
2519 W Maple Rd (48301-2750)
PHONE..................................248 594-1749
Karl Philip Woods, *Mng Member*
EMP: 6 **EST:** 2011
SALES (est): 300K **Privately Held**
WEB: www.shoptotaltennis.com
SIC: 3949 Strings, tennis racket

(G-1868)
TRIMAS COMPANY LLC (HQ)
39400 Woodward Ave # 130 (48304-5151)
PHONE..................................248 631-5450
Terry Collins, *President*
Omar Honegger, *Vice Pres*
Carlos Contreras, *Director*
EMP: 100 **EST:** 2007
SALES (est): 27.7MM
SALES (corp-wide): 769.9MM **Publicly Held**
WEB: www.trimascorp.com
SIC: 3715 Truck trailers
PA: Trimas Corporation
38505 Woodward Ave # 200
Bloomfield Hills MI 48304
248 631-5450

(G-1869)
TRIMAS CORPORATION (PA)
38505 Woodward Ave # 200 (48304-5096)
PHONE..................................248 631-5450
Samuel Valenti III, *Ch of Bd*
Thomas A Amato, *President*
Ryan Gladieux, *Vice Pres*
Sean Hoskins, *Vice Pres*
Al Malizia, *Vice Pres*
◆ **EMP:** 256 **EST:** 1986
SALES (est): 769.9MM **Publicly Held**
WEB: www.trimascorp.com
SIC: 3799 3714 3443 2672 Trailer hitches; motor vehicle parts & accessories; trailer hitches, motor vehicle; fabricated plate work (boiler shop); drums, knockout (reflux, etc.): metal plate; cylinders, pressure: metal plate; tape, pressure sensitive: made from purchased materials; bolts, nuts, rivets & washers; bolts, metal; screws, metal; machine tool accessories; drills (machine tool accessories); milling cutters

Boyne City - Charlevoix County (G-1898)

(G-1870)
TRUSS DEVELOPMENT
1573 S Telegraph Rd (48302-0048)
PHONE.....................248 624-8100
Basil Bacall, *Principal*
EMP: 8 **EST:** 2010
SALES (est): 185.3K **Privately Held**
SIC: 2439 Structural wood members

(G-1871)
TVDN GROUP LLC
1472 N Cranbrook Rd (48301-2313)
PHONE.....................248 255-6402
EMP: 4 **EST:** 2017
SALES (est): 112.6K **Privately Held**
SIC: 2759 Commercial printing

(G-1872)
V2SOFT INC (PA)
300 Enterprise Ct (48302-0376)
PHONE.....................248 904-1702
Varchasvi Shankar, *CEO*
Nandini S Varchasvi, *Vice Pres*
SAI Vallurupalli, *Project Mgr*
Kawalpreet Kaur, *Human Resources*
Parul Taylor, *Accounts Mgr*
EMP: 75 **EST:** 1998
SQ FT: 13,000
SALES (est): 63.5MM **Privately Held**
WEB: www.v2soft.com
SIC: 7379 7373 7372 8711 Computer related consulting services; computer integrated systems design; prepackaged software; engineering services; computer facilities management; management consulting services

(G-1873)
VIMAX PUBLISHING
600 Ridge Rd (48302-1558)
PHONE.....................248 563-2367
EMP: 5 **EST:** 2018
SALES (est): 112K **Privately Held**
WEB: www.vimaxmedia.com
SIC: 2741 Miscellaneous publishing

(G-1874)
WHEELHOUSE GRAPHIX LLC
445 Enterprise Ct (48302-0339)
PHONE.....................800 732-0815
Shauna Ryder, *President*
EMP: 17
SQ FT: 9,057
SALES (est): 1,000K **Privately Held**
WEB: www.wheelhousegraphix.com
SIC: 3993 Signs, not made in custom sign painting shops

(G-1875)
WOODCREEK CUSTOMS
3111 Woodcreek Way (48304-1865)
PHONE.....................248 761-5652
EMP: 4 **EST:** 2016
SALES (est): 88.3K **Privately Held**
SIC: 2431 Millwork

Bloomingdale
Van Buren County

(G-1876)
CTS WELDING
39065 County Road 388 (49026-9732)
PHONE.....................269 521-4481
Christopher Ssmith, *Principal*
EMP: 6 **EST:** 2011
SALES (est): 306.6K **Privately Held**
WEB: www.ctswelding.com
SIC: 7692 2514 3446 2599 Welding repair; metal household furniture; architectural metalwork; restaurant furniture, wood or metal

(G-1877)
NATHAN SHETLER
Also Called: Northern Building Components
44815 County Rd Ste 388 (49026)
PHONE.....................269 521-4554
Nathan Shetler, *Owner*
EMP: 10 **EST:** 2011
SALES (est): 3MM **Privately Held**
SIC: 3448 Prefabricated metal buildings

(G-1878)
PATHWAY PUBLISHING CORPORATION (DH)
Also Called: Pathway Publishers
43632 County Road 390 (49026-8755)
PHONE.....................269 521-3025
Lewis Lambright, *General Mgr*
Sarah Lambright, *Asst Mgr*
EMP: 10 **EST:** 2014
SQ FT: 1,500
SALES (est): 504.1K
SALES (corp-wide): 882.9K **Privately Held**
WEB: www.pathway-publishers.com
SIC: 5963 5192 2721 Newspapers, home delivery, not by printers or publishers; books, periodicals & newspapers; comic books: publishing & printing
HQ: Pcm
P C M Pcm Pumps Delasco Foodys
Levallois Perret 92300
177 683-100

(G-1879)
SOUTHWESTERN MICH DUST CTRL
110 E Spring St (49026-5109)
P.O. Box 152 (49026-0152)
PHONE.....................269 521-7638
Lew Baron Page, *President*
Carrol Page, *Vice Pres*
EMP: 28 **EST:** 1972
SQ FT: 1,800
SALES (est): 2.9MM **Privately Held**
WEB: www.lakesandcountry.com
SIC: 1611 1311 Highway & street maintenance; crude petroleum production

(G-1880)
SVF BLOOMINGDALE INC
43073 County Road 388 (49026-9728)
PHONE.....................269 521-3026
Raymond Biln, *Principal*
Sabina Saemann, *Controller*
EMP: 12 **EST:** 2020
SALES (est): 658.1K **Privately Held**
SIC: 2037 Frozen fruits & vegetables

Boon
Wexford County

(G-1881)
GJM PROPERTY LLC
8834 E 34 Rd Ste 131 (49618)
PHONE.....................248 592-7323
Gadoy Magee,
EMP: 10
SALES (est): 216.3K **Privately Held**
SIC: 1389 Construction, repair & dismantling services

Boyne City
Charlevoix County

(G-1882)
ARETE INDUSTRIES INC
1 Altair Dr (49712-9618)
PHONE.....................231 582-4470
Leon Tupper, *CEO*
Tom Monley, *President*
Michael Lange, *Vice Pres*
EMP: 10 **EST:** 2000
SQ FT: 67,000
SALES (est): 1.4MM **Privately Held**
WEB: www.aretenorth.com
SIC: 3714 Motor vehicle parts & accessories

(G-1883)
BOYNE AREA WLDG & FABRICATION
1095 Dam Rd (49712-9622)
PHONE.....................231 582-6078
Mike Markiewicz, *President*
EMP: 5 **EST:** 2007
SALES (est): 220K **Privately Held**
WEB: www.boyneareawelding.com
SIC: 7692 Welding repair

(G-1884)
BOYNE CITY GAZETTE
5 W Main St Unit 7 (49712-3700)
PHONE.....................231 582-2799
Chris Faulknor, *Principal*
EMP: 8 **EST:** 2011
SALES (est): 84.7K **Privately Held**
WEB: www.boynegazette.com
SIC: 2711 Newspapers, publishing & printing

(G-1885)
BULMANN ENTERPRISES INC
Also Called: Bulmann Dock & Lift
175 Magnet Dr (49712-8117)
PHONE.....................231 549-5020
Stephen Bulmann, *President*
Rebecca Bulmann, *Admin Sec*
EMP: 28 **EST:** 1998
SQ FT: 22,000
SALES (est): 2.5MM **Privately Held**
WEB: www.bulmanndock.com
SIC: 3536 3448 Boat lifts; docks: prefabricated metal

(G-1886)
CHRIS FAULKNOR
5 W Main St Unit 7 (49712-3700)
PHONE.....................231 645-1970
Chris Faulknor, *Principal*
EMP: 7 **EST:** 2016
SALES (est): 102.9K **Privately Held**
SIC: 2711 Newspapers, publishing & printing

(G-1887)
CLASSIC INSTRUMENTS INC
826 Moll Dr (49712-8112)
P.O. Box 411 (49712-0411)
PHONE.....................231 582-0461
Mike Stowe, *President*
John McLeod III, *General Mgr*
Jason Knight, *Engineer*
Ron Hanna, *Sales Mgr*
▲ **EMP:** 9 **EST:** 2001
SALES (est): 1.6MM **Privately Held**
WEB: www.classicinstruments.com
SIC: 3825 Instruments to measure electricity

(G-1888)
FLORIDA MACHINE & CASTING CO
926 N Lake St (49712-1185)
PHONE.....................561 655-3771
Andrew Darien, *President*
EMP: 3 **EST:** 1988
SALES (est): 1MM
SALES (corp-wide): 18.5MM **Privately Held**
WEB: www.tristatecast.com
SIC: 3599 Machine shop, jobbing & repair
PA: Tri-State Cast Technologies Co, Inc
926 N Lake St
Boyne City MI 49712
231 582-0452

(G-1889)
HONEYWELL INTERNATIONAL INC
375 N Lake St (49712-1101)
PHONE.....................231 582-5686
Barrett Bartelli, *Electrical Engi*
John Martenson, *Manager*
Rajani Gudipudi, *Senior Mgr*
John Martinson, *Administration*
EMP: 200
SALES (corp-wide): 32.6B **Publicly Held**
WEB: www.honeywell.com
SIC: 3728 3825 3823 3812 Aircraft parts & equipment; instruments to measure electricity; industrial instrmnts msrmnt display/control process variable; search & navigation equipment
PA: Honeywell International Inc.
855 S Mint St
Charlotte NC 28202
704 627-6200

(G-1890)
INDUSTRIAL MAGNETICS INC (PA)
1385 S M 75 (49712-9689)
PHONE.....................231 582-3100
Walter J Shear III, *CEO*
Robin Stanley, *CFO*
▲ **EMP:** 72 **EST:** 1961
SQ FT: 38,000
SALES (est): 54.9MM **Privately Held**
WEB: www.magnetics.com
SIC: 3499 Magnets, permanent: metallic

(G-1891)
J & J TRANSPORT LLC
4556 Lakeshore Rd (49712-9677)
PHONE.....................231 582-6083
Joyce Raveau,
James Raveau,
EMP: 5 **EST:** 2001
SALES (est): 342.6K **Privately Held**
SIC: 3537 Trucks: freight, baggage, etc.: industrial, except mining

(G-1892)
JEF-SCOT METAL INDUSTRIES
926 N Lake St (49712-1185)
PHONE.....................231 582-0452
Darien Andrew, *Administration*
EMP: 11 **EST:** 2015
SALES (est): 229.7K **Privately Held**
WEB: www.tristatecast.com
SIC: 3999 Manufacturing industries

(G-1893)
KIRTLAND PRODUCTS LLC
1 Altair Dr (49712-9618)
PHONE.....................231 582-7505
Leon Tupper, *Mng Member*
EMP: 11 **EST:** 2011
SALES (est): 1MM **Privately Held**
WEB: www.kirtlandproducts.com
SIC: 3484 Pellet & BB guns

(G-1894)
LEXAMAR CORPORATION
100 Lexamar Dr (49712-9799)
PHONE.....................231 582-3163
Al Powers, *President*
Grahame Burrow, *General Mgr*
Cheryl Savoix, *Traffic Mgr*
Craig Avery, *Engineer*
Rob Neumann, *Engineer*
EMP: 325 **EST:** 1985
SQ FT: 85,000
SALES (est): 92.6MM
SALES (corp-wide): 32.6B **Privately Held**
WEB: www.lexamar.com
SIC: 3089 Injection molding of plastics
HQ: Magna Exteriors Of America, Inc.
750 Tower Dr
Troy MI 48098
248 631-1100

(G-1895)
LOST CELLARS INC
745 High Pines Trl (49712-9061)
PHONE.....................734 626-0969
Willard Higdon, *Principal*
EMP: 6 **EST:** 2015
SALES (est): 66.1K **Privately Held**
WEB: www.lostdrawcellars.com
SIC: 2084 Wines

(G-1896)
MAGNETIC SYSTEMS INTL INC
Also Called: MSI
1095 Dam Rd (49712-9622)
PHONE.....................231 582-9600
Michael Markiewicz, *President*
▲ **EMP:** 23 **EST:** 1996
SQ FT: 27,000
SALES (est): 3MM **Privately Held**
WEB: www.msimagnets.com
SIC: 3499 Magnets, permanent: metallic

(G-1897)
MITCHELL COATES
5293 Korthase Rd (49712-9507)
PHONE.....................231 582-5878
EMP: 52
SALES (est): 3.1MM **Privately Held**
SIC: 3949 Mfg Sporting/Athletic Goods

(G-1898)
MOEKE FORESTY
710 Hull St (49712-9003)
PHONE.....................231 631-9600
EMP: 5 **EST:** 2018
SALES (est): 180.8K **Privately Held**
WEB: www.moekeforestry.com
SIC: 2411 Logging

Boyne City - Charlevoix County (G-1899)

(G-1899)
MORROW FOUNDRY
926 N Lake St (49712-1185)
PHONE 231 582-0452
EMP: 9 EST: 2019
SALES (est): 266.1K Privately Held
WEB: www.tristatecast.com
SIC: 3599 Machine shop, jobbing & repair

(G-1900)
PAINE PRESS LLC
209 S Lake St (49712-1398)
PHONE 231 645-1970
Faulknor Christopher, *Principal*
EMP: 5 EST: 2010
SALES (est): 102.3K Privately Held
SIC: 2741 Miscellaneous publishing

(G-1901)
PRECISION EDGE SRGCAL PDTS LLC
1448 Lexamar Dr (49712-9751)
PHONE 231 459-4304
John Truckey, *President*
EMP: 31 Privately Held
WEB: www.precisionedge.com
SIC: 3841 Surgical & medical instruments
PA: Precision Edge Surgical Products Company Llc
415 W 12th Ave
Sault Sainte Marie MI 49783

(G-1902)
TEMPREL INC
206 Industrial Parkway Dr (49712-9616)
PHONE 231 582-6585
John R Bertsch, *President*
EMP: 25 EST: 1965
SQ FT: 4,000
SALES (est): 4MM Privately Held
WEB: www.temprel.com
SIC: 3829 3823 3357 Thermocouples; industrial instrmnts msrmnt display/control process variable; nonferrous wiredrawing & insulating

(G-1903)
TIP OF MITT WELDING LLC
3058 Glenwood Beach Dr (49712-9058)
PHONE 231 582-2977
Chase Griffin, *Principal*
EMP: 5 EST: 2018
SALES (est): 33.6K Privately Held
SIC: 7692 Welding repair

(G-1904)
TRI-STATE CAST TECHNOLOGIES CO (PA)
926 N Lake St (49712-1185)
P.O. Box 230 (49712-0230)
PHONE 231 582-0452
J Andrew Darien, *President*
John Darien, *CFO*
EMP: 4 EST: 1978
SQ FT: 2,700
SALES (est): 18.5MM Privately Held
WEB: www.tristatecast.com
SIC: 3365 3599 Aluminum foundries; machine shop, jobbing & repair

(G-1905)
VAN DAM MARINE CO
Also Called: Van Dam Wood Craft
970 E Division St (49712-9609)
PHONE 231 582-2323
Stephen Van Dam, *President*
Ben Van, *Vice Pres*
Ben Vandam, *Vice Pres*
Jean Van Dam, *Treasurer*
Jean Dam, *Mktg Dir*
▲ EMP: 48 EST: 1977
SQ FT: 96,000
SALES (est): 1.1MM Privately Held
WEB: www.vandamboats.com
SIC: 3732 4493 Boat building & repairing; boat yards, storage & incidental repair

(G-1906)
WOOD SHOP INC
111 N East St (49712-1213)
PHONE 231 582-9835
Bruce Janssen, *President*
EMP: 5 EST: 1977
SALES (est): 409.9K Privately Held
WEB: www.thewoodshop.com
SIC: 2499 Signboards, wood

Boyne Falls
Charlevoix County

(G-1907)
FOGGY MOUNTAIN WOODWORKS
6959 Thumb Lake Rd (49713-9666)
PHONE 231 675-1757
Jeff Denise, *Administration*
EMP: 7 EST: 2013
SALES (est): 547.8K Privately Held
SIC: 2431 Millwork

(G-1908)
HEARTWOOD MILLS LLC
4740 Skop Rd Ste A (49713-9791)
PHONE 888 829-5909
Brad Baird, *Mng Member*
William Tudor,
▼ EMP: 12 EST: 2015
SALES (est): 1.7MM Privately Held
WEB: www.heartwoodmills.com
SIC: 2431 Millwork

(G-1909)
MATELSKI LUMBER COMPANY
2617 M 75 S (49713-9793)
PHONE 231 549-2780
Edward Matelski Jr, *President*
George Matelski, *Treasurer*
Marjorie Matelski, *Admin Sec*
EMP: 45 EST: 1987
SQ FT: 1,200
SALES (est): 4.9MM Privately Held
WEB: www.matelskilumbercompany.com
SIC: 2426 2448 Furniture dimension stock, hardwood; pallets, wood

(G-1910)
STRONGS WOODWORKING
76 Magee Rd N (49713-9739)
PHONE 989 350-9113
EMP: 4 EST: 2015
SALES (est): 85.2K Privately Held
WEB: www.strongswoodworking.com
SIC: 2431 Millwork

Breckenridge
Gratiot County

(G-1911)
INTEGRITY FAB & MACHINE INC
150 Enterprise Dr (48615-8724)
P.O. Box 456 (48615-0456)
PHONE 989 481-3200
Kirk Smith, *President*
Terry Geer, *Engineer*
Caryn Jenkins, *Sales Staff*
Mike Sparks, *Sales Staff*
Trent Holland, *Manager*
EMP: 11 EST: 2007
SQ FT: 15,000
SALES (est): 4.8MM Privately Held
WEB: www.ifabm.com
SIC: 7692 3544 Welding repair; special dies, tools, jigs & fixtures

(G-1912)
NUTRIEN AG SOLUTIONS INC
8263 N Ransom Rd (48615)
P.O. Box 157 (48615-0157)
PHONE 989 842-1185
Jeff Schulz, *Manager*
EMP: 9
SALES (corp-wide): 20.9B Privately Held
WEB: www.nutrienagsolutions.com
SIC: 2875 4221 4813 Fertilizers, mixing only; bean elevator; grain elevator, storage only;
HQ: Nutrien Ag Solutions, Inc.
3005 Rocky Mountain Ave
Loveland CO 80538
970 685-3300

(G-1913)
ORACLE BREWING COMPANY LLC
1411 W Pine River Rd (48615-9622)
PHONE 989 401-7446
Christopher Younk,
EMP: 11 EST: 2013
SALES (est): 59.4K Privately Held
WEB: www.oraclebeer.com
SIC: 5813 2082 5921 5181 Bars & lounges; ale (alcoholic beverage); beer (packaged); beer & ale

Bridgeport
Saginaw County

(G-1914)
AMIGO MOBILITY INTL INC (PA)
6693 Dixie Hwy (48722-9725)
PHONE 989 777-0910
Beth L Thieme, *CEO*
Tim Drumhiller, *President*
Al Thieme, *Chairman*
Christopher Hunter, *Production*
Jess Butler, *Purchasing*
◆ EMP: 66
SQ FT: 62,700
SALES (est): 13.2MM Privately Held
WEB: www.myamigo.com
SIC: 3842 3441 Wheelchairs; fabricated structural metal

(G-1915)
BRIDGEPORT MANUFACTURING INC
6689 Dixie Hwy (48722-9725)
PHONE 989 777-4314
Mel Shepard, *President*
Nancy Shepard, *Vice Pres*
EMP: 4 EST: 1990
SQ FT: 2,200
SALES (est): 572.8K Privately Held
WEB: www.myamigo.com
SIC: 3441 3599 Fabricated structural metal; machine shop, jobbing & repair

(G-1916)
GREAT LAKES GAUGE COMPANY
6950 Junction Rd (48722-9776)
PHONE 989 652-6136
Clint Bucholz, *General Mgr*
EMP: 31 EST: 1978
SALES (est): 3.2MM Privately Held
WEB: www.gle-precision.com
SIC: 3443 Cooling towers, metal plate

(G-1917)
ORCHID ORTHPD SOLUTIONS LLC
6688 Dixie Hwy (48722-9725)
PHONE 989 746-0780
Tracy Oldenburg, *Purchasing*
Heather Carolan, *Finance*
Carol Pershing, *Human Res Mgr*
Adam Ellison, *Branch Mgr*
Barry Torrey, *Manager*
EMP: 400
SALES (corp-wide): 496.9MM Privately Held
WEB: www.orchid-ortho.com
SIC: 3841 Surgical & medical instruments
HQ: Orchid Orthopedic Solutions Llc
1489 Cedar St
Holt MI 48842
517 694-2300

(G-1918)
STONEY CREST REGRIND SERVICE
6243 Dixie Hwy (48722-9513)
PHONE 989 777-7190
George Clauss III, *President*
Robin Gregory, *General Mgr*
EMP: 10 EST: 1979
SQ FT: 4,800
SALES (est): 951.1K Privately Held
WEB: www.stoneycrestregrind.com
SIC: 3545 3599 3541 Cutting tools for machine tools; machine shop, jobbing & repair; machine tools, metal cutting type

(G-1919)
WALTER JEROME LELO
5795 Roedel Rd (48722-9777)
PHONE 989 274-8895
Walter Jerome Lelo, *Principal*
EMP: 4 EST: 2010
SALES (est): 78.7K Privately Held
SIC: 3489 Ordnance & accessories

Bridgman
Berrien County

(G-1920)
APOLLO SEIKO LTD
3969 Lemon Creek Rd (49106-9503)
PHONE 269 465-3400
Rick G Schiffer, *CEO*
Connie Black, *Manager*
Stacey Barajas, *Executive Asst*
EMP: 12 EST: 2008
SALES (est): 1.6MM Privately Held
WEB: www.apolloseiko.com
SIC: 3549 Assembly machines, including robotic

(G-1921)
ART/FX SIGN CO
9751 Red Arrow Hwy (49106-9710)
P.O. Box 695 (49106-0695)
PHONE 269 465-5706
Doyle Rogers, *Owner*
EMP: 7 EST: 2008
SALES (est): 1MM Privately Held
WEB: www.artfxsign.com
SIC: 3993 Signs, not made in custom sign painting shops.

(G-1922)
BOSS OUTDOORS LLC
Also Called: Boss Shotshells
3385 Livingston Rd (49106-9509)
PHONE 269 465-3631
Brandon Cerecke, *Mng Member*
EMP: 9 EST: 2016
SALES (est): 356.2K Privately Held
SIC: 3482 Shot, steel (ammunition)

(G-1923)
D & F MOLD LLC
8088 Jericho Rd (49106-9519)
PHONE 269 465-6633
Gary Zech, *Design Engr*
Ed Lowe, *Sales Engr*
Richard Lockman,
EMP: 27 EST: 1969
SQ FT: 10,000
SALES (est): 1.1MM Privately Held
WEB: www.dnfmold.com
SIC: 3544 Special dies & tools

(G-1924)
DIES AND FIXTURES MOLD CORP
8088 Jericho Rd (49106-9566)
PHONE 269 465-6633
EMP: 8 EST: 2016
SALES (est): 93.6K Privately Held
WEB: www.dnfmold.com
SIC: 3544 Special dies & tools

(G-1925)
DLM HOLDING GROUP LLC
Also Called: Boss Shotshell Mfg.
3385 Livingston Rd (49106-9509)
PHONE 269 465-3631
EMP: 7 EST: 2010
SALES (est): 389.9K Privately Held
SIC: 3482 5032 Shotgun ammunition: empty, blank or loaded; asphalt mixture

(G-1926)
GAL GAGE CO
2953 Hinchman Rd (49106-9501)
P.O. Box 218, Stevensville (49127-0218)
PHONE 269 465-5750
Goodwin A Lycan, *President*
Isabella Valadez, *Principal*
Dieter Timm, *Vice Pres*
Sue Wolfram, *Sales Executive*
EMP: 15 EST: 1975
SQ FT: 5,000

GEOGRAPHIC SECTION **Brighton - Livingston County (G-1954)**

SALES (est): 1.4MM **Privately Held**
WEB: www.galgage.com
SIC: **3545** 3548 3429 3325 Gauges (machine tool accessories); welding & cutting apparatus & accessories; manufactured hardware (general); steel foundries

(G-1927)
GREAT LAKES METAL STAMPING INC
4607 Rambo Rd (49106-8700)
PHONE.................................269 465-4415
Keith Hettig, *President*
Joel Donovan, *Business Mgr*
Tim Eisengruber, *Plant Mgr*
Scott Ross, *Opers Staff*
Ben McGarvey, *Production*
▲ **EMP:** 26 **EST:** 1995
SQ FT: 38,000
SALES (est): 8.5MM **Privately Held**
WEB: www.glakesmetalstamping.com
SIC: **3469** Stamping metal for the trade

(G-1928)
GREAT LAKES STAIR & CASE CO
9155 Gast Rd (49106-9378)
PHONE.................................269 465-3777
Howard Klotz, *President*
Jim Woodsen, *Admin Sec*
EMP: 4 **EST:** 1986
SQ FT: 7,500
SALES (est): 400K **Privately Held**
WEB: www.greatlakesstair.com
SIC: **2431** Staircases & stairs, wood; doors, wood

(G-1929)
INDUSTRIAL FABRICATION LLC
9550 Mathieu St (49106-9575)
P.O. Box 458 (49106-0458)
PHONE.................................269 465-5960
Ronald Mikesell,
Jason Ross,
EMP: 35 **EST:** 1985
SQ FT: 50,000
SALES (est): 4.6MM **Privately Held**
WEB: www.indfabrication.com
SIC: **3441** Fabricated structural metal

(G-1930)
KATAI MACHINE SHOP
8632 Jericho Rd (49106-9518)
PHONE.................................269 465-6051
EMP: 15 **EST:** 1967
SQ FT: 1,200
SALES (est): 1.2MM **Privately Held**
SIC: **3544** Mfg Dies/Tools/Jigs/Fixtures

(G-1931)
LAZY BALLERINA WINERY LLC
4209 Lake St (49106-9113)
PHONE.................................269 759-8486
Melanie Owen, *Branch Mgr*
EMP: 12
SALES (corp-wide): 581.9K **Privately Held**
WEB: www.lazyballerinawinery.com
SIC: **2084** Wines
PA: Lazy Ballerina Winery Llc
 315 State St
 Saint Joseph MI 49085
 269 363-6218

(G-1932)
MINERAL VISIONS INC
3840 Livingston Rd (49106-9528)
P.O. Box 400 (49106-0400)
PHONE.................................800 255-7363
EMP: 4
SALES (est): 225.1K
SALES (corp-wide): 125.5MM **Privately Held**
SIC: **1442** Construction Sand/Gravel
HQ: Fairmount Santrol Inc.
 3 Summit Park Dr Ste 700
 Independence OH 44131
 404 214-3284

(G-1933)
PRATT INDUSTRIES INC
11365 Red Arrow Hwy (49106-9757)
PHONE.................................269 465-7676
Brian McPheely, *CEO*
Anthony Pratt, *Ch of Bd*
William F Pratt, *President*

David Dennis, *COO*
Cathy Foley, *Vice Pres*
▲ **EMP:** 60 **EST:** 1997
SQ FT: 1,500
SALES (est): 14.4MM **Privately Held**
WEB: www.prattinc.com
SIC: **3715** Truck trailer chassis

(G-1934)
ST JOE TOOL CO
11521 Red Arrow Hwy (49106)
P.O. Box 158, Sawyer (49125-0158)
PHONE.................................269 426-4300
Henry Braddock, *President*
Rose Braddock, *Vice Pres*
EMP: 27 **EST:** 1963
SQ FT: 25,000
SALES (est): 6MM **Privately Held**
WEB: www.meetmarqet.com
SIC: **3451** Screw machine products

Brighton
Livingston County

(G-1935)
A-1 ENGRAVING & SIGNS INC
397 Washington St Ste A (48116-1482)
PHONE.................................810 231-2227
Geoff Boltach, *President*
Trevor McElroy, *Vice Pres*
Gavin McElroy, *Manager*
EMP: 4 **EST:** 1989
SQ FT: 1,200
SALES (est): 389.7K **Privately Held**
WEB: www.a1engravingandsigns.com
SIC: **2796** 3993 Engraving on copper, steel, wood or rubber; printing plates; signs & advertising specialties

(G-1936)
AACCESS ENTERTAINMENT
11552 Eagle Way (48114-9019)
PHONE.................................734 260-1002
Brub Zamarron, *Owner*
EMP: 4 **EST:** 2010
SALES (est): 200.5K **Privately Held**
SIC: **3669** Communications equipment

(G-1937)
ACTION ASPHALT LLC
12809 Silver Lake Rd (48116-8516)
PHONE.................................734 449-8565
Daniel James Gee, *Partner*
EMP: 16 **EST:** 2013
SQ FT: 10,000
SALES (est): 1.5MM **Privately Held**
WEB: www.actionasphaltllc.com
SIC: **3479** 1771 Coating of metals & formed products; blacktop (asphalt) work

(G-1938)
ACTION TOOL & MACHINE INC
5976 Ford Ct (48116-8511)
PHONE.................................810 229-6300
San Miyamoto, *President*
Jamie Payne, *Purchasing*
Debra Cubr, *Controller*
Debra Eddie, *Officer*
EMP: 28 **EST:** 1993
SQ FT: 14,000
SALES (est): 3.6MM **Privately Held**
WEB: www.actiontoolmachine.com
SIC: **3544** 3545 3599 Special dies & tools; cutting tools for machine tools; machine shop, jobbing & repair

(G-1939)
AEROSPOKE INCORPORATED
5034 Walnut Hills Dr (48116-8880)
PHONE.................................248 685-9009
EMP: 6
SQ FT: 8,400
SALES (est): 1MM **Privately Held**
SIC: **3751** 5941 Motorcycles, Bicycles, And Parts, Nsk

(G-1940)
AFTERMARKET INDUSTRIES LLC
315 E Main St (48116-1613)
PHONE.................................810 229-3200
Dana Kraft, *Vice Pres*
Scott Kraft, *Mng Member*
EMP: 8 **EST:** 2010

SALES (est): 977.9K **Privately Held**
WEB: www.aftermarketindustriesllc.com
SIC: **3999** Atomizers, toiletry

(G-1941)
AIRMAN INC
6150 Whitmore Lake Rd (48116-1926)
PHONE.................................248 960-1354
Stephen Burke, *President*
Shane Lahousse, *Vice Pres*
Jeremy O'Neil, *Vice Pres*
Bob Allen, *Engineer*
John Keblaitis, *Manager*
EMP: 37 **EST:** 1995
SQ FT: 17,000
SALES (est): 5.5MM **Privately Held**
WEB: www.airmaninc.com
SIC: **3999** 3492 Atomizers, toiletry; control valves, aircraft: hydraulic & pneumatic

(G-1942)
AIRMAN PRODUCTS LLC
6150 Whitmore Lake Rd (48116-1926)
PHONE.................................248 960-1354
Ashley Reeves, *Materials Mgr*
Phil Bondi, *VP Finance*
Laura Drahms, *Manager*
Krissa Corkins,
▲ **EMP:** 45 **EST:** 2014
SALES (est): 6.1MM **Privately Held**
WEB: www.airmanproducts.com
SIC: **3492** 3593 Control valves, fluid power: hydraulic & pneumatic; fluid power actuators, hydraulic or pneumatic

(G-1943)
ALLOR MANUFACTURING INC
Also Called: Plesh Industries
12534 Emerson Dr (48116-8437)
P.O. Box 1540 (48116-5340)
PHONE.................................248 486-4500
Frederick M Allor, *President*
James J Newbold, *Corp Secy*
Bernard J Wendt, *Vice Pres*
Tyler Delong, *Engineer*
Jon Hatton, *Manager*
▲ **EMP:** 100
SQ FT: 25,000
SALES (est): 29.6MM **Privately Held**
WEB: www.allorpleshinc.com
SIC: **3462** 3568 3535 3444 Chains, forged steel; power transmission equipment; conveyors & conveying equipment; sheet metalwork; fabricated structural metal

(G-1944)
AMERICAN COMPOUNDING SPC LLC
Also Called: ACS
9984 Borderline Dr (48116-2082)
PHONE.................................810 227-3500
Dave Donie, *Mng Member*
EMP: 60 **EST:** 2011
SALES (est): 14.7MM
SALES (corp-wide): 1.9MM **Privately Held**
WEB: www.ravagomanufacturing.com
SIC: **2821** Plastics materials & resins
HQ: Ravago Americas Llc
 1900 Smmit Twr Blvd Ste 9
 Orlando FL 32810
 407 773-7777

(G-1945)
AMERIVET SERVICES LLC
12795 Silver Lake Rd (48116-8322)
PHONE.................................810 299-3095
EMP: 7 **EST:** 2009
SALES (est): 869.8K **Privately Held**
WEB: www.amerivetservices.biz
SIC: **7692** Welding repair

(G-1946)
AMPHENOL T&M ANTENNAS INC
Also Called: Amphenol Saa
7117 Fieldcrest Dr (48116-8607)
PHONE.................................847 478-5600
Craig Lampo, *CFO*
EMP: 5
SALES (corp-wide): 8.6B **Publicly Held**
WEB: www.amphenol-mcp.com
SIC: **3663** Antennas, transmitting & communications

HQ: Amphenol T&M Antennas, Inc.
 100 Tri State Intl # 255
 Lincolnshire IL 60069
 847 478-5600

(G-1947)
ASPEN TECHNOLOGIES INC (PA)
7963 Lochlin Dr (48116-8329)
PHONE.................................248 446-1485
Kyle Richardson, *Principal*
Dan Knezevich, *Principal*
April Jewell, *Purch Mgr*
Karl Szulczewski, *Manager*
Andy Matuszynski, *Consultant*
▲ **EMP:** 63 **EST:** 2003
SALES (est): 14.5MM **Privately Held**
WEB: www.aspen-tech.net
SIC: **3086** Plastics foam products

(G-1948)
BALOGH INC
3637 S Old Us 23 Ste 100 (48114-7668)
PHONE.................................810 360-0182
Jennifer Broadhurst, *Principal*
EMP: 6 **EST:** 2010
SALES (est): 238.4K **Privately Held**
WEB: www.baloghusa.com
SIC: **3663** Radio & TV communications equipment

(G-1949)
BARLOW CUSTOM WOODWORKING
1340 Baywood Cir (48116-6776)
PHONE.................................810 220-0648
Roger Barlow, *Principal*
EMP: 5 **EST:** 2009
SALES (est): 65.3K **Privately Held**
SIC: **2431** Millwork

(G-1950)
BELLAR INDUSTRIES INC
3447 Charlotte Dr (48114-7507)
PHONE.................................810 227-1574
Ronald Bellar, *Principal*
EMP: 6 **EST:** 2010
SALES (est): 139.9K **Privately Held**
SIC: **3999** Manufacturing industries

(G-1951)
BEST SELF STORAGE
7286 Grand River Rd (48114-7329)
PHONE.................................810 227-7050
Steve Krause, *Branch Mgr*
EMP: 6 **Privately Held**
WEB: www.beststorageintown.com
SIC: **2511** Storage chests, household: wood
PA: Best Self Storage
 700 N Old Us Highway 23
 Brighton MI 48114

(G-1952)
BRADHART PRODUCTS INC
7747 Lochlin Dr (48116-8329)
PHONE.................................248 437-3746
Karl Thiele, *President*
Bryan Mudge, *Production*
EMP: 35 **EST:** 1962
SQ FT: 30,000
SALES (est): 6.8MM **Privately Held**
WEB: www.bradhart.com
SIC: **3599** 3568 3444 3366 Machine shop, jobbing & repair; power transmission equipment; sheet metalwork; copper foundries; copper rolling & drawing

(G-1953)
BRIGHTON LABORATORIES INC
11871 Grand River Rd (48116-9618)
PHONE.................................810 225-9520
Gregory Yates, *President*
Denny Baker, *Engineer*
EMP: 10 **EST:** 1990
SQ FT: 35,000 **Privately Held**
WEB: www.brightonlabs.com
SIC: **2899** Chemical preparations

(G-1954)
BRYLLAN LLC
12501 Grand River Rd (48116-8389)
PHONE.................................248 442-7620
Allan Pfitzenmaier, *CEO*
Shelli Connelly, *Manager*

Brighton - Livingston County (G-1955) — GEOGRAPHIC SECTION

◆ EMP: 2 EST: 2009
SQ FT: 1,000
SALES (est): 2MM Privately Held
WEB: www.bryllan.com
SIC: 2834 Pharmaceutical preparations

(G-1955)
BUY BEST MANUFACTURING LLC
988 Rickett Rd Ste B (48116-1828)
PHONE.................................248 875-2491
Clifton Mahathey,
EMP: 10 EST: 2010
SALES (est): 468.1K Privately Held
SIC: 3444 Sheet metalwork

(G-1956)
BWI CHASSIS DYNAMICS NA INC (HQ)
12501 Grand River Rd (48116-8389)
PHONE.................................937 455-5308
Zijian Zhao, Admin Sec
EMP: 2 EST: 2018
SALES (est): 52.9MM Privately Held
WEB: www.bwigroup.com
SIC: 3714 Motor vehicle parts & accessories

(G-1957)
BWI NORTH AMERICA INC
Also Called: Brighton Technical Center
12501 Grand River Rd (48116-8389)
PHONE.................................810 494-4584
Matt Henry, Principal
Jeff Zhao, Vice Pres
EMP: 12 Privately Held
WEB: www.bwigroup.com
SIC: 3714 8734 8731 Motor vehicle parts & accessories; testing laboratories; commercial physical research
HQ: Bwi North America Inc.
3100 Res Blvd Ste 240
Kettering OH 45420

(G-1958)
C & C SPORTS INC
8090 Grand River Rd (48114-9372)
PHONE.................................810 227-7068
William Piggins, President
Robert Swackhamer, Sales Staff
EMP: 27 EST: 1972
SQ FT: 9,000
SALES (est): 5.1MM Privately Held
WEB: www.ccsport.com
SIC: 5571 5599 5261 5551 Motorcycles; motorcycle parts & accessories; snowmobiles; lawnmowers & tractors; motor boat dealers; motorcycle repair service; snowmobile repair; lawn mower repair shop; boat repair; boat building & repairing

(G-1959)
CABINETS EXPRESS
9325 Maltby Rd (48116-8213)
PHONE.................................810 494-0511
Dan Ramback, President
Matt Norton, Branch Mgr
EMP: 5 EST: 2014
SALES (est): 143.2K Privately Held
WEB: www.cabinets-express.com
SIC: 2434 Wood kitchen cabinets

(G-1960)
CAILLAU USA INC
7000 Kensington Rd (48116-8334)
PHONE.................................248 446-1900
Pierre Andre Fernandez, President
Martine Boucton, Vice Pres
Laurent Chapdelaine, Vice Pres
EMP: 6 EST: 2014
SQ FT: 6,000
SALES (est): 1.9MM
SALES (corp-wide): 849.5K Privately Held
WEB: www.caillau.com
SIC: 3429 Metal fasteners
HQ: Caillau
Etablissements Caillau Ets Caillau
Issy Les Moulineaux 92130
145 299-300

(G-1961)
CARL ZEISS NTS LLC
6826 Kensington Rd (48116-8513)
PHONE.................................248 486-7600
Jay Malack, Project Mgr
John Grzybowski, Natl Sales Mgr
Bart Newman, Regl Sales Mgr
Bill Bell, Branch Mgr
EMP: 31 Privately Held
SIC: 3827 Optical instruments & lenses
HQ: Carl Zeiss Nts, Llc
1 Corporate Pl Ste 3
Peabody MA 01960

(G-1962)
CARTIDGE WORLD
9864 E Grand River Ave (48116-1963)
PHONE.................................810 229-5599
Joe Martino, Owner
EMP: 5 EST: 2017
SALES (est): 143.2K Privately Held
SIC: 5734 2759 Computer & software stores; publication printing

(G-1963)
CE II HOLDINGS INC
12866 Sutherland Rd (48116-8515)
PHONE.................................248 305-7700
Robert H Edwards, President
Joseph C Cherup, Vice Pres
▲ EMP: 14 EST: 1971
SQ FT: 7,800
SALES (est): 1MM Privately Held
SIC: 3567 Industrial furnaces & ovens

(G-1964)
CHARTER COMMUNICATION
8180 Grand River Rd (48114-9376)
PHONE.................................810 360-2748
EMP: 4 EST: 2014
SALES (est): 63.3K Privately Held
SIC: 3651 Household audio & video equipment

(G-1965)
COMEC USA
7202 Whitmore Lake Rd (48116-8558)
PHONE.................................810 299-3000
John Moretti, Principal
EMP: 8 EST: 2010
SALES (est): 221.3K Privately Held
WEB: www.comec-usa.com
SIC: 3629 Electrical industrial apparatus

(G-1966)
COR-MET INC
12500 Grand River Rd (48116-8326)
PHONE.................................810 227-0004
J Peter Kiilunen, President
Mary Kiilunen, Corp Secy
David Kiilunen, Vice Pres
◆ EMP: 35 EST: 1972
SQ FT: 111,000
SALES (est): 8.7MM Privately Held
WEB: www.cor-met.com
SIC: 3496 3548 Miscellaneous fabricated wire products; welding wire, bare & coated

(G-1967)
CORNELL PUBLICATIONS LLC
11075 Shadywood Dr (48114-9248)
PHONE.................................810 225-3075
Abigail Mouat, Principal
EMP: 4 EST: 2009
SALES (est): 140.6K Privately Held
WEB: www.cornellpubs.com
SIC: 2741 Miscellaneous publishing

(G-1968)
CORNHOLE STOP LLC
6050 Sundance Trl (48116-7745)
PHONE.................................704 728-1550
Shirley Kowtko, Principal
EMP: 7 EST: 2016
SALES (est): 219.9K Privately Held
WEB: www.cornholestop.com
SIC: 3993 Signs & advertising specialties

(G-1969)
CORRIGAN ENTERPRISES INC
775 N 2nd St (48116-1218)
PHONE.................................810 229-6323
Michael B Corrigan, CEO
EMP: 50 EST: 2017
SALES (est): 5.2MM Privately Held
SIC: 2911 Oils, fuel

(G-1970)
CORTAR LASER AND FAB LLC
12828 Emerson Dr (48116-8560)
PHONE.................................248 446-1110
Livia Walker,
Robert Boroniec,
EMP: 4 EST: 2007
SQ FT: 16,000
SALES (est): 619.7K Privately Held
WEB: www.cortarlaser.com
SIC: 3699 Laser systems & equipment

(G-1971)
COXEN ENTERPRISES INC
12785 Emerson Dr (48116-8562)
PHONE.................................248 486-3800
Mike Lamarra, President
◆ EMP: 90 EST: 1937
SQ FT: 140,000
SALES (est): 21.4MM
SALES (corp-wide): 598.7MM Privately Held
WEB: www.kemkrest.com
SIC: 2992 7389 2842 Lubricating oils & greases; packaging & labeling services; specialty cleaning, polishes & sanitation goods
PA: Kem Krest Llc
3221 Magnum Dr
Elkhart IN 46516
574 389-2650

(G-1972)
DAKKOTA INTEGRATED SYSTEMS LLC (PA)
123 Brighton Lake Rd # 202 (48116-6773)
PHONE.................................517 694-6500
Jason Mullins, Superintendent
Andra Rush, Chairman
Michele Faeth, Business Mgr
David Wojie, Business Mgr
Mark McCauley, COO
▲ EMP: 297 EST: 2001
SALES (est): 242.2MM Privately Held
WEB: www.dakkota.com
SIC: 3711 Automobile assembly, including specialty automobiles

(G-1973)
DATA ACQUISITION CTRL SYSTEMS
7965 Kensington Ct Ste A2 (48116-6808)
PHONE.................................248 437-6096
Peter Collins, President
Pete Collins, Owner
EMP: 12 EST: 2008
SQ FT: 5,000
SALES (est): 692.3K Privately Held
WEB: www.dacsusa.com
SIC: 8711 3625 Consulting engineer; electric controls & control accessories, industrial

(G-1974)
DE LUXE DIE SET INC
5939 Ford Ct (48116-8511)
PHONE.................................810 227-2556
Bill L Andersen, President
Eileen K Andersen, Vice Pres
EMP: 6 EST: 1966
SQ FT: 20,000
SALES (est): 839K Privately Held
SIC: 3544 3312 Die sets for metal stamping (presses); plate, steel

(G-1975)
DISPENSE TECHNOLOGIES LLC
7036 Kensington Rd (48116-8334)
P.O. Box 1108 (48116-2708)
PHONE.................................248 486-6244
Mark D Perry, Mng Member
Mark Perry, Executive
Michelle Perry,
EMP: 8 EST: 2001
SQ FT: 10,000
SALES (est): 1.6MM Privately Held
WEB: www.dispensetech.com
SIC: 3586 3569 Measuring & dispensing pumps; liquid automation machinery & equipment

(G-1976)
DO RITE TOOL INC
2800 Van Amberg Rd (48114-9388)
PHONE.................................734 522-7510
David J Mc Donald, President
Lori Mc Donald, Vice Pres
EMP: 9 EST: 1969
SALES (est): 959.3K Privately Held
SIC: 3544 Special dies & tools; jigs & fixtures

(G-1977)
DR FORKLIFT
9870 Finnegan Dr (48116-6241)
PHONE.................................734 968-6576
Dale Russell, Principal
EMP: 5 EST: 2016
SALES (est): 154.2K Privately Held
SIC: 3537 Forklift trucks

(G-1978)
DR SCHNEIDER AUTO SYSTEMS INC
716 Advance St Ste A (48116-2925)
PHONE.................................270 858-5400
EMP: 4
SALES (corp-wide): 524MM Privately Held
SIC: 3089 Mfg Plastic Products
HQ: Dr. Schneider Automotive Systems, Inc.
223 Progress Dr
Russell Springs KY 42642
270 858-5400

(G-1979)
DUNNAGE ENGINEERING INC (PA)
721 Advance St (48116-1292)
PHONE.................................810 229-9501
David Joseph, President
Janet A Joseph, Treasurer
Edward Ward, Sr Project Mgr
Jim Banish, Manager
Robbi Raskin, Admin Mgr
▲ EMP: 49 EST: 1961
SQ FT: 36,000
SALES (est): 13MM Privately Held
WEB: www.dunnage-eng.com
SIC: 3089 3479 3441 Injection molding of plastics; coating of metals with plastic or resins; fabricated structural metal

(G-1980)
E B I INC
10454 Grand River Rd (48116-6524)
PHONE.................................810 227-8180
EMP: 5
SALES (est): 492.9K Privately Held
SIC: 2452 Mfg Prefabricated Wood Buildings

(G-1981)
EBERSPECHER CONTRLS N AMER INC
2035 Charles Orndorf Dr (48116)
PHONE.................................248 994-7010
Massimo Venturi, President
EMP: 40 EST: 2015
SQ FT: 200
SALES (est): 5.8MM
SALES (corp-wide): 5.4B Privately Held
WEB: www.eberspaecher.com
SIC: 3714 8711 Motor vehicle electrical equipment; electrical or electronic engineering
HQ: Eberspacher Climate Control Systems Gmbh
Eberspacherstr. 24
Esslingen Am Neckar BW 73730
711 939-00

(G-1982)
EBINGER MANUFACTURING COMPANY
Also Called: Jets Glove Manufacturing
7869 Kensington Rd (48116-8340)
PHONE.................................248 486-8880
Janny Lu, President
▲ EMP: 15 EST: 1966
SQ FT: 42,000
SALES (est): 2.9MM Privately Held
WEB: www.emcfasteners.com
SIC: 3965 3999 5084 Fasteners, glove; atomizers, toiletry; machine tools & accessories

GEOGRAPHIC SECTION
Brighton - Livingston County (G-2008)

(G-1983)
EDSTON PLASTICS COMPANY
8730 Riverside Dr (48116-8236)
PHONE.................................734 941-3750
Edward A Roberts Jr, *President*
EMP: 5 **EST:** 1954
SQ FT: 4,000
SALES (est): 750K **Privately Held**
SIC: 3089 3993 Injection molding of plastics; signs & advertising specialties

(G-1984)
ENER2 LLC
7685 Athlone Dr (48116-8847)
PHONE.................................248 842-2662
George Moser,
EMP: 8 **EST:** 2010
SALES (est): 104.7K **Privately Held**
SIC: 3511 Turbines & turbine generator sets

(G-1985)
EXCELLENCE LAWN LANDSCAPE
10379 Greenbrier (48114-9662)
PHONE.................................810 623-9742
EMP: 4 **EST:** 2015
SALES (est): 85.6K **Privately Held**
WEB: www.excellencelawnandlandscape.com
SIC: 5083 3524 Cultivating machinery & equipment; lawn & garden mowers & accessories

(G-1986)
EXECUTIVE OPERATIONS LLC
8391 Mallard Xing (48116-8402)
PHONE.................................313 312-0653
David Trader, *CEO*
EMP: 28 **EST:** 2007
SALES (est): 254.9K **Privately Held**
WEB: www.executive-operations.com
SIC: 7382 1731 4119 3715 Protective devices, security; safety & security specialization; local rental transportation; semitrailers for missile transportation; private investigator; information retrieval services

(G-1987)
EXPORT CORPORATION
6060 Whitmore Lake Rd (48116-1941)
PHONE.................................810 227-6153
Donald Peitz, *President*
David Peitz, *Vice Pres*
Tim Spickler, *Vice Pres*
Jeff Rauch, *Purch Mgr*
Megan Somers, *Controller*
◆ **EMP:** 223 **EST:** 1972
SQ FT: 175,000
SALES (est): 20.1MM **Privately Held**
WEB: www.exportcorporation.com
SIC: 2441 4783 Nailed wood boxes & shook; packing goods for shipping

(G-1988)
FARR & FARON ASSOCIATES INC
136 E Grand River Ave 3 (48116-1510)
PHONE.................................810 229-7730
Walter J Faron, *CEO*
Ryan Faron, *Vice Pres*
EMP: 3 **EST:** 1980
SALES (est): 3MM **Privately Held**
SIC: 3699 Electronic training devices

(G-1989)
FEDERAL SCREW WORKS
Also Called: Novex Tool Division
77 Advance St (48116)
PHONE.................................810 227-7712
Richard Klender, *Engineer*
Jeffrey Harness, *Sales & Mktg St*
Lynette Lynch, *Manager*
EMP: 87
SALES (corp-wide): 78.9MM **Privately Held**
WEB: www.federalscrewworks.com
SIC: 3451 3544 Screw machine products; special dies, tools, jigs & fixtures
PA: Federal Screw Works
34846 Goddard Rd
Romulus MI 48174
734 941-4211

(G-1990)
FLARETITE INC
7723 Kensington Ct (48116-8391)
P.O. Box 130, Fenton (48430-0130)
PHONE.................................810 750-4140
Norm Mathers, *President*
Vito Accetta, *Treasurer*
Kirk Smith, *Marketing Staff*
Kirk Lewandowski, *Director*
EMP: 8 **EST:** 2001
SQ FT: 2,500 **Privately Held**
WEB: www.flaretite.com
SIC: 3491 5085 Industrial valves; gaskets & seals
PA: Flaretite Pty Ltd
4 Forte Ct
Bridgeman Downs QLD

(G-1991)
FLEXDEX INC
Also Called: Flexdex Surgical
10421 Citation Dr Ste 900 (48116-6558)
PHONE.................................810 522-9009
Clark Barousse, *President*
Randall Sullivan, *COO*
Kin Cheung, *Vice Pres*
John Deyarmond, *Materials Mgr*
Eugene Thomas, *Sales Staff*
EMP: 12 **EST:** 2011
SALES (est): 1.5MM **Privately Held**
WEB: www.flexdex.com
SIC: 3841 Surgical & medical instruments

(G-1992)
FORTECH PRODUCTS INC
7600 Kensington Ct (48116-8392)
PHONE.................................248 446-9500
Creighton E Forester, *President*
Luis Madaleno, *COO*
Luis Madaleno, *COO*
Mike Nelson, *Project Mgr*
Jim McCrate, *Opers Mgr*
▲ **EMP:** 30 **EST:** 1994
SQ FT: 40,000
SALES (est): 8.8MM **Privately Held**
WEB: www.fortechproducts.com
SIC: 2992 2911 Lubricating oils & greases; fuel additives; fractionation products of crude petroleum, hydrocarbons

(G-1993)
FREEDOM TECHNOLOGIES CORP (PA)
10559 Citation Dr Ste 205 (48116-6546)
PHONE.................................810 227-3737
Brad Aldrich, *Ch of Bd*
Rick Scorey, *President*
Kay Maclean, *Office Admin*
Rodney Aldrich,
Sue Aldrich,
EMP: 30 **EST:** 1991
SQ FT: 6,400
SALES (est): 4.4MM **Privately Held**
WEB: www.freedomcorp.com
SIC: 7373 3575 5045 Computer integrated systems design; computer terminals, monitors & components; computers, peripherals & software

(G-1994)
FULL SPECTRUM TECH INC
6457 Brighton Rd (48116-9753)
PHONE.................................810 225-4760
Paul Weber, *President*
EMP: 9 **EST:** 2004
SALES (est): 570.3K **Privately Held**
WEB: www.fullspectec.com
SIC: 3826 Analytical instruments

(G-1995)
G P WOODWORKING L L C
2382 Woodvale Trl (48114-8184)
PHONE.................................313 600-9414
Gordon P Husted, *Principal*
Gordon Husted, *Principal*
EMP: 6 **EST:** 2011
SALES (est): 108.2K **Privately Held**
SIC: 2431 Millwork

(G-1996)
GARBAGE MAN LLC
5441 Ethel St (48116-1907)
P.O. Box 573 (48116-0573)
PHONE.................................810 225-3001
Josh Tinsley, *Mng Member*
EMP: 4 **EST:** 2013

SALES (est): 200K **Privately Held**
SIC: 3589 7389 Garbage disposers & compactors, commercial;

(G-1997)
GD ENTERPRISES LLC
7974 Lochlin Dr Ste B4 (48116-1664)
PHONE.................................248 486-9800
Rachel Boland, *Office Mgr*
Ron Gardner,
EMP: 6 **EST:** 2006
SALES (est): 528K **Privately Held**
WEB: www.gd-enterprises.net
SIC: 3559 Automotive related machinery

(G-1998)
GENERAL CHEMICAL CORPORATION
12336 Emerson Dr (48116-8343)
PHONE.................................248 587-5600
Mehul Shah, *CEO*
Andre Anderson II, *COO*
Dan Hill, *Plant Mgr*
Tim Fisher, *Controller*
Kailee Meisner, *Officer*
◆ **EMP:** 9 **EST:** 1980
SQ FT: 98,000
SALES (est): 2.6MM **Privately Held**
WEB: www.generalchem.com
SIC: 2851 2899 Paint removers; metal treating compounds; fluxes: brazing, soldering, galvanizing & welding; corrosion preventive lubricant; rust resisting compounds

(G-1999)
GENERAL MACHINE & BORING INC
5983 Ford Ct (48116-8511)
PHONE.................................810 220-1203
Allen Kastl Jr, *President*
Jerry Brown, *Manager*
EMP: 9 **EST:** 1984
SALES (est): 829.2K **Privately Held**
WEB: www.generalmachineandboring.synthasite.com
SIC: 3599 Machine shop, jobbing & repair

(G-2000)
GEORGE MOSES CO
Also Called: Marketeer, The
110 E North St (48116-1528)
P.O. Box 686 (48116-0686)
PHONE.................................810 227-1575
George Moses, *President*
Melanie Moses, *Corp Secy*
Peggy Neeley, *Accounts Exec*
Melanie Mazier, *Executive*
EMP: 1 **EST:** 1971
SQ FT: 2,000
SALES (est): 1MM **Privately Held**
WEB: www.georgemosesco.com
SIC: 2741 Guides: publishing only, not printed on site; shopping news: publishing only, not printed on site

(G-2001)
GLOBAL RETOOL GROUP AMER LLC
Also Called: Grg
7290 Kensington Rd (48116-8354)
PHONE.................................248 289-5820
Andreas Quak, *CEO*
Gino Longo, *Managing Dir*
Vincenzo Longo, *Vice Pres*
Stacey Nathanson, *Office Admin*
EMP: 40 **EST:** 2010
SQ FT: 46,000
SALES: 5.8MM
SALES (corp-wide): 88.3MM **Privately Held**
WEB: www.global-retool-group.com
SIC: 3545 Machine tool accessories
HQ: Wema Vogtland Technology Gmbh
Schenkendorfstr. 14
Plauen SN 08525
374 159-20

(G-2002)
GOLICH GLASS
7796 Boardwalk Rd (48116-8521)
PHONE.................................248 667-9084
EMP: 7 **EST:** 2019

SALES (est): 116.1K **Privately Held**
WEB: www.golich.com
SIC: 3211 Flat glass

(G-2003)
GOOD SENSE COFFEE LLC
7931 State St (48116-1346)
PHONE.................................810 355-2349
Ian Boyle,
EMP: 21 **EST:** 2013
SALES (est): 203.9K **Privately Held**
WEB: www.goodsensecoffee.com
SIC: 5812 2095 5149 Coffee shop; coffee roasting (except by wholesale grocers); coffee, green or roasted

(G-2004)
GRAPHIC ART SERVICE & SUPPLY
Also Called: Graphics Arts Service & Supply
1343 Rickett Rd (48116-1879)
PHONE.................................810 229-4700
Steve Tubergen, *President*
EMP: 5
SALES (corp-wide): 3.7MM **Privately Held**
WEB: www.gasupply.com
SIC: 5084 3554 7699 Printing trades machinery, equipment & supplies; cutting machines, paper; knife, saw & tool sharpening & repair
PA: Graphic Arts Service And Supply, Inc.
3933 S Greenbrooke Dr Se
Grand Rapids MI 49512
616 698-9300

(G-2005)
GREEN OAK TOOL AND SVCS INC
9449 Maltby Rd (48116-1665)
PHONE.................................586 531-2255
Henry W Dodson III, *Principal*
EMP: 14 **EST:** 2013
SALES (est): 291.4K **Privately Held**
WEB: www.greenoaktool.com
SIC: 3542 3545 Arbor presses; presses: forming, stamping, punching, sizing (machine tools); die casting machines; machine tool accessories; machine tool attachments & accessories; tools & accessories for machine tools

(G-2006)
GUIDOBONO CONCRETE INC
7474 Whitmore Lake Rd (48116-8536)
PHONE.................................810 229-2666
John Guidobono II, *President*
John Anthony Guidobono Jr, *Vice Pres*
EMP: 13 **EST:** 1980
SQ FT: 3,000
SALES (est): 1MM **Privately Held**
WEB: www.highgradematerials.com
SIC: 3273 5211 Ready-mixed concrete; concrete & cinder block

(G-2007)
H H BARNUM CO
12865 Silver Lake Rd (48116-8516)
PHONE.................................248 486-5982
EMP: 4
SALES (corp-wide): 25.1MM **Privately Held**
WEB: www.hhbarnum.com
SIC: 3613 Regulators, power
PA: H. H. Barnum Co.
7915 Lochlin Dr
Brighton MI 48116
248 486-7300

(G-2008)
HOFFMANN FILTER CORPORATION (PA)
7627 Kensington Ct (48116-8392)
PHONE.................................248 486-8430
Georg Hoffmann, *CEO*
Detlef Mieth, *President*
Annemarie Mieth, *VP Admin*
Bianca Gansler, *Project Mgr*
Alex Herrera, *Manager*
▲ **EMP:** 14 **EST:** 1984
SQ FT: 30,000
SALES (est): 2.9MM **Privately Held**
WEB: www.hoffmannfilter.com
SIC: 3569 5084 Filters, general line: industrial; industrial machinery & equipment

Brighton - Livingston County (G-2009)   GEOGRAPHIC SECTION

(G-2009)
HORN CORP
Also Called: Eclipse Tanning
2169 Corlett Rd (48114-8100)
PHONE................................248 358-8883
Matthew Horn, *President*
EMP: 4 **EST:** 1998
SALES (est): 65.5K **Privately Held**
WEB: www.horncorp.net
SIC: 7299 3111 Tanning salon; leather tanning & finishing

(G-2010)
HOWELL MACHINE PRODUCTS INC
6265 Grand River Rd # 100 (48114-5303)
PHONE................................517 546-0580
Irene C Vogt, *President*
Robert Vogt Jr, *Corp Secy*
Ronald Vogt, *Vice Pres*
EMP: 26 **EST:** 1953
SQ FT: 1,000
SALES (est): 1.1MM **Privately Held**
WEB: www.aboutbalancingbooks.com
SIC: 3599 Machine shop, jobbing & repair

(G-2011)
HUG-A-PLUG INC
2332 Pine Hollow Trl (48114-4900)
P.O. Box 2190 (48116-5990)
PHONE................................810 626-1224
Robert Green, *President*
EMP: 5 **EST:** 2006
SALES (est): 711.2K **Privately Held**
WEB: www.hugaplug.com
SIC: 3643 7389 Plugs, electric;

(G-2012)
HY CAPACITY INC
7567 Brighton Rd (48116-7722)
PHONE................................616 558-5690
EMP: 6 **EST:** 2019
SALES (est): 104.7K **Privately Held**
WEB: www.hy-capacity.com
SIC: 3523 Farm machinery & equipment

(G-2013)
INNOVATIVE PHARMACEUTICALS LLC
2250 Gnoa Bus Pk Dr Ste 1 (48114)
PHONE................................248 789-0999
Xhesika Tasi, *Mng Member*
EMP: 15 **EST:** 2016
SALES (est): 709K **Privately Held**
SIC: 2834 Pharmaceutical preparations

(G-2014)
J & J LAMINATE CONNECTION INC
10603 Grand River Rd (48116-9609)
PHONE................................810 227-1824
Jim Roy, *President*
John Roy, *Vice Pres*
EMP: 4 **EST:** 1988
SQ FT: 1,200
SALES (est): 303K **Privately Held**
SIC: 2541 1799 Counter & sink tops; kitchen & bathroom remodeling

(G-2015)
L & J PRODUCTS K HUNTINGTON
9954 Weber St (48116-1939)
PHONE................................810 919-3550
Kim Huntington, *Owner*
EMP: 5 **EST:** 2011
SALES (est): 89.9K **Privately Held**
WEB: www.allseasoning.com
SIC: 2099 Food preparations

(G-2016)
L A BURNHART INC (PA)
2095 Euler Rd (48114-7411)
PHONE................................810 227-4567
Gar Boling, *President*
EMP: 2
SQ FT: 14,000
SALES (est): 2MM **Privately Held**
SIC: 3498 3599 Tube fabricating (contract bending & shaping); boiler tube cleaners

(G-2017)
L4 MANUFACTURING LLC
6377 Wildflower Ln (48116-2211)
PHONE................................810 217-3407
Lloyd Dunlap, *Principal*
EMP: 5 **EST:** 2013
SALES (est): 66K **Privately Held**
SIC: 3999 Manufacturing industries

(G-2018)
LA GOLD MINE INC
Also Called: Continental Diamond
425 W Main St (48116-1484)
PHONE................................517 540-1050
Andre Duscio, *President*
EMP: 5
SQ FT: 1,600
SALES (est): 437.9K **Privately Held**
SIC: 5944 3911 Jewelry, precious stones & precious metals; jewelry apparel

(G-2019)
LADDERTECH LLC
7081 Dan Mcguire Dr (48116-8532)
PHONE................................248 437-7100
Anette Gaines, *President*
EMP: 10 **EST:** 2004
SALES (est): 1MM **Privately Held**
WEB: www.ladder-port.com
SIC: 3499 Metal ladders

(G-2020)
LAIRDS CUSTOM CABINETRY INC
11371 Eagle Way (48114-9019)
PHONE................................810 494-5164
William Topolsk, *Agent*
EMP: 4 **EST:** 2018
SALES (est): 46.6K **Privately Held**
SIC: 3482 Small arms ammunition

(G-2021)
LIVING ON ETCH
6132 Briggs Lake Dr (48116-9563)
PHONE................................810 229-7955
Paula Lee Shoulders, *Principal*
EMP: 7 **EST:** 2010
SALES (est): 229.6K **Privately Held**
SIC: 3229 Art, decorative & novelty glassware

(G-2022)
LIVINGSTON COUNTY CONCRETE INC
550 N Old Us Highway 23 (48114-7632)
PHONE................................810 632-3030
Mike Horan, *President*
Ron Lammy, *Vice Pres*
Diane Gregor, *Manager*
EMP: 35 **EST:** 1989
SQ FT: 7,500
SALES (est): 2.7MM **Privately Held**
WEB: www.livingstonconcrete.net
SIC: 3273 3271 Ready-mixed concrete; blocks, concrete: landscape or retaining wall

(G-2023)
LOWRY HOLDING COMPANY INC (PA)
Also Called: Lowry Solutions
9420 Maltby Rd (48116-8801)
PHONE................................810 229-7200
Michael Lowry, *CEO*
Sean Lowry, *Partner*
Bob Seitz, *General Mgr*
Steven R Lowry, *Exec VP*
Denis Bishop, *Vice Pres*
◆ **EMP:** 122 **EST:** 1974
SALES (est): 59.3MM **Privately Held**
WEB: www.lowrysolutions.com
SIC: 5045 2672 8742 7373 Computers, peripherals & software; coated & laminated paper; management consulting services; systems integration services; office equipment; computer & software stores

(G-2024)
MARCH COATINGS INC (PA)
160 Summit St (48116-2413)
PHONE................................810 229-6464
Steven E March, *CEO*
Bruce La Valley, *President*
Greg Criswell, *Opers Mgr*
EMP: 80 **EST:** 1997
SQ FT: 93,000
SALES (est): 12.5MM **Privately Held**
WEB: www.marchcoatings.com
SIC: 3479 7389 Painting of metal products; packaging & labeling services

(G-2025)
MARCIE ELECTRIC INC
8190 Boardwalk Rd Ste B (48116-8100)
PHONE................................248 486-1200
Mark Marcie, *President*
EMP: 5 **EST:** 1989
SQ FT: 3,600
SALES (est): 2MM **Privately Held**
WEB: www.marcie-electric.com
SIC: 3612 Control transformers

(G-2026)
MATRIX ENGINEERING INC
8830 Whitmore Lake Rd (48116-8325)
PHONE................................810 231-0212
Ralph Nalepa, *Treasurer*
EMP: 9 **EST:** 1984
SQ FT: 5,600
SALES (est): 761.8K **Privately Held**
WEB: www.matrixenginc.com
SIC: 3544 Special dies & tools

(G-2027)
MAXIM INTEGRATED PRODUCTS INC
10355 Citation Dr Ste 100 (48116-6578)
PHONE................................408 601-1000
Dale Schacht, *Branch Mgr*
EMP: 5
SALES (corp-wide): 5.6B **Publicly Held**
WEB: www.maximintegrated.com
SIC: 3674 Microcircuits, integrated (semiconductor)
HQ: Maxim Integrated Products, Inc.
160 Rio Robles
San Jose CA 95134
408 601-1000

(G-2028)
MC GUIRE SPRING CORPORATION
6135 Grand River Rd (48114-9329)
PHONE................................517 546-7311
Robert Puste, *President*
Andrea Puste, *Vice Pres*
Aaren Schwanitz, *Admin Sec*
EMP: 6 **EST:** 1964
SALES (est): 905K **Privately Held**
WEB: www.mcguiresprings.com
SIC: 3495 Wire springs

(G-2029)
MCS CONSULTANTS INC
1347 Rickett Rd (48116-1879)
PHONE................................810 229-4222
Dale Swystun, *President*
Buell Cash, *Vice Pres*
EMP: 9 **EST:** 1989
SQ FT: 7,650
SALES (est): 142.7K **Privately Held**
SIC: 3069 5047 Medical sundries, rubber; medical & hospital equipment

(G-2030)
MICHIGAN LASER MFG LLC
718 Advance St (48116-1238)
PHONE................................810 623-2783
EMP: 7 **EST:** 2019
SALES (est): 466.2K **Privately Held**
WEB: www.milaserman.com
SIC: 3999 Manufacturing industries

(G-2031)
MICRO GAUGE INC
7350 Kensington Rd (48116-8354)
PHONE................................248 446-3720
Jim Rourke, *Principal*
EMP: 190 **EST:** 1971
SQ FT: 8,700
SALES (est): 21MM **Publicly Held**
WEB: www.muellerindustries.com
SIC: 3599 Machine shop, jobbing & repair
HQ: Mueller Brass Co.
2199 Lapeer Ave
Port Huron MI 48060
810 987-7770

(G-2032)
MICROGAUGE MACHINING INC
7350 Kensington Rd (48116-8354)
PHONE................................248 446-3720
James Skivington, *President*
EMP: 1 **EST:** 1997
SQ FT: 10,000
SALES (est): 7.3MM **Publicly Held**
WEB: www.muellerindustries.com
SIC: 3465 Body parts, automobile: stamped metal
HQ: Mueller Brass Co.
2199 Lapeer Ave
Port Huron MI 48060
810 987-7770

(G-2033)
MID AMERICAN AEL LLC
1375 Rickett Rd (48116-2227)
PHONE................................810 229-5483
Craig Trojan,
EMP: 6 **EST:** 2011
SALES (est): 721.4K **Privately Held**
WEB: www.midamericanael.com
SIC: 3647 Vehicular lighting equipment

(G-2034)
MID-MICHIGAN BLINDS
7041 Grand River Rd # 250 (48114-3811)
PHONE................................810 225-8488
EMP: 4 **EST:** 2019
SALES (est): 57.3K **Privately Held**
SIC: 2591 Window blinds

(G-2035)
MOHR ENGINEERING INC
1351 Rickett Rd (48116-2227)
P.O. Box 779 (48116-0779)
PHONE................................810 227-4598
David R McDowell, *President*
Glen Howard, *Vice Pres*
EMP: 25 **EST:** 1988
SQ FT: 30,000
SALES (est): 6.4MM **Privately Held**
WEB: www.mohrengineering.com
SIC: 3089 3451 Injection molded finished plastic products; screw machine products

(G-2036)
MSR-PALLETS & PACKAGING LLC
1000 Lily Pond Dr (48116-0087)
PHONE................................810 360-0425
Michael Rutkowski, *President*
EMP: 4 **EST:** 2005
SALES (est): 240.3K **Privately Held**
WEB: www.msr-palletspkg.com
SIC: 2653 Corrugated & solid fiber boxes

(G-2037)
MUELLER INDUSTRIES INC
7350 Kensington Rd (48116-8354)
PHONE................................248 446-3720
Wendy Zobl, *Human Resources*
Lisa Lee, *Manager*
EMP: 7 **Publicly Held**
WEB: www.muellerindustries.com
SIC: 3351 3463 3494 3089 Copper & copper alloy pipe & tube; pipe, brass & bronze; tubing, copper & copper alloy; extruded shapes, copper & copper alloy; nonferrous forgings; aluminum forgings; valves & pipe fittings; plumbing & heating valves; fittings for pipe, plastic
PA: Mueller Industries, Inc.
150 Schilling Blvd # 100
Collierville TN 38017

(G-2038)
MY TEC-TRONICS LLC
Also Called: Livingston Lakes Live Bait & T
10894 Grand River Rd (48116-9539)
PHONE................................586 218-0118
Mike Flint, *Principal*
EMP: 6 **EST:** 2012
SALES (est): 89.6K **Privately Held**
SIC: 3949 Fishing equipment

(G-2039)
N C BRIGHTON MACHINE CORP
7300 Whitmore Lake Rd (48116-8558)
PHONE................................810 227-6190
Jack Clausnitzer, *President*
Bill Barton, *Principal*
Karl Barton, *Principal*

GEOGRAPHIC SECTION   Brighton - Livingston County (G-2065)

Tim Clausnitzer, *Principal*
Kim Sherman, *Safety Mgr*
▲ **EMP:** 140 **EST:** 1965
SQ FT: 200,000
SALES (est): 24.2MM **Privately Held**
WEB: www.brightonnc.com
SIC: 3599 Machine shop, jobbing & repair

(G-2040)
NATIONAL ELEMENT INC
7939 Lochlin Dr (48116-8329)
PHONE.................................248 486-1810
Lauren S Best, *President*
Jim Vance, *Purch Mgr*
Robert J Stevenson, *Treasurer*
Brenda Strong, *Finance Mgr*
Brian Aubert, *Info Tech Dir*
EMP: 35 **EST:** 1960
SQ FT: 30,000
SALES (est): 4.9MM **Privately Held**
WEB: www.nationalelement.com
SIC: 3567 3568 3535 8748 Heating units & devices, industrial: electric; drives, chains & sprockets; drives: belt, cable or rope; belt conveyor systems, general industrial use; systems analysis or design; electric housewares & fans

(G-2041)
NIKON METROLOGY INC (DH)
12701 Grand River Rd (48116-8506)
PHONE.................................810 220-4360
Kenji Yoshikawa, *CEO*
Ken Waterfield, *General Mgr*
Hideaki Okamoto, *Managing Dir*
Alex Lucas, *Business Mgr*
Peter Higgins, *Vice Pres*
◆ **EMP:** 50 **EST:** 1998
SQ FT: 100,000
SALES (est): 44.3MM **Privately Held**
WEB: www.nikonmetrology.com
SIC: 3829 Meteorological instruments
HQ: Nikon Metrology
   Geldenaaksebaan 329
   Leuven 3001
   167 401-01

(G-2042)
NIKON METROLOGY INC
12589 Grand River Rd (48116-8390)
PHONE.................................810 220-4347
EMP: 5 **Privately Held**
WEB: www.nikonmetrology.com
SIC: 3829 Measuring & controlling devices
HQ: Nikon Metrology, Inc.
   12701 Grand River Rd
   Brighton MI 48116
   810 220-4360

(G-2043)
NOVEL PUBLICITY LLC
5087 Canyon Oaks Dr (48114-7505)
PHONE.................................248 563-6637
Melissa Rayner, *Principal*
EMP: 7 **EST:** 2017
SALES (est): 293.6K **Privately Held**
WEB: www.novelpublicity.com
SIC: 2741 Miscellaneous publishing

(G-2044)
NOVI PRECISION PRODUCTS INC
11777 Grand River Rd (48116-9617)
PHONE.................................810 227-1024
Ronald Karaisz II, *President*
John Goit, *President*
James Reichel, *Vice Pres*
Jim Nagle, *Plant Mgr*
Diane Bennane, *Buyer*
▲ **EMP:** 24 **EST:** 1973
SQ FT: 36,000
SALES (est): 6MM **Privately Held**
WEB: www.noviprecision.com
SIC: 3549 3544 Assembly machines, including robotic; special dies, tools, jigs & fixtures

(G-2045)
NOVI SPRING INC
7735 Boardwalk Rd (48116-8521)
PHONE.................................248 486-4220
Jason Johnson, *President*
Sean Johnson, *President*
Kevin Howkins, *Vice Pres*
Monica Shaffer, *Purch Mgr*
Debbie Ryan, *Manager*

▲ **EMP:** 17 **EST:** 1960
SQ FT: 30,000
SALES (est): 2.5MM **Privately Held**
WEB: www.novispring.com
SIC: 3495 Wire springs

(G-2046)
PACKAGE DESIGN & MFG INC (PA)
Also Called: PDM
12424 Emerson Dr (48116-8343)
P.O. Box 596, Whitmore Lake (48189-0596)
PHONE.................................248 486-4390
David Rosser, *President*
Nick Ruitenberg, *CFO*
Elaine Taylor, *Director*
David Thomas, *Admin Sec*
EMP: 50
SQ FT: 26,000
SALES (est): 11.8MM **Privately Held**
WEB: www.pdmfoam.com
SIC: 2621 3053 3086 2821 Wrapping & packaging papers; packing materials; plastics foam products; plastics materials & resins

(G-2047)
PACKAGING ENGINEERING LLC
Also Called: Packaging Engineering-Brighton
7138 Kensington Rd (48116-8335)
PHONE.................................248 437-9444
James Rittmueller,
Jim Lantis,
Andy Wowianko,
EMP: 7 **EST:** 2004
SALES (est): 1.5MM **Privately Held**
WEB: www.pellc-brighton.com
SIC: 3086 Packaging & shipping materials, foamed plastic

(G-2048)
PDQ INK INC
Also Called: Big PDQ
7475 Grand River Rd (48114-9374)
PHONE.................................810 229-2989
Kirt Albrecht, *President*
Tammy Albrecht, *Owner*
Janet Rengers, *Plant Mgr*
EMP: 22 **EST:** 1970
SQ FT: 7,000
SALES (est): 2MM **Privately Held**
WEB: www.bigpdq.com
SIC: 2752 7334 Commercial printing, offset; blueprinting service

(G-2049)
PEAKER SERVICES INC
8080 Kensington Ct (48116-8570)
PHONE.................................248 437-4174
Ian Bradbury, *President*
Richard R Steele, *Chairman*
William Craft, *Vice Pres*
Dave Philips, *Sales Staff*
Rose Mary Stornes, *Manager*
▲ **EMP:** 72 **EST:** 1971
SQ FT: 37,000
SALES (est): 9.4MM **Privately Held**
WEB: www.peaker.com
SIC: 7699 3519 3743 3823 Engine repair & replacement, non-automotive; diesel engine rebuilding; streetcars & car equipment; industrial instrmnts msrmnt display/control process variable; relays & industrial controls
PA: Psi Holding Company
   8080 Kensington Ct
   Brighton MI 48116

(G-2050)
PENCHURA LLC
889 S Old US 23 (48114-7684)
PHONE.................................810 229-6245
Eric Sheffer, *Engineer*
Avis Sheffer, *Engineer*
Tony Shadwick, *Manager*
Tom Boren, *Consultant*
EMP: 10 **EST:** 2006
SQ FT: 2,000 **Privately Held**
WEB: www.penchura.com
SIC: 5941 3949 Playground equipment; playground equipment

(G-2051)
PETERSEN PRODUCTS INC
7915 Kensington Ct (48116-8597)
PHONE.................................248 446-0500
Peter Lyders, *President*
EMP: 21 **EST:** 1981
SQ FT: 10,500
SALES (est): 339K **Privately Held**
SIC: 3089 Injection molded finished plastic products; boxes, plastic

(G-2052)
PLESH INDUSTRIES INC (PA)
12534 Emerson Dr (48116-8437)
PHONE.................................716 873-4916
Ronald Plesh, *President*
EMP: 49 **EST:** 1969
SQ FT: 130,000
SALES (est): 4.6MM **Privately Held**
WEB: www.allorpleshinc.com
SIC: 3462 3599 3443 Chains, forged steel; machine shop, jobbing & repair; liners/lining

(G-2053)
POWER COOL SYSTEMS INC
2111 Euler Rd (48114-7411)
PHONE.................................317 852-4193
EMP: 9 **EST:** 2019
SALES (est): 716K **Privately Held**
WEB: www.powercoolsystems.com
SIC: 3714 Motor vehicle parts & accessories

(G-2054)
PRO LIGHTING GROUP INC
Also Called: Prolighting
716 Advance St Ste A (48116-2925)
PHONE.................................810 229-5600
Paul Kluska, *President*
Gary Bonk, *VP Sales*
Aaron Deakins, *Cust Mgr*
Marissa C N, *Sales Staff*
Kyle Semenok, *Sales Staff*
▼ **EMP:** 7 **EST:** 2001
SALES (est): 4MM **Privately Held**
SIC: 3646 Commercial indusl & institutional electric lighting fixtures

(G-2055)
PROMESS INC (PA)
Also Called: Promess Dimensions
11429 Grand River Rd (48116-9615)
P.O. Box 748 (48116-0748)
PHONE.................................810 229-9334
Larry E Stockline, *CEO*
Glenn Nausley, *Vice Pres*
Stefan Simeonov, *Engineer*
Gina Daavettila, *Marketing Staff*
Stephanie Price, *Software Engr*
EMP: 73 **EST:** 1984
SQ FT: 50,000
SALES (est): 15.1MM **Privately Held**
WEB: www.promessinc.com
SIC: 3829 Fatigue testing machines, industrial: mechanical

(G-2056)
PROMESS INCORPORATED
11475 Grand River Rd (48116-9615)
PHONE.................................810 229-9334
Brian Bethke, *Engineer*
Lauren Rall, *Mktg Dir*
EMP: 6 **EST:** 2016
SALES (est): 138.6K **Privately Held**
WEB: www.promessinc.com
SIC: 3829 Measuring & controlling devices

(G-2057)
PSI HOLDING COMPANY (PA)
Also Called: Peaker Services
8080 Kensington Ct (48116-8520)
PHONE.................................248 437-4174
Richard R Steele, *CEO*
Sherry Fust, *Engineer*
JW Harris, *Engineer*
Jim Logue, *Engineer*
Kurt Ulbick, *Sales Mgr*
▲ **EMP:** 72 **EST:** 1987
SQ FT: 45,500
SALES (est): 25.8MM **Privately Held**
WEB: www.peaker.com
SIC: 7699 3519 Engine repair & replacement, non-automotive; diesel engine rebuilding

(G-2058)
PUREM NOVI INC
2035 Orndorf Dr (48116-2398)
PHONE.................................810 225-4582
Dennis Berry, *Branch Mgr*
EMP: 101
SALES (corp-wide): 5.4B **Privately Held**
SIC: 3559 Automotive related machinery
HQ: Purem Novi Inc.
   29101 Haggerty Rd
   Novi MI 48377
   248 994-7010

(G-2059)
R F M INCORPORATED
2001 Orndorf Dr (48116-2398)
PHONE.................................810 229-4567
Motoharu Yamamoto, *President*
Rudolf F Meffert, *Vice Pres*
▲ **EMP:** 29 **EST:** 1978
SQ FT: 8,000
SALES (est): 10.1MM **Privately Held**
WEB: www.rfm-inc.com
SIC: 3541 3599 Machine tools, metal cutting type; machine shop, jobbing & repair
HQ: Mitsubishi Materials Usa Corp
   3535 Hyland Ave Ste 200
   Costa Mesa CA 92626
   714 352-6100

(G-2060)
R GARI SIGN STUDIO INC
9043 Buckhorn Ln (48116-8273)
PHONE.................................810 355-1245
Rebecca L Gary, *Administration*
EMP: 7 **EST:** 2010
SALES (est): 74.6K **Privately Held**
WEB: www.rgari.com
SIC: 3993 Signs & advertising specialties

(G-2061)
RAVAGO AMERICAS
7280 Forest Way (48116-4728)
PHONE.................................810 225-0029
EMP: 7 **EST:** 2016
SALES (est): 219K **Privately Held**
WEB: www.ravagomanufacturing.com
SIC: 2821 Plastics materials & resins

(G-2062)
RAVISHING WREATHS
3404 Watersedge Dr (48114-8119)
PHONE.................................248 613-6210
Christine Springhetti, *Principal*
EMP: 4 **EST:** 2017
SALES (est): 72.1K **Privately Held**
SIC: 3999 Wreaths, artificial

(G-2063)
RECYCLEDLPS COM
6320 Superior Dr (48116-9584)
PHONE.................................810 623-4498
Wendy Roberts, *Administration*
EMP: 5 **EST:** 2010
SALES (est): 62.2K **Privately Held**
WEB: www.recycledlps.com
SIC: 3999 Framed artwork

(G-2064)
REFRIGERATION RESEARCH INC (PA)
Also Called: Solar Research Division
525 N 5th St (48116-1293)
P.O. Box 869 (48116-0869)
PHONE.................................810 227-1151
Edward Bottum Jr, *President*
Tim Abramson, *Vice Pres*
Gladys L Bottum, *Vice Pres*
Mike Ramalia, *Vice Pres*
Nancy B Ramalia, *Vice Pres*
EMP: 80 **EST:** 1944
SQ FT: 60,000
SALES (est): 9.5MM **Privately Held**
WEB: www.refresearch.com
SIC: 3433 3585 3443 Solar heaters & collectors; refrigeration equipment, complete; heat pumps, electric; fabricated plate work (boiler shop)

(G-2065)
RFM MANUFACTURING
2001 Orndorf Dr (48116-2398)
PHONE.................................810 522-6922
Darlene Hall, *Director*
EMP: 7 **EST:** 2015

Brighton - Livingston County (G-2066)

SALES (est): 113.3K **Privately Held**
WEB: www.rfm-inc.com
SIC: 3999 Manufacturing industries

(G-2066)
ROAD TO FREEDOM
211 N 1st St (48116-1279)
PHONE..................810 775-0992
Michele Parker, *CEO*
Gerald Parker, *CEO*
EMP: 13 EST: 2007
SALES (est): 127.4K **Privately Held**
SIC: 8322 8331 8742 1389 Substance abuse counseling; job counseling; training & development consultant; construction, repair & dismantling services; plumbing, heating, air-conditioning contractors; electrical work

(G-2067)
RYSON TUBE INC
2095 Euler Rd (48114-7411)
PHONE..................810 227-4567
Gar Boling, *President*
EMP: 10 EST: 1980
SQ FT: 15,000
SALES (est): 1MM
SALES (corp-wide): 2MM **Privately Held**
SIC: 3498 7692 Tube fabricating (contract bending & shaping); welding repair
PA: L A Burnhart Inc
  2095 Euler Rd
  Brighton MI 48114
  810 227-4567

(G-2068)
SCARLET SPARTAN INC
Also Called: Fastsigns
533 W Grand River Ave (48116-1143)
PHONE..................810 224-5700
Christian Detombeur, *CEO*
EMP: 10 EST: 2017
SALES (est): 467.4K **Privately Held**
WEB: www.fastsigns.com
SIC: 3993 Signs & advertising specialties

(G-2069)
SHARP INDUSTRIES INCORPORATED
5975 Ford Ct (48116-8511)
PHONE..................810 229-6305
Dennis Robson, *President*
EMP: 7 EST: 1996
SQ FT: 1,500 **Privately Held**
WEB: www.sharpindinc.com
SIC: 3599 Machine shop, jobbing & repair

(G-2070)
SHIRT RAZOR LLC
126 E Grand River Ave (48116-1580)
PHONE..................810 623-7116
Rob Bates,
EMP: 5 EST: 2013
SALES (est): 77.5K **Privately Held**
SIC: 2759 Screen printing

(G-2071)
SIGN A RAMA INC
Also Called: Sign-A-Rama
5050 S Old Us Highway 23 # 200 (48114-7801)
PHONE..................810 494-7446
Kailee Marcom, *Manager*
EMP: 5 **Privately Held**
WEB: www.signarama.com
SIC: 3993 Signs & advertising specialties
HQ: Sign A Rama Inc.
  2121 Vista Pkwy
  West Palm Beach FL 33411
  561 640-5570

(G-2072)
SKF USA INC
9961 Hamburg Rd (48116-8225)
PHONE..................810 231-2400
Gus Darbringhaus, *President*
EMP: 26
SALES (corp-wide): 8.6B **Privately Held**
WEB: www.skf.com
SIC: 3541 Lathes
HQ: Skf Usa Inc.
  890 Forty Foot Rd
  Lansdale PA 19446
  267 436-6000

(G-2073)
SPAGNUOLO GEORGE & SONS
9903 Loch Lomond Dr (48116-8608)
PHONE..................810 229-4424
George K Spagnuolo, *Owner*
EMP: 4 EST: 1924
SALES (est): 70.9K **Privately Held**
SIC: 2064 Candy & other confectionery products

(G-2074)
SPIRAL-MATIC INC
7772 Park Pl (48116-8387)
PHONE..................248 486-5080
Daniel T Mc Phail, *President*
EMP: 9 EST: 1987
SQ FT: 20,000
SALES (est): 1.7MM **Privately Held**
WEB: www.spiralmatic.com
SIC: 3556 Food products machinery

(G-2075)
TECHNICAL ENVIRONMENTAL SVCS
775 N 2nd St (48116-1218)
PHONE..................810 229-6323
Michael Corrigan, *President*
Timothy Corrigan, *Vice Pres*
EMP: 20 EST: 1989
SALES (est): 1.4MM **Privately Held**
SIC: 1389 Removal of condensate gasoline from field (gathering) lines

(G-2076)
TEE
7673 Athlone Dr (48116-8847)
PHONE..................810 231-2764
EMP: 4 EST: 2010
SALES (est): 92.2K **Privately Held**
SIC: 2759 Screen printing

(G-2077)
TEMCOR SYSTEMS INC
1341 Rickett Rd (48116-1879)
PHONE..................810 229-0006
Joseph Kelly, *President*
EMP: 8 EST: 1989
SQ FT: 4,500
SALES (est): 970.7K **Privately Held**
SIC: 3625 Relays & industrial controls

(G-2078)
TG FLUID SYSTEMS USA CORP
Also Called: Tg North America
100 Brighton Interior Dr (48116-7469)
PHONE..................810 220-6161
Bryan Soddrill, *President*
Holland Rebeckah, *Buyer*
Gary Mudd, *Engineer*
Mark Allen, *Finance*
Steven Yurgalonis, *CIO*
◆ EMP: 350 EST: 2000
SQ FT: 70,000
SALES (est): 64.4MM **Privately Held**
WEB: www.toyodagosei.com
SIC: 3082 3089 Unsupported plastics profile shapes; plastic processing
PA: Toyoda Gosei Co., Ltd.
  1, Nagahata, Haruhi
  Kiyosu AIC 452-0

(G-2079)
TG FLUID SYSTEMS USA CORPORATI
7854 Lochlin Dr (48116-8329)
PHONE..................248 486-8950
Ron Buck, *President*
EMP: 7 EST: 2014
SALES (est): 170.6K **Privately Held**
SIC: 3714 Motor vehicle parts & accessories

(G-2080)
THINK SOCIAL MEDIA
209 W Main St (48116-1523)
PHONE..................810 360-0170
EMP: 4 EST: 2019
SALES (est): 112K **Privately Held**
WEB: www.4awtworks.com
SIC: 2741 Miscellaneous publishing

(G-2081)
THOMPSON ART GLASS INC
6815 Grand River Rd (48114-9345)
PHONE..................810 225-8766
Dirk Thompson III, *President*
Dirk J Thompson, *Corp Secy*
EMP: 6 EST: 1929
SQ FT: 5,000
SALES (est): 285K **Privately Held**
WEB: www.thompsonartglass.com
SIC: 3231 2499 Stained glass; made from purchased glass; decorative wood & woodwork

(G-2082)
TIMBERSTONE CSTM WOODWORKS LLC
4119 Buno Rd (48114-9269)
PHONE..................810 227-6404
Kurt Bart, *Principal*
EMP: 5 EST: 2016
SALES (est): 71.7K **Privately Held**
SIC: 2431 Millwork

(G-2083)
TORQUE 2020 CMA ACQSTION LLC D
Also Called: CMA Engineering Center
7015 Fieldcrest Dr (48116-8414)
P.O. Box 349 (48116-0349)
PHONE..................810 229-2534
Don Maybee, *Branch Mgr*
EMP: 14
SALES (corp-wide): 136.3MM **Privately Held**
WEB: www.cmacable.com
SIC: 3496 Miscellaneous fabricated wire products
PA: Oak Ridge Industries, Inc.
  10896 Industrial Pkwy Nw
  Bolivar OH 44612
  330 874-2900

(G-2084)
TRANSTAR AUTOBODY TECH LLC
2040 Heiserman Dr (48114-8969)
PHONE..................810 220-3000
Monte Ahuja, *Ch of Bd*
Charles E Fuqua, *President*
Douglas Cuneaz, *Mfg Spvr*
Rick Coy, *Maint Spvr*
Julie Ramirez, *Production*
◆ EMP: 120 EST: 1920
SQ FT: 71,000
SALES (est): 22.4MM **Privately Held**
WEB: www.tat-co.com
SIC: 7213 2891 2899 2819 Coat supply; adhesives & sealants; chemical preparations; industrial inorganic chemicals; specialty cleaning, polishes & sanitation goods
HQ: Transtar Group, Inc
  7350 Young Dr
  Walton Hills OH

(G-2085)
TUBE WRIGHT INC (PA)
2111 Euler Rd (48114-7411)
PHONE..................810 227-4567
Earl M Lemley, *CEO*
Doug Beck, *Sales Mgr*
EMP: 27 EST: 2000
SQ FT: 40,000
SALES (est): 5.9MM **Privately Held**
WEB: www.usgmfg.com
SIC: 3498 Tube fabricating (contract bending & shaping)

(G-2086)
ULTIMATE TUBE BENDER PART
3245 Sandpoint Dr (48114-7500)
PHONE..................810 599-7862
EMP: 6 EST: 2019
SALES (est): 173K **Privately Held**
WEB: www.benderpartsplus.com
SIC: 3599 Machine shop, jobbing & repair

(G-2087)
UNIFIED INDUSTRIES INC (HQ)
Also Called: Plastic Tool Company American
740 Advance St (48116-1238)
PHONE..................517 546-3220
Dana Bliss, *Production*
Jason Williams, *Engineer*
Jon C Adams, *Treasurer*
William Cuellar, *Sales Staff*
Anthony Alessi, *Marketing Staff*
▲ EMP: 54 EST: 1953
SQ FT: 34,700
SALES (est): 15MM
SALES (corp-wide): 809.1MM **Publicly Held**
WEB: www.columbusmckinnon.com
SIC: 3536 Cranes, overhead traveling
PA: Columbus Mckinnon Corporation
  205 Crosspoint Pkwy
  Getzville NY 14068
  716 689-5400

(G-2088)
UNIFLEX INC
7830 Lochlin Dr (48116-8329)
PHONE..................248 486-6000
Robert D Judge, *President*
Arthur J Bucki, *Vice Pres*
Lance Mitchell, *Purch Dir*
Nancy Wade, *Controller*
EMP: 9 EST: 1979
SQ FT: 2,000
SALES (est): 1.5MM **Privately Held**
WEB: www.uniflexinc.com
SIC: 3069 3089 5162 8711 Molded rubber products; injection molding of plastics; plastics products; engineering services; mechanical rubber goods; gaskets, packing & sealing devices

(G-2089)
UNILOCK MICHIGAN INC
12591 Emerson Dr (48116-8562)
PHONE..................248 437-7037
Edward Bryant, *President*
Tony Hooper, *Vice Pres*
Joseph C Kerr, *Vice Pres*
▲ EMP: 25 EST: 1988
SALES (est): 4.7MM **Privately Held**
WEB: www.unilock.com
SIC: 3281 Paving blocks, cut stone

(G-2090)
UNITED SYSTEMS GROUP LLC (PA)
2111 Euler Rd (48114-7411)
PHONE..................810 227-4567
Doug Beck, *Vice Pres*
Earl Lemley,
Douglas Beck,
EMP: 9 EST: 2014
SQ FT: 25,000
SALES (est): 2.3MM **Privately Held**
WEB: www.usgmfg.com
SIC: 3714 Radiators & radiator shells & cores, motor vehicle

(G-2091)
VALUABLE SERVICES LLC
9290 Lee Rd Ste 106 (48116-2142)
PHONE..................512 667-7490
EMP: 4 EST: 2019
SALES (est): 96.3K **Privately Held**
SIC: 2899 Chemical preparations

(G-2092)
VECTECH PHARMACEUTICAL CONS (PA)
12501 Grand River Rd (48116-8389)
PHONE..................248 478-5820
Allan F Pfitzenmaier, *President*
EMP: 10 EST: 1978
SQ FT: 13,000
SALES (est): 4.9MM **Privately Held**
SIC: 2834 6512 7363 Pharmaceutical preparations; commercial & industrial building operation; temporary help service

(G-2093)
VECTORALL MANUFACTURING INC
7675 Lochlin Dr (48116-8329)
PHONE..................248 486-4570
Brian Ledford, *President*
Dave Ringer, *Department Mgr*
EMP: 30 EST: 1988
SQ FT: 35,000
SALES (est): 3.6MM **Privately Held**
WEB: www.vectorallmfg.com
SIC: 3599 7389 5013 3462 Machine shop, jobbing & repair; inspection & testing services; automotive supplies & parts; iron & steel forgings

GEOGRAPHIC SECTION

Bronson - Branch County (G-2121)

(G-2094)
VIKING SALES INC
169 Summit St (48116-1834)
P.O. Box 639 (48116-0639)
PHONE...................810 227-2222
John Spitler, *Principal*
Kathleen Kramer, *Corp Secy*
Elizabeth H Spitler, *Vice Pres*
▲ **EMP:** 15 **EST:** 1973
SQ FT: 12,000
SALES (est): 2.1MM **Privately Held**
WEB: www.vikingmudflaps.com
SIC: 3799 Trailers & trailer equipment

(G-2095)
WEDGE MILL TOOL INC
7771 Kensington Ct (48116-8391)
PHONE...................248 486-6400
Craig Sloan, *Principal*
Brian Dzmelyk, *Engineer*
EMP: 9 **EST:** 2016
SALES (est): 1.1MM **Privately Held**
WEB: www.wedgemill.com
SIC: 3599 Machine shop, jobbing & repair

(G-2096)
WELK-KO FABRICATORS INC
Also Called: Kar Enterprises
11777 Grand River Rd (48116-9617)
PHONE...................810 227-7500
Ron Karaisz, *President*
EMP: 4
SALES (corp-wide): 2.5MM **Privately Held**
WEB: www.welk-ko.com
SIC: 3444 5013 Sheet metal specialties, not stamped; motor vehicle supplies & new parts
PA: Welk-Ko Fabricators, Inc.
  11885 Mayfield St
  Livonia MI 48150
  734 425-6840

(G-2097)
WMT PROPERTIES INC
7771 Kensington Ct (48116-8391)
PHONE...................248 486-6400
John Yaros, *President*
Brian S Dzmelyk, *Vice Pres*
Ronald J Lezotte Jr, *Vice Pres*
Elizabeth K Johnston, *Treasurer*
Beth Johnston, *Controller*
EMP: 19 **EST:** 1982
SQ FT: 12,000
SALES (est): 2.2MM **Privately Held**
WEB: www.wedgemill.com
SIC: 3599 Machine shop, jobbing & repair

(G-2098)
WOODLAND PARK & SALES
7993 Grand River Rd (48114-9365)
PHONE...................810 229-2397
EMP: 4 **EST:** 2013
SALES (est): 195.2K **Privately Held**
SIC: 2451 5271 6515 Mobile homes; mobile homes; mobile home site operators

(G-2099)
WYMAN-GORDON FORGINGS INC
7250 Whitmore Lake Rd (48116-8558)
PHONE...................810 229-9550
James Mulvihill, *Manager*
EMP: 294
SALES (corp-wide): 245.5B **Publicly Held**
WEB: www.standardmachine.com
SIC: 3462 Iron & steel forgings
HQ: Wyman-Gordon Forgings, Inc.
  10825 Telge Rd
  Houston TX 77095
  281 856-9900

Brimley
Chippewa County

(G-2100)
BIRCH POINT WOODWORKS
5586 W Birch Point Loop (49715-9120)
PHONE...................906 322-8761
EMP: 4 **EST:** 2014
SALES (est): 76.1K **Privately Held**
SIC: 2431 Millwork

(G-2101)
BOURQUE H JAMES & ASSOC INC
3060 W M 28 (49715)
P.O. Box 292, Sault Sainte Marie (49783-0292)
PHONE...................906 635-9191
H James Bourque, *President*
EMP: 5 **EST:** 1980
SALES (est): 402.2K **Privately Held**
WEB: www.hjamesbourque.com
SIC: 1481 Mine development, nonmetallic minerals

(G-2102)
CG LOGGING
11375 W Irish Line Rd (49715-9384)
PHONE...................906 322-1018
Traverse Carole Joan, *Owner*
EMP: 5 **EST:** 2015
SALES (est): 143.6K **Privately Held**
SIC: 2411 Logging

(G-2103)
CONTINENTAL AUTO SYSTEMS INC
9301 S M 221 (49715-9218)
PHONE...................906 248-6700
Ryan Alastan, *Manager*
Terin Salo, *Maintence Staff*
EMP: 7
SALES (corp-wide): 44.6B **Privately Held**
WEB: www.continental-automotive.com
SIC: 3714 Motor vehicle parts & accessories
HQ: Continental Automotive Systems, Inc.
  1 Continental Dr
  Auburn Hills MI 48326

(G-2104)
JASON LAPONSIE
8453 Old Brimley Grade Rd (49715-9434)
P.O. Box 186 (49715-0186)
PHONE...................906 440-3567
Jason Laponsie, *Principal*
EMP: 7 **EST:** 2011
SALES (est): 156.8K **Privately Held**
SIC: 2411 Logging

(G-2105)
ZF ACTIVE SAFETY US INC
21105 W M 28 Bldg 6 (49715-9126)
PHONE...................906 248-3882
EMP: 7
SALES (corp-wide): 216.2K **Privately Held**
WEB: www.zf.com
SIC: 3714 Motor vehicle parts & accessories
HQ: Zf Active Safety Us Inc.
  12025 Tech Center Dr
  Livonia MI 48150
  734 812-6979

Brockway
St. Clair County

(G-2106)
CENTER LINE GAGE INC
110 Commerce Dr (48097-3460)
PHONE...................810 387-4300
Matt Jurcak, *CEO*
EMP: 7 **EST:** 1989
SQ FT: 8,500
SALES (est): 500K **Privately Held**
SIC: 3545 3544 8711 Machine tool accessories; special dies, tools, jigs & fixtures; machine tool design

(G-2107)
IRON CLAD WELDING LLC
11076 Norman Rd (48097-4117)
PHONE...................810 304-1180
Jeffrey Brewer, *Principal*
EMP: 6 **EST:** 2014
SALES (est): 34.1K **Privately Held**
SIC: 7692 Welding repair

(G-2108)
YALE STEEL INC
13334 Jeddo Rd (48097-2309)
PHONE...................810 387-2567
Shane W Tesluck, *President*
Robert J Tesluck, *Vice Pres*
Thomas R Tesluck, *Treasurer*
EMP: 8 **EST:** 1983
SQ FT: 9,408
SALES (est): 1.6MM **Privately Held**
WEB: www.yalesteel.com
SIC: 5211 3443 Lumber & other building materials; fabricated plate work (boiler shop)

Brohman
Newaygo County

(G-2109)
WENSTROM DSIGN FABRICATION LLC
7525 N Woodbridge Ave (49312-5129)
PHONE...................269 760-2358
Thomas C Wenstrom,
EMP: 9 **EST:** 2012
SALES (est): 406.5K **Privately Held**
WEB: www.wenstromdesignfab.com
SIC: 3441 Fabricated structural metal

Bronson
Branch County

(G-2110)
D & L TOOLING INC
675 W Central Rd (49028-9297)
PHONE...................517 369-5655
Lynn Scott, *President*
Donald S Carpenter, *Vice Pres*
Shawn Scott, *Treasurer*
Margarette Scott, *Admin Sec*
EMP: 7 **EST:** 1977
SALES (est): 588.9K **Privately Held**
WEB: www.dltooling.com
SIC: 3544 Special dies & tools

(G-2111)
DOUGLAS AUTOTECH CORPORATION (DH)
300 Albers Rd (49028-1239)
PHONE...................517 369-2315
Etsutaka Ogusu, *CEO*
Vince Dault, *Purch Mgr*
Jason Wittenmyer, *Senior Buyer*
Brett Barrett, *Engineer*
Ryan Greenamyer, *Engineer*
◆ **EMP:** 80 **EST:** 1989
SQ FT: 125,000
SALES (est): 78.8MM **Privately Held**
WEB: www.douglasautotech.com
SIC: 3714 7361 Steering mechanisms, motor vehicle; employment agencies

(G-2112)
G & W DISPLAY FIXTURES INC
300 Mill St (49028-1018)
P.O. Box 6 (49028-0006)
PHONE...................517 369-7110
EMP: 30
SALES (corp-wide): 7.1MM **Privately Held**
SIC: 2542 3993 2541 5046 Partitions And Fixtures, Except Wood, Nsk
PA: G & W Display Fixtures, Inc.
  804 N Matteson St
  Bronson MI 49028
  517 369-7341

(G-2113)
GEIGER EDM INC
898 W Chicago Rd (49028-9426)
P.O. Box 185 (49028-0185)
PHONE...................517 369-9752
Rick Outwater, *President*
Kelly Outwater, *Corp Secy*
EMP: 12 **EST:** 1998
SQ FT: 5,000
SALES (est): 1.4MM **Privately Held**
WEB: www.geigeredm.com
SIC: 3599 Machine shop, jobbing & repair; electrical discharge machining (EDM)

(G-2114)
H G GEIGER MANUFACTURING CO
416 Mill St (49028-1098)
PHONE...................517 369-7357
Hubert G Geiger, *President*
Julie Geiger, *Corp Secy*
EMP: 28 **EST:** 1968
SQ FT: 20,000
SALES (est): 800K **Privately Held**
SIC: 3451 2542 3599 Screw machine products; fixtures: display, office or store: except wood; machine shop, jobbing & repair

(G-2115)
HARVEST OAK MANUFACTURING
804 N Matteson St (49028-1133)
PHONE...................517 781-4016
EMP: 6 **EST:** 2017
SALES (est): 442.7K **Privately Held**
WEB: www.harvestoakmanufacturing.com
SIC: 3999 Manufacturing industries

(G-2116)
HICE AND SUMMEY INC (PA)
Also Called: Protective Coating Associates
404 Union St (49028-1037)
PHONE...................269 651-6217
John Summey, *President*
Mike Brown, *Vice Pres*
Ruth Summey, *Vice Pres*
EMP: 14 **EST:** 1968
SQ FT: 19,000
SALES (est): 1.8MM **Privately Held**
WEB: www.pcoating.net
SIC: 3479 Coating of metals & formed products; coating of metals with plastic or resins

(G-2117)
K & W MANUFACTURING CO INC
555 W Chicago Rd (49028-9282)
P.O. Box 97 (49028-0097)
PHONE...................517 369-9708
Korinna Burke, *President*
Hank Burke, *COO*
Wendy Kehoe, *Vice Pres*
EMP: 36 **EST:** 1968
SQ FT: 4,900
SALES (est): 3MM **Privately Held**
WEB: www.customtoolboxes.com
SIC: 3599 3444 3443 3429 Machine shop, jobbing & repair; sheet metalwork; fabricated plate work (boiler shop); manufactured hardware (general)

(G-2118)
MADDOX INDUSTRIES INC
900 W Chicago Rd (49028-9426)
P.O. Box 190 (49028-0190)
PHONE...................517 369-8665
Steve Maddox, *President*
Shelly Maddox, *Admin Sec*
EMP: 24 **EST:** 1982
SQ FT: 13,000
SALES (est): 2.7MM **Privately Held**
SIC: 3544 Special dies & tools

(G-2119)
MSC BLINDS & SHADES INC
1241 W Chicago Rd (49028-9739)
PHONE...................269 489-5188
EMP: 4
SQ FT: 3,200
SALES (est): 380K **Privately Held**
SIC: 2591 Commercial Installations / Mfg Vertical Blinds

(G-2120)
SHIMP SAND & GRAVEL LLC
822 Snow Prairie Rd (49028-9221)
PHONE...................517 369-1632
Charles F Shimp, *Administration*
EMP: 10 **EST:** 2012
SALES (est): 579.3K **Privately Held**
SIC: 1442 Construction sand & gravel

(G-2121)
VANISHING POINT LURES
232 E Grant St (49028-1508)
PHONE...................260 316-7768
Timothy Cole, *Principal*
EMP: 4 **EST:** 2018
SALES (est): 47K **Privately Held**
SIC: 3949 Sporting & athletic goods

Brooklyn
Jackson County

(G-2122)
BROOKLYN PRODUCTS INTL
171 Wamplers Lake Rd (49230-9585)
PHONE 517 592-2185
Bob Linenfelser, *Principal*
Lisa Bascom, *Vice Pres*
Bob Reed, *Engineer*
Todd Wanty, *Accounts Mgr*
Laurie McLain, *Administration*
◆ **EMP:** 25 **EST:** 1955
SQ FT: 70,000
SALES (est): 4.8MM **Privately Held**
WEB: www.brooklynproducts.com
SIC: 3086 Padding, foamed plastic

(G-2123)
BROOKLYN SPECIAL TEES
11455 Brighton Hwy (49230-9215)
PHONE 623 521-3230
William Szentmiklosi, *Principal*
EMP: 5 **EST:** 2017
SALES (est): 131.5K **Privately Held**
WEB: www.brooklynspecialtees.com
SIC: 2759 Screen printing

(G-2124)
CHELSEA VLG CANDLES & GIFTS
12110 Silver Lake Hwy (49230-9063)
PHONE 734 385-6588
EMP: 4 **EST:** 2012
SALES (est): 118.4K **Privately Held**
SIC: 3999 Candles

(G-2125)
GOETZ CRAFT PRINTERS INC
121 Paula Dr (49230-9707)
PHONE 734 973-7604
J Larry Goetz, *President*
Britton L Goetz, *Vice Pres*
Troy Herrick, *Production*
Tasha Goetz, *Marketing Staff*
Paulette Goetz, *Admin Sec*
EMP: 16 **EST:** 1900
SQ FT: 12,000
SALES (est): 917.7K **Privately Held**
WEB: www.foresightgroup.net
SIC: 2752 Commercial printing, offset

(G-2126)
HOGLE SALES & MFG LLC
208 Irwin St (49230-9282)
P.O. Box 545, Michigan Center (49254-0548)
PHONE 517 592-1980
Gregory M Hogle,
EMP: 5 **EST:** 2001
SQ FT: 500
SALES (est): 752.1K **Privately Held**
WEB: www.hoglesales.com
SIC: 3544 Special dies & tools

(G-2127)
MAXABLE INC
202 Sherman St (49230-9261)
PHONE 517 592-5638
Anton Eichmuller, *President*
Darin Klann, *Manager*
▲ **EMP:** 14 **EST:** 1992
SQ FT: 25,000
SALES (est): 1MM **Privately Held**
WEB: www.maxableinc.com
SIC: 3714 7692 Motor vehicle parts & accessories; welding repair

(G-2128)
MID-AMERICA MACHINING INC
11530 Brooklyn Rd (49230-8486)
PHONE 517 592-4945
Robert Berry, *President*
Cheryl Berry, *Corp Secy*
Peter Lobbestael, *Vice Pres*
Dan Lobbestael, *Mfg Mgr*
Linda Norton, *Purchasing*
EMP: 75
SQ FT: 55,000
SALES (est): 14.9MM **Privately Held**
WEB: www.mid-americamachining.com
SIC: 3599 Machine shop, jobbing & repair

(G-2129)
NETWORK SIGN COMPANY INC
10958 Silver Lake Hwy (49230-8618)
PHONE 517 548-1232
Peter R Smoltz, *Administration*
EMP: 5 **EST:** 2013
SALES (est): 124.3K **Privately Held**
SIC: 3993 Signs & advertising specialties

(G-2130)
PLATFORMSH INC
106 S Main St Ste 4 (49230-8588)
P.O. Box 536 (49230-0536)
PHONE 734 707-9124
Frederic Plais, *CEO*
Erin Austin, *Office Mgr*
Matt Glaman, *Consultant*
Ryan Szrama, *CTO*
EMP: 65 **EST:** 2008
SQ FT: 400
SALES (est): 10.9MM
SALES (corp-wide): 1.6MM **Privately Held**
WEB: www.commerceguys.com
SIC: 7372 Business oriented computer software
PA: Platform.Sh Sas
131 Boulevard De Sebastopol
Paris 75002
140 093-000

(G-2131)
SALESMAN INC
129 S Main St (49230-9121)
PHONE 517 592-5886
Betty Watson, *Branch Mgr*
EMP: 5 **Privately Held**
WEB: www.salesmanpublications.com
SIC: 2741 Miscellaneous publishing
PA: The Salesman Inc
1101 Greenwood Ave
Jackson MI 49203

(G-2132)
SCHEPELER CORPORATION
Also Called: Exponent, The
160 S Main St (49230-8588)
PHONE 517 592-6811
Kris D Schepeler, *Principal*
Matthew B Schepeler, *Corp Secy*
Sharon Shepard, *Office Mgr*
EMP: 20 **EST:** 1881
SQ FT: 3,600
SALES (est): 5.4MM **Privately Held**
WEB: www.theexponent.com
SIC: 2711 2752 Newspapers: publishing only, not printed on site; commercial printing, offset

Brown City
Sanilac County

(G-2133)
AQUA SYSTEMS INC
7070 Enterprise Dr (48416-9002)
PHONE 810 346-2525
Jack Dempsey, *Vice Pres*
EMP: 6
SALES (corp-wide): 2MM **Privately Held**
WEB: www.aquasystemsinc.com
SIC: 3443 5999 Heat exchangers, condensers & components; aquarium supplies
PA: Aqua Systems, Inc.
289 Exeter Rd
Hampton Falls NH 03844
603 778-8796

(G-2134)
AUTOMATED TECHNIQUES LLC
7105 Enterprise Dr (48416-9084)
PHONE 810 346-4670
Raymond L Billig,
EMP: 7 **EST:** 2000
SALES (est): 747.7K **Privately Held**
WEB: www.automatedtechniques.com
SIC: 3599 Machine shop, jobbing & repair

(G-2135)
BECHTEL SAND & GRAVEL
5278 Churchill Rd (48416-9669)
PHONE 810 346-2041
Paul Bechtel, *Owner*
EMP: 8 **EST:** 1970

SALES (est): 591.4K **Privately Held**
WEB: www.midmichiganmaterials.com
SIC: 1442 Gravel mining

(G-2136)
EMMIE DIE AND ENGINEERING CORP
7254 Maple Valley Rd (48416-8247)
P.O. Box 66 (48416-0066)
PHONE 810 346-2914
George Emmi, *President*
Joseph Kipper, *Vice Pres*
Dawn Considine, *Office Mgr*
EMP: 8 **EST:** 1977
SQ FT: 34,000
SALES (est): 990.5K **Privately Held**
WEB: www.emmiedie.com
SIC: 3544 Special dies & tools; die sets for metal stamping (presses); jigs & fixtures

(G-2137)
FRANK INDUSTRIES INC
Also Called: Xplorer Motor Home Division
4467 Vine St (48416-8657)
P.O. Box 130 (48416-0130)
PHONE 810 346-3234
David Bockstanz, *Ch of Bd*
Joseph Murray, *Senior VP*
EMP: 22 **EST:** 1967
SQ FT: 50,000
SALES (est): 219.5K **Privately Held**
WEB: www.its-llc.net
SIC: 3711 3792 3714 3716 Motor vehicles & car bodies; travel trailers & campers; motor vehicle parts & accessories; recreational van conversion (self-propelled), factory basis

(G-2138)
J T EXPRESS LTD
4200 Van Dyke Rd (48416-9473)
P.O. Box 204, Imlay City (48444-0204)
PHONE 810 724-6471
Joyce Ann Treash, *President*
EMP: 6 **EST:** 1981
SALES (est): 1.1MM **Privately Held**
WEB: www.jtexp.com
SIC: 1442 4214 Construction sand & gravel; local trucking with storage

(G-2139)
LLINK TECHNOLOGIES LLC
3953 Burnsline Rd (48416-8473)
PHONE 586 336-9370
Jeff Goulet,
Joe Gamache,
Richard Knill,
Lisa Spencer,
▲ **EMP:** 44 **EST:** 1995
SQ FT: 40,000
SALES (est): 9.1MM **Privately Held**
WEB: www.llinktechnologies.com
SIC: 3442 3444 3449 3465 Metal doors, sash & trim; sheet metalwork; miscellaneous metalwork; automotive stampings; metal stampings; steel springs, except wire

(G-2140)
MAPLE VALLEY PLASTICS LLC
4119 Main St (48416-7713)
P.O. Box 130 (48416-0130)
PHONE 810 346-3040
George Rickman, *Opers Staff*
Bill Woodall, *Mng Member*
EMP: 47 **EST:** 2006
SALES (est): 11.7MM **Privately Held**
WEB: www.maplevalleyplastics.com
SIC: 3089 Injection molding of plastics

(G-2141)
RAYS GAME
Also Called: Ray's Big Game Processing
4101 Maple St (48416-8012)
PHONE 810 346-2628
Ray Dupuie, *Owner*
Linda Dupuie, *Owner*
EMP: 4 **EST:** 1975
SALES (est): 175.6K **Privately Held**
SIC: 2011 Meat packing plants

(G-2142)
SALVO TOOL & ENGINEERING CO (PA)
3948 Burnsline Rd (48416-8473)
P.O. Box 129 (48416-0129)
PHONE 810 346-2727
Sheri Robbins, *President*
Bruce Bedker, *President*
Beverly Zobay, *Vice Pres*
EMP: 11 **EST:** 1947
SALES (est): 2.4MM **Privately Held**
WEB: www.salvotool.com
SIC: 3542 Thread rolling machines

Brownstown
Wayne County

(G-2143)
BEST CONCRETE & SUPPLY INC
17200 Dix Toledo Hwy (48193-8415)
PHONE 734 283-7055
Gary Pachota, *President*
Richard Pachota, *Vice Pres*
EMP: 7 **EST:** 1954
SQ FT: 2,500
SALES (est): 687.9K **Privately Held**
WEB: www.bestconcretesupply.com
SIC: 3273 5032 Ready-mixed concrete; concrete building products; building blocks; sand, construction; stone, crushed or broken

(G-2144)
CONTRACT FURN SOLUTIONS INC
25069 Pine Ridge Dr (48134-9085)
PHONE 734 941-2750
Helen Wages-Duggan, *CEO*
EMP: 50
SALES (est): 1.2MM **Privately Held**
SIC: 2511 Kitchen & dining room furniture

(G-2145)
CUSTOM CABINETS & MORE LLC
22752 Donnelly Ave (48193-8225)
PHONE 734 231-9086
Glenn J Goldey, *Owner*
EMP: 4 **EST:** 2011
SALES (est): 203.6K **Privately Held**
SIC: 2434 Wood kitchen cabinets

(G-2146)
FORD MOTOR COMPANY
24999 Pennsylvania Rd (48174-9603)
PHONE 734 942-6248
EMP: 14
SALES (corp-wide): 127.1B **Publicly Held**
WEB: www.ford.com
SIC: 5511 3713 3714 6153 Automobiles, new & used; truck & bus bodies; motor vehicle parts & accessories; financing of dealers by motor vehicle manufacturers organ.; buying of installment notes; passenger car leasing
PA: Ford Motor Company
1 American Rd
Dearborn MI 48126
313 322-3000

(G-2147)
GENERAL MOTORS COMPANY
20001 Brownstown Ctr Dr (48183-1679)
PHONE 248 249-6347
Cheri Payne, *Business Mgr*
Nicole Wright, *Production*
Melinda Fondaw, *Senior Buyer*
Bonnie Ohman, *Buyer*
Al Cocco, *Engineer*
EMP: 14 **Publicly Held**
WEB: www.gm.com
SIC: 5511 3714 Automobiles, new & used; motor vehicle parts & accessories
PA: General Motors Company
300 Renaissance Ctr L1
Detroit MI 48243

(G-2148)
KENNY G MFG & SLS LLC
27275 Ritter Blvd (48134-0717)
PHONE 313 218-6297
Kenneth Cox,

GEOGRAPHIC SECTION

Bruce Twp - Macomb County (G-2173)

EMP: 4 EST: 2009
SALES (est): 269.4K **Privately Held**
SIC: 3999 Manufacturing industries

(G-2149)
LINCOLN PARK DIE & TOOL CO
Also Called: Lincoln Forge
18325 Dix Toledo Hwy (48193-8406)
PHONE.................................734 285-1680
Roger Magnusson, *President*
Bruce R Magnusson, *Vice Pres*
Monica Magnusson, *Vice Pres*
Patricia Magnusson, *Treasurer*
Leisa Wilson, *Human Resources*
▼ EMP: 40 EST: 1962
SQ FT: 39,000
SALES (est): 9.3MM **Privately Held**
WEB: www.lincolnforge.com
SIC: 3462 3463 3544 Horseshoes; aluminum forgings; special dies & tools

(G-2150)
MINDCHIP INDUSTRIES LLC
22684 Starling Dr (48183-1380)
PHONE.................................313 355-2447
Jason Heien, *Principal*
EMP: 4 EST: 2018
SALES (est): 48K **Privately Held**
SIC: 3999 Manufacturing industries

(G-2151)
MTU AMERICA INC
19771 Brownstown Ctr Dr (48183-1684)
PHONE.................................248 560-8298
Thomas Koenig, *President*
EMP: 5 EST: 2013
SALES (est): 96.8K **Privately Held**
SIC: 3519 Diesel, semi-diesel or duel-fuel engines, including marine

Brownstown Township
Wayne County

(G-2152)
FUEL CELL SYSTEM MFG LLC
20001 Brownstown Ctr Dr (48183-1679)
PHONE.................................313 319-5571
Suhed Haq, *President*
EMP: 8 EST: 2017
SALES (est): 443.9K **Privately Held**
SIC: 3674 Fuel cells, solid state

Brownstown Twp
Wayne County

(G-2153)
CERCO INC (PA)
Also Called: Northern Rfractories Insul Div
27301 Fort St (48183-4973)
PHONE.................................734 362-8664
Carl Rigg, *President*
EMP: 20 EST: 1985
SQ FT: 12,000
SALES (est): 2.6MM **Privately Held**
WEB: www.cercoinc.net
SIC: 1741 3441 3297 2899 Foundation building; bricklaying; concrete block masonry laying; refractory or acid brick masonry; fabricated structural metal; nonclay refractories; chemical preparations

(G-2154)
GEOFFREY MANUFACTURING INC
20080 Trentwood Ct (48183-1016)
P.O. Box 1050, Trenton (48183-6050)
PHONE.................................734 479-4030
Geoffrey A Havens, *President*
Nancy Havens, *Admin Sec*
EMP: 5 EST: 1981
SQ FT: 8,300
SALES (est): 454.4K **Privately Held**
SIC: 3592 Valves, engine

(G-2155)
INDUSTRIAL FABRICATING INC
28233 Fort St (48183-4909)
P.O. Box 277, Trenton (48183-0277)
PHONE.................................734 676-2710
Robert Joaquin, *President*
Robert E Joaquin, *President*

Joel Joaquin, *Vice Pres*
EMP: 10 EST: 1963
SQ FT: 30,000
SALES (est): 957.6K **Privately Held**
SIC: 3441 Fabricated structural metal

(G-2156)
LIMITED LBLTY CO COLORMEMINK
23211 Lorraine Blvd # 101 (48183-3029)
PHONE.................................313 707-3366
Armani Covington,
EMP: 4 EST: 2020
SALES (est): 39.6K **Privately Held**
SIC: 3999 Hair & hair-based products

(G-2157)
STEEL TOOL & ENGINEERING CO
28005 Fort St (48183-4909)
PHONE.................................734 692-8580
Peter C La Fond, *President*
Roy W Rapp III, *Chairman*
Joan Dunne, *Safety Mgr*
Pete Grunwald, *Mfg Staff*
Jennifer Smith, *Purchasing*
EMP: 70 EST: 1959
SQ FT: 17,200
SALES (est): 17.2MM
SALES (corp-wide): 36.6MM **Privately Held**
WEB: www.steeltool.com
SIC: 3724 3511 Aircraft engines & engine parts; turbines & turbine generator sets
PA: Rapp & Son, Inc.
3767 11th St
Wyandotte MI 48192
734 283-1000

(G-2158)
SUBURBAN INDUSTRIES INC
28093 Fort St (48183-4900)
PHONE.................................734 676-6141
William James Wilson, *President*
Gregory Wilson, *Vice Pres*
EMP: 10 EST: 1962
SQ FT: 36,000
SALES (est): 1.4MM **Privately Held**
WEB: www.suburbanindustries.org
SIC: 3544 Special dies & tools

(G-2159)
SYSTRAND MANUFACTURING CORP (PA)
19050 Allen Rd (48183-1002)
PHONE.................................734 479-8100
Sharon A Cannarsa, *President*
Anthony Cannarsa, *Vice Pres*
Luis Flores, *Production*
Sandy Pike, *Purch Agent*
Dennis Brushaber, *Engineer*
◆ EMP: 159 EST: 1982
SQ FT: 200,000
SALES (est): 23.7MM **Privately Held**
WEB: www.systrand.com
SIC: 3714 8742 Motor vehicle transmissions, drive assemblies & parts; motor vehicle body components & frame; management consulting services

(G-2160)
SYSTRAND PRSTA ENG SYSTEMS LLC
19050 Allen Rd Ste 200 (48183-1002)
PHONE.................................734 479-8100
Sharon Cannarsa, *CEO*
Rob Lidster, *Exec VP*
Carlos Dias, *Vice Pres*
Jim Meadows, *Finance*
Jose Morales, *Executive*
EMP: 14 EST: 2002
SQ FT: 400
SALES (est): 186.1K **Privately Held**
WEB: www.systrand.com
SIC: 3599 Crankshafts & camshafts, machining

(G-2161)
VAMP SCREW PRODUCTS COMPANY
Also Called: Vamp Company
28055 Fort St (48183-4909)
PHONE.................................734 676-8020
David Topolewski, *President*
Allan Topolewski, *Vice Pres*

▲ EMP: 24 EST: 1946
SQ FT: 18,500
SALES (est): 2.4MM **Privately Held**
WEB: www.vampcompany.com
SIC: 3452 Nuts, metal

Bruce Twp
Macomb County

(G-2162)
ALL SEASONS AGENCY INC
Also Called: All Seasons Communications
5455 34 Mile Rd (48065-2903)
P.O. Box 100, Romeo (48065-0100)
PHONE.................................586 752-6381
Kenneth Monicatti, *President*
Beth Monicatti, *Vice Pres*
Linda Monicatti, *Admin Sec*
EMP: 6 EST: 1976
SQ FT: 1,600
SALES (est): 200K **Privately Held**
WEB: www.allseasonscommunications.com
SIC: 8743 2721 7311 Public relations & publicity; magazines: publishing only, not printed on site; advertising agencies

(G-2163)
ARCTIC SOLUTIONS INC
Also Called: CBS
74100 Van Dyke Rd (48065-3215)
PHONE.................................586 331-2600
Michael Rice, *President*
Roderick De Greef, *CFO*
EMP: 35 EST: 2019
SALES (est): 8.4MM **Publicly Held**
WEB: www.biolifesolutions.com
SIC: 3443 Cryogenic tanks, for liquids & gases
PA: Biolife Solutions, Inc.
3303 Mnte Vlla Pkwy Ste 3
Bothell WA 98021

(G-2164)
AUTO CONNECTION
75903 Peters Dr (48065-2525)
PHONE.................................586 752-6371
Nick Batsikouras, *Owner*
EMP: 4 EST: 1991 **Privately Held**
WEB: www.autodealerads.com
SIC: 2721 Magazines: publishing only, not printed on site

(G-2165)
CUSTOM BLEND FEEDS INC
77500 Brown Rd (48065-2103)
PHONE.................................810 798-3265
Robert Harrow, *President*
Sidney Williams, *Treasurer*
EMP: 6
SQ FT: 10,000
SALES (est): 539.7K **Privately Held**
SIC: 2048 5191 Prepared feeds; animal feeds

(G-2166)
DECLARKS LANDSCAPING INC
13800 33 Mile Rd (48065-3901)
PHONE.................................586 752-7200
Mike Declark, *President*
Bryan Lingemann, *General Mgr*
Annette Declark, *Treasurer*
EMP: 50 EST: 1990
SALES (est): 5.4MM **Privately Held**
WEB: www.declarkslandscaping.com
SIC: 0781 3271 0782 Landscape services; landscape architects; blocks, concrete: landscape or retaining wall; fertilizing services, lawn; mowing services, lawn; mulching services, lawn; landscape contractors

(G-2167)
HARD MILLING SOLUTIONS INC
107 Peyerk Ct (48065-4921)
PHONE.................................586 286-2300
Corey Greenwald, *President*
Michelle Greenwald, *Agent*
EMP: 6 EST: 2004
SQ FT: 5,000
SALES (est): 1.3MM **Privately Held**
WEB: www.hardmillingsolutions.com
SIC: 3544 Special dies & tools

(G-2168)
INNOVATION FAB INC
77909 Pearl Dr (48065-1610)
PHONE.................................586 752-3092
Melvin McCartt, *President*
Eugene McKee, *Sales Mgr*
Sandie McCartt, *Manager*
EMP: 8 EST: 1996
SALES (est): 149.9K **Privately Held**
SIC: 3469 Electronic enclosures, stamped or pressed metal

(G-2169)
JOMAT INDUSTRIES LTD
131 Mclean (48065-4919)
PHONE.................................586 336-1801
Catherine Taylor, *CEO*
Blake Taylor, *President*
EMP: 10 EST: 1991
SQ FT: 20,000
SALES (est): 1.4MM **Privately Held**
WEB: www.jomat.com
SIC: 3829 5084 5085 Measuring & controlling devices; industrial machine parts; industrial tools

(G-2170)
KORTEN QUALITY INC
69069 Powell Rd (48065-4920)
P.O. Box 120, Romeo (48065-0120)
PHONE.................................586 752-6255
Chester Zochowski, *President*
◆ EMP: 51 EST: 1994
SQ FT: 5,000
SALES (est): 4.8MM
SALES (corp-wide): 19.5B **Privately Held**
WEB: www.dayrossgroup.com
SIC: 3565 4225 Packaging machinery; general warehousing & storage
HQ: Day & Ross Inc
398 Main St
Hartland NB E7P 1
506 375-4401

(G-2171)
L & L PRODUCTS INC (HQ)
160 Mclean (48065-4919)
PHONE.................................586 336-1600
John Ligon, *CEO*
Tom Klieno, *President*
Larry R Schmidt, *Chairman*
Robert M Ligon, *Treasurer*
Wilbur E Lane, *Admin Sec*
◆ EMP: 400 EST: 1958
SQ FT: 207,000
SALES (est): 171.3MM **Privately Held**
WEB: www.llproducts.com
SIC: 3053 Gaskets & sealing devices; gaskets, all materials

(G-2172)
L & L PRODUCTS INC
Also Called: Romeo North
160 Mclean (48065-4919)
PHONE.................................586 752-6681
Claude Dembey, *President*
Alan Lundquist, *Manager*
EMP: 304
SQ FT: 87,000 **Privately Held**
WEB: www.llproducts.com
SIC: 3053 2891 Gaskets, packing & sealing devices; adhesives & sealants
HQ: L & L Products, Inc.
160 Mclean
Bruce Twp MI 48065
586 336-1600

(G-2173)
L & L PRODUCTS INC
Also Called: Romeo South
159 Mclean (48065-4919)
PHONE.................................586 336-1600
Susan Deeb, *Branch Mgr*
EMP: 36 **Privately Held**
WEB: www.llproducts.com
SIC: 3053 Gaskets & sealing devices; gaskets, all materials
HQ: L & L Products, Inc.
160 Mclean
Bruce Twp MI 48065
586 336-1600

Bruce Twp - Macomb County (G-2174)

(G-2174)
LANZEN INCORPORATED (PA)
Also Called: Lanzen Fabricating
100 Peyerk Ct (48065-4921)
PHONE..................586 771-7070
Terry K Lanzen, *President*
Archie Coffman, *Exec VP*
Scott Cooper, *Vice Pres*
Anne Nicolazzo, *Vice Pres*
Joseph Borowy, *Manager*
▲ EMP: 48 EST: 1960
SQ FT: 32,000
SALES: 13.7MM **Privately Held**
WEB: www.lanzen.com
SIC: **3444** 3489 2531 Sheet metal specialties, not stamped; metal housings, enclosures, casings & other containers; ordnance & accessories; vehicle furniture

(G-2175)
LASL INC
74100 Van Dyke Rd (48065-3215)
PHONE..................586 331-2600
John Brothers, *President*
Shirley Brothers, *Principal*
▲ EMP: 35 EST: 1988
SQ FT: 47,000
SALES (est): 8.5MM **Privately Held**
SIC: **3443** Cryogenic tanks, for liquids & gases

(G-2176)
MAC-MOLD BASE INC
14921 32 Mile Rd (48065-4914)
PHONE..................586 752-1956
Michael Gustavus, *President*
EMP: 47 EST: 1990
SQ FT: 16,000
SALES (est): 5MM **Privately Held**
WEB: www.macmold.com
SIC: **3544** Industrial molds

(G-2177)
ROMEO MOLD TECHNOLOGIES INC
121 Mclean (48065-4919)
PHONE..................586 336-1245
Mark Suddon, *President*
Michael Fillo, *Corp Secy*
Bob Pulliam, *Vice Pres*
Geoffrey Watz, *Sales Staff*
EMP: 16 EST: 1996
SQ FT: 15,000
SALES (est): 1.5MM **Privately Held**
WEB: www.romeomold.com
SIC: **3544** Industrial molds

(G-2178)
ROMEO TECHNOLOGIES INC
101 Mclean (48065-4919)
PHONE..................586 336-5015
Mark Suddon, *President*
Pete Ellis, *General Mgr*
Peter Ellis, *Opers Mgr*
Mischele Makhlouf, *Purch Mgr*
Suzy Palmer, *Admin Asst*
EMP: 60 EST: 1991
SQ FT: 50,000
SALES (est): 7MM **Privately Held**
WEB: www.romeotech.com
SIC: **3544** 8711 Industrial molds; engineering services

(G-2179)
ROMEO-RIM INC
Also Called: RR
74000 Van Dyke Rd (48065-3208)
PHONE..................586 336-5800
Chris Morin, *CEO*
Tim Emmitt, *President*
Adam Ritchie, *Business Mgr*
Paul Condeelis, *Vice Pres*
R Mark Hamlin Jr, *Vice Pres*
▲ EMP: 240 EST: 1982
SQ FT: 151,000
SALES (est): 39.8MM **Privately Held**
WEB: www.romeorim.com
SIC: **3089** Blow molded finished plastic products; injection molding of plastics

(G-2180)
RONALD R WELLINGTON
Also Called: Bernal Products
141 Mclean (48065-4919)
PHONE..................586 488-3087
Ronald R Wellington, *Administration*
EMP: 12 EST: 2016
SALES (est): 1MM **Privately Held**
WEB: www.bernalpunches.com
SIC: **3544** Special dies & tools

(G-2181)
SCHIENKE PRODUCTS INC
Also Called: Schienke Electric & Mch Svcs I
120 Mclean (48065-4919)
PHONE..................586 752-5454
David Schienke, *President*
Fred Schienke, *Admin Sec*
EMP: 8 EST: 1987
SQ FT: 13,000
SALES (est): 1MM **Privately Held**
WEB: www.schienkeproducts.com
SIC: **3541** Numerically controlled metal cutting machine tools

(G-2182)
SHARP MODEL CO (PA)
Also Called: Sharp Tooling Solutions
70745 Powell Rd (48065-4918)
PHONE..................586 752-3099
Roger P Walker, *President*
Dave Weaver, *Project Mgr*
Timothy Kavanaugh, *Opers Mgr*
William Boston, *Accounts Mgr*
Eric Weidner, *Supervisor*
EMP: 69 EST: 1986
SQ FT: 3,000
SALES (est): 10.4MM **Privately Held**
WEB: www.sharptoolingsolutions.com
SIC: **3544** 3714 Special dies & tools; motor vehicle parts & accessories

(G-2183)
SMART DIET SCALE LLC
75903 Peters Dr (48065-2525)
PHONE..................586 383-6734
Nick Batsikouras,
EMP: 5 EST: 2013
SALES (est): 336K **Privately Held**
WEB: www.smartdietscale.com
SIC: **7371** 3569 7389 Computer software development & applications; blast cleaning equipment, dustless;

(G-2184)
TRW OCCUPANT SAFETY SYSTEMS
14761 32 Mile Rd (48065-4900)
PHONE..................586 752-1409
Dean Estenberg, *Manager*
EMP: 5 EST: 2016
SALES (est): 108.1K **Privately Held**
SIC: **3714** Motor vehicle parts & accessories

(G-2185)
ULTRAFORM INDUSTRIES INC
150 Peyerk Ct (48065-4921)
PHONE..................586 752-4508
Donald Frattaroli, *President*
Sheryl Frattaroli, *Principal*
Debra Westbrook, *Principal*
Mike Rosenmund, *QC Dir*
Curt Davis, *QC Mgr*
EMP: 66 EST: 1960
SQ FT: 29,000
SALES (est): 8.4MM **Privately Held**
WEB: www.ultraformindustries.com
SIC: **3496** 3469 Clips & fasteners, made from purchased wire; metal stampings

(G-2186)
WILLENBORG ASSOCIATES INC
Also Called: Leblond Lathe Service
5801 34 Mile Rd (48065-2906)
PHONE..................810 724-5678
Michael Willenborg, *President*
▲ EMP: 12 EST: 1983
SALES (est): 2.4MM **Privately Held**
SIC: **3599** Machine shop, jobbing & repair

(G-2187)
YOUR HOMETOWN SHOPPER LLC
Also Called: Creative Kids Publication
11453 Covered Bridge Ln (48065-3826)
PHONE..................586 412-8500
Pamela J Meadows,
EMP: 10 EST: 1991 **Privately Held**
WEB: www.hometownshopperllc.com
SIC: **7311** 2711 7331 Advertising agencies; newspapers: publishing only, not printed on site; mailing service

(G-2188)
ZEPHYROS INC (PA)
Also Called: L&L Products
160 Mclean (48065-4919)
P.O. Box 308, Romeo (48065-0308)
PHONE..................586 336-1600
John Ligon, *CEO*
Claude Z Demby, *President*
Larry R Schmidt, *Chairman*
Robert M Ligon, *Treasurer*
Wilbur E Lane, *Admin Sec*
EMP: 417 EST: 2006
SQ FT: 207,000
SALES (est): 171.3MM **Privately Held**
WEB: www.llproducts.com
SIC: **3053** Gaskets & sealing devices

Buchanan
Berrien County

(G-2189)
BERRIEN METAL PRODUCTS INC
460 Post Rd Ste A (49107-1070)
PHONE..................269 695-5000
Larry Barrett, *President*
Valore Barrett, *Vice Pres*
Joel S Barrett, *Plant Mgr*
EMP: 18 EST: 1985
SQ FT: 46,000
SALES (est): 4.8MM **Privately Held**
WEB: www.bmp.us
SIC: **3441** Fabricated structural metal

(G-2190)
BUCHANAN METAL FORMING INC (PA)
Also Called: B M F
103 W Smith St (49107-1548)
PHONE..................269 695-3836
Richard Tapper, *Ch of Bd*
Timothy Lewis, *Engineer*
▲ EMP: 33 EST: 1990
SQ FT: 30,000
SALES (est): 6.3MM **Privately Held**
WEB: www.bmfcorp.com
SIC: **3462** Iron & steel forgings

(G-2191)
C & S MACHINE PRODUCTS INC
248 Post Rd (49107-1021)
PHONE..................269 695-6859
Joe Saratoge, *Branch Mgr*
EMP: 7
SALES (corp-wide): 10.4MM **Privately Held**
WEB: www.candsmachine.com
SIC: **3599** Machine shop, jobbing & repair
PA: C & S Machine Products, Inc.
2929 Saratore Dr
Niles MI 49120
269 695-6859

(G-2192)
CHI CO/TABOR HILL WINERY (PA)
Also Called: Tabor Hill Winery & Restaurant
185 Mount Tabor Rd (49107-8326)
PHONE..................269 422-1161
Linda Upton, *President*
▲ EMP: 70 EST: 1970
SALES (est): 3.9MM **Privately Held**
WEB: www.taborhill.com
SIC: **2084** 5812 Wines; American restaurant

(G-2193)
FINE ARTS
108 W Roe St (49107-1514)
PHONE..................269 695-6263
Karen Falkenstein, *President*
Chad Winters, *Master*
EMP: 7 EST: 2001
SALES (est): 125K **Privately Held**
SIC: **3356** Tin

(G-2194)
G P MANUFACTURING INC
16689 Bakertown Rd (49107-9201)
PHONE..................269 695-1202
Brenda L Payton, *President*
Brenda Payton, *President*
Gordon L Payton, *Vice Pres*
EMP: 7 EST: 1993
SALES (est): 490K **Privately Held**
SIC: **3599** Machine shop, jobbing & repair

(G-2195)
GATOR GRAFIX & SIGNS
13747 N Red Bud Trl (49107-9129)
PHONE..................269 362-2039
Mario Palmisano, *Owner*
EMP: 4 EST: 2017
SALES (est): 59.8K **Privately Held**
WEB: www.gator-grafix-signs.ueniweb.com
SIC: **3993** Signs & advertising specialties

(G-2196)
GENERAL MACHINE SERVICES
Also Called: Gms Industries
807 W 4th St (49107)
P.O. Box 167 (49107-0167)
PHONE..................269 695-2244
Gerald M Smedley, *President*
Michael Smedley, *Vice Pres*
▲ EMP: 5 EST: 1983
SQ FT: 12,750
SALES (est): 452.3K **Privately Held**
WEB: www.joywinch.com
SIC: **3532** 3533 3599 Mining machinery; oil field machinery & equipment; machine shop, jobbing & repair

(G-2197)
JACK-POST CORPORATION
800 E 3rd St (49107-1803)
PHONE..................269 695-7000
John T Bycraft, *President*
Charles M Pomeroy III, *Treasurer*
Ronald J Jaicomo, *Admin Sec*
◆ EMP: 41 EST: 1988
SQ FT: 260,000
SALES (est): 3.3MM **Privately Held**
WEB: www.jack-post.com
SIC: **2514** 3446 2511 Metal lawn & garden furniture; architectural metalwork; flagpoles, metal; fences or posts, ornamental iron or steel; ornamental metalwork; wood household furniture

(G-2198)
K&S CONSULTANTS LLC
Also Called: Kilgore Industries
404 River St (49107-1483)
PHONE..................269 240-7767
Brian Kilgore, *Partner*
EMP: 4
SQ FT: 58,000
SALES (est): 60K **Privately Held**
WEB: www.kilgoreindustries.us
SIC: **3541** 3548 3536 Machine tool replacement & repair parts, metal cutting types; electric welding equipment; hoisting slings

(G-2199)
LEAN FACTORY AMERICA LLC
816 E 3rd St (49107-1468)
PHONE..................513 297-3086
Kelly Sullivan, *Engineer*
Jennifer Dickson, *Office Mgr*
Keith Chabut,
◆ EMP: 5 EST: 2008
SALES (est): 3.5MM
SALES (corp-wide): 10.5MM **Privately Held**
WEB: www.leanfactoryamerica.com
SIC: **3442** Window & door frames
PA: Orgatex Gmbh & Co. Kg
Albert-Einstein-Str. 19
Langenfeld (Rheinland) NW 40764
217 310-640

(G-2200)
OPTIMYSTIC ENTERPRISES INC
Also Called: Electric Steam Generator
600 S Oak St (49107-1564)
P.O. Box 21 (49107-0021)
PHONE..................269 695-7741
Carol L Roussin, *President*
F Thomas Roussin, *Vice Pres*
Mark C Lee, *Treasurer*

Caroline J Murphy, *Admin Sec*
EMP: 5 **EST:** 1946
SQ FT: 8,000
SALES (est): 961.2K **Privately Held**
WEB: www.esgcorp.com
SIC: 3629 Mercury arc rectifiers (electrical apparatus)

(G-2201)
RAMER PRODUCTS INC
400 Post Rd (49107-1052)
P.O. Box 1027, Niles (49120-1027)
PHONE 269 409-8583
Andrew Racine, *President*
EMP: 5 **EST:** 1969
SQ FT: 8,000
SALES (est): 782.2K **Privately Held**
WEB: www.ramerproducts.com
SIC: 3829 Measuring & controlling devices

(G-2202)
REDBUD ROOTS LAB I LLC
215 Post Rd (49107-1020)
PHONE 312 656-3823
Alexander Leonowicz, *Principal*
EMP: 12 **EST:** 2019
SALES (est): 1.3MM **Privately Held**
WEB: www.redbudroots.com
SIC: 3999

(G-2203)
RKA DESIGN BUILD
11337 Coveney Rd (49107-9372)
PHONE 269 362-5558
Richard Aguilera, *Owner*
EMP: 6 **EST:** 2001
SALES (est): 87.8K **Privately Held**
SIC: 3446 7389 Architectural metalwork; design services

Buckley
Wexford County

(G-2204)
AMERICAN DIE AND MOLD INC
141 S Industrial Dr (49620-9732)
PHONE 231 269-3788
Scott Flees, *President*
EMP: 5 **EST:** 2007 **Privately Held**
SIC: 3544 Industrial molds

(G-2205)
BRIDGE TOOL AND DIE LLC
125 S Industrial Dr (49620-9732)
PHONE 231 269-3200
Greg Mort, *Business Mgr*
Brent Bridgman, *Research*
Glenn Bridgman, *Mng Member*
EMP: 8 **EST:** 2007
SALES (est): 1MM **Privately Held**
WEB: www.bridgetoolanddie.com
SIC: 3544 Special dies & tools

(G-2206)
CARDBOARD ROBOT VISUALS LLC
10199 Samson Woods Dr (49620-9592)
PHONE 231 577-8710
Jake Burgess, *Principal*
EMP: 5 **EST:** 2017
SALES (est): 90.7K **Privately Held**
WEB: www.cardboardrobotvisuals.com
SIC: 2631 Cardboard

(G-2207)
MIDWEST TRACTOR & EQUIPMENT CO
10736 N M 37 (49620-9468)
P.O. Box 66 (49620-0066)
PHONE 231 269-4100
James Jurik, *President*
Larry Cade, *Treasurer*
EMP: 18 **EST:** 1979
SQ FT: 10,200
SALES (est): 3MM **Privately Held**
WEB: www.midwesttractor.com
SIC: 3537 5511 7538 Industrial trucks & tractors; trucks, tractors & trailers: new & used; truck engine repair, except industrial

(G-2208)
SEAL RIGHT SERVICES INC
141 W Wexford Ave (49620-8600)
PHONE 231 357-5595
Theodore Allen, *Principal*
EMP: 5 **EST:** 2013
SALES (est): 128K **Privately Held**
SIC: 1389 Oil field services

Burlington
Calhoun County

(G-2209)
HAMPTON COMPANY INC
12709 M 60 E (49029-9777)
PHONE 517 765-2222
Terry Hampton, *President*
EMP: 8 **EST:** 1970
SQ FT: 22,000
SALES (est): 714.8K **Privately Held**
WEB: www.hamptongames.com
SIC: 3944 Electronic game machines, except coin-operated

Burnips
Allegan County

(G-2210)
OLDCASTLE BUILDINGENVELOPE INC
4257 30th St (49314)
PHONE 616 896-8341
Brent Moomey, *Manager*
Kathryn Hutchins, *Executive*
EMP: 5
SALES (corp-wide): 27.5B **Privately Held**
WEB: www.obe.com
SIC: 5039 5013 3231 Glass construction materials; automobile glass; products of purchased glass
HQ: Oldcastle Buildingenvelope, Inc.
5005 Lyndon B Johnson Fwy # 1050
Dallas TX 75244
214 273-3400

Burr Oak
St. Joseph County

(G-2211)
C E B TOOLING INC
335 S 2nd St (49030-5142)
P.O. Box 12 (49030-0012)
PHONE 269 489-2251
Carl Baumeister, *President*
EMP: 5 **EST:** 1997
SQ FT: 4,900
SALES (est): 785.2K **Privately Held**
WEB: www.cebtooling.com
SIC: 3089 Injection molding of plastics

(G-2212)
LEEANN PLASTICS INC
300 Halfway Rd (49030-9792)
PHONE 269 489-5035
Gary L Kirtley, *President*
Sharry Kirtley, *Corp Secy*
EMP: 18 **EST:** 1979
SQ FT: 10,500
SALES (est): 1.1MM **Privately Held**
SIC: 3089 Injection molding of plastics

(G-2213)
NAKED SHIRT CUSTOM PRTG LLC
33246 Us 12 (49030-9602)
PHONE 269 625-7235
Donette Cooper, *Principal*
EMP: 6 **EST:** 2017
SALES (est): 83.9K **Privately Held**
WEB: www.the-naked-shirt-custom-printing.business.site
SIC: 2752 Commercial printing, lithographic

(G-2214)
VICTOR SCREW PRODUCTS CO
235 S 4th St (49030-5109)
P.O. Box 274 (49030-0274)
PHONE 269 489-2760
Fax: 269 489-2940
EMP: 4 **EST:** 1937
SQ FT: 7,500
SALES (est): 172.8K **Privately Held**
SIC: 3451 Mfg Screw Machine Products

Burt
Saginaw County

(G-2215)
GREGGS WOOD DUCK BOXES
3240 Fergus Rd (48417-9615)
PHONE 989 770-5204
Gregg Bishop, *Principal*
EMP: 4 **EST:** 2011
SALES (est): 74.3K **Privately Held**
WEB: www.woodducknestboxes.com
SIC: 2431 Millwork

(G-2216)
VILLANUEVO SOLEDAD
Also Called: El Acapulco Tamales
2855 E Burt Rd (48417-2341)
P.O. Box 128 (48417-0128)
PHONE 989 770-4309
Soledad Villanuevo, *Owner*
Annette Graves, *Exec Dir*
EMP: 8 **EST:** 1981
SALES (est): 739.9K **Privately Held**
SIC: 2099 Food preparations

(G-2217)
WENDE J PERIARD
2717 E Birch Run Rd (48417-9404)
PHONE 989 770-4542
Wende J Periard, *Principal*
EMP: 5 **EST:** 2004
SALES (est): 146K **Privately Held**
SIC: 3999 Manufacturing industries

Burtchville
St. Clair County

(G-2218)
COLUMBUS OIL & GAS LLC
6436 Lakeshore Rd (48059-2557)
P.O. Box 610158, Port Huron (48061-0158)
PHONE 810 385-9140
At Kuhns III, *COO*
Charles Lawrence,
EMP: 4 **EST:** 2008
SALES (est): 1.1MM **Privately Held**
SIC: 1389 1311 Gas field services; oil field services; crude petroleum & natural gas production; crude petroleum production

(G-2219)
D AND D WELDING
6111 Eastwood Dr (48059-2531)
PHONE 810 824-3622
EMP: 5 **EST:** 2016
SALES (est): 31.5K **Privately Held**
SIC: 7692 Welding repair

(G-2220)
GREAT LAKES WELDING CO
8117 State Rd (48059-1204)
PHONE 810 689-8182
Tim Petty, *Principal*
EMP: 5 **EST:** 2013
SALES (est): 40.5K **Privately Held**
WEB: www.greatlakesweldingandfab.com
SIC: 7692 Welding repair

(G-2221)
JEFFREY S ZIMMER
6117 Wildrose Ln (48059-4313)
PHONE 810 385-0726
Jeffrey S Zimmer, *Principal*
EMP: 4 **EST:** 2018
SALES (est): 92.3K **Privately Held**
SIC: 2752 Commercial printing, lithographic

(G-2222)
MARQUIS WOOD WORKS
8793 Lakeshore Rd (48059-1116)
PHONE 810 488-9406
EMP: 4 **EST:** 2014
SALES (est): 63.9K **Privately Held**
SIC: 2431 Millwork

(G-2223)
TOASTMASTERS INTERNATIONAL
6415 State Rd (48059-2411)
PHONE 810 385-5477
Rick Stone,
EMP: 7
SALES (corp-wide): 39.8MM **Privately Held**
WEB: www.toastmasters.org
SIC: 8299 2721 Educational service, non-degree granting; continuing educ.; magazines: publishing only, not printed on site
PA: Toastmasters International
9127 S Jamaica St Ste 400
Englewood CO 80112
949 858-8255

Burton
Genesee County

(G-2224)
ADAPTIVE MFG SOLUTIONS LLC
G4206 S Saginaw St (48529-1649)
PHONE 810 743-1600
Laurie S Moncrieff,
EMP: 7 **EST:** 2007
SQ FT: 21,000
SALES (est): 754.5K **Privately Held**
WEB: www.ams-miti.com
SIC: 3544 Special dies, tools, jigs & fixtures

(G-2225)
AFFORDABLE POOL AND SPA INC
3234 Associates Dr (48529-1302)
PHONE 810 422-5058
Edward McPheeters, *President*
EMP: 15 **EST:** 2012
SALES (est): 1.2MM **Privately Held**
WEB: www.affordablepoolandsparepair.com
SIC: 5261 2842 1799 5719 Nurseries & garden centers; specialty cleaning, polishes & sanitation goods; special trade contractors; miscellaneous home furnishings; swimming pools, above ground

(G-2226)
AMERICAN ELECTRIC MOTOR CORP (PA)
4102 Davison Rd (48509-1455)
PHONE 810 743-6080
Mark Lippincott, *President*
EMP: 13 **EST:** 1979
SQ FT: 17,000
SALES (est): 4.1MM **Privately Held**
WEB: www.americanelectricmotors.com
SIC: 7694 7699 Electric motor repair; hydraulic equipment repair

(G-2227)
BNB WELDING & FABRICATION INC
3140 E Hemphill Rd (48529-1456)
PHONE 810 820-1508
Jason Brewer, *President*
EMP: 8 **EST:** 2015
SALES (est): 587K **Privately Held**
WEB: www.bnbwelding.com
SIC: 7692 1799 3312 Welding repair; welding on site; structural shapes & pilings, steel

(G-2228)
BUCKS CEMENT INC
4299 Fenton Rd (48529)
PHONE 810 233-4141
Napoleon Groleau, *President*
Joyce Groleau, *Vice Pres*
EMP: 6 **EST:** 1993

Burton - Genesee County (G-2229)

SALES (est): 366.1K **Privately Held**
SIC: 3713 Cement mixer bodies

(G-2229)
C & D ENTERPRISES INC
G4349 S Dort Hwy (48529-1805)
PHONE..................................248 373-0011
Charles Farley, *President*
Craig Hefner, *Vice Pres*
Chris Hadden, *Sales Staff*
EMP: 26 EST: 1985
SQ FT: 15,400
SALES (est): 3.2MM **Privately Held**
WEB: www.c-d-enterprises.com
SIC: 2821 3543 Plastics materials & resins; industrial patterns

(G-2230)
C/W SOUTH INC
1220 N Center Rd (48509-1427)
PHONE..................................810 767-2806
Robert Sibilsky, *President*
EMP: 43 EST: 2000
SQ FT: 70,000
SALES (est): 465.9K **Privately Held**
WEB: www.compakwebcor.com
SIC: 2653 Boxes, corrugated: made from purchased materials

(G-2231)
CAMERON S ROAT
Also Called: Mid-Michigan Mailing & Prtg
4065 Manor Dr 190443 (48519-9991)
P.O. Box 190443 (48519-0443)
PHONE..................................810 620-7628
Cameron Roat, *Principal*
EMP: 4 EST: 2015
SALES (est): 63.1K **Privately Held**
SIC: 2752 Commercial printing, lithographic

(G-2232)
CENTURY ROLL INC
G4463 S Dort Hwy Ste C (48529-1837)
PHONE..................................810 743-5065
Donna Hedrick, *President*
EMP: 10 EST: 2015
SALES (est): 1.1MM **Privately Held**
WEB: www.centuryroll.com
SIC: 3441 Fabricated structural metal

(G-2233)
COMPAK INC
Also Called: Compac
1220 N Center Rd (48509-1427)
PHONE..................................989 288-3199
Clarence Koan, *Manager*
EMP: 5
SALES (corp-wide): 3.6MM **Privately Held**
WEB: www.compakinc.com
SIC: 2653 5113 Display items, corrugated: made from purchased materials; corrugated & solid fiber boxes
PA: Compak, Inc.
1220 N Center Rd
Burton MI 48509
810 767-2806

(G-2234)
CUSTOM COMPONENTS TRUSS CO
Also Called: Custom Wood Products
3109 E Bristol Rd (48529-1411)
PHONE..................................810 744-0771
Peter Bomireto, *President*
Patricia Bomireto, *Vice Pres*
EMP: 23 EST: 1984
SALES (est): 2.8MM **Privately Held**
SIC: 2439 Trusses, wooden roof

(G-2235)
FLINT BOXMAKERS INC
Also Called: Landahl Packaging Systems
G 2490 E Bristol Rd (48529)
P.O. Box 41, Flint (48501-0041)
PHONE..................................810 743-0400
Virginia R Landaal, *Ch of Bd*
Thomas Landaal, *President*
Stephen Landaal, *Exec VP*
Martha Jeanne Stetson, *Treasurer*
James Trembley, *Admin Sec*
EMP: 1 EST: 1959
SQ FT: 86,000

SALES (est): 1.2MM
SALES (corp-wide): 48.2MM **Privately Held**
WEB: www.landaal.com
SIC: 2653 Boxes, corrugated: made from purchased materials; boxes, solid fiber: made from purchased materials
PA: Delta Containers, Inc.
1400 Eddy St
Bay City MI 48708
810 742-2730

(G-2236)
GREAT LAKES EPOXY COATINGS LLC
1469 Casto Blvd (48509-2013)
PHONE..................................810 820-7073
Joel Hammon, *Principal*
EMP: 5 EST: 2016
SALES (est): 47.2K **Privately Held**
WEB: www.glcmich.com
SIC: 2851 Epoxy coatings

(G-2237)
KIRBY METAL CORPORATION
Also Called: Kirby Steel
4072 Flint Asphalt Dr (48529-1857)
PHONE..................................810 743-3360
James R Kirby, *President*
Michael Kirby, *Vice Pres*
EMP: 20 EST: 1994
SQ FT: 42,000
SALES (est): 3.3MM **Privately Held**
SIC: 3441 Fabricated structural metal

(G-2238)
KRAUS FIRE EQUIPMENT INC
G4080 S Dort Hwy (48529-1812)
P.O. Box 1063, Flint (48501-1063)
PHONE..................................810 744-4780
Milton McKinney, *President*
Richard Battstone, *Vice Pres*
EMP: 6 EST: 1948
SQ FT: 5,000
SALES (est): 750K **Privately Held**
SIC: 5099 7389 3999 Fire extinguishers; fire extinguisher servicing; fire extinguishers, portable

(G-2239)
METAL SPINNING SPECIALISTS
3217 Eastgate St (48519-1554)
PHONE..................................810 743-6797
Thomas Pierson, *Principal*
EMP: 7 EST: 2010
SALES (est): 105.8K **Privately Held**
WEB: www.precisionmetalspinning.com
SIC: 3469 Spinning metal for the trade

(G-2240)
MID WEST PALLET
2206 E Parkwood Ave (48529-1768)
PHONE..................................810 919-3072
Marcus Ellis, *Principal*
EMP: 4 EST: 2010
SALES (est): 151.3K **Privately Held**
SIC: 2448 Pallets, wood

(G-2241)
MJ MFG CO
2441 E Bristol Rd (48529-1304)
PHONE..................................810 744-3840
Edward P Arends, *President*
Zanita Arends, *Admin Sec*
EMP: 7 EST: 1978
SQ FT: 62,000
SALES (est): 997.4K **Privately Held**
SIC: 3714 Motor vehicle parts & accessories

(G-2242)
OMARA SPRUNG FLOORS INC
3130 Eugene St (48519-1655)
PHONE..................................810 743-8281
Edward J Omara, *President*
Mary Omara, *Vice Pres*
EMP: 7 EST: 1999
SQ FT: 5,000
SALES (est): 837.9K **Privately Held**
WEB: www.sprungfloors.com
SIC: 2426 Flooring, hardwood

(G-2243)
PRO-TECH MACHINE INC
3085 Joyce St (48529-1421)
PHONE..................................810 743-1854

David Currie, *President*
Scott Kamieniecki, *Controller*
EMP: 25 EST: 1996
SQ FT: 17,000
SALES (est): 4.6MM **Privately Held**
WEB: www.protechmachine.net
SIC: 3549 3544 Assembly machines, including robotic; special dies, tools, jigs & fixtures

(G-2244)
SCHMALD TOOL & DIE INC (PA)
G4206 S Saginaw St (48529-1695)
PHONE..................................810 743-1600
Laurie S Moncrieff, *President*
EMP: 15 EST: 1948
SQ FT: 30,000 **Privately Held**
WEB: www.ams-miti.com
SIC: 3544 Special dies & tools; dies & die holders for metal cutting, forming, die casting; forms (molds), for foundry & plastics working machinery

(G-2245)
SHAMROCK FABRICATING INC
2347 E Bristol Rd (48529-1304)
PHONE..................................810 744-0677
George Gilliam Jr, *President*
Tina Tomaszewski, *Corp Secy*
EMP: 10 EST: 1985
SQ FT: 5,800
SALES (est): 266K **Privately Held**
SIC: 3412 Pails, shipping: metal

(G-2246)
SOROC PRODUCTS INC
4349 S Dort Hwy (48529)
PHONE..................................810 743-2660
Dennis Cox, *CEO*
EMP: 49 EST: 1973
SQ FT: 24,000
SALES (est): 5.8MM **Privately Held**
WEB: www.sorocproducts.com
SIC: 3089 Molding primary plastic

(G-2247)
SUGAR SUGAR COTTON CANDY CO ◆
3300 S Center Rd (48519-1458)
P.O. Box 99402, Troy (48099-9402)
PHONE..................................248 847-0070
Amber Gray, *CEO*
EMP: 5 EST: 2021
SALES (est): 200K **Privately Held**
SIC: 2064 Candy & other confectionery products

(G-2248)
TERRA GREEN CERAMICS INC
1307 N Belsay Rd (48509-1602)
PHONE..................................810 742-4611
Bill Cokley, *Administration*
EMP: 6 EST: 2010
SALES (est): 108.1K **Privately Held**
SIC: 3269 Pottery products

(G-2249)
TYRONE TOOL COMPANY INC
Also Called: J T Products
3336 Associates Dr (48529-1302)
PHONE..................................810 742-4762
Dennis Conklin, *President*
Karen Conklin, *President*
EMP: 4 EST: 1974
SQ FT: 2,400
SALES (est): 50K **Privately Held**
SIC: 3599 Machine shop, jobbing & repair

(G-2250)
VERNS THREEDPRINTING
3336 Leta Ave (48529-1062)
PHONE..................................810 564-5184
Laverne Kingsbury III, *Principal*
EMP: 4 EST: 2019
SALES (est): 61.9K **Privately Held**
SIC: 2752 Commercial printing, lithographic

(G-2251)
WEBCOR PACKAGING CORPORATION (PA)
1220 N Center Rd (48509-1427)
PHONE..................................810 767-2806
William Martin, *Ch of Bd*
Luana Galbeno, *Project Engr*

Mark Blackburn, *Manager*
Megan Zahnow, *Manager*
John Goggins, *Shareholder*
▲ EMP: 3 EST: 1981
SQ FT: 70,000
SALES (est): 17.2MM **Privately Held**
WEB: www.compakcor.com
SIC: 2653 Boxes, corrugated: made from purchased materials

Byron
Shiawassee County

(G-2252)
ALL AMERICAN WELDING LLC
14392 Barnes Rd (48418-9738)
PHONE..................................517 294-2480
Lonnie Gene Lane Jr, *Principal*
EMP: 5 EST: 2015
SALES (est): 48.3K **Privately Held**
WEB: www.allamericanweldingllc.com
SIC: 7692 Welding repair

(G-2253)
FORSYTH MILLWORK AND FARMS
15315 Duffield Rd (48418-9543)
PHONE..................................810 266-4000
Michael Forsyth, *Owner*
EMP: 5 EST: 1985
SQ FT: 6,500
SALES (est): 257.3K **Privately Held**
SIC: 2431 Millwork

(G-2254)
GUILE & SON INC
11951 Rathbon Rd (48418-9614)
PHONE..................................517 376-2116
Ted Guile, *President*
EMP: 5 EST: 2008
SALES (est): 150K **Privately Held**
SIC: 3446 Architectural metalwork

(G-2255)
ON THE SIDE SIGN DSIGN GRPHICS
15216 Murray Rd (48418-9006)
PHONE..................................810 266-7446
Dan Rozboril, *Owner*
Steve Fairman, *Partner*
EMP: 4 EST: 1991
SQ FT: 5,500
SALES (est): 213.7K **Privately Held**
SIC: 3993 7532 3479 3353 Signs & advertising specialties; customizing services, non-factory basis; etching & engraving; aluminum sheet, plate & foil; products of purchased glass; commercial printing, lithographic

(G-2256)
PRECISION WELDING N FAB
10500 Rolston Rd (48418-9090)
PHONE..................................810 931-6853
Travis Alander, *Principal*
EMP: 4 EST: 2017
SALES (est): 54.2K **Privately Held**
SIC: 7692 Welding repair

Byron Center
Kent County

(G-2257)
ALAN BRUCE ENTERPRISES
4590 28th St Sw (49315-9609)
PHONE..................................616 262-4609
Bruce Breuker, *President*
EMP: 6 EST: 1979 **Privately Held**
SIC: 3312 Light oil crude from chemical recovery coke ovens

(G-2258)
ATW INDUSTRIES LLC
525 100th St Sw (49315-8539)
PHONE..................................616 318-6052
Andrew Walma, *Principal*
EMP: 4 EST: 2016
SALES (est): 92.7K **Privately Held**
WEB: www.atwindustries.com
SIC: 3999 Manufacturing industries

GEOGRAPHIC SECTION
Byron Center - Kent County (G-2286)

(G-2259)
BENNETT FUNERAL COACHES INC
584 76th St Sw B (49315-8307)
PHONE.................................616 538-8100
Rex Troost, *President*
W Rance Bennett, *Vice Pres*
EMP: 8 **EST:** 2006
SQ FT: 7,000
SALES (est): 760K **Privately Held**
WEB: www.bennettfuneralcoaches.com
SIC: 3711 Hearses (motor vehicles), assembly of

(G-2260)
BLIND SPOT AND MORE LLC
725 84th St Sw (49315-9307)
PHONE.................................616 828-6495
EMP: 6 **EST:** 2018
SALES (est): 148.6K **Privately Held**
WEB: www.myblindspot.org
SIC: 2591 Window blinds

(G-2261)
BPV LLC
Also Called: Bpv Environmental
511 76th St Sw (49315-8306)
PHONE.................................616 281-4502
Kevin Arnold, *General Mgr*
Laureen Hiscock, *Accounting Mgr*
Jody Black, *Mng Member*
Amber Eckert-Howe, *Manager*
Nicole Spain, *Manager*
EMP: 50 **EST:** 2001
SALES (est): 10MM
SALES (corp-wide): 48.2MM **Privately Held**
WEB: www.papergatorrecycling.com
SIC: 2611 Pulp manufactured from waste or recycled paper
HQ: Pestell Pet Products Inc
141 Hamilton Rd Suite 794
New Hamburg ON N3A 2
519 662-2877

(G-2262)
BREWTS LLC
1260 100th St Sw Ste 2 (49315-9342)
P.O. Box 429 (49315-0429)
PHONE.................................616 291-1117
EMP: 5 **EST:** 2015
SALES (est): 475.9K **Privately Held**
WEB: www.brewtsmix.com
SIC: 5149 2099 Dog food; sugar

(G-2263)
CHAMPION SCREEN PRINTERS
7355 Clyde Park Ave Sw (49315-6936)
PHONE.................................616 881-0760
EMP: 4 **EST:** 2018
SALES (est): 88.9K **Privately Held**
WEB: www.championscreenprinters.com
SIC: 2759 Screen printing

(G-2264)
CONSUMERS CONCRETE CORPORATION
8257 S Division Ave (49315-9031)
PHONE.................................616 827-0063
Gregg Ferguson, *Manager*
EMP: 8
SALES (corp-wide): 42.6MM **Privately Held**
WEB: www.consumersconcrete.com
SIC: 3273 Ready-mixed concrete
PA: Consumers Concrete Corporation
3506 Lovers Ln
Kalamazoo MI 49001
269 342-0136

(G-2265)
CUSTOM DOOR PARTS
8177 Clyde Park Ave Sw (49315-9585)
PHONE.................................616 949-5000
John H Brinkert Sr, *President*
EMP: 15 **EST:** 2017
SALES (est): 1.3MM **Privately Held**
WEB: www.customdoorparts.com
SIC: 2499 Laundry products, wood

(G-2266)
DIE CAD GROUP
8595 Byron Commerce Dr Sw (49315-9097)
PHONE.................................937 243-8357
EMP: 5 **EST:** 2019
SALES (est): 210K **Privately Held**
SIC: 3599 Machine shop, jobbing & repair

(G-2267)
DIOCESAN PUBLICATIONS (PA)
1050 76th St Sw (49315-8166)
P.O. Box 2461, Grand Rapids (49501-2461)
PHONE.................................616 878-5200
Robert Zielke, *Ch of Bd*
Carl Galant, *President*
Kevin Stapleton, *Exec VP*
Richard Wilterdink, *Vice Pres*
Beth Simon, *Production*
EMP: 40 **EST:** 1960
SQ FT: 11,000
SALES (est): 9.4MM **Privately Held**
WEB: www.diocesan.com
SIC: 2741 Business service newsletters: publishing & printing

(G-2268)
DUST & ASHES PUBLICATIONS
8940 Sorrento Ridge Dr Se (49315-9351)
PHONE.................................231 722-6657
EMP: 5 **EST:** 2008
SALES (est): 77.4K **Privately Held**
SIC: 2741 Miscellaneous publishing

(G-2269)
FABTEC ENTERPRISES INC
8538 Centre Indus Dr Sw (49315-9291)
PHONE.................................616 878-9288
Tim Stevens, *President*
Mitch Dalman, *Vice Pres*
Gregg Miller, *Project Mgr*
Jeremy Gress, *Manager*
EMP: 12 **EST:** 1995 **Privately Held**
WEB: www.fabtecent.com
SIC: 3316 Cold finishing of steel shapes

(G-2270)
FLOW-RITE CONTROLS LTD
960 74th St Sw (49315-7914)
PHONE.................................616 583-1700
Robert Burnetter, *CEO*
Dan Campau, *President*
Rob McKnight, *Regional Mgr*
Ashley Tobin, *Regional Mgr*
Steven Wong, *Business Mgr*
EMP: 35 **EST:** 1981
SQ FT: 25,000
SALES (est): 9.8MM **Privately Held**
WEB: www.flow-rite.com
SIC: 3494 3594 3728 3823 Valves & pipe fittings; fluid power pumps & motors; aircraft parts & equipment; industrial instrmnts msrmnt display/control process variable

(G-2271)
G & T INDUSTRIES INC (PA)
1001 76th St Sw (49315-7956)
PHONE.................................616 452-8611
Roland Grit, *President*
Dave Boggiano, *General Mgr*
John Bosch, *General Mgr*
Paul Wise, *General Mgr*
Kevin Kolesar, *Exec VP*
▲ **EMP:** 90 **EST:** 1954
SQ FT: 205,000
SALES (est): 53.5MM **Privately Held**
WEB: www.gtindustries.com
SIC: 3086 5072 Insulation or cushioning material, foamed plastic; packaging & shipping materials, foamed plastic; hardware

(G-2272)
GNAP LLC (PA)
Also Called: Surfaceprep
9000 Byron Commerce Dr Sw (49315-8077)
PHONE.................................616 583-5000
Michael Currie, *CEO*
Karen Thompson, *CFO*
Tyler Hitson, *Controller*
EMP: 5 **EST:** 2013
SALES (est): 11.8MM **Privately Held**
WEB: www.grandnorthernproducts.com
SIC: 5085 3272 Abrasives; concrete products

(G-2273)
GNASS MASONRY LLC
6612 Sunfield Dr Sw (49315-9451)
PHONE.................................616 530-3214
Scott Gnass, *Agent*
EMP: 6 **EST:** 2018
SALES (est): 223.6K **Privately Held**
SIC: 2024 Yogurt desserts, frozen

(G-2274)
GRABBER INC
365 84th St Sw Ste 4 (49315-7936)
P.O. Box 1191, Dalton GA (30722-1191)
PHONE.................................616 940-1914
John Bradley Wagner Jr, *President*
Gary Gerds, *Vice Pres*
John Weathers, *Treasurer*
Joe Vergona, *Director*
Takafumi Sakaguchi, *Admin Sec*
EMP: 32 **EST:** 2009
SALES (est): 2.9MM **Privately Held**
SIC: 2392 5023 Blankets, comforters & beddings; blankets

(G-2275)
GRAND RAPIDS CHAIR COMPANY
1250 84th St Sw (49315-8048)
PHONE.................................616 774-0561
Dave Miller, *CEO*
Geoff Miller, *COO*
Geoffrey Miller, *Vice Pres*
Tom Southwell, *Vice Pres*
Andrew Johnson, *Engineer*
▲ **EMP:** 120 **EST:** 1991
SQ FT: 150,000
SALES (est): 32MM **Privately Held**
WEB: www.grandrapidschair.com
SIC: 2511 Wood household furniture

(G-2276)
GRIFFEN FAB WORKS LLC
10195 S Kent Dr Sw (49315-6945)
P.O. Box 429 (49315-0429)
PHONE.................................616 890-0621
Mark Griffen, *Administration*
EMP: 6 **EST:** 2017
SALES (est): 155.1K **Privately Held**
SIC: 3441 Fabricated structural metal

(G-2277)
GROSS VENTURES INC
Also Called: Iroquois Hoods
6172 Valduga Dr Sw Ste B (49315-9614)
PHONE.................................231 767-1301
Mike Gross, *President*
EMP: 5 **EST:** 1964
SALES (est): 886.7K **Privately Held**
SIC: 3821 Laboratory apparatus & furniture

(G-2278)
INGLASS USA INC (DH)
Also Called: Hrsflow
920 74th St Sw (49315-7914)
PHONE.................................616 228-6900
Maurizio Bazzo, *Principal*
Marcello Simoncini, *Engineer*
Derric Tatum, *Engineer*
Tammy Baker, *Human Resources*
Tim Bruin, *Cust Mgr*
▲ **EMP:** 48 **EST:** 2014
SALES (est): 12.1MM **Privately Held**
WEB: www.hrsflow.com
SIC: 3544 Industrial molds
HQ: Inglass Spa
Via Piave 4
San Polo Di Piave TV 31020
042 275-0111

(G-2279)
KENTWOOD MANUFACTURING CO
6172 Valduga Dr Sw Ste F (49315-9614)
PHONE.................................616 698-6370
James Fennema Jr, *CEO*
Mike Fennema, *President*
Dawn Fennema, *Admin Sec*
▲ **EMP:** 25 **EST:** 1955
SALES (est): 4.1MM **Privately Held**
WEB: www.kentwoodmfg.com
SIC: 2426 2511 3231 Hardwood dimension & flooring mills; wood household furniture; products of purchased glass

(G-2280)
LAMON GROUP INC
Also Called: 3dx Tech
889 76th St Sw Unit 1 (49315-8400)
PHONE.................................616 710-3169
Matthew Howlett, *President*
Linda Dykstra, *Manager*
▲ **EMP:** 15 **EST:** 2008
SALES (est): 115.4K **Privately Held**
SIC: 2759 Commercial printing

(G-2281)
MAYVILLE ENGINEERING CO INC
990 84th St Sw (49315-9301)
PHONE.................................616 878-5235
Robert D Kamphuis, *CEO*
Amanda Overway, *Accounts Mgr*
Bob Borrink, *Supervisor*
EMP: 84
SALES (corp-wide): 357.6MM **Publicly Held**
WEB: www.mecinc.com
SIC: 3469 Stamping metal for the trade
PA: Mayville Engineering Co Inc
715 South St
Mayville WI 53050
920 387-4500

(G-2282)
MCDONALD ACQUISITIONS LLC
Also Called: Proficient Machine & Tool
8074 Clyde Park Ave Sw (49315-9332)
PHONE.................................616 878-7800
Thomas McDonald, *President*
EMP: 40 **EST:** 2013
SQ FT: 38,000
SALES (est): 4.7MM **Privately Held**
WEB: www.proficientmachineautomation.com
SIC: 3599 Machine shop, jobbing & repair

(G-2283)
MCM DISPOSAL LLC
978 64th St Sw (49315-8685)
PHONE.................................616 656-4049
Dan Strock,
Chad Arp,
EMP: 5 **EST:** 2011
SQ FT: 10,000
SALES (est): 588.3K **Privately Held**
WEB: www.mcmdisposal.com
SIC: 3443 4953 Dumpsters, garbage; recycling, waste materials; refuse collection & disposal services; rubbish collection & disposal; ashes, collection & disposal

(G-2284)
MICHAEL KORS
350 84th St Sw Ste 700 (49315-7003)
PHONE.................................616 730-7071
EMP: 5 **EST:** 2018
SALES (est): 42.5K **Privately Held**
WEB: www.locations.michaelkors.com
SIC: 2389 Apparel & accessories

(G-2285)
MICRO ENGINEERING INC
Also Called: Micro Belmont
257 Sorrento Dr Se (49315-9315)
PHONE.................................616 534-9681
James Jolliffe, *President*
EMP: 7 **EST:** 1967
SALES (est): 292.5K **Privately Held**
WEB: www.micro-belmont.com
SIC: 3842 3599 5012 5599 Traction apparatus; machine shop, jobbing & repair; snowmobiles; snowmobiles; special dies, tools, jigs & fixtures; hand & edge tools

(G-2286)
MIDWEST DIRECT TRANSPORT INC
1144 73rd St Sw Ste A (49315-6924)
PHONE.................................616 698-8900
David B Welsch, *President*
David Eninga, *President*
Jim Sterk, *Manager*
EMP: 15 **EST:** 2002
SALES (est): 2.4MM **Privately Held**
SIC: 3799 Trailers & trailer equipment

Byron Center - Kent County (G-2287)　　　　　　　　　　　　　　　　　　　　　　　　　　**GEOGRAPHIC SECTION**

(G-2287)
MIX MASTERS INC
530 76th St Sw Ste 400 (49315-8042)
PHONE..................................616 490-8520
Christopher Davey, *Principal*
EMP: 5 EST: 2016
SALES (est): 166.3K **Privately Held**
SIC: 3273 Ready-mixed concrete

(G-2288)
MODEL PATTERN COMPANY INC
Also Called: Mp Components
8499 Centre Indus Dr Sw (49315-9292)
PHONE..................................616 878-9710
Joseph Schlatter, *President*
Otto Schlatter, *Chairman*
John Schlatter, *Vice Pres*
Randy Veldhouse, *Plant Mgr*
Blair Bissell, *Project Mgr*
EMP: 40 EST: 1973
SQ FT: 32,000
SALES (est): 4.5MM **Privately Held**
WEB: www.mpcomponents.net
SIC: 3544 Industrial molds

(G-2289)
NIKE INC
Also Called: Unknown
350 84th St Sw Ste 300 (49315-7004)
PHONE..................................616 583-0754
Jessica Hirsh, *Engineer*
EMP: 5
SALES (corp-wide): 44.5B **Publicly Held**
WEB: www.nike.com
SIC: 3021 Rubber & plastics footwear
PA: Nike, Inc.
　1 Sw Bowerman Dr
　Beaverton OR 97005
　503 671-6453

(G-2290)
OFLOW-RITE CONTROLS LTD
960 74th St Sw (49315-7914)
PHONE..................................616 583-1700
Mike Semm, *Opers Staff*
Ashley Tobin, *Sales Staff*
EMP: 20 EST: 1999
SALES (est): 2.2MM **Privately Held**
WEB: www.flow-rite.com
SIC: 3823 Industrial instrmnts msrmnt display/control process variable

(G-2291)
PIONEER STEEL CORPORATION
Also Called: Pioneer Die Sets
8700 Byron Commerce Dr Sw (49315-8125)
PHONE..................................616 878-5800
Jeff Burk, *Project Mgr*
Greg Tapper, *Site Mgr*
Dave Smallridge, *Engineer*
Craig Elliott, *Sales Mgr*
James Shannon, *Regl Sales Mgr*
EMP: 32
SALES (corp-wide): 21.1MM **Privately Held**
WEB: www.pioneersteel.us
SIC: 3544 Die sets for metal stamping (presses)
PA: Pioneer Steel Corporation
　7447 Intervale St
　Detroit MI 48238
　313 933-9400

(G-2292)
PRO-VISION SOLUTIONS LLC
Also Called: Pro-Vision Video Systems
8625 Byron Commerce Dr Sw (49315-8249)
PHONE..................................616 583-1520
Michael Finn, *President*
Liz Peacock, *Vice Pres*
Adam Hinman, *Materials Mgr*
Steve Stanberry, *Human Res Mgr*
Andrew Beach, *Sales Staff*
▲ EMP: 90 EST: 2003
SALES (est): 24MM **Privately Held**
WEB: www.provisionusa.com
SIC: 3651 Household audio & video equipment

(G-2293)
PROVISION CNC LLC
1704 Kingsland Dr (49315-9551)
PHONE..................................616 309-4545
Kurt Tedford, *Principal*
EMP: 4 EST: 2018
SALES (est): 138.4K **Privately Held**
WEB: www.provisioncnc.com
SIC: 3599 Machine shop, jobbing & repair

(G-2294)
QUARRY RIDGE STONE INC
555 Ste B Sw (49315)
PHONE..................................616 827-8244
Daniel W Fox, *President*
Joe Fox, *Manager*
EMP: 10 EST: 2002
SALES (est): 1MM **Privately Held**
WEB: www.qrstone.com
SIC: 3281 Stone, quarrying & processing of own stone products

(G-2295)
SHOP MAKARIOS LLC
Also Called: MAKARIOS DECOR
4390 104th St Sw (49315-9713)
PHONE..................................800 479-0032
Maxwell Kolenda, *CEO*
Maxwell Kolend, *President*
Airika Kolenda, *Vice Pres*
EMP: 12 EST: 2014
SALES (est): 610.3K **Privately Held**
WEB: www.shopmakarios.com
SIC: 3993 7299 2511 5719 Signs, not made in custom sign painting shops; stitching, custom; wood household furniture; bedding (sheets, blankets, spreads & pillows); art & architectural supplies; factory furniture & fixtures

(G-2296)
TG MANUFACTURING LLC (PA)
Also Called: Dorr Industries
8197 Clyde Park Ave Sw (49315-9585)
PHONE..................................616 935-7575
Garret Strbik, *Vice Pres*
Sharma Ramasubramania, *Opers Mgr*
Patricia Rukundo, *Purchasing*
Joel Vandonkelaar, *Sales Mgr*
Tadas Anuzis, *Sales Staff*
EMP: 2 EST: 2008
SQ FT: 30,000
SALES (est): 13.6MM **Privately Held**
WEB: www.tg-manufacturing.com
SIC: 3498 3441 3469 Tube fabricating (contract bending & shaping); fabricated structural metal; metal stampings

(G-2297)
USHER TOOL & DIE INC
1015 84th St Sw (49315-9301)
PHONE..................................616 583-9160
Jay Usher, *President*
EMP: 21 EST: 1975
SQ FT: 10,000
SALES (est): 2.3MM **Privately Held**
WEB: www.usher-td.com
SIC: 3469 3544 Metal stampings; jigs & fixtures

(G-2298)
VAN BEEKS CUSTOM WOOD PRODUCTS
7950 Clyde Park Ave Sw (49315-7808)
PHONE..................................616 583-9002
Kevin Van Volkinburg, *President*
EMP: 12 EST: 1980
SQ FT: 8,500
SALES (est): 1.3MM **Privately Held**
WEB: www.vanbeekscwp.com
SIC: 2431 Doors, wood

(G-2299)
VISUAL WORKPLACE BYRON CTR INC
7381 Ardith Ct Sw Ste A (49315-8056)
PHONE..................................616 583-9400
Rhonda Kovera, *CEO*
Bruce Smith, *Business Mgr*
Amanda Powers, *Sales Staff*
▲ EMP: 2 EST: 2008
SQ FT: 5,000
SALES (est): 1.2MM **Privately Held**
WEB: www.visualworkplaceinc.com
SIC: 3993 Signs & advertising specialties

(G-2300)
VISUAL WORKPLACE LLC
1300 Richfield Ct Sw (49315-9493)
PHONE..................................616 583-9400
Rhonda Kovera, *Principal*
Melissa Brandt, *Accounts Mgr*
Laura Baker, *Sales Staff*
▲ EMP: 11 EST: 2003
SALES (est): 1.1MM **Privately Held**
WEB: www.visualworkplaceinc.com
SIC: 3993 Signs & advertising specialties

(G-2301)
WALTHER TROWAL LLC (HQ)
6147 Valduga Dr Sw Ste A (49315-9028)
PHONE..................................616 455-8940
Konrad Stadler, *President*
Ken Raby, *Vice Pres*
Greg Smolka, *Purch Mgr*
Jacob Gumowski, *Sales Staff*
Gregg Ottaway, *Manager*
◆ EMP: 12 EST: 2016
SALES: 7.9MM
SALES (corp-wide): 36MM **Privately Held**
WEB: www.walthertrowal.com
SIC: 3694 5084 3449 Engine electrical equipment; machine tools & metalworking machinery; miscellaneous metalwork
PA: Walther Trowal Gmbh & Co. Kg
　Rheinische Str. 35-37
　Haan NW 42781
　212 957-10

(G-2302)
WARMERSCOM
365 84th St Sw Ste 4 (49315-7936)
PHONE..................................800 518-0938
EMP: 5 EST: 2014
SALES (est): 79.6K **Privately Held**
WEB: www.warmers.com
SIC: 2252 Tights & leg warmers

(G-2303)
WOOD TECH INC
670 76th St Sw (49315-6959)
PHONE..................................616 455-0800
Mike Staples, *President*
Randy Franks, *Manager*
EMP: 21 EST: 1982
SQ FT: 22,000
SALES (est): 1.3MM **Privately Held**
SIC: 2439 Trusses, except roof: laminated lumber; trusses, wooden roof

(G-2304)
WYSER INNOVATIVE PRODUCTS LLC
6157 Valduga Dr Sw (49315-8637)
PHONE..................................616 583-9225
John Kyser,
EMP: 8 EST: 2002
SALES (est): 1.4MM **Privately Held**
WEB: www.wyserproducts.com
SIC: 3545 8748 Cutting tools for machine tools; business consulting

Cadillac
Wexford County

(G-2305)
AAR CORP
10732 Pine Shore Dr (49601-8257)
PHONE..................................231 779-4859
David Barber, *Principal*
Jean Langmesser, *Manager*
Clarence Martenies, *Info Tech Dir*
Stacie Tropf, *Technology*
EMP: 10
SALES (corp-wide): 1.6B **Publicly Held**
WEB: www.aarcorp.com
SIC: 3728 Aircraft parts & equipment
PA: Aar Corp.
　1100 N Wood Dale Rd
　Wood Dale IL 60191
　630 227-2000

(G-2306)
AAR MANUFACTURING INC
Also Called: AAR Mobility Systems
201 Haynes St (49601-1803)
P.O. Box 550 (49601-0550)
PHONE..................................231 779-8800
Mark McDonald, *Vice Pres*
Mark Platko, *Plant Mgr*
Roland Bowman, *Mfg Staff*
Michael Musta, *Project Engr*
Curt Rury, *Finance Mgr*
EMP: 48
SALES (corp-wide): 1.6B **Publicly Held**
WEB: www.aarcorp.com
SIC: 2448 2449 3537 3411 Wood pallets & skids; wood containers; industrial trucks & tractors; metal cans; aluminum rolling & drawing
HQ: Aar Manufacturing, Inc.
　1100 N Wood Dale Rd
　Wood Dale IL 60191
　630 227-2000

(G-2307)
ABLE HTNG CLNG & PLMBNG
9542 Peterson Dr (49601-9758)
PHONE..................................231 779-5430
James Huston, *Principal*
EMP: 5 EST: 2016
SALES (est): 93.8K **Privately Held**
SIC: 3567 Industrial furnaces & ovens

(G-2308)
ADVANCED RUBBER TECH INC
10640 W Cadillac Rd (49601-9415)
PHONE..................................231 775-3112
Erica Szegda, *President*
Philip West, *President*
Robert Stanhope, *Owner*
Thomas Boughner, *Maintence Staff*
EMP: 14 EST: 1987
SQ FT: 15,000
SALES (est): 2.4MM **Privately Held**
WEB: www.advanced-rubber.com
SIC: 3069 Molded rubber products; rubber automotive products

(G-2309)
AKWEL CADILLAC USA INC (DH)
Also Called: Avon Automotive-Orizaba
603 7th St (49601-1344)
PHONE..................................231 775-6571
Leland J Richards, *President*
Paul Tucker, *Plant Mgr*
William C Dircks, *CFO*
Scott Maresh, *Treasurer*
Roger Abrahamson, *Controller*
▲ EMP: 280 EST: 1959
SQ FT: 6,000
SALES (est): 96.3MM **Privately Held**
WEB: www.akwel-automotive.com
SIC: 3061 3089 Mechanical rubber goods; injection molded finished plastic products

(G-2310)
AKWEL MEXICO USA INC
603 7th St (49601-1344)
PHONE..................................231 775-6571
Leland Richards, *President*
Brent Dahlquist, *Manager*
EMP: 20 EST: 1991
SQ FT: 12,000
SALES (est): 6.1MM **Privately Held**
WEB: www.akwel-automotive.com
SIC: 3061 Automotive rubber goods (mechanical)
HQ: Akwel Cadillac Usa, Inc
　603 7th St
　Cadillac MI 49601
　231 775-6571

(G-2311)
AKWEL USA INC (DH)
Also Called: Avon Automotive
603 7th St (49601-1344)
PHONE..................................231 775-6571
Leland Richards, *President*
Lucien Alziari, *Senior VP*
Bryan Blasch, *Vice Pres*
Don Depault, *Vice Pres*
Paul Tucker, *Vice Pres*
▲ EMP: 15 EST: 2006
SALES (est): 104.5MM **Privately Held**
WEB: www.akwel-automotive.com
SIC: 3061 3089 Mechanical rubber goods; injection molded finished plastic products
HQ: Akwel Sa
　975 Route Des Burgondes
　Champfromier 01410
　450 480-588

GEOGRAPHIC SECTION

Cadillac - Wexford County (G-2334)

(G-2312)
AMERICAN BOTTLING COMPANY
Also Called: 7 Up Bottling Co
1481 Potthoff St (49601-9671)
PHONE..................................231 775-7393
Charlie Kelly, *Principal*
Tom Soltis, *Manager*
EMP: 14 **Publicly Held**
WEB: www.keurigdrpepper.com
SIC: 2086 Soft drinks: packaged in cans, bottles, etc.
HQ: The American Bottling Company
6425 Hall Of Fame Ln
Frisco TX 75034

(G-2313)
ARVCO CONTAINER CORPORATION
1355 Marty Paul St (49601-8244)
PHONE..................................231 876-0935
Kevin Hickman, *Vice Pres*
Justin Tonti, *Opers Staff*
Allen Andy, *Purchasing*
Andrea Arvanigian, *Sales Staff*
Lloyd Johnston, *Marketing Staff*
EMP: 30
SALES (corp-wide): 63.7MM **Privately Held**
WEB: www.arvco.com
SIC: 2653 Boxes, corrugated: made from purchased materials
PA: Arvco Container Corporation
845 Gibson St
Kalamazoo MI 49001
269 381-0900

(G-2314)
AVON PROTECTION SYSTEMS INC (DH)
503 8th St (49601-1370)
PHONE..................................231 779-6200
Michael Hamner, *President*
Scott Jesweak, *President*
Jamie Rogers, *General Mgr*
Katherine Boven, *Principal*
Brian Cooper, *COO*
◆ **EMP:** 163 **EST:** 2003
SALES (est): 109.1MM
SALES (corp-wide): 219.5MM **Privately Held**
WEB: www.avon-protection.com
SIC: 3842 Gas masks
HQ: Avon Rubber & Plastics, Inc.
503 8th St
Cadillac MI 49601
231 779-6290

(G-2315)
BIG FOOT MANUFACTURING CO
1480 Potthoff St (49601-9671)
PHONE..................................231 775-5588
R Lyle Matteson, *President*
Bernie Geers, *Treasurer*
EMP: 21 **EST:** 1984
SQ FT: 29,500
SALES (est): 6.1MM **Privately Held**
WEB: www.bigfootmanufacturing.com
SIC: 3531 3523 3498 3496 Wellpoint systems; farm machinery & equipment; fabricated pipe & fittings; miscellaneous fabricated wire products

(G-2316)
BORGWARNER INC
1100 Wright St (49601-9278)
PHONE..................................231 779-7500
Mark Reese, *Engineer*
Shelley Hurrell, *Human Res Mgr*
John Raasio, *Marketing Staff*
Jeff Addison, *Manager*
John Shoaf, *Manager*
EMP: 7
SALES (corp-wide): 10.1B **Publicly Held**
WEB: www.borgwarner.com
SIC: 3714 Motor vehicle parts & accessories
PA: Borgwarner Inc.
3850 Hamlin Rd
Auburn Hills MI 48326
248 754-9200

(G-2317)
BORGWARNER THERMAL SYSTEMS INC
Also Called: Borg Warner Automotive
1100 Wright St (49601-9278)
PHONE..................................231 779-7500
Jason Roderick, *Engineer*
Todd Bennington, *Manager*
EMP: 5
SALES (corp-wide): 10.1B **Publicly Held**
WEB: www.borgwarner.com
SIC: 3625 3568 3713 3564 Control equipment, electric; power transmission equipment; truck & bus bodies; blowers & fans
HQ: Borgwarner Thermal Systems Inc.
1507 S Kalamazoo Ave
Marshall MI 49068
269 781-1228

(G-2318)
BROOKS & PERKINS INC
Also Called: B & P Manufacturing
8051 E 34 Rd (49601-9013)
PHONE..................................231 775-2229
Keith Merchant, *CEO*
Jeff Olson, *President*
Lia Lipar, *General Mgr*
Debbie Bushor, *Buyer*
Tracy Hewett, *Buyer*
▲ **EMP:** 66 **EST:** 1995
SQ FT: 6,000
SALES (est): 20.2MM **Privately Held**
WEB: www.bpmfgdefense.com
SIC: 3355 Aluminum rail & structural shapes

(G-2319)
CADILLAC CASTING INC (PA)
1500 4th Ave (49601-9062)
PHONE..................................231 779-9600
John Hass, *President*
John Haas, *President*
Jim Weston, *Superintendent*
Alex Boosalis, *Vice Pres*
James Kamphouse, *Maint Spvr*
EMP: 276 **EST:** 1922
SQ FT: 280,000
SALES (est): 91.6MM **Privately Held**
WEB: www.cadillaccasting.com
SIC: 3321 Gray & ductile iron foundries; ductile iron castings

(G-2320)
CADILLAC CULVERT INC
5305 M 115 (49601-9659)
PHONE..................................231 775-3761
Chuck Thomas, *President*
Don Aldrich, *Vice Pres*
Darin Hower, *Office Mgr*
EMP: 12
SALES (est): 2.4MM **Privately Held**
WEB: www.cadillacculvert.com
SIC: 3498 Fabricated pipe & fittings

(G-2321)
CADILLAC ENGINEERED PLAS INC
Also Called: Fiamm Technologies
1550 Leeson Ave (49601-8975)
PHONE..................................231 775-2900
Stefano Roselini, *President*
Shawn Low, *Controller*
Ed Miller, *Sales Staff*
▲ **EMP:** 14 **EST:** 1997
SQ FT: 16,000
SALES (est): 5.5MM
SALES (corp-wide): 54.9MM **Privately Held**
WEB: www.fiamm.com
SIC: 3089 Injection molded finished plastic products
HQ: Fiamm Technologies, L.L.C.
23880 Industrial Park Dr
Farmington Hills MI 48335

(G-2322)
CADILLAC FABRICATION INC (PA)
Also Called: Yard King
1340 Marty Paul St (49601-8244)
PHONE..................................231 775-7386
Thomas D Bosscher, *President*
Susan Smith, *Human Res Mgr*
Carla Truman, *Info Tech Mgr*
Matt Thompson, *Representative*
EMP: 37 **EST:** 1983
SQ FT: 10,800
SALES (est): 5.3MM **Privately Held**
WEB: www.cadfab.com
SIC: 3441 Fabricated structural metal

(G-2323)
CADILLAC PRINTING COMPANY
214 S Mitchell St (49601-2140)
P.O. Box 157 (49601-0157)
PHONE..................................231 775-2488
Orren Tate, *President*
EMP: 10 **EST:** 1926
SQ FT: 15,000
SALES (est): 709.4K **Privately Held**
WEB: www.cadillacprintingco.com
SIC: 2752 5943 Commercial printing, offset; office forms & supplies

(G-2324)
CADILLAC TOOL AND DIE INC
1011 6th St (49601-9264)
PHONE..................................231 775-9007
Brian Ward, *President*
EMP: 8 **EST:** 2001
SQ FT: 1,000
SALES (est): 1.1MM **Privately Held**
WEB: www.cadillactoolanddie.com
SIC: 3544 Special dies & tools

(G-2325)
CALLAHAN SUPPLY LLC
10429 W Watergate Rd (49601-9427)
PHONE..................................231 878-9023
Chris Schepers, *President*
EMP: 5 **EST:** 2016
SALES (est): 94.3K **Privately Held**
WEB: www.callahansupply.com
SIC: 3273 Ready-mixed concrete

(G-2326)
CONCRETE STORE
8181 E 34 Rd (49601-9013)
PHONE..................................231 577-3433
Todd Schmid, *Manager*
EMP: 8 **EST:** 2017
SALES (est): 100.5K **Privately Held**
WEB: www.lcredimix.com
SIC: 3273 Ready-mixed concrete

(G-2327)
CRANDALL PRECISION INC
615 5th St (49601-1318)
P.O. Box 224 (49601-0224)
PHONE..................................231 775-7101
Lloyd Crandall, *President*
Gary Vandenboss, *President*
Martin Crandall, *Vice Pres*
EMP: 5 **EST:** 1977
SQ FT: 6,500
SALES (est): 771.9K **Privately Held**
WEB: www.crandallprecision.com
SIC: 3599 Machine shop, jobbing & repair

(G-2328)
DUMBARTON TOOL INC
151 Clay Dr (49601-8614)
PHONE..................................231 775-4342
Daniel Gray, *President*
Dan Gray, *Owner*
Robert King, *Vice Pres*
Paul Warner, *Treasurer*
EMP: 12 **EST:** 1986
SQ FT: 8,000
SALES (est): 2MM **Privately Held**
WEB: www.dumbartontool.com
SIC: 3545 Cutting tools for machine tools

(G-2329)
FIBERGLASS TECHNOLOGY INDS INC
1637 Marty Paul St (49601-9608)
PHONE..................................740 335-9400
Greg Solomon, *General Mgr*
Eric Lockhart, *Office Mgr*
Jerry Kroll, *Branch Mgr*
EMP: 6
SALES (corp-wide): 39.3MM **Privately Held**
WEB: www.fiber-tech.net
SIC: 3089 Panels, building: plastic
HQ: Fiberglass Technology Industries, Inc.
3808 N Sullivan Rd # 31
Spokane Valley WA 99216
509 928-8880

(G-2330)
FRANKE SALISBURY VIRGINIA
Also Called: Franke Septic Tank Service
11894 S Mackinaw Trl (49601-9082)
PHONE..................................231 775-7014
Virginia Franke Salisbury, *Owner*
EMP: 4 **EST:** 1947
SQ FT: 4,000
SALES (est): 347.3K **Privately Held**
SIC: 1794 3272 4212 7699 Excavation work; septic tanks, concrete; dump truck haulage; septic tank cleaning service; sewer cleaning & rodding

(G-2331)
GLASTRON LLC
925 Frisbie St (49601-9259)
PHONE..................................800 354-3141
Mary Neu, *Purch Mgr*
Linda Ackerman, *Sales Staff*
Roch Lambert, *Mng Member*
Al Kuebelbeck, *Mng Member*
▼ **EMP:** 65 **EST:** 2010
SALES (est): 1.9MM
SALES (corp-wide): 1.3MM **Privately Held**
WEB: www.glastron.com
SIC: 3732 Boat building & repairing
HQ: Rec Boat Holdings, Llc
925 Frisbie St
Cadillac MI 49601

(G-2332)
GOODWILL INDS NTHRN MICH INC
Also Called: Goodwill Cadillac Transition H
901 N Mitchell St Ste 15 (49601-1254)
PHONE..................................231 779-1311
Todd Salisbury, *Manager*
EMP: 4
SALES (corp-wide): 15.5MM **Privately Held**
WEB: www.goodwillnmi.org
SIC: 5932 8331 2431 8322 Clothing, secondhand; sheltered workshop; millwork; meal delivery program; settlement house
PA: Goodwill Industries Of Northern Michigan, Inc.
2279 S Airport Rd W
Traverse City MI 49684
231 922-4805

(G-2333)
GOODWILL INDS NTHRN MICH INC
Also Called: Goodwill Resale Store
610 S Mitchell St (49601-2510)
PHONE..................................231 779-1361
Ruth Blick, *Branch Mgr*
EMP: 6
SALES (corp-wide): 15.5MM **Privately Held**
WEB: www.goodwillnmi.org
SIC: 5932 8331 2431 8322 Clothing, secondhand; sheltered workshop; millwork; meal delivery program; settlement house
PA: Goodwill Industries Of Northern Michigan, Inc.
2279 S Airport Rd W
Traverse City MI 49684
231 922-4805

(G-2334)
HOPE NETWORK WEST MICHIGAN
Also Called: N O C Industries
1610 Corwin St (49601-8139)
PHONE..................................231 775-3425
Carol Wood, *Branch Mgr*
EMP: 20
SALES (corp-wide): 13.1MM **Privately Held**
WEB: www.hopenetwork.org
SIC: 3469 Metal stampings
HQ: Hope Network West Michigan
795 36th St Se
Grand Rapids MI 49548
616 248-5900

Cadillac - Wexford County (G-2335)

(G-2335)
HOSTESS CAKE ITT CONTNTL BKG
Also Called: Wonder Hostess Thrift Store
838 N Mitchell St (49601-1472)
PHONE................................231 775-4629
EMP: 9
SALES (est): 48.5K **Privately Held**
SIC: **2051** Mfg Bread/Related Products

(G-2336)
HUTCHNSON ANTVBRTION SYSTEMS I
Also Called: Paulstra C R C-Cadillac Div
600 7th St (49601-1345)
P.O. Box 209 (49601-0209)
PHONE................................231 775-9737
Thomas Kelley, *Plant Mgr*
Roger Wayt, *QC Mgr*
Lynn Osowski, *Engineer*
Jane Bigham, *Human Res Mgr*
Pamela Kinney, *Human Res Mgr*
EMP: 159
SALES (corp-wide): 4.6B **Publicly Held**
SIC: **3069** 3061 Molded rubber products; mechanical rubber goods
HQ: Hutchinson Antivibration Systems, Inc.
460 Fuller Ave Ne
Grand Rapids MI 49503
616 459-4541

(G-2337)
INLAND LAKES MACHINE INC
314 Haynes St (49601-1806)
PHONE................................231 775-6543
Carl Kuhn, *President*
Richard C Kuhn, *Corp Secy*
Rich Kuhn, *Vice Pres*
Trent Kuhn, *Production*
EMP: 44 EST: 1945
SQ FT: 60,000
SALES (est): 5.5MM **Privately Held**
WEB: www.inlandlakes.com
SIC: **3599** 3541 3451 3369 Machine shop, jobbing & repair; machine tools, metal cutting type; screw machine products; nonferrous foundries

(G-2338)
JANET KELLY
Also Called: Kel Graphics
110 W River St (49601-1816)
PHONE................................231 775-2313
Janet Kelly, *Owner*
Travis Butkovich, *Manager*
Liv Grover,
EMP: 10 EST: 1985
SQ FT: 6,000
SALES (est): 1.3MM **Privately Held**
WEB: www.kelgraphics.com
SIC: **2261** 2395 3993 2752 Finishing plants, cotton; embroidery products, except schiffli machine; signs & advertising specialties; commercial printing, lithographic; automotive & apparel trimmings

(G-2339)
KEURIG DR PEPPER INC
Also Called: Dr Pepper Snapple Group
1481 Potthoff St (49601-9671)
PHONE................................231 775-7393
Tom Soltis, *Branch Mgr*
EMP: 6 **Publicly Held**
WEB: www.keurigdrpepper.com
SIC: **2086** Soft drinks: packaged in cans, bottles, etc.
PA: Keurig Dr Pepper Inc.
53 South Ave
Burlington MA 01803

(G-2340)
KIDDER MACHINE COMPANY
702 8th St (49601)
P.O. Box 507 (49601-0507)
PHONE................................231 775-9271
Dean L Kidder, *President*
Michael Wylie, *Vice Pres*
Charles Kilpatrick, *Site Mgr*
EMP: 4 EST: 1948
SQ FT: 6,200
SALES (est): 339.3K **Privately Held**
WEB: www.kiddermfg.com
SIC: **3544** Industrial molds

(G-2341)
KYSOR INDUSTRIAL CORPORATION
Kysor Cadillac Division
1100 Wright St (49601-8275)
PHONE................................231 779-7500
Patrick Laine, *Branch Mgr*
EMP: 214
SALES (corp-wide): 1.1B **Publicly Held**
SIC: **3714** Motor vehicle parts & accessories
HQ: Kysor Industrial Corporation
2227 Welbilt Blvd
Trinity FL 34655
727 376-8600

(G-2342)
LC MATERIALS LLC (HQ)
Also Called: Cornillie Concrete
805 W 13th St (49601-9281)
PHONE................................231 946-5600
Richard Deneweth, *Partner*
Robert Cherry, *Partner*
Joe Cornilie, *Partner*
EMP: 5 EST: 2014
SALES (est): 2.5MM
SALES (corp-wide): 170.1MM **Privately Held**
WEB: www.smyrnareadymix.com
SIC: **3273** Ready-mixed concrete
PA: Srm Concrete, Llc
1136 2nd Ave N
Nashville TN 37208
615 355-1028

(G-2343)
LEWIS METALS LLC
850 Arbutus Dr (49601-9538)
PHONE................................231 468-3435
Joshua Wagner, *Administration*
EMP: 9 EST: 2015
SALES (est): 252.1K **Privately Held**
WEB: www.lewismetals.com
SIC: **3441** Fabricated structural metal

(G-2344)
MAHNKE MACHINE INC
1551 Filmore Ave Ste A (49601-1163)
PHONE................................231 775-0581
Bonnie Mahnke, *President*
Michael Mahnke, *Vice Pres*
EMP: 4 EST: 2004
SALES (est): 391.6K **Privately Held**
WEB: www.mahnkemachineinc.com
SIC: **3599** Machine shop, jobbing & repair

(G-2345)
MATTESON MANUFACTURING INC
1480 Potthoff St (49601-9671)
PHONE................................231 779-2898
R Lyle Matteson, *President*
EMP: 6 EST: 1978
SQ FT: 5,000
SALES (est): 871.3K **Privately Held**
SIC: **3599** 7692 Machine shop, jobbing & repair; welding repair

(G-2346)
METAL PUNCH CORPORATION
907 Saunders St (49601-9270)
PHONE................................231 775-8391
Irvin J Swider, *CEO*
Chuck Cooper, *Engineer*
Irvin Swider, *Sales Executive*
EMP: 16 EST: 1973
SQ FT: 20,000
SALES (est): 1MM **Privately Held**
WEB: www.metalpunch.com
SIC: **3544** 3545 Punches, forming & stamping; special dies & tools; machine tool accessories

(G-2347)
MILITARY VTRANS AFFIRS MICH DE
Army National Guard
415 Haynes St (49601-1807)
PHONE................................231 775-7222
Brian Lince, *Branch Mgr*
EMP: 106
SALES (corp-wide): 54.6B **Privately Held**
SIC: **3728** Military aircraft equipment & armament
HQ: Michigan Department Of Military And Veterans Affairs
3411 N Martin Luther King
Lansing MI 48906

(G-2348)
PIRANHA HOSE PRODUCTS INC
2500 Weigel St (49601-8106)
PHONE................................231 779-4390
Thomas Hanyok, *President*
Christina Beydoun, *Principal*
Brian Blake, *Plant Mgr*
Rohn Dean, *Maint Spvr*
▲ EMP: 30 EST: 2005
SQ FT: 38,000
SALES (est): 16MM **Privately Held**
WEB: www.piranhahose.com
SIC: **3052** Plastic hose
HQ: Kuriyama Of America, Inc.
360 E State Pkwy
Schaumburg IL 60173
847 755-0360

(G-2349)
PROCTOR LOGGING INC
298 Bramblewood (49601-8178)
PHONE................................231 775-3820
Kevin Proctor, *Principal*
EMP: 6 EST: 2013
SALES (est): 361.6K **Privately Held**
SIC: **2411** Logging camps & contractors

(G-2350)
REC BOAT HOLDINGS LLC (DH)
925 Frisbie St (49601-9259)
PHONE................................231 779-2616
Christophe Lavigne, *Vice Pres*
Joe Perrin, *Plant Mgr*
Melinda Hannula, *Purchasing*
Dave Wade, *Engineer*
Dianne Brian, *Controller*
◆ EMP: 415 EST: 2010
SALES (est): 71.6MM
SALES (corp-wide): 1.3MM **Privately Held**
WEB: www.recboatholdings.com
SIC: **3732** 5551 Boat building & repairing; motor boat dealers

(G-2351)
REMPCO ACQUISITION INC
251 Bell Ave (49601-1103)
P.O. Box 1020 (49601-6020)
PHONE................................231 775-0108
James F Clark, *President*
Gilbert Hall, *Superintendent*
Willard Lajoie, *Vice Pres*
Cathy Gray, *Buyer*
Susan Martin, *Office Mgr*
EMP: 25 EST: 1978
SQ FT: 19,500
SALES (est): 2.6MM **Privately Held**
WEB: www.rempco.com
SIC: **3451** 3542 5084 Screw machine products; machine tools, metal forming type; industrial machinery & equipment

(G-2352)
ROOTS INDUSTRIES
870 Holly Rd (49601-2424)
PHONE................................231 779-2865
Glenn Bathrick, *Principal*
EMP: 6 EST: 2012
SALES (est): 171.1K **Privately Held**
SIC: **3999** Manufacturing industries

(G-2353)
SIGN SCREEN
450 S Mackinaw Trl (49601-8512)
PHONE................................231 942-2273
EMP: 4 EST: 2019
SALES (est): 111.2K **Privately Held**
WEB: www.signscreen.com
SIC: **3993** Signs & advertising specialties

(G-2354)
SOUTHWEST BROACH
311 E Harris St (49601-2126)
PHONE................................714 356-2967
Michael Ochs, *Principal*
EMP: 5 EST: 2013
SALES (est): 78.8K **Privately Held**
SIC: **3545** Cutting tools for machine tools

(G-2355)
SPEEDWAY LLC
Also Called: Speedway Superamerica 3570
2010 N Mitchell St (49601-1138)
PHONE................................231 775-8101
EMP: 10
SALES (corp-wide): 100.2B **Publicly Held**
SIC: **1311** Crude Petroleum/Natural Gas Production
HQ: Speedway Llc
500 Speedway Dr
Enon OH 45323
937 864-3000

(G-2356)
SPENCER PLASTICS INC
2300 Gary E Schwach St (49601-8309)
PHONE................................231 942-7100
Thomas Spencer, *CEO*
Shannon Abraham, *Vice Pres*
EMP: 25 EST: 1998
SQ FT: 45,000
SALES (est): 6.7MM **Privately Held**
WEB: www.spencerplastics.com
SIC: **3089** Injection molding of plastics; molding primary plastic

(G-2357)
SRM CONCRETE LLC
8183 E 34 Rd (49601-9013)
PHONE................................231 775-9301
Dave Gilde, *President*
EMP: 8
SALES (corp-wide): 170.1MM **Privately Held**
WEB: www.smyrnareadymix.com
SIC: **3273** Ready-mixed concrete
PA: Srm Concrete, Llc
1136 2nd Ave N
Nashville TN 37208
615 355-1028

(G-2358)
SRP SOFTWARE
9372 E 50 Rd (49601-9521)
PHONE................................231 779-3602
Scott Peterson, *Principal*
EMP: 6 EST: 2010
SALES (est): 142.8K **Privately Held**
SIC: **7372** Prepackaged software

(G-2359)
STAGG MACHINE PRODUCTS INC
11711 W Cadillac Rd (49601-9412)
PHONE................................231 775-2355
Phillip Stagg, *President*
Cynthia Stagg, *Corp Secy*
EMP: 8 EST: 1976
SQ FT: 23,500
SALES (est): 947.6K **Privately Held**
WEB: www.staggmachine.com
SIC: **3451** Screw machine products

(G-2360)
TALLULAHS SATCHELS
615 White Pine Dr (49601-8515)
PHONE................................231 775-4082
Christine Samardich, *Administration*
EMP: 4 EST: 2014
SALES (est): 219.6K **Privately Held**
SIC: **3161** Satchels

(G-2361)
TRAININGMASK LLC
1140 Plett Rd (49601-1212)
PHONE................................888 407-7555
Casey Danford, *Principal*
Toby Danford, *Opers Staff*
Michael Gennusa, *Info Tech Mgr*
EMP: 10 EST: 2011
SALES (est): 674.9K **Privately Held**
WEB: www.trainingmask.com
SIC: **3949** Masks: hockey, baseball, football, etc.

(G-2362)
TRIPLE S PUBLICATIONS LLC
Also Called: Michigan Hooks & Bullets Mag
7416 S 33 Rd (49601-9307)
P.O. Box 251, Harrison (48625-0251)
PHONE................................231 775-6113
Kevin K Speer,
EMP: 5 EST: 2008

▲ = Import ▼ = Export
◆ = Import/Export

GEOGRAPHIC SECTION

Caledonia - Kent County (G-2390)

SALES (est): 67.5K **Privately Held**
WEB: www.hooksandbullets.com
SIC: **2741** Miscellaneous publishing

(G-2363)
WEDIN INTERNATIONAL INC (PA)
1111 6th Ave (49601-9276)
PHONE.................................231 779-8650
Jack N Rabun, *President*
Jack N Rabun Jr, *Vice Pres*
Mark Lemke, *Engineer*
Vickie Templeton, *Admin Asst*
EMP: **41** EST: 1938
SQ FT: 47,000
SALES (est): 8.3MM **Privately Held**
WEB: www.wedin.com
SIC: **3452** 3545 3535 3462 Screws, metal; rivets, metal; machine tool accessories; conveyors & conveying equipment; iron & steel forgings

(G-2364)
WILLIAM C FOX ENTERPRISES INC
Also Called: Printmasters
1215 N Mitchell St (49601-1260)
PHONE.................................231 775-2732
William C Fox, *President*
EMP: **14** EST: 1983
SQ FT: 9,000
SALES (est): 348.6K **Privately Held**
SIC: **2752** Commercial printing, offset

Caledonia
Kent County

(G-2365)
2 DONKEYS PUBLISHING
6550 Leisure Creek Dr Se (49316-8962)
PHONE.................................616 554-3958
Peter Scott, *Principal*
EMP: **4** EST: 2015
SALES (est): 49K **Privately Held**
SIC: **2741** Miscellaneous publishing

(G-2366)
ACTION PACKAGING LLC
Also Called: Opus Packaging
6995 Southbelt Dr Se (49316-7664)
PHONE.................................616 871-5200
Kevin Manor, *President*
Eric Stepnitz, *General Mgr*
Ralph B Stoner, *Principal*
Mike Seifert, *Vice Pres*
Doug Stoner, *Plant Mgr*
EMP: **40** EST: 1987
SQ FT: 80,000
SALES (est): 18.2MM **Privately Held**
WEB: www.opuspkg.com
SIC: **2653** 2655 Partitions, corrugated: made from purchased materials; fiber shipping & mailing containers
PA: Safeway Packaging, Inc.
   300 White Mountain Dr
   New Bremen OH 45869
   419 629-3200

(G-2367)
ACTIVE PLASTICS INC
125 Mill Ave Se (49316-9440)
PHONE.................................616 813-5109
Jeff Kusmierz, *President*
EMP: **10** EST: 2000
SALES (est): 298K **Privately Held**
WEB: www.activeplastics.com
SIC: **3999** 3089 Models, general, except toy; plastic processing

(G-2368)
BIG O SMOKEHOUSE INC
9740 Cherry Valley Ave Se (49316-9521)
P.O. Box 182 (49316-0182)
PHONE.................................616 891-5555
Keith Osterhaven, *Principal*
Seth Vanregenmorter, *Manager*
EMP: **20** EST: 1997
SQ FT: 35,000
SALES (est): 2.5MM **Privately Held**
WEB: www.bigosmokehouse.com
SIC: **2013** 2091 Smoked meats from purchased meat; fish, smoked

(G-2369)
BLACK BOX CORPORATION
8180 Broadmoor Ave Se A (49316-8526)
PHONE.................................616 246-1320
EMP: **11**
SALES (corp-wide): 855.7MM **Publicly Held**
SIC: **3577** Mfg Computer Peripheral Equipment
PA: Black Box Corporation
   1000 Park Dr
   Lawrence PA 15055
   724 746-5500

(G-2370)
BOAT CUSTOMS TRAILERS LLC
3678 68th St Se (49316-9130)
PHONE.................................517 712-3512
Chris Mills, *Principal*
EMP: **8** EST: 2017
SALES (est): 2.5MM **Privately Held**
WEB: www.boatcustoms.com
SIC: **3799** Boat trailers

(G-2371)
CIG JAN PRODUCTS LTD
3300 Hanna Lk Indus Dr Se (49316)
PHONE.................................616 698-9070
Jerome A Janssen, *President*
Richard Tolan, *Vice Pres*
EMP: **38** EST: 1975
SQ FT: 30,000
SALES (est): 4.9MM **Privately Held**
WEB: www.cig-jan.com
SIC: **3281** Cut stone & stone products

(G-2372)
CLEARFORM
5220 68th St Se Ste 8 (49316-7406)
PHONE.................................616 656-5359
Michael Bieker, *Principal*
Pete Robirds, *Engineer*
EMP: **9** EST: 2008
SALES (est): 2.4MM **Privately Held**
WEB: www.clear-form.com
SIC: **3089** Injection molding of plastics

(G-2373)
FUNCTION INC
Also Called: Function of Beauty
6610 Patterson Ave Se (49316-8473)
PHONE.................................570 317-0737
Zahir Dossa, *CEO*
EMP: **117**
SALES (corp-wide): 83.1MM **Privately Held**
SIC: **2844** Hair preparations, including shampoos
PA: Function Inc.
   116 W Houston St Apt 5
   New York NY 10012
   570 317-0737

(G-2374)
GEM INDUSTRIES INC
Also Called: Gem Industries & Fold A Cover
4045 Korona Ct Se (49316-8428)
PHONE.................................616 656-9779
Charles Steffens, *President*
Diane Steffens, *Accountant*
EMP: **25** EST: 1982
SQ FT: 40,000
SALES (est): 1.8MM **Privately Held**
WEB: www.gemindust.com
SIC: **3599** Machine shop, jobbing & repair

(G-2375)
GR X MANUFACTURING
7000 Dtton Indus Pk Dr Se (49316-8385)
PHONE.................................616 541-7420
EMP: **14** EST: 2015
SALES (est): 171.3K **Privately Held**
SIC: **3999** Manufacturing industries

(G-2376)
GRAND RAPIDS GRAPHIX LLC
3371 68th St Se Ste 1 (49316-7653)
PHONE.................................616 359-2383
EMP: **4** EST: 2019
SALES (est): 109.9K **Privately Held**
WEB: www.grandrapidsgraphix.com
SIC: **2759** Screen printing

(G-2377)
HARRIS OBRIEN WOODWORKS
7000 Dtton Indus Pk Dr Se (49316-8385)
PHONE.................................616 292-2613
EMP: **7** EST: 2018
SALES (est): 303.7K **Privately Held**
WEB: www.obrienharris.com
SIC: **2431** Millwork

(G-2378)
HELEN INC
Also Called: Chemical Specialties
6450 Hanna Lake Ave Se (49316-8365)
PHONE.................................616 698-8102
Michael McAllister, *President*
Mark Flint, *Vice Pres*
Jody Sarres, *Accountant*
Mark Foote, *Sales Staff*
▼ EMP: **16** EST: 1967
SQ FT: 55,000
SALES (est): 4.2MM **Privately Held**
WEB: www.envcoatings.com
SIC: **2851** Paints: oil or alkyd vehicle or water thinned; lacquers, varnishes, enamels & other coatings; enamels; varnishes

(G-2379)
HERITAGE RESOURCES INC
6490 68th St Se (49316-8964)
PHONE.................................616 554-9888
Kirk Velting, *President*
Gary Todd, *Consultant*
EMP: **8** EST: 1968
SQ FT: 200
SALES (est): 1.4MM **Privately Held**
WEB: www.portableriprap.com
SIC: **1442** Construction sand & gravel

(G-2380)
HIGH GRADE MATERIALS COMPANY
6869 E Paris Ave Se (49316-7630)
PHONE.................................616 554-8828
Stu Africa, *Manager*
EMP: **9**
SALES (corp-wide): 17.2MM **Privately Held**
WEB: www.highgradematerials.com
SIC: **3273** Ready-mixed concrete
PA: High Grade Materials Company
   9266 Snows Lake Rd
   Greenville MI 48838
   616 754-5545

(G-2381)
HILCO INDUSTRIAL PLASTICS LLC
Also Called: Hilco Technologies
3260 Hnna Lk Ind Pk Dr Se (49316-9190)
PHONE.................................616 554-8833
Joe Stoken, *Principal*
EMP: **6** EST: 1974
SALES (est): 80.9K **Privately Held**
SIC: **3089** Molding primary plastic

(G-2382)
HILCO INDUSTRIAL PLASTICS LLC
3260 Hanna Lake Ind Park (49316-9190)
PHONE.................................616 554-8833
Matthew Holwerda, *Branch Mgr*
Brad Ringelberg, *Supervisor*
EMP: **47**
SALES (corp-wide): 23.7MM **Privately Held**
WEB: www.hilcotech.com
SIC: **3089** 8711 Molding primary plastic; designing: ship, boat, machine & product
PA: Hilco Industrial Plastics, Llc
   4172 Danvers Ct Se
   Grand Rapids MI 49512
   616 957-1081

(G-2383)
HYDRO-CHEM SYSTEMS INC
6605 Broadmoor Ave Se (49316-9511)
PHONE.................................616 531-6420
Dave Presley, *President*
Jim Teague, *Principal*
June Heyn, *Vice Pres*
John Teague, *Vice Pres*
Ginger Travis, *Admin Sec*
EMP: **28** EST: 1971
SQ FT: 20,000 **Privately Held**
WEB: www.hydrochemsystems.com

SIC: **2841** 2842 Soap & other detergents; cleaning or polishing preparations

(G-2384)
J & J ENGINEERING AND MACHINE
3265 68th St Se (49316-7419)
PHONE.................................616 554-3302
Mark Scott, *President*
EMP: **7** EST: 1992
SQ FT: 3,000
SALES (est): 605.7K **Privately Held**
SIC: **3599** Machine shop, jobbing & repair

(G-2385)
JELD-WEN INC
Also Called: Karona
4100 Korona Ct Se (49316-8419)
PHONE.................................616 554-3551
Matt Waite, *Engineer*
Lee Donaldson, *Sales Staff*
Brent Wagner, *Director*
Harold Jewell, *Maintence Staff*
EMP: **150** **Publicly Held**
SIC: **2431** Doors, wood
HQ: Jeld-Wen, Inc.
   2645 Silver Crescent Dr
   Charlotte NC 28273
   800 535-3936

(G-2386)
JOHNSON SYSTEMS INC
7835 100th St Se (49316-9548)
PHONE.................................616 455-1900
John J Johnson, *President*
Loretta Johnson, *Corp Secy*
EMP: **5** EST: 1984
SQ FT: 8,000
SALES (est): 425K **Privately Held**
SIC: **1711** 3499 Mechanical contractor; machine bases, metal

(G-2387)
KOOIKER TOOL & DIE INC
3259 68th St Se (49316-8425)
PHONE.................................616 554-3630
Jason O'Krangley, *President*
Mercy Peterson, *Vice Pres*
EMP: **16** EST: 1985
SQ FT: 1,200
SALES (est): 1.2MM **Privately Held**
WEB: www.ktdmachining.com
SIC: **3545** Precision tools, machinists'

(G-2388)
MARKETLAB INC
6850 Southbelt Dr Se (49316-7680)
PHONE.................................866 237-3722
Mike Bieker, *CEO*
Steve Bosio, *President*
Pete Robirds, *Engineer*
Andre Lebaron, *CFO*
Bob Schmidt, *CFO*
EMP: **95** EST: 1993
SQ FT: 100,000
SALES (est): 54.8MM **Privately Held**
WEB: www.marketlab.com
SIC: **5047** 3841 3821 Medical laboratory equipment; medical instruments & equipment, blood & bone work; laboratory apparatus & furniture
PA: Water Street Healthcare Partners Llc
   444 W Lake St Ste 1800
   Chicago IL 60606

(G-2389)
MICRO MANUFACTURING INC
6900 Dtton Indus Pk Dr Se (49316-7323)
PHONE.................................616 554-9200
Donald Jolliffe, *President*
EMP: **25** EST: 1999
SQ FT: 45,000
SALES (est): 5.8MM **Privately Held**
WEB: www.micromfg.com
SIC: **3599** Machine shop, jobbing & repair

(G-2390)
NATIONAL PLASTEK INC
7050 Dtton Indus Pk Dr Se (49316-8900)
PHONE.................................616 698-9559
Mike Klein, *President*
Brad Whalen, *General Mgr*
Susan Demute, *Plant Mgr*
Dan Murphy, *Plant Mgr*
Michael Klein, *Prdtn Mgr*
EMP: **27** EST: 1987

Caledonia - Kent County (G-2391)

SQ FT: 60,000
SALES (est): 6MM **Privately Held**
WEB: www.plastek.com
SIC: 3089 Injection molding of plastics

(G-2391)
OPUS PACKAGING GROUP INC (PA)
6995 Southbelt Dr Se (49316-7664)
PHONE 616 871-5200
Ralph Stoner, *President*
Doug Stoner, *Sales Mgr*
Adriana Avila, *Sales Associate*
EMP: 62 **EST:** 2013
SALES (est): 24.2MM **Privately Held**
WEB: www.opuspkg.com
SIC: 2653 2673 2671 Boxes, corrugated: made from purchased materials; boxes, solid fiber: made from purchased materials; bags: plastic, laminated & coated; packaging paper & plastics film, coated & laminated

(G-2392)
PICKLED DOOR LLC
503 S Shore Dr (49316-9228)
PHONE 616 916-6836
Pamela Root, *Principal*
EMP: 4 **EST:** 2014
SALES (est): 80.2K **Privately Held**
SIC: 2035 Pickled fruits & vegetables

(G-2393)
PRESTIGE POWDER COATING
2811 84th St Se (49316-9121)
PHONE 616 401-0250
EMP: 4 **EST:** 2018
SALES (est): 108.1K **Privately Held**
WEB: www.prestigepowder.com
SIC: 3479 Coating of metals & formed products

(G-2394)
PRICE KOCH INDUSTRIES
5041 68th St Se (49316-9516)
PHONE 616 871-0263
Clarence Boeshart, *President*
EMP: 9 **EST:** 2016
SALES (est): 99.6K **Privately Held**
WEB: www.kochllc.com
SIC: 3999 Manufacturing industries

(G-2395)
R AND T WEST MICHIGAN INC
6955 E Paris Indus Ct Se (49316-7784)
PHONE 616 698-9931
Robert Wiegand, *President*
Thomas Wolfgang, *Vice Pres*
Steve Deem, *CFO*
Phil Hermenitt, *Sales Staff*
EMP: 22 **EST:** 2005
SQ FT: 20,000
SALES (est): 4.3MM **Privately Held**
WEB: www.rtmachineservices.com
SIC: 3542 Machine tools, metal forming type

(G-2396)
RATTUNDE CORPORATION (PA)
5080 Beltway Dr Se (49316-7465)
PHONE 616 940-3340
Ulrich Rattunde, *Principal*
Alec Banish, *Vice Pres*
Javier Lopez, *Sales Engr*
Sharon Stadler, *Office Mgr*
▲ **EMP:** 3 **EST:** 2006
SALES (est): 1.3MM **Privately Held**
WEB: www.rattunde.one
SIC: 3541 Saws & sawing machines

(G-2397)
RKP CONSULTING INC
Also Called: Industrial Powder Coating
3286 Hnna Lk Ind Pk Dr Se (49316-9190)
PHONE 616 698-0300
Robert E Price, *President*
▲ **EMP:** 30 **EST:** 1983
SQ FT: 30,000
SALES (est): 1.4MM **Privately Held**
SIC: 3441 Fabricated structural metal

(G-2398)
SHURCO LLC
7192 Bridge Town Ln Se (49316-9192)
PHONE 616 366-2367
Susan K Schreur, *Principal*
EMP: 16 **EST:** 2009
SALES (est): 72.9K **Privately Held**
WEB: www.shurco.com
SIC: 3429 Manufactured hardware (general)

(G-2399)
SIGNS THAT SCREAM
6570 Millstream Loop Se (49316-9182)
PHONE 616 698-6284
Dawn Drake, *Principal*
EMP: 5 **EST:** 2009
SALES (est): 55K **Privately Held**
SIC: 3993 Signs & advertising specialties

(G-2400)
SILICONATURE CORPORATION
4255 68th St Se (49316-9191)
P.O. Box 500 (49316-0500)
PHONE 312 987-1848
David Arado, *President*
EMP: 25 **EST:** 2017
SALES (est): 25MM **Privately Held**
SIC: 2671 Packaging paper & plastics film, coated & laminated

(G-2401)
SPECIALTY METAL FABRICATORS
6975 Dtton Indus Pk Dr Se (49316-9146)
PHONE 616 698-9020
James Harris, *Principal*
EMP: 7 **EST:** 2010
SALES (est): 901.4K **Privately Held**
WEB: www.specialtymetalfab.net
SIC: 3499 Fabricated metal products

(G-2402)
STRETCHY SCREENS
5969 Pidge Rdg Se (49316-9780)
PHONE 989 780-1624
EMP: 6 **EST:** 2013
SALES (est): 88.5K **Privately Held**
WEB: www.stretchyscreens.com
SIC: 3999 Manufacturing industries

(G-2403)
SUITE SPA MANUFACTURING LLC
464 Stanton Farms Dr (49316-9226)
PHONE 616 560-2713
Vickie Bennett, *CEO*
Victor Bennett, *CEO*
EMP: 5
SALES (est): 371.3K **Privately Held**
SIC: 2869 Perfumes, flavorings & food additives

(G-2404)
TILE BY BILL & SONDRA
6873 Rosecrest Dr Se (49316-9073)
PHONE 616 554-5413
William Vandergeld, *President*
EMP: 5 **EST:** 2002
SALES (est): 78.7K **Privately Held**
SIC: 3993 Signs & advertising specialties

(G-2405)
VAN DELLEN STEEL INC
6945 Dtton Indus Pk Dr Se (49316-9148)
PHONE 616 698-9950
Corey Van Dellen, *CEO*
James Devries, *President*
Sharon Van Dellen, *Owner*
Joel Bruin-Slot, *Plant Mgr*
Patricia Kolenda, *Treasurer*
EMP: 30 **EST:** 1968
SQ FT: 50,000
SALES (est): 4.8MM **Privately Held**
WEB: www.vandellensteel.com
SIC: 3441 Building components, structural steel

(G-2406)
VIKING GROUP INC (DH)
5150 Beltway Dr Se (49316-7447)
PHONE 616 432-6800
Kevin Ortyl, *President*
Steve Falke, *Business Mgr*
Karen Koop, *Engineer*
Janice Oshinski, *CFO*
Denise Fairbrother, *Human Res Mgr*
EMP: 8 **EST:** 2001
SALES (est): 884.2MM **Privately Held**
SALES (corp-wide): 177.9MM **Privately Held**
WEB: www.vikinggroupinc.com
SIC: 3569 5961 Sprinkler systems, fire: automatic; mail order house
HQ: Minimax Viking Gmbh
Industriestr. 10/
Bad Oldesloe SH 23843
453 180-30

(G-2407)
XL ENGINEERING LLC
6960 Hammond Ave Se (49316-8351)
PHONE 616 656-0324
Corrie Elsbrie, *Manager*
Kevin Swiderski,
EMP: 9 **EST:** 1995
SQ FT: 3,000
SALES (est): 1MM **Privately Held**
WEB: www.xl-engineering.com
SIC: 3599 Machine shop, jobbing & repair

Calumet
Houghton County

(G-2408)
BEAN COUNTER INC
25963 Cedar St (49913-1249)
PHONE 906 523-5027
Deborah Bean, *Principal*
EMP: 5 **EST:** 2010
SALES (est): 104.6K **Privately Held**
WEB: www.beancounter4hire.com
SIC: 3131 Counters

(G-2409)
DOUG ANDERSON LOGGING
54586 Oikarinen Rd (49913-9207)
PHONE 906 337-3707
Doug Anderson, *Owner*
Rebecca Anderson, *Co-Owner*
EMP: 5 **EST:** 1994
SALES (est): 449.8K **Privately Held**
SIC: 2411 Logging camps & contractors

(G-2410)
KIILUNEN MFG GROUP INC
Also Called: Superior Polymer Products
25280 Renaissance Rd (49913-2701)
PHONE 906 337-2433
Erik Kiilunen, *President*
Kurt Johnson, *General Mgr*
▲ **EMP:** 7 **EST:** 1987
SQ FT: 6,000
SALES (est): 2MM **Privately Held**
WEB: www.superiorpolymer.com
SIC: 2891 Adhesives & sealants

(G-2411)
LEONARD J HILL LOGGING CO
30980 Woodbush Rd (49913-9542)
PHONE 906 337-3435
EMP: 10
SALES (est): 739.8K **Privately Held**
SIC: 2411 Logging

(G-2412)
MQ OPERATING COMPANY
Also Called: Calumet Machine
416 6th St (49913-1412)
PHONE 906 337-1515
Eugene Loukus, *President*
Nancy Londo, *Office Mgr*
EMP: 21 **EST:** 1972
SQ FT: 16,000
SALES (est): 6.9MM **Privately Held**
SIC: 5084 7699 7629 3568 Machine tools & accessories; welding machinery & equipment; industrial machinery & equipment repair; electrical repair shops; power transmission equipment; mining machinery

(G-2413)
REL INC
57640 11th St (49913-3118)
PHONE 906 337-3018
Josh Loukus, *President*
Robert Loukus, *Founder*
Adam Loukus, *Vice Pres*
Steve Berg, *Engineer*
Bob Loukus, *Engineer*
EMP: 44 **EST:** 2006
SALES (est): 7.7MM **Privately Held**
WEB: www.relinc.com
SIC: 8711 3999 3829 3641 Engineering services; atomizers, toiletry; testing equipment: abrasion, shearing strength, etc.; ultraviolet lamps

(G-2414)
RIPPA PRODUCTS INC
25256 Renaissance Rd (49913-2701)
PHONE 906 337-0010
Robert Rippa, *President*
Chris Johnson, *Vice Pres*
EMP: 20 **EST:** 1980
SQ FT: 7,200
SALES (est): 1.8MM **Privately Held**
WEB: www.ripparodholder.com.au
SIC: 3452 Nuts, metal

(G-2415)
VOCATIONAL STRATEGIES INC
23390 Airpark Blvd (49913-9233)
PHONE 906 482-6142
Kevin Store, *Exec Dir*
EMP: 12 **EST:** 1970
SQ FT: 20,000
SALES (est): 255.7K **Privately Held**
WEB: www.vocstrat.org
SIC: 8331 3993 2448 2426 Sheltered workshop; signs & advertising specialties; wood pallets & skids; hardwood dimension & flooring mills

(G-2416)
WANDAS BARIUM COOKIE LLC
25770 Elm St (49913-1220)
P.O. Box 294 (49913-0294)
PHONE 906 281-1788
Wanda Kiiskila,
EMP: 5 **EST:** 2007
SALES (est): 391.7K **Privately Held**
WEB: www.bariumcookie.com
SIC: 2834 Proprietary drug products

(G-2417)
WARM RAIN CORPORATION (PA)
51675 Industrial Dr (49913-9235)
P.O. Box 600, Hancock (49930-0600)
PHONE 906 482-3750
George Kronschnabel, *President*
Brian Mayworm, *General Mgr*
Ted Kronschnabel, *Vice Pres*
William Kronschnabel, *Admin Sec*
EMP: 52 **EST:** 1972
SQ FT: 55,000
SALES (est): 5.9MM **Privately Held**
WEB: www.warmrain.com
SIC: 3088 Tubs (bath, shower & laundry), plastic; hot tubs, plastic or fiberglass; shower stalls, fiberglass & plastic

(G-2418)
WILLIAMS PARTS & SUPPLY CO
701 Oak St (49913-1633)
PHONE 906 337-3813
Patricia Timmons, *Manager*
EMP: 12
SALES (corp-wide): 3.5MM **Privately Held**
WEB: www.williamsparts.com
SIC: 2678 5084 Stationery products; industrial machinery & equipment
PA: Williams Parts & Supply Co.
720 Lake Linden Ave
Laurium MI 49913
906 337-3813

Camden
Hillsdale County

(G-2419)
CAMPUB INC (DH)
Also Called: Camden Publications
331 E Bell St (49232-9613)
P.O. Box 130 (49232-0130)
PHONE 517 368-0365
Julia Hite, *General Mgr*
EMP: 10 **EST:** 1898
SQ FT: 9,000

GEOGRAPHIC SECTION
Canton - Wayne County (G-2446)

SALES (est): 9.5MM
SALES (corp-wide): 3.4B **Publicly Held**
WEB: www.gannett.com
SIC: **2711** 2741 Newspapers: publishing only, not printed on site; art copy: publishing & printing
HQ: Gannett Media Corp.
7950 Jones Branch Dr
Mc Lean VA 22102
703 854-6000

(G-2420)
CURTIS COUNTRY CONNECTION LLC
338 E Bell St (49232-9613)
PHONE.................................517 368-5542
Dave Curtis, *CEO*
David Curtis, *General Mgr*
Steve Sanders, *Engineer*
EMP: **12** EST: **2007**
SALES (est): 562.7K **Privately Held**
SIC: **2448** Pallets, wood

(G-2421)
D P EQUIPMENT CO
10700 S Edon Rd (49232-9011)
P.O. Box 159 (49232-0159)
PHONE.................................517 368-5266
Dale R Pushee, *President*
Patricia D Pushee, *Corp Secy*
Sharon Gillen, *Office Mgr*
Dean EBY, *Manager*
EMP: **11** EST: **1968**
SQ FT: **11,000**
SALES (est): 2MM **Privately Held**
SIC: **3531** 7353 5261 7699 Construction machinery; earth moving equipment, rental or leasing; lawnmowers & tractors; lawn mower repair shop

(G-2422)
G & D WOOD PRODUCTS INC
Also Called: Page Pallet & Lumber
12860 Hillsdale Rd (49232-9030)
PHONE.................................517 254-4463
Glen Page, *President*
Denise Page, *Vice Pres*
EMP: **8** EST: **1995**
SALES (est): 1.8MM **Privately Held**
WEB: www.ganddwoodproducts.com
SIC: **2448** 2411 2449 Wood pallets & skids; logging; wood containers

(G-2423)
LAWSONS LOGGING
5251 E Territorial Rd (49232-9749)
PHONE.................................517 567-0025
Randy Lawson, *Principal*
EMP: **6** EST: **2016**
SALES (est): 309K **Privately Held**
WEB: www.lawsonfamilylogging.com
SIC: **2411** Logging camps & contractors

(G-2424)
RED HEADED HONEY LLC
14900 Woodbridge Rd (49232-9073)
PHONE.................................707 616-4278
Niki Backes, *Mng Member*
Jeffrey Dayton, *Mng Member*
EMP: **5** EST: **2014**
SALES (est): 97.1K **Privately Held**
WEB: www.redheadedhoney.com
SIC: **2099** Honey, strained & bottled

Canton
Wayne County

(G-2425)
3R INFO LLC (PA)
5840 N Canton Center Rd # 2 (48187-2684)
PHONE.................................201 221-6153
S Raju Nadimpalli, *Mng Member*
EMP: **18** EST: **2015**
SALES (est): 1.7MM **Privately Held**
WEB: www.3rinfo.com
SIC: **7371** 7372 7379 Computer software systems analysis & design, custom; prepackaged software; computer related consulting services

(G-2426)
A S A P MACHINE COMPANY
8575 Ronda Dr (48187-2003)
PHONE.................................734 459-2447
Mark Swain, *President*
EMP: **5** EST: **1984**
SQ FT: **2,500**
SALES (est): 411.3K **Privately Held**
WEB: www.asapmachineco.com
SIC: **3599** Machine shop, jobbing & repair

(G-2427)
ACCENT SIGNS
45721 Bryn Mawr Rd (48187-5431)
PHONE.................................860 693-6760
EMP: **7** EST: **2018**
SALES (est): 46K **Privately Held**
WEB: www.accentsignage.com
SIC: **3993** Signs & advertising specialties

(G-2428)
ACCORD SOFTWARE SOLUTIONS LLC
42565 Laird Ln (48187-3164)
PHONE.................................616 604-1699
Pardhava Vourganti, *Owner*
EMP: **4** EST: **2017**
SALES (est): 76.7K **Privately Held**
SIC: **7372** Prepackaged software

(G-2429)
ADVANCE ENGINEERING COMPANY (PA)
Also Called: Advance Engineering Co Mich
7505 Baron Dr (48187-2494)
PHONE.................................313 537-3500
George Helms, *President*
Dean Corra, *VP Opers*
Joe Stupnicki, *Executive*
EMP: **95** EST: **2004**
SALES (est): 42.7MM **Privately Held**
SIC: **3465** 3469 3823 Automotive stampings; metal stampings; thermal conductivity instruments, industrial process type

(G-2430)
ADVANCED MAGNET SOURCE CORP (PA)
Also Called: WHOLESALE
5033 Belleville Rd (48188-2407)
PHONE.................................734 398-7188
Yufang Shi, *President*
▲ EMP: **5** EST: **2006**
SALES (est): 9.9MM **Privately Held**
WEB: www.advancedmagnetsource.com
SIC: **3499** Magnets, permanent: metallic

(G-2431)
AESTHTIC AFFCTS STFFING AGCY L
50010 Cherry Hill Rd (48187-4876)
PHONE.................................734 436-1248
Latoya Lewis,
EMP: **5** EST: **2020**
SALES (est): 200K **Privately Held**
SIC: **3634** Massage machines, electric, except for beauty/barber shops

(G-2432)
AIRHUG LLC
47960 Red Run Dr (48187-5461)
PHONE.................................734 262-0431
Wayne Fung, *Partner*
Kam Lee, *Partner*
EMP: **4** EST: **2012**
SALES (est): 244.6K **Privately Held**
SIC: **2221** 3564 Broadwoven fabric mills, manmade; purification & dust collection equipment

(G-2433)
AMERICAN LABEL & TAG INC
41878 Koppernick Rd (48187-2409)
P.O. Box 85488, Westland (48185-0488)
PHONE.................................734 454-7600
Tim Gleason, *President*
Joe Kuzara, *Manager*
Brent Whalen, *Manager*
Paul Gubbins, *MIS Mgr*
Eric Marschner, *Shareholder*
EMP: **28** EST: **1988**
SQ FT: **52,000**
SALES (est): 6.3MM **Privately Held**
WEB: www.americanlabel.com
SIC: **2672** 3993 2789 2671 Labels (unprinted), gummed: made from purchased materials; name plates: except engraved, etched, etc.: metal; bookbinding & related work; packaging paper & plastics film, coated & laminated

(G-2434)
AMERITRONIX INC
777 Kings Way (48188-1132)
PHONE.................................724 956-2356
Sheetal Patel, *President*
Mittal Patel, *Vice Pres*
Hetal Patel, *Treasurer*
Divyal Amin, *Admin Sec*
EMP: **4** EST: **2019**
SALES (est): 307.7K **Privately Held**
WEB: www.ameritronixinc.com
SIC: **3672** Printed circuit boards

(G-2435)
ANTECH TOOL INC
7553 Baron Dr (48187-2494)
PHONE.................................734 207-3622
Anthony Szafraniec, *President*
Linda Szafraniec, *Treasurer*
Dennis Perry, *Supervisor*
EMP: **15** EST: **1991**
SQ FT: **13,000**
SALES (est): 3.7MM **Privately Held**
WEB: www.antechtool.com
SIC: **5084** 3541 Machine tools & accessories; drilling & boring machines

(G-2436)
APPGRAFT LLC
435 Innsbrook Dr (48188-3035)
PHONE.................................734 546-8458
Paul Bagadzinski, *Manager*
EMP: **6** EST: **2013**
SALES (est): 87.5K **Privately Held**
WEB: www.appgraft.com
SIC: **7372** Prepackaged software

(G-2437)
ATG PRECISION PRODUCTS LLC
7545 N Haggerty Rd (48187-2435)
PHONE.................................586 247-5400
Esad Kaknjo, *President*
Randy Link, *QC Mgr*
Sheryl Ziola, *Admin Asst*
EMP: **35** EST: **1942**
SQ FT: **78,000**
SALES (est): 9MM
SALES (corp-wide): 13MM **Privately Held**
WEB: www.atgpp.com
SIC: **3451** Screw machine products
PA: Dirksen Screw Products Co.
14490 23 Mile Rd
Shelby Township MI 48315
586 247-5400

(G-2438)
AUTOMATED MEDIA INC
Also Called: It Service
5711 Research Dr (48188-2261)
P.O. Box 87370 (48188-0370)
PHONE.................................313 937-5000
Gerald Gentile, *President*
Gerald A Gentile, *President*
Nancy Williamson, *Vice Pres*
Chris Horvath, *Controller*
Jaimi Temple, *Program Mgr*
EMP: **85** EST: **1989**
SQ FT: **12,000**
SALES (est): 30.2MM **Privately Held**
WEB: www.automatedmediainc.com
SIC: **5734** 7378 7372 Computer peripheral equipment; computer maintenance & repair; application computer software

(G-2439)
BCC DISTRIBUTION INC
7529 Baron Dr (48187-2494)
PHONE.................................734 737-9300
Jon Newman, *President*
Lisa Fritz, *Sales Staff*
Donna Newman, *Technology*
EMP: **12** EST: **2000**
SQ FT: **3,500**
SALES (est): 1.7MM **Privately Held**
WEB: www.bccdistribution.com
SIC: **3577** Bar code (magnetic ink) printers

(G-2440)
BERKSHIRE & ASSOCIATES INC
5840 N Canton Center Rd (48187-2684)
PHONE.................................734 719-1822
Anthony Morris, *President*
EMP: **10** EST: **2011**
SALES (est): 355K **Privately Held**
WEB: www.berkshireassociates.com
SIC: **8741** 3577 Management services; data conversion equipment, media-to-media: computer

(G-2441)
BOCH PUBLISHING LLC
41620 Pheasant Creek Dr (48188-5202)
PHONE.................................734 718-2973
Laura Bramer, *Principal*
EMP: **4** EST: **2018**
SALES (est): 81.7K **Privately Held**
SIC: **2741** Miscellaneous publishing

(G-2442)
BODYCOTE THERMAL PROC INC
8580 N Haggerty Rd (48187-2095)
PHONE.................................734 451-0338
Michael Harrison, *General Mgr*
EMP: **7**
SALES (corp-wide): 795.2MM **Privately Held**
WEB: www.bodycote.com
SIC: **3398** Brazing (hardening) of metal
HQ: Bodycote Thermal Processing, Inc.
12750 Merit Dr Ste 1400
Dallas TX 75251
214 904-2420

(G-2443)
BOYERS MEAT PROCESSING INC
4125 Barr Rd (48188-2103)
PHONE.................................734 495-1342
Robert Boyer, *President*
EMP: **4** EST: **1985**
SQ FT: **7,200**
SALES (est): 279.1K **Privately Held**
SIC: **2011** Meat packing plants

(G-2444)
BRICKERS BOX BOARD INC
2200 N Canton Center Rd # 120 (48187-5098)
P.O. Box 87116 (48187-0116)
PHONE.................................734 981-0828
Doug Bricker, *President*
Doug White, *Sales Staff*
Peggy Burke, *Office Mgr*
▼ EMP: **6** EST: **1989**
SQ FT: **1,800**
SALES (est): 6.1MM **Privately Held**
WEB: www.brickersbb.com
SIC: **2653** Boxes, corrugated: made from purchased materials

(G-2445)
CARRIGAN GRAPHICS INC
Also Called: AlphaGraphics 336
7994 N Lilley Rd (48187-2432)
PHONE.................................734 455-6550
Robert Carrigan, *President*
Mark Carrigan, *Vice Pres*
EMP: **7** EST: **1991**
SQ FT: **3,350**
SALES (est): 1.2MM **Privately Held**
WEB: www.alphagraphics.com
SIC: **2752** Commercial printing, lithographic

(G-2446)
CASUAL PTIO FURN RFNISHING INC
7851 Haverhill Ct N (48187-1047)
PHONE.................................586 254-1900
Michael Maloney, *President*
Ronald Lippard, *Vice Pres*
EMP: **7**
SQ FT: **10,000**
SALES (est): 1MM **Privately Held**
WEB: www.woodyspizzaplace.com
SIC: **3645** 5021 Garden, patio, walkway & yard lighting fixtures: electric; furniture

Canton - Wayne County (G-2447)

(G-2447)
CENTER MASS INC
6845 Woonsocket St (48187-2749)
PHONE..................................734 207-8934
Jeff Felts, *President*
▼ EMP: 7 EST: 1995
SALES (est): 929.7K **Privately Held**
WEB: www.shop.centermassinc.com
SIC: 3496 7389 Slings, lifting: made from purchased wire;

(G-2448)
CHAMPAGNE GRINDING & MFG CO
8600 Ronda Dr (48187-2005)
PHONE..................................734 459-1759
Leo E Champagne, *President*
Mark B Champagne, *Vice Pres*
Gernith Champagne, *Admin Sec*
EMP: 31 EST: 1956
SQ FT: 9,600
SALES (est): 725.3K **Privately Held**
WEB: www.champagnegrinding-mfg.com
SIC: 3545 Tools & accessories for machine tools; gauges (machine tool accessories)

(G-2449)
CHROMATECH INC (PA)
7723 Market Dr (48187-2445)
PHONE..................................734 451-1230
Roy Perlove, *CEO*
Lezlie Luceus, *Managing Dir*
Paul Stema, *Accountant*
Kimberly Dotson, *Cust Mgr*
Mary Mordue, *Manager*
▲ EMP: 14 EST: 1986
SQ FT: 39,000
SALES (est): 5.5MM **Privately Held**
WEB: www.chromatechcolors.com
SIC: 2865 5198 Color pigments, organic; colors & pigments

(G-2450)
CLEAN AIR TECHNOLOGY INC
41105 Capital Dr (48187-2444)
PHONE..................................734 459-6320
Jeffrey L Waller, *President*
Beverly A Favor, *Corp Secy*
Casey J Bell, *Vice Pres*
EMP: 24 EST: 1980
SQ FT: 18,400
SALES (est): 8.6MM **Privately Held**
WEB: www.cleanairtechnology.com
SIC: 1542 8711 3564 Nonresidential construction; engineering services; blowers & fans

(G-2451)
COMMAND PUBLISHING LLC
43311 Joy Rd Ste 201 (48187-2075)
PHONE..................................734 776-2692
Wade Meyers, *Principal*
EMP: 5 EST: 2008
SALES (est): 112.7K **Privately Held**
SIC: 2741 Miscellaneous publishing

(G-2452)
CPR INC
44029 S Umberland Cir (48187-2700)
PHONE..................................734 459-7251
EMP: 4 EST: 2016
SALES (est): 77.9K **Privately Held**
SIC: 3826 Analytical instruments

(G-2453)
D & L WATER CONTROL INC
7534 Baron Dr (48187-2493)
PHONE..................................734 455-6982
Douglas Day, *President*
Lilli Day, *Vice Pres*
Pete Weiland, *Opers Staff*
Ian Dow, *Sales Staff*
▲ EMP: 28 EST: 1990
SQ FT: 13,000
SALES (est): 5.1MM **Privately Held**
WEB: www.dlwater.com
SIC: 3589 Water treatment equipment, industrial

(G-2454)
DETROIT MARKING PRODUCTS CORP
8201 Ronda Dr (48187-2078)
PHONE..................................313 838-9760
William Foerg, *President*
Joseph R Foerg, *Vice Pres*
Thomas S Foerg, *Vice Pres*
EMP: 11 EST: 1918
SQ FT: 10,000
SALES (est): 701.1K **Privately Held**
WEB: www.dmpsignco.com
SIC: 3993 3953 Signs & advertising specialties; embossing seals & hand stamps

(G-2455)
DIAGKNOWSTICS TUTORING
44165 Vassar St (48188-1033)
PHONE..................................877 382-1133
Rohen Shah, *Principal*
EMP: 6 EST: 2014
SALES (est): 117.5K **Privately Held**
WEB: www.diagknowstics.com
SIC: 8299 7372 Tutoring school; educational computer software

(G-2456)
DUO-GARD INDUSTRIES INC
40442 Koppernick Rd (48187-4279)
PHONE..................................734 207-9700
Albert S Miller, *CEO*
David M Miller, *President*
Michael Arvidson, *Vice Pres*
Patrick Telford, *Project Mgr*
Fred Hankes, *Opers Staff*
▼ EMP: 68
SQ FT: 24,000
SALES (est): 11.5MM **Privately Held**
WEB: www.duo-gard.com
SIC: 3089 3083 3448 3444 Windows, plastic; laminated plastics plate & sheet; prefabricated metal buildings; sheet metalwork; metal doors, sash & trim; products of purchased glass

(G-2457)
DYNAMIC MTAL TREATING INTL INC
Also Called: Dynamic Surface Technologies
7784 Ronda Dr (48187-2447)
PHONE..................................734 459-8022
Loren J Epler, *President*
Jack Dewan, *Accounts Mgr*
Alex Koprivica, *Regl Sales Mgr*
John Dewitt, *Department Mgr*
▲ EMP: 25 EST: 1984
SALES (est): 2MM **Privately Held**
WEB: www.dynablue.com
SIC: 3398 Metal heat treating

(G-2458)
EMPATHETICBOT LLC
301 Roosevelt St (48188-6697)
PHONE..................................810 938-3168
Steven Ledsworth, *Principal*
EMP: 4 EST: 2019
SALES (est): 60.9K **Privately Held**
SIC: 7372 Application computer software

(G-2459)
ENGTECHNIK INC (PA)
40615 Koppernick Rd # 2 (48187-4280)
PHONE..................................734 667-4237
Jose Aldo Francioli, *CEO*
Mackenzie Wilson, *Manager*
EMP: 3 EST: 2014
SALES (est): 1.2MM **Privately Held**
WEB: www.engtechnik.com
SIC: 3089 7371 4911 Injection molding of plastics; software programming applications; electric services

(G-2460)
FAIRLANE GEAR INC
8182 N Canton Center Rd (48187-1305)
PHONE..................................734 459-2440
John Ptak, *President*
Stanley Z Ptak, *President*
Lydia Ptak, *Prdtn Mgr*
Michael Piatak, *Director*
EMP: 9 EST: 1965
SQ FT: 21,000
SALES (est): 972.7K **Privately Held**
WEB: www.fairlane-gear.com
SIC: 3462 Iron & steel forgings

(G-2461)
FARO SCREEN PROCESS INC
41805 Koppernick Rd (48187-2416)
PHONE..................................734 207-8400
EMP: 19
SQ FT: 31,000
SALES (est): 2.8MM **Privately Held**
SIC: 2759 Commercial Printing, Nec

(G-2462)
G AND R LASER SOLUTIONS INC
42035 Addison Ave (48187-3739)
PHONE..................................734 748-6603
Randy Cook, *Principal*
EMP: 5 EST: 2012
SALES (est): 80.6K **Privately Held**
SIC: 3699 Laser systems & equipment

(G-2463)
GIL-MAR MANUFACTURING CO (PA)
Also Called: GM
7925 Ronda Dr (48187-2456)
PHONE..................................248 640-4303
Gildo Ruicci, *President*
William L Martin, *Vice Pres*
William Martin, *Vice Pres*
Joseph Ruicci, *Vice Pres*
Dave Lavigne, *Plant Mgr*
▲ EMP: 70 EST: 1982
SQ FT: 50,000
SALES (est): 18.9MM **Privately Held**
WEB: www.gil-mar.com
SIC: 3599 Machine shop, jobbing & repair

(G-2464)
GIL-MAR MANUFACTURING CO
7777 Ronda Dr (48187-2448)
PHONE..................................734 459-4803
EMP: 7
SALES (corp-wide): 18.9MM **Privately Held**
WEB: www.gil-mar.com
SIC: 3599 Machine shop, jobbing & repair
PA: Gil-Mar Manufacturing Co.
7925 Ronda Dr
Canton MI 48187
248 640-4303

(G-2465)
GLADIATOR QUALITY SORTING LLC
43220 Oakbrook Ct (48187-2034)
PHONE..................................734 578-1950
Mary T Hulett, *President*
EMP: 6 EST: 2003
SQ FT: 800
SALES (est): 334.9K **Privately Held**
SIC: 3312 Pipes & tubes

(G-2466)
GNS CANTON LLC (HQ)
7261 Commerce Blvd (48187-4287)
PHONE..................................734 927-9520
Moon-Gyu Kong, *President*
Elie Mordavanaki, *Vice Pres*
Jacek Sznaza, *Vice Pres*
David Waynick, *Prdtn Mgr*
Tim Vervaeke, *Engineer*
▲ EMP: 199 EST: 2011
SQ FT: 116,000
SALES (est): 47.2MM
SALES (corp-wide): 52.1MM **Privately Held**
WEB: www.gnsauto.com
SIC: 3465 Body parts, automobile: stamped metal
PA: Gns North America, Inc.
13341 Quincy St
Holland MI 49424
616 796-0433

(G-2467)
GREAT LAKES CUSTOM EMBROIDERY
1356 N Beck Rd (48187-4813)
PHONE..................................734 844-7347
Matthew Ritzler, *Administration*
EMP: 5 EST: 2014
SALES (est): 77K **Privately Held**
WEB: www.glcembroidery.com
SIC: 2395 Embroidery products, except schiffli machine

(G-2468)
GROSSE POINTE NEWS
1167 Longfellow Dr (48187-5024)
PHONE..................................734 674-0131
Debra A Pascoe, *Principal*
EMP: 8 EST: 2011
SALES (est): 135.8K **Privately Held**
WEB: www.grossepointenews.com
SIC: 2711 Newspapers, publishing & printing

(G-2469)
GRUPO ANTOLIN PRIMERA AUTO SYS (DH)
Also Called: Grupo Antolin Wayne
47440 Mi Ave Ste 150 (48188-2215)
PHONE..................................734 495-9180
William Pickard, *President*
Garrett Roberson, *Mfg Staff*
Gerald McCabe, *Buyer*
Gary Clark, *Engineer*
Rosanne Friedrich, *Engineer*
▲ EMP: 85 EST: 1998
SQ FT: 170,000
SALES (est): 59.2MM
SALES (corp-wide): 2.6MM **Privately Held**
WEB: www.grupoantolin.com
SIC: 3714 Motor vehicle body components & frame
HQ: Grupo Antolin-Irausa Sa
Carretera Madrid-Irun (Burgos) (- Km 244,8)
Burgos 09007
947 474-847

(G-2470)
H W MOTOR HOMES INC
5390 Belleville Rd (48188-2424)
PHONE..................................734 394-2000
Toll Free:..................................888 -
Forest H White, *President*
Daniel White, *Vice Pres*
EMP: 8 EST: 1960
SQ FT: 3,000
SALES (est): 1.1MM **Privately Held**
WEB: www.hwmotorhomes.com
SIC: 3799 Recreational vehicles; automobile trailer chassis; carriages, horse drawn

(G-2471)
HORIBA INSTRUMENTS INC
5449 Research Dr (48188-2261)
PHONE..................................866 540-2715
Jai Hakhu, *Ch of Bd*
EMP: 51 **Privately Held**
WEB: www.horiba.com
SIC: 2869 Laboratory chemicals, organic
HQ: Horiba Instruments Incorporated
9755 Research Dr
Irvine CA 92618
949 250-4811

(G-2472)
HORIBA INSTRUMENTS INC
Also Called: Pointe Scientific
5449 Research Dr (48188-2261)
PHONE..................................734 487-8300
Jai Hakhu, *Ch of Bd*
EMP: 30 **Privately Held**
WEB: www.horiba.com
SIC: 3841 Diagnostic apparatus, medical
HQ: Horiba Instruments Incorporated
9755 Research Dr
Irvine CA 92618
949 250-4811

(G-2473)
IMPECCABLE MACHINING INC
42600 Executive Dr Unit 3 (48188-3600)
PHONE..................................734 844-3855
George J Harvey, *President*
EMP: 7 EST: 2002
SQ FT: 30,000
SALES (est): 165.5K **Privately Held**
WEB: www.impeccablemachining.com
SIC: 3469 Machine parts, stamped or pressed metal

(G-2474)
INDUSTRIAL TEMPERATURE CONTROL (PA)
7282 N Haggerty Rd (48187-2436)
PHONE..................................734 451-8740
Dale Robenault, *President*
EMP: 6 EST: 1952
SQ FT: 3,000

GEOGRAPHIC SECTION
Canton - Wayne County (G-2501)

SALES (est): 1.6MM Privately Held
SIC: 5075 3823 8734 3822 Warm air heating equipment & supplies; thermocouples, industrial process type; testing laboratories; auto controls regulating residntl & coml environmnt & applncs; relays & industrial controls; industrial furnaces & ovens

(G-2475)
INLAND VAPOR OF MICHIGAN LLC
125 N Haggerty Rd (48187-3901)
PHONE.................................734 738-6312
EMP: 9
SALES (corp-wide): 576.1K Privately Held
WEB: www.inlandvaporsmichigan.com
SIC: 3641 Electric lamps
PA: Inland Vapor Of Michigan Llc
33447 Ford Rd
Garden City MI 48135
734 237-4389

(G-2476)
INNKEEPER LLC
4902 Dewitt Rd Ste 104 (48188-2451)
PHONE.................................734 743-1707
Kevin Kretschmann, *Managing Dir*
Karen Brehob, *Project Mgr*
Christie Peters, *Manager*
EMP: 4 EST: 2006
SALES (est): 820.7K Privately Held
WEB: www.innkeeperllc.com
SIC: 3829 Testing equipment: abrasion, shearing strength, etc.

(G-2477)
INNOVATIVE SOLUTIONS TECH INC
Also Called: Starlite Coatings
41158 Koppernick Rd (48187-2405)
PHONE.................................734 335-6665
Danny J Werner, *President*
Gordon Brooks, *Vice Pres*
Timothy G Williams, *CFO*
EMP: 9 EST: 2008
SQ FT: 20,000
SALES (est): 1.6MM Privately Held
WEB: www.innsoltech.com
SIC: 2851 Paints & allied products

(G-2478)
INTERNATIONAL DOOR INC
Also Called: American Industrial Door
8001 Ronda Dr (48187-2090)
PHONE.................................248 547-7240
John Kaounas, *President*
Danny Degott, *Exec VP*
Gus Kaounas, *Vice Pres*
Chrisy Glavas, *Purch Agent*
Ron Barnett, *Engineer*
EMP: 30 EST: 1974
SQ FT: 27,000
SALES (est): 9.3MM Privately Held
WEB: www.international-door.com
SIC: 3442 3613 Metal doors; hangar doors, metal; switchgear & switchboard apparatus

(G-2479)
INTERNATIONAL MACHINE TOO
8460 Ronda Dr (48187-2002)
PHONE.................................810 588-9591
EMP: 7 EST: 2013
SALES (est): 273K Privately Held
WEB: www.imtsind.com
SIC: 3599 Machine shop, jobbing & repair

(G-2480)
JEP INDUSTRIES LLC
1965 Oakview Dr (48187-3140)
PHONE.................................734 844-3506
James Parks III, *Mng Member*
Lori Parks,
EMP: 4 EST: 2005
SALES (est): 34.7K Privately Held
SIC: 3498 Piping systems for pulp paper & chemical industries

(G-2481)
JRC FABRICATING SALES AND MFG
8539 Ronda Dr (48187-2003)
PHONE.................................734 459-6711
EMP: 4 EST: 2018
SALES (est): 102.8K Privately Held
WEB: www.jrclighthouse.com
SIC: 3441 Fabricated structural metal

(G-2482)
K & Y MANUFACTURING LLC
41880 Koppernick Rd (48187-2409)
PHONE.................................734 414-7000
Andrew Istvan, *President*
Mark Saker, *Engineer*
Kimberly Istvan, *Controller*
Diana Istvan, *Shareholder*
▲ EMP: 35 EST: 1948
SQ FT: 29,000
SALES (est): 3.5MM Privately Held
WEB: www.kymfg.com
SIC: 3451 Screw machine products

(G-2483)
K&S CUSTOM EMBROIDERY LLC
44234 Ardmore St (48188-1807)
PHONE.................................734 709-2689
Kristin Forster,
EMP: 5 EST: 2015
SALES (est): 58.4K Privately Held
WEB: www.kscustomembroidery.com
SIC: 2395 Embroidery products, except schiffli machine

(G-2484)
KRISTA MESSER
50619 Colchester Ct (48187-4464)
PHONE.................................734 459-1952
Krista Messer, *Principal*
EMP: 5 EST: 2010
SALES (est): 97.1K Privately Held
SIC: 3443 Fabricated plate work (boiler shop)

(G-2485)
L & R CENTERLESS GRINDING
5701 S Sheldon Rd (48188-2534)
PHONE.................................734 397-3031
EMP: 4 EST: 2017
SALES (est): 99.2K Privately Held
WEB: www.lrgrinding.com
SIC: 3599 Grinding castings for the trade

(G-2486)
LOTUS INTERNATIONAL COMPANY
6880 Commerce Blvd (48187-4457)
PHONE.................................734 245-0140
Madan M Sharma, *President*
Sam Venkat, *CFO*
Prasad Koppolu, *Sales Executive*
Al Lukas, *IT/INT Sup*
Amar Paul, *Director*
◆ EMP: 520
SQ FT: 295,000
SALES: 398.8MM Privately Held
WEB: www.licus.com
SIC: 8711 3651 1221 Consulting engineer; television receiving sets; bituminous coal & lignite-surface mining

(G-2487)
LYON MANUFACTURING INC
7121 N Haggerty Rd (48187-2452)
PHONE.................................734 359-3000
John Lyon, *President*
Jim Lyon, *Vice Pres*
Sean Fineran, *Opers Mgr*
Matthew Lyon, *Opers Staff*
James Lyon, *Treasurer*
EMP: 50 EST: 1955
SQ FT: 35,500
SALES (est): 8.7MM Privately Held
WEB: www.lyonmfg.com
SIC: 3451 Screw machine products

(G-2488)
MARIAS ITALIAN BAKERY INC
115 N Haggerty Rd (48187-3901)
PHONE.................................734 981-1200
Peter Koza, *President*
Jerome Mc Donald, *General Mgr*
Sam Abdal, *Vice Pres*
EMP: 11 EST: 1972
SQ FT: 11,000
SALES (est): 819.8K Privately Held
WEB: www.mariasitalianbakery.com
SIC: 5411 5921 2052 2051 Grocery stores, independent; beer (packaged); wine; hard liquor; cookies & crackers; bread, cake & related products; eating places

(G-2489)
MARIMBA AUTO LLC
41150 Van Born Rd (48188-2745)
PHONE.................................734 398-9000
Vijay M Patel, *Sales Staff*
Anurag Bajaj, *Mng Member*
▲ EMP: 60
SQ FT: 50,000
SALES (est): 12MM Privately Held
WEB: www.marimbaauto.com
SIC: 3714 Motor vehicle engines & parts

(G-2490)
MATERIAL SCIENCES CORPORATION (PA)
Also Called: MSC Canton
6855 Commerce Blvd (48187-4458)
PHONE.................................734 207-4444
Patrick Murley, *CEO*
Michael Noble, *Vice Pres*
Michael R Wilson, *Vice Pres*
Tim Levin, *Plant Mgr*
Jan Negrini, *Opers Mgr*
▲ EMP: 10 EST: 1982
SQ FT: 205,000
SALES (est): 120.8MM Privately Held
WEB: www.materialsciencescorp.com
SIC: 3479 3471 Painting of metal products; electroplating of metals or formed products

(G-2491)
MATRIX ENGINEERING AND SLS INC
44330 Duchess Dr (48187-3244)
PHONE.................................734 981-7321
Timothy Sylvester, *Principal*
EMP: 5 EST: 1996 Privately Held
WEB: www.matrixengineering.us
SIC: 3357 Automotive wire & cable, except ignition sets: nonferrous

(G-2492)
MEDTEST HOLDINGS INC
5449 Research Dr (48188-2261)
PHONE.................................866 540-2715
Hanjoon Ryu, *CEO*
Len Stigliano, *CFO*
EMP: 100 EST: 2011
SALES (est): 32.1MM Privately Held
WEB: www.medtestdx.com
SIC: 2869 Laboratory chemicals, organic
HQ: Horiba Instruments Incorporated
9755 Research Dr
Irvine CA 92618
949 250-4811

(G-2493)
MERCHANTS AUTOMATIC PDTS INC
Also Called: Mapco Manufacturing
5740 S Beck Rd (48188-2262)
PHONE.................................734 829-0020
George Merchant Jr, *President*
Brian Szewczyk, *Purch Agent*
Tina Baditoi, *Admin Mgr*
Dave Moon, *Prgrmr*
Bob Fields, *Maintence Staff*
▲ EMP: 38 EST: 1971
SQ FT: 30,000
SALES (est): 4.9MM Privately Held
WEB: www.mapcomfg.com
SIC: 3452 3451 3599 Dowel pins, metal; screw machine products; machine & other job shop work

(G-2494)
MERCHANTS INDUSTRIES INC
Also Called: L & R Grinding
5715 S Sheldon Rd (48188-2534)
PHONE.................................734 397-3031
George H Merchant Sr, *CEO*
George Merchant Jr, *President*
EMP: 6 EST: 1980
SQ FT: 4,400
SALES (est): 448K Privately Held
WEB: www.merchantsmetals.com
SIC: 3599 Machine shop, jobbing & repair

(G-2495)
METALTEC STEEL ABRASIVE CO (HQ)
41155 Joy Rd (48187-2094)
PHONE.................................734 459-7900
Gary Stevers, *President*
Gary Wood, *Treasurer*
Jim Allor, *Representative*
◆ EMP: 34 EST: 1980
SALES (est): 9.9MM Privately Held
WEB: www.metaltecsteel.com
SIC: 3291 Steel shot abrasive

(G-2496)
MICHIGAN PAVING AND MTLS CO (DH)
2575 S Haggerty Rd # 100 (48188-2673)
PHONE.................................734 397-2050
Dennis Rickard, *President*
Allen Lindstrom, *Division Mgr*
Jim Bliss, *Area Mgr*
Nick Ricketts, *Area Mgr*
Jason Vanpatten, *Area Mgr*
▲ EMP: 30 EST: 1925
SQ FT: 12,000
SALES (est): 224.4MM
SALES (corp-wide): 27.5B Privately Held
WEB: www.michiganpaving.com
SIC: 1522 1541 2911 Residential construction; industrial buildings, new construction; asphalt or asphaltic materials, made in refineries

(G-2497)
MOBILITY TRNSP SVCS INC
Also Called: Mobilitytrans
42000 Koppernick Rd A3 (48187-4282)
PHONE.................................734 453-6452
David Brown, *President*
Geralyn Brown, *Vice Pres*
Nick Brown, *Sales Staff*
EMP: 38 EST: 1993
SQ FT: 25,000
SALES (est): 28.5MM Privately Held
WEB: www.eftymarket.com
SIC: 7532 3713 Van conversion; van bodies

(G-2498)
MORNING STAR LAND COMPANY LLC
Also Called: Dynamic Metal Treating
7857 Ronda Dr (48187-2456)
PHONE.................................734 459-8022
Lauren Epler,
EMP: 12 EST: 2002
SALES (est): 924.5K Privately Held
WEB: www.dynablue.com
SIC: 2899 Metal treating compounds

(G-2499)
NATIONAL FUELS INC
40401 Michigan Ave (48188-2915)
PHONE.................................734 895-7836
Abbas Nasser, *Principal*
EMP: 8 EST: 2008
SALES (est): 388.8K Privately Held
SIC: 2869 Fuels

(G-2500)
NEW KEY PET LLC ✿
440 Lenox Dr (48188-1594)
PHONE.................................734 716-5357
Christopher M Tidwell, *Mng Member*
EMP: 5 EST: 2021
SALES (est): 150.7K Privately Held
SIC: 3999 Pet supplies

(G-2501)
NORD PUBLICATIONS INC
8115 Tillotson Ct (48187-1759)
PHONE.................................734 455-5271
Ilene Honiss, *Principal*
EMP: 5 EST: 2011
SALES (est): 133.5K Privately Held
SIC: 2741 Miscellaneous publishing

Canton - Wayne County (G-2502)

(G-2502)
NSS TECHNOLOGIES INC (DH)
Also Called: N S S Industries
8680 N Haggerty Rd (48187-2098)
PHONE....................734 459-9500
Mark Donegan, CEO
◆ EMP: 40 EST: 1970
SQ FT: 45,000
SALES (est): 44.3MM
SALES (corp-wide): 245.5B Publicly Held
WEB: www.pccfasteners.com
SIC: 3452 3316 Bolts, metal; cold finishing of steel shapes
HQ: Sps Technologies, Llc
  301 Highland Ave
  Jenkintown PA 19046
  215 572-3000

(G-2503)
OBDPROS LLC
45564 Baldwin Ct (48187-5263)
PHONE....................734 274-5315
Jay Shroff, Mng Member
Michael Schnieder,
Mita Shroff,
EMP: 5 EST: 2006
SALES (est): 440.6K Privately Held
WEB: www.obdpros.com
SIC: 3694 7389 Automotive electrical equipment;

(G-2504)
PANELCRAFT INC
8205 Ronda Dr (48187-2078)
PHONE....................734 646-2173
Jeff Whittaker, President
Chad Richert, Exec VP
EMP: 4 EST: 2014
SALES (est): 223.4K Privately Held
WEB: www.mypanelcraft.myshopify.com
SIC: 3999 Manufacturing industries

(G-2505)
PC TECHS ON WHEELS
8418 Brooke Park Dr # 111 (48187-5123)
PHONE....................734 262-4424
Craig Livingston, Partner
EMP: 4
SALES (est): 181.6K Privately Held
SIC: 3571 Electronic computers

(G-2506)
PERENNIAL SOFTWARE
45185 Joy Rd Ste 102 (48187-1729)
PHONE....................734 414-0760
Michael Marks, Owner
Erick Steckel, Accounts Exec
John Doyle, Sales Staff
Bob Esquerra, Manager
Lisa Gambatese, Training Spec
EMP: 10 EST: 1998
SALES (est): 547.4K Privately Held
WEB: www.boldgroup.com
SIC: 7372 Prepackaged software

(G-2507)
PILZ AUTOMTN SAFETY LTD PARTNR (HQ)
7150 Commerce Blvd (48187-4289)
PHONE....................734 354-0272
Thomas Pilz, CEO
Susanne Kunchert, Partner
Renate Pilz, Partner
Michal Neveril, General Mgr
Doug Burkmire, Regional Mgr
◆ EMP: 45 EST: 1995
SQ FT: 22,000
SALES (est): 15.1MM
SALES (corp-wide): 299.8MM Privately Held
WEB: www.pilz.com
SIC: 3625 Relays & industrial controls
PA: Pilz Gmbh & Co. Kg
  Felix-Wankel-Str. 2
  Ostfildern BW 73760
  711 340-90

(G-2508)
PLASTIPAK HOLDINGS INC
44564 Twyckingham Ln (48187-2643)
PHONE....................209 681-9919
William Schroeck, Branch Mgr
EMP: 755
SALES (corp-wide): 2.9B Privately Held
WEB: www.plastipak.com
SIC: 3089 Blow molded finished plastic products
PA: Plastipak Holdings, Inc.
  41605 Ann Arbor Rd E
  Plymouth MI 48170
  734 455-3600

(G-2509)
POCO INC
4850 S Sheldon Rd (48188-2527)
PHONE....................313 220-6752
Martin Powelson, President
Murray Powelson, Vice Pres
EMP: 31 EST: 1970
SALES (est): 4.2MM Privately Held
WEB: www.pocoinc.com
SIC: 3499 7359 3993 Barricades, metal; sign rental; signs & advertising specialties

(G-2510)
POLLARD BREWING
43636 Hanover Ct (48187-2221)
PHONE....................734 207-3886
Steve Pollard, Principal
EMP: 4 EST: 2016
SALES (est): 62.3K Privately Held
SIC: 2082 Malt beverages

(G-2511)
PRIME WHEEL CORPORATION
6250 N Haggerty Rd (48187-3605)
PHONE....................248 207-4739
Joseph Atwell, Engineer
Mike Dailey, Engineer
EMP: 8
SALES (corp-wide): 315.6MM Privately Held
WEB: www.primewheel.com
SIC: 3312 Wheels
PA: Prime Wheel Corporation
  17705 S Main St
  Gardena CA 90248
  310 516-9126

(G-2512)
PRIORITY ONE EMERGENCY INC
5755 Belleville Rd (48188-2425)
PHONE....................734 398-5900
Sarah Nolan, President
EMP: 5 EST: 1999
SQ FT: 5,000
SALES (est): 880K Privately Held
WEB: www.priority1emergency.com
SIC: 7549 2311 2399 Automotive customizing services, non-factory basis; firemen's uniforms: made from purchased materials; policemen's uniforms: made from purchased materials; emblems, badges & insignia

(G-2513)
PRITECH CORPORATION
46036 Michigan Ave # 188 (48188-2304)
PHONE....................248 488-9120
Warren Jiang, President
◆ EMP: 6 EST: 2000
SALES (est): 256K Privately Held
SIC: 3751 3714 Motorcycles & related parts; frames, motor vehicle

(G-2514)
PRO GEAR PRINTING LLC
48161 Park Lane Ct (48187-5469)
PHONE....................734 386-1105
EMP: 5 EST: 2019
SALES (est): 90.6K Privately Held
SIC: 2759 7389 Screen printing;

(G-2515)
PROSYS INDUSTRIES INC
7666 Market Dr (48187-2441)
PHONE....................734 207-3710
Phillipe Dupessey, CEO
Xaver Tomaszewski, General Mgr
Mathurin Braibant, Project Mgr
Michel Gaillet, Info Tech Mgr
EMP: 83 EST: 1994
SQ FT: 20,000
SALES (est): 7.8MM
SALES (corp-wide): 70.9K Privately Held
WEB: www.prosys-group.com
SIC: 3549 3677 Assembly machines, including robotic; coil windings, electronic
HQ: Prosys Sa
  Zae De Findrol
  Fillinges 74250
  450 362-940

(G-2516)
QUALITY CAVITY INC
3958 Napier Rd (48187-4628)
PHONE....................248 344-9995
Dennis J Craig, President
Barbara Craig, Vice Pres
EMP: 10 EST: 1976
SALES (est): 742K Privately Held
SIC: 3599 3312 Machine & other job shop work; tool & die steel

(G-2517)
RILAS & ROGERS LLC
44440 Meadowcreek Ln (48187-2471)
PHONE....................937 901-4228
Henry Washington, President
P F Thomas III, CFO
EMP: 10
SALES (est): 750K Privately Held
SIC: 3999 Manufacturing industries

(G-2518)
RND ENGINEERING LLC
46036 Michigan Ave # 201 (48188-2304)
PHONE....................734 328-8277
Richalin K Digue,
Richalin Dique,
EMP: 8 EST: 2004
SQ FT: 8,500
SALES (est): 744.6K Privately Held
WEB: www.rnd-engineering.com
SIC: 3541 Machine tools, metal cutting type

(G-2519)
S & N GRAPHIC SOLUTIONS LLC
1818 Stonebridge Way (48188-3273)
PHONE....................734 495-3314
Greg Jahn,
EMP: 7
SQ FT: 8,000
SALES (est): 780K Privately Held
SIC: 2752 Commercial printing, offset

(G-2520)
SALAD SPECIALIST LLC
46036 Michigan Ave # 135 (48188-2304)
PHONE....................734 325-4032
Jo Daniels,
EMP: 4 EST: 2020
SALES (est): 116.1K Privately Held
SIC: 2099 Salads, fresh or refrigerated

(G-2521)
SCHOOL OF ROCK CANTON
5810 N Sheldon Rd (48187-3153)
PHONE....................734 845-7448
EMP: 5 EST: 2020
SALES (est): 59.5K Privately Held
SIC: 8299 7929 7032 3931 Music school; entertainers & entertainment groups; sporting & recreational camps; musical instruments

(G-2522)
SCHULER INCORPORATED (DH)
Also Called: Schuler Hydroforming
7145 Commerce Blvd (48187-4288)
PHONE....................734 207-7200
Stefan Klebert, CEO
Klaus Hertell, General Mgr
Bob Rich, General Mgr
Peter Jost, COO
Tim Quinn, Vice Pres
◆ EMP: 73 EST: 1961
SQ FT: 53,160
SALES (est): 81.3MM
SALES (corp-wide): 7.9B Privately Held
WEB: www.schulergroup.com
SIC: 5084 3444 3599 Industrial machinery & equipment; sheet metal specialties, not stamped; custom machinery
HQ: Schuler Ag
  Schuler-Platz 1
  Goppingen BW 73033
  716 166-0

(G-2523)
SELECT DENTAL EQUIPMENT LLC
47118 N Pointe Dr (48187-1443)
PHONE....................734 667-1194
Naader Bazzi DDS, Principal
EMP: 6 EST: 2008
SALES (est): 142.4K Privately Held
SIC: 3843 Dental equipment

(G-2524)
SOFTWARE BOTS INC
2200 N Canton Center Rd # 220 (48187-5065)
PHONE....................734 730-6526
Shawn Nelson, Business Mgr
David Ramy, Manager
EMP: 8 EST: 2015
SALES (est): 155.4K Privately Held
WEB: www.swbots.com
SIC: 7372 Prepackaged software

(G-2525)
SPALDING
7298 Green Meadow Ln (48187-2484)
PHONE....................734 414-1567
Ronald Spalding, Principal
EMP: 6 EST: 2010
SALES (est): 63.7K Privately Held
WEB: www.powers-spalding.org
SIC: 2253 Jerseys, knit

(G-2526)
SPORTSWEAR SPECIALTIES INC
7930 N Lilley Rd (48187-2432)
PHONE....................734 416-9941
Brad Craig, President
EMP: 7 EST: 1995
SQ FT: 1,600
SALES (est): 706.1K Privately Held
WEB: www.sportswearspecialties.com
SIC: 2395 Embroidery & art needlework

(G-2527)
STAR RINGMASTER
1261 S Lotz Rd (48188-1345)
PHONE....................734 641-7147
Brian McElfresh, Owner
EMP: 5 EST: 1999
SALES (est): 238.5K Privately Held
WEB: www.starringmaster.com
SIC: 3545 Machine tool accessories

(G-2528)
STYLECRAFT PRINTING CO (PA)
Also Called: Stylecraft Printing & Graphics
8472 Ronda Dr (48187-2087)
PHONE....................734 455-5500
Richard A Pesci, President
Mark Hauser, Purch Mgr
Jeff Reichard, Technical Staff
▲ EMP: 75
SQ FT: 25,000
SALES (est): 10MM Privately Held
WEB: www.stylecraftprinting.com
SIC: 2752 Commercial printing, offset; business forms, lithographed

(G-2529)
SWISS AMERICAN SCREW PDTS INC
5740 S Sheldon Rd (48188-2507)
PHONE....................734 397-1600
Roland Leist, President
Mary Leist, Corp Secy
Robert Leist, Vice Pres
Lisa Rowe, Director
EMP: 23 EST: 1962
SQ FT: 8,200
SALES (est): 2.3MM Privately Held
WEB: www.sasp.biz
SIC: 3451 3769 3714 Screw machine products; guided missile & space vehicle parts & auxiliary equipment; motor vehicle parts & accessories

(G-2530)
TECHNICAL ILLUSTRATION CORP
Also Called: Ticglobal
46177 Windridge Ln (48188-6226)
PHONE....................313 982-9660
Peter Kapas, President
Anthony Kapas, Vice Pres

Colleen Kapas, *Treasurer*
Helen Kapas, *Admin Sec*
EMP: 18 **EST:** 1987
SQ FT: 3,800
SALES (est): 1.3MM **Privately Held**
WEB: www.ticglobal.com
SIC: 2741 Technical manuals: publishing only, not printed on site

(G-2531)
TECHNOLOGY PLUS TRAILERS INC
7780 Ronda Dr (48187-2447)
PHONE....................734 928-0001
Emory Buttermore, *President*
EMP: 10 **EST:** 2002
SQ FT: 22,000
SALES (est): 1.4MM **Privately Held**
SIC: 3792 5561 3715 Camping trailers & chassis; travel trailers: automobile, new & used; truck trailers

(G-2532)
TEEQ SPIRITS INC ✪
43311 Joy Rd Ste 273 (48187-2075)
PHONE....................866 877-1840
Nayana Ferguson, *COO*
EMP: 9 **EST:** 2021
SALES (est): 250K **Privately Held**
SIC: 2084 Wines

(G-2533)
TEESNITCH SCREEN PRINTING
8215 Ronda Dr (48187-2078)
PHONE....................734 667-1636
Ryan Hetkowski, *President*
EMP: 4 **EST:** 2017
SALES (est): 88.6K **Privately Held**
SIC: 2759 Screen printing

(G-2534)
TEKNIKUT CORPORATION
46036 Michigan Ave (48188-2304)
PHONE....................586 778-7150
Sean McNeilly, *President*
EMP: 5 **EST:** 1989
SQ FT: 2,000 **Privately Held**
WEB: www.teknikut.com
SIC: 3545 5084 Cutting tools for machine tools; machine tools & accessories

(G-2535)
TOMAS PLASTICS INC
42600 Cherry Hill Rd # 308 (48187-3782)
PHONE....................734 455-4706
Frank Tomaszycki, *President*
EMP: 5 **EST:** 2009
SALES (est): 63.3K **Privately Held**
SIC: 3089 Injection molding of plastics

(G-2536)
TWB COMPANY LLC
Also Called: Canton Manufacturing
7295 N Haggerty Rd (48187-2452)
PHONE....................734 454-4000
Kathy Henneman, *Branch Mgr*
Kalyan Palanisamy, *Director*
EMP: 77
SALES (corp-wide): 3.1B **Publicly Held**
WEB: www.twbcompany.com
SIC: 3465 Automotive stampings
HQ: Twb Company, L.L.C.
 1600 Nadeau Rd
 Monroe MI 48162

(G-2537)
VERSATILE SYSTEMS LLC
8347 Ronda Dr (48187-2079)
PHONE....................734 397-3957
EMP: 16
SQ FT: 2,400
SALES (est): 3MM **Privately Held**
SIC: 3625 Mfg Relays/Industrial Controls

(G-2538)
VIRA CLEAN LLC
5860 N Canton Center Rd # 3 (48187-2687)
PHONE....................313 455-1020
Christopher Shah,
EMP: 7 **EST:** 2020
SALES (est): 96.5K **Privately Held**
SIC: 2842 Sanitation preparations, disinfectants & deodorants

(G-2539)
VISTEON CORPORATION
45004 Lothrop Ct (48188-1077)
PHONE....................734 718-8927
EMP: 83
SALES (corp-wide): 7.5B **Publicly Held**
SIC: 3714 Mfg Motor Vehicle Parts/Accessories
PA: Visteon Corporation
 1 Village Center Dr
 Van Buren Twp MI 48111
 800 847-8366

(G-2540)
VITAL SIGNS INC (PA)
Also Called: VSI Archtectural Signs Systems
6753 Kings Mill Dr (48187-5478)
PHONE....................313 491-2010
Francis A Schmitt, *President*
EMP: 4 **EST:** 1988
SALES (est): 390K **Privately Held**
WEB: www.vitalsignsmichigan.com
SIC: 3993 Signs, not made in custom sign painting shops

(G-2541)
VOXELJET AMERICA INC
41430 Haggerty Cir S (48188-2227)
PHONE....................734 709-8237
Ingo Ederer, *CEO*
Michael Dougherty, *Managing Dir*
David Tait, *Managing Dir*
Rudolf Franz, *COO*
▲ **EMP:** 20 **EST:** 2014
SQ FT: 50,000
SALES (est): 5.5MM
SALES (corp-wide): 25.5MM **Privately Held**
WEB: www.voxeljet.com
SIC: 3555 Printing presses
PA: Voxeljet Ag
 Paul-Lenz-Str. 1a
 Friedberg BY 86316
 821 748-3100

(G-2542)
WINE AND CANVAS OF ANN ARBOR
44730 Ford Rd (48187-2942)
PHONE....................734 277-9253
EMP: 4 **EST:** 2019
SALES (est): 97K **Privately Held**
WEB: www.wineandcanvas.com
SIC: 2211 Canvas

(G-2543)
WORTHINGTON INDUSTRIES INC
5260 S Haggerty Rd (48188-2775)
PHONE....................734 397-6187
Justin Edgar, *Opers Staff*
Michael Maggard, *Branch Mgr*
Charles Kinney, *Manager*
EMP: 8
SALES (corp-wide): 3.1B **Publicly Held**
WEB: www.worthingtonindustries.com
SIC: 3316 Cold finishing of steel shapes
PA: Worthington Industries, Inc.
 200 W Old Wlson Bridge Rd
 Worthington OH 43085
 614 438-3210

(G-2544)
YAZAKI INTERNATIONAL CORP (HQ)
6801 N Haggerty Rd 4707e (48187-3538)
PHONE....................734 983-1000
Yutaka Inagaki, *Principal*
Ben Kwon, *Counsel*
Kim Ward, *Counsel*
James Romine, *Exec VP*
Angeles Fabianamador, *Vice Pres*
◆ **EMP:** 9 **EST:** 1992
SALES (est): 1.7B **Privately Held**
WEB: www.yazaki-europe.com
SIC: 5013 3643 Automotive supplies & parts; current-carrying wiring devices

(G-2545)
ZSI-FOSTER INC (HQ)
45065 Michigan Ave (48188-2441)
PHONE....................734 844-0055
Rick Stepien, *CEO*
David Sack, *Vice Pres*
John Waller, *Vice Pres*
Holly Fender, *Sales Staff*
Max Weger, *Sales Staff*
◆ **EMP:** 36 **EST:** 2014
SALES (est): 12MM
SALES (corp-wide): 224.6MM **Privately Held**
WEB: www.zsi-foster.com
SIC: 3429 Clamps, metal
PA: Ideal Tridon Holdings, Inc.
 8100 Tridon Dr
 Smyrna TN 37167
 615 459-5800

Capac
St. Clair County

(G-2546)
CELANI PRINTING CO
126 N Main St (48014-3142)
PHONE....................810 395-1609
Daniel Celani, *Principal*
EMP: 6 **EST:** 2008
SALES (est): 108.2K **Privately Held**
SIC: 2752 Commercial printing, lithographic

(G-2547)
MILLER BROACH INC
Also Called: MB
14510 Bryce Rd (48014-3179)
P.O. Box 99 (48014-0099)
PHONE....................810 395-8810
Jeffrey Miller, *President*
Ken Nemec, *Vice Pres*
John Robert, *Prdtn Mgr*
Cintia Villegas, *Purch Mgr*
Rick Vargo, *QC Mgr*
EMP: 80 **EST:** 1988
SQ FT: 58,000
SALES (est): 10MM **Privately Held**
WEB: www.millerbroach.com
SIC: 3545 3541 Broaches (machine tool accessories); machine tools, metal cutting type

(G-2548)
MILLER PROD & MACHINING INC
14510 Bryce Rd (48014-3179)
P.O. Box 99 (48014-0099)
PHONE....................810 395-8810
Krista Starna-Miller, *CEO*
Jeffrey Miller, *President*
EMP: 10 **EST:** 2016
SQ FT: 20,000
SALES (est): 122.6K **Privately Held**
WEB: www.millerbroach.com
SIC: 3599 Machine shop, jobbing & repair

Carleton
Monroe County

(G-2549)
A & L METAL PRODUCTS
Also Called: Detroit Mini Safe Co
11984 Telegraph Rd (48117-9045)
P.O. Box 135 (48117-0135)
PHONE....................734 654-8990
Fax: 734 654-0045
EMP: 5
SQ FT: 12,000
SALES (est): 520.6K **Privately Held**
SIC: 3613 3499 5072 Mfg Switchgear/Switchboards & Deposit Safes & Whol Security Hardware

(G-2550)
DAILY RECYCLING OF MICHIGAN
201 Matlin Rd (48117-9797)
PHONE....................734 654-9800
Nick Straub, *Manager*
EMP: 4 **EST:** 1990
SALES (est): 74.6K **Privately Held**
SIC: 2711 4953 Newspapers, publishing & printing; refuse systems

(G-2551)
DERU EXTRACTS LLC
12915 Sumpter Rd (48117-9553)
P.O. Box 300 (48117-0300)
PHONE....................734 497-2963
EMP: 4 **EST:** 2018
SALES (est): 74.4K **Privately Held**
WEB: www.deruextracts.com
SIC: 2836 Extracts

(G-2552)
DIAMOND ALTERNATIVES LLC
Also Called: Diamond Recyclers
11602 Finzel Rd (48117-9168)
PHONE....................734 755-1505
Gene Eswatek, *President*
EMP: 7 **EST:** 2014
SALES (est): 137.1K **Privately Held**
WEB: www.diamondrecyclers.net
SIC: 3545 Diamond cutting tools for turning, boring, burnishing, etc.

(G-2553)
FCX PERFORMANCE INC (PA)
Also Called: Renew Valve & Machine Co.
845 Monroe St (48117-9077)
PHONE....................734 654-2201
Sherry Champagne, *Sales Staff*
JB Rorick, *Mng Member*
Gerald Frey, *Info Tech Dir*
Carolyn Wasner, *Info Tech Mgr*
Glenn Goodnight, *Technical Staff*
EMP: 42 **EST:** 2010
SALES (est): 6.8MM **Privately Held**
WEB: www.renewvalve.com
SIC: 7699 3491 Valve repair, industrial; industrial valves

(G-2554)
GREEN FUELS LLC
715 Indian Trail Rd (48117-9315)
PHONE....................734 735-6802
Lauren L Smith, *Administration*
EMP: 5 **EST:** 2012
SALES (est): 133.9K **Privately Held**
SIC: 2869 Fuels

(G-2555)
GUARDIAN INDUSTRIES LLC
14600 Romine Rd (48117-9257)
PHONE....................734 654-4285
Gerry Hool, *Opers-Prdtn-Mfg*
Conrad Sobania, *QC Mgr*
Charles Buiocchi, *Manager*
Jim Salo, *Manager*
EMP: 500
SALES (corp-wide): 36.9B **Privately Held**
WEB: www.guardian.com
SIC: 3211 3231 3229 Flat glass; products of purchased glass; pressed & blown glass
HQ: Guardian Industries, Llc
 2300 Harmon Rd
 Auburn Hills MI 48326
 248 340-1800

(G-2556)
GUARDIAN INDUSTRIES LLC
Also Called: Guardian Science & Tech Ctr
14511 Romine Rd (48117-9647)
PHONE....................734 654-1111
Scott Thompson, *Branch Mgr*
EMP: 85
SALES (corp-wide): 36.9B **Privately Held**
WEB: www.guardian.com
SIC: 3211 Flat glass
HQ: Guardian Industries, Llc
 2300 Harmon Rd
 Auburn Hills MI 48326
 248 340-1800

(G-2557)
KACE LOGISTICS LLC (PA)
862 Will Carleton Rd (48117-9704)
PHONE....................734 946-8600
Kenyon S Calender, *CEO*
Joseph Parin, *President*
Jeff Carroll, *Vice Pres*
Paul Pavelich, *Vice Pres*
EMP: 25 **EST:** 1986
SALES (est): 21.7MM **Privately Held**
WEB: www.kclog.com
SIC: 4731 3577 Truck transportation brokers; bar code (magnetic ink) printers

Carleton - Monroe County (G-2558)

(G-2558)
LAKEWOOD MACHINE PRODUCTS CO
12429 Maxwell Rd (48117-8800)
P.O. Box 388 (48117-0388)
PHONE..................734 654-6677
Martin Lisowski, *President*
Howard J Morrin, *Vice Pres*
Lois Schafer Lisowski, *Treasurer*
Elizabeth Duvall, *Admin Sec*
EMP: 52 **EST:** 1956
SQ FT: 22,000
SALES (est): 10.8MM **Privately Held**
WEB: www.lakewoodmachineproducts.com
SIC: 3537 Platforms, stands, tables, pallets & similar equipment

(G-2559)
LV METALS INC
2094 Ready Rd (48117-9778)
PHONE..................734 654-8081
EMP: 5
SQ FT: 20,000
SALES (est): 346.1K **Privately Held**
SIC: 7389 5051 3444 Business Services Metals Service Center Mfg Sheet Metalwork

(G-2560)
MOSLEY
9628 Lazy Oak Dr (48117-9628)
PHONE..................734 654-2969
Kristie Mosley, *Principal*
EMP: 5 **EST:** 2010
SALES (est): 88.1K **Privately Held**
SIC: 3569 Baling machines, for scrap metal, paper or similar material

(G-2561)
PARSONS INDUSTRIAL MAINTENANCE
876 Indian Trail Rd (48117-9315)
P.O. Box 248, Rockwood (48173-0248)
PHONE..................734 236-4163
Wayne Parsons, *Owner*
Mathew Parsons, *Owner*
EMP: 6 **EST:** 2017
SALES (est): 476.2K **Privately Held**
WEB: www.pimindustrialmaintenance.com
SIC: 7692 Welding repair

(G-2562)
RVM COMPANY OF TOLEDO
Also Called: Dayton Precision Services
845 Monroe St (48117-9077)
PHONE..................734 654-2201
Tim Rorick, *President*
EMP: 5 **EST:** 1961
SQ FT: 30,000
SALES (est): 524.2K
SALES (corp-wide): 6.8MM **Privately Held**
WEB: www.renewvalve.com
SIC: 7699 5085 3599 Valve repair, industrial; valves & fittings; machine shop, jobbing & repair
PA: Fcx Performance Inc
845 Monroe St
Carleton MI 48117
734 654-2201

Carney
Menominee County

(G-2563)
JASPERS SUGAR BUSH LLC
W1867 County Road 374 (49821-9333)
PHONE..................906 639-2588
Mark Jasper, *Mng Member*
Bree Wicklund, *Analyst*
Brenda Jasper,
John Jasper,
EMP: 6 **EST:** 2001
SALES (est): 90K **Privately Held**
WEB: www.jaspermaple.com
SIC: 2099 Sugar, industrial maple; maple syrup

(G-2564)
SUPERIOR CEDAR PRODUCTS INC
N285 Us 41 S (49812)
P.O. Box 38 (49812-0038)
PHONE..................906 639-2132
Dwaine Mellen, *President*
Timothy Bruce, *Vice Pres*
Charles Olson, *Vice Pres*
Charles Dornfeld, *Treasurer*
EMP: 40 **EST:** 1998
SALES (est): 9.4MM **Privately Held**
WEB: www.superiorcedar.com
SIC: 3524 Lawn & garden equipment

Caro
Tuscola County

(G-2565)
ANDOOR CRAFTMASTER
3521 Lobdell Rd (48723-9552)
PHONE..................989 672-2020
Tracy Mazur, *Owner*
EMP: 7 **EST:** 1987
SALES (est): 390.7K **Privately Held**
SIC: 2431 3442 Doors, wood; metal doors, sash & trim

(G-2566)
CAROL PACKING HOUSE
1131 Weeden Rd (48723-9583)
PHONE..................989 673-2688
Dan Maurer, *Partner*
EMP: 6 **EST:** 1947
SQ FT: 5,000
SALES (est): 406.8K **Privately Held**
SIC: 2011 Meat packing plants

(G-2567)
CARRY MANUFACTURING INC
Also Called: Carry Pump Co.
1360 Prospect Ave (48723-9288)
PHONE..................989 672-2779
Del Nichols, *CEO*
James Nichols, *President*
Delmar Nichiols, *Vice Pres*
Gene Nichols, *Treasurer*
Jeanie Nichols, *Treasurer*
EMP: 3 **EST:** 1987
SQ FT: 11,000
SALES (est): 1.3MM **Privately Held**
WEB: www.32f.com
SIC: 3312 3914 Stainless steel; stainless steel ware

(G-2568)
CORLS KILN
2978 W Deckerville Rd (48723-9663)
PHONE..................989 673-4925
Bill Corl, *Principal*
EMP: 6 **EST:** 2008
SALES (est): 88.5K **Privately Held**
WEB: www.corlskiln.com
SIC: 3559 Kilns

(G-2569)
DR AND HI MOLD AND MCH INC
3266 Leix Rd (48723-9544)
PHONE..................989 672-2192
EMP: 4 **EST:** 2018
SALES (est): 66.2K **Privately Held**
SIC: 3544 Special dies & tools

(G-2570)
EDWARDS PUBLICATIONS IN
344 N State St (48723-1538)
PHONE..................864 882-3272
Tim Murphy, *Publisher*
EMP: 5 **EST:** 2009
SALES (est): 73K **Privately Held**
SIC: 2741 Miscellaneous publishing

(G-2571)
ENGINEERED TOOLS CORP
2710 W Caro Rd (48723-9609)
P.O. Box 209 (48723-0209)
PHONE..................989 673-8733
Glen Perkins, *President*
Ross Deneau, *Engineer*
Richard Perkins, *Mktg Dir*
Patricia Perkins, *Admin Sec*
EMP: 34 **EST:** 1949
SQ FT: 24,500
SALES (est): 2.2MM **Privately Held**
WEB: www.engineeredtools.com
SIC: 3545 8711 Cutting tools for machine tools; engineering services

(G-2572)
GREAT LAKES LIFT INC
1382 E Caro Rd (48723-9306)
PHONE..................989 673-2109
David J Sturtevant, *President*
Brenda Stein, *Admin Sec*
EMP: 4 **EST:** 1971
SQ FT: 10,000
SALES (est): 675.8K **Privately Held**
WEB: www.greatlakeslift.com
SIC: 3536 3448 3799 Boat lifts; docks: prefabricated metal; trailers & trailer equipment

(G-2573)
LASER MARKING TECHNOLOGIES LLC
1101 W Sanilac Rd (48723-9539)
PHONE..................989 673-6690
Staci Meyer, *Office Mgr*
Zach Brown, *Technical Staff*
Samuel Palmeter,
▲ **EMP:** 13 **EST:** 2006
SALES (est): 3.7MM **Privately Held**
WEB: www.lasermarktech.com
SIC: 3699 Laser systems & equipment

(G-2574)
MICHIGAN SUGAR COMPANY
725 S Almer St (48723-1812)
P.O. Box 107 (48723-0107)
PHONE..................989 673-3126
William Gough, *Manager*
EMP: 165
SALES (corp-wide): 189.4MM **Privately Held**
WEB: www.michigansugar.com
SIC: 2063 2062 Beet sugar from beet sugar refinery; cane sugar refining
PA: Michigan Sugar Company
122 Uptown Dr Unit 300
Bay City MI 48708
989 686-0161

(G-2575)
MICHIGAN SUGAR COMPANY
819 Peninsular St (48723)
P.O. Box 107 (48723-0107)
PHONE..................989 673-2223
Daniel Mashue, *Branch Mgr*
EMP: 118
SALES (corp-wide): 189.4MM **Privately Held**
WEB: www.michigansugar.com
SIC: 5149 2063 2061 Sugar, honey, molasses & syrups; beet sugar; raw cane sugar
PA: Michigan Sugar Company
122 Uptown Dr Unit 300
Bay City MI 48708
989 686-0161

(G-2576)
MIDWEST BUILD CENTER LLC
1750 Speirs Rd Ste 1 (48723-8212)
PHONE..................989 672-1388
Henry Rise, *Mng Member*
EMP: 7 **EST:** 2017
SALES (est): 417.8K **Privately Held**
WEB: www.mwskysports.com
SIC: 3721 Airplanes, fixed or rotary wing

(G-2577)
POET BIOREFINING - CARO LLC
Also Called: Michigan Ethanol, LLC
1551 Empire Dr (48723-8804)
PHONE..................989 672-1222
David Gloer, *General Mgr*
Jeffrey Broin, *Chairman*
EMP: 41
SALES (est): 10.4MM **Privately Held**
WEB: www.poet.com
SIC: 2869 Ethyl alcohol, ethanol
PA: Poet, Llc
4615 N Lewis Ave
Sioux Falls SD 57104

(G-2578)
QUALITY STEEL FABG & ERCT
2990 E Dayton Rd (48723-9449)
PHONE..................989 672-2873
EMP: 5 **EST:** 2019
SALES (est): 292.7K **Privately Held**
SIC: 3544 Special dies & tools

(G-2579)
R & S TOOL & DIE INC
545 Columbia St Ste B (48723-8935)
PHONE..................989 673-8511
Stephen Cotton, *President*
Robert H Cotton Sr, *President*
Ruth Cotton, *Corp Secy*
EMP: 9 **EST:** 1985
SQ FT: 5,000
SALES (est): 783.5K **Privately Held**
WEB: www.rstoolanddie.com
SIC: 3559 3549 3545 3544 Plastics working machinery; metalworking machinery; gauges (machine tool accessories); die sets for metal stamping (presses); machine shop, jobbing & repair

(G-2580)
S WOOD ENTERPRISES LLC
1549 E Deckerville Rd (48723-9109)
PHONE..................989 673-8150
Scott Wood, *Principal*
EMP: 5 **EST:** 2015
SALES (est): 99.3K **Privately Held**
WEB: www.wood-enterprises.com
SIC: 2499 Wood products

(G-2581)
TI GROUP AUTO SYSTEMS LLC
Also Called: Caro Test Center
630 Columbia St (48723-9502)
PHONE..................989 672-1200
Bill Learman, *Engineer*
Kurt Nickel, *Agent*
Kurt Mickel, *Agent*
EMP: 7
SALES (corp-wide): 3.3B **Privately Held**
WEB: www.tifluidsystems.com
SIC: 3714 Motor vehicle parts & accessories
HQ: Ti Group Automotive Systems, Llc
2020 Taylor Rd
Auburn Hills MI 48326
248 296-8000

(G-2582)
TI GROUP AUTO SYSTEMS LLC
630 Columbia St (48723-9502)
PHONE..................989 673-7727
Roger Affeldt, *Branch Mgr*
EMP: 7
SALES (corp-wide): 3.3B **Privately Held**
WEB: www.tifluidsystems.com
SIC: 3714 Motor vehicle parts & accessories
HQ: Ti Group Automotive Systems, Llc
2020 Taylor Rd
Auburn Hills MI 48326
248 296-8000

(G-2583)
TUSCOLA COUNTY ADVERTISER INC (PA)
344 N State St (48723-1538)
P.O. Box 106 (48723-0106)
PHONE..................989 673-3181
Bob Edwards, *President*
Joyce Edwards, *Corp Secy*
Jerry Edwards, *Vice Pres*
Steve Edwards, *Vice Pres*
Tim Murphy, *Director*
EMP: 35 **EST:** 1868
SQ FT: 9,000
SALES (est): 9.4MM **Privately Held**
WEB: www.tuscolatoday.com
SIC: 2711 2741 Newspapers: publishing only, not printed on site; miscellaneous publishing

(G-2584)
TUSCOLA COUNTY ADVERTISER INC
Also Called: Heritage Press
344 N State St (48723-1538)
PHONE..................517 673-3181
EMP: 438

GEOGRAPHIC SECTION
Cass City - Tuscola County (G-2610)

SALES (corp-wide): 9.4MM **Privately Held**
WEB: www.tuscolatoday.com
SIC: 2759 Commercial printing
PA: Tuscola County Advertiser, Inc.
344 N State St
Caro MI 48723
989 673-3181

(G-2585)
VARSITY MONTHLY THUMB
251 N State St (48723-1560)
PHONE.....................810 404-5297
Brenda Tomlinson, *Sales Staff*
EMP: 5 **EST:** 2017
SALES (est): 118.5K **Privately Held**
SIC: 2721 Magazines: publishing only, not printed on site

(G-2586)
WOW PRODUCTS USA
1111 S Colling Rd (48723-9238)
PHONE.....................989 672-1300
EMP: 8 **EST:** 2011
SALES (est): 132.2K **Privately Held**
WEB: www.wowplastics.net
SIC: 3089 Injection molding of plastics

Carrollton
Saginaw County

(G-2587)
CUSTOM DESIGN & MANUFACTURING
3673 Carrollton Rd (48724-5004)
P.O. Box 190 (48724-0190)
PHONE.....................989 754-9962
James Nuerminger, *President*
Dan Vesterfelt, *Vice Pres*
EMP: 15 **EST:** 1996
SQ FT: 5,000
SALES (est): 1.2MM **Privately Held**
SIC: 3441 7692 3444 1799 Fabricated structural metal; welding repair; sheet metalwork; welding on site

(G-2588)
DARLING INGREDIENTS INC
340 Tyler St (48724-5061)
P.O. Box 181 (48724-0181)
PHONE.....................989 752-4340
Jim Schmieder, *Sales Staff*
Sam Immel, *Manager*
Al Steiger, *Senior Mgr*
EMP: 10
SALES (corp-wide): 3.3B **Publicly Held**
WEB: www.darlingii.com
SIC: 2077 4212 Tallow rendering, inedible; local trucking, without storage
PA: Darling Ingredients Inc.
5601 N Macarthur Blvd
Irving TX 75038
972 717-0300

(G-2589)
ROCK REDI-MIX INC
Also Called: Rock Products, The
2820 Carrollton Rd (48724)
P.O. Box 39 (48724-0039)
PHONE.....................989 752-0795
EMP: 9
SALES (est): 1.2MM **Privately Held**
SIC: 3273 Mfg Ready-Mixed Concrete

(G-2590)
SAGINAW ASPHALT PAVING CO
2981 Carrollton Rd (48724)
PHONE.....................989 755-8147
Edward Levy, *President*
▲ **EMP:** 93 **EST:** 1952
SQ FT: 18,000
SALES (est): 32.9MM
SALES (corp-wide): 521.9MM **Privately Held**
WEB: www.ace-saginawpaving.com
SIC: 1611 8741 2951 Highway & street paving contractor; construction management; asphalt & asphaltic paving mixtures (not from refineries)
PA: Edw. C. Levy Co.
9300 Dix
Dearborn MI 48120
313 429-2200

Carson City
Montcalm County

(G-2591)
ALLEY T & GIFTS
118 E Main St (48811-9756)
PHONE.....................989 875-4793
Jenna Strong, *Sales Staff*
Janet Strong, *Branch Mgr*
EMP: 5
SALES (corp-wide): 778.9K **Privately Held**
WEB: www.alleyt.net
SIC: 2759 Screen printing
PA: Alley T & Gifts
103 S Jeffery Ave
Ithaca MI 48847
989 875-4793

(G-2592)
DUTCHMANS WELDING & REPAIR
6161 County Line Rd (48811)
PHONE.....................989 584-6861
Harvey Imhoff, *Owner*
Ruth Imhoff, *Co-Owner*
EMP: 4 **EST:** 2000
SALES (est): 258.4K **Privately Held**
SIC: 7692 Welding repair

(G-2593)
HARVEYS COMMODITIES LLC
729 W Main St (48811-8553)
PHONE.....................616 920-1805
Michael McCracking, *Administration*
Travis Marshall, *Merchandising*
Greg Thon, *Merchandising*
EMP: 11 **EST:** 2013
SALES (est): 5MM **Privately Held**
WEB: www.harveyscommodities.com
SIC: 2048 Prepared feeds

(G-2594)
PADDLE KING INC
7110 S Crystal Rd (48811-8503)
PHONE.....................989 235-6776
Mark Brusskoter, *President*
EMP: 14 **EST:** 1986
SALES (est): 5MM **Privately Held**
WEB: www.paddleking.com
SIC: 3732 2394 2499 Non-motorized boat, building & repairing; canvas & related products; floating docks, wood; ladders, wood

(G-2595)
PLASTICO INDUSTRIES INC (PA)
320 W Main St (48811-5116)
P.O. Box 325, Springville CA (93265-0325)
PHONE.....................616 304-6289
EMP: 13
SQ FT: 30,000
SALES (est): 1MM **Privately Held**
SIC: 3089 Mfg Injection Molded Plastic Point-Of-Purchase Displays

Carsonville
Sanilac County

(G-2596)
NATURES BEST TOP SOIL COMPOST
640 Old 51 (48419-9427)
PHONE.....................810 657-9528
Michael Davis, *Owner*
EMP: 5 **EST:** 2008
SALES (est): 312.2K **Privately Held**
WEB: www.naturesbesttopsoil.com
SIC: 2875 Compost

Casco
St. Clair County

(G-2597)
AFTERSHOCK MOTORSPORTS
5831 Church Rd (48064-4207)
PHONE.....................586 273-1333
Ruby Bishop, *Owner*
EMP: 5 **EST:** 2002
SQ FT: 7,200 **Privately Held**
WEB: www.aftershockmotorsports.com
SIC: 3711 5571 Automobile assembly, including specialty automobiles; motorcycle parts & accessories

(G-2598)
INNOVATED PORTABLE WELDIN
5221 Lois Ct (48064-4663)
PHONE.....................586 322-4442
EMP: 4 **EST:** 2009
SALES (est): 42K **Privately Held**
SIC: 7692 Welding repair

(G-2599)
JD EDWARDS MGT GROUP INC
4200 Bethuy Rd (48064-2315)
PHONE.....................586 727-4039
James B Edwards, *President*
Debra J Edwards, *Principal*
EMP: 5 **EST:** 2007
SQ FT: 2,500
SALES (est): 563K **Privately Held**
WEB: www.jdeei.com
SIC: 3544 7389 Die sets for metal stamping (presses); brokers' services

(G-2600)
MAGNETIC CHUCK SERVICES CO INC
Also Called: Industrial System Services
9391 Lindsey Rd (48064-2412)
PHONE.....................586 822-9441
James Ewald, *President*
EMP: 6 **EST:** 2003
SQ FT: 2,500
SALES (est): 411.2K **Privately Held**
WEB: www.magneticchuckservices.com
SIC: 7699 3545 Industrial machinery & equipment repair; chucks: drill, lathe or magnetic (machine tool accessories)

(G-2601)
NEW LIFE COP BRASS MINT FREE M
Also Called: All Metal Finishing
9984 Marine City Hwy (48064-4108)
PHONE.....................586 725-3286
Ken Hancock, *Mng Member*
EMP: 6 **EST:** 1983
SALES (est): 717.4K **Privately Held**
SIC: 5051 3471 Copper products; finishing, metals or formed products

(G-2602)
PACE SOFTWARE SYSTEMS INC
5345 Meldrum St (48064-3703)
P.O. Box 458, Fraser (48026-0458)
PHONE.....................586 727-3189
Roger Pace, *President*
EMP: 10 **EST:** 1988
SALES (est): 483.4K **Privately Held**
WEB: www.pacesoftwaresystems.com
SIC: 7372 Prepackaged software

Caseville
Huron County

(G-2603)
CASEVILLE VILLAGE GOVERNMENT
6685 Clay St (48725-9556)
PHONE.....................989 856-4407
David Quinn, *Manager*
EMP: 6 **EST:** 2009
SALES (est): 105.1K **Privately Held**
WEB: www.cityofcaseville.com
SIC: 3589 Water treatment equipment, industrial

(G-2604)
EVENHEAT KILN INC
6949 Legion Rd (48725-9575)
P.O. Box 399 (48725-0399)
PHONE.....................989 856-2281
John D Watson, *President*
Susan Siver, *Office Mgr*
Dave Graf, *CTO*
EMP: 20 **EST:** 1948
SQ FT: 20,000
SALES (est): 3.4MM **Privately Held**
WEB: www.evenheat-kiln.com
SIC: 3567 Ceramic kilns & furnaces

(G-2605)
STEADFAST TOOL & MACHINE INC
6601 Limerick Rd (48725-9724)
PHONE.....................989 856-8127
Chad Bohn, *President*
EMP: 4 **EST:** 1997 **Privately Held**
SIC: 3541 Brushing machines (metalworking machinery)

Casnovia
Muskegon County

(G-2606)
DANMARK GRAPHICS LLC
153 N Main St (49318-8704)
P.O. Box 96 (49318-0096)
PHONE.....................616 675-7499
Mark Vanderzanden, *Principal*
EMP: 7 **EST:** 2004
SALES (est): 404.3K **Privately Held**
WEB: www.danmarkgraphics.com
SIC: 7336 2759 5999 Commercial art & graphic design; letterpress & screen printing; banners, flags, decals & posters

(G-2607)
MARTENS LOGGING
2335 Canada Rd (49318-9605)
PHONE.....................616 675-5473
Douglas Martens, *Principal*
EMP: 5 **EST:** 2010
SALES (est): 148.4K **Privately Held**
SIC: 2411 Logging

Caspian
Iron County

(G-2608)
NORTHEASTERN PRODUCTS CORP
85 Brady Ave (49915-5115)
P.O. Box 467 (49915-0467)
PHONE.....................906 265-6241
Chris Gilbert, *Vice Pres*
Mark Stauber, *Manager*
EMP: 21
SALES (corp-wide): 11MM **Privately Held**
WEB: www.nep-co.com
SIC: 2493 Reconstituted wood products
PA: Northeastern Products Corp.
115 Sweet Rd
Warrensburg NY 12885
518 623-3161

(G-2609)
TECHNIMOLD INC
501 W Railroad (49915-5154)
P.O. Box 702 (49915-0702)
PHONE.....................906 284-1921
Dennis Crounse, *President*
EMP: 12 **EST:** 1972
SALES (est): 1.5MM **Privately Held**
WEB: www.technimolds.us
SIC: 3089 Injection molding of plastics

Cass City
Tuscola County

(G-2610)
ANROD SCREEN CYLINDER COMPANY
6160 Garfield Ave (48726-1309)
P.O. Box 117 (48726-0117)
PHONE.....................989 872-2101
Gregory A Biddinger, *President*
Richard Biddinger, *Treasurer*
Dan Post, *Executive*
EMP: 44 **EST:** 1950
SQ FT: 32,000
SALES (est): 5MM **Privately Held**
WEB: www.anrodscreen.com
SIC: 3496 3714 3564 3494 Cylinder wire cloth; motor vehicle parts & accessories; blowers & fans; valves & pipe fittings; metal stampings

Cass City - Tuscola County (G-2611)

(G-2611)
BATTELS SUGAR BUSH
7964 Daus Rd (48726-9714)
PHONE...................989 872-4794
Sue S Battel, *Principal*
EMP: 5 **EST:** 2015
SALES (est): 62.3K **Privately Held**
WEB: www.battelsyrup.weebly.com
SIC: 2099 Maple syrup

(G-2612)
CASS CITY CHRONICLE INC
6550 Main St (48726-1561)
P.O. Box 115 (48726-0115)
PHONE...................989 872-2010
Clarke Haire, *President*
John Haire, *Vice Pres*
EMP: 9 **EST:** 1940
SALES (est): 499.6K **Privately Held**
WEB: www.ccchronicle.net
SIC: 2711 Newspapers: publishing only, not printed on site

(G-2613)
COLE CARBIDE INDUSTRIES INC
6880 Cass City Rd (48726-9642)
PHONE...................989 872-4348
Scott Kelly, *General Mgr*
Dennis Kessler, *Site Mgr*
Tom Stimpfel, *Info Tech Mgr*
Nancy Pavlosky, *Admin Sec*
EMP: 8
SQ FT: 17,000
SALES (corp-wide): 10.2MM **Privately Held**
WEB: www.colecarbide.com
SIC: 3545 Cutting tools for machine tools
PA: Cole Carbide Industries, Inc.
  4930 S Lapeer Rd
  Lake Orion MI 48359
  248 276-1278

(G-2614)
ERLAS INC
Also Called: Erla's Food Center
6233 Church St (48726-1111)
PHONE...................989 872-2191
EMP: 100 **EST:** 1953
SQ FT: 30,000
SALES (est): 21.6MM **Privately Held**
SIC: 5147 5411 2013 2011 Whol Meats/Products Ret Groceries Mfg Prepared Meats Meat Packing Plant

(G-2615)
IDA D BYLER
4169 Moore Rd (48726-9506)
PHONE...................810 672-9355
Ida D Byler, *Principal*
EMP: 4 **EST:** 2013
SALES (est): 196.6K **Privately Held**
SIC: 2421 Sawmills & planing mills, general

(G-2616)
KAPPEN SAW MILL
4518 Hurds Corner Rd (48726-9473)
PHONE...................989 872-4410
Wallace Kappen, *Owner*
EMP: 4 **EST:** 1996
SALES (est): 186.3K **Privately Held**
SIC: 2421 Sawmills & planing mills, general

(G-2617)
LEGENDARY FABRICATION WLDG LLC
8260 Van Dyke Rd (48726-9636)
PHONE...................989 872-9353
Mark Neveau, *Mng Member*
EMP: 9 **EST:** 2017
SALES (est): 1.3MM **Privately Held**
WEB: www.legendaryweld.com
SIC: 3441 Fabricated structural metal

(G-2618)
MI-TECH TOOLING INC
6215 Garfield Ave (48726-1341)
PHONE...................989 912-2440
Joseph Langenburg, *President*
EMP: 26 **EST:** 2003
SQ FT: 7,500
SALES (est): 2.1MM **Privately Held**
WEB: www.mi-techtool.com
SIC: 3541 Home workshop machine tools, metalworking

(G-2619)
MICRO EDM CO LLC
6172 Main St (48726-1106)
PHONE...................989 872-4306
Lori Forman, *Office Mgr*
Robert Bredemeyer,
EMP: 6 **EST:** 1987
SALES (est): 669.4K **Privately Held**
WEB: www.microedm.com
SIC: 3599 5084 Electrical discharge machining (EDM); machine tools & metalworking machinery

(G-2620)
MILLENNIUM STEERING LLC
6285 Garfield Ave (48726-1341)
PHONE...................989 872-8823
Gary Vollmar,
▲ **EMP:** 75 **EST:** 2006
SQ FT: 5,000
SALES (est): 5.7MM **Privately Held**
SIC: 3714 Motor vehicle engines & parts

(G-2621)
TAKE CARE NATURAL PRODUCTS
3645 Cooklin Rd (48726-9341)
PHONE...................989 280-3947
Melissa Fritz, *Executive*
EMP: 4 **EST:** 2018
SALES (est): 79.1K **Privately Held**
SIC: 2841 Soap & other detergents

(G-2622)
WALBRO LLC
6242 Garfield Ave (48726-1325)
PHONE...................989 872-2131
Dave McNaughton, *General Mgr*
William Gaun, *Vice Pres*
Jerry Kibby, *Vice Pres*
Jeffrey Sensmeier, *Vice Pres*
Jorge Gastelum, *Opers Mgr*
EMP: 56 **Privately Held**
WEB: www.walbro.com
SIC: 3592 3714 3694 3561 Carburetors; motor vehicle parts & accessories; engine electrical equipment; pumps & pumping equipment; fabricated plate work (boiler shop)
HQ: Walbro Llc
  2015 W River Rd Ste 202
  Tucson AZ 85704

(G-2623)
WAVE TOOL LLC
6215 Garfield Ave (48726-1341)
PHONE...................989 912-2116
Joseph Langenburg,
EMP: 11 **EST:** 2014
SALES (est): 1.4MM **Privately Held**
WEB: www.mi-techtool.com
SIC: 3541 Drilling machine tools (metal cutting)

(G-2624)
WHITTAKER TIMBER CORPORATION
3623 Elmwood Rd (48726-9476)
PHONE...................989 872-3065
David A Whittaker, *President*
EMP: 4 **EST:** 1985
SALES (est): 451.2K **Privately Held**
WEB: www.preferredlegalcourier.com
SIC: 2411 Logging

Cassopolis
Cass County

(G-2625)
AMERI-KART(MI) CORP
19300 Grange St (49031-9501)
PHONE...................269 641-5811
Mike O'Brien, *General Mgr*
Lee Karn, *Plant Mgr*
Chris Sheeley, *Engineer*
Cindy Schneider, *Sales Staff*
Randy Shelton, *Maintence Staff*
▲ **EMP:** 195 **EST:** 1969
SQ FT: 200,000
SALES (est): 9.9MM
SALES (corp-wide): 510.3MM **Publicly Held**
WEB: www.myersindustries.com
SIC: 3089 Injection molding of plastics
PA: Myers Industries, Inc.
  1293 S Main St
  Akron OH 44301
  330 253-5592

(G-2626)
CHT USA INC (DH)
805 Wolfe Ave (49031-9777)
PHONE...................269 445-0847
Levi Cottington, *CEO*
Ken Kemerer, *COO*
Tom Gawlik, *CFO*
Kenneth Charboneau, *CTO*
Richard Hughes, *Director*
▲ **EMP:** 31 **EST:** 1989
SQ FT: 75,000
SALES (est): 62.2MM
SALES (corp-wide): 144.1K **Privately Held**
WEB: www.cht-silicones.com
SIC: 2819 2822 Chemicals, high purity: refined from technical grade; silicone rubbers
HQ: Cht Germany Gmbh
  Bismarckstr. 102
  Tubingen BW 72072
  707 115-40

(G-2627)
ENGINEERED CONCEPTS INC
67990 Milmc Ln (49031-7547)
PHONE...................574 333-9110
John McColley, *President*
EMP: 10 **EST:** 2010
SALES (est): 508.5K **Privately Held**
SIC: 3599 Custom machinery

(G-2628)
FRANKS PRODUCTS
Also Called: C N C Machining
66796 N Shore Dr (49031-9620)
PHONE...................269 350-7366
Frank Chmilewski, *Partner*
Freida Chmilewski, *Partner*
EMP: 5 **EST:** 1965
SQ FT: 3,600
SALES (est): 360.2K **Privately Held**
SIC: 3599 Machine shop, jobbing & repair

(G-2629)
HARBINGER LASER
708 Sherman Ln (49031-8711)
PHONE...................269 445-1499
EMP: 8 **EST:** 2013
SALES (est): 187.7K **Privately Held**
WEB: www.thirtyaxis.com
SIC: 2759 Commercial printing

(G-2630)
ICMP INC
805 Wolfe Ave (49031-9777)
PHONE...................269 445-0847
Kenneth Charboneau, *President*
Bobbi Post, *Principal*
Donna Charboneau, *Corp Secy*
Kent Charboneau, *Accountant*
Dana Baker, *Marketing Staff*
▲ **EMP:** 38 **EST:** 1989
SQ FT: 75,000
SALES (est): 19.3MM
SALES (corp-wide): 144.1K **Privately Held**
WEB: www.cht.com
SIC: 2819 Industrial inorganic chemicals
HQ: Cht Germany Gmbh
  Bismarckstr. 102
  Tubingen 72072
  707 115-40

(G-2631)
K & M MACHINE-FABRICATING INC
20745 M 60 (49031-9431)
P.O. Box 218 (49031-0218)
PHONE...................269 445-2495
Michael McLoughlin, *President*
▲ **EMP:** 250 **EST:** 1951
SQ FT: 335,000
SALES (est): 32.6MM **Privately Held**
WEB: www.k-mm.com
SIC: 3599 Machine shop, jobbing & repair

(G-2632)
MORGOLD INC
18409 Quaker Rd (49031-9482)
P.O. Box 26 (49031-0026)
PHONE...................269 445-3844
Robert Morgan, *President*
Phyllis Morgan, *Corp Secy*
EMP: 6 **EST:** 1981
SQ FT: 4,800
SALES (est): 509.4K **Privately Held**
WEB: www.4dtv.com
SIC: 3491 5085 Industrial valves; pistons & valves

(G-2633)
SCHWINTEK INC
310 Ranger Dr (49031-9810)
PHONE...................269 445-9999
Michael Schwindaman, *President*
Michael Howard, *Admin Sec*
◆ **EMP:** 6 **EST:** 2003
SQ FT: 13,000
SALES (est): 1.1MM **Privately Held**
WEB: www.schwintek.com
SIC: 3089 Automotive parts, plastic

(G-2634)
STEPHEN A JAMES
Also Called: Industrial Extrusion Belting
68730 Calvin Center Rd (49031-9570)
PHONE...................269 641-5879
Stephen A James, *Owner*
EMP: 5 **EST:** 1983
SQ FT: 8,000
SALES (est): 503.7K **Privately Held**
WEB: www.indexbelt.com
SIC: 3052 Rubber & plastics hose & beltings

(G-2635)
VIN-LEE-RON MEAT PACKING LLC
54501 Griffis Rd (49031-9759)
PHONE...................574 353-1386
Randy Cuthpert, *President*
Ron M Buncich, *President*
Vincent R Buncich, *Treasurer*
EMP: 12 **EST:** 1988
SALES (est): 344.8K **Privately Held**
SIC: 2011 Meat packing plants

Cedar
Leelanau County

(G-2636)
BULLETIN OF CONCERNED ASI
3693 S Bay Bluffs Dr (49621-9434)
PHONE...................231 228-7116
Martha K Winnacker, *Owner*
EMP: 5 **EST:** 2000 **Privately Held**
SIC: 2711 Newspapers, publishing & printing

(G-2637)
CENTURN MACHINE & TOOL INC
5588 S French Rd (49621-9640)
PHONE...................231 947-4773
EMP: 7
SALES (est): 663.7K **Privately Held**
SIC: 3599 Mfg Industrial Machinery

(G-2638)
CHERRY BEND TOOL & DIE
Hoxie Rd (49621)
P.O. Box 27 (49621-0027)
PHONE...................231 947-3046
Harold Lautner, *Owner*
Harold Lautner, *Owner*
EMP: 4 **EST:** 1974
SALES (est): 237.4K **Privately Held**
SIC: 3544 Special dies & tools

(G-2639)
FRENCH VALLEY VINEYARD L L C
3655 S French Rd (49621-9604)
PHONE...................231 228-2616
EMP: 4 **EST:** 2013

GEOGRAPHIC SECTION

Cedar Springs - Kent County (G-2667)

SALES (est): 106.3K **Privately Held**
SIC: 2084 Wines

(G-2640)
WEATHERVANE VINYARDS INC
Also Called: Bel Lago
6530 S Lake Shore Dr (49621-9615)
PHONE...................................231 228-4800
Charlie Charles Edson, *President*
Charles Edson, *President*
Amy F Iezzoni, *Treasurer*
Amy Iezzoni, *Treasurer*
Kathy Calcutt, *Manager*
EMP: 8 **EST:** 1996
SALES (est): 540.5K **Privately Held**
WEB: www.bellago.com
SIC: 2084 0762 Wines; vineyard management & maintenance services

Cedar Springs
Kent County

(G-2641)
ATWOOD FOREST PRODUCTS INC
1177 17 Mile Rd Ne (49319-7817)
P.O. Box 548 (49319-0548)
PHONE...................................616 696-0081
Ronald Atwood, *President*
Karen Atwood, *Vice Pres*
▼ **EMP:** 50 **EST:** 1977
SALES (est): 10MM **Privately Held**
WEB: www.atwoodforestproducts.com
SIC: 2411 2421 2426 Logging camps & contractors; sawmills & planing mills, general; hardwood dimension & flooring mills

(G-2642)
BETTER BUILT GATES CANVAS LLC
315 19 Mile Rd Ne (49319-8835)
PHONE...................................616 818-9103
Doug Fisk, *Principal*
EMP: 4 **EST:** 2018
SALES (est): 46.5K **Privately Held**
SIC: 2211 Canvas

(G-2643)
CEDAR MOBILE HOME SERVICE INC
4720 Russell St (49319-9111)
PHONE...................................616 696-1580
EMP: 6
SQ FT: 2,500
SALES: 475K **Privately Held**
SIC: 7699 4213 2451 5561 Repair Services Truck Operator-Nonlocal Mfg Mobile Homes Ret Recreational Vhcls

(G-2644)
CEDAR SPRINGS POST INC
Also Called: Cedar Springs Post Newspaper
36 E Maple (49319-5143)
P.O. Box 370 (49319-0370)
PHONE...................................616 696-3655
Lois Allen, *President*
Roger Allen, *Treasurer*
EMP: 8 **EST:** 1994
SALES (est): 646.5K **Privately Held**
WEB: www.cedarspringspost.com
SIC: 2711 Newspapers, publishing & printing

(G-2645)
CEDAR SPRINGS SALES LLC
Also Called: Cedar Springs Sales & Graphix
2571 20 Mile Rd Ne (49319-9615)
PHONE...................................616 696-2111
Mark Vanlangen, *Partner*
Gregg Vanlangen, *Partner*
Darlene Vanlangen, *Sales Staff*
Denise Vanlangen, *Office Mgr*
EMP: 6 **EST:** 2007
SQ FT: 4,000
SALES (est): 750K **Privately Held**
WEB: www.cedarcycleinc.com
SIC: 2396 2759 Fabric printing & stamping; printing & embossing on plastics fabric articles; letterpress & screen printing

(G-2646)
COMMERCIAL COATING SYSTEMS LLC
11760 Forestwood Dr Ne (49319-7953)
PHONE...................................616 490-6242
Blain Dayton, *Principal*
EMP: 6 **EST:** 2017
SALES (est): 122.9K **Privately Held**
WEB: www.commbldmaint.com
SIC: 3479 Coating of metals & formed products

(G-2647)
CS MANUFACTURING INC
299 W Cherry St (49319-8678)
P.O. Box K230 (49319-0930)
PHONE...................................616 696-2772
Tim Mabie, *President*
Brendan Fitzgerald, *Vice Pres*
Wil McClurken, *Vice Pres*
Christine Cramer, *Buyer*
Jason Ballard, *Project Engr*
◆ **EMP:** 350 **EST:** 1986
SQ FT: 82,000
SALES (est): 37.7MM **Privately Held**
WEB: www.csmanufacturing.us
SIC: 3089 Injection molding of plastics

(G-2648)
CS TOOL ENGINEERING INC
251 W Cherry St (49319-8678)
P.O. Box K210 (49319-0910)
PHONE...................................616 696-0940
Don Mabie, *President*
Thomas Mabie, *Principal*
Raymond Sova, *Project Mgr*
Jim Steenwyk, *Purch Agent*
James Steenwyk, *Project Engr*
EMP: 50 **EST:** 1967
SQ FT: 43,000
SALES (est): 5.5MM **Privately Held**
WEB: www.cste.com
SIC: 3544 Special dies & tools

(G-2649)
DISPLAY PACK INC (PA)
650 West St (49319-9699)
PHONE...................................616 451-3061
Victor Hansen, *President*
Jim Woodcock, *President*
Jon Hansen, *Vice Pres*
Jonathan Hansen, *Vice Pres*
Shannon Moorman, *Production*
EMP: 250
SQ FT: 375,000
SALES (est): 84MM **Privately Held**
WEB: www.displaypack.com
SIC: 3089 2759 7389 Plastic processing; commercial printing; packaging & labeling services

(G-2650)
DISPLAY PACK DISC VDH INC
650 West St (49319-9699)
PHONE...................................616 451-3061
EMP: 9 **EST:** 2015
SALES (est): 134.7K **Privately Held**
WEB: www.displaypack.com
SIC: 2631 Packaging board

(G-2651)
FLAUNT IT SPORTSWEAR
34 N Main Ste B (49319-5102)
P.O. Box 294 (49319-0294)
PHONE...................................616 696-9084
Karen Sudhoss, *Partner*
EMP: 8 **EST:** 1995
SALES (est): 539.5K **Privately Held**
WEB: www.flauntitsportswear.com
SIC: 2396 Screen printing on fabric articles

(G-2652)
GREAT LAKES RIGHT OF WAY LLC
1177 17 Mile Rd Ne (49319-7817)
PHONE...................................616 263-9898
Jolene Atwood, *CEO*
EMP: 9 **EST:** 2000
SALES (est): 842.7K **Privately Held**
SIC: 1629 1623 1611 2273 Heavy construction; pipeline construction; gravel or dirt road construction; mats & matting;

(G-2653)
HEAVENLY VINYARDS LLC
14155 Olin Lakes Dr (49319-9433)
PHONE...................................616 710-2751
EMP: 4 **EST:** 2014
SALES (est): 140.9K **Privately Held**
WEB: www.heavenlyvineyards.weebly.com
SIC: 2084 Wines

(G-2654)
LEANNE SOWA
10855 Sandy Oak Trl (49319-9260)
PHONE...................................616 225-8858
Richard J Sowa, *Principal*
EMP: 4 **EST:** 2010
SALES (est): 47.5K **Privately Held**
WEB: www.leanne-sowa.pixels.com
SIC: 3999 Framed artwork

(G-2655)
LIPSTICK JODI LLC
13638 Starflower Ln (49319-9139)
PHONE...................................616 430-5389
Karlena Morehouse, *Principal*
EMP: 4 **EST:** 2017
SALES (est): 67.6K **Privately Held**
WEB: www.lipstickjodi.bandcamp.com
SIC: 2844 Lipsticks

(G-2656)
LITE BRIGHT WELDING
5993 16 Mile Rd Ne (49319-8537)
PHONE...................................269 208-5698
Brett Gardell, *Principal*
EMP: 4 **EST:** 2018
SALES (est): 33.6K **Privately Held**
SIC: 7692 Welding repair

(G-2657)
MICHIGAN PROTEIN INC
15030 Stout Ave Ne (49319-9727)
PHONE...................................877 869-0630
Joseph Castine, *President*
Joe Castine, *Senior VP*
EMP: 14 **EST:** 2002
SALES (est): 2.2MM **Privately Held**
WEB: www.michiganprotein.com
SIC: 2077 Grease rendering, inedible

(G-2658)
PRACTICAL PAPER INC
Also Called: Print Metro
98 E Division St Sparta (49319)
P.O. Box 125, Sparta (49345-0125)
PHONE...................................616 887-1723
Thomas Owen, *President*
EMP: 10 **EST:** 1992
SQ FT: 14,000
SALES (est): 1.5MM **Privately Held**
SIC: 5113 2732 Paper & products, wrapping or coarse; book printing

(G-2659)
PRECISION JIG & FIXTURE INC
4030 Cedar Coml Dr Ne (49319)
PHONE...................................616 696-2595
Tom Oshinski, *Plant Mgr*
Dan Ketelaar, *Engineer*
Todd Nauta, *Program Mgr*
Sean Richards, *Manager*
David Schuiling, *Administration*
EMP: 45 **Privately Held**
WEB: www.pjfinc.com
SIC: 3544 Jigs: inspection, gauging & checking
PA: Peterson Jig & Fixture, Inc.
301 Rockford Park Dr Ne
Rockford MI 49341

(G-2660)
QUALITY GUEST PUBLISHING INC
Also Called: Heaven Is My Home
12920 Algoma Ave Ne (49319-9428)
P.O. Box 333, Rockford (49341-0333)
PHONE...................................616 894-1111
Gary Meyers, *Owner*
EMP: 10 **EST:** 2000
SALES (est): 250K **Privately Held**
SIC: 2741 Miscellaneous publishing

(G-2661)
SLY FOX PRINTS LLC (PA)
Also Called: Cornhole America
1321 17 Mile Rd Ne (49319-9692)
PHONE...................................616 900-9677
Jason Duflo, *Mng Member*
EMP: 4 **EST:** 2018
SALES (est): 619.6K **Privately Held**
WEB: www.cornholeamerica.com
SIC: 3944 7389 Board games, children's & adults'; fund raising organizations

(G-2662)
STEEL 21 LLC
11786 White Creek Ave Ne (49319-9417)
PHONE...................................616 884-2121
Andy Couturier, *Engineer*
Kimm E Slater, *Mng Member*
Lee Ringelberg, *Prgrmr*
EMP: 26 **EST:** 2014
SQ FT: 30,000
SALES (est): 4.8MM **Privately Held**
WEB: www.steel21.com
SIC: 3312 Plate, steel

(G-2663)
STEELTECH LTD
Also Called: Cedar Springs Castings
69 Maple (49319-8396)
PHONE...................................616 696-1130
Pell Jody, *Natl Sales Mgr*
Jordan Jensen, *Sales Staff*
EMP: 4
SALES (corp-wide): 12.5MM **Privately Held**
WEB: www.steeltechltd.com
SIC: 3325 3321 Alloy steel castings, except investment; gray & ductile iron foundries
PA: Steeltech, Ltd.
1251 Phillips Ave Sw
Grand Rapids MI 49507
616 243-7920

(G-2664)
TARGET CONSTRUCTION INC
3850 Russell St (49319-9422)
PHONE...................................616 866-7728
Kenneth Newman, *President*
Bridget Bigler, *Manager*
EMP: 35 **EST:** 1982
SALES (est): 2.7MM **Privately Held**
SIC: 3444 Sheet metalwork

(G-2665)
TEMPER INC
12333 Luyk Dr Ne (49319-8258)
P.O. Box 755, Rockford (49341-0755)
PHONE...................................616 293-1349
William Dykstra, *President*
EMP: 11 **EST:** 2001
SQ FT: 12,000
SALES (est): 2.2MM **Privately Held**
WEB: www.temperinc.com
SIC: 3721 Research & development on aircraft by the manufacturer

(G-2666)
WEFA CEDAR INC
104 W Beech St (49319-8679)
P.O. Box K209 (49319-0909)
PHONE...................................616 696-0873
Jon Veenstra, *President*
Vratislav Kern, *Managing Dir*
Ralf Huber, *Engineer*
Jaroslava Moravcova, *Sales Staff*
Udo Bene, *Manager*
EMP: 13 **EST:** 2009
SQ FT: 40,000
SALES (est): 3.3MM
SALES (corp-wide): 8.8MM **Privately Held**
WEB: www.wefa.com
SIC: 3544 Extrusion dies
PA: Wefa Singen Gmbh
Rudolf-Diesel-Str. 11
Singen (Hohentwiel) BW 78224
773 183-900

(G-2667)
WHEATONS WOODWORKING LLC
1010 Solon (49319-8475)
PHONE...................................616 288-8159
Nicholas Wheaton, *Principal*
EMP: 4 **EST:** 2019

Cedarville
Mackinac County

(G-2668)
CARMEUSE LIME INC
5093 E M 134 (49719-9511)
PHONE..................906 484-2201
Kursten G Walton, *Purchasing*
Todd Nyberg, *Branch Mgr*
EMP: 123
SALES (corp-wide): 177.9K **Privately Held**
SIC: 1422 Crushed & broken limestone
HQ: Carmeuse Lime, Inc.
11 Stanwix St Fl 21
Pittsburgh PA 15222
412 995-5500

(G-2669)
FLOATATION DOCKING INC (PA)
Also Called: CEDARVILLE MARINE
160 Hodeck St (49719)
P.O. Box 178 (49719-0178)
PHONE..................906 484-3422
Cody Carmichael, *Owner*
Teresa Carmichael, *Office Mgr*
Jeff Cason, *Manager*
EMP: 33 **EST:** 1974
SQ FT: 25,000
SALES: 5.5MM **Privately Held**
WEB: www.flotationdocking.com
SIC: 3731 5599 4493 Drydocks, floating; snowmobiles; marinas

(G-2670)
LES CHENEAUX DISTILLERS INC
172 S Meridian St (49719-5125)
P.O. Box 126 (49719-0126)
PHONE..................906 748-0505
Jason D Bowlby, *Mng Member*
EMP: 40 **EST:** 2017
SALES (est): 3.1MM **Privately Held**
WEB: www.lescheneaux.net
SIC: 2085 Distilled & blended liquors

(G-2671)
O N MINERALS
5093 E M 134 (49719-9511)
PHONE..................906 484-2201
Michael Lundin, *Principal*
EMP: 7 **EST:** 2008
SALES (est): 328.4K **Privately Held**
SIC: 1422 Crushed & broken limestone

(G-2672)
O-N MINERALS MICHIGAN COMPANY
Also Called: Aggregate
5093 E M 134 (49719-9511)
PHONE..................906 484-2201
Raymond Leclair, *Manager*
EMP: 125
SALES (corp-wide): 33.1MM **Privately Held**
SIC: 1422 Limestones, ground
PA: O-N Minerals (Michigan) Company
1035 Calcite Rd
Rogers City MI 49779
989 734-2131

(G-2673)
O-N MINERALS MICHIGAN COMPANY
Also Called: Carmeuse Lime & Stone
5093 E M 134 (49719-9511)
PHONE..................906 484-2201
EMP: 152
SALES (corp-wide): 177.9K **Privately Held**
SIC: 1422 Crushed & broken limestone
HQ: O-N Minerals (Michigan) Company
11 Stanwix St Fl 21
Pittsburgh PA 15222
412 995-5500

(G-2674)
TASSIER BOAT WORKS INC
1011 S Islington Rd (49719-9744)
PHONE..................906 484-2573
James Hart, *President*
Alice Smith, *Principal*
Martha Hart, *Corp Secy*
Dan Smith, *Vice Pres*
EMP: 7 **EST:** 1940
SQ FT: 1,200
SALES (est): 387.1K **Privately Held**
WEB: www.tassierboatworks.com
SIC: 7699 5551 3732 Boat repair; marine supplies & equipment; boat building & repairing

Cement City
Lenawee County

(G-2675)
ABRASIVE SOLUTIONS LLC
12875 Mack Ave (49233-9791)
PHONE..................517 592-2668
Nathan Baumann,
EMP: 5 **EST:** 2011
SQ FT: 3,800 **Privately Held**
WEB: www.abrasivesolutionsmi.com
SIC: 1721 3471 Commercial painting; sand blasting of metal parts

(G-2676)
ROSS DESIGN & ENGINEERING INC (PA)
14445 E Chicago Rd (49233-9677)
PHONE..................517 547-6033
Jack Plate, *President*
EMP: 20 **EST:** 1989
SQ FT: 31,000
SALES (est): 9.7MM **Privately Held**
WEB: www.rossdesign.net
SIC: 3544 8711 Special dies & tools; engineering services

Center Line
Macomb County

(G-2677)
AIRSERVE LLC
26770 Liberal (48015-1237)
P.O. Box 510, Warren (48090-0510)
PHONE..................586 427-5349
Ken Fasse, *President*
Nick Smith, *Opers Mgr*
EMP: 4 **EST:** 2002
SQ FT: 2,000
SALES (est): 628.1K **Privately Held**
SIC: 2813 Oxygen, compressed or liquefied

(G-2678)
ALL-COTE COATINGS COMPANY LLC
23896 Sherwood (48015-2011)
PHONE..................586 427-0062
George Shrock,
EMP: 6 **EST:** 1993
SALES (est): 892.5K **Privately Held**
WEB: www.allcote.com
SIC: 3479 Coating of metals & formed products

(G-2679)
AMERICAN DUMPSTER SERVICES LLC
6490 E 10 Mile Rd (48015-1144)
PHONE..................586 501-3600
Gary Smith,
EMP: 8 **EST:** 2016
SALES (est): 592.4K **Privately Held**
SIC: 3443 Dumpsters, garbage

(G-2680)
BINSON-BECKER INC
Also Called: Binsons Orthtic Prsthtics Svcs
26834 Lawrence (48015-1262)
PHONE..................888 246-7667
James Binson, *President*
Craig Boyles, *President*
Loretta Miller, *Admin Sec*
EMP: 10 **EST:** 1987
SQ FT: 5,000
SALES (est): 820K **Privately Held**
WEB: www.binsons.com
SIC: 5999 3842 Orthopedic & prosthesis applications; prosthetic appliances

(G-2681)
DONATO WOODWORKS
7287 Henry (48015-1014)
PHONE..................586 899-7430
Donato Mongelli, *Principal*
EMP: 4 **EST:** 2008
SALES (est): 116.6K **Privately Held**
SIC: 2431 Millwork

(G-2682)
LASER PRODUCT DEVELOPMENT LLC
24340 Sherwood (48015-1061)
PHONE..................800 765-4424
EMP: 4 **EST:** 2006
SALES (est): 310K **Privately Held**
SIC: 3699 Mfg Electrical Equipment/Supplies

(G-2683)
N A SODECIA INC
Also Called: Sodecia Group
24331 Sherwood (48015-1060)
PHONE..................586 879-8969
Rui Montero, *CEO*
Gary Easterly, *Vice Pres*
Hugo Rios, *Vice Pres*
George Alexopoulos, *Project Mgr*
Brian Wawrzynski, *CFO*
▲ **EMP:** 300 **EST:** 2010
SALES (est): 65.8MM
SALES (corp-wide): 225.3K **Privately Held**
WEB: www.sodecia.com
SIC: 3465 Body parts, automobile: stamped metal
HQ: Sodecia Automotive Detroit Corp.
24331 Sherwood
Center Line MI 48015
586 759-2200

(G-2684)
PALLET PROS LLC
8233 Sterling (48015-1715)
PHONE..................586 864-3353
Phillip Eddins, *Principal*
EMP: 4 **EST:** 2012
SALES (est): 232.4K **Privately Held**
WEB: www.palletpros.com
SIC: 2448 Pallets, wood

(G-2685)
PRIMA TECHNOLOGIES INC
24837 Sherwood (48015-1058)
PHONE..................586 759-0250
Arturo Desantes Jr, *President*
Richard Vansteenkiste, *General Mgr*
Richard Van Steenkiste, *Corp Secy*
EMP: 15 **EST:** 1996
SQ FT: 15,000
SALES (est): 1MM **Privately Held**
WEB: www.prima-tec.com
SIC: 3544 Dies, plastics forming

(G-2686)
SODECIA AUTO DETROIT CORP (DH)
Also Called: Sodecia USA
24331 Sherwood (48015-1060)
PHONE..................586 759-2200
Rui Montero, *CEO*
Don Bilyea, *Vice Pres*
Aloisio Monteiro, *Purchasing*
Kerry Fitzgerald, *Engineer*
Andrew Toth, *Engineer*
▲ **EMP:** 200 **EST:** 2002
SALES (est): 307.4MM
SALES (corp-wide): 225.3K **Privately Held**
WEB: www.sodecia.com
SIC: 3465 Body parts, automobile: stamped metal
HQ: Sodecia - ParticipaCOes Sociais, Sgps, S.A.
Rua Do Espido, 164f
Maia 4470-
220 101-920

(G-2687)
SOPHIAS TEXTILES & FURN INC
24170 Sherwood (48015-2027)
PHONE..................586 759-6231
Sofia Yousif, *Principal*
▲ **EMP:** 17 **EST:** 2010
SALES (est): 1.1MM **Privately Held**
WEB: www.sophiastextilesandfurnishings.com
SIC: 2591 Blinds vertical; venetian blinds; window shades

(G-2688)
TRIANON INDUSTRIES CORPORATION
24331 Sherwood (48015-1060)
P.O. Box 3067 (48015-0067)
PHONE..................586 759-2200
Francis Barge, *President*
Jean-Claude Garolla, *CFO*
EMP: 25 **EST:** 1986
SALES (est): 415.5K **Privately Held**
SIC: 3465 3544 Automotive stampings; special dies & tools

(G-2689)
WHITLAM GROUP INC (PA)
24800 Sherwood (48015-1059)
PHONE..................586 757-5100
Richard Shaieb, *President*
Debbie Price, *Vice Pres*
James Shaieb, *Vice Pres*
John Paul Shaieb, *Vice Pres*
Chris Denison, *Production*
EMP: 102 **EST:** 1969
SQ FT: 125,000
SALES: 26.7MM **Privately Held**
WEB: www.whitlam.com
SIC: 2759 Flexographic printing

(G-2690)
WICO METAL PRODUCTS COMPANY
24400 Sherwood (48015-2023)
PHONE..................586 755-9600
Brodie Richard, *Branch Mgr*
EMP: 13
SALES (corp-wide): 43.3MM **Privately Held**
WEB: www.wicometal.com
SIC: 3544 Special dies & tools
PA: Wico Metal Products Company Inc
23500 Sherwood Ave
Warren MI 48091
586 755-9600

Central Lake
Antrim County

(G-2691)
CENTRAL LAKE ARMOR EXPRESS INC
7915 Cameron St (49622-9458)
P.O. Box 516 (49622-0516)
PHONE..................231 544-6090
Matthew Davis, *President*
Glenn Katz, *President*
Frank Cappo, *Vice Pres*
Rick Dressler, *Vice Pres*
Jonathan Macneil, *Research*
◆ **EMP:** 105 **EST:** 2005
SQ FT: 15,000
SALES (est): 44.4MM
SALES (corp-wide): 7.4MM **Privately Held**
WEB: www.armorexpress.com
SIC: 3312 3842 Armor plate; bulletproof vests
PA: Praesidium Spa
Via Della Giustizia 10/A
Milano MI 20125
023 030-971

(G-2692)
CREATIVE CHARACTERS INC
7924 Cameron St (49622-9458)
P.O. Box 699 (49622-0699)
PHONE..................231 544-6084
Jack Bodis, *President*
EMP: 5 **EST:** 1989
SQ FT: 3,000
SALES (est): 348.8K **Privately Held**
SIC: 2752 2731 Commercial printing, offset; books; publishing & printing

GEOGRAPHIC SECTION

Charlevoix - Charlevoix County (G-2718)

(G-2693)
DEFOREST & BLOOM SEPTIC TANKS
7994 Houghton Rd (49622-9558)
PHONE..................................231 544-3599
Victor Bloom, *Owner*
EMP: 4 **EST:** 1945 **Privately Held**
SIC: 3272 1711 Septic tanks, concrete; septic system construction

(G-2694)
ECHO QUALITY GRINDING INC
3166 Muckle Rd (49622-9526)
PHONE..................................231 544-6637
James Kowal, *President*
EMP: 16 **EST:** 1978
SQ FT: 14,200
SALES (est): 1.7MM **Privately Held**
WEB: www.echoqualitygrinding.com
SIC: 3599 3469 Grinding castings for the trade; machine parts, stamped or pressed metal

(G-2695)
MAMMOTH DISTILLING LLC
1554 N East Torch Lake Dr (49622-9631)
P.O. Box 459 (49622-0459)
PHONE..................................773 841-4242
Chad Munger, *Mng Member*
EMP: 5 **EST:** 2015
SALES (est): 270.3K **Privately Held**
WEB: www.mammothdistilling.com
SIC: 2085 Applejack (alcoholic beverage)

Centreville
St. Joseph County

(G-2696)
BIRKHOLD PATTERN COMPANY INC
22921 S River Rd (49032-9757)
PHONE..................................269 467-8705
EMP: 7 **EST:** 1936
SQ FT: 15,000
SALES (est): 62.5K **Privately Held**
SIC: 3365 Aluminum Foundry

(G-2697)
HOCHSTETLER SAWMILL
24700 Walters Rd (49032-9760)
PHONE..................................269 467-7018
Vernon Hochstetler, *Principal*
EMP: 7 **EST:** 2011
SALES (est): 238.6K **Privately Held**
WEB: www.centreville-mi.michigan-bd.com
SIC: 2421 Sawmills & planing mills, general

(G-2698)
SUPERIOR RECEIPT BOOK CO INC
215 S Clark St (49032-5133)
P.O. Box 326 (49032-0326)
PHONE..................................269 467-8265
Cheryl Gilbert, *President*
Barbara J Taggart, *Vice Pres*
Barbara Taggart, *Vice Pres*
EMP: 13 **EST:** 1946
SQ FT: 2,400
SALES (est): 1MM **Privately Held**
WEB: www.receipts.com
SIC: 2782 Receipt books

(G-2699)
VAN EMON BRUCE
Also Called: A A A Machine
501 S Clark St (49032)
P.O. Box 19 (49032-0019)
PHONE..................................269 467-7803
Bruce Van Emon, *Owner*
Carl Ishito, *General Mgr*
EMP: 4 **EST:** 1990
SQ FT: 1,200
SALES (est): 252.8K **Privately Held**
SIC: 3545 3544 3316 Machine tool attachments & accessories; special dies, tools, jigs & fixtures; cold finishing of steel shapes

(G-2700)
WALDRONS ANTIQUE EXHAUST
Also Called: Waldron's Exhaust
208 W Main St (49032-9534)
P.O. Box 99 (49032-0099)
PHONE..................................269 467-7185
Joseph Tonetto, *President*
Ruth Frisbie, *Administration*
EMP: 5 **EST:** 1963
SQ FT: 2,400
SALES (est): 465.7K **Privately Held**
WEB: www.waldronexhaust.com
SIC: 3714 Motor vehicle parts & accessories

(G-2701)
WAYNE ALLEN LAMBERT
Also Called: Lambert Industries
231 N Clark St (49032-9590)
PHONE..................................269 467-4624
Wayne Lambert, *Owner*
EMP: 5 **EST:** 1999
SALES (est): 329.6K **Privately Held**
WEB: www.lambertmfg.com
SIC: 3544 Special dies, tools, jigs & fixtures

Ceresco
Calhoun County

(G-2702)
BEAR CREEK LOGGING
123 Court St (49033-9659)
PHONE..................................269 317-7475
Gary L Bauer, *Principal*
EMP: 6 **EST:** 2008
SALES (est): 261.7K **Privately Held**
SIC: 2411 Logging

(G-2703)
D&D DEFENSE LLC
10827 B Dr N (49033-9634)
PHONE..................................248 255-8765
Danielle Epps, *Principal*
EMP: 4 **EST:** 2014
SALES (est): 61.5K **Privately Held**
SIC: 3812 Defense systems & equipment

Champion
Marquette County

(G-2704)
EAGLE MINE LLC
4547 County Road 601 (49814-9475)
PHONE..................................906 339-7000
Brooke Routhier, *Project Engr*
Ben Rose, *CFO*
Paul Rhodea, *Manager*
Bob Mahin, *Exploration*
Paul Wisuri, *Technician*
EMP: 300
SALES (est): 57.6MM
SALES (corp-wide): 1.8B **Privately Held**
WEB: www.eaglemine.com
SIC: 1021 Copper ore milling & preparation
PA: Lundin Mining Corporation
150 King St W Suite 2200
Toronto ON M5H 1
416 342-5560

Channing
Dickinson County

(G-2705)
ADAMS HOLSTERS
W8941 Newberg Rd (49815-9748)
PHONE..................................906 662-4212
EMP: 7 **EST:** 2016
SALES (est): 49.1K **Privately Held**
SIC: 3199 Holsters, leather

(G-2706)
J CAREY LOGGING INC
Sawyer Lake Rd (49815)
PHONE..................................906 542-3420
James R Carey, *President*
EMP: 12 **EST:** 1980
SQ FT: 5,000
SALES (est): 2.3MM **Privately Held**
WEB: www.call-carey.com
SIC: 2411 Logging camps & contractors

Charlevoix
Charlevoix County

(G-2707)
ACAT GLOBAL LLC (PA)
5339 M 66 N (49720-9511)
PHONE..................................231 330-2553
Joseph Moch, *CEO*
Darrell Blackburn, *Vice Pres*
Benjamin Dimock, *Engineer*
Jim Lentz, *Controller*
Dennis Kraber, *Sales Staff*
EMP: 7 **EST:** 2011
SALES (est): 2.3MM **Privately Held**
WEB: www.acatglobal.com
SIC: 3714 Exhaust systems & parts, motor vehicle

(G-2708)
ALP LGHTING CMPNNTS CHARLEVOIX
10163 Us Highway 31 N (49720-9649)
PHONE..................................231 547-6584
EMP: 10 **EST:** 2019
SALES (est): 1.6MM **Privately Held**
WEB: www.alpadvantage.com
SIC: 3089 Injection molding of plastics

(G-2709)
ALP LIGHTING CEILING PDTS INC
Also Called: Lexalite
10163 Us Highway 31 N (49720-9649)
PHONE..................................231 547-6584
Tom Barnes, *Vice Pres*
Lana Garvelink, *Human Res Mgr*
EMP: 5
SALES (corp-wide): 120.3MM **Privately Held**
WEB: www.alpadvantage.com
SIC: 3089 Injection molding of plastics; extruded finished plastic products
PA: Alp Lighting & Ceiling Products, Inc.
6333 W Gross Point Rd
Niles IL 60714
773 774-9550

(G-2710)
BALDWIN PRECISION INC
Also Called: Oliver Racing Parts
5339 M 66 N (49720-9511)
PHONE..................................231 237-4515
Bruce B Baldwin, *President*
Ken Ondercin, *Vice Pres*
David Reynier, *Manager*
EMP: 49 **EST:** 1975
SQ FT: 102,000
SALES (est): 3MM **Privately Held**
WEB: www.oliverracingparts.com
SIC: 3714 Connecting rods, motor vehicle engine

(G-2711)
BDK GROUP NORTHERN MICH INC
Also Called: Hodgkiss & Douma
6795 Us Highway 31 N (49720-9416)
PHONE..................................574 875-5183
Thomas R Irwin, *President*
EMP: 15 **EST:** 1938
SQ FT: 8,000
SALES (est): 725K **Privately Held**
SIC: 1611 1442 1794 1623 General contractor, highway & street construction; highway & street paving contractor; construction sand mining; gravel mining; excavation & grading, building construction; sewer line construction; water main construction; concrete work; curb construction; blacktop (asphalt) work; asphalt paving mixtures & blocks

(G-2712)
CEMEX CEMENT INC
1600 Bells Bay Rd (49720)
P.O. Box 367 (49720-0367)
PHONE..................................231 547-9971
John Laney, *Manager*
EMP: 214 **Privately Held**
WEB: www.cemexusa.com
SIC: 3273 Ready-mixed concrete
HQ: Cemex Cement, Inc.
10100 Katy Fwy Ste 300
Houston TX 77043
713 650-6200

(G-2713)
CHARLEVOIX SCREEN MASTERS INC
12512 Taylor Rd (49720-1022)
PHONE..................................231 547-5111
Roger Nesburg, *President*
Annette Nesburg, *Treasurer*
Angela Behling, *Admin Sec*
EMP: 7 **EST:** 1984
SQ FT: 7,000
SALES (est): 904.6K **Privately Held**
WEB: www.screenmaster.net
SIC: 2261 2395 Screen printing of cotton broadwoven fabrics; embroidery products, except schiffli machine

(G-2714)
DCL INC (PA)
Also Called: Dust Control & Loading Systems
8660 Ance Rd (49720-2055)
P.O. Box 125 (49720-0125)
PHONE..................................231 547-5600
Tim English, *President*
Reinhard Matye, *President*
Werner Egger, *Vice Pres*
Kurt Danforth, *Electrical Engi*
▼ **EMP:** 129 **EST:** 1981
SQ FT: 45,000
SALES (est): 20.8MM **Privately Held**
WEB: www.dclinc.com
SIC: 3535 5084 3564 3494 Conveyors & conveying equipment; industrial machinery & equipment; blowers & fans; valves & pipe fittings

(G-2715)
GERBERS HOME MADE SWEETS
8218 Pincherry Rd (49720-9413)
PHONE..................................231 348-3743
Jerry J Gerber, *Owner*
EMP: 4 **EST:** 2003
SALES (est): 171.7K **Privately Held**
SIC: 2064 Candy & other confectionery products

(G-2716)
GIC LLC
Also Called: Gic Thermo Dynamics
12575 Us Highway 31 N (49720-1101)
PHONE..................................231 237-7000
Thomas Ray, *President*
Linda Clements, *General Mgr*
EMP: 12 **EST:** 2011
SALES (est): 1MM **Privately Held**
WEB: www.gicservicesllc.com
SIC: 3823 3829 Industrial instrmnts msrmnt display/control process variable; measuring & controlling devices

(G-2717)
HARBOR INDUSTRIES INC
100 Harbor View Ln (49720-1294)
P.O. Box 228 (49720-0228)
PHONE..................................231 547-3280
Walter Miranda, *Exec VP*
Greg Gavin, *Project Mgr*
Heather Henson, *Mfg Staff*
Al Corp, *QC Dir*
Raul Romeiro, *Engineer*
EMP: 96
SQ FT: 65,000
SALES (corp-wide): 55.6MM **Privately Held**
WEB: www.harborretail.com
SIC: 3993 2542 2541 Displays & cutouts, window & lobby; partitions & fixtures, except wood; wood partitions & fixtures
PA: Harbor Industries, Inc.
14130 172nd Ave
Grand Haven MI 49417
616 842-5330

(G-2718)
HARBOR INDUSTRIES INC
107 Airport Dr (49720-8904)
PHONE..................................616 842-5330
EMP: 96

SALES (corp-wide): 55.6MM **Privately Held**
WEB: www.harborretail.com
SIC: 2541 Display fixtures, wood
PA: Harbor Industries, Inc.
 14130 172nd Ave
 Grand Haven MI 49417
 616 842-5330

(G-2719)
IRISH BOAT SHOP INC
13000 Stover Rd (49720-9500)
PHONE...................................231 547-9967
Michael Esposito, *President*
John Hodge, *Vice Pres*
Jack Hodge, *Branch Mgr*
Ashley Hagen, *Manager*
EMP: 25
SALES (corp-wide): 12.6MM **Privately Held**
WEB: www.irishboatshop.com
SIC: 4493 5551 5561 4226 Boat yards, storage & incidental repair; boat dealers; recreational vehicle dealers; special warehousing & storage; boat building & repairing
PA: Irish Boat Shop, Inc.
 400 E Bay St
 Harbor Springs MI 49740
 231 526-6225

(G-2720)
MDC CONTRACTING LLC
5481 Us Highway 31 S (49720-8919)
PHONE...................................231 547-6595
Mark Manthei, *President*
Jacob Manthei, *Owner*
Abe Manthei, *Sales Executive*
Chris Pease, *Director*
Elissa Shafer, *Administration*
EMP: 1 EST: 2002
SALES (est): 4.8MM **Privately Held**
WEB: www.mantheiconstruction.com
SIC: 2951 Asphalt paving mixtures & blocks

(G-2721)
MICHIGAN SCIENTIFIC CORP
8500 Ance Rd (49720-2033)
PHONE...................................231 547-5511
Robert Popovczak, *Engineer*
John Suomi, *Engineer*
Randal Schnackenberg, *Sales Mgr*
Wanda Cogar, *Office Mgr*
Mike Castiglione, *Manager*
EMP: 65
SQ FT: 15,000
SALES (corp-wide): 16.7MM **Privately Held**
WEB: www.michsci.com
SIC: 3829 8734 3825 3469 Testing equipment: abrasion, shearing strength, etc.; testing laboratories; instruments to measure electricity; metal stampings
PA: Michigan Scientific Corporation
 321 E Huron St
 Milford MI 48381
 248 685-3939

(G-2722)
NORTHERN MICHIGAN LEATHER
6779 Bay Shore West Dr (49720-9369)
PHONE...................................231 675-4712
Thomas Hovie, *Principal*
EMP: 5 EST: 2011
SALES (est): 69K **Privately Held**
SIC: 3069 Rubber automotive products

(G-2723)
NORTHWEST CANVAS
5195 Us Highway 31 S (49720-9792)
PHONE...................................231 676-1757
Ryan Oliver, *Principal*
EMP: 4 EST: 2014
SALES (est): 161.6K **Privately Held**
WEB: www.northwestmichigancanvas.com
SIC: 2211 Canvas

(G-2724)
NU-CORE INC
8833 Gibbons Dr (49720-2056)
PHONE...................................231 547-2600
Bob Grove, *President*
Jesse Grove, *Engineer*
▲ EMP: 8 EST: 1998
SALES (est): 1.4MM **Privately Held**
WEB: www.nu-core.com
SIC: 3599 Machine shop, jobbing & repair

(G-2725)
OMNI UNITED (USA) INC (HQ)
9900 Two Lakes Trl (49720-2107)
PHONE...................................855 906-6646
Gajendra Sareen, *CEO*
Scott Rhodes, *Vice Pres*
Phillip D Caris, *Exec Dir*
Sagra Maceira De Rosen,
EMP: 9 EST: 2012
SQ FT: 55,000
SALES (est): 3.7MM **Privately Held**
WEB: www.omni-united.com
SIC: 3011 Tires & inner tubes

(G-2726)
OPTIC EDGE CORPORATION
6279 Us Highway 31 S (49720-8916)
P.O. Box 503 (49720-0503)
PHONE...................................231 547-6090
Dan Yenglin, *President*
EMP: 5 EST: 2003
SQ FT: 5,000
SALES (est): 500K **Privately Held**
WEB: www.mktec.com
SIC: 3641 Electric lamps & parts for generalized applications
PA: Market Technologies, Inc.
 6279 Us Highway 31 S
 Charlevoix MI 49720

(G-2727)
PARSONS CENTENNIAL FARM LLC
Also Called: Harwood Hritg Gold Maple Syrup
61 Parsons Rd (49720-8910)
PHONE...................................231 547-2038
David W Parsons, *Principal*
EMP: 6 EST: 2009
SALES (est): 210.3K **Privately Held**
WEB: www.harwoodgold.com
SIC: 2099 0831 Maple syrup; maple sap gathering

(G-2728)
PINE RIVER INC
5339 M 66 N (49720-9511)
PHONE...................................231 758-3400
Michael Way, *President*
EMP: 16 EST: 2006
SQ FT: 35,000
SALES (est): 530.6K **Privately Held**
WEB: www.pineriverrustics.com
SIC: 2952 Siding materials

(G-2729)
PRECISION PALLET LLC
17195 Beck Rd (49720-9736)
PHONE...................................252 943-5193
EMP: 4 EST: 2015
SALES (est): 109.3K **Privately Held**
WEB: www.palletnc.com
SIC: 2448 Pallets, wood & wood with metal

(G-2730)
RK WOJAN INC
6336 Us Highway 31 N (49720-9416)
P.O. Box 189 (49720-0189)
PHONE...................................231 347-1160
Robert Wojan, *President*
Keri Wojan, *Vice Pres*
EMP: 21 EST: 1965
SQ FT: 45,000
SALES (est): 336.7K **Privately Held**
WEB: www.wojan.com
SIC: 3535 3443 Bulk handling conveyor systems; fabricated plate work (boiler shop)

(G-2731)
RON PAIR ENTERPRISES INC
105 Stover Rd (49720-1756)
P.O. Box 438 (49720-0438)
PHONE...................................231 547-4000
Ronald Pair, *President*
EMP: 30 EST: 1965
SQ FT: 21,000
SALES (est): 1.3MM **Privately Held**
WEB: www.midwestmagic.com
SIC: 3564 Dust or fume collecting equipment, industrial

(G-2732)
RUF INTERNATIONAL MFG CORP
8020 Shrigley Rd (49720-9429)
PHONE...................................954 448-3454
Lia Arlt, *Principal*
EMP: 5 EST: 2016
SALES (est): 39.6K **Privately Held**
SIC: 3999 Manufacturing industries

(G-2733)
SPARE KEY WINERY LLC
6872 Upper Bay Shore Rd (49720-9412)
PHONE...................................231 250-7442
EMP: 4 EST: 2017
SALES (est): 88.7K **Privately Held**
WEB: www.sparekeywinery.com
SIC: 2084 Wines

(G-2734)
STEVEN CRANDELL
10436 Burnett Rd (49720-9183)
PHONE...................................231 582-7445
Steven Crandell, *Principal*
EMP: 5 EST: 2005
SALES (est): 109.4K **Privately Held**
SIC: 2411 Logging

(G-2735)
STITCH N LYDS EMBROIDERY
13929 Phelps Rd (49720-9201)
PHONE...................................231 675-1916
EMP: 4 EST: 2014
SALES (est): 60.4K **Privately Held**
SIC: 2395 Embroidery & art needlework

(G-2736)
THAT FRENCH PLACE
212 Bridge St (49720-1404)
PHONE...................................231 437-6037
Brian Freund, *Owner*
EMP: 10 EST: 2015
SALES (est): 682.8K **Privately Held**
WEB: www.thatfrenchplace.com
SIC: 2024 Ice cream & frozen desserts

Charlotte
Eaton County

(G-2737)
C S MOBILE WELDING LLC
516 N Washington St (48813-1138)
PHONE...................................517 543-2339
Corey Sanders, *Principal*
EMP: 4 EST: 2015
SALES (est): 27.2K **Privately Held**
SIC: 7692 Welding repair

(G-2738)
CARMEL TOWNSHIP
661 Beech Hwy (48813-1048)
PHONE...................................888 805-6182
EMP: 6 EST: 2018
SALES (est): 257K **Privately Held**
SIC: 3625 Motor controls & accessories

(G-2739)
CASS POLYMERS (HQ)
Also Called: Ad-Tech Plastics Systems
815 W Shepherd St Ste 2 (48813-2037)
PHONE...................................517 543-7510
Richard Bullock, *CEO*
Doug Frans, *President*
B J Goodrich, *Manager*
EMP: 44 EST: 1981
SQ FT: 6,400
SALES (est): 9.5MM
SALES (corp-wide): 17.8MM **Privately Held**
WEB: www.milamar.com
SIC: 2821 3087 2891 2851 Epoxy resins; polyesters; custom compound purchased resins; adhesives & sealants; paints & allied products
PA: Cass Polymers, Inc.
 311 Nw 122nd St Ste 100
 Oklahoma City OK 73114
 405 755-8448

(G-2740)
CATI ARMOR LLC
435 Packard Hwy Ste C (48813-7748)
PHONE...................................269 788-4322
Brian Moore, *President*
EMP: 5 EST: 2013
SALES (est): 591.2K **Privately Held**
WEB: www.catiarmor.com
SIC: 3711 Cars, armored, assembly of

(G-2741)
CHARLOTTE ANODIZING PDTS INC
591 Packard Hwy (48813-9701)
PHONE...................................517 543-1911
Ronald Mc Diarmid, *President*
EMP: 65 EST: 1991
SQ FT: 20,000
SALES (est): 5.7MM **Privately Held**
WEB: www.charlotte-anodizing.com
SIC: 3471 Electroplating of metals or formed products

(G-2742)
CHARLOTTE CABINETS INC
629 W Seminary St (48813-1883)
P.O. Box 132 (48813-0132)
PHONE...................................517 543-1522
John S Little, *President*
EMP: 6 EST: 1984
SQ FT: 8,000
SALES (est): 887.9K **Privately Held**
WEB: www.charlottecabinets.biz
SIC: 2434 2511 5211 1751 Wood kitchen cabinets; wood household furniture; cabinets, kitchen; cabinet & finish carpentry

(G-2743)
CITIZENS LLC
421 N Cochran Ave (48813-1125)
P.O. Box F (48813-0523)
PHONE...................................517 541-1449
Sam Hudnutt, *Owner*
EMP: 8
SALES (corp-wide): 10.9MM **Privately Held**
WEB: www.citizenselevator.com
SIC: 5153 2041 Grains; flour & other grain mill products
PA: Citizens L.L.C.
 870 S Main St
 Vermontville MI 49096
 517 726-0514

(G-2744)
CNI PLASTICS LLC
Also Called: Futuris Automotive
400 Parkland Dr (48813-8799)
PHONE...................................517 541-4960
EMP: 50
SALES (est): 7.5MM **Privately Held**
SIC: 3089 Plastics Products, Nec, Nsk
HQ: Cni Enterprises, Inc.
 1451 E Lincoln Ave
 Madison Heights MI 48071
 248 586-3300

(G-2745)
COUNTRY MILL FARMS LLC
4648 Otto Rd (48813-9723)
PHONE...................................517 543-1019
Bernard Tennes,
Steve Tennes,
EMP: 7
SQ FT: 10,000
SALES (est): 1.1MM **Privately Held**
WEB: www.countrymillfarms.com
SIC: 0175 2051 2033 5947 Apple orchard; bread, cake & related products; canned fruits & specialties; gift, novelty & souvenir shop; eating places

(G-2746)
COUNTY JOURNAL INC
Also Called: Flashes Advertising & News
241 S Cochran Ave Ste 1 (48813-1584)
PHONE...................................517 543-1099
Cindy Gaedert, *Administration*
EMP: 16 EST: 2006
SALES (est): 2.8MM **Privately Held**
WEB: www.county-journal.com
SIC: 2711 Commercial printing & newspaper publishing combined; newspapers, publishing & printing

GEOGRAPHIC SECTION

Chase - Lake County (G-2775)

(G-2747)
CRANDELL BROS TRUCKING CO
800 Island Hwy (48813-9359)
P.O. Box 370 (48813-0370)
PHONE..................517 543-2930
Randolph A Crandell, *President*
Daniel Crandell, *Vice Pres*
EMP: 40 **EST:** 1955
SQ FT: 7,200
SALES (est): 6.1MM **Privately Held**
SIC: 4212 1442 Dump truck haulage; construction sand mining

(G-2748)
CUSTOM CABINETS & MORE
3476 Mcconnell Hwy (48813-8738)
PHONE..................517 285-7286
Ken Waterman, *Principal*
EMP: 5 **EST:** 2013
SALES (est): 65.5K **Privately Held**
WEB: www.custom-kitchen-cabinets.com
SIC: 2434 Wood kitchen cabinets

(G-2749)
DANJOS FOODS INC
594 Tirrell Rd (48813-2106)
PHONE..................517 543-2260
Daniel Walker, *Principal*
EMP: 5 **EST:** 2010
SALES (est): 88.9K **Privately Held**
SIC: 2099 Food preparations

(G-2750)
DORNBOS SIGN INC
619 W Harris St (48813-1466)
PHONE..................517 543-4000
Robert Dornbos, *President*
Jeff Dornbos, *Vice Pres*
Andrea Johnston, *Office Mgr*
Pete Lahr, *Supervisor*
EMP: 15 **EST:** 1954
SQ FT: 10,000
SALES (est): 1.1MM **Privately Held**
WEB: www.dornbossign.com
SIC: 3993 Signs & advertising specialties

(G-2751)
ENOVAPREMIER LLC
403 Parkland Dr (48813-7733)
PHONE..................517 541-3200
George Gunlock, *Engineer*
EMP: 4 **Privately Held**
WEB: www.enovapremier.com
SIC: 3089 3714 Automotive parts, plastic; motor vehicle parts & accessories
PA: Enovapremier Llc
   1630 Lyndon Farm Ct Ste 1
   Louisville KY 40223

(G-2752)
ERIC ROGERS LLC
1101 Lipsey Dr (48813-7741)
P.O. Box 190 (48813-0190)
PHONE..................517 543-7126
EMP: 8 **EST:** 2019
SALES (est): 610.6K **Privately Held**
WEB: www.ericrogersllc.com
SIC: 0782 2951 Landscape contractors; asphalt paving mixtures & blocks

(G-2753)
FAMILY TRDTONS TREE STANDS LLC
202 Morrell St (48813-1136)
PHONE..................517 543-3926
Jack Turner,
EMP: 9 **EST:** 2004
SALES (est): 1MM **Privately Held**
WEB: www.familytraditiontreestands.com
SIC: 3949 Hunting equipment

(G-2754)
FARMERS EGG COOPERATIVE
Also Called: Grazing Fields
1300 W Mount Hope Hwy (48813-8631)
PHONE..................517 649-8957
Jane Bush, *CEO*
Sam Catey, *Director*
EMP: 7 **EST:** 1997
SALES (est): 300K **Privately Held**
WEB: www.grazingfields.org
SIC: 0252 2015 Chicken eggs; egg processing

(G-2755)
FAULKNER TECH INC
239 S Cochran Ave (48813-1550)
PHONE..................517 857-4241
Matt Ayotte, *Manager*
EMP: 9 **EST:** 2018
SALES (est): 876.6K **Privately Held**
WEB: www.faulknertech.com
SIC: 3652 Pre-recorded records & tapes

(G-2756)
FREDS JERKY PRODUCTS
436 Pleasant St (48813-1939)
PHONE..................517 202-1908
EMP: 4 **EST:** 2019
SALES (est): 106.3K **Privately Held**
SIC: 2013 Snack sticks, including jerky: from purchased meat

(G-2757)
G-FORCE TOOLING LLC (PA)
1325 Island Hwy (48813-9358)
PHONE..................517 541-2747
Julie Cotter, *Principal*
Todd Cotter, *Engineer*
EMP: 27 **EST:** 2010
SALES (est): 602.5K **Privately Held**
WEB: www.g-forcetooling.com
SIC: 3721 Helicopters

(G-2758)
GALE BRIGGS INC (PA)
311 State St (48813-1735)
PHONE..................517 543-1320
Steve Briggs, *President*
Gale Lee Briggs, *President*
Betty Briggs, *Corp Secy*
EMP: 8 **EST:** 1930
SQ FT: 16,900
SALES (est): 1.2MM **Privately Held**
WEB: www.galebriggs.com
SIC: 3273 1442 Ready-mixed concrete; sand mining; gravel mining

(G-2759)
GO CAT FEATHER TOYS
605 W Lovett St (48813-1427)
PHONE..................517 543-7519
Harriet Morier, *President*
▲ **EMP:** 4 **EST:** 1983
SALES (est): 415.6K **Privately Held**
WEB: www.go-cat.com
SIC: 5999 5199 3069 Pet supplies; cats; toys, rubber

(G-2760)
K-TEL CORPORATION
Also Called: Universal Brick System
518 W Lovett St Ste 1 (48813-1774)
PHONE..................517 543-6174
EMP: 10
SQ FT: 2,000
SALES (est): 1.2MM **Privately Held**
SIC: 3271 5039 Mfg Concrete Block/Brick Whol Construction Materials Ret Lumber/Building Materials

(G-2761)
LYON HIDE LEATHER GOODS LLC
106 W Lovett St (48813-1406)
PHONE..................517 997-6067
Travis Lyon, *Principal*
EMP: 4 **EST:** 2015
SALES (est): 72.1K **Privately Held**
SIC: 3199 Leather goods

(G-2762)
MEREDITH LEA SAND GRAVEL
6703 Lansing Rd (48813-9328)
P.O. Box 332, Dimondale (48821-0332)
PHONE..................517 930-3662
Meredith Smith, *Principal*
EMP: 6 **EST:** 2015
SALES (est): 489.2K **Privately Held**
SIC: 3273 Ready-mixed concrete

(G-2763)
NORTHERN CONCRETE PIPE INC
5281 Lansing Rd (48813-9374)
PHONE..................517 645-2777
Luke Wahr, *Project Mgr*
Bill Washabaugh, *Production*
Gary Frie, *Purchasing*
Eric Katje, *Engineer*
John Balogh, *Sales Staff*
EMP: 8
SALES (corp-wide): 20.6MM **Privately Held**
WEB: www.ncp-inc.com
SIC: 3272 5032 Pipe, concrete or lined with concrete; sewer pipe, clay
PA: Northern Concrete Pipe, Inc.
   401 Kelton St
   Bay City MI 48706
   989 892-3545

(G-2764)
PHALANX PRESS
4832 W Kalamo Hwy (48813-9539)
PHONE..................517 213-9393
Wj Lundy, *Principal*
EMP: 4 **EST:** 2018
SALES (est): 72.7K **Privately Held**
SIC: 2741 Miscellaneous publishing

(G-2765)
PLAINVIEW INDUSTRIES LLC
416 N Washington St (48813-1172)
PHONE..................517 652-1466
Christopher Hall, *Principal*
EMP: 4 **EST:** 2015
SALES (est): 60.6K **Privately Held**
SIC: 3999 Manufacturing industries

(G-2766)
S P KISH INDUSTRIES INC
600 W Seminary St (48813-1876)
P.O. Box C (48813-0802)
PHONE..................517 543-2650
Robert Kish, *President*
Mike Desai, *Director*
▼ **EMP:** 22 **EST:** 1966
SQ FT: 100,000
SALES (est): 4.7MM **Privately Held**
WEB: www.kishindustries.com
SIC: 2851 Paints & allied products

(G-2767)
SHYFT GROUP INC
Also Called: Spartan Motors
1541 Reynolds Rd (48813-2040)
PHONE..................517 543-6400
EMP: 26
SALES (corp-wide): 146.2MM **Publicly Held**
WEB: www.spartanmotors.com
SIC: 3711 3714 7519 Chassis, motor vehicle; motor vehicle parts & accessories; utility trailer rental
PA: The Shyft Group Inc
   41280 Bridge St
   Novi MI 48375
   517 543-6400

(G-2768)
SHYFT GROUP INC
1549 Mikesell St (48813-2021)
PHONE..................517 543-6400
EMP: 26
SALES (corp-wide): 146.2MM **Publicly Held**
WEB: www.spartanmotors.com
SIC: 3711 Chassis, motor vehicle; fire department vehicles (motor vehicles), assembly of; ambulances (motor vehicles), assembly of
PA: The Shyft Group Inc
   41280 Bridge St
   Novi MI 48375
   517 543-6400

(G-2769)
SHYFT GROUP USA INC (HQ)
1000 Reynolds Rd (48813-2018)
PHONE..................517 543-6400
Daryl M Adams, *CEO*
John Slawson, *President*
Frederick Sohm, *Treasurer*
Peter Robert, *Manager*
Thomas W Gorman, *Director*
◆ **EMP:** 100 **EST:** 1990
SQ FT: 100,000
SALES (est): 33.9MM
SALES (corp-wide): 146.2MM **Publicly Held**
WEB: www.spartanmotors.com
SIC: 3711 Fire department vehicles (motor vehicles), assembly of
PA: The Shyft Group Inc
   41280 Bridge St
   Novi MI 48375
   517 543-6400

(G-2770)
SILK SCREENSTUFF
2860 S Cochran Rd (48813-9177)
PHONE..................517 543-7716
Kevin Bowen, *Owner*
EMP: 4 **EST:** 1986
SALES (est): 1,400 **Privately Held**
WEB: www.silkscreenstuff.net
SIC: 2396 2759 2395 Screen printing on fabric articles; screen printing; embroidery products, except schiffli machine

(G-2771)
SLAYER OUTDOOR PRODUCTS
435 Packard Hwy Ste A (48813-7748)
P.O. Box 156 (48813-0156)
PHONE..................517 726-0221
EMP: 4 **EST:** 2017
SALES (est): 145K **Privately Held**
WEB: www.slayeroutdoorproducts.com
SIC: 3949 Sporting & athletic goods

(G-2772)
SPARTAN MOTORS CHASSIS INC
Also Called: Spartan Chassis
1541 Reynolds Rd (48813-2099)
PHONE..................517 543-6400
John E Sztykiel, *CEO*
Daryl M Adams, *COO*
Thomas T Kivell, *Vice Pres*
Dale Kroger, *Prdtn Mgr*
Jennifer Taylor, *Purchasing*
▼ **EMP:** 400 **EST:** 1998
SALES (est): 25.1MM
SALES (corp-wide): 146.2MM **Publicly Held**
WEB: www.spartaner.com
SIC: 3711 Chassis, motor vehicle
PA: The Shyft Group Inc
   41280 Bridge St
   Novi MI 48375
   517 543-6400

(G-2773)
ST REGIS CULVERT INC (PA)
202 Morrell St (48813-1198)
PHONE..................517 543-3430
John R Mooney, *President*
Christopher Mooney, *Vice Pres*
Brian Caldwell, *Sales Staff*
Jennifer Turner, *Admin Sec*
EMP: 15 **EST:** 1890
SQ FT: 20,000
SALES (est): 4.4MM **Privately Held**
WEB: www.stregisculvert.com
SIC: 3498 Fabricated pipe & fittings

(G-2774)
WALMART INC
1680 Packard Hwy (48813-9773)
PHONE..................517 541-1481
Terry Lantz, *Manager*
Dorothy Schroeder, *Executive*
EMP: 15
SQ FT: 189,173
SALES (corp-wide): 559.1B **Publicly Held**
WEB: www.corporate.walmart.com
SIC: 5311 5411 5812 5531 Department stores, discount; supermarkets, hypermarket; eating places; automotive & home supply stores; bread, cake & related products; drug stores & proprietary stores
PA: Walmart Inc.
   702 Sw 8th St
   Bentonville AR 72716
   479 273-4000

Chase
Lake County

(G-2775)
BROOKS MANUFACTURING
8457 E 64th St (49623-7704)
PHONE..................231 832-4961
EMP: 8 **EST:** 2008

Chassell - Houghton County (G-2776)

GEOGRAPHIC SECTION

SALES (est): 139.2K **Privately Held**
WEB: www.brooksmfg.com
SIC: 3999 Manufacturing industries

Chassell
Houghton County

(G-2776)
BODA CORPORATION
Us 41 (49916)
PHONE.................................906 353-7320
Allen M Boda, *President*
EMP: 5 EST: 1973
SQ FT: 1,800
SALES (est): 399.1K **Privately Held**
SIC: 3544 Special dies & tools

(G-2777)
ERICKSON LOGGING INC
40734 Lower Pike Rd (49916-9497)
PHONE.................................906 481-4021
Travis L Erickson, *Principal*
Michelle Erickson, *Admin Sec*
EMP: 5 EST: 2003
SALES (est): 583.2K **Privately Held**
WEB: www.ericksonlogging.com
SIC: 2411 Logging camps & contractors

Chatham
Alger County

(G-2778)
PORCUPINE PRESS INC
Also Called: Porky Press
3720 Munising St E (49816)
P.O. Box 200 (49816-0200)
PHONE.................................906 439-5111
Michael Van Denbranden, *President*
Michael Vandenbranden, *President*
Jeremy Williams, *Principal*
Robin Lindinberg, *Vice Pres*
EMP: 8 EST: 1989
SALES (est): 816K **Privately Held**
WEB: www.upmag.online
SIC: 2711 Newspapers: publishing only, not printed on site

Cheboygan
Cheboygan County

(G-2779)
1JOHNSON ERLING
Also Called: Black River Sanding Gravel
6564 N Black River Rd (49721-9526)
PHONE.................................231 625-2247
Erling Johnson, *Owner*
EMP: 7 EST: 2012
SALES (est): 179K **Privately Held**
SIC: 1794 1442 Excavation work; construction sand & gravel

(G-2780)
BECKMAN EQUIPMENT
12800 Airport Rd (49721-8436)
PHONE.................................231 420-4791
EMP: 5 EST: 2017
SALES (est): 67.6K **Privately Held**
WEB: www.beckman.com
SIC: 3826 Analytical instruments

(G-2781)
CHAMBERS OTTAWA INC
2064 Campbell Rd (49721-9305)
P.O. Box 173 (49721-0173)
PHONE.................................231 238-2122
Curtis Chambers,
EMP: 4 EST: 2010 **Privately Held**
WEB: www.chambersottawa.com
SIC: 2676 Sanitary paper products

(G-2782)
CHEBOYGAN CEMENT PRODUCTS INC (PA)
702 Lafayette Ave (49721-2199)
PHONE.................................231 627-5631
Ernest Gildner, *President*
Veronica Gildner, *Corp Secy*
Michael Gildner, *Vice Pres*
Ashley Ptasnik, *Treasurer*
Cathy Gildner, *Executive*
EMP: 50 EST: 1946
SALES (est): 8.7MM **Privately Held**
WEB: www.cheboygancement.com
SIC: 3273 3271 3272 1442 Ready-mixed concrete; blocks, concrete or cinder: standard; septic tanks, concrete; burial vaults, concrete or precast terrazzo; dry mixture concrete; construction sand & gravel

(G-2783)
CHEBOYGAN CNTY HBTAT FOR HMNIT
9385 N Straits Hwy (49721-9069)
PHONE.................................231 597-4663
Mandy Martin, *Exec Dir*
EMP: 6
SALES: 251.9K **Privately Held**
WEB: www.habitatcheboygan.org
SIC: 8399 1389 5999 Community development groups; construction, repair & dismantling services; miscellaneous retail stores

(G-2784)
GREAT LAKES CUSTOM METALWORKS
9656 N M 33 Hwy (49721-9450)
PHONE.................................231 818-5888
Gwynnette Aldrich, *Principal*
EMP: 4 EST: 2014
SALES (est): 127.3K **Privately Held**
WEB: www.miglcm.com
SIC: 3441 Fabricated structural metal

(G-2785)
GREAT LAKES TISSUE COMPANY
437 S Main St (49721-1999)
PHONE.................................231 627-0200
Clarence Roznowski, *CEO*
EMP: 100
SQ FT: 450,000
SALES (est): 26.2MM **Privately Held**
SIC: 2621 Towels, tissues & napkins: paper & stock

(G-2786)
INSCRIBD LLC
6050 Carey Rd (49721-7800)
PHONE.................................231 445-9104
William Ness,
EMP: 5 EST: 2016
SALES (est): 62.4K **Privately Held**
SIC: 2844 2834 Face creams or lotions; zinc ointment

(G-2787)
INVERNESS DAIRY INC
1631 Woiderski Rd (49721-8969)
PHONE.................................231 627-4655
EMP: 20 EST: 1922
SQ FT: 10,000
SALES (est): 213.8K **Privately Held**
SIC: 2026 2021 Mfg Fluid Milk Mfg Creamery Butter

(G-2788)
J B LUNDS & SONS INC
Also Called: Cheboygan Harbor Marine
707 Cleveland Ave (49721-2049)
P.O. Box 370 (49721-0370)
PHONE.................................231 627-9070
George E Lund, *Vice Pres*
Clayton Lund, *Treasurer*
Richard Lund, *Admin Sec*
EMP: 4 EST: 1902
SQ FT: 5,000
SALES (est): 355.9K **Privately Held**
SIC: 3599 5051 Machine shop, jobbing & repair; steel

(G-2789)
JARMANS PURE MAPLE SYRUP LLC
6856 Jarman Rd (49721-9033)
PHONE.................................231 818-5315
EMP: 4 EST: 2014
SALES (est): 62.3K **Privately Held**
SIC: 2099 Maple syrup

(G-2790)
KEEBLER COMPANY
10364 Neuman Rd (49721-8914)
PHONE.................................231 445-0335
Peter Chasse, *Principal*
EMP: 112
SALES (corp-wide): 13.7B **Publicly Held**
WEB: www.keebler.com
SIC: 2052 Cookies
HQ: Keebler Company
1 Kellogg Sq
Battle Creek MI 49017
269 961-2000

(G-2791)
LIEBNER ENTERPRISES LLC
Also Called: United States Ski Pole Company
1160 E State St Unit C (49721-2166)
PHONE.................................231 331-3076
Andrew Liebner, *Mng Member*
Roger Liebner, *Mng Member*
EMP: 5 EST: 2012
SALES (est): 575K **Privately Held**
WEB: www.usskipoles.com
SIC: 3949 Sporting & athletic goods

(G-2792)
MSHIIKENH RNWBLE RESOURCES LLC
8585 Swan Pointe Dr (49721-7802)
PHONE.................................231 818-9353
Daniel Uber, *Mng Member*
EMP: 4 EST: 2009
SALES (est): 225K **Privately Held**
SIC: 2611 Pulp mills

(G-2793)
NICHOLASS BLACK RIVER VINEYAR (PA)
Also Called: Nicholas Wine Sampling Room
6209 N Black River Rd (49721-9457)
PHONE.................................231 625-9060
Nick J Koklanaris, *President*
▲ EMP: 4 EST: 1999
SALES (est): 318.1K **Privately Held**
WEB: www.nicholasblackriverwinery.com
SIC: 2084 Wines

(G-2794)
NORTHERN MICH MMRALS MONUMENTS
2754 Old Mackinaw Rd (49721-9311)
PHONE.................................231 290-2333
Matthew Redmond, *Principal*
EMP: 4 EST: 2015
SALES (est): 128.2K **Privately Held**
WEB: www.northernmichiganmemorialsmonuments.com
SIC: 2435 Hardwood veneer & plywood

(G-2795)
PEPSI
Also Called: Pepsico
6303 N Straits Hwy (49721-9048)
PHONE.................................231 627-2290
EMP: 4
SALES (est): 139.6K **Privately Held**
SIC: 2086 Carb Sft Drnkbtlcn

(G-2796)
PRECISION THREADING CORP
Also Called: North Attleboro Taps
1306 Higgins Dr (49721-1061)
PHONE.................................231 627-3133
Arthur C Heintel, *President*
Paul Scheer, *Vice Pres*
Amy L Deeter, *CFO*
Amy Deeter, *CFO*
Dennis Bergstrom, *Manager*
▲ EMP: 7 EST: 1927
SQ FT: 28,000
SALES (est): 934K **Privately Held**
WEB: www.cheboygantap.com
SIC: 3545 Machine tool accessories

(G-2797)
R K C CORPORATION
600 Riggs Dr (49721-1066)
PHONE.................................231 627-9131
Reinhardt Jahn, *President*
C Reinhardt Jahn, *President*
EMP: 8 EST: 1972
SQ FT: 40,000
SALES (est): 822.7K **Privately Held**
WEB: www.rkc-corp.com
SIC: 3599 Custom machinery

(G-2798)
SCHWARTZ BOILER SHOP INC
Also Called: Schwartz Blast & Paint
850 Lahaie Rd (49721-1810)
P.O. Box 312 (49721-0312)
PHONE.................................231 627-2556
Jade Hunt, *President*
Roger A Schwartz, *Vice Pres*
Diane Schwartz, *Admin Sec*
EMP: 9 EST: 1902
SQ FT: 8,000
SALES (est): 794.9K **Privately Held**
WEB: www.schwartzboiler.com
SIC: 7699 3471 7353 Nautical repair services; ship boiler & tank cleaning & repair, contractors; sand blasting of metal parts; cranes & aerial lift equipment, rental or leasing

(G-2799)
SHOPPERS FAIR INC
Also Called: Cheboygan Tribune
308 N Main St (49721-1545)
P.O. Box 290 (49721-0290)
PHONE.................................231 627-7144
Gary Lambert, *President*
Janis Coryell, *Business Mgr*
Jennifer Fenstermaker, *Executive*
EMP: 20 EST: 1991
SALES (est): 934K **Privately Held**
WEB: www.cheboygannews.com
SIC: 2711 Commercial printing & newspaper publishing combined; newspapers, publishing & printing

(G-2800)
STRAITS AREA PRINTING CORP
313 Lafayette Ave (49721-2154)
P.O. Box 11 (49721-0011)
PHONE.................................231 627-5647
Charles Beard, *President*
Scott Beard, *General Mgr*
Sandra Beard, *Treasurer*
EMP: 9 EST: 1977
SQ FT: 2,100
SALES (est): 662.2K **Privately Held**
WEB: www.straitsprinting.com
SIC: 2752 2759 Commercial printing, offset; letterpress printing

Chelsea
Washtenaw County

(G-2801)
ABRASIVE FINISHING INC
Also Called: Burr Bench
11770 Dexter Chelsea Rd (48118-9539)
PHONE.................................734 433-9236
William Ackley, *Owner*
◆ EMP: 6 EST: 2006
SALES (est): 928.4K **Privately Held**
WEB: www.abrasivefinishing.com
SIC: 3291 Abrasive products

(G-2802)
ADVANCED INDUSTRIES INC
Also Called: Koolblast
3955 S Fletcher Rd (48118-9207)
PHONE.................................734 433-1800
Kevin Beckington, *President*
Michelle Monge, *Purch Mgr*
EMP: 24 EST: 1991
SQ FT: 15,000
SALES (est): 5.5MM **Privately Held**
WEB: www.advancedindustriesinc.com
SIC: 3599 Machine shop, jobbing & repair

(G-2803)
AFI ENTERPRISES INC
11770 Dexter Chelsea Rd (48118-9539)
PHONE.................................734 475-9111
William A Ackley, *President*
◆ EMP: 35 EST: 1954
SQ FT: 80,000
SALES (est): 700.9K **Privately Held**
WEB: www.abrasivefinishing.com
SIC: 3291 Grinding balls, ceramic; stones, abrasive

(G-2804)
AL CORP
Also Called: Phoenix Color
525 Glazier Rd (48118-9779)
PHONE.................................734 475-7357

▲ = Import ▼ =Export
◆ =Import/Export

GEOGRAPHIC SECTION   Chesaning - Saginaw County (G-2830)

EMP: 15
SALES (est): 941K **Privately Held**
SIC: 2759 2796 2791 Commercial Printing Platemaking Services Typesetting Services
PA: Access Bidco Incorporated
200 N Washington Sq # 440
Lansing MI 48933

(G-2805)
ALLOY INDUSTRIES CORPORATION
13500 Luick Dr (48118-9587)
PHONE 734 433-1112
Carl E Perry, *President*
EMP: 8 **EST:** 1990
SQ FT: 8,500
SALES (est): 669.9K **Privately Held**
WEB: www.alloyindustries.us
SIC: 3599 Machine shop, jobbing & repair

(G-2806)
CHELSEA MILLING COMPANY (PA)
201 W North St (48118-1297)
P.O. Box 460 (48118-0460)
PHONE 734 475-1361
Howdy S Holmes, *President*
Joseph Goryl, *General Mgr*
Leo Brintnall, *Business Mgr*
Doug Garriga, *Business Mgr*
Jay Hilscher, *Business Mgr*
EMP: 300 **EST:** 1901
SQ FT: 350,000
SALES (est): 86.6MM **Privately Held**
WEB: www.site.jiffymix.com
SIC: 2041 Flour: blended, prepared or self-rising

(G-2807)
CHELSEA TOOL INC
20401 W Old Us Highway 12 # 4
(48118-2300)
P.O. Box 178 (48118-0178)
PHONE 734 475-9679
Dennis Boos, *President*
EMP: 5 **EST:** 1986
SQ FT: 4,000
SALES (est): 471K **Privately Held**
WEB: www.chelsealumber.com
SIC: 3599 Machine shop, jobbing & repair

(G-2808)
DETROIT ABRASIVES COMPANY (PA)
11910 Dexter Chelsea Rd (48118-9539)
PHONE 734 475-1651
Richard G Wallace, *President*
Katherine A Wallace, *Corp Secy*
▲ **EMP:** 5 **EST:** 1937
SQ FT: 10,000
SALES (est): 1.5MM **Privately Held**
SIC: 3291 Aluminum oxide (fused) abrasives

(G-2809)
DEXTER CIDER MILL INC
4885 Kalmbach Rd (48118-9701)
PHONE 734 475-6419
EMP: 5 **EST:** 2019
SALES (est): 337.8K **Privately Held**
WEB: www.dextercidermill.com
SIC: 2099 Cider, nonalcoholic

(G-2810)
DEXTER MANUFACTURING INC
20401 W Old Us Highway 12 # 1
(48118-2300)
P.O. Box 114 (48118-0114)
PHONE 734 475-8046
Bill J Mikkelson, *President*
EMP: 5 **EST:** 1994
SQ FT: 3,500
SALES (est): 400.4K **Privately Held**
SIC: 3599 Machine shop, jobbing & repair

(G-2811)
FILTER PLUS INC
2442 Mckinley Rd (48118-9512)
PHONE 734 475-7403
John Temple, *President*
EMP: 7 **EST:** 1995
SALES (est): 157K **Privately Held**
SIC: 3841 Surgical & medical instruments

(G-2812)
GESTAMP WASHTENAW LLC
5800 Sibley Rd (48118-1262)
PHONE 734 593-9036
Jeffrey Wilson,
EMP: 30 **EST:** 2016
SALES (est): 14.8MM
SALES (corp-wide): 400.4MM **Privately Held**
WEB: www.gestamp.com
SIC: 3465 Body parts, automobile: stamped metal
HQ: Gestamp Automocion Sociedad Anonima
Barrio Lebario (Pg Industrial De Lebario), S/N
Abadino 48220

(G-2813)
GREENE MANUFACTURING INC
Also Called: GMI
3985 S Fletcher Rd (48118-9653)
PHONE 734 428-8304
Bruce Greene, *President*
Julie Greene, *Controller*
Lauren Aiuto, *Director*
Chris Stiman, *Relations*
EMP: 23 **EST:** 1969
SQ FT: 15,000
SALES (est): 5.5MM **Privately Held**
WEB: www.greenemfg.com
SIC: 3444 2531 Sheet metalwork; school furniture

(G-2814)
HATCH STAMPING COMPANY LLC (HQ)
635 E Industrial Dr (48118-1599)
PHONE 734 475-8628
Daniel Craig, *President*
Chris Parrott, *Exec VP*
Christopher Parrott, *Exec VP*
Christophe Parrott, *Exec VP*
Todd Fyall, *Vice Pres*
◆ **EMP:** 200 **EST:** 1965
SQ FT: 110,000
SALES (est): 313.8MM
SALES (corp-wide): 574.8MM **Privately Held**
WEB: www.hatchstamping.com
SIC: 3465 7692 Automotive stampings; automotive welding
PA: Prophet Equity Lp
1460 Main St Ste 200
Southlake TX 76092
817 898-1500

(G-2815)
INK FRENZY
420 N Main St Ste 400 (48118-1494)
PHONE 734 562-2621
EMP: 4 **EST:** 2015
SALES (est): 77.6K **Privately Held**
WEB: www.inkfrenzy.com
SIC: 2759 Screen printing

(G-2816)
JAYTEC LLC
5800 Sibley Rd (48118-1262)
PHONE 734 397-6300
Darryl Macneil, *General Mgr*
Robert Koss, *Vice Pres*
EMP: 10
SALES (corp-wide): 3.1B **Privately Held**
WEB: www.autokiniton.com
SIC: 3465 Automotive stampings
HQ: Jaytec, Llc
17757 Woodland Dr
New Boston MI 48164
517 451-8272

(G-2817)
JIFFY MIX
201 W North St (48118-1297)
PHONE 734 475-1361
Lori Reynolds, *Manager*
EMP: 6 **EST:** 2019
SALES (est): 259.1K **Privately Held**
WEB: www.site.jiffymix.com
SIC: 2099 Food preparations

(G-2818)
KERN AUTO SALES AND SVC LLC
1630 S Main St (48118-1411)
PHONE 734 475-2722
Thomas D Kern,
Vickie Kern,
EMP: 10 **EST:** 2007
SALES (est): 2.7MM **Privately Held**
SIC: 5521 7539 2869 5411 Automobiles, used cars only; automotive repair shops; fuels; convenience stores

(G-2819)
LUCKY BIRD CANDLE CO
139 Van Buren St (48118-1055)
PHONE 734 272-7338
Joel Boyce, *Principal*
EMP: 4 **EST:** 2019
SALES (est): 107.2K **Privately Held**
SIC: 3999 Candles

(G-2820)
MANLY INNOVATIONS LLC
19735 Deerfield Ct (48118-9316)
PHONE 734 548-0200
Joseph Manly,
EMP: 4 **EST:** 2013
SALES (est): 178.1K **Privately Held**
WEB: www.manlyinnovations.com
SIC: 3484 Guns (firearms) or gun parts, 30 mm. & below

(G-2821)
MUSICALIA PRESS
226 South St (48118-1238)
PHONE 734 433-1289
Wayne Petty, *Principal*
EMP: 4 **EST:** 2017
SALES (est): 37.5K **Privately Held**
WEB: www.musicaliapress.com
SIC: 2741 Miscellaneous publishing

(G-2822)
ORCHID MACDEE LLC
13800 Luick Dr (48118-9135)
PHONE 734 475-9165
Michael Zamiara, *Mng Member*
EMP: 220 **EST:** 2006
SALES (est): 2.9MM
SALES (corp-wide): 496.9MM **Privately Held**
WEB: www.orchid-ortho.com
SIC: 3841 Surgical & medical instruments
PA: Tulip Us Holdings, Inc.
1489 Cedar St
Holt MI 48842
517 694-2300

(G-2823)
PLOW POINT BREWING CO
6447 Stillwater Dr (48118-9166)
PHONE 734 562-9102
Don Smith, *Principal*
EMP: 5 **EST:** 2015
SALES (est): 68.6K **Privately Held**
WEB: www.plowpointbrewing.com
SIC: 2082 Malt beverages

(G-2824)
PRECISION HRDWOOD RSOURCES INC
Also Called: Hardwood Solutions
680 E Industrial Dr (48118-1285)
PHONE 734 475-0144
Jeffrey Hardcastle, *President*
Mike Myers, *General Mgr*
Bob Mendoza, *Vice Pres*
Robert Mendoza, *Vice Pres*
Debra Hardcastle, *Treasurer*
◆ **EMP:** 15 **EST:** 1996
SQ FT: 42,000
SALES (est): 3.8MM **Privately Held**
WEB: www.hardwoodsolutions.com
SIC: 2421 Sawmills & planing mills, general

(G-2825)
SAC LEGACY COMPANY LLC
Also Called: Spring Arbor Coatings, LLC
635 E Industrial Dr (48118-1538)
P.O. Box 582, Spring Arbor (49283-0582)
PHONE 517 750-2903
Dan Craig, *Mng Member*
Chris Parrott,
Pete Schira,
Charles Winters,
EMP: 60 **EST:** 2006
SQ FT: 25,000
SALES (est): 13.8MM
SALES (corp-wide): 574.8MM **Privately Held**
WEB: www.hatchstamping.com
SIC: 3471 Electroplating & plating
HQ: Hatch Stamping Company Llc
635 E Industrial Dr
Chelsea MI 48118
734 475-8628

(G-2826)
SHERIDAN BOOKS INC (DH)
613 E Industrial Dr (48118-1536)
P.O. Box 370 (48118-0370)
PHONE 734 475-9145
Robert Moore, *President*
Michal Seagram, *President*
Andrea Deljanovan, *Credit Mgr*
Jessica Ansorge, *Sales Staff*
◆ **EMP:** 402 **EST:** 1950
SALES (est): 85.6MM
SALES (corp-wide): 631.4MM **Privately Held**
WEB: www.sheridan.com
SIC: 2752 Commercial printing, offset

Chesaning
Saginaw County

(G-2827)
4 WHEELS INDUSTRIES
9980 Peet Rd (48616-1712)
PHONE 989 323-2191
Brett Taylor, *Principal*
EMP: 7 **EST:** 2015
SALES (est): 365.5K **Privately Held**
WEB: www.4wheelbuy.com
SIC: 3999 Manufacturing industries

(G-2828)
INTEGRATED BUILDING SOLUTIONS
13609 Larner Rd (48616-9445)
PHONE 616 889-3070
Kevin Damic, *Owner*
EMP: 10 **EST:** 2005
SQ FT: 3,000
SALES (est): 2.5MM **Privately Held**
SIC: 3822 Building services monitoring controls, automatic

(G-2829)
LIPPERT COMPONENTS MFG INC
Also Called: Hehr Michigan Division
1103 Pearl St (48616-1007)
P.O. Box 217 (48616-0217)
PHONE 989 845-3061
Douglas Gerding, *Branch Mgr*
EMP: 90
SALES (corp-wide): 2.8B **Publicly Held**
WEB: www.lci1.com
SIC: 3231 3714 3442 3354 Windshields, glass: made from purchased glass; motor vehicle parts & accessories; metal doors, sash & trim; aluminum extruded products; van conversion; doors & windows
HQ: Lippert Components Manufacturing, Inc.
3501 County Road 6 E
Elkhart IN 46514
574 535-1125

(G-2830)
SWARTZMILLER LUMBER COMPANY (PA)
802 W Broad St (48616-1002)
P.O. Box 126 (48616-0126)
PHONE 989 845-6625
Donald Swartzmiller, *Ch of Bd*
Annette Swartzmiller, *President*
Christopher Theily, *Vice Pres*
EMP: 6 **EST:** 1912
SQ FT: 40,000

(PA)=Parent Co (HQ)=Headquarters (DH)=Div Headquarters
✧ = New Business established in last 2 years

Chesaning - Saginaw County (G-2831)

SALES (est): 872.9K **Privately Held**
WEB: www.swartzmillerlumber.com
SIC: 5211 3271 3273 5961 Home centers; lumber products; concrete block & brick; ready-mixed concrete; catalog & mail-order houses; truck rental, without drivers

(G-2831)
VB CHESANING LLC
Also Called: High Life Farms
624 Brady St (48616-1155)
PHONE..........................989 323-2333
Tom Celani, *Mng Member*
EMP: 170 EST: 2018
SALES (est): 10.4MM **Privately Held**
WEB: www.villageofchesaning.org
SIC: 3999

Chesterfield
Macomb County

(G-2832)
1271 ASSOCIATES INC (PA)
Also Called: Welders and Presses
27295 Luckino Dr (48047-5229)
PHONE..........................586 948-4300
Robert Kohler, *President*
David Kohler, *Exec VP*
Shawn Hartman, *Plant Mgr*
EMP: 65 EST: 1989
SQ FT: 42,000
SALES (est): 7.6MM **Privately Held**
WEB: www.wpimfg.com
SIC: 3548 5085 7699 Resistance welders, electric; welding supplies; industrial machinery & equipment repair

(G-2833)
2-N-1 GRIPS INC
Also Called: Turbo Grips
46460 Continental Dr (48047-5206)
PHONE..........................800 530-9878
David A Bernhardt, *President*
Orman Bernhardt, *Corp Secy*
Alan Bernhardt, *Vice Pres*
▲ EMP: 14 EST: 1990
SQ FT: 70,000
SALES (est): 1.6MM **Privately Held**
WEB: www.turbogrips.com
SIC: 3949 Bowling equipment & supplies

(G-2834)
ACHATZS HAND MADE PIE CO (PA)
30301 Commerce Blvd (48051-1243)
PHONE..........................586 749-2882
David Achatz, *Owner*
Joann Austin, *Safety Mgr*
Renee Brown, *Human Res Mgr*
Ashley Bainbridge, *Manager*
Sandra Collias, *Manager*
EMP: 40 EST: 1993
SQ FT: 4,500
SALES (est): 11.4MM **Privately Held**
WEB: www.achatzpies.com
SIC: 2038 2051 5141 Frozen specialties; bread, cake & related products; groceries, general line

(G-2835)
ADM GRAPHICS & PRINT PROD LLC
48505 Carmine Ct (48051-2903)
PHONE..........................586 598-1821
David McKinney, *Principal*
EMP: 4 EST: 2015
SALES (est): 77.3K **Privately Held**
SIC: 2752 Commercial printing, lithographic

(G-2836)
ADVANCED INTEG TOOLING SOLNS
Also Called: Advanced Integration Tech Mich
29700 Commerce Blvd (48051-1244)
PHONE..........................586 749-5525
Edward J Chalupa, *Partner*
Robert Reno, *Vice Pres*
Frisch Dave, *Project Mgr*
Paul Schoenherr, *Analyst*
▲ EMP: 230 EST: 2010

SALES (est): 75.3MM
SALES (corp-wide): 188.2MM **Privately Held**
WEB: www.aint.com
SIC: 3544 Industrial molds
PA: Advanced Integration Technology, Lp
2805 E Plano Pkwy Ste 300
Plano TX 75074
972 423-8354

(G-2837)
ADVANCED INTEGRATION TECH LP
Also Called: Ait Tooling
29700 Commerce Blvd (48051-1244)
PHONE..........................586 749-5525
Michael Juricny, *Project Mgr*
Craig Schiffelbine, *Production*
Frank Dusett, *Engineer*
Keith Music, *Engineer*
Jennifer Weigel, *Controller*
EMP: 6
SALES (corp-wide): 188.2MM **Privately Held**
WEB: www.aint.com
SIC: 3728 8711 Aircraft parts & equipment; machine tool design
PA: Advanced Integration Technology, Lp
2805 E Plano Pkwy Ste 300
Plano TX 75074
972 423-8354

(G-2838)
AMERICAN BRAKE AND CLUTCH INC
Also Called: Superior Waterjet Service
50631 E Russell Schmidt (48051-2454)
PHONE..........................586 948-3730
Daniel C Breazeale, *President*
EMP: 10 EST: 1988
SQ FT: 55,000
SALES (est): 1.5MM **Privately Held**
WEB: www.americanbrake.com
SIC: 3625 3542 Electromagnetic clutches or brakes; plasma jet spray metal forming machines

(G-2839)
ANCHOR BAY FAB
50545 Metzen Dr (48051-3137)
PHONE..........................586 231-0295
EMP: 4 EST: 2018
SALES (est): 108.8K **Privately Held**
SIC: 3499 Fabricated metal products

(G-2840)
ANCHOR BAY MANUFACTURING CORP
50900 E Russell Schmidt (48051-2497)
PHONE..........................586 949-1195
EMP: 11
SALES (corp-wide): 2.8MM **Privately Held**
WEB: www.anchorbaypackaging.com
SIC: 2621 Wrapping & packaging papers
PA: Anchor Bay Packaging Corporation
30905 23 Mile Rd
Chesterfield MI 48047
586 949-4040

(G-2841)
ANCHOR BAY MANUFACTURING CORP (PA)
30905 23 Mile Rd (48047-5702)
PHONE..........................586 949-4040
Victoria Pierno, *Principal*
Robert Kebblish, *Design Engr*
EMP: 139 EST: 1979
SALES (est): 2.8MM **Privately Held**
WEB: www.anchorbaypackaging.com
SIC: 2621 Paper mills

(G-2842)
ANCHOR BAY PACKAGING CORP (PA)
Also Called: Phoenix Packaging
30905 23 Mile Rd (48047-5702)
PHONE..........................586 949-4040
Victoria L Pierno, *President*
Chris Hastings, *Principal*
Collin Tripp, *Principal*
Philip Taravella, *Vice Pres*
Robert Kebblish, *Design Engr*
▲ EMP: 27 EST: 1985
SQ FT: 40,000

SALES (est): 20.1MM **Privately Held**
WEB: www.anchorbaypackaging.com
SIC: 2653 8734 3565 Boxes, corrugated: made from purchased materials; testing laboratories; packaging machinery

(G-2843)
ANCHOR BAY PACKAGING CORP
30871 23 Mile Rd (48047-1894)
PHONE..........................586 949-1500
EMP: 5
SALES (corp-wide): 20.1MM **Privately Held**
WEB: www.anchorbaypackaging.com
SIC: 2653 2671 2631 Boxes, corrugated: made from purchased materials; packaging paper & plastics film, coated & laminated; paperboard mills
PA: Anchor Bay Packaging Corporation
30905 23 Mile Rd
Chesterfield MI 48047
586 949-4040

(G-2844)
ANDERSON-COOK INC (PA)
Also Called: L M Gear Company Division
50550 E Rssell Schmidt Bl (48051-2451)
PHONE..........................586 954-0700
Dennis Neagher, *CEO*
Kim Anderson, *Ch of Bd*
Matthew Richey, *General Mgr*
Walt Hudas, *Mfg Mgr*
Dominik Zaleski, *Opers Staff*
▲ EMP: 55 EST: 1970
SALES (est): 40.3MM **Privately Held**
WEB: www.andersoncook.com
SIC: 3542 3714 3599 3549 Spline rolling machines; gears, motor vehicle; machine shop, jobbing & repair; metalworking machinery; machine tool accessories

(G-2845)
ANKARA INDUSTRIES INCORPORATED
56359 N Bay Dr (48051-3738)
PHONE..........................586 749-1190
Richard B Moore, *President*
EMP: 22 EST: 1971
SQ FT: 35,000
SALES (est): 962.4K **Privately Held**
WEB: www.ankaraindustries.com
SIC: 3452 3465 Nuts, metal; automotive stampings

(G-2846)
ARNOLD TOOL & DIE CO (PA)
48800 Structural Dr (48051-2677)
PHONE..........................586 598-0099
Thomas A McKay, *President*
Tom Buerkle, *General Mgr*
Dan Swinyer, *Purchasing*
Nona Batkins, *Admin Sec*
EMP: 49 EST: 1964
SALES (est): 4.3MM **Privately Held**
WEB: www.arnoldtool.com
SIC: 3599 3544 3469 Machine shop, jobbing & repair; special dies, tools, jigs & fixtures; metal stampings

(G-2847)
ARO WELDING TECHNOLOGIES INC
Also Called: Savair
48500 Structural Dr (48051-2673)
PHONE..........................586 949-9353
Pierre Barthelemy, *President*
Jean- Yves David, *President*
Richard Gibson, *Managing Dir*
Albert Roland, *Principal*
Mike Dubay, *Plant Mgr*
▲ EMP: 99 EST: 1986
SQ FT: 80,000
SALES: 24.9MM
SALES (corp-wide): 906.8MM **Privately Held**
WEB: www.arotechnologies.com
SIC: 3548 Electric welding equipment
PA: Langley Holdings Plc
Enterprise Way Thrumpton Lane
Retford NOTTS DN22
177 770-0039

(G-2848)
AUTHORITY FLAME HRDNING STRGHT
49803 Leona Dr (48051-2480)
PHONE..........................586 598-5887
David Decook,
Darlene Decook,
Matthew Decook,
EMP: 34 EST: 2001
SQ FT: 11,000
SALES (est): 3.2MM **Privately Held**
SIC: 3398 Metal heat treating

(G-2849)
AUTO BUILDERS INC
46571 Continental Dr (48047-5207)
P.O. Box 180726, Utica (48318-0726)
PHONE..........................586 948-3780
EMP: 25 EST: 2003
SALES (est): 3.7MM **Privately Held**
SIC: 3599 Mfg Industrial Machinery

(G-2850)
BERG TOOL INC
56253 Precision Dr (48051-3736)
PHONE..........................586 646-7100
Colin Sutherland, *Principal*
Andy KAC, *Principal*
Glenn Burmeister, *Supervisor*
EMP: 15 EST: 1976
SQ FT: 14,000
SALES (est): 2.1MM **Privately Held**
WEB: www.bergtool.com
SIC: 3541 3544 Machine tools, metal cutting type; special dies, tools, jigs & fixtures

(G-2851)
BRICO WELDING & FAB INC
27057 Morelli Dr (48051-2033)
PHONE..........................586 948-8881
Brian W Coons, *President*
Bradford W Coons, *Vice Pres*
EMP: 22 EST: 1991
SQ FT: 27,500
SALES (est): 4.2MM **Privately Held**
WEB: www.bricowelding.com
SIC: 7692 Welding repair

(G-2852)
BRIGGS INDUSTRIES INC
54145 Bates Rd (48051-1617)
P.O. Box 160, New Baltimore (48047-0160)
PHONE..........................586 749-5191
Elmer Lee Briggs, *President*
Cynthia J Rogers, *Corp Secy*
EMP: 30 EST: 1972
SQ FT: 17,000
SALES (est): 2.8MM **Privately Held**
WEB: www.briggsind.com
SIC: 3545 3543 3544 3086 Tools & accessories for machine tools; industrial patterns; special dies, tools, jigs & fixtures; plastics foam products

(G-2853)
BROACHING INDUSTRIES INC
25755 Dhondt Ct (48051-2601)
PHONE..........................586 949-3775
Michael E Priehs Sr, *President*
EMP: 26 EST: 1977
SQ FT: 6,200
SALES (est): 1.1MM **Privately Held**
WEB: www.broachingindustries.com
SIC: 8711 3469 3452 3545 Engineering services; metal stampings; bolts, nuts, rivets & washers; machine tool accessories; blast furnaces & steel mills; machine tools, metal cutting type

(G-2854)
C & M MANUFACTURING CORP INC
30207 Commerce Blvd (48051-1241)
PHONE..........................586 749-3455
Mat Warren, *President*
Mark Warren, *Regional Mgr*
Linda Warren, *Vice Pres*
Troy Warren, *Plant Mgr*
EMP: 40
SQ FT: 50,000
SALES (est): 6.9MM **Privately Held**
WEB: www.candmmfg.com
SIC: 3465 3312 Automotive stampings; tool & die steel

GEOGRAPHIC SECTION
Chesterfield - Macomb County (G-2882)

(G-2855)
C W INDUSTRIES
27999 Hambeltonian Dr (48047-4896)
PHONE..................................586 465-4157
Bill Chicowlas, *President*
EMP: 5 **EST:** 1991
SALES (est): 118.3K **Privately Held**
WEB: www.a1customsigns.com
SIC: 3599 Machine shop, jobbing & repair

(G-2856)
CABINET INSTALL SHOP
50515 Metzen Dr (48051-3137)
PHONE..................................586 946-0500
EMP: 4 **EST:** 2017
SALES (est): 127.1K **Privately Held**
WEB: www.cabinetinstallshop.com
SIC: 2434 Wood kitchen cabinets

(G-2857)
CAMRYN FABRICATION LLC
Also Called: Pro-Weld
50625 Richard W Blvd (48051-2493)
PHONE..................................586 949-0818
Steve Remstad, *President*
Jim Comer,
Les Stansbery,
EMP: 10 **EST:** 2015
SALES (est): 367.3K **Privately Held**
SIC: 3441 Fabricated structural metal

(G-2858)
CHEEBA HUT SMOKE SHOP LLC
50189 Gratiot Ave (48051-3124)
PHONE..................................586 213-5156
Ronnie Moussa,
EMP: 5 **EST:** 2017
SALES (est): 109.9K **Privately Held**
WEB: www.cheebasmokeshopchesterfield.com
SIC: 5199 2111 Smokers' supplies; cigarettes

(G-2859)
CHESTERFIELD ENGINES INC
Also Called: Chesterfield Engines Nic
52402 Gratiot Ave (48051-2024)
PHONE..................................586 949-5777
Gerald Barylski, *President*
EMP: 6 **EST:** 1998
SALES (est): 755.5K **Privately Held**
WEB: www.chesterfieldengines.net
SIC: 7538 7699 7539 5084 Engine rebuilding: automotive; boat repair; machine shop, automotive; engines & parts, diesel; machine shop, jobbing & repair

(G-2860)
COLUMBIA MARKING TOOLS INC
27430 Luckino Dr (48047-5270)
PHONE..................................586 949-8400
Michelle Krembel, *President*
Brian Barbara, *Regl Sales Mgr*
Thomas Phipps, *Admin Sec*
EMP: 40 **EST:** 1960
SQ FT: 30,000
SALES (est): 6.2MM **Privately Held**
WEB: www.columbiamt.com
SIC: 3549 3953 3544 3542 Marking machines, metalworking; marking devices; special dies, tools, jigs & fixtures; machine tools, metal forming type; commercial printing

(G-2861)
COSTELLO MACHINE LLC
56358 Precision Dr (48051-3737)
PHONE..................................586 749-0136
Frank Keena, *Managing Dir*
Tom Orban, *Export Mgr*
Victor A Costello, *Mng Member*
Thomas Orban, *Information Mgr*
◆ **EMP:** 27 **EST:** 2000
SQ FT: 35,000
SALES (est): 4.4MM **Privately Held**
WEB: www.costellomachine.com
SIC: 3545 Comparators (machinists' precision tools); precision tools, machinists'

(G-2862)
COX INDUSTRIES INC (PA)
30800 26 Mile Rd (48051-1234)
P.O. Box 480366, New Haven (48048-0366)
PHONE..................................586 749-6650
Alice Cox, *President*
Charles Cox, *Vice Pres*
Dick Ventura, *Plant Mgr*
Richard Ventura, *Sales Mgr*
EMP: 11 **EST:** 1970
SALES (est): 2.7MM **Privately Held**
WEB: www.cox-industries.com
SIC: 3399 Metal fasteners

(G-2863)
CUSOLAR INDUSTRIES INC
28161 Kehrig St (48047-5218)
PHONE..................................586 949-3880
Thomas W Cusack, *President*
Nadine Cusack, *Vice Pres*
EMP: 27 **EST:** 1979
SQ FT: 12,000
SALES (est): 225.1K **Privately Held**
WEB: www.cusolar.com
SIC: 3672 3714 3677 3694 Printed circuit boards; filters: oil, fuel & air, motor vehicle; coil windings, electronic; engine electrical equipment; brakes, electromagnetic; molding primary plastic

(G-2864)
D & B METAL FINISHING
34537 Shorewood St (48047-4412)
PHONE..................................586 725-6056
Deana Ulman, *Owner*
Bruce Ulman, *Co-Owner*
EMP: 6 **EST:** 2001
SALES (est): 400K **Privately Held**
WEB: www.dandbmetalfinishing.com
SIC: 3471 Electroplating of metals or formed products

(G-2865)
DAJACO IND INC
49715 Leona Dr (48051-2478)
PHONE..................................586 949-1590
Denise Hardy, *Principal*
Alan Ziehm, *Engineer*
Tony Varnadore, *Engng Exec*
Christopher Leggett, *Accounts Mgr*
Karleigh Ziehm, *Accounts Mgr*
EMP: 10 **EST:** 2013
SALES (est): 4.7MM **Privately Held**
WEB: www.dajaco.com
SIC: 3469 Stamping metal for the trade

(G-2866)
DAJACO INDUSTRIES INC
49715 Leona Dr (48051-2478)
PHONE..................................586 949-1590
James M Ureel, *President*
James Ureel Jr, *President*
Jeffery Ureel, *Vice Pres*
Jeffrey Ureel, *Vice Pres*
Shantel White, *Engineer*
EMP: 56
SQ FT: 55,000
SALES (est): 10.2MM **Privately Held**
WEB: www.dajaco.com
SIC: 3469 3465 Stamping metal for the trade; body parts, automobile: stamped metal

(G-2867)
DANLYN CONTROLS INC
25090 Terra Industrial Dr (48051-2739)
P.O. Box 711, Mount Clemens (48046-0711)
PHONE..................................586 773-6797
James Zimmerman, *President*
EMP: 5 **EST:** 1994
SQ FT: 10,000
SALES (est): 666.3K **Privately Held**
SIC: 3613 Control panels, electric

(G-2868)
DAVALOR MOLD COMPANY LLC
46480 Continental Dr (48047-5206)
PHONE..................................586 598-0100
Frank Palazzolo, *Vice Pres*
Dale Trumble, *VP Opers*
Don Rospierski, *Plant Mgr*
Donald Rospierski, *Plant Mgr*
Ken Carlson, *Mfg Mgr*
EMP: 155 **EST:** 2016
SALES (est): 26.5MM **Privately Held**
WEB: www.davalor.com
SIC: 3089 Injection molding of plastics

(G-2869)
DEGELE MANUFACTURING INC
25700 Dhondt Ct (48051-2600)
PHONE..................................586 949-3550
John Degele, *President*
Mary Louise Degele, *Vice Pres*
EMP: 20 **EST:** 1980
SQ FT: 34,000
SALES (est): 2.3MM **Privately Held**
WEB: www.degelemfg.com
SIC: 3469 Stamping metal for the trade

(G-2870)
DESIGN SERVICES UNLIMITED INC
Also Called: DSU
25754 Dhondt Ct (48051-2600)
PHONE..................................586 463-3225
Craig Marsack, *President*
EMP: 6 **EST:** 1997
SALES (est): 774.1K **Privately Held**
WEB: www.dsumfg.com
SIC: 3541 Machine tools, metal cutting type

(G-2871)
DICO MANUFACTURING LLC
48605 Structural Dr (48051-2666)
PHONE..................................586 731-3008
Diane L Centofanti,
EMP: 4 **EST:** 2006
SALES (est): 830K **Privately Held**
WEB: www.dicomfg.com
SIC: 2891 Laminating compounds

(G-2872)
DYNAMIC PLASTICS INC
29831 Commerce Blvd (48051-1245)
PHONE..................................586 749-6100
Joe Doss, *President*
James Connell, *Vice Pres*
EMP: 23 **EST:** 1993
SQ FT: 13,500
SALES (est): 5.5MM **Privately Held**
WEB: www.dynamicplastics.com
SIC: 3544 Special dies & tools

(G-2873)
E M P MANUFACTURING CORP
28190 23 Mile Rd (48051-2318)
PHONE..................................586 949-8277
Randy Harm, *President*
Kris McClintock, *CFO*
EMP: 10 **EST:** 1981
SQ FT: 14,000
SALES (est): 3MM **Privately Held**
SIC: 3452 Bolts, metal; nuts, metal; screws, metal

(G-2874)
ELLSWORTH CUTTING TOOLS LTD
Also Called: Manufacturing
25190 Terra Industrial Dr (48051-2728)
PHONE..................................586 598-6040
Doug Ellsworth, *Partner*
Janis Baditoi, *Sales Staff*
Ellsworth Miller,
EMP: 17 **EST:** 1980
SALES (est): 2.2MM **Privately Held**
WEB: www.ellsworthtoolsusa.com
SIC: 3545 7699 Cutting tools for machine tools; knife, saw & tool sharpening & repair

(G-2875)
EMHART TEKNOLOGIES LLC
Also Called: Emhart Industries
50501 E Russell Schmidt B (48051-2452)
P.O. Box 868, Mount Clemens (48046-0868)
PHONE..................................586 949-0440
Daniel Lebeau, *Branch Mgr*
EMP: 10
SALES (corp-wide): 14.5B **Publicly Held**
SIC: 3541 Machine tools, metal cutting type
HQ: Emhart Teknologies Llc
 4 Shelter Rock Ln
 Danbury CT 06810
 800 783-6427

(G-2876)
EMHART TEKNOLOGIES LLC
Also Called: Stanley Engineered Fastening
49201 Gratiot Ave (48051-2521)
PHONE..................................800 783-6427
Anna Stayer, *Exec VP*
Gregg Chamberlain, *Vice Pres*
Bill Frederick, *Vice Pres*
Jennifer Ledonne, *Vice Pres*
Colette Bartos, *Opers Staff*
EMP: 17
SALES (corp-wide): 14.5B **Publicly Held**
SIC: 3541 Machine tools, metal cutting type
HQ: Emhart Teknologies Llc
 4 Shelter Rock Ln
 Danbury CT 06810
 800 783-6427

(G-2877)
EXCO EXTRUSION DIES INC
Also Called: Ets Exco Tooling Solutions
56617 N Bay Dr (48051-3746)
PHONE..................................586 749-5400
Bryan Robbins, *CEO*
Bonnie Cartwright, *President*
Mathew Robbins, *COO*
Matt Buchanan, *Plant Mgr*
Glenn Haigh, *Opers Mgr*
▲ **EMP:** 127 **EST:** 1977
SQ FT: 8,000
SALES (est): 38.4MM
SALES (corp-wide): 311.7MM **Privately Held**
WEB: www.etsdies.com
SIC: 3544 Dies, steel rule; special dies & tools
PA: Exco Technologies Limited
 130 Spy Crt Fl 2
 Markham ON L3R 5
 905 477-3065

(G-2878)
EXCO USA
56617 N Bay Dr (48051-3746)
PHONE..................................586 749-5400
Mari-Lynne Moroni, *Controller*
David Mrdjenovic, *Manager*
Marilynne L Moroni, *Manager*
Ben Martinez, *Technical Staff*
EMP: 11 **EST:** 2016
SALES (est): 1.6MM **Privately Held**
WEB: www.etsdies.com
SIC: 3544 Special dies, tools, jigs & fixtures

(G-2879)
FAB CONCEPTS
52826 Turnberry Dr (48051-3656)
PHONE..................................586 466-6411
James Szczesny, *President*
Lisa Szczesny, *Office Mgr*
EMP: 4 **EST:** 1997
SALES (est): 446.5K **Privately Held**
WEB: www.fabconceptsinc.com
SIC: 3312 1751 Structural shapes & pilings, steel; store fixture installation

(G-2880)
FINAZZO TOOL & DIE LLC
56335 Precision Dr (48051-3736)
PHONE..................................586 598-5806
EMP: 9 **EST:** 2008
SALES (est): 118.9K **Privately Held**
WEB: www.finazzotool.com
SIC: 3544 Special dies & tools

(G-2881)
FISHER KELLERING CO
30500 Commerce Blvd (48051-1212)
PHONE..................................586 749-6616
Fax: 586 749-9424
◆ **EMP:** 6
SQ FT: 18,500
SALES: 500K **Privately Held**
SIC: 3544 Mfg Progressive Dies

(G-2882)
FLAGLER CORPORATION
56513 Precision Dr (48051-3736)
PHONE..................................586 749-6300
Harley J Flagler, *President*
Ken Gasko, *Production*
Mary Lou Flagler, *Admin Sec*
EMP: 20 **EST:** 1949
SQ FT: 22,000

Chesterfield - Macomb County (G-2883)

SALES (est): 4.5MM **Privately Held**
WEB: www.flaglercorp.com
SIC: 3542 3544 3549 Sheet metalworking machines; special dies, tools, jigs & fixtures; metalworking machinery

(G-2883)
FLINT HYDROSTATICS INC (HQ)
48175 Gratiot Ave (48051-2604)
PHONE.................................901 794-2462
Shirish Pareek, *CEO*
David Kelley, *VP Opers*
Timm Flint, *CFO*
◆ EMP: 10 EST: 1977
SALES (est): 11.5MM **Privately Held**
WEB: www.hydraulex.com
SIC: 3594 3621 5084 Hydrostatic drives (transmissions); motors & generators; industrial machinery & equipment

(G-2884)
FORMA-KOOL MANUFACTURING INC
46880 Continental Dr (48047-5269)
PHONE.................................586 949-4813
Deanna Males, *President*
EMP: 24 EST: 1980
SQ FT: 18,000
SALES (est): 3.7MM **Privately Held**
SIC: 3585 3442 5078 3564 Refrigeration equipment, complete; metal doors, sash & trim; refrigerators, commercial (reach-in & walk-in); blowers & fans; household refrigerators & freezers

(G-2885)
FOURSLIDES INC
50801 E Rssell Schmidt Bl (48051-2457)
PHONE.................................313 564-5600
George Kofmeister, *President*
EMP: 16 EST: 1947
SQ FT: 44,800
SALES (est): 388.8K **Privately Held**
WEB: www.4slides.net
SIC: 3965 Fasteners

(G-2886)
FREAL FUEL INC
28230 23 Mile Rd (48051-2317)
PHONE.................................248 790-7202
Husam Sami, *Principal*
EMP: 8 EST: 2015
SALES (est): 823.9K **Privately Held**
WEB: www.freal.com
SIC: 2869 Fuels

(G-2887)
GLOBAL ADVANCED PRODUCTS LLC
30707 Commerce Blvd (48051-1231)
PHONE.................................586 749-6800
Ravinder Sandhu, *President*
Bruce Havel,
▲ EMP: 100 EST: 2005
SQ FT: 90,000
SALES (est): 20.9MM
SALES (corp-wide): 34.4MM **Privately Held**
WEB: www.aapincorp.com
SIC: 3469 Stamping metal for the trade
PA: Advanced Assembly Products, Inc.
1300 E 9 Mile Rd
Hazel Park MI 48030
248 543-2427

(G-2888)
GLOBAL ENTERPRISE LIMITED
Also Called: Global Chesterfield
50450 E Rssell Schmidt Bl (48051-2449)
PHONE.................................586 948-4100
Irving Thompson, *Principal*
EMP: 5 EST: 1990
SALES (est): 2.7MM
SALES (corp-wide): 50.5MM **Privately Held**
WEB: www.globalent.org
SIC: 3089 Plastic containers, except foam
PA: Polymerica Limited Company
26909 Woodward Ave
Huntington Woods MI 48070
248 542-2000

(G-2889)
GRACE PRODUCTION SERVICES LLC
52100 Sierra Dr (48047-1309)
PHONE.................................810 643-8070
Gracemary Allen, *CEO*
Leeann Hamilton, *Manager*
EMP: 6
SQ FT: 10,000
SALES (est): 451.7K **Privately Held**
SIC: 3089 Injection molding of plastics

(G-2890)
HERITAGE MFG INC
49787 Leona Dr (48051-2478)
PHONE.................................586 949-7446
Fax: 586 949-6143
EMP: 4
SQ FT: 6,250
SALES: 800K **Privately Held**
SIC: 3599 2821 Mfg Industrial Machinery Mfg Plastic Materials/Resins

(G-2891)
HYDRAULEX INTL HOLDINGS INC (PA)
Also Called: Hydraulex Global
48175 Gratiot Ave (48051-2604)
PHONE.................................914 682-2700
Shirish Pareek, *CEO*
Kevin Leary, *Vice Pres*
Derek Weyand, *Plant Mgr*
John Vanhollenbeck, *Opers Mgr*
Jerry Kolb, *Purchasing*
EMP: 25 EST: 2011
SALES (est): 76.4MM **Privately Held**
WEB: www.hydraulex.com
SIC: 3594 3621 5084 Hydrostatic drives (transmissions); motors & generators; industrial machinery & equipment

(G-2892)
INDEXABLE CUTTER ENGINEERING
Also Called: Ice Tools
50525 Metzen Dr (48051-3137)
PHONE.................................586 598-1540
Bob Lotz, *President*
Wade Dougherty, *Chairman*
EMP: 6 EST: 1995
SQ FT: 3,000
SALES (est): 521.7K **Privately Held**
WEB: www.icetools.net
SIC: 3541 Machine tools, metal cutting type

(G-2893)
INDUSTRIES UNLIMITED INC
49739 Leona Dr (48051-2478)
PHONE.................................586 949-4300
Scott Atchison, *President*
EMP: 17 EST: 1981
SQ FT: 6,500
SALES (est): 1.1MM **Privately Held**
WEB: www.industriesunlimited.com
SIC: 3496 3089 Clips & fasteners, made from purchased wire; injection molding of plastics

(G-2894)
INNOVATIVE TOOL INC
28195 Kehrig St (48047-5218)
PHONE.................................586 329-4922
Jeffrey S Rambow, *CEO*
Brian A Rambow, *President*
Steve Berkley, *Manager*
John Kulcharyk, *Manager*
EMP: 28 EST: 2003
SQ FT: 20,000
SALES (est): 5MM **Privately Held**
WEB: www.innovativetoolinc.com
SIC: 3599 Machine shop, jobbing & repair

(G-2895)
INNOVATIVE WORKS INC
28323 Anchor Dr (48047-5300)
PHONE.................................586 329-1557
Wendy Moran, *President*
Dennis Moran, *Engineer*
▼ EMP: 4 EST: 2007
SALES (est): 635.6K **Privately Held**
WEB: www.iwi-inc.com
SIC: 3599 Machine shop, jobbing & repair

(G-2896)
INOVISION SFTWR SOLUTIONS INC (PA)
50561 Chesterfield Rd (48051-3119)
PHONE.................................586 598-8750
David Treadwell, *President*
Curtis Goff, *President*
Brandon See, *Software Engr*
EMP: 6 EST: 1993
SQ FT: 1,400
SALES (est): 3MM **Privately Held**
SIC: 7373 7372 7371 Systems software development services; systems engineering, computer related; turnkey vendors, computer systems; application computer software; business oriented computer software; computer software development

(G-2897)
J & K INDUSTRIES LLC
28003 Graham Dr (48047-6402)
PHONE.................................586 948-2747
James Michajlyszyn, *Principal*
EMP: 4 EST: 2016
SALES (est): 39.6K **Privately Held**
SIC: 3999 Manufacturing industries

(G-2898)
JAG ENTERPRISES INC ◆
51915 Gratiot Ave (48051-2018)
P.O. Box 637, Richmond (48062-0637)
PHONE.................................586 784-4231
Harry Gann, *President*
EMP: 5 EST: 2021
SALES (est): 300K **Privately Held**
SIC: 3541 Gear cutting & finishing machines

(G-2899)
KALB & ASSOCIATES INC
Also Called: Applied Tech Industries
50271 E Rssell Schmidt Bl (48051-2446)
PHONE.................................586 949-2735
David Kalb, *President*
Michael Holloway, *General Mgr*
Matt Kucel, *Opers Staff*
Donna Holloway, *Office Mgr*
EMP: 40 EST: 2008
SQ FT: 50,000
SALES (est): 4MM **Privately Held**
WEB: www.appliedtechind.com
SIC: 3479 Coating of metals & formed products

(G-2900)
KEHRIG MANUFACTURING COMPANY
28151 William P Rosso Hwy (48047-5246)
PHONE.................................586 949-9610
Donald Kehrig Jr, *President*
Steve Kehrig, *Vice Pres*
EMP: 4 EST: 1943
SQ FT: 13,400
SALES (est): 464.9K **Privately Held**
WEB: www.kehrigmetalfab.com
SIC: 3444 Sheet metal specialties, not stamped

(G-2901)
KENT TOOL AND DIE INC
50605 Richard W Blvd (48051-2493)
P.O. Box 580, New Baltimore (48047-0580)
PHONE.................................586 949-6600
Steve Ellis, *President*
Joseph Duffey, *Corp Secy*
Neil Haske, *Vice Pres*
Patricia Graf, *CTO*
EMP: 29 EST: 1966
SQ FT: 34,000
SALES (est): 878.9K **Privately Held**
WEB: www.kentdie.com
SIC: 3544 Special dies & tools

(G-2902)
KIMASTLE CORPORATION
Also Called: Dager Systems
28291 Kehrig St (48047-5248)
PHONE.................................586 949-2355
Kirk Gilewski, *President*
Steven Gilewski, *Vice Pres*
Chris Zobl, *Engineer*
Mark Oliver, *Design Engr*
Scott West, *Sales Engr*
EMP: 82 EST: 1980
SQ FT: 17,000

SALES (est): 17.8MM **Privately Held**
WEB: www.kimastle.com
SIC: 3559 3544 Degreasing machines, automotive & industrial; special dies, tools, jigs & fixtures

(G-2903)
KNIGHT CARBIDE INC
48665 Structural Dr (48051-2666)
PHONE.................................586 598-4888
Bruce Kyle, *President*
Chris Kyle, *Vice Pres*
Jack Kroll, *Purchasing*
Teresa Rylee, *Human Resources*
John Hoh, *Sales Staff*
EMP: 46 EST: 1972
SQ FT: 24,000
SALES (est): 10.8MM **Privately Held**
WEB: www.knightcarbide.com
SIC: 3545 Tools & accessories for machine tools; cutting tools for machine tools

(G-2904)
KRAFTS & THINGZ
51382 Village Edge N (48047-3518)
PHONE.................................810 689-2457
EMP: 4
SALES (est): 226.5K **Privately Held**
SIC: 2022 Mfg Cheese

(G-2905)
LOFTIS MANUFACTURING INC
30103 Commerce Blvd (48051-1242)
PHONE.................................855 564-8665
EMP: 4 EST: 2020
SALES (est): 68.7K **Privately Held**
WEB: www.loftismfginc.com
SIC: 3999 Manufacturing industries

(G-2906)
M & W MANUFACTURING CO LLC
Also Called: M & W Tubing
46409 Continental Dr (48051-5251)
PHONE.................................586 741-8897
Ronald Misch, *General Mgr*
Dave Misch, *Vice Pres*
Robin Misch, *Vice Pres*
Jon Misch, *Mfg Staff*
EMP: 11 EST: 2015
SALES (est): 1.2MM **Privately Held**
WEB: www.mwmfg.co
SIC: 3317 Steel pipe & tubes

(G-2907)
MACOMB 4X4 LLC
28145 Kehrig St (48047-5218)
PHONE.................................586 744-0335
William A Walters, *Principal*
EMP: 4 EST: 2018
SALES (est): 121.4K **Privately Held**
WEB: www.macomb-4x4.business.site
SIC: 2711 Newspapers, publishing & printing

(G-2908)
MAYNARD L MACLEAN L C
50855 E Russell Schmidt (48047-2457)
PHONE.................................586 949-0471
Tim Taylor,
Greg Lasonde,
Robert B Loebs,
Frank Ruprich,
◆ EMP: 77 EST: 1964
SQ FT: 52,000
SALES (est): 14MM
SALES (corp-wide): 1.1B **Privately Held**
WEB: www.macleanfogg.com
SIC: 3452 3451 Screws, metal; bolts, metal; nuts, metal; screw machine products
PA: Mac Lean-Fogg Company
1000 Allanson Rd
Mundelein IL 60060
847 566-0010

(G-2909)
MERCURY PRODUCTS CORP
30707 Commerce Blvd (48051-1231)
PHONE.................................586 749-6800
Tom Chuminatto, *Vice Pres*
EMP: 11 EST: 1946
SALES (est): 257.9K **Privately Held**
SIC: 3469 Metal stampings

▲ = Import ▼ = Export
◆ = Import/Export

GEOGRAPHIC SECTION
Chesterfield - Macomb County (G-2939)

(G-2910)
METAL FORMING TECHNOLOGY INC
48630 Structural Dr (48051-2665)
PHONE.................586 949-4586
Fred Guimaraes, *CEO*
Andrea Spagnoli, *Plant Mgr*
Paolo Stasi, *Controller*
▲ **EMP:** 10 **EST:** 2006
SQ FT: 30,000
SALES (est): 2.3MM
SALES (corp-wide): 126.9K **Privately Held**
WEB: www.mftbrass.com
SIC: 3462 Iron & steel forgings
HQ: Gnutti Cirillo Spa
Via Ruca 96
Lumezzane BS 25065
030 892-8511

(G-2911)
METALBUILT LLC
50171 E Rssell Schmidt Bl (48051-2444)
PHONE.................586 786-9106
Ronald McCormick, *Mng Member*
EMP: 30 **EST:** 2007
SALES (est): 6.1MM **Privately Held**
WEB: www.metalbuilt.com
SIC: 3441 Fabricated structural metal

(G-2912)
METARIS HYDRAULICS
48175 Gratiot Ave (48051-2604)
PHONE.................586 949-4240
EMP: 6 **EST:** 2016
SALES (est): 174.7K **Privately Held**
SIC: 3594 5084 Fluid power pumps & motors; industrial machinery & equipment

(G-2913)
MICHIGAN METAL TECH INC
50250 E Russell Schmidt (48051-2445)
P.O. Box 85367, Westland (48185-0367)
PHONE.................586 598-7800
EMP: 23
SALES (corp-wide): 4.5MM **Privately Held**
SIC: 3544 Mfg Industrial Metal Molds
PA: Michigan Metal Technologies, Inc.
50320 E Russell Schmdt Bl
Chesterfield MI

(G-2914)
MODULATED METALS INC
56409 Precision Dr (48051-3736)
PHONE.................586 749-8400
James C Stelzer, *President*
Frank S Campo, *Vice Pres*
Jacqueline M Campo, *Treasurer*
Jacqueline Campo, *Info Tech Mgr*
Geraldine G Stelzer, *Admin Sec*
EMP: 14 **EST:** 1981
SQ FT: 13,400
SALES (est): 3.3MM **Privately Held**
WEB: www.modulatedmetals.com
SIC: 3444 Sheet metal specialties, not stamped

(G-2915)
MOTOR CITY STAMPINGS INC (PA)
47783 Gratiot Ave (48051-2721)
PHONE.................586 949-8420
Judith Kucway, *CEO*
Roger Kucway, *Vice Pres*
Bob Ritter, *Plant Mgr*
Steve Saunders, *Plant Mgr*
Beverly Hinton, *Opers Mgr*
▲ **EMP:** 328 **EST:** 1969
SQ FT: 225,000
SALES (est): 44.7MM **Privately Held**
WEB: www.mcstamp.com
SIC: 3465 3544 Body parts, automobile: stamped metal; special dies, tools, jigs & fixtures

(G-2916)
OAKLAND WELDING INDUSTRIES
28162 23 Mile Rd (48051-2318)
P.O. Box 732, New Baltimore (48047-0732)
PHONE.................586 949-4090
David M Prudhomme, *President*
Michael Prudhomme, *Vice Pres*
Gary Prudhomme, *Treasurer*
Lawrence Prudhomme, *Shareholder*
Richard M Prudhomme, *Admin Sec*
EMP: 20 **EST:** 1961
SALES (est): 2.5MM **Privately Held**
WEB: www.oaklandweldingindustries.com
SIC: 3567 3532 3443 Industrial furnaces & ovens; mining machinery; sheet metalwork; fabricated plate work (boiler shop); fabricated structural metal; blast furnaces & steel mills

(G-2917)
OFF SITE MFG TECH INC (PA)
50350 E Rssell Schmidt Bl (48051-2447)
PHONE.................586 598-3110
Michael C Wallace, *President*
▲ **EMP:** 68 **EST:** 1992
SALES (est): 11.9MM **Privately Held**
WEB: www.offsitemfg.com
SIC: 3713 Truck bodies & parts

(G-2918)
OFFSITE MANUFACTURING INC
Also Called: Off Site Manufacturing Tech
750 Structural Dr (48051)
PHONE.................586 598-8850
Michael C Wallace, *President*
EMP: 7 **Privately Held**
WEB: www.offsitemfg.com
SIC: 3714 Motor vehicle parts & accessories
PA: Off Site Manufacturing Technologies, Inc.
50350 E Rssell Schmidt Bl
Chesterfield MI 48051

(G-2919)
OGURA CORPORATION
55025 Gratiot Ave (48051-1249)
PHONE.................586 749-1900
Yasahiro Ogura, *Ch of Bd*
Masayoshi Takahashi, *Vice Ch Bd*
Hisashi Ukita, *President*
Keith Bentler, *Purchasing*
Robey Ledford, *Engineer*
▲ **EMP:** 105 **EST:** 1988
SQ FT: 111,000
SALES (est): 24.6MM **Privately Held**
WEB: www.oguracorp.com
SIC: 3714 5013 Clutches, motor vehicle; clutches
PA: Ogura Clutch Co., Ltd.
2-678, Aioicho
Kiryu GNM 376-0

(G-2920)
OTH CONSULTANTS INC
Also Called: Davalor Mold
46480 Continental Dr (48047-5206)
PHONE.................586 598-0100
James Puscas, *CEO*
Orman L Bernhardt, *Treasurer*
EMP: 200 **EST:** 1979
SQ FT: 100,000
SALES (est): 13.5MM **Privately Held**
SIC: 3089 Injection molding of plastics

(G-2921)
P D E SYSTEMS INC
37230 26 Mile Rd (48047-2909)
PHONE.................586 725-3330
Paul Painter, *President*
Donna M Painter, *Treasurer*
EMP: 11 **EST:** 2012
SALES (est): 645.1K **Privately Held**
WEB: www.pdesystems.com
SIC: 3599 Custom machinery

(G-2922)
PATRIOT BARS MFG LLC
51568 Stern Ln (48051-2346)
PHONE.................248 342-3319
Stephen Bertoncello, *Administration*
EMP: 4 **EST:** 2019
SALES (est): 43.6K **Privately Held**
SIC: 3999 Manufacturing industries

(G-2923)
PEDRI MOLD INC
46429 Continental Dr (48047-5251)
PHONE.................586 598-0882
Ernest Pedri, *President*
Ernest Pedri Jr, *Vice Pres*
Raymond Pedri, *Vice Pres*
EMP: 8 **EST:** 1991
SQ FT: 5,300
SALES (est): 765K **Privately Held**
SIC: 3544 Industrial molds

(G-2924)
PFG ENTERPRISES INC (PA)
Also Called: Bellevue Processing
50271 E Rssell Smith Blvd (48051)
PHONE.................586 755-1053
Kenneth Pape, *CEO*
Fred Pape, *President*
Sandra Pape, *Admin Sec*
EMP: 40 **EST:** 1999
SQ FT: 50,000
SALES (est): 27.3MM **Privately Held**
SIC: 3471 Cleaning, polishing & finishing

(G-2925)
PIN POINT WELDING INC
50505 Metzen Dr (48051-3137)
PHONE.................586 598-7382
Terry Yadon, *President*
Kim Yadon, *Corp Secy*
EMP: 4 **EST:** 1986
SQ FT: 2,400
SALES (est): 240K **Privately Held**
SIC: 7692 Welding repair

(G-2926)
POSEIDON INDUSTRIES INC
25700 Dhondt Ct (48051-2600)
PHONE.................586 949-3550
John Degele, *President*
Mary Degele, *Treasurer*
EMP: 7 **EST:** 1969
SQ FT: 12,000
SALES (est): 716.7K **Privately Held**
SIC: 3544 Special dies, tools, jigs & fixtures

(G-2927)
POWDER IT INC
46070 Edgewater St (48047-5325)
PHONE.................586 949-0395
Michael Ursem, *President*
EMP: 5 **EST:** 2000
SALES (est): 171.2K **Privately Held**
SIC: 2399 Powder puffs & mitts

(G-2928)
PRISM PLASTICS INC (DH)
52111 Sierra Dr (48047-1309)
PHONE.................810 292-6300
Brian Diaz, *President*
Rodney Bricker, *President*
Jeff Wolf, *Treasurer*
EMP: 12 **EST:** 1999
SQ FT: 28,000
SALES (est): 64.9MM
SALES (corp-wide): 245.5B **Publicly Held**
WEB: www.prismplastics.com
SIC: 3089 Injection molding of plastics
HQ: Marmon Engineered Components Company
181 W Madison St Fl 26
Chicago IL 60602
312 372-9500

(G-2929)
PRO TOOL & DIE LLC
25777 Dhondt Ct (48051-2601)
PHONE.................586 840-7040
Charles Johnson, *President*
EMP: 5 **EST:** 2015
SALES (est): 109.9K **Privately Held**
SIC: 3448 Prefabricated metal buildings

(G-2930)
PROBE-TEC
48454 Harbor Dr (48047-3469)
PHONE.................765 252-0257
Tom Houck, *Principal*
EMP: 4 **EST:** 2010
SALES (est): 300K **Privately Held**
WEB: www.probe-tec.com
SIC: 3429 Manufactured hardware (general)

(G-2931)
PROFILE MFG INC
50790 Richard W Blvd (48051-2496)
PHONE.................586 598-0007
James Gall, *President*
EMP: 30 **EST:** 1990
SQ FT: 30,000
SALES (est): 6.4MM **Privately Held**
WEB: www.profilemfg.com
SIC: 3089 Injection molding of plastics

(G-2932)
PROGRESSIVE FINISHING INC
50800 E Rssell Schmidt Bl (48051-2456)
PHONE.................586 949-6961
Paul R Hinderliter, *President*
Paul Hinderliter, *President*
Michael Stornant, *Mfg Mgr*
Mike Stornant, *Mfg Mgr*
Sandy Scott, *QC Mgr*
EMP: 23 **EST:** 1992
SQ FT: 42,000
SALES (est): 1.2MM **Privately Held**
WEB: www.progressivefinishinginc.com
SIC: 3599 Machine shop, jobbing & repair

(G-2933)
PROTOTECH LASER INC
Also Called: Plant 2
46340 Continental Dr (48047-5255)
PHONE.................586 948-3032
Mike Williams, *Branch Mgr*
EMP: 12 **Privately Held**
WEB: www.ptlaser.com
SIC: 3714 Motor vehicle parts & accessories
PA: Prototech Laser, Inc.
46340 Continental Dr
Chesterfield MI 48047

(G-2934)
PROTOTECH LASER INC (PA)
46340 Continental Dr (48047-5255)
PHONE.................586 598-6900
Ed Genord, *President*
Lori Williams, *Bookkeeper*
Dave Mayle, *Manager*
Larry Hallesy, *Supervisor*
EMP: 30 **EST:** 1990
SQ FT: 47,000
SALES (est): 5.5MM **Privately Held**
WEB: www.ptlaser.com
SIC: 3599 3444 3499 Machine shop, jobbing & repair; forming machine work, sheet metal; machine bases, metal

(G-2935)
QUALITY LUBE EXPRESS INC
50900 Donner Rd (48047-1753)
PHONE.................586 421-0600
Prab Putta, *Principal*
EMP: 9 **EST:** 2005
SALES (est): 457.5K **Privately Held**
WEB: www.prestonautorepair.com
SIC: 2992 Lubricating oils

(G-2936)
R C GRINDING AND TOOL COMPANY
49669 Leona Dr (48051-2476)
PHONE.................586 949-4373
Robert E Collinge, *President*
EMP: 6 **EST:** 1973
SQ FT: 6,000
SALES (est): 472.3K **Privately Held**
WEB: www.rcgrindingtoolcompany.tripod.com
SIC: 3599 Machine shop, jobbing & repair

(G-2937)
RAINBOW WRAP
46440 Jefferson Ave (48047-5365)
PHONE.................586 949-3976
Thomas Svoboda, *Owner*
EMP: 10 **EST:** 2001
SALES (est): 399.5K **Privately Held**
SIC: 2754 Wrapper & seal printing, gravure

(G-2938)
RESINS UNLIMITED LLC
52438 Silent Ridge Dr (48051-1986)
PHONE.................586 725-6873
Brent Cymbalski,
EMP: 8 **EST:** 2003
SALES (est): 576.7K **Privately Held**
WEB: www.resinsunlimited.com
SIC: 2821 Plastics materials & resins

(G-2939)
RICHMOND STEEL INC
50570 E Rssell Schmidt Bl (48051-2451)
PHONE.................586 948-4700
Christopher M Austin, *President*

Chesterfield - Macomb County (G-2940)

Krista McLaughlin, *General Mgr*
EMP: 26 **EST:** 1994
SQ FT: 28,000
SALES (est): 5.4MM **Privately Held**
WEB: www.richmondsteel.biz
SIC: 3353 Aluminum sheet, plate & foil

(G-2940)
ROCKTECH SYSTEMS LLC
50250 E Russell Schmidt (48051-2445)
PHONE.................................586 330-9031
John Stolz, *General Mgr*
Christopher Pierik, *QC Mgr*
John Griffith, *Project Engr*
Steve Pierik, *Mng Member*
Kristina Johnston, *Executive*
EMP: 50 **EST:** 2011
SALES (est): 10MM **Privately Held**
WEB: www.rocktech.com
SIC: 3089 Automotive parts, plastic

(G-2941)
RS PRODUCTS LLC
53416 Christy Dr (48051-1537)
P.O. Box 480545, New Haven (48048-0545)
PHONE.................................801 722-9746
Scot Hoskisson, *President*
EMP: 5 **EST:** 2011
SALES (est): 299.8K **Privately Held**
SIC: 3827 7699 3484 Gun sights, optical; gun parts made to individual order; guns (firearms) or gun parts, 30 mm. & below

(G-2942)
S & P FABRICATING INC
25201 Terra Industrial Dr A (48051-2772)
PHONE.................................586 421-1950
Richard Scullion, *Principal*
EMP: 8 **EST:** 2005
SALES (est): 738.9K **Privately Held**
WEB: www.spsteelfab.net
SIC: 3441 Fabricated structural metal

(G-2943)
S A S
33614 Lakeview St (48047-3486)
PHONE.................................586 725-6381
Thomas Yaschen, *Principal*
EMP: 5 **EST:** 2009
SALES (est): 122.9K **Privately Held**
SIC: 3131 Footwear cut stock

(G-2944)
SABRE-TEC INC
48705 Structural Dr (48051-2664)
PHONE.................................586 949-5386
Jose Villalobos, *President*
David Gault, *Vice Pres*
EMP: 15 **EST:** 1980
SQ FT: 16,000
SALES (est): 1.8MM **Privately Held**
SIC: 3599 Machine shop, jobbing & repair

(G-2945)
SAFIE SPECIALTY FOODS CO INC
25565 Terra Industrial Dr (48051-2734)
P.O. Box 46333, Mount Clemens (48046-6333)
PHONE.................................586 598-8282
Mary D Safie, *President*
EMP: 50 **EST:** 1994
SQ FT: 22,000
SALES (est): 8.6MM **Privately Held**
WEB: www.safiefoods.com
SIC: 2099 Food preparations

(G-2946)
SCHALLER CORPORATION (PA)
Also Called: Schaller Group
49495 Gratiot Ave (48051-2523)
PHONE.................................586 949-6000
Robert Schaller, *President*
Michael Evans, *General Mgr*
Albert Schaller, *Chairman*
Justin C Schaller, *Corp Secy*
Roger L Schaller, *Exec VP*
EMP: 110 **EST:** 1982
SQ FT: 92,000
SALES (est): 42.7MM **Privately Held**
WEB: www.schallergroup.com
SIC: 3469 Stamping metal for the trade

(G-2947)
SCHALLER TOOL & DIE CO
49505 Gratiot Ave (48051-2525)
PHONE.................................586 949-5500
Steven G Shaller, *President*
Steven Schaller, *President*
Albert L Schaller, *Vice Pres*
Roger L Schaller, *Treasurer*
Michele Guilbault, *Accountant*
EMP: 34 **EST:** 1945
SQ FT: 28,000
SALES (est): 742.3K **Privately Held**
WEB: www.schallergroup.com
SIC: 3544 3599 3545 Special dies & tools; jigs & fixtures; custom machinery; machine tool accessories

(G-2948)
SL HOLDINGS INC
Also Called: Protective Land & Sea Systems
50625 Richard W Blvd (48051-2493)
PHONE.................................586 949-0912
Rhonda Wendland, *President*
EMP: 23 **EST:** 1993
SALES (est): 449.1K **Privately Held**
SIC: 3441 Fabricated structural metal

(G-2949)
SONRIZE LLC
48051 Book Ct (48047-2252)
PHONE.................................586 329-3225
Charles Pope, *President*
EMP: 4 **EST:** 2010
SALES (est): 302K **Privately Held**
SIC: 3648 Lighting equipment

(G-2950)
STELMATIC INDUSTRIES INC
50575 Richard W Blvd (48051-2487)
PHONE.................................586 949-0160
Edward K Stelzer, *President*
Marjorie Stelzer, *Corp Secy*
EMP: 10 **EST:** 1962
SQ FT: 20,000
SALES (est): 1.7MM **Privately Held**
WEB: www.stelmaticind.com
SIC: 3444 Sheet metal specialties, not stamped

(G-2951)
SUR-FORM LLC
50320 E Rssell Schmidt Bl (48051-2447)
PHONE.................................586 221-1950
EMP: 41
SQ FT: 30,000
SALES (est): 2.1MM
SALES (corp-wide): 240.4MM **Publicly Held**
SIC: 3089 Mfg Plastic Products
HQ: Big 3 Precision Products, Inc.
  2923 S Wabash Ave
  Centralia IL 62801
  618 533-3251

(G-2952)
SUREFIT PARTS LLC
50400 Patricia St (48051-2481)
PHONE.................................586 416-9150
Ronald Devriendt,
EMP: 4 **EST:** 2020
SALES (est): 54.5K **Privately Held**
SIC: 3524 Lawn & garden equipment

(G-2953)
TACHYON CORPORATION
48705 Gratiot Ave (48051-2614)
PHONE.................................586 598-4320
David Nicholas, *President*
Gregory Mitchell, *Vice Pres*
Kenneth Young, *Treasurer*
Barry Thorp, *Admin Sec*
EMP: 11 **EST:** 1990
SQ FT: 3,000
SALES (est): 577.6K **Privately Held**
WEB: www.tachyonjobs.com
SIC: 1796 3625 Machinery installation; electric controls & control accessories, industrial

(G-2954)
TECHNICAL STAMPING INC
50600 E Russell Schmidt (48051-2453)
PHONE.................................586 948-3285
Timothy Schaffner, *President*
Larry Laporte, *Vice Pres*
EMP: 5 **EST:** 1988
SQ FT: 7,000
SALES (est): 683.6K **Privately Held**
WEB: www.technicalstamping.net
SIC: 3469 Stamping metal for the trade

(G-2955)
THEUT PRODUCTS INC
47875 Gratiot Ave (48051-2722)
PHONE.................................586 949-1300
Eric Theut, *Manager*
EMP: 7
SALES (corp-wide): 15.7MM **Privately Held**
WEB: www.theutproductsinc.com
SIC: 3273 Ready-mixed concrete
PA: Theut Products, Inc.
  73408 Van Dyke Rd
  Bruce Twp MI 48065
  586 752-4541

(G-2956)
TI GROUP AUTO SYSTEMS LLC
Also Called: TI Automotive Systems
30600 Commerce Blvd (48051-1228)
PHONE.................................586 948-6006
Charlie Cronenworth, *Manager*
EMP: 7
SALES (corp-wide): 3.3B **Privately Held**
WEB: www.tifluidsystems.com
SIC: 3714 3643 3429 Motor vehicle parts & accessories; current-carrying wiring devices; manufactured hardware (general)
HQ: Ti Group Automotive Systems, Llc
  2020 Taylor Rd
  Auburn Hills MI 48326
  248 296-8000

(G-2957)
TOOL COMPANY INC
48707 Gratiot Ave (48051-2614)
PHONE.................................586 598-1519
Don Artman, *President*
EMP: 6 **EST:** 1995
SQ FT: 5,000
SALES (est): 488.8K **Privately Held**
WEB: www.toolco.com
SIC: 3544 Special dies & tools

(G-2958)
TRI-TOOL BORING MACHINE CO
46440 Continental Dr (48047-5206)
PHONE.................................586 598-0036
Salvatore Riera, *President*
EMP: 15 **EST:** 1977
SQ FT: 8,500
SALES (est): 1.3MM **Privately Held**
WEB: www.tri-tool.com
SIC: 3599 Machine shop, jobbing & repair

(G-2959)
TROY TUBE & MANUFACTURING CO
50100 E Russell Schmidt B (48051-2443)
P.O. Box 696, New Baltimore (48047-0696)
PHONE.................................586 949-8700
John Maniaci, *President*
Joe M Maniaci, *Plant Mgr*
Dan Cutshaw, *Mfg Mgr*
Carlos Folino, *QC Mgr*
Fabio Folino, *Manager*
EMP: 100 **EST:** 1978
SQ FT: 70,000
SALES (est): 17.2MM **Privately Held**
WEB: www.troytube.com
SIC: 3498 7692 Tube fabricating (contract bending & shaping); welding repair

(G-2960)
UNITED MFG NETWRK INC
33717 Embassy St (48047-2064)
PHONE.................................586 321-7887
Gerald Sitek, *Vice Pres*
Jerry Sitek, *CFO*
EMP: 9 **EST:** 2013
SALES (est): 237.1K **Privately Held**
WEB: www.umninc.com
SIC: 3541 3999 Grinding machines, metalworking; custom pulverizing & grinding of plastic materials

(G-2961)
UTICA AEROSPACE INC
26950 23 Mile Rd (48051-1999)
PHONE.................................586 598-9300
Kathy Phillips, *Principal*
EMP: 10 **EST:** 2014
SALES (est): 778.6K **Privately Held**
SIC: 3812 Acceleration indicators & systems components, aerospace

(G-2962)
UTICA STEEL INC
48000 Structural Dr (48051-2629)
PHONE.................................586 949-1900
David Kraemer, *President*
Charles Lafontaine, *Vice Pres*
Ray Mach, *Vice Pres*
Chuck Lafontaine, *Plant Mgr*
Sherry Dawson, *Treasurer*
EMP: 75
SQ FT: 75,000
SALES (est): 26MM **Privately Held**
WEB: www.uticasteelinc.com
SIC: 3441 Fabricated structural metal

(G-2963)
VERSTAR GROUP INC (PA)
Also Called: Accurate Tooling Solutions
50305 Patricia St (48051-3803)
PHONE.................................586 465-5033
Derek Starks, *President*
David Hale, *QC Mgr*
Craig Beauvais, *Manager*
EMP: 16 **EST:** 1976
SALES (est): 4.9MM **Privately Held**
WEB: www.accuratewelding.us
SIC: 7692 Welding repair

(G-2964)
VISIONCRAFT
28161 Kehrig St (48047-5218)
PHONE.................................586 949-6540
Nick Sorvala, *Administration*
EMP: 5 **EST:** 2008
SALES (est): 659.9K **Privately Held**
SIC: 5048 3827 Optometric equipment & supplies; optical instruments & lenses

(G-2965)
WELDERS & PRESSES INC
27295 Luckino Dr (48047-5229)
PHONE.................................586 948-4300
EMP: 5
SALES (est): 264.5K **Privately Held**
SIC: 7692 Welding Repair

(G-2966)
Z MOLD & ENGINEERING INC
46390 Continental Dr (48047-5255)
PHONE.................................586 948-5000
Konrad Zuschlag, *President*
Sheryl Zuschlag, *Vice Pres*
EMP: 8 **EST:** 2006
SQ FT: 7,500
SALES (est): 1.8MM **Privately Held**
WEB: www.zmold.com
SIC: 3544 Industrial molds

(G-2967)
ZERILLI & SESI LLC
Also Called: Hydro Pros Indoor Garden Sup
30504 23 Mile Rd (48047-1845)
PHONE.................................586 741-8805
Sean Zerilli, *Principal*
Hansee Sesi,
EMP: 6 **EST:** 2009
SALES (est): 78K **Privately Held**
SIC: 3999 Hydroponic equipment

China
St. Clair County

(G-2968)
ANTOLIN ST CLAIR LLC
4662 Puttygut Rd (48054-2109)
PHONE.................................810 329-1045
Jeff Long, *Accounts Mgr*
Mark Wilsdon,
Ana Raquel Heredia,
EMP: 240 **EST:** 2020
SALES (est): 47.1MM
SALES (corp-wide): 2.6MM **Privately Held**
WEB: www.grupoantolin.com
SIC: 3089 Automotive parts, plastic
HQ: Grupo Antolin North America, Inc.
  1700 Atlantic Blvd
  Auburn Hills MI 48326
  248 373-1749

GEOGRAPHIC SECTION
Clare - Clare County (G-2998)

(G-2969)
BEWITCHING STITCHNG EMBROIDERY
4051 Starville Rd (48054-2313)
PHONE 810 289-3978
James Darga, *Principal*
EMP: 5 **EST:** 2016
SALES (est): 31.2K Privately Held
SIC: 2395 Embroidery & art needlework

(G-2970)
J G WELDING & MAINTENANCE INC
7059 Lindsey Rd (48054-2304)
PHONE 586 758-0150
Julius Gaffke, *President*
EMP: 4 **EST:** 1978
SQ FT: 6,000
SALES (est): 244.1K Privately Held
SIC: 7692 Welding repair

Clare
Clare County

(G-2971)
1ST RATE OFFICE SOLUTIONS LLC
1395 N Mcewan St (48617-1111)
PHONE 989 544-4009
John Sheets, *President*
EMP: 4 **EST:** 2015
SALES (est): 271.2K Privately Held
WEB: www.1strateoffice.com
SIC: 3589 Servicing machines, except dry cleaning, laundry: coin-oper.

(G-2972)
ADVANCED BATTERY CONCEPTS LLC
8 Consumers Energy Pkwy (48617-9540)
PHONE 989 424-6645
Edward O Shaffer II, *CEO*
David Barrie, *Ch of Bd*
Ronald Beebe, *Vice Chairman*
Michael Everett, *COO*
Gerald Mullis, *COO*
▲ **EMP:** 44 **EST:** 2008
SALES (est): 4.8MM Privately Held
WEB: www.advancedbatteryconcepts.com
SIC: 3691 Storage batteries

(G-2973)
ATHEY PRECISION INC
2021 S Athey Ave (48617-9776)
PHONE 989 386-4523
John Pirosko, *President*
Regina Pirosko, *Admin Sec*
EMP: 9 **EST:** 1983
SQ FT: 6,000
SALES (est): 833.4K Privately Held
WEB: www.atheyprecision.com
SIC: 3544 Special dies & tools

(G-2974)
BURNRITE PELLET CORPORATION
2495 E Rock Rd (48617-9424)
PHONE 989 429-1067
James Swan, *President*
Mark Ghile, *Vice Pres*
Jim Eckman, *Treasurer*
Tim Walker, *Shareholder*
EMP: 5 **EST:** 2006
SQ FT: 800
SALES (est): 500K Privately Held
SIC: 2448 Pallets, wood

(G-2975)
CLARE COUNTY REVIEW
105 W 4th St Ste 1 (48617-1458)
PHONE 989 386-4414
Patricia Maurer, *Owner*
Sherry Landon, *Graphic Designe*
Pat Maurer, *Correspondent*
EMP: 5 **EST:** 1991 Privately Held
WEB: www.wilcoxnewspapers.com
SIC: 2711 Newspapers, publishing & printing

(G-2976)
CLARE PRINT & PULP
409 N Mcewan St (48617-1402)
PHONE 989 386-3497
Pete Montini, *Owner*
EMP: 4 **EST:** 1975
SQ FT: 1,600
SALES (est): 296.8K Privately Held
WEB: www.clareprintandpulp.logomall.com
SIC: 5943 2752 5044 Office forms & supplies; lithographing on metal; office equipment

(G-2977)
DYNA- BIGNELL PRODUCTS LLC
201 W 3rd St (48617-1408)
PHONE 989 418-5050
EMP: 6 **EST:** 2016
SALES (est): 508.8K Privately Held
WEB: www.dynabignell.com
SIC: 3541 Machine tools, metal cutting type

(G-2978)
E & M CORES INC
Also Called: E and M Cores
9805 S Athey Ave (48617-9688)
PHONE 989 386-9223
Jeff Thomski, *Owner*
EMP: 4 **EST:** 2000
SALES (est): 247.1K Privately Held
SIC: 2655 3321 3272 Fiber cans, drums & similar products; gray & ductile iron foundries; concrete products

(G-2979)
FILCON INC
528 Pioneer Pkwy (48617-8812)
PHONE 989 386-2986
Nathan Rogers, *President*
Wesley Parker, *Corp Secy*
David Rogers, *Director*
▲ **EMP:** 10 **EST:** 1993
SALES (est): 2.1MM
SALES (corp-wide): 6MM Privately Held
WEB: www.filcon.com
SIC: 2671 3089 3081 Plastic film, coated or laminated for packaging; plastic processing; unsupported plastics film & sheet
PA: Rogers Group, Inc.
528 Pioneer Pkwy
Clare MI 48617
989 386-7393

(G-2980)
GREEN GABLES SAW MILL
5605 E Surrey Rd (48617-9793)
PHONE 989 386-7846
Andrew Byler, *Principal*
EMP: 5 **EST:** 2007
SALES (est): 106K Privately Held
SIC: 2421 Sawmills & planing mills, general

(G-2981)
INTEGRITY MACHINE SERVICES
Also Called: IMS
5615 S Clare Ave (48617-8608)
PHONE 989 386-0216
Larry Kleinhardt, *President*
Travis Wezensky, *Engineer*
Jason Manderbach, *Manager*
Judy Kleinhardt, *Admin Sec*
EMP: 7 **EST:** 1992
SALES (est): 590K Privately Held
WEB: www.imsmachines.net
SIC: 3599 Machine shop, jobbing & repair

(G-2982)
JD METALWORKS INC
635 Industrial Dr (48617-9225)
PHONE 989 386-3231
Duane Gottsclark, *President*
John Miller, *Founder*
Joe Haley, *Prdtn Mgr*
Jennifer Crystal, *Human Resources*
Wendy Wixson, *Services*
EMP: 70 **EST:** 1999
SQ FT: 30,000
SALES (est): 13.7MM Privately Held
WEB: www.jdmetalworks.com
SIC: 7692 Welding repair

(G-2983)
JT BAKERS
127 W 4th St Ste 2 (48617-1410)
PHONE 989 424-5102
EMP: 4 **EST:** 2011
SALES (est): 179.4K Privately Held
SIC: 2051 Bakery: wholesale or wholesale/retail combined

(G-2984)
KTR PRINTING INC
Also Called: Integrity Printing
801 Industrial Dr (48617-9140)
P.O. Box 809 (48617-0809)
PHONE 989 386-9740
Dale Smith, *President*
Kirk Smith, *Vice Pres*
Joe Mooney, *Opers Staff*
Emily Komperda, *Office Mgr*
▲ **EMP:** 15 **EST:** 1983
SQ FT: 29,000
SALES (est): 4MM Privately Held
WEB: www.integrityprinting.com
SIC: 2752 Commercial printing, offset

(G-2985)
LETHERER TRUSS INC (PA)
851 Industrial Dr (48617-9140)
PHONE 989 386-4999
Steven C Letherer, *President*
Steve Letherer, *Founder*
Bernard C Letherer, *Corp Secy*
Mary Rogers, *Office Mgr*
Christena Gotts, *Admin Sec*
EMP: 54 **EST:** 1984
SQ FT: 19,600
SALES (est): 7.6MM Privately Held
WEB: www.letherer.com
SIC: 2439 Trusses, except roof: laminated lumber; trusses, wooden roof

(G-2986)
MID-MICHIGAN INDUSTRIES INC
Also Called: Mid Michigan Industries
790 Industrial Dr (48617-9224)
PHONE 989 386-7707
Jori Coster, *Human Res Dir*
Chris Zeigler, *Manager*
EMP: 25
SALES (corp-wide): 5.1MM Privately Held
WEB: www.mmionline.com
SIC: 8331 3471 2396 Vocational training agency; plating & polishing; automotive & apparel trimmings
PA: Mid-Michigan Industries, Inc.
2426 Parkway Dr
Mount Pleasant MI 48858
989 773-6918

(G-2987)
MILLERS WOODWORKING
3378 E Beaverton Rd (48617-9430)
PHONE 989 386-8110
Mettie Miller, *Owner*
EMP: 6 **EST:** 1996
SALES (est): 334.6K Privately Held
SIC: 2449 Wood containers

(G-2988)
NATURAL WAY CHEESE
6060 E Beaverton Rd (48617-9653)
PHONE 989 935-9380
EMP: 4 **EST:** 2019
SALES (est): 136.8K Privately Held
SIC: 2022 Natural cheese

(G-2989)
NEVILL SUPPLY INCORPORATED
8415 S Eberhart Ave (48617-9736)
PHONE 989 386-4522
Donald Nevill, *President*
Andrew Nevill, *Vice Pres*
EMP: 9 **EST:** 1989
SQ FT: 5,000
SALES (est): 2.3MM Privately Held
WEB: www.nevillfencesupply.net
SIC: 5211 1799 2499 Fencing; fence construction; snow fence, wood

(G-2990)
NORTHERN LOGISTICS LLC
805 Industrial Dr (48617-9140)
PHONE 989 386-2389
Ron Kunse,
Tom Kunse,
Steve Stark,
EMP: 20 **EST:** 1996
SQ FT: 10,000
SALES (est): 2MM Privately Held
WEB: www.norloworld.com
SIC: 3089 4213 Plastic processing; trucking, except local

(G-2991)
NORTHERN PALLET
4915 E Colonville Rd (48617-8920)
P.O. Box 650 (48617-0650)
PHONE 989 386-7556
Steven Schunk, *Executive*
EMP: 5 **EST:** 2008
SALES (est): 132K Privately Held
SIC: 2448 Pallets, wood

(G-2992)
NORTHERN TANK LLC
805 Industrial Dr (48617-9140)
PHONE 989 386-2389
Thomas R Kunse,
EMP: 8 **EST:** 2017
SALES (est): 193.9K Privately Held
WEB: www.northerntank.com
SIC: 1389 Pipe testing, oil field service

(G-2993)
PACKARD FARMS LLC
6584 S Brand Ave (48617-9645)
PHONE 989 386-3816
Roger Packard, *President*
EMP: 21 **EST:** 2001
SQ FT: 3,500
SALES (est): 4.9MM Privately Held
SIC: 3523 Barn, silo, poultry, dairy & livestock machinery

(G-2994)
PIONEER POLE BUILDINGS N INC
7400 S Clare Ave (48617-8619)
PHONE 989 386-2570
Robert Griffor, *President*
Joan Griffor, *Vice Pres*
EMP: 17 **EST:** 1962
SALES (est): 2.7MM Privately Held
WEB: www.pioneerpole.com
SIC: 1542 3448 2452 7389 Farm building construction; prefabricated metal buildings; prefabricated wood buildings;

(G-2995)
ROBMAR PLASTICS INC
1385 E Maple Rd (48617-9455)
P.O. Box 326 (48617-0326)
PHONE 989 386-9600
Robert D Ohler, *President*
Nick Ohler, *Manager*
Martha Ohler, *Admin Sec*
EMP: 5 **EST:** 1988
SQ FT: 10,000
SALES (est): 864.2K Privately Held
WEB: www.robmarplastics.com
SIC: 3089 Injection molding of plastics

(G-2996)
ROGERS ATHLETIC
495 Pioneer Pkwy (48617-8813)
P.O. Box 208 (48617-0208)
PHONE 989 386-7393
EMP: 8
SALES (est): 199.7K Privately Held
SIC: 3949 Mfg Sporting/Athletic Goods

(G-2997)
SHARPCO WLDG & FABRICATION LLC
26 Consumers Energy Pkwy (48617-9540)
PHONE 989 915-0556
Seth Sharp, *Mng Member*
EMP: 4 **EST:** 2011
SALES (est): 392.4K Privately Held
WEB: www.sharpcowelding.com
SIC: 7692 Welding repair

(G-2998)
SOUND PRODUCTIONS ENTRMT
Also Called: Soundcase
1601 E Maple Rd (48617-8806)
P.O. Box 236 (48617-0236)
PHONE 989 386-2221

Clare - Clare County (G-2999)

James Paetschow, *President*
Baxter Lawson, *Sales Staff*
Devon Musselman, *Mktg Dir*
Brandin Evinger, *Technician*
EMP: 16 **EST:** 1980
SQ FT: 15,000
SALES (est): 1.6MM **Privately Held**
WEB: www.soundproductions.com
SIC: 3648 3161 7929 3663 Lighting equipment; cases, carrying; disc jockey service; radio & TV communications equipment; commercial indusl & institutional electric lighting fixtures

(G-2999)
STAGERIGHT CORPORATION (PA)
Also Called: Stage Right
495 Pioneer Pkwy (48617-8813)
PHONE.................989 386-7393
David Rogers, *President*
Wayne Saupe, *General Mgr*
Tim Hockemeyer, *Engineer*
Judy Fargher, *Sales Staff*
Nate Yarhouse, *Sales Staff*
◆ **EMP:** 179 **EST:** 1984
SQ FT: 150,000
SALES (est): 43.3MM **Privately Held**
WEB: www.stageright.com
SIC: 3999 3444 Stage hardware & equipment, except lighting; sheet metalwork

(G-3000)
TRANQUIL SYSTEMS INTL LLC
528 Pioneer Pkwy (48617-8812)
PHONE.................800 631-0212
Kevin Beavers, *President*
Wesley Parker, *CFO*
EMP: 10 **EST:** 2015
SQ FT: 15,000
SALES (est): 1.8MM
SALES (corp-wide): 6MM **Privately Held**
WEB: www.tranquilsystems.com
SIC: 2521 Wood office furniture
PA: Rogers Group, Inc.
528 Pioneer Pkwy
Clare MI 48617
989 386-7393

(G-3001)
WHITE PALLET CHAIR
4961 E Colonville Rd (48617-8920)
PHONE.................989 424-8771
Tammi L Beckley, *Principal*
EMP: 6 **EST:** 2016
SALES (est): 152K **Privately Held**
SIC: 2448 Pallets, wood

(G-3002)
XCAL TOOLS - CLARE LLC
314 E 4th St (48617-1500)
P.O. Box 298 (48617-0298)
PHONE.................989 386-5376
Tony Calandra, *President*
Scott Carter, *Principal*
Bruce Johnson, *Vice Pres*
Robbie A Maie, *Treasurer*
Gary Cotter, *Manager*
▲ **EMP:** 30 **EST:** 2005
SALES (est): 4.3MM **Privately Held**
WEB: www.xcaltools.com
SIC: 7692 Welding repair

Clarklake
Jackson County

(G-3003)
CLARKLAKE MACHINE INCORPORATED
9451 S Meridian Rd (49234-9613)
PHONE.................517 529-9454
Michael P De Karske, *President*
Mark H De Karske, *Vice Pres*
Mark Dekarske, *Plant Supt*
Debby Dekarske, *Materials Mgr*
Matt Dekarske, *Engineer*
EMP: 25 **EST:** 1968
SQ FT: 20,000
SALES (est): 2.6MM **Privately Held**
WEB: www.clarklakemachine.com
SIC: 3599 Machine shop, jobbing & repair

(G-3004)
CLEARWATER TREATMENT SYSTEMS
4700 Industrial Dr (49234-9636)
PHONE.................517 688-9316
Paul Gietek, *CEO*
EMP: 4 **EST:** 2004
SALES (est): 288.5K **Privately Held**
SIC: 2899 Water treating compounds

(G-3005)
CRAFT ELECTRIC
245 Hyde Rd (49234-9686)
PHONE.................517 529-7164
Carl Evenson, *President*
EMP: 4 **EST:** 2015
SALES (est): 149.2K **Privately Held**
SIC: 3699 1731 Electrical equipment & supplies; electrical work

(G-3006)
NU-ICE AGE INC
9700 Myers Rd (49234-9642)
PHONE.................517 990-0665
Edward L Cooper, *President*
EMP: 10 **EST:** 2007
SALES (est): 592.4K **Privately Held**
SIC: 3569 Ice crushers (machinery)

(G-3007)
PRODUCTION SAW & MACHINE CO
9091 S Meridian Rd (49234-9613)
PHONE.................517 529-4014
James M Vancalbergh, *CEO*
David C Bevier, *President*
Greg Vancalbergh, *Exec VP*
Terry Maynard, *Vice Pres*
Joe Zonts, *Purch Mgr*
EMP: 55 **EST:** 1975
SQ FT: 113,000
SALES (est): 12.7MM **Privately Held**
WEB: www.productionsaw.com
SIC: 3599 Machine shop, jobbing & repair

(G-3008)
SPEC CORPORATION
4701 Industrial Dr (49234-9636)
P.O. Box 333 (49234-0333)
PHONE.................517 529-4105
Ronald Miller, *President*
Bonita Miller, *Admin Sec*
EMP: 5 **EST:** 1972
SQ FT: 7,000
SALES (est): 534.7K **Privately Held**
SIC: 8711 3613 Electrical or electronic engineering; control panels, electric

(G-3009)
STONECRAFTERS INC
4807 Industrial Dr (49234-9636)
PHONE.................517 529-4990
Hunter Andrews, *President*
Kath Rhodes, *Admin Sec*
EMP: 10 **EST:** 1998
SALES (est): 374.5K **Privately Held**
SIC: 3281 2821 Table tops, marble; granite, cut & shaped; plastics materials & resins

(G-3010)
YOUR HOME TOWN USA INC
Also Called: Platemate
9301 Hyde Rd (49234-9023)
P.O. Box 335 (49234-0335)
PHONE.................517 529-9421
Sharon Jones, *President*
EMP: 9 **EST:** 1986
SQ FT: 2,400
SALES (est): 569.6K **Privately Held**
SIC: 7311 2759 2721 Advertising agencies; commercial printing; periodicals: publishing only

Clarkston
Oakland County

(G-3011)
ACME GROOVING TOOL CO
7409 S Village Dr (48346-5000)
PHONE.................800 633-8828
EMP: 17 **EST:** 1953
SQ FT: 9,000
SALES: 1.1MM **Privately Held**
SIC: 3545 Mfg Machine Tool Accessories

(G-3012)
ADE INC
8949 Dixie Hwy (48348-4246)
P.O. Box 660 (48347-0660)
PHONE.................248 625-7200
Bryan Ellis, *President*
Jim Haggerty, *Opers Staff*
Bridget McEvilly, *Marketing Mgr*
Craig Vallelunga, *IT/INT Sup*
EMP: 7 **EST:** 1983
SQ FT: 1,200
SALES (est): 908K **Privately Held**
WEB: www.adeincorp.com
SIC: 3695 Computer software tape & disks: blank, rigid & floppy

(G-3013)
ADVANCED DEF VHCL SYSTEMS CORP
Also Called: Advs
6716 Ridgeview Dr (48346-4461)
PHONE.................248 391-3200
James Leblanc Jr, *President*
Robert Samuelson, *Purchasing*
EMP: 18 **EST:** 2007
SALES (est): 1.7MM **Privately Held**
SIC: 3711 Motor vehicles & car bodies

(G-3014)
ADVANCED POLYMERS COMPOSITES
7111 Dixie Hwy 110 (48346-2077)
PHONE.................248 766-1507
Robert Bogart, *Principal*
EMP: 7 **EST:** 2001
SALES (est): 255.4K **Privately Held**
WEB: www.polymercompositesinc.com
SIC: 2821 Thermosetting materials

(G-3015)
ADVANCED TUBULAR TECH INC
1076 Blue Ridge Dr (48348-4091)
PHONE.................248 674-2059
Michael Cone, *President*
Dawne Baker, *Sales Staff*
EMP: 4 **EST:** 1993
SALES (est): 405.7K **Privately Held**
WEB: www.advancedtubulartech.com
SIC: 7371 7372 Computer software development; prepackaged software

(G-3016)
AMK IRONWORKS
5543 Chickadee Ln (48346-2902)
PHONE.................248 620-9027
Atticus McFadden Keesling, *Principal*
EMP: 5 **EST:** 2016
SALES (est): 185.9K **Privately Held**
WEB: www.amkironworks.org
SIC: 3462 Iron & steel forgings

(G-3017)
ANSCO PATTERN & MACHINE CO
7945 Perry Lake Rd (48348-4646)
PHONE.................248 625-1362
Brian Anderson, *Owner*
EMP: 4 **EST:** 1956
SALES (est): 270.3K **Privately Held**
WEB: www.ansco-machine.com
SIC: 3599 Machine shop, jobbing & repair

(G-3018)
ASPHALT SERVICES
5052 Clntonville Pines Dr (48346-4170)
PHONE.................313 971-5005
Vanessa Williams, *Principal*
EMP: 7 **EST:** 2015
SALES (est): 90.7K **Privately Held**
SIC: 2951 Asphalt paving mixtures & blocks

(G-3019)
BLANCK CANVAS PHOTOGRAPHY LLC
7022 Oakhurst Ridge Rd (48348-5075)
PHONE.................248 342-4935
Kasey Blanck, *Principal*
EMP: 4 **EST:** 2018
SALES (est): 46.5K **Privately Held**
WEB: www.blanckcanvas.com
SIC: 2211 Canvas

(G-3020)
BMU INTERNATIONAL LLC
6230 Ascension St (48348-4704)
PHONE.................248 342-4032
Brian Udebrock, *Administration*
EMP: 6 **EST:** 2012
SALES (est): 145.2K **Privately Held**
SIC: 2833 Medicinals & botanicals

(G-3021)
BRACELET SHACK
5193 Frankwill Ave (48346-3719)
PHONE.................312 656-9191
Ida Figueroa, *Principal*
EMP: 4 **EST:** 2014
SALES (est): 88.4K **Privately Held**
WEB: www.braceletshack.com
SIC: 3961 Bracelets, except precious metal

(G-3022)
CABINET ONE INC
4571 White Lake Ct (48346-2549)
PHONE.................248 625-9440
Joseph D Delude, *President*
Caroline Fredricks, *Vice Pres*
EMP: 4 **EST:** 1983
SQ FT: 10,440
SALES (est): 479.8K **Privately Held**
WEB: www.cabinetoneinc.com
SIC: 2434 Vanities, bathroom: wood

(G-3023)
CHASE PLASTIC SERVICES INC (PA)
Also Called: Cbk Warehouse & Distribution
6467 Waldon Center Dr # 200 (48346-4830)
P.O. Box 67000, Detroit (48267-0002)
PHONE.................248 620-2120
Kevin Chase, *President*
Carole Chase, *Vice Pres*
Doug Wright, *Vice Pres*
▲ **EMP:** 20 **EST:** 1992
SQ FT: 9,200
SALES (est): 30.2MM **Privately Held**
WEB: www.chaseplastics.com
SIC: 2821 Plastics materials & resins

(G-3024)
CLARKSTON CONTROL PRODUCTS
4809 Crestview Dr (48348-3946)
PHONE.................248 394-1430
Richard E Kopicko, *President*
Diana Kopicko, *Corp Secy*
EMP: 6 **EST:** 1992
SQ FT: 2,250
SALES (est): 600.8K **Privately Held**
WEB: www.clarkstoncontrols.com
SIC: 8711 3613 7699 Industrial engineers; control panels, electric; industrial equipment services

(G-3025)
CLARKSTON COURTS LLC
Also Called: Parker's Hilltop Brewery
6110 Dixie Hwy (48346-3409)
PHONE.................248 383-8444
Dave Parker, *President*
Nico Campbell, *Corp Secy*
Heather Karl, *Opers Mgr*
Joe Morin, *Controller*
EMP: 200 **EST:** 2013
SALES (est): 9.6MM **Privately Held**
WEB: www.hilltopbrew.com
SIC: 5181 2082 Beer & ale; ale (alcoholic beverage)

(G-3026)
CLAWSON CONTAINER COMPANY (PA)
4545 Clawson Tank Dr (48346-2581)
PHONE.................248 625-8700
Richard Harding II, *President*
Terrance Groh, *Vice Pres*
Robert Harding Jr, *Treasurer*
Robert E Harding, *Treasurer*
EMP: 50 **EST:** 1993
SQ FT: 25,000
SALES (est): 10.9MM **Privately Held**
WEB: www.highlandtank.com
SIC: 3443 Fabricated plate work (boiler shop)

▲ = Import ▼ = Export
◆ = Import/Export

GEOGRAPHIC SECTION
Clarkston - Oakland County (G-3058)

(G-3027)
CLAWSON TANK COMPANY (PA)
4701 White Lake Rd (48346-2554)
PHONE 248 625-8700
Terrance Groh, *President*
Robert Harding, *Buyer*
Dick Harding, *Treasurer*
Richard T Harding, *Treasurer*
Trisha Burke, *Bookkeeper*
EMP: 44 **EST:** 1953
SQ FT: 100,000
SALES (est): 6.1MM **Privately Held**
WEB: www.highlandtank.com
SIC: 3443 Tanks, standard or custom fabricated: metal plate

(G-3028)
COMPLEX TOOL & MACHINE INC
Also Called: J W Briney Products
6460 Sashabaw Rd (48346-2262)
PHONE 248 625-0664
John H Bender, *President*
Patricia A Bender, *Corp Secy*
EMP: 5 **EST:** 1983
SQ FT: 11,000
SALES (est): 427.6K **Privately Held**
SIC: 3599 3545 Machine shop, jobbing & repair; machine tool accessories

(G-3029)
CONTINENT WINES INC
7457 Deerview Ct (48348-2736)
PHONE 248 467-7383
John M Waddell, *President*
EMP: 7 **EST:** 2016
SALES (est): 228K **Privately Held**
SIC: 2084 Wines

(G-3030)
DEKES CONCRETE INC
6653 Andersonville Rd (48346-2701)
PHONE 810 686-5570
Sam Dekalita, *President*
EMP: 13 **EST:** 1959
SQ FT: 9,250
SALES (est): 344.4K **Privately Held**
SIC: 3273 Ready-mixed concrete

(G-3031)
E D C O PUBLISHING INC
Also Called: Edco Media
990 S Baldwin Rd (48348-3608)
PHONE 248 690-9184
Edna Stephens, *President*
EMP: 7 **EST:** 1997
SQ FT: 2,500
SALES (est): 553.1K **Privately Held**
WEB: www.edco.ie
SIC: 2741 2731 Miscellaneous publishing; book publishing

(G-3032)
ENDOSCOPIC SOLUTIONS
5701 Bow Pointe Dr (48346-3198)
PHONE 248 625-4055
M Veslav Stecevic, *Principal*
Christa Bright, *Admin Asst*
EMP: 14 **EST:** 2014
SALES (est): 590.9K **Privately Held**
WEB: www.mygicareteam.com
SIC: 3845 Endoscopic equipment, electromedical

(G-3033)
ERIC HENRY WOODWORKS
9496 Cedargrove Rd (48348-2106)
PHONE 248 613-5696
Eric Christie, *Owner*
EMP: 6 **EST:** 2013
SALES (est): 78.8K **Privately Held**
SIC: 2431 Millwork

(G-3034)
EYEWEAR DETROIT COMPANY
6466 Shappie Rd (48348-1960)
PHONE 248 396-2214
EMP: 5 **EST:** 2018
SALES (est): 272.6K **Privately Held**
SIC: 3827 Optical instruments & lenses

(G-3035)
FRUSHOUR PUBLISHERS
4871 Curtis Ln (48346-2727)
PHONE 248 701-2548
Randy Frushour, *Principal*
EMP: 5 **EST:** 2016
SALES (est): 64.2K **Privately Held**
SIC: 2711 Newspapers

(G-3036)
G & G METAL PRODUCTS INC
9575 Rattalee Lake Rd (48348-1531)
PHONE 248 625-8099
Gerald Rumph, *President*
Jerry Rumph, *General Mgr*
EMP: 4 **EST:** 1981
SALES (est): 200K **Privately Held**
SIC: 3599 Machine shop, jobbing & repair

(G-3037)
G G & D INC
Also Called: Print Shop, The
5911 Dixie Hwy (48346-3361)
PHONE 248 623-1212
Eugene Metzger, *President*
EMP: 8 **EST:** 1980
SQ FT: 1,800
SALES (est): 545.4K **Privately Held**
WEB: www.theprintshopclarkston.com
SIC: 2752 Commercial printing, offset

(G-3038)
HD SELCATING PAV SOLUTIONS LLC
8205 Valleyview Dr (48348-4042)
PHONE 248 241-6526
Alyssa Retsel,
David Retsel,
EMP: 2 **EST:** 2010
SALES (est): 1MM **Privately Held**
WEB: www.hdsealcoating.com
SIC: 2951 1611 1771 1799 Asphalt paving mixtures & blocks; surfacing & paving; resurfacing contractor; driveway, parking lot & blacktop contractors; parking lot maintenance

(G-3039)
HIDDEN LAKE CABINET TRIM
5254 Heath Ave (48346-3529)
PHONE 586 246-9119
Erik Carney, *CEO*
EMP: 5 **EST:** 2016
SALES (est): 240.1K **Privately Held**
WEB: www.hiddenlakecabinets.net
SIC: 2434 Wood kitchen cabinets

(G-3040)
HIGHLAND TANK & MFG CO
4701 White Lake Rd (48346-2554)
PHONE 248 795-2000
EMP: 15 **EST:** 2019
SALES (est): 961.7K **Privately Held**
WEB: www.highlandtank.com
SIC: 3999 Manufacturing industries

(G-3041)
I B P INC
Also Called: Industrial Building Panels
9295 Allen Rd (48348-2726)
PHONE 248 588-4710
Clarence E Johns, *President*
EMP: 17 **EST:** 1964
SQ FT: 25,000
SALES (est): 1MM **Privately Held**
WEB: www.ibpcustompanels.com
SIC: 3448 Panels for prefabricated metal buildings

(G-3042)
IBC NORTH AMERICA INC (HQ)
4545 Clawson Tank Dr (48346-2581)
PHONE 248 625-8700
Richard Harding, *President*
Dick Harding, *President*
Micheal Harding, *Exec VP*
Robert Harding Jr, *Treasurer*
Terrance Groh, *Admin Sec*
▲ **EMP:** 100 **EST:** 1998
SALES (est): 10.9MM **Privately Held**
WEB: www.mauserpackaging.com
SIC: 2631 Container, packaging & boxboard

(G-3043)
KIMBERLY LIGHTING LLC
Also Called: Kimberly Led Lighting
5827 Terex (48346-1717)
PHONE 888 480-0070
Laura Squier, *Mng Member*
Kim Jenkins, *Agent*
▲ **EMP:** 38 **EST:** 2008
SQ FT: 50,000
SALES (est): 5.8MM **Privately Held**
WEB: www.kimberlyledlighting.com
SIC: 3674 Light emitting diodes

(G-3044)
LAWRENCE PLASTICS LLC
6338 Sashabaw Rd (48346-2260)
PHONE 248 475-0186
Mike Bloomfield, *Managing Prtnr*
Ken George, *Managing Prtnr*
Rachel Hahnefeld, *Managing Prtnr*
Patrick Hobert, *Plant Mgr*
Allan Pearson, *Plant Mgr*
▼ **EMP:** 100 **EST:** 1946
SQ FT: 60,000
SALES (est): 10.4MM **Privately Held**
WEB: www.lawrenceplastics.com
SIC: 3089 Injection molding of plastics

(G-3045)
LOGOS AND LETTERS
6525 Dixie Hwy (48346-3499)
PHONE 248 795-2093
EMP: 4 **EST:** 2015
SALES (est): 155.9K **Privately Held**
WEB: www.logosnlettersmi.com
SIC: 2759 Screen printing

(G-3046)
MACHINING TECHNOLOGIES LLC
9635 Davisburg Rd (48348-4135)
PHONE 248 379-4201
Todd Horner, *Mng Member*
EMP: 4 **EST:** 2002
SQ FT: 6,500 **Privately Held**
SIC: 3545 Precision tools, machinists'

(G-3047)
MARELLI AUTOMOTIVE LTG LLC
5600 Bow Pointe Dr (48346-3115)
PHONE 248 418-3000
Mark Waggoner, *Engineer*
EMP: 5 **Publicly Held**
WEB: www.al.world
SIC: 3647 Headlights (fixtures), vehicular
HQ: Marelli Automotive Lighting Llc
26555 Northwestern Hwy
Southfield MI 48033
248 418-3000

(G-3048)
MAUSER
4750 Clawson Tank Dr (48346-0001)
PHONE 248 795-2330
Evan Dorries, *Sales Staff*
Brian Guiheen, *Manager*
▲ **EMP:** 28 **EST:** 2015
SALES (est): 4.6MM **Privately Held**
WEB: www.mauserpackaging.com
SIC: 3412 2655 Barrels, shipping: metal; fiber cans, drums & containers

(G-3049)
MELISS COMPANY INC
5020 White Lake Rd (48346-2641)
PHONE 248 398-1970
Margret Hambrick, *President*
EMP: 12 **EST:** 1969
SQ FT: 3,500
SALES (est): 1.8MM **Privately Held**
SIC: 5051 3599 Aluminum bars, rods, ingots, sheets, pipes, plates, etc.; machine shop, jobbing & repair

(G-3050)
MICHAELENES INC
Also Called: Michaelene's Gourmet Granola
7415 Deer Forest Ct (48348-2734)
PHONE 248 625-0156
Michaelene Hearn, *President*
Lawrence Hearn, *Vice Pres*
EMP: 5 **EST:** 1984
SQ FT: 1,200
SALES (est): 360.3K **Privately Held**
WEB: www.gourmetgranola.com
SIC: 2099 Food preparations

(G-3051)
MID COST GRASS CHOPPERS
5381 Frankwill Ave (48346-3725)
PHONE 985 445-7155
Benjamin Hawley, *Principal*
EMP: 4 **EST:** 2016
SALES (est): 61.3K **Privately Held**
SIC: 3751 Motorcycles & related parts

(G-3052)
MOBILE KNOWLEDGE GROUP LLC (PA)
Also Called: Mkg
5750 Bella Rosa Blvd # 100 (48348-4780)
PHONE 248 625-3327
Craig S Miller, *President*
Steve C Buchholz, *Principal*
Steve Buchholz, *VP Opers*
EMP: 4 **EST:** 2001
SQ FT: 2,200
SALES (est): 3.5MM **Privately Held**
WEB: www.mkgsource.com
SIC: 3679 3575 5084 Antennas, receiving; computer terminals; industrial machinery & equipment

(G-3053)
O FLEX GROUP INC
5780 Garnet Cir (48348-3060)
PHONE 248 505-0322
EMP: 6 **EST:** 2018
SALES (est): 119.9K **Privately Held**
SIC: 3714 Motor vehicle parts & accessories

(G-3054)
OBLUT LIMITED
Also Called: Unique Shape Fabricating
4511 Ennismore Dr (48346-3614)
PHONE 810 241-4029
George Cline, *President*
EMP: 14 **EST:** 1984
SALES (est): 6.5MM **Privately Held**
SIC: 3465 Automotive stampings

(G-3055)
PFIZER INC
7064 Oak Meadows Dr (48348-4254)
PHONE 248 867-9067
Josh Wiggins, *Principal*
EMP: 4
SALES (corp-wide): 41.9B **Publicly Held**
WEB: www.pfizer.com
SIC: 2834 Pharmaceutical preparations
PA: Pfizer Inc.
235 E 42nd St Rm 107
New York NY 10017
212 733-2323

(G-3056)
PINNACLE ENERGY LLC
5071 Timber Ridge Trl (48346-3850)
PHONE 248 623-6091
Jeffrey Crampton, *Vice Pres*
Howard Crampton,
EMP: 4 **EST:** 2004 **Privately Held**
WEB: www.pinnacleenergy.com
SIC: 1382 Oil & gas exploration services

(G-3057)
PONTIAC COIL INC (PA)
5800 Moody Dr (48348-4768)
PHONE 248 922-1100
Nick Najmolhoda, *CEO*
John Moody, *President*
Michael T Gidley, *Exec VP*
Mike Gidley, *Exec VP*
Jeff Reddy, *Exec VP*
▲ **EMP:** 114 **EST:** 1958
SQ FT: 77,000
SALES (est): 44.6MM **Privately Held**
WEB: www.pontiaccoil.com
SIC: 3498 3621 3677 3714 Fabricated pipe & fittings; motors & generators; coil windings, electronic; motor vehicle parts & accessories

(G-3058)
PPG INDUSTRIES INC
Also Called: PPG 5637
5860 Sashabaw Rd (48346-3152)
PHONE 248 625-7282
EMP: 4
SALES (corp-wide): 15.1B **Publicly Held**
WEB: www.ppg.com
SIC: 2851 Paints & allied products
PA: Ppg Industries, Inc.
1 Ppg Pl
Pittsburgh PA 15272
412 434-3131

Clarkston - Oakland County (G-3059)

(G-3059)
RECTICEL FOAM CORPORATION (HQ)
5600 Bow Pointe Dr (48346-3115)
P.O. Box 8985, Wilmington DE (19899-8985)
PHONE..................248 241-9100
Olivier Chapelle, *CEO*
Ralf Becker, *General Mgr*
Zena Taylor, *Hum Res Coord*
Michael Kurkowski, *Manager*
◆ EMP: 2 EST: 1979
SALES (est): 25MM
SALES (corp-wide): 292.1MM **Privately Held**
WEB: www.recticel.com
SIC: 2515 Mattresses, containing felt, foam rubber, urethane, etc.
PA: Recticel
Avenue Du Bourget 42
Bruxelles 1130
277 518-82

(G-3060)
REILLY & ASSOCIATES INC
7754 Parkcrest Cir (48348-2967)
PHONE..................248 605-9393
Daniel Reilly, *President*
EMP: 20 EST: 1995
SALES (est): 515.6K **Privately Held**
WEB: www.reilly-associates.com
SIC: 7372 Prepackaged software

(G-3061)
RUELLE INDUSTRIES INC
5756 Knob Hill Cir (48348-4861)
PHONE..................248 618-0333
Patrick Ruelle, *President*
EMP: 8 EST: 2008
SALES (est): 268.4K **Privately Held**
WEB: www.ruelleindustries.com
SIC: 3599 Machine shop, jobbing & repair

(G-3062)
SAFE N SIMPLE LLC
5827 Terex (48346-1717)
PHONE..................248 875-0840
Tyler Sajan, *Opers Staff*
Elizabet Sajan,
▲ EMP: 17 EST: 2007
SALES (est): 2.1MM **Privately Held**
WEB: www.sns-medical.com
SIC: 2834 Pharmaceutical preparations

(G-3063)
SEAL BOWLING BALLS LLC
5422 Bristol Parke Dr (48348-4800)
PHONE..................248 707-6482
Pamela Ritter, *Principal*
EMP: 4 EST: 2017
SALES (est): 65.6K **Privately Held**
SIC: 3949 Bowling balls

(G-3064)
SHEFFLER MANUFACTURING LLC
6338 Sashabaw Rd (48346-2260)
PHONE..................248 409-0966
John Sheffler, *President*
▲ EMP: 11 EST: 2005
SALES (est): 256.9K **Privately Held**
WEB: www.lgiinternational.com
SIC: 2499 Kitchen, bathroom & household ware: wood

(G-3065)
SHEFFLER MFG INTL LGISTICS LLC
6338 Sashabaw Rd (48346-2260)
PHONE..................248 409-0960
John T Sheffler,
Carol J Sheffler,
EMP: 23 EST: 2000
SQ FT: 30,000
SALES (est): 780.8K **Privately Held**
SIC: 3089 4731 Automotive parts, plastic; freight transportation arrangement

(G-3066)
SIGN GRAPHIX
8457 Andersonville Rd (48346-2575)
PHONE..................248 241-6531
William R Lutz III, *President*
EMP: 8 EST: 2017
SALES (est): 296K **Privately Held**
WEB: www.signgraphix.net
SIC: 3993 Signs & advertising specialties

(G-3067)
SKG INTERNATIONAL INC
7550 Deerhill Dr (48346-1236)
P.O. Box 1962 (48347-1962)
PHONE..................248 620-4139
Tony Kayyod, *CEO*
Steven Tarino, *Director*
EMP: 10 EST: 2013
SALES (est): 907.1K **Privately Held**
SIC: 3714 Air conditioner parts, motor vehicle

(G-3068)
ST PIERRE INC
9649 Northwest Ct (48346-1744)
PHONE..................248 620-2755
James C St Pierre, *President*
Joseph St Pierre, *Treasurer*
William J St Pierre, *Admin Sec*
EMP: 6 EST: 1969
SQ FT: 6,000
SALES (est): 464.2K **Privately Held**
SIC: 3599 Machine shop, jobbing & repair

(G-3069)
STEEL TANK & FABRICATING CO (PA)
Also Called: Clawson Tank
4701 White Lake Rd (48346-2554)
PHONE..................248 625-8700
Richard T Harding II, *President*
Robert E Harding Jr, *Treasurer*
◆ EMP: 75 EST: 1943
SQ FT: 15,000
SALES (est): 9.5MM **Privately Held**
SIC: 3443 Tanks, standard or custom fabricated: metal plate

(G-3070)
SUBWAY RESTAURANT
7743 Sashabaw Rd Ste B (48348-4775)
PHONE..................248 625-5739
Joe Grant, *Manager*
EMP: 9 EST: 2008
SALES (est): 488.9K **Privately Held**
WEB: www.subway.com
SIC: 5812 2099 Sandwiches & submarines shop; salads, fresh or refrigerated

(G-3071)
THOMAS ENGINEERING
9647 Rattalee Lake Rd (48348-1533)
PHONE..................248 620-7916
Robert Thomas, *Owner*
EMP: 8 EST: 1985
SALES (est): 580.1K **Privately Held**
WEB: www.rsthomasengineering.generacdealers.com
SIC: 3714 3711 Motor vehicle engines & parts; chassis, motor vehicle

(G-3072)
TRIPLE A CROCHET LLC
9271 Shamrock Ln (48348-2547)
PHONE..................248 534-0818
Lauren Gentges, *Principal*
EMP: 4 EST: 2017
SALES (est): 68.5K **Privately Held**
SIC: 2399 Hand woven & crocheted products

(G-3073)
TST TOOLING SOFTWARE TECH LLC (PA)
6547 Dixie Hwy (48346-5500)
PHONE..................248 922-9293
Devin White, *Engineer*
Patty Poma, *Info Tech Mgr*
Deb Kesteloot, *IT/INT Sup*
James Kesteloot,
Stacey Chatterson, *Admin Asst*
EMP: 10 EST: 2001 **Privately Held**
WEB: www.tst-software.com
SIC: 7372 Prepackaged software

(G-3074)
TWISTED SCISSOR
5907 Dixie Hwy Ste A (48346-3571)
PHONE..................248 620-2626
Tommy Evens, *Owner*
EMP: 4 EST: 2015
SALES (est): 115.4K **Privately Held**
WEB: www.twistedscissorsstudio.com
SIC: 3999 Candles

(G-3075)
UNION COMMISSARY LLC
Also Called: Union Kitchen
64 S Main St (48346-5303)
PHONE..................248 795-2483
Curt Catallo, *Mng Member*
EMP: 10 EST: 2016
SALES (est): 1.6MM
SALES (corp-wide): 4.2MM **Privately Held**
WEB: www.unionjoints.com
SIC: 2099 Food preparations
PA: Union Joints, Llc
90 N Main St
Clarkston MI 48346
248 795-2483

(G-3076)
WELDING & JOINING TECH LLC
Also Called: Weldpower
5439 Bristol Parke Dr (48348-4801)
PHONE..................734 926-9353
Stephen Boergert, *Mng Member*
EMP: 4 EST: 2013
SQ FT: 10,000
SALES (est): 359.6K **Privately Held**
WEB: www.weldpowercorp.com
SIC: 8742 8999 8748 7692 Business consultant; scientific consulting; business consulting; welding repair; fabricated plate work (boiler shop)

Clarksville
Ionia County

(G-3077)
BAD DAY INDUSTRIES LLC
9932 Bell Rd (48815-9765)
PHONE..................844 213-6541
EMP: 4 EST: 2019
SALES (est): 39.6K **Privately Held**
WEB: www.baddayindustries.com
SIC: 3999 Manufacturing industries

(G-3078)
BLOUGH HARDWOODS INC
9975 W Clarksville Rd (48815-9604)
PHONE..................616 693-2174
Marvin Blough, *President*
EMP: 8 EST: 1974
SQ FT: 3,200
SALES (est): 914K **Privately Held**
WEB: www.bloughhardwoods.com
SIC: 2421 Sawmills & planing mills, general

(G-3079)
MR CS CUSTOM TEES
151 Lind Ave (48815-9400)
PHONE..................989 965-2222
Cory Schutter, *Principal*
EMP: 4 EST: 2018
SALES (est): 82.7K **Privately Held**
SIC: 2759 Screen printing

(G-3080)
TIQ WOODWORKING LLC
11900 Nash Hwy (48815-9608)
PHONE..................616 206-9369
EMP: 4 EST: 2018
SALES (est): 56.4K **Privately Held**
WEB: www.tiqwoodworking.com
SIC: 2431 Millwork

(G-3081)
TITANIUM ELITE MTS GLOBAL LLC
9112 Elm Rd (48815-9784)
PHONE..................616 262-5222
EMP: 4 EST: 2017
SALES (est): 99.9K **Privately Held**
SIC: 3356 Titanium

(G-3082)
WEST MICHIGAN SAWMILL
7760 Nash Hwy (48815-9715)
PHONE..................616 693-0044
Jim Bough, *Owner*
EMP: 9 EST: 2007
SALES (est): 1.4MM **Privately Held**
WEB: www.wmsawmill.com
SIC: 2421 Lumber: rough, sawed or planed

Clawson
Oakland County

(G-3083)
ACOUFELT LLC
1238 Anderson Rd Fl 2 (48017-1002)
PHONE..................800 966-8557
Janelle Truan, *Business Mgr*
Bob Truan, *Opers Mgr*
Jessica Grace, *Sales Staff*
Alexander Trisha, *Sales Staff*
Ben Grace, *Mng Member*
EMP: 7 EST: 2017
SALES (est): 943.1K **Privately Held**
WEB: www.acoufelt.com
SIC: 2299 Acoustic felts

(G-3084)
ADAPTABLE TOOL SUPPLY LLC
309 N Chocolay Ave (48017-1379)
P.O. Box 120 (48017-0120)
PHONE..................248 439-0866
Libertee Chamberlin, *Mng Member*
EMP: 10 EST: 2009
SQ FT: 4,000
SALES (est): **Privately Held**
SIC: 3545 5084 Cutting tools for machine tools; machine tools & accessories

(G-3085)
AMERICAN FLAG & BANNER COMPANY
28 S Main St (48017-2088)
PHONE..................248 288-3010
William S Miles, *President*
Jane Miles, *Vice Pres*
EMP: 8 EST: 1940
SQ FT: 8,500
SALES (est): 900K **Privately Held**
WEB: www.afbco.com
SIC: 2399 5999 Flags, fabric; banners, made from fabric; flags; posters

(G-3086)
AMERICAN REPROGRAPHICS CO LLC
Also Called: Entire Rprdction Imging Sltion
1009 W Maple Rd (48017-1058)
PHONE..................248 299-8900
Dick Ricky, *Manager*
EMP: 4
SALES (corp-wide): 289.4MM **Publicly Held**
WEB: www.ryansallans.com
SIC: 7336 2791 2759 7334 Commercial art & graphic design; typesetting; commercial printing; blueprinting service
HQ: American Reprographics Company, L.L.C.
1981 N Broadway Ste 385
Walnut Creek CA 94596
925 949-5100

(G-3087)
BAYLUME INC
2832 High St (48017)
PHONE..................877 881-3641
Michael H Bay, *President*
EMP: 6 EST: 2002
SALES (est): 356.7K **Privately Held**
WEB: www.baylume.com
SIC: 3645 Garden, patio, walkway & yard lighting fixtures: electric

(G-3088)
BIRMINGHAM BENDERS CO
1271 W Maple Rd (48017-1060)
PHONE..................313 435-4200
Joan Walker, *Ch of Bd*
Lee Runk, *President*
Donald D Bush, *Vice Pres*
Joseph J Gagliardi, *Admin Sec*
EMP: 14 EST: 1986
SQ FT: 35,000
SALES (est): 1.1MM **Privately Held**
SIC: 3542 3544 Bending machines; special dies, tools, jigs & fixtures

Clay - St. Clair County (G-3117)

(G-3089)
BROWN FORMAN
1030 N Crooks Rd Ste B (48017-1020)
PHONE 248 464-2011
Jason Piwko, *Principal*
EMP: 8 **EST:** 2015
SALES (est): 106.4K **Privately Held**
WEB: www.brown-forman.com
SIC: 2085 Distilled & blended liquors

(G-3090)
CLAWSON CUSTOM WOODWORK LLC
295 Broadacre Ave (48017-1503)
PHONE 248 515-5336
Dwayne Back, *Principal*
EMP: 5 **EST:** 2015
SALES (est): 104.9K **Privately Held**
SIC: 2499 Wood products

(G-3091)
CORNELIUS SYSTEMS INC (PA)
1302 Anderson Rd (48017-1044)
PHONE 248 545-5558
Todd Cornelius, *CEO*
Michael A Cornelius, *CEO*
Michael T Cornelius, *President*
Dave Bentsen, *Regional Mgr*
David Cornelius, *Vice Pres*
EMP: 45 **EST:** 1971
SALES (est): 5MM **Privately Held**
WEB: www.mycornelius.com
SIC: 7629 3578 1731 7382 Business machine repair, electric; automatic teller machines (ATM); access control systems specialization; security systems services

(G-3092)
CREATIVE SOLUTIONS GROUP INC (PA)
1250 N Crooks Rd (48017-1047)
PHONE 248 288-9700
Thomas Valentine, *President*
Maatisak S Amenhetep, *Principal*
James Bailey, *Vice Pres*
David Burton, *Vice Pres*
Ken Fransson, *Vice Pres*
▲ **EMP:** 97 **EST:** 1998
SQ FT: 86,000
SALES (est): 12.3MM **Privately Held**
WEB: www.csgnow.com
SIC: 7389 2542 Advertising, promotional & trade show services; partitions & fixtures, except wood

(G-3093)
D & S ENGINE SPECIALIST INC
875 N Rochester Rd (48017-1731)
PHONE 248 583-9240
Michael N Henderson, *President*
EMP: 10 **EST:** 1983
SALES (est): 2MM **Privately Held**
WEB: www.dsengine.com
SIC: 5084 3519 7538 Engines & parts, air-cooled; gas engine rebuilding; engine rebuilding: automotive

(G-3094)
DETROIT HITCH CO
651 N Rochester Rd (48017-1729)
PHONE 248 379-0071
Joseph Volpe, *President*
Lana Volpe, *Corp Secy*
EMP: 15 **EST:** 1976
SQ FT: 25,000
SALES (est): 2.5MM **Privately Held**
WEB: www.detroithitch.com
SIC: 3714 Motor vehicle parts & accessories

(G-3095)
E & E MANUFACTURING CO INC
701 S Main St (48017-2017)
PHONE 248 616-1300
Matt Menchinger, *Business Mgr*
Wallace Smith, *Sales Staff*
Ethan Starr, *Manager*
Dylan McGowan, *Technology*
Jerry Hall, *Maintence Staff*
EMP: 23
SALES (corp-wide): 61.3MM **Privately Held**
WEB: www.eemfg.com
SIC: 3714 3465 3469 3452 Motor vehicle parts & accessories; automotive stampings; metal stampings; bolts, nuts, rivets & washers
PA: E & E Manufacturing Company, Inc.
300 400 Indus Drv Plymouth
Plymouth MI 48170
734 451-7600

(G-3096)
ELITE DEFENSE LLC
1332 Anderson Rd (48017-1044)
PHONE 734 424-9955
Dennis Finnegan, *President*
Theresa Helm, *Export Mgr*
Michelle Finnegan, *CFO*
Frank Moss, *Sales Staff*
Brittany Westcott, *Sales Staff*
EMP: 14 **EST:** 2007
SALES (est): 1.5MM **Privately Held**
WEB: www.elitedefense.com
SIC: 3949 5091 5136 Shooting equipment & supplies, general; firearms, sporting; uniforms, men's & boys'

(G-3097)
FOUR WAY INDUSTRIES INC
855 N Rochester Rd (48017-1731)
PHONE 248 588-5421
David Tye, *President*
Aaron T Tye, *Manager*
EMP: 10 **EST:** 1998
SALES (est): 1.4MM **Privately Held**
WEB: www.fourwayindustries.com
SIC: 3469 Patterns on metal

(G-3098)
GJ PREY COML & INDUS PNTG COV
710 N Crooks Rd (48017-1399)
PHONE 248 250-4792
Gary Prey, *Owner*
EMP: 5 **EST:** 1997 **Privately Held**
SIC: 1721 3471 Commercial painting; industrial painting; plating & polishing

(G-3099)
INTERNTNAL MNUTE PRESS CLAWSON
640 W 14 Mile Rd (48017-1967)
PHONE 248 629-4220
EMP: 6 **EST:** 2018
SALES (est): 37.5K **Privately Held**
WEB: www.clawson-mi.intlminutepress.com
SIC: 2752 Commercial printing, lithographic

(G-3100)
JULIAN BROTHERS INC
540 S Rochester Rd (48017-2124)
PHONE 248 588-0280
Richard P Julian, *President*
EMP: 16 **EST:** 1971
SQ FT: 3,000
SALES (est): 729.2K **Privately Held**
WEB: www.julianbrothers.com
SIC: 5461 2051 2053 Bread; bread, cake & related products; cakes, bakery: frozen

(G-3101)
ND INDUSTRIES INC (PA)
Also Called: ND Technologies
1000 N Crooks Rd (48017-1003)
PHONE 248 288-0000
Michael Garofalo, *President*
Richard Wallace, *Chairman*
Jim Barr, *Vice Pres*
John Cain, *Vice Pres*
Richard Foukes, *Vice Pres*
▲ **EMP:** 120
SALES (est): 59.9MM **Privately Held**
WEB: www.ndindustries.com
SIC: 2891 3479 Adhesives & sealants; coating of metals & formed products

(G-3102)
PEAKTRONICS INC
1363 Anderson Rd Ste A (48017-1051)
PHONE 248 542-5640
Jack M Leason, *President*
Peter W Mueller, *Exec VP*
Peter Mueller, *Exec VP*
Marion Spurlock, *Mfg Mgr*
◆ **EMP:** 8 **EST:** 1985
SQ FT: 10,000
SALES: 3.6MM **Privately Held**
WEB: www.peaktronics.com
SIC: 3823 Industrial instrmnts msrmnt display/control process variable

(G-3103)
PEPRO ENTERPRISES INC
Also Called: Gemini Plastics
53 W Maple Rd (48017-1109)
PHONE 248 435-7271
Tom McCurley, *Branch Mgr*
EMP: 7 **Privately Held**
WEB: www.geminigroup.net
SIC: 3089 Injection molding of plastics
HQ: Pepro Enterprises, Inc.
4385 Garfield St
Ubly MI 48475
989 658-3200

(G-3104)
PROFORMA PLTNUM PRTG PRMOTIONS
143 W Tacoma St (48017-1983)
PHONE 248 341-3814
Suzanne Ashcraft, *Owner*
EMP: 4 **EST:** 2007
SALES (est): 212.4K **Privately Held**
WEB: www.proformaplatinumprinting.espwebsite.com
SIC: 2752 Commercial printing, offset

(G-3105)
PROJECT ECHO LLC (PA)
Also Called: American Holoptics
1332 Anderson Rd (48017-1044)
PHONE 248 971-4027
Matthew Van Haaren,
EMP: 11 **EST:** 2020
SALES (est): 17.4MM **Privately Held**
SIC: 3812 Defense systems & equipment

(G-3106)
QUALITY PRESS
144 Roth Blvd (48017-2408)
PHONE 248 541-0753
Jim Palmer, *Principal*
EMP: 4 **EST:** 2016
SALES (est): 73.3K **Privately Held**
SIC: 2752 Commercial printing, offset

(G-3107)
QUALITY TOOL AND DIE LLC
934 Broadacre Ave (48017-1433)
PHONE 248 707-0060
Lorant Selimas,
EMP: 6 **EST:** 2013
SALES (est): 165.9K **Privately Held**
SIC: 3544 Special dies & tools

(G-3108)
RENEGADE SCREEN PRINTING
141 Fisher Ct (48017-1681)
PHONE 248 632-0207
Steven Barber, *Principal*
EMP: 5 **EST:** 2012
SALES (est): 138.8K **Privately Held**
WEB: www.screen-printing-services.cmac.ws
SIC: 2752 Commercial printing, lithographic

(G-3109)
RHODES WELDING INC
1206 W Selfridge Blvd (48017-1341)
PHONE 248 568-0857
James Rhodes, *Administration*
EMP: 7 **EST:** 2017
SALES (est): 441.8K **Privately Held**
WEB: www.rhodeswelding.com
SIC: 7692 Welding repair

(G-3110)
STIRNEMANN TOOL & MCH CO INC
1457 N Main St (48017-1199)
PHONE 248 435-4040
James Stirnemann, *President*
EMP: 5 **EST:** 1946
SQ FT: 5,000
SALES (est): 700K **Privately Held**
WEB: www.stirnemanninc.com
SIC: 7699 3599 Industrial equipment services; machine shop, jobbing & repair

(G-3111)
VISIONARY CABINETRY AND DESIGN
429 S Main St (48017-2011)
PHONE 248 850-7178
Richard Kastler, *Administration*
EMP: 5 **EST:** 2015
SALES (est): 134.7K **Privately Held**
WEB: www.visionarycabinetry.com
SIC: 2434 Wood kitchen cabinets

(G-3112)
WILSON TECHNOLOGIES INC
Also Called: Ologic
851 W Maple Rd (48017-1185)
PHONE 248 655-0005
John Parent, *President*
Blake Edwards, *Manager*
Salvador Holguin, *Software Dev*
EMP: 9 **EST:** 2004
SALES (est): 1MM **Privately Held**
WEB: www.wilsontechnologies.com
SIC: 7372 Business oriented computer software

Clay
St. Clair County

(G-3113)
ADVANCED AUTOMOTIVE GROUP LLC
8784 Folkert Rd (48001-3700)
PHONE 586 206-2478
Steven Bartolomucci, *President*
EMP: 10 **EST:** 1999
SQ FT: 8,000
SALES (est): 795K **Privately Held**
WEB: www.advancedautogrp.com
SIC: 3599 Machine & other job shop work

(G-3114)
ALGONAC MARINE CAST LLC
9300 Stone Rd (48001-4436)
PHONE 810 794-9391
Pam Wrightner, *Sales Mgr*
John Pugh,
EMP: 26 **EST:** 1921
SQ FT: 48,000
SALES (est): 988.4K **Privately Held**
WEB: www.algonacmarinecast.com
SIC: 3365 3369 Aluminum & aluminum-based alloy castings; nonferrous foundries

(G-3115)
AMERICAN DIE CORPORATION
6860 Holland Rd (48001-3722)
PHONE 810 794-4080
Steve Bartolomucci, *President*
EMP: 13 **EST:** 1999
SALES (est): 589.7K **Privately Held**
SIC: 3544 Special dies & tools

(G-3116)
AUTO CRAFT TOOL & DIE CO
Also Called: Eckhart USA
1800 Fruit St (48001-4503)
PHONE 810 794-4929
Michael Duvernay, *President*
Annalena Hullquist, *Business Mgr*
David Du Vernay, *Vice Pres*
David Duvernay, *Vice Pres*
Joseph Grover, *Engineer*
▲ **EMP:** 64 **EST:** 1958
SQ FT: 57,250
SALES (est): 13.2MM
SALES (corp-wide): 78MM **Privately Held**
WEB: www.eckhartusa.com
SIC: 3544 Special dies & tools
HQ: Eckhart Holdings, Inc.
16185 National Pkwy
Lansing MI 48906
517 321-7700

(G-3117)
AUTO CRAFT TOOL & DIE CO
1800 Fruit St (48001-4503)
PHONE 810 794-4929
EMP: 25
SALES (corp-wide): 17.2MM **Privately Held**
SIC: 3544 Mfg Dies/Tools/Jigs/Fixtures

Clay - St. Clair County (G-3118)

PA: Auto Craft Tool & Die Co.
1800 Fruit St
Clay MI 48001
810 794-4929

(G-3118)
CTC FABRICATORS LLC
8797 Stone Rd (48001-3819)
PHONE...................586 242-8809
Eugene Petrovich, *Mng Member*
EMP: 5 **EST:** 2017
SALES (est): 400K **Privately Held**
SIC: 3449 2431 5531 Fabricated bar joists & concrete reinforcing bars; brackets, wood; automotive parts

(G-3119)
ELECTRIC MOTOR & CONTG CO
7273 Flamingo St (48001-4131)
PHONE...................313 871-3775
Patricia Farris, *President*
Adam Ralston, *Division Mgr*
David Jager, *Vice Pres*
Ashley Bare, *Production*
Hakan Ertekin, *Project Engr*
EMP: 10 **EST:** 1965
SALES (est): 758.8K **Privately Held**
WEB: www.emc-co.com
SIC: 7694 7699 Electric motor repair; industrial machinery & equipment repair

(G-3120)
GREGS DOCKSIDE MARINE SVC LLC
6311 Benoit Rd (48001-3307)
PHONE...................810 874-8250
Greg Allison, *Principal*
EMP: 4 **EST:** 2018
SALES (est): 54.6K **Privately Held**
WEB: www.gregsmarineservice.com
SIC: 3732 Boat building & repairing

(G-3121)
J&M GROUP INDUSTRIAL SVCS INC
6354 Swartout Rd (48001-3327)
PHONE...................248 957-0006
Arthur Murray, *President*
EMP: 4 **EST:** 2019
SALES (est): 377.6K **Privately Held**
WEB: www.jmgrp.net
SIC: 3541 Machine tool replacement & repair parts, metal cutting types

(G-3122)
METAL WORXS INC
7374 Flamingo St (48001-4132)
PHONE...................586 484-9355
Robert Hamilton, *Principal*
EMP: 5 **EST:** 1999
SALES (est): 441.7K **Privately Held**
SIC: 7692 Welding repair

(G-3123)
NU-ERA HOLDINGS INC (PA)
Also Called: Monnier
2034 Fruit St (48001)
P.O. Box 409, Algonac (48001-0409)
PHONE...................810 794-4935
Patrick Nichols, *President*
Aaron Hodges, *Engineer*
EMP: 30 **EST:** 1996
SQ FT: 29,000
SALES (est): 10.9MM **Privately Held**
WEB: www.monnier.com
SIC: 3569 Filters, general line: industrial; lubricating equipment

(G-3124)
SCAFF-ALL INC
Also Called: Scott-Systems
7269 Cardinal St (48001-4107)
PHONE...................888 204-9990
Daniel Zempel, *Treasurer*
William Bowser, *Director*
Kimberly Bowser, *Director*
Elliott Clark, *Director*
Anthony Dayble, *Director*
EMP: 5 **EST:** 1994
SALES (est): 308.3K **Privately Held**
WEB: www.scaff-all.com
SIC: 3429 Manufactured hardware (general)

(G-3125)
SOFIA ROSE INDUSTRIES INC
9100 Island Dr (48001-4409)
PHONE...................810 278-4907
Elizabeth M Simons, *President*
EMP: 8 **EST:** 2020
SALES (est): 264.3K **Privately Held**
SIC: 3999 Manufacturing industries

(G-3126)
SUNSATION PRODUCTS INC
Also Called: Sunsation Boats
9666 Kretz Dr (48001-4622)
PHONE...................810 794-4888
Wayne Schaldenbrand, *President*
Kyle Miller, *Partner*
Joseph Schaldenbrand, *Vice Pres*
Jared Morris, *VP Mktg*
John Schaldenbrand, *Manager*
EMP: 38 **EST:** 1981
SQ FT: 12,000
SALES (est): 5.2MM **Privately Held**
WEB: www.sunsationboats.com
SIC: 3732 Boats, fiberglass: building & repairing

(G-3127)
THUMBPRINT NEWS
8061 Marsh Rd (48001-3401)
PHONE...................810 794-2300
Scott Zimmer, *Manager*
EMP: 7 **EST:** 2009
SALES (est): 170.8K **Privately Held**
WEB: www.thumbprintnews.com
SIC: 2711 Commercial printing & newspaper publishing combined; newspapers, publishing & printing

(G-3128)
ULTRA-TEMP CORPORATION
7270 Flamingo St (48001-4130)
P.O. Box 230035, Fair Haven (48023-0035)
PHONE...................810 794-4709
Thomas C Kershaw, *President*
Roy Lueth, *Vice Pres*
EMP: 9 **EST:** 1981
SALES (est): 624.6K **Privately Held**
SIC: 3567 Industrial furnaces & ovens

Clayton
Lenawee County

(G-3129)
FISCHELL MACHINERY LLC
6122 Whaley Hwy (49235-9632)
PHONE...................517 445-2828
James Fischer,
EMP: 7 **EST:** 2003
SALES (est): 553.2K **Privately Held**
WEB: www.fischellmachinery.com
SIC: 3599 Custom machinery

Clifford
Lapeer County

(G-3130)
ADVANCED DRAINAGE SYSTEMS INC
4800 Marlette Rd (48727-9743)
PHONE...................989 761-7610
Roger Corkins, *Branch Mgr*
EMP: 9
SALES (corp-wide): 1.9B **Publicly Held**
WEB: www.adspipe.com
SIC: 3084 Plastics pipe
PA: Advanced Drainage Systems, Inc.
4640 Trueman Blvd
Hilliard OH 43026
614 658-0050

(G-3131)
DECO ENGINEERING INC
Also Called: Newcor, Deco Division
9900 Main St (48727-9550)
PHONE...................989 761-7521
David S Segal, *Ch of Bd*
James Connor, *President*
EMP: 1 **EST:** 1942

SALES (est): 5.3MM
SALES (corp-wide): 146.6MM **Privately Held**
WEB: www.cieautomotive.com
SIC: 3599 Machine shop, jobbing & repair
HQ: Newcor, Inc.
1021 N Shiawassee St
Corunna MI 48817
248 537-0014

(G-3132)
MACHINE TOOL & GEAR INC
Also Called: Cie Newcor RGI
9900 Main St (48727-9550)
PHONE...................989 761-7521
EMP: 269
SALES (corp-wide): 146.6MM **Privately Held**
SIC: 3714 5051 3089 Motor vehicle parts & accessories; iron or steel flat products; automotive parts, plastic
HQ: Machine Tool & Gear, Inc.
1021 N Shiawassee St
Corunna MI 48817
989 743-3936

(G-3133)
ROCHESTER GEAR INC (DH)
9900 Main St (48727-9550)
PHONE...................989 659-2899
David Siegel, *President*
Bill Crane, *Controller*
EMP: 60 **EST:** 1944
SQ FT: 45,000
SALES (est): 35.4MM
SALES (corp-wide): 146.6MM **Privately Held**
SIC: 3714 Gears, motor vehicle
HQ: Newcor, Inc.
1021 N Shiawassee St
Corunna MI 48817
248 537-0014

Climax
Kalamazoo County

(G-3134)
BETZ CONTRACTING INC
Also Called: Betz Contracting and Machining
320 N Main St (49034-9502)
P.O. Box 156 (49034-0156)
PHONE...................269 746-3320
Sean Betz, *President*
Carol Ann Betz, *Corp Secy*
Rodney Betz, *Vice Pres*
Charles Betz, *Executive*
Carol Betz,
EMP: 6 **EST:** 1989
SALES (est): 1.1MM **Privately Held**
WEB: www.betzmachine.com
SIC: 3544 Special dies & tools

(G-3135)
BURKETT SIGNS CORP
15886 E Michigan Ave (49034-9710)
PHONE...................269 746-4285
Robb Perrin, *President*
Sean Perrin, *Admin Sec*
EMP: 16 **EST:** 1957
SQ FT: 2,400 **Privately Held**
WEB: www.burkettsigns.com
SIC: 3993 Signs & advertising specialties

Clinton
Lenawee County

(G-3136)
DST INDUSTRIES INC
11900 Tecumseh Clinton Rd (49236-9439)
PHONE...................734 941-0300
Dan Ulrich, *Manager*
EMP: 10
SQ FT: 174,000 **Privately Held**
WEB: www.dstindustries.com
SIC: 3714 Motor vehicle parts & accessories
HQ: Dst Industries, Inc.
34364 Goddard Rd
Romulus MI 48174
734 941-0300

(G-3137)
EDEN FOODS INC (PA)
Also Called: New Meridian
701 Tecumseh Rd (49236-9599)
PHONE...................517 456-7424
Michael Potter, *Ch of Bd*
Robert Andrews, *General Mgr*
John Ardrey, *General Mgr*
Nicholas Cannon, *General Mgr*
Jan Pfund, *COO*
◆ **EMP:** 70 **EST:** 1969
SQ FT: 40,000
SALES (est): 43.8MM **Privately Held**
WEB: www.edenfoods.com
SIC: 2099 Food preparations

(G-3138)
FORESTRY MANAGEMENT SVCS INC
Also Called: Hardwoods of Michigan
430 Division St (49236-9702)
P.O. Box 620 (49236-0620)
PHONE...................517 456-7431
Bob Vogel, *President*
Richard L Service, *Chairman*
John Binegar, *Vice Pres*
Jeff Mercy, *Vice Pres*
Ron Steele, *Safety Mgr*
◆ **EMP:** 140 **EST:** 1970
SQ FT: 3,000
SALES (est): 19.8MM **Privately Held**
WEB: www.hmilumber.com
SIC: 2421 2426 Kiln drying of lumber; furniture stock & parts, hardwood

(G-3139)
FRYE PRINTING COMPANY INC (PA)
11801 Tecumseh Clinton Rd (49236-9676)
PHONE...................517 456-4124
John R Frye, *President*
EMP: 15 **EST:** 1949
SQ FT: 10,700
SALES (est): 1.8MM **Privately Held**
WEB: www.fryeprinting.com
SIC: 2752 2789 2761 2759 Commercial printing, offset; bookbinding & related work; manifold business forms; commercial printing

(G-3140)
HAVERS HERITAGE
7500 Clinton Macon Rd (49236-9564)
PHONE...................517 423-3455
Sharon Haver, *Owner*
EMP: 5 **EST:** 1990
SALES (est): 231.8K **Privately Held**
WEB: www.leonelegal.com
SIC: 3999 Potpourri

(G-3141)
HMI HARDWOODS LLC
Also Called: Tri-County Logging
430 Division St (49236-9702)
P.O. Box 620 (49236-0620)
PHONE...................517 456-7431
Robert Vogel, *President*
John Binegar, *Vice Pres*
Jeffrey Mercy, *Vice Pres*
Ron Steele, *Safety Mgr*
Laura Gebhardt, *CFO*
EMP: 100 **EST:** 2004
SALES (est): 17.1MM
SALES (corp-wide): 950.6MM **Privately Held**
WEB: www.hmilumber.com
SIC: 2421 Sawmills & planing mills, general
PA: Hardwoods Distribution Inc
9440 202 St Unit 306
Langley BC V1M 4
604 881-1988

(G-3142)
STANSLEY MINERAL RESOURCES INC
Also Called: Adrian Sand & Stone
13500 Allen Rd (49236-9652)
PHONE...................517 456-6310
Dan White, *Manager*
EMP: 7
SALES (corp-wide): 5.9MM **Privately Held**
SIC: 1442 Construction sand & gravel

Clinton Township - Macomb County (G-3171)

PA: Stansley Mineral Resources, Inc.
3793 Silica Rd B
Sylvania OH 43560
419 843-2813

Clinton Township
Macomb County

(G-3143)
2 SG WOOKWORKS LLC
35360 Forton Ct (48035-5626)
PHONE..................586 884-7090
John Blumline, *Principal*
EMP: 4 **EST:** 2017
SALES (est): 54.1K **Privately Held**
WEB: www.2sgww.com
SIC: 2431 Millwork

(G-3144)
A & M INDUSTRIES INC
35590 Groesbeck Hwy (48035-2519)
PHONE..................586 791-5610
Frank Migliaczo, *President*
Royce C Sam, *General Mgr*
EMP: 14 **EST:** 1984
SQ FT: 12,000
SALES (est): 1.2MM **Privately Held**
WEB: www.amindustries.com
SIC: 3599 Machine shop, jobbing & repair

(G-3145)
A G CASE LLC
36227 Eaton Dr (48035-1446)
PHONE..................586 791-0125
Luigi Buccitelli, *Principal*
EMP: 4 **EST:** 2015
SALES (est): 132.4K **Privately Held**
SIC: 3523 Farm machinery & equipment

(G-3146)
A M T WELDING INC
21446 Carlo Dr (48038-1512)
PHONE..................586 463-7030
Joseph Ouimet, *President*
EMP: 8 **EST:** 1990
SQ FT: 5,000
SALES (est): 872.8K **Privately Held**
SIC: 7692 Welding repair

(G-3147)
A S A P TOOL INC
35660 Groesbeck Hwy (48035-2561)
PHONE..................586 790-6550
Thomas Smits, *President*
EMP: 4 **EST:** 1986
SQ FT: 6,400
SALES (est): 389.1K **Privately Held**
WEB: www.asaptoolinc.com
SIC: 3544 Special dies & tools

(G-3148)
A S PLUS INDUSTRIES INC
34728 Centaur Dr (48035-3701)
PHONE..................586 741-0400
Sarita Hingorani, *President*
Arun Hingorani, *Vice Pres*
EMP: 7 **EST:** 1992
SQ FT: 8,300
SALES (est): 792.2K **Privately Held**
SIC: 3089 Molding primary plastic

(G-3149)
A&D INDUSTRIES LLC
44645 Macomb Indus Dr (48036-1148)
PHONE..................586 291-6444
EMP: 5 **EST:** 2012
SALES (est): 156.5K **Privately Held**
SIC: 3999 Manufacturing industries

(G-3150)
AARON INCORPORATED
33674 Kelly Rd (48035-4844)
PHONE..................586 791-0320
Thomas A Dempsey, *President*
EMP: 8 **EST:** 1961
SQ FT: 8,000
SALES (est): 991.4K **Privately Held**
WEB: www.aaronincorporated.com
SIC: 3465 Body parts, automobile; stamped metal

(G-3151)
AARONS FABRICATION OF STEEL
21427 Carlo Dr (48038-1513)
PHONE..................586 883-0652
Sue Bursteinowicz, *President*
EMP: 7 **EST:** 2014
SALES (est): 592.4K **Privately Held**
WEB: www.aaronsfabrication.net
SIC: 3449 7359 Miscellaneous metalwork; home appliance, furniture & entertainment rental services

(G-3152)
ACCURATE INJECTION MOLDS INC
Also Called: A I M I
22264 Starks Dr (48036-1199)
PHONE..................586 954-2553
James P Jarrett, *President*
Debi Metcalfe, *Business Mgr*
EMP: 25 **EST:** 1988
SQ FT: 12,000
SALES (est): 2.2MM **Privately Held**
WEB: www.medbioinc.com
SIC: 3089 Injection molding of plastics

(G-3153)
ACHIEVE INDUSTRIES LLC
44421 N Groesbeck Hwy (48036-1117)
PHONE..................586 493-9780
Dave McGoffin,
EMP: 7 **EST:** 2011
SALES (est): 758.3K **Privately Held**
WEB: www.achieveind.com
SIC: 3999 Manufacturing industries

(G-3154)
ACME GEAR COMPANY INC
23402 Reynolds Ct (48036-1240)
PHONE..................586 465-7740
David P Kelly, *President*
Scott Kelly, *Vice Pres*
Jeffrey Kelly, *Treasurer*
EMP: 36 **EST:** 1960
SQ FT: 10,000
SALES (est): 1.2MM **Privately Held**
WEB: www.acmegearco.com
SIC: 3599 Machine shop, jobbing & repair

(G-3155)
ACTION WOOD TECHNOLOGIES INC
Also Called: Action Wood 360
44500 Reynolds Dr (48036-1246)
PHONE..................586 468-2300
Christopher A Grobbel, *CEO*
▲ **EMP:** 25 **EST:** 1984
SQ FT: 31,000
SALES (est): 5.5MM **Privately Held**
WEB: www.actionwood360.com
SIC: 2449 4783 Rectangular boxes & crates, wood; packing & crating

(G-3156)
ADMIRAL BROACH COMPANY INC
21391 Carlo Dr (48038-1511)
PHONE..................586 468-8411
Patrick W Considine, *President*
William Smith, *Vice Pres*
Debra Considine, *Office Mgr*
▲ **EMP:** 20 **EST:** 1976
SQ FT: 12,200
SALES (est): 4MM **Privately Held**
WEB: www.admiralbroach.com
SIC: 3545 Broaches (machine tool accessories)

(G-3157)
ADVANCED MOLD SOLUTIONS
43682 N Gratiot Ave (48036-3330)
PHONE..................586 468-6883
David Forner, *Owner*
EMP: 4 **EST:** 2004
SALES (est): 200.1K **Privately Held**
WEB: www.advancedmoldservices.com
SIC: 3544 Industrial molds

(G-3158)
ADVANTAGE DESIGN & TOOL INC
44319 Macomb Indus Dr (48036-1143)
PHONE..................586 463-2800
Michele Kerner, *President*
Joe Torre, *Vice Pres*
EMP: 7 **EST:** 1990
SALES (est): 800.2K **Privately Held**
WEB: www.advantagedesign.com
SIC: 3544 Special dies & tools

(G-3159)
AIM PLASTICS INC
22264 Starks Dr (48036-1199)
PHONE..................586 954-2553
Craig Fisher, *President*
Greg Dixon, *Engineer*
Kristina Palombo, *Art Dir*
James Jarrett, *Admin Sec*
EMP: 35 **EST:** 1993
SQ FT: 4,000
SALES (est): 9.1MM
SALES (corp-wide): 44.9MM **Privately Held**
WEB: www.medbioinc.com
SIC: 3089 Injection molding of plastics
PA: Medbio, Llc
5346 36th St Se
Grand Rapids MI 49512
616 245-0214

(G-3160)
ALADDIN MACHINING INC
21240 Carlo Dr (48038-1508)
PHONE..................586 465-4280
Linda Maskey, *President*
EMP: 6 **EST:** 1993
SQ FT: 4,200
SALES (est): 1MM **Privately Held**
WEB: www.aladdinmachining.com
SIC: 3542 Machine tools, metal forming type

(G-3161)
ALDEZ NORTH AMERICA
42463 Garfield Rd (48036-1651)
PHONE..................586 530-5314
Jeffrey Copek, *CEO*
Michael J Byrne, *Mng Member*
Jeffrey Copak,
EMP: 10 **EST:** 2007
SALES (est): 933K **Privately Held**
WEB: www.aldezna.com
SIC: 7389 4214 2653 3999 Industrial & commercial equipment inspection service; local trucking with storage; corrugated & solid fiber boxes; barber & beauty shop equipment; container, packaging & boxboard; packaging & shipping materials, foamed plastic

(G-3162)
ALLIED SIGNS INC
33650 Giftos Dr (48035-4241)
PHONE..................586 791-7900
Randy Schmitt, *President*
Carrie Howe, *Opers Staff*
Dominic Palazzolo, *Opers Staff*
Marie Smith, *CFO*
Art Conley, *Sales Staff*
EMP: 10 **EST:** 1994
SALES (est): 1MM **Privately Held**
WEB: www.alliedsignsinc.com
SIC: 3993 Electric signs

(G-3163)
AME INTERNATIONAL LLC
21481 Carlo Dr (48038-1513)
P.O. Box 182010, Shelby Township (48318-2010)
PHONE..................586 532-8981
EMP: 30
SALES (est): 950K **Privately Held**
SIC: 3999 Mfg Misc Products

(G-3164)
AMERICAN AIRCRAFT PARTS MFG CO
44801 Centre Ct E (48038-5512)
PHONE..................586 294-3300
Michael Thomas, *President*
James Tigani, *Vice Pres*
EMP: 26 **EST:** 1952
SQ FT: 33,267
SALES (est): 4.3MM **Privately Held**
WEB: www.aapmfg.com
SIC: 3728 Aircraft parts & equipment

(G-3165)
AMERICAN INK USA PRNTG & GRPHC
33812 Groesbeck Hwy (48035-3970)
PHONE..................586 790-2555
Karen Vaughn, *President*
Shannon Vaughn, *Controller*
EMP: 5 **EST:** 1999
SQ FT: 2,500
SALES (est): 372.2K **Privately Held**
WEB: www.americanink.biz
SIC: 2752 Commercial printing, offset

(G-3166)
AMERICAN LAZER CENTERS
16010 19 Mile Rd Ste 100 (48038-1141)
PHONE..................248 798-6552
Karen Harris, *Manager*
EMP: 5 **EST:** 2005
SALES (est): 69.4K **Privately Held**
SIC: 3845 Laser systems & equipment, medical

(G-3167)
AMERICHIP INTERNATIONAL INC
24700 Capital Blvd (48036-1350)
PHONE..................586 783-4598
William P Conlin, *Ch of Bd*
Richard Rossman, *President*
Edward D Rutkowski, *COO*
Richard Zyla, *Vice Pres*
Mark Shircliff, *VP Opers*
EMP: 32 **EST:** 2000
SALES (est): 2.6MM **Privately Held**
WEB: www.americhiplacc.com
SIC: 3541 Machine tools, metal cutting type

(G-3168)
AMOUR YOUR BODY LLC
Also Called: Ayb
16518 Festian Dr (48035-2229)
PHONE..................586 846-3100
Canetha Porter, *Mng Member*
EMP: 4 **EST:** 2017
SALES (est): 100K **Privately Held**
WEB: www.amouryourbody.com
SIC: 5999 2844 Cosmetics; lotions, shaving

(G-3169)
AMPHENOL CORPORATION
Also Called: Amphenol Sine Systems
44724 Morley Dr (48036-1357)
PHONE..................586 465-3131
Alma Vancamp, *Owner*
Scott Wilton, *General Mgr*
Chris Furman, *Buyer*
Dale Ryngaert, *Sales Staff*
EMP: 345
SALES (corp-wide): 8.6B **Publicly Held**
WEB: www.amphenol.com
SIC: 3678 Electronic connectors
PA: Amphenol Corporation
358 Hall Ave
Wallingford CT 06492
203 265-8900

(G-3170)
AMTEX INC
34680 Nova Dr (48035-3716)
PHONE..................586 792-7888
Daniel Cowie, *President*
Steven Schutz, *Vice Pres*
EMP: 7 **EST:** 1995
SQ FT: 5,000
SALES (est): 766.5K **Privately Held**
WEB: www.amtex-inc.com
SIC: 3625 8711 Electric controls & control accessories, industrial; engineering services

(G-3171)
ANBO TOOL & MANUFACTURING INC
22785 Macomb Indus Dr (48036-1181)
PHONE..................586 465-7610
Andrew Music, *President*
Bobby Ray Wiley, *Admin Sec*
EMP: 5 **EST:** 1989
SQ FT: 2,400
SALES (est): 534.7K **Privately Held**
SIC: 3545 Precision tools, machinists'

Clinton Township - Macomb County (G-3172)

(G-3172)
ANN BARRETTE
44381 Manitou Dr (48038-4436)
PHONE....................586 713-8145
Ann Barrette, *Principal*
EMP: 4 **EST:** 2010
SALES (est): 58.5K **Privately Held**
SIC: 3999 Barrettes

(G-3173)
ARC SERVICES OF MACOMB INC
44050 N Gratiot Ave (48036-1308)
PHONE....................586 469-1600
Lisa Lepine, *President*
Deborah Shirkey, *Human Resources*
Ron Kimball, *Exec Dir*
Matthew Peters, *Director*
Shelly Taras, *Representative*
EMP: 39 **EST:** 1953
SQ FT: 20,000
SALES (est): 3.3MM **Privately Held**
WEB: www.arcservices.org
SIC: 8331 3471 Sheltered workshop; plating & polishing

(G-3174)
AUDIA WOODWORKING & FINE FURN
16627 Millar Rd (48036-1639)
PHONE....................586 296-6330
Salvatore Audia, *President*
EMP: 12 **EST:** 1955
SQ FT: 30,000
SALES (est): 590.5K **Privately Held**
WEB: www.audiawoodworking.net
SIC: 2511 2431 Tables, household: wood; chairs, household, except upholstered: wood; desks, household: wood; millwork

(G-3175)
AUDIONET AMERICA INC
33900 Harper Ave Ste 101 (48035-4258)
PHONE....................586 944-0043
Colleen Shefferly, *Principal*
Rebecca Wagner, *Accounts Mgr*
Randall Dervishi, *Marketing Staff*
Dana Miriani, *Manager*
Brenda Thompson, *Executive Asst*
EMP: 13 **EST:** 2011
SALES (est): 4.6MM **Privately Held**
WEB: www.audionetamerica.com
SIC: 3842 Hearing aids

(G-3176)
AUTOMOTIVE PROTOTYPE STAMPING
17207 Millar Rd (48036-2071)
PHONE....................586 445-6792
EMP: 8
SALES (est): 1.1MM **Privately Held**
SIC: 3469 Mfg Metal Stampings

(G-3177)
AVATAR INC
44041 N Groesbeck Hwy (48036-1115)
PHONE....................586 846-3195
EMP: 6 **EST:** 2014
SALES (est): 98K **Privately Held**
SIC: 3312 Blast furnaces & steel mills

(G-3178)
AXALTA COATING SYSTEMS LLC
45000 River Ridge Dr # 200 (48038-5582)
PHONE....................586 846-4160
Michael Magdich, *Vice Pres*
William Dubose, *Technical Mgr*
Alex Klemens, *Research*
Alex McIntosh, *Research*
Jonathan Nguyen, *Research*
EMP: 4
SALES (corp-wide): 3.7B **Publicly Held**
WEB: www.axalta.com
SIC: 2851 Paints & allied products
HQ: Axalta Coating Systems, Llc
50 Applied Bank Blvd # 300
Glen Mills PA 19342
855 547-1461

(G-3179)
AXIS TMS CORP
Also Called: Blusys
36380 Garfield Rd Ste 2 (48035-1162)
P.O. Box 328, Royal Oak (48068-0328)
PHONE....................248 509-2440
Nick Nader Sr, *CFO*
Mike Dzopa, *Sales Staff*
EMP: 21 **EST:** 2013
SALES (est): 1.3MM **Privately Held**
WEB: www.axistms.com
SIC: 7371 3669 Computer software development; intercommunication systems, electric

(G-3180)
BECK INDUSTRIES INC
24454 Sorrentino Ct (48035-3258)
PHONE....................586 790-4060
Mike Beck, *President*
Mary Beck, *Vice Pres*
EMP: 5 **EST:** 1994
SQ FT: 8,500
SALES (est): 750K **Privately Held**
WEB: www.beckindustries.com
SIC: 3599 Machine shop, jobbing & repair; machine & other job shop work

(G-3181)
BELL FORKLIFTS
4660 Centaur Ave (48035)
PHONE....................586 469-7979
EMP: 4
SALES (est): 379.2K **Privately Held**
SIC: 3537 Forklift

(G-3182)
BENCHWORK INC
Also Called: Bench Works
34100 Kelly Rd (48035-3369)
PHONE....................586 464-6699
Joseph L Janis, *President*
Craig Janis, *Principal*
Jason Janis, *Principal*
Brenda Vujanic, *COO*
Thad Bench, *Manager*
EMP: 4 **EST:** 1988
SQ FT: 4,000
SALES (est): 381.8K **Privately Held**
SIC: 2599 Work benches, factory

(G-3183)
BEST TOOL & ENGINEERING CO
34730 Nova Dr (48035-3717)
PHONE....................586 792-4119
Jean Cherluck, *President*
Joe Cherluck, *Principal*
Jim Cherluck, *Vice Pres*
Joseph Cherluck, *Engineer*
EMP: 12 **EST:** 1981
SALES (est): 2.5MM **Privately Held**
WEB: www.bteplastics.com
SIC: 3544 Special dies & tools

(G-3184)
BIG BOY RESTAURANTS INTL LLC
16880 Hall Rd (48038-1205)
PHONE....................586 263-6220
Dave Newcomb, *Branch Mgr*
EMP: 54
SALES (corp-wide): 49.4MM **Privately Held**
WEB: www.bigboy.com
SIC: 5812 2051 5461 Restaurant, family chain; bread, cake & related products; bakeries
PA: Big Boy Restaurants International L.L.C.
26300 Telg Rd Ste 101
Southfield MI 48033
586 759-6000

(G-3185)
BLUE WATER FABRICATORS INC
21462 Carlo Dr (48038-1512)
PHONE....................586 307-3550
James Landuyt, *President*
EMP: 6 **EST:** 2020
SALES (est): 277.7K **Privately Held**
WEB: www.bluewaterfab.com
SIC: 3444 Sheet metalwork

(G-3186)
BOB G MACHINING LLC
44345 N Groesbeck Hwy (48036-1116)
PHONE....................586 285-1400
Bob Gjerovski, *Mng Member*
Jasmina Gjerovski,
EMP: 7 **EST:** 2010
SQ FT: 3,000
SALES (est): 650K **Privately Held**
WEB: www.bobgmachining.com
SIC: 3541 3545 Vertical turning & boring machines (metalworking); milling machine attachments (machine tool accessories)

(G-3187)
BORDER LINE RICH APPAREL LLC
15437 Lkside Vlg Dr Unit (48038)
PHONE....................866 959-3003
Charnita Hinton, *Mng Member*
EMP: 4 **EST:** 2020
SALES (est): 45K **Privately Held**
SIC: 2211 Apparel & outerwear fabrics, cotton

(G-3188)
BORDER LINE RICH CLOTHING LLC
Also Called: Retail
21396 Cass Ave (48036-1404)
PHONE....................586 267-5251
Charnita Hinton, *CEO*
EMP: 5 **EST:** 2020
SALES (est): 50K **Privately Held**
SIC: 2211 5999 5632 Apparel & outerwear fabrics, cotton; perfumes & colognes; apparel accessories

(G-3189)
BROWE INC
36359 Harper Ave (48035-2958)
PHONE....................248 877-3800
Brian K Browe, *President*
EMP: 5 **EST:** 2009
SALES (est): 521K **Privately Held**
WEB: www.browe-inc.com
SIC: 3827 Optical instruments & lenses

(G-3190)
BROWNLEE GROUP LLC
23333 Quinn Rd (48035-3732)
PHONE....................512 202-0568
Michael Brownlee, *Mng Member*
EMP: 4 **EST:** 2020
SALES (est): 180.7K **Privately Held**
SIC: 3537 Trucks: freight, baggage, etc.: industrial, except mining

(G-3191)
BURKARD INDUSTRIES INC
35300 Kelly Rd (48035-2446)
P.O. Box 81877, Rochester (48308-1877)
PHONE....................586 791-6520
John A Burkard, *CEO*
Jay Burkard, *President*
Patricia Moore, *Plant Mgr*
Cyndi Stahl, *Supervisor*
▲ **EMP:** 104 **EST:** 1933
SQ FT: 70,000
SALES (est): 9.7MM **Privately Held**
WEB: www.burkardind.com
SIC: 3479 Coating of metals & formed products

(G-3192)
C & J FABRICATION INC
34885 Groesbeck Hwy (48035-3366)
PHONE....................586 791-6269
EMP: 6
SALES (est): 894.2K **Privately Held**
SIC: 2221 3441 Manmade Broadwoven Fabric Mill Structural Metal Fabrication

(G-3193)
C & S MILLWORK INC
44163 N Groesbeck Hwy (48036-1179)
PHONE....................586 465-6470
Christopher Griebe, *Owner*
Steven Griebe, *Corp Secy*
EMP: 10 **EST:** 1993
SQ FT: 3,000
SALES (est): 898.1K **Privately Held**
SIC: 2431 Millwork

(G-3194)
CARBIDE SURFACE COMPANY (PA)
44336 Reynolds Dr (48036-1242)
PHONE....................586 465-6110
Hugh Vestal, *President*
Mary Vestal, *Vice Pres*
EMP: 7
SQ FT: 8,000
SALES (est): 1.7MM **Privately Held**
WEB: www.carbsurf.com
SIC: 3479 3545 Coating of metals & formed products; drill bushings (drilling jig)

(G-3195)
CARMAC TOOL LLC
22969 Rasch Dr (48035-3736)
PHONE....................586 649-7245
EMP: 5 **EST:** 2016
SALES (est): 146K **Privately Held**
WEB: www.carmactool.com
SIC: 3599 Machine shop, jobbing & repair

(G-3196)
CERTIFIED METAL PRODUCTS INC
22802 Morelli Dr (48036-1176)
PHONE....................586 598-1000
Paul Steinmetz, *President*
Ken McKen, *Manager*
Nadia Puglisi, *Executive*
EMP: 10 **EST:** 1989
SQ FT: 6,500
SALES (est): 1MM **Privately Held**
WEB: www.cmpinc.us
SIC: 3544 Special dies & tools

(G-3197)
CHATMAN WALKER PUBLISHING LLC
22456 Glen Oak Dr (48035-4115)
PHONE....................586 604-7534
Patricia Chatman, *Principal*
EMP: 4 **EST:** 2015
SALES (est): 55.8K **Privately Held**
SIC: 2741 Miscellaneous publishing

(G-3198)
CHIEFTAIN COATING LLC
35300 Kelly Rd (48035-2446)
PHONE....................586 791-1866
Mark Thompson, *CEO*
Debbie Wilkins, *Controller*
EMP: 50 **EST:** 2019
SALES (est): 3.5MM **Privately Held**
SIC: 3479 Coating of metals & formed products

(G-3199)
CHOICE CORPORATION
Also Called: Choice Mold Components
44383 Reynolds Dr (48036-1243)
PHONE....................586 783-5600
James W Humes, *President*
EMP: 28 **EST:** 1974
SALES (est): 900.1K **Privately Held**
WEB: www.choicemold.com
SIC: 3599 Machine shop, jobbing & repair

(G-3200)
CHOICE MOLD COMPONENTS INC
44383 Reynolds Dr (48036-1243)
PHONE....................586 783-5600
James W Humes, *President*
Kathryn Humes, *Vice Pres*
▲ **EMP:** 26 **EST:** 1994
SALES (est): 3.6MM **Privately Held**
WEB: www.choicemold.com
SIC: 3599 Machine shop, jobbing & repair

(G-3201)
CIGNET LLC (PA)
24601 Capital Blvd (48036-1345)
PHONE....................586 307-3790
Patrick Green, *CEO*
Tom Davidson, *COO*
Will Lianos, *CFO*
Richard S Crawford, *Manager*
Crawford Group LLC,
EMP: 40 **EST:** 1996
SQ FT: 1,500

GEOGRAPHIC SECTION
Clinton Township - Macomb County (G-3229)

SALES (est): 26.5MM **Privately Held**
WEB: www.cignet.net
SIC: 3694 Engine electrical equipment

(G-3202)
CIRCLES WAY TO GO AROUND INC
43508 Rivergate Dr (48038-1350)
PHONE.....................313 384-1193
EMP: 10
SALES (est): 450K **Privately Held**
SIC: 2397 Mfg Schiffli Embroideries

(G-3203)
COLONIAL BUSHINGS INC
44336 Reynolds Dr (48036-1242)
PHONE.....................586 954-3880
Hugh Vestal, *President*
Mary Vestal, *Vice Pres*
EMP: 24 EST: 1946
SQ FT: 8,000
SALES (est): 1.5MM
SALES (corp-wide): 1.7MM **Privately Held**
WEB: www.colonialbushings.com
SIC: 3545 3568 Drill bushings (drilling jig); power transmission equipment
PA: Carbide Surface Company
44336 Reynolds Dr
Clinton Township MI 48036
586 465-6110

(G-3204)
COLONIAL MOLD INC
Also Called: Colonial Group
44479 Reynolds Dr (48036-1245)
PHONE.....................586 469-4944
Cathy Roberts, *CEO*
Richard J Roberts, *President*
Rich Blasutig, *Plant Mgr*
Bill Mead, *Sales Staff*
Maureen Lambiris, *Admin Asst*
EMP: 35 EST: 1985
SQ FT: 45,000
SALES (est): 2.9MM **Privately Held**
WEB: www.colgrp.com
SIC: 3544 Industrial molds

(G-3205)
COLT - 7 CORPORATION
34859 Groesbeck Hwy (48035-3366)
PHONE.....................586 792-9050
Craig Bubka, *President*
EMP: 9 EST: 1977
SQ FT: 10,000
SALES (est): 158.2K **Privately Held**
WEB: www.colt7corp.com
SIC: 3599 Machine shop, jobbing & repair

(G-3206)
COMPLETE KITCHEN DESIGN LLC
33827 Harper Ave (48035-4217)
PHONE.....................586 790-2800
EMP: 4 EST: 2016
SALES (est): 56K **Privately Held**
WEB: www.completekitchen.design
SIC: 3639 Major kitchen appliances, except refrigerators & stoves

(G-3207)
COMPLETE PROTOTYPE SVCS INC (PA)
Also Called: C P S
44783 Morley Dr (48036-1357)
PHONE.....................586 690-8897
Chris Michayluk, *President*
Howard Madden, *General Mgr*
Aaron Malinowski, *General Mgr*
Don Miller, *Design Engr*
Benny Larocca, *CFO*
EMP: 150 EST: 1995
SQ FT: 24,000
SALES (est): 53.3MM **Privately Held**
WEB: www.completeprototype.com
SIC: 3543 3714 Industrial patterns; motor vehicle body components & frame

(G-3208)
COMPLETE SURFACE TECHNOLOGIES
21338 Carlo Dr (48038-1510)
PHONE.....................586 493-5800
Peter Ruggirello, *CEO*
Gordon Pinger, *President*

Bill Hickson, *Managing Dir*
Debbie Hagedorn, *Administration*
EMP: 38 EST: 1999
SQ FT: 42,000
SALES (est): 5.6MM **Privately Held**
WEB: www.cststudio.com
SIC: 3544 Dies, plastics forming; forms (molds), for foundry & plastics working machinery

(G-3209)
CONNER ENGINEERING LLC
21200 Carlo Dr (48038-1508)
PHONE.....................586 465-9590
Doyal Reich, *Engineer*
Tom Gerada, *Director*
Bill Middletown,
EMP: 20 EST: 1964
SQ FT: 22,000
SALES (est): 1.8MM **Privately Held**
WEB: www.connerengineering.com
SIC: 3599 Machine shop, jobbing & repair

(G-3210)
CONSTRUCTION RETAIL SVCS INC
Also Called: Llowds Retail Construction
38555 Moravian Dr (48036-1958)
PHONE.....................586 469-2289
Gregory Oakwood, *President*
Timothy Ozment, *Vice Pres*
Robert Moore, *Treasurer*
EMP: 6 EST: 2005
SALES (est): 393.1K **Privately Held**
SIC: 2542 7389 Fixtures, store: except wood;

(G-3211)
CONTINENTAL CARBIDE LTD INC
23545 Reynolds Ct (48036-1269)
PHONE.....................586 463-9577
Terrence Mc Quade, *President*
Karola Mc Quade, *Corp Secy*
EMP: 31 EST: 1982
SQ FT: 20,000
SALES (est): 626.2K **Privately Held**
WEB: www.mcquade-industries.com
SIC: 2819 5085 Carbides; industrial supplies

(G-3212)
COUGAR CUTTING TOOLS INC
23529 Reynolds Ct (48036-1269)
PHONE.....................586 469-1310
Vasko Stefanoski, *President*
Sue Stefanoski, *Vice Pres*
Andrew Stefanoski, *Opers Mgr*
Piyush Sharma, *Marketing Mgr*
EMP: 27 EST: 1987
SQ FT: 10,000
SALES (est): 2.8MM **Privately Held**
WEB: www.cougarct.com
SIC: 3545 Cutting tools for machine tools

(G-3213)
CREATIVE SURFACES INC
20500 Hall Rd (48036-5326)
PHONE.....................586 226-2950
Stella M Giannini, *President*
Tina Truman, *General Mgr*
EMP: 10 EST: 2007
SALES (est): 2MM **Privately Held**
WEB: www.cre8tivesurfaces.com
SIC: 3531 2851 Surfacers, concrete grinding; epoxy coatings

(G-3214)
CTS MANUFACTURING INC
44760 Trinity Dr (48038-1553)
PHONE.....................586 465-4594
Steven Sterrett, *President*
Kim Sterrett, *Vice Pres*
EMP: 8 EST: 1984
SQ FT: 5,000
SALES (est): 917.1K **Privately Held**
WEB: www.ctsmanufacturinginc.com
SIC: 3544 Special dies & tools

(G-3215)
CUMMINS INC
43575 N Gratiot Ave (48036-3327)
PHONE.....................586 469-2010
Susan Lake, *Manager*
EMP: 4

SALES (corp-wide): 19.8B **Publicly Held**
WEB: www.cummins.com
SIC: 5084 3519 Engines & parts, diesel; internal combustion engines
PA: Cummins Inc.
500 Jackson St
Columbus IN 47201
812 377-5000

(G-3216)
D-N-S INDUSTRIES INC
Also Called: American Roll Manufacturing
44805 Trinity Dr (48038-1557)
PHONE.....................586 465-2444
Dennis R Mc Quade, *President*
Carol Mc Quade, *Vice Pres*
EMP: 33 EST: 1980
SQ FT: 20,000
SALES (est): 2.4MM **Privately Held**
WEB: www.dnsind.com
SIC: 3599 3547 Machine shop, jobbing & repair; steel rolling machinery

(G-3217)
DATUM PRECISION MACHINE INC
35235 Automation Dr (48035-3115)
PHONE.....................586 790-1120
Raymond Alarie, *President*
Bonnie Alarie, *Vice Pres*
EMP: 7 EST: 1988
SQ FT: 8,000
SALES (est): 596.2K **Privately Held**
SIC: 3599 Machine shop, jobbing & repair

(G-3218)
DEJON CABINETRY INC
44310 N Groesbeck Hwy (48036-1110)
PHONE.....................586 468-8611
John Brunke, *President*
EMP: 4 EST: 2006
SALES (est): 233.5K **Privately Held**
WEB: www.dejoncabinetry.com
SIC: 2434 Wood kitchen cabinets

(G-3219)
DETROIT FLAME HARDENING CO
35674 Shook Ln (48035-3227)
PHONE.....................586 484-1726
Allen Leach, *Principal*
EMP: 9
SALES (corp-wide): 4.4MM **Privately Held**
WEB: www.detroitflame.com
SIC: 3398 Brazing (hardening) of metal
PA: Detroit Flame Hardening Company Inc
17644 Mount Elliott St
Detroit MI
313 891-2936

(G-3220)
DETROIT PRINTED PRODUCTS
42121 Brianna Dr (48038-5223)
PHONE.....................586 226-3860
Beverly Nowaczyk, *Principal*
EMP: 4 EST: 2015
SALES (est): 97.7K **Privately Held**
WEB: www.detroitprintshop.com
SIC: 2752 Commercial printing, lithographic

(G-3221)
DIAMOND DIE AND MOLD COMPANY
Also Called: Ddm
35401 Groesbeck Hwy (48035-2518)
PHONE.....................586 791-0700
Joann Hinds, *President*
Sharon Baldyga, *Vice Pres*
Patricia Quackenbush, *Treasurer*
EMP: 15 EST: 1956
SQ FT: 17,200
SALES (est): 1.8MM **Privately Held**
WEB: www.diamond-die.com
SIC: 3544 Special dies & tools

(G-3222)
DIAMOND RACING PRODUCTS
35075 Automation Dr (48035-3117)
PHONE.....................586 792-6620
Joe Dewey, *Manager*
EMP: 10 EST: 2015

SALES (est): 253.7K **Privately Held**
WEB: www.diamondracing.net
SIC: 3599 Machine shop, jobbing & repair

(G-3223)
DIAMOND RACING PRODUCTS INC
23003 Diamond Dr (48035-3126)
PHONE.....................586 792-6620
Vincent J Cavallaro, *President*
EMP: 17 EST: 2000
SALES (est): 681.8K **Privately Held**
WEB: www.diamondracing.net
SIC: 3599 Machine shop, jobbing & repair

(G-3224)
DIFFERENT MUSIC GROUP ENT LLC
42389 Clinton Place Dr (48038-1627)
PHONE.....................313 980-6159
Anthony Anderson, *Mng Member*
EMP: 5
SALES (est): 150K **Privately Held**
SIC: 2741 Music books: publishing & printing

(G-3225)
DIVERSIFIED FABRICATORS INC
Also Called: DFI
21482 Carlo Dr (48038-1512)
PHONE.....................586 868-1000
Robert Landuyt, *President*
Laura Winans, *Accounting Mgr*
EMP: 18 EST: 1981
SQ FT: 14,600
SALES (est): 3.2MM **Privately Held**
WEB: www.diversifiedfab.com
SIC: 3441 3444 Fabricated structural metal; housings for business machines, sheet metal; vats, sheet metal

(G-3226)
DRAKE ENTERPRISES INC
24800 Capital Blvd (48036-1351)
PHONE.....................586 783-3009
Leroy Stemple, *President*
Keith Stemple, *Exec VP*
Richard Stemple, *Vice Pres*
Joseph Sharp, *Engineer*
Jennifer Kathawa, *Human Resources*
▲ EMP: 45 EST: 1952
SQ FT: 38,000
SALES (est): 12MM **Privately Held**
WEB: www.drakeent.com
SIC: 3714 Motor vehicle body components & frame; steering mechanisms, motor vehicle

(G-3227)
E D M SHUTTLE INC
44695 Enterprise Dr (48038-1533)
PHONE.....................586 468-9880
Daniel Bruck, *President*
Jacqueline Bruck, *Manager*
EMP: 6 EST: 1988
SQ FT: 5,600
SALES (est): 541.3K **Privately Held**
SIC: 3599 Electrical discharge machining (EDM)

(G-3228)
EATON CORPORATION
19700 Hall Rd Ste B (48038-4451)
PHONE.....................586 228-2029
Cheryl Breza, *Principal*
EMP: 5 **Privately Held**
WEB: www.eatonelectrical.com
SIC: 3625 Relays & industrial controls
HQ: Eaton Corporation
1000 Eaton Blvd
Cleveland OH 44122
440 523-5000

(G-3229)
EDGEMEN SCREEN PRINTING
19757 15 Mile Rd (48035-3407)
PHONE.....................586 465-6820
James Lawson, *Principal*
EMP: 4 EST: 2018
SALES (est): 162.2K **Privately Held**
WEB: www.edgemenprinting.com
SIC: 2752 Commercial printing, lithographic

Clinton Township - Macomb County (G-3230)

(G-3230)
ELECTROPLATING INDUSTRIES INC
Also Called: E P I
21410 Carlo Dr (48038-1512)
PHONE................................586 469-2390
Jeffrey Curtis, *President*
EMP: 15 **EST:** 1981
SQ FT: 19,400
SALES (est): 2.1MM **Privately Held**
WEB: www.epiplating.com
SIC: 3471 Electroplating of metals or formed products; plating of metals or formed products

(G-3231)
ELITE MANUFACTURING TECH LLC
33670 Lipke St (48035-3617)
PHONE................................586 846-2055
EMP: 14
SALES (est): 2.9MM **Privately Held**
WEB: www.elitemanufacturingtechnologies.com
SIC: 3999 Manufacturing industries

(G-3232)
ENTREPRENEUR SOLUTIONS LLC
Also Called: Be At Ease Products
20235 Wybridge St Apt 201 (48036)
P.O. Box 841, Mount Clemens (48046-0841)
PHONE................................248 660-2858
Michelle Gibbs,
Patricia Gibbs,
EMP: 5 **EST:** 2020
SALES (est): 201.5K **Privately Held**
WEB: www.entrepsolutions.com
SIC: 2844 Toilet preparations

(G-3233)
EXTREME SIGNS INC
34853 S Gratiot Ave (48035-3546)
PHONE................................586 846-3251
Hussein Bazzi, *Principal*
EMP: 6 **EST:** 2015
SALES (est): 275.5K **Privately Held**
SIC: 3993 Signs & advertising specialties

(G-3234)
FAB-JET SERVICES LLC
44335 Macomb Indus Dr (48036-1143)
PHONE................................586 463-9622
Jason Glezman,
EMP: 5 **EST:** 2005
SALES (est): 500K **Privately Held**
WEB: www.fab-jet.com
SIC: 3496 3545 Miscellaneous fabricated wire products; cutting tools for machine tools

(G-3235)
FALCON INDUSTRY INC
44660 Macomb Indus Dr (48036-1185)
PHONE................................586 468-7010
Joe Azzopardi, *President*
Joseph Azzopardi, *President*
Erik Azzopardi, *Engineer*
EMP: 14 **EST:** 1983
SALES (est): 1.7MM **Privately Held**
WEB: www.falconindustry.com
SIC: 3544 Special dies & tools

(G-3236)
FEGA TOOL & GAGE COMPANY
44837 Macomb Indus Dr (48036-1140)
PHONE................................586 469-4400
Roy Usteski, *President*
Martha Ann Usteski, *Treasurer*
EMP: 14 **EST:** 1952
SQ FT: 11,000
SALES (est): 1.2MM **Privately Held**
WEB: www.fegatool.com
SIC: 3544 7389 3545 3599 Dies & die holders for metal cutting, forming, die casting; grinding, precision: commercial or industrial; machine tool attachments & accessories; gauges (machine tool accessories); machine shop, jobbing & repair

(G-3237)
FERRO FAB LLC
Also Called: Abz Steel Systems
23309 Quinn Rd (48035-3732)
PHONE................................586 791-3561
Gina Wolf, *CEO*
EMP: 10 **EST:** 2009
SALES (est): 2MM **Privately Held**
WEB: www.ferro-fab.com
SIC: 5051 2296 3441 Steel; steel tire cords & tire cord fabrics; fabricated structural metal

(G-3238)
FIDO ENTERPRISES INC
34692 Nova Dr (48035-3716)
PHONE................................586 790-8200
Philip L Edwards, *President*
Brenda Nemens, *Plant Mgr*
▲ **EMP:** 9
SQ FT: 7,500
SALES (est): 1.4MM **Privately Held**
WEB: www.fidobones.com
SIC: 3089 Injection molded finished plastic products

(G-3239)
FIVE LAKES MANUFACTURING INC
Also Called: F L M
24400 Capital Blvd (48036-1342)
PHONE................................586 463-4123
Roger Eger Jr, *CEO*
Patricia Tischbein, *President*
EMP: 50 **EST:** 1994
SQ FT: 40,000
SALES (est): 7.4MM **Privately Held**
WEB: www.fivelakesmfg.com
SIC: 2431 Doors, wood

(G-3240)
FLAMINGO LABEL CO
21428 Carlo Dr (48038-1512)
PHONE................................586 469-9587
Brian Klauss, *President*
Jason Ford, *Sales Staff*
EMP: 17 **EST:** 1988
SALES (est): 1.8MM **Privately Held**
WEB: www.flamingolabel.com
SIC: 2759 Labels & seals: printing

(G-3241)
FLEX MANUFACTURING INC
44805 Trinity Dr (48038-1557)
PHONE................................586 469-1076
David Gleason, *President*
Quin Gleason, *Vice Pres*
EMP: 17 **EST:** 1974
SQ FT: 4,000
SALES (est): 551.1K **Privately Held**
WEB: www.flexmfginc.com
SIC: 3599 Machine shop, jobbing & repair

(G-3242)
FLUID SYSTEMS ENGINEERING INC
18855 E 14 Mile Rd (48035-3901)
PHONE................................586 790-8880
Mark T Steiner, *President*
John Doll, *Vice Pres*
Paul Lipiec, *Foreman/Supr*
Philip Kubik, *Engineer*
Joseph A Baker, *Treasurer*
EMP: 27 **EST:** 1964
SQ FT: 19,700
SALES (est): 10MM **Privately Held**
WEB: www.fluidsystemsengineering.com
SIC: 5085 3561 5084 Valves & fittings; industrial pumps & parts; machine tools & accessories
HQ: Motion & Control Enterprises Llc
100 Williams Dr
Zelienople PA 16063
724 452-6000

(G-3243)
FREER TOOL & DIE INC
Also Called: Freer Tool and Supply
44675 Morley Dr (48036-1358)
PHONE................................586 463-3200
John Fulton, *President*
Bill Fulton, *General Mgr*
Joe Corneille, *Accounts Mgr*
Chai Vang, *Prgrmr*
▲ **EMP:** 31 **EST:** 1994
SQ FT: 22,280
SALES (est): 5.3MM **Privately Held**
WEB: www.freertool.com
SIC: 3544 Special dies & tools

(G-3244)
FREER TOOL & DIE INC
Also Called: Freer Tool & Supply
44675 Morley Dr (48036-1358)
PHONE................................586 741-5274
John Fulton, *Principal*
EMP: 7 **EST:** 1994
SALES (est): 519.3K **Privately Held**
WEB: www.freertool.com
SIC: 3544 Special dies & tools

(G-3245)
FRICTION COATING CORPORATION
44833 Centre Ct (48038-1316)
PHONE................................586 731-0990
Charles Neff, *President*
EMP: 27 **EST:** 1992
SALES (est): 2.1MM **Privately Held**
WEB: www.frictioncoating.com
SIC: 3599 Machine shop, jobbing & repair

(G-3246)
FRICTION CONTROL LLC
35360 Forton Ct (48035-5626)
PHONE................................586 741-8493
John Bireescu, *Mng Member*
Susan Bireescu,
EMP: 5 **EST:** 1996
SQ FT: 5,288
SALES (est): 966.9K **Privately Held**
WEB: www.frictioncontrol.com
SIC: 3568 Clutches, except vehicular

(G-3247)
GAGE BILT INC
44766 Centre Ct (48038-1315)
PHONE................................586 226-1500
Bruce Godfrey, *President*
Loree Godfrey, *Opers Mgr*
Tony Potts, *Engineer*
Bruce T Godfrey, *Administration*
EMP: 45 **EST:** 1956
SQ FT: 25,005
SALES: 4.2MM **Privately Held**
WEB: www.gagebilt.com
SIC: 3452 Rivets, metal; bolts, metal

(G-3248)
GARBARINO INDUSTRIES LLC
24100 Capital Blvd (48038-1338)
PHONE................................586 215-5479
EMP: 4 **EST:** 2017
SALES (est): 68.1K **Privately Held**
WEB: www.garbarinoind.com
SIC: 3999 Manufacturing industries

(G-3249)
GREENE METAL PRODUCTS INC (PA)
24500 Capital Blvd (48038-1348)
PHONE................................586 465-6800
Bruce Wilden, *President*
Tina Smith, *General Mgr*
Robert Wilden, *Chairman*
Jamie Schneider, *CFO*
Ann Smith, *Receptionist*
▲ **EMP:** 49 **EST:** 1975
SQ FT: 60,000
SALES (est): 14.3MM **Privately Held**
WEB: www.greene-metal-products-inc.sb-contract.com
SIC: 3444 3443 3441 Sheet metalwork; fabricated plate work (boiler shop); fabricated structural metal

(G-3250)
GRIND-ALL PRECISION TOOL CO
21300 Carlo Dr (48038-1510)
PHONE................................586 954-3430
M Dean McCreadie, *President*
EMP: 10 **EST:** 1967
SQ FT: 12,000
SALES (est): 1.3MM **Privately Held**
WEB: www.grindallprecisiontool.com
SIC: 3545 3599 Precision tools, machinists'; grinding castings for the trade

(G-3251)
HANDY BINDERY CO INC
23170 Giacoma Ct (48036-4608)
PHONE................................586 469-2240
Suzanne Canu, *President*
EMP: 22 **EST:** 1986
SQ FT: 8,000
SALES (est): 2.4MM **Privately Held**
WEB: www.handybindery.com
SIC: 2759 2789 Letterpress printing; bookbinding & related work

(G-3252)
HEATING INDUCTION SERVICES INC
24483 Sorrentino Ct (48036-3240)
PHONE................................586 791-3160
Ernest W Taylor, *President*
George Haddad, *Vice Pres*
Richard Barnes, *CIO*
Shirley Taylor, *Admin Sec*
EMP: 9 **EST:** 1980
SQ FT: 12,400
SALES (est): 1.9MM **Privately Held**
WEB: www.heatinginductionservices.com
SIC: 3567 7699 Induction heating equipment; industrial machinery & equipment repair

(G-3253)
HIGGINS LAKE FAMILY CAMPGROUND
37012 Charter Oaks Blvd (48036-2404)
PHONE................................989 821-6891
Monica Worman, *Owner*
EMP: 4 **EST:** 2017
SALES (est): 66.9K **Privately Held**
SIC: 2452 Prefabricated wood buildings

(G-3254)
HOUSTON FLAME HARDENING CO
35674 Shook Ln (48035-3227)
PHONE................................713 926-8017
EMP: 7 **EST:** 2019
SALES (est): 125.7K **Privately Held**
WEB: www.detroitflame.com
SIC: 3398 Metal heat treating

(G-3255)
HUSITE ENGINEERING CO INC
44831 N Groesbeck Hwy (48036-1124)
PHONE................................248 588-0337
Larry Huston, *President*
Jack T Huston, *Vice Pres*
EMP: 17 **EST:** 1957
SALES (est): 1.3MM **Privately Held**
WEB: www.husite.biz
SIC: 3543 3369 3363 Industrial patterns; nonferrous foundries; aluminum die-castings

(G-3256)
HYLITE TOOL & MACHINE INC
44685 Macomb Indus Dr (48036-1148)
PHONE................................586 465-7878
Holger Joost, *President*
Gary Romatz, *Vice Pres*
Harold Joost, *Treasurer*
EMP: 7 **EST:** 1987
SQ FT: 12,000
SALES (est): 750K **Privately Held**
WEB: www.transport-industry.com
SIC: 3599 Machine shop, jobbing & repair

(G-3257)
IDC INDUSTRIES INC
18901 15 Mile Rd (48035-2504)
PHONE................................586 427-4321
Jamie Pangborn, *President*
Michael Pangborn, *Vice Pres*
Andrew Janies, *Treasurer*
Chris Mansur, *Manager*
Rose Mattiacci, *Admin Asst*
EMP: 42 **EST:** 1968
SQ FT: 50,000
SALES (est): 12.7MM **Privately Held**
WEB: www.idcind.com
SIC: 3568 5085 Power transmission equipment; power transmission equipment & apparatus

▲ = Import ▼ = Export
◆ = Import/Export

GEOGRAPHIC SECTION

(G-3258)
INFINITY RECYCLING LLC
Also Called: Infinity Transportation
44057 N Groesbeck Hwy (48036-1123)
PHONE.....................248 939-2563
Peter Corrado, *Vice Pres*
EMP: 10 EST: 2014
SALES (est): 743.6K **Privately Held**
WEB: www.infinityrecycling.org
SIC: 2611 Pulp manufactured from waste or recycled paper

(G-3259)
INTEGRATED INDUSTRIES INC
33670 Lipke St (48035-3617)
PHONE.....................586 790-1550
Paul T Newman, *President*
EMP: 11 EST: 1989
SQ FT: 25,000
SALES (est): 438.9K **Privately Held**
WEB: www.integrated-ind.com
SIC: 3444 Ducts, sheet metal

(G-3260)
INTERNATIONAL MOLD CORPORATION (PA)
23224 Giacoma Ct (48036-4608)
PHONE.....................586 783-6890
James H Pelcher, *President*
Michael Lilla, *Treasurer*
Ben Pfropper, *Sales Staff*
Tim Cook, *Program Mgr*
Tim Malloy, *Program Mgr*
▲ EMP: 96 EST: 2005
SQ FT: 12,000
SALES (est): 22.9MM **Privately Held**
WEB: www.internationalmold.net
SIC: 3544 Industrial molds

(G-3261)
J & J METAL PRODUCTS INC
Also Called: J & J Sheet Metal
34145 Groesbeck Hwy (48035-3355)
PHONE.....................586 792-2680
Robert J Kehoe, *President*
Robert Kehole, *President*
EMP: 4 EST: 1945
SQ FT: 3,800
SALES (est): 463K **Privately Held**
WEB: www.jandjsheetmetal.com
SIC: 3444 Ducts, sheet metal

(G-3262)
J M MOLD & ENGINEERING
44910 Vic Wertz Dr (48036-1251)
PHONE.....................586 783-3300
Rene Bossio, *Vice Pres*
EMP: 5 EST: 2019
SALES (est): 85.2K **Privately Held**
SIC: 3541 Machine tools, metal cutting type

(G-3263)
JAM TIRE INC
36031 Groesbeck Hwy (48035-1542)
PHONE.....................586 772-2900
Kenny Weber, *Branch Mgr*
EMP: 27
SALES (corp-wide): 17.5MM **Privately Held**
WEB: www.jambestone.com
SIC: 7534 5531 5014 3011 Tire retreading & repair shops; automotive tires; tires & tubes; tires & inner tubes
PA: Jam Tire Inc
6202 Fairfield Dr
Northwood OH 43619
419 661-1800

(G-3264)
JEM COMPUTERS INC
Also Called: Jem Tech Group
23537 Lakepointe Dr (48036-3323)
PHONE.....................586 783-3400
James Miller, *CEO*
Jami M Moore, *President*
Denise Bonino, *Purchasing*
Carrie Senkowski, *Sales Staff*
Christie Rosso, *Marketing Staff*
EMP: 14 EST: 1988
SQ FT: 6,500
SALES (est): 8.7MM **Privately Held**
WEB: www.jemtechgroup.com
SIC: 5045 3629 3577 2522 Computer peripheral equipment; computer software; electronic generation equipment; power conversion units, a.c. to d.c.: static-electric; computer peripheral equipment; printers, computer; office furniture, except wood; computer peripheral equipment

(G-3265)
JOGGLE TOOL & DIE CO INC
24424 Kolleen Ln (48035-5438)
PHONE.....................586 792-7477
Thomas Platte, *President*
Frank Hiegel, *Vice Pres*
Terry Jelineck, *Admin Sec*
EMP: 4 EST: 1952
SQ FT: 6,000
SALES (est): 350.4K **Privately Held**
SIC: 3544 Special dies & tools

(G-3266)
JUST ADORABLE CROCHETING
17443 Kingsbrooke Cir # 103 (48038-3766)
PHONE.....................586 746-7137
Brenda J Carroll, *Principal*
EMP: 4 EST: 2012
SALES (est): 50K **Privately Held**
SIC: 2399 Hand woven & crocheted products

(G-3267)
JVIS - USA LLC
Also Called: Jvis USA LLC - Harper
34501 Harper Ave (48035-3708)
P.O. Box 530, Mount Clemens (48046-0530)
PHONE.....................586 803-6056
Nick Lewis, *Managing Prtnr*
Michael Alexander, *Vice Pres*
Gregory Kasinec, *Engineer*
Nicholas Allam, *Program Mgr*
Mark Frentner, *Program Mgr*
EMP: 400
SALES (corp-wide): 226.2MM **Privately Held**
WEB: www.jvis.us
SIC: 3559 Automotive related machinery
PA: Jvis - Usa, Llc
52048 Shelby Pkwy
Shelby Township MI 48315
586 884-5700

(G-3268)
JVIS MANUFACTURING LLC
Jvis Manufacturing-Harper
34501 Harper Ave (48035-3708)
PHONE.....................586 405-1950
EMP: 200
SALES (corp-wide): 226.2MM **Privately Held**
WEB: www.jvis.us
SIC: 3089 Automotive parts, plastic
HQ: Jvis Manufacturing Llc
1285 N Crystal Ave
Benton Harbor MI 49022

(G-3269)
K AND K MACHINE TOOLS INC
22393 Starks Dr (48036-1197)
PHONE.....................586 463-1177
Moritz C Cunha, *President*
Mark Cunha, *Vice Pres*
Susan Cunha, *Admin Sec*
EMP: 5 EST: 1995
SQ FT: 6,000
SALES (est): 484.6K **Privately Held**
SIC: 3561 3544 Industrial pumps & parts; special dies, tools, jigs & fixtures

(G-3270)
KATECH INC
Also Called: Katech Performance
24324 Sorrentino Ct (48035-3238)
PHONE.....................586 791-4120
Steve Spurr, *President*
EMP: 43 EST: 2014
SALES (est): 4.6MM **Privately Held**
WEB: www.katechengines.com
SIC: 3519 Parts & accessories, internal combustion engines

(G-3271)
KEN BUDOWICK FABRICATING LLC
42781 Heydenreich Rd (48038-2422)
PHONE.....................586 263-1318
Kenneth Budowick, *Principal*
EMP: 4 EST: 2015
SALES (est): 39.6K **Privately Held**
SIC: 3999 Manufacturing industries

(G-3272)
KENCOAT COMP
24500 Capital Blvd (48036-1348)
PHONE.....................586 754-1400
James L Schroth, *President*
Robert A Connelly, *Vice Pres*
EMP: 8 EST: 1955
SQ FT: 12,200
SALES (est): 1.1MM
SALES (corp-wide): 11.6MM **Privately Held**
SIC: 3479 Coating of metals & formed products
PA: Schroth Enterprises Inc
95 Tonnacour Pl
Grosse Pointe Farms MI 48236
586 759-4240

(G-3273)
KENNEDY SALES INC
19683 Tanglewood Cir (48038-4964)
PHONE.....................586 228-9390
James D Kennedy, *President*
Constance Kennedy, *Vice Pres*
EMP: 2 EST: 1991
SALES (est): 2.1MM **Privately Held**
WEB: www.kennedysales.com
SIC: 3949 Playground equipment

(G-3274)
KUHNHENN BREWING CO LLC
3600 Groes Beck Hwy (48035)
PHONE.....................586 231-0249
Emily Daum, *Branch Mgr*
EMP: 8
SALES (corp-wide): 2.7MM **Privately Held**
WEB: www.brewingworld.com
SIC: 2082 Brewers' grain
PA: Kuhnhenn Brewing Co., L.L.C.
5951 Chicago Rd
Warren MI 48092
586 979-8361

(G-3275)
L F M ENTERPRISES INC
Also Called: Laporte Industries
33256 Kelly Rd (48036-3982)
PHONE.....................586 792-7220
Dennis Laporte, *President*
Diane Hanson, *Corp Secy*
EMP: 30 EST: 1984
SQ FT: 20,000
SALES (est): 4.5MM **Privately Held**
SIC: 3599 Machine shop, jobbing & repair

(G-3276)
L LEWALLEN CO INC
22900 Interstate Dr (48036-3713)
P.O. Box 180176, Utica (48318-0176)
PHONE.....................586 792-9930
Lou Lewallen, *President*
Matt Hammond, *General Mgr*
Matthew Hammer, *Purchasing*
Robert Burke, *Sales Mgr*
Jason Lewallen, *Sales Staff*
EMP: 15 EST: 1991
SALES (est): 2.4MM **Privately Held**
WEB: www.llewallen.com
SIC: 2821 Plastics materials & resins

(G-3277)
L T C ROLL & ENGINEERING CO (PA)
23500 John Gorsuch Dr (48036-1215)
PHONE.....................586 465-1023
Andrew Ligda, *President*
Ned M Cavallaro, *Vice Pres*
Ned Cavallaro, *Vice Pres*
Drew Ligda, *Vice Pres*
Gene Moore, *Maint Spvr*
▲ EMP: 28 EST: 1967
SQ FT: 100,000
SALES (est): 19.9MM **Privately Held**
WEB: www.ltcroll.com
SIC: 3469 Metal stampings

(G-3278)
L&L PRINTING INC
Also Called: American Speedy Printing
42120 Garfield Rd (48038-1645)
PHONE.....................586 263-0060
Loren K Maurina, *President*
EMP: 6 EST: 1991
SQ FT: 1,600
SALES (est): 832.7K **Privately Held**
WEB: www.allegramarketingprint.com
SIC: 2752 Commercial printing, offset

(G-3279)
LEE PRINTING COMPANY
21222 Cass Ave (48036-1403)
P.O. Box 832, Mount Clemens (48046-0832)
PHONE.....................586 463-1564
Keith Lesperance, *President*
Ryan Lesperance, *Manager*
Beverly Lesperance, *Shareholder*
EMP: 10 EST: 1964
SQ FT: 4,800
SALES (est): 2MM **Privately Held**
WEB: www.golpc.com
SIC: 2752 Commercial printing, offset

(G-3280)
LODUCA WOODWORKS LLC
37151 Willow Ln (48036-3666)
PHONE.....................734 626-2525
Salvatore Loduca,
EMP: 4 EST: 2017
SALES (est): 306.8K **Privately Held**
WEB: www.loducawoodworks.com
SIC: 2431 Millwork

(G-3281)
LULULEMON USA INC
17360 Hall Rd Ste 183 (48038-4871)
PHONE.....................586 690-6001
EMP: 12
SALES (corp-wide): 3.2B **Privately Held**
SIC: 2339 Athletic clothing: women's, misses' & juniors'
HQ: Lululemon Usa Inc.
2201 140th Ave E
Sumner WA 98390
604 732-6124

(G-3282)
LUSH
17370 Hall Rd (48038-4873)
PHONE.....................586 228-1594
EMP: 4 EST: 2018
SALES (est): 74.4K **Privately Held**
SIC: 2844 Toilet preparations

(G-3283)
M & J MANUFACTURING INC
22711 Morelli Dr (48036-1154)
PHONE.....................586 778-6322
Michael Belkowski, *President*
EMP: 5 EST: 1999
SALES (est): 580.7K **Privately Held**
SIC: 3441 Fabricated structural metal

(G-3284)
M & M TURNING CO
19000 15 Mile Rd (48035-2506)
PHONE.....................586 791-7188
Dennis Irwin, *CEO*
Charlie J Laforest, *President*
Ron A Radlick, *Opers Mgr*
Lori Maslar, *Office Admin*
EMP: 28 EST: 1991
SALES (est): 5.9MM **Privately Held**
WEB: www.alphaprecisionaerospace.com
SIC: 3542 Spinning lathes

(G-3285)
M S MANUFACTURING INC
44431 Reynolds Dr (48036-1245)
PHONE.....................586 463-2788
Craig S Walworth, *President*
Terry Walworth, *Vice Pres*
EMP: 10 EST: 2010
SQ FT: 20,000
SALES (est): 2.2MM **Privately Held**
WEB: www.msmfg.net
SIC: 3714 Motor vehicle body components & frame

Clinton Township - Macomb County (G-3286) — GEOGRAPHIC SECTION

(G-3286)
MACOMB BUSINESS FORMS INC
Also Called: American Graphics Printing
34895 Groesbeck Hwy (48035-3366)
PHONE.................................586 790-8500
Robert A Hindman, *President*
Michael Grix, *General Mgr*
Virginia Hindman, *Vice Pres*
EMP: 16 **EST:** 1975
SQ FT: 10,000
SALES (est): 2.4MM **Privately Held**
SIC: 2752 Commercial printing, offset

(G-3287)
MACOMB COUNTY COUGARS
21673 Laurel St (48035-3611)
PHONE.................................586 231-5543
Scott Johnson, *President*
Keith Anderson, *Treasurer*
Shantell Mauldin, *Accountant*
Tanisha Garner, *Director*
Dwayne Arnold, *Bd of Directors*
EMP: 6 **EST:** 2014
SALES (est): 253.5K **Privately Held**
WEB: www.macombcountycougars.com
SIC: 2711 Newspapers, publishing & printing

(G-3288)
MACOMB PRINTING INC
Also Called: Macomb Marketing Media
44272 N Groesbeck Hwy (48036-1188)
PHONE.................................586 463-2301
Ronald J Bracali II, *President*
Ronald Bracali, *President*
Pam Bracali, *Vice Pres*
EMP: 25 **EST:** 1960
SQ FT: 35,000
SALES (est): 834.9K **Privately Held**
WEB: www.macombprinting.com
SIC: 2752 2791 2789 Commercial printing, offset; typesetting; bookbinding & related work

(G-3289)
MACOMB RESIDENTIAL OPPRTNTS
15780 17 Mile Rd (48038-2700)
PHONE.................................586 231-0363
Chassi Webster, *Manager*
EMP: 4 **EST:** 2019
SALES (est): 112.1K **Privately Held**
WEB: www.macombresidential.com
SIC: 2759 Commercial printing

(G-3290)
MACOMB SHEET METAL INC
35195 Forton Ct (48035-3132)
PHONE.................................586 790-4600
Richard Opatik, *President*
Kathy Opatik, *Vice Pres*
EMP: 27 **EST:** 1982
SQ FT: 20,000
SALES (est): 5.5MM **Privately Held**
WEB: www.msmetal.com
SIC: 3699 Laser welding, drilling & cutting equipment

(G-3291)
MAJIK GRAPHICS INC
19751 15 Mile Rd (48035-3407)
PHONE.................................586 792-8055
Marcetta Hurst, *President*
EMP: 9 **EST:** 1991
SQ FT: 4,000
SALES (est): 945K **Privately Held**
WEB: www.majikgraphics.com
SIC: 3993 Signs & advertising specialties

(G-3292)
MANOR INDUSTRIES INC
24400 Maplehurst Dr (48036-1323)
PHONE.................................586 463-4604
Ray Tokarczyk, *President*
Jerald Decker, *President*
Richard Decker, *Vice Pres*
Neal Hamel, *Sales Executive*
EMP: 56 **EST:** 1937
SQ FT: 33,000
SALES (est): 299K **Privately Held**
WEB: www.manorindustries.com
SIC: 3599 Machine shop, jobbing & repair

(G-3293)
MANOS AUTHENTIC LLC
22599 15 Mile Rd (48035-6020)
PHONE.................................800 242-2796
EMP: 5 **EST:** 2017
SALES (est): 253K **Privately Held**
WEB: www.manosauthentic.com
SIC: 2096 Potato chips & similar snacks

(G-3294)
MARINE MACHINING AND MFG
33475 Giftos Dr (48035-4242)
PHONE.................................586 791-8800
Brian A Jenich, *Owner*
Val Jenich, *Co-Owner*
▼ **EMP:** 6 **EST:** 1979
SQ FT: 1,000
SALES (est): 401.2K **Privately Held**
WEB: www.marinemachining.com
SIC: 3599 Machine shop, jobbing & repair

(G-3295)
MASTER MACHINE & TOOL CO INC
23414 Reynolds Ct (48036-1240)
PHONE.................................586 469-4243
Tom Mireau, *CEO*
Natalie Mireau, *President*
EMP: 8 **EST:** 1954
SQ FT: 8,900 **Privately Held**
WEB: www.mastermachineandtool.com
SIC: 3544 3545 Jigs & fixtures; precision tools, machinists'

(G-3296)
MAYCO INTERNATIONAL LLC
Also Called: Njt Enterprises LLC
34501 Harper Ave (48035-3708)
P.O. Box 180149, Utica (48318-0149)
PHONE.................................586 803-6000
Allen L Grajek, *CFO*
EMP: 210 **Privately Held**
WEB: www.maycointernational.com
SIC: 3089 Injection molding of plastics
PA: Mayco International Llc
    42400 Merrill Rd
    Sterling Heights MI 48314

(G-3297)
MECCOM INDUSTRIAL PRODUCTS CO
Also Called: Pebco Sales
22760 Macomb Indus Dr (48036-1137)
PHONE.................................586 463-2828
Paul Baltzer Jr, *CEO*
Philip Bearance, *President*
Glenn Ortez, *Vice Pres*
EMP: 14 **EST:** 1981
SALES (est): 3.5MM
SALES (corp-wide): 5MM **Privately Held**
WEB: www.meccomindustrial.com
SIC: 5085 3069 Valves & fittings; expansion joints, rubber
PA: Pebco Sales, Inc
    22760 Macomb Indus Dr
    Clinton Township MI 48036
    586 463-7850

(G-3298)
METALCRAFT CUTTING TOOLS LLC
37060 Garfield Rd Ste T-4 (48036-3647)
P.O. Box 757, Sterling Heights (48311-0757)
PHONE.................................586 243-5591
Sandra Tapper, *Sales Engr*
Greg Maison, *Mng Member*
EMP: 8 **EST:** 2010
SALES (est): 836K **Privately Held**
WEB: www.mc-tools.com
SIC: 3599 Machine shop, jobbing & repair

(G-3299)
METRO SIGN FABRICATORS INC
43984 N Groesbeck Hwy (48036-1107)
PHONE.................................586 493-0502
Timothy White, *President*
Bradley Cash, *Manager*
John Newman, *Manager*
Craig Baines, *Technician*
EMP: 5 **EST:** 2003
SALES (est): 570.3K **Privately Held**
WEB: www.signfabricators.com
SIC: 3993 Signs & advertising specialties

(G-3300)
MIDSTATES INDUSTRIAL GROUP INC
21299 Carlo Dr (48038-1509)
PHONE.................................586 307-3414
Arnold D Jones, *President*
Dean Jones, *Purchasing*
Joey Peters, *Purchasing*
Frank Soullier, *Engineer*
Barbara Hopkins, *Bookkeeper*
EMP: 24 **EST:** 1999
SQ FT: 18,500
SALES (est): 5.6MM **Privately Held**
WEB: www.midstatesind.com
SIC: 3465 3711 8711 Automotive stampings; automobile assembly, including specialty automobiles; engineering services

(G-3301)
MILLENNIUM MOLD & TOOL INC
35225 Automation Dr (48035-3115)
PHONE.................................586 791-1711
Michelle Fournier, *President*
Joseph R Fournier, *Vice Pres*
Molly Keesling, *Office Mgr*
EMP: 4 **EST:** 1997
SQ FT: 4,200
SALES (est): 521.2K **Privately Held**
WEB: www.millmold.com
SIC: 3544 Special dies & tools

(G-3302)
MINI-MIX INC
33600 Kelly Rd (48035-4844)
PHONE.................................586 792-2260
Joe Latorre, *President*
Sam Latorre, *Vice Pres*
EMP: 40 **EST:** 1973
SQ FT: 3,000
SALES (est): 3.3MM **Privately Held**
WEB: www.minimixinc.net
SIC: 3273 Ready-mixed concrete

(G-3303)
MJC TOOL & MACHINE CO INC
35806 Groesbeck Hwy (48035-2524)
PHONE.................................586 790-4766
Laura Clarkston, *CEO*
Michael Clarkston, *Admin Sec*
EMP: 7 **EST:** 2011
SQ FT: 5,000
SALES (est): 452.6K **Privately Held**
WEB: www.mjctoolmachine.com
SIC: 7699 3545 7539 Industrial machinery & equipment repair; machine tool accessories; machine shop, automotive

(G-3304)
MORLEY BRANDS LLC
23770 Hall Rd (48036-1275)
PHONE.................................586 468-4300
Ronald W Rapson, *Mng Member*
EMP: 48 **EST:** 2002
SALES (est): 2.5MM
SALES (corp-wide): 176.8MM **Privately Held**
WEB: www.morleycandy.com
SIC: 2064 5441 Candy & other confectionery products; candy
HQ: Sanders Candy, Llc
    23770 Hall Rd
    Clinton Township MI 48036
    800 651-7263

(G-3305)
MOUNT CLEMENS ORTHOPEDIC APPLS
Also Called: Mount Clmens Orthopaedic Appls
24432 Crocker Blvd (48036-3215)
PHONE.................................586 463-3600
Rolf Schroeter, *President*
Werner Schroeter, *President*
EMP: 5 **EST:** 1972
SALES (est): 427.2K **Privately Held**
SIC: 3842 5999 Orthopedic appliances; orthopedic & prosthesis applications

(G-3306)
MT CLEMENS GLASS & MIRROR CO
1231 S Gratiot Ave (48036-3595)
PHONE.................................586 465-1733
David Egge, *President*
EMP: 9 **EST:** 1972
SQ FT: 7,800
SALES (est): 960.8K **Privately Held**
WEB: www.mtclemensglass.org
SIC: 1793 3442 Glass & glazing work; window & door frames

(G-3307)
MY SECRET BUNDLES LLC
42491 Clinton Place Dr (48038-1634)
PHONE.................................586 610-2804
Nacole McKinney,
EMP: 5 **EST:** 2020
SALES (est): 150.7K **Privately Held**
SIC: 3999 Hair & hair-based products

(G-3308)
NORRIS GRAPHICS INC
Also Called: Signs By Tomorrow
33251 S Gratiot Ave (48035-4039)
PHONE.................................586 447-0646
Fax: 586 447-0650
EMP: 4
SALES (est): 260K **Privately Held**
SIC: 3993 Signsadv Specs

(G-3309)
NORTH-EAST GAGE INC
33398 Kelly Rd (48035-3983)
PHONE.................................586 792-6790
Harry James Freer, *President*
EMP: 7 **EST:** 1987
SQ FT: 5,000
SALES (est): 750K **Privately Held**
WEB: www.northeastgage.com
SIC: 3545 Gauges (machine tool accessories)

(G-3310)
OAKLEY INDUSTRIES INC (PA)
35166 Automation Dr (48035-3113)
PHONE.................................586 791-3194
Ronald Oakley, *CEO*
Michael Oakley, *President*
Brenda Oakley, *Corp Secy*
Don Gielespi, *Safety Mgr*
Michae Goniwicha, *Sales Mgr*
EMP: 30
SQ FT: 8,800
SALES (est): 16.8MM **Privately Held**
WEB: www.oakley-ind.com
SIC: 3465 3089 Automotive stampings; injection molding of plastics

(G-3311)
OAKLEY INDUSTRIES INC
35224 Automation Dr (48035-3114)
PHONE.................................586 792-1261
Ronald Oakley, *Manager*
EMP: 110
SALES (corp-wide): 16.8MM **Privately Held**
WEB: www.oakley-ind.com
SIC: 3465 Automotive stampings
PA: Oakley Industries, Inc.
    35166 Automation Dr
    Clinton Township MI 48035
    586 791-3194

(G-3312)
ODYSSEY TOOL LLC
22373 Starks Dr (48036-1197)
PHONE.................................586 468-6696
Carol Harris, *Manager*
George Tilli,
EMP: 12 **EST:** 2001
SALES (est): 2.7MM **Privately Held**
WEB: www.odysseytool.com
SIC: 3544 Special dies & tools

(G-3313)
OMEGA PLASTIC INC
24401 Capital Blvd (48036-1343)
PHONE.................................816 246-3115
Melvin Gross, *President*
Stan Wilson, *Treasurer*
EMP: 42 **EST:** 1992
SALES (est): 371.4K **Privately Held**
WEB: www.opinc.com
SIC: 3089 Injection molding of plastics

(G-3314)
OMEGA PLASTICS INC
24401 Capital Blvd (48036-1343)
PHONE.................................586 954-2100
Jeffrey Kaczperski, *President*
Brian Dimuzio, *Maint Spvr*

GEOGRAPHIC SECTION

Clinton Township - Macomb County (G-3342)

EMP: 92 EST: 1984
SALES (est): 24.2MM Privately Held
WEB: www.opinc.com
SIC: 3089 3544 Injection molded finished plastic products; industrial molds

(G-3315)
OMNICO AGV LLC
Also Called: L & J Omnico Agv
44538 Macomb Indus Dr (48036-1186)
PHONE..................586 268-7700
Gerald Vanneste,
EMP: 10 EST: 2012
SQ FT: 19,400
SALES (est): 822.2K Privately Held
SIC: 3711 Trucks, pickup, assembly of

(G-3316)
OXYGENPLUS LLC
15760 19 Mile Rd Ste E (48038-6319)
PHONE..................586 221-9112
Chad Moline, Vice Pres
Robert Rudowski, Mng Member
EMP: 5 EST: 2007
SALES (est): 406.1K Privately Held
SIC: 3841 Medical instruments & equipment, blood & bone work

(G-3317)
PCT SECURITY INC
34668 Nova Dr (48035-3716)
PHONE..................888 567-3287
EMP: 4
SALES (est): 979.7K Privately Held
SIC: 5065 7382 3699 Whol Electronic Parts/Equipment Security Systems Services Mfg Electrical Equipment/Supplies

(G-3318)
PERFORMANCE SAILING INC
Also Called: U K Sailmakers
24227 Sorrentino Ct (48035-3237)
PHONE..................586 790-7500
Alex J Declercq, President
EMP: 8 EST: 1987
SQ FT: 12,000
SALES (est): 259.1K Privately Held
WEB: www.californiarentsaver.com
SIC: 2394 2221 Sails: made from purchased materials; broadwoven fabric mills, manmade

(G-3319)
PLAST-O-FOAM LLC
24601 Capital Blvd (48036-1345)
PHONE..................586 307-3790
Mark Arrowood, QC Mgr
Lisa Antosh, Accountant
Andy Watts, Marketing Mgr
Jeremy Tom, Program Mgr
Steve Westfall, Manager
▲ EMP: 74 EST: 1980
SQ FT: 110,000
SALES (est): 23MM
SALES (corp-wide): 26.5MM Privately Held
WEB: www.plastofoam.com
SIC: 3089 Injection molding of plastics; pallets, plastic
PA: Cignet, L.L.C.
24601 Capital Blvd
Clinton Township MI 48036
586 307-3790

(G-3320)
PLASTIC SERVICE CENTERS INC
21445 Carlo Dr (48038-1513)
PHONE..................586 307-3900
Mike Youngblood, President
Arduino Carducci, Vice Pres
David Youngblood, Vice Pres
EMP: 13 EST: 1995
SQ FT: 25,000
SALES (est): 3.5MM Privately Held
WEB: www.plasticservice.com
SIC: 2821 Plastics materials & resins

(G-3321)
PLASTICOS INC
21445 Carlo Dr Ste B (48038-1513)
PHONE..................586 493-1908
Marcelino Ramirez III, President
Steve Anderson, President
EMP: 4 EST: 2012
SQ FT: 20,000
SALES (est): 385.5K Privately Held
WEB: www.plasticosinc.com
SIC: 2821 Plastics materials & resins

(G-3322)
POWERSCREEN OF MICHIGAN LLC
36639 Groesbeck Hwy (48045-1553)
PHONE..................586 690-7224
Donald Northey, Administration
EMP: 9 EST: 2014
SALES (est): 321.3K Privately Held
WEB: www.powerscreenofmi.com
SIC: 3531 Construction machinery

(G-3323)
PRECISION ADVANCED MACHINING
24400 Maplehurst Dr (48036-1323)
PHONE..................586 463-3900
Gerald R Decker, President
David Decker, General Mgr
Richard Decker Jr, Vice Pres
Dolf Burnham, Foreman/Supr
Jason Chumbler, Manager
▲ EMP: 53 EST: 1937
SQ FT: 35,000
SALES (est): 5.5MM Privately Held
WEB: www.precisionadvancedmachining.com
SIC: 3599 Machine shop, jobbing & repair

(G-3324)
PRECISIONCRAFT CO
44395 Reynolds Dr (48036-1243)
PHONE..................586 954-9510
Gary R Hartigan, President
Doug Hartigan, Vice Pres
Jack Hartigan, Vice Pres
Jim Hartigan, Vice Pres
EMP: 14 EST: 1964
SQ FT: 13,850
SALES: 2.2MM Privately Held
WEB: www.pcicraft.com
SIC: 3599 Machine shop, jobbing & repair

(G-3325)
PRESS-WAY INC
Also Called: Grant Industries
19101 15 Mile Rd (48035-2508)
PHONE..................586 790-3324
Robert Grant, President
Steven Grant, Vice Pres
Tim Schley, Human Res Mgr
Robert Schmitz, Manager
EMP: 41 EST: 1961
SALES (est): 2.7MM
SALES (corp-wide): 16.1MM Privately Held
WEB: www.pressway.it
SIC: 3465 3469 Body parts, automobile: stamped metal; metal stampings
PA: Grant Industries, Incorporated
33415 Groesbeck Hwy
Fraser MI 48026
586 293-9200

(G-3326)
PRIME MOLD LLC
44645 Macomb Indus Dr (48036-1148)
PHONE..................586 221-2512
Tim Whitmore, Sales Mgr
Timothy Whitmore,
EMP: 15 EST: 2016
SALES (est): 1.5MM Privately Held
WEB: www.primemold.com
SIC: 3544 Industrial molds

(G-3327)
PRIORITY WASTE LLC
42822 Garfield Rd (48038-1656)
PHONE..................586 228-1200
Pauline R Stamper,
EMP: 20 EST: 2018
SALES (est): 1.6MM Privately Held
WEB: www.prioritywaste.com
SIC: 4212 3443 Dump truck haulage; dumpsters, garbage

(G-3328)
PRO - TECH GRAPHICS LTD
34851 Groesbeck Hwy (48035-3366)
PHONE..................586 791-6363
David Hoffman, President
▲ EMP: 11 EST: 1987
SQ FT: 5,600
SALES (est): 1.3MM Privately Held
WEB: www.protechgraphics.com
SIC: 3479 Etching & engraving

(G-3329)
PRO-LINE DOORS LLC
24415 Maplehurst Dr (48036-1324)
PHONE..................586 765-1657
Keith Craig, President
EMP: 5 EST: 2012
SALES (est): 524.4K Privately Held
WEB: www.prolinedoors.com
SIC: 3442 Garage doors, overhead: metal

(G-3330)
R & R BROACH INC
21391 Carlo Dr (48038-1511)
PHONE..................586 779-2227
Patrick W Considine, President
EMP: 5 EST: 1960
SALES (est): 445.5K Privately Held
WEB: www.rrbroach.com
SIC: 3541 Machine tools, metal cutting type

(G-3331)
RECARO AUTOMOTIVE NORTH AMER (HQ)
24801 Capital Blvd (48036-1347)
PHONE..................586 210-2600
Emil Kreycik, President
James Koelzer, Vice Pres
Dave Quenneville, Senior Buyer
Alan Kowalewski, CFO
Brian Sabo, Sales Staff
◆ EMP: 80 EST: 1988
SQ FT: 110,000
SALES (est): 107.4MM Privately Held
SIC: 2531 8711 Seats, automobile; engineering services

(G-3332)
RECARO NORTH AMERICA INC
24801 Capital Blvd (48036-1347)
PHONE..................734 254-4704
EMP: 500
SALES (corp-wide): 844.4K Privately Held
SIC: 2531 Public Building And Related Furniture,Nsk
HQ: Recaro Automotive North America, Llc
24801 Capital Blvd
Clinton Township MI 48036

(G-3333)
REEF TOOL & GAGE CO
44800 Macomb Indus Dr (48036-1146)
PHONE..................586 468-3000
E Robert Langtry Jr, President
EMP: 23 EST: 1980
SALES (est): 1.2MM Privately Held
WEB: www.rtgcinc.com
SIC: 3544 3545 Special dies & tools; jigs: inspection, gauging & checking; gauges (machine tool accessories)

(G-3334)
REGENCY CONSTRUCTION CORP
Also Called: Regency Dki
35240 Forton Ct (48035-3131)
PHONE..................586 741-8000
Scott Stamper, President
EMP: 30 EST: 1991
SQ FT: 3,000
SALES (est): 4.4MM Privately Held
WEB: www.regencydrt.com
SIC: 7349 1521 8744 8748 Janitorial service, contract basis; general remodeling, single-family houses; ; business consulting; manufactured hardware (general)

(G-3335)
RELIABLE REASONABLE TL SVC LLC
21356 Carlo Dr (48038-1510)
PHONE..................586 630-6016
Jason Rhodes, CEO
Ronald Rhodes,
EMP: 16 EST: 2005
SQ FT: 16,000
SALES (est): 1.4MM Privately Held
WEB: www.reliableandreasonable.com
SIC: 3089 Injection molded finished plastic products

(G-3336)
RETURNABLE PACKAGING CORP
1917 S Riveerhill Dr (48038)
PHONE..................586 206-8050
Bruce Steffens, President
EMP: 10 EST: 1996
SALES (est): 270.8K Privately Held
SIC: 3443 Trash racks, metal plate

(G-3337)
RICHMOND INSTRS & SYSTEMS INC
21392 Carlo Dr (48038-1510)
PHONE..................586 954-3770
Dennis Mach, President
Marilyn Mach, Corp Secy
Mike Mach, Vice Pres
Aaron Fisher, Sales Mgr
EMP: 15 EST: 1989
SQ FT: 11,500
SALES (est): 2.8MM Privately Held
WEB: www.risi1.com
SIC: 3829 Measuring & controlling devices

(G-3338)
RITE MACHINE PRODUCTS INC
44795 Enterprise Dr (48038-1535)
PHONE..................586 465-9393
Gregory Hall, CEO
Regina Hall, Corp Secy
Kenneth Hall, Vice Pres
Michael Hall, Vice Pres
Cheryl Mc Guire, Vice Pres
EMP: 19 EST: 1974
SQ FT: 20,200
SALES (est): 2.1MM Privately Held
WEB: www.ritemachine.com
SIC: 3599 Machine shop, jobbing & repair

(G-3339)
RJL SCIENCES INC
Also Called: Rjl Systems
33939 Harper Ave (48035-4218)
PHONE..................800 528-4513
Rudolph J Liedtke, President
Paul Maletz, Prdtn Mgr
Michael Liedtke, Sales Staff
Josh Myers, Technician
EMP: 10 EST: 1979
SQ FT: 10,000
SALES (est): 1.6MM Privately Held
WEB: www.rjlsystems.com
SIC: 3841 Surgical & medical instruments

(G-3340)
ROBO-FENCE LLC
33646 Lipke St (48035-3617)
PHONE..................586 232-3909
Evis Kola,
EMP: 25 EST: 2017
SALES (est): 1.8MM Privately Held
WEB: www.robo-fence.com
SIC: 3444 Machine guards, sheet metal

(G-3341)
ROSATI SPECIALTIES LLC
24300 Capital Blvd (48036-1340)
PHONE..................586 783-3866
Donald R Rosati,
EMP: 3 EST: 2000
SALES (est): 1MM Privately Held
WEB: www.rosatispecialties.com
SIC: 2431 2435 Moldings, wood: unfinished & prefinished; panel work, wood; hardwood plywood, prefinished

(G-3342)
ROTH-WILLIAMS INDUSTRIES INC
Also Called: Lunar Industries
34335 Groesbeck Hwy (48035-3359)
PHONE..................586 792-0090
Patricia Williams, President
Tony Horner, General Mgr
Roger Roth, Chairman
EMP: 42 EST: 1966
SQ FT: 18,000
SALES (est): 1.8MM Privately Held
WEB: www.lunarind.com
SIC: 3544 3545 Special dies & tools; industrial molds; machine tool accessories

Clinton Township - Macomb County (G-3343) — GEOGRAPHIC SECTION

(G-3343)
ROURA ACQUISITION INC (PA)
Also Called: Roura Material Handling
35355 Forton Ct (48035-3133)
PHONE..................................586 790-6100
Mike Genter, *President*
Wes Bruner, *Opers Mgr*
Joe Frontera, *Engineer*
Janie Langston, *Sales Staff*
Susan Bush, *Administration*
▲ **EMP:** 14 **EST:** 1915
SQ FT: 25,000
SALES (est): 7.8MM **Privately Held**
WEB: www.rouramh.com
SIC: 3444 Metal housings, enclosures, casings & other containers

(G-3344)
RTS CUTTING TOOLS INC
24100 Capital Blvd (48036-1338)
PHONE..................................586 954-1900
Michael Disser, *President*
Greg Berentt, *Owner*
Gregg Berendt, *Partner*
Roger Ludlow, *Regional Mgr*
Daniel Hulgrave, *Corp Secy*
EMP: 35 **EST:** 1939
SALES (est): 2.8MM **Privately Held**
WEB: www.rtscut.com
SIC: 3545 3546 3541 3423 Cutting tools for machine tools; power-driven hand-tools; machine tools, metal cutting type; hand & edge tools

(G-3345)
RUBBER TUCKER LLC
41491 Mary Kay Dr (48038-1991)
PHONE..................................586 216-7071
Gregg McIntosh, *Principal*
EMP: 5 **EST:** 2018
SALES (est): 349.7K **Privately Held**
WEB: www.rubberhugger.com
SIC: 3069 Mattress protectors, rubber

(G-3346)
RUSSOS BAKERY INC
35160 Forton Ct (48035-3130)
PHONE..................................586 791-7320
Andjelko Stamevski, *President*
▲ **EMP:** 26 **EST:** 1980
SQ FT: 10,000
SALES (est): 1.3MM **Privately Held**
WEB: www.russobakeryinc.com
SIC: 2051 Bakery: wholesale or wholesale/retail combined

(G-3347)
RYDIN AND ASSOCIATES INC
Also Called: Rydin & Associates
44604 Macomb Indus Dr (48036-1185)
PHONE..................................586 783-9772
Bruce Rydin, *President*
David Peck, *Vice Pres*
EMP: 11 **EST:** 1993
SALES (est): 548.8K **Privately Held**
WEB: www.rydinassociates.com
SIC: 3699 Laser welding, drilling & cutting equipment

(G-3348)
SALDET SALES AND SERVICES INC
44810 Vic Wertz Dr (48036-1250)
PHONE..................................586 469-4312
Larry Sylvester, *President*
Fred Parker, *Owner*
EMP: 13 **EST:** 2005
SQ FT: 12,500
SALES (est): 240.7K **Privately Held**
WEB: www.ambitechbrakes.com
SIC: 3679 Harness assemblies for electronic use; wire or cable

(G-3349)
SANDERS CANDY LLC (HQ)
23770 Hall Rd (48036-1275)
PHONE..................................800 651-7263
Ronald Rapson, *President*
Lori Kellie, *Purch Agent*
Jennifer Szubelak, *Purch Agent*
Melissa Vanthournout, *Human Res Dir*
Michael Koch, *Maintence Staff*
▲ **EMP:** 100 **EST:** 1919
SQ FT: 70,000
SALES (est): 62MM
SALES (corp-wide): 176.8MM **Privately Held**
WEB: www.sanderscandy.com
SIC: 2064 2066 5441 Candy & other confectionery products; chocolate & cocoa products; candy
PA: Knpc Holdco, Llc
    1200 E 14 Mile Rd
    Madison Heights MI 48071
    248 588-1903

(G-3350)
SENSTRONIC INC
44990 Vic Wertz Dr Ste A (48036-1251)
PHONE..................................586 466-4108
Remy Kirchdoerffer, *President*
EMP: 16 **EST:** 2006
SQ FT: 3,000
SALES (est): 2.1MM **Privately Held**
WEB: www.senstronic.com
SIC: 3559 Electronic component making machinery

(G-3351)
SEQUOIA TOOL INC
44831 N Groesbeck Hwy (48036-1124)
PHONE..................................586 463-4400
Joseph Coates, *CEO*
Joe Coates, *President*
James Coates, *General Mgr*
Nimet Coates, *COO*
Frank Coates, *Vice Pres*
EMP: 82 **EST:** 1988
SQ FT: 14,000
SALES (est): 22.8MM **Privately Held**
WEB: www.sequoiatool.com
SIC: 3544 Special dies & tools

(G-3352)
SHORECREST ENTERPRISES INC
Also Called: Signs By Tomorrow
33251 S Gratiot Ave (48035-4039)
PHONE..................................586 948-9226
Bruce Slezak, *President*
Kenneth Slezak, *Vice Pres*
EMP: 5 **EST:** 2015
SALES (est): 502.7K **Privately Held**
WEB: www.signsbytomorrow.com
SIC: 3993 Signs & advertising specialties

(G-3353)
SHORES ENGINEERING CO INC
34632 Nova Dr (48035-3716)
PHONE..................................586 792-2748
Brian Quinlan, *President*
EMP: 21 **EST:** 1992
SQ FT: 2,400
SALES (est): 2.3MM **Privately Held**
WEB: www.shoresengineeringco.net
SIC: 3544 Special dies & tools

(G-3354)
SIGMA TOOL MFG INC
35280 Forton Ct (48035-3131)
PHONE..................................586 792-3300
Wolfgang Pfahl, *Owner*
EMP: 5 **EST:** 2005
SALES (est): 393.3K **Privately Held**
WEB: www.sigmatoolmfg.com
SIC: 3544 Special dies & tools

(G-3355)
SIGN-A-RAMA
36886 Harper Ave (48036-2014)
PHONE..................................586 792-7446
Bryan Duquet, *Owner*
EMP: 4 **EST:** 2004
SALES (est): 388.4K **Privately Held**
WEB: www.teamsignarama.com
SIC: 3993 Signs & advertising specialties

(G-3356)
SIGNS BY RHONDA LLC
39911 Day Dr (48038-3027)
PHONE..................................248 408-0552
Rhonda Nagle, *Principal*
EMP: 4 **EST:** 2017
SALES (est): 101.7K **Privately Held**
SIC: 3993 Signs & advertising specialties

(G-3357)
SIGNS OF LOVE INC
38490 Ammerst Dr (48038-3201)
PHONE..................................586 413-1269
Anne M Debruyne, *Principal*
EMP: 5 **EST:** 2008
SALES (est): 89.6K **Privately Held**
SIC: 3993 Signs & advertising specialties

(G-3358)
SIMS SOFTWARE II INC
44668 Morley Dr (48036-1358)
PHONE..................................586 491-0058
EMP: 5
SALES (est): 610K **Privately Held**
SIC: 7372 Prepackaged Software

(G-3359)
SINE SYSTEMS CORPORATION (HQ)
44724 Morley Dr (48036-1357)
P.O. Box Caller 2336, Mount Clemens (48046)
PHONE..................................586 465-3131
R Adam Norwitt, *CEO*
Wayne Spence, *Business Mgr*
John Blood, *Info Tech Mgr*
▲ **EMP:** 200 **EST:** 1967
SQ FT: 70,000
SALES (est): 55.9MM
SALES (corp-wide): 8.6B **Publicly Held**
WEB: www.amphenol-sine.com
SIC: 3643 3678 3357 3625 Connectors & terminals for electrical devices; electronic connectors; nonferrous wiredrawing & insulating; control circuit relays, industrial
PA: Amphenol Corporation
    358 Hall Ave
    Wallingford CT 06492
    203 265-8900

(G-3360)
SLATER TOOLS INC
44725 Trinity Dr (48038-1554)
PHONE..................................586 465-5000
John R Scaduto Jr, *President*
Kris Renner, *Sales Staff*
EMP: 25 **EST:** 1951
SQ FT: 22,000
SALES (est): 1.7MM **Privately Held**
WEB: www.slatertools.com
SIC: 3544 3451 Special dies, tools, jigs & fixtures; screw machine products

(G-3361)
SPARTAN PALLET LLC
22387 Starks Dr (48036-1197)
PHONE..................................586 291-8898
Mike Rubino, *Principal*
EMP: 4 **EST:** 2012
SALES (est): 246.5K **Privately Held**
SIC: 2448 Pallets, wood

(G-3362)
SRS MANUFACTURING INC
Also Called: Framar
18840 Kelly Ct (48035-3980)
PHONE..................................586 792-5693
Scott Stay, *President*
EMP: 11 **EST:** 1996
SQ FT: 10,000
SALES (est): 2MM **Privately Held**
WEB: www.srsmanufacturing.com
SIC: 3599 Machine shop, jobbing & repair

(G-3363)
STATISTICAL PROCESSED PRODUCTS (PA)
35409 Groesbeck Hwy (48035-2518)
PHONE..................................586 792-6900
Ernest Young, *President*
EMP: 19 **EST:** 1997
SALES (est): 1.7MM **Privately Held**
SIC: 2851 3465 3089 Paints & allied products; automotive stampings; blow molded finished plastic products

(G-3364)
STOKED & BEARDED LLC ◆
42533 Clinton Place Dr (48038-1640)
PHONE..................................248 513-2927
Earl Stokes,
EMP: 6 **EST:** 2021
SALES (est): 39.6K **Privately Held**
SIC: 3999 Hair & hair-based products

(G-3365)
SUPERIOR HEAT TREAT LLC
36125 Groesbeck Hwy (48035-1544)
PHONE..................................586 792-9500
Lue Bertha Brown, *Office Mgr*
Ralph J Kaiser Sr,
Mark Kaiser,
EMP: 25 **EST:** 1941
SQ FT: 17,300
SALES (est): 3.2MM **Privately Held**
WEB: www.superiorheattreat.com
SIC: 3398 Metal heat treating

(G-3366)
SUPREME MEDIA BLASTING AND POW
36427 Groesbeck Hwy (48035-1551)
PHONE..................................586 792-7705
John Feldpausch, *CEO*
Todd Nowak, *Director*
EMP: 4 **EST:** 2014
SQ FT: 11,500
SALES (est): 247.9K **Privately Held**
WEB: www.suprememediablasting.com
SIC: 3471 2851 Sand blasting of metal parts; epoxy coatings

(G-3367)
SWAROVSKI NORTH AMERICA LTD
17410 Hall Rd Ste 175 (48036-6918)
PHONE..................................586 226-4420
EMP: 4
SALES (corp-wide): 4.5B **Privately Held**
WEB: www.swarovski.com
SIC: 3961 Costume jewelry
HQ: Swarovski North America Limited
    1 Kenney Dr
    Cranston RI 02920
    401 463-6400

(G-3368)
SWEET SUGAS LLC
35598 Ashton Ct (48035-2175)
PHONE..................................313 444-8570
Dionne Morris,
EMP: 4 **EST:** 2020
SALES (est): 116.1K **Privately Held**
SIC: 2051 Bakery, for home service delivery

(G-3369)
SYNERGY ADDITIVE MFG LLC (HQ)
Also Called: Sam
22792 Macomb Indus Dr (48036-1137)
PHONE..................................248 719-2194
Marcus Stackpoole,
Kunal Varma,
EMP: 3 **EST:** 2016
SALES (est): 1MM
SALES (corp-wide): 5.3MM **Privately Held**
WEB: www.synergyadditive.com
SIC: 3441 Fabricated structural metal
PA: Synergy Prototype Stamping Llc
    22778 Macomb Indus Dr
    Clinton Township MI 48036
    586 961-6109

(G-3370)
SYNERGY PROTOTYPE STAMPING LLC (PA)
Also Called: Tool & Die
22778 Macomb Indus Dr (48036-1137)
PHONE..................................586 961-6109
Sheila Fante, *CFO*
Crystal Meesseman, *Accountant*
Ryan Willette, *VP Sales*
Kevin Stackpoole, *Manager*
Marcus Stackpoole,
EMP: 23 **EST:** 2011
SQ FT: 2,000
SALES (est): 5.3MM **Privately Held**
WEB: www.synergyprototype.com
SIC: 3469 Stamping metal for the trade

(G-3371)
T & K INDUSTRIES INC
18057 Gaylord Ct (48035-1306)
PHONE..................................586 212-9100
Dave Hogan, *President*
EMP: 5 **EST:** 2008
SQ FT: 1,200 **Privately Held**
SIC: 3089 Injection molding of plastics

▲ = Import ▼ = Export
◆ = Import/Export

GEOGRAPHIC SECTION

Clio - Genesee County (G-3399)

(G-3372)
TAMSCO INC
43175 W Kirkwood Dr (48038-1225)
PHONE..........................586 415-1500
Nancy Stachnik, *President*
EMP: 23 **EST:** 1972
SALES (est) 724.1K **Privately Held**
WEB: www.propakproductsltd.com
SIC: 7389 2448 Packaging & labeling services; cargo containers, wood & wood with metal

(G-3373)
TAPER-LINE INC (PA)
23426 Reynolds Ct (48036-1240)
PHONE..........................586 775-5960
James Finn, *President*
Pamela Montay, *Corp Secy*
EMP: 7 **EST:** 1975
SQ FT: 12,000 **Privately Held**
WEB: www.taperline.com
SIC: 3452 Nuts, metal

(G-3374)
TARPON AUTOMATION & DESIGN CO
44785 Macomb Indus Dr (48036-1147)
PHONE..........................586 774-8020
Robert Legeret, *President*
Robert Legeret Jr, *Sales Mgr*
Vanderdonck Scott, *Director*
▼ **EMP:** 50
SALES (est) 10MM **Privately Held**
WEB: www.tarponautomation.com
SIC: 3549 Assembly machines, including robotic

(G-3375)
TENIBAC-GRAPHION INC (HQ)
35155 Automation Dr (48035-3116)
PHONE..........................586 792-0150
Jim Deliz, *CEO*
Thomas Gusmano, *Vice Pres*
EMP: 75 **EST:** 1969
SQ FT: 45,000
SALES (est) 10.8MM
SALES (corp-wide): 656.2MM **Publicly Held**
WEB: www.tenibac.com
SIC: 3469 Patterns on metal
PA: Standex International Corporation
23 Keewaydin Dr Ste 300
Salem NH 03079
603 893-9701

(G-3376)
THUNDER BAY PATTERN WORKS INC
44345 Macomb Indus Dr (48036-1143)
PHONE..........................586 783-1126
Dorothy La Fleche, *CEO*
James Flom, *President*
George La Fleche, *Chairman*
Bruce La Fleche, *Vice Pres*
Georgene Hildebrand, *Treasurer*
EMP: 11 **EST:** 2000
SQ FT: 30,000
SALES (est) 1.1MM **Privately Held**
WEB: www.thunderbaypatternworks.com
SIC: 3089 Automotive parts, plastic

(G-3377)
TIJER INC
44326 Macomb Indus Dr (48036-1142)
PHONE..........................586 741-0308
Tim Taylor, *President*
Jerry Auclair, *Vice Pres*
EMP: 4 **EST:** 2002 **Privately Held**
SIC: 3544 Special dies & tools

(G-3378)
TOP CRAFT TOOL INC
33674 Giftos Dr (48035-4241)
PHONE..........................586 461-4600
Gary Kimmen, *President*
Kelley Kimmen, *Opers Staff*
Lloyd Kimmen, *Treasurer*
EMP: 24 **EST:** 1968
SQ FT: 10,000
SALES (est) 4.5MM **Privately Held**
WEB: www.topcrafttool.com
SIC: 3599 3544 Machine shop, jobbing & repair; special dies & tools

(G-3379)
TOWER ATMTIVE OPRTONS USA I LL
44850 N Groesbeck Hwy (48036-1121)
PHONE..........................586 465-5158
Jim Ruzzin, *Manager*
EMP: 100
SALES (corp-wide): 3.1B **Privately Held**
WEB: www.autokiniton.com
SIC: 3465 Automotive stampings
HQ: Tower Automotive Operations Usa I, Llc
17757 Woodland Dr
New Boston MI 48164

(G-3380)
TWEDDLE GROUP INC (PA)
24700 Maplehurst Dr (48036-1336)
PHONE..........................586 307-3700
Patrick Aubry, *CEO*
David Frisk, *Editor*
Tina Stuart, *COO*
Atul Kishore, *Exec VP*
Ryan Pike, *Exec VP*
▲ **EMP:** 250 **EST:** 1954
SQ FT: 120,000
SALES (est) 186MM **Privately Held**
WEB: www.tweddle.com
SIC: 2732 2791 2752 2759 Book printing; photocomposition, for the printing trade; typesetting, computer controlled; commercial printing, lithographic; commercial printing, technical manual & paper publishing; computer software development & applications

(G-3381)
ULTRA-SONIC EXTRUSION DIES INC
34863 Groesbeck Hwy (48035-3366)
PHONE..........................586 791-8550
David Schoenegge, *President*
Al Gwozdz, *Corp Secy*
Dave Nicholas, *Plant Mgr*
EMP: 38 **EST:** 1970
SQ FT: 10,000
SALES (est) 1.2MM **Privately Held**
WEB: www.usedies.com
SIC: 3544 Extrusion dies

(G-3382)
UNIFIED EQUIPMENT SYSTEMS INC
42950 Walnut St (48036-4352)
PHONE..........................586 307-3770
James E Sutton, *President*
Gordon Toward, *Vice Pres*
John Peck, *Engineer*
D Wirsu, *Engineer*
Edward Buckley, *Senior Engr*
EMP: 7 **EST:** 1994
SQ FT: 13,000
SALES (est) 336.9K **Privately Held**
SIC: 3443 3559 5084 Tanks, lined: metal plate; refinery, chemical processing & similar machinery; processing & packaging equipment

(G-3383)
UNIVERSAL MANUFACTURING CO
43900 N Groesbeck Hwy (48036-1107)
PHONE..........................586 463-2560
Sandra Kedzierski, *CEO*
William Kedzierski, *President*
Roy Seelbinder, *Treasurer*
▼ **EMP:** 24 **EST:** 1969
SQ FT: 18,000
SALES (est) 2.8MM **Privately Held**
WEB: www.universaltruss.com
SIC: 3648 3441 Lighting fixtures, except electric: residential; tower sections, radio & television transmission

(G-3384)
VERONICA K LLC
24204 Lotus Dr Apt 101 (48036-4306)
PHONE..........................248 251-5144
Erica King,
EMP: 4 **EST:** 2020
SALES (est) 100K **Privately Held**
SIC: 3861 Trays, photographic printing & processing

(G-3385)
VERSA-CRAFT INC
35117 Automation Dr (48035-3116)
PHONE..........................586 465-5999
Don Johnson, *President*
Karen Johnson, *Admin Sec*
EMP: 8 **EST:** 1984
SQ FT: 13,000
SALES (est) 966.9K **Privately Held**
SIC: 3535 Belt conveyor systems, general industrial use

(G-3386)
WARREN INDUSTRIES INC (PA)
22805 Interstate Dr (48036-3742)
PHONE..........................586 741-0420
Douglas Udicki, *President*
Stevan Udicki, *Vice Pres*
John Blaskowski, *Engineer*
Larry George, *Marketing Staff*
Sonja Avramovska, *Manager*
EMP: 153 **EST:** 1977
SQ FT: 95,000
SALES (est) 19.1MM **Privately Held**
WEB: www.warren-ind.com
SIC: 3541 Numerically controlled metal cutting machine tools; drilling & boring machines

(G-3387)
WARTROM MACHINE SYSTEMS INC
22786 Patmore Dr (48036-1191)
PHONE..........................586 469-1915
Terry A Ward, *CEO*
Martha L Ward, *Vice Pres*
Kevin Caperton, *Mfg Staff*
Kila Maison, *Purchasing*
Sue Miller, *Executive*
EMP: 35 **EST:** 1983
SQ FT: 21,000
SALES (est) 5.8MM **Privately Held**
WEB: www.wartrom.com
SIC: 3569 3544 Assembly machines, non-metalworking; special dies, tools, jigs & fixtures

(G-3388)
WIRCO INC
17001 19 Mile Rd Ste 1 (48038-4867)
P.O. Box 609, Avilla IN (46710-0609)
PHONE..........................586 267-1300
EMP: 8 **EST:** 2019
SALES (est) 73.4K **Privately Held**
WEB: www.wirco.com
SIC: 3465 Automotive stampings

(G-3389)
WOLVERINE PRODUCTS INC
35220 Groesbeck Hwy (48035-2513)
PHONE..........................586 792-3740
Matthew Chase, *President*
David Chase, *Vice Pres*
EMP: 12 **EST:** 1966
SQ FT: 23,000
SALES (est) 2.1MM **Privately Held**
WEB: www.wolverineproductsinc.com
SIC: 3544 3543 Industrial molds; jigs & fixtures; industrial patterns

(G-3390)
XCENTRIC MOLD & ENGRG LLC
24541 Maplehurst Dr (48036-1352)
PHONE..........................586 598-4636
Matt McIntosh, *CEO*
Brendan Weaver, *President*
John Sidorowicz, *Vice Pres*
Mark Strobel, *Vice Pres*
Tom Neill, *VP Opers*
EMP: 100
SQ FT: 13,500
SALES (est) 3.9MM **Privately Held**
WEB: www.xcentricmold.com
SIC: 3089 Injection molding of plastics

(G-3391)
YOE INDUSTRIES INC
24451 Sorrentino Ct (48035-3240)
PHONE..........................586 791-7660
Henry F Yoe, *President*
EMP: 5 **EST:** 1987
SQ FT: 10,000
SALES (est) 345K **Privately Held**
WEB: www.yoeconcreteindustrial.com
SIC: 7699 3561 Hydraulic equipment repair; cylinders, pump

(G-3392)
ZAJAC INDUSTRIES INC
Also Called: Zajac Packaging
21319 Carlo Dr (48038-1511)
PHONE..........................586 489-6746
Bob Zajac, *President*
EMP: 23 **EST:** 1994
SALES (est) 1.1MM **Privately Held**
WEB: www.zajacindustries.com
SIC: 2671 Paper coated or laminated for packaging

(G-3393)
ZUNAIRAH FUELS INC
37109 Harper Ave (48036-3013)
PHONE..........................647 405-1606
Asher Ahmed, *Principal*
EMP: 7 **EST:** 2014
SALES (est) 496.7K **Privately Held**
SIC: 2869 Fuels

Clio
Genesee County

(G-3394)
CARDINAL MACHINE CO
860 Tacoma Ct (48420-1581)
PHONE..........................810 686-1190
Brian Pennington, *President*
Linda Pennington, *Corp Secy*
Dan Wilson, *Project Mgr*
Jeremy Clontz, *Engineer*
Brent Koester, *Design Engr*
EMP: 27 **EST:** 1973
SQ FT: 24,000
SALES (est) 5.7MM **Privately Held**
WEB: www.cardinalmachine.biz
SIC: 3549 3545 Metalworking machinery; machine tool attachments & accessories

(G-3395)
CMG AMERICA INC
11424 N Saginaw Rd (48420-1679)
P.O. Box 178, Frankenmuth (48734-0178)
PHONE..........................810 686-3064
Vittiorio Martei, *President*
Stephen Myers, *Vice Pres*
▲ **EMP:** 6 **EST:** 2012
SQ FT: 14,000
SALES (est) 400K **Privately Held**
WEB: www.cmg.it
SIC: 3821 Granulators, laboratory

(G-3396)
DEMMEM ENTERPRISES LLC
Also Called: Perfect Fit Brdal Tuxedos Prom
4268 W Vienna Rd (48420-9454)
PHONE..........................810 564-9500
Daniel McKay, *Mng Member*
EMP: 10 **EST:** 2013
SALES (est) 421.2K **Privately Held**
WEB: www.perfectfitformalsonline.com
SIC: 7299 2335 7219 Tuxedo rental; wedding gowns & dresses; garment making, alteration & repair

(G-3397)
DODGE WEST JOE NICKEL
2219 E Farrand Rd (48420-9188)
PHONE..........................810 691-2133
Joseph Nickels, *Principal*
EMP: 6 **EST:** 2009
SALES (est) 382.3K **Privately Held**
SIC: 3356 Nickel

(G-3398)
FIRST CLASS TIRE SHREDDERS INC
7302 W Vienna Rd (48420-9448)
PHONE..........................810 639-4466
Harry Powell, *President*
EMP: 15 **EST:** 2000
SALES (est) 1MM **Privately Held**
WEB: www.fcshredsandsales.com
SIC: 3069 Reclaimed rubber & specialty rubber compounds

(G-3399)
GENESEE COUNTY HERALD INC
Also Called: Bridal Nook
10098 N Dort Hwy (48420-1670)
P.O. Box 127, Mount Morris (48458-0127)
PHONE..........................810 686-3840

Clio - Genesee County (G-3400)

Michael Harrington, *President*
EMP: 12 **EST:** 1967
SALES (est): 943K **Privately Held**
WEB: www.myherald.net
SIC: 2711 5621 3993 2791 Job printing & newspaper publishing combined; bridal shops; signs & advertising specialties; typesetting; commercial printing; commercial printing, lithographic

(G-3400)
HAMILTONS CUSTOM STAIRS
3024 Ridgelawn Dr (48420-9734)
PHONE 810 686-5698
Scott Hamilton, *Principal*
EMP: 6 **EST:** 2007
SALES (est): 85.6K **Privately Held**
SIC: 3446 Stairs, staircases, stair treads: prefabricated metal

(G-3401)
HOYT & COMPANY LLC
12555 N Saginaw Rd (48420-1012)
P.O. Box 182 (48420-0182)
PHONE 810 624-4445
Cassie Hoyt, *CEO*
EMP: 6 **EST:** 2010
SALES (est): 400K **Privately Held**
WEB: www.hoytcompany.com
SIC: 2395 2759 Embroidery products, except schiffli machine; screen printing

(G-3402)
KENS REDI MIX INC
14406 N Saginaw Rd (48420-8864)
PHONE 810 687-6000
Jeff Bailey, *President*
EMP: 10
SALES (corp-wide): 3MM **Privately Held**
WEB: www.kensredimix.com
SIC: 3273 Ready-mixed concrete
PA: Ken's Redi Mix, Inc.
8016 S State Rd
Goodrich MI 48438
810 636-2630

(G-3403)
KENYON SPECIALTIES INC
1153 Liberty St (48420)
P.O. Box 160, Mount Morris (48458-0160)
PHONE 810 686-3190
Peggy Duford, *President*
Margaret A Duford, *President*
Norman O Duford General, *Manager*
EMP: 8 **EST:** 1964
SQ FT: 14,600
SALES (est): 615.7K **Privately Held**
SIC: 3544 Special dies & tools

(G-3404)
MARQUEE ENGRAVING INC
600 S Mill St Ste A (48420-2317)
PHONE 810 686-7550
Jennifer Rendue, *President*
EMP: 4 **EST:** 1976
SALES (est): 125K **Privately Held**
WEB: www.marqueeengraving.com
SIC: 2759 5999 Engraving; trophies & plaques

(G-3405)
MICHIGAN CHIMNEYS
9341 Neff Rd (48420-1660)
PHONE 810 640-7961
Kenneth Nottingham, *Principal*
EMP: 5 **EST:** 2019
SALES (est): 106.3K **Privately Held**
WEB: www.michiganchimneys.net
SIC: 2842 Specialty cleaning, polishes & sanitation goods

(G-3406)
MICHIGAN SCREEN PRINTING
204 S Railway St (48420-1340)
PHONE 810 687-5550
Paul Gustafson, *Owner*
EMP: 5 **EST:** 1983
SALES (est): 301.9K **Privately Held**
WEB: www.screen-printing-services.cmac.ws
SIC: 2759 Screen printing

(G-3407)
MONTAGUE LATCH COMPANY
Also Called: Montague Tool
2000 W Dodge Rd (48420-1657)
PHONE 810 687-4242
Joel Stinedurf, *President*
Thad Hobson, *Controller*
▲ **EMP:** 18 **EST:** 1994
SQ FT: 10,000 **Privately Held**
WEB: www.montaguelatch.com
SIC: 3823 Industrial instrmnts msrmnt display/control process variable

(G-3408)
MONTAGUE TOOL AND MFG CO
Also Called: Paws Workholding
11533 Liberty St Ste 3 (48420-1493)
PHONE 810 686-0000
Jim Montague, *CEO*
John Montague, *President*
Joel Montague, *Vice Pres*
Linda Karnjate, *CFO*
Lois Montague, *Treasurer*
EMP: 35
SQ FT: 20,000
SALES (est): 7.9MM **Privately Held**
WEB: www.montaguemanufacturing.com
SIC: 3599 3545 Machine shop, jobbing & repair; machine tool accessories

(G-3409)
PERFECT STITCH INC
3422 W Wilson Rd (48420-1930)
PHONE 407 797-5527
Susan K Bettinger, *Principal*
EMP: 4 **EST:** 2017
SALES (est): 50.2K **Privately Held**
SIC: 2395 Embroidery & art needlework

(G-3410)
R J CHEMICAL MANUFACTURING LLC
920 Tacoma Ct (48420-1595)
PHONE 810 252-8425
Reta Johnson, *Principal*
EMP: 5 **EST:** 2011
SALES (est): 67.6K **Privately Held**
WEB: www.rjchemicals.com
SIC: 3999 Manufacturing industries

(G-3411)
SIGNATURE TRUCK SYSTEMS LLC ✪
13460 N Saginaw Rd (48420-1017)
PHONE 810 564-2294
Mike Vandenboom, *Mng Member*
EMP: 78 **EST:** 2021
SALES (est): 2.2MM **Privately Held**
SIC: 3714 Propane conversion equipment, motor vehicle

Clyde
St. Clair County

(G-3412)
DOW CHEMICAL COMPANY
3381 Woodview (48049-4330)
PHONE 810 966-9816
EMP: 68
SALES (corp-wide): 48.1B **Publicly Held**
SIC: 2821 Mfg Plastic Materials/Resins
PA: The Dow Chemical Company
2030 Dow Ctr
Midland MI 48642
989 636-1000

(G-3413)
HESS ASPHALT PAV SAND CNSTR CO
6330 Lapeer Rd (48049-4221)
PHONE 810 984-4466
Frederick T Hess, *President*
Thomas J Hess, *Treasurer*
Gloria Hess, *Admin Sec*
EMP: 22 **EST:** 1944
SQ FT: 3,200
SALES (est): 1.7MM **Privately Held**
WEB: www.hessasphalt.com
SIC: 1611 2951 Highway & street paving contractor; resurfacing contractor; asphalt & asphaltic paving mixtures (not from refineries)

(G-3414)
PLUSH PRODUCTS MFG LLC
3140 Nokomis Trl (48049-4529)
PHONE 586 871-8082
Debby Alighire, *Principal*
EMP: 4 **EST:** 2016
SALES (est): 49.1K **Privately Held**
WEB: www.jaagplush.com
SIC: 3999 Manufacturing industries

(G-3415)
REDLINE FABRICATIONS
4752 Walker Rd (48049-3939)
PHONE 810 984-5621
Barrie Rusch, *Owner*
EMP: 4 **EST:** 1991
SALES (est): 269.5K **Privately Held**
WEB: www.redlinefabrications.com
SIC: 3711 Automobile assembly, including specialty automobiles

(G-3416)
RUBY SAND & GRAVEL
6601 Imlay City Rd (48049-2935)
PHONE 810 364-6100
Tim Burgess, *Principal*
EMP: 4 **EST:** 2011
SALES (est): 87K **Privately Held**
SIC: 1442 Construction sand & gravel

Coldwater
Branch County

(G-3417)
4EVER ALUMINUM PRODUCTS INC
628 Pebblestone Dr (49036-7551)
PHONE 517 368-0000
James Starr, *President*
EMP: 15 **EST:** 2004
SQ FT: 14,000
SALES (est): 1.7MM **Privately Held**
WEB: www.4everaluminum.com
SIC: 5084 3448 Lift trucks & parts; docks: prefabricated metal

(G-3418)
ALERIS INTERNATIONAL INC
368 W Garfield Ave (49036-9711)
P.O. Box 338 (49036-0338)
PHONE 517 279-9596
Steven J Demetriou, *CEO*
Roeland Baan, *Exec VP*
Christopher R Clegg, *Exec VP*
Sean M Stack, *Exec VP*
Scott A McKinley, *Senior VP*
EMP: 11 **EST:** 2013
SALES (est): 255.9K **Privately Held**
SIC: 3334 Primary aluminum

(G-3419)
ANITOM AUTOMATION LLC
349 S Clay St (49036-2139)
P.O. Box 10 (49036-0010)
PHONE 517 278-6205
Thomas G Waller, *Co-Owner*
Rick F Morris, *Co-Owner*
EMP: 20 **EST:** 2004
SQ FT: 8,000
SALES (est): 1.9MM **Privately Held**
WEB: www.anitomautomation.com
SIC: 3544 Special dies & tools; jigs & fixtures

(G-3420)
ASAMA COLDWATER MFG INC (DH)
Also Called: Acm
180 Asama Pkwy (49036-1590)
PHONE 517 279-1090
Masao Yamaura, *President*
Frank Draper, *Buyer*
Dan Gilbert, *Engineer*
Niroop Matta, *Engineer*
Darrell Snyder, *Engineer*
▲ **EMP:** 294 **EST:** 1996
SQ FT: 400,000
SALES (est): 62.9MM **Privately Held**
WEB: www.asamacm.com
SIC: 3714 Motor vehicle steering systems & parts

(G-3421)
BDS COMPANY INC
491 W Garfield Ave (49036-8000)
PHONE 517 279-2135
Lonnie Avra, *CEO*
Steve Olmsted, *President*
▲ **EMP:** 19 **EST:** 1995
SQ FT: 60,000
SALES (est): 1.3MM **Privately Held**
WEB: www.bds-suspension.com
SIC: 3568 3713 3714 3711 Power transmission equipment; truck bodies & parts; motor vehicle parts & accessories; motor vehicles & car bodies; bolts, nuts, rivets & washers; manufactured hardware (general)

(G-3422)
BURNHAM & NORTHERN INC
169 Industrial Ave (49036-2168)
P.O. Box 481 (49036-0481)
PHONE 517 279-7501
Leslie Northern, *President*
Connie Voice, *Chairman*
Candace Northern, *Vice Pres*
EMP: 6
SQ FT: 10,000
SALES (est): 350K **Privately Held**
SIC: 3444 3498 3441 3312 Sheet metalwork; fabricated pipe & fittings; fabricated structural metal; blast furnaces & steel mills

(G-3423)
C & M MANUFACTURING INC
129 Industrial Ave (49036-2178)
PHONE 517 279-0013
Carl Albert, *President*
Michelle Albert, *Vice Pres*
EMP: 21 **EST:** 1970
SQ FT: 40,000
SALES (est): 2.1MM **Privately Held**
WEB: www.candmmfginc.com
SIC: 3441 Fabricated structural metal

(G-3424)
CAMOPLAST
25 Concept Dr (49036-1585)
PHONE 517 278-8567
Ed Bell, *President*
EMP: 5 **EST:** 2017
SALES (est): 53K **Privately Held**
SIC: 3999 Manufacturing industries

(G-3425)
CASE WELDING & FABRICATION INC
235 N Angola Rd (49036-8575)
PHONE 517 278-2729
Wayne Case, *President*
EMP: 4 **EST:** 1991
SQ FT: 3,000
SALES (est): 532.5K **Privately Held**
WEB: www.casewelding.com
SIC: 7692 1799 Welding repair; welding on site

(G-3426)
CLEMENS WELCOME CENTER
285 N Michigan Ave (49036-1528)
PHONE 517 278-2500
EMP: 9 **EST:** 2016
SALES (est): 163.2K **Privately Held**
WEB: www.cfgcoldwater.com
SIC: 2011 Meat packing plants

(G-3427)
COLDWATER VENEER INC (PA)
548 Race St (49036-2122)
PHONE 517 278-5676
Dean Calhoun, *CEO*
Dave Counterman, *President*
Sandy Calhoun, *Vice Pres*
Don Steffey, *Vice Pres*
Dan McCracken, *Buyer*
◆ **EMP:** 160 **EST:** 2015
SALES (est): 40MM **Privately Held**
WEB: www.coldwaterveneer.com
SIC: 2435 Hardwood veneer & plywood

(G-3428)
COLDWTER SINTERED MET PDTS INC
300 Race St (49036-2120)
PHONE 517 278-8750

GEOGRAPHIC SECTION
Coldwater - Branch County (G-3452)

Kenneth Bible, *President*
Michael Lange, *Vice Pres*
David Hodson, *Manager*
Sharolyn Brainard, *Admin Sec*
EMP: 20 **EST:** 1984
SQ FT: 68,000
SALES (est): 2MM **Privately Held**
WEB: www.sinteredmetalproducts.com
SIC: 3599 Machine shop, jobbing & repair

(G-3429)
COMMERCIAL GRAPHICS COMPANY
205 W Garfield Ave (49036-9711)
PHONE..................517 278-2159
Michael Liechty, *President*
Lynne Liechty, *Vice Pres*
EMP: 5 **EST:** 1981
SQ FT: 5,400
SALES (est): 489.6K **Privately Held**
WEB: www.g-three.com
SIC: 2752 7313 7336 Commercial printing, offset; printed media advertising representatives; graphic arts & related design

(G-3430)
DAILY REPORTER
Also Called: Gatehouse Publishing
15 W Pearl St (49036-1912)
PHONE..................517 278-2318
Dan Pollefson, *President*
Troy Tennyson, *Editor*
Karen Allard, *Manager*
Carla Ludwick, *Manager*
EMP: 23 **EST:** 1896
SALES (est): 2.2MM **Privately Held**
WEB: www.thedailyreporter.com
SIC: 2711 2752 Newspapers: publishing only, not printed on site; commercial printing, lithographic

(G-3431)
DARLING INGREDIENTS INC
600 Jay St (49036-2153)
PHONE..................517 279-9731
Jim Roth, *Manager*
EMP: 106
SALES (corp-wide): 3.3B **Publicly Held**
WEB: www.darlingii.com
SIC: 2077 2048 Grease rendering, inedible; prepared feeds
PA: Darling Ingredients Inc.
5601 N Macarthur Blvd
Irving TX 75038
972 717-0300

(G-3432)
ENVIROLITE LLC
421 Race St (49036-2119)
PHONE..................888 222-2191
Kasey Robinson, *Plant Mgr*
Renee Fenstermaker, *QC Mgr*
Vatche Tazian,
EMP: 60
SALES (corp-wide): 16.9MM **Privately Held**
WEB: www.envirolite.com
SIC: 3086 5999 5199 Plastics foam products; foam & foam products; foams & rubber
PA: Envirolite, Llc
1700 W Big Beavr Rd # 150
Troy MI 48084
248 792-3184

(G-3433)
EXO-S US LLC
Also Called: Coldwater Plant
25 Concept Dr (49036-1585)
PHONE..................517 278-8567
Craige Mohney, *Branch Mgr*
EMP: 135
SALES (corp-wide): 115.9MM **Privately Held**
WEB: www.exo-s.com
SIC: 3089 Injection molding of plastics
HQ: Exo-S Us Llc
6505 N State Road 9
Howe IN 46746

(G-3434)
GOKOH COLDWATER INCORPORATED
Also Called: GCI
100 Concept Dr (49036-1588)
PHONE..................517 279-1080
Kenji Iwato, *President*
EMP: 15 **EST:** 1996
SQ FT: 34,000
SALES (est): 3.2MM **Privately Held**
WEB: www.mycoldwater.com
SIC: 3559 3471 3444 3369 Foundry, smelting, refining & similar machinery; foundry machinery & equipment; plating & polishing; sheet metalwork; nonferrous foundries
HQ: Gokoh Corporation
1280 Archer Dr
Troy OH 45373
937 339-4977

(G-3435)
GRAPHICS 3 INC
205 W Garfield Ave (49036-8001)
PHONE..................517 278-2159
Larry Iverson, *President*
Michael Iverson, *Vice Pres*
Michael Liechty, *Vice Pres*
Terry Garn, *Prdtn Mgr*
Jacquelyn Iverson, *Treasurer*
EMP: 31
SQ FT: 11,900
SALES (est): 8.2MM **Privately Held**
WEB: www.g-three.com
SIC: 2752 Commercial printing, offset

(G-3436)
GROHOLSKI MFG SOLUTIONS LLC
Also Called: G M S
127 Industrial Ave (49036-2168)
P.O. Box 428 (49036-0428)
PHONE..................517 278-9339
Jim Ackerson, *Engineer*
Nathan Coy, *Design Engr*
Tom Crampton, *Sales Engr*
Ben Marcov, *Sales Engr*
Samuel Marcov, *Sales Engr*
EMP: 20 **EST:** 2001
SQ FT: 12,000
SALES (est): 4.6MM **Privately Held**
SIC: 3552 3545 Dyeing, drying & finishing machinery & equipment; tools & accessories for machine tools

(G-3437)
H C STARCK INC
460 Jay St (49036-2181)
PHONE..................517 279-9511
Jens Knoell, *COO*
Marius Pilz, *Vice Pres*
Greg Reitsma, *Engineer*
William Collins, *Plant Engr*
Kelly Cline, *Human Resources*
▲ **EMP:** 7
SALES (corp-wide): 355.8K **Privately Held**
WEB: www.hcstarcksolutions.com
SIC: 3339 3356 3313 Primary nonferrous metals; nonferrous rolling & drawing; electrometallurgical products
HQ: H. C. Starck Inc.
45 Industrial Pl
Newton MA 02461
617 630-5800

(G-3438)
HAROLD K SCHULTZ
Also Called: Shopper's Guide
15 W Pearl St (49036-1912)
PHONE..................517 279-9764
Harold K Schultz, *Owner*
EMP: 5 **EST:** 1954
SALES (est): 123.5K **Privately Held**
SIC: 2711 2752 Newspapers: publishing only, not printed on site; commercial printing, offset

(G-3439)
INVIS INC
Also Called: Seybert's Billiard Supply
702 E Chicago Rd (49036-9484)
PHONE..................517 279-7585
Toll Free:..................877 -
Sidney Kreis, *President*
James L Tong, *Vice Pres*
Paul Tong, *Treasurer*
Glynis Tong, *Admin Sec*
▲ **EMP:** 7 **EST:** 2000
SQ FT: 7,500
SALES (est): 982.7K **Privately Held**
WEB: www.seyberts.com
SIC: 3949 Sporting & athletic goods

(G-3440)
KIMBLE AUTO AND RV LLC
132 W Chicago Rd (49036-9390)
PHONE..................517 227-5089
Jeffrey M Kimble, *Administration*
EMP: 6 **EST:** 2016
SALES (est): 180.3K **Privately Held**
WEB: www.kimblerv.com
SIC: 3792 Travel trailers & campers

(G-3441)
KNAPP MANUFACTURING INC
555 Hillside Dr (49036-9787)
PHONE..................517 279-9538
Chris Knapp, *President*
Joyce Knapp, *Corp Secy*
EMP: 23 **EST:** 1973
SQ FT: 13,200
SALES (est): 2.2MM **Privately Held**
WEB: www.knappmanufacturing.com
SIC: 3599 Machine & other job shop work

(G-3442)
L & S PRODUCTS LLC
294 Block Rd (49036-9757)
PHONE..................517 238-4645
▲ **EMP:** 3 **EST:** 1954
SQ FT: 168,000
SALES (est): 1MM **Privately Held**
SIC: 5199 2542 Whol Nondurable Goods Mfg Partitions/Fixtures-Nonwood

(G-3443)
LONGSTREET GROUP LLC
Also Called: LONGSTREET LIVING
720 E Chicago Rd (49036-9404)
PHONE..................517 278-4487
EMP: 12 **EST:** 2007
SALES (est): 4.1MM **Privately Held**
WEB: www.longstreetlivingcoldwater.com
SIC: 3444 5712 Metal flooring & siding; beds & accessories

(G-3444)
MICHIGAN GRAPHIC ARTS
131 N Angola Rd (49036-8573)
PHONE..................517 278-4120
James Knisely, *Owner*
EMP: 5 **EST:** 1981
SQ FT: 8,000
SALES (est): 251.4K **Privately Held**
WEB: www.michigangraphicarts.com
SIC: 3993 2395 Signs & advertising specialties; embroidery products, except schiffli machine

(G-3445)
PEPSI-COLA METRO BTLG CO INC
101 Treat Dr (49036-9709)
PHONE..................517 279-8436
Brian Farmer, *Manager*
Candice Burgener, *Admin Asst*
EMP: 6
SALES (corp-wide): 70.3B **Publicly Held**
WEB: www.pepsico.com
SIC: 2086 5149 Soft drinks: packaged in cans, bottles, etc.; groceries & related products
HQ: Pepsi-Cola Metropolitan Bottling Company, Inc.
1111 Westchester Ave
White Plains NY 10604
914 767-6000

(G-3446)
PLEASANT VALLEY PACKING LLC
572 Newton Rd (49036-9465)
PHONE..................517 278-2500
EMP: 71
SALES (corp-wide): 648.5MM **Privately Held**
WEB: www.simplyhatfield.com
SIC: 2011 2013 Pork products from pork slaughtered on site; sausages & other prepared meats
HQ: Pleasant Valley Packing, Llc
2700 Clemens Rd
Hatfield PA 19440
215 368-2500

(G-3447)
PROTO SHAPES INC
125 Industrial Ave (49036-2168)
P.O. Box 143 (49036-0143)
PHONE..................517 278-3947
Robert C Small, *President*
Elaine Gray, *Office Mgr*
▲ **EMP:** 12 **EST:** 1995
SQ FT: 10,000
SALES (est): 2.1MM **Privately Held**
WEB: www.protoshapes.com
SIC: 3089 5162 Injection molding of plastics; plastics products

(G-3448)
PUTNAM MACHINE PRODUCTS INC
35 Cecil Dr (49036-9155)
PHONE..................517 278-2364
Glenna R Bartholomew, *CEO*
Rob Putnam, *General Mgr*
James Putnam, *Materials Mgr*
Jim Putnam, *Materials Mgr*
Paul Quiter, *Engineer*
EMP: 36 **EST:** 1954
SQ FT: 38,000
SALES (est): 3.9MM **Privately Held**
WEB: www.putnammachine.com
SIC: 3599 Machine shop, jobbing & repair

(G-3449)
QUALITY SPRING/TOGO INC
Also Called: Qsti
355 Jay St (49036-2176)
PHONE..................517 278-2391
Kazuyoski Murase, *CEO*
Mineo Muto, *President*
Nicki Ellis, *Purch Agent*
Ned Yearling, *Engineer*
Sandee Sawdey, *Accounting Mgr*
◆ **EMP:** 104 **EST:** 1988
SQ FT: 125,445
SALES (est): 24.9MM **Privately Held**
WEB: www.qsti.com
SIC: 3493 3714 5013 3495 Steel springs, except wire; motor vehicle parts & accessories; automotive supplies & parts; mechanical springs, precision
HQ: Togo Seisakusyo Corporation
1, Azahiruike, Haruki, Togocho
Aichi-Gun AIC 470-0

(G-3450)
REMNANT PUBLICATIONS INC
649 E Chicago Rd Ste B (49036-8444)
PHONE..................517 279-1304
Dwight Hall, *CEO*
David Berthiaume, *Marketing Staff*
Bill Yager, *Manager*
Dan Hall, *Admin Sec*
▲ **EMP:** 20 **EST:** 1987
SQ FT: 20,000
SALES (est): 4.2MM **Privately Held**
WEB: www.remnantpublications.com
SIC: 2731 8011 Textbooks: publishing & printing; offices & clinics of medical doctors

(G-3451)
RWS & ASSOCIATES LLC
Also Called: Excell Paving Plus
305 W Chicago Rd (49036-9334)
PHONE..................517 278-3134
Randy Sell, *Manager*
EMP: 25 **EST:** 2002
SQ FT: 400
SALES (est): 5.8MM **Privately Held**
WEB: www.excellpaving.com
SIC: 2951 1771 1611 Asphalt paving mixtures & blocks; blacktop (asphalt) work; surfacing & paving

(G-3452)
SCHMITZ FOAM PRODUCTS LLC
188 Treat Dr (49036-9709)
PHONE..................517 781-6615
Erguen Oezcan, *CEO*
Allen Hubbard, *Natl Sales Mgr*
EMP: 25 **EST:** 2017

Coldwater - Branch County (G-3453)

SALES (est): 4.5MM
SALES (corp-wide): 242.1K Privately Held
WEB: www.schmitzfoam.com
SIC: 3086 Padding, foamed plastic
HQ: Schmitz Foam Products B.V.
Produktieweg 6
Roermond 6045
475 370-270

(G-3453)
SEKISUI AMERICA CORPORATION
Voltek Division
17 Allen Ave (49036-2101)
PHONE.................517 279-7587
Shannon Damron, Sales Mgr
Joe Hughes, Manager
Katsuhiko Miki, Manager
Douglas Sands, Officer
Eric Dules,
EMP: 5 Privately Held
WEB: www.sekisui-corp.com
SIC: 3086 2821 Plastics foam products; plastics materials & resins
HQ: Sekisui America Corporation
333 Meadowlands Pkwy
Secaucus NJ 07094
201 423-7960

(G-3454)
SEKISUI VOLTEK LLC (DH)
17 Allen Ave (49036-2101)
PHONE.................800 225-0668
Yoshiyuki Hirai, CEO
Gustavo Morel, Mfg Mgr
Rob Knapp, Purchasing
Anh Le, Research
Brian Ng, Research
▲ EMP: 102 EST: 2003
SALES (est): 57.9MM Privately Held
WEB: www.sekisuivoltek.com
SIC: 2821 Plastics materials & resins
HQ: Sekisui America Corporation
333 Meadowlands Pkwy
Secaucus NJ 07094
201 423-7960

(G-3455)
SEKISUI VOLTEK LLC
17 Allen Ave (49036-2101)
PHONE.................517 279-7587
Auble Thomas, Prdtn Mgr
Kaitlyn Clark, Engineer
Gary Gray, Engineer
Terry Stanley, Engineer
Keiji Wakayama, Engineer
EMP: 180 Privately Held
WEB: www.sekisuivoltek.com
SIC: 3086 Plastics foam products
HQ: Sekisui Voltek, Llc
17 Allen Ave
Coldwater MI 49036

(G-3456)
ST USA HOLDING CORP (PA)
491 W Garfield Ave (49036-8000)
PHONE.................517 278-7144
Mark Meldrum, President
EMP: 100 EST: 2014
SALES (est): 70MM Privately Held
WEB: www.blog.sporttruckusainc.com
SIC: 3446 Acoustical suspension systems, metal

(G-3457)
ST USA HOLDING CORP
575 Race St (49036-2121)
PHONE.................800 637-3303
EMP: 170
SALES (corp-wide): 70MM Privately Held
WEB: www.blog.sporttruckusainc.com
SIC: 3446 Acoustical suspension systems, metal
PA: St Usa Holding Corp.
491 W Garfield Ave
Coldwater MI 49036
517 278-7144

(G-3458)
TRI STATE OPTICAL INC
350 Marshall St Ste B (49036-1176)
PHONE.................517 279-2701
Michael Sussex, President
Daniel J Casey, President
Robert Heath, Vice Pres
EMP: 8 EST: 1989
SQ FT: 750
SALES (est): 1MM Privately Held
WEB: www.tristateopticalinc.com
SIC: 5048 3851 5047 Ophthalmic goods; ophthalmic goods; medical equipment & supplies

(G-3459)
UNION PALLET & CONT CO INC
161 Race St (49036-2114)
PHONE.................517 279-4888
Jonathan Slack, President
Twyla Slack, Corp Secy
EMP: 24 EST: 1990
SQ FT: 36,000
SALES (est): 1.2MM Privately Held
WEB: www.unionpallet.com
SIC: 2449 2448 Wood containers; pallets, wood & wood with metal

(G-3460)
VACHON INDUSTRIES INC (PA)
Also Called: Koltec Div
580 Race St (49036-2122)
P.O. Box 383 (49036-0383)
PHONE.................517 278-2354
Douglas Mc Michael, President
▲ EMP: 18 EST: 1983
SQ FT: 35,000
SALES (est): 2MM Privately Held
WEB: www.wwwabrasiveproducts.net
SIC: 3291 5085 Abrasive wheels & grindstones, not artificial; buffing or polishing wheels, abrasive or nonabrasive; wheels, abrasive; abrasives; abrasives & adhesives

(G-3461)
WARNER OIL COMPANY
Also Called: Roost Oil Company
400 Race St (49036-2115)
P.O. Box 367 (49036-0367)
PHONE.................517 278-5844
Mark Loveberry, President
EMP: 14 EST: 1970
SQ FT: 17,500
SALES (est): 12MM Privately Held
WEB: www.warneroil.com
SIC: 2992 5172 Lubricating oils; petroleum products; fuel oil; diesel fuel; gasoline

Coleman
Midland County

(G-3462)
CHEMLOC INC
4996 N Dickenson Rd (48618-9643)
P.O. Box 169 (48618-0169)
PHONE.................989 465-6541
Ryan Roman, President
Tim Roman, Vice Pres
Jan Roman, Treasurer
EMP: 4 EST: 1987
SQ FT: 1,970 Privately Held
WEB: www.chemlocmi.net
SIC: 2842 Cleaning or polishing preparations

(G-3463)
DREAMBUILDER PUBLICATIONS
104 E Adams St (48618-9316)
PHONE.................989 465-1583
EMP: 5 EST: 2011
SALES (est): 102.7K Privately Held
SIC: 2741 Miscellaneous publishing

(G-3464)
HOMESTEAD PRODUCTS INC
2618 Coolidge Rd (48618-9402)
PHONE.................989 465-6182
Ben Robinson, President
Tim Ewert, Plant Mgr
Dan Wood, Manager
EMP: 14 EST: 1982
SQ FT: 2,400
SALES (est): 1MM Privately Held
WEB: www.bedgard.com
SIC: 3089 Plastic processing

(G-3465)
HOMESTEAD TOOL AND MACHINE
Also Called: Homestead Foundry
2618 Coolidge Rd (48618-9402)
PHONE.................989 465-6182
Bernard L Robinson, President
Jenny Ewert, Finance
Kim Brown, Office Mgr
Dan Wood, Info Tech Mgr
EMP: 50 EST: 1976
SQ FT: 2,400
SALES (est): 4.6MM Privately Held
SIC: 3544 3543 3363 Special dies & tools; dies, plastics forming; forms (molds), for foundry & plastics working machinery; industrial patterns; aluminum die-castings

(G-3466)
HPI
2618 Coolidge Rd (48618-9402)
PHONE.................989 465-6141
Nazali Wood, Manager
EMP: 7 EST: 2017
SALES (est): 126.1K Privately Held
SIC: 3089 Injection molding of plastics

(G-3467)
HUHTAMAKI INC
Also Called: Huhtamaki Plastics
5760 W Shaffer Rd (48618-9706)
PHONE.................989 633-8900
Michael Gross, Branch Mgr
EMP: 97
SALES (corp-wide): 3.9B Privately Held
WEB: www.huhtamaki.com
SIC: 3089 2656 Pallets, plastic; sanitary food containers
HQ: Huhtamaki, Inc.
9201 Packaging Dr
De Soto KS 66018
913 583-3025

(G-3468)
LP PRODUCTS (PA)
6680 M 18 (48618-8543)
PHONE.................989 465-0287
Larry Peters, Owner
EMP: 7 EST: 1983
SALES (est): 1.4MM Privately Held
WEB: www.lpproducts.co
SIC: 3544 Special dies & tools

(G-3469)
MIDDLETON WELL DRILLING
3890 W Mcnally Rd (48618-9730)
PHONE.................989 465-1078
William Middlet, Principal
EMP: 5 EST: 2018
SALES (est): 201.3K Privately Held
SIC: 1381 Drilling oil & gas wells

(G-3470)
QUALITY DOOR & MORE INC
135 Miles Pkwy (48618-9604)
PHONE.................989 317-8314
Ryan W Tebo, Administration
EMP: 9 EST: 2014
SALES (est): 2.5MM Privately Held
WEB: www.qualitydoorandmore.com
SIC: 5211 3699 Doors, wood or metal, except storm; door opening & closing devices, electrical

(G-3471)
RACE GRAPHICS PLUS
10751 E Rosebush Rd (48618-9624)
PHONE.................989 465-9117
Kenneth Germain, Principal
EMP: 5 EST: 2008
SALES (est): 141.1K Privately Held
WEB: www.racegraphicsplus.com
SIC: 5099 3993 Signs, except electric; signs & advertising specialties

(G-3472)
ROBINSON INDUSTRIES INC
3051 W Curtis Rd (48618-8549)
PHONE.................989 465-6111
Inez Kaleto, CEO
Bernard Robinson, President
Treva Robinson, Corp Secy
Tom Roberts, Production
Steve Zaske, Maintence Staff
▼ EMP: 190 EST: 1949
SQ FT: 78,300
SALES (est): 22.7MM Privately Held
WEB: www.robinsonind.com
SIC: 3089 Injection molded finished plastic products

(G-3473)
TIGNER PRINTING INC
221 E Railway St (48618-9799)
P.O. Box 289 (48618-0289)
PHONE.................989 465-6916
Jack Tigner, President
EMP: 5 EST: 1987
SQ FT: 3,000
SALES (est): 391.8K Privately Held
WEB: www.tigprint.com
SIC: 2752 Commercial printing, offset

Coloma
Berrien County

(G-3474)
AMHAWK LLC
236 N West St (49038-8407)
PHONE.................269 468-4141
Regi Kurien, Branch Mgr
EMP: 10
SALES (corp-wide): 6.6MM Privately Held
WEB: www.amhawk.com
SIC: 3441 Fabricated structural metal
PA: Amhawk, Llc
200 Dunbar St
Hartford MI 49057
269 468-4177

(G-3475)
COLOMA FROZEN FOODS INC (PA)
4145 Coloma Rd (49038-8967)
PHONE.................269 849-0500
Bradley Wendzel, President
Alton Wendzel, Chairman
Rodney Winkel, Vice Pres
Dennis Ostyn, Plant Mgr
Matthew Chudy, QC Mgr
EMP: 80 EST: 1952
SQ FT: 52,000
SALES (est): 21.7MM Privately Held
WEB: www.colomafrozen.com
SIC: 2037 Frozen fruits & vegetables

(G-3476)
CONTESSA WINE CELLARS
3235 Friday Rd (49038-8959)
PHONE.................269 468-5534
Tony Peterson, Owner
EMP: 6 EST: 2004
SALES (est): 109.1K Privately Held
WEB: www.contessawinecellars.com
SIC: 2084 Wines

(G-3477)
M&I MACHINE INC
5040 M 63 N (49038-9139)
PHONE.................269 849-3624
Mark Coons, President
EMP: 10 EST: 1981
SALES (est): 826.3K Privately Held
WEB: www.shotendtooling.com
SIC: 3599 Machine shop, jobbing & repair

(G-3478)
M&M POLISHING INC
320 Park St (49038-9485)
P.O. Box 71 (49038-0071)
PHONE.................269 468-4407
Brian G Bittner, Principal
EMP: 10 EST: 2008
SALES (est): 2.2MM Privately Held
WEB: www.mandmpolishing.com
SIC: 3544 Industrial molds

(G-3479)
MICHIGAN MOLD INC
500 Washington St (49038-9007)
P.O. Box 705 (49038-0705)
PHONE.................269 468-4407
Larry Bittner, President
Brian Bittner, Vice Pres
Rosanne Bittner, Director
EMP: 21 EST: 1991

SQ FT: 20,000
SALES (est): 2.3MM **Privately Held**
WEB: www.michmold.com
SIC: 3544 Industrial molds

(G-3480)
MIKES MEAT PROCESSING
5135 N Coloma Rd (49038-8828)
PHONE..................269 468-6173
Mary Anderson, *Principal*
EMP: 4 EST: 2010
SALES (est): 84.4K **Privately Held**
SIC: 2011 Meat packing plants

(G-3481)
NORTH SHORE MFG CORP
4706 M 63 N (49038-9140)
PHONE..................269 849-2551
Mark Frank, *President*
Christine Frank, *Vice Pres*
▲ **EMP: 30 EST:** 1969
SQ FT: 20,000
SALES (est): 2.4MM **Privately Held**
WEB: www.nshoremfg.com
SIC: 3363 3364 Aluminum die-castings; lead & zinc die-castings; zinc & zinc-base alloy die-castings

(G-3482)
REGAL FINISHING CO INC
3927 Bessemer Rd (49038-8979)
PHONE..................269 849-2963
Jim Kodis, *President*
Nancy Kodis, *Vice Pres*
Richard Hildebrand, *Production*
Eli Reybuck, *Purch Mgr*
Sharon Wallis, *Sales Mgr*
EMP: 27 EST: 1966
SQ FT: 40,000
SALES (est): 9.5MM **Privately Held**
WEB: www.regalfinishing.com
SIC: 3089 Injection molding of plastics

(G-3483)
SPI BLOW MOLDING LLC
3930 Bessemer Rd (49038-8979)
P.O. Box 359 (49038-0359)
PHONE..................269 849-3200
John Doster Sr, *President*
Susan Doster,
EMP: 31 EST: 2008
SQ FT: 46,000
SALES (est): 4.7MM **Privately Held**
WEB: www.moldedparts.com
SIC: 3089 Injection molding of plastics

(G-3484)
WHIRLPOOL CORPORATION
3694 Kerlikowske Rd (49038-9473)
PHONE..................269 849-0907
EMP: 175
SALES (corp-wide): 20.8B **Publicly Held**
SIC: 3633 3585 3632 Mfg Washing Machines Refrigerators Air Conditionin Units Dishwashers Vacuum Cleaners & Cooking Ranges
PA: Whirlpool Corporation
    2000 N M 63
    Benton Harbor MI 49022
    269 923-5000

(G-3485)
WITCHCRAFT TAPE PRODUCTS INC (PA)
Also Called: W T P
100 Klitchman Dr (49038-8749)
P.O. Box 937 (49038-0937)
PHONE..................269 468-3399
Henry Klitchman, *President*
Dave Pentridge, *Info Tech Mgr*
EMP: 59 EST: 1973
SQ FT: 16,000
SALES (est): 3.7MM **Privately Held**
WEB: www.shopwtp-inc.com
SIC: 2295 3949 2672 Tape, varnished: plastic & other coated (except magnetic); sporting & athletic goods; coated & laminated paper

Colon
St. Joseph County

(G-3486)
ABBOTTS MAGIC MANUFACTURING CO
Also Called: Abbott Magic
124 S Saint Joseph St (49040-9342)
PHONE..................269 432-3235
Greg W Bordner, *President*
Martin Bordner, *Treasurer*
EMP: 5 EST: 1934
SQ FT: 6,500
SALES (est): 528.8K **Privately Held**
SIC: 5945 3999 3944 Hobby, toy & game shops; magic equipment, supplies & props; games, toys & children's vehicles

(G-3487)
FULL SPECTRUM STAINED GL INC
31323 W Colon Rd (49040-9512)
PHONE..................269 432-2610
John McCartney, *President*
Valerie McCartney, *Vice Pres*
EMP: 8 EST: 1988
SALES (est): 654.1K **Privately Held**
WEB: www.fullspectrumstainedglass.com
SIC: 3231 5231 Stained glass: made from purchased glass; glass, leaded or stained

(G-3488)
MAXITROL COMPANY
1000 E State St (49040-9420)
PHONE..................269 432-3291
Jan Stoll, *Info Tech Dir*
EMP: 5
SQ FT: 51,000
SALES (corp-wide): 57MM **Privately Held**
WEB: www.mertik.net
SIC: 3822 3625 Gas burner, automatic controls; relays & industrial controls
PA: Maxitrol Company
    23555 Telegraph Rd
    Southfield MI 48033
    248 356-1400

(G-3489)
PANDIA INDUSTRIES LLC
160 Palmer Ave (49040-9302)
PHONE..................269 386-2110
Adam Baker, *Principal*
EMP: 4 EST: 2016
SALES (est): 79.8K **Privately Held**
SIC: 3999 Manufacturing industries

(G-3490)
PREMIER PASSIVATION SERVICES
1244 Blossom Rd (49040-9789)
PHONE..................269 432-2244
Ruben Haywood, *Owner*
EMP: 4 EST: 2015
SALES (est): 14.8K **Privately Held**
WEB: www.premierpassivation.com
SIC: 3679 7389 Passive repeaters;

(G-3491)
RIVERSIDE VANS INC
57951 Farrand Rd (49040-9513)
P.O. Box 44 (49040-0044)
PHONE..................269 432-3212
Ann Gilchrist, *President*
Harold Hemel, *Treasurer*
EMP: 10 EST: 1985
SQ FT: 9,000
SALES (est): 1.2MM **Privately Held**
SIC: 3716 Recreational van conversion (self-propelled), factory basis

(G-3492)
WHM INVESTMENTS INC
Also Called: Magic Pop Popcorn
29808 Brandt Rd (49040-9506)
P.O. Box 217, Burr Oak (49030-0217)
PHONE..................269 432-3251
William Macdaniels, *President*
Cindy Macdaniels, *Corp Secy*
EMP: 4 EST: 1981
SQ FT: 12,000
SALES (est): 24.6K **Privately Held**
SIC: 2096 Popcorn, already popped (except candy covered)

(G-3493)
WILLIE N EICHER
31534 Brandt Rd (49040-9558)
PHONE..................269 432-3707
Willie N Eicher, *Principal*
EMP: 7 EST: 2005
SALES (est): 70.3K **Privately Held**
SIC: 2273 Carpets & rugs

Columbiaville
Lapeer County

(G-3494)
NAUTICRAFT
3120 Levalley Rd (48421-9758)
PHONE..................810 356-2942
Steven Lentzer, *Owner*
EMP: 4 EST: 2015
SALES (est): 68.8K **Privately Held**
WEB: www.nauticraft.com
SIC: 3732 Boat building & repairing

(G-3495)
SKY INDUSTRIES
5007 Lonsberry Rd (48421-9334)
PHONE..................810 614-6044
Dawn Hubbard, *Owner*
EMP: 4 EST: 2012
SALES (est): 103.2K **Privately Held**
SIC: 3999 Manufacturing industries

Columbus
St. Clair County

(G-3496)
ARIZONA TOOLING INC
7964 Gratiot Ave (48063-3315)
PHONE..................810 533-8828
EMP: 6 EST: 2013
SALES (est): 154.1K **Privately Held**
WEB: www.arizonatoolingco.com
SIC: 3599 Machine shop, jobbing & repair

(G-3497)
BANDIT UTV SUSPENSION
1631 Palms Rd (48063-3320)
PHONE..................586 419-9574
Kelly Cates, *Administration*
EMP: 5 EST: 2016
SALES (est): 258.9K **Privately Held**
WEB: www.banditutvsuspension.com
SIC: 3714 Motor vehicle parts & accessories

(G-3498)
INTERNATIONAL MOLD
1618 Palms Rd (48063-3329)
PHONE..................586 727-7898
EMP: 7 EST: 2013
SALES (est): 142.9K **Privately Held**
WEB: www.internationalmold.net
SIC: 3544 Industrial molds

(G-3499)
JOHN T STOLIKER ENTERPRISES
9353 Gratiot Ave (48063-3611)
PHONE..................586 727-1402
John T Stoliker, *Owner*
EMP: 6 EST: 1995
SALES (est): 189.4K **Privately Held**
SIC: 1382 Oil & gas exploration services

(G-3500)
KGF ENTERPRISE INC
2141 Werner Rd (48063-3729)
PHONE..................586 430-4182
Kerry Fleury, *President*
Debra Fleury, *Treasurer*
EMP: 4 EST: 1977
SALES (est): 382.2K **Privately Held**
WEB: www.kgfenterprise.com
SIC: 3844 5047 X-ray apparatus & tubes; medical equipment & supplies

(G-3501)
PROTO-FORM ENGINEERING INC
10312 Gratiot Ave (48063-4007)
P.O. Box 174, Richmond (48062-0174)
PHONE..................586 727-9803
Frederick G Weeks, *President*
EMP: 16 EST: 1968
SQ FT: 6,000
SALES (est): 1.2MM **Privately Held**
SIC: 3442 Metal doors, sash & trim

(G-3502)
SHARK TOOL & DIE INC
9412 Gratiot Ave (48063-3612)
PHONE..................586 749-7400
David Gryspeerd, *President*
EMP: 6 EST: 1988
SALES (est): 530.6K **Privately Held**
WEB: www.sharktool.net
SIC: 3544 3429 Special dies & tools; metal fasteners

Comins
Oscoda County

(G-3503)
BILLS LOGGING INC
2482 Delano Rd (48619-9727)
PHONE..................989 546-7164
EMP: 6 EST: 2016
SALES (est): 315.4K **Privately Held**
SIC: 2411 Logging

(G-3504)
MICHIGAN LUMBER & WOOD FIBER I
4776 N Abbe Rd (48619-9730)
P.O. Box 97 (48619-0097)
PHONE..................989 848-2100
EMP: 21 EST: 2008
SALES (est): 8.3MM **Privately Held**
WEB: www.ml-wf.com
SIC: 2421 Sawmills & planing mills, general

Commerce Township
Oakland County

(G-3505)
ACCELL TECHNOLOGIES INC
4143 Pioneer Dr (48390-1355)
PHONE..................248 360-3762
Daniel R Helland, *President*
EMP: 5 EST: 1988
SQ FT: 5,200 **Privately Held**
WEB: www.accelltechnologies.com
SIC: 3545 Gauges (machine tool accessories)

(G-3506)
ACE FILTRATION INC
Also Called: Ace Purification
4123 Pioneer Dr (48390-1355)
PHONE..................248 624-6300
Robert McKay, *President*
◆ **EMP: 8 EST:** 2001
SQ FT: 3,000
SALES (est): 1MM **Privately Held**
SIC: 3699 Generators, ultrasonic

(G-3507)
ALADDIN PRINTING
1546 Union Lake Rd (48382-2238)
PHONE..................248 360-2842
Matt Mac Dermaid, *Owner*
EMP: 4 EST: 1982
SALES (est): 292.8K **Privately Held**
WEB: www.aladdin-printing.com
SIC: 2752 2791 2789 Commercial printing, offset; typesetting; bookbinding & related work

(G-3508)
ALL ABOUT DRAINAGE LLC
1940 Alton Cir (48390-2605)
PHONE..................248 921-0766
Keith Swan, *Partner*
Kody Swan, *Partner*
EMP: 7

Commerce Township - Oakland County (G-3509)

SALES (est): 500K **Privately Held**
SIC: 3272 1771 Concrete products used to facilitate drainage; concrete repair

(G-3509)
ALLIED WELDING INCORPORATED
8240 Goldie St (48390-4108)
PHONE 248 360-1122
Randy Horstmann, *President*
EMP: 4 EST: 1990
SALES (est): 261.9K **Privately Held**
SIC: 7692 7699 Welding repair; marine propeller repair

(G-3510)
AMERICAN MFG INNOVATORS INC
Also Called: A M I
1840 W West Maple Rd (48390-2951)
PHONE 248 669-5990
Conrad Lindstrom, *President*
Elizabeth Lindstrom, *Controller*
EMP: 11 EST: 1988
SQ FT: 15,000
SALES (est): 2.7MM **Privately Held**
WEB: www.amiusainc.com
SIC: 3599 Machine shop, jobbing & repair

(G-3511)
ARBOC LTD (PA)
3504 Car Dr (48382-1603)
PHONE 248 684-2895
James Bartel, *President*
Corrine Bartel, *Treasurer*
EMP: 9 EST: 1983
SALES (est): 911.3K **Privately Held**
WEB: www.arbocsv.com
SIC: 8711 3715 Consulting engineer; truck trailer chassis

(G-3512)
ARMALY SPONGE COMPANY (PA)
Also Called: Armaly Brands
1900 Easy St (48390-3220)
P.O. Box 611, Walled Lake (48390-0611)
PHONE 248 669-2100
John W Armaly Jr, *President*
Annmarie Armaly, *Corp Secy*
Gilbert C Armaly, *Vice Pres*
Kevin D Delaney, *Opers Staff*
Theresa Muzzi, *Controller*
◆ EMP: 31 EST: 1925
SQ FT: 69,000
SALES (est): 14.9MM **Privately Held**
WEB: www.armalybrands.com
SIC: 3089 3086 5199 Sponges, plastic; plastics foam products; sponges (animal)

(G-3513)
BASAN CORD INC
4170 Martin Rd (48390-4116)
PHONE 888 802-2726
Sam Cherrin, *CEO*
EMP: 5 EST: 2017
SALES (est): 254.6K **Privately Held**
WEB: www.basancord.com
SIC: 3999 Manufacturing industries

(G-3514)
BASC MANUFACTURING INC
4325 Martin Rd (48390-4121)
PHONE 248 360-2272
Michael J Burskey, *President*
Stephen Fricke, *COO*
Bruce Brown, *Sales Staff*
EMP: 5 EST: 1987
SALES (est): 791.2K **Privately Held**
WEB: www.bascmfg.com
SIC: 2542 Shelving, office & store: except wood

(G-3515)
BIELOMATIK INC
300 Eagle Pond Dr Apt 435 (48390-3070)
PHONE 248 446-9910
Ulrik Frodermann, *President*
Autumn Seymour, *Admin Sec*
▲ EMP: 28 EST: 1991

SALES (est): 10.2MM
SALES (corp-wide): 1.1MM **Privately Held**
WEB: www.bielomatik.us
SIC: 3548 Welding & cutting apparatus & accessories
HQ: Bielomatik Leuze Gmbh + Co. Kg
Daimlerstr. 6-10
Neuffen BW 72639
702 512-0

(G-3516)
BIELOMATIK USA INC
300 Eagle Pond Dr Apt 435 (48390-3070)
PHONE 248 446-9910
Porten Warnatsch, *President*
EMP: 50 EST: 2003
SALES (est): 9.7MM
SALES (corp-wide): 1.1MM **Privately Held**
WEB: www.bielomatik.us
SIC: 3541 Machine tools, metal cutting type
HQ: Bielomatik Leuze Gmbh + Co. Kg
Daimlerstr. 6-10
Neuffen BW 72639
702 512-0

(G-3517)
BOONES CANDLE CO
125 Liza Ln (48382-3177)
PHONE 248 444-0621
EMP: 4 EST: 2018
SALES (est): 41.6K **Privately Held**
SIC: 3999 Candles

(G-3518)
CHAMPION GASKET & RUBBER INC
3225 Haggerty Hwy (48390-1725)
PHONE 248 624-6140
Robin C Dubuc, *President*
Nathan Dubuc, *Vice Pres*
Jacob Dubuc, *QC Mgr*
EMP: 30 EST: 1971
SQ FT: 40,000
SALES (est): 5.4MM **Privately Held**
WEB: www.championgasket.com
SIC: 3053 Gaskets, all materials

(G-3519)
CRANKSHAFT CRAFTSMAN INC
1960 W West Maple Rd (48390-2950)
PHONE 313 366-0140
Russell Taylor, *President*
Susan P Taylor, *Corp Secy*
Timothy Taylor, *Vice Pres*
EMP: 4 EST: 1962
SQ FT: 17,500 **Privately Held**
WEB: www.crankshaftcraftsmen.com
SIC: 3599 Machine shop, jobbing & repair

(G-3520)
CUSTOM LINE CABINETS
482 Mulberry Dr (48390-3264)
PHONE 810 459-0414
Thomas Scalise, *Principal*
EMP: 5 EST: 2010
SALES (est): 153.8K **Privately Held**
SIC: 2434 Wood kitchen cabinets

(G-3521)
DAVIS IRON WORKS INC
1166 Benstein Rd (48390-2926)
P.O. Box 900, Walled Lake (48390-0900)
PHONE 248 624-5960
Frank G Nehr Sr, *President*
Frank G Nehr Jr, *Exec VP*
Elizabeth J Nehr, *Admin Sec*
EMP: 30 EST: 1945
SQ FT: 20,000
SALES (est): 6.2MM **Privately Held**
WEB: www.davisironworksinc.com
SIC: 1791 3446 Structural steel erection; architectural metalwork

(G-3522)
DIAMONDBACK CORP
Also Called: Diamondback Abrasive Co
3141 Old Farm Ln (48390-1655)
PHONE 248 960-8260
Douglas Menzies, *President*
EMP: 19 EST: 1998
SQ FT: 2,500

SALES (est): 1MM **Privately Held**
WEB: www.diamondbackabrasive.com
SIC: 3291 Wheels, grinding: artificial

(G-3523)
DKO INTL
39500 W 14 Mile Rd (48390-3908)
PHONE 248 926-9115
Dennis Kiraga, *Owner*
EMP: 10 EST: 1993
SALES (est): 669.9K **Privately Held**
SIC: 2499 Picture frame molding, finished

(G-3524)
E-LIGHT LLC
3144 Martin Rd (48390-1627)
PHONE 734 427-0600
EMP: 4
SALES (est): 197.9K **Privately Held**
SIC: 3646 Mfg Commercial Lighting Fixtures

(G-3525)
ECA EDUCATIONAL SERVICES INC
Also Called: Eca Educational Services Div
1981 Dallavo Dr (48390-1683)
PHONE 248 669-7170
Dennis J Harlan, *President*
Heidi Harlan, *Exec VP*
Claudia Harlan, *Vice Pres*
Miguel Delafuente, *Opers Staff*
EMP: 53 EST: 1981
SALES (est): 7.4MM **Privately Held**
WEB: www.eca.bz
SIC: 3944 7372 Science kits: microscopes, chemistry sets, etc.; educational computer software

(G-3526)
ELEGANT WOODWORKING
3711 Ellisia Rd (48382-1727)
PHONE 248 363-3804
Harold Canfield, *Owner*
EMP: 4 EST: 2014
SALES (est): 71.2K **Privately Held**
WEB: www.elegant-woodworking.com
SIC: 2431 Millwork

(G-3527)
EXIE SMITH PUBLICATIONS LLC
1829 Union Lake Rd (48382-2247)
PHONE 248 360-2917
Exie Smith, *President*
EMP: 5 EST: 2012
SALES (est): 88.7K **Privately Held**
SIC: 2741 Miscellaneous publishing

(G-3528)
EZM LLC
730 Welch Rd (48390-3812)
PHONE 248 861-2602
Tom V Esch,
Carine Woldanski,
EMP: 13 EST: 2007
SALES (est): 722.9K **Privately Held**
SIC: 3825 3829 Electrical energy measuring equipment; measuring & controlling devices

(G-3529)
FITZ-RITE PRODUCTS INC
Also Called: Special Tooling Service, Inc.
4228 Pioneer Dr (48390-1353)
PHONE 248 360-3730
Dean Ftizpatrick, *President*
EMP: 7 EST: 2003
SALES (est): 595.7K **Privately Held**
WEB: www.ststool.com
SIC: 3541 Machine tools, metal cutting type

(G-3530)
FKA DISTRIBUTING CO LLC (PA)
Also Called: Homedics
3000 N Pontiac Trl (48390-2720)
PHONE 248 863-3000
Saby Sen, *Vice Pres*
Kathy Stankewitz, *Vice Pres*
Andrea Vandekerkhoff, *Purch Mgr*
Jeff Deachin, *Purchasing*
Ben Dvir, *Purchasing*
◆ EMP: 236 EST: 1987
SQ FT: 400,000

SALES (est): 120.4MM **Privately Held**
WEB: www.homedics.com
SIC: 3679 3634 Headphones, radio; massage machines, electric, except for beauty/barber shops

(G-3531)
FLEXI DISPLAY MARKETING INC
Also Called: Awarenessideas.com
2156 Maplehurst Dr (48390-3248)
PHONE 800 875-1725
Marvin Weisenthal, *President*
Jeannie Hauser, *Sales Staff*
◆ EMP: 6 EST: 1996
SALES (est): 800K **Privately Held**
WEB: www.flexidisplaymarketing.com
SIC: 3999 Advertising display products

(G-3532)
FOUR STAR RUBBER INC
3185 Old Farm Ln (48390-1655)
PHONE 810 632-3335
Rosemary Voros, *President*
Dan Voros, *Treasurer*
EMP: 8 EST: 1988
SQ FT: 5,200
SALES (est): 1.3MM **Privately Held**
WEB: www.fourstarrubber.com
SIC: 3061 5085 Mechanical rubber goods; rubber goods, mechanical

(G-3533)
GOVRO-NELSON CO
1132 Ladd Rd (48390-3032)
PHONE 810 329-4727
Ann Schmidt, *President*
EMP: 5 EST: 1923 **Privately Held**
SIC: 3541 Drilling machine tools (metal cutting); tapping machines

(G-3534)
H-O-H WATER TECHNOLOGY INC
1013 Rig St (48390-2265)
PHONE 248 669-6667
Phil Davis, *Division Mgr*
Wallace Hood, *Division Mgr*
Flo Zeitler, *General Mgr*
Henry Becker, *Vice Pres*
Carl Cameron, *Sales Staff*
EMP: 46
SALES (corp-wide): 21.7MM **Privately Held**
WEB: www.hohwatertechnology.com
SIC: 2899 3589 Water treating compounds; water treatment equipment, industrial
PA: H-O-H Water Technology, Inc.
500 S Vermont St
Palatine IL 60067
847 358-7400

(G-3535)
HEINZMANN D TOOL & DIE INC
Also Called: D H Tool & Die
4335 Pineview Dr (48390-4129)
PHONE 248 363-5115
Dieter Heinzmann, *President*
Joanne Heinzmann, *Corp Secy*
EMP: 10 EST: 1979
SQ FT: 8,000
SALES (est): 991.1K **Privately Held**
WEB: www.centuryrealtyonline.com
SIC: 3544 3469 Special dies & tools; jigs & fixtures; metal stampings

(G-3536)
HERKULES EQUIPMENT CORPORATION
2760 Ridgeway Ct (48390-1662)
PHONE 248 960-7100
Todd Bacon, *President*
Scott Wilhelm, *Engineer*
Brian Abbott, *CFO*
Kevin Prost, *CFO*
Ruth Macdonald, *Controller*
▲ EMP: 25 EST: 1984
SQ FT: 32,000
SALES (est): 8.5MM **Privately Held**
WEB: www.herkules.us
SIC: 5084 3535 Paint spray equipment, industrial; conveyors & conveying equipment

GEOGRAPHIC SECTION
Commerce Township - Oakland County (G-3568)

(G-3537)
HIGHLAND MACHINE DESIGN INC
Also Called: Wojo Associates
3125 Old Farm Ln (48390-1655)
PHONE...................248 669-6150
Ian Joyce, *President*
EMP: 6 EST: 1995
SQ FT: 2,000
SALES (est): 400K Privately Held
WEB: www.highlandmachinedesigninc.com
SIC: 8711 3541 Machine tool design; machine tools, metal cutting type

(G-3538)
HOLD IT PRODUCTS CORPORATION
1900 Easy St (48390-3220)
P.O. Box 731, Walled Lake (48390-0731)
PHONE...................248 624-1195
John W Armaly Jr, *President*
▼ EMP: 5 EST: 1986
SQ FT: 3,000
SALES (est): 469.9K Privately Held
WEB: www.holditproducts.com
SIC: 3089 Plastic containers, except foam

(G-3539)
HOMEDICS USA LLC (HQ)
Also Called: Homedics Group Canada
3000 N Pontiac Trl (48390-2720)
PHONE...................248 863-3000
Joann Berg, *Benefits Mgr*
Alon Kaufman, *Mng Member*
Beth Harrison Meyer, *Director*
◆ EMP: 195 EST: 1987
SALES (est): 92.9MM
SALES (corp-wide): 120.4MM Privately Held
WEB: www.homedics.com
SIC: 2844 5047 5961 Toilet preparations; medical equipment & supplies; fitness & sporting goods, mail order
PA: Fka Distributing Co., Llc
   3000 N Pontiac Trl
   Commerce Township MI 48390
   248 863-3000

(G-3540)
HOUSE OF MARLEY LLC
Also Called: House of Marley Canada
3000 N Pontiac Trl (48390-2720)
PHONE...................248 863-3000
Alon Kaufman, *CEO*
Roman Ferber, *President*
Sam Vanderveer, *Senior VP*
▲ EMP: 5 EST: 2010
SALES (est): 3.9MM
SALES (corp-wide): 120.4MM Privately Held
WEB: www.thehouseofmarley.com
SIC: 3679 Headphones, radio
PA: Fka Distributing Co., Llc
   3000 N Pontiac Trl
   Commerce Township MI 48390
   248 863-3000

(G-3541)
HYDRO CHEM LABORATORIES INC
1565 Switzerland Dr (48382-4759)
PHONE...................248 348-1737
James V Boyd, *President*
Michael Trzos, *Vice Pres*
EMP: 4 EST: 1976
SALES (est): 449.9K Privately Held
WEB: www.hydrochemlabs.com
SIC: 2899 Water treating compounds

(G-3542)
INKPRESSIONS
3175 Martin Rd (48390-1628)
PHONE...................248 956-7974
EMP: 5 EST: 2017
SALES (est): 73.2K Privately Held
WEB: www.inkpressions.com
SIC: 2759 Screen printing

(G-3543)
INKPRESSIONS LLC
3175 Martin Rd (48390-1628)
PHONE...................248 461-2555
Tracey Chase,
EMP: 20 EST: 2017
SALES (est): 1MM Privately Held
WEB: www.inkpressions.com
SIC: 2395 2261 Emblems, embroidered; printing of cotton broadwoven fabrics

(G-3544)
INVEST BUY OWN LLC
1933 Forest View Ct (48390-3943)
PHONE...................248 467-2048
Jason Ridgeway,
EMP: 4 EST: 2019
SALES (est): 170.2K Privately Held
SIC: 3161 Clothing & apparel carrying cases

(G-3545)
IRENE INDUSTRIES LLC
866 Grandview Dr (48390-5932)
PHONE...................757 696-3969
Kelly Rankin, *Principal*
EMP: 7 EST: 2016
SALES (est): 318.6K Privately Held
SIC: 3999 Manufacturing industries

(G-3546)
J&J CUSTOM PRINT SERVICES
8436 Cascade St (48382-4705)
PHONE...................616 581-0545
EMP: 4 EST: 2015
SALES (est): 63.2K Privately Held
SIC: 2752 Commercial printing, lithographic

(G-3547)
JAMIE BYRNES
1775 Chateau Rd (48382-1910)
PHONE...................248 872-2513
Jamie Byrnes, *President*
EMP: 4 EST: 2016
SALES (est): 62.8K Privately Held
SIC: 2046 Wet corn milling

(G-3548)
K&S FUEL VENTURES
519 W Commerce Rd (48382-3924)
PHONE...................248 360-0055
EMP: 8 EST: 2005
SALES (est): 384.1K Privately Held
SIC: 2869 Fuels

(G-3549)
LANCAST URETHANE INC
1132 Ladd Rd (48390-3032)
PHONE...................517 485-6070
Dan Eckert, *President*
EMP: 5 EST: 1998 Privately Held
WEB: www.lancasturethane.com
SIC: 2851 Polyurethane coatings

(G-3550)
LEBUTT PUBLISHING LLC
5922 Strawberry Cir (48382-5508)
PHONE...................248 756-1613
Christian Lebutt, *Principal*
EMP: 5 EST: 2012
SALES (est): 63.9K Privately Held
SIC: 2741 Miscellaneous publishing

(G-3551)
LIQUID OTC LLC
Also Called: Lol
3250 Old Farm Ln Ste 1 (48390-1602)
P.O. Box 1351, Walled Lake (48390-5351)
PHONE...................248 214-7771
Thomas F Morse,
Alina Morse,
EMP: 6 EST: 2011
SQ FT: 3,000
SALES: 737.3K Privately Held
WEB: www.britenz.com
SIC: 2064 3843 Lollipops & other hard candy; dental equipment & supplies

(G-3552)
MANUFCTRING SOLUTIONS TECH LLC
Also Called: Vitullo & Associates
1975 Alpha St (48382-2302)
PHONE...................734 744-5050
David Townsend, *Mng Member*
Chris Jones,
EMP: 8
SQ FT: 16,100

(G-3553)
MAP TO ELOPAK PRECISION
1200 Benstein Rd (48390-2200)
PHONE...................417 467-7419
Marty R Idemiller, *Technology*
EMP: 8 EST: 2019
SALES (est): 89.6K Privately Held
SIC: 3599 Machine shop, jobbing & repair

(G-3554)
MARK TOOL & DIE COMPANY INC
Also Called: Mark Precision Tool and Engrg
4360 Haggerty Hwy (48390-1316)
PHONE...................248 363-1567
George Vidu, *President*
Rick Lloyd, *Project Mgr*
Kim Haislip, *Office Mgr*
Kimberly Hester, *Office Mgr*
EMP: 20 EST: 1966
SQ FT: 16,000
SALES (est): 3.4MM Privately Held
SIC: 3545 3544 Machine tool accessories; special dies & tools

(G-3555)
MAVERICK BUILDING SYSTEMS LLC
3190 Walnut Lake Rd (48390-1743)
PHONE...................248 366-9410
Brian Dittenber, *Sales Staff*
Kevin A Maguire,
Glenn Johnson,
EMP: 17 EST: 1996
SQ FT: 25,000
SALES (est): 2.1MM Privately Held
WEB: www.mavbldgsys.com
SIC: 2439 5031 Trusses, wooden roof; lumber, plywood & millwork

(G-3556)
MICHIGAN ROLL FORM INC (PA)
Also Called: American Eagle Systems
1132 Ladd Rd (48390-3032)
PHONE...................248 669-3700
Steven M Arens, *President*
EMP: 35 EST: 1986
SQ FT: 28,600
SALES (est): 6.4MM Privately Held
WEB: www.mrf-inc.com
SIC: 3542 3559 Spinning, spline rolling & winding machines; plastics working machinery

(G-3557)
NINJA PANTS PRESS LLC
1980 Blue Stone Ln (48390-4307)
PHONE...................248 669-6577
Robert Matthews, *Principal*
EMP: 5 EST: 2013
SALES (est): 84.1K Privately Held
SIC: 2741 Miscellaneous publishing

(G-3558)
NR RACING LLC
1960 W West Maple Rd # 200 (48390-2950)
PHONE...................248 767-0421
EMP: 6 EST: 2019
SALES (est): 432.8K Privately Held
WEB: www.nrracing.com
SIC: 3714 Motor vehicle parts & accessories

(G-3559)
OLD SAWMILL WOODWORKING CO
4552 Newcroft St (48382-3820)
PHONE...................248 366-6245
Robert Milkowski, *Manager*
EMP: 6 EST: 1991
SALES (est): 459.2K Privately Held
SIC: 2421 Sawmills & planing mills, general

(G-3560)
OPENALPR SOFTWARE SOLUTIONS L
324 Annison Dr (48382-3642)
PHONE...................800 935-1699
Matthew Hill, *Principal*
Erik Stafford, *Director*
EMP: 6 EST: 2019
SALES (est): 75K Privately Held
WEB: www.openalpr.com
SIC: 7372 Prepackaged software

(G-3561)
OPTIONS CABINETRY INC
2121 Easy St (48390-3225)
PHONE...................248 669-0000
Alan Edelson, *President*
EMP: 13 EST: 1992
SQ FT: 24,600
SALES (est): 1.5MM Privately Held
SIC: 3429 Cabinet hardware

(G-3562)
PETERSON AMERICAN CORPORATION
K P American Division
3285 Martin Rd Ste N106 (48390-1601)
PHONE...................248 799-5410
Carl Atwater, *Manager*
EMP: 6
SALES (corp-wide): 1.6B Privately Held
WEB: www.pspring.com
SIC: 3495 Wire springs
HQ: Peterson American Corporation
   21200 Telegraph Rd
   Southfield MI 48033
   248 799-5400

(G-3563)
PHOENIX TRAILER & BODY COMPANY
4751 Juniper Dr (48382-1512)
PHONE...................248 360-7184
Emory Buttermore, *President*
EMP: 10
SALES (est): 90K Privately Held
WEB: www.phoenixtrail.com
SIC: 3799 7389 Trailers & trailer equipment; design services

(G-3564)
PRECISION COATINGS INC (PA)
8120 Goldie St (48390-4107)
PHONE...................248 363-8361
Andrew W Rich, *President*
Delores Oneil, *Vice Pres*
Norman Sweet, *Vice Pres*
Jake Gill, *Engineer*
Robert F Wider, *CFO*
EMP: 94 EST: 1970
SQ FT: 50,000
SALES (est): 11.8MM Privately Held
WEB: www.pcicoatings.com
SIC: 3479 Coating of metals & formed products

(G-3565)
PREFERRED PRODUCTS INC
Also Called: Preferred Screen Printing
1200 Benstein Rd (48390-2200)
PHONE...................248 255-0200
Steve Steinway, *President*
Debra Steinway, *Vice Pres*
EMP: 16 EST: 1985
SQ FT: 10,600
SALES (est): 1.2MM Privately Held
SIC: 3842 2392 Orthopedic appliances; household furnishings

(G-3566)
QUANENERGY SYSTEMS INC
2655 E Oakley Park Rd # 105 (48390-1684)
PHONE...................248 859-5587
EMP: 8 EST: 2017
SALES (est): 213.8K Privately Held
SIC: 3812 Search & navigation equipment

(G-3567)
QUARTERS VENDING LLC
3174 Old Farm Ln (48390-1633)
PHONE...................313 510-5555
EMP: 6 EST: 2011
SALES (est): 200K Privately Held
SIC: 3131 Quarters

(G-3568)
R & J MANUFACTURING COMPANY
3200 Martin Rd (48390-1629)
PHONE...................248 669-2460

Commerce Township - Oakland County (G-3569)

Anabella Richardi, *President*
EMP: 15 **EST:** 1962
SQ FT: 25,000
SALES (est): 1.3MM **Privately Held**
WEB: www.rjman.com
SIC: 3053 3829 3061 Gaskets & sealing devices; testing equipment: abrasion, shearing strength, etc.; mechanical rubber goods

(G-3570)
REAL ESTATE ONE INC
Also Called: Real Estate One Licensing Co
3100 Old Farm Ln Ste 10 (48390-1652)
PHONE.................248 851-2600
Jeff Dixon, *Branch Mgr*
EMP: 4
SALES (corp-wide): 104.5MM **Privately Held**
WEB: www.realestateone.com
SIC: 2752 Promotional printing, lithographic
PA: Real Estate One, Inc.
   25800 Northwestern Hwy # 100
   Southfield MI 48075
   248 208-2900

(G-3570)
REAL GREEN SYSTEMS INC (DH)
4375 Pineview Dr (48390-4129)
PHONE.................888 345-2154
Donald F Brown, *CEO*
Joseph J Kucik, *President*
Dave Boulter, *Vice Pres*
Peter Brown, *Vice Pres*
Tony Buck, *Vice Pres*
▲ **EMP:** 60 **EST:** 1987
SQ FT: 18,000
SALES (est): 23.3MM
SALES (corp-wide): 805.8MM **Privately Held**
WEB: www.realgreen.com
SIC: 7331 2396 7371 0782 Direct mail advertising services; printing & embossing on plastics fabric articles; software programming applications; lawn & garden services; landscape services; carpet & rug cleaning & repairing plant
HQ: Workwave Llc
   101 Crawfords Corner Rd
   Holmdel NJ 07733
   866 794-1658

(G-3571)
RODAN TOOL & MOLD LLC
3185 Old Farm Ln (48390-1655)
PHONE.................248 926-9200
Dan Voros, *Mng Member*
EMP: 5 **EST:** 2003
SALES (est): 418.7K **Privately Held**
WEB: www.fourstarrubber.com
SIC: 3545 Tools & accessories for machine tools

(G-3572)
SCIENCEKITWARHOUSECOM
1981 Dallavo Dr (48390-1683)
PHONE.................800 992-8338
EMP: 5 **EST:** 2012
SALES (est): 94.7K **Privately Held**
SIC: 3231 Aquariums & reflectors, glass

(G-3573)
SKINNY KID RACE CARS
3170 E Oakley Park Rd A (48390-1661)
PHONE.................248 668-1040
Keith Engling, *Owner*
EMP: 5 **EST:** 2005
SALES (est): 484.8K **Privately Held**
WEB: www.skinnykidracecars.com
SIC: 3711 Automobile assembly, including specialty automobiles

(G-3574)
SPX CORPORATION
Also Called: Metal Forge
3160 Dallavo Ct (48390-1606)
PHONE.................248 669-5100
Dave Bruss, *Manager*
EMP: 102
SALES (corp-wide): 1.5B **Publicly Held**
WEB: www.spx.com
SIC: 3443 3363 Fabricated plate work (boiler shop); aluminum die-castings

PA: Spx Corporation
   6325 Ardrey Kell Rd # 400
   Charlotte NC 28277
   980 474-3700

(G-3575)
STORK INDUSTRIES CBD LLC
1699 Traditional Dr (48390-2973)
PHONE.................248 513-1778
William Vlasic, *Principal*
EMP: 5 **EST:** 2019
SALES (est): 298.2K **Privately Held**
SIC: 3599 Machine shop, jobbing & repair

(G-3576)
TECLA COMPANY INC (PA)
Also Called: Resco Pet Products
1250 Ladd Rd (48390-3067)
P.O. Box 1177, Walled Lake (48390-5177)
PHONE.................248 624-8200
Richard Clark, *President*
Richard N Clark, *President*
Jeffrey L Clark, *Corp Secy*
Robert W Clark, *Vice Pres*
▲ **EMP:** 23 **EST:** 1900
SQ FT: 23,000
SALES (est): 5MM **Privately Held**
WEB: www.teclausa.com
SIC: 3429 3999 3089 Marine hardware; pet supplies; plastic processing

(G-3577)
THREE M TOOL & MACHINE INC
Also Called: Ultra-Grip International Div
8135 Richardson Rd (48390-4131)
PHONE.................248 363-0982
Lori Holland, *Controller*
Sharon Medwid, *Manager*
EMP: 25
SALES (corp-wide): 9.5MM **Privately Held**
WEB: www.three-m.com
SIC: 3599 Machine shop, jobbing & repair
PA: Three M Tool & Machine, Inc.
   8155 Richardson Rd
   Commerce Township MI 48390
   248 363-1555

(G-3578)
TIMS CUSTOM CABINETS LLC
525 W Oakley Park Rd (48390-1240)
PHONE.................248 912-4154
Timothy Yehle, *Principal*
EMP: 5 **EST:** 2009
SALES (est): 164.7K **Privately Held**
WEB: www.timscustomcabinets.com
SIC: 2434 Wood kitchen cabinets

(G-3579)
TRIUNFAR INDUSTRIES INC I
2375 Bevin Ct (48382-2068)
PHONE.................248 993-9302
EMP: 5 **EST:** 2018
SALES (est): 373.8K **Privately Held**
SIC: 3999 Manufacturing industries

(G-3580)
TS CARBIDE INC
3131 Ruler Dr (48390-1675)
PHONE.................248 486-8330
Todd Temple, *Manager*
EMP: 5 **EST:** 2005
SALES (est): 580.7K **Privately Held**
SIC: 3545 Cutting tools for machine tools

(G-3581)
WIRE NETS
1873 Twin Sun Cir (48390-4403)
PHONE.................248 669-5312
Dennis Nufer, *Principal*
EMP: 6 **EST:** 2005
SALES (est): 246.6K **Privately Held**
SIC: 3312 Wire products, steel or iron

(G-3582)
WLW MUSICAL
850 Ladd Rd (48390-3021)
PHONE.................248 956-3060
EMP: 5 **EST:** 2018
SALES (est): 72.8K **Privately Held**
SIC: 3931 Musical instruments

(G-3583)
XCELL SOFTWARE INC
3830 Benstein Rd (48382-1815)
PHONE.................248 760-3160

Chris Baird, *Principal*
EMP: 5 **EST:** 2016
SALES (est): 125.9K **Privately Held**
SIC: 7372 Prepackaged software

Comstock Park
Kent County

(G-3584)
ABC PACKAGING EQP & MTLS INC
544 7 Mile Rd Nw (49321-8254)
P.O. Box 435 (49321-0435)
PHONE.................616 784-2330
Frank Peltz, *CEO*
Robert Brechting, *Co-Owner*
David Peltz, *Vice Pres*
Joan Peltz, *Admin Sec*
EMP: 11 **EST:** 1971
SALES (est): 915.3K **Privately Held**
SIC: 3089 5113 Molding primary plastic; industrial & personal service paper

(G-3585)
ABC-2100 INC
5320 6 Mile Ct Nw (49321-9634)
PHONE.................616 647-9200
Robert Baker, *President*
Kevin Grinnell, *President*
Dawn Meyer, *Production*
EMP: 41 **EST:** 1985
SQ FT: 25,000
SALES (est): 4.5MM **Privately Held**
SIC: 3599 Machine shop, jobbing & repair

(G-3586)
ADVANCED TOOLING SYSTEMS INC (HQ)
Also Called: Tsg Tooling Systems Group
1166 7 Mile Rd Nw (49321-9783)
PHONE.................616 784-7513
Drew Boresma, *President*
Rick Huisken, *General Mgr*
Dennis Simons, *Project Mgr*
Mike Klein, *Opers Mgr*
◆ **EMP:** 9 **EST:** 1983
SQ FT: 48,000
SALES (est): 7.6MM **Privately Held**
WEB: www.toolingsystemsgroup.com
SIC: 3544 Special dies & tools

(G-3587)
ALL PHASE WELDING SERVICE INC
950 Vitality Dr Nw Ste G (49321-7908)
PHONE.................616 235-6100
Dave Deweese, *President*
Jeffrey Vereeke, *Vice Pres*
EMP: 8 **EST:** 1996
SALES (est): 767.6K **Privately Held**
WEB: www.all-phase-welding-services.business.site
SIC: 7692 Welding repair

(G-3588)
ASELTINE CIDER COMPANY INC
533 Lamoreaux Dr Nw (49321-9204)
PHONE.................616 784-7676
John Klamt, *President*
Ronald Klamt, *Corp Secy*
EMP: 4 **EST:** 1953
SQ FT: 4,000
SALES (est): 436K **Privately Held**
SIC: 2099 Cider, nonalcoholic

(G-3589)
BAUBLE PATCH INC
5228 Alpine Ave Nw Ste A (49321-7802)
PHONE.................616 785-1100
Richard Kerkau, *President*
Erica Edwards, *Sales Associate*
EMP: 7 **EST:** 1994
SQ FT: 1,200
SALES (est): 1MM **Privately Held**
WEB: www.baublepatchjewelers.com
SIC: 5944 7631 5094 3911 Jewelry, precious stones & precious metals; jewelry repair services; jewelry; jewelry, precious metal; jewelry mountings & trimmings

(G-3590)
BIBLE DOCTRINES TO LIVE BY INC
Also Called: BIBLE DOCTRINES PUBLICATIONS
895 W River Center Dr Ne (49321-8955)
P.O. Box 564 (49321-0564)
PHONE.................616 453-0493
Joel McGarvey, *CEO*
S Lee Homoki, *President*
Darlene Homoki, *Corp Secy*
EMP: 6 **EST:** 1981
SQ FT: 1,000
SALES (est): 238.6K **Privately Held**
WEB: www.bibledoctrines.org
SIC: 2759 1761 Periodicals: printing; roofing, siding & sheet metal work

(G-3591)
BIER BARREL DISTILLERY LLC
5295 West River Dr Ne # 200 (49321-8030)
PHONE.................616 633-8601
Joel Bierling, *Administration*
EMP: 9 **EST:** 2016
SALES (est): 662.6K **Privately Held**
WEB: www.bierdistillery.com
SIC: 2085 Distilled & blended liquors

(G-3592)
CENTERLINE ENGINEERING INC
940 7 Mile Rd Nw (49321-7918)
P.O. Box 2 (49321-0002)
PHONE.................616 735-2506
Bob Haadsma, *CEO*
Dan Hansen, *President*
EMP: 91 **EST:** 2000
SQ FT: 6,600
SALES (est): 10.7MM **Privately Held**
WEB: www.centerlineeng.com
SIC: 3544 Special dies & tools

(G-3593)
CG AUTOMATION & FIXTURE INC
Also Called: Cg Automation
5352 Rusche Dr Nw (49321-9551)
PHONE.................616 785-5400
Douglas Alan Bouwman, *CEO*
Phil Knapp, *Project Engr*
Scott Jelsma, *Program Mgr*
Rick Cairns, *Manager*
EMP: 24 **EST:** 1991
SQ FT: 24,000
SALES (est): 7.7MM **Privately Held**
WEB: www.commercialtoolgroup.com
SIC: 3544 Special dies & tools

(G-3594)
CG PLASTICS INC
5349 Rusche Dr Nw (49321-9551)
PHONE.................616 785-1900
Jane A Bulkowski Bouwman, *President*
EMP: 7 **EST:** 1995
SQ FT: 18,000
SALES (est): 1.3MM **Privately Held**
WEB: www.commercialtoolgroup.com
SIC: 3089 Injection molding of plastics

(G-3595)
CHAMPION DIE INCORPORATED
5510 West River Dr Ne (49321-8914)
PHONE.................616 784-2397
Robert G Champion, *President*
Linda Champion, *Vice Pres*
EMP: 25 **EST:** 1987
SALES (est): 2.1MM **Privately Held**
WEB: www.championdie.com
SIC: 3544 Dies, steel rule; special dies & tools

(G-3596)
COMMERCIAL TOOL & DIE INC
Also Called: Commercial Tool Group
5351 Rusche Dr Nw (49321-9551)
PHONE.................616 785-8100
Doug Bouwman, *CEO*
Chris Ostosh, *President*
Dave Ketelaar, *General Mgr*
Keith Foster, *Vice Pres*
Scott Chase, *Project Mgr*
▲ **EMP:** 141
SQ FT: 47,000

GEOGRAPHIC SECTION
Comstock Park - Kent County (G-3625)

SALES (est): 29.8MM **Privately Held**
WEB: www.commercialtoolgroup.com
SIC: 3599 Machine shop, jobbing & repair

(G-3597)
CONCEPT METAL MACHINING LLC
5320 6 Mile Ct Nw (49321-9634)
PHONE.................................616 647-9200
Robert Baker, *President*
Rick Williams, *General Mgr*
EMP: 45 EST: 2019
SALES (est): 10.5MM **Privately Held**
WEB: www.conceptmetalsgroup.com
SIC: 3441 Fabricated structural metal
PA: Concept Metal Products, Inc.
    16928 148th Ave
    Spring Lake MI 49456

(G-3598)
CPJ COMPANY INC
3739 Laramie Dr Ne (49321-8973)
PHONE.................................616 784-6355
Charles Brickey, *President*
Pamela Brickey, *Vice Pres*
Peter Schamel, *Vice Pres*
Scott Johnson, *Manager*
EMP: 36 EST: 1974
SQ FT: 18,000
SALES (est): 4.8MM **Privately Held**
SIC: 3561 7699 7629 3593 Pumps & pumping equipment; hydraulic equipment repair; pumps & pumping equipment repair; electrical repair shops; fluid power cylinders & actuators; gaskets, packing & sealing devices

(G-3599)
CRETE DRY-MIX & SUPPLY CO
20 N Park St (49321)
PHONE.................................616 784-5790
Hilda Roede, *Ch of Bd*
Ronald R Roede, *President*
Mary Nixon, *Vice Pres*
EMP: 10 EST: 1952
SQ FT: 20,000
SALES (est): 822.1K **Privately Held**
SIC: 3273 Ready-mixed concrete

(G-3600)
D&M METAL PRODUCTS COMPANY
4994 West River Dr Ne (49321-8521)
PHONE.................................616 784-0601
Robert Buist, *President*
Russ Deviries, *Vice Pres*
Jerry Vonbroock, *Opers Spvr*
EMP: 50
SQ FT: 60,000
SALES (est): 13MM **Privately Held**
WEB: www.dmmetalproducts.com
SIC: 3441 Fabricated structural metal

(G-3601)
DADCO INC
848 W River Center Dr Ne C (49321-8010)
PHONE.................................616 785-2888
Michael Diebolt, *Owner*
EMP: 5
SALES (corp-wide): 15.1MM **Privately Held**
WEB: www.dadco.net
SIC: 3593 Fluid power cylinders & actuators
PA: Dadco, Inc.
    43850 Plymouth Oaks Blvd
    Plymouth MI 48170
    734 207-1100

(G-3602)
DIVERSIFIED MECH SVCS INC
844 W River Center Dr Ne (49321-8955)
PHONE.................................616 785-2735
EMP: 10
SQ FT: 6,000
SALES (est): 1.4MM **Privately Held**
SIC: 1711 3443 Plumbing/Heating/Air Cond Contractor Mfg Fabricated Plate Work

(G-3603)
DRAG FINISHING TECH LLC (PA)
Also Called: Advanced Finishing Tech
835 W River Center Dr Ne # 1 (49321-8017)
PHONE.................................616 785-0400

Mike Heller, *Vice Pres*
Elizabeth Hastings, *VP Sales*
Tim Dyer,
Terry Dyer,
▲ EMP: 4 EST: 2003
SQ FT: 100
SALES (est): 1.2MM **Privately Held**
WEB: www.advancedfinish.com
SIC: 3531 Finishers & spreaders (construction equipment)

(G-3604)
DUBOIS PRODUCTION SERVICES INC
30 N Park St Ne (49321)
P.O. Box 209 (49321-0209)
PHONE.................................616 785-0088
Kathleen Dubois, *President*
EMP: 17 EST: 1991
SQ FT: 70,000
SALES (est): 771.7K **Privately Held**
WEB: www.duboisproduction.com
SIC: 7692 3599 3544 3444 Welding repair; machine shop, jobbing & repair; special dies, tools, jigs & fixtures; sheet metalwork

(G-3605)
EAGLE INDUSTRIAL GROUP INC
847 W River Center Dr Ne (49321-8955)
PHONE.................................616 647-9904
Chad Boersma, *President*
Brandon Kuiphof, *Prgrmr*
EMP: 20 EST: 2009
SALES (est): 3.3MM **Privately Held**
WEB: www.toolingsystemsgroup.com
SIC: 5082 3728 5084 General construction machinery & equipment; military aircraft equipment & armament; tool & die makers' equipment

(G-3606)
ELK BREWING
400 Dodge Rd Ne (49321-8041)
PHONE.................................616 214-8172
EMP: 6 EST: 2017
SALES (est): 267.6K **Privately Held**
WEB: www.elkbrewing.com
SIC: 2082 Malt beverages

(G-3607)
GEN3 DEFENSE AND AEROSPACE LLC
285 Dodge Ct Ste E (49321-8052)
PHONE.................................616 345-8031
Edward Wells, *CFO*
Matthew Borisch, *Mng Member*
EMP: 10 EST: 2020
SALES (est): 1.1MM **Privately Held**
SIC: 3812 3365 Defense systems & equipment; aerospace castings, aluminum

(G-3608)
GLS ENTERPRISES INC
Also Called: GLS Promotional Specialties
960 W Rver Ctr Dr Ne Ste (49321)
PHONE.................................616 243-2574
Steve Williams, *President*
EMP: 4 EST: 1980
SQ FT: 3,200 **Privately Held**
WEB: www.glsenter.com
SIC: 5199 2389 Advertising specialties; handkerchiefs, except paper

(G-3609)
GR TOOLING & AUTOMATION INC
3670 Mill Creek Dr Ne (49321-9042)
PHONE.................................616 299-1521
Brad Meulenberg, *President*
EMP: 18 EST: 2020
SALES (est): 2MM **Privately Held**
SIC: 3569 Liquid automation machinery & equipment

(G-3610)
GREAT LAKES LABEL LLC
910 Metzgar Dr Nw (49321-9728)
PHONE.................................616 647-9880
John A Cook, *President*
Kandi Devos, *QC Mgr*
Ross Scholma, *Engineer*
Dan Basilius, *Controller*
Emily Surman, *Marketing Staff*

EMP: 38 EST: 2002
SALES (est): 7.6MM **Privately Held**
WEB: www.greatlakeslabel.com
SIC: 2759 Labels & seals: printing

(G-3611)
IMAGES2PRINTCOM
1094 11 Mile Rd Ne (49321-9676)
PHONE.................................616 821-7143
Kenneth Michael Hill, *Owner*
EMP: 5 EST: 2014
SALES (est): 68K **Privately Held**
SIC: 2752 Commercial printing, lithographic

(G-3612)
INTERLOCK DESIGN
5830 Comstock Park Dr Nw (49321-9593)
P.O. Box 453 (49321-0453)
PHONE.................................616 784-5901
Larry Roelofs, *President*
EMP: 10 EST: 1986
SALES (est): 907K **Privately Held**
WEB: www.interlockdesign.net
SIC: 3271 Concrete block & brick

(G-3613)
JAVA MANUFACTURING INC
4760 West River Dr Ne (49321-8927)
P.O. Box 546 (49321-0546)
PHONE.................................616 784-3873
Norine Smulders, *President*
EMP: 7 EST: 1983
SQ FT: 4,500
SALES (est): 695.7K **Privately Held**
WEB: www.javacontrolsmfg.com
SIC: 3613 Panelboards & distribution boards, electric

(G-3614)
KEN RODENHOUSE DOOR & WINDOW
Also Called: Rodenhouse Door & Window
5120 West River Dr Ne (49321-8522)
PHONE.................................616 784-3365
Fax: 616 784-7663
EMP: 10
SQ FT: 15,000
SALES: 900K **Privately Held**
SIC: 3442 Mfg Metal Doors/Sash/Trim

(G-3615)
KENTWATER TOOL & MFG CO
5516 West River Dr Ne (49321-8914)
PHONE.................................616 784-7171
Frank T Marek, *President*
Dave Marek, *Vice Pres*
Thomas Merek, *Admin Sec*
EMP: 9 EST: 1964
SQ FT: 13,000 **Privately Held**
WEB: www.kentwatertool.com
SIC: 3544 3599 Special dies & tools; custom machinery

(G-3616)
KIMBOW INC
901 Metzgar Dr Nw (49321-9728)
PHONE.................................616 774-4680
Tim Schelhaas, *President*
EMP: 17 EST: 1996
SALES (est): 3.6MM **Privately Held**
WEB: www.kimbowinc.com
SIC: 3444 Sheet metal specialties, not stamped

(G-3617)
KORE INC
5263 6 Mile Ct Nw (49321-9635)
PHONE.................................616 785-5900
Karl J Burdick, *President*
Ann Burdick, *Corp Secy*
▲ EMP: 20 EST: 1988
SQ FT: 12,000 **Privately Held**
WEB: www.koreinc.com
SIC: 3699 8731 Electrical equipment & supplies; electronic research

(G-3618)
KSB DUBRIC INC
3737 Laramie Dr Ne (49321-8973)
P.O. Box 43 (49321-0043)
PHONE.................................616 784-6355
Jeffrey Koeper, *CEO*
Casie Rain, *Cust Svc Mgr*
EMP: 35 EST: 1976

SALES (est): 6.1MM **Privately Held**
WEB: www.dubric.com
SIC: 5085 3561 7699 7629 Seals, industrial; packing, industrial; pumps & pumping equipment; hydraulic equipment repair; pumps & pumping equipment repair; electrical repair shops; fluid power cylinders & actuators; gaskets, packing & sealing devices

(G-3619)
LAKELAND ELEC MTR SVCS INC
3810 Mill Creek Dr Ne (49321-9044)
PHONE.................................616 647-0331
Steve Rokos, *President*
Ryan Schmader, *Opers Staff*
EMP: 38 EST: 1992
SALES (est): 3.8MM **Privately Held**
WEB: www.lakeland-electric.com
SIC: 3548 Electric welding equipment

(G-3620)
M & J ENTP GRND RAPIDS LLC
5304 Alpine Ave Nw (49321-9708)
PHONE.................................616 485-9775
Michael Granger,
EMP: 10 EST: 2013
SQ FT: 58,000
SALES (est): 50K **Privately Held**
SIC: 2631 Cardboard

(G-3621)
MAGNUM POWDER COATING INC
5500 West River Dr Ne (49321-8914)
PHONE.................................616 785-3155
Nancy Couturier, *President*
Steve Couturier, *Opers Staff*
EMP: 8 EST: 1992
SQ FT: 6,000
SALES (est): 1.3MM **Privately Held**
WEB: www.magnumpowdercoating.com
SIC: 3479 Coating of metals & formed products; painting, coating & hot dipping

(G-3622)
MAYCO TOOL
5880 Comstock Park Dr Nw (49321-9593)
PHONE.................................616 785-7350
Kurt May, *Owner*
EMP: 5 EST: 2004
SALES (est): 561K **Privately Held**
WEB: www.maycotool.com
SIC: 3544 Special dies & tools

(G-3623)
MBA PRINTING INC
Also Called: M B A Printing
90 Windflower St Ne (49321-8235)
PHONE.................................616 243-1600
Jerry Hofman, *President*
EMP: 9 EST: 1989
SALES (est): 470.1K **Privately Held**
SIC: 2752 Commercial printing, offset

(G-3624)
MEGA WALL INC
5340 6 Mile Ct Nw (49321-9634)
PHONE.................................616 647-4190
David McGinnis, *President*
Brad McGinnis, *CFO*
Mark McGinnis, *Manager*
▲ EMP: 17 EST: 2002
SQ FT: 41,000
SALES (est): 4.8MM **Privately Held**
WEB: www.megawall.com
SIC: 2542 Fixtures, store: except wood

(G-3625)
META4MAT LLC
320 Dodge Rd Ne Ste B (49321-8045)
PHONE.................................616 214-7418
Grant Cooper, *Principal*
Dan Norman, *Principal*
Ashley Rozeveld, *Production*
Brian Krueger, *Manager*
EMP: 8
SALES (est): 1.3MM **Privately Held**
WEB: www.meta4mat.com
SIC: 2759 Commercial printing

Comstock Park - Kent County (G-3626)

(G-3626)
MILL CREEK FABRICATION LLC
5402 Rusche Dr Nw (49321-9551)
PHONE..................................616 419-4857
Dennis Horn, *Mng Member*
Scott Dood,
EMP: 5 **EST:** 2020
SALES (est): 520.2K **Privately Held**
SIC: 3444 Sheet metalwork

(G-3627)
NBHX TRIM USA CORPORATION (DH)
1020 7 Mile Rd Nw (49321-9542)
PHONE..................................616 785-9400
Stefan Clemens, *President*
Tobias Engel, *General Mgr*
Michael Homrich, *Vice Pres*
Pete Walenta, *Vice Pres*
Nick Bailey, *Engineer*
▲ **EMP:** 409 **EST:** 1986
SQ FT: 125,000
SALES (est): 57.8MM
SALES (corp-wide): 2.5B **Privately Held**
WEB: www.nbhx-trim.com
SIC: 3714 Motor vehicle parts & accessories
HQ: Nbhx Trim Gmbh
Gutenbergstr. 30-32
Heilsbronn BY 91560
987 280-2280

(G-3628)
NEXT LEVEL MANUFACTURING LLC
5405 Pine Island Dr Ne (49321-9513)
PHONE..................................616 965-1913
David Warner, *Branch Mgr*
EMP: 5
SALES (corp-wide): 4MM **Privately Held**
WEB: www.nextlevelmfg.com
SIC: 3599 Machine & other job shop work
PA: Next Level Manufacturing, Llc
6778 18th Ave
Jenison MI 49428
269 397-1220

(G-3629)
NORTH WOODS INDUSTRIAL
3644 Mill Creek Dr Ne (49321-9042)
P.O. Box 141006, Grand Rapids (49514-1006)
PHONE..................................616 784-2840
David L Vandermolen, *President*
Carol Vandermolen, *Corp Secy*
David Vandermolen Jr, *Vice Pres*
EMP: 8 **EST:** 1996
SQ FT: 13,000 **Privately Held**
SIC: 3567 3535 3444 Industrial furnaces & ovens; conveyors & conveying equipment; sheet metalwork

(G-3630)
NUCRAFT FURNITURE COMPANY
5151 West River Dr Ne (49321-8938)
PHONE..................................616 784-6016
Matthew Schad, *President*
Chris Hawkins, *General Mgr*
Timothy Schad, *Chairman*
Bob Bockheim, *COO*
James Doletzky, *Vice Pres*
▼ **EMP:** 245 **EST:** 1936
SQ FT: 300,000
SALES (est): 49.2MM **Privately Held**
WEB: www.nucraft.com
SIC: 2521 Wood office furniture

(G-3631)
OPTISOURCE LLC
310 Dodge Rd Ne Ste A (49321-8043)
PHONE..................................616 554-9048
William Streng,
EMP: 5 **EST:** 2018
SALES (est): 62.3K **Privately Held**
SIC: 2064 Candy & other confectionery products

(G-3632)
OVER TOP STEEL COATING LLC
931 W River Center Dr Ne B (49321-8008)
PHONE..................................616 647-9140
Jason Hoek, *Mng Member*
EMP: 7 **EST:** 2005
SALES (est): 412.5K **Privately Held**
WEB: www.overthetopsealcoating.com
SIC: 2952 Asphalt felts & coatings

(G-3633)
PARKER EXCVTG GRAV & RECYCLE
295 Hayes Rd Nw (49321-9712)
PHONE..................................616 784-1681
Russell G Parker, *President*
Carolyn Parker, *Corp Secy*
Kevin Parker, *Vice Pres*
Ross Parker, *Vice Pres*
EMP: 13 **EST:** 1969
SQ FT: 3,376
SALES (est): 5.6MM **Privately Held**
SIC: 5032 1442 Gravel; gravel mining

(G-3634)
PATTEN MONUMENT COMPANY (PA)
Also Called: Pattern Monument
3980 West River Dr Ne (49321-8997)
P.O. Box 427 (49321-0427)
PHONE..................................616 785-4141
Eric Ericksen, *President*
Andy Bolt, *Corp Secy*
Chris Fortosis, *Vice Pres*
Alex Fortosis, *Sales Staff*
EMP: 60 **EST:** 1917
SQ FT: 55,000
SALES (est): 14.9MM **Privately Held**
WEB: www.pattenmonument.com
SIC: 5099 5999 3281 Monuments & grave markers; monuments & tombstones; cut stone & stone products

(G-3635)
PERRIN SCREEN PRINTING INC
5320 Rusche Dr Nw (49321-9551)
PHONE..................................616 785-9900
Randy Perrin, *President*
EMP: 18 **EST:** 1988
SQ FT: 39,000
SALES (est): 425.3K **Privately Held**
WEB: www.perrinwear.com
SIC: 2396 2261 Screen printing on fabric articles; screen printing of cotton broadwoven fabrics

(G-3636)
PERRIN SOUVENIR DISTRS INC
5320 Rusche Dr Nw (49321-9551)
PHONE..................................616 785-9700
Mitch Heiman, *President*
Randy Perrin, *President*
Rick Koster, *CFO*
Ron Jipping, *Representative*
▲ **EMP:** 300 **EST:** 1977
SQ FT: 120,000
SALES (est): 22.1MM **Privately Held**
WEB: www.perrinwear.com
SIC: 2759 2396 2395 7389 Labels & seals; printing; automotive & apparel trimmings; pleating & stitching; decoration service for special events

(G-3637)
PETAL PUSHERS BY LIZ LLC
5535 Division Ave N (49321-8214)
PHONE..................................616 481-9513
Elizabeth Antor, *Principal*
EMP: 6 **EST:** 2015
SALES (est): 101.6K **Privately Held**
SIC: 3545 Pushers

(G-3638)
PREFERRED TOOL & DIE CO INC
Also Called: Diebotics
5400 West River Dr Ne (49321-8925)
P.O. Box 386 (49321-0386)
PHONE..................................616 784-6789
Timothy R Launiere, *President*
Robert E Launiere, *Admin Sec*
▲ **EMP:** 30 **EST:** 1966
SQ FT: 20,000 **Privately Held**
SIC: 3544 Special dies & tools; jigs & fixtures

(G-3639)
PUMMILL PRINT SERVICES LC
960 W Rver Ctr Dr Ne Ste (49321)
P.O. Box 3249, Kalamazoo (49003-3249)
PHONE..................................616 785-7960
David R Pummill,
EMP: 4 **EST:** 2009 **Privately Held**
WEB: www.pummill.com
SIC: 2752 Commercial printing, offset

(G-3640)
QUALITY LIQUID FEEDS INC
5715 Comstock Park Dr Nw (49321-7200)
PHONE..................................616 784-2930
Kevin Pratt, *Branch Mgr*
EMP: 5
SALES (corp-wide): 150.7MM **Privately Held**
WEB: www.qlf.com
SIC: 2048 Feed supplements
PA: Quality Liquid Feeds, Inc.
3586 Hwy 23 N
Dodgeville WI 53533
608 935-2345

(G-3641)
R N B MACHINE & TOOL INC
5200 West River Dr Ne (49321-8523)
PHONE..................................616 784-6868
David Bogardus, *President*
Kenneth Bogardus, *Vice Pres*
Jady Bogardus, *Treasurer*
Ed Bogardus, *Admin Sec*
EMP: 5 **EST:** 1971
SQ FT: 6,600
SALES (est): 377.8K **Privately Held**
SIC: 3599 Machine shop, jobbing & repair

(G-3642)
RAPID ENGINEERING LLC (PA)
1100 7 Mile Rd Nw (49321-9782)
PHONE..................................616 784-0500
Bruce Bellamy,
Robert Gordon,
▲ **EMP:** 64 **EST:** 1962
SQ FT: 85,000
SALES (est): 14MM **Privately Held**
WEB: www.rapidengineering.com
SIC: 3585 3567 Heating equipment, complete; paint baking & drying ovens

(G-3643)
REFRIGERATION CONCEPTS INC
5959 Comstock Park Dr Nw (49321-8258)
PHONE..................................616 785-7335
Tom Cooper, *President*
Todd McCoy, *Engineer*
Rob Swem, *Treasurer*
Robert Swem, *Treasurer*
Nick Hankamp, *Manager*
EMP: 22 **EST:** 1994
SQ FT: 7,000
SALES (est): 6.6MM **Privately Held**
WEB: www.rcicold.com
SIC: 7389 1711 7623 3498 Design, commercial & industrial; refrigeration contractor; refrigeration repair service; piping systems for pulp paper & chemical industries

(G-3644)
SERVICE EXTRUSION DIE CO INC
3648 Mill Creek Dr Ne (49321-9042)
P.O. Box 44 (49321-0044)
PHONE..................................616 784-6933
Robert Warnes, *President*
EMP: 6 **EST:** 1956
SQ FT: 7,200 **Privately Held**
WEB: www.service-extrusion-die-co-inc.business.site
SIC: 3544 Extrusion dies

(G-3645)
SPECIFIED A SLTONS HLDINGS LLC (HQ)
1100 7 Mile Rd Nw (49321-9727)
P.O. Box 44, Buffalo NY (14240-0044)
PHONE..................................616 784-0500
Charley Brown, *CEO*
EMP: 100 **EST:** 2014
SALES (est): 140.5MM
SALES (corp-wide): 907.1MM **Privately Held**
WEB: www.robertsgordon.com
SIC: 3585 3567 Heating equipment, complete; paint baking & drying ovens
PA: Madison Industries Holdings Llc
444 W Lake St Ste 4400
Chicago IL 60606
312 277-0156

(G-3646)
SUGAR FREE SPECIALTIES LLC (PA)
Also Called: Dr. John's Candies
5320 West River Dr Ne (49321-8524)
PHONE..................................616 734-6999
Debra L Bruinsma, *VP Sales*
Michael McDonald, *Mng Member*
EMP: 15 **EST:** 1997
SALES (est): 2.7MM **Privately Held**
SIC: 2064 2066 Candy & other confectionery products; chocolate & cocoa products

(G-3647)
THINK CHROMATIC
3934 West River Dr Ne (49321-8997)
P.O. Box 342 (49321-0342)
PHONE..................................248 719-2058
EMP: 8 **EST:** 2018
SALES (est): 376.7K **Privately Held**
WEB: www.thinkchromatic.com
SIC: 3993 Signs, not made in custom sign painting shops

(G-3648)
TOTAL TOOLING CONCEPTS INC
4870 West River Dr Ne A (49321-8942)
PHONE..................................616 785-8402
David Walejewski, *President*
Ken Scholl, *General Mgr*
Jeff Rietman, *Sales Staff*
EMP: 7 **EST:** 2001
SQ FT: 6,300
SALES (est): 1.6MM **Privately Held**
WEB: www.totaltooling.net
SIC: 3545 Machine tool accessories

(G-3649)
VALLEY CITY SIGN COMPANY
5009 West River Dr Ne (49321-8961)
PHONE..................................616 784-5711
Judson L Kovalak Jr, *CEO*
Randy Czubko, *President*
Leslie Runyon, *Production*
Susan Sear, *Production*
Lynn Kiel, *CFO*
EMP: 50 **EST:** 1948
SQ FT: 75,000
SALES (est): 10.4MM **Privately Held**
WEB: www.valleycitysign.com
SIC: 3993 3446 Electric signs; architectural metalwork

(G-3650)
WARNER SOFTWARE CO LLC
3881 Yorkland Dr Nw Apt 8 (49321-8160)
PHONE..................................616 916-1182
James Warner, *Principal*
EMP: 4 **EST:** 2009
SALES (est): 145.7K **Privately Held**
SIC: 7372 Prepackaged software

(G-3651)
WEATHER-RITE LLC
1100 7 Mile Rd Nw (49321-9727)
PHONE..................................612 338-1401
Patrick Stone, *Mng Member*
▼ **EMP:** 44 **EST:** 1957
SQ FT: 85,000
SALES (est): 1.1MM **Privately Held**
WEB: www.weather-rite.com
SIC: 3585 3357 Heating equipment, complete; air conditioning equipment, complete; magnet wire, nonferrous

(G-3652)
WOODLAND PAVING CO (PA)
3566 Mill Creek Dr Ne (49321-9041)
P.O. Box 608 (49321-0608)
PHONE..................................616 784-5220
Old Castle,
EMP: 38 **EST:** 1969
SQ FT: 2,000
SALES (est): 5.3MM **Privately Held**
SIC: 1611 1771 2951 Surfacing & paving; parking lot construction; asphalt & asphaltic paving mixtures (not from refineries)

(G-3653)
YELLOWSTONE PRODUCTS INC
310 Dodge Rd Ne Ste C (49321-8043)
PHONE..................................616 299-7855
Michael Olman, *President*
Mike Olman, *Administration*
EMP: 6 **EST:** 2013
SALES (est): 1MM **Privately Held**
SIC: 3281 Granite, cut & shaped

Concord
Jackson County

(G-3654)
PRECISE MCHINING UNLIMITED LLC
505 Spring Arbor Rd (49237-9661)
P.O. Box 175, Homer (49245-0175)
PHONE..................................517 524-3104
Lloyd Mosher, *Mng Member*
EMP: 6 **EST:** 2010
SALES (est): 400.1K **Privately Held**
WEB: www.precisemachiningunlimited.com
SIC: 3599 Machine shop, jobbing & repair

(G-3655)
SPRY SIGN & GRAPHICS CO LLC
12123 Spring Arbor Rd (49237-9722)
P.O. Box 603 (49237-0603)
PHONE..................................517 524-7685
Kim Spry,
EMP: 4 **EST:** 2000
SALES (est): 346.7K **Privately Held**
WEB: www.sprysigngraphics.com
SIC: 3993 Signs & advertising specialties

(G-3656)
UNIQUE FABRICATING NA INC
13221 Allman Rd (49237-9813)
PHONE..................................517 524-9010
EMP: 5
SALES (corp-wide): 120.2MM **Publicly Held**
WEB: www.uniquefab.com
SIC: 3053 Gaskets, all materials
HQ: Unique Fabricating Na, Inc.
800 Standard Pkwy
Auburn Hills MI 48326
248 853-2333

(G-3657)
UNIQUE MOLDED FOAM TECH INC
13221 Allman Rd (49237-9813)
PHONE..................................517 524-9010
Tim Pecker, *General Mgr*
EMP: 19 **EST:** 2015
SALES (est): 3MM
SALES (corp-wide): 120.2MM **Publicly Held**
WEB: www.uniquefab.com
SIC: 3086 Plastics foam products
HQ: Unique Fabricating Na, Inc.
800 Standard Pkwy
Auburn Hills MI 48326
248 853-2333

(G-3658)
WOLVERINE STEEL AND WELDING
13300 Spring Arbor Rd (49237-9508)
P.O. Box 450 (49237-0450)
PHONE..................................517 524-7300
John Hoover, *President*
EMP: 20 **EST:** 1992
SQ FT: 15,000
SALES (est): 1.8MM **Privately Held**
WEB: www.wsw-inc.com
SIC: 3441 7692 Fabricated structural metal; welding repair

Conklin
Ottawa County

(G-3659)
APPLE QUEST INC
1380 Coolidge St (49403-8707)
PHONE..................................616 299-4834
Bruce E Rasch, *President*
EMP: 25 **EST:** 2005
SALES (est): 1MM **Privately Held**
SIC: 2034 Dehydrated fruits, vegetables, soups

(G-3660)
CAVEMAN PALLETS LLC
2382 Van Dyke St (49403-9596)
P.O. Box 116, Casnovia (49318-0116)
PHONE..................................616 675-7270
Tina E Rooks, *Mng Member*
EMP: 5 **EST:** 2012
SALES (est): 118.8K **Privately Held**
SIC: 2448 Pallets, wood

(G-3661)
MICHIGAN ORNAMENTAL IR & FABG
219 Roosevelt St (49403-9715)
P.O. Box 67 (49403-0067)
PHONE..................................616 899-2441
Mary Kay Menn, *President*
Stephen A Menn, *Principal*
EMP: 10 **EST:** 1963
SQ FT: 8,500
SALES (est): 840K **Privately Held**
WEB: www.michiganornamentaliron.com
SIC: 3446 Ornamental metalwork

(G-3662)
PHIL BROWN WELDING CORPORATION
4689 8 Mile Rd (49403-9604)
PHONE..................................616 784-3046
Phillip A Brown, *President*
Dorothy Brown, *Vice Pres*
▲ **EMP:** 15 **EST:** 1965
SQ FT: 15,000
SALES (est): 1.8MM **Privately Held**
WEB: www.philbrownwelding.com
SIC: 3523 7692 Farm machinery & equipment; welding repair

Constantine
St. Joseph County

(G-3663)
BERRY GLOBAL INC
700 Centreville St (49042-1273)
P.O. Box 187 (49042-0187)
PHONE..................................269 435-2425
Gayle Sears, *Branch Mgr*
EMP: 5 **Publicly Held**
WEB: www.berryplastics.com
SIC: 3089 3081 Bottle caps, molded plastic; unsupported plastics film & sheet
HQ: Berry Global, Inc.
101 Oakley St
Evansville IN 47710

(G-3664)
DENARCO INC
301 Industrial Park Dr (49042-9702)
P.O. Box 191 (49042-0191)
PHONE..................................269 435-8404
Dennis G Harr, *President*
EMP: 6 **EST:** 1974
SQ FT: 20,000
SALES (est): 791.3K **Privately Held**
WEB: www.denarcoinc.com
SIC: 2891 Sealants

(G-3665)
E L NICKELL CO
Also Called: Alnco
385 Centreville St (49042-1201)
P.O. Box 97 (49042-0097)
PHONE..................................269 435-2475
Shelby Nickell, *President*
Martin Eltzroth, *Professor*
EMP: 10 **EST:** 1944
SQ FT: 35,000 **Privately Held**
WEB: www.elnickell.com
SIC: 3443 Industrial vessels, tanks & containers

(G-3666)
FIBRE CONVERTERS INC (PA)
1 Industrial Park Dr (49042-8735)
P.O. Box 130 (49042-0130)
PHONE..................................269 279-1700
James D Stuck, *CEO*
Stephen N Reed, *Vice Pres*
EMP: 43 **EST:** 1949
SQ FT: 160,000
SALES (est): 11.4MM **Privately Held**
WEB: www.fibreconverters.com
SIC: 2671 2631 2396 Packaging paper & plastics film, coated & laminated; paperboard mills; automotive & apparel trimmings

(G-3667)
HELPING HEARTS HELPING HANDS
285 Mill St (49042-1025)
PHONE..................................248 980-5090
Nancy Sebring-Cale, *Principal*
EMP: 5 **EST:** 2010
SALES (est): 55.9K **Privately Held**
WEB: www.helpingheartshelpinghands.org
SIC: 2515 Foundations & platforms

(G-3668)
HIG RECOVERY FUND INC
485 Florence Rd (49042-1261)
P.O. Box 188 (49042-0188)
PHONE..................................269 435-8414
Angela Pollard, *Principal*
Steve Malinoski, *QC Mgr*
Jessica Arseneau, *Engineer*
Christopher Franke, *Accounts Mgr*
Blake Bailey, *Manager*
EMP: 4 **EST:** 2010
SALES (est): 206.6K **Privately Held**
SIC: 2295 Resin or plastic coated fabrics

(G-3669)
MARCON TECHNOLOGIES LLC
1 Industrial Park Dr (49042-8735)
P.O. Box 130 (49042-0130)
PHONE..................................269 279-1701
Jim Stuck, *Mng Member*
▲ **EMP:** 2 **EST:** 1999
SQ FT: 25,000
SALES (est): 1.7MM
SALES (corp-wide): 11.4MM **Privately Held**
WEB: www.fibreconverters.com
SIC: 3089 Extruded finished plastic products
PA: Fibre Converters, Inc.
1 Industrial Park Dr
Constantine MI 49042
269 279-1700

(G-3670)
MICHIANA RTATIONAL MOLDING LLC
950 Industrial Park Dr (49042-9763)
PHONE..................................574 849-7077
Stacy N Outman, *Treasurer*
Wayne D Roberts, *Mng Member*
EMP: 15 **EST:** 2019
SALES (est): 1.2MM **Privately Held**
WEB: www.michianamolding.com
SIC: 3089 Molding primary plastic

(G-3671)
MICHIGAN MILK PRODUCERS ASSN
Constantine Plant
125 Depot St (49042-1066)
P.O. Box 158 (49042-0158)
PHONE..................................269 435-2835
Thomas Carpenter, *Manager*
EMP: 68
SQ FT: 10,000
SALES (corp-wide): 75.4MM **Privately Held**
WEB: www.mimilk.com
SIC: 2021 2026 2023 Creamery butter; milk processing (pasteurizing, homogenizing, bottling); dry, condensed, evaporated dairy products
PA: Michigan Milk Producers Association
41310 Bridge St
Novi MI 48375
248 474-6672

(G-3672)
MONSANTO COMPANY
67760 Us 31 (49042)
PHONE..................................269 483-1300
Connie T Verberkmoes, *Vice Pres*
Travis Sharp, *Prdtn Mgr*
Hannah Z Wirz, *Opers Staff*
Seth Logan, *Research*
Michael R Litton, *Engineer*
EMP: 4
SALES (corp-wide): 48.9B **Privately Held**
WEB: www.monsanto.com
SIC: 2879 Agricultural chemicals
HQ: Monsanto Company
800 N Lindbergh Blvd
Saint Louis MO 63167
314 694-1000

(G-3673)
OX ENGINEERED PRODUCTS LLC
700 Centreville St (49042-1273)
PHONE..................................269 435-2425
EMP: 83
SALES (corp-wide): 25MM **Privately Held**
WEB: www.oxengineeredproducts.com
SIC: 2493 Wall tile, fiberboard
PA: Ox Engineered Products, Llc
22260 Haggerty Rd Ste 365
Northville MI 48167
248 289-9950

(G-3674)
OX PAPERBOARD MICHIGAN LLC
700 Centreville St (49042-1273)
PHONE..................................800 345-8881
EMP: 80
SALES (est): 34.7MM **Privately Held**
WEB: www.oxindustries.com
SIC: 2631 Paperboard Mills, Nsk

(G-3675)
RETRO ENTERPRISES INC
1045 Parkview St (49042-1278)
PHONE..................................269 435-8583
Ron Wetstone, *President*
EMP: 5 **EST:** 1997
SALES (est): 653.3K **Privately Held**
SIC: 3089 Injection molding of plastics

(G-3676)
TRIPLE CREEK SHIRTS AND MORE
420 Grove St (49042-1224)
PHONE..................................269 273-5154
Mandy Murphy, *Owner*
EMP: 4 **EST:** 2014
SALES (est): 170.3K **Privately Held**
WEB: www.triplecreekshirts.com
SIC: 2759 Screen printing

(G-3677)
VAUPELL MOLDING & TOOLING INC
Also Called: Vaupell Midwest
485 Florence Rd (49042-1261)
PHONE..................................269 435-8414
Ben Bauer, *Opers Staff*
Jordan Santos, *Manager*
Kerry Stump, *Network Enginr*
Rich Troyer, *Officer*
EMP: 16 **Privately Held**
WEB: www.vaupell.com
SIC: 3089 Injection molding of plastics
HQ: Vaupell Molding & Tooling, Inc.
1144 Nw 53rd St
Seattle WA 98107

Coopersville
Ottawa County

(G-3678)
A&A MANUFACTURING
18634 56th Ave (49404-9628)
PHONE..................................800 473-1730
James Fairbanks, *Principal*
EMP: 6 **EST:** 2017
SALES (est): 71.6K **Privately Held**
WEB: www.aa-mfg.com
SIC: 3999 Manufacturing industries

(G-3679)
AGGRESSIVE TOOL & DIE INC
728 Main St (49404-1363)
PHONE..................................616 837-1983
Gregory Wiersma, *President*
Tom Zuidema, *Vice Pres*
Jason Breen, *Foreman/Supr*

Coopersville - Ottawa County (G-3680)

James Smith, *Engineer*
EMP: 45 **EST:** 1993
SQ FT: 12,500 **Privately Held**
WEB: www.aggressivetooldie.com
SIC: 3544 Special dies & tools

(G-3680)
BAKKER WELDING & MECHANICS LLC (PA)
Also Called: BAKKER METAL FABRICATION
15031 84th Ave (49404-9787)
PHONE 616 828-8664
Sid Bakker,
EMP: 7 **EST:** 2007
SALES (est): 627K **Privately Held**
WEB: www.bakkermetalfabrication.com
SIC: 7692 Welding repair

(G-3681)
BROOKFIELD INC
8041 Leonard St (49404-9794)
PHONE 616 997-9663
Les Yoder, *President*
EMP: 6 **EST:** 1998
SQ FT: 10,000
SALES (est): 490.3K **Privately Held**
WEB: www.brookfieldcase.com
SIC: 2493 Reconstituted wood products

(G-3682)
CONTINENTAL DAR FACILITIES LLC
999 W Randall St (49404-1311)
PHONE 616 837-7641
Steve Cooper, *COO*
Rich Clark, *Plant Mgr*
Dustin Sarber, *Engineer*
Cheslie Stehouwer, *Sales Staff*
Shawn Storm, *Manager*
▲ **EMP:** 65 **EST:** 2008
SALES (est): 32.8MM **Privately Held**
WEB: www.continentaldfllc.com
SIC: 2023 Dry, condensed, evaporated dairy products

(G-3683)
CONVEYOR CONCEPTS MICHIGAN LLC
743 Main St (49404-1362)
PHONE 616 997-5200
Andrew Richard, *Engineer*
Aaron Weycker, *Engineer*
Mary Alice Brown, *Prgrmr*
Joy Weersma, *Executive*
James Malda,
EMP: 12 **EST:** 2003
SQ FT: 20,000
SALES (est): 3.2MM **Privately Held**
WEB: www.ccmich.com
SIC: 3535 Conveyors & conveying equipment

(G-3684)
COOPERSVILLE OBSERVER INC
1374 W Randall St (49404-9701)
P.O. Box 111 (49404-0111)
PHONE 616 997-5049
Kerri Snowdin, *President*
EMP: 4 **EST:** 1996 **Privately Held**
WEB: www.coopersvilleobserver.com
SIC: 2711 Newspapers, publishing & printing

(G-3685)
DEMEESTER WOOD PRODUCTS INC
15527 32nd Ave (49404-9636)
PHONE 616 677-5995
Daniel D Meester, *Owner*
EMP: 17 **EST:** 1994
SALES (est): 1.2MM **Privately Held**
SIC: 2426 2449 2448 2441 Furniture stock & parts, hardwood; frames for upholstered furniture, wood; wood containers; wood pallets & skids; nailed wood boxes & shook

(G-3686)
FLEXTRONICS AUTOMOTIVE USA INC (DH)
323 Skeels St (49404-1326)
PHONE 248 853-5724
Mike McNamara, *CEO*
Franois Barbier, *President*
Doug Britt, *President*
Paul Humphries, *President*
Avery Chumbley, *General Mgr*
▲ **EMP:** 100 **EST:** 1985
SQ FT: 68,000
SALES (est): 636.5MM **Privately Held**
WEB: www.flex.com
SIC: 3625 3714 3643 Control circuit relays, industrial; solenoid switches (industrial controls); switches, electronic applications; motor vehicle parts & accessories; vacuum brakes, motor vehicle; fuel systems & parts, motor vehicle; oil strainers, motor vehicle; current-carrying wiring devices

(G-3687)
FORERUNNER 3D PRINTING
411 64th Ave N (49404-1070)
PHONE 231 722-1144
EMP: 9 **EST:** 2017
SALES (est): 436.4K **Privately Held**
WEB: www.forerunner3d.com
SIC: 2752 Commercial printing, lithographic

(G-3688)
HEATH MANUFACTURING COMPANY (HQ)
Also Called: Heath Ultra Products
140 Mill St Ste A (49404-1269)
PHONE 616 997-8181
Jim Campbell, *President*
Ken Daly, *Prdtn Mgr*
Rich Johnson, *Opers Staff*
Jenna Burke, *Treasurer*
Andris Chapin, *Director*
▲ **EMP:** 50 **EST:** 1947
SQ FT: 82,500
SALES: 12.2MM
SALES (corp-wide): 108.2MM **Privately Held**
WEB: www.heathmfg.com
SIC: 2048 2499 3499 3523 Bird food, prepared; fencing, docks & other outdoor wood structural products; metal household articles; farm machinery & equipment
PA: Chapin Manufacturing, Inc.
700 Ellicott St Ste 3
Batavia NY 14020
585 343-3140

(G-3689)
KINNEY TOOL AND DIE INC
Also Called: Ranger Die
1300 W Randall St (49404-9701)
PHONE 616 997-0901
Leo Raap, *President*
Emily Raap, *Controller*
Stephen Raap, *Director*
Joseph Raap, *Admin Sec*
EMP: 100 **EST:** 1955
SQ FT: 105,000
SALES (est): 19.2MM **Privately Held**
SIC: 3544 3469 Special dies & tools; metal stampings

(G-3690)
LEATHER LORE
475 W Randall St (49404-1342)
P.O. Box 232 (49404-0232)
PHONE 269 548-7160
EMP: 4 **EST:** 2018
SALES (est): 48.9K **Privately Held**
WEB: www.leatherlore.com
SIC: 2741 Miscellaneous publishing

(G-3691)
MARK-PACK INC (PA)
Also Called: Accord Paper and Packaging
776 Main St (49404-1363)
P.O. Box 305 (49404-0305)
PHONE 616 837-5400
David Nielsen, *CEO*
Michael Marine, *President*
David Martel, *Vice Pres*
Donnis Pastor, *Purch Mgr*
Denise Bragg, *Accounts Mgr*
EMP: 20 **EST:** 1964
SQ FT: 31,000
SALES (est): 5.8MM **Privately Held**
WEB: www.markpackinc.com
SIC: 3953 5084 5113 Marking devices; processing & packaging equipment; industrial & personal service paper

(G-3692)
MAYROSE SIGN AND MKTG CO LLC
4035 Hayes St (49404-8409)
PHONE 616 837-1884
Philip Mayrose, *Principal*
EMP: 5 **EST:** 2018
SALES (est): 288.4K **Privately Held**
SIC: 3993 Signs & advertising specialties

(G-3693)
MIDWEST MACHINING INC
Also Called: Self Lube
526 Omalley Dr (49404-1372)
PHONE 616 837-0165
Phillip Allor, *President*
Jennifer Anderson, *Office Mgr*
Phil Allor, *Director*
Lauri Wagner,
EMP: 28 **EST:** 1990
SQ FT: 26,000
SALES (est): 5.5MM **Privately Held**
WEB: www.selflube.com
SIC: 3544 Special dies & tools

(G-3694)
NIEBOERS PIT STOP
288 Main St (49404-1233)
PHONE 616 997-2026
Gregg Nieboer, *Partner*
EMP: 4 **EST:** 2004
SALES (est): 241.7K **Privately Held**
SIC: 2541 Store & office display cases & fixtures

(G-3695)
PHILIPS MACHINING COMPANY
80 Mason Dr (49404-1354)
PHONE 616 997-7777
James Pleune, *President*
Randy Mosher, *General Mgr*
Jim Pleune, *Vice Pres*
Greg Osborn, *Finance Mgr*
Doug Tyink, *Supervisor*
EMP: 10 **EST:** 1987
SQ FT: 7,000
SALES (est): 1.6MM **Privately Held**
WEB: www.wireburn.com
SIC: 3545 3315 3544 Machine tool accessories; steel wire & related products; special dies, tools, jigs & fixtures

(G-3696)
REEVES PLASTICS LLC
507 Omalley Dr (49404-1373)
PHONE 616 997-0777
David A Reeves, *President*
Sharon L Reeves, *Corp Secy*
Mark Lempke, *Vice Pres*
Max Fahling, *Purchasing*
Jaret Shawl, *Sales Engr*
EMP: 25 **EST:** 1978
SQ FT: 20,000
SALES (est): 3.1MM **Privately Held**
WEB: www.reevesplastics.com
SIC: 3089 3544 Molding primary plastic; special dies, tools, jigs & fixtures

(G-3697)
STRAITOPLANE INC
7193 Arthur St (49404-9757)
PHONE 616 997-2211
Richard Fink, *President*
Steven Fink, *Vice Pres*
Theresa Fink, *Admin Sec*
EMP: 6 **EST:** 2001
SALES (est): 400K **Privately Held**
SIC: 3553 Planers, woodworking machines

Copemish
Manistee County

(G-3698)
M-R PRODUCTS INC (PA)
Also Called: Mr Chain
16612 Russo Dr (49625-8503)
P.O. Box 128 (49625-0128)
PHONE 231 378-2251
Mary Mulvoy, *President*
Ryan Schultz, *Controller*
EMP: 5 **EST:** 1960
SQ FT: 2,220
SALES (est): 5.2MM **Privately Held**
WEB: www.mrchain.com
SIC: 3089 Injection molded finished plastic products

Coral
Montcalm County

(G-3699)
JNS SAWMILL
4991 N Satterlee Rd (49322-9744)
PHONE 989 352-5430
John Hershberger, *Principal*
EMP: 4 **EST:** 2014
SALES (est): 233.4K **Privately Held**
SIC: 2411 7389 Saw logs;

(G-3700)
LIVING QUARTERS
14179 Meta Dr (49322-9793)
PHONE 616 874-6160
Paula Slopsema, *Principal*
EMP: 5 **EST:** 2007
SALES (est): 84.8K **Privately Held**
SIC: 3131 Footwear cut stock

Cornell
Delta County

(G-3701)
MARVIN NELSON FOREST PRODUCTS
9868 County 426 E Rd (49818-9348)
PHONE 906 384-6700
Marvin Nelson, *President*
Donna Nelson, *Vice Pres*
Brian Nelson, *Treasurer*
David Nelson, *Admin Sec*
EMP: 14 **EST:** 1972
SALES (est): 1.2MM **Privately Held**
SIC: 2411 4212 Logging camps & contractors; timber trucking, local

(G-3702)
R&H LOGGING INC
11435 Sa Rd (49818-9461)
PHONE 906 241-7248
EMP: 5 **EST:** 2016
SALES (est): 124.4K **Privately Held**
SIC: 2411 Logging

(G-3703)
USHER LOGGING LLC
14443 Sa Rd (49818-9442)
PHONE 906 238-4261
Denise Usher,
Terry W Usher,
EMP: 4 **EST:** 2000
SALES (est): 231K **Privately Held**
SIC: 2411 Logging camps & contractors

Corunna
Shiawassee County

(G-3704)
ADVANCED AIR TECHNOLOGIES INC
300 Sleeseman Dr (48817-1078)
PHONE 989 743-5544
Jerry A Dedic, *President*
▲ **EMP:** 8 **EST:** 1987
SQ FT: 9,500
SALES (est): 1.6MM **Privately Held**
WEB: www.advairtech.com
SIC: 3564 Air purification equipment

(G-3705)
BOURNE INDUSTRIES INC
491 S Comstock St (48817-1799)
PHONE 989 743-3461
Jeffrey Walters, *President*
Kim Rathburn, *Finance Mgr*
Tim Reid, *Manager*
Henry Phillips,
EMP: 22 **EST:** 1977
SQ FT: 57,000

GEOGRAPHIC SECTION

Croswell - Sanilac County (G-3731)

SALES (est): 4.2MM **Privately Held**
WEB: www.bourneindustries.com
SIC: 2521 2531 2493 2541 Wood office furniture; school furniture; particleboard, plastic laminated; store & office display cases & fixtures; display fixtures, wood; cabinets, lockers & shelving

(G-3706)
CITY ANIMATION CO
Also Called: Neway Manufacturing
1013 N Shiawassee St (48817-1151)
P.O. Box 188 (48817-0188)
PHONE.................................989 743-3458
James D Schultz, *Branch Mgr*
EMP: 10
SALES (corp-wide): 11.2MM **Privately Held**
WEB: www.cityeventsgroup.com
SIC: 5099 3993 7359 7812 Video & audio equipment; signs & advertising specialties; audio-visual equipment & supply rental; video tape production; machine tools, metal cutting type
PA: City Animation Co.
57 Park Dr
Troy MI 48083
248 589-0600

(G-3707)
CORUNNA MILLS FEED LLC
417 S Shiawassee St (48817-1643)
PHONE.................................989 743-3110
Chris Demerly, *Mng Member*
Dick Demerly,
Jamie Demerly,
EMP: 7 EST: 1992
SQ FT: 20,000
SALES (est): 568.9K **Privately Held**
WEB: www.corunnamills.yolasite.com
SIC: 5999 2048 5261 5153 Feed & farm supply; feed premixes; fertilizer; grains

(G-3708)
HANSON LEHIGH INC
3820 Serr Rd (48817-1146)
PHONE.................................989 233-5343
EMP: 11 EST: 2018
SALES (est): 197.9K **Privately Held**
WEB: www.lehighhanson.com
SIC: 3273 Ready-mixed concrete

(G-3709)
KELSHEIMER INDUSTRIES LLC
318 E State St (48817-1425)
PHONE.................................810 701-9455
Thomas M Kelsheimer, *Principal*
EMP: 4 EST: 2017
SALES (est): 52.1K **Privately Held**
SIC: 3999 Manufacturing industries

(G-3710)
LLOYD MILLER & SONS INC
3695 E M 21 (48817-9771)
P.O. Box 384, Webberville (48892-0384)
PHONE.................................517 223-3112
William Miller, *Owner*
EMP: 8 EST: 2009
SALES (est): 77.5K **Privately Held**
WEB: www.lloydmillerandsons.com
SIC: 3524 Lawn & garden equipment

(G-3711)
MACHINE TOOL & GEAR INC (DH)
Also Called: Mtg
1021 N Shiawassee St (48817-1151)
PHONE.................................989 743-3936
David Segal, *Ch of Bd*
EMP: 78 EST: 2002
SQ FT: 300,000
SALES (est): 51.7MM
SALES (corp-wide): 146.6MM **Privately Held**
SIC: 3714 5051 3089 Motor vehicle parts & accessories; iron or steel flat products; automotive parts, plastic
HQ: Newcor, Inc.
1021 N Shiawassee St
Corunna MI 48817
248 537-0014

(G-3712)
MONOGRAM ETC
231 N Shiawassee St (48817-1457)
PHONE.................................989 743-5999
Jeffery Bodary, *Owner*
Patricia Bodary, *Co-Owner*
EMP: 4 EST: 1995 **Privately Held**
WEB: www.monogramsetc.com
SIC: 2395 Embroidery products, except schiffli machine; embroidery & art needlework

(G-3713)
MOTORS ONLINE LLC
503 S Shiawassee St (48817-1663)
PHONE.................................989 723-8985
Steve Olmsted,
EMP: 10 EST: 2018
SALES (est): 115.2K **Privately Held**
SIC: 7694 Electric motor repair

(G-3714)
NEWAY MANUFACTURING INC
1013 N Shiawassee St (48817-1151)
P.O. Box 188 (48817-0188)
PHONE.................................989 743-3458
James Schultz, *President*
James D Schultz, *President*
Mary Eickholt, *Vice Pres*
▼ EMP: 6 EST: 1973
SALES (est): 852.6K **Privately Held**
WEB: www.newaymfg.com
SIC: 3541 Machine tools, metal cutting type

(G-3715)
NEWCOR INC (HQ)
Also Called: Bay City Division
1021 N Shiawassee St (48817-1151)
PHONE.................................248 537-0014
David Segal, *CEO*
Steve Nasceif, *Sales Staff*
Scott Wright, *Admin Sec*
EMP: 150 EST: 1969
SQ FT: 210,000
SALES (est): 116.5MM
SALES (corp-wide): 146.6MM **Privately Held**
WEB: www.cieautomotive.com
SIC: 3714 Motor vehicle transmissions, drive assemblies & parts; gears, motor vehicle; drive shafts, motor vehicle; transmission housings or parts, motor vehicle
PA: Cie Automotive, Sa
Alameda Mazarredo, 69 - Piso 8o
Bilbao 48009
946 054-835

(G-3716)
QUIRKY 3D PRINTING
5794 Hibbard Rd (48817-9314)
PHONE.................................810 247-6732
Tyler Quirk, *Principal*
EMP: 4 EST: 2015
SALES (est): 83.9K **Privately Held**
SIC: 2752 Commercial printing, lithographic

(G-3717)
S L H METALS INC
229 Sleeseman Dr (48817-1077)
PHONE.................................989 743-3467
Michael Sarrazin, *President*
Aimee Braeutigan, *Office Mgr*
EMP: 14 EST: 2006
SALES (est): 1.4MM **Privately Held**
WEB: www.slhmetals.com
SIC: 3441 7389 Fabricated structural metal;

(G-3718)
STRAUSS TOOL INC
410 S Shiawassee St (48817-1644)
PHONE.................................989 743-4741
Joseph Strauss, *President*
Joseph M Strauss Jr, *Vice Pres*
EMP: 4 EST: 1984
SQ FT: 6,000 **Privately Held**
WEB: www.strausscncmachining.com
SIC: 3599 Machine shop, jobbing & repair

(G-3719)
WINANS INC
Also Called: Winans Electric Motor Repair
494 S Comstock St (48817-1726)
P.O. Box 233 (48817-0233)
PHONE.................................810 744-1240
Barry Catrell, *President*
Lindsey Montpas, *General Mgr*
▼ EMP: 7 EST: 1980
SQ FT: 11,800 **Privately Held**
SIC: 7694 5063 Electric motor repair; motors, electric

Cottrellville
St. Clair County

(G-3720)
HOWELL ENGINE DEVELOPMENTS INC
6201 Industrial Way (48039-1326)
PHONE.................................810 765-5100
Matthew Howell, *President*
Jennifer Siegel Tallman, *Office Mgr*
EMP: 18 EST: 1988
SQ FT: 7,000
SALES (est): 4MM **Privately Held**
WEB: www.howellefi.com
SIC: 3714 7539 Automotive wiring harness sets; fuel system repair, motor vehicle

(G-3721)
I & G TOOL CO INC
7270 Starville Rd (48039-2425)
PHONE.................................586 777-7690
Sigfried Charow, *President*
EMP: 15 EST: 1984
SALES (est): 1.1MM **Privately Held**
WEB: www.igtool.com
SIC: 3545 3544 Cutting tools for machine tools; special dies, tools, jigs & fixtures

(G-3722)
INDUSTRIAL MTAL FBRICATORS LLC
Also Called: I M F
2700 Plank Rd (48039-1461)
PHONE.................................810 765-8960
Kenneth Teneyck,
EMP: 20 EST: 2002
SQ FT: 10,000
SALES (est): 2.9MM **Privately Held**
SIC: 3444 Sheet metalwork

(G-3723)
IROQUOIS INDUSTRIES INC
7177 Marine City Hwy (48039-1008)
PHONE.................................586 465-1023
Gene Moore, *Facilities Mgr*
Shally Ziarko, *Buyer*
Sharon Petrill, *Human Resources*
Dave Hoffmann, *Sales Staff*
Jim Mayworm, *Program Mgr*
EMP: 23
SALES (corp-wide): 54.4MM **Privately Held**
WEB: www.iroquoisind.com
SIC: 3465 Automotive stampings
PA: Iroquois Industries, Inc.
25101 Groesbeck Hwy
Warren MI 48089
586 771-5734

(G-3724)
L R OLIVER AND COMPANY INC
Also Called: Oliver Carbide Products
7445 Mayer Rd (48039-2410)
PHONE.................................810 765-1000
Rex Oliver, *President*
Steven Simasko, *Principal*
Scott Oliver, *Vice Pres*
Kris Grumbling, *Treasurer*
Paul Butler, *Sales Staff*
▲ EMP: 38 EST: 1962
SALES (est): 4.2MM **Privately Held**
WEB: www.olivercorp.com
SIC: 3291 Abrasive products

Covert
Van Buren County

(G-3725)
SENSIBLE VISION INC
40376 Wilderness Dunes Ln (49043-8563)
PHONE.................................734 478-1130
EMP: 8 EST: 2017
SALES (est): 140K **Privately Held**
WEB: www.sensiblevision.com
SIC: 7372 Prepackaged software

(G-3726)
SWING-LO SUSPENDED SCAFFOLD CO
Also Called: Swing-Lo System
75609 County Road 376 (49043-9794)
P.O. Box 128 (49043-0128)
PHONE.................................269 764-8989
George Saleeby, *CEO*
Stephen Leonard, *President*
EMP: 18 EST: 1955
SQ FT: 31,000
SALES (est): 3.3MM **Privately Held**
WEB: www.swing-lo.com
SIC: 3446 Scaffolds, mobile or stationary: metal

Covington
Baraga County

(G-3727)
YOUNGGREN FARM & FOREST INC
34392 Younggren Rd (49919-9021)
PHONE.................................906 355-2272
Francis Younggren, *President*
EMP: 8 EST: 1958
SQ FT: 2,000
SALES (est): 863.5K **Privately Held**
SIC: 2411 Logging camps & contractors

(G-3728)
YOUNGGREN TIMBER COMPANY
34392 Younggren Rd (49919-9021)
PHONE.................................906 355-2272
Greg Younggren, *Partner*
Daniel Younggren, *Partner*
Paul Younggren, *Partner*
EMP: 7 EST: 2010
SALES (est): 950K **Privately Held**
SIC: 2411 Logging

Croswell
Sanilac County

(G-3729)
BEADEN SCREEN INC
305 Melvin St (48422-1027)
P.O. Box 199 (48422-0199)
PHONE.................................810 679-3119
William O'Connor, *President*
Steven O'Connor, *Vice Pres*
Steve Oconnor, *Vice Pres*
EMP: 30 EST: 1961
SQ FT: 11,100
SALES (est): 3.3MM **Privately Held**
WEB: www.beadenscreen.com
SIC: 3496 3494 Cylinder wire cloth; valves & pipe fittings

(G-3730)
JAY & KAY MANUFACTURING LLC (PA)
72 Louise St (48422-1043)
PHONE.................................810 679-2333
James Essad, *Vice Pres*
Brian Wood, *Purch Mgr*
Karen Vanderhoss, *Human Res Mgr*
Messinger Clyde, *Info Tech Dir*
Mark Boone,
▼ EMP: 38 EST: 1984
SQ FT: 58,000
SALES (est): 6.7MM **Privately Held**
WEB: www.jaykaymfg.com
SIC: 3429 3714 Marine hardware; motor vehicle parts & accessories

(G-3731)
JAY & KAY MANUFACTURING LLC
141 E Sanborn Ave (48422-1404)
PHONE.................................810 679-3079
EMP: 5
SALES (est): 308.5K
SALES (corp-wide): 10.2MM **Privately Held**
SIC: 3429 3714 Mfg Hardware Mfg Motor Vehicle Parts/Accessories

Croswell - Sanilac County (G-3732) — GEOGRAPHIC SECTION

PA: Jay & Kay Manufacturing, Llc
72 Louise St
Croswell MI 48422
810 679-2333

(G-3732)
MATERIAL CONTROL INC (PA)
Also Called: Conveyor Components
130 Seltzer Rd (48422-9180)
PHONE..................630 892-4274
Clinton F Stimpson III, *President*
Keith Clayton, *Admin Sec*
▼ **EMP:** 3 **EST:** 1968
SALES (est): 48MM **Privately Held**
WEB: www.materialcontrolinc.com
SIC: 3535 Bucket type conveyor systems

(G-3733)
MICHIGAN SUGAR COMPANY
159 S Howard Ave (48422-1398)
PHONE..................810 679-2241
Gregory Soule, *Branch Mgr*
Alex Demeter, *Supervisor*
EMP: 165
SALES (corp-wide): 189.4MM **Privately Held**
WEB: www.michigansugar.com
SIC: 2063 Beet sugar from beet sugar refinery
PA: Michigan Sugar Company
122 Uptown Dr Unit 300
Bay City MI 48708
989 686-0161

(G-3734)
PEDMIC CONVERTING INC
7241 Wildcat Rd (48422-9012)
P.O. Box 226 (48422-0226)
PHONE..................810 679-9600
Dennis Pedler, *Ch of Bd*
William I Mc Comb, *President*
EMP: 16 **EST:** 1984
SQ FT: 30,000
SALES (est): 1.1MM **Privately Held**
SIC: 3086 Packaging & shipping materials, foamed plastic

(G-3735)
RENES INC
Also Called: Le'tush
3131 Mortimer Line Rd (48422-8738)
PHONE..................810 294-5008
Ren Ebner-Todd, *President*
Rene Ebner-Todd, *President*
Michelle Mueller, *Admin Sec*
EMP: 5 **EST:** 1988
SQ FT: 1,200
SALES (est): 492.8K **Privately Held**
SIC: 2361 2369 7389 Girls' & children's dresses, blouses & shirts; girls' & children's outerwear; design services

(G-3736)
SUPERIOR PRODUCTS MFG INC
124 Louise St (48422-1050)
PHONE..................810 679-4479
Jeffrey Stringer, *President*
Donna Stringer, *Corp Secy*
EMP: 5 **EST:** 1992
SALES (est): 819K **Privately Held**
SIC: 3544 3599 Special dies & tools; machine shop, jobbing & repair

(G-3737)
THEUT CONCRETE PRODUCTS INC
138 E Harrington Rd (48422-1121)
PHONE..................810 679-3376
EMP: 13 **EST:** 1920
SQ FT: 10,000
SALES (est): 126.8K **Privately Held**
SIC: 3271 5032 3273 Mfg Concrete Block/Brick Whol Brick/Stone Matrls Mfg Ready-Mixed Concrete

(G-3738)
VAN S FABRICATIONS INC
Also Called: Van's Fabrications
4446 Peck Rd (48422-9620)
PHONE..................810 679-2115
Gerrit Van Der Maas, *President*
EMP: 5 **EST:** 1984
SQ FT: 3,000

SALES (est): 396.8K **Privately Held**
WEB: www.lincolnvulcanizers.com
SIC: 3599 7389 3469 5984 Machine shop, jobbing & repair; metal slitting & shearing; stamping metal for the trade; propane gas, bottled; welding on site

Crystal
Montcalm County

(G-3739)
ACCESSORIES & SPECIALTIES INC
121 E Park St (48818)
P.O. Box 91 (48818-0091)
PHONE..................989 235-3331
Fax: 989 235-3859
EMP: 6
SALES (est): 310K **Privately Held**
SIC: 3949 Mfg Sporting/Athletic Goods

(G-3740)
AMERICAN UNDERCAR
10099 E Stanton Rd (48818-9758)
PHONE..................989 235-1427
Roger Wilson, *Principal*
EMP: 11 **EST:** 2013
SALES (est): 1.1MM **Privately Held**
WEB: www.thetireclub.com
SIC: 3714 Motor vehicle parts & accessories

Crystal Falls
Iron County

(G-3741)
CRYSTAL FALLS SPRINGS INC
Also Called: Cool Artesian Water
346 Rock Crusher Rd (49920-9041)
PHONE..................906 875-3191
Debra Rose, *President*
Brian Rose, *Vice Pres*
Dennis Rose, *VP Sales*
EMP: 5 **EST:** 2002
SQ FT: 10,000
SALES (est): 500K **Privately Held**
WEB: www.artesiapremiumwater.com
SIC: 2086 Water, pasteurized: packaged in cans, bottles, etc.

(G-3742)
DJW ENTERPRISES INC
324 N Light Lake Rd (49920-9607)
PHONE..................414 791-6192
Deborah Weis, *President*
EMP: 1 **EST:** 1987
SQ FT: 28,000
SALES (est): 6.2MM
SALES (corp-wide): 1.1B **Privately Held**
WEB: www.djwenterprises.com
SIC: 3089 7389 Injection molded finished plastic products;
HQ: Maclean-Fogg Component Solutions, L.L.C
1000 Allanson Rd
Mundelein IL 60060
248 853-2525

(G-3743)
MAGIGLIDE INC
Also Called: Land Quilts
257 Industrial Park Rd (49920-9643)
PHONE..................906 822-7321
Dennis Box, *President*
Leann Davis, *Manager*
EMP: 10 **EST:** 2004
SALES (est): 741.4K **Privately Held**
SIC: 2431 Doors, wood

(G-3744)
PRIME ASSEMBLIES INC
2525 Us Highway 2 (49920-9109)
P.O. Box 445, Iron Mountain (49801-0445)
PHONE..................906 875-6420
Cynthia Rahoi, *President*
Joseph Rahoi, *Vice Pres*
EMP: 28 **EST:** 1992
SALES (est): 300K **Privately Held**
WEB: www.primeassemblies.com
SIC: 3643 Current-carrying wiring devices

(G-3745)
R J MANUFACTURING INCORPORATED
110 Forest Gtwy (49920-8856)
P.O. Box 886, Iron Mountain (49801-0886)
PHONE..................906 779-9151
James W Flood, *President*
Joan Flood, *Corp Secy*
EMP: 9 **EST:** 1983
SALES (est): 1.8MM **Privately Held**
SIC: 3567 3991 Paint baking & drying ovens; brooms & brushes

(G-3746)
SUPERIOR SUPPLIERS NETWORK LLC
1307 Harrison Ave (49920-1022)
PHONE..................906 284-1561
EMP: 15
SALES (est): 950K **Privately Held**
SIC: 3441 Fabricated Structural Metal

(G-3747)
WILLIAMS REDDI MIX INC
1345 Us Highway 2 (49920-1048)
PHONE..................906 875-6952
Dennis Williams, *President*
EMP: 8 **EST:** 1973
SQ FT: 2,800
SALES (est): 750K **Privately Held**
SIC: 3273 Ready-mixed concrete

(G-3748)
WILLIAMS REDI MIX
170 Williams Rd (49920-9412)
PHONE..................906 875-6839
Dennis Williams, *Principal*
EMP: 5 **EST:** 2009
SALES (est): 173.8K **Privately Held**
SIC: 3273 Ready-mixed concrete

Curran
Alcona County

(G-3749)
4 GENERATION LOGGING INC
2335 N Curran Rd. (48728-9771)
PHONE..................989 350-0337
EMP: 6 **EST:** 2019
SALES (est): 974.6K **Privately Held**
SIC: 2411 Logging

Curtis
Mackinac County

(G-3750)
DUBERVILLE LOGGING
W16683 Sandtown Rd (49820-9606)
PHONE..................906 586-6267
Jake Duberville, *Principal*
EMP: 7 **EST:** 2006
SALES (est): 271.6K **Privately Held**
WEB: www.dubervillelogging.com
SIC: 2411 Logging camps & contractors

(G-3751)
ODIN INTERNATIONAL INC
Also Called: Thortarp
N9448 Manistique Lakes Rd (49820-9649)
P.O. Box 35 (49820-0035)
PHONE..................262 569-7171
Steven Wallace, *CEO*
EMP: 5 **EST:** 1996
SQ FT: 20,000
SALES (est): 442.5K **Privately Held**
WEB: www.thortarp.com
SIC: 2394 Canvas & related products

Custer
Mason County

(G-3752)
WATERS INDUSTRIES LLC
4960 Lookout Trl (49405-8770)
PHONE..................616 848-8050
Paul Waters, *Principal*
EMP: 4 **EST:** 2015

SALES (est): 43.6K **Privately Held**
SIC: 3999 Barber & beauty shop equipment

Daggett
Menominee County

(G-3753)
MOTTO CEDAR PRODUCTS INC
Us Hwy 41 & County Rd 360 (49821)
P.O. Box 56 (49821-0056)
PHONE..................906 753-4892
Gary Motto, *President*
Larry Motto, *Corp Secy*
Garland Motto, *Vice Pres*
Jody Motto, *Vice Pres*
EMP: 4 **EST:** 1958
SALES (est): 651.2K **Privately Held**
WEB: www.mottocedar.com
SIC: 2411 2426 5211 Posts, wood: hewn, round or split; furniture stock & parts, hardwood; lumber & other building materials

(G-3754)
US PRINTERS
W4763 Okwood Rd 30 (49821-9543)
PHONE..................906 639-3100
EMP: 5 **EST:** 2015
SALES (est): 168.5K **Privately Held**
SIC: 2752 Commercial printing, offset

Dansville
Ingham County

(G-3755)
CC EMBROIDERY VINYL DESIGNS
1435 E Mason St (48819-9661)
PHONE..................517 996-6030
Crystal Amon, *Owner*
EMP: 4 **EST:** 2013
SALES (est): 47.7K **Privately Held**
SIC: 2395 Embroidery & art needlework

Davisburg
Oakland County

(G-3756)
ALPHA DIRECTIONAL BORING
11910 Scott Rd (48350-3018)
PHONE..................586 405-0171
Kevin Pattison, *Principal*
EMP: 4 **EST:** 2010
SALES (est): 363K **Privately Held**
SIC: 1381 Directional drilling oil & gas wells

(G-3757)
ARL SERVICE LLC
10399 Enterprise Dr (48350-1312)
PHONE..................248 625-6160
Mark Pettit, *Engineer*
Albert R Lewellen,
Andrea Lewellen, *Assistant*
EMP: 7 **EST:** 2002
SQ FT: 5,000
SALES (est): 1.6MM **Privately Held**
WEB: www.arlservice.com
SIC: 3599 Machine shop, jobbing & repair

(G-3758)
AUTOMTION MDLAR COMPONENTS INC (PA)
Also Called: AMC
10301 Enterprise Dr (48350-1312)
PHONE..................248 922-4740
Richard A Shore Sr, *CEO*
D Ick Shore, *President*
Jeff Barrett, *Plant Mgr*
Braydon Laframboise, *Project Mgr*
John Welch, *Purch Agent*
▲ **EMP:** 75 **EST:** 1988
SQ FT: 63,000
SALES (est): 14.8MM **Privately Held**
WEB: www.amcautomation.com
SIC: 3535 Conveyors & conveying equipment

GEOGRAPHIC SECTION
Davison - Genesee County (G-3786)

(G-3759)
AWD ASSOCIATES INC
10560 Enterprise Dr Ste A (48350-1346)
P.O. Box 99, Clarkston (48347-0099)
PHONE.................................248 922-9898
Larry Littleson, *President*
Sharon Littleson, *Vice Pres*
EMP: 17 **EST:** 1991
SQ FT: 8,000
SALES (est): 431.2K **Privately Held**
WEB: www.awddrills.com
SIC: 3599 Machine shop, jobbing & repair

(G-3760)
BCS CREATIVE LLC
10012 Old Farm Trl (48350-2235)
PHONE.................................248 917-1660
Candice Layton,
EMP: 4 **EST:** 2014
SALES (est): 143.5K **Privately Held**
WEB: www.bcs-creative.com
SIC: 3993 7389 Signs, not made in custom sign painting shops;

(G-3761)
BULLDOG WELDING
4785 Ormond Rd (48350-3319)
PHONE..................................248 342-1189
EMP: 4 **EST:** 2014
SALES (est): 45.5K **Privately Held**
SIC: 7692 Welding repair

(G-3762)
C & D TOOL & DIE COMPANY INC
12395 Shaffer Rd (48350-3714)
PHONE.................................248 922-5937
Mike Bender, *President*
Pat Endres, *Vice Pres*
EMP: 20 **EST:** 1968
SQ FT: 15,000
SALES (est): 961.6K **Privately Held**
SIC: 3544 Special dies & tools

(G-3763)
CARBIDE FORM MASTER INC
10565 Dixie Hwy (48350-1309)
PHONE.................................248 625-9373
James L Stoglin, *President*
Richard Coburn, *Vice Pres*
Penny A Stoglin, *Admin Sec*
EMP: 8 **EST:** 1979
SQ FT: 6,280 **Privately Held**
SIC: 3545 Cutting tools for machine tools

(G-3764)
COLOMBO SALES & ENGRG INC
Also Called: Colombo Beverage Chase Systems
10421 Enterprise Dr Ste A (48350-1345)
PHONE.................................248 547-2820
Harry Colombo, *President*
Kevin Hedrich, *Accounts Mgr*
Ted Mangosh, *Accounts Mgr*
Jacob Hedrich, *Manager*
EMP: 10 **EST:** 1970
SQ FT: 9,500
SALES (est): 2MM **Privately Held**
WEB: www.colombopts.com
SIC: 3535 7699 Pneumatic tube conveyor systems; miscellaneous building item repair services

(G-3765)
EDW C LEVY CO
16255 Tindall Rd (48350-1035)
PHONE..................................248 634-0879
Rick Will, *Manager*
EMP: 5
SALES (corp-wide): 521.9MM **Privately Held**
WEB: www.edwclevy.com
SIC: 2951 Asphalt & asphaltic paving mixtures (not from refineries)
PA: Edw. C. Levy Co.
 9300 Dix
 Dearborn MI 48120
 313 429-2200

(G-3766)
EXCEL MACHINERY INTL CORP
13479 Neal Rd (48350-3308)
PHONE..................................810 348-9162
Humberto Serna, *Owner*
EMP: 5 **EST:** 2017

SALES (est): 89.6K **Privately Held**
SIC: 3599 Industrial machinery

(G-3767)
FABRICATION SPECIALTIES INC
9600 Melissa Ln (48350-1200)
PHONE.................................313 891-7181
Denise Mc Clain, *President*
Maryanne Mazzenga, *Admin Sec*
EMP: 5 **EST:** 1996
SALES (est): 412.2K **Privately Held**
WEB: www.fabricationspecialties.com
SIC: 3444 Sheet metalwork

(G-3768)
FALCON TRUCKING COMPANY
Also Called: Holly Sand & Gravel
16240 Tindall Rd (48350-1034)
PHONE.................................248 634-9471
Scott Bandkau, *Manager*
EMP: 25
SALES (corp-wide): 18.1MM **Privately Held**
SIC: 1442 5032 Sand mining; gravel mining; paving materials
PA: Falcon Trucking Company
 9300 Dix
 Dearborn MI 48120
 313 843-7200

(G-3769)
GENERAL INSPECTION LLC
10585 Enterprise Dr (48350-1338)
P.O. Box 189002, Utica (48318-9002)
PHONE.................................248 625-0529
Nathan Kujacznski, *Research*
Laura Poletti, *Mktg Coord*
Chris Alexander, *Mng Officer*
Mike Nygaard,
Greg Nygaard,
EMP: 12 **EST:** 1991
SALES (est): 3.6MM **Privately Held**
WEB: www.geninsp.com
SIC: 3829 Measuring & controlling devices

(G-3770)
GLOBAL SUPPLY INTEGRATOR LLC
10145 Creekwood Trl (48350-2059)
PHONE.................................586 484-0734
Shawn Oneill, *Engineer*
Randall Leach, *Sales Staff*
Randy Leach,
EMP: 6 **EST:** 2000
SQ FT: 4,000
SALES (est): 3.2MM **Privately Held**
SIC: 3089 8711 7371 Injection molded finished plastic products; engineering services; computer software development

(G-3771)
PRECISION RACE SERVICES INC
16749 Dixie Hwy Ste 9 (48350-1051)
PHONE.................................248 634-4010
James P Kelly, *President*
David L Decker, *Vice Pres*
EMP: 9 **EST:** 1992
SQ FT: 5,000
SALES (est): 937.2K **Privately Held**
WEB: www.p-r-s.com
SIC: 7539 3714 Electrical services; automotive wiring harness sets

(G-3772)
QUALITY FIRST SYSTEMS INC
10301 Enterprise Dr (48350-1312)
PHONE.................................248 922-4780
John Welch, *Vice Pres*
Robert Landry, *Purch Agent*
Joe Vitale, *Engineer*
Richard Shore Jr, *CFO*
Jere Hill, *Manager*
◆ **EMP:** 26 **EST:** 1981
SQ FT: 62,000
SALES (est): 5.2MM **Privately Held**
WEB: www.qualityfirstsystems.com
SIC: 3829 Fatigue testing machines, industrial: mechanical

(G-3773)
ZAREMBA & CO INC
10590 Enterprise Dr (48350-1339)
P.O. Box 695, Clarkston (48347-0695)
PHONE.................................248 922-3300
Patrick E Zaremba, *President*

Dave Novak, *Opers Staff*
EMP: 7 **EST:** 1998
SALES (est): 581.1K **Privately Held**
WEB: www.zarembaandco.com
SIC: 0781 3271 Landscape planning services; blocks, concrete: landscape or retaining wall

---

Davison
Genesee County

(G-3774)
BRISTOL MANUFACTURING INC
4416 N State Rd (48423-8538)
PHONE..................................810 658-9510
Victor Moody, *President*
Raymond Oliver, *Vice Pres*
Joyce Lawton, *Project Mgr*
EMP: 23 **EST:** 1998
SQ FT: 6,000
SALES (est): 2.4MM **Privately Held**
WEB: www.bristolmanufacturing.com
SIC: 7353 3537 Cranes & aerial lift equipment, rental or leasing; forklift trucks

(G-3775)
BRISTOL STEEL & CONVEYOR CORP
4416 N State Rd (48423-8538)
PHONE..................................810 658-9510
Raymond D Oliver, *President*
Michelle June, *Purch Agent*
Kevin Hicks, *Manager*
Matt Payne, *Manager*
Terry J Oliver, *Admin Sec*
EMP: 50 **EST:** 1979
SQ FT: 2,800
SALES (est): 13.3MM **Privately Held**
WEB: www.bristolsteel.com
SIC: 3441 3449 1791 3535 Building components, structural steel; miscellaneous metalwork; iron work, structural; conveyors & conveying equipment; sheet metalwork

(G-3776)
CHAD S SIGNS AND SHIRTS
9430 Tiger Run Trl (48423-8431)
PHONE..................................248 821-3087
Benny Willmore, *Principal*
EMP: 5 **EST:** 2010
SALES (est): 72.9K **Privately Held**
WEB: www.signandshirtstore.com
SIC: 3993 Signs & advertising specialties

(G-3777)
COLES MACHINE SERVICE INC
201 W Rising St (48423-1537)
PHONE..................................810 658-5373
Kenneth Cole, *President*
Keith Cole, *Vice Pres*
Kyle Cole, *Engineer*
Cora Cole, *Treasurer*
EMP: 20 **EST:** 1967
SQ FT: 14,000
SALES (est): 4.1MM **Privately Held**
WEB: www.colesmachine.com
SIC: 3544 3545 3599 Special dies & tools; machine tool accessories; custom machinery

(G-3778)
CONQUEST SCENTS
8399 E Bristol Rd (48423-8767)
PHONE..................................810 653-2759
Karen Roberts, *Principal*
EMP: 11 **EST:** 2011
SALES (est): 700.6K **Privately Held**
WEB: www.conquestscents.com
SIC: 2844 Toilet preparations

(G-3779)
D & W AWNING AND WINDOW CO
8068 E Court St (48423-2503)
PHONE..................................810 742-0340
David Wood, *President*
Derek Wood, *General Mgr*
Mark Wood, *Vice Pres*
EMP: 50 **EST:** 1959
SQ FT: 70,000

SALES (est): 4MM **Privately Held**
WEB: www.dwwindows.com
SIC: 3089 3444 3354 Window frames & sash, plastic; awnings & canopies; aluminum extruded products

(G-3780)
FASTBALL LLC
4302 Charter Oaks Dr (48423-3295)
PHONE..................................810 955-8510
Kori JP Garman,
EMP: 4 **EST:** 2010
SALES (est): 53.4K **Privately Held**
SIC: 3949 Sporting & athletic goods

(G-3781)
FERGUSON BLOCK CO INC
5430 N State Rd (48423-8596)
PHONE..................................810 653-2812
Lillian Diehl, *President*
Robert Ferguson, *Admin Sec*
EMP: 24 **EST:** 1927
SQ FT: 1,600
SALES (est): 5.4MM **Privately Held**
WEB: www.fergusonblock.com
SIC: 3271 3273 5211 Blocks, concrete or cinder: standard; ready-mixed concrete; concrete & cinder block

(G-3782)
FERNCO INC (PA)
Also Called: Fernco Joint Sealer Company
300 S Dayton St (48423-1564)
PHONE..................................810 503-9000
Chris Cooper, *CEO*
Mark Cooper, *President*
Darrell Cooper, *Chairman*
Glenn P Ginther, *Corp Secy*
Terry Oistad, *Design Engr*
◆ **EMP:** 140 **EST:** 1964
SQ FT: 75,000
SALES (est): 60.9MM **Privately Held**
WEB: www.fernco.com
SIC: 3432 3498 Plastic plumbing fixture fittings, assembly; fabricated pipe & fittings

(G-3783)
FILTRATION MACHINE
10049 N Hunt Ct (48423-3511)
PHONE..................................810 845-0536
Michael Ovadek, *Principal*
EMP: 6 **EST:** 2015
SALES (est): 120.6K **Privately Held**
SIC: 3724 Aircraft engines & engine parts

(G-3784)
GENOVA-MINNESOTA INC
7034 E Court St (48423-2504)
PHONE..................................810 744-4500
▼ **EMP:** 100
SALES (est): 19.1MM **Privately Held**
SIC: 3089 Mfg Plastic Products
HQ: Genova Products, Inc.
 7034 E Court St
 Davison MI 48423
 810 744-4500

(G-3785)
GLOBAL PUMP COMPANY LLC (PA)
10162 E Coldwater Rd (48423-8598)
PHONE..................................810 653-4828
Rod Mersino Jr,
David Tersignio,
◆ **EMP:** 4 **EST:** 1988
SQ FT: 70,000
SALES (est): 2.6MM **Privately Held**
WEB: www.globalpump.com
SIC: 7699 7359 5084 3561 Pumps & pumping equipment repair; equipment rental & leasing; pumps & pumping equipment; industrial pumps & parts

(G-3786)
HENSLEY MFG INC
1097 S State Rd Ste 3 (48423-1934)
PHONE..................................810 653-3226
Colin Connell, *President*
Terry Powell, *Partner*
▲ **EMP:** 19 **EST:** 1993
SQ FT: 1,200
SALES: 2.3MM **Privately Held**
WEB: www.hensleymfg.com
SIC: 3799 3231 Trailer hitches; mirrored glass

Davison - Genesee County (G-3787)

(G-3787)
HILTON SCREENERS INC
210 N Main St (48423-1432)
PHONE.................810 653-0711
Kent Elliott, *President*
Kim Elliott, *Vice Pres*
Rachel Miller, *Office Mgr*
EMP: 7 EST: 1984
SQ FT: 1,600
SALES (est): 604.8K **Privately Held**
WEB: www.hiltonscreeners.com
SIC: 2261 2759 Screen printing of cotton broadwoven fabrics; screen printing

(G-3788)
KELLOGG COMPANY
2166 Oak Shade Dr (48423-2105)
PHONE.................810 653-5625
Robin Kellogg, *Principal*
EMP: 4
SALES (corp-wide): 13.7B **Publicly Held**
WEB: www.kelloggcompany.com
SIC: 2043 Cereal breakfast foods
PA: Kellogg Company
1 Kellogg Sq
Battle Creek MI 49017
269 961-2000

(G-3789)
LVC TECHNOLOGIES INC
2200 S State Rd (48423-8799)
PHONE.................248 373-3778
Les Amon, *President*
EMP: 21 EST: 1999
SALES (est): 560.3K **Privately Held**
WEB: www.lvctechnologies.com
SIC: 7382 3612 Security systems services; feeder voltage boosters (electric transformers)

(G-3790)
MARC MOLINA
10122 E Stanley Rd (48423-9307)
PHONE.................810 701-3587
Hattie Molina, *Principal*
EMP: 4 EST: 2017
SALES (est): 74.4K **Privately Held**
SIC: 2844 Lipsticks

(G-3791)
MURPHYS WATER WELL BITS (PA)
Also Called: Murphys Bits
3340 S State Rd (48423-8755)
PHONE.................810 658-1554
Larry Murphy, *Owner*
◆ EMP: 5 EST: 1984
SALES (est): 420K **Privately Held**
WEB: www.murphysbits.com
SIC: 3533 Water well drilling equipment

(G-3792)
PARISEAUS PRINTING INC
218 Mill St (48423-1442)
PHONE.................810 653-8420
Alan Pariseau, *President*
Stephen Pariseau, *President*
EMP: 5 EST: 1968
SQ FT: 2,500
SALES (est): 225K **Privately Held**
WEB: www.pariseausprinting.com
SIC: 2752 Commercial printing, offset

(G-3793)
PIONEER CABINETRY INC
301 W Rising St Ste 2 (48423-1571)
P.O. Box 280 (48423-0280)
PHONE.................810 658-2075
Lawrence E Fox, *President*
Sandra Townsend, *QC Dir*
EMP: 100 EST: 1986
SQ FT: 74,000
SALES (est): 13.5MM **Privately Held**
WEB: www.pioneercabinetry.net
SIC: 2434 Vanities, bathroom: wood

(G-3794)
R J MANUFACTURING
4196 S Irish Rd (48423-8737)
PHONE.................810 610-0205
Richard Steel, *Owner*
EMP: 5 EST: 2007
SQ FT: 3,800
SALES (est): 180K **Privately Held**
SIC: 3999 Manufacturing industries

(G-3795)
RIEGLE PRESS INC (PA)
Also Called: Frankenmuth Printing
1282 N Gale Rd (48423-2552)
P.O. Box 207, Flint (48501-0207)
PHONE.................810 653-9631
Gerald R Carmody, *President*
Chester Parish, *Vice Pres*
David Young, *Vice Pres*
Candi Franzel, *Sales Staff*
EMP: 30 EST: 1962
SQ FT: 40,000
SALES (est): 3.4MM **Privately Held**
WEB: www.rieglepress.com
SIC: 2752 2759 2789 2761 Commercial printing, offset; business forms, lithographed; commercial printing; bookbinding & related work; manifold business forms

(G-3796)
SIGNS DIRECT LLC
2259 Wicklow South Dr (48423-8442)
PHONE.................810 732-5067
EMP: 5 EST: 2016
SALES (est): 63.6K **Privately Held**
WEB: www.signsdirect.com
SIC: 3993 Signs & advertising specialties

(G-3797)
SPECIAL T CUSTOM PRODUCTS
1492 Newcastle Dr (48423-8371)
PHONE.................810 654-9602
John McCrea, *Owner*
Terri McCrea, *Co-Owner*
EMP: 4 EST: 2003
SQ FT: 500
SALES (est): 130.8K **Privately Held**
SIC: 2395 Embroidery & art needlework

(G-3798)
STEPLEN COATINGS LLC
2234 S Irish Rd (48423-8361)
PHONE.................810 653-6418
Christine T Stephens, *Administration*
EMP: 4 EST: 2010
SALES (est): 74.2K **Privately Held**
SIC: 3479 Metal coating & allied service

(G-3799)
UNIVERSAL SFTWR SOLUTIONS INC
1334 S Irish Rd (48423-8313)
PHONE.................810 653-5000
Christopher Dobiesz, *President*
Dave Golen, *COO*
Michelle Dobiesz, *Treasurer*
Fred Lang, *Manager*
Jillian Miller, *Training Spec*
EMP: 30 EST: 2000
SQ FT: 5,000
SALES (est): 5MM **Privately Held**
WEB: www.universalss.com
SIC: 7372 Prepackaged software

(G-3800)
VEIT TOOL & GAGE INC
303 S Dayton St (48423-1501)
PHONE.................810 658-4949
Duane Veit, *President*
EMP: 25 EST: 1988
SQ FT: 7,000
SALES (est): 1.5MM **Privately Held**
WEB: www.veit-tool.com
SIC: 3544 3599 Special dies & tools; custom machinery

(G-3801)
WILLIAMS GUN SIGHT COMPANY
7389 Lapeer Rd (48423-2509)
P.O. Box 329 (48423-0329)
PHONE.................800 530-9028
Thomas Wright, *President*
Brian Wright, *COO*
Cary Morin, *Purch Mgr*
Diane Parker, *CFO*
▼ EMP: 67 EST: 1951
SQ FT: 78,500
SALES (est): 11.4MM **Privately Held**
WEB: www.williamsgunsight.com
SIC: 5941 3827 Firearms; gun sights, optical

De Tour Village
Chippewa County

(G-3802)
NETTLETON WOOD PRODUCTS INC
34882 S Mcadams Rd (49725-9586)
PHONE.................906 297-5791
Gerald Nettleton, *President*
Diane Nettleton, *Vice Pres*
EMP: 4 EST: 1971
SALES (est): 432.2K **Privately Held**
SIC: 2421 2426 Lumber: rough, sawed or planed; hardwood dimension & flooring mills

Dearborn
Wayne County

(G-3803)
1ST QUALITY LLC
6700 Wyoming St Ste A (48126-2345)
P.O. Box 519, Garden City (48136-0519)
PHONE.................313 908-4864
Dennis Lane, *Mng Member*
EMP: 5 EST: 2015
SQ FT: 1,500
SALES (est): 274.7K **Privately Held**
SIC: 3714 Transmissions, motor vehicle

(G-3804)
A E G M INC
Also Called: Artistic European Granich MBL
335 S Telegraph Rd (48124-1478)
PHONE.................313 304-5279
John Borota, *President*
EMP: 7 EST: 1985
SALES (est): 1MM **Privately Held**
SIC: 3281 Furniture, cut stone

(G-3805)
ACTIVE SOLUTIONS GROUP INC
Also Called: Data Center
4 Parklane Blvd Ste 170 (48126-4215)
PHONE.................313 278-4522
Frank Kadaf, *President*
Ilir Ala, *Vice Pres*
EMP: 5 EST: 2003
SQ FT: 1,900
SALES (est): 2.6MM **Privately Held**
WEB: www.activesolutionsmi.com
SIC: 7378 7373 5045 3357 Computer maintenance & repair; computer integrated systems design; computers, peripherals & software; nonferrous wiredrawing & insulating

(G-3806)
ALBASARA FUEL LLC
10419 Ford Rd (48126-3334)
PHONE.................313 443-6581
Al Mursalan, *Principal*
EMP: 5 EST: 2011
SALES (est): 161.7K **Privately Held**
SIC: 2869 Fuels

(G-3807)
AMERICO CORPORATION
25120 Trowbridge St (48124-2443)
PHONE.................313 565-6550
Lillian Wozniak, *President*
E Lillian Wozniak, *President*
John Carey, *Vice Pres*
Stan Lukasik, *Vice Pres*
EMP: 9 EST: 1963
SQ FT: 12,000
SALES (est): 1.6MM **Privately Held**
WEB: www.americo-corp.com
SIC: 3089 3069 Plastic processing; hard rubber & molded rubber products

(G-3808)
ANCHOR CONVEYOR PRODUCTS INC
6830 Kingsley St (48126-1941)
PHONE.................313 582-5045
William Farmer, *Owner*
Robert Farmer, *Purchasing*
Pam Moorman, *Controller*
Michael Lamarand, *Sales Staff*
▲ EMP: 5 EST: 1925
SALES (est): 1.2MM **Privately Held**
WEB: www.anchorconveyor.com
SIC: 3535 Conveyors & conveying equipment

(G-3809)
ARAB AMERICAN NEWS INC
5706 Chase Rd (48126-2102)
PHONE.................313 582-4888
Oussama Siblani, *President*
EMP: 9 EST: 1984
SALES (est): 754.3K **Privately Held**
WEB: www.arabamericannews.com
SIC: 2711 Newspapers, publishing & printing

(G-3810)
ARCTURIAN LLC
3319 Greenfield Rd 423 (48120-1212)
PHONE.................313 643-5326
Kevin Starks, *Managing Prtnr*
Anthony Evans, *Managing Prtnr*
Kim Rivers, *Managing Prtnr*
Neal Starks, *Managing Prtnr*
EMP: 4 EST: 2003
SALES (est): 250K **Privately Held**
WEB: www.arcturian.com
SIC: 3465 Body parts, automobile: stamped metal

(G-3811)
AT HOME
5901 Mercury Dr (48126-4162)
PHONE.................313 769-4200
EMP: 6 EST: 2015
SALES (est): 139.3K **Privately Held**
SIC: 2599 Furniture & fixtures

(G-3812)
BALLARD POWER SYSTEMS CORP
15001 N Commerce Dr (48120-1226)
PHONE.................313 583-5980
John Sheridan, *CEO*
Jinsong Zhang, *Principal*
Rob Campbell, *Vice Pres*
▲ EMP: 1100
SQ FT: 38,400
SALES (est): 101.6MM
SALES (corp-wide): 2.1B **Privately Held**
WEB: www.superiorplus.com
SIC: 3621 Electric motor & generator parts
PA: Superior Plus Corp
200 Wellington St W Suite 401
Toronto ON M5V 3
416 345-8050

(G-3813)
BENMAR COMMUNICATIONS LLC
1 Parklane Blvd Ste 1105e (48126-4256)
PHONE.................313 593-0690
Samuel A Dawson,
Lawrence Jackson,
EMP: 10 EST: 1997
SQ FT: 6,800
SALES (est): 1.1MM **Privately Held**
WEB: www.jacksondawson.com
SIC: 3555 Printing trades machinery

(G-3814)
BF FRANCHISING
1825 N Martha St (48128-1362)
PHONE.................313 565-2713
Bilal Karamali, *Principal*
EMP: 5 EST: 2010
SALES (est): 146.2K **Privately Held**
SIC: 3011 Tires & inner tubes

(G-3815)
BIG 3 PRECISION PRODUCTS INC
Also Called: Industrial Disgn Innvtions Div
10611 Haggerty St (48126-1908)
PHONE.................313 846-6601
Chuck McHugh, *Branch Mgr*
EMP: 11
SALES (corp-wide): 240.4MM **Publicly Held**
WEB: www.big3precision.com
SIC: 3544 Special dies & tools
HQ: Big 3 Precision Products, Inc.
2923 S Wabash Ave
Centralia IL 62801
618 533-3251

▲ = Import ▼ = Export ◆ = Import/Export

GEOGRAPHIC SECTION
Dearborn - Wayne County (G-3842)

(G-3816)
BREWS BROTHERS III INC
510 Crescent Dr (48124-1200)
PHONE..................228 255-5548
EMP: 4 **EST:** 2018
SALES (est): 96.8K **Privately Held**
WEB: www.brewsbrotherscraftbeer.com
SIC: 3993 Signs & advertising specialties

(G-3817)
CAMMENGA & ASSOCIATES LLC
2011 Bailey St (48124-2404)
PHONE..................313 914-7160
CJ Karchon, *General Mgr*
Christopher Karchon, *Principal*
Alex Karchon, *Vice Pres*
Michael A Alexander,
EMP: 14 **EST:** 1992
SQ FT: 15,000
SALES (est): 1.2MM **Privately Held**
WEB: www.cammenga.com
SIC: 3829 5084 Measuring & controlling devices; controlling instruments & accessories

(G-3818)
CARHARTT INC (PA)
5750 Mercury Dr (48126-4167)
P.O. Box 600 (48121-0600)
PHONE..................313 271-8460
Mark Valade, *CEO*
Linda P Hubbard, *President*
Kamiko Freeman, *General Mgr*
Andi Donovan, *Senior VP*
Jennifer Piscopink, *Vice Pres*
◆ **EMP:** 450 **EST:** 1889
SQ FT: 56,000
SALES (est): 1.9B **Privately Held**
WEB: www.carhartt.com
SIC: 2326 2325 2329 Overalls & coveralls; dungarees: men's, youths' & boys'; jeans: men's, youths' & boys'; men's & boys' leather, wool & down-filled outerwear; coats (oiled fabric, leatherette, etc.): men's & boys'; hunting coats & vests, men's

(G-3819)
CHANDAS ENGINEERING INC
4800 Curtis St (48126-4125)
P.O. Box 1583 (48121-1583)
PHONE..................313 582-8666
Philip Pettyjohn, *President*
EMP: 10 **EST:** 1954
SALES (est): 539.8K **Privately Held**
WEB: www.chandas.com
SIC: 3519 8711 Internal combustion engines; aviation &/or aeronautical engineering

(G-3820)
CLEVELAND-CLIFFS STEEL CORP
Also Called: Dearborn Works
14661 Rotunda Dr (48126-1256)
P.O. Box 1699 (48121-1699)
PHONE..................313 317-8900
Denise Johnson, *Vice Pres*
David Pray, *Safety Mgr*
Bashar Alzihery, *Engineer*
Walter Gembarski, *Engineer*
James R Wainscott, *Branch Mgr*
EMP: 500
SALES (corp-wide): 5.3B **Publicly Held**
WEB: www.clevelandcliffs.com
SIC: 3312 Blast furnaces & steel mills
HQ: Cleveland-Cliffs Steel Corporation
200 Public Sq Ste 3300
Cleveland OH 44114

(G-3821)
CLEVELAND-CLIFFS STEEL CORP
Also Called: Tube City AK
4001 Miller Rd Ste 12 (48120-1461)
P.O. Box 8750, West Chester OH (45071-8750)
PHONE..................800 532-8857
Bruce Black, *Branch Mgr*
EMP: 1600
SALES (corp-wide): 5.3B **Publicly Held**
WEB: www.clevelandcliffs.com
SIC: 3312 Stainless steel; sheet or strip, steel, cold-rolled: own hot-rolled
HQ: Cleveland-Cliffs Steel Corporation
200 Public Sq Ste 3300
Cleveland OH 44114

(G-3822)
COREY
3125 Walnut St (48124-4322)
PHONE..................313 565-8501
Jeffrey Corey, *Principal*
EMP: 5 **EST:** 2010
SALES (est): 85.8K **Privately Held**
SIC: 2741 Miscellaneous publishing

(G-3823)
CUMMINS INC
3760 Wyoming St (48120-1419)
PHONE..................313 843-6200
Craig Henrikson, *Manager*
EMP: 5
SALES (corp-wide): 19.8B **Publicly Held**
WEB: www.cummins.com
SIC: 7538 3519 Diesel engine repair: automotive; internal combustion engines
PA: Cummins Inc.
500 Jackson St
Columbus IN 47201
812 377-5000

(G-3824)
DEARBORN OFFSET PRINTING INC
1946 Monroe St (48124-2917)
PHONE..................313 561-1173
Tim Cote, *President*
Margaret Cote, *Admin Sec*
EMP: 6 **EST:** 1952
SQ FT: 2,500
SALES (est): 150K **Privately Held**
WEB: www.dearbornoffset.com
SIC: 2752 Commercial printing, offset

(G-3825)
DEARBORNE CUMMINS
3760 Wyoming St (48120-1419)
PHONE..................313 843-6200
Don Jones, *Principal*
EMP: 10 **EST:** 2013
SALES (est): 205.8K **Privately Held**
WEB: www.cummins.com
SIC: 3714 Motor vehicle parts & accessories

(G-3826)
DELACO STEEL CORPORATION (PA)
8111 Tireman Ave Ste 1 (48126-1789)
PHONE..................313 491-1200
Gerald F Diez, *President*
Chris Currie, *Vice Pres*
Paul Florkowski, *Plant Supt*
Joseph Jezioro, *Plant Mgr*
Glenn Hejna, *Facilities Mgr*
EMP: 114 **EST:** 1970
SQ FT: 200,000
SALES (est): 54.9MM **Privately Held**
WEB: www.thediezgroup.com
SIC: 5051 3465 3312 Steel; automotive stampings; blast furnaces & steel mills

(G-3827)
DELPHI CORP
5800 Mercury Dr (48126-2757)
PHONE..................313 996-3429
EMP: 12 **EST:** 2019
SALES (est): 950K **Privately Held**
WEB: www.borgwarner.com
SIC: 3714 Motor vehicle parts & accessories

(G-3828)
DIAMOND BOUTIQUE
3200 Greenfield Rd # 300 (48120-1802)
PHONE..................313 451-4217
Diamond Clay, *Principal*
EMP: 7 **EST:** 2017
SALES (est): 170.2K **Privately Held**
WEB: www.shopthediamond.com
SIC: 5621 5099 2339 Boutiques; sunglasses; women's & misses' accessories

(G-3829)
DIE-MOLD-AUTOMATION COMPONENT
Also Called: N Forcer
14300 Henn St Ste A (48126-4521)
PHONE..................313 581-6510
Jessica Martin, *President*
Paul J Martin, *Vice Pres*
EMP: 5 **EST:** 1986
SQ FT: 19,000
SALES (est): 550.3K **Privately Held**
WEB: www.n-forcer.com
SIC: 3544 3443 Special dies & tools; fabricated plate work (boiler shop)

(G-3830)
DOUBLE EAGLE DEFENSE LLC (PA)
25205 Trowbridge St (48124-2414)
PHONE..................313 562-5550
EMP: 3
SALES (est): 1.8MM **Privately Held**
SIC: 3599 Supplier Of Production Prototype Metal Components And Assemblies

(G-3831)
DOUBLE EAGLE STEEL COATING CO
3000 Miller Rd (48120-1400)
PHONE..................313 203-9800
Bill Boege, *President*
EMP: 140 **EST:** 1986
SQ FT: 300,000
SALES (est): 19.7MM **Privately Held**
WEB: www.ussteel.com
SIC: 3479 Galvanizing of iron, steel or end-formed products

(G-3832)
E C MOORE COMPANY (PA)
Also Called: Challenge Packaging Division
13325 Leonard St (48126-3633)
P.O. Box 353 (48121-0353)
PHONE..................313 581-7878
George G Aho, *President*
Dan Noble, *Opers Mgr*
Kathleen Douglas, *Director*
▲ **EMP:** 44 **EST:** 1894
SQ FT: 5,100
SALES (est): 8MM **Privately Held**
WEB: www.ecmoore.com
SIC: 3291 3843 Abrasive products; abrasive points, wheels & disks, dental

(G-3833)
EDDIES QUICK STOP INC
5517 Middlesex St (48126-5021)
PHONE..................313 712-1818
Daher Faraj, *Principal*
EMP: 4 **EST:** 2013
SQ FT: 3,000
SALES (est): 94.6K **Privately Held**
SIC: 3715 Truck trailers

(G-3834)
EDENS POLITICAL
360 Devonshire St (48124-1084)
PHONE..................313 277-0700
David Eden, *Owner*
Arlene Eden, *Co-Owner*
EMP: 4 **EST:** 1975
SQ FT: 1,000
SALES (est): 162.6K **Privately Held**
SIC: 2759 Screen printing

(G-3835)
EDW C LEVY CO (PA)
Also Called: Charleston Mill Services
9300 Dix (48120-1528)
PHONE..................313 429-2200
Edward C Levy Jr, *President*
Robert Scholz, *Vice Pres*
S E Weiner, *Vice Pres*
Joe Stachurski, *Plant Mgr*
Ryan Hyatt, *Production*
▲ **EMP:** 357 **EST:** 1946
SQ FT: 7,500
SALES (est): 521.9MM **Privately Held**
WEB: www.edwclevy.com
SIC: 5032 2951 3295 Aggregate; asphalt & asphaltic paving mixtures (not from refineries); blast furnace slag

(G-3836)
ENERGY DEVELOPMENT ASSOC LLC
15201 Century Dr (48120-1232)
PHONE..................313 354-2644
Kent Harmon, *CEO*
Thao Attard, *VP Sales*
Anil Tulandhar, *CTO*
Neil Tuldhar, *CTO*
Ken Farkas, *Officer*
EMP: 8 **EST:** 2009
SALES (est): 423.1K **Privately Held**
WEB: www.energydevelopmentassociates.com
SIC: 8711 3822 Electrical or electronic engineering; energy cutoff controls, residential or commercial types

(G-3837)
ENVISIONTEC US LLC
15162 S Commerce Dr (48120-1237)
PHONE..................313 436-4300
Ali El Siblani, *CEO*
Kent Lindbergh, *Partner*
Madalyne Ridella, *Engineer*
Michael Gasparovich, *Accountant*
Sheryl Kearney, *Human Resources*
EMP: 65 **EST:** 2003
SALES (est): 1.2MM
SALES (corp-wide): 16.4MM **Publicly Held**
WEB: www.envisiontec.com
SIC: 3577 2821 3544 7699 Plotters, computer; printers, computer; data conversion equipment, media-to-media: computer; plastics materials & resins; forms (molds), for foundry & plastics working machinery; professional instrument repair services
PA: Desktop Metal, Inc.
63 3rd Ave
Burlington MA 01803
978 224-1244

(G-3838)
EPPINGER MFG CO
6340 Schaefer Rd (48126-2285)
PHONE..................313 582-3205
Karen Eppinger, *President*
Jennifer Buftamante, *Admin Sec*
EMP: 18 **EST:** 1906
SQ FT: 9,000
SALES (est): 1.2MM **Privately Held**
WEB: www.dardevle.com
SIC: 3949 Fishing tackle, general

(G-3839)
FALCON TRUCKING COMPANY (PA)
9300 Dix (48120-1528)
PHONE..................313 843-7200
S Evan Weiner, *President*
Robert Flucker, *Treasurer*
EMP: 8 **EST:** 1967
SQ FT: 10,000
SALES (est): 18.1MM **Privately Held**
SIC: 1442 4212 Sand mining; local trucking, without storage

(G-3840)
FIRST RESPONSE MED SUPS LLC
2020 N Lafayette St (48128-1148)
PHONE..................313 731-2554
Mirza Salmaci, *President*
EMP: 10 **EST:** 2013
SALES (est): 345.1K **Privately Held**
SIC: 5661 3842 Shoes, orthopedic; foot appliances, orthopedic

(G-3841)
FORD INVESTMENT ENTPS CORP
1 American Rd (48126-2701)
PHONE..................973 764-8783
Samira Dghaily, *Principal*
EMP: 5 **EST:** 2016
SALES (est): 87.2K **Privately Held**
WEB: www.ford.com
SIC: 3711 Motor vehicles & car bodies

(G-3842)
FORD MOTOR COMPANY (PA)
1 American Rd (48126-2701)
P.O. Box 685 (48121-0685)
PHONE..................313 322-3000

Dearborn - Wayne County (G-3843)

GEOGRAPHIC SECTION

William Clay Ford Jr, *Ch of Bd*
James D Farley Jr, *President*
Anning Chen, *President*
Kumar Galhotra, *President*
Neale Hill, *President*
EMP: 8000 **EST:** 1903
SALES (est): 127.1B **Publicly Held**
WEB: www.ford.com
SIC: 3711 3713 3714 6153 Automobile assembly, including specialty automobiles; truck & bus bodies; motor vehicle parts & accessories; financing of dealers by motor vehicle manufacturers organ.; buying of installment notes; financing: automobiles, furniture, etc., not a deposit bank; automobile loans, including insurance; passenger car leasing

(G-3843)
FORD MOTOR COMPANY
3001 Miller Rd (48120-1496)
PHONE..................313 594-0050
Jim Padilla, *President*
Fnu Brinda, *Engineer*
Kenneth Cordry, *Engineer*
Mike Pollari, *Engineer*
Linda McCombs, *Finance Spvr*
EMP: 1297
SQ FT: 2,100,000
SALES (corp-wide): 127.1B **Publicly Held**
WEB: www.ford.com
SIC: 3714 Motor vehicle parts & accessories
PA: Ford Motor Company
1 American Rd
Dearborn MI 48126
313 322-3000

(G-3844)
FORD MOTOR COMPANY
21175 Oakwood Blvd (48124-4079)
P.O. Box 1899 (48121-1899)
PHONE..................313 322-7715
Ryan Haller, *Purchasing*
Jay Moore, *Purchasing*
Noori Pandit, *Engineer*
Brian Amidon, *Manager*
Michele Katynski, *Technology*
EMP: 7
SALES (corp-wide): 127.1B **Publicly Held**
WEB: www.ford.com
SIC: 3711 3713 Motor vehicles & car bodies; truck & bus bodies
PA: Ford Motor Company
1 American Rd
Dearborn MI 48126
313 322-3000

(G-3845)
FORUM AND LINK INC
12740 W Wrren Ave Ste 100 (48126)
PHONE..................313 945-5465
Muhannad Haimour, *CEO*
EMP: 8 **EST:** 2004
SALES (est): 408.2K **Privately Held**
WEB: www.forumandlink.com
SIC: 2711 8748 Newspapers, publishing & printing; communications consulting

(G-3846)
GLASS RECYCLERS LTD
6465 Wyoming St (48126-2341)
PHONE..................313 584-3434
Robert S Rahaim, *President*
Daniel Easterly, *Vice Pres*
Douglas Rahaim, *Vice Pres*
EMP: 34 **EST:** 1993
SQ FT: 35,000
SALES (est): 1.5MM **Privately Held**
WEB: www.glassrecyclers.net
SIC: 3231 4953 Products of purchased glass; recycling, waste materials

(G-3847)
GLOBAL RESTAURANT GROUP INC
13250 Rotunda Dr (48120-1230)
PHONE..................313 271-2777
Ahmad Hodroj, *President*
EMP: 9 **EST:** 2007

SALES (est): 196.3K **Privately Held**
SIC: 2032 2086 5141 5149 Ethnic foods: canned, jarred, etc.; carbonated beverages, nonalcoholic: bottled & canned; food brokers; beverages, except coffee & tea; soft drinks

(G-3848)
GLOBAL THREAD GAGE INC
25302 Trowbridge St (48124-2415)
PHONE..................313 438-6789
EMP: 8 **EST:** 2019
SALES (est): 250.7K **Privately Held**
WEB: www.globalthreadgage.com
SIC: 3545 Machine tool accessories

(G-3849)
GREAT LAKES MECHANICAL CORP (PA)
Also Called: Great Lkes Htg Colg Rfrgn Shtm
3800 Maple St (48126-3672)
PHONE..................313 581-1400
Mark Perpich, *President*
Harold J Perpich, *Chairman*
George Perpich II, *Vice Pres*
EMP: 150 **EST:** 1955
SQ FT: 50,000
SALES (est): 28.8MM **Privately Held**
WEB: www.greatlakesmechanical.com
SIC: 1711 3444 Mechanical contractor; sheet metalwork

(G-3850)
HOLLINGSWORTH CONTAINER LLC
14225 W Warren Ave (48126-1456)
PHONE..................313 768-1400
Daniel Cote, *Opers Staff*
Donna Randall, *Program Mgr*
Steven Barr,
Charles Angell,
Mike McNamara,
EMP: 4 **EST:** 1997
SALES (est): 2.6MM **Privately Held**
WEB: www.hollingsworthllc.com
SIC: 3499 Boxes for packing & shipping, metal
PA: Hollingsworth, Inc.
14225 W Warren Ave
Dearborn MI 48126

(G-3851)
HT COMPUTING SERVICES
23253 Edward St (48128-1357)
PHONE..................313 563-0087
J Dove, *Manager*
EMP: 7 **EST:** 2000
SALES (est): 373.8K **Privately Held**
SIC: 7372 Prepackaged software

(G-3852)
IBIDLTD-BLUE GREEN ENERGY (PA)
6659 Schaefer Rd Ste 110 (48126-1812)
PHONE..................909 547-5160
Kelley Elisabeth, *Principal*
EMP: 39 **EST:** 2018
SALES (est): 118.4K **Privately Held**
WEB: www.internationalbrandidltd.com
SIC: 2869 Fuels

(G-3853)
ILLUSION SIGNS & GRAPHIC INC
14241 Michigan Ave (48126-3524)
PHONE..................313 443-0567
Eihab Harazi, *CEO*
Shehad Harazi, *President*
EMP: 9 **EST:** 2018
SALES (est): 620.6K **Privately Held**
WEB: www.illusionsign.com
SIC: 3993 Signs, not made in custom sign painting shops

(G-3854)
INTELLIGENT DYNAMICS LLC
456 Berkley St (48124-1397)
PHONE..................313 727-9920
Michael A Staszel, *Mng Member*
Michael Staszel, *Manager*
EMP: 10 **EST:** 2009
SALES (est): 250K **Privately Held**
WEB: www.intelligentdynamics.com
SIC: 3829 Measuring & controlling devices

(G-3855)
IRIS DESIGN & PRINT INC
24730 Michigan Ave (48124-1750)
PHONE..................313 277-0505
EMP: 8
SQ FT: 5,600
SALES (est): 700K **Privately Held**
SIC: 2752 7336 2731 7389 Lithographic Coml Print Coml Art/Graphic Design Book-Publishing/Printing Business Services

(G-3856)
JIT STEEL CORP
8111 Tireman Ave Ste 1 (48126-1789)
PHONE..................313 491-3212
Gerald F Diez, *President*
EMP: 10 **EST:** 1985
SALES (est): 3.3MM
SALES (corp-wide): 54.9MM **Privately Held**
WEB: www.thediezgroup.com
SIC: 5051 3312 Steel; blast furnaces & steel mills
PA: Delaco Steel Corporation
8111 Tireman Ave Ste 1
Dearborn MI 48126
313 491-1200

(G-3857)
KENWAL PICKLING LLC
8223 W Warren Ave (48126-1615)
PHONE..................313 739-1040
Kenneth Eisenberg,
EMP: 50 **EST:** 2000
SQ FT: 130,000
SALES (est): 6.1MM **Privately Held**
WEB: www.kenwal.com
SIC: 3471 Plating & polishing

(G-3858)
KLANN
1439 S Telegraph Rd (48124-1808)
PHONE..................313 565-4135
Kennith Klann, *Principal*
Debbie Meadows, *Accounting Mgr*
Karla Pitsenberger, *Manager*
Jeff Burdettex, *Maintence Staff*
EMP: 6 **EST:** 2010
SALES (est): 75.2K **Privately Held**
SIC: 3089 Injection molding of plastics

(G-3859)
L A MARTIN COMPANY
14400 Henn St (48126-1887)
PHONE..................313 581-3444
Paul J Martin, *President*
Laura Martin, *Corp Secy*
Frank Wampler, *Manager*
EMP: 32 **EST:** 1928
SQ FT: 22,000
SALES (est): 1.6MM **Privately Held**
WEB: www.lamartincompany.com
SIC: 3451 Screw machine products

(G-3860)
LCA INTERNATIONAL PUBLISHING
5218 Royal Vale Ln (48124-4302)
PHONE..................313 908-4583
Cheryl Bologna, *Principal*
EMP: 5 **EST:** 2011
SALES (est): 133.2K **Privately Held**
SIC: 2741 Miscellaneous publishing

(G-3861)
LEVY ENVIRONMENTAL SERVICES CO
9300 Dix (48120-1528)
PHONE..................313 429-2272
S Evan Weiner, *President*
EMP: 23 **EST:** 1994
SALES (est): 3.8MM **Privately Held**
SIC: 1442 Construction sand & gravel

(G-3862)
LEVY INDIANA SLAG CO (HQ)
Also Called: Ashland Slag Company
9300 Dix (48120-1528)
PHONE..................313 843-7200
S Evan Weiner, *President*
Edward C Levy Jr, *Chairman*
Robert P Scholz, *CFO*
▲ **EMP:** 100 **EST:** 1997

SALES (est): 51.9MM
SALES (corp-wide): 521.9MM **Privately Held**
WEB: www.edwclevy.com
SIC: 1411 Limestone, dimension-quarrying
PA: Edw. C. Levy Co.
9300 Dix
Dearborn MI 48120
313 429-2200

(G-3863)
LITE N GO INC
5410 Argyle St (48126-3146)
PHONE..................248 414-7540
Hala Abdallah, *Owner*
EMP: 5 **EST:** 2006
SALES (est): 157.3K **Privately Held**
SIC: 3999 Cigarette & cigar products & accessories

(G-3864)
LYON SAND & GRAVEL CO (PA)
Also Called: Oakland Sand & Gravel
9300 Dix (48120-1528)
PHONE..................313 843-7200
S Evan Weiner, *President*
Robert Flucker, *Vice Pres*
Edward C Levy Jr, *Vice Pres*
Scott Carson, *Opers Mgr*
EMP: 3 **EST:** 1961
SQ FT: 5,000
SALES (est): 10MM **Privately Held**
SIC: 1442 Gravel mining

(G-3865)
M BEARD SOLUTIONS LLC ◯
3200 Greenfield Rd # 300 (48120-1802)
PHONE..................734 441-0660
Marcus Beard, *Principal*
EMP: 5 **EST:** 2021
SALES (est): 74.4K **Privately Held**
SIC: 2834 Solutions, pharmaceutical

(G-3866)
M M CUSTOM CANVAS SHRINK
5402 Reuter St (48126-3324)
PHONE..................734 658-0497
EMP: 4 **EST:** 2016
SALES (est): 46.5K **Privately Held**
SIC: 2211 Canvas

(G-3867)
MACOMB SMOKED MEATS LLC
2450 Wyoming St (48120-1518)
PHONE..................313 842-2375
Tony Kowalewski, *Sales Staff*
Clifford T Meier, *Mng Member*
Katherine Kosch, *Manager*
Amy Decapo, *Planning*
Justin Havlick,
EMP: 80 **EST:** 2011
SQ FT: 30,000
SALES (est): 8.9MM **Privately Held**
WEB: www.dearbornbrand.com
SIC: 2013 Sausages from purchased meat

(G-3868)
MARK LAND INDUSTRIES INC
5433 Miller Rd (48126-3351)
PHONE..................313 615-0503
Qais Alsawafy, *President*
Mike Sobosky, *Sales Staff*
EMP: 35 **EST:** 2000
SQ FT: 50,000
SALES (est): 5.5MM **Privately Held**
WEB: www.landmi.com
SIC: 5531 4226 7389 3714 Automotive parts; special warehousing & storage; packaging & labeling services; tie rods, motor vehicle

(G-3869)
MD HILLER CORP
2021 Monroe St Ste 103 (48124-2926)
PHONE..................877 751-9010
EMP: 5 **EST:** 2015
SALES (est): 262.6K **Privately Held**
WEB: www.mdhillerrx.com
SIC: 2834 Vitamin, nutrient & hematinic preparations for human use

(G-3870)
METAL PREP TECHNOLOGY INC
621 Nightingale St (48128-1562)
PHONE..................313 843-2890
Stanley S Luckow, *President*

▲ = Import ▼ = Export
◆ = Import/Export

Al Miller, *Vice Pres*
EMP: 5
SQ FT: 34,000
SALES (est): 80.8K **Privately Held**
SIC: 3471 3398 Finishing, metals or formed products; shot peening (treating steel to reduce fatigue)

(G-3871)
METALFAB INC (PA)
6900 Chase Rd (48126-4504)
PHONE.................................313 381-7579
James C Pinkney, *President*
EMP: 7 **EST:** 1995
SQ FT: 4,000
SALES (est): 1.6MM **Privately Held**
WEB: www.metalfabinc.org
SIC: 3441 Fabricated structural metal

(G-3872)
MICHELS INC (PA)
Also Called: M J Diamonds
18900 Michigan Ave K103 (48126-3929)
PHONE.................................313 441-3620
Michael Ansara, *President*
Hilda Ansara, *Admin Sec*
▲ **EMP:** 19 **EST:** 1976
SQ FT: 2,400
SALES (est): 4.5MM **Privately Held**
WEB: www.mjdiamonds.com
SIC: 5944 3911 Jewelry, precious stones & precious metals; jewelry apparel

(G-3873)
MILLER DESIGNWORKS LLC
Also Called: Spectrum Signs & Designs
3001 S Gulley Rd Ste D (48124-4534)
PHONE.................................313 562-4000
Don Boshaw, *Manager*
Roger L Miller,
EMP: 8 **EST:** 2002 **Privately Held**
SIC: 3993 Signs, not made in custom sign painting shops

(G-3874)
MOTOR CITY DESIGNS LLC
6659 Schaefer Rd Ste 1078 (48126-1812)
PHONE.................................313 686-1025
Charlton Boyer, *CEO*
Charlton E Boyer,
EMP: 4 **EST:** 2020
SALES (est): 10K **Privately Held**
SIC: 3161 Clothing & apparel carrying cases

(G-3875)
NATION WIDE FUEL INC
6341 Barrie St (48126-2033)
PHONE.................................734 721-7110
Ali Aboutaam, *Principal*
EMP: 4
SALES (est): 221.6K **Privately Held**
SIC: 2869 Fuels

(G-3876)
NEW YASMEEN DETROIT INC
Also Called: New Yasmeen Bakery
13900 W Warren Ave (48126-1455)
PHONE.................................313 582-6035
Mohamed Seblini, *President*
Hussain Seblini, *Corp Secy*
Ahmad Seblini, *Vice Pres*
EMP: 17 **EST:** 1985
SQ FT: 10,000
SALES (est): 773.8K **Privately Held**
WEB: www.yasmeenbakery.com
SIC: 5461 5149 2051 Bread; bakery products; bread, cake & related products

(G-3877)
NORTH STAR CANDLE COMPANY LLC
2030 Dacosta St (48128-1321)
PHONE.................................248 430-4321
EMP: 4 **EST:** 2016
SALES (est): 63K **Privately Held**
WEB: www.nscandleco.com
SIC: 3999 Candles

(G-3878)
NUTS & COFFEE GALLERY
13041 W Warren Ave (48126-1536)
PHONE.................................313 581-3212
Al Hashem, *Owner*
EMP: 5 **EST:** 1985
SQ FT: 360
SALES (est): 413.6K **Privately Held**
WEB: www.hashems.com
SIC: 4813 5149 5411 2099 ; spices & seasonings; grocery stores, independent; seasonings & spices; spices, including grinding; coffee; spices & herbs

(G-3879)
OAKWOOD METAL FABRICATING CO (PA)
Also Called: Oakwood Group, The
1100 Oakwood Blvd (48124-2820)
PHONE.................................313 561-7740
Richard Audi, *President*
Phil Biondi, *Business Mgr*
Jonathan Hsieh, *Purch Agent*
Simon Michalik, *Engineer*
Dane Winbigler, *Senior Engr*
▲ **EMP:** 25 **EST:** 1945
SQ FT: 17,000
SALES (est): 89.6MM **Privately Held**
WEB: www.theoakwoodgroup.com
SIC: 3441 3714 3089 Fabricated structural metal; motor vehicle engines & parts; injection molded finished plastic products; injection molding of plastics

(G-3880)
OFFICIAL BRAND LIMITED
Also Called: Official Media Solutions
3347 Heritage Pkwy (48124-3190)
PHONE.................................734 224-9942
Jordan Woods, *Owner*
Jordan R Woods, *Owner*
EMP: 5 **EST:** 2020
SALES (est): 56K **Privately Held**
SIC: 5734 3571 7336 Software, computer games; computers, digital, analog or hybrid; graphic arts & related design

(G-3881)
OPIO LLC
3 Parklane Blvd (48126-2506)
PHONE.................................313 433-1098
Basel Alyasin, *CEO*
Bilal Hashwi, *Mng Member*
EMP: 10 **EST:** 2018
SALES (est): 344K **Privately Held**
SIC: 7372 Application computer software

(G-3882)
PARAMOUNT SIGNS LLC
15145 Prospect St (48126-2921)
PHONE.................................734 548-1721
Karrar Al-Banawi, *Principal*
EMP: 5 **EST:** 2016
SALES (est): 81.6K **Privately Held**
WEB: www.paramountsigns.net
SIC: 3993 Signs & advertising specialties

(G-3883)
PEAK INDUSTRIES CO INC
5320 Oakman Blvd (48126-3394)
PHONE.................................313 846-8666
James Kostaroff, *CEO*
Timothy Kostaroff, *President*
EMP: 42 **EST:** 1965
SQ FT: 50,000
SALES (est): 1.3MM **Privately Held**
WEB: www.peakindustries.com
SIC: 3544 3535 3548 3822 Jigs & fixtures; conveyors & conveying equipment; welding apparatus; auto controls regulating residntl & coml environmt & applncs; relays & industrial controls; machine tool accessories

(G-3884)
PRC COMMERCIAL SERVICES LLC
3011 Syracuse St (48124-3303)
PHONE.................................313 445-1760
Christopher Paulsen, *Principal*
EMP: 5 **EST:** 2011
SALES (est): 42.8K **Privately Held**
SIC: 8999 1389 Artists & artists' studios; construction, repair & dismantling services

(G-3885)
PRICE INDUSTRIES LLC
3301 Lincoln St (48124-3507)
PHONE.................................313 706-9862
Benjamin Robert Price, *Principal*
EMP: 4 **EST:** 2015
SALES (est): 60.6K **Privately Held**
WEB: www.priceindustries.com
SIC: 3999 Manufacturing industries

(G-3886)
PRINT ZONE
23936 Michigan Ave (48124-1833)
PHONE.................................313 278-0800
EMP: 4 **EST:** 2017
SALES (est): 74.7K **Privately Held**
SIC: 2752 Commercial printing, lithographic

(G-3887)
PRINTXPRESS INC
7120 Chase Rd (48126-4505)
PHONE.................................313 846-1644
Ali Ashkar, *CEO*
EMP: 4 **EST:** 2002
SALES (est): 346.8K **Privately Held**
WEB: www.store.cmykusa.com
SIC: 7336 2759 Graphic arts & related design; commercial printing; promotional printing

(G-3888)
QUALITY PRECISION INC
5171 Miller Rd (48126-3736)
PHONE.................................313 254-9141
Walid Houssami, *Principal*
EMP: 7 **EST:** 2017
SALES (est): 138.9K **Privately Held**
WEB: www.qualityprecisioninc.com
SIC: 3599 Machine shop, jobbing & repair

(G-3889)
QUICK DRAW TARPAULIN SYSTEMS (PA)
10200 Ford Rd (48126-3333)
PHONE.................................313 945-0766
Walt Demonte, *President*
Sheri Le Blanc, *Vice Pres*
Sheri Leblanc, *Vice Pres*
Luc Billard, *Manager*
▲ **EMP:** 15 **EST:** 1999
SQ FT: 20,000
SALES (est): 9.3MM **Privately Held**
WEB: www.quickdrawtarps.com
SIC: 2394 Tarpaulins, fabric: made from purchased materials

(G-3890)
RHOMBUS ENERGY SOLUTIONS INC
15201 Century Dr (48120-1232)
PHONE.................................313 406-3292
Anil Tuladhar, *VP Engrg*
Kent Harmin, *Branch Mgr*
EMP: 7
SALES (corp-wide): 12.2MM **Privately Held**
WEB: www.rhombusenergysolutions.com
SIC: 8711 3822 Engineering services; energy cutoff controls, residential or commercial types
PA: Rhombus Energy Solutions, Inc
10915 Technology Pl
San Diego CA 92127
858 353-1002

(G-3891)
S& A FUEL LLC
10005 W Warren Ave (48126-1653)
PHONE.................................313 945-6555
Iman Zreik, *Principal*
EMP: 6 **EST:** 2010
SALES (est): 350.9K **Privately Held**
SIC: 2869 Fuels

(G-3892)
SAJA NATURAL HERBS
10820 W Warren Ave (48126-1516)
PHONE.................................313 769-6411
Ali Sobh, *Owner*
EMP: 4 **EST:** 2015
SALES (est): 146.8K **Privately Held**
WEB: www.sajaherbs.com
SIC: 2833 Drugs & herbs: grading, grinding & milling

(G-3893)
SAMS WELDING INC
6903 Hartwell St (48126-1884)
PHONE.................................313 350-5010
EMP: 4 **EST:** 2017
SALES (est): 28.1K **Privately Held**
SIC: 7692 Welding repair

(G-3894)
SECURE CROSSING RES & DEV INC
1122 Mason St (48124-2801)
PHONE.................................248 535-3800
Robert G Lorente, *President*
Kathleen Wantuck, *Marketing Staff*
Randall E Reeves, *CTO*
EMP: 14 **EST:** 2005
SALES (est): 700K **Privately Held**
WEB: www.securecrossing.com
SIC: 3699 Security devices

(G-3895)
SERVICES TO ENHANCE POTENTIAL (PA)
Also Called: Step
2941 S Gulley Rd (48124-3160)
PHONE.................................313 278-3040
Brent Mikulski, *President*
Timothy Kachmarik, *Mfg Staff*
Douglas Rousell, *CFO*
James Grice, *Exec Dir*
Cheryl Fregolle, *Director*
EMP: 8 **EST:** 1972
SQ FT: 20,000
SALES (est): 17MM **Privately Held**
WEB: www.stepcentral.org
SIC: 3999 5932 7349 8322 Bric-a-brac; used merchandise stores; building & office cleaning services; adult day care center; job training & vocational rehabilitation services

(G-3896)
SHATILA FOOD PRODUCTS INC (PA)
8505 W Warren Ave (48126-1617)
PHONE.................................313 934-1520
Riad Shatila, *President*
▲ **EMP:** 50 **EST:** 1990
SQ FT: 48,000
SALES (est): 22.6MM **Privately Held**
WEB: www.shatila.com
SIC: 5149 5461 2052 2051 Bakery products; bakeries; cookies & crackers; bread, cake & related products

(G-3897)
SMS TECHNICAL SERVICE LLC
4001 Miller Rd (48120-1461)
PHONE.................................313 322-4890
EMP: 11 **EST:** 2016
SALES (est): 168.4K **Privately Held**
SIC: 3547 Ferrous & nonferrous mill equipment, auxiliary

(G-3898)
SND MANUFACTURING LLC
23000 Arlington St (48128-1806)
PHONE.................................313 996-5088
Neil Shuell, *Mng Member*
EMP: 6 **EST:** 2006
SQ FT: 3,000
SALES (est): 400K **Privately Held**
SIC: 2431 Doors & door parts & trim, wood

(G-3899)
SOUTH PARK SALES & MFG INC
6900 Chase Rd (48126-4504)
PHONE.................................313 381-7579
James Pinkney, *President*
Antoinette Pinkney, *Corp Secy*
EMP: 5 **EST:** 1972
SQ FT: 2,000
SALES (est): 731K **Privately Held**
SIC: 5084 3498 3451 3441 Machine tools & accessories; tube fabricating (contract bending & shaping); screw machine products; fabricated structural metal; paperboard mills

(G-3900)
SPARKLING WOODSBY LLC
700 Claremont St (48124-1579)
PHONE.................................313 724-0455
Jonathon Husby, *Principal*
EMP: 5 **EST:** 2015
SALES (est): 41.5K **Privately Held**
SIC: 2499 Wood products

Dearborn - Wayne County (G-3901)

(G-3901)
STEVES BACKROOM LLC
13250 Rotunda Dr (48120-1230)
PHONE...................................313 527-7240
Andre Dixon, *General Mgr*
EMP: 10 **EST:** 2015
SQ FT: 7,000
SALES (est): 449.8K **Privately Held**
SIC: 2099 Ready-to-eat meals, salads & sandwiches

(G-3902)
SUPERIOR FUELS LLC
6833 Kingsley St (48126-1940)
PHONE...................................586 738-6851
Haykal Awad, *Administration*
EMP: 5 **EST:** 2015
SALES (est): 154.4K **Privately Held**
SIC: 2869 Fuels

(G-3903)
THERMO ARL US INC
15300 Rotunda Dr Ste 301 (48120-1239)
PHONE...................................313 336-3901
EMP: 12
SALES (corp-wide): 5.6MM **Privately Held**
SIC: 3826 3823 Mfg Analytical Instruments Mfg Process Control Instruments
PA: Thermo Arl U.S. Inc.
    1400 Northpoint Pkwy # 50
    West Palm Beach FL 33407
    800 532-4752

(G-3904)
THINK NORTH AMERICA INC (PA)
Also Called: Think NA
22226 Garrison St (48124-2208)
PHONE...................................313 565-6781
Barry Engle, *CEO*
Richard Canny, *Chairman*
EMP: 20 **EST:** 2009
SALES (est): 3.5MM **Privately Held**
SIC: 3711 Motor vehicles & car bodies

(G-3905)
THOMAS INDUSTRIAL ROLLS INC
8526 Brandt St (48126-2330)
PHONE...................................313 584-9696
Dennis Simpson, *President*
Debbie Simpson, *Vice Pres*
Stephanie Crain, *Manager*
John Boike, *Supervisor*
▲ **EMP:** 15 **EST:** 1990
SQ FT: 20,000
SALES (est): 3.3MM **Privately Held**
WEB: www.nccmco.com
SIC: 3469 Metal stampings

(G-3906)
UNIVESITY MICHIGAN-DEARBORN
Also Called: Michigan Journal, The
4901 Evergreen Rd # 2130 (48128-2406)
PHONE...................................313 593-5428
Domenico Grasso, *Chancellor*
Kristina Calvird, *Manager*
EMP: 10
SALES (corp-wide): 7.9B **Privately Held**
WEB: www.umdearborn.edu
SIC: 2711 8221 Newspapers, publishing & printing; university
HQ: Univesity Of Michigan-Dearborn
    4901 Evergreen Rd
    Dearborn MI 48128
    313 593-5000

(G-3907)
USA CUSTOM CABINET INC
5404 Maple St (48126-3202)
PHONE...................................313 945-9796
EMP: 4 **EST:** 2008
SALES (est): 13.3K **Privately Held**
SIC: 2434 Wood kitchen cabinets

(G-3908)
USA HEALTH LLC (PA)
Also Called: 24 Hr Health
9 Edgerton Ln (48120-1021)
PHONE...................................248 846-0575
Khoder Hamka, *Mng Member*
EMP: 5 **EST:** 2018
SALES (est): 401.6K **Privately Held**
SIC: 2834 Vitamin preparations

(G-3909)
VERTEX INDUSTRIES INC
15080 N Commerce Dr (48120-1251)
PHONE...................................248 838-1827
EMP: 5 **EST:** 2017
SALES (est): 49.9K **Privately Held**
WEB: www.hometheaterinstallerbirmingham.com
SIC: 3999 Manufacturing industries

(G-3910)
VISTEON SYSTEMS LLC
5500 Auto Club Dr (48126-2779)
PHONE...................................313 755-9500
Rich Wood, *Engineer*
Kevin Singer,
▲ **EMP:** 150 **EST:** 1999
SALES (est): 47.7MM
SALES (corp-wide): 2.5B **Publicly Held**
WEB: www.visteon.com
SIC: 3711 Motor vehicles & car bodies
PA: Visteon Corporation
    1 Village Center Dr
    Van Buren Twp MI 48111
    734 627-7384

(G-3911)
VITESCO TECHNOLOGIES USA LLC
15001 N Commerce Dr (48120-1226)
PHONE...................................313 583-5980
Gregory Razook, *Engineer*
EMP: 107
SALES (corp-wide): 8.8B **Privately Held**
SIC: 3714 Motor vehicle parts & accessories
HQ: Vitesco Technologies Usa, Llc
    2400 Executive Hills Dr
    Auburn Hills MI 48326
    248 209-4000

(G-3912)
VORTECH PHARMACEUTICAL LTD
6851 Chase Rd (48126-1748)
P.O. Box 189 (48121-0189)
PHONE...................................313 584-4088
John A Macneil, *President*
Viberta Macneil, *Vice Pres*
Brian Jones, *Marketing Staff*
Blair Harding, *General Counsel*
EMP: 15 **EST:** 1982
SQ FT: 12,000
SALES (est): 1.3MM **Privately Held**
WEB: www.vortechpharm.com
SIC: 2834 Pharmaceutical preparations

(G-3913)
W W WILLIAMS COMPANY LLC
4000 Stecker St (48126-3803)
PHONE...................................313 584-6150
Alan Gatlin, *CEO*
L Ed McIntyre, *Manager*
EMP: 7
SALES (corp-wide): 1.4B **Privately Held**
WEB: www.wwilliams.com
SIC: 3519 Internal combustion engines
HQ: The W W Williams Company Llc
    5025 Bradenton Ave # 130
    Dublin OH 43017
    614 228-5000

(G-3914)
WARREN CITY FUEL
134 N Silvery Ln (48128-1536)
PHONE...................................586 759-4759
Hussein Beydoun, *Principal*
EMP: 4 **EST:** 2010
SALES (est): 95.6K **Privately Held**
SIC: 2869 Fuels

(G-3915)
WATER DEPARTMENT
Also Called: Dearborn Water Department
2951 Greenfield Rd (48120-1318)
PHONE...................................313 943-2307
Samuel Smalley, *Manager*
EMP: 13 **EST:** 1989
SALES (est): 118.2K **Privately Held**
WEB: www.cityofdearborn.org
SIC: 3561 Pumps, domestic: water or sump

(G-3916)
WOLVERINE ADVANCED MTLS LLC (DH)
5850 Mercury Dr Ste 250 (48126-2980)
PHONE...................................313 749-6100
Grant Beard, *CEO*
Remi Riou, *General Mgr*
Abdul-Hafiz Afaneh, *Vice Pres*
Laurent Crosnier, *Vice Pres*
Brian Knox, *Vice Pres*
◆ **EMP:** 50 **EST:** 2006
SALES (est): 145.6MM
SALES (corp-wide): 2.4B **Publicly Held**
WEB: www.wamglobal.com
SIC: 3559 3694 Automotive related machinery; automotive electrical equipment
HQ: Itt Llc
    1133 Westchester Ave N-100
    White Plains NY 10604
    914 641-2000

(G-3917)
YOGURTOWN INC
22231 Watsonia St (48128-1415)
PHONE...................................313 908-9376
Mahmoud Nasser, *Principal*
EMP: 10 **EST:** 2012
SALES (est): 823.8K **Privately Held**
WEB: www.myyogurtown.com
SIC: 2026 Yogurt

Dearborn Heights
Wayne County

(G-3918)
ABC GRINDING INC
26950 Van Born Rd (48125-1206)
PHONE...................................313 295-1060
Mike Resetar, *Principal*
EMP: 7 **EST:** 2007
SALES (est): 302.9K **Privately Held**
SIC: 3599 Grinding castings for the trade

(G-3919)
ALLEGRA-MARKETING DESIGN PRINT
22250 Ford Rd (48127-2420)
PHONE...................................313 561-8000
Mike Hurite, *Owner*
EMP: 6 **EST:** 2007
SALES (est): 86.7K **Privately Held**
WEB: www.allegramarketingprint.com
SIC: 2752 Commercial printing, offset

(G-3920)
ARMORED GROUP LLC
2727 S Beech Daly St (48125-1156)
PHONE...................................602 840-2271
Robert Pazderka, *CEO*
Jeff Carnicom, *COO*
Jacque Hughes, *Vice Pres*
Jennifer Barnes-Spicer, *Controller*
Jennifer Spicer, *Controller*
◆ **EMP:** 50 **EST:** 2004
SQ FT: 144,000
SALES (est): 8.8MM **Privately Held**
WEB: www.armoredcars.com
SIC: 3711 Cars, armored, assembly of

(G-3921)
AUGUST COMMUNICATIONS INC
Also Called: Allegra-Marketingdesign Print
22250 Ford Rd (48127-2420)
PHONE...................................313 561-8000
Michael Hurite, *President*
EMP: 6 **EST:** 2008
SALES (est): 634.1K **Privately Held**
WEB: www.allegramarketingprint.com
SIC: 2752 7334 Commercial printing, offset; photocopying & duplicating services

(G-3922)
DEARBORN TOTAL AUTO SVC CTR
23416 Van Born Rd (48125-2353)
PHONE...................................313 291-6300
George Ascione, *President*
EMP: 10 **EST:** 1988
SALES (est): 447.4K **Privately Held**
WEB: www.dearborntotalautoservice.com
SIC: 7533 5531 7539 7538 Muffler shop, sale or repair & installation; automotive parts; electrical services; general automotive repair shops; motor vehicle parts & accessories

(G-3923)
DELICATE CREATIONS INC
25623 Pennie St (48125-1538)
PHONE...................................313 406-6268
William Rose, *Principal*
EMP: 4 **EST:** 2008
SALES (est): 47.9K **Privately Held**
SIC: 3299 7299 Architectural sculptures: gypsum, clay, papier mache, etc.; party planning service

(G-3924)
DIVINE DESSERT
25930 Ford Rd (48127-2936)
PHONE...................................313 278-3322
Ayman Akrouch, *Principal*
EMP: 8 **EST:** 2011
SALES (est): 383.1K **Privately Held**
SIC: 2051 Cakes, pies & pastries

(G-3925)
EASTERN POWER AND LIGHTING
5758 Hubbell St (48127-2444)
PHONE...................................248 739-0908
EMP: 5 **EST:** 2011
SALES (est): 238.1K **Privately Held**
SIC: 3612 Transformers, except electric

(G-3926)
ELSTON ENTERPRISES INC
22250 Ford Rd (48127-2420)
PHONE...................................313 561-8000
David Elston, *President*
Nancy Kimberlin, *Graphic Designe*
EMP: 10 **EST:** 1986
SQ FT: 2,000
SALES (est): 723.7K **Privately Held**
WEB: www.allegramarketingprint.com
SIC: 7334 2752 Photocopying & duplicating services; commercial printing, lithographic

(G-3927)
FIRE SAFETY DISPLAYS CO
20422 Van Born Rd (48125-3051)
PHONE...................................313 274-7888
David C Cox, *President*
Mary Ann Cox, *Treasurer*
EMP: 9 **EST:** 1981
SQ FT: 5,000
SALES (est): 1MM **Privately Held**
WEB: www.firesafetydisplays.com
SIC: 7389 3993 Fire protection service other than forestry or public; electric signs

(G-3928)
HASHEMS OF DEARBORN HEIGHTS
26509 Ford Rd (48127-2887)
PHONE...................................313 278-2000
Wessam Hashem, *Mng Member*
EMP: 13 **EST:** 2015
SALES (est): 698.1K **Privately Held**
WEB: www.hashems.com
SIC: 5421 5411 5499 2099 Meat markets, including freezer provisioners; grocery stores; coffee; spices & herbs; seasonings & spices; spices, including grinding

(G-3929)
J B EXPRESS LLC
8614 Appleton St (48127-1407)
PHONE...................................313 903-4601
EMP: 4 **EST:** 2016
SALES (est): 154.4K **Privately Held**
WEB: www.jbexpressgr.com
SIC: 2741 Miscellaneous publishing

(G-3930)
LEADER PRINTING AND DESIGN INC
25034 W Warren St (48127-2145)
PHONE...................................313 565-0061
Stephen P Henry, *President*
EMP: 10 **EST:** 2005

SALES (est): 600K **Privately Held**
WEB: www.leaderprintingandmailing.com
SIC: 2752 Commercial printing, offset

(G-3931)
M & K CABINETS LLC
20424 Ann Arbor Trl (48127-2660)
PHONE..............................313 744-2755
Mohamed Khandkani, *Principal*
EMP: 4 **EST:** 2018
SALES (est): 73.4K **Privately Held**
SIC: 2434 Wood kitchen cabinets

(G-3932)
M & R MACHINE COMPANY
5900 N Telegraph Rd (48127-3221)
PHONE..............................313 277-1570
Blazija Resetar, *President*
Ray Resetar, *Treasurer*
EMP: 6 **EST:** 1973
SQ FT: 12,000
SALES (est): 662.9K **Privately Held**
SIC: 3599 Machine shop, jobbing & repair

(G-3933)
MIDWEST TRANSPORTATION INC
7020 Plainfield St (48127-4602)
PHONE..............................313 615-7282
Qeithar Alhemuzi, *CEO*
EMP: 7 **EST:** 2011
SALES (est): 454.4K **Privately Held**
SIC: 3799 Transportation equipment

(G-3934)
MURRAY GRINDING INC
5441 Sylvia St (48125-1230)
PHONE..............................313 295-6030
Maurice Wrobleski, *President*
▲ **EMP:** 36 **EST:** 1952
SQ FT: 14,500
SALES (est): 2.5MM **Privately Held**
WEB: www.murraygrinding.com
SIC: 3599 Machine shop, jobbing & repair; grinding castings for the trade

(G-3935)
NB CEMENT CO
4203 Merrick St (48125-2849)
PHONE..............................313 278-8299
John Bossio, *Partner*
Mario Naccarito, *Partner*
EMP: 4 **EST:** 1998
SALES (est): 282.6K **Privately Held**
SIC: 3241 Cement, hydraulic

(G-3936)
PATRIOT TOOL INC
5310 Bayham St (48125-1300)
PHONE..............................313 299-1400
Randal A Manny, *President*
Ryan Teichmiller, *Vice Pres*
EMP: 5 **EST:** 1991
SQ FT: 14,000
SALES (est): 733.7K **Privately Held**
WEB: www.patriottool.com
SIC: 3599 Machine shop, jobbing & repair

(G-3937)
RESETAR EQUIPMENT INC
26950 Van Born Rd (48125-1206)
PHONE..............................313 291-0500
Balzija Resetar, *President*
Blazija Resetar, *President*
EMP: 5 **EST:** 1988
SALES (est): 1MM **Privately Held**
WEB: www.resetarequipment.com
SIC: 3599 3312 Machine shop, jobbing & repair; blast furnaces & steel mills

(G-3938)
RHEMA PRODUCTS INC
24141 Ann Arbor Trl Ste 5 (48127-1797)
PHONE..............................313 561-6800
Katherine M Lee, *President*
EMP: 5 **EST:** 1999
SALES (est): 325.6K **Privately Held**
SIC: 2841 Detergents, synthetic organic or inorganic alkaline

(G-3939)
SIGN PROS LLC
5671 Berwyn St (48127-2926)
PHONE..............................313 310-1010
Ali Zeidan, *Principal*

EMP: 4 **EST:** 2013
SALES (est): 66.1K **Privately Held**
SIC: 3993 Signs & advertising specialties

(G-3940)
T4 SOFTWARE
26300 Ford Rd (48127-2854)
PHONE..............................313 610-3297
Doug Thiele, *Principal*
EMP: 6 **EST:** 2009
SALES (est): 123K **Privately Held**
WEB: www.t4software.com
SIC: 7372 Prepackaged software

(G-3941)
TAIZ FUEL INC
4630 S Beech Daly St (48125-1571)
PHONE..............................313 485-2972
Gamila Kaid, *Principal*
EMP: 5 **EST:** 2014
SALES (est): 154K **Privately Held**
SIC: 2869 Fuels

(G-3942)
TOTAL SOURCE LED INC
3914 Mckinley St (48125-2505)
PHONE..............................313 575-8889
Ron Cimino, *Administration*
EMP: 5 **EST:** 2015
SALES (est): 110.9K **Privately Held**
WEB: www.totalsourceled.com
SIC: 3648 Lighting equipment

(G-3943)
UNITED PRECISION PDTS CO INC
25040 Van Born Rd (48125-2008)
PHONE..............................313 292-0100
Gary M Winkler, *President*
Brian Chichila, *Plant Supt*
Jennifer Hamilton, *Controller*
EMP: 36
SQ FT: 16,000
SALES (est): 6.9MM **Privately Held**
WEB: www.uppci.com
SIC: 3728 3724 3452 3451 Aircraft parts & equipment; aircraft engines & engine parts; bolts, nuts, rivets & washers; screw machine products

(G-3944)
Y NOT CANDLES
5115 Michael St (48125-1837)
PHONE..............................313 289-6299
Regina Wilson, *Principal*
EMP: 4 **EST:** 2018
SALES (est): 39.6K **Privately Held**
SIC: 3999 Candles

Decatur
Van Buren County

(G-3945)
CUBE TRACKER LLC
46980 86th Ave (49045-8821)
PHONE..............................269 436-1270
Chris Schaap,
EMP: 5 **EST:** 2015
SALES (est): 73.4K **Privately Held**
WEB: www.cubetracker.com
SIC: 3429 Manufactured hardware (general)

(G-3946)
DECATUR WOOD PRODUCTS INC
79201 M 51 (49045-8209)
P.O. Box 85, Paw Paw (49079-0085)
PHONE..............................269 657-6041
John Tapper Jr, *President*
▲ **EMP:** 35 **EST:** 1992
SQ FT: 42,000
SALES (est): 4.6MM **Privately Held**
SIC: 2435 2431 2421 Plywood, hardwood or hardwood faced; millwork; sawmills & planing mills, general

(G-3947)
DOLE PACKAGED FOODS LLC
Also Called: Dole Packaged Food Company
101 W Bronson St (49045-1259)
PHONE..............................269 423-6375
Kurt Wiese, *Manager*

EMP: 272 **Privately Held**
WEB: www.dolesunshine.com
SIC: 2037 Fruits, quick frozen & cold pack (frozen); vegetables, quick frozen & cold pack, excl. potato products
HQ: Dole Packaged Foods, Llc
3059 Townsgate Rd
Westlake Village CA 91361
805 601-5500

(G-3948)
KUNZMAN & ASSOCIATES WEST
18555 Warner Rd (49045-9414)
PHONE..............................269 663-8978
Micheal Kunzman, *President*
EMP: 4 **EST:** 2002
SALES (est): 230.5K **Privately Held**
WEB: www.kunzman.com
SIC: 3581 Mechanisms & parts for automatic vending machines

(G-3949)
KWK INDUSTRIES INC
56040 Territorial Rd (49045-9022)
PHONE..............................269 423-6213
Robert Weber, *President*
Kurt Weber, *Vice Pres*
Irene Weber, *Treasurer*
EMP: 5 **EST:** 1992
SQ FT: 5,000
SALES (est): 380K **Privately Held**
SIC: 3544 Dies & die holders for metal cutting, forming, die casting

(G-3950)
MOORMANN PRINTING INC
Also Called: Decatur Republican
121 S Phelps St (49045-1117)
P.O. Box 36 (49045-0036)
PHONE..............................269 423-2411
David D Moormann, *Owner*
Kimberly Babcock, *Treasurer*
EMP: 7
SALES (corp-wide): 725.1K **Privately Held**
WEB: www.marcellusnews.com
SIC: 2711 2791 2759 2752 Newspapers, publishing & printing; typesetting; commercial printing; commercial printing, lithographic
PA: Moormann Printing Inc
149 W Main St
Marcellus MI 49067
269 646-2101

(G-3951)
SPECIAL-LITE INC
860 S Williams St (49045-1258)
P.O. Box 6 (49045-0006)
PHONE..............................800 821-6531
Henry L Upjohn II, *Ch of Bd*
Kevin J Hanley, *President*
W Dow Ruch, *Vice Pres*
Cathy Ericksen, *CFO*
Megan Ogden, *Director*
EMP: 120 **EST:** 1971
SQ FT: 150,000
SALES (est): 30.3MM **Privately Held**
WEB: www.special-lite.com
SIC: 3089 3354 3442 Doors, folding: plastic or plastic coated fabric; aluminum extruded products; metal doors

(G-3952)
UNIVERSAL PULTRUSION
860 S Williams St (49045-1258)
P.O. Box 6 (49045-0006)
PHONE..............................269 423-7068
EMP: 8 **EST:** 2017
SALES (est): 55.1K **Privately Held**
WEB: www.special-lite.com
SIC: 3999 Manufacturing industries

Deckerville
Sanilac County

(G-3953)
DESTINY PLASTICS INCORPORATED
2121 Stoutenberg (48427)
P.O. Box 7 (48427-0007)
PHONE..............................810 622-0018

Todd Cristy, *President*
EMP: 15 **EST:** 1993
SQ FT: 25,000
SALES (est): 2.6MM **Privately Held**
WEB: www.destinyplasticsinc.com
SIC: 2821 Plastics materials & resins

(G-3954)
EMR CORP
3473 Main St (48427-7709)
P.O. Box 97 (48427-0097)
PHONE..............................810 376-4710
EMP: 7 **EST:** 2017
SALES (est): 143.7K **Privately Held**
WEB: www.emrcorp.com
SIC: 3663 Radio & TV communications equipment

(G-3955)
MIDWEST RUBBER COMPANY (PA)
3525 Range Line Rd (48427-9420)
P.O. Box 98 (48427-0098)
PHONE..............................810 376-2085
Kenneth L Jehle, *President*
Donald E Rose, *Vice Pres*
Richard Bezemek, *Manager*
EMP: 157 **EST:** 1946
SQ FT: 88,000
SALES (est): 14.6MM **Privately Held**
WEB: www.mwrco.com
SIC: 3069 Medical & laboratory rubber sundries & related products

(G-3956)
PROTO CRAFTS INC (PA)
4740 Shabbona Rd (48427-9364)
P.O. Box 36 (48427-0036)
PHONE..............................810 376-3665
Lowell Manley, *President*
Faith Manley, *Corp Secy*
EMP: 20 **EST:** 1970
SQ FT: 4,500
SALES (est): 3MM **Privately Held**
SIC: 3089 Injection molding of plastics

Deerfield
Lenawee County

(G-3957)
LIMO-REID INC
420 Carey St (49238-9741)
P.O. Box 164 (49238-0164)
PHONE..............................517 447-4164
James O'Brien II, *CEO*
EMP: 8 **EST:** 2004
SALES (est): 698.2K **Privately Held**
SIC: 3594 8711 Motors: hydraulic, fluid power or air; engineering services

(G-3958)
MERIDIAN MECHATRONICS LLC
120 W Keegan St (49238-9612)
PHONE..............................517 447-4587
Kevin Iott, *Owner*
EMP: 8 **EST:** 2011
SALES (est): 787.2K **Privately Held**
WEB: www.meridianmechatronics.com
SIC: 3827 Telescopes: elbow, panoramic, sighting, fire control, etc.

(G-3959)
OBRIEN ENGINEERED PRODUCTS
Also Called: Obep
420 Carey St (49238-9741)
P.O. Box 164 (49238-0164)
PHONE..............................517 447-3602
James A O'Brien II, *President*
Sharon A O'Brien, *Vice Pres*
EMP: 12 **EST:** 1997
SQ FT: 3,500
SALES (est): 271.7K **Privately Held**
WEB: www.obepsolutions.com
SIC: 3429 Door locks, bolts & checks

Deford
Tuscola County

(G-3960)
DEFORD ENGINE
65 N Crawford Rd (48729-9792)
PHONE..................989 872-3640
EMP: 4 EST: 2017
SALES (est): 125.9K **Privately Held**
WEB: www.defordengine.zumvu.com
SIC: 3599 Machine shop, jobbing & repair

Delton
Barry County

(G-3961)
ALLIED MACHINE & TOOL INC
3590 Hope Industry Dr (49046-9812)
PHONE..................269 623-7295
Rodney Morris, *President*
Troy Norris, *Vice Pres*
EMP: 10 EST: 2001
SQ FT: 12,000
SALES (est): 1.3MM **Privately Held**
WEB: www.allied-machine.com
SIC: 3599 Machine shop, jobbing & repair

(G-3962)
BOURDO LOGGING
5794 Mullen Ridge Dr (49046-8100)
PHONE..................269 623-4981
Gordon Bourdo, *Principal*
EMP: 5 EST: 2010
SALES (est): 73.2K **Privately Held**
SIC: 2411 Logging

(G-3963)
FREELANDS COUNTRY UPOLSTERY
4054 Osborne Rd (49046-9532)
PHONE..................269 330-2416
EMP: 4 EST: 2012
SALES (est): 59.1K **Privately Held**
SIC: 2431 Millwork

(G-3964)
LAWS & PONIES LOGGING SHOW
6805 Pine Lake Rd (49046-8495)
PHONE..................269 838-3942
Cheryl L Laws, *President*
EMP: 5 EST: 2013
SALES (est): 160K **Privately Held**
SIC: 2411 Logging

(G-3965)
LOCAL GRIND
117 S Grove St (49046-9470)
PHONE..................269 623-5777
Kristina Harrington, *Owner*
EMP: 6 EST: 2013
SALES (est): 326.6K **Privately Held**
SIC: 3599 Grinding castings for the trade

(G-3966)
SCRAPALOO
6590 S M 43 Hwy (49046-9627)
PHONE..................269 623-7310
John Carpenter, *Owner*
EMP: 4 EST: 2005
SALES (est): 255.6K **Privately Held**
WEB: www.myscrapaloo.com
SIC: 2782 Scrapbooks

(G-3967)
STEPHEN REX FETTERLEY JR
2550 W Cloverdale Rd (49046-9620)
PHONE..................269 215-2035
EMP: 4 EST: 2018
SALES (est): 81.7K **Privately Held**
WEB: www.deltontimber.com
SIC: 2411 Logging

Detroit
Oakland County

(G-3968)
WRIGHT & FILIPPIS LLC
23520 Woodward Ave (48220-1346)
PHONE..................248 336-8460
Kurt Schlau, *Manager*
EMP: 19
SALES (corp-wide): 77.5MM **Privately Held**
WEB: www.firsttoserve.com
SIC: 5999 7352 3842 3841 Hospital equipment & supplies; invalid supplies rental; surgical appliances & supplies; surgical & medical instruments
PA: Wright & Filippis, Llc
2845 Crooks Rd
Rochester Hills MI 48309
248 829-8292

Detroit
Wayne County

(G-3969)
2020 MOBILE DETAILING LLC
2493 S La Salle Gdns (48206-2509)
PHONE..................313 953-6363
Kenneth Davis,
EMP: 4
SALES (est): 100K **Privately Held**
SIC: 2842 Sanitation preparations, disinfectants & deodorants

(G-3970)
3M COMPANY
11900 E 8 Mile Rd (48205-1048)
P.O. Box 5130 (48205-0130)
PHONE..................313 372-4200
Ann Adams, *Business Mgr*
Brandon Campbell, *Engineer*
Jonathan Wood, *Human Res Mgr*
Donald Hess, *Personnel*
Wendell Smith, *Sales Mgr*
EMP: 30
SALES (corp-wide): 32.1B **Publicly Held**
WEB: www.3m.com
SIC: 3291 Abrasive products
PA: 3m Company
3m Center
Saint Paul MN 55144
651 733-1110

(G-3971)
A & R SPECIALTY SERVICES CORP
Also Called: United Metal Products
8101 Lyndon St (48238-2452)
PHONE..................313 933-8750
Fax: 313 933-1001
EMP: 24
SALES (est): 5.3MM **Privately Held**
SIC: 3469 Mfg Metal Stampings

(G-3972)
A K SERVICES INC
1604 Clay St Ste 137 (48211-1903)
PHONE..................313 972-1010
Alan Kaniarz, *President*
EMP: 4 EST: 1983
SQ FT: 6,600
SALES (est): 250K **Privately Held**
SIC: 2434 2511 3231 7699 Wood kitchen cabinets; wood household furniture; ornamental glass: cut, engraved or otherwise decorated; antique repair & restoration, except furniture, automobiles; antiques

(G-3973)
A N L SPRING MANUFACTURING
18307 Weaver St (48228-1153)
PHONE..................313 837-0200
Anthony Luna, *President*
Dave Cheedie, *Vice Pres*
EMP: 5 EST: 1976
SQ FT: 3,200
SALES (est): 474.5K **Privately Held**
WEB: www.anlspring.com
SIC: 3493 3495 Steel springs, except wire; wire springs

(G-3974)
A&M ASSEMBLY AND MACHINING LLC
6400 E Hildale St (48234-2594)
PHONE..................313 369-9475
Clint Cerny, *VP Opers*
Scott McAslan,
Angela Bove,
Cling Cerny,
Mark J Diponio,
EMP: 23 EST: 2005
SQ FT: 50,000
SALES (est): 2.3MM **Privately Held**
WEB: www.ptiam.com
SIC: 3714 Motor vehicle parts & accessories

(G-3975)
A-LINE PRODUCTS CORPORATION
2955 Bellevue St (48207-3502)
PHONE..................313 571-8300
Alger Laura, *CEO*
Kevin E Laura, *President*
Dave Laura, *Accounts Mgr*
EMP: 15 EST: 1965
SQ FT: 73,000
SALES (est): 1.4MM **Privately Held**
WEB: www.a-line.com
SIC: 2851 2822 2899 Lacquers, varnishes, enamels & other coatings; butyl rubber, isobutylene-isoprene rubbers; rust resisting compounds

(G-3976)
AAM INTERNATIONAL HOLDINGS INC (DH)
1 Dauch Dr (48211-1115)
PHONE..................313 758-2000
Richard E Dauch, *Ch of Bd*
EMP: 897 EST: 1998
SALES (est): 24.2MM
SALES (corp-wide): 4.7B **Publicly Held**
WEB: www.aam.com
SIC: 3714 Motor vehicle parts & accessories

(G-3977)
AAM MEXICO HOLDINGS LLC (DH)
1 Dauch Dr (48211-1115)
PHONE..................313 758-2000
EMP: 100 EST: 2015
SALES (est): 2.1MM
SALES (corp-wide): 4.7B **Publicly Held**
WEB: www.aam.com
SIC: 3711 3714 Motor vehicles & car bodies; motor vehicle parts & accessories
HQ: Aam International S.a R.L.
Rue De Koerich 68
Steinfort 8437
263 527-04

(G-3978)
AAM TRAVEL SERVICES LLC
1 Dauch Dr (48211-1115)
PHONE..................313 758-2000
David C Dauch, *Ch of Bd*
EMP: 8 EST: 2012
SALES (est): 2.2MM
SALES (corp-wide): 4.7B **Publicly Held**
WEB: www.aam.com
SIC: 3711 3714 Motor vehicles & car bodies; motor vehicle parts & accessories
HQ: American Axle & Manufacturing, Inc.
1 Dauch Dr
Detroit MI 48211

(G-3979)
ABB ENTERPRISE SOFTWARE INC
16503 Manor St (48221-2825)
PHONE..................313 863-1909
Bernice Early, *Branch Mgr*
EMP: 47
SALES (corp-wide): 26.1B **Privately Held**
WEB: www.global.abb
SIC: 3674 Microcircuits, integrated (semiconductor)
HQ: Abb Inc.
305 Gregson Dr
Cary NC 27511

(G-3980)
ABLE ENTITIES LLC
3330 Stockton St (48234-1735)
PHONE..................313 422-9555
Stanley Williams,
EMP: 12 EST: 2019
SALES (est): 366.5K **Privately Held**
SIC: 3842 Surgical appliances & supplies

(G-3981)
ACCUFORM PRTG & GRAPHICS INC
7231 Southfield Fwy (48228-3598)
PHONE..................313 271-5600
Helen Konczal, *President*
Gail Konczal, *Treasurer*
EMP: 19 EST: 1969
SQ FT: 5,500
SALES (est): 3MM **Privately Held**
WEB: www.accuformprint.com
SIC: 7389 3861 5112 Printers' services: folding, collating; photographic equipment & supplies; stationery & office supplies

(G-3982)
ACE-TEX ENTERPRISES INC (PA)
Also Called: Ace Wiping Cloth
7601 Central St (48210-1038)
PHONE..................313 834-4000
Martin Laker, *President*
Irving Laker, *President*
Daniel Chupinsky, *Treasurer*
▲ EMP: 40 EST: 1946
SQ FT: 122,000
SALES (est): 20.3MM **Privately Held**
WEB: www.ace-tex.com
SIC: 2621 2211 Toweling tissue, paper; scrub cloths

(G-3983)
ACME PLATING INC
18636 Fitzpatrick St (48228-1493)
PHONE..................313 838-3870
Kenneth J Jurban, *President*
Nancy Jurban, *Vice Pres*
EMP: 7 EST: 1958
SQ FT: 9,800
SALES (est): 562.5K **Privately Held**
SIC: 3471 Plating of metals or formed products

(G-3984)
ACME WIRE & IRON WORKS LLC
3527 E Canfield St (48207-1701)
PHONE..................313 923-7555
Robert A Galster, *President*
Barbara Galster, *General Mgr*
Marvin E Galster, *Vice Pres*
Una C Galster, *Admin Sec*
EMP: 12 EST: 1899
SQ FT: 50,000
SALES (est): 2.3MM **Privately Held**
WEB: www.acmewireandironworks.com
SIC: 3496 Miscellaneous fabricated wire products

(G-3985)
ACTIVERSE LLC
10577 Marne St (48224-1149)
PHONE..................313 463-9344
Antonio Hughes,
EMP: 5 EST: 2020
SALES (est): 203.2K **Privately Held**
SIC: 3161 Clothing & apparel carrying cases

(G-3986)
ADGRAVERS INC
269 Walker St (48207-4258)
PHONE..................313 259-3780
John T Flanagan, *President*
Kurt Flanagan, *Vice Pres*
EMP: 11 EST: 1969
SQ FT: 16,000
SALES (est): 317.6K **Privately Held**
SIC: 2796 2791 Lithographic plates, positives or negatives; typesetting

(G-3987)
ADHESIVE SYSTEMS INC
15477 Woodrow Wilson St (48238-1586)
PHONE..................313 865-4448
George H Hill, *President*

Arnold F Joseff, *Vice Pres*
Patrick Ohaka, *Technical Mgr*
Paul Borkosh, *CFO*
▲ **EMP:** 50 **EST:** 1986
SQ FT: 85,000
SALES (est): 14MM
SALES (corp-wide): 58.3MM **Privately Held**
WEB: www.dchem.com
SIC: 2891 Glue
PA: Diversified Chemical Technologies, Inc.
15477 Woodrow Wilson St
Detroit MI 48238
313 867-5444

(G-3988)
ADVANCED URETHANES INC
Also Called: Aldoa Company
12727 Westwood St (48223-3433)
PHONE.................................313 273-5705
Irfan Raza, *President*
Mahmood Farooqi, *Vice Pres*
Laura Mitchell, *Bookkeeper*
▲ **EMP:** 7 **EST:** 1957
SQ FT: 15,000
SALES (est): 1.6MM **Privately Held**
WEB: www.aldoaco.com
SIC: 2869 8731 Industrial organic chemicals; chemical laboratory, except testing

(G-3989)
AFRICAN AMERCN PARENT PUBG INC
Also Called: Blac Detroit
6200 2nd Ave (48202-3400)
PHONE.................................313 312-1611
Alexis Bourkoulas, *Vice Pres*
Chantel Wright, *Director*
EMP: 7 **EST:** 1998
SQ FT: 4,500
SALES (est): 645.8K **Privately Held**
WEB: www.blac.media
SIC: 2721 Magazines: publishing only, not printed on site

(G-3990)
AIR TIGHT SOLUTIONS LLC
18677 Robson St (48235-2808)
PHONE.................................248 629-0461
Frank Usher,
EMP: 5 **EST:** 2016
SALES (est): 120K **Privately Held**
SIC: 3559 Recycling machinery

(G-3991)
AIRTEC CORPORATION
17565 Wlter P Chrysler Fw (48203-2366)
PHONE.................................313 892-7800
James F Boettcher, *CEO*
Christopher Boettcher, *President*
James Boettcher, *General Mgr*
John Comai, *Controller*
EMP: 27 **EST:** 1936
SQ FT: 16,000
SALES (est): 6.8MM **Privately Held**
WEB: www.airteccorp.net
SIC: 3339 Babbitt metal (primary)

(G-3992)
AJAX METAL PROCESSING INC (PA)
4651 Bellevue St (48207-1713)
PHONE.................................313 267-2100
Derek J Stevens, *Ch of Bd*
Frank Buono, *President*
Gregory Wronkowicz, *Vice Pres*
Daniel L Morrell, *CFO*
Dave Krause, *Manager*
▲ **EMP:** 7 **EST:** 1914
SQ FT: 281,780
SALES (est): 21.8MM **Privately Held**
WEB: www.ajaxmetal.com
SIC: 3471 3398 3479 4783 Plating of metals or formed products; metal heat treating; coating of metals & formed products; packing goods for shipping

(G-3993)
AJM PACKAGING CORPORATION
6910 Dix St (48209-1269)
PHONE.................................313 842-7530
Kim Jess, *COO*
Keith Stillson, *Manager*
EMP: 93

SALES (corp-wide): 419.9MM **Privately Held**
WEB: www.ajmpack.com
SIC: 2656 2674 2676 Plates, paper: made from purchased material; paper bags: made from purchased materials; sanitary paper products
PA: A.J.M. Packaging Corporation
E-4111 Andover Rd
Bloomfield Hills MI 48302
248 901-0040

(G-3994)
ALAMIN SUPER MARKET LLC
11920 Conant St (48212-3142)
PHONE.................................313 305-7281
Moklasur Mukul, *Principal*
EMP: 5 **EST:** 2012
SALES (est): 98.1K **Privately Held**
SIC: 3421 Table & food cutlery, including butchers'

(G-3995)
ALBION AUTOMOTIVE LIMITED
1 Dauch Dr (48211-1115)
PHONE.................................313 758-2000
David C Dauch, *CEO*
EMP: 1 **EST:** 2015
SALES (est): 7.6MM
SALES (corp-wide): 4.7B **Publicly Held**
WEB: www.aam.com
SIC: 3714 Motor vehicle parts & accessories
PA: American Axle & Manufacturing Holdings, Inc.
1 Dauch Dr
Detroit MI 48211
313 758-2000

(G-3996)
ALCO PRODUCTS LLC
580 Saint Jean St (48214-3476)
PHONE.................................313 823-7500
Neil Jackson, *President*
Michael Vanwyngarden, *Vice Pres*
Trent Worden, *Opers Mgr*
Edward Karpinski, *Mng Member*
Lee Vandermyde,
EMP: 20 **EST:** 2009
SQ FT: 100,000
SALES (est): 11.2MM **Privately Held**
WEB: www.alco-products.com
SIC: 2952 3441 3255 2951 Roofing felts, cements or coatings; coating compounds, tar; fabricated structural metal; clay refractories; asphalt paving mixtures & blocks; adhesives & sealants

(G-3997)
ALINOSI FRENCH ICE CREAM CO
Also Called: Alinosi Ice Cream Co.
12748 E Mcnichols Rd (48205-3353)
PHONE.................................313 527-3195
Steven Di Maggio, *President*
Joseph Di Maggio, *Corp Secy*
Steve Di Maggio, *Human Res Dir*
EMP: 5 **EST:** 1921
SQ FT: 4,000
SALES (est): 937.6K **Privately Held**
SIC: 2024 2066 5451 5441 Ice cream, bulk; ice cream, packaged: molded, on sticks, etc.; chocolate candy, solid; ice cream (packaged); candy

(G-3998)
ALL AMERICAN WHSE & COLD STOR
14401 Dexter Ave (48238-2633)
P.O. Box 38368 (48238-0368)
PHONE.................................313 865-3870
Sophie Tatarian Nemeth, *President*
EMP: 10 **EST:** 1986
SQ FT: 80,000
SALES (est): 602.6K **Privately Held**
SIC: 4222 2037 Warehousing, cold storage or refrigerated; frozen fruits & vegetables

(G-3999)
ALL CARE TEAM INC
22341 Karl St (48219-2313)
PHONE.................................313 533-7057
Thelma Mitchell, *Principal*
EMP: 5 **EST:** 2016

SALES (est): 90.8K **Privately Held**
SIC: 3341 Secondary nonferrous metals

(G-4000)
ALL FOR LOVE PRINTS LLC
1205 Harding St (48214-3614)
PHONE.................................313 207-1547
Nathaniel Womack,
EMP: 4
SALES (est): 120K **Privately Held**
SIC: 2396 Printing & embossing on plastics fabric articles

(G-4001)
ALLIANCE ENGNRED SLTONS NA LTD
18615 Sherwood St (48234-2813)
PHONE.................................586 291-3694
Sekou Shorter, *General Mgr*
EMP: 200 **EST:** 2012
SQ FT: 125,000
SALES (est): 17.7MM **Privately Held**
SIC: 3442 Rolling doors for industrial buildings or warehouses, metal

(G-4002)
ALLIANCE PRINTS LLC
24502 W 7 Mile Rd (48219-1611)
PHONE.................................313 484-0700
Zechariah Gross,
EMP: 4 **EST:** 2020
SALES (est): 50K **Privately Held**
SIC: 2752 Commercial printing, lithographic

(G-4003)
ALLY SERVICING LLC (HQ)
Also Called: Semperian Collection Center
500 Woodward Ave Fl 1 (48226-3416)
PHONE.................................248 948-7702
Evan Noulas, *President*
Lee G McCarty, *Exec VP*
William C Ploog, *Exec VP*
Cathy L Quenneville, *Admin Sec*
EMP: 1347 **EST:** 1999
SQ FT: 20,486
SALES (est): 666.6MM
SALES (corp-wide): 10.7B **Publicly Held**
WEB: www.ally.com
SIC: 1389 Roustabout service
PA: Ally Financial Inc.
500 Woodward Ave Fl 10
Detroit MI 48226
866 710-4623

(G-4004)
ALO LLC
Also Called: Workshop Detroit
3011 W Grand Blvd Ste 105 (48202-3068)
PHONE.................................313 318-9029
Kevin Borsay,
EMP: 6 **EST:** 2015
SALES (est): 290.6K **Privately Held**
SIC: 2511 Wood household furniture

(G-4005)
ALTERED STONE REALTY CO LLC
16061 Fairmount Dr (48205-1449)
PHONE.................................313 800-0362
Angela McCants, *CEO*
Angela S McCants,
EMP: 10 **EST:** 2020
SALES (est): 140K **Privately Held**
SIC: 1389 7299 Construction, repair & dismantling services; home improvement & renovation contractor agency

(G-4006)
ALUMINUM ARCHITECTURAL MET CO
8711 Epworth St (48204-2957)
PHONE.................................313 895-2555
Frank J Mueth Jr, *President*
EMP: 5 **EST:** 1920
SQ FT: 20,500
SALES (est): 1.5MM
SALES (corp-wide): 4.7MM **Privately Held**
WEB: www.sconcepts.com
SIC: 3446 Architectural metalwork
PA: Dumas Concepts In Building, Inc.
8711 Epworth St
Detroit MI 48204
313 895-2555

(G-4007)
ALUMINUM SUPPLY COMPANY INC
14359 Meyers Rd (48227-3923)
PHONE.................................313 491-5040
Nancy Marshall, *President*
Veronica Larke, *Purchasing*
Eric Noe, *Sales Staff*
Lucas Zoll, *Marketing Staff*
EMP: 28 **EST:** 1948
SQ FT: 15,000 **Privately Held**
WEB: www.aluminumsupply.com
SIC: 3446 5051 Architectural metalwork; miscellaneous nonferrous products

(G-4008)
AMBASSADOR MAGAZINE
151 W Congress St 306 (48226-3204)
PHONE.................................313 965-6789
EMP: 5
SALES (est): 340K **Privately Held**
SIC: 2721 Periodicals-Publishing/Printing

(G-4009)
AMBER ENGINE LLC
711 Griswold St (48226-3276)
PHONE.................................313 373-4751
Daniel Bahr, *Vice Pres*
Austin Szelkowski, *Marketing Staff*
James Garner, *Software Engr*
Stacy Pitt, *Executive Asst*
EMP: 15 **EST:** 2017
SALES (est): 2.4MM **Privately Held**
WEB: www.amberengine.com
SIC: 3652 Pre-recorded records & tapes

(G-4010)
AMERICAN AXLE & MFG INC
Also Called: Detroit Gear & Axle Facility
1840 Holbrook St (48212-3442)
P.O. Box 12159 (48212-0159)
PHONE.................................810 772-8778
Richard Ragan, *Vice Pres*
Ed Klawender, *Production*
John Matton, *Purchasing*
Brian Hemker, *Engineer*
John Steinmetz, *Engineer*
EMP: 7
SALES (corp-wide): 4.7B **Publicly Held**
WEB: www.aam.com
SIC: 3714 Axles, motor vehicle
HQ: American Axle & Manufacturing, Inc.
1 Dauch Dr
Detroit MI 48211

(G-4011)
AMERICAN AXLE & MFG INC (HQ)
Also Called: AAMCO Transmissions
1 Dauch Dr (48211-1198)
PHONE.................................313 758-3600
Yogendra Rahangdale, *Vice Ch Bd*
Michael Simonte, *President*
Jon R Morrison, *President*
Tolga Oal, *President*
Amit Gupta, *Managing Dir*
▲ **EMP:** 325 **EST:** 1993
SALES (est): 1.5B
SALES (corp-wide): 4.7B **Publicly Held**
WEB: www.aam.com
SIC: 3714 Rear axle housings, motor vehicle
PA: American Axle & Manufacturing Holdings, Inc.
1 Dauch Dr
Detroit MI 48211
313 758-2000

(G-4012)
AMERICAN AXLE MFG HOLDINGS INC (PA)
Also Called: AAM
1 Dauch Dr (48211-1198)
PHONE.................................313 758-2000
David C Dauch, *Ch of Bd*
Gregory S Deveson, *President*
Michael K Simonte, *President*
Norman Willemse, *President*
John Geis, *Counsel*
EMP: 4218 **EST:** 1994
SALES (est): 4.7B **Publicly Held**
WEB: www.aam.com
SIC: 3714 3711 Axles, motor vehicle; axle housings & shafts, motor vehicle; chassis, motor vehicle

Detroit - Wayne County (G-4013)

GEOGRAPHIC SECTION

(G-4013)
AMERICAN METALLURGICAL SVCS
Also Called: Can-AM Metallurgical
2731 Jerome St (48212-1545)
PHONE................................313 893-8328
Rod Woodworth, *President*
Patty Woodworth, *Treasurer*
EMP: 10 **EST:** 1979
SQ FT: 17,000
SALES (est): 701.6K **Privately Held**
WEB: www.canamheattreat.com
SIC: 3398 Metal heat treating

(G-4014)
AMERICAN SEALANTS INC
26112 W 7 Mile Rd (48240-1847)
PHONE................................313 534-2500
Joseph W Miller, *Agent*
EMP: 9 **EST:** 1988
SALES (est): 405.1K **Privately Held**
WEB: www.americansealants.net
SIC: 2891 Adhesives

(G-4015)
AMESITE INC (PA)
607 Shelby St Ste 700 (48226-3282)
PHONE................................734 876-8141
Ann Marie Sastry, *Ch of Bd*
Rick Dibartolomeo, *CFO*
Madison Bush, *Administration*
EMP: 9 **EST:** 2017
SALES: 59.7K **Publicly Held**
WEB: www.amesite.com
SIC: 7372 Prepackaged software

(G-4016)
AMK AUTOMATION CORP
500 Woodward Ave Ste 4000 (48226-5403)
PHONE................................804 348-2125
Eberhard Mueller, *President*
Jurgen Steuer, *Exec VP*
EMP: 6 **EST:** 1993
SALES (est): 3.4MM
SALES (corp-wide): 1.7B **Privately Held**
WEB: www.amk-group.com
SIC: 3566 Speed changers, drives & gears
HQ: Amk Holding Gmbh & Co. Kg
Waldstr. 26-28
Aichwald BW 73773

(G-4017)
AMRICAN PETRO INC
Also Called: Allstate
9210 Freeland St (48228-2309)
PHONE................................313 520-8404
Malak Tarhini, *President*
Ahmad Abadi, *Vice Pres*
EMP: 7 **EST:** 2008
SALES (est): 628.6K **Privately Held**
SIC: 2911 7389 Gases & liquefied petroleum gases;

(G-4018)
ANAYAS PALLETS & TRANSPORT INC
163 Morrell St (48209-3129)
PHONE................................313 843-6570
Zeferino Anaya, *CEO*
Eli Galarza, *General Mgr*
EMP: 16 **EST:** 1995
SQ FT: 60,000
SALES (est): 521K **Privately Held**
WEB: www.anayaspallets.net
SIC: 2448 Pallets, wood

(G-4019)
ANCHOR WIPING CLOTH INC
3855 E Outer Dr (48234-2936)
PHONE................................313 892-4000
Scott L Baskin, *President*
Mike Osterwind, *General Mgr*
Marc Baskin, *Principal*
Sean Baskin, *Safety Mgr*
Mark Cook, *Sales Associate*
▲ **EMP:** 62 **EST:** 1982
SQ FT: 80,000
SALES (est): 9.2MM **Privately Held**
WEB: www.anchorwipingcloth.com
SIC: 2392 2842 Household furnishings; dusting cloths, chemically treated

(G-4020)
ANDERSEN EYE PROSTHETICS LLC
4719 Saint Antoine St (48201-1423)
PHONE................................989 249-1030
Gregory C Hazen, *Director*
EMP: 5 **EST:** 2018
SALES (est): 86.6K **Privately Held**
WEB: www.anderseneye.com
SIC: 3842 Prosthetic appliances

(G-4021)
ANGEL AFFECTS CANDLES LLC ◆
16250 Stansbury St (48235-4504)
PHONE................................313 288-6899
Cynthia Harris Murphy, *CEO*
EMP: 4 **EST:** 2021
SALES (est): 125.1K **Privately Held**
SIC: 3999 7389 Candles;

(G-4022)
ANNAS KITCHEN LLC
17910 Van Dyke St (48234-3954)
PHONE................................248 499-4774
Celestine Taylor, *Mng Member*
EMP: 6 **EST:** 2018
SALES (est): 100K **Privately Held**
WEB: www.nannaskitchen.com
SIC: 5461 2051 Cakes; cakes, pies & pastries

(G-4023)
APEX APPAREL LLC
22413 Lyndon St (48223-1856)
PHONE................................248 915-1073
James, *Principal*
EMP: 15
SALES (est): 400.1K **Privately Held**
SIC: 2326 Men's & boys' work clothing

(G-4024)
ARCELRMTTAL TLRED BLNKS AMRCAS
8650 Mount Elliott St (48211-1722)
PHONE................................313 332-5300
Todd Baker, *President*
Brian Aranaha, *Director*
Paul Liebenson, *Admin Sec*
EMP: 300 **EST:** 1997
SALES (est): 60MM **Privately Held**
SIC: 7692 Automotive welding

(G-4025)
ARCHER RECORD PRESSING CO
7401 E Davison St (48212-1912)
PHONE................................313 365-9545
Michael Archer, *Corp Secy*
Richard J Archer, *Manager*
EMP: 6 **EST:** 1965
SQ FT: 4,800
SALES (est): 380K **Privately Held**
WEB: www.archerrecordpressing.com
SIC: 3652 5735 7389 Phonograph record blanks; records; music & broadcasting services

(G-4026)
ARCO ALLOYS CORP
1891 Trombly St (48211-2195)
PHONE................................313 871-2680
David S Aronow, *Principal*
Roslyn Aronow, *Corp Secy*
Adria Aronow, *Vice Pres*
Scott Figures, *Vice Pres*
Randy Walla, *Production*
EMP: 30 **EST:** 1938
SALES (est): 5.4MM **Privately Held**
WEB: www.arcoalloys.com
SIC: 3339 3341 Zinc smelting (primary), including zinc residue; zinc smelting & refining (secondary)

(G-4027)
ARLINGTON DISPLAY INDS INC
19303 W Davison St (48223-3418)
PHONE................................313 837-1212
Fax: 313 837-3425
EMP: 8 **EST:** 1947
SQ FT: 37,500
SALES (est): 690K **Privately Held**
SIC: 3993 2542 Mfg Signs/Ad Specialties Mfg Nonwd Partition/Fixt

(G-4028)
ARROW CHEMICAL PRODUCTS INC
2067 Sainte Anne St (48216-1501)
P.O. Box 19968, Kalamazoo (49019-0968)
PHONE................................313 237-0277
Cynthia Schroeder, *President*
Caroline Brown, *Principal*
Nancy Wallace, *Vice Pres*
Jen Schroeder, *Store Mgr*
Lynda Harris, *Marketing Mgr*
EMP: 25 **EST:** 1928
SQ FT: 20,000
SALES (est): 4.3MM **Privately Held**
WEB: www.arrowchemicalproducts.com
SIC: 2842 Disinfectants, household or industrial plant; sanitation preparations, disinfectants & deodorants

(G-4029)
ARTED CHROME PLATING INC
38 Piquette St (48202-3512)
PHONE................................313 871-3331
Ronald F Borawski, *President*
Frank Borawski, *Vice Pres*
EMP: 15 **EST:** 1946
SQ FT: 9,000
SALES (est): 590.7K **Privately Held**
SIC: 3471 Electroplating of metals or formed products

(G-4030)
ASP HHI ACQUISITION CO INC (DH)
1 Dauch Dr (48211-1115)
PHONE................................313 758-2000
EMP: 5
SALES (est): 349MM
SALES (corp-wide): 4.7B **Publicly Held**
SIC: 3714 3711 Mfg Motor Vehicle Parts/Accessories Mfg Motor Vehicle Parts/Accessories
HQ: Asp Hhi Intermediate Holdings Ii, Inc.
1 Towne Sq Ste 550
Southfield MI
248 727-1800

(G-4031)
AUTOMATED BOOKKEEPING INC
1555 Broadway St (48226-2160)
PHONE................................866 617-3122
Steve Robert, *CEO*
Aaron Schmid, *COO*
EMP: 9 **EST:** 2015
SQ FT: 10,000
SALES (est): 200K **Privately Held**
WEB: www.autobooks.com
SIC: 7372 Business oriented computer software

(G-4032)
AUTOMOTIVE TUMBLING CO INC
3125 Meldrum St (48207-2404)
PHONE................................313 925-7450
Dale Webster, *President*
EMP: 8 **EST:** 1963
SQ FT: 6,000 **Privately Held**
SIC: 3471 Tumbling (cleaning & polishing) of machine parts; finishing, metals or formed products

(G-4033)
AVALON INTL NEW CTR LLC
Also Called: Avalon International Breads
4731 Bellevue St (48207-1301)
PHONE................................313 308-0150
Jaquelyn Victor, *CEO*
France Narowski, *CFO*
Ben Ackerman, *Manager*
Soh Suzuki, *Admin Asst*
EMP: 40 **EST:** 2013
SALES (est): 2.7MM **Privately Held**
SIC: 5461 2051 Bread; cakes, pies & pastries

(G-4034)
AVANTI PRESS INC (PA)
Also Called: Avanti Greeting Cards
155 W Congress St Ste 200 (48226-3261)
PHONE................................800 228-2684
Frederic G Ruffner III, *President*
Calvin Kerr, *Vice Pres*
Michael Quackenbush, *Vice Pres*
Scott Singelyn, *Vice Pres*
EMP: 45 **EST:** 1980
SALES (est): 18.5MM **Privately Held**
WEB: www.avantipress.com
SIC: 2771 2741 Greeting cards; miscellaneous publishing

(G-4035)
AWCOA INC
17210 Gable St (48212-1369)
PHONE................................313 892-4100
Randy Sandys, *President*
Monika Sandys, *Vice Pres*
EMP: 7 **EST:** 1989
SQ FT: 14,000
SALES (est): 814.1K **Privately Held**
WEB: www.awcoa.com
SIC: 3496 Miscellaneous fabricated wire products

(G-4036)
AYE MONEY PROMOTIONS PUBG LLC
20355 Plymouth Rd (48228-1272)
PHONE................................313 808-8173
Kell Y Durden,
EMP: 4 **EST:** 2015
SALES (est): 64.6K **Privately Held**
SIC: 2741 Miscellaneous publishing

(G-4037)
B & B ENTPS PRTG CNVRTING INC
17800 Filer St (48212-1408)
PHONE................................313 891-9840
Tim Barnett, *President*
Brian Barnett, *Vice Pres*
EMP: 9 **EST:** 1993
SQ FT: 40,000
SALES (est): 979.8K **Privately Held**
SIC: 2679 Book covers, paper

(G-4038)
B & B PRODUCTION LLC
10103 Kercheval St (48214-3118)
PHONE................................586 822-9960
Deane Benetti,
EMP: 7 **EST:** 1998
SQ FT: 24,000
SALES (est): 621.8K **Privately Held**
WEB: www.bbprollc.com
SIC: 3599 Machine shop, jobbing & repair

(G-4039)
B & H MACHINE SALES INC
Also Called: Speedreducer.com
9339 W Fort St (48209-2588)
P.O. Box 7340, Dearborn (48121-7340)
PHONE................................313 843-6720
Richard Bekolay, *President*
Mark Bekolay, *Vice Pres*
EMP: 25 **EST:** 1939
SQ FT: 35,000
SALES (est): 4.6MM **Privately Held**
WEB: www.bhmachine.com
SIC: 5084 3568 Industrial machinery & equipment; power transmission equipment

(G-4040)
B & J ENMELING INC A MICH CORP
6827 E Davison St (48212-1909)
PHONE................................313 365-6620
Judy Barkus, *President*
EMP: 17 **EST:** 1978
SQ FT: 13,000
SALES (est): 559.2K **Privately Held**
SIC: 3479 Coating of metals & formed products

(G-4041)
BABYBOPS MELANIN COLLECTION
607 Shelby St (48226-3268)
PHONE................................313 770-4997
De'asia General, *CEO*
EMP: 10 **EST:** 2018
SALES (est): 389K **Privately Held**
SIC: 2844 Face creams or lotions

(G-4042)
BAHWSE/BAHWSE BRAND LLC
2400 S Bassett St (48217-1651)
PHONE................................313 704-7376

Latesha Warren,
EMP: 6
SALES (est): 262.9K **Privately Held**
SIC: 2211 Apparel & outerwear fabrics, cotton

(G-4043)
BAZZI TIRE & WHEELS
8001 Schaefer Hwy (48228-2744)
PHONE.................................313 846-8888
Nick Bazzi, *Owner*
EMP: 4 **EST:** 2008
SALES (est): 440.7K **Privately Held**
WEB: www.bazzitires.com
SIC: 3312 Wheels

(G-4044)
BD DIAGNOSTIC SYSTEMS
920 Henry St (48201-2532)
PHONE.................................313 442-8800
Lee Bowling, *Director*
EMP: 7 **EST:** 2005
SALES (est): 128.2K **Privately Held**
SIC: 3841 Diagnostic apparatus, medical

(G-4045)
BEARD BALM LLC
1951 Temple St (48216-1279)
PHONE.................................313 451-3653
Nadine Beydoun, *Marketing Staff*
Jonathan Koller,
EMP: 8 **EST:** 2012
SALES (est): 559.3K **Privately Held**
WEB: www.beardbalm.us
SIC: 2844 Shampoos, rinses, conditioners: hair

(G-4046)
BEARING HOLDINGS LLC (DH)
1 Dauch Dr (48211-1115)
PHONE.................................313 758-2000
EMP: 1
SALES (est): 1.4MM
SALES (corp-wide): 4.7B **Publicly Held**
SIC: 3711 3714 Mfg Motor Vehicle/Car Bodies Mfg Motor Vehicle Parts/Accessories
HQ: Hhi Holdings, Llc
1 Dauch Dr
Detroit MI 48211
313 758-2000

(G-4047)
BECHARAS BROS COFFEE CO
14501 Hamilton Ave (48203-3788)
PHONE.................................313 869-4700
Dean Becharas, *Ch of Bd*
Nicholas Becharas, *President*
Stephanie Becharas, *Corp Secy*
Telmer Constan, *Vice Pres*
John Parks, *Vice Pres*
EMP: 20 **EST:** 1914
SQ FT: 20,000
SALES (est): 7.1MM **Privately Held**
WEB: www.becharas.com
SIC: 5149 2095 Coffee, green or roasted; roasted coffee

(G-4048)
BEDROCK MANUFACTURING CO LLC
485 W Milwaukee St (48202-3220)
PHONE.................................972 422-4372
Tom Kartsotis, *CEO*
Michele Santana, *CFO*
Shannon Washburn, *Manager*
EMP: 22 **EST:** 2014
SALES (est): 2.7MM **Privately Held**
SIC: 2389 2339 Men's miscellaneous accessories; women's & misses' accessories

(G-4049)
BELL FORK LIFT INC
13700 Mellon St (48217-1307)
PHONE.................................313 841-1220
Phil Beste, *Sales Staff*
Louie Henneman, *Sales Staff*
William McNeff, *Sales Staff*
Mike Berger, *Branch Mgr*
Eric Ruhlman, *Manager*
EMP: 10
SQ FT: 2,500
SALES (est): 40.5MM **Privately Held**
WEB: www.bellforklift.com
SIC: 7699 3537 Industrial machinery & equipment repair; forklift trucks
PA: Bell Fork Lift, Inc.
34660 Centaur Dr
Clinton Township MI 48035
586 469-7979

(G-4050)
BELLEVUE PROC MET PREP INC
Also Called: Parts Finishing Group
5143 Bellevue St (48211-3211)
PHONE.................................313 921-1931
Kenneth Pape, *CEO*
Fred Pape, *President*
EMP: 216 **EST:** 1932
SQ FT: 47,000
SALES (corp-wide): 27.3MM **Privately Held**
SIC: 3471 3398 Finishing, metals or formed products; metal heat treating
PA: Pfg Enterprises, Inc.
50271 E Rssell Smith Blvd
Chesterfield MI 48051
586 755-1053

(G-4051)
BERRY SNS-RBBEH ISLMIC SLGHTRH
2496 Orleans St (48207-4521)
PHONE.................................313 259-6925
Salah Rababeh, *President*
Harvey Wallace, *Managing Prtnr*
Yasseen Rababeh, *Treasurer*
EMP: 5 **EST:** 1979
SQ FT: 11,000
SALES (est): 982.1K **Privately Held**
WEB: www.berryandsonshalalmeat.com
SIC: 5159 0214 2011 Skins, raw; sheep & goats; lamb products from lamb slaughtered on site

(G-4052)
BEST NETWRK DESIGN & ASSOC LLC
18249 Wyoming St (48221-2031)
PHONE.................................313 680-2047
Eze Ejelonu, *CEO*
EMP: 20 **EST:** 2019
SALES (est): 1.5MM **Privately Held**
WEB: www.bestnetworkdesign.com
SIC: 7379 1623 1731 5065 ; telephone & communication line construction; access control systems specialization; security control equipment & systems; battery charging generators, automobile & aircraft; audio-visual program production

(G-4053)
BEST-BLOCK CO
14210 W Chicago St (48228-2368)
PHONE.................................313 933-8676
EMP: 7 **EST:** 2019
SALES (est): 258.8K **Privately Held**
WEB: www.bestblock.net
SIC: 3273 Ready-mixed concrete

(G-4054)
BETTER MADE SNACK FOODS INC
Also Called: Better Made Potato Chips
10148 Gratiot Ave (48213-3211)
PHONE.................................313 925-4774
Catherine Gusmano, *CEO*
Robert Marracino, *President*
Jeff Ienco, *District Mgr*
Elijah Larson, *District Mgr*
Rick Campbell, *Vice Pres*
EMP: 152 **EST:** 1932
SQ FT: 34,000
SALES (est): 48.1MM **Privately Held**
WEB: www.bettermade.com
SIC: 2099 2096 Food preparations; potato chips & other potato-based snacks

(G-4055)
BIRKS WORKS ENVIRONMENTAL LLC
19719 Mount Elliott St (48234-2726)
PHONE.................................313 891-1310
Jeffrey Heard, *President*
EMP: 6 **EST:** 1999
SQ FT: 2,000
SALES (est): 905.2K **Privately Held**
SIC: 8744 3589 ; vacuum cleaners & sweepers, electric: industrial

(G-4056)
BLAC INC
6200 2nd Ave (48202-3400)
PHONE.................................313 690-3372
EMP: 7
SALES (est): 262.1K **Privately Held**
WEB: www.blac.media
SIC: 2721 Magazines: publishing & printing

(G-4057)
BLACK BOTTOM BREWING CO INC
1055 Trumbull St (48216-1938)
PHONE.................................313 205-5493
Sean Murphy, *CEO*
EMP: 5 **EST:** 2016
SALES (est): 99.5K **Privately Held**
WEB: www.blackbottombrewing.com
SIC: 2082 Beer (alcoholic beverage)

(G-4058)
BLACKGIRLPERCEPTION LLC
14635 Penrod St (48223-2363)
PHONE.................................313 398-4275
Dominique Davis, *CEO*
EMP: 5 **EST:** 2020
SALES (est): 250.8K **Privately Held**
SIC: 2731 5942 Books: publishing only; book stores

(G-4059)
BLUE CIRCLE CEMENT
9333 Dearborn St (48209-9700)
PHONE.................................313 842-4600
EMP: 5 **EST:** 2017
SALES (est): 62.6K **Privately Held**
SIC: 3241 Cement, hydraulic

(G-4060)
BOLDEN INDUSTRIES INC
19231 Bretton Dr (48223-1363)
PHONE.................................248 387-9489
Kenneth Bolden II, *Principal*
Sakina Bolden, *Principal*
EMP: 10 **EST:** 2016
SALES (est): 506.4K **Privately Held**
SIC: 3999 Manufacturing industries

(G-4061)
BOND BAILEY AND SMITH COMPANY
Also Called: Bond, Bailey & Smith Machining
2707 W Fort St (48216-2000)
PHONE.................................313 496-0177
David D Smith, *President*
Dudley Smith, *President*
EMP: 7 **EST:** 1979
SALES (est): 449.4K **Privately Held**
WEB: www.signsforsandiego.com
SIC: 3599 7692 7629 Machine shop, jobbing & repair; welding repair; electrical repair shops

(G-4062)
BOND MANUFACTURING LLC
17910 Van Dyke St (48234-3954)
PHONE.................................313 671-0799
Arthur Cartwright,
EMP: 5 **EST:** 2019
SALES (est): 198.1K **Privately Held**
SIC: 3131 2389 Boot & shoe accessories; apparel & accessories

(G-4063)
BOOMER COMPANY (PA)
Also Called: Boomer Construction Materials
1940 E Forest Ave (48207-1119)
P.O. Box 07039 (48207-0039)
PHONE.................................313 832-5050
Robert Boomr, *Ch of Bd*
George Gill, *President*
Ed Basile, *Vice Pres*
John Formentin, *Vice Pres*
Chad Matthews, *Purchasing*
▲ **EMP:** 22 **EST:** 1903
SQ FT: 5,200
SALES (est): 10.3MM **Privately Held**
WEB: www.polkcountyconnect.una.io
SIC: 5032 3441 7359 5082 Brick, except refractory; building components, structural steel; equipment rental & leasing; general construction machinery & equipment

(G-4064)
BOULDING FILTRATION CO LLC
11900 E Mcnichols Rd (48205-3357)
PHONE.................................313 300-2388
Mercedes Boulding, *Principal*
EMP: 4 **EST:** 2017
SALES (est): 231K **Privately Held**
SIC: 3569 Filters

(G-4065)
BOVVY MKT LLC
14377 Warwick St (48223-2952)
PHONE.................................313 706-7922
Gregory Hall,
EMP: 4 **EST:** 2019
SALES (est): 116.1K **Privately Held**
SIC: 2099 Food preparations

(G-4066)
BRAIQ INC
2000 Brush St Ste 201 (48226-2269)
PHONE.................................858 729-4116
Sameer Saproo, *President*
Paul Sajda, *Bd of Directors*
Victor Shih, *Bd of Directors*
EMP: 4 **EST:** 2016
SQ FT: 5,000
SALES (est): 144K **Privately Held**
SIC: 7371 7372 8748 Computer software development; application computer software; systems engineering consultant, ex. computer or professional

(G-4067)
BRAMIN ENTERPRISES
2218 Ford St (48238-2934)
PHONE.................................313 960-1528
Thomas Hanifin, *Owner*
EMP: 5
SALES (est): 220K **Privately Held**
SIC: 2741 7389 ; business services

(G-4068)
BRANDON BERNARD COLLECTION LLC ✪
24444 W 7 Mile Rd (48219-1611)
PHONE.................................888 611-7011
Kevin Hayes, *Mng Member*
EMP: 5 **EST:** 2021
SALES (est): 250K **Privately Held**
SIC: 2389 Suspenders

(G-4069)
BREW DETROIT LLC
1401 Abbott St (48216-1946)
PHONE.................................313 974-7366
Jerry Kocak, *CEO*
Rob Nicholl, *Opers Mgr*
EMP: 17 **EST:** 2012
SALES (est): 5.2MM **Privately Held**
WEB: www.brewdetroit.com
SIC: 2082 5921 Beer (alcoholic beverage); beer (packaged)

(G-4070)
BRIDGEWATER INTERIORS LLC (DH)
4617 W Fort St (48209-3208)
PHONE.................................313 842-3300
Ron Hall, *President*
Cassandra Alston-Childs, *COO*
Carrie Elaine Tingle, *Exec VP*
Ronald Hall, *Vice Pres*
Lareshia Party, *Production*
▲ **EMP:** 200 **EST:** 1998
SQ FT: 155,871
SALES (est): 128.4MM **Privately Held**
WEB: www.bridgewater-interiors.com
SIC: 5013 2531 Motor vehicle supplies & new parts; public building & related furniture
HQ: Adient Us Llc
49200 Halyard Dr
Plymouth MI 48170
734 254-5000

Detroit - Wayne County (G-4071) — GEOGRAPHIC SECTION

(G-4071)
BRIGHT STAR SIGN INC
13300 Foley St (48227-3592)
PHONE.....................................313 933-4460
Ibrihim McAimech, *President*
EMP: 6 **EST:** 1995
SQ FT: 8,000
SALES (est): 332.5K **Privately Held**
SIC: 3993 Neon signs

(G-4072)
BRIGHTER SMILE BY TIERRA LLC
4291 17th St (48208-2508)
PHONE.....................................248 278-3117
Tierra Kimble,
EMP: 4 **EST:** 2020
SALES (est): 74.4K **Privately Held**
WEB: www.brightersmilebytierra.com
SIC: 2844 Cosmetic preparations

(G-4073)
BRIGHTLY TWISTED
1418 Michigan Ave (48216-1324)
PHONE.....................................313 303-1364
EMP: 4 **EST:** 2019
SALES (est): 270.3K **Privately Held**
WEB: www.brightlytwistedtiedye.com
SIC: 3999 Manufacturing industries

(G-4074)
BRINTLEY ENTERPRISES
Also Called: Original Stay Cool Cap, The
8660 Rosemont Ave (48228-3139)
PHONE.....................................248 991-4086
Carmen Brintley, *Principal*
Angelique Mathis, *Principal*
Monique Mathis, *Principal*
Temica Slay, *Principal*
EMP: 4 **EST:** 2016
SALES (est): 257.5K **Privately Held**
SIC: 5137 5131 5632 2339 Women's & children's clothing; hair accessories; apparel accessories; women's & misses' accessories

(G-4075)
BROADSIDE PRESS
20117 Monica St (48221-1236)
PHONE.....................................313 736-5338
EMP: 4 **EST:** 2018
SALES (est): 83.3K **Privately Held**
SIC: 2741 Miscellaneous publishing

(G-4076)
BROPHY ENGRAVING CO INC
626 Harper Ave (48202-3540)
PHONE.....................................313 871-2333
Howard Brophy, *President*
Greg Carr, *Production*
Darcie Grubba, *Controller*
Michael Sturtz, *Sales Dir*
EMP: 30 **EST:** 1939
SQ FT: 18,000
SALES (est): 4.1MM **Privately Held**
WEB: www.brophy.com
SIC: 2796 2791 2759 2752 Photoengraving plates, linecuts or halftones; typesetting; commercial printing; commercial printing, lithographic

(G-4077)
BURHANI LABS INC
18254 Livernois Ave (48221-4214)
PHONE.....................................313 212-3842
Taher Patrawala, *President*
EMP: 6 **EST:** 2013
SALES (est): 145.6K **Privately Held**
SIC: 2869 Laboratory chemicals, organic

(G-4078)
BUSTED BRA SHOP LLC
15 E Kirby St Ste A (48202-4047)
PHONE.....................................313 288-0449
Lee Padgett, *Mng Member*
EMP: 5 **EST:** 2013
SQ FT: 1,400 **Privately Held**
WEB: www.bustedbrashop.com
SIC: 2342 Brassieres

(G-4079)
BUTLER MILL SERVICE COMPANY
Also Called: Whitesville Mill Service Co
8800 Dix St (48209-1093)
PHONE.....................................313 429-2486
S Evan Weiner, *Principal*
EMP: 50 **Privately Held**
WEB: www.edwclevy.com
SIC: 3449 Miscellaneous metalwork
PA: Butler Mill Service Company
9300 Dix
Dearborn MI 48120

(G-4080)
BUTTERED BODY ESSENTIALS LLC
676 Lothrop Rd (48202-2731)
PHONE.....................................313 687-3847
Khadijah Ansari,
EMP: 5 **EST:** 2020
SALES (est): 74.4K **Privately Held**
SIC: 2844 Face creams or lotions

(G-4081)
BWJS PRINTING LLC
12610 Riad St (48224-1008)
PHONE.....................................248 678-3610
Brian Brooks-El, *CEO*
EMP: 4 **EST:** 2020
SALES (est): 146.3K **Privately Held**
SIC: 2752 7389 Commercial printing, lithographic;

(G-4082)
C & A WHOLESALE INC
18942 Hayes St (48205-2960)
PHONE.....................................248 302-3555
Ceaser Yaldo, *CEO*
EMP: 5
SALES (est): 950K **Privately Held**
SIC: 3663 Radio & TV communications equipment

(G-4083)
C & A WOOD PRODUCTS INC
17434 Cliff St (48212-1902)
PHONE.....................................313 365-8400
Archie Price, *President*
Vicky Price, *Vice Pres*
EMP: 10 **EST:** 1984
SQ FT: 10,600
SALES (est): 719.4K **Privately Held**
SIC: 2431 Millwork

(G-4084)
C F BURGER CREAMERY CO
Also Called: Twin Pines
8101 Greenfield Rd (48228-2296)
PHONE.....................................313 584-4040
Lawrence Angott, *Ch of Bd*
Thomas V Angott Sr, *Ch of Bd*
Dean Angott, *Vice Pres*
Laura Sawchuk, *Vice Pres*
Barbara Reark, *Treasurer*
◆ **EMP:** 57 **EST:** 1928
SQ FT: 100,000
SALES (est): 20.8MM **Privately Held**
WEB: www.cfburger.com
SIC: 5143 2026 5149 Dairy products, except dried or canned; milk processing (pasteurizing, homogenizing, bottling); half & half; cream, whipped; beverages, except coffee & tea

(G-4085)
CADILLAC OIL COMPANY
13650 Helen St (48212-2096)
PHONE.....................................313 365-6200
Roger Piceu, *President*
Tom Tilotti, *Purchasing*
Kenneth Litvin, *Sales Staff*
John G Piceu, *Mng Member*
Jim Lange, *Manager*
▼ **EMP:** 24 **EST:** 1921
SQ FT: 42,000
SALES (est): 5.1MM **Privately Held**
WEB: www.cadillacoil.com
SIC: 3479 2992 Coating, rust preventive; lubricating oils

(G-4086)
CAPITAL WELDING INC
20101 Hoover St (48205-1031)
PHONE.....................................248 355-0410
William C Warner, *CEO*
Robert W Warner, *President*
Ruth Warner, *Corp Secy*
EMP: 35 **EST:** 1988
SQ FT: 32,000
SALES (est): 7.4MM
SALES (corp-wide): 33.2MM **Privately Held**
WEB: www.futuramic.com
SIC: 3441 Fabricated structural metal
PA: Futuramic Tool & Engineering Company Inc
24680 Gibson D
Warren MI 48089
586 758-2200

(G-4087)
CARACO PHARMA INC
1150 Elijah Mccoy Dr (48202-3344)
PHONE.....................................313 871-8400
Jitendra N Doshi, *President*
G P Singh, *Senior VP*
Mukul Rathi, *CFO*
Jeff Brodsky, *Controller*
Andrew Bos, *Legal Staff*
▲ **EMP:** 3 **EST:** 2009
SALES (est): 5.1MM **Privately Held**
WEB: www.sunpharma.com
SIC: 2834 Pharmaceutical preparations
HQ: Sun Pharmaceutical Industries, Inc.
2 Independence Way
Princeton NJ 08540
609 495-2800

(G-4088)
CARAVAN TECHNOLOGIES INC
3033 Bourke St (48238-2170)
P.O. Box 2067, Dearborn (48123-2067)
PHONE.....................................313 632-8545
Robert Charleston, *Principal*
EMP: 14 **EST:** 1975
SQ FT: 2,000
SALES (est): 483.3K **Privately Held**
SIC: 2841 2899 2869 2842 Soap & other detergents; chemical preparations; industrial organic chemicals; specialty cleaning, polishes & sanitation goods; industrial inorganic chemicals

(G-4089)
CARCO INC
Also Called: Mike Haas
10333 Shoemaker St (48213-3313)
P.O. Box 13859 (48213-0859)
PHONE.....................................313 925-1053
Harvey Gordon, *President*
Mike Haas, *Corp Secy*
David Gordon, *Vice Pres*
EMP: 21 **EST:** 1946
SQ FT: 14,000
SALES (est): 1.1MM **Privately Held**
WEB: www.carcousa.com
SIC: 3953 2899 3951 Marking devices; ink or writing fluids; markers, soft tip (felt, fabric, plastic, etc.)

(G-4090)
CBP FABRICATION INC
12700 Mansfield St (48227-4901)
PHONE.....................................313 653-4220
Joseph Calcaterra, *President*
Robert Black, *Treasurer*
Michelle Calcaterra, *Controller*
EMP: 45 **EST:** 1999
SQ FT: 35,000
SALES (est): 9.1MM **Privately Held**
WEB: www.cbpfab.com
SIC: 3441 Fabricated structural metal

(G-4091)
CHEMTRADE CHEMICALS US LLC
800 Marion Ave (48218-1689)
PHONE.....................................313 842-5222
Ken Hayes, *Manager*
EMP: 4
SALES (corp-wide): 1B **Privately Held**
SIC: 2819 Industrial inorganic chemicals
HQ: Chemtrade Chemicals Us Llc
90 E Halsey Rd
Parsippany NJ 07054

(G-4092)
CHEWYS GOURMET KITCHEN LLC
2939 Russell St (48207-4825)
PHONE.....................................313 757-2595
Bertha Bowles, *Principal*
EMP: 10 **EST:** 2010
SQ FT: 3,000
SALES (est): 133.8K **Privately Held**
WEB: www.chewysgourmetkitchen.com
SIC: 2051 2052 Bakery: wholesale or wholesale/retail combined; bakery products, dry

(G-4093)
CHIIPSS
10229 Joseph Campau St (48212-3223)
PHONE.....................................248 345-6112
Patrick Miller, *Owner*
EMP: 4 **EST:** 2008
SALES (est): 179.2K **Privately Held**
SIC: 3949 Skateboards

(G-4094)
CISCO SYSTEMS INC
200 Renaissance Ctr (48243-1300)
PHONE.....................................800 553-6387
Tom Myers, *Partner*
Patrick Romzek, *Vice Pres*
Frank Misak, *Engineer*
Kelle Likly, *Accounts Mgr*
Jennifer Cichoski, *Sales Staff*
EMP: 5
SALES (corp-wide): 49.8B **Publicly Held**
WEB: www.cisco.com
SIC: 3577 Data conversion equipment, media-to-media: computer
PA: Cisco Systems, Inc.
170 W Tasman Dr
San Jose CA 95134
408 526-4000

(G-4095)
CLEANING UP DETROIT CITY LLC
4369 W Euclid St (48204-2442)
PHONE.....................................517 715-7010
Malcolm Parker, *President*
EMP: 10 **EST:** 2020
SALES (est): 419K **Privately Held**
SIC: 3639 Trash compactors, household

(G-4096)
COAT IT INC OF DETROIT
15400 Woodrow Wilson St (48238-1564)
PHONE.....................................313 869-8500
Arnold Joseff, *President*
EMP: 4 **EST:** 2005
SALES (est): 167.7K **Privately Held**
SIC: 2851 Paints: oil or alkyd vehicle or water thinned

(G-4097)
COLE KING FOODS
40 Clairmount St (48202-1507)
PHONE.....................................313 872-0220
Amir Bashir, *Owner*
EMP: 6 **EST:** 2013
SALES (est): 210.7K **Privately Held**
WEB: www.kingcolefoods.com
SIC: 2038 Ethnic foods, frozen

(G-4098)
COMMONWEALTH SEWING COMPANY
1314 Holden St (48202-3326)
PHONE.....................................313 319-2417
John Schmidt, *CEO*
EMP: 8 **EST:** 2018
SALES (est): 346.8K **Privately Held**
WEB: www.cws-det4.com
SIC: 2399 Fabricated textile products

(G-4099)
COMPOSITE FORGINGS LTD PARTNR
Also Called: Finkl Steel- Composite
2300 W Jefferson Ave (48216-2055)
P.O. Box 441457 (48244-1457)
PHONE.....................................313 496-1226
Charles Brian Hopper, *Partner*
Paul Budd, *Vice Pres*
Rob Allen, *Mfg Staff*
Michael John Hammerly, *VP Finance*
Janine Bullis, *Sales Staff*

▲ = Import ▼ = Export ◆ = Import/Export

GEOGRAPHIC SECTION
Detroit - Wayne County (G-4128)

▼ EMP: 76 EST: 1991
SQ FT: 100,000
SALES (est): 16.6MM
SALES (corp-wide): 3.3B Privately Held
WEB: www.finkl.com
SIC: 3462 Iron & steel forgings
HQ: A. Finkl & Sons Co.
    412 S Wells St Ste 500
    Chicago IL 60607
    773 975-2510

(G-4100)
COMPUWARE CORPORATION (HQ)
1 Campus Martius Fl 4 (48226-5099)
PHONE.................................313 227-7300
Chris O'Malley, *President*
Ken Baldwin, *President*
Christopher Omalley, *President*
Tommi White, *President*
Jim Langston, *Principal*
▲ EMP: 35 EST: 1973
SQ FT: 1,100,000
SALES (est): 87.3MM
SALES (corp-wide): 1.5B Privately Held
WEB: www.bmc.com
SIC: 7371 7372 Computer software development; prepackaged software
PA: Bmc Software, Inc.
    2103 Citywest Blvd
    Houston TX 77042
    713 918-8800

(G-4101)
CONANT GARDENERS
18621 San Juan Dr (48221-2173)
P.O. Box 21663 (48221-0663)
PHONE.................................313 863-2624
Clyde Hopkins, *Ch of Bd*
Orlin Jones, *Vice Pres*
Ray Chaney, *Treasurer*
Carol Carringdon, *Admin Sec*
EMP: 6 EST: 2001
SALES (est): 300K Privately Held
WEB: www.conantsda.org
SIC: 2731 Book publishing

(G-4102)
CONTRACTORS FENCE SERVICE
14900 Telegraph Rd (48239-3457)
PHONE.................................313 592-1300
Michael Novik, *CEO*
EMP: 35 EST: 1967
SQ FT: 12,000
SALES (est): 4.7MM Privately Held
WEB: www.contractorsfence.com
SIC: 1799 5211 2499 Fence construction; fencing; fencing, wood

(G-4103)
COOKIE MUSIC ENT LLC ✪
19400 Syracuse St (48234-2571)
PHONE.................................209 851-6383
Gino Morgan,
EMP: 5 EST: 2021
SALES (est): 90.4K Privately Held
SIC: 2782 Record albums

(G-4104)
COTTON CONCEPTS PRINTING LLC
1220 Longfellow St (48202-1545)
PHONE.................................313 444-3857
Ken Lemon,
EMP: 4 EST: 2010 Privately Held
WEB: www.ccpdetroit.com
SIC: 8099 3993 Health screening service; signs & advertising specialties

(G-4105)
COUNTS INVESTMENT GROUP LLC
18635 Ohio St (48221-2057)
PHONE.................................313 613-6866
Terrell Counts,
EMP: 14 EST: 2013
SALES (est): 400K Privately Held
SIC: 1389 Construction, repair & dismantling services

(G-4106)
CRAIN COMMUNICATIONS INC (PA)
Also Called: Genomeweb
1155 Gratiot Ave (48207-2732)
PHONE.................................313 446-6000
Kc Crain, *CEO*
Keith E Crain, *Ch of Bd*
Rance E Crain, *President*
Rory Carroll, *Publisher*
Josh Freed, *General Mgr*
EMP: 310 EST: 1916
SQ FT: 100,000
SALES (est): 249.1MM Privately Held
WEB: www.crain.com
SIC: 2721 2711 Magazines: publishing only, not printed on site; newspapers, publishing & printing

(G-4107)
CRC INDUSTRIES INC
Also Called: Weld-Aid Products
14650 Dequindre St (48212-1504)
PHONE.................................313 883-6977
EMP: 25
SALES (corp-wide): 1.8B Privately Held
WEB: www.crcindustries.com
SIC: 2899 Fluxes: brazing, soldering, galvanizing & welding
HQ: Crc Industries, Inc.
    800 Enterprise Rd Ste 101
    Horsham PA 19044
    215 674-4300

(G-4108)
CREATIVE POWER SYSTEMS INC
Also Called: Power Without Wires
1921 10th St (48216-1518)
PHONE.................................313 961-2460
Murray Davis, *CEO*
EMP: 13 EST: 1982
SQ FT: 8,000
SALES (est): 557.9K Privately Held
WEB: www.creativepowersystems.net
SIC: 3825 7539 Power measuring equipment, electrical; electrical services

(G-4109)
CROWN HEATING INC
24521 W Mcnichols Rd (48219-3654)
PHONE.................................248 352-1688
Floyd Caver, *President*
EMP: 4 EST: 2010
SALES (est): 545.1K Privately Held
WEB: www.crownheatinginc.com
SIC: 1542 1721 3585 1711 Commercial & office building contractors; residential wallcovering contractor; heating & air conditioning combination units; heating systems repair & maintenance; heating & air conditioning contractors; warm air heating & air conditioning contractor; boilers, low-pressure heating: steam or hot water

(G-4110)
CT CUSTOM COLLISION LLC ✪
8330 Pinehurst St (48204-3075)
PHONE.................................313 912-9776
Philip Norris,
EMP: 5 EST: 2021
SALES (est): 252.7K Privately Held
SIC: 3711 Automobile assembly, including specialty automobiles

(G-4111)
CTE PUBLISHING LLC
18451 Rosemont Ave (48219-2919)
PHONE.................................313 338-4335
Clarence Terrell, *President*
EMP: 5 EST: 2003
SALES (est): 192.3K Privately Held
SIC: 2721 Magazines: publishing & printing

(G-4112)
CUMMINGS-MOORE GRAPHITE CO
1646 N Green St (48209-2093)
PHONE.................................313 841-1615
Michael Mares, *President*
Debra L Nowacki, *General Mgr*
William T Meglaughlin, *Treasurer*
H Marvin Riddle III, *Admin Sec*
▲ EMP: 24 EST: 1916
SALES (est): 6.1MM
SALES (corp-wide): 130.9MM Privately Held
WEB: www.asbury.com
SIC: 3624 2992 2899 Carbon & graphite products; lubricating oils & greases; chemical preparations
PA: Asbury Carbons, Inc.
    405 Old Main St
    Asbury NJ 08802
    908 537-2155

(G-4113)
CUSTOM ARCHTCTRAL SHTMTL SPCLS
Also Called: Cass
5641 Conner St (48213-3407)
PHONE.................................313 571-2277
Glen Parvin, *President*
Sue Durocher, *Controller*
Greg Gietek, *Administration*
EMP: 15 EST: 1990
SQ FT: 12,000
SALES (est): 2.9MM Privately Held
WEB: www.casssheetmetal.com
SIC: 1761 3444 Architectural sheet metal work; sheet metalwork

(G-4114)
CUTE N CLASSY COLLECTION LLC
13311 Hurston Foster Ln (48215-3358)
PHONE.................................313 279-8217
Lakeisha Burnett, *CEO*
EMP: 5 EST: 2019
SALES (est): 50K Privately Held
WEB: www.cuteclassycollection.com
SIC: 2339 Women's & misses' athletic clothing & sportswear

(G-4115)
D & A WELDING & FABG LLC
19169 Northrop St (48219-1856)
PHONE.................................313 220-2277
Dijon Anderson, *Principal*
EMP: 4 EST: 2017
SALES (est): 43.4K Privately Held
SIC: 7692 Welding repair

(G-4116)
D & W SQUARE LLC
8932 Coyle St (48228-2359)
PHONE.................................313 493-4970
Willie Pitts,
Dennis Bright,
EMP: 5 EST: 2004
SALES (est): 60K Privately Held
SIC: 3612 Voltage regulators, transmission & distribution

(G-4117)
D AND WP RINTS LLC
16315 Grand River Ave (48227-1825)
PHONE.................................313 646-6571
William Haggins IV, *Principal*
EMP: 4 EST: 2019
SALES (est): 83.9K Privately Held
SIC: 2752 Commercial printing, lithographic

(G-4118)
D L W PUBLISHING CO
7739 Brace St (48228-3473)
PHONE.................................313 593-4554
David Watkins, *Manager*
EMP: 5 EST: 2011
SALES (est): 70.5K Privately Held
SIC: 2741 Miscellaneous publishing

(G-4119)
DAC INC
2930 S Dartmouth St (48217-1019)
PHONE.................................313 388-4342
Douglas Crouther, *President*
EMP: 5 EST: 1993
SALES (est): 60.5K Privately Held
WEB: www.dacinc.business.site
SIC: 2731 Book publishing

(G-4120)
DAMIONISHA 823 COSMETICS LLC
19705 Binder St (48234-1905)
PHONE.................................586 557-9893
Eddrena Garth, *Mng Member*
EMP: 5 EST: 2019
SALES (est): 75.6K Privately Held
SIC: 2844 Toilet preparations; shampoos, rinses, conditioners: hair; bleaches, hair; home permanent kits

(G-4121)
DAUGHTERY GROUP INC
16892 Parkside St (48221-3155)
PHONE.................................313 452-7918
Robert L Daughtery, *President*
EMP: 4 EST: 2010 Privately Held
SIC: 3449 Bars, concrete reinforcing: fabricated steel

(G-4122)
DAULINAS LLC
13877 Bringard Dr (48205-1237)
PHONE.................................313 258-0958
Constance Parker,
EMP: 4 EST: 2018
SALES (est): 47K Privately Held
SIC: 2329 Riding clothes:, men's, youths' & boys'

(G-4123)
DCR SERVICES & CNSTR INC (PA)
2200 Hunt St Ste 487 (48207-3210)
PHONE.................................313 297-6544
Dwight Belyue, *CEO*
EMP: 15 EST: 2007
SALES (est): 2.9MM Privately Held
WEB: www.dcr-services.com
SIC: 0782 8748 0781 1382 Lawn & garden services; business consulting; environmental consultant; landscape counseling & planning; oil & gas exploration services; surveying services; industrial buildings & warehouses

(G-4124)
DE WITT PRODUCTS CO
5860 Plumer St (48209-1398)
PHONE.................................313 554-0575
Donald D McClellan, *President*
Jack McClellan, *Exec VP*
Ed Rader, *VP Opers*
Jack D McClellan Jr, *CFO*
Michael Strube, *Sales Mgr*
▲ EMP: 22 EST: 1931
SQ FT: 60,000
SALES (est): 5.3MM Privately Held
WEB: www.dewittproducts.com
SIC: 2952 Roofing felts, cements or coatings

(G-4125)
DEADLINE DETROIT
66 Winder St Apt 443 (48201-3131)
PHONE.................................248 219-5985
Allan Lengel, *Administration*
EMP: 6 EST: 2013
SALES (est): 134.6K Privately Held
WEB: www.deadlinedetroit.com
SIC: 2711 Newspapers, publishing & printing

(G-4126)
DEADLINE DETROIT
615 Griswold St Lbby 7 (48226-3556)
PHONE.................................586 863-8397
Allan Lengel, *Principal*
EMP: 7 EST: 2019
SALES (est): 363.5K Privately Held
WEB: www.deadlinedetroit.com
SIC: 2711 Newspapers, publishing & printing

(G-4127)
DEADLINE DETROIT
15 E Kirby St Apt 526 (48202-4040)
PHONE.................................202 309-5555
Allan Lengel, *Principal*
EMP: 4 EST: 2019
SALES (est): 126.6K Privately Held
WEB: www.deadlinedetroit.com
SIC: 2711 Newspapers, publishing & printing

(G-4128)
DEALER AID ENTERPRISES
Also Called: A-Day Badge Co
8200 E Jefferson Ave # 60 (48214-3974)
PHONE.................................313 331-5800
Geraldine Tigner, *Owner*

Detroit - Wayne County (G-4129) — GEOGRAPHIC SECTION

EMP: 4
SQ FT: 3,800
SALES (est): 249.4K **Privately Held**
WEB: www.dealeraid.com
SIC: **3999** 5199 Badges, metal: policemen, firemen, etc.; advertising specialties

(G-4129)
DEARBORN MID WEST CONVEYOR CO
19440 Glendale St (48223-3426)
PHONE...................313 273-2804
Johnny Lindeman, *Principal*
▲ EMP: 8 EST: 2010
SALES (est): 312.4K **Privately Held**
SIC: **3535** Conveyors & conveying equipment

(G-4130)
DENIM & ROSES CHILDRENS CL LLC
16709 Rosemont Ave (48219-4116)
PHONE...................313 363-0387
Eboni Chavers, *Principal*
EMP: 5 EST: 2016
SALES (est): 73K **Privately Held**
SIC: **2211** Denims

(G-4131)
DENIM CITY LLC
15846 Murray Hill St (48227-1912)
PHONE...................313 270-2942
Calvin Wade Cornelious, *Agent*
EMP: 4 EST: 2016
SALES (est): 64.3K **Privately Held**
SIC: **2211** Denims

(G-4132)
DEPEREZ CONTRACTING LLC ◆
4192 31st St (48210-2553)
PHONE...................947 224-1999
Alexis Omar Perez, *Principal*
EMP: 5 EST: 2021
SALES (est): 50K **Privately Held**
SIC: **1389** Construction, repair & dismantling services

(G-4133)
DESLATAE
5522 Bluehill St (48224-2109)
PHONE...................313 820-4321
Laura Bragg, *Principal*
EMP: 5
SALES (est): 193.2K **Privately Held**
SIC: **2741** Miscellaneous publishing

(G-4134)
DETMAR CORPORATION
2001 W Alexandrine St (48208-2605)
P.O. Box 8098 (48208-0098)
PHONE...................313 831-1155
George A Wrigley, *President*
Dean Henkel, *Controller*
▲ EMP: 46 EST: 1958
SQ FT: 70,000
SALES (est): 1MM **Privately Held**
WEB: www.detmarcorp.com
SIC: **3429** Marine hardware; motor vehicle hardware

(G-4135)
DETROIT BIKES LLC (PA)
13639 Elmira St (48227-3015)
PHONE...................313 646-4109
John Richardson, *Production*
Tina Johnson, *Human Res Mgr*
Mike Kojis, *Sales Staff*
Vak Pashak, *Mng Member*
Stephen Cuomo, *Manager*
▲ EMP: 7 EST: 2011
SQ FT: 50,000
SALES (est): 1MM **Privately Held**
WEB: www.detroitbikes.com
SIC: **3751** 5941 Bicycles & related parts; bicycle & bicycle parts

(G-4136)
DETROIT BLOW PIPE & SHTMTL
7495 E Davison St (48212-1912)
P.O. Box 806300, Saint Clair Shores (48080-6300)
PHONE...................313 365-8970
John R Werden, *President*
EMP: 6 EST: 1972
SQ FT: 4,000
SALES (est): 501.1K **Privately Held**
SIC: **3444** Sheet metalwork

(G-4137)
DETROIT BOILER COMPANY (PA)
2931 Beaufait St (48207-3401)
PHONE...................313 921-7060
Ronald Johnson, *President*
Chris Lanzon, *President*
EMP: 15 EST: 1977
SQ FT: 23,000
SALES (est): 5.4MM **Privately Held**
WEB: www.detroitboilerco.com
SIC: **1711** 3443 Boiler maintenance contractor; fabricated plate work (boiler shop)

(G-4138)
DETROIT BUSINESS CENTERCOM INC
Also Called: Digimax Copy Store
18461 W Mcnichols Rd (48219-4113)
PHONE...................313 255-4300
Andre Bartell, *President*
EMP: 6 EST: 2006
SQ FT: 3,000
SALES (est): 250K **Privately Held**
WEB: www.detroitbusinesscenter.com
SIC: **2752** Commercial printing, offset

(G-4139)
DETROIT CHASSIS LLC
6501 Lynch Rd (48234-4140)
PHONE...................313 571-2100
Edwina Milligan, *Vice Pres*
Michael J Guthrie, *Mng Member*
Joseph W Gause, *Mng Member*
Carlton Guthrie, *Mng Member*
Craig Prisby, *Program Mgr*
▲ EMP: 4 EST: 1998
SQ FT: 218,000
SALES (est): 5.2MM
SALES (corp-wide): 21.1MM **Privately Held**
SIC: **3711** Chassis, motor vehicle
PA: Spectra Lmp, Llc
6501 Lynch Rd
Detroit MI 48234
313 571-2100

(G-4140)
DETROIT CHROME INC
Also Called: DCI Aerotech
7515 Lyndon St (48238-2481)
PHONE...................313 341-9478
Ronald N Nichols Sr, *President*
Bruce Nichols, *Vice Pres*
Bryan Nichols, *Vice Pres*
Ronald Nichols II, *Vice Pres*
Nick Lechman, *Opers Staff*
EMP: 48 EST: 1948
SQ FT: 100,000
SALES (est): 9.6MM **Privately Held**
WEB: www.dciaerotech.com
SIC: **3471** 7389 Electroplating of metals or formed products; plating of metals or formed products; finishing, metals or formed products; grinding, precision: commercial or industrial

(G-4141)
DETROIT CITY DISTILLERY LLC
Also Called: Spirits of Detroit, The
2462 Riopelle St (48207-4525)
PHONE...................313 338-3760
Chuck Gellasch, *Manager*
John Paul Jerone,
EMP: 11 EST: 2014
SALES (est): 1.7MM **Privately Held**
WEB: www.detroitcitydistillery.com
SIC: **2085** Distilled & blended liquors

(G-4142)
DETROIT CUSTOM CHASSIS LLC
6501 Lynch Rd (48234-4140)
PHONE...................313 571-2100
Anderson L Dobbins, *Vice Pres*
Anderson Dobbins, *VP Opers*
Joseph Gause, *CFO*
Michael J Guthrie, *Mng Member*
Carlton Guthrie, *Mng Member*
EMP: 225 EST: 2005
SQ FT: 200,000
SALES (est): 1.9MM
SALES (corp-wide): 21.1MM **Privately Held**
SIC: **3711** Chassis, motor vehicle
PA: Spectra Lmp, Llc
6501 Lynch Rd
Detroit MI 48234
313 571-2100

(G-4143)
DETROIT DENIM LLC
Also Called: Apparel Manufacturer
12811 Hillview St (48227-4086)
PHONE...................313 351-1040
Eric Yelsma, *President*
EMP: 4 EST: 2010
SALES (est): 356.2K **Privately Held**
WEB: www.detroitdenim.com
SIC: **2211** 2389 Denims; apparel & accessories

(G-4144)
DETROIT DIESEL CORPORATION (HQ)
Also Called: Detroit Diesel USA
13400 W Outer Dr (48239-1309)
PHONE...................313 592-5000
Eckhard Cordes, *Ch of Bd*
Sandeep Singh, *General Mgr*
Greg Stahl, *General Mgr*
Henry Laskos, *Superintendent*
Andrew Sablosky, *Principal*
◆ EMP: 3500 EST: 1987
SQ FT: 3,000,000
SALES (est): 1.9B
SALES (corp-wide): 182.4B **Privately Held**
WEB: www.demanddetroit.com
SIC: **3519** 3714 7538 Engines, diesel & semi-diesel or dual-fuel; diesel engine rebuilding; motor vehicle engines & parts; diesel engine repair: automotive
PA: Daimler Ag
Mercedesstr. 120
Stuttgart BW 70372
711 170-

(G-4145)
DETROIT DUMPSTER INC
8701 Grinnell St (48213-1152)
PHONE...................313 466-3174
EMP: 7 EST: 2015
SALES (est): 169.3K **Privately Held**
WEB: www.detroitdumpster.com
SIC: **3443** Dumpsters, garbage

(G-4146)
DETROIT EDGE TOOL COMPANY (PA)
Also Called: Michigan Flame Hardening
6570 E Nevada St (48234-2866)
PHONE...................313 366-4120
Raymond R Ebbing, *Ch of Bd*
John Ebbing, *Vice Pres*
Jerry Madynski, *Vice Pres*
▲ EMP: 100 EST: 1885
SQ FT: 35,000
SALES (est): 18.9MM **Privately Held**
WEB: www.detroitedge.com
SIC: **3599** 3545 3423 Machine shop, jobbing & repair; machine knives, metalworking; hand & edge tools

(G-4147)
DETROIT FD ENTRPRNRSHIP ACDEMY
Also Called: DETROIT FOOD ACADEMY
4444 2nd Ave (48201-1216)
PHONE...................248 894-8941
Jen Rusciano, *Exec Dir*
Angela Abiodun, *Program Dir*
Maria Cortes, *Admin Sec*
Joselyn Nava, *Admin Sec*
Charles Elswick, *Teacher*
EMP: 19 EST: 2013
SALES: 771.7K **Privately Held**
WEB: www.detroitfoodacademy.org
SIC: **8211** 8299 2064 Academy; cooking school; granola & muesli, bars & clusters

(G-4148)
DETROIT FREE PRESS INC (DH)
Also Called: Detroit News, The
160 W Fort St Fl 1 (48226-3700)
PHONE...................313 222-2300
Paul Bascobert, *President*
Brian Dickerson, *Editor*
Ryan Ford, *Editor*
Holly Griffin, *Editor*
Jeff Juterbock, *Editor*
EMP: 290 EST: 1877
SQ FT: 300,000
SALES (est): 74.7MM
SALES (corp-wide): 1.8B **Privately Held**
WEB: www.freep.com
SIC: **2711** 4833 Newspapers, publishing & printing; television broadcasting stations

(G-4149)
DETROIT FRENDS POTATO CHIP LLC
8230 E Forest Ave (48214-1156)
PHONE...................313 924-0085
Michael Wimberley,
EMP: 6 EST: 2017
SALES (est): 5K **Privately Held**
SIC: **2096** Potato chips & other potato-based snacks

(G-4150)
DETROIT LEGAL NEWS COMPANY (PA)
Also Called: Inland Press
2001 W Lafayette Blvd (48216-1880)
PHONE...................313 961-6000
Bradley L Thompson II, *President*
Michael Mc Masters, *Vice Pres*
Andy Thompson, *Engineer*
Steve Fowler, *CFO*
Marsha Johnson, *Bookkeeper*
▲ EMP: 60 EST: 1895
SQ FT: 65,000
SALES (est): 9MM **Privately Held**
WEB: www.inlandpress.com
SIC: **2711** 2721 Commercial printing & newspaper publishing combined; periodicals: publishing & printing

(G-4151)
DETROIT LITHO INC
8200 W Outer Dr (48219-3580)
PHONE...................313 993-6186
Rick McCarty, *President*
EMP: 4 EST: 1984
SQ FT: 3,000
SALES (est): 313.1K **Privately Held**
SIC: **2752** Commercial printing, offset

(G-4152)
DETROIT MFG SYSTEMS LLC (PA)
12701 Suthfield Rd Bldg A (48223)
PHONE...................313 243-0700
Andra M Rush, *CEO*
Tanya Geffrard, *Business Mgr*
Ben Meachem, *COO*
Matt Langton, *Exec VP*
Tony Pashigian, *Vice Pres*
EMP: 58 EST: 2011
SQ FT: 480,000
SALES (est): 45.7MM **Privately Held**
WEB: www.dmsna.com
SIC: **3711** Automobile bodies, passenger car, not including engine, etc.

(G-4153)
DETROIT NEWS INC
Also Called: Detroit News, The
600 W Fort St (48226-3138)
PHONE...................313 222-6400
Joyce Jenereaux, *President*
Robert Allen, *Editor*
Marlowe Alter, *Editor*
Nicole Avery, *Editor*
Kevin Bull, *Editor*
EMP: 300 EST: 1840
SALES (est): 63.8MM
SALES (corp-wide): 3.4B **Publicly Held**
WEB: www.gannett.com
SIC: **2711** Newspapers: publishing only, not printed on site
HQ: Gannett Media Corp.
7950 Jones Branch Dr
Mc Lean VA 22102
703 854-6000

▲ = Import ▼ = Export
◆ = Import/Export

GEOGRAPHIC SECTION
Detroit - Wayne County (G-4180)

(G-4154)
DETROIT NEWS INC
Also Called: Detroit News, The
615 W Lafayette Blvd (48226-3124)
PHONE..................313 222-6400
Kelly Root, *Manager*
EMP: 6
SALES (corp-wide): 1.8B **Privately Held**
WEB: www.detroitnews.com
SIC: 2711 Newspapers
HQ: Detroit Free Press, Inc.
160 W Fort St Fl 1
Detroit MI 48226
313 222-2300

(G-4155)
DETROIT NEWSPAPER PARTNR LP (DH)
Also Called: Detroit Media Partnership
160 W Fort St (48226-3700)
PHONE..................313 222-2300
Dean Krajewski, *President*
Joyce Jenereaux, *Partner*
David Hunke, *Partner*
Tracey M Medley, *Partner*
Mark Durling, *Division Mgr*
EMP: 700 **EST:** 1989
SQ FT: 300,000
SALES: 553.5MM
SALES (corp-wide): 3.4B **Publicly Held**
WEB: www.michigan.com
SIC: 2711 Newspapers: publishing only, not printed on site; newspapers, publishing & printing
HQ: Gannett Media Corp.
7950 Jones Branch Dr
Mc Lean VA 22102
703 854-6000

(G-4156)
DETROIT NEWSPAPER PARTNR LP
600 W Fort St (48226-3138)
PHONE..................313 222-6400
Frank J Vega, *President*
EMP: 668
SALES (corp-wide): 3.4B **Publicly Held**
WEB: www.michigan.com
SIC: 2711 Newspapers, publishing & printing
HQ: Detroit Newspaper Partnership, L.P.
160 W Fort St
Detroit MI 48226

(G-4157)
DETROIT NIPPLE WORKS INC (PA)
Also Called: Taylor Supply Company, The
6530 Beaubien St (48202-3226)
PHONE..................313 872-6370
Richard I Larsen, *President*
Michael Larsen, *Vice Pres*
Nancy Larsen, *Treasurer*
EMP: 12 **EST:** 1934
SQ FT: 41,000
SALES (est): 3.8MM **Privately Held**
WEB: www.detroitnippleworks.com
SIC: 5085 3498 Valves & fittings; fabricated pipe & fittings

(G-4158)
DETROIT PEANUTS LLC
1515 W Lafayette Blvd (48216-1926)
PHONE..................313 826-4327
Ricardo Copeland, *Administration*
EMP: 5 **EST:** 2017
SALES (est): 326.5K **Privately Held**
SIC: 7335 2099 Commercial photography; food preparations

(G-4159)
DETROIT PLATE FABRICATORS INC
2931 Beaufait St (48207-3401)
PHONE..................313 921-7020
Amante C Lanzon, *President*
EMP: 8 **EST:** 1986
SQ FT: 23,000
SALES (est): 1.2MM
SALES (corp-wide): 5.4MM **Privately Held**
WEB: www.detroitboilerco.com
SIC: 3443 Fabricated plate work (boiler shop)
PA: Detroit Boiler Company
2931 Beaufait St
Detroit MI 48207
313 921-7060

(G-4160)
DETROIT READY MIX CONCRETE
9189 Central St (48204-4323)
PHONE..................313 931-7043
Shel Wheatley, *President*
Shelby Wheatley, *General Mgr*
EMP: 12 **EST:** 1991
SALES (est): 2.3MM **Privately Held**
WEB: www.detroitreadymix.com
SIC: 3273 4212 Ready-mixed concrete; delivery service, vehicular

(G-4161)
DETROIT RECYCLED CONCRETE CO
Also Called: Negal Paving
14294 Meyers Rd (48227-3922)
PHONE..................313 934-7677
Bret Warstler, *Manager*
EMP: 7
SALES (corp-wide): 1.1MM **Privately Held**
WEB: www.novicrushedconcrete.com
SIC: 3273 Ready-mixed concrete
PA: Detroit Recycled Concrete Co Inc
39525 W 13 Mile Rd # 300
Novi MI 48377
248 553-0600

(G-4162)
DETROIT RENEWABLE ENERGY LLC
Also Called: Detroit Thermal
541 Madison St (48226-2356)
PHONE..................313 972-5700
Steven A White, *CEO*
Thomas Cinzori, *CFO*
James Royce, *CFO*
Loretta Workman, *Asst Controller*
Eric Vanhouten, *Director*
EMP: 151 **EST:** 2010
SALES (est): 1.1MM **Privately Held**
WEB: www.detroitthermal.com
SIC: 3612 5211 Power & distribution transformers; energy conservation products

(G-4163)
DETROIT RVRTOWN BRWING CMPAY L
Also Called: Atwater Brewery
237 Joseph Campau St (48207-4107)
PHONE..................313 877-9205
Chris Owens, *General Mgr*
Katherine Stevenson, *Marketing Staff*
Mark Rieth, *Mng Member*
Mark Reith, *Mng Member*
Danielle Leveque, *Manager*
EMP: 150 **EST:** 2004
SALES (est): 14.1MM **Privately Held**
WEB: www.atwaterbeer.com
SIC: 2082 5812 Malt beverages; American restaurant

(G-4164)
DETROIT SALT COMPANY LC (HQ)
12841 Sanders St (48217-1407)
PHONE..................313 554-0456
Janette Ferrantino, *President*
Thomas Joseph, *Vice Pres*
John Shook, *Vice Pres*
Michelle Dastagir, *Accountant*
Reginald Miller, *Sales Staff*
EMP: 40 **EST:** 1997
SALES (est): 42.8MM
SALES (corp-wide): 5MM **Privately Held**
WEB: www.detroitsalt.com
SIC: 1481 Nonmetallic mineral services
PA: Kissner Group Holdings Lp
148 Manitou Dr Suite 301
Kitchener ON N2C 1
519 279-4860

(G-4165)
DETROIT SAVINGS LLC
1509 Chateaufort Pl (48207-2717)
PHONE..................313 971-5696
EMP: 4 **EST:** 2017
SALES (est): 101K **Privately Held**
SIC: 2721 Magazines: publishing only, not printed on site

(G-4166)
DETROIT SIGN FACTORY LLC
2900 E Jefferson Ave B4 (48207-4244)
PHONE..................313 782-4667
Kay Stefanski, *Principal*
EMP: 6 **EST:** 2016
SALES (est): 50.6K **Privately Held**
SIC: 3993 Signs & advertising specialties

(G-4167)
DETROIT SIGNS LLC
2648 E Jefferson Ave B (48207-4152)
PHONE..................313 345-5858
Brent Walker,
EMP: 7 **EST:** 2018
SALES (est): 378.7K **Privately Held**
SIC: 3993 Signs & advertising specialties

(G-4168)
DETROIT TUBE PRODUCTS LLC
300 S Junction St (48209-3192)
PHONE..................313 841-0300
M Therese Bellaimey,
EMP: 25 **EST:** 1911
SQ FT: 37,000
SALES (est): 4.4MM **Privately Held**
WEB: www.detroittubeproducts.com
SIC: 3498 Tube fabricating (contract bending & shaping)

(G-4169)
DETROIT TUBING MILL INC
12301 Hubbell St (48227-3900)
PHONE..................313 491-8823
Kenneth Kokko, *President*
Rudolph Taylor, *President*
Peter G Corriveau, *Vice Pres*
Jimmie R Edwards, *Vice Pres*
Mary A James, *Sales Staff*
EMP: 48 **EST:** 1978
SQ FT: 100,000
SALES (est): 4.6MM **Privately Held**
WEB: www.detroittubingmill.com
SIC: 3317 Tubes, wrought: welded or lock joint

(G-4170)
DETROIT WILBERT VAULT CORP
20514 Woodingham Dr (48221-1256)
PHONE..................313 862-1616
Marcia Strickler, *President*
Diane Mac Leod, *Admin Sec*
EMP: 22 **EST:** 1919
SQ FT: 51,000
SALES (est): 2.6MM **Privately Held**
WEB: www.detroitwilbert.com
SIC: 3272 Burial vaults, concrete or precast terrazzo

(G-4171)
DETROIT WRECKER SALES LLC
19303 W Davison St (48223-3418)
PHONE..................313 835-8700
Mike Farrell, *CEO*
Laura Farrell, *Vice Pres*
Debbie Scheetz, *Office Mgr*
Rick Farrell, *Mng Member*
EMP: 6 **EST:** 1976
SQ FT: 12,100
SALES (est): 1.2MM **Privately Held**
WEB: www.detroitwrecker.com
SIC: 3799 5511 Towing bars & systems; pickups, new & used

(G-4172)
DETROITS VERY OWN CL CO LLC
15517 Appoline St (48227-4002)
PHONE..................313 614-1033
David Horton,
EMP: 4 **EST:** 2017
SALES (est): 63K **Privately Held**
SIC: 3999 Manufacturing industries

(G-4173)
DEVELOPMENTAL SERVICES INC
13621 Park Grove St (48205-2838)
PHONE..................313 653-1185
Johnnie Bennett, *Principal*
Miranda Sanders, *Principal*
Rhonda Sanders, *Agent*
EMP: 4 **EST:** 2016
SALES (est): 50K **Privately Held**
WEB: www.dsiservices.org
SIC: 2731 6531 7389 Books: publishing only; real estate brokers & agents; music recording producer

(G-4174)
DHS INC
1925 Elsmere St (48209-1436)
PHONE..................313 724-6566
EMP: 4
SALES (est): 240K **Privately Held**
SIC: 3543 Mfg Industrial Patterns

(G-4175)
DIETERT FOUNDRY TESTING EQP (PA)
9190 Roselawn St (48204-5903)
PHONE..................313 491-4680
David Miller, *President*
David E Miller, *President*
Raymond R Booth, *Treasurer*
Darlene T Miller, *Admin Sec*
EMP: 4 **EST:** 1983
SQ FT: 7,359
SALES (est): 757.3K **Privately Held**
WEB: www.dietertlab.com
SIC: 3829 Testing equipment: abrasion, shearing strength, etc.

(G-4176)
DIGIMAX BUSINESS CORPORATION
18461 W Mcnichols Rd (48219-4113)
PHONE..................313 255-4300
Ondreya Bartell, *Vice Pres*
EMP: 4 **EST:** 2017
SALES (est): 441.5K **Privately Held**
WEB: www.digimaxbusiness.com
SIC: 2752 Commercial printing, offset

(G-4177)
DIGITAL PRINT SPECIALTIES
6538 Russell St (48211-2005)
PHONE..................248 545-5888
EMP: 4 **EST:** 2017
SALES (est): 104.1K **Privately Held**
WEB: www.digitalprintspecialties.com
SIC: 2752 Commercial printing, lithographic

(G-4178)
DIOP COLLECTION LLC
Also Called: Vendor Ventures
16145 Ferguson St (48235-3440)
PHONE..................313 522-6029
Markia Diop, *Principal*
EMP: 4
SALES (est): 156.7K **Privately Held**
SIC: 2844 Toilet preparations

(G-4179)
DIVERSFIED CHEM TCHNLGIES OPRT
15477 Woodrow Wilson St (48238-1586)
PHONE..................313 867-5444
George H Hill, *President*
Arnold F Joseff, *Vice Pres*
Fawzi Tomey, *Vice Pres*
EMP: 1 **EST:** 1997
SQ FT: 51,000
SALES: 3.5MM
SALES (corp-wide): 58.3MM **Privately Held**
WEB: www.dchem.com
SIC: 2865 Cyclic crudes & intermediates
PA: Diversified Chemical Technologies, Inc.
15477 Woodrow Wilson St
Detroit MI 48238
313 867-5444

(G-4180)
DIVERSIFIED CHEMICAL TECH INC (PA)
15477 Woodrow Wilson St (48238-1586)
PHONE..................313 867-5444
George H Hill, *President*
Arnold F Joseff, *Vice Pres*
Jeanne Quick, *Controller*
Chris Fejes, *Manager*
EMP: 170 **EST:** 1971
SQ FT: 51,000

# Detroit - Wayne County (G-4181)	GEOGRAPHIC SECTION

SALES (est): 58.3MM **Privately Held**
WEB: www.dchem.com
SIC: **2891** 2992 2899 2842 Sealing compounds, synthetic rubber or plastic; glue; epoxy adhesives; lubricating oils & greases; chemical preparations; specialty cleaning, polishes & sanitation goods; soap & other detergents

(G-4181)
DIVERSITAK INC
15477 Woodrow Wilson St (48238-1586)
PHONE.................................313 869-8500
Pam Newton, *Manager*
Larry Braden, *Manager*
Jamillah Watkins, *Manager*
▲ EMP: 50 EST: 2010
SALES (est): 13.3MM **Privately Held**
WEB: www.dchem.com
SIC: **2891** Adhesives

(G-4182)
DLH WORLD LLC
2517 Hazelwood St (48206-2291)
PHONE.................................313 915-0274
Derek Higgins, *President*
EMP: 4 EST: 2016
SALES (est): 311.4K **Privately Held**
SIC: **3272** Sills, concrete

(G-4183)
DMC SERVICE GROUP
11111 Sturgis St (48234-3539)
PHONE.................................313 526-2431
Kasie Clifford, *Manager*
EMP: 8 EST: 2018
SALES (est): 763.2K **Privately Held**
WEB: www.dmcsgdetroit.com
SIC: **3444** Booths, spray; prefabricated sheet metal

(G-4184)
DO & CO DETROIT INC (PA)
5 Detroit Metro Airport (48242-1004)
PHONE.................................424 288-9025
Gottfried Neumeister, *CEO*
EMP: 53 EST: 2020
SALES (est): 1.4MM **Privately Held**
SIC: **2099** Food preparations

(G-4185)
DO-ALL PLASTIC INC
1265 Terminal St (48214-3444)
PHONE.................................313 824-6565
Gary Laduke, *President*
Gary La Duke, *President*
Melinda Stine, *QC Dir*
EMP: 9 EST: 1953
SQ FT: 20,000
SALES (est): 311.4K **Privately Held**
WEB: www.doallplastic.com
SIC: **3089** Injection molding of plastics

(G-4186)
DOORSTEP PRINTING LLC
7300 W 7 Mile Rd (48221-2122)
PHONE.................................248 470-9567
Ashley Smith, *CEO*
Carlos Bowen, *Mng Member*
EMP: 6 EST: 2015
SALES (est): 516K **Privately Held**
WEB: www.doorstepprinting.com
SIC: **2752** 2396 Commercial printing, lithographic; screen printing on fabric articles

(G-4187)
DORDEN & COMPANY INC
Also Called: Dorden Squeegees
7446 Central St (48210-1037)
P.O. Box 10247 (48210-0247)
PHONE.................................313 834-7910
Bruce Gale, *President*
▲ EMP: 7 EST: 1929
SQ FT: 10,000
SALES (est): 477.2K **Privately Held**
WEB: www.dordensqueegee.com
SIC: **3999** Window squeegees

(G-4188)
DOUGCO INDUSTRIES LLC
5119 Cadillac Ave (48213-3165)
PHONE.................................313 808-1689
Douglas Kuykendall, *Administration*
EMP: 4 EST: 2011
SALES (est): 135.7K **Privately Held**
SIC: **3999** Manufacturing industries

(G-4189)
DOUTHITT CORPORATION (PA)
245 Adair St (48207-4287)
PHONE.................................313 259-1565
Robert J Diehl, *Ch of Bd*
Douglas Diehl, *Co-President*
John Diehl, *Co-President*
Mark Diehl, *Co-President*
James Haggerty Jr, *Co-President*
▲ EMP: 40 EST: 1919
SQ FT: 26,000
SALES (est): 5.1MM **Privately Held**
WEB: www.douthittcorp.com
SIC: **3861** 3555 Printing equipment, photographic; printing trades machinery

(G-4190)
DOUTHITT CORPORATION
277 Adair St (48207-4246)
PHONE.................................313 259-1565
Robert J Diehl, *Branch Mgr*
EMP: 10
SALES (corp-wide): 5.1MM **Privately Held**
WEB: www.douthittcorp.com
SIC: **3861** Printing equipment, photographic
PA: Douthitt Corporation
    245 Adair St
    Detroit MI 48207
    313 259-1565

(G-4191)
DREAM CATCHERS PUBLISHING LLC
17165 Rutherford St (48235-3556)
PHONE.................................313 575-3933
EMP: 5 EST: 2019
SALES (est): 37.5K **Privately Held**
SIC: **2741** Miscellaneous publishing

(G-4192)
DSW HOLDINGS INC (PA)
400 Renaissance Ctr Ste (48243-1502)
PHONE.................................313 567-4500
Daniel S Weiss, *President*
Chris Fitch, *Vice Pres*
Jim Hart, *Vice Pres*
EMP: 31 EST: 1980
SQ FT: 3,000
SALES (est): 24MM **Privately Held**
SIC: **2899** Water treating compounds

(G-4193)
DTE ENERGY COMPANY (PA)
1 Energy Plz (48226-1221)
PHONE.................................313 235-4000
Gerard M Anderson, *Ch of Bd*
Gerardo Norcia, *President*
Trevor F Lauer, *President*
Matthew Paul, *President*
David Slater, *President*
▼ EMP: 20 EST: 1898
SALES (est): 12.1B **Publicly Held**
WEB: www.newlook.dteenergy.com
SIC: **4911** 4923 1311 ; generation, electric power; transmission, electric power; ; gas transmission & distribution; crude petroleum & natural gas

(G-4194)
DTE ENERGY TRUST II
2000 2nd Ave (48226-1279)
P.O. Box 44646 (48244-0646)
PHONE.................................313 235-8822
Michael A McNalley, *President*
Steve Hare, *Engineer*
EMP: 1 EST: 2001
SALES (est): 17.3MM **Publicly Held**
WEB: www.newlook.dteenergy.com
SIC: **4911** 4923 1311 ; gas transmission & distribution; crude petroleum & natural gas
PA: Dte Energy Company
    1 Energy Plz
    Detroit MI 48226

(G-4195)
DTE ENERGY VENTURES INC (HQ)
1 Energy Plz (48226-1221)
PHONE.................................313 235-8000
Anthony Early, *President*
Daniel Braker, *General Mgr*
Steve Hare, *Principal*

Bryan Yake, *Principal*
Anthony J Tomczak, *Vice Pres*
EMP: 1 EST: 1994
SALES (est): 75.1MM **Publicly Held**
WEB: www.newlook.dteenergy.com
SIC: **4911** 4923 1311 ; gas transmission & distribution; crude petroleum & natural gas

(G-4196)
DUMAS CONCEPTS IN BUILDING INC (PA)
8711 Epworth St (48204-2957)
PHONE.................................313 895-2555
Junius L Dumas, *President*
EMP: 10 EST: 1973
SQ FT: 3,200
SALES (est): 4.7MM **Privately Held**
WEB: www.dumasconceptsinc.com
SIC: **1542** 1791 1796 3535 Commercial & office building, new construction; commercial & office buildings, renovation & repair; structural steel erection; elevator installation & conversion; conveyors & conveying equipment; industrial machinery & equipment; fabricated structural metal

(G-4197)
DYNASTY MECHANICAL INC
18445 Greenlawn St (48221-2108)
PHONE.................................313 506-5504
Jesse H Butler Jr, *CEO*
EMP: 4 EST: 2008 **Privately Held**
SIC: **3585** Refrigeration & heating equipment

(G-4198)
E SMART FUELS AMERICA INC
1001 Brush St (48226-2908)
PHONE.................................248 687-8003
Michael McClean, *Principal*
EMP: 9
SALES (est): 500K **Privately Held**
SIC: **1311** Natural gas production

(G-4199)
EATON DETROIT SPRING SVC CO
1555 Michigan Ave (48216-1325)
PHONE.................................313 963-3839
Michael M Eaton, *President*
Kim Mitchell, *Vice Pres*
Sandy Eaton, *Office Mgr*
EMP: 10 EST: 1937
SQ FT: 8,200
SALES (est): 1.4MM **Privately Held**
WEB: www.eatondetroitspring.com
SIC: **3493** Leaf springs: automobile, locomotive, etc.

(G-4200)
ECLECTIC METAL ARTS LLC
20225 Livernois Ave (48221-1283)
PHONE.................................248 251-5924
Dennis Graham, *CEO*
EMP: 8 EST: 2016
SALES (est): 633.3K **Privately Held**
SIC: **3339** Primary nonferrous metals

(G-4201)
EDEN FOODS INC
Also Called: Eden Organic Pasta Company
9104 Culver St (48213-2237)
PHONE.................................313 921-2053
Steven Swaney, *Manager*
EMP: 34
SALES (corp-wide): 43.8MM **Privately Held**
WEB: www.edenfoods.com
SIC: **2099** Food preparations
PA: Eden Foods, Inc.
    701 Tecumseh Rd
    Clinton MI 49236
    517 456-7424

(G-4202)
EDW C LEVY CO
Also Called: Milford Sand & Gravel
8800 Dix St (48209-1093)
PHONE.................................313 843-7200
Edward C Levy Jr, *President*
Thomas Green, *Director*
EMP: 5

SALES (corp-wide): 521.9MM **Privately Held**
WEB: www.edwclevy.com
SIC: **3273** 3295 5032 2951 Ready-mixed concrete; minerals, ground or treated; aggregate; asphaltic & asphaltic paving mixtures (not from refineries); highway & street paving contractor
PA: Edw. C. Levy Co.
    9300 Dix
    Dearborn MI 48120
    313 429-2200

(G-4203)
ELLIS INFINITY LLC
1545 Clay St Unit 6 (48211-1911)
PHONE.................................313 570-0840
Nailah Ellis- Brown, *Mng Member*
EMP: 9 EST: 2008
SQ FT: 4,000
SALES (est): 105K **Privately Held**
WEB: www.ellisislandtea.com
SIC: **2086** 5149 Iced tea & fruit drinks, bottled & canned; tea

(G-4204)
ELMWOOD MANUFACTURING COMPANY
3925 Beaufait St (48207-1861)
PHONE.................................313 571-1777
Felix Zagumny, *President*
EMP: 4
SQ FT: 2,000
SALES (est): 330.1K **Privately Held**
WEB: www.elmwood-manufacturing-co-inc.hub.biz
SIC: **3714** Motor vehicle parts & accessories

(G-4205)
EMACULATE ENTERPRISES LLC
18300 Van Dyke St (48234-3610)
PHONE.................................313 805-0654
Martez Brown,
EMP: 4 EST: 2010
SALES (est): 120K **Privately Held**
SIC: **2396** Automotive & apparel trimmings

(G-4206)
EMBERS BALLSCREW REPAIR
10200 Grinnell St (48213-1167)
PHONE.................................586 216-8444
Ernie Williams, *Owner*
EMP: 9 EST: 2005
SQ FT: 6,000
SALES (est): 60K **Privately Held**
WEB: www.embersballscrewrepair.com
SIC: **3451** Screw machine products

(G-4207)
EMCO CHEMICAL INC
4470 Lawton St (48208-2198)
PHONE.................................313 894-7650
Emrys Davies, *President*
EMP: 12 EST: 1962
SQ FT: 21,000
SALES (est): 7MM **Privately Held**
WEB: www.emcochemical.net
SIC: **2899** Rust resisting compounds; metal treating compounds

(G-4208)
EMERSON PRCESS MGT PWR WTR SLT
3031 W Grand Blvd Ste 423 (48202-3008)
PHONE.................................313 874-0860
EMP: 35
SALES (corp-wide): 16.7B **Publicly Held**
SIC: **3823** Industrial instrmnts msrmnt display/control process variable
HQ: Emerson Process Management Power & Water Solutions, Inc.
    200 Beta Dr
    Pittsburgh PA 15238
    412 963-4000

(G-4209)
ENGINEERING REPRODUCTION INC (PA)
13550 Conant St (48212-1602)
PHONE.................................313 366-3390
Shawna Cornish, *President*
Jonathan Shuert, *General Mgr*
Paul Cornish, *Branch Mgr*

GEOGRAPHIC SECTION
Detroit - Wayne County (G-4236)

EMP: 6 EST: 1942
SQ FT: 8,700
SALES (est): 1.9MM Privately Held
WEB: www.eng-repro.com
SIC: 7334 7389 2399 3993 Blueprinting service; laminating service; banners, made from fabric; advertising novelties

(G-4210)
ENHANCEHER COLLECTION LLC
1420 Washington Blvd # 301 (48226-1718)
PHONE.................................313 279-7308
Diana Benks,
EMP: 5 EST: 2020
SALES (est): 30K Privately Held
SIC: 3999 Hair & hair-based products

(G-4211)
ENUF HAIRCARE AND LASHES LLC
4085 Hereford St (48224-3910)
PHONE.................................586 354-1798
Latasha Primus,
EMP: 4 EST: 2020
SALES (est): 39.6K Privately Held
SIC: 3999 Hair & hair-based products

(G-4212)
ENVIRODRONE INC
440 Burroughs St (48202-3429)
PHONE.................................226 344-5614
Ryan Cant, *CEO*
EMP: 5 EST: 2016
SALES (est): 265.2K Privately Held
WEB: www.envdrone.com
SIC: 3861 Aerial cameras

(G-4213)
EON PROJECT
14875 Penrod St (48223-2334)
PHONE.................................313 717-5976
Gregory Harvey, *Principal*
EMP: 6 EST: 2013
SALES (est): 189.6K Privately Held
SIC: 2752 Commercial printing, lithographic

(G-4214)
ESPINOZA BROS
2397 Stair St (48209-1209)
PHONE.................................313 468-7775
Enrique Espinoza, *Principal*
EMP: 6 EST: 2007
SALES (est): 222.2K Privately Held
SIC: 3272 Fireplace & chimney material: concrete

(G-4215)
ESSENTIAL SCREEN PRINTING LLC
Also Called: ESP
2630 Orleans St (48207-4507)
PHONE.................................313 300-6411
Scott Michalski, *Principal*
EMP: 4 EST: 2012
SQ FT: 1,300
SALES (est): 360K Privately Held
WEB: www.espdetroit.com
SIC: 2759 Screen printing

(G-4216)
EUCLID MANUFACTURING CO INC
1500 E Euclid St (48211-1310)
PHONE.................................734 397-6300
Scott Jones, *President*
Bob Koss, *CFO*
EMP: 20 EST: 2011
SALES (est): 5.4MM
SALES (corp-wide): 3.1B Privately Held
WEB: www.autokiniton.com
SIC: 3469 Metal stampings
HQ: L & W, Inc.
17757 Woodland Dr
New Boston MI 48164
734 397-6300

(G-4217)
EUGENE
Also Called: Realryteshop
22116 Grand River Ave (48219-3261)
PHONE.................................313 217-9297
EMP: 30 EST: 2020
SALES (est): 1MM Privately Held
SIC: 3612 Distribution transformers, electric

(G-4218)
EV ANYWHERE LLC
3011 W Grand Blvd # 1800 (48202-3096)
PHONE.................................313 653-9870
Kwabena Johnson, *Principal*
EMP: 7 EST: 2013
SALES (est): 90.7K Privately Held
WEB: www.evanywhere.org
SIC: 3621 Generators for gas-electric or oil-electric vehicles

(G-4219)
EVANS INDUSTRIES INC
Darnell Rose Div
12402 Hubbell St (48227-2757)
PHONE.................................313 272-8200
John Wood, *Enginr/R&D Mgr*
EMP: 5
SQ FT: 37,000
SALES (corp-wide): 39.4MM Privately Held
SIC: 3562 3568 3429 Casters; couplings, shaft: rigid, flexible, universal joint, etc.; manufactured hardware (general)
HQ: Evans Industries, Inc.
3150 Livernois Rd Ste 170
Troy MI 48083
313 259-2266

(G-4220)
EVERYTHING EDBL TRATS FOR STNE
6008 Scotten St (48210-1386)
PHONE.................................313 725-0118
Lanice Turner,
EMP: 4 EST: 2020
SALES (est): 171.1K Privately Held
SIC: 2631 Food board, special

(G-4221)
EXCLUSIVE HEATING & COOLG COMP
7725 W Mcnichols Rd (48221-2562)
P.O. Box 2328 (48202-0328)
PHONE.................................248 219-9528
Nathaniel Hall, *President*
EMP: 8 EST: 2004
SALES (est): 975K Privately Held
SIC: 3585 Refrigeration & heating equipment

(G-4222)
EXPEDITE FREIGHT LLC
19320 Braile St (48219-2572)
PHONE.................................313 502-7572
Brian Stokes, *Mng Member*
EMP: 7 EST: 2019
SALES (est): 267.7K Privately Held
WEB: www.expeditedfreight.com
SIC: 3799 Transportation equipment

(G-4223)
EXQUISE INC
Also Called: Fire Sfety Prtction Pdts / Svc
2512 W Grand Blvd (48208-1239)
PHONE.................................248 220-9048
Gerald W Parker, *President*
Jessica Parker, *Vice Pres*
Wilbert Parker, *Admin Sec*
Alice Knight,
Beverly Parker,
EMP: 5 EST: 2012
SALES (est): 516.4K Privately Held
SIC: 3829 1711 5099 3999 Fire detector systems, non-electric; fire sprinkler system installation; fire extinguishers; fire extinguishers, portable; fire extinguishers; electric alarms & signaling equipment

(G-4224)
FABRICATIONS UNLIMITED INC
4651 Beaufait St (48207-1711)
PHONE.................................313 567-9616
Lee Perrell, *President*
EMP: 5
SALES (corp-wide): 1.1MM Privately Held
WEB: www.fabrications-unlimited.com
SIC: 3443 Fabricated plate work (boiler shop)

PA: Fabrications Unlimited Inc
45757 Cornwall St
Shelby Township MI 48317
313 567-9616

(G-4225)
FAIRMONT SIGN COMPANY (PA)
3750 E Outer Dr (48234-2900)
PHONE.................................313 368-4000
Salim Haddad, *CEO*
David Haddad, *President*
Nick Hanna, *VP Mfg*
Kurt Stanley, *Opers Mgr*
John Rohloff, *Purch Agent*
EMP: 37 EST: 1979
SQ FT: 176,000
SALES (est): 6.3MM Privately Held
WEB: www.fairmontsign.com
SIC: 3993 Signs, not made in custom sign painting shops

(G-4226)
FASTSIGNS
2648 E Jefferson Ave # 1 (48207-4168)
PHONE.................................313 345-5858
EMP: 9 EST: 2019
SALES (est): 325.1K Privately Held
WEB: www.fastsigns.com
SIC: 3993 Signs & advertising specialties

(G-4227)
FAYGO BEVERAGES INC (DH)
3579 Gratiot Ave (48207-1892)
PHONE.................................313 925-1600
Nick A Caporella, *Ch of Bd*
Alan Chittaro, *President*
Stanley M Sheridan, *President*
Dan Ferrara, *Regional Mgr*
David Piontkowski, *Vice Pres*
EMP: 375 EST: 1907
SQ FT: 400,000
SALES (est): 98.9MM
SALES (corp-wide): 1B Publicly Held
WEB: www.faygo.com
SIC: 2086 Soft drinks: packaged in cans, bottles, etc.; mineral water, carbonated: packaged in cans, bottles, etc.

(G-4228)
FCA US LLC
Mt Elliott Tool & Die
3675 E Outer Dr (48234-2659)
PHONE.................................313 369-7312
Robert Vulaj, *Opers Mgr*
Patrick Toth, *Mfg Staff*
Ray Waelchli, *Branch Mgr*
Russ Wootton, *Sr Project Mgr*
Paul Bryant, *Manager*
EMP: 5
SALES (corp-wide): 102.5B Privately Held
WEB: www.chrysler.com
SIC: 3544 Special dies, tools, jigs & fixtures
HQ: Fca Us Llc
1000 Chrysler Dr
Auburn Hills MI 48326

(G-4229)
FCA US LLC
Also Called: Chrysler Engine Plant 2
4500 Saint Jean St (48214-4719)
PHONE.................................313 957-7000
Mike Lutsch, *Manager*
Catherine Towne, *Manager*
EMP: 4
SALES (corp-wide): 102.5B Privately Held
WEB: www.chrysler.com
SIC: 3519 Engines, diesel & semi-diesel or dual-fuel
HQ: Fca Us Llc
1000 Chrysler Dr
Auburn Hills MI 48326

(G-4230)
FCA US LLC
Also Called: Detroit Office & Warehouse
12501 Chrysler Dr (48203-3506)
PHONE.................................800 334-9200
Richard Steinberg, *Manager*
EMP: 7
SALES (corp-wide): 102.5B Privately Held
WEB: www.chrysler.com
SIC: 3711 Motor vehicles & car bodies

HQ: Fca Us Llc
1000 Chrysler Dr
Auburn Hills MI 48326

(G-4231)
FERRANTE MANUFACTURING CO
6626 Gratiot Ave (48207-1912)
PHONE.................................313 571-1111
Sante Ferrante, *President*
Tony Costa, *Vice Pres*
Daniel Friedel, *Vice Pres*
William Bonnell, *Treasurer*
Dale Durant, *Manager*
EMP: 50 EST: 1946
SQ FT: 60,000
SALES (est): 8.3MM Privately Held
WEB: www.ferrantemanufacturing.com
SIC: 2541 2542 Bar fixtures, wood; partitions & fixtures, except wood

(G-4232)
FIFE PEARCE ELECTRIC COMPANY
20201 Sherwood St (48234-2926)
PHONE.................................313 369-2560
Roger N Pearce, *President*
John Fracassa, *Vice Pres*
Debbi Hamlin, *Controller*
Brian Couey, *Sales Staff*
Chuck Jones, *Manager*
EMP: 19
SQ FT: 40,000
SALES (est): 5.6MM Privately Held
WEB: www.fifepearce.com
SIC: 7694 Electric motor repair

(G-4233)
FIRE EQUIPMENT COMPANY
Also Called: Michigan Fire Estinguishers
20100 John R St (48203-1138)
PHONE.................................313 891-3164
Mark Agar, *President*
Jim McMillan, *General Mgr*
Willis C Beard, *Chairman*
Ronald Laplante, *Vice Pres*
James McMillan, *CFO*
EMP: 28
SQ FT: 14,000
SALES (est): 3.2MM Privately Held
WEB: www.fireequipco.com
SIC: 3699 7389 Fire control or bombing equipment, electronic; fire extinguisher servicing

(G-4234)
FIRE-RITE INC
13801 Lyndon St (48227-3146)
P.O. Box 219, Davisburg (48350-0219)
PHONE.................................313 273-3730
Richard D Yovich, *President*
▲ EMP: 40 EST: 1975
SQ FT: 50,000
SALES (est): 4.8MM Privately Held
WEB: www.fire-rite.com
SIC: 3398 7389 3471 Metal heat treating; metal cutting services; plating & polishing

(G-4235)
FITZGERALD FINISHING LLC
17450 Filer St (48212-1908)
PHONE.................................313 368-3630
Safet Kurtovic, *Purch Mgr*
Sharon Halnyj, *CFO*
Thomas Melita, *Mng Member*
Derrell Bracy, *Manager*
Aaron Gant, *Manager*
EMP: 90 EST: 2003
SQ FT: 80,000
SALES (est): 9.9MM Privately Held
WEB: www.fitzgeraldfinishing.com
SIC: 3471 Electroplating of metals or formed products

(G-4236)
FLEX-N-GATE DETROIT LLC
9201 Saint Cyril St (48213-1012)
PHONE.................................586 759-8092
David Ekblad, *CFO*
Jeff Harrell, *Manager*
Shahid Khan,
EMP: 400 EST: 2016
SQ FT: 300,000

Detroit - Wayne County (G-4237) — GEOGRAPHIC SECTION

SALES (est): 105.7MM
SALES (corp-wide): 1.5B **Privately Held**
WEB: www.flex-n-gate.com
SIC: 3089 Automotive parts, plastic
PA: Flex-N-Gate Llc
1306 E University Ave
Urbana IL 61802
217 384-6600

(G-4237)
FLEXIBLE CONTROLS CORPORATION
Also Called: Fitzgerald Finishing
17450 Filer St (48212-1908)
PHONE...................313 368-3630
Thomas Melita, *President*
Larry Gutowsky, *Vice Pres*
James R Gitre, *Treasurer*
Sharon Halnyj, *Financial Exec*
EMP: 41 EST: 1959
SQ FT: 107,000
SALES (est): 1.8MM **Privately Held**
SIC: 3471 Decorative plating & finishing of formed products

(G-4238)
FLINT LIME INDUSTRIES INC
327 S Fordson St (48217-1314)
P.O. Box 133, Allen Park (48101-0133)
PHONE...................313 843-6050
Greg Sartor, *President*
EMP: 6 EST: 1979
SALES (est): 352.8K **Privately Held**
SIC: 1422 Crushed & broken limestone

(G-4239)
FMMB LLC
Also Called: Stanek Rack Company
4786 Bellevue St (48207-1302)
P.O. Box 7280 (48207-0280)
PHONE...................313 372-7420
Keith Labeau, *Sales Staff*
Pam Haddix, *Office Mgr*
Mark McClelland,
EMP: 27 EST: 1960
SQ FT: 20,000
SALES (est): 3.3MM **Privately Held**
WEB: www.stanekrack.com
SIC: 2542 Racks, merchandise display or storage: except wood

(G-4240)
FORD MOTOR COMPANY
300 Renaissance Ctr (48243-1402)
PHONE...................313 446-5945
Hari Annadi, *General Mgr*
Sandy Corbett, *COO*
Christohper Campo, *Project Mgr*
Jeremy Conrad, *Project Mgr*
Sree Gatti, *Project Mgr*
EMP: 1500
SALES (corp-wide): 127.1B **Publicly Held**
WEB: www.ford.com
SIC: 3211 8734 Window glass, clear & colored; product testing laboratory, safety or performance
PA: Ford Motor Company
1 American Rd
Dearborn MI 48126
313 322-3000

(G-4241)
FORGED TUBULAR
9339 W Fort St (48209-2555)
PHONE...................313 843-4870
Richard Bekolay, *Owner*
EMP: 6 EST: 2010
SALES (est): 187.1K **Privately Held**
SIC: 3714 Motor vehicle parts & accessories

(G-4242)
FORGED TUBULAR PRODUCTS INC (PA)
Also Called: B & H Machine Sales
9339 W Fort St (48209-2555)
PHONE...................313 843-6720
Richard Tm Bekolay, *President*
EMP: 13 EST: 1997
SALES (est): 1.4MM **Privately Held**
WEB: www.bhmachine.com
SIC: 3317 Seamless pipes & tubes

(G-4243)
FORGING HOLDINGS LLC (DH)
1 Dauch Dr (48211-1115)
PHONE...................313 758-2000
EMP: 5
SALES (est): 318.3MM
SALES (corp-wide): 4.7B **Publicly Held**
SIC: 3711 3714 Mfg Motor Vehicle/Car Bodies Mfg Motor Vehicle Parts/Accessories
HQ: Hhi Holdings, Llc
1 Dauch Dr
Detroit MI 48211
313 758-2000

(G-4244)
FORMER COMPANY LLC
Also Called: Gentleman
2920 E Jefferson Ave (48207-5028)
PHONE...................248 202-0473
EMP: 7 EST: 2016
SALES (est): 676.8K **Privately Held**
WEB: www.formerco.com
SIC: 3861 Motion picture film

(G-4245)
FPT SCHLAFER
Also Called: Schlafer Iron & Steel Co
1950 Medbury St (48211-2626)
PHONE...................313 925-8200
Barry Briskin, *President*
Anthony Benacquisto, *Corp Secy*
Steve Benacquisto, *Vice Pres*
Steven Benacquisto, *Vice Pres*
▲ EMP: 21 EST: 1986
SQ FT: 38,000
SALES (est): 1.9MM **Privately Held**
WEB: www.fptscrap.com
SIC: 5093 3341 Ferrous metal scrap & waste; secondary nonferrous metals

(G-4246)
FRESH START CMNTY INITIATIVE
535 Griswold St 111-19 (48226-3604)
PHONE...................941 225-9693
Jonel Gilmer, *President*
EMP: 5 EST: 2019
SALES (est): 65.1K **Privately Held**
SIC: 2741 Miscellaneous publishing

(G-4247)
FRITZ ENTERPRISES
Also Called: Fritz Products
255 Marion Ave (48218-1695)
PHONE...................313 841-9460
Al Seguin, *Safety Dir*
John Splan, *Plant Supt*
EMP: 6
SALES (corp-wide): 35.7MM **Privately Held**
WEB: www.fritzinc.com
SIC: 3567 3334 Smelting ovens; primary aluminum
HQ: Fritz Enterprises
1650 W Jefferson Ave
Trenton MI 48183
734 283-7272

(G-4248)
FUNCTIONAL FLUIDICS INC
440 Burroughs St Ste 641 (48202-3474)
PHONE...................410 493-8322
Patrick Hines,
John Cunningham,
EMP: 5 EST: 2014
SALES (est): 742.7K **Privately Held**
WEB: www.functionalfluidics.com
SIC: 3841 7389 Diagnostic apparatus, medical;

(G-4249)
G A MACHINE COMPANY INC
8851 Mark Twain St (48228-2310)
PHONE...................313 836-5646
Steven Kiss, *President*
Betty J Kiss, *Vice Pres*
EMP: 7 EST: 1946
SQ FT: 3,200
SALES (est): 400K **Privately Held**
SIC: 3544 3545 Special dies & tools; sockets (machine tool accessories)

(G-4250)
GANAS LLC
7400 E Davison St (48212-1913)
PHONE...................313 646-9966
Ted Sliwinski, *Opers Staff*
Richard Ganas, *Mng Member*
EMP: 11
SALES (est): 1.1MM **Privately Held**
WEB: www.ganasmfg.com
SIC: 2426 Carvings, furniture: wood

(G-4251)
GANNETT STLLITE INFO NTWRK INC
Also Called: USA Today
601 Rogell Dr (48242-1103)
PHONE...................734 229-1150
EMP: 117
SALES (corp-wide): 3.1B **Publicly Held**
SIC: 2711 Newspapers-Publishing/Printing
HQ: Gannett Satellite Information Network, Llc
7950 Jones Branch Dr
Mc Lean VA 22102
703 854-6000

(G-4252)
GEEKS OF DETROIT LLC
282 Newport St Ste 1a (48215-3170)
PHONE...................734 576-2363
Donnie Hall,
Tamara Canty,
Deshoun Smith,
EMP: 4 EST: 2008
SQ FT: 2,000
SALES (est): 213.3K **Privately Held**
SIC: 3575 7378 Computer terminals; computer maintenance & repair

(G-4253)
GENERAL HARDWOOD COMPANY (PA)
Also Called: All Overhead Door Operator Co
7201 E Mcnichols Rd (48212-2050)
PHONE...................313 365-7733
Ronald Ellerbrock, *President*
Mark Ellerbrock, *Vice Pres*
EMP: 15 EST: 1932
SQ FT: 3,200
SALES (est): 4.9MM **Privately Held**
WEB: www.generalhardwood.com
SIC: 5031 2431 Lumber: rough, dressed & finished; millwork

(G-4254)
GENERAL MOTORS CHINA LLC (DH)
300 Renaissance Ctr L1 (48243-1403)
P.O. Box 33122 (48232-5122)
PHONE...................313 556-5000
Lillian Orth, *CEO*
Matthew Tsien, *Exec VP*
Margaret Benton, *Supervisor*
EMP: 1 EST: 1991
SALES (est): 7.7MM **Publicly Held**
WEB: www.gm.com
SIC: 3714 Motor vehicle parts & accessories

(G-4255)
GENERAL MOTORS COMPANY (PA)
300 Renaissance Ctr L1 (48243-1403)
PHONE...................313 667-1500
Mary T Barra, *Ch of Bd*
Julian Blissett, *President*
Mark L Reuss, *President*
Craig B Glidden, *Exec VP*
Gerald Johnson, *Exec VP*
EMP: 51710 EST: 1908
SALES (est): 122.4B **Publicly Held**
WEB: www.gm.com
SIC: 3711 3714 Motor vehicles & car bodies; motor vehicle parts & accessories

(G-4256)
GENERAL MOTORS HOLDINGS LLC (HQ)
300 Renaissance Ctr L1 (48243-1403)
PHONE...................313 667-1500
Mary Barra, *CEO*
Mary T Barra, *CEO*
Mark L Reuss, *President*
Matt Tsien, *Exec VP*

Paul Jacobson, *CFO*
▲ EMP: 243 EST: 2009
SALES (est): 13.8B **Publicly Held**
WEB: www.gm.com
SIC: 5511 3714 Automobiles, new & used; motor vehicle parts & accessories

(G-4257)
GENERAL MOTORS LLC
2500 E Grand Blvd (48211-2006)
PHONE...................313 972-6000
EMP: 2000 **Publicly Held**
SIC: 3711 3714 6153 6141 Mfg Assemble And Sale Motor Vehicles Related Parts And Accessories Auto Financing Leasing Insur And Mtg Banking And Investmen
HQ: General Motors Llc
300 Renaissance Ctr L1
Detroit MI 48243

(G-4258)
GENERAL MOTORS LLC (HQ)
300 Renaissance Ctr L1 (48243-1403)
PHONE...................313 665-4919
Mary Barra, *CEO*
Dan Ammann, *President*
Jaime Ardila, *President*
Cathy Ehgotz, *General Mgr*
David Stillwell, *General Mgr*
▼ EMP: 2390 EST: 2012
SALES (est): 2.5B **Publicly Held**
WEB: www.gm.com
SIC: 5511 3714 Automobiles, new & used; motor vehicle parts & accessories

(G-4259)
GENERAL MOTORS LLC
2500 E Grand Blvd (48211-2006)
PHONE...................313 972-6000
Ryan Schutte, *Counsel*
Ann Cook, *Export Mgr*
Kendra Williams, *Engineer*
Troy Clarke, *Manager*
Patrick Foley, *Securities*
EMP: 2000 **Publicly Held**
WEB: www.gm.com
SIC: 3711 Motor vehicles & car bodies
HQ: General Motors Llc
300 Renaissance Ctr L1
Detroit MI 48243

(G-4260)
GENERAL MOTORS LLC
2500 E Grand Motors Blvd (48211)
PHONE...................313 556-5000
EMP: 2028 **Publicly Held**
SIC: 3711 3714 Mfg Motor Vehicle/Car Bodies Mfg Motor Vehicle Parts/Accessories
HQ: General Motors Llc
300 Renaissance Ctr L1
Detroit MI 48243

(G-4261)
GERALD HARRIS
Also Called: Domnmar Manufacturing Group
14846 Dexter Ave (48238-2123)
PHONE...................985 774-0261
Gerald Harris, *Owner*
EMP: 4 EST: 2010 **Privately Held**
SIC: 3541 Machine tools, metal cutting type

(G-4262)
GINKGOTREE INC
1555 Broadway St Ste 300 (48226-2159)
PHONE...................734 707-7191
Lida Hasbrouck, *CEO*
Scott Hasbrouck, *CEO*
Andrew Colchagoff, *Chief Engr*
EMP: 4 EST: 2012
SALES (est): 240.6K **Privately Held**
SIC: 7379 7371 7372 ; computer software development & applications; educational computer software

(G-4263)
GIONL LLC
15601 Schoolcraft St (48227-4607)
PHONE...................313 957-9247
Summer Grafton,
EMP: 5 EST: 2019
SALES (est): 100K **Privately Held**
SIC: 3161 Clothing & apparel carrying cases

▲ = Import ▼ = Export
◆ = Import/Export

GEOGRAPHIC SECTION
Detroit - Wayne County (G-4292)

(G-4264)
GLAMOUR GIRL HAIR LLC
1300 E Lafayette St # 1103 (48207-2920)
PHONE.................................313 204-4143
Dannis Mitchell, *Mng Member*
EMP: 10 **EST:** 2013
SALES (est): 530.5K **Privately Held**
SIC: 3999 Wigs, including doll wigs, toupees or wiglets

(G-4265)
GM COMPONENTS HOLDINGS LLC (DH)
Also Called: General Mtrs Cmpnents Holdings
300 Renaissance Ctr (48243-1402)
PHONE.................................870 594-0351
Daniel Milot, *District Mgr*
Brian King, *Business Mgr*
Niharika Taskar Ramdev, *Vice Pres*
David Bartoy, *Opers Mgr*
Jason Cummings, *Maint Spvr*
▲ **EMP:** 185 **EST:** 2009
SALES (est): 1.3B **Publicly Held**
WEB: www.gm.com
SIC: 5511 3714 Automobiles, new & used; motor vehicle parts & accessories

(G-4266)
GM DEFENSE LLC (DH)
300 Renaissance Ctr Fl 24 (48243-1402)
PHONE.................................313 462-8782
Stephen Dumont, *Mng Member*
EMP: 109 **EST:** 2017
SALES (est): 52.6MM **Publicly Held**
SIC: 3711 3714 Motor vehicles & car bodies; motor vehicle parts & accessories

(G-4267)
GM LAAM HOLDINGS LLC (DH)
300 Renaissance Ctr (48243-1402)
PHONE.................................313 556-5000
EMP: 100 **EST:** 2003
SALES (est): 2.9MM **Publicly Held**
WEB: www.gm.com
SIC: 3711 3714 Automobile assembly, including specialty automobiles; truck & tractor truck assembly; military motor vehicle assembly; motor vehicle parts & accessories

(G-4268)
GO FRAC LLC
Also Called: Gofrac
7000 Calmont Ave Ste 310 (48207)
PHONE.................................817 731-0301
Richard Crawford, *CEO*
Buddy Petersen, *COO*
Harlan Foster, *Vice Pres*
Kevin McGlinch, *CFO*
EMP: 7 **EST:** 2011
SALES (est): 455K **Privately Held**
SIC: 1389 Oil field services

(G-4269)
GOLDEN POINTE INC
Also Called: Golden Pointe Awning & Sign Co
16050 W Warren Ave (48228-3740)
PHONE.................................313 581-8284
Nouhad Elhajj, *President*
EMP: 7 **EST:** 1987
SQ FT: 3,200
SALES (est): 347.7K **Privately Held**
WEB: www.goldenpointeawningandsign.com
SIC: 3993 3089 Signs & advertising specialties; awnings, fiberglass & plastic combination

(G-4270)
GOOD GOD PRINTING
4215 Miracles Blvd (48201-1546)
PHONE.................................313 694-2985
Jerome Montgomery, *Principal*
EMP: 4 **EST:** 2016
SALES (est): 78K **Privately Held**
SIC: 2752 Commercial printing, lithographic

(G-4271)
GORDON METAL PRODUCTS INC
8101 Lyndon St (48238-2452)
PHONE.................................586 445-0960
EMP: 14 **EST:** 2004
SALES (est): 859.7K **Privately Held**
WEB: www.gordonmetalproducts.com
SIC: 3469 Stamping metal for the trade

(G-4272)
GRAHAMS PRINTING COMPANY INC
8620 Gratiot Ave (48213-2931)
PHONE.................................313 925-1188
Cecil Graham, *President*
Juanita Graham, *Vice Pres*
EMP: 4 **EST:** 1964
SQ FT: 3,000
SALES (est): 476.1K **Privately Held**
SIC: 2752 Commercial printing, offset

(G-4273)
GRANDKIDS EDCTED MOTIVATED GEM
18626 Wexford St (48234-1858)
PHONE.................................313 539-7330
EMP: 4 **EST:** 2011
SALES (est): 55.7K **Privately Held**
SIC: 3915 Jewelers' materials & lapidary work

(G-4274)
GRANDPAPAS INC
6500 E Davison St (48212-1422)
PHONE.................................313 891-6830
Mike Robin, *President*
▼ **EMP:** 25 **EST:** 1996
SQ FT: 45,000
SALES (est): 2.6MM **Privately Held**
WEB: www.grandpapasinc.com
SIC: 2096 Pork rinds

(G-4275)
GRAVITY SOFTWARE LLC
300 Rverfront Dr Unit 22a (48226)
PHONE.................................844 464-7284
Valerie Silvani, *Vice Pres*
Mandy Vogt, *Marketing Staff*
EMP: 8 **EST:** 2019
SALES (est): 285.2K **Privately Held**
WEB: www.gogravity.com
SIC: 7372 Prepackaged software

(G-4276)
GREAT LAKES DOCK & DOOR LLC
19345 John R St (48203-1660)
P.O. Box 128, Hazel Park (48030-0128)
PHONE.................................313 368-6300
C J Ruffing,
EMP: 20
SALES (est): 8MM **Privately Held**
WEB: www.gldock.com
SIC: 3537 Loading docks: portable, adjustable & hydraulic

(G-4277)
GREAT LAKES WOODWORKING CO INC
11345 Mound Rd (48212-2556)
PHONE.................................313 892-8500
Michael J Mancinelli, *President*
Tony Gatliff, *Partner*
Anthony Gatliff, *Corp Secy*
Paul La Croix, *Vice Pres*
John Shea, *Opers Staff*
EMP: 50 **EST:** 1986
SQ FT: 42,000
SALES (est): 10.8MM **Privately Held**
WEB: www.glwdetroit.com
SIC: 2521 5712 Wood office furniture; office furniture

(G-4278)
GREEN DAY MANAGEMENT LLC
607 Shelby St Ste 700-100 (48226-3268)
PHONE.................................313 652-1390
Erick Cromartie, *Mng Member*
Lashondra Cromartie, *Mng Member*
EMP: 10 **EST:** 2015
SALES (est): 824.2K **Privately Held**
WEB: www.greenday.com
SIC: 3524 5083 Snowblowers & throwers, residential; landscaping equipment

(G-4279)
GREEN DREAMZZ LLC
8587 Northlawn St (48204-3233)
PHONE.................................313 377-2926
Gregory Norman,
EMP: 4 **EST:** 2020
SALES (est): 100K **Privately Held**
SIC: 2099 Food preparations

(G-4280)
GREEN POLYMERIC MATERIALS INC
6031 Joy Rd (48204-2909)
PHONE.................................313 933-7390
Yogesh Goel, *President*
Irfan Raza, *President*
Lov Goel, *Vice Pres*
EMP: 50 **EST:** 2014
SQ FT: 70,000
SALES (est): 5MM **Privately Held**
WEB: www.gpmaterials.com
SIC: 3086 3069 3053 Plastics foam products; insulation or cushioning material, foamed plastic; padding, foamed plastic; reclaimed rubber (reworked by manufacturing processes); packing materials

(G-4281)
GREENFIELD NOODLE SPECIALTY CO
Also Called: Greenfeld Homemade Egg Noodles
600 Custer St (48202-3128)
PHONE.................................313 873-2212
Kenneth Michaels, *President*
Mary Michaels, *Vice Pres*
EMP: 11 **EST:** 1947
SQ FT: 13,000
SALES (est): 505.9K **Privately Held**
WEB: www.greenfieldnoodle.com
SIC: 2098 5149 Noodles (e.g. egg, plain & water), dry; groceries & related products

(G-4282)
GREENING INCORPORATED (PA)
19465 Mount Elliott St (48234-2742)
PHONE.................................313 366-7160
Charles W Greening Sr, *CEO*
Charles W Greening Jr, *President*
Brent D Greening, *Vice Pres*
Marilyn F Greening, *Admin Sec*
▲ **EMP:** 2 **EST:** 1979
SQ FT: 21,000
SALES (est): 7.2MM **Privately Held**
WEB: www.greeninginc.com
SIC: 3829 8734 Dynamometer instruments; product testing laboratory, safety or performance

(G-4283)
GREENING ASSOCIATES INC
Also Called: Greening Testing Laboratories
19465 Mount Elliott St (48234-2742)
PHONE.................................313 366-7160
Charles W Greening Sr, *Ch of Bd*
Brent D Greening, *President*
Charles W Greening Jr, *Vice Pres*
Niki Bidinger, *Purch Mgr*
Marilyn Greening, *Treasurer*
▲ **EMP:** 25 **EST:** 1965
SQ FT: 22,000
SALES (est): 5MM
SALES (corp-wide): 7.2MM **Privately Held**
WEB: www.greeninginc.com
SIC: 3825 3829 Instruments to measure electricity; dynamometer instruments
PA: Greening, Incorporated
19465 Mount Elliott St
Detroit MI 48234
313 366-7160

(G-4284)
GROUP 7500 INC
Also Called: Red Door Digital
7500 Oakland St (48211-1350)
PHONE.................................313 875-9026
Roger Robinson, *President*
EMP: 18 **EST:** 1990
SALES (est): 2.1MM **Privately Held**
WEB: www.reddoordigital.com
SIC: 2759 Commercial printing

(G-4285)
GSA DIRECT SUPPLY LLC
12908 W 7 Mile Rd (48235-1305)
PHONE.................................313 739-6375
Eldrick Brown,
EMP: 9 **EST:** 2017
SALES (est): 769.9K **Privately Held**
WEB: www.gsadirectsupply.com
SIC: 2434 Wood kitchen cabinets

(G-4286)
GUIDING OUR DESTINY MINISTRY
14811 Greenfield Rd A4 (48227-4115)
PHONE.................................313 212-9063
Elmira Robinson, *Exec Dir*
EMP: 5 **EST:** 2009
SALES (est): 145.3K **Privately Held**
SIC: 3799 Transportation equipment

(G-4287)
GUZMAN WOODWORKS
2740 Honorah St (48209-1118)
PHONE.................................313 436-1912
EMP: 5 **EST:** 2017
SALES (est): 212.7K **Privately Held**
WEB: www.guzman-wood-works.business.site
SIC: 2431 Millwork

(G-4288)
H M PRODUCTS INC
1435 E Milwaukee St (48211-2009)
PHONE.................................313 875-5148
Harry S Radcliff, *President*
Mitchell Radcliff, *Vice Pres*
EMP: 6 **EST:** 1981
SQ FT: 750
SALES (est): 365.9K **Privately Held**
SIC: 3914 2899 Silverware & plated ware; chemical preparations

(G-4289)
HACIENDA MEXICAN FOODS LLC (PA)
6100 Buchanan St (48210-2400)
P.O. Box 10678 (48210-0678)
PHONE.................................313 895-8823
Lydia Guttierrez, *President*
EMP: 80 **EST:** 1994
SQ FT: 33,000
SALES (est): 7.6MM **Privately Held**
WEB: www.haciendadegutierrez.com
SIC: 2096 5149 Tortilla chips; diet foods

(G-4290)
HACKETT BRASS FOUNDRY CO (PA)
1200 Lillibridge St (48214-3295)
PHONE.................................313 822-1214
Alan L Wright, *President*
Lucas Wright, *Vice Pres*
EMP: 20 **EST:** 1918
SQ FT: 25,000
SALES (est): 2.6MM **Privately Held**
WEB: www.hackettbrass.com
SIC: 3364 3363 Copper & copper alloy die-castings; aluminum die-castings

(G-4291)
HACKETT BRASS FOUNDRY CO
Also Called: Centro Division
45 Saint Jean St (48214-3491)
PHONE.................................313 331-6005
Joseph Butala, *Plant Supt*
Lucas Wright, *Manager*
EMP: 5
SQ FT: 22,729
SALES (corp-wide): 2.6MM **Privately Held**
WEB: www.hackettbrass.com
SIC: 3365 3369 3366 3325 Aluminum & aluminum-based alloy castings; nonferrous foundries; copper foundries; steel foundries
PA: Hackett Brass Foundry Co.
1200 Lillibridge St
Detroit MI 48214
313 822-1214

(G-4292)
HAMTRAMCK REVIEW INC
3020 Caniff St (48212-3019)
PHONE.................................313 874-2100
John Ulaj, *President*
EMP: 6 **EST:** 2009
SALES (est): 494.3K **Privately Held**
WEB: www.thehamtramckreview.com
SIC: 2711 Newspapers: publishing only, not printed on site

Detroit - Wayne County (G-4293)   GEOGRAPHIC SECTION

(G-4293)
HAND 2 HAND WHL & DIST LLC
11942 Roxbury St (48224-4114)
PHONE..................................313 574-2861
Vanessa Armstrong,
EMP: 5
SALES (est): 100K **Privately Held**
SIC: 2051 Bakery: wholesale or wholesale/retail combined

(G-4294)
HAPPY HOWIES INC
15510 Dale St (48223-1038)
P.O. Box 231837 (48223-8037)
PHONE..................................313 537-7200
Stan Dickson, *President*
David Collado, *Vice Pres*
Wayne Whitney, *Natl Sales Mgr*
Peggy Malarik, *Manager*
▲ **EMP:** 10 **EST:** 2006
SQ FT: 600,000
SALES (est): 700K **Privately Held**
WEB: www.happyhowies.com
SIC: 2047 Dog food

(G-4295)
HARPER ARRINGTON PUBG LLC
18701 Grand River Ave # 105
(48223-2214)
PHONE..................................313 282-6751
Michael Harper,
Jay Arrington,
EMP: 4 **EST:** 2004
SALES (est): 442K **Privately Held**
WEB: www.harperarringtonmedia.com
SIC: 7372 2731 Publishers' computer software; books: publishing only

(G-4296)
HATTIEGIRL ICE CREAM FOODS LLC
16159 Wyoming St (48221-2846)
PHONE..................................877 444-3738
James Render, *General Mgr*
James D Render, *Principal*
EMP: 6 **EST:** 2017
SQ FT: 1,000
SALES (est): 515.4K **Privately Held**
WEB: www.hattiegirlfoodproducts.com
SIC: 2024 Ice cream & frozen desserts

(G-4297)
HEALTHCURE LLC
6501 Lynch Rd (48234-4140)
PHONE..................................313 743-2331
John McIntyre, *President*
Carlton Guthrie, *Chairman*
Dave Taylor, *Opers Staff*
Joseph Gause, *CFO*
Michael Hinton, *Human Res Dir*
EMP: 10 **EST:** 2011
SALES (est): 653.8K **Privately Held**
WEB: www.healthcure.biz
SIC: 2842 Sanitation preparations

(G-4298)
HERCULES ELECTRIC MOBILITY INC
Also Called: Hercules Electric Vehicles
2875 E Grand Blvd (48202-3150)
PHONE..................................734 666-8078
James Breyer, *CEO*
EMP: 4 **EST:** 2018
SALES (est): 295.2K **Privately Held**
WEB: www.herculesev.com
SIC: 3711 Motor vehicles & car bodies

(G-4299)
HHI FUNDING II LLC
1 Dauch Dr (48211-1115)
PHONE..................................313 758-2000
EMP: 214
SALES (est): 5.6MM
SALES (corp-wide): 4.7B **Publicly Held**
SIC: 3714 3711 Mfg Motor Vehicle Parts/Accessories Mfg Motor Vehicle/Car Bodies
HQ: Hephaestus Holdings, Llc
39475 W 13 Mile Rd # 105
Novi MI 48377

(G-4300)
HHI HOLDINGS LLC (DH)
1 Dauch Dr (48211-1115)
PHONE..................................313 758-2000
EMP: 3
SALES (est): 328.8MM
SALES (corp-wide): 4.7B **Publicly Held**
SIC: 3714 3711 Mfg Motor Vehicle/Car Bodies Mfg Motor Vehicle Parts/Accessories
HQ: Asp Hhi Acquisition Co., Inc.
1 Dauch Dr
Detroit MI 48211
313 758-2000

(G-4301)
HIGH FREQUENCY HEALING CO LLC
17349 Stoepel St (48221-2611)
PHONE..................................313 938-9711
Brittney Williams,
EMP: 4 **EST:** 2020
SALES (est): 100.4K **Privately Held**
SIC: 2834 Vitamin preparations

(G-4302)
HMW CONTRACTING LLC
Also Called: H M White
12855 Burt Rd (48223-3316)
PHONE..................................313 531-8477
Jonathon B Ricker, *President*
Rob Keramidas, *Project Mgr*
Nicholas Konkle, *Project Engr*
Domenico E Colone, *Treasurer*
Jon Ricker, *CIO*
EMP: 150 **EST:** 2009
SQ FT: 35,000
SALES (est): 47.4MM **Privately Held**
WEB: www.hmwhite.com
SIC: 3444 Metal ventilating equipment

(G-4303)
HOME STYLE FOODS INC
5163 Edwin St (48212-3377)
PHONE..................................313 874-3250
Micheal Kowliski, *President*
EMP: 11 **EST:** 1953
SQ FT: 5,000
SALES (est): 4MM **Privately Held**
WEB: www.homestylefoods.com
SIC: 5148 5149 2099 Vegetables; groceries & related products; macaroni; ready-to-eat meals, salads & sandwiches

(G-4304)
HONEYWORKS LLC
17410 Northlawn St (48221-4511)
PHONE..................................313 575-0871
Leotis Brown, *Mng Member*
Aliyma Wakefeld,
EMP: 4
SALES (est): 20K **Privately Held**
SIC: 2844 5999 Lotions, shaving; toiletries, cosmetics & perfumes

(G-4305)
HOOVER TREATED WOOD PDTS INC
7500 E Davison St (48212-1925)
PHONE..................................313 365-4200
Thomas Spiekhout, *Manager*
EMP: 18
SALES (corp-wide): 2.8B **Publicly Held**
WEB: www.frtw.com
SIC: 2491 Structural lumber & timber, treated wood
HQ: Hoover Treated Wood Products, Inc.
154 Wire Rd
Thomson GA 30824
706 595-5058

(G-4306)
HOPE FOCUS
Also Called: Focus Hope Manufacturing
1400 Oakman Blvd (48238-2848)
PHONE..................................313 494-4500
Vanessa Davis, *Comms Dir*
Tim Sullivan, *Branch Mgr*
Ordie Hamilton, *Manager*
Judith Robinson, *Manager*
Debbie Fisher, *Director*
EMP: 35

SALES (corp-wide): 36.6MM **Privately Held**
WEB: www.focushope.edu
SIC: 3714 Motor vehicle parts & accessories
PA: Hope Focus
1400 Oakman Blvd
Detroit MI 48238
313 494-5500

(G-4307)
HOPE FOCUS (PA)
1400 Oakman Blvd (48238-2848)
PHONE..................................313 494-5500
Vernice Davis Anthony, *CEO*
Portia L Roberson, *President*
Lizebeth Ardisana, *Vice Chairman*
Rodney Smith, *Business Mgr*
Timothy M Duperron, *COO*
EMP: 170 **EST:** 1968
SQ FT: 16,000
SALES (est): 36.6MM **Privately Held**
WEB: www.focushope.edu
SIC: 8399 3714 8249 8299 Neighborhood development group; motor vehicle parts & accessories; vocational schools; educational services

(G-4308)
HOPE FOCUS COMPANIES INC (HQ)
Also Called: Focus Hope Logistics
1200 Oakman Blvd (48238-2998)
PHONE..................................313 494-5500
Timothy Duperron, *CEO*
Martha Schultz, *Treasurer*
Micheal Collins, *Info Tech Dir*
Carl T Weber, *Technology*
Ladawn White, *Asst Director*
▲ **EMP:** 20 **EST:** 1984
SALES (est): 29.3MM
SALES (corp-wide): 36.6MM **Privately Held**
WEB: www.focushope.edu
SIC: 3545 Precision tools, machinists'
PA: Hope Focus
1400 Oakman Blvd
Detroit MI 48238
313 494-5500

(G-4309)
HUNTERS JEWELRY REPAIR CTR INC
20250 Packard St (48234-4617)
PHONE..................................313 892-7621
Joseph Hunter Jr, *Owner*
EMP: 4 **EST:** 2012
SALES (est): 169.8K **Privately Held**
SIC: 3911 Jewelry mountings & trimmings

(G-4310)
HYDE SPRING AND WIRE COMPANY
14341 Schaefer Hwy (48227-5603)
PHONE..................................313 272-2201
John M Hyde, *Owner*
Bonnie Hyde, *Vice Pres*
Leona Lear, *Manager*
EMP: 10 **EST:** 1944
SQ FT: 22,000
SALES (est): 500K **Privately Held**
WEB: www.hydespring.com
SIC: 3495 Mechanical springs, precision

(G-4311)
IDEAL SHIELD LLC
2525 Clark St (48209-1337)
PHONE..................................866 825-8659
Richard Grove, *Sales Staff*
Frank Venegas,
Jesse Venegas,
Linzie Venegas,
Loren Venegas,
▼ **EMP:** 50 **EST:** 1997
SQ FT: 67,000
SALES (est): 11.5MM **Privately Held**
WEB: www.idealshield.com
SIC: 3089 3449 Plastic processing; miscellaneous metalwork
PA: The Ideal Group Inc
2525 Clark St
Detroit MI 48209

(G-4312)
IDEAL STEEL & BLDRS SUPS LLC
2525 Clark St (48209-9703)
PHONE..................................313 849-0000
Frank Venegas, *CEO*
Hector Romero, *Plant Mgr*
Stephen Pedley, *Project Mgr*
Rachel Johnson, *CFO*
EMP: 22 **EST:** 2015
SALES (est): 5.5MM **Privately Held**
WEB: www.idealsteel.com
SIC: 3441 Fabricated structural metal

(G-4313)
IHC INC
Also Called: International Hardcoat
12400 Burt Rd (48228-5500)
PHONE..................................313 535-3210
Jeffrey R Pernick, *President*
Joel Peltier, *General Mgr*
Joe Peltier, *Vice Pres*
James D Weil, *Vice Pres*
Al Harrell, *Prdtn Mgr*
EMP: 115 **EST:** 1962
SQ FT: 100,000
SALES (est): 17.8MM **Privately Held**
WEB: www.ihccorp.com
SIC: 3471 Electroplating of metals or formed products

(G-4314)
INDUSTRIAL CONTAINER INC
6671 French Rd (48213-3277)
PHONE..................................313 923-8778
Douglas Tito, *President*
Victoria Sumner, *Manager*
David Tito, *Admin Sec*
EMP: 18 **EST:** 1987
SQ FT: 36,000
SALES (est): 2.7MM **Privately Held**
WEB: www.indcontainer.com
SIC: 3443 Containers, shipping (bombs, etc.): metal plate

(G-4315)
INDUSTRIAL ELC CO DETROIT INC
Also Called: I.E. Communications
275 E Milwaukee St (48202-3233)
PHONE..................................313 872-1133
William M Darish, *President*
John T Darish, *Corp Secy*
Thomas R Darish, *Vice Pres*
John Darish, *Project Mgr*
Tom Darish, *Project Mgr*
EMP: 55 **EST:** 1934
SQ FT: 5,500
SALES (est): 9MM **Privately Held**
WEB: www.industrialelectric.net
SIC: 1731 7694 General electrical contractor; armature rewinding shops

(G-4316)
INDUSTRIAL SEW INNVTION CTR IS
5800 Cass Ave Ste 43 (48202-3452)
PHONE..................................313 870-1898
Jennifer Guarino, *Principal*
Dorothy Powers, *Principal*
Kimberly Sutherland, *Principal*
EMP: 6 **EST:** 2018
SALES (est): 748.9K **Privately Held**
WEB: www.isaic.org
SIC: 2389 Apparel & accessories

(G-4317)
INFOTEL
105 E Bethune St (48202-2810)
PHONE..................................313 879-0820
EMP: 6 **EST:** 2007
SALES (est): 50.1K **Privately Held**
SIC: 2791 Typesetting

(G-4318)
INLAND MANAGEMENT INC (HQ)
4086 Michigan Ave (48210-3261)
PHONE..................................313 899-3014
Jeffery Stark, *President*
Claude Kubrak, *President*
Dan Ford, *Vice Pres*
Andrea Stier, *Opers Mgr*
Tom Gray, *Sls & Mktg Exec*
▼ **EMP:** 2 **EST:** 1985

SQ FT: 43,000
SALES (est): 48.2MM **Privately Held**
WEB: www.teamipr.com
SIC: 3589 Sewer cleaning equipment, power

(G-4319)
INNOVATIVE GROUPS INC
400 Renaissance Ctr # 2600 (48243-1502)
PHONE.................................313 309-7064
Lemoyne Veney, *Principal*
Shawn Baek, *Principal*
EMP: 5 EST: 2019
SALES (est): 391K **Privately Held**
SIC: 3699 Electrical equipment & supplies

(G-4320)
INNOVATIVE MATERIAL HANDLING
18820 Woodward Ave (48203-1901)
PHONE.................................586 291-3694
Gregory Armstrong, *CEO*
EMP: 8 EST: 2014
SALES (est): 110.7K **Privately Held**
SIC: 2396 Automotive & apparel trimmings

(G-4321)
INOVATION SERVICES LLC
3750 Seminole St (48214-1193)
PHONE.................................586 932-7653
Lamar Fisher, *Principal*
EMP: 10 EST: 2020
SALES (est): 450.2K **Privately Held**
SIC: 2211 Broadwoven fabric mills, cotton

(G-4322)
INTEGRATED MFG & ASSEMBLY LLC (PA)
Also Called: I M A
6501 E Nevada St (48234-2833)
PHONE.................................734 530-5600
Mike Puckett, *Plant Mgr*
Adrian Boyer, *Opers Mgr*
Chauna Grigsby, *Finance*
Joi Silver, *Human Resources*
James Comer,
▲ EMP: 350 EST: 1996
SQ FT: 40,000
SALES (est): 46.9MM **Privately Held**
SIC: 2531 Seats, automobile

(G-4323)
INTELLIBEE INC
400 Renaissance Ctr # 2600 (48243-1502)
PHONE.................................313 586-4122
Prasad Beesabathuni, *President*
EMP: 50 EST: 2000
SALES (est): 6.7MM **Privately Held**
WEB: www.intellibee.com
SIC: 7379 7373 7371 7372 Computer related consulting services; computer integrated systems design; custom computer programming services; computer software development & applications; application computer software; minicomputers

(G-4324)
INTRAMODE LLC
1420 Brdwy St (48226)
PHONE.................................313 964-6990
Maureen Kraemer, *Principal*
Robert Kraemer,
EMP: 6 EST: 2000
SQ FT: 10,000
SALES (est): 515.5K **Privately Held**
WEB: www.intramode.structuredchannel.com
SIC: 2392 Household furnishings

(G-4325)
IPAX ATLANTIC LLC
8301 Lyndon St (48238-2444)
PHONE.................................313 933-4211
Evgeniia Taranova, *Controller*
Ledion Curi, *Accounting Mgr*
Irina Andrianova, *Mng Member*
EMP: 9 EST: 2012
SQ FT: 50,000
SALES (est): 1.3MM **Privately Held**
WEB: www.ipax.com
SIC: 2842 2843 2841 Cleaning or polishing preparations; degreasing solvent; surface active agents; textile soap

(G-4326)
IPAX CLEANOGEL INC
8301 Lyndon St (48238-2444)
PHONE.................................313 933-4211
Alla Katz, *President*
Igor Berger, *Vice Pres*
Paul Katz, *Vice Pres*
Ledion Curi, *Accountant*
Brian Taylor, *Sales Staff*
▼ EMP: 8 EST: 1982
SQ FT: 30,000
SALES (est): 1.5MM **Privately Held**
WEB: www.ipax.com
SIC: 2842 Cleaning or polishing preparations

(G-4327)
ITALIAN BTR BREAD STICKS BKY
4241 E Mcnichols Rd (48212-1717)
PHONE.................................313 893-4945
Veljko Djuric, *Partner*
Kosara Djuric, *Partner*
EMP: 4 EST: 1980
SQ FT: 3,000
SALES (est): 225.6K **Privately Held**
SIC: 2051 Bread, all types (white, wheat, rye, etc): fresh or frozen

(G-4328)
IVAN DOVERSPIKE
Also Called: E-Course Machinery
9501 Conner St (48213-1241)
PHONE.................................313 579-3000
Ivan D Doverspike, *President*
Judith Doverspike, *Vice Pres*
Gary Ede, *Safety Mgr*
Jill Doverspike Neal, *Treasurer*
Mark Spresser, *Manager*
EMP: 17
SQ FT: 4,000
SALES (est): 2.3MM **Privately Held**
SIC: 3312 5084 3541 Rods, iron & steel: made in steel mills; industrial machinery & equipment; machine tools, metal cutting type

(G-4329)
IVORY INDUSTRIES INC
2253 Burns St (48214-2895)
PHONE.................................313 821-3291
Frank I Cross, *Principal*
EMP: 4 EST: 2011
SALES (est): 123.3K **Privately Held**
SIC: 3999 Manufacturing industries

(G-4330)
IVY SNOW LLC
4110 Commonwealth St (48208-2909)
PHONE.................................248 842-1242
Hailey Myziuk, *Principal*
EMP: 4 EST: 2016
SALES (est): 64.9K **Privately Held**
SIC: 2754 Commercial printing, gravure

(G-4331)
J & G PALLETS INC (PA)
2971 Bellevue St (48207-3502)
PHONE.................................313 921-0222
Geraldine Givahen, *President*
EMP: 7 EST: 1995
SALES (est): 1.4MM **Privately Held**
WEB: www.jgpalletsandtrucking.com
SIC: 2448 Pallets, wood

(G-4332)
JAM ENTERPRISES
16349 E Warren Ave (48224-2715)
PHONE.................................313 417-9200
James Antwine, *Owner*
EMP: 4 EST: 1982
SQ FT: 1,400
SALES (est): 190.1K **Privately Held**
SIC: 2396 Screen printing on fabric articles

(G-4333)
JANUTOL PRINTING CO INC
9920 Conner St (48213-1245)
PHONE.................................313 526-6196
Peter Janutol, *President*
Charles Janutol, *Corp Secy*
Eleanor Janutol, *Vice Pres*
EMP: 5 EST: 1956
SQ FT: 9,000
SALES (est): 440.2K **Privately Held**
WEB: www.janutolprinting.com
SIC: 2752 Commercial printing, offset

(G-4334)
JAR-ME LLC
16801 Grand River Ave # 2 (48227-1421)
PHONE.................................313 319-7765
Bryanna Reed,
EMP: 4
SALES (est): 165.1K **Privately Held**
SIC: 2037 Frozen fruits & vegetables

(G-4335)
JASCO INTERNATIONAL LLC (PA)
7140 W Fort St (48209-2917)
PHONE.................................313 841-5000
Louis James, *President*
Pat Dennis, *CFO*
Eiichi Seto, *Treasurer*
EMP: 5 EST: 2002
SALES (est): 9.8MM **Privately Held**
WEB: www.mcljasco.com
SIC: 3711 4213 4214 7389 Automobile assembly, including specialty automobiles; trucking, except local; local trucking with storage; inventory stocking service

(G-4336)
JAYS FAMOUS FD HOTDOGS & MORE
18020 Bradford St (48205-2604)
PHONE.................................313 648-7225
Jeremiah Jones, *Owner*
EMP: 6 EST: 2014
SALES (est): 118.6K **Privately Held**
SIC: 2599 Food wagons, restaurant

(G-4337)
JGA PRESS/JACKSON GATES ASSOC
1115 W Boston Blvd (48202-1409)
PHONE.................................313 957-0200
Cynthia Reaves, *Principal*
EMP: 4 EST: 2018
SALES (est): 86.6K **Privately Held**
WEB: www.jacksongates.com
SIC: 2741 Miscellaneous publishing

(G-4338)
JO-MAR ENTERPRISES INC
7489 E Davison St (48212-1912)
PHONE.................................313 365-9200
Joseph R Joye, *President*
EMP: 6 EST: 1955
SQ FT: 3,600 **Privately Held**
WEB: www.jomarchrome.com
SIC: 3471 Electroplating of metals or formed products

(G-4339)
JOGUE INC
6349 E Palmer St (48211-3201)
PHONE.................................313 921-4802
Dr Warren McKlenden, *Principal*
EMP: 6
SALES (corp-wide): 14.8MM **Privately Held**
WEB: www.jogue.com
SIC: 2087 2844 Extracts, flavoring; toilet preparations
PA: Jogue, Inc.
    14731 Helm Ct
    Plymouth MI 48170
    734 207-0100

(G-4340)
JOHNICO LLC
Also Called: America's Green Line
400 Monroe St Ste 480 (48226-2960)
PHONE.................................248 895-7820
Brian Buchler, *Manager*
Ken Johnson, *Director*
Nico Gatzaros,
John Economy,
Maria Gatzaros,
EMP: 25 EST: 2014
SALES (est): 2.7MM **Privately Held**
WEB: www.americasgreenline.com
SIC: 3641 3646 3648 Tubes, electric light; commercial indusl & institutional electric lighting fixtures; public lighting fixtures; street lighting fixtures

(G-4341)
JOHNSON CONTROLS INC
4617 W Fort St (48209-3208)
PHONE.................................313 842-3300
Denise Stinson, *Manager*
EMP: 7 **Publicly Held**
WEB: www.johnsoncontrols.com
SIC: 3714 Motor vehicle parts & accessories
HQ: Johnson Controls, Inc.
    5757 N Green Bay Ave
    Glendale WI 53209
    800 382-2804

(G-4342)
JONES MUSIC CO
18982 Runyon St (48234-3751)
PHONE.................................313 521-6471
Chtrice Jones, *President*
Clark Jones, *Manager*
EMP: 4 EST: 2015
SALES (est): 122K **Privately Held**
SIC: 2741 Miscellaneous publishing

(G-4343)
JSP INTERNATIONAL LLC
13889 W Chicago St (48228-2525)
PHONE.................................724 477-5100
Donna Rouse, *Mfg Mgr*
Damion Gunn, *Production*
Joe Mihelich, *Sales Mgr*
Robert Doerr, *Sales Staff*
Stan Purnsley, *Manager*
EMP: 5 **Privately Held**
WEB: www.jsp.com
SIC: 3081 Polyethylene film; polypropylene film & sheet
HQ: Jsp International Llc
    1285 Drummers Ln Ste 301
    Wayne PA 19087

(G-4344)
JW LIESS MACHINE SHOP
20475 Woodingham Dr (48221-1260)
PHONE.................................248 219-0444
EMP: 4 EST: 2017
SALES (est): 81.4K **Privately Held**
SIC: 3599 Machine shop, jobbing & repair

(G-4345)
K & N TRANSPORT LLC ✪
10780 Duprey St (48224-1295)
PHONE.................................313 384-0037
Pierre Livingston,
EMP: 4 EST: 2021
SALES (est): 149.8K **Privately Held**
SIC: 3731 Transport vessels, troop: building & repairing

(G-4346)
K AND A PUBLISHING CO LLC
18085 Forrer St (48235-3114)
PHONE.................................734 743-1541
Kalio White,
EMP: 6 EST: 2017
SALES (est): 219.1K **Privately Held**
WEB: www.k-and-a-publishing-co-llc.business.site
SIC: 2721 Magazines: publishing & printing

(G-4347)
K G S SCREEN PROCESS INC
12650 Burt Rd (48223-3315)
PHONE.................................313 794-2777
EMP: 5
SQ FT: 15,000
SALES (est): 500K **Privately Held**
SIC: 2759 Screen Printing

(G-4348)
KAE ORGANICS LLC
6514 Greenview Ave (48228-4764)
PHONE.................................248 832-0403
Torrie Hill,
EMP: 4 EST: 2020
SALES (est): 156.7K **Privately Held**
WEB: www.doorganics.grubmarket.com
SIC: 2844 Hair preparations, including shampoos

(G-4349)
KAMPS INC
Also Called: Kamps Pallets
19001 Glendale St (48223-3423)
PHONE.................................313 381-2681
Savanna Kuhlow, *Natl Sales Mgr*

Detroit - Wayne County (G-4350) — GEOGRAPHIC SECTION

Clifton Cheek, *Manager*
EMP: 23
SALES (corp-wide): 1.7B **Privately Held**
WEB: www.kampspallets.com
SIC: 2448 2499 Pallets, wood; mulch, wood & bark
HQ: Kamps, Inc.
  2900 Peach Ridge Ave Nw
  Grand Rapids MI 49534
  616 453-9676

(G-4350)
KAR-BONES INC
8350 John Kronk St (48210-2101)
PHONE.................................313 582-5551
Hussain Al-Nassari, *Mng Member*
EMP: 7 **EST:** 2016
SALES (est): 466.5K **Privately Held**
SIC: 3714 Motor vehicle parts & accessories

(G-4351)
KASH ST JAMES LLC
4016 29th St (48210-2695)
PHONE.................................248 571-1160
Brian Morrison, *Mng Member*
EMP: 5
SALES (est): 227.5K **Privately Held**
SIC: 3161 7389 Clothing & apparel carrying cases;

(G-4352)
KATRINA LOVE-JONES LLC
12068 Littlefield St (48227-3439)
PHONE.................................248 779-6017
Katrina Love-Jones, *CEO*
EMP: 4 **EST:** 2020
SALES (est): 100K **Privately Held**
SIC: 2842 Disinfectants, household or industrial plant

(G-4353)
KAUL GLOVE AND MFG CO (PA)
Also Called: Choctaw-Kaul Distribution Co
3540 Vinewood St (48208-2363)
PHONE.................................313 894-9494
Kenny Tubby, *CEO*
Anthony C Naso, *Vice Pres*
Stephen Kovats, *Purch Agent*
Grace Lopiccolo, *Purchasing*
Michael G Conniff Jr, *CFO*
EMP: 30 **EST:** 1945
SQ FT: 110,000
SALES (est): 85.6MM **Privately Held**
WEB: www.choctawkaul.com
SIC: 2381 3151 5136 Fabric dress & work gloves; gloves, leather: work; work clothing, men's & boys'

(G-4354)
KAUTEX INC
Also Called: Kautex Detroit
2627 Clark St (48210-3265)
PHONE.................................313 633-2254
EMP: 280
SALES (corp-wide): 11.6B **Publicly Held**
WEB: www.kautex.com
SIC: 3089 Plastic containers, except foam; automotive parts, plastic
HQ: Kautex Inc.
  800 Tower Dr Ste 200
  Troy MI 48098
  248 616-5100

(G-4355)
KCI PRENTIS BUILDING
110 E Warren Ave (48201-1312)
PHONE.................................313 578-4400
Richard Pense, *Research*
Peggy Gulewicz, *Manager*
Diane Spezia, *Manager*
Shiela Summers, *Admin Asst*
Felicity Harper, *Assoc Prof*
EMP: 11 **EST:** 2019
SALES (est): 1.2MM **Privately Held**
SIC: 2599 Hospital beds

(G-4356)
KEETZ KLOSET KOLLECTION LLC
9461 Wayburn St (48224-2814)
PHONE.................................313 878-1032
Rickeita Hall,
EMP: 8 **EST:** 2020
SALES (est): 275.5K **Privately Held**
WEB: www.keetzkloset.com
SIC: 2339 Women's & misses' outerwear

(G-4357)
KELLYS RECYCLING SERVICE INC
14800 Castleton St (48227-2422)
PHONE.................................313 389-7870
Bert Kelly, *Principal*
EMP: 5 **EST:** 2000
SALES (est): 875.5K **Privately Held**
SIC: 2077 Tallow rendering, inedible

(G-4358)
KERRY INC
4444 52nd St (48210-2728)
PHONE.................................616 871-9940
EMP: 20 **Privately Held**
WEB: www.kerry.com
SIC: 2023 Dry, condensed, evaporated dairy products
HQ: Kerry Inc.
  3400 Millington Rd
  Beloit WI 53511
  608 363-1200

(G-4359)
KEURIG DR PEPPER INC
Also Called: Seven-Up of Detroit
12201 Beech Daly Rd (48239-2431)
PHONE.................................313 937-3500
Michael Nelson, *Branch Mgr*
EMP: 6 **Publicly Held**
WEB: www.keurigdrpepper.com
SIC: 2086 Soft drinks: packaged in cans, bottles, etc.
PA: Keurig Dr Pepper Inc.
  53 South Ave
  Burlington MA 01803

(G-4360)
KEYSTONE CABLE CORPORATION
8200 Lynch Rd (48234-4143)
P.O. Box 599, Saint Clair Shores (48080-0599)
PHONE.................................313 924-9720
Thomas A Scott, *President*
Marijore Scott, *Corp Secy*
Tim Scott, *Vice Pres*
Timothy Scott, *Vice Pres*
Debbie Serafino, *Opers Staff*
EMP: 6 **EST:** 1963
SQ FT: 13,000 **Privately Held**
WEB: www.keystonecable.net
SIC: 3694 Battery cable wiring sets for internal combustion engines

(G-4361)
KHEARMA GROUP LLC
8301 Saint Aubin St (48211-1330)
PHONE.................................248 513-5763
Raymond Conley, *Mng Member*
EMP: 15 **EST:** 2020
SALES (est): 576.3K **Privately Held**
SIC: 3462 Automotive forgings, ferrous: crankshaft, engine, axle, etc.

(G-4362)
KIMS MART INC
Also Called: Beauty Spot
20240 W 7 Mile Rd (48219-3469)
PHONE.................................313 592-4929
Hungwoo Kim, *President*
EMP: 4 **EST:** 2004
SALES (est): 257.9K **Privately Held**
SIC: 3999 Barber & beauty shop equipment

(G-4363)
KINGDOM BUILDING MERCHANDISE
20230 Ardmore St (48235-1575)
PHONE.................................313 334-3866
Janine Carter, *Principal*
EMP: 4 **EST:** 2007
SALES (est): 67.9K **Privately Held**
SIC: 2531 Church furniture

(G-4364)
KIRKS AUTOMOTIVE INCORPORATED (PA)
Also Called: R K Parts
9330 Roselawn St (48204-2749)
PHONE.................................313 933-7030
Robert E Kirkman, *President*
Stephen Allen Benish, *Vice Pres*
Micheal Kirkman, *Vice Pres*
▲ **EMP:** 34 **EST:** 1946
SQ FT: 52,000
SALES (est): 8.8MM **Privately Held**
WEB: www.kirksauto.com
SIC: 5013 3694 Automotive supplies & parts; engine electrical equipment

(G-4365)
KOLENE CORPORATION (PA)
12890 Westwood St (48223-3436)
PHONE.................................313 273-9220
Roger L Shoemaker, *CEO*
W Scott Schilling, *President*
Tom Strickland, *General Mgr*
Dennis J McCardle, *Exec VP*
Dennis McCardle, *Exec VP*
▼ **EMP:** 51 **EST:** 1939
SQ FT: 38,800
SALES (est): 13.5MM **Privately Held**
WEB: www.kolene.com
SIC: 2899 3567 Metal treating compounds; fuel-fired furnaces & ovens

(G-4366)
KOWALSKI COMPANIES INC (PA)
2270 Holbrook St (48212-3445)
PHONE.................................313 873-8200
Michael Kowalski, *President*
Ulrich Eggert, *Treasurer*
Patty Monette, *Human Res Mgr*
Greg Thayer, *Manager*
Linda Kowalski, *Admin Sec*
EMP: 116
SQ FT: 60,000
SALES (est): 38.4MM **Privately Held**
WEB: www.kowality.com
SIC: 2013 5421 Sausages from purchased meat; bacon, side & sliced: from purchased meat; meat extracts from purchased meat; meat & fish markets

(G-4367)
KREATIONS INC
15340 Dale St (48223-1036)
PHONE.................................313 255-1230
Elias Madi, *President*
Imad Madi, *Vice Pres*
EMP: 10 **EST:** 1987
SQ FT: 4,500
SALES (est): 1.4MM **Privately Held**
SIC: 2541 8712 Cabinets, except refrigerated: show, display, etc.: wood; architectural services

(G-4368)
KRUMBSNATCHER ENTERPRISES LLC
Also Called: Krumbsnatcher Cookies
11000 W Mcnic (48235)
PHONE.................................313 408-6802
Daryll Gray, *Mng Member*
Christine Gray,
Tonya Gray,
Tina Poole,
EMP: 10 **EST:** 2005
SALES (est): 500K **Privately Held**
WEB: www.krumbsnatcherenterprises.com
SIC: 2052 7389 Cookies; business services

(G-4369)
KUHLMAN CASTING CO INC
20415 Woodingham Dr (48221-1288)
PHONE.................................248 853-2382
Neal Norgrove, *President*
Thomas F Hanrahan, *Corp Secy*
Richard Hanrahan, *Vice Pres*
EMP: 18 **EST:** 1949
SQ FT: 6,900
SALES (est): 316.2K **Privately Held**
SIC: 3369 Machinery castings, nonferrous: ex. alum., copper, die, etc.

(G-4370)
KYKLOS HOLDINGS INC (DH)
1 Dauch Dr (48211-1115)
PHONE.................................313 758-2000
EMP: 3
SALES (est): 1.2MM
SALES (corp-wide): 4.7B **Publicly Held**
SIC: 3711 3714 Mfg Motor Vehicle/Car Bodies Mfg Motor Vehicle Parts/Accessories
HQ: Bearing Holdings Llc
  1 Dauch Dr
  Detroit MI 48211
  313 758-2000

(G-4371)
LA ROSA REFRIGERATION & EQP CO
19191 Filer St (48234-2883)
PHONE.................................313 368-6620
Sebastiano Grillo, *President*
Jerry Grillo, *Vice Pres*
Daniel Gudenau, *Design Engr*
Josh Compton, *VP Sls/Mktg*
EMP: 20 **EST:** 1970
SQ FT: 30,000
SALES (est): 4.2MM **Privately Held**
WEB: www.larosaequip.com
SIC: 3585 2599 Refrigeration equipment, complete; restaurant furniture, wood or metal

(G-4372)
LA SOLUCION CORP
19930 Conner St (48234-3227)
PHONE.................................313 893-9760
Patricia Maria Leon, *President*
◆ **EMP:** 5 **EST:** 1999
SALES (est): 708.6K **Privately Held**
WEB: www.la-solucion.com
SIC: 3677 Filtration devices, electronic

(G-4373)
LABOR EDUCATION AND RES PRJ
Also Called: Labor Notes
7435 Michigan Ave (48210-2227)
PHONE.................................313 842-6262
Samantha Winslow, *Managing Dir*
Mark Brenner, *Director*
Theresa El Amin, *Bd of Directors*
Barbara Madeloni, *Education*
EMP: 9 **EST:** 1978
SALES (est): 1MM **Privately Held**
WEB: www.labornotes.org
SIC: 2759 Publication printing

(G-4374)
LABTECH CORPORATION
7707 Lyndon St (48238-2465)
PHONE.................................313 862-1737
Corey Bryce, *President*
EMP: 11 **EST:** 1977
SQ FT: 75,000
SALES (est): 1.6MM **Privately Held**
WEB: www.labtechcorp.com
SIC: 2842 Cleaning or polishing preparations

(G-4375)
LAFARGE NORTH AMERICA INC
1301 Springwells Ct (48209-4608)
PHONE.................................313 842-9258
Jodie Weiss, *Manager*
EMP: 6
SALES (corp-wide): 25.3B **Privately Held**
WEB: www.lafarge-na.com
SIC: 3273 Ready-mixed concrete
HQ: Lafarge North America Inc.
  8700 W Bryn Mawr Ave # 30
  Chicago IL 60631
  773 372-1000

(G-4376)
LAKESIDE BUILDING PRODUCTS
9189 Central St (48204-4323)
P.O. Box 2900, Farmington Hills (48333-2900)
PHONE.................................248 349-3500
EMP: 4
SALES (est): 367.8K **Privately Held**
SIC: 3273 Mfg Ready-Mixed Concrete

GEOGRAPHIC SECTION — Detroit - Wayne County (G-4405)

(G-4377)
LAND STAR INC
Also Called: Michigan Masonry Materials
14284 Meyers Rd (48227-3922)
PHONE.................................313 834-2366
Fred Warstler, *President*
EMP: 4 **EST:** 1995
SALES (est): 608.5K **Privately Held**
WEB: www.landstar.com
SIC: 5211 3273 Lumber & other building materials; ready-mixed concrete

(G-4378)
LATINO PRESS INC
6301 Michigan Ave (48210-2954)
PHONE.................................313 361-3000
Elias Gutierrez, *President*
EMP: 7 **EST:** 1993
SQ FT: 4,000
SALES (est): 480K **Privately Held**
WEB: www.latinodetroit.com
SIC: 2711 Newspapers, publishing & printing

(G-4379)
LAUGHABITS LLC
9301 Dwight St (48214-2903)
PHONE.................................248 990-3011
Greg Robinson, *Mng Member*
EMP: 5 **EST:** 2006
SALES (est): 147.5K **Privately Held**
WEB: www.laughabits.com
SIC: 3993 Advertising artwork

(G-4380)
LEAR AUTOMOTIVE MFG LLC
6555 E Davison St (48212-1455)
PHONE.................................248 447-1603
EMP: 11
SALES (est): 556.8K
SALES (corp-wide): 20.4B **Publicly Held**
SIC: 3714 7532 Mfg Of Aftermarket Auto Parts And Leather Goods
PA: Lear Corporation
    21557 Telegraph Rd
    Southfield MI 48033
    248 447-1500

(G-4381)
LEAR AUTOMOTIVE MFG LLC
6555 E Davison St (48212)
PHONE.................................248 447-1603
Barney Theisen, *Vice Pres*
EMP: 11 **EST:** 2002
SALES (est): 1.9MM
SALES (corp-wide): 17B **Publicly Held**
WEB: www.lear.com
SIC: 3714 7532 Motor vehicle electrical equipment; instrument board assemblies, motor vehicle; automotive wiring harness sets; motor vehicle body components & frame; upholstery & trim shop, automotive
PA: Lear Corporation
    21557 Telegraph Rd
    Southfield MI 48033
    248 447-1500

(G-4382)
LEAR CORPORATION
Also Called: Lear Ima Detroit
6501 E Nevada St (48234-2833)
PHONE.................................313 731-0840
EMP: 200
SALES (corp-wide): 17B **Publicly Held**
WEB: www.lear.com
SIC: 3714 Motor vehicle parts & accessories
PA: Lear Corporation
    21557 Telegraph Rd
    Southfield MI 48033
    248 447-1500

(G-4383)
LEAR CORPORATION
119 State St (48226-1803)
PHONE.................................313 965-0507
Michael Modreski, *Engineer*
EMP: 7
SALES (corp-wide): 17B **Publicly Held**
WEB: www.lear.com
SIC: 3714 Motor vehicle electrical equipment
PA: Lear Corporation
    21557 Telegraph Rd
    Southfield MI 48033
    248 447-1500

(G-4384)
LEAR CORPORATION
9501 Conner St (48213-1241)
PHONE.................................248 447-1563
David Staples, *Branch Mgr*
EMP: 472
SALES (corp-wide): 17B **Publicly Held**
SIC: 2531 Seats, automobile
PA: Lear Corporation
    21557 Telegraph Rd
    Southfield MI 48033
    248 447-1500

(G-4385)
LEFTY LOVE LLC
17144 Plainview Ave (48219-3554)
PHONE.................................248 795-3858
Latonya Lobe,
EMP: 4 **EST:** 2020
SALES (est): 171.1K **Privately Held**
SIC: 2675 Photographic mats, mounts & folders

(G-4386)
LEGEND LLLYS PET GRMING RET SP ✪
3479 S Bassett St (48217-1560)
PHONE.................................734 346-6030
Lakeisha Jones,
EMP: 6 **EST:** 2021
SALES (est): 278K **Privately Held**
WEB: www.legendlillyspetshop.com
SIC: 3999 Pet supplies

(G-4387)
LEGGETT & PLATT INCORPORATED
1333 Gratiot Ave (48207-4542)
PHONE.................................417 358-8131
Milosz Niec, *Branch Mgr*
EMP: 6
SALES (corp-wide): 4.2B **Publicly Held**
WEB: www.leggett.com
SIC: 2515 Box springs, assembled
PA: Leggett & Platt, Incorporated
    1 Leggett Rd
    Carthage MO 64836
    417 358-8131

(G-4388)
LEMICA CORPORATION
11201 Manning St (48234-3538)
PHONE.................................313 839-2150
Gary L Brown, *CEO*
EMP: 28 **EST:** 1976
SQ FT: 28,000
SALES (est): 2.2MM **Privately Held**
WEB: www.lemicadoors.com
SIC: 2431 Doors, wood; moldings, wood: unfinished & prefinished

(G-4389)
LENOX BLOCK CLUB ASSN
1136 Lenox St (48215-3703)
PHONE.................................313 823-0941
Agnes Reid, *President*
EMP: 4 **EST:** 2017
SALES (est): 97.4K **Privately Held**
SIC: 3585 Refrigeration & heating equipment

(G-4390)
LEONARD FOUNTAIN SPC INC
Also Called: Leonard's Syrups
4601 Nancy St (48212-1213)
PHONE.................................313 891-4141
Leonard Bugajewski, *President*
Leonard Bugajewski III, *Vice Pres*
Sherri Bugajewski, *Admin Sec*
EMP: 54 **EST:** 1965
SQ FT: 75,000
SALES (est): 8.9MM **Privately Held**
WEB: www.leonardssyrups.com
SIC: 7359 2087 Equipment rental & leasing; syrups, drink

(G-4391)
LEONARDS NEWCORP INC
17350 Ryan Rd (48212-1116)
PHONE.................................313 366-9300
Leonard S Bugajewski Jr, *CEO*
EMP: 15 **EST:** 2003
SALES (est): 3.4MM **Privately Held**
SIC: 2891 Adhesives

(G-4392)
LETTS INDUSTRIES INC (PA)
1111 Bellevue St (48207-3683)
PHONE.................................313 579-1100
Charles E Letts Jr, *President*
Craig Pickard, *Treasurer*
Jeff Bolton, *Manager*
Sandy N Phillip, *Manager*
Sandy Phillip, *Manager*
▲ **EMP:** 3 **EST:** 1909
SQ FT: 83,000
SALES (est): 1.3MM **Privately Held**
SIC: 3714 3462 5084 Steering mechanisms, motor vehicle; automotive forgings, ferrous: crankshaft, engine, axle, etc.; machine tools & metalworking machinery; materials handling machinery

(G-4393)
LEVEL ELEVEN LLC
1520 Woodward Ave Fl 3 (48226-2040)
PHONE.................................313 662-2000
Robert Marsh, *CEO*
Lauren McMichael, *Partner*
Bill Johnson, *COO*
Bickley Craig, *Vice Pres*
David Leinweber, *Vice Pres*
EMP: 28 **EST:** 2012
SALES (est): 2.6MM **Privately Held**
WEB: www.leveleleven.com
SIC: 7372 Business oriented computer software

(G-4394)
LG ESSENTIALS LLC
8541 Birwood St (48204-3013)
PHONE.................................313 312-3813
Isiah Gilbert,
EMP: 6 **EST:** 2020
SALES (est): 185.1K **Privately Held**
SIC: 2051 Bakery: wholesale or wholesale/retail combined

(G-4395)
LGC GLOBAL INC
Also Called: Lakeshore Global
7310 Woodward Ave 500a (48202-3165)
PHONE.................................313 989-4141
Avinash Rachmale, *CEO*
Fred Feliciano, *Vice Pres*
Dan Heaps, *Opers Staff*
Jinansh Shah, *Opers Staff*
Shashidhar Shastri, *CFO*
EMP: 42 **EST:** 2003
SQ FT: 20,000
SALES (est): 14.9MM **Privately Held**
WEB: www.lgccorp.com
SIC: 8711 1623 1389 4931 Construction & civil engineering; water, sewer & utility lines; construction, repair & dismantling services; electric & other services combined; environmental consultant

(G-4396)
LGC GLOBAL ENERGY FM LLC
7310 Woodward Ave 500a (48202-3165)
PHONE.................................313 989-4141
Fred Feliciano, *Principal*
Tushar Patel, *Principal*
EMP: 1 **EST:** 2014
SALES (est): 1.1MM **Privately Held**
WEB: www.lgccorp.com
SIC: 1623 1382 Natural gas compressor station construction; oil & gas exploration services

(G-4397)
LIBERTY BURNISHING CO
18401 Sherwood St (48234-2832)
PHONE.................................313 366-7878
Jeffrey Davis, *President*
Rodney Pett, *Corp Secy*
Laura Davis, *Vice Pres*
Julie Pett, *Vice Pres*
EMP: 5 **EST:** 1961
SQ FT: 6,500
SALES (est): 639K **Privately Held**
WEB: www.libertyburnishingcompany.com
SIC: 3471 Tumbling (cleaning & polishing) of machine parts; finishing, metals or formed products

(G-4398)
LIGHTHOUSE DIRECT BUY LLC
Also Called: Lighthouse Cards and Gifts
16143 Wyoming St (48221-2846)
P.O. Box 21637 (48221-0637)
PHONE.................................313 340-1850
Jack Taylor Jones, *Mng Member*
Claudy E Jones,
Claudy Jones,
EMP: 5 **EST:** 2008
SQ FT: 3,100
SALES (est): 286.3K **Privately Held**
SIC: 5947 5999 5942 2752 Gift shop; religious goods; book stores; photolithographic printing; clothing accessories: men's & boys'; gifts & novelties

(G-4399)
LIGHTING ENTERPRISES INC
Also Called: Universal Led
16706 Telegraph Rd (48219-3729)
PHONE.................................313 693-9504
Mohammed Abueida, *CEO*
Khaled Abueida, *Principal*
Jeff Kovacs, *VP Bus Dvlpt*
John Bruton, *VP Sales*
▲ **EMP:** 8 **EST:** 1974
SALES (est): 1.8MM **Privately Held**
WEB: www.universalled.net
SIC: 3645 Table lamps; floor lamps

(G-4400)
LIMELITE PRINTING LLC
15285 Cedargrove St (48205-3631)
PHONE.................................313 839-7321
Carmella Lazzana, *Principal*
EMP: 4 **EST:** 2018
SALES (est): 97.9K **Privately Held**
SIC: 2752 Commercial printing, offset

(G-4401)
LIN ADAM FUEL INC
13330 Linwood St (48238-3448)
PHONE.................................313 733-6631
EMP: 6 **EST:** 2012
SALES (est): 401.5K **Privately Held**
SIC: 2869 Fuels

(G-4402)
LIVE TRACK PRODUCTIONS INC
848 Manistique St (48215-2974)
PHONE.................................313 704-2224
Robert Kelsey, *President*
EMP: 5 **EST:** 2014
SALES (est): 117K **Privately Held**
SIC: 2741 7389 Music book & sheet music publishing;

(G-4403)
LOCAL MEDIA GROUP INC
9 Alger Pl (48230-1908)
PHONE.................................313 885-2612
EMP: 98
SALES (corp-wide): 3.4B **Publicly Held**
WEB: www.gannett.com
SIC: 2711 Newspapers: publishing only, not printed on site
HQ: Local Media Group, Inc.
    90 Crystal Run Rd Ste 310
    Middletown NY 10941
    845 341-1100

(G-4404)
LOPEZ REPRODUCTIONS INC
645 Griswold St Ste 27 (48226-4013)
P.O. Box 94, Allen Park (48101-0094)
PHONE.................................313 386-4526
Leonard Lopez, *President*
Ronald Lopez, *Vice Pres*
EMP: 7 **EST:** 1976
SQ FT: 1,000
SALES (est): 362.2K **Privately Held**
SIC: 2752 7334 Commercial printing, offset; photocopying & duplicating services

(G-4405)
LORENZO WHITE
Also Called: Quality Lock & Door
20029 Cooley St (48219-1208)
PHONE.................................313 943-3667
Lorenzo White, *Owner*
EMP: 4 **EST:** 1999
SALES (est): 276.1K **Privately Held**
SIC: 3442 Metal doors, sash & trim

Detroit - Wayne County (G-4406) — GEOGRAPHIC SECTION

(G-4406)
LOTUS TECHNOLOGIES LLC
1420 Washington Blvd # 301 (48226-1718)
PHONE.................................313 550-1889
Juliana Moore, *CEO*
Juliana Lorita Moore,
Roderick Douglas Moore,
EMP: 10 **EST:** 2019
SALES (est): 446.8K **Privately Held**
SIC: 7389 2671 3081 5162 ; plastic film, coated or laminated for packaging; plastic film & sheet; plastics materials & basic shapes

(G-4407)
LOU JACK CITY PUBLISHING LLC
1603 Lawrence St (48206-1518)
PHONE.................................404 863-7124
Louis Jackson, *Principal*
EMP: 4 **EST:** 2015
SALES (est): 65.3K **Privately Held**
SIC: 2741 Miscellaneous publishing

(G-4408)
LOVE PUBLICITY
277 Gratiot Ave Ste 600 (48226-2211)
PHONE.................................313 288-8342
EMP: 4 **EST:** 2016
SALES (est): 38.8K **Privately Held**
WEB: www.lovepublicity.com
SIC: 2741 Miscellaneous publishing

(G-4409)
LOYALTY 1977 INK
18528 Margareta St (48219-2932)
PHONE.................................313 759-1006
Brandon Cunningham, *Partner*
EMP: 4 **EST:** 2011
SALES (est): 146.4K **Privately Held**
WEB: www.loyalty1977ink.com
SIC: 2396 Fabric printing & stamping

(G-4410)
LP INDUSTRIES LTD
15366 Coyle St (48227-2620)
PHONE.................................313 834-4847
Christine Pendleton, *Principal*
EMP: 4 **EST:** 2015
SALES (est): 128.9K **Privately Held**
SIC: 3999 Manufacturing industries

(G-4411)
LUSCIOUSLY SILKED LLC
1550 Cherboneau Pl # 204 (48207-2806)
PHONE.................................313 878-7058
Melissa Gadson,
EMP: 4 **EST:** 2019
SALES (est): 147.6K **Privately Held**
WEB: www.lusciouslysilked.com
SIC: 2211 Apparel & outerwear fabrics, cotton

(G-4412)
LYNDON FABRICATORS INC
12478 Beech Daly Rd (48239-2400)
PHONE.................................313 937-3640
John Largent, *President*
James Fee, *Sales Staff*
EMP: 6 **EST:** 1946
SQ FT: 4,500
SALES (est): 662.7K **Privately Held**
WEB: www.lyndonfab.com
SIC: 3441 Fabricated structural metal

(G-4413)
M AND A FUELS
13601 Plymouth Rd (48227-3026)
PHONE.................................313 397-7141
Mohammed Al, *Administration*
EMP: 5 **EST:** 2015
SALES (est): 179.2K **Privately Held**
SIC: 2869 Fuels

(G-4414)
MACKENZIE COMPANY
1600 Clay St (48211-1914)
PHONE.................................231 335-1997
Alexander Mackenzie, *Principal*
EMP: 4 **EST:** 2017
SALES (est): 159.6K **Privately Held**
WEB: www.mackenziecocpa.com
SIC: 2899 Chemical preparations

(G-4415)
MAGNA SEATING AMERICA INC
Also Called: Magna Seating Detroit
12800 Oakland Pkwy (48203-3587)
PHONE.................................313 422-6000
John Oilar, *VP Engrg*
Jeff Corkins, *Chief Engr*
Cindy Puchalski, *Engineer*
Arlene Alessi, *VP Human Res*
Laura Bryant, *HR Admin*
EMP: 420
SALES (corp-wide): 32.6B **Privately Held**
WEB: www.magna.com
SIC: 3714 Motor vehicle parts & accessories
HQ: Magna Seating Of America, Inc.
30020 Cabot Dr
Novi MI 48377

(G-4416)
MAGNI-INDUSTRIES INC (HQ)
2771 Hammond St (48209-1239)
PHONE.................................313 843-7855
David E Berry, *Ch of Bd*
Warren Knape, *Executive*
Zac Clouse, *Technician*
▲ **EMP:** 38 **EST:** 1978
SQ FT: 4,200
SALES (est): 30.2MM
SALES (corp-wide): 72.9MM **Privately Held**
WEB: www.magnicoatings.com
SIC: 2851 Paints & allied products
PA: The Magni Group Inc
390 Park St Ste 300
Birmingham MI 48009
248 647-4500

(G-4417)
MAJESTIC PATTERN COMPANY INC
20400 Sherwood St (48234-2986)
PHONE.................................313 892-5800
EMP: 7
SQ FT: 7,000
SALES (est): 700K **Privately Held**
SIC: 3543 Mfg Industrial Patterns

(G-4418)
MAJOR ONE ELECTRONICS LLC
18284 Ardmore St (48235-2530)
PHONE.................................313 652-3723
Lindsey Sargent, *President*
EMP: 5 **EST:** 2002
SALES (est): 50K **Privately Held**
SIC: 5999 7372 8748 Electronic parts & equipment; business oriented computer software; systems analysis & engineering consulting services

(G-4419)
MANSA DENIM COMPANY
607 Shelby St Ste 700 (48226-3282)
PHONE.................................313 384-3929
Ahmad Otler, *Principal*
EMP: 4 **EST:** 2015
SALES (est): 105K **Privately Held**
WEB: www.mansadc.com
SIC: 2211 Denims

(G-4420)
MANUFACTURERS HARDWARE COMPANY
17641 Filer St (48212-1405)
PHONE.................................313 892-6650
David M Griebe, *President*
Lawrence Griebe, *Corp Secy*
Edwin J Griebe, *Vice Pres*
EMP: 18 **EST:** 1960
SQ FT: 4,800
SALES (est): 1.5MM **Privately Held**
SIC: 3599 Machine & other job shop work

(G-4421)
MAVEN DRIVE LLC
300 Renaissance Ctr (48243-1402)
PHONE.................................313 667-1541
Julia Steyn, *CEO*
EMP: 90 **EST:** 2016
SALES (est): 14MM **Publicly Held**
WEB: www.gm.com
SIC: 3711 Motor vehicles & car bodies
HQ: General Motors Llc
300 Renaissance Ctr L1
Detroit MI 48243

(G-4422)
MCCLURES PICKLES LLC
8201 Saint Aubin St (48211-1301)
PHONE.................................248 837-9323
Dan McCreedy, *Opers Staff*
Catrina Derosia, *Controller*
Joseph McClure, *Mng Member*
Robert McCclure,
▼ **EMP:** 24 **EST:** 2006
SQ FT: 20,000
SALES (est): 4.7MM **Privately Held**
WEB: www.mcclures.com
SIC: 2099 2033 Food preparations; canned fruits & specialties

(G-4423)
MCDONALD WHOLESALE DISTRIBUTOR
19536 W Davison St (48223-3422)
PHONE.................................313 273-2870
Patricia McDonald, *President*
George McDonald, *Vice Pres*
EMP: 4 **EST:** 1917
SQ FT: 4,800 **Privately Held**
WEB:
www.mcdonaldwholesaledistributor.com
SIC: 5023 2591 Window furnishings; window shades

(G-4424)
MCL JASCO INC
Also Called: McL Jasco International
7140 W Fort St (48209-2917)
PHONE.................................313 294-7414
Louis James, *President*
EMP: 1 **EST:** 2007
SALES (est): 1.3MM
SALES (corp-wide): 9.8MM **Privately Held**
WEB: www.mcljasco.com
SIC: 3743 8741 Freight cars & equipment; management services
PA: Jasco International, Llc
7140 W Fort St
Detroit MI 48209
313 841-5000

(G-4425)
MD INVESTORS CORPORATION (DH)
Also Called: Metaldyne
1 Dauch Dr (48211-1115)
PHONE.................................734 207-6200
Thomas A Amato, *CEO*
Benjamin Schmidt, *Vice Pres*
Terry Iwasaki, *CFO*
Stephanie O'Connor, *Admin Sec*
EMP: 150 **EST:** 2012
SALES (est): 1.3B
SALES (corp-wide): 4.7B **Publicly Held**
SIC: 3714 Motor vehicle parts & accessories

(G-4426)
MECCOM CORPORATION
5945 Martin St (48210-1650)
PHONE.................................313 895-4900
James Steele, *President*
EMP: 8 **EST:** 1975
SQ FT: 25,000
SALES (est): 495.1K **Privately Held**
WEB: www.meccomcorp.com
SIC: 7692 3498 3441 Welding repair; fabricated pipe & fittings; expansion joints (structural shapes), iron or steel

(G-4427)
MEDIA SOLUTIONS INC
4715 Woodward Ave Fl 2 (48201-1307)
PHONE.................................313 831-3152
Lila Abraham, *President*
Odette Jones, *Vice Pres*
EMP: 4 **EST:** 1995
SQ FT: 1,500
SALES (est): 410.9K **Privately Held**
SIC: 7336 3993 Graphic arts & related design; signs & advertising specialties

(G-4428)
MEEZHERATI INDUSTRIES LLC
2037 Collingwood St (48206-1555)
PHONE.................................734 931-0466
Antonio Harris, *Principal*
EMP: 4 **EST:** 2016
SALES (est): 89.4K **Privately Held**
SIC: 3599 Industrial machinery

(G-4429)
MERIDIANRX LLC
1 Campus Martius Ste 750 (48226-5013)
PHONE.................................855 323-4580
Jon Cotton, *President*
Amy Krauss, *Editor*
Rene Acker, *COO*
Justin Bookmeier, *Opers Mgr*
Amanda Messer, *Opers Spvr*
EMP: 90 **EST:** 2009
SALES (est): 21.2MM **Publicly Held**
WEB: www.meridianrx.com
SIC: 2834 Pharmaceutical preparations
HQ: The Wellcare Management Group Inc
280 Broadway Ste 3
Newburgh NY
845 440-2400

(G-4430)
METAL DESIGN MANUFACTURING LLC
17891 Ryan Rd (48212-1121)
PHONE.................................313 893-9810
Roger Steyer, *General Mgr*
Teresa Disantis, *Mng Member*
EMP: 6 **EST:** 1996
SQ FT: 30,000
SALES (est): 1.6MM **Privately Held**
WEB: www.metaldesignmfg.com
SIC: 3444 Metal roofing & roof drainage equipment

(G-4431)
METAL DYNAMICS DETROIT
3100 Lonyo St (48209-1089)
PHONE.................................313 841-1800
EMP: 6 **EST:** 2019
SALES (est): 365.9K **Privately Held**
SIC: 3312 Blast furnaces & steel mills

(G-4432)
METAL TECH PRODUCTS INC
15720 Dale St (48223-1040)
PHONE.................................313 533-5277
Richard Mollick, *President*
Letitia Gordon, *Vice Pres*
EMP: 22 **EST:** 1987
SQ FT: 39,000
SALES (est): 2.5MM **Privately Held**
SIC: 3443 Weldments

(G-4433)
METALDYNE LLC (DH)
1 Dauch Dr (48211-1115)
PHONE.................................734 207-6200
David Dauch, *President*
Thomas V Chambers, *COO*
Robert Defauw, *Vice Pres*
Doug Grimm, *Vice Pres*
Christoph Guhe, *Vice Pres*
EMP: 150 **EST:** 2009
SALES (est): 1.3B
SALES (corp-wide): 4.7B **Publicly Held**
WEB: www.aam.com
SIC: 3714 Motor vehicle parts & accessories

(G-4434)
METALDYNE PWRTRAIN CMPNNTS INC (DH)
1 Dauch Dr (48211-1115)
PHONE.................................313 758-2000
Thomas A Amato, *CEO*
▲ **EMP:** 170 **EST:** 1977
SQ FT: 30,000
SALES (est): 35.4MM
SALES (corp-wide): 4.7B **Publicly Held**
WEB: www.aam.com
SIC: 3714 Motor vehicle parts & accessories

(G-4435)
METRIC TOOL COMPANY INC
17144 Mount Elliott St (48212-1361)
PHONE.................................313 369-9610
Peter Hayda, *President*
Andy Pensko, *Plant Mgr*
EMP: 10 **EST:** 1975
SQ FT: 32,000
SALES (est): 884.9K **Privately Held**
SIC: 3599 Machine shop, jobbing & repair

▲ = Import ▼ = Export
◆ = Import/Export

GEOGRAPHIC SECTION
Detroit - Wayne County (G-4464)

(G-4436)
METRO PIPING INC
1500b Trombly St (48211-2126)
PHONE.................................313 872-4330
Steven H Lowe, *President*
John Morrison, *Vice Pres*
EMP: 16 **EST:** 2000
SQ FT: 32,000
SALES (est): 2.3MM **Privately Held**
WEB: www.metropiping.com
SIC: 3494 Pipe fittings

(G-4437)
METRO POWDER COATING
18434 Fitzpatrick St (48228-1407)
PHONE.................................313 744-7134
EMP: 5 **EST:** 2017
SALES (est): 172.4K **Privately Held**
WEB: www.metropowdercoating.com
SIC: 3479 Coating of metals & formed products

(G-4438)
METROPOLITAN ALLOYS CORP
17385 Ryan Rd (48212-1196)
PHONE.................................313 366-4443
Murray Spilman, *President*
EMP: 20 **EST:** 1942
SQ FT: 18,000
SALES (est): 12.4MM
SALES (corp-wide): 24.6MM **Privately Held**
WEB: www.metroalloys.com
SIC: 5051 3643 3341 3339 Zinc; current-carrying wiring devices; secondary nonferrous metals; primary nonferrous metals
PA: Mac Group International Incorporated
17385 Ryan Rd
Detroit MI 48212
313 366-4444

(G-4439)
METROPOLITAN BAKING COMPANY
Also Called: Michigan Baking Co.
8579 Lumpkin St (48212-3622)
PHONE.................................313 875-7246
James G Kordas, *President*
Mike Zrimec, *General Mgr*
EMP: 65 **EST:** 1945
SQ FT: 75,000
SALES (est): 9.1MM **Privately Held**
WEB: www.metropolitanbaking.com
SIC: 2051 Bread, all types (white, wheat, rye, etc): fresh or frozen; rolls, bread type: fresh or frozen; buns, bread type: fresh or frozen

(G-4440)
MEXICO EXPRESS
7611 W Vernor Hwy (48209-1513)
PHONE.................................313 843-6717
Francisco Leon, *President*
EMP: 10 **EST:** 2001
SALES (est): 457.9K **Privately Held**
SIC: 3111 4822 Leather tanning & finishing; telegraph & other communications

(G-4441)
MEXTOR DISPOSABLE LLC ✪
607 Shelby St Ste 700 (48226-3282)
PHONE.................................313 921-6860
Michael Obidare,
EMP: 4 **EST:** 2021
SALES (est): 57.5K **Privately Held**
SIC: 2621 Packaging paper

(G-4442)
MGS HORTICULTURAL USA INC
Also Called: Plant Products
9900 Mount Elliott St (48211-1603)
PHONE.................................248 661-4378
Mike Dooley, *Technical Staff*
EMP: 24 **EST:** 2012
SALES (est): 1MM
SALES (corp-wide): 11.5MM **Privately Held**
WEB: www.plantproducts.com
SIC: 3999 Manufacturing industries
HQ: Plant Products Inc
50 Hazelton St
Leamington ON N8H 1
519 326-9037

(G-4443)
MH INDUSTRIES LTD
8101 Lyndon St (48238-2452)
PHONE.................................734 261-2600
EMP: 6 **EST:** 2017
SALES (est): 87.6K **Privately Held**
WEB: www.mhind.com
SIC: 3999 Manufacturing industries

(G-4444)
MICHIGAN BOX COMPANY (PA)
Also Called: Fontana Forest Products
1910 Trombly St (48211-2130)
PHONE.................................313 873-9500
Carl Fontana, *President*
Elaine Fontana, *President*
Louis Fontana, *Vice Pres*
Greg White, *Purch Mgr*
Bill Vasilofski, *CFO*
▼ **EMP:** 55
SQ FT: 160,000
SALES (est): 13.5MM **Privately Held**
WEB: www.michiganbox.com
SIC: 2441 2652 2653 Boxes, wood; filing boxes, paperboard: made from purchased materials; boxes, corrugated: made from purchased materials

(G-4445)
MICHIGAN BRUSH MFG CO
7446 Central St (48210-1037)
P.O. Box 10247 (48210-0247)
PHONE.................................313 834-1070
Bruce Gale, *President*
EMP: 38 **EST:** 1917
SQ FT: 55,000
SALES (est): 1.1MM **Privately Held**
WEB: www.mi-brush.com
SIC: 3991 Brushes, household or industrial; brooms; paint rollers

(G-4446)
MICHIGAN BTLG & CSTM PACK CO
13940 Tireman St (48228-2718)
PHONE.................................313 846-1717
Sal Landa, *President*
Chaker Aoun, *COO*
▲ **EMP:** 65 **EST:** 2005
SQ FT: 40,000
SALES (est): 3.8MM **Privately Held**
SIC: 2086 Bottled & canned soft drinks

(G-4447)
MICHIGAN CHRONICLE PUBG CO
1452 Randolph St Ste 400 (48226-2284)
PHONE.................................313 963-5522
Haram Jackson, *President*
EMP: 46 **EST:** 1936
SQ FT: 30,000
SALES (est): 1.7MM **Privately Held**
WEB: www.michiganchronicle.com
SIC: 2711 Newspapers, publishing & printing

(G-4448)
MICHIGAN CRUSHED CONCRETE INC
25012 Plymouth Rd (48239-1637)
PHONE.................................313 534-1500
Bruce Segur, *President*
Larry Brock, *Treasurer*
Joanne Brock, *Admin Sec*
EMP: 9
SQ FT: 200
SALES (est): 1.4MM **Privately Held**
WEB: www.micrushedconcrete.com
SIC: 3273 Ready-mixed concrete

(G-4449)
MICHIGAN FAB AND ENGRG LLC
12700 Mansfield St (48227-4901)
PHONE.................................248 297-5268
Michelle Calcaterra, *Administration*
EMP: 7 **EST:** 2014
SALES (est): 537.6K **Privately Held**
SIC: 3441 Fabricated structural metal

(G-4450)
MICHIGAN FRONT PAGE LLC
479 Ledyard St (48201-2641)
PHONE.................................313 963-5522
Sam Logan, *Publisher*
EMP: 8 **EST:** 2000
SALES (est): 1.1MM
SALES (corp-wide): 8.9MM **Privately Held**
WEB: www.chicagodefender.com
SIC: 2711 Newspapers, publishing & printing
PA: Real Times Ii Llc
4445 S Dr Mrtn Lther King Martin Luther King
Chicago IL 60653
312 225-2400

(G-4451)
MICHIGAN PAPER DIE INC
632 Harper Ave (48202-3540)
PHONE.................................313 873-0404
Mark Megie, *President*
Nick Bommarito, *Treasurer*
EMP: 28 **EST:** 1968
SQ FT: 10,000
SALES (est): 3.1MM **Privately Held**
WEB: www.michiganpaperdie.com
SIC: 2675 Die-cut paper & board

(G-4452)
MICHIGAN STEEL FINISHING CO
Also Called: Michigan Steel Spring Company
12850 Mansfield St (48227-1240)
PHONE.................................313 838-3925
John S Haine, *President*
Roger L Abram, *Vice Pres*
EMP: 13 **EST:** 1976
SQ FT: 18,000
SALES (est): 2.2MM **Privately Held**
WEB: www.michigansteelspring.com
SIC: 3452 3495 Washers; wire springs

(G-4453)
MICHIGAN TILE AND MARBLE CO (PA)
9317 Freeland St (48228-2300)
PHONE.................................313 931-1700
Maryann Brady, *President*
Katherine Vitto, *Treasurer*
James Lanzetta, *Admin Sec*
▲ **EMP:** 39 **EST:** 1943
SQ FT: 3,000
SALES (est): 3.1MM **Privately Held**
WEB: www.michigantileandmarble.com
SIC: 3281 1411 Cut stone & stone products; dimension stone

(G-4454)
MICRO PLATERS SALES INC
Also Called: Hajjar Plating
221 Victor St (48203-3131)
PHONE.................................313 865-2293
Howard Hicks, *President*
John Hicks, *Corp Secy*
Tammy T Packer, *Vice Pres*
▲ **EMP:** 41 **EST:** 1963
SALES (est): 1.7MM **Privately Held**
SIC: 3471 Plating of metals or formed products; polishing, metals or formed products

(G-4455)
MICRO RIM CORPORATION
221 Victor St (48203-3131)
PHONE.................................313 865-1090
Tammy Parker, *President*
Howard T Hicks II, *Vice Pres*
Donna De Michael, *Manager*
▲ **EMP:** 10 **EST:** 1991
SQ FT: 125,000
SALES (est): 2.5MM **Privately Held**
SIC: 3714 Bumpers & bumperettes, motor vehicle

(G-4456)
MIDWEST STEEL INC (PA)
2525 E Grand Blvd (48211-2001)
PHONE.................................313 873-2220
Gary R Broad, *President*
Dino Benedict, *Superintendent*
Mark Dungan, *Superintendent*
Bernie Osterberg, *Superintendent*
Bob Vellmure, *Superintendent*
EMP: 50 **EST:** 1968
SQ FT: 30,000
SALES (est): 74.3MM **Privately Held**
WEB: www.midweststeel.com
SIC: 3441 1791 Fabricated structural metal; structural steel erection

(G-4457)
MILANO BAKERY INC
3500 Russell St (48207-2030)
PHONE.................................313 833-3500
Dragoslav Janevski, *President*
EMP: 30 **EST:** 1978
SQ FT: 6,000
SALES (est): 2.5MM **Privately Held**
WEB: www.milanobakeryandcafe.com
SIC: 2051 Bread, all types (white, wheat, rye, etc): fresh or frozen

(G-4458)
MILTON MANUFACTURING INC
Also Called: Wayne Stmping Intrntnal- Sbsid
301 E Grixdale (48203-2073)
PHONE.................................313 366-2450
Shelly L Green, *President*
Jeff Benton, *General Mgr*
Lisa Grover, *General Mgr*
Jim Green Jr, *Vice Pres*
Devaughn Hoskins, *Engineer*
EMP: 50 **EST:** 1945
SQ FT: 350,000
SALES (est): 16.2MM **Privately Held**
WEB: www.miltonmfg.com
SIC: 3444 3496 3441 3429 Sheet metal specialties, not stamped; miscellaneous fabricated wire products; fabricated structural metal; manufactured hardware (general)

(G-4459)
MINTMESH INC
400 Renaissance Ctr # 2600 (48243-1502)
PHONE.................................888 874-3644
Sunil Chathaveetil, *CEO*
Neha Bhuradia, *Director*
EMP: 18 **EST:** 2015
SALES (est): 914.5K **Privately Held**
WEB: www.mintmesh.ai
SIC: 7372 Application computer software

(G-4460)
MIZJAYZBRAIDZ LLC
6115 Auburn St (48228-3986)
PHONE.................................313 799-7756
Jordan Hornshaw,
EMP: 4 **EST:** 2020
SALES (est): 15K **Privately Held**
SIC: 2844 Hair preparations, including shampoos

(G-4461)
MJC INDUSTRIES INC
Also Called: Hy-Vac Technologies
15701 Glendale St (48227-1708)
PHONE.................................313 838-2800
Kevan Johnston, *President*
Jim McClelland, *Vice Pres*
EMP: 34 **EST:** 1983
SQ FT: 20,000
SALES (est): 1MM **Privately Held**
WEB: www.hy-vac.com
SIC: 3398 Annealing of metal; brazing (hardening) of metal

(G-4462)
MLH SERVICES LLC
11310 Kenmoor St (48205-3284)
PHONE.................................313 768-4403
Stacey Horn,
Keith Horn,
EMP: 4 **EST:** 2008
SALES (est): 165.1K **Privately Held**
WEB: www.rbainc.com
SIC: 3953 Seal presses, notary & hand

(G-4463)
MODIFIED GEAR AND SPLINE INC
18300 Mount Elliott St (48234-2735)
PHONE.................................313 893-3511
Randall Dulecki, *President*
EMP: 10 **EST:** 1979
SQ FT: 12,000 **Privately Held**
SIC: 3599 Grinding castings for the trade

(G-4464)
MOOSE MFG & MACHINING LLC
440 Burroughs St Ste 692 (48202-3476)
PHONE.................................586 765-4686
Vladimir Yasnogorodskiy,
EMP: 4

Detroit - Wayne County (G-4465) — GEOGRAPHIC SECTION

SALES (est): 162.4K **Privately Held**
SIC: 3728 Aircraft parts & equipment

(G-4465)
MORGAN SOFA CO
2501 Russell St Ste 400 (48207-2632)
PHONE.................................347 262-5995
Justin Stein, *CEO*
EMP: 6 **EST:** 2018
SALES (est): 200.6K **Privately Held**
SIC: 2396 Furniture trimmings, fabric

(G-4466)
MOTOR CITY BENDING & ROLLING
17655 Filer St (48212-1495)
PHONE.................................313 368-4400
James Vanderjagt, *President*
James Vander Jagt, *President*
EMP: 8 **EST:** 1961
SQ FT: 9,600
SALES (est): 677.7K **Privately Held**
WEB: www.motorcitybending.com
SIC: 3498 3599 Fabricated pipe & fittings; machine shop, jobbing & repair

(G-4467)
MOTOR CITY ELECTRIC TECH INC
9440 Grinnell St (48213-1151)
PHONE.................................313 921-5300
Dale M Wieczorek, *President*
Denise Hodgins, *Vice Pres*
Justin Nelson, *Technician*
EMP: 95 **EST:** 1986
SQ FT: 60,000
SALES (est): 22.2MM
SALES (corp-wide): 101.6MM **Privately Held**
WEB: www.mceco.com
SIC: 3613 8711 Control panels, electric; engineering services
PA: Motor City Electric Co.
   9440 Grinnell St
   Detroit MI 48213
   313 921-5300

(G-4468)
MPC
1001 S Oakwood (48217-1319)
PHONE.................................313 297-6386
EMP: 6 **EST:** 2018
SALES (est): 102K **Privately Held**
SIC: 2911 Petroleum refining

(G-4469)
MR MCGOOZ PRODUCTS INC
18911 W 7 Mile Rd (48219-2764)
PHONE.................................313 693-4003
Ronald Husdon, *Principal*
EMP: 4 **EST:** 2014
SALES (est): 90K **Privately Held**
SIC: 3999 Manufacturing industries

(G-4470)
MRM IDA PRODUCTS CO INC
8385 Lyndon St (48238-2444)
PHONE.................................313 834-0200
Sanford Moser, *President*
David Soffer, *Vice Pres*
EMP: 8 **EST:** 1974
SQ FT: 8,500
SALES (est): 779.3K **Privately Held**
WEB: www.locatewindows.com
SIC: 5211 5031 3589 Windows, storm: wood or metal; sash, wood or metal; windows; metal doors, sash & trim; garbage disposers & compactors, commercial

(G-4471)
MSMAC DESIGNS LLC
11069 Nashville St (48205-3232)
PHONE.................................313 521-6289
Patrice Kathleen McDonald, *CEO*
EMP: 8 **EST:** 2004
SALES (est): 301.7K **Privately Held**
SIC: 3999 Manufacturing industries

(G-4472)
MUSIC
2647 Crane St (48214-1912)
PHONE.................................313 854-3606
EMP: 4 **EST:** 2013

SALES (est): 41.4K **Privately Held**
SIC: 2741 Music book & sheet music publishing

(G-4473)
MYLOCKERCOM LLC
Also Called: Customcat
1300 Rosa Parks Blvd (48216-1952)
PHONE.................................877 898-3366
Paul Domke, *Controller*
Jesse Mason, *Marketing Staff*
Alex Phillips, *Marketing Staff*
Robert Hake, *Mng Member*
Janice Winters, *Manager*
▲ **EMP:** 280 **EST:** 2006
SQ FT: 126,000
SALES (est): 37.4MM **Privately Held**
WEB: www.mylocker.net
SIC: 2759 Letterpress & screen printing

(G-4474)
NAIL TIME
8862 Greenfield Rd (48228-2237)
PHONE.................................313 837-3871
Phong Trang, *Manager*
EMP: 4 **EST:** 2007
SALES (est): 68.2K **Privately Held**
WEB: www.nail-care-services.cmac.ws
SIC: 2844 Manicure preparations

(G-4475)
NATIONAL BAKERY
736 E State Fair (48203-1115)
PHONE.................................313 891-7803
Chris Cvhokodki, *Owner*
EMP: 7 **EST:** 1978
SALES (est): 355.7K **Privately Held**
WEB: www.nationalbakery.com
SIC: 2051 Bakery: wholesale or wholesale/retail combined

(G-4476)
NATIONAL FLEET SERVICE LLC
10100 Grinnell St (48213-1142)
PHONE.................................313 923-1799
Monica Palmer, *Opers Staff*
James Konen, *Natl Sales Mgr*
Timothy Lariviere, *Mng Member*
Lee Scafidi, *Exec Dir*
▲ **EMP:** 20 **EST:** 1998
SALES (est): 5.5MM **Privately Held**
SIC: 3714 Motor vehicle parts & accessories

(G-4477)
NATIVE DETROITER PUBG INC
8200 E Jefferson Ave # 1204 (48214-3974)
PHONE.................................313 822-1958
Sherman Eaton, *Agent*
EMP: 5 **EST:** 2018
SALES (est): 37.5K **Privately Held**
WEB: www.nativedetroitermagazine.com
SIC: 2741 Miscellaneous publishing

(G-4478)
NAVARRE INC
Also Called: Michigan Motor Exchange
3500 E 8 Mile Rd (48234-1005)
PHONE.................................313 892-7300
Kenneth Navarre, *President*
Joyce R Fleck, *Vice Pres*
EMP: 7
SALES (corp-wide): 3.1MM **Privately Held**
WEB: www.michmo.com
SIC: 3714 3519 Rebuilding engines & transmissions, factory basis; internal combustion engines
PA: Navarre Inc
   6497 Highland Rd Ste B
   Waterford MI

(G-4479)
NEIGHBORHOOD ARTISANS INC
85 Oakman Blvd (48203-3051)
PHONE.................................313 865-5373
Mary Jane Karsinski, *Director*
EMP: 6
SQ FT: 10,000
SALES: 79K **Privately Held**
SIC: 8399 2396 Community development groups; automotive & apparel trimmings

(G-4480)
NELSON IRON WORKS INC
6350 Benham St (48211-1899)
PHONE.................................313 925-5355
John N Knill Jr, *President*
Sara Havlik, *Human Res Dir*
Diane Grabowski, *Administration*
EMP: 9 **EST:** 1947
SQ FT: 10,000
SALES (est): 2.1MM **Privately Held**
WEB: www.nelsonironworks.com
SIC: 3441 Fabricated structural metal

(G-4481)
NEW CENTER STAMPING INC
950 E Milwaukee St (48211-2008)
PHONE.................................313 872-3500
Ronald Hall, *CEO*
Ric Monkaba, *President*
Greg Smith, *COO*
Don Stein, *Vice Pres*
Chris Garvey, *CFO*
EMP: 110 **EST:** 1992
SQ FT: 200,000
SALES (est): 24.3MM **Privately Held**
WEB: www.newcenter.net
SIC: 3469 Stamping metal for the trade

(G-4482)
NEW HARPER SEASONING INC ◆
12715 Harper Ave (48213-1822)
PHONE.................................734 767-6290
Theo Burdine, *CEO*
EMP: 5 **EST:** 2021
SALES (est): 220.7K **Privately Held**
SIC: 2099 Seasonings & spices

(G-4483)
NEW MARTHA WASHINGTON BAKERY
10335 Joseph Campau St (48212-3259)
PHONE.................................313 872-1988
Petar Petrovic, *Owner*
EMP: 7 **EST:** 1925
SALES (est): 343.7K **Privately Held**
SIC: 2051 5461 Bakery: wholesale or wholesale/retail combined; bakeries

(G-4484)
NEXTEK POWER SYSTEMS INC (PA)
461 Burroughs St (48202-3419)
PHONE.................................313 887-1321
Paul Savage, *President*
Wayne Gutschow, *President*
Paul Wickett, *Engineer*
Brian Noble, *CFO*
Ben Hartman, *CTO*
▲ **EMP:** 9 **EST:** 1995
SQ FT: 5,000
SALES (est): 4.8MM **Privately Held**
WEB: www.nextekpower.com
SIC: 3612 8711 5063 Fluorescent ballasts; electrical or electronic engineering; lighting fixtures

(G-4485)
NIKKIS PRINTING & MORE LLC
20291 Kentfield St (48219-1425)
PHONE.................................313 532-0281
Nakia Campbell, *Principal*
EMP: 5 **EST:** 2015
SALES (est): 120K **Privately Held**
SIC: 2752 Commercial printing, lithographic

(G-4486)
NJE ENTERPRISES LLC
Also Called: Allegra Print Imaging Detroit
400 Renaissance Ctr Lbby (48243-1607)
PHONE.................................313 963-3600
Shelley Murphy, *Sales Dir*
N Eschenburg, *Mng Member*
Norma Eschenburg,
EMP: 5 **EST:** 1987
SQ FT: 2,700
SALES (est): 650K **Privately Held**
WEB: www.allegramarketingprint.com
SIC: 2752 2759 Commercial printing, offset; commercial printing

(G-4487)
NO LIMIT WIRELESS-MICHIGAN INC
6236 Michigan Ave (48210-2953)
PHONE.................................313 285-8402
EMP: 7 **EST:** 2009
SALES (est): 223.7K **Privately Held**
SIC: 4812 3679 8748 Cellular telephone services; headphones, radio; telecommunications consultant

(G-4488)
NORBROOK PLATING INC
19230 Mount Elliott St (48234-2723)
PHONE.................................313 369-9304
Gerald Plodzick, *Manager*
EMP: 8 **EST:** 2005
SALES (est): 490K **Privately Held**
SIC: 3471 Plating of metals or formed products

(G-4489)
NORTHERN LKES SAFOOD MEATS LLC
12301 Conant St (48212-2341)
PHONE.................................313 368-4234
Irwin Groskind, *Mng Member*
James Meyer,
EMP: 29 **EST:** 2004
SALES (est): 13MM **Privately Held**
WEB: www.northernlakesfoods.com
SIC: 5146 2077 Seafoods; marine fats, oils & meals

(G-4490)
NORTHERN MILLWORK CO
Also Called: General Hardwood Co
7201 E Mcnichols Rd (48212-2050)
PHONE.................................313 365-7733
Ronald Ellerbrock, *President*
Mark Ellerbrock, *Vice Pres*
EMP: 10 **EST:** 1984
SQ FT: 16,000
SALES (est): 1.5MM
SALES (corp-wide): 4.9MM **Privately Held**
WEB: www.generalhardwood.com
SIC: 2431 Millwork
PA: General Hardwood Company
   7201 E Mcnichols Rd
   Detroit MI 48212
   313 365-7733

(G-4491)
NORTRONIC COMPANY
20210 Sherwood St (48234-2952)
PHONE.................................313 893-3730
Timothy Butts, *President*
Alfred Krause, *Treasurer*
Maryann Arquette, *Admin Sec*
▲ **EMP:** 6 **EST:** 1964
SQ FT: 22,000
SALES (est): 996.2K **Privately Held**
SIC: 5084 3548 7699 Welding machinery & equipment; welding & cutting apparatus & accessories; welding equipment repair

(G-4492)
NOTES FROM MAN CAVE LLC
3680 Seminole St (48214-1124)
PHONE.................................586 604-1997
Theresa Zuber, *CEO*
Arika Ewell, *CFO*
EMP: 4 **EST:** 2016
SALES (est): 143.1K **Privately Held**
SIC: 2771 Greeting cards

(G-4493)
NSE PROPERTY GROUP LLC
1732 S Deacon St (48217-1633)
PHONE.................................313 605-1646
Johnathan Spencer,
EMP: 5 **EST:** 2020
SALES (est): 150K **Privately Held**
SIC: 1389 Construction, repair & dismantling services

(G-4494)
NUTCO INC (PA)
Also Called: Germack Nut Co
2140 Wilkins St (48207-2123)
PHONE.................................800 872-4006
Bill Gierman, *President*
Frank Germack III, *Corp Secy*
Suzanne Germack, *Shareholder*

GEOGRAPHIC SECTION Detroit - Wayne County (G-4525)

EMP: 21 EST: 1924
SALES (est): 13.4MM Privately Held
SIC: 5145 2068 5441 Nuts, salted or roasted; salted & roasted nuts & seeds; nuts

(G-4495)
OAKLAND BOLT & NUT CO LLC
8977 Lyndon St (48238-2355)
PHONE....................313 659-1677
Henry Wojcik II, *President*
Keith Williamson, *Treasurer*
David Lavoie, *Manager*
EMP: 4 EST: 2002
SQ FT: 15,000
SALES (est): 432.5K Privately Held
SIC: 3452 Bolts, nuts, rivets & washers

(G-4496)
OAKLAND STAMPING LLC (DH)
1200 Woodland St (48211-1071)
PHONE....................734 397-6300
Scott Jones, *President*
Robert Koss, *Treasurer*
▲ EMP: 250 EST: 2009
SALES (est): 44.4MM
SALES (corp-wide): 3.1B Privately Held
WEB: www.autokiniton.com
SIC: 3469 Stamping metal for the trade

(G-4497)
OMAHA AUTOMATION INC
8301 Saint Aubin St (48211-1330)
P.O. Box 81400, Rochester (48308-1400)
PHONE....................313 557-3565
Phillip M Cifuentes, *President*
Ronald Scott Muschong, *Vice Pres*
EMP: 7 EST: 2008
SQ FT: 10,000
SALES (est): 968.1K Privately Held
WEB: www.omahaautomation.com
SIC: 8711 3711 Engineering services; automobile assembly, including specialty automobiles

(G-4498)
ON SITE CAR WASH AND DETAIL
2744 W Davison (48238-3444)
PHONE....................313 350-8357
Sylvester Little, *President*
EMP: 6 EST: 2019
SALES (est): 130K Privately Held
WEB: www.starautowash.net
SIC: 3589 Car washing machinery

(G-4499)
ONE SOURCE TRUCKING LLC
Also Called: Expediting
20185 Washburn St (48221-1021)
PHONE....................855 999-7723
Michael Patterson, *Owner*
EMP: 4 EST: 2019
SALES (est): 120K Privately Held
SIC: 3537 Trucks: freight, baggage, etc.: industrial, except mining

(G-4500)
ONSTAR LLC
300 Renaissance Ctr (48243-1402)
PHONE....................313 300-0106
Jeff Millwood, *General Mgr*
EMP: 31 EST: 1999
SALES (est): 1.2MM Privately Held
SIC: 7372 Application computer software

(G-4501)
OSOWET COLLECTIONS INC
Also Called: Production, Publishing
5809 Bluehill St (48224-2015)
PHONE....................313 844-8171
Shanta Williams, *CEO*
EMP: 7 EST: 2017
SALES (est): 61.7K Privately Held
WEB: www.osowetcollections.com
SIC: 5812 5651 3861 3651 Fast food restaurants & stands; unisex clothing stores; sound recording & reproducing equipment, motion picture; music distribution apparatus

(G-4502)
OWNTHEPLAY INC
1401 Vermont St Ste 180 (48216-1884)
PHONE....................248 514-0352
Matthew Chatlin, *Principal*
EMP: 4 EST: 2015
SALES (est): 148.5K Privately Held
SIC: 7372 Prepackaged software

(G-4503)
PAINEXX CORPORATION
18307 James Couzens Fwy (48235-2504)
P.O. Box 35936 (48235-0936)
PHONE....................313 863-1200
Nicole Weldon, *CEO*
Douglas Sewell, *Chairman*
EMP: 6 EST: 2007
SALES (est): 100K Privately Held
SIC: 2834 Pharmaceutical preparations

(G-4504)
PAPA JOES GRMET MKT HNRY FORD
2799 W Grand Blvd (48202-2608)
PHONE....................248 609-5670
Anthony J Curtis,
Jeffrey Curtis,
Joseph Curtis,
Tony Curtis,
EMP: 11 EST: 2016
SALES (est): 975.2K Privately Held
SIC: 2011 Meat packing plants

(G-4505)
PAPER CHASE AMERICAN DREAM LLC
7174 Mackenzie St (48204-3349)
PHONE....................248 819-0939
Shanae Williams,
EMP: 5 EST: 2019
SALES (est): 126.2K Privately Held
WEB: www.iampaperchase.com
SIC: 2211 Apparel & outerwear fabrics, cotton

(G-4506)
PAPPAS CUTLERY-GRINDING INC
575 E Milwaukee St (48202-3237)
PHONE....................800 521-0888
John C Pappas, *President*
David La Motte, *Vice Pres*
John McMurdo, *Manager*
EMP: 6 EST: 1921
SQ FT: 7,200
SALES (est): 706K Privately Held
SIC: 3556 5084 Grinders, commercial, food; food industry machinery

(G-4507)
PARAGON VCISO GROUP LLC
Also Called: Cyber Data Lock
16777 Avon Ave (48219-4119)
PHONE....................248 895-9866
Larita Moore,
EMP: 4 EST: 2009 Privately Held
SIC: 7372 Prepackaged software

(G-4508)
PAURI RETAIL STORE LLC
2785 E Grand Blvd # 312 (48211-2003)
PHONE....................415 980-1525
Matthew Hall, *CEO*
EMP: 13
SALES (est): 519.6K Privately Held
SIC: 3944 Games, toys & children's vehicles

(G-4509)
PEARSON AUTO SERVICE INC
20800 W 7 Mile Rd (48219-1969)
PHONE....................313 538-6870
EMP: 5 EST: 2019
SALES (est): 285.5K Privately Held
SIC: 3471 Plating & polishing

(G-4510)
PEARSON INDUSTRIES LLC
18205 Marx St (48203-5401)
PHONE....................740 584-9080
Olivia Pearson, *Principal*
EMP: 4 EST: 2018
SALES (est): 39.6K Privately Held
WEB: www.pearsonindustries.com
SIC: 3999 Manufacturing industries

(G-4511)
PEARSON SOFTWARE COMPANY
21124 Schoolcraft Apt B1 (48223-2654)
PHONE....................313 878-2687
Casey Pearson, *Principal*
EMP: 4 EST: 2010
SALES (est): 125.7K Privately Held
SIC: 7372 Prepackaged software

(G-4512)
PEERLESS MTAL PWDERS ABRSIVE L
131 S Military St (48209-3032)
PHONE....................313 841-5400
Norma Bearce, *Manager*
EMP: 20
SALES (corp-wide): 3MM Privately Held
WEB: www.peerlessmetal.com
SIC: 3399 Powder, metal
PA: Peerless Metal Powders & Abrasive, Llc
124 S Military St
Detroit MI 48209
313 841-5400

(G-4513)
PEERLESS MTAL PWDERS ABRSIVE L
6307 W Fort St (48209-2940)
PHONE....................313 841-5400
Paul Tousley, *President*
EMP: 6
SALES (corp-wide): 3MM Privately Held
WEB: www.peerlessmetal.com
SIC: 3291 Abrasive products
PA: Peerless Metal Powders & Abrasive, Llc
124 S Military St
Detroit MI 48209
313 841-5400

(G-4514)
PEERLESS QUALITY PRODUCTS
7707 Lyndon St (48238-2465)
P.O. Box 480, Grand Blanc (48480-0480)
PHONE....................313 933-7525
EMP: 11
SQ FT: 27,000
SALES (est): 2MM Privately Held
SIC: 2842 Mfg Polish/Sanitation Goods

(G-4515)
PEGASUS TOOL LLC
12680 Farley (48239-2643)
PHONE....................313 255-5900
Arthur Scharr Sr,
EMP: 4 EST: 1999
SALES (est): 234.9K Privately Held
SIC: 3069 3089 Molded rubber products; injection molding of plastics

(G-4516)
PEPSI-COLA METRO BTLG CO INC
1555 Mack Ave (48207-4719)
PHONE....................313 832-0910
Tim Matson, *Plant Mgr*
Mike Henige, *Mfg Staff*
Katie Morris, *Human Res Dir*
Jamie Rush, *Sales Staff*
Robert Belisle, *Sales Associate*
EMP: 6
SQ FT: 365,694
SALES (corp-wide): 70.3B Publicly Held
WEB: www.pepsico.com
SIC: 2086 Carbonated soft drinks, bottled & canned
HQ: Pepsi-Cola Metropolitan Bottling Company, Inc.
1111 Westchester Ave
White Plains NY 10604
914 767-6000

(G-4517)
PERFECT EYES OPTICAL
15292 E 8 Mile Rd (48205-1353)
PHONE....................248 275-7861
EMP: 4 EST: 2019
SALES (est): 81K Privately Held
SIC: 3851 Ophthalmic goods

(G-4518)
PERFECTION INDUSTRIES INC (PA)
18571 Weaver St (48228-1187)
PHONE....................313 272-4040
Arthur G Ryan, *President*
EMP: 20 EST: 1951
SQ FT: 13,000
SALES (est): 2.2MM Privately Held
WEB: www.perfectionindustries.com
SIC: 3471 Electroplating of metals or formed products

(G-4519)
PERIGEE MANUFACTURING CO INC
7519 Intervale St (48238-2401)
PHONE....................313 933-4420
Michael F Topolewski, *President*
EMP: 12 EST: 1964
SQ FT: 20,000
SALES (est): 2MM Privately Held
WEB: www.perigeemfg.com
SIC: 3452 Nuts, metal

(G-4520)
PERSONAL TOUCH
8481 Stahelin Ave (48228-3026)
PHONE....................313 354-4255
Lakisha Fields, *Principal*
EMP: 4 EST: 2017
SALES (est): 58.2K Privately Held
SIC: 3999 Candles

(G-4521)
PETE PULLUM COMPANY INC
15330 Castleton St (48227-2016)
PHONE....................313 837-9440
John R Pullum Jr, *President*
EMP: 4 EST: 1940
SQ FT: 52,800
SALES (est): 750.4K Privately Held
WEB: www.pullumwindow.com
SIC: 2431 5031 Windows & window parts & trim, wood; door frames, wood; windows

(G-4522)
PEWABIC SOCIETY INC
Also Called: PEWABIC POTTERY
10125 E Jefferson Ave (48214-3138)
PHONE....................313 626-2000
Amanda Rogers, *Marketing Staff*
Mario Lopez, *Technical Staff*
Steve McBride, *Exec Dir*
Heather Simmet, *Director*
Alethea Davenport, *Technician*
EMP: 35 EST: 1979
SQ FT: 10,500
SALES: 2MM Privately Held
WEB: www.pewabic.org
SIC: 3255 8412 8299 Tile, clay refractory; museum; art gallery, noncommercial; arts & crafts schools

(G-4523)
PIETRZYK FOODS LLC
Also Called: Pietrzyk Pierogi
1429 Gratiot Ave Ste 109 (48207-2745)
PHONE....................313 614-9393
Erica Pietrzyk, *Principal*
EMP: 6 EST: 2017
SALES (est): 270.3K Privately Held
WEB: www.pietrzykpierogi.com
SIC: 2038 Frozen specialties

(G-4524)
PINGREE MFG L3C
Also Called: Pingree Detroit
15707 Livernois Ave (48238-1319)
PHONE....................313 444-8428
Jarret Schlaff, *CEO*
EMP: 4 EST: 2016
SALES (est): 233.6K Privately Held
WEB: www.pingreedetroit.com
SIC: 3999 Manufacturing industries

(G-4525)
PIONEER STEEL CORPORATION (PA)
7447 Intervale St (48238-2401)
PHONE....................313 933-9400
Donald R Sazama, *President*
Gil Hoard, *General Mgr*
Donald Seavey, *COO*

Detroit - Wayne County (G-4526) — GEOGRAPHIC SECTION

Ronald Bebes, *Vice Pres*
Michael R Small, *Vice Pres*
EMP: 43 **EST:** 1982
SQ FT: 38,000
SALES (est): 21.1MM **Privately Held**
WEB: www.pioneersteel.us
SIC: 5051 3544 Plates, metal; bars, metal; die sets for metal stamping (presses)

(G-4526)
PISTON AUTOMOTIVE LLC
4015 Michigan Ave (48210-3266)
PHONE................................313 541-8789
Myron Crowell, *General Mgr*
Robert Fisher, *Vice Pres*
Eric Schryer, *Opers Staff*
Kelvin Hutchins, *Production*
Vincenzo Nestico, *Engineer*
EMP: 600
SALES (corp-wide): 2.3B **Privately Held**
WEB: www.pistongroup.com
SIC: 3714 Motor vehicle parts & accessories
HQ: Piston Automotive, L.L.C.
   12723 Telegraph Rd Ste 1
   Redford MI 48239
   313 541-8674

(G-4527)
PISTON MODULES LLC
4015 Michigan Ave (48210-3266)
PHONE................................313 897-1540
Vincent Johnson, *CEO*
Kurt Hall, *President*
Brandon Tankesley, *Opers Mgr*
Sharon Johnson, *Human Res Mgr*
Kelly Slayton, *Human Res Mgr*
▲ **EMP:** 3599 **EST:** 2001
SQ FT: 22,000
SALES (est): 5.7MM
SALES (corp-wide): 2.3B **Privately Held**
WEB: www.pistongroup.com
SIC: 3592 Pistons & piston rings
HQ: Piston Automotive, L.L.C.
   12723 Telegraph Rd Ste 1
   Redford MI 48239
   313 541-8674

(G-4528)
PLASTICORE INC
200 Renaissance Ctr # 2682 (48243-1300)
PHONE................................877 573-3090
David Franklin, *Ch of Bd*
EMP: 16 **EST:** 2016
SALES (est): 860.3K **Privately Held**
SIC: 3069 Floor coverings, rubber

(G-4529)
POINT A ORGANIZATION
12091 Cloverlawn St (48204-1012)
PHONE................................313 971-4625
Latoya Mobley, *Principal*
EMP: 4 **EST:** 2017
SALES (est): 74.4K **Privately Held**
SIC: 3999 Candles

(G-4530)
POPPIN TOP HAT LLC
1376 Broadway St (48226-2202)
PHONE................................313 427-0400
Athena Hinojosa,
EMP: 4 **EST:** 2018
SALES (est): 100K **Privately Held**
WEB: www.poppintophat.com
SIC: 2099 Popcorn, packaged: except already popped

(G-4531)
PRANKSTER PRESS LLC
1492 Gratiot Ave (48207-2723)
PHONE................................616 550-3099
Elizabeth Luidens, *Principal*
EMP: 5 **EST:** 2016
SALES (est): 74.2K **Privately Held**
WEB: www.theprankterpress.com
SIC: 2741 Miscellaneous publishing

(G-4532)
PRECISION HONE & TOOL INC
13600 Evergreen Rd (48223-3441)
PHONE................................313 493-9760
Mark Behr, *President*
EMP: 12 **EST:** 2000
SALES (est): 795.4K **Privately Held**
WEB: www.honingmichigan.com
SIC: 3599 Machine shop, jobbing & repair

(G-4533)
PRESSURE VESSEL SERVICE INC (PA)
Also Called: PVS Chemicals
10900 Harper Ave (48213-3364)
PHONE................................313 921-1200
James B Nicholson, *President*
Patrick Collins, *Business Mgr*
Peter Messina, *Business Mgr*
Tim Nicholson, *COO*
Tom Bennett, *Vice Pres*
◆ **EMP:** 45 **EST:** 1945
SQ FT: 187,000
SALES (est): 651.4MM **Privately Held**
WEB: www.pvschemicals.com
SIC: 5169 2819 2899 4953 Acids; industrial chemicals; sulfuric acid, oleum; water treating compounds; acid waste, collection & disposal; conveyors & conveying equipment

(G-4534)
PRO KING TRUCKING INC
3241 Doris St (48238-2721)
PHONE................................909 800-7885
Terry Garvin, *Principal*
EMP: 4 **EST:** 2018
SALES (est): 164.7K **Privately Held**
SIC: 3799 Transportation equipment

(G-4535)
PRO SIGN AND AWNING INC
17627 W Warren Ave (48228-3508)
PHONE................................313 581-9333
Zaina Fardous, *President*
EMP: 6 **EST:** 2010
SALES (est): 248K **Privately Held**
WEB: www.signmi.com
SIC: 3993 Signs & advertising specialties

(G-4536)
PRODUCTION ACCESSORIES CO
123 E Golden Gate (48203-2053)
PHONE................................313 366-1500
John Else, *President*
William Else, *Manager*
EMP: 8 **EST:** 1940
SQ FT: 15,000
SALES (est): 850K **Privately Held**
WEB: www.productionaccessories.com
SIC: 3535 Unit handling conveying systems

(G-4537)
PRODUCTION TUBE COMPANY INC
481 Beaufait St (48207-4303)
PHONE................................313 259-3990
EMP: 8
SQ FT: 21,000
SALES (est): 750K **Privately Held**
SIC: 3498 3471 3444 3398 Mfg Fabrctd Pipe/Fitting Plating/Polishing Svcs Mfg Sheet Metalwork Metal Heat Treating Copper Foundry

(G-4538)
PRONTOPRINTING LLC
17145 Plainview Ave (48219-3529)
PHONE................................313 622-7565
EMP: 4 **EST:** 2018
SALES (est): 96.2K **Privately Held**
SIC: 2752 Commercial printing, lithographic

(G-4539)
PROP ART STUDIO INC
112 E Grand Blvd (48207-3713)
PHONE................................313 824-2200
Michael Stapleton, *President*
Denise Connolly, *Vice Pres*
EMP: 6 **EST:** 1988
SQ FT: 7,200
SALES (est): 907.9K **Privately Held**
WEB: www.propartstudio.com
SIC: 1799 2759 Float (parade) construction; prop, set or scenery construction, theatrical; posters, including billboards: printing

(G-4540)
PSC INDUSTRIAL OUTSOURCING LP
Also Called: Hydrochempsc
515 Lycaste St (48214-3473)
PHONE................................313 824-5859
Steve Snider, *Manager*
EMP: 44
SALES (corp-wide): 468MM **Privately Held**
WEB: www.hydrochempsc.com
SIC: 3443 Vessels, process or storage (from boiler shops): metal plate; reactor containment vessels, metal plate; heat exchangers: coolers (after, inter), condensers, etc.; columns (fractioning, etc.): metal plate
PA: Psc Industrial Outsourcing, Lp
   900 Georgia Ave
   Deer Park TX 77536
   713 393-5600

(G-4541)
PTI QLITY CNTNMENT SLTIONS LLC (PA)
18615 Sherwood St (48234-2813)
PHONE................................313 365-3999
Jamie Hamman, *Principal*
Deb Sorenson, *Principal*
Alla Timan, *Principal*
David Salazar, *COO*
Zack Iqbal, *Vice Pres*
EMP: 200 **EST:** 2004
SQ FT: 162,000
SALES (est): 35.6MM **Privately Held**
WEB: www.ptiqcs.com
SIC: 4785 8742 3479 5013 Inspection services connected with transportation; management consulting services; industry specialist consultants; painting, coating & hot dipping; automotive servicing equipment

(G-4542)
PUNKIN DSIGN SEDS ORGNLITY LLC
633 Burlingame St (48202-1004)
PHONE................................313 347-8488
Susan Y Jones,
EMP: 7 **EST:** 2010
SALES (est): 144K **Privately Held**
SIC: 2711 Newspapers

(G-4543)
PUZZLE ESCAPE
18727 Grandville Ave (48219-2894)
PHONE................................313 645-6405
Andre Morgan, *Principal*
EMP: 4 **EST:** 2016
SALES (est): 76K **Privately Held**
WEB: www.escapetheroom.com
SIC: 3944 Puzzles

(G-4544)
QT GLAMOUR COLLECTION LLC
14182 Collingham Dr (48205-1217)
PHONE................................248 605-5507
Tanisha Williams,
EMP: 4 **EST:** 2020
SALES (est): 39.6K **Privately Held**
SIC: 3999 Hair & hair-based products

(G-4545)
QUAKER HOUGHTON PA INC
Also Called: D.A. Stuart Company
9100 Freeland St (48228-2309)
PHONE................................313 273-7374
Taylor Libby, *Opers Staff*
Regan Seymur, *Manager*
Jim Stocking, *Supervisor*
EMP: 4
SALES (corp-wide): 1.4B **Publicly Held**
WEB: www.home.quakerhoughton.com
SIC: 2992 Cutting oils, blending: made from purchased materials; re-refining lubricating oils & greases
HQ: Quaker Houghton Pa, Inc.
   901 E Hector St
   Conshohocken PA 19428
   610 832-4000

(G-4546)
QUALITY BENDING THREADING INC
5100 Stanton St (48208-2064)
PHONE................................313 898-5100
Matthew J Seely, *President*
EMP: 10 **EST:** 1960
SQ FT: 35,000
SALES (est): 1.7MM **Privately Held**
WEB: www.qualitybending.com
SIC: 3441 Fabricated structural metal

(G-4547)
QUESTRON PACKAGING LLC
7650 W Chicago (48204-2862)
PHONE................................313 657-1630
Aiman Kawas, *President*
EMP: 8 **EST:** 2014
SQ FT: 50,000
SALES (est): 200K **Privately Held**
SIC: 2899 Fuel tank or engine cleaning chemicals

(G-4548)
QUIKRETE DETROIT
8951 Schaefer Hwy Ste 4 (48228-2515)
PHONE................................313 491-3500
Joe Boice, *Manager*
▲ **EMP:** 13 **EST:** 2007
SALES (est): 1MM **Privately Held**
WEB: www.quikrete.com
SIC: 3272 Concrete products

(G-4549)
R & L COLOR GRAPHICS INC
18709 Meyers Rd (48235-1310)
PHONE................................313 345-3838
Linda Davis, *Owner*
Richard Jackson, *Vice Pres*
EMP: 5 **EST:** 1994
SQ FT: 3,000
SALES (est): 495.3K **Privately Held**
WEB: www.randlcolor.com
SIC: 2752 Commercial printing, offset

(G-4550)
R B L PLASTICS INCORPORATED
Also Called: Kwik Paint Products
6040 Russell St (48211-2120)
PHONE................................313 873-8800
Ronald B Lipson, *President*
Brian K Lipson, *Vice Pres*
Rosalie Lipson, *Treasurer*
Tim Mclsaac, *Sales Staff*
Joni Lipson, *Admin Sec*
▲ **EMP:** 40 **EST:** 1979
SQ FT: 50,000
SALES (est): 4.4MM **Privately Held**
SIC: 3089 Injection molded finished plastic products; thermoformed finished plastic products

(G-4551)
R N E BUSINESS ENTERPRISES (PA)
Also Called: American Speedy Printing
400 Renaissance Ctr Lbby (48243-1607)
PHONE................................313 963-3600
Norma Eschenberg, *President*
Kurt Eschenberg, *Vice Pres*
EMP: 6 **EST:** 1981
SQ FT: 2,500
SALES (est): 917.2K **Privately Held**
WEB: www.americanspeedy.com
SIC: 2752 Commercial printing, offset

(G-4552)
RADIANT ELECTRIC SIGN CORP
14500 Schoolcraft St (48227-2874)
PHONE................................313 835-1400
Marty Weinstock, *President*
Paul Weinsock, *Vice Pres*
EMP: 6 **EST:** 1945
SQ FT: 5,000 **Privately Held**
SIC: 3993 Neon signs

(G-4553)
RANDYS LAWN CARE SERVICES LLC ✪
3392 S Ethel St (48217-1536)
PHONE................................313 447-9536
Randy Clark, *Mng Member*
EMP: 5 **EST:** 2021

▲ = Import ▼ = Export
◆ = Import/Export

GEOGRAPHIC SECTION

Detroit - Wayne County (G-4581)

SALES (est): 291.7K Privately Held
SIC: 3524 Lawn & garden mowers & accessories

(G-4554)
RBC ENTERPRISES INC (PA)
12301 Hubbell St (48227-2777)
P.O. Box 28159 (48228-0159)
PHONE..................313 491-3350
Rudy Taylor, *President*
EMP: 20 EST: 2007 Privately Held
WEB: www.rbc-enterprises.com
SIC: 3317 Steel pipe & tubes

(G-4555)
RBL PRODUCTS INC
6040 Russell St (48211-2120)
PHONE..................313 873-8806
Ronald P Lipson, *President*
Richard Limbacher, *Vice Pres*
▲ EMP: 17 EST: 1993
SQ FT: 49,610
SALES (est): 3.8MM Privately Held
WEB: www.rblproducts.com
SIC: 3089 Aquarium accessories, plastic

(G-4556)
REAL TIMES MEDIA LLC (PA)
1452 Randolph St Ste 400 (48226-2284)
PHONE..................313 963-8100
Hiram E Jackson, *CEO*
Britton H Cox, *Vice Pres*
Leonard Corbin, *Sales Staff*
Nelson Angelique, *Office Mgr*
Angelique Nelson, *Office Mgr*
EMP: 1 EST: 2006
SALES (est): 2MM Privately Held
WEB: www.realtimesmedia.com
SIC: 2711 Newspapers, publishing & printing

(G-4557)
REBEL NELL L3C
4731 Grand River Ave (48208-2250)
PHONE..................716 640-4267
Emily Peterson, *President*
EMP: 7 EST: 2013
SALES (est): 300K Privately Held
WEB: www.rebelnell.com
SIC: 3911 Jewelry, precious metal

(G-4558)
RECYCLED PAPERBOARD PDTS CORP
10400 Devine St (48213-3225)
PHONE..................313 579-6608
Joy Martinek, *President*
EMP: 6 EST: 1992
SQ FT: 18,000
SALES (est): 875.1K Privately Held
SIC: 2621 Paper mills

(G-4559)
RECYCLED POLYMETRIC MATERIALS
15477 Woodrow Wilson St (48238-1586)
PHONE..................313 957-6373
EMP: 9 EST: 2010
SALES (est): 342.4K Privately Held
WEB: www.gpmaterials.com
SIC: 2821 5169 Polyurethane resins; polyurethane products

(G-4560)
REED SPORTSWEAR MFG CO (PA)
1601 W Lafayette Blvd (48216-1927)
PHONE..................313 963-7980
Mark Silver, *Owner*
Eda Reed, *Vice Pres*
Roseann Silver, *Admin Sec*
▲ EMP: 35 EST: 1950
SQ FT: 37,000 Privately Held
WEB: www.reedsportswear.com
SIC: 2386 5136 Coats & jackets, leather & sheep-lined; leather & sheep lined clothing, men's & boys'

(G-4561)
REED SPORTSWEAR MFG CO
Also Called: Leather Unlimited
1601 W Lafayette Blvd (48216-1927)
PHONE..................313 963-7980
Rosco Mihajlovic, *Manager*
EMP: 6

SQ FT: 2,500 Privately Held
WEB: www.reedsportswear.com
SIC: 5611 5621 2339 Men's & boys' clothing stores; women's clothing stores; women's & misses' athletic clothing & sportswear
PA: Reed Sportswear Manufacturing Co.
1601 W Lafayette Blvd
Detroit MI 48216
313 963-7980

(G-4562)
RELIABLE GLASS COMPANY
Also Called: Reliable Architectural Mtls Co
9751 Erwin St (48213-1103)
PHONE..................313 924-9750
Douglas F Tarrance, *Owner*
Zach Havrilla, *QC Mgr*
Karen Havrilla, *Admin Sec*
EMP: 38 EST: 1960
SQ FT: 32,500
SALES (est): 4.8MM Privately Held
WEB: www.ramcometals.com
SIC: 5039 5031 3442 Structural assemblies, prefabricated: non-wood; glass construction materials; building materials, interior; metal doors; window & door frames

(G-4563)
RELIGIOUS COMMUNICATIONS LLC
5590 Coplin St (48213-3706)
PHONE..................313 822-3361
Kathleen Humprey, *Manager*
EMP: 5
SALES (corp-wide): 1.7MM Privately Held
SIC: 5049 2759 7374 7319 Religious supplies; commercial printing; computer graphics service; display advertising service
PA: Religious Communications Llc
2 Sun Ct Ste 300
Norcross GA

(G-4564)
REMACON COMPRESSORS INC
7939 Mcgraw St (48210-2156)
PHONE..................313 842-8219
Raymond G Mickiewicz, *President*
Laurie M Mickiewicz, *Corp Secy*
Charles J Mickiewicz, *Vice Pres*
EMP: 5 EST: 1981
SQ FT: 9,800
SALES (est): 728.8K Privately Held
WEB: www.semppes.com
SIC: 3585 Compressors for refrigeration & air conditioning equipment

(G-4565)
REMY GIRLS
19445 Livernois Ave (48221-1718)
PHONE..................313 397-2870
Shantel Roberts, *Principal*
EMP: 4 EST: 2015
SALES (est): 91.8K Privately Held
WEB: www.remygirls.com
SIC: 3999 Wigs, including doll wigs, toupees or wiglets

(G-4566)
REO HYDRAULIC & MFG INC
18475 Sherwood St (48234-2832)
PHONE..................313 891-2244
Robert E Obrecht, *President*
David Obrecht, *Vice Pres*
Rudy Vandenbroeck, *Engineer*
Kou Hang, *Design Engr*
Chris Utah, *Director*
EMP: 18 EST: 1972
SALES (est): 2.2MM Privately Held
WEB: www.reogroup.com
SIC: 5084 3594 Pneumatic tools & equipment; fluid power pumps & motors

(G-4567)
REO HYDRO-PIERCE INC
18475 Sherwood St (48234-2832)
PHONE..................313 891-2244
Robert Obrecht, *President*
Raymond E Obrecht, *Vice Pres*
▲ EMP: 21 EST: 1984
SQ FT: 32,000

SALES (est): 1.2MM Privately Held
WEB: www.reogroup.com
SIC: 3599 Machine shop, jobbing & repair

(G-4568)
REPAIR INDUSTRIES MICHIGAN INC
Also Called: Rim Custom Racks
6501 E Mcnichols Rd (48212-2027)
P.O. Box 290, Saint Clair Shores (48080-0290)
PHONE..................313 365-5300
Todd A Schorer, *President*
Michael Bahr, *Business Mgr*
Mike Skaff, *Accounting Mgr*
Thomas Dobek, *VP Sales*
Howard Schorer, *Manager*
EMP: 110 EST: 1978
SQ FT: 156,000
SALES (est): 28.7MM Privately Held
WEB: www.repair-industries.com
SIC: 5021 3412 3312 Racks; metal barrels, drums & pails; blast furnaces & steel mills

(G-4569)
RESTRICTED AREA LLC
15410 Young St (48205-3660)
PHONE..................419 975-8109
Solomon Wilson Jr,
EMP: 5
SALES (est): 100K Privately Held
SIC: 3161 Clothing & apparel carrying cases

(G-4570)
RESURGO LLC
786 W Grand Blvd (48216-1003)
PHONE..................313 559-2325
George Kyle, *Principal*
EMP: 4 EST: 2017
SALES (est): 54.1K Privately Held
WEB: www.resurgo.net
SIC: 2431 Millwork

(G-4571)
RICHARD BENNETT & ASSOCIATES
470 Brainard St (48201-1718)
PHONE..................313 831-4262
Richard Bennett, *President*
Betty Bennett, *Vice Pres*
EMP: 4 EST: 1984
SQ FT: 28,500
SALES (est): 379.5K Privately Held
WEB: www.richardbennettdesigns.com
SIC: 3441 Fabricated structural metal

(G-4572)
ROWSEY CONSTRUCTION & DEV LLC
607 Shelby St Ste 722 (48226-3282)
PHONE..................313 675-2464
Clyde Rowsey, *President*
EMP: 5 EST: 2016
SALES (est): 351.7K Privately Held
WEB: www.spacelabdetroit.com
SIC: 1799 1389 1742 1771 Waterproofing; oil field services; stucco work, interior; stucco, gunite & grouting contractors

(G-4573)
RTLF-HOPE LLC
Also Called: Hope Global of Detroit
1401 Abbott St (48216-1946)
PHONE..................313 538-1700
John Luca, *Vice Pres*
Robert L Ferdinand,
Cheryl Merchant,
EMP: 9 EST: 2003
SQ FT: 19,000
SALES (est): 255.9K Privately Held
SIC: 2396 Automotive & apparel trimmings

(G-4574)
S B C HOLDINGS INC
300 River Place Dr # 5000 (48207-5068)
PHONE..................313 446-2000
John W Stroh III, *Chairman*
George E Kuehn, *Exec VP*
Mark Tuttle, *Vice Pres*
EMP: 12 EST: 1850
SQ FT: 17,000

SALES (est): 1MM
SALES (corp-wide): 2.6MM Privately Held
WEB: www.strohbiz.com
SIC: 2082 2086 Beer (alcoholic beverage); fruit drinks (less than 100% juice): packaged in cans, etc.
PA: The Stroh Companies Inc
300 River Place Dr # 5000
Detroit MI 48207
313 446-2000

(G-4575)
SAA TECH INC
7420 Intervale St (48238-2460)
PHONE..................313 933-4960
Scott Apkarian, *President*
EMP: 9 EST: 1995
SALES (est): 2MM Privately Held
SIC: 3556 Meat processing machinery

(G-4576)
SAKTHI AUTO GROUP USA INC
100 American Way St (48209-2955)
PHONE..................313 551-6001
David Naboychik, *Manager*
EMP: 225 Privately Held
SIC: 3711 Chassis, motor vehicle
PA: Sakthi Automotive Group Usa, Inc.
6401 W Fort St
Detroit MI 48209

(G-4577)
SAKTHI AUTO GROUP USA INC
201 S Waterman St (48209-3065)
PHONE..................248 292-9328
Lalit Kumar, *Branch Mgr*
EMP: 225 Privately Held
SIC: 3711 Chassis, motor vehicle
PA: Sakthi Automotive Group Usa, Inc.
6401 W Fort St
Detroit MI 48209

(G-4578)
SAKTHI AUTO GROUP USA INC (PA)
Also Called: Sag USA
6401 W Fort St (48209-1271)
PHONE..................313 652-5254
Kevin English, *CEO*
Pete Ravenna, *Engineer*
Nalin Chaudhry, *Finance*
◆ EMP: 150 EST: 2010
SALES (est): 83.9MM Privately Held
SIC: 3711 Chassis, motor vehicle

(G-4579)
SALEM/SAVARD INDUSTRIES LLC
8561 W Chicago (48204-2623)
PHONE..................313 931-6880
John A Savard,
EMP: 10 EST: 2003
SQ FT: 25,000
SALES (est): 252.9K Privately Held
SIC: 3564 3567 3444 Blowers & fans; industrial furnaces & ovens; sheet metalwork

(G-4580)
SAVAGE SEAMOSS LLC
16250 Stansbury St (48235-4504)
PHONE..................313 288-6899
Cynthia Harris Murphy,
EMP: 4 EST: 2020
SALES (est): 229.8K Privately Held
SIC: 2833 Vitamins, natural or synthetic: bulk, uncompounded

(G-4581)
SAVARD CORPORATION
8561 W Chicago (48204-2623)
PHONE..................313 931-6880
John Savard, *President*
Charles Savard, *Vice Pres*
Chris Savard, *Vice Pres*
Frank Savard, *Vice Pres*
EMP: 14 EST: 1945
SQ FT: 20,000
SALES (est): 537.8K Privately Held
WEB: www.salemsavard.com
SIC: 3549 Metalworking machinery

Detroit - Wayne County (G-4582)   GEOGRAPHIC SECTION

(G-4582)
SAVS WELDING SERVICES INC
11811 Pleasant St (48217-1619)
P.O. Box 18417, River Rouge (48218-0417)
PHONE..................313 841-3430
Thomas Saville, *President*
Robert F Benso, *Vice Pres*
EMP: 14 **EST:** 1990
SQ FT: 4,000
SALES (est): 3.1MM **Privately Held**
WEB: www.savswelding.com
SIC: 7692 3441 Welding repair; fabricated structural metal

(G-4583)
SBOY LLC
1938 Franklin St Ste 106 (48207-4037)
PHONE..................313 350-0496
David Woods, *Principal*
EMP: 6 **EST:** 2013
SALES (est): 225.7K **Privately Held**
SIC: 2759 Commercial printing

(G-4584)
SCHAD BOILER SETTING COMPANY
Also Called: Schad Refractory Cnstr Co
15240 Castleton St (48227-2092)
PHONE..................313 273-2235
Richard Lee, *CEO*
Tyler Vanwinkle, *Regional Mgr*
James R Choate, *Vice Pres*
George Kitto, *Mktg Dir*
Michael Burak, *Manager*
EMP: 60 **EST:** 1942
SQ FT: 50,000
SALES (est): 11.8MM **Privately Held**
WEB: www.schadrefractory.com
SIC: 3255 3443 Tile & brick refractories, except plastic; fabricated plate work (boiler shop)

(G-4585)
SCOTTEN STEEL PROCESSING INC
Also Called: C & J Steel Processing
3545 Scotten St (48210-3159)
PHONE..................313 897-8837
Warren Chappel, *President*
Al Jones, *Vice Pres*
EMP: 18 **EST:** 1980
SQ FT: 65,000
SALES (est): 408.5K **Privately Held**
SIC: 7389 5051 3444 Scrap steel cutting; metals service centers & offices; sheet metalwork

(G-4586)
SEA FARE FOODS INC
2127 Brewster St (48207-2103)
P.O. Box 7587 (48207-0587)
PHONE..................313 568-0223
S A Lincoln Sack, *President*
Phillip Sack, *Vice Pres*
Dorothy Sack, *Treasurer*
EMP: 14 **EST:** 1959
SQ FT: 22,000
SALES (est): 3MM **Privately Held**
WEB: www.macohens.com
SIC: 2091 2092 Herring, cured; fresh or frozen packaged fish

(G-4587)
SESCO INC
Also Called: Sesko Incorporated
7800 Dix St (48209-1106)
PHONE..................313 843-7710
Werner Lehmann, *President*
Gerhard H Eckle, *COO*
Fritz Gauer, *Mfg Staff*
Otto Guencel, *Purchasing*
EMP: 58 **EST:** 1938
SQ FT: 55,000
SALES (est): 3.9MM **Privately Held**
WEB: www.sesco-inc.com
SIC: 3549 3542 Coiling machinery; machine tools, metal forming type

(G-4588)
SET DUCT MANUFACTURING LLC
7800 Intervale St (48238-2463)
PHONE..................313 491-4380
Thomas Pilkington, *Director*
Victor Edozien,
EMP: 50 **EST:** 2010
SALES (est): 12.5MM **Privately Held**
WEB: www.setduct.com
SIC: 3444 Sheet metalwork
PA: Set Enterprises, Inc.
29488 Woodward Ave 296
Royal Oak MI 48073

(G-4589)
SHAW & SLAVSKY INC (PA)
Also Called: Shaw Design Group
13821 Elmira St (48227-3099)
PHONE..................313 834-3990
Thomas G Smith, *President*
Reynaldo J Linares, *Vice Pres*
John J Debono, *CFO*
▲ **EMP:** 20 **EST:** 1932
SQ FT: 100,000
SALES (est): 8.2MM **Privately Held**
WEB: www.shawandslavsky.com
SIC: 2542 3993 Office & store showcases & display fixtures; signs & advertising specialties

(G-4590)
SHAW & SLAVSKY INC
Also Called: Shaw Design
13639 Elmira St (48227-3015)
PHONE..................313 834-3990
Tom Smith, *Manager*
EMP: 15
SALES (corp-wide): 8.2MM **Privately Held**
WEB: www.shawandslavsky.com
SIC: 2542 Stands, merchandise display: except wood
PA: Shaw & Slavsky, Inc.
13821 Elmira St
Detroit MI 48227
313 834-3990

(G-4591)
SHINOLA/DETROIT LLC (PA)
485 W Milwaukee St (48202-3220)
PHONE..................888 304-2534
Tom Lewand, *CEO*
Jacques Panis, *President*
Shannon Washburn, *President*
Matthew Duell, *Project Mgr*
Kirk Black, *Store Mgr*
▲ **EMP:** 250 **EST:** 2011
SQ FT: 100,000
SALES (est): 95MM **Privately Held**
WEB: www.shinola.com
SIC: 3751 5094 3651 3199 Bicycles & related parts; clocks, watches & parts; watches & parts; household audio equipment; straps, leather; watches, clocks, watchcases & parts; bicycles

(G-4592)
SIGMA WIRELESS LLC
8063 Coyle St (48228-2448)
PHONE..................313 423-2629
EMP: 4 **EST:** 2018
SALES (est): 92.4K **Privately Held**
SIC: 3661 Headsets, telephone

(G-4593)
SIGNAL-RETURN INC
1345 Division St Ste 102 (48207-2639)
PHONE..................313 567-8970
Lynne Avadenka, *Director*
Jane Hoehner, *Director*
EMP: 5 **EST:** 2014
SALES (est): 300.4K **Privately Held**
WEB: www.signalreturnpress.org
SIC: 2759 Letterpress printing

(G-4594)
SIMPLY SUZANNE LLC
200 River Place Dr Apt 10 (48207-4397)
PHONE..................917 364-4549
EMP: 8
SALES (est): 567.3K **Privately Held**
SIC: 2064 Mfg Candy/Confectionery

(G-4595)
SIMPLY ZARA S TREATS LLC
19928 Lindsay St (48235-2201)
PHONE..................313 327-5002
Leonna Weatherspoon,
EMP: 10 **EST:** 2020
SALES (est): 283.4K **Privately Held**
WEB: www.simplyzarastreats.com
SIC: 2051 Cakes, bakery: except frozen

(G-4596)
SISTA ROLES CUISINE LLC
3905 Bewick St (48214-1579)
PHONE..................313 588-1142
Portia Jackson,
EMP: 8 **EST:** 2019
SALES (est): 285.5K **Privately Held**
SIC: 2599 Food wagons, restaurant

(G-4597)
SKIN BAR VII LLC
18951 Livernois Ave (48221-2258)
PHONE..................313 397-9919
Kimberly Jones, *Mng Member*
EMP: 5 **EST:** 2014
SQ FT: 1,500
SALES (est): 263.1K **Privately Held**
WEB: www.skinbar7.com
SIC: 3999 7231 Sterilizers, barber & beauty shop; cosmetology & personal hygiene salons

(G-4598)
SMITH WA INC
Also Called: Brite Products
14650 Dequindre St (48212-1504)
PHONE..................313 883-6977
Steven Smith, *President*
Tony Zaccagni, *Vice Pres*
Sherry Sprks, *Manager*
EMP: 38 **EST:** 1958
SQ FT: 12,000
SALES (est): 1.6MM **Privately Held**
WEB: www.crcindustries.com
SIC: 2899 Chemical preparations

(G-4599)
SOPHIAS BAKERY INC
Also Called: Lebanon Baking Company
8421 Michigan Ave (48210-2076)
PHONE..................313 582-6992
Lazaros Kircos, *President*
David Depoy, *Vice Pres*
Clide Manion, *Vice Pres*
Clyde Manion, *Vice Pres*
Paula Kircos, *Treasurer*
EMP: 18 **EST:** 1980
SQ FT: 22,000
SALES (est): 623.8K **Privately Held**
WEB: www.sophiasbakery.com
SIC: 2051 Breads, rolls & buns

(G-4600)
SPECTRA LMP LLC (PA)
6501 Lynch Rd (48234-4140)
PHONE..................313 571-2100
Michael Hinton, *Human Res Dir*
Michael Guthrie, *Mng Member*
Carlton Guthrie, *Mng Member*
EMP: 3 **EST:** 2001
SALES (est): 21.1MM **Privately Held**
SIC: 3711 Chassis, motor vehicle

(G-4601)
SPIFFYS SLAY STATION LLC
18529 Anglin St (48234-1403)
PHONE..................313 401-8906
Breonia Anthony,
EMP: 5
SALES (est): 42.5K **Privately Held**
SIC: 2389 7389 Apparel & accessories;

(G-4602)
SPOONFUL PRESS
16617 Muirland St (48221-3079)
PHONE..................313 862-6579
Eric Fields, *Principal*
EMP: 5 **EST:** 2008
SALES (est): 88.6K **Privately Held**
SIC: 2741 Miscellaneous publishing

(G-4603)
ST JOHN
4100 John R St (48201-2013)
PHONE..................313 576-8212
Chris Fontichiaro, *Principal*
EMP: 5
SALES (est): 219.9K **Privately Held**
SIC: 2339 Sportswear, women's

(G-4604)
STAN SAX CORP (PA)
10900 Harper Ave (48213-3364)
PHONE..................248 683-9199
David Sax, *President*
Barry Weber, *CFO*
EMP: 12 **EST:** 1959
SQ FT: 25,000
SALES (est): 1.3MM **Privately Held**
WEB: www.stansaxcorp.com
SIC: 3291 Abrasive products

(G-4605)
STANDARD SCALE & SUPPLY CO (PA)
25421 Glendale (48239-4511)
P.O. Box 40720, Redford (48240-0720)
PHONE..................313 255-6700
Clarence W Bowman Jr, *President*
Bill Bowman, *Vice Pres*
Suzanne A Bowman, *Treasurer*
EMP: 2 **EST:** 1946
SQ FT: 12,000
SALES (est): 2.7MM **Privately Held**
WEB: www.standardscale.com
SIC: 5046 7699 3596 Scales, except laboratory; scale repair service; industrial scales

(G-4606)
STAR PAPER CONVERTERS INC
Also Called: Star Paper Products
1717 17th St (48216-1889)
P.O. Box 379, Allen Park (48101-0379)
PHONE..................313 963-5200
Richard A Nawrocki, *President*
Helen Jenks, *Vice Pres*
Mark Laske, *Vice Pres*
Janet G Nawrocki, *Admin Sec*
EMP: 10 **EST:** 1993
SQ FT: 50,000
SALES (est): 970.1K **Privately Held**
WEB: www.star-paper.com
SIC: 2621 Paper mills

(G-4607)
STARLITE TOOL & DIE WELDING
12091 Woodbine (48239-2417)
PHONE..................313 533-3462
Walter Milewski, *President*
EMP: 4 **EST:** 1974
SQ FT: 1,900
SALES (est): 175.4K **Privately Held**
WEB: www.starlitewelding.com
SIC: 7692 Welding repair

(G-4608)
STARTEC TRAINING INSTITUTE
20021 Carrie St (48234-3073)
PHONE..................313 808-7013
Michael Northen, *Principal*
EMP: 10 **EST:** 2020
SALES (est): 471.9K **Privately Held**
SIC: 3548 Welding apparatus

(G-4609)
STELLAR PLASTICS FABG LLC
14121 Gratiot Ave (48205-2865)
PHONE..................313 527-7337
Brad Franciosi,
EMP: 7 **EST:** 2008
SALES (est): 66.7K **Privately Held**
WEB: www.stellarplastics.com
SIC: 3089 Injection molding of plastics

(G-4610)
STITCHED NOW
18600 Eureka St (48234-2120)
PHONE..................586 460-6175
Laskhas Hill, *CEO*
EMP: 4
SALES (est): 115.8K **Privately Held**
SIC: 2399 Hand woven & crocheted products

(G-4611)
STREET DENIM & CO
15530 Grand River Ave (48227-2223)
PHONE..................313 837-1200
EMP: 4
SALES (est): 431.8K **Privately Held**
SIC: 2211 Cotton Broadwoven Fabric Mill

GEOGRAPHIC SECTION
Detroit - Wayne County (G-4643)

(G-4612)
STROH COMPANIES INC (PA)
300 River Place Dr # 5000 (48207-5068)
PHONE.................................313 446-2000
John W Stroh III, *Chairman*
Mark K Tuttle, *CFO*
Melissa Fenner, *Sales Mgr*
George E Kuehn, *Admin Sec*
EMP: 1 **EST:** 1850
SQ FT: 508,000
SALES (est): 2.6MM **Privately Held**
WEB: www.strohriverplace.com
SIC: 2082 2086 6552 6531 Beer (alcoholic beverage); malt liquors; near beer; fruit drinks (less than 100% juice): packaged in cans, etc.; tea, iced: packaged in cans, bottles, etc.; subdividers & developers; land subdividers & developers, commercial; real estate managers

(G-4613)
STRONG STEEL PRODUCTS LLC
6464 Strong St (48211-1862)
PHONE.................................313 267-3300
Jeffrey N Cole, *President*
EMP: 18 **EST:** 1996
SALES (est): 1.2MM **Privately Held**
WEB: www.fptscrap.com
SIC: 5093 3341 4953 3312 Ferrous metal scrap & waste; secondary nonferrous metals; refuse systems; blast furnaces & steel mills

(G-4614)
SUN TOOL COMPANY
18505 Weaver St (48228-1158)
PHONE.................................313 837-2442
EMP: 4
SALES (est): 260K **Privately Held**
SIC: 3599 Mfg Industrial Machinery

(G-4615)
SUPER FLUIDS LLC
Also Called: Good Juice
8838 3rd St (48202-1706)
P.O. Box 2334 (48202-0334)
PHONE.................................313 409-6522
EMP: 4 **EST:** 2015
SALES (est): 192.5K **Privately Held**
SIC: 2037 Fruit juices

(G-4616)
SUPER WOMAN PRODUCTIONS PUBG L
8539 Meyers Rd (48228-4018)
PHONE.................................313 491-6819
Angela Jones, *Principal*
EMP: 4 **EST:** 2015
SALES (est): 62.9K **Privately Held**
SIC: 2711 Newspapers

(G-4617)
SUPERIOR MTAL FINSHG RUSTPROOF
3510 E Mcnichols Rd (48212-1619)
PHONE.................................313 893-1050
EMP: 15
SALES (est): 2.2MM **Privately Held**
SIC: 3479 3471 Coating/Engraving Service Plating/Polishing Service

(G-4618)
SUPREME BAKING COMPANY
Also Called: Supreme Bakery & Deli
5401 Proctor St (48210-2221)
PHONE.................................313 894-0222
Dusko Filipovich, *Partner*
Stojko Filipovich, *Partner*
EMP: 9 **EST:** 1967
SQ FT: 8,000
SALES (est): 277.3K **Privately Held**
SIC: 5461 5411 5149 2051 Bakeries; grocery stores, independent; bakery products; bread, cake & related products; cookies & crackers

(G-4619)
SWEET N SPORTY TEES
20410 W 7 Mile Rd (48219-3471)
PHONE.................................313 693-9793
EMP: 4 **EST:** 2018
SALES (est): 73.2K **Privately Held**
SIC: 2759 Screen printing

(G-4620)
SWEETEST TABOO LLC
14091 Mark Twain St (48227-4811)
PHONE.................................313 575-4642
Alena Dinkins, *Principal*
EMP: 5 **EST:** 2019
SALES (est): 67.3K **Privately Held**
WEB: www.sweetesttaboobakery.com
SIC: 2051 Bakery: wholesale or wholesale/retail combined

(G-4621)
SWEETHEART BAKERY INC (PA)
19200 Kelly Rd (48225-1902)
PHONE.................................313 839-6330
Michael Gralewski, *President*
Amelia Gralewski, *Vice Pres*
EMP: 39 **EST:** 1950
SQ FT: 9,000
SALES (est): 1.1MM **Privately Held**
SIC: 5461 2051 Bakeries; bread, cake & related products

(G-4622)
SYNC TECHNOLOGIES INC (PA)
2727 2nd Ave Ste 107 (48201-2620)
PHONE.................................313 963-5353
Cliff Spallings, *CEO*
Donna Stallings, *President*
Arnold Derrick Stallings, *Vice Pres*
David Stallings, *Vice Pres*
Donald Stallings, *Vice Pres*
EMP: 49 **EST:** 1988
SQ FT: 3,000
SALES (est): 1.2MM **Privately Held**
SIC: 7373 7371 7372 7374 Computer integrated systems design; computer software development; prepackaged software; data processing & preparation

(G-4623)
T S M FOODS LLC
1241 Woodward Ave (48226-2006)
PHONE.................................313 262-6556
EMP: 6 **EST:** 2011
SALES (est): 314.1K **Privately Held**
SIC: 3421 Table & food cutlery, including butchers'

(G-4624)
T WIGLEY INC
1537 Hale St (48207-2008)
PHONE.................................313 831-6881
Tom Wigley, *President*
EMP: 12 **EST:** 1999
SQ FT: 4,500
SALES (est): 1.2MM **Privately Held**
WEB: www.wigleys.com
SIC: 5147 2013 Meats, fresh; corned beef from purchased meat

(G-4625)
TALON LLC
350 Talon Centre Dr (48207-5035)
PHONE.................................313 392-1000
Randolph J Agley, *Ch of Bd*
Michael T Timmis, *Vice Ch Bd*
Paul Sieloff, *CFO*
Paul Sielofff, *CFO*
Jeff Boyd, *Officer*
EMP: 16 **EST:** 1973
SALES (est): 1.2MM **Privately Held**
WEB: www.talon.us
SIC: 3544 8741 Industrial molds; business management; financial management for business; administrative management

(G-4626)
TDW CUSTOM APPAREL & MORE LLC
20466 Kentucky St (48221-1115)
PHONE.................................248 934-0312
Tiffany Walker,
EMP: 4 **EST:** 2020
SALES (est): 20K **Privately Held**
SIC: 3944 Craft & hobby kits & sets

(G-4627)
TEAM BREADWINNER LLC
14414 Mansfield St (48227-4907)
PHONE.................................313 460-0152
Bruce J Spearman,
EMP: 5 **EST:** 2013
SQ FT: 4,800
SALES (est): 198.3K **Privately Held**
WEB: www.breadwinner.com
SIC: 2731 Book publishing

(G-4628)
TECH TOOL COMPANY INC
18235 Weaver St (48228-1193)
PHONE.................................313 836-4131
Jeff Emerson, *President*
EMP: 6 **EST:** 1959
SQ FT: 8,880
SALES (est): 575.5K **Privately Held**
SIC: 3462 Gear & chain forgings

(G-4629)
TECHNICAL ENTERPRISES LLC ○
16519 Lawton St (48221-3147)
PHONE.................................313 333-1438
Julian Lee,
EMP: 5 **EST:** 2021
SALES (est): 131.6K **Privately Held**
SIC: 1389 7389 Construction, repair & dismantling services;

(G-4630)
TF ENTERTAINMENT LLC ○
16800 Birwood St (48221-2806)
PHONE.................................424 303-3407
Darius McCullum,
EMP: 15 **EST:** 2021
SALES (est): 587.6K **Privately Held**
SIC: 3651 Music distribution apparatus

(G-4631)
THOMAS PORCHEA COLLECTION LLC
18628 Greeley St (48203-2188)
PHONE.................................313 693-6308
Porchea Thomas,
EMP: 5 **EST:** 2014
SALES (est): 67K **Privately Held**
SIC: 2329 Men's & boys' clothing

(G-4632)
THOUGHT PRVOKING TEES PRTG LLC
19409 Revere St (48234-1766)
PHONE.................................313 673-6632
Aaron Pettway, *Principal*
EMP: 6 **EST:** 2013
SALES (est): 169.7K **Privately Held**
SIC: 2752 Commercial printing, lithographic

(G-4633)
TIPALOY INC
1435 E Milwaukee St (48211-2009)
PHONE.................................313 875-5145
Harry S Radcliff Jr, *President*
Mitchell Radcliff, *Vice Pres*
Rob Vella, *Mfg Staff*
Elizabeth C Radcliff, *Admin Sec*
▲ **EMP:** 11 **EST:** 1941
SQ FT: 13,500
SALES (est): 2.6MM **Privately Held**
WEB: www.tipaloy.com
SIC: 3548 Electrodes, electric welding

(G-4634)
TITAN SALES INTERNATIONAL LLC
Also Called: Titan Coatings International
1497 E Grand Blvd (48211-3451)
PHONE.................................313 469-7105
Sean Kelly, *President*
EMP: 4 **EST:** 1968
SALES (est): 699.6K **Privately Held**
SIC: 2851 Shellac (protective coating)

(G-4635)
TOLERANCE TOOL & ENGINEERING
20541 Glendale St (48223-3324)
PHONE.................................313 592-4011
Gerard J Fiorentino, *President*
Dave Bruckman, *COO*
Gerard Fiorentino, *Director*
Sheryl Fiorentino, *Admin Sec*
EMP: 20 **EST:** 1980
SQ FT: 14,000
SALES (est): 3.7MM **Privately Held**
WEB: www.toltool.com
SIC: 3544 3545 Special dies & tools; machine tool accessories

(G-4636)
TOMKINS PRODUCTS INC
1040 W Grand Blvd (48208-2337)
PHONE.................................313 894-2222
Charles S Tompkins, *President*
EMP: 19 **EST:** 1939
SALES (est): 139.3K **Privately Held**
WEB: www.tompkinsproducts.com
SIC: 3599 Machine shop, jobbing & repair

(G-4637)
TOMPKINS PRODUCTS INC (PA)
1040 W Grand Blvd (48208-2337)
PHONE.................................313 894-2222
Charles S Tompkins III, *President*
Joseph B Tompkins, *Vice Pres*
Ken Bailey, *Mfg Mgr*
Charles Tompkins, *Maint Spvr*
Steve Berger, *Engineer*
◆ **EMP:** 95 **EST:** 1939
SQ FT: 40,000
SALES (est): 23.3MM **Privately Held**
WEB: www.tompkinsproducts.com
SIC: 3451 Screw machine products

(G-4638)
TOPSYDEKENNEL LLC ○
16709 Rosemont Ave (48219-4116)
PHONE.................................313 655-5804
Javar Chavers,
EMP: 4 **EST:** 2021
SALES (est): 300K **Privately Held**
SIC: 3199 Dog furnishings: collars, leashes, muzzles, etc.: leather

(G-4639)
TOTAL PACKAGING SOLUTIONS LLC
615 Griswold St Ste 700 (48226-3535)
PHONE.................................248 519-2376
Elizabeth Dzuris,
EMP: 10 **EST:** 2005
SQ FT: 200
SALES (est): 555.2K **Privately Held**
WEB: www.totalpkgsolutions.com
SIC: 7389 2393 Packaging & labeling services; textile bags

(G-4640)
TOUCHED BY CUPIDS ○
10725 Mckinney St (48224-1824)
PHONE.................................313 704-6334
Starlet Jones, *Owner*
EMP: 4 **EST:** 2021
SALES (est): 40K **Privately Held**
SIC: 7335 2759 5999 Commercial photography; post cards, picture: printing; picture frames, ready made

(G-4641)
TPA INC
1360 Oakman Blvd (48238-4243)
P.O. Box 38778 (48238-0778)
PHONE.................................248 302-9131
James J Padilla Jr, *President*
EMP: 5 **EST:** 2006
SALES (est): 414.8K **Privately Held**
WEB: www.thepoweralternative.com
SIC: 2869 High purity grade chemicals, organic

(G-4642)
TRACTION TECH HOLDINGS LLC
Also Called: Slipnot
2545 Beaufait St (48207-3467)
PHONE.................................313 923-0400
William Davidson, *President*
Jeff Baker, *General Mgr*
Michael Schulte, *Project Mgr*
Destry Farner, *Sales Staff*
Melissa Hosner, *Sales Associate*
EMP: 44 **EST:** 1961
SQ FT: 35,500
SALES (est): 12.2MM **Privately Held**
WEB: www.slipnot.com
SIC: 3399 3479 Metal powders, pastes & flakes; etching & engraving

(G-4643)
TRANOR INDUSTRIES LLC
Also Called: Marwood International
19365 Sherwood St (48234-2820)
PHONE.................................313 733-4888
Karl Lund, *Prgrmr*

Detroit - Wayne County (G-4644)   GEOGRAPHIC SECTION

Sam Fodale,
Gregory E Burcz,
▲ **EMP:** 12 **EST:** 2009
SALES (est): 6.4MM
SALES (corp-wide): 56.4MM **Privately Held**
WEB: www.tranorindustries.com
SIC: 3544 Special dies & tools
HQ: Marwood International Inc
105 Spruce St
Tillsonburg ON N4G 5
519 688-1144

(G-4644)
TRI-VISION LLC (PA)
Also Called: Pic-Turn
12326 E Mcnichols Rd (48205-3328)
PHONE 313 526-6020
Paul Werner, *Mng Member*
Sean Powell, *Manager*
EMP: 9 **EST:** 1936
SQ FT: 5,000
SALES (est): 500K **Privately Held**
WEB: www.trivisioncreative.com
SIC: 3444 Sheet metalwork

(G-4645)
TRIANGLE BROACH COMPANY
18404 Fitzpatrick St (48228-1420)
PHONE 313 838-2150
Gary Hanton, *President*
Carter Elton, *Vice Pres*
EMP: 31 **EST:** 1946
SQ FT: 8,000
SALES (est): 761.7K **Privately Held**
WEB: www.trianglebroach.com
SIC: 3545 3544 3829 3541 Broaches (machine tool accessories); gauges (machine tool accessories); jigs & fixtures; measuring & controlling devices; machine tools, metal cutting type

(G-4646)
TRU POINT CORPORATION
6707 W Warren Ave (48210-1135)
PHONE 313 897-9100
Michael Mainsinger, *President*
Valerie Mainsinger, *Treasurer*
EMP: 4 **EST:** 1939
SQ FT: 4,600 **Privately Held**
WEB: www.trupointcorp.com
SIC: 3544 3545 Jigs & fixtures; collets (machine tool accessories)

(G-4647)
TRULY TEES & CO LLC
6421 Vaughan St (48228-4943)
PHONE 313 266-1819
Delorean Pierson,
EMP: 5 **EST:** 2020
SALES (est): 65K **Privately Held**
SIC: 2211 Apparel & outerwear fabrics, cotton

(G-4648)
TTADEVELOPMENT LLC
11687 Yellowstone St (48204-1425)
PHONE 626 399-4225
Terrence Brown, *CEO*
EMP: 4 **EST:** 2018
SALES (est): 276.8K **Privately Held**
SIC: 1389 0782 Construction, repair & dismantling services; landscape contractors

(G-4649)
TWEDDLE GROUP INC
2111 Woodward Ave 8f (48201-3421)
PHONE 586 840-3275
Jason Donovan, *Art Dir*
EMP: 4
SALES (corp-wide): 186MM **Privately Held**
WEB: www.tweddle.com
SIC: 7372 Prepackaged software
PA: Tweddle Group, Inc.
24700 Maplehurst Dr
Clinton Township MI 48036
586 307-3700

(G-4650)
TWO JAMES SPIRITS LLC
2445 Michigan Ave (48216-1366)
PHONE 313 964-4800
Terry Bishop, *Production*
Jake Zyrek, *Sales Staff*
David Landrum, *Mng Member*

Austin Furnas, *Manager*
Andreas Joseph,
▲ **EMP:** 9 **EST:** 2012
SALES (est): 1.4MM **Privately Held**
WEB: www.twojames.com
SIC: 5921 2085 Liquor stores; distilled & blended liquors

(G-4651)
U S ICE CORP
10625 W 8 Mile Rd (48221-1032)
PHONE 313 862-3344
Saad Abbo, *President*
Fida Abbo, *Admin Sec*
EMP: 20 **EST:** 1985
SQ FT: 9,000
SALES (est): 3.1MM **Privately Held**
WEB: www.usicecorp.com
SIC: 2097 Ice cubes

(G-4652)
UNCLE RAYS LLC (HQ)
14245 Birwood St (48238-2207)
PHONE 313 834-0800
Raymond Jenkins, *President*
Dennis Dapra, *Vice Pres*
Brian Gaggin, *Vice Pres*
Jennifer Jenkins, *Vice Pres*
David Boussie, *Warehouse Mgr*
◆ **EMP:** 141 **EST:** 1985
SQ FT: 75,000
SALES (est): 900.6K
SALES (corp-wide): 21.6MM **Privately Held**
WEB: www.unclerays.com
SIC: 2096 Potato chips & other potato-based snacks
PA: The H T Hackney Co
502 S Gay St Ste 300
Knoxville TN 37902
865 546-1291

(G-4653)
UNITED STATES GYPSUM COMPANY
10090 W Jefferson Ave (48218-1363)
PHONE 313 842-4455
Matt Craig, *Branch Mgr*
EMP: 70
SALES (corp-wide): 10.7B **Privately Held**
WEB: www.usg.com
SIC: 3275 Gypsum products
HQ: United States Gypsum Company
550 W Adams St Ste 1300
Chicago IL 60661
312 606-4000

(G-4654)
URBAN AGING L3C
1905 Hyde Park Rd (48207-3819)
PHONE 313 204-5140
Patricia Rencher,
EMP: 9 **EST:** 2015
SALES (est): 444.4K **Privately Held**
SIC: 2711 Newspapers: publishing only, not printed on site

(G-4655)
US WIRE ROPE SUPPLY INC
Also Called: U.S. Wire & Rope
6555 Sherwood St (48211-2475)
PHONE 313 925-0444
James R Dagostino, *President*
Charlene Egan, *Plant Mgr*
Claudia R Dagostino, *Finance*
Claudia Dagostino, *Executive*
▲ **EMP:** 23 **EST:** 1971
SQ FT: 40,000
SALES (est): 2.5MM **Privately Held**
SIC: 3496 Grocery carts, made from purchased wire

(G-4656)
USHER ENTERPRISES INC
Also Called: Usher Oil Company
9000 Roselawn St (48204-2747)
PHONE 313 834-7055
Matthew Usher, *President*
Lori Anne Usher, *Vice Pres*
EMP: 35 **EST:** 1932
SALES (est): 9.1MM **Privately Held**
WEB: www.usheroil.com
SIC: 5093 3559 Oil, waste; recycling machinery

(G-4657)
USM HOLDINGS LLC
1 Dauch Dr (48211-1115)
PHONE 313 758-2000
David C Dauch, *Ch of Bd*
EMP: 12 **EST:** 1999
SALES (est): 5.7MM
SALES (corp-wide): 4.7B **Publicly Held**
WEB: www.aam.com
SIC: 3714 3711 Motor vehicle parts & accessories; motor vehicles & car bodies
HQ: Aam International S.a R.L.
Rue De Koerich 68
Steinfort 8437
263 527-04

(G-4658)
USM HOLDINGS LLC II
1 Dauch Dr (48211-1115)
PHONE 313 758-2000
David C Dauch, *Ch of Bd*
EMP: 10 **EST:** 2005
SALES (est): 2.9MM
SALES (corp-wide): 4.7B **Publicly Held**
WEB: www.aam.com
SIC: 3714 3711 Motor vehicle parts & accessories; motor vehicles & car bodies
HQ: Aam International S.a R.L.
Rue De Koerich 68
Steinfort 8437
263 527-04

(G-4659)
UTICA WASHERS
3105 Beaufait St (48207-2401)
PHONE 313 571-1568
Bruce Jay, *Plant Mgr*
EMP: 11 **EST:** 2004
SALES (est): 80.9K **Privately Held**
WEB: www.mnp.com
SIC: 3452 Washers

(G-4660)
VALEO NORTH AMERICA INC
Valeo Front End Module
12240 Oakland Pkwy (48203-3543)
PHONE 313 883-8850
Carlos Jimenez, *Prdtn Dir*
Felipe Trejo, *Research*
EMP: 215
SALES (corp-wide): 177.9K **Privately Held**
SIC: 3714 Radiators & radiator shells & cores, motor vehicle
HQ: Valeo North America, Inc.
150 Stephenson Hwy
Troy MI 48083

(G-4661)
VAN PELT CORPORATION
13700 Sherwood St (48212-2060)
PHONE 313 733-0073
EMP: 9
SALES (corp-wide): 29.1MM **Privately Held**
WEB: www.servicesteel.com
SIC: 3441 Fabricated structural metal
PA: Van Pelt Corporation
36155 Mound Rd
Sterling Heights MI 48310
313 365-3600

(G-4662)
VAN PELT CORPORATION
Also Called: Service Steel Co - Detroit
13700 Sherwood St Ste 1 (48212-2060)
PHONE 313 365-6500
Edward Masar, *Branch Mgr*
EMP: 18
SALES (corp-wide): 29.1MM **Privately Held**
WEB: www.servicesteel.com
SIC: 3317 3441 Tubes, seamless steel; fabricated structural metal
PA: Van Pelt Corporation
36155 Mound Rd
Sterling Heights MI 48310
313 365-3600

(G-4663)
VAUGHAN INDUSTRIES INC
8490 Lyndon St (48238-2446)
PHONE 313 935-2040
Lawrence J Balash, *President*
Nancy J Balash, *Corp Secy*
Josh Ames, *Sales Staff*

Jon Bertolet, *Technical Staff*
EMP: 15 **EST:** 1977
SQ FT: 25,000
SALES (est): 2.4MM **Privately Held**
WEB: www.vaughanind.com
SIC: 2841 5084 2992 Soap & other detergents; meters, consumption registering; cutting oils, blending: made from purchased materials

(G-4664)
VENTURE LABEL INC
3380 Baseline Rd (48231)
PHONE 313 928-2545
EMP: 5
SALES (corp-wide): 2MM **Privately Held**
WEB: www.venturelabels.com
SIC: 2679 Labels, paper: made from purchased material
PA: Venture Labels
2120 Fasan Dr
Oldcastle ON N0R 1
519 966-9580

(G-4665)
VERDUYN TARPS DETROIT INC
19231 W Davison St (48223-3416)
PHONE 313 270-4890
Lloyd Verduyn, *President*
Terrance Watson, *Manager*
▲ **EMP:** 8 **EST:** 2005
SQ FT: 50,000
SALES (est): 1.1MM **Privately Held**
WEB: www.verduyntarps.com
SIC: 2399 5199 Automotive covers, except seat & tire covers; tarpaulins

(G-4666)
VERNDALE PRODUCTS INC
8445 Lyndon St (48238-2483)
PHONE 313 834-4190
Laverne E Johnson, *President*
Dale Johnson, *President*
Fred Kreger, *Vice Pres*
Marlene I Johnson, *Treasurer*
Marlene Johnson, *Finance Mgr*
EMP: 40 **EST:** 1958
SQ FT: 59,000
SALES (est): 9MM **Privately Held**
WEB: www.verndaleproducts.com
SIC: 2023 Powdered milk

(G-4667)
VERTICAL DETROIT
1538 Centre St (48226-2165)
PHONE 313 732-9463
EMP: 7 **EST:** 2015
SALES (est): 251.4K **Privately Held**
WEB: www.verticaldetroit.com
SIC: 2591 Blinds vertical

(G-4668)
VIRTUOSO CUSTOM CREATIONS LLC
1111 Bellevue St Unit 201 (48207-3687)
PHONE 313 332-1299
Mark Klimkowski,
EMP: 8 **EST:** 2018
SALES (est): 322.8K **Privately Held**
SIC: 2431 Millwork

(G-4669)
VISIONIT SUPPLIES AND SVCS INC
3031 W Grand Blvd Ste 600 (48202-3014)
PHONE 313 664-5650
David H Segura, *CEO*
Omar Mendez, *Vice Pres*
Tracie Tino, *Director*
EMP: 25 **EST:** 1997
SQ FT: 5,000
SALES (est): 646.6K **Privately Held**
WEB: www.visionit.com
SIC: 3577 3955 5734 Printers, computer; print cartridges for laser & other computer printers; printers & plotters: computers

(G-4670)
VISTAPRINT
645 Griswold St (48226-4105)
PHONE 260 615-0027
Gregory Paradise, *Principal*
EMP: 4 **EST:** 2018

▲ = Import ▼ = Export
◆ = Import/Export

GEOGRAPHIC SECTION

Detroit - Wayne County (G-4699)

SALES (est): 117.5K **Privately Held**
WEB: www.vistaprint.com
SIC: 2752 Commercial printing, lithographic

(G-4671)
VITEC LLC
2801 Clark St (48210-9716)
PHONE.................................313 633-2254
William F Pickard, *CEO*
JD Allen, *Opers Mgr*
Tim Desjardins, *Engineer*
Robert Meert, *Engineer*
Trinita Grayson, *Office Mgr*
▲ **EMP:** 290 **EST:** 1998
SQ FT: 150,000
SALES (est): 46.7MM **Privately Held**
WEB: www.vitec-usa.com
SIC: 3089 Plastic & fiberglass tanks; automotive parts, plastic

(G-4672)
VIVA SALON NOUVELLE LLC
16221 Grand River Ave (48227-1823)
PHONE.................................947 800-9115
McClendon Starks,
EMP: 10 **EST:** 2020
SALES (est): 120K **Privately Held**
SIC: 3161 Clothing & apparel carrying cases

(G-4673)
VIVICA MILLER LLC ✪
15466 Stansbury St (48227-3233)
PHONE.................................313 434-3280
Vivica Millerspencer,
EMP: 4 **EST:** 2021
SALES (est): 156.7K **Privately Held**
SIC: 2836 Culture media

(G-4674)
WALL STREET JOURNAL GATE A 20
1 Detroit Metro Airport (48242-1004)
PHONE.................................734 941-4139
Tim Stibers, *General Mgr*
EMP: 7 **EST:** 2013
SALES (est): 133.9K **Privately Held**
SIC: 2711 Newspapers, publishing & printing

(G-4675)
WATSON EMBROIDERY
17395 Livernois Ave (48221-2758)
PHONE.................................313 459-5070
EMP: 4 **EST:** 2018
SALES (est): 39.3K **Privately Held**
SIC: 2395 Embroidery & art needlework

(G-4676)
WAVE MUSIC AND PUBLISHING
12227 Findlay St (48205-3823)
PHONE.................................313 290-2193
EMP: 5 **EST:** 2015
SALES (est): 76.9K **Privately Held**
SIC: 2741 Miscellaneous publishing

(G-4677)
WESLEY FLOOR CARE COMPANY
19483 Hartwell St (48235-1251)
PHONE.................................313 978-4539
Jonathon Crosby, *Owner*
EMP: 8 **EST:** 2019
SALES (est): 310.7K **Privately Held**
SIC: 3589 Commercial cleaning equipment

(G-4678)
WESTCOTT DISPLAYS INC (PA)
Also Called: Westcott Paper Products
450 Amsterdam St (48202-3408)
PHONE.................................313 872-1200
Allan G Campbell III, *President*
Greg Campbell, *President*
George A Chirillo, *Vice Pres*
Robert Schwanitz, *Vice Pres*
Lori Webb, *Treasurer*
▲ **EMP:** 50
SQ FT: 100,000
SALES (est): 8.8MM **Privately Held**
WEB: www.westcottdisplays.com
SIC: 3993 Displays & cutouts, window & lobby

(G-4679)
WH FILTRATION INC
19 Clifford St Fl 8 (48226-1705)
PHONE.................................248 633-4001
Cheng Chang, *President*
EMP: 5 **EST:** 2016
SQ FT: 150
SALES (est): 79.7K **Privately Held**
SIC: 3564 Blower filter units (furnace blowers)

(G-4680)
WHIMSICAL FUSIONS LLC
2326 E 7 Mile Rd (48234-1304)
PHONE.................................248 956-0952
Angela Thornton,
EMP: 4 **EST:** 2018
SALES (est): 25K **Privately Held**
SIC: 2844 Toilet preparations

(G-4681)
WHITESIDE CONSULTING GROUP LLC
Also Called: Wcg Design
19341 Stansbury St (48235-1733)
P.O. Box 35174 (48235-0174)
PHONE.................................313 288-6598
Ronald Whiteside,
Candice Whiteside,
Rashard Whiteside,
Tanisha Whiteside,
EMP: 5 **EST:** 2012
SALES (est): 205.2K **Privately Held**
WEB: www.whitesideconsulting.com
SIC: 7374 7336 8742 2791 Computer graphics service; commercial art & graphic design; business consultant; typesetting, computer controlled; office computer automation systems integration;

(G-4682)
WHOLESALE WEAVE INC
3130 E 8 Mile Rd (48234-1019)
PHONE.................................800 762-2037
Shonny Beavers, *Vice Pres*
EMP: 10 **EST:** 2013
SALES (est): 454.2K **Privately Held**
SIC: 3999 7334 Doll wigs (hair); photocopying & duplicating services

(G-4683)
WHOS WHO PUBLISHING CO LLC
1452 Randolph St Ste 400 (48226-2284)
PHONE.................................614 481-7300
C Martin, *Owner*
EMP: 5 **EST:** 2012
SALES (est): 80.7K **Privately Held**
SIC: 2741 Miscellaneous publishing

(G-4684)
WILLIAMS MANAGEMENT GROUP LLC
19745 Ralston St (48203-1545)
PHONE.................................248 506-7967
Andrew Brewart, *Mng Member*
EMP: 7 **EST:** 2020
SALES (est): 500K **Privately Held**
SIC: 2499 Picture frame molding, finished

(G-4685)
WIRE FAB INC
18055 Sherwood St (48234-2812)
PHONE.................................313 893-8816
Michael Wehner, *President*
Annkaethe Wehner, *Corp Secy*
Richard Wehner, *Manager*
EMP: 10 **EST:** 1962
SQ FT: 11,500
SALES (est): 590.9K **Privately Held**
WEB: www.wirefabinc.com
SIC: 3496 3545 Miscellaneous fabricated wire products; tools & accessories for machine tools

(G-4686)
WLS PROCESSING LLC
6501 Mack Ave (48207-2306)
PHONE.................................313 378-5743
Ryan Lewicki,
EMP: 5 **EST:** 2019
SALES (est): 401.5K **Privately Held**
SIC: 3341 Aluminum smelting & refining (secondary)

(G-4687)
WOLVERINE CONCRETE PRODUCTS
9189 Central St (48204-4323)
PHONE.................................313 931-7189
Shel Wheatley, *President*
EMP: 4 **EST:** 1984
SQ FT: 15,000
SALES (est): 494.7K **Privately Held**
WEB: www.wolverineconcrete.com
SIC: 3272 4212 Concrete products, precast; delivery service, vehicular

(G-4688)
WOLVERINE PACKING CO (PA)
2535 Rivard St (48207-2621)
PHONE.................................313 259-7500
A James Bonahoom, *President*
Jay Bonahoom, *Vice Pres*
Jim Bonahoom, *Vice Pres*
Roger P Bonahoom, *Vice Pres*
Marvin Coleman, *Plant Mgr*
◆ **EMP:** 100
SQ FT: 55,000
SALES (est): 210.9MM **Privately Held**
WEB: www.wolverinepacking.com
SIC: 5147 2011 5142 Meats, fresh; veal from meat slaughtered on site; lamb products from lamb slaughtered on site; meat, frozen: packaged; poultry, frozen: packaged

(G-4689)
WOLVERING FUR
2937 Russell St (48207-4825)
PHONE.................................313 961-0620
Paul Petcoff, *President*
Clay Campbell, *Vice Pres*
Michael Van Buren, *Vice Pres*
EMP: 7
SALES (est): 416.4K **Privately Held**
WEB: www.wolverinefurs.com
SIC: 5632 2371 Furriers; apparel, fur

(G-4690)
WOODWARD ENERGY SOLUTIONS LLC
719 Griswold St Ste 720 (48226-3300)
PHONE.................................888 967-4533
Brandon Boudreau, *Co-Owner*
Matthew Goyette, *VP Bus Dvlpt*
EMP: 10 **EST:** 2015
SALES (est): 782K **Privately Held**
WEB: www.woodwardenergy.com
SIC: 3646 Commercial indusl & institutional electric lighting fixtures

(G-4691)
WORLD OF PALLETS AND TRUCKING
3420 Lovett St (48210-3135)
PHONE.................................313 899-2000
Fernando Anaya, *President*
Soledad Anaya, *Vice Pres*
EMP: 6 **EST:** 2016
SALES (est): 250.5K **Privately Held**
WEB: www.jgpalletsandtrucking.com
SIC: 2448 4731 Wood pallets & skids; freight transportation arrangement

(G-4692)
WRIGHT & FILIPPIS INC
4201 Saint Antoine St (48201-2153)
PHONE.................................313 832-5020
Steven Filippis, *Exec VP*
Dale Ferguson, *Director*
EMP: 6
SALES (corp-wide): 77.5MM **Privately Held**
WEB: www.firsttoserve.com
SIC: 3842 Prosthetic appliances
PA: Wright & Filippis, Llc
2845 Crooks Rd
Rochester Hills MI 48309
248 829-8292

(G-4693)
WRITE IDEA
613 Abbott St Ste 130e (48226-2508)
PHONE.................................313 967-5881
EMP: 4 **EST:** 2017
SALES (est): 100K **Privately Held**
SIC: 2752 Commercial printing, offset

(G-4694)
XENITH LLC
4333 W Fort St (48209-3221)
PHONE.................................866 888-2322
John Duerden, *CEO*
David Selby, *COO*
Kerry Hughes, *Controller*
Ivreet Takhar, *Human Resources*
Nura Wilkinson, *Sales Mgr*
▲ **EMP:** 28 **EST:** 2007
SALES (est): 13MM
SALES (corp-wide): 16.5B **Publicly Held**
WEB: www.xenith.com
SIC: 3949 Helmets, athletic
HQ: Rock Ventures Llc
1074 Woodward Ave
Detroit MI 48226

(G-4695)
XXTAR ASSOCIATES LLC (PA)
18100 Meyers Rd Ste L2 (48235-1426)
PHONE.................................888 946-6066
Bernard Porter, *Mng Member*
EMP: 4 **EST:** 2008
SALES (est): 278K **Privately Held**
WEB: www.xxtar.com
SIC: 3821 3089 5047 5049 Laboratory apparatus, except heating & measuring; plastic containers, except foam; hospital equipment & furniture; medical equipment & supplies; laboratory equipment, except medical or dental; scientific instruments; bandages; printing & writing paper

(G-4696)
XYTEK INDUSTRIES INC
19431 W Davison St (48223-3419)
PHONE.................................313 838-6961
Bob W Shipton, *President*
Carl T Lizut, *Vice Pres*
Blair Kergan, *Manager*
EMP: 15 **EST:** 1985
SQ FT: 7,500
SALES (est): 339.9K **Privately Held**
WEB: www.xytek-equip.com
SIC: 8711 8734 3694 Electrical or electronic engineering; testing laboratories; automotive electrical equipment

(G-4697)
YANFENG US AUTO INTR SYSTEMS I
Also Called: Plastech
2931 E Jefferson Ave (48207-4288)
PHONE.................................313 259-3226
Kevin Flores, *Program Mgr*
EMP: 5 **Privately Held**
WEB: www.yfai.com
SIC: 3089 Injection molding of plastics
HQ: Yanfeng Us Automotive Interior Systems I Llc
41935 W 12 Mile Rd
Novi MI 48377
248 319-7333

(G-4698)
YORE CREATIONS LLC ✪
415 Brainard St (48201-1794)
PHONE.................................313 463-8652
Yolonda Riley,
EMP: 5 **EST:** 2021
SALES (est): 67K **Privately Held**
SIC: 2339 Women's & misses' accessories

(G-4699)
YOUNG SUPPLY COMPANY
Also Called: Johnson Contrls Authorized Dlr
1177 W Baltimore St (48202-2905)
PHONE.................................313 875-3280
Ronald Vallan, *Owner*
Anthony Vallan, *Vice Pres*
Joe Bobzin, *Treasurer*
Brian Armour, *Sales Staff*
Bob Laho, *Sales Staff*
▲ **EMP:** 29 **EST:** 1943
SQ FT: 18,337
SALES (est): 2.8MM **Privately Held**
WEB: www.youngsupply.com
SIC: 3585 5078 5075 5074 Parts for heating, cooling & refrigerating equipment; refrigeration equipment & supplies; warm air heating & air conditioning; plumbing & hydronic heating supplies

Detroit - Wayne County (G-4700)   **GEOGRAPHIC SECTION**

(G-4700)
ZAK BROTHERS PRINTING LLC
Also Called: Palmer Printing Co
5480 Cass Ave (48202-3614)
PHONE.................................313 831-3216
William P Ganzak,
James J Ganzak,
EMP: 4 **EST:** 1938
SQ FT: 6,500
SALES (est): 440K **Privately Held**
WEB: www.palmerprintsdetroit.com
SIC: 2752 2759 Commercial printing, offset; letterpress printing

(G-4701)
ZAKOORS
3909 Woodward Ave (48201-2087)
PHONE.................................313 831-6969
Michael Zakoor, *Owner*
EMP: 5 **EST:** 2015
SALES (est): 116.2K **Privately Held**
SIC: 2759 Screen printing

(G-4702)
ZELLARS GROUP LLC
8615 Knodell St (48213-1124)
PHONE.................................313 828-2309
Jeffrey Zellars,
EMP: 9 **EST:** 2019
SALES (est): 320.8K **Privately Held**
SIC: 1389 Construction, repair & dismantling services

(G-4703)
ZEMIS 5 LLC
Also Called: Snake Island
13207 Santa Clara St (48235-2613)
Drawer 195 29488, Royal Oak (48073)
PHONE.................................317 946-7015
Emmanuel El-Amin, *Principal*
Isaac El-Amin El-Amin, *Principal*
Maurice El-Amin, *Principal*
Stanley El-Amin, *Principal*
Zachary El-Amin, *Principal*
EMP: 5
SALES (est): 319.8K **Privately Held**
SIC: 2426 2321 Carvings, furniture: wood; sport shirts, men's & boys': from purchased materials

(G-4704)
ZURN INDUSTRIES LLC
7431 W 8 Mile Rd (48221-1262)
P.O. Box 37317, Oak Park (48237-0317)
PHONE.................................313 864-2800
George Johnston, *Branch Mgr*
EMP: 10 **Publicly Held**
WEB: www.zurn.com
SIC: 5074 3431 Plumbing & hydronic heating supplies; sinks: enameled iron, cast iron or pressed metal
HQ: Zurn Industries, Llc
    1801 Pittsburgh Ave
    Erie PA 16502
    814 455-0921

Dewitt
Clinton County

(G-4705)
ANNIERAERV CO
13200 S Us Highway 27 (48820-7840)
PHONE.................................517 669-4103
Annie Rae, *Owner*
EMP: 6 **EST:** 2007
SALES (est): 148.7K **Privately Held**
SIC: 3799 Recreational vehicles

(G-4706)
BLTS WEARABLE ART INC
1541 W Round Lake Rd (48820-9799)
PHONE.................................517 669-9659
Ronald Baumgardner, *Partner*
Tammy Baumgardner, *Treasurer*
EMP: 7 **EST:** 1990
SQ FT: 3,000
SALES (est): 320K **Privately Held**
WEB: www.bltswearableart.com
SIC: 2759 2396 Screen printing; automotive & apparel trimmings

(G-4707)
BRANDONS DEFENSE
12583 Ro Dic Don Dr (48820-9350)
P.O. Box 8 (48820-0008)
PHONE.................................517 669-5272
Julie Gordon, *Principal*
EMP: 8 **EST:** 2009
SALES (est): 96.7K **Privately Held**
WEB: www.staystrongdoit.com
SIC: 3812 Defense systems & equipment

(G-4708)
CAPITAL EQUIPMENT CLARE LLC (PA)
12263 S Us Highway 27 (48820-8374)
PHONE.................................517 669-5533
Gary Holt, *Principal*
Kevin Holt, *Vice Pres*
Dick Mouser, *Manager*
EMP: 12 **EST:** 2007
SALES (est): 1.1MM **Privately Held**
WEB: www.cedealer.com
SIC: 7353 3531 Heavy construction equipment rental; tractors, construction

(G-4709)
CARHARTT INC
128 Spring Meadows Ln (48820-9598)
PHONE.................................517 282-4193
EMP: 5
SALES (corp-wide): 1.9B **Privately Held**
WEB: www.carhartt.com
SIC: 2326 Men's & boys' work clothing
PA: Carhartt, Inc.
    5750 Mercury Dr
    Dearborn MI 48126
    313 271-8460

(G-4710)
H & R ELECTRICAL CONTRS LLC
10588 S Us Highway 27 (48820-8428)
P.O. Box 467 (48820-0467)
PHONE.................................517 669-2102
Todd Rusnell, *President*
Amy C Rusnell, *Mng Member*
EMP: 24 **EST:** 2005
SALES (est): 2.5MM **Privately Held**
WEB: www.hrelectricllc.com
SIC: 3589 5063 1731 Commercial cooking & foodwarming equipment; lighting fixtures, commercial & industrial; general electrical contractor

(G-4711)
LOGAN BROTHERS PRINTING INC
13544 Blackwood Dr (48820-8106)
PHONE.................................517 485-3771
Ronald A Maiers, *President*
Ron Bollinger, *Representative*
EMP: 8 **EST:** 1951
SQ FT: 7,000
SALES (est): 313.9K **Privately Held**
WEB: www.foresightgroup.net
SIC: 2752 2789 Commercial printing, offset; bookbinding & related work

(G-4712)
MESA CORPORATION
1000 E Geneva Dr (48820-9569)
PHONE.................................517 669-5656
Paul J Potts, *Administration*
EMP: 6 **EST:** 2013
SALES (est): 148.4K **Privately Held**
SIC: 3571 Electronic computers

(G-4713)
MIDWEST WALL COMPANY LLC
13753 Cottonwood Dr (48820-8500)
PHONE.................................517 881-3701
Dean Bourdon, *Mng Member*
EMP: 10 **EST:** 2011
SALES (est): 859.3K **Privately Held**
WEB: www.mwwall.com
SIC: 3444 Sheet metalwork

(G-4714)
MONOGRAM MARKET LLC
1161 Clark Cors (48820)
PHONE.................................517 455-9083
Douglas Reed,
EMP: 4 **EST:** 2017
SALES (est): 39.6K **Privately Held**
SIC: 3999 Manufacturing industries

(G-4715)
SIGNS & WONDERS LLC
1378 Lacosta Dr (48820-8343)
PHONE.................................618 694-4960
Danielle Cox, *Principal*
EMP: 4 **EST:** 2018
SALES (est): 74.2K **Privately Held**
SIC: 3993 Signs & advertising specialties

(G-4716)
SWEETIE PIE PANTRY (PA)
108 N Bridge St (48820-8900)
PHONE.................................517 669-9300
Linda Hundt, *Mng Member*
EMP: 19 **EST:** 2005
SALES (est): 1.3MM **Privately Held**
WEB: www.sweetie-licious.com
SIC: 2052 Bakery products, dry

(G-4717)
TIN CAN DEWITT
13175 Schavey Rd (48820-9000)
PHONE.................................517 624-2078
EMP: 4 **EST:** 2012
SALES (est): 236.5K **Privately Held**
SIC: 3411 Tin cans

(G-4718)
TOUCHSTONE DISTRIBUTING INC
Also Called: Touchstone Pottery
103 S Bridge St Ste B (48820-8840)
PHONE.................................517 669-8200
Paul Hartleib, *President*
▲ **EMP:** 6 **EST:** 1983
SQ FT: 4,200
SALES (est): 515K **Privately Held**
WEB: www.touchstonepottery.net
SIC: 3911 Jewelry, precious metal

Dexter
Washtenaw County

(G-4719)
AA EDM CORPORATION
7455 Newman Blvd (48130-1558)
PHONE.................................734 253-2784
John Macgregor, *President*
George Barbulescu, *Vice Pres*
Nicky Borcea, *Vice Pres*
Carl Naudi, *Sales Mgr*
Bill Becker, *Technician*
EMP: 16 **EST:** 2009
SALES (est): 2.7MM **Privately Held**
WEB: www.aaedmcorp.com
SIC: 3599 Electrical discharge machining (EDM)

(G-4720)
ABLETECH INDUSTRIES LLC
8383 Millview Ct (48130-9475)
PHONE.................................734 677-2420
Michael Olson, *CEO*
EMP: 9 **EST:** 2014
SALES (est): 401.7K **Privately Held**
SIC: 3999 3829 Manufacturing industries; geophysical & meteorological testing equipment

(G-4721)
ADAIR PRINTING COMPANY (PA)
7850 2nd St (48130-1238)
PHONE.................................734 426-2822
Dennis Adair, *President*
Alisa Jenks, *Vice Pres*
William Crtitendon, *Accounts Mgr*
George Kurinsky, *Accounts Mgr*
Bernadette Quist, *Accounts Mgr*
EMP: 30 **EST:** 1928
SQ FT: 150,000
SALES (est): 6.1MM **Privately Held**
WEB: www.adairgraphic.com
SIC: 2759 2752 8742 7371 Catalogs: printing; commercial printing, lithographic; marketing consulting services; software programming applications

(G-4722)
ALCO MANUFACTURING CORP
8763 Dexter Chelsea Rd (48130-9782)
PHONE.................................734 426-3941
Christopher Morgan, *Mng Member*
EMP: 50 **EST:** 1995
SQ FT: 25,000
SALES (est): 10.6MM
SALES (corp-wide): 1.6B **Privately Held**
WEB: www.alco.com
SIC: 3492 3451 Fluid power valves & hose fittings; screw machine products
HQ: Alco Manufacturing Corporation Llc
    10584 Middle Ave
    Elyria OH 44035

(G-4723)
ALPHA METAL FINISHING CO
8155 Huron St (48130-1026)
PHONE.................................734 426-2855
Robert E Wood, *President*
Greg Wood, *COO*
Bob Wood, *Plant Mgr*
John Mc Keone, *Manager*
Carol B Wood, *Admin Sec*
EMP: 12 **EST:** 1966
SQ FT: 20,000
SALES (est): 2.7MM **Privately Held**
WEB: www.alphametal.com
SIC: 3471 Finishing, metals or formed products; anodizing (plating) of metals or formed products; chromium plating of metals or formed products

(G-4724)
APPLIED MOLECULES LLC
7275 Joy Rd Ste D (48130-9268)
PHONE.................................810 355-1475
Paul Snowwhite, *President*
EMP: 6 **EST:** 2014
SQ FT: 2,500
SALES (est): 712.7K **Privately Held**
WEB: www.appliedmolecules.com
SIC: 2891 8731 Adhesives & sealants; commercial research laboratory

(G-4725)
AUTOMATION CONTRLS & ENGRG LLC
Also Called: Ace
2105 Bishop Cir W (48130-1561)
PHONE.................................734 424-5500
Steve Moore, *Vice Pres*
Keith Johnson, *Project Mgr*
Andy Richards, *Project Mgr*
Chris Mackey, *VP Sales*
James Carey, *Mng Member*
EMP: 38 **EST:** 2014
SQ FT: 20,000
SALES (est): 5MM **Privately Held**
WEB: www.ace-automation.net
SIC: 8711 8742 3535 Engineering services; automation & robotics consultant; conveyors & conveying equipment

(G-4726)
BELJAN LTD INC
4635 Mcguiness Rd (48130-9546)
PHONE.................................734 426-3503
Faith Krug, *President*
Robin Janiszewski, *Vice Pres*
Sharon Denk, *Production*
John Johnson, *Finance*
EMP: 10 **EST:** 1956
SQ FT: 2,500
SALES (est): 280.7K **Privately Held**
WEB: www.beljan.com
SIC: 7374 2791 Data processing & preparation; typesetting

(G-4727)
BERRY & ASSOCIATES INC
2434 Bishop Cir E (48130-1570)
PHONE.................................734 426-3787
David Berry, *President*
Lana Berry, *Vice Pres*
Joe Repine, *Research*
Julie Olson, *Info Tech Mgr*
Connor Holm, *Technology*
EMP: 10 **EST:** 1988
SQ FT: 7,500
SALES (est): 6.2MM **Publicly Held**
WEB: www.shop.biosearchtech.com
SIC: 2869 Industrial organic chemicals
HQ: Lgc Limited
    Queens Road
    Teddington MIDDX

(G-4728)
BIG BORE SIGNS LLC
6335 Reinhard Dr (48130-9675)
PHONE.................................313 701-5900

▲ = Import ▼ = Export ◆ = Import/Export

GEOGRAPHIC SECTION
Dexter - Washtenaw County (G-4753)

EMP: 4 EST: 2018
SALES (est): 46K Privately Held
SIC: 3993 Signs & advertising specialties

(G-4729)
BTI MEASUREMENT TSTG SVCS LLC
2800 Zeeb Rd Dockk (48130-2204)
PHONE.................734 769-2100
Stephen Simon, Manager
EMP: 4
SALES (corp-wide): 1.1MM Privately Held
WEB: www.balancetechnology.com
SIC: 3829 Testing equipment: abrasion, shearing strength, etc.
PA: Bti Measurement & Testing Services Llc
7035 Jomar Dr
Whitmore Lake MI 48189
734 769-2100

(G-4730)
BURLY OAK BUILDERS INC
9980 Dexter Chelsea Rd (48130-9777)
PHONE.................734 368-4912
Richard Parr, President
EMP: 6 EST: 2003
SALES (est): 700K Privately Held
WEB: www.bob-barn.com
SIC: 1521 3523 New construction, single-family houses; barn, silo, poultry, dairy & livestock machinery

(G-4731)
CLARK-MXR INC
7300 Huron River Dr Ste 1 (48130-1209)
PHONE.................734 426-2803
William Clark, President
Tissa Gunaratne, Sales Dir
Taune De Bolt, Admin Asst
EMP: 20 EST: 1991
SQ FT: 10,000
SALES (est): 2.7MM Privately Held
WEB: www.cmxr.com
SIC: 3826 3827 8731 Laser scientific & engineering instruments; optical instruments & apparatus; medical research, commercial

(G-4732)
COMPLETE DSIGN AUTOMTN SYSTEMS (PA)
2117 Bishop Cir E (48130-1565)
PHONE.................734 424-2789
EMP: 7
SQ FT: 10,000
SALES (est): 1.7MM Privately Held
SIC: 8711 3625 Engineering Services Mfg Relays/Industrial Controls

(G-4733)
DESIGN & TEST TECHNOLOGY INC
2430 Scio Rd (48130-9716)
P.O. Box 1526, Ann Arbor (48106-1526)
PHONE.................734 665-4111
Michael Murphy, President
EMP: 8
SALES (corp-wide): 1.3MM Privately Held
WEB: www.designtest.com
SIC: 7373 3825 Computer systems analysis & design; test equipment for electronic & electric measurement
PA: Design & Test Technology, Inc
3744 Plaza Dr Ste 2
Ann Arbor MI 48108
734 665-4316

(G-4734)
DEXTER AUTOMATIC PRODUCTS CO
Also Called: Dapco Industries
2500 Bishop Cir E (48130-1566)
PHONE.................734 426-8900
Willis E Tupper, Ch of Bd
Ronald E Tupper, President
Kevin Pequet, Business Mgr
Jason Alderson, QC Mgr
Don Colliau, Engineer
EMP: 180 EST: 1952
SQ FT: 80,000
SALES (est): 25.6MM Privately Held
WEB: www.dapcoind.com
SIC: 3592 3564 3544 3494 Valves, engine; blowers & fans; special dies, tools, jigs & fixtures; valves & pipe fittings; screw machine products

(G-4735)
DEXTER CABINET WORKS INC
1084 Baker Rd (48130-1521)
PHONE.................734 426-5035
Del Young Jr, President
Iris Findlay Young, Corp Secy
EMP: 7 EST: 1984
SQ FT: 6,000
SALES (est): 487.3K Privately Held
WEB: www.dextercabinet.com
SIC: 2434 Wood kitchen cabinets

(G-4736)
DEXTER FASTENER TECH INC (PA)
Also Called: Dextech
2110 Bishop Cir E (48130-1594)
PHONE.................734 426-0311
J Sakatoa, Ch of Bd
Mike Frazier, President
Paul Godlewski, Plant Mgr
Wayne Stahl, Plant Mgr
Don Semones, Safety Mgr
▲ EMP: 225 EST: 1989
SQ FT: 350,000
SALES (est): 45.7MM Privately Held
WEB: www.dextech.net
SIC: 3452 Bolts, metal

(G-4737)
DEXTER FASTENER TECH INC
2103 Bishop Cir W (48130-1561)
PHONE.................734 426-5200
Mike Frazier, CEO
Cory Boomer, Sales Staff
EMP: 5 Privately Held
WEB: www.dextech.net
SIC: 3452 Bolts, nuts, rivets & washers
PA: Dexter Fastener Technologies, Inc.
2110 Bishop Cir E
Dexter MI 48130

(G-4738)
DEXTER PRINT & STITCH
3170 Baker Rd (48130-1119)
PHONE.................734 580-2181
Neil O'Brien, Principal
EMP: 5 EST: 2017
SALES (est): 255.1K Privately Held
WEB: www.dexterprint.com
SIC: 2752 Commercial printing, lithographic

(G-4739)
DEXTER RESEARCH CENTER INC
7300 Huron River Dr Ste 2 (48130-1086)
PHONE.................734 426-3921
Robert S Toth Jr, President
Kurt Hochrein, COO
EMP: 55
SQ FT: 21,680
SALES (est): 7MM Privately Held
WEB: www.dexterresearch.com
SIC: 3823 Infrared instruments, industrial process type

(G-4740)
DIECUTTING SERVICE INC
2415 Bishop Cir W (48130-1563)
P.O. Box 471 (48130-0471)
PHONE.................734 426-0290
Les Baxter, President
Scott Baxter, Vice Pres
EMP: 19 EST: 1990
SQ FT: 11,250
SALES (est): 2MM Privately Held
SIC: 2675 Paper die-cutting

(G-4741)
ELECTRO ARC MANUFACTURING CO
2055 N Lima Center Rd A (48130-9515)
PHONE.................734 483-4233
Harold W Stark Jr, President
EMP: 20 EST: 1926
SALES (est): 3.2MM Privately Held
WEB: www.electroarc.com
SIC: 3829 5084 3541 Hardness testing equipment; industrial machine parts; machine tools, metal cutting: exotic (explosive, etc.)

(G-4742)
GENESIS SERVICE ASSOCIATES LLC
3255 Central St Apt 1 (48130-1157)
PHONE.................734 994-3900
Michael Mason,
EMP: 5 EST: 1994
SALES (est): 450.7K Privately Held
WEB: www.genservassoc.com
SIC: 2752 7336 Commercial printing, lithographic; graphic arts & related design

(G-4743)
INTUITIVE TECHNOLOGY INC
3223 Boulder Ct (48130-9396)
PHONE.................602 249-5750
Chris Jones, CEO
Geoff Oslund, Director
EMP: 5 EST: 2015
SQ FT: 900
SALES (est): 1MM Privately Held
WEB: www.intuitivetechnology.com
SIC: 3999 5087 5999 Barber & beauty shop equipment; service establishment equipment; alarm & safety equipment stores

(G-4744)
K-SPACE ASSOCIATES INC
2182 Bishop Cir E (48130-1564)
PHONE.................734 426-7977
Darryl Barlett, CEO
Roy Clarke, President
Sandhya Johnson, Engineer
Kathy Wheeler, Sales Engr
Mike Bonnici, Technician
EMP: 34 EST: 1992
SQ FT: 2,780
SALES (est): 10.3MM Privately Held
WEB: www.k-space.com
SIC: 3829 5049 3823 Stress, strain & flaw detecting/measuring equipment; scientific & engineering equipment & supplies; industrial instrmnts msrmnt display/control process variable

(G-4745)
MERLIN SIMULATION INC
2135 Bishop Cir E Ste 6 (48130-1602)
P.O. Box 6110, Falls Church VA (22040-6110)
PHONE.................703 560-7203
Kenneth A Zimmerman, President
▲ EMP: 7 EST: 1996
SALES (est): 177.9K Privately Held
WEB: www.merlinsimulation.com
SIC: 3845 Transcutaneous electrical nerve stimulators (TENS)

(G-4746)
MIDWEST GRAPHICS & AWARDS INC
2135 Bishop Cir E Ste 8 (48130-1602)
PHONE.................734 424-3700
Kevin Crouch, President
Mary Didonato, Vice Pres
Adam Hernandez, Opers Staff
Abbie Buhr, Manager
EMP: 4 EST: 1992
SQ FT: 2,200
SALES (est): 541.6K Privately Held
WEB: www.midwestgraphicsa2.com
SIC: 2759 5999 5094 Screen printing; decals: printing; trophies & plaques; coins, medals & trophies; trophies

(G-4747)
NULL TAPHOUSE
2319 Bishop Cir E (48130-1567)
PHONE.................734 792-9124
EMP: 5 EST: 2015
SALES (est): 197.7K Privately Held
WEB: www.nulltaphouse.com
SIC: 2082 Malt beverages

(G-4748)
PALADIN BRANDS GROUP INC (HQ)
Also Called: Paladin Attachments
2800 Zeeb Rd (48130-2204)
PHONE.................319 378-3696
Steve Andrews, CEO
Matt Roney, President
Bob Ferguson, Vice Pres
Dan Schmidt, Vice Pres
Tom Carlson, Plant Mgr
◆ EMP: 17 EST: 1996
SALES (est): 324MM
SALES (corp-wide): 14.5B Publicly Held
WEB: www.paladinattachments.com
SIC: 3531 Finishers & spreaders (construction equipment); subgraders (construction equipment); drags, road (construction & road maintenance equipment)
PA: Stanley Black & Decker, Inc.
1000 Stanley Dr
New Britain CT 06053
860 225-5111

(G-4749)
PHOTO SYSTEMS INC (PA)
7200 Huron River Dr Ste B (48130-1099)
PHONE.................734 424-9625
Alan Fischer, President
Margaret Warden, Personnel
◆ EMP: 20 EST: 1968
SQ FT: 42,000
SALES (est): 12.8MM Privately Held
WEB: www.photosys.com
SIC: 5043 2899 Photographic equipment & supplies; chemical preparations

(G-4750)
PROTOMATIC INC
2125 Bishop Cir W (48130)
PHONE.................734 426-3655
Rita Jean Wetzel, President
Douglas Wetzel, Vice Pres
Brian Heldt, Finance Mgr
David Wetzel, Sales Mgr
Mark Novitsch, Sales Staff
EMP: 42 EST: 1971
SQ FT: 30,500
SALES (est): 3.7MM Privately Held
WEB: www.protomatic.com
SIC: 3599 Machine shop, jobbing & repair

(G-4751)
QED ENVMTL SYSTEMS INC (HQ)
Also Called: En Novative Technologies
2355 Bishop Cir W (48130-1592)
P.O. Box 3726, Ann Arbor (48106-3726)
PHONE.................734 995-2547
Mark Weinberger, President
▲ EMP: 69 EST: 1982
SQ FT: 50,000
SALES (est): 40.7MM
SALES (corp-wide): 1.6B Publicly Held
WEB: www.qedenv.com
SIC: 3561 3821 3826 3823 Industrial pumps & parts; sample preparation apparatus; water testing apparatus; controllers for process variables, all types
PA: Graco Inc.
88 11th Ave Ne
Minneapolis MN 55413
612 623-6000

(G-4752)
RICK OWEN & JASON VOGEL PARTNR
10475 N Territorial Rd (48130-8547)
PHONE.................734 417-3401
Rick Owen, Owner
EMP: 6 EST: 2010
SALES (est): 75.3K Privately Held
SIC: 3088 Plastics plumbing fixtures

(G-4753)
ROSE CORPORATION
Also Called: Doors & Drawers
2467 Bishop Cir E (48130-1567)
PHONE.................734 426-0005
Charles J Manitz, President
Rosemary L Manitz, Vice Pres
Dave Bennitt, Prdtn Mgr
Brian Manitz, Warehouse Mgr
Rose Manitz, CIO

Dexter - Washtenaw County (G-4754)

EMP: 25 EST: 1983
SQ FT: 10,000
SALES (est): 2.3MM **Privately Held**
WEB: www.doorsanddrawers.net
SIC: 5712 5211 2521 2434 Cabinet work, custom; counter tops; wood office furniture; wood kitchen cabinets

(G-4754)
SIKO PRODUCTS INC
Also Called: Jim Schnabelt
2155 Bishop Cir E (48130-1565)
P.O. Box 279 (48130-0279)
PHONE.................................734 426-3476
Darrell Davey, *President*
Lukas Dickele, *Manager*
Elvira Maurer, *Manager*
August Meyers, *Manager*
Mathias Roth, *Manager*
▲ EMP: 9 EST: 1981
SQ FT: 6,000
SALES (est): 1.4MM
SALES (corp-wide): 24.2MM **Privately Held**
WEB: www.siko-global.com
SIC: 3829 Measuring & controlling devices
PA: Siko Gmbh
   Weihermattenweg 2
   Buchenbach BW 79256
   766 139-40

(G-4755)
SIMPLY GREEN OUTDOOR SVCS LLC
1535 Baker Rd (48130-1601)
PHONE.................................734 385-6190
Richard E Olberg Jr,
EMP: 5 EST: 2018
SALES (est): 750K **Privately Held**
SIC: 0721 1771 3271 0782 Planting services; concrete work; blocks, concrete; landscape or retaining wall; lawn care services

(G-4756)
SOHNER PLASTICS LLC
Also Called: Ipr Automation Sohner Plastic
7275 Joy Rd Ste D (48130-9268)
PHONE.................................734 222-4847
Nicky Borcea, *President*
Laurie Loria, *Office Mgr*
Denny Pier, *Manager*
▲ EMP: 18 EST: 1990
SQ FT: 10,400
SALES (est): 2.6MM **Privately Held**
WEB: www.sohnerplastics.com
SIC: 3089 Injection molding of plastics

(G-4757)
SWEEPSTER ATTACHMENTS LLC
Also Called: Harley Attachments
2800 Zeeb Rd (48130-2204)
PHONE.................................734 996-9116
Matt Roney, *Principal*
Steve Brancheau, *Export Mgr*
Ananth Parameswaran, *VP Mktg*
◆ EMP: 1300 EST: 1945
SQ FT: 465,000
SALES (est): 198.1MM
SALES (corp-wide): 14.5B **Publicly Held**
WEB: www.paladinattachments.com
SIC: 3589 3991 Dirt sweeping units, industrial; brooms; street sweeping brooms, hand or machine; brushes, household or industrial
HQ: Paladin Brands Group, Inc.
   2800 Zeeb Rd
   Dexter MI 48130
   319 378-3696

(G-4758)
THOMSON-SHORE INC
7300 Joy Rd (48130-9492)
PHONE.................................734 426-3939
Peter Shima, *President*
Kevin Spall, *President*
Thomson Shore, *Principal*
Terri Barlow, *Vice Pres*
◆ EMP: 200 EST: 1972
SQ FT: 144,000
SALES (est): 52.3MM
SALES (corp-wide): 631.4MM **Privately Held**
WEB: www.thomsonshore.com
SIC: 2752 Commercial printing, offset

PA: Cjk Group, Inc.
   3323 Oak St
   Brainerd MN 56401
   800 328-0450

(G-4759)
TRUCENT INC (PA)
7400 Newman Blvd (48130-1557)
PHONE.................................734 426-9015
Tom Czartoski, *CEO*
David Weber, *General Mgr*
Jarred Barnes, *Regional Mgr*
Jason Hugie, *Project Mgr*
Chris Earls, *Safety Mgr*
EMP: 1 EST: 2004
SALES (est): 42.1MM **Privately Held**
WEB: www.trucent.com
SIC: 8742 3677 5084 Industrial consultant; filtration devices, electronic; industrial machinery & equipment

(G-4760)
TRUCENT SEPARATION TECH LLC
7400 Newman Blvd (48130-1557)
PHONE.................................734 426-9015
Tom Czartoski, *President*
Steve Atkinson, *General Mgr*
David Emrick, *General Mgr*
Creighton Holmes, *General Mgr*
Roger Wilson, *General Mgr*
EMP: 75 EST: 1996
SQ FT: 12,000
SALES (est): 20.8MM **Privately Held**
WEB: www.trucent.com
SIC: 8742 3677 Industrial consultant; filtration devices, electronic
PA: Trucent, Inc.
   7400 Newman Blvd
   Dexter MI 48130

(G-4761)
VARIETY DIE & STAMPING CO
2221 Bishop Cir E (48130-1595)
PHONE.................................734 426-4488
Kevin G Woods, *Principal*
Jonathan Woods, *Corp Secy*
Michael A Vernon, *Vice Pres*
Mike Vernon, *Vice Pres*
Greg Young, *Vice Pres*
▲ EMP: 75 EST: 1955
SQ FT: 50,000
SALES (est): 9.1MM **Privately Held**
WEB: www.varietydie.com
SIC: 3465 3469 Automotive stampings; metal stampings

(G-4762)
WAHOO COMPOSITES LLC
7190 Huron River Dr (48130-1066)
PHONE.................................734 424-0966
Anne Parker, *CEO*
EMP: 10 EST: 1999
SALES (est): 730K **Privately Held**
WEB: www.wahoocomposites.com
SIC: 3624 Carbon & graphite products

Dimondale
Eaton County

(G-4763)
GREEN PEAK INDUSTRIES LLC
10070 Harvest Park (48821)
PHONE.................................517 408-0178
Jeff Donahue, *Principal*
Cody Corkwell, *Purchasing*
Ember Osborn, *Office Mgr*
EMP: 1 EST: 2017
SALES (est): 1.1MM **Privately Held**
SIC: 3999 Manufacturing industries

(G-4764)
PROSTHETIC CENTER INC
7343 Dupre Ave (48821-9547)
PHONE.................................517 372-7007
Toll Free:................................877 -
EMP: 4
SQ FT: 2,200
SALES (est): 440.4K **Privately Held**
SIC: 3842 5999 Mfg Surgical Appliances/Supplies Ret Misc Merchandise

(G-4765)
TRIKALA INC
Also Called: Mackellar Screenworks
11546 Ransom Hwy (48821-8730)
PHONE.................................517 646-8188
Kirk Mackellar, *President*
EMP: 4 EST: 1996
SALES (est): 370K **Privately Held**
WEB: www.mackellarscreenworks.com
SIC: 2759 Screen printing

Dollar Bay
Houghton County

(G-4766)
YOUNG MANUFACTURING INC
Also Called: Central Vac International
23455 Hellman Ave (49922-9740)
P.O. Box 259 (49922-0259)
PHONE.................................906 483-3851
Mark Young, *President*
EMP: 5 EST: 2008
SALES (est): 499.1K **Privately Held**
WEB: www.centralvac.com
SIC: 3999 1761 Chairs, hydraulic, barber & beauty shop; sheet metalwork

Dorr
Allegan County

(G-4767)
BEST MFG TOOLING SOLUTIONS
4190 Pro Line Ct (49323-9055)
PHONE.................................616 877-5149
EMP: 4 EST: 2017
SALES (est): 51.1K **Privately Held**
SIC: 3999 Manufacturing industries

(G-4768)
INTEGRITY DOOR LLC
3010 143rd Ave (49323-9715)
PHONE.................................616 896-8077
Jared Dishinger,
EMP: 4 EST: 2014
SALES (est): 62K **Privately Held**
SIC: 3442 Garage doors, overhead: metal

(G-4769)
PDS PLASTICS INC
3297 140th Ave (49323-9530)
PHONE.................................616 896-1109
Stacy Demaray, *President*
EMP: 17 EST: 1995
SALES (est): 1.9MM **Privately Held**
WEB: www.pdsplastics.com
SIC: 3089 2759 Injection molding of plastics; commercial printing

(G-4770)
S & S MACHINE TOOL REPAIR LLC
Also Called: S & S Specialties
1664 144th Ave (49323-9777)
P.O. Box 61, Wayland (49348-0061)
PHONE.................................616 877-4930
Scott Ellens,
Doug Cook,
EMP: 4 EST: 2001
SALES (est): 390.9K **Privately Held**
SIC: 3541 Machine tool replacement & repair parts, metal cutting types

(G-4771)
WILLIAMS TOOLING & MFG
1856 142nd Ave (49323-9501)
P.O. Box 7 (49323-0007)
PHONE.................................616 681-2093
Jerry Williams, *Owner*
Rebecca Davis, *Vice Pres*
Pat Wells, *Supervisor*
Lorie Williams, *Admin Sec*
EMP: 29 EST: 1991
SQ FT: 4,000
SALES (est): 1.4MM **Privately Held**
WEB: www.williamstooling.com
SIC: 3544 Die sets for metal stamping (presses)

Douglas
Allegan County

(G-4772)
DOUGLAS MARINE CORPORATION
Also Called: Skater Boats
6780 Enterprise Dr (49406-5136)
P.O. Box 819 (49406-0819)
PHONE.................................269 857-1764
Peter C Hledin, *President*
▼ EMP: 28 EST: 1978
SQ FT: 51,000
SALES (est): 3.7MM **Privately Held**
WEB: www.skaterpowerboats.com
SIC: 3732 Motorboats, inboard or outboard: building & repairing

(G-4773)
ENTERPRISE HINGE INC
6779 Enterprise Dr (49406-5136)
P.O. Box 397 (49406-0397)
PHONE.................................269 857-2111
Brian Pearson, *President*
David Pearson, *President*
▲ EMP: 8 EST: 1946
SQ FT: 15,500
SALES (est): 958.7K **Privately Held**
WEB: www.enterprisehinge.com
SIC: 3429 Builders' hardware

(G-4774)
SAUGATUCK BREWING COMPANY INC
2948 Blue Star Hwy (49406-5207)
P.O. Box 856 (49406-0856)
PHONE.................................269 857-7222
Ric Gillette, *President*
Robert Klute, *General Ptnr*
Cathy Gillette, *Controller*
EMP: 35 EST: 1995
SALES (est): 6.3MM **Privately Held**
WEB: www.saugatuckbrewing.com
SIC: 2082 Beer (alcoholic beverage)

Dowagiac
Cass County

(G-4775)
AUTOCAM CORPORATION
Also Called: Autocam-Pax
201 Percy St (49047-1500)
PHONE.................................269 782-5186
Charles Laue, *CEO*
Verlin Bush, *Enginr/R&D Mgr*
Shane Garrow, *Technician*
Joe Gerhold, *Maintence Staff*
EMP: 7
SALES (corp-wide): 427.5MM **Publicly Held**
WEB: www.autocam.com
SIC: 3714 Motor vehicle engines & parts
HQ: Autocam Corporation
   4180 40th St Se
   Kentwood MI 49512
   616 698-0707

(G-4776)
AUTOCAM-PAX INC
201 Percy St (49047-1500)
PHONE.................................269 782-5186
John C Kennedy, *Ch of Bd*
Warren A Veltman, *CFO*
▲ EMP: 180 EST: 1946
SQ FT: 35,000
SALES (est): 1.5MM
SALES (corp-wide): 427.5MM **Publicly Held**
WEB: www.autocam.com
SIC: 3451 3592 3494 3398 Screw machine products; valves; valves & pipe fittings; metal heat treating; nonferrous rolling & drawing; blast furnaces & steel mills
HQ: Autocam Corporation
   4180 40th St Se
   Kentwood MI 49512
   616 698-0707

GEOGRAPHIC SECTION

Drummond Island - Chippewa County (G-4803)

(G-4777)
BAKERS RHAPSODY
144 S Front St (49047-1716)
PHONE.................................269 767-1368
Jordan A Anderson, *Principal*
EMP: 5 **EST:** 2013
SALES (est): 186.9K **Privately Held**
WEB: www.thebakersrhapsody.com
SIC: 2053 Frozen bakery products, except bread

(G-4778)
COMMERCIAL WELDING COMPANY INC
316 Cass Ave (49047-2146)
P.O. Box 505 (49047-0505)
PHONE.................................269 782-5252
Mark Smith, *President*
David Smith, *Vice Pres*
EMP: 4 **EST:** 1946
SQ FT: 11,000
SALES (est): 623.2K **Privately Held**
WEB: www.commercialwelding.com
SIC: 3443 5084 Tanks, standard or custom fabricated: metal plate; pumps & pumping equipment

(G-4779)
CREATIVE FOAM CORPORATION
55210 Rudy Rd (49047-9641)
P.O. Box 238 (49047-0238)
PHONE.................................269 782-3483
Kevin Honaker, *General Mgr*
Fred Estrada, *Vice Pres*
Dave Friend, *Vice Pres*
Mark Shepler, *Vice Pres*
Robert Spring, *Plant Mgr*
EMP: 5
SALES (corp-wide): 198.2MM **Privately Held**
WEB: www.creativefoam.com
SIC: 3086 Packaging & shipping materials, foamed plastic
PA: Creative Foam Corporation
300 N Alloy Dr
Fenton MI 48430
810 629-4149

(G-4780)
CYCLONE MANUFACTURING INC
56850 Woodhouse Dr (49047-7735)
P.O. Box 815 (49047-0815)
PHONE.................................269 782-9670
Dennis Day, *CEO*
EMP: 7 **EST:** 1988
SALES (est): 777.2K **Privately Held**
WEB: www.cycloneblasters.com
SIC: 3471 Plating & polishing

(G-4781)
DOREL HOME FURNISHINGS INC
202 Spaulding St (49047-1452)
PHONE.................................269 782-8661
Raymond Toal, *Vice Pres*
Terry Murray, *Opers Staff*
Kelly Weaver, *Production*
Tonya Jacobs, *Controller*
Pam Sida, *Credit Staff*
EMP: 157
SALES (corp-wide): 2.7B **Privately Held**
WEB: www.ameriwoodhome.com
SIC: 2511 2493 Console tables: wood; coffee tables: wood; tea wagons: wood; reconstituted wood products
HQ: Dorel Home Furnishings, Inc.
410 E 1st St S
Wright City MO 63390
636 745-3351

(G-4782)
DOWSETT SPRING COMPANY
27071 Marcellus Hwy (49047-7465)
PHONE.................................269 782-2138
Fax: 269 782-6283
EMP: 9
SQ FT: 15,000
SALES: 800.1K **Privately Held**
SIC: 3495 Mfg Wire Springs

(G-4783)
INNOVATIVE FAB INC
29160 Middle Crossing Rd (49047-8200)
PHONE.................................269 782-9154
Marty Mottweiler, *President*
EMP: 5 **EST:** 1995
SALES (est): 496.2K **Privately Held**
SIC: 3599 Machine shop, jobbing & repair

(G-4784)
JAC CUSTOM POUCHES INC
56525 Woodhouse Dr (49047-7710)
P.O. Box 29 (49047-0029)
PHONE.................................269 782-3190
Kimberly Sirovica, *President*
Steven Coleman, *Vice Pres*
George Bauer, *Shareholder*
Jean Bauer, *Shareholder*
Harry E Coleman, *Shareholder*
EMP: 27 **EST:** 1983
SQ FT: 2,300
SALES (est): 2.4MM **Privately Held**
WEB: www.jaccustompouches.com
SIC: 2393 2394 2221 Bags & containers, except sleeping bags: textile; canvas & related products; broadwoven fabric mills, manmade

(G-4785)
JERZ MACHINE TOOL CORPORATION
415 E Prairie Ronde St (49047-1348)
PHONE.................................269 782-3535
Fax: 269 782-1998
EMP: 8
SQ FT: 5,500
SALES: 1MM **Privately Held**
SIC: 3599 7692 Mfg Industrial Machinery Welding Repair

(G-4786)
LAYLIN WELDING INC
501 E Prairie Ronde St (49047-1545)
PHONE.................................269 782-2910
Gale Laylin, *President*
Shirley Laylin, *Corp Secy*
EMP: 4 **EST:** 1936
SQ FT: 6,000 **Privately Held**
SIC: 7692 Welding repair

(G-4787)
LYONS INDUSTRIES INC (PA)
30000 M 62 W (49047-9348)
P.O. Box 88 (49047-0088)
PHONE.................................269 782-3404
Donald D Lyons, *Ch of Bd*
Lance Lyons, *President*
Debbie Wright, *Vice Pres*
Richard Xouris, *CFO*
▼ **EMP:** 114 **EST:** 1968
SQ FT: 96,000
SALES (est): 27MM **Privately Held**
WEB: www.lyonsindustries.com
SIC: 3088 Bathroom fixtures, plastic

(G-4788)
MENNEL MILLING CO OF MICH INC
301 S Mill St (49047-1473)
PHONE.................................269 782-5175
Don Mennel, *President*
Frank Herbes, *General Mgr*
EMP: 40
SQ FT: 9,000
SALES (est): 6.6MM
SALES (corp-wide): 211.1MM **Privately Held**
WEB: www.mennel.com
SIC: 2041 Wheat flour
PA: The Mennel Milling Company
319 S Vine St
Fostoria OH 44830
419 435-8151

(G-4789)
MICHIGAN DIE CASTING LLC
51241 M 51 N (49047-9626)
PHONE.................................269 471-7715
Phil Munforde Jr, *President*
Brad Farver, *General Mgr*
Tony Krukowski, *Engineer*
Tricia Tibbitts, *Manager*
EMP: 60 **EST:** 2017

SALES (est): 13.2MM
SALES (corp-wide): 33.1MM **Privately Held**
WEB: www.mumfordmetalcasting.com
SIC: 3363 Aluminum die-castings
PA: Mumford Metal Casting Llc
2222 S Halsted St
Chicago IL 60608
312 733-2600

(G-4790)
MICHIGAN PRECISION TL & ENGRG
Also Called: Michigan Precision Tl & Engrg
613 Rudy Rd (49047-9668)
PHONE.................................269 783-1300
Tony Karasch, *President*
Edwin Karasch Jr, *Corp Secy*
Henry D Karasch, *Vice Pres*
Terri Karasch, *Office Mgr*
EMP: 20 **EST:** 1985
SQ FT: 17,000
SALES (est): 1MM **Privately Held**
WEB: www.michiganprecisiontool.com
SIC: 3544 Special dies & tools

(G-4791)
MV METAL PDTS & SOLUTIONS LLC
51241 M 51 N (49047-9626)
PHONE.................................269 462-4010
EMP: 60
SALES (corp-wide): 136.8MM **Privately Held**
SIC: 3364 3363 Nonferrous Die-Castings Expt Aluminum,Nsk
PA: Mv Metal Products & Solutions, Llc
3585 Bellflower Dr
Portage MI 49024
269 471-7715

(G-4792)
NATE RONALD
50317 W Lakeshore Dr (49047-8873)
PHONE.................................269 424-3777
Ronald Nate, *Owner*
EMP: 6 **EST:** 2001
SALES (est): 173.1K **Privately Held**
SIC: 2084 Wines

(G-4793)
PREFERRED PRINTING INC (PA)
304 E Division St (49047-1425)
PHONE.................................269 782-5488
Rich Mc Cormick, *President*
Sue Mc Cormick, *Vice Pres*
EMP: 14 **EST:** 1977
SQ FT: 3,500
SALES (est): 1MM **Privately Held**
WEB: www.preferredprintinginc.net
SIC: 2752 Commercial printing, offset

(G-4794)
ROSS JOSEPH
93264 Wolf Dr (49047-8861)
PHONE.................................269 424-5448
Joseph Ross, *Principal*
EMP: 4 **EST:** 2001
SALES (est): 71.5K **Privately Held**
SIC: 3537 Industrial trucks & tractors

(G-4795)
SCHOTT SAW CO
54813 M 51 N (49047-9679)
P.O. Box 513 (49047-0513)
PHONE.................................269 782-3203
Ronnie Pond, *President*
EMP: 6 **EST:** 1960
SQ FT: 4,700
SALES (est): 239.9K **Privately Held**
SIC: 7699 3425 Knife, saw & tool sharpening & repair; saw blades & handsaws

(G-4796)
SECURIT METAL PRODUCTS CO
55905 92nd Ave (49047-9505)
PHONE.................................269 782-7076
Clayton A Wiker, *President*
Craig A Wiker, *Vice Pres*
Shirley M Wiker, *Treasurer*
▼ **EMP:** 24 **EST:** 1952
SQ FT: 45,000
SALES (est): 2.7MM **Privately Held**
WEB: www.securitmetalproducts.com
SIC: 3452 Rivets, metal

(G-4797)
STEINBAUER PERFORMANCE LLC
22790 Fosdick St (49047-7463)
PHONE.................................704 587-0856
Sherie Jones, *Pub Rel Mgr*
Herbert Steinbauer, *Mng Member*
Matt Ausen, *Technician*
Diesel Performance Australia,
▲ **EMP:** 9 **EST:** 2010
SQ FT: 4,200
SALES (est): 956.4K **Privately Held**
WEB: www.steinbauer.cc
SIC: 3714 Motor vehicle parts & accessories

(G-4798)
SYMONDS MACHINE CO INC
414 West St (49047-1045)
P.O. Box 268 (49047-0268)
PHONE.................................269 782-8051
Bob Symonds, *President*
Don Symonds, *Corp Secy*
John Symonds, *Vice Pres*
EMP: 7 **EST:** 1998
SALES (est): 780K **Privately Held**
SIC: 3599 Machine shop, jobbing & repair

Dowling
Barry County

(G-4799)
TNR MACHINE INC
2050 W Dowling Rd (49050-9714)
PHONE.................................269 623-2827
Norman Watson, *President*
Ronald Watson, *Vice Pres*
Thomas Watson, *Treasurer*
EMP: 20 **EST:** 1987
SQ FT: 7,800
SALES (est): 2.2MM **Privately Held**
WEB: www.tnrmachine.com
SIC: 3544 Special dies & tools

Drummond Island
Chippewa County

(G-4800)
DI TEE PEE LLC
38336 S Glen Cove Rd (49726-9681)
PHONE.................................906 493-6929
Fredrick Guith II, *Administration*
EMP: 5 **EST:** 2017
SALES (est): 80.6K **Privately Held**
SIC: 2759 Screen printing

(G-4801)
HOLLOW HILL WOODWORKS
33486 S Center St (49726-9583)
PHONE.................................906 493-6913
Jorn Asztalos, *Principal*
EMP: 5 **EST:** 2011
SALES (est): 75.4K **Privately Held**
SIC: 2431 Millwork

(G-4802)
MANUFACTURERS SERVICES INDS (PA)
Also Called: MSI
40014 S Cream City Pt Rd (49726-8600)
PHONE.................................906 493-6685
David E Williams, *President*
EMP: 4
SQ FT: 23,000
SALES (est): 450.1K **Privately Held**
SIC: 3089 Plastic processing

(G-4803)
OSBORNE MATERIALS COMPANY
Also Called: Drummond Dolemite
23311 E Haul Rd (49726-9492)
PHONE.................................906 493-5211
Gilbert Aikey, *Manager*
EMP: 40 **Privately Held**
WEB: www.osbornecompaniesinc.com
SIC: 3273 Ready-mixed concrete
PA: Osborne Materials Company
1 Williams St
Grand River OH 44045

Dryden
Lapeer County

(G-4804)
DRYDEN MOLD SERVICES INC
2988 Walker Rd (48428-9747)
P.O. Box 71 (48428-0071)
PHONE................................810 614-8621
Greg Eastin, *CEO*
EMP: 12 **EST:** 2003
SALES (est) 576.1K **Privately Held**
SIC: 3544 Industrial molds

(G-4805)
DRYDEN STEEL LLC
5585 North St Bldg D (48428-7723)
PHONE................................586 777-7600
Michael Oddo,
EMP: 7 **EST:** 2017
SALES (est) 406.5K **Privately Held**
SIC: 3291 Abrasive metal & steel products

(G-4806)
METAL MASTER WELDING LLC
3857 Hollow Corners Rd (48428-9727)
PHONE................................810 706-0476
Timothy Barbret, *Principal*
EMP: 4 **EST:** 2018
SALES (est) 25K **Privately Held**
SIC: 7692 Welding repair

(G-4807)
NEWARK GRAVEL COMPANY
4290 Calkins Rd (48428-9608)
PHONE................................810 796-3072
EMP: 10
SQ FT: 2,400
SALES (est) 447.9K **Privately Held**
SIC: 1442 5032 Construction Sand/Gravel Whol Brick/Stone Material

(G-4808)
UNYTREX INC
5901 Dryden Rd (48428-9619)
PHONE................................810 796-9074
Gene Siemen, *President*
Cindy Stephens, *Treasurer*
Kathy Siemen, *Admin Sec*
EMP: 12 **EST:** 1994
SQ FT: 16,000
SALES (est) 588.7K **Privately Held**
WEB: www.unytrex.com
SIC: 3544 Industrial molds

Dundee
Monroe County

(G-4809)
AMBROSIA INC
Also Called: Swan Creek Candle
129 Riley St (48131-1025)
PHONE................................734 529-7174
Erica Morrison, *Manager*
EMP: 6
SALES (corp-wide): 7MM **Privately Held**
WEB: www.swancreekwholesale.com
SIC: 3999 Candles
PA: Ambrosia, Inc.
395 W Airport Hwy
Swanton OH 43558
419 825-1151

(G-4810)
BLUE COLLAR WINERY LLC
6112 Wilcox Rd (48131-9628)
PHONE................................419 344-4715
Brian Evans,
EMP: 4 **EST:** 2017
SALES (est): 98.9K **Privately Held**
SIC: 2084 Wines

(G-4811)
CLEAN TECH INC
500 Dunham St (48131-1159)
PHONE................................734 529-2475
EMP: 50
SALES (corp-wide): 2.9B **Privately Held**
WEB: www.cleantechrecycling.com
SIC: 4953 3087 Recycling, waste materials; custom lapound purchased resins
HQ: Clean Tech, Inc.
41605 Ann Arbor Rd E
Plymouth MI 48170

(G-4812)
CLEAN TECH INC
500 Dunham St (48131-1159)
PHONE................................734 529-2475
Clarice Hampson, *Accountant*
EMP: 5
SALES (corp-wide): 2.9B **Privately Held**
WEB: www.plastipak.com
SIC: 3087 Custom compound purchased resins
HQ: Clean Tech, Inc.
41605 Ann Arbor Rd E
Plymouth MI 48170

(G-4813)
DARBY READY MIX-DUNDEE LLC
7801 N Ann Arbor Rd (48131-9587)
PHONE................................734 529-7100
Kevin Luke, *Manager*
Joseph M Comstock,
EMP: 13 **EST:** 2007 **Privately Held**
WEB: www.darbyreadymix.com
SIC: 5211 3273 Cement; ready-mixed concrete

(G-4814)
DUFFERIN AGGREGATES
6211 N Ann Arbor Rd (48131-9527)
P.O. Box 122 (48131-0122)
PHONE................................734 529-2411
David Loomes, *Vice Pres*
Dawn Crawford, *Vice Pres*
Michel Moser, *Plant Mgr*
Greg Turner, *Engineer*
EMP: 9 **EST:** 2016
SALES (est): 818.9K **Privately Held**
SIC: 1422 Crushed & broken limestone

(G-4815)
DUNDEE CASTINGS COMPANY
500 Ypsilanti St (48131-1197)
PHONE................................734 529-2455
Edgar Crawley, *President*
Patricia Bradley, *Corp Secy*
Tim Maki, *Vice Pres*
Pat Bradley, *Controller*
Kathy Archer, *Admin Asst*
▲ **EMP:** 95 **EST:** 1946
SQ FT: 13,200
SALES (est): 8MM **Privately Held**
WEB: www.dundeecastings.com
SIC: 3365 3369 Aluminum foundries; nonferrous foundries

(G-4816)
DUNDEE MANUFACTURING CO INC
107 Fairchild Dr (48131-9585)
P.O. Box 143 (48131-0143)
PHONE................................734 529-2540
Peter Davis, *President*
Dale Davis, *Vice Pres*
Heather Cannon, *Marketing Staff*
EMP: 35 **EST:** 1979
SQ FT: 32,000
SALES (est): 9.5MM **Privately Held**
WEB: www.dundeemfg.com
SIC: 3429 Builders' hardware

(G-4817)
DUNDEE PRODUCTS COMPANY
14490 Stowell Rd (48131-9516)
PHONE................................734 529-2441
Lori Monagin, *President*
Mark Maschino, *Plant Mgr*
Brian Yensch, *Prdtn Mgr*
Darren Miller, *Sales Staff*
Marjorie Monagin, *Admin Sec*
EMP: 24 **EST:** 1955
SQ FT: 48,000
SALES (est): 5MM **Privately Held**
WEB: www.dundeeproducts.com
SIC: 3312 Blast furnaces & steel mills

(G-4818)
EOI PIONEER INC
110 Research Pkwy (48131-9777)
PHONE................................626 823-5639
Fanny Huang, *President*
EMP: 4

SALES (est): 200K **Privately Held**
WEB: www.eoi.com.tw
SIC: 3647 Automotive lighting fixtures

(G-4819)
FCA US LLC
5800 N Ann Arbor Rd (48131-9772)
PHONE................................734 478-5658
Tania Young, *Plant Mgr*
Martin Sanders, *Engineer*
EMP: 500
SALES (corp-wide): 102.5B **Privately Held**
WEB: www.chrysler.com
SIC: 3714 Motor vehicle parts & accessories
HQ: Fca Us Llc
1000 Chrysler Dr
Auburn Hills MI 48326

(G-4820)
FCAUS DUNDEE ENGINE PLANT
5800 N Ann Arbor Rd (48131-9772)
PHONE................................734 529-9256
Tanya Young, *Branch Mgr*
Ken Crawford, *Maintence Staff*
Jane Matthews, *Legal Staff*
EMP: 720
SALES (corp-wide): 102.5B **Privately Held**
WEB: www.stellantis.com
SIC: 3714 Motor vehicle parts & accessories
PA: Stellantis N.V.
Taurusavenue 1
Hoofddorp
203 421-707

(G-4821)
GAZELLE PUBLISHING
Also Called: Independent Newspapers, The
112 Park Pl Ste 3 (48131-1016)
P.O. Box 98 (48131-0098)
PHONE................................734 529-2688
Sean McClellan, *Partner*
EMP: 8 **EST:** 1987
SQ FT: 6,000
SALES (est): 552.5K **Privately Held**
WEB: www.dundeeonline.com
SIC: 2711 5943 Commercial printing & newspaper publishing combined; office forms & supplies

(G-4822)
GLOBAL ENGINE MFG ALIANCE LLC
Also Called: Gema
5800 N Ann Arbor Rd (48131-9772)
PHONE................................734 529-9888
Matthew Regalia, *Financial Analy*
Reid Bigland, *Sales Staff*
Pietro Gorlier, *Chief Mktg Ofcr*
Bruce Baumbach, *Manager*
Linda Knoll, *Officer*
EMP: 7 **EST:** 2004
SALES (est): 2.6MM **Privately Held**
SIC: 3462 Automotive & internal combustion engine forgings

(G-4823)
HOLCIM (US) INC
6211 N Ann Arbor Rd (48131-9527)
P.O. Box 122 (48131-0122)
PHONE................................734 529-2411
Paul A Yhouse, *President*
Robert Pawluk, *Terminal Mgr*
Scott Poaps, *QC Mgr*
Matt Branam, *Engineer*
Robert West, *Cust Mgr*
EMP: 100
SALES (corp-wide): 25.3B **Privately Held**
WEB: www.lafargeholcim.us
SIC: 3241 5032 Portland cement; brick, stone & related material
HQ: Holcim (Us) Inc.
8700 W Bryn Mawr Ave
Chicago IL 60631

(G-4824)
HOLCIM (US) INC
Also Called: Dundee Plant
15215 Day Rd (48131-9586)
P.O. Box 122 (48131-0122)
PHONE................................734 529-4600
Lisa Olsen, *Counsel*
Darren Dunn, *Opers Mgr*

Ken Farrar, *Opers Staff*
Chaz Rowser, *Engineer*
Charles Pillivant, *Credit Staff*
EMP: 4
SALES (corp-wide): 25.3B **Privately Held**
WEB: www.lafargeholcim.us
SIC: 3241 3272 Portland cement; concrete products
HQ: Holcim (Us) Inc.
8700 W Bryn Mawr Ave
Chicago IL 60631

(G-4825)
HOME WINERY SUPPLY LLC
208 Main St (48131-1204)
PHONE................................734 529-3296
William J Falk,
Joshua Fink,
EMP: 4 **EST:** 1929
SQ FT: 1,300
SALES (est): 330.7K **Privately Held**
WEB: www.homewinery.com
SIC: 2084 Wines

(G-4826)
L & W INC
Also Called: Axis Engineering Div
5461 Circle Seven Dr (48131-9561)
PHONE................................734 529-7290
Wayne D Jones, *Manager*
EMP: 10
SALES (corp-wide): 3.1B **Privately Held**
WEB: www.autokiniton.com
SIC: 3465 3469 Automotive stampings; stamping metal for the trade
HQ: L & W, Inc.
17757 Woodland Dr
New Boston MI 48164
734 397-6300

(G-4827)
LAFARGE NORTH AMERICA INC
6211 N Ann Arbor Rd (48131-9527)
PHONE................................703 480-3600
EMP: 4
SALES (corp-wide): 25.3B **Privately Held**
WEB: www.lafarge-na.com
SIC: 3273 3272 3271 1442 Ready-mixed concrete; concrete products; precast terrazo or concrete products; prestressed concrete products; cylinder pipe, prestressed or pretensioned concrete; blocks, concrete or cinder: standard; construction sand & gravel; construction sand mining; gravel mining; asphalt paving mixtures & blocks; paving mixtures; asphalt & asphaltic paving mixtures (not from refineries); portland cement
HQ: Lafarge North America Inc.
8700 W Bryn Mawr Ave # 30
Chicago IL 60631
773 372-1000

(G-4828)
LAFARGHLCIM ACM NWCO TX-LA LLC
6211 N Ann Arbor Rd (48131-9527)
PHONE................................972 837-2462
Anthony Bond, *President*
Anita Leiter, *Administration*
EMP: 8 **EST:** 2017
SALES (est): 2.4MM **Privately Held**
SIC: 3273 Ready-mixed concrete

(G-4829)
LATTIMORE MATERIAL
6211 N Ann Arbor Rd (48131-9527)
PHONE................................972 837-2462
Anthony Bond, *President*
EMP: 43 **EST:** 2015
SALES (est): 5.4MM **Privately Held**
WEB: www.lafargeholcim.us
SIC: 3273 Ready-mixed concrete

(G-4830)
MAC VALVES INC
5555 N Ann Arbor Rd (48131-9201)
PHONE................................734 529-5099
Dennis Ryan, *Plant Mgr*
Linda Wigner, *Buyer*
Grace Morse, *Engineer*
Charlie Townsend, *Engineer*
Jason Trost, *Engineer*
EMP: 5

SALES (corp-wide): 157.8MM **Privately Held**
WEB: www.macvalves.com
SIC: 5085 3494 3491 Valves & fittings; valves & pipe fittings; industrial valves
PA: Mac Valves, Inc.
30569 Beck Rd
Wixom MI 48393
248 624-7700

(G-4831)
MATT AND DAVE LLC
Also Called: Schultz Motors
4706 N Ann Arbor Rd (48131-9684)
PHONE 734 439-1988
Duane A Schultz,
EMP: 10 **EST:** 2015
SALES (est): 499.5K **Privately Held**
SIC: 3594 Motors, pneumatic; motors: hydraulic, fluid power or air

(G-4832)
MITCHELL EQUIPMENT CORPORATION
Also Called: Mitchell Rail Gear
5275 N Ann Arbor Rd (48131-9201)
PHONE 734 529-3400
Estel Lovitt Jr, *President*
Rob Hilton, *Prdtn Mgr*
▼ **EMP:** 25 **EST:** 1978
SQ FT: 44,000
SALES (est): 4MM **Privately Held**
WEB: www.mitchell-railgear.com
SIC: 3743 Railroad equipment

(G-4833)
REAU MANUFACTURING CO
100 Research Pkwy (48131-9777)
PHONE 734 823-5603
Dawn Reau, *President*
Rob Reau, *Manager*
EMP: 3 **EST:** 2013
SALES (est): 1MM **Privately Held**
WEB: www.reaumfg.com
SIC: 3699 3599 1799 Laser welding, drilling & cutting equipment; machine shop, jobbing & repair; welding on site

(G-4834)
SALENBIEN WELDING SERVICE INC
460 Roosevelt St (48131-9557)
P.O. Box 134 (48131-0134)
PHONE 734 529-3280
George J Salenbien, *President*
EMP: 10 **EST:** 1973
SQ FT: 10,000
SALES (est): 1.1MM **Privately Held**
WEB: www.salenbienwelding.com
SIC: 7692 Welding repair

(G-4835)
SEARCHLIGHT SAFETY LLC
15500 Old Dixon Rd (48131-9598)
PHONE 313 333-9200
Kevin Townsend, *Principal*
EMP: 5 **EST:** 2013
SALES (est): 159.9K **Privately Held**
WEB: www.searchlightsafetyllc.com
SIC: 3648 Searchlights

(G-4836)
ST JULIAN WINE COMPANY INC
700 Freedom Ct (48131-9572)
PHONE 734 529-3700
Nancie Oxley, *Vice Pres*
David Baraganini, *Branch Mgr*
Richard Barnes, *CIO*
EMP: 9
SALES (corp-wide): 13.2MM **Privately Held**
WEB: www.stjulian.com
SIC: 2084 Wines
PA: St. Julian Wine Company, Incorporated
716 S Kalamazoo St
Paw Paw MI 49079
269 657-5568

(G-4837)
TITANIUM SPORTS LLC
13705 Stowell Rd (48131-9735)
PHONE 734 818-0904
Richard M Williams IV, *Administration*
EMP: 5 **EST:** 2012
SALES (est): 86.5K **Privately Held**
SIC: 3356 Titanium

Durand
Shiawassee County

(G-4838)
2ND CHANCE WOOD COMPANY
7505 E M 71 Ste B (48429-9800)
PHONE 989 472-4488
▲ **EMP:** 5 **EST:** 2010
SALES (est): 1.2MM **Privately Held**
WEB: www.2ndchancewood.com
SIC: 2491 Structural lumber & timber, treated wood

(G-4839)
B & M MACHINE & TOOL COMPANY
Also Called: Co-Op Machine & Tool
7665 E M 71 (48429-9776)
PHONE 989 288-2934
Daniel L Brown, *President*
Jim Mahrle, *Vice Pres*
EMP: 6 **EST:** 1970
SQ FT: 13,500
SALES (est): 502K **Privately Held**
WEB: www.bm-machine.com
SIC: 3544 3599 Special dies & tools; machine shop, jobbing & repair

(G-4840)
BEECHCRAFT PRODUCTS INC
1100 N Saginaw St (48429-1215)
PHONE 989 288-2606
Richard D Misner, *President*
Dorothy Misner, *Corp Secy*
Tom Misner, *Vice Pres*
EMP: 33 **EST:** 1958
SQ FT: 40,000
SALES (est): 2.8MM **Privately Held**
WEB: www.beechcraftproducts.com
SIC: 3089 3442 3211 2431 Plastic hardware & building products; metal doors, sash & trim; flat glass; louver doors, wood

(G-4841)
EMPIRE MACHINE & CONVEYORS INC
5111 S Durand Rd (48429-1267)
PHONE 989 541-2060
Harry Oumedian, *President*
Gwenn Hollister, *Controller*
EMP: 11 **EST:** 1998
SQ FT: 22,000
SALES (est): 1.4MM **Privately Held**
WEB: www.empireconveyors.com
SIC: 3535 3441 1791 Conveyors & conveying equipment; trolley conveyors; overhead conveyor systems; fabricated structural metal; building components, structural steel; iron work, structural

(G-4842)
MICHIGAN REEF DEVELOPMENT
8252 E Lansing Rd (48429-1059)
PHONE 989 288-2172
Harry Mohney, *President*
EMP: 7 **EST:** 1975
SQ FT: 1,000
SALES (est): 875K **Privately Held**
SIC: 1311 Crude petroleum & natural gas

(G-4843)
MY-CAN LLC
989 N Saginaw St (48429-1265)
P.O. Box 185 (48429-0185)
PHONE 989 288-7779
Connie Leedle,
EMP: 4 **EST:** 2005
SALES (est): 217.8K **Privately Held**
SIC: 3949 Camping equipment & supplies

(G-4844)
PANCHECK LLC
Also Called: Shaw's Pharmacy
221 N Saginaw St (48429-1165)
PHONE 989 288-6886
Mark Pancheck,
EMP: 14 **EST:** 2018
SALES (est): 2MM **Privately Held**
WEB: www.shawspharmacy.com
SIC: 2834 5122 Pharmaceutical preparations; drugs, proprietaries & sundries

(G-4845)
POWERSCREEN USA LLC
Also Called: Terex Simplicity
212 S Oak St (48429-1621)
PHONE 989 288-3121
EMP: 4
SALES (corp-wide): 3B **Publicly Held**
WEB: www.powerscreen.com
SIC: 3535 Conveyors & conveying equipment
HQ: Powerscreen Usa Llc
11001 Electron Dr
Louisville KY 40299
502 736-5200

(G-4846)
RIPRAP
407 N Oak St (48429-1223)
PHONE 734 945-0892
Patrick Schaefer, *Principal*
James Schaefer, *Exec Dir*
EMP: 7 **EST:** 2016
SALES (est): 82.4K **Privately Held**
WEB: www.riprap.org
SIC: 3663 Radio & TV communications equipment

(G-4847)
SHIAWASSEE COUNTY 9/12 COMM
512 N Marquette St (48429-1332)
PHONE 989 288-5049
Kenneth A Themm, *Manager*
EMP: 6 **EST:** 2012
SALES (est): 122.1K **Privately Held**
WEB: www.owossoindependent.com
SIC: 2711 Newspapers

(G-4848)
SIMPLICITY ENGINEERING COMPANY
Also Called: Terex Simplicity
212 S Oak St (48429-1601)
PHONE 989 288-3121
Lou Grossi, *Engineer*
Alex Kayanga, *Finance*
EMP: 1 **EST:** 1979
SALES (est): 1.3MM
SALES (corp-wide): 3B **Publicly Held**
WEB: www.terex.com
SIC: 3531 Construction machinery
PA: Terex Corporation
45 Glover Ave Ste 2
Norwalk CT 06850
203 222-7170

(G-4849)
TEREX CORPORATION
Also Called: Terex Canica
212 S Oak St (48429-1621)
PHONE 360 993-0515
Josh Ellis, *Design Engr*
Mike Schultz, *Manager*
EMP: 7
SALES (corp-wide): 3B **Publicly Held**
WEB: www.terex.com
SIC: 3531 Cranes
PA: Terex Corporation
45 Glover Ave Ste 2
Norwalk CT 06850
203 222-7170

(G-4850)
WIESKE TOOL INC
202 S Hagle St (48429-1700)
P.O. Box 335 (48429-0335)
PHONE 989 288-2648
Dan Wieske, *President*
Roger Wieske, *Vice Pres*
EMP: 4 **EST:** 1966
SQ FT: 5,500
SALES (est): 447.7K **Privately Held**
SIC: 3544 Special dies & tools

Eagle
Clinton County

(G-4851)
C&D PALLETS INC
13777 S Jones Rd (48822-9609)
PHONE 517 285-5228
Dean Gross, *Principal*
EMP: 4 **EST:** 2011
SALES (est): 170.3K **Privately Held**
SIC: 2448 Pallets, wood

(G-4852)
PATTY RAYMOND
15680 S Niles Rd (48822-9708)
PHONE 517 256-6673
Patricia Raymond, *Executive*
EMP: 5 **EST:** 2006
SALES (est): 92K **Privately Held**
SIC: 2899 Chemical preparations

Eagle Harbor
Keweenaw County

(G-4853)
SOCIETY OF SAINT JOHN INC
Also Called: Jampot
6559 State Highway M26 (49950-9642)
PHONE 906 289-4484
Fr Nicholas Glenn, *President*
Fr Basil Paris, *Admin Sec*
EMP: 6 **EST:** 1983
SALES (est): 452.6K **Privately Held**
WEB: www.societystjohn.com
SIC: 8661 2033 Monastery; jams, jellies & preserves: packaged in cans, jars, etc.

East China
St. Clair County

(G-4854)
A M R INC
671 Hathaway St (48054-1539)
PHONE 810 329-9049
Mark A Achatz, *President*
Mark J Achatz, *Vice Pres*
EMP: 9 **EST:** 2006
SALES (est): 1MM **Privately Held**
WEB: www.amrmachine.com
SIC: 3089 Injection molding of plastics

(G-4855)
ADVANCED STAGE TOOLING LLC
4317 River Rd (48054-2913)
PHONE 810 444-9807
Jerry Eschenburg,
EMP: 7 **EST:** 2017
SALES (est): 344K **Privately Held**
SIC: 3541 Machine tools, metal cutting type

(G-4856)
BLOOMBERRY
6189 Pleasant St (48054-4726)
PHONE 586 212-9510
Jim Numbers, *Principal*
EMP: 6 **EST:** 2012
SALES (est): 97K **Privately Held**
SIC: 2026 Yogurt

(G-4857)
J & L TURNING INC
Also Called: Alliance Broach and Tool
5664 River Rd (48054-4176)
PHONE 810 765-5755
Helen Johnson, *President*
EMP: 10 **EST:** 1977
SQ FT: 28,000
SALES (est): 1.5MM **Privately Held**
WEB: www.alliancebroach.com
SIC: 3599 3545 Machine shop, jobbing & repair; broaches (machine tool accessories)

(G-4858)
KKSP PRECISION MACHINING LLC
650 Hathaway St (48054-1533)
PHONE 810 329-4731
Dave Beller, *Vice Pres*
Kent Damisch, *Sales Staff*
Jeff Haskell, *Sales Staff*
Ryan D Hathaway, *Sales Staff*
Craig Law, *Sales Staff*
EMP: 36
SALES (corp-wide): 41.9MM **Privately Held**
WEB: www.kksp.com
SIC: 3599 Machine shop, jobbing & repair

PA: Kksp Precision Machining, Llc
1688 Glen Ellyn Rd
Glendale Heights IL 60139
630 260-1735

(G-4859)
TRP ENTERPRISES INC
Also Called: Trp Sand & Gravel
6267 Saint Clair Hwy (48054-1209)
PHONE..................................810 329-4027
James Pieprzak, *President*
Terry Pieprzak, *Vice Pres*
EMP: 5 **EST:** 1995
SALES (est): 377.2K **Privately Held**
SIC: 1442 2875 Construction sand & gravel; potting soil, mixed

East Jordan
Charlevoix County

(G-4860)
BURNETTE FOODS INC
200 State St (49727-9799)
P.O. Box 887 (49727-0887)
PHONE..................................231 536-2284
Ted Sherman Jr, *Plant Mgr*
William Sherman, *Sales Executive*
EMP: 107
SALES (corp-wide): 95.5MM **Privately Held**
WEB: www.burnettefoods.com
SIC: 2033 Fruits: packaged in cans, jars, etc.; vegetables: packaged in cans, jars, etc.
PA: Burnette Foods, Inc.
701 S Us Highway 31
Elk Rapids MI 49629
231 264-8116

(G-4861)
CITY OF EAST JORDAN
218 N Lake St (49727-8823)
PHONE..................................231 536-2561
Troy Thomas, *Superintendent*
Roberta Nemecek, *Treasurer*
Tom Cannon, *Commissioner*
EMP: 7 **EST:** 2011
SALES (est): 1.2MM **Privately Held**
WEB: www.eastjordancity.org
SIC: 3321 Manhole covers, metal

(G-4862)
DOUBLE GUN JOURNAL
5014 Rockery School Rd (49727-9636)
P.O. Box 550 (49727-0550)
PHONE..................................231 536-7439
Daniel Cote, *Partner*
Joanna Cote, *Partner*
EMP: 5 **EST:** 1988
SALES (est): 1MM **Privately Held**
WEB: www.doublegunshop.com
SIC: 2721 Magazines: publishing only, not printed on site

(G-4863)
EJ AMERICAS LLC (HQ)
301 Spring St (49727-5128)
P.O. Box 439 (49727-0439)
PHONE..................................231 536-2261
Lori Willis, *Principal*
Chris Hale, *Sales Staff*
David Curtiss, *Marketing Staff*
EMP: 0 **EST:** 2009
SALES (est): 311.2MM **Privately Held**
WEB: www.ejco.com
SIC: 6719 3321 Investment holding companies, except banks; manhole covers, metal

(G-4864)
EJ ARDMORE INC
301 Spring St (49727-5128)
P.O. Box 477 (49727-0477)
PHONE..................................231 536-2261
Jack Poindexter, *CFO*
William Lorne, *Admin Sec*
EMP: 18 **EST:** 2001
SALES (est): 1.6MM **Privately Held**
SIC: 3272 Manhole covers or frames, concrete

(G-4865)
EJ ASIA-PACIFIC INC (HQ)
301 Spring St (49727-5128)
PHONE..................................231 536-2261
William Lorne, *Principal*
EMP: 301 **EST:** 2009
SALES (est): 3.3MM **Privately Held**
WEB: www.ejco.com
SIC: 3321 Manhole covers, metal

(G-4866)
EJ CO
5000 Airport Rd (49727-9094)
P.O. Box 439 (49727-0439)
PHONE..................................231 536-4527
Jodi Kirkpatrick, *Marketing Staff*
Caroline Vanhorn, *Marketing Staff*
Korinna Holt, *Manager*
EMP: 17 **EST:** 2013
SALES (est): 1.1MM **Privately Held**
WEB: www.ejps.org
SIC: 3321 Gray & ductile iron foundries

(G-4867)
EJ EUROPE LLC (HQ)
301 Spring St (49727-5128)
PHONE..................................231 536-2261
William Lorne, *Principal*
EMP: 213 **EST:** 2009
SALES (est): 3.2MM **Privately Held**
WEB: www.ejco.com
SIC: 3321 Manhole covers, metal

(G-4868)
EJ GROUP INC (PA)
301 Spring St (49727-5128)
P.O. Box 439 (49727-0439)
PHONE..................................231 536-2261
Tracey K Malpass, *CEO*
Florent Vernhes, *General Mgr*
Nick Astle, *Superintendent*
Gary Betz, *Superintendent*
Paul Burks, *Superintendent*
EMP: 25 **EST:** 2009
SALES (est): 506MM **Privately Held**
WEB: www.ejco.com
SIC: 3321 Manhole covers, metal

(G-4869)
EJ TIMBER PRODUCERS INC
972 Toby Rd (49727-9252)
PHONE..................................231 544-9866
Virgil Lavanway, *President*
EMP: 10 **EST:** 2003
SALES (est): 331.9K **Privately Held**
SIC: 2411 Logging

(G-4870)
EJ USA INC (DH)
301 Spring St (49727-5128)
P.O. Box 477 (49727-0477)
PHONE..................................800 874-4100
Fred Malpass, *President*
Adam Morgan, *Mfg Mgr*
Kristy Kelley, *Purch Agent*
Candace Rusinowski, *Purchasing*
Carl Barnum, *QC Mgr*
◆ **EMP:** 500 **EST:** 1883
SQ FT: 360,000
SALES (est): 224.8MM **Privately Held**
WEB: www.ejco.com
SIC: 3321 Gray iron castings

(G-4871)
EJ USA INC
5000 Airport Rd (49727-9094)
P.O. Box 842907, Boston MA (02284-2907)
PHONE..................................231 536-2261
EMP: 7 **Privately Held**
WEB: www.eastjordancity.org
SIC: 3321 Gray & ductile iron foundries
HQ: Ej Usa, Inc.
301 Spring St
East Jordan MI 49727
800 874-4100

(G-4872)
JAMES L BARNETT
2759 Finkton Rd (49727-8850)
PHONE..................................231 544-8118
James L Barnett, *Principal*
EMP: 5 **EST:** 2005
SALES (est): 67.5K **Privately Held**
SIC: 7692 Welding repair

(G-4873)
JORDAN VALLEY CONCRETE SERVICE
Also Called: North Land Septic Tank Service
126 Garner Rd (49727-8734)
PHONE..................................231 536-7701
EMP: 10
SQ FT: 600
SALES (est): 1.1MM **Privately Held**
SIC: 3273 3272 1794 Septic Tanks & Excavating Contractor

(G-4874)
JORDAN VALLEY GLASSWORKS
209 State St (49727-9799)
P.O. Box 362 (49727-0362)
PHONE..................................231 536-0539
Shelly Bavers, *President*
Jay Bavers, *Vice Pres*
Glenna Haney, *Vice Pres*
EMP: 4 **EST:** 1992
SALES (est): 421K **Privately Held**
WEB: www.jordanvalleyglassworks.com
SIC: 3231 3229 Stained glass: made from purchased glass; glassware, art or decorative

(G-4875)
MCCULLYS WLDG FABRICATION LLC
3916 E Old State Rd (49727-8713)
PHONE..................................231 499-3842
Mark McCully, *Principal*
EMP: 4 **EST:** 2015
SALES (est): 107.3K **Privately Held**
SIC: 7692 Welding repair

(G-4876)
MICHIGAN SNOWMOBILER INC
200 Main St Ste B (49727-5126)
P.O. Box 572 (49727-0572)
PHONE..................................231 536-2371
Patti Tisron, *President*
EMP: 4 **EST:** 2015
SALES (est): 160.2K **Privately Held**
WEB: www.michsnowmag.com
SIC: 2711 Newspapers, publishing & printing

(G-4877)
NEXT-LEVEL SANDBAG LLC
Also Called: Next Level Sandbag
2831 S M 66 (49727-9438)
P.O. Box 354 (49727-0354)
PHONE..................................231 350-6738
John C Strehl II,
EMP: 4 **EST:** 2020
SALES (est): 85K **Privately Held**
SIC: 1442 Sand mining

(G-4878)
NORTHWEST FABRICATION INC
Also Called: East Jordan Sandblasting
450 Griffin Rd (49727-5133)
P.O. Box 1148 (49727-1148)
PHONE..................................231 536-3229
Brian Stanek, *President*
Karen Stanek, *Treasurer*
EMP: 4 **EST:** 1998
SQ FT: 12,000
SALES (est): 275K **Privately Held**
WEB: www.nwfab.com
SIC: 3441 3471 3444 3443 Fabricated structural metal; sand blasting of metal parts; sheet metalwork; fabricated plate work (boiler shop)

(G-4879)
SIGNS LETTERS & GRAPHICS INC
4095 Jonathon Dr (49727-9637)
P.O. Box 832 (49727-0832)
PHONE..................................231 536-7929
Mark K Postma, *President*
EMP: 4 **EST:** 1997
SALES (est): 331.4K **Privately Held**
SIC: 3993 Signs & advertising specialties

(G-4880)
SOCKS KICK LLC
117 S Lake St (49727-9375)
P.O. Box 587 (49727-0587)
PHONE..................................231 222-2402
EMP: 4 **EST:** 2018

SALES (est): 154K **Privately Held**
WEB: www.sockskick.com
SIC: 2252 Socks

(G-4881)
STONEHEDGE FARM
2246 Pesek Rd (49727-8817)
PHONE..................................231 536-2779
Debra Mc Dermott, *Owner*
EMP: 8 **EST:** 2001
SALES (est): 749.2K **Privately Held**
WEB: www.stonehedgefibermill.com
SIC: 2231 Broadwoven fabric mills, wool

(G-4882)
WES CORP
5900 Airport Rd (49727-9071)
PHONE..................................231 536-2500
Richard Gotts, *Principal*
EMP: 4 **EST:** 2006
SALES (est): 428.3K **Privately Held**
SIC: 3399 Primary metal products

(G-4883)
WIT-SON CARBIDE TOOL INC
6490 Rogers Rd (49727-5140)
P.O. Box 339 (49727-0339)
PHONE..................................231 536-2247
Douglas Barrett, *President*
Ron Peck, *Sales Staff*
EMP: 21 **EST:** 1959
SQ FT: 12,000
SALES (est): 2MM **Privately Held**
WEB: www.wit-soncarbide.com
SIC: 3545 Cutting tools for machine tools

East Lansing
Ingham County

(G-4884)
AALPHA TINADAWN INC
Also Called: Budget Printing Center
974 Trwbrdge Rd Trwbrdge Trowbridge (48823)
P.O. Box 1331 (48826-1331)
PHONE..................................517 351-1200
Mina Saboury, *President*
EMP: 7 **EST:** 1985
SQ FT: 1,050
SALES (est): 854.2K **Privately Held**
WEB: www.nameworld.ca
SIC: 2752 Commercial printing, offset

(G-4885)
AI MACHINE SHOP
325 E Grand River Ave (48823-4384)
PHONE..................................615 855-1217
EMP: 4 **EST:** 2017
SALES (est): 162.5K **Privately Held**
SIC: 3599 Machine shop, jobbing & repair

(G-4886)
ARTEMIS TECHNOLOGIES INC
2501 Coolidge Rd Ste 503 (48823-6352)
P.O. Box 4948 (48826-4948)
PHONE..................................517 336-9915
John W Gilkey III, *President*
Olubunmi Akinyemiju, *Vice Pres*
EMP: 20 **EST:** 2004
SQ FT: 2,756
SALES (est): 607K **Privately Held**
SIC: 3571 Electronic computers

(G-4887)
BIOPOLYMER INNOVATIONS LLC
16647 Chandler Rd (48823-6111)
PHONE..................................517 432-3044
Laura Fisher,
Ramani Narayan,
EMP: 5 **EST:** 2003
SALES (est): 336K **Privately Held**
WEB: www.biopolymerinnovations.com
SIC: 2834 Pharmaceutical preparations

(G-4888)
BRAND LOGOED BARWARE
203 Mac Ave (48823-4353)
PHONE..................................517 763-1044
Brandon Cocke, *Principal*
EMP: 4 **EST:** 2014
SALES (est): 76K **Privately Held**
SIC: 3229 Barware

(G-4889)
CAPITAL SOFTWARE INC MICHIGAN
4660 S Hagadorn Rd # 100 (48823-5353)
PHONE..................................517 324-9100
Chris Nelson, *President*
EMP: 5 **EST:** 1982
SQ FT: 1,000
SALES (est): 430K **Privately Held**
WEB: www.evolution-rating.com
SIC: 7372 Application computer software

(G-4890)
CHERRY OAK LANDSCAPING LLC
16400 Upton Rd (48823-9304)
PHONE..................................517 339-2881
Brandon James Barrett, *Owner*
EMP: 16 **EST:** 2014
SALES (est): 1.1MM **Privately Held**
WEB: www.cherryoaklandscaping.com
SIC: 0781 0782 3271 7389 Landscape services; lawn services; blocks, concrete; landscape or retaining wall; business services

(G-4891)
EL 903 ELEMENT LLC
139 W Lake Lansing Rd # 21 (48823-8525)
PHONE..................................517 655-3492
EMP: 4 **EST:** 2018
SALES (est): 177.7K **Privately Held**
SIC: 2819 Elements

(G-4892)
FEDEX OFFICE & PRINT SVCS INC
626 Michigan Ave (48823-4219)
PHONE..................................517 332-5855
EMP: 6
SALES (corp-wide): 83.9B **Publicly Held**
SIC: 7334 2791 2789 Photocopying & duplicating services; typesetting; bookbinding & related work
HQ: Fedex Office And Print Services, Inc.
7900 Legacy Dr
Plano TX 75024
800 463-3339

(G-4893)
FIT FUEL BY KT LLC
16400 Upton Rd Lot 227 (48823-9306)
PHONE..................................517 643-8827
Kaitlyn Kelly,
EMP: 5 **EST:** 2016
SALES (est): 357K **Privately Held**
SIC: 2869 Fuels

(G-4894)
GREAT LAKES CRYSTAL TECH INC
4942 Dawn Ave Ste 118 (48823-5606)
PHONE..................................517 249-4395
Keith Evans, *CEO*
EMP: 4 **EST:** 2019
SALES (est): 655.5K **Privately Held**
WEB: www.glcrystal.com
SIC: 3674 Semiconductors & related devices

(G-4895)
HOHMANN & BARNARD INC
909 Abbot Rd Ste 2b (48823-3168)
PHONE..................................765 420-7940
EMP: 13
SALES (corp-wide): 245.5B **Publicly Held**
WEB: www.h-b.com
SIC: 3496 Clips & fasteners, made from purchased wire
HQ: Hohmann & Barnard, Inc.
30 Rasons Ct
Hauppauge NY 11788
631 234-0600

(G-4896)
HUNTSMAN ADVNCED MTLS AMRCAS L
4917 Dawn Ave (48823-5605)
PHONE..................................517 351-5900
Greg Benedict, *Project Engr*
Larry Klusack, *Manager*
Darlene Bommorito, *Manager*
George Sollner, *Manager*
EMP: 59
SALES (corp-wide): 6B **Publicly Held**
WEB: www.huntsman.com
SIC: 2821 Plastics materials & resins
HQ: Huntsman Advanced Materials Americas Llc
10003 Woodloch Forest Dr # 260
The Woodlands TX 77380
281 719-6000

(G-4897)
INPORE TECHNOLOGIES INC
Also Called: Claytec
5901 E Sleepy Hollow Ln (48823-9706)
PHONE..................................517 481-2270
Gerald Roston, *CEO*
Thomas Pinnavaia, *Vice Pres*
EMP: 6 **EST:** 1996
SQ FT: 2,000
SALES (est): 606.1K **Privately Held**
WEB: www.inpore.com
SIC: 2819 Silica compounds

(G-4898)
KATARINA NATURALS
2000 Merritt Rd (48823-2921)
PHONE..................................517 333-6880
Dianne Holman, *Principal*
EMP: 4 **EST:** 2014
SALES (est): 69.6K **Privately Held**
SIC: 2844 Toilet preparations

(G-4899)
LANSING LABOR NEWS INC
16910 Black Walnut Ln (48823-9656)
PHONE..................................517 484-7408
Nancy Sears, *Principal*
Mike Bestero, *Treasurer*
Harold Foster, *Director*
EMP: 4 **EST:** 1949
SALES (est): 168.1K **Privately Held**
WEB: www.lansinglabornews.org
SIC: 2711 Newspapers: publishing only, not printed on site

(G-4900)
LEE CLEANERS INC
2843 E Grnd Rvr Ave # 140 (48823-4989)
PHONE..................................517 351-5655
Sung Ki Lee, *CEO*
EMP: 5 **EST:** 2006
SALES (est): 300K **Privately Held**
SIC: 2842 Laundry cleaning preparations

(G-4901)
LUHU LLC
540 Glenmoor Rd (48823-3999)
PHONE..................................320 469-3162
Rueben Hewitt, *Mng Member*
Zwede Hewitt,
EMP: 6
SALES (est): 135.3K **Privately Held**
SIC: 7372 7389 Application computer software; business services

(G-4902)
MCLANAHAN CORPORATION
227 Chesterfield Pkwy (48823-4110)
PHONE..................................517 614-2007
EMP: 9 **EST:** 2017
SALES (est): 109K **Privately Held**
WEB: www.mclanahan.com
SIC: 3532 Mining machinery

(G-4903)
MICHIGAN SOFT WATER OF CENTR
Also Called: Wolverine Water Trtmnt Systems
2075 E M 78 (48823-9783)
PHONE..................................517 339-0722
Paul Mahaney, *President*
EMP: 100 **EST:** 1950
SQ FT: 10,000
SALES (est): 7.8MM **Privately Held**
SIC: 3589 5074 5999 1711 Water filters & softeners, household type; water treatment equipment, industrial; water purification equipment, household type; water softeners; water heaters & purification equipment; water purification equipment; plumbing, heating, air-conditioning contractors

(G-4904)
MICHIGAN STATE MEDICAL SOCIETY (PA)
Also Called: Michigan Medical Society
120 W Saginaw St (48823-2605)
PHONE..................................517 337-1351
Julie L Novak, *CEO*
Paula Richardson, *CFO*
Julie A Ozbun, *Agent*
Virginia Gibson, *Director*
EMP: 47 **EST:** 1910
SQ FT: 32,000
SALES (est): 5.7MM **Privately Held**
WEB: www.msms.org
SIC: 8621 2752 Health association; commercial printing, offset

(G-4905)
MICHIGAN STATE UNIV PRESS
Manly Mles Bldg 1405 S Hr (48823)
PHONE..................................517 355-9543
Anastasia Wraight, *Editor*
Gabriel M Dotto, *Director*
▲ **EMP:** 30 **EST:** 1949
SALES (est): 928.1K
SALES (corp-wide): 1.9B **Privately Held**
WEB: www.msupress.org
SIC: 2731 Book publishing
PA: Michigan State University
426 Auditorium Rd
East Lansing MI 48824
517 355-1855

(G-4906)
MICHIGAN STATE UNIVERSITY
Also Called: MSU Bakers
220 Service Rd (48824-7003)
PHONE..................................517 353-9310
Cynthia Baswell, *Branch Mgr*
EMP: 7
SALES (corp-wide): 1.9B **Privately Held**
WEB: www.msu.edu
SIC: 2051 Bakery: wholesale or wholesale/retail combined
PA: Michigan State University
426 Auditorium Rd
East Lansing MI 48824
517 355-1855

(G-4907)
O AND P SPARTON
2947 Eyde Pkwy (48823-5373)
PHONE..................................517 220-4960
Dean Woolcock, *Principal*
EMP: 7 **EST:** 2016
SALES (est): 1.2MM **Privately Held**
WEB: www.spartanoandp.com
SIC: 3842 Orthopedic appliances

(G-4908)
SENSUS
1612 Snyder Rd (48823-3748)
PHONE..................................517 230-1529
Jeff Miller, *Principal*
EMP: 4 **EST:** 2017
SALES (est): 64.2K **Privately Held**
WEB: www.sensus.com
SIC: 3824 Fluid meters & counting devices

(G-4909)
STATE NEWS INC
Also Called: Michigan State University Pape
435 E Grand River Ave # 100 (48823-4498)
PHONE..................................517 295-1680
Christopher Richert, *President*
Travis Ricks, *Prdtn Mgr*
Marty Sprigg, *Manager*
EMP: 90 **EST:** 1909
SALES (est): 1.3MM **Privately Held**
WEB: www.statenews.com
SIC: 2711 8742 7311 8999 Newspapers, publishing & printing; marketing consulting services; advertising agencies; advertising consultant; advertising copy writing; design services

(G-4910)
STUDENT BOOK STORE INC
Also Called: Spartan Corner
103 E Grand River Ave (48823-4322)
PHONE..................................517 351-6768
EMP: 7
SALES (corp-wide): 5.1MM **Privately Held**
SIC: 5942 2395 Ret Misc Apparel/Accessories Pleating/Stitching Services
PA: Student Book Store, Inc.
421 E Grand River Ave
East Lansing MI 48823
517 351-4210

(G-4911)
SUPERIOR BRASS & ALUM CAST CO
4893 Dawn Ave (48823-5694)
PHONE..................................517 351-7534
Chris W Edwards, *President*
Sally Edwards, *Vice Pres*
EMP: 18 **EST:** 1956
SQ FT: 20,000 **Privately Held**
SIC: 3369 Nonferrous foundries

(G-4912)
SUPPORTED INTELLIGENCE LLC
1555 Watertower Pl # 300 (48823-6394)
PHONE..................................517 908-4420
Matthew Irey, *CEO*
EMP: 5 **EST:** 2012
SALES (est): 288.1K **Privately Held**
WEB: www.supportedintelligence.com
SIC: 7372 Application computer software

(G-4913)
TRANSOLOGY ASSOCIATES
2915 Crestwood Dr (48823-2371)
PHONE..................................517 694-8645
John Darlington, *Partner*
Leo Defrain, *Partner*
EMP: 5 **EST:** 1993 **Privately Held**
WEB: www.transology.com
SIC: 3823 Industrial process measurement equipment

(G-4914)
USMFG INC (HQ)
601 Abbot Rd (48823-3366)
PHONE..................................262 993-9197
Bernd Blondin, *CEO*
EMP: 1 **EST:** 2013
SQ FT: 1,000
SALES (est): 5MM
SALES (corp-wide): 155.4MM **Privately Held**
WEB: www.arrandene-mfg.com
SIC: 3339 Precious metals
PA: Mfg Metall- Und Ferrolegierungsges.
Mbh Hafner, Blondin & Tidou
Rudolf-Diesel-Str. 9
Meerbusch NW 40670
215 969-630

East Leroy
Calhoun County

(G-4915)
VAN MACHINE CO
131 2nd St (49051-5100)
P.O. Box 185 (49051-0185)
PHONE..................................269 729-9540
Steven Van Middlesworth, *Partner*
Robert Van Middlesworth, *Partner*
EMP: 6 **EST:** 1992
SQ FT: 2,100
SALES (est): 700K **Privately Held**
SIC: 3599 Machine shop, jobbing & repair

East Tawas
Iosco County

(G-4916)
ALEXANDER DIRECTIONAL BORING
2395 Robinet Dr (48730)
P.O. Box 254 (48730-0254)
PHONE..................................989 362-9506
Randall Alexander, *President*
EMP: 6 **EST:** 1998
SALES (est): 481.1K **Privately Held**
SIC: 1381 Directional drilling oil & gas wells

East Tawas - Iosco County (G-4917) GEOGRAPHIC SECTION

(G-4917)
IOSCO NEWS PRESS PUBLISHING CO
Also Called: Iosco News County Herald
110 W State St (48730-1229)
P.O. Box 72 (48730-0072)
PHONE.................................989 362-3456
Natalie Rigg, *Bookkeeper*
EMP: 8 **Privately Held**
WEB: www.iosconews.com
SIC: 2711 Commercial printing & newspaper publishing combined
HQ: Iosco News Press Publishing Co
311 S State St
Oscoda MI 48750
989 739-2054

(G-4918)
LOS CUARTO AMIGOS
1626 E Us 23 (48730-9351)
PHONE.................................989 984-0200
EMP: 7 **Privately Held**
SIC: 3421 Mfg Cutlery
PA: Los Cuarto Amigos
4570 Bay Rd
Saginaw MI 48604

(G-4919)
PLASTIC TRIM INTERNATIONAL INC (DH)
935 Aulerich Rd (48730-9565)
PHONE.................................248 259-7468
Howard Boyer, *CEO*
Kathleen Burgess, *Vice Pres*
Denise Wirley, *Buyer*
Sharon Faubert,
▲ **EMP:** 332 **EST:** 2003
SQ FT: 11,500
SALES (est): 150MM **Privately Held**
WEB: www.minthgroup.com
SIC: 3465 Body parts, automobile: stamped metal

(G-4920)
PLASTIC TRIM INTERNATIONAL INC
Starboard Industries
935 Aulerich Rd (48730-9565)
P.O. Box 32 (48730-0032)
PHONE.................................989 362-4419
Paul Koroly, *Principal*
Jessica Lee, *Buyer*
Mark Fore, *QC Mgr*
Wangyang Wang, *Engineer*
Jinyun Duffy, *Finance*
EMP: 175 **Privately Held**
SIC: 3089 Extruded finished plastic products
HQ: Plastic Trim International, Inc.
935 Aulerich Rd
East Tawas MI 48730
248 259-7468

(G-4921)
PRINT N GO
1769 E Us 23 (48730-9393)
PHONE.................................989 362-6041
Larry D Stimson, *Partner*
Robin D Pelton, *Partner*
Larry Stimson, *Partner*
EMP: 5 **EST:** 1976
SQ FT: 2,800
SALES (est): 590.9K **Privately Held**
WEB: www.printngo.org
SIC: 2752 5943 Photo-offset printing; office forms & supplies

(G-4922)
REDBIRD WD PDTS BLDWIN TWNSHIP
776 Aulerich Rd (48730-9565)
PHONE.................................989 362-7670
Dave Hicks, *Owner*
EMP: 6 **EST:** 2007
SALES (est): 186.7K **Privately Held**
WEB: www.redbirdwoodproducts.com
SIC: 2431 Millwork

(G-4923)
STAR CUTTER COMPANY INC
980 Aulerich Rd (48730-9565)
PHONE.................................248 474-8200
MA Million, *Principal*
Mike Bergwall, *Purch Mgr*
Chris Cella, *Manager*
EMP: 20 **EST:** 1949
SALES (est): 362K **Privately Held**
WEB: www.starcutter.com
SIC: 3541 Machine tools, metal cutting type

(G-4924)
TAWAS TOOL CO INC (HQ)
756 Aulerich Rd (48730-9568)
PHONE.................................989 362-6121
Brad Lawton, *President*
Bradley L Lawton, *President*
Jeffrey Lawton, *Vice Pres*
Mark Timreck, *Plant Mgr*
William Cronk, *Engineer*
▲ **EMP:** 60 **EST:** 1972
SQ FT: 4,500
SALES (est): 12.8MM
SALES (corp-wide): 204.2MM **Privately Held**
WEB: www.tawas.com
SIC: 3545 Hobs
PA: Star Cutter Co.
23461 Industrial Park Dr
Farmington Hills MI 48335
248 474-8200

(G-4925)
TAWAS TOOL CO INC
Also Called: Tawas Tools Plant 2
980 Aulerich Rd (48730-9566)
PHONE.................................989 362-0414
Jim Santorum, *Manager*
John Thornton, *Supervisor*
EMP: 60
SALES (corp-wide): 204.2MM **Privately Held**
WEB: www.tawas.com
SIC: 3545 3541 Hobs; machine tools, metal cutting type
HQ: Tawas Tool Co Inc
756 Aulerich Rd
East Tawas MI 48730
989 362-6121

Eastpointe
Macomb County

(G-4926)
A-W CUSTOM CHROME INC
17726 E 9 Mile Rd (48021-2565)
PHONE.................................586 775-2040
Russ Brian Box, *President*
Steve Box, *Vice Pres*
Janet Box, *Treasurer*
EMP: 6 **EST:** 1977
SQ FT: 2,000
SALES (est): 775.8K **Privately Held**
SIC: 3471 Buffing for the trade; chromium plating of metals or formed products; polishing, metals or formed products

(G-4927)
AJ HOMETOWN LLC
Also Called: Bee Queen Dairy & Ice Cream
14700 E 9 Mile Rd (48021-2138)
PHONE.................................313 415-0843
Ameen Alhalemi, *Mng Member*
EMP: 5 **EST:** 2016
SALES (est): 62.3K **Privately Held**
SIC: 2024 5812 Ice cream & frozen desserts; eating places

(G-4928)
BOWTIE CATERING LLC
23123 Normandy Ave (48021-1878)
PHONE.................................313 989-3952
Asia Phillips, *Principal*
EMP: 4 **EST:** 2020
SALES (est): 116.1K **Privately Held**
SIC: 2099 Food preparations

(G-4929)
CANDLES BY JUGG
21712 Donald Ave (48021-2435)
PHONE.................................313 732-1349
Donnell Young, *Principal*
EMP: 4 **EST:** 2019
SALES (est): 39.6K **Privately Held**
SIC: 3999 Candles

(G-4930)
CAPACITY HOUSE PUBLISHING
18121 E 8 Mile Rd (48021-3245)
PHONE.................................586 209-3924
Kierra Jones, *Principal*
EMP: 5 **EST:** 2019
SALES (est): 37.5K **Privately Held**
SIC: 2741 Miscellaneous publishing

(G-4931)
CFE RACING PRODUCTS INC
16834 Chesterfield Ave (48021-3384)
PHONE.................................586 773-6310
Carl Foltz, *President*
EMP: 8 **EST:** 1983
SQ FT: 4,500
SALES (est): 5MM **Privately Held**
WEB: www.cferacing.com
SIC: 7389 3559 3714 Design, commercial & industrial; automotive related machinery; motor vehicle engines & parts

(G-4932)
CONTROLLER SYSTEMS CORPORATION
Also Called: Controller Security Systems
21363 Gratiot Ave (48021-2886)
PHONE.................................586 772-6100
Henry J Luks, *President*
Kent Muravchick, *Engineer*
EMP: 40 **EST:** 1970
SQ FT: 12,000
SALES (est): 1.4MM **Privately Held**
WEB: www.controlersecurity.com
SIC: 3669 Burglar alarm apparatus, electric; fire alarm apparatus, electric

(G-4933)
CRK LTD
Also Called: UPS Stores, The
23205 Gratiot Ave (48021-1641)
PHONE.................................586 779-5240
Joseph Solomon, *President*
EMP: 5 **EST:** 1992
SQ FT: 1,000
SALES (est): 582.6K **Privately Held**
WEB: www.theupsstore.com
SIC: 7389 3053 Mailbox rental & related service; packing materials

(G-4934)
CROWN GROUP CO
Also Called: Crown Group Detroit Plant
15794 Nicolai Ave (48021-1652)
PHONE.................................313 922-8433
EMP: 75
SALES (corp-wide): 15.3B **Publicly Held**
SIC: 3479 Coating/Engraving Service
HQ: The Crown Group Co
5875 New King Ct
Troy MI 48098
586 575-9800

(G-4935)
CUSTOM PTINT INK LLC
14943 E 9 Mile Rd (48021-2147)
PHONE.................................586 799-2465
Jeffrey Carter,
EMP: 4 **EST:** 2016
SALES (est): 100K **Privately Held**
SIC: 2396 Screen printing on fabric articles

(G-4936)
HERFERT SOFTWARE
Also Called: Herfert Chiropractic Software
15700 E 9 Mile Rd (48021-3905)
PHONE.................................586 776-2880
Richard Herfert, *Owner*
EMP: 5 **EST:** 1980
SALES (est): 372.5K **Privately Held**
WEB: www.herfertsoftware.com
SIC: 7372 Prepackaged software

(G-4937)
INDUSTRIAL IMPRNTNG & DIE CTNG
15291 E 10 Mile Rd (48021-1009)
PHONE.................................586 778-9470
Ronald Baluch, *Principal*
EMP: 4 **EST:** 1969
SQ FT: 3,300
SALES (est): 362.2K **Privately Held**
WEB: www.industrialimprinting.com
SIC: 7389 2752 2796 2759 Printers' services: folding, collating; commercial printing, lithographic; platemaking services; commercial printing; die-cut paper & board

(G-4938)
JS ORIGINAL SILKSCREENS LLC
18132 E 10 Mile Rd (48021-1345)
PHONE.................................586 779-5456
Julia Cadotte-Capps, *Owner*
EMP: 7 **EST:** 1981
SQ FT: 2,450
SALES (est): 589.6K **Privately Held**
WEB: www.jssilkscreens.com
SIC: 2396 5699 Screen printing on fabric articles; customized clothing & apparel; belts, apparel: custom

(G-4939)
LITHO PRINTING SERVICE INC
21541 Gratiot Ave (48021-2892)
PHONE.................................586 772-6067
Dale Heid, *President*
Carole C Heid, *Admin Sec*
EMP: 9 **EST:** 1966
SQ FT: 5,000
SALES (est): 2MM **Privately Held**
WEB: www.lithoprinting.com
SIC: 2752 Commercial printing, offset

(G-4940)
LITTLE LEGENDS CREATIONS LLC
17431 Juliana Ave (48021-3143)
PHONE.................................313 828-7292
Na'shai Johnson,
EMP: 5 **EST:** 2020
SALES (est): 269.7K **Privately Held**
SIC: 2329 Men's & boys' clothing

(G-4941)
MPRESS DESIGHNS LLC
19030 Veronica Ave (48021-2757)
PHONE.................................313 627-9727
Mark Mtcalf, *Principal*
EMP: 4 **EST:** 2018
SALES (est): 37.5K **Privately Held**
SIC: 2741 Miscellaneous publishing

(G-4942)
MUNRO PRINTING
16145 E 10 Mile Rd (48021-1131)
PHONE.................................586 773-9579
John Laforest, *Owner*
EMP: 4 **EST:** 1984
SQ FT: 1,600
SALES (est): 417K **Privately Held**
WEB: www.munroprint.com
SIC: 2752 Commercial printing, offset

(G-4943)
REEMARKABLE EYES LLC ✪
18121 E 8 Mile Rd 321a (48021-3245)
PHONE.................................313 461-3006
Shareese Simpson, *Mng Member*
EMP: 5 **EST:** 2021
SALES (est): 150.7K **Privately Held**
SIC: 3999 Eyelashes, artificial

(G-4944)
SCS FASTENERS LLC
23205 Gratiot Ave (48021-1641)
PHONE.................................586 563-0865
Shirley Warne, *Administration*
EMP: 5 **EST:** 2016
SALES (est): 293.3K **Privately Held**
SIC: 3965 Fasteners

(G-4945)
TRUE WELDING LLC
16242 Bell Ave (48021-1151)
PHONE.................................586 822-5398
EMP: 4 **EST:** 2010
SALES (est): 45.1K **Privately Held**
WEB: www.truewelding.com
SIC: 7692 Welding repair

(G-4946)
UNIT CITY WIGS LLC
24836 Dale Ave (48021-1023)
PHONE.................................313 264-8112

▲ = Import ▼ =Export
◆ =Import/Export

Teeya Wells,
EMP: 4 **EST:** 2020
SALES (est): 50.2K **Privately Held**
SIC: 3999 Wigs, including doll wigs, toupees or wiglets

(G-4947)
VALADE PRECISION MACHINING INC
Also Called: V.P.M.
17155 Stephens Dr (48021-1767)
PHONE 586 771-7705
EMP: 5
SQ FT: 5,000
SALES (est): 320.7K **Privately Held**
SIC: 3599 Mfg Machining Service

(G-4948)
VISUAL CHIMERA
Also Called: Golden Dental Solutions
23082 Saxony Ave (48021-1846)
PHONE 586 585-1210
Michael Pavlak, *Owner*
EMP: 10 **EST:** 2015
SALES (est): 305.5K **Privately Held**
SIC: 3843 Dental equipment & supplies

Eastport
Antrim County

(G-4949)
BROWNWOOD ACRES FOODS INC
4819 Us 31 (49627)
P.O. Box 486 (49627-0486)
PHONE 231 599-3101
Stephen Detar, *President*
Dana Detar, *Treasurer*
Ken Shepley, *Regl Sales Mgr*
EMP: 10 **EST:** 1981
SQ FT: 8,000
SALES (est): 988.1K **Privately Held**
WEB: www.fruitfast.com
SIC: 2033 5411 Canned fruits & specialties; grocery stores

Eaton Rapids
Eaton County

(G-4950)
ADTEK GRAPHICS INC
Also Called: Crg Directories
228 1/2 S Main St (48827-1256)
P.O. Box 305 (48827-0305)
PHONE 517 663-2460
D Ed Shotwell, *President*
Jane Degrow, *Vice Pres*
Sue Steward, *Opers Mgr*
Kim Frarey, *Accounts Exec*
Dan Trubak, *Accounts Exec*
EMP: 10 **EST:** 1988
SQ FT: 1,200
SALES (est): 918.2K **Privately Held**
WEB: www.totallocal.com
SIC: 2741 Directories, telephone: publishing only, not printed on site

(G-4951)
ANGEL EMBROIDERY
9100 Deer Run Dr (48827-8518)
PHONE 517 515-4836
Marjorie Morden, *Principal*
EMP: 4 **EST:** 2017
SALES (est): 49.2K **Privately Held**
SIC: 2395 Embroidery & art needlework

(G-4952)
AUTOMATED PRECISION EQP LLC
770 Jackson St Ste A (48827-1872)
PHONE 517 481-2414
Kurt Norgaard, *CEO*
EMP: 6 **EST:** 2010
SALES (est): 400K **Privately Held**
WEB: www.apecnc.com
SIC: 3553 7389 Woodworking machinery; grinding, precision: commercial or industrial

(G-4953)
AXSON TECH US INC
1611 Hults Dr (48827-9500)
PHONE 517 663-8191
Charles Churet, *Principal*
EMP: 50
SALES (corp-wide): 8.6B **Privately Held**
SIC: 2851 Lacquers, varnishes, enamels & other coatings
HQ: Sika Automotive Eaton Rapids, Inc.
30800 Stephenson Hwy
Madison Heights MI 48071
248 588-2270

(G-4954)
B L TOOL PRODUCTS
6407 Ferris Rd (48827-9659)
PHONE 517 896-1624
William Bruce Sweet Jr, *Administration*
EMP: 5 **EST:** 2018
SALES (est): 199K **Privately Held**
SIC: 3541 Machine tools, metal cutting type

(G-4955)
BARTZ MFG LLC
1215 N Smith Rd (48827-9327)
PHONE 517 281-2571
EMP: 4 **EST:** 2016
SALES (est): 79.7K **Privately Held**
SIC: 3999 Manufacturing industries

(G-4956)
BRIAN M FOWLER PIPE ORGANS
Also Called: Fowler Organ Co
215 Dexter Rd (48827-1129)
PHONE 517 485-3748
Brian M Fowler, *Owner*
EMP: 6 **EST:** 1978
SALES (est): 500K **Privately Held**
WEB: www.fowlerorgan.com
SIC: 7699 3931 Organ tuning & repair; organs, all types: pipe, reed, hand, electronic, etc.

(G-4957)
CARDBOARD PROPHETS
5472 Oak Hills Dr (48827-8743)
PHONE 517 512-1267
Michael D Karl, *Agent*
EMP: 4 **EST:** 2017
SALES (est): 84.7K **Privately Held**
WEB: www.cardboardprophets.org
SIC: 2631 Cardboard

(G-4958)
DOWDING INDUSTRIES
503 Marilin Ave (48827-1843)
PHONE 319 294-9094
EMP: 18 **EST:** 2015
SALES (est): 623.8K **Privately Held**
WEB: www.dowdingindustries.com
SIC: 3999 Manufacturing industries

(G-4959)
DOWDING INDUSTRIES INC (PA)
449 Marilin Ave (48827-1841)
PHONE 517 663-5455
G Christine Dowding, *President*
Jeff Metts, *President*
Maurice H Dowding, *Chairman*
Mike Gonser, *Exec VP*
Donald Harper, *Plant Mgr*
▲ **EMP:** 20 **EST:** 1965
SQ FT: 160,000
SALES (est): 24MM **Privately Held**
WEB: www.dowdingindustries.com
SIC: 3429 3441 3444 3449 Manufactured hardware (general); fabricated structural metal; sheet metalwork; miscellaneous metalwork; machine & other job shop work

(G-4960)
DOWDING INDUSTRIES INC
502 Marilin Ave (48827-1867)
PHONE 517 663-5455
Mike Gonser, *Branch Mgr*
EMP: 120

SALES (corp-wide): 24MM **Privately Held**
WEB: www.dowdingindustries.com
SIC: 3465 7692 3714 3713 Automotive stampings; welding repair; motor vehicle parts & accessories; truck & bus bodies; fabricated structural metal
PA: Dowding Industries, Inc.
449 Marilin Ave
Eaton Rapids MI 48827
517 663-5455

(G-4961)
DOWDING MACHINING LLC
503 Marilin Ave (48827-1843)
PHONE 517 663-5455
Amber Loch, *Human Res Mgr*
Chris Dowding,
Maurice H Dowding,
Jeff Metts,
▲ **EMP:** 10 **EST:** 2008
SALES (est): 18MM **Privately Held**
WEB: www.dowdingindustries.com
SIC: 3545 3511 Machine tool accessories; turbines & turbine generator set units, complete

(G-4962)
EDGEWATER APARTMENTS
223 N Main St (48827-1280)
PHONE 517 663-8123
Merri Domer, *Manager*
Kristine Jackson, *Manager*
EMP: 5 **EST:** 1999
SALES (est): 296.1K **Privately Held**
WEB: www.edgewaterapartments.com
SIC: 6513 2675 Apartment building operators; die-cut paper & board

(G-4963)
FRESH WATER BUYER II LLC
5260 S Clinton Trl (48827-8901)
P.O. Box 503 (48827-0503)
PHONE 517 914-8284
Jeff Matzen, *President*
EMP: 14 **EST:** 1987
SQ FT: 12,000
SALES (est): 2.4MM **Privately Held**
WEB: www.ranchlife.com
SIC: 3496 1799 1521 Miscellaneous fabricated wire products; fence construction; patio & deck construction & repair

(G-4964)
G & F TOOL PRODUCTS
7127 E 5 Point Hwy (48827-9053)
PHONE 517 663-3646
George Goodnoe Jr, *Owner*
Bill St Andrew, *QC Mgr*
EMP: 14 **EST:** 1970
SQ FT: 35,000
SALES (est): 1.1MM **Privately Held**
SIC: 3544 Special dies & tools

(G-4965)
HOAG & SONS BOOK BINDERY INC
Also Called: Media Tecnologies
145 N Main St (48827-1225)
P.O. Box 162, Springport (49284-0162)
PHONE 517 857-2033
Dave Wiltus, *President*
Dorci Franks, *Manager*
EMP: 10 **EST:** 1893
SALES (est): 558.8K **Privately Held**
WEB: www.hoagandsons.com
SIC: 2789 Binding only: books, pamphlets, magazines, etc.

(G-4966)
MARKDOM OF AMERICA INC (PA) ✪
2285 S Michigan Rd (48827-9206)
PHONE 716 681-8306
Joseph Greco, *President*
EMP: 3 **EST:** 2021
SALES (est): 25MM **Privately Held**
SIC: 3089 Automotive parts, plastic

(G-4967)
PRECISION PROTOTYPE & MFG INC
500 Marilin Ave (48827-1844)
PHONE 517 663-4114
Ronald Taylor, *President*

Jason Beeler, *Safety Mgr*
EMP: 15 **EST:** 1993
SQ FT: 6,500
SALES (est): 6.7MM **Privately Held**
WEB: www.precisionprototype.com
SIC: 3469 3444 Metal stampings; sheet metalwork

(G-4968)
PRO FLOOR SERVICE
11636 Columbia Hwy (48827-9278)
PHONE 517 663-5012
Tony Williams, *Owner*
EMP: 4 **EST:** 2000
SALES (est): 344.4K **Privately Held**
SIC: 3996 Hard surface floor coverings

(G-4969)
QUALITY DECALS & SIGNS
7340 E Nye Hwy (48827-9067)
PHONE 517 441-1200
David Wick, *Principal*
EMP: 4 **EST:** 2015
SALES (est): 62.7K **Privately Held**
SIC: 3993 Signs & advertising specialties

(G-4970)
RAPIDS TOOL & ENGINEERING
Also Called: Rapids Tool & Engnrng
10618 Petrieville Hwy (48827-9205)
PHONE 517 663-8721
Ronald Goodnoe, *Owner*
EMP: 8 **EST:** 1966
SQ FT: 12,000
SALES (est): 670.6K **Privately Held**
SIC: 3544 Special dies & tools; dies & die holders for metal cutting, forming, die casting

(G-4971)
RICKS MEAT PROCESSING LLC
Also Called: Rick's Deer Processing
3320 Onondaga Rd (48827-9608)
PHONE 517 628-2263
EMP: 4
SALES (est): 170K **Privately Held**
SIC: 2011 Meat Packing Plant

(G-4972)
TETRA CORPORATION
1606 Hults Dr (48827-8955)
P.O. Box 10 (48827-0010)
PHONE 401 529-1630
George Cioe, *President*
John Dutka, *Regl Sales Mgr*
EMP: 21 **EST:** 2009
SALES (est): 6.5MM **Privately Held**
WEB: www.thetetracorp.com
SIC: 5999 2834 Cosmetics; emulsions, pharmaceutical

(G-4973)
TIME TRAVELING DJS
615 S Main St (48827-1425)
PHONE 517 402-0976
Joel Krupa, *Principal*
EMP: 4 **EST:** 2019
SALES (est): 87.2K **Privately Held**
SIC: 2741 Miscellaneous publishing

(G-4974)
TOTAL LOCAL ACQUISITIONS LLC
Also Called: Crg Directories
117 E Knight St (48827-1219)
P.O. Box 305 (48827-0305)
PHONE 517 663-2405
Teresa Miller, *President*
EMP: 7 **EST:** 2018
SALES (est): 760K **Privately Held**
WEB: www.totallocal.com
SIC: 7311 2741 Advertising agencies; telephone & other directory publishing

(G-4975)
VON WEISE LLC (DH)
402 Haven St Ste H (48827-1870)
PHONE 517 618-9763
Scott Abright, *Purchasing*
Alan Signer, *Engineer*
Kevin Hein, *CFO*
▲ **EMP:** 9 **EST:** 2009

Eau Claire - Berrien County (G-4976)

GEOGRAPHIC SECTION

SALES (est): 3MM
SALES (corp-wide): 54.5MM **Privately Held**
WEB: www.vonweise.com
SIC: 3714 3625 Gears, motor vehicle; actuators, industrial
HQ: Maradyne Corporation
4540 W 160th St
Cleveland OH 44135
216 362-0755

Eau Claire
Berrien County

(G-4976)
ENGINEERED POLYMER PRODUCTS
7988 W Eureka Rd (49111-9691)
PHONE..................................269 461-6955
Robert Dorstewitz, *Owner*
EMP: 25 EST: 1980
SQ FT: 21,000
SALES (est): 4.2MM **Privately Held**
SIC: 3089 Injection molding of plastics

(G-4977)
FLAMM PICKLE AND PACKAGING CO
4502 Hipps Hollow Rd (49111-9781)
P.O. Box 500 (49111-0500)
PHONE..................................269 461-6916
Gina D Flamm, *President*
Dorothy Munao, *General Mgr*
EMP: 15 EST: 1924
SQ FT: 38,000
SALES (est): 4MM **Privately Held**
WEB: www.flammpickle.com
SIC: 2035 Relishes, fruit & vegetable

Eben Junction
Alger County

(G-4978)
HALLSTROM COMPANY
M-94 W (49825)
P.O. Box 185 (49825-0185)
PHONE..................................906 439-5439
Edward Hallstrom, *President*
Ruth Hallstrom, *Vice Pres*
EMP: 7 EST: 1965
SQ FT: 3,500
SALES (est): 490.9K **Privately Held**
SIC: 3599 Machine shop, jobbing & repair

Ecorse
Wayne County

(G-4979)
A & S REEL & TACKLE INC
4420 High St (48229-1582)
PHONE..................................313 928-1667
Paul Rakecky, *President*
EMP: 5 EST: 1990
SQ FT: 1,500
SALES (est): 402.5K **Privately Held**
SIC: 3469 Metal stampings

(G-4980)
BLACKBERRY PUBLICATIONS
3915 11th St (48229-1303)
PHONE..................................313 627-1520
Darlene Runnels, *Owner*
EMP: 5 EST: 2007
SALES (est): 25K **Privately Held**
SIC: 2741 Miscellaneous publishing

(G-4981)
CDS SPECIALTY COATINGS LLC
4015 16th St (48229-1308)
PHONE..................................313 300-8997
Curtis Tamlin, *Mng Member*
Yvette Tamlin,
EMP: 7 EST: 2006
SALES (est): 518.7K **Privately Held**
WEB: www.danpolpainting.com
SIC: 3471 Plating & polishing

(G-4982)
DAMONDS MOBILE WELDING
36 Ridge St (48229-1723)
PHONE..................................313 932-4135
Damond Smith, *Principal*
EMP: 4 EST: 2019
SALES (est): 25K **Privately Held**
SIC: 7692 Welding repair

(G-4983)
LA AZTECA FOODS LLC
3748 W Jefferson Ave (48229-1898)
PHONE..................................313 413-2014
Hector Estrada,
EMP: 6 EST: 2011
SALES (est): 287.5K **Privately Held**
WEB: www.laaztecafoods.wordpress.com
SIC: 2051 Bakery: wholesale or wholesale/retail combined

(G-4984)
PAK-RITE INDUSTRIES INC
4270 High St (48229-1572)
PHONE..................................313 388-6400
Rory Renaud, *CEO*
Charles Lefler, *President*
Mike Lefler, *Corp Secy*
Joseph W Lefler, *Vice Pres*
James M Lefler, *Admin Sec*
◆ EMP: 80 EST: 1949
SQ FT: 3,000
SALES (est): 35.2MM **Privately Held**
WEB: www.pakrite.com
SIC: 4783 2674 Packing goods for shipping; crating goods for shipping; shipping bags or sacks, including multiwall & heavy duty

(G-4985)
SECORD SOLUTIONS LLC
240 Southfield Rd (48229-1130)
P.O. Box 456, Grosse Ile (48138-0456)
PHONE..................................734 363-8887
Alexandria Sroca, *Mng Member*
EMP: 5 EST: 2009
SALES (est): 262.2K **Privately Held**
WEB: www.secordsolutions.com
SIC: 8748 8711 3571 Systems engineering consultant, ex. computer or professional; consulting engineer; electronic computers

(G-4986)
STAR PAPER CONVERTERS
100 Labadie St (48229-1540)
PHONE..................................313 254-9833
EMP: 5 EST: 2016
SALES (est): 88.1K **Privately Held**
SIC: 2611 Pulp manufactured from waste or recycled paper

(G-4987)
TMS INTERNATIONAL LLC
1 Quality Dr (48229-1819)
PHONE..................................313 378-6502
EMP: 6 **Privately Held**
SIC: 3312 Blast Furnace-Steel Works
HQ: Tms International, Llc
Southside Wrks Bldg 1 3f
Pittsburgh PA 15203
412 678-6141

(G-4988)
TOMAR INC
3827 16th St (48229-1378)
PHONE..................................313 382-2293
Ronald Jones, *Principal*
EMP: 6 EST: 2017
SALES (est): 94.4K **Privately Held**
WEB: www.quartermasterusa.com
SIC: 3714 Motor vehicle parts & accessories

(G-4989)
XTRA-ORDINARY-YOU LLC ✪
4000 18th St (48229-1668)
PHONE..................................313 285-4472
Jamcia Basley,
EMP: 4 EST: 2021
SALES (est): 75K **Privately Held**
SIC: 2335 Women's, juniors' & misses' dresses

Edmore
Montcalm County

(G-4990)
CAMPBELL INDUSTRIAL FORCE LLC
Also Called: C I F
1380 Industrial Park Dr (48829-8399)
PHONE..................................989 427-0011
Rick Campbell, *Mng Member*
EMP: 23 EST: 2005 **Privately Held**
WEB: www.cifpackaging.com
SIC: 2631 Boxboard

(G-4991)
DOYLEN ALBRING JR
Also Called: Albring Auto Salvage
3873 E Edgar Rd (48829-9768)
PHONE..................................989 427-2919
Doyln Albring Jr, *President*
EMP: 4 EST: 1979
SALES (est): 249.6K **Privately Held**
SIC: 3312 Blast furnaces & steel mills

(G-4992)
EDMORE TOOL & GRINDING INC
Also Called: Cannon Vibrator Div
4255 E Hward Cy Edmore Rd (48829-9758)
PHONE..................................989 427-3790
Vic Johnson, *President*
EMP: 13 EST: 1978
SQ FT: 30,000
SALES (est): 1.9MM **Privately Held**
WEB: www.edmoretool.com
SIC: 3599 3451 3822 Grinding castings for the trade; screw machine products; pneumatic relays, air-conditioning type

(G-4993)
LAKELAND MILLS INC
1 Lakeland Pl (48829-8404)
PHONE..................................989 427-5133
Jason Hunt, *Vice Pres*
Keith Hunt, *Safety Mgr*
Jim Lahti, *Purch Mgr*
Teresa Hunt, *Finance Mgr*
Calvin Hunt, *Chief Mktg Ofcr*
▼ EMP: 49 EST: 1991
SQ FT: 113,000
SALES (est): 3.4MM **Privately Held**
WEB: www.lakelandmills.com
SIC: 3423 2511 Hand & edge tools; wood lawn & garden furniture

(G-4994)
PACKAGING CORPORATION AMERICA
Also Called: PCA/Edmore 321a
1106 Industrial Park Dr (48829-8396)
PHONE..................................989 427-2130
Connie Garner, *Controller*
Alan Garner, *Branch Mgr*
EMP: 8
SALES (corp-wide): 6.6B **Publicly Held**
WEB: www.packagingcorp.com
SIC: 2653 Boxes, corrugated: made from purchased materials
PA: Packaging Corporation Of America
1 N Field Ct
Lake Forest IL 60045
847 482-3000

(G-4995)
PACKAGING CORPORATION AMERICA
Also Called: PCA/Edmore 321
1106 Industrial Park Dr (48829-8396)
P.O. Box 80 (48829-0080)
PHONE..................................989 427-5129
Michael Tusing, *General Mgr*
Scott Gillespie, *Safety Mgr*
EMP: 5
SALES (corp-wide): 6.6B **Publicly Held**
WEB: www.packagingcorp.com
SIC: 2653 Boxes, corrugated: made from purchased materials
PA: Packaging Corporation Of America
1 N Field Ct
Lake Forest IL 60045
847 482-3000

(G-4996)
PRINT AND SAVE NOW
518 E Forest St (48829-9404)
PHONE..................................989 352-8171
James Cairns, *Principal*
EMP: 4 EST: 2015
SALES (est): 118.6K **Privately Held**
SIC: 2752 Commercial printing, lithographic

(G-4997)
RYANS EQUIPMENT INC
111 Quicksilver Ln (48829-7306)
P.O. Box 387 (48829-0387)
PHONE..................................989 427-2829
Don Ryan, *President*
Jill Ryan, *Vice Pres*
◆ EMP: 25 EST: 1996
SQ FT: 20,400
SALES (est): 3.7MM **Privately Held**
WEB: www.ryansequip.com
SIC: 3531 Construction machinery attachments

Edwardsburg
Cass County

(G-4998)
AB CUSTOM FABRICATING LLC
27531 May St (49112-9632)
PHONE..................................269 663-8100
Mike Brumitt,
EMP: 15 EST: 2005
SQ FT: 5,600
SALES (est): 1MM **Privately Held**
WEB: www.abcustomfabricating.com
SIC: 3479 3441 Coating of metals & formed products; fabricated structural metal

(G-4999)
BENTZER ENTERPRISES
26601 May St (49112-9652)
PHONE..................................269 663-2289
Karl Bentzer, *Principal*
EMP: 5 EST: 2005
SALES (est): 153.7K **Privately Held**
WEB: www.bentzerinc.com
SIC: 2295 Resin or plastic coated fabrics

(G-5000)
BENTZER INCORPORATED
69953 Section St (49112-8655)
PHONE..................................269 663-3649
Karl Bentzer, *President*
Ryan Bentzer, *Officer*
Kelsey Moreno, *Administration*
EMP: 17 EST: 2005
SALES (est): 4.7MM **Privately Held**
WEB: www.bentzerinc.com
SIC: 3089 Injection molding of plastics

(G-5001)
BROTHERS BAKING COMPANY
27260 Max St (49112-7615)
P.O. Box 680 (49112-0680)
PHONE..................................269 663-8591
Donald Wegner, *President*
Thomas Wegner, *Vice Pres*
EMP: 45 EST: 1987
SQ FT: 30,000
SALES (est): 13.3MM **Privately Held**
SIC: 2051 Cakes, bakery: except frozen

(G-5002)
CFB MICHIGAN INC
27450 May St (49112-8682)
PHONE..................................269 663-8855
John Ray, *CEO*
Tony Triplet, *Controller*
EMP: 8 EST: 2010
SALES (est): 496.6K **Privately Held**
SIC: 2911 Oils, lubricating

(G-5003)
CHRISTIANSON INDUSTRIES INC
27328 May St (49112-8681)
P.O. Box 549 (49112-0723)
PHONE..................................269 663-8502
Walter Smiles, *President*
Susan Klemm, *President*
EMP: 25 EST: 1973

▲ = Import ▼ = Export
◆ = Import/Export

GEOGRAPHIC SECTION
Elk Rapids - Antrim County (G-5029)

SQ FT: 15,000
SALES (est): 16.6MM **Privately Held**
WEB: www.skyox.com
SIC: 3354 Aluminum extruded products

(G-5004)
DANCORP INC
27496 Max St (49112-9664)
P.O. Box 157, Mead NE (68041-0157)
PHONE.................................269 663-5566
Dan Daniels, *President*
Lisa Lopez, *Principal*
EMP: 12 **EST:** 1991
SQ FT: 14,000
SALES (est): 2.2MM **Privately Held**
WEB: www.dancoh2o.com
SIC: 3589 Water treatment equipment, industrial

(G-5005)
DUO-FORM ACQUISITION CORP
Also Called: Duo-Form Plastics
69836 Kraus Rd (49112-9692)
PHONE.................................269 663-8525
George G Thomas, *President*
Glenn L Duncan, *Principal*
EMP: 151 **EST:** 1971
SQ FT: 5,000
SALES (est): 24.6MM **Privately Held**
WEB: www.duoformplastics.com
SIC: 3088 Tubs (bath, shower & laundry), plastic

(G-5006)
EXPRESSIVE WINDOW FASHIONS
69351 M 62 (49112-8676)
PHONE.................................269 663-8833
John Cesena, *Owner*
EMP: 4 **EST:** 2005
SALES (est): 50K **Privately Held**
SIC: 2591 5031 Window blinds; doors & windows

(G-5007)
MAJESTIC FORMED PLASTICS
69815 Brizendine St (49112-9178)
PHONE.................................269 663-2870
David Rheinheimer, *President*
EMP: 7 **EST:** 2016
SALES (est): 84.2K **Privately Held**
WEB: www.duoformplastics.com
SIC: 3089 Injection molding of plastics

(G-5008)
MALACHI PRINTING LLC
69936 Elkhart Rd (49112-8405)
PHONE.................................517 395-4813
Derek Fankhauser, *Owner*
EMP: 4 **EST:** 2016
SALES (est): 127.2K **Privately Held**
SIC: 2759 Screen printing

(G-5009)
MERCURY DISPLACEMENT INDS INC
Also Called: M D I
25028 Us 12 E (49112)
P.O. Box 710 (49112-0711)
PHONE.................................269 663-8574
Randy Brewers, *President*
▲ **EMP:** 75
SQ FT: 25,500
SALES (est): 16.2MM **Privately Held**
WEB: www.mdius.com
SIC: 3625 3822 3643 Relays, for electronic use; float controls, residential or commercial types; current-carrying wiring devices

(G-5010)
MICHIANA FORKLIFT
69735 Brizendine St (49112-8698)
P.O. Box 614 (49112-0614)
PHONE.................................269 663-2700
EMP: 5 **EST:** 2018
SALES (est): 109.4K **Privately Held**
WEB: www.michianaforklift.com
SIC: 3537 Forklift trucks

(G-5011)
MIDWEST TIMBER INC
190 Kraus Rd (49112)
P.O. Box 599 (49112-0579)
PHONE.................................269 663-5315

Edwin C Finley, *President*
Dick Opperman, *Vice Pres*
Richard L Opperman, *Vice Pres*
Dave Biek, *CFO*
Tiffany Jaynes, *Manager*
EMP: 50 **EST:** 1990
SALES (est): 18.6MM **Privately Held**
WEB: www.midwesttimber.com
SIC: 2421 Sawmills & planing mills, general; chipper mill

(G-5012)
MINLAND MACHINE INC
19801 Old 205 (49112-9756)
PHONE.................................269 641-7998
Fax: 269 641-7793
EMP: 8
SALES: 900K **Privately Held**
SIC: 3599 3559 Mfg Industrial Machinery Mfg Misc Industry Machinery

(G-5013)
NORTH AMERICAN FOREST PRODUCTS (HQ)
27263 May St (49112-8680)
P.O. Box 600 (49112-0580)
PHONE.................................269 663-8500
Jonh Robert Wiley II, *President*
Bob Wiley, *President*
Andrew Clark, *COO*
Mark Hardin, *Purchasing*
Tom Yoder, *Controller*
▲ **EMP:** 214 **EST:** 1989
SQ FT: 130,000
SALES (est): 52.3MM
SALES (corp-wide): 2.4B **Publicly Held**
WEB: www.nafpinc.com
SIC: 2421 5031 Resawing lumber into smaller dimensions; lumber: rough, sawed or planed; building & structural materials, wood; lumber: rough, dressed & finished
PA: Patrick Industries, Inc.
107 W Franklin St
Elkhart IN 46516
574 294-7511

(G-5014)
NORTH AMERICAN FOREST PRODUCTS
69708 Kraus Rd (49112-8474)
PHONE.................................269 663-8500
Tom Yoder, *Controller*
Larry Crandall, *Accountant*
Robert Wiley, *Manager*
Paul Probst, *Manager*
EMP: 6
SALES (corp-wide): 2.4B **Publicly Held**
WEB: www.nafpinc.com
SIC: 2421 2439 2431 2426 Sawmills & planing mills, general; structural wood members; millwork; hardwood dimension & flooring mills
HQ: North American Forest Products Liquidation, Inc.
27263 May St
Edwardsburg MI 49112
269 663-8500

(G-5015)
NORTH AMRCN MLDING LQDTION LLC (DH)
Also Called: North Amrcn Frest Pdts Lqdtion
70151 April St (49112-8485)
P.O. Box 600 (49112-0580)
PHONE.................................269 663-5300
Brett Lamont,
▲ **EMP:** 40 **EST:** 2002
SQ FT: 91,000
SALES (est): 26.6MM
SALES (corp-wide): 2.4B **Publicly Held**
WEB: www.nafpinc.com
SIC: 2431 Moldings, wood: unfinished & prefinished
HQ: North American Forest Products Liquidation, Inc.
27263 May St
Edwardsburg MI 49112
269 663-8500

(G-5016)
SINDELAR FINE WOODWORKING CO
69953 Section St (49112-8655)
PHONE.................................269 663-8841

EMP: 4 **EST:** 2019
SALES (est): 95.6K **Privately Held**
SIC: 2431 Millwork

(G-5017)
ST EVANS INC
27383 May St (49112-8681)
PHONE.................................269 663-6100
Ronald Evans, *President*
▲ **EMP:** 8 **EST:** 1981
SQ FT: 6,400
SALES (est): 773.3K **Privately Held**
WEB: www.fireworksplus.com
SIC: 5092 2899 Toys & games; toy novelties & amusements; fireworks; fireworks

(G-5018)
SUNSET COAST PUBLISHING LLC
25526 Joelle Ct (49112-8212)
PHONE.................................574 440-3228
Donald Harty, *Principal*
EMP: 4 **EST:** 2017
SALES (est): 59.2K **Privately Held**
SIC: 2741 Miscellaneous publishing

(G-5019)
T AND A WELDING
21660 Mason St (49112-9744)
PHONE.................................269 228-1268
EMP: 4 **EST:** 2019
SALES (est): 141K **Privately Held**
SIC: 7692 Welding repair

(G-5020)
VILLAGE AUTOMATICS INC
69576 Section St (49112-8607)
P.O. Box 617 (49112-0617)
PHONE.................................269 663-8521
Kenneth Strickland, *President*
Patty Strickland, *Treasurer*
EMP: 8 **EST:** 1989
SQ FT: 14,000
SALES (est): 418.2K **Privately Held**
WEB: www.villageautomatics.com
SIC: 3599 Machine shop, jobbing & repair

Elk Rapids
Antrim County

(G-5021)
BOKHARA PET CARE CENTERS (PA)
Also Called: Bokhara's Grooming
11535 S Elk Lake Rd (49629)
P.O. Box 175 (49629-0175)
PHONE.................................231 264-6667
Richard Smith, *Owner*
Shen Smith, *Co-Owner*
EMP: 11 **EST:** 1974
SQ FT: 15,000
SALES (est): 500K **Privately Held**
WEB: www.bokharapetresort.com
SIC: 0752 7372 Boarding services, kennels; grooming services, pet & animal specialties; application computer software

(G-5022)
BURNETTE FOODS INC (PA)
701 S Us Highway 31 (49629-9525)
P.O. Box 128 (49629-0128)
PHONE.................................231 264-8116
William R Sherman, *President*
John Pelizzari, *COO*
Theresa Bott, *Vice Pres*
Robert Sherman, *Vice Pres*
Clint Warren, *Plant Mgr*
◆ **EMP:** 60 **EST:** 1969
SALES (est): 95.5MM **Privately Held**
WEB: www.burnettefoods.com
SIC: 2033 Fruit juices: packaged in cans, jars, etc.

(G-5023)
ELK LAKE TOOL CO
203 Ec Loomis Dr (49629-9501)
P.O. Box 79 (49629-0079)
PHONE.................................231 264-5616
Jerald C Rives, *President*
Sharon Rives, *Admin Sec*
EMP: 26 **EST:** 1965
SQ FT: 7,500

SALES (est): 1.3MM **Privately Held**
WEB: www.elklaketool.com
SIC: 3545 3555 Cutting tools for machine tools; printing trades machinery

(G-5024)
ELK RAPIDS ENGINEERING INC
210 Industrial Park Dr (49629-9452)
P.O. Box 728 (49629-0728)
PHONE.................................231 264-5661
Bradley Lawton, *President*
Martin Woodhouse, *Vice Pres*
EMP: 19 **EST:** 1969
SQ FT: 25,000
SALES (est): 2.8MM
SALES (corp-wide): 204.2MM **Privately Held**
WEB: www.elkrapids.org
SIC: 3541 Machine tools, metal cutting type
PA: Star Cutter Co.
23461 Industrial Park Dr
Farmington Hills MI 48335
248 474-8200

(G-5025)
GRACE METAL PRODUCTS INC
Also Called: Grace USA
115 Ames St (49629-9800)
P.O. Box 67 (49629-0067)
PHONE.................................231 264-8133
Daniel D Morrison, *President*
Linda K Morrison, *Vice Pres*
EMP: 4 **EST:** 1940
SQ FT: 1,500
SALES (est): 401.1K **Privately Held**
WEB: www.graceusatools.com
SIC: 3423 Tools or equipment for use with sporting arms

(G-5026)
GREAT LAKES PWR GENERATION LLC
112 N Brand St (49629-9752)
PHONE.................................231 492-3764
Kaid Brookshire, *Principal*
EMP: 5 **EST:** 2019
SALES (est): 306.8K **Privately Held**
SIC: 3621 Power generators

(G-5027)
MICHIGAN MAPS INC
104 Dexter St (49629-5102)
P.O. Box 885 (49629-0885)
PHONE.................................231 264-6800
Mark Stone, *Principal*
EMP: 8 **EST:** 2011
SALES (est): 184.5K **Privately Held**
WEB: www.michiganmaps.net
SIC: 2711 Newspapers, publishing & printing

(G-5028)
NORTH COUNTRY POWER GENERATION
121 Ames St (49629-9739)
PHONE.................................231 499-3951
Jim Brookshaire, *Manager*
EMP: 7 **EST:** 2018
SALES (est): 253.2K **Privately Held**
WEB: www.ncpgeneration.com
SIC: 3621 Power generators

(G-5029)
TRAVERSE BAY MANUFACTURING INC
8980 Cairn Hwy (49629-9453)
P.O. Box 548 (49629-0548)
PHONE.................................231 264-8111
Mark Toteff, *President*
Chad Toteff, *Exec VP*
Deb Stoianoff, *QC Mgr*
EMP: 79 **EST:** 1989
SQ FT: 16,000
SALES (est): 5.6MM **Privately Held**
WEB: www.tbmfg.com
SIC: 2326 2329 2339 Men's & boys' work clothing; men's & boys' sportswear & athletic clothing; men's & boys' leather, wool & down-filled outerwear; women's & misses' outerwear

Elk Rapids - Antrim County (G-5030)

(G-5030)
TRELLEBORG SEALING SOLUTIONS
222 Industrial Park Dr (49629-9452)
PHONE....................231 264-0087
EMP: 85
SALES (corp-wide): 3.8B Privately Held
WEB: www.trelleborg.com
SIC: 3841 Surgical & medical instruments
HQ: Trelleborg Sealing Solutions Us, Inc.
   2761 Walnut Ave
   Tustin CA 92780

Elkton
Huron County

(G-5031)
HOT RODS BBQ SERVICES
2726 Hartsell Rd (48731-9713)
PHONE....................989 375-2191
Rodney Husk, *Owner*
EMP: 5 EST: 2017
SALES (est): 76.7K Privately Held
WEB: www.hotrodscatering.com
SIC: 2656 Sanitary food containers

(G-5032)
SCHUETTE FARMS
2679 N Elkton Rd (48731-9730)
PHONE....................989 550-0563
Dale Schuette,
EMP: 9 EST: 2014
SALES (est): 459K Privately Held
SIC: 3523 2063 2051 2046 Planting, haying, harvesting & processing machinery; granulated sugar from sugar beets; bread, all types (white, wheat, rye, etc); fresh or frozen; wet corn milling; soybeans

(G-5033)
TOWER ATMTIVE OPRTONS USA I LL
81 Drettman St (48731-5109)
P.O. Box 67 (48731-0067)
PHONE....................989 375-2201
Ellen Moorman, *Branch Mgr*
EMP: 100
SQ FT: 500,000
SALES (corp-wide): 3.1B Privately Held
WEB: www.autokiniton.com
SIC: 3465 Automotive stampings
HQ: Tower Automotive Operations Usa I, Llc
   17757 Woodland Dr
   New Boston MI 48164

(G-5034)
WELDALL CORPORATION
2295 Hartsell Rd (48731-9601)
PHONE....................989 375-2251
Gary Gardner, *President*
James Neurath, *Treasurer*
Ellis Gardner, *Admin Sec*
EMP: 5 EST: 1962
SQ FT: 9,000
SALES (est): 268K Privately Held
WEB: www.weldallcorp.com
SIC: 3356 Nonferrous rolling & drawing

Ellsworth
Antrim County

(G-5035)
DTS ENTERPRISES INC
Also Called: Time Machines Unlimited
9910 N Us Highway 31 (49729-9720)
PHONE....................231 599-3123
David L Draper, *President*
EMP: 38 EST: 1989
SALES (est): 4.8MM Privately Held
WEB: www.dts-marine.com
SIC: 7538 8711 3499 3444 General automotive repair shops; marine engineering; marine horns, compressed air or steam; restaurant sheet metalwork; upholstery & trim shop, automotive

(G-5036)
GRAND TRAVERSE ASSEMBLY INC
Also Called: Grand Traverse Pallet
7161 Essex Rd (49729-9713)
PHONE....................231 588-2406
Michael Rottman, *President*
EMP: 20 EST: 2000
SQ FT: 20,000
SALES (est): 1.3MM Privately Held
WEB: www.gtpallet.net
SIC: 2421 Sawmills & planing mills, general

(G-5037)
THOMAS COOPER
Also Called: Rocky Top Farm's
11486 Essex Rd (49729-9650)
PHONE....................231 599-2251
EMP: 4
SQ FT: 5,000
SALES (est): 313.9K Privately Held
SIC: 5961 2033 0171 0175 Mfg Canned Fruits/Vegetables Ret Mail-Order House Fruit Tree Orchard Berry Crop Farm

Elmira
Otsego County

(G-5038)
BEISHLAG WELDING LLC
3935 Buell Rd (49730-9734)
PHONE....................231 881-5023
Garret Beishlag, *Principal*
EMP: 6 EST: 2016
SALES (est): 88.7K Privately Held
SIC: 7692 Welding repair

(G-5039)
MAXIMUM OILFIELD SERVICE INC
7929 Alba Hwy (49730-8767)
PHONE....................989 731-0099
Randy Odell, *President*
EMP: 40 EST: 1996
SALES (est): 2.5MM Privately Held
SIC: 1389 Oil field services

(G-5040)
PARIS NORTH HARDWOOD LUMBER
Also Called: Silvery Sawmill
542 Tobias Rd (49730-8234)
PHONE....................231 584-2500
William Lenau, *President*
EMP: 16 EST: 1990
SQ FT: 35,000
SALES (est): 1.6MM Privately Held
WEB: www.silverleafsawmill.business.site
SIC: 2421 2491 2426 Lumber: rough, sawed or planed; wood preserving; hardwood dimension & flooring mills

Elwell
Gratiot County

(G-5041)
NELSON FARMS
7530 Madison Rd (48832-9732)
PHONE....................989 560-1303
Thomas R Nelson, *Owner*
EMP: 6 EST: 1973
SALES (est): 108.9K Privately Held
SIC: 3523 Driers (farm): grain, hay & seed

Empire
Leelanau County

(G-5042)
STEEL APPEAL
12100 S Plowman Rd (49630-8501)
PHONE....................231 326-6116
EMP: 6 EST: 2016
SALES (est): 348.3K Privately Held
WEB: www.steelappeal.com
SIC: 3499 Fabricated metal products

Engadine
Mackinac County

(G-5043)
FERGIN & ASSOCIATES INC
Pk N9263 Kraus Rd (49827)
PHONE....................906 477-0040
Glenn E Fergin, *President*
Earl G Fergin, *Vice Pres*
Dorothy J Burgett, *Treasurer*
Ruth A Fergin, *Admin Sec*
EMP: 4 EST: 1993
SALES (est): 300K Privately Held
WEB: www.fergin.com
SIC: 3569 Filters

Erie
Monroe County

(G-5044)
AUTOMATIC HANDLING INTL INC
360 La Voy Rd (48133-9436)
PHONE....................734 847-0633
David J Pienta, *President*
David Baldwin, *Principal*
Lee Brockman, *Exec VP*
Amy Flowers, *Vice Pres*
Andy Pienta, *Vice Pres*
▲ EMP: 75 EST: 2000
SQ FT: 100,000
SALES (est): 21.3MM Privately Held
WEB: www.automatichandling.com
SIC: 3535 Conveyors & conveying equipment

(G-5045)
BEDFORD MACHINERY INC
9899 Telegraph Rd (48133-9750)
PHONE....................734 848-4980
Vincent Fuleky, *President*
Donna Fuleky, *Corp Secy*
EMP: 5 EST: 1969
SQ FT: 2,000
SALES (est): 525.5K Privately Held
SIC: 3799 3599 Trailers & trailer equipment; automobile trailer chassis; boat trailers; machine shop, jobbing & repair

(G-5046)
CONCENTRIC INDUSTRIES INC
Also Called: R D Tool & Mfg
720 La Voy Rd (48133-9665)
PHONE....................734 848-5133
Thomas Lingle, *President*
Michael Penn, *Vice Pres*
Tom L Lingle, *Manager*
Mark Lingle, *Maintence Staff*
EMP: 29 EST: 1987
SQ FT: 36,000
SALES (est): 1.5MM Privately Held
WEB: www.rdtoolmfg.com
SIC: 3599 Machine shop, jobbing & repair

(G-5047)
ECOQUEST INTL INDEPENDENT
10950 Strasburg Rd (48133-9796)
PHONE....................734 854-6080
Luanne Rogoff, *Principal*
EMP: 5 EST: 2005
SALES (est): 128.8K Privately Held
SIC: 3564 Air cleaning systems

(G-5048)
INSTACOTE INC
160 La Voy Rd Ste C (48133-9412)
PHONE....................734 847-5260
Tom Nachtman, *President*
EMP: 4 EST: 1992
SALES (est): 491.2K Privately Held
WEB: www.instacote.com
SIC: 3479 Coating of metals with plastic or resins

(G-5049)
LIEDEL POWER CLEANING
2850 Luna Pier Rd (48133)
PHONE....................734 848-2827
Brad Liedel, *Owner*
Beth Liedel, *Co-Owner*
EMP: 5 EST: 1987
SALES (est): 370K Privately Held
WEB: www.liedelpowerwashingandpainting.com
SIC: 2842 7349 8999 Specialty cleaning preparations; cleaning service, industrial or commercial; artists & artists' studios

(G-5050)
M & F MACHINE & TOOL INC
6555 S Dixie Hwy (48133-9691)
PHONE....................734 847-0571
Mark D Milano, *President*
Robert J Milano, *Corp Secy*
Michael A Milano, *Vice Pres*
EMP: 20 EST: 1972
SQ FT: 40,000
SALES (est): 1.2MM Privately Held
WEB: www.mfmachine.com
SIC: 3599 3544 3549 Custom machinery; special dies, tools, jigs & fixtures; metalworking machinery

(G-5051)
MATNEY MODELS
10765 Victory Rd (48133-9324)
PHONE....................734 848-8195
Candy Matney, *Principal*
EMP: 5 EST: 2008
SALES (est): 98.3K Privately Held
SIC: 3999 Manufacturing industries

(G-5052)
ORT TOOL & DIE CORPORATION (PA)
Also Called: O R T
6555 S Dixie Hwy (48133-9691)
P.O. Box 5008, Toledo OH (43611-0008)
PHONE....................419 242-9553
Jim Shock, *CEO*
Angelo J Milano, *Ch of Bd*
Robert Milano, *President*
Michael A Milano, *Vice Pres*
Matt Baird, *Project Engr*
EMP: 70 EST: 1958
SQ FT: 100,000
SALES (est): 25.5MM Privately Held
WEB: www.orttool.com
SIC: 8711 3544 3469 Machine tool design; industrial engineers; special dies, tools, jigs & fixtures; machine parts, stamped or pressed metal

(G-5053)
PRECISION MASKING INC
721 La Voy Rd (48133-9665)
PHONE....................734 848-4200
Mary F Waters, *Corp Secy*
Richard D Waters, *Vice Pres*
EMP: 20 EST: 1985
SQ FT: 9,600
SALES (est): 3.7MM Privately Held
WEB: www.precisionmasking.com
SIC: 3544 3563 Special dies & tools; spraying & dusting equipment

(G-5054)
PROSERVICE MACHINE LTD
10835 Telegraph Rd (48133-9749)
PHONE....................734 317-7266
James Francis, *Owner*
Brandon Bihn,
EMP: 18 EST: 2004
SQ FT: 2,600
SALES (est): 2MM Privately Held
WEB: www.proservicemachine.com
SIC: 3312 Tool & die steel & alloys

(G-5055)
TNT PIPE AND TUBE LLC
640 Lavoy Rd (48133)
PHONE....................419 466-1144
Nick Williams, *President*
Michael Dustmann, *Treasurer*
Josh Dotson, *Asst Sec*
EMP: 20 EST: 2019
SALES: 3.6MM
SALES (corp-wide): 230MM Privately Held
WEB: www.heidtmantubular.com
SIC: 3312 Pipes & tubes
HQ: Heidtman Steel Products, Inc.
   2401 Front St
   Toledo OH 43605
   419 691-4646

GEOGRAPHIC SECTION

Escanaba - Delta County (G-5083)

Escanaba
Delta County

(G-5056)
ANDEX INDUSTRIES INC
Also Called: Andex Printing Division
2300 20th Ave N (49829-9317)
PHONE..................906 786-7588
Joel Sargent, *Engineer*
Lori Brayak, *Sales Staff*
Joseph Menard, *Sales Executive*
Tom Uelmen, *Branch Mgr*
Laura Lemire, *Representative*
EMP: 30
SALES (corp-wide): 12MM **Privately Held**
WEB: www.andex.net
SIC: 2752 2671 Commercial printing, offset; packaging paper & plastics film, coated & laminated
PA: Andex Industries, Inc.
1911 4th Ave N
Escanaba MI 49829
800 338-9882

(G-5057)
ANTHONY AND COMPANY
1503 N 23rd St (49829-1848)
P.O. Box 887 (49829-0887)
PHONE..................906 786-7573
David Anthony, *President*
Mary A Sherman, *Shareholder*
Eileen Vocke, *Shareholder*
John T Anthony, *Admin Sec*
◆ **EMP:** 15 **EST:** 1946
SQ FT: 22,349
SALES (est): 1.5MM **Privately Held**
WEB: www.anthonyco.com
SIC: 2499 Paint sticks, wood; yard sticks, wood

(G-5058)
APS MACHINE LLC
2501 Danforth Rd (49829-2566)
PHONE..................906 212-5600
Christopher Doyle, *President*
Sarah Doyle, *Opers Staff*
EMP: 10 **EST:** 2012
SQ FT: 10,000
SALES (est): 2.1MM **Privately Held**
WEB: www.apsmachine.com
SIC: 2295 Metallizing of fabrics

(G-5059)
BACH MOBILITIES INC
1617 N 28th St (49829-2513)
PHONE..................906 789-9490
Donald Fehrenbach, *President*
Bernice Fehrenbach, *Corp Secy*
EMP: 4
SALES (est): 300K **Privately Held**
WEB: www.bachmobilitiesinc.com
SIC: 3999 Wheelchair lifts

(G-5060)
BELLS BREWERY INC
Upper Hand Brewery
3525 Airport Rd (49829-1096)
PHONE..................906 233-5002
Sam Reese, *Director*
EMP: 16
SALES (corp-wide): 21.6MM **Privately Held**
WEB: www.bellsbeer.com
SIC: 2082 Beer (alcoholic beverage)
PA: Bell's Brewery, Inc.
8690 Krum Ave
Galesburg MI 49053
269 382-2338

(G-5061)
BELTONE SKORIC HEARNG AID CNTR
3600 Ludington St (49829-4220)
PHONE..................906 553-4660
EMP: 4 **EST:** 2015
SALES (est): 94.1K **Privately Held**
WEB: www.beltoneskorichearing.com
SIC: 7629 3842 Lamp repair & mounting; absorbent cotton, sterilized

(G-5062)
BICHLER GRAVEL & CONCRETE CO
6851 County 426 M.5 Rd (49829-9559)
P.O. Box 263 (49829-0263)
PHONE..................906 786-0343
Thomas L Brayak, *President*
Terry Brayak, *Vice Pres*
Karen Meiers, *Admin Sec*
EMP: 10 **EST:** 1900
SALES (est): 3.4MM **Privately Held**
WEB: www.bichlerconcrete.com
SIC: 3273 5032 Ready-mixed concrete; stone, crushed or broken; sand, construction; gravel

(G-5063)
BINKS COCA-COLA BOTTLING CO (PA)
3001 Danforth Rd (49829-2576)
PHONE..................906 786-4144
Robert N Bink, *President*
Mildred Bink, *Corp Secy*
Nicolas Bink, *Corp Secy*
EMP: 23 **EST:** 1903
SQ FT: 45,000
SALES (est): 5.2MM **Privately Held**
WEB: www.binksbeverages.com
SIC: 2086 Bottled & canned soft drinks

(G-5064)
CAL GRINDING INC (PA)
1401 N 26th St Stop 16 (49829-2500)
PHONE..................906 786-8749
Marc Calouette, *President*
Fred Caluhette, *Vice Pres*
Mike Calouette, *Treasurer*
EMP: 32 **EST:** 1988
SQ FT: 50,000
SALES (est): 3MM **Privately Held**
WEB: www.calvalves.com
SIC: 3592 3494 3471 Valves, engine; valves & pipe fittings; plating & polishing

(G-5065)
CLARE BEDDING MFG CO
433 Stephenson Ave (49829-2733)
P.O. Box 528 (49829-0528)
PHONE..................906 789-9902
Donald Balsavich, *President*
Tim Angsten, *Corp Secy*
Mike Angsten, *Vice Pres*
Evelyn St Ours, *Manager*
EMP: 33 **EST:** 1936
SQ FT: 49,000
SALES (est): 6.2MM **Privately Held**
WEB: www.clarebedding.com
SIC: 2515 Mattresses, innerspring or box spring; furniture springs

(G-5066)
DELTA WELDING SERVICES
411413 75th Rd (49829)
PHONE..................906 786-4348
Art A Menard, *Principal*
EMP: 5 **EST:** 2002
SALES (est): 35K **Privately Held**
SIC: 7692 Welding repair

(G-5067)
EMP ADVANCED DEVELOPMENT LLC
Also Called: Research and Development Off
2701 N 30th St (49829-9318)
PHONE..................906 789-7497
Brian Larche,
David Allen,
Paul Harvey,
EMP: 1 **EST:** 2005
SALES (est): 1.4MM **Privately Held**
WEB: www.emp-corp.com
SIC: 8711 3561 Engineering services; pumps & pumping equipment
PA: Engineered Machined Products, Inc.
3111 N 28th St
Escanaba MI 49829

(G-5068)
EMP RACING INC
Also Called: Stewart Components
2701 N 30th St (49829-9318)
P.O. Box 1246 (49829-6246)
PHONE..................906 786-8404
Brian Larche, *Ch of Bd*
▲ **EMP:** 6 **EST:** 2000
SALES (est): 746.6K **Privately Held**
WEB: www.stewartcomponents.com
SIC: 3519 3694 Internal combustion engines; ignition systems, high frequency

(G-5069)
ENGINEERED MACHINED PDTS INC (PA)
Also Called: E M P
3111 N 28th St (49829-9324)
P.O. Box 1246 (49829-6246)
PHONE..................906 786-8404
Brian K Larche, *CEO*
Mark Bader, *Vice Pres*
Jerry Guindon, *Vice Pres*
Ray Lanarche, *CFO*
Paul Harvey, *Admin Sec*
◆ **EMP:** 350 **EST:** 1981
SQ FT: 250,000
SALES (est): 103.7MM **Privately Held**
WEB: www.emp-corp.com
SIC: 3519 3714 3568 3599 Internal combustion engines; water pump, motor vehicle; pulleys, power transmission; air intake filters, internal combustion engine, except auto; pumps & pumping equipment

(G-5070)
ESCANABA AND LK SUPERIOR RR CO
Also Called: Car Shop
1401 N 26th St Bldg 20 (49829-2500)
PHONE..................906 786-9399
Mike Pratt, *Manager*
EMP: 9
SALES (corp-wide): 8.6MM **Privately Held**
WEB: www.elsrr.com
SIC: 4789 7692 Railroad car repair; welding repair
PA: Escanaba And Lake Superior Railroad Company
1 Larkin Plz
Wells MI 49894
906 786-0693

(G-5071)
EXPRESS WELDING INC
2525 14th Ave N (49829-1776)
PHONE..................906 786-8808
Duane Scheuren, *President*
Patricia Scheuren, *Corp Secy*
EMP: 4 **EST:** 1983
SQ FT: 44,000
SALES (est): 464.6K **Privately Held**
WEB: www.express-welding.com
SIC: 7692 3715 3523 Welding repair; truck trailers; farm machinery & equipment

(G-5072)
GENESIS GRAPHICS INC
1823 7th Ave N Ste 7 (49829-1421)
PHONE..................906 786-4913
Michael Olsen, *President*
EMP: 7 **EST:** 1976
SALES (est): 539K **Privately Held**
WEB: www.genesisgraphicsinc.com
SIC: 2759 Screen printing

(G-5073)
GIGUERE LOGGING INC
3200 5th Ave S (49829-4324)
PHONE..................906 786-3975
Edward Giguere, *President*
EMP: 8 **EST:** 1978
SALES (est): 813.7K **Privately Held**
SIC: 2411 Logging camps & contractors

(G-5074)
GREGG PUBLISHING CO
413 S 7th St (49829-3715)
PHONE..................906 789-1139
Robert Gregg, *Principal*
EMP: 5 **EST:** 2016
SALES (est): 37.5K **Privately Held**
SIC: 2741 Miscellaneous publishing

(G-5075)
HEED INDUSTRIES
2520 1st Ave S (49829-1311)
PHONE..................906 233-7192
Travis Godfrey, *Principal*
EMP: 5 **EST:** 2014
SALES (est): 47.5K **Privately Held**
SIC: 3999 Manufacturing industries

(G-5076)
HJ MANUFACTURING INC
Also Called: Delta Manufacturing
3707 19th Ave N (49829-2525)
PHONE..................906 233-1500
Harold Ross, *CEO*
Jean R Ross, *President*
Steve Coble, *Sales Staff*
▲ **EMP:** 11 **EST:** 2006
SALES (est): 2.4MM **Privately Held**
WEB: www.deltawheeltruingsolutions.net
SIC: 3479 8711 5088 3743 Painting of metal products; engineering services; railroad equipment & supplies; railroad equipment

(G-5077)
INDEPENDENT MACHINE CO INC
Also Called: IMC
2501 Danforth Rd (49829-2566)
PHONE..................906 428-4524
Chris Doyle, *President*
Jim Calouette, *Vice Pres*
Dave Phalen, *Plant Mgr*
Todd Palzewicz, *Prdtn Mgr*
Mark Wyman, *Controller*
EMP: 30 **EST:** 2014
SQ FT: 50,000
SALES (est): 4.4MM **Privately Held**
WEB: www.imc-info.com
SIC: 3537 3531 3599 Pallets, metal; railroad related equipment; machine & other job shop work

(G-5078)
JD MACHINE
6614 N.75 Dr (49829-9325)
PHONE..................906 233-7420
EMP: 12 **EST:** 2013
SALES (est): 125.3K **Privately Held**
WEB: www.jdmachine.com
SIC: 3599 Machine shop, jobbing & repair

(G-5079)
JOHNSTON PRINTING & OFFSET
711 Ludington St (49829-3802)
PHONE..................906 786-1493
James Mc Donough, *President*
Bonnie Mc Donough, *Corp Secy*
EMP: 4 **EST:** 1929
SQ FT: 2,400
SALES (est): 400K **Privately Held**
WEB: www.johnstonprinting.net
SIC: 2752 Commercial printing, offset

(G-5080)
LEIGHS GARDEN WINERY INC
209 S 12th St (49829-3427)
PHONE..................906 553-7799
Leigh Schmidt, *Principal*
EMP: 5 **EST:** 2008
SALES (est): 256.7K **Privately Held**
WEB: www.leighsgarden.com
SIC: 2084 Wines

(G-5081)
LLOYD JOHNSON LIVESTOCK INC
3697 18th Rd (49829-9715)
PHONE..................906 786-4878
Lloyd Johnson, *President*
EMP: 13 **EST:** 1990
SALES (est): 139.6K **Privately Held**
SIC: 2011 Meat packing plants

(G-5082)
MEAD WESTVACO PAPER DIV
1800 20th Ave N (49829-9500)
P.O. Box 757 (49829-0757)
PHONE..................906 233-2362
Keith Vanscotter, *President*
EMP: 9 **EST:** 1987
SALES (est): 136.5K **Privately Held**
SIC: 2672 Coated & laminated paper

(G-5083)
MECHANCAL SUP A DIV NTHRN MCHN
1701 N 26th St (49829-2558)
PHONE..................906 789-0355
John Liss, *President*

Escanaba - Delta County (G-5084)

EMP: 10 EST: 1981
SQ FT: 2,200
SALES (est): 285.2K Privately Held
WEB: www.northernmachining.com
SIC: 5085 7692 Seals, industrial; packing, industrial; welding repair

(G-5084)
MEIERS SIGNS INC
1717 N Lincoln Rd (49829-2504)
P.O. Box 441 (49829-0441)
PHONE..................................906 786-3424
Joseph Twa, *Owner*
Karen Twa, *Partner*
EMP: 6 EST: 1925
SQ FT: 5,000
SALES (est): 631.3K Privately Held
WEB: www.meiers-signs.com
SIC: 1731 7389 1799 3993 Electrical work; sign painting & lettering shop; sign installation & maintenance; electric signs

(G-5085)
MERCHANT HOLDINGS INC
440 N 10th St (49829-3837)
PHONE..................................906 786-7120
Terrie Peters, *Exec Dir*
EMP: 5 EST: 2009
SALES (est): 227.7K Privately Held
SIC: 3731 Shipbuilding & repairing

(G-5086)
NEUMEIER LOGGING INC
700 Stephenson Ave (49829-1418)
P.O. Box 278 (49829-0278)
PHONE..................................906 786-5242
EMP: 6
SALES (est): 385.6K Privately Held
SIC: 2411 Logging

(G-5087)
NK DOCKSIDE SERVICE & REPAIR
1014 8th Ave S (49829-3214)
PHONE..................................906 420-0777
Nicholas Kobasic, *Partner*
EMP: 6 EST: 2012
SALES (est): 232.4K Privately Held
SIC: 3731 Shipbuilding & repairing

(G-5088)
NORTHERN MACHINING & REPR INC
1701 N 26th St (49829-2558)
PHONE..................................906 786-0526
Jon Liss, *President*
Melisa Johnson, *General Mgr*
Jason Lofquist, *Vice Pres*
Andy Butryn, *Sales Mgr*
Dick Liberty, *Sales Mgr*
EMP: 39 EST: 1999
SQ FT: 40,000
SALES (est): 9.5MM Privately Held
WEB: www.northernmachining.com
SIC: 3599 3443 7692 3444 Machine shop, jobbing & repair; fabricated plate work (boiler shop); welding repair; sheet metalwork; fabricated structural metal

(G-5089)
PHOTO OFFSET INC
Also Called: Photo-Offset Printing
109 S Lincoln Rd (49829-1339)
P.O. Box 128 (49829-0128)
PHONE..................................906 786-5800
EMP: 5 EST: 1951
SQ FT: 1,200
SALES (est): 490K Privately Held
SIC: 2752 Offset Printer

(G-5090)
PLUM CREEK TIMBER COMPANY INC
Also Called: Nepko Lake Nursery
2831 N Lincoln Rd (49829-9569)
PHONE..................................715 453-7952
EMP: 6
SALES (corp-wide): 1.4B Publicly Held
SIC: 5099 2411 Whol Durable Goods Logging
PA: Plum Creek Timber Company Inc
601 Union St Ste 3100
Seattle WA 98101
206 467-3600

(G-5091)
PRECISION PLUS
6911 County 426 M.5 Rd (49829-8500)
PHONE..................................906 553-7900
Travis Gogfrey, *Owner*
EMP: 6 EST: 2012
SALES (est): 241.5K Privately Held
WEB: www.precisionplusmfg.com
SIC: 3549 Metalworking machinery

(G-5092)
PRS & PIP FTRS L 506
2601 N 30th St (49829-9204)
PHONE..................................906 789-9784
EMP: 8 EST: 2010
SALES (est): 76.9K Privately Held
WEB: www.lu111.com
SIC: 2741 Miscellaneous publishing

(G-5093)
QUARRYSTONE INC
6851 County 426 M.5 Rd (49829-9559)
PHONE..................................906 786-0343
Leonora Doonan, *President*
Cory Pangborn, *President*
EMP: 21 EST: 2018
SALES (est): 1.2MM Privately Held
SIC: 3273 Ready-mixed concrete

(G-5094)
RACE RAMPS LLC
Also Called: Brute Industries
2003 23rd Ave N Ste A (49829-2533)
PHONE..................................866 464-2788
David Buslee, *CFO*
Eric Lucas, *Technology*
EMP: 15 EST: 2019
SALES (est): 2MM Privately Held
WEB: www.raceramps.com
SIC: 3559 Automotive related machinery

(G-5095)
RICHARDS PRINTING
718 Ludington St (49829-3829)
PHONE..................................906 786-3540
Bette L Richards, *Owner*
EMP: 4 EST: 1909
SQ FT: 1,900
SALES (est): 303.3K Privately Held
SIC: 2752 Commercial printing, offset

(G-5096)
RNJ SERVICES INC
2003 23rd Ave N Ste A (49829-2533)
PHONE..................................906 786-0585
Richard Heinz, *President*
EMP: 16 EST: 2004
SALES (est): 2.5MM Privately Held
SIC: 3559 Automotive maintenance equipment

(G-5097)
RT MANUFACTURING INC
2522 14th Ave N (49829-1792)
PHONE..................................906 233-9158
Robert Triest, *President*
EMP: 10 EST: 2004
SQ FT: 35,000
SALES (est): 1MM Privately Held
WEB: www.rtmanufacturing.net
SIC: 3441 Fabricated structural metal

(G-5098)
SHESKI LOGGING
2875 18th Rd (49829-9737)
PHONE..................................906 786-1886
John Sheski, *Principal*
EMP: 5 EST: 2009
SALES (est): 110.1K Privately Held
SIC: 2411 Logging

(G-5099)
SIGN UP INC
Also Called: Sign Up Schumann Outdoor Arts
1300 Ludington St (49829-2844)
PHONE..................................906 789-7446
Peggy Schumann, *President*
Terry Schumann, *Vice Pres*
EMP: 5 EST: 1986
SALES (est): 125K Privately Held
WEB: www.signupprinting.espwebsite.com
SIC: 3993 Signs, not made in custom sign painting shops

(G-5100)
SM & AM ENTERPRISE INC
Also Called: Northern Screen Printing & EMB
1001 Ludington St (49829-3501)
PHONE..................................906 786-0373
Frank Bink, *Partner*
EMP: 5 EST: 1995
SALES (est): 470.5K Privately Held
WEB: www.northernscreen.com
SIC: 5699 2759 Miscellaneous apparel & accessories; screen printing

(G-5101)
STEWART KNIVES LLC
6911 County 426 M.5 Rd (49829-8500)
PHONE..................................906 789-1801
Lesley Stewart, *Mng Member*
Mike Stewart, *Mng Member*
Jackilyn Stewart,
James Stewart,
EMP: 40 EST: 2008
SQ FT: 17,000
SALES (est): 4MM Privately Held
SIC: 3421 5091 Knives: butchers', hunting, pocket, etc.; hunting equipment & supplies

(G-5102)
T D VINETTE COMPANY
Also Called: Vinette Boatworks
1212 N 19th St (49829-1630)
P.O. Box 416 (49829-0416)
PHONE..................................906 786-1884
Dan Branson, *President*
EMP: 6 EST: 1947
SQ FT: 26,500
SALES (est): 380K Privately Held
SIC: 3732 4493 Boat building & repairing; boat yards, storage & incidental repair

(G-5103)
UPPER PENINSULA CON PIPE CO (PA)
Also Called: U P Concrete Pipe
6480 Us Hwy 2 (49829)
P.O. Box 313 (49829-0313)
PHONE..................................906 786-0934
John G Kloet Jr, *President*
Gabriel Kloet, *General Mgr*
Harland Courllard, *Vice Pres*
Jordan Lacombe, *Plant Mgr*
Dave Ross, *Sales Staff*
EMP: 15 EST: 1950
SQ FT: 110,800
SALES (est): 3.3MM Privately Held
WEB: www.upconcretepipe.net
SIC: 3272 Sewer pipe, concrete; culvert pipe, concrete

(G-5104)
UPPER PENINSULA RUBBER CO INC
Also Called: Tunnel Vision Pipeline Svcs
2101 N 19th St Bldg B (49829-9573)
P.O. Box 541 (49829-0541)
PHONE..................................906 786-0460
John Kloet, *President*
James Laughbaum, *General Mgr*
Harland Couillard, *Vice Pres*
Harland Couillard, *Vice Pres*
Steven Delaire, *Engineer*
EMP: 5 EST: 1958
SALES (est): 666.7K
SALES (corp-wide): 3.3MM Privately Held
WEB: www.tvpipeservices.com
SIC: 3053 Gasket materials; gaskets, all materials
PA: Upper Peninsula Concrete Pipe Co
6480 Us Hwy 2
Escanaba MI 49829
906 786-0934

(G-5105)
VERSO CORPORATION
Also Called: Escanaba Paper Company
7100 County 426 M.5 Rd (49829-8501)
P.O. Box 757 (49829-0757)
PHONE..................................906 786-1660
Mark Harris, *Maint Spvr*
Pete Madaski, *Maint Spvr*
Jon Lafreniere, *Mfg Staff*
Jack Hakkola, *Engineer*
Sherri Peterson, *Human Res Dir*
EMP: 1165 Publicly Held
WEB: www.versoco.com
SIC: 2621 Paper mills
PA: Verso Corporation
8540 Gander Creek Dr
Miamisburg OH 45342

(G-5106)
VIAUS SUPER MARKET
1519 Sheridan Rd (49829-1826)
PHONE..................................906 786-1950
Wallace Viau, *President*
Jeanette Viau, *Corp Secy*
EMP: 8 EST: 1926
SQ FT: 6,100
SALES (est): 429.3K Privately Held
SIC: 5421 2013 5411 Meat markets, including freezer provisioners; sausages from purchased meat; smoked meats from purchased meat; grocery stores, independent

(G-5107)
WELDING WIZARD
6444 Marie L.45 Ln (49829-9771)
PHONE..................................906 786-4745
EMP: 4 EST: 2014
SALES (est): 48.2K Privately Held
SIC: 7692 Welding repair

Essexville
Bay County

(G-5108)
AMERICAN GOURMET SNACKS LLC
1211 Woodside Ave (48732-1269)
PHONE..................................989 892-4856
Robert Jaenicke, *Mng Member*
EMP: 9 EST: 1969
SALES (est): 500K Privately Held
WEB: www.americangourmetpretzel.com
SIC: 2064 5461 5441 Candy & other confectionery products; pretzels; popcorn, including caramel corn

(G-5109)
BAY ARCHERY SALES CO
2713 Center Ave (48732-1749)
PHONE..................................989 894-5800
Jere Brunette, *President*
James Brunette, *Vice Pres*
EMP: 7 EST: 1980
SQ FT: 4,200
SALES (est): 832.5K Privately Held
WEB: www.bayarchery.com
SIC: 5941 3999 Archery supplies; backpacking equipment; camping equipment; wind chimes

(G-5110)
BAY COMPOSITES INC
1801 Jarman Rd (48732-9800)
PHONE..................................989 891-9159
Glen Sonza, *President*
Brittany O 'loughlin, *Human Resources*
▲ EMP: 28 EST: 2008
SALES (est): 3MM Privately Held
WEB: www.baycomposites.com
SIC: 3624 Carbon & graphite products

(G-5111)
BAY MACHINE TOOL CO INC
110 Woodside Ave (48732-1110)
P.O. Box 78 (48732-0078)
PHONE..................................989 894-2863
William R Voigt, *President*
John R Lash, *Corp Secy*
EMP: 14 EST: 1952
SQ FT: 10,000
SALES (est): 224.6K Privately Held
SIC: 3599 Machine shop, jobbing & repair

(G-5112)
BAY TOOL INC
110 Woodside Ave (48732-1110)
P.O. Box 78 (48732-0078)
PHONE..................................989 894-2863
William Clark, *Vice Pres*
EMP: 7 EST: 1968
SQ FT: 10,000
SALES (est): 514.7K Privately Held
SIC: 3599 Machine shop, jobbing & repair

GEOGRAPHIC SECTION

Farmington - Oakland County (G-5140)

(G-5113)
EBERHARD AND FATHER SIGNWORKS
108 Woodside Ave (48732-1110)
PHONE...................989 892-5566
Kathy Washabaugh, *Partner*
Greg Brown, *Partner*
EMP: 6 EST: 1957
SQ FT: 5,000
SALES (est): 471.9K **Privately Held**
SIC: 3993 Signs, not made in custom sign painting shops

(G-5114)
JCS TOOL & MFG CO INC
Also Called: J C S
193 N Powell Rd (48732-1714)
PHONE...................989 892-8975
Roger Felske, *President*
Roger Fleske, *Principal*
Kevin Socier, *Vice Pres*
Allan Badour, *Treasurer*
EMP: 22 EST: 1984
SQ FT: 40,000
SALES (est): 4.8MM **Privately Held**
WEB: www.jcstool.com
SIC: 3544 3498 Special dies & tools; fabricated pipe & fittings

(G-5115)
K-C WELDING SUPPLY INC
1309 Main St (48732-1251)
PHONE...................989 893-6509
Keith Carolan II, *President*
Maureen A Carolan, *Treasurer*
Maureen Carolan, *Treasurer*
Marty Ulrey, *Manager*
EMP: 14 EST: 1954
SQ FT: 12,000
SALES (est): 3MM **Privately Held**
WEB: www.kcwelding.biz
SIC: 7692 5084 5085 Welding repair; welding machinery & equipment; industrial supplies

(G-5116)
LAFARGE NORTH AMERICA INC
Also Called: Lafargeholcim
1500 Main St (48732-1292)
PHONE...................989 894-0157
Isabel Suarez, *Marketing Staff*
Tami Clewley, *Administration*
EMP: 4
SALES (corp-wide): 25.3B **Privately Held**
WEB: www.lafarge-na.com
SIC: 3241 Cement, hydraulic
HQ: Lafarge North America Inc.
8700 W Bryn Mawr Ave # 300
Chicago IL 60631
773 372-1000

(G-5117)
LAFARGE NORTH AMERICA INC
1500 Main St (48732-1292)
PHONE...................216 566-0545
EMP: 4
SALES (corp-wide): 25.3B **Privately Held**
WEB: www.lafarge-na.com
SIC: 3273 Ready-mixed concrete
HQ: Lafarge North America Inc.
8700 W Bryn Mawr Ave # 300
Chicago IL 60631
773 372-1000

Evart
Osceola County

(G-5118)
A1 UTILITY CONTRACTOR INC
8399 Evergreen Rd (49631-9605)
PHONE...................989 324-8581
Troy Lyons, *President*
EMP: 56 EST: 2012
SALES (est): 7.5MM **Privately Held**
WEB: www.a1utilitycontractor.com
SIC: 1623 1311 Electric power line construction; natural gas production

(G-5119)
AFFORDABLE PRINTS
125 N Main St (49631-9416)
PHONE...................231 679-2606
EMP: 6 EST: 2013
SALES (est): 144.2K **Privately Held**
SIC: 2752 Commercial printing, lithographic

(G-5120)
AMALGAMATED UAW
Also Called: Amalgamated Uaw Local 2270
601 W 7th St (49631-9408)
P.O. Box 1037 (49631-1037)
PHONE...................231 734-9286
Dana Sible, *President*
EMP: 9 EST: 1989
SALES (est): 204.4K **Privately Held**
SIC: 8631 3714 Labor unions & similar labor organizations; motor vehicle parts & accessories

(G-5121)
BENNETT SAWMILL
4161 90th Ave (49631-8010)
PHONE...................231 734-5733
Kenneth Bennett, *Partner*
Kevin Bennett, *Partner*
Mark Bennett, *Partner*
EMP: 7 EST: 1960
SALES (est): 494.9K **Privately Held**
SIC: 2421 2411 Sawmills & planing mills, general; logging

(G-5122)
CHERRY CREEK POST LLC
Also Called: Cherry Creek Post Co
5882 7 Mile Rd (49631-8270)
PHONE...................231 734-2466
Omer Miller, *Partner*
Dewayne Miller, *Partner*
EMP: 6 EST: 1986
SALES (est): 1MM **Privately Held**
SIC: 5031 2499 Fencing, wood; fencing, wood

(G-5123)
HUFF MACHINE & TOOL CO INC
5469 85th Ave (49631-8763)
P.O. Box 638 (49631-0638)
PHONE...................231 734-3291
Fax: 231 734-5833
EMP: 12
SQ FT: 1,200
SALES (est): 1.5MM **Privately Held**
SIC: 3599 Job Machine Shop

(G-5124)
INTERNTNAL AUTO CMPNNTS GROUP
601 W 7th St (49631-9408)
PHONE...................231 734-9000
JD Smith, *QA Dir*
Steve Tipton, *Program Mgr*
EMP: 5 **Privately Held**
WEB: www.iacgroup.com
SIC: 3647 Automotive lighting fixtures
HQ: International Automotive Components Group North America, Inc.
27777 Franklin Rd # 2000
Southfield MI 48034

(G-5125)
LIBERTY DAIRY COMPANY
302 N River St (49631-9359)
PHONE...................800 632-5552
Fax: 231 734-3880
EMP: 125
SALES (est): 13.3MM **Publicly Held**
SIC: 2026 2022 Mfg Fluid Milk Mfg Cheese
HQ: Dean Holding Company
2711 N Haskell Ave
Dallas TX 75204
214 303-3400

(G-5126)
MECHANIC EVLTION CRTFCTION FOR
1620 70th Ave (49631-8722)
PHONE...................231 734-3483
John Hohman, *Exec Dir*
EMP: 7 EST: 2010
SALES (est): 12.7K **Privately Held**
WEB: www.mech-certification.org
SIC: 7692 7699 7623 Welding repair; boiler & heating repair services; refrigeration service & repair

(G-5127)
RKAA BUSINESS LLC
Also Called: Chippewa Plastics
5843 100th Ave (49631-8421)
PHONE...................231 734-5517
Albert Rohe, *President*
Ravi Kapur, *Managing Prtnr*
Derek Wade, *General Mgr*
John Holmes, *Vice Pres*
Dee Wade, *Purchasing*
▲ EMP: 35 EST: 1977
SQ FT: 75,000
SALES (est): 7.9MM **Privately Held**
SIC: 3089 3544 Injection molding of plastics; special dies & tools

(G-5128)
VENTRA EVART LLC
601 W 7th St (49631-9468)
PHONE...................231 734-9000
Amy Kellogg, *President*
Harold Stieber,
▲ EMP: 2 EST: 2007
SALES (est): 6.9MM **Privately Held**
SIC: 3089 5531 Injection molding of plastics; automobile & truck equipment & parts

Fairview
Oscoda County

(G-5129)
COOPER-STANDARD AUTOMOTIVE INC
2799 E Miller Rd (48621-9802)
P.O. Box 219 (48621-0219)
PHONE...................989 848-2272
Larry Wasnock, *Branch Mgr*
David Clover, *Telecom Exec*
EMP: 7
SALES (corp-wide): 2.3B **Publicly Held**
WEB: www.cooperstandard.com
SIC: 3714 Power steering equipment, motor vehicle
HQ: Cooper-Standard Automotive Inc.
40300 Traditions Dr
Northville MI 48168
248 596-5900

(G-5130)
FAIRVIEW SAWMILL INC
1901 Kneeland Rd (48621-9737)
PHONE...................989 848-5238
Dallas Hendrich, *Partner*
Dawson Oaks, *Partner*
EMP: 5 EST: 1998
SALES (est): 436.8K **Privately Held**
WEB: www.visitoscodacounty.com
SIC: 2421 Sawmills & planing mills, general

Falmouth
Missaukee County

(G-5131)
ADVANCED MANUFACTURING LLC
311 E Prosper Rd (49632-9528)
PHONE...................231 826-3859
Gary Gladu, *CEO*
EMP: 4 EST: 2011
SALES (est): 210.2K **Privately Held**
SIC: 3061 Mechanical rubber goods

(G-5132)
EBELS EQUIPMENT LLC
490 E Prosper Rd (49632-9521)
PHONE...................231 826-3334
Paul Ebel, *Principal*
EMP: 6
SALES (est): 106K **Privately Held**
SIC: 3559 Special industry machinery

(G-5133)
EBELS HARDWARE INC
490 E Prosper Rd (49632-9521)
P.O. Box 100 (49632-0100)
PHONE...................231 826-3334
Dave Ebels, *President*
Paul Ebels, *Vice Pres*
Gayle Ebels, *Treasurer*
Vicki Ebels, *Admin Sec*
EMP: 15 EST: 2009
SALES (est): 3.1MM **Privately Held**
WEB: www.ebelshardware.com
SIC: 5251 3546 3523 3524 Hardware; chain saws, portable; tractors, farm; grass catchers, lawn mower; lawnmowers & tractors; lawn mower repair shop

Farmington
Oakland County

(G-5134)
CASTINE COMMUNICATIONS INC
Also Called: Hockey Weekly
22658 Brookdale St (48336-4118)
P.O. Box 279 (48332-0279)
PHONE...................248 477-1600
John Castine, *President*
EMP: 4 EST: 2000
SALES (est): 336.8K **Privately Held**
WEB: www.hockeyweekly.com
SIC: 2721 Magazines: publishing only, not printed on site

(G-5135)
CHASSIS BRAKES INTL USA (PA)
34500 Grand River Ave (48335-3310)
PHONE...................248 957-9997
Dennis Berry, *President*
EMP: 7 EST: 2015
SALES (est): 2.2MM **Privately Held**
WEB: www.chassisbrakes.com
SIC: 3714 Motor vehicle brake systems & parts

(G-5136)
DETROIT MATERIALS INC
Also Called: Wayne Steel Tech
33203 Grand River Ave (48336-3123)
PHONE...................248 924-5436
Pedro Guillen, *CEO*
Nick Moroz, *CTO*
EMP: 4 EST: 2013
SALES (est): 319.9K **Privately Held**
WEB: www.detroitmaterials.com
SIC: 3325 8742 Steel foundries; management engineering

(G-5137)
E & D MACHINE COMPANY INC
32777 Chesley Dr (48336-5115)
PHONE...................248 473-0255
EMP: 30 EST: 1988
SQ FT: 2,500
SALES (est): 2.4MM **Privately Held**
SIC: 3544 Special dies & tools

(G-5138)
FRESH HEIR LLC
23994 Earl Ct (48335-3404)
PHONE...................313 312-4492
Matthew Hollis, *Mng Member*
EMP: 5 EST: 2016
SALES (est): 273.5K **Privately Held**
WEB: www.fresherheir.com
SIC: 2844 2241 Toilet preparations; shoe laces, except leather

(G-5139)
HTI USA INC
33106 W 8 Mile Rd (48336-5400)
PHONE...................248 358-5533
Herschel S Wright, *President*
▲ EMP: 1 EST: 1985
SQ FT: 40,000
SALES (est): 3.1MM
SALES (corp-wide): 194MM **Privately Held**
WEB: www.htiusa.com
SIC: 3826 Analytical instruments
HQ: Sam Brown Sales, Llc
33106 W 8 Mile Rd
Farmington MI 48336
248 358-2626

(G-5140)
JAY CEE SALES & RIVET INC
32861 Chesley Dr (48336-5117)
P.O. Box 1150 (48332-1150)
PHONE...................248 478-2150

Farmington - Oakland County (G-5141)

Michael Clinton, *President*
Allan Weitzman, *Principal*
Greg Weitzman, *Principal*
Cary B Weitzman, *Vice Pres*
Tina Pierzynski, *Admin Sec*
▲ **EMP:** 18 **EST:** 1944
SQ FT: 32,740
SALES (est): 7.3MM **Privately Held**
WEB: www.rivetsinstock.com
SIC: 5072 3429 5085 Rivets; metal fasteners; abrasives & adhesives

(G-5141)
KELLER SPORTS-OPTICS
35797 Smithfield Rd (48335-3144)
PHONE 248 894-0960
Howard Keller, *Principal*
EMP: 4 **EST:** 2010
SALES (est): 61.1K **Privately Held**
SIC: 3949 Sporting & athletic goods

(G-5142)
MAHLE AFTERMARKET INC (DH)
23030 Mahle Dr (48335-2606)
PHONE 248 347-9700
Arnd Franz, *Ch of Bd*
Heinz Junker, *Chairman*
Ted Hughes, *Mng Member*
William Foutch Jr, *Admin Sec*
▲ **EMP:** 100 **EST:** 2007
SALES (est): 122.4MM
SALES (corp-wide): 504.6K **Privately Held**
WEB: www.mahle-aftermarket.com
SIC: 3714 Motor vehicle parts & accessories
HQ: Mahle Gmbh
Pragstr. 26-46
Stuttgart BW 70376
711 501-0

(G-5143)
MOORE PRODUCTION TOOL SPC
Also Called: Moore Production Tool Spc
37531 Grand River Ave (48335-2879)
PHONE 248 476-1200
Richard E Moore, *CEO*
Durk Moore, *President*
Jack Newcombe, *Treasurer*
EMP: 16
SQ FT: 40,000
SALES (est): 1.1MM **Privately Held**
SIC: 3541 3542 Machine tools, metal cutting type; machine tools, metal forming type

(G-5144)
PLUSKATE BOARDING COMPANY
33335 Grand River Ave (48336-3194)
PHONE 248 426-0899
Robert Woelkers, *Principal*
EMP: 4 **EST:** 2004
SALES (est): 450.1K **Privately Held**
WEB: www.pluskateboarding.com
SIC: 3949 Skateboards

(G-5145)
ROUSH ENTERPRISES INC (PA)
34300 W 9 Mile Rd (48335-4706)
PHONE 734 805-4400
Evan Lyall, *CEO*
Geoffrey Smith, *President*
Jack Roush, *Chairman*
Patrick Oneil, *Area Mgr*
Doug Smith, *COO*
EMP: 125 **EST:** 1976
SQ FT: 67,000
SALES (est): 584.1MM **Privately Held**
WEB: www.roush.com
SIC: 8711 3714 7948 8734 Consulting engineer; motor vehicle engines & parts; motor vehicle transmissions, drive assemblies & parts; race car owners; stock car racing; automobile proving & testing ground

(G-5146)
ROUSH MANUFACTURING INC
Also Called: Rouch Enterprises
34300 W 9 Mile Rd (48335-4706)
PHONE 734 805-4400
Mark Slack, *Branch Mgr*
EMP: 70 **Privately Held**
WEB: www.roush.com
SIC: 3714 Motor vehicle parts & accessories
HQ: Roush Manufacturing, Inc.
12447 Levan Rd
Livonia MI 48150

(G-5147)
SAM BROWN SALES LLC (DH)
Also Called: Hi-Tech Industries
33106 W 8 Mile Rd (48336-5400)
PHONE 248 358-2626
Herschel S Wright, *President*
Hyman Brown, *Treasurer*
▲ **EMP:** 25 **EST:** 1983
SQ FT: 44,000
SALES (est): 19MM
SALES (corp-wide): 194MM **Privately Held**
WEB: www.sambrownsales.com
SIC: 5087 5013 3714 3291 Carwash equipment & supplies; motor vehicle supplies & new parts; motor vehicle parts & accessories; abrasive products
HQ: Niteo Products, Llc
5949 Sherry Ln Ste 540
Dallas TX 75225
214 245-5000

(G-5148)
SEIFERT CITY-WIDE PRINTING CO
30789 Shiawassee Rd # 12 (48336-4372)
PHONE 248 477-9525
George Kourtakis, *President*
Demetrios Kourtakis, *Vice Pres*
Audrey Kourtakis, *Admin Sec*
EMP: 4 **EST:** 1967
SQ FT: 10,000
SALES (est): 452.1K **Privately Held**
WEB: www.citywide.ws
SIC: 2752 Commercial printing, offset

(G-5149)
SIGN AND BANNER WORLD
31178 Grand River Ave (48336-4277)
PHONE 248 957-1240
EMP: 4 **EST:** 2016
SALES (est): 119.5K **Privately Held**
WEB: www.signandbannerworld.com
SIC: 3993 Signs & advertising specialties

(G-5150)
SIGNARAMA FARMINGTON
31178 Grand River Ave (48336-4277)
PHONE 248 957-1240
EMP: 6 **EST:** 2018
SALES (est): 140.7K **Privately Held**
WEB: www.signarama.com
SIC: 3993 Signs & advertising specialties

(G-5151)
SOFTWARE ASSOC INC
Also Called: UPS Store 093
35560 Grand River Ave (48335-3123)
PHONE 248 477-6112
Roopa Injeti,
EMP: 12 **EST:** 2005
SALES (est): 313.2K **Privately Held**
SIC: 7372 Prepackaged software

(G-5152)
SUPERFLY MANUFACTURING CO
31505 Grand River Ave 7c (48336-4231)
PHONE 313 454-1492
Justin Draplin, *President*
▲ **EMP:** 10 **EST:** 2011
SALES (est): 950K **Privately Held**
WEB: www.superflykids.com
SIC: 2389 Apparel & accessories

(G-5153)
TEKSID INC
36524 Grand River Ave B-1 (48335-3011)
PHONE 734 846-5492
Raniero Cucchiari, *CEO*
Rogerio Silva, *President*
Guido Topini, *CFO*
Karen McKinnon, *Admin Sec*
◆ **EMP:** 25 **EST:** 1979
SQ FT: 7,400
SALES (est): 22.5MM
SALES (corp-wide): 102.5B **Privately Held**
WEB: www.teksid.com
SIC: 3714 3322 5051 Motor vehicle parts & accessories; malleable iron foundries; castings, rough: iron or steel
HQ: Teksid Spa
Via Umberto Ii 5
Carmagnola TO 10022
011 979-4111

(G-5154)
WEATHER KING WINDOWS DOORS INC (PA)
Also Called: Weather King of Indiana
20775 Chesley Dr (48336-5111)
P.O. Box 3483 (48333-3483)
PHONE 313 933-1234
William Earl King, *President*
Elizabeth Oliver, *Vice Pres*
Greg Henderson, *Plant Mgr*
Barry Breshgold, *Accounting Mgr*
Beth Oliver, *Credit Mgr*
▲ **EMP:** 75 **EST:** 1948
SQ FT: 90,215
SALES (est): 10.2MM **Privately Held**
WEB: www.weatherkingdoors.com
SIC: 3089 3442 Window frames & sash, plastic; storm doors or windows, metal

(G-5155)
WEATHER KING WINDOWS DOORS INC
20775 Chesley Dr (48336-5111)
PHONE 248 478-7788
EMP: 48
SQ FT: 46,300
SALES (corp-wide): 13.2MM **Privately Held**
SIC: 3089 3442 Mfg Plastic Products Mfg Metal Door/Sash/Trim
PA: Weather King Windows And Doors, Inc.
20775 Chesley Dr
Farmington MI 48336
313 933-1234

Farmington Hills
Oakland County

(G-5156)
4 DETROITERS LIQUOR LLC
Also Called: 8 Mile Vodka
24125 Drake Rd Ste 102 (48335-3108)
PHONE 248 756-3678
Michael Tomey,
EMP: 4 **EST:** 2020
SALES (est): 62.3K **Privately Held**
SIC: 2085 Vodka (alcoholic beverage)

(G-5157)
ABB INC
23629 Industrial Park Dr (48335-2857)
PHONE 248 471-0888
Tom Wilson, *Branch Mgr*
EMP: 79
SALES (corp-wide): 26.1B **Privately Held**
WEB: www.global.abb
SIC: 3823 Controllers for process variables, all types
HQ: Abb Inc.
305 Gregson Dr
Cary NC 27511

(G-5158)
ACE CONTROLS INC (DH)
23435 Industrial Park Dr (48335-2855)
PHONE 248 476-0213
David Raguckas, *President*
Keith Szukalowski, *Vice Pres*
Mike Lees, *Opers Mgr*
Pete Satkowiak, *Safety Mgr*
Darryl Carlson, *QC Dir*
◆ **EMP:** 150 **EST:** 1962
SQ FT: 85,000
SALES (est): 47.2MM
SALES (corp-wide): 428.8K **Privately Held**
WEB: www.acecontrols.com
SIC: 3594 3714 3593 3559 Fluid power pumps; motor vehicle engines & parts; fluid power cylinders, hydraulic or pneumatic; sewing machines & hat & zipper making machinery; fire- or burglary-resistive products
HQ: Stabilus Gmbh
Wallersheimer Weg 100
Koblenz RP 56070
261 890-00

(G-5159)
AEES INC (DH)
Also Called: Pkc Group
36555 Corp Dr Ste 300 (48331)
PHONE 248 489-4700
Frank Sovis, *President*
Julie Bellamy, *Senior VP*
Rico Mutone, *Vice Pres*
Cortney Wilson, *Engineer*
John Shepp, *Senior Engr*
EMP: 4724 **EST:** 1984
SALES (est): 1.9B **Privately Held**
WEB: www.aeesinc.com
SIC: 3679 Electronic loads & power supplies
HQ: Pkc Group Usa Inc.
36555 Corp Dr Ste 300
Farmington Hills MI 48331
248 489-4700

(G-5160)
AEES POWER SYSTEMS LTD PARTNR
Also Called: Engineered Plastic Components
36555 Corp Dr Ste 300 (48331)
PHONE 269 668-4429
Chris Wooten, *Branch Mgr*
EMP: 5 **Privately Held**
SIC: 3089 3841 3694 3678 Injection molding of plastics; surgical & medical instruments; engine electrical equipment; electronic connectors; current-carrying wiring devices
HQ: Aees Power Systems Limited Partnership
999 Republic Dr
Allen Park MI 48101

(G-5161)
AGELESSMAGE FCIAL ASTHTICS LLC
28499 Orchard Lake Rd (48334-3702)
PHONE 269 998-5547
McKenzie Zientek,
EMP: 6 **EST:** 2012
SALES (est): 361.8K **Privately Held**
WEB: www.agelessimage.com
SIC: 3842 Cosmetic restorations

(G-5162)
AGM AUTOMOTIVE LLC (HQ)
27755 Stansbury Blvd # 300 (48334-3837)
PHONE 248 776-0600
Robert M Blinstrub, *President*
Richard Cook, *General Mgr*
Robert Grananta, *Exec VP*
William Lang, *Production*
Venkat Koneru, *Buyer*
▲ **EMP:** 90 **EST:** 2001
SQ FT: 45,000
SALES (est): 45.1MM **Privately Held**
WEB: www.agmautomotive.com
SIC: 2399 3357 2396 Automotive covers, except seat & tire covers; automotive wire & cable, except ignition sets; nonferrous; automotive trimmings, fabric

(G-5163)
AGM AUTOMOTIVE MEXICO LLC (DH)
27755 Stansbury Blvd # 300 (48334-3837)
PHONE 248 925-4152
Chris O'Connell, *Mng Member*
EMP: 150 **EST:** 2015
SALES (est): 3MM **Privately Held**
WEB: www.agmautomotive.com
SIC: 3714 Motor vehicle parts & accessories

GEOGRAPHIC SECTION
Farmington Hills - Oakland County (G-5191)

HQ: Agm Automotive, Llc
27755 Stansbury Blvd # 300
Farmington Hills MI 48334
248 776-0600

(G-5164)
AIR SOLUTION COMPANY
23857 Industrial Park Dr (48335-2860)
PHONE..................................800 819-2869
Kenneth Simmons, *Principal*
EMP: 11 **EST:** 1993
SALES (est): 237.2K **Privately Held**
WEB: www.airsolutioncompany.com
SIC: 3564 1711 Purification & dust collection equipment; plumbing, heating, air-conditioning contractors

(G-5165)
AKEBONO BRAKE CORPORATION (HQ)
34385 W 12 Mile Rd (48331-3375)
PHONE..................................248 489-7400
Wilm Uhlenbecker, *President*
William Gleeson, *Treasurer*
Brandon Kessinger, *Admin Sec*
◆ **EMP:** 123 **EST:** 1998
SQ FT: 12,000
SALES (est): 378.3MM **Privately Held**
WEB: www.akebonobrakes.com
SIC: 3714 Air brakes, motor vehicle

(G-5166)
AKWEL CADILLAC USA INC
Also Called: Detroit Sls & Engrg Ctr Div of
39205 Country Club Dr C1 (48331-3495)
PHONE..................................248 848-9599
Birgig Villeminey, *Branch Mgr*
EMP: 5 **Privately Held**
WEB: www.akwel-automotive.com
SIC: 3089 3052 Battery cases, plastic or plastic combination; rubber & plastics hose & beltings
HQ: Akwel Cadillac Usa, Inc
603 7th St
Cadillac MI 49601
231 775-6571

(G-5167)
ALLGRAPHICS CORP
28960 E King William Dr (48331-2578)
PHONE..................................248 994-7373
Frank Alspector, *President*
EMP: 4 **EST:** 1974
SQ FT: 3,000
SALES (est): 229.3K **Privately Held**
SIC: 2261 2759 Screen printing of cotton broadwoven fabrics; screen printing

(G-5168)
AMERICAN LASER CENTERS LLC
24555 Hallwood Ct (48335-1667)
PHONE..................................248 426-8250
Gregory Segall, *President*
EMP: 1572 **EST:** 2006
SALES (est): 3MM **Privately Held**
WEB: www.americanlaser.com
SIC: 3999 3841 Hair & hair-based products; skin grafting equipment; cannulae
PA: Versa Capital Management, Llc
10 Penn Ctr 1801 Mkt St
Philadelphia PA 19103

(G-5169)
AMERICAN SILK SCREEN & EMB
Also Called: Sportcap
24601 Hallwood Ct (48335-1604)
PHONE..................................248 474-1000
Michael R Lamb, *President*
Diana Lamb, *Vice Pres*
Todd Lamb, *Vice Pres*
EMP: 17 **EST:** 1967
SQ FT: 42,000
SALES (est): 375.6K **Privately Held**
WEB: www.americansilkscreenmi.com
SIC: 2396 5136 5137 Screen printing on fabric articles; sportswear, men's & boys'; sportswear, women's & children's

(G-5170)
AMERICAN STANDARD WINDOWS
30281 Pipers Ln (48334-4731)
PHONE..................................734 788-2261
Martin Szelag, *President*
EMP: 12 **EST:** 1986
SQ FT: 24,000
SALES (est): 381.1K **Privately Held**
SIC: 3089 Windows, plastic

(G-5171)
ARCONIC AUTOMOTIVE CASTINGS
37000 W 12 Mile Rd Ste 11 (48331-3032)
PHONE..................................248 489-4900
Jacques Vanier, *President*
Joe Kerkhove, *President*
Graeme Bottger, *Vice Pres*
John Kenna, *Vice Pres*
Sue Zemba, *Vice Pres*
▲ **EMP:** 109 **EST:** 1993
SQ FT: 150,000
SALES (est): 2.5MM
SALES (corp-wide): 5.6B **Publicly Held**
WEB: www.arconic.com
SIC: 3353 Aluminum sheet, plate & foil
PA: Arconic Corporation
201 Isabella St Ste 400
Pittsburgh PA 15212
412 992-2500

(G-5172)
ARCONIC CORPORATION
37000 W 12 Mile Rd Ste 11 (48331-3032)
PHONE..................................248 489-4900
Gerald Faunt, *Vice Pres*
Prashant Sopory, *Project Mgr*
Mark Finley, *Buyer*
Misha Pesic, *Engineer*
Julie Bellamy, *Human Resources*
EMP: 7
SALES (corp-wide): 5.6B **Publicly Held**
WEB: www.arconic.com
SIC: 3354 Aluminum extruded products
PA: Arconic Corporation
201 Isabella St Ste 400
Pittsburgh PA 15212
412 992-2500

(G-5173)
ARMORCLAD
24285 Indoplex Cir (48335-2523)
PHONE..................................248 477-7785
Gloria Chater, *Chairman*
EMP: 6 **EST:** 2017
SALES (est): 69.9K **Privately Held**
SIC: 3471 Plating & polishing

(G-5174)
ASW AMERCA INC
24762 Crestview Ct (48335-1506)
PHONE..................................248 957-9638
Markus Weber, *President*
Severin Beck, *Manager*
EMP: 4 **EST:** 2015
SALES (est): 249.3K **Privately Held**
SIC: 3569 5962 Assembly machines, non-metalworking; merchandising machine operators

(G-5175)
ATLAS THREAD GAGE INC
30990 W 8 Mile Rd (48336-5323)
PHONE..................................248 477-3230
Doug Hamer, *President*
Lisa Sheldon, *Manager*
EMP: 9 **EST:** 1951
SQ FT: 4,000
SALES (est): 712.6K **Privately Held**
WEB: www.atlasthreadgage.com
SIC: 3545 Machine tool accessories

(G-5176)
AUTONEUM NORTH AMERICA INC
38555 Hills Tech Dr (48331-3423)
PHONE..................................248 848-0100
Steve Kelchner, *Engineer*
Dustin Sabo, *Engineer*
Dave Kopelcheck, *Controller*
Jim Nemeth, *Human Res Dir*
Chad Stock, *Accounts Mgr*
EMP: 4
SALES (corp-wide): 1.9B **Privately Held**
WEB: www.autoneum.com
SIC: 8748 3489 3296 Business consulting; ordnance & accessories; mineral wool
HQ: Autoneum North America, Inc.
29293 Haggerty Rd
Novi MI 48377
248 848-0100

(G-5177)
AUTOWARES INC
23240 Industrial Park Dr (48335-2850)
PHONE..................................248 473-0928
EMP: 4
SALES (est): 298.9K **Privately Held**
SIC: 3465 Mfg Automotive Stampings

(G-5178)
AVANZADO LLC
25330 Interchange Ct (48335-1022)
P.O. Box 3435 (48333-3435)
PHONE..................................248 615-0538
Craig Frye, *CEO*
Leocadio J Padilla, *Ch of Bd*
Cathy Ferrel, *Exec VP*
Peter Ransome, *Exec VP*
Gregg Gabbana, *Vice Pres*
▲ **EMP:** 39 **EST:** 2004
SQ FT: 28,000
SALES (est): 6.7MM **Privately Held**
WEB: www.phoenixinnovate.com
SIC: 2752 Promotional printing, lithographic; color lithography

(G-5179)
AVIV GLOBAL LLC
32430 Northwestern Hwy (48334-1400)
PHONE..................................248 737-5777
Christopher Edwards, *Manager*
▲ **EMP:** 4 **EST:** 2008
SALES (est): 317.1K **Privately Held**
WEB: www.zazasink.com
SIC: 3431 Bathroom fixtures, including sinks

(G-5180)
BALIKO POS INC
22338 Tredwell Ave (48336-3871)
PHONE..................................248 470-4652
Ronald Bakilo, *Principal*
EMP: 4 **EST:** 2011
SALES (est): 55.8K **Privately Held**
SIC: 3578 Cash registers

(G-5181)
BIRDSALL TOOL & GAGE CO
24735 Crestview Ct (48335-1507)
PHONE..................................248 474-5150
David Birdsall, *President*
Kurt Baron, *Treasurer*
Marge Goward, *Controller*
John Robson, *Sales Staff*
Brian Closkey, *CTO*
▼ **EMP:** 30 **EST:** 1970
SQ FT: 13,700
SALES (est): 2.7MM **Privately Held**
WEB: www.birdsalltool.com
SIC: 3674 3542 Strain gages, solid state; machine tools, metal forming type

(G-5182)
BLUEWATER TECH GROUP INC
37900 Interchange Dr (48335-1034)
PHONE..................................248 356-4399
EMP: 6
SALES (corp-wide): 78.5MM **Privately Held**
WEB: www.bluewatertech.com
SIC: 3669 3651 Visual communication systems; audio electronic systems
HQ: Bluewater Technologies Group, Inc.
30303 Beck Rd
Wixom MI 48393
248 356-4399

(G-5183)
BMC SOFTWARE INC
27555 Executive Dr # 155 (48331-3568)
PHONE..................................248 888-4600
EMP: 11
SALES (corp-wide): 1.3B **Privately Held**
SIC: 7372 Prepackaged Software Services
HQ: Bmc Software, Inc.
2103 Citywest Blvd # 2100
Houston TX 77042
713 918-8800

(G-5184)
BODY CONTOUR VENTURES LLC
Also Called: Light-Rx
34405 W 12 Mile Rd # 200 (48331-5627)
PHONE..................................248 579-6772
Richard C Morgan, *Principal*
EMP: 32 **EST:** 2014
SALES (est): 4MM **Privately Held**
SIC: 7991 3999 Spas; massage machines, electric: barber & beauty shops

(G-5185)
BOHR MANUFACTURING LLC
23206 Commerce Dr (48335-2724)
PHONE..................................734 261-3010
EMP: 5 **EST:** 2018
SALES (est): 291.3K **Privately Held**
SIC: 3999 Manufacturing industries

(G-5186)
BROTHERS INDUSTRIALS INC
38844 Steeple Chase # 27101 (48331-4935)
PHONE..................................248 794-5080
Atheer Ibrahim, *Principal*
▲ **EMP:** 5 **EST:** 2008
SALES (est): 72.4K **Privately Held**
WEB: www.brothersindustrialsinc.com
SIC: 3559 Special industry machinery

(G-5187)
BRUCE KANE ENTERPRISES LLC (PA)
Also Called: Passport Health of Michigan
28200 Orchard Lake Rd # 107 (48334-3761)
PHONE..................................410 727-0637
Bruce Kane,
EMP: 5 **EST:** 2001
SALES (est): 693.7K **Privately Held**
WEB: www.passporthealthofmi.com
SIC: 2836 Vaccines & other immunizing products

(G-5188)
BURST LED
29412 Windmill Ct (48334-3110)
PHONE..................................248 321-6262
Gary Gozmamian, *Manager*
EMP: 8 **EST:** 2016
SALES (est): 95.9K **Privately Held**
WEB: www.burstled.com
SIC: 3646 Commercial indusl & institutional electric lighting fixtures

(G-5189)
BWB LLC
Also Called: Cornillie Concrete
33469 W 14 Mile Rd Ste 10 (48331-1521)
P.O. Box 2900 (48333-2900)
PHONE..................................231 439-9200
Nathan Sommer, *Principal*
Karen Giles, *Corp Secy*
Sommer Nate, *Manager*
EMP: 17 **EST:** 2010
SALES (est): 950K **Privately Held**
SIC: 3273 Ready-mixed concrete

(G-5190)
C L DESIGN INC
Also Called: Craig EDM
20739 Sunnydale St (48336-5254)
PHONE..................................248 474-4220
Marc J Craig, *President*
EMP: 4 **EST:** 1984
SQ FT: 6,400
SALES (est): 540.8K **Privately Held**
SIC: 3613 3599 Control panels, electric; electrical discharge machining (EDM)

(G-5191)
C L MAILING PRINTING
24980 Creekside Dr (48336-2020)
PHONE..................................248 471-3330
Chong So, *Principal*
EMP: 4 **EST:** 2010
SALES (est): 80.3K **Privately Held**
SIC: 2752 Commercial printing, offset

Farmington Hills - Oakland County (G-5192)

(G-5192)
C S M MANUFACTURING CORP (PA)
Also Called: CSM Cold Heading
24650 N Industrial Dr (48335-1553)
PHONE..................................248 471-0700
William A Fleury, *President*
Gail A Fleury, *Vice Pres*
Steve Klaserner, *Opers Mgr*
EMP: 80 EST: 1978
SALES (est): 13.6MM Privately Held
WEB: www.csmmfg.net
SIC: 3451 3599 Screw machine products; machine shop, jobbing & repair

(G-5193)
CABINET FINISHERS
21002 Orchard Lake Rd (48336-5227)
PHONE..................................248 635-7584
Timothy Knoppe, *Principal*
EMP: 4 EST: 2014
SALES (est): 281.6K Privately Held
WEB: www.thecabinetfinishers.com
SIC: 2434 Wood kitchen cabinets

(G-5194)
CAM PUBLISHING INC
38800 Country Club Dr (48331-3439)
PHONE..................................248 848-3148
EMP: 5 EST: 2018
SALES (est): 115.2K Privately Held
SIC: 2741 Miscellaneous publishing

(G-5195)
CAMACO LLC (HQ)
37000 W Twlve Mile Rd Ste (48331)
PHONE..................................248 442-6800
Arvind Pradhan, *CEO*
Sue Barber, *Production*
Jeremiah Bear, *Production*
Delano Farmer, *Engineer*
Dennis Walsh, *Engineer*
▲ EMP: 25 EST: 1998
SQ FT: 5,000
SALES (est): 267.5MM
SALES (corp-wide): 494.7MM Privately Held
WEB: www.camacollc.com
SIC: 3565 3499 Packaging machinery; automobile seat frames, metal
PA: P & C Group I, Inc.
37000 W 12 Mile Rd Ste 10
Farmington Hills MI 48331
248 442-6800

(G-5196)
CAPITAL BILLING SYSTEMS INC
33533 W 12 Mile Rd # 131 (48331-5634)
PHONE..................................248 478-7298
Diane Amendt, *President*
EMP: 7 EST: 1994
SALES (est): 640.3K Privately Held
SIC: 7372 Prepackaged software

(G-5197)
CAPITAL STAMPING & MACHINE INC (PA)
24650 N Industrial Dr (48335-1553)
PHONE..................................248 471-0700
William A Fleury, *President*
Gail A Fleury, *Admin Sec*
EMP: 2 EST: 1987
SQ FT: 35,000
SALES (est): 3.4MM Privately Held
WEB: www.csmmfg.net
SIC: 3465 Automotive stampings

(G-5198)
CARLESIMO PRODUCTS INC
29800 W 8 Mile Rd (48336-5506)
PHONE..................................248 474-0415
John Carlesimo, *President*
Elizabeth Carlesimo, *Vice Pres*
EMP: 27 EST: 1923
SQ FT: 3,200
SALES (est): 1.3MM Privately Held
WEB: www.takenote.com
SIC: 3272 3271 Pipe, concrete or lined with concrete; manhole covers or frames, concrete; concrete block & brick

(G-5199)
CARRIER & GABLE INC (PA)
24110 Research Dr (48335-2633)
PHONE..................................248 477-8700
Dan Carrier, *President*
Gerald W Carrier, *Chairman*
Sally Carrier, *Vice Pres*
Geri M Schmidt, *Vice Pres*
Jules Altvater, *CFO*
EMP: 22 EST: 1945
SQ FT: 16,000
SALES: 10.4MM Privately Held
WEB: www.carriergable.com
SIC: 5063 5099 3993 Signaling equipment, electrical; reflective road markers; signs & advertising specialties

(G-5200)
CASPER CORPORATION
24081 Research Dr (48335-2632)
PHONE..................................248 442-9000
Jim Casper Jr, *President*
Siobhan Strickland, *Marketing Staff*
EMP: 25
SALES (corp-wide): 5.5MM Privately Held
WEB: www.caspercorp.com
SIC: 2542 Shelving, office & store; except wood
PA: The Casper Corporation
24081 Research Dr
Farmington Hills MI
248 442-9000

(G-5201)
CG DETROIT
26970 Haggerty Rd Ste 200 (48331-3450)
PHONE..................................248 553-0202
Jason Weiss, *Vice Pres*
Amy Lauter, *Executive*
EMP: 7 EST: 2019
SALES (est): 284.8K Privately Held
WEB: www.cgdetroit.com
SIC: 3993 Signs & advertising specialties

(G-5202)
CHALLENGER MANUFACTURING LLC
20733 Sunnydale St (48336-5254)
PHONE..................................248 930-9920
Thomas Kolar, *Partner*
Jeff Kolar, *Principal*
EMP: 11 EST: 2017
SALES (est): 976.9K Privately Held
WEB: www.challenger-mfg.com
SIC: 3499 Furniture parts, metal

(G-5203)
CLARION CORPORATION AMERICA
Also Called: Clarion Group
31440 Northwestern Hwy (48334-5418)
PHONE..................................248 991-3100
Jean-Noel Bahar, *Branch Mgr*
EMP: 50
SALES (corp-wide): 41.2MM Privately Held
SIC: 5064 3651 Radios, motor vehicle; household audio equipment
HQ: Clarion Corporation Of America
2800 High Meadow Cir
Auburn Hills MI 48326
248 724-5100

(G-5204)
COCA-COLA REFRESHMENTS USA INC
26777 Halsted Rd (48331-3577)
PHONE..................................313 897-5000
Stephen Orselli, *Branch Mgr*
EMP: 6
SALES (corp-wide): 33B Publicly Held
WEB: www.coca-cola.com
SIC: 2086 Bottled & canned soft drinks
HQ: Coca-Cola Refreshments Usa, Inc.
2500 Windy Ridge Pkwy Se
Atlanta GA 30339
770 989-3000

(G-5205)
COMMON SENSORS LLC
27520 W 8 Mile Rd (48336-6224)
PHONE..................................248 722-8556
Mark Boyd, *Owner*
EMP: 6 EST: 2010
SALES (est): 243.3K Privately Held
SIC: 3829 Fatigue testing machines, industrial: mechanical

(G-5206)
COMPTEK INC
37450 Enterprise Ct (48331-3437)
PHONE..................................248 477-5215
Richard B Gentry, *President*
Monica Kakos, *Project Engr*
William Wisniewski, *VP Sales*
EMP: 24 EST: 1983
SQ FT: 15,000
SALES (est): 1.3MM Privately Held
WEB: www.comptekinc.com
SIC: 7373 3699 3625 3577 Turnkey vendors, computer systems; electrical equipment & supplies; relays & industrial controls; computer peripheral equipment

(G-5207)
COMPTON PRESS INDUSTRIES LLC
23079 Commerce Dr (48335-2721)
PHONE..................................248 473-8210
Brian Michaels, *Prdtn Mgr*
Jeff Angelosante, *Accounts Exec*
Joe Fetter, *Accounts Exec*
Eric Michaels, *Accounts Exec*
Larry Willis, *Accounts Exec*
EMP: 2 EST: 2007
SALES (est): 1.3MM Privately Held
WEB: www.comptonpress.com
SIC: 2752 Commercial printing, offset

(G-5208)
CONTEMPORARY INDUSTRIES INC (PA)
24037 Research Dr (48335-2632)
PHONE..................................248 478-8850
Michael Wilczewski, *President*
Josh Pawlovich, *General Mgr*
Leslie Wilczewski, *Vice Pres*
EMP: 6 EST: 1974
SALES (est): 799K Privately Held
WEB: www.contemporaryindustries.com
SIC: 3499 8742 Trophies, metal, except silver; marketing consulting services

(G-5209)
D2 INK INC
Also Called: N2 Publishing
37933 Glengrove Dr (48331-1197)
PHONE..................................248 590-7076
Danny Deddeh, *Principal*
EMP: 5 EST: 2017
SALES (est): 125K Privately Held
WEB: www.n2pub.com
SIC: 2741 Miscellaneous publishing

(G-5210)
DAL-TILE CORPORATION
24640 Drake Rd (48335-2504)
PHONE..................................248 471-7150
Jeff Glazier, *Manager*
EMP: 10
SQ FT: 1,500 Publicly Held
WEB: www.daltile.com
SIC: 2824 5032 Organic fibers, noncellulosic; ceramic wall & floor tile
HQ: Dal-Tile Corporation
7834 C F Hawn Fwy
Dallas TX 75217
214 398-1411

(G-5211)
DEFENSE COMPONENTS AMERICA LLC
30955 Northwestern Hwy (48334-2580)
PHONE..................................248 789-1578
James Carlton,
EMP: 6 EST: 2016
SALES (est): 451.4K Privately Held
SIC: 3599 Machine shop, jobbing & repair

(G-5212)
DERBY HATS BY RACHELLE
35945 Fredericksburg Rd (48331-2574)
PHONE..................................248 489-0971
Rachelle Willnus, *Principal*
EMP: 5 EST: 2009
SALES (est): 135.3K Privately Held
WEB: www.derbyhatsbyrachelle.com
SIC: 2353 Hats, caps & millinery

(G-5213)
DETROIT JEWISH NEWS LTD PARTNR (PA)
Also Called: Jewish News, The
32255 Northwestern Hwy (48334-1566)
PHONE..................................248 354-6060
Arthur Horwitz, *Partner*
EMP: 57 EST: 1942
SALES (est): 7MM Privately Held
WEB: www.thejewishnews.com
SIC: 2711 Newspapers: publishing only, not printed on site; newspapers, publishing & printing

(G-5214)
DETROIT LASER CO LLC
24770 Crestview Ct (48335-1506)
PHONE..................................313 338-9494
EMP: 4 EST: 2015
SALES (est): 106.8K Privately Held
WEB: www.detroitlaserco.com
SIC: 3479 Metal coating & allied service

(G-5215)
DIAMOND ELECTRIC MFG CORP
23065 Commerce Dr (48335-2721)
P.O. Box 830, Eleanor WV (25070-0830)
PHONE..................................734 995-5525
Lloyd Ayers, *General Mgr*
Kunihiko Ishikawa, *Exec VP*
Gene Bialy, *Vice Pres*
Tatsuo Ikenaga, *Opers Staff*
Teresa Ranck, *Purchasing*
EMP: 15 Privately Held
WEB: www.diamond-us.com
SIC: 3694 3621 Ignition coils, automotive; motors & generators
HQ: Diamond Electric Mfg Corp
State Rt 62 Elnor Indus P
Eleanor WV 25070

(G-5216)
DIAMOND MOBA AMERICAS INC
Also Called: Diamond Systems
23400 Haggerty Rd (48335-2613)
P.O. Box 930639, Wixom (48393-0639)
PHONE..................................248 476-7100
Richard Litman, *Vice Pres*
Gale Wegela, *Production*
Cort Murdock, *Engineer*
Chadwick Wierenga, *Engineer*
Jeff Day, *CFO*
◆ EMP: 135 EST: 1934
SQ FT: 150,000
SALES (est): 39.4MM
SALES (corp-wide): 392.5K Privately Held
WEB: www.moba.net
SIC: 3523 Farm machinery & equipment
HQ: Moba Group B.V.
Stationsweg 117
Barneveld 3771
342 455-655

(G-5217)
DIFFERENT BY DESIGN INC
38611 Cedarbrook Ct (48331-2919)
PHONE..................................248 588-4840
Yvette M Mortz, *President*
EMP: 9 EST: 1983
SALES (est): 381.8K Privately Held
SIC: 2791 7336 Typesetting; graphic arts & related design

(G-5218)
DIGESTED ORGANICS LLC
23745 Research Dr (48335-2625)
P.O. Box 3386, Ann Arbor (48106-3386)
PHONE..................................844 934-4378
Robert Levine, *CEO*
Ian Charles, *Ch of Bd*
Chris Maloney, *COO*
EMP: 5 EST: 2013
SALES (est): 1.2MM Privately Held
WEB: www.digestedorganics.com
SIC: 1629 3589 Waste water & sewage treatment plant construction; water treatment equipment, industrial

(G-5219)
DOLPHIN DUMPSTERS LLC
30650 River Gln (48336-4739)
PHONE..................................734 272-8981
Douglas Wischmeyer, *Principal*

▲ = Import ▼ = Export
◆ = Import/Export

GEOGRAPHIC SECTION
Farmington Hills - Oakland County (G-5244)

EMP: 5 EST: 2010
SALES (est): 205.3K **Privately Held**
SIC: 3443 Dumpsters, garbage

(G-5220)
DYNAMIC COLOR PUBLICATIONS
Also Called: Real Estate Book
32905 W 12 Mile Rd # 210 (48334-3344)
PHONE.................................248 553-3115
Tom Hartman, *President*
Tobie Hartman, *Admin Sec*
EMP: 5 EST: 1989
SALES (est): 373.8K **Privately Held**
WEB: www.thomaslhartman.com
SIC: 2721 Periodicals: publishing only

(G-5221)
E Z LOGIC DATA SYSTEMS INC
Also Called: EZ Logic
31455 Northwestern Hwy (48334-2574)
PHONE.................................248 817-8800
Ali Koumaiha, *President*
Omar Azrag, *COO*
EMP: 30 EST: 2013
SALES (est): 2MM **Privately Held**
WEB: www.rtpos.com
SIC: 7371 7372 Computer software systems analysis & design, custom; computer software development & applications; application computer software; business oriented computer software

(G-5222)
EAST COAST FINISHERS
30300 Nwestern Hwy # 113 (48334-3212)
PHONE.................................844 366-9966
EMP: 30 EST: 2014
SALES (est): 1.3MM **Privately Held**
WEB: www.eastcoastfinishers.com
SIC: 3531 Finishers & spreaders (construction equipment)

(G-5223)
ELECTRO-MATIC INTEGRATED INC
23410 Industrial Park Ct (48335-2848)
PHONE.................................248 478-1182
Mario Barraco, *President*
▲ EMP: 20 EST: 2014
SQ FT: 23,180
SALES (est): 5MM **Privately Held**
WEB: www.electro-matic.com
SIC: 3679 Harness assemblies for electronic use: wire or cable

(G-5224)
ELECTRO-MATIC PRODUCTS INC (HQ)
Also Called: Electro-Matic Company
23409 Industrial Park Ct (48335-2849)
PHONE.................................248 478-1182
Richar Laramee, *President*
Derek Klanke, *Accounts Mgr*
Brett Nowak, *Accounts Mgr*
Scott Nuyttens, *Accounts Mgr*
Tom Tubaugh, *Accounts Mgr*
EMP: 1 EST: 1969
SALES (est): 57MM
SALES (corp-wide): 101.4MM **Privately Held**
WEB: www.electro-matic.com
SIC: 3694 5063 Distributors, motor vehicle engine; electrical apparatus & equipment
PA: Electro-Matic Ventures, Inc.
23409 Industrial Park Ct
Farmington Hills MI 48335
248 478-1182

(G-5225)
ELECTRO-MATIC VENTURES INC (PA)
23409 Industrial Park Ct (48335-2849)
PHONE.................................248 478-1182
James C Baker Jr, *President*
Charles Stone, *Engineer*
Thomas Weeks, *Engineer*
David Scaglione, *Treasurer*
Andrew Sornig, *Sales Engr*
▲ EMP: 188 EST: 1972
SQ FT: 42,000

SALES (est): 101.4MM **Privately Held**
WEB: www.electro-matic.com
SIC: 3674 Electrical supplies; semiconductors & related devices

(G-5226)
ELECTRO-MATIC VISUAL INC
23660 Industrial Park Dr (48335-2856)
PHONE.................................248 478-1182
Jim Baker, *CEO*
Rich Laramee, *President*
EMP: 18 EST: 2014
SALES (est): 1.8MM **Privately Held**
WEB: www.electro-matic.com
SIC: 3699 Cleaning equipment, ultrasonic, except medical & dental

(G-5227)
EMAG LLC (DH)
38800 Grand River Ave (48335-1526)
PHONE.................................248 477-7440
Yang Ning, *Sales Mgr*
Hou Qing, *Regl Sales Mgr*
Samantha Chapman, *Mng Member*
M Hessbrueggen,
◆ EMP: 47 EST: 1994
SQ FT: 46,000
SALES (est): 10.1MM
SALES (corp-wide): 601.3MM **Privately Held**
WEB: www.emag.com
SIC: 3541 3999 Grinding machines, metalworking; atomizers, toiletry
HQ: Emag Systems Gmbh
Austr. 24
Salach BW 73084
716 217-0

(G-5228)
EMAG USA CORPORATION
38800 Grand River Ave (48335-1526)
PHONE.................................248 477-7440
M Hessbrueggen, *President*
EMP: 124 EST: 1993
SALES (est): 9.3MM **Privately Held**
SIC: 3541 Grinding machines, metalworking

(G-5229)
EMC CORPORATION
36555 Corporate Dr # 200 (48331-3567)
PHONE.................................248 957-5800
Monica Ransom, *Project Mgr*
John Manera, *Engineer*
Tony McCoy, *Branch Mgr*
Dan Benson, *Consultant*
John Pedrie, *Technology*
EMP: 5 **Publicly Held**
WEB: www.emc.com
SIC: 3572 7372 Computer storage devices; prepackaged software
HQ: Emc Corporation
176 South St
Hopkinton MA 01748
508 435-1000

(G-5230)
EMESA FOODS COMPANY
29790 Palmer Ct (48336-1328)
PHONE.................................248 982-3908
Rakan Chabaan, *CEO*
EMP: 5 EST: 2016
SALES (est): 107.4K **Privately Held**
WEB: www.emesafood.com
SIC: 5499 2032 2051 Gourmet food stores; ethnic foods: canned, jarred, etc.; bakery: wholesale or wholesale/retail combined

(G-5231)
EMM INC
23409 Industrial Park Ct (48335-2849)
PHONE.................................248 478-1182
James C Baker Jr, *President*
Raymond J Persia, *Founder*
Robert Waldie, *Vice Pres*
Thomas C Moore, *Treasurer*
EMP: 9
SQ FT: 42,000
SALES (est): 1.3MM **Privately Held**
SIC: 3643 Connectors & terminals for electrical devices

(G-5232)
EMPIRE PRINTING
28535 Orchard Lake Rd # 400 (48334-2918)
PHONE.................................248 547-9223
Asgar Ismailji, *Partner*
Salma Ismailji, *Partner*
EMP: 4 EST: 1988
SALES (est): 338.1K **Privately Held**
WEB: www.empireprinting.net
SIC: 2752 Commercial printing, offset

(G-5233)
ENCORE COMMERCIAL PRODUCTS INC
Also Called: Postguard
37525 Interchange Dr (48335-1027)
PHONE.................................248 354-4090
Bruce Liebowitz, *President*
Stuart Bernstein, *Vice Pres*
Ronald Klein, *Vice Pres*
▲ EMP: 12 EST: 2002
SQ FT: 2,500
SALES (est): 3.4MM **Privately Held**
WEB: www.postguard.com
SIC: 3081 Unsupported plastics film & sheet

(G-5234)
ENERTROLS INC
Also Called: Boretti Div
23435 Industrial Park Dr (48335-2855)
PHONE.................................734 595-4500
EMP: 40 EST: 1974
SQ FT: 10,000
SALES (est): 4MM **Privately Held**
SIC: 3714 Mfg Industrial Shock Absorbers

(G-5235)
ERA TOOL & ENGINEERING CO
28175 Wingfield Way (48331-3073)
PHONE.................................734 464-7788
Douglas E Thorwall, *President*
Daniel E Thorwall, *Treasurer*
EMP: 10 EST: 1956
SALES (est): 1.2MM **Privately Held**
SIC: 3544 Special dies & tools; jigs & fixtures

(G-5236)
ETERON INC
23944 Freeway Park Dr (48335-2816)
PHONE.................................248 478-2900
John C Kim II, *President*
EMP: 21 EST: 2001
SALES (est): 922.5K **Privately Held**
WEB: www.eteroninc.com
SIC: 2655 Drums, fiber: made from purchased material

(G-5237)
EUKO DESIGN-SIGNS INC
Also Called: Euko Signs
24849 Hathaway St (48335-1552)
PHONE.................................248 478-1330
Eugene Diachenko, *President*
Andrea Diachenko, *Vice Pres*
EMP: 4 EST: 1976
SQ FT: 4,500
SALES (est): 599.9K **Privately Held**
WEB: www.eukosigns.com
SIC: 3993 Electric signs; neon signs; advertising artwork

(G-5238)
EVEREST MANUFACTURING INC
23800 Research Dr (48335-2627)
P.O. Box 51951, Livonia (48151-5951)
PHONE.................................313 401-2608
Mark Hendrickson, *President*
Mike Miller, *Vice Pres*
Steve Miller, *Treasurer*
Dave Morehead, *Sales Staff*
EMP: 12 EST: 2009
SALES (est): 1.2MM **Privately Held**
WEB: www.everestpack.com
SIC: 2679 3086 Building, insulating & packaging paper; insulation or cushioning material, foamed plastic

(G-5239)
EVIEW 360 LLC
39255 Country Club Dr B (48331-3486)
PHONE.................................248 306-5191

Wael Berrached, *President*
Elie Elirany, *Project Mgr*
Evan Veit, *Project Mgr*
Amy Tafilaj, *Treasurer*
Pete Saules, *Program Mgr*
EMP: 34 EST: 2001
SQ FT: 2,000
SALES (est): 4.2MM **Privately Held**
WEB: www.eview360.com
SIC: 7374 7372 8712 Computer graphics service; application computer software; architectural services

(G-5240)
FARAGO & ASSOCIATES LLC
30600 Northwestern Hwy # 105 (48334-3150)
PHONE.................................248 546-7070
Peter J Farago, *Mng Member*
Bruce Macdonald,
Mike Schofding,
Scott Schofding,
EMP: 15 EST: 1994
SALES (est): 2.2MM **Privately Held**
WEB: www.faragoassoc.com
SIC: 2721 Magazines: publishing only, not printed on site

(G-5241)
FASTSIGNS
27615 Halsted Rd (48331-3511)
PHONE.................................248 488-9010
Gregory C Woelfel, *President*
Sue Woelfel, *Treasurer*
Kevin Carrithers, *Accounts Mgr*
Wesley Bekins, *Accounts Exec*
Reghan Moore, *Accounts Exec*
EMP: 7 EST: 1992
SALES (est): 902.6K **Privately Held**
WEB: www.fastsigns.com
SIC: 3993 Signs & advertising specialties

(G-5242)
FENDT BUILDERS SUPPLY INC (PA)
22005 Gill Rd (48335-4646)
P.O. Box 418 (48332-0418)
PHONE.................................248 474-3211
Alan D Fendt, *President*
Junior L Fendt, *Chairman*
Bob Schuessler, *VP Sales*
Jim Gendron, *Sales Staff*
Kurt Weber, *Sales Staff*
EMP: 35 EST: 1924
SQ FT: 42,000
SALES (est): 8MM **Privately Held**
WEB: www.fendtproducts.com
SIC: 5211 3271 3272 2951 Masonry materials & supplies; blocks, concrete or cinder: standard; paving blocks, concrete; blocks, concrete: landscape or retaining wall; concrete products; asphalt paving mixtures & blocks

(G-5243)
FIAMM TECHNOLOGIES LLC (HQ)
23880 Industrial Park Dr (48335-2871)
PHONE.................................248 427-3200
John Defrances, *CEO*
Shercoara Shepard, *Purch Agent*
Dianne Vickrey, *Purchasing*
Jeremy Au, *Sales Mgr*
Ed Miller, *Sales Staff*
◆ EMP: 175 EST: 1990
SQ FT: 80,000
SALES (est): 61.2MM
SALES (corp-wide): 54.9MM **Privately Held**
WEB: www.fiamm.com
SIC: 3714 Horns, motor vehicle
PA: Elettra 1938 Spa
Viale Europa 75
Montecchio Maggiore VI 36075
044 472-5511

(G-5244)
FIVES CINETIC CORP (DH)
23400 Halsted Rd (48335-2840)
PHONE.................................248 477-0800
Michael Dimichele, *President*
Case Vandenkieboom, *Project Mgr*
Dominic Rozario, *Opers Staff*
Janet Driscoll, *Purch Agent*
Eric Boyd, *Buyer*
EMP: 194 EST: 1999

Farmington Hills - Oakland County (G-5245)

SALES (est): 32.9MM
SALES (corp-wide): 2.3MM **Privately Held**
WEB: www.fivesgroup.com
SIC: 3549 Assembly machines, including robotic
HQ: Fives Inc.
23400 Halsted Rd
Farmington Hills MI 48335
248 477-0800

(G-5245)
FORGE DIE & TOOL CORP
31800 W 8 Mile Rd (48336-5210)
PHONE.................248 477-0020
Eric Kchikian, *President*
Van Kchikian, *President*
Roger Bolman, *QC Mgr*
EMP: 52 EST: 1968
SQ FT: 35,000
SALES (est): 2.6MM **Privately Held**
WEB: www.forgeprecision.com
SIC: 3544 Dies & die holders for metal cutting, forming, die casting; special dies & tools

(G-5246)
FORGE PRECISION COMPANY
31800 W 8 Mile Rd (48336-5210)
PHONE.................248 477-0020
Van Kchikian, *President*
Eric Kchikian, *Treasurer*
EMP: 26 EST: 1991
SQ FT: 20,000
SALES (est): 2.8MM **Privately Held**
WEB: www.forgeprecision.com
SIC: 3599 Machine shop, jobbing & repair

(G-5247)
FUJIKURA AUTOMOTIVE AMER LLC (DH)
Also Called: F A A
27555 Executive Dr # 150 (48331-3554)
PHONE.................248 957-0130
Kirk McCardell, *Mng Member*
◆ EMP: 20 EST: 2005
SQ FT: 5,100
SALES (est): 42MM **Privately Held**
WEB: www.fujikura.com
SIC: 3714 Motor vehicle parts & accessories
HQ: America Fujikura Ltd
170 Ridgeview Cir
Duncan SC 29334
800 235-3423

(G-5248)
GABRIEL RIDE CONTROL LLC
39300 Country Club Dr (48331-3473)
PHONE.................248 247-7600
Sesha Peeramsetty, *Senior Engr*
Deborah Passero, *Human Res Mgr*
Stephen Das, *Sales Staff*
Samiayah Crowder, *Sales Executive*
Wanyun Yang, *Business Anlyst*
EMP: 38 EST: 2009
SALES (est): 12.5MM **Privately Held**
WEB: www.gabriel.com
SIC: 3714 Motor vehicle parts & accessories
HQ: Ride Control, Llc
39300 Country Club Dr
Farmington Hills MI 48331

(G-5249)
GEEKS AND GURUS INC
24305 Broadview St (48336-1809)
PHONE.................313 549-2796
Stephen J Bodnar, *Administration*
EMP: 4 EST: 2015
SALES (est): 141.9K **Privately Held**
WEB: www.geeksandgurus.com
SIC: 3652 Pre-recorded records & tapes

(G-5250)
GEHRING CORPORATION
24800 Drake Rd (48335-2506)
PHONE.................248 478-8060
Robert Van Dermolen, *President*
Moreen Durkin, *Principal*
Heinz Gehring, *Chairman*
Dorothy Stein, *Principal*
Tom Newbrough, *Materials Mgr*
EMP: 81 EST: 1976
SQ FT: 43,500
SALES (est): 12.9MM **Privately Held**
WEB: www.gehring-group.com
SIC: 6512 3541 Nonresidential building operators; machine tools, metal cutting type

(G-5251)
GEHRING HONING MACHS
24800 Drake Rd (48335-2506)
PHONE.................248 478-8061
Olas Tessarzyk, *Principal*
Jeff Steinaway, *Project Mgr*
Kristina Conger, *Purchasing*
Jay McIntosh, *Sales Staff*
Wayne Starosciak, *Manager*
EMP: 80 EST: 2001
SALES (est): 4.5MM **Privately Held**
WEB: www.gehring-group.com
SIC: 3599 Grinding castings for the trade

(G-5252)
GLOBAL TECHNOLOGY VENTURES INC (PA)
Also Called: Globaltech Ventures
37408 Hills Tech Dr (48331-3414)
PHONE.................248 324-3707
Steven Willis, *President*
John Schmidt, *Vice Pres*
John Reider, *Representative*
▲ EMP: 7 EST: 2003
SQ FT: 2,500
SALES (est): 1.3MM **Privately Held**
WEB: www.gtvinc.com
SIC: 8711 3089 3321 Designing: ship, boat, machine & product; casting of plastic; ductile iron castings

(G-5253)
GM BASSETT PATTERN INC
31162 W 8 Mile Rd (48336-5201)
PHONE.................248 477-6454
Gerald Bassett, *President*
Scott Defrank, *Principal*
EMP: 5 EST: 1962
SQ FT: 3,200 **Privately Held**
WEB: www.gmbassettpattern.com
SIC: 3543 Industrial patterns

(G-5254)
GRASSHOPPER SIGNS GRAPHICS LLC
Also Called: Identicom
24655 Halsted Rd (48335-1611)
PHONE.................248 946-8475
Giovanni Dinunzio, *Mng Member*
EMP: 10 EST: 2015
SALES (est): 579.2K **Privately Held**
SIC: 3993 Signs & advertising specialties

(G-5255)
GREEN ROOM MICHIGAN LLC
32000 Northwestern Hwy (48334-1565)
PHONE.................248 289-3288
Joseph Rogewitz,
EMP: 10
SALES (est): 250K **Privately Held**
WEB: www.michiganshandyman.com
SIC: 2023 Dietary supplements, dairy & non-dairy based

(G-5256)
GREENMANS SPEEDY PRINTING
30650 W 8 Mile Rd (48336-5302)
PHONE.................248 478-2600
William M Greenman, *President*
EMP: 9 EST: 2015
SALES (est): 122.8K **Privately Held**
WEB: www.gpidirect.com
SIC: 2752 Commercial printing, offset

(G-5257)
HARMAN BECKER AUTO SYSTEMS INC (DH)
Also Called: Harman Consumer Group
39001 W 12 Mile Rd (48331-2912)
P.O. Box 550, Farmington (48332-0550)
PHONE.................248 785-2361
Klaus Blickle, *President*
Herbert K Parker, *President*
Mark Quint, *Vice Pres*
Lori Duprey, *Mfg Staff*
Arndt Hensgens, *Chief Engr*
◆ EMP: 500 EST: 1981
SQ FT: 182,000
SALES (est): 530.5K **Privately Held**
WEB: www.harman.com
SIC: 3812 3931 Navigational systems & instruments; autophones (organs with perforated music rolls)
HQ: Harman International Industries Incorporated
400 Atlantic St
Stamford CT 06901
203 328-3500

(G-5258)
HARMONIE INTERNATIONAL LLC
30201 Orchard Lake Rd (48334-2235)
PHONE.................248 737-9933
William Donahue,
EMP: 11 EST: 1901
SALES (est): 212.2K **Privately Held**
WEB: www.harmonieinternational.com
SIC: 1389 Gas field services

(G-5259)
HEXON CORPORATION
26050 Orchard Lake Rd # 10 (48334-4407)
PHONE.................248 585-7585
Abdullah Zubi, *President*
EMP: 25 EST: 1969
SQ FT: 40,000
SALES (est): 1.3MM **Privately Held**
SIC: 2675 7389 2782 3993 Die-cut paper & board; printers' services: folding, collating; looseleaf binders & devices; signs & advertising specialties; automotive & apparel trimmings

(G-5260)
HIGH IMPACT SOLUTIONS INC
20793 Farmington Rd # 13 (48336-5182)
PHONE.................248 473-9804
Bill Strobridge, *President*
Roy Sexton, *Marketing Staff*
EMP: 3 EST: 1988
SQ FT: 800
SALES (est): 1MM **Privately Held**
WEB: www.highimpact.us
SIC: 2754 7389 8742 Commercial printing, gravure; product endorsement service; marketing consulting services

(G-5261)
HITACHI AMERICA LTD
Farmington Hills Tchncal Ctr Di
34500 Grand River Ave (48335-3373)
PHONE.................248 477-5400
Osumu Abe, *General Mgr*
Craig Fisher, *Vice Pres*
Rob Sharpe, *Vice Pres*
Tom Bieniek, *Facilities Mgr*
Amy Barlow, *Production*
EMP: 4 **Privately Held**
WEB: www.hitachi.us
SIC: 5082 5065 5063 5084 Construction & mining machinery; electronic parts & equipment; electrical apparatus & equipment; industrial machinery & equipment; motor vehicle parts & accessories; petroleum refining
HQ: Hitachi America Ltd
707 Westchester Ave LI7
White Plains NY 10604
914 332-5800

(G-5262)
HLC INDUSTRIES INC
38880 Grand River Ave (48335-1526)
PHONE.................810 477-9600
Kevin Morrow, *President*
James Darling, *Vice Pres*
EMP: 72 EST: 1991
SQ FT: 42,000
SALES (est): 6.7MM **Privately Held**
WEB: www.hlcindustries.com
SIC: 3492 3496 3498 Hose & tube fittings & assemblies, hydraulic/pneumatic; wire cloth & woven wire products; tube fabricating (contract bending & shaping)

(G-5263)
HUF NORTH AMERICA AUTOMOTI
24860 Hathaway St (48335-1513)
PHONE.................248 213-4605
Randy Kingsley, *Branch Mgr*
Adam Jambeck, *Manager*
EMP: 7 **Privately Held**
SIC: 3714 Motor vehicle parts & accessories
HQ: Huf North America Automotive Parts Manufacturing, Corp.
395 T Elmer Cox Rd
Greeneville TN 37743

(G-5264)
HUMANTICS INNVTIVE SLTIONS INC (HQ)
Also Called: First Technology Safety System
23300 Haggerty Rd (48335-2603)
PHONE.................734 451-7878
Christopher O'Connor, *President*
Lin Pan, *General Mgr*
Jim Davis, *Vice Pres*
Michael Jarouche, *Vice Pres*
Mike Van Horn, *Vice Pres*
◆ EMP: 200 EST: 2010
SQ FT: 34,000
SALES (est): 97.4MM **Privately Held**
WEB: www.humanetics.humaneticsgroup.com
SIC: 3829 Testing equipment: abrasion, shearing strength, etc.
PA: Safety Technology Holdings, Inc.
23300 Haggerty Rd
Farmington Hills MI 48335
415 983-2706

(G-5265)
ID ENTERPRISES
24333 Indoplex Cir (48335-2525)
PHONE.................248 442-4849
EMP: 7 EST: 2019
SALES (est): 272.6K **Privately Held**
WEB: www.id-enterprises.com
SIC: 3993 Signs & advertising specialties

(G-5266)
IDEATION INTERNATIONAL INC
32000 Northwestern Hwy # 145 (48334-1565)
PHONE.................248 737-8854
EMP: 15
SQ FT: 1,500
SALES (est): 1.3MM **Privately Held**
SIC: 7371 8742 7372 Custom Computer Programming Services, Nsk

(G-5267)
IDENTICOM SIGN SOLUTIONS LLC
24657 Halsted Rd (48335-1611)
PHONE.................248 344-9590
John Dinunzio, *Principal*
Amanda Scott, *Project Mgr*
Sarah Moore, *Office Admin*
EMP: 10 EST: 2011
SALES (est): 1.7MM **Privately Held**
WEB: www.identicomsigns.com
SIC: 3993 Electric signs

(G-5268)
IFM EFECTOR
39340 Country Club Dr (48331-3434)
PHONE.................800 441-8246
EMP: 5 EST: 2007
SALES (est): 84K **Privately Held**
WEB: www.ifm.com
SIC: 3829 Measuring & controlling devices

(G-5269)
INNOVATIVE SURFACE WORKS
23206 Commerce Dr (48335-2724)
PHONE.................734 261-3010
Gary Bohr, *Owner*
Tony Norris, *Sales Mgr*
Don McFarland, *Sales Staff*
EMP: 18 EST: 2013
SALES (est): 2.3MM **Privately Held**
WEB: www.innovativesurfaceworks.com
SIC: 3996 Hard surface floor coverings

(G-5270)
INOAC INTERIOR SYSTEMS LLC (DH)
Also Called: Inoac Automotive
22670 Haggerty Rd Ste 150 (48335-2637)
PHONE.................248 488-7610
Britney Netherland, *Production*
John Showalter, *Chief Engr*
David Cutting, *Accounts Mgr*
Tony Clemons, *Sales Staff*
Roger Dawes, *Mng Member*

▲ = Import ▼ = Export
◆ = Import/Export

GEOGRAPHIC SECTION   **Farmington Hills - Oakland County (G-5296)**

EMP: 16 EST: 2014
SALES (est): 9.7MM Privately Held
WEB: www.inoacusa.com
SIC: 3069 3089 8711 Rubber automotive products; automotive parts, plastic; engineering services
HQ: Inoac Usa, Inc.
1515 Equity Dr Ste 200
Troy MI 48084
248 619-7031

(G-5271)
INTERNATIONAL WHEEL & TIRE INC (PA)
23255 Commerce Dr (48335-2705)
PHONE................................248 298-0207
Richard Kerwin, *President*
Kevin Kerwin, *Vice Pres*
Mohamad Hassan, *Plant Mgr*
▼ EMP: 29 EST: 2004
SALES (est): 5.1MM Privately Held
WEB: www.iwt-global.com
SIC: 3559 Wheel balancing equipment, automotive

(G-5272)
INTERTEC SYSTEMS LLC (DH)
22670 Haggerty Rd Ste 150 (48335-2637)
PHONE................................248 488-7610
Randy Dunn, *Plant Mgr*
Don Dollens, *Controller*
Robert Depotter, *Mng Member*
Dave Rubin,
▲ EMP: 10 EST: 1996
SQ FT: 70,000
SALES (est): 9.7MM Privately Held
WEB: www.intertecsystems.com
SIC: 3714 Instrument board assemblies, motor vehicle
HQ: Inoac Interior Systems, Llc
22670 Haggerty Rd Ste 150
Farmington Hills MI 48335
248 488-7610

(G-5273)
IRISO USA INC (HQ)
34405 W 12 Mile Rd # 237 (48331-5627)
PHONE................................248 324-9780
Akihiko Ohira, *CEO*
▲ EMP: 27 EST: 1994
SQ FT: 10,281
SALES: 66.5MM Privately Held
WEB: www.irisoconnectors.com
SIC: 3678 Electronic connectors

(G-5274)
JING-JIN ELECTRIC N AMER LLC
34700 Grand River Ave (48335-3375)
PHONE................................248 554-7247
Ping Yu, *President*
Clinton Lockhart, *Principal*
EMP: 2 EST: 2012
SALES (est): 2.1MM Privately Held
WEB: www.jjecn.com
SIC: 3694 Motors, starting: automotive & aircraft
PA: Jing-Jin Electric Technologies Co., Ltd.
103b-4, Floor 1, Building 106, Lize Zhongyuan, Chaoyang District
Beijing 10001

(G-5275)
JOMARK INC
Also Called: Greenman's Printing & Imaging
30650 W 8 Mile Rd (48336-5302)
PHONE................................248 478-2600
William Greenman, *President*
EMP: 20 EST: 1978
SQ FT: 3,600
SALES (est): 1MM Privately Held
SIC: 2752 7338 2791 2759 Commercial printing, offset; secretarial & court reporting; typesetting; commercial printing

(G-5276)
JST SALES AMERICA INC
37879 Interchange Dr (48335-1024)
PHONE................................248 324-1957
Nishi Moto, *President*
Sari Wren, *Sales Staff*
▲ EMP: 15 EST: 2007
SALES (est): 1MM Privately Held
SIC: 3643 Electric connectors

(G-5277)
JUST RITE BRACKET
21565 Verdun St (48336-6070)
PHONE................................248 477-0592
Gary Justice, *Owner*
EMP: 6 EST: 1989
SALES (est): 377.4K Privately Held
WEB: www.justritebracket.com
SIC: 3861 Cameras & related equipment

(G-5278)
JUST WRITE INVITES LLC
30409 Mirlon Dr (48331-2069)
PHONE................................248 797-7844
Kimberly Kraus, *Principal*
EMP: 5 EST: 2012
SALES (est): 166.4K Privately Held
SIC: 2754 Stationery & invitation printing, gravure

(G-5279)
KAYCEE LUX LLC
32031 Middlebelt Rd (48334-1712)
PHONE................................248 461-7117
Kilen Marcie Craig,
EMP: 4 EST: 2017
SALES (est): 56.2K Privately Held
SIC: 5941 3949 5091 Sporting goods & bicycle shops; sporting & athletic goods; sporting & recreation goods

(G-5280)
KERN-LIEBERS PIERON INC
24505 Indoplex Cir (48335-9991)
PHONE................................248 427-1100
Frank Foembacher, *President*
John Hennessey, *Engineer*
Daniel Marvin, *Engineer*
Marcus Marzetti, *Engineer*
Oscar Ortiz, *Sales Mgr*
EMP: 53 EST: 1998
SQ FT: 15,000
SALES (est): 9.1MM
SALES (corp-wide): 694.7MM Privately Held
WEB: www.kern-liebers-north-america.com
SIC: 3446 Architectural metalwork
PA: Hugo Kern Und Liebers Gmbh & Co. Kg Platinen- Und Federnfabrik
Dr.-Kurt-Steim-Str. 35
Schramberg BW 78713
742 251-10

(G-5281)
KINGSTON EDUCATIONAL SOFTWARE
38452 Lynwood Ct (48331-3749)
PHONE................................248 895-4803
Elan Benford, *President*
Sheila Wrightbenford, *General Mgr*
EMP: 5 EST: 2014
SALES (est): 156.6K Privately Held
SIC: 7372 7371 Prepackaged software; computer software development & applications

(G-5282)
KISTLER INSTRUMENT CORP
Also Called: Kistler Automotive
39205 Country Club Dr C20 (48331-3495)
PHONE................................248 489-1090
John Kubler, *President*
EMP: 6 EST: 2002
SALES (est): 18.2K Privately Held
WEB: www.kistler.com
SIC: 3861 Photographic equipment & supplies

(G-5283)
KONRAD TECHNOLOGIES INC (HQ)
Also Called: Konrad Technologies USA
27300 Haggerty Rd F-10 (48331-5702)
PHONE................................248 489-1200
Diane Tibbs, *CEO*
EMP: 3 EST: 2013
SALES (est): 11.4MM
SALES (corp-wide): 23MM Privately Held
WEB: www.konrad-technologies.com
SIC: 3825 Test equipment for electronic & electrical circuits
PA: Konrad Gmbh
Fritz-Reichle-Ring 12
Radolfzell Am Bodensee 78315
773 298-150

(G-5284)
KURABE AMERICA CORPORATION
37735 Interchange Dr (48335-1030)
PHONE................................248 939-5803
Yasuto Kanazawa, *CEO*
Takenobu Kanazawa, *President*
Bram Davis, *Accounts Mgr*
▲ EMP: 16 EST: 2006
SQ FT: 13,800
SALES (est): 1.7MM Privately Held
WEB: www.kurabe.co.jp
SIC: 3357 5531 3714 Automotive wire & cable, except ignition sets: nonferrous; automotive parts; heaters, motor vehicle

(G-5285)
KURE PRODUCTS DISTRIBUTION INC
37460 Hills Tech Dr (48331-3414)
PHONE................................248 330-3933
Aniss Shayota, *Principal*
EMP: 7 EST: 2020
SALES (est): 74.4K Privately Held
SIC: 2834 Proprietary drug products

(G-5286)
KURTZ GRAVEL COMPANY INC (HQ)
33469 W 14 Mile Rd Ste 10 (48331-1521)
PHONE................................810 787-6543
Jeff Sparr, *Principal*
EMP: 40 EST: 1920
SQ FT: 3,500
SALES (est): 23.6MM Privately Held
WEB: www.superiormaterials.net
SIC: 3273 1442 3272 3271 Ready-mixed concrete; gravel mining; concrete products; concrete block & brick
PA: Superior Materials Inc.
585 Stewart Ave
Farmington Hills MI 48333
248 788-8000

(G-5287)
L&W PRODUCTS
34150 Old Timber Ct (48331-1541)
PHONE................................248 661-3889
Wendy Glaser, *Principal*
EMP: 4 EST: 2006
SALES (est): 47.3K Privately Held
SIC: 3999 Manufacturing industries

(G-5288)
LA JALISCIENSE INC (PA)
31048 Applewood Ln (48331-1211)
PHONE................................313 237-0008
Sergio Abundis, *President*
Gloria Cavarell, *Vice Pres*
Myrna Alge, *Treasurer*
Norma Abundes, *Admin Sec*
EMP: 15 EST: 1946
SQ FT: 6,000
SALES (est): 1.4MM Privately Held
SIC: 2099 Tortillas, fresh or refrigerated

(G-5289)
LAMINA INC
Also Called: Anchor Danly
38505 Country Club Dr # 100 (48331-3403)
P.O. Box 2540 (48333-2540)
PHONE................................248 489-9122
Roy Verstraete, *President*
Todd Castile, *Vice Pres*
Steve Zerio, *CFO*
Craig Swoish, *Treasurer*
Zana Kurtovic, *Credit Staff*
EMP: 74 EST: 1992
SQ FT: 130,000
SALES (est): 20.5MM Privately Held
WEB: www.daytonlamina.com
SIC: 3545 3546 Machine tool attachments & accessories; drills, portable, except rock: electric or pneumatic
HQ: Anchor Lamina America, Inc.
3650 S Derenzy Rd
Bellaire MI 49615
248 489-9122

(G-5290)
LAW OFFICES TOWANA TATE PC
30300 Northwestern Hwy (48334-3212)
PHONE................................248 560-7250
EMP: 4 EST: 2019
SALES (est): 162.1K Privately Held
WEB: www.lawfix.com
SIC: 2331 Women's & misses' blouses & shirts

(G-5291)
LINE PRECISION INC
31666 W 8 Mile Rd (48336-5207)
PHONE................................248 474-5280
Stanley R Clarke, *President*
Dave Mertz, *Vice Pres*
EMP: 28 EST: 1966
SQ FT: 28,000
SALES (est): 3.2MM Privately Held
WEB: www.lineprecision.com
SIC: 3599 3545 3544 3369 Grinding castings for the trade; precision tools, machinists'; special dies, tools, jigs & fixtures; nonferrous foundries; aluminum foundries

(G-5292)
LINTECH GLOBAL INC
34119 W 12 Mile Rd # 200 (48331-3300)
PHONE................................248 553-8033
Michael Lin, *President*
Liza Lin, *Vice Pres*
Reagan Blanton, *Human Res Mgr*
Kelly Atwell, *Program Mgr*
Sogand Rahmani, *Manager*
EMP: 100 EST: 2007
SQ FT: 2,000
SALES (est): 13.5MM Privately Held
WEB: www.lintechglobal.com
SIC: 7371 7372 7373 Computer software systems analysis & design, custom; prepackaged software; systems software development services

(G-5293)
LIVONIA MAGNETICS CO INC
23801 Industrial Park Dr # 210 (48335-2822)
PHONE................................734 397-8844
Kenneth Kobmann, *CEO*
Larry Farr, *President*
Glenn R Stork, *Vice Pres*
EMP: 25 EST: 1969
SALES (est): 6.1MM Privately Held
WEB: www.livoniamagnetics.com
SIC: 3535 3264 3695 Conveyors & conveying equipment; belt conveyor systems, general industrial use; magnets, permanent: ceramic or ferrite; magnetic disks & drums

(G-5294)
LOGGING-IN COM INC
32770 Grand River Ave # 2 (48336-3159)
PHONE................................248 466-0708
EMP: 5 EST: 2018
SALES (est): 202.7K Privately Held
WEB: www.logging-in.com
SIC: 2411 Logging camps & contractors

(G-5295)
LOGGING-INCOM LLC
37085 Grand River Ave # 3 (48335-2830)
PHONE................................248 662-7864
Keith Anderson, *Sales Mgr*
Sunitha Pasala,
SAI Loggingin, *Recruiter*
EMP: 10 EST: 2018
SALES (est): 1MM Privately Held
WEB: www.logging-in.com
SIC: 2411 Logging camps & contractors

(G-5296)
LUMECON LLC
23107 Commerce Dr (48335-2723)
PHONE................................248 505-1090
Harrison Brigham, *Prdtn Mgr*
Mike Verleger, *Natl Sales Mgr*
Chris Leonard, *Regl Sales Mgr*
Sharon Shaw, *Manager*
Kurtis Vanderlind, *CIO*
▲ EMP: 3 EST: 2006

Farmington Hills - Oakland County (G-5297)

SALES: 10.4MM Privately Held
WEB: www.lumecon.com
SIC: 3229 5063 Bulbs for electric lights; light bulbs & related supplies; lighting fixtures, commercial & industrial
PA: Carrier & Gable, Inc.
24110 Research Dr
Farmington Hills MI 48335
248 477-8700

(G-5297)
LUMILEDS LLC
34119 W 12 Mile Rd Ste 10 (48331-3308)
PHONE..............................248 553-9080
Hazwani Hidayatul, *Engineer*
Hossein Lotfi, *Senior Engr*
Christine Millgard, *Branch Mgr*
Leslie Bowman, *Manager*
Tran Nguyen, *Technician*
EMP: 40
SALES (corp-wide): 133.6MM Privately Held
WEB: www.lumileds.com
SIC: 3825 3674 Instruments to measure electricity; semiconductors & related devices
HQ: Lumileds Llc
370 W Trimble Rd
San Jose CA 95131
408 964-2900

(G-5298)
MACLEAN ROYAL OAK LLC
23400 Haggerty Rd (48335-2613)
PHONE..............................248 840-0880
EMP: 9
SALES (est): 90K
SALES (corp-wide): 1.1B Privately Held
WEB: www.macleanfogg.com
SIC: 3678 Electronic connectors
PA: Mac Lean-Fogg Company
1000 Allanson Rd
Mundelein IL 60060
847 566-0010

(G-5299)
MAGAZINES IN MOTION INC
35451 Valley Crk (48335-3947)
PHONE..............................248 310-7647
Thomas Ledermann, *Principal*
EMP: 6 EST: 2005
SALES (est): 135.8K Privately Held
SIC: 2721 Periodicals

(G-5300)
MAGNECOR AUSTRALIA LIMITED
24581 Crestview Ct (48335-1503)
PHONE..............................248 471-9505
EMP: 10
SQ FT: 20,000
SALES (est): 1.8MM Privately Held
SIC: 3694 Mfg Engine Electrical Equipment

(G-5301)
MAHLE INC
23030 Mahle Dr (48335-2606)
PHONE..............................248 305-8200
EMP: 37
SALES (est): 10.1MM Privately Held
SIC: 3714 Mfg Motor Vehicle Parts/Accessories

(G-5302)
MAHLE ENG COMPONENTS USA INC
23030 Haggerty Rd (48335-2602)
PHONE..............................248 305-8200
Chris Wright, *Opers Staff*
Alex Schaub, *Production*
John Lusk, *Chief Engr*
Marcio Coenca, *Engineer*
Gary Goedtel, *Engineer*
EMP: 4
SALES (corp-wide): 504.6K Privately Held
WEB: www.us.mahle.com
SIC: 3592 3443 Pistons & piston rings; cylinders, pressure; metal plate
HQ: Mahle Engine Components Usa, Inc.
23030 Mahle Dr
Farmington Hills MI 48335
248 305-8200

(G-5303)
MAHLE INDUSTRIES INCORPORATED (DH)
23030 Mahle Dr (48335-2606)
PHONE..............................248 305-8200
EMP: 50
SQ FT: 100,000
SALES (est): 11.9MM Privately Held
SIC: 3714 7699 Mfg Motor Vehicle Parts/Accessories Repair Services
HQ: Mahle Gmbh
Pragstr. 26-46
Stuttgart 70376
711 501-0

(G-5304)
MAHLE INDUSTRIES INCORPORATED (DH)
23030 Mahle Dr (48335-2606)
P.O. Box 748, Morristown TN (37815-0748)
PHONE..............................248 305-8200
Heinz Junker, *Ch of Bd*
Scott Ferriman, *President*
Pat Bond, *Buyer*
Dawn Jasenas, *Buyer*
Philipp Schurig, *Buyer*
▲ EMP: 1 EST: 1998
SALES (est): 494.5MM
SALES (corp-wide): 504.6K Privately Held
WEB: www.us.mahle.com
SIC: 3714 Motor vehicle parts & accessories
HQ: Mahle Gmbh
Pragstr. 26-46
Stuttgart BW 70376
711 501-0

(G-5305)
MAHLE INDUSTRIES INCORPORATED
23030 Haggerty Rd (48335-2602)
PHONE..............................248 473-6511
Wolfgang Rein, *Branch Mgr*
EMP: 25
SALES (corp-wide): 504.6K Privately Held
WEB: www.mahle-powertrain.com
SIC: 3714 Motor vehicle parts & accessories
HQ: Mahle Industries, Incorporated
23030 Mahle Dr
Farmington Hills MI 48335

(G-5306)
MAHLE MANUFACTURING MGT INC (DH)
23030 Mahle Dr (48335-2606)
PHONE..............................248 735-3623
Bruce Moorehouse, *CEO*
Justin Zakrzewski, *Analyst*
▼ EMP: 5 EST: 2015
SQ FT: 100
SALES (est): 27.3MM
SALES (corp-wide): 504.6K Privately Held
WEB: www.us.mahle.com
SIC: 3714 Motor vehicle parts & accessories

(G-5307)
MAHLE POWERTRAIN LLC (DH)
23030 Mahle Dr (48335-2606)
PHONE..............................248 305-8200
Bruce Fandel, *Plant Mgr*
Tracey Patalon, *Purch Agent*
Austin Coffman, *Engineer*
Paul Windisch, *Engineer*
Amit Meghani, *Senior Engr*
EMP: 90 EST: 2005
SQ FT: 36,500
SALES (est): 51.2MM
SALES (corp-wide): 504.6K Privately Held
WEB: www.mahle-powertrain.com
SIC: 8711 3825 3823 3625 Engineering services; engine electrical test equipment; industrial instrmnts msrmnt display/control process variable; relays & industrial controls

(G-5308)
MAK PRESS & MACHINERY CO
29322 Hemlock Dr (48336-2119)
PHONE..............................734 266-3044
Mark A Krausman, *President*
EMP: 5 EST: 1995
SALES (est): 329.5K Privately Held
WEB: www.makpress.com
SIC: 3542 Machine tools, metal forming type

(G-5309)
MANUFACTURING & INDUS TECH INC
Also Called: Mit
30445 Northwestern Hwy (48334-3158)
PHONE..............................248 522-6959
Ashwini Patil, *President*
Robert Folts, *Vice Pres*
Prabhu Patil, *Vice Pres*
EMP: 50 EST: 1999 Privately Held
WEB: www.mfgind.com
SIC: 7373 7371 3724 7363 Computer-aided engineering (CAE) systems service; computer software development & applications; aircraft engines & engine parts; temporary help service

(G-5310)
MARKETING DISPLAYS INC
Also Called: Marketing Displays Intl
38271 W 12 Mile Rd (48335-3041)
P.O. Box 576, Farmington (48332-0576)
PHONE..............................248 553-1900
Lisa Sarkisian, *President*
John Sarkisian, *COO*
Jason Carr, *Project Mgr*
Phyllis Herrick, *Mfg Spvr*
Ed Parkyn, *Maint Spvr*
◆ EMP: 165 EST: 1965
SQ FT: 87,500
SALES (est): 35.4MM
SALES (corp-wide): 1.6MM Privately Held
WEB: www.mdiworldwide.com
SIC: 3993 3354 2396 Signs, not made in custom sign painting shops; aluminum extruded products; automotive & apparel trimmings
PA: Mdi France
Parc Icade Immeuble Paprika
Rungis 94150
155 531-630

(G-5311)
MAYA JIG GRINDING & GAGE CO
Also Called: Maya Gage Co.
20770 Parker St (48336-5150)
PHONE..............................248 471-0820
Kim S Beier, *President*
Tony Cucci, *Purch Mgr*
Steve Yeager, *QC Mgr*
Vic Adams, *Engineer*
EMP: 16 EST: 1974
SQ FT: 7,000
SALES (est): 2.4MM Privately Held
WEB: www.mayagage.com
SIC: 3544 Special dies & tools

(G-5312)
MCELROYS AUTOMOTIVE SVC LLC
30863 W 10 Mile Rd (48336-2607)
PHONE..............................248 427-0501
Patrick Elroy, *Principal*
EMP: 7 EST: 2009
SALES (est): 296.8K Privately Held
WEB: www.mcelroyauto.com
SIC: 7694 7549 5531 Armature rewinding shops; lubrication service, automotive; automobile & truck equipment & parts

(G-5313)
MEDICAL SYSTEMS RESOURCE GROUP
26105 Orchard Lake Rd (48334-4576)
PHONE..............................248 476-5400
Raymond Malover, *Sales Staff*
Roger Avie
EMP: 7 EST: 2010
SALES (est): 378.6K Privately Held
WEB: www.msrgp.com
SIC: 7372 7373 7378 Application computer software; business oriented computer software; systems integration services; turnkey vendors, computer systems; computer maintenance & repair

(G-5314)
MEDSKER ELECTRIC INC
28650 Grand River Ave (48336-5824)
PHONE..............................248 855-3383
Robert P Medsker, *President*
EMP: 16 EST: 1971
SQ FT: 38,000
SALES (est): 503.5K Privately Held
WEB: www.medskerelectric.com
SIC: 7694 5084 8734 Electric motor repair; instruments & control equipment; testing laboratories

(G-5315)
MERCEDES-BENZ EXTRA LLC
36455 Corp Dr Ste 175 (48331)
PHONE..............................205 747-8006
EMP: 35
SALES (est): 1.1MM Privately Held
SIC: 3423 Mfg Hand/Edge Tools

(G-5316)
METALWORKING INDUSTRIES OF MI
27750 Stansbury Blvd # 100 (48334-3803)
PHONE..............................248 538-0680
Robert Dewey, *Opers Staff*
Mark Sledzinski, *Manager*
Patricia Wehrung, *Manager*
Janet Dobryden, *Consultant*
EMP: 8 EST: 2014
SALES (est): 85.3K Privately Held
WEB: www.mimfund.com
SIC: 3999 Manufacturing industries

(G-5317)
METER DEVICES COMPANY INC
23847 Industrial Park Dr (48335-2860)
PHONE..............................330 455-0301
Jack Roessner, *President*
John T Hanft, *Vice Pres*
▲ EMP: 72 EST: 1918
SQ FT: 70,000
SALES (est): 2.9MM
SALES (corp-wide): 470.6MM Privately Held
WEB: www.tydenbrooks.com
SIC: 3625 3644 3643 3444 Switches, electric power; noncurrent-carrying wiring services; current-carrying wiring devices; sheet metalwork
HQ: E.J. Brooks Company
409 Hoosier Dr
Angola IN 46703
800 348-4777

(G-5318)
MICHIGAN INDUSTRIAL FINISHES
Also Called: Mif Custom Coatings
29463 Shenandoah Dr (48331-2464)
PHONE..............................248 553-7014
Norman Solomon, *President*
Sandra Felisiak, *Purch Agent*
EMP: 15 EST: 1949
SQ FT: 40,000
SALES (est): 443.9K Privately Held
SIC: 2851 Paints & paint additives

(G-5319)
MICHIGAN WHOLESALE PRTG INC
24653 Halsted Rd (48335-1611)
PHONE..............................248 350-8230
Andrew Petty, *President*
EMP: 8 EST: 1986
SQ FT: 5,500
SALES (est): 619.9K Privately Held
WEB: www.mwprinting.com
SIC: 2752 Commercial printing, offset

(G-5320)
MICROTEMP FLUID SYSTEMS LLC
23900 Haggerty Rd (48335-2618)
PHONE..............................248 703-5056
Robert Schoenfeldt,
EMP: 7 EST: 2008 Privately Held
SIC: 3585 Refrigeration & heating equipment

(G-5321)
MILLENNIUM CABINETRY
24748 Crestview Ct (48335-1506)
PHONE..............................248 477-4420

Andy Sallen, *Principal*
Andrew Sallan, *Vice Pres*
EMP: 10 **EST:** 2011
SALES (est): 537.3K **Privately Held**
WEB: www.millenniumcabinetry.com
SIC: 2434 Wood kitchen cabinets

(G-5322)
MILLENNIUM PLANET LLC
Also Called: Millennium Filters
27300 Haggerty Rd Ste F28 (48331-5704)
PHONE 248 835-2331
Robert Oneill, *Principal*
EMP: 6 **EST:** 2013
SALES (est): 586.1K **Privately Held**
WEB: www.millennium-filters.com
SIC: 3569 3533 3563 5085 Filters; filters, general line: industrial; oil field machinery & equipment; air & gas compressors; filters, industrial

(G-5323)
MILLENNM-THE INSIDE SLTION INC
Also Called: Futuristic Furnishings
24748 Crestview Ct (48335-1506)
PHONE 248 645-9005
Andrew Sallan, *President*
Jeff Melloh, *Sales Staff*
EMP: 19 **EST:** 1985
SQ FT: 20,000
SALES (est): 1.2MM **Privately Held**
SIC: 2517 2541 2511 2434 Home entertainment unit cabinets, wood; wood partitions & fixtures; wood household furniture; wood kitchen cabinets

(G-5324)
MLS AUTOMOTIVE INCORPORATED
27280 Haggerty Rd Ste C-9 (48331-3433)
PHONE 844 453-3669
Ahmad Sameh Jwania, *President*
Sam Jwania, *Vice Pres*
Ghath Jouanieh, *Controller*
Ghath Joueniah, *Controller*
EMP: 10 **EST:** 2013
SALES (est): 2.6MM **Privately Held**
WEB: www.mls-automotive.com
SIC: 3647 Automotive lighting fixtures

(G-5325)
MODA MANUFACTURING LLC
39255 Country Club Dr B1 (48331-3486)
PHONE 586 204-5120
EMP: 10 **EST:** 2015
SALES (est): 271.5K **Privately Held**
SIC: 3553 5712 Cabinet makers' machinery; cabinet work, custom

(G-5326)
MOLDEX3D NORTHERN AMERICA INC (HQ)
27725 Stansbury Blvd # 1 (48334-3807)
PHONE 248 946-4570
Anthony Yang, *President*
Michael Dai, *President*
Prabhakar Vallury, *Vice Pres*
Stephen Chung, *Senior Engr*
Kiki Kratzer, *Sales Staff*
EMP: 14 **EST:** 2011
SALES (est): 3.7MM **Privately Held**
WEB: www.moldex3d.com
SIC: 3089 8742 Injection molding of plastics; industry specialist consultants

(G-5327)
MPS TRADING GROUP LLC
38755 Hills Tech Dr (48331-3408)
PHONE 313 841-7588
Edward L Schwartz, *Principal*
EMP: 28 **EST:** 2007
SALES (est): 296.1K **Privately Held**
WEB: www.mpsgrp.com
SIC: 2851 Paint removers

(G-5328)
MR SOGS CREATURES
29700 Citation Cir # 14205 (48331-5829)
PHONE 901 413-0291
Joelle Medici, *Principal*
Emily Doyle, *Principal*
EMP: 4 **EST:** 2013

SALES (est): 129.3K **Privately Held**
WEB: www.mrsogs.com
SIC: 2771 3942 Greeting cards; stuffed toys, including animals

(G-5329)
NABTESCO MOTION CONTROL INC
23976 Freeway Park Dr (48335-2816)
PHONE 248 553-3020
Jason Lazar, *President*
James Gruszczynski, *Sales Staff*
Paul Lugauer, *Sales Staff*
Rosemarie Cook, *Manager*
Kazuhisa Katayama, *Manager*
▲ **EMP:** 16 **EST:** 1999
SALES (est): 2.7MM **Privately Held**
WEB: www.nabtescomotioncontrol.com
SIC: 5084 3593 3566 3594 Industrial machinery & equipment; fluid power cylinders & actuators; speed changers, drives & gears; fluid power pumps & motors; fluid power valves & hose fittings

(G-5330)
NADEX OF AMERICA CORPORATION (PA)
Also Called: W T C
24775 Crestview Ct (48335-1507)
PHONE 248 477-3900
Durrell G Miller, *President*
David Androvich, *Vice Pres*
Steve Connors, *Vice Pres*
▲ **EMP:** 34 **EST:** 1939
SQ FT: 33,000
SALES (est): 25.6MM **Privately Held**
SIC: 3625 3825 8711 3548 Control equipment, electric; current measuring equipment; electrical or electronic engineering; welding apparatus

(G-5331)
NATIONWIDE LASER TECHNOLOGIES
Also Called: Nationwide Toner Cartridge
27600 Farmington Rd B1 (48334-3363)
PHONE 248 488-0155
Omar Tame, *Owner*
EMP: 4 **EST:** 1991
SALES (est): 150K **Privately Held**
WEB: www.toneronline.tv
SIC: 3861 7699 Toners, prepared photographic (not made in chemical plants); photocopy machine repair

(G-5332)
NDEX
31440 Northwestern Hwy (48334-5418)
PHONE 248 432-9000
Scott Goldstein, *CEO*
John Smith, *COO*
EMP: 10 **EST:** 2010
SALES (est): 346.3K **Privately Held**
SIC: 2711 Newspapers, publishing & printing

(G-5333)
NEAPCO HOLDINGS LLC (DH)
38900 Hills Tech Dr (48331-3430)
PHONE 248 699-6500
Kenneth Hopkins, *CEO*
Lynn Barrett, *General Mgr*
Gerald Coster, *COO*
Christopher A Fenton, *Vice Pres*
Erik Leenders, *Vice Pres*
◆ **EMP:** 200 **EST:** 2010
SQ FT: 350,000
SALES (est): 742.6MM **Privately Held**
WEB: www.neapco.com
SIC: 3568 3714 Power transmission equipment; motor vehicle parts & accessories

(G-5334)
NORMAN A LEWIS
Also Called: Global Auditing Solutions
27268 Pembridge Ln (48331-3671)
PHONE 248 219-5736
Norman A Lewis, *Owner*
EMP: 5 **EST:** 2019
SALES (est): 258.5K **Privately Held**
SIC: 2834 Pharmaceutical preparations

(G-5335)
NORTHWEST PATTERN COMPANY
29473 Medbury St (48336-2124)
P.O. Box 403 (48332-0403)
PHONE 248 477-7070
John H Dutton, *President*
EMP: 6 **EST:** 1957
SQ FT: 7,500 **Privately Held**
WEB: www.northwestpattern.com
SIC: 3553 3469 Pattern makers' machinery, woodworking; patterns on metal

(G-5336)
NPI
23910 Freeway Park Dr (48335-2816)
PHONE 248 478-0010
Michael K Hamzey, *President*
EMP: 5 **EST:** 1976
SQ FT: 4,000
SALES (est): 335K
SALES (corp-wide): 12MM **Privately Held**
WEB: www.npiprofile.com
SIC: 7699 3594 3593 3494 Hydraulic equipment repair; fluid power pumps & motors; fluid power cylinders & actuators; valves & pipe fittings
PA: The R M Wright Company Inc
23910 Freeway Park Dr
Farmington Hills MI 48335
248 476-9800

(G-5337)
NU-ERA HOLDINGS INC
32613 Folsom Rd (48336-4424)
PHONE 248 477-2288
Pete Coulter, *Branch Mgr*
EMP: 15
SALES (corp-wide): 10.9MM **Privately Held**
WEB: www.monnier.com
SIC: 3593 Fluid power cylinders, hydraulic or pneumatic
PA: Nu-Era Holdings, Inc.
2034 Fruit St
Clay MI 48001
810 794-4935

(G-5338)
OCUPHIRE PHARMA INC (PA)
37000 Grand River Ave # 1 (48335-2868)
PHONE 248 681-9815
CAM Gallagher, *Ch of Bd*
Mina Sooch, *President*
Bernhard Hoffmann, *Vice Pres*
Richard Rodgers, *Director*
EMP: 6 **EST:** 2001
SQ FT: 1,600 **Publicly Held**
WEB: www.ocuphire.com
SIC: 2834 Pharmaceutical preparations; druggists' preparations (pharmaceuticals); drugs acting on the central nervous system & sense organs

(G-5339)
OFFICE CONNECTION INC (PA)
37676 Enterprise Ct (48331-3440)
PHONE 248 871-2003
Karen Minc, *CEO*
Joseph Minc, *President*
John Johannes, *Accounts Exec*
Jennifer Henderson, *Info Tech Mgr*
EMP: 25 **EST:** 1982
SQ FT: 15,100
SALES (est): 16.8MM **Privately Held**
WEB: www.smartofficedeals.com
SIC: 5112 5021 2752 Office supplies; office furniture; commercial printing, offset

(G-5340)
OXID
24730 Crestview Ct (48335-1506)
PHONE 248 474-9817
Jeffrey Hocking, *Executive*
EMP: 9 **EST:** 2014
SALES (est): 75.9K **Privately Held**
WEB: www.oxid.com
SIC: 3599 Machine shop, jobbing & repair

(G-5341)
P & C GROUP I INC (PA)
Also Called: Camaco
37000 W 12 Mile Rd Ste 10 (48331-3032)
PHONE 248 442-6800
Arvind Pradhan, *President*

Vishal Pradhan, *Purchasing*
Shawn Kerns, *Manager*
George Husted, *Director*
▲ **EMP:** 35 **EST:** 1996
SQ FT: 3,000
SALES (est): 494.7MM **Privately Held**
SIC: 3465 3499 Automotive stampings; automobile seat frames, metal

(G-5342)
PARAMETER DRIVEN SOFTWARE INC (PA)
32605 W 12 Mile Rd # 275 (48334-3337)
PHONE 248 553-6410
Patrick K Comeaux, *President*
Linda Comeaux, *Admin Sec*
EMP: 10 **EST:** 1981
SQ FT: 1,700
SALES (est): 894.8K **Privately Held**
SIC: 7373 7372 Local area network (LAN) systems integrator; business oriented computer software

(G-5343)
PAT RO PUBLISHING
32364 Nottingwood St (48334-2744)
PHONE 248 553-4935
Patrick Byrnes, *Principal*
EMP: 4 **EST:** 2004
SALES (est): 105.6K **Privately Held**
SIC: 2741 Miscellaneous publishing

(G-5344)
PCB LOAD & TORQUE INC
24350 Indoplex Cir (48335-2524)
PHONE 248 471-0065
Mike Lally, *President*
EMP: 20 **EST:** 2009
SALES (est): 5.6MM
SALES (corp-wide): 8.6B **Publicly Held**
WEB: www.pcb.com
SIC: 3829 Physical property testing equipment
HQ: Pcb Piezotronics, Inc.
3425 Walden Ave
Depew NY 14043
716 684-0001

(G-5345)
PCB PIEZOTRONICS INC
24350 Indoplex Cir (48335-2524)
PHONE 716 684-0001
Kirk Hinkins, *Administration*
EMP: 8
SALES (corp-wide): 8.6B **Publicly Held**
WEB: www.larsondavis.com
SIC: 3829 Measuring & controlling devices
HQ: Pcb Piezotronics, Inc.
3425 Walden Ave
Depew NY 14043
716 684-0001

(G-5346)
PHILIPS NORTH AMERICA LLC
Also Called: Philips Automotive Ltg N Amer
34119 W 12 Mile Rd Ste 10 (48331-3308)
PHONE 248 553-9080
Dennis Samsioippo, *Manager*
EMP: 101
SALES (corp-wide): 133.6MM **Privately Held**
WEB: www.usa.philips.com
SIC: 3641 Electric lamps
HQ: Philips North America Llc
222 Jacobs St Fl 3
Cambridge MA 02141
978 659-3000

(G-5347)
PIEDMONT CONCRETE INC
29934 W 8 Mile Rd (48336-5507)
PHONE 248 474-7740
David Guidobono, *President*
Anthony Guidobono, *Vice Pres*
EMP: 26 **EST:** 1959
SQ FT: 9,916
SALES (est): 2.2MM **Privately Held**
WEB: www.piedmontconcreteinc.com
SIC: 3273 Ready-mixed concrete

(G-5348)
PKC GROUP USA INC (DH)
36555 Corp Dr Ste 300 (48331)
PHONE 248 489-4700
Frank Sovis, *President*
Kieran Sheehy, *General Mgr*

Farmington Hills - Oakland County (G-5349)

Ivo Volkov, *General Mgr*
Rose Mendoza, *Opers Staff*
Jason Collins, *Production*
EMP: 1398 **EST:** 1997
SALES (est): 1.9B **Privately Held**
WEB: www.pkcgroup.com
SIC: 3679 Harness assemblies for electronic use: wire or cable

(G-5349)
POLY FLEX PRODUCTS INC (PA)
23093 Commerce Dr (48335-2721)
PHONE..................734 458-4194
Mark Kirchmer, *CEO*
Ken Bylo, *Vice Pres*
Ken Przbylowicz, *Vice Pres*
Aaron Fedewa, *Plant Mgr*
Bob Hatherley, *Plant Mgr*
◆ **EMP:** 48 **EST:** 2003
SQ FT: 20,000
SALES (est): 12.9MM **Privately Held**
WEB: www.polyflexpro.com
SIC: 3089 Injection molding of plastics

(G-5350)
POSA-CUT CORPORATION
23600 Haggerty Rd (48335-2615)
PHONE..................248 474-5620
Kevin B O Brien, *President*
Chris O Brien, *Vice Pres*
Donna O Brien, *Treasurer*
Ellen Obrien, *Office Mgr*
Janet Soderberg, *Admin Sec*
EMP: 20 **EST:** 1959
SQ FT: 12,000
SALES (est): 3.5MM **Privately Held**
WEB: www.posacut.com
SIC: 3541 3545 5084 Machine tools, metal cutting type; machine tool accessories; industrial machinery & equipment

(G-5351)
POWER CONTROLLERS LLC
23900 Freeway Park Dr (48335-2816)
PHONE..................248 888-9896
David Backus, *CEO*
Mark Stanczak, *President*
Kym Croucher, *Office Mgr*
EMP: 4
SALES (est): 154.1K **Privately Held**
WEB: www.pwrcontrollers.com
SIC: 3613 3621 Power connectors, electric; power switching equipment; motors & generators; electric motor & generator parts; control equipment for electric buses & locomotives

(G-5352)
PRIDE SOURCE CORPORATION
Also Called: Between The Lines
33608 Edmonton St (48335-5226)
PHONE..................734 293-7200
Susan Horowitz, *Publisher*
Janet R Stevenson, *CFO*
EMP: 19 **EST:** 1995
SALES (est): 3.4MM **Privately Held**
WEB: www.pridesource.com
SIC: 2721 Magazines: publishing only, not printed on site

(G-5353)
PRINT HOUSE INC
23014 Commerce Dr (48335-2720)
PHONE..................248 473-1414
Kenneth D Manko, *Vice Pres*
Barry J Melamed, *Vice Pres*
Shane Fisher, *Graphic Designe*
EMP: 19 **EST:** 1975
SQ FT: 7,200
SALES (est): 3.4MM **Privately Held**
WEB: www.theprinthouse.com
SIC: 2752 7331 Commercial printing, offset; mailing service

(G-5354)
PRINTED IMPRESSIONS INC
32210 W 8 Mile Rd (48336-5100)
PHONE..................248 473-5333
Thomas Mullen, *President*
Douglas Mullen, *Vice Pres*
Evelyn Mullen, *Treasurer*
EMP: 4 **EST:** 1987
SQ FT: 2,500 **Privately Held**
WEB: www.printedimpressions.com
SIC: 2752 Commercial printing, offset

(G-5355)
PROSTHETIC & IMPLANT DENTISTRY
31396 Northwestern Hwy (48334-2534)
PHONE..................248 254-3945
Furat George, *Principal*
EMP: 8 **EST:** 2018
SALES (est): 370.2K **Privately Held**
WEB: www.enameldentalstudio.com
SIC: 3842 Prosthetic appliances

(G-5356)
PTM-ELECTRONICS INC
39205 Country Club Dr C40 (48331-5701)
PHONE..................248 987-4446
Jeffery Cohen, *President*
Jim McGrew, *Vice Pres*
▲ **EMP:** 12 **EST:** 1989
SQ FT: 6,000
SALES (est): 2.4MM **Privately Held**
WEB: www.ptmelec.com
SIC: 3825 8711 Test equipment for electronic & electrical circuits; designing: ship, boat, machine & product

(G-5357)
PURE LUXE LLC
22541 Maywood Ct (48335-3940)
PHONE..................248 987-8734
Jacinta Thompson, *CEO*
EMP: 7 **EST:** 2013
SALES (est): 259.1K **Privately Held**
SIC: 2339 5122 Women's & misses' accessories; cosmetics, perfumes & hair products

(G-5358)
PUTNAM CABINETRY
29233 Scotten St (48336-5568)
PHONE..................248 442-0118
Dennis Putnam, *Principal*
EMP: 4 **EST:** 2007
SALES (est): 131.4K **Privately Held**
SIC: 2434 Wood kitchen cabinets

(G-5359)
QAD INC
27555 Executive Dr # 155 (48331-3554)
PHONE..................248 324-9890
Michael Blough, *Vice Pres*
Tracy Turnbull, *Branch Mgr*
Seema Jain, *Analyst*
EMP: 4
SALES (corp-wide): 307.8MM **Publicly Held**
WEB: www.qad.com
SIC: 7372 Business oriented computer software
PA: Qad Inc.
100 Innovation Pl
Santa Barbara CA 93108
805 566-6000

(G-5360)
QUESTYME USA INC
26878 Wembley Ct (48331-3529)
PHONE..................832 912-4994
Zainab Boxwala, *President*
Yusuf Bhindarwala, *Principal*
EMP: 7 **EST:** 2009
SALES (est): 1.2MM **Privately Held**
WEB: www.questyme.com
SIC: 3629 Electronic generation equipment

(G-5361)
QUIGLEY INDUSTRIES INC (HQ)
38880 Grand River Ave (48335-1526)
PHONE..................248 426-8600
Carol C Quigley, *President*
Alice Flynn, *Vice Pres*
Shana Degroff, *Prdtn Mgr*
Paul Vu, *Engineer*
Christine McCanham, *Bookkeeper*
EMP: 50 **EST:** 1947
SQ FT: 42,000
SALES (est): 8.6MM
SALES (corp-wide): 10.9MM **Privately Held**
WEB: www.quigleyind.com
SIC: 3469 3465 3443 Stamping metal for the trade; automotive stampings; fabricated plate work (boiler shop)
PA: Quigley Manufacturing, Inc.
38880 Grand River Ave
Farmington Hills MI 48335
248 426-8600

(G-5362)
QUIGLEY MANUFACTURING INC (PA)
38880 Grand River Ave (48335-1526)
PHONE..................248 426-8600
Carol C Quigley, *President*
Alice Flynn, *Vice Pres*
Robert A Moug, *Treasurer*
EMP: 5 **EST:** 1954
SQ FT: 42,000
SALES (est): 10.9MM **Privately Held**
WEB: www.quigleyind.com
SIC: 3465 3469 3498 3829 Automotive stampings; metal stampings; tube fabricating (contract bending & shaping); gauges, motor vehicle: oil pressure, water temperature

(G-5363)
R M WRIGHT COMPANY INC (PA)
23910 Freeway Park Dr (48335-2816)
P.O. Box 382, Farmington (48332-0382)
PHONE..................248 476-9800
Michael K Hamzey, *Principal*
EMP: 22 **EST:** 1940
SQ FT: 15,000
SALES (est): 12MM **Privately Held**
WEB: www.rmwrightco.com
SIC: 5085 5084 3593 3494 Valves & fittings; industrial machinery & equipment; fluid power cylinders & actuators; valves & pipe fittings; manufactured hardware (general)

(G-5364)
RACELOGIC USA CORPORATION
27260 Haggerty Rd Ste A2 (48331-3400)
PHONE..................248 994-9050
Reid Scott, *President*
EMP: 9 **EST:** 2012
SALES (est): 984.6K **Privately Held**
WEB: www.racelogic.co.uk
SIC: 3825 Instruments to measure electricity

(G-5365)
READY MOLDS INC (PA)
Also Called: Ready Boring & Tooling
32645 Folsom Rd (48336-4424)
P.O. Box 655, Farmington (48332-0655)
PHONE..................248 474-4007
Lawrence P Nussio, *President*
EMP: 15 **EST:** 1972
SQ FT: 9,000
SALES (est): 2.2MM **Privately Held**
WEB: www.readyboring.com
SIC: 3544 Industrial molds

(G-5366)
REESE BUSINESS GROUP LLC
29236 Fieldstone (48334-4102)
PHONE..................246 216-2605
William Reese,
EMP: 4 **EST:** 2020
SALES (est): 120K **Privately Held**
SIC: 3559 Ozone machines

(G-5367)
RENAISSANCE MEDIA LLC
Also Called: Detroit Jewish New
32255 Northwestern Hwy # 205 (48334-1574)
PHONE..................248 354-6060
Craig Cphipps, *Controller*
Arthur M Horwitz,
Hazel Bender, *Analyst*
Kevin Browett,
Arthur Horwitz,
EMP: 14 **EST:** 2002
SALES (est): 2.4MM **Privately Held**
WEB: www.jewishrenaissancemedia.com
SIC: 2721 Magazines: publishing only, not printed on site

(G-5368)
REYNOLDS WATER CONDITIONING CO
24545 Hathaway St (48335-1549)
PHONE..................248 888-5000
James A Reynolds Sr, *President*
Elizabeth Reynolds, *Admin Sec*
▲ **EMP:** 15 **EST:** 1931
SQ FT: 10,000
SALES (est): 2.4MM **Privately Held**
WEB: www.reynoldswater.com
SIC: 3589 5999 Water treatment equipment, industrial; water filters & softeners, household type; water purification equipment

(G-5369)
RIDE CONTROL LLC (HQ)
39300 Country Club Dr (48331-3473)
PHONE..................248 247-7600
Lisa J Bahash, *CEO*
Anna Christensen, *Managing Dir*
John Gabriel, *Principal*
Jennifer McKheen, *Vice Pres*
Lily Ng, *Project Mgr*
◆ **EMP:** 100 **EST:** 1919
SQ FT: 20,000
SALES (est): 171.4MM **Privately Held**
WEB: www.gabriel.com
SIC: 3714 Shock absorbers, motor vehicle

(G-5370)
ROBERT BOSCH BTRY SYSTEMS LLC (HQ)
38000 Hills Tech Dr (48331-3418)
PHONE..................248 620-5700
Matt Jonas, *President*
John Lieske, *Engineer*
Chris Millon, *Engineer*
Priscilla Stephan, *Engineer*
Reinhardt Peper,
▲ **EMP:** 100 **EST:** 1994
SALES (est): 25MM
SALES (corp-wide): 297.8MM **Privately Held**
WEB: www.cobasys.com
SIC: 3691 3692 Storage batteries; primary batteries, dry & wet
PA: ROBERTBOSCHSTIFTUNG Gesellschaft Mit Beschrankter Haftung
Heidehofstr. 31
Stuttgart BW 70184
711 460-840

(G-5371)
ROBERT BOSCH LLC (DH)
Also Called: Robert Bosch GMBH
38000 Hills Tech Dr (48331-3418)
P.O. Box 2609 (48333-2609)
PHONE..................248 876-1000
Tim Frasier, *President*
Gad Toren, *Partner*
Todd Hertzler, *Vice Pres*
Kurt Person, *Vice Pres*
Ed Prange, *Vice Pres*
◆ **EMP:** 1 **EST:** 1906
SALES (est): 220.7MM
SALES (corp-wide): 297.8MM **Privately Held**
WEB: www.bosch.us
SIC: 3694 5013 5064 3565 Motors, starting: automotive & aircraft; distributors, motor vehicle engine; automotive supplies & parts; automotive engines & engine parts; automotive brakes; radios, motor vehicle; packaging machinery; deburring machines; motor vehicle brake systems & parts
HQ: Robert Bosch North America Corporation
1 Tower Ln Ste 3100
Oakbrook Terrace IL 60181
708 865-5200

(G-5372)
ROGER ZATKOFF COMPANY (PA)
Also Called: Zatkoff Seals-Farmington
23230 Industrial Park Dr (48335-2850)
P.O. Box 486, Farmington (48332-0486)
PHONE..................248 478-2400
Gary Zatkoff, *CEO*
Patty Anson, *General Mgr*
David Zatkoff, *Vice Pres*
Erin Bydash, *Purchasing*
Sue Pasquantonio, *Purchasing*
▲ **EMP:** 42 **EST:** 1959
SQ FT: 25,000
SALES (est): 102.1MM **Privately Held**
WEB: www.zatkoff.com
SIC: 5085 3053 Seals, industrial; gaskets, packing & sealing devices; gaskets & sealing devices

GEOGRAPHIC SECTION
Farmington Hills - Oakland County (G-5398)

(G-5373)
ROUTEONE HOLDINGS LLC (HQ)
Also Called: Maximtrak
31500 Northwestern Hwy # 300 (48334-2501)
PHONE..................800 282-6308
Justin Oesterle, *CEO*
Janice Basile, *CFO*
EMP: 35 **EST:** 2016
SALES (est): 11.2MM
SALES (corp-wide): 149MM **Privately Held**
WEB: www.routeone.com
SIC: 7372 Business oriented computer software
PA: Routeone Llc
31500 Nrthwstrn Hwy 200
Farmington Hills MI 48334
866 768-8201

(G-5374)
RS TECHNOLOGIES LTD
25286 Witherspoon St (48335-1369)
P.O. Box 2959 (48333-2959)
PHONE..................248 888-8260
Ralph S Shoberg, *President*
Jo Ellen Prior, *Admin Asst*
EMP: 13 **EST:** 1991
SALES (est): 868.8K **Privately Held**
SIC: 3829 Physical property testing equipment

(G-5375)
SAFETY TECHNOLOGY HOLDINGS INC (PA)
23300 Haggerty Rd (48335-2603)
PHONE..................415 983-2706
Christopher J Oconnor, *President*
Bryan J Brown, *Development*
James Habel, *CFO*
Janis E Major, *Human Resources*
EMP: 17 **EST:** 2009
SALES (est): 97.4MM **Privately Held**
SIC: 3829 Testing equipment: abrasion, shearing strength, etc.

(G-5376)
SBSI SOFTWARE INC (PA)
23570 Haggerty Rd (48335-2614)
PHONE..................248 567-3044
Kristen Bye, *Principal*
Anastasia Kennebrew, *Controller*
Kelly Kizyma, *Accounts Mgr*
Julie Haarala, *Manager*
Russ Bergendahl, *Director*
EMP: 14 **EST:** 2011
SALES (est): 276.8K **Privately Held**
WEB: www.digitalsignup.net
SIC: 7372 Application computer software

(G-5377)
SFI ACQUISITION INC
Also Called: State Fabricators
30550 W 8 Mile Rd (48336-5301)
PHONE..................248 471-1500
Charles S Peltz, *CEO*
Matt Peltz, *President*
Robert Cureton, *Vice Pres*
Roy Rodriguez, *Facilities Mgr*
Mark Ransley, *Supervisor*
EMP: 50 **EST:** 1946
SQ FT: 25,000
SALES (est): 15.1MM **Privately Held**
WEB: www.statefab.com
SIC: 3537 2542 3443 3544 Pallets, metal; skids, metal; dollies (hand or power trucks), industrial except mining; pallet racks: except wood; weldments; special dies, tools, jigs & fixtures; sheet metalwork; wood pallets & skids

(G-5378)
SIGNATURE DESIGNS INC
24357 Indoplex Cir (48335-2525)
PHONE..................248 426-9735
Robert Pietila, *President*
Bernard Hurwitz, *Vice Pres*
Rebecca Rakowski, *Admin Sec*
▲ **EMP:** 5 **EST:** 1994
SQ FT: 3,600
SALES (est): 1.5MM **Privately Held**
SIC: 2591 2391 Window blinds; draperies, plastic & textile: from purchased materials

(G-5379)
SIGNS IN LLC
34705 W 12 Mile Rd (48331-3259)
P.O. Box 3253 (48333-3253)
PHONE..................248 939-7446
Richard Daguanno, *Administration*
EMP: 8 **EST:** 2015
SALES (est): 407.8K **Privately Held**
SIC: 3993 Signs & advertising specialties

(G-5380)
SIGNS OF PROSPERITY LLC
27615 Halsted Rd (48331-3511)
PHONE..................248 488-9010
Jay Newby, *Principal*
EMP: 9 **EST:** 2011
SALES (est): 909.7K **Privately Held**
SIC: 3993 Signs & advertising specialties

(G-5381)
SIGNTEXT INCORPORATED
Also Called: Signtext 2
24333 Indoplex Cir (48335-2525)
PHONE..................248 442-9080
Michael Frasier, *President*
EMP: 24 **EST:** 1984
SQ FT: 12,500
SALES (est): 3MM **Privately Held**
WEB: www.signtext.com
SIC: 3993 Signs, not made in custom sign painting shops; letters for signs, metal

(G-5382)
SIMPLIFY INVENTIONS LLC
38955 Hills Tech Dr (48331-3431)
PHONE..................248 960-1700
Michael Rehrauer, *CEO*
EMP: 100 **EST:** 2018
SALES (est): 3MM **Privately Held**
SIC: 7379 2086 Computer related services; bottled & canned soft drinks

(G-5383)
SOFTWARE FINESSE LLC (PA)
31224 Mulfordton St # 200 (48334-1408)
P.O. Box 250673, West Bloomfield (48325-0673)
PHONE..................248 737-8990
Ivan Avramov, *CEO*
Galia Avramov, *Principal*
EMP: 7 **EST:** 1997
SALES (est): 925.8K **Privately Held**
WEB: www.softwarefinesse.com
SIC: 7371 7374 7372 Computer software systems analysis & design, custom; computer software writing services; optical scanning data service; prepackaged software; application computer software

(G-5384)
SPECIALTY STEEL TREATING INC
31610 W 8 Mile Rd (48336-5207)
PHONE..................586 293-5355
Justin Kollmorgen, *General Mgr*
Tony Richey, *General Mgr*
Mark Sosnowski, *Vice Pres*
Brandon Scruggs, *Plant Supt*
Denmis Kollmorgen, *Facilities Mgr*
EMP: 52
SQ FT: 42,000
SALES (corp-wide): 56.3MM **Privately Held**
WEB: www.sst.net
SIC: 3398 Metal heat treating
PA: Specialty Steel Treating, Inc.
34501 Commerce
Fraser MI 48026
586 293-5355

(G-5385)
SPRAYING SYSTEMS CO
39340 Country Club Dr # 100 (48331-3434)
P.O. Box 587, Farmington (48332-0587)
PHONE..................248 473-1331
Rick Maxwell, *CFO*
Richard Maxwell, *Manager*
EMP: 10
SALES (corp-wide): 348.1MM **Privately Held**
WEB: www.spray.com
SIC: 3499 Nozzles, spray: aerosol, paint or insecticide
PA: Spraying Systems Co.
200 W North Ave
Glendale Heights IL 60139
630 665-5000

(G-5386)
STANLEY ELECTRIC SALES AMERICA
37000 Grand River Ave (48335-2868)
PHONE..................248 471-1300
Sidney Alenander, *Owner*
EMP: 6 **EST:** 2014
SALES (est): 128K **Privately Held**
SIC: 3699 1731 Electrical equipment & supplies; electrical work

(G-5387)
STAR CUTTER CO (PA)
Also Called: Star Cutter Company
23461 Industrial Park Dr (48335-2855)
P.O. Box 376, Farmington (48332-0376)
PHONE..................248 474-8200
Bradley L Lawton, *President*
Julie Grimm, *Business Mgr*
Thomas Bel, *Vice Pres*
Mike Billiel, *Vice Pres*
David W Goodfellow, *Vice Pres*
◆ **EMP:** 30 **EST:** 1927
SQ FT: 25,000
SALES (est): 204.2MM **Privately Held**
WEB: www.starcutter.com
SIC: 3545 3479 3546 3541 Cutting tools for machine tools; hobs; reamers, machine tool; drilling machine attachments & accessories; painting, coating & hot dipping; power-driven handtools; machine tools, metal cutting type

(G-5388)
STAR SU COMPANY LLC
23461 Industrial Park Dr (48335-2855)
P.O. Box 376 (48332-0376)
PHONE..................248 474-8200
David Goodfellow, *General Mgr*
Tessa Johnson, *Sales Staff*
Dan Kalafut, *Sales Staff*
John Brandon, *Supervisor*
Andy Kobs, *Supervisor*
EMP: 5
SALES (corp-wide): 44.2MM **Privately Held**
WEB: www.star-su.com
SIC: 3541 Machine tools, metal cutting type
PA: Star Su Company, Llc
5200 Prairie Stone Pkwy
Hoffman Estates IL 60192
847 649-1450

(G-5389)
STERLING MILLWORK INC
Also Called: Sterling Contracting
24000 Research Dr (48335-2600)
PHONE..................248 427-1400
Mark A Bolitho, *President*
Nancy Bolitho, *Vice Pres*
EMP: 70 **EST:** 1981
SALES (est): 12.3MM **Privately Held**
WEB: www.sterlingmillwork.com
SIC: 2541 2431 1542 2517 Wood partitions & fixtures; millwork; commercial & office buildings, renovation & repair; commercial & office building, new construction; wood television & radio cabinets

(G-5390)
STEWART STEEL SPECIALTIES
20755 Whitlock St (48336-5169)
PHONE..................248 477-0680
John C Stewart, *Partner*
Rick Stewart, *Partner*
EMP: 5 **EST:** 1911
SQ FT: 2,000
SALES (est): 469.3K **Privately Held**
WEB: www.stewartsteel.us
SIC: 3444 Sheet metalwork

(G-5391)
STYROLUTION
29247 Glencastle Ct (48336-1416)
PHONE..................248 320-7230
John Fialka, *President*
EMP: 7 **EST:** 2018
SALES (est): 256.7K **Privately Held**
WEB: www.ineos-styrolution.com
SIC: 2821 Plastics materials & resins

(G-5392)
SUMIKA POLYMERS NORTH AMER LLC (DH)
27555 Executive Dr # 300 (48331-3555)
PHONE..................248 284-4797
Osanu Sugasawa, *President*
Brian Weider, *President*
Joe Johnson, *CFO*
Andrew Johnston, *Sales Staff*
▲ **EMP:** 37 **EST:** 2011
SQ FT: 3,000
SALES (est): 29MM **Privately Held**
WEB: www.sumikapna.com
SIC: 2821 Polyoxymethylene resins
HQ: Sumitomo Chemical America, Inc.
150 E 42nd St Rm 701
New York NY 10017
212 572-8200

(G-5393)
SUN PHARMACEUTICAL INDS INC
29714 Orion Ct (48334-4114)
PHONE..................248 346-7302
Anup Kulkarni, *General Mgr*
Jitendra Doshi, *Principal*
Ed Barnes, *Vice Pres*
Phanindranat Punji, *Vice Pres*
Melissa Sorrentino, *Vice Pres*
EMP: 15 **EST:** 2011
SALES (est): 404K **Privately Held**
SIC: 2834 Pharmaceutical preparations

(G-5394)
SUPERIOR MATERIALS LLC (PA)
30701 W 10 Mile Rd (48336-2617)
P.O. Box 2900 (48333-2900)
PHONE..................248 788-8000
Jeff Spahr, *President*
Gary Lowell, *VP Opers*
Pat Joyce, *Cust Mgr*
Alex Blakeman, *Surgery Dir*
EMP: 99 **EST:** 2007
SALES (est): 8.5MM **Privately Held**
WEB: www.superiormaterialsllc.com
SIC: 3273 Ready-mixed concrete

(G-5395)
SUPERIOR MATERIALS INC (PA)
585 Stewart Ave (48333)
P.O. Box 2900 (48333-2900)
PHONE..................248 788-8000
Gary Lowell, *President*
Bruce Schimmel, *Sales Staff*
EMP: 2 **EST:** 2005
SALES (est): 23.6MM **Privately Held**
WEB: www.superiormaterials.net
SIC: 3273 Ready-mixed concrete

(G-5396)
SUPERIOR MTLS HOLDINGS LLC
30701 W 10 Mile Rd (48336-2617)
P.O. Box 2900 (48333-2900)
PHONE..................248 788-8000
Jeff Spahr, *President*
Karen Giles, *CFO*
Marc Robinson, *CIO*
EMP: 32 **EST:** 2011
SALES (est): 1MM **Privately Held**
WEB: www.superiormaterialsllc.com
SIC: 3273 Ready-mixed concrete

(G-5397)
TACHI-S ENGINEERING USA INC (HQ)
23227 Commerce Dr (48335-2705)
PHONE..................248 478-5050
Kenji Kajihata, *President*
Paula G Thompson, *Publisher*
Mary Britton, *Senior Buyer*
Christopher Robles, *Buyer*
Michael Muzzin, *Purchasing*
▲ **EMP:** 85 **EST:** 1986
SQ FT: 57,400
SALES (est): 173MM **Privately Held**
WEB: www.tachi-s.com
SIC: 2531 Seats, automobile

(G-5398)
THERMO FLEX LLC
23093 Commerce Dr (48335-2721)
PHONE..................734 458-4194

Farmington Hills - Oakland County (G-5399)

EMP: 9 EST: 2019
SALES (est): 715.2K **Privately Held**
WEB: www.polyflexpro.com
SIC: 3089 Injection molding of plastics

(G-5399)
THREAD GRINDING SERVICE INC
32420 W 8 Mile Rd (48336-5104)
PHONE.................................248 474-5350
Donna Dancik, *President*
EMP: 8 EST: 1965
SQ FT: 2,000
SALES (est): 567.2K **Privately Held**
SIC: 3599 Machine shop, jobbing & repair

(G-5400)
THREADS INVISABLE
31535 W 13 Mile Rd (48334-2103)
PHONE.................................248 516-5051
EMP: 6 EST: 2018
SALES (est): 85.8K **Privately Held**
WEB: www.invisible-thread.com
SIC: 2395 Embroidery products, except schiffli machine

(G-5401)
TITUS WELDING COMPANY
20750 Sunnydale St (48336-5251)
PHONE.................................248 476-9366
Joseph F Cavanaugh, *President*
Paul E Centers, *Vice Pres*
EMP: 12 EST: 1946
SQ FT: 7,000
SALES (est): 1.8MM **Privately Held**
WEB: www.tituswelding.com
SIC: 1791 7692 Structural steel erection; welding repair

(G-5402)
TMJ MANUFACTURING LLC
26842 Haggerty Rd (48331-5715)
PHONE.................................248 987-7857
EMP: 4 EST: 2014
SALES (est): 64K **Privately Held**
SIC: 3841 Surgical & medical instruments

(G-5403)
TOPAS ADVANCED POLYMES INC
27240 Haggerty Rd E-20 (48331-5716)
PHONE.................................859 746-6447
EMP: 7 EST: 2019
SALES (est): 270.6K **Privately Held**
WEB: www.topas.com
SIC: 2821 Plastics materials & resins

(G-5404)
TOUCH WORLD INC
31500 W 13 Mile Rd # 101 (48334-2172)
PHONE.................................248 539-3700
Eric Morton, *Business Mgr*
Madhusudan Duggi, *Exec Dir*
Gordon McKenna, *Director*
EMP: 40 EST: 1996
SALES (est): 1.2MM **Privately Held**
WEB: www.touchworld.com
SIC: 7371 7379 7372 Software programming applications; ; application computer software

(G-5405)
TRW AUTOMOTIVE US LLC
23855 Research Dr (48335-2628)
PHONE.................................248 426-3901
Fax: 248 426-3953
EMP: 45 **Privately Held**
SIC: 3469 Mfg Plastic Fastners
HQ: Trw Automotive U.S. Llc
12001 Tech Center Dr
Livonia MI 48150
734 855-2600

(G-5406)
TRYCO INC
23800 Research Dr (48335-2627)
P.O. Box 530188, Livonia (48153-0188)
PHONE.................................734 953-6800
Dave Moorehead, *President*
Sarah Ketelhut, *General Mgr*
Steve Miller, *Corp Secy*
Mark Henderickson, *Vice Pres*
Justin Schneider, *Sales Staff*
EMP: 14 EST: 2001
SQ FT: 7,500

SALES (est): 6.2MM **Privately Held**
WEB: www.trycoinc.com
SIC: 2671 5169 5085 Paper coated or laminated for packaging; chemical additives; mill supplies

(G-5407)
V & T PAINTING LLC
29585 Gramercy Ct (48336-1339)
PHONE.................................248 497-1494
Vasel Malaj, *Mng Member*
EMP: 1 EST: 2001
SQ FT: 7,000
SALES (est): 1.3MM **Privately Held**
SIC: 1721 3589 Painting & paper hanging; vacuum cleaners & sweepers, electric: industrial

(G-5408)
VAN-MARK PRODUCTS CORPORATION
24145 Industrial Park Dr (48335-2864)
PHONE.................................248 478-1200
Jeff Van Cleave, *President*
Carol L Van Cleave, *Corp Secy*
Bryan Brillhart, *Sales Mgr*
Gary Weinert, *Sales Mgr*
Reine Gordon, *Office Mgr*
▼ EMP: 40 EST: 1964
SQ FT: 26,000
SALES (est): 7.9MM **Privately Held**
WEB: www.van-mark.com
SIC: 3549 3541 3542 Rotary slitters (metalworking machines); machine tools, metal cutting type; beaders, metal (machines)

(G-5409)
VERIMATION TECHNOLOGY INC
23883 Industrial Park Dr (48335-2860)
PHONE.................................248 471-0000
Kenneth Law Sr, *Ch of Bd*
Bob Reuter, *Vice Pres*
Jon Anderson, *Manager*
Robert Perry, *CIO*
Eric Marry, *Prgrmr*
EMP: 20 EST: 2002
SQ FT: 6,000
SALES (est): 3.9MM **Privately Held**
WEB: www.verimation.com
SIC: 3829 Gauging instruments, thickness ultrasonic

(G-5410)
VIBRACOUSTIC NORTH AMERICA LP
32605 W 12 Mile Rd # 350 (48334-3379)
PHONE.................................248 410-5066
EMP: 6 EST: 2016
SALES (est): 282.8K **Privately Held**
SIC: 2821 Plastics materials & resins

(G-5411)
VIRGILS VINEYARD LLC
Also Called: Rgils Vineyard
27044 Hampstead Blvd (48331-3674)
PHONE.................................248 719-2808
John F Hanhauser, *Principal*
EMP: 4 EST: 2010
SALES (est): 71.4K **Privately Held**
WEB: www.virgilsvineyard.com
SIC: 2084 Wines

(G-5412)
WATERSONG PUBLICATIONS
29711 Sierra Pointe Cir (48331-1493)
PHONE.................................248 592-0109
John Shanteau, *Principal*
EMP: 6 EST: 2008
SALES (est): 87.6K **Privately Held**
SIC: 2741 Miscellaneous publishing

(G-5413)
WELDING TECHNOLOGY CORP
Also Called: W T C
24775 Crestview Ct (48335-1507)
PHONE.................................248 477-3900
Wakami Narisako, *CEO*
David Androvich, *Vice Pres*
Steve Connors, *Vice Pres*
◆ EMP: 110 EST: 1999
SQ FT: 55,000

SALES (est): 20.4MM
SALES (corp-wide): 25.6MM **Privately Held**
WEB: www.weldtechcorp.com
SIC: 3823 3548 3625 Industrial instrmnts msrmnt display/control process variable; welding & cutting apparatus & accessories; resistance welder controls
PA: Nadex Of America Corporation
24775 Crestview Ct
Farmington Hills MI 48335
248 477-3900

(G-5414)
WON-DOOR CORP
25629 Westmoreland Dr (48336-1281)
PHONE.................................248 478-5757
Mike Stankovich, *Manager*
EMP: 9 EST: 2018
SALES (est): 153.5K **Privately Held**
WEB: www.wondoor.com
SIC: 3446 Architectural metalwork

(G-5415)
WOODCRAFT CUSTOMS LLC
24790 Crestview Ct (48335-1506)
PHONE.................................248 987-4473
Christopher Sentowski,
EMP: 6 EST: 2017
SALES (est): 400.1K **Privately Held**
WEB: www.miwoodcraft.com
SIC: 2511 Wood household furniture

(G-5416)
WREATHINKINGBYKATHIE LLC
29554 Colony Circle Dr (48334-1914)
PHONE.................................248 432-7312
Kathleen M Boguslawski, *Principal*
EMP: 4 EST: 2018
SALES (est): 134.2K **Privately Held**
SIC: 3999 Wreaths, artificial

(G-5417)
ZF ACTIVE SAFETY & ELEC US LLC
ZF TRW Automotive Electronics
24175 Research Dr (48335-2634)
PHONE.................................248 478-7210
Neil Das, *Software Engr*
EMP: 339
SALES (corp-wide): 216.2K **Privately Held**
WEB: www.zf.com
SIC: 3714 Motor vehicle parts & accessories
HQ: Zf Active Safety & Electronics Us Llc
12001 Tech Center Dr
Livonia MI 48150
734 855-2600

(G-5418)
ZF ACTIVE SAFETY US INC
Also Called: TRW Parts & Service America
24175 Research Dr (48335-2634)
PHONE.................................248 478-7210
Dan Borsodi, *Engineer*
Howard Heyl, *Engineer*
Greg Ratcliffe, *Engineer*
Mariusz Skowron, *Engineer*
Ewa Kedzierska, *Controller*
EMP: 7
SALES (corp-wide): 216.2K **Privately Held**
WEB: www.zf.com
SIC: 3714 Motor vehicle parts & accessories
HQ: Zf Active Safety Us Inc.
12025 Tech Center Dr
Livonia MI 48150
734 812-6979

(G-5419)
ZUME IT INC
34405 W 12 Mile Rd # 137 (48331-5627)
PHONE.................................248 522-6868
Sudhakar Nimmagadda, *President*
Shraddha Yelwande, *Human Resources*
SAI Krishna, *Technology*
EMP: 5 EST: 2009
SALES (est): 810.6K **Privately Held**
WEB: www.zumeit.com
SIC: 7372 Prepackaged software

Farwell
Clare County

(G-5420)
ALLSTATE SIGN COMPANY INC
1291 E Surrey Rd (48622-8400)
PHONE.................................989 386-4045
Michel Denoyer, *Owner*
EMP: 5 EST: 2004
SALES (est): 258.3K **Privately Held**
WEB: www.allstatesignco.com
SIC: 3993 Signs, not made in custom sign painting shops

(G-5421)
BOUCHEY AND SONS INC
750 Kapplinger Dr (48622-9478)
PHONE.................................989 588-4118
Elizabeth Bouchey, *President*
Jack Bouchey, *Vice Pres*
Denise Bouchey, *Admin Sec*
EMP: 5 EST: 1993
SALES (est): 898.5K **Privately Held**
WEB: www.boucheyinc.com
SIC: 1794 1442 5211 4212 Excavation & grading, building construction; construction sand & gravel; sand & gravel; dump truck haulage; truck rental with drivers

(G-5422)
CMC PLASTYK LLC
176 E Ludington Dr (48622-9447)
PHONE.................................989 588-4468
Norman Myers,
Jeff Crandall,
Dave O'Dell,
EMP: 6
SQ FT: 18,000
SALES (est): 600K **Privately Held**
WEB: www.cmcplastyk.com
SIC: 2821 Molding compounds, plastics

(G-5423)
FUTURE MOLD CORPORATION
215 S Webber St (48622-8415)
PHONE.................................989 588-9948
Melvin Otto, *President*
Marlene G Otto, *Vice Pres*
Michael Otto, *Vice Pres*
Nancy Densmore, *Purch Agent*
David Cote, *Sales Engr*
EMP: 60 EST: 1970
SQ FT: 33,000
SALES (est): 10.5MM **Privately Held**
WEB: www.futuremoldcorp.com
SIC: 3544 Special dies & tools

(G-5424)
JAMES JOY LLC
Also Called: Four Leaf Brewing
412 N Mcewan St (48622)
PHONE.................................989 317-6629
Amy Shindorf, *Principal*
Brad Bellinger, *Principal*
EMP: 6 EST: 2014
SQ FT: 2,200
SALES (est): 292.8K **Privately Held**
WEB: www.fourleafbrewing.com
SIC: 2082 Beer (alcoholic beverage)

(G-5425)
LEAR CORPORATION
Also Called: Renosol Seating
505 Hoover St (48622-9114)
P.O. Box 249 (48622-0249)
PHONE.................................989 588-6181
Koron Dorsett, *Manager*
Robert Webster, *Director*
EMP: 278
SALES (corp-wide): 17B **Publicly Held**
WEB: www.lear.com
SIC: 3714 Motor vehicle electrical equipment
PA: Lear Corporation
21557 Telegraph Rd
Southfield MI 48033
248 447-1500

(G-5426)
MELLING PRODUCTS NORTH LLC
333 Grace St (48622-9772)
PHONE.................................989 588-6147
Mark Melling, *Owner*

▲ = Import ▼=Export
◆ =Import/Export

Thomas C Evanson, *Corp Secy*
David Dent, *Vice Pres*
Kim Tomaski, *Purch Mgr*
Pam Yurga, *Engineer*
EMP: 75 **EST:** 1981
SQ FT: 44,000
SALES (est): 23.6MM
SALES (corp-wide): 206.3MM **Privately Held**
WEB: www.melling.com
SIC: 3498 3465 3714 Tube fabricating (contract bending & shaping); body parts, automobile; stamped metal; motor vehicle parts & accessories
PA: Melling Tool Co.
  2620 Saradan Dr
  Jackson MI 49202
  517 787-8172

(G-5427)
ROGERS ATHLETIC COMPANY INC
3760 W Ludington Dr (48622-9795)
PHONE..................800 457-5337
Nathan D Rogers, *President*
Joel Brown, *Regl Sales Mgr*
Gary McMurry, *Regl Sales Mgr*
Dan Shula, *Regl Sales Mgr*
Ashley Cunningham, *Sales Staff*
EMP: 20 **EST:** 1936
SALES (est): 4.4MM **Privately Held**
WEB: www.rogersathletic.com
SIC: 3949 Football equipment & supplies, general

(G-5428)
S AND S WELDING
1011 Florence Dr (48622-9633)
PHONE..................989 588-6916
Stephen Sysak, *Principal*
EMP: 4 **EST:** 2018
SALES (est): 25K **Privately Held**
SIC: 7692 Welding repair

(G-5429)
SWAIN COMPANY INC
220 E Ludington Dr (48622-8413)
PHONE..................989 773-3700
Kirk Gillespie, *President*
EMP: 5 **EST:** 2019
SALES (est): 366.5K **Privately Held**
WEB: www.swainmeter.com
SIC: 3825 Instruments to measure electricity

(G-5430)
SWAIN METER COMPANY
220 E Ludington Dr (48622-8413)
PHONE..................989 773-3700
Greg Gillespie, *CEO*
Brian Horanoff, *COO*
Tim Menjoulet, *Mfg Staff*
EMP: 5 **EST:** 2006
SALES (est): 1MM **Privately Held**
WEB: www.swainmeter.com
SIC: 3825 Ammeters

Felch
Dickinson County

(G-5431)
JACOBSON LOGGING INC
W4193 Lantz Dr (49831-8857)
P.O. Box 182 (49831-0182)
PHONE..................906 246-3497
Jeffrey Jacobson, *Principal*
EMP: 10 **EST:** 2001
SALES (est): 506.9K **Privately Held**
SIC: 2411 Logging camps & contractors

(G-5432)
LE-Q FABRICATORS LTD
W4106 M 69 (49831)
P.O. Box 4, Niagara WI (54151-0004)
PHONE..................906 246-3402
Mary Quick, *President*
Tim Quick, *Vice Pres*
EMP: 7 **EST:** 1972
SALES (est): 622.7K **Privately Held**
SIC: 3599 Machine shop, jobbing & repair

Fennville
Allegan County

(G-5433)
ABILITY MFG & ENGRG CO
Also Called: Ameco
1585 68th St (49408-9733)
P.O. Box 694, Saugatuck (49453-0694)
PHONE..................269 227-3292
Jeff W Johnson, *President*
Elizabeth Johnson, *Vice Pres*
EMP: 51 **EST:** 1990
SQ FT: 16,000
SALES (est): 1MM **Privately Held**
WEB: www.ameco.org
SIC: 7692 3441 3599 5084 Welding repair; fabricated structural metal; custom machinery; industrial machinery & equipment

(G-5434)
BIRDS EYE FOODS INC
100 Sherman Rd (49408)
P.O. Box 1050 (49408-1050)
PHONE..................269 561-8211
Kim Baiers, *Branch Mgr*
EMP: 60
SALES (corp-wide): 312.2MM **Privately Held**
SIC: 2033 Canned fruits & specialties
PA: Birds Eye Foods, Inc.
  121 Woodcrest Rd
  Cherry Hill NJ 08003

(G-5435)
FENN VALLEY VINEYARDS INC (PA)
6130 122nd Ave (49408-9457)
PHONE..................269 561-2396
Douglas Welsch, *President*
Robin Blake, *CFO*
Gwen Lesperance, *Manager*
Matthew Jannette, *Associate*
EMP: 19 **EST:** 1950
SQ FT: 17,000
SALES (est): 3.1MM **Privately Held**
WEB: www.fennvalley.com
SIC: 2084 Wines

(G-5436)
GLENN VINEYARDS LLC
2128 62nd St (49408-9407)
PHONE..................269 330-2350
EMP: 4 **EST:** 2018
SALES (est): 286.3K **Privately Held**
SIC: 2084 Wines

(G-5437)
HARRINGTON CONSTRUCTION CO
Also Called: Metal Fbrication Machining Div
6720 124th Ave (49408-9632)
PHONE..................269 543-4251
Thomas L Harrington, *President*
Ed Miller, *Sales Executive*
EMP: 5 **EST:** 1942
SQ FT: 32,400
SALES (est): 769.6K **Privately Held**
WEB: www.harringtonmarine.com
SIC: 3441 3599 Fabricated structural metal; machine shop, jobbing & repair

(G-5438)
HI TEC STAINLESS INC
6790 124th Ave (49408-9632)
PHONE..................269 543-4205
Walter Radzinski, *President*
Gary Leonardis, *Vice Pres*
Lee Wagner, *Vice Pres*
EMP: 20 **EST:** 1988
SALES (est): 3.2MM **Privately Held**
SIC: 3429 Marine hardware

(G-5439)
KENKRAFT INDUSTRIAL WELDI
6889 120th Ave (49408-9759)
PHONE..................269 543-3153
Kenneth Sisson, *Administration*
EMP: 5 **EST:** 2010
SALES (est): 285.9K **Privately Held**
WEB: www.kenkraftwelding.com
SIC: 7692 Welding repair

(G-5440)
METALLURGICAL HIGH VACUUM CORP
6708 124th Ave (49408-9632)
PHONE..................269 543-4291
Geoffrey Humberstone, *President*
Scott Wieczorkowski, *Opers Staff*
Kristy Young, *Purchasing*
Deborah Humberstone, *Treasurer*
EMP: 17 **EST:** 1981
SQ FT: 20,000
SALES (est): 3.5MM **Privately Held**
WEB: www.methivac.com
SIC: 3599 3563 Machine shop, jobbing & repair; air & gas compressors including vacuum pumps

(G-5441)
PGI OF SAUGATUCK INC
Also Called: Palazzolo's Gelato
413 3rd St (49408-8671)
PHONE..................800 443-5286
Pete Palazzolo, *CEO*
Peter V Palazzolo, *President*
Marie Palazzo, *Shareholder*
EMP: 30 **EST:** 1986
SALES (est): 6.1MM **Privately Held**
WEB: www.palazzolosdairy.com
SIC: 2024 Ice cream, bulk

(G-5442)
SYSTEMS DESIGN & INSTALLATION
2091 66th St (49408-9779)
PHONE..................269 543-4204
Paul Zehner, *President*
EMP: 4 **EST:** 2010
SALES (est): 213.7K **Privately Held**
SIC: 1799 2522 Athletic & recreation facilities construction; office furniture, except wood

(G-5443)
TRANSPORT TRAILERS CO
2166 68th St (49408-8603)
PHONE..................269 543-4405
Joel Johnson, *Owner*
EMP: 7 **EST:** 1973
SQ FT: 8,000
SALES (est): 576.5K **Privately Held**
SIC: 3715 7539 Trailer bodies; trailer repair

(G-5444)
VIRTUE CIDER
2180 62nd St (49408-9407)
PHONE..................269 455-0526
Gregory Hall, *Principal*
Michelle McDonnell, *Marketing Staff*
Robert Kenney, *Manager*
Kevin Northrup, *Manager*
EMP: 15 **EST:** 2012
SALES (est): 1.8MM **Privately Held**
WEB: www.virtuecider.com
SIC: 2084 Wines

Fenton
Genesee County

(G-5445)
589 FABRICATION LLC
10105 Gordon Rd (48430-9312)
PHONE..................313 402-0586
Thomas Ramm, *Principal*
EMP: 6 **EST:** 2017
SALES (est): 318.6K **Privately Held**
SIC: 7692 Welding repair

(G-5446)
ALLIED INDUS FABRICATION LLC
3061 W Thompson Rd (48430-9705)
PHONE..................810 422-5093
Mark Kramer,
EMP: 20 **EST:** 2018
SALES (est): 1.7MM **Privately Held**
WEB: www.alliedindgroup.com
SIC: 3548 Welding & cutting apparatus & accessories

(G-5447)
ALLIED INDUS SOLUTIONS LLC
Also Called: Ally Equipment Solutions
3061 W Thompson Rd Ste 1 (48430-9705)
PHONE..................810 422-5093
Kevin Kramer, *Controller*
Mark Kramer,
EMP: 12 **EST:** 2017
SQ FT: 5,000
SALES (est): 1.8MM **Privately Held**
SIC: 3535 Conveyors & conveying equipment

(G-5448)
ALLIED MAILING AND PRTG INC
Also Called: Allied Media.net
240 N Fenway Dr (48430-2699)
PHONE..................810 750-8291
Christine Veit, *Project Mgr*
Bryan Harper, *Consultant*
Duane Zalewski, *Consultant*
Richard Rockman Jr, *Admin Sec*
Craig Rockman, *Shareholder*
EMP: 20 **EST:** 1997
SQ FT: 10,000
SALES (est): 3.8MM **Privately Held**
WEB: www.alliedunionservices.com
SIC: 2752 Commercial printing, offset

(G-5449)
ALLY EQUIPMENT LLC
3061 W Thompson Rd Ste 1 (48430-9705)
PHONE..................810 422-5093
Thomas Adams, *Mng Member*
David King,
EMP: 7 **EST:** 2009
SQ FT: 5,000
SALES (est): 858.8K **Privately Held**
SIC: 3535 Conveyors & conveying equipment

(G-5450)
AMERICANDIECAST RELEASANTS
2040 W Thompson Rd (48430-9798)
PHONE..................810 714-1964
James Kauserud, *General Mgr*
Olav Kauserud, *Principal*
EMP: 6 **EST:** 2010
SALES (est): 100K **Privately Held**
SIC: 3842 Welders' hoods

(G-5451)
ATLAS TECHNOLOGIES LLC
Also Called: Material Cnversion Systems Div
14165 N Fenton Rd 102c (48430-1587)
PHONE..................810 629-6663
Robert Bloomfield, *Mfg Staff*
Cathy Nagy, *Buyer*
Kwabena Peltier, *Engineer*
Bill Lockard, *Human Res Dir*
Tim McLaughlan, *Sales Staff*
▲ **EMP:** 55 **EST:** 1972 **Privately Held**
WEB: www.atlastechnologies.com
SIC: 3542 3549 3541 Sheet metalworking machines; assembly machines, including robotic; machine tools, metal cutting type
PA: Productivity Technologies Corp
  3100 Copper Ave
  Fenton MI 48430

(G-5452)
ATLAS TECHNOLOGIES INC
2100 Upper Ave (48430)
PHONE..................810 629-6663
Shirquirlin Wilson, *Finance*
Padget Cowan, *Human Resources*
Richard Davis, *Human Resources*
Hal Potts, *Regl Sales Mgr*
John Dillon, *Branch Mgr*
EMP: 4 **Privately Held**
WEB: www.atlas-packaging.com
SIC: 3569 Liquid automation machinery & equipment
PA: Atlas Technologies Inc
  1000 Tuscarawas St E
  Canton OH

(G-5453)
AUTONERTIA INC
6456 Hartland Rd (48430-9578)
PHONE..................810 882-1002
Christopher Hiler, *Ch of Bd*
EMP: 10 **EST:** 2020

Fenton - Genesee County (G-5454)

SALES (est): 544K **Privately Held**
WEB: www.autonertia.com
SIC: 3315 Wire, steel: insulated or armored

(G-5454)
B & J TOOL CO
11289 Quality Dr (48430-9739)
PHONE......................810 629-8577
Larry Shafer, *President*
Tim Le Cureux, *Vice Pres*
EMP: 12 **EST:** 1985
SQ FT: 7,000
SALES (est): 405.8K **Privately Held**
WEB: www.bandjtoolservices.com
SIC: 3599 Machine shop, jobbing & repair

(G-5455)
B & J TOOL SERVICES INC
11289 Quality Way Dr (48430)
PHONE......................810 629-8577
Michael Wagner, *President*
EMP: 14 **EST:** 2007
SALES (est): 1MM **Privately Held**
SIC: 3559 Automotive maintenance equipment

(G-5456)
BAY WOOD HOMES INC
1393 Eden Gardens Dr (48430-9623)
PHONE......................989 245-4156
Richard W Haight, *President*
Bruce Holder, *Vice Pres*
EMP: 12 **EST:** 1976
SQ FT: 14,000
SALES (est): 270.8K **Privately Held**
SIC: 2452 3537 2541 2439 Prefabricated buildings, wood; industrial trucks & tractors; wood partitions & fixtures; structural wood members; hardwood veneer & plywood; millwork

(G-5457)
BENECOR INC
400 S Fenway Dr (48430-2667)
PHONE......................248 437-4337
Brendan Foster, *President*
▲ **EMP:** 14 **EST:** 2008
SALES (est): 2.2MM **Privately Held**
WEB: www.benecor.com
SIC: 3561 Pumps & pumping equipment

(G-5458)
BENTLY SAND & GRAVEL
9220 Bennett Lake Rd (48430-9053)
PHONE......................810 629-6172
Amma B Bentley, *Owner*
EMP: 4 **EST:** 1966
SALES (est): 772K **Privately Held**
WEB: www.bentleysandandgravel.com
SIC: 1442 5032 Gravel mining; gravel; sand, construction

(G-5459)
BOMAUR QUALITY PLASTICS INC
10388 Jayne Valley Ln (48430-3521)
PHONE......................810 629-9701
Fax: 810 629-5183
EMP: 11
SQ FT: 9,000
SALES (est): 930K **Privately Held**
SIC: 3089 Plastic Injection Molding

(G-5460)
BREMEN CORP
300 N Alloy Dr (48430-2648)
PHONE......................574 546-4238
David T Swallow, *President*
EMP: 12 **EST:** 2015
SALES (est): 1MM **Privately Held**
WEB: www.creativefoam.com
SIC: 3086 Plastics foam products

(G-5461)
BURGAFLEX NORTH AMERICA LLC
Also Called: D & D Investments Equipment
1101 Copper Ave (48430-1770)
P.O. Box 435 (48430-0285)
PHONE......................810 714-3285
Erik Roeren, *CEO*
David Kennedy, *President*
Jeremy Sheppard, *General Mgr*
Steve Collins, *Opers Staff*
Richard Reid, *Opers Staff*
▲ **EMP:** 32 **EST:** 2001
SQ FT: 13,000
SALES (est): 10.1MM
SALES (corp-wide): 257.2K **Privately Held**
WEB: www.burgaflexna.com
SIC: 3492 Hose & tube fittings & assemblies, hydraulic/pneumatic
HQ: Andre Bout Holding B.V.
Mon Plaisir 112
Etten-Leur

(G-5462)
BUSINESS SIGNS OF AMERICA
14250 North Rd (48430-1395)
PHONE......................810 814-3987
Daniel Myers, *Principal*
EMP: 4 **EST:** 2011
SALES (est): 82.4K **Privately Held**
SIC: 3993 Signs & advertising specialties

(G-5463)
CENTURY TOOL & GAGE LLC
200 S Alloy Dr (48430-1704)
PHONE......................810 629-0784
Robert Rich, *President*
Scott Barrie, *General Mgr*
David Cummings, *Vice Pres*
Mike Swiecicki, *Purch Mgr*
Tim Cummings, *Engineer*
EMP: 75 **EST:** 1973
SQ FT: 72,000
SALES (est): 19.3MM
SALES (corp-wide): 49.5MM **Privately Held**
WEB: www.toolingtechgroup.com
SIC: 3544 Special dies & tools; jigs & fixtures
PA: Tooling Technology, Llc
51223 Quadrate Dr
Macomb MI 48042
937 381-9211

(G-5464)
CLASSFCATION FLOTATION SYSTEMS
Also Called: C F S
235 Industrial Way (48430-1719)
PHONE......................810 714-5200
Thomas Swaninger, *President*
▼ **EMP:** 5 **EST:** 1990
SALES (est): 713.4K **Privately Held**
WEB: www.cfs-web.com
SIC: 3532 Mining machinery

(G-5465)
CMI-SCHNEIBLE GROUP (HQ)
Also Called: C M I
3061 W Thompson Rd Ste 1 (48430-9705)
PHONE......................810 354-0404
William Goetz, *CEO*
Ray H Witt, *Director*
EMP: 105 **EST:** 1990
SQ FT: 30,000
SALES (est): 8MM
SALES (corp-wide): 13.3MM **Privately Held**
WEB: www.saginawvalleyafs.org
SIC: 3443 Vessels, process or storage (from boiler shops): metal plate
PA: Cmi- Management Services Inc.
29580 Northwestern Hwy # 100
Southfield MI 48034
248 415-3950

(G-5466)
COMPATIBLE LASER PRODUCTS INC
1045 Grant St (48430-1715)
PHONE......................810 629-0459
Susan Cave, *CEO*
Tony Cave, *President*
EMP: 13 **EST:** 1990
SQ FT: 9,000
SALES (est): 565.4K **Privately Held**
WEB: www.compatiblelaser.com
SIC: 3955 5943 3861 Print cartridges for laser & other computer printers; office forms & supplies; photographic equipment & supplies

(G-5467)
CREATIVE FOAM CORPORATION (PA)
Also Called: S P P D
300 N Alloy Dr (48430-2648)
PHONE......................810 629-4149
Roger Morgan, *Ch of Bd*
Peter Swallow, *Vice Ch Bd*
Wayne Blessing, *President*
Paul Junk, *General Mgr*
Bruce Graham, *Exec VP*
▲ **EMP:** 200 **EST:** 1969
SQ FT: 102,500
SALES (est): 198.2MM **Privately Held**
WEB: www.creativefoam.com
SIC: 3061 3089 3053 3086 Mechanical rubber goods; injection molded finished plastic products; gaskets, packing & sealing devices; plastics foam products; foam rubber

(G-5468)
CREATIVE FOAM CORPORATION
Also Called: Fenway Business Unit
555 N Fenway Dr (48430-2636)
PHONE......................810 714-0140
Greg Graham, *Engineer*
Paul Jonik, *Manager*
EMP: 5
SALES (corp-wide): 198.2MM **Privately Held**
WEB: www.creativefoam.com
SIC: 3089 3053 2671 3086 Injection molded finished plastic products; laminating of plastic; gaskets, packing & sealing devices; packaging paper & plastics film, coated & laminated; packaging & shipping materials, foamed plastic
PA: Creative Foam Corporation
300 N Alloy Dr
Fenton MI 48430
810 629-4149

(G-5469)
CREATIVE FORM CORP
1100 Copper Ave (48430-1771)
PHONE......................810 714-5860
EMP: 8 **EST:** 2017
SALES (est): 192.7K **Privately Held**
SIC: 3089 Injection molding of plastics

(G-5470)
DIBBLEVILLE WOODWORK CO
12272 N Fenton Rd Ste 3 (48430-9614)
PHONE......................810 750-1139
Terry Steffey, *Owner*
EMP: 5 **EST:** 1989
SQ FT: 3,000
SALES (est): 327.6K **Privately Held**
WEB: www.dibblevillewoodworks.com
SIC: 2434 Wood kitchen cabinets

(G-5471)
DOMICO MED-DEVICE LLC
14241 N Fenton Rd (48430-1541)
PHONE......................810 750-5300
Jeremy Weidner, *Sales Staff*
Michael Czop,
EMP: 84 **EST:** 2018
SALES (est): 11MM **Privately Held**
WEB: www.domicomed.com
SIC: 3841 Surgical & medical instruments

(G-5472)
ENERGY CONTROL SOLUTIONS INC
Also Called: Control Pak International
11494 Delmar Dr Ste 100 (48430-9018)
PHONE......................810 735-2800
Timothy Glinke, *President*
Chris Ptaszynski, *Vice Pres*
EMP: 9 **EST:** 1976
SQ FT: 8,000
SALES (est): 603.2K **Privately Held**
WEB: www.controlpak.com
SIC: 3822 Thermostats & other environmental sensors

(G-5473)
EPIC MACHINE INC
201 Industrial Way Ste A (48430-1719)
PHONE......................810 629-9400
Mike Parker, *President*
Michael Parker, *President*
Nicholas Popa, *Chairman*
Daniel Whaley, *Vice Pres*
EMP: 20 **EST:** 1953
SALES (est): 3.4MM **Privately Held**
WEB: www.epicmachine.com
SIC: 3599 3544 Machine shop, jobbing & repair; special dies, tools, jigs & fixtures

(G-5474)
EZBAKE TECHNOLOGIES LLC
Also Called: Bakery Ingredient Mfg
7244 Driftwood Dr (48430-4308)
P.O. Box 270527, Flower Mound TX (75027-0527)
PHONE......................817 430-1621
Shaena Sparrow, *Vice Pres*
Rita Tolvanen,
EMP: 3 **EST:** 1993
SALES (est): 1.8MM **Privately Held**
WEB: www.ezbaketechnologies.com
SIC: 8742 7389 2045 Industry specialist consultants; ; prepared flour mixes & doughs

(G-5475)
FENTON CONCRETE INC
10513 Old Us 23 (48430-9385)
P.O. Box 497 (48430-0497)
PHONE......................810 629-0783
Curtis M Schupbach, *President*
EMP: 7 **EST:** 1975
SQ FT: 4,800
SALES (est): 695.7K **Privately Held**
WEB: www.fentonconcreteinc.com
SIC: 3273 5211 Ready-mixed concrete; lumber & other building materials

(G-5476)
FENTON CORPORATION (PA)
3236 Owen Rd (48430-1758)
PHONE......................810 629-2858
Bobby D Butts, *President*
Brian Kelly, *Purchasing*
EMP: 6 **EST:** 1980
SQ FT: 2,400
SALES (est): 5.5MM **Privately Held**
WEB: www.fentonglass.com
SIC: 6553 3272 5999 5099 Cemeteries, real estate operation; concrete products, precast; monuments & tombstones; monuments & grave markers

(G-5477)
FENTON MEMORIALS & VAULTS INC
3236 Owen Rd (48430-1758)
P.O. Box 289 (48430-0289)
PHONE......................810 629-2858
Gregory Duberg, *President*
EMP: 1 **EST:** 1945
SQ FT: 1,800
SALES (est): 3MM
SALES (corp-wide): 5.5MM **Privately Held**
WEB: www.fentonmemorials.com
SIC: 3272 5099 5999 Burial vaults, concrete or precast terrazzo; monuments & grave markers; monuments & tombstones
PA: Fenton Corporation
3236 Owen Rd
Fenton MI 48430
810 629-2858

(G-5478)
FENTON RADIATOR & GARAGE INC
1542 N Leroy St Ste 4 (48430-1972)
PHONE......................810 629-0923
Daniel Phalen, *President*
Tina Phalen, *Admin Sec*
EMP: 4 **EST:** 1965
SQ FT: 4,000
SALES (est): 428.9K **Privately Held**
WEB: www.partsplus.org
SIC: 7539 7538 5531 3599 Radiator repair shop, automotive; general automotive repair shops; automobile air conditioning equipment, sale, installation; flexible metal hose, tubing & bellows

(G-5479)
FOX FIRE GLASS LLC
3071 W Thompson Rd (48430-9705)
PHONE......................248 332-2442
Donna Stiefel, *Mng Member*
EMP: 4 **EST:** 2011

GEOGRAPHIC SECTION
Fenton - Genesee County (G-5508)

SALES (est): 374.4K **Privately Held**
WEB: www.foxfireglass.com
SIC: **3231** Products of purchased glass

(G-5480)
FRENCH PRESS KNITS LLC
10631 Oakhill St (48430-9489)
PHONE.................................810 623-0650
Melynda Bernardi, *Principal*
EMP: 4 EST: 2009
SALES (est): 78.9K **Privately Held**
WEB: www.frenchpressknits.com
SIC: **2741** Miscellaneous publishing

(G-5481)
GLOBAL FMI LLC
17195 Silver Pkwy Ste 111 (48430-3426)
PHONE.................................810 964-5555
Deane Nash, *Mng Member*
Tim Kruszka,
EMP: 70
SALES (est): 3MM **Privately Held**
SIC: **3463** 3714 3465 3519 Nonferrous forgings; motor vehicle parts & accessories; automotive stampings; internal combustion engines

(G-5482)
GREAT LAKES TECH & MFG LLC
201 S Alloy Dr Ste C (48430-4435)
P.O. Box 550 (48430-0550)
PHONE.................................810 593-0257
Mark Russell, *Opers Staff*
Charles Rice,
EMP: 4 EST: 2008
SALES (est): 900K **Privately Held**
WEB: www.greatlakestech.net
SIC: **3541** Machine tools, metal cutting type

(G-5483)
H & H POWDERCOATING INC
300 S Fenway Dr (48430-2657)
PHONE.................................810 750-1800
Brett Hammond, *Principal*
EMP: 15 EST: 2005
SALES (est): 2.3MM **Privately Held**
WEB: www.hhpowdercoating.com
SIC: **3479** Coating of metals & formed products

(G-5484)
HARROUN ENTERPRISES INC
1111 Fenway Cir (48430-2644)
PHONE.................................810 629-9885
Hugh D Harroun, *President*
▲ EMP: 6 EST: 1978
SQ FT: 30,000
SALES (est): 1.2MM **Privately Held**
WEB: www.harroun.com
SIC: **3545** Boring machine attachments (machine tool accessories); bits for use on lathes, planers, shapers, etc.; milling cutters

(G-5485)
HPC HOLDINGS INC
1101 Copper Ave (48430-1770)
PHONE.................................810 714-9213
Paul Bubnar, *Manager*
EMP: 24
SALES (corp-wide): 5.1MM **Privately Held**
SIC: **3471** Electroplating of metals or formed products
PA: Hpc Holdings, Inc.
   111 Rosette St
   Holly MI 48442
   248 634-9361

(G-5486)
IMAGE PROJECTIONS INC
1470 Torrey Rd (48430-1360)
PHONE.................................810 629-0700
Richard F Waldchen, *President*
Cheryl Waldchen, *Partner*
Rick Waldchen, *Partner*
Mike Abrusio, *Contractor*
EMP: 10 EST: 1980
SQ FT: 5,800
SALES (est): 656K **Privately Held**
WEB: www.imageprojections.net
SIC: **2396** 2759 Screen printing on fabric articles; screen printing

(G-5487)
KENEWELL GROUP
3031 W Thompson Rd (48430-9771)
PHONE.................................810 714-4290
Blair Kenewell, *Owner*
EMP: 8 EST: 2004
SALES (est): 558.7K **Privately Held**
WEB: www.kenewellgroup.com
SIC: **2759** 7319 7334 7336 Commercial printing; advertising; photocopying & duplicating services; graphic arts & related design

(G-5488)
KUKA ASSEMBLY AND TEST CORP
255 S Fenway Dr (48430-2628)
P.O. Box 1968, Saginaw (48605-1968)
PHONE.................................810 593-0350
Lev Mondrusov, *Vice Pres*
Joe Burgess, *Project Mgr*
Scott Green, *Sr Project Mgr*
Scott Orendach, *Manager*
Brent Garbuschewski, *Manager*
EMP: 10 **Privately Held**
WEB: www.kuka-at.com
SIC: **3826** Environmental testing equipment
HQ: Kuka Assembly And Test Corp.
   5675 Dixie Hwy
   Saginaw MI 48601
   989 220-3088

(G-5489)
LINEAR MEASUREMENT INSTRS CORP
Also Called: L M I
101 N Alloy Dr Ste B (48430-1794)
PHONE.................................810 714-5811
Ernest Booker, *President*
Martha Knobler, *COO*
Tim Martin, *Project Engr*
Steve Hearing, *Sales Mgr*
Rebecca Rodgers, *Manager*
EMP: 21 EST: 1985
SQ FT: 12,500
SALES (est): 3.4MM **Privately Held**
WEB: www.lmicorporation.com
SIC: **3599** Machine shop, jobbing & repair

(G-5490)
MACHINE SHOP BEER COMPANY LLC
14194 Landings Way (48430-1316)
PHONE.................................810 577-4202
Johanna Hoelzle, *Principal*
EMP: 4 EST: 2015
SALES (est): 108.4K **Privately Held**
SIC: **3599** Machine shop, jobbing & repair

(G-5491)
MELISSA FOWLER
Also Called: Crimson Craft Co
1020 N Lemen St (48430-1590)
PHONE.................................818 447-9903
Melissa Fowler, *Owner*
EMP: 5 EST: 2020
SALES (est): 100K **Privately Held**
SIC: **3944** Craft & hobby kits & sets

(G-5492)
MOTT MEDIA LLC (PA)
Also Called: Living Hope Books & More
1130 Fenway Cir (48430-2641)
PHONE.................................810 714-4280
William P Hoetger,
Jacqueline M Hoetger,
EMP: 8 EST: 1974
SQ FT: 15,900
SALES (est): 1.4MM **Privately Held**
WEB: www.mottmedia.com
SIC: **2731** 5192 Books: publishing only; books

(G-5493)
PARAGON MANUFACTURING CORP
2046 W Thompson Rd (48430-9798)
PHONE.................................810 629-4100
Robert A Booher, *President*
EMP: 23 EST: 1991
SQ FT: 8,000
SALES (est): 1.6MM **Privately Held**
WEB: www.pmc-cnc.com
SIC: **3599** Machine shop, jobbing & repair

(G-5494)
PARSHALLVILLE CIDER MILL
8507 Parshallville Rd (48430-9239)
P.O. Box 353, Clarkston (48347-0353)
PHONE.................................810 629-9079
EMP: 6
SALES (est): 44.2K **Privately Held**
SIC: **2099** Mfg Food Preparations

(G-5495)
PHOENIX DENTAL INC
3452 W Thompson Rd (48430-9635)
PHONE.................................810 750-2328
Jeffrey Cox, *President*
EMP: 5 EST: 1998 **Privately Held**
WEB: www.phoenixdental.com
SIC: **3843** Compounds, dental

(G-5496)
PRODUCTIVITY TECHNOLOGIES (PA)
3100 Copper Ave (48430-1778)
PHONE.................................810 714-0200
Samuel N Seidman, *Ch of Bd*
Arthur Stupay, *Principal*
Michael D Austin, *Senior VP*
Jesse A Levine, *Vice Pres*
Mike Clement, *Purchasing*
EMP: 8
SALES (est): 15.2MM **Privately Held**
WEB: www.productivitytech.com
SIC: **3542** 3541 3545 Machine tools, metal forming type; machine tools, metal cutting type; machine tool accessories

(G-5497)
PUSHMAN MANUFACTURING CO INC
1044 Grant St (48430-1716)
PHONE.................................810 629-9688
Michael D Pushman, *Ch of Bd*
Marie E Foguth, *Corp Secy*
Gerald Bidelman, *Vice Pres*
James W Pushman, *Vice Pres*
EMP: 25 EST: 1965
SQ FT: 18,000
SALES (est): 1.2MM **Privately Held**
WEB: www.pushmanmanufacturing.com
SIC: **3599** 7692 Machine shop, jobbing & repair; welding repair

(G-5498)
R & B EDM INC
1065 Grant St (48430-1715)
PHONE.................................810 714-5050
Ryan Booker, *Principal*
EMP: 17 EST: 2009
SALES (est): 616.4K **Privately Held**
WEB: www.rbedm.com
SIC: **3599** Machine shop, jobbing & repair

(G-5499)
ROCKMAN & SONS PUBLISHING LLC
240 N Fenway Dr (48430-2699)
PHONE.................................810 750-6011
Mark Rockwood, *Info Tech Dir*
Craig Rockman,
Richard Rockman Jr,
EMP: 10 EST: 1990
SQ FT: 5,500
SALES (est): 530K **Privately Held**
WEB: www.rockmanpublishing.com
SIC: **2711** 2731 2721 Newspapers, publishing & printing; books: publishing only; periodicals

(G-5500)
ROCKMAN COMMUNICATIONS INC
Also Called: Tri-County Times
256 N Fenway Dr (48430-2699)
P.O. Box 1125 (48430-5125)
PHONE.................................810 433-6800
Tim Jagielo, *Editor*
John Evans, *Business Mgr*
Craig Rockman, *Vice Pres*
Jillian Banish, *Marketing Staff*
EMP: 27 EST: 1994
SALES (est): 2MM **Privately Held**
WEB: www.tctimes.com
SIC: **2711** 4813 Newspapers, publishing & printing;

(G-5501)
SADDLE UP MAGAZINE
8415 Hogan Rd (48430-9049)
PHONE.................................810 714-9000
Cindy Couturier, *Principal*
EMP: 4 EST: 2009
SALES (est): 88.5K **Privately Held**
WEB: www.saddleupmag.com
SIC: **2721** Magazines: publishing only, not printed on site

(G-5502)
SANDYS CONTRACTING
10464 Circle J Ct (48430-9515)
PHONE.................................810 629-2259
Sandy Meade, *Owner*
EMP: 5 EST: 2002
SALES (est): 188.5K **Privately Held**
SIC: **1429** Crushed & broken stone

(G-5503)
SHOUSE TOOL INC
290 N Alloy Dr (48430-2645)
PHONE.................................810 629-0391
Virgil Shouse, *President*
Haney Shouse, *Corp Secy*
Bill Shouse, *Vice Pres*
Mike Shouse, *VP Opers*
Kurt Mosher, *Sales Executive*
EMP: 18 EST: 1974
SALES (est): 2.4MM **Privately Held**
WEB: www.shousetool.com
SIC: **3545** Cutting tools for machine tools

(G-5504)
STANDALE SMOOTHIE LLC
1028 N Leroy St (48430-2756)
PHONE.................................810 691-9625
Dianne Lemieux, *Principal*
EMP: 6 EST: 2015
SALES (est): 274.9K **Privately Held**
SIC: **2037** Frozen fruits & vegetables

(G-5505)
STONEBRDGE TECHNICAL ENTPS LTD
Also Called: Stonebridge Technical Services
14165 N Fenton Rd 102c (48430-1587)
PHONE.................................810 750-0040
David Hense, *President*
Bill Rogner, *Opers Mgr*
Brad Austin, *Engineer*
EMP: 12 EST: 2008
SALES (est): 1.9MM **Privately Held**
WEB: www.stonebridgetech.com
SIC: **8748** 3492 3625 8711 Systems analysis or design; control valves, fluid power: hydraulic & pneumatic; electric controls & control accessories, industrial; machine tool design

(G-5506)
TELMAR MANUFACTURING COMPANY
2121 W Thompson Rd (48430-9704)
PHONE.................................810 577-7050
Paul Martel, *Owner*
EMP: 6 EST: 1992
SQ FT: 1,600
SALES (est): 420K **Privately Held**
SIC: **3714** Motor vehicle parts & accessories

(G-5507)
TELO
707 Hickory St (48430-1880)
PHONE.................................810 845-8051
EMP: 5
SQ FT: 1,800
SALES (est): 162.6K **Privately Held**
SIC: **2051** Mfg Bread/Related Products

(G-5508)
TIG ENTITY LLC
Also Called: Thompson I.g
3196 W Thompson Rd (48430-9799)
PHONE.................................810 629-9558
Lorne Flaig, *Vice Pres*
Cory Duso, *Production*
Zakk Dekalita, *Engineer*
Greg Hajec, *Controller*
Debra Snow, *Credit Staff*
EMP: 48 EST: 2012

Fenton - Genesee County (G-5509)

SALES (est): 8.4MM Privately Held
WEB: www.thompsonig.com
SIC: 3229 Industrial-use glassware

(G-5509)
TRELLBORG SLING SLTIONS US INC
2111 W Thompson Rd (48430-9704)
PHONE..................810 655-3900
Tim Callison, *Branch Mgr*
EMP: 5
SALES (corp-wide): 3.8B Privately Held
WEB: www.trelleborg.com
SIC: 3089 Plastic containers, except foam
HQ: Trelleborg Sealing Solutions Us, Inc.
2531 Bremer Rd
Fort Wayne IN 46803
260 749-9631

(G-5510)
TRUSTED TOOL MFG INC
8075 Old Us 23 (48430-9309)
PHONE..................810 750-6000
John K Martin, *President*
EMP: 7 EST: 1988
SQ FT: 5,000
SALES (est): 1.1MM Privately Held
WEB: www.trustedtoolmfg.com
SIC: 3545 3599 Gauges (machine tool accessories); custom machinery

(G-5511)
TTS OLDCO LLC (DH)
Also Called: Tritec Performance Solutions
2111 W Thompson Rd (48430-9704)
PHONE..................810 655-3900
Marcus Pillion, *CEO*
Lisa Gee, *Manager*
Alice Studer, *Representative*
▲ EMP: 31 EST: 2012
SALES (est): 14MM
SALES (corp-wide): 3.8B Privately Held
WEB: www.tritec-ps.com
SIC: 3053 3566 Gaskets, all materials; gears, power transmission, except automotive
HQ: Trelleborg Sealing Solutions Us, Inc.
2531 Bremer Rd
Fort Wayne IN 46803
260 749-9631

(G-5512)
VALMEC INC
12487 Thornbury Dr (48430-9558)
P.O. Box 1069 (48430-5069)
PHONE..................810 629-8750
Krystn Tatus, *CEO*
Bradley Van Leuven, *President*
Colin Van Leuven, *Vice Pres*
Larry Van Leuven, *Treasurer*
EMP: 6 EST: 1972
SALES (est): 1.5MM Privately Held
WEB: www.valmecinc.com
SIC: 5084 5199 3625 7389 Conveyor systems; packaging materials; electric controls & control accessories, industrial;

(G-5513)
WHALEY WELDING AND MECHINE LLC
211 Industrial Way (48430-1719)
PHONE..................810 835-5804
EMP: 4 EST: 2020
SALES (est): 97.6K Privately Held
SIC: 7692 Welding repair

(G-5514)
ZANDER COLLOIDS LC
Also Called: Adcr
2040 W Thompson Rd (48430-9798)
P.O. Box 1095 (48430-5095)
PHONE..................810 714-1623
Doug Brumbill,
▲ EMP: 5
SQ FT: 3,400
SALES (est): 1.2MM Privately Held
WEB: www.zandercolloids.com
SIC: 2821 Silicone resins

(G-5515)
ZF ACTIVE SAFETY US INC
9475 Center Rd (48430-9388)
PHONE..................810 750-1036
Bob Holman, *Manager*
Fernando Mesa, *Manager*
EMP: 7

SALES (corp-wide): 216.2K Privately Held
WEB: www.zf.com
SIC: 3714 Motor vehicle parts & accessories
HQ: Zf Active Safety Us Inc.
12025 Tech Center Dr
Livonia MI 48150
734 812-6979

Fenwick
Montcalm County

(G-5516)
APEX COMPETITION ENGINES
119 E South Cnty Line Rd (48834-9721)
PHONE..................616 761-4010
Dan Minikey, *Principal*
EMP: 7 EST: 2014
SALES (est): 58.8K Privately Held
SIC: 3519 Internal combustion engines

Ferndale
Oakland County

(G-5517)
3 TEN DENIM KO LLC
195 W 9 Mile Rd (48220-2914)
PHONE..................248 556-1725
Koria Ampey, *CEO*
EMP: 4 EST: 2020
SALES (est): 180.7K Privately Held
SIC: 2211 Denims

(G-5518)
AEROBEE ELECTRIC INC
3030 Hilton Rd (48220-1019)
PHONE..................248 549-2044
Timothy Craddock, *President*
EMP: 12 EST: 1986
SALES (est): 1.1MM Privately Held
WEB: www.aerobeeinc.com
SIC: 1731 3699 General electrical contractor; electrical equipment & supplies

(G-5519)
AEROFAB COMPANY INC
2335 Goodrich St (48220-1440)
PHONE..................248 542-0051
Robert M Eckerman, *Ch of Bd*
Jules Bols III, *President*
EMP: 10 EST: 1991
SQ FT: 30,000
SALES (est): 1.7MM Privately Held
WEB: www.aerofab-corp.com
SIC: 3069 Molded rubber products

(G-5520)
AIRGAS USA LLC
1200 Farrow St (48220-1960)
PHONE..................248 545-9353
Bill Henderson, *Accounts Exec*
Irving Sparage, *Branch Mgr*
EMP: 5
SALES (corp-wide): 102.6MM Privately Held
WEB: www.airgas.com
SIC: 5085 3548 Industrial supplies; welding apparatus
HQ: Airgas Usa, Llc
259 N Radnor Chester Rd
Radnor PA 19087
216 642-6600

(G-5521)
ALL KIDS CNSDRED PUBG GROUP IN
Also Called: Metro Parent Media Group
22041 Woodward Ave (48220-2520)
PHONE..................248 398-3400
Alyssa R Martina, *President*
Ruth Robbins, *Publisher*
Alexia Bourkoulas, *Vice Pres*
Chantel Maloney, *Opers Mgr*
Kim Kovelle, *Assoc Editor*
EMP: 44 EST: 1986
SALES (est): 4.1MM Privately Held
SIC: 2721 Magazines: publishing only, not printed on site

(G-5522)
ALL KIDS CONSIDERED PUBG GROUP
22041 Woodward Ave (48220-2520)
PHONE..................248 398-3400
Linda Holland, *Sales Staff*
Alyssa R Martina, *Administration*
EMP: 9 EST: 2011
SALES (est): 505.5K Privately Held
SIC: 2741 Miscellaneous publishing

(G-5523)
ALLIED PRINTING CO INC (PA)
Also Called: Allied Distribution
2035 Hilton Rd (48220-1574)
PHONE..................248 541-0551
Robert Straub, *CEO*
Paul Zimmer, *Ch of Bd*
David Bader, *President*
Tony Pelc, *COO*
Tony Pelc - Vp, *Opers Staff*
EMP: 21
SQ FT: 255,000
SALES (est): 12.3MM Privately Held
WEB: www.alliedprintingcompany.com
SIC: 2752 4212 Commercial printing, offset; mail carriers, contract

(G-5524)
ALLIED PRINTING CO INC
965 Wanda St (48220-2959)
PHONE..................248 514-7394
Joe Wegher, *Branch Mgr*
EMP: 50
SALES (corp-wide): 12.3MM Privately Held
WEB: www.alliedprintingcompany.com
SIC: 2752 4212 Commercial printing, offset; local trucking, without storage
PA: Allied Printing Co., Inc.
2035 Hilton Rd
Ferndale MI 48220
248 541-0551

(G-5525)
AMANDA PRODUCTS LLC
Also Called: UNI-Bond Brake
1350 Jarvis St (48220-2011)
PHONE..................248 547-3870
Jim Langley, *Vice Pres*
Anne Reynaud, *Controller*
Lisa Moore, *Info Tech Dir*
Robert Gruschow,
Michael B Grattan,
▲ EMP: 50 EST: 1952
SQ FT: 102,000
SALES (est): 10MM
SALES (corp-wide): 109.1MM Privately Held
WEB: www.unibond.net
SIC: 3714 3469 3446 Motor vehicle brake systems & parts; metal stampings; architectural metalwork
PA: Deshler Group, Inc.
34450 Industrial Rd
Livonia MI 48150
734 525-9100

(G-5526)
ANGEL KISSES INC
513 Allen St (48220-2444)
PHONE..................248 219-8577
Dawn Lyman, *Principal*
EMP: 4 EST: 2020
SALES (est): 93.1K Privately Held
WEB: www.angelkisses.org
SIC: 2034 Dehydrated fruits, vegetables, soups

(G-5527)
ARC MIT
660 E 10 Mile Rd (48220-1036)
PHONE..................248 399-4800
EMP: 8
SALES (est): 671.6K Privately Held
SIC: 3312 Blast Furnace-Steel Works

(G-5528)
ARTIFCIAL INTLLGNCE TECH SLTON
10800 Galaxie Ave (48220-2132)
PHONE..................877 787-6268
Steven Reinharz, *CEO*
Anthony Brenz, *CFO*
EMP: 50 EST: 2010

SALES: 360.8K Privately Held
SIC: 7372 Prepackaged software

(G-5529)
AXLE OF DEARBORN INC (PA)
Also Called: Detroit Axle
2000 W 8 Mile Rd (48220-2215)
PHONE..................248 543-5995
Mouhamad Musheinesh, *President*
Gilbert Jones, *Auditor*
Abdul Musheinesh, *Director*
▲ EMP: 148 EST: 2000
SQ FT: 175,000
SALES (est): 179.3MM Privately Held
WEB: www.detroitaxle.com
SIC: 5013 5531 3312 Automotive hardware; automotive supplies; automotive parts; axles, rolled or forged: made in steel mills

(G-5530)
B NEKTAR LLC
Also Called: B Nektar Meadery
1511 Jarvis St (48220-2025)
PHONE..................313 744-6323
Laura Hayes, *Sales Staff*
Brad Dahlhofer, *Mng Member*
Kerry Trusewicz, *Graphic Designe*
EMP: 15 EST: 2006
SALES (est): 100K Privately Held
WEB: www.bnektar.com
SIC: 2084 Wines

(G-5531)
BATTERY CENTER OF AMERICA
1805 E 9 Mile Rd (48220-2063)
PHONE..................248 399-5999
EMP: 5 EST: 2013
SALES (est): 129.3K Privately Held
SIC: 3691 Storage batteries

(G-5532)
CAMPBELL SOUP COMPANY
1220 E 9 Mile Rd (48220-1972)
PHONE..................248 336-8486
EMP: 6
SALES (corp-wide): 8.4B Publicly Held
WEB: www.campbellsoupcompany.com
SIC: 5461 2038 2033 2052 Bakeries; frozen specialties; canned fruits & specialties; cookies & crackers; bread, cake & related products; potato chips & similar snacks
PA: Campbell Soup Company
1 Campbell Pl
Camden NJ 08103
856 342-4800

(G-5533)
CANDLE WICK
175 W 9 Mile Rd (48220-1730)
PHONE..................248 547-2987
Eric Paquette, *Owner*
EMP: 4 EST: 2007
SALES (est): 254.2K Privately Held
WEB: www.candlewickshoppe.com
SIC: 3999 Candles

(G-5534)
CNC TOOLING SOLUTIONS LLC
1211 Rosewood St (48220-1926)
PHONE..................248 890-5625
Jeffrey Schmidt, *Principal*
Mike Butler, *Sales Staff*
EMP: 6 EST: 2014
SALES (est): 61.6K Privately Held
WEB: www.gradcoinc.com
SIC: 3599 Machine shop, jobbing & repair

(G-5535)
CONTEXT FURNITURE L L C
1054 W Lewiston Ave (48220-1286)
P.O. Box 2385, Sequim WA (98382-4341)
PHONE..................248 200-0724
Carrie Moore, *President*
Bryce Moore, *Vice Pres*
EMP: 4 EST: 2002
SALES (est): 250.9K Privately Held
SIC: 2511 Dining room furniture: wood

(G-5536)
COVENTRY CREATIONS INC (PA)
195 W 9 Mile Rd (48220-2914)
PHONE..................248 547-2987
EMP: 28 EST: 2014

GEOGRAPHIC SECTION
Ferndale - Oakland County (G-5563)

SALES (est): 1.7MM **Privately Held**
WEB: www.coventrycreations.com
SIC: 3999 Candles

(G-5537)
COVENTRY CREATIONS INC
930 E Lewiston Ave (48220-1451)
PHONE.....................248 545-8360
Jacqueline Smith, *Principal*
Patty Shaw, *Vice Pres*
EMP: 14
SALES (corp-wide): 1.7MM **Privately Held**
WEB: www.coventrycreations.com
SIC: 2759 Screen printing
PA: Coventry Creations Inc
 195 W 9 Mile Rd
 Ferndale MI 48220
 248 547-2987

(G-5538)
DARSON CORPORATION
10610 Galaxie Ave (48220-2171)
PHONE.....................313 875-7781
Mary Ellen Darge, *President*
EMP: 10 EST: 1973
SQ FT: 15,000
SALES (est): 726.8K **Privately Held**
WEB: www.dnpe.com
SIC: 2759 Screen printing

(G-5539)
DAVID EPSTEIN INC
Also Called: Better-Form
1135 E 9 Mile Rd (48220-1936)
PHONE.....................248 542-0802
David Epstein, *President*
Valerie Epstein, *Project Mgr*
Jake Hickey, *Info Tech Dir*
▲ EMP: 10 EST: 1992
SQ FT: 3,000
SALES (est): 1.5MM **Privately Held**
SIC: 3842 3841 3131 Orthopedic appliances; surgical & medical instruments; footwear cut stock

(G-5540)
DETAIL PRECISION PRODUCTS INC
1480 E 9 Mile Rd (48220-2040)
PHONE.....................248 544-3390
Michael W Fox, *President*
Linda J Fox, *Vice Pres*
EMP: 29 EST: 1984
SQ FT: 12,000
SALES (est): 3MM **Privately Held**
SIC: 3728 3545 3462 Aircraft parts & equipment; machine tool accessories; iron & steel forgings

(G-5541)
DETAIL PRODUCTION COMPANY INC
1480 E 9 Mile Rd (48220-2040)
PHONE.....................248 544-3390
Clifford J Seeger, *President*
Linda J Fox, *Corp Secy*
EMP: 15 EST: 1942
SQ FT: 12,000
SALES (est): 142.1K **Privately Held**
SIC: 3714 Gears, motor vehicle; drive shafts, motor vehicle

(G-5542)
DETROIT BUBBLE TEA COMPANY
22821 Woodward Ave (48220-1738)
PHONE.....................248 239-1131
EMP: 6 EST: 2014
SALES (est): 406.6K **Privately Held**
WEB: www.detroitbubbletea.com
SIC: 2086 Tea, iced: packaged in cans, bottles, etc.

(G-5543)
DETROIT COIL CO
2435 Hilton Rd (48220-1599)
PHONE.....................248 658-1543
Robert Dugan, *President*
David Gohlke, *CFO*
Kevin Browning, *Shareholder*
William Buban, *Shareholder*
Don Eichderger, *Shareholder*
▲ EMP: 33 EST: 1912
SQ FT: 22,000

SALES (est): 665.3K **Privately Held**
WEB: www.rossdecco.com
SIC: 3625 3728 3621 Solenoid switches (industrial controls); aircraft parts & equipment; motors & generators

(G-5544)
DETROIT CORNICE & SLATE CO INC
1315 Academy St (48220-2001)
PHONE.....................248 398-7690
Doneen Hesse, *President*
Kurt Hesse, *Vice Pres*
Stephanie Madurski, *Office Mgr*
Dawn Hesse, *Admin Sec*
EMP: 20 EST: 1888
SQ FT: 11,200
SALES (est): 5.6MM **Privately Held**
WEB: www.detroitcornice.com
SIC: 1761 3444 2952 Roofing contractor; sheet metalwork; sheet metalwork; asphalt felts & coatings

(G-5545)
DETROIT ELEVATOR COMPANY
2121 Burdette St Ste A (48220-1992)
PHONE.....................248 591-7484
Donald Purdie, *President*
Sheri Depifanio, *Principal*
Don Purdie Jr, *Vice Pres*
EMP: 50 EST: 1914
SQ FT: 100,000
SALES (est): 8.1MM **Privately Held**
WEB: www.detroitelevator.com
SIC: 1796 3534 7699 Elevator installation & conversion; elevators & equipment; elevators: inspection, service & repair

(G-5546)
DETROIT FINE PRODUCTS LLC
Also Called: Detroit Grooming Company LLC
2615 Wolcott St Ste E (48220-1422)
PHONE.....................877 294-5826
Steve Henes, *Managing Prtnr*
EMP: 6 EST: 2017
SALES (est): 485.3K **Privately Held**
WEB: www.detroitgrooming.com
SIC: 2844 5122 Hair preparations, including shampoos; cosmetics, perfumes & hair products

(G-5547)
DETROIT NAME PLATE ETCHING INC
10610 Galaxie Ave (48220-2171)
PHONE.....................248 543-5200
Gregory Rivard, *President*
David Rivard, *Plant Mgr*
Chin Rivard, *Sales Staff*
John B Peabody, *Shareholder*
Brian Raden, *Administration*
▲ EMP: 31 EST: 1986
SQ FT: 11,000
SALES (est): 6.1MM **Privately Held**
WEB: www.dnpe.com
SIC: 3479 2396 3993 Name plates: engraved, etched, etc.; automotive & apparel trimmings; signs & advertising specialties

(G-5548)
DIVERSFIED PRCUREMENT SVCS LLC
1530 Farrow St (48220-1907)
PHONE.....................248 821-1147
Donald John O Connell,
EMP: 4 EST: 2006
SALES (est): 281.4K **Privately Held**
SIC: 5047 3443 3469 3465 Medical equipment & supplies; metal parts; machine parts, stamped or pressed metal; automotive stampings; motor vehicle supplies & new parts; automotive supplies & parts

(G-5549)
DIVERSIFIED METAL FABRICATORS
2351 Hilton Rd (48220-1570)
PHONE.....................248 541-0500
Gary W Dulong, *President*
EMP: 22 EST: 1993

SALES (est): 3.8MM **Privately Held**
WEB: www.dmfdetroit.com
SIC: 3444 Sheet metal specialties, not stamped

(G-5550)
E-SNAP PUBLICATIONS LLC
23211 Woodward Ave (48220-1361)
PHONE.....................708 740-0910
Anita Tharpe, *Principal*
EMP: 5 EST: 2018
SALES (est): 137K **Privately Held**
SIC: 2741 Miscellaneous publishing

(G-5551)
ENGINEERED ALUM FABRICATORS CO
Also Called: Engineered Alum Fabricators
1530 Farrow St (48220-1907)
PHONE.....................248 582-3430
Donald John O'Connell, *President*
▲ EMP: 7 EST: 2008
SALES (est): 500K **Privately Held**
WEB: www.eafab.com
SIC: 3441 Fabricated structural metal

(G-5552)
ENOVATE IT
1250 Woodward Hts (48220-1427)
PHONE.....................248 721-8104
Fred Calero, *COO*
EMP: 11 EST: 2007
SALES (est): 400.9K **Privately Held**
SIC: 3571 Electronic computers

(G-5553)
FERNDALE LABORATORIES INC (HQ)
Also Called: Ferndale Contract Mfg
780 W 8 Mile Rd (48220-2498)
PHONE.....................248 548-0900
James T McMillan II, *CEO*
Michael Burns, *President*
Joey West, *Business Mgr*
Leon Dupuis, *Vice Pres*
Scott Mason, *Vice Pres*
▲ EMP: 180
SQ FT: 105,600
SALES (est): 56.6MM
SALES (corp-wide): 63.9MM **Privately Held**
WEB: www.ferndalelabsmfg.com
SIC: 2834 Pharmaceutical preparations
PA: Ferndale Pharma Group, Inc.
 780 W 8 Mile Rd
 Ferndale MI 48220
 248 548-0900

(G-5554)
FERNDALE PHARMA GROUP INC (PA)
780 W 8 Mile Rd (48220-2422)
PHONE.....................248 548-0900
James McMillan, *CEO*
Michael Burns, *President*
Elliott Milstein, *Vice Pres*
Ann Smith, *Vice Pres*
Eric Debus, *Project Mgr*
EMP: 260 EST: 1897
SALES (est): 63.9MM **Privately Held**
WEB: www.ferndalepharmagroup.com
SIC: 2834 3841 Pharmaceutical preparations; surgical & medical instruments

(G-5555)
GAGE CORPORATION (PA)
821 Wanda St Ste 1 (48220-2944)
PHONE.....................248 541-3824
Michael J Gage, *Ch of Bd*
Donald R Dixon, *President*
Raymond D Gage III, *Director*
EMP: 10 EST: 1985
SALES (est): 28.8MM **Privately Held**
WEB: www.gageproducts.com
SIC: 2869 Solvents, organic

(G-5556)
GAGE GLOBAL SERVICES INC (PA)
Also Called: Gage Products Company
821 Wanda St Ste 2 (48220-2944)
PHONE.....................248 541-3824
Donald Dixon, *President*
Mike Baaso, *Production*
Dan Macgregor, *Controller*

Scott Bischoff, *Accounts Mgr*
Theodore Finkiewicz, *Sales Staff*
EMP: 91 EST: 1991
SALES (est): 8.6MM **Privately Held**
WEB: www.gageproducts.com
SIC: 2841 Scouring compounds

(G-5557)
GAGE PRODUCTS COMPANY
625 Wanda St (48220-2690)
PHONE.....................248 541-3824
EMP: 4
SALES (corp-wide): 28.8MM **Privately Held**
WEB: www.gageproducts.com
SIC: 2869 Industrial organic chemicals
HQ: Gage Products Company
 821 Wanda St
 Ferndale MI 48220
 248 541-3824

(G-5558)
GARDEN FRESH GOURMET LLC (HQ)
1220 E 9 Mile Rd (48220-1972)
PHONE.....................866 725-7239
Jack Aronson,
EMP: 77 EST: 2015
SALES (est): 55MM
SALES (corp-wide): 8.4B **Publicly Held**
WEB: www.campbellsoupcompany.com
SIC: 2035 Pickles, sauces & salad dressings
PA: Campbell Soup Company
 1 Campbell Pl
 Camden NJ 08103
 856 342-4800

(G-5559)
GOLDEN SIGN CO
841 Farmdale St (48220-1872)
PHONE.....................313 580-4094
Jordan Zielke, *Principal*
EMP: 4 EST: 2014
SALES (est): 103K **Privately Held**
WEB: www.goldensignco.tumblr.com
SIC: 3993 Signs & advertising specialties

(G-5560)
I PARTH INC
Also Called: Midwest Circuits
2206 Burdette St (48220-1404)
PHONE.....................248 548-9722
Rajanber Patel, *President*
Jay Patel, *Vice Pres*
▲ EMP: 7 EST: 1999
SQ FT: 14,000
SALES (est): 960.6K **Privately Held**
WEB: www.mcledlighting.com
SIC: 3672 3648 Printed circuit boards; lighting equipment

(G-5561)
JEFFERSON IRON WORKS INC
2441 Wolcott St (48220-1446)
PHONE.....................248 542-3554
Daniel Blake, *President*
EMP: 7
SQ FT: 18,000
SALES (est): 845.8K **Privately Held**
WEB: www.jeffersonironworks.com
SIC: 3599 Machine shop, jobbing & repair

(G-5562)
K-TEC SYSTEMS INC (PA)
2615 Wolcott St (48220-1422)
PHONE.....................248 414-4100
Catherine Koch, *President*
Michael Martin, *Vice Pres*
Shayna Tigani, *Accounting Dir*
EMP: 12
SALES (est): 3.9MM **Privately Held**
WEB: www.k-tecsystems.com
SIC: 3823 Temperature instruments: industrial process type

(G-5563)
L BARGE & ASSOCIATES INC
Also Called: Midwest Diversified Products
1530 Farrow St (48220-1907)
PHONE.....................248 582-3430
Lloyd H Barge, *President*
Donald J O Connell, *Corp Secy*
EMP: 24 EST: 1982
SQ FT: 30,000

Ferndale - Oakland County (G-5564)

GEOGRAPHIC SECTION

SALES (est): 1.9MM **Privately Held**
WEB: www.lbarge.com
SIC: 3443 3469 3465 5013 Metal parts; machine parts, stamped or pressed metal; automotive stampings; motor vehicle supplies & new parts; automotive supplies & parts

(G-5564)
LADY LAZARUS LLC
22801 Woodward Ave (48220-1738)
PHONE 810 441-9115
Christopher Best, *Principal*
EMP: 8 **EST:** 2014
SALES (est): 223.8K **Privately Held**
WEB: www.ladylazarusdetroit.com
SIC: 2741 Miscellaneous publishing

(G-5565)
LE HOST LLC
Also Called: Lehost Hair & Wigs
305 W 9 Mile Rd (48220-1767)
PHONE 248 546-4247
Haith Johnson, *Partner*
Henry Johnson, *Vice Pres*
Orena Perry, *Admin Sec*
EMP: 6 **EST:** 2010
SQ FT: 2,000
SALES (est): 686.4K **Privately Held**
WEB: www.lehosthair.com
SIC: 2844 3999 Hair preparations, including shampoos; wigs, including doll wigs, toupees or wiglets

(G-5566)
MACDERMID INCORPORATED
Also Called: Macdermid Ferndale Facility
1221 Farrow St (48220-1918)
PHONE 248 399-3553
David Bruce, *Director*
Deveco Bridges, *Technician*
EMP: 5
SQ FT: 10,000
SALES (corp-wide): 1.8B **Publicly Held**
WEB: www.macdermid.com
SIC: 2899 Metal treating compounds
HQ: Macdermid, Incorporated
   245 Freight St
   Waterbury CT 06702
   203 575-5700

(G-5567)
MAYER ALLOYS CORPORATION (PA)
10711 Northend Ave (48220-2130)
PHONE 248 399-2233
Steven Ruzumna, *President*
Ilene R Lubell, *Vice Pres*
Barbara Morton, *Vice Pres*
Phyllis Mertins, *Controller*
EMP: 3 **EST:** 1981
SQ FT: 2,400
SALES (est): 1.2MM **Privately Held**
WEB: www.mayeralloys.com
SIC: 3339 Lead smelting & refining (primary); tin-base alloys (primary)

(G-5568)
MICHIGAN METRO TIMES INC
1100 Woodward Hts (48220-1425)
PHONE 313 961-4060
Chris Xexson, *Principal*
Bernadette Brown, *Principal*
Danielle Smith-Elliott, *Accounts Exec*
Danielle Smith, *Sales Staff*
EMP: 220 **EST:** 1980
SALES (est): 2.1MM
SALES (corp-wide): 63.5MM **Privately Held**
WEB: www.metrotimes.com
SIC: 2711 Newspapers, publishing & printing
PA: The Scranton Times L P
   149 Penn Ave Ste 1
   Scranton PA 18503
   570 348-9100

(G-5569)
MOTOR CITY MANUFACTURING LTD
23440 Woodward Ave (48220-1344)
PHONE 586 731-1086
Fred Berg, *President*
Paul Berg, *Vice Pres*
EMP: 7 **EST:** 1994

SALES (est): 541.5K **Privately Held**
WEB: www.motorcitymfg.com
SIC: 3993 Signs & advertising specialties

(G-5570)
NALCOR LLC (PA)
Also Called: Nalpac Enterprises
1365 Jarvis St (48220-2025)
PHONE 248 541-1140
Ralph S Caplan, *President*
Andy Craig, *COO*
Glenn Leboeuf, *Opers Staff*
Kimberly Cowens, *Buyer*
Jerry Nardecchia, *Asst Controller*
▲ **EMP:** 70 **EST:** 1971
SQ FT: 200,000
SALES (est): 29.1MM **Privately Held**
SIC: 5199 5099 3993 2759 Gifts & novelties; advertising specialties; sunglasses; signs & advertising specialties; commercial printing; automotive & apparel trimmings

(G-5571)
NEW UNISON CORPORATION
1601 Wanda St (48220-2022)
PHONE 248 544-9500
David A Swider, *President*
▲ **EMP:** 30 **EST:** 1999
SQ FT: 35,000
SALES (est): 4.9MM **Privately Held**
WEB: www.unisonemail.com
SIC: 3541 3549 Grinding machines, metalworking; metalworking machinery

(G-5572)
NEW YORK BAGEL BAKING CO (PA)
23316 Woodward Ave (48220-1302)
PHONE 248 548-2580
Howard Goldsmith, *President*
Harvey Goldsmith, *Vice Pres*
EMP: 15 **EST:** 1934
SQ FT: 5,000
SALES (est): 9.7MM **Privately Held**
WEB: www.newyorkbagel-detroit.com
SIC: 5149 5461 2051 Bakery products; bagels; bread, cake & related products

(G-5573)
NODEL-CO
2615 Wolcott St (48220-1422)
PHONE 248 543-1325
Norm Dell, *President*
Lynne Prudden, *Vice Pres*
EMP: 10 **EST:** 2002
SALES (est): 918.4K **Privately Held**
SIC: 3999 3714 Cigarette filters; motor vehicle parts & accessories

(G-5574)
OVERHEAD CONVEYOR COMPANY (PA)
Also Called: OCC Systems
1330 Hilton Rd (48220-2898)
PHONE 248 547-3800
Tom Woodbeck, *President*
Mike Sherman, *Superintendent*
Glenn Toombs, *Superintendent*
Ted Woodbeck, *Vice Pres*
Len Bochenek, *Project Mgr*
EMP: 40 **EST:** 1945
SALES (est): 53.4MM **Privately Held**
WEB: www.occsystems.com
SIC: 3535 Conveyors & conveying equipment

(G-5575)
PAK MAIL CENTER OF AMERICA
23211 Woodward Ave (48220-1361)
PHONE 248 543-3097
Bob Zellers, *Principal*
EMP: 5 **EST:** 2016
SALES (est): 424K **Privately Held**
WEB: www.pakmail.com
SIC: 3499 2752 5113 Boxes for packing & shipping, metal; color lithography; shipping supplies

(G-5576)
PARALLAX PRINTING LLC
2615 Wolcott St (48220-1422)
PHONE 248 397-5156
EMP: 5 **EST:** 2020

SALES (est): 94.6K **Privately Held**
WEB: www.parallaxprinting.com
SIC: 2752 Commercial printing, lithographic

(G-5577)
PC COMPLETE INC
Also Called: Pos Complete
742 Livernois St (48220-2307)
PHONE 248 545-4211
Marshall Miller, *President*
Jenifer Miller, *Corp Secy*
Jennifer Miller,
EMP: 9 **EST:** 1995
SQ FT: 7,500
SALES (est): 967.8K **Privately Held**
WEB: www.pchomecare.com
SIC: 3578 Point-of-sale devices

(G-5578)
PK FABRICATING INC
1975 Hilton Rd (48220-1501)
PHONE 248 398-4500
Kathleen Kaiafas, *President*
Peter Kaiafas, *Vice Pres*
EMP: 12 **EST:** 1996
SALES (est): 1MM **Privately Held**
WEB: www.pkfab.com
SIC: 3441 Building components, structural steel

(G-5579)
PLASTI-FAB INC
2305 Hilton Rd (48220-1570)
PHONE 248 543-1415
Richard P Melin, *President*
Harold R Melin, *Corp Secy*
EMP: 30
SQ FT: 15,000
SALES (est): 3.5MM **Privately Held**
WEB: www.plasti-fabinc.com
SIC: 3089 2672 2396 Plastic processing; coated & laminated paper; automotive & apparel trimmings

(G-5580)
POWERTRAN CORPORATION
1605 Bonner St (48220-1909)
PHONE 248 399-4300
Thomas M Schalk, *President*
Ramesh Naik, *Vice Pres*
EMP: 21 **EST:** 1956
SQ FT: 10,000
SALES (est): 3.4MM **Privately Held**
WEB: www.powertran.com
SIC: 3612 Transformers, except electric

(G-5581)
PRECISION SPINDLE SERVICE CO
836 Woodward Hts (48220-1431)
PHONE 248 544-0100
David Marschick, *President*
Bill Foy, *President*
EMP: 10 **EST:** 1946
SQ FT: 6,000
SALES (est): 2.2MM **Privately Held**
WEB: www.spindlerebuilding.com
SIC: 3552 Spindles, textile

(G-5582)
PRO PET L L C
2313 Garfield St (48220-1159)
PHONE 248 930-2880
Michael Prentice, *Principal*
EMP: 5 **EST:** 2017
SALES (est): 78.1K **Privately Held**
WEB: www.propet.com
SIC: 2047 Dog & cat food

(G-5583)
PROGRESS CUSTOM SCREEN PRTG
Also Called: Progress Custom Screen Prtg
364 Hilton Rd (48220-2548)
PHONE 248 982-4247
Grant Gamlaski,
EMP: 5 **EST:** 2010
SALES (est): 226.5K **Privately Held**
WEB: www.printwithprogress.com
SIC: 2759 Screen printing

(G-5584)
SCHRAMMS MEAD
327 W 9 Mile Rd (48220-1767)
PHONE 248 439-5000
Owen Nikki, *Accountant*
James Naeger, *Assistant*
EMP: 7 **EST:** 2013
SALES (est): 341.1K **Privately Held**
WEB: www.schrammsmead.com
SIC: 2084 Wines

(G-5585)
SLAUGHTERHOUSE COLLECTIVE LLC
1604 Jewell St (48220-2695)
PHONE 248 259-5257
Cassandra Litten,
Brittany Alyse,
Kyle Parker,
EMP: 4 **EST:** 2018
SALES (est): 73.4K **Privately Held**
SIC: 2721 Magazines: publishing & printing

(G-5586)
SPRAYTEK INC (HQ)
2535 Wolcott St (48220-1446)
PHONE 248 546-3551
Dave Berry, *President*
Steven Ross, *Sales Mgr*
Laurie Alfonso, *Manager*
Eric Swisher, *Manager*
▲ **EMP:** 13 **EST:** 2004
SALES (est): 4.5MM
SALES (corp-wide): 72.9MM **Privately Held**
WEB: www.spraytekinc.com
SIC: 3479 Coating of metals & formed products
PA: The Magni Group Inc
   390 Park St Ste 300
   Birmingham MI 48009
   248 647-4500

(G-5587)
STRUCTURAL EQUIPMENT CO
Also Called: Overhead Conveyer
1330 Hilton Rd (48220-2837)
PHONE 248 547-3800
Milford E Woodbeck Sr, *CEO*
Milford E Woodbeck Jr, *Vice Pres*
EMP: 15 **EST:** 1958
SQ FT: 4,000
SALES (est): 1MM **Privately Held**
WEB: www.occsystems.com
SIC: 3535 Conveyors & conveying equipment

(G-5588)
TEE QUILTERS
3308 Inman St (48220-1092)
PHONE 248 336-9779
EMP: 4 **EST:** 2019
SALES (est): 87.4K **Privately Held**
SIC: 2759 Screen printing

(G-5589)
TROY HAYGOOD
Also Called: Plush Apparel Cstm Impressions
2871 Hilton Rd (48220-1066)
PHONE 313 478-3308
Troy Haygood, *Owner*
EMP: 4 **EST:** 2011 **Privately Held**
SIC: 2759 Commercial printing

(G-5590)
TRU-THREAD CO INC
1600 Hilton Rd (48220-1911)
P.O. Box 20255 (48220-0255)
PHONE 248 399-0255
Milford Messer, *President*
Thomas Messer, *Vice Pres*
EMP: 8 **EST:** 1961
SQ FT: 14,000
SALES (est): 954.9K **Privately Held**
WEB: www.truthreadco.com
SIC: 3599 Machine shop, jobbing & repair

(G-5591)
TUBESOURCE MANUFACTURING INC
1600 E 9 Mile Rd (48220-2028)
PHONE 248 543-4746
James A Bery, *President*
Sandy Koelzer, *General Mgr*
▲ **EMP:** 20 **EST:** 1942

GEOGRAPHIC SECTION　　　　　　　　　　　　　　　　　　　　　　　　　　　　　　　　Flat Rock - Wayne County (G-5617)

SQ FT: 23,000
SALES (est): 1.3MM **Privately Held**
WEB: www.tubesource.net
SIC: 3498 Tube fabricating (contract bending & shaping)

(G-5592)
UBER HAIR AND NAILS LLC
990 W 8 Mile Rd (48220-2321)
PHONE..................................248 268-3227
Chanh Lanoi, *Mng Member*
EMP: 4
SALES (est): 74.4K **Privately Held**
SIC: 2844 Manicure preparations

(G-5593)
UNI-VUE INC
2424 Wolcott St (48220-1424)
P.O. Box 1558, Troy (48099-1558)
PHONE..................................248 564-3251
Chris Mytnik, *President*
Pamela Lee, *Marketing Staff*
▼ EMP: 20 EST: 1980
SALES (est): 1.4MM **Privately Held**
WEB: www.uni-vue.com
SIC: 3531 Mud jacks

(G-5594)
UNIVERSAL CONTAINER CORP
10750 Galaxie Ave (48220-2132)
PHONE..................................248 543-2788
Leonard W Horton II, *President*
J Anthony Mooter, *Corp Secy*
John Madigan, *Vice Pres*
Ron Roelofson, *Sales Mgr*
Brian Mathew, *Accounts Mgr*
EMP: 45 EST: 1975
SQ FT: 80,000
SALES (est): 7.4MM **Privately Held**
WEB: www.packpros.net
SIC: 2653 Boxes, corrugated: made from purchased materials

(G-5595)
VALENTINE DISTILLING
161 Vester St (48220-1711)
PHONE..................................248 629-9951
Rifino Valentine, *Owner*
Heather Deliso, *General Mgr*
EMP: 7 EST: 2016
SALES (est): 152.5K **Privately Held**
WEB: www.valentinedistilling.com
SIC: 2085 Vodka (alcoholic beverage)

(G-5596)
VALENTINE DISTILLING CO
965 Wanda St (48220-2959)
PHONE..................................646 286-2690
Rifino Valentine, *Owner*
EMP: 6
SALES (est): 396K **Privately Held**
WEB: www.valentinedistilling.com
SIC: 2085 Distilled & blended liquors

(G-5597)
VAN INDUSTRIES INC
1285 Wordsworth St (48220-2675)
PHONE..................................248 398-6990
Don La Flamboy, *President*
William H Howard, *Vice Pres*
Doug La Flamboy, *Vice Pres*
EMP: 10 EST: 1964
SQ FT: 13,000
SALES (est): 936.2K **Privately Held**
SIC: 3291 Abrasive buffs, bricks, cloth, paper, stones, etc.

(G-5598)
WINDING ROAD PUBLISHING INC
2355 Wolcott St (48220-1420)
PHONE..................................248 545-8360
P Yvonne, *Agent*
EMP: 5 EST: 2008
SALES (est): 39.4K **Privately Held**
WEB: www.windingroadpublishing.com
SIC: 2741 Miscellaneous publishing

(G-5599)
ZOYES EAST INC
Also Called: Architectural Model Studios
1280 Hilton Rd (48220-2837)
PHONE..................................248 584-3300
Dean Zoyes, *President*
Amee Zoyes, *Vice Pres*
Anna Kunnath, *Business Dir*

Shelby Caverly, *Account Dir*
EMP: 5 EST: 1996
SQ FT: 3,700
SALES (est): 555.9K **Privately Held**
WEB: www.zoyescreative.com
SIC: 8712 3999 Architectural engineering; models, except toy

Ferrysburg
Ottawa County

(G-5600)
ADVANCED SIGNS INCORPORATED
401 2nd St (49409-5133)
P.O. Box 67 (49409-0067)
PHONE..................................616 846-4667
Bernard Wade, *President*
EMP: 11 EST: 1985
SQ FT: 12,500
SALES (est): 2.1MM **Privately Held**
WEB: www.adsigns.com
SIC: 3993 Signs, not made in custom sign painting shops; electric signs

(G-5601)
BUCKEYE TERMINALS LLC
17806 N Shore Rd (49409)
PHONE..................................616 842-2450
EMP: 7 EST: 2008
SALES (est): 464.9K **Privately Held**
SIC: 2911 Liquefied petroleum gases, LPG

(G-5602)
EPS INDUSTRIES INC
585 Second St (49409)
P.O. Box 502, Spring Lake (49456-0502)
PHONE..................................616 844-9220
Ed Summers, *President*
Ryan Elliston, *Vice Pres*
EMP: 25 EST: 2000
SQ FT: 10,000
SALES (est): 2.8MM **Privately Held**
WEB: www.epsind.com
SIC: 3324 3366 3365 Aerospace investment castings, ferrous; commercial investment castings, ferrous; copper foundries; bronze foundry; aluminum foundries

(G-5603)
JOHNSTON BOILER COMPANY
300 Pine St (49409-5131)
P.O. Box 300 (49409-0300)
PHONE..................................616 842-5050
David Reinink, *President*
Rick Ewing, *Vice Pres*
Marci Marry, *Engineer*
Tim Nick, *Engineer*
Rick Slater, *Project Engr*
EMP: 45 EST: 1864
SQ FT: 93,800
SALES (est): 14.7MM
SALES (corp-wide): 177.4MM **Privately Held**
WEB: www.johnstonboiler.com
SIC: 3443 Boilers: industrial, power, or marine
PA: Hines Corporation
　　1218 E Pontaluna Rd Ste B
　　Norton Shores MI 49456
　　231 799-6240

(G-5604)
PORTENGA MANUFACTURING COMPANY
220 5th St (49409)
P.O. Box 26 (49409-0026)
PHONE..................................616 846-2691
Chad Portenga, *President*
Jay Schuitema, *Vice Pres*
EMP: 7 EST: 1981
SQ FT: 5,400 **Privately Held**
WEB: www.portenga.com
SIC: 3543 Industrial patterns

Fife Lake
Kalkaska County

(G-5605)
DOLLARS SENSE
7850 Scotch Blf Sw (49633-8289)
PHONE..................................231 369-3610
EMP: 4 EST: 2010
SALES (est): 214.3K **Privately Held**
SIC: 3643 Outlets, electric: convenience

(G-5606)
FOREST BLAKE PRODUCTS INC
10723 Shippy Rd Sw (49633-9103)
PHONE..................................231 879-3913
Frank Blake, *President*
EMP: 9 EST: 1980
SALES (est): 723.7K **Privately Held**
SIC: 2411 2611 4213 4212 Logging; pulp mills; trucking, except local; local trucking, without storage; sawmills & planing mills, general

(G-5607)
GUSTOS QUALITY SYSTEMS
11655 Gusto Dr (49633-9091)
PHONE..................................231 409-0219
John Gustafson, *Owner*
EMP: 8 EST: 2008
SALES (est): 151K **Privately Held**
SIC: 7692 7694 Automotive welding; hermetics repair

(G-5608)
HAYES MANUFACTURING INC
6875 Us Highway 131 (49633-9765)
P.O. Box 220 (49633-0220)
PHONE..................................231 879-3372
Holly Miller, *President*
Raymond J Hayes, *President*
Carol Ann Hayes, *Corp Secy*
Penny Challende, *Vice Pres*
Charles James Hayes, *Vice Pres*
▲ EMP: 30 EST: 1962
SQ FT: 24,000
SALES (est): 8.7MM **Privately Held**
WEB: www.hayescouplings.com
SIC: 3568 Couplings, shaft: rigid, flexible, universal joint, etc.

(G-5609)
WADE LOGGING
7108 W Sharon Rd Sw (49633-9208)
PHONE..................................231 463-0363
Jim Wade, *Owner*
EMP: 7 EST: 2013
SALES (est): 215.9K **Privately Held**
WEB: www.wadelogging.com
SIC: 2411 Logging

Filer City
Manistee County

(G-5610)
PACKAGING CORPORATION AMERICA
Also Called: PCA/Filer City 640
2246 Udell St (49634-9801)
P.O. Box 5 (49634-0005)
PHONE..................................231 723-1442
Kenneth Holman, *Maint Spvr*
Greg Fessenden, *Electrical Engi*
Colleen Kenny, *Finance Mgr*
Sonny Rice, *Sales Staff*
Robert Peritin, *Branch Mgr*
EMP: 350
SALES (corp-wide): 6.6B **Publicly Held**
WEB: www.packagingcorp.com
SIC: 2653 Boxes, corrugated: made from purchased materials
PA: Packaging Corporation Of America
　　1 N Field Ct
　　Lake Forest IL 60045
　　847 482-3000

(G-5611)
TES FILER CY STN LTD PARTNR
700 Mee St (49634-8800)
PHONE..................................231 723-6573
Catherine M Reynolds, *Partner*
EMP: 2 EST: 1988

SALES (est): 2.1MM
SALES (corp-wide): 6.6B **Publicly Held**
SIC: 1311 Coal gasification
HQ: Cms Generation Filer City, Inc.
　　1 Energy Plaza Dr
　　Jackson MI 49201

Filion
Huron County

(G-5612)
D R W SYSTEMS
4484 N Van Dyke Rd (48432-9727)
PHONE..................................989 874-4663
David Rushing, *Owner*
EMP: 4 EST: 2004
SALES (est): 170K **Privately Held**
SIC: 3291 Synthetic abrasives

Flat Rock
Wayne County

(G-5613)
AMERICAN INDUSTRIAL TRAINING
23851 Vreeland Rd (48134-9409)
PHONE..................................734 789-9099
EMP: 5 EST: 2019
SALES (est): 281.8K **Privately Held**
SIC: 3496 Miscellaneous fabricated wire products

(G-5614)
AUTO PALLETS-BOXES INC
27945 Cooke St (48134-1201)
PHONE..................................734 782-1110
EMP: 9
SALES (corp-wide): 6.9MM **Privately Held**
SIC: 2448 Mfg Wood Pallets/Skids
PA: Auto Pallets-Boxes, Inc.
　　28000 Southfield Rd Fl 2
　　Lathrup Village MI 48076
　　248 559-7744

(G-5615)
AUTOALLIANCE MANAGEMENT CO
1 International Dr (48134-9401)
PHONE..................................734 782-7800
Tim Young, *President*
Rodney Haynes, *CFO*
◆ EMP: 81 EST: 1985
SALES (est): 4.6MM **Privately Held**
SIC: 3711 Motor vehicles & car bodies

(G-5616)
BAR PROCESSING CORPORATION (HQ)
Also Called: Flat Rock
26601 W Huron River Dr (48134-1134)
P.O. Box 1090 (48134-2090)
PHONE..................................734 782-4454
Paul Lanzon, *CEO*
Brian Drozdowski, *General Mgr*
Rick Kern, *General Mgr*
Jeff Kolbus, *General Mgr*
Fritz Michalk, *General Mgr*
▲ EMP: 200 EST: 1970
SALES (est): 39.9MM **Privately Held**
WEB: www.barprocessingcorp.com
SIC: 3471 Finishing, metals or formed products; polishing, metals or formed products
PA: Shields Acquisition Company, Inc.
　　26601 W Huron River Dr
　　Flat Rock MI 48134
　　734 782-4454

(G-5617)
CUSTOM COATING TECHNOLOGIES
26601 W Huron River Dr (48134-1134)
PHONE..................................734 244-3610
EMP: 5 EST: 2015
SALES (est): 403.2K **Privately Held**
WEB: www.customcoatingtech.com
SIC: 3479 Coating of metals & formed products

Flat Rock - Wayne County (G-5618)

(G-5618)
FLAT ROCK METAL INC
Also Called: Flatrock Metal Bar and Proc
26601 W Huron River Dr (48134-1134)
P.O. Box 1090 (48134-2090)
PHONE..................734 782-4454
Keith King, *CEO*
Paul Lanzon, *CEO*
Terry Moran, *President*
Dan Crippen, *General Mgr*
Jeff Kolbus, *General Mgr*
EMP: 200 EST: 1981
SALES (est): 26.4MM Privately Held
WEB: www.frm.com
SIC: 3471 3316 Plating & polishing; cold finishing of steel shapes

(G-5619)
FLATROCK TIRE
24599 Gibraltar Rd (48134-1347)
PHONE..................734 783-0100
EMP: 4 EST: 2020
SALES (est): 83.1K Privately Held
SIC: 5531 5014 2296 Automotive tires; tires & tubes; tire cord & fabrics

(G-5620)
FORD MOTOR COMPANY
1 International Dr (48134-9401)
PHONE..................734 782-7800
EMP: 7
SALES (corp-wide): 127.1B Publicly Held
WEB: www.ford.com
SIC: 3711 Automobile assembly, including specialty automobiles
PA: Ford Motor Company
  1 American Rd
  Dearborn MI 48126
  313 322-3000

(G-5621)
FOUR WAY PALLET SERVICE
3988 Will Carleton Rd (48134-9659)
P.O. Box 304 (48134-0304)
PHONE..................734 782-5914
Daniel E Gerhardi, *Owner*
EMP: 6 EST: 1991
SQ FT: 6,000
SALES (est): 243.3K Privately Held
SIC: 2448 Pallets, wood

(G-5622)
INNOVATIVE FABRICATION LLC
23851 Vreeland Rd (48134-9409)
PHONE..................734 789-9099
Kristy Stapula,
EMP: 40 EST: 2017
SALES (est): 1.8MM Privately Held
SIC: 3999 Manufacturing industries

(G-5623)
MESSINA CONCRETE INC
14675 Telegraph Rd (48134-9655)
P.O. Box 1173 (48134-2173)
PHONE..................734 783-1020
Vince Messina, *Manager*
EMP: 22
SALES (corp-wide): 3.7MM Privately Held
WEB: www.messinaconcrete.com
SIC: 3273 Ready-mixed concrete
PA: Messina Concrete, Inc.
  725 N Dixie Hwy
  Monroe MI
  734 241-8380

(G-5624)
OT DYNAMICS LLC
27100 Hall Rd (48134-1195)
PHONE..................734 984-7022
Bill Corbett, *Business Mgr*
Ernie Clark, *Sales Mgr*
EMP: 10 EST: 2016
SQ FT: 30,000
SALES (est): 2.3MM Privately Held
WEB: www.otdynamics.com
SIC: 2851 Paints & allied products

(G-5625)
POLYTEK MICHIGAN INC
24601 Vreeland Rd Ste 2 (48134-1810)
PHONE..................734 782-0378
Mark Wingfield, *Principal*
EMP: 5 EST: 2010

SALES (est): 87.6K Privately Held
SIC: 3011 Tires & inner tubes

(G-5626)
QUALITY ALUM ACQUISITION LLC
14544 Telegraph Rd Ste 1 (48134-8910)
P.O. Box 269, Hastings (49058-0269)
PHONE..................734 783-0990
Robert Clark, *CEO*
Blaze Tomich, *Finance Mgr*
Aaron Erdman, *Manager*
EMP: 10 Privately Held
WEB: www.qualityaluminum.com
SIC: 3444 3354 Sheet metalwork; aluminum extruded products
PA: Quality Aluminum Acquisition Llc
  429 S Michigan Ave
  Hastings MI 49058

(G-5627)
QUALITY CLUTCHES INC
3966 Dauncy Rd (48134-9608)
PHONE..................734 782-0783
Ricky Leigh Kargel, *President*
Judy Kargel, *Admin Sec*
EMP: 6 EST: 1984
SQ FT: 4,000
SALES (est): 492.3K Privately Held
SIC: 3714 Transmission housings or parts, motor vehicle

(G-5628)
ROYAL ARC WELDING COMPANY (PA)
Also Called: Royal ARC Crane Service
23851 Vreeland Rd (48134-9409)
P.O. Box 419, Lincoln Park (48146-0419)
PHONE..................734 789-9099
Robert Siemens, *President*
Helen Murphy, *Sales Staff*
David Lee, *Manager*
Elizabeth McClain, *Personnel Assit*
EMP: 35
SQ FT: 60,000
SALES (est): 15.8MM Privately Held
WEB: www.royalarc.com
SIC: 3536 3441 3412 8299 Cranes, industrial plant; fabricated structural metal; metal barrels, drums & pails; educational services; vocational schools

(G-5629)
SHIELDS ACQUISITION CO INC (PA)
26601 W Huron River Dr (48134-1134)
PHONE..................734 782-4454
Keith S King, *President*
EMP: 2 EST: 1970
SALES (est): 39.9MM Privately Held
SIC: 3471 Finishing, metals or formed products; polishing, metals or formed products

(G-5630)
SINGLE SOURCE INC
Also Called: C.P.
27100 Hall Rd (48134-1195)
PHONE..................765 825-4111
Ernest Clark, *Sales Mgr*
Dan Boboltz, *Manager*
EMP: 6 Privately Held
WEB: www.ncssi.com
SIC: 5013 2851 Automotive servicing equipment; paints & allied products
PA: Single Source, Inc.
  4900 Fls Of Neuse Rd # 150
  Raleigh NC 27609

(G-5631)
TO Z A MANUFACTURING
24685 Telegraph Rd (48134-9225)
PHONE..................734 782-3911
Donald Morton, *Principal*
EMP: 4 EST: 2001
SALES (est): 62.4K Privately Held
SIC: 3999 Manufacturing industries

Flint
Genesee County

(G-5632)
4D SYSTEMS LLC
4130 Market Pl (48507-3205)
PHONE..................800 380-9165
Jean-Pierre Rasaiah, *President*
Martin Barker, *Vice Pres*
Fay Tanner, *Project Mgr*
Leonardo Sawaya, *Engineer*
Ryan Glogowski, *Design Engr*
EMP: 25 EST: 2007
SQ FT: 1,500
SALES (est): 4.7MM Privately Held
WEB: www.4dsysco.com
SIC: 7372 8711 Prepackaged software; engineering services

(G-5633)
A I FLINT LLC
4444 W Maple Ave (48507-3128)
PHONE..................810 732-8760
Darrel Reece,
EMP: 1100 EST: 2000
SQ FT: 240,000
SALES (est): 94.3MM
SALES (corp-wide): 474.4MM Privately Held
WEB: www.android-ind.com
SIC: 3714 Motor vehicle parts & accessories
PA: Android Industries, L.L.C.
  2155 Executive Hills Dr
  Auburn Hills MI 48326
  248 454-0500

(G-5634)
ACCU-SHAPE DIE CUTTING INC
4050 Market Pl (48507-3203)
PHONE..................810 230-2445
Preston D Means, *President*
Joe Brooks, *COO*
Emma Brooks, *CFO*
▲ **EMP: 44 EST: 1998**
SQ FT: 45,000
SALES (est): 7.1MM Privately Held
WEB: www.accushapediecutting.com
SIC: 2675 3554 3544 Die-cut paper & board; paper industries machinery; special dies, tools, jigs & fixtures

(G-5635)
ACE OUTDOOR SERVICES LLC
5249 Miller Rd (48507-1067)
P.O. Box 779, Grand Blanc (48480-0779)
PHONE..................810 820-8313
Aron Whitener, *Mng Member*
EMP: 40 EST: 2007
SALES (est): 1MM Privately Held
WEB: www.aceoutdoorservices.com
SIC: 0782 3524 Landscape contractors; snowblowers & throwers, residential

(G-5636)
ACI PLASTICS INC
2945 Davison Rd (48506-3928)
PHONE..................810 767-3800
Lynne Krupp, *COO*
Bill McCaffrey, *COO*
Tony McGee, *Plant Mgr*
Mark Lieberman, *Manager*
EMP: 21
SALES (corp-wide): 36.5MM Privately Held
WEB: www.aciplastics.com
SIC: 4953 3087 5162 Recycling, waste materials; custom compound purchased resins; plastics resins
PA: Aci Plastics, Inc.
  2945 Davison Rd
  Flint MI 48506
  810 767-3800

(G-5637)
ACI PLASTICS INC (PA)
Also Called: A C I Plastics
2945 Davison Rd (48506-3928)
PHONE..................810 767-3800
Mark Lieberman, *CEO*
Scott Melton, *Vice Pres*
Lynne Krupp, *Controller*
Jennifer Jarman, *Sales Staff*
Robert Bailey, *Manager*

▲ **EMP: 50 EST: 1984**
SQ FT: 125,000
SALES (est): 36.5MM Privately Held
WEB: www.aciplastics.com
SIC: 4953 3087 5162 Recycling, waste materials; custom compound purchased resins; plastics resins

(G-5638)
ACI/WIPAG RECYCLING LLC
2945 Davison Rd (48506-3928)
PHONE..................810 767-4424
Mark Lieberman,
M Scott Melton,
EMP: 14 EST: 2000
SQ FT: 45,000
SALES (est): 743.9K Privately Held
WEB: www.aciplastics.com
SIC: 2821 Plastics materials & resins

(G-5639)
ADVANCED MAINTENANCE TECH
3118 S Dye Rd (48507-1004)
PHONE..................810 820-2554
Thomas Walker, *President*
EMP: 6 EST: 2011
SALES (est): 265.8K Privately Held
WEB: www.amtvibrationanalysis.com
SIC: 3541 Lathes

(G-5640)
AERO TRAIN CORP
5083 Miller Rd (48507-1075)
PHONE..................810 230-8096
EMP: 6 EST: 2011
SALES (est): 122.2K Privately Held
WEB: www.aerotrain.aero
SIC: 3728 Aircraft parts & equipment

(G-5641)
AI-GENESEE LLC
4400 Matthew (48507-3152)
PHONE..................810 720-4848
Darrel Reece,
Dave Donnay,
Marti Komer,
Keith Masserang,
Richard Niazy,
EMP: 15 EST: 2001
SQ FT: 280,000
SALES (est): 530.3K Privately Held
SIC: 3711 Automobile assembly, including specialty automobiles

(G-5642)
ALLIANCE AUTOMATION LLC
4072 Market Pl (48507-3203)
PHONE..................810 953-9539
Bruce Cranston, *Founder*
Hillary Herbruck, *Sales Staff*
▲ **EMP: 14 EST: 2006**
SALES (est): 2MM Privately Held
WEB: www.allianceautomationllc.com
SIC: 5531 3463 3559 Automotive accessories; automotive forgings, nonferrous; automotive maintenance equipment

(G-5643)
ALLIED ASP SEALCOAT & REPR LLC
913 Markham St (48507-2568)
PHONE..................810 797-6080
Adam J Adrian, *Principal*
EMP: 4 EST: 2019
SALES (est): 96.3K Privately Held
WEB: www.alliedasphalt.com
SIC: 2951 Asphalt & asphaltic paving mixtures (not from refineries)

(G-5644)
AMERICA WIRELESS
4205 Miller Rd (48507-1260)
PHONE..................810 820-3273
EMP: 6 EST: 2017
SALES (est): 134.8K Privately Held
SIC: 3312 Ammonia & liquor, from chemical recovery coke ovens

(G-5645)
ASSENMACHER LIGHTWEIGHT CYCLES
Also Called: Assemacher's Cycling Center
1272 W Hill Rd (48507-4762)
PHONE..................810 232-2994

▲ = Import ▼ = Export
◆ = Import/Export

GEOGRAPHIC SECTION

Flint - Genesee County (G-5674)

Lee Frantz, *Manager*
EMP: 5
SALES (corp-wide): 993.2K **Privately Held**
WEB: www.assenmachers.com
SIC: 3949 5941 Exercising cycles; sporting goods & bicycle shops
PA: Assenmacher Lightweight Cycles
8053 Miller Rd
Swartz Creek MI 48473
810 635-7844

(G-5646)
ATTENTIVE INDUSTRIES INC
1301 Alabama Ave (48505-3985)
PHONE 810 233-7077
Brien Lord, *Branch Mgr*
EMP: 10 **Privately Held**
WEB: www.attentiveindustries.com
SIC: 3444 Sheet metalwork
PA: Attentive Industries, Inc.
502 Kelso St
Flint MI 48506

(G-5647)
ATTENTIVE INDUSTRIES INC (PA)
502 Kelso St (48506-4033)
PHONE 810 233-7077
Tom Brown, *President*
Brien Lord, *Vice Pres*
▲ **EMP:** 6 **EST:** 1994
SQ FT: 7,500
SALES (est): 10.7MM **Privately Held**
WEB: www.attentiveindustries.com
SIC: 3444 Sheet metalwork

(G-5648)
AUTOMOTIVE PLASTICS RECYCLING
Also Called: American Commodities
2945 Davison Rd (48506-3928)
PHONE 810 767-3800
Mark Lieberman, *President*
M Scott Milton, *COO*
Scott Melton, *CFO*
EMP: 13 **EST:** 1984
SQ FT: 45,000
SALES (est): 611.6K **Privately Held**
WEB: www.aciplastics.com
SIC: 3089 4953 Plastic processing; refuse systems

(G-5649)
BANACOM INSTANT SIGNS
4463 Miller Rd (48507-1123)
PHONE 810 230-0233
Craig Hatch, *Owner*
EMP: 4 **EST:** 1987
SALES (est): 187.4K **Privately Held**
WEB: www.jdprint.com
SIC: 3993 Signs, not made in custom sign painting shops

(G-5650)
BARRETTE OUTDOOR LIVING INC
3200 Rbert T Longway Blvd (48506-4043)
PHONE 810 235-0400
Lisa Miller, *Prdtn Mgr*
Shannon Byrd, *Export Mgr*
Tammy May, *Accountant*
Christine McCann, *Human Res Mgr*
Jill Barnette, *VP Mktg*
EMP: 8
SALES (corp-wide): 322.9MM **Privately Held**
WEB: www.barretteoutdoorliving.com
SIC: 3315 Fence gates posts & fittings: steel
PA: Barrette Outdoor Living, Inc.
7830 Freeway Cir
Middleburg Heights OH 44130
440 891-0790

(G-5651)
BARRYS SIGN COMPANY
Also Called: Benmark Advertising
3501 Blackington Ave (48503-4962)
PHONE 810 234-9919
Barry D Wiselogle, *President*
Sandra K Wiselogle, *Admin Sec*
EMP: 4 **EST:** 1972
SQ FT: 6,000
SALES (est): 433.4K **Privately Held**
WEB: www.barryssigncompany.com
SIC: 3993 Signs, not made in custom sign painting shops

(G-5652)
BAUMANS RUNNING CENTER INC
Also Called: Baumans Running & Walking Shop
1473 W Hill Rd (48507-4709)
PHONE 810 238-5981
Mark E Bauman, *President*
Ryan Garland, *Sales Staff*
EMP: 8 **EST:** 1974
SQ FT: 1,600 **Privately Held**
WEB: www.werunthistown.com
SIC: 5661 5699 2261 Footwear, athletic; sports apparel; screen printing of cotton broadwoven fabrics

(G-5653)
BEATTIE SPRING & WELDING SVC
2840 Rbert T Longway Blvd (48506-4038)
PHONE 810 239-9151
Matthew Beattie, *President*
EMP: 5 **EST:** 1965
SALES (est): 499.5K **Privately Held**
WEB: www.beattiespring.com
SIC: 7539 7692 Automotive springs, rebuilding & repair; welding repair

(G-5654)
BENTLEY INDUSTRIES
1105 University Ave (48504-6223)
PHONE 810 625-0400
Steve Bentley, *Principal*
EMP: 4 **EST:** 2016
SALES (est): 117.7K **Privately Held**
SIC: 3999 Manufacturing industries

(G-5655)
BILL CARR SIGNS INC
719 W 12th St (48503-3851)
P.O. Box 7340 (48507-0340)
PHONE 810 232-1569
Jeremy Elfstrom, *President*
Ronald P Elfstrom, *President*
Jim Niestroy, *General Mgr*
Vince Brooks, *Sales Staff*
Tya Tallieu, *Office Mgr*
EMP: 10 **EST:** 1919
SQ FT: 16,000
SALES (est): 1.5MM **Privately Held**
WEB: www.billcarrsigns.com
SIC: 3993 7389 Signs, not made in custom sign painting shops; lettering & sign painting services

(G-5656)
BLADE EXCAVATING INC
2910 Wilton Pl (48506-1386)
PHONE 810 287-6457
Bobby Blade, *Director*
EMP: 4 **EST:** 2018
SALES (est): 66K **Privately Held**
SIC: 1081 Metal mining exploration & development services

(G-5657)
BLEVINS SCREW PRODUCTS INC
1838 Remell St (48503-4432)
PHONE 810 744-1820
Bruce Blevins, *President*
Mark Blevins, *Vice Pres*
Larry Craney, *Prdtn Mgr*
Kathrine Perdue, *Office Mgr*
Roger Blevins, *Admin Sec*
EMP: 21 **EST:** 1958
SQ FT: 9,000
SALES (est): 1.7MM **Privately Held**
WEB: www.blevinsscrew.com
SIC: 3599 Machine shop, jobbing & repair

(G-5658)
BOBIER TOOL SUPPLY INC
Also Called: Precision Metrology Inspection
G4163 Corunna Rd (48532-4360)
PHONE 810 732-4030
Melville D Bobier, *President*
Devere Bobier Jr, *President*
Mary Bobier, *Vice Pres*
Kim Bobier, *Technology*
EMP: 20 **EST:** 1948
SQ FT: 12,000
SALES (est): 2.6MM **Privately Held**
WEB: www.bobiermetrologysolutions.com
SIC: 5084 3569 Industrial machinery & equipment; robots, assembly line: industrial & commercial

(G-5659)
BORNEMAN & PETERSON INC
1810 Remell St (48503-4432)
PHONE 810 744-1890
Roger Blevins, *President*
Bruce Blevins, *Admin Sec*
EMP: 10 **EST:** 1943
SQ FT: 12,500
SALES (est): 803.3K **Privately Held**
WEB: www.bornemanandpeterson.com
SIC: 3451 3312 3599 1531 Screw machine products; blast furnaces & steel mills; machine shop, jobbing & repair; ; robots, assembly line: industrial & commercial

(G-5660)
BREMER PROSTHETIC DESIGN INC (PA)
3487 S Linden Rd Ste U (48507-3020)
PHONE 810 733-3375
Nathan Kapa, *President*
Jackie Bremer, *Administration*
EMP: 5 **EST:** 1993
SALES (est): 942K **Privately Held**
WEB: www.bremerprosthetics.com
SIC: 5999 3842 Orthopedic & prosthesis applications; prosthetic appliances

(G-5661)
BRIDGEWATER INDUSTRIES
4023 W Pierson Rd (48504-1334)
PHONE 810 228-3963
EMP: 4 **EST:** 2017
SALES (est): 81.9K **Privately Held**
SIC: 3999 Manufacturing industries

(G-5662)
CANVAS SHOPPE INC
3198 One Half S Dye Rd (48507)
PHONE 810 733-1841
Michael Gargliano, *Owner*
EMP: 5 **EST:** 1976
SQ FT: 2,600
SALES (est): 735.5K **Privately Held**
WEB: www.skiboatcovers.com
SIC: 2394 Liners & covers, fabric: made from purchased materials

(G-5663)
CAROLYNS PUBLICATION
909 Carton St (48505-5512)
PHONE 810 787-4114
Carolyn White, *Principal*
EMP: 4 **EST:** 2005
SALES (est): 57.1K **Privately Held**
SIC: 2741 Miscellaneous publishing

(G-5664)
CARRIAGE TOWN PRESS
703 Mason St (48503-2421)
PHONE 810 410-5113
Phillip Barnhart, *Principal*
EMP: 6 **EST:** 2019
SALES (est): 37.5K **Privately Held**
WEB: www.carriagetown.org
SIC: 2741 Miscellaneous publishing

(G-5665)
CASE ISLAND GLASS LLC
1120 Beach St (48502-1407)
PHONE 810 252-1704
Suellen Parker, *Principal*
EMP: 6 **EST:** 2005
SALES (est): 120.4K **Privately Held**
WEB: www.caseislandglass.weebly.com
SIC: 3231 Products of purchased glass

(G-5666)
CHARTER COMMUNICATION
4370 Miller Rd (48507-1127)
PHONE 810 515-8418
EMP: 5 **EST:** 2014
SALES (est): 70.1K **Privately Held**
SIC: 3651 Household audio & video equipment

(G-5667)
CHRISTIAN UNITY PRESS INC
5195 Exchange Dr Ste A (48507-2976)
PHONE 810 732-1831
Kurt Heinze, *Director*
EMP: 5 **EST:** 1928
SALES (est): 366.3K **Privately Held**
WEB: www.thechurchofgod.cc
SIC: 2759 Commercial printing

(G-5668)
COKE BOTTLE
2515 Lapeer Rd (48503-4350)
PHONE 810 424-3352
Bryan Misenheimer, *Manager*
EMP: 6 **EST:** 2014
SALES (est): 135.5K **Privately Held**
WEB: www.coca-cola.com
SIC: 2086 Bottled & canned soft drinks

(G-5669)
COLORADO PAVERS & WALLS INC
3328 Torrey Rd (48507-3252)
PHONE 517 881-1704
Chris Matthew Stalo, *Principal*
EMP: 13 **EST:** 2016
SALES (est): 824.6K **Privately Held**
WEB: www.michiganpavers.com
SIC: 2951 Asphalt paving mixtures & blocks

(G-5670)
COMPLETE HEALTH SYSTEM
5084 Vlla Lnde Pkwy Ste 7 (48532)
PHONE 810 720-3891
Muhanad Jondy, *President*
EMP: 6 **EST:** 2004
SALES (est): 797.6K **Privately Held**
WEB: www.completehs.net
SIC: 3841 Diagnostic apparatus, medical

(G-5671)
CONCRETE STEP CO
G5491 Clio Rd (48504-1238)
PHONE 810 789-3061
Archie Gerstenberger, *President*
EMP: 5 **EST:** 1958
SALES (est): 489K **Privately Held**
SIC: 3272 Concrete products, precast

(G-5672)
CORSAIR ENGINEERING INC (PA)
3020 Airpark Dr S (48507-3477)
PHONE 810 233-0440
Howard W Campbell Jr, *President*
Todd Campbell, *Vice Pres*
EMP: 12 **EST:** 1982
SQ FT: 30,000
SALES (est): 9.3MM **Privately Held**
WEB: www.richfieldindustries.com
SIC: 7359 3496 Shipping container leasing; miscellaneous fabricated wire products

(G-5673)
CORSAIR ENGINEERING INC
2702 N Dort Hwy (48506-2958)
PHONE 810 234-3664
Richard Clark, *Manager*
EMP: 188
SALES (corp-wide): 9.3MM **Privately Held**
WEB: www.richfieldindustries.com
SIC: 3496 3441 Miscellaneous fabricated wire products; fabricated structural metal
PA: Corsair Engineering Incorporated
3020 Airpark Dr S
Flint MI 48507
810 233-0440

(G-5674)
COUNTRY HOME CREATIONS INC
5132 Richfield Rd (48506-2121)
P.O. Box 126, Goodrich (48438-0126)
PHONE 810 244-7348
Shirley Ann Kautman Jones, *President*
EMP: 27 **EST:** 1980
SQ FT: 6,000

Flint - Genesee County (G-5675) — GEOGRAPHIC SECTION

SALES (est): 1.7MM Privately Held
WEB: www.countryhomecreations.com
SIC: 2099 5499 5947 2022 Spices, including grinding; spices & herbs; gift shop; cheese, natural & processed

(G-5675)
COZART PRODUCERS
3130 Mcclure Ave (48506-2536)
PHONE.....................810 736-1046
A C Cozart, Owner
EMP: 4 EST: 1974
SALES (est): 77.8K Privately Held
SIC: 2079 Edible oil products, except corn oil

(G-5676)
CREATIVE FOAM CMPSITE SYSTEMS
6401 Taylor Dr (48507-0500)
PHONE.....................810 629-4149
David Swallow, President
Nark Shepler, Vice Pres
Terri Hamlet, Controller
EMP: 9 EST: 2008
SALES (est): 255.1K Privately Held
SIC: 3086 Plastics foam products

(G-5677)
CREATIVE PRINTING & GRAPHICS
430 S Dort Hwy (48503-2847)
PHONE.....................810 235-8815
Cindy Barnes, President
Daniel Barnes, Vice Pres
EMP: 5 EST: 1983
SQ FT: 2,000
SALES (est): 366.7K Privately Held
WEB: www.creativeprinting.org
SIC: 2752 Commercial printing, offset

(G-5678)
CURBCO INC
3145 S Dye Rd (48507-1003)
P.O. Box 70, Swartz Creek (48473-0070)
PHONE.....................810 232-2121
Keith Kirby, President
Carol Cruz, Sales Staff
Ashley Barajas, Manager
David Wurtz, Manager
Archie Canterbury, CIO
EMP: 60 EST: 1996
SALES (est): 7.3MM Privately Held
WEB: www.curbco2121.com
SIC: 7699 2952 8742 Fountain pen repair shop; asphalt felts & coatings; construction project management consultant

(G-5679)
CURTIS PRINTING INC
2171 Lodge Rd (48532-4949)
PHONE.....................810 230-6711
Elaine Sass, President
Marilyn Alvord, Corp Secy
EMP: 5 EST: 1930
SQ FT: 5,600 Privately Held
WEB: www.curtisfinepapers.com
SIC: 2752 Commercial printing, offset

(G-5680)
CUSTOM SIGNS BY HUNTLEY
1416 Ida St (48503-3586)
PHONE.....................810 399-8185
Cynthia Huntley, Principal
EMP: 4 EST: 2017
SALES (est): 49.6K Privately Held
SIC: 3993 Signs & advertising specialties

(G-5681)
D M J CORP
Also Called: One Stop Store 15
3910 Fenton Rd Ste 15 (48507-2469)
PHONE.....................810 239-9071
Diane Wehby, General Mgr
EMP: 7
SALES (corp-wide): 40.3MM Privately Held
SIC: 2869 5411 Fuels; convenience stores
PA: D M J Corp
710 N State Rd
Davison MI
810 658-2414

(G-5682)
DALLAS DESIGN INC
3432 S Saginaw St (48503-4146)
PHONE.....................810 238-4546
Dallas Tiensivu, President
EMP: 5 EST: 1975
SALES (est): 500K Privately Held
WEB: www.dallasdesigncabinets.com
SIC: 2541 5211 Cabinets, except refrigerated: show, display, etc.: wood; cabinets, kitchen

(G-5683)
DANA OFF-HGHWAY COMPONENTS LLC
3040 S Dye Rd (48507-1002)
PHONE.....................586 467-1600
Jim Kamsickas, CEO
EMP: 29 EST: 2019
SALES (est): 12.4MM Publicly Held
WEB: www.dana.com
SIC: 3714 Rear axle housings, motor vehicle
HQ: Dana Limited
3939 Technology Dr
Maumee OH 43537

(G-5684)
DAVISMADE INC
Also Called: Standing Dani
4400 S Saginaw St # 1470 (48507-2645)
PHONE.....................810 743-5262
EMP: 10
SALES (est): 810K Privately Held
SIC: 3842 Mfg Orthopedic Appliances

(G-5685)
DELTA PAVING INC
4186 Holiday Dr (48507-3513)
PHONE.....................810 232-0220
Charles K Owens, President
Coyanne Owens, Corp Secy
Terry L Owens, Vice Pres
EMP: 19 EST: 1991
SQ FT: 4,000
SALES (est): 2.6MM Privately Held
SIC: 2951 1771 Asphalt paving mixtures & blocks; driveway contractor; parking lot construction

(G-5686)
DELTA TUBE & FABRICATING CORP
2610 N Dort Hwy (48506-2960)
PHONE.....................810 239-0154
Terry Brown, Human Res Mgr
Howard W Campbell Jr, Branch Mgr
EMP: 147
SALES (corp-wide): 20.6MM Privately Held
SIC: 3441 Fabricated structural metal
PA: Delta Tube & Fabricating Corporation
4149 Grange Hall Rd
Holly MI 48442
248 634-8267

(G-5687)
DELTA TUBE & FABRICATION
3020 Airpark Dr S Bldg A (48507-3477)
PHONE.....................810 233-0440
EMP: 13 EST: 2017
SALES (est): 123.7K Privately Held
WEB: www.richind.com
SIC: 3441 Fabricated structural metal

(G-5688)
DIPLOMAT SPCLTY PHRM FLINT LLC
4100 S Saginaw St (48507-2683)
PHONE.....................810 768-9000
Phil Hagerman, CEO
Eric Hill, Vice Pres
Jeanne Ann Stasny, Vice Pres
Michelle Schultz, Finance Dir
Leslie Suciu, Human Resources
EMP: 387 EST: 2005
SALES (est): 63.7MM
SALES (corp-wide): 257.1B Publicly Held
WEB: www.diplomatpharmacy.com
SIC: 5912 5122 2834 Drug stores; pharmaceuticals; pharmaceutical preparations
HQ: Diplomat Pharmacy, Inc.
4100 S Saginaw St Ste A
Flint MI 48507
888 720-4450

(G-5689)
DONS QUALITY TOOLS LLC
2560 Tyrone St (48504-7705)
PHONE.....................248 701-5154
Don Heverly Jr, Principal
EMP: 4 EST: 2016
SALES (est): 121.7K Privately Held
SIC: 3541 Machine tools, metal cutting type

(G-5690)
EARL DAUP SIGNS
Also Called: EDS Enterprises
6060 Birch Rd (48507-4648)
PHONE.....................810 767-2020
Gerald Daup, President
Daniel Daup, Vice Pres
EMP: 11 EST: 1948
SQ FT: 18,000
SALES (est): 1.5MM Privately Held
WEB: www.earldaupsigns.com
SIC: 3993 Electric signs; neon signs

(G-5691)
ECM MANUFACTURING INC
4301 Western Rd (48506-1805)
PHONE.....................810 736-0299
Randy Wharram, President
EMP: 7 EST: 2007
SALES (est): 309K Privately Held
SIC: 3999 Manufacturing industries

(G-5692)
ECM SPECIALTIES INC
4301 Western Rd (48506-1805)
PHONE.....................810 736-0299
Randy Wharram, President
Gary Krueger, Principal
EMP: 7 EST: 1981
SALES (est): 663.5K Privately Held
SIC: 3451 Screw machine products

(G-5693)
ED CUMINGS INC
2305 Branch Rd (48506-2910)
P.O. Box 90118, Burton (48509-0118)
PHONE.....................810 736-0130
Jeffrey Powell, President
Brenda Defoy, Sales Staff
Richard Powell, Admin Sec
▲ EMP: 21 EST: 1933
SQ FT: 28,000
SALES (est): 1.7MM Privately Held
WEB: www.cumingsnets.com
SIC: 2399 3949 Fishing nets; fishing equipment

(G-5694)
EDM WIRE TEK
4155 Holiday Dr (48507-3512)
PHONE.....................810 235-5344
Paul Schaeffer, Owner
EMP: 6 EST: 1987
SALES (est): 116.6K Privately Held
WEB: www.edmwiretek.wordpress.com
SIC: 3599 Machine shop, jobbing & repair

(G-5695)
EMD WIRE TEK
4155 Holiday Dr (48507-3512)
PHONE.....................810 235-5344
Paul E Schaeffer, President
Sandra Schaeffer, Corp Secy
EMP: 8
SQ FT: 6,700
SALES (est): 829.4K Privately Held
WEB: www.edmwiretek.wordpress.com
SIC: 3599 3544 Electrical discharge machining (EDM); special dies, tools, jigs & fixtures

(G-5696)
ENGINEERED PRODUCTS COMPANY (PA)
Also Called: Byron Manufacturing
601 Kelso St (48506-4034)
P.O. Box 108 (48501-0108)
PHONE.....................810 767-2050
Treg Scott, President
Mike Scannell, Opers Staff
▲ EMP: 23 EST: 1940

SQ FT: 30,000
SALES (est): 2.1MM Privately Held
WEB: www.epcohardware.com
SIC: 3429 Builders' hardware; cabinet hardware; door opening & closing devices, except electrical

(G-5697)
ETNA DISTRIBUTORS LLC
2395 Lapeer Rd (48503-4220)
PHONE.....................810 232-4760
EMP: 10
SALES (corp-wide): 184.2MM Privately Held
WEB: www.etnasupply.com
SIC: 5074 3432 Plumbing fittings & supplies; plumbing fixture fittings & trim
PA: Etna Distributors, Llc
4901 Clay Ave Sw
Grand Rapids MI 49548
616 245-4373

(G-5698)
EXTREME PRECISION SCREW PDTS
1838 Remell St (48503-4499)
PHONE.....................810 744-1980
Mark Blevins, President
Vicki Blevins, Corp Secy
Amanda Cornell, Office Mgr
EMP: 24 EST: 1965
SQ FT: 9,500
SALES (est): 3.4MM Privately Held
WEB: www.epspinc.com
SIC: 3599 3728 3451 Machine shop, jobbing & repair; aircraft parts & equipment; screw machine products

(G-5699)
EZ FUEL INC
1330 E Atherton Rd (48507-2820)
PHONE.....................810 744-4452
Aldabyani Dahan, Manager
EMP: 7 EST: 2012
SALES (est): 448.1K Privately Held
SIC: 2869 Fuels

(G-5700)
FERRIS WHEEL INNOVATION CENTER
615 S Saginaw St (48502-1505)
PHONE.....................810 213-4720
Brandee Cooke, Opers Staff
Darrell Williams, Finance Mgr
Kayla Laird, CIO
EMP: 6 EST: 2018
SALES (est): 982.3K Privately Held
WEB: www.100kideas.org
SIC: 3599 Ferris wheels

(G-5701)
FLINT OPTICAL COMPANY INC
Also Called: Julie Opticians
518 S Saginaw St (48502-1804)
P.O. Box 819 (48501-0819)
PHONE.....................810 235-4607
Julia Peachovich, President
EMP: 6 EST: 1965
SQ FT: 4,800
SALES (est): 592.1K Privately Held
WEB: www.flintoptical.biz
SIC: 5995 3851 Opticians; ophthalmic goods

(G-5702)
FLINT STOOL & CHAIR CO INC
1517 N Dort Hwy (48506-3915)
PHONE.....................810 235-7001
Thomas Walter, President
Jeneffer Walter, Admin Sec
EMP: 4 EST: 1985
SQ FT: 3,800
SALES (est): 500K Privately Held
WEB: www.flintstoolandchair.com
SIC: 2531 Seats, miscellaneous public conveyances

(G-5703)
GARRISONS HITCH CENTER INC
1050 Meida St (48532-5046)
PHONE.....................810 239-5728
Jack R Johnson Jr, President
EMP: 4
SQ FT: 4,200

▲ = Import ▼ = Export
◆ = Import/Export

GEOGRAPHIC SECTION

Flint - Genesee County (G-5727)

SALES (est): 401.2K **Privately Held**
WEB: www.flinttrailerhitch.com
SIC: 3714 7353 Trailer hitches, motor vehicle; heavy construction equipment rental

(G-5704)
GENERAL MOTORS LLC
G-2238 W Bristol Rd (48553-0001)
PHONE..................................810 234-2710
Thomas V McLean, *Production*
Thomas Braun, *Engineer*
Don Mayton, *Branch Mgr*
EMP: 14 **Publicly Held**
WEB: www.gm.com
SIC: 5511 3465 3444 Automobiles, new & used; automotive stampings; sheet metalwork
HQ: General Motors Llc
300 Renaissance Ctr L1
Detroit MI 48243

(G-5705)
GENERAL MOTORS LLC
2238 W Bristol Rd (48507-3272)
PHONE..................................810 234-2710
Max Miller, *Manager*
EMP: 14 **Publicly Held**
WEB: www.gm.com
SIC: 5511 3465 Automobiles, new & used; automotive stampings
HQ: General Motors Llc
300 Renaissance Ctr L1
Detroit MI 48243

(G-5706)
GENERAL MOTORS LLC
425 S Stevenson St (48503-1259)
P.O. Box 1730 (48501-1730)
PHONE..................................810 236-1970
David Koepf, *Engineer*
Tony Suggs, *Branch Mgr*
EMP: 8 **Publicly Held**
WEB: www.gm.com
SIC: 3312 3544 3465 Tool & die steel; special dies, tools, jigs & fixtures; automotive stampings
HQ: General Motors Llc
300 Renaissance Ctr L1
Detroit MI 48243

(G-5707)
GENESEE GROUP INC
Also Called: Genesee Packaging
1102 N Averill Ave (48506-3905)
PHONE..................................810 235-6120
Jane Worthing, *CEO*
Veronica Artis, *COO*
EMP: 23
SALES (corp-wide): 20.6MM **Privately Held**
WEB: www.genpackaging.com
SIC: 2653 Corrugated & solid fiber boxes
PA: The Genesee Group Inc
2022 North St
Flint MI 48505
810 235-8041

(G-5708)
GREAT LAKES AERO PRODUCTS
915 Kearsley Park Blvd (48503-4807)
PHONE..................................810 235-1402
John A Zofko, *President*
John Zofko, *President*
Heather Z Bills, *Corp Secy*
Heather Zofko-Wiles, *Admin Sec*
EMP: 12 **EST:** 1973
SQ FT: 20,000
SALES (est): 500K **Privately Held**
WEB: www.aircraftwindshieldstore.com
SIC: 3229 5599 5088 Pressed & blown glass; aircraft instruments, equipment or parts; aircraft equipment & supplies

(G-5709)
GREAT PUT ON INC
3240 W Pasadena Ave (48504-2330)
PHONE..................................810 733-8021
Raji Salomon, *President*
Taylor Salomon, *Sales Staff*
EMP: 9 **EST:** 1979
SQ FT: 10,000

SALES (est): 1MM **Privately Held**
WEB: www.greatputon.com
SIC: 2261 7389 Screen printing of cotton broadwoven fabrics; textile & apparel services

(G-5710)
GROUND EFFECTS LLC (DH)
3435 Vanslyke Rd (48507)
PHONE..................................810 250-5560
Jim Scott, *President*
David Condon, *Plant Mgr*
Mark Kupko, *VP Finance*
EMP: 200 **EST:** 2012
SALES (est): 315.3MM **Privately Held**
WEB: www.gfxltd.com
SIC: 3714 Motor vehicle parts & accessories
HQ: Ground Effects Ltd
4505 Rhodes Dr
Windsor ON N8W 5
519 944-3800

(G-5711)
GROUND EFFECTS LLC
2501 Lippincott Blvd (48507-2019)
PHONE..................................810 250-5560
EMP: 275 **Privately Held**
WEB: www.gfxltd.com
SIC: 3714 Motor vehicle parts & accessories
HQ: Ground Effects Llc
3435 Vanslyke Rd
Flint MI 48507
810 250-5560

(G-5712)
HAAS GROUP INTERNATIONAL LLC
G3100 Van Slyke Rd (48551-0001)
PHONE..................................810 236-0032
Lisa Perkette, *Branch Mgr*
EMP: 5
SALES (corp-wide): 1.7B **Privately Held**
WEB: www.incora.com
SIC: 2899 Metal treating compounds; water treating compounds
HQ: Haas Group International, Llc
1475 Phnxvlle Pike Ste 20
West Chester PA 19380
484 564-4500

(G-5713)
HERALD NEWSPAPERS COMPANY INC
Also Called: Saginaw News
540 S Saginaw St 3 (48502-1855)
PHONE..................................989 752-7171
Renee Hampton, *Sales Staff*
Paul Chafee, *Branch Mgr*
EMP: 6
SALES (corp-wide): 2.8B **Privately Held**
WEB: www.advancemediany.com
SIC: 2711 7313 Newspapers, publishing & printing; newspaper advertising representative
HQ: The Herald Newspapers Company Inc
220 S Warren St
Syracuse NY 13202
315 470-0011

(G-5714)
HERALD NEWSPAPERS COMPANY INC
Also Called: Flint Journal, The
540 S Saginaw St Ste 101 (48502-1813)
PHONE..................................810 766-6100
Matthew Sharp, *Publisher*
EMP: 6
SQ FT: 65,000
SALES (corp-wide): 2.8B **Privately Held**
WEB: www.advancemediany.com
SIC: 2711 5192 Newspapers: publishing only, not printed on site; newspapers
HQ: The Herald Newspapers Company Inc
220 S Warren St
Syracuse NY 13202
315 470-0011

(G-5715)
HERALD NEWSPAPERS COMPANY INC
Also Called: Bay City Times
540 S Saginaw St Ste 101 (48502-1813)
PHONE..................................989 895-8551

C K Dykema, *Publisher*
Khalil Alhajal, *Editor*
Darren Bennett, *Accounts Exec*
Michelle Demink, *Accounts Exec*
Tracey Koperski, *Accounts Exec*
EMP: 6
SALES (corp-wide): 2.8B **Privately Held**
WEB: www.advancemediany.com
SIC: 2711 7313 2759 Newspapers: publishing only, not printed on site; newspaper advertising representative; commercial printing
HQ: The Herald Newspapers Company Inc
220 S Warren St
Syracuse NY 13202
315 470-0011

(G-5716)
IRWIN ENTERPRISES INC
Also Called: Instant Copy Center
3030 W Pasadena Ave (48504-2365)
PHONE..................................810 732-0770
Larry J Irwin, *CEO*
EMP: 26 **EST:** 1970
SQ FT: 2,000
SALES (est): 1.3MM **Privately Held**
WEB: www.fax-a-ticketaaa.v4.pressero.com
SIC: 2752 2759 Commercial printing, offset; commercial printing

(G-5717)
ISLAND SUN TIMES INC
5152 Commerce Rd (48507-2939)
PHONE..................................810 230-1735
Vince Lorraine, *President*
Sherron Barden, *Editor*
Kim Davis, *Controller*
EMP: 22 **EST:** 1999
SQ FT: 10,000
SALES (est): 1MM **Privately Held**
WEB: www.istmagazine.com
SIC: 2711 Newspapers, publishing & printing

(G-5718)
JAMES GLOVE & SUPPLY
3422 W Pasadena Ave (48504-2353)
PHONE..................................810 733-5780
Gail A McKone-Burns, *President*
Judith R McKone, *Treasurer*
EMP: 10 **EST:** 1972 **Privately Held**
WEB: www.tqauto.com
SIC: 3842 5099 Personal safety equipment; gloves, safety; safety equipment & supplies

(G-5719)
JUDAH SCENTS
1825 Rockcreek Ln (48502-2233)
PHONE..................................810 219-9956
Loretta Kenebrew-Cox, *Principal*
EMP: 4 **EST:** 2017
SALES (est): 88.9K **Privately Held**
SIC: 2844 Toilet preparations

(G-5720)
KEARSLEY LAKE TERRACE LLC
3400 Benmark Pl Ofc (48506-1946)
PHONE..................................810 736-7000
Stanley Benmark,
EMP: 6 **EST:** 1960
SALES (est): 434.1K **Privately Held**
WEB: www.israeli.rr.4wnp.pw
SIC: 6515 3714 1522 5271 Mobile home site operators; motor vehicle parts & accessories; apartment building construction; mobile homes

(G-5721)
KENDALL & COMPANY INC
Also Called: Kendall Printing
1624 Lambden Rd (48532-4552)
PHONE..................................810 733-7330
Scott K Brown, *President*
Todd Sneed, *Production*
EMP: 7 **EST:** 1989
SQ FT: 2,800
SALES (est): 1MM **Privately Held**
WEB: www.printingbykendall.com
SIC: 2752 5112 7336 Commercial printing, offset; business forms; graphic arts & related design

(G-5722)
KOEGEL MEATS INC (PA)
3400 W Bristol Rd (48507-3199)
PHONE..................................810 238-3685
John C Koegel, *President*
Kathryn Koegel, *Vice Pres*
Albert J Koegel, *Treasurer*
Kathlyn Koegel, *Human Res Dir*
Jeffry Rocco, *Admin Sec*
EMP: 109 **EST:** 1916
SQ FT: 96,000
SALES: 34MM **Privately Held**
WEB: www.koegelmeats.com
SIC: 2013 5712 Frankfurters from purchased meat; furniture stores

(G-5723)
LEAR CORPORATION
902 E Hamilton Ave (48550-0001)
PHONE..................................313 731-0833
Tim Reedy, *Branch Mgr*
EMP: 700
SALES (corp-wide): 17B **Publicly Held**
WEB: www.lear.com
SIC: 3714 Motor vehicle electrical equipment; instrument board assemblies, motor vehicle; automotive wiring harness sets; motor vehicle body components & frame
PA: Lear Corporation
21557 Telegraph Rd
Southfield MI 48033
248 447-1500

(G-5724)
LIBERTY FABRICATORS INC
2229 W Hill Rd (48507-4654)
PHONE..................................810 877-7117
David Shemansky, *President*
Jack Hedrick, *Vice Pres*
EMP: 16 **EST:** 2004
SQ FT: 45,000
SALES (est): 1.7MM **Privately Held**
WEB: www.libertyfab.com
SIC: 3559 3441 Automotive maintenance equipment; fabricated structural metal

(G-5725)
LOCKETT ENTERPRISES LLC
Also Called: Janitorial
607 E 2nd Ave Ste 30 (48502-2042)
P.O. Box 427 (48501-0427)
PHONE..................................810 407-6644
Corey Lockett, *CEO*
EMP: 5 **EST:** 2008
SQ FT: 1,210
SALES (est): 369.6K **Privately Held**
WEB: www.lockettenterprises.com
SIC: 7349 5137 5136 5722 Janitorial service, contract basis; underwear: women's, children's & infants'; underwear, men's & boys'; household appliance stores; convection ovens, including portable: household

(G-5726)
LOGISTICS INSIGHT CORP
3311 Torrey Rd (48507-3251)
PHONE..................................810 424-0511
Mike Townley, *Principal*
EMP: 66
SALES (corp-wide): 1.3B **Publicly Held**
WEB: www.universallogistics.com
SIC: 3537 Tractors, used in plants, docks, terminals, etc.: industrial
HQ: Logistics Insight Corp.
12755 E 9 Mile Rd
Warren MI 48089

(G-5727)
LOGOFIT LLC
3202 Lapeer Rd (48503-4424)
PHONE..................................810 715-1980
Lindsey Ayotte, *Sales Staff*
Jon Kraut,
Dave Kraut,
▲ **EMP:** 24 **EST:** 1992
SQ FT: 12,000
SALES (est): 2.9MM **Privately Held**
WEB: www.logofit.com
SIC: 2389 2396 Men's miscellaneous accessories; automotive & apparel trimmings

Flint - Genesee County (G-5728) — GEOGRAPHIC SECTION

(G-5728)
LORBEC METALS - USA LTD
3415 Western Rd (48504-2327)
PHONE.....................810 736-0961
Jay Goldstein, *President*
Lawrence Leibov, *Corp Secy*
Lawrence Lifshitz, *Vice Pres*
▼ **EMP:** 47 **EST:** 1991
SQ FT: 110,000
SALES (est): 17.8MM **Privately Held**
WEB: www.lorbecusa.com
SIC: 5093 3341 Ferrous metal scrap & waste; secondary nonferrous metals

(G-5729)
MACARTHUR CORP
3202 Lapeer Rd (48503-4424)
PHONE.....................810 744-1380
Jill Close, *Owner*
EMP: 7 **EST:** 2015
SALES (est): 284.9K **Privately Held**
WEB: www.macarthurcorp.com
SIC: 2672 Coated & laminated paper

(G-5730)
MACHINING SPECIALISTS INC MICH
2712 N Saginaw St Ofc (48505-4408)
PHONE.....................517 881-2863
Duane Dahl, *President*
EMP: 5
SQ FT: 3,150
SALES (est): 430K **Privately Held**
SIC: 3599 Machine shop, jobbing & repair

(G-5731)
MICHIGAN -BSED FRDMAN DSCNDNTS
2406 Thom St (48506-2862)
PHONE.....................810 820-3017
Steven Thomas, *Administration*
EMP: 6 **EST:** 2020
SALES (est): 46.5K **Privately Held**
SIC: 2273 Finishers of tufted carpets & rugs

(G-5732)
MICHIGAN STEEL FABRICATORS INC
5225 Energy Dr (48505-1836)
PHONE.....................810 785-1478
Richard Webster, *President*
Chris Webster, *Vice Pres*
EMP: 20 **EST:** 1991
SQ FT: 15,000
SALES (est): 4.9MM **Privately Held**
WEB: www.michigansteel.com
SIC: 3441 Fabricated structural metal

(G-5733)
MID-STATE PLATING CO INC
602 Kelso St (48506-4057)
PHONE.....................810 767-1622
Charles J Stokes, *CEO*
David Stokes, *President*
Caitlin Stokes, *Office Mgr*
Tim Stokes, *Technician*
EMP: 30 **EST:** 1967
SQ FT: 30,000
SALES (est): 4.2MM **Privately Held**
WEB: www.midstateplating.com
SIC: 3471 Electroplating of metals or formed products

(G-5734)
MIDWEST FLEX SYSTEMS INC
415 Sb Chavez Dr (48503-1910)
PHONE.....................810 424-0060
Daniel Sternbergh, *President*
EMP: 10 **EST:** 1994
SQ FT: 4,000
SALES (est): 1.7MM **Privately Held**
WEB: www.midwestflex.com
SIC: 3829 Measuring & controlling devices

(G-5735)
MODERN INDUSTRIES INC
Also Called: Modern Concrete Products
3275 W Pasadena Ave (48504-2386)
PHONE.....................810 767-3330
Ronald D Lammy II, *President*
Joseph Genova, *Program Mgr*
EMP: 8 **EST:** 1963
SALES (est): 1.9MM **Privately Held**
WEB: www.modernconcreteproducts.com
SIC: 7353 3273 1442 Heavy construction equipment rental; ready-mixed concrete; construction sand & gravel

(G-5736)
MONROE TRUCK EQUIPMENT INC (PA)
Also Called: M T E
2400 Reo Dr (48507-6359)
PHONE.....................810 238-4603
Tom Ninneman, *CEO*
David Quade, *President*
Andrea Brown, *General Mgr*
Scott Hanewall, *General Mgr*
Tom Johnson, *CFO*
EMP: 28 **EST:** 1970
SQ FT: 1,000
SALES (est): 12MM **Privately Held**
WEB: www.monroetruck.com
SIC: 3713 5013 Truck & bus bodies; truck parts & accessories

(G-5737)
MOORE BROTHERS ELECTRICAL CO
2602 Leith St (48506-2826)
P.O. Box 90062, Burton (48509-0062)
PHONE.....................810 232-2148
Rhex Moore, *President*
EMP: 5 **EST:** 1946
SQ FT: 7,000
SALES (est): 983.4K **Privately Held**
WEB: www.moorebrotherselectric.com
SIC: 5074 7694 Heating equipment (hydronic); electric motor repair

(G-5738)
NICKELS BOAT WORKS INC
1871 Tower St (48503-4435)
PHONE.....................810 767-4050
Hugh Armbruster, *President*
EMP: 10 **EST:** 1999
SQ FT: 15,000 **Privately Held**
WEB: www.windrider.com
SIC: 2221 2519 Dress fabrics, manmade fiber & silk; fiberglass furniture, household; padded or plain

(G-5739)
OAKLEY INDS SUB ASSMBLY DIV IN (PA)
4333 Matthew (48507-3160)
PHONE.....................810 720-4444
Ronald Oakley, *President*
Arthur Meisels, *Principal*
Michael Oakley, *Corp Secy*
Moshe Kraus, *COO*
Robert O Trygstad, *Vice Pres*
EMP: 44 **EST:** 1984
SQ FT: 80,000
SALES (est): 89MM **Privately Held**
WEB: www.oakleysubassembly.com
SIC: 3714 Motor vehicle wheels & parts; motor vehicle body components & frame

(G-5740)
OAKLEY SUB ASSEMBLY INC
Also Called: Oakley Inds Sub Assmbly Div In
4333 Matthew (48507-3160)
PHONE.....................810 720-4444
Ronald Oakley, *President*
Patrick Gerow, *Engineer*
EMP: 54 **EST:** 2003
SALES (est): 10.6MM
SALES (corp-wide): 89MM **Privately Held**
WEB: www.oakleysubassembly.com
SIC: 3714 Motor vehicle wheels & parts
PA: Oakley Industries Sub Assembly Division, Inc.
4333 Matthew
Flint MI 48507
810 720-4444

(G-5741)
OAKLEY SUB ASSEMBLY INTL INC
4333 Matthew (48507-3160)
PHONE.....................810 720-4444
Ronald Oakley, *President*
EMP: 13 **EST:** 2015
SALES (est): 346.4K
SALES (corp-wide): 89MM **Privately Held**
WEB: www.oakleysubassembly.com
SIC: 3714 Motor vehicle parts & accessories
PA: Oakley Industries Sub Assembly Division, Inc.
4333 Matthew
Flint MI 48507
810 720-4444

(G-5742)
OIL CHEM INC
711 W 12th St (48503-3851)
PHONE.....................810 235-3040
Robert Massey, *President*
Beverly Bryers, *Purch Agent*
Barney Ellingson, *Research*
Bob Massey, *Engineer*
Brandon Massey, *Manager*
EMP: 20
SQ FT: 61,272
SALES (est): 24.7MM **Privately Held**
WEB: www.oilcheminc.com
SIC: 5172 2841 2992 Lubricating oils & greases; detergents, synthetic organic or inorganic alkaline; lubricating oils & greases

(G-5743)
PANTER MASTER CONTROLS INC
3060 S Dye Rd Ste A (48507-1078)
PHONE.....................810 687-5600
Ronald Panter, *President*
Gloria Burns, *Supervisor*
Allen Panter, *Director*
EMP: 12 **EST:** 1985
SALES (est): 1.7MM **Privately Held**
WEB: www.pantermastercontrols.com
SIC: 3599 7371 Custom machinery; computer software development

(G-5744)
PEPSI-COLA METRO BTLG CO INC
6200g Taylor Dr (48507-4681)
PHONE.....................810 232-3925
John Ankey, *Manager*
Mark Levy, *Manager*
EMP: 6
SALES (corp-wide): 70.3B **Publicly Held**
WEB: www.pepsico.com
SIC: 2086 5149 Soft drinks: packaged in cans, bottles, etc.; soft drinks
HQ: Pepsi-Cola Metropolitan Bottling Company, Inc.
1111 Westchester Ave
White Plains NY 10604
914 767-6000

(G-5745)
POSTAL SAVINGS DIRECT MKTG
Also Called: Postal Savers
1035 Ann Arbor St (48503-3603)
PHONE.....................810 238-8866
Charles J Koory, *President*
EMP: 10 **EST:** 1981
SQ FT: 3,000
SALES (est): 791.8K **Privately Held**
WEB: www.theprintshopofflint.com
SIC: 7331 2752 Mailing list compilers; commercial printing, offset

(G-5746)
PPG INDUSTRIES INC
Also Called: PPG Automotive
3601 James P Cole Blvd (48505-3954)
PHONE.....................810 767-8030
John P Holewinski, *Branch Mgr*
EMP: 6
SALES (corp-wide): 15.1B **Publicly Held**
WEB: www.ppg.com
SIC: 2851 Paints & allied products
PA: Ppg Industries, Inc.
1 Ppg Pl
Pittsburgh PA 15272
412 434-3131

(G-5747)
PRECISION INDUSTRIES INC
3002 E Court St (48506-4093)
PHONE.....................810 239-5816
Jeffrey Swanson, *CEO*
Terri Daly, *CFO*
EMP: 15 **EST:** 1945
SQ FT: 10,500
SALES (est): 2.6MM **Privately Held**
WEB: www.precisionindinc.com
SIC: 3089 Injection molding of plastics

(G-5748)
PREMIERE PACKAGING INC (PA)
Also Called: Ppi
6220 Lehman Dr (48507-4678)
PHONE.....................810 239-7650
Mark Drolet, *President*
Alex Garrett, *Sales Staff*
Rob Lynch, *IT/INT Sup*
Kathy Elsworth, *Admin Sec*
▲ **EMP:** 74 **EST:** 1987
SQ FT: 100,000
SALES (est): 56.4MM **Privately Held**
WEB: www.premierepkg.com
SIC: 2842 Polishing preparations & related products

(G-5749)
PRINTCOMM INC (PA)
Also Called: Marketing Impact
3040 S Dye Rd (48507-1002)
PHONE.....................810 239-5763
Kevin E Naughton, *President*
Gerald F Minarik, *President*
Eric Bauer, *Plant Mgr*
Julie Stehle, *Human Resources*
Jeff Spears, *Accounts Mgr*
EMP: 51 **EST:** 1958
SALES (est): 25.1MM **Privately Held**
WEB: www.printcomm.com
SIC: 5112 2752 2791 2789 Business forms; commercial printing, offset; typesetting; bookbinding & related work; commercial printing

(G-5750)
PSA COURIER C
109 Welch Blvd (48503-1159)
PHONE.....................810 234-8770
EMP: 5 **EST:** 2019
SALES (est): 138.1K **Privately Held**
WEB: www.cpsaflint.com
SIC: 2711 Newspapers, publishing & printing

(G-5751)
QFD RECYCLING
4450 Linden Creek Pkwy (48507-2943)
PHONE.....................810 733-2335
Nancy Trump, *Accounts Mgr*
Douglas C Carlton,
Dr Anup Sud,
EMP: 30 **EST:** 1995
SQ FT: 10,000
SALES (est): 1.6MM **Privately Held**
WEB: www.qfdrecycling.com
SIC: 3089 Plastic hardware & building products; downspouts, plastic

(G-5752)
QUALITY FIRST FIRE ALARM
4286 Pheasant Dr (48506-1742)
P.O. Box 618, Davison (48423-0618)
PHONE.....................810 736-4911
Greg Lauderbaugh, *Principal*
EMP: 7 **EST:** 2008
SALES (est): 140.2K **Privately Held**
SIC: 3711 Fire department vehicles (motor vehicles), assembly of

(G-5753)
QUANTUM DIFFEREENCE CORP
5321 Gateway Ctr (48507-3980)
PHONE.....................810 845-8765
David Ewing, *Principal*
EMP: 6 **EST:** 2013
SALES (est): 144.5K **Privately Held**
WEB: www.thequantumdifference.com
SIC: 3572 Computer storage devices

(G-5754)
RELIANCE ELECTRIC MACHINE CO
2601 Leith St (48506-2825)
PHONE.....................810 232-3355
Michael Gavroski, *President*
Olga Gavroski, *Vice Pres*
EMP: 12 **EST:** 1996

GEOGRAPHIC SECTION

Flint - Genesee County (G-5785)

SQ FT: 12,000
SALES (est): 1MM Privately Held
WEB: www.relianceelectricmachine.com
SIC: 7694 5063 Electric motor repair; motors, electric

(G-5755)
RODZINA INDUSTRIES INC
Also Called: Ameriplastic Imprinting Co
3518 Fenton Rd (48507-1567)
PHONE............................810 235-2341
Robert E Cross Jr, *President*
Ronald K Cross, *Vice Pres*
EMP: 4 **EST:** 1983
SQ FT: 2,000
SALES (est): 500K Privately Held
WEB: www.rodzinaindustries.net
SIC: 3953 3999 2759 3993 Embossing seals & hand stamps; identification badges & insignia; engraving; signs & advertising specialties; gaskets, packing & sealing devices

(G-5756)
ROGERS FOAM AUTOMOTIVE CORP (HQ)
501 W Kearsley St (48503-2647)
PHONE............................810 820-6323
David P Marotta, *President*
David Backer, *Business Mgr*
Tim Nyman, *QC Mgr*
Adam Partaledis, *Sales Staff*
Paul Leaf, *Manager*
▲ **EMP:** 50 **EST:** 2009
SALES (est): 35.3MM
SALES (corp-wide): 89.7MM Privately Held
WEB: www.rogersfoam.com
SIC: 3086 Plastics foam products
PA: Rogers Foam Corporation
 20 Vernon St Ste 1
 Somerville MA 02145
 617 623-3010

(G-5757)
ROHMANN IRON WORKS INC
201 Kelso St (48506-4087)
PHONE............................810 233-5611
Jack Quinn, *President*
Jeff Quinn, *Vice Pres*
EMP: 31 **EST:** 1953
SQ FT: 16,000
SALES (est): 6.7MM Privately Held
WEB: www.rohmanniron.com
SIC: 3441 Building components, structural steel

(G-5758)
ROYAL PUBLISHING
5608 Maplebrook Ln (48507-4134)
PHONE............................810 768-3057
Alexander Royal, *Principal*
EMP: 4 **EST:** 2015
SALES (est): 73.7K Privately Held
SIC: 2741 Miscellaneous publishing

(G-5759)
SALES MFG
1113 University Ave (48504-6203)
PHONE............................810 597-7707
EMP: 4 **EST:** 2019
SALES (est): 83.9K Privately Held
SIC: 2752 Commercial printing, lithographic

(G-5760)
SCHNEIDER ELECTRIC USA INC
4110 Pier North Blvd D (48504-1486)
PHONE............................810 733-9400
EMP: 4
SALES (corp-wide): 177.9K Privately Held
WEB: www.se.com
SIC: 3613 Switchgear & switchboard apparatus
HQ: Schneider Electric Usa, Inc.
 201 Wshngton St Ext Ste 2
 Boston MA 02108
 978 975-9600

(G-5761)
SEMTRON INC
6465 Corunna Rd (48532-5350)
PHONE............................810 732-9080
Paul Semerad, *President*
Steve Lafon, *General Mgr*
Matt Post, *General Mgr*
G Ruth Semerad, *Vice Pres*
Katie Lafon, *Sales Staff*
▲ **EMP:** 12 **EST:** 1980
SQ FT: 6,700
SALES (est): 1.8MM Privately Held
WEB: www.semtron.com
SIC: 3661 3643 Telephones & telephone apparatus; electric switches; connectors & terminals for electrical devices

(G-5762)
SIGN SCREEN INC
408 S Center Rd (48506-4128)
PHONE............................810 239-1100
Gilbert L McCord, *President*
Gilbert McCord Jr, *Executive*
EMP: 7 **EST:** 1994
SQ FT: 5,300
SALES (est): 943.1K Privately Held
WEB: www.signscreen.com
SIC: 2759 7336 7389 3993 Screen printing; silk screen design; embroidering of advertising on shirts, etc.; signs & advertising specialties; automotive & apparel trimmings

(G-5763)
SIGNS AND MORE
3295 S Linden Rd (48507-3005)
PHONE............................810 820-9955
EMP: 4 **EST:** 2019
SALES (est): 46K Privately Held
SIC: 3993 Signs & advertising specialties

(G-5764)
SIGNS BY CRANNIE INC (PA)
4145 Market Pl (48507-3204)
PHONE............................810 487-0000
Daniel C Crannie Jr, *President*
EMP: 25 **EST:** 1991
SQ FT: 17,000
SALES (est): 5.8MM Privately Held
WEB: www.signsbycrannie.com
SIC: 3993 Electric signs

(G-5765)
SPEN-TECH MACHINE ENGRG CORP
2851 James P Cole Blvd (48505-4500)
PHONE............................810 275-6800
Troy S Spence, *CEO*
Craig Spence, *Purchasing*
Wanda Angus, *Sales Staff*
Dale Doran, *Med Doctor*
Glenn Grossbauer, *Executive*
EMP: 90
SQ FT: 165,000
SALES (est): 27.2MM Privately Held
WEB: www.spentechusa.com
SIC: 3549 8711 3599 Assembly machines, including robotic; consulting engineer; machine shop, jobbing & repair

(G-5766)
SPINFORM INC
1848 Tower St (48503-4436)
PHONE............................810 767-4660
Michael A Howells, *President*
EMP: 9 **EST:** 1995
SQ FT: 7,500
SALES (est): 1.5MM Privately Held
WEB: www.spinform.com
SIC: 3444 3469 Sheet metalwork; metal stampings

(G-5767)
SPOILER WING KING
5042 Exchange Dr (48507-2906)
PHONE............................810 733-9464
Christina Burns, *Owner*
EMP: 9 **EST:** 2009
SALES (est): 416.5K Privately Held
WEB: www.spoilerandwingking.com
SIC: 3465 Body parts, automobile: stamped metal

(G-5768)
STAINED GLASS AND GIFTS
4290 N Genesee Rd (48506-1504)
PHONE............................810 736-6766
Susan Godfrey, *Owner*
EMP: 4 **EST:** 1975
SALES (est): 60K Privately Held
SIC: 3231 Products of purchased glass

(G-5769)
STANSLEY INDUSTRIES INC
4171 Holiday Dr (48507-3512)
PHONE............................810 515-1919
EMP: 5 **EST:** 2015
SALES (est): 64.6K Privately Held
SIC: 3999 Manufacturing industries

(G-5770)
STNJ LLC (PA)
Also Called: Sign-A-Rama
4297 Miller Rd (48507-1227)
PHONE............................810 230-6445
Beth Powers, *Mng Member*
EMP: 14 **EST:** 2018
SALES (est): 1MM Privately Held
WEB: www.signarama.com
SIC: 3993 Signs & advertising specialties

(G-5771)
STOKES STEEL TREATING COMPANY
624 Kelso St (48506-4095)
PHONE............................810 235-3573
Robb Stokes, *President*
Ted Stokes, *Vice Pres*
Todd Stokes, *Vice Pres*
Wayne Stokes, *Shareholder*
EMP: 38 **EST:** 1950
SQ FT: 8,000
SALES (est): 1.9MM Privately Held
WEB: www.stokessteel.com
SIC: 3398 Metal heat treating

(G-5772)
SUBTERRANEAN PRESS
913 Beard St (48503-5370)
P.O. Box 190106, Burton (48519-0106)
PHONE............................810 232-1489
Timothy K Holt, *Principal*
EMP: 9 **EST:** 2000
SALES (est): 657.1K Privately Held
WEB: www.subterraneanpress.com
SIC: 2741 Miscellaneous publishing

(G-5773)
SUPPLY PRO
5402 Hill 23 Dr (48507-3967)
PHONE............................810 239-8658
EMP: 8 **EST:** 2015
SALES (est): 123.4K Privately Held
WEB: www.supplypro.com
SIC: 3589 Service industry machinery

(G-5774)
SXS GEAR
6075 Birch Rd (48507-4647)
PHONE............................810 265-7219
Chris Keeter, *Administration*
EMP: 7 **EST:** 2015
SALES (est): 294.2K Privately Held
SIC: 3714 Motor vehicle parts & accessories

(G-5775)
T AND RC ANVAS AWNING LLC
2153 Lodge Rd (48532-4908)
PHONE............................810 230-1740
EMP: 6 **EST:** 2018
SALES (est): 318.8K Privately Held
SIC: 2211 Canvas

(G-5776)
T SHIRT SHOP
G5082 N Saginaw St (48505-1674)
PHONE............................810 285-8857
EMP: 4 **EST:** 2016
SALES (est): 107.7K Privately Held
SIC: 2759 Screen printing

(G-5777)
TECHNICHEM
4289 E Coldwater Rd (48506-1051)
P.O. Box 186, Genesee (48437-0186)
PHONE............................810 744-3770
EMP: 4 **EST:** 2016
SALES (est): 498.1K Privately Held
SIC: 5169 2899 Chemicals & allied products; chemical preparations

(G-5778)
TGI DIRECT INC (PA)
5365 Hill 23 Dr (48507-3906)
P.O. Box 354 (48501-0354)
PHONE............................810 239-5553
Monica Weaver, *President*
Renee Kowal, *Business Mgr*
Alex Torre, *Business Mgr*
Linda Bacon, *Corp Secy*
Deb Holbeck, *Vice Pres*
▲ **EMP:** 40 **EST:** 1964
SQ FT: 35,000
SALES (est): 13.3MM Privately Held
WEB: www.tgidirect.com
SIC: 2759 7389 7374 7331 Business forms: printing; packaging & labeling services; data processing service; mailing service

(G-5779)
TOP QUALITY CLEANING LLC
Also Called: Top Quality Records
2718 Mallery St (48504-7367)
PHONE............................810 493-4211
Zanando Jacobs, *Principal*
Lydell Brown Jr, *Principal*
Katrina Clark, *Principal*
Orlando Jacobs Sr, *Principal*
Theophilus Jacobs, *Principal*
EMP: 12 **EST:** 2006
SALES (est): 105.9K Privately Held
SIC: 7699 2782 0783 2851 Cleaning services; record albums; removal services, bush & tree; removers & cleaners; records, audio discs & tapes; records

(G-5780)
TRANE US INC
5335 Hill 23 Dr (48507-3906)
PHONE............................800 245-3964
EMP: 50 Privately Held
SIC: 3585 Mfg Refrigeration/Heating Equipment
HQ: Trane U.S. Inc.
 3600 Pammel Creek Rd
 La Crosse WI 54601
 608 787-2000

(G-5781)
TRANSPORTATION TECH GROUP INC (PA)
Also Called: Richfield Industries
3020 Airpark Dr S (48507-3477)
PHONE............................810 233-0440
Howard W Campbell, *President*
John Cuddeback, *General Mgr*
Dennis Murphy, *General Mgr*
Betty L Campell, *Corp Secy*
Eric Wiltse, *Project Mgr*
EMP: 15 **EST:** 1996
SQ FT: 12,000
SALES (est): 10.8MM Privately Held
SIC: 3315 3317 Baskets, steel wire; steel pipe & tubes

(G-5782)
TRAVIS FULMORE LLC
413 Garland St (48503-2573)
PHONE............................810 701-6981
Travis Fulmore,
EMP: 12 **EST:** 2020
SALES (est): 400K Privately Held
SIC: 3161 Clothing & apparel carrying cases

(G-5783)
TREASURE ENTERPRISE LLC
1161 N Ballenger Hwy # 7 (48504-7543)
PHONE............................810 233-7128
Larry Holley, *President*
EMP: 11 **EST:** 1994
SALES (est): 464.2K Privately Held
WEB: www.treasurereceiver.com
SIC: 2711 Newspapers

(G-5784)
TROUT ENTERPRISES LLC
1840 Groveland Ave (48505-3079)
PHONE............................810 309-4289
Antonio Troutman, *Mng Member*
EMP: 5 **EST:** 2020
SALES (est): 258.1K Privately Held
WEB: www.trout-enterprises.com
SIC: 1422 Agricultural limestone, ground

(G-5785)
TRU CUSTOM BLENDS INC
2321 Branch Rd (48506-2910)
PHONE............................810 407-6207
Roland Urch, *CEO*
Timothy Urch, *COO*

Flint - Genesee County (G-5786)

EMP: 15 EST: 2008
SALES (est): 1MM Privately Held
SIC: 2851 Paints & allied products

(G-5786)
TRUTH TRAXX LLC
3123 Stevenson St (48504-3246)
PHONE..................800 792-2239
Tiandra Ellis, *CEO*
EMP: 11 EST: 2018
SALES (est): 369.3K Privately Held
SIC: 3999 Hair & hair-based products

(G-5787)
U S SPEEDO INC
Also Called: Motor City Products
6050 Birch Rd (48507-4648)
PHONE..................810 244-0909
Terri Brink, *President*
Harry Brink, *Vice Pres*
John Lance, *Sales Dir*
Jeremy White, *Graphic Designe*
▲ EMP: 28 EST: 2000
SQ FT: 15,000
SALES (est): 2.8MM Privately Held
WEB: www.usspeedo.com
SIC: 3824 Speedometers

(G-5788)
UNIVERSAL COATING INC
5204 Energy Dr (48505-1837)
PHONE..................810 785-7555
Henry Johnson, *President*
Tim Johnson, *Treasurer*
Mary Ann Zaruba, *Manager*
EMP: 55 EST: 1984
SQ FT: 20,000
SALES (est): 10MM Privately Held
WEB: www.universalcoating.com
SIC: 3479 Coating of metals & formed products

(G-5789)
UPF INC
Also Called: UPF Group PLC
2851 James P Cole Blvd (48505-4500)
PHONE..................810 768-0001
David Wolgast, *CEO*
EMP: 26 EST: 1998
SQ FT: 100,000
SALES (est): 1.2MM Privately Held
SIC: 3711 Chassis, motor vehicle

(G-5790)
VEHICLE CY WLDG FBRICATION LLC
2085 Diamond Ave (48532-4535)
PHONE..................810 836-2385
Timothy Pelky, *Administration*
EMP: 4 EST: 2019
SALES (est): 27.6K Privately Held
WEB: www.vehiclecitywelding.wixsite.com
SIC: 7692 Welding repair

(G-5791)
VENTUOR LLC
336 W 1st St Ste 113 (48502-1382)
PHONE..................248 790-8700
Hesham Dean, *CEO*
EMP: 4 EST: 2013
SALES (est): 92.4K Privately Held
SIC: 7371 7372 7389 Computer software development & applications; application computer software;

(G-5792)
WGS GLOBAL SERVICES LC (PA)
6350 Taylor Dr (48507-4680)
PHONE..................810 239-4947
Adam Satkowiak, *Purchasing*
Ron Williams, *CFO*
Casey Goetz, *Manager*
Mary Haney, *Manager*
Ghaffan M Saab,
▲ EMP: 349 EST: 2008
SALES (est): 49.5MM Privately Held
WEB: www.wgsglobalservices.com
SIC: 3711 Automobile assembly, including specialty automobiles

(G-5793)
WINSOL ELECTRONICS LLC
2000 N Saginaw St (48505-4770)
PHONE..................810 767-2987
EMP: 5
SALES: 63.5K Privately Held
SIC: 3999 Mfg Misc Products

(G-5794)
WOODWORTH INC
4201 Pier North Blvd (48504-1360)
PHONE..................810 820-6780
Matt Woodworth, *General Mgr*
EMP: 34 Privately Held
WEB: www.woodworthheattreating.com
SIC: 3398 Metal heat treating
PA: Woodworth, Inc.
500 Centerpoint Pkwy N
Pontiac MI 48341

(G-5795)
WOOLEY INDUSTRIES INC
3034 S Ballenger Hwy (48507-1380)
PHONE..................810 341-8823
Dennis Allen, *Principal*
EMP: 8 EST: 2008
SALES (est): 936.3K Privately Held
SIC: 3498 Tube fabricating (contract bending & shaping)

(G-5796)
WPW INC
Also Called: Steel Fab
5225 Energy Dr (48505-1836)
PHONE..................810 785-1478
Chris Webster, *President*
Richard Webster, *President*
Brad Payne, *Vice Pres*
EMP: 14 EST: 1996
SQ FT: 15,000
SALES (est): 384.7K Privately Held
SIC: 3441 Fabricated structural metal

(G-5797)
WRIGHT TIME FOODS LLC
1414 S Graham Rd (48532-3539)
PHONE..................810 835-9219
Travis Wright,
EMP: 4 EST: 2020
SALES (est): 80K Privately Held
SIC: 2599 Food wagons, restaurant

(G-5798)
X-TREME PRINTING INC
2638 Corunna Rd (48503-3316)
PHONE..................810 232-3232
Jean Benton, *President*
Gail Benedettini, *Vice Pres*
EMP: 5 EST: 1969
SQ FT: 2,300
SALES (est): 336.4K Privately Held
SIC: 2752 Commercial printing, offset

(G-5799)
ZYGOT OPERATIONS LIMITED
4301 Western Rd (48506-1805)
PHONE..................810 736-2900
Ronald D Wharram, *President*
EMP: 48 EST: 1991
SQ FT: 25,000
SALES (est): 3.6MM Privately Held
SIC: 3451 3644 3469 Screw machine products; noncurrent-carrying wiring services; metal stampings

Flushing
Genesee County

(G-5800)
ADS PLUS PRINTING LLC
767 E Main St (48433-2009)
PHONE..................810 659-7190
John Sanders,
EMP: 5 EST: 1989
SQ FT: 3,000
SALES (est): 515.8K Privately Held
WEB: www.adsplusprinting.com
SIC: 2759 7331 Screen printing; direct mail advertising services

(G-5801)
ALMAR ORCHARDS LLC
1431 Duffield Rd (48433-9764)
PHONE..................810 659-6568
James Koan,
Zachary Koan,
Monique Lapinski,
EMP: 12 EST: 1944
SALES (est): 1.1MM Privately Held
WEB: www.almarorchards.com
SIC: 0175 2051 2033 Apple orchard; bread, cake & related products; canned fruits & specialties

(G-5802)
ARTISTIC FLAIR EMB & PRTG
11070 Potter Rd (48433-9737)
PHONE..................810 487-9074
EMP: 4 EST: 2014
SALES (est): 111.6K Privately Held
SIC: 2752 Commercial printing, lithographic

(G-5803)
BEAMER LASER MARKING
7136 Sheridan Rd (48433-9610)
PHONE..................810 471-3044
Allen Warren, *Manager*
EMP: 89 EST: 2005
SALES (est): 2MM Privately Held
SIC: 2759 7389 Laser printing; business services

(G-5804)
CENTRAL CONCRETE PRODUCTS INC
4067 Commerce Dr (48433-2311)
PHONE..................810 659-7488
Rene Adkins, *President*
Larry C Adkins, *Treasurer*
EMP: 32 EST: 1993
SQ FT: 10,000
SALES (est): 2.4MM Privately Held
WEB: www.central-concrete.net
SIC: 3273 Ready-mixed concrete

(G-5805)
COFFEE BEANERY LTD (HQ)
3429 Pierson Pl (48433-2498)
PHONE..................810 733-1020
Joanne Shaw, *President*
Kevin Shaw, *President*
Julius Shaw, *Chairman*
Kurt Shaw, *Vice Pres*
David Thorin, *Marketing Staff*
▲ EMP: 40 EST: 1976
SQ FT: 45,000
SALES (est): 11.8MM Privately Held
WEB: www.coffeebeanery.com
SIC: 5812 5149 6794 2099 Coffee shop; coffee, green or roasted; franchises, selling or licensing; food preparations; roasted coffee; flavoring extracts & syrups

(G-5806)
COLOR FACTORY
8034 N Mckinley Rd (48433-8801)
PHONE..................810 577-2974
Diane Fondren, *Principal*
EMP: 7 EST: 2012
SALES (est): 263.2K Privately Held
SIC: 3479 Painting, coating & hot dipping

(G-5807)
DARLA NAGEL
7080 Stanley Rd (48433-9069)
PHONE..................810 624-9043
Darla Nagel, *Principal*
EMP: 4 EST: 2018
SALES (est): 147.6K Privately Held
WEB: www.darlanagel.com
SIC: 3841 Surgical & medical instruments

(G-5808)
FLATLANDER SIGNS
10427 Potter Rd (48433-9783)
PHONE..................810 867-2207
EMP: 4 EST: 2016
SALES (est): 62.5K Privately Held
WEB: www.flatlandersigns.com
SIC: 3993 Electric signs

(G-5809)
FUEL TOBACCO STOP
Also Called: Marathon Oil
226 E Main St (48433-2026)
PHONE..................810 487-2040
Shukri Abdulla, *Owner*
EMP: 5 EST: 2011
SALES (est): 147.9K Privately Held
WEB: www.marathonoil.com
SIC: 2869 Fuels

(G-5810)
KING PAR LLC
Also Called: K P
5140 Flushing Rd (48433-2667)
P.O. Box 757, Ortonville, (48462-0757)
PHONE..................810 732-2470
Ryan Coffell, *CFO*
Amanda Jones, *Mktg Dir*
John Runyon,
Richard Williams, *Admin Sec*
▲ EMP: 54 EST: 2009
SALES (est): 9.4MM Privately Held
WEB: www.kingparsuperstore.com
SIC: 5091 3949 Golf & skiing equipment & supplies; golf equipment

(G-5811)
MB LIQUIDATING CORPORATION
Also Called: Ultra-Dex Tooling Systems
7162 Sheridan Rd (48433-9610)
PHONE..................810 638-5388
Pat Mulzahy, *President*
Gregg Bishop, *Opers Staff*
Jennifer Krupp, *Purch Mgr*
Meg Koos, *Human Res Mgr*
Duane Cornella, *Manager*
EMP: 100 EST: 1988
SQ FT: 12,000
SALES (est): 23.7MM Privately Held
WEB: www.archcuttingtools.com
SIC: 3545 3541 Machine tool accessories; machine tools, metal cutting type

(G-5812)
MOTOR CITY SIGNS LLC
10427 Potter Rd (48433-9783)
PHONE..................810 867-2207
Kevin McQuigg, *Principal*
EMP: 5 EST: 2016
SALES (est): 104.3K Privately Held
SIC: 3993 Signs & advertising specialties

(G-5813)
STAR LINE COMMERCIAL PRINTING
6122 W Pierson Rd Unit 5 (48433-3104)
PHONE..................810 733-1152
Cheryl Schultz, *Owner*
EMP: 5 EST: 2005
SALES (est): 66.5K Privately Held
SIC: 2759 Post cards, picture: printing

(G-5814)
ULTRA-DEX USA LLC
7144 Sheridan Rd (48433-9610)
PHONE..................810 638-5388
Eli Crotzer, *President*
Pat Mulcahy, *Vice Pres*
Joe Krupp, *Engineer*
EMP: 5 EST: 2013
SALES (est): 426.8K Privately Held
WEB: www.archcuttingtools.com
SIC: 3541 Machine tool replacement & repair parts, metal cutting types

(G-5815)
VETS ACCESS LLC
Also Called: Cor Health
1449 E Pierson Rd Ste B (48433-1885)
PHONE..................810 639-2222
Holli Beckett, *Director*
Darren Corcoran, *Officer*
Daniel P Corcoran,
Jenna Richmond, *Nurse*
EMP: 8 EST: 2005
SALES (est): 1MM Privately Held
WEB: www.vetsaccessllc.com
SIC: 3448 5047 7699 Ramps: prefabricated metal; medical & hospital equipment; technical aids for the handicapped; hospital equipment repair services

(G-5816)
WECO INTERNATIONAL INC
235 S Seymour Rd (48433-2618)
P.O. Box 189, Clio (48420-0189)
PHONE..................810 686-7221
Brett Wehner, *President*
Tony Tenore, *Opers Staff*
Grainne Wilson, *Admin Mgr*
▲ EMP: 11 EST: 1991

SALES (est): 1MM **Privately Held**
WEB: www.wecointernational.com
SIC: 3634 Heating units, for electric appliances

(G-5817)
WILLIES WICKS
1315 Kapp Ct (48433-1403)
P.O. Box 16 (48433-0016)
PHONE.................................810 730-4176
William Francis Kumpon Jr, *Owner*
EMP: 4 **EST:** 2015
SALES (est): 181.7K **Privately Held**
WEB: www.willieswicks.com
SIC: 3999 Candles

Fort Gratiot
St. Clair County

(G-5818)
BRITT MFG
5150 Lakeshore Rd (48059-3115)
PHONE.................................810 966-0223
EMP: 4 **EST:** 2018
SALES (est): 158.9K **Privately Held**
WEB: www.brittmfg.com
SIC: 3999 Manufacturing industries

(G-5819)
C W ENTERPRISES INC
Also Called: Allegra Print Imging Port Hron
4137 24th Ave (48059-3802)
PHONE.................................810 385-9100
Chuck Warczynsky, *President*
Chris Warczinsky, *Admin Sec*
Cara Furness, *Representative*
EMP: 6 **EST:** 1986
SQ FT: 2,500
SALES (est): 1MM **Privately Held**
WEB: www.allegramarketingprint.com
SIC: 2752 Commercial printing, offset

(G-5820)
CAMPBELL AND CO PUBLISHING LLC
4340 Greenview Cir (48059-3928)
PHONE.................................810 320-0224
Joseph Campbell, *Owner*
EMP: 5 **EST:** 2000
SALES (est): 70.4K **Privately Held**
SIC: 2741 Miscellaneous publishing

(G-5821)
FERGUSON STEEL INC
3755 N River Rd (48059-4146)
PHONE.................................810 984-3918
William White, *President*
EMP: 10 **EST:** 1941
SQ FT: 18,000
SALES (est): 700K **Privately Held**
WEB: www.fergusonsteel.net
SIC: 3441 1791 Fabricated structural metal; structural steel erection

(G-5822)
NOBBY INC
Also Called: Forsports
3950 Pine Grove Ave (48059-4218)
PHONE.................................810 984-3300
Scott Forster, *President*
William Forster, *Vice Pres*
Sonya Dye, *Purch Mgr*
Carl Haas, *Treasurer*
Daniel Hartwick, *Manager*
EMP: 18 **EST:** 1975
SQ FT: 16,000
SALES (est): 4.4MM **Privately Held**
WEB: www.fs4sports.com
SIC: 5999 5941 2396 2395 Trophies & plaques; sporting goods & bicycle shops; automotive & apparel trimmings; pleating & stitching

(G-5823)
PORT HURON MEDICAL ASSOC
3825 24th Ave (48059-4100)
PHONE.................................810 982-0100
Richard Covart, *Manager*
EMP: 5 **EST:** 1993
SALES (est): 575.2K **Privately Held**
WEB: www.phalrentals.com
SIC: 2834 Medicines, capsuled or ampuled

(G-5824)
SEPHORA INSIDE JCPENNEY
4400 24th Ave (48059-3809)
PHONE.................................810 385-9800
EMP: 4 **EST:** 2019
SALES (est): 100K **Privately Held**
SIC: 2844 Toilet preparations

Fostoria
Tuscola County

(G-5825)
NORTH BRANCH MACHINING & ENGRG
9318 Beech St (48435-7709)
P.O. Box 186 (48435-0186)
PHONE.................................989 795-2324
Michael P Grimes, *President*
Roxanne M Grimes, *Vice Pres*
EMP: 7 **EST:** 1977
SQ FT: 3,000
SALES (est): 475.2K **Privately Held**
SIC: 3599 Machine shop, jobbing & repair

Fountain
Mason County

(G-5826)
ADVANCED ECO PRINT
5884 E Ford Lake Dr (49410-9634)
PHONE.................................231 292-1688
Keith Michael Bott, *Owner*
EMP: 5 **EST:** 2018
SALES (est): 256.2K **Privately Held**
SIC: 2752 Commercial printing, lithographic

(G-5827)
MICHIGAN FARM CHEESE DAIRY
4295 E Millerton Rd (49410-9583)
PHONE.................................231 462-3301
Lu Andrulis, *President*
EMP: 4 **EST:** 1937
SQ FT: 8,000
SALES (est): 453.5K **Privately Held**
WEB: www.andrulischeese.com
SIC: 2022 Natural cheese

(G-5828)
TIMELESS PICTURE FRAMING
6161 E Millerton Rd (49410-9747)
PHONE.................................231 233-2221
Robert Randle, *Principal*
EMP: 5 **EST:** 2016
SALES (est): 150K **Privately Held**
SIC: 2499 Picture frame molding, finished

Fowler
Clinton County

(G-5829)
J J WOHLFERTS CUSTOM FURNITURE
10691 W M 21 (48835-5139)
PHONE.................................989 593-3283
Jerry J Wohlfert, *President*
Catherine Wohlfert, *Vice Pres*
EMP: 10 **EST:** 1980
SQ FT: 16,000
SALES (est): 752.7K **Privately Held**
WEB: www.jjwohlferts.com
SIC: 2431 Millwork

(G-5830)
MILLERS REDI-MIX INC
6218 S Wright Rd (48835)
PHONE.................................989 587-6511
Joseph Miller, *President*
Dale Fedewa, *Vice Pres*
EMP: 22 **EST:** 1960
SQ FT: 200
SALES (est): 2.1MM **Privately Held**
SIC: 3273 Ready-mixed concrete

(G-5831)
POHLS CUSTOM COUNTER TOPS
Also Called: Pohl's Cstm Cnter Tops Cbnetry
12185 W Colony Rd (48835-9760)
PHONE.................................989 593-2174
Russ Pohl, *Owner*
EMP: 4 **EST:** 2002
SALES (est): 139.6K **Privately Held**
WEB: www.pohlccc.blogspot.com
SIC: 2541 Counters or counter display cases, wood

Fowlerville
Livingston County

(G-5832)
ARMOURED RSSTNCE MCHANISMS INC
Also Called: Armi
345 W Frank St (48836-7960)
P.O. Box 329 (48836-0329)
PHONE.................................517 223-7618
Susan Pretty, *President*
Steven Pretty, *Admin Sec*
EMP: 16 **EST:** 2002
SQ FT: 12,600 **Privately Held**
WEB: www.banditproof.com
SIC: 3089 Flat panels, plastic

(G-5833)
ASAHI KASEI PLAS N AMER INC (HQ)
1 Thermofil Way (48836-7936)
PHONE.................................517 223-2000
Ramesh Iyer, *President*
Todd Glogovsky, *President*
John Moyer, *Principal*
Michael Hayden, *Business Mgr*
Yuta Kume, *Corp Secy*
◆ **EMP:** 119 **EST:** 1967
SALES (est): 78MM **Privately Held**
WEB: www.akplastics.com
SIC: 2821 Thermoplastic materials

(G-5834)
ASAHI KASEI PLASTICS AMER INC
1 Thermofil Way (48836-7936)
PHONE.................................517 223-2000
Nobuyuki Shunaga, *President*
Jefferey Bishop, *Production*
Mike Franchy, *Marketing Staff*
Erin Martin, *Planning*
▲ **EMP:** 62 **EST:** 2000
SQ FT: 150,000
SALES (est): 22.9MM **Privately Held**
WEB: www.akplastics.com
SIC: 2821 Thermoplastic materials
PA: Asahi Kasei Corporation
1-1-2, Yurakucho
Chiyoda-Ku TKY 100-0

(G-5835)
BIGOS PRECAST
555 E Van Riper Rd (48836-7909)
P.O. Box 726 (48836-0726)
PHONE.................................517 223-5000
Dave Bigos, *Owner*
EMP: 5 **EST:** 1996
SALES (est): 716.3K **Privately Held**
WEB: www.bigosequipmentrental.com
SIC: 3273 Ready-mixed concrete

(G-5836)
BULLDOG INNOVATIVE MFG LLC
925 Garden Ln (48836-9056)
PHONE.................................517 223-2500
John Dedoes, *Owner*
Phyllis Dedoes, *Vice Pres*
EMP: 24 **EST:** 2004
SALES (est): 2.9MM **Privately Held**
SIC: 3441 Boat & barge sections, prefabricated metal

(G-5837)
ECKERT MFG CO
3820 Nicholson Rd (48836-8296)
P.O. Box 828 (48836-0828)
PHONE.................................517 521-4905
William C Eckert, *Ch of Bd*
Jo Ann Eckert, *President*
Jean Westerby, *Corp Secy*
David Eckert, *Vice Pres*
Sherri Davis, *Manager*
EMP: 6 **EST:** 1966
SQ FT: 8,000
SALES (est): 500K **Privately Held**
SIC: 3089 Injection molding of plastics

(G-5838)
EXCELDA MFG HOLDG LLC
900 Garden Ln (48836-9053)
PHONE.................................517 223-8000
Chris Ferris, *Production*
Eric Dandrea, *Engineer*
Mike Mansfield, *Branch Mgr*
EMP: 10
SALES (corp-wide): 598.7MM **Privately Held**
SIC: 2992 7389 Lubricating oils & greases; packaging & labeling services
HQ: Excelda Manufacturing Holding, Llc
12785 Emerson Dr Bldg A
Brighton MI 48116
248 486-3800

(G-5839)
FOWLERVILLE FEED & PET SUPS
120 Hale St (48836-9076)
P.O. Box 374 (48836-0374)
PHONE.................................517 223-9115
Robert Esch, *President*
Duane Herbert, *Manager*
Richard Peckens, *Admin Sec*
EMP: 6 **EST:** 1919
SALES (est): 622.1K **Privately Held**
WEB: www.fowlervillefeed.com
SIC: 3999 Pet supplies; hair clippers for human use, hand & electric; hair driers, designed for beauty parlors

(G-5840)
FOWLERVILLE MACHINE TOOL INC
5010 W Grand River Rd (48836-8547)
PHONE.................................517 223-8871
William David Mink, *President*
EMP: 9 **EST:** 1964
SQ FT: 4,000
SALES (est): 605K **Privately Held**
SIC: 3544 Dies, steel rule

(G-5841)
FOWLERVILLE NEWS & VIEWS
Also Called: H & H Publications
206 E Grand River Ave (48836-8634)
P.O. Box 937 (48836-0937)
PHONE.................................517 223-8760
Steven Horton, *Partner*
Steve Horton, *Info Tech Mgr*
EMP: 4 **EST:** 1985
SALES (est): 332.7K **Privately Held**
WEB: www.fowlervillenewsandviews.com
SIC: 2711 7313 Newspapers: publishing only, not printed on site; newspaper advertising representative

(G-5842)
IEC FABRICATION LLC
Also Called: Chip Enterprises Sole Member
144 National Park Dr (48836-9672)
PHONE.................................810 623-1546
Bradley Salutes, *Principal*
EMP: 13 **EST:** 2017
SALES (est): 3.5MM **Privately Held**
WEB: www.iec-jpn.co.jp
SIC: 3441 Fabricated structural metal

(G-5843)
INVENTION EVOLUTION COMP LLC
Also Called: IEC N.A.
144 National Park Dr (48836-9672)
PHONE.................................517 219-0180
Don Redford, *Controller*
Michael B McLean, *Manager*
EMP: 22 **EST:** 2010
SALES (est): 6.7MM **Privately Held**
SIC: 3465 Body parts, automobile: stamped metal

Fowlerville - Livingston County (G-5844)

(G-5844)
J AMERICA LICENSED PDTS INC (PA)
Also Called: J America
445 E Van Riper Rd (48836-7931)
PHONE................................517 655-8800
Jeffrey Radway, *President*
Tara Kirsch, *Production*
David Salters, *Engineer*
Ryan Wall, *Regl Sales Mgr*
Salina Krawczak, *Technology*
▲ **EMP:** 3 **EST:** 2009
SALES (est): 1.4MM **Privately Held**
SIC: 5949 5131 2221 Fabric stores piece goods; silk piece goods, woven; broadwoven fabric mills, manmade

(G-5845)
J N B MACHINERY LLC
9119 W Grand River Rd (48836-9608)
P.O. Box 362 (48836-0362)
PHONE................................517 223-0725
Dennis Russ,
Brian Manson,
John Manson,
EMP: 8 **EST:** 2005
SQ FT: 30,000
SALES (est): 2.6MM **Privately Held**
WEB: www.jnbmach.com
SIC: 3599 Machine shop, jobbing & repair
PA: J.N.B. Machining Company, Inc.
9119 W Grand River Rd
Fowlerville MI 48836

(G-5846)
JNB MACHINING COMPANY INC (PA)
9119 W Grand River Rd (48836-9608)
P.O. Box 362 (48836-0362)
PHONE................................517 223-0725
John Manson, *President*
Brian Manson, *Vice Pres*
Nancy Manson, *Treasurer*
Evelyn Valeri, *Bookkeeper*
▲ **EMP:** 22 **EST:** 1991
SQ FT: 17,000
SALES (est): 11.9MM **Privately Held**
WEB: www.jnbmach.com
SIC: 3599 Machine shop, jobbing & repair

(G-5847)
JOHN FULLER LOGGING
6318 Nicholson Rd (48836-9671)
PHONE................................517 304-3298
John Fuller, *President*
EMP: 4 **EST:** 2017
SALES (est): 88.8K **Privately Held**
SIC: 2411 Logging camps & contractors

(G-5848)
KRAFT OUTDOOR SVC
6320 W Grand River Rd (48836-8567)
PHONE................................517 404-8023
EMP: 7 **EST:** 2020
SALES (est): 229.2K **Privately Held**
SIC: 2022 Processed cheese

(G-5849)
LUCASVARITY INC
500 E Van Riper Rd (48836-7908)
PHONE................................517 223-8330
Tom Sliwa, *Principal*
EMP: 7 **EST:** 2006
SALES (est): 158.4K **Privately Held**
SIC: 3711 Motor vehicles & car bodies

(G-5850)
MAGNUS SOFTWARE INC
3883 Hogback Rd (48836-9543)
P.O. Box 358 (48836-0358)
PHONE................................517 294-0315
Shane Merem, *President*
EMP: 5 **EST:** 1994
SQ FT: 4,000
SALES (est): 471.1K **Privately Held**
WEB: www.magnusoft.com
SIC: 7372 Prepackaged software

(G-5851)
MICHIGAN DIVERSIFIED METALS
144 Veterans Dr (48836-9050)
P.O. Box 508 (48836-0508)
PHONE................................517 223-7730
Dan Ordan, *President*
EMP: 7 **EST:** 1989
SQ FT: 3,000
SALES (est): 652.1K **Privately Held**
SIC: 3441 Fabricated structural metal

(G-5852)
QUALITY COATINGS
5323 Meadowlawn Rd (48836-9368)
PHONE................................517 294-0394
EMP: 4 **EST:** 2016
SALES (est): 119.6K **Privately Held**
WEB: www.qualitycoatingsmi.com
SIC: 3479 Metal coating & allied service

(G-5853)
RAVAGO AMERICAS LLC
Also Called: Industrial Resin Recycling
705 E Van Riper Rd (48836-8971)
PHONE................................517 548-4140
EMP: 28
SALES (corp-wide): 1.9MM **Privately Held**
WEB: www.amcopolymers.com
SIC: 2821 Plastics materials & resins
HQ: Ravago Americas Llc
1900 Smmit Twr Blvd Ste 9
Orlando FL 32810
407 773-7777

(G-5854)
RDZ RACING INCORPORATED
9642 Sober Rd (48836-9394)
PHONE................................517 468-3254
Robert Earls, *Principal*
EMP: 4 **EST:** 2011
SALES (est): 167.6K **Privately Held**
WEB: www.rdzracing.com
SIC: 3799 All terrain vehicles (ATV)

(G-5855)
RHE-TECH LLC
9201 W Grand River Rd (48836-9608)
PHONE................................517 223-4874
EMP: 5
SALES (corp-wide): 1.5B **Privately Held**
WEB: www.hexpol.com
SIC: 3087 2821 Custom compound purchased resins; plastics materials & resins
HQ: Rhe-Tech, Llc
1500 E N Territorial Rd
Whitmore Lake MI 48189
734 769-0585

(G-5856)
SEAN MICHAEL BRINES
11539 Owosso Rd (48836-9571)
P.O. Box 446, Howell (48844-0446)
PHONE................................517 404-5481
Sean Michael Brines, *Principal*
EMP: 5 **EST:** 2008
SALES (est): 175.9K **Privately Held**
SIC: 2819 Brine

(G-5857)
VENTRA FOWLERVILLE LLC
8887 W Grand River Rd (48836-9208)
PHONE................................517 223-5900
Shahid R Khan, *Mng Member*
Norm Addair, *Maintence Staff*
Dave Edblad,
▲ **EMP:** 270 **EST:** 2009
SQ FT: 250,000
SALES (est): 68.9MM
SALES (corp-wide): 1.5B **Privately Held**
WEB: www.flex-n-gate.com
SIC: 3714 Motor vehicle parts & accessories
PA: Flex-N-Gate Llc
1306 E University Ave
Urbana IL 61802
217 384-6600

(G-5858)
ZF ACTIVE SAFETY US INC
500 E Van Riper Rd (48836-7908)
PHONE................................517 223-8330
Kathy Grostelia, *Branch Mgr*
EMP: 7
SALES (corp-wide): 216.2K **Privately Held**
WEB: www.zf.com
SIC: 3714 Motor vehicle parts & accessories
HQ: Zf Active Safety Us Inc.
12025 Tech Center Dr
Livonia MI 48150
734 812-6979

Frankenmuth
Saginaw County

(G-5859)
BERNTHAL PACKING INC
9378 Junction Rd (48734-9539)
PHONE................................989 652-2648
Herbert Bernthal, *CEO*
Philip Bernthal, *President*
Frances Bernthal, *Corp Secy*
EMP: 11 **EST:** 1966
SQ FT: 6,000
SALES (est): 737.7K **Privately Held**
WEB: www.bernthalpacking.com
SIC: 5421 0751 2013 2011 Meat markets, including freezer provisioners; slaughtering: custom livestock services; sausages & other prepared meats; meat packing plants

(G-5860)
BRONNER DISPLAY SIGN ADVG INC
Also Called: Bronner Christmas Decorations
25 Christmas Ln (48734-1807)
P.O. Box 176 (48734-0176)
PHONE................................989 652-9931
Wayne Bronner, *President*
Carla Bronner Spletzer, *Vice Pres*
Carla Spletzer, *Vice Pres*
Maria Bronner Sutorik, *Vice Pres*
Tammy Hall, *Buyer*
◆ **EMP:** 250 **EST:** 1945
SQ FT: 320,000
SALES (est): 24.1MM **Privately Held**
WEB: www.bronners.com
SIC: 5999 5199 3699 Christmas lights & decorations; Christmas novelties; Christmas tree lighting sets, electric; Christmas tree ornaments, electric

(G-5861)
FRANKENMUTH BREWERY LLC
425 S Main St (48734-1615)
P.O. Box 226 (48734-0226)
PHONE................................989 262-8300
Clark Bien, *Treasurer*
Karen Partlo, *Human Res Mgr*
Randall E Heine,
Steve Buszka, *Master*
EMP: 50 **EST:** 1987
SQ FT: 50,000
SALES (est): 7.9MM **Privately Held**
WEB: www.frankenmuthbrewery.com
SIC: 2082 Ale (alcoholic beverage)

(G-5862)
FRANKENMUTH INDUSTRIAL SVCS
310 List St (48734-1910)
P.O. Box 357 (48734-0357)
PHONE................................989 652-3322
George Anscomb, *President*
George A Anscomb, *President*
Michelle L Anscomb, *Vice Pres*
EMP: 20 **EST:** 1988
SQ FT: 20,000
SALES (est): 2.6MM **Privately Held**
WEB: www.frankenmuthindustrial.com
SIC: 7692 3441 Welding repair; fabricated structural metal

(G-5863)
FRANKENMUTH NEWS LLC
527 N Franklin St Ste A (48734-2011)
P.O. Box 252 (48734-0252)
PHONE................................989 652-3246
Steven Grainger, *President*
Gretchen Rau, *Office Mgr*
EMP: 9 **EST:** 1946
SQ FT: 3,200
SALES (est): 516K **Privately Held**
WEB: www.frankenmuthnews.com
SIC: 2711 Newspapers, publishing & printing

(G-5864)
GLAXOSMITHKLINE LLC
1331 S Dehmel Rd (48734-9150)
PHONE................................989 450-9859
EMP: 4
SALES (corp-wide): 45.3B **Privately Held**
WEB: www.us.gsk.com
SIC: 2834 Pharmaceutical preparations
HQ: Glaxosmithkline Llc
5 Crescent Dr
Philadelphia PA 19112
215 751-4000

(G-5865)
GRASEL GRAPHICS INC
9710 Junction Rd (48734-9502)
P.O. Box 385 (48734-0385)
PHONE................................989 652-5151
Steven Grasel, *President*
Amy Grasel, *Admin Sec*
EMP: 9 **EST:** 1995
SQ FT: 5,500
SALES (est): 1.2MM **Privately Held**
WEB: www.graselgraphics.com
SIC: 2759 2395 Screen printing; embroidery products, except schiffli machine

(G-5866)
KERNEL BENNYS
701 Mill St (48734-1629)
PHONE................................989 928-3950
EMP: 5 **EST:** 2018
SALES (est): 98.7K **Privately Held**
WEB: www.kernelbenny.com
SIC: 2064 Candy & other confectionery products

(G-5867)
KERNS SAUSAGES INC
110 W Jefferson St (48734-1898)
PHONE................................989 652-2684
Ronald Kern, *President*
Kevin Kern, *Vice Pres*
EMP: 18 **EST:** 1949
SALES (est): 750K **Privately Held**
WEB: www.kernssausage.com
SIC: 5421 5411 2013 2011 Meat markets, including freezer provisioners; grocery stores, independent; sausages & other prepared meats

(G-5868)
KREMIN INC
235 Keystone Way (48734-9629)
PHONE................................989 790-5147
Michael Kremin Jr, *President*
Andrew Agans, *Project Mgr*
Gary Hiltz, *Production*
EMP: 27 **EST:** 1983
SQ FT: 20,000
SALES (est): 4.8MM **Privately Held**
WEB: www.kremininc.com
SIC: 3599 3544 Machine shop, jobbing & repair; special dies, tools, jigs & fixtures

(G-5869)
MEMTRON TECHNOLOGIES CO
Also Called: Esterline Mmtron Input Cmpnnts
530 N Franklin St (48734-1000)
PHONE................................989 652-2656
Denis Staver, *President*
▲ **EMP:** 82 **EST:** 1974
SQ FT: 30,000
SALES (est): 17.6MM **Privately Held**
WEB: www.advancedinput.com
SIC: 3679 Electronic circuits

(G-5870)
MICHIGAN BRAND INC
320 Heinlein Strasse (48734-1940)
PHONE................................989 395-4345
Adam Keyes, *Principal*
EMP: 9
SALES (corp-wide): 3.1MM **Privately Held**
WEB: www.michiganbrand.net
SIC: 2011 Meat packing plants
PA: Michigan Brand, Inc
1313 S Farragut St
Bay City MI 48708
989 893-9589

(G-5871)
MILLER MOLD CO
690 Wren Rd (48734-9320)
PHONE................................989 793-8881

Robert J Piesko, *President*
EMP: 35 **EST:** 1951
SALES (est): 3.2MM **Privately Held**
WEB: www.millermold.com
SIC: 3559 3544 Plastics working machinery; special dies, tools, jigs & fixtures

(G-5872)
ST JULIAN WINE COMPANY INC
127 S Main St (48734-1611)
PHONE.................................989 652-3281
Gordon Lockhart, *Manager*
EMP: 7
SALES (corp-wide): 13.2MM **Privately Held**
WEB: www.stjulian.com
SIC: 5921 2086 2084 Wine; bottled & canned soft drinks; wines, brandy & brandy spirits
PA: St. Julian Wine Company, Incorporated
716 S Kalamazoo St
Paw Paw MI 49079
269 657-5568

(G-5873)
STAR OF WEST MILLING COMPANY (PA)
121 E Tuscola St (48734-1731)
P.O. Box 146 (48734-0146)
PHONE.................................989 652-9971
Gary Rummel, *Ch of Bd*
William A Zehnder III, *Vice Ch Bd*
Arthur A Loeffler, *President*
Michael Fassezke, *Vice Pres*
Mike Fassezke, *Vice Pres*
▼ **EMP:** 71 **EST:** 1870
SQ FT: 45,000
SALES: 380.1MM **Privately Held**
WEB: www.starofthewest.com
SIC: 2041 5153 5191 Flour; grains; beans, dry: bulk; fertilizer & fertilizer materials; seeds: field, garden & flower; feed

(G-5874)
ZEILINGER WOOL CO LLC
1130 Weiss St (48734-1995)
PHONE.................................989 652-2920
Kathy Zeilinger, *President*
Kathy Ann Zeilinger, *President*
EMP: 22
SQ FT: 7,000
SALES (est): 850K **Privately Held**
WEB: www.zwool.com
SIC: 2299 5949 7219 Batts & batting: cotton mill waste & related material; roves, flax & jute; sewing, needlework & piece goods; reweaving textiles (mending service)

Frankfort
Benzie County

(G-5875)
BENZIE MANUFACTURING LLC
401 Parkview Ln (49635-9492)
PHONE.................................231 631-0498
Tami Scott,
Kevin Scott,
EMP: 3 **EST:** 2013
SALES (est): 1MM **Privately Held**
WEB: www.benzie.net
SIC: 3599 Machine & other job shop work; custom machinery; machine shop, jobbing & repair

(G-5876)
FRANKFORT MANUFACTURING INC
1105 Main St (49635-9020)
P.O. Box 273 (49635-0273)
PHONE.................................231 352-7551
Donald Surber, *President*
Tom Weber, *Sales Staff*
EMP: 38 **EST:** 1990
SQ FT: 15,000
SALES (est): 2.9MM **Privately Held**
WEB: www.frankfortmfg.com
SIC: 3544 Special dies & tools

(G-5877)
GRACELAND FRUIT INC
1123 Main St (49635-9341)
PHONE.................................231 352-7181
Alan Devore, *CEO*
Jeff Seeley, *President*
James Nugent, *Chairman*
Dan Engler, *COO*
Steve Nugent, *COO*
◆ **EMP:** 180 **EST:** 1973
SQ FT: 110,000
SALES (est): 31.5MM **Privately Held**
WEB: www.gracelandfruit.com
SIC: 2034 2037 Fruits, dried or dehydrated, except freeze-dried; fruits, quick frozen & cold pack (frozen)

(G-5878)
H W JENCKS INCORPORATED
Detroit Coil Company
1339 Elm St (49635-9674)
P.O. Box 1097 (49635-1097)
PHONE.................................231 352-4422
Fax: 231 352-4024
EMP: 35
SALES (corp-wide): 2.2MM **Privately Held**
SIC: 3677 3643 3621 Mfg Electronic Coils/Transformers Mfg Conductive Wiring Devices Mfg Motors/Generators
PA: H W Jencks Incorporated
2435 Hilton Rd
Ferndale MI

(G-5879)
PRACTICE MANAGEMENT TECH
541 Lake St (49635-9738)
P.O. Box 1787 (49635-1787)
PHONE.................................231 352-9844
Gary Rice, *President*
EMP: 6 **EST:** 2001
SALES (est): 130.7K **Privately Held**
WEB: www.pmtechweb.com
SIC: 7372 Prepackaged software

(G-5880)
ROGER MIX STORAGE
1218 Elm St (49635-9338)
P.O. Box 2231 (49635-2231)
PHONE.................................231 352-9762
Roger Mix, *President*
EMP: 4 **EST:** 1989
SALES (est): 226.2K **Privately Held**
SIC: 3273 4225 Ready-mixed concrete; general warehousing & storage

(G-5881)
SMELTZER COMPANIES INC
Also Called: Smeltzer Orchard Company
6032 Joyfield Rd (49635-9163)
PHONE.................................231 882-4421
Tim Brian, *President*
James H Brian, *Vice Pres*
Mike Henschell, *Director*
Clinton Smeltzer, *Director*
Donald Smeltzer, *Director*
▼ **EMP:** 110 **EST:** 1942
SQ FT: 106,150
SALES (est): 16MM **Privately Held**
WEB: www.smeltzerorchards.com
SIC: 2037 2034 Fruits, quick frozen & cold pack (frozen); dehydrated fruits, vegetables, soups

Franklin
Oakland County

(G-5882)
CIRCLEBUILDER SOFTWARE LLC
Also Called: Circlebuilder .com
24811 Franklin Park Dr (48025-1237)
P.O. Box 250656 (48025-0656)
PHONE.................................248 770-3191
Steve Schwartz, *Director*
Julie Snyder, *Director*
Howard Brown,
EMP: 4 **EST:** 2006
SALES (est): 200.7K **Privately Held**
WEB: www.circlebuilder.com
SIC: 7372 Prepackaged software

(G-5883)
MY LITTLE PRINTS
26645 Normandy Rd (48025-1033)
PHONE.................................248 613-8439
Julie Goldstein, *Principal*
EMP: 6 **EST:** 2010
SALES (est): 76.8K **Privately Held**
SIC: 2752 Commercial printing, lithographic

(G-5884)
OPTIONS
32696 Ravine Dr (48025-1137)
PHONE.................................248 855-6151
EMP: 5 **EST:** 2015
SALES (est): 101.2K **Privately Held**
SIC: 2434 Wood kitchen cabinets

(G-5885)
TALBOT & ASSOCIATES INC
Also Called: Tai Consulting
30400 Telg Rd Ste 479 (48025)
PHONE.................................248 723-9700
Michael R Talbot, *President*
Michele Kandt, *Treasurer*
Linda Lavin, *Admin Sec*
EMP: 10 **EST:** 1997
SALES (est): 922.9K **Privately Held**
WEB: www.taiconsulting.com
SIC: 7372 Business oriented computer software

Fraser
Macomb County

(G-5886)
A B RUSGO INC (PA)
Also Called: Labor World
32064 Utica Rd (48026-2207)
PHONE.................................586 296-7714
Alan B Rusgo, *President*
Julienne Rusgo, *Admin Sec*
EMP: 7 **EST:** 1995
SQ FT: 2,800
SALES (est): 725.1K **Privately Held**
WEB: www.allegiancestaffing.com
SIC: 2711 Newspapers: publishing only, not printed on site

(G-5887)
A-1 STAMPINGS INC
33381 Kelly Rd (48026-1533)
PHONE.................................586 294-7790
Edmund Kirkman, *President*
EMP: 5 **EST:** 1962
SQ FT: 15,200
SALES (est): 610.2K **Privately Held**
WEB: www.a1stampings.com
SIC: 3469 3465 Stamping metal for the trade; automotive stampings

(G-5888)
ADVANCED INTEGRATED MFG
34673 Bennett (48026-3413)
PHONE.................................586 439-0300
Jeffrey R Siciliano, *President*
Michael W See, *Vice Pres*
EMP: 3 **EST:** 1982
SQ FT: 5,000
SALES (est): 2.1MM **Privately Held**
WEB: www.aimcom.com
SIC: 3824 3823 3577 3571 Fluid meters & counting devices; industrial instrmnts msrmnt display/control process variable; computer peripheral equipment; electronic computers; systems software development services
PA: A S A P Computer Services, Inc
34673 Bennett
Fraser MI 48026

(G-5889)
AFFINITY ELECTRONICS INC
33710 Doreka (48026-3430)
PHONE.................................586 477-4920
John Hogan, *President*
EMP: 6 **EST:** 2009
SQ FT: 5,000
SALES (est): 971.1K **Privately Held**
WEB: www.affinityelectronicsinc.com
SIC: 3679 Loads, electronic

(G-5890)
AMBER MANUFACTURING INC
18320 Malyn Blvd (48026-3494)
PHONE.................................586 218-6080
Lyle J Atcton, *President*
Lyle J Acton, *President*
Janice Acton, *Vice Pres*
EMP: 7 **EST:** 1974
SQ FT: 7,200
SALES (est): 871.6K **Privately Held**
SIC: 3544 Special dies & tools

(G-5891)
AMERICAN AXLE & MFG INC
Also Called: AAM Fraser Mfg Fcilty
18450 15 Mile Rd (48026-3460)
PHONE.................................586 415-2000
EMP: 7
SALES (corp-wide): 4.7B **Publicly Held**
WEB: www.aam.com
SIC: 3714 Motor vehicle engines & parts
HQ: American Axle & Manufacturing, Inc.
1 Dauch Dr
Detroit MI 48211

(G-5892)
AMERICAN PRIDE MACHINING INC
34062 James J Pompo Dr (48026-3408)
PHONE.................................586 294-6404
Susan Kolatski, *CEO*
EMP: 4 **EST:** 2010
SALES (est): 1MM **Privately Held**
WEB: www.apmincorp.com
SIC: 7699 3541 Industrial machinery & equipment repair; machine tool replacement & repair parts, metal cutting types

(G-5893)
AMERICAS FINEST PRTG GRAPHICS (PA)
17060 Masonic Ste 101 (48026-2561)
PHONE.................................586 296-1312
Judy Hill, *President*
Joseph Hill, *Corp Secy*
Jason Hill, *Vice Pres*
EMP: 5 **EST:** 1995
SQ FT: 1,200
SALES (est): 768.2K **Privately Held**
WEB: www.americasfinestprint.com
SIC: 2759 7338 2791 2789 Screen printing; secretarial & court reporting; typesetting; bookbinding & related work; commercial printing, lithographic

(G-5894)
AMERISTEEL INC
33900 Doreka (48026-1611)
PHONE.................................586 585-5250
Warren Damman, *President*
Pat Burke, *Opers Staff*
EMP: 20 **EST:** 1985
SQ FT: 20,000
SALES (est): 9.8MM **Privately Held**
WEB: www.ameristeelonline.com
SIC: 2541 5051 Store & office display cases & fixtures; steel

(G-5895)
ANDERSON-COOK INC
Also Called: Anderson Cook Machine Tool
17650 15 Mile Rd (48026-3450)
P.O. Box 26509 (48026-6509)
PHONE.................................586 293-0800
Brent Chartier, *Vice Pres*
Kurt Karlstorm, *Purch Mgr*
Shane Koch, *Engineer*
Thomas Millie, *Asst Controller*
Craig Everlove, *Manager*
EMP: 5
SALES (corp-wide): 40.3MM **Privately Held**
WEB: www.andersoncook.com
SIC: 3542 3714 3599 3549 Spline rolling machines; gears, motor vehicle; machine shop, jobbing & repair; metalworking machinery; machine tool accessories
PA: Anderson-Cook, Inc.
50550 E Rssell Schmidt Bl
Chesterfield MI 48051
586 954-0700

(G-5896)
ARISTO-COTE INC
Also Called: Aristo Industries
32100 Groesbeck Hwy (48026-3144)
PHONE.................................586 447-9049
Matt Murray, *President*
Brian Murray, *General Mgr*
EMP: 70 **Privately Held**
WEB: www.aristoind.com

SIC: 3479 Coating of metals & formed products; coating of metals with plastic or resins; coating of metals with silicon; coating or wrapping steel pipe
PA: Aristo-Cote, Inc.
24951 Henry B Joy Blvd
Harrison Township MI 48045

(G-5897)
AUTO/CON CORP
33842 James J Pompo Dr (48026-3468)
PHONE..................586 791-7474
Ronald R Matheson, *President*
Cheryl Cargill, *Corp Secy*
Daniel Hucul, *Vice Pres*
Gerald Stehlin, *Vice Pres*
EMP: 53 **EST:** 1981
SQ FT: 70,900
SALES (est): 7.3MM **Privately Held**
WEB: www.autoconcorp.com
SIC: 3549 Assembly machines, including robotic

(G-5898)
AUTO/CON SERVICES LLC
Also Called: ACS
33661 James J Pompo Dr (48026-3467)
PHONE..................586 791-7474
Chris Michayluk, *CEO*
EMP: 5 **EST:** 2012
SQ FT: 30,000
SALES (est): 260.6K **Privately Held**
WEB: www.autoconservices.com
SIC: 7389 3569 3535 Design services; assembly machines, non-metalworking; robots, assembly line: industrial & commercial; overhead conveyor systems

(G-5899)
AUTOMATED PROD ASSEMBLIES
33957 Doreka (48026-1612)
PHONE..................586 293-3990
Thomas Monroe, *President*
EMP: 23 **EST:** 1973
SQ FT: 10,900
SALES (est): 685.4K **Privately Held**
WEB: www.tappingonline.com
SIC: 3599 Machine shop, jobbing & repair

(G-5900)
BARNES GROUP INC
Also Called: Kaller Gas Springs
33280 Groesbeck Hwy (48026-1597)
PHONE..................586 415-6377
Michael Ambrogio, *General Mgr*
Rick Bastow, *Regl Sales Mgr*
EMP: 8
SALES (corp-wide): 1.4B **Publicly Held**
WEB: www.barnesgroupinc.com
SIC: 3495 3469 Wire springs; metal stampings
PA: Barnes Group Inc.
123 Main St
Bristol CT 06010
860 583-7070

(G-5901)
BAY DESIGN INC
17800 15 Mile Rd (48026-1601)
PHONE..................586 296-7130
Milton Bayagich, *President*
Thomas Bayagich, *Vice Pres*
John Bayagich, *Treasurer*
Robert Bayagich, *Admin Sec*
EMP: 25 **EST:** 1982
SQ FT: 8,000
SALES (est): 600.4K **Privately Held**
WEB: www.bayproductsinc.com
SIC: 3599 Machine shop, jobbing & repair

(G-5902)
BAY PRODUCTS INC
17800 15 Mile Rd (48026-1601)
PHONE..................586 296-7130
Thomas Bayagich, *Vice Pres*
EMP: 42 **EST:** 1983
SQ FT: 18,000
SALES (est): 9.9MM **Privately Held**
WEB: www.bayproductsinc.com
SIC: 3544 Special dies & tools; jigs & fixtures

(G-5903)
BERMONT GAGE & AUTOMATION INC
Also Called: Bermont Technologies
34500 Klein Rd (48026-3022)
PHONE..................586 296-1103
Vincent Dudek, *President*
Herg Langegger, *Vice Pres*
▼ **EMP:** 27 **EST:** 2001
SQ FT: 24,000
SALES (est): 1.7MM **Privately Held**
WEB: www.bermontgage.com
SIC: 3599 Machine shop, jobbing & repair

(G-5904)
BEST IMPRESSIONS INC
32680 Newman (48026-3210)
PHONE..................313 839-9000
Robin Nadolski, *President*
Mark F Nadolski, *Vice Pres*
EMP: 5 **EST:** 1977
SQ FT: 1,000
SALES (est): 527.7K **Privately Held**
WEB: www.bestimpressionsdaylighting.com
SIC: 3089 Panels, building: plastic

(G-5905)
BMT AEROSPACE USA INC
Also Called: Orwood Precision Pdts Caratron
18559 Malyn Blvd (48026-1606)
PHONE..................586 285-7700
Robert J Puckett, *President*
Michael S Wilson, *COO*
Brian Schoenrock, *Buyer*
Peter Praet, *QC Mgr*
Muhammad Ali-Khan, *Engineer*
◆ **EMP:** 100 **EST:** 2007
SQ FT: 56,638
SALES (est): 32.9MM
SALES (corp-wide): 183.7K **Privately Held**
WEB: www.bmtaerospace.com
SIC: 3728 3541 Gears, aircraft power transmission; gear cutting & finishing machines
HQ: Bmt Aerospace International
Handelsstraat 6
Oostkamp 8020
502 490-00

(G-5906)
BOLYEA INDUSTRIES
33847 Doreka (48026-1646)
PHONE..................586 293-8700
Rick Bolyea, *President*
James Bolyea, *Shareholder*
Joseph O'Brien, *Admin Sec*
EMP: 10 **EST:** 1972
SQ FT: 15,000
SALES (est): 1MM **Privately Held**
WEB: www.flamesprayusa.com
SIC: 3479 Coating of metals & formed products

(G-5907)
BUDDIES FOODS LLC
Also Called: Chuck and Dave's Salsa
17445 Malyn Blvd (48026-1634)
PHONE..................586 776-4036
Susan Maiorana, *Vice Pres*
Dave Kernya,
Cathy Kernya,
Vincent C Maiorana,
EMP: 35 **EST:** 2002
SQ FT: 21,000
SALES (est): 6.5MM **Privately Held**
WEB: www.chuckanddaves.net
SIC: 2099 Sauces: gravy, dressing & dip mixes

(G-5908)
C & N MANUFACTURING INC
33722 James J Pompo Dr (48026-1645)
PHONE..................586 293-9150
Gerald A Naski, *President*
Patricia Naski, *Vice Pres*
EMP: 20 **EST:** 1980
SQ FT: 14,100
SALES (est): 3.5MM **Privately Held**
WEB: www.cnmfginc.com
SIC: 3599 3544 Machine shop, jobbing & repair; special dies, tools, jigs & fixtures

(G-5909)
C & S AUTOMATED SYSTEMS LLC
31784 Groesbeck Hwy (48026-3911)
PHONE..................586 265-1416
Douglas Cesar, *CEO*
EMP: 4 **EST:** 2014
SALES (est): 377.1K **Privately Held**
SIC: 3599 Custom machinery

(G-5910)
CARBIDE TECHNOLOGIES INC
18101 Malyn Blvd (48026-3493)
PHONE..................586 296-5200
Bernice Souris, *Principal*
Nicholas T Souris, *Vice Pres*
Nicholas Souris, *Vice Pres*
Nick Souris, *Opers Mgr*
Joanne Kastoris, *Purchasing*
EMP: 50 **EST:** 1978
SQ FT: 70,000
SALES (est): 12MM **Privately Held**
WEB: www.carbidetechnologies.com
SIC: 3356 3545 3546 Tungsten, basic shapes; cutting tools for machine tools; reamers, machine tool; power-driven handtools

(G-5911)
CARDINAL CUSTOM DESIGNS INC
31469 Utica Rd (48026-2533)
PHONE..................586 296-2060
Clarence Bury, *President*
EMP: 5 **EST:** 1989
SQ FT: 3,800
SALES (est): 150K **Privately Held**
SIC: 2391 Draperies, plastic & textile: from purchased materials

(G-5912)
CDK ENTERPRISES LLC
Also Called: Apollo E.D.M. Company
16601 E 13 Mile Rd (48026-2554)
PHONE..................586 296-9300
Christopher Kain,
EMP: 27 **EST:** 1969
SQ FT: 15,000
SALES (est): 4.4MM **Privately Held**
SIC: 3599 Machine shop, jobbing & repair

(G-5913)
CENTURY TOOL WELDING INC
32873 Groesbeck Hwy (48026-3128)
PHONE..................586 293-8130
Carl Wolschon, *President*
Stephen Wolschon, *Vice Pres*
Marilyn Wolschon, *Admin Sec*
EMP: 6 **EST:** 1976
SALES (est): 592.3K **Privately Held**
WEB: www.centurytoolwelding.com
SIC: 7692 Welding repair

(G-5914)
CONSOLDTED DCMENT SLUTIONS LLC
17601 Malyn Blvd (48026-3487)
P.O. Box 187 (48026-0187)
PHONE..................586 293-8100
Charles Ftorm, *Mng Member*
Michele Hall, *Graphic Designe*
EMP: 12 **EST:** 1989
SALES (est): 2.4MM **Privately Held**
WEB: www.cdocsolutions.com
SIC: 2759 5112 Business forms: printing; stationery & office supplies

(G-5915)
CONTINENTAL CRANE & SERVICE
33681 Groesbeck Hwy (48026-1542)
PHONE..................586 294-7900
Edward Dungan Jr, *President*
Christian Dungan, *Vice Pres*
Joseph Dungan, *Vice Pres*
Susan Hood, *Treasurer*
Judy Hamilton, *Admin Sec*
EMP: 22 **EST:** 1973
SQ FT: 4,500
SALES (est): 1.4MM **Privately Held**
SIC: 3535 7389 Conveyors & conveying equipment; crane & aerial lift service

(G-5916)
CW CREATIVE WELDING INC
33360 Groesbeck Hwy (48026-1545)
PHONE..................586 294-1050
Rich Bursteinowicz, *President*
EMP: 5 **EST:** 1998
SALES (est): 290.1K **Privately Held**
WEB: www.cwcreativewelding.com
SIC: 7692 Welding repair

(G-5917)
DELTA PRECISION INC
33214 Janet (48026-4303)
PHONE..................248 585-2344
Mark Detheridge, *President*
Donald Baross, *Vice Pres*
EMP: 4 **EST:** 1970
SQ FT: 3,000
SALES (est): 280.9K **Privately Held**
WEB: www.deltaprecisionsystems.com
SIC: 3544 Industrial molds

(G-5918)
DELUXE TECHNOLOGIES LLC
34537 Bennett (48026-1691)
P.O. Box 180149, Utica (48318-0149)
PHONE..................586 294-2340
Nick Demiro, *President*
Patricia A Stephens, *Vice Pres*
EMP: 21 **EST:** 2007
SQ FT: 40,000
SALES (est): 1.5MM **Privately Held**
WEB: www.dlxtech.net
SIC: 3999 Dock equipment & supplies, industrial

(G-5919)
DORRIS COMPANY
17430 Malyn Blvd (48026-1635)
PHONE..................586 293-5260
Robert Diez, *President*
Peter Osadczuk, *General Mgr*
Kristin Williams, *Officer*
EMP: 16 **EST:** 1980
SQ FT: 70,000
SALES (est): 4MM
SALES (corp-wide): 9.6MM **Privately Held**
WEB: www.dorrisco.com
SIC: 3566 3769 3724 3462 Speed changers, drives & gears; guided missile & space vehicle parts & auxiliary equipment; aircraft engines & engine parts; iron & steel forgings; sheet metalwork; gears, aircraft power transmission
PA: Supreme Gear Co.
17430 Malyn Bvld
Fraser MI 48026
586 775-6325

(G-5920)
DREAM CUSTOM CABINETS
33314 Duncan (48026-1958)
PHONE..................586 718-4812
Huber Ochoa, *Principal*
EMP: 4 **EST:** 2016
SALES (est): 75.2K **Privately Held**
SIC: 2434 Wood kitchen cabinets

(G-5921)
DYTRON CORPORATION
17000 Masonic (48026-3948)
PHONE..................586 296-9600
Richard C Donovan, *President*
Lois J Donovan, *Vice Pres*
EMP: 17 **EST:** 1964
SQ FT: 8,000
SALES (est): 1MM **Privately Held**
WEB: www.dytroncorp.com
SIC: 3548 5084 Welding wire, bare & coated; welding machinery & equipment

(G-5922)
EDRICH PRODUCTS INC
Also Called: Aquarich Water Treatment Pdts
33672 Doreka (48026-1609)
PHONE..................586 296-3350
Howard A Smith, *President*
Dianna M Smith, *Corp Secy*
Debby Andy, *Vice Pres*
Gregory Benfatti, *Accounts Mgr*
EMP: 12 **EST:** 1972
SQ FT: 15,000

GEOGRAPHIC SECTION

Fraser - Macomb County (G-5950)

SALES (est): 3MM **Privately Held**
WEB: www.edrichproducts.com
SIC: 2992 Cutting oils, blending: made from purchased materials; rust arresting compounds, animal or vegetable oil base

(G-5923)
EIFEL MOLD & ENGINEERING INC
31071 Fraser Dr (48026-2504)
P.O. Box 190 (48026-0190)
PHONE..................586 296-9640
Richard A Hecker, *President*
Wendy Tabor, *Controller*
Ann Sulkowski, *Human Resources*
Gary Schulz, *Marketing Mgr*
EMP: 20 EST: 1973
SQ FT: 10,000
SALES (est): 2.9MM **Privately Held**
WEB: www.eifel-inc.com
SIC: 3544 Industrial molds; jigs & fixtures

(G-5924)
ELECTROLABS INC
18503 E 14 Mile Rd (48026-1551)
P.O. Box 456 (48026-0456)
PHONE..................586 294-4150
Dennis Suddon, *President*
Scott Sutton, *Vice Pres*
Robert Rein, *Treasurer*
Denise Dawson, *Admin Sec*
EMP: 10 EST: 1962
SQ FT: 7,500
SALES (est): 1MM **Privately Held**
WEB: www.elabsmetalfab.com
SIC: 3444 Sheet metalwork

(G-5925)
ENMARK TOOL COMPANY
18100 Cross (48026-1666)
PHONE..................586 293-2797
Gary M Enmark, *President*
Tim Krauss, *General Mgr*
John Enmark, *Vice Pres*
Denice Baur, *Human Res Mgr*
Dolores Enmark, *Admin Sec*
EMP: 50 EST: 1951
SQ FT: 46,000
SALES (est): 8.9MM **Privately Held**
WEB: www.enmarktool.com
SIC: 3544 3545 Special dies & tools; gauges (machine tool accessories)

(G-5926)
FAIRLANE CO
33792 Doreka (48026-3430)
PHONE..................586 294-6100
Justin Gordon, *CEO*
Bill Leto, *Marketing Staff*
EMP: 33 EST: 2011
SALES (est): 4.9MM **Privately Held**
WEB: www.fairlaneproducts.com
SIC: 3544 Special dies & tools

(G-5927)
FENIXX TECHNOLOGIES LLC
17009 Masonic (48026-3927)
PHONE..................586 254-6000
Lawrence Schaller, *President*
EMP: 12 EST: 2008
SALES (est): 752.1K **Privately Held**
WEB: www.fenixxtech.com
SIC: 3999 Manufacturing industries

(G-5928)
FIXTUREWORKS LLC
33792 Doreka (48026-3430)
PHONE..................586 294-6100
Delores Ferland, *Bookkeeper*
Laura Kisch, *Sales Staff*
Tammy Labine, *Office Mgr*
Mark Gordon,
Justin Gordon,
▲ EMP: 6 EST: 2003
SQ FT: 12,000
SALES (est): 784.8K **Privately Held**
WEB: www.fixtureworks.com
SIC: 3544 5072 5085 Special dies & tools; hardware; industrial fittings

(G-5929)
FOUR-SLIDE TECHNOLOGY INC
33946 Doreka (48026-1611)
PHONE..................586 755-7778
Roger Pelc, *President*
Brian Pelc, *Vice Pres*
Brian Lamphier, *Engineer*
EMP: 15 EST: 1999
SQ FT: 22,000
SALES (est): 2MM **Privately Held**
WEB: www.four-slide.com
SIC: 3469 Stamping metal for the trade

(G-5930)
FRASER GRINDING CO (PA)
34235 Riviera (48026-1624)
PHONE..................586 293-6060
Rudolf F Lipski, *President*
Marjory Lipski, *Vice Pres*
Kenneth York, *Vice Pres*
EMP: 10 EST: 1959
SQ FT: 90,000
SALES (est): 5.2MM **Privately Held**
WEB: www.sharpcutter.com
SIC: 3599 Machine shop, jobbing & repair

(G-5931)
GRANT INDUSTRIES INCORPORATED (PA)
33415 Groesbeck Hwy (48026-4203)
PHONE..................586 293-9200
Robert Grant, *President*
Kathy Peterson, *Vice Pres*
Timothy Schley, *Vice Pres*
Steven Grant, *Admin Sec*
EMP: 45
SQ FT: 82,000
SALES (est): 16.1MM **Privately Held**
WEB: www.grantgrp.com
SIC: 3465 3469 3452 3429 Body parts, automobile: stamped metal; metal stampings; bolts, nuts, rivets & washers; manufactured hardware (general); cold finishing of steel shapes; blast furnaces & steel mills

(G-5932)
GROSSEL TOOL CO
34190 Doreka (48026-3434)
PHONE..................586 294-3660
Kurt Kowal, *President*
Mark Kowal, *Vice Pres*
Laura Casano, *Human Resources*
Marilyn E Kowal, *Shareholder*
Dyana Jones, *Admin Sec*
EMP: 36 EST: 1946
SQ FT: 20,000
SALES (est): 3.5MM **Privately Held**
WEB: www.grosseltool.com
SIC: 3548 3443 Welding apparatus; fabricated plate work (boiler shop)

(G-5933)
HAYNIE AND HESS REALTY CO LLC
33670 Riviera (48026-1621)
PHONE..................586 296-2750
Jeff Hess, *Mktg Dir*
William Hess,
Gary Hess,
EMP: 11 EST: 1969
SQ FT: 23,500
SALES (est): 450.8K **Privately Held**
SIC: 3555 Type casting, founding or melting machines

(G-5934)
HERCULES MACHINE TL & DIE LLC
33901 James J Pompo Dr (48026-3471)
PHONE..................586 778-4120
EMP: 7 **Privately Held**
WEB: www.hmtd.com
SIC: 3544 Special dies, tools, jigs & fixtures
HQ: Hercules Machine Tool & Die Llc
13920 E 10 Mile Rd
Warren MI 48089
586 778-4120

(G-5935)
HHI FORMTECH LLC
Also Called: Fraser Mfg Facility
18450 15 Mile Rd (48026-3460)
PHONE..................586 415-2000
EMP: 40
SALES (corp-wide): 4.7B **Publicly Held**
SIC: 3714 3544 3463 3462 Motor Vehicle Parts And Accessories
HQ: Hhi Formtech, Llc
1 Dauch Dr
Detroit MI

(G-5936)
HI-CRAFT ENGINEERING INC
Also Called: Frost Division
33105 Kelly Rd Ste B (48026-4212)
PHONE..................586 293-0551
Kevin Andre, *President*
Don Nemens, *Vice Pres*
Bill Duke, *CFO*
Karen Speelman, *Accountant*
Maggie Czanstke, *Manager*
EMP: 60
SQ FT: 100,000
SALES (est): 10MM **Privately Held**
WEB: www.hicraftengineering.com
SIC: 3544 3089 Forms (molds), for foundry & plastics working machinery; injection molding of plastics

(G-5937)
HILL MACHINE WORKS LLC
33950 Riviera (48026-1627)
PHONE..................586 238-2897
Nicole Johnson, *Manager*
Walter Hill,
EMP: 10 EST: 2013
SALES (est): 846.1K **Privately Held**
WEB: www.hillmachineworks.com
SIC: 3399 3541 2899 3599 Laminating steel; machine tools, metal cutting type; electrochemical milling machines; fluxes: brazing, soldering, galvanizing & welding; electrical discharge machining (EDM)

(G-5938)
HMR FABRICATION UNLIMITED INC
33830 Riviera (48026-4807)
PHONE..................586 569-4288
Mark Blanchard, *President*
Samantha Klein, *Office Mgr*
EMP: 12 EST: 2015
SALES (est): 3.5MM **Privately Held**
WEB: www.hmrfab.com
SIC: 3548 Welding & cutting apparatus & accessories

(G-5939)
HONEYWELL INTERNATIONAL INC
31807 Utica Rd (48026-3945)
PHONE..................586 777-7870
EMP: 6
SALES (corp-wide): 32.6B **Publicly Held**
WEB: www.honeywell.com
SIC: 3724 Aircraft engines & engine parts
PA: Honeywell International Inc.
855 S Mint St
Charlotte NC 28202
704 627-6200

(G-5940)
HOT TOOL CUTTER GRINDING CO
33545 Groesbeck Hwy (48026-4205)
PHONE..................586 790-4867
George Juncaj, *Owner*
EMP: 9 EST: 1994
SQ FT: 12,000
SALES (est): 447K **Privately Held**
WEB: www.htcmfg.com
SIC: 3541 7699 Machine tools, metal cutting type; knife, saw & tool sharpening & repair

(G-5941)
IANNUZZI MILLWORK INC
33877 Doreka (48026-3473)
PHONE..................586 285-1000
Dominic Iannuzzi, *President*
EMP: 21 EST: 1980
SQ FT: 20,000
SALES (est): 2MM **Privately Held**
WEB: www.iannuzzimillwork.com
SIC: 2431 Interior & ornamental woodwork & trim

(G-5942)
IMAGE MACHINE & TOOL INC
34501 Bennett (48026-1691)
PHONE..................586 466-3400
Kevin Kayne, *President*
EMP: 4 EST: 1995
SALES (est): 373.6K **Privately Held**
WEB: www.imagemachinetool.com
SIC: 3545 Precision tools, machinists'

(G-5943)
INSIDE ENGLISH
16272 Pine Ridge Dr N (48026-5004)
PHONE..................586 801-4351
Sandy Schuman, *Principal*
EMP: 5 EST: 2010
SALES (est): 44.8K **Privately Held**
SIC: 2741 Miscellaneous publishing

(G-5944)
INTER-LAKES BASES INC
17480 Malyn Blvd (48026-1671)
PHONE..................586 294-8120
Barbara Kasper, *President*
David Moore, *Vice Pres*
EMP: 40 EST: 1966
SQ FT: 40,000
SALES (est): 4.9MM **Privately Held**
WEB: www.interlakesbases.com
SIC: 3441 Fabricated structural metal

(G-5945)
INTERPOWER INDUCTION SVCS INC
34197 Doreka (48026-3435)
PHONE..................586 296-7697
Gary M Gariglio, *CEO*
Mike Rugg, *Manager*
EMP: 15 EST: 1991
SALES (est): 2MM **Privately Held**
WEB: www.interpowerinduction.com
SIC: 3567 Induction heating equipment

(G-5946)
JET GAGE & TOOL INC
31265 Kendall (48026-2590)
PHONE..................586 294-3770
Annete C Braun, *President*
Annette C Braun, *President*
Irma Braun, *Corp Secy*
EMP: 4 EST: 1967
SQ FT: 9,500
SALES (est): 517K **Privately Held**
SIC: 3544 Special dies & tools; jigs & fixtures

(G-5947)
JF HUBERT ENTERPRISES INC (PA)
Also Called: Sharp Tooling and Assembly
34480 Commerce (48026-1649)
PHONE..................586 293-8660
Christopher J Hubertt, *CEO*
Christopher J Hubert, *President*
EMP: 14 EST: 1983
SALES (est): 4MM **Privately Held**
SIC: 8711 3541 Machine tool design; machine tools, metal cutting type

(G-5948)
JPS MFG INC
17640 15 Mile Rd (48026-3450)
PHONE..................586 415-8702
Joseph Szacon, *Principal*
EMP: 7 EST: 2011
SALES (est): 833.8K **Privately Held**
WEB: www.jpsmfg.com
SIC: 3541 Machine tools, metal cutting type

(G-5949)
K & F ELECTRONIC INC
Also Called: K&F Electronics
33041 Groesbeck Hwy (48026-1514)
PHONE..................586 294-8720
Richard Kincaid, *President*
Kurt Jogwick, *Maintence Staff*
EMP: 25 EST: 1972
SQ FT: 25,000
SALES (est): 4.1MM **Privately Held**
WEB: www.circuitboards.com
SIC: 3672 Circuit boards, television & radio printed

(G-5950)
KENDOR STEEL RULE DIE INC
31275 Fraser Dr (48026-2572)
PHONE..................586 293-7111
Kenneth Dale Eltringham, *President*
Sean Eltringham, *Purch Mgr*

Kathie McCarthy, *Office Mgr*
EMP: 12 **EST:** 1978
SQ FT: 30,000
SALES (est): 1.9MM **Privately Held**
WEB: www.kendor.com
SIC: 7389 3544 3469 3462 Metal cutting services; dies, steel rule; metal stampings; iron & steel forgings

(G-5951)
KLEINS 3D PRTG SOLUTIONS LLC
15330 Cambridge Dr (48026-2364)
PHONE 586 212-9763
Steven Klein, *Principal*
EMP: 4 **EST:** 2018
SALES (est): 99.5K **Privately Held**
SIC: 2752 Commercial printing, lithographic

(G-5952)
KOCH LIMITED
Also Called: K & K Tool & Die
34230 Riviera (48026-1623)
PHONE 586 296-3103
Joseph J Koch, *President*
Lea Timpf, *Controller*
EMP: 8 **EST:** 2003
SQ FT: 5,000
SALES (est): 774K **Privately Held**
WEB: www.kktdi.com
SIC: 3541 3544 Machine tools, metal cutting type; special dies & tools

(G-5953)
KURT MACHINE TOOL CO INC
33910 Riviera (48026-1627)
P.O. Box 68 (48026-0068)
PHONE 586 296-5070
Michael Phillips, *President*
Christine Phillips, *Corp Secy*
EMP: 10 **EST:** 1975
SQ FT: 11,000
SALES (est): 958.6K **Privately Held**
WEB: www.kurtmachinetool.com
SIC: 3599 Machine shop, jobbing & repair

(G-5954)
L T C ROLL & ENGINEERING CO
31140 Kendall (48026-2501)
PHONE 586 465-1023
Deborah Stephens, *Controller*
EMP: 10
SALES (corp-wide): 19.9MM **Privately Held**
WEB: www.ltcroll.com
SIC: 3714 Motor vehicle parts & accessories
PA: L. T. C. Roll & Engineering Co.
 23500 John Gorsuch Dr
 Clinton Township MI 48036
 586 465-1023

(G-5955)
LASER FAB INC
33901 Riviera (48026-1614)
PHONE 586 415-8090
EMP: 4
SQ FT: 9,000
SALES (est): 480K **Privately Held**
SIC: 3699 3444 Mfg Electrical Equipment/Supplies Mfg Sheet Metalwork

(G-5956)
LASER SPECIALISTS INC
Also Called: LSI
17921 Malyn Blvd Plant 1 1 Plant (48026)
P.O. Box 26189 (48026-6189)
PHONE 586 294-8830
Nicholas J Paquin, *President*
Jon Paquin, *Vice Pres*
EMP: 20 **EST:** 1986
SQ FT: 24,000
SALES (est): 3.5MM **Privately Held**
WEB: www.laserspecialists.com
SIC: 3444 Sheet metalwork

(G-5957)
LEE SPRING COMPANY LLC
34137 Doreka (48026-3435)
P.O. Box 388 (48026-0388)
PHONE 586 296-9850
Steve Kempf, *Branch Mgr*
EMP: 17

SALES (corp-wide): 86.8MM **Privately Held**
WEB: www.leespring.com
SIC: 3495 3493 3315 5085 Wire springs; steel springs, except wire; steel wire & related products; industrial supplies
PA: Lee Spring Company Llc
 140 58th St Ste 3c
 Brooklyn NY 11220
 888 777-4647

(G-5958)
LUMBEE CUSTOM PAINTING LLC
31725 Fraser Dr (48026-2595)
PHONE 586 296-5083
Debra A Garrison,
EMP: 4 **EST:** 2008
SALES (est): 182.2K **Privately Held**
SIC: 3559 Special industry machinery

(G-5959)
M P PUMPS INC
Also Called: Gardner Denver Mp Pumps
34800 Bennett (48026-1694)
PHONE 586 293-8240
Greg Peabody, *President*
Dee Gudenau, *Supervisor*
▲ **EMP:** 90 **EST:** 1989
SQ FT: 90,000
SALES (est): 21.5MM
SALES (corp-wide): 4.9B **Publicly Held**
WEB: www.gardnerdenver.com
SIC: 3594 3561 Fluid power pumps & motors; pumps & pumping equipment
PA: Ingersoll Rand Inc.
 800 Beaty St Ste A
 Davidson NC 28036
 704 896-4000

(G-5960)
MADISON ELECTRIC COMPANY
Madison Electronics Division
17930 E 14 Mile Rd (48026-2291)
PHONE 586 294-8300
Scott Lemaster, *Principal*
Scott Leemaster, *Vice Pres*
Ben Rosenthal, *CFO*
Jim Aras, *Accounts Mgr*
Joel Gibb, *Accounts Mgr*
EMP: 35
SALES (corp-wide): 91.4MM **Privately Held**
WEB: www.madisonelectric.com
SIC: 3355 3357 Aluminum wire & cable; nonferrous wiredrawing & insulating
PA: Madison Electric Company
 31855 Van Dyke Ave
 Warren MI 48093
 586 825-0200

(G-5961)
MAGNUS PRECISION TOOL LLC
34082 James J Pompo Dr (48026-3409)
PHONE 586 285-2500
Christopher Alfastsen,
Pete Pizzimenti,
EMP: 4 **EST:** 1997
SQ FT: 4,800
SALES (est): 400.1K **Privately Held**
WEB: www.magnusprecision.com
SIC: 3599 Machine shop, jobbing & repair

(G-5962)
MARTEN MODELS & MOLDS INC
18291 Mike C Ct (48026-1613)
PHONE 586 293-2260
Steve Marten, *President*
Tom Ruehlete, *Vice Pres*
EMP: 15 **EST:** 1988
SQ FT: 17,000
SALES (est): 2.7MM **Privately Held**
WEB: www.martenmodels.com
SIC: 3544 3543 Industrial molds; industrial patterns

(G-5963)
MILO BORING & MACHINING INC
34275 Riviera (48026-1624)
PHONE 586 293-8611
Ilija Milosavlevski, *President*
EMP: 4 **EST:** 1996
SALES (est): 440.6K **Privately Held**
WEB: www.cbsboring.com
SIC: 3599 Machine shop, jobbing & repair

(G-5964)
MODERN TOOL AND TAPPING INC
33517 Kelly Rd (48026-4231)
PHONE 586 777-5144
Cynthia Gohlke, *President*
EMP: 7 **EST:** 2004
SALES (est): 500K **Privately Held**
WEB: www.moderntooltapping.com
SIC: 3549 Metalworking machinery

(G-5965)
MOLD-RITE LLC (PA)
33830 Riviera (48026-4807)
PHONE 586 296-3970
Barry Daggett, *Vice Pres*
Keith Kelble, *Vice Pres*
Eric Zeisloft, *Vice Pres*
Erica Miglets, *Human Res Mgr*
Matt Baker, *Sales Mgr*
EMP: 6 **EST:** 2009
SQ FT: 5,000
SALES (est): 1.2MM **Privately Held**
WEB: www.mold-rite.com
SIC: 3089 Injection molding of plastics; molding primary plastic

(G-5966)
MS CHIP INC
34137 Doreka (48026-3435)
P.O. Box 388 (48026-0388)
PHONE 586 296-9850
W E Tillinger Sr, *President*
Joseph Tillinger, *Treasurer*
W E Tillinger Jr, *Shareholder*
EMP: 17 **EST:** 1961
SQ FT: 15,000
SALES (est): 3.2MM
SALES (corp-wide): 86.8MM **Privately Held**
WEB: www.msspring.com
SIC: 3493 3495 Flat springs, sheet or strip stock; instrument springs, precision
PA: Lee Spring Company Llc
 140 58th St Ste 3c
 Brooklyn NY 11220
 888 777-4647

(G-5967)
NEW METHOD STEEL STAMPS INC
17801 Helro (48026-3818)
P.O. Box 338 (48026-0338)
PHONE 586 293-0200
Charles Brown II, *President*
Lavonda Cary, *Sales Staff*
▼ **EMP:** 6 **EST:** 1931
SQ FT: 10,000
SALES (est): 866.3K **Privately Held**
WEB: www.newmethod.com
SIC: 3953 Embossing seals & hand stamps

(G-5968)
NEW WORLD ETCHING N AMER VE
Also Called: World Etching North America Ve
33870 Riviera (48026-4807)
PHONE 586 296-8082
Vic Barbu,
EMP: 6 **EST:** 2010
SALES (est): 410.2K **Privately Held**
WEB: www.nwe-na.com
SIC: 2759 Engraving

(G-5969)
NEW-MATIC INDUSTRIES INC
31256 Fraser Dr (48026-2571)
PHONE 586 415-9801
Ronald Secord, *President*
Greg Karlichek, *Vice Pres*
EMP: 7 **EST:** 1983
SQ FT: 8,000
SALES (est): 656.6K **Privately Held**
SIC: 3559 Automotive related machinery

(G-5970)
NOVA INDUSTRIES INC
34180 Klein Rd (48026-3020)
PHONE 586 294-9182
Thomas Kruger, *CEO*
EMP: 38 **EST:** 1993
SALES (est): 9.2MM **Privately Held**
WEB: www.nova-ind.net
SIC: 3089 Injection molding of plastics

(G-5971)
ORLANDI GEAR COMPANY INC
17755 Masonic (48026-3158)
PHONE 586 285-9900
Michael Schiavi, *President*
Carlos Hernandez, *Plant Mgr*
Mark Berlin, *Mfg Staff*
Mike Kelmigian, *Treasurer*
Linda Baysdell, *Office Mgr*
EMP: 47 **EST:** 1944
SQ FT: 33,000
SALES (est): 8.5MM **Privately Held**
WEB: www.orlandigear.com
SIC: 3566 Gears, power transmission, except automotive

(G-5972)
OSBORNE TRANSFORMER CORP
33258 Groesbeck Hwy (48026-1597)
P.O. Box 70 (48026-0070)
PHONE 586 218-6900
James R Osborne, *President*
Suzanne Osborne, *Vice Pres*
EMP: 10 **EST:** 1932
SALES (est): 1MM **Privately Held**
WEB: www.osbornetransformer.com
SIC: 3612 5063 3677 Power transformers, electric; electrical apparatus & equipment; electronic coils, transformers & other inductors

(G-5973)
PALMER DISTRIBUTORS INC
Also Called: Palmer Promotional Products
33525 Groesbeck Hwy (48026-4205)
PHONE 586 772-4225
Jim Palmer, *President*
Jim Wennechuk, *Vice Pres*
Al Vespa, *Mfg Staff*
Bruce Barr, *Production*
Alex Felmlee, *Purch Mgr*
◆ **EMP:** 100 **EST:** 1953
SQ FT: 66,000
SALES (est): 18.9MM **Privately Held**
WEB: www.palmermetropcs.com
SIC: 3089 2821 Molding primary plastic; plastics materials & resins

(G-5974)
PARAGON MOLDS CORPORATION
33997 Riviera (48026-1670)
PHONE 586 294-7630
Daniel V Smoger, *President*
David M Smoger, *Vice Pres*
EMP: 31 **EST:** 1973
SQ FT: 15,200
SALES (est): 1MM **Privately Held**
WEB: www.kiefel.com
SIC: 3544 3999 3543 Industrial molds; models, general, except toy; industrial patterns

(G-5975)
PATMAI COMPANY INC
31425 Fraser Dr (48026-2584)
PHONE 586 294-0370
Edwin S Maddox, *President*
James Defer, *Vice Pres*
Tamita Weigand, *Office Mgr*
▲ **EMP:** 14 **EST:** 1963
SQ FT: 14,000
SALES (est): 1.1MM **Privately Held**
WEB: www.patmai-co.com
SIC: 3471 Buffing for the trade; polishing, metals or formed products

(G-5976)
PCS COMPANY (DH)
34488 Doreka (48026-3438)
PHONE 586 294-7780
Ed Mohrbach, *President*
Randy S Wissinger, *VP Finance*
Bruce Konopinski, *Sales Mgr*
Tom Berchulc, *Sales Staff*
Kory Kline, *Marketing Mgr*
▲ **EMP:** 94 **EST:** 1960
SQ FT: 40,000
SALES (est): 29.4MM **Privately Held**
WEB: www.pcs-company.com
SIC: 3544 Special dies, tools, jigs & fixtures

HQ: Dayton Progress Corporation
500 Progress Rd
Dayton OH 45449
937 859-5111

(G-5977)
POETRY FACTORY LTD
34028 James J Pompo Dr (48026-1643)
PHONE.................................586 296-3125
Symella S Chengges, *President*
EMP: 5 **EST:** 2009
SQ FT: 3,000 **Privately Held**
WEB: www.thepoetryfactory.net
SIC: 3499 Novelties & giftware, including trophies

(G-5978)
POLARIS ENGINEERING INC
17540 15 Mile Rd (48026-1603)
PHONE.................................586 296-1603
Michael Burns, *President*
EMP: 10 **EST:** 1968
SQ FT: 12,000
SALES (est): 1.5MM **Privately Held**
WEB: www.polarisenginc.com
SIC: 3599 Machine shop, jobbing & repair

(G-5979)
PRIMA WLDG & EXPERIMENTAL INC
31000 Fraser Dr (48026-2503)
PHONE.................................586 415-8873
Dale Lohr, *President*
EMP: 7 **EST:** 1977
SQ FT: 5,200
SALES (est): 532.2K **Privately Held**
WEB: www.primawelding.com
SIC: 7692 Welding repair

(G-5980)
PRODUCT AND TOOLING TECH INC
Also Called: P T T
33957 Riviera (48026-1614)
PHONE.................................586 293-1810
Mark Fritz, *President*
Candice Calabrese, *General Mgr*
Luke Fritz, *Vice Pres*
Chad Romanelli, *Vice Pres*
Jon Deimel, *Controller*
EMP: 40 **EST:** 1996
SALES (est): 8.8MM **Privately Held**
WEB: www.pttech.us
SIC: 3544 3542 Special dies & tools; die casting & extruding machines

(G-5981)
PROTOJET LLC
17850 E 14 Mile Rd (48026-2271)
PHONE.................................810 956-8000
Eric J Gunderson, *President*
Tim Legato, *General Mgr*
Stephen Gunderson, *Mfg Dir*
Steve Gunderson, *Mfg Staff*
Mark Rohloff, *Sales Staff*
EMP: 13 **EST:** 2007
SQ FT: 9,000
SALES (est): 4.2MM **Privately Held**
WEB: www.protojet.com
SIC: 3089 3999 Synthetic resin finished products; models, general, except toy

(G-5982)
PT TECH STAMPING INC
33222 Groesbeck Hwy (48026-1597)
PHONE.................................586 293-1810
Mark Fritz, *CEO*
Jerry Swims, *President*
EMP: 25 **EST:** 2003
SALES (est): 4.9MM **Privately Held**
WEB: www.pttech.us
SIC: 3465 3542 Automotive stampings; machine tools, metal forming type

(G-5983)
QUALITY GRINDING INC
33950 Riviera (48026-1627)
PHONE.................................586 293-3780
Fax: 586 293-3782
EMP: 4
SQ FT: 10,000
SALES (est): 320K **Privately Held**
SIC: 3599 Machine Shop

(G-5984)
QUANTUM CUSTOM DESIGNS LLC
Also Called: Qcd
33771 Groesbeck Hwy (48026-4207)
PHONE.................................989 293-7372
Dorothy Kubisz, *CEO*
EMP: 4 **EST:** 2016
SALES (est): 100K **Privately Held**
WEB: www.qcdx4.com
SIC: 3999 3469 Manufacturing industries; metal stampings

(G-5985)
R T GORDON INC
33792 Doreka (48026-3430)
PHONE.................................586 294-6100
Mark Gordon, *Vice Pres*
EMP: 21 **EST:** 1975
SQ FT: 40,000
SALES (est): 1MM **Privately Held**
SIC: 3545 3544 3429 Machine tool accessories; special dies, tools, jigs & fixtures; manufactured hardware (general)

(G-5986)
REGER MANUFACTURING COMPANY
31375 Fraser Dr (48026-2552)
PHONE.................................586 293-5096
Gale English, *CEO*
Gale W English, *CEO*
Alfred English, *President*
Matthew English, *Vice Pres*
Brandon Purcell, *Vice Pres*
EMP: 9 **EST:** 1949
SALES (est): 1.7MM **Privately Held**
WEB: www.regermfg.com
SIC: 3544 3549 Special dies & tools; jigs & fixtures; metalworking machinery

(G-5987)
RENAS FUDGE SHOPS INC
31181 Kendall (48026-3917)
P.O. Box 1410, Mackinac Island (49757-1410)
PHONE.................................586 293-0600
Rena Callewaert, *President*
Lillian Schaldenbrand, *Treasurer*
EMP: 15 **EST:** 1988
SALES (est): 1.2MM **Privately Held**
SIC: 2064 5145 5441 2066 Candy & other confectionery products; confectionery; candy, nut & confectionery stores; chocolate & cocoa products

(G-5988)
REVERE PLASTICS SYSTEMS LLC
18401 Malyn Blvd (48026-1628)
PHONE.................................586 415-4823
Dawn Shotts, *Office Mgr*
Kevin Stolzenfeld, *Director*
Josephine Schutt, *Executive*
Dave Wesner, *Maintence Staff*
EMP: 200
SALES (corp-wide): 21.1MM **Privately Held**
WEB: www.revereindustries.com
SIC: 3089 Injection molding of plastics
HQ: Revere Plastics Systems, Llc
39555 Orchard Hill Pl # 155
Novi MI 48375

(G-5989)
RICHTER PRECISION INC
17741 Malyn Blvd (48026-1632)
PHONE.................................586 465-0500
Mark Good, *Production*
Ming Peng, *Engineer*
Randy Badger, *Regl Sales Mgr*
Jackie Fenton, *Sales Staff*
Thomas Grammer, *Sales Staff*
EMP: 30
SALES (corp-wide): 24.5MM **Privately Held**
WEB: www.richterprecision.com
SIC: 3479 3398 2851 Coating of metals & formed products; metal heat treating; paints & allied products
PA: Richter Precision, Inc.
1021 Commercial Ave
East Petersburg PA 17520
717 560-9990

(G-5990)
RX-RITE OPTICAL CO
32925 Groesbeck Hwy (48026-3155)
PHONE.................................586 293-8888
Anthony C Stefani, *President*
Corine Stefani, *Treasurer*
EMP: 9 **EST:** 1973
SQ FT: 1,500
SALES (est): 548.6K **Privately Held**
SIC: 3851 8042 Lens grinding, except prescription: ophthalmic; offices & clinics of optometrists

(G-5991)
SCORPION RELOADS LLC
34054 James J Pompo Dr (48026-3408)
PHONE.................................586 214-3843
Jeff Doolin III, *Principal*
EMP: 9 **EST:** 2010
SALES (est): 289.1K **Privately Held**
WEB: www.scorpionreloads.com
SIC: 3482 Cartridge cases for ammunition, 30 mm. & below; pellets & BB's, pistol & air rifle ammunition

(G-5992)
SGC INDUSTRIES INC
17430 Malyn Blvd (48026-1635)
PHONE.................................586 293-5260
Robert Diez, *President*
EMP: 7 **EST:** 2008
SALES (est): 238.4K **Privately Held**
WEB: www.dorrisco.com
SIC: 3728 3724 3711 3841 Gears, aircraft power transmission; aircraft engines & engine parts; universal carriers, military, assembly of; surgical & medical instruments; automotive related machinery; guided missile & space vehicle parts & auxiliary equipment

(G-5993)
SHARP DIE & MOLD CO
Also Called: Hubert Group
34480 Commerce (48026-1649)
PHONE.................................586 293-8660
Josef Hubert, *President*
Brian Lorenz, *Corp Secy*
John Hubert, *Vice Pres*
EMP: 10 **EST:** 1967
SQ FT: 24,000
SALES (est): 680K **Privately Held**
SIC: 3544 3549 Industrial molds; special dies & tools; metalworking machinery

(G-5994)
SOYAD BROTHERS TEXTILE CORP
Also Called: Quality Socks
34272 Doreka (48026-1659)
PHONE.................................586 755-5700
Toufic Soyad, *President*
Leba Soyad, *Vice Pres*
George Soyad, *Treasurer*
Joseph Soyad, *Admin Sec*
▲ **EMP:** 20 **EST:** 1977
SQ FT: 26,000
SALES (est): 1.1MM **Privately Held**
WEB: www.soyadsocks.com
SIC: 2252 Socks

(G-5995)
SPARTAN CARBIDE INC
34110 Riviera (48026-4811)
PHONE.................................586 285-9786
Mark Maron, *President*
Thomas Haaberski, *Vice Pres*
Kevin Haberski, *Sales Staff*
Nanci Wishon, *Office Mgr*
EMP: 50 **EST:** 1973
SQ FT: 20,000
SALES (est): 6.5MM **Privately Held**
WEB: www.spartancarbide.com
SIC: 3545 Cutting tools for machine tools

(G-5996)
SPECIAL TOOL & ENGINEERING INC (PA)
33910 James J Pompo Dr (48026-3470)
PHONE.................................586 285-5900
Andre F Special, *President*
Enrico Gualtieri, *Vice Pres*
Jodi Baxter, *Prdtn Mgr*
Bob Currie, *Manager*
EMP: 75 **EST:** 1993

SQ FT: 43,000
SALES (est): 10.1MM **Privately Held**
WEB: www.specialtool.net
SIC: 3544 Special dies & tools

(G-5997)
SPECIALTY COATINGS INC (PA)
33835 Kelly Rd (48026-1503)
PHONE.................................586 294-8343
Dan Brownlee, *President*
Larry Alexander, *Sales Staff*
Curtis Esch, *Sales Staff*
Anthony Citraro, *Administration*
▼ **EMP:** 9 **EST:** 1997
SQ FT: 17,280
SALES (est): 1.3MM **Privately Held**
WEB: www.specialtycoatingsinc.com
SIC: 2851 Epoxy coatings

(G-5998)
SPECIALTY STEEL TREATING INC (PA)
34501 Commerce (48026-1692)
PHONE.................................586 293-5355
Martha Parker, *CEO*
Harold Cox, *President*
Mary Verhelle, *President*
Anthony Richey, *General Mgr*
Brandon Couture, *Business Mgr*
EMP: 45 **EST:** 1956
SQ FT: 30,000
SALES (est): 56.3MM **Privately Held**
WEB: www.sst.net
SIC: 5051 3423 3715 3339 Metals service centers & offices; hand & edge tools; aluminum foundries; primary nonferrous metals; primary copper; brazing (hardening) of metal

(G-5999)
SPLIT SECOND DEFENSE LLC
34024 James J Pompo Dr (48026-1643)
PHONE.................................586 709-1385
Jeff Doolin, *Principal*
EMP: 5 **EST:** 2017
SALES (est): 126.9K **Privately Held**
SIC: 3812 Defense systems & equipment

(G-6000)
STANDEX INTERNATIONAL CORP
Also Called: Mold Tech Michigan
34497 Kelly Rd (48026-3404)
PHONE.................................586 296-5500
Omar Ahmed, *Research*
Robert Hamood, *Branch Mgr*
EMP: 45
SALES (corp-wide): 656.2MM **Publicly Held**
WEB: www.standex.com
SIC: 2796 Engraving on copper, steel, wood or rubber; printing plates
PA: Standex International Corporation
23 Keewaydin Dr Ste 300
Salem NH 03079
603 893-9701

(G-6001)
SUPREME GEAR CO (PA)
17430 Malyn Blvd (48026)
PHONE.................................586 775-6325
Robert A Diez, *President*
Thom Bone, *Purchasing*
Michael Sigman, *QC Mgr*
Dwight Merrill, *Engineer*
Stephan Nieman, *Engineer*
EMP: 29 **EST:** 1951
SQ FT: 70,000
SALES (est): 9.6MM **Privately Held**
SIC: 3724 3711 3795 3841 Aircraft engines & engine parts; motor vehicles & car bodies; tanks & tank components; surgical & medical instruments; power transmission equipment

(G-6002)
T & M MACHINING INC
18110 E 14 Mile Rd (48026-2295)
PHONE.................................586 294-5781
Tim Wolf, *President*
EMP: 7 **EST:** 1996
SQ FT: 5,000
SALES (est): 919K **Privately Held**
WEB: www.tmmachining.com
SIC: 3599 Machine shop, jobbing & repair

(G-6003)
TOOL SERVICE COMPANY INC
34150 Riviera (48026-4811)
PHONE..............................586 296-2500
Bruce Bellard, *President*
EMP: 8 **EST:** 1929
SQ FT: 12,000
SALES (est): 1.6MM **Privately Held**
SIC: 3545 Cutting tools for machine tools

(G-6004)
TOP SHELF PAINTER INC
34400 Klein Rd (48026-3009)
PHONE..............................586 465-0867
Peter Rinaldi, *Principal*
EMP: 18 **EST:** 2014
SALES (est): 653.6K **Privately Held**
WEB: www.topshelfus.com
SIC: 1721 1389 1522 Residential painting; construction, repair & dismantling services; residential construction

(G-6005)
TRINITY INDUSTRIES INC
33910 James J Pompo Dr (48026-3470)
PHONE..............................586 285-1692
Lee Powers, *Superintendent*
Martin Erwin, *Vice Pres*
Robert Chandler, *Warehouse Mgr*
Jazmin Tillman, *HR Admin*
Alexandra Priputen, *Sales Staff*
EMP: 5
SALES (corp-wide): 2B **Publicly Held**
WEB: www.trin.net
SIC: 3743 Freight cars & equipment
PA: Trinity Industries, Inc.
 14221 Dallas Pkwy # 1100
 Dallas TX 75254
 214 631-4420

(G-6006)
TRINITY TOOL CO
Also Called: Trinco
34600 Commerce (48026-1690)
P.O. Box 98 (48026-0098)
PHONE..............................586 296-5900
Katherine Boyle, *President*
William Boyle, *Vice Pres*
Karen Boyle, *Treasurer*
Todd Johnson, *Mng Member*
▼ **EMP:** 25 **EST:** 1951
SQ FT: 44,000
SALES (est): 4.2MM **Privately Held**
WEB: www.trinco.com
SIC: 3569 3549 3291 Blast cleaning equipment, dustless; metalworking machinery; abrasive products

(G-6007)
TURN TECH INC
33901 Riviera (48026-1614)
PHONE..............................586 415-8090
Leonard Johnson, *President*
Jillian Harris, *Assistant*
EMP: 20 **EST:** 1988
SQ FT: 9,000
SALES (est): 580.8K **Privately Held**
SIC: 3599 Machine shop, jobbing & repair

(G-6008)
UNICOTE CORPORATION
33165 Groesbeck Hwy (48026-1596)
P.O. Box 426 (48026-0426)
PHONE..............................586 296-0700
Thomas G Kury, *President*
Chuck Gietzen, *Engineer*
Adam Horetski, *Administration*
EMP: 35 **EST:** 1966
SQ FT: 35,000
SALES (est): 1.3MM **Privately Held**
WEB: www.unicotecorporation.com
SIC: 3479 Coating of metals & formed products

(G-6009)
UNITED STTES SCKET SCREW MFG C (PA)
Also Called: United Dowel Pin Mfg Co
33891 Doreka (48026-3473)
PHONE..............................586 469-8871
Jac A Roth, *President*
Andrew Roth, *Vice Pres*
▲ **EMP:** 14 **EST:** 1961

SALES (est): 5.7MM **Privately Held**
SIC: 5072 3542 Screws; nuts (hardware); bolts; miscellaneous fasteners; punching & shearing machines

(G-6010)
VAN-DIES ENGINEERING INC
17525 Helro (48026-2252)
P.O. Box 408, Roseville (48066-0408)
PHONE..............................586 293-1430
Gary Vanhoorne, *President*
EMP: 20 **EST:** 2007
SQ FT: 10,000
SALES (est): 2.3MM **Privately Held**
SIC: 3469 Stamping metal for the trade

(G-6011)
VISIONEERING INC
17085 Masonic (48026-3927)
PHONE..............................248 622-5600
Brad Hallett, *Branch Mgr*
EMP: 30
SALES (corp-wide): 60.6MM **Privately Held**
WEB: www.vistool.com
SIC: 3728 Aircraft assemblies, subassemblies & parts
PA: Visioneering, Inc.
 2055 Taylor Rd
 Auburn Hills MI 48326
 248 622-5600

(G-6012)
WIRE DYNAMICS INC
18210 Malyn Blvd (48026-1631)
PHONE..............................586 879-0321
George Kozel, *President*
Jeff Kozel, *Vice Pres*
EMP: 5 **EST:** 1977
SQ FT: 2,400
SALES (est): 540K **Privately Held**
WEB: www.wiredynamics.com
SIC: 3544 Jigs & fixtures

(G-6013)
YARBROUGH PRECISION SCREWS LLC
17722 Rainbow (48026-2420)
PHONE..............................586 776-0752
EMP: 11
SALES (est): 2MM **Privately Held**
SIC: 3451 Mfg Precision Ball Screw

Frederic
Crawford County

(G-6014)
AUSABLE WOODWORKING CO INC
6677 Frederic St (49733-8761)
P.O. Box 108 (49733-0108)
PHONE..............................989 348-7086
EMP: 35
SALES: 1MM **Privately Held**
SIC: 2499 3993 3873 Mfg Wood Products Mfg Signs/Ad Specialties Mfg Watches/Clocks/Parts

(G-6015)
FLUIDTHERM CORP MICHIGAN
7730 Old 27 N (49733-9732)
PHONE..............................989 344-1500
Roger L Brummel, *President*
Brenda Brummel, *Admin Sec*
EMP: 4 **EST:** 1972
SQ FT: 5,000
SALES (est): 260K **Privately Held**
WEB: www.fluid-therm.com
SIC: 3567 Industrial furnaces & ovens

(G-6016)
NORTHERN WOODCRAFTERS
8449 W Hulbert Rd (49733-9775)
PHONE..............................989 348-2553
Scott Page, *Owner*
EMP: 6 **EST:** 2006
SALES (est): 433.7K **Privately Held**
WEB: www.northernwoodcrafters.com
SIC: 3553 Furniture makers' machinery, woodworking

Freeland
Saginaw County

(G-6017)
ACCURATE SAFETY DISTRS INC
Also Called: A S D
10320 Thor Dr (48623-8804)
PHONE..............................989 695-6446
Dennis Peden, *President*
Nancy Lantz, *Controller*
Sarah Pierce, *Sales Mgr*
Mike Corner, *Sales Staff*
EMP: 9 **EST:** 1974
SQ FT: 12,000
SALES (est): 1.6MM **Privately Held**
WEB: www.accsafety.com
SIC: 5084 3842 Safety equipment; surgical appliances & supplies

(G-6018)
ALLEN MODELS OF MICHIGAN LLC
9961 Buck Rd (48623-8602)
PHONE..............................989 284-8866
Karen Knox, *Principal*
EMP: 6 **EST:** 2012
SALES (est): 100.3K **Privately Held**
WEB: www.allenmodels.com
SIC: 3999 Manufacturing industries

(G-6019)
BUSCH MACHINE TOOL SUPPLY LLC
7251 Midland Rd (48623-8760)
PHONE..............................989 798-4794
Greg Busch, *President*
EMP: 4 **EST:** 2007
SQ FT: 12,000 **Privately Held**
WEB: www.buschmachinetool.com
SIC: 3999 5251 5085 Atomizers, toiletry; tools; tools

(G-6020)
DESIGNTECH CUSTOM INTERIORS
8570 Carter Rd (48623-9008)
PHONE..............................989 695-6306
Greg Awad, *Owner*
Joseph Rutkiewicz, *Vice Pres*
EMP: 4 **EST:** 1987
SQ FT: 6,000 **Privately Held**
WEB: www.designtechonline.com
SIC: 1751 5712 2434 Cabinet building & installation; customized furniture & cabinets; vanities, bathroom; wood

(G-6021)
DOW CHEMICAL COMPANY
M B S Intl Hngr 5 (48623)
PHONE..............................989 695-2584
Daniel Grohol, *Research*
Dan Carroll, *Manager*
Keith Macdonald, *Manager*
David Born, *Director*
Stacy Kontranowski, *Admin Asst*
EMP: 4
SALES (corp-wide): 38.5B **Publicly Held**
WEB: www.dow.com
SIC: 2869 Industrial organic chemicals
HQ: The Dow Chemical Company
 2211 H H Dow Way
 Midland MI 48642
 989 636-1000

(G-6022)
EGGERS EXCAVATING LLC
7832 Kochville Rd Ste 1 (48623-8003)
P.O. Box 5908, Saginaw (48603-0908)
PHONE..............................989 695-5205
Chadwick Eggers, *Mng Member*
Russell Eggers, *Mng Member*
EMP: 11 **EST:** 2013
SALES (est): 2.4MM **Privately Held**
SIC: 1794 6531 1499 1422 Excavation work; real estate leasing & rentals; asphalt mining & bituminous stone quarrying; crushed & broken limestone; industrial sand

(G-6023)
EOVATIONS LLC (HQ)
12629 Whisper Ridge Dr (48623-9548)
PHONE..............................989 671-1460

Claude Brown, *President*
John Teller, *General Mgr*
EMP: 1 **EST:** 2010
SQ FT: 75,000
SALES (est): 1.7MM
SALES (corp-wide): 5.1B **Publicly Held**
WEB: www.eovationsllc.com
SIC: 2821 Thermoplastic materials
PA: Ufp Industries, Inc.
 2801 E Beltline Ave Ne
 Grand Rapids MI 49525
 616 364-6161

(G-6024)
FRONT LINE SERVICES INC
Also Called: Slsi
8588 Carter Rd (48623-9008)
PHONE..............................989 695-6633
Jeffrey T Simon, *President*
Wendy Simon, *Vice Pres*
Dale Rottman, *Technician*
EMP: 13 **EST:** 1990
SQ FT: 6,500
SALES (est): 2.5MM **Privately Held**
WEB: www.flsi.net
SIC: 7538 5087 5012 3569 General automotive repair shops; firefighting equipment; fire trucks; firefighting apparatus & related equipment

(G-6025)
MJBCUSTOMWOODWORKING
8850 N Orr Rd (48623-9508)
PHONE..............................989 695-2737
Michael J Bain, *Principal*
EMP: 5 **EST:** 2011
SALES (est): 158.5K **Privately Held**
SIC: 2431 Millwork

(G-6026)
MMGG INC
Also Called: Falcon Asphalt Repair Eqp
2600 Salzburg Rd (48623-9324)
PHONE..............................989 324-7319
Mark Groulx, *Principal*
EMP: 9 **EST:** 2004
SALES (est): 539.6K **Privately Held**
SIC: 1499 Asphalt mining & bituminous stone quarrying

(G-6027)
R & M MACHINE TOOL INC
7920 Webster Rd (48623-8400)
P.O. Box 746 (48623-0746)
PHONE..............................989 695-6601
Ronald Miller Jr, *President*
EMP: 23 **EST:** 1995
SQ FT: 7,000
SALES (est): 3.5MM **Privately Held**
WEB: www.rmmachine.com
SIC: 3599 Machine shop, jobbing & repair

(G-6028)
RIDGE LOCOMOTIVE
9961 Buck Rd (48623-8602)
PHONE..............................989 714-4671
EMP: 5 **EST:** 2019
SALES (est): 95.4K **Privately Held**
WEB: www.ridgeboiler.com
SIC: 7692 Welding repair

(G-6029)
SAGINAW KNITTING MILLS INC
8788 Carter Rd (48623-8679)
P.O. Box 218 (48623-0218)
PHONE..............................989 695-2481
Terry W Grenell, *President*
Marie Grenell, *Vice Pres*
EMP: 15 **EST:** 1974
SALES (est): 1.7MM **Privately Held**
WEB: www.saginawkm.com
SIC: 2396 2395 Screen printing on fabric articles; embroidery products, except schiffli machine

(G-6030)
TODD R LRCQUE PNTG WLLCVRING L
Also Called: Todd R Larocque Home Imprv
8521 Pierce Rd (48623-9043)
PHONE..............................989 252-9424
Todd Larocque, *President*
EMP: 6 **EST:** 2019

SALES (est): 360.3K **Privately Held**
WEB: www.larocquepainting.com
SIC: 1721 3479 Exterior residential painting contractor; exterior commercial painting contractor; commercial wallcovering contractor; residential wallcovering contractor; painting of metal products

(G-6031)
WILLSIE LUMBER COMPANY
9770 Pierce Rd (48623-8101)
P.O. Box 603 (48623-0603)
PHONE..........................989 695-5094
Denny Willsie, *President*
EMP: 10 **EST:** 1935
SQ FT: 20,000
SALES (est): 2.6MM **Privately Held**
WEB: www.willsielumber.com
SIC: 2421 Planing mills; furniture dimension stock, softwood

Freeport
Barry County

(G-6032)
BUSKIRK LUMBER COMPANY
319 Oak St (49325-9472)
P.O. Box 11 (49325-0011)
PHONE..........................616 765-5103
Paul Kamps, *Owner*
Ken Jones, *General Mgr*
Robert Zandstra, *Executive*
EMP: 21 **EST:** 2008
SALES (est): 2.5MM **Privately Held**
WEB: www.buskirklumber.com
SIC: 2421 Sawmills & planing mills, general

(G-6033)
FREEPORT MILLING
223 Division St (49325-9757)
P.O. Box 1 (49325-0001)
PHONE..........................616 765-8421
Dan Fighter, *Principal*
EMP: 6 **EST:** 2009
SALES (est): 323.7K **Privately Held**
WEB: www.freeportmichigan.org
SIC: 2041 Flour & other grain mill products

(G-6034)
KETCHUM MACHINE CORPORATED
219 Oak St (49325-9471)
P.O. Box 26 (49325-0026)
PHONE..........................616 765-5101
Geoffrey G Ketchum, *President*
Duane Alerding, *Vice Pres*
Cynthia S Ketchum, *Treasurer*
Lucinda B Ketchum, *Admin Sec*
EMP: 18 **EST:** 1957
SQ FT: 18,500
SALES (est): 734.7K **Privately Held**
WEB: www.ketchummachine.com
SIC: 3544 3599 Special dies & tools; custom machinery

(G-6035)
MUNN MANUFACTURING COMPANY
312 County Line Rd (49325-5108)
P.O. Box 24 (49325-0024)
PHONE..........................616 765-3067
Steve Buehler, *President*
Wendy Buehler, *Treasurer*
EMP: 46 **EST:** 1967
SQ FT: 12,500
SALES (est): 5.1MM **Privately Held**
WEB: www.munnman.com
SIC: 3599 3469 Machine shop, jobbing & repair; custom machinery; metal stampings

(G-6036)
PARAGON MODEL SHOP INC
10083 Thompson Rd (49325-9623)
PHONE..........................616 693-3224
Janet Mc Intyre, *President*
Randy McIntyre, *Vice Pres*
EMP: 4 **EST:** 1984
SQ FT: 12,000
SALES (est): 685.9K **Privately Held**
WEB: www.paragonmodelshop.com
SIC: 3599 Machine shop, jobbing & repair

Fremont
Newaygo County

(G-6037)
CONSUMERS CONCRETE CORPORATION
4550 W 72nd St (49412-7316)
PHONE..........................231 924-6131
Mike Woodward, *Director*
EMP: 12
SALES (corp-wide): 42.6MM **Privately Held**
WEB: www.consumersconcrete.com
SIC: 3273 Ready-mixed concrete
PA: Consumers Concrete Corporation
  3506 Lovers Ln
  Kalamazoo MI 49001
  269 342-0136

(G-6038)
CR FORGE LLC
1914 S Comstock Ave (49412-8034)
PHONE..........................231 924-2033
Christopher Ellesson, *Principal*
EMP: 11 **EST:** 2005
SALES (est): 1.2MM **Privately Held**
WEB: www.crforge.com
SIC: 3446 Architectural metalwork

(G-6039)
DUS OPERATING INC
Also Called: Dura Automotive Systems
502 Connie Ave (49412-1812)
PHONE..........................231 924-0930
Tim Stevens, *Branch Mgr*
Laura Flanagan, *Exec Dir*
EMP: 7
SALES (corp-wide): 847.6MM **Privately Held**
SIC: 3714 Motor vehicle parts & accessories
HQ: Dus Operating Inc.
  1780 Pond Run
  Auburn Hills MI 48326
  248 299-7500

(G-6040)
FLAT-TO-FORM METAL SPC INC
9577 W 40th St (49412-8017)
PHONE..........................231 924-1288
Patrick Brown, *President*
Kevin Dummer, *Admin Sec*
EMP: 10 **EST:** 1995
SQ FT: 9,000
SALES (est): 600K **Privately Held**
WEB: www.flattoform.com
SIC: 3441 Fabricated structural metal

(G-6041)
FREMONT GENERATE DIGESTER LLC
Also Called: Fremont Regional Digester
1634 Locust St (49412-1870)
PHONE..........................231 924-9401
Matthew Goodman, *Principal*
EMP: 8 **EST:** 2016
SALES (est): 417K **Privately Held**
WEB: www.fremontdigester.com
SIC: 2834 Pharmaceutical preparations

(G-6042)
GERBER PRODUCTS COMPANY
405 State St (49412-1056)
PHONE..........................231 928-2076
Thomas Boerger, *Plant Mgr*
Jennifer Larkey, *Safety Mgr*
Seth Braafhart, *Train & Dev Mgr*
Craig Thompson, *Branch Mgr*
Trisha Shoemaker, *Director*
EMP: 20
SALES (corp-wide): 92.3B **Privately Held**
WEB: www.gerber.com
SIC: 2023 Dry, condensed, evaporated dairy products
HQ: Gerber Products Company
  12 Vreeland Rd Fl 2
  Florham Park NJ 07932
  973 593-7500

(G-6043)
GERBER PRODUCTS COMPANY
Also Called: Nestle Infant Nutrition
445 State St (49413-0001)
PHONE..........................231 928-2000
Craig Thompson, *Branch Mgr*
Cecile Smith, *Analyst*
Rolando Patino, *Maintence Staff*
EMP: 20
SALES (corp-wide): 92.3B **Privately Held**
WEB: www.gerber.com
SIC: 2023 Baby formulas
HQ: Gerber Products Company
  12 Vreeland Rd Fl 2
  Florham Park NJ 07932
  973 593-7500

(G-6044)
GIBBIES DEER PROCESSING
215 Jerrette Ave (49412-1025)
PHONE..........................231 924-6042
Jeff Gibbie, *Owner*
EMP: 7 **EST:** 1985
SALES (est): 92.9K **Privately Held**
SIC: 2011 Meat packing plants

(G-6045)
HI-LITES GRAPHIC INC (PA)
Also Called: Hi-Lites Shoppers Guide
1212 Locust St (49412-1858)
PHONE..........................231 924-0630
Jon Sovinski, *President*
Thomas Kowalski, *Corp Secy*
Mike McMillan, *Vice Pres*
Mary Justian, *Executive Asst*
Stacie Ramirez, *Graphic Designe*
EMP: 30 **EST:** 1948
SQ FT: 15,000
SALES (est): 2.7MM **Privately Held**
WEB: www.hi-litesgraphics.com
SIC: 2752 2741 7336 2791 Commercial printing, offset; shopping news: publishing only, not printed on site; silk screen design; typesetting; bookbinding & related work

(G-6046)
K-MAR STRUCTURES LLC
Also Called: Mast Mini Barns
7960 Meinert Rd (49412-9162)
PHONE..........................231 924-3895
Marvin Mast, *Mng Member*
Katie Mast, *Mng Member*
EMP: 10 **EST:** 2005
SQ FT: 17,000
SALES (est): 1.3MM **Privately Held**
SIC: 3272 5999 Solid containing units, concrete; sales barn

(G-6047)
M-B-M MANUFACTURING INC
9576 W 40th St (49412-8017)
PHONE..........................231 924-9614
William C Murphy, *President*
Jeffrey Murphy, *Vice Pres*
Troy Roberson, *Vice Pres*
David Murphy, *Treasurer*
Sandra Kilbourne, *Admin Sec*
EMP: 7 **EST:** 1977
SQ FT: 5,000
SALES (est): 460.1K **Privately Held**
SIC: 3949 3569 Bowling pin machines, automatic; lubrication equipment, industrial

(G-6048)
NESTLE USA INC
445 State St (49413-1000)
PHONE..........................231 928-2000
Steven Medema, *Project Mgr*
EMP: 208
SALES (corp-wide): 92.3B **Privately Held**
WEB: www.nestleusa.com
SIC: 2023 Evaporated milk
HQ: Nestle Usa, Inc.
  1812 N Moore St Ste 118
  Rosslyn VA 22209
  440 264-7249

(G-6049)
NIEBOER ELECTRIC INC
502 E Main St (49412-9788)
PHONE..........................231 924-0960
Doug Nieboer, *President*
Douglas Nieboer, *Owner*
Nancy Nieboer, *Corp Secy*
Harry J Nieboer, *Vice Pres*
EMP: 18 **EST:** 1958
SQ FT: 5,000
SALES (est): 578.4K **Privately Held**
WEB: www.thebodyworksinc.com
SIC: 1731 5999 7694 General electrical contractor; motors, electric; electric motor repair

(G-6050)
OPCO LUBRICATION SYSTEMS INC
9569 W 40th St (49412-8017)
PHONE..........................231 924-6160
Patrick A Brown, *President*
Tyler Thompson, *Sales Staff*
ABI Dodge,
▼**EMP:** 8 **EST:** 2009
SQ FT: 2,500
SALES (est): 1.2MM **Privately Held**
WEB: www.opcolube.com
SIC: 3569 Lubrication equipment, industrial

(G-6051)
PARVOX TECHNOLOGY
531 Chippewa Dr (49412-1761)
PHONE..........................231 924-4366
EMP: 4 **EST:** 2020
SALES (est): 93.6K **Privately Held**
WEB: www.parvox.com
SIC: 3663 Radio & TV communications equipment

(G-6052)
PARVOX TECHNOLOGY
14 W Main St (49412-1136)
P.O. Box 39 (49412-0039)
PHONE..........................231 924-4366
Thomas Korenstra, *General Mgr*
EMP: 4 **EST:** 1994
SQ FT: 3,600
SALES (est): 465.8K **Privately Held**
WEB: www.parvox.com
SIC: 3663 Radio receiver networks

(G-6053)
PEARCE PLASTICS LLC
4898 W 80th St (49412-7321)
PHONE..........................231 519-5994
Mark Pearce, *Principal*
EMP: 10 **EST:** 2010
SALES (est): 444.5K **Privately Held**
WEB: www.pearceplastics.com
SIC: 3089 Injection molding of plastics

(G-6054)
PIONEER TECHNOLOGIES CORP
7998 W 90th St (49412-9164)
PHONE..........................702 806-3152
Michael Agin, *President*
Marta Agin, *Admin Sec*
EMP: 5 **EST:** 1997
SALES (est): 101.8K **Privately Held**
SIC: 8711 8748 3826 Aviation &/or aeronautical engineering; systems analysis & engineering consulting services; systems engineering consultant, ex. computer or professional; laser scientific & engineering instruments

(G-6055)
PROGRESSIVE MANUFACTURING LLC
425 Connie Ave (49412-1809)
PHONE..........................231 924-9975
Gordon Lucies,
John Lucus,
EMP: 4 **EST:** 2002
SQ FT: 75,000
SALES (est): 500K **Privately Held**
WEB: www.progmfg.com
SIC: 3444 Casings, sheet metal; ducts, sheet metal

(G-6056)
TIMES INDICATOR PUBLICATIONS
44 W Main St (49412-1176)
P.O. Box 7 (49412-0007)
PHONE..........................231 924-4400
Tony Komlance, *Owner*
EMP: 7

Fremont - Newaygo County (G-6057) GEOGRAPHIC SECTION

SALES (est): 342.2K **Privately Held**
WEB: www.timesindicator.com
SIC: 2711 Newspapers, publishing & printing

(G-6057)
WHITE RIVER KNIFE AND TOOL
Also Called: Reid Manufacturing
515 Industrial Dr (49412-1867)
PHONE....................................616 997-0026
Jeffery Cothery, *President*
EMP: 5 EST: 2002
SALES (est): 678K **Privately Held**
WEB: www.whiteriverknives.com
SIC: 3544 Special dies & tools

Fruitport
Muskegon County

(G-6058)
ARE YOU READY
281 N 3rd Ave (49415-8843)
PHONE....................................616 935-1133
Sheila A Prenger, *Administration*
EMP: 5 EST: 2008
SALES (est): 88.8K **Privately Held**
SIC: 3273 Ready-mixed concrete

(G-6059)
AUTOMATED INDUS MOTION INC
Also Called: Aim Mail Centers
5627 Airline Rd (49415-8753)
PHONE....................................231 865-1800
Kurt Witham, *President*
Floyd Howe, *Vice Pres*
Rocky Howe, *VP Engrg*
Dick Lague, *Admin Sec*
EMP: 6 EST: 1985
SQ FT: 10,000
SALES (est): 1.8MM **Privately Held**
WEB: www.aimcoil.com
SIC: 3542 3599 Spinning, spline rolling & winding machines; custom machinery

(G-6060)
BASCH OLOVSON ENGINEERING CO
3438 E Mount Garfield Rd (49415-9209)
PHONE....................................231 865-2027
Roy Olovson Jr, *President*
Joni Olovson, *Vice Pres*
EMP: 6 EST: 1970
SQ FT: 4,600
SALES (est): 916.3K **Privately Held**
WEB: www.basch-machinekeys.com
SIC: 3452 Machine keys

(G-6061)
BRALYN INC
Also Called: Ram Electronics
259 N 3rd Ave (49415-8843)
PHONE....................................231 865-3186
Robert Bradley Davis, *President*
Lynne Bosgraaf, *Vice Pres*
EMP: 5 EST: 2015
SQ FT: 8,800
SALES (est): 372.8K **Privately Held**
SIC: 3672 Printed circuit boards

(G-6062)
ELITE CANVAS LLC
294 Pine St (49415-8735)
P.O. Box 123 (49415-0123)
PHONE....................................231 343-7649
EMP: 4 EST: 2019
SALES (est): 56.3K **Privately Held**
WEB: www.elitecustomcanvas.com
SIC: 2211 Canvas

(G-6063)
INDUSTRIAL ASSEMBLIES INC
3130 Farr Rd (49415-8774)
PHONE....................................231 865-6500
Jerry Hanson, *CEO*
Scott Hanson, *President*
Marsha Hanson, *Corp Secy*
EMP: 25 EST: 1996
SQ FT: 80,000
SALES (est): 2.7MM **Privately Held**
WEB: www.industrial-assemblies.com
SIC: 2431 Millwork

(G-6064)
JBS COATING
3158 Farr Rd (49415-8774)
PHONE....................................231 366-7159
John McCaul, *Principal*
EMP: 12 EST: 2015
SALES (est): 1.2MM **Privately Held**
WEB: www.jbs-coating.com
SIC: 3479 Metal coating & allied service

(G-6065)
LEE MANUFACTURING INC
6406 Airline Rd (49415-8934)
PHONE....................................231 865-3359
Bruce Gaultney, *President*
Arloa Gaultney, *Vice Pres*
Cindy Gaultney, *Vice Pres*
EMP: 15 EST: 1979
SQ FT: 12,000
SALES (est): 1.8MM **Privately Held**
SIC: 3599 Machine shop, jobbing & repair

(G-6066)
MARHAR SNOWBOARDS LLC
5693 Airline Rd (49415-8753)
PHONE....................................616 432-3104
Nathan Morse, *Partner*
Josh Skiles, *Partner*
EMP: 6 EST: 2009
SALES (est): 382.9K **Privately Held**
WEB: www.marharsnowboards.com
SIC: 3949 Skateboards

(G-6067)
MODULAR SYSTEMS INC
169 Park St (49415-8896)
P.O. Box 399 (49415-0399)
PHONE....................................231 865-3167
Montgomery J Welch, *President*
James Knapp, *Vice Pres*
Al Engle, *Manager*
Joann Jarvi, *Manager*
Harry Knudson, *Admin Sec*
▲ EMP: 8 EST: 1966
SQ FT: 50,000
SALES: 1.1MM **Privately Held**
WEB: www.mod-eez.com
SIC: 3452 2541 Screws, metal; shelving, office & store, wood

(G-6068)
MOTION DYNAMICS CORPORATION
5621 Airline Rd (49415-8753)
PHONE....................................231 865-7400
Chris Witham, *President*
Steven Dufon, *Vice Pres*
John McManus, *Vice Pres*
Norm Moss, *Opers Mgr*
Michael Erpenbeck, *Research*
EMP: 65 EST: 2016
SQ FT: 12,000
SALES (est): 14.1MM **Privately Held**
WEB: www.motiondc.com
SIC: 3495 Precision springs

(G-6069)
RAM ELECTRONICS INC
259 N 3rd Ave (49415-8843)
PHONE....................................231 865-3186
Donald R Neidlinger, *President*
Teresa Vargo, *Purchasing*
Shawn Gibson, *Shareholder*
EMP: 12 EST: 1970
SQ FT: 8,800
SALES (est): 2.1MM **Privately Held**
WEB: www.ramelectronics.com
SIC: 8611 3672 3699 Manufacturers' institute; printed circuit boards; electrical equipment & supplies

(G-6070)
SHIPSTON ALUM TECH MICH INC
Also Called: Busche Aluminum Technologies
14638 Apple Dr (49415-9511)
PHONE....................................616 842-3500
Joseph Perkins, *President*
Bethany Aebli, *Engineer*
Tom Jennings, *Engineer*
David Ralstin, *Treasurer*
Robert Eckheart, *Manager*
◆ EMP: 7 EST: 2007
SQ FT: 230,000
SALES (est): 6.6MM
SALES (corp-wide): 332.2MM **Privately Held**
WEB: www.mobexglobal.com
SIC: 3365 Aluminum foundries
HQ: Shipston Aluminum Technologies International, Inc.
22122 Telegraph Rd
Southfield MI 48033

(G-6071)
WILLIS ENGINE & MACHINING SVC
19092 144th Ave (49415-9504)
PHONE....................................616 842-4366
David Willis, *Principal*
EMP: 4 EST: 2016
SALES (est): 89.6K **Privately Held**
WEB: www.search.fergusfallsjournal.com
SIC: 3599 Machine shop, jobbing & repair

Fulton
Kalamazoo County

(G-6072)
RAYS PURE MPLE SYRUP PDTS LLC
14399 S 47th St (49052-9709)
PHONE....................................269 601-7694
EMP: 4 EST: 2016
SALES (est): 62.3K **Privately Held**
SIC: 2099 Maple syrup

Galesburg
Kalamazoo County

(G-6073)
ALUMILITE CORPORATION
1458 S 35th St (49053-9679)
PHONE....................................269 488-4000
Mike Faupel, *President*
▲ EMP: 12 EST: 1975
SALES (est): 2.5MM
SALES (corp-wide): 49.5MM **Privately Held**
WEB: www.alumilite.com
SIC: 3089 3087 2821 Casting of plastic; custom compound purchased resins; plastics materials & resins
PA: Polytek Development Corp.
55 Hilton St
Easton PA 18042
610 559-8620

(G-6074)
CLASSIC GUTTER SYSTEMS LLC
155 Mccollum (49053-9509)
P.O. Box 2319, Kalamazoo (49003-2319)
PHONE....................................269 665-2700
Kathy Hord, *Manager*
Charles Crookston,
◆ EMP: 15 EST: 1998
SALES (est): 2.4MM **Privately Held**
WEB: www.classicgutters.com
SIC: 3444 Gutters, sheet metal

(G-6075)
DRIVE MEDICAL
1446 S 35th St (49053-9679)
PHONE....................................404 349-0280
EMP: 5 EST: 2018
SALES (est): 115.9K **Privately Held**
WEB: www.drivemedical.com
SIC: 3841 Surgical & medical instruments

(G-6076)
EATON CORPORATION
13100 E Michigan Ave (49053-9201)
PHONE....................................269 342-3000
Michael Sikorski, *Division Mgr*
Chand Tailor, *Exec VP*
Stephen Noble, *Vice Pres*
Kathleen Davis, *Plant Mgr*
Brendan Butler, *Project Mgr*
EMP: 400 **Privately Held**
WEB: www.eatonelectrical.com
SIC: 3714 Motor vehicle transmissions, drive assemblies & parts
HQ: Eaton Corporation
1000 Eaton Blvd
Cleveland OH 44122
440 523-5000

(G-6077)
EATON CORPORATION
Also Called: Eaton Fuller Reman Center
13100 E Michigan Ave (49053-9201)
PHONE....................................269 342-3000
Ricardo Collaco, *Engineer*
Sara Berglund, *Senior Engr*
Michele Nemedi, *Credit Staff*
Dave Karnes, *VP Sales*
Gustavo Cruz, *Manager*
EMP: 7 **Privately Held**
WEB: www.eatonelectrical.com
SIC: 3714 Motor vehicle transmissions, drive assemblies & parts
HQ: Eaton Corporation
1000 Eaton Blvd
Cleveland OH 44122
440 523-5000

(G-6078)
GROUPER WILD LLC
Also Called: Shiloh Inds Hot Stamping LLC
9000 E Michigan Ave (49053-8509)
PHONE....................................269 665-4261
William Curtis, *Engineer*
Jennifer Piotrowicz, *Human Res Mgr*
Bill Nieboer, *Branch Mgr*
EMP: 7
SALES (corp-wide): 1.6B **Privately Held**
WEB: www.benteler.com
SIC: 3714 Axles, motor vehicle
HQ: Grouper Wild, Llc
1780 Pond Run
Auburn Hills MI 48326
248 299-7500

(G-6079)
IMPACT LABEL CORPORATION (PA)
Also Called: Vari-Data Co.
8875 Krum Ave (49053-9552)
PHONE....................................269 381-4280
Susan Fogleson, *President*
Abdullah Alyousif, *Engineer*
Lindsey Swaney, *Human Resources*
Brenda Battle, *Sales Staff*
Justin Paulton, *Sales Staff*
EMP: 55 EST: 1964
SQ FT: 35,000
SALES (est): 13.4MM **Privately Held**
WEB: www.impactlabel.com
SIC: 2759 2672 2671 2395 Labels & seals: printing; coated & laminated paper; packaging paper & plastics film, coated & laminated; pleating & stitching

(G-6080)
MICHIGAN GROWER PRODUCTS INC
251 Mccollum (49053-9509)
P.O. Box 373 (49053-0373)
PHONE....................................269 665-7071
Richard Derks, *President*
Dean Cramer, *Vice Pres*
Gregory D Bonnema, *Treasurer*
Gregory Bonnema, *Treasurer*
Lorence Wenke, *Admin Sec*
EMP: 11 EST: 1979
SQ FT: 43,000
SALES (est): 1.4MM **Privately Held**
WEB: www.surefill.com
SIC: 2875 Fertilizers, mixing only

(G-6081)
PHARMACEUTICAL SPECIALTIES LLC
Also Called: Pharmspec
1541 N 30th St (49053-8740)
P.O. Box 2135, Kalamazoo (49003-2135)
PHONE....................................269 382-6402
Jerry M Shorb, *Mng Member*
Karen Shorb,
▲ EMP: 10 EST: 1992
SQ FT: 15,000
SALES (est): 1.9MM **Privately Held**
SIC: 5122 3829 3842 Pharmaceuticals; thermometers, including digital: clinical; canes, orthopedic

GEOGRAPHIC SECTION

(G-6082)
PULVERDRYER USA INC
139 Vanbruggen St (49053-9565)
PHONE...................................269 552-5290
EMP: 6 EST: 2019
SALES (est): 164.8K Privately Held
WEB: www.pulverdryerusa.com
SIC: 3559 Special industry machinery

(G-6083)
SMITHS MACHINE & GRINDING INC
203 E Battle Creek St (49053-9412)
PHONE...................................269 665-4231
Scott Ogden, President
John Wunderlin, Purch Mgr
◆ EMP: 34 EST: 1952
SQ FT: 24,000
SALES (est): 3.2MM Privately Held
WEB: www.smithsmachinegrinding.com
SIC: 3599 Machine shop, jobbing & repair

(G-6084)
SOUPCAN INC
Also Called: Wet N Rugged Sports
9406 E K Ave Ste 5 (49053-8522)
PHONE...................................269 381-2101
EMP: 12
SQ FT: 2,800
SALES: 3MM Privately Held
SIC: 3949 Mfg Sporting/Athletic Goods

(G-6085)
TECNIQ INC
9100 E Michigan Ave (49053-8539)
PHONE...................................269 629-4440
Mark Pruss, CEO
Patrick Condon, President
John Vitek, Vice Pres
Sheila Hawkins, Manager
▲ EMP: 42 EST: 2005
SALES (est): 16.5MM Privately Held
WEB: www.tecniqinc.com
SIC: 3647 Taillights, motor vehicle

(G-6086)
VEL-KAL MANUFACTURING INC
283 Vanbruggen St (49053-9564)
PHONE...................................269 344-1204
Martin Velten, President
EMP: 11 EST: 2020
SALES (est): 714.7K Privately Held
SIC: 3499 Machine bases, metal

Galien
Berrien County

(G-6087)
CAST COATINGS INC (PA)
203 W Southeastern St (49113-9688)
P.O. Box 216 (49113-0216)
PHONE...................................269 545-8373
Robert Anstey, President
Roxy Scheer, Plant Mgr
EMP: 25 EST: 1987
SQ FT: 18,200
SALES (est): 3.8MM Privately Held
WEB: www.castcoatings.com
SIC: 3479 Coating of metals & formed products

(G-6088)
KRUGER PLASTIC PRODUCTS LLC
117 S Grant St (49113-5116)
P.O. Box 258 (49113-0258)
PHONE...................................269 545-3311
Thomas Slifer, Maint Spvr
Brian Fee, Opers Staff
Jim Machacek, Purchasing
EMP: 215
SALES (corp-wide): 10.1MM Privately Held
WEB: www.springboardmfg.com
SIC: 3089 Injection molding of plastics
PA: Kruger Plastic Products Llc
   5681 Cleveland Rd 1
   South Bend IN 46628
   269 465-6404

(G-6089)
KRUMRIE SAW MILL SERVICES
1986 Us Highway 12 (49113-9748)
PHONE...................................269 838-9060
EMP: 4 EST: 2017
SALES (est): 146.9K Privately Held
WEB: www.krumriesms.com
SIC: 2431 Millwork

(G-6090)
LOUD N CLEAR EXTRACTS LLC
18201 Cleveland Ave (49113-9654)
PHONE...................................312 320-4970
Tracie Hurst, Agent
EMP: 4 EST: 2018
SALES (est): 74.4K Privately Held
SIC: 2836 Extracts

Garden City
Wayne County

(G-6091)
ALL AROUND BEAUTY SHOP LLC
30106 Ford Rd (48135-2370)
PHONE...................................313 704-2494
Latoya Carrell,
EMP: 4 EST: 2020
SALES (est): 131K Privately Held
SIC: 2051 Bakery: wholesale or wholesale/retail combined

(G-6092)
ALLISON
1219 Farmington Rd (48135-1186)
PHONE...................................734 261-3735
EMP: 5 EST: 2010
SALES (est): 91.3K Privately Held
SIC: 3714 Motor vehicle parts & accessories

(G-6093)
E AND P FORM TOOL COMPANY INC
31759 Block St Ste A (48135-1538)
PHONE...................................734 261-3530
Joseph F Podzikowski, President
Mary J Podzikowski, Treasurer
EMP: 19 EST: 1968
SQ FT: 7,000
SALES (est): 760.9K Privately Held
WEB: www.eptoolco.com
SIC: 3451 Screw machine products

(G-6094)
FRANKLIN ELECTRIC CORPORATION
32606 Industrial Rd (48135-1523)
P.O. Box 12408, Detroit (48212-0408)
PHONE...................................248 442-8000
Russ D Gorden, President
EMP: 10 EST: 1998
SALES (est): 1.2MM Privately Held
WEB: www.franklin-electric.com
SIC: 7699 7629 7694 Industrial equipment services; electrical equipment repair, high voltage; electric motor repair

(G-6095)
HITE TOOL CO INC
32127 Block St Ste 200 (48135-1537)
PHONE...................................734 422-1777
Jack Hite, President
Todd Hite, Vice Pres
EMP: 5 EST: 1977
SQ FT: 3,200
SALES (est): 446.2K Privately Held
WEB: www.hitetool.com
SIC: 3544 Dies & die holders for metal cutting, forming, die casting

(G-6096)
I D MERCH
153 Merriman Rd (48135-1342)
PHONE...................................734 237-4111
EMP: 4 EST: 2017
SALES (est): 91.7K Privately Held
SIC: 2759 Screen printing

(G-6097)
INKORPORATE
6841 Middlebelt Rd (48135-2148)
PHONE...................................734 261-4657
Jim Neve, Owner
EMP: 6 EST: 2008
SALES (est): 727.9K Privately Held
WEB: www.inkorporategraphics.com
SIC: 2759 Screen printing

(G-6098)
INLAND VAPOR OF MICHIGAN LLC (PA)
33447 Ford Rd (48135-1154)
PHONE...................................734 237-4389
Ken Dobozy, Manager
EMP: 53 EST: 2013
SQ FT: 1,270
SALES (est): 576.1K Privately Held
WEB: www.inlandvaporsmichigan.com
SIC: 3822 3641 Vapor heating controls; lamps, vapor

(G-6099)
INTEGRITY MARKETING PRODUCTS
5905 Middlebelt Rd (48135-2478)
P.O. Box 668, Dearborn Heights (48127-0668)
PHONE...................................734 522-5050
Daniel Seguin, President
EMP: 6 EST: 1998
SQ FT: 4,600
SALES (est): 653.7K Privately Held
WEB: www.integritypromos.com
SIC: 2759 Screen printing

(G-6100)
INTERNATIONAL EXTRUSION
32841 Parklane St Ste 6 (48135-1529)
PHONE...................................734 427-1934
EMP: 6 EST: 2019
SALES (est): 211.2K Privately Held
WEB: www.extrusion.net
SIC: 3354 Aluminum extruded products

(G-6101)
INTERNATIONAL EXTRUSIONS
32416 Industrial Rd (48135-1523)
PHONE...................................734 956-6841
George Gazepis, CFO
EMP: 18 EST: 2018
SALES (est): 28.7MM Privately Held
WEB: www.extrusion.net
SIC: 3354 Aluminum extruded products

(G-6102)
INTERNATIONAL EXTRUSIONS INC (PA)
Also Called: Excrution Painting
5800 Venoy Rd (48135-1655)
PHONE...................................734 427-8700
Nicholas Noecker, President
George Gazepis, CFO
David Brokos, Info Tech Dir
Gregory Stangler, Admin Sec
EMP: 164 EST: 1971
SQ FT: 12,000
SALES (est): 35.9MM Privately Held
WEB: www.extrusion.net
SIC: 3354 3441 Aluminum extruded products; fabricated structural metal

(G-6103)
JWG INDUSTRIES
30762 Ford Rd (48135-1803)
PHONE...................................734 881-0312
Greg Klopp, Principal
EMP: 4 EST: 2017
SALES (est): 105.4K Privately Held
WEB: www.jwg-industries.com
SIC: 3999 Manufacturing industries

(G-6104)
MOM OF SHIRE APOTHECARY LLC
30550 Pierce St (48135-1431)
PHONE...................................734 751-9443
Michelle M Nixon,
EMP: 4 EST: 2016
SALES (est): 94.3K Privately Held
SIC: 2841 Soap & other detergents

(G-6105)
ORIN JEWELERS INC (PA)
29317 Ford Rd (48135-2887)
P.O. Box 549 (48136-0549)
PHONE...................................734 422-7030
Orin J Mazzoni Jr, President
Joshua Summers, Cust Mgr
Margo Kasbarian, Sales Staff
Jennifer Strong, Sales Staff
Tobin Allen, Manager
EMP: 17 EST: 1954
SQ FT: 3,500
SALES (est): 3.5MM Privately Held
WEB: www.orinjewelers.com
SIC: 5944 7631 3911 Jewelry, precious stones & precious metals; watches; jewelry repair services; watch repair; jewelry, precious metal

(G-6106)
PUFF BABY LLC
6250 Middlebelt Rd (48135-2409)
PHONE...................................734 620-9991
EMP: 4 EST: 2014
SALES (est): 179.8K Privately Held
SIC: 3671 Gas or vapor tubes

(G-6107)
SAF-AIR PRODUCTS INC
32839 Manor Park (48135-1526)
PHONE...................................734 522-8360
Patricia Lescoe, President
Bob Lescoe, Vice Pres
EMP: 6 EST: 1959
SQ FT: 5,000
SALES (est): 737.8K Privately Held
WEB: www.saf-air.com
SIC: 3728 Aircraft parts & equipment

(G-6108)
SCHAEFER SCREW PRODUCTS CO
32832 Indl Rd (48135)
PHONE...................................734 522-0020
Sanford Szalay, President
David McManus, General Mgr
Michael Szalay, Vice Pres
Brett Belda, Human Res Mgr
▲ EMP: 27 EST: 1944
SQ FT: 16,000
SALES (est): 3.4MM Privately Held
WEB: www.schaeferscrew.com
SIC: 3599 Machine shop, jobbing & repair

(G-6109)
SIDLEY DIAMOND TOOL COMPANY (PA)
32320 Ford Rd (48135-1507)
PHONE...................................734 261-7970
Michael J Sidley, President
▲ EMP: 29 EST: 1956
SQ FT: 15,000
SALES (est): 2.5MM Privately Held
WEB: www.sidleydiamond.com
SIC: 3291 3545 Abrasive products; diamond cutting tools for turning, boring, burnishing, etc.; diamond dressing & wheel crushing attachments

(G-6110)
SIGN-A-RAMA INC
6641 Middlebelt Rd (48135-2146)
PHONE...................................734 522-6661
Gregory Solovey, CEO
EMP: 5 EST: 1981
SALES (est): 512.6K Privately Held
WEB: www.signarama.com
SIC: 3993 5099 Signs & advertising specialties; signs, except electric

(G-6111)
STIMMEL CONSTRUCTION LLC (PA)
32176 Chester St (48135-1742)
PHONE...................................734 263-8949
Steven Stimmel, Principal
EMP: 8 EST: 2018
SALES (est): 46K Privately Held
WEB: www.stimmelconstruction.com
SIC: 3993 Signs & advertising specialties

(G-6112)
TEL-X CORPORATION
32400 Ford Rd (48135-1512)
PHONE...................................734 425-2225

Gary Gillard, *President*
Mike Logan, *COO*
Keith Speck, *Vice Pres*
Tammy Carol, *Controller*
Jennifer Lauer, *Marketing Staff*
EMP: 31
SQ FT: 21,000
SALES (est): 6.6MM **Privately Held**
WEB: www.telxcorp.com
SIC: 3444 3465 Sheet metal specialties, not stamped; automotive stampings

(G-6113)
TRANS PARTS PLUS INC
32816 Manor Park (48135-1545)
P.O. Box 51655, Livonia (48151-5655)
PHONE......................734 427-6844
Bruce Zarbaugh, *President*
EMP: 5 **EST:** 1991
SQ FT: 5,000
SALES (est): 660.3K **Privately Held**
SIC: 3714 Transmission housings or parts, motor vehicle

(G-6114)
US TRADE LLC
29145 Warren Rd (48185-2144)
PHONE......................800 676-0208
EMP: 7 **EST:** 2014
SALES (est): 792.9K **Privately Held**
SIC: 3674 Light emitting diodes

(G-6115)
VIKING INDUSTRIES INC
6012 Hubbard St (48185-1520)
PHONE......................734 421-5416
Frank Klem, *President*
EMP: 10 **EST:** 1984
SALES (est): 932.9K **Privately Held**
WEB: www.vikingpackaging.com
SIC: 3334 Primary aluminum

Gaylord
Otsego County

(G-6116)
AKSTON HUGHES INTL LLC
1865 Orourke Blvd Ste A (49735-8030)
PHONE......................989 448-2322
Daniel Walsh, *CEO*
EMP: 15 **EST:** 2011
SALES (est): 1.3MM **Privately Held**
SIC: 2131 Smoking tobacco

(G-6117)
ALBIES FOOD PRODUCTS LLC
1534 Orourke Blvd (49735-9565)
PHONE......................989 732-2800
Paul Lochinski, *Principal*
EMP: 16 **EST:** 2018
SALES (est): 932.3K **Privately Held**
WEB: www.albies.com
SIC: 2099 Food preparations

(G-6118)
AMERICAN BOTTLING COMPANY
Also Called: 7-Up of Gaylord
1923 Orourke Blvd (49735-8029)
PHONE......................989 731-5392
EMP: 20 **Publicly Held**
SIC: 2086 Mfg Bottled/Canned Soft Drinks
HQ: The American Bottling Company
  5301 Legacy Dr
  Plano TX 75034

(G-6119)
BAKER HUGHES HOLDINGS LLC
Unichem
526 Barnyard (49735)
PHONE......................989 732-2082
Gary Gallup, *Branch Mgr*
EMP: 6
SALES (corp-wide): 20.7B **Publicly Held**
WEB: www.bakerhughes.com
SIC: 1389 Acidizing wells; oil field services
HQ: Baker Hughes Holdings Llc
  17021 Aldine Westfield Rd
  Houston TX 77073
  713 439-8600

(G-6120)
BOZZER BROTHERS INC
1252 Krys Rd (49735-8211)
PHONE......................989 732-9684
Nelson Bozzer, *President*
Gino Bozzer, *Admin Sec*
EMP: 8 **EST:** 1974
SQ FT: 5,000
SALES (est): 647.7K **Privately Held**
SIC: 3273 5211 Ready-mixed concrete; lumber & other building materials

(G-6121)
BUSTEDTEES LLC
1782 Orourke Blvd (49735-8009)
PHONE......................989 448-3179
Josh Kent,
EMP: 4 **EST:** 2018
SALES (est): 46.5K **Privately Held**
SIC: 2253 Hats & headwear, knit

(G-6122)
CHOICE PUBLICATIONS INC
112 E 6th St (49735-2015)
P.O. Box 382 (49734-0382)
PHONE......................989 732-8160
David Baragrey Sr, *President*
Chad Baragrey, *Manager*
David G Baragrey Jr, *Shareholder*
EMP: 4 **EST:** 2003
SQ FT: 10,000 **Privately Held**
WEB: www.weeklychoice.com
SIC: 2711 Newspapers, publishing & printing

(G-6123)
COMPLETE TRUCK AND TRAILER
184 Meecher Rd (49735-9374)
PHONE......................989 732-9000
EMP: 6 **EST:** 2019
SALES (est): 1.3MM **Privately Held**
SIC: 3715 Truck trailers

(G-6124)
CROSSROADS INDUSTRIES INC
2464 Silver Fox Trl (49735-7440)
P.O. Box 1337 (49734-5337)
PHONE......................989 732-1233
William Marshall, *CEO*
Rikkard Rambo, *Mng Member*
Vicky Otto, *Assistant*
EMP: 44 **EST:** 1972
SQ FT: 15,000
SALES (est): 473.4K **Privately Held**
WEB: www.crossroadsindustries.com
SIC: 8331 2431 2441 Vocational rehabilitation agency; door frames, wood; boxes, wood

(G-6125)
CUSTOM MARINE AND MCH SERVIC
1440 Beaver Dam Rd (49735-9586)
PHONE......................989 732-5455
EMP: 4 **EST:** 2019
SALES (est): 143.8K **Privately Held**
WEB: www.custommarinemachine.com
SIC: 3599 Custom machinery

(G-6126)
DIVERSIFIED METAL PRODUCTS INC
1489 Oorouk Blvd (49735)
PHONE......................989 448-7120
Richard Ericson, *President*
Dennis Holden, *Admin Sec*
EMP: 20 **EST:** 2009
SQ FT: 20,000
SALES (est): 4.1MM **Privately Held**
WEB: www.diversifiedmp.com
SIC: 3542 Die casting machines

(G-6127)
ELENZ INC (PA)
1829 Calkins Dr (49735-8008)
PHONE......................989 732-7233
Edward Elenz, *President*
Joan Elenz, *Corp Secy*
EMP: 7 **EST:** 1978
SALES (est): 831.6K **Privately Held**
SIC: 2411 2421 Pulpwood contractors engaged in cutting; wooden logs; wood chips, produced at mill

(G-6128)
ELENZ INC
1455 Dickerson Rd (49735-7448)
PHONE......................989 732-7233
Edward Elenz, *President*
EMP: 10
SALES (corp-wide): 831.6K **Privately Held**
SIC: 2421 Wood chips, produced at mill
PA: Elenz, Inc
  1829 Calkins Dr
  Gaylord MI 49735
  989 732-7233

(G-6129)
FORREST BROTHERS INC (PA)
1272 Millbocker Rd (49735-9507)
PHONE......................989 356-4011
Matthew Forrest, *President*
John Forrest, *Vice Pres*
EMP: 245 **EST:** 1991
SQ FT: 62,000
SALES (est): 8MM **Privately Held**
SIC: 1796 3564 3823 Pollution control equipment installation; dust or fume collecting equipment, industrial; industrial instrmnts msrmnt display/control process variable

(G-6130)
GAYLORD MCH & FABRICATION LLC
2758 Dickerson Rd (49735-7453)
PHONE......................989 732-0817
Bob Pruitt,
EMP: 14 **EST:** 1994
SQ FT: 8,400
SALES (est): 2MM **Privately Held**
WEB: www.gaylordmachine.com
SIC: 3599 Machine shop, jobbing & repair

(G-6131)
GREAT LKES TEX RESTORATION LLC
651 Expressway Ct (49735-8117)
P.O. Box 1821 (49734-5821)
PHONE......................989 448-8600
Douglas Bailey,
EMP: 5 **EST:** 2014
SALES (est): 332.1K **Privately Held**
WEB: www.greatlakestextilerestoration.com
SIC: 2211 Laundry fabrics, cotton

(G-6132)
GTM STEAMER SERVICE INC
647 Poplar Dr (49735-9406)
P.O. Box 171 (49734-0171)
PHONE......................989 732-7678
EMP: 4
SALES (est): 230K **Privately Held**
SIC: 1381 1799 4959 1389 Oil/Gas Well Drilling Special Trade Contractor Sanitary Services Oil/Gas Field Services

(G-6133)
H & S MOLD INC
1640 Orourke Blvd (49735-9565)
PHONE......................989 732-3566
Douglas Hancock, *President*
Todd Hancock, *Corp Secy*
EMP: 10 **EST:** 1974
SQ FT: 10,000
SALES (est): 1MM **Privately Held**
WEB: www.hs-mold.biz
SIC: 3544 Forms (molds), for foundry & plastics working machinery; industrial molds

(G-6134)
HRF EXPLORATION & PROD LLC
990 S Wisconsin Ave (49735-1781)
PHONE......................989 732-6950
Harry Fruehauf, *Branch Mgr*
EMP: 28 **Privately Held**
SIC: 1382 Oil & gas exploration services
PA: Hrf Exploration & Production, L.L.C.
  250 El Dorado Ln
  Palm Beach FL 33480

(G-6135)
IMAGE FACTORY INC
870 N Center Ave (49735-1510)
P.O. Box 1234 (49734-5234)
PHONE......................989 732-2712
Ronald Grendel, *President*
EMP: 5 **EST:** 1979
SQ FT: 2,400
SALES (est): 441K **Privately Held**
WEB: www.imagefactoryinc.net
SIC: 2752 5199 Commercial printing, offset; advertising specialties

(G-6136)
JET SUBSURFACE ROD PUMPS CORP
450 Sides Dr (49735-7503)
P.O. Box 250, Rapid City (49676-0250)
PHONE......................989 732-7513
Dave Findley, *President*
Randy Cherwinski, *General Mgr*
Lyle Benaway, *Purchasing*
EMP: 6 **EST:** 1995
SQ FT: 5,600
SALES (est): 1MM **Privately Held**
WEB: www.jetsubsurfacepumps.com
SIC: 5251 1389 Pumps & pumping equipment; oil field services

(G-6137)
KARPS KITCHENS & BATHS INC
10683 Old Us Highway 27 S (49735-9471)
P.O. Box 74, Waters (49797-0074)
PHONE......................989 732-7676
Dennis Karp, *Owner*
EMP: 5 **EST:** 2008
SALES (est): 69K **Privately Held**
SIC: 2599 Furniture & fixtures

(G-6138)
KASPER INDUSTRIES INC
356 Expressway Ct (49735-8111)
PHONE......................989 705-1177
Tim Kasper, *President*
Collin Wilcox, *Sales Staff*
EMP: 25 **EST:** 1953
SQ FT: 26,000
SALES (est): 2.6MM **Privately Held**
WEB: www.kasperindustries.com
SIC: 3599 Machine shop, jobbing & repair

(G-6139)
KEAYS FAMILY TRUCKIN
Also Called: Kft
1658 Ashley Ln (49735-8116)
PHONE......................231 838-6430
Dannan Keays, *Principal*
EMP: 4 **EST:** 2014
SALES (est): 64.2K **Privately Held**
SIC: 3523 4212 Driers (farm): grain, hay & seed; animal & farm product transportation services

(G-6140)
KRAFT POWER CORPORATION
2852 D And M Dr (49735-7417)
PHONE......................989 748-4040
Tom Rogers, *Branch Mgr*
EMP: 21
SALES (corp-wide): 98.6MM **Privately Held**
WEB: www.kraftpower.com
SIC: 5084 3621 Engines & parts, diesel; industrial machine parts; power generators
PA: Kraft Power Corporation
  199 Wildwood Ave
  Woburn MA 01801
  781 938-9100

(G-6141)
LAKEVIEW QUALITY TOOL INC
696 Alpine Rd (49735-9531)
PHONE......................989 732-6417
Albert L Quaal, *President*
Jerry Cattaneo, *Vice Pres*
Regen Quaal, *Vice Pres*
Jerry C Cattaneo, *Manager*
EMP: 7 **EST:** 1985
SQ FT: 5,500
SALES (est): 250K **Privately Held**
SIC: 3544 3599 Special dies & tools; jigs & fixtures; machine shop, jobbing & repair

(G-6142)
LAPPANS OF GAYLORD INC
Also Called: John Deere Authorized Dealer
4085 Old Us Highway 27 S (49735-9596)
PHONE......................989 732-3274
James Lappan, *President*
James A Lappan II, *Vice Pres*

GEOGRAPHIC SECTION

Germfask - Schoolcraft County (G-6169)

Rusty Maxwell, *Sales Staff*
Barbara Lappan, *Admin Sec*
EMP: 7 **EST:** 1976
SQ FT: 2,000
SALES (est): 1MM **Privately Held**
WEB: www.lappans.com
SIC: 3679 5082 Power supplies, all types: static; construction & mining machinery

(G-6143)
LOSHAW BROS INC
231 Meecher Rd (49735-9372)
P.O. Box 1761 (49734-5761)
PHONE......................989 732-7263
Thomas Loshaw, *President*
Brenda Loshaw, *Vice Pres*
Stacy Loshaw, *Office Mgr*
EMP: 5 **EST:** 1990
SQ FT: 2,000
SALES (est): 1.4MM **Privately Held**
WEB: www.loshawcrane.com
SIC: 1389 7389 Oil field services; crane & aerial lift service

(G-6144)
MAKE IT MINE DSIGN EMB SCREEN
147 W Main St (49735-1384)
PHONE......................989 448-8678
EMP: 4 **EST:** 2019
SALES (est): 96.1K **Privately Held**
SIC: 2759 Screen printing

(G-6145)
MARK ONE CORPORATION
517 Alpine Rd (49735-9531)
PHONE......................989 732-2427
Francis J Kestler, *President*
Keith Crandall, *Vice Pres*
Philip Shelton, *Vice Pres*
Timothy Schmidt, *Design Engr*
Kirby Robertson, *VP Bus Dvlpt*
EMP: 100 **EST:** 1968
SQ FT: 50,000
SALES (est): 20MM **Privately Held**
WEB: www.markonecorp.com
SIC: 3549 3569 3535 Assembly machines, including robotic; lubricating equipment; conveyors & conveying equipment

(G-6146)
MAYFAIR ACCESSORIES INC
1639 Calkins Dr (49735-9501)
PHONE......................989 732-8400
John Behnke, *President*
EMP: 4 **EST:** 1990
SALES (est): 347.9K **Privately Held**
WEB: www.mayfairaccessoriesonline.com
SIC: 2759 Imprinting

(G-6147)
MAYFAIR GOLF ACCESSORIES
1639 Calkins Dr (49735-9501)
PHONE......................989 732-8400
Kevin Alread, *Owner*
John Benke, *Senior VP*
▲ **EMP:** 8 **EST:** 1991
SALES (est): 147.5K **Privately Held**
WEB: www.mayfairaccessoriesonline.com
SIC: 2396 3993 Printing & embossing on plastics fabric articles; signs & advertising specialties

(G-6148)
MAYFAIR PLASTICS INC
845 Dickerson Rd (49735-9204)
P.O. Box 995 (49734-0995)
PHONE......................989 732-2441
Carl R Janssens, *CEO*
Scott Weir, *President*
Michelle Schwarz, *Vice Pres*
▲ **EMP:** 85
SQ FT: 40,000
SALES (est): 30.9MM **Privately Held**
WEB: www.mayfair.net
SIC: 3089 Injection molding of plastics

(G-6149)
MID-STATES BOLT & SCREW CO
1069 Orourke Blvd (49735-9505)
PHONE......................989 732-3265
Charles Schepperley, *Branch Mgr*
EMP: 16

SALES (corp-wide): 73MM **Privately Held**
WEB: www.midstatesbolt.com
SIC: 5072 3452 Miscellaneous fasteners; bolts, nuts, rivets & washers
PA: Mid-States Bolt & Screw Co.
4126 Somers Dr
Burton MI 48529
810 744-0123

(G-6150)
NORTHERN MICHIGAN REVIEW INC (PA)
Also Called: Petoskey News Review
2058 S Otsego Ave (49735-9422)
P.O. Box 528, Petoskey (49770-0528)
PHONE......................231 547-6558
Doug Caldwell, *President*
Paul Gunderson, *General Mgr*
Bob Reedy, *Consultant*
EMP: 49
SALES (est): 9MM **Privately Held**
WEB: www.petoskeynews.com
SIC: 2711 Commercial printing & newspaper publishing combined

(G-6151)
NORTHERN TANK TRUCK SERVICE
10764 Old Us Highway 27 S (49735)
P.O. Box 8, Waters (49797-0008)
PHONE......................989 732-7531
Gary Courtright, *President*
Donald Niceswander, *President*
Dorothy Courtright, *Corp Secy*
EMP: 8 **EST:** 1969
SALES (est): 1.5MM **Privately Held**
WEB: www.northerntank.com
SIC: 1389 1794 Oil field services; excavation work

(G-6152)
P I W CORPORATION
Also Called: Waterjetplus
1492 Orourke Blvd (49735-9506)
PHONE......................989 448-2501
Todd Shepherd, *President*
EMP: 8 **EST:** 1983
SALES (est): 770.3K **Privately Held**
WEB: www.piwcorp.com
SIC: 2221 3441 Fiberglass fabrics; fabricated structural metal

(G-6153)
PAYNE & DOLAN INC
1029 Gornick Ave Ste 105 (49735-1775)
PHONE......................989 731-0700
Penny Derenzy, *Branch Mgr*
EMP: 9
SALES (corp-wide): 27.3MM **Privately Held**
WEB: www.walbecgroup.com
SIC: 2951 Asphalt paving mixtures & blocks
PA: Payne & Dolan, Inc.
N3w23650 Badinger Rd
Waukesha WI 53188
262 524-1700

(G-6154)
PERFECTO INDUSTRIES INC (PA)
1567 Calkins Dr (49735-9501)
PHONE......................989 732-2941
Kevin Roberts, *President*
Mike Skop, *Engineer*
◆ **EMP:** 45
SQ FT: 50,000
SALES (est): 12.9MM **Privately Held**
WEB: www.perfectoindustries.com
SIC: 3547 3549 3599 3537 Rolling mill machinery; coiling machinery; custom machinery; industrial trucks & tractors

(G-6155)
RLH INDUSTRIES INC
1574 Calkins Dr (49735-9501)
PHONE......................989 732-0493
Robert Huta, *President*
Lisa Huta, *Vice Pres*
EMP: 10 **EST:** 1984
SQ FT: 7,800

SALES (est): 1.8MM **Privately Held**
WEB: www.rlhindustriesinc.com
SIC: 3433 3443 Heating equipment, except electric; liners/lining

(G-6156)
ROXBURY CREEK LLC
207 Arrowhead Trl (49735-9013)
PHONE......................989 731-2062
Keitrh R Martell Jr,
EMP: 4 **EST:** 2010
SALES (est): 5K **Privately Held**
SIC: 2411 Logging

(G-6157)
RUSSELL R PETERS CO LLC
1370 Pineview St (49735-7400)
PHONE......................989 732-0660
Kasey Bourcier, *Office Mgr*
Penny Banaszak, *Manager*
William T Peters, *President*
EMP: 5 **EST:** 1930
SQ FT: 21,000
SALES (est): 524K **Privately Held**
SIC: 2653 3086 5113 2675 Corrugated boxes, partitions, display items, sheets & pad; packaging & shipping materials, foamed plastic; insulation or cushioning material, foamed plastic; padding, foamed plastic; corrugated & solid fiber boxes; containers, paper & disposable plastic; die-cut paper & board; fiber cans, drums & similar products

(G-6158)
SCENTMATCHERS LLC
514 Camp Ten Rd (49735-9229)
P.O. Box 1550 (49734-5550)
PHONE......................231 878-9918
Adam Schultz, *President*
EMP: 4 **EST:** 2007
SALES (est): 444.1K **Privately Held**
WEB: www.scentmatchers.com
SIC: 2844 7389 Perfumes & colognes;

(G-6159)
SHIRT WORKS
1196 Energy Dr (49735-7957)
PHONE......................989 448-8889
EMP: 8 **EST:** 2020
SALES (est): 169K **Privately Held**
WEB: www.shirtworksracewear.com
SIC: 2396 Automotive & apparel trimmings

(G-6160)
SILVERSMITH INC
1370 Millbocker Rd (49735-7425)
P.O. Box 1934 (49734-5934)
PHONE......................989 732-8988
EMP: 38
SALES (est): 9.5MM **Privately Held**
WEB: www.silversmithdata.com
SIC: 3824 Mfg Fluid Meter/Counting Devices

(G-6161)
STELLAR COMPUTER SERVICES LLC
633 Crestwood Dr (49735-9141)
PHONE......................989 732-7153
Robert Erat,
EMP: 4 **EST:** 1994
SQ FT: 18,000
SALES (est): 293.8K **Privately Held**
WEB: www.stellarcomputerservices.com
SIC: 7378 3571 Computer & data processing equipment repair/maintenance; computers, digital, analog or hybrid

(G-6162)
TANK TRUCK SERVICE & SALES INC
1981 Engel Ave (49735-7416)
PHONE......................989 731-4887
Jeff Czerwinski, *Purch Mgr*
Jeff Lawer, *Manager*
EMP: 5
SALES (corp-wide): 8.9MM **Privately Held**
WEB: www.tanktruckservice.com
SIC: 3541 Machine tools, metal cutting type
PA: Tank Truck Service & Sales, Inc.
25150 Dequindre Rd
Warren MI 48091
586 757-6500

(G-6163)
TIMBERLINE LOGGING INC
855 Dickerson Rd (49735-9204)
P.O. Box 395, Johannesburg (49751-0395)
PHONE......................989 731-2794
James Payne Jr, *President*
EMP: 29 **EST:** 1987
SQ FT: 1,000
SALES (est): 1.9MM **Privately Held**
SIC: 2411 Logging camps & contractors

(G-6164)
TOP OMICHIGAN RECLAIMERS INC
620 E Main St (49735-8519)
PHONE......................989 705-7983
Philip J Mason, *President*
Henry Mason, *Vice Pres*
Lisa H Mason, *Treasurer*
Sarah Butler, *Admin Sec*
EMP: 4 **EST:** 1991
SALES (est): 150K **Privately Held**
SIC: 1442 Gravel mining

(G-6165)
UPPER MICHIGAN NEWSPAPERS LLC
Also Called: Star Publication
1966 S Otsego Ave (49735-8489)
PHONE......................989 732-5125
John Sherlock, *Controller*
◆ **EMP:** 7 **EST:** 1968
SQ FT: 3,000
SALES (est): 108.9K **Privately Held**
SIC: 2741 Guides: publishing only, not printed on site

(G-6166)
WARD LAKE DRILLING INC (DH)
Also Called: Ward Lake Energy
685 E M 32 Ste 201 (49735-7775)
P.O. Box 977 (49734-0977)
PHONE......................989 732-8499
Donald A Rutishauser, *Treasurer*
Jeffrey Raleigh, *Manager*
Joseph M Vitale, *Admin Sec*
EMP: 44 **EST:** 1985
SQ FT: 10,000
SALES (est): 2.1MM **Privately Held**
SIC: 1311 1381 Natural gas production; crude petroleum production; drilling oil & gas wells
HQ: Belden & Blake Corporation
1001 Fannin St Ste 800
Houston TX 77002
713 659-3500

(G-6167)
WODER CONSTRUCTION INC
3661 Nowak Rd (49735-9312)
P.O. Box 993 (49734-0993)
PHONE......................989 731-6371
Timothy Woder, *President*
EMP: 10 **EST:** 1997
SALES (est): 576.2K **Privately Held**
WEB: www.dehaanracing.com
SIC: 1389 Oil field services

Genesee
Genesee County

(G-6168)
HATCHBACK PUBLISHING
7138 Ridgeview Dr (48437-7724)
P.O. Box 494 (48437-0494)
PHONE......................810 394-8612
Cynthia Hatcher, *Principal*
EMP: 6 **EST:** 2007
SALES (est): 125.3K **Privately Held**
WEB: www.hatchbackpublishing.com
SIC: 2741 Miscellaneous publishing

Germfask
Schoolcraft County

(G-6169)
ZELLAR FOREST PRODUCTS
Also Called: John Zellar Jr Forest Products
462 Lustila Rd (49836-9041)
PHONE......................906 586-9817
John Zellar Jr, *Owner*

(PA)=Parent Co (HQ)=Headquarters (DH)=Div Headquarters
✪ = New Business established in last 2 years

EMP: 9 EST: 1958
SALES (est): 920.6K Privately Held
SIC: 2411 1794 Logging; excavation work

Gibraltar
Wayne County

(G-6170)
GILSBACH FABRICATING LLC
19484 Homestead Ln (48173-1287)
PHONE..................................734 379-9169
EMP: 4 EST: 2018
SALES (est): 97K Privately Held
SIC: 3089 Plastics products

(G-6171)
HYCAL CORP
Also Called: Ferrous Cal Co.
27800 W Jefferson Ave (48173-9796)
PHONE..................................216 671-6161
Eduardo Gonzalez, *President*
Reed McGivney, *Exec VP*
Anthony Potelicki, *Vice Pres*
David Hill, *CFO*
EMP: 15 EST: 2014
SQ FT: 560,000
SALES (est): 2.3MM
SALES (corp-wide): 49.1MM Privately Held
WEB: www.hycalcorp.com
SIC: 3398 Annealing of metal
PA: Ferragon Corporation
    11103 Memphis Ave
    Cleveland OH 44144
    216 671-6161

(G-6172)
MAG MACHINE TOOL
14127 Middle Gibraltar Rd (48173-9772)
PHONE..................................734 281-1700
John Grietsell, *Owner*
EMP: 5 EST: 1976
SALES (est): 447.9K Privately Held
WEB: www.mag-machineandtoo.com
SIC: 3599 Industrial machinery

Gladstone
Delta County

(G-6173)
BAYSIDE ENGINEERING AND MFG
80 Delta Ave (49837-1904)
PHONE..................................906 420-8770
EMP: 7 EST: 2019
SALES (est): 132.1K Privately Held
WEB: www.baysideengineering.com
SIC: 3999 Manufacturing industries

(G-6174)
BRAMCO CONTAINERS INC
824 Clark Dr (49837-8966)
PHONE..................................906 428-2855
John O'Driscoll, *President*
Stephen O'Driscoll, *Vice Pres*
EMP: 8 EST: 1990
SQ FT: 11,500
SALES (est): 800K Privately Held
WEB: www.bramcocontainers.com
SIC: 2653 Boxes, corrugated: made from purchased materials

(G-6175)
BUCKS SPORTS PRODUCTS INC
Also Called: Thesnowmobilestore.com
7721 Lake Bluff 19.4 Rd (49837-2448)
PHONE..................................763 229-1331
David Buckland, *President*
EMP: 5 EST: 2002
SQ FT: 60
SALES (est): 500K Privately Held
SIC: 3949 Sporting & athletic goods

(G-6176)
BUGAY LOGGING
8409 N P.11 Dr (49837-2654)
PHONE..................................906 428-2125
Joe Bugay, *Principal*
EMP: 6 EST: 2013
SALES (est): 231.3K Privately Held
SIC: 2411 Logging

(G-6177)
CRL INC
Also Called: Marbels Outdoors
623 Rains Dr (49837-1156)
PHONE..................................906 428-3710
George Brinkley, *CEO*
Craig Lauerman, *President*
James Lauerman, *Vice Pres*
▲ EMP: 38 EST: 1964
SQ FT: 20,000
SALES (est): 1.3MM Privately Held
WEB: www.marblearms.com
SIC: 3484 3949 3827 3421 Shotguns or shotgun parts, 30 mm. & below; sporting & athletic goods; optical instruments & lenses; cutlery

(G-6178)
DAVID HIRN CABINETS AND CONTG
1319 Delta Ave (49837-1315)
PHONE..................................906 428-1935
David Hirn, *President*
EMP: 5
SALES (est): 367.3K Privately Held
SIC: 2434 Wood kitchen cabinets

(G-6179)
DAWZYE EXCAVATION INC
7575 Rays M.7 Cir 7m (49837-9022)
PHONE..................................906 786-5276
Michael Bruce, *Principal*
EMP: 6 EST: 2006
SALES (est): 118.8K Privately Held
SIC: 2411 Logging

(G-6180)
DELFAB INC
103 N 12th St (49837-1423)
P.O. Box 144 (49837-0144)
PHONE..................................906 428-9570
William Westlund, *President*
EMP: 23 EST: 2003
SALES (est): 2.9MM Privately Held
WEB: www.delfab.com
SIC: 3548 Soldering equipment, except hand soldering irons

(G-6181)
HAWORTH HONG KONG LLC (PA)
1 Haworth Ctr (49837)
PHONE..................................616 393-3484
Matthew Haworth,
EMP: 5 EST: 1995
SALES (est): 98K Privately Held
SIC: 2522 2521 Office furniture, except wood; wood office furniture

(G-6182)
K & M INDUSTRIAL LLC
80 Delta Ave (49837-1904)
PHONE..................................906 420-8770
Josh King, *President*
Sarah Hoffmeyer, *Controller*
EMP: 6 EST: 2009
SALES (est): 3.8MM Privately Held
WEB: www.kmindusa.com
SIC: 3441 2411 1629 8711 Boat & barge sections, prefabricated metal; timber, cut at logging camp; dredging contractor; building construction consultant; industrial buildings, new construction; cylinders, pump

(G-6183)
LITTLE BAY CONCRETE PRODUCTS
119 N 9th St (49837-1644)
P.O. Box 342 (49837-0342)
PHONE..................................906 428-9859
EMP: 6
SQ FT: 1,000
SALES (est): 770.3K Privately Held
SIC: 3273 Mfg Ready Mix Concrete

(G-6184)
NORTHERN MICHIGAN VENEERS INC
710 Rains Dr (49837-1129)
P.O. Box 352 (49837-0352)
PHONE..................................906 428-1082
John D Besse, *President*
Melissa Besse, *Treasurer*
Greg Besse, *Admin Sec*
▲ EMP: 65 EST: 1966
SQ FT: 40,000
SALES (est): 9.5MM Privately Held
WEB: www.bessegroup.com
SIC: 2435 Veneer stock, hardwood
PA: Forest Besse Products Inc
    933 N 8th St
    Gladstone MI 49837

(G-6185)
PARDON INC
3510 State Highway M35 (49837-2652)
PHONE..................................906 428-3494
James Pardon, *President*
Jim Pardon, *General Mgr*
Richard Barnes, *CIO*
EMP: 40 EST: 1964
SQ FT: 7,200
SALES (est): 1.7MM Privately Held
WEB: www.pardoninc.net
SIC: 3714 3444 Hydraulic fluid power pumps for auto steering mechanism; cylinder heads, motor vehicle; sheet metalwork

(G-6186)
PISCES FISH MACHINERY INC (PA)
7036 Us Highway 2 41 M35 (49837-2503)
P.O. Box 189, Wells (49894-0189)
PHONE..................................906 789-1636
Trevor Wastell, *President*
Mathew Wastell, *Vice Pres*
▲ EMP: 21
SQ FT: 9,500
SALES (est): 3.3MM Privately Held
WEB: www.pisces-ind.com
SIC: 3556 Fish & shellfish processing machinery; poultry processing machinery

(G-6187)
VANAIRE INC
Also Called: Gladstone Metals
840 Clark Dr (49837-8966)
PHONE..................................906 428-4656
Steven Soderman, *CEO*
William Vandevusse, *President*
Bob McFarlane, *Manager*
Jodi Possi, *Manager*
Walt H Wiesmiller, *Manager*
EMP: 82
SQ FT: 48,000
SALES (est): 18.7MM Privately Held
WEB: www.vanaireinc.com
SIC: 3589 Water treatment equipment, industrial

Gladwin
Gladwin County

(G-6188)
ACCURATE MACHINING & FABG INC
1650 S M 30 (48624-8474)
PHONE..................................989 426-5400
Marshall Grimmett, *CEO*
EMP: 4 EST: 2004
SQ FT: 6,880
SALES (est): 372.6K Privately Held
WEB: www.accurate-machining.com
SIC: 3599 Machine shop, jobbing & repair

(G-6189)
BOAT GUARD INC
3577 N West Branch Dr (48624-7933)
PHONE..................................989 424-1490
John Highfield, *President*
▲ EMP: 4 EST: 2010
SALES (est): 206.7K Privately Held
WEB: www.theboatguard.com
SIC: 2394 7389 Convertible tops, canvas or boat: from purchased materials;

(G-6190)
BOBCAT OIL & GAS INC (PA)
901 E Cedar Ave (48624-2252)
P.O. Box 483 (48624-0483)
PHONE..................................989 426-4375
Gordon Tuck, *President*
Joyce Tuck, *Admin Sec*
EMP: 6 EST: 1992
SALES (est): 2.8MM Privately Held
SIC: 1382 Oil & gas exploration services

(G-6191)
CAM PACKAGING LLC
705 Weaver Ct (48624-1718)
PHONE..................................989 426-1200
Robert Oberloier, *President*
Dave Andrist, *Plant Mgr*
Dayna Bittner, *Controller*
EMP: 12 EST: 2013
SQ FT: 48,000
SALES (est): 2MM Privately Held
WEB: www.cam-pack.com
SIC: 2671 Packaging paper & plastics film, coated & laminated

(G-6192)
CAMERON KIRK FOREST PDTS INC
1467 S Shearer Rd (48624-9442)
PHONE..................................989 426-3439
Judy Cameron, *President*
Kirk Cameron, *Vice Pres*
EMP: 5 EST: 2001 Privately Held
SIC: 3713 Truck & bus bodies

(G-6193)
CHRIS MUMA FOREST PRODUCTS
1154 W 1st St (48624-1017)
P.O. Box 17 (48624-0017)
PHONE..................................989 426-5916
Chris Muma, *President*
Jamie Shell, *Admin Sec*
EMP: 29 EST: 1976
SALES (est): 3MM Privately Held
SIC: 2411 Wood chips, produced in the field; logging camps & contractors

(G-6194)
D&W FINE PACK LLC
1191 Wolfson Ct (48624-7026)
PHONE..................................866 296-2020
EMP: 52
SALES (corp-wide): 900.4MM Privately Held
WEB: www.dwfinepack.com
SIC: 3089 Plastic kitchenware, tableware & houseware
HQ: D&W Fine Pack Llc
    777 Mark St
    Wood Dale IL 60191

(G-6195)
E & D ENGINEERING SYSTEMS LLC
890 Industrial Dr (48624-1704)
PHONE..................................989 246-0770
Ed Wark, *Partner*
Debby Wark, *Partner*
▼ EMP: 4 EST: 2002
SALES (est): 667K Privately Held
WEB: www.e-dengineering.com
SIC: 3089 3599 Plastic processing; machine & other job shop work; custom machinery

(G-6196)
GLADWIN COUNTY NEWSPAPERS LLC
700 E Cedar Ave (48624-2218)
PHONE..................................989 426-9411
Stephanie Buffman, *Editor*
Carissa Petherbridge, *Prdtn Mgr*
Mark Schaefer, *Accounts Exec*
Dawn Laidlaw, *Office Mgr*
EMP: 8 EST: 2018
SALES (est): 348.3K Privately Held
WEB: www.gladwinmi.com
SIC: 2711 Newspapers: publishing only, not printed on site

(G-6197)
GLADWIN MACHINE INC
535 S M 18 (48624-9333)
PHONE..................................989 426-8753
EMP: 8
SQ FT: 6,000
SALES (est): 800K Privately Held
SIC: 3544 3599 Mfg Dies/Tools/Jigs/Fixtures Mfg Industrial Machinery

GEOGRAPHIC SECTION

(G-6198)
GLADWIN METAL PROCESSING INC
795 E Maple St (48624-1717)
PHONE 989 426-9038
Lloyd R Bowen, *President*
Jean Bowen, *Vice Pres*
Carole Govitz, *Admin Sec*
EMP: 7 **EST:** 1972
SQ FT: 16,000 **Privately Held**
WEB: www.gladwinmetalprocessing.com
SIC: 3471 3479 Electroplating of metals or formed products; lacquering of metal products

(G-6199)
GLADWIN TANK MANUFACTURING INC
207 Industrial Park Ave (48624-1799)
PHONE 989 426-4768
Beverly Grove, *President*
Thane Grove, *Vice Pres*
Keith Cotton, *Sales Staff*
EMP: 17
SQ FT: 28,500
SALES: 3.3MM **Privately Held**
WEB: www.gladwintank.com
SIC: 3443 3444 Tanks, standard or custom fabricated: metal plate; sheet metalwork

(G-6200)
LOOSE PLASTICS INC
1016 E 1st St (48624-1268)
PHONE 989 246-1880
Scott C Loose, *CEO*
Joshua Loose, *Vice Pres*
Mike Orr, *Vice Pres*
Wade Strickland, *QC Mgr*
Jamie A Loose, *Treasurer*
EMP: 120 **EST:** 1985
SQ FT: 144,000
SALES (est): 17.5MM **Privately Held**
WEB: www.blingbyjasco.com
SIC: 3089 Injection molding of plastics

(G-6201)
R V WOLVERINE
1088 N M 18 (48624-9202)
PHONE 989 426-9241
Howard Smith, *Owner*
EMP: 10 **EST:** 1958
SALES (est): 507.7K **Privately Held**
SIC: 3792 3711 Campers, for mounting on trucks; motor homes, self-contained, assembly of

(G-6202)
ROLL RITE CORPORATION
650 Indl Pk Ave (48624)
PHONE 989 345-3434
Rob Neering, *Principal*
John Orr Jr, *Engineer*
Matthew Hanson, *CFO*
Bernie Vogel, *Manager*
Timothy Searfoss, *Info Tech Dir*
▲ **EMP:** 46
SQ FT: 53,000
SALES (est): 10.7MM **Privately Held**
WEB: www.rollrite.com
SIC: 3466 Closures, stamped metal

(G-6203)
ROLL RITE GROUP HOLDINGS LLC (HQ)
650 Industrial Dr (48624-1708)
PHONE 989 345-3434
Brad G Templeman, *CEO*
Robert Neering, *CFO*
EMP: 100 **EST:** 2011
SALES: 30.5MM
SALES (corp-wide): 186.2MM **Privately Held**
WEB: www.rollrite.com
SIC: 3713 Truck bodies & parts
PA: Safe Fleet Holdings Llc
  6800 E 163rd St
  Belton MO 64012
  816 318-8000

(G-6204)
ROLL-RITE LLC (DH)
Also Called: Roll Rite Group Holdings
650 Industrial Dr (48624-1708)
PHONE 989 345-3434
Brad Templeman, *CEO*
Keith Searfoss, *President*
Stephen Hunter, *General Mgr*
Jim Kenyon, *Vice Pres*
Robert Neering, *CFO*
▲ **EMP:** 49 **EST:** 2004
SALES (est): 15.1MM
SALES (corp-wide): 186.2MM **Privately Held**
WEB: www.rollrite.com
SIC: 3713 Truck bodies & parts
HQ: Roll Rite Group Holdings Llc
  650 Industrial Dr
  Gladwin MI 48624
  989 345-3434

(G-6205)
SHAWN MUMA
2315 Dassay Rd (48624-9761)
PHONE 989 426-9505
Shawn Muma, *Owner*
EMP: 5 **EST:** 2010
SALES (est): 210.9K **Privately Held**
SIC: 2411 Logging

(G-6206)
SHAWN MUMA LOGGING
2315 Dassay Rd (48624-9761)
PHONE 989 426-6852
Shawn Muma, *Owner*
EMP: 8 **EST:** 2012
SALES (est): 1.1MM **Privately Held**
WEB: www.centerforlifetransitions.com
SIC: 2411 Logging camps & contractors

(G-6207)
SILVER CREEK CABINETS
1775 Chappel Dam Rd (48624-8722)
PHONE 989 387-0858
Daniel O Bontrager, *Owner*
EMP: 4 **EST:** 2018
SALES (est): 126.6K **Privately Held**
WEB: www.silvercreekcabinets.com
SIC: 2434 Wood kitchen cabinets

(G-6208)
WILLIAM R HALL KIMBERLY
Also Called: Hall Mat
4083 Cassidy Rd (48624-8900)
PHONE 989 426-4605
William R Hall, *Principal*
EMP: 8 **EST:** 2010
SALES (est): 1.4MM **Privately Held**
WEB: www.hallmac1.com
SIC: 1311 Crude petroleum & natural gas

Glen Arbor
Leelanau County

(G-6209)
CHERRY REPUBLIC INC (PA)
6026 S Lake St (49636-5115)
P.O. Box 677 (49636-0677)
PHONE 231 334-3150
Robert Sutherland, *President*
Terry Hornbaker, *Prdtn Mgr*
Rick Burbee, *Marketing Staff*
Brian Kindt, *Network Enginr*
Veronica Hazelton, *Director*
EMP: 68 **EST:** 1990
SALES (est): 13.4MM **Privately Held**
WEB: www.cherryrepublic.com
SIC: 2052 2033 5499 5812 Cookies; barbecue sauce: packaged in cans, jars, etc.; gourmet food stores; snack shop

(G-6210)
KOMMAR INDUSTRIES
6137 Bay Ln (49636-5133)
P.O. Box 25 (49636-0025)
PHONE 231 334-3475
Kerry R Kotila, *Administration*
EMP: 5 **EST:** 2015
SALES (est): 86.2K **Privately Held**
SIC: 3999 Manufacturing industries

(G-6211)
NORTHWODS PRPERTY HOLDINGS LLC
Also Called: Northwoods Hardware
6053 S Glen Lake Rd (49636-9771)
PHONE 231 334-3000
Jeff Gietzen, *General Mgr*
Kyle Lautner, *Mng Member*
EMP: 5 **EST:** 2013
SALES (est): 1MM **Privately Held**
WEB: www.northwoodshardware.com
SIC: 5251 3559 7699 Hardware; glass cutting machinery; locksmith shop

Glennie
Alcona County

(G-6212)
GRIFF & SON TREE SERVICE INC
2921 Lakeshore Dr (48737-9396)
PHONE 989 735-5160
Gary Griffith, *President*
EMP: 5 **EST:** 1972 **Privately Held**
SIC: 0783 3531 Removal services, bush & tree; chippers: brush, limb & log

(G-6213)
LONE WOLF CUSTOM BOWS
3893 Gray St (48737-9371)
PHONE 989 735-3358
Moira Maus, *Owner*
EMP: 4 **EST:** 1989
SALES (est): 140.3K **Privately Held**
WEB: www.lonewolfcustombows.com
SIC: 3949 Bows, archery

(G-6214)
MC GUIRE MILL & LUMBER
4499 Ford Rd (48737-9749)
PHONE 989 735-3851
Richard Mc Guire, *Owner*
EMP: 4 **EST:** 1975
SALES (est): 395.1K **Privately Held**
SIC: 2421 5211 Sawmills & planing mills, general; lumber & other building materials

(G-6215)
NORTHERN CANVAS & UPHOLSTERY
7995 State Rd (48737-9600)
PHONE 989 735-2150
Michelle L Pinko, *Principal*
EMP: 4 **EST:** 2015
SALES (est): 51.5K **Privately Held**
SIC: 2211 Canvas

Gobles
Van Buren County

(G-6216)
ALLOY STEEL TREATING COMPANY
22138 M 40 (49055-8708)
P.O. Box 28 (49055-0028)
PHONE 269 628-2154
Scott Wesler, *President*
Cheryl Wesler, *Manager*
EMP: 22 **EST:** 1963
SQ FT: 15,000
SALES (est): 1MM **Privately Held**
SIC: 3398 Metal heat treating

(G-6217)
H & R WOOD SPECIALTIES INC
20783 County Road 653 (49055-9241)
PHONE 269 628-2181
Jim Hurst, *President*
Kevin McMahon, *General Mgr*
Paul Haluch, *Project Engr*
Karen Case, *Manager*
James Hurst, *Manager*
EMP: 20 **EST:** 1983
SQ FT: 36,000
SALES (est): 3.5MM **Privately Held**
WEB: www.hrwood.com
SIC: 3083 2426 2541 2431 Plastic finished products, laminated; furniture stock & parts, hardwood; display fixtures, wood; trim, wood

(G-6218)
PILLAR MANUFACTURING INC
35620 County Road 388 (49055-8618)
P.O. Box 414 (49055-0414)
PHONE 269 628-5605
Beth Pillar, *President*
Greg Pillar, *Vice Pres*
▲ **EMP:** 15 **EST:** 1985
SQ FT: 12,000
SALES (est): 2.5MM **Privately Held**
WEB: www.pillarmfg.com
SIC: 3532 Mining machinery

(G-6219)
RENDON & SONS MACHINING INC
21870 M 40 (49055-8621)
PHONE 269 628-2200
Jesse Rendon, *President*
James Rendon, *Vice Pres*
EMP: 10 **EST:** 1979
SQ FT: 7,000
SALES (est): 892.8K **Privately Held**
WEB: www.rendonandsons.com
SIC: 3599 3443 Machine shop, jobbing & repair; weldments

(G-6220)
WAHMHOFF FARMS LLC
11121 M 40 (49055-8639)
PHONE 269 628-4308
Ken Wahmhoff, *Partner*
Dan Wahmhoff, *Partner*
Dan Mulhern, *Governor*
Lorie Wahmhoff, *Manager*
EMP: 10 **EST:** 1962
SQ FT: 600
SALES (est): 845.4K **Privately Held**
WEB: www.mitrees.com
SIC: 0811 3441 0782 0181 Christmas tree farm; fabricated structural metal; lawn & garden services; ornamental nursery products; nurseries & garden centers; flowers & florists' supplies

Goodrich
Genesee County

(G-6221)
ALLIED DEFENSE
10420 Valley Creek Dr (48438-8734)
PHONE 810 252-9232
Jonathan Swartz, *Principal*
EMP: 4 **EST:** 2018
SALES (est): 84.6K **Privately Held**
SIC: 3812 Defense systems & equipment

(G-6222)
BURKLAND INC (PA)
6520 S State Rd (48438-8710)
PHONE 810 636-2233
Scott P Nelson, *President*
Mike McHugh, *Production*
Nathan Pahl, *Buyer*
Robert Alm, *Controller*
Julie Thornsberry, *Human Res Mgr*
▲ **EMP:** 137 **EST:** 1961
SQ FT: 77,000
SALES (est): 18MM **Privately Held**
WEB: www.burklandinc.com
SIC: 3465 3469 3544 Automotive stampings; stamping metal for the trade; special dies, tools, jigs & fixtures

(G-6223)
FENTON SYSTEMS INC
7160 S State Rd Ste B (48438-8757)
PHONE 810 636-6318
James F Schembri, *President*
Kathy Thompson, *Prdtn Mgr*
James Crone, *Director*
Stanley Siddall, *Director*
Rick Rathke, *Technician*
EMP: 7 **EST:** 1986
SQ FT: 5,000
SALES (est): 987.1K **Privately Held**
WEB: www.fentonsystems.com
SIC: 3625 7373 Relays & industrial controls; systems integration services

(G-6224)
KENS REDI MIX INC (PA)
8016 S State Rd (48438-8864)
P.O. Box 339 (48438-0339)
PHONE 810 636-2630
Jayme Simmonds, *Principal*
Jeff Bailey, *Comptroller*
EMP: 8 **EST:** 1951
SQ FT: 1,500

Goodrich - Genesee County (G-6225)

SALES (est): 3MM **Privately Held**
WEB: www.kensredimix.com
SIC: **3273** Ready-mixed concrete

(G-6225)
PIFERS AIRMOTIVE INC
11080 Bendix Dr (48438-9445)
PHONE.................248 674-0909
Richard S Pifer, *President*
Lois M Pifer, *Vice Pres*
EMP: 6 EST: 1970
SALES (est): 653.5K **Privately Held**
WEB: www.pifersinc.com
SIC: **3728** Aircraft assemblies, subassemblies & parts

(G-6226)
PORTERS ORCHARDS FARM MARKET
12160 Hegel Rd (48438-9271)
PHONE.................810 636-7156
Raymond Porter, *Owner*
Maxine Porter, *Co-Owner*
EMP: 9 EST: 1921
SQ FT: 4,000
SALES (est): 416.7K **Privately Held**
WEB: www.portersorchard.com
SIC: **0175** 2099 5431 Apple orchard; cider, nonalcoholic; fruit & vegetable markets

(G-6227)
SCHNEIDER NATIONAL INC
10316 Gale Rd (48438-9046)
PHONE.................810 636-2220
Mark Schall, *Branch Mgr*
EMP: 10
SALES (corp-wide): 4.5B **Publicly Held**
WEB: www.schneider.com
SIC: **3559** Automotive related machinery
PA: Schneider National, Inc.
3101 Packerland Dr
Green Bay WI 54313
920 592-2000

Gould City
Mackinac County

(G-6228)
WRIGHT WAY FABRICATION & WELDI
W15383 Us Highway 2 (49838-9054)
PHONE.................602 703-1393
Robert Wright, *Owner*
EMP: 5 EST: 2006
SALES (est): 214.1K **Privately Held**
WEB: www.thewrightwayfab.com
SIC: **7692** Welding repair

Gowen
Kent County

(G-6229)
FIVE COUNT PUBLISHING LLC
16543 Lake Shore Dr (49326-9513)
PHONE.................616 308-6148
Ritchard Rahn Bentley, *Administration*
EMP: 5 EST: 2015
SALES (est): 41.3K **Privately Held**
WEB: www.fivecountpub.com
SIC: **2741** Miscellaneous publishing

(G-6230)
THOMPSON WELL DRILLING
12944 Lincoln Lake Ave (49326-9404)
PHONE.................616 754-5032
Daniel Thompson, *Owner*
Dan Thompson, *Contractor*
EMP: 6 EST: 1965
SALES (est): 844.3K **Privately Held**
WEB: www.thompson-welldrilling.com
SIC: **1381** 1781 Drilling oil & gas wells; water well drilling

Grand Blanc
Genesee County

(G-6231)
ALRO STEEL CORPORATION
3000 Tri Park Dr (48439-7020)
PHONE.................810 695-7300
William McMurphy, *Manager*
EMP: 4
SQ FT: 70,000
SALES (corp-wide): 1.9B **Privately Held**
WEB: www.alrosteel.com
SIC: **5051** 3441 Steel; fabricated structural metal
PA: Alro Steel Corporation
3100 E High St
Jackson MI 49203
517 787-5500

(G-6232)
AMPED ELECTRIC LLC
5384 Silverton Dr (48439-4348)
PHONE.................419 436-1818
EMP: 4 EST: 2018
SALES (est): 88.9K **Privately Held**
WEB: www.ampedelectric.biz
SIC: **2752** Commercial printing, lithographic

(G-6233)
AUXANT SOFTWARE LLC
8340 Loon Ln (48439-7241)
PHONE.................810 584-5947
Raymond Booms, *Principal*
Raymond Powers, *Programmer Anys*
EMP: 4 EST: 2010
SALES (est): 71.9K **Privately Held**
WEB: www.auxant.com
SIC: **7372** Prepackaged software

(G-6234)
BARRON PRECISION INSTRUMENTS
8170 Embury Rd (48439-8192)
P.O. Box 973 (48480-0973)
PHONE.................810 695-2080
Mark Barron, *President*
EMP: 28 EST: 1947
SALES (est): 3.2MM **Privately Held**
WEB: www.bpic.com
SIC: **3841** Skin grafting equipment

(G-6235)
BCT INTERNET LLC
6076 Dort Hwy (48439-8100)
PHONE.................810 771-9117
Bryan Tomczyk, *Principal*
EMP: 4 EST: 2018
SALES (est): 83.9K **Privately Held**
WEB: www.bctinternet.com
SIC: **2752** Commercial printing, lithographic

(G-6236)
BEHIND SHUTTER LLC
7070 Anna St (48439-8571)
PHONE.................248 467-7237
Jessica Butterworth, *Principal*
EMP: 4 EST: 2018
SALES (est): 93.5K **Privately Held**
WEB: www.behindtheshutterllc.com
SIC: **3442** Shutters, door or window: metal

(G-6237)
BURGAFLEX NORTH AMERICA INC
8186 Industrial Park Dr (48439-1865)
PHONE.................810 584-7296
▼ EMP: 12 EST: 2012
SALES (est): 1.6MM **Privately Held**
WEB: www.burgaflexna.com
SIC: **3317** Steel pipe & tubes

(G-6238)
COMET INFORMATION SYSTEMS LLC
Also Called: Carefluence
8359 Office Park Dr (48439-2078)
PHONE.................248 686-2600
Lloyd Williams, *COO*
Aditya Ayyagari, *CTO*
EMP: 15 EST: 2012
SQ FT: 5,000
SALES (est): 971.8K **Privately Held**
WEB: www.carefluence.com
SIC: **7372** Prepackaged software

(G-6239)
CRAZY METALS LLC
6279 Porter Rd (48439-8536)
PHONE.................810 730-9489
Michael A Fox, *Principal*
EMP: 7 EST: 2002
SALES (est): 251.2K **Privately Held**
SIC: **2514** Metal household furniture

(G-6240)
DAG TECHNOLOGY INC
10168 N Holly Rd (48439)
PHONE.................586 276-9310
Dale Hadel, *President*
EMP: 5
SALES (est): 100K **Privately Held**
SIC: **3089** Automotive parts, plastic

(G-6241)
EMBROIDERY HUTCH
10248 Beacon Ct (48439-9484)
PHONE.................810 459-8728
Melanie Hutchinson, *Principal*
EMP: 5 EST: 2016
SALES (est): 41K **Privately Held**
WEB: www.therabbithutchembroidery.com
SIC: **2395** Embroidery & art needlework

(G-6242)
GENESEE CUT STONE & MARBLE CO (PA)
5276 S Saginaw Rd (48507-4493)
PHONE.................810 743-1800
David K Stites, *Managing Prtnr*
Richard J Bouck, *Partner*
Eva Hempel, *Partner*
Douglas Howes, *Partner*
Robert Paul, *Partner*
▲ EMP: 24 EST: 1953
SQ FT: 35,600
SALES (est): 5MM **Privately Held**
WEB: www.gcsm.biz
SIC: **5211** 5032 3281 1423 Masonry materials & supplies; building stone; dimension stone for buildings; crushed & broken granite; crushed & broken limestone

(G-6243)
GLOBAL IMPACT GROUP LLC
Also Called: Global Vehicle Works
9082 S Saginaw Rd (48439-9577)
PHONE.................248 895-9900
Daniel Kocks,
EMP: 6 EST: 2008
SALES (est): 981.1K **Privately Held**
WEB: www.theglobalimpactgroup.org
SIC: **8748** 3711 Business consulting; automobile assembly, including specialty automobiles

(G-6244)
GRAND BLANC CEMENT PDTS INC (PA)
10709 Center Rd (48439-1032)
P.O. Box 585 (48480-0585)
PHONE.................810 694-7500
Kenneth E Minnock, *Ch of Bd*
Norman A Nelson, *President*
Steven K Minnock, *Exec VP*
Michael J Hicks, *Vice Pres*
EMP: 45 EST: 1926
SQ FT: 14,320
SALES (est): 9.9MM **Privately Held**
WEB: www.grandblanccementproducts.com
SIC: **3271** 5211 Blocks, concrete or cinder: standard; brick; concrete & cinder block

(G-6245)
GRAND BLANC PRINTING INC
9449 Holly Rd (48439-8396)
PHONE.................810 694-1155
Morton Stebbins, *President*
EMP: 37 EST: 1968
SQ FT: 14,000
SALES (est): 4.8MM **Privately Held**
WEB: www.grandblancprinting.com
SIC: **2752** 2759 2791 2789 Commercial printing, offset; newspapers: printing; typesetting; bookbinding & related work

(G-6246)
GREAT PUT ON INC
12235 S Saginaw St (48439-1471)
PHONE.................810 771-4174
EMP: 5 EST: 2019
SALES (est): 93.3K **Privately Held**
WEB: www.greatputon.com
SIC: **2759** Screen printing

(G-6247)
HERRMANN AEROSPACE
5202 Moceri Ln (48439-4330)
PHONE.................810 695-1758
Robert Herrmann, *Principal*
EMP: 5 EST: 2007
SALES (est): 73.1K **Privately Held**
SIC: **3812** Aircraft/aerospace flight instruments & guidance systems

(G-6248)
INFECTION PREVENTION TECH LLC
1245 E Grand Blanc Rd (48439-6325)
PHONE.................248 340-8800
Mark Statham,
EMP: 8 EST: 2010
SALES (est): 621K **Privately Held**
WEB: www.skytron.com
SIC: **3648** Lighting equipment

(G-6249)
INNOVATIVE PROGRAMMING SYSTEMS
Also Called: Computer Assistanc
8210 S Saginaw St Ste 1 (48439-2463)
PHONE.................810 695-9332
Duane Zimmer, *President*
Douglas Zimmer, *CIO*
EMP: 5 EST: 1993
SALES (est): 667.8K **Privately Held**
WEB: www.ipsdev.com
SIC: **7372** 7371 Prepackaged software; computer software systems analysis & design, custom

(G-6250)
KING STEEL CORPORATION (PA)
Also Called: American Rod Consumers
5225 E Cook Rd Ste K (48439-8388)
PHONE.................800 638-2530
John King, *CEO*
Doug King, *Principal*
Dave Scribner, *Vice Pres*
Jerry Sudderth, *Vice Pres*
Jon Schnebel, *Opers Staff*
▲ EMP: 20
SQ FT: 2,000
SALES (est): 23.1MM **Privately Held**
WEB: www.kingsteelcorp.com
SIC: **5051** 3312 Steel; bar, rod & wire products

(G-6251)
LLOYD TOOL & MFG CORP
5505 Chatham Ln (48439-9742)
PHONE.................810 694-3519
Richard R Lloyd, *President*
Tamara Garleff, *Corp Secy*
Edwin R Lloyd, *Vice Pres*
EMP: 13 EST: 1969
SQ FT: 21,000
SALES (est): 571.4K **Privately Held**
SIC: **3542** 3548 3544 3541 Presses: hydraulic & pneumatic, mechanical & manual; welding & cutting apparatus & accessories; special dies, tools, jigs & fixtures; machine tools, metal cutting type

(G-6252)
MACARTHUR CORP (PA)
3190 Tri Park Dr (48439-7088)
P.O. Box 10 (48480-0010)
PHONE.................810 606-1777
Christie Wong, *CEO*
Tom Barrett, *President*
Omer Sanjay, *Engineer*
Joshua Schlegelmilch, *Engineer*
Stephanie Blanchard, *Controller*
EMP: 48 EST: 1963
SQ FT: 39,000

GEOGRAPHIC SECTION

Grand Haven - Ottawa County (G-6280)

SALES (est): 11.8MM Privately Held
WEB: www.macarthurcorp.com
SIC: **2672** 2679 2671 2675 Coated & laminated paper; labels, paper: made from purchased material; packaging paper & plastics film, coated & laminated; die-cut paper & board; commercial printing; gaskets, packing & sealing devices

(G-6253)
MICHIGAN HIGHWAY SIGNS INC (PA)
5182 S Saginaw Rd (48507-4470)
PHONE..................................810 695-7529
Timothy Peake, *President*
EMP: 8 EST: 1999
SQ FT: 6,000
SALES (est): 935.4K Privately Held
WEB: www.michigan-highway-signs.com
SIC: **3993** Signs, not made in custom sign painting shops

(G-6254)
NEW TECHNOLOGIES TOOL & MFG
4380 E Baldwin Rd (48439)
P.O. Box 97 (48480-0097)
PHONE..................................810 694-5426
Andrew Bentley, *President*
John Lively, *Vice Pres*
Donald Schopieray, *Vice Pres*
Karen Bentley, *Financial Exec*
Bob Carbary, *Sales Staff*
EMP: 13 EST: 1986
SQ FT: 15,000 Privately Held
WEB: www.newtechnologiesinc.com
SIC: **3599** 3535 Machine shop, jobbing & repair; conveyors & conveying equipment

(G-6255)
PANTHER PUBLISHING
5341 Northwood Rd (48439-3434)
PHONE..................................586 202-9814
EMP: 4 EST: 2017
SALES (est): 85.2K Privately Held
SIC: **2741** Miscellaneous publishing

(G-6256)
PINK PALLET LLC
4176 Knollwood Dr (48439-2025)
PHONE..................................586 873-2982
Suzanne Perreault, *Principal*
EMP: 4 EST: 2014
SALES (est): 59.6K Privately Held
SIC: **2448** Pallets, wood

(G-6257)
PRIME PDIATRICS ADOLESCENT PLC
2291 Lake Ridge Dr (48439-7365)
PHONE..................................281 259-5785
EMP: 4 EST: 2018
SALES (est): 82.3K Privately Held
WEB: www.primepediatricsandadolescent.com
SIC: **7372** Prepackaged software

(G-6258)
PROPRIDE INC
8538 Old Plank Rd (48439-2045)
PHONE..................................810 695-1127
Sean Woodruff, *Principal*
EMP: 5 EST: 2007
SALES (est): 445.3K Privately Held
WEB: www.propridehitch.com
SIC: **3714** Motor vehicle parts & accessories

(G-6259)
PROPRIDE INC
8137 Embury Rd Unit 7 (48439-2710)
PHONE..................................810 962-0219
EMP: 5 EST: 2018
SALES (est): 2.4MM Privately Held
WEB: www.propridehitch.com
SIC: **3714** Motor vehicle parts & accessories

(G-6260)
RDC MACHINE INC
Also Called: Kuntz Tool & Die
11891 Shell Bark Ln (48439-3305)
PHONE..................................810 695-5587
EMP: 4

SALES (est): 200K Privately Held
SIC: **3599** 3544 Machine Shop

(G-6261)
ROCKY MTN CHOCLAT FCTRY INC
12821 S Saginaw St (48439-2457)
PHONE..................................810 606-8550
EMP: 59
SALES (corp-wide): 39.1MM Publicly Held
SIC: **2066** 2064 2026 6794 Mfg Chocolate/Cocoa Prdt Mfg Candy/Confectionery Mfg Fluid Milk Patent Owner/Lessor
PA: Rocky Mountain Chocolate Factory, Inc.
265 Turner Dr
Durango CO 81303
949 579-3000

(G-6262)
RYAN DAUP
11294 Grand Oak Dr Apt 3 (48439-1250)
PHONE..................................810 240-6016
Ryan Daup, *Principal*
EMP: 4 EST: 2018
SALES (est): 63.9K Privately Held
SIC: **3993** Signs & advertising specialties

(G-6263)
SELMURO LTD
Also Called: Premier Tooling Systems
3111 Tri Park Dr (48439-7088)
PHONE..................................810 603-2117
Thomas Self, *CEO*
Richard Ouellette, *President*
Ben Vick, *Engineer*
Matthew Henion, *Design Engr*
EMP: 27 EST: 1992
SQ FT: 17,000
SALES (est): 2.5MM Privately Held
SIC: **3545** 3542 Cutting tools for machine tools; counterbores, metalworking; reamers, machine tool; die casting machines

(G-6264)
STEEL MASTER LLC
8018 Embury Rd (48439-8186)
PHONE..................................810 771-4943
James M Shook, *Mng Member*
Gus Andreopoulos, *Mng Member*
Gus Bisbikis, *Mng Member*
Charles Seitz,
EMP: 30 EST: 1978
SQ FT: 52,000
SALES (est): 2.5MM Privately Held
WEB: www.steelmasterllc.com
SIC: **3535** 3452 Unit handling conveying systems; washers

(G-6265)
UNYPOS MANUFACTURING INC
6203 Westview Dr (48439-9747)
PHONE..................................810 701-8719
Joseph James, *Agent*
EMP: 6 EST: 2018
SALES (est): 86.8K Privately Held
WEB: www.unypos.com
SIC: **3999** Manufacturing industries

(G-6266)
VINYL SASH OF FLINT INC (PA)
5433 Fenton Rd G (48507-4022)
PHONE..................................810 234-4831
Robert Bloss, *President*
Peggy J Bloss, *Admin Sec*
EMP: 40 EST: 1982
SQ FT: 11,600
SALES (est): 4.6MM Privately Held
WEB: www.vinylsash.co
SIC: **1751** 1521 1761 3442 Window & door (prefabricated) installation; patio & deck construction & repair; siding contractor; metal doors, sash & trim

(G-6267)
VISION SOLUTIONS INC
4417 Brighton Dr (48439-8086)
PHONE..................................810 695-9569
David Vanitvelt, *Owner*
EMP: 5 Privately Held
WEB: www.visionsolutions-optometrist.business.site
SIC: **2621** Printing paper

PA: Vision Solutions, Inc.
15300 Barranca Pkwy
Irvine CA 92618

(G-6268)
WGS GLOBAL SERVICES LC
7075 Dort Hwy (48439-8217)
P.O. Box 876 (48480-0876)
PHONE..................................810 694-3843
Anna Whippie, *Plant Mgr*
Pat Goetz, *Branch Mgr*
EMP: 80 Privately Held
WEB: www.wgsglobalservices.com
SIC: **3711** Automobile assembly, including specialty automobiles
PA: Wgs Global Services, L.C.
6350 Taylor Dr
Flint MI 48507

(G-6269)
WICKED WLDG & FABRICATION LLC
8137 Embury Rd Unit 8 (48439-2710)
PHONE..................................517 304-3709
EMP: 4 EST: 2016
SALES (est): 45K Privately Held
WEB: www.wickedweldingandfab.com
SIC: **7692** Welding repair

Grand Haven
Ottawa County

(G-6270)
AALL AMERICAN FASTENERS
1730 Airpark Dr (49417-8981)
PHONE..................................616 414-7688
EMP: 6 EST: 2019
SALES (est): 64.6K Privately Held
WEB: www.aallamericanfasteners.com
SIC: **3965** Fasteners

(G-6271)
AGC GRAND HAVEN LLC
16750 Comstock St (49417-7949)
PHONE..................................616 842-1820
Yongping Gu, *Mng Member*
▲ EMP: 6 EST: 2007
SALES (est): 10MM Privately Held
SIC: **3559** 3463 Automotive maintenance equipment; pump, compressor, turbine & engine forgings, except auto

(G-6272)
ALTERNATE NUMBER FIVE INC (PA)
Also Called: Ultimate Highway Solutions
11095 W Olive Rd (49417-9682)
PHONE..................................616 842-2581
John Carlyle, *Ch of Bd*
Ronald Nienhouse, *President*
Leon Span, *President*
Shawn Howley, *Vice Pres*
Greg Nienhouse, *Vice Pres*
EMP: 73 EST: 1988
SQ FT: 52,000
SALES (est): 21.4MM Privately Held
SIC: **3469** Metal stampings

(G-6273)
ASP PLATING COMPANY
211 N Griffin St (49417-1125)
P.O. Box 227 (49417-0227)
PHONE..................................616 842-8080
Gary Rowe, *President*
EMP: 7 EST: 1947
SALES (est): 505.4K Privately Held
WEB: www.aspplating.com
SIC: **3471** Electroplating of metals or formed products

(G-6274)
ASPC INTERNATIONAL INC
803 Taylor Ave (49417-2159)
PHONE..................................616 842-7800
Steven Moreland, *Principal*
EMP: 5 EST: 2016
SALES (est): 126.5K Privately Held
SIC: **3496** Miscellaneous fabricated wire products

(G-6275)
ASSEM-TECH INC
1600 Kooiman St (49417-2529)
PHONE..................................616 846-3410
Michael Wilson, *President*
Kristine Wentworth, *QC Mgr*
EMP: 50 EST: 1984
SQ FT: 28,000
SALES (est): 7.7MM Privately Held
WEB: www.assem-tech.com
SIC: **3679** 3672 Harness assemblies for electronic use: wire or cable; printed circuit boards

(G-6276)
ASSEMBLY SOURCE ONE INC
17169 Hayes St Ste B (49417-8988)
PHONE..................................616 844-5250
Philip Paul, *President*
Ruth Anne, *Manager*
EMP: 8
SQ FT: 30,000
SALES (est): 670K Privately Held
SIC: **3441** Fabricated structural metal

(G-6277)
ATCOFLEX INC
Also Called: Atco Rubber Products
14261 172nd Ave (49417-9462)
P.O. Box 118 (49417-0118)
PHONE..................................616 842-4661
William H Tuggle, *President*
Darlene Graska, *Opers Mgr*
Jon Graska, *QC Mgr*
Jon E Graska, *Electrical Engi*
Scot Tuggle, *Sales Staff*
EMP: 13 EST: 1978
SQ FT: 65,000
SALES (est): 2.3MM Privately Held
WEB: www.atcoflexinc.com
SIC: **3052** Rubber & plastics hose & beltings

(G-6278)
AUTOMATIC SPRING PRODUCTS CORP (PA)
803 Taylor Ave (49417-2159)
PHONE..................................616 842-2284
Steven Moreland, *President*
Pat Deshaw, *COO*
Bradley Diamond, *Maint Spvr*
Dave Wooden, *Engineer*
Michael Miller, *CFO*
EMP: 155 EST: 1950
SQ FT: 105,000
SALES (est): 28.8MM Privately Held
WEB: www.automaticspring.com
SIC: **3496** 3465 3469 3493 Clips & fasteners, made from purchased wire; automotive stampings; metal stampings; torsion bar springs

(G-6279)
BIGSIGNSCOM
22 S Harbor Dr Unit 101 (49417-1581)
PHONE..................................800 790-7611
Corey Leonard, *President*
Michelle R Alvarez, *Principal*
Tom Suszka, *Sales Staff*
David Luttrull, *Manager*
John P Morales, *Manager*
EMP: 13 EST: 2009
SALES (est): 2.9MM Privately Held
WEB: www.bigsigns.com
SIC: **3993** Signs, not made in custom sign painting shops

(G-6280)
BIOSOLUTIONS LLC
1800 Industrial Dr Ste F (49417-9496)
PHONE..................................616 846-1210
Dave Kittel, *Purchasing*
Gary Verplank,
Budd Brink,
Mark James Lackner,
Peter Sturrus,
EMP: 13 EST: 1996
SQ FT: 10,000
SALES (est): 2.1MM Privately Held
WEB: www.biosolutionsllc.com
SIC: **2842** Specialty cleaning preparations

Grand Haven - Ottawa County (G-6281)

(G-6281)
BRILLIANCE PUBLISHING INC
Also Called: Brilliance Audio
1704 Eaton Dr (49417-2820)
P.O. Box 887 (49417-0887)
PHONE.................616 846-5256
Jeffrey L Belle, *President*
Margaret Carroll, *Dean*
Ted Widmer, *Dean*
Jessi Reuwer, *Human Resources*
Jim Marshall, *Marketing Staff*
▲ EMP: 150
SQ FT: 40,000
SALES (est): 47.5MM **Publicly Held**
WEB: www.brilliancepublishing.com
SIC: 3652 Magnetic tape (audio): prerecorded
PA: Amazon.Com, Inc.
410 Terry Ave N
Seattle WA 98109

(G-6282)
C & M COATINGS INC
1730 Airpark Dr Ste C (49417-8981)
PHONE.................616 842-1925
David Van Portfliet, *President*
EMP: 13 EST: 1959
SQ FT: 10,000
SALES (est): 2.2MM **Privately Held**
WEB: www.conveyor-roller-covers.com
SIC: 3479 Coating of metals with plastic or resins; coating of metals & formed products

(G-6283)
CARLON METER INC
1710 Eaton Dr (49417-2820)
PHONE.................616 842-0420
Bill Hildebrand, *President*
▲ EMP: 9 EST: 1962
SQ FT: 16,000
SALES (est): 1.8MM **Privately Held**
WEB: www.carlonmeter.com
SIC: 3824 Water meters; electromechanical counters

(G-6284)
CHADKO LLC
725 Taylor Ave Ste B (49417-2180)
P.O. Box 965 (49417-0965)
PHONE.................616 402-9207
Carrie Frifeldt, *Mng Member*
EMP: 4 EST: 2002
SQ FT: 4,500
SALES (est): 440.8K **Privately Held**
WEB: www.chadkollc.com
SIC: 3089 Organizers for closets, drawers, etc.: plastic

(G-6285)
CITY AUTO GLASS CO (PA)
Also Called: Glassource
295 N Beechtree St (49417-1158)
PHONE.................616 842-3235
Jim Arnold, *President*
Rose Arnold, *Vice Pres*
Josh Leonard, *Regl Sales Mgr*
Chloe Arnold, *Producer*
Jim Arnolds, *Executive*
▲ EMP: 5 EST: 1974
SALES (est): 1.4MM **Privately Held**
WEB: www.glassource.net
SIC: 3229 3231 Industrial-use glassware; doors, glass: made from purchased glass

(G-6286)
CLASSIC IMAGES EMBROIDERY
15774 Ronny Rd (49417-2946)
PHONE.................616 844-1702
Barbara Lankes,
Michael Lankes,
EMP: 4 EST: 2003
SALES (est): 215.9K **Privately Held**
SIC: 2395 5199 Embroidery products, except schiffli machine; advertising specialties

(G-6287)
COMMERCIAL MFG & ASSEMBLY INC
17087 Hayes St (49417-8990)
PHONE.................616 847-9980
John Geneva, *President*
Chris Geneva, *Principal*
Michael Voss, *Vice Pres*
Jim Platt, *Project Mgr*
Don Silvis, *Treasurer*
▲ EMP: 50
SQ FT: 65,000
SALES (est): 29.1MM **Privately Held**
WEB: www.callcma.com
SIC: 5085 3544 7692 3469 Packing, industrial; punches, forming & stamping; welding repair; metal stampings; sheet metalwork

(G-6288)
CORE-LITE INDUSTRIES LLC
13354 Greenleaf Ln (49417-9453)
PHONE.................616 843-5993
EMP: 4 EST: 2018
SALES (est): 189.6K **Privately Held**
WEB: www.featherblock.net
SIC: 3999 Manufacturing industries

(G-6289)
CORE-LITE INDUSTRIES LLC
13750 172nd Ave Ste A (49417-8979)
PHONE.................616 822-7587
EMP: 4 EST: 2019
SALES (est): 114.4K **Privately Held**
WEB: www.featherblock.net
SIC: 3999 Manufacturing industries

(G-6290)
CORLIN COMPANY
1640 Marion Ave (49417-2366)
P.O. Box 50, Spring Lake (49456-0050)
PHONE.................616 842-7093
John Atherton, *Owner*
EMP: 7 EST: 1984
SQ FT: 6,400
SALES (est): 432.1K **Privately Held**
SIC: 3479 Coating of metals & formed products

(G-6291)
DEPOTTEY ACQUISITION INC
Also Called: Econoline Abrasive Products
401 N Griffin St (49417-1129)
P.O. Box 229 (49417-0229)
PHONE.................616 846-4150
Daniel D Depottey, *President*
Diane Fortenbacher, *Controller*
Tracey Inso, *Accountant*
EMP: 17 EST: 2001
SQ FT: 21,000
SALES (est): 4MM **Privately Held**
SIC: 3449 Miscellaneous metalwork

(G-6292)
DIMENSION PRODUCTS CORPORATION
13746 172nd Ave (49417-8909)
PHONE.................616 842-6050
Ralph J Abraham, *President*
EMP: 10 EST: 1985
SALES (est): 686.3K **Privately Held**
SIC: 3829 Measuring & controlling devices

(G-6293)
DMI SHEET METAL LLC
740 Taylor Ave Ste A (49417-2158)
PHONE.................517 242-6005
EMP: 4 EST: 2018
SALES (est): 188.1K **Privately Held**
SIC: 3444 Sheet metalwork

(G-6294)
EARTHWERKS LLC
319 S 2nd St (49417-1314)
PHONE.................800 275-7943
Henry J Werksma, *Principal*
EMP: 7 EST: 2014
SALES (est): 75.3K **Privately Held**
WEB: www.earthwerks.com
SIC: 5032 3253 Ceramic wall & floor tile; floor tile, ceramic

(G-6295)
ECON-O-LINE ABRASIVE PRODUCTS
401 N Griffin St (49417-1129)
P.O. Box 229 (49417-0229)
PHONE.................616 846-4150
Dan Depottey, *President*
EMP: 11 EST: 1996
SALES (est): 234K **Privately Held**
SIC: 3449 Bars, concrete reinforcing: fabricated steel

(G-6296)
EMERSON ELECTRIC CO
15399 Hofma Dr (49417-9678)
PHONE.................616 846-3950
EMP: 49
SALES (corp-wide): 24.5B **Publicly Held**
SIC: 3823 Mfg Process Control Instruments
PA: Emerson Electric Co.
8000 W Florissant Ave
Saint Louis MO 63136
314 553-2000

(G-6297)
ENGINE POWER COMPONENTS INC
Also Called: Engine Parts Grinding
1333 Fulton Ave (49417-1593)
P.O. Box 837 (49417-0837)
PHONE.................616 846-0110
Mark Quigg, *President*
Duane L Quigg, *Chairman*
Peter Grose, *Vice Pres*
Jeff Ferguson, *Mfg Mgr*
Jackie Vanderweg, *Purch Mgr*
◆ EMP: 300 EST: 1979
SQ FT: 200,000
SALES (est): 36.2MM **Privately Held**
WEB: www.engpwr.com
SIC: 3714 Camshafts, motor vehicle

(G-6298)
ERVOTT TOOL CO LLC
13951 132nd Ave (49417-8722)
PHONE.................616 842-3688
Rob Young, *Partner*
Robin Young,
Mike Ott,
EMP: 5 EST: 1976
SQ FT: 2,000
SALES (est): 250K **Privately Held**
SIC: 3599 Machine shop, jobbing & repair

(G-6299)
FUTURE INDUSTRIES INC
1729 Airpark Dr (49417-9424)
P.O. Box 806 (49417-0806)
PHONE.................616 844-0772
David Schultz, *President*
EMP: 24 EST: 1993
SALES (est): 3.8MM **Privately Held**
WEB: www.futureind.com
SIC: 3469 3498 Stamping metal for the trade; fabricated pipe & fittings

(G-6300)
GHSP INC
Also Called: Kds Controls
1250 S Beechtree St (49417-2840)
PHONE.................248 588-5095
Paul Doyle, *President*
EMP: 7
SALES (corp-wide): 1B **Privately Held**
WEB: www.ghsp.com
SIC: 3714 3625 Motor vehicle parts & accessories; electric controls & control accessories, industrial
HQ: Ghsp, Inc.
701 S Waverly Rd Ste 100
Holland MI 49423
616 842-5500

(G-6301)
GHSP INC
Also Called: Electronics Tech Center
1250 S Beechtree St (49417-2840)
PHONE.................248 581-0890
Kathi Lewis, *COO*
EMP: 7
SALES (corp-wide): 1B **Privately Held**
WEB: www.ghsp.com
SIC: 3714 Motor vehicle parts & accessories
HQ: Ghsp, Inc.
701 S Waverly Rd Ste 100
Holland MI 49423
616 842-5500

(G-6302)
GRAND HAVEN CUSTOM MOLDING LLC
1500 S Beechtree St (49417-2846)
PHONE.................616 935-3160
Karl R Chapel, *Principal*
Matt Whitney, *Purch Mgr*
Bob Chapel, *Engineer*
Alyson Sybesma, *Human Res Mgr*
Dan McFadden, *Clerk*
EMP: 95 EST: 2010
SALES (est): 15.8MM **Privately Held**
WEB: www.ghcmolding.com
SIC: 3089 Injection molding of plastics

(G-6303)
GRAND HAVEN GASKET COMPANY
1701 Eaton Dr (49417-2824)
P.O. Box 671 (49417-0671)
PHONE.................616 842-7682
Ruth Suchecki, *CEO*
Kent Suchecki, *President*
Brad Suchecki, *Vice Pres*
Bradley Suchecki, *Vice Pres*
Douglas Suchecki, *Vice Pres*
EMP: 21 EST: 1969
SQ FT: 45,000
SALES (est): 4.7MM **Privately Held**
WEB: www.ghgc
SIC: 2672 3086 Adhesive backed films, foams & foils; plastics foam products

(G-6304)
GRAND HAVEN POWDER COATING INC
1710 Airpark Dr (49417-9476)
PHONE.................616 850-8822
John Denhartigh, *President*
Sue Rollins, *Corp Secy*
Pete Denhartigh, *Vice Pres*
Deb Zellar, *Manager*
EMP: 30 EST: 2000
SQ FT: 70,000
SALES (est): 3.5MM **Privately Held**
WEB: www.ghpowdercoating.com
SIC: 3479 Coating of metals & formed products

(G-6305)
GRAND HAVEN PUBLISHING CORP
Also Called: Grand Haven Tribune
101 N 3rd St (49417-1209)
PHONE.................616 842-6400
David Rau, *President*
Alice W Rau, *Treasurer*
Alan Rowe, *Accounts Exec*
Susan White, *Admin Sec*
EMP: 5 EST: 1885
SQ FT: 9,000
SALES (est): 2.9MM
SALES (corp-wide): 5.9MM **Privately Held**
WEB: www.grandhaventribune.com
SIC: 2711 2752 Newspapers: publishing only, not printed on site; commercial printing, lithographic
PA: Herald Reflector Inc
61 E Monroe St
Norwalk OH 44857
419 668-3771

(G-6306)
GRAND HAVEN STEEL PRODUCTS INC
Also Called: Dawson Grinding
1627 Marion Ave (49417-2365)
PHONE.................616 842-2740
Barry King, *President*
William Belcher, *Plant Supt*
EMP: 61
SALES (est): 13.5MM **Privately Held**
WEB: www.grandhavensteel.com
SIC: 3451 Screw machine products

(G-6307)
GRAND INDUSTRIES INC
1700 Airpark Dr (49417-9424)
P.O. Box 535 (49417-0535)
PHONE.................616 846-7120
Brad Billinghurst, *President*
Mardy Carr, *General Mgr*
Dave Billinghurst, *Vice Pres*
Beth Norwick, *Office Mgr*
EMP: 35 EST: 1980
SQ FT: 55,000
SALES (est): 7.2MM **Privately Held**
WEB: www.grandindustriesinc.com
SIC: 7389 2448 Packaging & labeling services; cargo containers, wood

GEOGRAPHIC SECTION
Grand Haven - Ottawa County (G-6332)

(G-6308)
GREAT LAKES CONTRACTING INC
14370 172nd Ave (49417-9000)
PHONE..................................616 846-8888
Raymond Buikema, *President*
Jane Kalavitz, *Business Mgr*
EMP: 30 **EST:** 1992
SQ FT: 20,000
SALES (est): 3.2MM **Privately Held**
WEB: www.glccontracting.com
SIC: 3441 Fabricated structural metal

(G-6309)
GTI LIQUIDATING INC (PA)
Also Called: Texas Transformer
1500 Marion Ave (49417-2368)
P.O. Box 799 (49417-0799)
PHONE..................................616 842-5430
Ed Smith, *COO*
EMP: 56 **EST:** 1951
SQ FT: 50,000
SALES (est): 14.6MM **Privately Held**
SIC: 3612 Transformers, except electric

(G-6310)
GTI POWER ACQUISITION LLC (PA)
Also Called: Grand Power Systems
1500 Marion Ave (49417-2368)
P.O. Box 799 (49417-0799)
PHONE..................................616 842-5430
Ed Smith, *CEO*
Chris Donnelly, *Vice Pres*
Jody Hanson, *Human Resources*
James Baughman, *Manager*
Lisa Horton, *Manager*
EMP: 115 **EST:** 2014
SALES (est): 46.1MM **Privately Held**
WEB: www.grandpowersystems.com
SIC: 3612 Autotransformers, electric (power transformers); control transformers; distribution transformers, electric

(G-6311)
GYRO POWDER COATING INC
1624 Marion Ave (49417-2366)
PHONE..................................616 846-2580
Peter Van Oordt, *President*
EMP: 12 **EST:** 1973
SQ FT: 30,000
SALES (est): 1.3MM **Privately Held**
WEB: www.ghpowdercoating.com
SIC: 3479 Coating of metals & formed products

(G-6312)
HARBOR INDUSTRIES INC (PA)
Also Called: Harbor Retail
14130 172nd Ave (49417-9446)
PHONE..................................616 842-5330
Henry T Parker Jr, *President*
Timothy Parker, *President*
Mike Blaskovich, *Managing Dir*
Michael Detenber, *Vice Pres*
Bill Emrich, *Vice Pres*
◆ **EMP:** 70 **EST:** 1950
SQ FT: 190,000
SALES (est): 55.6MM **Privately Held**
WEB: www.harborretail.com
SIC: 2541 3993 Display fixtures, wood; signs & advertising specialties

(G-6313)
HARBOR INDUSTRIES INC
14170 172nd Ave (49417-9446)
PHONE..................................616 842-5330
Henry Parker Jr, *President*
Todd Rose, *Sr Project Mgr*
Ron Kuperus, *Manager*
EMP: 96
SALES (corp-wide): 55.6MM **Privately Held**
WEB: www.harborretail.com
SIC: 2541 Wood partitions & fixtures
PA: Harbor Industries, Inc.
   14130 172nd Ave
   Grand Haven MI 49417
   616 842-5330

(G-6314)
HARDING ENERGY INC
725 Taylor Ave Ste A (49417-2180)
PHONE..................................231 798-7033
Stev Morgan, *President*
Ed Hanenburg, *Chairman*
◆ **EMP:** 32 **EST:** 1987
SALES (est): 4.8MM **Privately Held**
WEB: www.hardingenergy.com
SIC: 3691 Storage batteries

(G-6315)
HAVEN INNOVATION INC
1705 Eaton Dr (49417-2824)
PHONE..................................616 935-1040
Donald Wisner, *President*
Tom Broene, *Controller*
Bayard Saunders, *VP Mktg*
Sammie Baker, *Admin Asst*
▲ **EMP:** 25 **EST:** 2010
SALES (est): 3.1MM **Privately Held**
WEB: www.haveninnovation.com
SIC: 3569 Assembly machines, non-metalworking

(G-6316)
HAVEN MANUFACTURING COMPANY
13720 172nd Ave (49417-8909)
PHONE..................................616 842-1260
James Warners, *President*
EMP: 35 **EST:** 1966
SQ FT: 9,000
SALES (est): 1MM **Privately Held**
WEB: www.havenmanufacturing.com
SIC: 3599 Machine shop, jobbing & repair

(G-6317)
HEYBOER TRANSFORMERS INC (PA)
17382 Hayes St (49417-9305)
PHONE..................................616 842-5830
Arlyn Arendson, *President*
Alden Arendson, *Principal*
Philip Dannenburg, *Vice Pres*
EMP: 24 **EST:** 1957
SQ FT: 13,200 **Privately Held**
WEB: www.heyboertransformers.com
SIC: 3612 Power transformers, electric

(G-6318)
HOLLAND PLASTICS CORPORATION (PA)
Also Called: Anderson Technologies
14000 172nd Ave (49417-9431)
PHONE..................................616 844-2505
Glenn C Anderson, *President*
Jim Morren, *COO*
Steve Bosch, *Vice Pres*
Jim Brown, *Opers Staff*
Chuck Cell, *Engineer*
▲ **EMP:** 50 **EST:** 1948
SQ FT: 80,000
SALES (est): 20.1MM **Privately Held**
WEB: www.andtec.com
SIC: 3089 3544 Injection molding of plastics; special dies, tools, jigs & fixtures; industrial molds; dies, plastics forming

(G-6319)
HOT LOGIC LLC
1705 Eaton Dr (49417-2824)
PHONE..................................616 935-1040
Donald Wisner, *Mng Member*
Kristie Burns, *Director*
EMP: 8 **EST:** 2007
SALES (est): 272.6K **Privately Held**
WEB: www.hotlogic.com
SIC: 3589 Food warming equipment, commercial

(G-6320)
I DO SIGNS
312 S 2nd St (49417-1315)
PHONE..................................616 604-0431
EMP: 4 **EST:** 2017
SALES (est): 47.8K **Privately Held**
WEB: www.i-do-signs.com
SIC: 3993 Signs & advertising specialties

(G-6321)
JOHNSONS FABRICATION AND WLDG
740 Taylor Ave (49417-2158)
PHONE..................................616 607-2202
EMP: 4 **EST:** 2014
SALES (est): 64.4K **Privately Held**
WEB: www.johnsonsfab.com
SIC: 7692 Welding repair

(G-6322)
JOST INTERNATIONAL CORP (DH)
1770 Hayes St (49417-9428)
PHONE..................................616 846-7700
Lee Brace, *President*
Greg Laarman, *President*
Rich Carroll, *Vice Pres*
Richard Carroll, *Vice Pres*
Israel Hildebrandt, *Vice Pres*
◆ **EMP:** 227 **EST:** 1956
SQ FT: 65,000
SALES (est): 105MM
SALES (corp-wide): 939.4MM **Privately Held**
WEB: www.jostinternational.com
SIC: 3714 Motor vehicle parts & accessories
HQ: Jost-Werke International Beteiligungsverwaltung Gmbh
   Siemensstr. 2
   Neu-Isenburg HE 63263
   610 229-50

(G-6323)
JSJ CORPORATION
Also Called: Ghsp
1250 S Beechtree St (49417-2840)
PHONE..................................616 842-5500
Joe Martella, *President*
Anil Mandala, *Business Mgr*
Thomas J Rizzi, *COO*
Bethany Grossman, *Project Mgr*
Dale Harken, *Facilities Mgr*
EMP: 7
SQ FT: 160,000
SALES (corp-wide): 1B **Privately Held**
WEB: www.jsjcorp.com
SIC: 3714 Motor vehicle parts & accessories
PA: Jsj Corporation
   700 Robbins Rd
   Grand Haven MI 49417
   616 842-6350

(G-6324)
JSJ CORPORATION (PA)
700 Robbins Rd (49417-2603)
PHONE..................................616 842-6350
Nelson Jacobson, *President*
James Campbell, *Business Mgr*
Dan Haverstock, *COO*
Barry Lemay, *COO*
Thomas J Rizzi, *COO*
◆ **EMP:** 25 **EST:** 1919
SQ FT: 12,000
SALES (est): 1B **Privately Held**
WEB: www.jsjcorp.com
SIC: 3465 3469 3366 3089 Automotive stampings; metal stampings; castings (except die); brass; injection molded finished plastic products; plastics foam products; chairs, office: padded or plain, except wood

(G-6325)
JSJ DC HOLDINGS INC
724 Robbins Rd (49417-2603)
PHONE..................................616 842-7110
Jason Riemersma, *President*
Susan Brentana, *Buyer*
Eryn Leedy, *Mktg Coord*
Alex Rltzema, *Manager*
Chris Streng, *Manager*
▲ **EMP:** 58 **EST:** 2007
SALES (est): 10MM
SALES (corp-wide): 41.6MM **Privately Held**
WEB: www.lagunatools.com
SIC: 3549 Metalworking machinery
PA: Laguna Tools, Inc.
   7291 Heil Ave
   Huntington Beach CA 92647
   949 474-1200

(G-6326)
JSJ FURNITURE CORPORATION (HQ)
Also Called: Izzy
700 Robbins Rd (49417-2603)
PHONE..................................616 847-6534
Chuck Saylor, *CEO*
Nancy Dallinger, *President*
Rick Glasser, *President*
Gregg Masenthin, *President*
Joan Hill, *COO*
◆ **EMP:** 354 **EST:** 2000
SALES (est): 96.9MM
SALES (corp-wide): 1B **Privately Held**
WEB: www.homewaresinsider.com
SIC: 2521 Cabinets, office: wood
PA: Jsj Corporation
   700 Robbins Rd
   Grand Haven MI 49417
   616 842-6350

(G-6327)
LAKESHORE CUSTOM POWDR COATING
411 N Griffin St (49417-1129)
PHONE..................................616 296-9330
Craig Pitts, *Owner*
EMP: 4 **EST:** 2007
SALES (est): 405.3K **Privately Held**
WEB: www.lakeshorecustompowdercoating.com
SIC: 3479 Coating of metals & formed products

(G-6328)
LAKESHORE FITTINGS INC
Also Called: Cascade Manufacturing
1865 Industrial Park Dr (49417-7970)
PHONE..................................616 846-5090
Albert R Hoffman, *President*
Scott Reus, *General Mgr*
Chris Hendrix, *Engineer*
Luanne Colley, *Sales Mgr*
Albert Hoffman, *Marketing Staff*
EMP: 51 **EST:** 1980
SQ FT: 40,000
SALES (est): 11.4MM
SALES (corp-wide): 1.6B **Privately Held**
WEB: www.alco.com
SIC: 3451 Screw machine products
HQ: Alco Manufacturing Corporation Llc
   10584 Middle Ave
   Elyria OH 44035

(G-6329)
LIGHT CORP INC (PA)
14800 172nd Ave (49417-8969)
PHONE..................................616 842-5100
Gary Verplank, *CEO*
Bradley Davis, *President*
Budd Brink, *Vice Pres*
Ted Dekker, *Engineer*
Shannon Westveld, *Engineer*
▲ **EMP:** 149 **EST:** 1986
SQ FT: 100,000
SALES (est): 30MM **Privately Held**
WEB: www.lightcorp.com
SIC: 3646 Desk lamps, commercial

(G-6330)
LOFTIS ALUMI-TEC INC
13888 172nd Ave (49417-8910)
P.O. Box 753 (49417-0753)
PHONE..................................616 846-1990
James Loftis, *President*
EMP: 9 **EST:** 1989
SQ FT: 13,000
SALES (est): 426.4K **Privately Held**
WEB: www.alumitecmanifolds.com
SIC: 3498 3594 3494 3354 Manifolds, pipe: fabricated from purchased pipe; fluid power pumps & motors; valves & pipe fittings; aluminum extruded products

(G-6331)
LOFTIS MACHINE COMPANY
13888 172nd Ave (49417-8910)
P.O. Box 753 (49417-0753)
PHONE..................................616 846-1990
James Loftis, *President*
EMP: 15 **EST:** 1962
SQ FT: 15,000
SALES (est): 485.8K **Privately Held**
WEB: www.loftismachine.com
SIC: 3599 3444 Machine shop, jobbing & repair; sheet metalwork

(G-6332)
MAGNA DONNELLY CORP
1800 Hayes St (49417-9428)
PHONE..................................616 844-8257
EMP: 9 **EST:** 2019
SALES (est): 486.2K **Privately Held**
SIC: 3714 Motor vehicle parts & accessories

(PA)=Parent Co (HQ)=Headquarters (DH)=Div Headquarters
✪ = New Business established in last 2 years

Grand Haven - Ottawa County (G-6333)

(G-6333)
MAGNA MIRRORS AMERICA INC
Service Parts Division
1800 Hayes St (49417-9428)
PHONE 616 786-7000
Jeff Westbrook, *Engineer*
Terry Bekins, *Project Engr*
Scott Brownlie, *Senior Engr*
Dave Willmore, *Design Engr*
Darin Loveland, *Electrical Engi*
EMP: 5
SQ FT: 50,000
SALES (corp-wide): 32.6B **Privately Held**
WEB: www.magna.com
SIC: 3231 Mirrored glass
HQ: Magna Mirrors Of America, Inc.
5085 Kraft Ave Se
Grand Rapids MI 49512
616 786-7000

(G-6334)
MAPLE LEAF PRESS INC
1215 S Beechtree St (49417-2839)
PHONE 616 846-8844
Vicki Patterson, *President*
Doug Patterson, *Vice Pres*
EMP: 6 **EST:** 1975
SALES (est): 957.5K **Privately Held**
WEB: www.mapleleafpress.com
SIC: 3555 Printing presses

(G-6335)
MECA-SYSTEME USA INC
101 Washington Ave (49417-1302)
PHONE 616 843-5566
William Butch, *Manager*
Alain Gatard, *Director*
▲ **EMP:** 7 **EST:** 2013
SALES (est): 131.3K **Privately Held**
WEB: www.meca-systeme.com
SIC: 3565 Packaging machinery

(G-6336)
MIRUS INDUSTRIES INC
736 Woodlawn Ave (49417-2142)
PHONE 616 402-3256
Philip M Gilbertson, *Principal*
EMP: 6 **EST:** 2010
SALES (est): 134.2K **Privately Held**
SIC: 3999 Manufacturing industries

(G-6337)
MOLDING SOLUTIONS INC (PA)
Also Called: Advanced Molding Solutions
1734 Airpark Dr Ste F (49417-8943)
PHONE 616 847-6822
Robert Buresh, *President*
Bob Buresh, *General Mgr*
Brad Ahrens, *Treasurer*
▲ **EMP:** 20 **EST:** 1999
SQ FT: 10,000
SALES (est): 8.3MM **Privately Held**
SIC: 3089 Injection molding of plastics

(G-6338)
MONTINA MANUFACTURING INC
13740 172nd Ave (49417-8909)
P.O. Box 505, Spring Lake (49456-0505)
PHONE 616 846-1080
Gary Cobb, *President*
Dawn Cobb, *Treasurer*
EMP: 7 **EST:** 1981
SQ FT: 7,000
SALES (est): 1MM **Privately Held**
WEB: www.montinamanufacturing.com
SIC: 3599 Machine shop, jobbing & repair

(G-6339)
NAUTICAL KNOTS
301 N Harbor Dr Ste 12 (49417-1078)
PHONE 231 206-0400
Jeff Gundy, *Owner*
Connie Gundy, *Co-Owner*
EMP: 9 **EST:** 2005
SALES (est): 386.3K **Privately Held**
SIC: 2052 Pretzels

(G-6340)
NETSHAPE INTERNATIONAL LLC
1900 Hayes St (49417-8937)
PHONE 616 846-8700
Gary Verplank, *Ch of Bd*
Michelle Barrett, *Supervisor*
EMP: 55 **EST:** 2000
SALES (est): 5.4MM **Privately Held**
WEB: www.shapecorp.com
SIC: 3449 Miscellaneous metalwork

(G-6341)
OUT ON A LIMB PLAYHOUSES
13104 116th Ave (49417-8899)
PHONE 616 502-4251
Mike A Fraser, *Administration*
EMP: 4 **EST:** 2012
SALES (est): 138.1K **Privately Held**
SIC: 3842 Limbs, artificial

(G-6342)
OUTDOOR LINES LLC
13334 Hidden Creek Dr (49417-8964)
PHONE 616 844-7351
Tricia Gardner, *Principal*
EMP: 6 **EST:** 2013
SALES (est): 168.6K **Privately Held**
WEB: www.outdoorlines.com
SIC: 3949 Sporting & athletic goods

(G-6343)
PARKER PROPERTY DEV INC
Also Called: Stoneway Marble Granite & Tile
12589 104th Ave (49417-9732)
PHONE 616 842-6118
G Kevin Parker, *President*
Karen Parker, *Vice Pres*
EMP: 11 **EST:** 1994
SQ FT: 10,200
SALES (est): 966.6K **Privately Held**
WEB: www.stonewaymarble.com
SIC: 3281 Cut stone & stone products

(G-6344)
POLYPLY COMPOSITES LLC
1540 Marion Ave (49417-2368)
PHONE 616 842-6330
Kip Downhour, *General Mgr*
Tracy Archer, *Plant Mgr*
Dan Lockard, *Director*
Thomas White,
EMP: 40
SQ FT: 70,000
SALES (est): 9MM **Privately Held**
WEB: www.polyplycomposites.com
SIC: 3083 3089 Laminated plastics plate & sheet; plastic processing

(G-6345)
PPG INDUSTRIAL COATINGS
14295 172nd Ave (49417-9431)
PHONE 616 844-4391
EMP: 6 **EST:** 2015
SALES (est): 76K **Privately Held**
WEB: www.corporate.ppg.com
SIC: 2851 Paints & allied products

(G-6346)
PPG INDUSTRIES INC
Also Called: I.V.C. Industrial
1855 Industrial Park Dr (49417-7970)
PHONE 616 846-4400
Jim Holtel, *Human Res Dir*
David McMurtry, *Sales Staff*
Shekhar Nanivadekar, *Manager*
Robert Dyga, *Supervisor*
Kelly Shillings, *Assistant*
EMP: 50
SALES (corp-wide): 15.1B **Publicly Held**
WEB: www.ppg.com
SIC: 2851 Paints & paint additives; enamels; varnishes; lacquer; bases, dopes, thinner
PA: Ppg Industries, Inc.
1 Ppg Pl
Pittsburgh PA 15272
412 434-3131

(G-6347)
PRO SOURCE MANUFACTURING INC
12880 N Cedar Dr (49417-8446)
PHONE 616 607-2990
Kris Rillema, *President*
Keith Rillema, *Engineer*
EMP: 8 **EST:** 2012
SALES (est): 521K **Privately Held**
WEB: www.pro-sourcemfg.com
SIC: 3599 Machine shop, jobbing & repair

(G-6348)
PRO TOOL LLC
14714 Indian Trails Dr (49417-9126)
PHONE 616 850-0556
Jeff Friedgen,
Julie Friedgen,
EMP: 8 **EST:** 2004
SALES (est): 931.7K **Privately Held**
WEB: www.pro-tool-llc.com
SIC: 3544 Special dies & tools

(G-6349)
R A MILLER INDUSTRIES INC (PA)
Also Called: Rami
14500 168th Ave (49417-9460)
P.O. Box 858 (49417-0858)
PHONE 888 845-9450
Paul E Miller, *President*
Jillane Payne, *Vice Pres*
Mark Price, *Opers Staff*
Travis Dahlman, *Buyer*
Kurt Bareham, *Purchasing*
EMP: 119 **EST:** 1956
SQ FT: 110,000
SALES (est): 21.7MM **Privately Held**
WEB: www.rami.com
SIC: 3669 3663 3812 Intercommunication systems, electric; antennas, transmitting & communications; antennas, radar or communications

(G-6350)
RAP ELECTRONICS & MACHINES
13353 Green St (49417-8720)
PHONE 616 846-1437
Rex Pease, *Owner*
Janice Pease, *Treasurer*
EMP: 10 **EST:** 1983
SALES (est): 60K **Privately Held**
SIC: 7378 3824 Computer maintenance & repair; controls, revolution & timing instruments

(G-6351)
REED YACHT SALES LLC
1333 Madison St Blgd A St (49417)
P.O. Box 730 (49417-0730)
PHONE 616 842-8899
EMP: 9
SALES (corp-wide): 1MM **Privately Held**
WEB: www.reedyachtsales.com
SIC: 3732 Yachts, building & repairing
PA: Reed Yacht Sales, Llc
11840 Toledo Beach Rd
La Salle MI 48145
419 304-4405

(G-6352)
REFAB METAL FABRICATION LLC
1811 Hayes St Ste D (49417-9493)
PHONE 616 842-9705
Andrew Dewys, *President*
EMP: 20 **EST:** 2020
SALES (est): 4MM
SALES (corp-wide): 29.5MM **Privately Held**
WEB: www.refabmetalfab.com
SIC: 3441 Fabricated structural metal
PA: Dewys Manufacturing, Inc.
15300 8th Ave
Marne MI 49435
616 677-5281

(G-6353)
RENUCELL
41 Washington Ave Ste 345 (49417-3303)
PHONE 888 400-6032
EMP: 4 **EST:** 2017
SALES (est): 238.8K **Privately Held**
WEB: www.renucell.com
SIC: 2834 Pharmaceutical preparations

(G-6354)
RIDGID SLOTTING LLC
12046 120th Ave (49417-9621)
PHONE 616 847-0332
Jim Bourque,
EMP: 5 **EST:** 1997
SQ FT: 12,000
SALES (est): 185.9K **Privately Held**
WEB: www.ridgidslotting.com
SIC: 3498 Tube fabricating (contract bending & shaping)

(G-6355)
RML INDUSTRIES LLC
14500 168th Ave (49417-9454)
PHONE 616 935-3839
Robert Lynas, *President*
EMP: 6 **EST:** 2012
SALES (est): 141.5K **Privately Held**
SIC: 3663 Radio & TV communications equipment

(G-6356)
RSS BAKER LLC
Also Called: Baker Metal Products Corp.
11118 Us 31 (49417-8808)
PHONE 616 844-5429
Brett Zeerip, *Mng Member*
Dave Willet, *Manager*
Melissa Rookus, *Administration*
EMP: 50 **EST:** 1988
SQ FT: 98,000
SALES (est): 8.1MM **Privately Held**
SIC: 3443 3498 7692 Metal parts; tube fabricating (contract bending & shaping); welding repair
PA: Reliance Service Solutions Llc
11118 Us 31
Grand Haven MI

(G-6357)
SCRUBS MYWAY LLC
13976 Johnson St (49417-8733)
PHONE 616 201-8366
Kimberly S Duerr,
EMP: 5 **EST:** 2019
SALES (est): 99.3K **Privately Held**
SIC: 2326 Medical & hospital uniforms, men's

(G-6358)
SEAVER FINISHING INC
Also Called: E Coat Division
16900 Hayes St (49417-8989)
PHONE 616 844-4360
Craig Seaver, *President*
Andy Bereza, *Opers Mgr*
David L Seaver, *Shareholder*
EMP: 26 **EST:** 1996
SQ FT: 45,000
SALES (est): 870.8K **Privately Held**
WEB: www.seaverfinishing.com
SIC: 3479 Painting of metal products

(G-6359)
SEAVER INDUSTRIAL FINISHING CO
1645 Marion Ave (49417-2365)
P.O. Box 857 (49417-0857)
PHONE 616 842-8560
David L Seaver, *CEO*
Craig Seaver, *President*
EMP: 70 **EST:** 1953
SQ FT: 33,000
SALES (est): 465.7K
SALES (corp-wide): 10.9MM **Privately Held**
WEB: www.seaverfinishing.com
SIC: 3479 3471 Coating of metals & formed products; plating & polishing
PA: Seaver-Smith, Inc.
1645 Marion Ave
Grand Haven MI 49417
616 842-8560

(G-6360)
SEAVER-SMITH INC (PA)
Also Called: Seaver Finishing
1645 Marion Ave (49417-2365)
P.O. Box 857 (49417-0857)
PHONE 616 842-8560
David L Seaver, *CEO*
Craig Seaver, *President*
Jack Blessman, *Plant Mgr*
EMP: 50 **EST:** 1953
SQ FT: 33,000
SALES (est): 10.9MM **Privately Held**
WEB: www.seaverfinishing.com
SIC: 3479 Coating of metals & formed products

GEOGRAPHIC SECTION

Grand Ledge - Eaton County (G-6386)

(G-6361)
SHAPE CORP (PA)
1900 Hayes St (49417-8937)
P.O. Box 369 (49417-0369)
PHONE................................616 846-8700
Gary Verplank, *Ch of Bd*
Mark Butterfield, *Managing Dir*
Pam Obrien, *Editor*
Pete Sturrus, *Vice Chairman*
Shawn Moline, *Regional Mgr*
◆ **EMP:** 300 **EST:** 1974
SQ FT: 225,000
SALES (est): 597.1MM **Privately Held**
WEB: www.shapecorp.com
SIC: 3449 3089 Miscellaneous metalwork; molding primary plastic

(G-6362)
SHAPE CORP
16344 Comstock St (49417-9423)
PHONE................................616 846-8700
Gary Verplank, *Ch of Bd*
EMP: 129
SALES (corp-wide): 597.1MM **Privately Held**
WEB: www.shapecorp.com
SIC: 3449 Miscellaneous metalwork
PA: Shape Corp.
1900 Hayes St
Grand Haven MI 49417
616 846-8700

(G-6363)
SNAP DISPLAY FRAMES
101 Washington Ave (49417-1302)
PHONE................................616 846-7747
EMP: 4 **EST:** 2016
SALES (est): 160.4K **Privately Held**
WEB: www.snapdisplayframes.com
SIC: 3993 Signs & advertising specialties

(G-6364)
SOS ENGINEERING INC
1901 Hayes St (49417-8937)
PHONE................................616 846-5767
David Suchecki, *President*
Brett Suchecki, *Vice Pres*
EMP: 16 **EST:** 1973
SQ FT: 25,000
SALES (est): 2.3MM **Privately Held**
WEB: www.sosengineering.net
SIC: 3469 Stamping metal for the trade

(G-6365)
SPRIK CUSTOM WOODWORKS LLC
13139 Sikkema Dr (49417-8913)
PHONE................................616 826-0858
Joshua Sprik, *Principal*
EMP: 6 **EST:** 2017
SALES (est): 54.1K **Privately Held**
WEB: www.sprikcw.com
SIC: 2431 Millwork

(G-6366)
STANCO METAL PRODUCTS INC (PA)
Also Called: Stanco Metal Products Company
2101 168th Ave (49417-9396)
PHONE................................616 842-5000
Gerald Slagel, *President*
Benjamin Slagel, *Vice Pres*
Dennis Bayle, *QC Mgr*
Steve Zimmer, *Engineer*
Kevin Fortier, *Project Engr*
◆ **EMP:** 45 **EST:** 1917
SQ FT: 135,000
SALES (est): 38.6MM **Privately Held**
WEB: www.stancometal.com
SIC: 3465 3469 Automotive stampings; stamping metal for the trade

(G-6367)
STAR BOARD MULTI MEDIA INC
Also Called: Star Board ATT Tev
41 Washington Ave Ste 395 (49417-3305)
PHONE................................616 296-0823
Kevin Galbavi, *President*
EMP: 5 **EST:** 1999
SALES (est): 406.3K **Privately Held**
WEB: www.starboardappdev.com
SIC: 3674 7336 7374 7372 Read-only memory (ROM); graphic arts & related design; computer graphics service; application computer software

(G-6368)
STEADFAST ENGINEERED PDTS LLC
775 Woodlawn Ave (49417-2141)
PHONE................................616 846-4747
Allan J Westmaas II,
Jay Cutie,
EMP: 15 **EST:** 1996
SQ FT: 10,000
SALES (est): 609K **Privately Held**
WEB: www.steadfastep.com
SIC: 3451 Screw machine products

(G-6369)
SWEET TMPTTONS ICE CREAM PRLOR
1003 S Beacon Blvd (49417-2585)
PHONE................................616 842-8108
Ray Marine, *Owner*
EMP: 4 **EST:** 2001
SALES (est): 277.7K **Privately Held**
WEB: www.sweet-temptations.com
SIC: 2024 Ice cream & frozen desserts

(G-6370)
TELESCOPIC SEATING SYSTEMS LLC (PA)
335 N Griffin St (49417-1127)
P.O. Box 1556, Holland (49422-1556)
PHONE................................855 713-0118
Denise Jacobs, *President*
Fred Jacobs, *Vice Pres*
EMP: 12 **EST:** 2012
SALES (est): 1.6MM **Privately Held**
WEB: www.telescopicseatingsystems.com
SIC: 5021 2531 3999 Theater seats; public building & related furniture; barber & beauty shop equipment

(G-6371)
TRAINER METAL FORMING CO INC
Also Called: Steel Forming Systems
14080 172nd Ave (49417-9431)
P.O. Box 139 (49417-0139)
PHONE................................616 844-9982
D J Trainer, *President*
Jeffrey W Harms, *Principal*
EMP: 33 **EST:** 1988
SQ FT: 79,000
SALES (est): 3.6MM **Privately Held**
WEB: www.steelformingsystems.com
SIC: 3544 Special dies & tools

(G-6372)
TRANSFER TOOL SYSTEMS LLC
Also Called: Transfer Tool Products
14444 168th Ave (49417-9454)
PHONE................................616 846-8510
James Raterink, *President*
John M Fiore, *Vice Pres*
Heath Verstraete, *Opers Staff*
Amanda Montgomery, *Senior Buyer*
Randy Barnhard, *Engineer*
EMP: 103
SQ FT: 45,000
SALES (est): 19.1MM **Privately Held**
WEB: www.transfertool.com
SIC: 3469 3541 3965 Stamping metal for the trade; machine tool replacement & repair parts, metal cutting types; fasteners, buttons, needles & pins

(G-6373)
TRUSTED TOOL MFG GRAND HAVEN
1800 Industrial Dr (49417-9496)
PHONE................................616 607-2023
EMP: 9 **EST:** 2014
SALES (est): 90.2K **Privately Held**
WEB: www.trustedtoolmfg.com
SIC: 3599 Machine shop, jobbing & repair

(G-6374)
UNISLAT LLC
13660 172nd Ave (49417-8908)
PHONE................................616 844-4211
Jeff Berry,
EMP: 4 **EST:** 2009
SQ FT: 5,000
SALES (est): 408.6K **Privately Held**
WEB: www.unislat.com
SIC: 2541 Display fixtures, wood

(G-6375)
UNIVERSAL COATING TECHNOLOGY
16891 Johnson St Ste A (49417-8461)
PHONE................................616 847-6036
Timothy Widner, *Owner*
Tim Widener, *Sales Staff*
EMP: 6 **EST:** 1991
SQ FT: 6,000
SALES (est): 650.9K **Privately Held**
WEB: www.universalcoatingtech.com
SIC: 3479 Coating of metals & formed products

(G-6376)
UV PARTNERS INC (PA)
Also Called: Uv Angel
233 Washington Ave (49417-1374)
PHONE................................888 277-2596
Paul Byrne, *Vice Pres*
Luke Platz, *Engineer*
Douglas Sharp, *Administration*
EMP: 7 **EST:** 2015
SALES (est): 1.2MM **Privately Held**
WEB: www.uvangel.com
SIC: 3845 5731 Electromedical equipment; consumer electronic equipment

(G-6377)
V & V INC
Also Called: Harbor Deburring & Finshg Co
1703 Eaton Dr (49417-2824)
P.O. Box 547 (49417-0547)
PHONE................................616 842-8611
Steven Vink, *President*
EMP: 24 **EST:** 1962
SQ FT: 37,500
SALES (est): 578.1K **Privately Held**
SIC: 3471 Finishing, metals or formed products; tumbling (cleaning & polishing) of machine parts

(G-6378)
VAN PELT INDUSTRIES LLC
720 Taylor Ave (49417-2158)
P.O. Box 541 (49417-0541)
PHONE................................616 842-1200
Holly Bacon,
Kevin Bacon,
EMP: 4 **EST:** 2011
SQ FT: 18,000
SALES (est): 306.2K **Privately Held**
SIC: 3498 Tube fabricating (contract bending & shaping)

(G-6379)
WARNER INSTRUMENTS
Also Called: Fireight Controls
1320 Fulton Ave (49417-1534)
PHONE................................616 843-5342
Gene L Warner, *Owner*
EMP: 7 **EST:** 1976
SQ FT: 4,600
SALES (est): 510K **Privately Held**
WEB: www.warneronline.com
SIC: 3823 3822 3625 Temperature instruments: industrial process type; auto controls regulating residntl & coml environmt & applncs; relays & industrial controls

(G-6380)
WARNER POWER ACQUISITION LLC (HQ)
1500 Marion Ave (49417-2368)
PHONE................................603 456-3111
Nick Hoiles, *Principal*
Souheil Benzerrouk, *Vice Pres*
Maryann Burout, *Vice Pres*
Scott Everett, *Vice Pres*
Kevin Shannon, *Vice Pres*
◆ **EMP:** 135 **EST:** 1999
SALES (est): 46.1MM **Privately Held**
WEB: www.grandpowersystems.com
SIC: 3699 5063 Electrical equipment & supplies; transformers, electric
PA: Gti Power Acquisition, Llc
1500 Marion Ave
Grand Haven MI 49417
616 842-5430

(G-6381)
WARNER POWER CONVERSION LLC
1500 Marion Ave (49417-2368)
PHONE................................603 456-3111
Nick Hoiles, *CEO*
EMP: 39 **EST:** 1999
SALES (est): 4MM
SALES (corp-wide): 46.1MM **Privately Held**
WEB: www.grandpowersystems.com
SIC: 3629 Power conversion units, a.c. to d.c.: static-electric
HQ: Warner Power Acquisition, Llc
1500 Marion Ave
Grand Haven MI 49417
603 456-3111

(G-6382)
WEST MICHIGAN MOLDING INC
Also Called: Grand Haven Nursery Products
1425 Aerial View Dr (49417-9400)
PHONE................................616 846-4950
Alan Chapel, *President*
Karl Chapel, *Vice Pres*
Mark Lulofs, *VP Mfg*
Rick Boes, *Purch Mgr*
Wayne Brummitt, *Purch Mgr*
▲ **EMP:** 103 **EST:** 1983
SALES (est): 22.6MM **Privately Held**
WEB: www.wmmolding.com
SIC: 3089 Injection molded finished plastic products; injection molding of plastics

Grand Junction
Van Buren County

(G-6383)
SOLLMAN & SON MOLD & TOOL
Also Called: S & S Mold & Tool
254 58th St (49056-9534)
PHONE................................269 236-6700
Todd Sollman, *President*
EMP: 4 **EST:** 1996
SALES (est): 350.5K **Privately Held**
WEB: www.sandsmold.com
SIC: 3599 Machine shop, jobbing & repair

Grand Ledge
Eaton County

(G-6384)
AMERICAN BOTTLING COMPANY
Also Called: 7 Up Lansing
1145 Comet Ln (48837-9363)
PHONE................................517 622-8605
Jim Willett, *Manager*
EMP: 14 **Publicly Held**
WEB: www.keurigdrpepper.com
SIC: 2086 5149 Soft drinks: packaged in cans, bottles, etc.; groceries & related products
HQ: The American Bottling Company
6425 Hall Of Fame Ln
Frisco TX 75034

(G-6385)
ARCHER-DANIELS-MIDLAND COMPANY
Also Called: ADM
16994 Wright Rd (48837-9258)
PHONE................................517 627-4017
Don Seidl, *Branch Mgr*
EMP: 4
SALES (corp-wide): 64.3B **Publicly Held**
WEB: www.adm.com
SIC: 2041 Flour & other grain mill products
PA: Archer-Daniels-Midland Company
77 W Wacker Dr Ste 4600
Chicago IL 60601
312 634-8100

(G-6386)
BITZENBURGER MACHINE & TOOL
13060 Lawson Rd (48837-9701)
PHONE................................517 627-8433
Jerry Anderson, *Owner*
Bill Anderson, *Manager*
EMP: 4 **EST:** 1996
SALES (est): 291.4K **Privately Held**
WEB: www.bitzenburger.com
SIC: 3949 Archery equipment, general

Grand Ledge - Eaton County (G-6387)

GEOGRAPHIC SECTION

(G-6387)
CORE TECHNOLOGY CORPORATION
11518 Millstone Dr (48837-2290)
PHONE 517 627-1521
David Hadsall, *President*
Jill McCready, *Controller*
Sarah Lee, *Accounts Mgr*
EMP: 15 **EST:** 1981
SQ FT: 7,000
SALES (est): 5.7MM **Privately Held**
WEB: www.coretechcorp.com
SIC: 7372 7371 Business oriented computer software; custom computer programming services
PA: Harris Systems Usa, Inc

    Jersey City NJ
    613 226-5511

(G-6388)
DANS CONCRETE LLC
9202 Riverside Dr (48837-9273)
PHONE 517 242-0754
Daniel Rahall,
EMP: 9
SALES (est): 250K **Privately Held**
SIC: 2951 Asphalt paving mixtures & blocks

(G-6389)
E-T-M ENTERPRISES I INC (PA)
920 N Clinton St (48837-1106)
PHONE 517 627-8461
David Mohnke, *Ch of Bd*
Troy Ward, *Opers Mgr*
Tony Fitzpatrick, *Engineer*
Scott Wallas, *CFO*
Jim Sundstrom, *Sales Staff*
▲ **EMP:** 163 **EST:** 1970
SQ FT: 100,000
SALES (est): 28.2MM **Privately Held**
WEB: www.etmenterprises.com
SIC: 3544 3089 3714 3713 Special dies & tools; spouting, plastic & glass fiber reinforced; motor vehicle parts & accessories; truck & bus bodies

(G-6390)
ENERCO CORPORATION (PA)
317 N Bridge St (48837-1632)
PHONE 517 627-1669
Robert T Othmer, *President*
Jo Ann Cranson, *Vice Pres*
Jo Cranson, *Vice Pres*
Rudy Othmer, *Vice Pres*
Kay Taylor, *Treasurer*
EMP: 18 **EST:** 1977
SALES (est): 2.9MM **Privately Held**
WEB: www.enercocorp.com
SIC: 2899 Water treating compounds

(G-6391)
GRAND APPS LLC
13150 Lawson Rd (48837-9649)
P.O. Box 128 (48837-0099)
PHONE 517 927-5140
David Kreager, *Principal*
EMP: 8 **EST:** 2010
SALES (est): 264.1K **Privately Held**
SIC: 2752 2759 7336 Promotional printing, lithographic; screen printing; silk screen design

(G-6392)
GREAT LAKES NEON
9861 W Grand River Hwy (48837-9259)
PHONE 517 582-7451
Sain Robert, *Principal*
EMP: 5 **EST:** 2016
SALES (est): 123.2K **Privately Held**
SIC: 2813 Neon

(G-6393)
KENS CARBURETOR SERVICE INC
13828 Hartel Rd (48837-9301)
PHONE 517 627-1417
EMP: 4 **EST:** 2019
SALES (est): 121K **Privately Held**
SIC: 3592 Carburetors

(G-6394)
L & W INC
Also Called: L & W, Engineering
13112 Oneida Rd (48837-9772)
PHONE 517 627-7333
Jeanne Blasciuc, *Senior Buyer*
Ron Buchanan, *QC Mgr*
EMP: 10
SALES (corp-wide): 3.1B **Privately Held**
WEB: www.autokiniton.com
SIC: 3469 Stamping metal for the trade
HQ: L & W, Inc.
    17757 Woodland Dr
    New Boston MI 48164
    734 397-6300

(G-6395)
LEDGES SIGN COMPANY
136 N Clinton St (48837-1637)
PHONE 517 925-1139
EMP: 4 **EST:** 2009
SALES (est): 11.9K **Privately Held**
SIC: 3993 Signs & advertising specialties

(G-6396)
MICHIGAN POLY PIPE INC
Also Called: Michigan Pipe Company
10242 W Grand River Hwy (48837-9204)
PHONE 517 709-8100
Chad Cadwell, *President*
EMP: 7 **EST:** 2018
SQ FT: 3,000
SALES (est): 6MM **Privately Held**
WEB: www.michiganpoly.com
SIC: 3321 Cast iron pipe & fittings

(G-6397)
PITCHFORD BERTIE
Also Called: Pitchfords Auto Parts & Svc
7821 W Grand River Hwy (48837-8212)
PHONE 517 627-1151
Bertie Pitchford, *Owner*
David Pitchford, *Principal*
EMP: 6 **EST:** 1985
SQ FT: 4,400
SALES (est): 493.5K **Privately Held**
SIC: 7538 7539 3546 General automotive repair shops; machine shop, automotive; saws & sawing equipment

(G-6398)
RT SWANSON INC
1030 Tulip St (48837-2045)
PHONE 517 627-4955
Richard Swanson, *President*
EMP: 6 **EST:** 1989
SALES (est): 387.4K **Privately Held**
WEB: www.churchorgantrader.com
SIC: 3931 Organ parts & materials

(G-6399)
SPECIALTY WELDING
12703 Melody Rd (48837-8940)
PHONE 517 627-5566
Jim Westwood, *Owner*
EMP: 6 **EST:** 1979
SALES (est): 137.8K **Privately Held**
WEB: www.specialtyweldingfl.com
SIC: 7692 1799 Welding repair; welding on site

(G-6400)
VIETH CONSULTING LLC
209 S Bridge St (48837-1526)
PHONE 517 622-3090
Billy Jean, *Sales Mgr*
Christopher Vieth, *Mng Member*
EMP: 16 **EST:** 2000
SALES (est): 1.1MM **Privately Held**
WEB: www.viethconsulting.com
SIC: 7372 Prepackaged software

(G-6401)
ZION INDUSTRIES INC
1180 Comet Ln (48837-9321)
PHONE 517 622-3409
Jonathan Holman, *Plant Mgr*
Lou Ghinga, *Prdtn Mgr*
Mark Shoemaker, *Opers Staff*
Bradly Cardwell, *Sales Staff*
Steve Sandstedt, *Manager*
EMP: 10
SALES (corp-wide): 11MM **Privately Held**
WEB: www.zioninduction.com
SIC: 3398 Metal heat treating
PA: Zion Industries, Inc.
    6229 Grafton Rd
    Valley City OH 44280
    330 225-3246

Grand Rapids
Kent County

(G-6402)
2 GEN MANUFACTURING LLC
3025 Madison Ave Se (49548-1209)
PHONE 616 443-7886
EMP: 7 **EST:** 2019
SALES (est): 463.3K **Privately Held**
SIC: 3999 Manufacturing industries

(G-6403)
20/20 PRINTING
1702 Glenvale Ct Sw (49519-4994)
PHONE 616 635-9690
Tim Powell, *Principal*
EMP: 6 **EST:** 2007
SALES (est): 127.7K **Privately Held**
SIC: 2752 Commercial printing, lithographic

(G-6404)
3D PRINTED PARTS
4355 Airwest Dr Se (49512-3920)
PHONE 616 516-3074
Mike McLean, *General Mgr*
EMP: 6 **EST:** 2017
SALES (est): 158.3K **Privately Held**
WEB: www.3dprintedparts.com
SIC: 2752 Commercial printing, lithographic

(G-6405)
3DM SOURCE INC
555 Plymouth Ave Ne (49505-6029)
PHONE 616 647-9513
Brian Huff, *President*
Drew Boersma, *Treasurer*
EMP: 16 **EST:** 2006
SQ FT: 6,000
SALES (est): 265.8K **Privately Held**
SIC: 3842 5999 Surgical appliances & supplies; business machines & equipment

(G-6406)
3DXTECH LLC
904 36th St Se Ste B (49508-2532)
PHONE 616 717-3811
Matthew Howlett, *President*
EMP: 12 **EST:** 2015
SALES (est): 3.4MM **Privately Held**
WEB: www.3dxtech.com
SIC: 3672 Printed circuit boards

(G-6407)
A & K FINISHING INC
4175 Danvers Ct Se (49512-4041)
P.O. Box 888159 (49588-8159)
PHONE 616 949-9100
Jerry Posthumus, *Business Mgr*
Vincent Larkin, *Production*
Richard Barnes, *QC Mgr*
Steve Levingston, *Marketing Staff*
Don Bolt, *Manager*
EMP: 12 **Privately Held**
WEB: www.akfinishing.com
SIC: 3479 Etching & engraving; painting, coating & hot dipping
PA: A & K Finishing, Inc.
    4436 Donkers Ct Se
    Grand Rapids MI 49512

(G-6408)
A A A MAILING & PACKG SUPS LLC
Also Called: D N D Business Machines
3148 Plainfield Ave Ne # 258 (49525-3285)
PHONE 616 481-9120
Joe Feller, *Mng Member*
EMP: 4 **EST:** 2009
SALES (est): 200K **Privately Held**
SIC: 3579 Mailing, letter handling & addressing machines

(G-6409)
A C MACHINING LLC
7490 Division Ave S (49548-7162)
PHONE 616 455-3870
Ann Timmer, *Principal*
Allen Timmer,
EMP: 5 **EST:** 1998
SALES (est): 250K **Privately Held**
SIC: 3599 Machine shop, jobbing & repair

(G-6410)
A K OIL LLC DBA SPEEDY OIL AND
925 Leonard St Nw (49504-4153)
PHONE 616 233-9505
Alex Kanaan, *Principal*
EMP: 4 **EST:** 2010
SALES (est): 270.5K **Privately Held**
SIC: 2992 Lubricating oils

(G-6411)
A TASTE OF LEONE LLC
736 Cherry St Se (49503-4745)
PHONE 616 238-8881
Yohan Aharon,
EMP: 5 **EST:** 2020
SALES (est): 50K **Privately Held**
SIC: 2836 Culture media

(G-6412)
A-PAC MANUFACTURING COMPANY
2719 Courier Dr Nw (49534-1247)
PHONE 616 791-7222
Leonard J Fouty, *President*
David Kraai, *Corp Secy*
Tim Takken, *Plant Mgr*
Sara Collins, *Purchasing*
Michael Janiga, *Marketing Mgr*
EMP: 48 **EST:** 1984
SQ FT: 34,000
SALES (est): 8.2MM **Privately Held**
WEB: www.polybags.com
SIC: 3081 2673 Packing materials, plastic sheet; bags; plastic, laminated & coated

(G-6413)
A1 POWDER COATING
3460 Fruit Ridge Ave Nw (49544-9707)
PHONE 616 238-0683
EMP: 4 **EST:** 2016
SALES (est): 79.8K **Privately Held**
WEB: www.a1powdercoatingmi.com
SIC: 3479 Coating of metals & formed products

(G-6414)
A2Z COATING
200 Garden St Se (49507-1711)
PHONE 616 805-3281
EMP: 5 **EST:** 2015
SALES (est): 133K **Privately Held**
SIC: 3479 Metal coating & allied service

(G-6415)
ABC COATING COMPANY INC
Also Called: ABC Coating Company Michigan
1503 Burlingame Ave Sw (49509-1001)
P.O. Box 9484 (49509-0484)
PHONE 616 245-4626
Marcella Acuna, *President*
EMP: 10
SALES (corp-wide): 8.1MM **Privately Held**
SIC: 3312 Blast furnaces & steel mills
PA: Abc Coating Company, Inc.
    2236 S Yukon Ave
    Tulsa OK 74107
    918 585-2587

(G-6416)
ABC NAILS LLC
20 Monroe Center St Ne # 110 (49503-3276)
PHONE 616 776-6000
Charlie Vu, *Mng Member*
EMP: 4 **EST:** 2006
SALES (est): 185.7K **Privately Held**
WEB: www.abcnailsmi.com
SIC: 2824 Anidex fibers

(G-6417)
ABLE MANUFACTURING INC
601 Crosby St Nw (49504-3104)
PHONE 616 235-3322
Russ Golemba, *President*
Jeff Miller, *Manager*
Richard Barnes, *CIO*
EMP: 47 **EST:** 1960

▲ = Import ▼ = Export
♦ = Import/Export

GEOGRAPHIC SECTION
Grand Rapids - Kent County (G-6442)

SQ FT: 20,000
SALES (est): 2.9MM **Privately Held**
WEB: www.ablemanufacturing.com
SIC: 3599 Grinding castings for the trade; machine shop, jobbing & repair

(G-6418)
ACCELERATED TOOLING LLC
2909 Buchanan Ave Sw (49548-1027)
PHONE 616 293-9612
Scott Oshinski, *Mng Member*
Chris Brooker,
EMP: 13 **EST:** 2005
SALES (est): 2.1MM **Privately Held**
WEB: www.acceltool.com
SIC: 3599 Machine shop, jobbing & repair

(G-6419)
ACCUFORM INDUSTRIES INC (PA)
1701 Broadway Ave Nw (49504-2049)
PHONE 616 363-3801
Mark Holleman, *President*
EMP: 11 **EST:** 1966
SQ FT: 20,000
SALES (est): 2.1MM **Privately Held**
WEB: www.accuformgr.com
SIC: 3444 Sheet metal specialties, not stamped

(G-6420)
ACCUFORM INDUSTRIES INC
Also Called: Accu-Form Metal Products
1701 Broadway Ave Nw (49504-2049)
PHONE 616 363-3801
Mark Holleman, *Manager*
EMP: 4
SALES (corp-wide): 2.1MM **Privately Held**
WEB: www.accuformgr.com
SIC: 3444 Sheet metal specialties, not stamped
PA: Accuform Industries, Inc.
   1701 Broadway Ave Nw
   Grand Rapids MI 49504
   616 363-3801

(G-6421)
ACCURATE COATING INC
955 Godfrey Ave Sw (49503-5003)
P.O. Box 1214 (49501-1214)
PHONE 616 452-0016
Dave Kasper, *Principal*
EMP: 5 **EST:** 2007
SALES (est): 663.9K **Privately Held**
WEB: www.accuratecoatinginc.com
SIC: 3471 Electroplating of metals or formed products

(G-6422)
ACE VENDING SERVICE INC
Also Called: Kent Commerce Center
3417 Rger B Chffee Mem Bl (49548-2358)
PHONE 616 243-7983
Thomas Lileikis, *Vice Pres*
EMP: 10 **EST:** 1955
SQ FT: 77,000
SALES (est): 4MM **Privately Held**
WEB: www.acevendingservice.com
SIC: 5962 6512 5963 2099 Sandwich & hot food vending machines; commercial & industrial building operation; direct selling establishments; food preparations

(G-6423)
ACTION FABRICATORS INC
Also Called: Boyd
3760 East Paris Ave Se (49512-3903)
PHONE 616 957-2032
Matt Alferink, *President*
Donald Armbrester, *Exec VP*
Don Armbrester, *Vice Pres*
Bruce Barthuly, *Plant Supt*
Robin Hay, *Purch Mgr*
EMP: 150
SQ FT: 105,000
SALES (est): 47.8MM **Privately Held**
WEB: www.boydcorp.com
SIC: 3053 3086 2891 Gaskets, all materials; plastics foam products; adhesives
PA: Lti Holdings, Inc.
   5960 Inglewood Dr Ste 115
   Pleasanton CA 94588

(G-6424)
ACTION MOLD & MACHINING INC
3120 Ken O Sha Ind Pk Ct (49508-1360)
PHONE 616 452-1580
Michael Paul Fassbender, *President*
Becky Lytle, *Advisor*
▲ **EMP:** 45 **EST:** 1997
SALES (est): 7.8MM **Privately Held**
WEB: www.actionmold.net
SIC: 3544 Special dies & tools

(G-6425)
ACTT MANAGEMENT LLC
Also Called: Crumbl Cookies Grand Rapids
3577 28th St Se Ste G4 (49512-1603)
PHONE 616 803-8734
Berry Lemay,
EMP: 30 **EST:** 2020
SALES (est): 1.1MM **Privately Held**
SIC: 2052 Cookies

(G-6426)
ADAC AUTOMOTIVE TRIM INC (HQ)
5690 Eagle Dr Se (49512-2057)
P.O. Box 888375 (49588-8375)
PHONE 616 957-0311
Kenneth G Hungerford, *CEO*
Jim Teets, *President*
Stokes Jeff, *Program Mgr*
▲ **EMP:** 39 **EST:** 2000
SALES (est): 18MM
SALES (corp-wide): 285.6MM **Privately Held**
WEB: www.adacautomotive.com
SIC: 3714 Motor vehicle parts & accessories
PA: Adac Plastics, Inc.
   5690 Eagle Dr Se
   Grand Rapids MI 49512
   616 957-0311

(G-6427)
ADAC DOOR COMPONENTS INC
Also Called: Adac Automotive
5690 Eagle Dr Se (49512-2057)
P.O. Box 888375 (49588-8375)
PHONE 616 957-0311
Jim Teets, *President*
Ken Hungerford II, *Chairman*
Evan Dewitt, *Engineer*
Jeff Dolbee, *CFO*
Ben Hartstock, *Program Mgr*
▲ **EMP:** 434 **EST:** 1998
SALES (est): 1.9MM
SALES (corp-wide): 285.6MM **Privately Held**
WEB: www.adacautomotive.com
SIC: 3089 3711 Injection molding of plastics; motor vehicles & car bodies
PA: Adac Plastics, Inc.
   5690 Eagle Dr Se
   Grand Rapids MI 49512
   616 957-0311

(G-6428)
ADAC PLASTICS INC (PA)
Also Called: Adac Automotive
5690 Eagle Dr Se (49512-2057)
P.O. Box 888375 (49588-8375)
PHONE 616 957-0311
Jim Teets, *CEO*
Kenneth G Hungerford, *Ch of Bd*
Adam Smith, *Business Mgr*
Peter Hungerford, *COO*
Jeff Ackerman, *Exec VP*
▲ **EMP:** 40 **EST:** 1975
SQ FT: 13,000
SALES (est): 285.6MM **Privately Held**
WEB: www.adacautomotive.com
SIC: 3089 Injection molding of plastics

(G-6429)
ADAC PLASTICS INC
Also Called: Adac Automotive
2929 32nd St Se (49512-1771)
PHONE 616 957-0311
David Lovelace, *Branch Mgr*
EMP: 10
SALES (corp-wide): 285.6MM **Privately Held**
WEB: www.adacautomotive.com
SIC: 3089 Injection molding of plastics
PA: Adac Plastics, Inc.
   5690 Eagle Dr Se
   Grand Rapids MI 49512
   616 957-0311

(G-6430)
ADCO SPECIALTIES INC
4331 E Beltline Ave Ne (49525-9784)
PHONE 616 452-6882
Matthew Coash, *President*
EMP: 7 **EST:** 1992
SQ FT: 1,400
SALES (est): 1MM **Privately Held**
WEB: www.shopadco.com
SIC: 5199 7389 2261 Advertising specialties; embroidering of advertising on shirts, etc.; embossing cotton broadwoven fabrics

(G-6431)
ADVANCE BCI INC (PA)
Also Called: Advance Newspapers
3102 Walker Ridge Dr Nw (49544-9125)
PHONE 616 669-1366
Joel Holland, *Publisher*
Mike Winegarden, *Manager*
EMP: 75 **EST:** 1966
SQ FT: 12,000
SALES (est): 11.3MM **Privately Held**
WEB: www.advancenewspapers.com
SIC: 2741 2752 2711 Shopping news: publishing & printing; commercial printing, offset; newspapers

(G-6432)
ADVANCE PACKAGING ACQUISITION (HQ)
Also Called: Colonial Packaging
4450 36th St Se (49512-1917)
P.O. Box 888311 (49588-8311)
PHONE 616 949-6610
Carol Hoyt, *CEO*
Donald W Crossley, *President*
▲ **EMP:** 80 **EST:** 2000
SALES (est): 24.5MM
SALES (corp-wide): 67.3MM **Privately Held**
WEB: www.advancepkg.com
SIC: 2653 Boxes, corrugated: made from purchased materials; sheets, corrugated: made from purchased materials
PA: Advance Packaging Corporation
   4459 40th St Se
   Grand Rapids MI 49512
   616 949-6610

(G-6433)
ADVANCE PACKAGING CORPORATION (PA)
4459 40th St Se (49512-4036)
P.O. Box 888311 (49588-8311)
PHONE 616 949-6610
Carol Hoyt, *CEO*
Don Crossley, *President*
Sue Albrecht, *Vice Pres*
Pat Reynolds, *Vice Pres*
Dan Boucher, *CFO*
EMP: 185 **EST:** 1966
SQ FT: 170,700
SALES (est): 67.3MM **Privately Held**
WEB: www.advancepkg.com
SIC: 2653 3412 Boxes, corrugated: made from purchased materials; metal barrels, drums & pails

(G-6434)
ADVANCED FOOD TECHNOLOGIES INC
Also Called: Rothbury Farms
1140 Butterworth St Sw (49504-6104)
P.O. Box 300 (49501-0300)
PHONE 616 574-4144
Robert Roskam, *CEO*
Tom Okke, *Manager*
▲ **EMP:** 65 **EST:** 1997
SQ FT: 70,000
SALES (est): 13.3MM
SALES (corp-wide): 453.5MM **Privately Held**
WEB: www.rothburyfarms.com
SIC: 2045 2041 Prepared flour mixes & doughs; flour mixes
PA: Roskam Baking Company
   4880 Corp Exch Blvd Se
   Grand Rapids MI 49512
   616 574-5757

(G-6435)
ADVANTAGE LABEL AND PACKG INC
Also Called: Advantage Label & Packg Pdts
5575 Executive Pkwy Se (49512-5509)
PHONE 616 656-1900
Brad Knoth, *President*
Todd Geglio, *Vice Pres*
John Long, *Production*
Debbie Tavolacci, *Purch Mgr*
Thomas J Long, *Treasurer*
EMP: 46 **EST:** 1996
SQ FT: 14,000
SALES (est): 12MM **Privately Held**
WEB: www.advantagelabel.com
SIC: 2754 2759 Labels: gravure printing; commercial printing

(G-6436)
AFTECH INC
3056 Walker Ridge Dr Nw A (49544-9133)
PHONE 616 866-1650
EMP: 7 **EST:** 2013
SALES (est): 275K **Privately Held**
WEB: www.aftech-intl.com
SIC: 3714 Motor vehicle parts & accessories

(G-6437)
AGAPE PLASTICS INC
11474 1st Ave Nw (49534-3399)
PHONE 616 735-4091
Cynthia Alt, *CEO*
David Cornelius, *President*
Mike Straayer, *Purchasing*
Christopher Davis, *Engineer*
Philip Shea, *Engineer*
EMP: 175
SQ FT: 67,000
SALES (est): 44MM **Privately Held**
WEB: www.agapeplastics.com
SIC: 3089 Injection molding of plastics

(G-6438)
AGENDA 2020 INC
Also Called: La Familia Stop 'n' Shop
555 Cascade West Pkwy Se (49546-2105)
PHONE 616 581-6271
Jose Flores, *President*
EMP: 11 **EST:** 1985
SALES (est): 1.4MM **Privately Held**
SIC: 5411 2721 Convenience stores; magazines: publishing only, not printed on site

(G-6439)
AGROPUR INC
Also Called: Parmalat Grand Rapids
5252 Clay Ave Sw (49548-5658)
PHONE 616 538-3822
Mark Sherman, *Branch Mgr*
EMP: 20
SALES (corp-wide): 4.5B **Privately Held**
WEB: www.agropur.com
SIC: 2022 Natural cheese
HQ: Agropur Inc.
   3500 E Destination Dr # 200
   Appleton WI 54915
   920 944-0990

(G-6440)
AJS MANUFACTURING LLC
1940 Turner Ave Nw Ste D (49504-2045)
PHONE 616 916-6521
EMP: 5 **EST:** 2013
SALES (est): 100.9K **Privately Held**
WEB: www.ajsmanufacturingllc.com
SIC: 3999 Manufacturing industries

(G-6441)
AKILAHS BEAUTY SALON LLC
509 Diamond Ave Se (49506-2520)
PHONE 602 607-8503
EMP: 4
SALES (est): 28K **Privately Held**
SIC: 2844 Hair preparations, including shampoos

(G-6442)
ALEXANDER DODDS COMPANY
3000 Walkent Dr Nw (49544-1453)
PHONE 616 784-6000
Bernard Campbell, *CEO*
Bob Linner, *Director*
▲ **EMP:** 8 **EST:** 1882
SQ FT: 27,600

Grand Rapids - Kent County (G-6443)

GEOGRAPHIC SECTION

SALES (est): 2.1MM Privately Held
WEB: www.dodds.com
SIC: 3553 Woodworking machinery

(G-6443)
ALGOMA PRODUCTS INC
4201 Brockton Dr Se (49512-4051)
PHONE..................616 285-6440
Trevor Wolfe, *President*
EMP: 10 EST: 1991
SQ FT: 23,000
SALES (est): 2MM Privately Held
WEB: www.broadmoorproducts.com
SIC: 2819 Industrial inorganic chemicals

(G-6444)
ALL ABOUT INTERIORS
974 Front Ave Nw Ste 1 (49504-4456)
PHONE..................616 452-8998
Sue Mickelson, *Principal*
EMP: 6 EST: 2016
SALES (est): 66.8K Privately Held
WEB: www.draperyservices.com
SIC: 2591 Drapery hardware & blinds & shades

(G-6445)
ALL AROUND MOBIL WELDING
3926 Edinboro St Nw (49534-4543)
PHONE..................616 481-4267
Keith Copeland, *Principal*
EMP: 5 EST: 2011
SALES (est): 116.6K Privately Held
WEB: www.allaroundweldinggr.com
SIC: 7692 Welding repair

(G-6446)
ALL BENDING & TUBULAR PDTS LLC
430 Cummings Ave Nw Ste G (49534-7984)
PHONE..................616 333-2364
Carol Willet, *Mng Member*
Dave Willet, *Mng Member*
EMP: 12 EST: 2010
SQ FT: 10,000
SALES (est): 1.3MM Privately Held
WEB: www.allbendingandtubularproducts.com
SIC: 3317 Steel pipe & tubes

(G-6447)
ALLEGRA PRINT AND IMAGING
929 Alpine Commerce Park (49544-8232)
PHONE..................616 784-6699
Eric Vetter, *Principal*
EMP: 9 EST: 1982
SALES (est): 458.6K Privately Held
WEB: www.allegramarketingprint.com
SIC: 8741 2752 Business management; commercial printing, offset

(G-6448)
ALLIANCE CNC LLC
Also Called: Alliance Cnc Ctter Grnding Svc
3987 Brockton Dr Se Ste A (49512-4070)
PHONE..................616 971-4700
Richard Czarniecki, *President*
EMP: 14 EST: 1995
SQ FT: 10,000
SALES (est): 1.5MM
SALES (corp-wide): 40.3MM Privately Held
WEB: www.gwstoolgroup.com
SIC: 3599 Machine shop, jobbing & repair
PA: Gws Tool Holdings, Llc
595 County Road 448
Tavares FL 32778
352 343-8778

(G-6449)
ALLIANT ENTERPRISES LLC
Also Called: Alliant Healthcare Products
2140 Oak Industrial Dr Ne (49505-6014)
PHONE..................269 629-0300
Robert W Taylor, *CEO*
Rick Lariviere, *Vice Pres*
Mark McKinney, *Vice Pres*
Rebecca Parise, *Vice Pres*
Amanda Deakin, *Opers Staff*
▲ EMP: 60 EST: 2002
SQ FT: 60,000
SALES (est): 10MM Privately Held
WEB: www.allianthealthcare.com
SIC: 3841 Surgical & medical instruments

(G-6450)
ALLIED FINISHING INC
4100 Broadmoor Ave Se (49512-3933)
P.O. Box 3728 (49501-3728)
PHONE..................616 698-7550
Bruce Stone, *President*
Jerry Vandersloot, *Materials Mgr*
Jeremy Crego, *Mfg Spvr*
Scott Franzen, *QC Mgr*
Jacob Dolecki, *Engineer*
EMP: 145 EST: 1977
SQ FT: 96,000
SALES (est): 23.9MM Privately Held
WEB: www.alliedfinishinginc.com
SIC: 3471 Plating of metals or formed products

(G-6451)
ALLSALES ENTERPRISES INC
Also Called: Ag-Pro
1013 Country Gdns Nw (49534-7919)
PHONE..................616 437-0639
Roger De Haan, *President*
Chad Morton, *Principal*
Todd Rose, *Principal*
David Vandervelde, *Principal*
Roger Dehaan, *Vice Pres*
EMP: 10 EST: 1994
SQ FT: 1,200
SALES (est): 1.1MM Privately Held
SIC: 2671 5999 Packaging paper & plastics film, coated & laminated; packaging materials: boxes, padding, etc.

(G-6452)
AMERICAN COOLING SYSTEMS LLC
3099 Wilson Dr Nw (49534-7565)
PHONE..................616 954-0280
Greg Westbrook, *Plant Mgr*
Ryan Hanson, *Engineer*
Robert A Rosin, *Manager*
John Jahns, *Exec Dir*
Robert Rosin,
▼ EMP: 38 EST: 1999
SALES (est): 6.7MM Privately Held
WEB: www.americancooling.com
SIC: 3714 Motor vehicle parts & accessories

(G-6453)
AMERICAN LEAR
2150 Alpine Ave Nw (49544-1921)
PHONE..................616 252-3643
Melissa Bishop, *Asst Controller*
Jason Helmus, *Technology*
EMP: 15 EST: 2016
SALES (est): 153.6K Privately Held
WEB: www.lear.com
SIC: 3714 Motor vehicle parts & accessories

(G-6454)
AMERICAN SEATING COMPANY (PA)
801 Broadway Ave Nw # 200 (49504-4499)
PHONE..................616 732-6561
Edward J Clark, *CEO*
Thomas E Bush, *President*
Jonathan Dinsmore, *Area Mgr*
Kevin Koehler, *Vice Pres*
Keith A McDowell, *Vice Pres*
◆ EMP: 425 EST: 1886
SQ FT: 640,000
SALES (est): 125.7MM Privately Held
WEB: www.americanseating.com
SIC: 2522 2531 Office furniture, except wood; vehicle furniture; stadium seating

(G-6455)
AMERICAN SEATING COMPANY
801 Broadway Ave Nw # 200 (49504-4499)
PHONE..................616 732-6600
Edward J Clark, *CEO*
Allen Fox, *Vice Pres*
Roger Skorupski, *Human Res Dir*
Jodi Ross, *Human Resources*
Stacey Snider, *Accounts Mgr*
EMP: 17
SALES (corp-wide): 125.7MM Privately Held
WEB: www.americanseating.com
SIC: 2522 Office furniture, except wood

PA: American Seating Company
801 Broadway Ave Nw # 200
Grand Rapids MI 49504
616 732-6561

(G-6456)
AMERICAN T-MOULD LLC
5090 Weeping Willow Dr Se (49546-7908)
PHONE..................616 617-2422
Wilhelm Kliewer, *Manager*
EMP: 7 EST: 2011
SALES (est): 183K Privately Held
SIC: 3714 Motor vehicle parts & accessories

(G-6457)
AMERIKAM INC
1337 Judd Ave Sw (49509-1096)
PHONE..................616 243-5833
Stephanie Leonardos, *President*
Roberta Warren, *General Mgr*
Helen Popovich, *Corp Secy*
Michael Ragon, *Plant Mgr*
Michael Regelbrugge, *Research*
EMP: 90
SQ FT: 55,000
SALES (est): 17.6MM Privately Held
WEB: www.amerikam.com
SIC: 3451 3441 Screw machine products; fabricated structural metal

(G-6458)
AMPHENOL BORISCH TECH INC (HQ)
Also Called: Borisch Mfg
4511 East Paris Ave Se (49512-5314)
PHONE..................616 554-9820
Jonathan Borisch, *President*
Eric Johr, *General Mgr*
Marc Wetsig, *General Mgr*
Ariel Koblenz, *Business Mgr*
Philip Provost, *Business Mgr*
▲ EMP: 107 EST: 2011
SALES (est): 59.9MM
SALES (corp-wide): 8.6B Publicly Held
WEB: www.borisch.com
SIC: 3679 3599 Harness assemblies for electronic use: wire or cable; electronic circuits; machine shop, jobbing & repair
PA: Amphenol Corporation
358 Hall Ave
Wallingford CT 06492
203 265-8900

(G-6459)
ANGSTROM ALUMINUM CASTINGS LLC
3559 Kraft Ave Se (49512-2033)
PHONE..................616 309-1208
Lalitha Gadiraju, *Finance Dir*
Nagesh K Palakurthi,
EMP: 39 EST: 2015
SALES (est): 6.1MM Privately Held
WEB: www.angstrom-usa.com
SIC: 3363 Aluminum die-castings
PA: Angstrom Automotive Group, Llc
2000 Town Ctr Ste 100
Southfield MI 48075

(G-6460)
ANTELLS CUSTOM CABINETRY
2581 Maguire Ave Ne (49525-9732)
PHONE..................616 318-8637
David Holmden, *Owner*
EMP: 4 EST: 2010
SALES (est): 110K Privately Held
SIC: 2434 Wood kitchen cabinets

(G-6461)
APEM SOLUTIONS LLC ○
2508 Hufford Ave Nw (49544-1935)
PHONE..................616 848-5393
Pamela Lett,
EMP: 4 EST: 2021
SALES (est): 950K Privately Held
SIC: 3663 Satellites, communications

(G-6462)
APEX SPRING & STAMPING CORP
11420 1st Ave Nw (49534-3399)
PHONE..................616 453-5463
Dennis K Bhaskaran, *CEO*
Dennis Bhaskaran, *CEO*
Chase Olsen, *Plant Mgr*

Tom Walkons, *Sales Engr*
David Holtrop, *Sales Staff*
EMP: 67
SQ FT: 78,000
SALES (est): 19MM Privately Held
WEB: www.apexspring.com
SIC: 3496 3469 3544 3495 Miscellaneous fabricated wire products; metal stampings; special dies, tools, jigs & fixtures; wire springs; bolts, nuts, rivets & washers; manufactured hardware (general)

(G-6463)
APOLLO TOOL & ENGINEERING INC
3020 Wilson Dr Nw (49534-7564)
PHONE..................616 735-4934
Mike Hartley, *President*
Floyd Hoyt, *Corp Secy*
EMP: 17 EST: 1984
SQ FT: 2,500
SALES (est): 1.4MM Privately Held
SIC: 3545 Cutting tools for machine tools

(G-6464)
APPLIED MECHANICS CORPORATION
Also Called: Amcor
14122 Ironwood Dr Nw (49534-1034)
PHONE..................616 677-1355
Theodore Vecchio, *President*
G M Minnhaar-Tomatis, *Vice Pres*
M Minnhaar Tomatis, *Purchasing*
Laurie Deschaine, *Manager*
EMP: 5 EST: 1954
SQ FT: 5,500
SALES (est): 1.1MM Privately Held
WEB: www.amcortooling.com
SIC: 3544 Special dies & tools

(G-6465)
APPROPOS LLC
Also Called: Appropos Digital
678 Front Ave Nw Ste 100 (49504-5323)
PHONE..................844 462-7776
Jon Faber, *CEO*
Todd Slager, *COO*
Brandon Merritt, *CFO*
Steve Dabbs, *Manager*
EMP: 30 EST: 2012
SQ FT: 9,000
SALES (est): 2.7MM Privately Held
WEB: www.envoyb2b.com
SIC: 7372 7335 Business oriented computer software; commercial photography

(G-6466)
ARBOR GAGE & TOOLING INC
2031 Calvin Ave Se (49507-3305)
PHONE..................616 454-8266
Edward Heerema Jr, *President*
Ruth Heerema, *Vice Pres*
Emily Koning, *Opers Staff*
Dale McClure, *Prgrmr*
EMP: 35 EST: 1978
SQ FT: 37,000
SALES (est): 3.9MM Privately Held
WEB: www.arborgage.com
SIC: 2542 3544 3543 Office & store showcases & display fixtures; special dies, tools, jigs & fixtures; industrial patterns

(G-6467)
ARCANUM STEEL TECHNOLOGIES INC
265 Auburn Ave Se (49506-1623)
PHONE..................630 715-4899
Adam Thomas, *CEO*
EMP: 44
SALES (corp-wide): 91.8K Privately Held
SIC: 3312 Rods, iron & steel: made in steel mills
PA: Arcanum Steel Technologies Inc.
4460 44th St Se Ste F
Kentwood MI 49512
630 715-4899

(G-6468)
ARCTEL CORP
4707 40th St Se (49512-4076)
PHONE..................616 241-6001
Kurg Bouna, *President*
EMP: 12 EST: 2008

▲ = Import ▼ = Export
◆ = Import/Export

GEOGRAPHIC SECTION

Grand Rapids - Kent County (G-6495)

SALES (est): 1.3MM **Privately Held**
WEB: www.arctel.com
SIC: 2431 Millwork

(G-6469)
ARGUS TECHNOLOGIES LLC
Also Called: C2 Group The
560 5th St Nw Ste 100 (49504-5243)
PHONE 616 538-9895
Kelly Maichele, *Bookkeeper*
Brian Beaupied, *Mktg Dir*
Michael Kunzler, *Mng Member*
David Stielstra, *Technical Staff*
David Fewless, *Software Dev*
EMP: 25 **EST:** 2015
SALES (est): 3.3MM **Privately Held**
WEB: www.c2experience.com
SIC: 7372 Application computer software

(G-6470)
ARKEMA INC
Also Called: Arkema Coating Resins
1415 Steele Ave Sw (49507-1562)
PHONE 616 243-4578
Chuck Bennett, *CEO*
Jeff Mills, *Plant Mgr*
EMP: 43
SALES (corp-wide): 117MM **Privately Held**
WEB: www.arkema.com
SIC: 2819 Industrial inorganic chemicals
HQ: Arkema Inc.
    900 1st Ave
    King Of Prussia PA 19406
    610 205-7000

(G-6471)
ART OPTICAL CONTACT LENS INC
3175 3 Mile Rd Nw (49534-1325)
P.O. Box 1848 (49501-1848)
PHONE 616 453-1888
Thomas Anastor, *President*
Sheryl Pine, *General Mgr*
Chad Boyce, *COO*
Jill Anastor, *Vice Pres*
Beverly Behrens, *Human Res Dir*
EMP: 110
SQ FT: 30,000
SALES (est): 23.1MM **Privately Held**
WEB: www.artoptical.com
SIC: 3851 Contact lenses

(G-6472)
ARTESIAN DISTILLERS
955 Ken O Sha Ind Park (49508-8246)
P.O. Box 43, Burnips (49314-0043)
PHONE 616 252-1700
EMP: 5
SALES (est): 419.6K **Privately Held**
SIC: 2085 Mfg Distilled/Blended Liquor

(G-6473)
ARTIFLEX MANUFACTURING LLC
I T S
731 Broadway Ave Nw (49504-5247)
PHONE 616 459-8285
Jason Ware, *Project Mgr*
Tom Eveland, *Maint Spvr*
Jim Hammel, *Opers Staff*
Tim Reed, *Opers Staff*
Jeff Dies, *Purch Agent*
EMP: 160
SALES (corp-wide): 177.3MM **Privately Held**
WEB: www.artiflexmfg.com
SIC: 3544 Die sets for metal stamping (presses)
PA: Artiflex Manufacturing, Llc
    1425 E Bowman St
    Wooster OH 44691
    330 262-2015

(G-6474)
ARVRON INC
4720 Clay Ave Sw (49548-3071)
PHONE 616 530-1888
Marvin Wynalda, *President*
Doug Oostdyk, *Plant Mgr*
▲ **EMP:** 30 **EST:** 1978
SQ FT: 63,000
SALES (est): 18.9MM **Privately Held**
WEB: www.arvron.com
SIC: 2821 Polyurethane resins

(G-6475)
ASCRIBE
100 Grandville Ave Sw (49503-4055)
PHONE 616 726-2490
Kelley Hogan, *Sr Consultant*
EMP: 5 **EST:** 2017
SALES (est): 37.5K **Privately Held**
SIC: 2741 Miscellaneous publishing

(G-6476)
ASIAN NOODLE LLC
201 Fulton St W Apt 1415 (49503-2678)
PHONE 989 316-2380
EMP: 5 **EST:** 2014
SALES (est): 246.7K **Privately Held**
SIC: 2098 Noodles (e.g. egg, plain & water), dry

(G-6477)
ASSOCIATED RACK CORPORATION
4910 Kraft Ave Se (49512-9708)
PHONE 616 554-6004
W L Faulman, *President*
EMP: 5
SALES (corp-wide): 30.6MM **Privately Held**
WEB: www.associatedrack.com
SIC: 2542 Racks, merchandise display or storage: except wood
PA: Associated Rack Corporation
    70 Athens Dr
    Mount Juliet TN 37122
    615 288-4204

(G-6478)
ASTELLAS PHARMA US INC
5905 Kraft Ave Se (49512-9684)
PHONE 616 698-8825
Arla Boot, *Owner*
EMP: 9 **Privately Held**
WEB: www.astellas.com
SIC: 2834 Vitamin, nutrient & hematinic preparations for human use
HQ: Astellas Pharma Us, Inc.
    1 Astellas Way
    Northbrook IL 60062

(G-6479)
AUSTEMPER INC
341 Grant St Sw (49503-4921)
PHONE 616 458-7061
Lee Price, *Manager*
EMP: 30
SALES (corp-wide): 23.6MM **Privately Held**
WEB: www.austemperinc.com
SIC: 3398 Annealing of metal
HQ: Austemper, Inc.
    30760 Century Dr
    Wixom MI 48393
    586 293-4554

(G-6480)
AUTO-MASTERS INC
6521 Division Ave S (49548-7891)
PHONE 616 455-4510
Gordon Gillman, *President*
Ralph Bos, *Vice Pres*
EMP: 18 **EST:** 1978
SQ FT: 16,000
SALES (est): 2.3MM **Privately Held**
WEB: www.automastersgr.com
SIC: 5531 5013 7538 3716 Automotive accessories; automotive parts; automotive supplies & parts; general automotive repair shops; motor homes

(G-6481)
AUTOCAM CORP
4180 40th St Se (49512-4122)
PHONE 616 698-0707
David Thompson, *Principal*
John Kennedy, *Manager*
EMP: 63 **EST:** 1992
SALES (est): 140.9K **Privately Held**
WEB: www.autocam.com
SIC: 3599 3841 3714 3694 Machine shop, jobbing & repair; surgical & medical instruments; motor vehicle parts & accessories; engine electrical equipment; carburetors, pistons, rings, valves

(G-6482)
AUTOCAM MEDICAL DEVICES LLC (HQ)
4152 East Paris Ave Se (49512-3911)
PHONE 877 633-8080
John C Kennedy, *CEO*
Jeff Goodman, *General Mgr*
Scott Koester, *Purch Mgr*
Ricardo Cardenas, *Engineer*
Ralf Sherrill, *Engineer*
EMP: 25 **EST:** 2009
SQ FT: 190,000
SALES (est): 55MM **Privately Held**
WEB: www.autocam-medical.com
SIC: 3842 3841 Implants, surgical; surgical & medical instruments

(G-6483)
AUTODIE LLC
44 Coldbrook St Nw (49503-1046)
PHONE 616 454-9361
Warren Miller, *CEO*
David Crandall, *COO*
Mark Battle, *Vice Pres*
Charlie Murphy, *CFO*
Jam Bertsch, *Treasurer*
▲ **EMP:** 250 **EST:** 2006
SALES (est): 47.5MM
SALES (corp-wide): 102.5B **Privately Held**
WEB: www.autodie-llc.com
SIC: 3544 Special dies & tools
HQ: Fca Us Llc
    1000 Chrysler Dr
    Auburn Hills MI 48326

(G-6484)
AUTOEXEC INC
4477 East Paris Ave Se (49512-5312)
PHONE 616 971-0080
Charles Lippert, *CEO*
David Lippert, *President*
Kevin Smallegan, *Manager*
Priscilla Carrick, *Director*
▲ **EMP:** 5 **EST:** 1993
SALES (est): 821K **Privately Held**
WEB: www.autoexec.com
SIC: 2522 Office desks & tables: except wood

(G-6485)
AUVESY INC
146 Monroe Center St Nw # 1210 (49503-2821)
PHONE 616 888-3770
Robert Glaser, *CEO*
Emma Baranowski, *Office Mgr*
EMP: 5 **EST:** 2018
SALES (est): 308.3K **Privately Held**
WEB: www.auvesy.us
SIC: 7372 Prepackaged software

(G-6486)
AVANTIS INC
5441 36th St Se (49512-2015)
PHONE 616 285-8000
Douglas Oosterman, *Vice Pres*
Joe Brophy, *Manager*
▲ **EMP:** 5 **EST:** 2004
SALES (est): 250K **Privately Held**
SIC: 2522 Office furniture, except wood

(G-6487)
AWARD CUTTER COMPANY INC
5577 Crippen Ave Sw (49548-5716)
PHONE 616 531-0430
Mark Beilfuss, *President*
Brenda Vanreenens, *Vice Pres*
EMP: 10 **EST:** 1959
SQ FT: 6,000
SALES (est): 840.2K **Privately Held**
WEB: www.awardcutter.com
SIC: 3545 End mills

(G-6488)
B & G PRODUCTS INC
3631 44th St Se Ste E (49512-3971)
PHONE 616 698-9050
Kathleen Geddes, *President*
Jacci Harding, *Vice Pres*
Caleb Woodwyk, *Engineer*
Rich Wellington, *Supervisor*
EMP: 17 **EST:** 2000
SQ FT: 5,000

SALES (est): 2.5MM **Privately Held**
WEB: www.bgproducts.com
SIC: 3565 3443 Bottling machinery: filling, capping, labeling, bottling & canning machinery; metal parts

(G-6489)
B&B HAIR&CO LLC ◯
625 Kenmoor Ave Se # 301 (49546-2395)
PHONE 616 600-4568
Lenika Wilson, *Mng Member*
EMP: 5 **EST:** 2021
SALES (est): 257.2K **Privately Held**
SIC: 3999 Hair & hair-based products

(G-6490)
B-QUICK INSTANT PRINTING
3120 Division Ave S (49548-1133)
PHONE 616 243-6562
Gary Ball, *Owner*
EMP: 5 **EST:** 1974
SQ FT: 1,600
SALES (est): 250K **Privately Held**
WEB: www.bquickprint.com
SIC: 2752 Commercial printing, offset

(G-6491)
BAINBRIDGE MANUFACTURING INC
1931 Will Ave Nw Ste 1 (49504-2013)
PHONE 616 447-7631
Eugene Bainbridge, *President*
Barbara Bainbridge, *Corp Secy*
William Bainbridge, *Vice Pres*
EMP: 7 **EST:** 1999
SQ FT: 10,000
SALES (est): 547.6K **Privately Held**
WEB: www.bainbridgemfg.com
SIC: 2499 Carved & turned wood

(G-6492)
BAKER PERKINS INC
3223 Kraft Ave Se (49512-2063)
PHONE 616 784-3111
Dan Smith, *General Mgr*
John Cowx, *Principal*
Jeff Noordyke, *Project Mgr*
Larry Tyron, *Buyer*
Jerry Jaquish, *Engineer*
◆ **EMP:** 55 **EST:** 2006
SQ FT: 25,000
SALES (est): 13.7MM
SALES (corp-wide): 56MM **Privately Held**
WEB: www.bakerperkins.com
SIC: 3556 Smokers, food processing equipment
PA: Baker Perkins Limited
    Manor Drive
    Peterborough CAMBS PE4 7
    173 328-3000

(G-6493)
BAKING COMPANY LLC ◯
Also Called: Savory Foods
1880 Turner Ave Nw Ste C (49504-2032)
PHONE 616 241-2583
Carey Brechting, *Mng Member*
EMP: 50 **EST:** 2021
SALES (est): 2.8MM **Privately Held**
SIC: 2051 Bakery: wholesale or wholesale/retail combined

(G-6494)
BANTA FURNITURE COMPANY
Also Called: Banta Management Resources
3390 Broadmoor Ave Se A (49512-8181)
PHONE 616 575-8180
Theodore Banta, *President*
EMP: 11 **EST:** 1993
SQ FT: 13,500
SALES (est): 860K **Privately Held**
WEB: www.bantafurniture.com
SIC: 2599 7641 Factory furniture & fixtures; furniture upholstery repair

(G-6495)
BARE BULB COMPANIES LLC
2090 Celebration Dr Ne # 204 (49525-9200)
PHONE 616 644-8251
Michael Bodell, *Principal*
Matthew Dressel, *Principal*
EMP: 7 **EST:** 2004
SALES (est): 390.9K **Privately Held**
SIC: 3229 Bulbs for electric lights

Grand Rapids - Kent County (G-6496)

GEOGRAPHIC SECTION

(G-6496)
BATTS GROUP LTD (PA)
3855 Sparks Dr Se Ste 222 (49546-2427)
PHONE.................................616 956-3053
John H Batts, *President*
EMP: 3 **EST:** 1998
SQ FT: 1,400
SALES (est): 2.6MM **Privately Held**
SIC: 3089 6282 6211 Clothes hangers, plastic; investment advice; security brokers & dealers

(G-6497)
BAUER PRODUCTS INC
702 Evergreen St Se (49507-1890)
PHONE.................................616 245-4540
Jon Bacon, *President*
J Norman, *Vice Pres*
Bruce Bacon, *Treasurer*
▲ **EMP:** 25 **EST:** 1957
SQ FT: 10,000
SALES (est): 4.8MM **Privately Held**
WEB: www.bauerproducts.com
SIC: 3429 Metal fasteners

(G-6498)
BELT-TECH USA INC
200 Ottawa Ave Nw Ste 900 (49503-2427)
PHONE.................................450 372-5826
Robert Belanger, *President*
EMP: 175 **EST:** 2014
SALES (est): 10.7MM **Privately Held**
WEB: www.belt-tech.com
SIC: 2399 Seat belts, automobile & aircraft

(G-6499)
BENMILL LLC
Also Called: Kent Design & Manufacturing
3522 Lousma Dr Se (49548-2259)
PHONE.................................616 243-7555
Chuck Bennett, *Principal*
Mike Miller, *VP Opers*
Lori Stream, *CFO*
David Faulkner, *Sales Staff*
Larry Miller,
▲ **EMP:** 35 **EST:** 1999
SQ FT: 79,500
SALES (est): 4.5MM **Privately Held**
WEB: www.kentdesign.com
SIC: 3496 Grilles & grillework, woven wire; woven wire products

(G-6500)
BENNETT STEEL LLC
1239 Randolph Ave Sw (49507-1517)
PHONE.................................616 401-5271
Steven J Entingh, *Principal*
EMP: 10 **EST:** 2010
SALES (est): 2.4MM **Privately Held**
WEB: www.bennett-steel.com
SIC: 3441 Fabricated structural metal

(G-6501)
BENTELER AUTOMOTIVE CORP
Also Called: Tubular Products Division
3721 Hagen Dr Se (49548-2331)
PHONE.................................616 245-4607
Steve Bates, *Plant Mgr*
Terry Scofield, *Technical Mgr*
Miakel Bixler, *Engineer*
Jonathan Quint, *Marketing Staff*
Christoph Kreiter, *Manager*
EMP: 485
SALES (corp-wide): 7.5B **Privately Held**
WEB: www.benteler.com
SIC: 3714 3317 Exhaust systems & parts, motor vehicle; steel pipe & tubes
HQ: Benteler Automotive Corporation
2650 N Opdyke Rd Ste B
Auburn Hills MI 48326
248 364-7190

(G-6502)
BEST METAL PRODUCTS CO INC
3570 Raleigh Dr Se (49512-2064)
PHONE.................................616 942-7141
David Faasse, *CEO*
Jonathan Bras, *Opers Mgr*
Noel Dreyer, *Maint Spvr*
David Dooge, *Purch Mgr*
Kelly Kik, *Engineer*
▲ **EMP:** 115 **EST:** 1950
SQ FT: 30,000
SALES (est): 22.2MM **Privately Held**
WEB: www.bestmetalproducts.com
SIC: 3599 3593 Machine shop, jobbing & repair; fluid power cylinders & actuators

(G-6503)
BEST PORTABLE SIGN
4932 Stauffer Ave Se (49508-5147)
PHONE.................................616 291-2911
Joel Pounders, *Principal*
EMP: 5 **EST:** 2010
SALES (est): 80.5K **Privately Held**
WEB: www.bestportablesign.com
SIC: 3993 Signs & advertising specialties

(G-6504)
BETZ INDUSTRIES INC
Also Called: Betz Castings
2121 Bristol Ave Nw (49504-1403)
PHONE.................................616 453-4429
Karl Betz, *Principal*
David Moorhead, *Vice Pres*
Robin Boire, *Purchasing*
Catherine Jenkins, *Research*
Dan Scott, *Human Res Dir*
▲ **EMP:** 90
SQ FT: 500,000
SALES (est): 30.4MM **Privately Held**
WEB: www.betzindustries.com
SIC: 3321 Ductile iron castings; gray iron castings

(G-6505)
BEYOND EMBROIDERY
2013 E Wyndham Hill Dr Ne # 102 (49505-7105)
PHONE.................................616 726-7000
Steve Mieras, *Owner*
EMP: 5 **EST:** 2006
SALES (est): 198.4K **Privately Held**
SIC: 2759 Screen printing

(G-6506)
BICO MICHIGAN INC (HQ)
Also Called: Bico Steel Service Centers
99 Steele St Nw (49534-8737)
PHONE.................................616 453-2400
Michael A Ensminger, *President*
Tom Vanlopik, *Opers Mgr*
▲ **EMP:** 30 **EST:** 1986
SQ FT: 33,000
SALES: 41MM
SALES (corp-wide): 75.3MM **Privately Held**
SIC: 5051 3444 3325 Steel; sheet metalwork; steel foundries
PA: Bico Buyer, Inc.
3100 Gilchrist Rd
Mogadore OH 44260
330 794-1716

(G-6507)
BIG DOME HOLDINGS INC
3044 Wilson Dr Nw (49534-7564)
PHONE.................................616 735-6228
Nat Rich, *President*
Brian Morrissey, *Vice Pres*
Erik Winger, *Engineer*
▲ **EMP:** 55 **EST:** 1989
SQ FT: 25,000
SALES (est): 8.6MM **Privately Held**
SIC: 3543 Industrial patterns

(G-6508)
BIG RAPIDS PRINTING
2801 Oak Industrial Dr Ne (49505-6046)
PHONE.................................231 796-8588
EMP: 6
SALES (est): 250K **Privately Held**
SIC: 2759 5943 Commercial Printing Ret Stationery

(G-6509)
BIOLYTE LABORATORIES LLC
Also Called: Biolyte Labs
310 Northern Dr Nw (49534-3700)
PHONE.................................616 350-9055
Joni Kaline, *COO*
Daniel Kaline, *Mng Member*
EMP: 12 **EST:** 2012
SALES (est): 1MM **Privately Held**
WEB: www.biolytelabs.com
SIC: 2834 Pharmaceutical preparations

(G-6510)
BISSELL BETTER LIFE LLC
Also Called: Better Life Cleaning Products
2345 Walker Ave Nw (49544-2597)
P.O. Box 1888 (49501-1888)
PHONE.................................800 237-7691
James S Nicholson, *CFO*
Rebecca Hafner, *Administration*
EMP: 5 **EST:** 2017
SALES (est): 1.1MM
SALES (corp-wide): 1B **Privately Held**
WEB: www.bissell.com
SIC: 2842 3589 3635 Specialty cleaning, polishes & sanitation goods; vacuum cleaners & sweepers, electric: industrial; household vacuum cleaners
HQ: Bissell Inc.
2345 Walker Ave Nw
Grand Rapids MI 49544
616 453-4451

(G-6511)
BISSELL HOMECARE INC (DH)
2345 Walker Ave Nw (49544-2597)
P.O. Box 3606 (49501-3606)
PHONE.................................800 237-7691
Mark J Bissell, *President*
Mike Freeman, *Regional Mgr*
Jaclyn Ahearne, *Vice Pres*
Michael Gannon, *Vice Pres*
Ryan McLean, *Vice Pres*
◆ **EMP:** 789 **EST:** 1999
SQ FT: 600,000
SALES: 505.3MM
SALES (corp-wide): 1B **Privately Held**
WEB: www.global.bissell.com
SIC: 3635 Household vacuum cleaners
HQ: Bissell Inc.
2345 Walker Ave Nw
Grand Rapids MI 49544
616 453-4451

(G-6512)
BIVINS GRAPHICS
808 Carpenter Ave Nw (49504-3723)
PHONE.................................616 453-2211
Fred Bivins, *Owner*
EMP: 4 **Privately Held**
WEB: www.vinecroft.com
SIC: 2759 2396 Commercial printing; automotive & apparel trimmings
PA: Bivins Graphics
1614 Vinecroft St Nw
Grand Rapids MI 49544

(G-6513)
BLACK & DECKER (US) INC
3040 28th St Se (49512-1627)
PHONE.................................410 716-3900
EMP: 4
SALES (corp-wide): 14.5B **Publicly Held**
WEB: www.dewalt.com
SIC: 3546 Power-driven handtools
HQ: Black & Decker (U.S.) Inc.
1000 Stanley Dr
New Britain CT 06053
860 225-5111

(G-6514)
BLACK OWL DISTILLERY LLC
4717 Broadmoor Ave Se F (49512-9330)
PHONE.................................616 901-9003
EMP: 4 **EST:** 2017
SALES (est): 93.4K **Privately Held**
SIC: 2084 Wines

(G-6515)
BLISS & VINEGAR LLC
888 Forest Hill Ave Se (49546-2326)
PHONE.................................616 970-0732
Mark McNamara, *Principal*
EMP: 7 **EST:** 2014
SALES (est): 212.2K **Privately Held**
WEB: www.blissandvinegar.net
SIC: 2099 Vinegar

(G-6516)
BLOOM INDUSTRIES LLC (PA)
2218 Ashcreek Ct Nw (49534-2716)
PHONE.................................616 453-2946
Kristen R Inbody, *Principal*
EMP: 8 **EST:** 2017
SALES (est): 280.4K **Privately Held**
SIC: 3999 Manufacturing industries

(G-6517)
BLUEWATER TECH GROUP INC
4245 44th St Se Ste 1 (49512-4053)
PHONE.................................616 656-9380
Nick Marino, *Vice Pres*
Douglas Wack, *Vice Pres*
Jim Moceri, *Project Mgr*
Paul Villamil, *Project Mgr*
Tj Frasier, *Opers Staff*
EMP: 5
SALES (corp-wide): 78.5MM **Privately Held**
WEB: www.bluewatertech.com
SIC: 3651 5064 7622 7359 Household audio & video equipment; electrical appliances, television & radio; radio & television repair; equipment rental & leasing
HQ: Bluewater Technologies Group, Inc.
30303 Beck Rd
Wixom MI 48393
248 356-4399

(G-6518)
BOB-O-LINK ASSOCIATES LLC (PA)
570 Market Ave Sw (49503-4831)
PHONE.................................616 891-6939
David Maas,
Daniel Timmer,
EMP: 4 **EST:** 1996
SALES (est): 376.4K **Privately Held**
SIC: 3531 Asphalt plant, including gravelmix type

(G-6519)
BODYCOTE THERMAL PROC INC
3700 Eastern Ave Se (49508-2413)
PHONE.................................616 245-0465
Lisa Van Schelven, *General Mgr*
Tom Williams, *General Mgr*
Dean Smith, *Branch Mgr*
EMP: 7
SALES (corp-wide): 795.2MM **Privately Held**
WEB: www.bodycote.com
SIC: 3398 Metal heat treating
HQ: Bodycote Thermal Processing, Inc.
12750 Merit Dr Ste 1400
Dallas TX 75251
214 904-2420

(G-6520)
BOLD ENDEAVORS LLC
Also Called: Boldsocks
17 Division Ave S Ste 100 (49503-4231)
PHONE.................................616 389-3902
Ryan Preisner, *Manager*
EMP: 9 **EST:** 2014
SALES (est): 199.3K **Privately Held**
SIC: 2252 Socks

(G-6521)
BOND STREET SOFTWARE
820 Monroe Ave Nw (49503-1442)
PHONE.................................616 847-8377
EMP: 4 **EST:** 2008
SALES (est): 149.8K **Privately Held**
SIC: 7372 Prepackaged software

(G-6522)
BOOMERANG EXHIBITS
3223 Kraft Ave Se (49512-2063)
PHONE.................................315 525-6973
EMP: 7 **EST:** 2015
SALES (est): 409.7K **Privately Held**
WEB: www.boomerangexhibits.com
SIC: 3949 Boomerangs

(G-6523)
BRECK GRAPHICS INCORPORATED (PA)
Also Called: Allegra Print & Imaging
3983 Linden Ave Se (49548-3431)
PHONE.................................616 248-4110
Eric Vetter, *CEO*
Ron Vetter, *CEO*
Beverly Vetter, *Corp Secy*
Debbie Guertler, *Project Mgr*
Lori Heimburger, *Project Mgr*
EMP: 20 **EST:** 1979
SQ FT: 17,000

GEOGRAPHIC SECTION   **Grand Rapids - Kent County (G-6550)**

SALES (est): 3.1MM **Privately Held**
WEB: www.allegramarketingprint.com
SIC: 2752 2796 2791 2789 Commercial printing, offset; platemaking services; typesetting; bookbinding & related work

(G-6524)
BRIGHTFORMAT INC
5300 Corprte Grv Dr Se (49512-5514)
PHONE..........................616 247-1161
Peter Houlihan, *President*
Tom Zeitter, *Plant Supt*
Sheryl Ringler, *Project Mgr*
Staci Weaver, *Project Mgr*
Linda Pearman, *Sr Project Mgr*
EMP: 20 EST: 2012
SALES (est): 2.2MM **Privately Held**
WEB: www.brightformat.com
SIC: 2759 7331 Commercial printing; mailing service

(G-6525)
BRILLIANT INDUSTRIES LLC
Also Called: Hansen Towing and Recovery
4864 Glen Meadow Ct Se (49546-7916)
PHONE..........................616 954-9209
David Hansen, *Partner*
David B Hansen,
EMP: 5 EST: 2005
SALES (est): 360.9K **Privately Held**
SIC: 3999 7549 Manufacturing industries; towing service, automotive

(G-6526)
BRITISH CARBURETORS LLC
1556 Philadelphia Ave Se (49507-2236)
PHONE..........................616 920-0203
Mathew Fortier, *Principal*
EMP: 4 EST: 2017
SALES (est): 136.5K **Privately Held**
SIC: 3592 Carburetors

(G-6527)
BRUN LABORATORIES INC
1120 Monroe Ave Nw # 180 (49503-1075)
P.O. Box 2663 (49501-2663)
PHONE..........................616 456-1114
EMP: 4
SQ FT: 4,000
SALES (est): 300K **Privately Held**
SIC: 2844 Mfg & Distributor & Ret Cream Products

(G-6528)
BUCHER HYDRAULICS INC (DH)
1363 Michigan St Ne (49503-2003)
PHONE..........................616 458-1306
Dan Vaughan, *President*
Robert Gordon, *General Mgr*
Greg Bergman, *Engineer*
Nathan Brandeberry, *Engineer*
Kevin Hall, *Engineer*
▲ EMP: 140 EST: 1856
SQ FT: 100,000
SALES (est): 84.9MM
SALES (corp-wide): 3B **Privately Held**
WEB: www.bucherhydraulics.com
SIC: 3594 3492 Pumps, hydraulic power transfer; fluid power valves & hose fittings
HQ: Bucher Hydraulics Ag
Industriestrasse 15
Neuheim ZG 6345
417 570-333

(G-6529)
BUITER TOOL & DIE INC
8187 Division Ave S (49548-7233)
PHONE..........................616 455-7410
John Buiter, *President*
Petronella Buiter, *Corp Secy*
Edward Buiter, *Vice Pres*
Steve Star, *Prgrmr*
EMP: 22 EST: 1962
SQ FT: 18,600
SALES (est): 2.2MM **Privately Held**
WEB: www.buitertool.com
SIC: 3544 7692 Special dies & tools; welding repair

(G-6530)
BULL HN INFO SYSTEMS INC
2620 Horizon Dr Se D1 (49546-7520)
PHONE..........................616 942-7126
Paul Miller, *Branch Mgr*
EMP: 5

SALES (corp-wide): 146.7MM **Privately Held**
WEB: www.bull.us
SIC: 3571 3577 7378 7373 Mainframe computers; computer peripheral equipment; computer & data processing equipment repair/maintenance; computer peripheral equipment repair & maintenance; systems integration services
HQ: Bull Hn Information Systems Inc.
285 Billerica Rd
Chelmsford MA 01824
978 294-6000

(G-6531)
BULMAN PRODUCTS INC
1650 Mcreynolds Ave Nw (49504-2091)
PHONE..........................616 363-4416
Ann Kirkwood Hall, *President*
Rita Kirkwood, *Vice Pres*
Dini Sahitolli, *Production*
John R Kirkwood, *Treasurer*
Cary Anderson, *Info Tech Dir*
EMP: 31 EST: 1905
SQ FT: 26,000
SALES (est): 4.3MM **Privately Held**
WEB: www.bulmanproducts.com
SIC: 3499 Metal household articles

(G-6532)
BURCO INC
2936 S Wilson Ct Nw (49534-7567)
PHONE..........................616 453-7771
Michael Mervenne, *President*
James F Mervenne, *President*
Michael J Mervenne, *Vice Pres*
Jeff Vander, *Design Engr*
Elisabeth Mervenne, *CFO*
EMP: 26 EST: 1952
SQ FT: 21,000
SALES (est): 4.2MM **Privately Held**
WEB: www.burcoinc.com
SIC: 3231 Products of purchased glass; mirrors, truck & automobile: made from purchased glass; mirrored glass

(G-6533)
BURGE INCORPORATED
Also Called: Burge Chemical Products
2751 Westbrook Dr Nw (49504-2348)
PHONE..........................616 791-2214
Terry L Wisner, *President*
Craig Wisner, *Vice Pres*
EMP: 6
SQ FT: 18,000
SALES (est): 400K **Privately Held**
SIC: 2842 Cleaning or polishing preparations

(G-6534)
BURGER IRON CO
99 Steele St Nw (49534-8737)
PHONE..........................330 794-1716
Ed Bobko, *Plant Mgr*
EMP: 5 EST: 2018
SALES (est): 54.1K **Privately Held**
SIC: 3547 Rolling mill machinery

(G-6535)
BURKE E PORTER MACHINERY CO (PA)
Also Called: Burke Porter Machinery Co
730 Plymouth Ave Ne (49505-6034)
PHONE..........................616 234-1200
David Deboer, *CEO*
Jim Lehman, *Vice Pres*
Brian Westerhof, *Engineer*
Ali Tanade, *Controller*
Seth Berghorst, *Human Res Dir*
◆ EMP: 168 EST: 1980
SQ FT: 105,000
SALES (est): 104.3MM **Privately Held**
WEB: www.bepco.com
SIC: 3826 3559 3549 3825 Analytical instruments; automotive maintenance equipment; metalworking machinery; instruments to measure electricity; industrial instrmnts msrmnt display/control process variable

(G-6536)
BURKK INC
4455 Airwest Dr Se (49512-3939)
PHONE..........................616 365-0354
Brett Burkhardt, *President*
EMP: 13 EST: 2001

SALES (est): 391.9K **Privately Held**
SIC: 3398 Metal heat treating

(G-6537)
BURLINGAME INDUSTRIES INC
6757 Cascade Rd Se (49546-6849)
PHONE..........................616 682-5691
Mark Bruinius, *Principal*
EMP: 5 EST: 2011
SALES (est): 312.2K **Privately Held**
WEB: www.tankshield.com
SIC: 3999 Manufacturing industries

(G-6538)
BURNSIDE ACQUISITION LLC (PA)
1060 Kenosha Indus Dr Se (49508)
PHONE..........................616 243-2800
Matt Andreychuk, *Opers Mgr*
John Boll, *Mng Member*
Lori Farkas, *Manager*
Kevin Williams, *Executive*
Brian Burnside,
EMP: 2 EST: 2006
SQ FT: 1,000
SALES (est): 7.8MM **Privately Held**
WEB: www.garichards.com
SIC: 3469 Stamping metal for the trade

(G-6539)
BUSCH INDUSTRIES INC
900 East Paris Ave Se # 304 (49546-3676)
PHONE..........................616 957-3737
Fax: 616 957-9951
EMP: 5
SQ FT: 1,500
SALES (est): 688.3K **Privately Held**
SIC: 8742 3441 Management Consulting Services

(G-6540)
BUSINESS CONNECT L3C
Also Called: Business Connect World
2146 Division Ave S (49507-3031)
PHONE..........................833 229-6753
Natalie Thue, *Manager*
Jereme Lambert,
Jeffrey Haveman,
Lou Haveman,
EMP: 5 EST: 2014
SALES (est): 849.6K **Privately Held**
WEB: www.businessconnectworld.com
SIC: 3589 5074 Water purification equipment, household type; water purification equipment

(G-6541)
BUTTERBALL FARMS INC
1435 Buchanan Ave Sw (49507-1699)
PHONE..........................616 243-0105
Mark Peters, *CEO*
David Riemersma, *President*
David O 'hagan, *COO*
Lela Honicutt, *Manager*
Elinor Fultz, *Supervisor*
EMP: 135 EST: 1983
SQ FT: 125,000
SALES (est): 36.8MM **Privately Held**
WEB: www.butterballfarms.com
SIC: 2099 5143 Butter, renovated & processed; butter

(G-6542)
C D TOOL AND GAGE
3223 3 Mile Rd Nw (49534-1223)
PHONE..........................616 682-1111
EMP: 7 EST: 2017
SALES (est): 859.4K **Privately Held**
WEB: www.cdgage.com
SIC: 3599 Machine shop, jobbing & repair

(G-6543)
C G WITVOET & SONS COMPANY
356 Crown St Sw (49548-4279)
PHONE..........................616 534-6677
Brian Witvoet, *President*
Pete Musser, *CFO*
Mike Brackett, *Director*
EMP: 25 EST: 1932
SALES (est): 4.2MM **Privately Held**
WEB: www.cgwitvoet.com
SIC: 3993 Signs & advertising specialties

(G-6544)
CAD CAM SERVICES INC
4017 Brockton Dr Se (49512-4084)
PHONE..........................616 554-5222
Michael Haverkamp, *President*
Bob Kleinsteiber, *Sales Staff*
EMP: 10 EST: 1991
SQ FT: 20,000
SALES (est): 954.9K **Privately Held**
WEB: www.c2machining.com
SIC: 3544 Special dies & tools

(G-6545)
CALUMET ABRASIVES CO INC
Also Called: Cabco
3890 Buchanan Ave Sw (49548-3111)
PHONE..........................219 844-2695
John G Anderson, *Principal*
Gayle Labus, *Manager*
▼ EMP: 30 EST: 1943
SALES (est): 4.3MM **Privately Held**
SIC: 3291 Abrasive wheels & grindstones, not artificial

(G-6546)
CANNON MACHINE INC
1641 Davis Ave Nw (49504-2001)
PHONE..........................616 363-4014
Brian Meester, *President*
Ray Shalle Roberts, *Manager*
EMP: 9 EST: 1987
SALES (est): 857.7K **Privately Held**
WEB: www.cannonmachine.com
SIC: 3599 Machine shop, jobbing & repair

(G-6547)
CARAUSTAR CSTM PACKG GROUP INC
Grand Rapids Plant
1957 Beverly Ave Sw (49519-1720)
PHONE..........................616 247-0330
Ben Ora, *General Mgr*
Paul Curtis, *Vice Pres*
Don Aardema, *Engineer*
Larry Howard, *Maintence Staff*
EMP: 87
SALES (corp-wide): 4.5B **Publicly Held**
SIC: 2653 2657 Boxes, corrugated: made from purchased materials; folding paperboard boxes
HQ: Caraustar Custom Packaging Group, Inc.
5000 Austell Powder Sprin
Austell GA 30106

(G-6548)
CARTER PRODUCTS COMPANY INC
2871 Northridge Dr Nw (49544-9109)
PHONE..........................616 647-3380
Peter Perez, *President*
Carroll Perez, *Corp Secy*
Terry Camp, *Vice Pres*
▲ EMP: 34 EST: 1929
SQ FT: 16,000
SALES (est): 7.6MM **Privately Held**
WEB: www.carterproducts.com
SIC: 3553 3549 Woodworking machinery; metalworking machinery

(G-6549)
CARTERS INC
Also Called: Carter's Children's Store
3390 Alpine Ave Nw (49544-1672)
PHONE..........................616 647-9452
EMP: 9
SALES (corp-wide): 3B **Publicly Held**
WEB: www.carters.com
SIC: 5641 5137 2369 Children's wear; children's goods; girls' & children's outerwear
PA: Carter's, Inc.
3438 Peachtree Rd Ne # 18
Atlanta GA 30326
678 791-1000

(G-6550)
CASCADE DIE CASTING GROUP INC (DH)
7441 Division Ave S A1 (49548-7979)
PHONE..........................616 281-1774
Theodore C Hohman, *Ch of Bd*
Patrick J Greene, *Vice Pres*
Jim Moran, *Vice Pres*
Rodney Manns, *QC Mgr*

Grand Rapids - Kent County (G-6551)

Heidi Lacey, *Human Res Mgr*
▲ **EMP:** 9
SQ FT: 2,700
SALES (est): 87.9MM **Privately Held**
WEB: www.cascade-cdc.com
SIC: 3364 3363 Zinc & zinc-base alloy die-castings; aluminum die-castings
HQ: T C H Industries Incorporated
7441 Div Ave S Ste A1
Grand Rapids MI 49548
616 942-0505

(G-6551)
CASCADE DIE CASTING GROUP INC
Also Called: Cascade Die Casting/Mid-State
7750 Division Ave S (49548-7226)
PHONE.................................616 455-4010
Dick Evans, *Branch Mgr*
EMP: 7
SALES (corp-wide): 79.1MM **Privately Held**
WEB: www.cascade-cdc.com
SIC: 3369 3364 White metal castings (lead, tin, antimony), except die; nonferrous die-castings except aluminum
HQ: Cascade Die Casting Group Inc
7441 Division Ave S A1
Grand Rapids MI 49548
616 281-1660

(G-6552)
CASCADE ENGINEERING INC (PA)
Also Called: Cascade Cart Solutions
3400 Innovation Ct Se (49512-2085)
P.O. Box 888405 (49588-8405)
PHONE.................................616 975-4800
Christina Keller, *President*
Frederick P Keller, *Chairman*
Kenyatta Brame, *Exec VP*
Steve Bushong, *Vice Pres*
Mike Jorritsma, *Vice Pres*
◆ **EMP:** 850 **EST:** 1973
SQ FT: 300,000
SALES (est): 432.2MM **Privately Held**
WEB: www.cascadeng.com
SIC: 3089 Injection molding of plastics

(G-6553)
CASCADE ENGINEERING INC
3739 Patterson Ave Se (49512-4024)
PHONE.................................616 975-4767
EMP: 5
SALES (corp-wide): 432.2MM **Privately Held**
WEB: www.cascadeng.com
SIC: 3089 Injection molding of plastics
PA: Cascade Engineering, Inc.
3400 Innovation Ct Se
Grand Rapids MI 49512
616 975-4800

(G-6554)
CASCADE ENGINEERING INC
4950 37th St Se (49512-4072)
PHONE.................................616 975-4965
Jo Perkins, *Vice Pres*
EMP: 7
SALES (corp-wide): 432.2MM **Privately Held**
WEB: www.cascadecartsolutions.com
SIC: 3714 Motor vehicle parts & accessories
PA: Cascade Engineering, Inc.
3400 Innovation Ct Se
Grand Rapids MI 49512
616 975-4800

(G-6555)
CASCADE PAPER CONVERTERS LLC
Also Called: Greif
4935 Starr St Se (49546-6350)
PHONE.................................616 974-9165
Tom Natale, *General Mgr*
Lori Natale,
Jodey Barnes,
John Falkenhagen,
EMP: 18 **EST:** 2007
SQ FT: 40,000
SALES (est): 4.7MM **Privately Held**
WEB: www.cascadetwp.com
SIC: 2655 2298 2631 Tubes, fiber or paper: made from purchased material; binder & baler twine; packaging board

(G-6556)
CASCADE PRTG & GRAPHICS INC
Also Called: Budget Print Center
6504 28th St Se Ste A (49546-6929)
PHONE.................................616 222-2937
Brian Ebbers, *President*
Diane Ebbers, *Vice Pres*
EMP: 4 **EST:** 1984
SALES (est): 393.1K **Privately Held**
WEB: www.cascadeprint.com
SIC: 2752 Commercial printing, offset

(G-6557)
CASCADES ENVIROPAC HPM LLC
236 Stevens St Sw (49507-1566)
PHONE.................................616 243-4870
E Deillette, *General Mgr*
Mikael Avequin, *Plant Mgr*
John Sawyer, *Warehouse Mgr*
Tina Combs, *Human Res Mgr*
EMP: 57 **EST:** 2007
SALES (est): 10.7MM
SALES (corp-wide): 3.9B **Privately Held**
WEB: www.cascades.com
SIC: 2621 Paper mills
PA: Cascades Inc
404 Boul Marie-Victorin
Kingsey Falls QC J0A 1
819 363-5100

(G-6558)
CASE-FREE INC
Also Called: Coye's Canvas & Awnings
240 32nd St Se (49548-2221)
PHONE.................................616 245-3136
David Smith, *President*
EMP: 8 **EST:** 2004 **Privately Held**
WEB: www.awningsnow.com
SIC: 2394 3089 3444 Awnings, fabric: made from purchased materials; canvas awnings & canopies; awnings, fiberglass & plastic combination; awnings & canopies

(G-6559)
CASTLETON VILLAGE CENTER INC
Also Called: Hightech Signs
3580 Rgr B Chaffee Mem Dr (49548-2328)
PHONE.................................616 247-8100
Mike Abramowski, *Vice Pres*
EMP: 4 **Privately Held**
SIC: 3993 Signs, not made in custom sign painting shops
PA: Castleton Village Center Inc
6321 Huguenard Rd Ste A
Fort Wayne IN 46818

(G-6560)
CENTRAL INDUSTRIAL CORPORATION
Also Called: Central Industrial Packaging
2916 Walkent Dr Nw (49544-1483)
PHONE.................................616 784-9612
Lawrence Larsen, *President*
EMP: 9 **EST:** 2015
SALES (est): 717.4K **Privately Held**
WEB: www.rsmask.com
SIC: 3492 Hose & tube fittings & assemblies, hydraulic/pneumatic

(G-6561)
CERVA SCREEN PRINTING
3125 Rypens Dr Nw (49504-2467)
PHONE.................................616 272-2635
Jose Cervantes, *Principal*
EMP: 5 **EST:** 2018
SALES (est): 241.6K **Privately Held**
WEB: www.cervaimprints.com
SIC: 2759 Screen printing

(G-6562)
CHALLENGE MFG COMPANY LLC
3200 Fruit Ridge Ave Nw (49544-9707)
PHONE.................................616 735-6500
Bruce Vor Broker, *President*
EMP: 196
SALES (corp-wide): 781.8MM **Privately Held**
WEB: www.challenge-mfg.com
SIC: 3465 Automotive stampings

PA: Challenge Mfg. Company, Llc
3200 Fruit Ridge Ave Nw
Walker MI 49544
616 735-6500

(G-6563)
CHALLENGE MFG HOLDINGS LLC
3200 Fruit Ridge Ave Nw (49544-9707)
PHONE.................................616 735-6500
EMP: 23 **EST:** 2018
SALES (est): 1.2MM **Privately Held**
WEB: www.challenge-mfg.com
SIC: 3542 Machine tools, metal forming type

(G-6564)
CHAMES LLC
Also Called: Five Star Window Coatings
163 Ann St Ne Ste 1 (49505-6261)
PHONE.................................616 363-0000
Nicholas Tebos, *Sales Staff*
Randall K Hutson, *Mng Member*
Randall Hutson, *Manager*
Melinda Hutson,
EMP: 8 **EST:** 1999
SQ FT: 2,000
SALES (est): 1MM **Privately Held**
WEB: www.fiveswc.com
SIC: 1751 2899 Window & door (prefabricated) installation; household tints or dyes

(G-6565)
CHARLES GROUP INC (PA)
7441 Div Ave S Ste A1 (49548)
PHONE.................................336 882-0186
Theodore C Hohman, *President*
Patrick Greene, *Vice Pres*
EMP: 275 **EST:** 1985
SALES (est): 79.1MM **Privately Held**
SIC: 3364 3363 Zinc & zinc-base alloy die-castings; aluminum die-castings

(G-6566)
CHASE PLASTIC SERVICES INC
1115 Cadillac Dr Se (49506-6503)
PHONE.................................616 246-7190
EMP: 4 **Privately Held**
SIC: 2821 Mfg Plastic Materials/Resins
PA: Chase Plastic Services, Inc.
6467 Waldon Center Dr # 200
Clarkston MI 48346

(G-6567)
CHEEZE KURLS LLC
2915 Walkent Dr Nw (49544-1400)
PHONE.................................616 784-6095
Jaime Colbourne, *CEO*
Robert Franzak, *Vice Pres*
Dave Krombeen, *Vice Pres*
Christopher Dedinas, *Production*
Laura Vanvuuren, *Controller*
▲ **EMP:** 90 **EST:** 1965
SQ FT: 100,000
SALES (est): 24MM **Privately Held**
WEB: www.cheezekurls.com
SIC: 2099 2096 Food preparations; potato chips & similar snacks

(G-6568)
CHILDRENS BIBLE HOUR INC
Also Called: KEYS FOR KIDS MINISTRIES
2060 43rd St Se (49508-5099)
P.O. Box 1001 (49501-1001)
PHONE.................................616 647-4500
Davin Malin, *Business Mgr*
Dave Carpenter, *Accounts Mgr*
Greg Yoder, *Exec Dir*
Gary Feenstra, *Director*
Jessica Kogelshatz, *Director*
EMP: 15 **EST:** 1942
SQ FT: 12,000
SALES (est): 1.2MM **Privately Held**
WEB: www.keysforkids.org
SIC: 7922 8699 2731 Radio producers; charitable organization; book publishing

(G-6569)
CHRISTY VAULT COMPANY INC
3669 Bridgehampton Dr Ne (49546-1444)
P.O. Box 717, Parkton MD (21120-0717)
PHONE.................................415 994-1378
EMP: 9 **EST:** 2014

SALES (est): 221.8K **Privately Held**
WEB: www.christyvault.com
SIC: 3272 Burial vaults, concrete or precast terrazzo

(G-6570)
CLASSIC DIE INC
610 Plymouth Ave Ne (49505-6040)
PHONE.................................616 454-3760
Daniel J Parmeter Sr, *President*
Todd Verwys, *President*
Joyce Parmeter, *Corp Secy*
Andy Bourn, *Project Mgr*
Mike Wright, *Engineer*
▲ **EMP:** 21 **EST:** 1975
SQ FT: 12,000
SALES (est): 3.9MM **Privately Held**
WEB: www.classicdie.com
SIC: 3089 3544 Injection molding of plastics; special dies, tools, jigs & fixtures

(G-6571)
CLEAN ROOMS INTERNATIONAL INC
4939 Starr St Se (49546-6350)
PHONE.................................616 452-8700
Timothy D Werkema, *President*
Nelson G Werkema, *President*
Keith Weber, *Vice Pres*
Ted Eastway, *Mfg Staff*
Melissa Wise, *Manager*
EMP: 30 **EST:** 1982
SQ FT: 36,000
SALES (est): 11.4MM **Privately Held**
WEB: www.cleanroomsint.com
SIC: 3564 Ventilating fans: industrial or commercial

(G-6572)
CLEANING SOLUTIONS INC
1250 Ramona St Se (49507-2164)
PHONE.................................616 243-0555
Ronald L Balk, *Branch Mgr*
EMP: 4 **Privately Held**
WEB: www.cleaningsolutionsinc.com
SIC: 2842 2899 Specialty cleaning preparations; chemical preparations
PA: Cleaning Solutions Inc
48080 Roger B Chaffee
Grand Rapids MI

(G-6573)
CLEAR CUT WATER JET MACHINING
4515 Patterson Ave Se (49512-5304)
PHONE.................................616 534-9119
EMP: 5
SALES (est): 457.3K **Privately Held**
SIC: 3541 Mfg Machine Tools-Cutting

(G-6574)
CLIPPER BELT LACER COMPANY
1995 Oak Industrial Dr Ne (49505-6009)
PHONE.................................616 459-3196
Rick White, *President*
Joseph Dickson, *Engineer*
John Collier, *Administration*
▲ **EMP:** 90 **EST:** 1890
SQ FT: 90,000
SALES (est): 16MM
SALES (corp-wide): 106.6MM **Privately Held**
WEB: www.flexco.com
SIC: 3496 3599 Miscellaneous fabricated wire products; custom machinery
PA: Flexible Steel Lacing Company Inc
2525 Wisconsin Ave
Downers Grove IL 60515
800 323-3444

(G-6575)
CLOUD APPS CONSULTING LLC
1406 Laurel Ave Se (49506-4123)
PHONE.................................616 528-0528
Jonathan A Reifler,
EMP: 4 **EST:** 2015
SALES (est): 71.2K **Privately Held**
SIC: 7372 Application computer software

(G-6576)
CND PRODUCTS LLC
1642 Broadway Ave Nw 3n (49504-2046)
PHONE.................................616 361-1000
Jeffrey D Tyner,

GEOGRAPHIC SECTION
Grand Rapids - Kent County (G-6602)

EMP: 5 **EST:** 1991
SQ FT: 1,000
SALES (est): 373.2K Privately Held
WEB: www.point-o-care.com
SIC: 3841 Surgical & medical instruments

(G-6577)
COATINGS PLUS INC
675 Chestnut St Sw (49503-4938)
PHONE..................................616 451-2427
Jeff Stegmeier, *President*
Jim Vanos, *General Mgr*
Bob Rabe, *Vice Pres*
EMP: 25 **EST:** 2007
SQ FT: 40,000
SALES (est): 2.2MM Privately Held
WEB: www.coatingsplus.com
SIC: 3479 Coating of metals & formed products

(G-6578)
COCA-COLA REFRESHMENTS USA INC
1208 Butterworth St Sw (49504-6059)
PHONE..................................616 913-0400
Don Harkness, *Manager*
EMP: 6
SALES (corp-wide): 33B Publicly Held
WEB: www.coca-cola.com
SIC: 2086 2033 5149 Soft drinks: packaged in cans, bottles, etc.; canned fruits & specialties; groceries & related products
HQ: Coca-Cola Refreshments Usa, Inc.
2500 Windy Ridge Pkwy Se
Atlanta GA 30339
770 989-3000

(G-6579)
COCA-COLA REFRESHMENTS USA INC
1440 Butterworth St Sw (49504-6094)
PHONE..................................616 458-4536
Marty Piet, *Branch Mgr*
Matt Barribou, *Manager*
Jim Clark, *Manager*
EMP: 6
SALES (corp-wide): 33B Publicly Held
WEB: www.coca-cola.com
SIC: 2086 Bottled & canned soft drinks
HQ: Coca-Cola Refreshments Usa, Inc.
2500 Windy Ridge Pkwy Se
Atlanta GA 30339
770 989-3000

(G-6580)
COFFMAN ELECTRICAL EQP CO
3300 Jefferson Ave Se (49548-2242)
PHONE..................................616 452-8708
Richard E Coffman, *President*
Marcia Coffman, *Corp Secy*
Steve Coffman, *Technology*
EMP: 20 **EST:** 1948
SQ FT: 27,000
SALES (est): 5.3MM Privately Held
WEB: www.steadypower.com
SIC: 5063 3524 Generators; snowblowers & throwers, residential

(G-6581)
COIT AVENUE GRAVEL CO INC
4772 Coit Ave Ne (49525-1198)
PHONE..................................616 363-7777
Greg Jaaueowski, *President*
EMP: 22 **EST:** 1948
SQ FT: 6,000
SALES (est): 4.7MM Privately Held
WEB: www.coitgravel.com
SIC: 3273 Ready-mixed concrete

(G-6582)
COLES QUALITY FOODS INC (PA)
4079 Park East Ct Se A (49546-8815)
PHONE..................................231 722-1651
Wesley S Devon Jr, *CEO*
Cynthia A Havard, *COO*
Monte Nis, *Plant Mgr*
Janelle Johnston, *Controller*
Jane Kendall, *Accountant*
EMP: 10 **EST:** 1943
SALES (est): 52.2MM Privately Held
WEB: www.coles.com
SIC: 2051 Bakery: wholesale or wholesale/retail combined

(G-6583)
COLOR HOUSE GRAPHICS INC
3505 Eastern Ave Se (49508-2408)
PHONE..................................616 241-1916
Ken Postema, *President*
Phil Knight, *General Mgr*
Steve Landheer, *Corp Secy*
Derek Landheer, *Prdtn Mgr*
Dan Roest, *Purch Agent*
▲ **EMP:** 45 **EST:** 1986
SQ FT: 27,000
SALES (est): 8.7MM Privately Held
WEB: www.colorhousegraphics.com
SIC: 2752 Commercial printing, offset

(G-6584)
COLORHUB LLC
4950 Kraft Ave Se (49512-9708)
PHONE..................................616 333-4411
Tim Harris, *CEO*
Claire Niemeier, *Graphic Designe*
EMP: 19 **EST:** 2016
SALES (est): 5.5MM Privately Held
WEB: www.colorhubprint.com
SIC: 2752 Commercial printing, lithographic

(G-6585)
COLUMBUS PRINTING INC
4920 Starr St Se (49546-6351)
PHONE..................................614 534-0266
EMP: 4 **EST:** 2018
SALES (est): 87K Privately Held
SIC: 2752 Commercial printing, lithographic

(G-6586)
COMPETITIVE EDGE DESIGNS INC
4506 R B Chaffee Mem Dr S (49548)
PHONE..................................616 257-0565
James Houda, *President*
EMP: 5 **EST:** 1994
SQ FT: 3,500
SALES (est): 442.8K Privately Held
WEB: www.comp-edge.com
SIC: 8711 3599 Mechanical engineering; designing: ship, boat, machine & product; machine shop, jobbing & repair

(G-6587)
COMPLETE SOURCE INC
4455 44th St Se (49512-4010)
PHONE..................................616 285-9110
Paul Schweitze, *President*
Robert Carpenter, *Sales Staff*
Robin Furman, *Sales Staff*
Bridget Start, *Marketing Staff*
EMP: 7 **EST:** 1989
SALES (est): 1.3MM Privately Held
WEB: www.completesource.com
SIC: 2759 7319 Screen printing; display advertising service

(G-6588)
COMPONENT ENGRG SOLUTIONS LLC
1740 Chicago Dr Sw (49519-1207)
PHONE..................................616 514-1343
John Lallo, *President*
Vicki Veen, *Controller*
Kevin Beutler, *Sales Staff*
Geoffrey Boutelier, *Sales Staff*
EMP: 27 **EST:** 1998
SQ FT: 15,000
SALES (est): 5.4MM Privately Held
WEB: www.tpprobes.com
SIC: 3599 Machine shop, jobbing & repair

(G-6589)
COMPOSITE TECHNIQUES INC
3345 Brook Trl Se (49508-2676)
PHONE..................................616 878-9795
Jeff Cable, *President*
EMP: 10 **EST:** 1995
SALES (est): 965.4K Privately Held
SIC: 3089 8711 Injection molding of plastics; structural engineering; industrial engineers

(G-6590)
COMPRESSOR TECHNOLOGIES INC
Also Called: CTI
4420 40th St Se (49512-4035)
PHONE..................................616 949-7000
Tom Russell, *President*
EMP: 19 **EST:** 1991
SQ FT: 25,000
SALES (est): 4.3MM Privately Held
SIC: 5084 3564 7699 5075 Compressors, except air conditioning; blowers & fans; compressor repair; dehumidifiers, except portable

(G-6591)
CONCEPT TOOLING SYSTEMS INC
555 Plymouth Ave Ne (49505-6029)
PHONE..................................616 301-6906
Mark Eberlein, *President*
EMP: 32 **EST:** 2005
SALES (est): 2.1MM Privately Held
WEB: www.toolingsystemsgroup.com
SIC: 3544 Special dies & tools

(G-6592)
CONFORM AUTOMOTIVE LLC
5505 52nd St Sw (49512)
PHONE..................................248 647-0400
Gary Stantis, *Branch Mgr*
EMP: 10 Privately Held
WEB: www.conformgroup.com
SIC: 3714 Motor vehicle parts & accessories
PA: Conform Automotive, Llc
32500 Telg Rd Ste 207
Bingham Farms MI 48025

(G-6593)
CONICAL CUTTING TOOLS INC
Also Called: Conical Tool Company
3890 Buchanan Ave Sw (49548-3111)
PHONE..................................616 531-8500
Robert M Shindors, *President*
EMP: 49 **EST:** 1944
SQ FT: 10,000
SALES (est): 3.4MM Privately Held
WEB: www.conicalendmills.com
SIC: 3545 End mills

(G-6594)
CONLEY COMPOSITES LLC
Also Called: An Andronaco Industries Co
4855 Broadmoor Ave Se (49512-5360)
PHONE..................................918 299-5051
Ronald V Andronaco, *CEO*
Adam Hanson, *Engineer*
Ben Parkhurst, *Engineer*
Ron Woltjer, *Engineer*
Scott Palmitier, *CFO*
▲ **EMP:** 45 **EST:** 2015
SALES (est): 19MM
SALES (corp-wide): 144.6MM Privately Held
WEB: www.conleyfrp.com
SIC: 3084 3089 3491 2891 Plastics pipe; fittings for pipe, plastic; industrial valves; adhesives, plastic; epoxy adhesives; valves & pipe fittings
PA: Andronaco, Inc.
4855 Broadmoor Ave Se
Kentwood MI 49512
616 554-4600

(G-6595)
CONSOLDTED RSOURCE IMAGING LLC
2943 S Wilson Ct Nw (49534-7567)
PHONE..................................616 735-2080
Nathan Crawford, *Owner*
Rodney Davis, *COO*
John Schroeder, *Electrical Engi*
Edward Elsner, *Controller*
EMP: 31 **EST:** 2004
SALES (est): 4.8MM Privately Held
WEB: www.cri.us.com
SIC: 8731 7629 8999 3812 Electronic research; electronic equipment repair; scientific consulting; infrared object detection equipment; electrical or electronic engineering

(G-6596)
CONSOLIDATED METAL PDTS INC
3831 Clay Ave Sw (49548-3012)
PHONE..................................616 538-1000
Gary Becker, *President*
John Becker, *Treasurer*
David Becker, *Admin Sec*
EMP: 5 **EST:** 1974
SQ FT: 4,800
SALES (est): 729.5K Privately Held
WEB: www.cmpincorp.com
SIC: 3469 3599 7692 3452 Stamping metal for the trade; machine shop, jobbing & repair; welding repair; bolts, nuts, rivets & washers; sheet metalwork

(G-6597)
CONTECH (US) INC
Also Called: Pherotech
314 Straight Ave Sw (49504-6439)
PHONE..................................616 459-4139
Mark Grambart, *President*
◆ **EMP:** 17 **EST:** 1992
SALES (est): 991K Privately Held
WEB: www.loudartdesign.com
SIC: 3524 Lawn & garden equipment

(G-6598)
CONTRACT FLAVORS INC
Also Called: CFC
3855 Linden Ave Se (49548-3429)
PHONE..................................616 454-5950
Frederick High, *President*
EMP: 10 **EST:** 1962
SQ FT: 2,000
SALES (est): 614.2K Privately Held
SIC: 2087 Syrups, drink

(G-6599)
CONTRACT SOURCE & ASSEMBLY INC
Also Called: C S A
5230 33rd St Se (49512-2070)
PHONE..................................616 897-2186
Chris Cooper, *President*
▲ **EMP:** 16 **EST:** 2001
SQ FT: 30,000
SALES (est): 3.2MM Privately Held
WEB: www.contractmi.com
SIC: 2522 Office furniture, except wood

(G-6600)
CONTRACTORS STEEL COMPANY
2768 Dormax St Sw (49519-2406)
PHONE..................................616 531-4000
Keith D Ford, *Opers-Prdtn-Mfg*
Gary Herrold, *Credit Mgr*
James Bokas, *Sales Staff*
EMP: 46
SALES (corp-wide): 575.6MM Privately Held
WEB: www.upgllc.com
SIC: 5051 3542 Steel; machine tools, metal forming type
HQ: Contractors Steel Company
36555 Amrhein Rd
Livonia MI 48150
734 464-4000

(G-6601)
CONTRIBUTE A VERSE PUBLISHING
2862 Leelanau Dr Ne (49525-1903)
PHONE..................................616 447-2271
Tyler Richardson, *Principal*
EMP: 5 **EST:** 2008
SALES (est): 66.4K Privately Held
SIC: 2741 Miscellaneous publishing

(G-6602)
CONTROLLED PLATING TECH INC
1100 Godfrey Ave Sw (49503-5008)
PHONE..................................616 243-6622
Steve Slot, *President*
Dennis Matthews, *Manager*
Douglas Slot, *Manager*
Glenn Schuemann, *Supervisor*
EMP: 36 **EST:** 1991
SQ FT: 30,000

Grand Rapids - Kent County (G-6603)
GEOGRAPHIC SECTION

SALES (est): 5.2MM Privately Held
WEB: www.controlledplating.com
SIC: 3471 Electroplating of metals or formed products

(G-6603)
CONWAY PRODUCTS CORPORATION
Also Called: Emerald Spa
4150 East Paris Ave Se # 1 (49512-3995)
PHONE..................................616 698-2601
Paul Slagh, President
Duncan McColl, Opers Staff
Tracy Kempkers, Controller
John Kennedy, Shareholder
♦ EMP: 25 EST: 1988
SQ FT: 84,000
SALES (est): 3.6MM Privately Held
SIC: 3999 3088 3949 Hot tubs; plastics plumbing fixtures; sporting & athletic goods

(G-6604)
CONWAY-CLEVELAND CORP (PA)
2320 Oak Industrial Dr Ne (49505-6090)
PHONE..................................616 458-0056
Daniel Conway, President
Linda Conway, Vice Pres
▲ EMP: 4 EST: 1965
SQ FT: 7,000
SALES (est): 1.1MM Privately Held
WEB: www.conwaycleveland.com
SIC: 3829 2851 3553 3546 Measuring & controlling devices; wood fillers or sealers; woodworking machinery; power-driven handtools; gum & wood chemicals

(G-6605)
CORIUM INC
4558 50th St Se (49512-5401)
PHONE..................................616 656-4563
Christina Dickerson, Vice Pres
Bobby Singh, Vice Pres
Mike Sayfie, Mfg Dir
Michelle Looyenga, Project Mgr
Jennifer Loniewski, Opers Staff
EMP: 30
SALES (corp-wide): 75.8MM Privately Held
WEB: www.corium.com
SIC: 2834 Adrenal pharmaceutical preparations
HQ: Corium, Inc.
    4558 50th St Se
    Grand Rapids MI 49512

(G-6606)
CORIUM INC (HQ)
4558 50th St Se (49512-5401)
PHONE..................................650 298-8255
Perry Sternberg, President
Parminder Singh, Vice Pres
Jason Vines, Opers Staff
Edward Marcoux, Mfg Staff
Melanie Caruano, Research
EMP: 150 EST: 1995
SALES (est): 31.8MM
SALES (corp-wide): 75.8MM Privately Held
WEB: www.corium.com
SIC: 2834 8731 2836 Pharmaceutical preparations; biological research; biological products, except diagnostic
PA: Gurnet Point Capital Llc
    55 Cambridge Pkwy Ste 401
    Cambridge MA 02142
    617 588-4902

(G-6607)
CORLETT-TURNER CO
Also Called: G. A. Rchards - Corlett Turner
1060 Kn O Sha Indus Dr Se (49508)
PHONE..................................616 772-9082
EMP: 18 EST: 2009
SALES (est): 695.1K Privately Held
WEB: www.garichards.com
SIC: 3444 Sheet metalwork

(G-6608)
CORVAC COMPOSITES LLC
4450 36th St Se (49512-1917)
PHONE..................................616 281-2430
Jeff Wilson, Engineer
James Sitzell, Mng Member
Katie Irons, Program Mgr
EMP: 250
SALES (corp-wide): 190MM Privately Held
WEB: www.corvaccomposites.com
SIC: 3559 Automotive related machinery
HQ: Corvac Composites, Llc
    4450 36th St Se
    Kentwood MI 49512

(G-6609)
COUNCIL FOR EDCTL TRVL US AMER
Also Called: Cetusa
678 Front Ave Nw Ste 91a (49504-5323)
PHONE..................................949 940-1140
Susan Doughty, QC Dir
Jie Chui James, Branch Mgr
Karissa Marson, Manager
Kevin Watson, Program Dir
Tricia Lyon, Assistant
EMP: 49
SALES (corp-wide): 4.8MM Privately Held
WEB: www.cetusa.org
SIC: 3851 Spectacles
PA: Council For Educational Travel United States Of America
    903 Calle Amanecer # 200
    San Clemente CA 92673
    949 940-1140

(G-6610)
CREATIVE STEEL RULE DIES INC
4157 Stafford Ave Sw (49548-3053)
PHONE..................................630 307-8880
Larry T Corriere, President
Sandra Corriere, Admin Sec
EMP: 6 EST: 1982
SALES (est): 137.7K Privately Held
SIC: 3544 Dies, steel rule

(G-6611)
CREEK DIESEL SERVICES INC
Also Called: Van Eck Diesel Services
3748 Water Leaf Ct Ne (49525-8604)
PHONE..................................800 974-4600
Tracey Garrett, Manager
EMP: 10 EST: 1990
SQ FT: 8,250
SALES (est): 130.2K Privately Held
SIC: 7538 7699 3519 Engine repair; general truck repair; marine engine repair; internal combustion engines

(G-6612)
CROP MARKS PRINTING
128 Coldbrook St Ne (49503-1010)
PHONE..................................616 356-5555
Russ Colter, Owner
EMP: 8 EST: 2009
SALES (est): 522.2K Privately Held
WEB: www.cropmarksprinting.com
SIC: 3993 Signs & advertising specialties

(G-6613)
CROSS PATHS CORP
955 Ken O Sha Ind Park Dr (49508-8246)
PHONE..................................616 248-5371
Clifford Cross, President
Steve Siekman, Treasurer
EMP: 7 EST: 1997
SQ FT: 3,000
SALES (est): 605K Privately Held
WEB: www.crosspathscorp.com
SIC: 3545 3599 Gauges (machine tool accessories); machine shop, jobbing & repair

(G-6614)
CROWN EQUIPMENT CORPORATION
Also Called: Crown Lift Trucks
4131 Roger Chaffee Mem Se (49548)
PHONE..................................616 530-3000
Rachael Horton, Sales Staff
Eric McNutt, Manager
EMP: 46
SALES (corp-wide): 3.6B Privately Held
WEB: www.crown.com
SIC: 3537 Lift trucks, industrial: fork, platform, straddle, etc.
PA: Crown Equipment Corporation
    44 S Washington St
    New Bremen OH 45869
    419 629-2311

(G-6615)
CROZE NEST COOPERAGE LLC
Also Called: Croze Nest Oak Barrels
316 Collindale Ave Sw (49534-5821)
PHONE..................................616 805-9132
EMP: 5 EST: 2016
SALES (est): 55K Privately Held
WEB: www.crozenest.com
SIC: 2449 Barrels, wood: coopered

(G-6616)
CS VENDETTA PUB LLC
2330 Valleywood Dr Se K5 (49546-7749)
PHONE..................................616 422-7555
Vernal Shaw, Mng Member
EMP: 4
SALES (est): 90K Privately Held
SIC: 2721 Comic books: publishing only, not printed on site

(G-6617)
CSN MANUFACTURING INC
1750 Elizabeth Ave Nw (49504-2060)
PHONE..................................616 364-0027
Fax: 616 364-0082
EMP: 35
SQ FT: 25,000
SALES (est): 5.1MM Privately Held
SIC: 2821 Mfg Plastic Materials/Resins

(G-6618)
CUMMINS INC
3715 Clay Ave Sw (49548-3010)
PHONE..................................616 538-2250
Dan Zammitt, General Mgr
Ashley Dunstan, Technician
EMP: 5
SALES (corp-wide): 19.8B Publicly Held
WEB: www.cummins.com
SIC: 5063 3519 Generators; internal combustion engines
PA: Cummins Inc.
    500 Jackson St
    Columbus IN 47201
    812 377-5000

(G-6619)
CUP ACQUISITION LLC (PA)
Also Called: Custom Profile
2535 Waldorf Ct Nw (49544-1469)
PHONE..................................616 735-4410
Kevin Richardson, Plant Mgr
Tony Dykhouse, Engineer
Rick Portone, Engineer
Jim Lynema, Project Engr
Jim Gorant, CFO
EMP: 222 EST: 2013
SALES (est): 62.2MM Privately Held
WEB: www.custom-profile.com
SIC: 3089 Injection molding of plastics

(G-6620)
CUSTOM GEARS INC
3761 Linden Ave Se Ste B (49548-3459)
PHONE..................................616 243-2723
Ronald C Deyoung, President
EMP: 6 EST: 1989
SALES (est): 563.5K Privately Held
SIC: 3566 Gears, power transmission, except automotive

(G-6621)
CUSTOM POWDER AND FABRICATORS
2100 Nelson Ave Se (49507-3355)
PHONE..................................616 915-9995
EMP: 11 EST: 2016
SALES (est): 1MM Privately Held
WEB: www.custompowderandfabricators.com
SIC: 3441 Fabricated structural metal

(G-6622)
CUSTOM POWDER COATING LLC
1601 Madison Ave Se Ste 1 (49507-2566)
PHONE..................................616 454-9730
Paul Sapp, Manager
Jonathan Hunsberger, Technology
Jori Bennett, Exec Dir
Lynda Vanos,
EMP: 5 EST: 2007
SALES (est): 496.7K Privately Held
WEB: www.custompowderandfabricators.com
SIC: 3399 3479 Silver powder; metal coating & allied service

(G-6623)
CUSTOM PRINTERS INC
Also Called: Pageworks
2801 Oak Industrial Dr Ne (49505-6046)
PHONE..................................616 454-9224
Daniel M Goris, President
Debra Goris, Vice Pres
Nathan Kooienga, Marketing Staff
Amanda Gracey, Account Dir
EMP: 60 EST: 1946
SQ FT: 35,000
SALES (est): 12.2MM Privately Held
WEB: www.customprinters.com
SIC: 2752 2789 2759 Commercial printing, offset; bookbinding & related work; commercial printing

(G-6624)
CUT ONCE LLC
Also Called: Coye's Canvas and Awning
240 32nd St Se (49548-2221)
PHONE..................................616 245-3136
Amy Lodenstein, Principal
EMP: 9 EST: 2017
SALES (est): 113.7K Privately Held
WEB: www.awningsnow.com
SIC: 2211 Canvas

(G-6625)
D & B HEAT TRANSFER PDTS INC
8031 Division Ave S Ste C (49548-7205)
PHONE..................................616 827-0028
Dale Deboer, President
Brian Amante, Vice Pres
Mark De Groot, Manager
EMP: 10 EST: 2004
SQ FT: 18,000
SALES (est): 1.6MM Privately Held
WEB: www.dbheattransfer.com
SIC: 5013 3585 Radiators; evaporative condensers, heat transfer equipment

(G-6626)
D & D BUILDING INC
Also Called: Advantage Millwork
3959 Linden Ave Se (49548-3431)
PHONE..................................616 248-7908
Jim Keuning, Branch Mgr
EMP: 10
SALES (corp-wide): 36.7MM Privately Held
WEB: www.dndbuilding.com
SIC: 5031 2431 Millwork; millwork
PA: D & D Building, Inc.
    3264 Union Ave Se
    Wyoming MI 49548
    616 243-5633

(G-6627)
D & D BUSINESS MACHINES INC
Also Called: Neopost Mailing Equipment
3545 Brandau Dr Ne (49525-2881)
PHONE..................................616 364-8446
Ron Weidenfeller, President
EMP: 6 EST: 1975
SALES (est): 482.9K Privately Held
SIC: 2893 Duplicating ink

(G-6628)
D & D PRINTING CO
342 Market Ave Sw Unit 1 (49503-4000)
PHONE..................................616 454-7710
Mike Bardwell, President
Scott McCardy, Vice Pres
Larry Bardwell, Treasurer
Jason Bardwell, Sales Staff
Richard McCarty, Admin Sec
EMP: 27 EST: 1968
SQ FT: 20,000
SALES (est): 4.2MM Privately Held
WEB: www.ghprintlocal.com
SIC: 2752 Commercial printing, offset

(G-6629)
D A C INDUSTRIES INC
600 11th St Nw (49504-4458)
PHONE..................................616 235-0140

GEOGRAPHIC SECTION
Grand Rapids - Kent County (G-6657)

Dan W Hickey, *President*
EMP: 5 **EST:** 1985
SQ FT: 400
SALES (est): 850.9K Privately Held
WEB: www.dacindustries.com
SIC: 3429 Door opening & closing devices, except electrical

(G-6630)
DAGENHAM MILLWORKS LLC
4525 Airwest Dr Se (49512-3951)
PHONE..................616 698-8883
Doug Deeder, *President*
EMP: 4 **EST:** 2009
SALES (est): 460.7K Privately Held
WEB: www.tmcfurniture.com
SIC: 2431 Millwork

(G-6631)
DAMAR MACHINERY CO
3389 3 Mile Rd Nw (49534-1221)
PHONE..................616 453-4655
David Crysler, *President*
Douglas Crysler, *Vice Pres*
Becky Crysler, *Admin Sec*
EMP: 15 **EST:** 1977
SQ FT: 20,000
SALES (est): 2.6MM Privately Held
WEB: www.damarmachinery.com
SIC: 3599 Machine shop, jobbing & repair

(G-6632)
DANLY IEM
4300 40th St Se (49512-4101)
PHONE..................800 243-2659
James Skalitzky, *Purch Mgr*
Harvey Van Huizen, *VP Sales*
EMP: 5 **EST:** 2011
SALES (est): 346.3K Privately Held
WEB: www.danly.com
SIC: 3544 Die sets for metal stamping (presses)

(G-6633)
DATUM INDUSTRIES LLC
4740 44th St Se (49512-4017)
PHONE..................616 977-1995
David Grieve, *General Mgr*
Matthew Lockwood, *Sales Staff*
Scott Leasure,
▲ **EMP:** 34 **EST:** 2001
SQ FT: 50,000
SALES (est): 6.2MM Privately Held
WEB: www.datumindustries.com
SIC: 3544 Special dies & tools

(G-6634)
DAWN FOOD PRODUCTS INC
2885 Clydon Ave Sw (49519-2401)
P.O. Box 14391, Louisville KY (40214)
PHONE..................800 654-4843
Jerry Hoogterp, *Manager*
Taylor Wilson, *Master*
EMP: 4
SALES (corp-wide): 1.7B Privately Held
WEB: www.dawnfoods.com
SIC: 2045 Doughs & batters: from purchased flour
HQ: Dawn Food Products, Inc.
3333 Sargent Rd
Jackson MI 49201

(G-6635)
DC BYERS CO/GRAND RAPIDS INC (PA)
Also Called: Byers, D C Company
5946 Clay Ave Sw (49548-5768)
PHONE..................616 538-7300
Bernard L Bouma, *CEO*
Douglas Lectka, *Exec VP*
John Stevenson Jr, *VP Sales*
EMP: 15 **EST:** 1903
SQ FT: 10,000
SALES (est): 3.4MM Privately Held
WEB: www.dcbyers.com
SIC: 1799 3471 Caulking (construction); plating & polishing

(G-6636)
DE VRU PRINTING CO
1446 Eastern Ave Se (49507-2054)
PHONE..................616 452-5451
Carl Huisman, *Owner*
EMP: 4 **EST:** 1969
SQ FT: 6,500

SALES (est): 374.2K Privately Held
WEB: www.brownagency.net
SIC: 2752 2759 2791 2789 Commercial printing, offset; letterpress printing; typesetting; bookbinding & related work

(G-6637)
DECADE PRODUCTS LLC (PA)
Also Called: Dolav
3400 Innovation Ct Se (49512-2085)
PHONE..................616 975-4965
Frederick Keller, *CEO*
Raphael Harris, *President*
Matt Kramer, *Opers Staff*
Dave Gargett, *Sales Mgr*
Steven Hobson, *Sales Mgr*
◆ **EMP:** 14 **EST:** 1999
SALES (est): 8.6MM Privately Held
WEB: www.decadeproducts.com
SIC: 3089 Plastic containers, except foam

(G-6638)
DECC COMPANY INC
Also Called: Cascade Rental Centers
1266 Wallen Ave Sw (49507-1586)
PHONE..................616 245-0431
Fred Mellema, *President*
Calista Phillips, *Manager*
Renee Warfield, *Manager*
Melissa Bass, *Technology*
▼ **EMP:** 50 **EST:** 1964
SQ FT: 100,000
SALES (est): 11MM Privately Held
WEB: www.decc.com
SIC: 3479 Coating of metals & formed products

(G-6639)
DECORATIVE CONCRETE BY JOHN
5000 Fruit Ridge Ave Nw (49544-9789)
PHONE..................616 862-7152
John McCleary, *Owner*
EMP: 7 **EST:** 2015
SALES (est): 122.5K Privately Held
SIC: 3272 Concrete products

(G-6640)
DECORATIVE FINISHES DIVISION
13 Mcconnell St Sw (49503-5126)
PHONE..................616 450-4918
EMP: 9 **EST:** 2017
SALES (est): 93.5K Privately Held
WEB: www.spectrumindustries.com
SIC: 3479 Coating of metals & formed products

(G-6641)
DERK PIETER CO INC
Also Called: Sir Speedy
4513 Broadmoor Ave Se A (49512-5313)
PHONE..................616 554-7777
Rudy Dykhuis, *President*
EMP: 4 **EST:** 1995
SQ FT: 2,000
SALES (est): 399.5K Privately Held
WEB: www.sirspeedygr.com
SIC: 2752 7338 2791 2789 Commercial printing, lithographic; secretarial & court reporting; typesetting; bookbinding & related work

(G-6642)
DESIGN CONVERTING INC
3470 Raleigh Dr Se (49512-2042)
PHONE..................616 942-7780
Randy Stout, *President*
Arthur Brand, *Vice Pres*
Peggy Schweitzer, *Vice Pres*
Tom Linck, *Prdtn Mgr*
EMP: 17 **EST:** 1995
SQ FT: 23,000
SALES (est): 4.5MM Privately Held
WEB: www.designconverting.com
SIC: 2675 3714 Paperboard die-cutting; motor vehicle body components & frame

(G-6643)
DESIGN DESIGN INC (PA)
Also Called: As
19 La Grave Ave Se (49503-4225)
P.O. Box 2266 (49501-2266)
PHONE..................866 935-2648
Donald J Kallil, *President*
Gregory Devries, *Vice Pres*

Jennifer Kallil, *Vice Pres*
Lauren Kallil, *Project Mgr*
Maria Van Portfliet, *Purch Mgr*
◆ **EMP:** 152 **EST:** 1986
SQ FT: 5,700
SALES (est): 39.8MM Privately Held
WEB: www.designdesign.us
SIC: 2771 Greeting cards

(G-6644)
DEWITT PACKAGING CORPORATION
5080 Kraft Ave Se (49512-9707)
PHONE..................616 698-0210
Steven Dewitt, *President*
Gordon Jack Dewitt, *Vice Pres*
Jill Dewitt, *Treasurer*
Dorothy Dewitt, *Admin Sec*
EMP: 48 **EST:** 1983
SQ FT: 35,000
SALES (est): 8.2MM Privately Held
WEB: www.dewittpackaging.com
SIC: 2653 Boxes, corrugated: made from purchased materials

(G-6645)
DI-ANODIC FINISHING CORP
736 Ottawa Ave Nw 38 (49503-1428)
PHONE..................616 454-0470
A James Wanczuk, *President*
EMP: 16 **EST:** 1953
SQ FT: 7,500
SALES (est): 171.2K Privately Held
WEB: www.dianodicfinishing.com
SIC: 3471 Electroplating of metals or formed products

(G-6646)
DIE-NAMIC TOOL CORP
4541 Patterson Ave Se (49512-5304)
PHONE..................616 954-7882
Rogelio A Ramirez, *President*
Stephen Paulin, *Manager*
EMP: 6 **EST:** 1998
SQ FT: 6,000
SALES (est): 988.9K Privately Held
WEB: www.dienamictc.com
SIC: 3544 Special dies & tools

(G-6647)
DIE-TECH AND ENGINEERING INC
4620 Herman Ave Sw (49509-5140)
PHONE..................616 530-9030
William H Berry III, *President*
Sandra Berry, *Corp Secy*
Thomas Gray, *Vice Pres*
EMP: 41 **EST:** 1984
SQ FT: 25,000
SALES (est): 3.7MM Privately Held
SIC: 3544 Special dies & tools

(G-6648)
DIMENSION GRAPHICS INC
800 Burton St Se (49507-3320)
PHONE..................616 245-1447
Ken Blessing, *President*
Donna Blessing, *Treasurer*
EMP: 8 **EST:** 1970
SQ FT: 8,200
SALES (est): 697.8K Privately Held
WEB: www.dimensiongraphics.com
SIC: 3993 Signs, not made in custom sign painting shops

(G-6649)
DIRECT AIM MEDIA LLC
1778 Grand Ct Ne (49525-7040)
PHONE..................800 817-7101
Robert Raff, *Mng Member*
EMP: 20 **EST:** 2015
SALES (est): 671.7K Privately Held
WEB: www.directaimmedia.com
SIC: 7319 2741 Advertising;

(G-6650)
DISCOUNT PALLETS
4580 Airwest Dr Se (49512-3950)
PHONE..................616 453-5455
Randy Vanderveen, *President*
EMP: 5 **EST:** 1991
SQ FT: 7,500
SALES (est): 455.5K Privately Held
WEB: www.discountpallet.com
SIC: 2448 Pallets, wood

(G-6651)
DISCOVERY HOUSE PUBLISHERS
Also Called: D H P
3000 Kraft Ave Se (49512-2024)
P.O. Box 2222 (49501-2222)
PHONE..................616 942-9218
Martin Dehaan, *President*
Dave Branon, *Editor*
Robert K De Vries, *Vice Pres*
Max E Smith, *CFO*
Anne Bauman, *Marketing Staff*
▲ **EMP:** 76 **EST:** 1988
SQ FT: 65,000
SALES: 4.8MM
SALES (corp-wide): 51.2MM Privately Held
WEB: www.ourdailybreadpublishing.org
SIC: 2741 Miscellaneous publishing
PA: Rbc Ministries
3000 Kraft Ave Se
Grand Rapids MI 49512
616 942-6770

(G-6652)
DN PLASTICS CORPORATION
1415 Steele Ave Sw Ste 2 (49507-1562)
P.O. Box 586, Ada (49301-0586)
PHONE..................616 942-6060
Sunita Agrawal, *CEO*
EMP: 15 **EST:** 2000
SALES (est): 183.7K Privately Held
WEB: www.dnplasticscorp.com
SIC: 2821 Plastics materials & resins

(G-6653)
DOMART LLC
3923 28th St Se (49512-1805)
PHONE..................616 285-9177
Martin Doorn, *Owner*
EMP: 4 **EST:** 2010
SALES (est): 256.2K Privately Held
SIC: 4783 2759 7331 7389 Packing goods for shipping; commercial printing; mailing service; packaging & labeling services

(G-6654)
DONALD SCHILSTRA
1452 Trentwood St Sw (49509-5037)
PHONE..................616 534-1897
Donald Schilstra, *Owner*
EMP: 5 **EST:** 2016
SALES (est): 70.3K Privately Held
WEB: www.nutritionbeat.com
SIC: 3572 Computer storage devices

(G-6655)
DOOR SEC SOLUTIONS OF MICH
6757 Cascade Rd Se 304 (49546-6849)
PHONE..................616 301-1991
Jim Grondin, *President*
EMP: 10 **EST:** 2003
SQ FT: 958
SALES (est): 980K Privately Held
WEB: www.dss-mi.com
SIC: 3429 Door locks, bolts & checks

(G-6656)
DOUBLE OTIS INC
Also Called: Doubleo O Supply & Craftsmen
1415 Division Ave S (49507-1601)
PHONE..................616 878-3998
Michael F Otis, *President*
Linda N Otis, *Corp Secy*
Doug Pingel, *Opers Dir*
Donn Deemter, *Project Mgr*
Tom Ralya, *Sales Mgr*
EMP: 35
SQ FT: 40,000
SALES: 8MM Privately Held
WEB: www.doubleoinc.com
SIC: 5031 2431 1793 Windows; windows & window parts & trim, wood; windows, wood; glass & glazing work

(G-6657)
DOVER PMPS PRCESS SLTONS SGMEN
Blackmer Pump
1809 Century Ave Sw (49503-8017)
PHONE..................616 241-1611
Jim Walker, *Engineer*
Mike Hedgecock, *Design Engr*

Grand Rapids - Kent County (G-6658)

Bob Lauson, *Branch Mgr*
Tim Brookens, *Manager*
Doug Chapman, *Manager*
EMP: 260
SALES (corp-wide): 6.6B **Publicly Held**
WEB: www.psgdover.com
SIC: 3594 3561 Motors: hydraulic, fluid power or air; pumps & pumping equipment
HQ: Dover Pumps & Process Solutions Segment, Inc.
1815 S Meyers Rd
Oakbrook Terrace IL 60181
630 487-2240

(G-6658)
DOWN INC
635 Evergreen St Se (49507-1891)
PHONE..................................616 241-3922
Donna McLin, *General Mgr*
◆ **EMP:** 30 **EST:** 1980
SQ FT: 8,700
SALES (est): 5.3MM
SALES (corp-wide): 218.8MM **Privately Held**
WEB: www.downinc.com
SIC: 2392 Comforters & quilts: made from purchased materials; pillows, bed: made from purchased materials
HQ: Eurasia Feather, Inc.
635 Evergreen St Se
Grand Rapids MI 49507
616 245-5496

(G-6659)
DYNA PLATE INC
344 Mart St Sw (49548-1015)
PHONE..................................616 452-6763
Craig Hill, *President*
Richard Hill, *Vice Pres*
EMP: 21 **EST:** 1979
SQ FT: 40,000
SALES (est): 1.7MM **Privately Held**
WEB: www.dynaplate.com
SIC: 3471 Electroplating of metals or formed products

(G-6660)
EAGILE INCORPORATED
1880 Turner Ave Nw Ste A (49504-2032)
PHONE..................................616 243-1200
Gary Burns, *CEO*
Peter Phaneuf, *President*
Matthew Wiersum, *Materials Mgr*
Jon Ryskamp, *Production*
Bob Vorpagel, *CFO*
▼ **EMP:** 15 **EST:** 2009
SQ FT: 40,000
SALES (est): 4.3MM **Privately Held**
WEB: www.eagile.com
SIC: 3825 2754 Radio frequency measuring equipment; labels: gravure printing

(G-6661)
EAGLE INDUS GROUP FEDERAL LLC
555 Plymouth Ave Ne (49505-6029)
PHONE..................................616 863-8623
Chad Boersma,
EMP: 6 **EST:** 2009
SALES (est): 523.2K **Privately Held**
WEB: www.toolingsystemsgroup.com
SIC: 3544 Special dies & tools

(G-6662)
EARTHBOUND INC
1116 Plnfeld Ave Ne Ste 2 (49503)
PHONE..................................616 774-0096
EMP: 4
SALES (est): 300K **Privately Held**
SIC: 2759 2395 Commercial Printing Pleating/Stitching Services

(G-6663)
EATON AEROSPACE LLC
3675 Patterson Ave Se (49512-4022)
PHONE..................................616 949-1090
Brian Woloszyk, *Project Dir*
Rose Hummel, *Project Mgr*
Matthew Lytle, *Materials Mgr*
Denise Mann, *Mfg Staff*
Robert Bishop, *Engineer*
EMP: 300

SALES (corp-wide): 385.8MM **Privately Held**
SIC: 3625 3714 3594 3559 Motor controls & accessories; motor starters & controllers, electric; actuators, industrial; motor vehicle engines & parts; motor vehicle transmissions, drive assemblies & parts; motor vehicle steering systems & parts; pumps, hydraulic power transfer; motors: hydraulic, fluid power or air; semiconductor manufacturing machinery; personal computers (microcomputers)
PA: Eaton Aerospace Llc
1000 Eaton Blvd
Cleveland OH 44122
216 523-5000

(G-6664)
ECOPRINT SERVICES LLC
549 Ottawa Ave Nw Ste 103 (49503-1474)
PHONE..................................616 254-8019
Joe Lawrence, *Software Dev*
Paul Bott,
EMP: 6 **EST:** 2005
SALES (est): 447.8K **Privately Held**
WEB: www.ecoprintgr.com
SIC: 2759 Commercial printing

(G-6665)
EDGE INDUSTRIES INC
Also Called: Edge-Sweets Company
2887 3 Mile Rd Nw (49534-1319)
PHONE..................................616 453-5458
Richard Hungerford Sr, *President*
Stephen Hoffman, *Vice Pres*
T Heethuis, *Mfg Staff*
Kelly Wender, *Production*
Angie Bissell, *Purch Mgr*
▼ **EMP:** 1 **EST:** 1895
SQ FT: 80,000
SALES (est): 2.9MM
SALES (corp-wide): 12.8MM **Privately Held**
WEB: www.edge-sweets.com
SIC: 3559 3586 3545 3541 Plastics working machinery; measuring & dispensing pumps; machine tool accessories; machine tools, metal cutting type; conveyors & conveying equipment; saw blades & handsaws
PA: Esco Group, Inc.
2887 3 Mile Rd Nw
Grand Rapids MI 49534
616 453-5458

(G-6666)
EL VOCERO HISPANO INC
2818 Vineland Ave Ne (49508-1453)
P.O. Box 7287 (49510-7287)
PHONE..................................616 246-6023
Andres Abreu, *President*
EMP: 10 **EST:** 1993
SQ FT: 2,000
SALES (est): 1.4MM **Privately Held**
WEB: www.elvocerous.com
SIC: 2711 Newspapers, publishing & printing

(G-6667)
EL-MILAGRO OF MICHIGAN INC (PA)
1846 Clyde Park Ave Sw (49509-1502)
PHONE..................................616 452-6625
Jesse Lopez, *CEO*
Minerva Duran, *CEO*
Melissa Rincones, *President*
Rafael Lopez, *Admin Sec*
EMP: 8 **EST:** 1988
SALES (est): 991.4K **Privately Held**
WEB: www.el-milagro.com
SIC: 2099 Tortillas, fresh or refrigerated

(G-6668)
ELECTRIC SOUL TATTOO AND FINE
876 Grandville Ave Sw (49503-5152)
PHONE..................................616 930-3113
Philip Kosman, *Principal*
EMP: 4 **EST:** 2015
SALES (est): 55.9K **Privately Held**
SIC: 8412 3699 Art gallery; electrical equipment & supplies

(G-6669)
ELECTRO CHEMICAL FINISHING CO
379 44th St Sw (49548-4122)
PHONE..................................616 531-1250
Carla Rock, *Opers Staff*
Mark Sismour, *VP Sales*
Judy Lee, *Manager*
Lisa Volkema, *Personnel Assit*
Larry Keeney, *Maintence Staff*
EMP: 68
SALES (corp-wide): 15.6MM **Privately Held**
WEB: www.ecfinc.com
SIC: 3471 Electroplating of metals or formed products
PA: Electro Chemical Finishing Co.
2973 Dormax St Sw
Grandville MI 49418
616 531-0670

(G-6670)
ELEMENT 80 ENGRAVING LLC
519 Macomb Ave Nw (49534-3570)
PHONE..................................616 318-7407
Alfred Hartl, *Principal*
EMP: 5 **EST:** 2013
SALES (est): 153.8K **Privately Held**
SIC: 2819 Industrial inorganic chemicals

(G-6671)
ELEMENTAL ARTISTRY LLC
957 Leonard St Nw (49504-4153)
PHONE..................................616 326-1758
Juliana Kaio, *Principal*
EMP: 8 **EST:** 2018
SQ FT: 2,000
SALES (est): 415.7K **Privately Held**
SIC: 3446 3429 3499 3442 Architectural metalwork; furniture builders' & other household hardware; furniture parts, metal; metal doors, sash & trim

(G-6672)
ELEVATED TECHNOLOGIES INC
Also Called: Metro Elevator
817 Ottawa Ave Nw (49503-1429)
PHONE..................................616 288-9817
Nathan McFabden, *President*
Brett Cone, *General Mgr*
Scott Miller, *General Mgr*
Mary Kersjes, *Manager*
Emily McFadden, *Administration*
EMP: 40 **EST:** 1987
SQ FT: 2,500
SALES (est): 8.4MM **Privately Held**
SIC: 1796 7699 1541 1791 Elevator installation & conversion; elevators: inspection, service & repair; industrial buildings & warehouses; structural steel erection; sheet metalwork; stair elevators, motor powered

(G-6673)
EMACK MANUFACTURING
1012 Ken O Sha Ind Pk Dr (49508-8216)
PHONE..................................616 241-3040
EMP: 5 **EST:** 2014
SALES (est): 161.6K **Privately Held**
WEB: www.emackmfg.com
SIC: 3999 Manufacturing industries

(G-6674)
EMBRACELETS
1422 Margaret Ave Se (49507-2226)
PHONE..................................616 719-3545
Javonne Granderson, *Principal*
EMP: 4 **EST:** 2012
SALES (est): 46.3K **Privately Held**
WEB: www.embracelets.org
SIC: 3961 Bracelets, except precious metal

(G-6675)
EMBROIDME GRAND RAPIDS
6161 28th St Se Ste 3 (49546-6931)
PHONE..................................616 974-1033
Ray Titus, *Owner*
EMP: 7 **EST:** 2016
SALES (est): 130.3K **Privately Held**
WEB: www.fullypromoted.com
SIC: 2395 Embroidery & art needlework

(G-6676)
EMERALD GRAPHICS INC
4949 W Greenbrooke Dr Se (49512-5400)
PHONE..................................616 871-3020
Ann Kennedy, *President*
Mark Kennedy, *President*
Nicole Taylor, *Opers Staff*
EMP: 6 **EST:** 1995
SALES (est): 670K **Privately Held**
WEB: www.emeraldcorporation.com
SIC: 2759 Screen printing

(G-6677)
EMPIRICAL BIOSCIENCE INC
2007 Eastcastle Dr Se (49508-8773)
PHONE..................................877 479-9949
Craig Pippel, *Principal*
Jingwei Yan, *Mfg Staff*
Elisabeth Reus, *Accountant*
EMP: 5 **EST:** 2012
SALES (est): 2.5MM **Privately Held**
WEB: www.empiricalbioscience.com
SIC: 2819 Chemicals, reagent grade: refined from technical grade

(G-6678)
ENERSAVE LLC
3716 Dykstra Dr Nw (49544-9745)
PHONE..................................616 785-1800
Frank Vankempen,
EMP: 10 **EST:** 2003
SALES (est): 124.5K **Privately Held**
SIC: 3585 Refrigeration & heating equipment

(G-6679)
ENERTEMP INC
3961 Eastern Ave Se (49508-2416)
PHONE..................................616 243-2752
Clair D Norder, *President*
Joel T Teft, *Vice Pres*
Phil Vandenheuvel, *Engineer*
Michael Schellenboom, *Sales Engr*
Diane Braun, *Office Mgr*
EMP: 23 **EST:** 1981
SQ FT: 5,000
SALES (est): 3.4MM **Privately Held**
WEB: www.enertemp.com
SIC: 3822 Auto controls regulating residntl & coml environmt & applncs

(G-6680)
ENGINEERED PRFMCE COATINGS INC
4881 Kendrick St Se (49512-9602)
PHONE..................................616 988-7927
Matthew Wolfe, *General Mgr*
Maryann Gillespie, *Administration*
EMP: 3 **EST:** 2016
SQ FT: 7,500
SALES (est): 3MM
SALES (corp-wide): 1.3MM **Privately Held**
WEB: www.ep-coatings.com
SIC: 3479 Coating of metals & formed products
HQ: Engineered Performance Coatings Ltd
Lanesborough House
Cardiff S GLAM CF3 2
292 166-0155

(G-6681)
ENGINEERED TOOLING SYSTEMS INC
Also Called: Tsg Tooling Systems Group.com
2780 Courier Dr Nw (49534-1247)
PHONE..................................616 647-5063
Jim Grotenrath, *President*
Kurtis Van Vels, *Vice Pres*
Chad Gould, *Project Mgr*
Drew Boresma, *Admin Sec*
▲ **EMP:** 12 **EST:** 1996
SQ FT: 16,000
SALES (est): 6.1MM **Privately Held**
WEB: www.toolingsystemsgroup.com
SIC: 3544 Special dies & tools
HQ: Advanced Tooling Systems, Inc.
1166 7 Mile Rd Nw
Comstock Park MI 49321
616 784-7513

(G-6682)
EOVATIONS LLC
2801 E Beltline Ave Ne (49525-9680)
PHONE..................................616 361-7136

GEOGRAPHIC SECTION

Grand Rapids - Kent County (G-6708)

Patrick Lockwood, *Owner*
EMP: 10 **EST:** 2010
SALES (est): 310.4K **Privately Held**
WEB: www.eovationsllc.com
SIC: 2421 Sawmills & planing mills, general

(G-6683)
ERWIN QUARDER INC
5101 Kraft Ave Se Ste B (49512-9737)
PHONE 616 575-1600
Martin Quarder, *President*
Shanna Brown, *Purchasing*
Adnan Dizdarevic, *QC Dir*
Ron Roys, *Engineer*
Scott Brown, *Sales Engr*
▲ **EMP:** 95 **EST:** 1998
SQ FT: 80,000
SALES (est): 32.1MM
SALES (corp-wide): 149MM **Privately Held**
WEB: www.quarder.de
SIC: 3089 3544 3714 7692 Injection molding of plastics; special dies, tools, jigs & fixtures; motor vehicle parts & accessories; welding repair
HQ: Erwin Quarder Systemtechnik Gmbh
   Fritz-Souchon-Str. 2
   Espelkamp NW 32339
   577 291-140

(G-6684)
ESCO COMPANY LLC
2330 East Paris Ave Se (49546-6131)
PHONE 231 726-3106
▲ **EMP:** 60
SALES (est): 17.2MM **Privately Held**
SIC: 2865 Cyclic Crudes And Intermediates, Nsk
HQ: Mitsui Chemicals America, Inc.
   800 Westchester Ave N607
   Rye Brook NY 10573

(G-6685)
ESCO GROUP INC (PA)
2887 3 Mile Rd Nw (49534-1319)
PHONE 616 453-5458
Richard Hungerford Jr, *CEO*
EMP: 12 **EST:** 2003
SALES (est): 12.8MM **Privately Held**
WEB: www.edge-sweets.com
SIC: 3599 3541 Air intake filters, internal combustion engine, except auto; drilling & boring machines

(G-6686)
ETO MAGNETIC CORP (DH)
5925 Patterson Ave Se (49512-9618)
PHONE 616 957-2570
Stefan Jacob, *CEO*
Michael Ignaczak, *President*
Greg Peters, *Vice Pres*
Dave Powers, *Prdtn Mgr*
John Merrill, *Purchasing*
▲ **EMP:** 151 **EST:** 2000
SQ FT: 70,000
SALES (est): 31.1MM
SALES (corp-wide): 267.9K **Privately Held**
WEB: www.etogruppe.com
SIC: 3679 3625 3647 Solenoids for electronic applications; solenoid switches (industrial controls); automotive lighting fixtures
HQ: Eto Magnetic Gmbh
   Hardtring 8
   Stockach BW 78333
   777 180-90

(G-6687)
EVANS TEMPCON DELAWARE LLC
3260 Eagle Park Dr Ne Ne100 (49525-4569)
PHONE 616 361-2681
Mark L Smith, *President*
Rodney Roderick, *CFO*
EMP: 8 **EST:** 2018
SALES (est): 1.6MM
SALES (corp-wide): 113.8MM **Privately Held**
SIC: 3585 Air conditioning, motor vehicle
HQ: Proair Holdings Corporation
   6630 E State Highway 114
   Haslet TX 76052
   817 636-2308

(G-6688)
EVANS TOOL & ENGINEERING INC
4287 3 Mile Rd Nw (49534-1144)
PHONE 616 791-6333
Michael Evans, *CEO*
Jacquelin Evans, *Vice Pres*
EMP: 12 **EST:** 1988
SQ FT: 12,000
SALES (est): 1.9MM **Privately Held**
WEB: www.evanstool.com
SIC: 3545 Cutting tools for machine tools

(G-6689)
EVEN-CUT ABRASIVE COMPANY
3890 Buchanan Ave Sw (49548-3111)
PHONE 216 881-9595
Arthur Ellison, *President*
▲ **EMP:** 70
SQ FT: 65,000
SALES (est): 9.7MM **Privately Held**
WEB: www.evencut.com
SIC: 3291 Abrasive products

(G-6690)
EVOLVE LONGBOARDS USA LLC
1959 Will Ave Nw (49504-2035)
PHONE 616 915-3876
Bruce Bubin, *Principal*
EMP: 5 **EST:** 2014
SALES (est): 145.6K **Privately Held**
SIC: 3949 5941 Skateboards; skateboarding equipment

(G-6691)
EXCELLENCE MANUFACTURING INC
629 Ionia Ave Sw (49503-5148)
PHONE 616 456-9928
John P Carrier, *President*
David Collins, *Vice Pres*
David Savage, *Vice Pres*
Jim Sumners, *Vice Pres*
EMP: 27 **EST:** 1989
SQ FT: 40,000
SALES (est): 1.3MM **Privately Held**
SIC: 3714 Motor vehicle parts & accessories

(G-6692)
EXPECTANCY LEARNING LLC
3152 Peregrine Dr Ne # 110 (49525-9723)
PHONE 866 829-9533
Tom Koziol, *Marketing Staff*
Brad Pennington, *Manager*
Jeremy Erard, *Executive*
EMP: 7 **EST:** 2015
SQ FT: 3,000
SALES (est): 458.9K **Privately Held**
WEB: www.expectancylearning.com
SIC: 7372 Educational computer software

(G-6693)
EXPERT COATING COMPANY INC
2855 Marlin Ct Nw (49534-1293)
PHONE 616 453-8261
Erik Klimek, *President*
Walter Klimek, *Vice Pres*
Mennow Klimek, *Treasurer*
Patricia Lesinski, *Admin Sec*
EMP: 10 **EST:** 1940
SQ FT: 15,000
SALES: 1.1MM **Privately Held**
WEB: www.expertcoating-mi.net
SIC: 3471 3479 Plating of metals or formed products; coating of metals with plastic or resins

(G-6694)
EXTREME SCREEN PRINTS
3723 Burlingame Ave Sw (49509-3701)
PHONE 616 889-8305
Daniel Lund, *Owner*
EMP: 4 **EST:** 2008
SALES (est): 605.5K **Privately Held**
WEB: www.extremescreenprints.com
SIC: 2759 Screen printing

(G-6695)
EXTRUDE HONE LLC
Thermoburr Michigan West
2882 Northridge Dr Nw (49544-9109)
PHONE 616 647-9050

EMP: 10
SALES (corp-wide): 174.2MM **Privately Held**
SIC: 3541 Mfg Machine Tools-Cutting
HQ: Extrude Hone Llc
   235 Industry Blvd
   Irwin PA 15642
   724 863-5900

(G-6696)
EXTRUSIONS DIVISION INC
201 Cottage Grove St Se (49507-1701)
PHONE 616 247-3611
James Azzar, *President*
Linda Azzar, *Admin Sec*
EMP: 5 **EST:** 1974
SALES (est): 605.7K **Privately Held**
WEB: www.extrudedpolymers.com
SIC: 3089 Extruded finished plastic products

(G-6697)
EZE PRINTS A DIV ALLIED
517 32nd St Se (49548-2303)
PHONE 616 281-2406
Donald Price, *Owner*
EMP: 5 **EST:** 2013
SALES (est): 59.4K **Privately Held**
SIC: 2752 Commercial printing, lithographic

(G-6698)
FAITH ALIVE CHRISTN RESOURCES (PA)
1700 28th St Se (49508-1414)
PHONE 800 333-8300
Paul Faber, *Editor*
Jane Hilbrand, *Opers Staff*
Mike Dykema, *Finance Mgr*
Gary Mulder, *Exec Dir*
▲ **EMP:** 35 **EST:** 1915
SQ FT: 22,000
SALES (est): 5.1MM **Privately Held**
WEB: www.faithaliveresources.org
SIC: 2721 2731 5049 Periodicals: publishing only; books: publishing & printing; pamphlets: publishing & printing; religious supplies

(G-6699)
FALK PRODUCTION LLC
Also Called: Falk Panel
1782 Northridge Dr Nw (49544-9130)
PHONE 616 540-1053
Boudewijn Haase, *Principal*
Pete Tuitel, *Sales Mgr*
EMP: 14 **EST:** 2018
SALES (est): 1.4MM **Privately Held**
WEB: www.falkpanel.com
SIC: 3448 Prefabricated metal buildings

(G-6700)
FASTCO INDUSTRIES INC (PA)
2685 Mullins Ct Nw (49534-1219)
P.O. Box 141427 (49514-1427)
PHONE 616 453-5428
Arvin L Tap, *Ch of Bd*
Bruce Tap, *President*
Rick Smith, *Principal*
Scott Smith, *Vice Pres*
Phil Kowalczyk, *Prdtn Mgr*
▲ **EMP:** 124 **EST:** 1968
SQ FT: 46,000
SALES (est): 17.3MM **Privately Held**
WEB: www.fastcoindustries.com
SIC: 3452 Bolts, nuts, rivets & washers

(G-6701)
FASTCO INDUSTRIES INC
2700 Courier Dr Nw (49534-1247)
PHONE 616 389-1390
Emily Bradfield, *Manager*
Andy Ike, *Manager*
Brennan Ursell, *Manager*
EMP: 8
SALES (corp-wide): 17.3MM **Privately Held**
WEB: www.fastcoindustries.com
SIC: 3452 Bolts, nuts, rivets & washers
PA: Fastco Industries, Inc.
   2685 Mullins Ct Nw
   Grand Rapids MI 49534
   616 453-5428

(G-6702)
FASTCO INDUSTRIES INC
2759 Mullins Ave (49534)
PHONE 616 453-5428
Jane Fuller, *Branch Mgr*
EMP: 7
SALES (corp-wide): 17.3MM **Privately Held**
WEB: www.fastcoindustries.com
SIC: 3452 Bolts, nuts, rivets & washers
PA: Fastco Industries, Inc.
   2685 Mullins Ct Nw
   Grand Rapids MI 49534
   616 453-5428

(G-6703)
FATHOM DRONES INC
401 Hall St Sw Ste 213 (49503-4997)
PHONE 586 216-7047
Matthew Gira, *CEO*
EMP: 4 **EST:** 2017
SQ FT: 100
SALES (est): 200.9K **Privately Held**
WEB: www.shop.fathomdrone.com
SIC: 3429 Marine hardware

(G-6704)
FD LAKE COMPANY
3313 Lousma Dr Se (49548-2278)
PHONE 616 241-5639
Caryl Carlsen, *CEO*
Michael W Posey, *President*
Dennis Dilley, *Engineer*
Sue Elyn Johnson, *Controller*
Brian Finkbeiner, *Sales Staff*
▲ **EMP:** 14 **EST:** 1947
SQ FT: 12,000
SALES (est): 5MM **Privately Held**
WEB: www.fdlake.com
SIC: 1796 3731 Machine moving & rigging; marine rigging

(G-6705)
FIDO & STITCH
820 Monroe Ave Nw (49503-1442)
PHONE 616 288-7992
Allison Marie McDonough, *Principal*
EMP: 5 **EST:** 2016
SALES (est): 410.1K **Privately Held**
WEB: www.fidoandstitch.com
SIC: 2395 Embroidery & art needlework

(G-6706)
FIREBOY-XINTEX INC (HQ)
Also Called: Aetna Engineering
O-379 Lake Michigan Dr Nw (49534-3355)
PHONE 616 735-9380
Larry Akins, *CEO*
Tim Shively, *President*
Ron Wiersum, *Controller*
▲ **EMP:** 29 **EST:** 1973
SQ FT: 30,000
SALES (est): 11.5MM
SALES (corp-wide): 126.5MM **Privately Held**
WEB: www.fireboy-xintex.com
SIC: 3531 Marine related equipment
PA: W. S. Darley & Co.
   325 Spring Lake Dr
   Itasca IL 60143
   630 735-3500

(G-6707)
FIREHOUSE WOODWORKS LLC
1945 Kalamazoo Ave Se (49507-2832)
PHONE 616 285-2300
Troy Yarbrough,
EMP: 5 **EST:** 2015
SQ FT: 1,200
SALES (est): 252K **Privately Held**
SIC: 2599 Factory furniture & fixtures

(G-6708)
FIRSTRONIC LLC
1655 Michigan St Ne (49503-2015)
PHONE 616 456-9220
Merry Maiani, *Ch of Bd*
John Sammut, *President*
Jochen Lipp, *COO*
Steve Fraser, *Vice Pres*
Wally Johnson, *Vice Pres*
▲ **EMP:** 500 **EST:** 2009

Grand Rapids - Kent County (G-6709) GEOGRAPHIC SECTION

SALES (est): 228.8MM
SALES (corp-wide): 6.8MM **Privately Held**
WEB: www.firstronic.com
SIC: 3559 Electronic component making machinery
PA: Lacroix Group
17 Rue Oceane
St Herblain 44800

(G-6709)
FIXALL ELECTRIC MOTOR SERVICE
737 Butterworth St Sw (49504-6394)
PHONE 616 454-6863
Chuck Baar, *President*
EMP: 7 **EST:** 1950
SQ FT: 2,500
SALES (est): 911.2K **Privately Held**
WEB: www.fixallelectric.com
SIC: 7694 Electric motor repair

(G-6710)
FLEX-N-GATE LLC
3075 Breton Rd Se (49512-1747)
PHONE 616 222-3296
Donald Griffin, *Project Mgr*
Darryl Matthews, *Mfg Staff*
William Dustman, *Engineer*
Martha Nava, *Engineer*
Karen Hahnthornton, *Controller*
EMP: 7
SALES (corp-wide): 1.5B **Privately Held**
WEB: www.flex-n-gate.com
SIC: 3714 Bumpers & bumperettes, motor vehicle
PA: Flex-N-Gate Llc
1306 E University Ave
Urbana IL 61802
217 384-6600

(G-6711)
FLEXFAB LLC
5333 33rd St Se (49512-2022)
PHONE 269 945-3533
Matthew Decamp, *Branch Mgr*
EMP: 25
SALES (corp-wide): 129.3MM **Privately Held**
WEB: www.flexfab.com
SIC: 3052 Rubber & plastics hose & beltings
HQ: Flexfab, Llc
1699 W M 43 Hwy
Hastings MI 49058
800 331-0003

(G-6712)
FLOORCOVERING ENGINEERS LLC
2489 Maplevalley Dr Se (49512-3801)
PHONE 616 299-1007
John Quillan,
EMP: 1 **EST:** 1988
SALES (est): 5MM **Privately Held**
WEB: www.qmsconsulting.com
SIC: 5023 3996 Carpets; hard surface floor coverings

(G-6713)
FLURESH LLC (PA)
1213 Phillips Ave Sw (49507-1516)
PHONE 616 600-0420
Scott Asiala, *Vice Pres*
Jacob Fein, *Controller*
Alexis Tuffs, *Accountant*
Chris Anderson, *General Counsel*
EMP: 57 **EST:** 2018
SALES (est): 9.6MM **Privately Held**
WEB: www.fluresh.com
SIC: 3999

(G-6714)
FLYING PIG COATINGS LLC
3529 3 Mile Rd Nw (49534-1229)
PHONE 616 947-1118
EMP: 6 **EST:** 2017
SALES (est): 76.9K **Privately Held**
WEB: www.flyingpigcoatings.com
SIC: 3479 Coating of metals & formed products; aluminum coating of metal products

(G-6715)
FOREMOST GRAPHICS LLC
Also Called: Dana Trading
2921 Wilson Dr Nw (49534-7565)
PHONE 616 453-4747
Brian Vanderhooning, *COO*
Tim Karel, *Vice Pres*
Donna Perschbacher, *Controller*
Sarah Devries Phr, *Human Res Mgr*
Jeff Christians, *Sales Staff*
EMP: 70 **EST:** 1968
SQ FT: 80,000
SALES (est): 15MM **Privately Held**
WEB: www.foremostgraphics.com
SIC: 2752 2791 2789 Lithographing on metal; typesetting; bookbinding & related work

(G-6716)
FORMAX MANUFACTURING CORP
168 Wealthy St Sw (49503-4019)
PHONE 616 456-5458
Andrew Johnston, *President*
Gordon Johnston, *VP Mfg*
EMP: 40 **EST:** 1938
SQ FT: 50,000
SALES (est): 2.7MM **Privately Held**
WEB: www.formaxmfg.com
SIC: 3291 2842 Buffing or polishing wheels, abrasive or nonabrasive; abrasive buffs, bricks, cloth, paper, stones, etc.; sticks, abrasive; specialty cleaning, polishes & sanitation goods

(G-6717)
FORWARD METAL CRAFT INC
329 Summer Ave Nw (49504-5316)
PHONE 616 459-6051
Ward Schenck, *President*
Scot Schenck, *President*
EMP: 10 **EST:** 1978
SQ FT: 40,000
SALES (est): 1.8MM **Privately Held**
WEB: www.forwardmetalcraft.com
SIC: 3465 3469 Automotive stampings; furniture components, porcelain enameled

(G-6718)
FOXYS LEOTARDS
4540 East Paris Ave Se A (49512-5444)
PHONE 616 949-1847
EMP: 7 **EST:** 1985
SALES (est): 42.5K **Privately Held**
WEB: www.foxysleos.com
SIC: 2389 Apparel & accessories

(G-6719)
FRANKLIN PRESS INC
2426 28th St Sw (49519-2188)
PHONE 616 538-5320
Vic Helder, *President*
Amanda Buiter, *Graphic Designe*
EMP: 15 **EST:** 1943
SQ FT: 5,500
SALES (est): 1.4MM **Privately Held**
WEB: www.franklinpressinc.com
SIC: 2752 Commercial printing, offset

(G-6720)
FRONTLINES PUBLISHING
Also Called: Pregnancy Resource Center
72 Ransom Ave Ne Ofc (49503-3217)
PHONE 616 887-6256
EMP: 21
SALES (est): 1.1MM **Privately Held**
SIC: 2741 Misc Publishing

(G-6721)
FROST INC (PA)
2020 Bristol Ave Nw (49504-1402)
PHONE 616 785-9030
Charles C Frost, *President*
Fred Sytsema, *Vice Pres*
EMP: 2 **EST:** 1950
SALES (est): 18.5MM **Privately Held**
WEB: www.frostlinks.com
SIC: 3535 3536 Overhead conveyor systems; trolley conveyors; hoists, cranes & monorails; hand hoists

(G-6722)
FROST INCORPORATED (HQ)
Also Called: CMS
2020 Bristol Ave Nw (49504-1402)
PHONE 616 453-7781
Chad Frost, *President*
John Yahmpun, *Vice Pres*
◆ **EMP:** 50 **EST:** 1915
SALES (est): 18.5MM **Privately Held**
WEB: www.frostinc.com
SIC: 3535 3562 3537 3536 Overhead conveyor systems; trolley conveyors; ball & roller bearings; industrial trucks & tractors; hand hoists
PA: Frost Inc.
2020 Bristol Ave Nw
Grand Rapids MI 49504
616 785-9030

(G-6723)
FROST INCORPORATED
2020 Bristol Ave Nw (49504-1402)
PHONE 616 453-7781
Chad Frost, *President*
EMP: 9
SALES (corp-wide): 18.5MM **Privately Held**
WEB: www.frostinc.com
SIC: 3536 Hoists, cranes & monorails
HQ: Frost Incorporated
2020 Bristol Ave Nw
Grand Rapids MI 49504
616 453-7781

(G-6724)
FROST INCORPORATED
Also Called: CMS Conveyor Maint & Sup Div
2020 Bristol Ave Nw (49504-1402)
PHONE 616 785-9030
Chad Frost, *Branch Mgr*
EMP: 9
SALES (corp-wide): 18.5MM **Privately Held**
WEB: www.frostinc.com
SIC: 3535 Conveyors & conveying equipment
HQ: Frost Incorporated
2020 Bristol Ave Nw
Grand Rapids MI 49504
616 453-7781

(G-6725)
FROST LINKS (PA)
2020 Bristol Ave Nw (49504-1402)
PHONE 616 785-9030
Paula Miller, *President*
▲ **EMP:** 7 **EST:** 1997
SALES (est): 7.1MM **Privately Held**
WEB: www.frostlinks.com
SIC: 3535 Conveyors & conveying equipment

(G-6726)
FULCRUM INDUSTRIES INC
4849 Barden Ct Se (49512-5456)
PHONE 888 818-5121
EMP: 6 **EST:** 2017
SALES (est): 59.4K **Privately Held**
SIC: 3999 Manufacturing industries

(G-6727)
FULLY PROMOTED
6161 28th St Se Ste 2 (49546-6931)
PHONE 616 285-8009
EMP: 4 **EST:** 2018
SALES (est): 144.4K **Privately Held**
WEB: www.fullypromoted.com
SIC: 2395 Embroidery & art needlework

(G-6728)
FURNITURE CITY GLASS CORP
1012 Ken O Sha Ind Pk Dr (49508-8216)
PHONE 616 784-5500
Michael Greengard, *President*
EMP: 13 **EST:** 1973
SQ FT: 40,000
SALES (est): 357.5K **Privately Held**
SIC: 3211 3231 Building glass, flat; products of purchased glass

(G-6729)
G & W MACHINE CO
2107 Merlin St Ne (49525-2855)
PHONE 616 363-4435
Steven Wojciakowski, *Partner*
Thomas Wojciakowski, *Partner*
EMP: 4
SQ FT: 6,000
SALES (est): 457.3K **Privately Held**
WEB: www.gwmachinery.com
SIC: 3541 Machine tools, metal cutting type

(G-6730)
G A RICHARDS COMPANY (PA)
1060 Ken O Sha Ind Pk Dr (49508-8220)
PHONE 616 243-2800
John Boll, *President*
Marty Dewyn, *Mfg Staff*
Paul Meeter, *Buyer*
Jay Pearson, *Purchasing*
Brooke Schreur, *Purchasing*
▲ **EMP:** 70
SQ FT: 75,000
SALES (est): 17.1MM **Privately Held**
WEB: www.garichards.com
SIC: 3444 Sheet metalwork

(G-6731)
G DEFENSE COMPANY B
823 Ottawa Ave Nw (49503-1429)
PHONE 616 202-4500
EMP: 4 **EST:** 2017
SALES (est): 167.9K **Privately Held**
WEB: www.bgdefense.com
SIC: 3812 Defense systems & equipment

(G-6732)
GATEWAY ENGINEERING INC
6534 Clay Ave Sw (49548-7832)
PHONE 616 284-1425
Dan Owen, *President*
EMP: 16 **EST:** 1989
SQ FT: 4,000
SALES (est): 626.1K **Privately Held**
WEB: www.gateway-engineering.com
SIC: 3568 Power transmission equipment

(G-6733)
GE AVIATION SYSTEMS LLC
3290 Patterson Ave Se (49512-1934)
PHONE 616 241-7000
EMP: 10
SALES (corp-wide): 79.6B **Publicly Held**
WEB: www.geaviation.com
SIC: 3812 Search & navigation equipment
HQ: Ge Aviation Systems Llc
1 Aviation Way
Cincinnati OH 45215
937 898-9600

(G-6734)
GE AVIATION SYSTEMS LLC
Also Called: GE Edison Works
3290 Patterson Ave Se (49512-1934)
PHONE 616 224-6480
Lacey Fyan, *General Mgr*
Keith Sanderson, *Vice Pres*
Leblanc Jerry, *Mfg Staff*
Amanda Murphy, *Buyer*
Marie Partridge, *QC Mgr*
EMP: 25
SALES (corp-wide): 79.6B **Publicly Held**
WEB: www.geaviation.com
SIC: 3812 Aircraft control systems, electronic
HQ: Ge Aviation Systems Llc
1 Aviation Way
Cincinnati OH 45215
937 898-9600

(G-6735)
GEELHOED PERFORMANCE
2400 Turner Ave Nw Ste E (49544-2004)
PHONE 616 837-6666
Doug Geelhoed, *President*
EMP: 6 **EST:** 2012
SALES (est): 60K **Privately Held**
WEB: www.saberboats.com
SIC: 3732 Boat building & repairing

(G-6736)
GEM PLASTICS INC
2533 Thornwood St Sw (49519-2148)
PHONE 616 538-5966
Michael Deyman, *President*
Jody Roane, *Manager*
EMP: 6 **EST:** 1985
SQ FT: 15,000
SALES (est): 1.2MM **Privately Held**
WEB: www.gemplasticsinc.com
SIC: 3089 Injection molding of plastics

▲ = Import ▼ = Export
◆ = Import/Export

GEOGRAPHIC SECTION

Grand Rapids - Kent County (G-6763)

(G-6737)
GEMINI CORPORATION
Also Called: Gemini Publications
401 Hall St Sw Ste 331a (49503-6501)
PHONE.................................616 459-4545
John Zwarensteyn, *CEO*
Charlsie Dewey, *Editor*
Jennifer Maksimowski, *Sales Mgr*
Karla Jeltema, *Advt Staff*
Susan Smalley, *Advt Staff*
◆ **EMP:** 46 **EST:** 1979
SALES (est): 5.3MM **Privately Held**
WEB: www.grmag.com
SIC: 2721 2711 2741 Magazines: publishing only, not printed on site; newspapers: publishing only, not printed on site; miscellaneous publishing

(G-6738)
GENERAL DIE & ENGINEERING INC (PA)
6500 Clay Ave Sw (49548-7832)
PHONE.................................616 698-6961
Leon McCudden, *CEO*
Charles Kukulis, *President*
Doug Kukulis, *COO*
Craig Karman, *Vice Pres*
John Rose, *Vice Pres*
◆ **EMP:** 51 **EST:** 1971
SQ FT: 68,000
SALES (est): 6.8MM **Privately Held**
WEB: www.gendie.com
SIC: 3544 Special dies & tools

(G-6739)
GENESIS SEATING INC (HQ)
Also Called: Genesis Seating 0519
3445 East Paris Ave Se (49512-2960)
PHONE.................................616 954-1040
Kevin Kuske, *CEO*
Christopher Barnes, *Engineer*
◆ **EMP:** 79 **EST:** 1994
SQ FT: 129,000
SALES (est): 25.4MM
SALES (corp-wide): 4.2B **Publicly Held**
WEB: www.lpworkfurniture.com
SIC: 5021 2521 2511 2426 Office & public building furniture; wood office furniture; wood household furniture; hardwood dimension & flooring mills
PA: Leggett & Platt, Incorporated
1 Leggett Rd
Carthage MO 64836
417 358-8131

(G-6740)
GILL CORPORATION (DH)
Also Called: GRS&s
5271 Plainfield Ave Ne (49525-1046)
PHONE.................................616 453-4491
James J Zawacki, *President*
Ted Hohman, *Treasurer*
Erin Whitney, *Controller*
▲ **EMP:** 280 **EST:** 1961
SALES (est): 93.7MM
SALES (corp-wide): 17B **Publicly Held**
WEB: www.lear.com
SIC: 3469 3312 3495 3493 Metal stampings; tool & die steel; wire springs; steel springs, except wire; miscellaneous fabricated wire products; automotive stampings
HQ: Gill Holding Company, Inc.
5271 Plainfield Ave Ne
Grand Rapids MI 49525
616 559-2700

(G-6741)
GILL HOLDING COMPANY INC (HQ)
5271 Plainfield Ave Ne (49525-1046)
PHONE.................................616 559-2700
Richard Perreault, *CEO*
J Timothy Gargaro, *CFO*
EMP: 100 **EST:** 2011
SALES (est): 331.3MM
SALES (corp-wide): 17B **Publicly Held**
WEB: www.lear.com
SIC: 3465 3544 Automotive stampings; special dies & tools
PA: Lear Corporation
21557 Telegraph Rd
Southfield MI 48033
248 447-1500

(G-6742)
GILL INDUSTRIES INC (DH)
5271 Plainfield Ave Ne (49525-1046)
PHONE.................................616 559-2700
Rita Williams, *CEO*
Joe Gill, *Vice Pres*
Charles Scholfield, *Vice Pres*
Bob Sutter, *Vice Pres*
Rita Woodruff, *Vice Pres*
◆ **EMP:** 112 **EST:** 1964
SQ FT: 150,000
SALES (est): 232.2MM
SALES (corp-wide): 17B **Publicly Held**
WEB: www.lear.com
SIC: 3465 3544 Automotive stampings; special dies & tools
HQ: Gill Holding Company, Inc.
5271 Plainfield Ave Ne
Grand Rapids MI 49525
616 559-2700

(G-6743)
GILL INDUSTRIES INC
Also Called: Gill Manufacturing
5271 Plainfield Ave Nw (49525)
PHONE.................................616 559-2700
John Woodruff, *Branch Mgr*
EMP: 5
SALES (corp-wide): 17B **Publicly Held**
WEB: www.lear.com
SIC: 3423 Hand & edge tools
HQ: Gill Industries, Inc.
5271 Plainfield Ave Ne
Grand Rapids MI 49525
616 559-2700

(G-6744)
GINSAN LIQUIDATING COMPANY LLC
Also Called: Trusco
3611 3 Mile Rd Nw (49534-1251)
PHONE.................................616 791-8100
Sigrid Valk-Feeney, *President*
Barbara Botbyl, *Buyer*
Marlene Redner, *Credit Staff*
Dan Kamsickas, *Technical Staff*
◆ **EMP:** 95 **EST:** 1992
SQ FT: 45,000
SALES (est): 18.6MM **Privately Held**
WEB: www.ginsan.com
SIC: 3589 2899 Car washing machinery; water treating compounds

(G-6745)
GMD INDUSTRIES INC
1464 28th St Se (49508-1410)
PHONE.................................616 245-1215
Kurt Hein, *Administration*
EMP: 7 **EST:** 2015
SALES (est): 284.6K **Privately Held**
WEB: www.gmdindustries.com
SIC: 3999 Candles

(G-6746)
GO BEYOND HEALTHY LLC
2290 Christine Ct Se (49546-6468)
PHONE.................................407 255-0314
Scott Graves, *Mng Member*
EMP: 4 **EST:** 2011
SALES (est): 105.7K **Privately Held**
SIC: 2076 7922 5149 Coconut oil; beauty contest production; juices

(G-6747)
GOLDEN FASHION
1949 Eastern Ave Se (49507-2770)
PHONE.................................616 288-9465
Osman Abduulrahman Sakin, *Principal*
EMP: 5 **EST:** 2016
SALES (est): 46.4K **Privately Held**
SIC: 5651 2299 Family clothing stores; jute & flax textile products

(G-6748)
GONZALEZ JR PALLETS LLC
1601 Madison St Sw (49507)
PHONE.................................616 885-0201
Valentin Gonzalez,
EMP: 7 **EST:** 2013
SQ FT: 16,000
SALES (est): 350K **Privately Held**
SIC: 2448 Pallets, wood

(G-6749)
GONZALEZ UNIVERSAL PALLETS LLC
955 Godfrey Ave Sw (49503-5003)
PHONE.................................616 243-5524
Alfonso Gonzalez Ortiz,
EMP: 8 **EST:** 2006
SALES (est): 849.4K **Privately Held**
WEB: www.gonzalezuniversalpallets.com
SIC: 2448 Pallets, wood

(G-6750)
GOODALE ENTERPRISES LLC (PA)
21 Fennessey St Sw (49534-5896)
PHONE.................................616 453-7690
Patrick Goodale, *Mng Member*
EMP: 7 **EST:** 1973
SALES (est): 4.9MM **Privately Held**
SIC: 1311 Crude petroleum production

(G-6751)
GOSSAMER PRESS LLC
940 Knapp St Ne (49505-4349)
PHONE.................................616 363-4608
EMP: 4 **EST:** 2018
SALES (est): 88.4K **Privately Held**
WEB: www.gossamerpress.com
SIC: 2741 Miscellaneous publishing

(G-6752)
GPI-X LLC
11310 1st Ave Nw (49534-3399)
PHONE.................................616 453-4170
Ed Geskus, *Principal*
EMP: 6 **EST:** 2016
SALES (est): 37.5K **Privately Held**
SIC: 2741 Miscellaneous publishing

(G-6753)
GR PSP LLC
3593 Alpine Ave Nw (49544-1635)
PHONE.................................616 785-1070
EMP: 5 **EST:** 2017
SALES (est): 48.3K **Privately Held**
WEB: www.petsuppliespluscares.com
SIC: 3999 Manufacturing industries

(G-6754)
GRAND RAPIDS CARVERS INC
4465 Rger B Chffee Mem Dr (49548-7522)
PHONE.................................616 538-0022
Kevin J Slagter, *President*
Robert Buehler, *Vice Pres*
Tammy Buehler, *CFO*
Rhonda Slagter, *Treasurer*
EMP: 32 **EST:** 1940
SQ FT: 42,000
SALES (est): 5.1MM **Privately Held**
WEB: www.grcarvers.com
SIC: 2431 2426 3543 2531 Millwork; furniture dimension stock, hardwood; frames for upholstered furniture, wood; industrial patterns; public building & related furniture; wood office furniture; wood household furniture

(G-6755)
GRAND RAPIDS ELC MTR SVC LLC
1057 Cottage Grove St Se (49507-2003)
PHONE.................................616 243-8866
Trent Bremer,
EMP: 8 **EST:** 2016
SALES (est): 587.5K **Privately Held**
WEB: www.grandrapidstransmission.com
SIC: 7694 Electric motor repair

(G-6756)
GRAND RAPIDS ELC MTR SVCS LLC
Also Called: Ems Grand Rapids
1057 Cottage Grove St Se (49507-2003)
PHONE.................................616 243-8866
Brent Pelishek, *Principal*
Cindy Klompstra, *Sales Staff*
EMP: 8 **EST:** 2020
SALES (est): 542.6K **Privately Held**
WEB: www.emsgrandrapids.com
SIC: 7694 Electric motor repair

(G-6757)
GRAND RAPIDS EMBROIDERY
4223 Valley Side Dr Ne (49525-9692)
PHONE.................................616 451-2827
Cynthia Lehman, *Principal*
EMP: 6 **EST:** 2016
SALES (est): 91.2K **Privately Held**
WEB: www.grandrapids-embroidery.com
SIC: 2395 Embroidery products, except schiffli machine; embroidery & art needlework

(G-6758)
GRAND RAPIDS GRAPHIX LLC
1360 Canary Grass Dr Se (49508-7870)
PHONE.................................616 359-2383
Adam Lamos, *Principal*
EMP: 6 **EST:** 2014
SALES (est): 114.9K **Privately Held**
WEB: www.grandrapidsgraphix.com
SIC: 2759 Screen printing

(G-6759)
GRAND RAPIDS GRAVEL COMPANY (PA)
Also Called: Port City Redi-Mix
2700 28th St Sw (49519-2110)
P.O. Box 9160 (49509-0160)
PHONE.................................616 538-9000
Andrew Dykema, *President*
James Dykema, *Admin Sec*
EMP: 10 **EST:** 1920
SQ FT: 10,000
SALES (est): 23.9MM **Privately Held**
WEB: www.grgravel.com
SIC: 3273 1422 8741 1442 Ready-mixed concrete; calcareous tufa, crushed & broken-quarrying; cement rock, crushed & broken-quarrying; management services; construction sand & gravel

(G-6760)
GRAND RAPIDS LABEL COMPANY
Also Called: Grlabel
2351 Oak Industrial Dr Ne (49505-6017)
PHONE.................................616 459-8134
William M Muir, *President*
Steve Allen, *Vice Pres*
Bill Bergstrom, *Vice Pres*
Elizabeth J Crosby, *Vice Pres*
John Crosby, *Vice Pres*
EMP: 72
SQ FT: 103,000
SALES (est): 13.8MM **Privately Held**
WEB: www.grlabel.com
SIC: 2759 7389 Flexographic printing; packaging & labeling services

(G-6761)
GRAND RAPIDS LEGAL NEWS
1430 Monroe Ave Nw # 140 (49505-4678)
PHONE.................................616 454-9293
Ben Piseo, *Principal*
EMP: 8 **EST:** 2011
SALES (est): 168.4K **Privately Held**
WEB: www.legalnews.com
SIC: 2711 Newspapers, publishing & printing

(G-6762)
GRAND RAPIDS LETTER SERVICE
315 Fuller Ave Ne (49503-3630)
PHONE.................................616 459-4711
EMP: 4
SQ FT: 3,500
SALES (est): 300K **Privately Held**
SIC: 2752 2759 Offset Printing Shop

(G-6763)
GRAND RAPIDS MACHINE REPAIR
3710 Linden Ave Se (49548-3428)
PHONE.................................616 248-4760
Ron Brow Jr, *President*
EMP: 8 **EST:** 2005
SALES (est): 171.4K **Privately Held**
WEB: www.grmr.com
SIC: 3599 Machine shop, jobbing & repair

Grand Rapids - Kent County (G-6764)

(G-6764)
GRAND RAPIDS MACHINE REPR INC
4000 Eastern Ave Se (49508-3402)
PHONE.................................616 245-9102
Ronald Brow Sr, *President*
EMP: 34 **EST:** 1979
SQ FT: 15,000
SALES (est): 3.8MM **Privately Held**
WEB: www.grmr.com
SIC: 7699 3812 Aircraft & heavy equipment repair services; aircraft flight instruments

(G-6765)
GRAND RAPIDS METALTEK INC
2860 Marlin Ct Nw (49534-1217)
PHONE.................................616 791-2373
Paul Bultinck, *President*
Karla Cook, *Vice Pres*
Kris Hurley, *Project Mgr*
Trena Bresky, *Treasurer*
Michael Romain, *Manager*
EMP: 49 **EST:** 1979
SQ FT: 23,000
SALES (est): 8.5MM **Privately Held**
WEB: www.grmetaltek.com
SIC: 7692 3599 7389 3545 Welding repair; machine shop, jobbing & repair; grinding, precision: commercial or industrial; precision tools, machinists'

(G-6766)
GRAND RAPIDS POLSG & BUFFING
3000 Hillcroft Ave Sw (49513-1035)
P.O. Box 9297, Wyoming (49509-0297)
PHONE.................................616 241-2233
Ben Bishop Jr, *President*
EMP: 25 **EST:** 1964
SQ FT: 16,000
SALES (est): 1.3MM **Privately Held**
WEB: www.grpolishingandbuffing.com
SIC: 3471 3398 Buffing for the trade; polishing, metals or formed products; metal heat treating

(G-6767)
GRAND RAPIDS PRESS INC
3102 Walker Ridge Dr Nw (49544-9125)
PHONE.................................616 459-1400
Sheri Compton, *Principal*
EMP: 29 **EST:** 2008
SALES (est): 2.4MM **Privately Held**
SIC: 2711 Newspapers, publishing & printing

(G-6768)
GRAND RAPIDS PRINTING INK CO (PA)
4920 Starr St Se (49546-6351)
PHONE.................................616 241-5681
John Toigo, *President*
Joe Toigo, *Treasurer*
John Osborne, *Manager*
Miles Ranke, *Manager*
▲ **EMP:** 9 **EST:** 1954
SQ FT: 17,000
SALES (est): 2.8MM **Privately Held**
WEB: www.grpi.net
SIC: 2893 5085 Printing ink; ink, printers'

(G-6769)
GRAND RAPIDS SALSA
1301 Benjamin Ave Se (49506-3228)
PHONE.................................616 780-1801
Tom Carrick, *Principal*
EMP: 4 **EST:** 2017
SALES (est): 104.3K **Privately Held**
SIC: 2099 Dips, except cheese & sour cream based

(G-6770)
GRAND RAPIDS STRIPPING CO
1933 Will Ave Nw (49504-2035)
P.O. Box 3730 (49501-3730)
PHONE.................................616 361-0794
Michael Murphy, *President*
Phyllis Murphy, *Corp Secy*
EMP: 5
SQ FT: 8,000
SALES (est): 462.6K **Privately Held**
SIC: 3471 Cleaning & descaling metal products

(G-6771)
GRAND RAPIDS TECHNOLOGIES INC
3133 Madison Ave Se Ste B (49548-1277)
PHONE.................................616 245-7700
Gregory R Toman, *President*
EMP: 8 **EST:** 1991
SQ FT: 5,000
SALES (est): 1MM **Privately Held**
WEB: www.grtavionics.com
SIC: 3728 Aircraft parts & equipment

(G-6772)
GRAND RAPIDS TIMES INC
2016 Eastern Ave Se (49507-3235)
P.O. Box 7258 (49510-7258)
PHONE.................................616 245-8737
Patricia Pulliam, *President*
Sallie Calloway, *Director*
EMP: 16 **EST:** 1957
SALES (est): 624.9K **Privately Held**
WEB: www.grtimes.com
SIC: 2711 Commercial printing & newspaper publishing combined; newspapers, publishing & printing

(G-6773)
GRAND RAPIDS WOODWORKING
3993 Roger B Chaffee Mem (49548-3404)
PHONE.................................616 780-7137
EMP: 4 **EST:** 2018
SALES (est): 54.1K **Privately Held**
WEB: www.grandrapidswoodworking.com
SIC: 2431 Millwork

(G-6774)
GRAND RAPIDS WOODWORKING LLC
247 Dickinson St Se (49507-2559)
PHONE.................................616 301-8719
James Hutchinson, *Manager*
EMP: 4 **EST:** 2014
SALES (est): 68.6K **Privately Held**
WEB: www.grandrapidswoodworking.com
SIC: 2431 Millwork

(G-6775)
GRAND RIVER ASEPTIC MFG
524 Butterworth St Sw (49504-6420)
PHONE.................................616 678-2400
Amela Nesimovic, *Associate*
EMP: 4 **EST:** 2020
SALES (est): 194.9K **Privately Held**
SIC: 3999 Manufacturing industries

(G-6776)
GRAND RIVER ASEPTIC MFG INC (PA)
Also Called: Gram
140 Front Ave Sw (49504-6426)
PHONE.................................616 678-2400
Tom Ross, *President*
Val Pannell, *Business Mgr*
Jason Steele, *Business Mgr*
Nick Bykerk, *Vice Pres*
Steven Nole, *Vice Pres*
EMP: 165 **EST:** 2010
SALES (est): 50.2MM **Privately Held**
WEB: www.grandriverasepticmfg.com
SIC: 5047 2834 Medical equipment & supplies; solutions, pharmaceutical

(G-6777)
GRAND RIVER INTERIORS INC
Also Called: Echo Etching
974 Front Ave Nw Ste 2 (49504-4456)
PHONE.................................616 454-2800
David Wiest, *CEO*
Charles Luepnitz, *President*
MO Hill, *Cust Mgr*
John Hogenson, *VP Mktg*
Troy Vincent, *Manager*
EMP: 20 **EST:** 1981
SQ FT: 30,000
SALES (est): 2.9MM **Privately Held**
WEB: www.grandriverinteriors.com
SIC: 1752 5023 3231 Carpet laying; linoleum installation; ceramic floor tile installation; floor coverings; decorated glassware: chipped, engraved, etched, etc.

(G-6778)
GRAND RPIDS WILBERT BURIAL VLT
2500 3 Mile Rd Nw (49534-1314)
PHONE.................................616 453-9429
William F Sturrus, *President*
Dave Sturrus, *General Mgr*
David Sturrus, *Vice Pres*
Todd Sturrus, *Treasurer*
Greg Veltema, *Sales Staff*
EMP: 25 **EST:** 1936
SQ FT: 12,000
SALES (est): 4.5MM **Privately Held**
WEB: www.grandvalleyconcrete.com
SIC: 3272 Burial vaults, concrete or precast terrazzo; septic tanks, concrete; manhole covers or frames, concrete; covers, catch basin: concrete

(G-6779)
GRAND VALLEY WOOD PRODUCTS INC
Also Called: Sunstone Granite & Marble Co
4030 Eastern Ave Se (49508-3402)
PHONE.................................616 475-5890
Terry Idema, *President*
Nick Eubank, *Sr Project Mgr*
EMP: 50 **EST:** 1978
SALES (est): 7.8MM **Privately Held**
WEB: www.grandvalleywoodproducts.com
SIC: 2431 2542 2541 3442 Millwork; counters or counter display cases: except wood; cabinets, except refrigerated: show, display, etc.: wood; display fixtures, wood; table or counter tops, plastic laminated; metal doors, sash & trim; wood office furniture

(G-6780)
GRANITEONECOM INC
639 Hoyt St Se (49507-3213)
P.O. Box 5050, Pine Ridge SD (57770-5050)
PHONE.................................616 452-8372
EMP: 4 **EST:** 2003
SALES: 100K **Privately Held**
SIC: 1423 Crushed/Broken Granite

(G-6781)
GRAPHIC ARTS SERVICE & SUP INC (PA)
Also Called: Speciality Grinding Co.
3933 S Greenbrooke Dr Se (49512-5382)
PHONE.................................616 698-9300
Brian Tubergen, *President*
Jeff Hansel, *Vice Pres*
▲ **EMP:** 10
SQ FT: 5,000
SALES (est): 3.7MM **Privately Held**
WEB: www.gasupply.com
SIC: 5084 3554 7699 Printing trades machinery, equipment & supplies; cutting machines, paper; knife, saw & tool sharpening & repair

(G-6782)
GRAPHIC IMPRESSIONS INC
Also Called: Matrix Printing & Mailing
6621 Division Ave S (49548-7805)
PHONE.................................616 455-0303
Matthew Van Dore, *President*
EMP: 5 **EST:** 1995
SQ FT: 2,200 **Privately Held**
WEB: www.matrixgr.com
SIC: 2759 2789 2752 Commercial printing; bookbinding & related work; commercial printing, lithographic

(G-6783)
GRAPHIC SPECIALTIES INC (PA)
Also Called: G S I
2350 Brton Indus Pk Dr Se (49508-1548)
PHONE.................................616 247-0060
Dale Hutchins, *President*
Don Corey, *Vice Pres*
Mathew Hutchins, *Vice Pres*
Tj Moran, *Sales Dir*
EMP: 38 **EST:** 1989
SQ FT: 6,000

SALES (est): 4.7MM **Privately Held**
WEB: www.gs-sg.com
SIC: 3497 2675 2759 2796 Metal foil & leaf; die-cut paper & board; embossing on paper; platemaking services; bookbinding & related work

(G-6784)
GRAPHICS EMBOSSED IMAGES INC
1975 Waldorf St Nw Ste A (49544-1404)
PHONE.................................616 791-0404
Ron Feenstra, *President*
Meredyth Hasenjaeger, *Vice Pres*
Michele Matthews, *Vice Pres*
EMP: 9 **EST:** 1974
SALES (est): 688.5K **Privately Held**
WEB: www.geifinishing.com
SIC: 2759 Embossing on paper

(G-6785)
GRAY SKIES DISTILLERY
700 Ottawa Ave Nw (49503-1428)
PHONE.................................616 437-1119
Stephen Vanderpol, *Mng Member*
EMP: 10 **EST:** 2015
SALES (est): 788.4K **Privately Held**
WEB: www.grayskiesdistillery.com
SIC: 2085 Distilled & blended liquors

(G-6786)
GREAT LAKES BINDERY INC
3741 Linden Ave Se (49548-3427)
PHONE.................................616 245-5264
Stephen W Landheer, *President*
Dan Dafoe, *Vice Pres*
Brian Willemstyn, *Plant Mgr*
EMP: 18 **EST:** 1978
SQ FT: 5,000 **Privately Held**
WEB: www.greatlakesbindery.com
SIC: 2789 Binding only: books, pamphlets, magazines, etc.

(G-6787)
GREAT LAKES GRILLING CO
2685 Northridge Dr Nw C (49544-9111)
PHONE.................................616 791-8600
Randy Barnard, *President*
Julie Van Horn, *Purchasing*
EMP: 10 **EST:** 2002
SALES (est): 1.6MM **Privately Held**
WEB: www.greatlakesgrilling.com
SIC: 3496 Grilles & grillework, woven wire

(G-6788)
GREAT LAKES-TRIAD PLASTIC (PA)
Also Called: Glt Packaging
3939 36th St Se (49512-2917)
PHONE.................................616 241-6441
Brian Burns, *President*
Kevin Burns, *Corp Secy*
Steven White, *CFO*
Jack Jenerou, *Sales Staff*
Lori Meyers, *Sales Staff*
EMP: 80 **EST:** 1974
SQ FT: 83,000
SALES (est): 11.4MM **Privately Held**
SIC: 2653 Boxes, corrugated: made from purchased materials

(G-6789)
GREAT LKES FSTIDA HOLDINGS INC
Also Called: Festida Foods
219 Canton St Sw Ste A (49507-1098)
PHONE.................................616 241-0400
Joseph Riley, *CEO*
Kyle Curtiss, *President*
Gloria Vega, *Vice Pres*
Travis Tomaszewski, *Opers Mgr*
Laurie Steinbrecher, *Prdtn Mgr*
▲ **EMP:** 15 **EST:** 1988
SQ FT: 150,000
SALES (est): 9.6MM **Privately Held**
SIC: 2099 Food preparations

(G-6790)
GREYSTONE IMAGING LLC
5510 33rd St Se Ste 1 (49512-2060)
PHONE.................................616 742-3810
Frederick Nagle Jr, *Bd of Directors*
EMP: 5 **EST:** 2009
SALES (est): 87.4K **Privately Held**
SIC: 2759 Commercial printing

GEOGRAPHIC SECTION
Grand Rapids - Kent County (G-6817)

(G-6791)
GRM AUTOMATION INC
5271 Plainfield Ave Ne (49525-1046)
PHONE..................................616 559-2700
Bob Sutter, *Vice Pres*
Brad Meulenberg, *Manager*
EMP: 15 **EST:** 2014
SQ FT: 15,150
SALES (est): 295.9K **Privately Held**
WEB: www.grmautomation.com
SIC: 3544 Special dies, tools, jigs & fixtures

(G-6792)
GRW TECHNOLOGIES INC
4460 44th St Se Ste B (49512-4096)
PHONE..................................616 575-8119
Walter Soehner, *President*
Joechim Hollimius, *Vice Pres*
Juan Zavala, *Production*
Julia Heiche, *Engineer*
Erica Wagner, *Sales Associate*
▲ **EMP:** 160 **EST:** 2008
SQ FT: 24,000
SALES (est): 41.6MM
SALES (corp-wide): 177.9K **Privately Held**
WEB: www.soehnergroup.com
SIC: 3544 3089 Special dies, tools, jigs & fixtures; injection molding of plastics
PA: Sohnergroup Gmbh
  Daimlerstr. 13
  Schwaigern BW
  713 822-0

(G-6793)
GRX MANUFACTURING
3800 36th St Se (49512-2912)
PHONE..................................616 570-0832
EMP: 14 **EST:** 2018
SALES (est): 500.5K **Privately Held**
WEB: www.grxmfg.com
SIC: 3999 Manufacturing industries

(G-6794)
GUILFORD OF MAINE MARKETING CO
5300 Corprte Grv Dr Se # 200 (49512-5512)
PHONE..................................616 554-2250
Brian Demoura, *President*
Amy Robertson, *Accounts Exec*
Renee Mascolo, *Manager*
EMP: 51 **EST:** 1996
SALES (est): 4.2MM
SALES (corp-wide): 300K **Privately Held**
WEB: www.guilfordofmaine.com
SIC: 2299 Upholstery filling, textile
HQ: Duvaltex (Us), Inc.
  9 Oak St
  Guilford ME 04443
  207 873-3331

(G-6795)
GUO JI TOOLING SYSTEMS LLC
555 Plymouth Ave Ne (49505-6029)
PHONE..................................616 301-6906
EMP: 14 **EST:** 2014
SALES (est): 502.4K **Privately Held**
WEB: www.toolingsystemsgroup.com
SIC: 3544 Special dies & tools

(G-6796)
GWINNETT PLASTICS INC
2233 Mapleton St Ne (49505-6394)
PHONE..................................765 215-6593
EMP: 5 **EST:** 2018
SALES (est): 117.4K **Privately Held**
SIC: 3089 Injection molding of plastics

(G-6797)
GWS TOOL LLC
3987 Brockton Dr Se (49512-4070)
PHONE..................................616 971-4700
EMP: 7 **EST:** 2019
SALES (est): 284.7K **Privately Held**
WEB: www.gwstoolgroup.com
SIC: 3599 Machine shop, jobbing & repair

(G-6798)
H & R INDUSTRIES INC (PA)
3020 Stafford Ave Sw (49548-1098)
PHONE..................................616 247-1165
Janet L Herr, *President*
Christine Page, *Vice Pres*
David A Herr, *Admin Sec*
EMP: 14 **EST:** 1964
SQ FT: 6,000
SALES (est): 4.7MM **Privately Held**
WEB: www.handr-industries.com
SIC: 5084 3699 3561 Cleaning equipment, high pressure, sand or steam; pumps & pumping equipment; cleaning equipment, ultrasonic, except medical & dental; pumps & pumping equipment

(G-6799)
H S DIE & ENGINEERING INC
2640 Mullins Ct Nw (49534-1220)
PHONE..................................616 453-5451
Steve Bussing, *Project Mgr*
Mike Tuttle, *Branch Mgr*
Dave Baker, *Manager*
Phil Tanis, *Supervisor*
Deanna Hart, *Receptionist*
EMP: 9
SALES (corp-wide): 50MM **Privately Held**
WEB: www.hsinc.us
SIC: 3544 Special dies, tools, jigs & fixtures
PA: H.S. Inc.
  O-215 Lake Michigan Dr Nw
  Grand Rapids MI 49534
  616 453-5451

(G-6800)
HANDICAP SIGN INC
1142 Wealthy St Se (49506-1543)
PHONE..................................616 454-9416
Charles J Tasma, *President*
Kim Tasma, *Treasurer*
EMP: 8 **EST:** 1956
SQ FT: 5,500
SALES (est): 791.5K **Privately Held**
WEB: www.hsisign.com
SIC: 7389 3993 Sign painting & lettering shop; signs & advertising specialties

(G-6801)
HANDORN INC
Also Called: Custom Counters By Handorn
636 Crofton St Se (49507-1819)
PHONE..................................616 241-6181
Seth Erlandson, *President*
EMP: 20 **EST:** 1987
SQ FT: 20,000
SALES (est): 2.3MM **Privately Held**
WEB: www.handorn.com
SIC: 2434 Wood kitchen cabinets

(G-6802)
HANSON INC
Also Called: Dpi In Mold Applications
1340 Monroe Ave Nw (49505-4604)
PHONE..................................616 451-3061
Victor Hanson, *CEO*
EMP: 13 **EST:** 2008
SALES (est): 181.3K **Privately Held**
SIC: 3544 Industrial molds

(G-6803)
HARDWARE EXCHANGE INC
3854 Broadmoor Ave Se # 101 (49512-3967)
PHONE..................................440 449-8006
Mark Borlin, *President*
EMP: 5 **EST:** 1993
SALES (est): 864K **Privately Held**
WEB: www.serviceexpress.com
SIC: 3571 Electronic computers

(G-6804)
HARPERCOLLINS CHRISTN PUBG INC
3900 Sparks Dr Se (49546-6146)
PHONE..................................616 698-3230
Doug Lockhart, *Senior VP*
Londa Alderink, *Vice Pres*
Bev Stout, *Production*
Jason Short, *Sales Staff*
Robert Barnett, *Pub Rel Staff*
EMP: 14
SALES (corp-wide): 9.3B **Publicly Held**
WEB: www.harpercollinschristian.com
SIC: 2741 Miscellaneous publishing
HQ: Christian Harpercollins Publishing Inc
  501 Nelson Pl
  Nashville TN 37214
  615 889-9000

(G-6805)
HART & COOLEY LLC (DH)
5030 Corp Exch Blvd Se (49512)
P.O. Box 2930, Milwaukee WI (53201-2930)
PHONE..................................616 656-8200
Jeffrey Stark, *CEO*
Brenda Emmons, *Buyer*
Charles Dewildt, *Engineer*
Keith Page, *VP Sls/Mktg*
Mary De Vree, *Credit Mgr*
◆ **EMP:** 130 **EST:** 1999
SALES (est): 503.4MM
SALES (corp-wide): 148MM **Privately Held**
WEB: www.hartandcooleyllc.com
SIC: 3446 3822 Registers (air), metal; auto controls regulating residntl & coml environmt & applncs
HQ: Duravent, Inc.
  877 Cotting Ct
  Vacaville CA 95688
  800 835-4429

(G-6806)
HARVEST ENERGY INC
2820 Division Ave S (49548-1127)
PHONE..................................269 838-4595
Thomas O'Hara, *President*
EMP: 20 **EST:** 2008
SALES (est): 4.9MM **Privately Held**
WEB: www.harvestenergy.com
SIC: 3823 Industrial process measurement equipment

(G-6807)
HEB DEVELOPMENT LLC (PA)
1946 Turner Ave Nw (49504-2034)
PHONE..................................616 363-3825
Bill Mast, *Managing Prtnr*
Heath Baxter, *Managing Prtnr*
Bruce G Visser, *Managing Prtnr*
Eric Todd Visser, *Managing Prtnr*
EMP: 47 **EST:** 2003
SALES (est): 2.6MM **Privately Held**
SIC: 3251 Structural brick & blocks

(G-6808)
HEL INC
Also Called: Hastings Equipment
450 Market Ave Sw (49503-4943)
PHONE..................................616 774-9032
Richard Van Dam, *President*
Randall Van Dam, *Treasurer*
John Van Dam, *Admin Sec*
EMP: 15 **EST:** 1974
SQ FT: 43,000
SALES (est): 1.2MM **Privately Held**
WEB: www.helinc.com
SIC: 7699 7692 7629 Industrial machinery & equipment repair; welding repair; electrical repair shops

(G-6809)
HELLO LIFE INC (PA)
Also Called: Vetionx
4655 Patterson Ave Se C (49512-5337)
PHONE..................................616 808-3290
Albert Duoibes, *CEO*
Curtis Hagberg, *Principal*
Fekadu Tonna, *Principal*
▲ **EMP:** 37 **EST:** 2010
SQ FT: 2,800
SALES (est): 4.8MM **Privately Held**
WEB: www.hellolife.net
SIC: 5499 2834 Dietetic foods; pharmaceutical preparations; cough medicines

(G-6810)
HERALD NEWSPAPERS COMPANY INC
Grand Rapids Paper, The
3102 Walker Ridge Dr Nw (49544-9125)
P.O. Box 2168 (49501-2168)
PHONE..................................616 222-5400
Nancy Clay, *Manager*
Rick Sullivan, *Exec Dir*
EMP: 6
SALES (corp-wide): 2.8B **Privately Held**
WEB: www.advancemediany.com
SIC: 2711 Newspapers, publishing & printing
HQ: The Herald Newspapers Company Inc
  220 S Warren St
  Syracuse NY 13202
  315 470-0011

(G-6811)
HERALD NEWSPAPERS COMPANY INC
Also Called: Ann Arbor News
3102 Walker Ridge Dr Nw (49544-9125)
PHONE..................................734 834-6376
Laurel Champion, *Exec Dir*
EMP: 6
SALES (corp-wide): 2.8B **Privately Held**
WEB: www.advancemediany.com
SIC: 2711 Newspapers, publishing & printing
HQ: The Herald Newspapers Company Inc
  220 S Warren St
  Syracuse NY 13202
  315 470-0011

(G-6812)
HERITAGE WDWRKS GRND RPIDS LLC
318 Paris Ave Se (49503-4717)
PHONE..................................616 780-9499
Carl Johnson, *Principal*
EMP: 6 **EST:** 2015
SALES (est): 99.7K **Privately Held**
WEB: www.heritagewoodworks.info
SIC: 2431 Millwork

(G-6813)
HI-TECH/FPA INC
4585 40th St Se (49512-4036)
PHONE..................................616 942-0076
Steven Sawyer, *Engineer*
Don Setsma, *Manager*
EMP: 5 **EST:** 2020
SALES (est): 168.4K **Privately Held**
WEB: www.hitechengineering.com
SIC: 3559 Special industry machinery

(G-6814)
HIGH GRADE MATERIALS COMPANY
10561 Linden Dr Nw (49534-9647)
PHONE..................................616 677-1271
Curt Hanson, *Manager*
EMP: 10
SALES (corp-wide): 17.2MM **Privately Held**
WEB: www.highgradematerials.com
SIC: 3273 Ready-mixed concrete
PA: High Grade Materials Company
  9266 Snows Lake Rd
  Greenville MI 48838
  616 754-5545

(G-6815)
HILCO FIXTURE FINDERS LLC
Also Called: Supermarket Liquidation
1345 Monroe Ave Nw # 321 (49505-4673)
PHONE..................................616 453-1300
Scott Hoek, *CEO*
▼ **EMP:** 40 **EST:** 2006
SALES (est): 8.4MM **Privately Held**
WEB: www.hilcoffe.com
SIC: 2541 Store fixtures, wood
HQ: Hilco Merchant Resources, Llc
  5 Revere Dr Ste 206
  Northbrook IL 60062

(G-6816)
HILL BROTHERS
Also Called: Hill Bros Orchards
6159 Peach Ridge Ave Nw (49544-9110)
PHONE..................................616 784-2767
Walter Hill, *Partner*
David Hill, *Partner*
Arlene Hill, *Principal*
EMP: 5
SALES (est): 373.1K **Privately Held**
WEB: www.hillbrosorchards.com
SIC: 0175 2099 2086 Apple orchard; cider, nonalcoholic; bottled & canned soft drinks

(G-6817)
HILL MACHINERY CO
4585 Danvers Dr Se (49512-4040)
PHONE..................................616 940-2800
Donald V Bos Jr, *President*
Shane O'Neill, *Vice Pres*
Greg Zmudka, *Purch Mgr*
Jerry Falicki, *Engineer*
Jeff Senn, *Controller*
EMP: 60 **EST:** 1897
SQ FT: 45,000

Grand Rapids - Kent County (G-6818)

GEOGRAPHIC SECTION

SALES: 21.9MM **Privately Held**
WEB: www.hillmachinery.com
SIC: **3544** 3494 Special dies & tools; jigs & fixtures; valves & pipe fittings

(G-6818)
HIPPIES CHIPPIES INC
2322 Lake Michigan Dr Nw (49504-5967)
PHONE..................616 259-2133
Melissa Puplis, *President*
EMP: 5 EST: 2019
SALES (est): 62.3K **Privately Held**
WEB: www.hippieschippies.com
SIC: **2096** Potato chips & similar snacks

(G-6819)
HOMAG MACHINERY NORTH AMER INC
4577 Patterson Ave Se (49512-5308)
PHONE..................616 254-8181
Frank Wegener, *President*
Jens Fahlbusch, *Corp Comm Staff*
Chris Jones, *Manager*
▲ EMP: 19 EST: 2008
SQ FT: 32,000
SALES (est): 4.6MM
SALES (corp-wide): 3.9B **Privately Held**
WEB: www.homag.com
SIC: **3553** Woodworking machinery
PA: Durr Ag
  Carl-Benz-Str. 34
  Bietigheim-Bissingen BW 74321
  714 278-0

(G-6820)
HORMEL FOODS CORPORATION
801 Broadway Ave Nw (49504-4462)
PHONE..................616 454-0418
EMP: 6
SALES (corp-wide): 9.6B **Publicly Held**
WEB: www.hormelfoods.com
SIC: **2011** Meat packing plants
PA: Hormel Foods Corporation
  1 Hormel Pl
  Austin MN 55912
  507 437-5611

(G-6821)
HOWE US INC
401 Hall St Sw Ste 458 (49503-5098)
PHONE..................616 419-2226
Michael Jacobsen, *President*
Brian Christiansen, *Accounting Mgr*
Debbie King, *Sales Mgr*
EMP: 52 EST: 2013
SALES (est): 5.9MM
SALES (corp-wide): 9.3MM **Privately Held**
WEB: www.howe.com
SIC: **2521** Wood office furniture
PA: Howe A/S
  Filosofgangen 18
  Odense 5000
  634 164-00

(G-6822)
HOWIES HOCKEY INCORPORATED
Also Called: Howies Hockey Tape
3445 36th St Se Ste B (49512-2811)
PHONE..................616 643-0594
Harry Sipelinga, *Principal*
Jason Koole, *Finance*
Luke Lanham, *Sales Staff*
▲ EMP: 2 EST: 2004
SALES (est): 1MM **Privately Held**
WEB: www.howieshockeytape.com
SIC: **3949** 5961 5091 Sporting & athletic goods; ; sporting & recreation goods

(G-6823)
HS INC (PA)
O-215 Lake Michigan Dr Nw (49534-3357)
PHONE..................616 453-5451
Marcia Steele, *CEO*
Jeff Hearn, *COO*
Bill Kindt, *Vice Pres*
Steve Bussing, *Plant Mgr*
Garison Jewett, *Opers Mgr*
▼ EMP: 214 EST: 1969
SQ FT: 90,000
SALES (est): 50MM **Privately Held**
WEB: www.hsinc.us
SIC: **3544** Special dies & tools

(G-6824)
HUDSONVILLE PRODUCTS LLC
1735 Elizabeth Ave Nw (49504-2003)
P.O. Box 140501 (49514-0501)
PHONE..................616 836-1904
Ben Douzman, *Mng Member*
EMP: 6 EST: 2017
SALES (est): 436.1K **Privately Held**
SIC: **2541** 5046 Store & office display cases & fixtures; store fixtures & display equipment

(G-6825)
HUTCHINSON CORPORATION (DH)
460 Fuller Ave Ne (49503-1912)
P.O. Box 1886 (49501-1886)
PHONE..................616 459-4541
Yves Rene Manot, *Ch of Bd*
Gerard Gehin, *President*
Mike Degraaf, *Purchasing*
Franck Larmande, *VP Engrg*
Toan Nguyen, *Draft/Design*
◆ EMP: 5 EST: 1974
SQ FT: 305,868
SALES (est): 1B
SALES (corp-wide): 4.6B **Publicly Held**
WEB: www.hutchinsonna.com
SIC: **3069** 3011 Molded rubber products; mittens, rubber; tires, cushion or solid rubber
HQ: Hutchinson
  2 Rue Balzac
  Paris 75008
  140 748-300

(G-6826)
HUTCHNSON ANTVBRTION SYSTEMS I (DH)
Also Called: Hutchnson Auto Anti Vbrtion Sy
460 Fuller Ave Ne (49503-1912)
PHONE..................616 459-4541
Jacques Maigne, *Ch of Bd*
Monica Draper, *Buyer*
Tammi Doolittle, *Accountant*
▲ EMP: 350 EST: 1930
SALES (est): 250MM
SALES (corp-wide): 4.6B **Publicly Held**
WEB: www.hutchinsonna.com
SIC: **3069** 3061 Molded rubber products; mechanical rubber goods
HQ: Hutchinson Corporation
  460 Fuller Ave Ne
  Grand Rapids MI 49503
  616 459-4541

(G-6827)
I C S CORPORATION AMERICA INC
Also Called: Ics Filtration Products
4675 Talon Ct Se (49512-5408)
PHONE..................616 554-9300
Sherwin D Doorn, *President*
Norman Hoekman, *Treasurer*
EMP: 17 EST: 1988
SQ FT: 14,500
SALES (est): 3.4MM **Privately Held**
WEB: www.icscorporation.net
SIC: **2819** Nonmetallic compounds

(G-6828)
I D MEDICAL SYSTEMS INC
3954 44th St Se (49512-3942)
PHONE..................616 698-0535
Robert O'Connor, *President*
EMP: 4 EST: 1985
SQ FT: 3,500
SALES (est): 503.4K **Privately Held**
WEB: www.medid.com
SIC: **3844** 0742 X-ray apparatus & tubes; veterinary services, specialties

(G-6829)
ICON INDUSTRIES INC
1522 Madison Ave Se (49507-1715)
PHONE..................616 241-1877
Thomas D Jacques, *President*
Robert J Zieger, *Vice Pres*
EMP: 6 EST: 1986
SQ FT: 80,000
SALES (est): 2MM **Privately Held**
WEB: www.iconindustries.com
SIC: **5084** 7389 3089 Industrial machinery & equipment; design, commercial & industrial; plastic processing

(G-6830)
IDEAL PRINTING
2059 Lake Michigan Dr Nw (49504-4742)
PHONE..................616 453-5556
EMP: 6 EST: 2019
SALES (est): 88.9K **Privately Held**
WEB: www.idealprinting.net
SIC: **2752** Commercial printing, offset

(G-6831)
IDEAL PRINTING COMPANY (PA)
2801 Oak Industrial Dr Ne (49505-6046)
PHONE..................616 454-9224
Howard Goris, *Ch of Bd*
Dan Goris, *President*
Marian Goris, *Treasurer*
Debbie Goris, *Admin Sec*
EMP: 20 EST: 1956
SQ FT: 8,000
SALES (est): 2.3MM **Privately Held**
WEB: www.idealprinting.net
SIC: **2752** Lithographing on metal; commercial printing, offset

(G-6832)
IGA ABRASIVES LLC
3011 Hillcroft Ave Sw (49548-1099)
PHONE..................616 243-5566
SL Munson,
▼ EMP: 35 EST: 2006
SQ FT: 35,000
SALES (est): 2.4MM **Privately Held**
WEB: www.igaabrasives.com
SIC: **3291** Abrasive products

(G-6833)
IHS INC
2851 Charlevoix Dr Se # 314 (49546-7092)
PHONE..................616 464-4224
EMP: 4 **Privately Held**
SIC: **3537** Mfg Industrial Trucks/Tractors
HQ: Ihs Inc.
  15 Inverness Way E
  Englewood CO 80112
  303 790-0600

(G-6834)
ILLMATIK INDUSTRIES
50 Valley Ave Nw (49504-7202)
PHONE..................714 767-1296
Juan Garcia, *Principal*
EMP: 5 EST: 2016
SALES (est): 80K **Privately Held**
SIC: **3599** Industrial machinery

(G-6835)
IMAGESOFT
100 Morningside Dr Se (49506-2404)
PHONE..................919 462-8505
Steve Dale, *Accounts Exec*
EMP: 8 EST: 2017
SALES (est): 79.6K **Privately Held**
WEB: www.imagesoftinc.com
SIC: **7372** Prepackaged software

(G-6836)
IMPERIAL CLINICAL RES SVCS INC
Also Called: Imperial Graphics
3100 Walkent Dr Nw (49544-1402)
PHONE..................616 784-0100
Matthew Bissell, *President*
Steven Balk, *Vice Pres*
Chris Howard, *Sales Mgr*
Brandon Bissell, *Manager*
Ryan Seeley, *Manager*
▼ EMP: 150 EST: 1965
SQ FT: 100,000
SALES (est): 36.7MM **Privately Held**
WEB: www.imperialcrs.com
SIC: **2761** 5112 2759 2732 Manifold business forms; stationery & office supplies; commercial printing; book printing; medical research

(G-6837)
IMPERIAL LASER INC
11473 1st Ave Nw (49534-3364)
PHONE..................616 735-9315
Mark Meade, *President*
EMP: 5 EST: 1999
SQ FT: 5,000
SALES (est): 549.1K **Privately Held**
WEB: www.imperiallaser.com
SIC: **3699** Laser systems & equipment

(G-6838)
IMPERIAL METAL PRODUCTS CO
835 Hall St Sw (49503-4820)
PHONE..................616 452-1700
Jeff Dean, *President*
Richard Dean, *General Mgr*
Adam Dean, *Vice Pres*
Ken Preston, *Vice Pres*
Greg Collins, *Engineer*
EMP: 45 EST: 1993
SQ FT: 49,000
SALES (est): 7.9MM **Privately Held**
WEB: www.imperialmetalproducts.com
SIC: **3599** Machine shop, jobbing & repair

(G-6839)
IN THE ZONE SPORTS CAMPS
260 Langlois Dr Se (49546-2296)
PHONE..................616 889-5571
EMP: 7 EST: 2010
SALES (est): 181.1K **Privately Held**
WEB: www.inthezonetennis.com
SIC: **3949** Sporting & athletic goods

(G-6840)
INCREASE ENTERPRISES LLC
1940 Fruitwood Dr Nw (49504-6009)
PHONE..................616 550-8553
John Jannereth, *Administration*
EMP: 5 EST: 2019
SALES (est): 94.5K **Privately Held**
WEB: www.grandrapidscity.com
SIC: **2711** Newspapers, publishing & printing

(G-6841)
INDELCO PLASTICS CORPORATION
3322 Lousma Dr Se (49548-2200)
PHONE..................616 452-7077
EMP: 8 EST: 2016
SALES (est): 182.7K **Privately Held**
WEB: www.indelco.com
SIC: **2821** Molding compounds, plastics

(G-6842)
INDEPENDENT DIE CUTTING INC
1265 Godfrey Ave Sw (49503-5009)
PHONE..................616 452-3197
EMP: 10
SQ FT: 25,000
SALES (est): 1.9MM **Privately Held**
SIC: **2672** Die Cut Pressure Sensitive Tapes Mylar Foam Ect

(G-6843)
INDUSTRIAL SERVICE TECH INC
Also Called: International Sports Timing
3286 Kentland Ct Se (49548-2310)
PHONE..................616 247-1033
Richard Farnsworth, *President*
Jennifer Farnsworth, *Treasurer*
EMP: 15 EST: 1982
SQ FT: 4,800
SALES (est): 3.1MM **Privately Held**
WEB: www.industrialservicetech.com
SIC: **7629** 3569 8711 5734 Electronic equipment repair; robots, assembly line: industrial & commercial; engineering services; computer software & accessories

(G-6844)
INFOR (US) LLC
Also Called: Ssa Global
3040 Charlevoix Dr Se # 200 (49546-7065)
PHONE..................616 258-3311
Premkumar Panjikunje, *Finance*
Carmen Reilly, *Manager*
Keith Kapera, *Consultant*
Mary Rekucki, *Consultant*
Susan Clark, *Senior Mgr*
EMP: 4
SALES (corp-wide): 36.9B **Privately Held**
WEB: www.infor.com
SIC: **7372** Application computer software
HQ: Infor (Us), Llc
  641 Ave Of The Americas
  New York NY 10011
  866 244-5479

GEOGRAPHIC SECTION
Grand Rapids - Kent County (G-6872)

(G-6845)
INNOVATIVE CLEANING EQP INC
Also Called: Foam-It
3833 Soundtech Ct Se (49512-4116)
PHONE..................616 656-9225
Dan Jacques, *President*
Matt Mandsager, *General Mgr*
Brian Scharp, *Marketing Staff*
Brad Devries, *Manager*
Ann Jacques,
◆ EMP: 25 EST: 1985
SQ FT: 20,000
SALES (est): 18.5MM **Privately Held**
WEB: www.foamit.com
SIC: 3559 Chemical machinery & equipment

(G-6846)
INNOVATIVE IRON INC
3370 Jefferson Ave Se (49548-2242)
PHONE..................616 248-4250
John Versluys, *President*
Thomas Hoffman, *Vice Pres*
EMP: 6 EST: 2001
SQ FT: 9,000
SALES (est): 872.5K **Privately Held**
WEB: www.innovativeiron.com
SIC: 3441 Fabricated structural metal

(G-6847)
INNOVATIVE SFTWR SOLUTIONS LTD
4300 Plnfeld Ave Ne Ste H (49525)
PHONE..................616 785-0745
John Stallmer, *President*
Kari Vandermaas, *Opers Staff*
Luke Swope, *Sales Staff*
Ben Vlietstra, *Manager*
Mitchell Taylor, *Consultant*
EMP: 23 EST: 1991
SQ FT: 2,800
SALES (est): 2MM **Privately Held**
WEB: www.growpicas.com
SIC: 7372 Prepackaged software

(G-6848)
INTAGLIO LLC
Also Called: Dialogue
3106 3 Mile Rd Nw (49534-1326)
PHONE..................616 243-3300
Rich Tomlinson, *Design Engr*
Kirk Grimshaw, *Mng Member*
Ethan Brown, *Technical Staff*
Douglas Kenney, *Prgrmr*
Theresa Gray, *Administration*
EMP: 49 EST: 2006
SALES (est): 5.8MM **Privately Held**
WEB: www.intaglioav.com
SIC: 3651 7622 4899 Household audio equipment; radio repair & installation; data communication services

(G-6849)
INTERNAL GRINDING ABRASIVES
3011 Hillcroft Ave Sw (49548-1099)
PHONE..................616 243-5566
Susan Smith, *President*
Donald Kranenberg Sr, *President*
Jim Menerick, *Project Engr*
John Hoekstra, *Treasurer*
EMP: 23 EST: 1958
SQ FT: 25,000
SALES (est): 525.5K **Privately Held**
WEB: www.iga-abrasives.com
SIC: 3291 3541 Grinding balls, ceramic; hones; coated abrasive products; machine tools, metal cutting type

(G-6850)
INTERNATIONAL MET SYSTEMS INC
Also Called: Intermet Systems
4767 Broadmoor Ave Se # 7 (49512-9397)
PHONE..................616 971-1005
Frederick Clowney, *President*
Joseph Parini, *Chairman*
Joe Barnes, *Vice Pres*
▲ EMP: 15 EST: 1997
SQ FT: 5,000
SALES (est): 3MM **Privately Held**
WEB: www.intermetsystems.com
SIC: 3829 Meteorologic tracking systems; meteorological instruments

(G-6851)
INTERNATIONAL WOOD INDS INC
2801 E Beltline Ave Ne (49525-9680)
PHONE..................800 598-9663
Patrick M Webster, *Principal*
EMP: 8 EST: 2008
SALES (est): 143.1K **Privately Held**
WEB: www.iwiproducts.com
SIC: 3999 Manufacturing industries

(G-6852)
IONXHEALTH INC
Also Called: Vetionx
4635 40th St Se (49512-4038)
PHONE..................616 808-3290
EMP: 40 EST: 2007
SALES: 1MM **Privately Held**
SIC: 0752 2834 5499 Animal Services Mfg Pharmaceutical Preparations Ret Misc Foods

(G-6853)
IORIO GELATO KENTWOOD LLC
4455 Breton Rd Se (49508-5273)
PHONE..................517 927-9928
Nicolas Lemmer, *Mng Member*
EMP: 12 EST: 2019
SALES (est): 250K **Privately Held**
WEB: www.ioriosgelato.com
SIC: 2024 Ice cream & frozen desserts

(G-6854)
IRWIN SEATING HOLDING COMPANY (PA)
3251 Fruit Ridge Ave Nw (49544-9748)
P.O. Box 2429 (49501-2429)
PHONE..................616 574-7400
Earle S Irwin, *President*
Dale I Tanis, *Senior VP*
Dale Tanis, *Senior VP*
Damon Duckworth, *Prdtn Mgr*
Chad Adams, *Engineer*
◆ EMP: 400 EST: 1975
SQ FT: 400,000
SALES (est): 110.4MM **Privately Held**
WEB: www.irwinseating.com
SIC: 7641 2531 Furniture repair & maintenance; school furniture

(G-6855)
J HANSEN-BALK STL TREATING CO
1230 Monroe Ave Nw (49505-4620)
PHONE..................616 458-1414
James Balk II, *President*
Steve Fuller, *Engineer*
Eleazar Lopez, *Info Tech Mgr*
Shirley Balk, *Admin Sec*
EMP: 35 EST: 1955
SQ FT: 60,000
SALES (est): 4.2MM **Privately Held**
WEB: www.hansenbalk.com
SIC: 3398 Metal heat treating

(G-6856)
J KALTZ & CO
3987 Brockton Dr Se Ste C (49512-4070)
PHONE..................616 942-6070
Sue Bothwell, *Manager*
EMP: 7
SALES (corp-wide): 4.3MM **Privately Held**
WEB: www.jkaltzco.com
SIC: 5251 3083 Hardware; laminated plastics plate & sheet
PA: J. Kaltz & Co.
 730 E 9 Mile Rd
 Ferndale MI 48220
 248 541-8800

(G-6857)
J MARK SYSTEMS INC
3696 Northridge Dr Nw # 10 (49544-9002)
PHONE..................616 784-6005
Mark Zeilbeck, *President*
Todd McNulty, *General Mgr*
EMP: 7 EST: 1984
SQ FT: 6,400
SALES (est): 933.4K **Privately Held**
WEB: www.jmarksystems.com
SIC: 3589 Water treatment equipment, industrial

(G-6858)
J W HOLDINGS INC
Also Called: U S Engineering
2530 Thornwood St Sw B (49519-2178)
PHONE..................616 530-9889
Dennis Madden, *President*
EMP: 40 EST: 1991
SQ FT: 33,000
SALES (est): 6.9MM **Privately Held**
SIC: 3548 3549 3541 Resistance welders, electric; assembly machines, including robotic; machine tools, metal cutting type

(G-6859)
JACKSONS INDUSTRIAL MFG
4310 Willow Lane Dr Ne (49525-7207)
PHONE..................616 531-1820
Gerald Grooters, *CEO*
Susan Latham, *President*
Barbara Grooters, *Vice Pres*
EMP: 10 EST: 1974
SALES (est): 700K **Privately Held**
WEB: www.jacksonsindustrial.com
SIC: 3561 Pumps & pumping equipment

(G-6860)
JAMES E SULLIVAN & ASSOCIATES
Also Called: Carpet Crafters
4617 Sundial Dr Ne (49525-9492)
PHONE..................616 453-0345
James E Sullivan, *Owner*
EMP: 4
SALES (est): 2.4MM **Privately Held**
SIC: 5023 2273 Carpets; carpets, textile fiber

(G-6861)
JANELLE PETERSON
Also Called: Pages In Time
5274 Plainfield Ave Ne (49525-1047)
PHONE..................616 447-9070
Fax: 616 457-8425
EMP: 7 EST: 1997
SQ FT: 2,300
SALES (est): 310K **Privately Held**
SIC: 2782 Mfg Blankbooks/Binders

(G-6862)
JAPHIL INC
Also Called: Postema Sign Co
7475 Division Ave S (49548-7137)
PHONE..................616 455-0260
Sandy Postema, *President*
Jim Vantol, *Sales Mgr*
Mark Postema, *Office Mgr*
EMP: 9 EST: 1965
SQ FT: 4,900
SALES (est): 821.2K **Privately Held**
SIC: 3993 Electric signs

(G-6863)
JBL ENTERPRISES
Also Called: Abl Enterprises
3535 Wentworth Dr Sw (49519-3161)
PHONE..................616 530-8647
Jeffrey R Godfrey, *Owner*
EMP: 5 EST: 1981
SALES (est): 327.2K **Privately Held**
WEB: www.jbl-enterprises.com
SIC: 3479 2396 5199 Engraving jewelry silverware, or metal; screen printing on fabric articles; badges

(G-6864)
JC AND ASSOCIATES
1904 Leonard St Nw (49504-3956)
PHONE..................616 401-5798
Ronald Ray Barrett, *Owner*
EMP: 6 EST: 2011
SALES (est): 66.4K **Privately Held**
WEB: www.jcandassoc.com
SIC: 3799 Recreational vehicles

(G-6865)
JCR INDUSTRIES INC
2471 Pineview Dr Ne (49525-6701)
PHONE..................616 364-4856
Jack A Roersma, *Principal*
EMP: 4 EST: 2010
SALES (est): 56.6K **Privately Held**
WEB: www.jcrindustries.com
SIC: 3999 Manufacturing industries

(G-6866)
JEAN SMITH DESIGNS
2704 Boston St Se (49506-4718)
PHONE..................616 942-9212
Jean Smith, *Owner*
EMP: 4 EST: 1979
SALES (est): 76.3K **Privately Held**
SIC: 2395 2396 Embroidery & art needlework; automotive & apparel trimmings

(G-6867)
JEDCO INC (PA)
1615 Broadway Ave Nw (49504-2026)
PHONE..................616 459-5161
Daniel Szymanski, *Ch of Bd*
Raymond Weston, *General Mgr*
John Boeschenstein, *Vice Pres*
Traci Grose, *Vice Pres*
Robert Nyquist, *Vice Pres*
EMP: 150
SQ FT: 75,000
SALES (est): 32.5MM **Privately Held**
WEB: www.jedinc.com
SIC: 3728 Aircraft parts & equipment

(G-6868)
JELD-WEN INC
Jeld-Wen Doors
4200 Roger B Chaffee Se (49548-3446)
PHONE..................616 531-5440
Jeff Koger, *Manager*
EMP: 80 **Publicly Held**
SIC: 2431 Doors, wood
HQ: Jeld-Wen, Inc.
 2645 Silver Crescent Dr
 Charlotte NC 28273
 800 535-3936

(G-6869)
JERKY STOCK LLC
3220 Dawes Ave Se (49508-1538)
PHONE..................616 481-2329
Terrell Tyms,
EMP: 5 EST: 2019
SALES (est): 282.9K **Privately Held**
SIC: 2013 Snack sticks, including jerky: from purchased meat

(G-6870)
JETCO PACKAGING SOLUTIONS LLC
Also Called: Jetco Federal Supply
5575 Kraft Ave Se Ste 100 (49512-9653)
PHONE..................616 588-2492
Susan Tellier, *President*
Jon Tellier, *Vice Pres*
Sue Tellier, *Vice Pres*
Ashley Julien, *Opers Staff*
Michelle Gauthier, *Research*
EMP: 12 EST: 2006
SALES (est): 2MM **Privately Held**
WEB: www.jetcofederal.com
SIC: 2671 2653 Packaging paper & plastics film, coated & laminated; boxes, corrugated: made from purchased materials

(G-6871)
JOAN ARNOUDSE
2499 Omega Dr Ne (49525-6710)
PHONE..................616 364-9075
Joan Arnoudse, *Owner*
EMP: 5 EST: 2001
SALES (est): 217.9K **Privately Held**
SIC: 2211 Laundry fabrics, cotton

(G-6872)
JOHN H DEKKER & SONS INC
Also Called: Dekker Bookbinding
2941 Clydon Ave Sw (49519-2403)
PHONE..................616 257-4120
John M Dekker Jr, *President*
Chris Dekker, *Vice Pres*
Corbin Dekker, *Vice Pres*
Noel Hentschel, *Plant Mgr*
Beth Pitsch, *Purchasing*
▼ EMP: 60 EST: 1928
SQ FT: 95,000
SALES (est): 8MM **Privately Held**
WEB: www.dekkerbook.com
SIC: 2789 Binding only: books, pamphlets, magazines, etc.

Grand Rapids - Kent County (G-6873)

(G-6873)
JONATHAN STEVENS MATTRESS CO (PA)
Also Called: Acme Bedding Company
3800 Division Ave S (49548-3275)
PHONE..................................616 243-4342
Ronald Zagel, *President*
Dick Westrate, *General Mgr*
John Huff, *Vice Pres*
EMP: 3 **EST:** 1945
SQ FT: 10,000
SALES (est): 4.7MM **Privately Held**
WEB: www.jonathanstevens.com
SIC: 5712 2515 Bedding & bedsprings; mattresses, innerspring or box spring

(G-6874)
JUST SIGNS SOMETIMES T-SHIRTS
101 Fuller Ave Ne (49503-3628)
PHONE..................................616 401-1215
John Howland, *Principal*
EMP: 4 **EST:** 2012
SALES (est): 57.2K **Privately Held**
SIC: 3993 Signs & advertising specialties

(G-6875)
K C M INC
1010 Chicago Dr Sw (49509-1108)
PHONE..................................616 245-8599
Bruno Unzens, *President*
EMP: 10 **EST:** 1984
SQ FT: 6,000
SALES (est): 445.4K **Privately Held**
SIC: 2841 Soap & other detergents

(G-6876)
K-BUR ENTERPRISES INC
Also Called: Sign-A-Rama
5120 Plainfield Ave Ne (49525-2084)
PHONE..................................616 447-7446
Brian Burmanai, *President*
Kevin Curtiss, *Vice Pres*
EMP: 4 **EST:** 1999
SQ FT: 960
SALES (est): 329.5K **Privately Held**
WEB: www.signarama.com
SIC: 3993 Signs & advertising specialties

(G-6877)
KALAMAZOO PACKAGING SYSTEMS
900 47th St Sw Ste I (49509-5142)
P.O. Box 88141 (49518-0141)
PHONE..................................616 534-2600
Charles Rencurrel, *President*
Penny Rencurrel, *Corp Secy*
EMP: 5 **EST:** 1978
SQ FT: 6,000
SALES (est): 555.4K **Privately Held**
WEB: www.kalpack.com
SIC: 3565 Packaging machinery

(G-6878)
KAMPS INC (HQ)
Also Called: Kamps Wood Resources
2900 Peach Ridge Ave Nw (49534-1333)
PHONE..................................616 453-9676
Bernard Kamps, *President*
Ken Haines, *CFO*
John Carpenter, *Manager*
Lydia Slusher, *Executive Asst*
EMP: 60 **EST:** 1973
SQ FT: 19,600
SALES: 105.5MM
SALES (corp-wide): 1.7B **Privately Held**
WEB: www.kampspallets.com
SIC: 2448 2499 Pallets, wood; mulch, wood & bark
PA: Freeman Spogli & Co. Llc
    11100 Santa Monica Blvd # 1900
    Los Angeles CA 90025
    310 444-1822

(G-6879)
KAWASAKI PRCISION MCHY USA INC
3838 Broadmoor Ave Se (49512-3932)
PHONE..................................616 975-3100
Noriaki Kanekiyo, *President*
Matt Bol, *Engineer*
Chris Hoffbeck, *Engineer*
Takashi Miki, *Engineer*
Jeremy Spillane, *Engineer*
▲ **EMP:** 32 **EST:** 2006
SALES (est): 8.3MM **Privately Held**
WEB: www.kpm-usa.com
SIC: 3594 Fluid power pumps & motors; fluid power motors
PA: Kawasaki Heavy Industries, Ltd.
    1-1-3, Higashikawasakicho, Chuo-Ku
    Kobe HYO 650-0

(G-6880)
KEANE SAUNDERS & ASSOCIATES
6350 Cascade Pointe Dr Se (49546-8711)
PHONE..................................616 954-7088
John Keane, *Owner*
EMP: 4 **EST:** 1998
SALES (est): 327.7K **Privately Held**
WEB: www.keanesales.com
SIC: 3569 General industrial machinery

(G-6881)
KELLOGG COMPANY
310 28th St Se (49548-1108)
P.O. Box 8881011 (49588-1011)
PHONE..................................616 247-4841
Rodney Dodson, *Opers Mgr*
Cory Robinson, *Human Res Mgr*
John Post, *Branch Mgr*
William Bush, *Manager*
Dan Yousef, *Info Tech Mgr*
EMP: 29
SALES (corp-wide): 13.7B **Publicly Held**
WEB: www.kelloggcompany.com
SIC: 2043 Cereal breakfast foods
PA: Kellogg Company
    1 Kellogg Sq
    Battle Creek MI 49017
    269 961-2000

(G-6882)
KELLOGGS CORPORATION
5300 Patterson Ave Se (49512-5663)
PHONE..................................616 219-6100
Kris Bahner, *Vice Pres*
Alistair Hirst, *Vice Pres*
EMP: 105 **EST:** 2015
SALES (est): 20.3MM
SALES (corp-wide): 13.7B **Publicly Held**
WEB: www.kelloggccu.org
SIC: 2041 Flour & other grain mill products
PA: Kellogg Company
    1 Kellogg Sq
    Battle Creek MI 49017
    269 961-2000

(G-6883)
KENDRICK PLASTICS INC
5050 Kendrick St Se (49512-9205)
PHONE..................................616 975-4000
Andrew Masterson, *Administration*
Ray Dittenber, *Maintence Staff*
Josh Schulze,
EMP: 400 **EST:** 2019
SALES (est): 57.9MM **Privately Held**
WEB: www.kendrickplastics.com
SIC: 3711 Motor vehicles & car bodies

(G-6884)
KENNEDY ACQUISITION INC (PA)
Also Called: Emerald Graphics
4949 W Greenbrooke Dr Se (49512-5400)
PHONE..................................616 871-3020
John Kennedy, *President*
Daniel Orent, *Engineer*
Paul Slagh, *Treasurer*
Patrick Kennedy, *Program Mgr*
Stu Cheney, *Admin Sec*
EMP: 3 **EST:** 2003
SALES (est): 13.1MM **Privately Held**
SIC: 2759 Screen printing

(G-6885)
KENONA INDUSTRIES LLC
3044 Wilson Dr Nw (49534-7564)
PHONE..................................616 735-6228
Bryan Morrissey, *President*
Chris Afendoulis, *CFO*
EMP: 140 **EST:** 2018
SALES (est): 50MM **Privately Held**
WEB: www.kenona.net
SIC: 3714 Motor vehicle parts & accessories

(G-6886)
KENT COMMUNICATIONS INC
Also Called: Kci Printsource
3901 East Paris Ave Se (49512-3906)
PHONE..................................616 957-2120
Joe Wujkowski, *CEO*
Brian Quist, *President*
Ericka Clement, *Accounts Mgr*
Miriam Franken, *Accounts Mgr*
Lisa Needham, *Accounts Mgr*
EMP: 62 **EST:** 1975
SQ FT: 32,000
SALES (est): 9.3MM **Privately Held**
WEB: www.kentcommunications.com
SIC: 7331 2752 2789 7336 Mailing list compilers; mailing service; commercial printing, lithographic; bookbinding & related work; commercial art & graphic design

(G-6887)
KENT COUNTY
Also Called: Board of Commissioners
300 Monroe Ave Nw (49503-2206)
PHONE..................................616 632-7580
Jason Cramer, *Administration*
EMP: 17
SALES (corp-wide): 412.8MM **Privately Held**
WEB: www.accesskent.com
SIC: 9121 9311 2759 9211 County commissioner; finance, taxation & monetary policy; publication printing
PA: Kent County
    300 Monroe Ave Nw
    Grand Rapids MI 49503
    616 632-7580

(G-6888)
KENT DOOR & SPECIALTY INC
Also Called: Kent Door Supply
2535 28th St Sw (49519-2105)
PHONE..................................616 534-9691
David Hees, *President*
David Homrich, *Vice Pres*
EMP: 25 **EST:** 1982
SQ FT: 85,000
SALES (est): 8.8MM **Privately Held**
WEB: www.kentdoor.com
SIC: 5031 2431 Doors; millwork

(G-6889)
KENT MANUFACTURING COMPANY
2200 Oak Industrial Dr Ne (49505-6016)
PHONE..................................616 454-9495
Kenneth Muraski, *President*
Tom Muraski, *Exec VP*
Michael Muraski, *Vice Pres*
Thomas Muraski, *Vice Pres*
Mary Rott, *Vice Pres*
EMP: 60 **EST:** 1940
SQ FT: 45,000
SALES (est): 19.6MM **Privately Held**
WEB: www.kent-mfg.com
SIC: 2672 3053 3069 2891 Tape, pressure sensitive: made from purchased materials; adhesive papers, labels or tapes: from purchased material; gaskets & sealing devices; gasket materials; medical & laboratory rubber sundries & related products; tape, pressure sensitive: rubber; foam rubber; adhesives; plastics foam products; laminated plastics plate & sheet

(G-6890)
KENT WELDING INC
1915 Sterling Ave Nw (49504-2023)
PHONE..................................616 363-4414
Mathew Delano, *President*
EMP: 4 **EST:** 1945
SQ FT: 5,200
SALES (est): 362.5K **Privately Held**
SIC: 7692 Welding repair

(G-6891)
KENTWOOD POWDER COAT INC
3900 Swank Dr Se (49512-3961)
PHONE..................................616 698-8181
Leonard Vining, *President*
EMP: 36 **EST:** 1988
SALES (est): 4.8MM **Privately Held**
WEB: www.kentwoodpowder.com
SIC: 3479 Coating of metals & formed products; painting, coating & hot dipping

(G-6892)
KERKSTRA MECHANICAL LLC
4345 44th St Se Ste C (49512-4089)
PHONE..................................616 532-6100
Keith Swann, *Purchasing*
Lisa England, *Human Res Dir*
Ray Simmons, *Manager*
Chad Timmer, *Manager*
Mark Harmsel, *CIO*
EMP: 7 **EST:** 2007
SALES (est): 811K **Privately Held**
WEB: www.kerkstra.com
SIC: 3714 Water pump, motor vehicle

(G-6893)
KERRY FOODS
4444 52nd St Se (49512-9674)
P.O. Box 8846, Kentwood (49518-8846)
PHONE..................................616 871-9940
Rhonda Gonzalez, *Principal*
Mat Stephany, *Manager*
EMP: 11 **EST:** 2010
SALES (est): 1.3MM **Privately Held**
WEB: www.kerry.com
SIC: 2099 Food preparations

(G-6894)
KESSEBOHMER ERGONOMIE AMER INC
3900 Linden Ave Se (49548-3406)
PHONE..................................616 202-1239
Scot Jonker, *Principal*
Robert Van Driel, *Vice Pres*
EMP: 9 **EST:** 2018
SALES (est): 356.6K **Privately Held**
WEB: www.kessebohmerergonomics.com
SIC: 2522 Benches, office: except wood

(G-6895)
KIND CRUMBS LLC
4751 3 Mile Rd Nw Ste I (49534-1274)
PHONE..................................616 881-6388
Rebecca Duiven, *Mng Member*
EMP: 8 **EST:** 2010
SALES (est): 511.7K **Privately Held**
WEB: www.kindcrumbs.com
SIC: 7389 2051 ; bakery: wholesale or wholesale/retail combined

(G-6896)
KINDEL FURNITURE COMPANY LLC (PA)
Also Called: Karges Furniture Co
4047 Eastern Ave Se (49508-3401)
PHONE..................................616 243-3676
Robert Burch, *CEO*
James Fisher, *President*
Dennis Patterson, *Vice Pres*
▲ **EMP:** 160 **EST:** 1901
SQ FT: 150,000
SALES (est): 20.8MM **Privately Held**
WEB: www.kindelfurniture.com
SIC: 2511 7641 Dining room furniture: wood; reupholstery & furniture repair

(G-6897)
KINGS SELF DEFENSE LLC
6769 Bent Grass Dr Se (49508-7873)
PHONE..................................910 890-4322
Jared Reyes, *Principal*
EMP: 4 **EST:** 2016
SALES (est): 199.2K **Privately Held**
SIC: 3812 Defense systems & equipment

(G-6898)
KITCHEN JOY
887 Bailey Park Dr Ne (49525-2111)
PHONE..................................616 682-7327
Amanda McGovern, *Principal*
EMP: 5 **EST:** 2019
SALES (est): 91.5K **Privately Held**
SIC: 2741 Miscellaneous publishing

(G-6899)
KLISE MANUFACTURING COMPANY
Also Called: Tanis Custom Grills
11450 3rd Ave Nw (49534-3500)
PHONE..................................616 459-4283
Phillip Veen, *President*

GEOGRAPHIC SECTION
Grand Rapids - Kent County (G-6923)

Allan Veen, *Vice Pres*
Dave Delany, *Safety Mgr*
EMP: 48 **EST:** 1910
SQ FT: 72,000
SALES (est): 4.7MM **Privately Held**
WEB: www.klisemfg.com
SIC: 2431 Moldings, wood: unfinished & prefinished

(G-6900)
KNAPE & VOGT MANUFACTURING CO (DH)
2700 Oak Industrial Dr Ne (49505-6081)
PHONE..................616 459-3311
Peter Martin, *President*
Morgan Hitson, *Business Mgr*
Linda Carron, *Counsel*
Jon P Elordi, *Vice Pres*
Gordon Kirsch, *Vice Pres*
◆ **EMP:** 582 **EST:** 1898
SQ FT: 444,000
SALES (est): 154.6MM
SALES (corp-wide): 3B **Privately Held**
WEB: www.knapeandvogt.com
SIC: 2541 3429 2542 Wood partitions & fixtures; shelving, office & store, wood; display fixtures, wood; furniture builders' & other household hardware; shelving, office & store: except wood

(G-6901)
KNICKERBOCKER
417 Bridge St Nw (49504-5305)
PHONE..................616 345-5642
EMP: 7 **EST:** 2016
SALES (est): 89.5K **Privately Held**
WEB: www.newhollandbrew.com
SIC: 2082 Malt beverages

(G-6902)
KOEZE COMPANY (PA)
Also Called: Koeze Direct
2555 Burlingame Ave Sw (49509-2237)
P.O. Box 9470 (49509-0470)
PHONE..................616 724-2601
Jeffrey Koeze, *Ch of Bd*
William E Malpass, *Corp Secy*
John Feenstra, *Purch Mgr*
Mark Minkus, *Controller*
Martin Andree, *Marketing Mgr*
◆ **EMP:** 33 **EST:** 1910
SQ FT: 92,000
SALES (est): 10.7MM **Privately Held**
WEB: www.koeze.com
SIC: 5441 2068 2095 Candy; salted & roasted nuts & seeds; roasted coffee

(G-6903)
KOLENDA TECHNOLOGIES LLC
2544 Garfield Ave Nw (49544-1822)
PHONE..................616 299-0126
David Kolenda, *Administration*
EMP: 6 **EST:** 2019
SALES (est): 92.3K **Privately Held**
WEB: www.kolendatechnologies.com
SIC: 3599 Machine shop, jobbing & repair

(G-6904)
KRAFT HEINZ FOODS COMPANY
Also Called: Kraft Foods
3950 Sparks Dr Se (49546-6146)
PHONE..................616 447-0481
Drew Fries, *Manager*
EMP: 7
SALES (corp-wide): 26.1B **Publicly Held**
WEB: www.kraftheinzcompany.com
SIC: 2099 Food preparations
HQ: Kraft Heinz Foods Company
   1 Ppg Pl Ste 3400
   Pittsburgh PA 15222
   412 456-5700

(G-6905)
KRIEGER CRAFTSMEN INC
2758 3 Mile Rd Nw (49534-1318)
PHONE..................616 735-9200
Tim Krieger, *President*
EMP: 26 **EST:** 1994
SQ FT: 5,000
SALES (est): 3.7MM **Privately Held**
WEB: www.kriegercraftsmen.com
SIC: 3544 Special dies & tools

(G-6906)
L3 AVIATION PRODUCTS INC (DH)
Also Called: L3 Commnctons Avionics Systems
5353 52nd St Se (49512-9702)
PHONE..................616 949-6600
Christopher E Kubasik, *CEO*
Jay Lafoy, *President*
Dan Oomkes, *Engineer*
Eric Smead, *Engineer*
Kacie Byard, *Sales Staff*
EMP: 300 **EST:** 1968
SQ FT: 110,000
SALES (est): 149.2MM
SALES (corp-wide): 18.1B **Publicly Held**
WEB: www.avionics.cas.l3harris.com
SIC: 3812 Aircraft flight instruments; gyroscopes; automatic pilots, aircraft; radar systems & equipment
HQ: L3 Technologies, Inc.
   600 3rd Ave Fl 34
   New York NY 10016
   321 727-9100

(G-6907)
LACH DIAMOND
4350 Airwest Dr Se Ofc A (49512-3969)
PHONE..................616 698-0101
Horst Lach, *President*
Randall Prafke, *General Mgr*
Sue Wilder, *Finance Spvr*
Lonn Beaver, *Manager*
Randy Prafke, *CIO*
EMP: 26 **EST:** 1982
SQ FT: 12,000
SALES (est): 5MM **Privately Held**
WEB: www.lach-diamond.com
SIC: 3423 7699 Hand & edge tools; knife, saw & tool sharpening & repair

(G-6908)
LACKS ENTERPRISES INC (PA)
5460 Cascade Rd Se (49546-6406)
PHONE..................616 949-6570
Richard Lacks, *President*
Jeff Lacross, *General Mgr*
John Lacks, *Principal*
Chris Walker, *Principal*
Kurt Lacks, *Exec VP*
EMP: 60 **EST:** 1985
SQ FT: 19,000
SALES (est): 562.2MM **Privately Held**
WEB: www.lacksenterprises.com
SIC: 3089 Molding primary plastic

(G-6909)
LACKS EXTERIOR SYSTEMS LLC (HQ)
Also Called: Lacks Trim Systems
5460 Cascade Rd Se (49546-6406)
PHONE..................616 949-6570
Beb Bieri, *General Mgr*
Kurt Lacks, *Vice Pres*
Joe Sullivan, *Site Mgr*
Lisa Pond, *Purch Agent*
Emila Aganovic, *Engineer*
▲ **EMP:** 1000 **EST:** 1966
SALES (est): 307.6MM **Privately Held**
WEB: www.lacksenterprises.com
SIC: 3089 Plastic hardware & building products

(G-6910)
LACKS EXTERIOR SYSTEMS LLC
5010 52nd St Se (49512-9731)
PHONE..................616 949-6570
Courtney Bockover, *Branch Mgr*
EMP: 21 **Privately Held**
WEB: www.lacksenterprises.com
SIC: 3089 Plastic hardware & building products
HQ: Lacks Exterior Systems, Llc
   5460 Cascade Rd Se
   Grand Rapids MI 49546
   616 949-6570

(G-6911)
LACKS EXTERIOR SYSTEMS LLC
5711 Kraft Ave Se (49512-9607)
PHONE..................616 949-6570
Dan Centille, *Branch Mgr*
EMP: 21 **Privately Held**
WEB: www.lacksenterprises.com
SIC: 3089 Automotive parts, plastic
HQ: Lacks Exterior Systems, Llc
   5460 Cascade Rd Se
   Grand Rapids MI 49546
   616 949-6570

(G-6912)
LACKS EXTERIOR SYSTEMS LLC
5801 Kraft Ave Se (49512-9683)
PHONE..................616 949-6570
Joel Goward, *Branch Mgr*
EMP: 125 **Privately Held**
WEB: www.lacksenterprises.com
SIC: 3089 Automotive parts, plastic
HQ: Lacks Exterior Systems, Llc
   5460 Cascade Rd Se
   Grand Rapids MI 49546
   616 949-6570

(G-6913)
LACKS EXTERIOR SYSTEMS LLC
4315 52nd St Se (49512-9673)
PHONE..................616 949-6570
Jason Fogelsonger, *Branch Mgr*
EMP: 225 **Privately Held**
WEB: www.lacksenterprises.com
SIC: 3089 Automotive parts, plastic
HQ: Lacks Exterior Systems, Llc
   5460 Cascade Rd Se
   Grand Rapids MI 49546
   616 949-6570

(G-6914)
LACKS EXTERIOR SYSTEMS LLC
3703 Patterson Sw (49512)
PHONE..................616 949-6570
Jeff Reest, *Manager*
EMP: 25 **Privately Held**
WEB: www.lacksenterprises.com
SIC: 2396 Automotive & apparel trimmings
HQ: Lacks Exterior Systems, Llc
   5460 Cascade Rd Se
   Grand Rapids MI 49546
   616 949-6570

(G-6915)
LACKS INDUSTRIES INC
Kentwood Division
4260 Airwest Dr Se (49512-3948)
PHONE..................616 698-6890
Joe Sullivan, *Manager*
EMP: 166 **Privately Held**
WEB: www.lacksenterprises.com
SIC: 3089 3714 3429 Molding primary plastic; motor vehicle parts & accessories; manufactured hardware (general)
HQ: Lacks Industries, Inc.
   5460 Cascade Rd Se
   Grand Rapids MI 49546
   616 949-6570

(G-6916)
LACKS INDUSTRIES INC
4375 52nd St Se (49512-9673)
PHONE..................616 698-3600
Joe Sullivan, *Manager*
EMP: 166 **Privately Held**
WEB: www.lacksenterprises.com
SIC: 3089 Molding primary plastic
HQ: Lacks Industries, Inc.
   5460 Cascade Rd Se
   Grand Rapids MI 49546
   616 949-6570

(G-6917)
LACKS INDUSTRIES INC
Also Called: Lacks Trim Systems
4090 Barden Dr (49512)
PHONE..................616 698-6854
Steve Morrissey, *Plant Mgr*
Betty Brown, *QC Mgr*
Jennifer Bosscher, *Personnel*
Bill Mull, *Manager*
Tracy Bartlebaugh, *Manager*
EMP: 166 **Privately Held**
WEB: www.lacksenterprises.com
SIC: 3089 Molding primary plastic
HQ: Lacks Industries, Inc.
   5460 Cascade Rd Se
   Grand Rapids MI 49546
   616 949-6570

(G-6918)
LACKS INDUSTRIES INC
4260 Airlane Dr Se (49512-3959)
PHONE..................616 698-9852
Jim Morsey, *Manager*
EMP: 200 **Privately Held**
WEB: www.lacksenterprises.com
SIC: 2396 3471 Automotive trimmings, fabric; plating & polishing
HQ: Lacks Industries, Inc.
   5460 Cascade Rd Se
   Grand Rapids MI 49546
   616 949-6570

(G-6919)
LACKS INDUSTRIES INC
Also Called: Lacks Wheel Trim Systems
3505 Kraft Ave Se (49512-2033)
PHONE..................616 554-7134
Jim Stratton, *Project Engr*
Lary O'Tool, *Branch Mgr*
Bob Tice, *Manager*
Garry Van Houten, *Technology*
EMP: 166 **Privately Held**
WEB: www.lacksenterprises.com
SIC: 3089 Plastic containers, except foam
HQ: Lacks Industries, Inc.
   5460 Cascade Rd Se
   Grand Rapids MI 49546
   616 949-6570

(G-6920)
LACKS INDUSTRIES INC
Also Called: Airwest Engineering
4275 Airwest Dr Se (49512-3949)
PHONE..................616 698-2776
Doug Reams, *Principal*
Dave Walters, *COO*
Jason Fogelsonger, *Plant Mgr*
Clayton Powers, *Production*
Betty Brown, *QC Mgr*
EMP: 166 **Privately Held**
WEB: www.lacksenterprises.com
SIC: 3089 Molding primary plastic
HQ: Lacks Industries, Inc.
   5460 Cascade Rd Se
   Grand Rapids MI 49546
   616 949-6570

(G-6921)
LACKS INDUSTRIES INC
4365 52nd St Se (49512-9673)
PHONE..................616 656-2910
Chris Ober, *Manager*
EMP: 166 **Privately Held**
WEB: www.lacksenterprises.com
SIC: 3089 3714 Plastic hardware & building products; motor vehicle parts & accessories
HQ: Lacks Industries, Inc.
   5460 Cascade Rd Se
   Grand Rapids MI 49546
   616 949-6570

(G-6922)
LACKS WHEEL TRIM SYSTEMS LLC (PA)
5460 Cascade Rd Se (49546-6406)
PHONE..................616 949-6570
Doug Phelps, *Plant Mgr*
Jenny Skelonc, *Purch Agent*
Joseph Senneker, *Engineer*
Mike Clover, *CFO*
Scott Elsbrie, *Supervisor*
EMP: 50 **EST:** 1998
SQ FT: 40,000
SALES (est): 9.9MM **Privately Held**
WEB: www.lacksenterprises.com
SIC: 3089 Injection molding of plastics

(G-6923)
LAKELAND FINISHING CORPORATION
5400 36th St Se (49512-2016)
PHONE..................616 949-8001
Thomas A Smith, *President*
Denise Mogg, *Production*
Cindy Veurink, *Human Res Mgr*
Kabrina Alcorn, *Program Mgr*
John Behrend, *Technical Staff*
EMP: 110 **EST:** 1990
SQ FT: 85,000

Grand Rapids - Kent County (G-6924)

SALES (est): 17.6MM
SALES (corp-wide): 17.6MM **Privately Held**
WEB: www.lakelandmonroe.com
SIC: 3714 Motor vehicle parts & accessories
PA: Monroe Group Holdings, Llc
4490 44th St Se
Grand Rapids MI 49512
616 942-9820

(G-6924)
LAKELAND PALLETS INC (PA)
3801 Kraft Ave Se (49512-2039)
PHONE.................................616 949-9515
Joel Bodbyl, *President*
Jordan Koole, *Office Mgr*
EMP: 40 **EST:** 1986
SALES (est): 5.3MM **Privately Held**
WEB: www.lakelandpalletsinc.com
SIC: 2448 Pallets, wood; pallets, wood & wood with metal

(G-6925)
LAKESHORE PAINTS & COATING
761 Baylis St Sw (49503-1573)
PHONE.................................616 831-6990
David Jasperse, *President*
EMP: 4 **EST:** 1996
SQ FT: 5,000
SALES (est): 591.8K **Privately Held**
WEB: www.lakeshorepaints.com
SIC: 2851 Paints & allied products

(G-6926)
LAMININ MEDICAL PRODUCTS INC
3760 East Paris Ave Se (49512-3903)
PHONE.................................616 871-3390
Jon Rudolph, *President*
Don Armbrester, *Exec VP*
▲ **EMP:** 8 **EST:** 2011
SALES (est): 236.8K **Privately Held**
WEB: www.lamininmedical.com
SIC: 2672 Adhesive backed films, foams & foils

(G-6927)
LAND & HOMES INC
1701 Porter St Sw Ste 6 (49519-1771)
PHONE.................................616 534-5792
Paul Land, *President*
Roger Lucas, *Vice Pres*
Daniel Hibma, *Treasurer*
Dan Himba, *Treasurer*
EMP: 4 **EST:** 1991
SALES (est): 584.2K **Privately Held**
WEB: www.txlandlocator.com
SIC: 2721 Periodicals

(G-6928)
LASER ACCESS INC
3691 Northridge Dr Nw # 1 (49544-9006)
PHONE.................................616 459-5496
Daniel Szymanski, *President*
Glenn Jarrell, *Controller*
Kay Ostrowski, *Technology*
EMP: 120
SALES (est): 18.3MM
SALES (corp-wide): 32.5MM **Privately Held**
WEB: www.laseraccess.com
SIC: 3699 7692 Laser welding, drilling & cutting equipment; welding repair
PA: Jedco, Inc.
1615 Broadway Ave Nw
Grand Rapids MI 49504
616 459-5161

(G-6929)
LASERCUTTING SERVICES INC
Also Called: Michigan Lasercut
4101 40th St Se Ste 7 (49512-4124)
PHONE.................................616 975-2000
Steve Schroder, *President*
Les Wong, *Chairman*
Brian Curtis, *Vice Pres*
Michele Schilling, *Executive Asst*
EMP: 28 **EST:** 1978
SQ FT: 12,500
SALES (est): 6.1MM **Privately Held**
SIC: 3544 Dies, steel rule

(G-6930)
LASERS RESOURCE INC
5555 Glnwood Hlls Pkwy Se (49512-2091)
PHONE.................................616 554-5555
Thomas Senecal, *President*
Joe Greene, *Accounts Mgr*
Adrian Lopez, *Sales Staff*
Debra Senecal, *Admin Sec*
Emily Lopez, *Administration*
EMP: 20 **EST:** 1991
SALES (est): 4.2MM **Privately Held**
WEB: www.appliedimaging.com
SIC: 3861 7378 Toners, prepared photographic (not made in chemical plants); computer peripheral equipment repair & maintenance

(G-6931)
LASERS UNLIMITED INC
4600 36th St Se (49512-1920)
PHONE.................................616 977-2668
Alan Bush, *President*
EMP: 19 **EST:** 1996
SQ FT: 41,000
SALES (est): 2.7MM **Privately Held**
WEB: www.lasersunlimited.net
SIC: 3441 Fabricated structural metal

(G-6932)
LATIN AMERICAN INDUSTRIES LLC
3120 Kn O Sha Indus Ct Se (49508)
PHONE.................................616 301-1878
Olivia Benitez, *Mng Member*
EMP: 7 **EST:** 2000
SALES (est): 788.9K **Privately Held**
WEB: www.laiinc.net
SIC: 3089 3544 Molding primary plastic; special dies, tools, jigs & fixtures

(G-6933)
LEATHERCRAFTS BY BEAR
751 Brownwood Ave Nw (49504-3645)
PHONE.................................616 453-8308
John Downer, *Owner*
Maureen Downer, *Co-Owner*
EMP: 4 **EST:** 1982
SALES (est): 123K **Privately Held**
SIC: 3199 Leather garments

(G-6934)
LEEDY MANUFACTURING CO LLC
210 Hall St Sw (49507-1034)
PHONE.................................616 245-0517
Paul Cape, *President*
Steve Traynor, *Vice Pres*
Gary King, *Opers Mgr*
Chris Hoke, *Mfg Staff*
Joe Mantooth, *VP Engrg*
▲ **EMP:** 70 **EST:** 1947
SQ FT: 75,000
SALES (est): 22.4MM **Privately Held**
WEB: www.leedymfg.com
SIC: 3714 3531 3568 3536 Gears, motor vehicle; transmissions, motor vehicle; winches; sprockets (power transmission equipment); pulleys, power transmission; hoists, cranes & monorails

(G-6935)
LEGACY BARRICADES INC
4320 Airwest Dr Se Ste B (49512-3921)
PHONE.................................616 656-9600
Debra Kelch, *Principal*
EMP: 5 **EST:** 2018
SALES (est): 81K **Privately Held**
WEB: www.legacybarricades.com
SIC: 3999 Manufacturing industries

(G-6936)
LEGACY METAL FABRICATING LLC
21 N Park St Nw (49544-6932)
PHONE.................................616 258-8406
Ryan McComb, *Vice Pres*
James McComb, *Sales Staff*
Dave Vandenberg, *Sales Staff*
Mary McComb, *Office Mgr*
Kim McComb,
EMP: 20 **EST:** 2009
SQ FT: 12,000
SALES (est): 4.8MM **Privately Held**
WEB: www.legacymetalfab.com
SIC: 3444 Sheet metalwork

(G-6937)
LEGEND SIGN COMPANY
5120 Plainfield Ave Ne (49525-2084)
PHONE.................................616 447-7446
EMP: 5 **EST:** 2017
SALES (est): 104.4K **Privately Held**
WEB: www.legendsigngr.com
SIC: 3993 Signs & advertising specialties

(G-6938)
LEICA GEO SYSTEMS GR LLC
6330 28th St Se (49546-6916)
PHONE.................................616 949-7430
Darrell Mortensen, *Principal*
EMP: 5 **EST:** 2016
SALES (est): 147.8K **Privately Held**
WEB: www.ceolaseralignment.com
SIC: 3531 Construction machinery

(G-6939)
LEIF DISTRIBUTION LLC
Also Called: Leif Led
3529 3 Mile Rd Nw (49534-1229)
PHONE.................................517 481-2122
Toby Leifker, *Mng Member*
▲ **EMP:** 25 **EST:** 2014
SALES (est): 1.6MM **Privately Held**
WEB: www.leifled.com
SIC: 3648 3646 Street lighting fixtures; outdoor lighting equipment; commercial indusl & institutional electric lighting fixtures; ornamental lighting fixtures, commercial; fluorescent lighting fixtures, commercial

(G-6940)
LEITZ TOOLING SYSTEMS LP
4301 East Paris Ave Se (49512-3980)
PHONE.................................616 698-7010
Terry Jacks, *Branch Mgr*
EMP: 4
SALES (corp-wide): 142MM **Privately Held**
WEB: www.leitz.org
SIC: 5084 3541 Industrial machinery & equipment; machine tools, metal cutting type
HQ: Leitz Tooling Systems Lp
4301 East Paris Ave Se
Grand Rapids MI 49512
800 253-6070

(G-6941)
LEITZ TOOLING SYSTEMS LP
4301 East Paris Ave Se (49512-3980)
PHONE.................................616 698-7010
Terry Jacks, *President*
Mark Alster, *Sales Mgr*
Viktor Yaremchuk, *Technical Staff*
EMP: 4
SALES (corp-wide): 142MM **Privately Held**
WEB: www.leitz.org
SIC: 5084 3541 Industrial machinery & equipment; machine tools, metal cutting type
HQ: Leitz Tooling Systems Lp
4301 East Paris Ave Se
Grand Rapids MI 49512
800 253-6070

(G-6942)
LIFESTYLE KITCHEN STUDIO
222 Fulton St E (49503-3211)
PHONE.................................616 454-2563
Susan Bloss, *President*
David Bloss, *Vice Pres*
Kristina B Sisk, *Opers Staff*
Kelly Barnes, *Assistant*
EMP: 6 **EST:** 2004
SALES (est): 683.1K **Privately Held**
WEB: www.lifestylekitchenstudio.com
SIC: 2434 Wood kitchen cabinets

(G-6943)
LIGHT SPEED USA LLC
Also Called: Phenosynthesis LLC
1971 E Beltlin Ave Ne 106-130 (49525-7045)
PHONE.................................616 308-0054
Anthony Cairo, *Managing Dir*
EMP: 895 **EST:** 2014

(G-6944)
SALES (est): 5MM **Privately Held**
SIC: 3229 8999 8748 Reflectors for lighting equipment, pressed or blown glass; scientific consulting; systems analysis & engineering consulting services

LILY PRODUCTS MICHIGAN INC
2070 Calvin Ave Se (49507-3373)
PHONE.................................616 245-9193
Steven Popma, *CEO*
Jason Popma, *President*
Ryan Murray, *Vice Pres*
EMP: 6 **EST:** 1968
SQ FT: 18,000
SALES (est): 1MM **Privately Held**
WEB: www.lilyproducts.com
SIC: 2819 Industrial inorganic chemicals

(G-6945)
LINAK US INC
678 Front Ave Nw Ste 175 (49504-5300)
PHONE.................................502 413-0387
EMP: 7 **EST:** 2017
SALES (est): 312.4K **Privately Held**
WEB: www.linak-us.com
SIC: 3625 Relays & industrial controls

(G-6946)
LIPP AMERICA TANK SYSTEMS LLC
4246 Kalamazoo Ave Se (49508-3607)
PHONE.................................616 201-6761
Manuel Lipp, *Ch of Bd*
Al Lettinga, *President*
EMP: 10 **EST:** 2016
SQ FT: 1,000
SALES (est): 2.2MM
SALES (corp-wide): 17.8MM **Privately Held**
WEB: www.lipp-ats.com
SIC: 3795 Tanks & tank components
PA: Lipp Gesellschaft Mit Beschrankter Haftung
Industriestr. 27
Tannhausen BW 73497
796 490-030

(G-6947)
LIVESPACE LLC
Also Called: Audiospace
4995 Starr St Se (49546-6350)
PHONE.................................616 929-0191
C Ben, *Project Mgr*
Bryan Campbell, *Engineer*
Jason McCleon, *CFO*
Todd Ernst, *Sales Staff*
Richards Bacans, *Mng Member*
EMP: 15 **EST:** 2005
SQ FT: 16,000
SALES: 3.2MM **Privately Held**
WEB: www.livespace.com
SIC: 3663 7941 Studio equipment, radio & television broadcasting; stadium event operator services

(G-6948)
LONG ROAD DISTILLERS LLC
537 Leonard St Nw Ste A (49504-4263)
PHONE.................................616 356-1770
Kyle Van Strien, *Owner*
Taylor Remy, *Manager*
EMP: 14 **EST:** 2014
SALES (est): 2.1MM **Privately Held**
WEB: www.longroaddistillers.com
SIC: 2085 Distillers' dried grains & solubles & alcohol

(G-6949)
LOWERY CORPORATION (PA)
Also Called: Applied Imaging
5555 Glnwood Hlls Pkwy Se (49512-2091)
PHONE.................................616 554-5200
John Lowery, *President*
Sandra Lowery, *Corp Secy*
John Konyonbelt, *Vice Pres*
Josh Gauthier, *Opers Staff*
Jenna Wassink, *Opers Staff*
EMP: 150 **EST:** 1986
SQ FT: 13,000
SALES (est): 134.1MM **Privately Held**
WEB: www.appliedimaging.com
SIC: 5044 7379 2759 Copying equipment; ; commercial printing

GEOGRAPHIC SECTION
Grand Rapids - Kent County (G-6978)

(G-6950)
LUB-TECH INC
Also Called: Lt Global
470 Market Ave Sw Unit 13 (49503-4981)
PHONE.................................616 299-3540
▲ **EMP:** 4
SALES (est): 342.1K **Privately Held**
SIC: 2992 5085 Mfg Lubricating Oils/Greases & Filters

(G-6951)
LUDWICKS FROZEN DONUTS INC
Also Called: Ludwick's Sour Cream Donuts
3217 3 Mile Rd Nw (49534-1223)
PHONE.................................616 453-6880
Tom Ludwick, *President*
EMP: 14 **EST:** 1957
SQ FT: 11,000
SALES (est): 1.4MM **Privately Held**
WEB: www.ludwicksbakery.com
SIC: 2053 2052 Doughnuts, frozen; cookies & crackers

(G-6952)
LUMICHRON INC
2215 29th St Se Ste B4 (49508-1580)
PHONE.................................616 245-8888
Ian Macartney, *President*
Karen Macartney, *Vice Pres*
◆ **EMP:** 4 **EST:** 2011
SQ FT: 3,500
SALES (est): 560.1K **Privately Held**
WEB: www.lumichron.com
SIC: 3873 Clocks, except timeclocks

(G-6953)
LUXURY RICHLAND LLC ✪
1444 Michigan St Ne Ste 5 (49503-2028)
PHONE.................................269 222-7979
Valentin Williams,
EMP: 10 **EST:** 2021
SALES (est): 514K **Privately Held**
SIC: 3861 Motion picture film

(G-6954)
LWHS LTD
Also Called: Bata Plastics
1001 40th St Se (49508-2401)
PHONE.................................616 452-5300
W Lee Hammond, *President*
Barbara Hammond, *CFO*
Matt Hammond, *Sales Executive*
Jason Rance, *Manager*
EMP: 55 **EST:** 1988
SQ FT: 50,000
SALES (est): 13.8MM **Privately Held**
WEB: www.bataplastics.com
SIC: 4953 3083 Recycling, waste materials; laminated plastics plate & sheet

(G-6955)
MACHINE STAR LLC
4674 Clay Ave Sw Ste D (49548-3039)
PHONE.................................616 245-6400
Brant Hendler, *Mng Member*
EMP: 1 **EST:** 2007
SALES (est): 1.1MM **Privately Held**
WEB: www.machinestar.com
SIC: 3089 Injection molding of plastics

(G-6956)
MAGNA MIRRORS AMERICA INC (DH)
Also Called: Magna Engineered Glass
5085 Kraft Ave Se (49512-9707)
PHONE.................................616 786-7000
John O'Hara, *President*
Aaron D McCarthy, *Exec VP*
Niall Lynam, *Senior VP*
James Brodie, *Vice Pres*
Andre Ertl, *Vice Pres*
◆ **EMP:** 20 **EST:** 1905
SALES (est): 1.4B
SALES (corp-wide): 32.6B **Privately Held**
WEB: www.magna.com
SIC: 3231 Products of purchased glass

(G-6957)
MALIBU SKATEBOARDS LLC
917 Pinecrest Ave Se (49506-3436)
PHONE.................................616 243-3154
Donald Tuitel, *Principal*
EMP: 4 **EST:** 2008

SALES (est): 102K **Privately Held**
WEB: www.malibuboards.net
SIC: 3949 Skateboards

(G-6958)
MAR-MED INC
333 Fuller Ave Ne (49503-3630)
PHONE.................................616 454-3000
Joseph Marogil, *President*
Anthony Giacona, *Business Mgr*
Joel Marogil, *Treasurer*
Jerry Marogil, *Admin Sec*
▲ **EMP:** 40 **EST:** 1987
SALES (est): 5.2MM **Privately Held**
WEB: www.marmed.com
SIC: 5047 3841 Medical equipment & supplies; surgical & medical instruments

(G-6959)
MARK MAKER COMPANY INC (PA)
4157 Stafford Ave Sw (49548-3053)
PHONE.................................616 538-6980
Robert Pettijohn, *President*
Charles Bobeldyk, *Vice Pres*
Steven Stout, *Vice Pres*
Ronna Schultz, *Treasurer*
Tim Workman, *Sales Staff*
EMP: 38 **EST:** 1970
SQ FT: 15,000
SALES (est): 6.4MM **Privately Held**
WEB: www.mark-makerco.com
SIC: 3953 3544 2796 Printing dies, rubber or plastic, for marking machines; dies & die holders for metal cutting, forming, die casting; platemaking services

(G-6960)
MARKIT PRODUCTS
2430 Turner Ave Nw Ste D (49544-2005)
PHONE.................................616 458-7881
Heather Grimes, *Owner*
Susan Deboer, *Production*
Janice Sherwood, *Sales Staff*
EMP: 4 **EST:** 2010
SALES (est): 472.3K **Privately Held**
WEB: www.markitmerchandise.com
SIC: 2395 Embroidery products, except schiffli machine

(G-6961)
MARSHALL RYERSON CO
7440 Lime Hollow Dr Se (49546-7437)
PHONE.................................616 299-1751
Marshall Ryerson, *President*
EMP: 10 **EST:** 2004
SALES (est): 489.8K **Privately Held**
SIC: 8742 3826 2851 2952 Marketing consulting services; instruments measuring thermal properties; polyurethane coatings; roofing felts, cements or coatings; waterproofing compounds; insulation, thermal

(G-6962)
MARTIN AND HATTIE RASCHE INC
Also Called: Valley City Plating Company
3353 Eastern Ave Se (49508-2404)
PHONE.................................616 245-1223
Jon Rasche, *President*
Jeff Rasche, *Vice Pres*
David Lammers, *Purchasing*
Frank Hapner, *QC Mgr*
John Soddy, *QC Mgr*
EMP: 65 **EST:** 1988
SQ FT: 75,000
SALES (est): 7.5MM **Privately Held**
WEB: www.valleycityplating.com
SIC: 3471 2514 Buffing for the trade; polishing, metals or formed products; plating of metals or formed products; metal household furniture

(G-6963)
MARY PALASZEK DR
1636 Leonard St Nw (49504-3950)
PHONE.................................616 453-2255
Mary Palaszek, *Principal*
EMP: 6 **EST:** 1995
SALES (est): 73K **Privately Held**
SIC: 3843 Enamels, dentists'

(G-6964)
MASS MOUNTAIN TECHNOLOGIES
3341 Ashton Rd Se (49546-2155)
PHONE.................................855 722-7900
Lisa Newell, *President*
Bryan Newell, *Finance Dir*
EMP: 6 **EST:** 1996
SALES (est): 591.5K **Privately Held**
WEB: www.massmountain.com
SIC: 3572 Computer storage devices

(G-6965)
MASTER FINISH CO
2100 Nelson Ave Se (49507-3355)
PHONE.................................877 590-5819
Dale Mulder, *President*
Douglas Roetman, *Vice Pres*
Gordon Lozic, *QC Mgr*
Matt Lomasney, *Engineer*
Steve Nanninga, *Sales Staff*
EMP: 150 **EST:** 1959
SALES (est): 13.5MM **Privately Held**
WEB: www.masterfinishco.com
SIC: 3471 Plating of metals or formed products; polishing, metals or formed products

(G-6966)
MATRIX MANUFACTURING INC
862 47th St Sw Ste B2 (49509-5141)
PHONE.................................616 532-6000
Jeffrey J Rodgers, *President*
Pam Rodgers, *CFO*
Ed Atanasoff, *Manager*
▲ **EMP:** 6 **EST:** 2001
SALES (est): 1MM **Privately Held**
WEB: www.matrixmanufacturing.net
SIC: 3089 Injection molding of plastics

(G-6967)
MATTSON TOOL & DIE CORP
4174 5 Mile Rd Ne (49525-9570)
PHONE.................................616 447-9012
EMP: 5 **EST:** 2013
SALES (est): 375.8K **Privately Held**
SIC: 3544 Mfg Dies/Tools/Jigs/Fixtures

(G-6968)
MAXAIR TRAMPOLINE
5161 Woodfield Ct Ne # 1 (49525-1027)
PHONE.................................616 929-0882
Christine Skeba, *Office Mgr*
EMP: 5 **EST:** 2017
SALES (est): 247.8K **Privately Held**
WEB: www.maxairtrampolines.com
SIC: 3949 Sporting & athletic goods

(G-6969)
MBWWPRODUCTS INC
825 Buchanan Ave Sw (49507-1004)
P.O. Box 501, Cannonsburg (49317-0501)
PHONE.................................616 464-1650
Michael D Petersen, *President*
EMP: 12 **EST:** 2008
SALES (est): 1MM **Privately Held**
SIC: 2499 Dishes, wood, carved & turned wood; decorative wood & woodwork; furniture inlays (veneers)

(G-6970)
MCCARTHY GROUP INCORPORATED (PA)
5505 52nd St Se (49512-9700)
PHONE.................................616 977-2900
John McCarthy, *President*
Derrick McCarthy, *Vice Pres*
Theressa Henderson, *Finance*
◆ **EMP:** 12 **EST:** 1980
SQ FT: 2,000
SALES (est): 1.1MM **Privately Held**
WEB: www.mccarthygrp.com
SIC: 2399 2843 4226 Automotive covers, except seat & tire covers; textile processing assistants; textile warehousing

(G-6971)
MCCLURE METALS GROUP INC
6161 28th St Se Ste 5 (49546-6931)
PHONE.................................616 957-5955
Steve McClure, *President*
Darren Nordquist, *Sales Staff*
Roger Schiefler, *Sales Staff*
▲ **EMP:** 4 **EST:** 1988 **Privately Held**
WEB: www.mccluremetals.com

SIC: 3315 Steel wire & related products

(G-6972)
MCCOY CRAFTSMAN LLC
1642 Broadway Ave Nw (49504-2046)
PHONE.................................616 634-7455
Jeffrey Bystry,
EMP: 12 **EST:** 2019
SALES (est): 738.7K **Privately Held**
WEB: www.mccoy-craftsman.business.site
SIC: 2431 Millwork

(G-6973)
MCGRAW HILL CO
3195 Wilson Dr Nw (49534-7565)
PHONE.................................616 802-3000
Leigh Brougher, *Sales Staff*
John Donneli, *Manager*
EMP: 7 **EST:** 2018
SALES (est): 33.3K **Privately Held**
SIC: 2731 Book publishing

(G-6974)
MDM ENTERPRISES INC
Also Called: Enamelite Industries
3829 Rger B Chffee Mem Dr (49548-3437)
PHONE.................................616 452-1591
Roger Rollman, *President*
Janet Miller, *QC Mgr*
EMP: 15 **EST:** 1967
SQ FT: 20,000
SALES (est): 2.5MM
SALES (corp-wide): 16MM **Privately Held**
WEB: www.enamelitefinishing.com
SIC: 3479 Coating of metals with plastic or resins
PA: Model Die & Mold, Inc.
3859 Roger B Chaffee Se
Grand Rapids MI
616 243-6996

(G-6975)
MEDBIO LLC (PA)
5346 36th St Se (49512-2014)
PHONE.................................616 245-0214
Christopher Williams, *President*
Ronald A Williams, *Chairman*
Rajesh Kothari, *Corp Secy*
Merri Jo Fey, *Production*
Ethan Bruyn, *Engineer*
▲ **EMP:** 70 **EST:** 2002
SQ FT: 65,000
SALES (est): 44.9MM **Privately Held**
WEB: www.medbioinc.com
SIC: 3089 Injection molding of plastics

(G-6976)
MEDTRONIC INC
620 Watson St Sw (49504-6340)
PHONE.................................616 643-5200
Fax: 616 643-1017
EMP: 8 **Publicly Held**
SIC: 3841 3845 3842 Mfg Surgical/Medical Instruments Mfg Electromedical Equipment Mfg Surgical Appliances/Supplies
HQ: Medtronic, Inc.
710 Medtronic Pkwy
Minneapolis MN 55432
763 514-4000

(G-6977)
METABOLIC SOLUTIONS DEV CO LLC
3133 Orchard Vista Dr Se (49546-7033)
PHONE.................................269 343-6732
Stephen C Benoit, *CEO*
Jerry Colca, *President*
Rolf Kletzien, *Senior VP*
Angeline Shashlo, *Vice Pres*
EMP: 22 **EST:** 2006
SALES (est): 1.1MM **Privately Held**
WEB: www.msdrx.com
SIC: 2833 8731 Medicinals & botanicals; biological research

(G-6978)
METAL COMPONENTS LLC (PA)
Also Called: M C
3281 Roger B (49548)
PHONE.................................616 252-1900
Craig Balow, *General Mgr*
▲ **EMP:** 80 **EST:** 1985
SQ FT: 85,000

(PA)=Parent Co (HQ)=Headquarters (DH)=Div Headquarters
✪ = New Business established in last 2 years

Grand Rapids - Kent County (G-6979)

SALES (est): 19.4MM **Privately Held**
WEB: www.metalcomp.us
SIC: **2522** 3444 Office furniture, except wood; metal housings, enclosures, casings & other containers

(G-6979)
METAL COMPONENTS LLC
3281 Rger B Chffee Mem Dr (49548-2321)
PHONE..................................616 252-1900
Todd Schreiber, *Branch Mgr*
EMP: 86
SALES (corp-wide): 19.4MM **Privately Held**
WEB: www.metalcomp.us
SIC: **3444** Sheet metalwork
PA: Metal Components, Llc
3281 Roger B
Grand Rapids MI 49548
616 252-1900

(G-6980)
METAL PLUS LLC
3711 Dykstra Dr Nw (49544-9745)
PHONE..................................616 459-7587
David Zimmer, *President*
Becky Pennell, *General Mgr*
Andy Papes, *Prdtn Mgr*
Seth Miller, *Manager*
EMP: 19 EST: 1999
SQ FT: 20,000
SALES (est): 2.4MM **Privately Held**
WEB: www.metalplusonline.com
SIC: **3444** Sheet metal specialties, not stamped

(G-6981)
METRO ENGRG OF GRND RAPIDS
845 Ottawa Ave Nw (49503-1429)
PHONE..................................616 458-2823
John Taylor, *President*
Todd Doyle, *Prgrmr*
EMP: 15 EST: 1992
SQ FT: 24,000
SALES (est): 1.2MM **Privately Held**
WEB: www.metroengineering.net
SIC: **3999** Models, general, except toy

(G-6982)
METRO GRAPHIC ARTS INC
900 40th St Se (49508-2401)
PHONE..................................616 245-2271
David Gaebel, *President*
William B Clifford, *Vice Pres*
Diane Gaebel, *Treasurer*
Linda Clifford, *Admin Sec*
EMP: 10 EST: 1945
SQ FT: 15,000
SALES (est): 120.6K **Privately Held**
WEB: www.metrographicarts.com
SIC: **2741** 5999 5199 Maps: publishing & printing; maps & charts; maps & charts

(G-6983)
METZGAR CONVEYOR CO
5801 Clay Ave Sw Ste A (49548-3033)
PHONE..................................616 784-0930
Patricia Metzgar, *Ch of Bd*
D Robert Metzgar, *President*
Russ Price, *General Mgr*
Jon Goeman, *Manager*
EMP: 40 EST: 1947
SALES (est): 6.2MM **Privately Held**
WEB: www.metzgarconveyors.com
SIC: **3535** 5084 3537 Conveyors & conveying equipment; industrial machinery & equipment; industrial trucks & tractors

(G-6984)
MEXAMERICA FOODS LLC
219 Canton St Sw Ste A (49507-1098)
PHONE..................................814 781-1447
Raymond Gunn, *CEO*
▲ EMP: 12 EST: 2010
SQ FT: 25,000
SALES (est): 511.3K **Privately Held**
SIC: **2099** 2096 5812 Tortillas, fresh or refrigerated; ready-to-eat meals, salads & sandwiches; potato chips & similar snacks; eating places

(G-6985)
MICHAEL E NIPKE LLC
51 Monroe Center St Nw # 201 (49503-2934)
PHONE..................................616 350-0200
Kristin Nipke, *Principal*
EMP: 4 EST: 2013
SALES (est): 77.5K **Privately Held**
SIC: **2211** Denims

(G-6986)
MICHCOR CONTAINER INC
1151 Sheldon Ave Se (49507-1135)
PHONE..................................616 452-7089
John Pettengill, *President*
Charity Dawson, *CFO*
Luann Shepardson, *Controller*
Robert Austin, *Sales Staff*
EMP: 27 EST: 1983
SQ FT: 40,000
SALES (est): 4.3MM **Privately Held**
WEB: www.michcor.com
SIC: **2653** Boxes, corrugated: made from purchased materials

(G-6987)
MICHIGAN COATING PRODUCTS INC
3761 Eastern Ave Se (49508-2412)
PHONE..................................616 456-8800
Tom Lilley, *President*
EMP: 9 EST: 1991
SQ FT: 15,000
SALES (est): 1.6MM **Privately Held**
WEB: www.michigancoatings.com
SIC: **2851** Paints & paint additives

(G-6988)
MICHIGAN ENVELOPE INC
6650 Clay Ave Sw (49548-7833)
PHONE..................................616 554-3404
Lloyd H De Vries, *President*
Phyllis De Vries, *Vice Pres*
EMP: 7 EST: 1987
SQ FT: 12,000
SALES (est): 840.9K **Privately Held**
SIC: **2677** Envelopes

(G-6989)
MICHIGAN FOAM PRODUCTS INC
1820 Chicago Dr Sw (49519-1209)
PHONE..................................616 452-9611
Jack Goodale, *President*
Scot Van Airsdale, *Sales Engr*
▲ EMP: 15 EST: 1972
SQ FT: 450,000
SALES (est): 3MM **Privately Held**
WEB: www.michiganfoam.com
SIC: **3086** 5199 Insulation or cushioning material, foamed plastic; packaging & shipping materials, foamed plastic; plastics foam

(G-6990)
MICHIGAN GENERAL GRINDING LLC
328 Winter Ave Nw (49504-5348)
PHONE..................................616 454-5089
Dan Huver,
EMP: 6 EST: 1965
SQ FT: 14,000
SALES (est): 813.1K **Privately Held**
WEB: www.michigangeneralgrinding.com
SIC: **3599** Grinding castings for the trade

(G-6991)
MICHIGAN INSTRUMENTS LLC
4717 Talon Ct Se (49512-5409)
PHONE..................................616 554-9696
Christopher Blanker, *Principal*
Matthew Maatman, *Prdtn Mgr*
Victor Frigo, *Sales Mgr*
EMP: 9 EST: 2017
SALES (est): 988.4K **Privately Held**
WEB: www.michiganinstruments.com
SIC: **3841** Surgical & medical instruments

(G-6992)
MICHIGAN LIGHTNING PROTECTION
2401 O Brien Rd Sw (49534-7009)
PHONE..................................866 712-4071
Terrence K Portfleet, *President*
EMP: 5 EST: 1936

SALES (est): 492.4K **Privately Held**
WEB: www.michiganlightning.com
SIC: **3648** Lighting equipment

(G-6993)
MICHIGAN PATTERN WORKS INC
872 Grandville Ave Sw (49503-5152)
PHONE..................................616 245-9259
Randy Toppel, *President*
Gary Rauser, *Treasurer*
Mary Kay Toppel, *Office Mgr*
EMP: 24 EST: 1945
SQ FT: 10,500
SALES (est): 2.4MM **Privately Held**
WEB: www.mipattern.com
SIC: **3543** Industrial patterns

(G-6994)
MICHIGAN TRKEY PRDCERS COOP IN (PA)
1100 Hall St Sw (49503-4861)
PHONE..................................616 245-2221
Dan Lennon, *President*
Teresa Vanloon, *Regional Mgr*
Brian Boerigter, *CFO*
Ed Harriman, *Manager*
EMP: 450 EST: 1998
SQ FT: 192,000
SALES (est): 81.5MM **Privately Held**
WEB: www.miturkey.com
SIC: **2015** Turkey processing & slaughtering

(G-6995)
MICHIGAN TURKEY PRODUCERS LLC
1100 Hall St (49501)
PHONE..................................616 243-4186
Stan McLean, *Principal*
Jeniffer Muniz, *Human Res Mgr*
Doreen Redder, *Supervisor*
EMP: 14 EST: 2015
SALES (est): 1.5MM **Privately Held**
WEB: www.miturkey.com
SIC: **2015** Poultry slaughtering & processing

(G-6996)
MICHIGAN WHEEL CORP
2685 Northridge Dr Nw E (49544-9111)
PHONE..................................616 647-1078
Chip Gerlach, *Principal*
EMP: 6 EST: 2010
SALES (est): 85K **Privately Held**
WEB: www.miwheel.com
SIC: **3312** Wheels

(G-6997)
MICHIGAN WHEEL OPERATIONS LLC (DH)
Also Called: Michigan Wheel Marine
1501 Buchanan Ave Sw (49507-1697)
PHONE..................................616 452-6941
Kenneth Creech, *CFO*
Susan Gray, *Cust Mgr*
Stan Heide, *Mng Member*
Nicholas Graham, *Supervisor*
◆ EMP: 65 EST: 2009
SQ FT: 157,480
SALES (est): 15.3MM **Privately Held**
WEB: www.miwheel.com
SIC: **3366** 3429 3599 Propellers; ship: cast brass; manufactured hardware (general); ties, form: metal

(G-6998)
MICHIGAN WIRE EDM SERVICES
1246 Scribner Ave Nw (49504-3230)
PHONE..................................616 742-0940
Khoa Tran, *President*
EMP: 9 EST: 2004
SALES (est): 662.2K **Privately Held**
WEB: www.michiganwiredm.com
SIC: **3599** Machine shop, jobbing & repair

(G-6999)
MICO INDUSTRIES INC (PA)
2929 32nd St Se Ste 8 (49512-1784)
PHONE..................................616 245-6426
Terence Sammon, *CEO*
Henry Visser, *President*
M Christina De La Garza, *Vice Pres*
EMP: 100
SQ FT: 50,000

SALES (est): 24.1MM **Privately Held**
WEB: www.micoindustries.com
SIC: **3469** 7692 3711 Stamping metal for the trade; automotive welding; automobile assembly, including specialty automobiles

(G-7000)
MICO INDUSTRIES INC
2725 Prairie St Sw (49519-2458)
PHONE..................................616 245-6426
Terence Sammon, *Manager*
Bryan Henderson, *Manager*
EMP: 10
SALES (corp-wide): 24.1MM **Privately Held**
WEB: www.micoindustries.com
SIC: **3469** Stamping metal for the trade
PA: Mico Industries, Inc.
2929 32nd St Se Ste 8
Grand Rapids MI 49512
616 245-6426

(G-7001)
MICO INDUSTRIES INC
219 Canton St Sw Ste B (49507-1098)
PHONE..................................616 514-1143
EMP: 50
SALES (corp-wide): 32.7MM **Privately Held**
SIC: **3469** Metal Stampings, Nec, Nsk
PA: Mico Industries, Inc.
2929 32nd St Se
Grand Rapids MI 49512
616 245-6426

(G-7002)
MICRON MFG COMPANY
1722 Kloet St Nw (49504-1421)
P.O. Box 141667 (49514-1667)
PHONE..................................616 453-5486
Michael Preston, *President*
Jaqueline Preston, *Treasurer*
Jim Wila, *Sales Staff*
Katie Preston, *Office Mgr*
Brian Hoff, *Manager*
EMP: 47 EST: 1952
SQ FT: 30,000
SALES (est): 7.1MM **Privately Held**
WEB: www.systemicron.com
SIC: **3599** Machine shop, jobbing & repair

(G-7003)
MID MICHIGAN PIPE INC
977 Ada Place Dr Se Ste A (49546-8412)
P.O. Box 123, Mount Pleasant (48804-0123)
PHONE..................................989 772-5664
Doug Darnell, *President*
Donald Campbell, *Vice Pres*
EMP: 7 EST: 1991
SQ FT: 6,000
SALES (est): 994.5K **Privately Held**
WEB: www.mid-michiganpipe.com
SIC: **1623** 5051 3544 3441 Pipeline construction; pipe & tubing, steel; special dies & tools; fabricated structural metal; excavation work; snowplowing

(G-7004)
MIDDLETON PRINTING INC
Also Called: Campaign-Stickers.com
200 32nd St Se Ste A (49548-2269)
PHONE..................................616 247-8742
Steven Middleton, *President*
Blake Middleton, *Opers Mgr*
Troy Wymer, *Graphic Designe*
EMP: 7 EST: 1956
SQ FT: 14,000
SALES (est): 1.1MM **Privately Held**
WEB: www.gomiddleton.com
SIC: **2759** 2679 Flexographic printing; letterpress printing; tags & labels, paper

(G-7005)
MIDWEST PLATING COMPANY INC
613 North Ave Ne (49503-1695)
PHONE..................................616 451-2007
Brian L Wortman, *President*
Beth McCullough, *Corp Secy*
Doug Wortman, *Vice Pres*
Garry Wortman, *VP Opers*
Thomas Wortman, *VP Prdtn*
EMP: 20 EST: 1945
SQ FT: 35,000

GEOGRAPHIC SECTION
Grand Rapids - Kent County (G-7034)

SALES (est): 1.3MM Privately Held
WEB: www.midwest-plating.com
SIC: 3471 Electroplating of metals or formed products

(G-7006)
MIDWEST SAFETY PRODUCTS INC
4929 East Paris Ave Se (49512-5351)
PHONE.................................616 554-5155
Banah Miller, *President*
Kurt Solomon, *Vice Pres*
Theresa Wheeler, *Purchasing*
Jerry Vongphasouk, *Sales Staff*
Deborah Bump, *Manager*
EMP: 25 EST: 1984
SQ FT: 40,000
SALES (est): 8.8MM Privately Held
WEB: www.midwestsafety.com
SIC: 5099 3993 Safety equipment & supplies; signs & advertising specialties

(G-7007)
MIDWEST SEATING SOLUTIONS INC
2234 Burning Tree Dr Se (49546-5513)
P.O. Box 6159 (49516-6159)
PHONE.................................616 222-0636
EMP: 10
SALES (est): 1MM Privately Held
SIC: 2531 Mfg Public Building Furniture

(G-7008)
MIEN COMPANY INC
2547 3 Mile Rd Nw Ste F (49534-1358)
PHONE.................................616 818-1970
Johan Bergsma, *President*
Jacob Vanderlaan, *Principal*
Jason Deweerd, *Vice Pres*
Erin Bronkella, *Opers Staff*
Lacey Steward, *Sales Staff*
◆ EMP: 13 EST: 2012
SALES (est): 3.9MM Privately Held
WEB: www.miencompany.com
SIC: 2511 Wood household furniture

(G-7009)
MII DISPOSITION INC
4717 Talon Ct Se (49512-5408)
PHONE.................................616 554-9696
Joseph Baldwin, *President*
Vic Frigo, *Sales Mgr*
Eric Hadesh, *Executive*
Angie Kulesza, *Admin Sec*
EMP: 20 EST: 1964
SQ FT: 20,000
SALES (est): 2.9MM Privately Held
SIC: 3845 3842 Electromedical equipment; surgical appliances & supplies

(G-7010)
MILL STEEL CO (PA)
Also Called: Steel Plus Solutions
2905 Lucerne Dr Se # 100 (49546-7160)
PHONE.................................616 949-6700
Pam Heglund, *President*
Chase Canning, *President*
William Buck, *Vice Chairman*
Joe Poot, *Senior VP*
Wil Bertot, *Plant Supt*
EMP: 60 EST: 1959
SALES (est): 175.4MM Privately Held
WEB: www.millsteel.com
SIC: 5051 3312 Ferrous metals; blast furnaces & steel mills

(G-7011)
MILLERKNOLL INC
2915 Stonewood St Nw (49504-8003)
PHONE.................................616 453-5995
Ross Vanderklok, *Branch Mgr*
EMP: 5
SALES (corp-wide): 2.4B Publicly Held
WEB: www.hermanmiller.com
SIC: 3429 Furniture hardware
PA: Millerknoll, Inc.
    855 E Main Ave
    Zeeland MI 49464
    616 654-3000

(G-7012)
MILLERKNOLL INC
5460 44th St Se (49512-4093)
PHONE.................................616 949-3660
John Londo, *Technician*
EMP: 7

SALES (corp-wide): 2.4B Publicly Held
WEB: www.hermanmiller.com
SIC: 2521 Wood office furniture
PA: Millerknoll, Inc.
    855 E Main Ave
    Zeeland MI 49464
    616 654-3000

(G-7013)
MITTEN MADE WOODCRAFTS LLC
3215 Lake Michigan Dr Nw (49534-5862)
PHONE.................................616 430-2762
Renee Kennedy, *Principal*
EMP: 4 EST: 2015
SALES (est): 88.3K Privately Held
SIC: 2499 Wood products

(G-7014)
MITTLER SUPPLY
1000 Scribner Ave Nw (49504-4212)
PHONE.................................616 451-3055
Steve Luter, *President*
EMP: 4 EST: 2017
SALES (est): 119.3K Privately Held
SIC: 3599 Industrial machinery

(G-7015)
MIYACHI UNITEK CORP
1382 Glen Ellyn Dr Se (49546-3887)
PHONE.................................616 676-2634
EMP: 5 EST: 2012
SALES (est): 70.4K Privately Held
WEB: www.amadaweldtech.com
SIC: 3548 Welding apparatus

(G-7016)
MOBILE OFFICE VEHICLE INC
Also Called: Go Office.com
4053 Brockton Dr Se Ste A (49512-4071)
PHONE.................................616 971-0080
Charles E Lippert, *President*
◆ EMP: 4
SQ FT: 10,000
SALES (est): 57.5K Privately Held
SIC: 2522 Office furniture, except wood

(G-7017)
MOD SIGNS INC
Also Called: Postema Signs & Graphics
7475 Division Ave S (49548-7137)
PHONE.................................616 455-0260
Olga Dubois, *President*
EMP: 11 EST: 2018
SALES (est): 771.1K Privately Held
WEB: www.postemasign.com
SIC: 3993 Signs & advertising specialties

(G-7018)
MODERN ENGRG SOLUTIONS LLC
4985 52nd St Se (49512-9731)
PHONE.................................616 835-2711
Charles Huizinga,
EMP: 5 EST: 2020
SALES (est): 487.8K Privately Held
SIC: 3441 Fabricated structural metal

(G-7019)
MOELLER MFG COMPANY LLC
Also Called: Moeller Manufacturing Co
3757 Broadmoor Ave Se (49512-3908)
PHONE.................................616 285-5012
Kevin Atkinson, *President*
EMP: 4
SALES (corp-wide): 1B Privately Held
WEB: www.moelleraircraft.com
SIC: 3599 Machine shop, jobbing & repair
HQ: Moeller Mfg. Company, Llc
    30100 Beck Rd
    Wixom MI 48393
    248 960-3999

(G-7020)
MOL BELTING SYSTEMS INC
Also Called: Mol Belting Company
2532 Waldorf Ct Nw (49544-1478)
P.O. Box 141095 (49514-1095)
PHONE.................................616 453-2484
Edward Mol, *President*
David Hathaway, *Vice Pres*
Dan Mol, *Vice Pres*
Tim Jousma, *Engineer*
Jim Anderson, *Sales Staff*
◆ EMP: 75 EST: 1986

SQ FT: 52,000
SALES (est): 15.3MM Privately Held
WEB: www.molbelting.com
SIC: 3052 3535 3446 Rubber belting; conveyors & conveying equipment; architectural metalwork

(G-7021)
MOLD TOOLING SYSTEMS INC
4315 3 Mile Rd Nw (49534-1136)
PHONE.................................616 735-6653
Daniel Jay Vanenk, *President*
Jeff Momber, *General Mgr*
Drew Boersma, *Vice Pres*
EMP: 10 EST: 1995
SALES (est): 1.4MM Privately Held
WEB: www.toolingsystemsgroup.com
SIC: 3544 Special dies & tools

(G-7022)
MOLLERS NORTH AMERICA INC
5215 52nd St Se (49512-9702)
P.O. Box 888820 (49588-8820)
PHONE.................................616 942-6504
Thomas Wagner, *Exec VP*
Tom Wagner, *Exec VP*
Peter Engelhardt, *Admin Sec*
▲ EMP: 65 EST: 1978
SQ FT: 100,000
SALES (est): 14.3MM
SALES (corp-wide): 355.8K Privately Held
WEB: www.mollersna.com
SIC: 3537 7389 Palletizers & depalletizers; packaging & labeling services
PA: Birkenfeld Holding Gmbh
    Sudhoferweg 93
    Beckum
    252 188-0

(G-7023)
MONARCH METAL MFG INC
3303 Union Ave Se (49548-2311)
PHONE.................................616 247-0412
Gordon Sironen, *President*
Jane Sironen, *Vice Pres*
EMP: 6 EST: 1987
SQ FT: 5,500
SALES (est): 599.4K Privately Held
WEB: www.sheet-metal-contractors.cmac.ws
SIC: 3444 Sheet metalwork

(G-7024)
MONDRELLA PROCESS SYSTEMS LLC
2049 Innwood Dr Se (49508-5078)
PHONE.................................616 281-9836
Michael J Mondrella, *Administration*
EMP: 6 EST: 2000
SALES (est): 219.8K Privately Held
WEB: www.mondrellaprocess.com
SIC: 3535 Conveyors & conveying equipment

(G-7025)
MONROE LLC
4490 44th St Se Ste A (49512-4064)
PHONE.................................616 942-9820
Chad Vanhaun, *Engineer*
Adam Nixon, *Controller*
Michael Plont, *Human Res Mgr*
Chris Blanker,
Dee Levalley,
EMP: 285 EST: 2006
SALES (est): 44.1MM Privately Held
WEB: www.lakelandmonroe.com
SIC: 3089 3542 3544 Molding primary plastic; machine tools, metal forming type; special dies, tools, jigs & fixtures

(G-7026)
MONROE INC
4490 44th St Se Ste A (49512-4064)
PHONE.................................616 284-3358
Evan Lavigne, *QC Mgr*
Ted Maier, *Supervisor*
EMP: 7 EST: 2015
SALES (est): 129.5K Privately Held
WEB: www.lakelandmonroe.com
SIC: 3089 Injection molding of plastics

(G-7027)
MOONLIGHT GRAPHICS INC
3144 Broadmoor Ave Se (49512-1845)
PHONE.................................616 243-3166
Paul J Block, *President*
Micah Block, *Sales Staff*
Brian Vigna, *Director*
EMP: 6 EST: 1989
SQ FT: 3,500
SALES (est): 822.5K Privately Held
WEB: www.moonlight-graphics.com
SIC: 2752 Commercial printing, offset

(G-7028)
MOORECO INC
Also Called: Vanerum Stelter
549 Ionia Ave Sw (49503-5138)
PHONE.................................616 451-7800
EMP: 25 Privately Held
SIC: 2521 2522 5021 Manufactures Wood Office Furniture Office Furniture-Nonwood Wholesales Furniture
HQ: Mooreco, Inc.
    2885 Lorraine Ave
    Temple TX 76501

(G-7029)
MORTON INDUSTRIES LLC
1125 Covell Ave Nw (49504-3815)
PHONE.................................616 453-7121
Raymond Watkoski, *Principal*
EMP: 14 EST: 2010
SALES (est): 148.8K Privately Held
WEB: www.mortonind.com
SIC: 3999 Manufacturing industries

(G-7030)
MOSS AUDIO CORPORATION
Also Called: Moss Telecommunications Svcs
561 Century Ave Sw (49503-4903)
PHONE.................................616 451-9933
Jerry Schaefer, *CEO*
Gerard J Schaefer, *President*
Ethan Brown, *Project Mgr*
Jeff Schaefer, *Opers Mgr*
Bob Kelley, *Opers Staff*
EMP: 65 EST: 1977
SQ FT: 16,000
SALES (est): 15.4MM Privately Held
WEB: www.mosstele.com
SIC: 3651 Speaker systems

(G-7031)
MPD WELDING - GRAND RAPIDS INC
Also Called: Fire-Kote
1903 Clyde Park Ave Sw (49509-1592)
P.O. Box 9341 (49509-0341)
PHONE.................................616 248-9353
David Sinquefield, *President*
Ryan A Stambaugh, *Corp Secy*
EMP: 29 EST: 1985
SQ FT: 30,000
SALES (est): 2.8MM Privately Held
WEB: www.mpdwelding.com
SIC: 7692 3398 Welding repair; metal heat treating

(G-7032)
MULTI TECH PRECISION INC
3403 Lousma Dr Se (49548-2265)
PHONE.................................616 514-1415
Steve Steketee, *President*
EMP: 5 EST: 1992
SQ FT: 15,000
SALES (est): 460.9K Privately Held
SIC: 3599 Machine shop, jobbing & repair

(G-7033)
MY ELECTRICIAN GRAND RAPIDS
19 Jordan St Sw (49548-3124)
PHONE.................................616 208-4113
EMP: 5 EST: 2020
SALES (est): 239.7K Privately Held
WEB: www.myelectriciangrandrapids.com
SIC: 3825 Instruments to measure electricity

(G-7034)
N-K MANUFACTURING TECH LLC (PA)
1134 Freeman Ave Sw (49503-4816)
PHONE.................................616 248-3200
Rachel Miles-Williams, *Purchasing*

Saumil Joshi, *Project Engr*
Bonnie Kettner, *Controller*
Ann Kassouni, *Human Res Mgr*
Jacob Kassouni, *Sales Engr*
▲ **EMP:** 37 **EST:** 1995
SQ FT: 75,000
SALES (est): 8.4MM **Privately Held**
WEB: www.nkmfgtech.com
SIC: 3089 Injection molding of plastics

(G-7035)
N-K SEALING TECHNOLOGIES LLC (PA)
Also Called: Caldwell Gasket Company
1134 Freeman Ave Sw (49503-4816)
PHONE................................616 248-3200
Bonnie Kettner, *Comptroller*
Haig Kassouni,
Armen Kassouni,
EMP: 7 **EST:** 2016
SQ FT: 15,000
SALES (est): 939.8K **Privately Held**
WEB: www.nkmfgtech.com
SIC: 3053 Gaskets & sealing devices

(G-7036)
NATIONAL NAIL CORP (PA)
Also Called: West Michigan Nail & Wire Co
2964 Clydon Ave Sw (49519-2497)
PHONE................................616 538-8000
Roger Bruins, *Ch of Bd*
Scott Baker, *President*
Chip Manger, *President*
Richard Bilton, *General Mgr*
Chris Baker, *Vice Pres*
◆ **EMP:** 150 **EST:** 1967
SQ FT: 130,000
SALES (est): 52.3MM **Privately Held**
WEB: www.nationalnail.com
SIC: 3315 3442 Nails, steel: wire or cut; storm doors or windows, metal

(G-7037)
NB MEDIA SOLUTIONS LLC
6907 Cascade Rd Se (49546-7360)
PHONE................................616 724-7175
Nicholas Noe, *President*
EMP: 7 **EST:** 2010
SALES (est): 511K **Privately Held**
WEB: www.nbmsllc.com
SIC: 8742 7389 7374 4813 Marketing consulting services; ; computer graphics service; ; ;

(G-7038)
NELSONITE CHEMICAL PDTS INC
2320 Oak Industrial Dr Ne (49505-6018)
PHONE................................616 456-7098
Daniel Conway, *President*
Linda Conway, *Vice Pres*
EMP: 4
SQ FT: 8,000
SALES (est): 1.1MM **Privately Held**
WEB: www.nelsonite.com
SIC: 2819 2899 Chemicals, high purity: refined from technical grade; chemical preparations
PA: Conway-Cleveland Corp
 2320 Oak Industrial Dr Ne
 Grand Rapids MI 49505
 616 458-0056

(G-7039)
NEPTUNE CHEMICAL PUMP COMPANY (HQ)
Also Called: Neptune Mixer
1809 Century Ave Sw (49503-8017)
PHONE................................215 699-8700
Michael Dowse, *CEO*
Sivasankaran Somasundaram, *President*
William Barton, *Corp Secy*
John Allen, *Vice Pres*
▲ **EMP:** 128 **EST:** 1961
SALES (est): 20.7MM
SALES (corp-wide): 6.6B **Publicly Held**
WEB: www.psgdover.com
SIC: 3561 3586 Industrial pumps & parts; measuring & dispensing pumps
PA: Dover Corporation
 3005 Highland Pkwy # 200
 Downers Grove IL 60515
 630 541-1540

(G-7040)
NEW 9 INC
Also Called: G W I Engineering Division
1411 Michigan St Ne (49503-2005)
PHONE................................616 459-8274
Peter Cordes, *President*
Mark Blanding, *Vice Pres*
Christopher Cordes, *Vice Pres*
Jerry Coeling, *Chief Engr*
Bruce Gilbert, *Engineer*
EMP: 50 **EST:** 1955
SQ FT: 47,000
SALES (est): 11.5MM **Privately Held**
WEB: www.gwiengineering.com
SIC: 3569 Firefighting apparatus & related equipment

(G-7041)
NEW CLASSICS PRESS LLC
2400 Ridgecroft Ave Se (49546-8036)
PHONE................................616 975-9070
Mark Rizik, *Owner*
EMP: 4 **EST:** 2017
SALES (est): 61.1K **Privately Held**
SIC: 2741 Miscellaneous publishing

(G-7042)
NEW HOLLAND BREWERY
427 Bridge St Nw (49504-5305)
PHONE................................616 202-7200
Joel Petersen, *Vice Pres*
EMP: 11 **EST:** 2016
SALES (est): 411.9K **Privately Held**
WEB: www.newhollandbrew.com
SIC: 2082 Malt beverages

(G-7043)
NEXT CHAPTER MFG CORP
4221 Edinburgh Dr Se (49546-8310)
PHONE................................616 773-1200
Jason Murphy, *Principal*
EMP: 7 **EST:** 2017
SALES (est): 340.3K **Privately Held**
WEB: www.nxcmfg.com
SIC: 3999 Manufacturing industries

(G-7044)
NN INC
4180 40th St Se (49512-4122)
PHONE................................269 591-6951
EMP: 27 **EST:** 2018
SALES (est): 6.3MM **Privately Held**
WEB: www.nninc.com
SIC: 3542 Machine tools, metal forming type

(G-7045)
NOBLE POLYMERS LLC
4855 37th St Se (49512-4068)
P.O. Box 888405 (49588-8405)
PHONE................................616 975-4800
Frederick P Keller,
EMP: 17 **EST:** 1997
SALES (est): 3MM
SALES (corp-wide): 432.2MM **Privately Held**
WEB: www.noblepolymers.com
SIC: 3089 Automotive parts, plastic
PA: Cascade Engineering, Inc.
 3400 Innovation Ct Se
 Grand Rapids MI 49512
 616 975-4800

(G-7046)
NORDIC PRODUCTS INC
Also Called: NORDIC HOT TUBS
4655 Patterson Ave Se B (49512-5237)
PHONE................................616 940-4036
Maurizio Vozza, *CEO*
Andrew Krause, *President*
Todd Gibson, *COO*
Barbara Sisung, *Exec VP*
Tom Kribs, *CFO*
▼ **EMP:** 115 **EST:** 1995
SQ FT: 85,000
SALES (est): 19.6MM **Privately Held**
WEB: www.nordichottubs.com
SIC: 3088 Plastics plumbing fixtures

(G-7047)
NORTEK INC
2547 3 Mile Rd Nw Ste A (49534-1358)
PHONE................................616 719-5588
EMP: 4
SALES (corp-wide): 11.6B **Privately Held**
WEB: www.nortek.com
SIC: 3585 Refrigeration & heating equipment
HQ: Nortek, Inc.
 8000 Phoenix Pkwy
 O Fallon MO 63368

(G-7048)
NORTH AMER FUEL SYSTEMS RMNFCT
4232 Brockton Dr Se (49512-4048)
PHONE................................616 541-1100
Beth Adelsperger, *Materials Mgr*
Bill Reedy, *Engineer*
Stephen Rose, *IT/INT Sup*
Jeff Lecklich,
Laurina McCabe, *Executive Asst*
EMP: 140 **EST:** 1998
SQ FT: 52,000
SALES (est): 23.3MM
SALES (corp-wide): 182.4B **Privately Held**
WEB: www.nafsreman.com
SIC: 3714 Motor vehicle parts & accessories
HQ: Detroit Diesel Corporation
 13400 W Outer Dr
 Detroit MI 48239
 313 592-5000

(G-7049)
NORTHWEST METAL PRODUCTS INC
Also Called: Transet
2055 Walker Ct Nw (49544-1411)
PHONE................................616 453-0556
Mark Scholten, *President*
EMP: 10 **EST:** 1980
SQ FT: 12,500
SALES (est): 1.5MM **Privately Held**
WEB: www.northwestmetalproducts.com
SIC: 3429 Furniture hardware

(G-7050)
NOTIONS MARKETING INTL CORP
517 Crofton St Se (49507-1862)
PHONE................................616 243-8424
Steve Pietentol, *President*
Eric Meister, *Vice Pres*
Tom Nakfoor, *Vice Pres*
Melissa Saganski, *Buyer*
Gina Greenlee, *Sales Staff*
EMP: 500 **EST:** 2011
SALES (est): 43.4MM **Privately Held**
SIC: 2284 Hand knitting thread

(G-7051)
NOVARES US LLC
Also Called: Key Plastics
5375 Intl Pkwy Se (49512)
PHONE................................616 554-3555
Jackie Wesche, *Human Res Mgr*
John Choponis, *Maintence Staff*
EMP: 5
SALES (corp-wide): 113.4MM **Privately Held**
WEB: www.novaresteam.com
SIC: 3089 3714 3085 Injection molded finished plastic products; motor vehicle parts & accessories; plastics bottles
HQ: Novares Us Llc
 19575 Victor Pkwy Ste 400
 Livonia MI 48152
 248 449-6100

(G-7052)
NUWAVE TECHNOLOGY PARTNERS LLC
4079 Park East Ct Se B (49546-8815)
PHONE................................616 942-7520
Kyle Paalman, *Owner*
EMP: 16 **Privately Held**
WEB: www.nuwavepartners.com
SIC: 3661 7371 Telephone & telegraph apparatus; custom computer programming services
PA: Nuwave Technology Partners, Llc
 5268 Azo Dr
 Kalamazoo MI 49048

(G-7053)
NUWAY TOOL
3365 36th St Se (49512-2809)
PHONE................................616 452-4366
Bob Hannah, *Manager*
EMP: 6 **EST:** 1997
SALES (est): 64.7K **Privately Held**
SIC: 3599 Machine shop, jobbing & repair

(G-7054)
OBRIEN HARRIS WOODWORKS LLC
1125 41st St Se Ste A (49508-3666)
PHONE................................616 248-0779
Stephen Chausow, *Mng Member*
EMP: 25 **EST:** 2015
SQ FT: 33,000
SALES (est): 1.1MM **Privately Held**
SIC: 2434 Wood kitchen cabinets

(G-7055)
OH SO CHEESY LLC
435 Ionia Ave Sw (49503-5161)
PHONE................................616 835-1249
Mathias Schmitt, *CEO*
Blair Schwarz, *COO*
EMP: 5 **EST:** 2018
SALES (est): 120K **Privately Held**
SIC: 2022 Spreads, cheese

(G-7056)
OKTOBER LLC
5 Colfax St Ne (49505-4908)
PHONE................................231 750-1998
Joshua Van Den Heuvel, *Mng Member*
Dennis Grumm,
Clint Leatrea,
▼ **EMP:** 9 **EST:** 2016
SQ FT: 3,500
SALES (est): 1MM **Privately Held**
WEB: www.oktoberdesign.com
SIC: 3411 Aluminum cans

(G-7057)
OLIVER HEALTHCARE PACKAGING CO (HQ)
445 6th St Nw (49504-5253)
PHONE................................616 456-7711
Mike Benevento, *President*
Aldin Velic, *General Mgr*
Gregg Metcalf, *Regional Mgr*
Ken Pouliot, *Regional Mgr*
Temple Phipps, *Business Mgr*
EMP: 128 **EST:** 1890
SALES (est): 169.8MM
SALES (corp-wide): 1.8B **Privately Held**
WEB: www.oliverhcp.com
SIC: 5084 5199 3053 Processing & packaging equipment; packaging materials; packing materials
PA: Berwind Corporation
 2929 Walnut St Ste 900
 Philadelphia PA 19104
 215 563-2800

(G-7058)
OMEGA INDUSTRIES MICHIGAN LLC
3744 Linden Ave Se (49548-3428)
P.O. Box 818, Rockford (49341-0818)
PHONE................................616 460-0500
Lori Maher,
Jeff Twyman,
EMP: 6 **EST:** 2002
SALES (est): 1MM **Privately Held**
WEB: www.omegaindustriesmi.com
SIC: 5085 3559 5075 Filters, industrial; metal finishing equipment for plating, etc.; air filters

(G-7059)
ONE BEER AT A TIME LLC
Also Called: Brewery Vivant
925 Cherry St Se Ste 1-2 (49506-1403)
PHONE................................616 719-1604
Marco Ruiz, *General Mgr*
Chris Stoffel, *General Mgr*
Jonathan Ward, *Vice Pres*
Jason Spaulding, *Mng Member*
EMP: 45 **EST:** 2008
SQ FT: 9,000
SALES (est): 5.5MM **Privately Held**
WEB: www.breweryvivant.com
SIC: 5921 2082 Beer (packaged); brewers' grain

GEOGRAPHIC SECTION   Grand Rapids - Kent County (G-7085)

(G-7060)
ONION CROCK OF MICHIGAN INC
1221 Mcreynolds Ave Nw (49504-3116)
PHONE..............................616 458-2922
Eugene Lacroix, *President*
EMP: 4 EST: 1991
SALES (est): 250K **Privately Held**
WEB: www.onioncrock.com
SIC: 2032 2099 Soups & broths: canned, jarred, etc.; sauces: gravy, dressing & dip mixes

(G-7061)
OPERATOR SPECIALTY COMPANY INC
Also Called: Osco
2547 3 Mile Rd Nw (49534-1358)
PHONE..............................616 675-5050
William Hildebrand, *President*
▲ EMP: 54 EST: 1975
SQ FT: 25,000
SALES (est): 13.2MM **Privately Held**
WEB: www.nortekcontrol.com
SIC: 3699 Door opening & closing devices, electrical
HQ: Nortek Security & Control Llc
    5919 Sea Otter Pl Ste 100
    Carlsbad CA 92010
    760 438-7000

(G-7062)
ORANGEBOX US INC
4595 Broadmoor Ave Se # 120 (49512-5393)
PHONE..............................616 988-8624
Remo Vernaschi, *Principal*
Kayleigh Bower, *Admin Asst*
EMP: 3 EST: 2014
SALES (est): 3.3MM
SALES (corp-wide): 2.6B **Publicly Held**
WEB: www.orangebox.com
SIC: 2599 Boards: planning, display, notice
HQ: Orangebox Group Limited
    Heol Y Gamlas Parc Nantgarw
    Cardiff S GLAM CF15
    144 381-6604

(G-7063)
ORTHOPAEDIC ASSOCIATES MICH (PA)
Also Called: Orthopaedic Associates Mich
4665 44th St Se Ste A190 (49512-4135)
PHONE..............................616 459-7101
Patrick Reid, *CEO*
Paul Schutt, *Principal*
Chris Lafave, *COO*
Nick Malec, *Buyer*
Corey Herr, *Senior Engr*
EMP: 78 EST: 1949
SQ FT: 19,000
SALES (est): 25.1MM **Privately Held**
WEB: www.oamichigan.com
SIC: 8011 3842 Orthopedic physician; surgeon; surgical appliances & supplies

(G-7064)
OTTAWA TOOL & MACHINE LLC
2188 Leonard St Nw (49534-9514)
PHONE..............................616 677-1743
Charles Chambers,
EMP: 4 EST: 2009
SALES (est): 15K **Privately Held**
SIC: 3499 Fabricated metal products

(G-7065)
PAC-CNC INC
4045 Remembrance Rd Nw (49534-1109)
PHONE..............................616 288-3389
Roger Hoogewind, *President*
Randy Hoogewind, *Business Mgr*
Ross Kooienga, *Facilities Mgr*
Dj Degraaf, *Sales Staff*
EMP: 34
SQ FT: 15,000
SALES: 5.1MM **Privately Held**
WEB: www.paccnc.com
SIC: 3469 Stamping metal for the trade

(G-7066)
PACIFIC EPOXY POLYMERS INC
3450 Charlevoix Dr Se (49546-7054)
PHONE..............................616 949-1634
Charles E Bennett, *President*
Micky Burnham, *General Mgr*

Gholi Darehshori, *Shareholder*
EMP: 9 EST: 1993
SQ FT: 45,000
SALES (est): 545.9K **Privately Held**
SIC: 2821 2851 Epoxy resins; paints & allied products

(G-7067)
PADNOS LEITELT INC
Also Called: Leitelt Iron Works
2301 Turner Ave Nw (49544-2002)
PHONE..............................616 363-3817
Douglas Kesler, *Principal*
Francis Abrahams, *Vice Pres*
Joe Brechting, *Vice Pres*
Eda Lynn Sandstorm, *Manager*
EMP: 87 EST: 1862
SQ FT: 90,000
SALES (est): 2.9MM
SALES (corp-wide): 520.8MM **Privately Held**
WEB: www.padnos.com
SIC: 7699 3599 5051 Industrial machinery & equipment repair; machine shop, jobbing & repair; steel
PA: Louis Padnos Iron And Metal Company
    185 W 8th St
    Holland MI 49423
    800 442-3509

(G-7068)
PALADIN IND INC
4990 W Greenbrooke Dr Se (49512-5400)
PHONE..............................616 698-7495
Larry E Bell, *CEO*
Craig C Bell, *President*
Thad Bell, *Vice Pres*
Jeff Bouwens, *Project Mgr*
Barbara Bell, *Admin Mgr*
EMP: 30 EST: 1985
SQ FT: 54,000
SALES (est): 4.5MM **Privately Held**
WEB: www.paladinind.com
SIC: 2599 2521 Factory furniture & fixtures; wood office furniture

(G-7069)
PAPER AND PRINT USA LLC
3400 Raleigh Dr Se (49512-2042)
PHONE..............................616 940-8311
EMP: 7 EST: 2011
SALES (est): 264.6K **Privately Held**
SIC: 2752 Commercial printing, lithographic

(G-7070)
PARAGON DIE & ENGINEERING CO (PA)
Also Called: Paragon D&E
5225 33rd St Se (49512-2071)
PHONE..............................616 949-2220
Dave Muir, *CEO*
Charlie Frederick, *Vice Pres*
Dave Van Rooyen, *Vice Pres*
Chad Burger, *Project Mgr*
Patricia Cisler, *Purchasing*
▲ EMP: 187 EST: 1954
SQ FT: 180,000
SALES (est): 47.2MM **Privately Held**
WEB: www.paragonde.com
SIC: 3544 Special dies & tools

(G-7071)
PARKER TOOLING & DESIGN INC
Also Called: Vacuum Farm Tools
2563 3 Mile Rd Nw (49534-1313)
PHONE..............................616 791-1080
John Ervine, *President*
EMP: 15 EST: 1985
SQ FT: 10,000
SALES (est): 2.1MM **Privately Held**
WEB: www.parkertooling.net
SIC: 7692 3544 3543 Welding repair; special dies, tools, jigs & fixtures; industrial patterns

(G-7072)
PATRIOT SOLUTIONS LLC
5575 Kraft Ave Se Ste 100 (49512-9653)
PHONE..............................616 240-8164
Chad Boersma, *President*
Jon Tellier, *Vice Pres*
EMP: 4 EST: 2008

SALES (est): 286.2K **Privately Held**
WEB: www.patriotsol.com
SIC: 2653 Boxes, corrugated: made from purchased materials

(G-7073)
PAW PRINT GARDENS
601 Kinney Ave Nw (49534-4512)
PHONE..............................616 791-4758
James Dubridge, *Principal*
EMP: 5 EST: 2010
SALES (est): 100.9K **Privately Held**
SIC: 2752 Commercial printing, lithographic

(G-7074)
PAZZEL INC
100 Stevens St Sw (49507-1526)
PHONE..............................616 291-0257
Aaron Vandergalien, *President*
Joshua Conran, *Admin Sec*
EMP: 9 EST: 2007
SQ FT: 7,000
SALES (est): 850K **Privately Held**
WEB: www.pazzel.com
SIC: 2434 2521 2517 Wood kitchen cabinets; cabinets, office: wood; wood television & radio cabinets

(G-7075)
PENINSLAR OIL GAS CMPNY-MCHGAN
3196 Kraft Ave Se Ste 305 (49512-2065)
PHONE..............................616 676-2090
Gary McAleenan, *Partner*
EMP: 5 EST: 1959
SALES (est): 351.6K **Privately Held**
SIC: 1382 1389 Oil & gas exploration services; oil field services

(G-7076)
PENINSULAR TECHNOLOGIES LLC
3196 Kraft Ave Se Ste 305 (49512-2065)
P.O. Box 728, Ada (49301-0728)
PHONE..............................616 676-9811
Kevin Paul, *Vice Pres*
Laurie Hans, *Manager*
Jamie Taggart, *CTO*
Gary F McAleenan,
EMP: 21 EST: 1998
SALES (est): 821.5K **Privately Held**
WEB: www.pent.com
SIC: 7372 Prepackaged software

(G-7077)
PEPSI-COLA METRO BTLG CO INC
3700 Kraft Ave Se (49512-0704)
PHONE..............................616 285-8200
Will Warren, *Manager*
Sarah Heiner, *Manager*
EMP: 6
SALES (corp-wide): 70.3B **Publicly Held**
WEB: www.pepsico.com
SIC: 2086 4225 5149 Carbonated soft drinks, bottled & canned; general warehousing; groceries & related products
HQ: Pepsi-Cola Metropolitan Bottling Company, Inc.
    1111 Westchester Ave
    White Plains NY 10604
    914 767-6000

(G-7078)
PERFECTED GRAVE VAULT CO
2500 3 Mile Rd Nw (49534-1314)
PHONE..............................616 243-3375
Kenneth Komoelje Jr, *President*
EMP: 7 EST: 1921
SQ FT: 15,000
SALES (est): 628.1K **Privately Held**
SIC: 3559 3272 Parking facility equipment & supplies; grave markers, concrete

(G-7079)
PERFORMANCE FABRICS INC
Also Called: Hexarmor
640 Leffingwell Ave Ne (49505-6050)
PHONE..............................616 459-4144
Steven Van Ermen, *President*
Katie Heydenberk, *Partner*
Josh Nagelkerke, *Regional Mgr*
Brent Lohrmann, *Vice Pres*
Benjamin Stuart, *Prdtn Mgr*

▲ EMP: 141 EST: 2002
SQ FT: 10,000
SALES (est): 49.3MM **Privately Held**
WEB: www.hexarmor.com
SIC: 5099 3842 3851 Safety equipment & supplies; clothing, fire resistant & protective; ear plugs; noise protectors, personal; protectors, eye

(G-7080)
PERFORMANCE SYSTEMATIX LLC (DH)
5569 33rd St Se (49512-2061)
PHONE..............................616 949-9090
Karlis Vizulis, *CEO*
Glenn Dunn, *President*
Metra Krautmanis, *Vice Pres*
John Grover, *Manager*
▲ EMP: 46 EST: 1995
SQ FT: 64,000
SALES (est): 20MM
SALES (corp-wide): 1.7B **Privately Held**
WEB: www.psix.com
SIC: 3089 3841 Plastic containers, except foam; plastic hardware & building products; surgical & medical instruments
HQ: Selig Sealing Products, Inc.
    342 E Wabash Ave
    Forrest IL 61741
    815 785-2100

(G-7081)
PERFORMNCE DCUTTING FINSHG LLC
955 Godfrey Ave Sw (49503-5003)
PHONE..............................616 245-3636
Wayne Vanderlaan, *Administration*
EMP: 11 EST: 2008
SALES (est): 596.4K **Privately Held**
WEB: www.pdfdiecutting.com
SIC: 3423 Cutting dies, except metal cutting

(G-7082)
PERRIGO PRINTING INC
3852 44th St Se (49512-3944)
PHONE..............................616 454-6761
P Richard Perrigo, *President*
David Kirunda, *Research*
EMP: 4 EST: 1976
SALES (est): 550K **Privately Held**
WEB: www.perrigoprinting.com
SIC: 2752 Commercial printing, offset

(G-7083)
PET SUPPLIES PLUS
6159 Kalamazoo Ave Se (49508-7805)
PHONE..............................616 554-3600
Steve Adams, *Owner*
Mike Klothe, *Owner*
Jessica Yakima, *Marketing Staff*
Danielle Saltarski, *Manager*
Stephanie Vanoost, *Manager*
EMP: 9 EST: 2010
SALES (est): 165.4K **Privately Held**
WEB: www.petsuppliespluscares.com
SIC: 5999 3999 Pets & pet supplies; pet supplies

(G-7084)
PHASE III GRAPHICS INC (PA)
255 Colrain St Sw Ste 1 (49548-1057)
PHONE..............................616 949-9290
Jeffrey Veine, *President*
Janet Veine, *Vice Pres*
Chris Landis, *Marketing Mgr*
EMP: 5 EST: 1974
SALES (est): 622.1K **Privately Held**
WEB: www.phase3graphics.com
SIC: 2752 2791 2789 Commercial printing, offset; typesetting; bookbinding & related work

(G-7085)
PHIL ELENBAAS MILLWORK INC (PA)
3000 Wilson Dr Nw (49534-7564)
PHONE..............................616 791-1616
Ben Elenbaas, *President*
Jason Rybinski, *Manager*
EMP: 29 EST: 1990
SQ FT: 10,000

Grand Rapids - Kent County (G-7086)   GEOGRAPHIC SECTION

SALES (est): 2.6MM Privately Held
WEB: www.elenbaasmillwork.com
SIC: 2431 5211 Moldings, wood: unfinished & prefinished; millwork & lumber

(G-7086)
PHOTONICS PRODUCTS GROU
4375 Donkers Ct Se (49512-4054)
PHONE...................................616 301-7800
Chad Bacon, *Engineer*
EMP: 4 EST: 2015
SALES (est): 68.6K Privately Held
WEB: www.inrad-inc.com
SIC: 3841 Surgical & medical instruments

(G-7087)
PIONEER MOLDED PRODUCTS INC
5505 52nd St Se (49512-9700)
PHONE...................................616 977-4172
John McCarthy, *Ch of Bd*
Derrick McCarthy, *President*
▲ EMP: 45 EST: 2005
SALES (est): 8.8MM Privately Held
WEB: www.pioneermoldedproducts.com
SIC: 3089 Injection molding of plastics

(G-7088)
PITNEY BOWES INC
4460 44th St Se Ste D (49512-4096)
PHONE...................................616 285-9590
EMP: 100
SALES (corp-wide): 3.2B Publicly Held
SIC: 3579 Mfg Office Machines
PA: Pitney Bowes Inc.
   3001 Summer St
   Stamford CT 06905
   203 356-5000

(G-7089)
PLASTIC MOLD TECHNOLOGY INC
Also Called: Woldering Plastic Mold Tech
3870 Model Ct Se (49512-3938)
PHONE...................................616 698-9810
Gary Proos, *Owner*
EMP: 4
SALES (corp-wide): 12MM Privately Held
WEB: www.plasticmold.com
SIC: 3089 3544 Injection molding of plastics; special dies, tools, jigs & fixtures
PA: Plastic Mold Technology, Inc.
   4201 Broadmoor Ave Se
   Kentwood MI 49512
   616 698-9810

(G-7090)
PLASTIC PLATE LLC (HQ)
3500 Raleigh Dr Se (49512-2064)
PHONE...................................616 455-5240
Richard Lacks Jr, *President*
Ryan Lacks, *Accounts Mgr*
Jeff Merryman, *Maintence Staff*
EMP: 50 EST: 1964
SQ FT: 35,000
SALES (est): 32.5MM Privately Held
WEB: www.lacksenterprises.com
SIC: 3714 Motor vehicle parts & accessories

(G-7091)
PLASTIC PLATE LLC
5357 52nd St Se Ste B (49512-9709)
PHONE...................................616 455-5288
Ric Bouwma, *Manager*
EMP: 20 Privately Held
SIC: 3089 Automotive parts, plastic
HQ: Plastic Plate, Llc
   3500 Raleigh Dr Se
   Grand Rapids MI 49512
   616 455-5240

(G-7092)
PLASTIC-PLATE INC
5460 Cascade Rd Se (49546-6406)
PHONE...................................616 698-2030
Richard Lacks, *Principal*
Jeff Chiu, *Business Mgr*
Dale Frens, *Plant Mgr*
Erin Jimenez, *QC Mgr*
Tom Hawkins, *Engineer*
EMP: 32 EST: 2013

SALES (est): 5.1MM Privately Held
WEB: www.lacksenterprises.com
SIC: 3544 Forms (molds), for foundry & plastics working machinery

(G-7093)
POPPYSEED PRESS LLC
105 Oswego St Nw (49504-6047)
PHONE...................................616 450-8521
Megan Streng, *Principal*
EMP: 4 EST: 2018
SALES (est): 78K Privately Held
WEB: www.poppyseedpress.com
SIC: 2741 Miscellaneous publishing

(G-7094)
POSITECH INC
4134 36th St Se (49512-2903)
P.O. Box 888250 (49588-8250)
PHONE...................................616 949-4024
Charles W Boelkins, *President*
EMP: 6 EST: 1993
SQ FT: 8,000
SALES (est): 651.2K Privately Held
WEB: www.positech.com
SIC: 3569 Lubrication machinery, automatic

(G-7095)
PRATT (BELL PACKAGING) INC
2000 Beverly Ave Sw (49519-1719)
PHONE...................................616 452-2111
Brian McPheely, *President*
EMP: 53 EST: 2004
SALES (est): 1.6MM Privately Held
SIC: 3554 Box making machines, paper

(G-7096)
PRATT INDUSTRIES INC
Also Called: Corrugating Division
2000 Beverly Ave Sw (49519-1719)
PHONE...................................616 452-2111
Jamie Waltermire, *General Mgr*
Lisa Tschoerner-Pete, *Controller*
Linda Bulich, *Cust Mgr*
Kent Crass, *Manager*
EMP: 5 Privately Held
WEB: www.prattindustries.com
SIC: 2653 Boxes, corrugated: made from purchased materials
PA: Pratt Industries, Inc.
   1800 Sarasot Bus Pkwy Ne S
   Conyers GA 30013

(G-7097)
PRECISE CNC ROUTING INC
2605 Thornwood St Sw A (49519-2179)
PHONE...................................616 538-8608
Richard Lemson, *President*
Laura Lemson, *Corp Secy*
EMP: 20 EST: 1995
SQ FT: 66,000
SALES (est): 2.4MM Privately Held
WEB: www.precisecompanies.com
SIC: 3545 Precision tools, machinists'

(G-7098)
PRECISION AEROSPACE CORP
5300 Corporate Grv (49512-5514)
PHONE...................................616 243-8112
William R Hoyer, *President*
Roger Heyboer, *Vice Pres*
Lisa Bowe, *Production*
Michael Andrews, *Engineer*
Chris Schapka, *Engineer*
EMP: 158 EST: 1966
SQ FT: 80,000
SALES (est): 44.1MM
SALES (corp-wide): 57.3MM Privately Held
WEB: www.precision-aerospace.com
SIC: 3599 Machine shop, jobbing & repair
PA: Tribus Aerospace Llc
   10 S Wacker Dr Ste 3300
   Chicago IL 60606
   312 876-7267

(G-7099)
PRECISION FINISHING CO INC
1010 Chicago Dr Sw (49509-1199)
PHONE...................................616 245-2255
Bruno Unzens, *President*
Rory Giles, *Sales Staff*
Sean Dutty, *Technology*
EMP: 15 EST: 1967
SQ FT: 10,000

SALES (est): 1.1MM Privately Held
WEB: www.precisionfinishingcompany.com
SIC: 3471 Finishing, metals or formed products

(G-7100)
PRECISION WIRE EDM SERVICE
3180 3 Mile Rd Nw (49534-1326)
PHONE...................................616 453-4360
Frank Kruzel, *President*
EMP: 24 EST: 1991
SQ FT: 12,000
SALES (est): 1.2MM Privately Held
WEB: www.pwedm.com
SIC: 3599 Machine shop, jobbing & repair

(G-7101)
PREMACH ENGINEERING LTD
Also Called: Precision Machine & Engrg
750 Curve St Sw (49503-4891)
PHONE...................................616 247-3750
Mike Vonk, *President*
EMP: 5 EST: 1997
SQ FT: 6,200
SALES (est): 650K Privately Held
WEB: www.premacheng.com
SIC: 3599 Machine shop, jobbing & repair

(G-7102)
PREMIER FINISHING INC
3180 Fruit Ridge Ave Nw (49544-9707)
PHONE...................................616 785-3070
Andy Ribbens, *President*
Carin Ribbens, *Vice Pres*
Josh Ribbens, *Exec Dir*
EMP: 26 EST: 1997
SQ FT: 22,000
SALES (est): 1.9MM Privately Held
WEB: www.premierfinishinginc.com
SIC: 3471 Finishing, metals or formed products

(G-7103)
PRESSURE RELEASES CORPORATION (PA)
Also Called: Status Transportation
2035 Porter St Sw (49519-2271)
PHONE...................................616 531-8116
Len Collins, *President*
Daniel R Collins, *Senior VP*
Daniel Collins, *Vice Pres*
Priscilla Elaine Myers, *VP Mktg*
EMP: 10 EST: 1986
SALES (est): 1.3MM Privately Held
WEB: www.whitecapcomics.com
SIC: 4212 2721 Delivery service, vehicular; periodicals: publishing only

(G-7104)
PRESTIGE PRINTING INC
4437 Eastern Ave Se Ste 1 (49508-7530)
PHONE...................................616 532-5133
Fax: 616 532-1128
EMP: 6
SALES (est): 300K Privately Held
SIC: 2752 Lithographic Commercial Printing Service

(G-7105)
PREUSSER JEWELERS
125 Ottawa Ave Nw Ste 195 (49503-2840)
PHONE...................................616 458-1425
David H Kammeraad, *President*
Sharon Straight, *Accountant*
EMP: 8 EST: 1850
SQ FT: 2,300
SALES (est): 1.3MM Privately Held
WEB: www.preusserjewelers.com
SIC: 5944 7631 3961 Jewelry, precious stones & precious metals; watches; silverware; watch repair; jewelry repair services; costume jewelry

(G-7106)
PRIDGEON & CLAY INC (PA)
50 Cottage Grove St Sw (49507-1685)
PHONE...................................616 241-5675
Robert Earl Clay, *Ch of Bd*
Julie Church-Krafft, *COO*
Rick Martin, *Vice Pres*
Dwight Wells, *Vice Pres*
Keith O' Brien, *VP Opers*
▲ EMP: 575 EST: 1948
SQ FT: 285,000

SALES (est): 153.6MM Privately Held
WEB: www.pridgeonandclay.com
SIC: 3714 3465 Motor vehicle parts & accessories; automotive stampings

(G-7107)
PRIME PRODUCTS INC
2755 Remico St Sw (49519-2494)
PHONE...................................616 531-8970
James Mc Kenzie, *President*
Chrissie Jacobs, *QC Mgr*
Jj McKenzie, *VP Sales*
Amanda Miner, *Cust Mgr*
Debbie Nol, *Manager*
EMP: 40 EST: 1975
SQ FT: 17,000
SALES (est): 7MM Privately Held
WEB: www.primeproductsinc.com
SIC: 3728 Aircraft parts & equipment

(G-7108)
PRINTING CONSOLIDATION CO LLC (PA)
190 Monroe Ave Nw Ste 600 (49503-2628)
PHONE...................................616 233-3161
Aaron Day, *CEO*
John Ruther, *CFO*
EMP: 48 EST: 2015
SALES (est): 5.6MM Privately Held
SIC: 2759 Commercial printing

(G-7109)
PRINTING PRODUCTIONS INK
4183 40th St Se (49512-4121)
PHONE...................................616 871-9292
Shawn Wylie, *President*
Mike Cooper, *Production*
Tiffany Armitage, *Manager*
EMP: 5 EST: 1993
SALES (est): 125K Privately Held
WEB: www.printprodink.com
SIC: 2752 Commercial printing, offset

(G-7110)
PRO SEALANTS
3683 Maplebrook Dr Nw (49534-2709)
PHONE...................................616 318-6067
Jason Hendricks, *President*
EMP: 5 EST: 2012
SALES (est): 196.3K Privately Held
SIC: 2891 Sealants

(G-7111)
PRO STAMP PLUS LLC
1988 Alpine Ave Nw (49504-2808)
PHONE...................................616 447-2988
Shawn Tilstra, *General Mgr*
Sally Moyers, *QC Mgr*
Clark Schuiteman,
EMP: 8 EST: 2008
SALES (est): 1.2MM Privately Held
WEB: www.prostampllc.com
SIC: 3469 Metal stampings

(G-7112)
PRO-FINISH POWDER COATING INC
1000 Kn O Sha Indus Dr Se (49508)
PHONE...................................616 245-7550
Jeff Hutchinson,
EMP: 29 EST: 1993
SQ FT: 17,000
SALES (est): 3MM Privately Held
WEB: www.pro-finish.net
SIC: 3479 Coating of metals & formed products

(G-7113)
PROFESSIONAL FABRICATING INC
Also Called: Professional Fabricating & Mfg
902 47th St Sw Ste A (49509-5143)
PHONE...................................616 531-1240
John Moran, *President*
Mandy Walston, *Purch Agent*
Mark Postiech, *CFO*
Kim Moran, *Human Resources*
Robin Monroe, *CIO*
EMP: 35 EST: 1993
SQ FT: 20,000
SALES (est): 8.5MM Privately Held
WEB: www.profabgr.com
SIC: 3444 Sheet metal specialties, not stamped

GEOGRAPHIC SECTION
Grand Rapids - Kent County (G-7140)

(G-7114)
PROFESSIONAL METAL FINISHERS
2474 Turner Ave Nw Ste 4 (49544-2060)
PHONE..................................616 365-2620
Bepsy Boss, *President*
EMP: 24 EST: 1983
SQ FT: 10,000
SALES (est): 1.3MM **Privately Held**
WEB: www.pmfpowder.com
SIC: 3471 Anodizing (plating) of metals or formed products; electroplating of metals or formed products

(G-7115)
PROFICIENT MACHINING INC
3455 3 Mile Rd Nw (49534-1227)
PHONE..................................616 453-9496
Lawrence Rozendaal, *President*
Kristie Rozenbaal, *Vice Pres*
Lawrence R Rozendaal, *Purch Mgr*
EMP: 12 EST: 2003
SALES (est): 2.6MM **Privately Held**
WEB: www.proficientmach.com
SIC: 3599 Machine shop, jobbing & repair

(G-7116)
PROFILE INDUSTRIAL PACKG CORP
Also Called: Profile Films
1976 Avastar Pkwy Nw (49544-1936)
PHONE..................................616 245-7260
Steve Hansen, *President*
Jennifer B Coffman, *Vice Pres*
Brian Hoeksema, *Vice Pres*
Lora Dykstra, *Cust Mgr*
Nury Duque-Feghali, *Manager*
EMP: 150
SQ FT: 100,000
SALES (est): 39.5MM **Privately Held**
WEB: www.profilefilms.com
SIC: 2821 2671 Acrylic resins; plastic film, coated or laminated for packaging

(G-7117)
PROGRESSIVE SURFACE INC (PA)
4695 Danvers Dr Se (49512-4077)
PHONE..................................616 957-0871
Lewis Van Kuiken, *President*
Gerald Molitor, *Vice Pres*
James Whalen, *Vice Pres*
Alex Keizer, *Engineer*
Jill Machuta, *Accountant*
▼ EMP: 52
SQ FT: 80,500
SALES (est): 17.2MM **Privately Held**
WEB: www.progressivesurface.com
SIC: 3569 7699 Blast cleaning equipment, dustless; industrial machinery & equipment repair

(G-7118)
PROGRESSIVE SURFACE INC
4671 Danvers Dr Se (49512-4018)
PHONE..................................616 957-0871
Lewis Van Kuiken, *President*
EMP: 12
SALES (corp-wide): 17.2MM **Privately Held**
WEB: www.progressivesurface.com
SIC: 3569 7699 Blast cleaning equipment, dustless; industrial machinery & equipment repair
PA: Progressive Surface, Inc.
    4695 Danvers Dr Se
    Grand Rapids MI 49512
    616 957-0871

(G-7119)
PROJECT DIE AND MOLD INC
228 Wesley St Se (49548-1258)
PHONE..................................616 862-8689
Scott Garber, *President*
EMP: 6 EST: 2000
SALES (est): 739.4K **Privately Held**
SIC: 3544 Industrial molds

(G-7120)
PRONG HORN
Also Called: Pronghorn Imprinting Co
6757 Cascade Rd Se # 164 (49546-6849)
PHONE..................................616 456-1903
David Horn, *Owner*
David Prong, *Co-Owner*
EMP: 7 EST: 1979
SALES (est): 244.3K **Privately Held**
SIC: 2261 Screen printing of cotton broad-woven fabrics

(G-7121)
PROOS MANUFACTURING LLC
2555 Oak Industrial Dr Ne Ae (49505-6057)
PHONE..................................616 454-5622
Bryan Howard, *CEO*
Tyler Cook, *COO*
Joshua Punches, *Project Mgr*
Jason Vanderklok, *Opers Mgr*
Amy Proos, *Mfg Staff*
EMP: 140 EST: 2011
SALES (est): 58.4MM **Privately Held**
WEB: www.proos.com
SIC: 3469 8711 Stamping metal for the trade; engineering services
PA: Westbourne Capital Partners Llc
    30 N La Salle St
    Chicago IL 60602

(G-7122)
PROSPECTORS LLC
Also Called: Prospectors Cold Brew Coffee
5035 W Greenbrooke Dr Se # 2 (49512-5491)
PHONE..................................616 634-8260
David Wentworth, *Principal*
EMP: 5 EST: 2015
SALES (est): 752.5K **Privately Held**
WEB: www.drinkprospectors.com
SIC: 5046 7389 2095 Coffee brewing equipment & supplies; coffee service; freeze-dried coffee

(G-7123)
PROTO-CAM INC
1009 Ottawa Ave Nw (49503-1407)
PHONE..................................616 454-9810
William Tingley, *President*
Daniel Bradley, *Vice Pres*
Amanda Metzner, *Admin Asst*
EMP: 10 EST: 1983
SQ FT: 10,000 **Privately Held**
WEB: www.bendtooling.com
SIC: 3599 Machine shop, jobbing & repair

(G-7124)
PRS MANUFACTURING INC
3745 Dykstra Dr Nw (49544-9745)
PHONE..................................616 784-4409
Dennis Kowalczyk, *President*
Chad Kowalczyk, *Vice Pres*
EMP: 7 EST: 1961
SQ FT: 8,200
SALES (est): 850K **Privately Held**
SIC: 3499 3471 Fire- or burglary-resistive products; plating & polishing

(G-7125)
PUMP HOUSE
2090 Celebration Dr Ne # 120 (49525-9200)
PHONE..................................616 647-5481
Karen Avrey, *Owner*
EMP: 5 EST: 2015
SALES (est): 203.6K **Privately Held**
WEB: www.morepumpy.com
SIC: 2024 Ice cream & frozen desserts

(G-7126)
PWV STUDIOS LTD
1650 Broadway Ave Nw (49504-2027)
PHONE..................................616 361-5659
Carol Vsoske, *President*
Paul Vsoske, *Vice Pres*
Judy Smith, *Info Tech Mgr*
EMP: 23 EST: 1983
SALES (est): 2.3MM
SALES (corp-wide): 30MM **Privately Held**
WEB: www.pwvstudios.com
SIC: 2273 Carpets & rugs
PA: Scott Group Custom Carpets, Llc
    3232 Kraft Ave Se Ste A
    Grand Rapids MI 49512
    616 954-3200

(G-7127)
QUALITY DRAFT SYSTEMS LLC
3876 East Paris Ave Se # 16 (49512-3974)
PHONE..................................616 259-9852
EMP: 5 EST: 2017
SALES (est): 768K **Privately Held**
WEB: www.qualitydraftsystems.com
SIC: 3585 Refrigeration & heating equipment

(G-7128)
QUALITY METAL FABRICATING
1324 Burke Ave Ne (49505-5543)
PHONE..................................616 901-5510
Ernest Altman, *Principal*
EMP: 4 EST: 2008
SALES (est): 426.1K **Privately Held**
WEB: www.qualitymetalfabricating.com
SIC: 3441 Fabricated structural metal

(G-7129)
QUALITY MODEL & PATTERN CO
2663 Elmridge Dr Nw (49534-1329)
PHONE..................................616 791-1156
Ed Doyle, *President*
Kristin Adams, *Business Mgr*
Mary Tuttle, *Corp Secy*
Donald Tuttle, *Vice Pres*
EMP: 24 EST: 1983
SQ FT: 10,000
SALES (est): 3.9MM **Privately Held**
WEB: www.qualitymodel.com
SIC: 3543 3544 3354 Foundry pattern-making; special dies, tools, jigs & fixtures; aluminum extruded products

(G-7130)
QUALITY PRINTING & GRAPHICS
Also Called: Abby's Printing
3109 Broadmoor Ave Se (49512-1877)
PHONE..................................616 949-3400
Maher Karadsheh, *President*
Mark Karachy, *Manager*
Aubrey Kopytko, *Manager*
EMP: 5
SQ FT: 3,200
SALES (est): 400K **Privately Held**
WEB: www.abbysprinting.com
SIC: 2752 Commercial printing, offset

(G-7131)
QUICK PRINTING COMPANY INC
2642 Division Ave S (49507-3467)
PHONE..................................616 241-0506
Lori Weyers, *President*
Mark Weyers, *Vice Pres*
EMP: 4 EST: 1972
SQ FT: 3,000
SALES (est): 348.9K **Privately Held**
WEB: www.qpco.com
SIC: 2752 2791 Commercial printing, offset; typesetting

(G-7132)
QUIKTAP LLC
Also Called: Keg Guys
702 Hall St Sw (49503-4819)
PHONE..................................855 784-5827
EMP: 7 EST: 2017
SALES (est): 547K **Privately Held**
WEB: www.quiktap.com
SIC: 3412 Metal barrels, drums & pails

(G-7133)
R HOUSE INDUSTRIES LLC
929 Alpine Commerce Park (49544-1696)
PHONE..................................616 890-7125
Matthew Rich, *Principal*
EMP: 11 EST: 2017
SALES (est): 1.1MM **Privately Held**
WEB: www.rhouseindustries.com
SIC: 3999 Manufacturing industries

(G-7134)
R L ADAMS PLASTICS INC
5955 Crossroads Commerce (49519-9572)
PHONE..................................616 261-4400
Craig Adams, *CEO*
Trevor Matthew, *Production*
Duane Berends, *Purchasing*
Sean Fey, *Engineer*
Cathy Taylor, *CFO*
EMP: 100 EST: 1978
SALES (est): 21.8MM **Privately Held**
WEB: www.goadams.com
SIC: 3089 Trays, plastic

(G-7135)
R T LONDON COMPANY (PA)
Also Called: Rt London
1642 Broadway Ave Nw # 1 (49504-2046)
PHONE..................................616 364-4800
Richard Postma, *President*
Steve Eldserveld, *COO*
Dale Haley, *VP Opers*
Scott Christie, *Regl Sales Mgr*
Anthony Ferranti, *Regl Sales Mgr*
▲ EMP: 80 EST: 1989
SQ FT: 275,000
SALES (est): 18MM **Privately Held**
WEB: www.rtlondon.com
SIC: 2531 2521 Public building & related furniture; wood office furniture

(G-7136)
RADLEY CORPORATION
Also Called: Radley Corp of Grand Rapids
4595 Broadmoor Ave Se # 115 (49512-5300)
PHONE..................................616 554-9060
David Barks, *Vice Pres*
David Teitsma, *Sales Staff*
Dave Ley, *Branch Mgr*
Juan Cruz, *Manager*
Paula Simpson, *Consultant*
EMP: 23
SALES (corp-wide): 5.6MM **Privately Held**
WEB: www.radley.com
SIC: 7371 5045 7372 Computer software development; computers, peripherals & software; prepackaged software
PA: Radley Corporation
    23077 Greenfield Rd # 440
    Southfield MI 48075
    248 559-6858

(G-7137)
RAENELL PRESS LLC
3637 Clyde Park Ave Sw # 6 (49509-4095)
PHONE..................................616 534-8890
Daniel Britten, *Partner*
Gerald R Britten, *Partner*
Jack Britten, *Partner*
Kevin Britten, *Partner*
Gerald Britten, *Mng Member*
EMP: 5 EST: 1946
SQ FT: 1,000
SALES (est): 378.3K **Privately Held**
SIC: 2752 2759 Commercial printing, offset; letterpress printing

(G-7138)
RAM DIE CORP
Also Called: Rdc
2980 3 Mile Rd Nw (49534-1322)
PHONE..................................616 647-2855
Matt Alcumbrack, *President*
Chad Boersma, *Principal*
Rich Alflen, *Vice Pres*
Matthew Alcumbrack, *Foreman/Supr*
Jon Demeester, *Program Mgr*
EMP: 11 EST: 2002
SALES (est): 1.6MM **Privately Held**
WEB: www.ramdiecorp.com
SIC: 7389 3312 Design services; tool & die steel

(G-7139)
RANIR LLC (HQ)
Also Called: Perrigo Grand Rapids Mfg
4701 East Paris Ave Se (49512-5353)
P.O. Box 8877 (49518-8877)
PHONE..................................616 698-8880
Rich Sororta, *President*
Kari Caruso, *President*
Mark McCumby, *Senior VP*
Kim Babusik, *Vice Pres*
Landon Bonte, *Vice Pres*
▲ EMP: 420 EST: 2005
SQ FT: 150,000
SALES (est): 104.7MM **Privately Held**
WEB: www.ranir.com
SIC: 3843 3991 Dental equipment & supplies; toothbrushes, except electric

(G-7140)
RANIR GLOBAL HOLDINGS LLC
4701 East Paris Ave Se (49512-5353)
P.O. Box 8877 (49518-8877)
PHONE..................................616 698-8880
Rich Sorota, *President*
Julie Nass, *Vice Pres*

Grand Rapids - Kent County (G-7141)   GEOGRAPHIC SECTION

EMP: 650 EST: 2008
SALES (est): 42.7MM Privately Held
WEB: www.ranir.com
SIC: 3843 Dental equipment & supplies
PA: Perrigo Company Public Limited Company
Treasury Building
Dublin 2

(G-7141)
RAPID-PACKAGING CORPORATION
5151 52nd St Se (49512-9718)
PHONE..................................616 949-0950
James R Spees, Ch of Bd
Russell H Spees II, President
Jerry Shepard, Vice Pres
Jim Spees, Plant Mgr
Pat Flynn, Accounts Mgr
EMP: 35 EST: 1961
SQ FT: 60,000
SALES (est): 4.2MM Privately Held
WEB: www.rapidpkg.us
SIC: 2657 Folding paperboard boxes

(G-7142)
RBC MINISTRIES (PA)
Also Called: MIDWEST MEDIA MANAGEMENT DIV
3000 Kraft Ave Se (49512-2092)
P.O. Box 2222 (49555-0001)
PHONE..................................616 942-6770
Doug Bekkering, President
Katy Pent, President
Max Smith, President
Karlene Schmid, Partner
Anne Cetas, Editor
▲ EMP: 254 EST: 1938
SQ FT: 110,000
SALES: 51.2MM Privately Held
SIC: 7922 2731 Radio producers; pamphlets: publishing & printing

(G-7143)
REAL VIEW LLC
Also Called: Pro Kitchen Software
2505 East Paris Ave Se # 140 (49546-2436)
PHONE..................................616 524-5243
Andrew Waid, Vice Pres
Chris Midgley, VP Sls/Mktg
Jason Ellis, Sales Mgr
Dave Cross, Accounts Mgr
Christine Poortvliet, Accounts Mgr
EMP: 13 EST: 2017
SALES (est): 512.7K Privately Held
WEB: www.prokitchensoftware.com
SIC: 7372 Prepackaged software

(G-7144)
REARDEN DEVELOPMENT CORP
5960 Tahoe Dr Se Ste 103 (49546-7124)
PHONE..................................616 464-4434
Michael Neuhaus, President
EMP: 5 EST: 1996
SALES (est): 367.7K Privately Held
SIC: 7372 Prepackaged software

(G-7145)
RECON TECHNOLOGIES LLC
1522 Madison Ave Se (49507-1715)
PHONE..................................616 241-1877
Thomas Jacques,
EMP: 4 EST: 2011
SALES (est): 484.7K Privately Held
WEB: www.recontechusa.com
SIC: 3523 Dairy equipment (farm)

(G-7146)
RECYCLING CONCEPTS W MICH INC
5015 52nd St Se (49512-9731)
PHONE..................................616 942-8888
John Dewitt, President
Tim White, Vice Pres
EMP: 55 EST: 2003
SQ FT: 90,133
SALES (est): 25.4MM Privately Held
WEB: www.recyclingconceptsmi.com
SIC: 5162 2611 5085 5093 Plastics materials & basic shapes; pulp manufactured from waste or recycled paper; glass bottles; metal scrap & waste materials

(G-7147)
RED STAMP INC
3800 Patterson Ave Se (49512-4027)
PHONE..................................616 878-7771
Timothy Vetter, President
Jack Spaans, Opers Mgr
Steven Stomel, Treasurer
Barbara Frost, Accounting Mgr
Scott Dutton, Regl Sales Mgr
EMP: 35 EST: 1998
SQ FT: 4,700
SALES (est): 8.7MM Privately Held
WEB: www.redstampinc.com
SIC: 3565 Packing & wrapping machinery

(G-7148)
RELIANCE FINISHING CO
1236 Judd Ave Sw (49509-1094)
PHONE..................................616 241-4436
Michael Mosey, CEO
Mary Mosey, Vice Pres
EMP: 75 EST: 1954
SQ FT: 40,000
SALES (est): 9.8MM Privately Held
WEB: www.reliancefinishing.com
SIC: 3479 Aluminum coating of metal products; coating of metals & formed products

(G-7149)
RELIANCE PLASTISOL COATING CO
1240 Judd Ave Sw (49509-1019)
PHONE..................................616 245-2297
James C Blok, Vice Pres
C Blok, Vice Pres
Glen Borre, Admin Sec
EMP: 16 EST: 1964
SQ FT: 50,000
SALES (est): 622.1K Privately Held
WEB: www.reliancefinishing.com
SIC: 3479 Coating of metals & formed products

(G-7150)
RELIANCE SPRAY MASK CO INC
2825 Northridge Dr Nw (49544-9109)
PHONE..................................616 784-3664
Timothy Blanch, President
Richard Blanch, Vice Pres
Terri Lynn Blanch, Admin Sec
EMP: 11 EST: 1964
SQ FT: 7,200
SALES (est): 500K Privately Held
WEB: www.rsmask.com
SIC: 5013 3544 Body repair or paint shop supplies, automotive; special dies, tools, jigs & fixtures

(G-7151)
REVUE HOLDING COMPANY
Also Called: Revue Magazine
2422 Burton St Se (49546-4809)
PHONE..................................616 608-6170
Brian Edwards, Principal
EMP: 8 EST: 2008
SQ FT: 1,500 Privately Held
WEB: www.revuewm.com
SIC: 2721 Magazines: publishing only, not printed on site

(G-7152)
RHINO LININGS OF GRAND RAPIDS
1520 Rupert St Ne (49525-2817)
PHONE..................................616 361-9786
Steve French, General Mgr
EMP: 7 EST: 2012
SALES (est): 286K Privately Held
WEB: www.rhinogr.com
SIC: 2842 Automobile polish

(G-7153)
RICHARDS QUALITY BEDDING CO
3443 Manderley Dr Ne (49525-2033)
PHONE..................................616 363-0070
EMP: 30
SQ FT: 75,000
SALES: 2.8MM Privately Held
SIC: 2515 5712 Mfg Mattresses/Bedsprings Ret Furniture

(G-7154)
RICHWOOD INDUSTRIES INC (PA)
2700 Buchanan Ave Sw (49548-1040)
PHONE..................................616 243-2700
Rick Start, President
Lisa V Schelven, Exec VP
Rich Rivera, Engineer
Amy Huismann, Controller
Jim Bennor, Manager
▲ EMP: 44 EST: 1988
SQ FT: 110,000
SALES (est): 11.3MM Privately Held
WEB: www.richwoodind.com
SIC: 2499 5021 2426 Handles, poles, dowels & stakes: wood; furniture; hardwood dimension & flooring mills

(G-7155)
RIDGEFIELD COMPANY LLC
2601 Elmridge Dr Nw (49534-1329)
PHONE..................................888 226-8665
Debra De Clark,
EMP: 7 EST: 2019
SALES (est): 905.9K Privately Held
WEB: www.ridgefieldcompany.com
SIC: 3441 3599 Fabricated structural metal; machine & other job shop work

(G-7156)
RIDGEVIEW INDUSTRIES INC
2727 3 Mile Rd Nw (49534-1317)
PHONE..................................616 453-8636
Gil Rushlau, Manager
Kurt Christensen, Planning
EMP: 275
SALES (corp-wide): 87.6MM Privately Held
WEB: www.ridgeviewindustries.com
SIC: 3469 Stamping metal for the trade
PA: Ridgeview Industries, Inc.
3093 Northridge Dr Nw
Grand Rapids MI 49544
616 453-8636

(G-7157)
RIDGEVIEW INDUSTRIES INC (PA)
3093 Northridge Dr Nw (49544-9132)
PHONE..................................616 453-8636
David Nykamp, President
Jerry Deshaw, Vice Pres
Troy Hendges, Vice Pres
Jon Anderson, Maint Spvr
Linda Lafountain, Production
▲ EMP: 200 EST: 1975
SQ FT: 200,000
SALES (est): 87.6MM Privately Held
WEB: www.ridgeviewindustries.com
SIC: 3469 7692 Stamping metal for the trade; welding repair

(G-7158)
RISE HEALTH LLC ◆
555 3 Mile Rd Nw (49544-8223)
PHONE..................................616 451-2775
Jeffrey Bennett,
EMP: 5 EST: 2021
SALES (est): 100K Privately Held
SIC: 7372 Application computer software

(G-7159)
RIVER CITY METAL PRODUCTS INC (PA)
655 Godfrey Ave Sw Ste 5 (49503-4900)
P.O. Box 7187 (49510-7187)
PHONE..................................616 235-3746
Ben Rietema, President
Dan Rietema, Engineer
Jerry Radle, Controller
EMP: 100 EST: 1984
SQ FT: 100,000
SALES (est): 17.1MM Privately Held
WEB: www.rcmpinc.com
SIC: 3441 Fabricated structural metal

(G-7160)
RIVERSIDE PRTG OF GRND RAPIDS
1375 Monroe Ave Nw (49505-4621)
PHONE..................................616 458-8011
Gregg Cobb, President
Rich Van Ess, Vice Pres
Ken Van Ess, Treasurer
Matt Cobb, Admin Sec
EMP: 5 EST: 1976
SQ FT: 8,000
SALES (est): 950K Privately Held
WEB: www.riverside1375.comcastbiz.net
SIC: 2752 Commercial printing, offset

(G-7161)
ROBB MACHINE TOOL CO
4301 Clyde Park Ave Sw (49509-4036)
PHONE..................................616 532-6642
Phillip Parsh, President
EMP: 5
SQ FT: 5,000
SALES (est): 595.6K Privately Held
WEB: www.robbtool.com
SIC: 3544 Special dies & tools

(G-7162)
ROCK RIVER FABRICATIONS INC
7670 Caterpillar Ct Sw (49548-7203)
PHONE..................................616 281-5769
Chris Kowalski, Principal
John Herweyer, Safety Mgr
EMP: 28 EST: 1994
SQ FT: 75,000
SALES (est): 1.6MM Privately Held
SIC: 3498 3317 Tube fabricating (contract bending & shaping); steel pipe & tubes

(G-7163)
RODENHOUSE INC
130 Graham St Sw (49503-5102)
PHONE..................................616 454-3100
Robert H Rodenhouse, President
Jason Wigboldy, General Mgr
EMP: 4 EST: 1993
SALES (est): 532.7K Privately Held
WEB: www.trufastwalls.com
SIC: 3965 Fasteners

(G-7164)
ROLLSTOCK INC
3680 44th St Se Ste 100a (49512-3966)
PHONE..................................616 803-5370
James D Azzar, President
EMP: 9 EST: 2015
SALES (est): 153.8K Privately Held
WEB: www.rollstock.com
SIC: 3565 Packaging machinery

(G-7165)
ROSE TECHNOLOGIES COMPANY
Also Called: Rose Medical
1440 Front Ave Nw (49504-3221)
PHONE..................................616 233-3000
Todd Grimm, President
Eric Vroegop, Vice Pres
Brent Wybenga, Facilities Mgr
Brooke Draggoo, Engineer
Elliot Slenk, Engineer
EMP: 24 EST: 1998
SQ FT: 35,000
SALES (est): 7.1MM Privately Held
WEB: www.rosemedical.com
SIC: 3841 Surgical & medical instruments

(G-7166)
ROSKAM BAKING COMPANY (PA)
Also Called: Starr Puff Factory
4880 Corp Exch Blvd Se (49512)
P.O. Box 202 (49501-0202)
PHONE..................................616 574-5757
Robert Roskam, President
Brandon Heiser, COO
Gerald Slater, Vice Pres
Jesse Chavez, Foreman/Supr
Cindy Pena, Production
▲ EMP: 200 EST: 1918
SALES (est): 453.5MM Privately Held
WEB: www.rothburyfarms.com
SIC: 2051 2043 7389 Bread, cake & related products; cereal breakfast foods; packaging & labeling services

(G-7167)
ROSKAM BAKING COMPANY
Also Called: M1 Plant
3225 32nd St Se (49512-1870)
PHONE..................................616 574-5757
EMP: 289

GEOGRAPHIC SECTION

Grand Rapids - Kent County (G-7195)

SALES (corp-wide): 453.5MM **Privately Held**
WEB: www.rothburyfarms.com
SIC: **2051** Bread, cake & related products
PA: Roskam Baking Company
4880 Corp Exch Blvd Se
Grand Rapids MI 49512
616 574-5757

(G-7168)
ROSKAM BAKING COMPANY
Also Called: M2 Plant
3035 32nd St Se (49512-1753)
PHONE 616 574-5757
EMP: 289
SALES (corp-wide): 453.5MM **Privately Held**
WEB: www.rothburyfarms.com
SIC: **2051** Bread, cake & related products
PA: Roskam Baking Company
4880 Corp Exch Blvd Se
Grand Rapids MI 49512
616 574-5757

(G-7169)
ROSKAM BAKING COMPANY
Also Called: Doughnut World
4855 52nd St Se (49512-9701)
PHONE 616 554-9160
Pete Roessler, *QC Dir*
Bob Roskam, *Branch Mgr*
Chris Outman, *Manager*
EMP: 289
SALES (corp-wide): 453.5MM **Privately Held**
WEB: www.rothburyfarms.com
SIC: **2051** Bakery: wholesale or wholesale/retail combined
PA: Roskam Baking Company
4880 Corp Exch Blvd Se
Grand Rapids MI 49512
616 574-5757

(G-7170)
ROSKAM BAKING COMPANY
Also Called: S1 Plant
5353 Broadmoor Ave Se (49512-9601)
PHONE 616 574-5757
Chris Brading, *Production*
Cindy Wood, *Production*
Dave Dunn, *Purchasing*
Carrie Schneider, *Research*
Terry Brandon, *Engineer*
EMP: 289
SALES (corp-wide): 453.5MM **Privately Held**
WEB: www.rothburyfarms.com
SIC: **2051** Bread, cake & related products
PA: Roskam Baking Company
4880 Corp Exch Blvd Se
Grand Rapids MI 49512
616 574-5757

(G-7171)
ROTHBURY FARMS INC
3061 Shaffer Ave Se (49512-1709)
P.O. Box 202 (49501-0202)
PHONE 616 574-5757
Robert O Roskam, *President*
EMP: 21 EST: 1985
SALES (est): 12.5MM **Privately Held**
WEB: www.rothburyfarms.com
SIC: **5149** **2051** **2043** Bakery products; bread, cake & related products; cereal breakfast foods

(G-7172)
ROWSTER COFFEE INC
100 Stevens St Sw (49507-1526)
PHONE 616 780-7777
Kurt Stauffer, *President*
EMP: 20 EST: 2008
SALES (est): 671.8K **Privately Held**
WEB: www.rowstercoffee.com
SIC: **2095** Coffee roasting (except by wholesale grocers)

(G-7173)
ROYCE ROLLS RINGER COMPANY
16 Riverview Ter Ne (49505-6245)
P.O. Box 1831 (49501-1831)
PHONE 616 361-9266
Charles Royce Jr, *CEO*
Matthew L Royce, *President*
Bill Swartz, *Manager*
Angelica M Tant, *Technology*
EMP: 66 EST: 1925
SQ FT: 32,000
SALES (est): 9.4MM **Privately Held**
WEB: www.roycerolls.net
SIC: **3589** Mop wringers; janitors' carts

(G-7174)
S & S TOOL INC
2522 Bristol Ave Nw (49544-1412)
PHONE 616 458-3219
EMP: 5
SALES (est): 400K **Privately Held**
SIC: **3599** Mfg Industrial Machinery

(G-7175)
S F GILMORE INC
Also Called: Cumberland Furniture
321 Terminal St Sw (49548-1018)
PHONE 616 475-5100
Scott F Gilmore, *President*
Michael Emley, *Engineer*
Robert Clark, *Information Mgr*
Amanda Powell,
▲ EMP: 120 EST: 1983
SQ FT: 50,000
SALES (est): 19.7MM **Privately Held**
WEB: www.gilmorefurnitureinc.com
SIC: **2521** Wood office furniture

(G-7176)
S SHEREE COLLECTION LLC
432 Storrs St Se (49507-2636)
PHONE 616 930-1416
Shaniece Marie Green,
EMP: 4
SALES (est): 100K **Privately Held**
SIC: **3999** Hair & hair-based products

(G-7177)
S&G GROUP LLC
Also Called: West Michigan Cerakote
3876 East Paris Ave Se # 8 (49512-3974)
PHONE 616 719-3124
EMP: 8 EST: 2015
SALES (est): 622.1K **Privately Held**
SIC: **3479** Coating of metals & formed products

(G-7178)
SAGE DIRECT INC
3400 Raleigh Dr Se (49512-2042)
PHONE 616 940-8311
Gary Sage, *President*
Ann Marie Priddy, *General Mgr*
Pamela Sage, *Vice Pres*
EMP: 17 EST: 1995
SQ FT: 12,000
SALES (est): 3MM **Privately Held**
WEB: www.sagedirect.com
SIC: **8742** **7374** **2759** Marketing consulting services; data processing service; laser printing

(G-7179)
SALTER LABS LLC (DH)
2710 Northridge Dr Nw A (49544-9112)
PHONE 847 739-3224
Greg Pritchard, *CEO*
Joshua Bennett, *Vice Pres*
Mark Landgren, *Vice Pres*
Theresa Hewitt, *Opers Staff*
Angela Perkins, *CFO*
◆ EMP: 18 EST: 1975
SALES (est): 39.9MM
SALES (corp-wide): 118.5MM **Privately Held**
WEB: www.salterlabs.com
SIC: **3841** Surgical & medical instruments
HQ: Sunmed, Llc
2710 Northridge Dr Nw A
Grand Rapids MI 49544
616 259-8400

(G-7180)
SALTER MEDICAL HOLDINGS CORP
Also Called: Salter Labs
2710 Northridge Dr Nw A (49544-9112)
PHONE 800 421-0024
EMP: 51 EST: 2010
SALES (est): 1MM **Privately Held**
SIC: **3841** Surgical & medical instruments

(G-7181)
SAVORY FOODS INC
900 Hynes Ave Sw Ofc (49507-1091)
P.O. Box 2583 (49501-2583)
PHONE 616 241-2583
Dan Abraham, *President*
Gerald Abraham, *Principal*
Kathy Abraham, *Vice Pres*
Dien Le, *Vice Pres*
Natalya Grounin, *Accounting Mgr*
▲ EMP: 55 EST: 1971
SQ FT: 54,000
SALES (est): 13MM **Privately Held**
WEB: www.savoryfoods.com
SIC: **2051** **2099** **2053** **2052** Bakery: wholesale or wholesale/retail combined; food preparations; frozen bakery products, except bread; cookies & crackers

(G-7182)
SAW TUBERGEN SERVICE INC
Also Called: Tubergen Cutting Tools
5252 Division Ave S (49548-5606)
PHONE 616 534-0701
Andrew Tubergen, *President*
EMP: 6 EST: 1907
SQ FT: 2,500
SALES (est): 609.6K **Privately Held**
WEB: www.tubergen.net
SIC: **3425** **7699** Saw blades, chain type; knife, saw & tool sharpening & repair

(G-7183)
SCHNITZELSTEIN BAKING CO
1305 Fulton St E (49503-3851)
PHONE 616 988-2316
Brian De Bries, *Principal*
EMP: 4 EST: 2004
SALES (est): 140.1K **Privately Held**
SIC: **2051** Bread, all types (white, wheat, rye, etc): fresh or frozen

(G-7184)
SCHREIBER FOODS INC
5252 Clay Ave Sw (49548-5658)
PHONE 616 538-3822
EMP: 29
SALES (corp-wide): 1.6B **Privately Held**
WEB: www.schreiberfoods.com
SIC: **2022** Processed cheese; natural cheese
PA: Schreiber Foods, Inc.
400 N Washington St
Green Bay WI 54301
920 437-7601

(G-7185)
SCHWARZEROBITEC INC
3566 Roger B Chaffee Mem (49548-2328)
PHONE 616 278-3971
Chris Dorgan, *President*
EMP: 7 EST: 2017
SALES (est): 219.6K **Privately Held**
WEB: www.schwarze-robitec.com
SIC: **3714** Motor vehicle parts & accessories

(G-7186)
SCIACCESS PUBLISHERS
3039 Ledgestone Pl Ne (49525-7066)
PHONE 616 676-7012
EMP: 5 EST: 2015
SALES (est): 60.9K **Privately Held**
SIC: **2711** Newspapers: publishing only, not printed on site

(G-7187)
SCOTT GROUP CUSTOM CARPETS LLC (PA)
Also Called: Scott Group Studio
3232 Kraft Ave Se Ste A (49512-2040)
PHONE 616 954-3200
Mike Ruggeri, *President*
Rachel Janowitz, *Regional Mgr*
John Hart, *Exec VP*
Tim Hill, *Vice Pres*
Paul Hudson, *Vice Pres*
▲ EMP: 195 EST: 1969
SQ FT: 140,000
SALES (est): 30MM **Privately Held**
WEB: www.scottgroupstudio.com
SIC: **2273** Carpets, textile fiber

(G-7188)
SCREEN IDEAS INC
3257 Union Ave Se (49548-2311)
PHONE 616 458-5119
Mark Schumaker, *President*
Jeremy Schumaker, *Prdtn Mgr*
Susan Schumaker, *Treasurer*
EMP: 4 EST: 1989
SQ FT: 10,000
SALES (est): 792.1K **Privately Held**
WEB: www.screenideas.net
SIC: **5199** **5099** **2759** Advertising specialties; signs, except electric; screen printing

(G-7189)
SCREEN PRINT DEPARTMENT
1181 Taylor Ave N (49503-1000)
PHONE 616 235-2200
Carl Perrin, *President*
Mary Perrin, *Officer*
Maryjo Perrin, *Officer*
Mary J Perrin, *Executive*
EMP: 20 EST: 1999
SALES (est): 1.9MM **Privately Held**
WEB: www.tspd.net
SIC: **2759** Screen printing

(G-7190)
SELKIRK CORPORATION (DH)
5030 Corp Exch Blvd Se (49512)
PHONE 616 656-8200
Brooks F Sherman,
◆ EMP: 50 EST: 1925
SALES (est): 98.1MM **Publicly Held**
WEB: www.selkirkcorp.com
SIC: **3444** Metal ventilating equipment
HQ: Johnson Controls, Inc.
5757 N Green Bay Ave
Glendale WI 53209
800 382-2804

(G-7191)
SHAWNIEBOY ENTERPRISES INC
Also Called: Printing Productions Ink
4183 40th St Se (49512-4121)
PHONE 616 871-9292
Shawn Wylie, *Principal*
EMP: 10 EST: 2002
SALES (est): 933.3K **Privately Held**
SIC: **2752** Commercial printing, offset

(G-7192)
SHELTER CARPET SPECIALTIES
2025 Calvin Ave Se (49507-3305)
PHONE 616 475-4944
EMP: 4 EST: 2009
SALES (est): 173K **Privately Held**
SIC: **2273** Carpets & rugs

(G-7193)
SHERIDAN PUBG GRND RAPIDS INC
5100 33rd St Se (49512-2062)
PHONE 616 957-5100
Chris Kurtzman, *President*
Ben Matalamaki, *CFO*
EMP: 100 EST: 2018
SALES (est): 18.4MM
SALES (corp-wide): 631.4MM **Privately Held**
WEB: www.sheridan.com
SIC: **2732** Book printing
PA: Cjk Group, Inc.
3323 Oak St
Brainerd MN 56401
800 328-0450

(G-7194)
SHORT BOOKS INC
955 Godfrey Ave Sw (49503-5003)
PHONE 231 796-2167
Pat Patton, *Principal*
EMP: 4 EST: 2007
SALES (est): 128.6K **Privately Held**
WEB: www.theshortbooks.com
SIC: **2731** Books: publishing only

(G-7195)
SHOULDER INNOVATIONS INC
1535 Steele Ave Sw Ste B (49507-1530)
PHONE 616 294-1026
Matt Ahearn, *COO*
Jeff Ondrla, *Exec VP*
Matthew Ahearn, *Exec Dir*

(PA)=Parent Co (HQ)=Headquarters (DH)=Div Headquarters
✿ = New Business established in last 2 years

Grand Rapids - Kent County (G-7196)   GEOGRAPHIC SECTION

EMP: 13 **EST:** 2016
SALES (est): 1.1MM **Privately Held**
WEB: www.shoulderinnovations.com
SIC: 3841 Surgical & medical instruments

(G-7196)
SIGNCOMP LLC
Also Called: Signtech
3032 Walker Ridge Dr Nw (49544-9129)
PHONE..................616 784-0405
Peter Lamberts, *CEO*
Jason Lamberts, *President*
Gordon Poliquin, *QC Mgr*
Dave Breihof, *Sales Mgr*
Jeremy Breihof, *Regl Sales Mgr*
◆ **EMP:** 37 **EST:** 1982
SQ FT: 50,000
SALES (est): 7.9MM **Privately Held**
WEB: www.signcomp.com
SIC: 3993 Signs & advertising specialties

(G-7197)
SIGNMAKERS LTD
7290 Division Ave S Ste A (49548-7237)
PHONE..................616 455-4220
Eric Sheler, *President*
Michelle Sheler, *Vice Pres*
EMP: 4 **EST:** 1983
SQ FT: 3,600
SALES (est): 442.5K **Privately Held**
WEB: www.signmakersltd.com
SIC: 3993 Signs, not made in custom sign painting shops

(G-7198)
SIGNWORKS OF MICHIGAN INC (PA)
4612 44th St Se (49512-4015)
PHONE..................616 954-2554
Ann Frass, *President*
EMP: 6 **EST:** 2004
SALES (est): 959.5K **Privately Held**
WEB: www.signworksofmi.com
SIC: 3993 Signs, not made in custom sign painting shops

(G-7199)
SIMCO AUTOMOTIVE TRIM INC
Also Called: Ufp Technologies
3831 Patterson Ave Se (49512-4026)
PHONE..................616 608-9818
R Jeffrey Bailly, *President*
Kathy Wagner, *Buyer*
Andrew Beyer, *Project Engr*
Ronald J Lataille, *Treasurer*
David Brownell, *Accounts Mgr*
▲ **EMP:** 20 **EST:** 1961
SQ FT: 70,000
SALES (est): 4.5MM
SALES (corp-wide): 179.3MM **Publicly Held**
WEB: www.ufpmedtech.com
SIC: 3086 Packaging & shipping materials, foamed plastic
PA: Ufp Technologies, Inc.
100 Hale St
Newburyport MA 01950
978 352-2200

(G-7200)
SIMMONS CRTRGHT PLSTIC CTNGS L
Also Called: S & C Plastic Coating
2701a West River Dr Nw (49544-2013)
PHONE..................616 365-0045
Gary Courtright, *CFO*
Sam Simmons, *Mng Member*
EMP: 7 **EST:** 2004
SQ FT: 25,000
SALES (est): 983.2K **Privately Held**
WEB: www.scplasticcoating.com
SIC: 3479 Coating of metals & formed products

(G-7201)
SK ENTERPRISES INC
Also Called: Pets Supplys Plus
3593 Alpine Ave Nw (49544-1635)
PHONE..................616 785-1070
Jan Gandy, *Manager*
EMP: 8 **EST:** 1996
SALES (est): 133.3K **Privately Held**
WEB: www.petsuppliespluscares.com
SIC: 3999 3569 Pet supplies; general industrial machinery

(G-7202)
SMARTCOAST LLC
3200 Broadmoor Ave Se (49512-2865)
PHONE..................231 571-2020
Greg Vandenbosch,
EMP: 5 **EST:** 2013
SALES (est): 341.6K **Privately Held**
WEB: www.thesmartcoast.com
SIC: 3549 Assembly machines, including robotic

(G-7203)
SMITH AND NEPHEW
3 Leonard St Ne (49503-1064)
PHONE..................616 288-6153
Janice Monforton, *Accounts Mgr*
Andy Jones, *Sales Staff*
Scott Nemode, *Sales Staff*
Dave Rumney, *Sales Staff*
Ben Taylor, *Manager*
EMP: 11 **EST:** 2014
SALES (est): 710.5K **Privately Held**
SIC: 3841 Surgical & medical instruments

(G-7204)
SOURCEONE IMAGING LLC
Also Called: Vizcom Media
4500 Broadmoor Ave Se (49512-5398)
PHONE..................616 452-2001
Emili Kozminske, *Project Mgr*
Joe Steis, *Production*
Jon Vandergraaf, *Production*
Jacob Wurm, *Production*
Rick Overway, *Accounts Exec*
EMP: 7 **EST:** 2002
SALES (est): 1.4MM **Privately Held**
WEB: www.vizcomprints.com
SIC: 2752 Commercial printing, offset

(G-7205)
SOUTHWESTERN FOAM TECH INC (HQ)
1700 Alpine Ave Nw (49504-2810)
PHONE..................616 726-1677
Richard W Amann, *President*
EMP: 5 **EST:** 1994
SALES (est): 4.7MM
SALES (corp-wide): 119.3MM **Privately Held**
WEB: www.grft.com
SIC: 3086 Plastics foam products
PA: Grand Rapids Foam Technologies, Inc.
2788 Remico St Sw
Wyoming MI 49519
616 726-1677

(G-7206)
SPARKS BELTING COMPANY INC
5005 Kraft Ave Se Ste A (49512-9707)
PHONE..................800 451-4537
Bob Johnson, *Regional Mgr*
EMP: 9
SALES (corp-wide): 1B **Privately Held**
WEB: www.sparksbelting.com
SIC: 3535 Conveyors & conveying equipment
HQ: Sparks Belting Company, Inc.
5005 Kraft Ave Se
Grand Rapids MI 49512

(G-7207)
SPARKS BELTING COMPANY INC (HQ)
5005 Kraft Ave Se (49512-9707)
PHONE..................616 949-2750
Nelson C Jacobson, *President*
John Grasmeyer, *Vice Pres*
Timothy Wallace, *Natl Sales Mgr*
Bruce Dieleman, *VP Sales*
Skip Storer, *Sales Staff*
▲ **EMP:** 78 **EST:** 2007
SALES (est): 33.5MM
SALES (corp-wide): 1B **Privately Held**
WEB: www.sparksbelting.com
SIC: 3535 3052 Conveyors & conveying equipment; rubber belting
PA: Jsj Corporation
700 Robbins Rd
Grand Haven MI 49417
616 842-6350

(G-7208)
SPARTA SHEET METAL INC
2200 Bristol Ave Nw (49544-1406)
PHONE..................616 784-9035
Melvin Stoepker, *President*
Michele Kelly, *Business Mgr*
Linda Stoepker, *Vice Pres*
EMP: 15 **EST:** 1956
SALES (est): 2.5MM **Privately Held**
WEB: www.spartasheetmetal.com
SIC: 3444 1799 Sheet metalwork; welding on site

(G-7209)
SPARTAN CENTRAL KITCHEN
463 44th St Se (49548-4327)
PHONE..................616 878-8940
Gary Sputfky, *Manager*
EMP: 6 **EST:** 2010
SALES (est): 371.2K **Privately Held**
SIC: 2099 Food preparations

(G-7210)
SPEC INTERNATIONAL INC
739 Cottage Grove St Se (49507-1815)
PHONE..................616 248-9116
Kim McComb, *Manager*
EMP: 75 **Privately Held**
WEB: www.specinternational.com
SIC: 2392 Sheets, fabric: made from purchased materials
PA: Spec International, Inc.
840 Cottage Grove St Se
Grand Rapids MI 49507

(G-7211)
SPEC INTERNATIONAL INC (PA)
840 Cottage Grove St Se (49507-2060)
PHONE..................616 248-3022
J Marcus Stephenson, *President*
Orlando Stephenson III, *Corp Secy*
EMP: 10 **EST:** 1992
SALES (est): 7.2MM **Privately Held**
WEB: www.specinternational.com
SIC: 3999 2514 Coin-operated amusement machines; slot machines; metal household furniture

(G-7212)
SPECIALTY TOOL & MOLD INC
4542 Rger B Chffee Mem Dr (49548-7522)
PHONE..................616 531-3870
Erik Rogenbuck, *President*
EMP: 7 **EST:** 1967
SQ FT: 5,500
SALES (est): 850.1K **Privately Held**
WEB: www.specialtytoolandmold.com
SIC: 3544 Special dies & tools

(G-7213)
SPECIALTY TOOLING SYSTEMS INC
Also Called: STS
4315 3 Mile Rd Nw (49534-1136)
PHONE..................616 784-2353
Dave Ruthven, *President*
Paul Martin, *Engineer*
Drew Boersma, *Treasurer*
Jane Langeweg, *Financial Analy*
EMP: 36 **EST:** 2000
SALES (est): 14.6MM **Privately Held**
WEB: www.toolingsystemsgroup.com
SIC: 3544 Special dies & tools
PA: Tooling Systems Group Inc.
555 Plymouth Ave Ne
Grand Rapids MI 49505

(G-7214)
SPECIALTY TUBE LLC
Also Called: Beverlin Manufacturing
3515 Raleigh Dr Se (49512-2041)
PHONE..................616 949-5990
Richard Watson, *President*
John Watson,
Michael Watson,
EMP: 30 **EST:** 1976
SQ FT: 50,000
SALES (est): 8MM **Privately Held**
WEB: www.beverlin.com
SIC: 3469 Metal stampings

(G-7215)
SPECIATION ARTISAN ALES LLC
Also Called: Brewery
928 Wealthy St Se (49506-1515)
PHONE..................616 279-3929
Mitchell Ermatinger,
EMP: 8 **EST:** 2016
SALES (est): 884.6K **Privately Held**
WEB: www.speciationartisanales.com
SIC: 2084 2082 Wines; beer (alcoholic beverage)

(G-7216)
SPECTRUM INDUSTRIES INC (PA)
Also Called: Spectrum Cubic
700 Wealthy St Sw (49544-6440)
PHONE..................616 451-0784
I Jay Bassett, *President*
Keith Bassett, *Vice Pres*
Robert Wilder, *Vice Pres*
Eric Bassett, *Project Engr*
Steve Creasap, *VP Sales*
▲ **EMP:** 83 **EST:** 1984
SQ FT: 122,000
SALES (est): 19.2MM **Privately Held**
WEB: www.spectrumindustries.com
SIC: 3479 3471 Enameling, including porcelain, of metal products; plating & polishing

(G-7217)
SPINDEL CORP SPECIALIZED
Also Called: Spindel Electronics
4517 Broadmoor Ave Se (49512-5339)
PHONE..................616 554-2200
Boris Polic, *President*
Otto M Muller, *Vice Pres*
Paul Azar, *Buyer*
Jeff Jareo, *Technical Staff*
EMP: 10 **EST:** 1995
SALES (est): 1.1MM **Privately Held**
WEB: www.spindel.com
SIC: 3566 Speed changers, drives & gears

(G-7218)
SPINNAKER CORP
554 Prestwick Ave Se (49546-2250)
PHONE..................616 956-7677
Guy Combs, *Owner*
EMP: 5 **EST:** 2010
SALES (est): 80.3K **Privately Held**
WEB: www.spinnaker-e.com
SIC: 2761 Manifold business forms

(G-7219)
SPINNAKER FORMS SYSTEMS CORP
6812 Old 28th St Se Ste L (49546-6933)
PHONE..................616 956-7677
EMP: 4 **EST:** 1983
SQ FT: 400
SALES: 300K **Privately Held**
SIC: 5112 2752 5199 Whol Business Forms

(G-7220)
SPIRE MICHIGAN ACQUISITION LLC
Also Called: Precision Poly LLC
2500 Oak Industrial Dr Ne (49505-6022)
PHONE..................616 458-4924
Parnell Olson, *President*
EMP: 2 **EST:** 2011
SALES (est): 1.3MM
SALES (corp-wide): 290.2MM **Privately Held**
WEB: www.precisionpoly.com
SIC: 3081 Plastic film & sheet
PA: Transcendia, Inc.
9201 Belmont Ave Ste 100a
Franklin Park IL 60131
847 678-1800

(G-7221)
SPRING AIR CO
630 Myrtle St Nw (49504-3129)
PHONE..................616 459-8234
Ken Clapp, *President*
EMP: 4 **EST:** 2015
SALES (est): 140K **Privately Held**
WEB: www.springair.com
SIC: 5712 3999 Mattresses; atomizers, toiletry

▲ = Import ▼ = Export
◆ = Import/Export

GEOGRAPHIC SECTION
Grand Rapids - Kent County (G-7246)

(G-7222)
STATE HEAT TREATING COMPANY
520 32nd St Se (49548-2304)
PHONE..................................616 243-0178
Susan Boll, *President*
Paul Meengs, *Vice Pres*
Derek Huizinga, *Engineer*
EMP: 30 EST: 1946
SQ FT: 50,000
SALES (est): 1.5MM **Privately Held**
WEB: www.stateheattreating.com
SIC: 3398 Tempering of metal

(G-7223)
STEEL SUPPLY & ENGINEERING CO (PA)
Also Called: SS&e Metalcraft
2020 Newark Ave Se (49507-3356)
PHONE..................................616 452-3281
R Jeffrey Dean, *President*
Steve J Entingh, *Vice Pres*
Roy P Lorenz, *Vice Pres*
Jim Schueler, *Vice Pres*
Joel Sietsema, *Project Mgr*
EMP: 45 EST: 1996
SQ FT: 76,000
SALES (est): 12.9MM **Privately Held**
WEB: www.steelsupplyengineering.com
SIC: 1791 3441 Structural steel erection; fabricated structural metal

(G-7224)
STEELCASE INC (PA)
901 44th St Se (49508-7594)
P.O. Box 1967 (49501-1967)
PHONE..................................616 247-2710
Robert C Pew III, *Ch of Bd*
James P Keane, *President*
Ulrich H E Gwinner, *President*
Luke Nangle, *Business Mgr*
Sara E Armbruster, *Exec VP*
◆ EMP: 583 EST: 1912
SALES: 2.6B **Publicly Held**
WEB: www.steelcase.com
SIC: 2522 2521 3648 8748 Office furniture, except wood; chairs, office: padded or plain, except wood; desks, office: except wood; cabinets, office: except wood; wood office furniture; chairs, office: padded, upholstered or plain: wood; desks, office: wood; cabinets, office: wood; lighting equipment; business consulting

(G-7225)
STEELTECH LTD (PA)
1251 Phillips Ave Sw (49507-1589)
PHONE..................................616 243-7920
Gary L Salerno, *President*
John Decker, *Vice Pres*
Derek Price, *CFO*
Kevin Bozym, *Sales Staff*
Michael Olger, *Sales Staff*
▲ EMP: 66 EST: 1986
SQ FT: 40,000
SALES (est): 12.5MM **Privately Held**
WEB: www.steeltechltd.com
SIC: 3325 3321 Alloy steel castings, except investment; gray iron castings; ductile iron castings

(G-7226)
STEPHENS PIPE & STEEL LLC
Also Called: Stephens Fence Supply
3400 Rger B Chffee Mem Dr (49548-2326)
PHONE..................................616 248-3433
Terry Powell, *Manager*
EMP: 36 **Privately Held**
WEB: www.spsfence.com
SIC: 5051 3315 3523 Pipe & tubing, steel; steel wire & related products; farm machinery & equipment
HQ: Stephens Pipe & Steel, Llc
    2224 E Highway 619
    Russell Springs KY 42642
    270 866-3331

(G-7227)
STONEY CREEK COLLECTION INC
Also Called: Marilyn's Needlework
4336 Plnfeld Ave Ne Ste H (49525)
PHONE..................................616 363-4858
Marilynn Vredevelt, *President*
Sally Smith, *Corp Secy*
EMP: 17 EST: 1983
SQ FT: 35,000
SALES (est): 1.2MM **Privately Held**
WEB: www.stoneycreek.com
SIC: 2731 5949 2721 Books: publishing only; sewing, needlework & piece goods; periodicals

(G-7228)
STOVALL WELL DRILLING CO
Also Called: Stovall Drilling
2132 4 Mile Rd Ne (49525-2449)
PHONE..................................616 364-4144
Howard Stovall, *President*
Doris A Stovall, *Corp Secy*
EMP: 8 EST: 1951
SALES (est): 388.1K **Privately Held**
SIC: 1389 1381 Oil & gas wells: building, repairing & dismantling; drilling oil & gas wells

(G-7229)
STRIDE INC
678 Front Ave Nw (49504-5325)
PHONE..................................616 309-1600
EMP: 23
SALES (corp-wide): 1.5B **Publicly Held**
WEB: www.k12.com
SIC: 3999 Education aids, devices & supplies
PA: Stride, Inc.
    2300 Corporate Park Dr
    Herndon VA 20171
    703 483-7000

(G-7230)
STUMP SCHLELE SOMAPPA SPRNG
Also Called: SSS Spring & Wire
5161 Woodfield Ct Ne (49525-1027)
PHONE..................................616 361-2791
Derek Saynor, *General Mgr*
Ravi Machani, *Mng Member*
Raj Oak, *Manager*
Patrick Ladd,
▲ EMP: 22 EST: 2008
SQ FT: 30,000
SALES (est): 3MM **Privately Held**
WEB: www.sss-sw.com
SIC: 3495 Wire springs

(G-7231)
STUMPP SCHUELE SOMAPPA USA INC
5161 Woodfield Ct Ne (49525-1027)
PHONE..................................616 361-2791
Derek Saynor,
EMP: 11 EST: 2007
SALES (est): 346.4K **Privately Held**
WEB: www.sss-sw.com
SIC: 3495 Wire springs

(G-7232)
SULUGU CORPORATION USA INC
Also Called: Agribusiness
448 Oakdale St Se (49507-1806)
PHONE..................................478 714-0325
Jakaila Key, *CEO*
EMP: 57 EST: 2019
SALES (est): 3.4MM **Privately Held**
SIC: 5039 8742 1542 6799 Prefabricated structures; retail trade consultant; agricultural building contractors; commodity contract trading companies; commodity contract exchanges; gold ores mining

(G-7233)
SUMMIT TRAINING SOURCE INC (PA)
4170 Embassy Dr Se (49546-2417)
P.O. Box 809298, Chicago IL (60680-9298)
PHONE..................................800 842-0466
Bill Clendenen, *CEO*
Valerie R Overheul, *President*
Dave Myers, *CFO*
EMP: 44 EST: 1981
SQ FT: 15,000
SALES (est): 2.8MM **Privately Held**
WEB: www.summit.hsi.com
SIC: 8331 2741 3652 Skill training center; miscellaneous publishing; pre-recorded records & tapes

(G-7234)
SUNHILL AMERICA LLC (PA)
Also Called: American Trading International
5300 Broadmoor Ave Se B (49512-9654)
PHONE..................................616 249-3600
Raymond Wiedenfeller, *Ch of Bd*
Faye Meyer, *Opers Mgr*
▲ EMP: 29 EST: 2004
SALES (est): 2.8MM **Privately Held**
WEB: www.sunhillglobal.com
SIC: 3562 5084 Ball & roller bearings; materials handling machinery

(G-7235)
SUNMED HOLDINGS LLC (PA)
2710 Northridge Dr Nw (49544-9112)
PHONE..................................616 259-8400
Suzie Oosting, *Opers Staff*
Cameron Minch, *Production*
John Sommerdyke, *Mng Member*
EMP: 20 EST: 2013
SALES (est): 118.5MM **Privately Held**
WEB: www.sun-med.com
SIC: 3841 6719 Surgical & medical instruments; investment holding companies, except banks

(G-7236)
SUPERIOR DISTRIBUTION SVCS LLC
4001 3 Mile Rd Nw (49534-1132)
P.O. Box 1768 (49501-1768)
PHONE..................................616 453-6358
James Leonard, *Mng Member*
EMP: 3 EST: 2010
SALES (est): 1.7MM
SALES (corp-wide): 120.9MM **Privately Held**
WEB: www.superiordistribution.net
SIC: 3537 4212 Trucks: freight, baggage, etc.: industrial, except mining; local trucking, without storage
HQ: S. Abraham & Sons, Inc.
    4001 3 Mile Rd Nw
    Grand Rapids MI 49534
    616 453-6358

(G-7237)
SUPERIOR FIXTURE & TOOLING LLC
425 36th St Se (49548-2313)
PHONE..................................616 828-1566
Mark Mastbergen, *CEO*
EMP: 7 EST: 2015
SALES (est): 695.6K **Privately Held**
WEB: www.superiorfixture.com
SIC: 2599 Factory furniture & fixtures

(G-7238)
SUPERIOR STEEL COMPONENTS INC (PA)
180 Monroe Ave Nw Ste 2r (49503-2626)
P.O. Box 68, Marne (49435-0068)
PHONE..................................616 866-4759
Eric Greenfield, *President*
Titus R Hager, *Chairman*
Dennis Van Wyk, *Treasurer*
EMP: 45
SQ FT: 16,000
SALES (est): 5.1MM **Privately Held**
WEB: www.lgst.com
SIC: 3443 Truss plates, metal

(G-7239)
SUPERTRAMP CSTM TRMPLINE LLC D
5161 Woodfield Ct Ne # 1 (49525-1027)
PHONE..................................616 634-2010
Paul Hagan, *Owner*
EMP: 8 EST: 2011
SQ FT: 400
SALES (est): 352.4K **Privately Held**
WEB: www.maxairtrampolines.com
SIC: 3949 Trampolines & equipment

(G-7240)
SUSPA INCORPORATED (DH)
3970 Rger B Chffee Mem Dr (49548-3497)
PHONE..................................616 241-4200
Steve Garvelink, *President*
Stuart Atwater, *General Mgr*
Penny Drougal, *General Mgr*
Tracie Glupker, *General Mgr*
Tyler Hernden, *Engineer*
▲ EMP: 181 EST: 1974
SQ FT: 165,000
SALES (est): 27.7MM
SALES (corp-wide): 83.5K **Privately Held**
WEB: www.suspa.com
SIC: 3593 Fluid power cylinders & actuators

(G-7241)
SWIFT PRINTING CO
Also Called: Swift Printing and Comm
404 Bridge St Nw (49504-5379)
PHONE..................................616 459-4263
Walter D Gutowski, *CEO*
Walter Gutowski Jr, *Treasurer*
Kathy Schramski, *Corp Comm Staff*
Steve Hale, *Graphic Designe*
EMP: 10 EST: 1955
SQ FT: 6,000
SALES (est): 1.7MM **Privately Held**
WEB: www.swiftprintshop.com
SIC: 2759 2752 Screen printing; commercial printing, lithographic

(G-7242)
SWOBODA INC
4108 52nd St Se (49512-9636)
PHONE..................................616 554-6161
Thomas Hecksel, *CEO*
Michael Follmann Ceo, *Principal*
Erina Hanka, *Principal*
Christoph Hirt, *Principal*
John Fuhs, *Vice Pres*
▲ EMP: 120 EST: 1998
SQ FT: 60,000
SALES (est): 26.1MM
SALES (corp-wide): 226.5K **Privately Held**
WEB: www.swoboda.com
SIC: 3714 Motor vehicle engines & parts
HQ: Swoboda Wiggensbach Kg
    Max-Swoboda-Str. 1
    Wiggensbach BY 87487
    837 091-00

(G-7243)
SYNOD OF GREAT LAKES
4500 60th St Se (49512-9685)
PHONE..................................616 698-7071
Dave Schutt, *Director*
West Graneerg-Michaelson, *Director*
EMP: 34 EST: 1955
SQ FT: 5,000
SALES (est): 730.9K **Privately Held**
WEB: www.rca.org
SIC: 8661 2741 8741 Reformed Church; newsletter publishing; management services

(G-7244)
SYSTEM 2/90 INC
Also Called: 2/90 Sign Systems
5350 Corprte Grv Dr Se (49512-5500)
P.O. Box 888289 (49588-8289)
PHONE..................................616 656-4310
Albert J Perry, *President*
Chris Douma, *President*
Michael A Benedict, *Vice Pres*
Michael Herweyer, *Vice Pres*
Kathleen Kluck, *Vice Pres*
▼ EMP: 95 EST: 1978
SQ FT: 88,000
SALES (est): 11.2MM **Privately Held**
WEB: www.290signs.com
SIC: 3993 Electric signs

(G-7245)
T C H INDUSTRIES INCORPORATED (HQ)
7441 Div Ave S Ste A1 (49548)
PHONE..................................616 942-0505
Theodore C Hohman, *President*
Patrick J Greene, *Vice Pres*
EMP: 100 EST: 1982
SALES (est): 79.1MM **Privately Held**
WEB: www.tchindustries.com
SIC: 3364 3363 Zinc & zinc-base alloy die-castings; aluminum die-castings
PA: Charles Group, Inc.
    7441 Div Ave S Ste A1
    Grand Rapids MI 49548
    336 882-0186

(G-7246)
TABLETTING INC
4201 Danvers Ct Se (49512-4041)
PHONE..................................616 957-0281

Grand Rapids - Kent County (G-7247)

Bryan Koster, *President*
Dale Koster, *Vice Pres*
EMP: 7 **EST:** 1971
SQ FT: 5,000
SALES (est): 791.6K **Privately Held**
WEB: www.tablettinginc.com
SIC: 2834 Tablets, pharmaceutical

(G-7247)
TACK ELECTRONICS INC
5030 Kraft Ave Se Ste A (49512-9720)
PHONE..................616 698-0960
Todd Maines, *CEO*
George Maines, *President*
Jeffrey Austhof, *General Mgr*
Rachel Brand, *Purch Mgr*
EMP: 64 **EST:** 1996
SQ FT: 10,000 **Privately Held**
WEB: www.tackelectronics.com
SIC: 3357 Aircraft wire & cable, nonferrous

(G-7248)
TALISMAN
2033 Oak Industrial Dr Ne (49505-6011)
PHONE..................616 458-1391
EMP: 5 **EST:** 2018
SALES (est): 41K **Privately Held**
WEB: www.talismancompany.com
SIC: 3911 Jewelry, precious metal

(G-7249)
TAYLOR FREEZER MICHIGAN INC
2111 Walker Ct Nw (49544-1411)
PHONE..................616 453-0531
Rick Senica, *Vice Pres*
EMP: 13
SALES (corp-wide): 16.6MM **Privately Held**
WEB: www.taylorfreezermi.com
SIC: 3556 5046 5078 Ice cream manufacturing machinery; commercial equipment; ice cream cabinets
PA: Taylor Freezer Of Michigan, Inc.
 13341 Stark Rd
 Livonia MI
 800 292-0031

(G-7250)
TECH FORMS METAL LTD
2437 Coit Ave Ne (49505-4017)
PHONE..................616 956-0430
Timothy G Gleason, *President*
▲ **EMP:** 8 **EST:** 2003
SALES (est): 106.7K **Privately Held**
SIC: 3353 Aluminum sheet & strip

(G-7251)
TEKTON INC
Also Called: Michigan Industrial Tools
3707 Rger B Chffee Mem Dr (49548-3435)
PHONE..................616 243-2443
Attallah Amash, *President*
Marie Amash, *Vice Pres*
Greg Hawkins, *Opers Mgr*
Brent McBride, *Prdtn Mgr*
Jordan Flickinger, *QC Mgr*
◆ **EMP:** 90
SQ FT: 140,000
SALES (est): 16.8MM **Privately Held**
WEB: www.tekton.com
SIC: 3423 5072 Hand & edge tools; hand tools

(G-7252)
TEN X PLASTICS LLC
610 Maryland Ave Ne Ste A (49505-6052)
PHONE..................616 813-3037
EMP: 7
SALES (est): 894.9K **Privately Held**
SIC: 3089 Plastics Products, Nec, Nsk

(G-7253)
TER MOLEN & HART INC
3056 Eastern Ave Se Ste C (49508-8250)
PHONE..................616 458-4832
Steve Van Zytveld, *President*
EMP: 8 **EST:** 1927
SQ FT: 3,000
SALES (est): 892.9K **Privately Held**
WEB: www.termolenhart.com
SIC: 3444 Sheet metalwork

(G-7254)
TERRYBERRY COMPANY LLC (PA)
Also Called: Stange Company
2033 Oak Industrial Dr Ne (49505-6011)
P.O. Box 502 (49501-0502)
PHONE..................616 458-1391
Tad Evans, *Plant Mgr*
Jon Nemeth, *Sales Mgr*
Ed Lomonaco, *Software Dev*
Mike Byam,
David Beemer,
▲ **EMP:** 196 **EST:** 1918
SQ FT: 30,000
SALES (est): 40.8MM **Privately Held**
WEB: www.terryberry.com
SIC: 3911 Rings, finger: precious metal

(G-7255)
TG MANUFACTURING LLC
Aim Industries
4720 44th St Se Ste B (49512-4013)
PHONE..................616 842-1503
Jeanne Duthler, *Principal*
EMP: 30 **Privately Held**
WEB: www.tg-manufacturing.com
SIC: 3469 Stamping metal for the trade
PA: Tg Manufacturing, Llc
 8197 Clyde Park Ave Sw
 Byron Center MI 49315

(G-7256)
TGW SYSTEMS INC (DH)
3001 Orchard Vista Dr Se # 3 (49546-7094)
PHONE..................616 888-2595
Mario Hernel, *CEO*
Harald Stallinger, *Managing Dir*
Lynn Metzger, *Business Mgr*
Mario Herndl, *COO*
Markus Sturm, *Vice Pres*
◆ **EMP:** 207 **EST:** 1964
SALES (est): 64.2MM
SALES (corp-wide): 242.1K **Privately Held**
WEB: www.tgw-conveyor.com
SIC: 3535 Conveyors & conveying equipment

(G-7257)
THIERICA INC (HQ)
Also Called: Thierica Display Products
900 Clancy Ave Ne (49503-1599)
PHONE..................616 458-1538
Forrest Frank, *CEO*
James Stein, *President*
Delfino Garza, *General Mgr*
Tim Huffman, *General Mgr*
Sandra Frank, *Vice Pres*
▲ **EMP:** 84 **EST:** 1946
SQ FT: 57,000
SALES (est): 24.8MM **Privately Held**
WEB: www.thierica.com
SIC: 3812 3479 3829 Aircraft flight instruments; coating of metals & formed products; measuring & controlling devices

(G-7258)
THIERICA CONTROLS INC
Also Called: Automatrics
4400 Donkers Ct Se (49512-4054)
PHONE..................616 956-5500
Forrest Frank, *President*
Jim Jongekryg, *Opers Mgr*
Scott Strait, *Engineer*
Keith Rollenhagen, *Electrical Engi*
Krista Tanner, *Office Mgr*
EMP: 1 **EST:** 1998
SALES (est): 2.6MM **Privately Held**
SIC: 3613 Control panels, electric
PA: Thi Incorporated
 900 Clancy Ave Ne
 Grand Rapids MI 49503

(G-7259)
THIERICA EQUIPMENT CORPORATION (HQ)
Also Called: Thi Equipment
3147 N Wilson Ct Nw (49534-7566)
PHONE..................616 453-6570
Forrest Frank, *CEO*
James Stein, *President*
Sandra Frank, *Vice Pres*
Dan Van, *Purchasing*
Travis Kaylor, *Engineer*
▼ **EMP:** 44 **EST:** 1993
SQ FT: 57,000
SALES (est): 12.1MM **Privately Held**
WEB: www.thiequip.com
SIC: 3599 3991 3842 3563 Machine & other job shop work; brooms & brushes; surgical appliances & supplies; air & gas compressors; sheet metalwork

(G-7260)
THOMPSON CUSTOM WOODWORKING
1635 Acacia Dr Nw (49504-2301)
PHONE..................616 446-1058
Jim Thompson, *Principal*
EMP: 5 **EST:** 2010
SALES (est): 177K **Privately Held**
SIC: 2431 Millwork

(G-7261)
THORN APPLE BREWING COMPANY
6262 28th St Se (49546-6902)
PHONE..................616 288-6907
EMP: 8 **EST:** 2017
SALES (est): 398.1K **Privately Held**
WEB: www.thornapplebrewing.com
SIC: 5181 2082 Beer & ale; malt beverages

(G-7262)
THREE SHEEP LLC (PA)
Also Called: Three Sheep and A Mill LLC
625 Kenmoor Ave Se (49546-2395)
PHONE..................616 215-1848
Sarah Noble,
EMP: 14 **EST:** 2016
SALES (est): 138.1K **Privately Held**
SIC: 2221 Textile mills, broadwoven: silk & manmade, also glass

(G-7263)
TK ELEVATOR CORPORATION
5169 Northland Dr Ne (49525-1015)
PHONE..................616 942-4710
Scott Barron, *Manager*
EMP: 40
SALES (corp-wide): 1B **Privately Held**
WEB: www.tkelevator.com
SIC: 3534 1796 Elevators & moving stairways; installing building equipment
HQ: Tk Elevator Corporation
 11605 Haynes Bridge Rd
 Alpharetta GA 30009
 678 319-3240

(G-7264)
TON-TEX CORPORATION
4245 44th St Se Ste 1 (49512-4053)
PHONE..................616 957-3200
Robert Beaman, *Branch Mgr*
EMP: 20
SALES (corp-wide): 2MM **Privately Held**
WEB: www.tontex.com
SIC: 3568 Power transmission equipment
PA: Ton-Tex Corporation
 4029 E Grv Unit 7
 Greenville MI 48838
 616 957-3200

(G-7265)
TOOLING SYSTEMS GROUP INC (PA)
Also Called: Tooling Systems Enterprises
555 Plymouth Ave Ne (49505-6029)
P.O. Box 152053 (49515-2053)
PHONE..................616 863-8623
Julie Boersma, *CEO*
Drew Boersma, *President*
Leroy Bulson, *General Mgr*
Tony Baker, *Vice Pres*
Todd Kolasa, *QC Mgr*
▲ **EMP:** 12 **EST:** 2008
SALES (est): 22.7MM **Privately Held**
WEB: www.toolingsystemsgroup.com
SIC: 3544 Special dies & tools

(G-7266)
TOWER ATMTIVE OPRTONS USA I LL
4695 44th St Se Ste B175 (49512-4140)
PHONE..................616 802-1600
Orrie Jones, *Manager*
EMP: 52
SALES (corp-wide): 3.1B **Privately Held**
WEB: www.autokiniton.com
SIC: 3465 Automotive stampings
HQ: Tower Automotive Operations Usa I, Llc
 17757 Woodland Dr
 New Boston MI 48164

(G-7267)
TOWER INTERNATIONAL INC
4695 44th St Se Ste B175 (49512-4140)
PHONE..................616 802-1600
Linda Fryc, *Manager*
Katrina Moten, *Supervisor*
Phil Parker, *Analyst*
EMP: 4
SALES (corp-wide): 3.1B **Privately Held**
WEB: www.autokiniton.com
SIC: 3441 Fabricated structural metal
HQ: Tower International, Inc.
 17672 N Laurel Park Dr 400e
 Livonia MI 48152

(G-7268)
TRACKCORE INC
25 Commerce Ave Sw # 200 (49503-4100)
PHONE..................616 632-2222
Ross Macgregor, *Vice Pres*
Brent Maring, *Vice Pres*
Susan Zadel, *Controller*
Jesse Liebler, *Sales Mgr*
Courtney Macgregor, *Marketing Staff*
EMP: 10 **EST:** 2017
SALES (est): 1.4MM **Privately Held**
WEB: www.trackcoreinc.com
SIC: 3842 Implants, surgical

(G-7269)
TRANE US INC
5005 Corporate Exchange B (49512-5505)
PHONE..................616 971-1400
Andrew Tjoelker, *Project Mgr*
Mike Gumowski, *Project Engr*
Chad Nyenhuis, *Sales Staff*
Jon Suggitt, *Sales Staff*
Robert Katerberg, *Branch Mgr*
EMP: 4 **Privately Held**
WEB: www.trane.com
SIC: 3585 Refrigeration & heating equipment
HQ: Trane U.S. Inc.
 3600 Pammel Creek Rd
 La Crosse WI 54601
 608 787-2000

(G-7270)
TRANSFIGURE PRINT CO
1020 Sibley St Nw (49504-5458)
PHONE..................810 404-4569
Bailey Sell, *Principal*
EMP: 4 **EST:** 2019
SALES (est): 72.7K **Privately Held**
WEB: www.transfigureprintco.com
SIC: 2752 Commercial printing, lithographic

(G-7271)
TREAT OF DAY LLC
Also Called: Totd
2540 Ridgemoor Dr Se (49512-1635)
PHONE..................616 706-1717
Bakeer Muhammad,
Clifton Jura,
EMP: 7 **EST:** 2012
SALES (est): 267.8K **Privately Held**
SIC: 2095 Coffee roasting (except by wholesale grocers)

(G-7272)
TRECE ADHESIVE DIVISION
Also Called: Tad
314 Straight Ave Sw (49504-6439)
PHONE..................918 785-3061
EMP: 6 **EST:** 2018
SALES (est): 262.8K **Privately Held**
WEB: www.adhesives.com
SIC: 3829 Measuring & controlling devices

(G-7273)
TREE LINE MAPLE SYRUP
7220 Baumhoff Ave Nw (49544-9730)
PHONE..................616 889-6016
Karen Cordes, *Principal*
EMP: 4 **EST:** 2019
SALES (est): 62.3K **Privately Held**
SIC: 2099 Maple syrup

GEOGRAPHIC SECTION
Grand Rapids - Kent County (G-7300)

(G-7274)
TREND SOFTWARE LLC
2935 Pioneer Club Rd Se (49506-2037)
PHONE..................................616 452-8032
EMP: 4 EST: 2010
SALES (est): 96K Privately Held
SIC: 7372 Prepackaged software

(G-7275)
TRI-C PUBLICATIONS INC
2710 Hickorywood Ln Se (49546-7433)
PHONE..................................616 581-7967
Carolyn Brown, *Manager*
EMP: 7 EST: 1993
SALES (est): 33.3K Privately Held
SIC: 2731 Book publishing

(G-7276)
TRIDENT LIGHTING LLC
2929 32nd St Se (49512-1771)
PHONE..................................616 957-9500
Anthony Shaw, *CEO*
Carol Levy,
▲ EMP: 53 EST: 1895
SQ FT: 330,000
SALES (est): 3.2MM Privately Held
SIC: 3647 3714 3641 Automotive lighting fixtures; motor vehicle parts & accessories; electric lamps

(G-7277)
TRITON 3D LLC
904 36th St Se Ste B (49508-2532)
PHONE..................................616 405-8662
Matthew Howlett, *Principal*
Linda Dykstra, *Manager*
EMP: 6 EST: 2017
SALES (est): 101.3K Privately Held
WEB: www.triton3d.com
SIC: 2759 Commercial printing

(G-7278)
TRUE TEKNIT INC
5300 Corprte Grv Dr Se (49512-5514)
PHONE..................................616 656-5111
Alain Dueal, *CEO*
Brent Early, *Manager*
Pietro Miloro, *Technical Staff*
EMP: 10 EST: 2006
SQ FT: 40,000
SALES (est): 167K Privately Held
WEB: www.teknit.com
SIC: 2281 Knitting yarn, spun

(G-7279)
TRUE TOOL CNC REGRINDING & MFG
14110 Ironwood Dr Nw (49534-1034)
PHONE..................................616 677-1751
Tom Balzeski, *President*
Lisa Belzeski, *Admin Sec*
EMP: 4 EST: 1989
SQ FT: 3,000
SALES (est): 518.2K Privately Held
WEB: www.truetoolcnc.com
SIC: 3599 Grinding castings for the trade

(G-7280)
TUFF AUTOMATION INC
2751 Courier Dr Nw (49534-1247)
PHONE..................................616 735-3939
Monte R Tuffs, *President*
Ryan Dewey, *Project Mgr*
Erik Salisbury, *Opers Mgr*
Scott V Buren, *Info Tech Dir*
▲ EMP: 25 EST: 1992
SQ FT: 12,000
SALES (est): 4.5MM Privately Held
WEB: www.tuffautomation.com
SIC: 3599 Custom machinery

(G-7281)
TURNKEY FABRICATION LLC
840 Cottage Grove St Se (49507-2060)
PHONE..................................616 248-9116
EMP: 16 EST: 2012
SALES (est): 332.1K Privately Held
WEB: www.turnkeyfab.com
SIC: 1761 3444 Sheet metalwork; sheet metalwork

(G-7282)
TUSCOLA LOGGING
1138 Luce St Sw (49534-9615)
PHONE..................................517 231-2905
EMP: 5 EST: 2018
SALES (est): 89.8K Privately Held
SIC: 2411 Logging

(G-7283)
TVB INC
544 Richmond St Nw (49504-2007)
P.O. Box 651, Howard City (49329-0651)
PHONE..................................616 456-9629
Tom Van Blooys, *President*
EMP: 8 EST: 1917
SQ FT: 16,000
SALES (est): 1.1MM Privately Held
WEB: www.tvb-inc.com
SIC: 2522 5712 Office furniture, except wood; furniture stores

(G-7284)
TWINLAB HOLDINGS INC
3133 Orchard Vista Dr Se (49546-7033)
PHONE..................................800 645-5626
Marc Stover, *Vice Pres*
Niki Simoneaux, *Marketing Staff*
Joseph Sopracasa, *Director*
Al Gever, *Officer*
EMP: 4
SALES (corp-wide): 87.3MM Privately Held
WEB: www.twinlab.tlcchealth.com
SIC: 2099 Tea blending
PA: Twinlab Holdings, Inc.
 4800 T Rex Ave Ste 305
 Boca Raton FL 33431
 800 645-5626

(G-7285)
UEI INC
Also Called: U E I
2771 West River Dr Nw (49544-2013)
PHONE..................................616 361-6093
Greg Usher, *President*
Jeanine Usher, *Treasurer*
EMP: 30 EST: 1994
SQ FT: 16,000
SALES (est): 5.4MM Privately Held
WEB: www.ueitool.com
SIC: 3469 3544 Metal stampings; special dies & tools

(G-7286)
UFP ATLANTIC LLC
2801 E Beltline Ave Ne (49525-9680)
PHONE..................................616 364-6161
Michael Cole, *Principal*
EMP: 9 EST: 2011
SALES (est): 2.6MM
SALES (corp-wide): 5.1B Publicly Held
WEB: www.ufpi.com
SIC: 2421 5031 1796 Sawmills & planing mills, general; lumber, plywood & millwork; installing building equipment
PA: Ufp Industries, Inc.
 2801 E Beltline Ave Ne
 Grand Rapids MI 49525
 616 364-6161

(G-7287)
UFP EASTERN DIVISION INC (HQ)
Also Called: Universal Forest Products
2801 E Beltline Ave Ne (49525-9680)
PHONE..................................616 364-6161
C Scott Greene, *President*
◆ EMP: 452 EST: 1996
SALES (est): 362.9MM
SALES (corp-wide): 5.1B Publicly Held
WEB: www.ufpi.com
SIC: 2421 Sawmills & planing mills, general
PA: Ufp Industries, Inc.
 2801 E Beltline Ave Ne
 Grand Rapids MI 49525
 616 364-6161

(G-7288)
UFP GRAND RAPIDS LLC
825 Buchanan Ave Sw (49507-1004)
PHONE..................................616 464-1650
EMP: 16
SALES (est): 2.8MM
SALES (corp-wide): 5.1B Publicly Held
SIC: 2421 Mfg Wood Building Products
PA: Ufp Industries, Inc.
 2801 E Beltline Ave Ne
 Grand Rapids MI 49525
 616 364-6161

(G-7289)
UFP INDUSTRIES INC (PA)
Also Called: Universal Forest Products
2801 E Beltline Ave Ne (49525-9680)
PHONE..................................616 364-6161
Matthew J Missad, *CEO*
William G Currie, *Ch of Bd*
Patrick M Webster, *President*
Rick Dorman, *General Mgr*
Ken Klimek, *General Mgr*
▼ EMP: 120 EST: 1955
SALES (est): 5.1B Publicly Held
WEB: www.ufpi.com
SIC: 2421 1796 Building & structural materials, wood; lumber: rough, sawed or planed; installing building equipment

(G-7290)
UFP INTERNATIONAL LLC (HQ)
2801 E Beltline Ave Ne (49525-9680)
PHONE..................................770 472-3050
Mike Mordell, *CEO*
EMP: 14 EST: 2016
SALES (est): 21.9MM
SALES (corp-wide): 5.1B Publicly Held
WEB: www.ufpinternational.com
SIC: 5031 3272 Building materials, exterior; building materials, except block or brick: concrete
PA: Ufp Industries, Inc.
 2801 E Beltline Ave Ne
 Grand Rapids MI 49525
 616 364-6161

(G-7291)
UFP LANSING LLC
2801 E Beltline Ave Ne (49525-9680)
PHONE..................................517 325-5572
Tara Vereeke, *Principal*
EMP: 5 EST: 2019
SALES (est): 947K
SALES (corp-wide): 5.1B Publicly Held
WEB: www.ufpinvestor.com
SIC: 2426 Lumber, hardwood dimension
PA: Ufp Industries, Inc.
 2801 E Beltline Ave Ne
 Grand Rapids MI 49525
 616 364-6161

(G-7292)
UFP SAUK RAPIDS LLC
Also Called: Custom Caseworks
2801 E Beltline Ave Ne (49525-9680)
PHONE..................................320 259-5190
John Lindholm, *CEO*
Dennis Mohs, *Purchasing*
EMP: 50 EST: 2013
SALES (est): 9.7MM
SALES (corp-wide): 5.1B Publicly Held
WEB: www.ufpi.com
SIC: 2435 Panels, hardwood plywood
PA: Ufp Industries, Inc.
 2801 E Beltline Ave Ne
 Grand Rapids MI 49525
 616 364-6161

(G-7293)
UFP SOUTHWEST LLC
2801 E Beltline Ave Ne (49525-9680)
PHONE..................................616 364-6161
Allen Peters, *Manager*
EMP: 1 EST: 2009
SALES (est): 2.4MM
SALES (corp-wide): 5.1B Publicly Held
WEB: www.ufpi.com
SIC: 2421 Building & structural materials, wood
PA: Ufp Industries, Inc.
 2801 E Beltline Ave Ne
 Grand Rapids MI 49525
 616 364-6161

(G-7294)
UFP TECHNOLOGIES INC
Also Called: United Foam Products
3831 Patterson Ave Se (49512-4026)
PHONE..................................616 949-8100
R Jeffrey Bailly, *Branch Mgr*
◆ EMP: 100
SALES (corp-wide): 179.3MM Publicly Held
WEB: www.ufpmedtech.com
SIC: 3086 3714 3296 2821 Plastics foam products; motor vehicle parts & accessories; mineral wool; plastics materials & resins; packaging paper & plastics film, coated & laminated
PA: Ufp Technologies, Inc.
 100 Hale St
 Newburyport MA 01950
 978 352-2200

(G-7295)
UFP WEST CENTRAL LLC
2801 E Beltline Ave Ne (49525-9680)
PHONE..................................616 364-6161
David Tutas,
EMP: 62 EST: 2009
SALES (est): 1.4MM Privately Held
WEB: www.ufpi.com
SIC: 2421 5031 1796 Sawmills & planing mills, general; lumber, plywood & millwork; installing building equipment

(G-7296)
UNIBAND USA LLC
2555 Oak Industrial Dr Ne (49505-6056)
PHONE..................................616 676-6011
Sarah Waidelich, *Accountant*
Milco Marchetti, *Mng Member*
Jason Moy, *Manager*
Shae Husted, *Assistant*
Ben Valk, *Assistant*
▲ EMP: 18 EST: 2009
SALES (est): 4.8MM Privately Held
WEB: www.unibandusa.com
SIC: 7374 3535 Data processing service; belt conveyor systems, general industrial use

(G-7297)
UNIST INC (PA)
4134 36th St Se (49512-2903)
PHONE..................................616 949-0853
Wally Boelkins, *CEO*
Charles Boelkins, *President*
Linda Waring, *Principal*
Tim Walker, *Vice Pres*
Alexander Boelkins, *Opers Mgr*
EMP: 25 EST: 1957
SALES (est): 5.5MM Privately Held
WEB: www.unist.com
SIC: 3523 5172 3563 3494 Sprayers & spraying machines, agricultural; lubricating oils & greases; air & gas compressors; valves & pipe fittings; manufactured hardware (general)

(G-7298)
UNIVERSAL SIGN INC
5001 Falcon View Ave Se (49512-5405)
PHONE..................................616 554-9999
Michael Penkevich, *President*
Mark Koster, *Foreman/Supr*
Jack Vos, *Sales Associate*
EMP: 20 EST: 1996
SQ FT: 24,000
SALES (est): 5.2MM Privately Held
WEB: www.universalsignsystems.com
SIC: 3993 Electric signs

(G-7299)
UNIVERSAL SPIRAL AIR NPP
2735 West River Dr Nw (49544-2013)
PHONE..................................616 475-5905
EMP: 9 EST: 2019
SALES (est): 970.5K Privately Held
WEB: www.usaduct.com
SIC: 3444 Sheet metalwork

(G-7300)
URGENT TOOL AND MACHINE INC
625 Chestnut St Sw (49503-4938)
PHONE..................................616 288-5000
Jamine Noordhoeck, *Principal*
Benjamin Noordhoeck, *Principal*
Nerl Ruster, *Principal*
Jon Mollema, *Accounts Mgr*
Ben Noordhoek, *Manager*
EMP: 20 EST: 1957
SALES (est): 5MM Privately Held
SIC: 3599 Machine shop, jobbing & repair

Grand Rapids - Kent County (G-7301)   GEOGRAPHIC SECTION

(G-7301)
VACLOVERS INC
3611 3 Mile Rd Nw (49534-1231)
PHONE..................................616 246-1700
Dewey I Doyle III, *President*
Joseph P Doyle, *Corp Secy*
EMP: 14 **EST:** 1990
SQ FT: 25,000
SALES (est): 443.3K **Privately Held**
SIC: 3589 Vacuum cleaners & sweepers, electric: industrial

(G-7302)
VALLEY PUBLISHING
3100 Walker Ridge Dr Nw (49544-9125)
PHONE..................................989 671-1200
David Roberts, *Branch Mgr*
EMP: 8 **EST:** 2007
SALES (est): 613.8K **Privately Held**
SIC: 2741 Miscellaneous publishing

(G-7303)
VALLEY TRUCK PARTS INC (PA)
Also Called: Valley Trck Parts-Grand Rapids
1900 Chicago Dr Sw (49519-1211)
PHONE..................................616 241-5431
Jack Goodale, *President*
Rex Troost, *Vice Pres*
EMP: 100 **EST:** 1954
SQ FT: 15,000
SALES (est): 49.1MM **Privately Held**
WEB: www.valleytruckparts.com
SIC: 5013 5015 5012 7539 Automotive supplies & parts; automotive parts & supplies, used; trucks, commercial; automotive repair shops; truck & tractor truck assembly; armature rewinding shops

(G-7304)
VAN DAM IRON WORKS LLC
1813 Chicago Dr Sw (49519-1250)
PHONE..................................616 452-8627
James Stickland, *President*
Jack Goodale, *Owner*
Neal Stickland, *Vice Pres*
Ron Housler, *Project Mgr*
Austin Whitman, *Project Mgr*
EMP: 44 **EST:** 1930
SQ FT: 42,000
SALES (est): 5.5MM **Privately Held**
WEB: www.vdiw.net
SIC: 3441 Fabricated structural metal

(G-7305)
VAN ZEE ACQUISITIONS INC
Also Called: Superior Furniture Company
4047 Eastern Ave Se (49508-3401)
PHONE..................................616 855-7000
Sue Ann Burns, *Ch of Bd*
William J Lee II, *President*
▲ **EMP:** 12 **EST:** 1936
SQ FT: 65,000
SALES (est): 361.1K **Privately Held**
WEB: www.superiorfurnitureco.com
SIC: 2511 Wood household furniture

(G-7306)
VAN ZEE CORPORATION
Also Called: Taylor Company, The
4047 Eastern Ave Se (49508-3401)
PHONE..................................616 245-9000
John Van Zee, *President*
Clarence Medema, *Shareholder*
EMP: 29 **EST:** 1972
SQ FT: 90,000
SALES (est): 1.1MM **Privately Held**
WEB: www.thetaylorco.com
SIC: 2541 Wood partitions & fixtures

(G-7307)
VANDER MILL LLC
505 Ball Ave Ne (49503-2011)
PHONE..................................616 259-8828
Amanda Vander Heide, *Mng Member*
Paul Vander Heide, *Mng Member*
Stuart Vander Heide, *Mng Member*
EMP: 85 **EST:** 2005
SQ FT: 55,000
SALES (est): 8.2MM **Privately Held**
WEB: www.vandermill.com
SIC: 2084 Wines

(G-7308)
VECTOR DISTRIBUTION LLC
1642 Broadway Ave Nw (49504-2046)
PHONE..................................616 361-2021
Geoffrey Alpizar, *President*
Tom Korest,
▲ **EMP:** 6 **EST:** 2003
SALES (est): 1.1MM **Privately Held**
WEB: www.vectordist.com
SIC: 2759 Screen printing

(G-7309)
VELOCITY WORLDWIDE INC
Also Called: Velocity USA
2280 29th St Se (49508-1560)
PHONE..................................616 243-3400
Tom Black, *President*
Linda Black, *Vice Pres*
Dave Deyoung, *Manager*
▲ **EMP:** 17 **EST:** 2006
SALES (est): 1.6MM **Privately Held**
WEB: www.velocityusa.com
SIC: 3751 Bicycles & related parts

(G-7310)
VENTRA GRAND RAPIDS 5 LLC
3075 Breton Rd Se (49512-1747)
PHONE..................................616 222-3296
Jim Zsebok, *Treasurer*
Laura Kenndy, *Controller*
Shahid R Khan,
EMP: 300 **EST:** 2009
SALES (est): 88.1MM
SALES (corp-wide): 1.5B **Privately Held**
WEB: www.flex-n-gate.com
SIC: 3714 Motor vehicle parts & accessories
PA: Flex-N-Gate Llc
   1306 E University Ave
   Urbana IL 61802
   217 384-6600

(G-7311)
VENTURE WOODWORKS
349 Scott Ave Nw (49504-4980)
PHONE..................................616 262-1930
Martin Gedris, *President*
EMP: 4 **EST:** 2017
SALES (est): 59.5K **Privately Held**
WEB: www.venturewoodworks.net
SIC: 2431 Millwork

(G-7312)
VERSATILITY INC
Also Called: Union First Promotions
2610 Berwyck Rd Se (49506-4816)
PHONE..................................616 957-5555
Stephen Zain, *President*
Tommy Karrip, *Prdtn Mgr*
EMP: 5 **EST:** 1984
SALES (est): 526.6K **Privately Held**
WEB: www.versatilityinc.com
SIC: 3993 Advertising novelties

(G-7313)
VERSTRAETE CONVEYABILITY INC
2889 Northridge Dr Nw (49544-9109)
PHONE..................................800 798-0410
Pete Verstraete, *President*
Teresa M Sokorai, *Vice Pres*
Bob Sokorai, *Sales Mgr*
Seth Warfield, *Regl Sales Mgr*
Dianne Taylor, *Manager*
EMP: 15 **EST:** 1980
SQ FT: 24,000
SALES (est): 3.7MM **Privately Held**
WEB: www.conveyability.com
SIC: 3535 Conveyors & conveying equipment

(G-7314)
VI-CHEM CORP
55 Cottage Grove St Sw (49507-1646)
PHONE..................................616 247-8501
Leonard Slott, *President*
Michael Murphy, *Prdtn Mgr*
Taryn Laverdiere, *QC Mgr*
Derek Fountaine, *Research*
Mike Lourim, *CFO*
▲ **EMP:** 102 **EST:** 1981
SQ FT: 120,000
SALES (est): 35.7MM
SALES (corp-wide): 188.6MM **Privately Held**
WEB: www.americhem.com
SIC: 2821 Polyvinyl chloride resins (PVC)

PA: Americhem, Inc.
   2000 Americhem Way
   Cuyahoga Falls OH 44221
   330 929-4213

(G-7315)
VIANT MEDICAL LLC
620 Watson St Sw (49504-6340)
PHONE..................................616 643-5200
Luis Quesada, *Opers Staff*
Bryan Jennings, *Production*
Dan Croteau, *Branch Mgr*
Anant Gohil, *Manager*
Dennis Gilkey, *Director*
EMP: 32
SALES (corp-wide): 1.1B **Privately Held**
WEB: www.viantmedical.com
SIC: 3841 Surgical & medical instruments
HQ: Viant Medical, Llc
   2 Hampshire St
   Foxborough MA 02035

(G-7316)
VICRODESIGNS GLOBAL LLC
6026 Kalamazoo Ave Se (49508-7018)
PHONE..................................616 307-3701
Michael Morris,
EMP: 5 **EST:** 2011
SALES (est): 82.9K **Privately Held**
SIC: 2721 Magazines: publishing only, not printed on site

(G-7317)
VIERSON BOILER & REPAIR CO
3700 Patterson Ave Se (49512-4097)
PHONE..................................616 949-0500
Lydia Vierson, *Treasurer*
Christopher Castillo, *Manager*
EMP: 10 **EST:** 1934
SQ FT: 8,000
SALES (est): 1.7MM **Privately Held**
WEB: www.viersonboiler.com
SIC: 1711 1796 3443 Boiler maintenance contractor; installing building equipment; boiler & boiler shop work; process vessels, industrial: metal plate

(G-7318)
VINEYARD ON PLAINFIELD
3418 Plainfield Ave Ne (49525-2717)
PHONE..................................616 570-0659
EMP: 4 **EST:** 2017
SALES (est): 104.8K **Privately Held**
SIC: 2084 Wines

(G-7319)
VINTAGE VIEWS PRESS
959 Ogden Ave Se (49506-3560)
PHONE..................................616 475-7662
Thomas Wilson, *Principal*
EMP: 4 **EST:** 2015
SALES (est): 137.3K **Privately Held**
WEB: www.vintageviewsprints.com
SIC: 2711 Newspapers

(G-7320)
VITAL CONCEPTS INC
5090 Kendrick Ct Se (49512-9649)
PHONE..................................616 954-2890
Douglas Sheehan, *Owner*
EMP: 5 **EST:** 2018
SALES (est): 86.6K **Privately Held**
SIC: 3841 Surgical & medical instruments

(G-7321)
VN INDUSTRIES INC
4635 40th St Se (49512-4038)
P.O. Box 8145 (49518-8145)
PHONE..................................616 540-2812
Todd Hennink, *President*
EMP: 6 **EST:** 2015
SALES (est): 320.1K **Privately Held**
SIC: 3599 Custom machinery

(G-7322)
W H GREEN & ASSOCIATES
703 Cambridge Blvd Se (49506-2812)
PHONE..................................616 682-5202
William Green, *Owner*
EMP: 6 **EST:** 2005
SALES (est): 104.7K **Privately Held**
SIC: 2679 Converted paper products

(G-7323)
WALKER TOOL & DIE INC
2411 Walker Ave Nw (49544-1377)
PHONE..................................616 453-5471
David N Hendricks, *CEO*
Todd Finley, *President*
Jeff Umlor, *Plant Mgr*
Robert Huisken, *Project Mgr*
Dick Pierce, *Facilities Mgr*
♦ **EMP:** 95
SQ FT: 100,000
SALES (est): 20MM **Privately Held**
WEB: www.walkertool.com
SIC: 3544 Special dies & tools

(G-7324)
WALTHER TROWAL GMBH & CO KG
4540 East Paris Ave Se (49512-5444)
PHONE..................................616 871-0031
Joshua Vanduinen, *Regl Sales Mgr*
Karen Zaccaro, *Sales Staff*
▲ **EMP:** 12 **EST:** 2009
SALES (est): 608.1K **Privately Held**
WEB: www.walthertrowal.com
SIC: 3714 Motor vehicle parts & accessories

(G-7325)
WAX POETIC
1423 Lake Dr Se (49506-1709)
PHONE..................................616 272-4693
EMP: 5 **EST:** 2017
SALES (est): 109.3K **Privately Held**
WEB: www.waxpoeticcandlebar.com
SIC: 3999 Candles

(G-7326)
WEALTHY STREET CORPORATION (PA)
Also Called: Crown Coat
700 Wealthy St Sw (49504-6440)
PHONE..................................616 451-0784
I Jay Bassett, *President*
Keith Bassett, *Vice Pres*
Kevin Bassett, *Vice Pres*
EMP: 44 **EST:** 1992
SQ FT: 144,000
SALES (est): 7.6MM **Privately Held**
WEB: www.spectrumindustries.com
SIC: 3479 Coating of metals & formed products

(G-7327)
WEAVER INSTRUCTIONAL SYSTEMS
6161 28th St Se Ste 9 (49546-6931)
PHONE..................................616 942-2891
Harry Weaver, *President*
EMP: 5
SALES (est): 486.5K **Privately Held**
WEB: www.wisesoft.com
SIC: 7372 5049 5046 5087 Application computer software; school supplies; teaching machines, electronic; service establishment equipment

(G-7328)
WEDO CUSTOM SCREEN PRINTING
1077 Leonard St Ne Ste 1 (49503-1286)
PHONE..................................616 965-7332
Lisa Farren, *Principal*
EMP: 4 **EST:** 2011
SALES (est): 215.5K **Privately Held**
WEB: www.wedoprint.org
SIC: 2752 Commercial printing, lithographic

(G-7329)
WEISS TECHNIK NORTH AMER INC (DH)
Also Called: Envirotronics
3881 N Greenbrooke Dr Se (49512-5328)
PHONE..................................616 554-5020
Robert Levert, *CEO*
Daryl Penfold, *President*
Cheryl Martin, *Buyer*
Kevin Boring, *Engineer*
Nate Dierlam, *Engineer*
▲ **EMP:** 100 **EST:** 1979
SQ FT: 50,000

SALES (est): 76.9MM
SALES (corp-wide): 1.2B **Privately Held**
WEB: www.weiss-na.com
SIC: 8734 3569 Testing laboratories; testing chambers for altitude, temperature, ordnance, power
HQ: Weiss Technik Gmbh
Greizer Str. 41-49
Reiskirchen HE 35447
640 884-0

(G-7330)
WERKEMA MACHINE COMPANY INC
7300 Division Ave S (49548-7136)
PHONE 616 455-7650
Thomas Werkema, *President*
Steven Werkema, *Superintendent*
Kathleen Werkema, *Corp Secy*
Harry L Werkema, *Plant Mgr*
Grant Allison, *Design Engr*
EMP: 16 **EST:** 1970
SQ FT: 10,000
SALES (est): 1MM **Privately Held**
WEB: www.werkemamachine.com
SIC: 3599 Machine shop, jobbing & repair

(G-7331)
WEST MICH FLCKING ASSEMBLY LLC
977 Ada Place Dr Se (49546-8412)
PHONE 269 639-1634
Melvin Fox, *President*
Glenda Chadwick, *Accountant*
Alexander Fergus,
EMP: 39 **EST:** 1977
SALES (est): 1.9MM **Privately Held**
WEB: www.wmflocking.com
SIC: 3999 3569 Flocking metal products; assembly machines, non-metalworking

(G-7332)
WEST MICH PRCSION MCHINING INC
2500 Waldorf Ct Nw (49544-1416)
PHONE 616 791-1970
Phil Allen, *CEO*
EMP: 17 **EST:** 2003
SALES (est): 2.1MM **Privately Held**
WEB: www.wmpminc.com
SIC: 3599 Machine shop, jobbing & repair

(G-7333)
WEST MICHIGAN COATING LLC
3150 Fruit Ridge Ave Nw (49544-9707)
PHONE 616 647-9509
Jeff Momber, *Manager*
David H Nykamp,
EMP: 35 **EST:** 2000
SQ FT: 50,000
SALES (est): 3.1MM **Privately Held**
WEB: www.westmichigancoating.com
SIC: 3479 Coating of metals & formed products

(G-7334)
WEST MICHIGAN GL COATINGS INC
4047 Mission St Nw (49534-2123)
PHONE 616 970-4863
Joe Bockheim, *Principal*
Joseph Bockheim, *Principal*
EMP: 9 **EST:** 1987
SALES (est): 608.1K **Privately Held**
WEB: www.westmgc.com
SIC: 3479 Coating of metals & formed products

(G-7335)
WEST MICHIGAN TAG & LABEL INC
Also Called: Wmtl
5300 Broadmoor Ave Se F (49512-9654)
PHONE 616 235-0120
Richard Rice, *President*
Lou Robach, *Sales Staff*
EMP: 20 **EST:** 1987
SQ FT: 13,000
SALES (est): 2.7MM **Privately Held**
WEB: www.wmtlprinting.com
SIC: 2752 5199 Commercial printing, offset; tags, lithographed; packaging materials

(G-7336)
WEST THOMAS PARTNERS LLC
Also Called: The Gluten Free Bar, The
4053 Brockton Dr Se Ste A (49512-4071)
PHONE 616 430-7585
Anastasia Pennington, *Plant Mgr*
Lisa Koller, *Bookkeeper*
Amanda Dorda, *Business Anlyst*
Ben Wahl,
Marshall Rader,
▼ **EMP:** 40 **EST:** 2013
SALES (est): 7.8MM **Privately Held**
SIC: 2051 Bakery: wholesale or wholesale/retail combined

(G-7337)
WH MANUFACTURING INC
2606 Thornwood St Sw (49519-2151)
PHONE 616 534-7560
Debbie Williams, *President*
Mary Bolt, *Office Mgr*
EMP: 25 **EST:** 1993
SQ FT: 4,500
SALES (est): 2.9MM **Privately Held**
SIC: 3679 5063 Harness assemblies for electronic use: wire or cable; electronic wire & cable

(G-7338)
WHOLESALEMILLWORKCOM
4707 40th St Se (49512-4076)
PHONE 616 241-6011
EMP: 6 **EST:** 2017
SALES (est): 131.1K **Privately Held**
WEB: www.wholesalemillwork.com
SIC: 2431 Millwork

(G-7339)
WIKOFF COLOR CORPORATION
3410 Jefferson Ave Se (49548-2244)
PHONE 616 245-3930
James Withers, *Prdtn Mgr*
Gary Hildebrand, *Branch Mgr*
Gary Meyer, *Technical Staff*
EMP: 20
SALES (corp-wide): 156.4MM **Privately Held**
WEB: www.wikoff.com
SIC: 2893 Printing ink
PA: Wikoff Color Corporation
1886 Merritt Rd
Fort Mill SC 29715
803 548-2210

(G-7340)
WILLIAM B EERDMANS PUBG CO
4035 Park East Ct Se (49546-8818)
PHONE 616 459-4591
Anita Eerdmans, *President*
David Bratt, *Editor*
Jennifer Tornga, *COO*
James Ernest, *Vice Pres*
Klaas Wolterstorff, *Vice Pres*
▲ **EMP:** 42 **EST:** 1911
SQ FT: 80,000
SALES (est): 7MM **Privately Held**
WEB: www.eerdmans.com
SIC: 2731 2732 Books: publishing only; textbooks: publishing only, not printed on site; pamphlets: publishing only, not printed on site; books: printing & binding; textbooks: printing & binding, not publishing; pamphlets: printing & binding, not published on site

(G-7341)
WINE ND CANVAS GRAND RAPIDS
2675 East Paris Ave Se # 3 (49546-6138)
PHONE 616 970-1082
EMP: 4 **EST:** 2018
SALES (est): 55.5K **Privately Held**
WEB: www.wineandcanvas.com
SIC: 2211 Canvas

(G-7342)
WIZ WHEELZ INC
Also Called: Terratrike
4460 40th St Se (49512-4035)
PHONE 616 455-5988
Jack Wiswell, *CEO*
Scott Johnson, *Warehouse Mgr*
Jayant Lamba, *Engineer*
Wayne Oom, *CFO*
Luke Lindgren, *Sales Staff*
▲ **EMP:** 30 **EST:** 1996
SQ FT: 8,000
SALES (est): 5.2MM **Privately Held**
WEB: www.terratrike.com
SIC: 3751 5941 Bicycles & related parts; sporting goods & bicycle shops

(G-7343)
WNC OF GRAND RAPIDS 2 LLC
2675 East Paris Ave Se # 3 (49546-6138)
PHONE 269 986-5066
Nechole Culp, *Administration*
EMP: 7 **EST:** 2017
SALES (est): 472.2K **Privately Held**
SIC: 2211 Canvas

(G-7344)
WOLVERINE COIL SPRING COMPANY
818 Front Ave Nw (49504-4495)
PHONE 616 459-3504
Jay Dunwell, *President*
Jerry Walker, *Plant Mgr*
Douglas Miron, *CFO*
Jim Bennett, *Sales Mgr*
Brian Risch, *Sales Staff*
EMP: 70 **EST:** 1946
SQ FT: 45,000
SALES (est): 14.1MM **Privately Held**
WEB: www.wolverinecoilspring.com
SIC: 3495 Wire springs

(G-7345)
WOLVERINE CRANE & SERVICE INC (PA)
2557 Thornwood St Sw (49519-2148)
PHONE 616 538-4870
Rich Kelps, *President*
Carrie Raby, *Controller*
Dennis Okler, *Sales Staff*
▲ **EMP:** 20 **EST:** 1994
SQ FT: 60,000
SALES (est): 8.4MM **Privately Held**
WEB: www.wolverinecrane.com
SIC: 3536 7699 Cranes, overhead traveling; industrial equipment services

(G-7346)
WOLVERINE GAS AND OIL CORP (PA)
1 Rivrfront Plz 55 Cmpau (49503)
PHONE 616 458-1150
Sidney J Jansma Jr, *President*
David Rozendal, *Business Mgr*
Gary Bleeker, *Vice Pres*
Sidney Jansma Jr III, *Vice Pres*
Richard Moritz, *Vice Pres*
EMP: 25 **EST:** 1997
SALES (est): 9.9MM **Privately Held**
WEB: www.wolverinegasandoil.com
SIC: 1382 Oil & gas exploration services

(G-7347)
WOLVERINE PRINTING COMPANY LLC
Also Called: Spectrum Graphics
315 Grandville Ave Sw (49503-4098)
PHONE 616 451-2075
Bob Goeldel, *Purchasing*
Ray Boisvenue, *VP Human Res*
Kurt Burmeister, *Sales Staff*
Mike Fauble, *Sales Staff*
Julie Kreger, *Marketing Staff*
EMP: 32 **EST:** 1963
SQ FT: 36,000
SALES (est): 4.1MM **Privately Held**
WEB: www.wolverineprinting.com
SIC: 2791 2789 2752 Typesetting; bookbinding & related work; commercial printing, offset

(G-7348)
WOLVERINE SPECIAL TOOL INC
1857 Waldorf St Nw (49544-1433)
PHONE 616 791-1027
Guy Chilton, *President*
Paul Tenbrock, *Corp Secy*
Joe Stewart, *Sales Staff*
EMP: 20 **EST:** 1987
SQ FT: 5,500 **Privately Held**
WEB: www.wolverinespecialtool.com
SIC: 3545 7389 5084 Cutting tools for machine tools; grinding, precision: commercial or industrial; machine tools & metalworking machinery

(G-7349)
WONDERLAND GRAPHICS INC
4030 Eastern Ave Se (49508-3402)
PHONE 616 452-0712
Mark Hoover, *President*
Diane Krugh, *Corp Secy*
Tom Hooper, *Manager*
Shene Smith, *Director*
Marge Crischer, *Admin Sec*
EMP: 6 **EST:** 1986
SQ FT: 17,000
SALES (est): 157K **Privately Held**
WEB: www.reflectiveartinc.com
SIC: 3299 Art goods: plaster of paris, papier mache & scagliola

(G-7350)
WOODWAYS INDUSTRIES LLC (PA)
Also Called: Woodways Custom Built
4265 28th St Se Ste A (49512-5670)
PHONE 616 956-3070
Aaron Graft, *Prdtn Mgr*
Charles Feak, *Engineer*
Samuel Martonosi, *Project Engr*
Ben Telgenhof, *Project Engr*
Sarah Schwartz, *Sales Mgr*
EMP: 47 **EST:** 2007
SQ FT: 22,000
SALES (est): 5MM **Privately Held**
WEB: www.woodwayscustom.com
SIC: 2434 2511 1751 Wood kitchen cabinets; wood household furniture; carpentry work

(G-7351)
WYKE DIE & ENGINEERING INC
4334 Brockton Dr Se Ste I (49512-4117)
PHONE 616 871-1175
Robert Wykoski, *President*
EMP: 8 **EST:** 1993
SQ FT: 3,000
SALES (est): 623.5K **Privately Held**
WEB: www.wykedie.com
SIC: 3544 Special dies & tools

(G-7352)
X-EDGE PRODUCTS INC
2727 Elmridge Dr Nw (49534-1327)
PHONE 866 591-9991
Robert Bepristis Sr, *President*
EMP: 5 **EST:** 2016
SALES (est): 500K **Privately Held**
SIC: 3545 Tools & accessories for machine tools

(G-7353)
X-RITE INCORPORATED (HQ)
Also Called: X-Rite Company, The
4300 44th St Se (49512-4009)
PHONE 616 803-2100
Thomas J Vacchiano Jr, *CEO*
Ondrej Kruk, *President*
Jan-Paul V Maaren, *President*
Iris Mangelschots, *President*
Francis Lamy, *Exec VP*
▲ **EMP:** 149 **EST:** 1958
SALES (est): 80.5MM
SALES (corp-wide): 22.2B **Publicly Held**
WEB: www.xrite.com
SIC: 3823 3827 3613 3826 Industrial instrmnts msrmnt display/control process variable; optical instruments & lenses; switchgear & switchboard apparatus; analytical instruments; densitometers
PA: Danaher Corporation
2200 Penn Ave Nw Ste 800w
Washington DC 20037
202 828-0850

(G-7354)
YARD & HOME LLC
2801 E Beltline Ave Nw (49525)
PHONE 844 927-3466
EMP: 10 **EST:** 2017
SALES (est): 1MM
SALES (corp-wide): 5.1B **Publicly Held**
WEB: www.yardandhome.com
SIC: 2421 1796 Building & structural materials, wood; lumber: rough, sawed or planed; installing building equipment

Grand Rapids - Kent County (G-7355)   GEOGRAPHIC SECTION

PA: Ufp Industries, Inc.
2801 E Beltline Ave Ne
Grand Rapids MI 49525
616 364-6161

(G-7355)
YELLO DUMPSTER
1505 Steele Ave Sw (49507-1522)
PHONE..................616 915-0506
EMP: 6 EST: 2017
SALES (est): 164.4K Privately Held
WEB: www.yellodumpster.com
SIC: 3443 Dumpsters, garbage

(G-7356)
ZAYNA LLC
Also Called: Harnel Company
1600 Marshall Ave Se Side (49507-2069)
PHONE..................616 452-4522
James Tuffs, *President*
EMP: 5 EST: 1978
SQ FT: 30,000
SALES (est): 450.8K Privately Held
WEB: www.harnelcustomcase.com
SIC: 3089 3412 Plastic containers, except foam; metal barrels, drums & pails

(G-7357)
ZINGER SHEET METAL INC
4005 Rger B Chffee Mem Dr (49548-3441)
PHONE..................616 532-3121
Nelson Capestany, *President*
Denise Devries, *Office Mgr*
Sandra Capestany, *Admin Sec*
EMP: 18 EST: 1954
SQ FT: 10,200
SALES (est): 1.2MM Privately Held
WEB: www.zingersheetmetal.com
SIC: 3444 Sheet metal specialties, not stamped

(G-7358)
ZONDERVAN CORPORATION LLC (DH)
Also Called: Zondervan Publishing House
3900 Sparks Dr Se (49546-6146)
PHONE..................616 698-6900
Rich Tatum, *Publisher*
Stephanie S Smith, *Editor*
Randy Bishop, *Vice Pres*
Dennis Thompson, *Vice Pres*
Angel Grit, *Production*
◆ EMP: 315 EST: 1976
SQ FT: 306,000
SALES (est): 123.1MM
SALES (corp-wide): 9.3B Publicly Held
WEB: www.zondervan.com
SIC: 2741 Miscellaneous publishing; posters: publishing only, not printed on site
HQ: Harpercollins Publishers L.L.C.
195 Broadway
New York NY 10007
212 207-7000

(G-7359)
ZOOMER DISPLAY LLC
522 Stocking Ave Nw (49504-5504)
PHONE..................616 734-0300
Jackson Martin, *President*
EMP: 5 EST: 2012
SQ FT: 40,000
SALES (est): 409.7K Privately Held
WEB: www.zoomerdisplay.com
SIC: 2741 2653 7389 Miscellaneous publishing; display items, solid fiber: made from purchased materials; packaging & labeling services

Grandville
Kent County

(G-7360)
A KOPPEL COLOR IMAGE COMPANY
Also Called: Koppel A Color Image
4025 Chicago Dr Sw (49418-1201)
PHONE..................616 534-3600
John Koppel, *Partner*
Kim Koppel, *Partner*
Kim Kopple, *Records Dir*
EMP: 6 EST: 1989
SALES (est): 532.9K Privately Held
WEB: www.koppelprint.com
SIC: 2752 2791 2789 Commercial printing, offset; typesetting; bookbinding & related work

(G-7361)
ACCURATE AUTOMOTIVE ENGS INC
Also Called: Accurate Engines
2840 Dormax St Sw (49418-1121)
PHONE..................616 531-2050
Stephen Hassell, *President*
Brittany Parker, *Receptionist*
▼ EMP: 21 EST: 1980
SALES (est): 4.3MM Privately Held
WEB: www.accurateengines.com
SIC: 3714 Motor vehicle parts & accessories

(G-7362)
ACTION DIE & TOOL INC
4621 Spartan Indus Dr Sw (49418-2511)
PHONE..................616 538-2326
Tim Vandeclock, *President*
EMP: 8 EST: 1983
SQ FT: 3,500
SALES (est): 861.5K Privately Held
WEB: www.actiondie.com
SIC: 3544 Special dies & tools

(G-7363)
ADVANCED CNC MACHINING LLC
3086 Dixie Ave Sw Ste E (49418-1196)
PHONE..................616 226-6706
James Kozak,
EMP: 9 EST: 2007
SQ FT: 4,000
SALES (est): 800K Privately Held
WEB: www.cncmichigan.com
SIC: 3599 Machine shop, jobbing & repair

(G-7364)
ALUMINUM TEXTURES INC
2925 Remico St Sw Ste A (49418-2722)
PHONE..................616 538-3144
G T Boylan, *President*
Tom Dykstra, *Vice Pres*
EMP: 31 EST: 1968
SQ FT: 25,000
SALES (est): 5.7MM Privately Held
SIC: 3089 3469 3442 3354 Plastic processing; metal stampings; metal doors, sash & trim; aluminum extruded products

(G-7365)
APEX RACK AND COATING CO
Also Called: Quality Sandblasting
3434 Busch Dr Sw (49418-1098)
P.O. Box 337 (49468-0337)
PHONE..................616 530-6811
Dennis Carlon, *CEO*
EMP: 21 EST: 1961
SQ FT: 27,400
SALES (est): 559.2K Privately Held
WEB: www.apexrack.com
SIC: 3443 Trash racks, metal plate

(G-7366)
BAY HOME MEDICAL AND REHAB INC (PA)
5752 Stonebridge Dr Sw (49418-3239)
PHONE..................231 933-1200
Timothy Keller, *President*
Karen Keller, *Treasurer*
EMP: 17 EST: 1995
SQ FT: 4,500
SALES (est): 2.2MM Privately Held
WEB: www.bayhomemedical.com
SIC: 5999 5047 3999 Medical apparatus & supplies; hospital equipment & furniture; wheelchair lifts

(G-7367)
BELWITH PRODUCTS LLC
3100 Broadway Ave Sw (49418-1581)
PHONE..................616 247-4000
Andy Sidor, *President*
EMP: 10
SQ FT: 340,000 Privately Held
WEB: www.belwith-keeler.com
SIC: 3469 3429 3452 3366 Metal stampings; furniture hardware; bolts, nuts, rivets & washers; copper foundries

PA: Belwith Products, Llc
3100 Broadway Ave Sw
Grandville MI 49418

(G-7368)
BMC BIL-MAC CORPORATION
Also Called: BMC Bil-Mac Company
2995 44th St Sw (49418-2565)
PHONE..................616 538-1930
Mike Bowen, *President*
Nicholas Bowen, *Vice Pres*
Alex Calverley, *Engineer*
Marilyn Field, *Office Mgr*
Ellen Olson, *Office Mgr*
EMP: 77 EST: 1947
SQ FT: 65,000
SALES (est): 8.3MM Privately Held
WEB: www.bmcbil-mac.com
SIC: 3451 Screw machine products

(G-7369)
CHRISTIAN SCHOOLS INTL
2969 Pririe St Sw Ste 102 (49418)
PHONE..................616 957-1070
John Wolters, *CFO*
Todd Schilthuis, *Accounts Mgr*
Terry Kok, *Consultant*
Karen Sharda, *Admin Asst*
Val Avink, *Assistant*
EMP: 37
SALES: 1.8MM Privately Held
WEB: www.csionline.org
SIC: 8742 2731 Management consulting services; books: publishing & printing

(G-7370)
DEPPE MOLD & TOOLING INC
2814 Franklin Ave Sw (49418-1262)
PHONE..................616 530-1331
Jeff Deppe, *President*
Sheryl Deppe, *Admin Sec*
EMP: 23 EST: 1997
SQ FT: 4,000
SALES (est): 3MM Privately Held
WEB: www.deppemold.com
SIC: 3544 Special dies & tools

(G-7371)
DIGITAL TOOL & DIE INC
2606 Sanford Ave Sw (49418-1069)
PHONE..................616 532-8020
Michael Gill, *President*
Dennis Gill, *Vice Pres*
Nancy Allen, *Manager*
▲ EMP: 47 EST: 1989
SQ FT: 20,000
SALES (est): 9.7MM Privately Held
WEB: www.digitaltooldie.com
SIC: 3544 Special dies & tools

(G-7372)
ELECTRO CHEMICAL FINISHING CO (PA)
2973 Dormax St Sw (49418-1165)
PHONE..................616 531-0670
Terry Vollmer, *President*
Don Post, *President*
Eric Romero, *COO*
Dan Trapp, *VP Admin*
Tony Cockrill, *Engineer*
EMP: 15
SQ FT: 64,000
SALES (est): 15.6MM Privately Held
WEB: www.ecfinc.com
SIC: 3471 3479 Electroplating of metals or formed products; coating of metals & formed products

(G-7373)
ENERGY ACQUISITION
2992 28th St Sw (49418-2703)
PHONE..................616 350-9129
EMP: 5 EST: 2013
SALES (est): 232.8K Privately Held
WEB: www.energyacquisitionsgroup.com
SIC: 1311 Crude petroleum production

(G-7374)
ENTERPRISE TOOL & DIE LLC
4270 White St Sw (49418-1254)
PHONE..................616 538-0920
Doug Groom, *CEO*
Leslie Larsen, *President*
Richard W Schweikert, *Vice Pres*
Dan Hipp, *Project Mgr*
Eric Smith, *Project Mgr*

EMP: 55 EST: 1961
SQ FT: 45,000
SALES (est): 8.8MM Privately Held
WEB: www.enterprisedie.com
SIC: 3544 Special dies & tools

(G-7375)
EXTREME SCREENPRINTS
3030 Sangra Ave Sw (49418-2723)
PHONE..................616 889-8305
EMP: 5 EST: 2016
SALES (est): 376K Privately Held
WEB: www.extremescreenprints.com
SIC: 2759 Publication printing

(G-7376)
EXTREME WIRE EDM SERVICE INC
3636 Busch Dr Sw (49418-1340)
PHONE..................616 249-3901
Carl Berndt, *President*
Brian Berndt, *Vice Pres*
EMP: 8 EST: 1998
SALES (est): 711.2K Privately Held
WEB: www.extremewireedm.com
SIC: 3544 Special dies & tools

(G-7377)
FAMILY SAFETY PRODUCTS INC
2879 Remico St Sw (49418-1139)
PHONE..................616 530-6540
Jim Workman, *Chairman*
Connie Beles, *Accounting Mgr*
EMP: 9 EST: 1996
SALES (est): 978.5K Privately Held
WEB: www.familysafetyproductsinc.com
SIC: 3829 Gas detectors

(G-7378)
GECKOBRANDS LLC
2950 Pririe St Sw Ste 1000 (49418)
PHONE..................561 704-8400
Bryan Oconnell, *Administration*
EMP: 8 EST: 2015
SALES (est): 622.7K Privately Held
WEB: www.geckobrands.com
SIC: 2385 Waterproof outerwear

(G-7379)
GIVE-EM A BRAKE SAFETY LLC
2610 Sanford Ave Sw (49418-1069)
PHONE..................616 531-8705
Darrin Kelly, *Sales Staff*
Larry Booth, *Sales Executive*
Chris Heyboer, *Branch Mgr*
Dan Babcock, *Mng Member*
Shane Lemke, *Manager*
EMP: 20 EST: 2003
SQ FT: 10,000
SALES (est): 4MM Privately Held
WEB: www.gebsafety.com
SIC: 3499 3669 Barricades, metal; traffic signals, electric

(G-7380)
GRAND RAPIDS WOOD WORKS
3818 Bruce Dr Sw (49418-2432)
PHONE..................616 690-2889
Robert Powers, *Principal*
EMP: 5 EST: 2015
SALES (est): 62.4K Privately Held
WEB: www.woodtv.com
SIC: 2431 Millwork

(G-7381)
GRANDVILLE INDUSTRIES INC
4270 White St Sw (49418-1254)
P.O. Box 439 (49468-0439)
PHONE..................616 538-0920
Robert C Johnson, *CEO*
Russell Wiersma, *President*
John Szot, *Treasurer*
EMP: 27 EST: 1977
SQ FT: 45,000
SALES (est): 375.2K Privately Held
WEB: www.goodwillgr.org
SIC: 3544 Special dies & tools; dies, plastics forming

(G-7382)
GRANDVILLE PRINTING CO
4719 Ivanrest Ave Sw (49418-9141)
P.O. Box 247 (49468-0247)
PHONE..................616 534-8647
Jeffrey C Brewer, *Ch of Bd*
Patrick J Brewer, *President*

▲ = Import ▼ = Export
◆ = Import/Export

GEOGRAPHIC SECTION

Grandville - Kent County (G-7408)

Rickard A Durham, *Vice Pres*
Curtis J Cooke, *CFO*
Josh Waclawski, *Technology*
▼ **EMP:** 222 **EST:** 1956
SQ FT: 157,000
SALES (est): 53.3MM **Privately Held**
WEB: www.gpco.com
SIC: 2752 Commercial printing, offset

(G-7383)
GRANDVILLE TRACTOR SVCS LLC
3408 Busch Dr Sw Ste E (49418-3422)
PHONE................................616 530-2030
EMP: 17
SALES (est): 1.9MM **Privately Held**
SIC: 3524 Mfg Lawn/Garden Equipment

(G-7384)
H & L ADVANTAGE INC
3500 Busch Dr Sw (49418-1321)
PHONE................................616 532-1012
Brad Alkema, *President*
Lawrence Hobbie, *Vice Pres*
Larry Hobbie, *VP Engrg*
Lori Darcy, *Manager*
▲ **EMP:** 50
SQ FT: 36,000
SALES (est): 11.5MM **Privately Held**
WEB: www.hladvantage.com
SIC: 3429 5162 Furniture hardware; plastics materials & basic shapes; plastics products

(G-7385)
HADLEY PRODUCTS CORPORATION (HQ)
Also Called: B & R Manufacturing Division
2851 Prairie St Sw Ste A (49418-2179)
PHONE................................616 530-1717
James Humphrey, *CEO*
John W Humphrey, *Ch of Bd*
Robert Dubsky, *President*
Larry Leece, *COO*
Paul Blaicher, *Vice Pres*
◆ **EMP:** 138 **EST:** 1996
SQ FT: 117,000
SALES (est): 34.6MM
SALES (corp-wide): 190MM **Privately Held**
WEB: www.hadleyadvantage.com
SIC: 3714 Motor vehicle parts & accessories
PA: Humphrey Companies Llc
2851 Prairie St Sw
Grandville MI 49418
616 530-1717

(G-7386)
HARBOR FOAM INC
2950 Pririe St Sw Ste 300 (49418)
PHONE................................616 855-8150
Laura Kuperus, *President*
Ryan Dyke, *Vice Pres*
Ryan Van Dyke, *Vice Pres*
Scott Miller, *Engineer*
Patricia Van Dyke, *Sales Mgr*
▲ **EMP:** 8 **EST:** 2007
SALES (est): 1.5MM **Privately Held**
WEB: www.harborfoam.com
SIC: 3086 Insulation or cushioning material, foamed plastic

(G-7387)
HARLO CORPORATION (PA)
4210 Ferry St Sw (49418-1573)
P.O. Box 129 (49468-0129)
PHONE................................616 538-0550
Mary Helen Crooks, *CEO*
Craig Crooks, *Chairman*
Richard G Crooks, *Vice Pres*
Jim Johnson, *Controller*
EMP: 98 **EST:** 1938
SQ FT: 84,000
SALES (est): 18.2MM **Privately Held**
WEB: www.harlocorporation.com
SIC: 3537 3613 Lift trucks, industrial: fork, platform, straddle, etc.; control panels, electric

(G-7388)
HARLO PRODUCTS CORPORATION (HQ)
4210 Ferry St Sw (49418-1545)
P.O. Box 129 (49468-0129)
PHONE................................616 538-0550
Mary Helen Crooks, *CEO*
Craig Crooks, *Chairman*
Richard G Crooks, *Exec VP*
▲ **EMP:** 30 **EST:** 1958
SQ FT: 63,000
SALES (est): 16.3MM
SALES (corp-wide): 18.2MM **Privately Held**
WEB: www.harloproducts.com
SIC: 3537 Forklift trucks
PA: Harlo Corporation
4210 Ferry St Sw
Grandville MI 49418
616 538-0550

(G-7389)
HUMPHREY COMPANIES LLC (PA)
2851 Prairie St Sw (49418-2179)
PHONE................................616 530-1717
James A Humphrey, *CEO*
John W Humphrey, *Chairman*
Gary Schafer, *Engineer*
James D Green, *CFO*
Scott Finkhouse, *Manager*
EMP: 195 **EST:** 1984
SALES (est): 190MM **Privately Held**
WEB: www.humphreyenterprises.com
SIC: 3537 3714 3089 5023 Industrial trucks & tractors; motor vehicle parts & accessories; molding primary plastic; home furnishings; plastics sheets & rods

(G-7390)
I2 INTERNATIONAL DEV LLC
2905 Wilson Ave Sw # 200 (49418-1295)
PHONE................................616 534-8100
Bill Stewart, *President*
David Byker, *Owner*
Abdul Swalhah, *Vice Pres*
EMP: 6 **EST:** 2015
SQ FT: 3,000
SALES (est): 119.2K **Privately Held**
WEB: www.i2intl.net
SIC: 3211 5039 Construction glass; glass construction materials

(G-7391)
IFCA INTERNATIONAL INC (PA)
3520 Fairlanes Ave Sw (49418-1536)
P.O. Box 810 (49468-0810)
PHONE................................616 531-1840
Royce Sprague, *President*
Tom Olson, *Finance*
Les Lofquist, *Exec Dir*
EMP: 5 **EST:** 1930
SQ FT: 6,000
SALES (est): 1.1MM **Privately Held**
WEB: www.ifca.org
SIC: 2741 8661 Miscellaneous publishing; religious organizations

(G-7392)
INDUSTRIAL INNOVATIONS INC
Also Called: Spray Right
2936 Dormax St Sw (49418-1166)
PHONE................................616 249-1525
Troy W Turnbull, *President*
John W Hayes, *Vice Pres*
EMP: 10 **EST:** 1980
SQ FT: 10,000
SALES (est): 2.6MM **Privately Held**
WEB: www.industrialinnovations.com
SIC: 3542 3469 Die casting machines; metal stampings

(G-7393)
JIREH METAL PRODUCTS INC (PA)
3635 Nardin St Sw (49418-1066)
PHONE................................616 531-7581
Michael Davenport, *President*
Jim Kroll, *QC Mgr*
EMP: 93 **EST:** 2014
SQ FT: 114,000
SALES (est): 10.9MM **Privately Held**
WEB: www.jirehmetal.com
SIC: 3469 Stamping metal for the trade

(G-7394)
JUSTICE
3700 Rvrtwn Pkwy Sw # 2144 (49418-3091)
PHONE................................616 531-4534
EMP: 4 **EST:** 2019
SALES (est): 106.4K **Privately Held**
SIC: 2361 Girls' & children's dresses, blouses & shirts

(G-7395)
KERKSTRA PRECAST LLC
Also Called: Spancrete Great Lakes
3373 Busch Dr Sw (49418-1341)
PHONE................................616 457-4920
Greg Kerkstra, *CEO*
Derek Hunderman, *President*
Steve Haskill, *Vice Pres*
Susan Rollins, *Safety Dir*
Andy Eustice, *Project Mgr*
◆ **EMP:** 150 **EST:** 1962
SALES (est): 36.1MM **Privately Held**
WEB: www.kerkstra.com
SIC: 3432 3272 Plumbing fixture fittings & trim; septic tanks, concrete
HQ: Fabcon Precast, Llc
6111 Highway 13 W
Savage MN 55378
952 890-4444

(G-7396)
KREGEL INC (PA)
Also Called: Kregel Parable Christn Stores
4014 Chicago Dr Sw (49418-1202)
PHONE................................616 531-7707
James Kregel, *Ch of Bd*
Catherine Devries, *Publisher*
Dennis Hillman, *Publisher*
Janyre Tromp, *Editor*
Rachel Bono, *Production*
◆ **EMP:** 46 **EST:** 1909
SQ FT: 75,000
SALES (est): 18.8MM **Privately Held**
WEB: www.kregel.com
SIC: 2731 Books: publishing only

(G-7397)
LEGACY PRECISION MOLDS INC
4668 Spartan Indus Dr Sw (49418-2512)
PHONE................................616 532-6536
Tom Van Ree, *Owner*
EMP: 7 **EST:** 1999
SQ FT: 4,000
SALES (est): 850.3K **Privately Held**
WEB: www.legacyprecisionmolds.com
SIC: 3544 Industrial molds

(G-7398)
LEJ INVESTMENTS LLC
Also Called: Nanoplas
2950 Pririe St Sw Ste 900 (49418)
PHONE................................616 452-3707
Joe Coretti, *Sales Staff*
John B Hoff,
EMP: 10 **EST:** 2012
SALES (est): 949.6K **Privately Held**
SIC: 2821 Molding compounds, plastics

(G-7399)
M AND L FABRICATION LLC
3408 Busch Dr Sw Ste D (49418-3422)
P.O. Box 951 (49468-0951)
PHONE................................616 259-7754
EMP: 7 **EST:** 2012
SALES (est): 355.3K **Privately Held**
WEB: www.mlfabrication.com
SIC: 7692 Welding repair

(G-7400)
MICHIGAN LEGAL PUBLISHING LTD
2885 Sanford Ave Sw (49418-1342)
PHONE................................877 525-1990
Jeff Steinport, *Principal*
EMP: 11 **EST:** 2016
SALES (est): 902.4K **Privately Held**
SIC: 2741 Miscellaneous publishing

(G-7401)
MIDWEST VIBRO INC
Also Called: H & M Vibro
3715 28th St Sw (49418-1314)
P.O. Box 245 (49468-0245)
PHONE................................616 532-7670

Edwin Haverkamp, *President*
Douglas Haverkamp, *Vice Pres*
Nancy Haverkamp, *Admin Sec*
EMP: 5 **EST:** 1980
SQ FT: 10,500
SALES (est): 816.5K **Privately Held**
WEB: www.midwestvibro.com
SIC: 3531 7359 7699 Vibrators for concrete construction; equipment rental & leasing; professional instrument repair services

(G-7402)
MIEDEMA REALTY INC
4072 Chicago Dr Sw Ste 3 (49418-1291)
PHONE................................616 538-4800
David Miedema, *Director*
EMP: 4 **EST:** 1999
SALES (est): 81.4K **Privately Held**
WEB: www.communityfuelsinc.com
SIC: 3599 Industrial machinery

(G-7403)
MULL-IT-OVER PRODUCTS LLC
4275 White St Sw (49418-1253)
PHONE................................616 730-2162
Bruce Brugess,
EMP: 7 **EST:** 2011
SALES (est): 1.7MM **Privately Held**
WEB: www.mullitoverproducts.com
SIC: 3531 Construction machinery

(G-7404)
MULTIAX INTERNATIONAL INC
3000 Remico St Sw (49418-1189)
PHONE................................616 534-4530
Eduard Dauthier, *Managing Dir*
Darin De Clark, *Principal*
EMP: 5 **EST:** 2005
SALES (est): 471.7K **Privately Held**
WEB: www.multiax.com
SIC: 8741 3661 Management services; modems

(G-7405)
MUSICAL SNEAKERS INCORPORATED (PA)
2885 Snford Ave Sw 3533 (49418)
P.O. Box 310, New York NY (10029-0241)
PHONE................................888 410-7050
EMP: 16
SALES (est): 2.8MM **Privately Held**
SIC: 3021 Mfg Rubber/Plastic Footwear

(G-7406)
OFFICE STATION ENTERPRISES INC
4370 Chicago Dr Sw Ste B (49418-1694)
PHONE................................616 633-3339
Brian Herbst, *Principal*
EMP: 16 **EST:** 2005
SALES (est): 652.2K **Privately Held**
WEB: www.officestation.com
SIC: 2522 Office furniture, except wood

(G-7407)
PACKAGING CORPORATION AMERICA
Also Called: PCA Grandville
3251 Chicago Dr Sw (49418-1003)
PHONE................................616 530-5700
Mary Newmarch, *Principal*
Robin Pearson, *Sales Staff*
Bob Park, *Branch Mgr*
Darcy Pucilowski, *Executive*
EMP: 5
SALES (corp-wide): 6.6B **Publicly Held**
WEB: www.packagingcorp.com
SIC: 2653 Boxes, corrugated: made from purchased materials; boxes, solid fiber: made from purchased materials
PA: Packaging Corporation Of America
1 N Field Ct
Lake Forest IL 60045
847 482-3000

(G-7408)
PEERLESS STEEL COMPANY
3280 Century Center St Sw (49418-3101)
PHONE................................616 530-6695
Linda Arnold, *Sales Staff*
Ashley Betlejewski, *Sales Staff*
Michael Dixon, *Sales Staff*
Doug Guy, *Sales Staff*
Bill Brewer, *Marketing Staff*

EMP: 26
SALES (corp-wide): 78.7MM **Privately Held**
WEB: www.peerlesssteel.com
SIC: 5051 3322 3316 3312 Steel; malleable iron foundries; cold finishing of steel shapes; blast furnaces & steel mills
PA: Peerless Steel Company
2450 Austin Dr
Troy MI 48083
248 528-3200

(G-7409)
PLASMA BIOLIFE SERVICES L P
6331 Kenowa Ave Sw (49418-9414)
PHONE 616 667-0264
EMP: 6 **Privately Held**
SIC: 2834 3841 2835 3842 Pharmaceutical preparations; intravenous solutions; solutions, pharmaceutical; surgical & medical instruments; catheters; medical instruments & equipment, blood & bone work; surgical instruments & apparatus; blood derivative diagnostic agents; surgical appliances & supplies
HQ: Biolife Plasma Services L.P.
1200 Lakeside Dr
Bannockburn IL 60015
224 940-2000

(G-7410)
POWERMAT INC
2885 Sanford Ave Sw # 40939 (49418-1342)
PHONE 616 259-4867
Elad Dubzinsky, *CEO*
Micha Catran, *President*
Aya Kantor, *Vice Pres*
Eric Caldwell, *Marketing Staff*
EMP: 23 **EST:** 2008
SALES (est): 1MM **Privately Held**
WEB: www.powermat.com
SIC: 3694 Battery charging alternators & generators

(G-7411)
PRAISE SIGN COMPANY
3404 Busch Dr Sw Ste F (49418-1000)
PHONE 616 439-0315
John Vanocker, *Owner*
EMP: 9 **EST:** 2013
SALES (est): 1MM **Privately Held**
WEB: www.praisesign.com
SIC: 3993 1731 Signs & advertising specialties; general electrical contractor

(G-7412)
PRECISION LABEL INC
4181 Spartan Indus Dr Sw (49418-2553)
PHONE 616 534-9935
David Greiner, *President*
Tom Pikaart, *General Mgr*
Greg Glenn, *Mktg Coord*
EMP: 7 **EST:** 1994
SQ FT: 5,000
SALES (est): 877.8K **Privately Held**
WEB: www.timbertagger.com
SIC: 2759 Labels & seals: printing

(G-7413)
RAND WORLDWIDE SUBSIDIARY INC
4445 Wilson Ave Sw Ste 4 (49418-2351)
PHONE 616 261-8183
EMP: 4
SALES (corp-wide): 81MM **Publicly Held**
SIC: 3131 Mfg Footwear Cut Stock
HQ: Rand Worldwide Subsidiary, Inc.
11201 Dlfeld Blvd Ste 112
Owings Mills MD 21117
877 726-3243

(G-7414)
RIVER CITY STEEL SVC
2989 Chicago Dr Sw (49418-1116)
PHONE 616 301-7227
Harvey Wierenga, *President*
EMP: 6 **EST:** 2005
SALES (est): 215.6K **Privately Held**
WEB: www.rivercityss.com
SIC: 3441 Fabricated structural metal

(G-7415)
ROYAL PALLETS INC
3570 Viaduct St Sw (49418-1058)
P.O. Box 507 (49468-0507)
PHONE 616 261-2884
George Bodbyl Sr, *President*
Michelle Bodbyl, *Admin Sec*
EMP: 21 **EST:** 1988
SQ FT: 27,000
SALES (est): 2.4MM **Privately Held**
WEB: www.royalpallets.com
SIC: 2448 Pallets, wood

(G-7416)
S AND L ASSOCIATES
4341 Applewood Ct Sw (49418-8781)
PHONE 616 608-6583
Valerie Semaan, *Principal*
EMP: 5 **EST:** 2010
SALES (est): 119.1K **Privately Held**
SIC: 3842 Wheelchairs

(G-7417)
SCOTTS SIGNS
3386 Olivet St Sw (49418-1088)
P.O. Box 827 (49468-0827)
PHONE 616 532-2034
Scott Bouma, *Owner*
EMP: 4 **EST:** 1977
SQ FT: 3,750
SALES (est): 402.6K **Privately Held**
WEB: www.scottssigngallery.com
SIC: 7389 3993 Sign painting & lettering shop; signs & advertising specialties

(G-7418)
SPLASH OF VINYL
3257 Larue St Sw (49418-1013)
PHONE 616 723-0311
Nick Guppy, *Principal*
EMP: 4 **EST:** 2014
SALES (est): 155.6K **Privately Held**
SIC: 2752 Commercial printing, lithographic

(G-7419)
STANDALE LUMBER AND SUPPLY CO
2971 Franklin Ave Sw (49418-1266)
PHONE 616 530-8200
Buzz Holtvluwer, *Vice Pres*
Lori Pearce, *Human Res Dir*
Matt McClure, *Sales Staff*
Trent Moulton, *Sales Staff*
Tom Powers, *Manager*
EMP: 75
SALES (corp-wide): 35.8MM **Privately Held**
WEB: www.standalelumber.com
SIC: 5713 2431 5211 Floor covering stores; carpets; millwork; lumber products
PA: Standale Lumber And Supply Company
4100 Lake Michigan Dr Nw
Grand Rapids MI 49534
616 453-8207

(G-7420)
TAPESTRY INC
3700 Rvrtwn Pkwy Sw (49418-3085)
PHONE 616 538-5802
Mike Krueger, *Branch Mgr*
EMP: 7 **Publicly Held**
WEB: www.tapestry.com
SIC: 3199 5699 Embossed leather goods; customized clothing & apparel
PA: Tapestry, Inc.
10 Hudson Yards Fl 18
New York NY 10001

(G-7421)
THERM TECHNOLOGY CORP
2879 Remico St Sw (49418-1139)
PHONE 616 530-6540
Jim Workman, *Ch of Bd*
▲ **EMP:** 8 **EST:** 1987
SQ FT: 25,000
SALES (est): 873.2K **Privately Held**
SIC: 3634 Heaters, space electric

(G-7422)
VAN DYKEN MECHANICAL INC
4275 Spartan Indus Dr Sw (49418-2503)
PHONE 616 224-7030
Arnold Van Dyken, *Ch of Bd*
Randal Van Dyken, *President*
Joe Vandenberg, *Exec VP*
Bill Barrett, *Vice Pres*
William Barrett, *Vice Pres*
EMP: 85
SQ FT: 6,000
SALES (est): 16.8MM **Privately Held**
WEB: www.vdminc.com
SIC: 1711 8711 3499 Warm air heating & air conditioning contractor; mechanical contractor; engineering services; fire- or burglary-resistive products

(G-7423)
VITA TALALAY
2885 Sanford Ave Sw # 26440 (49418-1342)
PHONE 425 214-4732
EMP: 4 **EST:** 2019
SALES (est): 52.2K **Privately Held**
WEB: www.vitatalalay.com
SIC: 2519 Household furniture

(G-7424)
WOOD-CUTTERS TOOLING INC
4685 Spartan Indus Dr Sw (49418-2511)
PHONE 616 257-7930
Charlie Bosscher, *President*
EMP: 6 **EST:** 1980
SQ FT: 4,400
SALES (est): 841.5K **Privately Held**
WEB: www.woodcutterstooling.com
SIC: 3545 7699 Cutting tools for machine tools; knife, saw & tool sharpening & repair

Grant
Newaygo County

(G-7425)
ALLIED MACHINE INC
11171 Spruce Ave (49327-9342)
PHONE 231 834-0050
Kenneth Cronk, *President*
David Thompson, *Vice Pres*
Bill Dine, *Supervisor*
Stephanie Clark, *Prgrmr*
EMP: 18 **EST:** 1992
SQ FT: 19,600
SALES (est): 2.3MM **Privately Held**
SIC: 3599 7692 3444 Machine shop, jobbing & repair; welding repair; sheet metalwork

(G-7426)
AMERICAN PALLET COMPANY LLC
11421 S Peach Ave (49327-8759)
PHONE 231 834-5056
Henry Dehaan,
EMP: 6 **EST:** 2012
SALES (est): 117.1K **Privately Held**
WEB: www.american-pallet-company-mi.hub.biz
SIC: 2448 Pallets, wood

(G-7427)
BLACK LABEL CUSTOMS LLC
11833 S Fitzgerald Ave (49327-9061)
PHONE 231 924-8044
Brett Walton, *Owner*
EMP: 4 **EST:** 2017
SALES (est): 59.9K **Privately Held**
SIC: 2759 Commercial printing

(G-7428)
CHIVIS SPORTSMAN CASES
1192 E 112th St (49327-7423)
PHONE 231 834-1162
Gary Chivis, *President*
EMP: 5
SALES (est): 203.6K **Privately Held**
SIC: 2499 Wood products

(G-7429)
KEITH FALAN
14097 S Mason Dr (49327-9645)
PHONE 231 834-7358
Keith Falan, *Principal*
EMP: 5 **EST:** 2005
SALES (est): 66.2K **Privately Held**
SIC: 2411 Logging

(G-7430)
MIDWEST STEEL CARPORTS INC (PA)
13479 S Mason Dr (49327-8848)
PHONE 877 235-5210
Adbeel Cabrera, *President*
Hector Aguilar, *Treasurer*
Rodolfo Castillo, *Admin Sec*
EMP: 5 **EST:** 2013
SALES (est): 1MM **Privately Held**
WEB: www.midweststeelcarports.com
SIC: 3448 Prefabricated metal buildings

(G-7431)
QUALITY FINISHING SYSTEMS
333 W 136th St (49327-9646)
P.O. Box 372 (49327-0372)
PHONE 231 834-9131
Loren Courson, *President*
Brent Courson, *Accountant*
EMP: 18 **EST:** 1998
SALES (est): 3.5MM **Privately Held**
WEB: www.qualityfinishingsystems.com
SIC: 3441 3444 Fabricated structural metal; sheet metalwork

(G-7432)
RIDGE CIDER
351 W 136th St (49327-8456)
PHONE 231 674-2040
Matt Delong, *Owner*
EMP: 5 **EST:** 2015
SALES (est): 175.8K **Privately Held**
WEB: www.ridgecider.com
SIC: 2099 Cider, nonalcoholic

(G-7433)
TIMBERWOLF FURNACE CO
12727 Van Wagoner Ave (49327-9737)
PHONE 231 924-6654
James Powles, *President*
EMP: 7 **EST:** 2004
SALES (est): 258.4K **Privately Held**
WEB: www.timberwolffurnace.com
SIC: 3499 3999 Aerosol valves, metal; atomizers, toiletry

Grass Lake
Jackson County

(G-7434)
AGGREGATE INDUSTRIES - MWR INC
4950 Loveland Rd (49240-9106)
PHONE 734 475-2531
Randy Allen, *Manager*
EMP: 6
SALES (corp-wide): 25.3B **Privately Held**
SIC: 3273 Ready-mixed concrete
HQ: Aggregate Industries - Mwr, Inc.
2815 Dodd Rd
Eagan MN 55121

(G-7435)
AMERICAN TOOLING CENTER INC (PA)
4111 Mount Hope Rd (49240-9513)
PHONE 517 522-8411
John J Basso, *President*
Steve Doolan, *Business Mgr*
Linda Garrisi, *Vice Pres*
Donn Helfer, *Plant Supt*
Chris Butterwick, *Plant Mgr*
▲ **EMP:** 73 **EST:** 1992
SQ FT: 65,000
SALES (est): 18.5MM **Privately Held**
WEB: www.americantoolingcenter.com
SIC: 3544 Special dies & tools

(G-7436)
COY LABORATORY PRODUCTS INC
14500 Coy Dr (49240-9207)
PHONE 734 433-9296
Richard A Coy, *President*
Brian Coy, *President*
Carol Ann Coy, *Corp Secy*
Kevin Coy, *Corp Secy*
Ashley Coy, *Director*
▼ **EMP:** 22 **EST:** 1969
SQ FT: 20,000

GEOGRAPHIC SECTION
Grayling - Crawford County (G-7462)

SALES (est): 5.2MM **Privately Held**
WEB: www.coylab.com
SIC: 3821 Laboratory apparatus & furniture

(G-7437)
DOERKEN CORPORATION
11200 Cedar Knoll Dr (49240-9622)
P.O. Box 429 (49240-0429)
PHONE.................517 522-4600
Frederick A Schultz, *President*
Dennis Mulalic, *Director*
▲ **EMP:** 4 **EST:** 2001
SQ FT: 24,000
SALES (est): 1.8MM
SALES (corp-wide): 336.8MM **Privately Held**
WEB: www.doerkenusa.com
SIC: 2899 Corrosion preventive lubricant
PA: Ewald DOrken Ag
    Wetterstr. 58
    Herdecke NW 58313
    233 063-0

(G-7438)
GRASS LAKE COMMUNITY PHARMACY
Also Called: Indispensable Health
116 E Michigan Ave (49240-9685)
PHONE.................517 522-4100
Todd Raehtz, *President*
EMP: 8 **EST:** 2015
SALES (est): 1.6MM **Privately Held**
WEB: www.indispensablehealth.com
SIC: 2834 8742 Druggists' preparations (pharmaceuticals); hospital & health services consultant

(G-7439)
K & L MANUFACTURING LTD
4720 Clear Lake Shore Dr (49240-9240)
PHONE.................734 475-1009
Kenneth Richard, *Administration*
EMP: 4 **EST:** 2009
SALES (est): 110.6K **Privately Held**
SIC: 3999 Manufacturing industries

(G-7440)
LOVEN SPOONFUL
119 E Main St (49240)
PHONE.................517 522-3953
Shelly Hart, *Owner*
EMP: 5 **EST:** 2010
SALES (est): 86.1K **Privately Held**
WEB: www.missysgrassshack.com
SIC: 2024 Ice cream & frozen desserts

(G-7441)
MJ PRINT & IMAGING
4501 Jacob Rd (49240-9610)
PHONE.................734 216-6273
Julia Jensen, *Principal*
EMP: 4 **EST:** 2013
SALES (est): 148.2K **Privately Held**
WEB: www.mjprint-imaging.net
SIC: 2752 Commercial printing, offset

(G-7442)
P L SCHMITT CRBIDE TOOLING LLC
8865 Seymour Rd (49240-9565)
PHONE.................313 706-5756
Paul Schmitt,
EMP: 5 **EST:** 2014
SALES (est): 330.9K **Privately Held**
SIC: 3545 End mills

(G-7443)
PDF MFG INC
11000 Cedar Knoll Dr (49240-9811)
P.O. Box 186 (49240-0186)
PHONE.................517 522-8431
Lee Declaire, *President*
Glen A Primrose, *Corp Secy*
Bruce Fielder, *Shareholder*
EMP: 5 **EST:** 1992
SQ FT: 5,500
SALES (est): 774.9K **Privately Held**
SIC: 3599 3312 3544 Electrical discharge machining (EDM); tool & die steel; special dies, tools, jigs & fixtures

(G-7444)
PL SCHMITT CRBIDE TOLING LLC
133 Drake St (49240-8302)
PHONE.................517 522-6891
Paul Schmitt, *Mng Member*
EMP: 8 **EST:** 2014
SALES (est): 902.8K **Privately Held**
WEB: www.plsct.com
SIC: 3545 Cutting tools for machine tools

(G-7445)
SOLID MANUFACTURING INC
125 W Michigan Ave (49240-9188)
P.O. Box 280 (49240-0280)
PHONE.................517 522-5895
George T Husak II, *CEO*
George Husak Jr, *President*
Connie Husak, *Vice Pres*
George Husak Sr, *Vice Pres*
EMP: 20 **EST:** 1991
SQ FT: 15,000
SALES (est): 2.1MM **Privately Held**
SIC: 3599 Machine shop, jobbing & repair

(G-7446)
STR COMPANY
6442 Wooster Rd (49240-9505)
PHONE.................517 206-6058
Susann K Moore, *Owner*
EMP: 4 **EST:** 1993
SALES (est): 190K **Privately Held**
WEB: www.str.com
SIC: 2679 Paperboard products, converted

(G-7447)
TENNECO AUTOMOTIVE OPER CO INC
3901 Willis Rd (49240-9791)
P.O. Box 157 (49240-0157)
PHONE.................517 522-5520
Joe Czarnecki, *Opers-Prdtn-Mfg*
Rich Harms, *Program Mgr*
EMP: 245
SQ FT: 50,000
SALES (corp-wide): 15.3B **Publicly Held**
SIC: 3714 Motor vehicle parts & accessories
HQ: Tenneco Automotive Operating Company, Inc.
    500 N Field Dr
    Lake Forest IL 60045
    847 482-5000

Grawn
Grand Traverse County

(G-7448)
ALTUS BRANDS LLC (PA)
6893 Sullivan Rd (49637-9542)
PHONE.................231 421-3810
Shannon Plamondon, *Office Mgr*
Brian Breneman, *Mng Member*
◆ **EMP:** 11 **EST:** 2007
SALES (est): 2.8MM **Privately Held**
WEB: www.altusbrands.com
SIC: 3999 Advertising display products

(G-7449)
APPLE FENCE CO
1893 Pine Tree (49637-9776)
PHONE.................231 276-9888
Gary Sheffer, *President*
Scott Sheffer, *Corp Secy*
EMP: 12 **EST:** 1982
SQ FT: 2,560
SALES (est): 1.3MM **Privately Held**
WEB: www.applefence.com
SIC: 5211 2499 1799 Fencing; fencing, wood; drapery track installation

(G-7450)
EAGLE EXPLORATION INC
4287 S M 37 (49637-9745)
P.O. Box 89 (49637-0089)
PHONE.................231 252-4624
EMP: 6 **EST:** 2015
SALES (est): 247.6K **Privately Held**
WEB: www.eagleexplorationservices.com
SIC: 1382 Oil & gas exploration services

(G-7451)
GREAT LAKES WELLHEAD INC (PA)
4243 S M 37 (49637-9745)
PHONE.................231 943-9100
Bruce Rosema, *President*
Kyle Fitzpatrick, *Vice Pres*
Larry Sinkler Jr, *Facilities Mgr*
Buddy Sheffer, *Sales Staff*
Lisa Hernandez, *Branch Mgr*
EMP: 3 **EST:** 1985
SQ FT: 4,000
SALES (est): 5.2MM **Privately Held**
WEB: www.glwinc.us
SIC: 1389 7353 5082 Oil & gas wells: building, repairing & dismantling; oil equipment rental services; oil field equipment

(G-7452)
MATERNE NORTH AMERICA CORP
Also Called: Gogosqueez
6331 Us Highway 31 (49637-9620)
P.O. Box 268 (49637-0268)
PHONE.................231 346-6600
Michel Larroche, *CEO*
Jonathan Bailey, *Manager*
Jake Tanaka, *Manager*
Justin Meeder, *Maintence Staff*
EMP: 50
SALES (corp-wide): 6.2MM **Privately Held**
WEB: www.gogosqueez.com
SIC: 2033 Apple sauce: packaged in cans, jars, etc.
HQ: Materne North America, Corp.
    20 W 22nd St Fl 12
    New York NY 10010
    212 675-7881

(G-7453)
RIETH-RILEY CNSTR CO INC
4435 S M 37 (49637-9745)
PHONE.................231 263-2100
Jeff Saylor, *Manager*
EMP: 10
SQ FT: 864
SALES (corp-wide): 174.4MM **Privately Held**
WEB: www.rieth-riley.com
SIC: 1611 2951 Surfacing & paving; asphalt paving mixtures & blocks
PA: Rieth-Riley Construction Co., Inc.
    3626 Elkhart Rd
    Goshen IN 46526
    574 875-5183

Grayling
Crawford County

(G-7454)
A J D FOREST PDTS LTD PARTNR
4440 W 4 Mile Rd (49738-9779)
P.O. Box 629 (49738-0629)
PHONE.................989 348-5412
David J Stephenson, *Partner*
A D F 1 Corp, *Partner*
Fred Fisher, *Partner*
Albert L Quaal, *Partner*
EMP: 55 **EST:** 1974
SQ FT: 54,000
SALES (est): 2.8MM
SALES (corp-wide): 6.6B **Publicly Held**
WEB: www.ajdforestproducts.com
SIC: 2421 Lumber: rough, sawed or planed
PA: Cms Energy Corporation
    1 Energy Plaza Dr
    Jackson MI 49201
    517 788-0550

(G-7455)
AIR WAY AUTOMATION INC
2268 Industrial Dr (49738-7849)
P.O. Box 563 (49738-0563)
PHONE.................989 348-1802
Robert G Toms, *President*
David Starkey, *Corp Secy*
John Ammond, *Vice Pres*
Matt Birk, *Project Mgr*
Jason Graziano, *Project Mgr*
◆ **EMP:** 44

SQ FT: 51,700
SALES (est): 13.4MM **Privately Held**
WEB: www.airwayautomation.com
SIC: 3599 Machine shop, jobbing & repair

(G-7456)
ARAUCO NORTH AMERICA INC
5851 Arauco Rd (49738-9707)
PHONE.................800 261-4896
EMP: 200 **Privately Held**
SIC: 2493 Flakeboard
HQ: Arauco North America, Inc.
    400 Prmter Ctr Ter Ste 75
    Atlanta GA 30346

(G-7457)
BREITBURN OPERATING LP
8892 W 7 Mile Rd (49738-9796)
PHONE.................989 348-8459
Ed Blake, *Principal*
EMP: 6 **EST:** 2010
SALES (est): 425.4K **Privately Held**
SIC: 1311 Crude petroleum production

(G-7458)
CRAWFORD COUNTY AVALANCHE
108 E Michigan Ave (49738-1741)
P.O. Box 490 (49738-0490)
PHONE.................989 348-6811
Ann Marie Milliman, *President*
EMP: 5
SALES (est): 547.7K **Privately Held**
SIC: 2711 Job printing & newspaper publishing combined

(G-7459)
CSI EMERGENCY APPARATUS LLC
2332 Dupont St (49738-7836)
PHONE.................989 348-2877
Jim Wagner, *Purchasing*
Scott Patchin, *Sales Staff*
Joan Morley, *Office Mgr*
Chuck Quiney, *Mng Member*
Mark Brown,
EMP: 16 **EST:** 2002
SQ FT: 16,000
SALES (est): 3.4MM **Privately Held**
WEB: www.csiea.com
SIC: 3713 Truck bodies (motor vehicles)

(G-7460)
ENDLESS POSSIBILITIES INC
1169 S I 75 Business Loop (49738-2030)
PHONE.................248 262-7443
Joyce Murphy, *Owner*
▲ **EMP:** 7 **EST:** 2014
SALES (est): 388.4K **Privately Held**
SIC: 3999 Education aids, devices & supplies

(G-7461)
GEORGIA-PACIFIC LLC
4113 W 4 Mile Rd (49738-9779)
PHONE.................989 348-7275
Katie DOE, *Engineer*
Steve Randall, *Manager*
EMP: 5
SALES (corp-wide): 36.9B **Privately Held**
WEB: www.gp.com
SIC: 3087 2869 2821 Custom compound purchased resins; industrial organic chemicals; plastics materials & resins
HQ: Georgia-Pacific Llc
    133 Peachtree St Nw
    Atlanta GA 30303
    404 652-4000

(G-7462)
GRAYLING OUTDOOR PRODUCTS INC
2075 Industrial Dr (49738-7849)
P.O. Box 192 (49738-0192)
PHONE.................989 348-2956
Raymond Priebe, *President*
Sharon Priebe, *Vice Pres*
Kimberly Tinker, *Officer*
EMP: 10 **EST:** 1980
SQ FT: 5,000
SALES (est): 535.3K **Privately Held**
WEB: www.graylingoutdoorproducts.com
SIC: 3949 Archery equipment, general

Grayling - Crawford County (G-7463)

(G-7463)
IMM INC
758 Isenhauer Rd (49738-8638)
P.O. Box 747 (49738-0747)
PHONE 989 344-7662
Elizabeth Doering, *President*
Mark Saxton, *Vice Pres*
Mark Zumbaugh, *Project Mgr*
Dave Andrews, *Sales Mgr*
EMP: 40 **EST:** 2015
SQ FT: 45,000
SALES (est): 3.3MM **Privately Held**
WEB: www.immmi.com
SIC: 3441 1791 Fabricated structural metal; structural steel erection

(G-7464)
JACK MILLIKIN INC
4680 W N Down River Rd (49738-7892)
PHONE 989 348-8411
JC M Millikin, *Corp Secy*
Brian Pratt, *Vice Pres*
EMP: 9 **EST:** 1941
SQ FT: 12,400
SALES (est): 1.4MM **Privately Held**
WEB: www.jackmillikin.com
SIC: 1794 1442 5039 Excavation work; common sand mining; gravel mining; septic tanks

(G-7465)
MAY-DAY WINDOW MANUFACTURING
403 N Wilcox Bridge Rd (49738-8613)
PHONE 989 348-2809
Mark Swiercz, *President*
David Swiercz, *Vice Pres*
EMP: 4 **EST:** 1980
SQ FT: 12,000
SALES (est): 390.2K **Privately Held**
SIC: 3089 Windows, plastic

(G-7466)
MICHIGAN WOOD PELLET LLC
2211 Industrial Dr (49738-7849)
PHONE 989 348-4100
EMP: 10
SALES (est): 1.4MM **Privately Held**
SIC: 3532 Pellets

(G-7467)
MONARCH MILLWORK INC (PA)
2211 Industrial Dr (49738-7849)
PHONE 989 348-8292
Michael D Hees, *President*
EMP: 8 **EST:** 1992
SQ FT: 20,000
SALES (est): 1.9MM **Privately Held**
WEB: www.michiganwoodpellet.com
SIC: 2431 Doors, wood

(G-7468)
PADDLE HARD DISTRIBUTING LLC
118 E Michigan Ave (49738-1741)
PHONE 513 309-1192
Dave Vargo,
EMP: 5 **EST:** 2016
SQ FT: 3,000
SALES (est): 483.3K **Privately Held**
SIC: 2082 Beer (alcoholic beverage)

(G-7469)
SRM CONCRETE LLC
3881 W 4 Mile Rd (49738-8079)
PHONE 989 344-0235
Dave Gildey, *President*
EMP: 6
SALES (corp-wide): 170.1MM **Privately Held**
WEB: www.smyrnareadymix.com
SIC: 3273 Ready-mixed concrete
PA: Srm Concrete, Llc
1136 2nd Ave N
Nashville TN 37208
615 355-1028

(G-7470)
UNION OIL CO
8892 W 7 Mile Rd (49738-9796)
PHONE 989 348-8459
Steve Wallington, *Principal*
EMP: 5 **EST:** 2010
SALES (est): 164.1K **Privately Held**
SIC: 1389 Oil & gas field services

(G-7471)
WEYERHAEUSER COMPANY
4111 W 4 Mile Rd (49738-9702)
PHONE 989 348-2881
Phil Dennett, *Opers-Prdtn-Mfg*
Donna Alschbach, *Buyer*
Courtney Ryan, *Maintence Staff*
EMP: 4
SALES (corp-wide): 7.5B **Publicly Held**
WEB: www.weyerhaeuser.com
SIC: 2421 2493 Lumber: rough, sawed or planed; reconstituted wood products
PA: Weyerhaeuser Company
220 Occidental Ave S
Seattle WA 98104
206 539-3000

Greenbush
Alcona County

(G-7472)
HAVERCROFT TOOL & DIE INC
5002 Main St (48738-9698)
PHONE 989 724-5913
Timothy Havercroft, *CEO*
EMP: 5 **EST:** 2005
SALES (est): 473.1K **Privately Held**
WEB: www.havercrofttool.com
SIC: 3544 Special dies & tools

(G-7473)
W & S DEVELOPMENT INC
4957 Main St (48738-9696)
PHONE 989 724-5463
Thomas L Stojsik, *President*
EMP: 15 **EST:** 1970
SQ FT: 12,000
SALES (est): 1.1MM **Privately Held**
SIC: 3531 Dredging machinery

Greenville
Montcalm County

(G-7474)
AGA MARVEL
1260 E Van Deinse St (48838-1400)
PHONE 616 754-5601
EMP: 8 **EST:** 2015
SALES (est): 263.1K **Privately Held**
WEB: www.agamarvel.com
SIC: 3632 Household refrigerators & freezers

(G-7475)
AGGRESSIVE TOOLING INC
608 Industrial Park Dr (48838-9792)
PHONE 616 754-1404
Richard Jones, *President*
Jon Heaton, *Vice Pres*
Gabe Moore, *Vice Pres*
Jason Bigelow, *Engineer*
Mike Williamson, *Electrical Engi*
EMP: 96
SQ FT: 16,000
SALES (est): 27MM **Privately Held**
WEB: www.aggtool.com
SIC: 3544 7692 Special dies & tools; welding repair

(G-7476)
BELDING BLEACHER ERECTORS INC
Also Called: Jakeway
11467 Hart St Ne (48838-9327)
PHONE 616 794-3126
Roger Scheiern, *President*
EMP: 7 **EST:** 1996
SALES (est): 161.7K **Privately Held**
SIC: 3552 Bleaching machinery, textile

(G-7477)
BLACKSMITH SHOP LLC
809 Callaghan St (48838-7146)
PHONE 616 754-4719
Loie Byville, *Office Mgr*
William Byville,
EMP: 5 **EST:** 1981
SQ FT: 10,000
SALES (est): 546.2K **Privately Held**
SIC: 3446 Architectural metalwork

(G-7478)
CITY OF GREENVILLE
Also Called: Silent Observer
415 S Lafayette St (48838-2353)
PHONE 616 754-0100
EMP: 27 **Privately Held**
SIC: 2711 Newspapers-Publishing/Printing
PA: City Of Greenville
411 S Lafayette St
Greenville MI 48838
616 754-5644

(G-7479)
CLARION TECHNOLOGIES INC
501 S Cedar St (48838-2003)
PHONE 616 754-1199
Jody Fleet, *Purchasing*
Fred Gradisher, *Manager*
EMP: 33
SALES (corp-wide): 68.4MM **Privately Held**
WEB: www.clariontechnologies.com
SIC: 3089 Molding primary plastic
PA: Clarion Technologies, Inc.
238 S River Ave Fl 2
Holland MI 49423
616 698-7277

(G-7480)
D-M-E USA INC
Also Called: Mud Quick Change Tooling
1117 E Fairplains St (48838-2808)
PHONE 616 754-4601
Dennis Smith, *CEO*
Ken Jasina, *General Mgr*
Mary Wall, *Principal*
◆ **EMP:** 61 **EST:** 1958
SALES (est): 12.9MM **Publicly Held**
WEB: www.milacron.com
SIC: 3544 3443 Forms (molds), for foundry & plastics working machinery; fabricated plate work (boiler shop)
HQ: Dme Company Llc
29111 Stephenson Hwy
Madison Heights MI 48071

(G-7481)
DAILY NEWS
109 N Lafayette St (48838-1882)
P.O. Box 340 (48838-0340)
PHONE 616 754-9301
Darrin Clark, *Manager*
EMP: 7 **EST:** 2020
SALES (est): 233K **Privately Held**
WEB: www.thedailynews.cc
SIC: 2741 Miscellaneous publishing

(G-7482)
DICASTAL NORTH AMERICA INC (HQ)
1 Dicastal Dr (48838-9594)
PHONE 616 619-7500
Michael Lewis, *President*
Steve Evans, *Production*
Leona Lake, *Production*
Adam Rose, *Production*
Keith Spikes, *QC Mgr*
EMP: 430 **EST:** 2014
SQ FT: 623,749
SALES (est): 145.6MM **Privately Held**
WEB: www.dicastalna.com
SIC: 3714 Wheels, motor vehicle

(G-7483)
EAGLE GROUP II LTD
8384 Peck Rd (48838-9715)
PHONE 616 754-7777
Roy Ferguson Jr, *President*
Roy J Ferguson III, *President*
Roy J Ferguson Sr, *President*
Hal Soucie, *Vice Pres*
Beatrice Rosario, *Controller*
EMP: 25 **EST:** 1991
SQ FT: 16,000
SALES (est): 6.8MM **Privately Held**
WEB: www.eaglegroupltd.com
SIC: 3523 Farm machinery & equipment

(G-7484)
FABX INDUSTRIES INC (PA)
Also Called: Aquest Machining & Assembly
715 Callaghan St (48838-7157)
PHONE 616 225-1724
Gopikrishna Ganta, *President*
John Petersen, *Plant Mgr*
Josh Bishop, *Manager*
EMP: 13 **EST:** 2017
SALES (est): 3.5MM **Privately Held**
WEB: www.aquestmachining.com
SIC: 3599 Machine shop, jobbing & repair

(G-7485)
FEDERAL-MOGUL POWERTRAIN LLC
510 E Grove St (48838-1881)
PHONE 616 754-5681
Louise Swiatek, *Purchasing*
Damien Vezol, *Branch Mgr*
Ned Springsteen, *Maintence Staff*
EMP: 350
SALES (corp-wide): 15.3B **Publicly Held**
SIC: 3714 3568 Bearings, motor vehicle; power transmission equipment
HQ: Federal-Mogul Powertrain Llc
27300 W 11 Mile Rd # 100
Southfield MI 48034

(G-7486)
GRAPHITE ENGINEERING & SLS CO
712 Industrial Park Dr (48838-9792)
P.O. Box 637 (48838-0637)
PHONE 616 754-5671
Todd N Taylor, *Principal*
Lindsey Shelden, *IT/INT Sup*
EMP: 15 **EST:** 2011
SALES (est): 489.7K **Privately Held**
WEB: www.graphite-eng.com
SIC: 3599 Machine shop, jobbing & repair

(G-7487)
GREENVILLE CABINET DISTRI
1323 Callaghan St (48838-7152)
PHONE 616 225-2424
Byron Reynolds, *Owner*
EMP: 8 **EST:** 2007
SALES (est): 429.6K **Privately Held**
WEB: www.greenvillecabinet.com
SIC: 2434 Wood kitchen cabinets

(G-7488)
GREENVILLE TOOL & DIE CO
1215 S Lafayette St (48838-9386)
P.O. Box 310 (48838-0310)
PHONE 616 754-5693
Larry Caverley, *President*
Ted Bush, *Exec VP*
Joe Winters, *Plant Mgr*
Rob Rahn, *Design Engr*
Gregg Peters, *Controller*
◆ **EMP:** 140
SQ FT: 109,000
SALES: 24.6MM **Privately Held**
WEB: www.gtd.com
SIC: 3544 Special dies & tools

(G-7489)
GREENVILLE TRCK WLDG SUPS LLC (PA)
Also Called: Greenville Truck and Welding
201 W Greenville West Dr (48838-1162)
P.O. Box 933 (48838-0933)
PHONE 616 754-6120
Jeffrey Loding, *President*
Peter Gibson, *Vice Pres*
Pete Gibson, *Sales Staff*
Brenda Ladermann, *Office Mgr*
Richard Barnes, *CIO*
EMP: 12 **EST:** 1998
SALES (est): 1.7MM **Privately Held**
WEB: www.gtwsupplies.com
SIC: 5999 2813 Welding supplies; acetylene

(G-7490)
GREENVILLE VENTR PARTNERS LLC
6501 Fitzner Rd (48838-9783)
PHONE 616 303-2400
Michael Doyle, *President*
EMP: 30 **EST:** 2015
SALES (est): 3.5MM **Privately Held**
WEB: www.foremostfarms.com
SIC: 2022 2026 2023 2021 Cheese, natural & processed; fluid milk; condensed milk; evaporated whey; powdered milk; creamery butter
PA: Foremost Farms Usa Cooperative
E10889 Penny Ln
Baraboo WI 53913

(G-7491)
HEATSINKUSA LLC
801 Industrial Park Dr (48838-8779)
PHONE..................800 901-2395
Amy Mason, *Mng Member*
Russell Boss,
EMP: 7 **EST:** 2009
SALES (est): 1.2MM **Privately Held**
WEB: www.heatsinkusa.com
SIC: 3354 Aluminum extruded products

(G-7492)
HIGH GRADE MATERIALS COMPANY (PA)
9266 Snows Lake Rd (48838-8753)
PHONE..................616 754-5545
James Sturrus, *President*
Jared Watson, *Safety Dir*
Dave Cole, *Controller*
Patty Sturrus, *Human Res Mgr*
Sharon Schultz, *IT/INT Sup*
EMP: 27 **EST:** 1964
SQ FT: 34,000
SALES (est): 17.2MM **Privately Held**
WEB: www.highgradematerials.com
SIC: 3273 3272 1442 Ready-mixed concrete; concrete products; construction sand & gravel

(G-7493)
HUNTINGTON FOAM LLC
1323 Moore St (48838-8767)
PHONE..................661 225-9951
Scott Gloskey, *Prdtn Mgr*
Matthew Snyder, *Engineer*
Jeff Redding, *Sales Staff*
Sidney Montes, *Branch Mgr*
Robert Staffo, *Manager*
EMP: 140
SALES (corp-wide): 154.5MM **Privately Held**
WEB: www.hunt-sol.com
SIC: 3086 Plastics foam products
HQ: Huntington Foam, Llc
125 Caliber Ridge Dr # 200
Greer SC 29651

(G-7494)
JORGENSENS INC
Also Called: Jorgensen's Supermarket
1325 W Washington St (48838-2191)
PHONE..................989 831-8338
EMP: 30
SALES (corp-wide): 6.3MM **Privately Held**
SIC: 5411 5912 5812 2051 Grocery Stores, Nsk
PA: Jorgensen's Inc
215 N State St
Stanton MI 48888
989 831-8345

(G-7495)
K&W TOOL AND MACHINE INC
1216 Shearer Rd Ste A (48838-9102)
PHONE..................616 754-7540
Joseph H Kohn, *President*
Camren Kring, *Project Mgr*
Stacy Swindell, *QC Mgr*
Laura Kohn, *Human Resources*
EMP: 19 **EST:** 2000
SQ FT: 105,000 **Privately Held**
WEB: www.kwtoolinc.com
SIC: 3599 7389 Custom machinery; metal cutting services

(G-7496)
KENT FOUNDRY COMPANY
1413 Callaghan St (48838-8127)
P.O. Box 187 (48838-0187)
PHONE..................616 754-1100
Gerald A Poorman, *President*
Jim Perski, *General Mgr*
Jo Ann Poorman, *Corp Secy*
Kathy Porter, *Purch Mgr*
Richard Dykhouse, *QC Mgr*
EMP: 46 **EST:** 1934
SQ FT: 33,000
SALES (est): 7.7MM **Privately Held**
WEB: www.kentfoundry.com
SIC: 3321 Gray iron castings

(G-7497)
KNAPP PRINTING SERVICES INC
Also Called: Arrow Swift Prtg & Copy Ctr
6540 S Greenville Rd (48838-1021)
PHONE..................616 754-9159
Mike Knapp, *President*
April Sorrell, *Graphic Designe*
EMP: 7 **EST:** 1978
SQ FT: 2,500
SALES (est): 716.9K **Privately Held**
WEB: www.arrow-swift.net
SIC: 2752 Commercial printing, offset

(G-7498)
MANUFACTURERS SOLUTIONS LLC
108 N Irving St (48838-1742)
PHONE..................616 894-2964
Mark Lorenz, *Administration*
EMP: 4 **EST:** 2019
SALES (est): 43.6K **Privately Held**
SIC: 3999 Manufacturing industries

(G-7499)
MASTER PRECISION PRODUCTS INC
Also Called: Master Precision Molds
1212 E Fairplains St (48838-2809)
P.O. Box 70 (48838-0070)
PHONE..................616 754-5483
Stephen D Drake Jr, *President*
Mike Crandell, *Vice Pres*
Marcus Hansen, *Project Mgr*
Melinda Ross, *Purch Agent*
Rick Gunderson, *Engineer*
◆ **EMP:** 30
SQ FT: 30,000
SALES (est): 5.7MM **Privately Held**
WEB: www.masterprecision.com
SIC: 3544 Forms (molds), for foundry & plastics working machinery

(G-7500)
MERSEN USA GS CORP
Also Called: Mersen USA Gs - Greenville
712 Industrial Park Dr (48838-9792)
PHONE..................616 754-5671
Shannon Pettit, *Manager*
◆ **EMP:** 100
SALES (corp-wide): 889.5K **Privately Held**
WEB: www.graphite-eng.com
SIC: 3624 Carbon & graphite products
HQ: Mersen Usa Gs Corp.
215 Stackpole St
Saint Marys PA 15857
814 781-1234

(G-7501)
MERSEN USA GS CORP
Also Called: Mersen USA Gs - Greenville
712 Industrial Park Dr (48838-9792)
PHONE..................616 754-5671
EMP: 115
SALES (corp-wide): 1.5MM **Privately Held**
SIC: 3624 Carbon And Graphite Products
HQ: Mersen Usa Gs Corp.
215 Stackpole St
Saint Marys PA 15857
814 781-1234

(G-7502)
NORTHLAND CORPORATION
Also Called: Marvel Industries
1260 E Van Deinse St (48838-1400)
P.O. Box 400 (48838-0400)
PHONE..................616 754-5601
William Harris, *Plant Mgr*
Robert Ailes, *Purch Agent*
Richard Burns, *Purch Agent*
Richard Detrick, *Engineer*
Erskine Ratchford, *Engineer*
EMP: 27
SALES (corp-wide): 2.5B **Publicly Held**
WEB: www.agamarvel.com
SIC: 3444 Sheet metalwork
HQ: Northland Corporation
1260 E Van Deinse St
Greenville MI 48838
616 754-5601

(G-7503)
NORTHLAND CORPORATION (DH)
Also Called: Northland Refrigeration
1260 E Van Deinse St (48838-1400)
PHONE..................616 754-5601
William McGrath, *CEO*
Bradley S Stauffer, *Senior VP*
Shelly Giesseman, *Clerk*
◆ **EMP:** 148 **EST:** 1892
SQ FT: 175,000
SALES (est): 28.7MM
SALES (corp-wide): 2.5B **Publicly Held**
WEB: www.agamarvel.com
SIC: 3632 3444 Freezers, home & farm; sheet metalwork
HQ: Aga Rangemaster Group Limited
Meadow Lane
Nottingham NOTTS NG10
115 946-4000

(G-7504)
P C S COMPANIES INC
Also Called: Powder Coating Services
1251 Callaghan St (48838-8178)
PHONE..................616 754-2229
Patrick J Emerson, *President*
Jim Bullinger, *Vice Pres*
EMP: 7 **EST:** 1986
SQ FT: 10,000
SALES (est): 605.2K **Privately Held**
SIC: 1721 1521 3479 Industrial painting; single-family housing construction; coating of metals & formed products

(G-7505)
STAFFORD MEDIA INC (PA)
Also Called: Newsweb
109 N Lafayette St (48838-1853)
P.O. Box 340 (48838-0340)
PHONE..................616 754-9301
Chris Loiselle, *CEO*
Robert Stafford, *President*
Richard Ellafrits, *CPA*
John Moy, *VP Sales*
EMP: 40 **EST:** 1900
SQ FT: 10,000
SALES (est): 20.6MM **Privately Held**
WEB: www.go-stafford.com
SIC: 2791 2711 2752 2741 Typesetting; commercial printing & newspaper publishing combined; commercial printing, lithographic; miscellaneous publishing

(G-7506)
STAFFORD MEDIA INC
1005 E Fairplains St (48838-2806)
PHONE..................616 754-1178
John Moy, *Manager*
Peter Meade, *Executive*
EMP: 71
SALES (corp-wide): 20.6MM **Privately Held**
WEB: www.go-stafford.com
SIC: 2791 Typesetting
PA: Stafford Media, Inc.
109 N Lafayette St
Greenville MI 48838
616 754-9301

(G-7507)
TAW PLASTICS LLC (PA)
1118 S Edgewood St (48838-2522)
PHONE..................616 302-0954
Timothy A Weaver, *Mng Member*
EMP: 3 **EST:** 2002
SALES (est): 1.4MM **Privately Held**
SIC: 3089 Molding primary plastic; injection molding of plastics

(G-7508)
TON-TEX CORPORATION (PA)
4029 E Grv Unit 7 (48838)
P.O. Box 397 (48838-0397)
PHONE..................616 957-3200
Robert H Beaman, *Ch of Bd*
Robert L Fox, *President*
EMP: 17 **EST:** 1926
SQ FT: 32,500
SALES (est): 2MM **Privately Held**
WEB: www.tontex.com
SIC: 3568 3535 3052 2296 Power transmission equipment; conveyors & conveying equipment; rubber & plastics hose & beltings; tire cord & fabrics; conveyor belts

(G-7509)
US GBC WM
12199 Hart St Ne (48838-9320)
PHONE..................616 691-1340
EMP: 6 **EST:** 2019
SALES (est): 90.7K **Privately Held**
WEB: www.usgbcwm.org
SIC: 2653 Corrugated & solid fiber boxes

(G-7510)
WMC LLC
Also Called: West Michigan Compounding
1300 Moore St (48838-8768)
PHONE..................616 560-4142
Ashley Everin, *CFO*
Lorenda Davis, *Human Res Mgr*
Bill Thompson, *Manager*
Scott Barnard,
▲ **EMP:** 20 **EST:** 2005
SALES (est): 9.7MM **Privately Held**
WEB: www.wmcompounding.com
SIC: 2821 Plastics materials & resins

(G-7511)
WOODS GRAPHICS
Also Called: Wood Graphics Signs
9180 Wabasis Ave Ne (48838-9331)
PHONE..................616 691-8025
John Frueh, *Owner*
EMP: 10 **EST:** 1994
SALES (est): 393.9K **Privately Held**
SIC: 3993 Signs & advertising specialties

Greenwood
St. Clair County

(G-7512)
WITCO INC
6401 Bricker Rd (48006-2521)
PHONE..................810 387-4231
Georgina Witt, *CEO*
Kevin Witt, *President*
David E Witt, *Vice Pres*
David Witt, *Vice Pres*
Shane Koch, *Sales Mgr*
EMP: 52 **EST:** 1970
SQ FT: 45,000
SALES (est): 9MM **Privately Held**
WEB: www.witcoinc.com
SIC: 3599 Machine shop, jobbing & repair

Gregory
Livingston County

(G-7513)
BOOS PRODUCTS INC
Also Called: Michigan Gear & Engineering
20416 Kaiser Rd (48137-9713)
PHONE..................734 498-2207
Bill Jewell, *President*
Darwin Snider, *Vice Pres*
Tim Boos, *Admin Sec*
EMP: 19 **EST:** 1952
SQ FT: 14,500
SALES (est): 644.1K **Privately Held**
WEB: www.michigangear.com
SIC: 3599 3462 Machine shop, jobbing & repair; gears, forged steel

(G-7514)
EDT WELDING & FABRICATION LLC
5952 Iosco Mountain Rd (48137-9494)
PHONE..................978 257-4700
Eric Tracy, *Principal*
EMP: 5 **EST:** 2017
SALES (est): 242.3K **Privately Held**
SIC: 7692 Welding repair

(G-7515)
P & M INDUSTRIES INC
5901 Weller Rd (48137-9523)
P.O. Box 141 (48137-0141)
PHONE..................517 223-1000
Glen V Pantke, *President*
Susan C Pantke, *Vice Pres*
EMP: 10 **EST:** 1982
SQ FT: 6,000
SALES (est): 961.5K **Privately Held**
WEB: www.pm-industries.com
SIC: 3599 Machine shop, jobbing & repair

Grosse Ile
Wayne County

(G-7516)
ASSOCIATED PRINT & GRAPHICS
9617 Island Dr (48138-1464)
PHONE.................................734 676-8896
Charlotte Williams, *Owner*
EMP: 6 **EST:** 1990
SALES (est): 239K **Privately Held**
WEB: www.associatedprint.com
SIC: 2752 Commercial printing, offset

(G-7517)
CUSTARD CORNER INC
2972 W Jefferson Ave (48138)
PHONE.................................734 771-4396
Nicole Gall, *President*
EMP: 7 **EST:** 2014
SALES (est): 324.2K **Privately Held**
SIC: 2024 Ice cream & frozen desserts

(G-7518)
DAILY CONTRACTS LLC
7779 Grays Dr (48138-1505)
PHONE.................................734 676-0903
Dan Daily, *Principal*
EMP: 6 **EST:** 2009
SALES (est): 171.2K **Privately Held**
SIC: 2711 Newspapers, publishing & printing

(G-7519)
DIVERSIFIED TOOL & ENGINEERING
10340 Ruthmere Ave (48138-2133)
PHONE.................................734 692-1260
Patrick Manick, *President*
Kyle Beck, *Vice Pres*
EMP: 10 **EST:** 1986
SQ FT: 6,000
SALES (est): 572.5K **Privately Held**
SIC: 3544 3599 Special dies & tools; jigs & fixtures; machine shop, jobbing & repair

(G-7520)
DOUGLAS WEST COMPANY INC
Also Called: Sharewell
9177 Groh Rd Bldg 43 (48138-1950)
PHONE.................................734 676-8882
Douglas Bodrie, *President*
EMP: 7 **EST:** 1977
SALES (est): 482.4K **Privately Held**
WEB: www.douglasswest.com
SIC: 3444 Sheet metal specialties, not stamped

(G-7521)
EIKLAE PRODUCTS
10286 Boucher Rd (48138-2002)
PHONE.................................734 671-0752
Clayton Brundage, *Owner*
Clayton Grundage, *Owner*
EMP: 4 **EST:** 1987
SALES (est): 169.4K **Privately Held**
SIC: 2741 Business service newsletters: publishing & printing

(G-7522)
FUEL SOURCE LLC
29112 E River Rd (48138-1941)
PHONE.................................313 506-0448
Klaus P Uhse, *Administration*
EMP: 8 **EST:** 2003
SALES (est): 242.3K **Privately Held**
SIC: 2992 Re-refining lubricating oils & greases

(G-7523)
GREAT LAKES TECHNOLOGIES
17900 Parke Ln (48138-1042)
PHONE.................................734 362-8217
Brett Stachak, *Principal*
EMP: 7 **EST:** 2010
SALES (est): 96.3K **Privately Held**
WEB: www.greatlakestech.net
SIC: 7372 Prepackaged software

(G-7524)
NORTHERN PACKAGING MI INC
27665 Elba Dr (48138-1905)
PHONE.................................734 692-4700
Scott Wright, *President*
EMP: 16 **EST:** 1996
SQ FT: 20,000
SALES (est): 594.6K **Privately Held**
SIC: 2449 Rectangular boxes & crates, wood

(G-7525)
PFIZER INC
18141 Meridian Rd (48138-1088)
PHONE.................................734 679-7368
John Poslajko, *Branch Mgr*
EMP: 4
SALES (corp-wide): 41.9B **Publicly Held**
WEB: www.pfizer.com
SIC: 2834 Pharmaceutical preparations
PA: Pfizer Inc.
235 E 42nd St Rm 107
New York NY 10017
212 733-2323

(G-7526)
SOLAR CONTROL SYSTEMS
8463 Thorntree Dr (48138-1587)
PHONE.................................734 671-6899
Thomas Llewelyn, *Owner*
EMP: 5 **EST:** 1977
SALES (est): 278.7K **Privately Held**
SIC: 3433 Solar heaters & collectors

Grosse Pointe
Wayne County

(G-7527)
CHRYSLER & KOPPIN COMPANY
868 Lakeland Ct (48230-1285)
PHONE.................................313 491-7100
Douglas Koppin, *President*
Dale Koppin, *Vice Pres*
Karen Oakley, *CFO*
Donna Hutton, *Admin Sec*
EMP: 17 **EST:** 1883
SALES (est): 1.3MM **Privately Held**
WEB: www.chryslerkoppin.com
SIC: 3585 Refrigeration equipment, complete

(G-7528)
CUSTOM WHEEL SOLUTIONS
482 Rivard Blvd (48230-1631)
PHONE.................................248 547-9587
Dan Lezotte, *President*
EMP: 4 **EST:** 2018
SALES (est): 236.6K **Privately Held**
WEB: www.cwsheels.com
SIC: 3714 Motor vehicle parts & accessories

(G-7529)
DELTA IRON WORKS INC
558 Lincoln Rd (48230-1218)
PHONE.................................313 579-1445
Chris Manor, *President*
Lorraine L Manos, *President*
Kathy Manor, *Vice Pres*
Chris Manos, *President*
Kathy Manos, *Vice Pres*
EMP: 21 **EST:** 1957
SALES (est): 3.4MM **Privately Held**
SIC: 3444 3443 Sheet metalwork; fabricated plate work (boiler shop)

(G-7530)
DEWEYS LUMBERVILLE INC
757 Notre Dame St (48230-1239)
PHONE.................................313 885-0960
Joseph A Dewey Jr, *President*
EMP: 5 **EST:** 1939
SQ FT: 12,500
SALES (est): 487.1K **Privately Held**
SIC: 5211 2511 Lumber & other building materials; unassembled or unfinished furniture, household: wood

(G-7531)
NYMAN INDUSTRIES LLC
1458 Wayburn St (48230-1067)
PHONE.................................702 290-9433
Thomas Nyman, *Principal*
EMP: 4 **EST:** 2016
SALES (est): 66.3K **Privately Held**
SIC: 3999 Manufacturing industries

(G-7532)
PAGE LITHO INC
7 Wellington Pl (48230-1919)
PHONE.................................313 885-8555
Joy Pecherski, *President*
Denise Pecherski, *Vice Pres*
Jeff Pecherski, *Vice Pres*
Timothy Clement, *CFO*
EMP: 18 **EST:** 1981
SQ FT: 60,000
SALES (est): 1.1MM **Privately Held**
SIC: 2789 2752 Binding only: books, pamphlets, magazines, etc.; commercial printing, lithographic

(G-7533)
SEQUOIA MOLDING
820 Lakeland St (48230-1273)
PHONE.................................586 463-4400
EMP: 9 **EST:** 2009
SALES (est): 226.4K **Privately Held**
SIC: 3089 Molding primary plastic

Grosse Pointe Farms
Wayne County

(G-7534)
ARIANA PRESS INC
123 Cloverly Rd (48236-3312)
PHONE.................................313 885-7581
Larry Chengges, *Principal*
EMP: 7 **EST:** 2015
SALES (est): 153.3K **Privately Held**
SIC: 2741 Miscellaneous publishing

(G-7535)
FISHER MCCALL OIL GAS
18640 Mack Ave Ste 1133 (48236-7700)
PHONE.................................616 318-9155
EMP: 4 **EST:** 2017
SALES (est): 114.7K **Privately Held**
SIC: 1389 Oil & gas field services

(G-7536)
J HOUSE LLC
71 Lake Shore Rd (48236-3765)
PHONE.................................313 220-4449
Jennifer Dunbar, *Principal*
EMP: 6 **EST:** 2014
SALES (est): 353.1K **Privately Held**
SIC: 2033 Vegetable juices: fresh

(G-7537)
MH PUBLISHING LLC
166 Hillcrest Ln (48236-3017)
PHONE.................................313 881-3724
Melissa K King, *Principal*
EMP: 4 **EST:** 2015
SALES (est): 37.5K **Privately Held**
SIC: 2741 Miscellaneous publishing

(G-7538)
MODERN HARD CHROME SERVICE CO
376 Chalfonte Ave (48236-2910)
PHONE.................................586 445-0330
EMP: 14 **EST:** 1954
SALES (est): 251.2K **Privately Held**
SIC: 3471 Electroplating of metals or formed products

(G-7539)
P&K SOCKS LLC
244 Mckinley Ave (48236-3507)
PHONE.................................586 295-5427
Krista Ward, *Principal*
EMP: 4 **EST:** 2017
SALES (est): 92.8K **Privately Held**
SIC: 2252 Socks

(G-7540)
SCHROTH ENTERPRISES INC (PA)
95 Tonnacour Pl (48236-3032)
PHONE.................................586 759-4240
James L Schroth, *President*
Robert A Connelly, *Vice Pres*
EMP: 20 **EST:** 1976
SALES (est): 11.6MM **Privately Held**
SIC: 3398 3496 3069 3479 Metal heat treating; woven wire products; molded rubber products; hard rubber & molded rubber products; painting of metal products

(G-7541)
SIGN-ON CONNECT
296 Lothrop Rd (48236-3406)
PHONE.................................313 539-3246
Ashlee Trempus, *Principal*
EMP: 4 **EST:** 2015
SALES (est): 61.3K **Privately Held**
WEB: www.signonconnect.com
SIC: 3993 Signs & advertising specialties

(G-7542)
WARDLAW PRESS LLC
100 Hall Pl (48236-3815)
PHONE.................................313 806-4603
Susan Stapleton, *Principal*
EMP: 4 **EST:** 2017
SALES (est): 37.5K **Privately Held**
SIC: 2741 Miscellaneous publishing

Grosse Pointe Park
Wayne County

(G-7543)
AJAXX DESIGN INC
Also Called: Ajaxx 63
869 Whittier Rd (48230-1850)
PHONE.................................206 522-4545
William Sherman, *President*
Andrew Fraser, *Vice Pres*
◆ **EMP:** 4 **EST:** 1997
SALES (est): 261.5K **Privately Held**
WEB: www.ajaxx63.com
SIC: 2253 5699 5136 T-shirts & tops, knit; shirts, custom made; T-shirts, custom printed; caps, men's & boys'; shirts, men's & boys'

(G-7544)
ALLEGRA MARKETING PRINT MAIL
1201 Audubon Rd (48230-1151)
PHONE.................................586 335-2596
EMP: 6 **EST:** 2019
SALES (est): 205K **Privately Held**
WEB: www.allegramarketingprint.com
SIC: 2752 Commercial printing, offset

(G-7545)
ALTERNATIVE FUEL TECH LLC
1350 Buckingham Rd (48230-1140)
PHONE.................................313 417-9212
EMP: 4
SALES (est): 362.3K **Privately Held**
SIC: 8731 3714 Commercial Physical Research Mfg Motor Vehicle Parts/Accessories

(G-7546)
ANTEEBO PUBLISHERS INC
Also Called: Grosse Pointe News
16980 Kercheval Pl (48230-1554)
PHONE.................................313 882-6900
Robert G Edgar, *President*
Robert G Liggett Jr, *Publisher*
John Minnis, *Publisher*
Jody McVeigh, *Editor*
Julie R Sutton, *Accounts Exec*
EMP: 47 **EST:** 1940
SQ FT: 4,000
SALES (est): 2MM **Privately Held**
WEB: www.grossepointenews.com
SIC: 2711 2791 Newspapers: publishing only, not printed on site; typesetting

(G-7547)
APPLIED GENOMICS
702 Middlesex Rd (48230-1742)
PHONE.................................313 458-7318
EMP: 4 **EST:** 2018
SALES (est): 95.7K **Privately Held**
SIC: 2835 Microbiology & virology diagnostic products

(G-7548)
ATWATER IN PARK
1175 Lakepointe St (48230-1319)
PHONE 313 344-5104
Brady Hunt, *President*
EMP: 6 EST: 2014
SALES (est): 168.2K Privately Held
WEB: www.atwaterinthepark.com
SIC: 2082 Beer (alcoholic beverage)

(G-7549)
BARKSHANTY HOPS LLC
1231 Bishop Rd (48230-1143)
PHONE 810 300-8049
EMP: 9
SALES (corp-wide): 94.4K Privately Held
WEB: www.elkstreetbrewery.com
SIC: 2082 Malt beverages
PA: Barkshanty Hops Llc
340 S Lake St
Port Sanilac MI

(G-7550)
COLD STONE CREAMERY
16823 Kercheval Ave (48230-1532)
PHONE 313 886-4020
EMP: 12 EST: 2007
SALES (est): 247.4K Privately Held
WEB: www.coldstonecreamery.com
SIC: 2024 5143 5812 Ice cream & frozen desserts; ice cream & ices; ice cream stands or dairy bars

(G-7551)
DETROIT IMPRESSION COMPANY INC
1351 Three Mile Dr (48230-1123)
PHONE 313 921-9077
Edward W Godsalve, *President*
EMP: 5 EST: 2011
SALES (est): 399.2K Privately Held
WEB: www.detroitprinter.net
SIC: 2759 Screen printing

(G-7552)
DETROIT SOCK & STOCKING CO LLC
1465 Lakepointe St (48230-1015)
PHONE 313 409-8735
Juanita Francis, *Principal*
EMP: 6 EST: 2014
SALES (est): 96.6K Privately Held
WEB: www.detroitstockings.com
SIC: 2252 Socks

(G-7553)
ELECTRIC BEACH TANNING CO
15797 Mack Ave (48224-3479)
PHONE 313 423-6539
EMP: 4 EST: 2019
SALES (est): 44.4K Privately Held
SIC: 7299 3699 Tanning salon; electrical equipment & supplies

(G-7554)
FRASER TOOL & GAUGE LLC
1352 Harvard Rd (48230-1134)
PHONE 313 882-9192
Dave Lawrence, *Managing Dir*
David Lawrence, *Managing Dir*
Geoff Lawrence, *Sales Staff*
Ralph Lawrence, *Mng Member*
Jeffrey Lawrence, *Mng Member*
▲ EMP: 5 EST: 2005
SALES (est): 4MM Privately Held
WEB: www.frasergauge.com
SIC: 3545 Gauges (machine tool accessories)

(G-7555)
GENUS INC
767 Grand Marais St (48230-1848)
PHONE 810 580-9197
Joseph Gleason, *CEO*
Biju Jacob, *CTO*
Karen Hopman, *Director*
Cindy Bauer, *Advisor*
EMP: 5 EST: 2015
SQ FT: 1,200
SALES (est): 189.5K Privately Held
WEB: www.genusconnect.org
SIC: 7372 Application computer software

(G-7556)
HIGH WINDS GRAPHIX
15108 Kercheval Ave (48230-1360)
PHONE 313 363-3434
EMP: 4 EST: 2017
SALES (est): 128.7K Privately Held
WEB: www.hwgfx.com
SIC: 2759 Screen printing

(G-7557)
JAMCAT CANDLES LLC
1029 Audubon Rd (48230-1406)
PHONE 313 319-3125
Janet Dabney, *Principal*
EMP: 4 EST: 2017
SALES (est): 39.6K Privately Held
WEB: www.jamcatcandles.com
SIC: 3999 Candles

(G-7558)
POINTE PRINTING INC
1103 Balfour St (48230-1326)
PHONE 313 821-0030
James M Odell, *President*
James A Odell, *Owner*
EMP: 9 EST: 1949
SQ FT: 4,200
SALES (est): 594.2K Privately Held
SIC: 2752 2759 Commercial printing, offset; letterpress printing

(G-7559)
SIMPLY WOODWORKING LLC
1352 Maryland St (48230-1006)
PHONE 586 405-1080
EMP: 4 EST: 2018
SALES (est): 71K Privately Held
SIC: 2431 Millwork

(G-7560)
SIRIONLABS INC
1129 Yorkshire Rd (48230-1435)
PHONE 313 300-0588
EMP: 7 EST: 2014
SALES (est): 159.1K Privately Held
SIC: 7372 Prepackaged software

Grosse Pointe Shores
Wayne County

(G-7561)
DYNAMIC SUPPLY SOLUTIONS INC
56 Sunningdale Dr (48236-1664)
PHONE 248 987-2205
Debbie Mifsud, *Vice Pres*
Bill Bolton, *Vice Pres*
Will Bolton, *Vice Pres*
EMP: 5 EST: 2007
SALES (est): 333K Privately Held
WEB: www.dynamicsupplysolutions.com
SIC: 3679 Antennas, receiving

(G-7562)
HARPER DERMATOLOGY PC
21 Stillmeadow Ln (48236-1117)
PHONE 586 776-7546
Usha Sood, *President*
EMP: 4 EST: 1986
SALES (est): 256.1K Privately Held
SIC: 8011 2834 Dermatologist; dermatologicals

(G-7563)
M-SEAL PRODUCTS CO LLC
55 Fairford Rd (48236-2617)
PHONE 313 884-6147
Paul Van Der Hoeven, *Principal*
EMP: 6 EST: 2008
SALES (est): 105.6K Privately Held
WEB: www.msealproducts.com
SIC: 3053 Gaskets, packing & sealing devices

Grosse Pointe Woods
Wayne County

(G-7564)
BLOODLINE RICH LLC
18941 Alstead St (48236-2001)
PHONE 734 719-1650
Marvin Jackson, *Mng Member*
EMP: 5
SALES (est): 202.2K Privately Held
SIC: 3799 7389 Transportation equipment;

(G-7565)
CIRCUITS OF SOUND
840 Shoreham Rd (48236-2446)
PHONE 313 886-5599
Edward Bartos, *Principal*
EMP: 6 EST: 2007
SALES (est): 154.8K Privately Held
SIC: 3679 Electronic circuits

(G-7566)
CONTINNTAL BLDG SVCS OF CNCNNA
Also Called: Blue Flash Supply Co
580 Cook Rd (48236-2708)
PHONE 313 336-8543
Richard E Beck, *President*
Dave Divozzo, *Vice Pres*
Anna Beck, *Admin Sec*
EMP: 10 EST: 1980
SQ FT: 3,600
SALES (est): 315.8K Privately Held
SIC: 7349 2841 Building maintenance, except repairs; soap & other detergents

(G-7567)
FUR BRAINED IDEAS
1405 Brys Dr (48236-1016)
PHONE 248 830-0764
Charo Tobian, *Principal*
EMP: 4 EST: 2010
SALES (est): 58K Privately Held
SIC: 3999 Furs

(G-7568)
JOSEFS FRENCH PASTRY SHOP CO
21150 Mack Ave (48236-1044)
PHONE 313 881-5710
Joseph Bogosian, *President*
Eileen Bogosian, *Vice Pres*
Rebecca Brown, *Admin Sec*
EMP: 9 EST: 1971
SQ FT: 2,600
SALES (est): 341.4K Privately Held
WEB: www.josefspastryshop.com
SIC: 5461 2051 Pastries; bread, cake & related products

(G-7569)
JOSEPH A DIMAGGIO
Also Called: Dimaggio Jseph A Mstr Gldsmith
19876 Mack Ave (48236-2363)
PHONE 313 881-5353
Joseph A Dimaggio, *Owner*
EMP: 4 EST: 1960
SALES (est): 450.3K Privately Held
SIC: 7353 3911 Cranes & aerial lift equipment, rental or leasing; jewelry, precious metal

(G-7570)
LITTLE BLUE BOOK INC
Also Called: Ble Book Publishing
19803 Mack Ave (48236-2505)
PHONE 313 469-0052
Kim Towar, *President*
Brandy Towar, *Vice Pres*
Heidi Getman, *Accounts Exec*
Dorrie Brennan, *Sales Staff*
Brandi Towar, *Office Mgr*
EMP: 11 EST: 1948
SQ FT: 3,000
SALES (est): 1.4MM Privately Held
WEB: www.bluebooklocal.com
SIC: 2741 Telephone & other directory publishing

(G-7571)
MICHIGAN FUELS
20700 Mack Ave (48236-1436)
PHONE 313 886-7110
Atto Assi, *Manager*
EMP: 7 EST: 2009
SALES (est): 155.7K Privately Held
SIC: 2869 Fuels

(G-7572)
MONOGRAM LADY
1841 Lancaster St (48236-1608)
PHONE 313 649-2160
EMP: 4 EST: 2015
SALES (est): 56.3K Privately Held
SIC: 2395 Embroidery & art needlework

(G-7573)
PRINT XPRESS
20373 Mack Ave (48236-1610)
PHONE 313 886-6850
Tony Alfonsi, *Partner*
Terrie Mc Lauchlan, *Partner*
EMP: 7 EST: 1981
SQ FT: 2,800
SALES (est): 613.7K Privately Held
WEB: www.printxpressgp.com
SIC: 2752 Commercial printing, offset

(G-7574)
PUCK HOGS PRO SHOP INC
562 Heather Ln (48236-1509)
PHONE 419 540-1388
Jeremy Gould, *President*
EMP: 4 EST: 2017
SALES (est): 250K Privately Held
SIC: 5941 2329 3949 Hockey equipment, except skates; hockey uniforms: men's, youths' & boys'; sticks: hockey, lacrosse, etc.

(G-7575)
SHAMROCK PUBLISHING
1523 N Renaud Rd (48236-1762)
PHONE 313 881-1721
Charles Copus, *Principal*
EMP: 6 EST: 1997
SALES (est): 141.8K Privately Held
SIC: 2741 Miscellaneous publishing

(G-7576)
SPECTRA LINK
21885 River Rd (48236-1139)
PHONE 313 417-3723
Mike Moore, *Principal*
EMP: 5 EST: 2010
SALES (est): 219.9K Privately Held
WEB: www.link.enbridge.com
SIC: 3661 Telephone & telegraph apparatus

(G-7577)
TEMPERANCE FUEL STOP INC
2110 Anita Ave (48236-1430)
PHONE 734 206-2676
EMP: 5 EST: 2013
SALES (est): 245.7K Privately Held
SIC: 2869 Fuels

Gulliver
Schoolcraft County

(G-7578)
TUTTLE FOREST PRODUCTS
1964 W Hwy Us 2 (49840)
PHONE 906 283-3871
Betty Tuttle, *Owner*
EMP: 4 EST: 1950
SALES (est): 373.4K Privately Held
SIC: 2411 Logging camps & contractors; pulpwood contractors engaged in cutting; wooden logs

(G-7579)
UP SEAL-COATING
2521w Quarry Rd (49840-9058)
PHONE 906 283-3433
EMP: 5 EST: 2018
SALES (est): 101K Privately Held
SIC: 2952 Asphalt felts & coatings

Gwinn
Marquette County

(G-7580)
ARGONICS INC (PA)
520 9th St (49841-3110)
PHONE 906 226-9747
Robert Flood, *President*
Mike Brinker, *Plant Mgr*
Brett Koski, *Production*
Douglas Maves, *Engineer*
Jeremy Nylund, *Engineer*
▼ EMP: 70 EST: 1993

Gwinn - Marquette County (G-7581)

SQ FT: 10,040
SALES (est): 11.3MM **Privately Held**
WEB: www.argonics.com
SIC: 2821 Elastomers, nonvulcanizable (plastics)

(G-7581)
ARGONICS INC
Also Called: Kryptane Systems
520 9th St (49841-3110)
PHONE.................................303 664-9467
Robert Flood Jr, *President*
Jake Gervais, *Technical Staff*
▲ **EMP:** 15 **EST:** 1997
SALES (est): 2.8MM **Privately Held**
WEB: www.argonics.com
SIC: 2822 3714 Synthetic rubber; motor vehicle parts & accessories
PA: Argonics, Inc.
520 9th St
Gwinn MI 49841

(G-7582)
AVERY COLOR STUDIOS INC
511 Avenue D (49841-3307)
PHONE.................................906 346-3908
Wells Chapin, *President*
Amy Chapin, *Vice Pres*
EMP: 4 **EST:** 1998
SALES (est): 345K **Privately Held**
WEB: www.averycolorstudios.com
SIC: 2752 2741 Commercial printing, offset; miscellaneous publishing

(G-7583)
CANUSA INC
Also Called: Canusa Wood Products
502 2nd St (49841-3301)
PHONE.................................906 446-3327
Francis Fournier, *President*
Sherry Fournier, *Vice Pres*
EMP: 8 **EST:** 2001
SALES (est): 300K **Privately Held**
SIC: 2431 Planing mill, millwork

(G-7584)
FRONTIER MEDICAL DEVICES INC
512 4th St (49841-3312)
PHONE.................................906 232-1200
John Sonderegger, *CFO*
EMP: 13 **EST:** 2010
SQ FT: 10,000
SALES (est): 832.4K **Privately Held**
SIC: 3841 Surgical instruments & apparatus

(G-7585)
NATIONAL CARBON TECH LLC
513 4th St (49841-3304)
PHONE.................................651 330-4063
EMP: 37
SALES (corp-wide): 2.7MM **Privately Held**
WEB: www.national-carbon.com
SIC: 3624 Carbon specialties for electrical use
PA: National Carbon Technologies, Llc
3510 Hopkins Pl N
Saint Paul MN 55128
651 330-4063

(G-7586)
RED BARN MAPS
410 Avenue A (49841-3006)
PHONE.................................906 346-2226
Gerald Happel, *Owner*
EMP: 5 **EST:** 2008
SALES (est): 148.6K **Privately Held**
SIC: 3577 Printers & plotters

(G-7587)
SUPERIOR EXTRUSION INC
Also Called: SEI
118 Avenue G (49841-3107)
PHONE.................................906 346-7308
Daniel Amberg, *President*
Dan Amberg, *Plant Mgr*
Shannon Devooght, *Production*
Ron Fenton, *Purchasing*
Dean Borlace, *CFO*
◆ **EMP:** 170 **EST:** 1996
SQ FT: 103,000
SALES (est): 54.4MM **Privately Held**
WEB: www.superiorextrusion.com
SIC: 3354 Aluminum extruded products

Hale
Iosco County

(G-7588)
CONTAINER SPECIALTIES INC
Darton Archery Div
3540 Darton Rd (48739-8500)
P.O. Box 68 (48739-0068)
PHONE.................................989 728-4231
Ted Harpham, *Sales Mgr*
Rex Darlington, *Branch Mgr*
EMP: 22
SALES (corp-wide): 2.7MM **Privately Held**
WEB: www.dartonarchery.com
SIC: 3949 5941 Bows, archery; arrows, archery; skateboards; archery supplies
PA: Container Specialties, Inc
G3261 Flushing Rd
Flint MI

(G-7589)
FROM LOG UP LLC
1872 M 65 (48739-9017)
PHONE.................................989 728-0611
David A Bain
EMP: 5 **EST:** 2010
SALES (est): 90.1K **Privately Held**
SIC: 2411 Logging camps & contractors

(G-7590)
SOY D-LIGHTS & SCENTSATIONS
7731 Hillsdale Dr (48739-8955)
PHONE.................................989 728-5947
EMP: 4 **EST:** 2016
SALES (est): 68.4K **Privately Held**
SIC: 3999 Candles

Hamburg
Livingston County

(G-7591)
FLEXIBLE METAL INC
7495 E M 36 (48139-1001)
PHONE.................................810 231-1300
Joseph Baxter, *Manager*
EMP: 75
SALES (corp-wide): 94.6MM **Privately Held**
WEB: www.flexiblemetal.com
SIC: 3498 Fabricated pipe & fittings
HQ: Flexible Metal, Inc.
1685 Brandywine Ave
Chula Vista CA 91911

(G-7592)
NATIONAL CONTROL SYSTEMS INC
10737 Hamburg Rd (48139-1216)
P.O. Box 266 (48139-0266)
PHONE.................................810 231-2901
Thomas Treiber, *Ch of Bd*
Robert Socia, *President*
Mike Arpi, *Vice Pres*
Jan Kuklewski, *Train & Dev Mgr*
Patrick Jeski, *Admin Sec*
EMP: 7 **EST:** 1986
SQ FT: 5,000
SALES (est): 855.9K **Privately Held**
WEB: www.nationalcontrolsystems.com
SIC: 3625 Relays & industrial controls

(G-7593)
PICKO FERRUM FABRICATING LLC
10800 Featherly Dr (48139-1212)
PHONE.................................810 626-7086
Mike Jecks, *President*
EMP: 6 **EST:** 2017
SALES (est): 692.8K **Privately Held**
SIC: 3498 Tube fabricating (contract bending & shaping)

Hamilton
Allegan County

(G-7594)
ADVANCE CNC MACHINE INC
3051 Lincoln Rd (49419-9527)
P.O. Box 272 (49419-0272)
PHONE.................................269 751-7005
Lyle Lugten, *President*
Douglas Boals, *Vice Pres*
EMP: 7 **EST:** 1990
SQ FT: 5,500
SALES (est): 509.1K **Privately Held**
SIC: 3599 Machine shop, jobbing & repair

(G-7595)
ALLEGAN METAL FABRICATORS INC
3280 Lincoln Rd (49419-9531)
P.O. Box 251 (49419-0251)
PHONE.................................269 751-7130
Eric Nyhof, *President*
Henry M Nyhof, *Admin Sec*
EMP: 6 **EST:** 1967
SQ FT: 25,200
SALES (est): 585.2K **Privately Held**
WEB: www.alleganmetalfab.com
SIC: 7692 3441 Welding repair; fabricated structural metal

(G-7596)
AMERIVET ENGINEERING LLC
3146 53rd St (49419-9626)
PHONE.................................269 751-9092
Scott Russell,
EMP: 4 **EST:** 2012
SALES (est): 190.2K **Privately Held**
SIC: 8711 3559 Consulting engineer; automotive related machinery

(G-7597)
DARLING INGREDIENTS INC
5900 Old Allegan Rd (49419-9314)
PHONE.................................269 751-0560
Terry Pfannestill, *Principal*
EMP: 7
SALES (corp-wide): 3.3B **Publicly Held**
WEB: www.darlingii.com
SIC: 2077 2076 2048 2013 Animal & marine fats & oils; vegetable oil mills; prepared feeds; sausages & other prepared meats; commodity brokers, contracts
PA: Darling Ingredients Inc.
5601 N Macarthur Blvd
Irving TX 75038
972 717-0300

(G-7598)
HAMILTON BLOCK & READY MIX CO
4510 132nd Ave (49419-9530)
P.O. Box 7 (49419-0007)
PHONE.................................269 751-5129
Curt Pieper, *President*
Paul Haverdink, *Vice Pres*
Dorothy Motman, *Treasurer*
Margaret Scharf, *Admin Sec*
EMP: 21 **EST:** 1914
SQ FT: 2,500
SALES (est): 4.5MM **Privately Held**
WEB: www.hamiltonbr.com
SIC: 3273 Ready-mixed concrete

(G-7599)
HAMILTON INDUSTRIAL PRODUCTS
4555 134th Ave (49419-8579)
P.O. Box 157 (49419-0157)
PHONE.................................269 751-5153
Reinhold Petry, *President*
Eva Petry, *Vice Pres*
Eva J Petry, *Admin Sec*
EMP: 23 **EST:** 1972
SQ FT: 56,000
SALES (est): 254.2K **Privately Held**
WEB: www.glswalls.com
SIC: 3599 7629 3542 Machine shop, jobbing & repair; custom machinery; electrical repair shops; machine tools, metal forming type

(G-7600)
HAMILTON STEEL FABRICATIONS
3290 Lincoln Rd (49419-9531)
PHONE.................................269 751-8757
Rudy Lampen, *President*
Blake Lampen, *General Mgr*
EMP: 7 **EST:** 1984
SQ FT: 18,000
SALES (est): 1MM **Privately Held**
WEB: www.hamiltonsteelfab.com
SIC: 3441 Fabricated structural metal

(G-7601)
LEANN KELLEY ENTERPRISES LLC
5030 136th Ave (49419-9607)
PHONE.................................505 270-5687
Josephh M Cardamone, *Principal*
EMP: 4 **EST:** 2016
SALES (est): 129.9K **Privately Held**
WEB: www.leannkelley.com
SIC: 2741 Miscellaneous publishing

(G-7602)
LENWAY MACHINE COMPANY INC
Also Called: Len-Way Machine & Tool
3165 60th St (49419-9657)
PHONE.................................269 751-5183
Jeanette Sluis, *President*
EMP: 9 **EST:** 1976
SQ FT: 4,000
SALES (est): 641.4K **Privately Held**
WEB: www.lenwaymachine.com
SIC: 3599 3544 Machine shop, jobbing & repair; special dies, tools, jigs & fixtures

(G-7603)
LITE LOAD SERVICES LLC
3866 40th St (49419-9737)
PHONE.................................269 751-6037
Jeff Garvelink, *Mng Member*
EMP: 10 **EST:** 1997
SALES (est): 914.4K **Privately Held**
WEB: www.liteload.com
SIC: 1771 2951 Blacktop (asphalt) work; asphalt paving mixtures & blocks

(G-7604)
POST HARDWOODS INC
3544 38th St (49419-9500)
PHONE.................................269 751-2221
Robert Post, *President*
August Jay Post, *Vice Pres*
EMP: 29 **EST:** 1981
SQ FT: 10,000
SALES (est): 1.5MM **Privately Held**
WEB: www.posthardwoods.com
SIC: 2421 Lumber: rough, sawed or planed

(G-7605)
PROTOTYPES PLUS INC
3537 Lincoln Rd (49419-9601)
PHONE.................................269 751-7141
James H Lemson, *President*
EMP: 5 **EST:** 1991
SALES (est): 945.9K **Privately Held**
WEB: www.proto-plus.com
SIC: 3714 Motor vehicle parts & accessories

(G-7606)
R & D CNC MACHINING INC
3506 Lincoln Rd (49419-9601)
P.O. Box 218 (49419-0218)
PHONE.................................269 751-4171
Rienhold Petry, *Owner*
EMP: 10 **EST:** 2004
SALES (est): 569.6K **Privately Held**
WEB: www.randdcnc.com
SIC: 3599 Machine shop, jobbing & repair

(G-7607)
T-PRINT USA
3410 136th Ave (49419-9543)
PHONE.................................269 751-4603
Chris Malley, *Executive Asst*
EMP: 9 **EST:** 2008
SALES (est): 255K **Privately Held**
WEB: www.tprintusa.com
SIC: 2752 Commercial printing, offset

GEOGRAPHIC SECTION
Harbor Beach - Huron County (G-7636)

(G-7608)
TRESTLE PLASTIC SERVICES LLC
3393 Lincoln Rd (49419-8588)
P.O. Box 142 (49419-0142)
PHONE..................................616 262-5484
Rick Evstile, *Mng Member*
EMP: 4 **EST:** 2006
SQ FT: 6,000
SALES (est): 276.8K **Privately Held**
SIC: 3089 Injection molding of plastics

(G-7609)
WEBER BROS & WHITE METAL WORKS
4715 136th Ave (49419-9722)
P.O. Box 187 (49419-0187)
PHONE..................................269 751-5193
Stuart W White, *President*
Sara S Van Doornik, *Vice Pres*
Betty White, *Treasurer*
Harold Kirke White Jr, *Shareholder*
EMP: 4 **EST:** 1958
SQ FT: 15,000 **Privately Held**
WEB: www.weberbros-white.com
SIC: 3469 Spinning metal for the trade; stamping metal for the trade

Hamtramck
Wayne County

(G-7610)
18TH STREET DELI INC
8800 Conant St (48211-1401)
PHONE..................................313 921-7710
David Salerno, *President*
EMP: 5 **EST:** 1987
SALES (est): 1.8MM **Privately Held**
WEB: www.nuvuefoods.com
SIC: 2099 5141 Food preparations; groceries, general line

(G-7611)
AROMA TABA
10009 Joseph Campau St (48212-3221)
PHONE..................................313 782-4076
EMP: 4 **EST:** 2015
SALES (est): 71.7K **Privately Held**
SIC: 2844 Cosmetic preparations

(G-7612)
MELIX SERVICES INC
2359 Livernois Rd Ste 300 (48212)
PHONE..................................248 387-9303
Melis Lejlic, *President*
EMP: 7 **EST:** 2015
SALES (est): 200K **Privately Held**
SIC: 1389 6531 Construction, repair & dismantling services; real estate leasing & rentals

(G-7613)
SEVEN MILE AND GRND RIVER FUEL
Also Called: BP
5099 Fredro St (48212-2838)
PHONE..................................313 535-3000
EMP: 6 **EST:** 2015
SALES (est): 360.2K **Privately Held**
SIC: 2869 Fuels

Hancock
Houghton County

(G-7614)
A & S INDUSTRIAL LLC
19273 Kiiskila Rd (49930-9668)
PHONE..................................906 482-8007
Larry Anderson, *Principal*
EMP: 4 **EST:** 2017
SALES (est): 595.4K **Privately Held**
SIC: 3441 Fabricated structural metal

(G-7615)
B B WHEELCHAIR SERVICES
1215 Jasberg St (49930-1408)
PHONE..................................906 281-7202
EMP: 4 **EST:** 2018
SALES (est): 95.3K **Privately Held**
SIC: 3842 Wheelchairs

(G-7616)
BRENT BASTIAN LOGGING LLC
54215 Salo Rd (49930-9651)
PHONE..................................906 482-6378
Brent Bastian, *Principal*
EMP: 6 **EST:** 2010
SALES (est): 509.4K **Privately Held**
SIC: 2411 Logging camps & contractors

(G-7617)
CELEBRATIONS
Also Called: Celebrations Bridal & Formal
110 E Quincy St (49930-2138)
PHONE..................................906 482-4946
Diane Eshbach, *Owner*
EMP: 4 **EST:** 1990
SQ FT: 2,000
SALES (est): 165K **Privately Held**
WEB: www.celebrationsbridal.net
SIC: 5621 7221 7299 5699 Bridal shops; photographic studios, portrait; tuxedo rental; formal wear; shoes, orthopedic; invitation & stationery printing & engraving

(G-7618)
HANCOCK BOTTLING CO INC
Also Called: Coca-Cola
1800 Birch St (49930-1067)
PHONE..................................906 482-3701
Robert L Scholie Jr, *President*
Gary Scholie, *Vice Pres*
EMP: 21 **EST:** 1925
SALES (est): 1.6MM **Privately Held**
WEB: www.hancockcoke.com
SIC: 2086 Bottled & canned soft drinks

(G-7619)
HOME INSPECTION PROTECTION
25599 Pt Mills Estates Rd (49930-9525)
PHONE..................................906 370-6704
Sally Koppana, *Admin Sec*
EMP: 5 **EST:** 2017
SALES (est): 74.9K **Privately Held**
SIC: 2452 Prefabricated wood buildings

(G-7620)
INFRARED TELEMETRICS INC
Also Called: Ir Telemetrics
1780 Birch St (49930-1072)
P.O. Box 70, Houghton (49931-0070)
PHONE..................................906 482-0012
Glen L Barna, *President*
Carl L Anderson, *Corp Secy*
Paul La Vigne, *Vice Pres*
EMP: 12 **EST:** 1991
SQ FT: 5,000
SALES (est): 1.3MM **Privately Held**
WEB: www.irtelemetrics.com
SIC: 3829 3825 3823 8711 Measuring & controlling devices; instruments to measure electricity; industrial instrmnts msrmnt display/control process variable; professional engineer

(G-7621)
LIFE OTREACH CTR HOUGHTON CNTY
300b Quincy St (49930-1802)
PHONE..................................906 482-8681
Mark A Cavis, *Principal*
EMP: 9 **EST:** 1981
SALES (est): 74.4K **Privately Held**
WEB: www.lifeoutreachcenter.org
SIC: 2835 8742 Pregnancy test kits; hospital & health services consultant

(G-7622)
NORTH POST INC
Also Called: Northwoods Trading Post
120 Quincy St (49930-1856)
PHONE..................................906 482-5210
Richard Freeman, *President*
Carol Freeman, *Corp Secy*
EMP: 7 **EST:** 1957
SQ FT: 6,500
SALES (est): 664.9K **Privately Held**
WEB: www.northpostinc.com
SIC: 3949 Fishing equipment; hunting equipment

(G-7623)
VANDCO INCORPORATED
Also Called: Vollwerth & Co
200 Hancock St (49930-2004)
P.O. Box 239 (49930-0239)
PHONE..................................906 482-1550
Adam M Manderfield, *President*
Jared Manderfield, *Vice Pres*
James Schaaf, *Vice Pres*
Jim Schaaf, *Vice Pres*
Adam Manderfield, *Prdtn Mgr*
EMP: 35 **EST:** 1915
SQ FT: 20,000
SALES (est): 3.9MM **Privately Held**
WEB: www.vollwerth.com
SIC: 2013 5141 Sausages from purchased meat; smoked meats from purchased meat; groceries, general line

Hanover
Jackson County

(G-7624)
GREAT LAKE FOAM TECHNOLOGIES
104 W Main St (49241-9811)
PHONE..................................517 563-8030
William Maccready, *President*
EMP: 13 **EST:** 1996
SQ FT: 9,000
SALES (est): 596.3K **Privately Held**
SIC: 3069 Foam rubber

(G-7625)
LEVY MACHINING LLC
11901 Strait Rd (49241-9781)
P.O. Box 5 (49241-0005)
PHONE..................................517 563-2013
Ryan Levy,
Michael Levy,
Sherilene Levy,
EMP: 5 **EST:** 2002
SALES (est): 250K **Privately Held**
SIC: 3599 Machine shop, jobbing & repair

(G-7626)
SKW AUTOMATION INC
6422 Hanover Rd Ste 105 (49241-9666)
PHONE..................................517 563-8288
Kevin Wood, *CEO*
Shanna A Wood, *CFO*
Jennifer Denig, *Manager*
Jacob Wood,
EMP: 6 **EST:** 2002
SQ FT: 51,000
SALES (est): 678.9K **Privately Held**
WEB: www.skwautomation.com
SIC: 3549 Assembly machines, including robotic

(G-7627)
TRI-STATE TECHNICAL SERVICES
9659 Grover Rd (49241-9776)
PHONE..................................517 563-8743
Wendy Valentine,
Ross Valentine,
EMP: 4 **EST:** 1994
SALES (est): 376.6K **Privately Held**
WEB: www.usetsts.com
SIC: 3552 Embroidery machines

Harbor Beach
Huron County

(G-7628)
AG MANUFACTURING INC
319 Industrial Dr (48441-1014)
PHONE..................................989 479-9590
Victor Edozien, *CEO*
Stephanie Redman, *Opers Mgr*
John Hardy, *Maint Spvr*
Diane Hartman, *Engineer*
Mike Onianwah, *CFO*
▲ **EMP:** 30 **EST:** 2004
SQ FT: 55,000
SALES (est): 8.1MM **Privately Held**
WEB: www.agmanufacturing.com
SIC: 3315 Steel wire & related products

(G-7629)
CLASSY THREADZ
1529 Eppenbrock Rd (48441-8300)
PHONE..................................989 479-9595
Cindy Simen, *Owner*
EMP: 4 **EST:** 2008
SALES (est): 174.8K **Privately Held**
WEB: www.classythreadz.vpweb.com
SIC: 2395 Embroidery products, except schiffli machine

(G-7630)
CORTEVA AGRISCIENCE LLC
305 N Huron Ave (48441-1120)
PHONE..................................989 479-3245
Janet Chavous, *Finance Mgr*
Nicole Greyerbiehl, *Supervisor*
Michael Mermuys, *Maintence Staff*
EMP: 5
SALES (corp-wide): 14.2B **Publicly Held**
WEB: www.corteva.com
SIC: 2879 Agricultural chemicals
HQ: Corteva Agriscience Llc
    9330 Zionsville Rd
    Indianapolis IN 46268

(G-7631)
HARBOR BEACH TIMES
123 N 1st St (48441-1102)
PHONE..................................989 479-3605
Fax: 989 479-9697
EMP: 4
SALES (est): 177.2K **Privately Held**
SIC: 2711 Newspapers-Publishing/Printing

(G-7632)
HARBOR TOOL AND MACHINE
225 Hunter Industrial Dr (48441-9346)
PHONE..................................989 479-6708
Bob Glaza, *Partner*
Lucille Glaza, *Corp Secy*
Dennis Glaza, *Vice Pres*
Gary Glaza, *Manager*
EMP: 10 **EST:** 1996
SALES (est): 817.2K **Privately Held**
WEB: www.kalscustomservices.com
SIC: 3599 Machine shop, jobbing & repair

(G-7633)
JUPITER MANUFACTURING
8661 Sand Beach Rd (48441-9435)
PHONE..................................989 551-0519
Thomas Booms, *Manager*
EMP: 9 **EST:** 2014
SALES (est): 247K **Privately Held**
WEB: www.jupitermanufacturing.com
SIC: 3999 Manufacturing industries

(G-7634)
LEADER TOOL COMPANY - HB INC
630 N Huron Ave (48441-1007)
P.O. Box 66 (48441-0066)
PHONE..................................989 479-3281
Bryan Gunn, *President*
Allen D Gunn, *President*
Joan Gunn, *Vice Pres*
EMP: 42 **EST:** 1968
SQ FT: 30,000
SALES (est): 1.6MM **Privately Held**
SIC: 3544 3452 Special dies & tools; bolts, nuts, rivets & washers

(G-7635)
PRIME LAND FARM
7442 Toppin Rd (48441-9446)
PHONE..................................989 550-6120
Darrin Siemen, *Owner*
EMP: 9 **EST:** 2001
SALES (est): 305.5K **Privately Held**
WEB: www.primelandfarm.com
SIC: 0191 0133 2051 2046 General farms, primarily crop; sugarcane & sugar beets; bread, all types (white, wheat, rye, etc): fresh or frozen; wet corn milling; alfalfa or alfalfa meal, prepared as animal feed; planting, haying, harvesting & processing machinery

(G-7636)
SENSIENT FLAVORS LLC
79 State St (48441-1255)
PHONE..................................989 479-3211
EMP: 26 **EST:** 2008

Harbor Beach - Huron County (G-7637)

(G-7637)
SENSIENT TECHNOLOGIES CORP
79 State St (48441-1255)
PHONE...................989 479-3211
Jim Tenbusch, *Branch Mgr*
EMP: 7
SALES (corp-wide): 1.3B **Publicly Held**
WEB: www.sensient.com
SIC: **2099** 2087 Yeast; seasonings & spices; chili pepper or powder; seasonings: dry mixes; beverage bases
PA: Sensient Technologies Corporation
777 E Wisconsin Ave # 1100
Milwaukee WI 53202
414 271-6755

SALES (est): 3.6MM **Privately Held**
WEB: www.sensientflavorsandextracts.com
SIC: **2087** 2099 Flavoring extracts & syrups; yeast

(G-7638)
WOOD CONTRACTING LLC
265 Whitcomb St (48441-1176)
PHONE...................989 479-6037
Adam Wood, *Principal*
EMP: 7 EST: 2016
SALES (est): 368.6K **Privately Held**
SIC: **2499** Wood products

Harbor Springs
Emmet County

(G-7639)
AMERICAN GATOR TOOL COMPANY
1225 W Conway Rd Unit C (49740-9604)
PHONE...................231 347-3222
Donald Berg, *President*
Carol Berg, *Vice Pres*
EMP: 5
SQ FT: 6,000
SALES (est): 270K **Privately Held**
WEB: www.americangator.com
SIC: **3541** 3545 5084 Tapping machines; machine tool attachments & accessories; metalworking tools (such as drills, taps, dies, files); tapping attachments

(G-7640)
AMERICAN LAP COMPANY
220 Franklin Park (49740-9614)
P.O. Box 106 (49740-0106)
PHONE...................231 526-7121
Alan Hackman, *CEO*
Arthur J Hackman Jr, *CEO*
Alan T Hackman, *President*
Mary Alice Hackman, *Corp Secy*
EMP: 5 EST: 1944
SQ FT: 5,000
SALES (est): 470K **Privately Held**
WEB: www.americanlap.com
SIC: **3541** Machine tools, metal cutting type

(G-7641)
BEAR CUB HOLDINGS INC
8761 M 119 (49740-9586)
P.O. Box 291 (49740-0291)
PHONE...................231 242-1152
Mike Walda, *President*
Emylee Walda, *Vice Pres*
EMP: 4 EST: 2005
SALES (est): 483.3K **Privately Held**
SIC: **2891** Sealing compounds for pipe threads or joints

(G-7642)
BOYER GLASSWORKS INC
207 State St (49740-1528)
P.O. Box 733 (49740-0733)
PHONE...................231 526-6359
Harry Boyer, *President*
EMP: 4 EST: 1994
SALES (est): 218.7K **Privately Held**
WEB: www.northernmichiganeventscalendar.com
SIC: **3231** Art glass: made from purchased glass

(G-7643)
CEEFLOW INC
5334 S Lake Shore Dr (49740-9199)
PHONE...................231 526-5579
Peter A Cummings, *President*
David Cummings, *Admin Sec*
EMP: 4 EST: 1986
SQ FT: 5,000
SALES (est): 475.2K **Privately Held**
WEB: www.ceeflow.com
SIC: **3444** Skylights, sheet metal

(G-7644)
CENTRAL INDUSTRIAL MFG INC
Also Called: Walls Holding Company
1211 W Conway Rd (49740-9683)
PHONE...................231 347-5920
Erika Walls, *President*
EMP: 11 EST: 1965
SQ FT: 5,700
SALES (est): 2.8MM **Privately Held**
WEB: www.centralindustrialmanufacturing.com
SIC: **3544** Special dies & tools

(G-7645)
CORNILLIE CONCRETE
710 W Conway Rd (49740-9585)
PHONE...................231 439-9200
Rick Deneweth, *Owner*
EMP: 7 EST: 1997
SALES (est): 132.7K **Privately Held**
SIC: **3273** Ready-mixed concrete

(G-7646)
EQUUS MAGNIFICUS
526 S Lamkin Rd (49740-9182)
PHONE...................651 407-0023
Jeannette Roesner, *Principal*
EMP: 5 EST: 2019
SALES (est): 253.9K **Privately Held**
SIC: **2048** Prepared feeds

(G-7647)
HARBOR SPRNG VNYRDS WINERY LLC
Also Called: Tunnel Vision Brewery
5699 S Lake Shore Dr (49740-9784)
PHONE...................231 242-4062
James Palmer,
James Spencer IV,
Sharon Spencer,
EMP: 6 EST: 2010
SQ FT: 2,000
SALES (est): 338.8K **Privately Held**
WEB: www.pondhill.com
SIC: **2084** Wines

(G-7648)
HARRISON INDUSTRIES
7223 Lightfoot Rd (49740-9310)
PHONE...................231 881-4704
Leonard Harrison, *Principal*
EMP: 4 EST: 2010
SALES (est): 49.9K **Privately Held**
SIC: **3999** Manufacturing industries

(G-7649)
LC MATERIALS LLC
710 W Conway Rd (49740-9585)
PHONE...................817 835-4100
Robert Cherry, *Branch Mgr*
EMP: 204
SALES (corp-wide): 170.1MM **Privately Held**
WEB: www.lcredimix.com
SIC: **3273** Ready-mixed concrete
HQ: Lc Materials, Llc
805 W 13th St
Cadillac MI 49601
231 946-5600

(G-7650)
LUCKY PRESS LLC
4929 Turfway Trl (49740-9273)
PHONE...................614 309-0048
Janice Phelps, *Principal*
EMP: 4 EST: 2011
SALES (est): 63.4K **Privately Held**
SIC: **2741** Miscellaneous publishing

(G-7651)
MOELLER AEROSPACE TECH INC
8725 Moeller Dr (49740-9583)
PHONE...................231 347-9575
Jerilyn George, *Buyer*
Jeff Beaubien, *Manager*
Tony Budzinski, *Manager*
David Gervais, *Prgrmr*
EMP: 225 EST: 1988
SQ FT: 19,000
SALES (est): 42.1MM **Privately Held**
WEB: www.moeller-aerospace.com
SIC: **3724** Aircraft engines & engine parts

(G-7652)
MONOGRAM GOODS NAPLES LLC
261 E Main St (49740-1511)
PHONE...................231 526-7700
Laura Melges, *Principal*
EMP: 4 EST: 2016
SALES (est): 66.9K **Privately Held**
WEB: www.monogramgoods.com
SIC: **2395** Embroidery & art needlework

(G-7653)
NORTH COUNTRY PUBLISHING CORP
Also Called: Harbor Light Newspaper
211 E 3rd St (49740-1534)
P.O. Box 4545 (49740-4545)
PHONE...................231 526-2191
Kevin Oneill, *Publisher*
Ruth Oneill, *Treasurer*
EMP: 4
SQ FT: 2,500
SALES (est): 351.3K **Privately Held**
WEB: www.harborlightnews.com
SIC: **2759** Newspapers: printing; invitations: printing

(G-7654)
PHG AVIATION LLC
380 Franklin Park Ste 1 (49740-8669)
P.O. Box 10038, Phoenix AZ (85064-0038)
PHONE...................231 526-7380
Lacy Tippett, *CFO*
Gerald Haan, *Mng Member*
Benjamin Ide, *Director*
EMP: 4 EST: 2014
SALES (est): 63.4K **Privately Held**
SIC: **8711** 3812 Aviation &/or aeronautical engineering; aircraft/aerospace flight instruments & guidance systems

(G-7655)
PHIL ELENBAAS MILLWORK INC
341 Franklin Park (49740-9628)
PHONE...................231 526-8399
Yli Rabeiro, *Branch Mgr*
EMP: 7 **Privately Held**
WEB: www.elenbaasmillwork.com
SIC: **2431** Millwork
PA: Phil Elenbaas Millwork, Inc.
3000 Wilson Dr Nw
Grand Rapids MI 49534

(G-7656)
SEALEX INC
8850 Moeller Dr (49740-9461)
PHONE...................231 348-5020
Robert Hagen, *President*
Peter R Hagen, *Chairman*
Matthias Hagan, *Vice Pres*
EMP: 7 EST: 1991
SQ FT: 10,000
SALES (est): 764.8K **Privately Held**
SIC: **2891** Adhesives & sealants

(G-7657)
SMART SWATTER LLC
3229 Valleyview Trl (49740-9325)
P.O. Box 96, Alanson (49706-0096)
PHONE...................989 763-2626
Rod McDonald,
EMP: 4 EST: 2016
SALES (est): 25K **Privately Held**
WEB: www.smartswatter.com
SIC: **3999** Flyswatters

(G-7658)
TIMBERTECH INC
8796 Moeller Dr (49740-9583)
P.O. Box 546 (49740-0546)
PHONE...................231 348-2750
John F Phillips, *President*
Deborah Baker, *Sales Mgr*
Angie Olson, *Graphic Designe*
EMP: 12 EST: 1985
SQ FT: 13,500
SALES (est): 1.1MM **Privately Held**
WEB: www.timbertech.net
SIC: **2752** 2761 2759 2671 Business forms, lithographed; manifold business forms; commercial printing; packaging paper & plastics film, coated & laminated; automotive & apparel trimmings

(G-7659)
TRAVERSE BAY CANVAS INC
787 W Conway Rd (49740-9585)
PHONE...................231 347-3001
Carol E Kleinert, *President*
Carol Kleinert, *President*
EMP: 8 EST: 1979
SQ FT: 6,000
SALES (est): 785.8K **Privately Held**
WEB: www.traversebaycanvas.com
SIC: **2394** Awnings, fabric: made from purchased materials

(G-7660)
TREMCO INC SEALEX MFG PLA
8850 Moeller Dr (49740-9461)
PHONE...................231 348-5020
EMP: 4 EST: 2019
SALES (est): 90.7K **Privately Held**
SIC: **3999** Manufacturing industries

(G-7661)
VENTILATION + PLUS EQP INC
670 W Conway Rd 1 (49740-9489)
P.O. Box 811 (49740-0811)
PHONE...................231 487-1156
Gary Teffens, *President*
EMP: 4 EST: 2006
SALES (est): 724.7K **Privately Held**
WEB: www.proventilation.com
SIC: **3444** Metal ventilating equipment

Harper Woods
Wayne County

(G-7662)
AVIDASPORTS LLC
20844 Harper Ave Ste 300 (48225-1172)
PHONE...................313 447-5670
Bruce Burton, *Principal*
EMP: 10 EST: 2009
SALES (est): 289.8K **Privately Held**
WEB: www.avidasports.com
SIC: **2329** Bathing suits & swimwear: men's & boys'

(G-7663)
BELLA SKYY LLC
20441 Danbury Ln (48225-1118)
PHONE...................313 623-9296
Chantelle Johnson-Mosley, *Owner*
EMP: 5 EST: 2015
SALES (est): 71.4K **Privately Held**
WEB: www.bellaskyy.bigcartel.com
SIC: **7231** 2844 Hairdressers; hair preparations, including shampoos

(G-7664)
BORDER CITY TOOL AND MFG CO
19211 Tyrone St (48225-2425)
PHONE...................586 758-5574
Don Rothburn, *President*
EMP: 16 EST: 1955
SALES (est): 5.4MM **Privately Held**
SIC: **3531** Construction machinery

(G-7665)
CBD WITH B WELLNESS LTD LBLTY
21731 Bournemouth St (48225-2331)
PHONE...................248 595-3583
Brandy Lee,
EMP: 5 EST: 2020

GEOGRAPHIC SECTION

Harrison Township - Macomb County (G-7693)

SALES (est): 347K **Privately Held**
SIC: 2833 Vitamins, natural or synthetic: bulk, uncompounded

(G-7666)
EXPRESS EXPEDITING
20614 Washtenaw St (48225-2257)
PHONE.................................313 347-9975
EMP: 4 EST: 2014
SALES (est): 44.8K **Privately Held**
SIC: 2741 Miscellaneous publishing

(G-7667)
MASLIN CORPORATION (PA)
Also Called: Sir Speedy
20304 Harper Ave (48225-1733)
PHONE.................................586 777-7500
Thomas J Coughlin, *President*
Catherine Coughlin, *Corp Secy*
EMP: 4 EST: 1988
SALES (est): 846.8K **Privately Held**
WEB: www.sirspeedy.com
SIC: 2752 Commercial printing, lithographic

(G-7668)
OEM WHEELS
20416 Harper Ave (48225-1644)
PHONE.................................248 556-9993
EMP: 7 EST: 2011
SALES (est): 146.6K **Privately Held**
SIC: 3312 Wheels

(G-7669)
PACIFIC DOOR & TRIM
20125 Balfour St (48225-1734)
PHONE.................................619 887-1786
Christopher Isaac Reed, *Principal*
EMP: 4 EST: 2009
SALES (est): 97.6K **Privately Held**
WEB: www.pacificmutualdoor.com
SIC: 2431 Millwork

(G-7670)
PRINT SHOP
18000 Vernier Rd Ste 626 (48225-1030)
PHONE.................................313 499-8444
EMP: 4 EST: 2014
SALES (est): 73.5K **Privately Held**
WEB: www.arkansasgraphics.com
SIC: 2752 Commercial printing, offset

(G-7671)
REFINERY CORPORATION AMERICA
20008 Kelly Rd (48225-1919)
P.O. Box 361420, Grosse Pointe (48236-5420)
PHONE.................................877 881-0336
Ashia Paul, *President*
EMP: 6 EST: 2012
SQ FT: 4,000
SALES (est): 260.8K **Privately Held**
SIC: 1311 Gas & hydrocarbon liquefaction from coal

(G-7672)
SIX COLLECTION LLC
19179 Kenosha St (48225-2131)
PHONE.................................313 516-9999
Dacia Maiden,
EMP: 4 EST: 2019
SALES (est): 50K **Privately Held**
SIC: 2299 Towels & towelings, linen & linen-and-cotton mixtures

(G-7673)
SWEETHEART BAKERY OF MICHIGAN
Also Called: Michelle's Restaurant
19200 Kelly Rd (48225-1902)
P.O. Box 88, Roseville (48066-0088)
PHONE.................................586 795-1660
Michael Gralewski, *President*
Amelia Gralewski, *Vice Pres*
EMP: 12 EST: 1991
SQ FT: 13,000
SALES (est): 316K **Privately Held**
SIC: 5812 5461 2051 Family restaurants; bakeries; bread, cake & related products

(G-7674)
WE ARE URBAN TECHNOLOGY LLC
20325 Van Antwerp St (48225-1401)
PHONE.................................313 779-4406
Dashaun G Huston, *Principal*
EMP: 10 EST: 2020
SALES (est): 578.7K **Privately Held**
WEB: www.bulliontooltech.com
SIC: 3599 Machine shop, jobbing & repair

Harrison
Clare County

(G-7675)
CLARE COUNTY CLEAVER INC
183 W Main St (48625)
P.O. Box 436 (48625-0436)
PHONE.................................989 539-7496
Glen Bucholz, *President*
Martin Bucholz, *Vice Pres*
Mable Bucholz, *Treasurer*
EMP: 8 EST: 1881
SALES (est): 599.5K **Privately Held**
WEB: www.clarecountycleaver.net
SIC: 2711 Newspapers, publishing & printing; job printing & newspaper publishing combined

(G-7676)
FEDERAL BROACH & MCH CO LLC
1961 Sullivan Dr (48625-9455)
PHONE.................................989 539-7420
Dan Dennis, *Vice Pres*
Susan Langley, *Purch Agent*
Ken Kernen, *Engineer*
Don Mast, *Electrical Engi*
Alex Strawn, *Electrical Engi*
▲ EMP: 116 EST: 1985
SQ FT: 82,000
SALES (est): 23.7MM **Privately Held**
WEB: www.federalbroach.com
SIC: 3541 3545 Broaching machines; broaches (machine tool accessories)
HQ: Mitsubishi Heavy Industries America, Inc.
20 Greenway Plz Ste 83
Houston TX 77046
346 308-8800

(G-7677)
GAMBLES REDI-MIX INC
1415 N Clare Ave (48625-8218)
P.O. Box 692 (48625-0692)
PHONE.................................989 539-6460
Walter W Gamble, *President*
Cathy Gamble, *Vice Pres*
EMP: 20 EST: 1945
SQ FT: 2,400
SALES (est): 2.7MM **Privately Held**
WEB: www.gamblesredimix.com
SIC: 3273 3272 Ready-mixed concrete; concrete products

(G-7678)
IMPRESSIONS CUSTOM GRAPHICS
4195 N Clare Ave (48625-8030)
PHONE.................................989 429-0079
Veto Giannola, *Principal*
EMP: 4 EST: 2016
SALES (est): 76.6K **Privately Held**
SIC: 2759 Screen printing

(G-7679)
JAMES L MILLER
Also Called: Runnin Gears
2500 Major Mountain Rd (48625-8211)
PHONE.................................989 539-5540
James L Miller, *Owner*
EMP: 4 EST: 1995
SQ FT: 10,000
SALES (est): 481K **Privately Held**
WEB: www.runninggearsinc.com
SIC: 2411 5082 Logging; logging & forestry machinery & equipment

(G-7680)
MARINE AUTOMATED DOC SYSTEM
2900 Doc Dr (48625-7329)
PHONE.................................989 539-9010
Greg Heintz, *President*
Tom Dewey, *Vice Pres*
EMP: 13 EST: 1999
SALES (est): 1.1MM **Privately Held**
WEB: www.madsdocks.com
SIC: 3448 Docks: prefabricated metal

(G-7681)
SABERTOOTH ENTERPRISES LLC
Also Called: Billsby Lumber Company
2725 Larch Rd (48625-9211)
P.O. Box 530 (48625-0530)
PHONE.................................989 539-9842
Ray Billsby, *President*
Pamela Brown, *Principal*
Doris Billsby, *Vice Pres*
Joel Woodruff,
EMP: 16 EST: 1972
SQ FT: 6,240
SALES (est): 2.2MM **Privately Held**
WEB: www.billsbylumber.com
SIC: 2421 Sawmills & planing mills, general

(G-7682)
STITCHES AND STEEL
8600 Timberline Trl (48625-7613)
PHONE.................................248 330-6302
EMP: 4 EST: 2017
SALES (est): 154.8K **Privately Held**
SIC: 2395 Embroidery & art needlework

Harrison Township
Macomb County

(G-7683)
A & C ELECTRIC COMPANY
Also Called: A & C Electric Motor Sls & Svc
41225 Irwin Dr (48045-1330)
PHONE.................................586 773-2746
Jewell Arker, *President*
Daniel Arker, *Vice Pres*
Nancy Fountain, *Treasurer*
Lisa Jacobson, *Admin Sec*
John Kandt, *Maintence Staff*
EMP: 21 EST: 1952
SQ FT: 15,000
SALES (est): 4.2MM **Privately Held**
WEB: www.acelectricmotorservice.com
SIC: 7694 5063 Electric motor repair; motors, electric

(G-7684)
ACCURATE HOME INSPTN SVCS INC
38457 Huron Pointe Dr (48045-2840)
PHONE.................................303 530-9600
EMP: 4 EST: 2018
SALES (est): 76.5K **Privately Held**
SIC: 3823 Industrial instrmnts msrmnt display/control process variable

(G-7685)
ALLIANCE TOOL
41239 Irwin Dr (48045-1330)
PHONE.................................586 465-3960
Cynthia Thompson, *Owner*
EMP: 5 EST: 1990
SQ FT: 5,000
SALES (est): 417.3K **Privately Held**
WEB: www.alliancetool.net
SIC: 3541 Machine tools, metal cutting type

(G-7686)
AMP INNOVATIVE TECH LLC
42050 Executive Dr (48045-1311)
PHONE.................................586 465-2700
EMP: 25
SALES (est): 2.7MM **Privately Held**
SIC: 3089 Mfg Plastic Products

(G-7687)
AQUARIUS RECREATIONAL PRODUCTS
41201 Production Dr (48045-1353)
PHONE.................................586 469-4600
Josephine Adas, *President*
EMP: 4 EST: 1973
SQ FT: 4,000
SALES (est): 100K **Privately Held**
WEB: www.aquariusrec.com
SIC: 3499 3446 Ladders, portable: metal; furniture parts, metal; railings, prefabricated metal

(G-7688)
ARISTO-COTE INC (PA)
Also Called: Aristo Industries
24951 Henry B Joy Blvd (48045-1115)
PHONE.................................586 447-9049
Matt Murray, *President*
Nic Murray, *Supervisor*
EMP: 30 EST: 1999
SQ FT: 42,515
SALES (est): 29.2MM **Privately Held**
WEB: www.aristoind.com
SIC: 3479 3449 Coating of metals & formed products; coating of metals with plastic or resins; coating of metals with silicon; coating or wrapping steel pipe; miscellaneous metalwork

(G-7689)
ARTHUR R SOMMERS
Also Called: Sommers Marine
41700 Conger Bay Dr (48045-1432)
PHONE.................................586 469-1280
Arthur R Sommers, *Owner*
EMP: 6 EST: 1955
SALES (est): 532.3K **Privately Held**
WEB: www.shmarinas.com
SIC: 7699 3568 3566 Marine engine repair; power transmission equipment; speed changers, drives & gears

(G-7690)
BREITEN BOX & PACKAGING CO INC
42828 Executive Dr (48045-1317)
P.O. Box 576, Mount Clemens (48046-0576)
PHONE.................................586 469-0800
Tom Szajna, *President*
Kim Szajna, *Vice Pres*
EMP: 7 EST: 1961
SQ FT: 10,900 **Privately Held**
SIC: 2448 5031 Pallets, wood; lumber: rough, dressed & finished

(G-7691)
CAMBRO PRODUCTS INC
41135 Irwin Dr (48045-1329)
PHONE.................................586 468-8847
Kevin Cameron, *President*
Cheryl Cameron, *Treasurer*
EMP: 19 EST: 1977
SQ FT: 31,000
SALES (est): 3.9MM **Privately Held**
WEB: www.cambroproducts.com
SIC: 3714 Motor vehicle brake systems & parts

(G-7692)
CF PLASTIC FABRICATING INC
41590 Production Dr (48045-1357)
PHONE.................................586 954-1296
Charles Fowler, *President*
Dennis Fowler, *Vice Pres*
Margaret Fowler, *Admin Sec*
EMP: 7 EST: 1976
SQ FT: 4,500
SALES (est): 665.1K **Privately Held**
SIC: 2542 Fixtures: display, office or store: except wood

(G-7693)
CLASSIC BOAT DECKS LLC
31469 N River Rd (48045-1466)
PHONE.................................586 465-3606
Thomas Robinson, *Mng Member*
EMP: 7 EST: 2002
SALES (est): 384.1K **Privately Held**
WEB: www.boatcarpetguy.com
SIC: 5091 2273 Boat accessories & parts; carpets & rugs

Harrison Township - Macomb County (G-7694)

(G-7694)
CRANE 1 SERVICES INC
Also Called: Mt. Clemens Crane
42827 Irwin Dr (48045-1342)
PHONE..................586 468-0909
Matthew Milton, *President*
William Janssen, *Division Mgr*
Lisa Miketich, *CFO*
Louis Hyde, *Manager*
EMP: 25
SALES (corp-wide): 258.7MM **Privately Held**
WEB: www.crane1.com
SIC: 7699 5084 3536 Industrial machinery & equipment repair; cranes, industrial; hoists, cranes & monorails
HQ: Crane 1 Services, Inc.
1027 Byers Rd
Miamisburg OH 45342
937 704-9900

(G-7695)
D M C INTERNATIONAL INC
42470 Executive Dr (48045-1313)
PHONE..................586 465-1112
William Schneider, *Vice Pres*
▲ **EMP:** 6 **EST:** 1970
SQ FT: 8,200
SALES (est): 966.4K **Privately Held**
SIC: 3599 Machine shop, jobbing & repair

(G-7696)
DOCKSIDE CANVAS CO INC
29939 S River Rd (48045-3031)
PHONE..................586 463-1231
John P Bowen, *President*
EMP: 17 **EST:** 1982
SQ FT: 7,500
SALES (est): 4MM **Privately Held**
WEB: www.docksidecanvas.com
SIC: 2394 Awnings, fabric: made from purchased materials; convertible tops, canvas or boat: from purchased materials

(G-7697)
EMERALD GROWTH PARTNERS LLC
41900 Executive Dr (48045-1310)
PHONE..................248 756-0286
Randall J Buchman, *CEO*
Michael Yassay, *Mng Member*
EMP: 11 **EST:** 2018
SALES (est): 18.8MM **Privately Held**
SIC: 3999

(G-7698)
FAST TECH MFG INC
41601 Irwin Dr (48045-1333)
PHONE..................586 783-1741
Timothy Tripi, *President*
EMP: 5 **EST:** 1998
SQ FT: 4,200
SALES (est): 473.3K **Privately Held**
SIC: 3469 Metal stampings

(G-7699)
FERRO INDUSTRIES INC
35200 Union Lake Rd (48045-6100)
P.O. Box 86, Mount Clemens (48046-0086)
PHONE..................586 792-6001
Joseph V Clemente, *President*
Marilyn Clemente, *Vice Pres*
Dean Clemente, *Marketing Mgr*
Becky Durlock, *Manager*
EMP: 45 **EST:** 1962
SQ FT: 30,000
SALES (est): 5.8MM **Privately Held**
WEB: www.ferroind.com
SIC: 3291 3089 Abrasive products; injection molding of plastics

(G-7700)
FOX MFG CO
32535 S River Rd (48045-5703)
PHONE..................586 468-1421
Richard Fox, *President*
Steven Fox, *President*
Eunice Fox, *Treasurer*
Anne Fox, *Admin Sec*
EMP: 27 **EST:** 1933
SQ FT: 12,000
SALES (est): 1.1MM **Privately Held**
WEB: www.foxmfg.com
SIC: 3451 Screw machine products

(G-7701)
HENRY PLAMBECK
Also Called: American Dowel & Fastener
40962 Production Dr (48045-1352)
PHONE..................586 463-3410
Henry Plambeck, *Owner*
EMP: 6 **EST:** 1990
SALES (est): 1MM **Privately Held**
SIC: 3452 Dowel pins, metal

(G-7702)
J E ENTERPRISES
Also Called: River Bend Driving Range
38154 Willowmere St (48045-5327)
PHONE..................586 463-5129
EMP: 5
SALES: 210K **Privately Held**
SIC: 3599 Machine Shop

(G-7703)
JENE HOLLY DESIGNS INC
39876 Shoreline Dr (48045-1638)
PHONE..................586 954-0255
Christine Ewald, *President*
Leslie Ewald, *Vice Pres*
EMP: 6 **EST:** 1985 **Privately Held**
WEB: www.hollyjenedesigns.com
SIC: 2395 7389 5231 Embroidery products, except schiffli machine; advertising, promotional & trade show services; glass

(G-7704)
KRING PIZZA INC
35415 Jefferson Ave (48045-3240)
PHONE..................586 792-0049
John Kring, *President*
EMP: 8 **EST:** 1997
SALES (est): 424.4K **Privately Held**
SIC: 2099 2038 5812 Spices, including grinding; frozen specialties; pizza restaurants

(G-7705)
LASER CUTTING CO
42300 Executive Dr (48045-1312)
PHONE..................586 468-5300
Cheryl A Scullion, *President*
Melissa Pizzo, *Vice Pres*
Melissa R Scullion, *Vice Pres*
Mathew Henkel, *Opers Mgr*
Matt Henkel, *QC Mgr*
EMP: 27 **EST:** 1967
SQ FT: 37,432
SALES (est): 2.9MM **Privately Held**
WEB: www.lasercuttinginc.com
SIC: 3599 3469 3465 Machine shop, jobbing & repair; metal stampings; automotive stampings

(G-7706)
LESS PAY PALLETS INC
36750 Jefferson Ave (48045-2918)
PHONE..................586 649-3800
EMP: 7 **EST:** 2019
SALES (est): 200.8K **Privately Held**
WEB: www.paylesspallets.com
SIC: 2448 Pallets, wood

(G-7707)
LIBERTYS HIGH PRFMCE PDTS INC
41775 Production Dr (48045-1370)
PHONE..................586 469-1140
Craig Liberty, *President*
Jennifer Plutschuck, *Principal*
Casey Patterson, *Vice Pres*
▼ **EMP:** 12 **EST:** 1968
SQ FT: 8,800
SALES (est): 2MM **Privately Held**
WEB: www.libertysgears.com
SIC: 3714 Gears, motor vehicle

(G-7708)
MARDAN FABRICATION INC
41001 Production Dr (48045-1377)
PHONE..................586 466-6401
EMP: 6 **EST:** 2019
SALES (est): 487.8K **Privately Held**
WEB: www.mardanfab.com
SIC: 3444 Sheet metalwork

(G-7709)
MASTERLINE DESIGN & MFG
41580 Production Dr (48045-1357)
PHONE..................586 463-5888
Kathleen Pomaville, *President*
Dennis Pomaville, *Vice Pres*
EMP: 28 **EST:** 1972
SQ FT: 7,000
SALES (est): 3.2MM **Privately Held**
WEB: www.masterlinedesigninc.com
SIC: 3568 Shafts, flexible

(G-7710)
MILLERS CUSTOM BOAT TOP INC
41700 Conger Bay Dr (48045-1432)
PHONE..................586 468-5533
Dennis Miller, *President*
Cheryl Miller, *Vice Pres*
EMP: 6 **EST:** 1985
SQ FT: 3,000
SALES (est): 513.4K **Privately Held**
WEB: www.shmarinas.com
SIC: 2394 Liners & covers, fabric: made from purchased materials

(G-7711)
MRD AEROSPACE
37729 Elmlane (48045-2712)
PHONE..................586 468-1196
EMP: 5 **EST:** 2013
SALES (est): 122K **Privately Held**
WEB: www.mrdaerospace.com
SIC: 3721 Aircraft

(G-7712)
NORTHERN INDUSTRIAL MFG CORP
41000 Executive Dr (48045-1303)
PHONE..................586 468-2790
Harvey Hohlfeldt, *CEO*
Dale Hohlfeldt, *President*
Howard Powell, *Vice Pres*
Jeff Hohlfeldt, *Sales Staff*
Kaye Hohlfeldt, *Webmaster*
EMP: 45 **EST:** 1979
SALES (est): 9.7MM **Privately Held**
WEB: www.northernindmfg.com
SIC: 3465 3469 3452 Automotive stampings; metal stampings; bolts, nuts, rivets & washers

(G-7713)
OERLIKON BLZERS CATING USA INC
42728 Executive Dr (48045-1316)
PHONE..................586 465-0412
Fax: 586 465-1968
EMP: 50
SALES (corp-wide): 3.3B **Privately Held**
SIC: 3479 Coating/Engraving Service
HQ: Oerlikon Balzers Coating Usa Inc.
1475 E Wdfield Rd Ste 201
Schaumburg IL 60173
847 619-5541

(G-7714)
ONE PLUS BOATS INC
36301 Jefferson Ave (48045-2907)
PHONE..................586 493-9900
Earl Robert Velger, *Administration*
EMP: 8 **EST:** 2016
SALES (est): 451K **Privately Held**
SIC: 3089 Plastic boats & other marine equipment

(G-7715)
PINK DIAMOND LLC
35131 Brittany Park St (48045-3637)
PHONE..................586 298-7863
Demettrea Buchanan,
EMP: 5 **EST:** 2020
SALES (est): 20K **Privately Held**
WEB: www.pkdiamondllc.com
SIC: 2731 Books: publishing only

(G-7716)
POWER INDUSTRIES CORP
41901 Irwin Dr (48045-1336)
PHONE..................586 783-3818
Karen Lee Johnston, *President*
Glenn Johnston, *Vice Pres*
EMP: 6 **EST:** 1996
SALES (est): 532.1K **Privately Held**
SIC: 3462 3443 3441 Machinery forgings, ferrous; fabricated plate work (boiler shop); fabricated structural metal

(G-7717)
POWER MARINE LLC
38303 Mast St (48045-2751)
PHONE..................586 344-1192
Gerald Knotts, *Principal*
EMP: 7 **EST:** 2005
SALES (est): 190.6K **Privately Held**
SIC: 3443 Boilers: industrial, power, or marine

(G-7718)
R AND T SPORTING CLAYS INC
37853 Elmlane (48045-2713)
P.O. Box 46701, Mount Clemens (48046-6701)
PHONE..................586 215-9861
Tom Shather, *President*
Rick Stover, *Vice Pres*
EMP: 6 **EST:** 1996
SALES (est): 240.8K **Privately Held**
SIC: 3949 Hunting equipment

(G-7719)
RA PRCSION GRNDING MTLWRKS INC
40801 Irwin Dr (48045-1326)
PHONE..................586 783-7776
Roger Belanger, *President*
Linda Belanger, *Vice Pres*
EMP: 18 **EST:** 2015
SALES (est): 1.4MM **Privately Held**
SIC: 3541 Grinding machines, metalworking

(G-7720)
RELIABLE SIGN SERVICE INC
26701 Ponchartrain St (48045-2597)
PHONE..................586 465-6829
Peter Mc Laughlin, *President*
Wayne Milodrwski, *Vice Pres*
Mark Williams, *Sales Staff*
EMP: 4 **EST:** 1976
SQ FT: 9,600
SALES (est): 317.9K **Privately Held**
WEB: www.reliablesigns.com
SIC: 3993 Electric signs

(G-7721)
RIVERSIDE TOOL
37909 Sunnybrook St (48045-2786)
PHONE..................586 980-7630
EMP: 5 **EST:** 2016
SALES (est): 72.8K **Privately Held**
SIC: 3599 Machine shop, jobbing & repair

(G-7722)
ROCHESTER MACHINE PRODUCTS
41530 Production Dr (48045-1357)
PHONE..................586 466-6190
Henry August, *Principal*
EMP: 6 **EST:** 2007
SALES (est): 202.9K **Privately Held**
SIC: 3545 Machine tool accessories

(G-7723)
ROUSSIN M & UBELHOR R INC
Also Called: Shores Tool and Mfg
41903 Irwin Dr (48045-1336)
PHONE..................586 783-6015
Mark Roussin, *President*
EMP: 4 **EST:** 1988
SQ FT: 2,500
SALES (est): 300K **Privately Held**
SIC: 3541 Machine tools, metal cutting: exotic (explosive, etc.)

(G-7724)
SELFRIDGE PLATING INC
Also Called: Selfridge Technologies
42081 Irwin Dr (48045-1337)
PHONE..................586 469-3141
Howard Staudaker, *CEO*
Craig Studaker, *President*
Elyce Rausch, *Vice Pres*
Wanda Staudaker, *Treasurer*
EMP: 55 **EST:** 1970
SQ FT: 34,000
SALES (est): 5.5MM **Privately Held**
WEB: www.selfridgeplating.com
SIC: 3471 Electroplating of metals or formed products

GEOGRAPHIC SECTION

Hart - Oceana County (G-7752)

(G-7725)
SIGN FABRICATORS INC
38140 Circle Dr (48045-2815)
PHONE..................586 468-7360
Timothy White, *Principal*
EMP: 9 **EST:** 2010
SALES (est): 271.5K **Privately Held**
WEB: www.signfabricators.com
SIC: 3993 Signs & advertising specialties

(G-7726)
SR INJECTION MOLDING INC
41565 Production Dr (48045-1358)
PHONE..................586 260-2360
Scott Rheeder, *President*
EMP: 5 **EST:** 2016
SALES (est): 987.8K **Privately Held**
WEB: www.srinjectionmolding.com
SIC: 3089 Injection molding of plastics

(G-7727)
STERLING PROD MACHINING LLC
42522 Executive Dr (48045-1314)
PHONE..................586 493-0633
Stevo Sljivic, *Mng Member*
Donna Sljivic,
EMP: 4 **EST:** 1998
SQ FT: 13,000 **Privately Held**
WEB:
  www.sterlingproductionmachining.com
SIC: 3599 Machine shop, jobbing & repair

(G-7728)
TAZZ BROACH AND MACHINE INC
41565 Production Dr (48045-1358)
PHONE..................586 296-7755
Fax: 586 294-5850
EMP: 9
SQ FT: 2,800
SALES (est): 730K **Privately Held**
SIC: 3545 7389 Mfg Broaches & Precision Grinding Service

(G-7729)
TEMP RITE STEEL TREATING INC
42386 Executive Dr (48045-1312)
PHONE..................586 469-3071
Delphine Decook, *President*
David De Cook, *Vice Pres*
Paul De Cook, *Vice Pres*
Doreen Dulics, *Treasurer*
Debra Decook, *Manager*
EMP: 20 **EST:** 1985
SQ FT: 20,000
SALES (est): 2.4MM **Privately Held**
WEB: www.tempritesteeltreating.com
SIC: 3398 Shot peening (treating steel to reduce fatigue); brazing (hardening) of metal

(G-7730)
TRI MATICS MFG INC
25500 Henry B Joy Blvd (48045-1322)
PHONE..................586 469-3150
Robert Saunders, *President*
EMP: 7 **EST:** 1977
SQ FT: 4,000
SALES (est): 707.9K **Privately Held**
SIC: 3599 Machine shop, jobbing & repair

(G-7731)
WILD MANUFACTURING
39201 Townhall St (48045-5628)
PHONE..................586 719-2028
William Wildner, *Principal*
EMP: 4 **EST:** 2018
SALES (est): 58.5K **Privately Held**
SIC: 3999 Manufacturing industries

(G-7732)
WILSON-GARNER COMPANY
40935 Production Dr (48045-1351)
P.O. Box 1167, Mount Clemens (48046-1167)
PHONE..................586 466-5880
Timothy Pinchback, *President*
Joe Pinchback, *General Mgr*
Tyrus Pinchback, *Chairman*
Keith Pinchback, *Vice Pres*
Marion Claucherty, *Sales Executive*
EMP: 20 **EST:** 1948
SQ FT: 26,000 **Privately Held**

WEB: www.wilsongarner.com
SIC: 3452 Bolts, metal

(G-7733)
WOLVERINE BROACH CO INC (PA)
41200 Executive Dr (48045-1305)
PHONE..................586 468-4445
Bernard Aude, *President*
EMP: 24 **EST:** 1972
SQ FT: 11,600
SALES: 5.6MM **Privately Held**
WEB: www.wolverinebroach.com
SIC: 3545 Broaches (machine tool accessories)

(G-7734)
WOLVERINE PRODUCTION & ENGRG
40960 Production Dr (48045-1352)
PHONE..................586 468-2890
Bernard Aude Jr, *President*
John R Ferguson, *Plant Mgr*
EMP: 29 **EST:** 1982
SALES (est): 1.1MM **Privately Held**
WEB: www.wolverinebroach.com
SIC: 3545 Machine tool accessories

(G-7735)
YANFENG US AUTO INTR SYSTEMS I
Also Called: Yanfeng Automotive Interiors
42150 Executive Dr (48045-1376)
PHONE..................586 354-2101
Jerry Byrd, *Production*
Mark Salisbury, *Technical Mgr*
Martin Forrest, *Engineer*
Mark Kaiser, *Engineer*
Cinzia Miksitz, *Engineer*
EMP: 7 **Privately Held**
WEB: www.yfai.com
SIC: 3714 Motor vehicle parts & accessories
HQ: Yanfeng Us Automotive Interior Systems I Llc
  41935 W 12 Mile Rd
  Novi MI 48377
  248 319-7333

(G-7736)
YANFENG USA AUTO TRIM SYSTEMS (DH)
42150 Executive Dr (48045-1376)
PHONE..................586 354-2101
Johannes Roters, *CEO*
David Wang, *President*
Michael Caringi, *Opers Mgr*
Ronald Pashak, *Engineer*
Michael Kleinheksel, *CFO*
▲ **EMP:** 45 **EST:** 2010
SQ FT: 1,000
SALES (est): 15.3MM **Privately Held**
WEB: www.yfai.com
SIC: 2396 Automotive & apparel trimmings

Harrison Twp
Macomb County

(G-7737)
ABLE MACHINE TOOLING
40875 Irwin Dr (48045-1326)
PHONE..................586 783-7776
Ronald Balanger, *Principal*
EMP: 5 **EST:** 2017
SALES (est): 139K **Privately Held**
WEB: www.ablegrinding.webs.com
SIC: 3479 Metal coating & allied service

(G-7738)
BELLA GROUP LLC
24770 Trombley St (48045-3377)
PHONE..................586 789-7700
EMP: 6 **EST:** 2014
SALES (est): 66.1K **Privately Held**
WEB: www.bellagroupdesign.com
SIC: 3993 Signs & advertising specialties

(G-7739)
SARNS INDUSTRIES INC
Also Called: Sarns Machine
41451 Irwin Dr (48045-1331)
PHONE..................586 463-5829
Jerry Flowers, *President*

EMP: 24 **EST:** 1904
SQ FT: 13,000
SALES (est): 561.7K **Privately Held**
WEB: www.sarnsindustries.com
SIC: 7699 3559 Hydraulic equipment repair; automotive related machinery

Harrisville
Alcona County

(G-7740)
ALCONA COUNTY REVIEW
111 N Lake St (48740-9696)
P.O. Box 548 (48740-0548)
PHONE..................989 724-6384
Cheryl L Peterson, *Owner*
John Boufford, *Co-Owner*
EMP: 8 **EST:** 1876
SQ FT: 2,250
SALES (est): 853.8K **Privately Held**
WEB: www.alconareview.com
SIC: 2711 Newspapers: publishing only, not printed on site

(G-7741)
ALCONA TOOL & MACHINE INC (PA)
3040 E Carbide Dr (48740-9610)
P.O. Box 340, Lincoln (48742-0340)
PHONE..................989 736-8151
Monty L Kruttlin, *President*
Joe James, *Treasurer*
EMP: 48 **EST:** 1976
SQ FT: 12,000
SALES (est): 7.3MM **Privately Held**
WEB: www.alconatool.com
SIC: 3544 3599 Special dies & tools; machine shop, jobbing & repair

(G-7742)
ESR
2225 E Tait Rd (48740-9532)
PHONE..................989 619-7160
Craig Stoley, *President*
EMP: 4 **EST:** 2010
SALES (est): 373.3K **Privately Held**
WEB: www.esrenterprisesinc.com
SIC: 3541 Machine tools, metal cutting type

(G-7743)
LINCOLN TOOL CO INC
3140 E M 72 (48740-9714)
PHONE..................989 736-8711
Kenneth G Manning, *President*
Florence V Manning, *Corp Secy*
EMP: 4 **EST:** 1984
SQ FT: 5,000
SALES (est): 517.8K **Privately Held**
WEB: www.lincolntool.com
SIC: 3544 7699 Special dies, tools, jigs & fixtures; industrial tool grinding

(G-7744)
MANUS TOOL INC
510 S 3rd St (48740-9319)
P.O. Box 248 (48740-0248)
PHONE..................989 724-7171
Keith Nedo, *President*
Guy Holm, *Vice Pres*
EMP: 25 **EST:** 1996
SQ FT: 5,000
SALES (est): 1.6MM **Privately Held**
SIC: 3599 Machine shop, jobbing & repair

(G-7745)
SUNRISE TOOL PRODUCTS INC
604 S 3rd St (48740-9320)
P.O. Box 373 (48740-0373)
PHONE..................989 724-6688
Kevin Johnson, *President*
Michelle Johnson, *President*
Timothy Sutton, *Vice Pres*
Jaymie Sutton, *Treasurer*
EMP: 14 **EST:** 1990
SQ FT: 6,200
SALES (est): 1.9MM **Privately Held**
WEB: www.sunrisetoolproducts.com
SIC: 3541 Machine tools, metal cutting type

(G-7746)
WEISER METAL PRODUCTS INC
3040 E Carbide Dr (48740-9610)
P.O. Box 370, Lincoln (48742-0370)
PHONE..................989 736-6055
Terry Lenard, *President*
Joe James, *Corp Secy*
Keith Karuttlin, *Vice Pres*
EMP: 8 **EST:** 2000
SQ FT: 7,000
SALES (est): 1MM **Privately Held**
WEB: www.weisermetal.com
SIC: 2819 Carbides

(G-7747)
WIT-SON QUALITY TOOL & MFG LLC
230 N Barlow Rd (48740-9653)
PHONE..................989 335-4342
EMP: 7 **EST:** 2020
SALES (est): 697.6K **Privately Held**
WEB: www.wit-sonquality.com
SIC: 3545 Machine tool attachments & accessories

Harsens Island
St. Clair County

(G-7748)
BEARDSLEE INVESTMENTS INC
2256 N Channel Dr (48028-9790)
PHONE..................810 748-9951
Richard Engle, *CEO*
John Falkiewicz, *President*
John Salkiewicz, *General Mgr*
Steven Popkie, *Vice Pres*
EMP: 20 **EST:** 1971
SQ FT: 26,000
SALES (est): 1.3MM **Privately Held**
WEB: www.wcbeardslee.com
SIC: 3731 3732 Shipbuilding & repairing; yachts, building & repairing

(G-7749)
HOLLOWAY EQUIPMENT CO INC
4856 Middle Channel Dr (48028-9667)
PHONE..................810 748-9577
Paul J Hollowaty, *President*
Shirley A Hollowaty, *Admin Sec*
EMP: 8 **EST:** 1957
SQ FT: 26,000
SALES (est): 408.5K **Privately Held**
SIC: 3599 Custom machinery

Hart
Oceana County

(G-7750)
DALE ROUTLEY LOGGING
1870 N 100th Ave (49420-8826)
PHONE..................231 861-2596
Dale R Routley, *Principal*
EMP: 6 **EST:** 2008
SALES (est): 104.6K **Privately Held**
SIC: 2411 Logging camps & contractors

(G-7751)
ELEGANT WOOD CRAFTSMANSHIP
1260 W Polk Rd (49420-8111)
PHONE..................231 742-0706
EMP: 4 **EST:** 2015
SALES (est): 118.1K **Privately Held**
WEB: www.elegantwoodcraftsmanship.com
SIC: 2431 Millwork

(G-7752)
GHSP INC
Also Called: Ghsp Hart Plant
1500 Industrial Park Dr (49420-8148)
PHONE..................231 873-3300
Jeff Ducharme, *Principal*
Ana Rodriguez, *Mfg Staff*
Mario Romanelli, *Production*
Don Knebl, *QC Mgr*
Jim Becker, *Engineer*
EMP: 5

SALES (corp-wide): 1B Privately Held
WEB: www.ghsp.com
SIC: 3089 3714 Injection molded finished plastic products; motor vehicle parts & accessories
HQ: Ghsp, Inc.
   701 S Waverly Rd Ste 100
   Holland MI 49423
   616 842-5500

(G-7753)
GRAY & COMPANY (HQ)
3325 W Polk Rd (49420-8149)
PHONE..................................231 873-5628
James G Reynolds, *Ch of Bd*
Joshua E Reynolds, *Exec VP*
Ray Hacker, *Purch Agent*
Katie Visger, *Controller*
Holly Jaekel, *Accounting Mgr*
◆ EMP: 150 EST: 1908
SQ FT: 5,000
SALES (est): 72.4MM
SALES (corp-wide): 1.4B Publicly Held
WEB: www.grayandcompany.us
SIC: 2033 Maraschino cherries: packaged in cans, jars, etc.
PA: Seneca Foods Corporation
   3736 S Main St
   Marion NY 14505
   315 926-8100

(G-7754)
HART FREEZE PACK LLC
Also Called: Michigan Freeze Pack
835 S Griswold St (49420-9756)
P.O. Box 30 (49420-0030)
PHONE..................................231 873-2175
Lee Ball, *Production*
Vicki Spear, *QC Mgr*
Larissa Vanderputte, *Controller*
Mary Riddell, *Manager*
Frank Camehl, *Supervisor*
EMP: 10 EST: 2001
SQ FT: 100,000
SALES (est): 3.3MM Privately Held
WEB: www.michiganfreezepack.com
SIC: 2037 Fruits, quick frozen & cold pack (frozen); vegetables, quick frozen & cold pack, excl. potato products

(G-7755)
INDIAN SUMMER COOPERATIVE INC
409 Wood St (49420-1351)
P.O. Box 31 (49420-0031)
PHONE..................................231 873-7504
Denny Spear, *Plant Mgr*
Doreen Fenner, *Opers Mgr*
Scott Quillan, *Purch Agent*
Roger Warrmuskerkem, *Manager*
Jerome Betts, *Manager*
EMP: 120
SALES (corp-wide): 74.8MM Privately Held
SIC: 3556 2099 Dehydrating equipment, food processing; food preparations
PA: Indian Summer Cooperative Inc
   3958 W Chauvez Rd Ste 1
   Ludington MI 49431
   231 845-6248

(G-7756)
JSJ CORPORATION
1500 Industrial Park Dr (49420-8377)
PHONE..................................231 873-3300
Doyle Paul, *Branch Mgr*
EMP: 5
SALES (corp-wide): 1B Privately Held
WEB: www.jsjcorp.com
SIC: 3089 Plastic containers, except foam
PA: Jsj Corporation
   700 Robbins Rd
   Grand Haven MI 49417
   616 842-6350

(G-7757)
MAKKEDAH MT PROC & BULK FD STR
1813 N 136th Ave (49420-8809)
PHONE..................................231 873-2113
Ronald Marks, *President*
EMP: 7 EST: 2007
SALES (est): 34.4K Privately Held
SIC: 2011 Meat packing plants

(G-7758)
NORTHLAND CASTINGS CORPORATION
4130 W Tyler Rd (49420-8213)
P.O. Box 472 (49420-0472)
PHONE..................................231 873-4974
John L Orzechowski, *President*
Kirk Dow, *Vice Pres*
Charmaine Orzechowski, *Vice Pres*
Lynne Coverly, *Office Mgr*
EMP: 25 EST: 1974
SQ FT: 15,000
SALES (est): 2.5MM Privately Held
SIC: 3321 Gray iron castings

(G-7759)
OCEANAS HERALD-JOURNAL INC
Also Called: Freeway
123 S State St (49420-1124)
P.O. Box 190 (49420-0190)
PHONE..................................231 873-5602
James Young, *President*
Mary Sanford, *Editor*
Andrew Skinner, *Editor*
Lance Corey, *Branch Mgr*
Amanda Jagniecki, *Manager*
EMP: 18 EST: 1980
SQ FT: 3,000
SALES (est): 1.1MM Privately Held
WEB: www.shorelinemedia.net
SIC: 2711 2741 Job printing & newspaper publishing combined; shopping news: publishing only, not printed on site

(G-7760)
RAN-MARK CO
2978 E Hazel Rd (49420-8807)
PHONE..................................231 873-5103
Randy Fedo, *Owner*
EMP: 10 EST: 1974
SQ FT: 3,200
SALES (est): 739.4K Privately Held
WEB: www.fastbottles.com
SIC: 3544 0161 Special dies, tools, jigs & fixtures; asparagus farm

Hartford
Van Buren County

(G-7761)
AMHAWK LLC (PA)
200 Dunbar St (49057-8748)
PHONE..................................269 468-4177
Regi Kurien, *Mng Member*
EMP: 23 EST: 1973
SQ FT: 800,000
SALES (est): 6.6MM Privately Held
WEB: www.amhawk.com
SIC: 3443 3444 3441 Fabricated plate work (boiler shop); sheet metalwork; fabricated structural metal

(G-7762)
BURNETTE FOODS INC
87171 County Road 687 (49057-8602)
PHONE..................................269 621-3181
William Sherman Jr, *Plant Mgr*
Scott Corliss, *Maint Spvr*
Ashlee Kuenzli, *QC Mgr*
Mike Dorland, *Research*
John Wyatt, *Engineer*
EMP: 107
SALES (corp-wide): 95.5MM Privately Held
WEB: www.burnettefoods.com
SIC: 2033 Fruits: packaged in cans, jars, etc.; vegetable juices: packaged in cans, jars, etc.; fruit juices: packaged in cans, jars, etc.
PA: Burnette Foods, Inc.
   701 S Us Highway 31
   Elk Rapids MI 49629
   231 264-8116

(G-7763)
ELIASON CORPORATION
County Rd Cr 65 1/2 (49057)
PHONE..................................269 621-2100
M Woolsey, *Marketing Staff*
Dan Ekstron, *Manager*
EMP: 22

SALES (corp-wide): 1.3B Privately Held
WEB: www.eliasoncorp.com
SIC: 3442 3873 3444 2431 Window & door frames; timers for industrial use, clockwork mechanism only; sheet metalwork; millwork
HQ: Eliason Corporation
   9229 Shaver Rd
   Portage MI 49024
   269 327-7003

(G-7764)
KEELER-GLASGOW COMPANY INC
80444 County Road 687 (49057-8606)
P.O. Box 158 (49057-0158)
PHONE..................................269 621-2415
Ernest Glasgow, *President*
EMP: 10 EST: 1985
SQ FT: 15,000
SALES (est): 1MM Privately Held
WEB: www.keeler-glasgow.com
SIC: 3448 3231 1542 Greenhouses: prefabricated metal; products of purchased glass; nonresidential construction

(G-7765)
MANN METAL FINISHING INC
200 Prospect St (49057-1057)
PHONE..................................269 621-6359
Jewell D Mann Sr, *President*
Greg Collins, *Vice Pres*
Tammy Collins, *Vice Pres*
Tammy Ackerman, *Personnel*
Shirley Mann, *Admin Sec*
EMP: 70 EST: 1973
SQ FT: 100,000
SALES (est): 8.5MM Privately Held
WEB: www.mannmetal.com
SIC: 3471 5051 Polishing, metals or formed products; buffing for the trade; finishing, metals or formed products; metals service centers & offices

(G-7766)
PRO SLOT LTD
12 W Main St (49057-1005)
PHONE..................................616 897-6000
Daniel De Bella, *President*
Sherly De Bella, *Corp Secy*
Dan Debella, *Manager*
▲ EMP: 6 EST: 1971
SQ FT: 5,000
SALES (est): 923.1K Privately Held
WEB: www.proslot.com
SIC: 3621 3089 3451 Motors, electric; injection molding of plastics; screw machine products

Hartland
Livingston County

(G-7767)
CARDS4HEROESCOM LLC
3093 N Tipsico Lake Rd (48353-2319)
PHONE..................................877 640-8206
Donna Nakagiri, *President*
EMP: 5 EST: 2005
SALES (est): 223K Privately Held
WEB: www.cards4heroes.com
SIC: 2771 Greeting cards

(G-7768)
DENALI INCORPORATED
11600 Maxfield Blvd (48353-3425)
PHONE..................................517 574-0047
Ryan James Kincaid, *Branch Mgr*
EMP: 5
SALES (corp-wide): 6B Publicly Held
WEB: www.denali-inc.com
SIC: 3089 Air mattresses, plastic
HQ: Denali Incorporated
   9910 E 56th St N
   Tulsa OK 74117

(G-7769)
HECK INDUSTRIES INCORPORATED
1498 Old Us 23 Hwy (48353)
P.O. Box 425 (48353-0425)
PHONE..................................810 632-5400
Philip H Heck, *President*
Deborah Heck, *Treasurer*

▲ EMP: 18 EST: 1970
SQ FT: 10,000
SALES (est): 4.3MM Privately Held
WEB: www.heckind.net
SIC: 5084 3546 Industrial machinery & equipment; power-driven handtools

(G-7770)
INTERNATIONAL MCH TL SVCS LLC
4028 Hartland Rd (48353-1004)
PHONE..................................734 667-2233
Carol Passmore,
Dave Passmore,
EMP: 8 EST: 2008
SALES (est): 521.3K Privately Held
SIC: 3599 Machine shop, jobbing & repair

(G-7771)
J W MANCHESTER COMPANY INC
3552 Hartland Rd Ste 201 (48353-5500)
P.O. Box 159 (48353-0159)
PHONE..................................810 632-5409
John W Manchester, *Ch of Bd*
Doug Steele, *President*
John Manchester, *CFO*
Susane Nurnberger, *Admin Sec*
EMP: 7 EST: 1986
SQ FT: 1,400
SALES (est): 1.6MM Privately Held
WEB: www.manchesterbag.com
SIC: 5199 2671 Packaging materials; packaging paper & plastics film, coated & laminated

(G-7772)
TNT MARBLE AND STONE INC
1240 Bogie Lake Rd (48353)
PHONE..................................248 887-8237
Robert Taylor, *President*
EMP: 5 EST: 1992
SALES (est): 530.1K Privately Held
WEB: www.granitebytnt.com
SIC: 3281 1411 Table tops, marble; granite, cut & shaped; dimension stone

(G-7773)
VILLAGE & CNTRY WTR TRTMNT INC (PA)
Also Called: Cgc Water
2875 Old Us 23 (48353)
P.O. Box 448 (48353-0448)
PHONE..................................810 632-7880
Richard Abel, *President*
John Beauchamp, *President*
EMP: 12 EST: 1974
SALES (est): 2.9MM Privately Held
SIC: 5999 7389 4971 3432 Water purification equipment; water softener service; water distribution or supply systems for irrigation; plastic plumbing fixture fittings, assembly

(G-7774)
YOUR BIG SIGN
3440 Fenton Rd (48353-2208)
PHONE..................................248 881-9505
EMP: 5 EST: 2017
SALES (est): 46K Privately Held
WEB: www.yourbigsign.com
SIC: 3993 Signs & advertising specialties

Haslett
Ingham County

(G-7775)
MERIDIAN ENERGY CORPORATION
6009 Marsh Rd (48840-8988)
PHONE..................................517 339-8444
Richard B Patterson, *President*
James Patterson, *Manager*
Michelle Rich, *Info Tech Mgr*
James R Patterson, *Admin Sec*
Roberta Black, *Analyst*
EMP: 38 EST: 1983
SQ FT: 3,000
SALES (est): 6MM Privately Held
WEB: www.meridianlandgroup.com
SIC: 1382 6541 Oil & gas exploration services; title abstract offices

GEOGRAPHIC SECTION

(G-7776)
PIGEON RIVER PUBLISHING LLC
5566 Coral Way (48840-9736)
PHONE.................................616 528-4027
Robert H Rademacher, *Agent*
EMP: 4 **EST:** 2017
SALES (est): 58.8K Privately Held
WEB: www.pigeonriver.org
SIC: 2741 Miscellaneous publishing

(G-7777)
PROFESSIONAL METAL WORKS INC
8109 Old M 78 (48840-9307)
PHONE.................................517 351-7411
Fred Boling, *President*
Jerry McKenna, *Vice Pres*
Dan Plowman, *Manager*
EMP: 30 **EST:** 2000
SQ FT: 12,000
SALES (est): 4.9MM Privately Held
WEB: www.prometalworks.com
SIC: 3441 Fabricated structural metal

(G-7778)
SLIDING SYSTEMS INC
8080 E Old M (48840)
PHONE.................................517 339-1455
Wayne Humphrey, *Controller*
Duane A Swenson, *Administration*
Duane Swenson, *Administration*
EMP: 18 Privately Held
WEB: www.slidingsystems.com
SIC: 3714 Motor vehicle body components & frame
PA: Sliding Systems, Inc.
   N163w19743 Songbird Cir
   Jackson WI 53037

(G-7779)
SPARTANS FINISHING LLC ✪
8060 Old M 78 (48840-9337)
PHONE.................................517 528-5510
Nicholas Bartshe,
EMP: 5 **EST:** 2021
SALES (est): 500K Privately Held
SIC: 2842 3545 Metal polish; measuring tools & machines, machinists' metalworking type

Hastings
Barry County

(G-7780)
ALL ACCESS LIFT LLC
407 Woods Edge Dr (49058-7654)
PHONE.................................616 250-1084
Barry M Mol, *Principal*
EMP: 6 **EST:** 2013
SALES (est): 132.2K Privately Held
WEB: www.allaccesslift.com
SIC: 3534 5084 7699 1796 Elevators & equipment; elevators; elevators: inspection, service & repair; elevator installation & conversion

(G-7781)
AWEBA TOOL & DIE CORP
1004 E State St (49058-9166)
PHONE.................................478 296-2002
▲ **EMP:** 15
SALES (est): 500K
SALES (corp-wide): 7.3B Privately Held
SIC: 3312 Blast Furnaces And Steel Mills, Nsk
HQ: Aweba Werkzeugbau Gmbh Aue
   Damaschkestr. 7
   Aue 08280
   377 127-30

(G-7782)
BLISS MUNITIONS EQUIPMENT ✪
1004 E State St (49058-9166)
PHONE.................................269 953-6655
EMP: 6 **EST:** 2021
SALES (est): 73.4K Privately Held
WEB: www.blissmunitions.com
SIC: 3483 Ammunition components

(G-7783)
CNB INTERNATIONAL INC
Also Called: Niagara Machine
1004 S East St (49058)
PHONE.................................269 948-3300
Pete Straube, *CEO*
Charles Bahr, *CFO*
Richard J Laski, *President*
Michael Ponsetto, *Design Engr*
Michael Cygan, *CFO*
EMP: 100 **EST:** 1879
SQ FT: 400,000
SALES (est): 8.8MM Privately Held
WEB: www.bcntechserv.com
SIC: 3542 Bending machines

(G-7784)
CORNERSTONE FURNITURE INC
1035 E State St (49058-9166)
P.O. Box 276, Middleville (49333-0276)
PHONE.................................269 795-3379
Quentin Mulder, *President*
Jim Fairbrother, *Manager*
David Vantil, *Manager*
EMP: 4 **EST:** 1993
SQ FT: 8,000
SALES (est): 656.5K Privately Held
WEB: www.cornerstonefurniture.com
SIC: 2521 Desks, office: wood

(G-7785)
COURT-SIDE INC
122 W Mill St (49058-1430)
PHONE.................................269 948-2811
EMP: 4 **EST:** 2018
SALES (est): 48.7K Privately Held
WEB: www.courtsideinc.com
SIC: 2395 Embroidery products, except schiffli machine

(G-7786)
CROW FORGE
2563 N Charlton Park Rd (49058-9446)
PHONE.................................269 948-5346
EMP: 5 **EST:** 2007
SALES (est): 175.7K Privately Held
SIC: 3541 Milling machines

(G-7787)
CUTTING EDGE POLY
175 S M 37 Hwy (49058-9624)
PHONE.................................269 953-2866
Marc Waller, *Principal*
EMP: 5 **EST:** 2017
SALES (est): 146.1K Privately Held
WEB: www.cuttingedgepoly.com
SIC: 3531 Construction machinery

(G-7788)
D T R SIGN CO LLC
6315 Thornapple Valley Dr (49058-8287)
PHONE.................................616 889-8927
Ted Reidsma, *Principal*
EMP: 5 **EST:** 2014
SALES (est): 166.4K Privately Held
SIC: 3993 Signs & advertising specialties

(G-7789)
DIAMOND PRESS SOLUTIONS LLC
1611 S Hanover St (49058-2604)
PHONE.................................269 945-1997
Steve Diamond, *President*
EMP: 5 **EST:** 1994
SQ FT: 1,200
SALES (est): 496.4K Privately Held
WEB: www.diamondpresses.com
SIC: 3469 Metal stampings

(G-7790)
DIMOND MACHINERY COMPANY INC
922 N M 37 Hwy (49058-8266)
PHONE.................................269 945-5908
Russell Dimond, *President*
EMP: 12 **EST:** 1964
SQ FT: 15,680
SALES (est): 1MM Privately Held
WEB: www.dandimondequipment.com
SIC: 3541 3542 5084 5082 Machine tools, metal cutting type; mechanical (pneumatic or hydraulic) metal forming machines; industrial machinery & equipment; construction & mining machinery

(G-7791)
FLEXFAB HORIZONS INTL INC (PA)
Also Called: Fhi Family of Companies
102 Cook Rd (49058-9629)
PHONE.................................269 945-4700
Matt Decamp, *CEO*
Douglas A Decamp, *Ch of Bd*
Brian Kloeckner, *Materials Mgr*
Rita Brasseur, *Engineer*
Brad Brownell, *Engineer*
▲ **EMP:** 50 **EST:** 1961
SQ FT: 52,000
SALES (est): 129.3MM Privately Held
WEB: www.flexfab.com
SIC: 3599 3052 3053 2822 Flexible metal hose, tubing & bellows; rubber & plastics hose & beltings; gaskets, packing & sealing devices; synthetic rubber

(G-7792)
FLEXFAB LLC (HQ)
Also Called: Flexfab De Mexico
1699 W M 43 Hwy (49058-9285)
PHONE.................................800 331-0003
Martin Walsh, *Vice Pres*
Jeff Weiden, *Vice Pres*
Nikole Duliban-Shafer, *Buyer*
Derek Chandler, *Engineer*
Joshua Haywood, *Engineer*
▲ **EMP:** 8 **EST:** 1961
SQ FT: 120,000
SALES (est): 129.3MM Privately Held
WEB: www.flexfab.com
SIC: 3052 2822 Rubber & plastics hose & beltings; synthetic rubber
PA: Flexfab Horizons International, Inc.
   102 Cook Rd
   Hastings MI 49058
   269 945-4700

(G-7793)
GIBBYS TRANSPORT LLC
719 E Woodlawn Ave (49058-8455)
PHONE.................................269 838-2794
Timmy Allen Rosenberg, *Mng Member*
EMP: 4
SQ FT: 1,742,400
SALES (est): 260K Privately Held
SIC: 3792 Travel trailers & campers

(G-7794)
GLOBAL MANUFACTURING INDS (PA)
128 W Calgary Dr (49058-3022)
PHONE.................................513 271-2180
Jim Tusing, *Principal*
Rumen Berov, *Sales Mgr*
Michael Schwartz, *CIO*
EMP: 8 **EST:** 2010
SALES (est): 269.7K Privately Held
WEB: www.globalmfgind.com
SIC: 3999 Chairs, hydraulic, barber & beauty shop

(G-7795)
HASTINGS FIBER GLASS PDTS INC
1301 W Green St (49058-1718)
P.O. Box 218 (49058-0218)
PHONE.................................269 945-9541
Larry Baum, *CEO*
Earl L Mc Mullin, *Ch of Bd*
David Baum, *President*
Earlene Baum, *Corp Secy*
Kevin Dates, *Plant Mgr*
◆ **EMP:** 93
SQ FT: 52,500
SALES (est): 26.3MM Privately Held
WEB: www.hfgp.com
SIC: 3423 Hand & edge tools

(G-7796)
HASTINGS MANUFACTURING COMPANY
325 N Hanover St (49058-1598)
PHONE.................................269 945-2491
Ken Holbrook, *CEO*
Jeffrey P Guenther, *Vice Pres*
Danny Pickett, *Finance*
▲ **EMP:** 260 **EST:** 2013
SALES (est): 45.4MM Privately Held
WEB: www.hastingspistonrings.com
SIC: 3592 Carburetors, pistons, rings, valves

(G-7797)
HURLESS MACHINE SHOP INC
2450 Lower Lake Rd (49058-8406)
PHONE.................................269 945-9362
Mark Hurless, *President*
Danise Regan, *Treasurer*
EMP: 9 **EST:** 1978
SQ FT: 6,000
SALES (est): 831.1K Privately Held
SIC: 3599 Machine shop, jobbing & repair

(G-7798)
I-94 ENTERPRISES
2195 Tamarack Cove Dr (49058-7735)
PHONE.................................269 945-3185
Melanie Winfree, *Principal*
EMP: 5 **EST:** 2008
SALES (est): 169.9K Privately Held
WEB: www.i-94enterprises.com
SIC: 2759 Publication printing

(G-7799)
IRON EAGLE LOGGING
317 E High St (49058-1534)
PHONE.................................269 945-9617
Rex Jarman III, *Owner*
EMP: 5 **EST:** 2002
SALES (est): 110K Privately Held
SIC: 2411 Logging camps & contractors

(G-7800)
J-AD GRAPHICS INC (PA)
Also Called: Reminder, The
1351 N M 43 Hwy (49058-8499)
P.O. Box 188 (49058-0188)
PHONE.................................800 870-7085
John Jacobs, *President*
Brett Bremer, *Editor*
Shelly Sulser, *Editor*
Fred Jacobs, *Vice Pres*
Bobbie Wilkins, *Human Res Dir*
EMP: 85 **EST:** 1971
SQ FT: 100,000
SALES (est): 15.1MM Privately Held
WEB: www.hastingsprintshop.com
SIC: 2741 2711 2752 2791 Guides: publishing & printing; newspapers, publishing & printing; commercial printing, offset; typesetting; bookbinding & related work; commercial printing

(G-7801)
JMJ INC
1029 Enterprise Dr (49058-7804)
PHONE.................................269 948-2828
Mick Suter, *President*
▼ **EMP:** 18 **EST:** 1993
SALES (est): 2.8MM Privately Held
WEB: www.jmjinc.net
SIC: 2542 Partitions & fixtures, except wood

(G-7802)
K & E TACKLE INC
2530 Barber Rd (49058-9416)
PHONE.................................269 945-4496
James Sprague, *President*
Jennifer Sprague, *Treasurer*
Kenneth Sprague, *Director*
EMP: 17 **EST:** 1963
SQ FT: 4,560
SALES (est): 1.9MM Privately Held
WEB: www.anglersmart.com
SIC: 3949 Bait, artificial: fishing; fishing tackle, general

(G-7803)
KASTEN MACHINERY INC
1611 S Hanover St Ste 107 (49058-2604)
PHONE.................................269 945-1999
Steve Diamond, *President*
Carmen Solano, *Vice Pres*
▼ **EMP:** 4 **EST:** 2000
SALES (est): 241.4K Privately Held
SIC: 3542 Presses: forming, stamping, punching, sizing (machine tools)

(G-7804)
MENSCH MANUFACTURING LLC
2333 S M 37 Hwy (49058-9370)
P.O. Box 418 (49058-0418)
PHONE.................................269 945-5300
Donald Mensch, *President*
Sarah Mensch, *Manager*

Hastings - Barry County (G-7805)

EMP: 19 EST: 2010
SALES (est): 5.7MM **Privately Held**
WEB: www.menschmfg.com
SIC: 3523 Farm machinery & equipment

(G-7805)
MENSCH MFG MAR DIV INC
Also Called: Rubber Round-Up
2499 S M 37 Hwy (49058-9369)
P.O. Box 418 (49058-0418)
PHONE.................................269 945-5300
Donald L Mensch, *President*
EMP: 25 EST: 1985
SQ FT: 16,000
SALES (est): 4MM **Privately Held**
WEB: www.menschmfg.com
SIC: 3523 Farm machinery & equipment

(G-7806)
PROGRESSIVE GRAPHICS
115 S Jefferson St (49058-1825)
PHONE.................................269 945-9249
Doug Acker, *Owner*
EMP: 5 EST: 1982
SQ FT: 1,200
SALES (est): 363.5K **Privately Held**
SIC: 2759 Screen printing

(G-7807)
QUALITY ALUM ACQUISITION LLC (PA)
429 S Michigan Ave (49058-2250)
PHONE.................................800 550-1667
Bob Clark, *Plant Mgr*
Mike Clark, *Plant Mgr*
Chad Metzger, *Production*
Jason Boye, *Purch Mgr*
Robert Clark, *Treasurer*
EMP: 90 EST: 1990
SQ FT: 30,000
SALES (est): 41MM **Privately Held**
WEB: www.qualityaluminum.com
SIC: 3444 3354 Siding, sheet metal; aluminum extruded products

(G-7808)
SABRE MANUFACTURING
2324 S M 37 Hwy (49058-9370)
PHONE.................................269 945-4120
Steve Reaser, *President*
Larry Monroe, *General Mgr*
EMP: 8 EST: 1985
SALES (est): 300K **Privately Held**
WEB: www.usalogisticsinc.com
SIC: 3312 Tool & die steel

(G-7809)
SANINOCENCIO LOGGING
2900 Roush Rd (49058-8817)
PHONE.................................269 945-3567
James R Dull, *Principal*
EMP: 4 EST: 2011
SALES (est): 164.8K **Privately Held**
SIC: 2411 Logging

(G-7810)
SOARING CONCEPTS AEROSPACE LLC
3001 W Airport Rd (49058-9774)
PHONE.................................574 286-9670
Galen Geigley, *Mng Member*
EMP: 16 EST: 2016
SALES (est): 3.2MM **Privately Held**
WEB: www.soaringconceptsaerospace.com
SIC: 3721 3541 Aircraft; numerically controlled metal cutting machine tools

(G-7811)
VIKING CORPORATION (DH)
210 Industrial Park Dr (49058-9631)
PHONE.................................269 945-9501
Thomas G Deegan, *President*
Paul Coble, *General Mgr*
Karl Barton, *Business Mgr*
Gary W Buckley, *Vice Pres*
Delwin G Dornbos, *Vice Pres*
◆ EMP: 100 EST: 1897
SQ FT: 180,000
SALES (est): 250.2MM
SALES (corp-wide): 177.9K **Privately Held**
WEB: www.vikinggroupinc.com
SIC: 3499 Fire- or burglary-resistive products

(G-7812)
VIKING FABRICATION SVCS LLC (DH)
210 Industrial Park Dr (49058-9706)
PHONE.................................269 945-9501
Mike Dosma, *President*
Tom Deegan, *Vice Pres*
Martin Workman, *Vice Pres*
Jennifer McKeever, *Analyst*
▲ EMP: 400 EST: 2002
SALES (est): 57.1MM
SALES (corp-wide): 177.9K **Privately Held**
WEB: www.vikinggroupinc.com
SIC: 3499 Fire- or burglary-resistive products
HQ: Minimax Viking Gmbh
Industriestr. 10/
Bad Oldesloe SH 23843
453 180-30

(G-7813)
VIKING GROUP INC
210 Industrial Park Dr (49058-9706)
PHONE.................................616 831-6448
EMP: 135
SALES (corp-wide): 177.9K **Privately Held**
WEB: www.vikinggroupinc.com
SIC: 3569 Sprinkler systems, fire: automatic
HQ: Viking Group, Inc.
5150 Beltway Dr Se
Caledonia MI 49316

Hawks
Presque Isle County

(G-7814)
ALPENA ANTIQ TRCTR STM ENG CL
3219 Darga Hwy (49743-9720)
PHONE.................................989 734-3859
Angela Krajniak, *Principal*
EMP: 7 EST: 2009
SALES (est): 110.4K **Privately Held**
SIC: 3511 Steam engines

(G-7815)
PRELLS SAW MILL INC
Also Called: Prell's Sawmill
8571 F-21 Hwy (49743-8723)
P.O. Box 121 (49743-0121)
PHONE.................................989 734-2939
Joseph C Kuznizki, *President*
Linda K Kuznizki, *Admin Sec*
EMP: 25 EST: 1994
SQ FT: 400
SALES (est): 1.4MM **Privately Held**
WEB: www.prellssawmill.com
SIC: 2421 5211 Sawmills & planing mills, general; custom sawmill; kiln drying of lumber; lumber products

(G-7816)
RECOLLECTIONS CO
7956 F-21 Hwy (49743-8716)
PHONE.................................989 734-0566
Steven Koenig, *Partner*
Donna Klein, *Mktg Dir*
EMP: 11 EST: 1980
SALES (est): 597.7K **Privately Held**
WEB: www.recollections.biz
SIC: 2335 5621 Dresses, paper: cut & sewn; women's clothing stores

Hazel Park
Oakland County

(G-7817)
ADVANCED ASSEMBLY PRODUCTS INC (PA)
Also Called: A A P
1300 E 9 Mile Rd (48030-1959)
PHONE.................................248 543-2427
Ravinder Sandhu, *President*
Martin Sherree, *Opers Staff*
Melanie Hatzfeld, *Controller*
Vicki Duda, *Asst Controller*
Ron Waring, *Technology*
▲ EMP: 6 EST: 1963
SQ FT: 20,000
SALES (est): 34.4MM **Privately Held**
WEB: www.aapincorp.com
SIC: 3714 Motor vehicle parts & accessories

(G-7818)
AKASOL INC
1400 E 10 Mile Rd Ste 150 (48030-1263)
PHONE.................................248 259-7843
Roy Schulde, *President*
EMP: 20 EST: 2017
SALES (est): 2.5MM **Privately Held**
WEB: www.akasol.com
SIC: 3691 Storage batteries

(G-7819)
AMCOL CORPORATION
Also Called: American Charcoal
21435 Dequindre Rd (48030-2350)
PHONE.................................248 414-5700
James Dyla, *President*
Patty Craig, *Production*
Chris Dyla, *Sales Staff*
Mark Vangilder, *Sales Staff*
Michelle Vaughn, *Sales Staff*
◆ EMP: 25 EST: 1902
SQ FT: 27,000
SALES (est): 5.3MM **Privately Held**
WEB: www.amcolcorp.com
SIC: 2992 3569 Oils & greases, blending & compounding; lubricating equipment

(G-7820)
AVANCEZ LLC
1430 E 10 Mile Rd Ste 30 (48030-1258)
PHONE.................................313 404-1962
Monika Wojick, *VP Finance*
EMP: 90
SALES (corp-wide): 57.9MM **Privately Held**
WEB: www.avancezassembly.com
SIC: 3559 Automotive related machinery
PA: Avancez, Llc
27767 George Merrelli Dr
Warren MI 48092
248 789-0674

(G-7821)
BRONCO PRINTING COMPANY
21841 Dequindre Rd (48030-2103)
PHONE.................................248 544-1120
Walter Ziemniak, *President*
Mary Ann Toporek, *Vice Pres*
Sharon Zelmanski, *Treasurer*
EMP: 6 EST: 1947
SQ FT: 2,200
SALES (est): 500K **Privately Held**
WEB: www.broncoprinting.com
SIC: 2752 3993 2791 2789 Commercial printing, offset; signs & advertising specialties; typesetting; bookbinding & related work; commercial printing

(G-7822)
DAKKOTA INTEGRATED SYSTEMS LLC
1420 E 10 Mile Rd Ste 200 (48030-1258)
PHONE.................................517 694-6500
EMP: 7
SALES (corp-wide): 242.2MM **Privately Held**
WEB: www.dakkota.com
SIC: 3711 Automobile assembly, including specialty automobiles
PA: Dakkota Integrated Systems, Llc
123 Brighton Lake Rd # 202
Brighton MI 48116
517 694-6500

(G-7823)
DISCOVER YOUR MOBILITY INC
32 E 10 Mile Rd (48030-1135)
PHONE.................................866 868-9694
Claudette Langbeen, *Principal*
◆ EMP: 7 EST: 2013
SALES (est): 233.6K **Privately Held**
WEB: www.discovermymobility.com
SIC: 3751 Motor scooters & parts

(G-7824)
DIVERSIFIED PROF RLTY SVCS
Also Called: Diversified Prof Svcs Group
950 E 9 Mile Rd (48030-1839)
PHONE.................................313 215-1840
Marcus A Smith, *President*

EMP: 4 EST: 2005
SALES (est): 192K **Privately Held**
SIC: 6531 6411 1799 1389 Real estate brokers & agents; insurance agents, brokers & service; post-disaster renovations; construction, repair & dismantling services; general remodeling, single-family houses

(G-7825)
EXLTERRA INC
618 E 10 Mile Rd (48030-1259)
PHONE.................................248 268-2336
Frank Muller, *CEO*
Denis Gobet, *Vice Pres*
Nathan Rose, *Manager*
EMP: 7 EST: 2016
SALES (est): 883.7K **Privately Held**
WEB: www.exlterra.com
SIC: 3541 Drilling machine tools (metal cutting)

(G-7826)
FOX ALUMINUM PRODUCTS INC
Also Called: Weldore Manufacturing
1355 E Woodward Hts Blvd (48030-1628)
PHONE.................................248 399-4288
James Fox, *President*
Judith Fox, *Corp Secy*
▲ EMP: 25 EST: 1964
SQ FT: 42,000
SALES (est): 3.3MM **Privately Held**
WEB: www.foxweldoor.com
SIC: 3442 5211 Storm doors or windows, metal; windows, storm: wood or metal; doors, storm: wood or metal

(G-7827)
KC JONES PLATING CO
Jones, K C Plating Division
321 W 10 Mile Rd (48030-1184)
PHONE.................................248 399-8500
Marty Hartrick, *Branch Mgr*
Michael McLennan, *Manager*
Khalid Shafiq, *Manager*
EMP: 40
SQ FT: 25,000
SALES (corp-wide): 15.3MM **Privately Held**
WEB: www.kcjplating.com
SIC: 3471 Electroplating of metals or formed products
PA: K.C. Jones Plating Co.
2845 E 10 Mile Rd
Warren MI 48091
586 755-4900

(G-7828)
LG ELCTRNICS VHCL CMPNNTS USA (DH)
1400 E 10 Mile Rd Ste 100 (48030-1278)
PHONE.................................248 268-5851
Kenneth Cheng, *President*
EMP: 140 EST: 2017
SALES (est): 2.6B **Privately Held**
WEB: www.lg.com
SIC: 3694 Automotive electrical equipment
HQ: Lg Electronics U.S.A., Inc.
111 Sylvan Ave
Englewood Cliffs NJ 07632
201 816-2000

(G-7829)
LG ENERGY SOLUTION MICH INC
1400 E 10 Mile Rd Ste 100 (48030-1278)
PHONE.................................616 494-7153
Bonchul Koo, *President*
EMP: 179 **Privately Held**
WEB: www.lgenergymi.com
SIC: 3691 Batteries, rechargeable
HQ: Lg Energy Solution Michigan, Inc.
1 Lg Way
Holland MI 49423

(G-7830)
M C M FIXTURE COMPANY INC
Also Called: M C M Stainless Fabricating
21306 John R Rd (48030-2211)
PHONE.................................248 547-9280
Gary Brown, *President*
Jean L Walker, *Office Mgr*
Seymour Brown, *Shareholder*
EMP: 17 EST: 1953

GEOGRAPHIC SECTION

Hemlock - Saginaw County (G-7857)

SQ FT: 20,000
SALES (est): 2.3MM **Privately Held**
WEB: www.mcmstainless.com
SIC: **3444** 2514 2511 Restaurant sheet metalwork; metal household furniture; wood household furniture

(G-7831)
METRA INC
24211 John R Rd (48030-1110)
PHONE..................................248 543-3500
Mary Sappington, *President*
Henry Stafij, *Vice Pres*
Kenneth Lamparski, *Admin Sec*
EMP: 4 EST: 1979
SQ FT: 3,000
SALES (est): 500K **Privately Held**
WEB: www.metramagazine.com
SIC: **2741** Miscellaneous publishing

(G-7832)
MICHIGAN PLATING LLC
21733 Dequindre Rd (48030-2102)
PHONE..................................248 544-3500
Patrick Smith,
EMP: 6 EST: 2013
SALES (est): 408.8K **Privately Held**
WEB: www.signaturemetalfinishing.com
SIC: **3471** Plating of metals or formed products

(G-7833)
MICHIGAN SPLINE GAGE CO INC
1626 E 9 Mile Rd (48030-1937)
P.O. Box 69 (48030-0069)
PHONE..................................248 544-7303
Bernard Hagen, *President*
Cathy Bongilrno, *Admin Sec*
EMP: 18 EST: 1950
SQ FT: 10,000
SALES (est): 2.4MM **Privately Held**
WEB: www.michiganspline.com
SIC: **3545** Machine tool accessories

(G-7834)
MICRO GRIND CO INC
Also Called: Micro Gind
1648 E 9 Mile Rd (48030-1937)
PHONE..................................248 398-9770
Daniel Fiantaco, *President*
Barbara Fiantaco, *Vice Pres*
EMP: 4 EST: 1981
SQ FT: 2,500
SALES (est): 200K **Privately Held**
SIC: **3599** Machine shop, jobbing & repair

(G-7835)
MOTWON SIGN COMPANY LLC
428 E Harry Ave (48030-2071)
PHONE..................................313 580-4094
Jordan Zielke, *Principal*
EMP: 4 EST: 2017
SALES (est): 50.6K **Privately Held**
SIC: **3993** Signs & advertising specialties

(G-7836)
NEW MONITOR
23082 Reynolds Ave (48030-1441)
PHONE..................................248 439-1863
EMP: 4 EST: 2010
SALES (est): 81.1K **Privately Held**
SIC: **2711** Newspapers, publishing & printing

(G-7837)
NINJA TEES N MORE
505 W 9 Mile Rd Ste B (48030-1714)
PHONE..................................248 541-2547
Shawn Loiko, *Partner*
Mike Wilamowski, *Partner*
EMP: 5
SALES (est): 156.9K **Privately Held**
WEB: www.ninjateesnmore.com
SIC: **2759** Screen printing

(G-7838)
R E D INDUSTRIES INC
1671 E 9 Mile Rd (48030-1957)
PHONE..................................248 542-2211
Lila Elmhirst, *President*
Debbie White, *Buyer*
EMP: 14 EST: 1984
SQ FT: 10,000
SALES (est): 1.1MM **Privately Held**
WEB: www.redprototype.com
SIC: **3469** Stamping metal for the trade

(G-7839)
RAZE-IT PRINTING
24221 John R Rd (48030-1110)
PHONE..................................248 543-3813
Barbara Schmitz, *Principal*
EMP: 9 EST: 2004
SALES (est): 261.9K **Privately Held**
SIC: **2752** Commercial printing, offset

(G-7840)
ROCON LLC
1755 E 9 Mile Rd (48030-1939)
P.O. Box 249 (48030-0249)
PHONE..................................248 542-9635
Lars Rosaen, *Principal*
Erik Rosaen,
EMP: 7 EST: 1997
SALES (est): 1.6MM
SALES (corp-wide): 10.9MM **Privately Held**
WEB: www.flowmeters.com
SIC: **3491** 5084 Water works valves; industrial machinery & equipment
PA: Universal Flow Monitors, Inc.
1755 E 9 Mile Rd
Hazel Park MI 48030
248 542-9635

(G-7841)
SCOTT IRON WORKS INC
24529 John R Rd (48030-1141)
PHONE..................................248 548-2822
John H Petit, *President*
Virginia Petit, *Corp Secy*
Robert Petit, *Vice Pres*
Laura Van Almen, *Sales Staff*
Arthur Petit, *Shareholder*
EMP: 10 EST: 1960
SQ FT: 30,000
SALES (est): 934.5K **Privately Held**
WEB: www.scottiron.com
SIC: **3446** 3442 Gates, ornamental metal; railings, bannisters, guards, etc.: made from metal pipe; storm doors or windows, metal

(G-7842)
SHELLBACK MANUFACTURING CO
1320 E Elza Ave (48030-2354)
PHONE..................................248 544-4600
William Nielsen, *President*
EMP: 9 EST: 1934
SQ FT: 1,664
SALES (est): 1MM **Privately Held**
WEB: www.shellbackpumps.com
SIC: **3561** Pumps, domestic: water or sump

(G-7843)
STEADFAST LAB
22018 John R Rd (48030-1713)
PHONE..................................248 242-2291
EMP: 8 EST: 2018
SALES (est): 560.1K **Privately Held**
WEB: www.steadfastlabs.com
SIC: **3999**

(G-7844)
TOP NOTCH PRINTING LLC
24055 Dequindre Rd (48030-1251)
PHONE..................................248 268-3257
Yolanda Merrill, *Principal*
EMP: 4 EST: 2017
SALES (est): 80.8K **Privately Held**
SIC: **2752** Commercial printing, lithographic

(G-7845)
UNIVERSAL FLOW MONITORS INC (PA)
Also Called: Ufm
1755 E 9 Mile Rd (48030-1939)
P.O. Box 249 (48030-0249)
PHONE..................................248 542-9635
Lars O Rosaen, *President*
Erik Rosaen, *Principal*
EMP: 43 EST: 1963
SQ FT: 42,000
SALES (est): 10.9MM **Privately Held**
WEB: www.flowmeters.com
SIC: **3823** Flow instruments, industrial process type

(G-7846)
US MOLD LLC
608 E 10 Mile Rd (48030-1259)
PHONE..................................586 719-7239
Ronnie Hirmaz,
EMP: 5 EST: 2019
SALES (est): 301.1K **Privately Held**
SIC: **3089** Injection molding of plastics

(G-7847)
VISCOUNT EQUIPMENT CO INC
24443 John R Rd (48030-1113)
PHONE..................................586 293-5900
James Warda, *President*
Kenneth J Warda, *Vice Pres*
Daniel J Warda, *Admin Sec*
EMP: 5 EST: 1970
SQ FT: 10,000
SALES (est): 968.4K **Privately Held**
WEB: www.viscountequipment.com
SIC: **5084** 3541 Machine tools & accessories; drilling machine tools (metal cutting); tapping machines

(G-7848)
WALLACE PUBLISHING LLC
1127 E Pearl Ave (48030-1922)
P.O. Box 162 (48030-0162)
PHONE..................................248 416-7259
EMP: 28 EST: 2010
SALES (est): 1.7MM **Privately Held**
SIC: **2741** Misc Publishing

Hemlock
Saginaw County

(G-7849)
ANDERSONS INC
485 S Hemlock Rd (48626-8784)
PHONE..................................989 642-5291
Ashley Wilga, *Office Admin*
EMP: 4
SALES (corp-wide): 8.2B **Publicly Held**
WEB: www.andersonsinc.com
SIC: **5153** 0723 5191 2874 Grains; crop preparation services for market; farm supplies; phosphatic fertilizers; rental of railroad cars
PA: The Andersons Inc
1947 Briarfield Blvd
Maumee OH 43537
419 893-5050

(G-7850)
CORNERSTONE FABG & CNSTR INC (PA)
667 Watson Rd (48626-9795)
PHONE..................................989 642-5241
Robert Bishop, *President*
Tony Mansfield, *Opers Mgr*
EMP: 29 EST: 1987
SQ FT: 3,600
SALES (est): 7.6MM **Privately Held**
WEB: www.cornerstonefab.com
SIC: **3535** 3441 Conveyors & conveying equipment; fabricated structural metal

(G-7851)
DOUGLAS KING INDUSTRIES INC
Also Called: Dki
16425 Northern Pintail Dr (48626-8787)
P.O. Box 6575, Saginaw (48608-6575)
PHONE..................................989 642-2865
Douglas W King, *President*
Deborah King, *Vice Pres*
Gerry Mueller, *Vice Pres*
Gene Slachta, *Vice Pres*
EMP: 9 EST: 1990
SALES (est): 228.8K **Privately Held**
SIC: **3599** 3441 3544 3444 Machine shop, jobbing & repair; fabricated structural metal; special dies, tools, jigs & fixtures; sheet metalwork; nonferrous foundries; steel investment foundries

(G-7852)
DOW SILICONES CORPORATION
Also Called: Healthcare Inds Mtls Site
1635 N Gleaner Rd (48626)
P.O. Box 20 (48626-0020)
PHONE..................................800 248-2481
Jim Cross, *Branch Mgr*
EMP: 150
SALES (corp-wide): 38.5B **Publicly Held**
SIC: **2869** Industrial organic chemicals
HQ: Dow Silicones Corporation
2200 W Salzburg Rd
Auburn MI 48611
989 496-4000

(G-7853)
HEMLOCK SEMICONDUCTOR LLC
12334 Geddes Rd (48626-9409)
P.O. Box 80 (48626-0080)
PHONE..................................989 301-5000
Mark Bassett, *CEO*
Arabinda Ghosh, *COO*
Tania Ridley, *Project Mgr*
Mark Jardis, *Mfg Staff*
Justin Buckley, *Purchasing*
EMP: 2 EST: 2008
SALES (est): 16.2MM
SALES (corp-wide): 11.3B **Publicly Held**
WEB: www.hscpoly.com
SIC: **3674** Semiconductors & related devices
PA: Corning Incorporated
1 Riverfront Plz
Corning NY 14831
607 974-9000

(G-7854)
HEMLOCK SMCNDCTOR OPRTIONS LLC
12334 Geddes Rd (48626-9409)
P.O. Box 80 (48626-0080)
PHONE..................................989 301-5000
Mark Bassett, *CEO*
Arabinda Ghosh, *COO*
Andy Ault, *VP Mfg*
Christopher Roka, *Facilities Mgr*
Teresa Datz-Siegel, *Opers Staff*
▲ EMP: 400 EST: 1961
SALES (est): 223.1MM
SALES (corp-wide): 11.3B **Publicly Held**
WEB: www.hscpoly.com
SIC: **3674** Semiconductors & related devices
PA: Corning Incorporated
1 Riverfront Plz
Corning NY 14831
607 974-9000

(G-7855)
SOLARFALL INDUSTRIES LLC
16331 Blue Teal Trl (48626-8780)
PHONE..................................269 274-6108
Gabriel James Faubert, *Principal*
EMP: 4 EST: 2012
SALES (est): 61.9K **Privately Held**
SIC: **3999** Manufacturing industries

(G-7856)
SUES SCENTED SOY CANDLES
2991 Laporte Rd (48626-9512)
PHONE..................................989 642-3352
Susan Marie Krueger, *Principal*
EMP: 4 EST: 2018
SALES (est): 61.8K **Privately Held**
WEB: www.suesscents.com
SIC: **3999** Candles

(G-7857)
URS ENERGY & CONSTRUCTION INC
12334 Geddes Rd (48626-9409)
PHONE..................................989 642-4190
EMP: 235
SALES (corp-wide): 10.9B **Publicly Held**
SIC: **1622** 1629 1081 4953 Bridge/Tunnel Cnstn Heavy Construction Metal Mining Services Refuse Systems
HQ: Urs Energy & Construction, Inc.
7800 E Union Ave Ste 100
Denver CO 29801
303 843-2000

(G-7858)
WHITE KNIGHT FLUID HDLG INC
1077 Watson Rd (48626-9796)
PHONE..............................435 783-6040
Tom Simmons, *Principal*
EMP: 6 **EST:** 2016
SALES (est): 159.4K **Privately Held**
WEB: www.wkfluidhandling.com
SIC: 3531 Construction machinery

Henderson
Shiawassee County

(G-7859)
AJ LOGGING
8203 N M 52 (48841-9714)
PHONE..............................989 725-9610
Alan Sjoberg, *Owner*
EMP: 6 **EST:** 1990
SALES (est): 658.9K **Privately Held**
SIC: 2411 Logging camps & contractors

Hermansville
Menominee County

(G-7860)
BELLMORE LOGGING
N15312 M3 Rd (49847-9627)
PHONE..............................906 498-2528
Larry Bellmore, *Principal*
EMP: 4 **EST:** 2017
SALES (est): 101K **Privately Held**
SIC: 2411 Logging

(G-7861)
DUGREES SAND AND GRAVEL
W6017 Us Highway 2 (49847-9564)
PHONE..............................906 295-1569
Travis Dugree, *Principal*
EMP: 6 **EST:** 2018
SALES (est): 571.6K **Privately Held**
SIC: 1442 Construction sand & gravel

(G-7862)
STEWART MANUFACTURING LLC
N16415 Earle Dr (49847)
P.O. Box 219 (49847-0219)
PHONE..............................906 498-7600
Harry Bergquist, *Engineer*
Linda Laviolette, *Manager*
Gregory Stewart,
▲ **EMP:** 85 **EST:** 1969
SQ FT: 77,000
SALES (est): 19.5MM **Privately Held**
WEB: www.stewart-mfg.com
SIC: 3999 Barber & beauty shop equipment

(G-7863)
SUPERIOR WELDING & MFG INC
5704 Old Us 2 Rd 43 (49847)
P.O. Box 145 (49847-0145)
PHONE..............................906 498-7616
Kelly Plunger, *President*
Nick Arduin, *Treasurer*
Rick Arduin, *Admin Sec*
◆ **EMP:** 27 **EST:** 2004
SALES (est): 3.6MM **Privately Held**
WEB: www.upwelding.com
SIC: 7692 Welding repair

(G-7864)
WENDRICKS TRUSS INC (PA)
W5728 Old Us 2 Road No 43 (49847-9553)
P.O. Box 160 (49847-0160)
PHONE..............................906 498-7709
Kelly Plunger, *President*
Robin Newlin, *Manager*
EMP: 40 **EST:** 1975
SQ FT: 40,000
SALES (est): 8.3MM **Privately Held**
WEB: www.wendrickstruss.com
SIC: 2439 Trusses, wooden roof

(G-7865)
WHITENS KILN & LUMBER INC
125801 Coney Rd (49847)
P.O. Box 154 (49847-0154)
PHONE..............................906 498-2116
Russell Jay Whitens, *President*
Roger A Whitens, *Vice Pres*
EMP: 10 **EST:** 1985
SQ FT: 31,596
SALES (est): 919.4K **Privately Held**
SIC: 2421 2426 Lumber: rough, sawed or planed; kiln drying of lumber; hardwood dimension & flooring mills

Hersey
Osceola County

(G-7866)
ENERTECH CORPORATION
210 S Division St (49639-5117)
P.O. Box 183 (49639-0183)
PHONE..............................231 832-5587
Pamela J Hall, *President*
EMP: 10 **EST:** 1975
SQ FT: 18,000
SALES (est): 1.5MM **Privately Held**
WEB: www.enertechcorp.com
SIC: 3679 Electronic circuits

(G-7867)
LAIDCO SALES INC
4753 175th Ave (49639-8790)
PHONE..............................231 832-1327
Patrick Laidlaw, *President*
Bill Bondy, *Vice Pres*
EMP: 5 **EST:** 2006
SQ FT: 2,000 **Privately Held**
WEB: www.laidco.com
SIC: 3229 Glass lighting equipment parts

(G-7868)
MOSIAC POTASH HERSEY LLC
1395 135th Ave (49639-8746)
PHONE..............................231 832-3755
EMP: 8
SALES (est): 168.8K **Privately Held**
SIC: 1474 Potash/Soda/Borate Mining

(G-7869)
RIDGEWOOD STOVES LLC
1293 170th Ave (49639-8451)
PHONE..............................989 488-3397
EMP: 5 **EST:** 2012
SALES (est): 70.7K **Privately Held**
SIC: 2421 Outdoor wood structural products

Hesperia
Oceana County

(G-7870)
LOWRY JOANELLEN
Also Called: Cj's Smoked Spc Dom Game Proc
7833 Lincoln St (49421)
PHONE..............................231 873-2323
Joanellen Lowry, *Owner*
EMP: 6 **EST:** 2015
SALES (est): 100K **Privately Held**
SIC: 3556 Meat processing machinery

(G-7871)
NORTHERN LABEL INC
265 S Division St (49421-9601)
PHONE..............................231 854-6301
William P Walch, *President*
Sandy Kilborne, *Corp Secy*
Desmer Walch, *Vice Pres*
EMP: 7 **EST:** 1995
SQ FT: 11,100
SALES (est): 787.9K **Privately Held**
WEB: www.northernlabelinc.com
SIC: 2759 Labels & seals: printing

(G-7872)
SUBLIME PRINTS
283 Munn St (49421-9713)
PHONE..............................231 335-7799
Ken Brogan, *Owner*
EMP: 5 **EST:** 2005
SALES (est): 132.9K **Privately Held**
WEB: www.sublimeprints.com
SIC: 2759 Screen printing

Hessel
Mackinac County

(G-7873)
BAILEY ELECTRICAL INC
4070 E Simmons Rd (49745-9527)
PHONE..............................906 478-8000
Andrew Bailey, *CEO*
EMP: 6 **EST:** 2008
SALES (est): 254.2K **Privately Held**
SIC: 3699 Electrical equipment & supplies

(G-7874)
MAPLES SAWMILL INC
2736 Chard Rd (49745-9115)
P.O. Box 185 (49745-0185)
PHONE..............................906 484-3926
Luke Jaroche, *President*
Lynelle Jaroche, *Admin Sec*
EMP: 27 **EST:** 1963
SQ FT: 9,500
SALES (est): 1.9MM **Privately Held**
WEB: www.maplessawmill.com
SIC: 2421 Lumber: rough, sawed or planed

Hickory Corners
Barry County

(G-7875)
PENDER BOATWORKS LLC
15226 Marshfield Rd (49060-9535)
PHONE..............................269 207-0627
Henry Pender, *Principal*
EMP: 5 **EST:** 2014
SALES (est): 93.8K **Privately Held**
SIC: 3732 Boat building & repairing

Higgins Lake
Roscommon County

(G-7876)
CLASSIC LOG HOMES INCORPORATED
Also Called: Richard L Martin Construction
7340 Hillcrest Rd (48627)
P.O. Box 125 (48627-0125)
PHONE..............................989 821-6118
Richard Martin, *President*
EMP: 10 **EST:** 1971
SALES (est): 1.4MM **Privately Held**
WEB: www.richardlmartinconstruction.com
SIC: 2452 Log cabins, prefabricated, wood

Highland
Oakland County

(G-7877)
A B C PRINTING INC
2983 E Highland Rd (48356-2811)
PHONE..............................248 887-0010
Tim Camble, *President*
Tim Campbell, *Accounts Mgr*
EMP: 4 **EST:** 1981
SQ FT: 800
SALES (est): 352.6K **Privately Held**
WEB: www.printwithabc.com
SIC: 2752 2759 Commercial printing, offset; letterpress printing

(G-7878)
A TO Z SIGNS
2680 Morel Dr (48356-2769)
P.O. Box 372 (48357-0372)
PHONE..............................248 887-7737
Dennis M Cyporyn, *Owner*
EMP: 4 **EST:** 1974
SALES (est): 93.5K **Privately Held**
SIC: 7389 3993 Sign painting & lettering shop; signs & advertising specialties

(G-7879)
ABC PRINTING CORPORATION INC
2983 E Highland Rd (48356-2811)
PHONE..............................248 887-0010
Tim Campbell, *President*
EMP: 7 **EST:** 1991
SALES (est): 92.3K **Privately Held**
WEB: www.printwithabc.com
SIC: 2752 2759 2711 2741 Commercial printing, offset; letterpress printing; commercial printing & newspaper publishing combined; directories, telephone: publishing & printing

(G-7880)
ADVANCE CONCRETE PRODUCTS CO
975 N Milford Rd (48357-4551)
P.O. Box 549 (48357-0549)
PHONE..............................248 887-4173
Ronald P Kirchner, *President*
Richard Kirschner, *Exec VP*
Greg Pollard, *Vice Pres*
EMP: 30 **EST:** 1966
SQ FT: 32,000
SALES (est): 4.5MM **Privately Held**
WEB: www.advanceconcreteproducts.com
SIC: 3272 5211 Concrete products, precast; masonry materials & supplies

(G-7881)
ARMSTRONG MILLWORKS INC
3039 W Highland Rd (48357-4222)
PHONE..............................248 887-1037
Dennis W Armstrong, *President*
Susan M Armstrong, *Corp Secy*
Adam Armstrong, *Vice Pres*
EMP: 6 **EST:** 1948
SQ FT: 2,000
SALES (est): 1.2MM **Privately Held**
WEB: www.armstrongmillworks.com
SIC: 2431 Millwork

(G-7882)
ARTISTS PALLET
203 S Milford Rd (48357-4646)
PHONE..............................248 889-2440
Karen Beardsley, *Manager*
EMP: 5 **EST:** 2014
SALES (est): 68.5K **Privately Held**
SIC: 2448 Pallets, wood & wood with metal

(G-7883)
BETTERLIFE
1935 Oakland (48356-1354)
PHONE..............................248 889-3245
Gayle O'Brien, *President*
EMP: 4 **EST:** 2016
SALES (est): 56.5K **Privately Held**
SIC: 7372 Prepackaged software

(G-7884)
BIG DOG MARINE LLC
2986 White Oak Bch (48356-2448)
PHONE..............................248 705-2875
Sean Whelan, *President*
EMP: 4 **EST:** 2019
SALES (est): 431.4K **Privately Held**
SIC: 3429 Marine hardware

(G-7885)
BOESCH BUILT LLC
1730 W Wardlow Rd (48357-4321)
PHONE..............................248 318-2136
Matthew Boesch, *Principal*
EMP: 6 **EST:** 2009
SALES (est): 228.8K **Privately Held**
SIC: 3714 Motor vehicle parts & accessories

(G-7886)
C&P HOOVER LLC
Also Called: Allegra Print Imaging Highland
1100 S Milford Rd Ste 100 (48357-4892)
PHONE..............................248 887-2400
David Andrus, *Accounts Mgr*
Patrick Hoover, *Sales Staff*
Charles Hoover,
EMP: 2 **EST:** 2007
SALES (est): 1.2MM **Privately Held**
WEB: www.allegramarketingprint.com
SIC: 2752 Commercial printing, offset

(G-7887)
COMMERCIAL FABRICATING & ENGRG (PA)
1395 Energy Way (48357-3801)
P.O. Box 503 (48357-0503)
PHONE..............................248 887-1595
James W Shoner, *President*

GEOGRAPHIC SECTION
Hillman - Montmorency County (G-7914)

Dennis R Baker, *Vice Pres*
EMP: 10 **EST:** 1989
SQ FT: 25,000
SALES (est): 4.6MM **Privately Held**
WEB: www.commercialfab.us
SIC: 3444 Metal housings, enclosures, casings & other containers; sheet metal specialties, not stamped

(G-7888)
COMPLETE METALCRAFT LLC
184 W Wardlow Rd (48357-3841)
PHONE.................................248 952-8002
Ron Hassen, *COO*
Jason Swider, *Mng Member*
EMP: 5 **EST:** 2016
SALES (est): 409.9K **Privately Held**
WEB: www.completemetalcraft.com
SIC: 3469 Metal stampings

(G-7889)
CONSIDINE SALES & MARKETING
611 S Milford Rd (48357-4846)
P.O. Box 1208 (48357-1208)
PHONE.................................248 889-7887
James Considine Jr, *President*
James W Considine III, *Vice Pres*
Jim Bell, *Sales Staff*
Thom Bernheisel, *Admin Sec*
EMP: 8 **EST:** 1971
SALES (est): 2.1MM **Privately Held**
WEB: www.considinesales.com
SIC: 8742 3559 5531 Sales (including sales management) consultant; automotive maintenance equipment; automotive parts

(G-7890)
D T M 1 INC
1450 N Milford Rd Ste 101 (48357-4505)
PHONE.................................248 889-9210
Michael Denton, *President*
Drew Sweetman, *Vice Pres*
Glenn Sprague, *Engineer*
▲ **EMP:** 33 **EST:** 2002
SQ FT: 20,000
SALES (est): 4.9MM **Privately Held**
SIC: 3465 2821 3089 Body parts, automobile; stamped metal; thermoplastic materials; injection molding of plastics

(G-7891)
DT MANUFACTURING ONE LLC
Also Called: Dt Manufacturing Company
1450 N Milford Rd Ste 101 (48357-4505)
PHONE.................................248 889-9210
Michael Denton, *President*
Ray Gallatin, *Mfg Mgr*
Scott Denton, *Sales Engr*
Michael Finetti, *Manager*
EMP: 100 **EST:** 2011
SALES (est): 8.9MM **Privately Held**
WEB: www.dtmanufacturing.com
SIC: 3714 Thermostats, motor vehicle

(G-7892)
HIGHLAND SUPPLY INC
1415 Enterprise Dr (48357-0020)
P.O. Box 1041 (48357-1041)
PHONE.................................248 714-8355
Todd Hess, *President*
EMP: 12 **EST:** 2010
SQ FT: 6,000
SALES (est): 1.9MM **Privately Held**
WEB: www.highlandsupply.net
SIC: 2631 Container, packaging & boxboard

(G-7893)
JANET AND COMPANY INC
1385 Clyde Rd (48357-2216)
PHONE.................................248 887-2050
Janet M Pray, *President*
▲ **EMP:** 4 **EST:** 1980
SALES (est): 248.2K **Privately Held**
SIC: 2396 5699 Screen printing on fabric articles; clothing, hand painted

(G-7894)
LIBERTY BELL POWDR COATING LLC
Also Called: Liberty Powder Coating
1408 Enterprise Dr (48357-0020)
PHONE.................................586 557-6328
Timothy Garavaglia, *Mng Member*

EMP: 4 **EST:** 2012
SALES (est): 300K **Privately Held**
SIC: 3479 Coating of metals & formed products

(G-7895)
MAC MATERIAL ACQUISITION CO
1197 Craven Dr (48356-1130)
PHONE.................................248 685-8393
Kevin McDunnough, *Vice Pres*
Lynn McDunnough, *Administration*
EMP: 5 **EST:** 2008
SALES (est): 319.1K **Privately Held**
WEB: www.macmaterials.com
SIC: 2821 5149 7699 5084 Molding compounds, plastics; soft drinks; industrial machinery & equipment repair; industrial machinery & equipment

(G-7896)
MAGNETIC PRODUCTS INC
Also Called: Mpi
683 Town Center Dr (48356-2965)
P.O. Box 529 (48356-0529)
PHONE.................................248 887-5600
Keith Rhodes, *President*
Richard Barnes, *Plant Mgr*
Matthew Wiggins, *Opers Mgr*
Tim Anderson, *Engineer*
Stephen Heath, *Controller*
▲ **EMP:** 60 **EST:** 1981
SQ FT: 40,000
SALES (est): 15.8MM **Privately Held**
WEB: www.mpimagnet.com
SIC: 3535 5085 3559 3444 Conveyors & conveying equipment; industrial supplies; separation equipment, magnetic; sheet metalwork; fabricated plate work (boiler shop)

(G-7897)
NEPTECH INC
2000 E Highland Rd (48356-3058)
PHONE.................................810 225-2222
Michael P Seacord Sr, *CEO*
Nelson Zaragoza, *Engineer*
Brian Church, *Sales Engr*
EMP: 20 **EST:** 2006
SQ FT: 20,000
SALES (est): 5.5MM **Privately Held**
WEB: www.neptechinc.com
SIC: 3491 3634 3829 3826 Process control regulator valves; blankets, electric; thermocouples; coulometric analyzers, except industrial process type

(G-7898)
PICK ENERGY SAVINGS LLC
3625 Tara Dr (48356-1764)
P.O. Box 80, Prudenville (48651-0080)
PHONE.................................248 343-8354
Paul Pickell, *Principal*
EMP: 4 **EST:** 2017
SALES (est): 135.6K **Privately Held**
WEB: www.pickenergysavings.com
SIC: 2741 Miscellaneous publishing

(G-7899)
RANDY & SANDY DAVIS
557 Harvey Lake Rd (48356-2910)
PHONE.................................248 887-7124
Randy Davis, *Owner*
EMP: 4 **EST:** 2017
SALES (est): 70.3K **Privately Held**
SIC: 2499 Wood products

(G-7900)
SURGITECH SURGICAL SVCS INC
1477 Schooner Cv (48356-2259)
PHONE.................................248 593-0797
Garret Smith, *President*
EMP: 15 **EST:** 2000
SQ FT: 1,300
SALES (est): 1MM **Privately Held**
WEB: www.surgitechservices.com
SIC: 3841 Surgical & medical instruments

(G-7901)
UNITED FABRICATING COMPANY
160 N Saint John Rd (48357-4648)
P.O. Box 8 (48357-0008)
PHONE.................................248 887-7289

Gordon Langlois, *President*
Jeffrey Langlois, *Vice Pres*
EMP: 6 **EST:** 1959
SQ FT: 8,000
SALES (est): 595.8K **Privately Held**
WEB: www.unitedfabricating.com
SIC: 3441 Fabricated structural metal

Highland Park
Wayne County

(G-7902)
COCA-COLA BOTTLING CO
12225 Oakland Pkwy (48203-3500)
PHONE.................................313 868-2167
Kathy Cole, *Manager*
EMP: 12 **EST:** 2015
SALES (est): 537.6K **Privately Held**
WEB: www.coca-cola.com
SIC: 2086 Bottled & canned soft drinks

(G-7903)
DESIGNS BY D LLC
107 Geneva St (48203-2735)
PHONE.................................313 629-3617
Dareishia Gaut, *Mng Member*
EMP: 5 **EST:** 2018
SALES (est): 107.7K **Privately Held**
SIC: 3944 5945 Craft & hobby kits & sets; hobby, toy & game shops

(G-7904)
DETROIT DENIM COMPANY LLC
109 Eason St (48203-2787)
PHONE.................................313 626-9216
Stephen J Carson, *Principal*
EMP: 5 **EST:** 2015
SALES (est): 51.2K **Privately Held**
WEB: www.detroitdenim.com
SIC: 2211 Twills, drills, denims & other ribbed fabrics: cotton

(G-7905)
FAURECIA AUTO SEATING LLC
13000 Oakland Park Blvd (48203)
PHONE.................................248 563-9241
Dan Hodgins, *Branch Mgr*
EMP: 390
SALES (corp-wide): 41.2MM **Privately Held**
SIC: 2531 Seats, automobile
HQ: Faurecia Automotive Seating, Llc
 2800 High Meadow Cir
 Auburn Hills MI 48326
 248 288-1000

(G-7906)
FAURECIA AUTO SEATING LLC
12900 Oakland Park Blvd (48203)
PHONE.................................248 563-9241
Dan Hodgins, *Branch Mgr*
EMP: 174
SALES (corp-wide): 41.2MM **Privately Held**
SIC: 2531 Seats, automobile
HQ: Faurecia Automotive Seating, Llc
 2800 High Meadow Cir
 Auburn Hills MI 48326
 248 288-1000

(G-7907)
FTE AUTOMOTIVE USA INC
12700 Oakland Park Blvd (48203)
PHONE.................................248 209-8239
Uwe Krueger, *President*
Robert A Stead, *Corp Secy*
◆ **EMP:** 188 **EST:** 1985
SALES (est): 83.6MM
SALES (corp-wide): 177.9M **Privately Held**
WEB: www.fte.de
SIC: 3714 Motor vehicle transmissions, drive assemblies & parts
HQ: Fte Automotive Gmbh
 Andreas-Humann-Str. 2
 Ebern BY 96106
 953 181-0

(G-7908)
GREAT LAKES WINE & SPIRITS LLC (PA)
Also Called: J. Lewis Cooper Co.
373 Victor St (48203-3117)
PHONE.................................313 278-5400

Lew Cooper III, *CEO*
Syd Ross, *CEO*
J Lewis Cooper Jr, *Ch of Bd*
Mark Sabatini, *Division Mgr*
Ernie Almeranti, *Exec VP*
▲ **EMP:** 185 **EST:** 1946
SQ FT: 40,000
SALES (est): 356.2MM **Privately Held**
WEB: www.glwas.com
SIC: 5182 2084 Wine; wine coolers, alcoholic; liquor; wines, brandy & brandy spirits

(G-7909)
SHAKES AND CAKES LLC
13806 Woodward Ave (48203-3653)
PHONE.................................313 707-0923
Taessia Bursey,
EMP: 6 **EST:** 2017
SALES (est): 80K **Privately Held**
SIC: 2051 Bakery: wholesale or wholesale/retail combined

(G-7910)
SHERWOOD PROTOTYPE INC
124 Victor St (48203-3130)
P.O. Box 422, Willow Spring NC (27592-0422)
PHONE.................................313 883-3880
Peter Paxton, *President*
EMP: 19 **EST:** 1986
SALES (est): 1MM **Privately Held**
WEB: www.sherwoodprototype.com
SIC: 3599 Machine shop, jobbing & repair

Hillman
Montmorency County

(G-7911)
CHEBOYGAN CEMENT PRODUCTS INC
Also Called: Gilners Concrete
800 E Progress St (49746-8942)
PHONE.................................989 742-4107
Rick Hopp, *Finance Mgr*
Eugene Jameson, *Manager*
Paul Nowosad, *Manager*
EMP: 4
SALES (corp-wide): 8.7MM **Privately Held**
WEB: www.cheboygancement.com
SIC: 3272 3273 Concrete products; ready-mixed concrete
PA: Cheboygan Cement Products Inc
 702 Lafayette Ave
 Cheboygan MI 49721
 231 627-5631

(G-7912)
CRAWFORD FOREST PRODUCTS
705 E Progress St (49746-8942)
P.O. Box 458 (49746-0458)
PHONE.................................989 742-3855
Mike Mattish, *President*
Allan Crawford, *Vice Pres*
EMP: 11 **EST:** 1972
SALES (est): 360.9K **Privately Held**
SIC: 2411 2421 Pulpwood contractors engaged in cutting; wood chips, produced in the field; sawmills & planing mills, general

(G-7913)
LANCE SAFFORD WELDING LLC
230 S County St (49746-9663)
PHONE.................................989 464-7841
EMP: 4 **EST:** 2014
SALES (est): 55.4K **Privately Held**
SIC: 7692 Welding repair

(G-7914)
MICHIGAN TIMBER SAWMILL LLC
21909 County Road 624 (49746-7983)
PHONE.................................989 266-2417
Aaron Moody,
Lance Safford,
Zachary Safford,
EMP: 18 **EST:** 2016
SALES (est): 1.7MM **Privately Held**
WEB: www.mitimberservices.com
SIC: 2421 Sawmills & planing mills, general

Hillman - Montmorency County (G-7915) — GEOGRAPHIC SECTION

(G-7915)
PATCHWOOD PRODUCTS INC (PA)
14797 State St (49746-8034)
PHONE..................989 742-2605
Jim Paczkowski, *President*
Noreen Leon, *Manager*
Grace Liney, *Manager*
EMP: 5 EST: 2014
SALES (est): 1.6MM **Privately Held**
WEB: www.patchwood.nfshost.com
SIC: 2448 Pallets, wood

(G-7916)
RIPE HARVEST FOODS LLC ◆
24291 Veterans Mem Hwy (49746-8667)
PHONE..................630 863-2440
Aysha Chaudary,
EMP: 10 EST: 2021
SALES (est): 283.4K **Privately Held**
WEB: www.breadsfromanna.com
SIC: 2051 Bakery: wholesale or wholesale/retail combined

(G-7917)
WAYNE WIRE CLOTH PRODUCTS INC
Hillman Division
221 Garfield St (49746-9206)
PHONE..................989 742-4591
Alice Thompson, *Plant Mgr*
Steve Waugh, *Branch Mgr*
Zack Krantz, *Technology*
EMP: 16
SALES (corp-wide): 30.5MM **Privately Held**
WEB: www.waynewire.com
SIC: 3569 3564 3496 3494 Filters; blowers & fans; miscellaneous fabricated wire products; valves & pipe fittings
PA: Wayne Wire Cloth Products Inc
200 E Dresden St
Kalkaska MI 49646
231 258-9187

(G-7918)
WIDELL INDUSTRIES INC
24601 Veterans Mem Hwy (49746-8671)
PHONE..................989 742-4528
Laurie Standen, *Sales Staff*
Chuck Lisowe, *Manager*
EMP: 21
SQ FT: 11,000
SALES (corp-wide): 9.8MM **Privately Held**
WEB: www.widell.com
SIC: 3545 3544 5251 Taps, machine tool; special dies & tools; tools
PA: Widell Industries, Inc.
6622 Industrial Ave
Port Richey FL 34668
800 237-5963

Hillsdale
Hillsdale County

(G-7919)
ACME MILLS COMPANY
Also Called: Fairway Products Division
301 Arch Ave (49242-1080)
PHONE..................517 437-8940
Matt Utley, *Vice Pres*
Michael Rafe, *Accounts Mgr*
Scott Hill, *Sales Staff*
Brian Annis, *Marketing Staff*
Alex Sierra, *Branch Mgr*
EMP: 35
SALES (corp-wide): 75.1MM **Privately Held**
WEB: www.acmemills.com
SIC: 5131 3429 2674 2394 Textile converters; manufactured hardware (general); bags: uncoated paper & multiwall; canvas & related products; textile bags; men's & boys' work clothing
PA: Acme Mills Company
33 Blmfeld Hlls Pkwy Ste
Bloomfield Hills MI 48304
248 203-2000

(G-7920)
ACME MILLS COMPANY
Great Lakes Filter
301 Arch Ave (49242-1080)
PHONE..................517 437-8940
Brian Balliet, *Manager*
EMP: 21
SALES (corp-wide): 75.1MM **Privately Held**
WEB: www.acmemills.com
SIC: 3569 Filters
PA: Acme Mills Company
33 Blmfeld Hlls Pkwy Ste
Bloomfield Hills MI 48304
248 203-2000

(G-7921)
ACT TEST PANELS LLC
273 Industrial Dr (49242-1078)
PHONE..................517 439-1485
Frank Lutze, *CEO*
Scott Crosley, *Vice Pres*
Brad Kimpell, *Vice Pres*
Burt Johns, *Opers Mgr*
Craig Armstrong, *Maint Spvr*
▲ EMP: 33
SQ FT: 74,000
SALES (est): 5.3MM **Privately Held**
WEB: www.acttestpanels.com
SIC: 3479 Coating of metals & formed products

(G-7922)
AD ASTRA ROASTERS LLC
106 N Broad St (49242-1618)
Rural Route 106 N Broad St (49242)
PHONE..................517 914-2487
Patrick Whalen, *Mng Member*
EMP: 5
SALES (est): 62.3K **Privately Held**
WEB: www.adastraroasters.com
SIC: 2095 Roasted coffee

(G-7923)
AUTORACK TECHNOLOGIES INC
20 Superior St (49242-1735)
P.O. Box 672 (49242-0672)
PHONE..................517 437-4800
Scott Bowerman, *President*
EMP: 16 EST: 2004
SQ FT: 21,000
SALES (est): 1MM **Privately Held**
WEB: www.autoracktech.com
SIC: 7692 Welding repair

(G-7924)
BECKER & SCRIVENS CON PDTS INC
3340 Beck Rd (49242-9406)
PHONE..................517 437-4250
Gordon Scrivens, *President*
Aaron Scrivens, *Treasurer*
EMP: 24 EST: 1940
SQ FT: 3,000
SALES (est): 3.5MM **Privately Held**
WEB: www.beckerscrivens.com
SIC: 3273 3272 Ready-mixed concrete; septic tanks, concrete

(G-7925)
BIOLOGCAL MDIATION SYSTEMS LLC
200 Industrial Dr (49242-1075)
P.O. Box 650, Fort Collins CO (80522-0650)
PHONE..................970 221-5949
EMP: 10 EST: 2011
SALES (est): 236.7K **Privately Held**
WEB: www.biologicalmediation.com
SIC: 3448 Prefabricated metal buildings

(G-7926)
BOB EVANS FARMS INC
200 N Wolcott St (49242-1762)
P.O. Box 226 (49242-0226)
PHONE..................517 437-3349
Grant Fann, *General Mgr*
Kenneth Howe, *General Mgr*
Nick Newark, *General Mgr*
Stephanie Sanders, *General Mgr*
John Yorio, *Opers Staff*
EMP: 1136
SQ FT: 18,000 **Publicly Held**
WEB: www.bobevans.com
SIC: 2011 Sausages from meat slaughtered on site
HQ: Bob Evans Farms, Inc.
8111 Smiths Mill Rd
New Albany OH 43054
614 491-2225

(G-7927)
BUNDY CORPORATION
200 Arch Ave (49242-1079)
PHONE..................517 439-1132
Tom Neill, *Principal*
EMP: 4 EST: 2009
SALES (est): 61.5K **Privately Held**
SIC: 3498 Fabricated pipe & fittings

(G-7928)
CAMBRIA TOOL AND MACHINE INC
121 Mechanic Rd (49242-5025)
P.O. Box 248 (49242-0248)
PHONE..................517 437-3500
Troy Balser, *President*
Andrea Daniels, *Admin Sec*
EMP: 10 EST: 1953
SQ FT: 14,250
SALES (est): 1MM **Privately Held**
WEB: www.cambriatool.com
SIC: 3544 3599 3714 Special dies & tools; jigs & fixtures; custom machinery; drive shafts, motor vehicle

(G-7929)
CARDINAL GROUP INDUSTRIES CORP
266 Industrial Dr (49242-1077)
PHONE..................517 437-6000
Tracy McCullough, *President*
EMP: 15 EST: 2014
SQ FT: 10,000
SALES (est): 407.2K **Privately Held**
WEB: www.thecardinalgroupindustries.com
SIC: 7389 8742 3451 Brokers' services; management consulting services; screw machine products

(G-7930)
COBRA AERO LLC
240 Uran St (49242-1087)
PHONE..................517 437-9100
Sheena Sigler, *General Mgr*
Harold Hilbert, *Principal*
H Sean Hilbert, *Principal*
Sean Hilbert, *Engineer*
EMP: 6 EST: 2016
SALES (est): 600.8K **Privately Held**
WEB: www.cobra-aero.com
SIC: 3519 Internal combustion engines

(G-7931)
DAYCO PRODUCTS LLC
215 Industrial Dr (49242-1076)
PHONE..................517 439-0689
John Traylor, *Vice Pres*
David Kelly, *Vice Pres*
Sam Trego, *Vice Pres*
Del Melloch, *Purchasing*
William Oteney, *Purchasing*
EMP: 6
SQ FT: 15,000
SALES (corp-wide): 211.2MM **Privately Held**
WEB: www.daycoproducts.com
SIC: 3559 3714 Automotive related machinery; motor vehicle parts & accessories
HQ: Dayco Products, Llc
1650 Research Dr Ste 100
Troy MI 48083

(G-7932)
DDP SPCLTY ELCTRNIC MTLS US LL
Also Called: Ddp Hillsdale Shipping
190 Uran St (49242-1087)
PHONE..................517 439-4440
Paul Bowman, *Branch Mgr*
EMP: 84
SALES (corp-wide): 20.4B **Publicly Held**
SIC: 2869 Industrial organic chemicals
HQ: Ddp Specialty Electronic Materials Us, Llc
974 Centre Rd
Wilmington DE 19805
610 244-6000

(G-7933)
DOW CHEMICAL COMPANY
195 Uran St (49242-1087)
PHONE..................517 439-4400
Tim Dill, *Manager*
EMP: 5
SALES (corp-wide): 38.5B **Publicly Held**
WEB: www.dow.com
SIC: 5085 2899 2891 Industrial supplies; chemical preparations; adhesives & sealants
HQ: The Dow Chemical Company
2211 H H Dow Way
Midland MI 48642
989 636-1000

(G-7934)
FOUST ELECTRO MOLD INC
277 Industrial Dr (49242-1078)
PHONE..................517 439-1062
Alan Foust, *President*
Jeffrey Foust, *Agent*
EMP: 9 EST: 1976
SQ FT: 7,500
SALES (est): 938.3K **Privately Held**
WEB: www.foustelectromold.com
SIC: 3544 Special dies & tools; industrial molds

(G-7935)
FRANK CONDON INC
Also Called: Hillsdale Terminal
250 Industrial Dr (49242-1075)
PHONE..................517 849-2505
Frank Condon, *President*
Tom Condon, *Corp Secy*
Jim Condon, *Vice Pres*
John Condon, *Vice Pres*
Kurtis Condon, *Plant Mgr*
▲ EMP: 40 EST: 1976
SQ FT: 35,000
SALES (est): 7.9MM **Privately Held**
SIC: 3469 Stamping metal for the trade

(G-7936)
GENERAL AUTOMATIC MCH PDTS CO
Also Called: Gampco
266 Industrial Dr (49242-1077)
PHONE..................517 437-6000
Tracy McCullough, *President*
Ralph Schafer, *Chairman*
Scott Schafer, *Treasurer*
Sally Scott, *Planning*
EMP: 50 EST: 1944
SQ FT: 79,287
SALES (est): 8.1MM **Privately Held**
SIC: 3495 Mechanical springs, precision

(G-7937)
HILLSDALE PALLET LLC
1242 E Montgomery Rd (49242-8504)
PHONE..................517 254-4777
Shannon Miller,
EMP: 11 EST: 2008
SALES (est): 509.2K **Privately Held**
WEB: www.hillsdalepalletllc.com
SIC: 2448 Pallets, wood

(G-7938)
J & K SPRATT ENTERPRISES INC
Also Called: Precision Gage
256 Industrial Dr (49242-1077)
P.O. Box 277 (49242-0277)
PHONE..................517 439-5010
John Spratt, *President*
Eric Lewis, *Vice Pres*
Kenette Spratt, *Treasurer*
EMP: 56 EST: 1982
SQ FT: 56,000
SALES (est): 8.3MM **Privately Held**
SIC: 3599 3714 3545 3544 Machine shop, jobbing & repair; motor vehicle body components & frame; machine tool accessories; special dies, tools, jigs & fixtures; strain gages, solid state; prosthetic appliances

(G-7939)
KINGDOM GEEKDOM LLC
81 S Wolcott St (49242-1736)
PHONE..................517 610-5016
Alison McDowell, *Administration*
EMP: 4 EST: 2018

▲ = Import ▼=Export
◆ =Import/Export

GEOGRAPHIC SECTION

Holland - Ottawa County (G-7965)

SALES (est): 80.6K **Privately Held**
SIC: 2759 Screen printing

(G-7940)
MAR-VO MINERAL COMPANY INC
115 E Bacon St (49242-1655)
P.O. Box 86, Osseo (49266-0086)
PHONE...................517 523-2669
David Wheeler, *President*
Jana Wheeler, *Vice Pres*
EMP: 4 EST: 1996 **Privately Held**
WEB: www.lucky-buck.com
SIC: 2048 Mineral feed supplements

(G-7941)
PARAGON METALS LLC (PA)
Also Called: New Venture Foundry
3010 Mechanic Rd (49242-1095)
PHONE...................517 639-4629
Michael Smith, *CEO*
David Smith, *Vice Pres*
Jason Woodard, *Opers Staff*
Sheila Winner, *Buyer*
Lori Kosmerick, *Purchasing*
▲ **EMP: 7 EST:** 1991
SQ FT: 10,000
SALES (est): 27.7MM **Privately Held**
WEB: www.paragonmetals.com
SIC: 3321 3322 3324 3363 Gray & ductile iron foundries; malleable iron foundries; steel investment foundries; aluminum die-castings; nonferrous foundries; steel foundries

(G-7942)
PROFESSIONAL HEARING SERVICES
1231 Hudson Rd (49242-2092)
PHONE...................517 439-1610
EMP: 4 EST: 2020
SALES (est): 138.7K **Privately Held**
WEB: www.professional-hearing.com
SIC: 8062 3841 General medical & surgical hospitals; surgical & medical instruments

(G-7943)
QUALITE INC
Also Called: Qualite Sports Lighting
215 W Mechanic St (49242-5042)
P.O. Box 765 (49242-0765)
PHONE...................517 439-4316
Dwight C Shaneour Jr, *Ch of Bd*
Russ McCoy, *President*
Georgia Clark, *Corp Secy*
Mike Boorom, *Vice Pres*
Nic Page, *Vice Pres*
▲ **EMP: 20 EST:** 1982
SQ FT: 20,000
SALES (est): 8.4MM
SALES (corp-wide): 95MM **Privately Held**
WEB: www.qualite.com
SIC: 3648 Area & sports luminaries
HQ: The Shane Group Llc
215 W Mechanic St
Hillsdale MI 49242
517 439-4316

(G-7944)
QUALITY INDUSTRIES INC
215 W Mechanic St (49242-5042)
P.O. Box 765 (49242-0765)
PHONE...................517 439-1591
Robert Kuchowicz, *CEO*
Keith Addleman, *President*
Gary Van Deusen, *Vice Pres*
EMP: 36 EST: 1986
SQ FT: 85,000
SALES (est): 2.1MM
SALES (corp-wide): 95MM **Privately Held**
WEB: www.qualityindustries.com
SIC: 3949 Playground equipment
HQ: The Shane Group Llc
215 W Mechanic St
Hillsdale MI 49242
517 439-4316

(G-7945)
RICHARD D MATZKE
1844 Ferndale Dr (49242-9427)
PHONE...................517 320-0964
Richard D Matzke, *Principal*
EMP: 5 EST: 2013
SALES (est): 111.9K **Privately Held**
SIC: 2841 Soap & other detergents

(G-7946)
RON WATKINS
Also Called: H & R Enterprises
4080 State Rd (49242-9753)
PHONE...................517 439-5451
EMP: 5
SQ FT: 2,000
SALES (est): 260K **Privately Held**
SIC: 3751 Mfg Motorcycle Safety And Touring Equipment

(G-7947)
RUMLER BROTHERS INC
Also Called: Arrow Swift Printing
72 W Carleton Rd (49242-1202)
PHONE...................517 437-2990
Jerry Rumler, *President*
Steve Rumler, *Vice Pres*
EMP: 5 EST: 1984
SQ FT: 1,800
SALES (est): 423.4K **Privately Held**
WEB: www.cartridgeworldusa.com
SIC: 2752 7334 Commercial printing, offset; photocopying & duplicating services

(G-7948)
SCRANTON MACHINE INC
266 Industrial Dr (49242-1077)
PHONE...................517 437-6000
Scott Schafer, *CEO*
Ralph Schafer, *President*
EMP: 19 EST: 1996
SQ FT: 80,000
SALES (est): 228.8K **Privately Held**
SIC: 3599 Machine shop, jobbing & repair

(G-7949)
SHANE GROUP LLC (HQ)
215 W Mechanic St (49242-5042)
P.O. Box 765 (49242-0765)
PHONE...................517 439-4316
Eric Boorom, *President*
Alan Dimmers, *Corp Secy*
Dwight Shaneour Jr, *Exec VP*
Marci Bates, *Human Res Dir*
▲ **EMP: 3 EST:** 1974
SQ FT: 20,000
SALES (est): 80.4MM
SALES (corp-wide): 95MM **Privately Held**
WEB: www.worth-investments.com
SIC: 5074 3949 3429 Plumbing fittings & supplies; playground equipment; animal traps, iron or steel
PA: Worth Investment Group, Llc
3634 Mccain Rd Ste 8
Jackson MI 49203
517 750-9900

(G-7950)
SWISS INDUSTRIES INC
305 Arch Ave (49242-1080)
PHONE...................517 437-3682
Robert P Krick, *President*
Irene Krick, *Corp Secy*
William E Krick, *Vice Pres*
EMP: 8 EST: 1957
SQ FT: 8,000 **Privately Held**
SIC: 3451 Screw machine products

Holland
Ottawa County

(G-7951)
A & B PACKING EQUIPMENT INC
414 E 40th St (49423-5383)
PHONE...................616 294-3539
Michael Williamson, *CEO*
EMP: 4
SALES (corp-wide): 22.7MM **Privately Held**
WEB: www.abpacking.com
SIC: 3565 Packaging machinery
PA: A & B Packing Equipment, Inc.
732 W Saint Joseph St
Lawrence MI 49064
269 539-4700

(G-7952)
ABCOR INDUSTRIES LLC
4690 128th Ave (49424-8028)
PHONE...................616 994-9577
Ed Kleinjan, *Prdtn Mgr*
Josh Foreman, *Cust Mgr*
Jay T Weis, *Mng Member*
Rex Yancy, *Mng Member*
EMP: 16 EST: 2005
SQ FT: 67,000
SALES (est): 2.4MM **Privately Held**
WEB: www.abcorindustries.com
SIC: 2493 Reconstituted wood products

(G-7953)
ABCOR PARTNERS LLC
4690 128th Ave (49424-8028)
PHONE...................616 994-9577
Jt Weis, *CEO*
EMP: 24 EST: 2012
SALES (est): 2.8MM **Privately Held**
WEB: www.abcorindustries.com
SIC: 2411 Wooden logs

(G-7954)
ACCU TECH MICHIGAN
9652 Black River Ct # 10 (49424-8124)
PHONE...................616 953-0256
Loren Brouwer, *Administration*
EMP: 5 EST: 2017
SALES (est): 217.2K **Privately Held**
WEB: www.accutechmi.com
SIC: 3599 Machine shop, jobbing & repair

(G-7955)
ACCURATE ENGINEERING & MFG LLC
13569 New Holland St (49424-8467)
PHONE...................616 738-1261
Larry Koyers, *Principal*
EMP: 10 EST: 2016
SALES (est): 1.8MM **Privately Held**
WEB: www.accurateengmfg.com
SIC: 3599 Machine shop, jobbing & repair

(G-7956)
ACME PALLET INC
Also Called: Acme Small Log Sawmill
13450 New Holland St (49424-9407)
P.O. Box 1438 (49422-1438)
PHONE...................616 738-6452
Asher L Tourison, *President*
James Vandervoord, *Corp Secy*
Dan Lampe, *Vice Pres*
Majlis Johnston, *Executive*
EMP: 40 EST: 1963
SQ FT: 90,000
SALES (est): 6MM **Privately Held**
WEB: www.acmepallet.com
SIC: 2448 Pallets, wood

(G-7957)
ADRIANS SCREEN PRINT
Also Called: Adrian's T-Shirt Printery
3735 Hollywood Dr (49424-1134)
PHONE...................734 994-1367
Adrian J Cleypool, *Owner*
EMP: 4 EST: 1973
SQ FT: 2,100
SALES (est): 350K **Privately Held**
SIC: 2759 Screen printing

(G-7958)
AGRITEK INDUSTRIES INC
4211 Hallacy Dr (49424-8723)
PHONE...................616 786-9200
Larry Kooiker, *President*
Sid Widmayer, *Prdtn Mgr*
Peter Venlet, *Production*
Dave Fossen, *QC Mgr*
David Venlet, *QC Mgr*
▲ **EMP: 100 EST:** 1987
SQ FT: 70,000
SALES (est): 24.9MM **Privately Held**
WEB: www.agritek.com
SIC: 3523 3714 2522 Farm machinery & equipment; motor vehicle parts & accessories; office furniture, except wood

(G-7959)
AHS LLC (DH)
Also Called: Almost Heaven Saunas
11261 James St (49424-8627)
PHONE...................888 355-3050
Colleen Raymond, *Bookkeeper*
Richard M Mouw, *Mng Member*
EMP: 8 EST: 2007
SQ FT: 600
SALES (est): 4.6MM
SALES (corp-wide): 129MM **Privately Held**
WEB: www.almostheaven.com
SIC: 2452 5999 Sauna rooms, prefabricated, wood; sauna equipment & supplies
HQ: Harvia Us Inc.
11261 James St
Holland MI 49424
888 355-3050

(G-7960)
ALL METAL DESIGNS INC
Also Called: A M D
13131 Reflections Dr (49424-7262)
PHONE...................616 392-3696
Russell Fincher, *President*
Mike Kragt, *Vice Pres*
EMP: 7 EST: 1969
SQ FT: 12,000
SALES (est): 1.1MM **Privately Held**
WEB: www.allmetal.com
SIC: 3599 Custom machinery; machine shop, jobbing & repair

(G-7961)
ALSENTIS LLC
1261 S Waverly Rd (49423-9332)
PHONE...................616 395-8254
David Caldwell, *President*
EMP: 6 EST: 2008
SALES (est): 1MM
SALES (corp-wide): 1B **Publicly Held**
WEB: www.alsentis.com
SIC: 3674 Light sensitive devices
PA: Methode Electronics, Inc
8750 W Bryn Mawr Ave # 1000
Chicago IL 60631
708 867-6777

(G-7962)
AMERICAN BOTTLING COMPANY
545 E 32nd St (49423-5411)
PHONE...................616 396-1281
Drake Eckert, *Branch Mgr*
EMP: 14 Publicly Held
WEB: www.keurigdrpepper.com
SIC: 2086 Soft drinks: packaged in cans, bottles, etc.
HQ: The American Bottling Company
6425 Hall Of Fame Ln
Frisco TX 75034

(G-7963)
AMERICAN BOTTLING COMPANY
Also Called: 7 Up Holland
900 Brooks Ave Ste 1 (49423-5337)
PHONE...................616 392-2124
Ellen Jolley, *Office Mgr*
Ken Gerrits, *Manager*
EMP: 14 Publicly Held
WEB: www.keurigdrpepper.com
SIC: 2086 Soft drinks: packaged in cans, bottles, etc.
HQ: The American Bottling Company
6425 Hall Of Fame Ln
Frisco TX 75034

(G-7964)
AMERICAN CLASSIC HOMES INC
Also Called: Select Building Supplies
13352 Van Buren St (49424-9248)
PHONE...................616 594-5900
Scott Christopher, *CEO*
EMP: 8 EST: 1982
SQ FT: 2,500
SALES (est): 2MM **Privately Held**
SIC: 2421 Sawmills & planing mills, general

(G-7965)
AMNEON ACQUISITIONS LLC
Also Called: Jdti
199 E 17th St (49423-4385)
PHONE...................616 895-6640
Reggie Vanden Bosch, *President*
EMP: 13 EST: 2008
SQ FT: 49,000

Holland - Ottawa County (G-7966) GEOGRAPHIC SECTION

SALES (est): 1.5MM Privately Held
WEB: www.jdti.com
SIC: 2522 Office furniture, except wood

(G-7966)
AUTOFORM DEVELOPMENT INC
Also Called: Pro Body
257 E 32nd St Ste 2 (49423-5413)
PHONE..................................616 392-4909
Steve Dreyer, President
Anette Goozman, Manager
EMP: 10
SQ FT: 6,000
SALES (est): 650K Privately Held
WEB: www.autoformgroup.com
SIC: 7532 3714 3711 Top & body repair & paint shops; motor vehicle parts & accessories; motor vehicles & car bodies

(G-7967)
AUTOMATION SPECIALISTS INC
12555 Superior Ct (49424-8287)
PHONE..................................616 738-8288
Mitch Weener, President
Chad Weener, Purch Agent
Rick Berens, Engineer
Jacob Straus, Marketing Staff
Jeff Padding, Manager
EMP: 15 EST: 1988
SQ FT: 20,000
SALES (est): 2.2MM Privately Held
WEB: www.automationspecialistsinc.com
SIC: 3599 Machine shop, jobbing & repair

(G-7968)
AXIS MACHINE & TOOL INC
7217 W Olive Rd (49424-9415)
PHONE..................................616 738-2196
Timothy Ebels, President
EMP: 5 EST: 1996
SQ FT: 5,000
SALES (est): 573K Privately Held
WEB: www.axismt.com
SIC: 3544 Special dies & tools

(G-7969)
B & W WOODWORK INC
11362 James St (49424-8627)
PHONE..................................616 772-4577
Bruce Kruithoff, President
EMP: 8 EST: 1987
SQ FT: 17,000 Privately Held
SIC: 2431 2599 5211 Doors, wood; door trim, wood; cabinets, factory; millwork & lumber

(G-7970)
BARTON BOATWORKS
4328 52nd St (49423-9566)
P.O. Box 3156 (49422-3156)
PHONE..................................616 240-5562
Kyle Barton, Principal
EMP: 5 EST: 2011
SALES (est): 98K Privately Held
WEB: www.bartonboatworks.com
SIC: 3732 Boat building & repairing

(G-7971)
BAYSHORE CUSTOM ASSEMBLY LLC
13055 Riley St Ste 40 (49424-7240)
P.O. Box 8455 (49422-8455)
PHONE..................................616 396-5502
Stanley Szymanski, Mng Member
Chris Martin,
Hassel J Savard,
EMP: 4 EST: 2002
SQ FT: 2,000
SALES (est): 100K Privately Held
SIC: 8711 3569 Engineering services; assembly machines, non-metalworking

(G-7972)
BEECHBED MIX
120 James St (49424-1824)
PHONE..................................616 263-7422
Charles German, Principal
EMP: 5 EST: 2015
SALES (est): 171.3K Privately Held
SIC: 3273 Ready-mixed concrete

(G-7973)
BEI INTERNATIONAL LLC
10753 Macatawa Dr (49424-9572)
PHONE..................................616 204-8274
Richard McKibben, Vice Pres

▼ EMP: 15 EST: 1959
SQ FT: 28,000
SALES (est): 549.4K Privately Held
SIC: 3523 Harvesters, fruit, vegetable, tobacco, etc.; sprayers & spraying machines, agricultural; planting, haying, harvesting & processing machinery

(G-7974)
BENTELER AUTO HOLLAND INC
Also Called: Benteler Alumnium Systems Mich
533 Ottawa Ave (49423-5903)
PHONE..................................616 396-6591
Dirk Feidler, President
Jeton Lapi, Opers Mgr
Elena Sgroia, Finance Mgr
◆ EMP: 195 EST: 1993
SQ FT: 450,000
SALES (est): 51.2MM
SALES (corp-wide): 7.5B Privately Held
WEB: www.benteler.com
SIC: 3341 3354 Secondary nonferrous metals; aluminum extruded products
PA: Benteler International Aktiengesellschaft
SchillerstraBe 25
Salzburg 5020
662 228-30

(G-7975)
BIG DUTCHMAN INC (HQ)
Also Called: Cyclone International
3900 John F Donnelly Dr (49424-7277)
P.O. Box 1017 (49422-1017)
PHONE..................................616 392-5981
Clovis Rayzel, President
Thomas Wallace, General Mgr
John Bussema, Vice Pres
Steve Langley, Vice Pres
Steve Walcott, Vice Pres
◆ EMP: 84 EST: 1975
SQ FT: 94,000
SALES (est): 28MM
SALES (corp-wide): 1.1B Privately Held
WEB: www.bigdutchmanusa.com
SIC: 3523 Poultry brooders, feeders & waterers
PA: Big Dutchman Aktiengesellschaft
Auf Der Lage 2
Vechta NI 49377
444 780-10

(G-7976)
BILLCO ACQUISITION LLC
Also Called: Billco Products
1373 Lincoln Ave (49423-9389)
PHONE..................................616 928-0637
Tom Sligh, President
Jeff Sheridan, Plant Mgr
▲ EMP: 25 EST: 1965
SQ FT: 45,000
SALES (est): 4.4MM Privately Held
WEB: www.drgilcrest.com
SIC: 2599 Restaurant furniture, wood or metal; hotel furniture

(G-7977)
BLUE PRINT STUDIO
26 Holly Ct (49423-5236)
PHONE..................................616 283-2893
Lena Stob, Principal
EMP: 4 EST: 2019
SALES (est): 71.2K Privately Held
WEB: www.bpslakeshore.com
SIC: 2752 Commercial printing, lithographic

(G-7978)
BOARS HEAD PROVISIONS CO INC
284 Roost Ave (49424-2032)
PHONE..................................941 955-0994
Van Ayvazain, President
Valerie Danneffel, Hum Res Coord
Esmeralda Leon, Supervisor
Jim Monroe, Supervisor
EMP: 229
SALES (corp-wide): 401.8MM Privately Held
WEB: www.boarshead.com
SIC: 5147 2013 2011 Meats, fresh; luncheon meat from purchased meat; meat packing plants

PA: Boar's Head Provisions Co., Inc.
1819 Main St Ste 800
Sarasota FL 34236
941 955-0994

(G-7979)
BODYCOTE THERMAL PROC INC
3270 John F Donnelly Dr (49424-8222)
PHONE..................................616 399-6880
Pam Champion, Office Mgr
Pamela Champion, Office Mgr
Jodi Underhill, Office Mgr
Harrison Tiemann, Manager
EMP: 7
SALES (corp-wide): 795.2MM Privately Held
WEB: www.bodycote.com
SIC: 3398 Metal heat treating
HQ: Bodycote Thermal Processing, Inc.
12750 Merit Dr Ste 1400
Dallas TX 75251
214 904-2420

(G-7980)
BRACY & ASSOCIATES LTD
965 N Baywood Dr (49424-2585)
PHONE..................................616 298-8120
Arnold Bracey, Partner
EMP: 5 EST: 1983
SALES (est): 343.2K Privately Held
WEB: www.bracyassociates.com
SIC: 2531 Altars & pulpits

(G-7981)
BRADFORD COMPANY (PA)
Also Called: Bradford Packaging
13500 Quincy St (49424-9460)
P.O. Box 1199 (49422-1199)
PHONE..................................616 399-3000
Judson A Bradford, Ch of Bd
Thomas R Bradford, President
Mark Feenstra, Vice Pres
Amanda Raven, Opers Staff
Maynard Viersen, Engineer
◆ EMP: 160 EST: 1924
SQ FT: 184,000
SALES (est): 38.2MM Privately Held
WEB: www.bradfordcompany.com
SIC: 2653 3535 2675 Partitions, solid fiber: made from purchased materials; unit handling conveying systems; die-cut paper & board

(G-7982)
BRAWN MIXER INC
12838 Stainless Dr (49424-8218)
PHONE..................................616 399-5600
Jerry Fleishman, President
Dan Keller, General Mgr
George McIntosh, Vice Pres
Ben Searle, Mfg Staff
Aaron Beavers, Engineer
EMP: 27 EST: 1993
SQ FT: 21,000
SALES (est): 2.9MM Privately Held
WEB: www.brawnmixer.com
SIC: 3531 5084 Mixers: ore, plaster, slag, sand, mortar, etc.; industrial machinery & equipment

(G-7983)
BREWERS CITY DOCK INC
24 Pine Ave (49423-2838)
PHONE..................................616 396-6563
Phillip Brewer, President
Ronald Lucas, Vice Pres
EMP: 25 EST: 1946
SQ FT: 28,000
SALES (est): 3.4MM Privately Held
WEB: www.brewerscitydock.com
SIC: 3273 5032 Ready-mixed concrete; sand, construction

(G-7984)
BRON MACHINE INC
821 Productions Pl (49423-9168)
PHONE..................................616 392-5320
Ron Grenadier, President
EMP: 13 EST: 1965
SQ FT: 8,500
SALES (est): 499K Privately Held
WEB: www.bronmachines.com
SIC: 3599 Machine shop, jobbing & repair

(G-7985)
BUFFOLI NORTH AMERICA CORP
4508 128th Ave (49424-9257)
PHONE..................................616 610-4362
William Damian, Principal
Sharon Brower, Controller
EMP: 11 EST: 2018
SALES (est): 1.5MM Privately Held
WEB: www.buffoli.us
SIC: 3599 Industrial machinery

(G-7986)
BUHLERPRINCE INC (DH)
670 Windcrest Dr (49423-5410)
PHONE..................................616 394-8248
Mark Los, President
Robert Aylsworth, Vice Pres
Jeff Warner, Purch Mgr
Mark Hackney, QC Mgr
Naveen Gajula, Engineer
▲ EMP: 177 EST: 1985
SQ FT: 700,000
SALES (est): 49.7MM
SALES (corp-wide): 2.9B Privately Held
SIC: 3542 Die casting machines
HQ: Buhler Us Holding Inc.
13105 12th Ave N
Plymouth MN 55441
763 847-0237

(G-7987)
BUILT SYSTEMS LLC
11511 James St (49424-8962)
PHONE..................................616 834-5099
Michael Krueger, Design Engr
Joshua Rodriguez,
EMP: 12 EST: 2013
SALES (est): 2.2MM Privately Held
WEB: www.builtsystems.net
SIC: 3559 Special industry machinery

(G-7988)
BUSSCHER SEPTIC TANK SERVICE
Also Called: Busscher Septic Tank Company
11305 E Lakewood Blvd (49424-9605)
PHONE..................................616 392-9653
Verne J Lubbers, President
Virginia Lubbers, Vice Pres
EMP: 9
SALES (est): 14.1K Privately Held
WEB: www.teambusschers.com
SIC: 3272 7699 Septic tanks, concrete; burial vaults, concrete or precast terrazzo; septic tank cleaning service

(G-7989)
C T L ENTERPRISES INC
Also Called: Signs Now
832 Productions Pl (49423-9168)
PHONE..................................616 392-1159
Leslie Louisell, President
Timothy Louisell, President
Jackie Smith, Production
Mitchell Kroll, Engineer
Leslie A Louisell, Treasurer
EMP: 12 EST: 1990
SQ FT: 9,600
SALES (est): 1.7MM Privately Held
WEB: www.signsnow.com
SIC: 3993 Signs & advertising specialties

(G-7990)
CANVAS INNOVATIONS LLC
11276 E Lakewood Blvd (49424-8601)
PHONE..................................616 393-4400
Christopher Ritsema, Principal
EMP: 8 EST: 2010
SALES (est): 974.3K Privately Held
WEB: www.canvasinnovations.us
SIC: 2211 Canvas

(G-7991)
CARRY-ALL PRODUCTS INC
Also Called: Mobile Installations
4498 128th Ave (49424-9257)
PHONE..................................616 399-8080
Chuck Rademacher, President
Kenneth Rademacher, Vice Pres
Bruce Williams, Manager
EMP: 9 EST: 1983
SQ FT: 7,500

▲ = Import ▼ = Export
◆ = Import/Export

GEOGRAPHIC SECTION
Holland - Ottawa County (G-8017)

SALES (est): 1MM **Privately Held**
WEB: www.carry-allproducts.com
SIC: 2211 3552 Canvas; silk screens for textile industry

(G-7992)
CENTURY LANES INC
Also Called: Bam
478 E 16th St (49423-3793)
PHONE.................................616 392-7086
Phil Huffman, *President*
Philip Huffman, *Director*
EMP: 57 EST: 1977
SQ FT: 8,000
SALES (est): 3.1MM **Privately Held**
WEB: www.gobamgo.com
SIC: 5812 7993 2082 7933 Restaurant, family: independent; amusement arcade; beer (alcoholic beverage); bowling centers

(G-7993)
CHALLENGE MFG COMPANY LLC
1401 Washington Ave (49423-8747)
PHONE.................................616 396-2079
Ronald Mapes, *President*
Sulabh Gupta, *Project Mgr*
Brian Wilkinson, *Production*
Christine Chappell, *Purchasing*
Billy Roddy, *Purchasing*
EMP: 196
SALES (corp-wide): 781.8MM **Privately Held**
WEB: www.challenge-mfg.com
SIC: 3465 3469 Automotive stampings; metal stampings
PA: Challenge Mfg. Company, Llc
   3200 Fruit Ridge Ave Nw
   Walker MI 49544
   616 735-6500

(G-7994)
CHARLES BOWMAN & COMPANY
3328 John F Donnelly Dr (49424-9294)
PHONE.................................616 786-4000
John Ripley, *CEO*
Brett Helgeson, *Vice Pres*
Cara Larsen, *Vice Pres*
Anthony Evans, *VP Sls/Mktg*
Randy Watt, *Technical Staff*
◆ EMP: 19 EST: 1946
SQ FT: 20,000
SALES (est): 4.3MM **Privately Held**
WEB: www.charlesbowman.com
SIC: 2834 Druggists' preparations (pharmaceuticals)

(G-7995)
CHRISTENSEN FIBERGLASS LLC
126 Aniline Ave N (49424-6407)
PHONE.................................616 738-1219
Shelly Christensen, *Office Mgr*
Bill Christensen, *Mng Member*
EMP: 20 EST: 2001
SALES (est): 1.8MM **Privately Held**
WEB: www.christensenfiberglasstooling.com
SIC: 3544 Industrial molds

(G-7996)
CHROMATIC GRAPHICS INC
654 E Lakewood Blvd (49424-2025)
PHONE.................................616 393-0034
Glen Windemuller, *President*
Judy Windemuller, *Corp Secy*
Steve Windemuller, *Vice Pres*
EMP: 8 EST: 1985
SQ FT: 6,000
SALES (est): 1MM **Privately Held**
WEB: www.chromaticgraphics.net
SIC: 2396 2397 Screen printing on fabric articles; schiffli machine embroideries

(G-7997)
CIRCUS PROCESSION LLC
622 Graafschap Rd (49423-4549)
PHONE.................................616 834-8048
EMP: 5 EST: 2012
SALES (est): 218.3K **Privately Held**
SIC: 2084 Wines

(G-7998)
CLARION TECHNOLOGIES INC (PA)
238 S River Ave Fl 2 (49423-3144)
PHONE.................................616 698-7277
John Brownlow, *CEO*
Mark Alexander, *General Mgr*
Craig A Wierda, *Chairman*
Joe Ball, *Vice Pres*
Tony Norko, *Vice Pres*
◆ EMP: 110 EST: 1998
SQ FT: 130,000
SALES (est): 68.4MM **Privately Held**
WEB: www.clariontechnologies.com
SIC: 3089 Injection molding of plastics

(G-7999)
COASTAL CONTAINER CORPORATION
Also Called: Coastal Energy
1201 Industrial Ave (49423-5318)
PHONE.................................616 355-9800
Brent E Patterson, *President*
Bill Baumgartner, *Vice Pres*
Tamara Jalving, *Vice Pres*
Mark McConnell, *CFO*
Thomas Doyle, *Human Resources*
EMP: 75 EST: 2007
SQ FT: 235,000
SALES (est): 18.9MM **Privately Held**
WEB: www.coastal-container.com
SIC: 2653 Boxes, corrugated: made from purchased materials

(G-8000)
CODE BLUE CORPORATION
259 Hedcor St Ste 1 (49423-9314)
PHONE.................................616 392-8296
Kenneth Genzink, *Ch of Bd*
David Cook, *COO*
Roberto Zanotta, *Sales Mgr*
Michael Zuidema, *Marketing Staff*
Doug Vanderveen, *Technical Staff*
▲ EMP: 36 EST: 1989
SQ FT: 35,000
SALES (est): 8.5MM **Privately Held**
WEB: www.codeblue.com
SIC: 3669 5065 3661 Emergency alarms; security control equipment & systems; telephone & telegraph apparatus

(G-8001)
COMPAC SPECIALTIES INC
13444 Barry St (49424-8495)
PHONE.................................616 786-9100
Donald Schutt, *Ch of Bd*
Mike Schutt, *President*
Rick Schutt, *Vice Pres*
Elaine Zwagerman, *Office Mgr*
EMP: 10 EST: 1971
SALES (est): 739.7K **Privately Held**
WEB: www.bmeyers.net
SIC: 3559 Recycling machinery

(G-8002)
COMPOSITE BUILDERS LLC
430 W 18th St (49423-3904)
PHONE.................................616 377-7767
Matt Lepard, *General Mgr*
Pamela Lubbers, *Office Mgr*
Danielle Macinnes,
Brian Macinnes,
EMP: 4 EST: 2014
SALES (est): 691.3K **Privately Held**
WEB: www.compositebuilders.com
SIC: 3624 Carbon & graphite products

(G-8003)
CONAGRA BRANDS INC
147 E 6th St (49423-2911)
PHONE.................................616 392-2359
EMP: 23
SALES (corp-wide): 11.1B **Publicly Held**
WEB: www.conagrabrands.com
SIC: 2099 Food preparations
PA: Conagra Brands, Inc.
   222 Mdse Mart Plz Ste 1
   Chicago IL 60654
   312 549-5000

(G-8004)
CONSUMERS CONCRETE CORPORATION
4312 M 40 (49423)
PHONE.................................616 392-6190

Bill Kirby, *Manager*
EMP: 7
SALES (corp-wide): 42.6MM **Privately Held**
WEB: www.consumersconcrete.com
SIC: 3273 Ready-mixed concrete
PA: Consumers Concrete Corporation
   3506 Lovers Ln
   Kalamazoo MI 49001
   269 342-0136

(G-8005)
COPPERCRAFT DISTILLERY LLC
196 120th Ave (49424-3309)
PHONE.................................616 796-8274
Brandon Joldersma, *General Mgr*
Jason Mahar, *Principal*
EMP: 41 EST: 2020
SALES (est): 3.3MM **Privately Held**
WEB: www.coppercraftdistillery.com
SIC: 2085 Distillers' dried grains & solubles & alcohol

(G-8006)
CRAFTWOOD INDUSTRIES INC
2530 Kamar Dr (49424-8964)
P.O. Box 2068 (49422-2068)
PHONE.................................616 796-1209
Terry W Beckering, *President*
Roger Steensma, *Treasurer*
Kathy Prominski, *Admin Sec*
EMP: 35 EST: 1995
SQ FT: 32,750
SALES (est): 2.6MM **Privately Held**
WEB: www.craftwoodindustries.com
SIC: 2522 2531 2426 2511 Office furniture, except wood; public building & related furniture; hardwood dimension & flooring mills; wood household furniture; wood office furniture

(G-8007)
CREATIVE PRODUCTS INTL
Also Called: CPI Creative Products
A-4699 61st St Unit H (49423)
PHONE.................................616 335-3333
Dave Maurer, *President*
Maritza Voorhurst, *Business Mgr*
Derek Rieley, *Client Mgr*
Rob Carli, *Mktg Dir*
Scott Siegersma, *Manager*
▲ EMP: 12 EST: 2003
SALES (est): 554.5K **Privately Held**
WEB: www.creativeidea.net
SIC: 7699 5087 3589 Cleaning services; carpet & rug cleaning equipment & supplies, commercial; vacuum cleaning systems; commercial cleaning equipment; janitors' carts

(G-8008)
CUSACK MUSIC LLC
Also Called: Westshore Design
514 Lincoln Ave (49423-4249)
PHONE.................................616 546-8888
Jon Cusack, *CEO*
▲ EMP: 20 EST: 2002
SALES (est): 4.5MM **Privately Held**
WEB: www.cusackmusic.com
SIC: 7389 3651 Design services; audio electronic systems

(G-8009)
CUTTING EDGE TECHNOLOGIES INC
13305 New Holland St B (49424-7442)
PHONE.................................616 738-0800
Jim Dirette, *Vice Pres*
Pete Kornoelje, *Vice Pres*
Craig Kane, *Treasurer*
EMP: 14 EST: 2001
SQ FT: 14,000
SALES (est): 671.4K **Privately Held**
SIC: 3544 Special dies, tools, jigs & fixtures

(G-8010)
CWK INTERNATIONAL CORP
Also Called: Yost Vises
2221 Sunset Bluff Dr (49424-2385)
PHONE.................................616 396-2063
Patrick Nelis, *CEO*
Kevin Nelis, *President*
Fred Nelis, *Corp Secy*
▲ EMP: 6 EST: 2004

SALES (est): 650.7K **Privately Held**
SIC: 3545 Machine tool accessories

(G-8011)
D B INTERNATIONAL LLC
650 Riley St Ste C (49423-1592)
PHONE.................................616 796-0679
Khamtanh Sayavong, *Mng Member*
EMP: 6 EST: 2014
SALES (est): 150.2K **Privately Held**
SIC: 3089 Plastics products

(G-8012)
D SIGN LLC
Also Called: D-Sign
511 Chicago Dr (49423-2939)
PHONE.................................616 392-3841
Joy Smith, *MIS Staff*
Douglas Smith,
EMP: 5 EST: 1978
SQ FT: 2,000
SALES (est): 401.2K **Privately Held**
WEB: www.dsignllc.com
SIC: 3993 Neon signs

(G-8013)
DANIEL PRUITOFF
Also Called: Holland Automotive Machine
271 E 26th St (49423-5445)
PHONE.................................616 392-1371
Daniel Pruitoff, *Owner*
EMP: 5 EST: 1984
SQ FT: 3,000
SALES (est): 600K **Privately Held**
WEB: www.hollandautomotivemachine.com
SIC: 7538 7539 3599 Engine rebuilding: automotive; machine shop, automotive; crankshafts & camshafts, machining

(G-8014)
DIVERSIFIED PDTS & SVCS LLC
500 E 8th St (49423-3770)
P.O. Box 2081 (49422-2081)
PHONE.................................616 836-6600
EMP: 8 EST: 2014
SALES (est): 480K **Privately Held**
SIC: 2421 2441 2448 2449 Sawmill/Planing Mill Mfg Wood Boxes/Shooks Mfg Wood Pallets/Skids Mfg Wood Containers

(G-8015)
DIVERSIFIED WELDING & FABG
12813 Riley St (49424-9201)
PHONE.................................616 738-0400
Calvin Lawson, *President*
Jeff Genzink, *General Mgr*
Karen Lawson, *Vice Pres*
EMP: 5 EST: 1986
SQ FT: 5,000
SALES (est): 501.8K **Privately Held**
WEB: www.dwfab.com
SIC: 7692 Welding repair

(G-8016)
DR PEPPER SNAPPLE GROUP
777 Brooks Ave (49423-5340)
PHONE.................................616 393-5800
Henry Rockafellow, *Sales Staff*
EMP: 14 EST: 2018
SALES (est): 2.4MM **Privately Held**
WEB: www.snapple.com
SIC: 2086 Soft drinks: packaged in cans, bottles, etc.

(G-8017)
DRI-DESIGN INC
12480 Superior Ct Ste 1 (49424-7241)
P.O. Box 1286 (49422-1286)
PHONE.................................616 355-2970
Bradley J Zeeff, *President*
Bradley Zeeff, *Vice Pres*
Dana Beaudoin, *Project Mgr*
Leroy Douglass, *Project Mgr*
Leif Haugen, *Project Mgr*
EMP: 22 EST: 1996
SQ FT: 20,000
SALES (est): 12MM **Privately Held**
WEB: www.dri-design.com
SIC: 3444 Siding, sheet metal
HQ: Kingspan Insulated Panels Inc.
   726 Summerhill Dr
   Deland FL 32724
   386 626-6789

Holland - Ottawa County (G-8018)   GEOGRAPHIC SECTION

(G-8018)
DYNAMIC CORPORATION (PA)
Also Called: Dynamic Metrology Services
2565 Van Ommen Dr (49424-8208)
PHONE..................................616 399-2200
Hugh F Broersma, *President*
Ray Atwood, *Vice Pres*
Steve Connelly, *Vice Pres*
Samantha Kandler, *Manager*
Cheryl Moulder, *Asst Admin*
EMP: 19 **EST:** 1983
SQ FT: 10,000
SALES (est): 6MM **Privately Held**
WEB: www.dynamicinc.com
SIC: 8711 8744 8734 3544 Consulting engineer; facilities support services; product certification, safety or performance; calibration & certification; special dies, tools, jigs & fixtures; metal stampings; screw machine products

(G-8019)
DYNAMIC STAFFING SOLUTIONS (PA)
2565 Van Ommen Dr (49424-8208)
PHONE..................................616 399-5220
Hugh Broersma, *President*
Steve Connelly, *Vice Pres*
EMP: 8 **EST:** 1995
SQ FT: 14,000
SALES (est): 1.3MM **Privately Held**
WEB: www.dynamicstaffingsolutions.com
SIC: 2869 Laboratory chemicals, organic

(G-8020)
E M I CONSTRUCTION PRODUCTS
526 E 64th St (49423-8717)
PHONE..................................616 392-7207
Edward Shidler, *President*
Marlene Shidler, *Corp Secy*
▼ **EMP:** 19 **EST:** 1985
SALES (est): 2.1MM **Privately Held**
WEB: www.emisupplies.com
SIC: 5082 5211 3531 3496 Masonry equipment & supplies; masonry materials & supplies; construction machinery; miscellaneous fabricated wire products; hand & edge tools

(G-8021)
EBW ELECTRONICS INC
Also Called: Ebwe
13110 Ransom St (49424-8715)
PHONE..................................616 786-0575
Leo Leblanc, *CEO*
James Cory Steeby, *President*
Patrick Leblanc, *Chairman*
Tom Clark, *Vice Pres*
Phil De Vries, *Engineer*
▲ **EMP:** 322 **EST:** 1992
SQ FT: 12,000
SALES (est): 51.3MM **Privately Held**
WEB: www.ebw-electronics.com
SIC: 3679 3612 8731 Electronic circuits; transformers, except electric; electronic research

(G-8022)
ECO - COMPOSITES LLC
Also Called: Ccd Holdings
845 Allen Dr (49423-4501)
PHONE..................................616 395-8902
Fred Pettinga, *Business Mgr*
Becky Bonnell, *Project Mgr*
Mike Wells, *Mfg Staff*
Dave Hooker, *Engineer*
Tyler Nicholson, *Engineer*
EMP: 5 **EST:** 2002
SALES (est): 496K **Privately Held**
SIC: 3089 Molding primary plastic

(G-8023)
EDMAR MANUFACTURING INC
Also Called: EMI Construction Products
526 E 64th St (49423-8717)
PHONE..................................616 392-7218
Dave Shidler, *President*
Edward Shidler, *President*
David Van Hekken, *Vice Pres*
Jerry Higgins, *Mfg Dir*
Chuck Rhoda, *Purch Mgr*
▲ **EMP:** 52 **EST:** 1975

SALES (est): 19.7MM **Privately Held**
WEB: www.edmarmfg.com
SIC: 3469 3544 Metal stampings; special dies, tools, jigs & fixtures

(G-8024)
EDSTROM PROTOTYPE LLC
356 Roosevelt Ave (49424-2630)
PHONE..................................616 566-4361
EMP: 4 **EST:** 2005
SALES (est): 69K **Privately Held**
WEB: www.e-prototype.com
SIC: 3599 Machine shop, jobbing & repair

(G-8025)
EGEMIN AUTOMATION INC
Also Called: Egemin Group, Inc.
11818 James St (49424-7789)
PHONE..................................616 393-0101
Jan Vercammen, *CEO*
Craig Hoeve, *Purchasing*
Seth Cooper, *Engineer*
Marc Guns, *Ch Credit Ofcr*
Brad Byl, *Sr Software Eng*
▲ **EMP:** 180 **EST:** 2003
SQ FT: 58,000
SALES (est): 42.9MM
SALES (corp-wide): 9.8B **Privately Held**
WEB: www.dematic.com
SIC: 3535 7371 3537 Conveyors & conveying equipment; custom computer programming services; industrial trucks & tractors
PA: Kion Group Ag
Thea-Rasche-Str. 8
Frankfurt Am Main HE 60549
692 011-00

(G-8026)
ELDEAN YACHT BASIN LTD (PA)
Also Called: Yach Basin Marina
1862 Ottawa Beach Rd (49424-2444)
PHONE..................................616 786-2205
Herbert Eldean, *President*
Tom Denherder, *Treasurer*
EMP: 25 **EST:** 1990
SALES (est): 2MM **Privately Held**
WEB: www.yachtbasinmarina.com
SIC: 4493 3732 Boat yards, storage & incidental repair; boat building & repairing

(G-8027)
ELITE INDUSTRIAL MFG LLC
12764 Greenly St Ste 40 (49424-8021)
PHONE..................................616 377-7769
Adam Vanderwal, *Mng Member*
EMP: 9 **EST:** 2010
SALES (est): 110K **Privately Held**
SIC: 3612 Voltage regulating transformers, electric power; transmission & distribution voltage regulators

(G-8028)
ENSIGN EQUIPMENT INC
12523 Superior Ct (49424-8287)
PHONE..................................616 738-9000
David Pulver, *President*
Al Grollem, *Vice Pres*
Brian Sjoerdsma, *Supervisor*
EMP: 8 **EST:** 1990
SALES (est): 2.7MM
SALES (corp-wide): 32.3MM **Privately Held**
WEB: www.ensigneq.com
SIC: 3535 Bulk handling conveyor systems
PA: Excalibur Group L.L.C.
1160 Amboy Ave
Perth Amboy NJ 08861
732 442-8425

(G-8029)
ENVISION MACHINE AND MFG LLC
Also Called: Envision Machine & Mfg
741 Waverly Ct (49423-9387)
PHONE..................................616 953-8580
Tim Vander Toorn, *President*
Josh Vander Toorn, *Vice Pres*
Eric Jones, *Sales Staff*
Dan Camfferman, *Prgrmr*
EMP: 8 **EST:** 2011
SQ FT: 9,000 **Privately Held**
WEB: www.envisionmachine.com
SIC: 3599 Machine shop, jobbing & repair

(G-8030)
EPOCH ROBOTICS
13365 Tyler St (49424-9421)
PHONE..................................616 820-3369
Bill Yeck, *Manager*
EMP: 15 **EST:** 2018
SALES (est): 288.3K **Privately Held**
WEB: www.jrautomation.com
SIC: 3599 Industrial machinery

(G-8031)
ESS TEC INC
3347 128th Ave (49424-9263)
PHONE..................................616 394-0230
Constance S Essenburg, *President*
James Davis, *Vice Pres*
Elliot Essenburg, *Vice Pres*
Travis Chambers, *Materials Mgr*
Jose Gomez, *QC Mgr*
EMP: 89 **EST:** 1992
SQ FT: 20,000
SALES (est): 15.6MM **Privately Held**
WEB: www.ess-tec.com
SIC: 3089 3559 Injection molded finished plastic products; plastics working machinery

(G-8032)
EVEREST EXPEDITION LLC
Also Called: Worden Company, The
199 E 17th St (49423-4385)
PHONE..................................616 392-1848
Steve Deloof, *President*
Jim Hendrickson, *Purch Mgr*
Scott Van Zile, *Design Engr*
Paul Huesdash, *Manager*
Randy Johnson, *Technology*
EMP: 99 **EST:** 2013
SQ FT: 25,000
SALES (est): 15.9MM **Privately Held**
WEB: www.wordencompany.com
SIC: 2531 Library furniture

(G-8033)
EVIA LEARNING INC
720 E 8th St Ste 4 (49423-3079)
PHONE..................................616 393-8803
Lee Sorester, *President*
Claire Knowles, *Sales Staff*
EMP: 7 **EST:** 2008
SALES (est): 574.3K **Privately Held**
WEB: www.evialearning.com
SIC: 2731 Books: publishing & printing

(G-8034)
EVOQUA WATER TECHNOLOGIES LLC
2155 112th Ave (49424-9609)
PHONE..................................616 772-9011
Doug McFarland, *Regional Mgr*
Ken Hollidge, *Branch Mgr*
Thom Hourani, *CIO*
Robin Tushek, *IT/INT Sup*
Chris Knudsen, *Analyst*
EMP: 100
SALES (corp-wide): 1.4B **Publicly Held**
WEB: www.evoqua.com
SIC: 3589 Water treatment equipment, industrial
HQ: Evoqua Water Technologies Llc
210 6th Ave Ste 3300
Pittsburgh PA 15222
724 772-0044

(G-8035)
FLASHES PUBLISHERS INC
Also Called: Allegan Flashes
54 W 8th St (49423-3104)
PHONE..................................269 673-2141
John P Morgan, *President*
Hendrik G Meijer, *Treasurer*
EMP: 21 **EST:** 1934
SALES (est): 1.1MM **Privately Held**
WEB: www.flashesprinting.com
SIC: 2752 2741 Commercial printing, offset; shopping news: publishing & printing; directories, telephone: publishing & printing

(G-8036)
FLEXPOST INC
2236 112th Ave Ste 80 (49424-8502)
PHONE..................................616 928-0829
Thomas Stanley, *CEO*
John Kandra, *President*
EMP: 8 **EST:** 2006

SALES (est): 1.4MM **Privately Held**
WEB: www.flexpostinc.com
SIC: 3315 Fence gates posts & fittings: steel

(G-8037)
FOCUS MARKETING
2495 112th Ave Ste 8 (49424-9657)
PHONE..................................616 355-4362
EMP: 20
SALES (est): 1.6MM **Privately Held**
SIC: 2759 Commercial Printing

(G-8038)
FOREFRONT CONTROL SYSTEMS LLC
4314 136th Ave Ste 200 (49424-7467)
PHONE..................................616 796-3495
Garryl Roon, *Owner*
Susan Roon, *Administration*
EMP: 5 **EST:** 2000
SALES (est): 869.2K **Privately Held**
WEB: www.forefrontcontrols.com
SIC: 3823 Controllers for process variables, all types

(G-8039)
FORMED SOLUTIONS INC
1900 Lamar Ct (49423-8750)
PHONE..................................616 395-5455
Lyle Schut, *President*
Heather Rosencrans, *Office Mgr*
◆ **EMP:** 15 **EST:** 1998
SQ FT: 37,500
SALES (est): 2.5MM **Privately Held**
WEB: www.formedsolutions.com
SIC: 3089 Thermoformed finished plastic products; injection molding of plastics

(G-8040)
FORTRESS STBLZTION SYSTEMS LLC
184 W 64th St (49423-9302)
PHONE..................................616 355-1421
Karen Barnes, *Accountant*
Edward Wheatley,
EMP: 8 **EST:** 2001
SQ FT: 25,000
SALES (est): 1.3MM **Privately Held**
WEB: www.fortressstabilization.com
SIC: 3624 Fibers, carbon & graphite

(G-8041)
FRESH COAST CANDLES
6445 146th Ave (49423-8944)
PHONE..................................616 405-8518
Rebecca Dubois, *Principal*
EMP: 4 **EST:** 2016
SALES (est): 74.1K **Privately Held**
WEB: www.freshcoastcandles.com
SIC: 3999 Candles

(G-8042)
FROSTYS ICE CREAM MACHINE RETN
2080 Ottawa Beach Rd (49424-2457)
PHONE..................................616 886-1418
Kim Wojahn, *Principal*
EMP: 4 **EST:** 2016
SALES (est): 89.6K **Privately Held**
WEB: www.frostymachinerental.com
SIC: 3599 Industrial machinery

(G-8043)
FSI LABEL COMPANY
Also Called: Argo Systems
6227 136th Ave (49424-8289)
P.O. Box 36480, Grosse Pointe (48236-0480)
PHONE..................................586 776-4110
Emily Kopko, *President*
Christopher Roman, *Vice Pres*
Jason Ford, *Marketing Staff*
Matt Kopko, *Representative*
EMP: 20 **EST:** 1971
SQ FT: 30,000
SALES (est): 3.4MM **Privately Held**
WEB: www.fsilabel.com
SIC: 2759 5112 Labels & seals: printing; office filing supplies; file folders

(G-8044)
FURNITURE PARTNERS LLC
199 E 17th St (49423-4385)
PHONE..................................616 355-3051

▲ = Import ▼ = Export
◆ = Import/Export

GEOGRAPHIC SECTION
Holland - Ottawa County (G-8070)

James Weaver, *President*
Kenneth Filippini, *Principal*
EMP: 6 **EST:** 2015
SQ FT: 135,000
SALES (est): 540.1K **Privately Held**
SIC: 2531 Public building & related furniture

(G-8045)
G P REEVES INC
4551 Holland Ave (49424-9200)
PHONE 616 399-8893
Gordon P Reeves, *President*
Shirley Reeves, *Vice Pres*
Brad Alvesteffer, *Engineer*
Benjamin Keirn, *Project Engr*
Larry Jackson, *Sales Mgr*
EMP: 25 **EST:** 1971
SQ FT: 27,000
SALES (est): 3.8MM **Privately Held**
WEB: www.gpreeves.com
SIC: 3569 Lubrication equipment, industrial

(G-8046)
GENERAL PROCESSING SYSTEMS INC
Also Called: Product Saver
12838 Stainless Dr (49424-8218)
PHONE 630 554-7804
EMP: 10 **EST:** 1966
SQ FT: 10,000
SALES (est): 897.1K **Privately Held**
SIC: 3599 5084 Mfg Industrial Machinery Whol Industrial Equipment

(G-8047)
GENERAL TECHNOLOGY INC
4521 48th St (49423-9515)
PHONE 269 751-7516
Gregory Laarman, *President*
Betty Laarman, *Admin Sec*
EMP: 14 **EST:** 1984
SQ FT: 600
SALES (est): 750K **Privately Held**
SIC: 3599 Machine shop, jobbing & repair

(G-8048)
GENERATION PRESS INC
Also Called: Schreur Printing
10861 Paw Paw Dr (49424-8991)
PHONE 616 392-4405
Tim Schreur, *President*
Mary Jane Schreur, *Vice Pres*
Angela O 'brien, *Graphic Designe*
EMP: 9 **EST:** 1945
SALES (est): 500K **Privately Held**
WEB: www.schreurprinting.com
SIC: 2752 7331 Commercial printing, offset; mailing service

(G-8049)
GENESIS INNOVATION GROUP LLC
13827 Port Sheldon St (49424-9413)
PHONE 616 294-1026
Robert Ball, *Mng Member*
Jeff Ondrla,
Don Running,
EMP: 20 **EST:** 2016
SALES (est): 1.8MM **Privately Held**
WEB: www.genesisinnovationgroup.com
SIC: 3841 Diagnostic apparatus, medical

(G-8050)
GHSP INC (HQ)
Also Called: Convergence Technologies
701 S Waverly Rd Ste 100 (49423-9121)
PHONE 616 842-5500
Paul Doyle, *CEO*
Nelson Jacobson, *President*
Jerry Scott, *Chairman*
Mike Hnatiuk, *Project Mgr*
Dave Allison, *Mfg Staff*
▲ **EMP:** 350 **EST:** 1924
SQ FT: 200,000
SALES (est): 290.7MM
SALES (corp-wide): 1B **Privately Held**
WEB: www.ghsp.com
SIC: 3714 Motor vehicle parts & accessories
PA: Jsj Corporation
  700 Robbins Rd
  Grand Haven MI 49417
  616 842-6350

(G-8051)
GLOBAL BATTERY SOLUTIONS LLC
Also Called: Maufacturing
581 Ottawa Ave Ste 100 (49423-4088)
PHONE 800 456-4265
Hank Sybesma, *Managing Prtnr*
Ellington Ellis, *Mng Member*
EMP: 30 **EST:** 2014
SALES (est): 8.2MM **Privately Held**
WEB: www.globalbatterysolutions.com
SIC: 3691 1531 1711 Alkaline cell storage batteries; ; solar energy contractor

(G-8052)
GLW FINISHING
741 Waverly Ct (49423-9387)
P.O. Box 1738 (49422-1738)
PHONE 616 395-0112
EMP: 25
SQ FT: 33,000
SALES (est): 2.3MM **Privately Held**
SIC: 3479 Coating/Engraving Service

(G-8053)
GNS HOLLAND INC
Also Called: Gns America Co.
13341 Quincy St (49424-9460)
PHONE 616 796-0433
Sukje Lee, *President*
Morey Wagenmaker, *Business Mgr*
Earl Smith, *Materials Mgr*
Steve Fitzgerald, *Production*
Neal Dalman, *QC Mgr*
▲ **EMP:** 2 **EST:** 2009
SQ FT: 100,000
SALES: 4.8MM
SALES (corp-wide): 52.1MM **Privately Held**
WEB: www.gnsauto.com
SIC: 3469 Perforated metal, stamped
PA: Gns North America, Inc.
  13341 Quincy St
  Holland MI 49424
  616 796-0433

(G-8054)
GNS NORTH AMERICA INC (PA)
13341 Quincy St (49424-9460)
PHONE 616 796-0433
Moon Gyu-Kong, *President*
Todd Dale, *COO*
Ed Holub, *Vice Pres*
Lukasz Borowicz, *CFO*
Scott Fitzgerald, *Manager*
EMP: 6 **EST:** 2009
SQ FT: 1,750
SALES (est): 52.1MM **Privately Held**
WEB: www.gnsauto.com
SIC: 6719 3465 Investment holding companies, except banks; body parts, automobile: stamped metal

(G-8055)
GRAND RAPIDS GRAVEL COMPANY
Kalkman Redi-Mix Division
13180 Quincy St (49424-9474)
P.O. Box 9160, Wyoming (49509-0160)
PHONE 616 538-9000
Randy Venhuizen, *Office Mgr*
EMP: 27
SQ FT: 10,000
SALES (corp-wide): 23.9MM **Privately Held**
WEB: www.grgravel.com
SIC: 3273 8611 Ready-mixed concrete; business associations
PA: Grand Rapids Gravel Company
  2700 28th St Sw
  Grand Rapids MI 49519
  616 538-9000

(G-8056)
GRAPHIX SIGNS & EMBROIDERY
Also Called: Mle
11223 E Lakewood Blvd (49424-8601)
PHONE 616 396-0009
Marcia Essenburg, *Partner*
Beth Essenburg, *Partner*
Kari Weener, *Graphic Designe*
EMP: 8 **EST:** 1991
SQ FT: 5,200
SALES (est): 693.7K **Privately Held**
WEB: www.graphixsignsandembroidery.com
SIC: 3993 7299 Signs & advertising specialties; stitching, custom

(G-8057)
GREAT LAKE WOODS INC
3303 John F Donnelly Dr (49424-9207)
P.O. Box 1738 (49422-1738)
PHONE 616 399-3300
▼ **EMP:** 150
SQ FT: 103,000
SALES (est): 30.9MM **Privately Held**
WEB: www.greatlakewoods.com
SIC: 2851 2431 Paints And Allied Products, Nec

(G-8058)
GREAT LAKES CASTINGS LLC
12970 Ransom St (49424-9277)
PHONE 616 399-9710
Vince Palavcolo, *Branch Mgr*
Bryan Holmes, *Manager*
EMP: 50 **Privately Held**
WEB: www.greatlakescastings.com
SIC: 3321 Gray iron castings
HQ: Great Lakes Castings Llc
  800 N Washington Ave
  Ludington MI 49431
  231 843-2501

(G-8059)
GREAT LAKES NCW LLC
386 Bay Park Dr Ste 10 (49424-2083)
PHONE 616 355-2626
Steve Guillory, *President*
EMP: 5 **EST:** 2007
SALES (est): 287.2K **Privately Held**
SIC: 3589 Car washing machinery

(G-8060)
GREAT LEGS WNERY BRWRY DIST LL
2478 Nuttall Ct (49424-6499)
PHONE 616 298-7600
EMP: 4 **EST:** 2017
SALES (est): 132.8K **Privately Held**
SIC: 2085 5813 Distilled & blended liquors; bars & lounges

(G-8061)
GREEN PLASTICS LLC
13370 Barry St Ste A (49424-7451)
PHONE 616 295-2718
Dan English, *Mng Member*
Holly Bouwens,
Nick English,
EMP: 13 **EST:** 2010
SALES (est): 212.7K **Privately Held**
SIC: 3089 Injection molding of plastics

(G-8062)
GT SOLUTIONS LLC
Also Called: Matech Lighting Systems
31 E 8th St Ste 310 (49423-3541)
PHONE 616 259-0700
Jeffery Teroller, *Mng Member*
Julie Mesman, *Admin Asst*
EMP: 4 **EST:** 2012
SALES (est): 1.5MM **Privately Held**
WEB: www.vegalightcontrolsystems.com
SIC: 8748 3648 3646 Business consulting; lighting equipment; commercial indusl & institutional electric lighting fixtures

(G-8063)
GVD INDUSTRIES LLC
217 E 24th St Ste 140 (49423-4973)
PHONE 616 836-4067
EMP: 5 **EST:** 2018
SALES (est): 50.5K **Privately Held**
WEB: www.gvdindustries.com
SIC: 3999 Manufacturing industries

(G-8064)
GVD INDUSTRIES LLC
373 Highbanks Ct (49424-6372)
PHONE 616 298-7243
Gary Van Dyke, *Administration*
EMP: 7 **EST:** 2011
SALES (est): 144.2K **Privately Held**
WEB: www.gvdindustries.com
SIC: 3999 Manufacturing industries

(G-8065)
H E MORSE CO
Also Called: Morse-Hemco
455 Douglas Ave (49423-2772)
PHONE 616 396-4604
Christopher A Wysong, *President*
Laurence Wysong, *Chairman*
Michael Hop, *Vice Pres*
Renee Wilson, *Human Res Mgr*
Nancy Wennersten, *Admin Sec*
EMP: 60 **EST:** 1944
SQ FT: 36,000
SALES (est): 8.6MM **Privately Held**
WEB: www.hemcogages.com
SIC: 3545 Gauges (machine tool accessories)

(G-8066)
HARBOR PACKAGING
342 E 40th St (49423-5345)
PHONE 616 494-9913
EMP: 6 **EST:** 2019
SALES (est): 90.7K **Privately Held**
WEB: www.harborpackaging.com
SIC: 2671 Packaging paper & plastics film, coated & laminated

(G-8067)
HAWORTH INC (HQ)
1 Haworth Ctr (49423-8820)
PHONE 616 393-3000
Franco Bianchi, *President*
Matthew Haworth, *Chairman*
Allison Harris, *Business Mgr*
Paul Hirschberg, *Business Mgr*
Jos Amaral, *Vice Pres*
◆ **EMP:** 3200 **EST:** 1959
SQ FT: 1,550,000
SALES (est): 1.5B
SALES (corp-wide): 1.8B **Privately Held**
WEB: www.haworth.com
SIC: 2522 2521 Office furniture, except wood; wood office furniture
PA: Haworth International, Ltd.
  1 Haworth Ctr
  Holland MI 49423
  616 393-3000

(G-8068)
HAWORTH INTERNATIONAL LTD (PA)
1 Haworth Ctr (49423-8820)
PHONE 616 393-3000
Matthew Haworth, *Ch of Bd*
Frankco Bianchi, *President*
Heather Graham, *Business Mgr*
Tom Manikowski, *Business Mgr*
Jean Stepnicka, *Business Mgr*
◆ **EMP:** 3000 **EST:** 1948
SQ FT: 1,500,000
SALES: 1.8B **Privately Held**
WEB: www.haworth.com
SIC: 2522 2521 Office furniture, except wood; wood office furniture

(G-8069)
HEMP GLOBAL PRODUCTS INC
503 Essenburg Dr (49424-1623)
PHONE 616 617-6476
Israel Quintanilla, *President*
Bryce Taylor, *Treasurer*
EMP: 4
SQ FT: 3,000
SALES (est): 250K **Privately Held**
SIC: 2329 5199 2339 5136 Athletic (warmup, sweat & jogging) suits: men's & boys'; general merchandise, non-durable; women's & misses' outerwear; men's & boys' clothing; women's & children's clothing

(G-8070)
HGC WESTSHORE LLC
Also Called: Westshore Design
3440 Windquest Dr (49424-8069)
PHONE 616 796-1218
Jon Skekloff, *General Mgr*
Charles Isaac-Samuel, *Info Tech Mgr*
Gary Van Dyke,
EMP: 61 **EST:** 2018
SALES (est): 6.7MM **Privately Held**
WEB: www.westshoredesign.com
SIC: 3672 Printed circuit boards

Holland - Ottawa County (G-8071)

(G-8071)
HIGH Q LIGHTING INC
11439 E Lakewood Blvd (49424-9663)
P.O. Box 2817 (49422-2817)
PHONE...............616 396-3591
Michael A Goheen, *President*
Michael Serr, *Vice Pres*
Karen Marshall, *Purch Mgr*
Carlyle Serr, *Treasurer*
EMP: 19 **EST:** 1993
SQ FT: 20,000
SALES (est): 2.7MM **Privately Held**
WEB: www.hql.net
SIC: 3646 3648 3641 Fluorescent lighting fixtures, commercial; lighting equipment; electric lamps

(G-8072)
HIGH-TECH INDS OF HOLLAND
3269 John F Donnelly Dr (49424-8223)
PHONE...............616 399-5430
David Tenbrink, *President*
EMP: 40 **EST:** 1983
SQ FT: 20,000
SALES (est): 2.3MM **Privately Held**
SIC: 3369 Castings, except die-castings, precision

(G-8073)
HOLLAND ALLOYS INC
534 Chicago Dr (49423-2940)
P.O. Box 2459 (49422-2459)
PHONE...............616 396-6444
Richard O Hagen, *President*
Carolyn Hagen, *Vice Pres*
Bonnie De Kleine, *Admin Sec*
EMP: 32 **EST:** 1973
SQ FT: 1,000
SALES (est): 2.1MM
SALES (corp-wide): 5.2MM **Privately Held**
WEB: www.hollandalloys.com
SIC: 3369 3366 3365 3325 Castings, except die-castings, precision; copper foundries; aluminum foundries; steel foundries; malleable iron foundries; gray & ductile iron foundries
PA: Holland Pattern Co
534 Chicago Dr
Holland MI 49423
616 396-6348

(G-8074)
HOLLAND BAR STOOL COMPANY
Also Called: Holland Honey Cake Co.
12839 Corporate Circle Pl (49424-7267)
PHONE...............616 399-5530
Larry Bensink, *President*
Ling Bensink, *Vice Pres*
◆ **EMP:** 17 **EST:** 1940
SQ FT: 60,000
SALES (est): 4.6MM **Privately Held**
WEB: www.hollandbarstool.com
SIC: 2599 Bar, restaurant & cafeteria furniture

(G-8075)
HOLLAND BOWL MILL
120 James St (49424-1824)
P.O. Box 2102 (49422-2102)
PHONE...............616 396-6513
Donna B Phillips, *Partner*
Dave Gier, *Partner*
EMP: 12 **EST:** 1975
SQ FT: 18,000
SALES (est): 1.2MM **Privately Held**
WEB: www.hollandbowlmill.com
SIC: 2499 Bowls, wood

(G-8076)
HOLLAND COMMUNITY HOSP AUX INC
Also Called: Behavioral Health
854 Wshington Ave Ste 330 (49423)
PHONE...............616 355-3926
Steve Sorenson, *Branch Mgr*
Nathan Silva, *Software Engr*
Thomas Kuhn, *Psychiatry*
EMP: 5
SALES (corp-wide): 267.6MM **Privately Held**
WEB: www.hollandhospital.org
SIC: 3821 8734 8071 Clinical laboratory instruments, except medical & dental; testing laboratories; medical laboratories
PA: Holland Community Hospital Auxiliary, Inc.
602 Michigan Ave
Holland MI 49423
616 748-9346

(G-8077)
HOLLAND CUSTOM SIGNS
4047 56th St (49423-9344)
PHONE...............616 566-4783
EMP: 5 **EST:** 2018
SALES (est): 46K **Privately Held**
WEB: www.hollandcustomsigns.com
SIC: 3993 Signs & advertising specialties

(G-8078)
HOLLAND ELECTRIC MOTOR CO
11598 E Lakewood Blvd B (49424-7932)
PHONE...............616 392-1115
James Achterhof, *President*
Paul Achterhof, *Vice Pres*
Philip Holtrop, *Treasurer*
Mike Vanderwall, *Manager*
Delwyn Mokma, *Asst Sec*
EMP: 5 **EST:** 1988
SQ FT: 3,300
SALES (est): 563.8K **Privately Held**
WEB: www.hollandelectricmotor.com
SIC: 7694 5063 Electric motor repair; generators

(G-8079)
HOLLAND HOUSE CANDLES INC (PA)
16656 Riley St (49424-5811)
PHONE...............800 238-8467
Valerie Nichols, *President*
William Nichols, *Treasurer*
EMP: 7 **EST:** 1974
SALES (est): 840K **Privately Held**
WEB: www.hollandhousecandles.com
SIC: 3999 5999 Candles; candle shops

(G-8080)
HOLLAND PALLET REPAIR INC
13370 Barry St Ste A (49424-7451)
PHONE...............616 875-8642
John Breslin, *President*
Dave Mason, *Corp Secy*
EMP: 45 **EST:** 1991
SQ FT: 7,000
SALES (est): 5.1MM **Privately Held**
WEB: www.hollandpalletrepair.com
SIC: 2448 Pallets, wood

(G-8081)
HOLLAND PANEL PRODUCTS INC
615 E 40th St (49423-5314)
PHONE...............616 392-1826
Eric Smith, *President*
Bill Kok, *General Mgr*
Kristine Elders, *HR Admin*
EMP: 26 **EST:** 2005
SALES (est): 8.5MM
SALES (corp-wide): 91.6MM **Privately Held**
WEB: www.panel.com
SIC: 2431 Millwork
PA: Panel Processing, Inc.
1030 Devere Dr
Alpena MI 49707
800 433-7142

(G-8082)
HOLLAND PATTERN CO (PA)
534 Chicago Dr (49423-2999)
P.O. Box 2459 (49422-2459)
PHONE...............616 396-6348
Richard O Hagen, *President*
Carolyn Hagen, *Vice Pres*
Randy Schutt, *Engineer*
Beth Denbleyker, *Controller*
Bonnie Dekleine, *Admin Sec*
EMP: 5
SQ FT: 6,000
SALES (est): 5.2MM **Privately Held**
WEB: www.hollandpattern.com
SIC: 3543 3369 Industrial patterns; castings, except die-castings, precision

(G-8083)
HOLLAND PRINTING CENTER INC (PA)
Also Called: Allegra Print & Imaging
4314 136th Ave Ste 100 (49424-7467)
PHONE...............616 786-3101
Richard Schwander, *President*
Jeff Schwander, *Vice Pres*
EMP: 16 **EST:** 1987
SQ FT: 10,000
SALES (est): 1MM **Privately Held**
WEB: www.allegramarketingprint.com
SIC: 2752 Commercial printing, offset

(G-8084)
HOLLAND SCREEN PRINT INC
4665 44th St (49423-9031)
PHONE...............616 396-7630
Steve Dickerson, *President*
Tom Dickerson, *General Mgr*
Amy Dickerson, *Vice Pres*
EMP: 7 **EST:** 1967
SQ FT: 20,000
SALES (est): 593.5K **Privately Held**
WEB: www.hollandscreenprint.com
SIC: 2759 Screen printing

(G-8085)
HOLLAND STITCHCRAFT INC
13163 Reflections Dr (49424-7262)
PHONE...............616 399-3868
Tami Jo Beltman, *Owner*
Ernest Overkamp, *Principal*
Brian Beltman, *Vice Pres*
EMP: 17 **EST:** 1982
SQ FT: 12,000
SALES (est): 3.5MM **Privately Held**
WEB: www.hollandstitchcraft.com
SIC: 2521 2599 Wood office furniture; bar, restaurant & cafeteria furniture

(G-8086)
HOLLAND TRANSPLANTER CO INC
510 E 16th St (49423-3702)
P.O. Box 1527 (49422-1527)
PHONE...............616 392-3579
Howard Poll, *President*
Ken Poll, *VP Sales*
EMP: 15 **EST:** 1927
SQ FT: 100,000
SALES (est): 3MM **Privately Held**
WEB: www.transplanter.com
SIC: 3523 Transplanters

(G-8087)
HOLLAND VISION SYSTEMS INC
11301 James St (49424-8627)
PHONE...............616 494-9974
Bryan Mc Cranner, *CEO*
Dan Bennett, *Project Engr*
EMP: 30 **EST:** 1996
SALES (est): 4.3MM **Privately Held**
WEB: www.hollandvisionsystems.com
SIC: 3699 5083 3663 7389 Security devices; farm & garden machinery; television closed circuit equipment; design services

(G-8088)
HORNSHAW WOOD WORKS LLC
15774 Ransom St (49424-5539)
PHONE...............616 566-0720
Timothy Hornshaw, *Principal*
EMP: 6 **EST:** 2009
SALES (est): 87.8K **Privately Held**
WEB: www.hornshawwoodworks.com
SIC: 2431 Millwork

(G-8089)
HTI ASSOCIATES LLC
Also Called: High-Tech Industries
3269 John F Donnelly Dr (49424-8223)
PHONE...............616 399-5430
Kevin Stein, *General Mgr*
Jodi Wszolek, *QC Mgr*
Leonor De Ochoteco, *Human Res Mgr*
David Tenbrink, *Mng Member*
EMP: 30 **EST:** 1983
SALES (est): 3.5MM **Privately Held**
SIC: 3469 5084 Machine parts, stamped or pressed metal; industrial machine parts

(G-8090)
HTTM LLC
300 E 48th St (49423-5301)
PHONE...............616 820-2500
Patrick A Thompson, *Mng Member*
EMP: 4 **EST:** 2010
SALES (est): 1.2MM
SALES (corp-wide): 50.8MM **Privately Held**
WEB: www.transmatic.com
SIC: 3691 Storage batteries
PA: Trans-Matic Mfg Co Incorporated
300 E 48th St
Holland MI 49423
616 820-2500

(G-8091)
I S TWO
262 E 26th St (49423-5457)
PHONE...............616 396-5634
Rick Obbink, *Owner*
EMP: 7 **EST:** 2010
SALES (est): 337.9K **Privately Held**
SIC: 2434 Wood kitchen cabinets

(G-8092)
ICON SHELTERS INC
Also Called: Icon Shelter Systems
1455 Lincoln Ave (49423-9389)
PHONE...............616 396-0919
Davi Dayton, *President*
Richardl Lubbers, *Vice Pres*
Ellen Fisher, *VP Mfg*
Tim Postma, *CFO*
Danielle V Heide, *Receptionist*
EMP: 24 **EST:** 2004
SQ FT: 18,000
SALES (est): 8.7MM **Privately Held**
WEB: www.iconshelters.com
SIC: 3448 Buildings, portable: prefabricated metal

(G-8093)
IMPACT FAB INC
3440 John F Donnelly Dr (49424-9294)
PHONE...............616 399-9970
Dave Haan, *President*
Ross Haan, *Vice Pres*
EMP: 10 **EST:** 1994
SALES (est): 2MM **Privately Held**
WEB: www.impactfab.com
SIC: 3599 Machine shop, jobbing & repair

(G-8094)
IMPRES ENGINEERING SVCS LLC
Also Called: Machine Shop
147 Douglas Ave (49424-6584)
P.O. Box 8518 (49422-8518)
PHONE...............616 796-8976
Sarah Eldred, *Opers Staff*
Ross Hoek, *Mng Member*
EMP: 18 **EST:** 1995
SQ FT: 14,000
SALES (est): 1.4MM **Privately Held**
WEB: www.impresengineering.com
SIC: 3599 Machine shop, jobbing & repair

(G-8095)
IN-DEPTH EDITIONS LLC
1134 Goodwood Ct (49424-2795)
PHONE...............616 566-6009
Valerie Van Heest, *Mng Member*
Valerie Vanheest, *Manager*
EMP: 4 **EST:** 2010
SALES (est): 64.7K **Privately Held**
WEB: www.in-deptheditions.com
SIC: 2731 Book publishing

(G-8096)
INTERIOR SPC OF HOLLAND
262 E 26th St (49423-5457)
PHONE...............616 396-5634
Arthur Wormet, *President*
EMP: 12 **EST:** 1977
SQ FT: 14,000
SALES (est): 601.1K **Privately Held**
SIC: 5211 2434 Cabinets, kitchen; wood kitchen cabinets

GEOGRAPHIC SECTION
Holland - Ottawa County (G-8122)

(G-8097)
INTERNATIONAL MATERIAL CO
Also Called: Imcs
510 E 40th St (49423-5313)
PHONE 616 355-2800
Rodney Webb, *President*
David Geschwendt, *Vice Pres*
EMP: 12 **EST:** 1976
SQ FT: 30,000
SALES (est): 3.7MM **Privately Held**
WEB: www.imcs.solutions
SIC: 3535 Conveyors & conveying equipment

(G-8098)
IXL MACHINE SHOP INC
117 W 7th St (49423-2823)
P.O. Box 1979 (49422-1979)
PHONE 616 392-9803
Stuart B Padnos, *President*
EMP: 108 **EST:** 1902
SQ FT: 10,000
SALES (est): 1.3MM
SALES (corp-wide): 520.8MM **Privately Held**
WEB: www.padnos.com
SIC: 3599 Machine shop, jobbing & repair
PA: Louis Padnos Iron And Metal Company
185 W 8th St
Holland MI 49423
800 442-3509

(G-8099)
JAMESWAY TOOL AND DIE INC
401 120th Ave (49424-2119)
PHONE 616 396-3731
James Rozeboom, *President*
Mark Rozeboom, *Corp Secy*
David Rozeboom, *Vice Pres*
EMP: 35 **EST:** 1976
SQ FT: 17,400
SALES (est): 1.3MM **Privately Held**
WEB: www.jameswaytool.com
SIC: 3544 Dies & die holders for metal cutting, forming, die casting

(G-8100)
JMS OF HOLLAND INC
1010 Productions Ct (49423-9122)
PHONE 616 796-2727
Harold Jordan, *President*
Leon Jordan, *Vice Pres*
Travis Stevens, *QC Mgr*
Rodney Culver, *Treasurer*
Jason Raak, *Sales Mgr*
▼ **EMP:** 100 **EST:** 1994
SQ FT: 64,000
SALES (est): 21.1MM **Privately Held**
WEB: www.jmsincorporated.com
SIC: 3469 Stamping metal for the trade

(G-8101)
JOHN A VAN DEN BOSCH CO (PA)
Also Called: V D B
4511 Holland Ave (49424-9200)
P.O. Box 1786 (49422-1786)
PHONE 616 848-2000
David V Den Bosch, *CEO*
Jim D Bosch, *Vice Pres*
Amber Latchaw, *Asst Controller*
Michael V Bosch, *Accounting Mgr*
Mark Sorge, *Accounts Mgr*
EMP: 27
SQ FT: 118,000
SALES (est): 7.6MM **Privately Held**
WEB: www.vboschhome.com
SIC: 2048 Livestock feeds

(G-8102)
JOHNSON CONTROLS INC
88 E 48th St (49423-9404)
PHONE 616 394-6818
EMP: 6 **Privately Held**
SIC: 3714 Mfg Motor Vehicle Parts/Accessories
HQ: Johnson Controls, Inc.
5757 N Green Bay Ave
Glendale WI 53209
800 382-2804

(G-8103)
JOHNSON CONTROLS INC
1 Prince Ctr (49423-5486)
PHONE 616 392-5151
Bob Bieri, *Manager*

EMP: 7 **Publicly Held**
WEB: www.johnsoncontrols.com
SIC: 3714 Motor vehicle parts & accessories
HQ: Johnson Controls, Inc.
5757 N Green Bay Ave
Glendale WI 53209
800 382-2804

(G-8104)
JR AUTOMATION TECH LLC (DH)
Also Called: Jr Automation
13365 Tyler St (49424-9421)
PHONE 616 399-2168
Mike Dubose, *CEO*
Amy Briones, *Partner*
Bryan Jones, *Co-CEO*
Randy Bethke, *Vice Pres*
Kevin Bowe, *Vice Pres*
▲ **EMP:** 250 **EST:** 2004
SQ FT: 120,000
SALES (est): 322.1MM **Privately Held**
WEB: www.jrautomation.com
SIC: 3549 Assembly machines, including robotic
HQ: Hitachi Industrial Holdings Americas, Inc.
8700 W Bryn Mawr Ave
Chicago IL 60631
914 333-2994

(G-8105)
JR TECHNOLOGY GROUP LLC (DH)
Also Called: Jr Automation Technologies
13365 Tyler St (49424-9421)
PHONE 616 399-2168
Bryan Jones, *CEO*
Barry Kohn, *CFO*
Jim Kramer, *VP Sales*
EMP: 250 **EST:** 2015
SALES (est): 105.1MM **Privately Held**
WEB: www.jrautomation.com
SIC: 3549 Assembly machines, including robotic
HQ: Hitachi Industrial Holdings Americas, Inc.
8700 W Bryn Mawr Ave
Chicago IL 60631
914 333-2994

(G-8106)
K M S COMPANY
5072 Lakeshore Dr (49424-1068)
P.O. Box 34, Ferrysburg (49409-0034)
PHONE 616 994-7000
Kirk M Schutter, *President*
EMP: 4 **EST:** 1976
SALES (est): 255.3K **Privately Held**
WEB: www.kmscompany.com
SIC: 3546 Guns, pneumatic: chip removal

(G-8107)
KAM PLASTICS CORP
935 E 40th St (49423-5384)
PHONE 616 355-5900
Peter Prouty, *President*
Dan Rietveld, *Vice Pres*
Erik Salisbury, *Opers Mgr*
Chad Wiersma, *Opers Staff*
Christina Baker, *Production*
▲ **EMP:** 65
SALES (est): 10MM **Privately Held**
WEB: www.kamplastics.com
SIC: 3089 Injection molding of plastics

(G-8108)
KAMEX MOLDED PRODUCTS LLC (PA)
611 Ottawa Ave (49423-4068)
PHONE 616 355-5900
Mary Clawson, *Engineer*
Raul Ramirez, *Engineer*
Dan Tanis, *Engineer*
Trenton Dykstra, *Project Engr*
Linda Morris, *Hum Res Coord*
EMP: 183 **EST:** 2007
SALES (est): 1MM **Privately Held**
WEB: www.kamplastics.com
SIC: 3089 Injection molded finished plastic products

(G-8109)
KARR SPRING COMPANY (PA)
Also Called: Omni Die & Engineering
966 Brooks Ave (49423-5337)
PHONE 616 394-1277
Henry Vugteveen, *President*
Henry Vugteveen, *President*
Mark Perkins, *Vice Pres*
Doug Vugteveen, *Production*
Gregg Insley, *Sales Mgr*
EMP: 21 **EST:** 1928
SQ FT: 12,000
SALES (est): 4.1MM **Privately Held**
WEB: www.omnidie.com
SIC: 3545 Machine tool accessories

(G-8110)
KEGLOVE LLC
6403 Sand Castle Vw (49423-8527)
P.O. Box 396, Saugatuck (49453-0396)
PHONE 616 610-7289
Mark Young,
Bridget Young,
EMP: 7 **EST:** 2007
SALES (est): 866.8K **Privately Held**
WEB: www.keglove.com
SIC: 5084 5078 5046 3429 Brewery products manufacturing machinery, commercial; beverage coolers; commercial cooking & food service equipment; ice chests or coolers, portable, except foam plastic

(G-8111)
KENOWA INDUSTRIES INC (PA)
11405 E Lakewood Blvd (49424-9663)
PHONE 616 392-7080
Ed Amaya, *President*
Douglas Devries, *Principal*
Michael Devries, *Principal*
Sally Root, *Human Res Dir*
Nick Klaassen, *Sales Engr*
EMP: 40 **EST:** 1979
SQ FT: 38,000
SALES (est): 5.6MM **Privately Held**
WEB: www.kenowa.com
SIC: 3449 7692 Miscellaneous metalwork; welding repair

(G-8112)
KENRIE INC
500 E 8th St Ste 1100 (49423-4751)
PHONE 616 494-3200
Kenneth Vennesland, *President*
EMP: 18 **EST:** 2005
SALES (est): 2.1MM **Privately Held**
WEB: www.kenrie.com
SIC: 3545 5084 Precision tools, machinists'; industrial machine parts

(G-8113)
KESKA LLC
87 Chriscraft Ln (49424-6680)
PHONE 616 283-7056
Steven Hoek, *President*
EMP: 4 **EST:** 2015
SQ FT: 1,000
SALES (est): 252.1K **Privately Held**
WEB: www.keskacorp.com
SIC: 3672 Printed circuit boards

(G-8114)
KOETJE WOOD PRODUCTS INC
11743 Greenway Dr (49424-8654)
PHONE 616 393-9191
Terry Koetje, *President*
Jeff Bussler, *Treasurer*
EMP: 4
SQ FT: 6,000 **Privately Held**
WEB: www.curvedwood.info
SIC: 2499 Decorative wood & woodwork

(G-8115)
KRAFT HEINZ FOODS COMPANY
431 W 16th St (49423-3445)
PHONE 616 396-6557
Jerry Shoup, *Plant Mgr*
Ronald Ross, *Maintence Staff*
EMP: 7
SALES (corp-wide): 26.1B **Publicly Held**
WEB: www.kraftheinzcompany.com
SIC: 2032 2099 2033 Canned specialties; vinegar; canned fruits & specialties

HQ: Kraft Heinz Foods Company
1 Ppg Pl Ste 3400
Pittsburgh PA 15222
412 456-5700

(G-8116)
KROSS KRAFT LLC
4731 N 168th Ave (49424-1058)
PHONE 616 399-9167
Don Kross, *Principal*
EMP: 4 **EST:** 2014
SALES (est): 166.4K **Privately Held**
SIC: 2022 Natural cheese

(G-8117)
KYLER INDUSTRIES INC
192 E 48th St (49423-9307)
PHONE 616 392-1042
Thomas J Bratt, *President*
EMP: 5 **EST:** 1995
SALES (est): 807.2K **Privately Held**
WEB: www.kyler-industries.com
SIC: 2591 Blinds vertical; mini blinds

(G-8118)
L & W INC
Also Called: L & W Engineering Co
808 E 32nd St (49423-9128)
PHONE 616 394-9665
Trent Kauffman, *Vice Pres*
Maureen Mc Nabb, *Production*
Jim Swanston, *Branch Mgr*
Ginger Erickson, *Manager*
Roger Huffman, *Anesthesiology*
EMP: 7
SALES (corp-wide): 3.1B **Privately Held**
WEB: www.autokiniton.com
SIC: 3465 3443 Automotive stampings; bins, prefabricated metal plate
HQ: L & W, Inc.
17757 Woodland Dr
New Boston MI 48164
734 397-6300

(G-8119)
L PERRIGO COMPANY
13295 Reflections Dr (49424-8220)
PHONE 616 738-0150
David Gibbons, *Ch of Bd*
Matthew Laduke, *Research*
John Anderson, *Engineer*
Brian Conrad, *Plant Engr*
Jack Dang, *Financial Analy*
EMP: 4 **Privately Held**
WEB: www.perrigo.com
SIC: 2834 Vitamin, nutrient & hematinic preparations for human use
HQ: L. Perrigo Company
515 Eastern Ave
Allegan MI 49010
269 673-8451

(G-8120)
LAKE EFFECT ALPACAS
4266 60th St (49423-9329)
PHONE 616 836-7906
EMP: 4 **EST:** 2017
SALES (est): 76.9K **Privately Held**
SIC: 2231 Alpacas, mohair: woven

(G-8121)
LAKE MICHIGAN WIRE LLC
4211 Hallacy Dr (49424-8723)
PHONE 616 786-9200
Eric Anderson, *Mng Member*
EMP: 15 **EST:** 2009
SALES (est): 2.8MM **Privately Held**
WEB: www.lakemichiganwire.com
SIC: 3312 Wire products, steel or iron

(G-8122)
LAKESIDE PROPERTY SERVICES
14250 Ottawa Creek Ln (49424-8534)
PHONE 863 455-9038
Andrew Fikoski, *President*
EMP: 5
SALES (est): 111.6K **Privately Held**
WEB: www.lakeshorepropertymanagement.com
SIC: 0782 3953 4959 Mowing services, lawn; stencils, painting & marking; road, airport & parking lot maintenance services

Holland - Ottawa County (G-8123)   GEOGRAPHIC SECTION

(G-8123)
LANDSCAPE STONE SUPPLY INC
5960 136th Ave (49424-9477)
PHONE..................................616 953-2028
Brian Drabczyk, *Sales Staff*
EMP: 8 EST: 2011
SALES (est): 426.2K **Privately Held**
WEB: www.silverridgestone.com
SIC: 3281 Cut stone & stone products

(G-8124)
LAS BRAZAS TORTILLAS
3416 Crystal Valley Ct (49424-8517)
PHONE..................................616 886-0737
Isaias Sanchez, *Partner*
Juligta Rodriguez, *Partner*
EMP: 7 EST: 1998
SQ FT: 3,500
SALES (est): 475K **Privately Held**
WEB: www.las-brazas-tortilla-factory.hub.biz
SIC: 2099 Tortillas, fresh or refrigerated

(G-8125)
LEON INTERIORS INC (DH)
Also Called: Leon Automotive Interiors
88 E 48th St (49423-9307)
PHONE..................................616 422-7557
Shannon White, *CEO*
Roger Nelson, *Business Mgr*
Beth Haseley, *Opers Staff*
Kyler Diekevers, *Engineer*
Dave Scheidmantel, *VP Sales*
◆ EMP: 370 EST: 1984
SALES (est): 191.6MM
SALES (corp-wide): 316MM **Privately Held**
WEB: www.motusintegrated.com
SIC: 3089 3714 3086 Molding primary plastic; motor vehicle parts & accessories; plastics foam products
HQ: Motus Llc
    88 E 48th St
    Holland MI 49423
    616 422-7557

(G-8126)
LG ENERGY SOLUTION MICH INC (HQ)
Also Called: Lg Chem Battery Co
1 Lg Way (49423-8574)
PHONE..................................616 494-7100
Prabhakar Patil, *CEO*
Bon Chul Koo, *President*
Jae Wook Jung, *Corp Secy*
Jang Woo Park, *CFO*
◆ EMP: 248 EST: 2005
SQ FT: 618,000
SALES (est): 396.9MM **Privately Held**
WEB: www.lgchem.com
SIC: 3691 Storage batteries

(G-8127)
LIBERTY AUTOMOTIVE TECH LLC
4554 128th Ave (49424-9257)
PHONE..................................269 487-8114
Scott Irwin,
EMP: 5
SALES (est): 150.7K **Privately Held**
WEB: www.libertyautotech.net
SIC: 3999 Manufacturing industries

(G-8128)
LIBERTY PLASTICS INC
13170 Ransom St (49424-8715)
PHONE..................................616 994-7033
Richard Lynema, *President*
Matt Lynema, *Prdtn Mgr*
Larry Bruursema, *Maintence Staff*
EMP: 7 EST: 2000
SQ FT: 2,500
SALES (est): 1.2MM **Privately Held**
WEB: www.libertyplastics.com
SIC: 3089 Injection molding of plastics

(G-8129)
LIGHTNING MACHINE HOLLAND LLC
128 Manufacturers Dr (49424-1893)
PHONE..................................616 786-9280
Rich Tanis,
EMP: 10 EST: 1990
SQ FT: 8,600
SALES (est): 1.7MM **Privately Held**
WEB: www.lightningmachine.com
SIC: 3545 3599 Boring machine attachments (machine tool accessories); precision measuring tools; machine shop, jobbing & repair

(G-8130)
LOTUS CORPORATION
100 Aniline Ave N Ste 180 (49424-6682)
PHONE..................................616 494-0112
Anthony Ho, *President*
Anh Ho, *Exec VP*
EMP: 7 EST: 1989
SQ FT: 14,000
SALES (est): 475K **Privately Held**
WEB: www.lotuscorporation.com
SIC: 3544 Special dies, tools, jigs & fixtures

(G-8131)
MACHINE GUARD & COVER CO
6187 136th Ave (49424-8290)
PHONE..................................616 392-8188
William Labarge III, *President*
W Labarge Jr, *Vice Pres*
EMP: 6 EST: 1994
SALES (est): 1MM **Privately Held**
WEB: www.machineguard.com
SIC: 3432 Plastic plumbing fixture fittings, assembly

(G-8132)
MACHINE SHOP SERVICES LLC
4211 Hallacy Dr (49424-8723)
PHONE..................................616 396-4898
EMP: 6 EST: 2020
SALES (est): 368.9K **Privately Held**
SIC: 3599 Machine shop, jobbing & repair

(G-8133)
MAGNA
3401 128th Ave (49424-9263)
PHONE..................................616 786-7403
Aaron McCarthy, *Exec VP*
Eric Wilds, *Exec VP*
David McInerney, *QC Mgr*
Michael Baur, *Manager*
Leigh Rebone, *Manager*
EMP: 19 EST: 2015
SALES (est): 726.8K **Privately Held**
WEB: www.magna.com
SIC: 3231 3442 Products of purchased glass; metal doors, sash & trim

(G-8134)
MAGNA MIRRORS AMERICA INC
40th Street Divison
414 E 40th St (49423-5383)
PHONE..................................616 786-7300
John Roberts, *General Mgr*
EMP: 5
SALES (corp-wide): 32.6B **Privately Held**
WEB: www.magna.com
SIC: 3231 3647 3827 Mirrors, truck & automobile: made from purchased glass; windshields, glass: made from purchased glass; dome lights, automotive; automotive lighting fixtures; optical instruments & lenses
HQ: Magna Mirrors Of America, Inc.
    5085 Kraft Ave Se
    Grand Rapids MI 49512
    616 786-7000

(G-8135)
MAGNA MIRRORS AMERICA INC
Also Called: Jfd North
3601 John F Donnelly Dr (49424-9338)
PHONE..................................616 738-0115
Jim Brodie, *Branch Mgr*
EMP: 5
SALES (corp-wide): 32.6B **Privately Held**
WEB: www.magna.com
SIC: 3231 Mirrored glass
HQ: Magna Mirrors Of America, Inc.
    5085 Kraft Ave Se
    Grand Rapids MI 49512
    616 786-7000

(G-8136)
MAGNA MIRRORS AMERICA INC
3401 128th Ave (49424-9263)
PHONE..................................616 786-7000
Michael Baur, *Branch Mgr*
EMP: 6
SQ FT: 25,000
SALES (corp-wide): 32.6B **Privately Held**
WEB: www.magna.com
SIC: 5013 3231 Automotive servicing equipment; mirrors, truck & automobile: made from purchased glass
HQ: Magna Mirrors Of America, Inc.
    5085 Kraft Ave Se
    Grand Rapids MI 49512
    616 786-7000

(G-8137)
MAGNA MIRRORS AMERICA INC
3501 John F Donnelly Dr (49424-9284)
PHONE..................................616 786-7772
Edward Scott, *Engineer*
Matt Tumey, *Engineer*
Stacey Burroughs, *Branch Mgr*
EMP: 800
SALES (corp-wide): 32.6B **Privately Held**
WEB: www.magna.com
SIC: 3231 Mirrors, truck & automobile: made from purchased glass
HQ: Magna Mirrors Of America, Inc.
    5085 Kraft Ave Se
    Grand Rapids MI 49512
    616 786-7000

(G-8138)
MAJESTIC SONRISE ALPACAS
1189 Sorrento Ct (49423-6617)
PHONE..................................616 848-7414
EMP: 4 EST: 2015
SALES (est): 59.9K **Privately Held**
WEB: www.majesticsonrisealpacas.com.cutestat.com
SIC: 2231 Alpacas, mohair: woven

(G-8139)
MASLO FABRICATION LLC
155 Manufacturers Dr (49424-1894)
PHONE..................................616 298-7700
Jim England, *Mng Member*
EMP: 4 EST: 2010 **Privately Held**
WEB: www.maslofab.com
SIC: 3441 4492 Fabricated structural metal; towing & tugboat service

(G-8140)
MB FLUID SERVICES LLC
11372 E Lakewood Blvd (49424-9605)
PHONE..................................616 392-7036
Mike Boes,
EMP: 10 EST: 2017
SALES (est): 772.6K **Privately Held**
WEB: www.mbfluids.com
SIC: 2992 Lubricating oils & greases

(G-8141)
MECA SYSTEME USA
11846 Greenway Dr (49424-8956)
PHONE..................................616 294-1439
EMP: 7 EST: 2017
SALES (est): 87.3K **Privately Held**
WEB: www.meca-systeme.com
SIC: 2621 Paper mills

(G-8142)
MECHANICAL TRANSPLANTER CO LLC
1150 Central Ave (49423-5230)
PHONE..................................616 396-8738
Steve Van Loo, *Mng Member*
Dan Timmer,
▲ EMP: 20
SQ FT: 58,000
SALES: 4.5MM **Privately Held**
WEB: www.mechanicaltransplanter.com
SIC: 3523 Transplanters

(G-8143)
METAL FLOW CORPORATION
11694 James St (49424-8963)
PHONE..................................616 392-7976
Leslie Brown, *Ch of Bd*
Robert K Knittel, *President*
Kelly Springer, *COO*
Chuck Caesar, *Exec VP*
Kirk Bush, *Vice Pres*
▼ EMP: 230 EST: 1978
SQ FT: 150,000
SALES (est): 70MM **Privately Held**
WEB: www.metalflow.com
SIC: 3469 Stamping metal for the trade

(G-8144)
METAL STANDARD CORP
286 Hedcor St (49423-9364)
PHONE..................................616 396-6356
Mike Wiersema, *CEO*
Troy Thompson, *Engineer*
Brian Scalabrino, *Finance Dir*
Beth Lundquist, *HR Admin*
Chris McNicholas, *Technology*
▲ EMP: 90 EST: 1947
SQ FT: 36,000
SALES (est): 9.7MM **Privately Held**
WEB: www.metalstandard.com
SIC: 3444 Sheet metalwork

(G-8145)
METALUTION TOOL DIE
60 W 64th St (49423-9356)
PHONE..................................616 355-9700
Mike Finsky, *Principal*
EMP: 11 EST: 2010
SALES (est): 530.9K **Privately Held**
WEB: www.metalution.net
SIC: 3599 Machine shop, jobbing & repair

(G-8146)
MHR INC
Also Called: Mix Head Repair
78 Veterans Dr (49423-7813)
PHONE..................................616 394-0191
Doug Breuker, *President*
Larry Dyke, *General Mgr*
Julie Lynema, *Manager*
Patricia Breuker, *Admin Sec*
EMP: 10 EST: 1989
SQ FT: 6,400
SALES (est): 1.5MM **Privately Held**
WEB: www.mhr-inc.com
SIC: 7699 3569 5084 Industrial machinery & equipment repair; pumps & pumping equipment repair; assembly machines, non-metalworking; industrial machinery & equipment

(G-8147)
MICHIGAN WOOD FUELS LLC
1125 Industrial Ave (49423-5318)
PHONE..................................616 355-4955
Benjamin Rose, *CEO*
James Ackerson, *Plant Mgr*
Robert Oswald, *Plant Mgr*
Randall Grinwis, *Safety Mgr*
Dalemarie James, *Administration*
EMP: 16 EST: 2012
SALES (est): 4.5MM **Privately Held**
WEB: www.mipellets.com
SIC: 2499 Mulch or sawdust products, wood
PA: Northern Biomass Fuels Llc
    341 W Belden Ave
    Chicago IL 60614
    773 697-7186

(G-8148)
MIDWEST HEAT TREAT INC
Also Called: Midwest Pallet
2127 112th Ave (49424-9626)
P.O. Box 2097 (49422-2097)
PHONE..................................616 395-9763
David B Sligh, *CEO*
Tim Vandort, *President*
EMP: 20 EST: 2005
SQ FT: 45,000 **Privately Held**
SIC: 2448 3398 Wood pallets & skids; metal heat treating

(G-8149)
MOTUS HOLDINGS LLC (DH)
88 E 48th St (49423-9307)
PHONE..................................616 422-7557
Shannon White, *Mng Member*
EMP: 0 EST: 2014

Holland - Ottawa County (G-8175)

SALES (est): 262.9MM
SALES (corp-wide): 316MM Privately Held
WEB: www.motusintegrated.com
SIC: 6719 3465 Investment holding companies, except banks; body parts, automobile: stamped metal
HQ: Motus Us Holding B.V.
Prof. J.H. Bavincklaan 2
Amstelveen
205 214-777

(G-8150)
MOTUS LLC (DH)
Also Called: Motus Integrated Technologies
88 E 48th St (49423-9307)
PHONE.................................616 422-7557
Lisa Carter, President
Adam Badders, Opers Staff
Gabe Strickler, Senior Buyer
James Kaiser, Purchasing
Dan Buchanan, Engineer
▲ EMP: 180 EST: 2013
SALES (est): 262.9MM
SALES (corp-wide): 316MM Privately Held
WEB: www.motusintegrated.com
SIC: 3465 Body parts, automobile: stamped metal
HQ: Motus Holdings Llc
88 E 48th St
Holland MI 49423
616 422-7557

(G-8151)
NATIONAL BULK EQUIPMENT INC (PA)
12838 Stainless Dr (49424-8218)
PHONE.................................616 399-2220
Todd Reed, President
Dic K Dykema, Vice Pres
Ellen Kaines, Vice Pres
Chad Mitchem, Project Mgr
Mark Walli, Safety Mgr
◆ EMP: 109 EST: 1976
SQ FT: 65,000
SALES (est): 29.2MM Privately Held
WEB: www.nbe-inc.com
SIC: 3599 5084 Custom machinery; industrial machinery & equipment

(G-8152)
NELSON STEEL PRODUCTS INC
410 E 48th St (49423-8535)
PHONE.................................616 396-1515
Wallace Ryzenga Jr, President
Derek Helmholdt, Accountant
Paul Zeman, Sales Staff
Mark Ryzenga, Manager
EMP: 55 EST: 1963
SQ FT: 57,000
SALES (est): 9.9MM Privately Held
WEB: www.nelsonsteelproducts.com
SIC: 3444 7692 3469 3443 Sheet metalwork; welding repair; stamping metal for the trade; fabricated plate work (boiler shop)

(G-8153)
NEW 11 INC
Also Called: Power Manufacturing
1886 Russel Ct (49423-8749)
PHONE.................................616 494-9370
Todd Mulder, Owner
Troy Dokter, General Mgr
EMP: 33 EST: 1990
SQ FT: 40,000
SALES (est): 1.4MM Privately Held
WEB: www.powermanufacturing.net
SIC: 3469 3317 Stamping metal for the trade; steel pipe & tubes

(G-8154)
NEW HOLLAND BREWING CO LLC
684 Commerce Ct (49424-2913)
PHONE.................................616 355-2941
Shawna Cantu, General Mgr
Eli Harper, General Mgr
Joel Petersen, Vice Pres
Brad Kamphuis, Opers Staff
Jason Salas, Production
▲ EMP: 200 EST: 1996

SALES (est): 44.8MM Privately Held
WEB: www.newhollandbrew.com
SIC: 2082 5813 5812 Beer (alcoholic beverage); drinking places; eating places

(G-8155)
NEW PRODUCT DEVELOPMENT LLC
785 Mary Ave (49424-1615)
PHONE.................................616 399-6253
Jack Hartman, Owner
EMP: 5 EST: 2001
SALES (est): 246.6K Privately Held
SIC: 3089 Flower pots, plastic

(G-8156)
NORTEK AIR SOLUTIONS LLC
Also Called: Mammoth
4433 Holland Ave (49424-8279)
PHONE.................................616 738-7148
EMP: 60
SALES (corp-wide): 1B Privately Held
SIC: 3585 3567 3564 3561 Mfg Refrig/Heat Equip Indstl Furnace/Ovens Blowers/Fans Pumps/Pumping Equip
HQ: Nortek Air Solutions, Llc
4001 Valley Indus Blvd S
Shakopee MN 63368
952 358-6600

(G-8157)
NUVAR INC
895 E 40th St (49423-5397)
PHONE.................................616 394-5779
Mark Kuyper, President
Jeff Minarik, VP Opers
Dan Diedrich, Purch Agent
Sam Hansen, Engineer
Don Karaus, Engineer
◆ EMP: 30 EST: 1989
SQ FT: 40,000
SALES (est): 10.3MM Privately Held
WEB: www.nuvar.com
SIC: 2511 Wood household furniture

(G-8158)
OMT VEYHL
4430 136th Ave Ste 3 (49424-8499)
PHONE.................................616 738-6688
David Guy, Vice Pres
Jordan Sloan, Production
Pat Winters, Purch Mgr
Mark Johnson, Purch Agent
Brian Kooshian, Purch Agent
▲ EMP: 5 EST: 2006
SALES (est): 1.2MM Privately Held
WEB: www.omt-veyhl.com
SIC: 3499 Furniture parts, metal

(G-8159)
PANDA KING EXPRESS
520 Butternut Dr Ste 30 (49424-1587)
PHONE.................................616 796-3286
Yong Lin, Principal
EMP: 4 EST: 2005
SALES (est): 170.2K Privately Held
WEB: www.pandaexpress.com
SIC: 2741 Miscellaneous publishing

(G-8160)
PARKWAY ELC COMMUNICATIONS LLC (PA)
Also Called: Westshore Testing
11952 James St Ste A (49424-9618)
PHONE.................................616 392-2788
Doug Mitchell, COO
Joshua Emmons, Warehouse Mgr
EMP: 70 EST: 1945
SQ FT: 20,000
SALES (est): 23.1MM Privately Held
WEB: www.parkway.us
SIC: 1731 3679 General electrical contractor; voice controls

(G-8161)
PEERLESS WASTE SOLUTIONS LLC
510 E 40th St (49423-5313)
PHONE.................................616 355-2800
Donald Pellegrini, President
David Geschwendt,
EDP PWS LLC,
Rodney Webb,
EMP: 7 EST: 2008
SQ FT: 30,000 Privately Held

SIC: 3821 Sterilizers

(G-8162)
PERMALOC CORPORATION
Also Called: Permaloc Aluminum Edging
13505 Barry St (49424-9411)
PHONE.................................616 399-9600
Dan Zwier, President
Sally Zwier, Vice Pres
Dennis Klingenberg, Plant Mgr
Adam Zwier, Administration
▼ EMP: 13 EST: 1983
SQ FT: 14,000
SALES (est): 2.8MM Privately Held
WEB: www.permaloc.com
SIC: 3469 3353 Stamping metal for the trade; aluminum sheet, plate & foil

(G-8163)
PERRIGO COMPANY
3896 58th St (49423-9348)
PHONE.................................616 396-0941
Richard Waldschmidt, Opers Staff
Sarah Rodriguez, Manager
Peter Miller, Technology
Gretchen Starr, Commercial
EMP: 4 Privately Held
WEB: www.perrigo.com
SIC: 2834 Pharmaceutical preparations
HQ: Perrigo Company
515 Eastern Ave
Allegan MI 49010
269 673-8451

(G-8164)
PERRIGO COMPANY
Also Called: Holland Intrchnge Drv Dist Ctr
796 Interchange Dr (49423-9592)
PHONE.................................269 686-1782
EMP: 4 Privately Held
WEB: www.perrigo.com
SIC: 2834 Pharmaceutical preparations
HQ: Perrigo Company
515 Eastern Ave
Allegan MI 49010
269 673-8451

(G-8165)
PETRA ELECTRONIC MFG INC
3440 Windquest Dr (49424-8069)
PHONE.................................616 877-1991
Jack Doornbos, President
Jamie Vanderhaar, Accounting Mgr
EMP: 18 EST: 1996
SALES (est): 3.6MM Privately Held
WEB: www.westshoredesign.com
SIC: 3672 Printed circuit boards

(G-8166)
PLASMA-TEC INC
455 Douglas Ave (49424-2772)
PHONE.................................616 455-2593
Laurence A Wysong, CEO
Christopher Wysong, President
Mike Schroeder, Vice Pres
EMP: 31 EST: 1981
SALES (est): 4.6MM Privately Held
WEB: www.avonmachining.com
SIC: 3599 3479 3561 3511 Machine shop, jobbing & repair; coating of metals & formed products; pumps & pumping equipment; turbines & turbine generator sets

(G-8167)
PORTER CORP
Also Called: Poligon
4240 136th Ave (49424-8442)
PHONE.................................616 399-1963
Gary Vandyke, President
Tom Gold, Business Mgr
Mitch Harsevoort, Production
Steve Asselin, Engineer
Brad Fritz, CIO
EMP: 92 EST: 1964
SQ FT: 112,000
SALES (est): 18.9MM Privately Held
WEB: www.portercorp.com
SIC: 3448 Panels for prefabricated metal buildings; prefabricated metal buildings

(G-8168)
PRE-CUT PATTERNS
26 W 6th St (49423-2820)
PHONE.................................616 392-4415
Lori Corbat-Appel, President

EMP: 5 EST: 2002
SALES (est): 74.1K Privately Held
WEB: www.pre-cut.com
SIC: 3479 Metal coating & allied service

(G-8169)
PREFERRED WELDING LLC
4552 136th Ave (49424-9452)
PHONE.................................616 294-1068
EMP: 8 EST: 2019
SALES (est): 747.8K Privately Held
WEB: www.preferredweld.com
SIC: 7692 Welding repair

(G-8170)
PRIME WOOD PRODUCTS INC (PA)
Also Called: De Antigua
308 N River Ave (49424-2146)
PHONE.................................616 399-4700
Herman Raad, President
EMP: 9 EST: 1984
SQ FT: 7,500
SALES (est): 871.9K Privately Held
SIC: 2431 5023 2511 2434 Interior & ornamental woodwork & trim; mirrors & pictures, framed & unframed; wood household furniture; wood kitchen cabinets

(G-8171)
PRINT HAUS
295 120th Ave Ste 10 (49424-2192)
PHONE.................................616 786-4030
William Maclean, President
EMP: 5 EST: 1985
SALES (est): 408.9K Privately Held
WEB: www.printhaus.com
SIC: 2752 Commercial printing, offset

(G-8172)
PRINTERY INC
79 Clover St (49423-2941)
PHONE.................................616 396-4655
Robert Hydenberk, President
EMP: 35 EST: 1940
SALES (est): 1.3MM
SALES (corp-wide): 17.5B Publicly Held
WEB: www.printeryonline.com
SIC: 2752 2791 2789 2759 Commercial printing, offset; typesetting; bookbinding & related work; commercial printing
HQ: Mps Holdco, Inc.
5800 W Grand River Ave
Lansing MI 48906

(G-8173)
QUALITY MACHINE & AUTOMATION
184 Manufacturers Dr (49424-1893)
PHONE.................................616 399-4415
Scott Steggerda, President
Steve Meyaard, COO
Ben Baker, Purch Agent
Logan Kroll, Engineer
Kara Van Bronkhorst, Office Mgr
EMP: 16 EST: 1991
SQ FT: 12,000
SALES (est): 3.6MM Privately Held
WEB: www.qmautomation.com
SIC: 3599 Machine shop, jobbing & repair

(G-8174)
QUINCY STREET INC
13350 Quincy St (49424-9460)
PHONE.................................616 399-3330
Douglas M Miller, CEO
Philip A Holtrop, CFO
EMP: 165 EST: 1992
SQ FT: 100,000
SALES (est): 27.4MM Privately Held
WEB: www.quincystreetinc.com
SIC: 2013 Prepared pork products from purchased pork
HQ: Indiana Packers Corporation
6755 W 100 N
Delphi IN 46923

(G-8175)
R S L TOOL LLC
13417 New Hlland St Ste 2 (49424)
PHONE.................................616 786-2880
Robert Jacobs, Mng Member
Lauralee L Jacobs,
EMP: 5 EST: 1998
SQ FT: 1,800 Privately Held

Holland - Ottawa County (G-8176) — GEOGRAPHIC SECTION

WEB: www.rsltool.com
SIC: 3544 Special dies & tools

(G-8176)
RARE BIRD HOLDINGS LLC
849 Allen Dr (49423-4501)
PHONE 616 335-9463
Leon Devisser, *Principal*
EMP: 5 **EST:** 2016
SALES (est): 73.3K **Privately Held**
SIC: 2082 Malt beverages

(G-8177)
RECURSIVE LLC
14595 Jamesway Ave (49424-1474)
PHONE 904 449-2386
EMP: 4 **EST:** 2019
SALES (est): 98.1K **Privately Held**
SIC: 7372 Prepackaged software

(G-8178)
REKMAKKER MILLWORK INC
6035 145th Ave (49423-8905)
PHONE 616 546-3680
Randy Spykerman, *Principal*
EMP: 4 **EST:** 2010
SALES (est): 486.9K **Privately Held**
WEB: www.rekmakkermillwork.com
SIC: 2431 Millwork

(G-8179)
REPCOLITE PAINTS INC (PA)
Also Called: Repcolite Decorating Center
473 W 17th St (49423-3495)
PHONE 616 396-5213
Daniel Altena, *President*
David Altena, *Vice Pres*
Victor Vigil, *Production*
Rob Dale, *Controller*
Dave Helmholdt, *Cust Mgr*
EMP: 52 **EST:** 1948
SQ FT: 22,000
SALES (est): 12.4MM **Privately Held**
WEB: www.repcolite.com
SIC: 2851 5231 Paints & paint additives; paint

(G-8180)
REQUEST FOODS INC (PA)
3460 John F Donnelly Dr (49424-9569)
P.O. Box 2577 (49422-2577)
PHONE 616 786-0900
Jack Dewitt, *President*
Thong Chau, *Vice Pres*
Connie Knap, *Vice Pres*
Larry Vanderkolk, *Vice Pres*
Cheryl Zouwen, *Purchasing*
◆ **EMP:** 371 **EST:** 1988
SQ FT: 350,000
SALES (est): 176.2MM **Privately Held**
WEB: www.requestfoods.com
SIC: 3556 2038 Food products machinery; frozen specialties

(G-8181)
RJ CORP
Also Called: Red Wing Bags
2127 112th Ave (49424-9626)
P.O. Box 2877 (49422-2877)
PHONE 616 396-0552
Randy Lamer, *President*
Lisa Lamer, *Vice Pres*
▲ **EMP:** 9 **EST:** 2004
SQ FT: 5,000
SALES (est): 487K **Privately Held**
WEB: www.redwingbags.com
SIC: 2396 Printing & embossing on plastics fabric articles

(G-8182)
ROD CHOMPER INC
4249 58th St (49423-9315)
PHONE 616 392-9677
Wayne A Bouwman, *President*
Harold Tanis, *Sales Mgr*
▼ **EMP:** 16 **EST:** 1984
SQ FT: 2,800
SALES (est): 629.5K **Privately Held**
WEB: www.rodchomper.com
SIC: 3549 3547 3541 3496 Metalworking machinery; rolling mill machinery; machine tools, metal cutting type; miscellaneous fabricated wire products; blast furnaces & steel mills

(G-8183)
ROL USA INC
Also Called: Rol Group
694 E 40th St (49423-5327)
PHONE 616 499-8484
Norman Chambers, *Principal*
Bowman Brent, *Engineer*
Mark Walburn, *CFO*
Toni Zacker-Houseman, *Accountant*
▲ **EMP:** 2 **EST:** 2014
SALES (est): 1.2MM
SALES (corp-wide): 181.7MM **Privately Held**
SIC: 3999 Barber & beauty shop equipment
PA: Livan Holding Ab
   Flygplatsv 1
   Jonkoping 555 9
   363 688-00

(G-8184)
RUSSELLS TECHNICAL PDTS INC
1883 Russel Ct (49423-8749)
PHONE 616 392-3161
Gary Molenaar, *President*
Bill Bench, *Vice Pres*
William J Bench, *Vice Pres*
Ray Resseguie, *Plant Mgr*
Dave Jolly, *Engineer*
EMP: 45 **EST:** 1972
SQ FT: 31,000
SALES (est): 11.4MM **Privately Held**
WEB: www.russells-tech.com
SIC: 3829 Measuring & controlling devices

(G-8185)
RUTHERFORD & ASSOCIATES INC
1009 Productions Ct (49423-9122)
PHONE 616 392-5000
Mike Rutherford, *President*
John Bonney, *Vice Pres*
John Ross, *Vice Pres*
Brian Rutherford, *Vice Pres*
Todd Clevenger, *Project Mgr*
EMP: 25 **EST:** 1985
SALES (est): 5MM **Privately Held**
WEB: www.eostar.com
SIC: 3695 5734 5961 7372 Computer software tape & disks: blank, rigid & floppy; software, business & non-game; software, computer games; computer software, mail order; prepackaged software

(G-8186)
SAF-HOLLAND INC
430 W 18th St (49423-3904)
PHONE 616 396-6501
Richard Muzzy, *CEO*
Simon Low, *General Mgr*
Samuel Martin, *Branch Mgr*
Ken Griswold, *Director*
EMP: 7
SALES (corp-wide): 1.1B **Privately Held**
WEB: www.safholland.us
SIC: 3714 3715 Motor vehicle parts & accessories; trailer bodies
HQ: Saf-Holland, Inc.
   1950 Industrial Blvd
   Muskegon MI 49442
   231 773-3271

(G-8187)
SEBRIGHT MACHINING INC
613 Commerce Ct (49424-2924)
PHONE 616 399-0445
Gerald E Sebright, *President*
Carolyn E Sebright, *Corp Secy*
EMP: 15 **EST:** 1990
SQ FT: 6,000
SALES (est): 780.4K **Privately Held**
WEB: www.sebrightmachining.com
SIC: 3599 Machine shop, jobbing & repair

(G-8188)
SEKISUI KYDEX LLC
1305 Lincoln Ave (49423-9381)
PHONE 616 394-3810
Nik Taritas, *Vice Pres*
Mike Karr, *VP Opers*
Dave Hebda, *Plant Mgr*
Jake Vanderploeg, *Project Mgr*
Peggy Reeder, *Buyer*
EMP: 100 **Privately Held**
WEB: www.kydex.com
SIC: 2821 Plastics materials & resins
HQ: Sekisui Kydex, Llc
   6685 Lowe St
   Bloomsburg PA 17815
   570 389-5814

(G-8189)
SHAMROCK INDUSTRIES LLC
15720 Ryan Dr (49424-5513)
PHONE 616 566-6214
Connor Sweeney, *Principal*
EMP: 10 **EST:** 2014
SALES (est): 108.4K **Privately Held**
WEB: www.shamrockdiecast.com
SIC: 3999 Manufacturing industries

(G-8190)
SHERMAN DAIRY PRODUCTS CO INC
Also Called: Sherman Dairy Bar
345 E 48th St Ste 200 (49423-5381)
PHONE 269 637-8251
Robert V Eisenman, *President*
Jeanine Eisenman, *Vice Pres*
EMP: 29 **EST:** 1972
SALES (est): 2.4MM **Privately Held**
WEB: www.shermanicecream.com
SIC: 2024 Ice cream, bulk

(G-8191)
SHORELINE CONTAINER LLC (PA)
Also Called: Shoreline Container and Packg
4450 136th Ave (49424-9452)
P.O. Box 1993 (49422-1993)
PHONE 616 399-2088
Bruce Patterson, *President*
Bob Zuker, *VP Opers*
Rick Vandyke, *Purch Mgr*
Carolyn Bos, *Human Res Mgr*
Doug Temple, *VP Sales*
EMP: 163 **EST:** 1963
SQ FT: 203,000
SALES (est): 47.6MM **Privately Held**
WEB: www.shorelinecontainer.com
SIC: 2653 2671 Boxes, corrugated: made from purchased materials; partitions, corrugated: made from purchased materials; packaging paper & plastics film, coated & laminated

(G-8192)
SHORELINE CREATIONS LTD (PA)
Also Called: Group Tour Magazines
2465 112th Ave (49424-9657)
PHONE 616 393-2077
Carl Wassink, *President*
Ruth Wassink, *Exec VP*
Mark Dryer, *Prdtn Mgr*
Jamie Cannon, *Sales Staff*
Cannon Jamie, *Sales Staff*
EMP: 23 **EST:** 1981
SQ FT: 7,500
SALES (est): 2.3MM **Privately Held**
WEB: www.grouptour.com
SIC: 2721 2741 Magazines: publishing only, not printed on site; guides: publishing only, not printed on site

(G-8193)
SHORELINE MANUFACTURING LLC
11867 Greenway Dr (49424-8971)
PHONE 616 834-1503
Patti Klingenberg, *Office Mgr*
EMP: 8 **EST:** 2017
SALES (est): 1.1MM **Privately Held**
WEB: www.shorelinemanufacturing.com
SIC: 3999 Manufacturing industries

(G-8194)
SHORELINE MANUFACTURING LLC
155 Manufacturers Dr (49424-1894)
PHONE 616 834-1503
EMP: 4 **EST:** 2014
SALES (est): 191.8K **Privately Held**
WEB: www.shorelinemanufacturing.com
SIC: 3999 Manufacturing industries

(G-8195)
SHORES CREMATION & BURIAL
11939 James St (49424-9658)
PHONE 616 395-3630
EMP: 4 **EST:** 2011
SALES (est): 87.8K **Privately Held**
WEB: www.shorescb.com
SIC: 3272 Burial vaults, concrete or precast terrazzo

(G-8196)
SIGVARIS INC
13055 Riley St Ste 30 (49424-7240)
PHONE 616 741-4281
Dan Karadsheh, *Manager*
EMP: 25
SALES (corp-wide): 392.5K **Privately Held**
WEB: www.sigvaris.com
SIC: 3842 Surgical appliances & supplies
HQ: Sigvaris Inc
   1119 Highway 74 S
   Peachtree City GA 30269
   770 631-1778

(G-8197)
SLOAN TRANSPORTATION PDTS INC
534 E 48th St (49423-9502)
PHONE 616 395-5600
Thomas Bronz, *President*
▲ **EMP:** 33 **EST:** 1973
SQ FT: 105,000
SALES (est): 5.1MM **Privately Held**
WEB: www.tramecsloan.com
SIC: 3625 3561 3491 3714 Relays & industrial controls; pumps & pumping equipment; industrial valves; fuel systems & parts, motor vehicle

(G-8198)
SMW TOOLING INC
Also Called: S M W
11781 Greenway Dr (49424-8654)
PHONE 616 355-9822
Steve Zeerip, *President*
Elizabeth Zeerip, *Treasurer*
EMP: 10 **EST:** 1990
SQ FT: 12,000
SALES (est): 1.1MM **Privately Held**
WEB: www.smwtooling.com
SIC: 3599 Machine shop, jobbing & repair

(G-8199)
SOLAR STREET LIGHTS USA LLC
169 Manufacturers Dr # 1 (49424-1904)
PHONE 269 983-6361
Craig Brumels,
◆ **EMP:** 6 **EST:** 2009
SALES (est): 546.5K **Privately Held**
WEB: www.solarstreetlightsusa.com
SIC: 3829 Solarimeters

(G-8200)
SOLID LOGIC LLC
Also Called: Smooth Logics
3455 John F Donnelly Dr (49424-9207)
PHONE 616 738-8922
Jill Streur, *Manager*
Benjamin Fogg,
EMP: 13 **EST:** 2010
SALES (est): 806.7K **Privately Held**
WEB: www.counterpart-erp.com
SIC: 7372 Business oriented computer software

(G-8201)
STARBUCK MACHINING INC
13413 New Holland St (49424-9407)
PHONE 616 399-9720
Richard Starbuck, *President*
Amy Starbuck, *Purch Mgr*
EMP: 38 **EST:** 2002
SQ FT: 12,000
SALES (est): 2.6MM **Privately Held**
WEB: www.starbuckmachining.com
SIC: 3599 Ties, form: metal; machine shop, jobbing & repair

(G-8202)
STEKETEE-VAN HUIS INC
Also Called: MPS Holland
13 W 4th St (49423-2886)
PHONE 616 392-2326

▲ = Import ▼ = Export ◆ = Import/Export

Marc Shore, *CEO*
Theodore Etheridge, *President*
Dennis Kaltman, *President*
Gary Kremers, *COO*
William Ockerland, *CFO*
EMP: 252 **EST:** 1920
SQ FT: 69,000
SALES (est): 18.3MM
SALES (corp-wide): 17.5B **Publicly Held**
SIC: 2657 2752 Folding paperboard boxes; commercial printing, offset
HQ: Mps Holdco, Inc.
5800 W Grand River Ave
Lansing MI 48906

(G-8203)
STITCH ALLEY CUSTOMS
11140 Watertower Ct # 140 (49424-8506)
PHONE 616 377-7082
Jorge A Fuentes, *Administration*
EMP: 4 **EST:** 2017
SALES (est): 59.7K **Privately Held**
SIC: 2395 Embroidery & art needlework

(G-8204)
STM MFG INC (PA)
Also Called: S T M
494 E 64th St (49423-9324)
PHONE 616 392-4656
Roger Blauwkamp, *President*
Jacquelyn Blauwkamp, *Corp Secy*
Kevin Dannenberg, *Vice Pres*
Tim Machiele, *Vice Pres*
Steven Koning, *Maint Spvr*
EMP: 43 **EST:** 1977
SQ FT: 22,000
SALES (est): 13.8MM **Privately Held**
WEB: www.stmtooling.com
SIC: 3544 Special dies & tools

(G-8205)
STOW COMPANY (PA)
130 Central Ave Ste 400 (49423-2852)
PHONE 616 399-3311
Frank Newman, *President*
Elisabeth Devos, *Chairman*
Richard Devos, *Chairman*
Randy Tallman, *Exec VP*
Scott Sliva, *Vice Pres*
▲ **EMP:** 125 **EST:** 1984
SQ FT: 186,000
SALES (est): 79.7MM **Privately Held**
WEB: www.thestowcompany.com
SIC: 2511 Wood household furniture

(G-8206)
STUS WELDING & FABRICATION
4249 58th St (49423-9315)
PHONE 616 392-8459
EMP: 8
SQ FT: 18,750
SALES (est): 1MM **Privately Held**
SIC: 7692 3599 3446 3469 Welding Repair Mfg Industrial Machinery Mfg Architectural Mtlwrk Mfg Metal Stampings Mfg Sheet Metalwork

(G-8207)
SUBASSEMBLY PLUS INC
11359 James St (49424-8627)
PHONE 616 395-2075
Rick Zuverink, *President*
David Beckman, *Corp Secy*
David Baur, *Opers Staff*
EMP: 45 **EST:** 1996
SALES (est): 7.1MM **Privately Held**
WEB: www.subassemblyplus.com
SIC: 2531 Assembly hall furniture

(G-8208)
SUN RAY SIGN GROUP INC
376 Roost Ave (49424-2032)
PHONE 616 392-2824
Harvey Streur, *President*
Scott Tardiff, *Vice Pres*
EMP: 4 **EST:** 1973
SQ FT: 6,000
SALES (est): 275K **Privately Held**
WEB: www.sunraysigngroupinc.net
SIC: 3993 7389 Electric signs; sign painting & lettering shop

(G-8209)
SUPERIOR CUTTING SERVICE INC
4740 136th Ave (49424-8413)
PHONE 616 796-0114
Jack Van Voorst, *President*
Norman Veldhof, *Treasurer*
Randy Soper, *Admin Sec*
Bill Klomparens, *Maintence Staff*
EMP: 14 **EST:** 1991
SQ FT: 12,000
SALES (est): 2.1MM **Privately Held**
WEB: www.superiorcutting.com
SIC: 3599 Electrical discharge machining (EDM); machine shop, jobbing & repair

(G-8210)
SURE-LOC ALUMINUM EDGING INC
Also Called: Sure -Loc Edging-Wolverine Tls
310 E 64th St (49423-8731)
PHONE 616 392-3209
Roger Blauwkamp, *Principal*
Richard Haverdink, *Sales Staff*
Phil Johnson, *Sales Staff*
Tammy Knight, *Sales Staff*
Tara Nieboer, *Advt Staff*
◆ **EMP:** 7 **EST:** 1992
SALES (est): 2.9MM
SALES (corp-wide): 13.8MM **Privately Held**
WEB: www.surelocedging.com
SIC: 3524 0781 3423 Edgers, lawn; landscape planning services; shovels, spades (hand tools)
PA: Stm Mfg., Inc.
494 E 64th St
Holland MI 49423
616 392-4656

(G-8211)
T & T TOOLS INC
Also Called: T and T Tools
4470 128th Ave (49424-9257)
P.O. Box 531, Spring Lake (49456-0531)
PHONE 800 521-6893
Bob Thompson, *President*
EMP: 15 **EST:** 1989
SALES (est): 1.6MM **Privately Held**
SIC: 3544 Special dies & tools

(G-8212)
TANIS TECHNOLOGIES LLC
645 Commerce Ct Ste 10 (49424-2934)
PHONE 616 796-2712
Richard Tanis,
Jamie Tanis,
EMP: 6 **EST:** 2008
SQ FT: 10,000
SALES (est): 837.7K **Privately Held**
WEB: www.tanistechnologies.com
SIC: 3564 Air purification equipment; filters, air: furnaces, air conditioning equipment, etc.

(G-8213)
TECHNO-COAT INC
861 E 40th St (49423-5397)
PHONE 616 396-6446
Ike Vande Wege, *President*
Michael Wiersema, *Vice Pres*
Scott Eisen, *Engineer*
Norma V Wege, *Financial Exec*
Steve Martin, *Sales Staff*
EMP: 135
SQ FT: 90,000
SALES (est): 19.5MM **Privately Held**
WEB: www.technocoat.com
SIC: 3479 Coating of metals & formed products

(G-8214)
TELESCOPIC SEATING SYSTEMS LLC
190 E 8th St Unit 1556 (49422-0028)
PHONE 616 566-9232
Fred Jacobs, *Owner*
Denise Jacobs, *Principal*
EMP: 6 **EST:** 2017
SALES (est): 214.3K **Privately Held**
WEB: www.telescopicseatingsystems.com
SIC: 2399 Fabricated textile products

(G-8215)
TENNANT COMMERCIAL
12875 Ransom St (49424-9273)
PHONE 616 994-4000
Debby Davis, *Principal*
◆ **EMP:** 70 **EST:** 2009
SQ FT: 250,000
SALES (est): 4.4MM
SALES (corp-wide): 1B **Publicly Held**
WEB: www.tennantco.com
SIC: 3589 2842 Commercial cleaning equipment; specialty cleaning, polishes & sanitation goods
PA: Tennant Company
10400 Clean St
Eden Prairie MN 55344
763 540-1200

(G-8216)
TENNANT COMPANY
12875 Ransom St (49424-9273)
PHONE 616 994-4000
Pamela Maurer, *Materials Mgr*
Jay Nery, *Opers Spvr*
Blake Flemming, *Opers Staff*
Kent Vandewalker, *QC Mgr*
Dave Horn, *Engineer*
EMP: 6
SALES (corp-wide): 1B **Publicly Held**
WEB: www.tennantco.com
SIC: 3589 Commercial cleaning equipment
PA: Tennant Company
10400 Clean St
Eden Prairie MN 55344
763 540-1200

(G-8217)
TES AMERICA LLC
215 Central Ave 250 (49423-3231)
PHONE 616 786-5353
Mark Littlefield, *President*
Adam Renico, *Accounts Mgr*
EMP: 21 **EST:** 1977
SALES (est): 9.2MM **Privately Held**
SIC: 3571 Electronic computers
HQ: Tes Technology (Hong Kong) Limited
15/F Boc Group Life Assurance Twr
Central District HK

(G-8218)
THERMOTRON INDUSTRIES INC
875 Brooks Ave (49423-5338)
PHONE 616 928-9044
EMP: 35
SALES (corp-wide): 0 **Privately Held**
WEB: www.thermotron.com
SIC: 3599 Machine & other job shop work; custom machinery
HQ: Thermotron Industries, Inc.
291 Kollen Park Dr
Holland MI 49423

(G-8219)
THERMOTRON INDUSTRIES INC (HQ)
291 Kollen Park Dr (49423-3487)
PHONE 616 392-1491
Ron Lampen, *President*
Brian Nahey, *Principal*
Kevin Ewing, *Vice Pres*
Elaine Johnson, *Vice Pres*
Lynn Ternan, *Vice Pres*
▼ **EMP:** 340 **EST:** 1962
SALES (est): 126.2MM
SALES (corp-wide): 0 **Privately Held**
WEB: www.thermotron.com
SIC: 3829 Measuring & controlling devices
PA: Venturedyne, Ltd.
600 College Ave
Pewaukee WI 53072
262 691-9900

(G-8220)
TIARA YACHTS INC (PA)
725 E 40th St (49423-5315)
PHONE 616 392-7163
Leon R Slikkers, *Ch of Bd*
Robert L Slikkers, *President*
David A Slikkers, *COO*
Andy Marzolf, *Vice Pres*
June Kuiper, *Materials Mgr*
◆ **EMP:** 600 **EST:** 1974
SQ FT: 450,000 **Privately Held**
WEB: www.tiarayachts.com
SIC: 3732 Boats, fiberglass: building & repairing

(G-8221)
TIARA YACHTS INC
Tiara Yachts Corp Yachts Ctr
2081 Lakeway Dr (49423-4327)
PHONE 616 335-3594
EMP: 175 **Privately Held**
WEB: www.tiarayachts.com
SIC: 3732 Boat building & repairing
PA: Tiara Yachts, Inc.
725 E 40th St
Holland MI 49423
616 392-7163

(G-8222)
TOTAL INNOVATIVE MFG LLC
13395 Tyler St (49424-9421)
PHONE 616 399-9903
Kenneth Assink, *Owner*
EMP: 13 **EST:** 1999
SQ FT: 48,000
SALES (est): 404K **Privately Held**
SIC: 2522 Panel systems & partitions, office: except wood

(G-8223)
TPK AMERICA LLC
Also Called: TOUCH REVOLUTION
215 Central Ave Ste 200 (49423-3237)
PHONE 616 786-5300
Gene Halfy, *Mng Member*
▲ **EMP:** 12
SQ FT: 1,600
SALES: 65MM **Privately Held**
WEB: www.tpk-america.com
SIC: 3669 Visual communication systems
HQ: Tpk U.S.A., Llc
999 Baker Way Ste 120
San Mateo CA 94404

(G-8224)
TRAMEC SLOAN LLC (HQ)
Also Called: Sloan Transportation Products
534 E 48th St (49423-9502)
PHONE 616 395-5600
Mark A Holm, *President*
▲ **EMP:** 38 **EST:** 2013
SALES (est): 24.4MM
SALES (corp-wide): 110MM **Privately Held**
WEB: www.tramecsloan.com
SIC: 3714 3625 3561 Motor vehicle parts & accessories; relays & industrial controls; pumps & pumping equipment
PA: Tramec, L.L.C.
30 Davis St
Iola KS 66749
620 365-6977

(G-8225)
TRANS-MATIC MFG CO INC (PA)
300 E 48th St (49423-5391)
PHONE 616 820-2500
Patrick A Thompson, *CEO*
Patrick J Thompson, *President*
Bob Stander, *Vice Pres*
Dale Stinson, *Production*
Mary Wiley, *Production*
▲ **EMP:** 225 **EST:** 1968
SQ FT: 150,000
SALES (est): 50.8MM **Privately Held**
WEB: www.transmatic.com
SIC: 3465 3469 Automotive stampings; stamping metal for the trade

(G-8226)
TRENDWAY CORPORATION (HQ)
13467 Quincy St (49424-9484)
P.O. Box 9016 (49422-9016)
PHONE 616 399-3900
John Fellowes, *CEO*
Mark Rhoades, *President*
Douglas Dinkins, *Vice Pres*
Jeff Jalving, *Facilities Mgr*
Tim V Haitsma, *Buyer*
◆ **EMP:** 310 **EST:** 1968
SQ FT: 650,000
SALES (est): 54.7MM
SALES (corp-wide): 734.4MM **Privately Held**
WEB: www.trendway.com
SIC: 2522 2521 Panel systems & partitions, office: except wood; panel systems & partitions (free-standing), office: wood

Holland - Ottawa County (G-8227)

PA: Fellowes, Inc.
1789 Norwood Ave
Itasca IL 60143
630 893-1600

(G-8227)
TRENDWAY SVCS ORGANIZATION LLC
Also Called: Catapult Business Services
13467 Quincy St (49424-9460)
P.O. Box 9016 (49422-9016)
PHONE.................................616 994-5327
Eva Meekhof, *CEO*
Benjamin Lampen, *Controller*
EMP: 4 **EST:** 2016
SALES (est): 447.8K **Privately Held**
WEB: www.trendway.com
SIC: 2522 Office furniture, except wood

(G-8228)
TRI TECH TOOLING INC
11615 Greenway Dr (49424-7701)
P.O. Box 1137 (49422-1137)
PHONE.................................616 396-6000
Michael Bouma, *President*
Chris Schaefer, *Vice Pres*
Harwyn Berens, *Treasurer*
▲ **EMP:** 10 **EST:** 1995
SALES (est): 835.7K **Privately Held**
WEB: www.tritechtooling.com
SIC: 3544 Special dies & tools

(G-8229)
TRIANGLE PRODUCT DISTRIBUTORS
5750 Lakeshore Dr (49424-1021)
PHONE.................................970 609-9001
Charles Hozer, *CEO*
Charles L Hozer II, *President*
◆ **EMP:** 32 **EST:** 1975
SQ FT: 4,800
SALES (est): 141.9K **Privately Held**
SIC: 3577 5045 5074 Computer peripheral equipment; computer software; heating equipment & panels, solar

(G-8230)
TRIC TOOL LTD
3760 John F Donnelly Dr (49424-7278)
PHONE.................................616 395-1530
Thomas Jackson, *President*
James Carden, *Vice Pres*
Jim Carden, *Vice Pres*
Bill Bergsma, *Project Engr*
Barb Bosman, *Office Mgr*
EMP: 28 **EST:** 1994
SQ FT: 20,000
SALES (est): 5.6MM **Privately Held**
WEB: www.trictool.com
SIC: 3544 3599 Special dies & tools; machine shop, jobbing & repair

(G-8231)
TRIGON STEEL COMPONENTS INC
1448 Lincoln Ave (49423-9389)
PHONE.................................616 834-0506
Isaac Koert, *President*
Cortney Sluiter, *Vice Pres*
Alec Bobko, *Manager*
EMP: 4 **EST:** 2013
SQ FT: 8,200
SALES (est): 707.6K **Privately Held**
WEB: www.trigonsteel.com
SIC: 3448 Prefabricated metal components

(G-8232)
TWO CUPS COFFEE CO LLC
Also Called: Simpatico Coffee
490 Lincoln Ave Ste 10 (49423-4242)
PHONE.................................616 953-0534
Alexander Fink,
EMP: 19 **EST:** 2011
SALES (est): 605.7K **Privately Held**
SIC: 5812 2095 Coffee shop; coffee roasting (except by wholesale grocers)

(G-8233)
UNITED MANUFACTURING INC
Also Called: Umi
4150 Sunnyside Dr (49424-8716)
PHONE.................................616 738-8888
Randall Bezile, *President*
Mark Chase, *Vice Pres*
Keith Fox, *Vice Pres*

Bob Hanson, *Vice Pres*
EMP: 35 **EST:** 1998
SQ FT: 30,000
SALES (est): 6MM **Privately Held**
WEB: www.unitedmfginc.com
SIC: 3469 Stamping metal for the trade

(G-8234)
VARATECH INC
1141 Ambertrace Ln Apt 8 (49424-5335)
PHONE.................................616 393-6408
Robert Gardner Jr, *President*
Sridhar Nandula, *Business Mgr*
Gary Crispin, *CFO*
EMP: 10 **EST:** 1993
SALES (est): 850K **Privately Held**
WEB: www.varatech.com
SIC: 8711 7373 7372 Consulting engineer; systems software development services; prepackaged software

(G-8235)
VELDHEER TULIP GARDEN INC
Also Called: De Klomp Wden Shoe Delft Fctry
12755 Quincy St (49424-8285)
PHONE.................................616 399-1900
Vernon Veldheer, *CEO*
James Veldheer, *President*
▲ **EMP:** 25 **EST:** 1950
SALES (est): 578.3K **Privately Held**
WEB: www.veldheer.com
SIC: 0181 3269 2499 5191 Bulbs, growing of; flowers: grown under cover (e.g. greenhouse production); art & ornamental ware, pottery; shoe & boot products, wood; flower & field bulbs; flowers, fresh; men's footwear, except athletic

(G-8236)
VENNTIS TECHNOLOGIES LLC
1261 S Waverly Rd (49423-9332)
PHONE.................................616 395-8254
Erich Roehl, *Partner*
Jay Caldwell, *Opers Mgr*
Robert Bos, *Engineer*
Marla Venard, *Bookkeeper*
David Caldwell,
EMP: 18 **EST:** 2008
SALES (est): 1.8MM **Privately Held**
WEB: www.totalgrowlight.com
SIC: 3679 8711 Electronic circuits; consulting engineer

(G-8237)
VENTUREDYNE LTD
Thermotron Industries
836 Brooks Ave (49423-5339)
PHONE.................................616 392-6550
Dan O'Keefe, *Manager*
John Harbison, *Analyst*
EMP: 5
SALES (corp-wide): 0 **Privately Held**
WEB: www.venturedyne.com
SIC: 3826 Environmental testing equipment
PA: Venturedyne, Ltd.
600 College Ave
Pewaukee WI 53072
262 691-9900

(G-8238)
VERSE CHOCOLATE LLC
180 E 40th St Ste 400 (49423-5393)
PHONE.................................816 325-0208
Kerry Scott Walker,
EMP: 7 **EST:** 2020
SALES (est): 533.3K **Privately Held**
WEB: www.versechocolate.com
SIC: 2066 Chocolate bars, solid

(G-8239)
VIVATAR INC
935 E 40th St (49423-5384)
PHONE.................................616 928-0750
Brian Schelstraete, *CEO*
John Mugridge, *CFO*
EMP: 41 **EST:** 2007
SALES (est): 1.1MM **Privately Held**
WEB: www.vivatarinc.com
SIC: 3089 Injection molding of plastics

(G-8240)
W-LOK CORPORATION
861 Productions Pl (49423-9168)
PHONE.................................616 355-4015
Rudell Broekhuis, *President*

Waterson Chen, *Vice Pres*
Nana Wang, *Treasurer*
EMP: 4 **EST:** 1998
SALES (est): 284.6K **Privately Held**
SIC: 3429 Keys, locks & related hardware

(G-8241)
WALTERS SEED CO LLC
Also Called: Promogarden.com
65 Veterans Dr (49423-7813)
PHONE.................................616 355-7333
EMP: 10
SALES (est): 999.9K **Privately Held**
SIC: 5261 2679 Ret Nursery/Garden Supplies Mfg Converted Paper Products

(G-8242)
WAY2GO TECH LLC
425 142nd Ave (49424-6629)
PHONE.................................616 294-1301
Beate Ulrich,
EMP: 6 **EST:** 2013
SALES (est): 251.2K **Privately Held**
WEB: www.way2gotech.com
SIC: 3585 Humidifiers & dehumidifiers

(G-8243)
WELCHDRY INC
4270 Sunnyside Dr (49424-8653)
PHONE.................................616 399-2711
Dave Vander Heide, *President*
Sean Schaap, *Vice Pres*
Frank Kazda, *Director*
▲ **EMP:** 29 **EST:** 1989
SQ FT: 60,000
SALES (est): 6MM **Privately Held**
WEB: www.welchdry.com
SIC: 2834 Powders, pharmaceutical

(G-8244)
WEST MICHIGAN ALPACAS
15747 Greenly St (49424-5947)
PHONE.................................616 990-0556
Rhonda Faber, *Principal*
EMP: 6 **EST:** 2010
SALES (est): 87K **Privately Held**
WEB: www.michigan-alpacas.com
SIC: 2231 Alpacas, mohair: woven

(G-8245)
WEST MICHIGAN CANVAS COMPANY
Also Called: West Mich Awning
11041 Paw Paw Dr (49424-8992)
PHONE.................................616 355-7855
Karen De Jonge, *President*
Jay Win, *President*
EMP: 9 **EST:** 1988
SALES (est): 885.1K **Privately Held**
WEB: www.westmichigancanvasandawning.com
SIC: 2221 Manmade & synthetic broadwoven fabrics; vinal broadwoven fabrics

(G-8246)
WEST MICHIGAN SPLINE INC
156 Manufacturers Dr (49424-1893)
PHONE.................................616 399-4078
Gary R Hill, *President*
Marie Hill, *Treasurer*
▲ **EMP:** 12 **EST:** 1987
SQ FT: 11,750
SALES (est): 1.3MM **Privately Held**
WEB: www.westmichiganspline.com
SIC: 3542 Spline rolling machines

(G-8247)
WESTERN MICHIGAN PLASTICS
5745 143rd Ave (49423-8746)
PHONE.................................616 394-9269
Gregory Cook, *President*
Tom O'Neal, *Vice Pres*
Brianna Santellan, *Purchasing*
Bryan Tomberlin, *QC Mgr*
▲ **EMP:** 12 **EST:** 1988
SALES (est): 2.5MM **Privately Held**
WEB: www.wmiplastics.com
SIC: 3089 Injection molding of plastics

(G-8248)
WESTERN PEGASUS INC (PA)
728 E 8th St Ste 3 (49423-3080)
PHONE.................................616 393-9580
Heather Wincel, *President*
James Mc Gurk, *Owner*
EMP: 6 **EST:** 1980

SQ FT: 2,000
SALES (est): 4.4MM **Privately Held**
WEB: www.westpeg.com
SIC: 3545 Gauges (machine tool accessories)

(G-8249)
WHITTAKER ORGNAME ASSOC INC
1889 Ottawa Beach Rd (49424-2480)
PHONE.................................616 786-2255
Dean Whittaker, *Principal*
EMP: 6 **EST:** 2018
SALES (est): 252.2K **Privately Held**
WEB: www.whittakerassociates.com
SIC: 3433 Heating equipment, except electric

(G-8250)
WINDOW DESIGNS INC (PA)
Also Called: Great Lakes Draperies
753 Lincoln Ave (49423-5482)
PHONE.................................616 396-5295
Dorothy Willemstyn, *President*
Chet Willemstyn Sr, *Corp Secy*
Chet Willemstyn Jr, *Vice Pres*
Renee Milbridge, *Sales Staff*
EMP: 10 **EST:** 1965
SQ FT: 7,000
SALES (est): 1.4MM **Privately Held**
SIC: 5714 7389 2211 2221 Draperies; design services; draperies & drapery fabrics, cotton; draperies & drapery fabrics, manmade fiber & silk

(G-8251)
WOODEN RUNABOUT CO
4261 58th St (49423-9315)
PHONE.................................616 396-7248
Mike Teusink, *Owner*
EMP: 5 **EST:** 2010
SALES (est): 366.4K **Privately Held**
WEB: www.woodenrunabout.com
SIC: 3732 Boat building & repairing

(G-8252)
WORDEN GROUP LLC
199 E 17th St (49423-4385)
PHONE.................................616 392-1848
James Weaver, *President*
Kenneth Filippini, *Principal*
EMP: 99 **EST:** 2012
SQ FT: 25,000
SALES (est): 4.5MM **Privately Held**
WEB: www.wordencompany.com
SIC: 2531 Library furniture

(G-8253)
WORLD CLASS PROTOTYPES INC
400 Center St (49423-3717)
PHONE.................................616 355-0200
James Leonard, *President*
Susan Leonard, *Vice Pres*
Alice Leonard, *Purchasing*
Kevin Gagnon, *Sales Staff*
EMP: 10 **EST:** 1992
SQ FT: 2,000
SALES (est): 1.2MM **Privately Held**
WEB: www.worldclassprototypes.com
SIC: 3089 Injection molding of plastics

(G-8254)
YANFENG US AUTO INTR SYSTEMS I
915 E 32nd St (49423-9120)
PHONE.................................616 394-1567
Jeffrey Stout, *Engineer*
Duane Lemke, *Finance*
Dan White, *Branch Mgr*
Alejandro Chavez, *Manager*
Bryan Fredrick, *Director*
EMP: 7 **Privately Held**
WEB: www.yfai.com
SIC: 3714 5531 Motor vehicle parts & accessories; automotive parts
HQ: Yanfeng Us Automotive Interior Systems I Llc
41935 W 12 Mile Rd
Novi MI 48377
248 319-7333

▲ = Import ▼ = Export
◆ = Import/Export

GEOGRAPHIC SECTION

Holly - Oakland County (G-8282)

(G-8255)
YANFENG US AUTO INTR SYSTEMS I
Also Called: Yanfeng Auto Intr Systems
1598 Washington Ave (49423-9309)
PHONE.................616 283-1349
Brian Rogalske, *Engineer*
Chris Prestridge, *Controller*
Michal Stehlik, *Finance*
Tyler Carley, *Manager*
Joseph Derrico, *Manager*
EMP: 7 Privately Held
WEB: www.yfai.com
SIC: 3714 Motor vehicle parts & accessories
HQ: Yanfeng Us Automotive Interior Systems I Llc
41935 W 12 Mile Rd
Novi MI 48377
248 319-7333

(G-8256)
YANFENG US AUTO INTR SYSTEMS I
Also Called: Yanfeng Global Auto Interiors
921 E 32nd St 69 (49423-9160)
PHONE.................616 392-5151
Michael Driver, *General Mgr*
Robb Vanderkamp, *Managing Dir*
Tory Bowman, *Mfg Dir*
Eric Asselin, *Engrg Dir*
Dale Chamberlain, *Engineer*
EMP: 7 Privately Held
WEB: www.yfai.com
SIC: 3714 Motor vehicle parts & accessories
HQ: Yanfeng Us Automotive Interior Systems I Llc
41935 W 12 Mile Rd
Novi MI 48377
248 319-7333

(G-8257)
YANFENG US AUTOMOTIVE
Yanfeng Virtual City
915 32nd St Tech Ctr (49423)
PHONE.................616 394-1523
Court Manns, *Branch Mgr*
EMP: 4 Privately Held
WEB: www.yfai.com
SIC: 8741 2531 Management services; seats, automobile
HQ: Yanfeng Us Automotive Interior Systems I Llc
41935 W 12 Mile Rd
Novi MI 48377
248 319-7333

(G-8258)
YOST VISES LLC
2221 Sunset Bluff Dr (49424-2385)
PHONE.................616 396-2063
Fred J Nelis Jr, *President*
Kevin Nelis, *Vice Pres*
Ryan Nelis, *Sales Staff*
Patrick Nelis, *Admin Sec*
▲ **EMP:** 7 **EST:** 1908
SALES (est): 865.5K Privately Held
WEB: www.yostvises.com
SIC: 3545 Vises, machine (machine tool accessories)

(G-8259)
ZOET POULTRY
4847 140th Ave (49423-9546)
PHONE.................269 751-2776
John Zoet, *President*
Tim Zweering, *Opers Mgr*
◆ **EMP:** 25 **EST:** 1992
SALES (est): 1.2MM Privately Held
SIC: 0252 2015 Chicken eggs; egg processing

Holly
Oakland County

(G-8260)
AFCO MANUFACTURING CORP
428 Cogshall St (48442-1756)
P.O. Box 230 (48442-0230)
PHONE.................248 634-4415
Dawn Holbrook, *President*
Alicia Hardacre, *Manager*
EMP: 16
SQ FT: 35,000
SALES (est): 5.2MM Privately Held
WEB: www.afcomfg.com
SIC: 3441 Building components, structural steel

(G-8261)
APPLIED SYNERGISTICS INC
926 Running Brook Dr (48442-1579)
PHONE.................248 634-0151
Larry Gaffke, *Agent*
EMP: 4 **EST:** 2018
SALES (est): 75.6K Privately Held
SIC: 3823 Industrial instrmnts msrmnt display/control process variable

(G-8262)
BARS PRODUCTS INC (PA)
Also Called: Insealator
10386 N Holly Rd (48442-9302)
P.O. Box 187 (48442-0187)
PHONE.................248 634-8278
Robert Mermuys, *President*
Carrie Mermuys, *Exec VP*
Michael Mermuys, *Vice Pres*
Clayton Parks, *Vice Pres*
Fred Mannix, *QC Mgr*
▲ **EMP:** 32 **EST:** 1947
SQ FT: 45,000
SALES (est): 8.2MM Privately Held
WEB: www.barsproducts.com
SIC: 2899 2891 Chemical preparations; sealants

(G-8263)
COVENTRY INDUSTRIES LLC
313 E Sherman St (48442-1656)
PHONE.................248 761-8462
Michael Coventry, *Principal*
EMP: 10 **EST:** 2013
SALES (est): 1.1MM Privately Held
WEB: www.coventryind.com
SIC: 3999 Barber & beauty shop equipment

(G-8264)
CUPCAKES AND KISSES
108 S Saginaw St (48442-1610)
PHONE.................248 382-5314
EMP: 5 **EST:** 2015
SALES (est): 73.1K Privately Held
WEB: www.cupcakesandkisses19.com
SIC: 2051 Bread, cake & related products

(G-8265)
DAVE LEWISHCKY FANTSY CAMP
2040 Ranch Rd (48442-8027)
PHONE.................248 328-0891
Dave Lewis, *Owner*
EMP: 6 **EST:** 2001
SALES (est): 82.6K Privately Held
SIC: 3949 Camping equipment & supplies

(G-8266)
DAVID LEE NATURALS
113 Battle Aly (48442-1609)
PHONE.................248 328-1131
EMP: 5 **EST:** 2016
SALES (est): 109.9K Privately Held
SIC: 2844 Toilet preparations

(G-8267)
DELTA TUBE & FABRICATING CORP (PA)
4149 Grange Hall Rd (48442-1113)
PHONE.................248 634-8267
Howard W Campbell Jr, *President*
Betty Campbell, *Corp Secy*
Todd Campbell, *Vice Pres*
EMP: 20 **EST:** 1973
SQ FT: 12,000
SALES (est): 20.6MM Privately Held
SIC: 3496 3743 3317 Miscellaneous fabricated wire products; railroad car rebuilding; steel pipe & tubes

(G-8268)
DELTA TUBE & FABRICATING CORP
Also Called: Delta Rail Division
4149 Grange Hall Rd (48442-1113)
PHONE.................248 634-8267
Howard Campbell, *Owner*
Richard Clark, *Manager*
EMP: 183
SALES (corp-wide): 20.6MM Privately Held
SIC: 3547 3537 3444 3412 Pipe & tube mills; industrial trucks & tractors; sheet metalwork; metal barrels, drums & pails; metal cans; railroad & subway construction
PA: Delta Tube & Fabricating Corporation
4149 Grange Hall Rd
Holly MI 48442
248 634-8267

(G-8269)
FALCON MOTORSPORTS INC
Also Called: A P Engineering
255 Elm St (48442-1404)
PHONE.................248 328-2222
Carl D Lemke, *President*
Jeffery Lemke, *Vice Pres*
Kathleen Lemke, *Treasurer*
EMP: 7 **EST:** 1995
SQ FT: 2,200
SALES (est): 994.1K Privately Held
WEB: www.falconv7.com
SIC: 3541 7699 3545 Machine tools, metal cutting type; marine propeller repair; machine tool accessories

(G-8270)
GARCIA COMPANY
10255 Fish Lake Rd (48442-8626)
PHONE.................248 459-0952
John Garcia, *President*
EMP: 5 **EST:** 1991
SALES (est): 339.5K Privately Held
SIC: 2441 Cases, wood

(G-8271)
GD ENTERPRISES LLC
6496 Milford Rd (48442-8648)
PHONE.................248 207-1366
Ron Gardner, *Principal*
Ron G Gardner, *Purch Mgr*
EMP: 6 **EST:** 2005
SALES (est): 213.7K Privately Held
WEB: www.gd-enterprises.net
SIC: 3448 Prefabricated metal buildings

(G-8272)
GENESEE VALLEY VAULT INC
10510 N Holly Rd (48442-9323)
PHONE.................810 629-3909
Alton T Rice, *President*
Michael J Medor, *Vice Pres*
EMP: 5 **EST:** 1984
SQ FT: 9,625
SALES (est): 800K Privately Held
WEB: www.geneseevault.com
SIC: 3272 Burial vaults, concrete or precast terrazzo

(G-8273)
GENOAK MATERIALS INC (PA)
14300 Shields Rd (48442-9731)
P.O. Box 182 (48442-0182)
PHONE.................248 634-8276
Bernhard Rumbold, *President*
Hugh Carr, *Corp Secy*
Scott Mc Kay, *Vice Pres*
EMP: 131
SALES (est): 16.8MM Privately Held
SIC: 1442 4212 1611 1623 Gravel mining; local trucking, without storage; highway & street paving contractor; water, sewer & utility lines

(G-8274)
GIBRALTAR NATIONAL CORPORATION
Also Called: Quikrete Gibraltar National
14311 Cmi Dr (48442-9752)
PHONE.................248 634-8257
Paul Robbins, *Manager*
EMP: 24
SQ FT: 8,000 Privately Held
SIC: 3272 Concrete products
HQ: Gibraltar National Corporation
8951 Schaefer Hwy
Detroit MI 48228
313 491-3500

(G-8275)
GRAND BLANC PROCESSING LLC
10151 Gainey Rd (48442-9313)
PHONE.................810 694-6000
Matt Takahashi, *President*
Takashi Ono, *Financial Exec*
Jeff Newbill, *Technology*
Erica Crabb, *Executive*
Greg Edwards, *Maintence Staff*
▲ **EMP:** 58
SALES (est): 14.3MM Privately Held
WEB: www.shinsho.com
SIC: 3398 Metal heat treating
HQ: The Shinsho American Corporation
26200 Town Center Dr # 220
Novi MI 48375
248 675-0058

(G-8276)
HOLY ART FRAMING
201 S Saginaw St (48442-1613)
PHONE.................248 634-8190
EMP: 5 **EST:** 2016
SALES (est): 112K Privately Held
SIC: 2499 Picture frame molding, finished

(G-8277)
HPC HOLDINGS INC (PA)
111 Rosette St (48442-1304)
P.O. Box 158 (48442-0158)
PHONE.................248 634-9361
David Bubnar, *President*
Paul J Bubnar III, *Vice Pres*
Nancy Bubnar, *Treasurer*
EMP: 25 **EST:** 1969
SQ FT: 20,000
SALES (est): 5.1MM Privately Held
SIC: 3471 Electroplating of metals or formed products

(G-8278)
INK CHEMISTRY SCREEN PRINTING
4019 Baldwin Rd (48442-9303)
PHONE.................810 429-9095
EMP: 4 **EST:** 2019
SALES (est): 88.6K Privately Held
WEB: www.inkchemistry.com
SIC: 2759 Screen printing

(G-8279)
IRONMANN INDUSTRIES
407 Hadley St (48442-1637)
PHONE.................810 695-9177
EMP: 5 **EST:** 2017
SALES (est): 57.2K Privately Held
WEB: www.ironmannindustries.com
SIC: 3999 Manufacturing industries

(G-8280)
LANGS INC
5469 Jacobs Dr (48442-9566)
PHONE.................248 634-6048
Scott Lang, *President*
EMP: 8 **EST:** 1990
SQ FT: 1,000
SALES (est): 910K Privately Held
SIC: 2026 5143 Fermented & cultured milk products; cheese

(G-8281)
MAGNA E-CAR USA LLC
10410 N Holly Rd (48442-9332)
PHONE.................248 606-0600
Jim Kane, *Vice Pres*
Burge Young, *Vice Pres*
Mike Smalley, *Director*
Ted Robertson,
EMP: 89 **EST:** 2010
SALES (est): 6.8MM
SALES (corp-wide): 32.6B Privately Held
WEB: www.magna.com
SIC: 3621 Motors & generators
PA: Magna International Inc
337 Magna Dr
Aurora ON L4G 7
905 726-2462

(G-8282)
MAGNA ELECTRONICS INC
10345 N Holly Rd (48442-9302)
PHONE.................810 606-8683
Jeff Gary, *General Mgr*
EMP: 21

Holly - Oakland County (G-8283)

SALES (corp-wide): 32.6B **Privately Held**
WEB: www.magna.com
SIC: 3679 Electronic circuits
HQ: Magna Electronics Inc.
   2050 Auburn Rd
   Auburn Hills MI 48326

(G-8283)
MAGNA ELECTRONICS TECH INC (DH)
10410 N Holly Rd (48442-9332)
PHONE..................810 606-0145
David Turnbull, *President*
Kenneth Wagner, *Treasurer*
Chris Dewey, *Manager*
Jayson Wolkove, *Admin Sec*
▲ EMP: 100 EST: 2001
SALES (est): 54.4MM
SALES (corp-wide): 32.6B **Privately Held**
WEB: www.magna.com
SIC: 3714 Motor vehicle parts & accessories

(G-8284)
METROPOULOS AMPLIFICATION INC
10460 N Holly Rd (48442-9319)
PHONE..................810 614-3905
Scott Smith, *Chief*
George Metropoulos, *Administration*
EMP: 7 EST: 2008
SALES (est): 598.8K **Privately Held**
WEB: www.metropoulos.net
SIC: 3699 Electrical equipment & supplies

(G-8285)
NORTHERN OAK BREWERY INC
806 N Saginaw St (48442-1347)
PHONE..................248 634-7515
Ed Krupa, *President*
Andrew Stark, *Vice Pres*
EMP: 11 EST: 2014
SALES (est): 400K **Privately Held**
WEB: www.northernoakbrewery.com
SIC: 5813 2082 Bars & lounges; beer (alcoholic beverage)

(G-8286)
PRO SHOT BASKETBALL INC
407 Hadley St (48442-1637)
PHONE..................877 968-3865
EMP: 6 EST: 2018
SALES (est): 611.3K **Privately Held**
SIC: 3949 Sporting & athletic goods

(G-8287)
QUALITY WAY PRODUCTS LLC
407 Hadley St (48442-1637)
PHONE..................248 634-2401
Brian D Mann Jr,
EMP: 10 EST: 2004
SALES (est): 3.1MM **Privately Held**
WEB: www.qualitywayproducts.com
SIC: 3272 Columns, concrete

(G-8288)
QUANTUM LIFE LLC
3013 Oak Dr (48442-8305)
PHONE..................248 634-2784
Raymond J McConnell, *Principal*
EMP: 4 EST: 2019
SALES (est): 85.6K **Privately Held**
SIC: 3572 Computer storage devices

(G-8289)
QUANTUM VENTURES LLC
Also Called: Uantum Lifecare
18055 Fish Lake Rd (48442-8624)
PHONE..................248 325-8380
Pamelia M Jobes, *Principal*
EMP: 5 EST: 2015
SALES (est): 439K **Privately Held**
WEB: www.quantumlifecare.com
SIC: 3572 Computer storage devices

(G-8290)
RANKIN BIOMEDICAL CORPORATION
14515 Mackey Rd (48442-9738)
PHONE..................248 625-4104
Robert Rankin, *CEO*
Terry Sullivan, *Opers Mgr*
Joe Osentoski, *Marketing Mgr*
Kerry Goodman, *Director*
▼ EMP: 15 EST: 1995

SQ FT: 10,400
SALES (est): 4.3MM **Privately Held**
WEB: www.rankinbiomed.com
SIC: 5047 5049 3821 Medical equipment & supplies; laboratory equipment, except medical or dental; microtomes

(G-8291)
RAVEN ACQUISITION LLC
428 Cogshall St (48442-1756)
PHONE..................734 254-5000
Michael W Benoit, *Mng Member*
EMP: 450 EST: 2019 **Privately Held**
SIC: 6719 2531 8711 Investment holding companies, except banks; seats, automobile; engineering services

(G-8292)
RING SCREW LLC
Holly Operations At Baldwin
4146 Baldwin Rd (48442-9328)
PHONE..................810 695-0800
EMP: 90
SQ FT: 32,000 **Privately Held**
SIC: 3452 Mfg Bolts/Screws/Rivets
HQ: Ring Screw Llc
   6125 18 Mile Rd
   Sterling Heights MI 48314
   586 997-5600

(G-8293)
RUSH AIR INC
Also Called: Rush Technologies
200 Quality Way (48442-9480)
PHONE..................810 694-5763
Kelly Rushmore, *President*
Diane L Rushmore, *Admin Sec*
EMP: 19 EST: 1996
SQ FT: 36,000
SALES (est): 1.5MM **Privately Held**
SIC: 3585 Air conditioning equipment, complete

(G-8294)
S T A INC
4150 Grange Hall Rd (48442-1112)
PHONE..................248 328-5000
Charles E Phyle, *Chairman*
Dave Kahler, *Vice Pres*
Dan Ross, *Design Engr*
Rich Stoolmaker, *Design Engr*
Pat Brendle, *Sales Staff*
EMP: 47 EST: 1980
SQ FT: 25,000
SALES (est): 4.2MM **Privately Held**
SIC: 3571 7378 Electronic computers; computer maintenance & repair

(G-8295)
SOUTH FLINT GRAVEL INC
Also Called: Aldridge Trucking
6090 Belford Rd (48442-9443)
PHONE..................810 232-8911
Robert Aldridge, *Owner*
EMP: 6 EST: 2010
SALES (est): 470K **Privately Held**
WEB: www.aldridgetruckingco.com
SIC: 1442 Gravel mining

(G-8296)
STRUCTURAL PLASTICS INC
3401 Chief (48442-9333)
PHONE..................810 953-9400
Stephen Aho, *President*
Bree Cady, *Finance Mgr*
Monica March, *Credit Staff*
Leann Cradit, *Marketing Mgr*
Jonathan Scott, *Marketing Staff*
EMP: 46 EST: 1981
SQ FT: 4,000
SALES (est): 11.1MM **Privately Held**
WEB: www.spcindustrial.com
SIC: 2542 Partitions & fixtures, except wood

(G-8297)
TMI CLIMATE SOLUTIONS INC (DH)
200 Quality Way (48442-9400)
PHONE..................810 694-5763
Jim Huff, *CEO*
Ryan Whaley, *Vice Pres*
EMP: 150 EST: 1982
SQ FT: 160,000

SALES (est): 64.7MM
SALES (corp-wide): 245.5B **Publicly Held**
WEB: www.tmiclimatesolutions.com
SIC: 3585 Refrigeration & heating equipment
HQ: Mitek Industries, Inc.
   16023 Swinly Rdg
   Chesterfield MO 63017
   314 434-1200

(G-8298)
TRI-CITY AGGREGATES INC
14300 Shields Rd (48442-9731)
P.O. Box 182 (48442-0182)
PHONE..................248 634-8276
Bernhard C Rumbold, *President*
Hugh Carr, *Corp Secy*
Scott Mc Kay, *Vice Pres*
EMP: 24 EST: 1958
SQ FT: 5,000
SALES (est): 8.2MM **Privately Held**
SIC: 1442 4212 2951 Sand mining; gravel & pebble mining; local trucking, without storage; asphalt paving mixtures & blocks
PA: Genoak Materials Inc
   14300 Shields Rd
   Holly MI 48442

(G-8299)
V AND F TRANSFORMER
10703 W Braemar (48442-8694)
PHONE..................248 328-6288
EMP: 4 EST: 2017
SALES (est): 97.1K **Privately Held**
SIC: 3677 Electronic coils, transformers & other inductors

(G-8300)
VINYL TECH WINDOW SYSTEMS INC
405 Cogshall St (48442-1736)
PHONE..................248 634-8900
Paul Baker, *President*
EMP: 22 EST: 1990
SQ FT: 6,500
SALES (est): 987.2K **Privately Held**
SIC: 3089 Windows, plastic

(G-8301)
WOLVERINE MACHINE PRODUCTS CO
319 Cogshall St (48442-1761)
P.O. Box 209 (48442-0209)
PHONE..................248 634-9952
Brian K Hickman, *CEO*
Kenneth H Walker, *President*
Blaine Walker, *Vice Pres*
Bruce H Walker, *Vice Pres*
Frank Dean, *Opers Staff*
EMP: 22 EST: 1923
SQ FT: 1,200
SALES (est): 2.6MM **Privately Held**
WEB: www.wolverinemachine.com
SIC: 3568 3541 3451 Power transmission equipment; machine tools, metal cutting type; screw machine products

(G-8302)
YANKEE SCRW PRODUCTS COMPANY
212 Elm St (48442-1403)
PHONE..................248 634-3011
Michael Yankee, *President*
EMP: 9 EST: 1944
SQ FT: 40,000
SALES (est): 722.1K **Privately Held**
WEB: www.yankeescrew.com
SIC: 3451 Screw machine products

Holt
Ingham County

(G-8303)
APPLAUSE INC
Also Called: On-The-Spot-engraving
1655 Tuscany Ln (48842-6002)
PHONE..................517 485-9880
John Williams, *President*
Betty Williams, *Vice Pres*
EMP: 4 EST: 1976

SALES (est): 508.9K **Privately Held**
WEB: www.applauseinc.com
SIC: 7389 2396 Engraving service; automotive & apparel trimmings

(G-8304)
CAPITAL STEEL & BUILDERS SUP
3897 Holt Rd (48842-9774)
P.O. Box 279 (48842-0279)
PHONE..................517 694-0451
William A Buyak, *President*
EMP: 28 EST: 1968
SQ FT: 13,000
SALES (est): 3.2MM **Privately Held**
SIC: 3441 5051 5211 Fabricated structural metal; steel; lumber & other building materials

(G-8305)
D & M SILKSCREENING
4202 Charlar Dr Ste 3 (48842-6808)
PHONE..................517 694-4199
Michael Denison, *Owner*
Lynn Denison, *Principal*
EMP: 6 EST: 1990
SALES (est): 200K **Privately Held**
WEB: www.pcdoctormn.com
SIC: 2759 2395 Screen printing; embroidery products, except schiffli machine

(G-8306)
D D QUALITY SERVICING
1596 Witherspoon Way (48842-9568)
PHONE..................517 709-3705
David Davidoski, *Principal*
EMP: 8 EST: 2013
SALES (est): 1.3MM **Privately Held**
SIC: 1389 Roustabout service

(G-8307)
DAKKOTA INTEGRATED SYSTEMS LLC
4147 Keller Rd (48842-1253)
PHONE..................517 694-6500
Jim Gervers, *Transportation*
Scott Bassett, *Engineer*
Norman Moore, *Engineer*
Aaron Ewart, *Accountant*
Arthur Wakeford, *Accountant*
EMP: 7
SALES (corp-wide): 242.2MM **Privately Held**
WEB: www.dakkota.com
SIC: 3711 3714 Automobile assembly, including specialty automobiles; motor vehicle parts & accessories
PA: Dakkota Integrated Systems, Llc
   123 Brighton Lake Rd # 202
   Brighton MI 48116
   517 694-6500

(G-8308)
DAKKOTA LIGHTING TECH LLC (HQ)
4147 Keller Rd (48842-1253)
PHONE..................517 694-2823
Andra Rush, *Chairman*
Mark Licovitch, *Vice Pres*
Gary Caldwell,
Michael McCarthy,
Linda McMahan,
EMP: 24 EST: 2012
SQ FT: 150,000
SALES (est): 4.7MM
SALES (corp-wide): 242.2MM **Privately Held**
WEB: www.dakota.com
SIC: 3648 Lighting equipment
PA: Dakkota Integrated Systems, Llc
   123 Brighton Lake Rd # 202
   Brighton MI 48116
   517 694-6500

(G-8309)
DART CONTAINER MICHIGAN LLC
2148 Depot St (48842-1816)
PHONE..................517 694-9455
Larry McCaffrey, *Plant Mgr*
Randy Robinson, *Project Engr*
Aaron Eibl, *Manager*
EMP: 2628 **Privately Held**
WEB: www.dartcontainer.com

GEOGRAPHIC SECTION   Holt - Ingham County (G-8336)

SIC: 3086 2656 Cups & plates, foamed plastic; paper cups, plates, dishes & utensils
HQ: Dart Container Of Michigan Llc
500 Hogsback Rd
Mason MI 48854
800 248-5960

(G-8310)
ENERGY ACQUISITION CORP
2385 Delhi Commerce Dr # 5 (48842-2192)
PHONE.............................517 339-0249
EMP: 10
SQ FT: 800
SALES (est): 780.3K **Privately Held**
SIC: 1382 Oil/Gas Exploration Services

(G-8311)
FEMUR BUYER INC
Also Called: Orchid Orthopedic Solutions
1489 Cedar St (48842-1875)
PHONE.............................517 694-2300
Jerome Jurkiewicz, *President*
Louis Pace, *Treasurer*
EMP: 25 **EST:** 2018
SALES (est): 3.3MM
SALES (corp-wide): 496.9MM **Privately Held**
WEB: www.orchid-ortho.com
SIC: 3841 Surgical & medical instruments
HQ: Orchid Orthopedic Solutions Llc
1489 Cedar St
Holt MI 48842
517 694-2300

(G-8312)
FRISCOS MECHANICAL & FABG
3932 Berry Ridge Dr (48842-9715)
PHONE.............................517 719-3933
Francisco Godinez, *Principal*
EMP: 4 **EST:** 2015
SALES (est): 72.9K **Privately Held**
SIC: 3999 Manufacturing industries

(G-8313)
GARDEN OF EDYN
4075 Holt Rd Lot 248 (48842-6007)
PHONE.............................517 410-9931
Jadda Holmes, *Owner*
Jadda Williams, *Director*
EMP: 4 **EST:** 2016
SALES (est): 79.8K **Privately Held**
WEB: www.mygardenofedyn.com
SIC: 2844 3999 5963 7231 Face creams or lotions; candles; home related products, direct sales; cosmetology & personal hygiene salons;

(G-8314)
INDUSTRIAL MARKING PRODUCTS
1415 Grovenburg Rd (48842-8613)
P.O. Box 314 (48842-0314)
PHONE.............................517 699-2160
Gale Wilson, *President*
Larry Osborn, *Vice Pres*
EMP: 6 **EST:** 1988
SQ FT: 2,500
SALES (est): 494.1K **Privately Held**
WEB: www.industrialmarking.com
SIC: 3312 Plate, steel

(G-8315)
INNOVATIVE PACKG SOLUTIONS LLC
2075 Dean Ave Ste 2 (48842-1314)
PHONE.............................517 213-3169
EMP: 4
SALES (est): 249.1K **Privately Held**
SIC: 3089 7389 Mfg Plastic Products Business Services At Non-Commercial Site

(G-8316)
LASERS PLUS LLC
4421 Hyacinth (48842-8778)
PHONE.............................734 926-1030
Joshua Stephens, *Mng Member*
EMP: 6 **EST:** 2018
SALES (est): 182.1K **Privately Held**
SIC: 3479 Etching & engraving

(G-8317)
MANTISSA INDUSTRIES INC
2362 Jarco Dr (48842-1210)
PHONE.............................517 694-2260
Jeffrey Holoweiko, *President*
Samuel Holoweiko, *Info Tech Mgr*
EMP: 5 **EST:** 1988
SQ FT: 7,000
SALES (est): 871.4K **Privately Held**
WEB: www.mantissainds.com
SIC: 3089 3543 Injection molding of plastics; industrial patterns

(G-8318)
MOLDED PLASTIC INDUSTRIES INC
Also Called: Mpi
2382 Jarco Dr (48842-1210)
P.O. Box 70 (48842-0070)
PHONE.............................517 694-7434
Frank Phillips Jr, *President*
Steven A Carlson, *CFO*
Scott Parker, *Shareholder*
EMP: 37 **EST:** 1975
SQ FT: 55,000
SALES (est): 7.4MM **Privately Held**
WEB: www.moldedplastic.com
SIC: 3089 Injection molding of plastics

(G-8319)
MOLDED PLASTICS & TOOLING
2200 Depot St (48842-1818)
PHONE.............................517 268-0849
Frank Phillips, *Owner*
EMP: 18 **EST:** 2008
SALES (est): 204.1K **Privately Held**
SIC: 3089 Injection molding of plastics

(G-8320)
OCCASIONS (PA)
3575 Scholar Ln (48842-9423)
PHONE.............................517 694-6437
Mary Bower, *Owner*
EMP: 12 **EST:** 2005
SALES (est): 90.4K **Privately Held**
WEB: www.occasionsandinvites.com
SIC: 2754 Stationery & invitation printing, gravure

(G-8321)
ORCHID MPS HOLDINGS LLC
1489 Cedar St (48842-1875)
PHONE.............................517 694-2300
Nate Folkert, *Mng Member*
EMP: 2743 **EST:** 2007
SALES (est): 48.1MM **Privately Held**
WEB: www.orchid-ortho.com
SIC: 3841 Surgical & medical instruments

(G-8322)
ORCHID ORTHPD SLTONS ORGAN INC
Also Called: Orchid Connecticut
1489 Cedar St (48842-1875)
PHONE.............................203 877-3341
Michael E Miller, *President*
Ted Bloomfield, *Vice Pres*
Derrick Phillips, *Engineer*
Joe Zuzula, *Sales Staff*
Jorge Ramos, *Admin Sec*
EMP: 212 **EST:** 2012
SALES (est): 2.3MM
SALES (corp-wide): 496.9MM **Privately Held**
WEB: www.orchid-ortho.com
SIC: 3841 Bone plates & screws
PA: Tulip Us Holdings, Inc.
1489 Cedar St
Holt MI 48842
517 694-2300

(G-8323)
ORCHID ORTHPD SOLUTIONS LLC (HQ)
Also Called: Orchid Lansing
1489 Cedar St (48842-1875)
PHONE.............................517 694-2300
Michael E Miller, *President*
Clay Clayton, *General Mgr*
Matt Burba, *Exec VP*
Matthew Burba, *Vice Pres*
Bill Ditty, *Vice Pres*
EMP: 366 **EST:** 2005
SQ FT: 65,000
SALES (est): 220.1MM
SALES (corp-wide): 496.9MM **Privately Held**
WEB: www.orchid-ortho.com
SIC: 3841 Surgical & medical instruments
PA: Tulip Us Holdings, Inc.
1489 Cedar St
Holt MI 48842
517 694-2300

(G-8324)
PAGEANT HOMES INC
Also Called: Lumbertown
4000 Holt Rd (48842-1844)
P.O. Box 39 (48842-0039)
PHONE.............................517 694-0431
Kenneth Hope, *President*
Louis Legg Jr, *Treasurer*
Bruce Korstange, *Admin Sec*
EMP: 9 **EST:** 1957
SQ FT: 11,500
SALES (est): 860.6K **Privately Held**
WEB: www.legglumber.com
SIC: 2452 2541 Prefabricated buildings, wood; wood partitions & fixtures

(G-8325)
PRATT & WHITNEY AUTOAIR INC
Also Called: Auto-Air Composites
1781 Holloway Dr (48842-9795)
PHONE.............................517 348-1416
EMP: 26
SALES (corp-wide): 56.5B **Publicly Held**
WEB: www.prattwhitney.com
SIC: 3724 3544 Aircraft engines & engine parts; special dies, tools, jigs & fixtures
HQ: Pratt & Whitney Autoair, Inc.
5640 Enterprise Dr
Lansing MI 48911
517 393-4040

(G-8326)
PRINTING CENTRE INC
Also Called: Paper Image Printing Centres
1900 Cedar St (48842-1806)
PHONE.............................517 694-2400
Cindy Heister, *President*
Todd Wallis, *Senior Mgr*
EMP: 10 **EST:** 1974
SQ FT: 2,000
SALES (est): 808.8K **Privately Held**
WEB: www.paperimage.net
SIC: 2752 2791 7334 Commercial printing, offset; typesetting; photocopying & duplicating services

(G-8327)
ROSE DENIM
2301 Tiffany Ln (48842-9778)
PHONE.............................517 694-3020
Denise Rowe, *Principal*
EMP: 5 **EST:** 2007
SALES (est): 133.9K **Privately Held**
SIC: 2211 Denims

(G-8328)
SANITATION STRATEGIES LLC
1798 Holloway Dr Ste A (48842-7726)
PHONE.............................517 268-3303
Sherman McDonald, *President*
Steve Barrons, *Vice Pres*
Linda McDonald, *Vice Pres*
Melissa Massie, *Opers Mgr*
EMP: 11 **EST:** 2003
SQ FT: 2,000
SALES (est): 2.4MM **Privately Held**
WEB: www.sanitationstrategies.com
SIC: 2841 Soap & other detergents

(G-8329)
SCITEX LLC
Also Called: Trick Titanium
2046 Depot St Bldg B (48842-1814)
PHONE.............................517 694-7449
Michael Miller, *President*
Kip Harrison, *Sales Executive*
EMP: 7 **EST:** 2010
SALES (est): 776.7K **Privately Held**
WEB: www.tricktitanium.com
SIC: 3356 Titanium

(G-8330)
SCITEX LLC
Also Called: Trick Titanium
3982 Holt Rd (48842-9701)
P.O. Box 428 (48842-0428)
PHONE.............................517 694-7449
Eric Muska, *General Mgr*
Scott Cunningham, *Controller*
Ed McDyer, *Manager*
Mike Miller,
EMP: 20 **EST:** 2008
SALES (est): 2MM **Privately Held**
WEB: www.tricktitanium.com
SIC: 3356 Titanium

(G-8331)
SET LIQUIDATION INC (PA)
Also Called: Stealth Medical Technologies
1489 Cedar St (48842-1875)
PHONE.............................517 694-2300
Michael E Miller, *Ch of Bd*
Lawrence Peek, *President*
Mary Callaghan, *Corp Secy*
▲ **EMP:** 70 **EST:** 1993
SQ FT: 12,800
SALES (est): 5.1MM **Privately Held**
WEB: www.orchid-ortho.com
SIC: 3842 3494 8711 Implants, surgical; valves & pipe fittings; engineering services

(G-8332)
SHAYLESLIE CORPORATION
Also Called: Gaffey & Associates
2385 Delhi Commerce Dr # 1 (48842-2192)
P.O. Box 137 (48842-0137)
PHONE.............................517 694-4115
David J Gaffey, *President*
Shay Leslie Gaffey, *Vice Pres*
EMP: 4 **EST:** 1980
SQ FT: 10,000
SALES (est): 863.4K **Privately Held**
WEB: www.gogaffey.com
SIC: 5112 5199 2752 Business forms; office supplies; data processing supplies; advertising specialties; commercial printing, offset

(G-8333)
STINKN PRETTY LLC
1624 Gunn Rd (48842-9602)
PHONE.............................517 694-8659
Mary Parker, *Principal*
EMP: 5 **EST:** 2010
SALES (est): 103.3K **Privately Held**
SIC: 2844 Toilet preparations

(G-8334)
STONE CIRCLE BAKEHOUSE LLC
3647 Willoughby Rd (48842-9409)
PHONE.............................517 881-0603
Kevin Cosgrove,
EMP: 4 **EST:** 2006
SALES (est): 250K **Privately Held**
WEB: www.stonecirclebakehouse.com
SIC: 2051 Bakery: wholesale or wholesale/retail combined

(G-8335)
THUNDER BAY PRESS INC
2325 Jarco Dr (48842-1209)
P.O. Box 637 (48842-0637)
PHONE.............................517 694-3205
▲ **EMP:** 25
SQ FT: 30,000
SALES (est): 1.5MM
SALES (corp-wide): 123.2MM **Privately Held**
SIC: 2731 Publishing
PA: Partners Book Distributing, Inc.
2325 Jarco Dr
Holt MI 48842
517 694-3205

(G-8336)
TULIP US HOLDINGS INC (PA)
Also Called: Orchid Orthopedic Solutions
1489 Cedar St (48842-1875)
PHONE.............................517 694-2300
Jerome Jurkiewicz, *CEO*
Gina Feathers, *Opers Staff*
Billy Lu, *Engineer*
John Mathews, *Engineer*
Mitch Monahan, *Engineer*

Holton - Muskegon County (G-8337) — GEOGRAPHIC SECTION

EMP: 40 EST: 2011
SALES (est): 496.9MM **Privately Held**
WEB: www.orchid-ortho.com
SIC: 3841 Surgical & medical instruments

Holton
Muskegon County

(G-8337)
BEAVER CREEK CABINETS LLC
8636 Skeels Rd (49425-9794)
PHONE 231 821-2861
Johnnie Troyer Jr, *Administration*
EMP: 4 EST: 2016
SALES (est): 103K **Privately Held**
WEB: www.beavercreekcabinets.com
SIC: 2434 Wood kitchen cabinets

(G-8338)
H & M PALLET LLC
9148 S 200th Ave (49425-9656)
PHONE 231 821-8800
Melvin Miller, *Partner*
Jerry Miller,
EMP: 10 EST: 1998
SQ FT: 18,000
SALES (est): 1.1MM **Privately Held**
SIC: 2448 Pallets, wood

(G-8339)
JOSEPH MILLER
Also Called: Summit Truss
7781 Brickyard Rd (49425-9516)
PHONE 231 821-2430
Joseph Miller, *Principal*
EMP: 3 EST: 2006
SQ FT: 7,700
SALES (est): 1.3MM **Privately Held**
SIC: 2439 Trusses, wooden roof

(G-8340)
LAUGHING NEEDLES EMB LLC
6471 Holton Duck Lake Rd (49425-9523)
PHONE 231 720-5789
Debra Daunt, *Principal*
EMP: 4 EST: 2015
SALES (est): 45.8K **Privately Held**
WEB: www.mtneedlesembroidery.com
SIC: 2395 Embroidery & art needlework

(G-8341)
MAST MINI BARNS LLC
7680 Meinert Rd (49425-9706)
PHONE 231 924-3895
Alvin F Mast,
EMP: 4 EST: 1988
SQ FT: 5,000
SALES (est): 475.8K **Privately Held**
WEB: www.minibarnsonline.com
SIC: 3448 Prefabricated metal buildings

(G-8342)
VOGEL ENGINEERING INC
6688 Maple Island Rd (49425-7547)
PHONE 231 821-2125
Wayne Vogel, *President*
David Vogel, *Vice Pres*
Karen Vogel, *Treasurer*
EMP: 9 EST: 1977
SQ FT: 35,000
SALES (est): 2.1MM **Privately Held**
WEB: www.vogel-engineering.com
SIC: 3561 Pumps & pumping equipment

(G-8343)
WOOD HAVEN TRUSS
7950 Brunswick Rd (49425-9574)
PHONE 231 821-0252
EMP: 4 EST: 2017
SALES (est): 72K **Privately Held**
WEB: www.woodhaventruss.com
SIC: 3999 Manufacturing industries

Homer
Calhoun County

(G-8344)
AMSTED RAIL COMPANY INC
124 W Platt St (49245-1033)
PHONE 517 568-4161
EMP: 8 EST: 2016
SALES (est): 526.5K **Privately Held**
WEB: www.amstedrail.com
SIC: 3743 Railroad equipment

(G-8345)
BREMBO
6259 30 Mile Rd (49245-9764)
PHONE 517 568-4398
EMP: 18 EST: 2017
SALES (est): 2.1MM **Privately Held**
WEB: www.brembo.com
SIC: 3714 Motor vehicle parts & accessories

(G-8346)
BREMBO NORTH AMERICA INC
5851 30 Mile Rd (49245-9524)
PHONE 517 568-4398
Katrina Marsh, *Principal*
Johnny Wilson, *Engineer*
Mark Costa, *Human Res Mgr*
Angela Burton, *Program Mgr*
Melissa Radzi, *Manager*
EMP: 7 **Privately Held**
WEB: www.siti.com
SIC: 3714 Motor vehicle brake systems & parts
HQ: Brembo North America, Inc.
47765 Halyard Dr
Plymouth MI 48170

(G-8347)
BREMBO NORTH AMERICA INC
29991 E M 60 (49245-9753)
PHONE 517 568-3301
Stephanie Houser, *Purch Mgr*
Jason Burkhart, *Purchasing*
Mark Olson, *Engineer*
Trent Degrazia, *Sales Staff*
Thomas Leblanc, *Sales Staff*
EMP: 4
SQ FT: 250,000 **Privately Held**
WEB: www.siti.com
SIC: 3599 Machine shop, jobbing & repair
HQ: Brembo North America, Inc.
47765 Halyard Dr
Plymouth MI 48170

(G-8348)
BREMBO NORTH AMERICA HOMER INC
29991 E M 60 (49245-9753)
PHONE 517 568-4398
Dan Sandeburg, *CEO*
EMP: 30 EST: 1993
SALES (est): 3.6MM **Privately Held**
WEB: www.siti.com
SIC: 3599 Machine shop, jobbing & repair
HQ: Brembo North America, Inc.
47765 Halyard Dr
Plymouth MI 48170

(G-8349)
CALHOUN FOUNDRY COMPANY INC
506 S Clay St (49245-1359)
P.O. Box 218 (49245-0218)
PHONE 517 568-4415
George J Petredean, *Ch of Bd*
Micheal Hamaker, *President*
Melodie Avery, *Engineer*
Suzanne Nelson, *Treasurer*
Walt Bowers, *Sales Staff*
EMP: 62 EST: 1943
SQ FT: 70,000
SALES (est): 8.9MM **Privately Held**
WEB: www.calhounfoundry.com
SIC: 3321 Gray iron castings

(G-8350)
D J S SYSTEMS INC
801 S Hillsdale St (49245-9701)
P.O. Box 70 (49245-0070)
PHONE 517 568-4444
Dave Swope, *President*
Jeff Shermann, *Vice Pres*
▲ EMP: 40 EST: 2003
SQ FT: 20,000
SALES (est): 6.7MM **Privately Held**
WEB: www.djssystems.com
SIC: 3565 Packaging machinery

(G-8351)
F M T PRODUCTS INC
140 W Main St (49245-1046)
PHONE 517 568-3373
Thomas Grant, *President*
▲ EMP: 9 EST: 1984
SQ FT: 10,000
SALES (est): 1.2MM **Privately Held**
WEB: www.fmtproducts.com
SIC: 5013 3647 Automotive supplies & parts; motor vehicle lighting equipment

(G-8352)
HOMER INDEX
122 E Main St (49245-1137)
P.O. Box 236 (49245-0236)
PHONE 517 568-4646
Michael Warner, *Partner*
Sharon Warner, *Partner*
EMP: 4 EST: 1872
SALES (est): 281.5K **Privately Held**
WEB: www.homerindex.com
SIC: 2711 Newspapers, publishing & printing

(G-8353)
MCCONNELL & SCULLY INC (PA)
146 W Main St (49245-1046)
PHONE 517 568-4104
Ron Mc Connell, *President*
Elaine M Seitz, *Corp Secy*
Tom Mc Nicholas, *Vice Pres*
EMP: 2 EST: 1966
SQ FT: 11,000
SALES (est): 6MM **Privately Held**
WEB: www.mcconnell-scully-inc.business.site
SIC: 1389 Oil field services

(G-8354)
MCS INDUSTRIES INC
Also Called: Steel Products
124 W Platt St (49245-1033)
P.O. Box 217 (49245-0217)
PHONE 517 568-4161
Chris Miller, *President*
EMP: 11 EST: 1991
SQ FT: 8,000
SALES (est): 1.4MM **Privately Held**
WEB: www.steelproducts-mcs.com
SIC: 3441 Fabricated structural metal

(G-8355)
NAGEL MEAT PROCESSING
3265 22 Mile Rd (49245-9647)
PHONE 517 568-5035
Joseph Nagel, *Owner*
EMP: 7 EST: 1992
SALES (est): 932.6K **Privately Held**
SIC: 2011 7299 Meat packing plants; butcher service, processing only

(G-8356)
RSB TRANSMISSIONS NA INC (DH)
24425 W M 60 (49245-9651)
P.O. Box 68 (49245-0068)
PHONE 517 568-4171
Paul Metzbar, *General Mgr*
Priya Ranjan, *Vice Pres*
Durga Das, *Opers Staff*
Jerry Odell, *Purch Agent*
Karen Manus, *Engineer*
▲ EMP: 81 EST: 1990
SQ FT: 75,000
SALES (est): 24.8MM **Privately Held**
WEB: www.rsbna.com
SIC: 3599 Machine shop, jobbing & repair

(G-8357)
TEKKRA SYSTEMS INC
300 S Elm St (49245-1337)
PHONE 517 568-4121
Nels E Vorm, *President*
EMP: 26 EST: 2005
SQ FT: 20,000
SALES (est): 407.5K **Privately Held**
WEB: www.texwrap.com
SIC: 3565 Packaging machinery

(G-8358)
TROJAN HEAT TREAT INC
809 S Byron St (49245-9761)
P.O. Box 97 (49245-0097)
PHONE 517 568-4403
Ronald Di Salvio, *President*
Kristine Tracy, *QC Mgr*
Jeff Jones, *Plant Engr*
EMP: 62 EST: 1959
SQ FT: 46,000
SALES (est): 5.4MM
SALES (corp-wide): 26MM **Privately Held**
WEB: www.htsmi.com
SIC: 3398 Metal heat treating
PA: Heat Treating Services Corporation Of America
217 Central Ave
Pontiac MI 48341
248 858-2230

Honor
Benzie County

(G-8359)
FIELD CRAFTS INC (PA)
Also Called: Bookwear
9930 Honor Hwy (49640-9534)
PHONE 231 325-1122
John Gyr, *President*
EMP: 12 EST: 1977
SQ FT: 9,400
SALES (est): 2.1MM **Privately Held**
WEB: www.fieldcrafts.com
SIC: 2396 2759 Screen printing on fabric articles; commercial printing

(G-8360)
RAK WELDING
7739 Valley Rd (49640-9732)
PHONE 231 651-0732
Roger Kerby, *Principal*
EMP: 4 EST: 2018
SALES (est): 57.2K **Privately Held**
SIC: 7692 Welding repair

Hope
Midland County

(G-8361)
INTERNATIONAL ENGRG & MFG INC
Also Called: IEM
6054 N Meridian Rd (48628-9786)
P.O. Box 316, Edenville (48620-0316)
PHONE 989 689-4911
Robert Musselman, *President*
Ken Pincumbe, *Purchasing*
Serena Gardener, *Human Res Dir*
Larry Tiede, *Sales Dir*
Steve Piechocki, *Manager*
▲ EMP: 96 EST: 1968
SQ FT: 27,640
SALES (est): 12.3MM **Privately Held**
WEB: www.internationalengineeringinc.com
SIC: 3429 Manufactured hardware (general)

(G-8362)
L & M MFG INC
6016 N Meridian Rd (48628-9786)
PHONE 989 689-4010
Mark Wilkins, *President*
EMP: 4 EST: 1986
SQ FT: 6,800
SALES (est): 336K **Privately Held**
WEB: www.lmmfg.com
SIC: 3536 Boat lifts

(G-8363)
ROSES SUSIES FEATHER
7191 Middle Rd (48628-9307)
PHONE 989 689-6570
Mark Stewart, *Owner*
EMP: 4
SALES (est): 157.5K **Privately Held**
SIC: 3999 Flowers, artificial & preserved

(G-8364)
TRI-CITY REPAIR COMPANY
6700 Middle Rd (48628-9306)
PHONE 989 835-4784
Melvin R Vanmeter, *President*
Chris R Vanmeter, *Vice Pres*
Beverly J Riggie, *Treasurer*
Betty L Vanmeter, *Admin Sec*
EMP: 5 EST: 1983
SQ FT: 2,400

SALES (est): 275K **Privately Held**
SIC: 7699 3599 Industrial machinery & equipment repair; machine shop, jobbing & repair

(G-8365)
YACKS DRY DOCK
6227 N Meridian Rd (48628-9740)
PHONE 989 689-6749
EMP: 4 **EST:** 2010
SALES (est): 210K **Privately Held**
SIC: 3421 Mfg Cutlery

Hopkins
Allegan County

(G-8366)
MATERIAL HDLG TECHNIQUES INC
2782 134th Ave (49328-9528)
PHONE 616 890-1475
Steve Brunsink, *President*
Ron Brunsink, *Vice Pres*
EMP: 6 **EST:** 1995
SALES (est): 659.9K **Privately Held**
WEB: www.mht.works
SIC: 3535 Conveyors & conveying equipment

(G-8367)
MILLER SAND & GRAVEL COMPANY
1466 120th Ave (49328-9626)
PHONE 269 672-5601
Tom E Miller, *President*
Marvin Miller, *Vice Pres*
Helena Miller, *Treasurer*
Mary Carlson, *Admin Sec*
EMP: 8
SQ FT: 2,500
SALES (est): 520K **Privately Held**
WEB: www.millersand.com
SIC: 1442 3273 4212 Common sand mining; gravel mining; ready-mixed concrete; dump truck haulage

(G-8368)
REG PUBLISHERS LLC
2191 Walker Ridge Rd (49328-9536)
PHONE 616 889-4232
AMI Walker, *Principal*
EMP: 5 **EST:** 2012
SALES (est): 88K **Privately Held**
SIC: 2741 Miscellaneous publishing

(G-8369)
SEBRIGHT PRODUCTS INC (PA)
127 N Water St (49328-5116)
P.O. Box 296 (49328-0296)
PHONE 269 793-7183
David Sebright, *Ch of Bd*
Brent Sebright, *President*
Stuart Sebright, *General Mgr*
Lee Murray, *Vice Pres*
Ed Rewa, *Parts Mgr*
EMP: 20
SQ FT: 5,100
SALES (est): 16.1MM **Privately Held**
WEB: www.sebrightproducts.com
SIC: 3589 5084 Garbage disposers & compactors, commercial; industrial machinery & equipment

(G-8370)
SHRED-PAC INC
Also Called: Sp Industries
2982 22nd St (49328-9783)
PHONE 269 793-7978
Dennis Pool, *President*
Roger Arndt, *Exec VP*
Elise Dones, *Treasurer*
EMP: 37 **EST:** 1980
SQ FT: 45,000
SALES (est): 7.6MM **Privately Held**
WEB: www.bestcompactors.com
SIC: 3589 3531 Garbage disposers & compactors, commercial; construction machinery

(G-8371)
SMITH LOGGING LLC
2717 134th Ave (49328-9528)
PHONE 616 558-0729

Dudley Smith, *Principal*
EMP: 4 **EST:** 2016
SALES (est): 70.5K **Privately Held**
WEB: www.joesmithlogging.com
SIC: 2411 Logging camps & contractors

Horton
Jackson County

(G-8372)
CHOCOLATE VAULT LLC
8475 Chicago Rd (49246-9684)
PHONE 517 688-3388
Barb McCann, *CTO*
James McCann,
Barbara McCann,
Robert McCann,
EMP: 7 **EST:** 1983
SALES (est): 697.7K **Privately Held**
WEB: www.chocolatevault.com
SIC: 2026 5441 2064 Milk, chocolate; candy; candy bars, including chocolate covered bars; chocolate candy, except solid chocolate

(G-8373)
LOMAR MACHINE & TOOL CO
5931 Coats Rd (49246-9405)
PHONE 517 563-8136
Jason Dorian, *Project Mgr*
Eric Page, *Design Engr*
Mark Cuff, *Sales Mgr*
Matt Murphy, *Program Mgr*
Ronald Geisman, *Manager*
EMP: 21
SALES (corp-wide): 24.3MM **Privately Held**
WEB: www.lomar.com
SIC: 3599 Machine shop, jobbing & repair
PA: Lomar Machine & Tool Co.
    135 Main St
    Horton MI 49246
    517 563-8136

(G-8374)
LOMAR MACHINE & TOOL CO (PA)
135 Main St (49246-9540)
P.O. Box 128 (49246-0128)
PHONE 517 563-8136
Ronald E Geisman, *CEO*
Charles Murphy, *Vice Pres*
Mark Gladstone, *Plant Mgr*
Jason Dorian, *Project Mgr*
Tim Murphy, *Mfg Mgr*
EMP: 21 **EST:** 1976
SQ FT: 630,000
SALES (est): 24.3MM **Privately Held**
WEB: www.lomar.com
SIC: 3549 3544 Assembly machines, including robotic; special dies & tools; jigs & fixtures

(G-8375)
LOMAR MACHINE & TOOL CO
7595 Moscow Rd (49246-9301)
PHONE 517 563-8136
Barb Meyers, *Controller*
EMP: 8 **EST:** 2019
SALES (est): 259.7K **Privately Held**
WEB: www.lomar.com
SIC: 3599 Machine shop, jobbing & repair

(G-8376)
LOMAR MACHINE & TOOL CO
Also Called: Low Mar
7595 Moscow Rd (49246-9301)
PHONE 517 563-8800
Ron Geisman, *President*
EMP: 21
SALES (corp-wide): 24.3MM **Privately Held**
WEB: www.lomar.com
SIC: 3599 Machine shop, jobbing & repair
PA: Lomar Machine & Tool Co.
    135 Main St
    Horton MI 49246
    517 563-8136

(G-8377)
MEDICAL ENGINEERING & DEV
4910 Dancer Rd (49246-9016)
PHONE 517 563-2352
Bruce Harshe, *President*

Sharon Harshe, *Vice Pres*
EMP: 4 **EST:** 1985
SQ FT: 200
SALES (est): 298.1K **Privately Held**
SIC: 8731 3841 Commercial physical research; surgical & medical instruments

(G-8378)
RACK & PINION INC
7595 Moscow Rd (49246-9301)
P.O. Box 128 (49246-0128)
PHONE 517 563-8872
James L Geisman, *President*
Ron E Geisman, *Vice Pres*
Chuck Murphy, *Treasurer*
EMP: 7 **EST:** 1989
SQ FT: 11,000
SALES (est): 860.9K **Privately Held**
WEB: www.lomar.com
SIC: 3714 3462 Motor vehicle body components & frame; iron & steel forgings

Houghton
Houghton County

(G-8379)
6DF RESEARCH LLC
101 W Lkshore Dr Ste 101g (49931)
PHONE 906 281-1170
Dorothy Ruohonen, *Principal*
Jay Ruohonen, *Principal*
EMP: 4 **EST:** 2020
SALES (est): 49.1K **Privately Held**
SIC: 3861 Sensitometers, photographic

(G-8380)
ANDERSON WELDING & MFG INC
301 W Edwards Ave (49931-2229)
PHONE 906 523-4661
Ron Anderson, *CEO*
EMP: 13 **EST:** 1986
SALES (est): 1.1MM **Privately Held**
WEB: www.andweld.com
SIC: 3715 3443 3444 5083 Truck trailers; weldments; sheet metalwork; livestock equipment; machine shop, jobbing & repair; welding on site

(G-8381)
CONSISTACOM INC
47420 State Highway M26 # 2 (49931-2819)
P.O. Box 293 (49931-0293)
PHONE 906 482-7653
Steven C Fitzgerald, *President*
EMP: 6 **EST:** 2004
SALES (est): 494.2K **Privately Held**
WEB: www.consistacom.com
SIC: 7372 Business oriented computer software

(G-8382)
GREENFORCES LLC
600 E Lkshore Dr Ste 111 (49931)
PHONE 906 231-7769
Melvin Cooke, *Principal*
EMP: 5 **EST:** 2016
SALES (est): 119.7K **Privately Held**
WEB: www.greenforcesllc.com
SIC: 3599 Machine shop, jobbing & repair

(G-8383)
HOUGHTON CMNTY BRDCSTG CORP
313 E Montezuma Ave (49931-2112)
PHONE 906 482-7700
EMP: 9 **EST:** 2019
SALES (est): 557.3K **Privately Held**
WEB: www.thewolf.fm
SIC: 2711 Newspapers

(G-8384)
LAWRENCE J JULIO LLC
Also Called: Lawrence Co
47212 Main St (49931-9753)
P.O. Box 604 (49931-0604)
PHONE 906 483-4781
EMP: 5
SALES (est): 80K **Privately Held**
SIC: 3531 Whol Industrial Equipment

(G-8385)
LITEBRAKE TECH LLC
406 2nd St (49931-2206)
PHONE 906 523-2007
Scott Huang, *Mng Member*
Xiaodi Huang, *Manager*
Nannon Huang,
EMP: 5 **EST:** 2012
SALES (est): 277.7K **Privately Held**
WEB: www.litebrake.com
SIC: 3714 Motor vehicle brake systems & parts

(G-8386)
LITSENBERGER PRINT SHOP
Also Called: Print Shop, The
224 Shelden Ave (49931-2134)
PHONE 906 482-3903
Thomas A Litsenberger, *Owner*
Bobbie Jean Litsenberger, *Co-Owner*
Bobbi Jean Litsenberger, *Graphic Designe*
EMP: 8 **EST:** 1976
SQ FT: 3,000
SALES (est): 476.4K **Privately Held**
WEB: www.theprintshophoughton.com
SIC: 2752 2791 2789 2672 Commercial printing, offset; typesetting; bookbinding & related work; coated & laminated paper

(G-8387)
NANO INNOVATIONS LLC
22151 Ridge Rd (49931-9010)
PHONE 906 231-2101
Yoke Khin Yap,
John Diebel,
EMP: 4 **EST:** 2012
SALES (est): 178.1K **Privately Held**
SIC: 3299 Ceramic fiber

(G-8388)
ORBION SPACE TECHNOLOGY INC
101 W Lakeshore Dr Ste 4 (49931-2274)
PHONE 906 362-2509
Lyon King, *CEO*
Sam Baxendale, *Electrical Engi*
EMP: 23 **EST:** 2017
SALES (est): 2.6MM **Privately Held**
WEB: www.orbionspace.com
SIC: 3764 Guided missile & space vehicle propulsion unit parts; propulsion units for guided missiles & space vehicles

(G-8389)
PEPSI COLA BOTLING CO HOUGHTON
Also Called: Pepsico
309 E Sharon Ave (49931-1908)
PHONE 906 482-0161
William Harvey, *Owner*
Jim Holmquest, *General Mgr*
EMP: 16 **EST:** 1986
SALES (est): 2MM **Privately Held**
WEB: www.pepsico.com
SIC: 2086 Carbonated soft drinks, bottled & canned

(G-8390)
QUINCY WOODWRIGHTS LLC (PA)
408 E Montezuma Ave (49931-2115)
PHONE 808 397-0818
Jonathan D Julien, *Principal*
EMP: 4 **EST:** 2013
SQ FT: 26,000
SALES (est): 295.3K **Privately Held**
SIC: 2435 Veneer stock, hardwood

(G-8391)
SCOTT JOHNSON FOREST PDTS CO
43850 Superior Rd (49931-9770)
PHONE 906 482-3978
Scott Johnson, *President*
EMP: 7 **EST:** 2004
SALES (est): 451.6K **Privately Held**
SIC: 2411 Logging camps & contractors

(G-8392)
SUPERIOR BLOCK COMPANY INC
100 Isle Royale St (49931)
P.O. Box 6 (49931-0006)
PHONE 906 482-2731

Joan Lorenzetti, *CEO*
EMP: 21 **EST:** 1946
SQ FT: 12,000
SALES (est): 3.3MM **Privately Held**
WEB: www.superiorblock.com
SIC: 3271 Blocks, concrete or cinder: standard

(G-8393)
THOMAS J MOYLE JR INCORPORATED (PA)
Also Called: Moyle Lumber
46702 Hwy M 26 (49931)
P.O. Box 414 (49931-0414)
PHONE..................906 482-3000
Tom Moyle, *CEO*
Andy Moyle, *President*
Kimberly Moyle, *Treasurer*
Gary Moyle, *Manager*
EMP: 18 **EST:** 1978
SQ FT: 3,200
SALES (est): 7.1MM **Privately Held**
WEB: www.moyleusa.com
SIC: 1542 1521 3531 5211 Commercial & office building, new construction; new construction, single-family houses; concrete plants; lumber products; gravel

Houghton Lake
Roscommon County

(G-8394)
BOS FIELD MACHINING INC
Also Called: Beano's On Site Machining
1750 Maywood Rd (48629-9238)
P.O. Box 913 (48629-0913)
PHONE..................517 204-1688
Beano Sterns, *CEO*
Trish Stearns, *Office Mgr*
EMP: 6 **EST:** 1999
SALES (est): 504.9K **Privately Held**
SIC: 3599 Machine shop, jobbing & repair

(G-8395)
CHAMPION FORTUNE CORPORATION
387 S Harrison Rd (48629-8613)
P.O. Box 849 (48629-0849)
PHONE..................989 422-6130
Gregg Hetzinger, *President*
EMP: 15 **EST:** 1974
SQ FT: 30,000
SALES (est): 640.7K **Privately Held**
WEB: www.championfortune.com
SIC: 3599 Machine shop, jobbing & repair

(G-8396)
CLIFFS SAND & GRAVEL INC
1128 Federal Ave (48629-8945)
PHONE..................989 422-3463
Clifton Halliday, *President*
EMP: 6 **EST:** 1973
SALES (est): 412.7K **Privately Held**
SIC: 1442 Construction sand mining; gravel mining

(G-8397)
HALLIDAY SAND & GRAVEL INC
1128 Federal Ave (48629-8945)
PHONE..................989 422-3463
Clifton Halliday, *President*
Edah Halliday, *Corp Secy*
EMP: 40 **EST:** 1963
SALES (est): 4.7MM **Privately Held**
SIC: 1442 Construction sand mining; gravel mining

(G-8398)
HAMP
126 Winding Dr (48629-9153)
PHONE..................989 366-5341
Eric M Hamp, *Principal*
EMP: 8 **EST:** 2010
SALES (est): 71.1K **Privately Held**
SIC: 2711 Newspapers, publishing & printing

(G-8399)
HL OUTDOORS
308 Huron St (48629-9756)
P.O. Box 1013 (48629-1013)
PHONE..................989 422-3264
Steven L Johnston, *Owner*

EMP: 4 **EST:** 2001
SALES (est): 149.8K **Privately Held**
WEB: www.hloutdoors.com
SIC: 5091 3949 Fishing tackle; fishing tackle, general

(G-8400)
HOUGHTON LAKE RESORTER INC
4049 W Houghton Lake Dr (48629-9208)
P.O. Box 248 (48629-0248)
PHONE..................989 366-5341
Thoams W Hamp, *President*
Thomas W Hamp, *President*
Eric Hamp, *Editor*
Patricia Hamp, *Corp Secy*
Robert J Hamp Jr, *Vice Pres*
EMP: 18 **EST:** 1961
SQ FT: 5,000
SALES (est): 1.5MM **Privately Held**
WEB: www.houghtonlakeresorter.com
SIC: 2711 2752 2759 Newspapers: publishing only, not printed on site; commercial printing, offset; letterpress printing

(G-8401)
KUZIMSKI ENTERPRISES INC
Also Called: North Central Machine
9100 Knapp Rd (48629-8800)
PHONE..................989 422-5377
Kurt Kuzimski, *Principal*
EMP: 8 **EST:** 1995
SALES (est): 962.3K **Privately Held**
WEB: www.northcentralmachine.com
SIC: 3599 Machine shop, jobbing & repair

(G-8402)
PACKYS PET SUPPLIES LLC
9437 E Houghton Lake Dr (48629-8325)
PHONE..................989 422-5484
Peter Bush, *Administration*
EMP: 5 **EST:** 2019
SALES (est): 278.7K **Privately Held**
WEB: www.packyspetsupplies.com
SIC: 3999 Pet supplies

(G-8403)
SPICERS BOAT CY HUGHTON LK INC
4165 W Houghton Lake Dr (48629-8277)
PHONE..................989 366-8384
Phillip Spicer, *President*
Mike Trent, *Sales Staff*
Don Wigard, *Sales Staff*
EMP: 50 **EST:** 1959
SQ FT: 16,500
SALES (est): 7.9MM **Privately Held**
WEB: www.spicersboatcity.com
SIC: 5551 5599 4493 3732 Motor boat dealers; marine supplies; snowmobiles; boat yards, storage & incidental repair; boat building & repairing

(G-8404)
SRM CONCRETE LLC
9142 Knapp Rd (48629-8800)
PHONE..................989 422-4202
Steve Diss, *Branch Mgr*
EMP: 8
SALES (corp-wide): 170.1MM **Privately Held**
WEB: www.lcredimix.com
SIC: 3273 Ready-mixed concrete
PA: Srm Concrete, Llc
   1136 2nd Ave N
   Nashville TN 37208
   615 355-1028

(G-8405)
STAR BUYERS GUIDE
4772 W Houghton Lake Dr (48629-8221)
PHONE..................989 366-8341
EMP: 4 **EST:** 2011
SALES (est): 150K **Privately Held**
SIC: 2741 Misc Publishing

(G-8406)
SUPERIOR AUTO GLASS OF MICH
7006 W Houghton Lake Dr (48629-9715)
PHONE..................989 366-9691
Allyn C Packman, *President*
Albert J Taylor, *Vice Pres*
EMP: 5 **EST:** 1984

SALES (est): 425.3K **Privately Held**
SIC: 7536 3211 Automotive glass replacement shops; tempered glass

(G-8407)
VISION AIR
5187 W Houghton Lake Dr (48629-8268)
PHONE..................989 202-4100
Chris Putnam, *Principal*
EMP: 8 **EST:** 2009
SALES (est): 167.6K **Privately Held**
SIC: 3564 Air purification equipment

Howard City
Montcalm County

(G-8408)
CUSTOM DESIGN COMPONENTS INC
19569 W Edgar Rd (49329-9207)
PHONE..................231 937-6166
Robert Deurloo, *President*
Robert E Deurloo, *President*
Richard Barnes, *CIO*
EMP: 25 **EST:** 1993
SQ FT: 3,024
SALES (est): 1MM **Privately Held**
WEB: www.cdc-hydraulics.com
SIC: 3599 Machine shop, jobbing & repair

(G-8409)
HUSH PUPPIES RETAIL LLC
214 Washburn St (49329-9012)
PHONE..................231 937-1004
Steve Johnston, *Director*
EMP: 29
SALES (corp-wide): 1.7B **Publicly Held**
WEB: www.hushpuppies.com
SIC: 3143 5139 Men's footwear, except athletic; footwear
HQ: Hush Puppies Retail, Llc
   9341 Courtland Dr Ne
   Rockford MI 49351
   616 866-5500

(G-8410)
INFLATABLE MARINE PRODUCTS INC
Also Called: Sea Wolf
9485 N Reed Rd Ste C (49329-8621)
PHONE..................616 723-8140
Robert Johnson, *President*
David Johnson, *President*
EMP: 5 **EST:** 2012
SALES (est): 229.3K **Privately Held**
WEB: www.seawolf.biz
SIC: 3089 5551 Plastic boats & other marine equipment; inflatable boats

(G-8411)
LINDY PRESS INC
9794 Locust Ave (49329-9641)
PHONE..................231 937-6169
Deborah Sturgeon, *President*
EMP: 4
SQ FT: 3,000
SALES (est): 270K **Privately Held**
WEB: www.lindypressgr.com
SIC: 2752 Commercial printing, offset

(G-8412)
MIDNIGHT LOGGING LLC
7588 E 112th St (49329-9603)
PHONE..................202 521-1484
Chad Johnson, *Principal*
EMP: 4 **EST:** 2013
SALES (est): 89.8K **Privately Held**
SIC: 2411 Logging

(G-8413)
NORTHERN CABLE & AUTOMTN LLC (PA)
Also Called: Flex Cable
5822 Henkel Rd (49329-8668)
PHONE..................231 937-8000
Jerry Everts, *Mfg Mgr*
Mark Moore, *Engineer*
Cathey Kinney, *Controller*
Stuart Borman, *Mng Member*
Erwin Kroulik, *Manager*
EMP: 60
SQ FT: 50,000

SALES (est): 16.6MM **Privately Held**
WEB: www.flex-cable.com
SIC: 3496 Miscellaneous fabricated wire products

(G-8414)
NORTHERN MOLD
21051 Dewey Rd (49329-8920)
PHONE..................231 629-1342
Bradley K Merchant, *Owner*
Lisa Merchant, *Co-Owner*
EMP: 4 **EST:** 2003
SALES (est): 376.2K **Privately Held**
WEB: www.northernmoldinc.com
SIC: 3089 Injection molding of plastics; plastic processing

(G-8415)
PRECISE MACHINING INC
17279 Almy Rd (49329-9588)
PHONE..................231 937-7957
Carol Deurloo, *CEO*
John Deurloo, *President*
EMP: 5 **EST:** 1993
SALES (est): 307K **Privately Held**
SIC: 3599 Machine shop, jobbing & repair

(G-8416)
RATTLE TOP PRECISION ASSEMBLY
6342 Henkel Rd (49329-8622)
PHONE..................231 937-5333
Edna Holdridge, *Owner*
EMP: 6 **EST:** 2012
SALES (est): 121.5K **Privately Held**
SIC: 3711 Automobile assembly, including specialty automobiles

(G-8417)
RIVERSIDE PLASTIC CO
138 Washburn St (49329-9008)
PHONE..................231 937-7333
Chuck Freeman, *President*
Wesely Freeman, *Shareholder*
EMP: 12 **EST:** 1989
SQ FT: 20,000
SALES (est): 1.6MM **Privately Held**
WEB: www.riversideplastics.com
SIC: 3089 Injection molding of plastics

(G-8418)
ROUHAN SIGNS LLC
23667 Atikwa Trl (49329-9796)
PHONE..................406 202-2369
Andrea Stnson, *Principal*
EMP: 4 **EST:** 2009
SALES (est): 145.6K **Privately Held**
SIC: 3993 Electric signs

(G-8419)
STYX & TWIGS LLC
20912 Almy Rd (49329-9749)
PHONE..................231 245-6083
Dennis Johnson, *Principal*
EMP: 4 **EST:** 2019
SALES (est): 81.7K **Privately Held**
SIC: 2411 Logging

(G-8420)
UNIVERSAL MAGNETICS INC
5555 N Amy School Rd (49329-9722)
PHONE..................231 937-5555
George H Ravell, *President*
Dorothy Ravell, *Corp Secy*
EMP: 7 **EST:** 1975
SQ FT: 4,400
SALES (est): 694.3K **Privately Held**
WEB: www.univmag.com
SIC: 3559 3812 3499 Separation equipment, magnetic; electronic field detection apparatus (aeronautical); magnets, permanent: metallic

Howell
Livingston County

(G-8421)
305 N 3RD LLC
140 Skyline Dr (48843-8678)
PHONE..................517 404-1212
Craig Mincy, *Principal*
EMP: 4 **EST:** 2017

GEOGRAPHIC SECTION
Howell - Livingston County (G-8447)

SALES (est): 53.5K **Privately Held**
SIC: 3949 Winter sports equipment

(G-8422)
A & M MOBILE WELDING & FAB LLC
159 Groveland Dr (48843-9622)
PHONE................................517 672-0289
Al Charbonneau, *Principal*
EMP: 4 **EST:** 2018
SALES (est): 126.4K **Privately Held**
SIC: 7692 Welding repair

(G-8423)
A S R C INC
4285 Westhill Dr (48843-9492)
PHONE................................517 545-7430
Richard M Keough, *President*
Jennifer Keough, *Corp Secy*
John Keough, *Vice Pres*
EMP: 3 **EST:** 1995
SQ FT: 1,500
SALES (est): 1MM **Privately Held**
WEB: www.asrc.com
SIC: 3554 Folding machines, paper

(G-8424)
AA GEAR LLC
Also Called: Ann Arbor Gear
1045 Durant Dr (48843-9536)
PHONE................................517 552-3100
Pete Lazik, *Principal*
EMP: 18 **EST:** 2009
SQ FT: 112,000
SALES (est): 2.5MM **Privately Held**
SIC: 3714 Gears, motor vehicle

(G-8425)
AARON JAGT
3321 Sesame Dr (48843-9508)
PHONE................................517 304-4844
Aaron Jagt, *Principal*
EMP: 4 **EST:** 2016
SALES (est): 72.3K **Privately Held**
WEB: www.dollarhomeschool.com
SIC: 2741 Miscellaneous publishing

(G-8426)
ALPHA TECHNOLOGY CORPORATION
Also Called: Altec
1450 Mcpherson Park Dr (48843-1936)
P.O. Box 168 (48844-0168)
PHONE................................517 546-9700
Stephen Sweda, *President*
Shigeki Nagano, *President*
Mark Goodman, *General Mgr*
Akio Kobayashi, *Vice Pres*
▲ **EMP:** 21 **EST:** 1956
SQ FT: 6,000
SALES (est): 8.3MM **Privately Held**
WEB: www.altec-us.com
SIC: 3714 5013 3429 Motor vehicle parts & accessories; automotive supplies & parts; keys, locks & related hardware
PA: Alpha Corporation
  1-6-8, Fukuura, Kanazawa-Ku
  Yokohama KNG 236-0

(G-8427)
ALUDYNE NORTH AMERICA INC
2280 W Grand River Ave (48843-8515)
PHONE................................248 728-8642
Matthew Householder, *Opers Mgr*
David F Wells, *Engineer*
Kelly Seychel, *Controller*
Jamie Ulman, *Controller*
Katherine Bruning, *HR Admin*
EMP: 120
SALES (corp-wide): 1.5B **Privately Held**
WEB: www.aludyne.com
SIC: 3714 Motor vehicle parts & accessories
HQ: Aludyne North America Inc.
  300 Galleria Ofcntr Ste 5
  Southfield MI 48034

(G-8428)
AMERICAN CHEMICAL TECH INC (PA)
1892 Hydralic Dr (48855-7309)
PHONE................................866 945-1041
Kevin Kovanda, *President*
Kevin P Kovanda, *President*
James Kovanda, *Vice Pres*
Ross Kovanda, *Vice Pres*
Liz Jordan, *Project Mgr*
▲ **EMP:** 24 **EST:** 1977
SQ FT: 65,000
SALES (est): 33.3MM **Privately Held**
WEB: www.americanchemtech.com
SIC: 5172 2869 Lubricating oils & greases; hydraulic fluids, synthetic base

(G-8429)
ANTOLIN INTERIORS USA INC
Antolin Howell
3705 W Grand River Ave (48855-8792)
PHONE................................517 548-0052
Matt Edwards, *General Mgr*
Robert Stammler, *Engineer*
Nasr Azzi, *Manager*
Michael Moore, *Manager*
Todd Van Bynen, *Executive*
EMP: 718
SALES (corp-wide): 2.6MM **Privately Held**
SIC: 3714 3429 Motor vehicle parts & accessories; manufactured hardware (general)
HQ: Antolin Interiors Usa, Inc.
  1700 Atlantic Blvd
  Auburn Hills MI 48326
  248 373-1749

(G-8430)
BOA SOFTWARE LLC
2541 Birchwood Dr (48855-7664)
PHONE................................517 540-0681
Bill Bobbing, *Principal*
EMP: 4 **EST:** 2010
SALES (est): 96K **Privately Held**
SIC: 7372 Prepackaged software

(G-8431)
BOB MAXEY FORD HOWELL INC
2798 E Grand River Ave (48843-8545)
PHONE................................517 545-5700
Steve Shipley, *Principal*
Dan Duey, *Finance Mgr*
Steve Azar, *Sales Staff*
Michael Cain, *Sales Staff*
Cheri Cash, *Sales Staff*
EMP: 2 **EST:** 2012
SALES (est): 1.6MM **Privately Held**
WEB: www.bobmaxeyfordhowell.com
SIC: 7549 7694 Do-it-yourself garages; motor repair services

(G-8432)
BOTTLING GROUP INC
755 Mcpherson Park Dr (48843-1933)
PHONE................................517 545-2624
EMP: 5 **EST:** 2017
SALES (est): 437K **Privately Held**
SIC: 2086 Bottled & canned soft drinks

(G-8433)
C & D GAGE INC
8736 Glen Haven Dr (48843-8116)
PHONE................................517 548-7049
Dennis J Colegrove, *President*
Harold D Kaupp, *Vice Pres*
EMP: 5
SQ FT: 1,600
SALES (est): 486.5K **Privately Held**
SIC: 3543 Industrial patterns

(G-8434)
CARCOSTICS TECH CTR N AMER INC
1400 Durant Dr (48843-8572)
PHONE................................248 251-1737
Peter Schwibinger, *CEO*
Dietmar Stollenwerk, *COO*
Fiona Baer, *Food Svc Dir*
EMP: 8 **EST:** 2002
SALES (est): 2.5MM
SALES (corp-wide): 514.4MM **Privately Held**
WEB: www.carcoustics.com
SIC: 8711 3089 Acoustical engineering; automotive parts, plastic
HQ: Carcoustics Deutschland Gmbh
  Neuenkamp 8
  Leverkusen NW 51381
  217 190-00

(G-8435)
CARCOUSTICS USA INC
1400 Durant Dr (48843-8572)
PHONE................................517 548-6700
Alexander Elsing, *Business Mgr*
Thomas Sundermann, *Vice Pres*
Burkhard Graske, *Opers Mgr*
Jeff Dych, *Engineer*
Katherine Folk, *Engineer*
▲ **EMP:** 100 **EST:** 1995
SQ FT: 25,000
SALES (est): 21.9MM
SALES (corp-wide): 514.4MM **Privately Held**
WEB: www.carcoustics.com
SIC: 3086 Padding, foamed plastic
HQ: Carcoustics International Gmbh
  Neuenkamp 8
  Leverkusen 51381
  217 190-00

(G-8436)
CENTECH INC
1325 Grand Oaks Dr (48843-8579)
PHONE................................517 546-9185
Keith E Burrison, *President*
EMP: 12 **EST:** 1999
SQ FT: 4,240
SALES (est): 1.5MM **Privately Held**
WEB: www.centechinc.us
SIC: 3599 Machine shop, jobbing & repair

(G-8437)
CHEM-TREND HOLDING INC
1445 Mcpherson Park Dr (48843-3999)
PHONE................................517 545-7980
Devanir Moraes, *President*
Amy Bartrum, *Sales Mgr*
Lori Davis, *Sales Staff*
◆ **EMP:** 1 **EST:** 2001
SALES (est): 2.1MM
SALES (corp-wide): 10.4B **Privately Held**
WEB: www.chemtrend.com
SIC: 2899 Chemical preparations
PA: Freudenberg & Co. Kg
  Hohnerweg 2-4
  Weinheim BW 69469
  620 180-0

(G-8438)
CHEM-TREND LIMITED PARTNERSHIP (HQ)
1445 Mcpherson Park Dr (48843-3999)
P.O. Box 860 (48844-0860)
PHONE................................517 546-4520
Devanir Moraes, *Partner*
Mark Marshall, *COO*
Carl Poslusdny, *Exec VP*
Subramanian Hariharan, *Vice Pres*
Ritesh Nair, *Vice Pres*
◆ **EMP:** 150 **EST:** 1962
SQ FT: 70,000
SALES (est): 63.5MM
SALES (corp-wide): 10.4B **Privately Held**
WEB: www.chemtrend.com
SIC: 2899 2869 Chemical preparations; hydraulic fluids, synthetic base
PA: Freudenberg & Co. Kg
  Hohnerweg 2-4
  Weinheim BW 69469
  620 180-0

(G-8439)
CHEM-TREND LIMITED PARTNERSHIP
3205 E Grand River Ave (48843-8552)
PHONE................................517 546-4520
Mitchell H Berger, *Principal*
EMP: 5
SALES (corp-wide): 10.4B **Privately Held**
WEB: www.chemtrend.com
SIC: 2899 Chemical preparations
HQ: Chem-Trend Limited Partnership
  1445 Mcpherson Park Dr
  Howell MI 48843
  517 546-4520

(G-8440)
CJ CHEMICALS LLC
3469 E Grand River Ave # 112 (48843-8504)
PHONE................................888 274-1044
Cathy Lee, *President*
Hanna Lee, *General Mgr*
Josh Lee, *CFO*
David Lyons, *Sales Mgr*
Eric Earl, *Regl Sales Mgr*
EMP: 18 **EST:** 2010
SALES (est): 10.1MM **Privately Held**
WEB: www.cjchemicals.net
SIC: 2869 Industrial organic chemicals

(G-8441)
CRASH TOOL INC
1225 Fendt Dr (48843-7594)
PHONE................................517 552-0250
Joseph M Goers, *President*
EMP: 12 **EST:** 1988
SQ FT: 10,800
SALES (est): 575.7K **Privately Held**
SIC: 3544 Special dies & tools; jigs & fixtures

(G-8442)
CRB CRANE SERVICES INC (PA)
1194 Austin Ct (48843-9556)
PHONE................................517 552-5699
Craig Bendidict, *President*
Patrica Benedict, *Shareholder*
EMP: 20 **EST:** 1985
SQ FT: 24,000
SALES (est): 5MM **Privately Held**
WEB: www.crbcrane.com
SIC: 3536 Hoists, cranes & monorails

(G-8443)
CREATIVE STITCHING
1155 Purdy Ln (48843-8074)
PHONE................................248 210-9584
EMP: 4 **EST:** 2016
SALES (est): 31.2K **Privately Held**
SIC: 2395 Embroidery & art needlework

(G-8444)
DEWITTS RADIATOR LLC
1275 Grand Oaks Dr (48843-8578)
P.O. Box 288 (48844-0288)
PHONE................................517 548-0600
Jeff Scales, *President*
Shree Cameron, *Prdtn Mgr*
Shree A Cameron, *Production*
EMP: 12 **EST:** 2008
SQ FT: 3,000
SALES (est): 1.8MM **Privately Held**
WEB: www.dewitts.com
SIC: 3714 Radiators & radiator shells & cores, motor vehicle

(G-8445)
DIAMOND CHROME PLATING INC
604 S Michigan Ave (48843-2605)
P.O. Box 557 (48844-0557)
PHONE................................517 546-0150
John L Raymond, *President*
April Smith, *Vice Pres*
EMP: 60 **EST:** 1953
SQ FT: 30,000
SALES (est): 9.8MM
SALES (corp-wide): 20MM **Privately Held**
WEB: www.diamondchromeplating.com
SIC: 3471 Electroplating of metals or formed products
PA: Superior Technology Corp.
  Lacey Pl
  Southport CT 06890
  203 255-1501

(G-8446)
DMI AUTOMOTIVE INC
1200 Durant Dr (48843-9539)
PHONE................................517 548-1414
Dieter Schormann, *President*
Michael Ambrose, *Opers Staff*
EMP: 18 **EST:** 1996
SQ FT: 14,000
SALES (est): 1.2MM **Privately Held**
WEB: www.dmiautomotive.com
SIC: 3471 Chromium plating of metals or formed products

(G-8447)
DONALYN ENTERPRISES INC
Also Called: First Impression Prtg Howell
907 Fowler St (48843-2320)
PHONE................................517 546-9798
Donald Cortez, *President*
Sandie Cortez, *Vice Pres*
EMP: 15 **EST:** 1989
SQ FT: 6,000

Howell - Livingston County (G-8448)
GEOGRAPHIC SECTION

SALES (est): 2.5MM **Privately Held**
WEB: www.fipprint.com
SIC: **2752** 4783 Commercial printing, offset; packing goods for shipping

(G-8448)
DONTECH SOLUTIONS LLC
4755 Treasure Lake Dr (48843-9473)
P.O. Box 5021, Dearborn (48128-0021)
PHONE..................................248 789-3086
Mike Derry, *Manager*
Edward Parpart,
EMP: 13 EST: 2000
SALES (est): 3.5MM **Privately Held**
WEB: www.dontechsolutions.com
SIC: **3714** Automotive wiring harness sets

(G-8449)
DOWN HOME INC (PA)
Also Called: Down & Associates
110 W Grand River Ave (48843-2237)
PHONE..................................517 545-5955
William Down, *President*
EMP: 4 EST: 1983
SALES (est): 583.8K **Privately Held**
WEB: www.downhomeinteriors.com
SIC: **3499** Novelties & giftware, including trophies

(G-8450)
DRATHS CORPORATION
236 Crystal Ct (48843-6141)
PHONE..................................517 349-0668
Willard D Brown, *President*
EMP: 15 EST: 2006
SQ FT: 12,500
SALES (est): 1.1MM **Privately Held**
SIC: **2869** Industrial organic chemicals

(G-8451)
DUSEVOIR ACQUISITIONS LLC
Also Called: Dusevoir Metal Products
1609 White Blossom Ln (48843-8215)
PHONE..................................313 562-5550
Fax: 313 562-7731
EMP: 16
SALES (est): 1.8MM
SALES (corp-wide): 1.8MM **Privately Held**
SIC: **3599** Supplier Of Production Prototype And Experimental Manufactured Metal Components
PA: Double Eagle Defense, Llc
25205 Trowbridge St
Dearborn MI 48124
313 562-5550

(G-8452)
ELEMENT SERVICES LLC
3650 Norton Rd (48843-8909)
PHONE..................................517 672-1005
Steven Tinskey, *Principal*
EMP: 7 EST: 2015
SALES (est): 202.9K **Privately Held**
WEB: www.element.com
SIC: **2819** Elements

(G-8453)
FALCON STAMPING INC
1201 Fendt Dr (48843-7594)
PHONE..................................517 540-6197
Mark Mobley, *President*
Cheryl Swaim, *Corp Secy*
▼ EMP: 9 EST: 2000 **Privately Held**
WEB: www.falconstampinginc.com
SIC: **3469** Stamping metal for the trade

(G-8454)
FIORE CONSTRUCTION
936 Pingree Rd (48843-7695)
PHONE..................................517 404-0000
Melissa Sambiagio, *Owner*
EMP: 8 EST: 2000
SALES (est): 500K **Privately Held**
SIC: **1389** Construction, repair & dismantling services

(G-8455)
FIXTURE MAX INC
327 Catrell Dr (48843-1703)
PHONE..................................517 376-6421
Susan Domen, *Administration*
EMP: 7 EST: 2012
SALES (est): 266.8K **Privately Held**
WEB: www.displaymaxinc.com
SIC: **2542** Partitions & fixtures, except wood

(G-8456)
FRAGRANCE OUTLET INC
1475 N Burkhart Rd E115 (48855-8288)
PHONE..................................517 552-9545
EMP: 5
SALES (corp-wide): 42.4MM **Privately Held**
SIC: **2844** Mfg Toilet Preparations
PA: The Fragrance Outlet Inc
11920 Miramar Pkwy
Miramar FL 33025
305 654-8015

(G-8457)
GUESS INC
Also Called: Guess Factory Store 185
1475 N Burkhart Rd B100 (48855-7325)
PHONE..................................517 546-2933
Brandi Pendle, *Manager*
EMP: 7
SALES (corp-wide): 1.8B **Publicly Held**
WEB: www.guess.com
SIC: **5611** 5621 2325 2339 Clothing, sportswear, men's & boys'; women's sportswear, men's & boys' jeans & dungarees; women's & misses' outerwear
PA: Guess , Inc.
1444 S Alameda St
Los Angeles CA 90021
213 765-3100

(G-8458)
H & B MACHINING LLC
4392 Musson Rd (48855-8055)
PHONE..................................810 986-2423
Anthony Pasienza,
EMP: 4 EST: 2017
SALES (est): 39.6K **Privately Held**
SIC: **3999** Manufacturing industries

(G-8459)
HAND CAST COVERS
425 Mystic Meadows Ct (48843-6341)
PHONE..................................810 225-7770
EMP: 4 EST: 2015
SALES (est): 71.4K **Privately Held**
SIC: **3999** Manufacturing industries

(G-8460)
HIGHLAND ENGINEERING INC
Also Called: HEI
1153 Grand Oaks Dr (48843-8511)
PHONE..................................517 548-4372
Ralph S Beebe, *President*
Sally Beebe, *General Mgr*
Stephanie Rife, *Vice Pres*
Jacob Schumacher, *Project Mgr*
Raymond A Beebe Jr, *CFO*
▼ EMP: 45
SQ FT: 50,000
SALES: 7.9MM **Privately Held**
WEB: www.high-eng.com
SIC: **3535** 3599 3441 3469 Conveyors & conveying equipment; machine shop, jobbing & repair; fabricated structural metal; stamping metal for the trade; special dies, tools, jigs & fixtures; fabricated plate work (boiler shop)

(G-8461)
HOLE INDUSTRIES INCORPORATED
600 Chukker Cv (48843-8685)
PHONE..................................517 548-4229
Scott Hole, *President*
EMP: 7 EST: 1964
SQ FT: 3,500
SALES (est): 750K **Privately Held**
WEB: www.holeindustries.com
SIC: **3568** 3825 Power transmission equipment; instruments to measure electricity

(G-8462)
HORIZON BROS PAINTING CORP
1053 Kendra Ln (48843-8434)
PHONE..................................810 632-3362
Dino Djolaj, *President*
EMP: 8 EST: 1998
SQ FT: 3,000
SALES (est): 2.3MM **Privately Held**
SIC: **1721** 3589 Commercial painting; sandblasting equipment

(G-8463)
HOWELL GEAR COMPANY LLC ✪
1045 Durant Dr (48843-9536)
PHONE..................................517 273-5202
Benjamin Kendzicky, *Controller*
Chad Fietsam, *Mng Member*
EMP: 58 EST: 2021
SALES (est): 25MM **Privately Held**
SIC: **3542** Gear rolling machines

(G-8464)
HOWELL PENNCRAFT INC
3333 W Grand River Ave (48855-7602)
PHONE..................................517 548-2250
EMP: 9 EST: 2019
SALES (est): 133.8K **Privately Held**
WEB: www.ptgtools.com
SIC: **3599** Machine shop, jobbing & repair

(G-8465)
HOWELL TOOL SERVICE INC
5818 Sterling Dr (48843-8861)
PHONE..................................517 548-1114
EMP: 15
SQ FT: 19,000
SALES (est): 1MM **Privately Held**
SIC: **3291** 3545 Mfg Abrasive Products Mfg Machine Tool Accessories

(G-8466)
HOWELLS MAINSTREET WINERY
201 W Grand River Ave (48843-2238)
PHONE..................................517 545-9463
Sandy Vyletel, *Owner*
EMP: 6 EST: 2008
SALES (est): 605.6K **Privately Held**
WEB: www.howellsmainstreetwinery.com
SIC: **5921** 2084 Wine; wines

(G-8467)
JESS ENTERPRISES LLC
Also Called: Lectra Tool Company
5776 E Grand River Ave (48843-9106)
PHONE..................................517 546-5818
Joseph Patrell,
EMP: 9 EST: 1970
SQ FT: 4,000
SALES (est): 904K **Privately Held**
WEB: www.lectratool.com
SIC: **3599** Machine shop, jobbing & repair

(G-8468)
JJ JINKLEHEIMER & CO INC
2705 E Grand River Ave (48843-6634)
P.O. Box 446 (48844-0446)
PHONE..................................517 546-4345
Art Coloma, *President*
Joe Durbin, *Opers Staff*
Brad Austin, *Production*
Mike Cochran, *Production*
Kevin Partain, *Production*
EMP: 17 EST: 1991
SQ FT: 5,000
SALES (est): 2.5MM **Privately Held**
WEB: www.jjjink.com
SIC: **2395** 7389 Embroidery products, except schiffli machine; advertising, promotional & trade show services

(G-8469)
JT GENERAL INDUSTRIES LLC
2837 E Grand River Ave (48843-8548)
PHONE..................................517 712-8481
Jim Jabara, *Principal*
EMP: 4 EST: 2014
SALES (est): 56.6K **Privately Held**
SIC: **3999** Manufacturing industries

(G-8470)
KOPPERT BIOLOGICAL SYSTEMS INC
1502 N Old Us 23 (48843-9036)
PHONE..................................734 641-3763
Paul Koppert, *President*
Henri Oosthoek, *Managing Dir*
Tom Stall, *Prdtn Mgr*
Robert Burroughs, *Facilities Mgr*
Laura Tackett, *Opers Staff*
◆ EMP: 50 EST: 1994
SQ FT: 22,000
SALES (est): 10.6MM
SALES (corp-wide): 183.7K **Privately Held**
WEB: www.koppertus.com
SIC: **2836** Biological products, except diagnostic
HQ: Koppert B.V.
Veilingweg 14
Berkel En Rodenrijs 2651
105 140-444

(G-8471)
KVGA PUBLISHING
804 Spring St (48843-1443)
PHONE..................................517 545-0841
Lorne McKenzie, *Principal*
EMP: 5 EST: 2009
SALES (est): 78.3K **Privately Held**
SIC: **2741** Miscellaneous publishing

(G-8472)
LIVINGSTON MACHINE INC
7445 Schrepfer Rd (48855-9392)
PHONE..................................517 546-4253
James Philburn, *President*
Linda Philburn, *Vice Pres*
EMP: 16 EST: 1979
SQ FT: 16,000
SALES (est): 347.2K **Privately Held**
SIC: **3599** Machine shop, jobbing & repair

(G-8473)
LIVINGSTON STAIRWAY
2521 Bowen Rd (48855-7711)
PHONE..................................517 546-7132
Alan Klais, *Owner*
EMP: 5 EST: 2010
SALES (est): 132.8K **Privately Held**
SIC: **2431** Staircases, stairs & railings

(G-8474)
M S MACHINING SYSTEMS INC (PA)
5833 Fisher Rd (48855-8228)
PHONE..................................517 546-1170
Leo Voglrieder, *President*
Greg Cook, *Purchasing*
EMP: 14 EST: 1979
SQ FT: 20,000
SALES (est): 1.6MM **Privately Held**
WEB: www.machiningsystems.com
SIC: **3541** Numerically controlled metal cutting machine tools

(G-8475)
MAGNATRON NC PATTERN AND MFG
325 Roosevelt St (48843-1861)
PHONE..................................810 522-7520
EMP: 6 EST: 2019
SALES (est): 373.3K **Privately Held**
WEB: www.magnatronrp.com
SIC: **3999** Manufacturing industries

(G-8476)
MASONITE INTERNATIONAL CORP
Also Called: A & F Wood Products
5665 Sterling Dr (48843-9555)
PHONE..................................517 545-5811
Steve Korte, *Treasurer*
EMP: 19
SALES (corp-wide): 2.2B **Publicly Held**
WEB: www.masonite.com
SIC: **2431** Doors, wood
PA: Masonite International Corporation
1242 E 5th Ave
Tampa FL 33605
800 895-2723

(G-8477)
MERCHANTS METALS LLC
830 Grand Oaks Dr (48843-8512)
PHONE..................................810 227-3036
Alexander Baturlin, *Financial Analy*
Christopher Desm, *Manager*
Samuel Hughes, *Manager*
EMP: 10 **Privately Held**
WEB: www.merchantsmetals.com
SIC: **3496** Fencing, made from purchased wire

▲ = Import ▼ = Export
◆ = Import/Export

GEOGRAPHIC SECTION
Howell - Livingston County (G-8505)

HQ: Merchants Metals Llc
211 Perimeter Center Pkwy
Atlanta GA 30346
770 741-0300

(G-8478)
MERITOR SPECIALTY PRODUCTS LLC
Also Called: Aa Gear & Manufacturing
1045 Durant Dr (48843-9536)
PHONE................517 545-5800
EMP: 94 Publicly Held
SIC: 3714 Transmission housings or parts, motor vehicle; gears, motor vehicle
HQ: Meritor Specialty Products Llc
2135 W Maple Rd
Troy MI 48084
248 435-1000

(G-8479)
MICA CRAFTERS INC
3845 W Grand River Ave (48855-7798)
PHONE................517 548-2924
Terrance Newman, *President*
Pat Newman, *Corp Secy*
EMP: 14 EST: 1989
SALES (est): 1MM Privately Held
WEB: www.thriftypenguin.com
SIC: 2541 1799 Counter & sink tops; counter top installation

(G-8480)
MICCUS INC
Also Called: Blubridge
3336 Lakewood Shores Dr (48843-7858)
PHONE................616 604-4449
Jeremy S Kovacs, *President*
Karin Rautiola, *Corp Secy*
Karin Kovacs, *Treasurer*
Christian Groves, *Director*
▲ **EMP: 10 EST: 2008**
SQ FT: 4,000
SALES (est): 788.6K Privately Held
WEB: www.miccus.com
SIC: 3313 Electrometallurgical products

(G-8481)
MICHIGAN ROD PRODUCTS INC (PA)
1326 Grand Oaks Dr (48843-8579)
PHONE................517 552-9812
Edward Lumm, *President*
Jerry Bendert, *Principal*
John Allen, *Vice Pres*
Timothy F Brown, *Vice Pres*
Dave Niec, *Vice Pres*
▲ **EMP: 89 EST: 1981**
SQ FT: 128,000
SALES (est): 20.2MM Privately Held
WEB: www.michrod.com
SIC: 3496 3469 3452 3312 Miscellaneous fabricated wire products; metal stampings; bolts, nuts, rivets & washers; blast furnaces & steel mills

(G-8482)
MICHIGAN TOOL & GAUGE INC
1010 Packard Dr (48843-7338)
PHONE................517 548-4604
Wesley Brown, *President*
Glenda Brown, *Vice Pres*
Jason Kile, *Purchasing*
Jason Stiles, *Marketing Staff*
EMP: 22 EST: 1990
SQ FT: 13,000
SALES (est): 2.3MM Privately Held
WEB: www.michigantool.com
SIC: 3544 Special dies & tools; jigs & fixtures

(G-8483)
NESCO TOOL & FIXTURE LLC
530 Fowler St (48843-2367)
PHONE................517 618-7052
Bryan Norris, *Branch Mgr*
EMP: 9
SALES (corp-wide): 94.4K Privately Held
WEB: www.nescotool.com
SIC: 3544 Special dies & tools
PA: Nesco Tool & Fixture Llc
20830 Cass St
Farmington Hills MI

(G-8484)
NORTHSTAR WHOLESALE
5818 Sterling Dr (48843-8861)
P.O. Box 2273, Brighton (48116-6073)
PHONE................517 545-2379
Dennis Norwood, *President*
▲ **EMP: 12 EST: 1971**
SALES (est): 1MM Privately Held
SIC: 3585 Heating & air conditioning combination units

(G-8485)
NOVARES US LLC
1301 Mcpherson Park Dr (48843-1935)
PHONE................517 546-1900
Joe McKinley, *General Mgr*
John Burke, *Mfg Staff*
Eddie Durfee, *Mfg Staff*
Cheryl Bacarella, *Buyer*
EMP: 5
SQ FT: 26,000
SALES (corp-wide): 113.4MM Privately Held
WEB: www.novaresteam.com
SIC: 3089 Injection molded finished plastic products; coloring & finishing of plastic products
HQ: Novares Us Llc
19575 Victor Pkwy Ste 400
Livonia MI 48152
248 449-6100

(G-8486)
NUGENTEC OILFIELD CHEM LLC
1105 Grand Oaks Dr (48843-8511)
PHONE................517 518-2712
Kelley Behrendt, *Principal*
EMP: 6 EST: 2015
SALES (est): 191.2K Privately Held
SIC: 2819 Industrial inorganic chemicals

(G-8487)
NYATEX CHEMICAL COMPANY
2112 Industrial Dr (48843-2406)
P.O. Box 124 (48844-0124)
PHONE................517 546-4046
William H Hulbert, *President*
Augustus Tanner, *Manager*
EMP: 10 EST: 1970
SQ FT: 12,000
SALES (est): 1.7MM Privately Held
WEB: www.nyatex.com
SIC: 2891 Adhesives

(G-8488)
OAKLAND TACTICAL SUPPLY LLC
1818 N Old Us 23 (48843-7192)
PHONE................810 991-1436
Mike Paige,
EMP: 6 EST: 2003
SALES (est): 607.8K Privately Held
WEB: www.oaklandtactical.com
SIC: 5699 5941 3482 3484 Military goods & regalia; firearms; small arms ammunition; guns (firearms) or gun parts, 30 mm. & below

(G-8489)
OVIDON MANUFACTURING LLC
1200 Grand Oaks Dr (48843-8578)
P.O. Box 189002, Utica (48318-9002)
PHONE................517 548-4005
Dave Marshall, *Manager*
Elizabeth McDonald,
EMP: 56 EST: 2005
SQ FT: 52,000
SALES (est): 8.6MM Privately Held
WEB: www.ovidon.com
SIC: 3544 3469 Extrusion dies; metal stampings

(G-8490)
PASSENGER INC
1940 Olympia Dr (48843-9468)
PHONE................323 556-5400
EMP: 7 EST: 2019
SALES (est): 156.9K Privately Held
WEB: www.enjoyyourlingo.com
SIC: 3652 Pre-recorded records & tapes

(G-8491)
PATRICK CARBIDE DIE LLC
840 Victory Dr Ste 200 (48843-6633)
PHONE................517 546-5646
Mark Cook, *Mng Member*
EMP: 6 EST: 1992
SQ FT: 4,000
SALES (est): 850K Privately Held
SIC: 3544 Special dies, tools, jigs & fixtures

(G-8492)
PDL LLC
8767 Bergin Rd (48843-8045)
PHONE................810 844-3209
Patrick Holihan,
EMP: 5 EST: 2017
SALES (est): 95.3K Privately Held
SIC: 3843 Teeth, artificial (not made in dental laboratories)

(G-8493)
PEPSI BOTTLING GROUP
Also Called: Pepsico
404 Mason Rd (48843-3928)
PHONE................517 546-2777
Kelvin Greene, *Plant Mgr*
Garry Doherty, *Sales Staff*
Lars Murray, *Sales Staff*
Dale Pruitt, *Manager*
Martin Ryzak, *Supervisor*
EMP: 17 EST: 2010
SALES (est): 4.3MM Privately Held
WEB: www.pepsico.com
SIC: 2086 Carbonated soft drinks, bottled & canned

(G-8494)
PEPSI-COLA METRO BTLG CO INC
725 Mcpherson St (48843-1472)
PHONE................517 546-2777
Chuck Frame, *Branch Mgr*
EMP: 6
SALES (corp-wide): 70.3B Publicly Held
WEB: www.pepsico.com
SIC: 2086 Carbonated soft drinks, bottled & canned
HQ: Pepsi-Cola Metropolitan Bottling Company, Inc.
1111 Westchester Ave
White Plains NY 10604
914 767-6000

(G-8495)
PEPSI-NEW BERN-HOWELL-151
Also Called: Pepsico
755 Mcpherson Park Dr (48843-1933)
PHONE................517 546-7542
Andre El-Khoury, *Principal*
EMP: 13 EST: 2010
SALES (est): 1MM Privately Held
WEB: www.core.rm.4nme.pw
SIC: 2086 Carbonated soft drinks, bottled & canned

(G-8496)
PLASTICS RECYCLING TECH INC
Also Called: Uniplas
1145 Sutton St (48843-1715)
PHONE................248 486-1449
Donald C Root, *President*
Al Froehlich, *Opers Mgr*
Joe Romano, *Sales Mgr*
EMP: 7 EST: 1989
SQ FT: 8,000
SALES (est): 1.3MM Privately Held
WEB: www.uniplasinc.com
SIC: 2821 Plastics materials & resins

(G-8497)
PLUGS TO PANELS ELECTRICAL LLC
1471 Crest Rd (48843-1203)
PHONE................248 318-5915
EMP: 4 EST: 2019
SALES (est): 165.8K Privately Held
WEB: www.plugstopanelselectrical.com
SIC: 3643 Plugs, electric

(G-8498)
PR PLASTIC WELDING SERVICE
2553 Clivedon Rd (48843-6989)
PHONE................734 355-3341
Patrick Raquepaw, *Principal*
EMP: 5 EST: 2017
SALES (est): 34.5K Privately Held
SIC: 7692 Welding repair

(G-8499)
PRECISE FINISHING SYSTEMS INC (PA)
1650 N Burkhart Rd (48855-9690)
PHONE................517 552-9200
Michael McLean, *President*
Frank A Taube III, *Principal*
Cary Lyons, *Vice Pres*
Michelle Loiselle, *Purch Agent*
McGregor Neville, *Treasurer*
EMP: 22 EST: 1945
SQ FT: 23,000
SALES (est): 6.2MM Privately Held
WEB: www.preciseusa.com
SIC: 3823 3443 Temperature measurement instruments, industrial; industrial vessels, tanks & containers

(G-8500)
PRECISION STAMPING CO INC
1244 Grand Oaks Dr (48843-8578)
PHONE................517 546-5656
John P Parke Jr, *President*
John P Parke Sr, *Chairman*
EMP: 50 EST: 1946
SQ FT: 50,000
SALES (est): 11.4MM Privately Held
WEB: www.precisionstamping.com
SIC: 3465 3469 Body parts, automobile: stamped metal; appliance parts, porcelain enameled

(G-8501)
PREFERRED AVIONICS INSTRS LLC
3679 Bowen Rd (48855-7755)
PHONE................800 521-5130
Randy Weller, *Business Mgr*
Wendy Loruss, *Manager*
Christopher Turner,
EMP: 40 EST: 2009
SALES (est): 3.5MM
SALES (corp-wide): 96.3MM Privately Held
WEB: www.preferredavionics.com
SIC: 3812 Aircraft/aerospace flight instruments & guidance systems
PA: Construction Helicopters, Inc.
3679 Bowen Rd
Howell MI 48855
800 521-5130

(G-8502)
R & D SCREW PRODUCTS INC
810 Fowler St (48843-2319)
PHONE................517 546-2380
Norman C Dymond, *President*
Bob Dymond, *Vice Pres*
Robert J Dymond, *Vice Pres*
Helen N Dymond, *Admin Sec*
EMP: 42 EST: 1945
SQ FT: 10,000
SALES (est): 4.6MM Privately Held
WEB: www.rdscrew.com
SIC: 3451 Screw machine products

(G-8503)
R & K WOODWORKING
413 Browning Dr (48843-2000)
PHONE................734 741-3664
Richard Gubbins, *Principal*
EMP: 4 EST: 2018
SALES (est): 54.1K Privately Held
SIC: 2431 Millwork

(G-8504)
R AND J DUMPSTERS LLC
5886 Lange Rd (48843-9611)
PHONE................248 863-8579
Robert Ellwart, *Principal*
EMP: 6 EST: 2017
SALES (est): 220.5K Privately Held
SIC: 3443 Dumpsters, garbage

(G-8505)
R CONCEPTS INCORPORATED
10083 Bergin Rd (48843-7049)
PHONE................810 632-4857
Ray Sinke, *President*
Thomas Karr, *Engineer*
EMP: 7 EST: 2007

Howell - Livingston County (G-8506)

SALES (est): 661.8K Privately Held
WEB: www.rconceptsinc.com
SIC: 3569 3823 5084 Robots, assembly line: industrial & commercial; industrial instrmnts msrmnt display/control process variable; industrial machinery & equipment

(G-8506)
RADIOLGICAL FABRICATION DESIGN
Also Called: Rf Design
10187 Bergin Rd (48843-7048)
PHONE................................810 632-6000
Paul Price, *President*
EMP: 5 **EST:** 1993
SQ FT: 3,000
SALES (est): 388.6K Privately Held
WEB: www.rfdesigninc.com
SIC: 3842 5047 3356 Radiation shielding aprons, gloves, sheeting, etc.; X-ray film & supplies; nonferrous rolling & drawing

(G-8507)
RETRO-A-GO-GO LLC
214 S Michigan Ave (48843-2215)
PHONE................................734 476-0300
Kirsten Pagacz, *Principal*
Richard Barnes, *CIO*
Jen Delamielleure, *Analyst*
▲ **EMP:** 8 **EST:** 2005
SALES (est): 424.7K Privately Held
WEB: www.retroagogo.com
SIC: 2389 7389 Apparel & accessories; apparel designers, commercial

(G-8508)
REULAND ELECTRIC CO
4500 E Grand River Ave (48843-7567)
PHONE................................517 546-4400
Albert Matias, *VP Opers*
Abdulrahim Ayesh, *Engineer*
Don Jones, *Sales Staff*
Bobby Moody, *Branch Mgr*
Jeanie Brown, *Manager*
EMP: 10
SALES (corp-wide): 35.6MM Privately Held
WEB: www.reulandfoundry.com
SIC: 3621 Motors, electric
PA: Reuland Electric Co.
  17969 Railroad St
  City Of Industry CA 91748
  626 964-6411

(G-8509)
REX MATERIALS INC (PA)
1600 Brewer Rd (48855-8760)
PHONE................................517 223-3787
David D Rex, *President*
Robert Cravens, *Vice Pres*
Brad Valentine, *Vice Pres*
Abe Forbeck, *Engineer*
Steven Stanislaw, *Regl Sales Mgr*
EMP: 20 **EST:** 2001
SALES (est): 16.5MM Privately Held
WEB: www.rexmaterials.com
SIC: 3599 5033 3297 Oil filters, internal combustion engine, except automotive; insulation materials; nonclay refractories

(G-8510)
ROOTO CORPORATION
3505 W Grand River Ave (48855-9610)
PHONE................................517 546-8330
Joon S Moon, *President*
EMP: 10 **EST:** 1946
SQ FT: 5,000
SALES (est): 1.7MM Privately Held
WEB: www.rootocorp.com
SIC: 2842 2899 Drain pipe solvents or cleaners; cleaning or polishing preparations; sanitation preparations; concrete curing & hardening compounds

(G-8511)
ROSEMARY FELICE
335 Norlynn Dr (48843-9026)
PHONE................................517 861-7434
Rosemary Felice, *Principal*
EMP: 6 **EST:** 2010
SALES (est): 161.3K Privately Held
SIC: 2741 Miscellaneous publishing

(G-8512)
RUSTOP TECHNOLOGIES LLC (PA)
4831 W Grand River Ave (48855-8713)
PHONE................................517 223-5098
Robert Daymon,
John C Cook,
▼ **EMP:** 7 **EST:** 2002
SQ FT: 20,000
SALES (est): 875K Privately Held
SIC: 2899 Anti-glare material

(G-8513)
S & G ERECTION COMPANY
2055 N Lima Center Dr (48843)
PHONE................................517 546-9240
Tom Good, *President*
EMP: 21 **EST:** 1979
SQ FT: 5,000
SALES (est): 509.4K Privately Held
SIC: 3441 Fabricated structural metal

(G-8514)
SAEGERTOWN MANUFACTURING INC
1175 Callaway Ct (48843-5201)
PHONE................................517 281-9789
EMP: 8 **EST:** 2009
SALES (est): 68.1K Privately Held
WEB: www.macleanfoggcs.com
SIC: 3999 Manufacturing industries

(G-8515)
SCHWARTZ MANUFACTURING
1045 Durant Dr (48843-9536)
PHONE................................517 552-3100
EMP: 9 **EST:** 2011
SALES (est): 256.5K Privately Held
WEB: www.schwartzmfg.com
SIC: 3999 Manufacturing industries

(G-8516)
SERVICE CONTROL INC
Also Called: Systems Control
2852 Amberwood Trl (48855-8756)
PHONE................................248 478-1133
Robert Howe, *President*
Debbie Howe, *Corp Secy*
EMP: 30 **EST:** 1977
SALES (est): 2.5MM Privately Held
WEB: www.servicecontrolinc.com
SIC: 3585 Air conditioning equipment, complete

(G-8517)
SIGN WORKS INC
5380 E Grand River Ave (48843-9101)
PHONE................................517 546-3620
Daniel Haberl, *President*
Robert Haberl, *Corp Secy*
Andy Haberl, *Vice Pres*
EMP: 6 **EST:** 1986
SQ FT: 3,000
SALES (est): 804.5K Privately Held
WEB: www.thesignworks.org
SIC: 3993 Electric signs; neon signs

(G-8518)
SKS INDUSTRIES INC (PA)
Also Called: Armor Protective Packaging
1551 N Burkhart Rd (48855-9603)
P.O. Box 828 (48844-0828)
PHONE................................517 546-1117
John Holden, *CEO*
Robin McConnell, *President*
David Yancho, *Vice Pres*
Jan Camden, *Project Mgr*
Jeff Goodsall, *Opers Mgr*
▼ **EMP:** 10
SQ FT: 16,000
SALES (est): 15.5MM Privately Held
WEB: www.armorvci.com
SIC: 2899 2679 Corrosion preventive lubricant; paper products, converted

(G-8519)
SMART LABEL SOLUTIONS LLC
1100 Durant Dr (48843-9510)
PHONE................................800 996-7343
Morgan Hudson, *Project Mgr*
Kris Hudson, *Opers Mgr*
Cheryl Pearson, *Manager*
Jeff Hudson,
Kaye Pearson,
EMP: 6 **EST:** 2005

SALES (est): 1.8MM Privately Held
WEB: www.slsrfid.com
SIC: 3825 7373 Radio frequency measuring equipment; systems integration services

(G-8520)
SMULLEN FIRE APP SALES & SVCS
3680 W Grand River Ave (48855-7605)
P.O. Box 530 (48844-0530)
PHONE................................517 546-8898
Jim Smullen, *General Mgr*
Estelle Kirby, *Principal*
James Smullen,
EMP: 6 **EST:** 2000 Privately Held
WEB: www.smullensinc.com
SIC: 3569 General industrial machinery

(G-8521)
SPIRAL INDUSTRIES INC
1572 N Old Hwy Us23 (48843)
PHONE................................810 632-6300
Harry Linfield, *CEO*
Brandon Shouse, *Plant Mgr*
Dustin Lowe, *Engineer*
Don Schellenberg, *Sales Staff*
Holly St Pierre, *Manager*
EMP: 50
SQ FT: 50,000
SALES (est): 10.5MM Privately Held
WEB: www.spiralindustries.com
SIC: 3492 3498 3429 Hose & tube fittings & assemblies, hydraulic/pneumatic; fabricated pipe & fittings; manufactured hardware (general)

(G-8522)
SPIRIT OF LIVINGSTON INC
3280 W Grand River Ave (48855-9605)
PHONE................................517 545-8831
Carol Maczik, *President*
Daniel Maczik, *Vice Pres*
EMP: 4 **EST:** 2002
SALES (est): 356.7K Privately Held
WEB: www.spiritoflivingston.com
SIC: 2395 Embroidery products, except schiffli machine

(G-8523)
STEEL SKINZ LLC
Also Called: Steel Skinz Graphics
4836 Pinckney Rd (48843-7807)
PHONE................................517 545-9955
EMP: 6
SALES (est): 521K Privately Held
SIC: 7312 7336 3993 Outdoor Advertising Svcs Coml Art/Graphic Design Mfg Signs/Ad Specialties

(G-8524)
SYD ENTERPRISES
Also Called: We're Rolling Pretzel Company
3850 E Grand River Ave (48843-8593)
PHONE................................517 719-2740
Bob Dedarmo, *Owner*
Stacey Degarmo, *Co-Owner*
EMP: 7 **EST:** 2005
SALES (est): 442.8K Privately Held
WEB: www.wererolling.com
SIC: 2052 Pretzels

(G-8525)
TAIT GRINDING SERVICE INC
1940 Olympia Dr (48843-9468)
P.O. Box 158, New Hudson (48165-0158)
PHONE................................248 437-5100
Richard H Tait, *President*
EMP: 5 **EST:** 1966
SALES (est): 481K Privately Held
WEB: www.kelly-grinding-llc.hub.biz
SIC: 3599 Grinding castings for the trade

(G-8526)
TCH SUPPLY INC
895 Grand Oaks Dr (48843-8512)
PHONE................................517 545-4900
Chris Pagett, *Mng Member*
EMP: 6 **EST:** 2015
SALES (est): 220.6K Privately Held
WEB: www.tchsupply.com
SIC: 3531 5085 Construction machinery; fasteners & fastening equipment

(G-8527)
TECHNCAL AUDIO VIDEO SOLUTIONS
5695 Whispering Oaks Dr (48855-9791)
PHONE................................810 899-5546
EMP: 4 **EST:** 2010
SALES (est): 190K Privately Held
SIC: 3669 Mfg Communications Equipment

(G-8528)
TESMA INSTRUMENTS LLC
8770 Giovanni Ct (48855-6300)
P.O. Box 274, Hartland (48353-0274)
PHONE................................517 940-1362
Kaitlin Mattes, *Principal*
EMP: 5 **EST:** 2016
SALES (est): 69.3K Privately Held
SIC: 3841 Medical instruments & equipment, blood & bone work

(G-8529)
THAI SUMMIT AMERICA CORP (DH)
1480 Mcpherson Park Dr (48843-1936)
PHONE................................517 548-4900
Wiwat Laichuthai, *President*
Woody Iddhibhakdibong, *VP Admin*
Greg Haremski, *Opers Staff*
Brian Miller, *Opers Staff*
Steve Peca, *Mfg Staff*
◆ **EMP:** 100 **EST:** 1985
SQ FT: 1,000,000
SALES (est): 148.4MM Privately Held
WEB: www.thaisummit.us
SIC: 3469 Metal stampings

(G-8530)
THOMPSON JOHN
Also Called: Thompson Glass Co
5345 Crooked Lake Rd (48843-8806)
PHONE................................810 225-8780
John Thompson, *Owner*
EMP: 6 **EST:** 1929
SALES (est): 271.2K Privately Held
WEB: www.thompsonglass1929.com
SIC: 3229 1793 Glass fiber products; glass & glazing work

(G-8531)
THOMSON PLASTICS INC
3970 Parsons Rd (48855-9617)
PHONE................................517 545-5026
Rick Kibbey, *Principal*
EMP: 31 Privately Held
WEB: www.thomsonplastics.com
SIC: 3949 3089 Sporting & athletic goods; plastic containers, except foam
PA: Thomson Plastics, Inc.
  130 Quality Dr
  Thomson GA 30824

(G-8532)
THREE 60 ROTO LLC
741 Victory Dr (48843-7591)
PHONE................................517 545-3600
Jeff Oelslager, *President*
Bruce P Barton Jr, *President*
▲ **EMP:** 15 **EST:** 1983
SQ FT: 12,200
SALES (est): 2.9MM Privately Held
WEB: www.360roto.com
SIC: 3089 Injection molding of plastics

(G-8533)
TITAN SPRINKLER LLC
1987 Sundance Rdg (48843-7999)
PHONE................................517 540-1851
Timothy Kandow, *Mng Member*
EMP: 4 **EST:** 2002
SALES (est): 442.2K Privately Held
WEB: www.orchardplace.net
SIC: 3432 Lawn hose nozzles & sprinklers

(G-8534)
TK HOLDINGS INC
1199 Austin Ct (48843-9556)
PHONE................................517 545-9535
EMP: 570
SALES (corp-wide): 7.2B Privately Held
SIC: 2399 Seat belts, automobile & aircraft
HQ: Tk Holdings Inc.
  4611 Wiseman Blvd
  San Antonio TX 78251
  210 509-0762

GEOGRAPHIC SECTION

Hudson - Lenawee County (G-8562)

(G-8535)
TRI-MATIC SCREW PRODUCTS CO
5684 E Highland Rd (48843-9735)
PHONE..................................517 548-6414
Robert M Race Jr, *President*
Joseph F Race, *Vice Pres*
EMP: 20 EST: 1982
SQ FT: 6,000
SALES (est): 2MM **Privately Held**
WEB: www.trimatic.net
SIC: 3451 Screw machine products

(G-8536)
TRIBAR MANUFACTURING LLC (HQ)
2211 Grand Commerce Dr (48855-7320)
PHONE..................................248 516-1600
Mike Roemer, *Partner*
Frank Gray, *COO*
Bob Bretz, *VP Opers*
Joseph Vinson, *Opers Spvr*
Carol Brozek, *QC Mgr*
EMP: 350 EST: 1995
SQ FT: 65,000
SALES (est): 310.7MM
SALES (corp-wide): 318MM **Privately Held**
WEB: www.tribar.com
SIC: 3089 Injection molded finished plastic products
PA: Tribar Technologies, Inc.
    48668 Alpha Dr
    Wixom MI 48393
    248 516-1600

(G-8537)
UPCYCLE POLYMERS LLC
1145 Sutton St (48843-1715)
PHONE..................................248 446-8750
Dan Root,
EMP: 3 EST: 2012
SQ FT: 24,000
SALES (est): 2MM **Privately Held**
WEB: www.upcyclepolymers.com
SIC: 2611 5093 Pulp mills, chemical & semichemical processing; plastics scrap

(G-8538)
VANDELAY SERVICES LLC
10051 E Highland Rd (48843-6317)
PHONE..................................810 279-8550
Amy Pasienza, *Principal*
EMP: 7
SALES (est): 173.9K **Privately Held**
SIC: 2621 3315 3496 5039 Towels, tissues & napkins: paper & stock; steel wire & related products; wire & fabricated wire products; fencing, made from purchased wire; wire fence, gates & accessories

(G-8539)
VISION QUEST EMBROIDERY LLC
4900 Preston Rd (48855-7372)
PHONE..................................517 375-1518
Paul Mobbs, *Principal*
EMP: 4 EST: 2013
SALES (est): 31.2K **Privately Held**
SIC: 2395 Embroidery products, except schiffli machine

(G-8540)
VOCO AMERICA INC
280 Summer Shade Dr (48843-6001)
PHONE..................................248 568-0964
Allan Manser, *Principal*
Nichole Adams, *Sales Staff*
Kathy Gentile, *Sales Staff*
Henry Paszkiewicz, *Sales Staff*
Brian Roberge, *Sales Staff*
EMP: 6 EST: 2010
SALES (est): 116.7K **Privately Held**
WEB: www.voco.dental
SIC: 3843 Dental materials

(G-8541)
WIDE EYED 3D PRINTING
5343 Edgewood Shores Dr (48843-6848)
PHONE..................................517 376-6612
Nichole Haefner, *Principal*
EMP: 4 EST: 2014
SALES (est): 70.4K **Privately Held**
SIC: 2752 Commercial printing, offset

(G-8542)
WOODS 2 G LOGGING LLC
7700 Golf Club Rd (48843-8044)
PHONE..................................248 469-7416
Richard Valko Jr, *Principal*
EMP: 5 EST: 2016
SALES (est): 380.4K **Privately Held**
SIC: 2411 Logging

(G-8543)
WOW FACTOR TABLES AND EVENTS
4337 E Grand River Ave (48843-6583)
PHONE..................................248 550-5922
Cincarla Goddard, *Owner*
EMP: 4 EST: 2015
SQ FT: 500
SALES (est): 165.9K **Privately Held**
WEB: www.wow-factors.com
SIC: 2051 Bakery, for home service delivery

(G-8544)
ZENITH GLOBAL LLC
1100 Sutton St (48843-1716)
PHONE..................................517 546-7402
Suman Tetarbe,
EMP: 6 EST: 2007
SALES (est): 5MM
SALES (corp-wide): 1.7B **Privately Held**
WEB: www.zenithglobal.net
SIC: 3081 Unsupported plastics film & sheet
HQ: Pmc, Inc.
    12243 Branford St
    Sun Valley CA 91352
    818 896-1101

(G-8545)
ZF ACTIVE SAFETY US INC
1055 Packard Dr (48843-7303)
PHONE..................................956 491-9036
Allan Howe, *Branch Mgr*
EMP: 9
SALES (corp-wide): 216.2K **Privately Held**
WEB: www.zf.com
SIC: 3714 Motor vehicle parts & accessories
HQ: Zf Active Safety Us Inc.
    12025 Tech Center Dr
    Livonia MI 48150
    734 812-6979

Hubbard Lake
Alpena County

(G-8546)
FAIR & SQUARE PALLET & LBR CO
5700 Ratz Rd (49747-9547)
PHONE..................................989 727-3949
Robin Wilke, *Partner*
Randolph Wilke, *Partner*
Richard Wilke, *Partner*
Rory Wilke, *Partner*
Rudolph Wilke, *Partner*
EMP: 4 EST: 1991 **Privately Held**
SIC: 2448 Pallets, wood

Hudson
Lenawee County

(G-8547)
ARC GROUP WORLDWIDE INC
4111 Munson Hwy (49247-9551)
PHONE..................................517 448-8954
EMP: 9 EST: 2018
SALES (est): 953.5K **Privately Held**
WEB: www.arcw.com
SIC: 3089 Injection molding of plastics

(G-8548)
ARC METAL STAMPING LLC
Also Called: Kecy Metal Technologies
4111 Munson Hwy (49247-9551)
PHONE..................................517 448-8954
EMP: 90 EST: 2014
SALES (est): 8.2MM **Privately Held**
WEB: www.kecymetals.com
SIC: 3469 Stamping metal for the trade

(G-8549)
ARC-KECY LLC
4111 Munson Hwy (49247-9551)
PHONE..................................517 448-8954
Alan Quasha,
Eli Davidai,
Aaron Willman,
EMP: 70 EST: 2014
SALES (est): 5.9MM **Privately Held**
WEB: www.kecymetals.com
SIC: 3465 Automotive stampings

(G-8550)
HERALD BI-COUNTY INC
115 S Church St (49247-1301)
PHONE..................................517 448-2201
John W Monohan, *President*
Geri Monohan, *Vice Pres*
Karen Downing, *Treasurer*
EMP: 6 EST: 1947
SALES (est): 453.7K **Privately Held**
SIC: 2741 2752 Shopping news: publishing only, not printed on site; commercial printing, lithographic

(G-8551)
HI-LEX CONTROLS INCORPORATED
15780 Steger Indus Dr (49247-9574)
PHONE..................................517 448-2752
John Wyllie, *Engineer*
Takuju Murayama, *Manager*
Trevor Medley, *Asst Mgr*
Steve Battle, *Executive*
Jeff Bliss, *Analyst*
EMP: 165 **Privately Held**
SIC: 3714 3625 Motor vehicle parts & accessories; relays & industrial controls
HQ: Hi-Lex Controls Incorporated
    152 Simpson Dr
    Litchfield MI 49252

(G-8552)
HUDSON POST GAZETTE
113 S Market St (49247-1317)
P.O. Box 70 (49247-0070)
PHONE..................................517 448-2611
Edward Potter, *Owner*
EMP: 4 EST: 1858
SQ FT: 2,000 **Privately Held**
WEB: www.hudsonpg.com
SIC: 2711 Newspapers: publishing only, not printed on site

(G-8553)
KECY CORPORATION
4111 Munson Hwy (49247-9551)
PHONE..................................517 448-8954
Ray Cox, *President*
Dave Zerbey, *Vice Pres*
▲ EMP: 9 EST: 2009
SALES (est): 720.1K **Privately Held**
WEB: www.kecycorporation.com
SIC: 3469 Metal stampings

(G-8554)
KECY PRODUCTS INC
4111 Munson Hwy (49247-9551)
P.O. Box 150 (49247-0150)
PHONE..................................517 448-8954
Jack Donaldson, *President*
Minoru Kitsuda, *Vice Pres*
▲ EMP: 22 EST: 1987
SQ FT: 26,000
SALES (est): 4.6MM **Privately Held**
SIC: 3465 5084 3469 Body parts, automobile: stamped metal; industrial machinery & equipment; metal stampings

(G-8555)
MALABAR MANUFACTURING INC
4255 Munson Hwy (49247-9551)
P.O. Box 128 (49247-0128)
PHONE..................................517 448-2155
Bart Malarney, *President*
John W Malarney, *Principal*
EMP: 15 EST: 1981
SQ FT: 13,000
SALES (est): 1.9MM **Privately Held**
WEB: www.malabarmfg.com
SIC: 3451 Screw machine products

(G-8556)
MALMAC TOOL AND FIXTURE INC
4255 Munson Hwy (49247-9551)
P.O. Box 128 (49247-0128)
PHONE..................................517 448-8244
John W Malarney, *President*
Dale Mc Faul, *Vice Pres*
EMP: 5 EST: 1987
SQ FT: 3,500
SALES (est): 300K **Privately Held**
SIC: 3545 3544 Tools & accessories for machine tools; special dies, tools, jigs & fixtures

(G-8557)
NORTHSHORE PONTOON
3985 Munson Hwy (49247-9800)
PHONE..................................517 547-8877
Doug Haskell, *Owner*
EMP: 5 EST: 2015
SALES (est): 283.3K **Privately Held**
WEB: www.northshorepontoon.com
SIC: 3732 5551 Boats, fiberglass: building & repairing; motor boat dealers

(G-8558)
PASCHAL BURIAL VAULT SVC LLC
Also Called: Paschal Burial Vaults
431 School St (49247-1427)
PHONE..................................517 448-8868
Lee Paschal, *Mng Member*
EMP: 5 EST: 1980 **Privately Held**
SIC: 3272 Burial vaults, concrete or precast terrazzo

(G-8559)
PRO SHOP THE/P S GRAPHICS
309 W Main St (49247-1051)
P.O. Box 27 (49247-0027)
PHONE..................................517 448-8490
Dave Sheeley, *Owner*
Janet Sheely, *Owner*
EMP: 8 EST: 1979
SQ FT: 2,500 **Privately Held**
WEB: www.theproshop.imprintableapparel.com
SIC: 2261 5941 5999 2759 Screen printing of cotton broadwoven fabrics; sporting goods & bicycle shops; trophies & plaques; screen printing

(G-8560)
PURITY FOODS INC
417 S Meridian Rd (49247-9709)
PHONE..................................517 448-7440
Jaclyn Bowen, *Principal*
◆ EMP: 30 EST: 1979
SQ FT: 3,000
SALES (est): 5.4MM
SALES (corp-wide): 8.2B **Publicly Held**
WEB: www.natureslegacyforlife.com
SIC: 5153 5191 5149 2041 Grains; seeds: field, garden & flower; pasta & rice; flour & other grain mill products
PA: The Andersons Inc
    1947 Briarfield Blvd
    Maumee OH 43537
    419 893-5050

(G-8561)
RIMA MANUFACTURING COMPANY (PA)
3850 Munson Hwy (49247-9804)
PHONE..................................517 448-8921
Edward J Engle Jr, *President*
Jed Engle, *Vice Pres*
Jim Prestidge, *Supervisor*
Laura Tomasello, *Officer*
EMP: 159 EST: 1955
SQ FT: 50,000
SALES (est): 25.6MM **Privately Held**
WEB: www.rimamfg.com
SIC: 3451 3599 Screw machine products; machine shop, jobbing & repair

(G-8562)
SOLUTIONS FOR INDUSTRY INC
13240 Egypt Rd (49247-9237)
PHONE..................................517 448-8608
Kevin V Kuhn, *President*
Jane Stewart, *Vice Pres*
EMP: 6 EST: 1995

Hudson - Lenawee County (G-8563)   GEOGRAPHIC SECTION

SALES (est): 541.8K **Privately Held**
SIC: 3625 7539 8711 Control equipment, electric; electrical services; machine tool design

(G-8563)
VARNERS PWR COATING & SNDBLST
14935 Hemlock St (49247-9607)
PHONE 517 448-3425
EMP: 4 EST: 2018
SALES (est): 67.4K **Privately Held**
SIC: 3479 Coating of metals & formed products

Hudsonville
Ottawa County

(G-8564)
ADVANTAGE SIGN SUPPLY INC (PA)
Also Called: Advantage Sign Grphic Slutions
4182 Royal Ct (49426-7957)
P.O. Box 888684, Grand Rapids (49588-8684)
PHONE 877 237-4464
Gary Van Dyke, *CEO*
Steve Kloosterman, *President*
Dan Irrer, *Vice Pres*
Katy Kloosterman, *Admin Sec*
▲ EMP: 50 EST: 1990
SQ FT: 50,000
SALES (est): 55MM **Privately Held**
WEB: www.grimco.com
SIC: 3993 Signs & advertising specialties

(G-8565)
ALTRON AUTOMATION INC
3523 Highland Dr (49426-1916)
PHONE 616 669-7711
Ronald G McNees, *President*
Arnold Lacombe, *Vice Pres*
Ken Zost, *Foreman/Supr*
Tyler Lacombe, *Opers Staff*
Larry Forster, *Engineer*
EMP: 60 EST: 1989
SQ FT: 60,000
SALES (est): 13.8MM **Privately Held**
WEB: www.altronautomation.com
SIC: 3535 Unit handling conveying systems

(G-8566)
ALTRON AUTOMATION GROUP INC
3523 Highland Dr (49426-1916)
PHONE 616 669-7711
Ron McNees, *President*
Arnold Lacombe, *Vice Pres*
EMP: 146 EST: 1989
SALES (est): 6.6MM **Privately Held**
SIC: 8711 3535 Engineering services; conveyors & conveying equipment

(G-8567)
APTIV SERVICES US LLC
4254 Oak Meadow Dr (49426-8656)
PHONE 248 813-2000
EMP: 7
SALES (corp-wide): 14.3B **Privately Held**
SIC: 3714 Motor vehicle parts & accessories
HQ: Aptiv Services Us, Llc
5725 Innovation Dr
Troy MI 48098

(G-8568)
B PRETTY HATS LLC
4474 Equestrian Dr (49426-7490)
PHONE 616 726-0002
Brooke Harvey, *Agent*
EMP: 4 EST: 2017
SALES (est): 72.5K **Privately Held**
SIC: 2353 Hats, caps & millinery

(G-8569)
BAKER FASTENING SYSTEMS INC
5030 40th Ave (49426-9481)
PHONE 616 669-7400
Rick Sousley, *President*
▲ EMP: 7 EST: 1989

SALES (est): 645.3K **Privately Held**
WEB: www.baker-fasteners.business.site
SIC: 3965 Fasteners

(G-8570)
BDGN CORPORATION
3565 Highland Dr (49426-1916)
PHONE 616 669-9040
Brad Ward, *President*
Mike Valz, *COO*
Dawn Ward, *Vice Pres*
Joel Smith, *Engineer*
Ken Taylor, *Engineer*
EMP: 130 EST: 2001
SQ FT: 95,000
SALES (est): 18.4MM **Privately Held**
SIC: 7532 3089 3714 Paint shop, automotive; automotive parts, plastic; motor vehicle parts & accessories

(G-8571)
BLOEM LLC (PA)
Also Called: Bloem Living
3301 Hudson Trail Dr (49426-7401)
P.O. Box 583 (49426-0583)
PHONE 616 622-6344
Donald Lundberg, *Vice Pres*
Kevin Wilson, *Vice Pres*
James Warkentien, *Mfg Staff*
Brian Rudy, *CFO*
Brian Wierenga, *Controller*
EMP: 27 EST: 2012
SALES (est): 11.4MM **Privately Held**
WEB: www.bloemliving.com
SIC: 3089 Planters, plastic

(G-8572)
BLUE PONY LLC
Also Called: Joleado
3479 8th Ave (49426-9639)
PHONE 616 291-5554
Michael Emaus, *Managing Prtnr*
EMP: 8 EST: 2009
SQ FT: 5,000
SALES (est): 648.4K **Privately Held**
SIC: 7372 8748 8742 Business oriented computer software; communications consulting; marketing consulting services; financial consultant

(G-8573)
BORCHERS SHEET METAL
6521 Bradenwood Dr (49426-8228)
PHONE 260 413-0632
Valerie Borchers, *Principal*
EMP: 6 EST: 2017
SALES (est): 179.9K **Privately Held**
WEB: www.borcherssheetmetal.com
SIC: 3444 Sheet metalwork

(G-8574)
CK TECHNOLOGIES
3360 Allen St (49426-1630)
PHONE 616 836-6384
Kelli Sterley, *Principal*
EMP: 5 EST: 2016
SALES (est): 101.8K **Privately Held**
SIC: 3089 Injection molding of plastics

(G-8575)
CREME CURLS BAKERY INC
5292 Lawndale Ave (49426-1213)
P.O. Box 276 (49426-0276)
PHONE 616 669-6230
Gary A Bierling, *President*
Paul H Bierling, *Vice Pres*
EMP: 120 EST: 1966
SQ FT: 66,000
SALES (est): 11.7MM **Privately Held**
WEB: www.cremecurls.com
SIC: 2051 Bakery: wholesale or wholesale/retail combined

(G-8576)
CUSTOM MACHINING BY FARLEY
2792 24th Ave (49426-9603)
PHONE 616 896-8469
Robert Van Farowe, *President*
Marene Van Farowe, *Vice Pres*
EMP: 4 EST: 1995
SQ FT: 2,400
SALES (est): 307.9K **Privately Held**
SIC: 3599 Machine shop, jobbing & repair

(G-8577)
CUSTOM TOOL & DIE SERVICE INC
5090 40th Ave Ste A (49426-9595)
PHONE 616 662-1068
Jacob Broekema, *President*
Beverly Broekema, *Treasurer*
EMP: 8 EST: 1976
SQ FT: 10,000
SALES (est): 1.2MM **Privately Held**
WEB: www.customtoolanddieservice.com
SIC: 3544 Special dies & tools

(G-8578)
D&JS PLASTICS LLC
2322 Edson Dr (49426-7789)
PHONE 616 745-5798
Doug Reams,
Jon Price,
Justin Price,
Colin Reams,
Tom Reams,
EMP: 10 EST: 2006
SALES (est): 227.3K **Privately Held**
SIC: 3089 2673 Battery cases, plastic or plastic combination; garment bags (plastic film); made from purchased materials

(G-8579)
DAVON MANUFACTURING COMPANY
3531 Perry St (49426-9657)
PHONE 616 896-7888
Laurie Vonk, *President*
David Vonk, *Vice Pres*
EMP: 8 EST: 1990
SQ FT: 10,000
SALES (est): 1MM **Privately Held**
WEB: www.davonmfg.com
SIC: 3496 Clips & fasteners, made from purchased wire

(G-8580)
DIAMOND TOOL MANUFACTURING
6075 Taylor St (49426-9714)
PHONE 616 895-4007
EMP: 11 EST: 2017
SALES (est): 81K **Privately Held**
WEB: www.diamondtoolmfg.com
SIC: 3999 3599 Manufacturing industries; machine shop, jobbing & repair

(G-8581)
EMERGENCY TECHNOLOGY INC (PA)
Also Called: Sound-Off Signal
3900 Central Pkwy (49426-7884)
P.O. Box 206 (49426-0206)
PHONE 616 896-7100
Mark Litke, *President*
George Boerigter, *Chairman*
Douglas Baker, *Vice Pres*
Greg Leatherman, *Prdtn Mgr*
Ed Hedgecock, *Mfg Mgr*
▲ EMP: 96 EST: 1972
SQ FT: 40,000
SALES (est): 35.7MM **Privately Held**
WEB: www.soundoffsignal.com
SIC: 3648 3625 3699 3647 Lighting equipment; control circuit devices, magnet & solid state; electric sound equipment; motor vehicle lighting equipment; emergency alarms

(G-8582)
ESPEC CORP
4141 Central Pkwy (49426-7828)
PHONE 616 896-6100
Brandon Dinsmore, *Electrical Engi*
Judy Lambert, *Manager*
EMP: 21 EST: 2005
SALES (est): 8.7MM **Privately Held**
WEB: www.espec.com
SIC: 3826 Environmental testing equipment

(G-8583)
FASTSIGNS
6374 Eaglewood Dr (49426-9114)
PHONE 616 377-7491
EMP: 7 EST: 2019
SALES (est): 196.3K **Privately Held**
WEB: www.fastsigns.com
SIC: 3993 Signs & advertising specialties

(G-8584)
FOREST GROVE POWER EQP LLC
3188 32nd Ave (49426-9685)
PHONE 616 896-8344
Dave Isenga, *Administration*
EMP: 5
SALES (est): 569.3K **Privately Held**
WEB: www.forestgrovepe.net
SIC: 3524 Lawn & garden equipment

(G-8585)
HARBOR MASTER LTD
3127 Highland Blvd (49426-7934)
PHONE 616 669-3170
Tim Contreras, *President*
EMP: 10 EST: 1980
SQ FT: 24,000
SALES (est): 1.5MM **Privately Held**
WEB: www.harbor-master.com
SIC: 3536 Boat lifts

(G-8586)
INNOVTIVE DSPLAY SOLUTIONS LLC
Also Called: IDS
4256 Corp Exch Dr Ste A (49426)
PHONE 616 896-6080
Brian Newenhouse,
EMP: 10 EST: 2007
SALES (est): 2MM **Privately Held**
WEB: www.idsmfg.com
SIC: 2431 2499 Doors & door parts & trim, wood; laundry products, wood

(G-8587)
ITC INCORPORATED (PA)
3030 Corp Grove Dr Ste A (49426)
PHONE 616 396-1355
Michael V Camarota, *President*
Michael Camarota, *President*
Jordan Strehlke, *Electrical Engi*
Owen Welch, *CFO*
Alice A Camarota, *Treasurer*
▲ EMP: 24 EST: 1981
SQ FT: 25,000
SALES (est): 16.8MM **Privately Held**
WEB: www.itc-us.com
SIC: 5085 5088 3646 Industrial supplies; marine supplies; ceiling systems, luminous

(G-8588)
JEMAR TOOL INC
3523 Highland Dr (49426-1916)
PHONE 586 726-6960
▲ EMP: 23 **Privately Held**
SIC: 3544 Mfg Dies/Tools/Jigs/Fixtures

(G-8589)
KENT QUALITY FOODS INC
3426 Quincy St (49426-7835)
PHONE 616 459-4595
Charles M Soet, *President*
Karl Soet, *Vice Pres*
Gregg Rozycki, *Production*
Erik Stepanovich, *Production*
Trevor Vassallo, *Regl Sales Mgr*
EMP: 145 EST: 1916
SALES (est): 42.2MM **Privately Held**
WEB: www.kqf.com
SIC: 2011 2013 Meat packing plants; sausages & other prepared meats

(G-8590)
LINDE INC
Also Called: Praxair
1578 36th Ave (49426-7612)
PHONE 269 317-7225
EMP: 20 **Privately Held**
WEB: www.praxair.com
SIC: 2813 Industrial gases
HQ: Linde Inc.
10 Riverview Dr
Danbury CT 06810
203 837-2000

(G-8591)
M&D DUMPSTERS LLC
6117 Polk St (49426-8545)
P.O. Box 676, Jenison (49429-0676)
PHONE 616 299-0234
Mike Oosterhouse, *Principal*
EMP: 6 EST: 2015

SALES (est): 164.4K Privately Held
WEB: www.mddumpster.com
SIC: 3443 Dumpsters, garbage

(G-8592)
MARKED TOOL INC
2934 Highland Blvd (49426-9455)
PHONE................................616 669-3201
Mark W Overway, *President*
Sally Rae Overway, *Corp Secy*
EMP: 8 EST: 1988
SQ FT: 7,000
SALES (est): 1.1MM Privately Held
WEB: www.markedtool.com
SIC: 3544 Special dies & tools

(G-8593)
MESSENGER PRINTING & COPY SVC
5300 Plaza Ave (49426-1491)
P.O. Box 302 (49426-0302)
PHONE................................616 669-5620
Martin De Young, *President*
Kenneth Jipping, *Vice Pres*
EMP: 5 EST: 1977
SQ FT: 1,500
SALES (est): 474.9K Privately Held
WEB: www.messengerprinting.com
SIC: 2752 Commercial printing, offset

(G-8594)
MFP AUTOMATION ENGINEERING INC
4404 Central Pkwy (49426-7831)
PHONE................................616 538-5700
Roger Betten, *CEO*
Roger L Betten Jr, *President*
Brad Kirk, *COO*
Rod Kowalski, *Vice Pres*
Joe Tidd, *Warehouse Mgr*
EMP: 68 EST: 1991
SQ FT: 47,500
SALES (est): 39.2MM Privately Held
WEB: www.mifp.com
SIC: 5084 3594 Hydraulic systems equipment & supplies; fluid power pumps & motors

(G-8595)
MICHIGAN CELERY PROMOTION COOP
5009 40th Ave (49426-9481)
P.O. Box 306 (49426-0306)
PHONE................................616 669-1250
Gary Wruble, *General Mgr*
Duane Frens, *General Mgr*
EMP: 17 EST: 1951
SALES (est): 5.8MM Privately Held
WEB: www.michigancelery.com
SIC: 5148 2099 Vegetables; food preparations

(G-8596)
MICHIGAN VEAL INC
3007 Van Buren St (49426-1524)
P.O. Box 155 (49426-0155)
PHONE................................616 669-6688
Ed Deyoung, *President*
Ed De Young, *President*
Lisa De Young, *Admin Sec*
EMP: 22 EST: 1920
SQ FT: 30,000
SALES (est): 15MM Privately Held
SIC: 2011 Lamb products from lamb slaughtered on site; boxed beef from meat slaughtered on site; veal from meat slaughtered on site

(G-8597)
MIDWEST SIGN INSTALL INC
2900 Barry St (49426-9492)
PHONE................................616 862-7568
Sally Lucas, *Principal*
EMP: 4 EST: 2017
SALES (est): 50.6K Privately Held
SIC: 3993 Signs & advertising specialties

(G-8598)
MIGHTY CO
Also Called: Mighty In The Midwest
50 Louis St Nw 520 (49426)
PHONE................................616 822-1013
Clifton Wegner, *President*
Derek Mohr, *Software Dev*
Cliff Wegner, *Director*
EMP: 24
SALES (est): 1.6MM Privately Held
WEB: www.mightyinthemidwest.com
SIC: 7372 Prepackaged software

(G-8599)
NEW WAKE INC
7873 Mooring Ct (49426-9799)
PHONE................................800 957-5606
John Manilla, *President*
EMP: 6 EST: 2013
SALES (est): 735.5K Privately Held
WEB: www.wakeinc.com
SIC: 3823 3531 3829 Temperature measurement instruments, industrial; construction machinery; weather tracking equipment

(G-8600)
PETER DEHAAN PUBLISHING INC
2386 Outback Dr (49426-7715)
P.O. Box 563 (49426-0563)
PHONE................................616 284-1305
Peter Dehaan, *Principal*
EMP: 4 EST: 2016
SALES (est): 45.4K Privately Held
WEB: www.peterdehaanpublishing.com
SIC: 2741 Miscellaneous publishing

(G-8601)
PRINT RAPIDS LLC
4254 Central Pkwy (49426-7860)
PHONE................................616 202-6508
Maxwell Deyoung, *Principal*
EMP: 4 EST: 2016
SALES (est): 90.5K Privately Held
SIC: 2752 Commercial printing, lithographic

(G-8602)
PROCESS PARTNERS INC
3770 Chicago Dr (49426-1637)
PHONE................................616 875-2156
James Breslin, *President*
Sheila Breslin, *CFO*
EMP: 8 EST: 2000
SALES (est): 1.8MM Privately Held
WEB: www.processpartnersinc.com
SIC: 8711 3556 Consulting engineer; food products machinery

(G-8603)
RAPIDTEK LLC
Also Called: Rapid-Veyor
3825 Central Pkwy Ste A (49426-7844)
PHONE................................616 662-0954
H Alan Denning, *President*
Quinn Denning, *Mng Member*
Alan Denning,
▼ EMP: 8 EST: 1994
SQ FT: 11,000
SALES (est): 1.1MM Privately Held
WEB: www.rapidtekllc.com
SIC: 3799 5084 Towing bars & systems; industrial machinery & equipment

(G-8604)
ROYAL PLASTICS LLC
3765 Quincy St (49426-8836)
PHONE................................616 669-3393
Paul Vanderlaan, *President*
EMP: 24 EST: 2011
SALES (est): 169K Privately Held
WEB: www.royaltechnologies.com
SIC: 3089 Injection molding of plastics

(G-8605)
ROYAL TECHNOLOGIES CORPORATION
3614 Quincy St (49426-8519)
PHONE................................616 669-3393
Michael Buitenhuis, *Branch Mgr*
EMP: 68
SALES (corp-wide): 204MM Privately Held
WEB: www.royaltechnologies.com
SIC: 3089 Injection molded finished plastic products
PA: Royal Technologies Corporation
    3765 Quincy St
    Hudsonville MI 49426
    616 669-3393

(G-8606)
ROYAL TECHNOLOGIES CORPORATION
3133 Highland Blvd (49426-7495)
PHONE................................616 667-4102
Doyle Gerrig, *Branch Mgr*
EMP: 291
SALES (corp-wide): 204MM Privately Held
WEB: www.royaltechnologies.com
SIC: 3089 Injection molding of plastics
PA: Royal Technologies Corporation
    3765 Quincy St
    Hudsonville MI 49426
    616 669-3393

(G-8607)
ROYAL TECHNOLOGIES CORPORATION (PA)
Also Called: Hi-Tech Plastics
3765 Quincy St (49426-8408)
PHONE................................616 669-3393
James Vanderkolk, *President*
Alexander Bomers, *Vice Pres*
Perry Franco, *Vice Pres*
Richard Klamer, *Vice Pres*
Kirk Lambers, *Vice Pres*
◆ EMP: 60 EST: 2007
SQ FT: 82,000
SALES (est): 204MM Privately Held
WEB: www.royaltechnologies.com
SIC: 3089 Injection molded finished plastic products; injection molding of plastics

(G-8608)
ROYAL TECHNOLOGIES CORPORATION
3712 Quincy St (49426-8408)
PHONE................................616 667-4102
Jim Scott, *Manager*
EMP: 291
SALES (corp-wide): 204MM Privately Held
WEB: www.royaltechnologies.com
SIC: 3089 Injection molded finished plastic products
PA: Royal Technologies Corporation
    3765 Quincy St
    Hudsonville MI 49426
    616 669-3393

(G-8609)
ROYAL TECHNOLOGIES CORPORATION
2905 Corporate Grove Dr (49426-8020)
PHONE................................616 669-3393
Andy Knowlton, *Plant Mgr*
Chaunda Devries, *Technical Mgr*
Marc Kooi, *Technical Mgr*
Wayne Cumberworth, *Engineer*
Rodney De Went, *Project Engr*
EMP: 291
SALES (corp-wide): 204MM Privately Held
WEB: www.royaltechnologies.com
SIC: 3089 Injection molding of plastics
PA: Royal Technologies Corporation
    3765 Quincy St
    Hudsonville MI 49426
    616 669-3393

(G-8610)
RT BALDWIN ENTERPRISES INC
Also Called: R.T. Baldwin Hardwood Floors
4322 Cent Pkwy Ste A (49426)
PHONE................................616 669-1626
Lance Baldwin, *President*
EMP: 8 EST: 2005
SALES (est): 1MM Privately Held
WEB: www.rtbaldwin.com
SIC: 2426 Flooring, hardwood

(G-8611)
SHEFIT OPERATING COMPANY LLC
4400 Central Pkwy (49426-7831)
PHONE................................616 209-7003
Robert Moylan, *Mng Member*
EMP: 9 EST: 2010
SALES (est): 76.3K Privately Held
WEB: www.shefit.com
SIC: 2369 2342 5621 Leggings: girls', children's & infants'; brassieres; women's sportswear

(G-8612)
SIGNS BY TOMORROW
5657 Marlin Ave (49426-1003)
PHONE................................616 647-7446
Skip Lorimer, *Owner*
EMP: 7 EST: 2010
SALES (est): 76.3K Privately Held
WEB: www.signsbytomorrow.com
SIC: 3993 Signs & advertising specialties

(G-8613)
SVK MEDIA AND PUBLISHING LLC
5480 Alberta Dr Ste 1 (49426-8982)
P.O. Box 586 (49426-0586)
PHONE................................616 379-4001
EMP: 8 EST: 2015
SALES (est): 146K Privately Held
WEB: www.svkmp.com
SIC: 2741 Miscellaneous publishing

(G-8614)
US SUBURBAN PRESS
4675 32nd Ave Ste B (49426-8012)
PHONE................................616 662-6420
Philip Miller, *President*
EMP: 5 EST: 2015
SALES (est): 73.5K Privately Held
WEB: www.ussuburbanpress.com
SIC: 2741 Miscellaneous publishing

(G-8615)
WB PALLETS INC
4440 Chicago Dr (49426-9483)
PHONE................................616 669-3000
Warren Busscher, *President*
Diane Joy Busscher, *Vice Pres*
EMP: 24 EST: 1989
SQ FT: 32,000
SALES (est): 4.3MM Privately Held
WEB: www.wbpallets.com
SIC: 2448 Pallets, wood

(G-8616)
WESMAN DESIGNS
5489 32nd Ave (49426-2402)
PHONE................................616 669-3290
David West, *Owner*
EMP: 6 EST: 2001
SALES (est): 105K Privately Held
SIC: 2759 Menus: printing

(G-8617)
WEST MICHIGAN CABINET SUPPLY
Also Called: Wmcs
4366 Central Pkwy (49426-7830)
PHONE................................616 896-6990
Steve Sterk, *President*
Roland Hoezee, *Vice Pres*
EMP: 10 EST: 1994
SQ FT: 5,000 Privately Held
WEB: www.wmcabinetdoors.com
SIC: 2434 Wood kitchen cabinets

(G-8618)
WHATS SCOOP
3667 Baldwin St (49426-9767)
PHONE................................616 662-6423
Chandler Bullheis, *Owner*
EMP: 7 EST: 2008
SALES (est): 202.2K Privately Held
WEB: www.whatsthescoop.food94.com
SIC: 2024 Ice cream, bulk

(G-8619)
XRS HOLDINGS INC
Also Called: Shefit
4400 Central Pkwy (49426-7831)
P.O. Box 396 (49426-0396)
PHONE................................616 209-7003
Robert Moylan, *President*
Rachelle Tuttleman, *Controller*
Sara Moylan, *Shareholder*
EMP: 16 EST: 2013
SQ FT: 3,000
SALES (est): 2.5MM Privately Held
WEB: www.shefit.com
SIC: 2342 Brassieres

Huntington Woods
Oakland County

(G-8620)
COMMON EARTH PRESS LLC
10000 Nadine Ave (48070-1516)
PHONE..................313 407-2919
Nancy Jones, *Principal*
EMP: 4 **EST:** 2017
SALES (est): 80.2K **Privately Held**
WEB: www.commonearthpress.com
SIC: 2741 Miscellaneous publishing

(G-8621)
CURB APPAREL LLC
13340 Victoria Ave (48070-1721)
PHONE..................248 548-2324
Vicki Howard,
EMP: 4 **EST:** 2018
SALES (est): 198.4K **Privately Held**
SIC: 2389 Apparel & accessories

(G-8622)
LORNE HANLEY
Also Called: Custom Workroom
10085 Lincoln Dr (48070-1507)
PHONE..................248 547-9865
Lorne Hanley, *Owner*
EMP: 6 **EST:** 1989
SALES (est): 368.2K **Privately Held**
SIC: 2391 2591 Curtains & draperies; drapery hardware & blinds & shades

(G-8623)
POLYMERICA LIMITED COMPANY (PA)
Also Called: Global Enterprises
26909 Woodward Ave (48070-1365)
PHONE..................248 542-2000
William Kunz, *Managing Prtnr*
Manuel Gueterrez, *Partner*
Chris Cormier, *Partner*
Patricia Kladzyk, *Partner*
Marilyn Kunz, *Partner*
▲ **EMP:** 20 **EST:** 1998
SQ FT: 2,400
SALES (est): 50.5MM **Privately Held**
WEB: www.globalent.org
SIC: 3089 Extruded finished plastic products

Ida
Monroe County

(G-8624)
SOURCE 1 CNC LLC
7007 Todd Rd (48140-9747)
PHONE..................734 269-3381
Stephen Staszek, *President*
EMP: 7 **EST:** 2010
SALES (est): 176.8K **Privately Held**
SIC: 3599 Crankshafts & camshafts, machining

(G-8625)
TRUE ANLYTICS MFG SLUTIONS LLC
5400 Douglas Rd (48140-9512)
PHONE..................517 902-9700
John Murphy, *CEO*
EMP: 4 **EST:** 2016
SALES (est): 264.2K **Privately Held**
SIC: 7372 7389 Application computer software;

Imlay City
Lapeer County

(G-8626)
ALL SIZE PALLETS
4005 N Van Dyke Rd (48444-8902)
PHONE..................810 721-1999
Carman Daly, *Owner*
EMP: 27 **EST:** 2002
SALES (est): 2.3MM **Privately Held**
WEB: www.allsizepallets.com
SIC: 2448 Pallets, wood

(G-8627)
ANAND NVH NORTH AMERICA INC
2083 Reek Rd (48444-9203)
PHONE..................810 724-2400
Mark R Selleke, *President*
Kraig L Selleke, *Vice Pres*
Jai Singh, *Vice Pres*
Jennifer McKelvie, *Manager*
Miguel Rodriguez, *Maintence Staff*
▲ **EMP:** 244 **EST:** 1985
SQ FT: 105,057
SALES (est): 33.8MM **Privately Held**
WEB: www.rubberenterprises.com
SIC: 3069 3714 3061 3052 Molded rubber products; motor vehicle parts & accessories; mechanical rubber goods; rubber & plastics hose & beltings; metal stampings
PA: Anand Nvh Products Private Limited
F-3/5,Vasant Vihar,
New Delhi DL 12200

(G-8628)
CHAMPION BUS INC
331 Graham Rd (48444-9738)
P.O. Box 158 (48444-0158)
PHONE..................810 724-1753
John Resnik, *President*
Shawn Yopp, *Engineer*
◆ **EMP:** 300 **EST:** 1998
SQ FT: 172,000
SALES (est): 41.3MM **Publicly Held**
WEB: www.championbus.com
SIC: 3711 Motor vehicles & car bodies
PA: Rev Group, Inc.
245 S Executive Dr # 100
Brookfield WI 53005

(G-8629)
CONAGRA BRANDS INC
415 S Blacks Corners Rd (48444-9761)
PHONE..................810 724-2715
EMP: 7
SALES (corp-wide): 11.1B **Publicly Held**
WEB: www.conagrabrands.com
SIC: 2099 Food preparations
PA: Conagra Brands, Inc.
222 Mdse Mart Plz Ste 1
Chicago IL 60654
312 549-5000

(G-8630)
DIETECH TOOL & MFG INC
385 Industrial Dr (48444-1337)
PHONE..................810 724-0505
Arthur Adam, *Ch of Bd*
Gary Adam, *President*
Ronald Adam, *Vice Pres*
Norman Adam, *Treasurer*
Nick Kline, *Manager*
EMP: 94
SQ FT: 30,000
SALES (est): 18.7MM **Privately Held**
WEB: www.dietechtool.com
SIC: 3469 Stamping metal for the trade

(G-8631)
ESV PRECISION LLC
1353 N Van Dyke Rd (48444-9479)
PHONE..................810 441-0953
EMP: 5 **EST:** 2015
SALES (est): 76.2K **Privately Held**
SIC: 2621 Business form paper

(G-8632)
G & L MFG INC
2 Mountain Dr (48444-8819)
PHONE..................810 724-4101
Pete Lutz, *President*
EMP: 6 **EST:** 2012
SALES (est): 25.5K **Privately Held**
SIC: 3999 Manufacturing industries

(G-8633)
GENERAL COACH AMERICA INC (HQ)
275 Graham Rd (48444-9738)
PHONE..................810 724-6474
John Resnik, *President*
Theresa Smith, *Vice Pres*
Dominic Romeo, *Treasurer*
T Michael Pangburn, *Admin Sec*
EMP: 100 **EST:** 1993
SALES (est): 731.2K **Publicly Held**
WEB: www.revgroup.com
SIC: 3711 Buses, all types, assembly of

(G-8634)
GRAPENTIN SPECIALTIES INC
Also Called: Xstream Tackle
5599 Bowers Rd (48444-8919)
PHONE..................810 724-0636
Diane L Grapentin, *President*
Laura Vradelis, *Managing Dir*
Jeffrey Grapentin, *Vice Pres*
EMP: 4 **EST:** 1984
SQ FT: 4,000
SALES (est): 350K **Privately Held**
WEB: www.grapentin.com
SIC: 5091 5941 3949 Fishing tackle; hunting equipment & supplies; camping equipment & supplies; fishing equipment; camping equipment; fishing tackle, general

(G-8635)
HYPONEX CORPORATION
Scotts- Hyponex
332 Graham Rd (48444-9600)
PHONE..................810 724-2875
Nick Prusakiewicz, *Plant Mgr*
Mary Davis, *Manager*
Jill Rowe, *Manager*
Melissa Tatro, *Admin Sec*
EMP: 235
SALES (corp-wide): 4.1B **Publicly Held**
WEB: www.scotts.com
SIC: 2873 2875 Plant foods, mixed: from plants making nitrog. fertilizers; fertilizers, mixing only
HQ: Hyponex Corporation
14111 Scottslawn Rd
Marysville OH 43040
937 644-0011

(G-8636)
IMLAY CITY CONCRETE INC (PA)
Also Called: Homer Concrete Products
205 S Cedar St (48444-1389)
PHONE..................810 724-3905
James Homer, *President*
Jeremy Homer, *Vice Pres*
EMP: 13 **EST:** 1946
SQ FT: 30,000
SALES (est): 3MM **Privately Held**
WEB: www.imlaycitychamberofcommerce.org
SIC: 3273 3272 Ready-mixed concrete; septic tanks, concrete

(G-8637)
IMLAY CITY MOLDED PDTS CORP
593 S Cedar St (48444-1333)
PHONE..................810 721-9100
Charles Tesnow, *President*
Corey Drayer, *Principal*
Coleen Felstow, *Corp Secy*
Mary Theresa Justice, *Vice Pres*
Bonita Liebler, *Vice Pres*
EMP: 48 **EST:** 2000
SQ FT: 30,000
SALES (est): 5.3MM **Privately Held**
WEB: www.imlaycitymolded.com
SIC: 3089 Injection molded finished plastic products; injection molding of plastics

(G-8638)
JEFF SCHALLER TRANSPORT INC
2835 N Van Dyke Rd (48444-8985)
PHONE..................810 724-7640
Jeffrey Schaller, *President*
Wendy Schaller, *Vice Pres*
EMP: 5 **EST:** 1991
SALES (est): 450.3K **Privately Held**
WEB: www.jeffschaller.com
SIC: 3711 Motor vehicles & car bodies

(G-8639)
LEGACY METAL SERVICES INC
2073 S Almont Ave (48444-9732)
PHONE..................810 721-7775
Terry Moore, *President*
Sherry Moore, *Admin Sec*
EMP: 9 **EST:** 2017
SQ FT: 9,000
SALES (est): 900K **Privately Held**
WEB: www.legacymetalservices.com
SIC: 3441 Fabricated structural metal

(G-8640)
LUMBERJACK SHACK INC
7230 Webster Rd (48444-9655)
PHONE..................810 724-7230
Dave Zgnilec, *President*
EMP: 8 **EST:** 1976
SQ FT: 1,200
SALES (est): 1.2MM **Privately Held**
WEB: www.lumberjackshack.com
SIC: 5261 5571 7538 3546 Lawn & garden supplies; all-terrain vehicles; recreational vehicle repairs; saws & sawing equipment

(G-8641)
MIG MOLDING LLC
611 Industrial Park Dr (48444-1351)
PHONE..................810 724-7400
Jim Schoonover,
Brad Johnson,
Weizhong Mu,
EMP: 4
SQ FT: 70,000
SALES (est): 567.8K **Privately Held**
SIC: 3449 Custom roll formed products

(G-8642)
PAGE ONE INC
Also Called: Tri City Times
594 N Almont Ave (48444-1000)
P.O. Box 278 (48444-0278)
PHONE..................810 724-0254
Dolores Heim, *President*
EMP: 21 **EST:** 1980
SALES (est): 1.6MM **Privately Held**
WEB: www.tricitytimes-online.com
SIC: 2711 Newspapers, publishing & printing

(G-8643)
PINNACLE FOODS GROUP LLC
415 S Blacks Corners Rd (48444-9761)
PHONE..................810 724-6144
EMP: 300
SALES (corp-wide): 11B **Publicly Held**
SIC: 2038 Frozen Specialties, Nec
HQ: Pinnacle Foods Group Llc
399 Jefferson Rd
Parsippany NJ 07054

(G-8644)
PRINT SHOP 4U LLC
Also Called: Print Shop, The
110 N Almont Ave (48444-1003)
PHONE..................810 721-7500
Rebecca Homer,
EMP: 7 **EST:** 2018
SALES (est): 577.1K **Privately Held**
WEB: www.theprintshop4u.com
SIC: 2759 Publication printing

(G-8645)
RUBBER ENTERPRISES INC
2093 Reek Rd (48444-9203)
PHONE..................810 724-9200
Mark Selleke, *President*
EMP: 7 **EST:** 2016
SALES (est): 93.7K **Privately Held**
WEB: www.rubberenterprises.com
SIC: 3069 Bags, rubber or rubberized fabric

(G-8646)
SPRINGFIELD INDUSTRIES LLC
609 Folk Ct (48444-1355)
PHONE..................248 601-1445
EMP: 10
SQ FT: 4,500
SALES (est): 4.6MM **Privately Held**
SIC: 2821 Mfg Plastic Materials/Resins

(G-8647)
THOR INDUSTRIES INC
331 Graham Rd (48444-9738)
PHONE..................810 724-6474
EMP: 5 **EST:** 2018
SALES (est): 102.4K **Privately Held**
SIC: 3711 Motor vehicles & car bodies

GEOGRAPHIC SECTION

(G-8648)
TOYO SEAT USA CORPORATION (HQ)
2155 S Almont Ave (48444-9732)
PHONE.................................810 724-0300
Seizo Yamaguchi, *President*
Brian Fike, *Exec VP*
Mike Major, *Plant Mgr*
Mariann Jonas, *Purch Agent*
Joe Metzger, *Engineer*
▲ **EMP:** 200 **EST:** 1988
SQ FT: 125,000
SALES (est): 73.5MM **Privately Held**
WEB: www.toyoseat.com
SIC: 2531 8742 3714 3429 Seats, automobile; management consulting services; motor vehicle parts & accessories; manufactured hardware (general); automotive supplies & parts

(G-8649)
VALTEC LLC
565 S Cedar St (48444-1333)
PHONE.................................810 724-5048
Larry J Winget Jr, *President*
Nick Demiro, *Partner*
Christa Louks, *Purchasing*
Cody Buchanan, *Program Mgr*
Joe Winget, *Manager*
EMP: 120 **EST:** 2004
SALES (est): 14.7MM **Privately Held**
WEB: www.valtecplastics.com
SIC: 3089 Injection molding of plastics

(G-8650)
VINTECH INDUSTRIES INC (PA)
Also Called: M & S Extrusions
611 Industrial Park Dr (48444-1351)
PHONE.................................810 724-7400
Jim Schoonover, *President*
Doug Pender, *General Mgr*
Frank Mu, *Vice Pres*
Terri Lebow, *QC Mgr*
Giles Kathleen, *Human Resources*
▲ **EMP:** 160 **EST:** 2004
SQ FT: 72,500
SALES (est): 37.7MM **Privately Held**
WEB: www.vintechplastics.com
SIC: 3089 Extruded finished plastic products

(G-8651)
WITTOCK SUPPLY COMPANY
350 E 2nd St (48444-1318)
PHONE.................................810 721-8000
EMP: 7 **EST:** 2016
SALES (est): 80.8K **Privately Held**
WEB: www.wittock.com
SIC: 3432 Plumbing fixture fittings & trim

Indian River
Cheboygan County

(G-8652)
G B WOLFGRAM AND SONS INC
Also Called: Indian River Custom Log Homes
6083 River St (49749-5129)
P.O. Box 876 (49749-0876)
PHONE.................................231 238-4638
Gerald Wolfgram, *President*
Bob Davis, *Vice Pres*
Faye Wolfgram, *Admin Sec*
EMP: 10 **EST:** 1988
SQ FT: 1,000
SALES (est): 1MM **Privately Held**
SIC: 2452 1521 Log cabins, prefabricated, wood; single-family housing construction

(G-8653)
G L NELSON INC
Also Called: Today Publications
290 Patrick Dr (49749-9174)
PHONE.................................630 682-5958
Sharon Nelson, *President*
Gerald L Nelson, *President*
Sharon R Nelson, *Corp Secy*
EMP: 4
SALES (est): 350K **Privately Held**
SIC: 2741 2721 Shopping news: publishing & printing; periodicals

(G-8654)
LINK MANUFACTURING INC
Also Called: Link Industries
2208 S Straits Hwy (49749-9792)
PHONE.................................231 238-8741
Jeffrey Veryer, *Manager*
EMP: 5 **Privately Held**
WEB: www.linkeng.com
SIC: 3545 Drills (machine tool accessories)
HQ: Link Manufacturing, Inc.
43855 Plymouth Oaks Blvd
Plymouth MI 48170
734 453-0800

(G-8655)
MICHIGAN PURE ICE CO LLC
126 N Straits Hwy (49749-9147)
PHONE.................................231 420-9896
Crystal Schley, *CEO*
EMP: 5
SQ FT: 6,000
SALES (est): 70K **Privately Held**
SIC: 2097 Ice cubes

(G-8656)
SCREEN GRAPHICS CO INC
5859 S Straits Hwy (49749-8430)
PHONE.................................231 238-4499
Wes Allen, *President*
Maxwell Allen, *President*
Leigh Allen, *Vice Pres*
Wesley Allen, *Vice Pres*
EMP: 5 **EST:** 1980
SQ FT: 16,500
SALES (est): 523.6K **Privately Held**
WEB: www.screengraphic.com
SIC: 2759 Screen printing

Ingalls
Menominee County

(G-8657)
DON MACHALK SONS FENCING CORP
N7396 Us Highway 41 (49848-9202)
P.O. Box 117 (49848-0117)
PHONE.................................906 753-4002
Donald Machalk Jr, *President*
EMP: 20 **EST:** 1964
SQ FT: 5,000
SALES (est): 1.5MM **Privately Held**
WEB: www.machalkfence.com
SIC: 2499 5261 Fencing, wood; poles, wood; nurseries

(G-8658)
LAPOINTE CEDAR PRODUCTS INC
N7247 17.75 Ln (49848-9215)
PHONE.................................906 753-4072
Joseph Lapointe, *President*
EMP: 8 **EST:** 1975
SALES (est): 496.1K **Privately Held**
SIC: 2511 Lawn furniture: wood

Inkster
Wayne County

(G-8659)
BIRLON GROUP LLC
Also Called: Birlon Sacs
3801 Inkster Rd Ste 2 (48141-3069)
PHONE.................................313 551-5341
Gina Allen,
EMP: 7 **EST:** 2017
SALES (est): 319.1K **Privately Held**
WEB: www.birlonsacs.com
SIC: 3161 2393 3172 3199 Clothing & apparel carrying cases; canvas bags; leather money holders; equestrian related leather articles; fur apparel; leather goods, except luggage & shoes

(G-8660)
CABINETS BY H & K INC
1111 Inkster Rd (48141-1827)
PHONE.................................313 903-8500
Hussein Khater, *Principal*
EMP: 5 **EST:** 2016
SALES (est): 129.3K **Privately Held**
SIC: 2434 Wood kitchen cabinets

(G-8661)
COPPERTEC INC
Also Called: Nu-Core
2424 Beech Daly Rd (48141-2449)
PHONE.................................313 278-0139
Ted Fells, *CEO*
Bob Grove, *President*
Deanna Hohn, *Principal*
Martin Bochenek, *Engineer*
◆ **EMP:** 50 **EST:** 1982
SQ FT: 12,000
SALES (est): 9.7MM **Privately Held**
SIC: 7692 3643 3357 Welding repair; current-carrying wiring devices; nonferrous wiredrawing & insulating

(G-8662)
DONBAR LLC
Also Called: Cleardot Info
4224 John Daly St (48141-3119)
PHONE.................................313 784-3519
Bennie Barnes,
Bennie R Barnes,
EMP: 15 **EST:** 2008
SALES (est): 648.1K **Privately Held**
WEB: www.donbar-llc.com
SIC: 5961 2396 Novelty merchandise, mail order; automotive trimmings, fabric

(G-8663)
ECA ENTERPRISES LLC
1712 Heatherwood Dr # 102 (48141-4969)
PHONE.................................313 828-4098
EMP: 7 **EST:** 2019
SALES (est): 80.8K **Privately Held**
WEB: www.ecaenterprises.com
SIC: 3599 Machine shop, jobbing & repair

(G-8664)
GILMORE LOGISTICS LLC ✪
1461 Crescent St (48141-1819)
PHONE.................................586 488-9895
James Gilmore,
EMP: 6 **EST:** 2021
SALES (est): 268.5K **Privately Held**
SIC: 3537 Trucks, tractors, loaders, carriers & similar equipment

(G-8665)
HASSAN SONS SPCIAL HM SVCS LLC ✪
27631 Michigan Ave (48141-4149)
PHONE.................................313 558-1031
Hassan Powell,
EMP: 5 **EST:** 2021
SALES (est): 140K **Privately Held**
SIC: 1389 Construction, repair & dismantling services

(G-8666)
INKSTER FUEL & FOOD INC
1021 Inkster Rd (48141-1825)
PHONE.................................313 565-8230
Paula Abdul, *Owner*
EMP: 8 **EST:** 2009
SALES (est): 2MM **Privately Held**
WEB: www.cityofinkster.com
SIC: 2869 Fuels

(G-8667)
JOY CARPET CLEANING LLC ✪
28948 York St (48141-2821)
PHONE.................................734 656-8827
Darryl East, *CEO*
EMP: 6 **EST:** 2021
SALES (est): 100K **Privately Held**
SIC: 2842 Rug, upholstery, or dry cleaning detergents or spotters

(G-8668)
LARRYS TARPAULIN SHOP LLC
3452 Beech Daly Rd (48141-2625)
PHONE.................................313 563-2292
Larry C Smith,
EMP: 4 **EST:** 1974
SQ FT: 3,260
SALES (est): 210.6K **Privately Held**
SIC: 2394 Tarpaulins, fabric: made from purchased materials

(G-8669)
OIL EXCHANGE 6 INC
140 Middlebelt Rd (48141-1171)
PHONE.................................734 641-4310
EMP: 5
SALES (est): 370K **Privately Held**
SIC: 1389 Oil/Gas Field Services

(G-8670)
PLASTEEL CORPORATION
26970 Princeton St (48141-2314)
P.O. Box 555 (48141-0555)
PHONE.................................313 562-5400
William E Ohlsson, *President*
Jane Ohlsson, *Vice Pres*
Bill Ohlsson, *VP Mktg*
Wendy Langlois, *Admin Sec*
▲ **EMP:** 39 **EST:** 1941
SQ FT: 14,500
SALES (est): 9MM **Privately Held**
WEB: www.smoothfoam.com
SIC: 3086 2821 Insulation or cushioning material, foamed plastic; plastics materials & resins

(G-8671)
PRECISION MTL HDLG EQP LLC (HQ)
26700 Princeton St (48141-2310)
PHONE.................................313 789-8101
Edward Walker, *CEO*
Leona Burja, *President*
Chris Burja, *Vice Pres*
Phillip Fascetti, *Supervisor*
EMP: 97 **EST:** 2015
SQ FT: 90,000
SALES (est): 10.1MM
SALES (corp-wide): 20.3MM **Privately Held**
WEB: www.w-international.com
SIC: 3441 Fabricated structural metal
PA: W International, Llc
31720 Stephenson Hwy
Madison Heights MI 48071
248 577-0364

(G-8672)
PROTO-CAST INC
2699 John Daly St (48141-3704)
PHONE.................................313 565-5400
William H Covington, *President*
Don E Clapham, *Vice Pres*
Chaitanya Mitta, *Engineer*
EMP: 45 **EST:** 1973
SQ FT: 31,000
SALES (est): 5.2MM **Privately Held**
WEB: www.protocast.com
SIC: 3364 3543 3369 Zinc & zinc-base alloy die-castings; industrial patterns; nonferrous foundries

(G-8673)
QUALITY CUSTOMS CONS LLC
4134 Spruce St (48141-2924)
PHONE.................................313 564-9327
Preston Bowers, *Principal*
Marvin Paschall, *Principal*
EMP: 10 **EST:** 2004
SALES (est): 580.5K **Privately Held**
SIC: 3714 Motor vehicle parts & accessories

(G-8674)
QUICK DRAW TARPAULIN SYSTEMS
26125 Trowbridge St (48141-2408)
PHONE.................................313 561-0554
EMP: 13 **Privately Held**
WEB: www.quickdrawtarps.com
SIC: 2394 Tarpaulins, fabric: made from purchased materials
PA: Quick Draw Tarpaulin Systems Inc
10200 Ford Rd
Dearborn MI 48126

(G-8675)
S HASAN PUBLISHING LLC
3655 Henry St (48141-3079)
PHONE.................................734 858-8800
Shahidah Hasan, *Principal*
EMP: 4 **EST:** 2013
SALES (est): 37.5K **Privately Held**
SIC: 2741 Miscellaneous publishing

(G-8676)
TORESON INDUSTRIES INC
410 Biltmore St (48141-1388)
PHONE.................................818 261-7249
EMP: 4 **EST:** 2017

Inkster - Wayne County (G-8677)   **GEOGRAPHIC SECTION**

SALES (est): 68.6K **Privately Held**
WEB: www.toreson.com
SIC: 3999 Manufacturing industries

(G-8677)
W W J FORM TOOL COMPANY INC
26122 Michigan Ave (48141-2462)
PHONE.................................313 565-0015
Arthur Tykoski Jr, *President*
Jennifer Tykoski, *Treasurer*
Suzanne Baughman, *Manager*
EMP: 6 **EST:** 1959
SQ FT: 1,600
SALES (est): 250K **Privately Held**
SIC: 3541 Machine tools, metal cutting: exotic (explosive, etc.)

Interlochen
Grand Traverse County

(G-8678)
5 14 CANDLES
2801 Timber Ridge Rd (49643-9331)
PHONE.................................231 944-9585
Emily Pangborn, *Principal*
EMP: 4 **EST:** 2018
SALES (est): 39.6K **Privately Held**
WEB: www.514candles.com
SIC: 3999 Candles

(G-8679)
BENZIE PRINTING
9780 Innwood W (49643-9128)
PHONE.................................231 714-7565
EMP: 5 **EST:** 2013
SALES (est): 156.7K **Privately Held**
WEB: www.benzie.org
SIC: 2752 Commercial printing, lithographic

(G-8680)
CARPENTERS FRIEND WOODWORKING
3189 El Shaddai Ln (49643-8420)
PHONE.................................231 218-2736
Scott M Cynthia, *Owner*
EMP: 4 **EST:** 2016
SALES (est): 54.1K **Privately Held**
SIC: 2431 Millwork

(G-8681)
CONVENTIONAL GRAPHICS INC
11682 Us Highway 31 (49643-9357)
PHONE.................................231 943-4301
Robert Allard, *President*
Linda Marie Allard, *Vice Pres*
EMP: 5 **EST:** 1979
SALES (est): 230K **Privately Held**
SIC: 2752 Commercial printing, offset

(G-8682)
DEERINGS JERKY CO LLC
2015 Sandy Dr (49643-9388)
PHONE.................................231 590-5687
Paul M Deering, *Mng Member*
EMP: 5 **EST:** 2013
SALES (est): 454.4K **Privately Held**
SIC: 2013 Snack sticks, including jerky: from purchased meat

(G-8683)
FISH ON SPORTS INC
11838 Us Highway 31 (49643-9365)
PHONE.................................231 342-5231
EMP: 9 **EST:** 2011
SALES (est): 131.7K **Privately Held**
WEB: www.fishonsports.com
SIC: 3949 Fishing equipment; rods & rod parts, fishing

(G-8684)
SAWMILL BILL LUMBER INC
18657 Us Highway 31 (49643-9394)
PHONE.................................231 275-3000
William Reitz, *Owner*
Denise Reitz, *Vice Pres*
EMP: 5 **EST:** 1981
SQ FT: 22,000
SALES (est): 458.3K **Privately Held**
SIC: 2431 Millwork

(G-8685)
SIX LUGS LLC
19718 Platte River Jct (49643-9635)
P.O. Box 523 (49643-0523)
PHONE.................................231 275-0600
Sheryl Umulis, *Branch Mgr*
EMP: 12
SALES (corp-wide): 69.2K **Privately Held**
WEB: www.sixlugs.com
SIC: 2099 Dressings, salad: dry mixes
PA: Six Lugs Llc
  200 Wooded Valley Dr
  Traverse City MI
  231 270-0600

(G-8686)
WILLOW MFG INC
11455 Us Highway 31 (49643-9355)
PHONE.................................231 275-1026
Jerry A Carlson, *President*
EMP: 7 **EST:** 2003
SALES (est): 317.5K **Privately Held**
SIC: 3999 Barber & beauty shop equipment

Ionia
Ionia County

(G-8687)
BUSH POLISHING BUFFING LLC
5624 E Charles Rd (48846-9751)
PHONE.................................989 855-2248
EMP: 4 **EST:** 2019
SALES (est): 161.6K **Privately Held**
SIC: 3471 Plating & polishing

(G-8688)
CUSTOM COMPONENTS CORPORATION
1111 E Main St Ionia (48846)
PHONE.................................616 523-1111
Ryan Pawloski, *CEO*
David Leonard, *President*
Jenna Hurless, *Principal*
Tammy Pawloski, *Principal*
Collin Pawloski, *Engineer*
EMP: 15 **EST:** 1974
SQ FT: 96,000
SALES (est): 2.1MM **Privately Held**
WEB: www.cccsolution.com
SIC: 2599 2521 2522 5047 Hotel furniture; wood office furniture; office furniture, except wood; hospital furniture; table or counter tops, plastic laminated

(G-8689)
FOUR SEASONS MOBILE PRESS
417 Morse St (48846-1319)
PHONE.................................616 902-6233
Kirk Wolthuis, *Principal*
EMP: 5 **EST:** 2010
SALES (est): 76.2K **Privately Held**
SIC: 2741 Miscellaneous publishing

(G-8690)
MATCOR AUTOMOTIVE MICHIGAN INC
401 S Steele St (48846-9401)
P.O. Box 503 (48846-0503)
PHONE.................................616 527-4050
Art Artuso, *President*
Gilliano Tiberini, *Vice Pres*
Dave Singh, *Materials Mgr*
Tim Lee, *Manager*
EMP: 120 **EST:** 2009
SALES (est): 15.8MM **Privately Held**
WEB: www.matcor-matsu.com
SIC: 3465 5013 Body parts, automobile: stamped metal; automotive stampings

(G-8691)
ORION MANUFACTURING INC
480 Apple Tree Dr (48846-8512)
PHONE.................................616 527-5994
Joseph D Stewart, *President*
Scott Stewart, *COO*
Tony Sorsen, *Plant Mgr*
EMP: 16 **EST:** 1993
SQ FT: 25,000
SALES (est): 2.2MM **Privately Held**
WEB: www.orionmfg.net
SIC: 3465 3429 Automotive stampings; manufactured hardware (general); furniture builders' & other household hardware

(G-8692)
UNIPRAX LLC
Also Called: MI Probation
215 W Main St (48846-1638)
PHONE.................................616 522-3158
Christopher Staggs,
Christopher Vanstee,
Timothy Zylstra,
EMP: 4 **EST:** 2017
SALES (est): 74K **Privately Held**
SIC: 7372 Prepackaged software

(G-8693)
VENTRA IONIA MAIN LLC (HQ)
14 Beardsley St (48846-9789)
PHONE.................................616 597-3220
Gary Roe, *Engineer*
Shahid R Khan, *Mng Member*
Julie Brady, *Analyst*
John Atkinson,
Harold Stieber,
▲ **EMP:** 558 **EST:** 2009
SALES (est): 113.8MM
SALES (corp-wide): 1.5B **Privately Held**
WEB: www.ioniacounty.org
SIC: 3469 3089 5198 Metal stampings; molding primary plastic; paints
PA: Flex-N-Gate Llc
  1306 E University Ave
  Urbana IL 61802
  217 384-6600

(G-8694)
VOLCOR FINISHING INC
510 Apple Tree Dr (48846-8512)
PHONE.................................616 527-5555
David Doug, *Ch of Bd*
John Fisher, *President*
Jim Erickson, *Maintence Staff*
EMP: 20 **EST:** 1993
SQ FT: 25,000
SALES (est): 2.7MM **Privately Held**
WEB: www.volcor.com
SIC: 3479 Coating of metals & formed products

Ira
St. Clair County

(G-8695)
EST TOOLS AMERICA INC
10138 Radiance Dr (48023-1424)
PHONE.................................810 824-3323
Catherine Chen, *CEO*
EMP: 10 **EST:** 2016
SALES (est): 536.4K **Privately Held**
WEB: www.est-us.com
SIC: 3545 Machine tool accessories

(G-8696)
EVERSHARP TOOLS INC
10138 Radiance Dr (48023-1424)
PHONE.................................810 824-3323
EMP: 7 **EST:** 2017
SALES (est): 188.5K **Privately Held**
WEB: www.est-us.com
SIC: 3599 Machine shop, jobbing & repair

(G-8697)
G & G DIE AND ENGINEERING INC
6091 Corporate Dr (48023-1423)
PHONE.................................586 716-8099
William Gilley, *President*
▲ **EMP:** 20 **EST:** 1989
SQ FT: 10,000
SALES (est): 1.7MM **Privately Held**
SIC: 3544 Dies & die holders for metal cutting, forming, die casting

(G-8698)
HTC SALES CORPORATION
Also Called: Htc Products
6560 Bethuy Rd (48023-1810)
PHONE.................................800 624-2027
Charles Russell, *President*
▲ **EMP:** 14 **EST:** 2006
SQ FT: 38,000
SALES (est): 426.3K **Privately Held**
WEB: www.affinitytool.com
SIC: 3545 5084 Machine tool accessories; industrial machinery & equipment

(G-8699)
IIG-DSS TECHNOLOGIES LLC
6100 Bethuy Rd (48023-1120)
PHONE.................................586 725-5300
Francis G N Leo, *Mng Member*
Doug Dawson,
Sekou Shorter,
Greg Yezback,
▲ **EMP:** 11 **EST:** 2004
SQ FT: 68,000
SALES (est): 552K **Privately Held**
SIC: 3089 Injection molded finished plastic products

(G-8700)
KEHRIG STEEL INC
9279 Marine City Hwy (48023-1222)
PHONE.................................586 716-9700
Robert Kehrig, *President*
EMP: 4 **EST:** 1987
SQ FT: 8,000
SALES (est): 1MM **Privately Held**
WEB: www.kehrigmetalfab.com
SIC: 3441 Fabricated structural metal

(G-8701)
MATERIAL HANDLING TECH INC
9023 Marine City Hwy B (48023-1225)
PHONE.................................586 725-5546
David Vavro, *President*
Don Robert Vavro, *Vice Pres*
▲ **EMP:** 70 **EST:** 1986
SQ FT: 66,000
SALES (est): 10.2MM **Privately Held**
SIC: 3444 7692 5084 Hoppers, sheet metal; welding repair; materials handling machinery

(G-8702)
MOD INTERIORS INC
9301 Marine City Hwy (48023-1223)
PHONE.................................586 725-8227
Donald Megie, *President*
Matthew Gaglio, *Vice Pres*
Mason Gill, *Project Dir*
Donna Faucher, *Purch Agent*
Kennita Megie, *Controller*
EMP: 27 **EST:** 1982
SQ FT: 20,000
SALES (est): 12.7MM **Privately Held**
WEB: www.modinteriors.com
SIC: 2431 1751 Millwork; cabinet building & installation

(G-8703)
MODIFIED TECHNOLOGIES INC
6500 Bethuy Rd (48023-1810)
PHONE.................................586 725-0448
Charles Russell, *President*
Colleen Kowalski, *Manager*
Donna Russell, *Admin Sec*
EMP: 52 **EST:** 1991
SQ FT: 44,000
SALES (est): 3.8MM **Privately Held**
WEB: www.modifiedtech.com
SIC: 3544 Special dies, tools, jigs & fixtures

(G-8704)
MONROE SATTLER LLC
Also Called: Sattler Ira
6024 Corporate Dr (48023-1422)
PHONE.................................586 725-1140
Paul Sattler, *Mng Member*
EMP: 20 **EST:** 2020
SALES (est): 5MM **Privately Held**
SIC: 3599 Machine shop, jobbing & repair

(G-8705)
MURLEYS MARINE
8174 Dixie Hwy (48023-2513)
PHONE.................................586 725-7446
Michael Murley, *Owner*
EMP: 4 **EST:** 1975
SQ FT: 3,600
SALES (est): 283.3K **Privately Held**
WEB: www.dolphinmarineengineco.com
SIC: 3732 7699 Motorized boat, building & repairing; marine engine repair

GEOGRAPHIC SECTION

Iron Mountain - Dickinson County (G-8732)

(G-8706)
P D Q PRESS INC
7752 Dixie Hwy (48023-2728)
PHONE..................................586 725-1888
Thomas Gratopp, *President*
William Gratopp, *Corp Secy*
Willard Gratopp, *Vice Pres*
EMP: 5 EST: 1973
SALES (est): 467.2K **Privately Held**
WEB: www.pdqpress.com
SIC: 2759 2791 7331 7384 Ready prints; typesetting, computer controlled; direct mail advertising services; film developing & printing

(G-8707)
P T M CORPORATION (PA)
Also Called: Quasar Prototype and Tool Co.
6560 Bethuy Rd (48023-1810)
PHONE..................................586 725-2211
Charles T Russell, *President*
Donna Russell, *Vice Pres*
Steve Kuhr, *Opers Staff*
Tammy Redman, *Production*
Parlin Sitohang, *Engineer*
EMP: 88 EST: 1965
SQ FT: 121,500
SALES (est): 24.7MM **Privately Held**
WEB: www.ptmcorporation.com
SIC: 3714 3545 Motor vehicle parts & accessories; tools & accessories for machine tools

(G-8708)
P T M CORPORATION
6520 Bethuy Rd (48023-1810)
PHONE..................................586 725-2733
Mike Guilian, *Branch Mgr*
Jim Boelstler, *Manager*
Eugene Rosiek, *Manager*
Mike Kohlhoff, *Maintence Staff*
EMP: 8
SALES (corp-wide): 24.7MM **Privately Held**
WEB: www.ptmcorporation.com
SIC: 3545 3714 Tools & accessories for machine tools; motor vehicle parts & accessories
PA: P. T. M. Corporation
    6560 Bethuy Rd
    Ira MI 48023
    586 725-2211

(G-8709)
R E GALLAHER CORP
9601 Marine City Hwy (48023-1116)
PHONE..................................586 725-3333
James A Gallaher III, *President*
James A Gallaher IV, *Vice Pres*
EMP: 8 EST: 1969
SQ FT: 20,000
SALES (est): 153.8K **Privately Held**
SIC: 3451 Screw machine products

(G-8710)
RICHMOND MILLWORK INC
10134 Radiance Dr (48023-1424)
PHONE..................................586 727-6747
Mark Huss, *President*
Jim Vannuck, *Vice Pres*
Kenneth Huss, *Treasurer*
EMP: 13 EST: 2004
SALES (est): 1.8MM **Privately Held**
WEB: www.richmondmillwork.com
SIC: 2431 Millwork

(G-8711)
RIVERHILL PUBLICATIONS & PRTG
8850 Dixie Hwy (48023-2489)
PHONE..................................586 468-6011
Louis Cattaneo, *Vice Pres*
EMP: 10 EST: 1971
SQ FT: 6,000
SALES (est): 633.3K **Privately Held**
SIC: 2759 Commercial printing

(G-8712)
SATTLER INC
6024 Corporate Dr (48023-1422)
PHONE..................................586 725-1140
EMP: 10
SALES (est): 1.5MM **Privately Held**
SIC: 3599 Mfg Industrial Machinery

(G-8713)
SEJASMI INDUSTRIES INC
Also Called: Bosch
6100 Bethuy Rd (48023-1120)
PHONE..................................586 725-5300
Samir Patel, *President*
D S Patel, *Vice Pres*
Keith Conner, *Opers Mgr*
Norman Shelton, *Engineer*
Wayne Brockley, *Manager*
▲ EMP: 125 EST: 2007
SALES (est): 21.7MM **Privately Held**
WEB: www.sejasmi.com
SIC: 3052 Automobile hose, plastic

(G-8714)
SKILL-CRAFT COMPANY INC
10125 Radiance Dr (48023-1424)
PHONE..................................586 716-4300
James E Thurman, *President*
Donald P Thurman, *Vice Pres*
Dave Thurman, *Engineer*
EMP: 10 EST: 1952
SQ FT: 7,000
SALES (est): 1.5MM **Privately Held**
WEB: www.skill-craftcompany.com
SIC: 3545 Chucks: drill, lathe or magnetic (machine tool accessories); collets (machine tool accessories)

(G-8715)
SUPREME INDUSTRIES LLC
6015 Corporate Dr (48023-1423)
PHONE..................................586 725-2500
Rick Winarski
EMP: 5 EST: 2001
SALES (est): 595.3K **Privately Held**
WEB: www.supremeindllc.com
SIC: 3089 Injection molding of plastics

(G-8716)
TOTAL LIFE CHANGES LLC (PA)
6094 Corporate Dr (48023-1422)
PHONE..................................810 471-3812
Maria Randolph, *Sales Staff*
Jack Fallon, *Mng Member*
Jamie Harris, *Consultant*
Ron Rose, *Director*
Scott Bania, *Officer*
▲ EMP: 425 EST: 2001
SALES (est): 62.2MM **Privately Held**
WEB: www.totallifechanges.com
SIC: 5499 2834 Health foods; vitamin preparations

Iron Mountain
Dickinson County

(G-8717)
BERTOLDI OIL SERVICE INC
N2395 Cemetary Ln (49801)
P.O. Box 646 (49801-0646)
PHONE..................................906 774-1707
James Bertoldi, *President*
John Bertoldi, *Vice Pres*
George Bertoldi, *Treasurer*
EMP: 9 EST: 1988
SQ FT: 10,000
SALES (est): 668.1K **Privately Held**
SIC: 2911 Petroleum refining

(G-8718)
BINKS COCA-COLA BOTTLING CO
617 Industrial Dr (49801-1423)
PHONE..................................906 774-3202
Todd Charpier, *Manager*
EMP: 19
SALES (corp-wide): 5.2MM **Privately Held**
WEB: www.binksbeverages.com
SIC: 2086 Bottled & canned soft drinks
PA: Bink's Coca-Cola Bottling Co
    3001 Danforth Rd
    Escanaba MI 49829
    906 786-4144

(G-8719)
CHAMPION CHARTER SLS & SVC INC
180 Traders Mine Rd (49801-1447)
P.O. Box 490 (49801-0490)
PHONE..................................906 779-2300
Gary Benjamin, *Ch of Bd*
Thomas Jacko, *President*
Jim Rose, *Safety Dir*
Derek Thomas, *Engineer*
Daniel Wentarmini, *Treasurer*
EMP: 27 EST: 2007
SALES (est): 15.3MM **Privately Held**
WEB: www.champion-charter.com
SIC: 3491 3543 Industrial valves; industrial patterns

(G-8720)
CUMMINS INC
1901 N Stephenson Ave (49801-1483)
P.O. Box 5070, De Pere WI (54115-5070)
PHONE..................................906 774-2424
Krishna Chaitanya Belli, *Engineer*
Dan Carlson, *Branch Mgr*
EMP: 7
SALES (corp-wide): 19.8B **Publicly Held**
WEB: www.cummins.com
SIC: 3714 Fuel systems & parts, motor vehicle
PA: Cummins Inc.
    500 Jackson St
    Columbus IN 47201
    812 377-5000

(G-8721)
CUSTOMER METAL FABRICATION INC (PA)
W8762 Lakeview Dr (49801-9320)
P.O. Box 669 (49801-0669)
PHONE..................................906 774-3216
Richard Sparapani, *President*
Lori Machus, *Corp Secy*
David Ethington, *Vice Pres*
Thomas Wickman, *Vice Pres*
EMP: 35 EST: 1973
SQ FT: 16,000
SALES (est): 5.2MM **Privately Held**
WEB: www.customermetal.com
SIC: 3599 7692 3444 Machine shop, jobbing & repair; welding repair; sheet metalwork

(G-8722)
IMECO INC
1401 Carpenter Ave (49801-4768)
P.O. Box 2130, Kingsford (49802-2130)
PHONE..................................906 774-0202
Peter Anderson, *Vice Pres*
Jim Laydon, *Prdtn Mgr*
Matthew Fultz, *Admin Sec*
Billie Johnson, *Admin Asst*
EMP: 9 EST: 2019
SALES (est): 1.6MM **Privately Held**
WEB: www.tridentllc.com
SIC: 3822 Auto controls regulating residntl & coml environmt & applncs

(G-8723)
JERED LLC
821 East Blvd (49802-4435)
PHONE..................................906 776-1800
Mike Gerard, *Branch Mgr*
EMP: 4
SALES (corp-wide): 656MM **Privately Held**
SIC: 3625 3536 Marine & navy auxiliary controls; hoists, cranes & monorails
HQ: Jered Llc
    3000 Sidney Lanier Dr
    Brunswick GA 31525
    912 262-2000

(G-8724)
LAYDON ENTERPRISES INC (PA)
Also Called: Eagle Tool
101 Woodward Ave (49802-4736)
P.O. Box 459 (49801-0459)
PHONE..................................906 774-4633
John G Laydon, *President*
Dan Wender, *Vice Pres*
EMP: 42 EST: 1980
SQ FT: 15,000
SALES (est): 8.4MM **Privately Held**
WEB: www.eaglebroach.com
SIC: 3545 3398 3599 3541 Broaches (machine tool accessories); metal heat treating; machine shop, jobbing & repair; machine tools, metal cutting type

(G-8725)
MILLER PRODUCTS & SUPPLY CO
1801 N Stephenson Ave (49801-1407)
PHONE..................................906 774-1243
Robert Fayas, *President*
Alan Perla, *Manager*
Ryan Fayas, *Supervisor*
EMP: 10 EST: 1956
SQ FT: 6,000
SALES (est): 4MM **Privately Held**
SIC: 5032 3271 Concrete & cinder block; concrete block & brick

(G-8726)
NELSON PAINT COMPANY MICH INC
1 Nelson Dr (49802-4561)
P.O. Box 2040 (49802-2040)
PHONE..................................906 774-5566
EMP: 8
SALES (est): 667.2K **Privately Held**
SIC: 2851 5231 Mfg Paints/Allied Products Ret Paint/Glass/Wallpaper

(G-8727)
NORTHERN PRODUCTS OF WISCONSIN
W8969 Frei Dr (49801-9449)
PHONE..................................715 589-4417
David Lavarnway, *President*
EMP: 8 EST: 1985
SALES (est): 540K **Privately Held**
SIC: 2421 Sawmills & planing mills, general

(G-8728)
NORTHSIDE NOODLE COMPANY
609 Vulcan St (49801-2351)
PHONE..................................906 779-2181
Michael P Celello, *Administration*
EMP: 8 EST: 2011
SALES (est): 467.7K **Privately Held**
SIC: 2098 Noodles (e.g. egg, plain & water), dry

(G-8729)
ORBIT TECHNOLOGY INC
100 W Brown St (49801-2802)
P.O. Box 1043 (49801-8043)
PHONE..................................906 776-7248
Gary Marsden, *President*
Gary Unrein, *Vice Pres*
Amanda Harvath, *Office Mgr*
EMP: 7 EST: 1997
SALES (est): 679.1K **Privately Held**
WEB: www.orbittec.com
SIC: 7372 5044 Prepackaged software; copying equipment

(G-8730)
RICE JUICE COMPANY INC
873 Evergreen Ct (49802-1107)
PHONE..................................906 774-1733
Larry Rice, *President*
EMP: 7 EST: 1950
SQ FT: 13,050
SALES (est): 756.3K **Privately Held**
SIC: 2033 5149 Fruit juices: packaged in cans, jars, etc.; juices; soft drinks

(G-8731)
RRR TRAINING & PUBLISHING
1040 E Grant St (49801-1732)
PHONE..................................906 396-9546
Barbara J Reisner, *Principal*
EMP: 5 EST: 2010
SALES (est): 107.5K **Privately Held**
SIC: 2741 Miscellaneous publishing

(G-8732)
SCHNEIDER IRON & METAL INC
Also Called: East Kingsford Iron & Metal Co
100 E Superior St (49801)
PHONE..................................906 774-0644
Ronald Schneider, *Owner*
EMP: 9
SQ FT: 1,800
SALES (corp-wide): 5.3MM **Privately Held**
SIC: 5093 3444 3341 Ferrous metal scrap & waste; culverts, sheet metal; secondary nonferrous metals

Iron Mountain - Dickinson County (G-8733)

PA: Schneider Iron & Metal Inc
1929 Elmer St
Niagara WI 54151
906 774-0644

(G-8733)
SMITH CASTINGS INC
Ford Plant (49802)
PHONE..................906 774-4956
Eric Frantz, *President*
Rick Sadler, *Facilities Mgr*
EMP: 16 **EST:** 1996
SQ FT: 35,000
SALES (est): 573.4K **Privately Held**
WEB: www.smithcastings.com
SIC: 3321 3366 3369 3325 Gray iron castings; castings (except die); nonferrous foundries; steel foundries; malleable iron foundries

(G-8734)
SUPERIOR EQUIPMENT & SUPPLY CO
1515 S Stephenson Ave (49801-3633)
P.O. Box 339 (49801-0339)
PHONE..................906 774-1789
David Johnson, *President*
Mary Johnson, *Corp Secy*
EMP: 5 **EST:** 1986
SQ FT: 2,200
SALES (est): 846.1K **Privately Held**
WEB: www.supeq.com
SIC: 5084 3537 5082 Materials handling machinery; lift trucks, industrial: fork, platform, straddle, etc.; mining machinery & equipment, except petroleum

(G-8735)
SYSTEMS CONTROL INC
3201 E Industrial Dr (49801-1406)
P.O. Box 788 (49801-0788)
PHONE..................906 774-0440
Brad Lebouef, *CEO*
David Chiesa, *Vice Pres*
Bob Elsey, *Project Mgr*
Daniel George, *Project Mgr*
Anthony Pericolosi, *Project Mgr*
EMP: 700 **EST:** 1962
SALES (est): 132.9MM **Privately Held**
WEB: www.systemscontrol.com
SIC: 3613 Panelboards & distribution boards, electric
PA: Comvest Group Holdings Lp
525 Okeechobee Blvd # 1050
West Palm Beach FL 33401

(G-8736)
TIMBER PDTS MICH LTD PARTNR (PA)
104 E B St (49801-3468)
P.O. Box 378, Munising (49862-0378)
PHONE..................906 779-2000
Joseph Gonyea, *Partner*
EMP: 2 **EST:** 1962
SALES (est): 13.5MM **Privately Held**
SIC: 2435 2426 Veneer stock, hardwood; lumber, hardwood dimension

(G-8737)
WOODY HOLLOW CANDLES
507 Kent St (49801-6815)
PHONE..................906 774-7839
Charlie Ciantar, *Principal*
EMP: 4 **EST:** 2017
SALES (est): 60K **Privately Held**
SIC: 3999 Candles

(G-8738)
Z & R ELECTRIC SERVICE INC
619 Industrial Park Dr (49801)
P.O. Box 740, Schofield WI (54476-0740)
PHONE..................906 774-0468
Ricki Bieti, *President*
EMP: 30 **EST:** 1952
SQ FT: 20,000
SALES (est): 2.2MM **Privately Held**
SIC: 5063 7694 5999 3599 Motors, electric; electric motor repair; electronic parts & equipment; machine shop, jobbing & repair; motors & generators

Iron River
Iron County

(G-8739)
ALEXA FOREST PRODUCTS
137 Dirkman Rd (49935)
PHONE..................906 265-2347
David Alexa, *Owner*
EMP: 6 **EST:** 1971
SALES (est): 519.3K **Privately Held**
SIC: 2411 Logging camps & contractors

(G-8740)
DINA MIA KITCHENS INC
751 N 4th Ave (49935-1394)
PHONE..................906 265-9082
Peter Saving, *President*
Linda Saving, *Corp Secy*
EMP: 20 **EST:** 1961
SQ FT: 5,000
SALES (est): 2.2MM **Privately Held**
WEB: www.dinamiakitchens.com
SIC: 2038 2098 2035 2013 Pizza, frozen; spaghetti & meatballs, frozen; macaroni & spaghetti; pickles, sauces & salad dressings; sausages & other prepared meats
PA: Linda Mia Inc
751 N 4th Ave
Iron River MI 49935

(G-8741)
IRON RIVER MFG CO INC
Also Called: Lester Detterbeck Enterprises
3390 Us Highway 2 (49935-8578)
PHONE..................906 265-5121
John Detterbeck, *President*
EMP: 1 **EST:** 1973
SQ FT: 20,000
SALES (est): 1.1MM
SALES (corp-wide): 3.4MM **Privately Held**
WEB: www.lesterdetterbeck.com
SIC: 3541 5084 Machine tools, metal cutting type; industrial machinery & equipment
PA: Lester Detterbeck Enterprises, Ltd.
3390 Us Highway 2
Iron River MI 49935
906 265-5121

(G-8742)
J AND K LUMBER INC
100 Homer Rd (49935-9673)
PHONE..................906 265-9130
Paulette Frame, *Owner*
EMP: 5 **EST:** 2015
SALES (est): 258.4K **Privately Held**
SIC: 2421 Sawmills & planing mills, general

(G-8743)
JAMES SPICER INC
Also Called: Spicer's
1571 W Adams St (49935-1266)
PHONE..................906 265-2385
Tony Spicer, *President*
EMP: 6 **EST:** 1971
SALES (est): 705.8K **Privately Held**
SIC: 4212 2411 Local trucking, without storage; logging camps & contractors

(G-8744)
JKL HARDWOODS INC
1101 Homer Rd (49935-9692)
P.O. Box 428 (49935-0428)
PHONE..................906 265-9130
John Ricker, *President*
EMP: 13 **EST:** 2003
SQ FT: 100
SALES (est): 87.7K **Privately Held**
SIC: 2491 Structural lumber & timber, treated wood

(G-8745)
LAKE SHORE SYSTEMS INC
1520 W Adams St (49935-1265)
P.O. Box 467 (49935-0467)
PHONE..................906 265-5414
Dan Bruso, *Exec VP*
Joel Ambrioso, *Train & Dev Mgr*
EMP: 24
SALES (corp-wide): 77MM **Privately Held**
WEB: www.lakeshoresys.com
SIC: 3534 3731 3532 Elevators & moving stairways; shipbuilding & repairing; mining machinery
PA: Lake Shore Systems, Inc.
2141 Woodward Ave
Kingsford MI 49802
906 774-1500

(G-8746)
LESTER DETTERBECK ENTPS LTD (PA)
3390 Us Highway 2 (49935-8578)
PHONE..................906 265-5121
John Detterbeck, *President*
EMP: 24 **EST:** 1952
SALES (est): 3.4MM **Privately Held**
WEB: www.lesterdetterbeck.com
SIC: 3541 3545 3544 3451 Machine tools, metal cutting: exotic (explosive, etc.); machine tool accessories; special dies, tools, jigs & fixtures; screw machine products

(G-8747)
LINDA MIA INC (PA)
751 N 4th Ave (49935-1303)
PHONE..................906 265-9082
Peter Saving, *President*
Linda Saving, *Treasurer*
EMP: 2
SQ FT: 5,000
SALES (est): 2.3MM **Privately Held**
SIC: 2038 Pizza, frozen; spaghetti & meatballs, frozen

(G-8748)
LOW IMPACT LOGGING INC
3172 Us Highway 2 (49935-8568)
PHONE..................906 250-5117
Ted R Benson, *Principal*
EMP: 6 **EST:** 2007
SALES (est): 581.2K **Privately Held**
SIC: 2411 Logging camps & contractors

(G-8749)
MOTTES MATERIALS INC
4084 Us Highway 2 (49935-7972)
P.O. Box 112 (49935-0112)
PHONE..................906 265-9955
Eugene Mottes, *President*
EMP: 9 **EST:** 1977
SQ FT: 5,000
SALES (est): 271.1K **Privately Held**
SIC: 1442 3273 Sand mining; gravel mining; ready-mixed concrete

(G-8750)
NICOLET SIGN & DESIGN
Also Called: Nicolet Sign & Construction
612 W Adams St (49935-1322)
PHONE..................906 265-5220
Kris Hughes, *Owner*
EMP: 8 **EST:** 2016
SALES (est): 307.7K **Privately Held**
WEB: www.nicoletsign.com
SIC: 3993 Signs & advertising specialties

(G-8751)
NORTHLAND PUBLISHERS INC
Also Called: Reporter & Shoppers Guide
801 W Adams St (49935-1218)
P.O. Box 311 (49935-0311)
PHONE..................906 265-9927
Eugene A Halker, *President*
EMP: 10 **EST:** 1968
SALES (est): 124.5K **Privately Held**
WEB: www.ironcountyreporter.com
SIC: 2711 5943 Newspapers, publishing & printing; office forms & supplies

(G-8752)
PIWARSKI BROTHERS LOGGING INC
941 Gibbs City Rd (49935-9632)
PHONE..................906 265-2914
Larry Piwarski, *President*
Leonard Piwarski, *Partner*
Dell Piwarski, *Vice Pres*
EMP: 5 **EST:** 1970
SALES (est): 581.4K **Privately Held**
SIC: 2411 Logging camps & contractors

(G-8753)
SHAMCO INC
4128 Us Highway 2 (49935-7976)
P.O. Box 436 (49935-0436)
PHONE..................906 265-5065
Jerry Shamion, *President*
Todd Shamion, *Vice Pres*
Chris Shamion, *Treasurer*
Eric Shamion, *Treasurer*
Scott Shamion, *Treasurer*
EMP: 4 **EST:** 1997
SALES (est): 810K **Privately Held**
SIC: 2411 Logging camps & contractors

(G-8754)
SHAMCO LUMBER INC
4128 Us Highway 2 (49935-7976)
PHONE..................906 265-5065
Jonathan Richter, *President*
Ryan Shamion, *Vice Pres*
Scott Shamion, *Treasurer*
Todd Shamion, *Director*
Eric Shamion, *Admin Sec*
EMP: 8 **EST:** 2018
SALES (est): 508.4K **Privately Held**
SIC: 2411 Logging

(G-8755)
SHAMION BROTHERS
4128 Us Highway 2 (49935-7976)
P.O. Box 454 (49935-0454)
PHONE..................906 265-5065
Jerry Shamion, *Partner*
Richard Shamion, *Partner*
Ronald Shamion, *Partner*
EMP: 14 **EST:** 1967
SQ FT: 9,000
SALES (est): 314.5K **Privately Held**
SIC: 2411 Logging camps & contractors

(G-8756)
SV LOGGING LLC
102 Mattson Rd (49935-7858)
P.O. Box 500 (49935-0500)
PHONE..................715 360-0035
Steve Vandehey, *Principal*
EMP: 4 **EST:** 2019
SALES (est): 98.8K **Privately Held**
SIC: 2411 Logging

Irons
Lake County

(G-8757)
ROTHIG FOREST PRODUCTS INC
3600 N M 37 (49644)
P.O. Box 340, Luther (49656-0340)
PHONE..................231 266-8292
Ross Rothig, *President*
Robert Morgan, *Vice Pres*
Julie Morgan, *Admin Sec*
EMP: 12 **EST:** 1976
SALES (est): 1.7MM **Privately Held**
SIC: 5031 0851 2411 Lumber: rough, dressed & finished; forest management services; logging

Ironwood
Gogebic County

(G-8758)
BURTON INDUSTRIES INC
1260 Wall St (49938-1763)
P.O. Box 279, Goodrich (48438-0279)
PHONE..................906 932-5970
Clark E Johnson, *President*
Mike De Vries, *CPA*
Rosemary Kazik, *Human Res Dir*
▲ **EMP:** 50 **EST:** 1966
SQ FT: 50,000
SALES (est): 6.3MM **Privately Held**
WEB: www.burtonindustries.com
SIC: 3549 3559 Assembly machines, including robotic; automotive maintenance equipment

(G-8759)
BURTON INDUSTRIES INC
1260 Wall St (49938-1763)
PHONE..................906 932-5970

GEOGRAPHIC SECTION

Gary Burett, *Manager*
EMP: 22
SALES (corp-wide): 31.8MM **Privately Held**
WEB: www.burtonindustries.com
SIC: 3672 Printed circuit boards
PA: Burton Industries, Inc.
9821 Cedar Falls Rd
Hazelhurst WI 54531
906 932-5970

(G-8760)
CRAMBLITS WELDING LLC
Also Called: Fine Art Metalwork
1215 Wall St (49938-1764)
PHONE.................................906 932-3773
Ron Tankka, *Mng Member*
Julann Cramblit,
EMP: 5 **EST:** 1987
SQ FT: 19,200
SALES (est): 486K **Privately Held**
WEB: www.cramblits.com
SIC: 7692 1799 5999 Welding repair; ornamental metal work; welding supplies

(G-8761)
EVERSON TOOL & MACHINE LTD
620 Easy St (49938-1766)
P.O. Box 466 (49938-0466)
PHONE.................................906 932-3440
Michael Key, *Principal*
EMP: 19 **EST:** 1970
SQ FT: 12,000
SALES (est): 242.3K **Privately Held**
WEB: www.eversontool.com
SIC: 3544 Industrial molds

(G-8762)
FABRIC PATCH LTD
100 W Mcleod Ave (49938-2526)
PHONE.................................906 932-5260
Joanne Kuula, *President*
EMP: 4 **EST:** 1981
SQ FT: 1,000
SALES (est): 372.2K **Privately Held**
WEB: www.fabricpatch.com
SIC: 3496 5722 Fabrics, woven wire; sewing machines

(G-8763)
GLOBE INDUSTRIES INCORPORATED
Also Called: Globe Sand & Gravel
121 Mill St (49938-3025)
PHONE.................................906 932-3540
Mark Ruppe, *President*
EMP: 11 **EST:** 1969
SALES (est): 371.9K **Privately Held**
WEB: www.globeind.net
SIC: 3531 Bituminous, cement & concrete related products & equipment

(G-8764)
IRONWOOD PLASTICS INC (DH)
1235 Wall St (49938-1764)
PHONE.................................906 932-5025
Victor A Mancinelli, *President*
Edward Howe, *General Mgr*
John Lorenson, *General Mgr*
Marc Vike, *General Mgr*
Dave Zielinski, *Business Mgr*
▲ **EMP:** 155 **EST:** 1980
SQ FT: 54,000
SALES (est): 28.2MM
SALES (corp-wide): 245.5B **Publicly Held**
WEB: www.ironwood.com
SIC: 3089 Injection molding of plastics
HQ: Ctb, Inc.
611 N Higbee St
Milford IN 46542
574 658-4191

(G-8765)
JACQUART FABRIC PRODUCTS INC
1238 Wall St (49938-1763)
PHONE.................................906 932-1339
Robert J Jacquart, *President*
Bob Jacquart, *President*
Becky Maki, *Engineer*
Suzanne Pazdernik, *Human Res Mgr*
Al Gustafson, *Manager*
▲ **EMP:** 141 **EST:** 1956
SQ FT: 63,600
SALES (est): 17.5MM **Privately Held**
WEB: www.jacquarts.com
SIC: 2394 2392 7389 3842 Awnings, fabric: made from purchased materials; pillows, bed: made from purchased materials; sewing contractor; surgical appliances & supplies; furniture upholstery repair

(G-8766)
KAUFMAN CSTM SHTMTL FBRCTION L
400 W Aurora St (49938-2537)
PHONE.................................906 932-2130
Otto Gebhardt Jr,
EMP: 5 **EST:** 1949
SQ FT: 6,000
SALES (est): 432.4K **Privately Held**
WEB: www.scoopsandrakes.com
SIC: 3531 1761 Snow plow attachments; sheet metalwork

(G-8767)
MENDOTA MANTELS LLC
E6638 Maple Creek Rd (49938)
PHONE.................................651 271-7544
Tom Schoeller, *Manager*
EMP: 4 **EST:** 2004
SALES (est): 176.4K **Privately Held**
WEB: www.mendotamantels.com
SIC: 2431 Mantels, wood

(G-8768)
NORTH COUNTRY SUN INC
216 E Aurora St Ste 4 (49938-2146)
P.O. Box 425 (49938-0425)
PHONE.................................906 932-3530
Gary La Pean, *President*
Richard Barringer, *General Mgr*
Kay La Pean, *Vice Pres*
Teri Hoffman, *Manager*
EMP: 4 **EST:** 1978
SALES (est): 342.4K **Privately Held**
WEB: www.apg-wi.com
SIC: 2711 Newspapers, publishing & printing

(G-8769)
OTTAWA FOREST PRODUCTS INC
1243 Wall St (49938-1764)
P.O. Box 99 (49938-0099)
PHONE.................................906 932-9701
Charles Baxter, *President*
Aaron Somero, *General Mgr*
James Sweet, *VP Mfg*
Val Mower, *VP Sales*
Tony Neill, *Supervisor*
EMP: 40
SALES (est): 7.7MM **Privately Held**
WEB: www.ottawaforestproducts.com
SIC: 2421 2426 2448 Lumber: rough, sawed or planed; hardwood dimension & flooring mills; wood pallets & skids

(G-8770)
PRECISION TOOL & MOLD LLC
620 Easy St (49938-1766)
P.O. Box 466 (49938-0466)
PHONE.................................906 932-3440
Michael Key, *President*
Mark Maccani, *Production*
EMP: 19 **EST:** 2005
SQ FT: 12,000
SALES (est): 1MM **Privately Held**
WEB: www.precisiontoolmold.com
SIC: 3089 Injection molding of plastics

(G-8771)
RUPPE MANUFACTURING COMPANY (PA)
Also Called: Ironwood Testing & Design Div
100 Mill St (49938-3002)
PHONE.................................906 932-3540
Mark Ruppe, *President*
EMP: 20 **EST:** 1932
SQ FT: 30,000
SALES (est): 3.6MM **Privately Held**
SIC: 1442 3273 1794 3271 Construction sand mining; gravel mining; ready-mixed concrete; excavation & grading, building construction; blocks, concrete or cinder: standard

(G-8772)
SAWDUST BIN INC
629 W Cloverland Dr Ste 5 (49938-1006)
PHONE.................................906 932-5518
Jeff Wesenberg, *President*
EMP: 11 **EST:** 1985
SQ FT: 3,000
SALES (est): 1.4MM **Privately Held**
WEB: www.sawdustbin.openfos.com
SIC: 2434 2511 Wood kitchen cabinets; wood stands & chests, except bedside stands; tables, household: wood

(G-8773)
WOODTECH BUILDERS INC
219 E Frederick St (49938-2013)
PHONE.................................906 932-8055
Rick Tippett, *President*
EMP: 18 **EST:** 1995
SALES (est): 676.9K **Privately Held**
WEB: www.wausauhomes.com
SIC: 1521 2452 New construction, single-family houses; single-family home remodeling, additions & repairs; prefabricated wood buildings

Ishpeming
Marquette County

(G-8774)
A LINDBERG & SONS INC (PA)
599 Washington St (49849-1239)
P.O. Box 308 (49849-0308)
PHONE.................................906 485-5705
Roger Crimmins, *President*
David J Crimmins, *Vice Pres*
Daniel Saari, *Project Mgr*
Shirley Crimmins, *Treasurer*
Jon Pacl, *Supervisor*
EMP: 45 **EST:** 1920
SQ FT: 3,600
SALES (est): 10.8MM **Privately Held**
WEB: www.lindberginc.com
SIC: 1442 1611 1794 1623 Gravel mining; highway & street construction; excavation work; water main construction; sewer line construction

(G-8775)
CLEVELAND-CLIFFS INC
Cleveland Cliffs Nichigan Oper
101 Tilden Mine Rd (49849)
P.O. Box 2000 (49849-0901)
PHONE.................................906 475-3547
Joe Carrabba, *Branch Mgr*
EMP: 700
SALES (corp-wide): 5.3B **Publicly Held**
WEB: www.clevelandcliffs.com
SIC: 1011 Iron ores
PA: Cleveland-Cliffs Inc.
200 Public Sq Ste 3300
Cleveland OH 44114
216 694-5700

(G-8776)
GLOBE PRINTING & SPECIALTIES
200 W Division St (49849-2301)
P.O. Box 378 (49849-0378)
PHONE.................................906 485-1033
Curt Gronvall, *President*
Stacey Willey, *Treasurer*
EMP: 10 **EST:** 1953
SQ FT: 3,325
SALES (est): 663.2K **Privately Held**
WEB: www.globeprinting.net
SIC: 2752 2759 Commercial printing, offset; screen printing

(G-8777)
HOLLI FOREST PRODUCTS
900 Cooper Lake Rd (49849-3350)
P.O. Box 117 (49849-0117)
PHONE.................................906 486-9352
David Holli, *President*
EMP: 14 **EST:** 1965
SALES (est): 1.7MM **Privately Held**
WEB: www.holliforest.com
SIC: 2411 Logging

(G-8778)
LARSON TACTICAL ARMS
914 N Main St (49849-1630)
PHONE.................................906 204-8228
Terry Larson, *Principal*
EMP: 4 **EST:** 2016
SALES (est): 81.5K **Privately Held**
SIC: 3484 Guns (firearms) or gun parts, 30 mm. & below

(G-8779)
NORTHERN TIRE INC
1880 Us Highway 41 W (49849-3168)
PHONE.................................906 486-4463
Lee T Woods, *President*
Elizabeth A Woods, *Vice Pres*
EMP: 10 **EST:** 1961
SQ FT: 17,600
SALES (est): 3.1MM **Privately Held**
WEB: www.northerntire.com
SIC: 5014 3069 7534 Automobile tires & tubes; rubber automotive products; tire retreading & repair shops

(G-8780)
PEPIN-IRECO INC
9045 County Road 476 (49849-8996)
P.O. Box 8 (49849-0008)
PHONE.................................906 486-4473
Joseph A Pepin, *President*
Kathleen Pepin, *Admin Sec*
EMP: 9 **EST:** 1988
SALES (est): 857.1K **Privately Held**
WEB: www.pepinireco.com
SIC: 5169 2892 Explosives; explosives

(G-8781)
RUSSO BROS INC
1710 Us Highway 41 W (49849-3197)
PHONE.................................906 485-5250
John Korhonen, *President*
Jean Korhonen, *Admin Sec*
EMP: 11
SALES (est): 745.8K **Privately Held**
WEB: www.mamarusso.com
SIC: 2099 5421 5921 Emulsifiers, food; meat markets, including freezer provisioners; beer (packaged); wine

(G-8782)
T J NORTHWOODS SERVICES LLC
120 N Daisy St (49849-3003)
PHONE.................................906 250-3509
Timothy Nault, *Principal*
EMP: 4 **EST:** 2016
SALES (est): 61.7K **Privately Held**
SIC: 2499 Wood products

(G-8783)
TILDEN MINING COMPANY LC
Also Called: Tilden Mine
2 Miles S Of Ishpeming (49849)
P.O. Box 2000 (49849-0901)
PHONE.................................906 475-3400
David B Brake, *Manager*
EMP: 820
SALES (corp-wide): 5.3B **Publicly Held**
SIC: 1011 Iron ores
HQ: Tilden Mining Company L.C.
200 Public Sq Ste 3300
Cleveland OH 44114
216 694-5700

Ithaca
Gratiot County

(G-8784)
A B PUBLISHING INC
Also Called: Angela's Book Shelf
3039 S Bagley Rd (48847-9570)
P.O. Box 83, North Star (48862-0083)
PHONE.................................989 875-4985
Mike Foster, *President*
Katya Foster, *Admin Sec*
▲ **EMP:** 5 **EST:** 1987
SQ FT: 16,000
SALES (est): 1.9MM **Privately Held**
WEB: www.abpub.com
SIC: 5192 2731 Books; books: publishing only

Ithaca - Gratiot County (G-8785) GEOGRAPHIC SECTION

(G-8785)
AIRCRAFT PRECISION PDTS INC
185 Industrial Pkwy (48847-9476)
P.O. Box 340 (48847-0340)
PHONE.................................989 875-4186
William Henderson III, *President*
Gary Henderson, *Corp Secy*
Gary King, *QC Mgr*
EMP: 60
SQ FT: 58,000
SALES (est): 11MM **Privately Held**
WEB: www.aircraftprecision.net
SIC: 3592 3728 3053 3492 Carburetors, pistons, rings, valves; aircraft parts & equipment; gaskets, packing & sealing devices; fluid power valves & hose fittings; aircraft engines & engine parts

(G-8786)
ANCHOR DANLY INC
255 Indtl Pkwy (48847)
PHONE.................................989 875-5400
EMP: 5
SALES (corp-wide): 155.3MM **Privately Held**
WEB: www.anchordanly.com
SIC: 3544 Die sets for metal stamping (presses)
HQ: Anchor Danly Inc
2590 Ouellette Ave
Windsor ON N8X 1
519 966-4431

(G-8787)
CAU ACQUISITION COMPANY LLC (PA)
Also Called: Cartridges Are US
100 Raycraft Dr (48847-1762)
PHONE.................................989 875-8133
Daniel Ruhl,
James Cerkleski,
William Saracco,
▲ **EMP:** 52 **EST:** 1997
SALES (est): 21.9MM **Privately Held**
WEB: www.cartridgesareus.com
SIC: 3955 2899 Print cartridges for laser & other computer printers; chemical preparations

(G-8788)
CENTRAL MICH MET FBRCATION LLC
4476 W Saint Charles Rd (48847-9749)
PHONE.................................989 875-9172
Luke T Kelly, *Administration*
EMP: 6 **EST:** 2015
SALES (est): 298.2K **Privately Held**
SIC: 3499 Fabricated metal products

(G-8789)
CONNELL LIMITED PARTNERSHIP
Danly Die Set
255 Industrial Pkwy (48847-9476)
PHONE.................................989 875-5135
Rich Overla, *Manager*
EMP: 5
SQ FT: 60,000
SALES (corp-wide): 500MM **Privately Held**
WEB: www.connell-lp.com
SIC: 3544 3363 Die sets for metal stamping (presses); aluminum die-castings
PA: Connell Limited Partnership
1 International Pl Fl 31
Boston MA 02110
617 737-2700

(G-8790)
E & S GRAPHICS INC
300 Industrial Pkwy (48847-9489)
P.O. Box 98 (48847-0098)
PHONE.................................989 875-2828
Scott Gray, *President*
Douglas Sias, *Vice Pres*
John Gille, *Info Tech Dir*
EMP: 9 **EST:** 1979
SQ FT: 5,000
SALES (est): 869.7K **Privately Held**
WEB: www.esgraphics.com
SIC: 2752 2759 Commercial printing, offset; letterpress printing

(G-8791)
ITHACA MANUFACTURING CORP
1210 Avenue A (48847-8400)
P.O. Box 78 (48847-0078)
PHONE.................................989 875-4949
Scott Merchant, *President*
Jason Ebright, *Corp Secy*
Benjamin Cooley, *Vice Pres*
EMP: 7 **EST:** 2013 **Privately Held**
WEB: www.ithacamfg.com
SIC: 7692 Welding repair

(G-8792)
M & E PLASTICS LLC
205 Industrial Pkwy (48847-9476)
PHONE.................................989 875-4191
John Kungz,
EMP: 10 **EST:** 2018
SALES (est): 675K **Privately Held**
WEB: www.meplastics.com
SIC: 3089 Injection molding of plastics

(G-8793)
MACDONALD PUBLICATIONS INC
Also Called: Gratiot County Herald
123 N Main St (48847-1131)
P.O. Box 10 (48847-0010)
PHONE.................................989 875-4151
Patricia Macdonald, *President*
Tom Macdonald, *Publisher*
Thomas Macdonald, *Vice Pres*
Mary Rohrs, *Sales Staff*
EMP: 11
SQ FT: 4,200
SALES (est): 2.4MM **Privately Held**
WEB: www.gcherald.com
SIC: 2711 2741 2752 Newspapers, publishing & printing; shopping news: publishing & printing; commercial printing, offset

(G-8794)
MID-STATE PRINTING INC
145 Industrial Pkwy (48847-9476)
P.O. Box 277. (48847-0277)
PHONE.................................989 875-4163
Tom McDonald, *Principal*
John Belles, *Vice Pres*
EMP: 10 **EST:** 1981
SQ FT: 9,000
SALES (est): 376.4K **Privately Held**
WEB: www.mid-stateprinting.net
SIC: 2752 2791 2789 2759 Newspapers, lithographed only; typesetting; bookbinding & related work; commercial printing

(G-8795)
STAGE STOP
Also Called: Columbus Tree The
5348 Us 127 S (48847)
PHONE.................................989 838-4039
Beverly Nelson, *President*
Ronald Nelson, *Owner*
EMP: 8 **EST:** 1990
SQ FT: 9,000
SALES (est): 648K **Privately Held**
WEB: www.columbustree.com
SIC: 3312 Forgings, iron & steel

(G-8796)
TRIDENT MFG LLC
301 Industrial Pkwy (48847-9489)
PHONE.................................989 875-5145
EMP: 19 **EST:** 2018
SALES (est): 3.4MM **Privately Held**
SIC: 3999 Manufacturing industries

Jackson
Jackson County

(G-8797)
127 BREWING
3090 Shirley Dr (49201-7010)
PHONE.................................517 258-1346
Jeff Tolonen, *Owner*
EMP: 4 **EST:** 2016
SALES (est): 75.4K **Privately Held**
SIC: 2082 Malt beverages

(G-8798)
A J TOOL CO
3525 Scheele Dr Ste A (49201-1284)
PHONE.................................517 787-5755
EMP: 12
SALES (est): 1.1MM **Privately Held**
SIC: 3544 Mfg Dies/Tools/Jigs/Fixtures

(G-8799)
ABSOLUTE MACHINE LLC
3233 Gregory Rd (49202-2613)
PHONE.................................517 745-5905
EMP: 6 **EST:** 2013
SALES (est): 130.1K **Privately Held**
WEB: www.absolutemachine.net
SIC: 3599 Machine shop, jobbing & repair

(G-8800)
ACCUBILT AUTOMATED SYSTEMS LLC
2365 Research Dr (49203-6407)
P.O. Box 844 (49204-0844)
PHONE.................................517 787-9353
Rob Rooney, *President*
John Cross, *Treasurer*
EMP: 22 **EST:** 1988
SQ FT: 24,000
SALES (est): 7.8MM **Privately Held**
WEB: www.accubilt.com
SIC: 3544 3541 Special dies, tools, jigs & fixtures; machine tool replacement & repair parts, metal cutting types

(G-8801)
ACTION MOLD REMOVAL
129 Sagamore St (49203-5359)
PHONE.................................517 960-1928
Scott Hiller, *Principal*
EMP: 4 **EST:** 2015
SALES (est): 123.9K **Privately Held**
WEB: www.actionmoldremoval.com
SIC: 3544 Industrial molds

(G-8802)
ADVANCE TURNING AND MFG INC (PA)
4005 Morrill Rd (49201-7013)
PHONE.................................517 783-2713
John Macchia Jr, *CEO*
John Rappleye, *President*
John Macchia Sr, *Chairman*
Scott Halstead, *Vice Pres*
Joe Sorenson, *Vice Pres*
EMP: 101 **EST:** 1972
SQ FT: 38,000
SALES: 24.9MM **Privately Held**
WEB: www.advanceturning.com
SIC: 3769 3599 3451 3728 Guided missile & space vehicle parts & auxiliary equipment; machine shop, jobbing & repair; machine & other job shop work; screw machine products; aircraft power transmission equipment; aircraft engines & engine parts

(G-8803)
ADVANCE TURNING AND MFG INC
Also Called: McDivitt Road Facility
4901 James Mcdevitt St (49201-8958)
PHONE.................................517 750-3580
Scott Halstead, *Vice Pres*
Joe Sorenson, *Vice Pres*
Steve Ganton, *Purch Mgr*
Nicole Burks, *Accountant*
Shelley Zonts, *Manager*
EMP: 64
SQ FT: 22,500
SALES (corp-wide): 24.9MM **Privately Held**
WEB: www.advanceturning.com
SIC: 3599 Machine shop, jobbing & repair
PA: Advance Turning And Manufacturing, Inc.
4005 Morrill Rd
Jackson MI 49201
517 783-2713

(G-8804)
AERTECH MACHINING & MFG INC
2020 Micor Dr (49203-3448)
PHONE.................................517 782-4644
Michael D Macchia, *CEO*
Todd Cochrane, *President*
Adam Bauerly, *QC Mgr*
Jenny Griffis, *CFO*
Jay Gallant, *Manager*
EMP: 30 **EST:** 1982
SQ FT: 10,000
SALES (est): 4.1MM **Privately Held**
WEB: www.aertechmfg.com
SIC: 3599 3812 Machine shop, jobbing & repair; search & navigation equipment

(G-8805)
AFX INDUSTRIES LLC
4111 County Farm Rd (49201-4100)
PHONE.................................517 768-8993
D Sommerville, *Vice Pres*
Maria Sustaita, *Engineer*
Kathy Loftus, *Sales Staff*
EMP: 7
SALES (corp-wide): 311.7MM **Privately Held**
WEB: www.afxindustries.com
SIC: 3111 Cutting of leather
HQ: Afx Industries, L.L.C.
1411 3rd St Ste G
Port Huron MI 48060
810 966-4650

(G-8806)
AIR-HYDRAULICS INC
545 Hupp Ave (49203-1929)
P.O. Box 831 (49204-0831)
PHONE.................................517 787-9444
Joseph R Miller, *President*
David C Miller, *Vice Pres*
Joseph Leo Miller, *Vice Pres*
Philip G Miller, *Vice Pres*
Howard C Patch, *Admin Sec*
EMP: 18 **EST:** 1945
SQ FT: 13,000
SALES (est): 1.2MM **Privately Held**
WEB: www.airhydraulics.com
SIC: 3542 3559 3544 3537 Presses: hydraulic & pneumatic, mechanical & manual; automotive related machinery; plastics working machinery; punches, forming & stamping; tables, lift: hydraulic

(G-8807)
AIRMETAL CORPORATION
1309 Bagley Ave (49203-3303)
PHONE.................................517 784-6000
Bruce Rogers, *President*
Steve Marcinkiewicz, *Vice Pres*
EMP: 10 **EST:** 1952
SQ FT: 8,800
SALES (est): 968.5K **Privately Held**
SIC: 3599 3544 Machine shop, jobbing & repair; special dies & tools

(G-8808)
AIRWAY WELDING INC
2415 E High St (49203-3421)
PHONE.................................517 789-6125
Douglas R Rogers, *President*
Rick L Rogers, *Treasurer*
EMP: 11 **EST:** 1962
SQ FT: 23,500
SALES (est): 2.1MM **Privately Held**
WEB: www.airwaywelding.com
SIC: 7692 Welding repair

(G-8809)
ALLEGRA MARKETING PRINT MAIL
1232 S West Ave (49203-2959)
PHONE.................................517 879-2444
EMP: 4 **EST:** 2020
SALES (est): 155.8K **Privately Held**
WEB: www.allegramarketingprint.com
SIC: 2752 Commercial printing, offset

(G-8810)
ALLIED CHUCKER AND ENGRG CO (PA)
Also Called: Acecd
3529 Scheele Dr (49202-1296)
PHONE.................................517 787-1370
Melvin Schalhamer, *Ch of Bd*
William P Schomer, *President*
Morris Thorrez, *Corp Secy*
Patrick McCann, *Vice Pres*
Albert Thorrez, *Vice Pres*
EMP: 140 **EST:** 1965
SQ FT: 15,000

GEOGRAPHIC SECTION

Jackson - Jackson County (G-8838)

SALES (est): 18.5MM Privately Held
WEB: www.alliedchucker.com
SIC: 3599 Machine shop, jobbing & repair

(G-8811)
ALLIED CHUCKER AND ENGRG CO
3525 Scheele Dr (49202-1284)
PHONE 517 787-1370
Frank Zielinski, *Branch Mgr*
EMP: 90
SALES (corp-wide): 18.5MM Privately Held
WEB: www.alliedchucker.com
SIC: 3599 Machine shop, jobbing & repair
PA: Allied Chucker And Engineering Company
    3529 Scheele Dr
    Jackson MI 49202
    517 787-1370

(G-8812)
ALPHA OMEGA PUBLISHING
322 Madison St (49202-2270)
PHONE 517 879-1286
EMP: 5 EST: 2019
SALES (est): 321.7K Privately Held
WEB: www.omegapublishing.org
SIC: 2741 Miscellaneous publishing

(G-8813)
ALRO RIVERSIDE LLC
Also Called: Riverside Grinding Co
829 Belden Rd (49203-2189)
PHONE 517 782-8322
E G Miller, *Principal*
Steve Anspaugh, *Vice Pres*
Phill Miller,
Kathy Brady,
EMP: 6 EST: 1983
SQ FT: 10,000
SALES (est): 592.8K Privately Held
SIC: 3599 3443 Grinding castings for the trade; fabricated plate work (boiler shop)

(G-8814)
ALYNN INDUSTRIES
414 N Jackson St 97-11 (49201-1249)
P.O. Box 484 (49204-0484)
PHONE 517 764-7783
Debra Deskins, *Administration*
EMP: 5 EST: 2005
SALES (est): 94.5K Privately Held
WEB: www.alynnindustries.com
SIC: 3999 Manufacturing industries

(G-8815)
AMERICAN TOOLING CENTER INC
11505 Elm St (49202)
PHONE 517 522-8411
John J Basso, *President*
EMP: 9
SALES (corp-wide): 18.5MM Privately Held
WEB: www.americantoolingcenter.com
SIC: 3544 Special dies & tools
PA: American Tooling Center, Inc.
    4111 Mount Hope Rd
    Grass Lake MI 49240
    517 522-8411

(G-8816)
ANDERTON MACHINING LLC
2400 Enterprise St Ste 1 (49203-6414)
PHONE 517 905-5155
Dave Curl, *Production*
Craig Ledyard, *Engineer*
Melissa Hancock, *Admin Mgr*
Richard A Walawender,
EMP: 5 EST: 2015
SALES (est): 1MM Privately Held
WEB: www.andertonmachining.com
SIC: 3599 Machine shop, jobbing & repair
PA: Anderton Industries, Inc.
    3001 W Big Beavr Rd # 310
    Troy MI 48084
    248 430-6650

(G-8817)
ASSET TRACK TECHNOLOGIES LLC
Also Called: Asset Track Gps Systems
510 W Michigan Ave (49201-2034)
PHONE 517 745-3879
Gregory Schultz, *Mng Member*
EMP: 5 EST: 2011
SQ FT: 3,000
SALES (est): 1.8MM Privately Held
WEB: www.assettrackgps.com
SIC: 3663

(G-8818)
AUTOMOTIVE SERVICE CO
603 E Washington Ave (49203-6110)
P.O. Box 129 (49204-0129)
PHONE 517 784-6131
Toll Free: .... 888 -
Duane R Zwick Jr, *President*
Charlie Zwick, *Vice Pres*
Craig D Zwick, *Vice Pres*
EMP: 10 EST: 1927
SQ FT: 32,000
SALES (est): 1MM Privately Held
WEB: www.automotiveserviceco.com
SIC: 3715 3713 5531 5013 Truck trailers; truck bodies (motor vehicles); truck equipment & parts; trailer hitches, automotive; truck parts & accessories; trailer parts & accessories

(G-8819)
B & R GEAR COMPANY INC
2102 River St (49202-1719)
PHONE 517 787-8381
Michael Null, *President*
EMP: 16 EST: 1959
SQ FT: 8,000
SALES (est): 328.6K Privately Held
SIC: 3599 Machine shop, jobbing & repair

(G-8820)
BAILEY SAND & GRAVEL CO
6505 W Michigan Ave (49201-8997)
PHONE 517 750-4889
Jerald Bailey, *President*
Jeffery Bailey, *Vice Pres*
James Bailey, *Treasurer*
EMP: 16 EST: 1985
SQ FT: 8,000
SALES (est): 2MM Privately Held
WEB: www.baileysandandgravel.com
SIC: 1442 Sand mining; gravel & pebble mining

(G-8821)
BAKERS GAS AND WELDING SUPS
3151 Cooper St (49201-7523)
PHONE 517 539-5047
EMP: 5 EST: 2017
SALES (est): 96.1K Privately Held
WEB: www.bakersgas.com
SIC: 7692 5999 5085 Welding repair; welding supplies; industrial supplies

(G-8822)
BAXTER MACHINE & TOOL CO
103 N Horton St (49202-3719)
P.O. Box 530 (49204-0530)
PHONE 517 782-2808
Larry G Baxter, *President*
Sandra K Baxter, *Vice Pres*
Andy Piper, *QC Mgr*
Michael Baxter, *Engineer*
Michael V Baxter, *Engineer*
EMP: 35 EST: 1974
SQ FT: 25,000
SALES (est): 5.7MM Privately Held
WEB: www.baxtermachine.com
SIC: 3544 3599 3545 Special dies & tools; industrial molds; machine shop, jobbing & repair; machine tool accessories

(G-8823)
BISBEE INFRARED SERVICES INC
569 Wildwood Ave Unit 2 (49201-1048)
P.O. Box 51 (49204-0051)
PHONE 517 787-4620
Penny Wilson-Chrzan, *President*
EMP: 9 EST: 1978
SQ FT: 400
SALES (est): 978.4K Privately Held
SIC: 3823 Industrial instrmnts msrmnt display/control process variable

(G-8824)
BOBBYS MOBILE SERVICE LLC
1188 Herbert J Ave (49202-1928)
PHONE 517 206-6026
Roberty Holmes, *Principal*
EMP: 5 EST: 2012
SALES (est): 144.6K Privately Held
WEB: www.bobbysmobileservice.biz
SIC: 3715 Bus trailers, tractor type

(G-8825)
BOONES WELDING & FABRICATING
1309 Westlane St (49203-5024)
PHONE 517 782-7461
Stephen A Boone, *President*
Deborah H Boone, *Corp Secy*
EMP: 7 EST: 1982
SALES (est): 558.1K Privately Held
WEB: www.booneswelding.com
SIC: 3441 Fabricated structural metal

(G-8826)
BOYERS TOOL AND DIE INC
1729 W Ganson St (49202-4030)
PHONE 517 782-7869
R Tucker Boyers, *President*
Robert D Boyers, *Treasurer*
EMP: 8 EST: 1945
SQ FT: 6,000
SALES (est): 934.4K Privately Held
WEB: www.boyers-tool.com
SIC: 3544 Special dies & tools

(G-8827)
BRIGGS MOLD & DIE INC
414 N Jackson St 97-12 (49201-1249)
PHONE 517 784-6908
Howard Briggs, *President*
EMP: 4 EST: 1997
SALES (est): 403.3K Privately Held
SIC: 3544 Special dies & tools

(G-8828)
BROCKIE FABRICATING & WLDG LLC
1027 Hurst Rd (49201-8905)
PHONE 517 750-7500
Joshua Collins, *Purchasing*
Brian Burt, *Engineer*
EMP: 10 EST: 2017
SALES (est): 785.7K Privately Held
WEB: www.brockiefab.com
SIC: 7692 3443 Welding repair; fabricated plate work (boiler shop)

(G-8829)
C & H STAMPING INC
205 Obrien Rd (49201-8919)
PHONE 517 750-3600
David T Parshall, *President*
John Parshall, *President*
Lynne Parshall, *Vice Pres*
EMP: 30 EST: 1968
SQ FT: 36,000
SALES (est): 4.7MM Privately Held
WEB: www.chstamping.com
SIC: 3465 3544 Automotive stampings; special dies & tools

(G-8830)
C & K BOX COMPANY INC
423 Barrett Ave (49202-3901)
P.O. Box 1817 (49204-1817)
PHONE 517 784-1779
Robert C Stevens, *CEO*
Mark Stevens, *President*
Amy Stevens, *Corp Secy*
EMP: 18 EST: 1960
SQ FT: 35,000
SALES (est): 1.3MM Privately Held
WEB: www.ckboxco.com
SIC: 2448 2441 2449 Pallets, wood; boxes, wood; wood containers

(G-8831)
C THORREZ INDUSTRIES INC (PA)
4909 W Michigan Ave (49201-7909)
PHONE 517 750-3160
Albert F Thorrez, *Ch of Bd*
Camiel E Thorrez, *President*
Henry C Thorrez, *Vice Pres*
Michael Thorrez, *Vice Pres*
Jim Mackew, *QC Mgr*
▲ EMP: 54 EST: 1968
SQ FT: 48,000
SALES (est): 28.3MM Privately Held
WEB: www.thorrez.com
SIC: 3451 Screw machine products

(G-8832)
CAMSHAFT ACQUISITION INC
Also Called: Camshaft Machine Company
717 Woodworth Rd (49202-1636)
PHONE 517 787-2040
Jeremy Lumbrezer, *President*
EMP: 14 EST: 2014
SALES (est): 2.2MM Privately Held
WEB: www.camshaftmachine.com
SIC: 3714 Camshafts, motor vehicle

(G-8833)
CAMSHAFT MACHINE COMPANY LLC (PA)
717 Woodworth Rd (49202-1636)
PHONE 517 787-2040
Travis Hearn, *General Mgr*
Rodney Delong, *COO*
Todd Taylor, *Opers Mgr*
Chris Easterday, *Buyer*
Jacqueline Fagan, *QC Mgr*
EMP: 44 EST: 2002
SALES (est): 5MM Privately Held
WEB: www.camshaftmachine.com
SIC: 3714 Camshafts, motor vehicle

(G-8834)
CARB-A-TRON TOOL CO
4615 S Jackson Rd (49201-8382)
PHONE 517 782-2249
John Trammell, *President*
Joan Fayette, *Vice Pres*
EMP: 9 EST: 1948
SQ FT: 7,800
SALES (est): 721.9K Privately Held
SIC: 3541 3556 Machine tools, metal cutting: exotic (explosive, etc.); cutting, chopping, grinding, mixing & similar machinery

(G-8835)
CASALBI COMPANY INC
Also Called: Globe Tumbling Barrel Eqp
540 Wayne St (49202-4099)
PHONE 517 782-0345
Steven J Sparks, *President*
William Bregg, *Treasurer*
EMP: 16 EST: 1902
SQ FT: 10,000
SALES (est): 596.1K Privately Held
WEB: www.eyesee2020.com
SIC: 3541 Deburring machines

(G-8836)
CDGJL INC (PA)
Also Called: Comfort-Aire
1900 Wellworth (49203-6428)
PHONE 517 787-2100
Donald Peck, *Ch of Bd*
Lou Rasmussen, *Vice Pres*
David Duane, *CFO*
Tracy Volz, *Credit Mgr*
Suzanne Kanalas, *Marketing Staff*
◆ EMP: 45 EST: 1933
SQ FT: 175,000
SALES (est): 13.2MM Privately Held
WEB: www.comfortaire-hvac.com
SIC: 3585 3634 3564 Air conditioning equipment, complete; humidifiers, electric: household; dehumidifiers, electric: room; air purification equipment

(G-8837)
CERTAINTEED LLC
Wolverine Vinyl Siding
701 E Washington Ave (49203-6132)
PHONE 517 787-8898
Sheldon Thorpe, *Branch Mgr*
EMP: 5
SQ FT: 550,000
SALES (corp-wide): 77.7K Privately Held
WEB: www.certainteed.com
SIC: 3089 3444 Siding, plastic; sheet metalwork
HQ: Certainteed Llc
    20 Moores Rd
    Malvern PA 19355
    610 893-5000

(G-8838)
CERTAINTEED LLC
803 Belden Rd (49203-1908)
PHONE 517 787-1737

Jackson - Jackson County (G-8839) GEOGRAPHIC SECTION

Dave Beck, *Manager*
EMP: 4
SALES (corp-wide): 77.7K **Privately Held**
WEB: www.certainteed.com
SIC: 8731 3444 Commercial research laboratory; sheet metalwork
HQ: Certainteed Llc
  20 Moores Rd
  Malvern PA 19355
  610 893-5000

(G-8839)
CHANDELIER & MORE LLC ◆
209 E Washington Ave (49201-2393)
PHONE.................................248 214-1525
Mindy Kay Altamirano,
EMP: 20 EST: 2021
SALES (est): 1.4MM **Privately Held**
SIC: 3646 Commercial indusl & institutional electric lighting fixtures

(G-8840)
CHATEAU ARONAUTIQUE WINERY LLC
101 Chief Dr (49201-8154)
PHONE.................................517 569-2132
Lorenzo Lizarralde,
EMP: 5 EST: 2008
SALES (est): 409.3K **Privately Held**
WEB: www.chateauaeronautiquewinery.com
SIC: 2084 Wines

(G-8841)
CHEMETALL US INC
Also Called: Chemetall Americas
1100 Technology Dr (49201-2256)
PHONE.................................517 787-4846
Dan Winn, *Director*
EMP: 6
SALES (corp-wide): 69.9B **Privately Held**
WEB: www.chemetallna.com
SIC: 2842 2899 2851 Bleaches, household: dry or liquid; chemical preparations; paints & allied products
HQ: Chemetall U.S., Inc.
  675 Central Ave
  New Providence NJ 07974

(G-8842)
CLASSIC METAL FINISHING INC
Also Called: Precision Metal Finishing
2500 W Argyle St (49202-1900)
PHONE.................................517 990-0011
Scott A Brockie, *President*
Bradely E Nall, *Vice Pres*
Brett Brockie, *QC Mgr*
Herb Mahony, *QC Mgr*
Sam Absher, *Engineer*
EMP: 29
SALES (est): 5.9MM **Privately Held**
WEB: www.cmfpro.com
SIC: 3599 3471 Machine shop, jobbing & repair; anodizing (plating) of metals or formed products

(G-8843)
CLASSIC TURNING INC (PA)
Also Called: Cnc
3000 E South St (49201-8741)
PHONE.................................517 764-1335
Alex Webster, *President*
Philip J Curtis, *Owner*
EMP: 55 EST: 1982
SQ FT: 65,000
SALES (est): 21.8MM **Privately Held**
WEB: www.classicturning.com
SIC: 3599 Amusement park equipment

(G-8844)
CLDD LLC
1255 Falahee Rd (49203-3509)
PHONE.................................517 748-9376
EMP: 6 EST: 2017
SALES (est): 268.4K **Privately Held**
SIC: 2869 Fuels

(G-8845)
CMS ENTERPRISES COMPANY (HQ)
1 Energy Plaza Dr (49201-2357)
PHONE.................................517 788-0550
Thomas W Elward, *President*
Cathy Reynolds, *Senior VP*
Carol A Isles, *Vice Pres*
M Clifford Lawrenso, *Vice Pres*

William H Stephens, *Vice Pres*
▼EMP: 145 EST: 1987
SALES (est): 568.7MM
SALES (corp-wide): 6.6B **Publicly Held**
WEB: www.cmsenergy.com
SIC: 4911 1382 Generation, electric power; geophysical exploration, oil & gas field
PA: Cms Energy Corporation
  1 Energy Plaza Dr
  Jackson MI 49201
  517 788-0550

(G-8846)
CODO MACHINE & TOOL INC
1418 Lewis St (49203-3326)
PHONE.................................517 789-5113
David C Brautigam, *President*
Dorothy L Brautigam, *Corp Secy*
Corey O Brautigam, *Vice Pres*
EMP: 4 EST: 1983
SQ FT: 3,000
SALES (est): 340.9K **Privately Held**
WEB: www.codomachine.com
SIC: 3599 Machine shop, jobbing & repair

(G-8847)
COLLECTORS ZONE
1425 Wildwood Ave (49202-4026)
PHONE.................................517 788-8498
EMP: 8 EST: 2019
SALES (est): 265.8K **Privately Held**
WEB: www.thecollectorszone.net
SIC: 3914 Silverware & plated ware

(G-8848)
COLONIAL CHEMICAL CORP
720 E Mansion St (49203-4400)
P.O. Box 459, Canal Fulton OH (44614-0459)
PHONE.................................517 789-8161
Wayne F Aben, *President*
Pat Thibert, *Vice Pres*
▲EMP: 4 EST: 1974
SQ FT: 8,500
SALES (est): 440.2K **Privately Held**
WEB: www.met-all.com
SIC: 2842 Cleaning or polishing preparations

(G-8849)
COMMONWEALTH ASSOCIATES INC (PA)
2700 W Argyle St (49202-1975)
P.O. Box 1124 (49204-1124)
PHONE.................................517 788-3000
Richard N Collins, *President*
Matt Iadipaolo, *Business Mgr*
Stephen Arnold, *Senior VP*
Samuel R Barnes, *Vice Pres*
Linda Gray, *Vice Pres*
EMP: 170 EST: 1988
SQ FT: 49,000
SALES: 37MM **Privately Held**
WEB: www.cai-engr.com
SIC: 8711 3822 Consulting engineer; auto controls regulating residntl & coml environmt & applncs

(G-8850)
COMTRONICS
4909 W Michigan Ave (49201-7909)
PHONE.................................517 750-3160
EMP: 7 EST: 2017
SALES (est): 150.3K **Privately Held**
WEB: www.comtronics.com
SIC: 3451 Screw machine products

(G-8851)
CONCEN GRINDING INC (HQ)
2620 Saradan Dr (49202-1214)
P.O. Box 1188 (49204-1188)
PHONE.................................517 787-8172
Mark S Melling, *President*
Thomas C Evanson, *Corp Secy*
▲EMP: 1 EST: 1983
SALES (est): 22.2MM
SALES (corp-wide): 206.3MM **Privately Held**
WEB: www.melling.com
SIC: 3714 Motor vehicle parts & accessories
PA: Melling Tool Co.
  2620 Saradan Dr
  Jackson MI 49202
  517 787-8172

(G-8852)
CONSUMERS CONCRETE CORPORATION
3342 Page Ave (49203-2259)
PHONE.................................517 784-9108
Roger Butterfield, *Manager*
EMP: 10
SALES (corp-wide): 42.6MM **Privately Held**
WEB: www.consumersconcrete.com
SIC: 1771 3273 3272 Concrete work; ready-mixed concrete; concrete products
PA: Consumers Concrete Corporation
  3506 Lovers Ln
  Kalamazoo MI 49001
  269 342-0136

(G-8853)
CONTOUR TOOL AND MACHINE INC
2393 Research Dr (49203-6407)
PHONE.................................517 787-6806
Richard Johnson, *President*
Jeff Schutte, *Engineer*
EMP: 7 EST: 1978
SQ FT: 12,800
SALES (est): 847.8K **Privately Held**
WEB: www.contourtoolinc.com
SIC: 3545 3599 Tools & accessories for machine tools; machine shop, jobbing & repair

(G-8854)
CONTROLLED TURNING INC
1607 S Gorham St (49203-3412)
P.O. Box 1364 (49204-1364)
PHONE.................................517 782-0517
Jerome Broughman, *President*
Carol Broughman, *Vice Pres*
EMP: 9 EST: 1976
SQ FT: 10,000
SALES (est): 1.4MM **Privately Held**
WEB: www.controlledturning.com
SIC: 3599 Machine shop, jobbing & repair

(G-8855)
COX BROTHERS MACHINING INC
2300 E Ganson St (49202-3770)
PHONE.................................517 796-4662
Russell E Cox, *Owner*
Teri Cox, *Corp Secy*
EMP: 20
SQ FT: 2,400
SALES (est): 3.5MM **Privately Held**
WEB: www.coxbro.com
SIC: 3441 3479 Fabricated structural metal; coating of metals & formed products

(G-8856)
CRANKSHAFT MACHINE COMPANY (HQ)
Also Called: Lindberg Fluid Power Division
314 N Jackson St (49201-1246)
P.O. Box 1127 (49204-1127)
PHONE.................................517 787-3791
Craig Little, *President*
Ken Mackenzie, *Manager*
EMP: 33 EST: 1916
SQ FT: 50,000
SALES (est): 5.9MM
SALES (corp-wide): 474.5MM **Privately Held**
WEB: www.crankshaft.net
SIC: 3593 3541 Fluid power cylinders, hydraulic or pneumatic; crankshaft regrinding machines; grinding machines, metalworking; broaching machines
PA: Avis Industrial Corporation
  1909 S Main St
  Upland IN 46989
  765 998-8100

(G-8857)
CREATIVE GRAPHICS INC
430 N Mechanic St (49201-1307)
PHONE.................................517 784-0391
Gary Bailey, *President*
Nancy Vandworth, *Admin Sec*
EMP: 7 EST: 1978
SQ FT: 7,500
SALES (est): 903.8K **Privately Held**
SIC: 2732 Books: printing only; pamphlets: printing & binding, not published on site

(G-8858)
CROWN INDUSTRIAL SERVICES INC
Also Called: Miwi
2080 Brooklyn Rd (49203-4744)
P.O. Box 970197, Ypsilanti (48197-0026)
PHONE.................................517 905-5300
Kari Stanley, *Human Resources*
Steven Bullock, *Branch Mgr*
Judy McIntyre, *Manager*
EMP: 7
SALES (corp-wide): 10.4MM **Privately Held**
WEB: www.crownindservices.com
SIC: 3471 Cleaning, polishing & finishing
PA: Crown Industrial Services Inc
  2480 Airport Dr
  Ypsilanti MI 48198
  734 483-7270

(G-8859)
D W MACHINE INC
2501 Precision St (49202-3925)
PHONE.................................517 787-9929
Fax: 517 787-2151
EMP: 10
SQ FT: 8,500
SALES: 450K **Privately Held**
SIC: 3544 3541 Tool & Die Shop & Mfg Turrets

(G-8860)
DAWLEN CORPORATION
2029 Micor Dr (49203-3448)
P.O. Box 884 (49204-0884)
PHONE.................................517 787-2200
Faith F Small, *President*
Donna Burns, *Vice Pres*
Kevin Cummings, *Vice Pres*
Patricia A Lykins, *Vice Pres*
John Lynch, *Senior Engr*
▼EMP: 49 EST: 1942
SQ FT: 100,000
SALES (est): 3.7MM **Privately Held**
WEB: www.dawlen.com
SIC: 3451 3549 Screw machine products; metalworking machinery

(G-8861)
DAWN EQUIPMENT COMPANY INC
Also Called: Dawn Food Products
2021 Micor Dr (49203-3473)
PHONE.................................517 789-4500
Carrie Barber Jones, *President*
Gina Troutman, *Senior VP*
Fraser Lockhart, *Vice Pres*
Jean Rauchholz, *Vice Pres*
Mike Bowers, *Production*
EMP: 120 EST: 1987
SALES (est): 89.6MM
SALES (corp-wide): 1.7B **Privately Held**
WEB: www.dawnfoods.com
SIC: 5046 3556 Bakery equipment & supplies; bakery machinery
PA: Dawn Foods, Inc.
  3333 Sargent Rd
  Jackson MI 49201
  517 789-4400

(G-8862)
DAWN FOOD PRODUCTS INC
Also Called: Brothers Baking
3333 Sargent Rd (49201-8847)
PHONE.................................517 789-4400
Christi Oreilly, *Sales Staff*
Tom Wegner, *Manager*
Luis Sanchez, *Manager*
Penny McDonough, *Supervisor*
Corning David, *Technical Staff*
EMP: 4
SALES (corp-wide): 1.7B **Privately Held**
WEB: www.dawnfoods.com
SIC: 2045 Doughnut mixes, prepared: from purchased flour; cake mixes, prepared: from purchased flour
HQ: Dawn Food Products, Inc.
  3333 Sargent Rd
  Jackson MI 49201

(G-8863)
DAWN FOOD PRODUCTS INC (HQ)
3333 Sargent Rd (49201-8847)
PHONE.................................517 789-4400

GEOGRAPHIC SECTION
Jackson - Jackson County (G-8888)

Carrie L Barber, *CEO*
Miles E Jones, *Ch of Bd*
Ronald L Jones, *Ch of Bd*
Phil Batty, *President*
Carey Dassatti, *President*
◆ **EMP:** 200 **EST:** 1993
SQ FT: 95,000
SALES (est): 754.7MM
SALES (corp-wide): 1.7B **Privately Held**
WEB: www.dawnfoods.com
SIC: 2045 5046 3556 Doughnut mixes, prepared: from purchased flour; cake mixes, prepared: from purchased flour; bakery equipment & supplies; bakery machinery
PA: Dawn Foods, Inc.
3333 Sargent Rd
Jackson MI 49201
517 789-4400

(G-8864)
DAWN FOODS INC (PA)
3333 Sargent Rd (49201-8847)
PHONE..............................517 789-4400
Carrie Jones-Barber, *CEO*
Serhat Unsal, *CEO*
John Schmitz, *President*
Miles E Jones, *Chairman*
Jim Antrup, *Vice Pres*
◆ **EMP:** 200 **EST:** 1925
SALES (est): 1.7B **Privately Held**
WEB: www.dawnfoods.com
SIC: 2053 2045 3556 5046 Cakes, bakery: frozen; doughnut mixes, prepared: from purchased flour; bakery machinery; bakery equipment & supplies; investment holding companies, except banks

(G-8865)
DAWN FOODS INTERNATIONAL CORP
3333 Sargent Rd (49201-8847)
PHONE..............................517 789-4400
Ronald L Jones, *President*
Miles Jones, *COO*
Jerry Baglien, *CFO*
Marvel Jones, *Admin Sec*
EMP: 148 **EST:** 1993
SALES (est): 2.7MM
SALES (corp-wide): 1.7B **Privately Held**
WEB: www.dawnfoods.com
SIC: 2045 Prepared flour mixes & doughs
PA: Dawn Foods, Inc.
3333 Sargent Rd
Jackson MI 49201
517 789-4400

(G-8866)
DEXTER STAMPING COMPANY LLC
1013 Thorrez Rd (49201-8903)
PHONE..............................517 750-3414
Tracey Swarthout, *Vice Pres*
Tom Knox, *Purchasing*
Ken Lowry, *Engineer*
Denise Moeckel, *Controller*
Kenson Wilberding, *Auditor*
▲ **EMP:** 52
SQ FT: 100,000
SALES (est): 12.3MM **Privately Held**
WEB: www.dexterstamping.com
SIC: 3469 Stamping metal for the trade

(G-8867)
DIE-NAMIC TOOL & DESIGN LLC
147 Hobart St (49202-2497)
PHONE..............................517 787-4900
Robert Whiting,
Chad Whiting,
EMP: 13 **EST:** 2002
SQ FT: 7,000
SALES (est): 1.2MM **Privately Held**
WEB: www.dntdesign.com
SIC: 3544 Special dies & tools

(G-8868)
DIVERSIFIED ENGRG & PLAS LLC
1801 Wildwood Ave (49202-4044)
PHONE..............................517 789-8118
Anita-Mara Quillen, *President*
Anita Quillen, *Vice Pres*
Bruce Miller, *Plant Mgr*
Kathy Lamphere, *QC Mgr*
Kathy Miles, *QC Mgr*
EMP: 80 **EST:** 2010

SALES (est): 18.2MM **Privately Held**
WEB: www.deplastics.com
SIC: 3089 Injection molding of plastics

(G-8869)
DOME PRODUCTION LLC
1415 W Argyle St Ste B (49202-1978)
PHONE..............................517 787-9178
EMP: 5 **EST:** 2015
SALES (est): 102.1K **Privately Held**
WEB: www.domeproductions.com
SIC: 2759 Commercial printing

(G-8870)
DOROTHY DAWSON FOOD PRODUCTS
251 W Euclid Ave (49203-4101)
P.O. Box 312 (49204-0312)
PHONE..............................517 788-9830
Pj Dawson, *President*
John Kerrigan, *Opers Staff*
Troy Ghent, *Purchasing*
Brett Crosthwaite, *CFO*
William Kuhl, *Treasurer*
EMP: 32 **EST:** 1954
SQ FT: 10,000
SALES (est): 5.3MM **Privately Held**
WEB: www.dawsonfoods.com
SIC: 2099 2045 2051 2041 Food preparations; prepared flour mixes & doughs; bakery products, partially cooked (except frozen); flour & other grain mill products

(G-8871)
DRUSHAL FABRICATING LLC
3900 Francis St (49203-5434)
PHONE..............................517 539-5921
EMP: 9 **EST:** 2019
SALES (est): 547.7K **Privately Held**
WEB: www.drushalfabricating.com
SIC: 3441 7373 Fabricated structural metal; computer-aided design (CAD) systems service

(G-8872)
EAGLE POWDER COATING
2218 E High St Ste C (49203-3553)
PHONE..............................517 784-2556
Matthew Olinyk, *Owner*
EMP: 9 **EST:** 2002
SQ FT: 65,000
SALES (est): 1.3MM **Privately Held**
WEB: www.epcpowder.com
SIC: 3479 Coating of metals & formed products

(G-8873)
EATON AEROQUIP LLC
Also Called: Aerospace Group
300 S East Ave (49203-1973)
PHONE..............................949 452-9575
Scott Thompson, *General Mgr*
Terri Vernon Cleary, *Contract Law*
EMP: 350 **Privately Held**
SIC: 3492 3593 3494 Fluid power valves for aircraft; aircraft parts & equipment; fluid power pumps & motors; valves & pipe fittings; manufactured hardware (general); rubber & plastics hose & beltings
HQ: Eaton Aeroquip Llc
1000 Eaton Blvd
Cleveland OH 44122
440 523-5000

(G-8874)
EATON AEROSPACE LLC
300 S East Ave (49203-1973)
PHONE..............................517 787-8121
Nicholas Goerke, *President*
Jerry Hayball, *Analyst*
EMP: 111
SALES (corp-wide): 385.8MM **Privately Held**
SIC: 3721 Aircraft
PA: Eaton Aerospace Llc
1000 Eaton Blvd
Cleveland OH 44122
216 523-5000

(G-8875)
EATON CORPORATION
Jackson Plant
2425 W Michigan Ave (49202-3964)
PHONE..............................517 789-1148
Lisa Baarns, *Buyer*

Tameko Watts, *Buyer*
Kristen Assadi, *Engineer*
Robert Davis, *Branch Mgr*
Tina Davis, *Manager*
EMP: 4
SQ FT: 116,624 **Privately Held**
WEB: www.eatonelectrical.com
SIC: 3594 3593 3494 Fluid power pumps & motors; fluid power cylinders & actuators; valves & pipe fittings
HQ: Eaton Corporation
1000 Eaton Blvd
Cleveland OH 44122
440 523-5000

(G-8876)
EDWARDS MACHINING INC
Also Called: Edwards Machine & Tool Co
2335 Research Dr (49203-6407)
PHONE..............................517 782-2568
Scott Penrod, *President*
Kevin Immonen, *Manager*
Robert Moats, *Manager*
EMP: 22 **EST:** 2002
SALES (est): 4.5MM **Privately Held**
WEB: www.edwardsmachining.com
SIC: 3544 Special dies & tools

(G-8877)
EILER BROTHERS INC
2201 Brooklyn Rd (49203-4797)
PHONE..............................517 784-0970
Jeffrey Stout, *President*
Jeanetta Stout, *Corp Secy*
EMP: 19 **EST:** 1968
SQ FT: 15,000
SALES (est): 1.5MM **Privately Held**
WEB: www.eilerbrothersinc.com
SIC: 3599 Machine shop, jobbing & repair

(G-8878)
ELCO ENTERPRISES INC
Also Called: Wire Wizard Welding Products
5750 Marathon Dr Ste B (49201-7711)
PHONE..............................517 782-8040
Edward Cooper, *President*
John Sander, *Regl Sales Mgr*
▲ **EMP:** 20 **EST:** 1986
SQ FT: 23,000
SALES (est): 7.4MM **Privately Held**
WEB: www.wire-wizard.com
SIC: 3315 Wire & fabricated wire products

(G-8879)
ELITE MACHINING LLC
3832 Thorncrest Dr (49203-7102)
PHONE..............................517 784-0986
Nicholas Arcaro, *Principal*
EMP: 5 **EST:** 2016
SALES (est): 108.4K **Privately Held**
SIC: 3599 Machine shop, jobbing & repair

(G-8880)
ENDLESS ENGRAVINGS
319 S Maurice Ave (49203-5954)
PHONE..............................517 962-4293
Ralph Hansel IV, *Principal*
EMP: 5 **EST:** 2016
SALES (est): 73.2K **Privately Held**
SIC: 2759 Commercial printing

(G-8881)
F & H MANUFACTURING CO INC
149 W Porter St (49202-2319)
PHONE..............................517 783-2311
Scott Kellenberger, *President*
EMP: 35 **EST:** 1986
SQ FT: 20,000
SALES (est): 3.3MM **Privately Held**
WEB: www.fhmanufacturing.com
SIC: 3599 Machine shop, jobbing & repair

(G-8882)
F & S TOOL & GAUGE CO INC
1027 E South St (49203-4404)
PHONE..............................517 787-2661
Andrew Essenmacher, *President*
EMP: 8 **EST:** 1956
SQ FT: 3,000
SALES (est): 904.6K **Privately Held**
WEB: www.fstool.com
SIC: 3545 Machine tool attachments & accessories; gauges (machine tool accessories)

(G-8883)
FAB-ALLOY COMPANY
1163 E Morrell St (49203-1986)
P.O. Box 1429 (49204-1429)
PHONE..............................517 787-4313
Philip H Clark, *President*
Kathleen M Levy, *Treasurer*
Kathleen Levy, *Treasurer*
Jeff Reimers, *Accounting Dir*
Dorothea Clark, *Admin Sec*
EMP: 9 **EST:** 1917
SQ FT: 20,000
SALES (est): 841.8K **Privately Held**
WEB: www.fab-alloy.com
SIC: 3499 3444 3443 Fire- or burglary-resistive products; sheet metalwork; fabricated plate work (boiler shop)

(G-8884)
FITNESS FINDERS INC
1007 Hurst Rd (49201-8905)
PHONE..............................517 750-1500
Richard Fairbanks, *COO*
EMP: 12 **EST:** 2008 **Privately Held**
WEB: www.fitnessfinders.net
SIC: 5961 3089 Catalog sales; novelties, plastic

(G-8885)
FORSONS INC
Also Called: Insty-Prints
139 S Mechanic St (49201-2325)
PHONE..............................517 787-4562
Carolyn Matteson, *President*
EMP: 8 **EST:** 1969
SQ FT: 1,400
SALES (est): 944.1K **Privately Held**
WEB: www.allegramarketingprint.com
SIC: 2752 2791 2789 8743 Commercial printing, offset; typesetting; bookbinding & related work; sales promotion; advertising, promotional & trade show services; presorted mail service; business service newsletters: publishing & printing

(G-8886)
FOURWAY MACHINERY SALES CO
3215 Gregory Rd (49202-2613)
PHONE..............................517 782-9371
Lynn Hinkley Sr, *President*
Mark Vancalo, *Owner*
Mark Vancalbergh, *Vice Pres*
Steve Friend, *Sales Staff*
EMP: 13
SQ FT: 52,000
SALES (est): 2.6MM **Privately Held**
WEB: www.fourway.com
SIC: 5084 3541 Machine tools & accessories; machine tools, metal cutting type

(G-8887)
FRY KRISP FOOD PRODUCTS INC
Also Called: Fry Krisp Company, The
3514 Wayland Dr (49202-1234)
PHONE..............................517 784-8531
Richard G Neuenfeldt, *President*
Richard J Neuenfeldt, *President*
Steve Artz, *Vice Pres*
Steve Hartz, *Vice Pres*
Cheryl Czurak, *Sales Mgr*
EMP: 12 **EST:** 1950
SQ FT: 8,000
SALES (est): 3MM **Privately Held**
WEB: www.frykrisp.com
SIC: 2045 Prepared flour mixes & doughs

(G-8888)
FULL SPECTRUM SOLUTIONS INC (PA)
2021 Wellworth (49203-3451)
P.O. Box 1087 (49204-1087)
PHONE..............................517 783-3800
Michael Nevins, *President*
Justin Baldwin, *Vice Pres*
Ralph Hubbs, *Engineer*
Joelle Kolhagen, *Mktg Dir*
Alex Orr, *Marketing Staff*
▲ **EMP:** 30 **EST:** 1997
SQ FT: 72,000
SALES (est): 7.4MM **Privately Held**
WEB: www.fullspectrumsolutions.com
SIC: 3645 5063 Residential lighting fixtures; lighting fixtures

Jackson - Jackson County (G-8889)

(G-8889)
GAUS
3123 Catalpa Dr (49203-3501)
PHONE..............................517 764-6178
Jill Gaus, *Principal*
EMP: 4 **EST:** 2010
SALES (est): 100.8K **Privately Held**
SIC: 2741 Miscellaneous publishing

(G-8890)
GERDAU MACSTEEL INC
Macsteel Division
3100 Brooklyn Rd (49203-4809)
P.O. Box 1101 (49204-0411)
PHONE..............................517 764-0311
John Fisher, *Vice Pres*
Jerry Martin, *Production*
EMP: 350 **Privately Held**
WEB: www.gerdau-macsteel.com
SIC: 3312 3316 Bars & bar shapes, steel, cold-finished: own hot-rolled; cold finishing of steel shapes
HQ: Gerdau Macsteel, Inc.
5591 Morrill Rd
Jackson MI 49201

(G-8891)
GERDAU MACSTEEL INC (HQ)
Also Called: Nitro Steel
5591 Morrill Rd (49201-7084)
PHONE..............................517 782-0415
Mark Marcucci, *President*
Darrell Moore, *General Mgr*
Adam Tabor, *Regional Mgr*
Yuan Wang, *Vice Pres*
Joe Doskocil, *Production*
◆ **EMP:** 50 **EST:** 1968
SQ FT: 20,000
SALES (est): 533.4MM **Privately Held**
WEB: www.gerdau-macsteel.com
SIC: 3316 3312 Cold finishing of steel shapes; bars & bar shapes, steel, cold-finished: own hot-rolled

(G-8892)
GLOBAL MFG & ASSEMBLY CORP
1801 Wildwood Ave (49202-4044)
P.O. Box 983 (49204-0983)
PHONE..............................517 789-8116
Armida Pearse, *CEO*
Travis Pearse Jr, *President*
EMP: 21 **EST:** 2001
SALES (est): 1.3MM **Privately Held**
SIC: 3089 Plastic containers, except foam

(G-8893)
GREAT ATLANTIC NEWS LLC
Also Called: News Group, The
2571 Saradan Dr (49202-1211)
PHONE..............................517 784-7163
John Swett, *Owner*
Richard Ritter, *Opers Mgr*
Sheri Ward, *Human Res Dir*
Sue Kent, *Supervisor*
Valerie McDow, *Supervisor*
EMP: 241
SALES (corp-wide): 19B **Privately Held**
SIC: 2711 Newspapers, publishing & printing
HQ: Great Atlantic News L.L.C.
1962 Highway 160 W # 102
Fort Mill SC 29708

(G-8894)
GREAT LAKES GRAPHICS INC
209 E Washington Ave # 355 (49201-2398)
PHONE..............................517 783-5500
Micky Vanlake, *President*
EMP: 4 **EST:** 2001
SALES (est): 553.2K **Privately Held**
WEB: www.glgprint.com
SIC: 2752 Commercial printing, offset

(G-8895)
GREAT LAKES INDUSTRY INC
Also Called: G I
1927 Wildwood Ave (49202-4061)
PHONE..............................517 784-3153
Lawrence Schultz, *President*
Michael D Dwyer, *Vice Pres*
Don Werner, *Vice Pres*
Jim Dettloff, *Purchasing*
Carey Pace, *Purchasing*
▲ **EMP:** 45 **EST:** 1959
SQ FT: 52,000
SALES (est): 15MM **Privately Held**
WEB: www.greatlakesind.com
SIC: 3568 3462 Clutches, except vehicular; couplings, shaft: rigid, flexible, universal joint, etc.; sprockets (power transmission equipment); iron & steel forgings

(G-8896)
GREAT LAKES METAL FINSHG LLC
3000 E South St (49201-8741)
PHONE..............................517 764-1335
Philip J Curtis,
EMP: 69 **EST:** 2012
SALES (est): 748.5K
SALES (corp-wide): 21.8MM **Privately Held**
WEB: www.greatlakesmetalfinishing.com
SIC: 3471 Electroplating of metals or formed products
PA: Classic Turning, Inc.
3000 E South St
Jackson MI 49201
517 764-1335

(G-8897)
H & M WELDING AND FABRICATING
3600 Page Ave (49203-2322)
PHONE..............................517 764-3630
Richard Miller, *President*
EMP: 5 **EST:** 1969
SQ FT: 14,000
SALES (est): 700K **Privately Held**
SIC: 7692 3444 3443 3441 Welding repair; sheet metalwork; fabricated plate work (boiler shop); fabricated structural metal

(G-8898)
HANDLEY INDUSTRIES INC
2101 Brooklyn Rd (49203-4792)
PHONE..............................517 787-8821
Robert E Handley, *President*
Rick Harbaugh, *Plant Mgr*
Howard Patch, *Treasurer*
Barbara D Huggett, *Admin Sec*
▲ **EMP:** 10 **EST:** 1925
SQ FT: 55,000
SALES (est): 2.2MM **Privately Held**
WEB: www.handleyind.com
SIC: 3089 Boxes, plastic

(G-8899)
HANDS THAT HEAL
1144 Herbert J Ave (49202-1928)
PHONE..............................517 740-6930
EMP: 5 **EST:** 2008
SALES (est): 76.9K **Privately Held**
SIC: 3634 Massage machines, electric, except for beauty/barber shops

(G-8900)
HAYES-ALBION CORPORATION
1999 Wildwood Ave (49202-4046)
PHONE..............................517 629-2141
Chad Baase, *President*
EMP: 16 **EST:** 1979
SQ FT: 7,000
SALES (est): 510.4K **Privately Held**
SIC: 3714 3471 3711 2396 Motor vehicle parts & accessories; cleaning, polishing & finishing; motor vehicles & car bodies; automotive trimmings, fabric

(G-8901)
HEAT CONTROLLER LLC
1900 Wellworth (49203-6416)
PHONE..............................517 787-2100
Edward Chernoff, *President*
David Duane, *CFO*
Tracy Lee Volz, *Credit Mgr*
Lou Rasmussen,
EMP: 18 **EST:** 2013
SALES (est): 1.5MM
SALES (corp-wide): 69.8MM **Privately Held**
WEB: www.marsm-a.com
SIC: 3585 Air conditioning condensers & condensing units
PA: Motors & Armatures, Inc.
250 Rabro Dr
Hauppauge NY 11788
631 348-0200

(G-8902)
HERALD NEWSPAPERS COMPANY INC
Also Called: Jackson Citizen Patriot
1750 S Cooper St (49203-4417)
PHONE..............................517 787-2300
Sandy Petykiewicz, *Director*
EMP: 6
SALES (corp-wide): 2.8B **Privately Held**
WEB: www.advancemediany.com
SIC: 2711 Newspapers, publishing & printing
HQ: The Herald Newspapers Company Inc
220 S Warren St
Syracuse NY 13202
315 470-0011

(G-8903)
HI-TECH FLEXIBLE PRODUCTS INC
2000 Townley St (49203-4414)
PHONE..............................517 783-5911
Ron Phillips, *President*
Stephanie Cronkright, *Office Admin*
EMP: 21 **EST:** 1989
SQ FT: 8,000
SALES (est): 6.3MM **Privately Held**
WEB: www.htfp.com
SIC: 3069 Molded rubber products

(G-8904)
HOLIDAY DISTRIBUTING CO
Also Called: Addison Awning Co
3990 Francis St (49203-5434)
PHONE..............................517 782-7146
Anthony J Krupa Jr, *President*
Gary L Krupa, *President*
Tamyra Macfarlane, *Executive*
Ashley Tackett, *Admin Asst*
Aaron Rockwell, *Associate*
EMP: 40 **EST:** 1955
SQ FT: 26,000
SALES (est): 8.7MM **Privately Held**
WEB: www.addisonawning.com
SIC: 5551 2394 Marine supplies; awnings, fabric: made from purchased materials

(G-8905)
HORSE CREEK CANDLES LLC
2429 Smiley Way (49203-3624)
PHONE..............................517 962-1476
EMP: 4 **EST:** 2014
SALES (est): 69.2K **Privately Held**
SIC: 3999 Candles

(G-8906)
HYTROL MANUFACTURING INC
4005 Morrill Rd (49201-7013)
PHONE..............................734 261-8030
Fred R Waldecker, *CEO*
Scott Lawson, *President*
Steve Leger, *Vice Pres*
EMP: 31 **EST:** 1968
SQ FT: 15,000
SALES (est): 2.1MM **Privately Held**
WEB: www.advanceturning.com
SIC: 3728 3764 3812 Aircraft parts & equipment; engines & engine parts, guided missile; search & navigation equipment

(G-8907)
IMAGECRAFT
100 Robinson Rd (49203-1053)
PHONE..............................517 750-0077
John F Dawson, *Owner*
EMP: 5 **EST:** 1977 **Privately Held**
WEB: www.imagecraft.biz
SIC: 5999 3479 Trophies & plaques; engraving jewelry silverware, or metal

(G-8908)
INDUSTRIAL STEEL TREATING CO
Also Called: Ist
613 Carroll Ave (49202-3169)
P.O. Box 98 (49204-0098)
PHONE..............................517 787-6312
Timothy Levy, *President*
Rich Polin, *Vice Pres*
Doug Scott, *Human Res Mgr*
Jim Tarpley, *Manager*
Jeff Thomas, *Officer*
EMP: 85 **EST:** 1950
SQ FT: 175,000
SALES (est): 22.2MM **Privately Held**
WEB: www.indstl.com
SIC: 3398 Metal heat treating

(G-8909)
INTERN METALS AND ENERGY (PA)
Also Called: Imet
522 Hupp Ave (49203-1974)
PHONE..............................248 765-7747
Julius J Rim, *President*
Elena Rim, *Vice Pres*
EMP: 6 **EST:** 1980
SQ FT: 200,000
SALES (est): 1MM **Privately Held**
SIC: 7549 4226 3341 Emissions testing without repairs, automotive; special warehousing & storage; secondary nonferrous metals

(G-8910)
INTERNATIONAL SMART TAN NETWRK
Also Called: Tanning Trends
3101 Page Ave (49203-2254)
P.O. Box 1630 (49204-1630)
PHONE..............................517 841-4920
Dale Parrott, *President*
Ashley Laabs, *Manager*
EMP: 21 **EST:** 1985
SQ FT: 6,000
SALES (est): 2MM **Privately Held**
WEB: www.tanningtruth.com
SIC: 2721 Magazines: publishing only, not printed on site

(G-8911)
J & J INDUSTRIES INC
260 W Euclid Ave (49203-4161)
PHONE..............................517 784-3586
Jim Maes, *President*
Regina Maes, *Manager*
EMP: 6 **EST:** 1997
SALES (est): 821.4K **Privately Held**
WEB: www.jjindustriesinc.net
SIC: 3714 3451 Oil pump, motor vehicle; screw machine products

(G-8912)
JACKSON ARCHTCTRAL MET FBRCTOR
1421 S Cooper St (49203-4410)
PHONE..............................517 782-8884
Mike Mason, *Principal*
EMP: 7 **EST:** 2012
SALES (est): 1.2MM **Privately Held**
WEB: www.jacksonamf.com
SIC: 3444 Sheet metalwork

(G-8913)
JACKSON CANVAS COMPANY
2100 Brooklyn Rd (49203-4746)
PHONE..............................517 768-8459
Thedore Mac Cready, *President*
David Herman, *Vice Pres*
John Rappleye, *Treasurer*
Josh Dingee, *Manager*
EMP: 26 **EST:** 1943
SQ FT: 9,000
SALES (est): 4.5MM **Privately Held**
WEB: www.jacksoncanvas.com
SIC: 2394 Awnings, fabric: made from purchased materials

(G-8914)
JACKSON GRINDING CO INC
1300 Bagley Ave (49203-3304)
P.O. Box 964 (49204-0964)
PHONE..............................517 782-8080
Michael Alexander, *President*
Thomas Evanson, *Corp Secy*
EMP: 10 **EST:** 1979
SQ FT: 9,000
SALES (est): 776K **Privately Held**
WEB: www.jacksongrindingcompany.com
SIC: 3599 Machine shop, jobbing & repair

(G-8915)
JACKSON INDUSTRIAL COATING SVC
3600 Scheele Dr Ste A (49202-1283)
PHONE..............................517 782-8169
Richard Friedlund, *President*
Ron Markowski, *Treasurer*
EMP: 6 **EST:** 1985

GEOGRAPHIC SECTION

Jackson - Jackson County (G-8941)

SQ FT: 31,000
SALES (est): 675.2K Privately Held
WEB: www.jacksonpowdercoating.com
SIC: 3479 Coating of metals & formed products

(G-8916)
JACKSON OVEN SUPPLY INC
3507 Wayland Dr (49202-1233)
PHONE.................................517 784-9660
Dennis Cones, *CEO*
Jean Cones, *Controller*
EMP: 10 EST: 2002
SALES (est): 2MM Privately Held
WEB: www.jacksonoven.com
SIC: 3567 Industrial furnaces & ovens

(G-8917)
JACKSON PRECISION INDS INC
1900 Cooper St (49202-1710)
PHONE.................................517 782-8103
John Ziemba, *President*
Patricia Ziemba, *Vice Pres*
Steven Ziemba, *Admin Sec*
EMP: 48 EST: 1974
SQ FT: 75,000
SALES (est): 8MM Privately Held
WEB: www.jacksonprecision.com
SIC: 3469 Stamping metal for the trade

(G-8918)
JACKSON TUMBLE FINISH CORP
1801 Mitchell St (49203-3393)
P.O. Box 4007 (49204-4007)
PHONE.................................517 787-0368
Denise Losey, *President*
EMP: 47 EST: 1956
SQ FT: 40,000
SALES (est): 6MM Privately Held
WEB: www.jacksontumble.com
SIC: 3471 Electroplating of metals or formed products; buffing for the trade

(G-8919)
JANSEN INDUSTRIES INC
2400 Enterprise St (49203-6414)
PHONE.................................517 788-6800
James P Jansen, *President*
Thomas Jansen, *Vice Pres*
EMP: 32 EST: 1974
SQ FT: 440,000
SALES (est): 841K Privately Held
SIC: 3599 Machine shop, jobbing & repair

(G-8920)
JFP ACQUISITION LLC
Also Called: Jackson Flexible Products
7765 Clinton Rd (49201-9418)
PHONE.................................517 787-8877
Tim Dickerson, *CEO*
Ken Trupke, *President*
Lacey Fausneaucht, *COO*
Cody Shepherd, *QC Mgr*
EMP: 25 EST: 1969
SQ FT: 35,000
SALES (est): 4.9MM Privately Held
WEB: www.jacksonflex.com
SIC: 3069 Molded rubber products
PA: Tillerman Jfp, Llc
    10451 W Garbow Rd
    Middleville MI 49333
    616 443-8346

(G-8921)
JLC PRINT AND SHIP INC
Also Called: PostNet
156 W Michigan Ave (49201-1302)
PHONE.................................517 544-0404
Jeffrey L Case, *Principal*
EMP: 6 EST: 2018
SALES (est): 432.3K Privately Held
WEB: www.postnet.com
SIC: 7336 2752 7389 Commercial art & graphic design; commercial printing, lithographic; mailbox rental & related service

(G-8922)
JOHN CROWLEY INC (PA)
703 S Cooper St (49203-1886)
P.O. Box 925 (49204-0925)
PHONE.................................517 782-0491
Tom Clark, *President*
EMP: 16 EST: 1908
SQ FT: 60,000
SALES (est): 1.1MM Privately Held
WEB: www.johncrowley.com
SIC: 3443 3531 Weldments; buckets, excavating: clamshell, concrete, dragline, etc.

(G-8923)
JOHNSON SIGN COMPANY INC
2240 Lansing Ave (49202-1641)
PHONE.................................517 784-3720
James Jay Johnson, *President*
Jim Johnson, *Vice Pres*
Quinn Miller, *Foreman/Supr*
Dan Showalter, *Foreman/Supr*
Brion Martin, *Human Resources*
EMP: 16 EST: 1964
SQ FT: 12,000
SALES (est): 3.9MM Privately Held
WEB: www.johnsonsign.com
SIC: 3993 Signs, not made in custom sign painting shops; electric signs

(G-8924)
JSP INTERNATIONAL LLC
4335 County Farm Rd (49201-9078)
PHONE.................................517 748-5200
Rob Doerr, *Branch Mgr*
EMP: 4 Privately Held
WEB: www.jsp.com
SIC: 2821 Polypropylene resins
HQ: Jsp International Llc
    1285 Drummers Ln Ste 301
    Wayne PA 19087

(G-8925)
JTC INC
Also Called: Jackson Typesetting Company
1820 W Ganson St (49202-4033)
PHONE.................................517 784-0576
Jay Foust, *President*
Dan Fals, *Vice Pres*
EMP: 9 EST: 1946
SQ FT: 20,000
SALES (est): 185.6K Privately Held
SIC: 2791 Typesetting

(G-8926)
JUSTICE
1850 W Michigan Ave # 774 (49202-4007)
PHONE.................................517 780-4035
EMP: 4 EST: 2019
SALES (est): 93.6K Privately Held
WEB: www.justice.gov
SIC: 2361 Girls' & children's dresses, blouses & shirts

(G-8927)
K&A MACHINE AND TOOL INC
4821 W Michigan Ave (49201-8902)
P.O. Box 1173 (49204-1173)
PHONE.................................517 750-9244
Karl P Fridd, *President*
Constance M Fridd, *Vice Pres*
Melissa Heydenburg, *Prdtn Mgr*
Tina Dullock, *QC Mgr*
Connie Fridd, *Admin Mgr*
EMP: 68 EST: 1981
SQ FT: 19,000
SALES (est): 10MM Privately Held
WEB: www.kamachine.com
SIC: 3599 Machine shop, jobbing & repair

(G-8928)
KELLOGG CRANKSHAFT CO
3524 Wayland Dr (49202-1294)
PHONE.................................517 788-9200
Allen E Spiess Jr, *President*
E Leroy Kincaid, *Production*
Dexiao Hao, *Engineer*
Allen E Spiess Sr, *Treasurer*
Amy Phillips, *Financial Analy*
EMP: 89 EST: 1956
SQ FT: 100,000
SALES (est): 7.2MM Privately Held
WEB: www.kelloggcrankshaft.com
SIC: 3714 Crankshaft assemblies, motor vehicle

(G-8929)
KMAK INC
Also Called: American Speedy Printing
1232 S West Ave (49203-2959)
PHONE.................................517 784-8800
Amy Lienhard, *President*
Jim Yekle, *Manager*
EMP: 4 EST: 1988
SQ FT: 2,200
SALES (est): 459.5K Privately Held
WEB: www.allegramarketingprint.com
SIC: 2752 7334 Commercial printing, offset; photocopying & duplicating services

(G-8930)
KRT PRECISION TOOL & MFG CO
1300 Mitchell St (49203-3341)
PHONE.................................517 783-5715
Tim Hawkins, *President*
EMP: 5 EST: 1955
SQ FT: 7,200
SALES (est): 471.7K Privately Held
WEB: www.krtmfg.com
SIC: 3599 3544 Machine shop, jobbing & repair; special dies & tools

(G-8931)
LABOR AIDING SYSTEMS CORP
3101 Hart Rd (49201-8746)
PHONE.................................517 768-7478
Joseph Simon, *CEO*
EMP: 28 EST: 2013
SALES (est): 4.7MM Privately Held
WEB: www.laboraidingsystems.com
SIC: 3544 Special dies, tools, jigs & fixtures

(G-8932)
LAMPCO INDUSTRIES OF MI INC
1635 Losey Ave (49203-3439)
PHONE.................................517 783-3414
Phil Lewan, *President*
Diana Beveridge, *Treasurer*
EMP: 4 EST: 1994
SQ FT: 2,800
SALES (est): 432.6K Privately Held
WEB: www.lampcoindustries.com
SIC: 3569 3549 5084 Filters; metalworking machinery; metalworking tools (such as drills, taps, dies, files)

(G-8933)
LE WARREN INC
1600 S Jackson St (49203-4295)
PHONE.................................517 784-8701
Leo E Warren, *President*
Paul Devine, *Manager*
Tom Duncan, *Executive*
EMP: 21 EST: 1941
SQ FT: 22,500
SALES (est): 663.7K Privately Held
WEB: www.lewarren.com
SIC: 3599 Machine shop, jobbing & repair

(G-8934)
LEMATIC INC
2410 W Main St (49203-1099)
P.O. Box 787 (49204-0787)
PHONE.................................517 787-3301
Dale J Le Crone, *CEO*
John Hamilton, *President*
Mick Smith, *Production*
James Webb, *Engineer*
Tammy Sanford, *CFO*
◆ EMP: 60
SQ FT: 35,000
SALES (est): 19.7MM Privately Held
WEB: www.lematic.com
SIC: 3556 Bakery machinery

(G-8935)
LIBRA INDUSTRIES INC MICHIGAN (PA)
Also Called: Work Apparel Division
1435 N Blackstone St (49202-2227)
P.O. Box 1105 (49204-1105)
PHONE.................................517 787-5675
Beth Yoxheimer, *President*
John Matthews, *Accounts Mgr*
Matt Hanert, *Manager*
EMP: 4 EST: 1969
SQ FT: 70,000
SALES (est): 24.3MM Privately Held
WEB: www.librami.com
SIC: 5084 3559 1741 Recycling machinery & equipment; recycling machinery; tuckpointing or restoration

(G-8936)
LINDBERG HYDRAULIC SYSTEMS
314 N Jackson St (49201-1221)
PHONE.................................517 787-3791
John Mykala, *President*
Wendell Mowcomber, *Plant Mgr*
EMP: 11 EST: 2007
SALES (est): 167.2K Privately Held
WEB: www.crankshaft.net
SIC: 3599 Machine shop, jobbing & repair

(G-8937)
M & M AUTOMATIC PRODUCTS INC
420 Ingham St (49201-1251)
PHONE.................................517 782-0577
Joseph Miller, *President*
Mary Lynn Miller, *Admin Sec*
EMP: 10 EST: 1991
SQ FT: 10,000
SALES: 714.3K
SALES (corp-wide): 13.2MM Privately Held
WEB: www.mmautomatic.com
SIC: 3599 Machine shop, jobbing & repair
PA: Trinity Holding, Inc.
    420 Ingham St
    Jackson MI 49201
    517 787-3100

(G-8938)
M AND G LAMINATED PRODUCTS
507 W Michigan Ave (49201-2033)
PHONE.................................517 784-4974
Chet Malone, *CEO*
Dale Gazlay, *President*
EMP: 7 EST: 1995
SQ FT: 10,000
SALES (est): 437K Privately Held
SIC: 2599 5031 2541 2434 Cabinets, factory; kitchen cabinets; wood partitions & fixtures; wood kitchen cabinets

(G-8939)
M P JACKSON LLC
1824 River St (49202-1755)
PHONE.................................517 782-0391
Rich Regole, *President*
James C Allison, *Vice Pres*
R Mark Baker, *CFO*
Bob Holmes, *Manager*
▲ EMP: 19 EST: 1942
SQ FT: 55,000
SALES (est): 152.3K Privately Held
SIC: 3625 3613 Control circuit devices, magnet & solid state; power circuit breakers

(G-8940)
MAES TOOL & DIE CO INC
1074 Toro Dr (49201-8946)
PHONE.................................517 750-3131
Joseph Maes, *President*
Jerome Maes, *Vice Pres*
EMP: 19 EST: 1954
SQ FT: 25,500
SALES (est): 2.1MM Privately Held
WEB: www.maestoolanddie.com
SIC: 3544 3823 3545 3541 Special dies & tools; industrial instrmnts msrmnt display/control process variable; machine tool accessories; machine tools, metal cutting type

(G-8941)
MAG-TEC CASTING CORPORATION
2411 Research Dr (49203-6409)
PHONE.................................517 789-8505
Allen F Schroeder, *President*
James R Malloch, *Vice Pres*
Bill Wilson, *Vice Pres*
Sara Proctor, *CFO*
▲ EMP: 20 EST: 1990
SQ FT: 27,500
SALES (est): 4.7MM Privately Held
WEB: www.mag-teccasting.com
SIC: 3364 3363 Magnesium & magnesium-base alloy die-castings; aluminum die-castings

Jackson - Jackson County (G-8942)   GEOGRAPHIC SECTION

(G-8942)
MAIN & COMPANY
2700 Cooper St (49201-9555)
PHONE..................517 789-7183
Gerald Brown, *President*
Frank Main, *Chairman*
Herb Maskell, *Materials Mgr*
Rick Hood, *QC Mgr*
Howard Patch, *Admin Sec*
EMP: 21
SQ FT: 12,592
SALES (est): 5.6MM **Privately Held**
WEB: www.mainandcompany.com
SIC: 3599 Machine shop, jobbing & repair

(G-8943)
MAKE IT YOURS
6982 Surrey Ln (49201-2443)
PHONE..................517 990-6799
Peggy Hill, *Owner*
EMP: 6 **EST:** 2006
SALES (est): 194.9K **Privately Held**
WEB: www.makeityoursonline.net
SIC: 3269 Art & ornamental ware, pottery

(G-8944)
MARATHON WELD GROUP LLC
5750 Marathon Dr (49201-7711)
PHONE..................517 782-8040
Michelle Cooper, *COO*
Edward Cooper,
EMP: 11 **EST:** 2004
SALES (est): 555.3K **Privately Held**
SIC: 5084 3315 Welding machinery & equipment; wire & fabricated wire products

(G-8945)
MARSHALL FLORAL PRODUCTS
710 Wildwood Ave (49201-1017)
PHONE..................517 787-7620
Michael Kusisto, *Principal*
EMP: 6 **EST:** 2004
SALES (est): 141.1K **Privately Held**
WEB: www.marshallfloralproducts.com
SIC: 2679 Tags, paper (unprinted): made from purchased paper

(G-8946)
MATTHEWS PLATING INC
405 N Mechanic St (49201-1306)
PHONE..................517 784-3535
Brandon Niceswander, *Vice Pres*
EMP: 21 **EST:** 2008
SALES (est): 2.5MM **Privately Held**
WEB: www.matthewsplating.com
SIC: 3471 Finishing, metals or formed products

(G-8947)
MAX MANUFACTURING
205 Watts Rd (49203-2324)
PHONE..................517 990-9180
O Donnell Docks, *Owner*
EMP: 15 **EST:** 2008
SALES (est): 550.4K **Privately Held**
WEB: www.maxdock.com
SIC: 3732 Boat building & repairing

(G-8948)
MELLING DO BRASIL LLC
2620 Saradan Dr (49202-1214)
PHONE..................517 787-8172
EMP: 12 **EST:** 2008
SALES (est): 1MM
SALES (corp-wide): 206.3MM **Privately Held**
WEB: www.melling.com
SIC: 3714 3451 Oil pump, motor vehicle; screw machine products
PA: Melling Tool Co.
2620 Saradan Dr
Jackson MI 49202
517 787-8172

(G-8949)
MELLING INDUSTRIES INC
2620 Saradan Dr (49202-1214)
P.O. Box 1188 (49204-1188)
PHONE..................517 787-8172
Mark Melling, *President*
Dan McDonell, *General Mgr*
Pat Richardson, *Vice Pres*
Teresa Fouchey, *Production*
John Shellberg, *Purch Agent*
EMP: 50 **EST:** 1966
SQ FT: 27,000
SALES (est): 10.3MM
SALES (corp-wide): 206.3MM **Privately Held**
WEB: www.melling.com
SIC: 3599 Machine shop, jobbing & repair
PA: Melling Tool Co.
2620 Saradan Dr
Jackson MI 49202
517 787-8172

(G-8950)
MELLING MANUFACTURING INC
4901 James Mcdevitt St (49201-8958)
PHONE..................517 750-3580
Mark Melling, *President*
Thomas C Evanson, *Corp Secy*
David K Horthrop, *Vice Pres*
EMP: 70 **EST:** 1968
SALES (est): 603.5K
SALES (corp-wide): 206.3MM **Privately Held**
WEB: www.melling.com
SIC: 3599 3841 3728 Machine shop, jobbing & repair; surgical & medical instruments; aircraft parts & equipment
PA: Melling Tool Co.
2620 Saradan Dr
Jackson MI 49202
517 787-8172

(G-8951)
MELLING TOOL CO (PA)
Also Called: Melling Automotive Products
2620 Saradan Dr (49202-1258)
P.O. Box 1188 (49204-1188)
PHONE..................517 787-8172
Mark Melling, *President*
Brian Shaughnessy, *General Mgr*
Tim Risner, *Buyer*
Rick Edwards, *QC Mgr*
Wayne Long, *Engineer*
◆ **EMP:** 320 **EST:** 1956
SQ FT: 275,000
SALES (est): 206.3MM **Privately Held**
WEB: www.melling.com
SIC: 3451 3714 3625 3568 Screw machine products; oil pump, motor vehicle; relays & industrial controls; power transmission equipment; pumps & pumping equipment; valves & pipe fittings

(G-8952)
MELLING TOOL CO
Also Called: Melling Tool J4
3700 Scheele Dr (49202-1247)
PHONE..................517 787-8172
Kevin Harner, *Branch Mgr*
EMP: 7
SALES (corp-wide): 206.3MM **Privately Held**
WEB: www.melling.com
SIC: 3714 Fuel pumps, motor vehicle
PA: Melling Tool Co.
2620 Saradan Dr
Jackson MI 49202
517 787-8172

(G-8953)
MERRIMAN PRODUCTS INC
1302 W Ganson St (49202-4298)
PHONE..................517 787-1825
Jacque J Lake, *President*
Robert Kingsbury, *Vice Pres*
James Peters, *Vice Pres*
Janet E Putman, *Admin Secy*
EMP: 4 **EST:** 1951
SQ FT: 2,000
SALES (est): 420.3K **Privately Held**
WEB: www.merrimanproducts.com
SIC: 3544 Jigs & fixtures

(G-8954)
METALFORM LLC
2223 Rives Eaton Rd (49201-8222)
PHONE..................517 569-3313
Clifford Hanchett, *Owner*
EMP: 5 **EST:** 1981
SQ FT: 12,000
SALES (est): 411.6K **Privately Held**
SIC: 3544 Special dies, tools, jigs & fixtures

(G-8955)
METRO DUCT INC
485 E South St (49203-4440)
PHONE..................517 783-2646
Joanne Applegate, *President*
EMP: 11 **EST:** 1999
SQ FT: 45,000
SALES (est): 309K **Privately Held**
SIC: 3444 Sheet metalwork

(G-8956)
MICHIGAN PAVING AND MTLS CO
1600 N Elm Ave (49202-1745)
P.O. Box 1134 (49204-1134)
PHONE..................517 787-4200
Mike Jackson, *Division Mgr*
John Peters, *General Mgr*
EMP: 20
SALES (corp-wide): 27.5B **Privately Held**
WEB: www.michiganpaving.com
SIC: 7549 2952 2951 Road service, automotive; asphalt felts & coatings; asphalt paving mixtures & blocks
HQ: Michigan Paving And Materials Company
2575 S Haggerty Rd # 100
Canton MI 48188
734 397-2050

(G-8957)
MICROMATIC SCREW PRODUCTS INC
825 Carroll Ave (49202-3142)
PHONE..................517 787-3666
Harold A Burke, *President*
Carolyn Burke, *General Mgr*
EMP: 23
SQ FT: 8,000
SALES (est): 1MM **Privately Held**
SIC: 3451 Screw machine products

(G-8958)
MICROTECH MACHINE COMPANY
4801 W Michigan Ave (49201-8902)
PHONE..................517 750-4422
Robert C Ekin, *President*
Kathleen L Ekin, *Vice Pres*
EMP: 7 **EST:** 1990
SQ FT: 9,500
SALES (est): 772K **Privately Held**
WEB: www.microtechmachineandgaging.com
SIC: 3599 Machine shop, jobbing & repair

(G-8959)
MIDBROOK INC (PA)
2621 E Kimmel Rd (49201-8724)
PHONE..................800 966-9274
Milton F Lutz II, *Ch of Bd*
Joanne Houghton, *President*
Ernest Houghton, *Vice Pres*
Ernie Houghton, *Mfg Mgr*
Brian Rockwell, *Foreman/Supr*
▲ **EMP:** 97 **EST:** 1976
SQ FT: 200,000
SALES (est): 10MM **Privately Held**
WEB: www.midbrook.com
SIC: 3559 3444 Degreasing machines, automotive & industrial; sheet metalwork

(G-8960)
MIDBROOK LLC
1300 Falahee Rd Ste 51 (49203-4700)
PHONE..................800 966-9274
EMP: 9 **EST:** 2015
SALES (est): 3.4MM **Privately Held**
WEB: www.midbrook.com
SIC: 3351 Tubing, copper & copper alloy

(G-8961)
MIDWAY STRL PIPE & SUP INC (PA)
Also Called: Lannis Fence Systems
1611 Clara St (49203-3471)
P.O. Box 742 (49204-0742)
PHONE..................517 787-1350
Robin Brannan, *President*
Alan Brannan, *COO*
Douglas Murray, *CFO*
EMP: 8 **EST:** 2007
SQ FT: 6,000
SALES (est): 7.4MM **Privately Held**
WEB: www.midwaysupply.com
SIC: 3317 5039 5051 Steel pipe & tubes; wire fence, gates & accessories; pipe & tubing, steel

(G-8962)
MILLER INDUSTRIAL PRODUCTS INC
801 Water St (49203-1963)
PHONE..................517 783-2756
William R Miller, *President*
Bernie F Miller, *Exec VP*
EMP: 30 **EST:** 1942
SQ FT: 150,000
SALES (est): 3.1MM **Privately Held**
WEB: www.millerindustrialproductsmi.com
SIC: 3429 3714 Motor vehicle hardware; motor vehicle parts & accessories

(G-8963)
MILLER TOOL & DIE CO
Also Called: Miller Machine & Technologies
829 Belden Rd (49203-1994)
PHONE..................517 782-0347
Philip G Miller, *President*
Emmanuel G Miller, *Chairman*
Steven B Anspaugh, *Vice Pres*
Patrick G Miller, *Vice Pres*
Nick Arcaro, *Mfg Mgr*
▼ **EMP:** 43 **EST:** 1930
SQ FT: 60,000
SALES (est): 7.6MM **Privately Held**
WEB: www.millertd.com
SIC: 3542 3541 3544 3545 Machine tools, metal forming type; machine tools, metal cutting type; special dies, tools, jigs & fixtures; machine tool accessories

(G-8964)
MILLERS SHOE PARLOR INC
103 W Michigan Ave (49201-1368)
PHONE..................517 783-1258
James E Shotwell Jr, *President*
James E Shotwell Sr, *Vice Pres*
Letha Shotwell, *Admin Sec*
EMP: 5 **EST:** 1912
SQ FT: 4,200 **Privately Held**
WEB: www.millersshoeparlor.com
SIC: 5661 3143 3144 Men's shoes; women's shoes; children's shoes; shoes, orthopedic; orthopedic shoes, men's; orthopedic shoes, women's

(G-8965)
MILSCO LLC
Milsco Michigan Seat
2313 Brooklyn Rd (49203-4776)
PHONE..................517 787-3650
Fmm Fields, *Vice Pres*
Mark Perry, *Mfg Staff*
Jeremy Houchins, *Production*
Brian Budd, *Engineer*
Bryan Murray, *Engineer*
EMP: 42
SALES (corp-wide): 717.5MM **Privately Held**
WEB: www.milsco.com
SIC: 3069 2531 3537 3524 Foam rubber; vehicle furniture; industrial trucks & tractors; lawn & garden equipment
HQ: Milsco, Llc
1301 W Canal St
Milwaukee WI 53233
414 354-0500

(G-8966)
MLIVE COM
214 S Jackson St (49201-2267)
PHONE..................517 768-4984
Scott Hagen, *Principal*
EMP: 5 **EST:** 2015
SALES (est): 101.8K **Privately Held**
WEB: www.mlive.com
SIC: 2711 Newspapers, publishing & printing

(G-8967)
MMP MOLDED MAGNESIUM PDTS LLC
2336 E High St (49203-3422)
PHONE..................517 789-8505
Zach Lankton, *Opers Mgr*
Gavin McGraw, *Controller*
Bill Wilson, *Mng Member*
EMP: 8 **EST:** 2006

SALES (est): 2MM **Privately Held**
WEB: www.mmpmg.com
SIC: **3575** 5251 Computer terminals, monitors & components; tools

(G-8968)
MODERN BUILDERS SUPPLY INC
Also Called: Mbs
2401 Brooklyn Rd (49203-4803)
PHONE.................................517 787-3633
Larry Leggett, *President*
EMP: 7
SALES (corp-wide): 346.2MM **Privately Held**
WEB: www.modernbuilderssupply.com
SIC: **5072** 3089 Builders' hardware; windows, plastic; doors, folding; plastic or plastic coated fabric
PA: Modern Builders Supply, Inc.
3500 Phillips Ave
Toledo OH 43608
419 241-3961

(G-8969)
MODERN MACHINE TOOL CO
2005 Losey Ave (49203-3499)
PHONE.................................517 788-9120
Steven G Walker, *President*
Gregory Walker, *Vice Pres*
EMP: 16 EST: 1916
SQ FT: 42,000
SALES (est): 4.3MM **Privately Held**
WEB: www.modernmachinetool.com
SIC: **3541** Cutoff machines (metalworking machinery)

(G-8970)
MP HOLLYWOOD LLC (PA)
Also Called: Mechanical Products Co
1824 River St (49202-1755)
PHONE.................................517 782-0391
Rich Regole, *COO*
Ronald Prokup, *Vice Pres*
Jim Allison, *VP Engrg*
John Morrissey, *Engineer*
Mark Baker, *CFO*
▲ EMP: 18 EST: 1960
SQ FT: 20,000
SALES (est): 2.5MM **Privately Held**
SIC: **3613** Power circuit breakers

(G-8971)
MULTIMATIC MICHIGAN LLC
2400 Enterprise St (49203-6425)
PHONE.................................517 962-7190
Peter Czapka, *President*
EMP: 25 EST: 2015
SQ FT: 100,000
SALES (est): 5.9MM
SALES (corp-wide): 6.2MM **Privately Held**
WEB: www.multimatic.com
SIC: **3465** Automotive stampings
PA: Multimatic Holdings Inc
8688 Woodbine Ave Suite 200
Markham ON L3R 8
905 470-9149

(G-8972)
MUSIC BOX
300 W North St (49202-3311)
PHONE.................................517 539-5069
John Andrew Smith, *Administration*
EMP: 5 EST: 2016
SALES (est): 84.6K **Privately Held**
SIC: **3999** Music boxes

(G-8973)
MVP SPORTS STORE
5000 Ann Arbor Rd (49201-8801)
PHONE.................................517 764-5165
Raymond Hines, *President*
Ray Hines, *Owner*
Mark Buckland, *Vice Pres*
Kelley Hines, *Treasurer*
Brad Wait, *Sales Staff*
EMP: 4 EST: 2004
SALES (est): 405.9K **Privately Held**
WEB: www.mvpsportsjackson.com
SIC: **2396** 5137 Screen printing on fabric articles; uniforms, women's & children's

(G-8974)
MYRTLE INDUSTRIES INC
1810 E High St Ste 2 (49203-6433)
PHONE.................................517 784-8579
James Jenks, *President*
Russell Lyke, *Vice Pres*
▲ EMP: 10 EST: 1983
SQ FT: 5,000
SALES (est): 849K **Privately Held**
SIC: **3429** Clamps & couplings, hose

(G-8975)
NATIONWIDE COMMUNICATIONS LLC
5263 Thames Ct (49201-8347)
PHONE.................................517 990-1223
EMP: 4
SALES (est): 390K **Privately Held**
SIC: **3669** Mfg Communications Equipment

(G-8976)
NELSON COMPANY
654 Hupp Ave (49203-1930)
PHONE.................................517 788-6117
Amber Harrell, *Manager*
EMP: 7
SALES (corp-wide): 21.7MM **Privately Held**
WEB: www.nelsoncompany.com
SIC: **2448** Pallets, wood
PA: The Nelson Company
4517 North Point Blvd
Baltimore MD 21219
410 477-3000

(G-8977)
NORTHWEST MARKET
7051 Standish Rd (49201-9417)
PHONE.................................517 787-5005
Jack Milligan, *Owner*
EMP: 5 EST: 1967
SQ FT: 2,000
SALES (est): 305.8K **Privately Held**
WEB: www.nwmarket.com
SIC: **5421** 5921 2011 Meat markets, including freezer provisioniers; beer (packaged); wine; meat packing plants

(G-8978)
NORTHWEST TOOL & MACHINE INC
1014 Hurst Rd (49203-8905)
P.O. Box 201 (49204-0201)
PHONE.................................517 750-1332
Kent A Pickett, *President*
Kent Pickett Jr, *Vice Pres*
Jennifer Dysert, *Admin Sec*
EMP: 25 EST: 1984
SQ FT: 20,000 **Privately Held**
WEB: www.nwtool.biz
SIC: **3544** 3599 3549 5047 Special dies & tools; machine shop, jobbing & repair; metalworking machinery; medical & hospital equipment

(G-8979)
OFFICE DESIGN & FURN LLC
Also Called: Office Ways
710 Webb St (49202-3261)
PHONE.................................734 217-2717
Fred W Crandal III, *President*
EMP: 4 EST: 2010
SQ FT: 500
SALES (est): 973.9K **Privately Held**
WEB: www.officedesignllc.com
SIC: **2522** Office furniture, except wood

(G-8980)
ORBITFORM GROUP LLC
1600 Executive Dr (49203-3469)
PHONE.................................800 957-4838
Michael J Shirkey, *CEO*
Phil Sponsler, *President*
EMP: 96 EST: 1984
SQ FT: 107,000
SALES (est): 24MM
SALES (corp-wide): 40MM **Privately Held**
WEB: www.orbitform.com
SIC: **3542** Riveting machines
PA: Smsg, L.L.C.
1600 Executive Dr
Jackson MI 49203
517 787-9447

(G-8981)
OVERKILL RESEARCH & DEV LABS
2010 Micor Dr (49203-3448)
PHONE.................................517 768-8155
Martin D Sears, *President*
Mike Vogel, *Vice Pres*
EMP: 8 EST: 1992
SQ FT: 15,000
SALES (est): 100K **Privately Held**
WEB: www.overkillarchery.net
SIC: **3949** Archery equipment, general

(G-8982)
PAINLESS PRINTING
4796 Trumble Rd (49201-7650)
PHONE.................................517 812-6852
EMP: 4 EST: 2019
SALES (est): 343.8K **Privately Held**
SIC: **2752** Commercial printing, lithographic

(G-8983)
PC SOLUTIONS
Also Called: PC Solutions of Michigan
1200 S West Ave (49203-2959)
PHONE.................................517 787-9934
Allen Huber, *Owner*
Chris Ham, *Regional Mgr*
Kathy Richter, *Vice Pres*
Erin Anderson, *Accounting Mgr*
David Messing, *Regl Sales Mgr*
EMP: 25 EST: 1991
SALES (est): 6.9MM **Privately Held**
WEB: www.pcsolutionsnow.com
SIC: **7372** Prepackaged software

(G-8984)
PENTAR STAMPING INC
1821 Wildwood Ave (49202-4044)
P.O. Box 1449 (49204-1449)
PHONE.................................517 782-0700
Joe Tippins, *Partner*
Robert Moore, *Partner*
Dale Moretz, *Partner*
Todd Ostrander, *Mfg Dir*
Harley Burch, *Engineer*
EMP: 30 EST: 1998
SQ FT: 14,369
SALES (est): 4MM **Privately Held**
WEB: www.pentarstamping.com
SIC: **3469** Machine parts, stamped or pressed metal; stamping metal for the trade

(G-8985)
PETTY MACHINE & TOOL INC
4035 Morrill Rd (49201-7013)
PHONE.................................517 782-9355
Bobby Petty, *President*
Sandra Petty, *Vice Pres*
Sandy Petty, *Vice Pres*
Terri Obrien, *QC Mgr*
Chris Variell, *Supervisor*
EMP: 32 EST: 1984
SQ FT: 13,000
SALES (est): 3.4MM **Privately Held**
WEB: www.pettymachine.com
SIC: **3541** Machine tools, metal cutting type

(G-8986)
PIONEER FOUNDRY COMPANY INC
606 Water St (49203-1980)
P.O. Box 1425 (49204-1425)
PHONE.................................517 782-9469
James A Lefere, *CEO*
Bob Lefere, *President*
Kevin Evans, *Superintendent*
Ted Lefere, *Manager*
Howard Patch, *Admin Sec*
EMP: 14 EST: 1905
SQ FT: 60,000
SALES (est): 1.2MM **Privately Held**
WEB: www.pioneerfoundry.com
SIC: **3321** Gray iron castings

(G-8987)
PLASTGAGE CSTM FABRICATION LLC
250 W Monroe St (49202-2252)
PHONE.................................517 817-0719
Lisa Minor, *Office Mgr*
Dennis Minor,
EMP: 4 EST: 2004
SALES (est): 430.4K **Privately Held**
WEB: www.plastigagejackson.com
SIC: **3496** Miscellaneous fabricated wire products

(G-8988)
PLATING SYSTEMS AND TECH INC
Also Called: PS & T
317 N Mechanic St (49201-1305)
PHONE.................................517 783-4776
Thomas Rochester, *President*
David Rochester, *Vice Pres*
Kevin Wright, *Production*
Stacy Richardson, *Manager*
Stacey Richardson, *Associate*
▲ EMP: 7 EST: 1985
SQ FT: 15,000
SALES (est): 1.6MM **Privately Held**
SIC: **2899** Plating compounds

(G-8989)
PPG INDUSTRIES INC
Also Called: PPG 9356
167 W North St (49202-3362)
PHONE.................................517 784-6138
Craig Tingley, *Branch Mgr*
EMP: 4
SALES (corp-wide): 15.1B **Publicly Held**
WEB: www.ppg.com
SIC: **2851** Paints & allied products
PA: Ppg Industries, Inc.
1 Ppg Pl
Pittsburgh PA 15272
412 434-3131

(G-8990)
PRECISE MACHINE & TOOL CO
2921 Wildwood Ave Ste A (49202-3972)
PHONE.................................517 787-7699
Paul R Bolenbaugh, *President*
Tom Uebrick, *General Mgr*
Tom Vebrick, *Project Mgr*
EMP: 6 EST: 1979
SQ FT: 7,000
SALES (est): 549.5K **Privately Held**
WEB: www.precisemachine.com
SIC: **3544** Special dies & tools

(G-8991)
PRIME CUTS OF JACKSON LLC
1821 Horton Rd (49203-5130)
PHONE.................................517 768-8090
Walt McGaskey,
EMP: 20 EST: 2007
SALES (est): 2.2MM **Privately Held**
WEB: www.primecutsofjackson.com
SIC: **2011** Meat by-products from meat slaughtered on site

(G-8992)
PT&T PRECISE MACHINING LLC
Also Called: PT&t Properties
325 Watts Rd (49203-2326)
PHONE.................................517 748-9325
Phillip Vincent, *Mng Member*
Ted Kenell, *Mng Member*
EMP: 8 EST: 2004
SQ FT: 8,500
SALES (est): 850K **Privately Held**
WEB: www.pttprecise.com
SIC: **3599** Machine shop, jobbing & repair

(G-8993)
R J MICHAELS INC
Also Called: R J M
515 S West Ave (49201-1639)
P.O. Box 1467 (49204-1467)
PHONE.................................517 783-2637
Bonnie Gretzner, *Editor*
Andrea Gillmore, *Marketing Staff*
EMP: 27 EST: 1980
SQ FT: 2,000
SALES (est): 1.7MM **Privately Held**
WEB: www.rjm.marketing
SIC: **7311** 2721 Advertising consultant; periodicals

(G-8994)
RAY PRINTING COMPANY INC
201 Brookley Ave (49202-2399)
PHONE.................................517 787-4130
Gary Emerson, *President*
Gary Lewis, *Vice Pres*
EMP: 16

Jackson - Jackson County (G-8995)

SQ FT: 7,000
SALES (est): 1.7MM **Privately Held**
WEB: www.rayprinting.com
SIC: 2752 7331 2759 Commercial printing, offset; direct mail advertising services; letterpress printing

(G-8995)
REFRIGERATION SALES INC
1810 E High St Ste 2 (49203-6433)
PHONE.................................517 784-8579
Russell Lyke, *President*
Vern R Lyke, *Vice Pres*
James Burch, *Opers Mgr*
Melissa Cozart, *Controller*
▲ **EMP:** 9 **EST:** 1974
SQ FT: 2,000
SALES (est): 1.6MM **Privately Held**
WEB: www.refsales.com
SIC: 3429 Manufactured hardware (general)

(G-8996)
RIVMAX MANUFACTURING INC
2218 E High St Ste C (49203-3553)
PHONE.................................517 784-2556
Matthew Olinyk, *President*
EMP: 10 **EST:** 2005
SALES (est): 487.3K **Privately Held**
SIC: 2514 Cabinets, radio & television: metal

(G-8997)
ROE PUBLISHING DEPARTMENT
2535 Grey Tower Rd (49201-9120)
P.O. Box 309, Grass Lake (49240-0309)
PHONE.................................517 522-3598
Nathaniel Pop, *Owner*
EMP: 6 **EST:** 2000
SALES (est): 256.8K **Privately Held**
SIC: 2741 Miscellaneous publishing

(G-8998)
ROTARY VALVE SYSTEMS LLC
807 Airport Rd (49202-1862)
PHONE.................................517 780-4002
John Cassidy, *General Mgr*
Dale Moretz, *Principal*
Shawn Kahnert, *Prdtn Mgr*
Levi Cann, *Sales Engr*
Avery Oppegard, *Sales Engr*
EMP: 8 **EST:** 2007
SALES (est): 206.8K **Privately Held**
SIC: 3592 Valves

(G-8999)
ROYAL CABINET INC
Also Called: Kitchen Supply Co
3900 Francis St (49203-5434)
P.O. Box 177 (49204-0177)
PHONE.................................517 787-2940
Richard W Ehnis, *President*
Beverly A Ehnis, *Vice Pres*
EMP: 12 **EST:** 1985
SQ FT: 18,000
SALES (est): 323.7K **Privately Held**
WEB: www.kitchensupply.biz
SIC: 2541 Cabinets, except refrigerated: show, display, etc.: wood; table or counter tops, plastic laminated

(G-9000)
ROYALTEES GOLF LLC
2000 Townley St (49203-4414)
PHONE.................................517 783-5911
Ronald Phillips, *Marketing Mgr*
EMP: 7 **EST:** 2007
SALES (est): 180.7K **Privately Held**
WEB: www.royalteesgolf.com
SIC: 3949 Golf equipment

(G-9001)
RSM & ASSOCIATES CO
Also Called: RSM Auto Co.
4107 W Michigan Ave (49202-1830)
PHONE.................................517 750-9330
Robert Martens, *CEO*
▲ **EMP:** 26 **EST:** 1996
SALES (est): 3.9MM **Privately Held**
WEB: www.newminitrucks.com
SIC: 3799 5511 Midget autos, power driven; automobiles, new & used

(G-9002)
RTD MANUFACTURING INC
1150 S Elm Ave (49203-3306)
PHONE.................................517 783-1550
Bryant Ramsey, *President*
Donna Ramsey, *Corp Secy*
BJ Ramsey, *Vice Pres*
Dave Smith, *Executive*
EMP: 22 **EST:** 1985
SQ FT: 120,000
SALES (est): 4.6MM **Privately Held**
WEB: www.rtdtool.com
SIC: 3599 7389 Machine shop, jobbing & repair; design, commercial & industrial

(G-9003)
S R P INC
1927 Wildwood Ave (49202-4046)
PHONE.................................517 784-3153
Lawrence H Schultz, *President*
Douglas H Dold, *Admin Sec*
EMP: 14 **EST:** 1979
SQ FT: 52,000
SALES (est): 192.8K **Privately Held**
SIC: 3568 Clutches, except vehicular

(G-9004)
SALCO ENGINEERING AND MFG INC
2030 Micor Dr (49203-3448)
PHONE.................................517 789-9010
James Flack, *President*
Walter J Michner, *Corp Secy*
Rick Harbaugh, *Plant Mgr*
EMP: 17 **EST:** 1962
SQ FT: 60,000
SALES (est): 2.4MM **Privately Held**
WEB: www.salcoeng.com
SIC: 3496 Miscellaneous fabricated wire products

(G-9005)
SALESMAN INC (PA)
Also Called: Salesman Publications
1101 Greenwood Ave (49203-3113)
P.O. Box 205, Concord (49237-0205)
PHONE.................................517 783-4080
Betty Watson, *Manager*
Jim Clifton, *Executive*
EMP: 4 **EST:** 1994
SALES (est): 2.6MM **Privately Held**
WEB: www.salesmanpublications.com
SIC: 2741 Miscellaneous publishing

(G-9006)
SANDHILL CRANE VINEYARDS LLC
4724 Walz Rd (49201-9613)
PHONE.................................517 764-0679
Norman Moffatt, *Manager*
EMP: 5 **EST:** 2002
SALES (est): 364.7K **Privately Held**
WEB: www.sandhillcranevineyards.com
SIC: 2084 Wines

(G-9007)
SCHUTTE CORPORATION
4055 Morrill Rd (49201-7013)
PHONE.................................517 782-3600
Jeffery Reinert, *President*
Matt Morgan, *Regl Sales Mgr*
Brittany Parks, *Sales Staff*
◆ **EMP:** 15 **EST:** 1996
SQ FT: 15,000
SALES (est): 3.6MM **Privately Held**
WEB: www.schutteusa.com
SIC: 5084 3541 Machine tools & accessories; machine tools, metal cutting type

(G-9008)
SCOTT MACHINE INC
4025 Morrill Rd (49201-7013)
P.O. Box 468 (49204-0468)
PHONE.................................517 787-6616
Tom Dobbin, *President*
Edward R Scott, *Chairman*
Charles Donall, *Exec VP*
Tom Dwyer, *Vice Pres*
Michael Embury, *Vice Pres*
EMP: 50 **EST:** 1946
SQ FT: 27,000
SALES (est): 9.2MM **Privately Held**
WEB: www.scottmachineinc.com
SIC: 3728 3494 3492 Aircraft parts & equipment; valves & pipe fittings; fluid power valves & hose fittings

(G-9009)
SHAFER REDI-MIX INC
5405 E Michigan Ave (49201-8406)
PHONE.................................517 764-0517
Jerry Shafer, *Principal*
EMP: 55
SQ FT: 5,000
SALES (corp-wide): 12.5MM **Privately Held**
WEB: www.shaferbros.com
SIC: 3273 Ready-mixed concrete
PA: Shafer Redi-Mix, Inc.
29150 C Dr N
Albion MI 49224
517 629-4800

(G-9010)
SLED SHED ENTERPRISES LLC
1150 S Elm Ave (49203-3306)
PHONE.................................517 783-5136
Bryant Ramsey, *Mng Member*
EMP: 6
SQ FT: 25,000
SALES (est): 490.7K **Privately Held**
WEB: www.sledshed.net
SIC: 3799 Recreational vehicles

(G-9011)
SMSG LLC (PA)
Also Called: Orbitform Group
1600 Executive Dr (49203-3469)
PHONE.................................517 787-9447
Mark Shirkey, *CFO*
Mike Shirkey,
EMP: 2 **EST:** 2001
SALES (est): 40MM **Privately Held**
WEB: www.orbitform.com
SIC: 3452 Rivets, metal

(G-9012)
SPENCER ZDANOWITZ INC
120 S Dwight St (49203-2083)
PHONE.................................517 841-9380
John Spencer, *CEO*
Dennis L Zdanowitz, *COO*
EMP: 4 **EST:** 1999
SQ FT: 14,000
SALES (est): 519.8K
SALES (corp-wide): 21.8MM **Privately Held**
WEB: www.greatlakesmetalfinishing.com
SIC: 3471 Electroplating of metals or formed products
PA: Classic Turning, Inc.
3000 E South St
Jackson MI 49201
517 764-1335

(G-9013)
STEINKE-FENTON FABRICATORS
1355 Page Ave (49203-2158)
PHONE.................................517 782-8174
Robert D Chatfield, *President*
Todd Chatfield, *Vice Pres*
EMP: 15 **EST:** 1939
SQ FT: 18,000
SALES (est): 1.6MM **Privately Held**
WEB: www.steinkefenton.com
SIC: 3444 Sheet metal specialties, not stamped

(G-9014)
TAC MANUFACTURING INC (DH)
4111 County Farm Rd (49201-9065)
PHONE.................................517 789-7000
Hiro Ysui, *President*
Kiyoshi Sasaki, *President*
Y Hirai, *Vice Pres*
Corey Prior, *Buyer*
Arron Alexander, *Engineer*
▲ **EMP:** 290 **EST:** 1991
SQ FT: 110,000
SALES (est): 99.8MM **Privately Held**
WEB: www.tacmfg.com
SIC: 3714 3625 Motor vehicle engines & parts; relays & industrial controls
HQ: Tram, Inc.
47200 Port St
Plymouth MI 48170
734 254-8500

(G-9015)
TALKIN TACKLE LLC
205 S Sandstone Rd (49201-8925)
PHONE.................................517 474-6241
Ronald Kerver, *President*
Ralph McGonegal, *Managing Prtnr*
Kay Kerver, *Vice Pres*
Laurie Miller, *Admin Sec*
EMP: 4 **EST:** 2007
SALES (est): 242K **Privately Held**
WEB: www.talkingtackledepthwhisperer.com
SIC: 3812 7389 Sonar systems & equipment; business services

(G-9016)
TECH TOOLING SPECIALTIES INC
1708 Cooper St (49202)
PHONE.................................517 782-8898
Robert Woodard, *President*
EMP: 13 **EST:** 1989
SQ FT: 12,000
SALES (est): 1MM **Privately Held**
WEB: www.techtoolingjackson.com
SIC: 3544 3541 3599 3542 Special dies & tools; machine tools, metal cutting type; machine shop, jobbing & repair; machine tools, metal forming type

(G-9017)
TECHNIQUE INC
1500 Technology Dr (49201-2700)
P.O. Box 4010 (49204-4010)
PHONE.................................517 789-8988
Ronnie Johncox, *President*
Andrew Fisher, *Project Mgr*
Ryan McClain, *Engineer*
Laura Wright, *Human Resources*
Paul Brockie, *Accounts Mgr*
EMP: 75
SQ FT: 126,000
SALES (est): 17MM **Privately Held**
WEB: www.techniqueinc.com
SIC: 3469 3465 7692 3751 Metal stampings; automotive stampings; automotive welding; frames, motorcycle & bicycle; exhaust systems (mufflers, tail pipes, etc.); exhaust systems & parts, motor vehicle

(G-9018)
TENNECO AUTOMOTIVE OPER CO INC
2701 N Dettman Rd (49201-8883)
PHONE.................................517 522-5525
Bill Dreyer, *Principal*
Anthony Bartotti, *Engineer*
Heather Stewart, *Engineer*
Rick Veneziano, *Engineer*
Trent Hudson, *Program Mgr*
EMP: 7
SALES (corp-wide): 15.3B **Publicly Held**
SIC: 3714 Motor vehicle parts & accessories
HQ: Tenneco Automotive Operating Company, Inc.
500 N Field Dr
Lake Forest IL 60045
847 482-5000

(G-9019)
TERRY TOOL & DIE CO
1080 Toro Dr (49201-8946)
PHONE.................................517 750-1771
Janet Schrader, *President*
Ryan Schrader, *Vice Pres*
Ron Markowski, *Treasurer*
John Dobben, *Admin Sec*
EMP: 10 **EST:** 1973
SQ FT: 18,000
SALES (est): 731.1K **Privately Held**
WEB: www.terrytool.com
SIC: 3451 3544 Screw machine products; special dies, tools, jigs & fixtures

(G-9020)
THE SUN
214 S Jackson St (49201-2267)
PHONE.................................800 878-6397
Susan Allen, *Administration*
EMP: 4 **EST:** 2010

GEOGRAPHIC SECTION

Jenison - Ottawa County (G-9047)

SALES (est): 83K **Privately Held**
SIC: **2711** Newspapers, publishing & printing

(G-9021)
TMS INTERNATIONAL LLC
3100 Brooklyn Rd (49203-4809)
PHONE.................................517 764-5123
EMP: **4 Privately Held**
SIC: **3312** Blast Furnace-Steel Works
HQ: Tms International, Llc
Southside Wrks Bldg 1 3f
Pittsburgh PA 15203
412 678-6141

(G-9022)
TREGETS TOOL & ENGINEERING CO
1021 Airport Rd (49202-1850)
PHONE.................................517 782-0044
Steven Dygert, *President*
George Dygert, *Treasurer*
Dorothy Dygert, *Admin Sec*
EMP: **8** EST: 1979
SQ FT: 15,680
SALES (est): 842.7K **Privately Held**
WEB: www.tregets.com
SIC: **3544** Special dies & tools

(G-9023)
TRICO INCORPORATED
7401 Foxworth Ct (49201-8486)
PHONE.................................517 764-1780
Harold Jones, *President*
Shelley Jones, *Vice Pres*
EMP: **7** EST: 1943
SALES (est): 826.1K **Privately Held**
WEB: www.tricocylinders.com
SIC: **2796** Gravure printing plates or cylinders, preparation of

(G-9024)
TRINITY HOLDING INC (PA)
420 Ingham St (49201-1251)
PHONE.................................517 787-3100
Joseph R Miller, *President*
Phyllis L Miller, *Chairman*
Mary Lynn Miller, *Corp Secy*
EMP: **11** EST: 1986
SQ FT: 40,000
SALES: 13.2MM **Privately Held**
WEB: www.trinityholding.com
SIC: **5084** 4214 6531 3451 Industrial machinery & equipment; local trucking with storage; real estate agents & managers; screw machine products

(G-9025)
TRUFORM MACHINE INC
2510 Precision St (49202-3967)
PHONE.................................517 782-8523
Frank Phillips, *CEO*
Jeff Risk, *President*
Mike Zotter, *Vice Pres*
Regina Swab, *QC Mgr*
EMP: **35** EST: 1981
SQ FT: 12,000
SALES (est): 4.5MM **Privately Held**
WEB: www.truformmachine.com
SIC: **3599** 3841 3812 3769 Machine shop, jobbing & repair; surgical & medical instruments; search & navigation equipment; guided missile & space vehicle parts & auxiliary equipment; fluid power pumps & motors

(G-9026)
TRULIFE INC (DH)
Also Called: Discount Vitamin Store
2010 E High St (49203-3416)
PHONE.................................800 492-1088
Noel J Murphy, *CEO*
Alan Cooke, *CEO*
Chris Henry, *Research*
Kristi M Caddell, *Sales Staff*
Donna Robertson, *Manager*
▲ EMP: **50** EST: 1982
SQ FT: 75,000
SALES (est): 48.5MM **Privately Held**
WEB: www.trulife.com
SIC: **3842** 8011 Belts: surgical, sanitary & corrective; braces, orthopedic; supports: abdominal, ankle, arch, kneecap, etc.; offices & clinics of medical doctors

(G-9027)
TRUTH & TIDINGS
2030 Jeffrey Ct (49203-3826)
PHONE.................................517 782-9798
EMP: **4** EST: 2018
SALES (est): 93.7K **Privately Held**
WEB: www.truthandtidings.com
SIC: **2731** Book publishing

(G-9028)
UNIFIED TOOL AND DIE INC
2010 Micor Dr (49203-3448)
PHONE.................................517 768-8070
Michael Vogel, *President*
Marty Sears, *Treasurer*
EMP: **7** EST: 1981
SQ FT: 2,700
SALES (est): **Privately Held**
WEB: www.unifiedtool.com
SIC: **3544** Special dies & tools

(G-9029)
UNITED METAL TECHNOLOGY INC
144 W Monroe St (49202-2398)
PHONE.................................517 787-7940
Dennis G Rulewicz, *President*
Stephen G Rulewicz, *Vice Pres*
EMP: **22** EST: 1981
SQ FT: 18,500
SALES (est): 2.3MM **Privately Held**
WEB: www.unitedmetaltech.com
SIC: **3714** 3533 Motor vehicle parts & accessories; oil field machinery & equipment

(G-9030)
VERITAS VINEYARD LLC (PA)
Also Called: Grand River Brewery
117 W Louis Glick Hwy (49201-1304)
PHONE.................................517 962-2427
John Burtka,
Denise E Burtka,
EMP: **36** EST: 2002
SQ FT: 12,500
SALES (est): 5.9MM **Privately Held**
WEB: www.grandriverbrewery.com
SIC: **2084** 8741 5921 Wines; restaurant management; wine & beer

(G-9031)
VERSAH LLC
2000 Spring Arbor Rd B (49203-2887)
PHONE.................................844 711-5585
Jessica Rando, *Vice Pres*
EMP: **7** EST: 2019
SALES (est): 781.3K **Privately Held**
WEB: www.versah.com
SIC: **3841** Surgical & medical instruments

(G-9032)
W2 INC
Also Called: Gilbert's Chocolates
233 N Jackson St (49201-1203)
PHONE.................................517 764-3141
William R Blakemore, *President*
EMP: **7** EST: 1900
SQ FT: 1,500
SALES (est): 567.2K **Privately Held**
WEB: www.gilbertchocolates.com
SIC: **5441** 5145 2064 Candy; candy; candy & other confectionery products

(G-9033)
WAY BAKERY (HQ)
2100 Enterprise St (49203-6412)
PHONE.................................517 787-6720
John F Popp, *President*
Jay E Miller, *Vice Pres*
EMP: **230** EST: 1884
SQ FT: 62,000
SALES: 73.4MM
SALES (corp-wide): 457.7MM **Privately Held**
WEB: www.auntmillies.com
SIC: **2051** Buns, bread type: fresh or frozen
PA: Perfection Bakeries, Inc.
350 Pearl St
Fort Wayne IN 46802
260 424-5245

(G-9034)
WEATHERPROOF INC
385 Watts Rd (49203-2333)
PHONE.................................517 764-1330

Terri Jo, *President*
Carol Goldsmith, *President*
Lisa Haynes, *Vice Pres*
Terri Nichols, *Vice Pres*
EMP: **34** EST: 1964
SQ FT: 15,000
SALES (est): 6.8MM **Privately Held**
WEB: www.weatherproof.net
SIC: **2821** 3442 3211 2431 Vinyl resins; storm doors or windows, metal; insulating glass, sealed units; awnings, blinds & shutters, wood

(G-9035)
WILLBEE CONCRETE PRODUCTS CO
2323 Brooklyn Rd (49203-4751)
PHONE.................................517 782-8246
EMP: **14** EST: 1922
SQ FT: 15,000
SALES (est): 2MM **Privately Held**
SIC: **3272** 7261 5087 Mfg Concrete Products Funeral Service/Crematory Whol Service Establishment Equipment

(G-9036)
WILLBEE TRANSIT-MIX CO INC
2323 Brooklyn Rd (49203-4749)
P.O. Box 427 (49204-0427)
PHONE.................................517 782-9493
Andrew Willbee, *President*
Gregory Sherwood, *Vice Pres*
EMP: **25** EST: 1907
SQ FT: 1,300
SALES (est): 4MM **Privately Held**
WEB: www.willbeetransit-mix.com
SIC: **3273** 5032 Ready-mixed concrete; brick, stone & related material

(G-9037)
WOLVERINE TRAILERS INC
1500 Chanter Rd (49201-9563)
P.O. Box 1829 (49204-1829)
PHONE.................................517 782-4950
Lyle Johnson, *Branch Mgr*
EMP: **5**
SALES (corp-wide): 5MM **Privately Held**
WEB: www.wolverinetrailers.com
SIC: **3715** Truck trailers
PA: Wolverine Trailers, Inc.
116 Frost St
Jackson MI 49202
517 782-4950

(G-9038)
WOODIE MANUFACTURING INC
1400 Wildwood Ave (49202-4027)
PHONE.................................517 782-7663
John Flannery, *President*
EMP: **8** EST: 1992
SQ FT: 3,000
SALES (est): 933.3K **Privately Held**
WEB: www.woodiemanufacturing.com
SIC: **3599** Machine shop, jobbing & repair

(G-9039)
XYRESIC LLC
4905 James Mcdevitt St (49201-8958)
PHONE.................................906 281-0021
Robert Henderson,
EMP: **5** EST: 2020
SALES (est): 435.4K **Privately Held**
SIC: **3555** Printing trade parts & attachments

(G-9040)
YOXHEIMER TILE CO
919 E South St (49203-4404)
PHONE.................................517 788-7542
Scott Yoxheimer, *President*
EMP: **16** EST: 1992
SQ FT: 1,260
SALES (est): 3.7MM **Privately Held**
WEB: www.yoxheimertile.com
SIC: **1743** 3253 5032 Tile installation, ceramic; floor tile, ceramic; granite building stone

(G-9041)
ZIMMER MARBLE CO INC
1812 River St (49202-1755)
PHONE.................................517 787-1500
Joseph A Campau, *President*
Philip F Campau, *Vice Pres*
Karen Spaan, *Technology*
EMP: **14** EST: 1975

SQ FT: 54,000
SALES (est): 2.2MM **Privately Held**
WEB: www.zimmermarble.com
SIC: **3281** 3088 Marble, building: cut & shaped; plastics plumbing fixtures

Jenison
Ottawa County

(G-9042)
ADVANTAGE INDUSTRIES INC
2196 Port Sheldon St (49428-9315)
PHONE.................................616 669-2400
Kirk Klynstra, *President*
William Bos, *President*
Morris Kolff, *Vice Pres*
Bryan Galloway, *Project Engr*
Doug Dornbos, *Treasurer*
EMP: **40** EST: 1992
SQ FT: 20,000
SALES (est): 5MM **Privately Held**
WEB: www.advind.com
SIC: **3543** 3544 7373 1731 Industrial patterns; industrial molds; jigs: inspection, gauging & checking; computer-aided design (CAD) systems service; electrical work

(G-9043)
AGRI BLOWERS EXPRESS
6665 Marcan Ave Ste 1 (49428-7135)
PHONE.................................616 662-9999
Leslie Kamps, *Principal*
EMP: **7** EST: 2006
SALES (est): 99K **Privately Held**
SIC: **2741** Miscellaneous publishing

(G-9044)
APEX TOOLING SOLUTIONS LLC
6854 Valley View Ave (49428-8175)
PHONE.................................616 283-7439
Mitchell Stahl,
EMP: **5** EST: 2017
SALES (est): 90.8K **Privately Held**
SIC: **3312** Tool & die steel & alloys

(G-9045)
APPAREL SALES INC
2712 Edward St Ste A (49428-8187)
PHONE.................................616 842-5650
Jon Johnson, *President*
Robert Dykstra, *Vice Pres*
▲ EMP: **5** EST: 1969
SQ FT: 28,000
SALES (est): 751.3K **Privately Held**
SIC: **5136** 2759 2395 Sportswear, men's & boys'; screen printing; embroidery & art needlework

(G-9046)
AUTOMATED MACHINE SYSTEMS INC
6651 Pine Ridge Ct Sw (49428-9254)
PHONE.................................616 662-1309
Kris Chayer, *President*
Kevin Grinwis, *Vice Pres*
Kevan Grinwis, *Manager*
Michael Poff, *Technology*
Micah Farraher, *Technical Staff*
EMP: **23** EST: 1997
SQ FT: 5,000
SALES (est): 7.5MM **Privately Held**
WEB: www.automatedmachinesystems.com
SIC: **3537** Palletizers & depalletizers

(G-9047)
BOYNE MACHINE COMPANY INC
2169 Pine Ridge Dr Sw A (49428-8202)
PHONE.................................616 669-7178
Michael Blackmer, *President*
Russell Parker, *Vice Pres*
EMP: **15** EST: 1970
SQ FT: 18,000
SALES (est): 2.1MM **Privately Held**
WEB: www.boynemachine.com
SIC: **3599** Machine shop, jobbing & repair

Jenison - Ottawa County (G-9048) — GEOGRAPHIC SECTION

(G-9048)
CABINETS CUNTERTOPS DIRECT LLC
1225 Baldwin St (49428-8907)
PHONE 616 238-6608
Anthony Boonstra,
EMP: 5 **EST:** 2012
SALES (est): 63.5K **Privately Held**
WEB: www.cabinetsntops.com
SIC: 2434 Wood kitchen cabinets

(G-9049)
CELLULOSE MTL SOLUTIONS LLC
Also Called: CMS
2472 Port Sheldon St (49428-9342)
PHONE 616 669-2990
Matt Henderson, *Vice Pres*
Brandon Fenske, *Opers Staff*
Mark Henderson, *Mng Member*
EMP: 7 **EST:** 2006
SALES (est): 1MM **Privately Held**
WEB: www.cmsgreen.com
SIC: 2392 Blankets: made from purchased materials

(G-9050)
CORE LITE INDUSTRIES LLC
8901 Cedar Lake Dr (49428-9462)
PHONE 616 481-3940
EMP: 6 **EST:** 2014
SALES (est): 136.9K **Privately Held**
WEB: www.coreliteindustries.com
SIC: 3999 Manufacturing industries

(G-9051)
DENTON BOBELDYK
2711 Thrush Dr (49428-9172)
PHONE 616 669-2076
Bobeldyk Denton, *Executive*
EMP: 4 **EST:** 2016
SALES (est): 80.4K **Privately Held**
SIC: 2721 Periodicals

(G-9052)
DEWENT REDI-MIX LLC
1601 Chicago Dr (49428-9740)
PHONE 616 457-2100
Cheryl Zwagerman, *Principal*
EMP: 5 **EST:** 2019
SALES (est): 370.8K **Privately Held**
WEB: www.de-went-redi-mix.business.site
SIC: 3273 Ready-mixed concrete

(G-9053)
DSM ENGINEERING MATERIALS INC
7784 Steele Ave (49428-7937)
PHONE 616 667-2643
Douglas Bosch, *Principal*
EMP: 6
SALES (corp-wide): 9.9B **Privately Held**
WEB: www.dsm.com
SIC: 2834 Pharmaceutical preparations
HQ: Dsm Engineering Materials, Inc.
2267 W Mill Rd
Evansville IN 47720

(G-9054)
EMBROIDERY HOUSE INC
2688 Edward St (49428-8187)
PHONE 616 669-6400
Kurt Vander Loon, *President*
Derek Stark, *Sales Staff*
EMP: 7 **EST:** 1986
SQ FT: 5,200
SALES (est): 1MM **Privately Held**
WEB: www.embroideryhouseinc.com
SIC: 2395 2396 5199 2752 Embroidery products, except schiffli machine; emblems, embroidered; screen printing on fabric articles; advertising specialties; business form & card printing, lithographic

(G-9055)
FABRI-TECH INC (PA)
Also Called: Anterior Quest
6719 Pine Ridge Ct Sw (49428-9253)
PHONE 616 662-0150
Dennis Jonker, *President*
Scott Bowron, *Vice Pres*
Daniel Holtrop, *Vice Pres*
Nate Koster, *Sales Staff*
David Brandsen, *Chief Mktg Ofcr*
▲ **EMP:** 29 **EST:** 2000
SQ FT: 22,000
SALES (est): 7.3MM **Privately Held**
WEB: www.fabritech.biz
SIC: 3552 5949 Embroidery machines; sewing, needlework & piece goods

(G-9056)
ICON CHOPPERS
1538 Beechwood Dr (49428-8359)
PHONE 616 292-0536
Matthew Nelson, *Principal*
EMP: 5 **EST:** 2010
SALES (est): 134.5K **Privately Held**
SIC: 3751 Motorcycles & related parts

(G-9057)
INCOME WAXCOM
7702 Harold Ave (49428-7917)
PHONE 616 457-4277
Laurie Ayers, *Principal*
EMP: 4 **EST:** 2010
SALES (est): 69.6K **Privately Held**
WEB: www.thrivingcandlebusiness.com
SIC: 3999 Candles

(G-9058)
INHE MANUFACTURING LLC
904 Chicago Dr (49428-9351)
PHONE 616 863-2222
EMP: 6 **EST:** 2019
SALES (est): 456.9K **Privately Held**
SIC: 3999 Manufacturing industries

(G-9059)
INNOVATIVE MACHINES INC
1811 Chicago Dr (49428-9740)
PHONE 616 669-1649
Arlen Van Os, *President*
Don Ogle, *Vice Pres*
Lois Ogle, *Opers Staff*
▲ **EMP:** 8 **EST:** 1991
SQ FT: 90,000
SALES (est): 1.4MM **Privately Held**
WEB: www.innovative-machines.com
SIC: 3555 Printing trades machinery

(G-9060)
LARKHITE DEVELOPMENT SYSTEM
1501 Port Sheldon St (49428-9320)
P.O. Box 989 (49429-0989)
PHONE 616 457-6722
David Maier, *President*
EMP: 7 **EST:** 1992
SALES (est): 651.5K **Privately Held**
SIC: 2451 Mobile homes

(G-9061)
MCCLURE TABLES INC (PA)
6661 Roger Dr Ste C (49428-9248)
PHONE 616 662-5974
Todd McClure, *CEO*
Judy McClure, *President*
▲ **EMP:** 6 **EST:** 1985
SQ FT: 5,000
SALES (est): 1.2MM **Privately Held**
WEB: www.mccluretables.com
SIC: 3949 Shuffleboards & shuffleboard equipment

(G-9062)
MICHIGAN HERBAL REMEDIES LLC (PA)
904 Chicago Dr (49428-9351)
PHONE 616 818-0823
EMP: 8
SALES (est): 790.2K **Privately Held**
SIC: 5499 2023 1541 Miscellaneous Food Stores, Nsk

(G-9063)
NEXT LEVEL DIE CUTTING LLC
6778 18th Ave (49428-8385)
PHONE 888 819-9959
EMP: 11 **EST:** 2017
SALES (est): 579.9K **Privately Held**
WEB: www.nextleveldiecutting.com
SIC: 3423 Cutting dies, except metal cutting

(G-9064)
NEXT LEVEL MANUFACTURING LLC (PA)
6778 18th Ave (49428-8385)
PHONE 269 397-1220
David Warner, *President*
Tim Creamer, *Engineer*
EMP: 25 **EST:** 2011
SALES (est): 4MM **Privately Held**
WEB: www.nextlevelmfg.com
SIC: 3999 Atomizers, toiletry

(G-9065)
NU-WOOL CO INC
Also Called: Business Software Services
2472 Port Sheldon St (49428-9342)
PHONE 800 748-0128
Mark Henderson, *President*
Matt Henderson, *Vice Pres*
Valerie Henderson, *Vice Pres*
Bob Devries, *Technical Mgr*
Mercy Schaab, *Controller*
▲ **EMP:** 68 **EST:** 1949
SQ FT: 90,000
SALES (est): 13.9MM **Privately Held**
WEB: www.nuwool.com
SIC: 2499 2493 Mulch, wood & bark; insulation board, cellular fiber

(G-9066)
PRECISION SEALANT
8855 Cedar Lake Dr (49428-9461)
PHONE 616 667-9447
EMP: 4 **EST:** 2019
SALES (est): 125.7K **Privately Held**
SIC: 2891 Sealants

(G-9067)
PREFERRED MACHINE LLC
6673 Pine Ridge Ct Sw C (49428-9278)
PHONE 616 272-6334
Mitchell Steere, *Engineer*
Nathan Holstege, *Mng Member*
Aaron Fisher, *Department Mgr*
Ben Smith, *Manager*
Corey Westra, *Manager*
EMP: 30 **EST:** 2009
SALES (est): 4.6MM **Privately Held**
WEB: www.preferredmachinellc.com
SIC: 3599 Machine shop, jobbing & repair

(G-9068)
PROTXS INC (PA)
7974 Parkside Ct (49428-9100)
PHONE 989 255-3836
Nathan Blury, *President*
Dr Michael Halliday, *Founder*
▼ **EMP:** 217 **EST:** 2015
SQ FT: 4,556
SALES (est): 3.2MM **Privately Held**
SIC: 3571 Electronic computers

(G-9069)
R & R HARWOOD INC
Also Called: Hardwoods Prtg & Advg Servic
2688 Edward St (49428-8187)
PHONE 616 669-6400
Morton Harwood Sr, *President*
Morton Harwood Jr, *President*
Mabel Harwood, *Principal*
Randy Harwood, *Vice Pres*
EMP: 5 **EST:** 1939
SQ FT: 2,000
SALES (est): 1MM **Privately Held**
SIC: 2741 2752 2759 2789 Miscellaneous publishing; commercial printing, lithographic; commercial printing; bookbinding & related work; signs & advertising specialties; advertising specialties

(G-9070)
SCHRIER PLASTICS CORP
2019 Pine Ridge Dr Sw (49428-9228)
PHONE 616 669-7174
Jeffrey Schrier, *President*
Pamela Schrier, *Corp Secy*
EMP: 24 **EST:** 1995
SQ FT: 15,000
SALES (est): 1.2MM **Privately Held**
WEB: www.schrierplastics.com
SIC: 3089 Plastic hardware & building products; plastic processing

(G-9071)
SERVISCREEN INC
1765 Chicago Dr (49428-9740)
PHONE 616 669-1640
Allen Van Os, *CEO*
Ariah Van Os, *General Mgr*
Lowell Vanos, *Exec VP*
Allen Os, *Vice Pres*
Arlen Van Os, *Vice Pres*
EMP: 100 **EST:** 1962
SQ FT: 53,645
SALES (est): 23.6MM **Privately Held**
WEB: www.serviscreen.com
SIC: 2759 3479 Screen printing; painting, coating & hot dipping; painting of metal products

(G-9072)
STEPHANIES UNLIMITED CREAT LLC
6613 Center Industrial Dr (49428-8303)
PHONE 616 379-5392
Stephanie Walker, *Principal*
EMP: 5 **EST:** 2017
SALES (est): 328.4K **Privately Held**
WEB: www.stephaniesunlimitedcreations.com
SIC: 2395 Embroidery & art needlework

(G-9073)
TANNEWITZ INC
Also Called: Ramco
794 Chicago Dr (49428-9195)
PHONE 616 457-5999
Morry Pysarchik, *President*
David Oltouse, *Vice Pres*
◆ **EMP:** 24 **EST:** 1890
SQ FT: 21,000
SALES (est): 4.8MM **Privately Held**
WEB: www.tannewitz.com
SIC: 3549 3553 Metalworking machinery; woodworking machinery

(G-9074)
TRUSSWAY
8450 Winona Dr (49428-9540)
P.O. Box 27, Sparta (49345-0027)
PHONE 713 691-6900
Ron Wiersum, *Principal*
EMP: 15 **EST:** 2010
SALES (est): 170.5K **Privately Held**
WEB: www.trussway.com
SIC: 2439 Trusses, wooden roof

(G-9075)
USA SIGN FRAME & STAKE INC
2150 Center Industrial Ct (49428-8347)
PHONE 616 662-9100
Gary Moshluk, *President*
Brian Kronemeyer, *President*
EMP: 5 **EST:** 2009
SQ FT: 8,000
SALES (est): 850K **Privately Held**
WEB: www.usasignframeandstake.com
SIC: 3993 Signs, not made in custom sign painting shops

(G-9076)
VANEX MOLD INC
2240 Pine Ridge Dr Sw (49428-9229)
PHONE 616 662-4100
Tom Vanek, *President*
Ken Vanek, *Vice Pres*
EMP: 4 **EST:** 1996
SQ FT: 9,000
SALES (est): 680.3K **Privately Held**
SIC: 3544 Industrial molds

(G-9077)
VIBRATION RESEARCH CORPORATION
1294 Chicago Dr (49428-9308)
PHONE 616 669-3028
John Van Baren, *President*
Kevin Popering, *Engineer*
Curtis Fredricks, *CFO*
Casey Dubois, *Sales Engr*
Jeff Ludwig, *Sales Engr*
EMP: 20 **EST:** 1995
SQ FT: 8,000
SALES (est): 3.3MM **Privately Held**
WEB: www.vibrationresearch.com
SIC: 3829 Measuring & controlling devices

GEOGRAPHIC SECTION

Jonesville - Hillsdale County (G-9103)

Jerome
Hillsdale County

(G-9078)
LAKESIDE CUSTOM PRINTING LLC
11581 Bradley Dr (49249-9740)
PHONE.....................517 936-5904
Thomas Arnold, *Principal*
EMP: 4 **EST:** 2018
SALES (est): 83.9K **Privately Held**
SIC: 2752 Commercial printing, lithographic

(G-9079)
MICHIGAN AGGREGATES CORP
996 E Chicago Rd (49249)
PHONE.....................517 688-4414
Richard A Davidson, *President*
Mary Wendorf, *Corp Secy*
H Norman Jones, *Vice Pres*
EMP: 15 **EST:** 1952
SQ FT: 2,000
SALES (est): 2.6MM **Privately Held**
SIC: 1442 Gravel mining

Johannesburg
Otsego County

(G-9080)
BDR INC
9319 M 32 E (49751-9548)
PHONE.....................989 732-1608
Steven Tomaski, *President*
Mary Tomaski, *Vice Pres*
EMP: 5 **EST:** 1986
SALES (est): 816.7K **Privately Held**
SIC: 1389 Oil field services

(G-9081)
EASTPORT GROUP INC
9301 M 32 E (49751-9548)
P.O. Box 277 (49751-0277)
PHONE.....................989 732-0030
William C Myler Jr, *President*
Thomas J Myler, *Vice Pres*
EMP: 14 **EST:** 1991
SALES (est): 1.8MM **Privately Held**
SIC: 1389 Gas field services; oil field services

(G-9082)
RCS SERVICES COMPANY LLC
10850 Hetherton Rd (49751-8730)
P.O. Box 38 (49751-0038)
PHONE.....................989 732-7999
Dennis Marelich, *Prdtn Mgr*
Robert Jones, *Mng Member*
Richard Barnes, *CIO*
Connie Madej, *Administration*
EMP: 10 **EST:** 2004
SALES (est): 1.1MM **Privately Held**
WEB: www.rcsmi.com
SIC: 1389 Oil field services

Jones
Cass County

(G-9083)
DANIEL OLSON
Also Called: Maple Row Sugarhouse
12646 Born St (49061-9735)
PHONE.....................269 816-1838
Daniel Olson, *Owner*
EMP: 5 **EST:** 2014
SALES (est): 135.1K **Privately Held**
WEB: www.maplerowsugarhouse.com
SIC: 2099 Maple syrup

(G-9084)
ODONNELLS DOCKS
12097 M 60 (49061-8768)
P.O. Box 1 (49061-0001)
PHONE.....................269 244-1446
Shawn Odonnell, *Principal*
EMP: 4 **EST:** 2003
SALES (est): 354.2K **Privately Held**
WEB: www.odonnellsdocks.com
SIC: 3536 4491 Boat lifts; docks, incl. buildings & facilities: operation & maintenance

Jonesville
Hillsdale County

(G-9085)
BAY ALPHI MANUFACTURING INC
576 Beck St (49250-9472)
P.O. Box 9229, Green Bay WI (54308-9229)
PHONE.....................517 849-9945
Daniel A Schmidt, *CEO*
Ronn Kleinschmidt, *CFO*
Philip Marshallsay, *CFO*
Eric Maystead, *Manager*
Gloria J Schmidt, *Director*
EMP: 50 **EST:** 2018
SALES (est): 11.7MM **Privately Held**
WEB: www.bayfabrication.com
SIC: 3714 Mufflers (exhaust), motor vehicle
PA: Aws/Gb Corporation
2929 Walker Dr
Green Bay WI 54311

(G-9086)
CUSTOM BUILT HOLSTERS LLC
517 Crest Ln (49250-1207)
PHONE.....................517 825-9856
Adam Burlew, *Principal*
EMP: 4 **EST:** 2016
SALES (est): 58.6K **Privately Held**
SIC: 3199 Holsters, leather

(G-9087)
EXPRESS CNC & FABRICATION LLC
3041 North Adams Rd (49250-9200)
PHONE.....................517 937-8760
Tommy Schuette, *Vice Pres*
EMP: 7 **EST:** 2014
SQ FT: 145,000
SALES (est): 718.7K **Privately Held**
SIC: 3599 Machine shop, jobbing & repair

(G-9088)
GONZALEZ GROUP JONESVILLE LLC
3980 Beck Rd (49250-8400)
P.O. Box 360, Litchfield (49252-0360)
PHONE.....................517 849-9908
EMP: 50
SALES (corp-wide): 8.4MM **Privately Held**
SIC: 3498 Fabricated Pipe And Fittings
PA: Gonzalez Group, Llc
935 Anderson Rd
Litchfield MI 49252
517 542-2928

(G-9089)
INTERDYNE INC
530 Industrial Pkwy (49250-9006)
P.O. Box 165 (49250-0165)
PHONE.....................517 849-2281
Antonin Slovacek, *President*
Matt Slovacek, *Admin Sec*
Travis Berlin, *Administration*
EMP: 16 **EST:** 1976
SQ FT: 62,500
SALES (est): 3.1MM **Privately Held**
WEB: www.interdyneinc.com
SIC: 3069 Molded rubber products

(G-9090)
JT MANUFACTURING INC
Also Called: Jonesville Tool and Mfg
540 Industrial Pkwy (49250-9004)
P.O. Box 4364, Jackson (49204-4364)
PHONE.....................517 849-2923
Neil Caulkins, *President*
Cary Addleman, *Vice Pres*
Jim Parker, *Vice Pres*
Tim Westfall, *Purchasing*
Dan Waterstraut, *QC Mgr*
EMP: 48 **EST:** 2001
SQ FT: 32,500
SALES (est): 7.5MM **Privately Held**
WEB: www.jonesvilletool.com
SIC: 3599 3545 Machine shop, jobbing & repair; precision tools, machinists'

(G-9091)
K & K TANNERY LLC
561 Industrial Pkwy (49250-9004)
PHONE.....................517 849-9720
Gary Kies, *Owner*
EMP: 4 **EST:** 1995
SALES (est): 188.7K **Privately Held**
WEB: www.kandktannery.com
SIC: 3111 Hides: tanning, currying & finishing

(G-9092)
MACK ANDREW & SON BRUSH CO
216 E Chicago St (49250-1003)
P.O. Box 157 (49250-0157)
PHONE.....................517 849-9272
Jon M Fast, *President*
Betty J Fast, *Vice Pres*
Jonathan C Fast, *Vice Pres*
EMP: 9 **EST:** 1891
SQ FT: 1,500
SALES (est): 1.1MM **Privately Held**
WEB: www.mackbrush.com
SIC: 5231 3991 Paint brushes, rollers, sprayers & other supplies; paint brushes

(G-9093)
MARTINREA JONESVILLE LLC (HQ)
260 Gaige St (49250-9431)
PHONE.....................517 849-2195
Nick Orlando, *CEO*
Sheryl Miller, *Buyer*
Tim Seimet, *Technician*
Andre Larosa,
▲ **EMP:** 694 **EST:** 2009
SQ FT: 500,000
SALES (est): 88.1MM
SALES (corp-wide): 2.5B **Privately Held**
WEB: www.jonesville.org
SIC: 3465 Body parts, automobile: stamped metal
PA: Martinrea International Inc
3210 Langstaff Rd
Vaughan ON
416 749-0314

(G-9094)
MEGA SCREEN CORP
549 Industrial Pkwy (49250-9004)
P.O. Box 152 (49250-0152)
PHONE.....................517 849-7057
Mark L Domack, *President*
Stacy Domack, *Treasurer*
EMP: 6 **EST:** 1985
SQ FT: 9,000
SALES (est): 450.7K **Privately Held**
SIC: 2759 3089 3549 Screen printing; plastic processing; injection molding of plastics; metalworking machinery

(G-9095)
NORTH EAST FABRICATION CO INC
Also Called: Nefco
113 Deal Pkwy (49250-9351)
P.O. Box 231 (49250-0231)
PHONE.....................517 849-8090
Steve Harding, *President*
EMP: 18 **EST:** 2000
SQ FT: 5,000
SALES (est): 1.9MM **Privately Held**
SIC: 3499 5999 Welding tips, heat resistant: metal; welding supplies

(G-9096)
NORTHERN LASER CREATIONS
6482 Moreland Rd (49250-9724)
PHONE.....................517 581-7699
Randy Francis, *Principal*
EMP: 4 **EST:** 2017
SALES (est): 75.1K **Privately Held**
SIC: 3993 Signs & advertising specialties

(G-9097)
NYLONCRAFT OF MICHIGAN LLC
1640 E Chicago Rd (49250-9110)
P.O. Box 35 (49250-0035)
PHONE.....................517 849-9911
James Krzyzewski, *President*
Glenn Scolnik, *Chairman*
Roland Erb, *Vice Pres*
Terry Rensberger, *Vice Pres*
Tom Smith, *Plant Mgr*
▲ **EMP:** 260 **EST:** 1970
SQ FT: 145,000
SALES (est): 70.7MM
SALES (corp-wide): 445.3MM **Privately Held**
WEB: www.techniplas.com
SIC: 3089 Injection molding of plastics
HQ: Tp Remainco In, Inc.
616 W Mckinley Ave
Mishawaka IN 46545
574 256-1521

(G-9098)
PELHAMS CONSTRUCTION LLC
10800 Concord Rd (49250-9635)
PHONE.....................517 549-8276
Terry R Pelham, *Mng Member*
EMP: 4 **EST:** 1999
SALES (est): 500K **Privately Held**
SIC: 1389 Gas field services

(G-9099)
QUICKMITT INC
2400 E Chicago Rd (49250-9749)
PHONE.....................517 849-2141
Scott D Smith, *President*
EMP: 4 **EST:** 1986
SALES (est): 374.5K **Privately Held**
WEB: www.quickmitt.com
SIC: 2298 Slings, rope; cordage: abaca, sisal, henequen, hemp, jute or other fiber

(G-9100)
RITZ-CRAFT CORP PA INC
Also Called: Ritz Craft Corp of Michigan
118 Deal Pkwy (49250-9351)
PHONE.....................517 849-7425
Paul Lindley, *General Mgr*
Steve Jackson, *Principal*
Paul Lindsley, *Vice Pres*
Tedd Brungard, *Production*
Paul Troutman, *Purchasing*
EMP: 101
SALES (corp-wide): 86.3MM **Privately Held**
WEB: www.ritz-craft.com
SIC: 5211 2452 Modular homes; modular homes, prefabricated, wood
PA: Ritz-Craft Corporation Of Pennsylvania, Inc.
15 Industrial Park Rd
Mifflinburg PA 17844
570 966-1053

(G-9101)
S K D L P
260 Gaige St (49250-9431)
PHONE.....................517 849-2166
Steve Orey, *Plant Mgr*
EMP: 7 **EST:** 2010
SALES (est): 127.4K **Privately Held**
WEB: www.aspensnowmasshomes.com
SIC: 3714 Motor vehicle parts & accessories

(G-9102)
SA INDUSTRIES 2 INC
651 Beck St (49250-9473)
PHONE.....................248 391-5705
Bonnie Schulz, *Branch Mgr*
EMP: 13 **Privately Held**
WEB: www.saind2.com
SIC: 3452 Screws, metal
PA: Sa Industries 2, Inc.
1081 Indianwood Rd
Lake Orion MI 48362

(G-9103)
TECHNIPLAS LLC
1640 E Chicago Rd (49250-9110)
PHONE.....................517 849-9911
EMP: 260

Jonesville - Hillsdale County (G-9104)

SALES (corp-wide): 445.3MM **Privately Held**
WEB: www.techniplas.com
SIC: **3089** Plastic processing
PA: Techniplas, Llc
N44 W33341 Wtrtown Plank
Nashotah WI 53058
262 369-5555

(G-9104)
TILLER TOOL AND DIE INC
Also Called: Versacut Industries
551 Industrial Pkwy (49250-9004)
PHONE.................................517 458-6602
Gerald T Tiller, *President*
Cyndi Tiller, *Vice Pres*
EMP: 15 EST: 1983
SALES (est): 1.3MM **Privately Held**
WEB: www.geraldprecision.com
SIC: **3544** Special dies & tools

Kalamazoo
Kalamazoo County

(G-9105)
1-800-HANSONS
6475 Technology Ave Ste E (49009-7112)
PHONE.................................269 234-1670
EMP: 6 EST: 2019
SALES (est): 166.3K **Privately Held**
WEB: www.hansons.com
SIC: **3442** Metal doors, sash & trim

(G-9106)
A D JOHNSON ENGRAVING CO INC
2129 Portage St (49001-6145)
PHONE.................................269 385-0044
EMP: 12
SQ FT: 2,000
SALES (est): 250K **Privately Held**
SIC: **7389 3446 3993 3544** Business Services Mfg Architectural Mtlwrk Mfg Signs/Ad Specialties Mfg Dies/Tools/Jigs/Fixt Platemaking Services

(G-9107)
A&S INDUSTRIES
5743 N 20th St (49004-1472)
PHONE.................................269 903-1081
Nathaniel Simmons, *Principal*
EMP: 4 EST: 2018
SALES (est): 66.7K **Privately Held**
SIC: **3999** Manufacturing industries

(G-9108)
AJM MANUFACTURING SALES INC
8731 Mountain Pine Ln (49009-4989)
PHONE.................................269 447-2087
EMP: 4 EST: 2019
SALES (est): 39.6K **Privately Held**
SIC: **3999** Manufacturing industries

(G-9109)
ALLNEX USA INC
2715 Miller Rd (49001-4138)
PHONE.................................269 385-1205
William Doukas, *Opers Mgr*
Carl Walker, *Engineer*
Dan Kersting, *Manager*
EMP: 62
SALES (corp-wide): 177.9K **Privately Held**
WEB: www.allnex.com
SIC: **2821** Acrylic resins
HQ: Allnex Usa Inc.
9005 Westside Pkwy
Alpharetta GA
800 433-2873

(G-9110)
ALLYNN CORP
7868 Douglas Ave (49009-6327)
PHONE.................................269 383-1199
Larry Loviska, *President*
Kevin Marcy, *Vice Pres*
EMP: 9 EST: 1988
SQ FT: 3,000
SALES (est): 824.3K **Privately Held**
WEB: www.allynncorp.com
SIC: **3599 7692** Machine shop, jobbing & repair; welding repair

(G-9111)
ALTERNATIVE SYSTEMS INC
5519 E Cork St Ste A (49048-8634)
PHONE.................................269 384-2008
Daniel J Olinger, *President*
Troy Butler, *Vice Pres*
Linda Olinger, *Admin Sec*
EMP: 10 EST: 1997
SQ FT: 10,000
SALES (est): 1.7MM **Privately Held**
WEB: www.alternativesysteminc.com
SIC: **3089** Plates, plastic

(G-9112)
ALUMINUM FINISHING COMPANY
615 W Ransom St (49007-3311)
PHONE.................................269 382-4010
Duane Bass, *General Mgr*
Jahan Assadi, *Principal*
EMP: 4 EST: 1987
SQ FT: 10,000
SALES (est): 295.7K **Privately Held**
WEB: www.afcanodizing.com
SIC: **3471** Electroplating of metals or formed products

(G-9113)
AMERICAN BREWERS INC
Also Called: Kalamazoo Meadery
3408 Miller Rd Ste D (49001-4111)
PHONE.................................616 318-9230
Hunter R Dodge, *President*
Thomas McGuire, *Exec Dir*
Thomas Ostrowski, *Admin Sec*
EMP: 10 EST: 2012
SALES (est): 479.5K **Privately Held**
WEB: www.americanbrewers.us
SIC: **5813 2082 2084** Bars & lounges; beer (alcoholic beverage); wines

(G-9114)
APPLE BLOSSOM WINERY LLC
Also Called: Texas Corners Brewing Company
6970 Texas Dr (49009-9795)
PHONE.................................269 668-3724
Denise Schultz, *Principal*
EMP: 7 EST: 2012
SQ FT: 200
SALES (est): 246K **Privately Held**
WEB: www.texascornersbrewing.com
SIC: **2082 2083** Malt liquors; malt

(G-9115)
APPLIED COATINGS SOLUTIONS LLC
1830 Reed Ave (49001-4049)
PHONE.................................269 341-9757
Gary Yost,
EMP: 5 EST: 1986
SALES (est): 597.9K
SALES (corp-wide): 9.7MM **Privately Held**
WEB: www.weberspecialties.com
SIC: **3479** Coating of metals & formed products
PA: Weber Specialties Company
15230 Us Highway 131 S
Schoolcraft MI 49087
269 679-5160

(G-9116)
AQUAPRINTINGCOM
410 The Dells (49048-2013)
PHONE.................................269 779-2734
Shannon Goolsby, *Principal*
EMP: 5 EST: 2016
SALES (est): 57.8K **Privately Held**
WEB: www.store.aquaprinting.com
SIC: **2752** Lithographing on metal

(G-9117)
AQUEOUS ORBITAL SYSTEMS LLC
301 N 26th St (49048-4830)
PHONE.................................269 501-7461
James D Sutton,
EMP: 7 EST: 2017
SALES (est): 741.7K **Privately Held**
WEB: www.orbitalsystems.com
SIC: **3714** Motor vehicle transmissions, drive assemblies & parts

(G-9118)
ARCHITECTURAL GLASS & MTLS INC (PA)
604 S 8th St (49009-8041)
P.O. Box 19067 (49019-0067)
PHONE.................................269 375-6165
Bob Fujawa, *President*
Robin Wendland, *Corp Secy*
Jonathan Mutual, *Vice Pres*
Loretta Gill, *Bookkeeper*
EMP: 15 EST: 1991
SQ FT: 20,000
SALES (est): 9.9MM **Privately Held**
WEB: www.agm-michigan.com
SIC: **1751 3442** Window & door (prefabricated) installation; window & door frames

(G-9119)
ARETE PRODUCTS & MFG LLC ◆
Also Called: Pinto Products & Company
2525 Miller Rd (49001-4141)
PHONE.................................269 383-0015
Kevin McNab, *Principal*
EMP: 6 EST: 2021
SALES (est): 262.9K **Privately Held**
SIC: **3599** Industrial machinery

(G-9120)
ARGYLE SOCKS LLC
3800 Winding Way (49004-3738)
PHONE.................................269 615-0097
Craig Pennings, *Principal*
EMP: 5 EST: 2012
SALES (est): 78.7K **Privately Held**
WEB: www.argylesocks.co
SIC: **2252** Socks

(G-9121)
ARK WOODWORKS LLC
2016 Lakeway Ave (49001-5124)
PHONE.................................269 364-1397
Joseph Swabash, *Principal*
EMP: 4 EST: 2017
SALES (est): 54K **Privately Held**
WEB: www.arklwc.com
SIC: **2431** Millwork

(G-9122)
ARTIGY PRINTING
5285 E Fg Ave (49004-9638)
PHONE.................................269 373-6591
Roger Jackson, *Owner*
Sean Campbell, *Manager*
Kevin Muraszewski, *Manager*
EMP: 5 EST: 1994
SQ FT: 1,750
SALES (est): 247.7K **Privately Held**
SIC: **2752** Commercial printing, offset

(G-9123)
ARVCO CONTAINER CORPORATION (PA)
Also Called: Arvco Speciality Packaging
845 Gibson St (49001-2573)
PHONE.................................269 381-0900
Joann Arvanigian, *CEO*
Greg Arvanigian, *President*
Chuck Pearson, *Regional Mgr*
Bob Ford, *Vice Pres*
John Vrbensky, *Vice Pres*
▲ EMP: 25 EST: 1971
SQ FT: 170,000
SALES (est): 63.7MM **Privately Held**
WEB: www.arvco.com
SIC: **2653** Boxes, corrugated: made from purchased materials

(G-9124)
ARVCO CONTAINER CORPORATION
Also Called: Arvan Specialty Products
845 Gibson St (49001-2573)
PHONE.................................269 381-0900
Greg Arvanigian, *Branch Mgr*
EMP: 30
SALES (corp-wide): 63.7MM **Privately Held**
WEB: www.arvco.com
SIC: **2653** Boxes, corrugated: made from purchased materials; sheets, corrugated: made from purchased materials
PA: Arvco Container Corporation
845 Gibson St
Kalamazoo MI 49001
269 381-0900

(G-9125)
ARVCO CONTAINER CORPORATION
351 Rochester Ave (49007-4932)
PHONE.................................269 381-0900
Greg Arvanigian, *Branch Mgr*
EMP: 30
SALES (corp-wide): 63.7MM **Privately Held**
WEB: www.arvco.com
SIC: **2653** Boxes, corrugated: made from purchased materials; sheets, corrugated: made from purchased materials
PA: Arvco Container Corporation
845 Gibson St
Kalamazoo MI 49001
269 381-0900

(G-9126)
ARVCO CONTAINER CORPORATION
148 Parkway Dr (49007-4900)
PHONE.................................269 381-0900
Greg Arvanigian, *President*
Sierra McNee, *Administration*
EMP: 23
SALES (corp-wide): 63.7MM **Privately Held**
WEB: www.arvco.com
SIC: **2653** Corrugated & solid fiber boxes
PA: Arvco Container Corporation
845 Gibson St
Kalamazoo MI 49001
269 381-0900

(G-9127)
AUREOGEN INC
Also Called: Aureogen Biosciences
4717 Campus Dr Ste 2300 (49008-5620)
PHONE.................................269 353-3805
Ake Elhemmer, *CEO*
Jerry Slighten, *COO*
EMP: 8 EST: 2003
SQ FT: 4,000 **Privately Held**
WEB: www.aureogen.com
SIC: **2833** Antibiotics

(G-9128)
AXONIA MEDICAL INC
4321 Roxbury Ln (49008-3314)
PHONE.................................269 615-6632
Harry C Ledebur Jr, *CEO*
EMP: 5 EST: 2011
SALES (est): 275K **Privately Held**
WEB: www.axoniamedical.com
SIC: **2836** Biological products, except diagnostic

(G-9129)
AZON USA INC (PA)
643 W Crosstown Pkwy (49008-1910)
PHONE.................................269 385-5942
David Mills, *President*
Margaret Roberts, *COO*
Matt Deittrick, *Vice Pres*
Patrick Muessig, *Vice Pres*
Steve Beck, *Production*
▲ EMP: 18
SQ FT: 18,000
SALES (est): 10.7MM **Privately Held**
WEB: www.azonintl.com
SIC: **3087 3599** Custom compound purchased resins; custom machinery

(G-9130)
AZON USA INC
2204 Ravine Rd (49004-3506)
PHONE.................................269 385-5942
Jeff Hollenbeck, *COO*
Jeff Schlabach, *Purchasing*
Alex Labus, *Marketing Mgr*
David Mills, *Branch Mgr*
EMP: 5
SALES (corp-wide): 10.7MM **Privately Held**
WEB: www.azonintl.com
SIC: **3087 3599** Custom compound purchased resins; custom machinery

▲ = Import ▼ = Export
◆ = Import/Export

GEOGRAPHIC SECTION

Kalamazoo - Kalamazoo County (G-9156)

PA: Azon Usa, Inc.
643 W Crosstown Pkwy
Kalamazoo MI 49008
269 385-5942

(G-9131)
B L HARROUN AND SON INC (PA)
1018 Staples Ave (49007-2319)
PHONE..................................269 345-8657
Carole Ritcey, *President*
Willard S Harroun, *President*
Craig Harroun, *Vice Pres*
Todd Harroun, *Treasurer*
Carole Holmes, *Admin Sec*
EMP: 20 **EST:** 1940
SQ FT: 40,000
SALES (est): 4.8MM **Privately Held**
WEB: www.blharroun.com
SIC: 3498 1711 8741 Fabricated pipe & fittings; fire sprinkler system installation; management services

(G-9132)
BECKAN INDUSTRIES INC
2700 N Pitcher St (49004-3490)
PHONE..................................269 381-6984
Graham Ouding, *President*
EMP: 27 **EST:** 1978
SALES (est): 3.8MM **Privately Held**
WEB: www.gobeckan.com
SIC: 3599 Machine shop, jobbing & repair

(G-9133)
BECKTOLD ENTERPRISES INC
Also Called: Michigan Power Cleaning
2101 Palmer Ave (49001-4129)
PHONE..................................269 349-3656
Bryon Becktold, *President*
▲ **EMP:** 5 **EST:** 1989
SQ FT: 3,500
SALES (est): 800K **Privately Held**
WEB: www.michiganpowercleaning.com
SIC: 3561 5084 Industrial pumps & parts; industrial machinery & equipment

(G-9134)
BELLS BREWERY INC
355 E Kalamazoo Ave (49007-3807)
PHONE..................................269 382-1402
Angie Bell, *Vice Pres*
Josh Vigansky, *Project Mgr*
Brita Boer, *Human Resources*
Chelsea White, *Human Resources*
Brian Duprey, *Accounts Mgr*
EMP: 7
SALES (corp-wide): 21.6MM **Privately Held**
WEB: www.bellsbeer.com
SIC: 2082 Beer (alcoholic beverage)
PA: Bell's Brewery, Inc.
8690 Krum Ave
Galesburg MI 49053
269 382-2338

(G-9135)
BENSON DISTRIBUTION INC
5792 Stoney Brook Rd (49009-7705)
PHONE..................................269 344-5529
Chris Benson, *President*
EMP: 4 **EST:** 1999
SALES (est): 302.6K **Privately Held**
SIC: 2711 Newspapers, publishing & printing

(G-9136)
BIO KLEEN PRODUCTS INC
810 Lake St (49001-3045)
PHONE..................................269 567-9400
Tim Kowalski, *President*
Tracy Hall, *Natl Sales Mgr*
▼ **EMP:** 16 **EST:** 1988
SQ FT: 15,000
SALES (est): 2.4MM **Privately Held**
WEB: www.biokleen.com
SIC: 2842 5087 Specialty cleaning preparations; service establishment equipment

(G-9137)
BKM FUELS LLC
5566 Gull Rd (49048-1017)
PHONE..................................269 342-9576
Robert Willmarth, *Principal*
EMP: 7 **EST:** 2009
SALES (est): 439.1K **Privately Held**
SIC: 2869 Fuels

(G-9138)
BLENDCO LLC
5713 Venture Park Dr (49009-1847)
PHONE..................................269 350-2914
Leigh Ann Sayen,
EMP: 12 **EST:** 2013
SALES (est): 2.5MM **Privately Held**
WEB: www.blendco-llc.com
SIC: 2047 Dog & cat food

(G-9139)
BORROUGHS LLC (PA)
3002 N Burdick St (49004-3458)
PHONE..................................269 342-0161
Tim Tyler, *President*
Jeff Vaughn, *Regional Mgr*
Zac Sweetland, *Vice Pres*
Greg Worsnop, *VP Opers*
Dale Voelz, *Engineer*
◆ **EMP:** 100 **EST:** 1987
SQ FT: 465,000
SALES (est): 65MM **Privately Held**
WEB: www.borroughs.com
SIC: 2542 Partitions & fixtures, except wood

(G-9140)
BRADEEN SPECIALTIES LLC
3450 Claxton St (49048-8611)
PHONE..................................269 349-0276
EMP: 5 **EST:** 2016
SALES (est): 130.3K **Privately Held**
WEB: www.bradeenspecialtiesllc.com
SIC: 7692 Welding repair

(G-9141)
BRITISH CNVRTNG SLTNS NRTH AME
259 E Michigan Ave # 305 (49007-3949)
PHONE..................................281 764-6651
▲ **EMP:** 24 **EST:** 2013
SQ FT: 300
SALES (est): 2.3MM
SALES (corp-wide): 16.9MM **Privately Held**
SIC: 3565 Mfg Packaging Machinery
HQ: British Converting Solutions Limited
Townsend Industrial Estate
Dunstable BEDS LU5 5
152 537-9359

(G-9142)
BUSINESS DIRECT REVIEW
Also Called: Business Review
401 S Burdick St (49007-6215)
PHONE..................................269 373-7100
Michael Castranova, *Manager*
EMP: 7
SALES (est): 115.2K **Privately Held**
WEB: www.bdwnews.com
SIC: 2721 Periodicals

(G-9143)
CALCOMCO INC (PA)
5544 S Red Pine Cir (49009-4087)
PHONE..................................313 885-9228
Edwin Frederickson, *President*
EMP: 11 **EST:** 1986
SALES (est): 12.8MM **Privately Held**
SIC: 2711 Newspapers, publishing & printing

(G-9144)
CLAUSING INDUSTRIAL INC
Also Called: Clausing Industrial Svc Ctr
3963 Emerald Dr (49001-7923)
PHONE..................................269 345-7155
Greg Chidister, *Branch Mgr*
EMP: 10
SALES (corp-wide): 24.1MM **Privately Held**
WEB: www.clausing-industrial.com
SIC: 5084 3541 3546 Machine tools & accessories; drill presses; saws & sawing machines; power-driven handtools
PA: Clausing Industrial, Inc.
3963 Emerald Dr
Kalamazoo MI 49001
269 345-7155

(G-9145)
CLAUSING INDUSTRIAL INC (PA)
Also Called: Pratt Burnerd America
3963 Emerald Dr (49001-7923)
PHONE..................................269 345-7155
Donald J Haselton, *CEO*
Paul Peters, *District Mgr*
B J Lillibridge, *Vice Pres*
Kevin F Mungovan, *Vice Pres*
Dennis W Pepper, *Vice Pres*
▲ **EMP:** 57 **EST:** 1980
SQ FT: 150,000
SALES (est): 24.1MM **Privately Held**
WEB: www.clausing-industrial.com
SIC: 5084 3541 3546 Machine tools & accessories; drill presses; saws & sawing machines; power-driven handtools

(G-9146)
CLM VIBETECH INC
Also Called: Custom Lining and Molding
7025 E K Ave (49048-6047)
PHONE..................................269 344-3878
William Money, *President*
Ralph Hubbs, *Engineer*
Jason Petracek, *Sales Staff*
EMP: 16 **EST:** 1994
SQ FT: 46,000 **Privately Held**
WEB: www.clmvibetech.com
SIC: 3541 Deburring machines

(G-9147)
COMMERCIAL INDUS A SLTIONS LLC
6830 E Michigan Ave (49048-9532)
PHONE..................................269 373-8797
EMP: 4 **EST:** 2006
SALES (est): 340K **Privately Held**
SIC: 3444 Mfg Sheet Metalwork

(G-9148)
COMMUNITY ACCESS CENTER
359 S Kalamazoo Mall # 300 (49007-4845)
PHONE..................................269 343-2211
Jerry Brown, *Chairman*
Harry Haach, *Exec Dir*
EMP: 15 **EST:** 1983
SQ FT: 5,600
SALES (est): 248.6K **Privately Held**
SIC: 4841 3663 Cable & other pay television services; studio equipment; radio & television broadcasting

(G-9149)
COMPLETE AUTOMATION CMF
4301 Manchester Rd Ste A (49001-0833)
PHONE..................................269 343-0500
Bradford Neumann, *Manager*
EMP: 5 **EST:** 2019
SALES (est): 69.9K **Privately Held**
SIC: 3471 Electroplating of metals or formed products

(G-9150)
COMPLETE METAL FINISHING INC
4301 Manchester Rd Ste A (49001-0833)
PHONE..................................269 343-0500
Ken Matheis, *President*
Partrick Greene, *Vice Pres*
EMP: 10 **EST:** 2003
SALES (est): 902.9K **Privately Held**
WEB: www.completemetalfinishing.com
SIC: 3471 Finishing, metals or formed products

(G-9151)
CONSORT CORPORATION (PA)
Also Called: Consort Display Group
2129 Portage St (49001-6145)
P.O. Box 3597 (49003-3597)
PHONE..................................269 388-4532
Roger M Lepley, *President*
Judy Little, *General Mgr*
Steven Hanson, *Mfg Staff*
Jeff Belew, *Production*
Fern Taylor, *Accountant*
EMP: 24 **EST:** 1983
SQ FT: 13,500

SALES (est): 3.4MM **Privately Held**
WEB: www.consort.com
SIC: 2399 3429 3993 2599 Banners, made from fabric; metal fasteners; signs & advertising specialties; factory furniture & fixtures

(G-9152)
CONSUMERS CONCRETE CORP
3809 E Michigan Ave (49048-2417)
P.O. Box 2229 (49003-2229)
PHONE..................................269 384-0977
Tom W Thomas, *President*
Stephen A Thomas, *Vice Pres*
Gregory Thomas, *Treasurer*
Randy Parsons, *Executive*
Donald B Thomas, *Admin Sec*
EMP: 47
SQ FT: 4,000
SALES (est): 4.3MM
SALES (corp-wide): 42.6MM **Privately Held**
WEB: www.consumersconcrete.com
SIC: 3271 3273 Blocks, concrete or cinder: standard; ready-mixed concrete
PA: Consumers Concrete Corporation
3506 Lovers Ln
Kalamazoo MI 49001
269 342-0136

(G-9153)
CONSUMERS CONCRETE CORPORATION (PA)
Also Called: Consumers Concrete Products
3506 Lovers Ln (49001-4891)
P.O. Box 2229 (49003-2229)
PHONE..................................269 342-0136
Stephen A Thomas, *President*
Steve Thomas, *President*
Tom W Thomas, *Chairman*
Donald B Thomas Jr, *Vice Pres*
Gregory A Thomas, *Vice Pres*
EMP: 21 **EST:** 1946
SQ FT: 12,000
SALES (est): 42.6MM **Privately Held**
WEB: www.consumersconcrete.com
SIC: 3273 3271 5032 Ready-mixed concrete; blocks, concrete or cinder: standard; gravel

(G-9154)
CONSUMERS CONCRETE CORPORATION
700 Nazareth Rd (49048-1100)
P.O. Box 2229 (49003-2229)
PHONE..................................269 342-5983
Ken Baker, *Manager*
EMP: 12
SALES (corp-wide): 42.6MM **Privately Held**
WEB: www.consumersconcrete.com
SIC: 3273 Ready-mixed concrete
PA: Consumers Concrete Corporation
3506 Lovers Ln
Kalamazoo MI 49001
269 342-0136

(G-9155)
COOPER FOUNDRY INC
8216 Douglas Ave (49009-5255)
PHONE..................................269 343-2808
David Hollerbach, *President*
EMP: 29 **EST:** 1942
SQ FT: 18,000
SALES (est): 2.8MM **Privately Held**
WEB: www.cooperfoundryinc.com
SIC: 3364 3363 Brass & bronze die-castings; aluminum die-castings

(G-9156)
CORNERS LIMITED (PA)
Also Called: Esto Connectors
628 S 8th St (49009-8041)
PHONE..................................269 353-8311
James J Pestoor, *President*
Grace Pestoor, *Vice Pres*
EMP: 5 **EST:** 1981
SALES (est): 1MM **Privately Held**
WEB: www.estoconnectors.com
SIC: 3496 Cages, wire; shelving, made from purchased wire

Kalamazoo - Kalamazoo County (G-9157)

(G-9157)
COXLINE INC
Also Called: Wellsaw
2829 N Burdick St (49004-3457)
PHONE...........................269 345-1132
Robert Boyle, *President*
Mary Gucma, *Principal*
Delores Boyle, *Corp Secy*
EMP: 20 **EST:** 1911
SALES (est): 3.4MM **Privately Held**
WEB: www.wellsaw.com
SIC: 3553 3444 3546 Bandsaws, woodworking; metal housings, enclosures, casings & other containers; saws & sawing equipment

(G-9158)
CREW FAMILY REST & BKY LLC
Also Called: Crew, The
3810 E Cork St (49001-4612)
PHONE...........................269 337-9800
Robert Hren,
Richard Taylor,
EMP: 9 **EST:** 2013
SALES (est): 592.6K **Privately Held**
WEB:
www.thecrewrestaurantandbakery.com
SIC: 5812 2051 Restaurant, family: independent; bread, cake & related products

(G-9159)
CUMMINS LABEL COMPANY
2230 Glendenning Rd (49001-4115)
PHONE...........................269 345-3386
Phil Nagle, *President*
Debbie Hamming, *Corp Secy*
EMP: 25 **EST:** 1972
SQ FT: 26,000
SALES (est): 2.8MM **Privately Held**
WEB: www.cumminslabel.com
SIC: 2759 2671 2672 Flexographic printing; packaging paper & plastics film, coated & laminated; coated & laminated paper

(G-9160)
CYPRESS INDUSTRIES INC
3535 Bronson Blvd (49008-2925)
PHONE...........................269 381-2160
Richard K Lee, *Manager*
EMP: 10 **EST:** 2012
SALES (est): 251.6K **Privately Held**
WEB: www.cypressindustries.com
SIC: 3999 Manufacturing industries

(G-9161)
CYTEC INDUSTRIES INC
3115 Miller Rd (49001-4103)
PHONE...........................269 349-6677
Ed Elsinore, *Branch Mgr*
EMP: 5
SALES (corp-wide): 13MM **Privately Held**
WEB: www.solvay.com
SIC: 2899 2821 2824 2672 Chemical preparations; plastics materials & resins; acrylic fibers; adhesive backed films, foams & foils; industrial inorganic chemicals; aerospace castings, aluminum
HQ: Cytec Industries Inc.
4500 Mcginnis Ferry Rd
Alpharetta GA 30005

(G-9162)
DANA
6938 Elm Valley Dr # 101 (49009-7438)
PHONE...........................419 887-3000
EMP: 21 **EST:** 2019
SALES (est): 4.9MM **Privately Held**
WEB: www.dana.com
SIC: 3714 Motor vehicle parts & accessories

(G-9163)
DANA INCORPORATED
6938 Elm Valley Dr # 101 (49009-7438)
PHONE...........................269 567-1537
Steve Byrne, *Chief Engr*
Cedomir Eterovic, *Manager*
Rob Knapp, *Administration*
Robin Knapp, *Administration*
EMP: 200 **Publicly Held**
WEB: www.dana.com
SIC: 3714 Motor vehicle parts & accessories

PA: Dana Incorporated
3939 Technology Dr
Maumee OH 43537

(G-9164)
DAVIS STEEL RULE DIE
2222 Glendenning Rd 9b (49001-4159)
PHONE...........................269 492-9908
Mike Davis, *Owner*
EMP: 5 **EST:** 2003
SALES (est): 287.8K **Privately Held**
WEB: www.davissteelruledie.com
SIC: 3544 Special dies & tools

(G-9165)
DEKOFF & SONS INC
Also Called: D & D Printing
2531 Azo Dr (49048-9540)
PHONE...........................269 344-5816
John Dekoff, *President*
John De Koff, *President*
EMP: 5 **EST:** 1970
SQ FT: 4,000
SALES (est): 499.7K **Privately Held**
WEB: www.danddprinting.com
SIC: 2752 2759 2791 Commercial printing, offset; letterpress printing; typesetting

(G-9166)
DIAGNOSTIC SYSTEMS ASSOC INC
6190 Technology Ave (49009-8179)
P.O. Box 467, Oshtemo (49077-0467)
PHONE...........................269 544-9000
Robert Mitchell, *President*
EMP: 10 **EST:** 1997
SQ FT: 10,000
SALES (est): 1.1MM **Privately Held**
WEB: www.dsa-us.com
SIC: 7549 3825 Emissions testing without repairs, automotive; engine electrical test equipment

(G-9167)
DIAMOND GRAPHICS INC
2328 Lake St (49048-3270)
PHONE...........................269 345-1164
Fax: 269 345-3026
EMP: 6 **EST:** 1975
SQ FT: 4,230
SALES (est): 540K **Privately Held**
SIC: 2796 Mfg Engraved Printing Plates

(G-9168)
DIGITAL IMPACT DESIGN INC
Also Called: Fastsigns
403 Balch St (49001-2769)
PHONE...........................269 337-4200
Steve Trottier, *President*
Dee Trottier, *Corp Secy*
EMP: 5 **EST:** 1998
SQ FT: 2,400
SALES (est): 460.6K **Privately Held**
WEB: www.fastsigns.com
SIC: 3993 Signs & advertising specialties

(G-9169)
DIMPLEX THERMAL SOLUTIONS INC (HQ)
2625 Emerald Dr (49001-4542)
PHONE...........................269 349-6800
William Bohr, *President*
Katlyn Terburg, *Partner*
Kristin Anderson, *Vice Pres*
Keith Roberts, *Vice Pres*
Randy Hastings, *Opers Mgr*
▲ **EMP:** 174 **EST:** 1988
SALES (est): 73MM
SALES (corp-wide): 3.6MM **Privately Held**
WEB: www.dimplexthermal.com
SIC: 3585 Refrigeration & heating equipment
PA: Glen Dimplex Unlimited Company
Old Airport Road
Dublin K67 V
185 234-00

(G-9170)
DISTILLED KALAMAZOO LLC
3903 Devonshire Ave (49006-2703)
PHONE...........................269 993-2859
Joanna Merrill, *Principal*
EMP: 4 **EST:** 2014

SALES (est): 195K **Privately Held**
WEB: www.kalamazoostillhouse.com
SIC: 2085 Distilled & blended liquors

(G-9171)
DMS ELECTRIC APPARATUS SERVICE
630 Gibson St (49007-4921)
P.O. Box 50644 (49005-0644)
PHONE...........................269 349-7000
Tim Fielding, *CEO*
EMP: 32
SQ FT: 35,000
SALES (est): 9.4MM **Privately Held**
SIC: 5063 7694 3599 3621 Motors, electric; electric motor repair; machine shop, jobbing & repair; motors & generators

(G-9172)
DN-LAWRENCE INDUSTRIES INC
423 Walbridge St (49007-3625)
P.O. Box 141, Plainwell (49080-0141)
PHONE...........................269 552-4999
Ruth Lovelace Murphy, *President*
Michael Lovelace, *Treasurer*
EMP: 18 **EST:** 1964
SQ FT: 12,000
SALES (est): 1.1MM **Privately Held**
SIC: 3471 Plating of metals or formed products; polishing, metals or formed products

(G-9173)
DOMER INDUSTRIES LLC
Also Called: Agio Imaging
3434 S Burdick St (49001-4836)
PHONE...........................269 226-4000
Robert Lihosit, *President*
Jonathan Rykse, *Vice Pres*
Marc Androsky, *Accounts Exec*
Jake Wakeland, *Accounts Exec*
John Capotosto, *Sales Staff*
EMP: 14 **EST:** 2001
SQ FT: 11,000
SALES (est): 2.7MM **Privately Held**
WEB: www.agioimaging.com
SIC: 2759 7336 Screen printing; commercial art & graphic design

(G-9174)
DUNKLEY INTERNATIONAL INC
1910 Lake St (49001-3274)
PHONE...........................269 343-5583
Richard L Bogard, *President*
Nick Hatzinikolis, *General Mgr*
Kami Prince, *Controller*
Dave Walton, *Finance Mgr*
EMP: 115 **EST:** 1909
SQ FT: 36,400
SALES (est): 16.3MM
SALES (corp-wide): 47.5MM **Privately Held**
WEB: www.dunkleyinternational.net
SIC: 3556 3535 Juice extractors, fruit & vegetable: commercial type; conveyors & conveying equipment
PA: Cherry Central Cooperative, Inc.
1771 N Us Highway 31 S
Traverse City MI 49685
231 946-1860

(G-9175)
ELEMENT 22 COML GROUP LLC
2425 S 11th St Ste D (49009-2113)
PHONE...........................269 910-6739
Kenneth Leonard, *Principal*
EMP: 7 **EST:** 2018
SALES (est): 630.8K **Privately Held**
SIC: 2819 Elements

(G-9176)
ELENBAAS HARDWOOD INCORPORATED
3751 Alvan Rd (49001-4652)
PHONE...........................269 343-7791
Craig Dobbs, *Manager*
EMP: 5
SALES (corp-wide): 2.6MM **Privately Held**
WEB: www.elenbaas.com
SIC: 2431 Moldings, wood: unfinished & prefinished
PA: Elenbaas Hardwood, Incorporated
2363 Port Sheldon Ct
Jenison MI 49428
616 669-3085

(G-9177)
ELITE PRCSION MCHINING TOOLING
Also Called: Elite Tooling L.L.C.
3816 Miller Rd (49001-4637)
P.O. Box 3534 (49003-3534)
PHONE...........................269 383-9714
EMP: 7
SALES (est): 1.2MM
SALES (corp-wide): 3.5MM **Privately Held**
SIC: 3541 3812 Machine Tools, Metal Cutting Type
PA: Fabx Industries, Inc.
715 Callaghan St
Greenville MI 48838
616 225-1724

(G-9178)
ELKAY INDUSTRIES INC
Also Called: Elkay Fastening Systems
1804 Reed Ave (49001-4049)
PHONE...........................269 381-4266
Shirley A Knapp, *President*
Roger Knapp, *Vice Pres*
EMP: 10 **EST:** 1968
SQ FT: 50,000
SALES (est): 804.9K **Privately Held**
WEB: www.energydc.com
SIC: 5072 3965 Miscellaneous fasteners; rivets; washers (hardware); screws; fasteners

(G-9179)
ENCORE PUBLICATIONS
117 W Cedar St Ste A (49007-5205)
PHONE...........................269 488-3143
Alexis Stubelt, *Principal*
EMP: 6 **EST:** 2019
SALES (est): 366.4K **Privately Held**
WEB: www.encorekalamazoo.com
SIC: 2741 Miscellaneous publishing

(G-9180)
ENERGY SUPPLIERS LLC
Also Called: Michigan Biofuels
2813 W Main St (49006-2901)
PHONE...........................269 342-9482
Mark Meulendyk,
EMP: 10 **EST:** 2010
SQ FT: 5,000
SALES (est): 1.6MM **Privately Held**
SIC: 3559 Refinery, chemical processing & similar machinery

(G-9181)
ENVIRODYNE TECHNOLOGIES INC
Also Called: Kalamazoo Fabricating
7574 E Michigan Ave (49048-9531)
P.O. Box 2121 (49003-2121)
PHONE...........................269 342-1918
Tim Hanna, *President*
Michael Wicks,
▲ **EMP:** 31 **EST:** 1983
SQ FT: 30,000
SALES (est): 7.7MM
SALES (corp-wide): 44.7MM **Privately Held**
WEB: www.kalfab.com
SIC: 3441 Fabricated structural metal
PA: Kalamazoo Manufacturing Corporation Global
5944 E N Ave
Kalamazoo MI 49048
269 382-8200

(G-9182)
EX SOLI LLC (PA)
3680 Stadium Park Way (49009)
PHONE...........................800 525-2431
Dan Hinkle, *President*
Jim Willard, *VP Sales*
▼ **EMP:** 7 **EST:** 2012
SALES (est): 5.3MM **Privately Held**
WEB: www.flavorsum.com
SIC: 2869 Perfumes, flavorings & food additives

(G-9183)
FABRI-KAL CORPORATION
4141 Manchester Rd (49001-1893)
PHONE...........................269 385-5050
Rick Collins, *Principal*
Tom Bush, *Vice Pres*

Kerry Rasmussen, *QC Mgr*
Rodger Gibson, *Design Engr*
Todd Rhodes, *Controller*
EMP: 12 **Publicly Held**
WEB: www.fabri-kal.com
SIC: 3089 Thermoformed finished plastic products
HQ: Fabri-Kal Llc
   600 Plastics Pl
   Kalamazoo MI 49001
   269 385-5050

(G-9184)
FERGUSON ENTERPRISES LLC
Also Called: Ferguson Waterworks
2900 Millcork St (49001-4640)
PHONE.....................269 383-1200
EMP: 5
SALES (corp-wide): 21.8B **Privately Held**
WEB: www.ferguson.com
SIC: 5074 3432 Plumbing fittings & supplies; plumbing fixture fittings & trim
HQ: Ferguson Enterprises, Llc
   12500 Jefferson Ave
   Newport News VA 23602
   757 874-7795

(G-9185)
FERNAND CORPORATION
Also Called: Comfoot Shoes
326 W Kalamazoo Ave # 105 (49007-3361)
PHONE.....................231 882-9622
Steven Fernand, *President*
EMP: 4 **EST:** 1983
SALES (est): 325.5K **Privately Held**
WEB: www.smfernand.com
SIC: 3021 Shoes, rubber or plastic molded to fabric

(G-9186)
FIBERS OF KALAMAZOO INC
436 W Willard St Ste A (49007-3369)
P.O. Box 51028 (49005-1028)
PHONE.....................269 344-3122
Robert Boyle, *CEO*
William Boyle, *President*
Buddy Peterson, *President*
Colin Raymond, *Chairman*
Mike Horton, *Vice Pres*
EMP: 40 **EST:** 1981
SQ FT: 92,600
SALES (est): 9.7MM **Privately Held**
WEB: www.fibersofkzoo.com
SIC: 2679 5113 Paper products, converted; industrial & personal service paper

(G-9187)
FLARE FITTINGS INCORPORATED
2980 Interstate Pkwy (49048-9600)
PHONE.....................269 344-7600
Bernard F Havlock, *President*
Mary Ann Havlock, *Treasurer*
▲ **EMP:** 33 **EST:** 1981
SQ FT: 18,000
SALES (est): 3.1MM **Privately Held**
WEB: www.flarefittings.net
SIC: 3364 5941 Brass & bronze die-castings; sporting goods & bicycle shops

(G-9188)
FLAVORSUM LLC (PA)
3680 Stadium Pkwy (49009-9743)
PHONE.....................800 525-2431
Brian Briggs,
EMP: 28 **EST:** 2020
SALES (est): 6MM **Privately Held**
WEB: www.flavorsum.com
SIC: 2087 Flavoring extracts & syrups

(G-9189)
FLOWSERVE US INC
2100 Factory St (49001-4161)
PHONE.....................269 381-2650
Chuck Kruzan, *General Mgr*
Tyler Harden, *District Mgr*
Cory Griffin, *Project Mgr*
Joe Parker, *Project Mgr*
Ron Klatt, *Facilities Mgr*
EMP: 250
SALES (corp-wide): 3.7B **Publicly Held**
WEB: www.flowserve.com
SIC: 3053 Gaskets, packing & sealing devices

HQ: Flowserve Us Inc.
   5215 N Ocnnor Blvd Ste 23 Connor
   Irving TX 75039
   972 443-6500

(G-9190)
FORREST COMPANY
7877 N 12th St (49009-9084)
PHONE.....................269 384-6120
Jann Forrest, *President*
EMP: 7 **EST:** 1999
SQ FT: 4,500 **Privately Held**
WEB: www.forrestcompany.com
SIC: 3544 Special dies & tools

(G-9191)
GAISHIN MANUFACTURING
330 W Mosel Ave (49004-3472)
PHONE.....................269 459-6996
EMP: 4 **EST:** 2017
SALES (est): 67.6K **Privately Held**
WEB: www.gaishinmanufacturing.com
SIC: 3999 Manufacturing industries

(G-9192)
GENCO ALLIANCE LLC
630 Gibson St (49007-4921)
PHONE.....................269 216-5500
Douglas Gipson, *CEO*
Timothy Fielding, *COO*
▲ **EMP:** 8 **EST:** 2012
SQ FT: 60,000
SALES (est): 569.7K **Privately Held**
WEB: www.gencoalliance.com
SIC: 5063 3621 3441 7629 Electrical apparatus & equipment; motors & generators; fabricated structural metal; electrical repair shops

(G-9193)
GENERAL MILLS INC
6805 Beatrice Dr (49009-9559)
PHONE.....................763 764-7600
Steve Pearcowski, *Branch Mgr*
EMP: 4
SALES (corp-wide): 18.1B **Publicly Held**
WEB: www.generalmills.com
SIC: 2043 Cereal breakfast foods
PA: General Mills, Inc.
   1 General Mills Blvd
   Minneapolis MN 55426
   763 764-7600

(G-9194)
GENERAL MILLS INC
3800 Midlink Dr (49048-8802)
PHONE.....................269 337-0288
Edith Tuddel, *Manager*
Mekhi Stribling, *Associate*
EMP: 15
SALES (corp-wide): 18.1B **Publicly Held**
WEB: www.generalmills.com
SIC: 5143 2041 4225 Yogurt; flour mixes; general warehousing & storage
PA: General Mills, Inc.
   1 General Mills Blvd
   Minneapolis MN 55426
   763 764-7600

(G-9195)
GENX CORPORATION
2911 Emerald Dr (49001-4530)
PHONE.....................269 341-4242
Russ Ureel, *President*
EMP: 4 **EST:** 2009
SALES (est): 392.3K **Privately Held**
WEB: www.genxcomparators.com
SIC: 3827 Optical comparators

(G-9196)
GILLIGAN STEELE TASTINGS LLC
432 E Paterson St (49007-2599)
PHONE.....................269 808-3455
EMP: 6 **EST:** 2019
SALES (est): 611.5K **Privately Held**
SIC: 2082 Malt beverages

(G-9197)
GINGER TREE PRESS
3609 Olney Rd (49006-2835)
PHONE.....................269 779-5780
Anna Tomlonson, *Principal*
EMP: 4 **EST:** 2010
SALES (est): 67.1K **Privately Held**
SIC: 2741 Miscellaneous publishing

(G-9198)
GLASSMASTER CONTROLS CO INC
831 Cobb Ave (49007-2444)
PHONE.....................269 382-2010
Steven Trewhella, *President*
Wayne Nicolen, *General Mgr*
Michael Geschwendt, *Purch Mgr*
Brandon Dasher, *Engineer*
Alan Comensoli, *Controller*
▲ **EMP:** 45 **EST:** 1988
SQ FT: 90,000
SALES (est): 8.4MM
SALES (corp-wide): 136.3MM **Privately Held**
WEB: www.gcontrols.com
SIC: 3496 3812 3714 3672 Miscellaneous fabricated wire products; search & navigation equipment; motor vehicle parts & accessories; printed circuit boards; relays & industrial controls; nonferrous wire-drawing & insulating
PA: Oak Ridge Industries, Inc.
   10896 Industrial Pkwy Nw
   Bolivar OH 44612
   330 874-2900

(G-9199)
GRAND TRAVERSE DIST TASTING RM
224 E Michigan Ave (49007-3973)
PHONE.....................269 254-8113
EMP: 4 **EST:** 2018
SALES (est): 120.1K **Privately Held**
WEB: www.grandtraversedistillery.com
SIC: 2085 Distilled & blended liquors

(G-9200)
GRAPHIC PACKAGING INTL LLC
1421 N Pitcher St (49007-2579)
PHONE.....................269 343-6104
Gary Leeman, *Branch Mgr*
Randy Tiesman, *Manager*
Carol Sulka, *Supervisor*
EMP: 5 **Publicly Held**
WEB: www.graphicpkg.com
SIC: 5199 2657 Packaging materials; folding paperboard boxes
HQ: Graphic Packaging International, Llc
   1500 Riveredge Pkwy # 100
   Atlanta GA 30328

(G-9201)
GRAPHICS & PRINTING CO INC
5356 N Riverview Dr (49004-1543)
PHONE.....................269 381-1482
Gayle Bullard, *President*
Larry Bullard, *Admin Sec*
EMP: 6 **EST:** 1986
SQ FT: 3,000
SALES (est): 411.4K **Privately Held**
SIC: 2752 Commercial printing, offset

(G-9202)
GREEN BAY PACKAGING INC
Kalamazoo Container Division
5350 E N Ave (49048-9776)
P.O. Box 3007 (49003-3007)
PHONE.....................269 552-1000
Dean Murphy, *General Mgr*
Loren Smith, *Human Res Mgr*
Jankowski Brenda, *Relations*
EMP: 140
SALES (corp-wide): 1.8B **Privately Held**
WEB: www.gbpcoated.com
SIC: 2653 3412 Boxes, corrugated: made from purchased materials; metal barrels, drums & pails
PA: Green Bay Packaging Inc.
   1700 N Webster Ave
   Green Bay WI 54302
   920 433-5111

(G-9203)
GREEN DOOR DISTILLING CO LLC
429 E North St (49007-3506)
PHONE.....................269 207-2298
Josh Cook, *Principal*
EMP: 12 **EST:** 2016
SALES (est): 728.5K **Privately Held**
WEB: www.greendoordistilling.com
SIC: 2085 Distilled & blended liquors

(G-9204)
GREEN LINK INC
5519 E Cork St Ste A (49048-8634)
PHONE.....................269 216-9229
Phillip Georgeau, *CEO*
EMP: 10 **EST:** 2016
SALES (est): 2.1MM **Privately Held**
WEB: www.greenlinkengineering.com
SIC: 2952 Roofing materials

(G-9205)
GREG SOCHA
Also Called: Redline Manufacturing
5611 King Hwy (49048-5931)
PHONE.....................269 344-1204
Greg Socha, *Owner*
EMP: 20 **EST:** 1993
SALES (est): 1.2MM **Privately Held**
SIC: 3599 Machine shop, jobbing & repair

(G-9206)
GSB & ASSOCIATES INC
3680 Stadium Pkwy (49009-9743)
PHONE.....................770 424-1886
Corinne Baskin Buday, *CEO*
Paula Lawson, *Controller*
Ann Woolley, *Human Res Dir*
Jo Ivey, *Cust Mgr*
EMP: 9 **EST:** 1984
SALES (est): 2.4MM
SALES (corp-wide): 5.3MM **Privately Held**
WEB: www.flavorsum.com
SIC: 8742 2087 Business consultant; extracts, flavoring
PA: Ex. Soli, Llc
   3680 Stadium Park Way
   Kalamazoo MI 49009
   800 525-2431

(G-9207)
HAMMOND MACHINERY INC
1600 Douglas Ave (49007-1630)
PHONE.....................269 345-7151
Robert E Hammond, *President*
EMP: 78 **EST:** 1881
SQ FT: 145,000
SALES (est): 14.4MM
SALES (corp-wide): 29.8MM **Privately Held**
WEB: www.hammondroto.com
SIC: 3541 3564 3291 Deburring machines; grinding machines, metalworking; buffing & polishing machines; robots for drilling, cutting, grinding, polishing, etc.; dust or fume collecting equipment, industrial; abrasive products
PA: The Kalamazoo Company
   1600 Douglas Ave
   Kalamazoo MI 49007
   269 345-7151

(G-9208)
HAPMAN
5944 E N Ave (49048-9776)
PHONE.....................269 382-8257
Ned Thompson, *Owner*
Jeffrey Flees, *Engineer*
Dan Haugh, *Manager*
Lois Standley, *Admin Asst*
EMP: 17 **EST:** 2014
SALES (est): 4MM **Privately Held**
WEB: www.hapman.com
SIC: 3535 Conveyors & conveying equipment

(G-9209)
HARRISON PACKING CO INC (PA)
3420 Stadium Pkwy (49009-6767)
PHONE.....................269 381-3837
Rush Harrison, *President*
Bradley Harrison, *Admin Sec*
EMP: 13 **EST:** 1945
SQ FT: 40,000
SALES (est): 4MM **Privately Held**
WEB: www.harrisonpacking.com
SIC: 2035 Pickles, vinegar; vegetables, pickled

(G-9210)
HECO INC (PA)
Also Called: Hatfield Elc Indus Apprtus Rep
3509 S Burdick St (49001-4835)
PHONE.....................269 381-7200
Terrell Lee Hatfield, *Ch of Bd*

Mark S Hatfield, *President*
Joyce Hatfield, *Principal*
Kathy Bishop, *Vice Pres*
Brad S Hatfield, *Vice Pres*
EMP: 39 **EST:** 1959
SQ FT: 80,000
SALES (est) 27.9MM **Privately Held**
WEB: www.hecoinc.com
SIC: 5063 7694 3699 3677 Motors, electric; armature rewinding shops; electric motor repair; electrical equipment & supplies; electronic coils, transformers & other inductors; motors & generators; scales & balances, except laboratory

(G-9211)
HELION INDUSTRIES LLC
9860 Stadium Dr (49009-7941)
PHONE 618 303-0214
Kevin Johnson, *Administration*
EMP: 4 **EST:** 2016
SALES (est) 64.5K **Privately Held**
WEB: www.helionindustries.com
SIC: 3999 Manufacturing industries

(G-9212)
HELIOS SOLAR LLC
248 W Michigan Ave (49007-3735)
PHONE 269 343-5581
Connor Field, *CEO*
Samuel Field, *CFO*
EMP: 4 **EST:** 2009 **Privately Held**
WEB: www.helios-solar.com
SIC: 8711 3674 Engineering services; solar cells

(G-9213)
HERALD NEWSPAPERS COMPANY INC
Also Called: Kalamazoo Gazette
6825 Beatrice Dr Ste C (49009-7263)
PHONE 269 345-3511
Jim Stephanak, *Manager*
EMP: 6
SALES (corp-wide) 2.8B **Privately Held**
WEB: www.advancemediany.com
SIC: 2711 Newspapers, publishing & printing
HQ: The Herald Newspapers Company Inc
220 S Warren St
Syracuse NY 13202
315 470-0011

(G-9214)
HERALD NEWSPAPERS COMPANY INC
Also Called: Kalamazoo Gazette
401 S Burdick St (49007-6215)
PHONE 269 388-8501
EMP: 100
SALES (corp-wide) 2B **Privately Held**
SIC: 2711 Newspapers-Publishing/Printing
HQ: The Herald Newspapers Company Inc
1 Clinton Sq
Syracuse NY 13202
315 470-0011

(G-9215)
HERCULES LLC
5325 Autumn Glen St (49009-8184)
P.O. Box 118 (49004-0118)
PHONE 269 388-8676
John Prevost, *Branch Mgr*
EMP: 4
SALES (corp-wide) 2.3B **Publicly Held**
WEB: www.hercules.com
SIC: 2869 2899 Chemical warfare gases: phosgene, mustard gas, tear gas; chemical preparations
HQ: Hercules Llc
500 Hercules Rd
Wilmington DE 19808
302 594-5000

(G-9216)
HERITAGE GUITAR INC
225 Parsons St Ste 286 (49007-3593)
PHONE 269 385-5721
J P Moats, *President*
Daniel Struve, *Opers Mgr*
Bill Paige, *Treasurer*
James Deurloo, *Shareholder*
Marvin Lamb, *Shareholder*
EMP: 17 **EST:** 1985
SQ FT: 22,000
SALES (est) 2.2MM **Privately Held**
WEB: www.heritageguitars.com
SIC: 3931 5736 Fretted instruments & parts; guitars & parts, electric & nonelectric; mandolins & parts; banjos & parts; musical instrument stores

(G-9217)
HIBISKUS BIOPHARMA INC
4717 Campus Dr Ste 100 (49008-5602)
PHONE 616 234-2841
Andre Bachmann, *President*
Michael Purring, *Treasurer*
Marquicia Pierce, *Manager*
EMP: 4 **EST:** 2017
SALES (est) 1.8MM
SALES (corp-wide) 13.2MM **Publicly Held**
WEB: www.zymergen.com
SIC: 2834 Pharmaceutical preparations
HQ: Lodo Therapeutics Corporation
430 E 29th St Ste 625
New York NY 10016
646 828-5990

(G-9218)
HIGH GRADE MATERIALS COMPANY
2700 E Cork St (49001-4648)
PHONE 269 349-8222
Wyatt Brown, *Executive*
EMP: 9
SALES (corp-wide) 17.2MM **Privately Held**
WEB: www.highgradematerials.com
SIC: 3273 Ready-mixed concrete
PA: High Grade Materials Company
9266 Snows Lake Rd
Greenville MI 48838
616 754-5545

(G-9219)
HYCORR LLC
3654 Midlink Dr (49048-8806)
PHONE 269 381-6349
Robert Shafer, *President*
Lance Head, *Director*
EMP: 11 **EST:** 2012
SALES (est) 763.9K **Privately Held**
WEB: www.hycorr.com
SIC: 3554 7336 Paper mill machinery: plating, slitting, waxing, etc.; graphic arts & related design

(G-9220)
HYDRO EXTRUSION NORTH AMER LLC
Sapa Kalamazoo
5575 N Riverview Dr (49004-1547)
PHONE 269 349-6626
Samone Harper, *Safety Mgr*
Sat Adufumill, *Manager*
EMP: 300
SALES (corp-wide) 16.1B **Privately Held**
SIC: 3354 3444 Aluminum extruded products; sheet metalwork
HQ: Hydro Extrusion North America, Llc
6250 N River Rd
Rosemont IL 60018
877 710-7272

(G-9221)
IDEA MNP COM LLC
505 E Kalamazoo Ave (49007-3873)
PHONE 269 459-8955
EMP: 4 **EST:** 2016
SALES (est) 145.5K **Privately Held**
WEB: www.idealedsigns.com
SIC: 3993 Signs & advertising specialties

(G-9222)
IDEA SIGNS VISUALLY
1110 Engleman Ave (49048-1717)
PHONE 269 779-9163
EMP: 4 **EST:** 2016
SALES (est) 55.7K **Privately Held**
WEB: www.idealedsigns.com
SIC: 3993 Signs & advertising specialties

(G-9223)
INITIAL ATTRACTION
3021 Oakland Dr Ste A (49008-5904)
PHONE 269 341-4444
Bree Bennett, *Owner*
EMP: 6 **EST:** 2004

SALES (est) 341K **Privately Held**
WEB: www.shopinitialattraction.com
SIC: 2395 Embroidery products, except schiffli machine

(G-9224)
INTERKAL LLC (DH)
5981 E Cork St (49048-9638)
P.O. Box 2107 (49003-2107)
PHONE 269 349-1521
Brian Ellis, *Traffic Mgr*
Phil Miller, *Opers Staff*
Bob Mihelich, *Purch Mgr*
Lisa M Miniat, *Buyer*
Lisa Miniat, *Buyer*
◆ **EMP:** 149 **EST:** 1958
SQ FT: 190,000
SALES (est) 18.6MM **Privately Held**
WEB: www.interkal.com
SIC: 2531 Stadium seating
HQ: Kotocorp (Usa), Inc.
5981 E Cork St
Kalamazoo MI 49048
269 349-1521

(G-9225)
INTERSRCE RECOVERY SYSTEMS INC (PA)
1470 S 8th St (49009-9327)
PHONE 269 375-5100
William D Nemedi, *President*
Robert J Nemedi, *Treasurer*
EMP: 25 **EST:** 1985
SALES (est) 2.8MM **Privately Held**
WEB: www.inter-source.com
SIC: 3569 3535 Lubricating equipment; unit handling conveying systems

(G-9226)
INVITATIONS BY DESIGN
223 S Kalamazoo Mall (49007-4812)
PHONE 269 342-8551
Patrica Hirsch, *Mng Member*
EMP: 4 **EST:** 2004
SALES (est) 267.7K **Privately Held**
WEB: www.invitationbydesign.net
SIC: 2759 Invitation & stationery printing & engraving

(G-9227)
J B M TECHNOLOGY
4155 S 9th St (49009-8120)
PHONE 269 344-5716
James Creamer, *President*
EMP: 7 **EST:** 2000
SALES (est) 134.6K **Privately Held**
WEB: www.jbmtech.biz
SIC: 2759 Screen printing

(G-9228)
J STERLING INDUSTRIES LLC
6825 Beatrice Dr Ste A (49009-7263)
PHONE 269 492-6922
David Van Slingerland, *CEO*
Erik Humes, *General Mgr*
Tara Vandestreek, *Accounts Mgr*
Libni Cano, *Manager*
EMP: 15 **EST:** 2008
SQ FT: 30,000
SALES (est) 6.5MM **Privately Held**
WEB: www.sterlingindustries.com
SIC: 3841 Medical instruments & equipment, blood & bone work

(G-9229)
J STERLING INDUSTRIES LTD
6825 Beatrice Dr (49009-7263)
PHONE 269 492-6920
Erik Humes, *Opers Mgr*
Jeremy Schumann, *Branch Mgr*
EMP: 8
SALES (corp-wide) 590.1K **Privately Held**
WEB: www.sterlingindustries.com
SIC: 3841 Surgical & medical instruments
PA: J. Sterling Industries Ltd
295 Connie Cres Unit 1
Concord ON L4K 5
905 264-6657

(G-9230)
JBT BOTTLING LLC
8322 Waterwood Dr (49048-4832)
PHONE 269 377-4905
Nelson H Tansey, *President*
EMP: 7 **EST:** 2015

SALES (est) 389.6K **Privately Held**
WEB: www.jbtbottling.com
SIC: 2086 Bottled & canned soft drinks

(G-9231)
JIRGENS MODERN TOOL CORP
3536 Gembrit Cir (49001-4616)
PHONE 269 381-5588
Maija Jirgens, *President*
EMP: 10 **EST:** 1975
SQ FT: 10,000
SALES (est) 717K **Privately Held**
SIC: 3544 Special dies & tools

(G-9232)
JK MACHINING INC
5955 W D Ave (49009-9012)
PHONE 269 344-0870
Henry Kalkman, *President*
Mitch Willis, *Manager*
EMP: 16 **EST:** 1980
SQ FT: 6,125 **Privately Held**
WEB: www.jkmachining.com
SIC: 3089 Injection molding of plastics

(G-9233)
JOHN L HINKLE HOLDING CO INC
1206 E Crosstown Pkwy (49001-2563)
P.O. Box 2153 (49003-2153)
PHONE 269 344-3640
John Hinkle, *President*
◆ **EMP:** 41 **EST:** 1941
SQ FT: 10,000
SALES (est) 3.3MM **Privately Held**
SIC: 2087 Extracts, flavoring

(G-9234)
KAISER ALUMINUM CORPORATION
5205 Midlink Dr (49048-9648)
PHONE 269 488-0957
Charles Eyster, *Buyer*
Karena Pulver, *Associate*
EMP: 7
SALES (corp-wide) 1.1B **Publicly Held**
WEB: www.kaiseraluminum.com
SIC: 3354 Aluminum extruded products
PA: Kaiser Aluminum Corporation
27422 Portola Pkwy # 350
Foothill Ranch CA 92610
949 614-1740

(G-9235)
KAISER ALUMINUM FAB PDTS LLC
5205 Kaiser Dr (49048-8804)
PHONE 269 250-8400
Jeffrey Gurney, *Production*
EMP: 7
SALES (corp-wide) 1.1B **Publicly Held**
WEB: www.kaiseraluminum.com
SIC: 3334 3353 3354 Primary aluminum; aluminum sheet, plate & foil; aluminum rod & bar
HQ: Kaiser Aluminum Fabricated Products, Llc
27422 Portola Pkwy # 200
Foothill Ranch CA 92610

(G-9236)
KALAMAZOO CANDLE COMPANY
5111 E MI Ave Ste A15 (49048-8581)
PHONE 269 532-9816
Amy Bobo, *Manager*
Adam McFarlin,
EMP: 10 **EST:** 2018
SALES (est) 792.5K **Privately Held**
SIC: 3999 Candles

(G-9237)
KALAMAZOO COMPANY (PA)
Also Called: Hammound Roto-Finish
1600 Douglas Ave (49007-1630)
PHONE 269 345-7151
Robert E Hammond, *President*
Brenda Long, *General Mgr*
Dean Frantz, *Vice Pres*
Susan Sweerin, *Safety Mgr*
Adrian Iurea, *Engineer*
EMP: 50 **EST:** 1987
SQ FT: 115,000

GEOGRAPHIC SECTION
Kalamazoo - Kalamazoo County (G-9265)

SALES (est): 29.8MM Privately Held
WEB: www.hammondroto.com
SIC: 3541 5085 3291 Deburring machines; grinding machines, metalworking; buffing & polishing machines; robots for drilling, cutting, grinding, polishing, etc.; abrasives; abrasive products

(G-9238)
KALAMAZOO ELECTRIC MOTOR INC
414 Mills St (49001-2529)
PHONE.................................269 345-7802
Kristen Salvesen, President
Rick Curtis, Manager
EMP: 5 EST: 1949
SQ FT: 5,880
SALES (est): 568.9K Privately Held
WEB: www.kalamazooelectricmotor.com
SIC: 5999 5251 7694 5063 Motors, electric; hardware; tools, hand; electric motor repair; motors, electric

(G-9239)
KALAMAZOO ENGRG & MFG LLC
2525 Miller Rd (49001-4141)
PHONE.................................269 569-5205
George Philopoulos,
EMP: 8 EST: 2020
SALES (est): 840K Privately Held
SIC: 3545 Gauges (machine tool accessories)

(G-9240)
KALAMAZOO HOLDINGS INC (PA)
Also Called: Kalazack
3713 W Main St (49006-2842)
P.O. Box 50511 (49005-0511)
PHONE.................................269 349-9711
George Todd, President
Paul Todd, Chairman
Gary Hainrihar, Vice Pres
Braden Rhoda, Production
William Faro, Engineer
◆ EMP: 4 EST: 1979
SQ FT: 85,000
SALES (est): 128MM Privately Held
WEB: www.kzoo.edu
SIC: 2099 Spices, including grinding

(G-9241)
KALAMAZOO MECHANICAL INC
Also Called: Honeywell Authorized Dealer
5507 E Cork St (49048-9668)
PHONE.................................269 343-5351
Irving Cornish, President
Carson Cornish, Vice Pres
EMP: 19 EST: 1984
SQ FT: 6,500
SALES (est): 8.9MM Privately Held
WEB: www.kalamazoomechanical.com
SIC: 1711 3444 1761 Warm air heating & air conditioning contractor; sheet metalwork; sheet metalwork

(G-9242)
KALAMAZOO METAL FINISHERS INC
2019 Glendenning Rd (49001-4112)
P.O. Box 2650 (49003-2650)
PHONE.................................269 382-1611
Lisa Halliday, CEO
Richard Halliday, President
Michael Smith, Opers Staff
EMP: 15 EST: 1982
SQ FT: 22,000
SALES (est): 2.2MM Privately Held
WEB: www.kmfi.com
SIC: 3471 Electroplating of metals or formed products

(G-9243)
KALAMAZOO MFG CORP GLOBL (PA)
Also Called: Hatman
5944 E N Ave (49048-9776)
P.O. Box 2121 (49003-2121)
PHONE.................................269 382-8200
Edward Thompson, President
Carl Baker, Plant Mgr
Jennifer Woods, Mfg Spvr
Robert W Klinge, CFO
Teresa Phillips, Sales Staff

EMP: 128 EST: 2003
SALES (est): 44.7MM Privately Held
SIC: 3535 5084 Conveyors & conveying equipment; industrial machinery & equipment

(G-9244)
KALAMAZOO ORTHOTICS & DBTC
Also Called: Corey's Bootery
1016 E Cork St (49001-4823)
PHONE.................................269 349-2247
James F Bloomfield III, President
Kim Brust, Office Mgr
EMP: 10 EST: 2004
SQ FT: 1,200
WEB: www.coreysbootery.com
SIC: 3143 5139 5661 Orthopedic shoes, men's; shoes; custom & orthopedic shoes

(G-9245)
KALAMAZOO PHOTO COMP SVCS
Also Called: Kpc Graphics
701 Commerce Ln (49004-1128)
P.O. Box 614, Richland (49083-0614)
PHONE.................................269 345-3706
Judy Appelgren, President
EMP: 5 EST: 1961
SQ FT: 6,600
SALES (est): 354.1K Privately Held
WEB: www.universalphoto.net
SIC: 2791 7336 2796 Typesetting; graphic arts & related design; platemaking services

(G-9246)
KALAMAZOO PRTG & PROMOTIONS
533 Whitcomb St (49008-2389)
PHONE.................................269 818-1122
EMP: 4 EST: 2018
SALES (est): 83.9K Privately Held
WEB: www.frontdoorpromotions.com
SIC: 2752 Commercial printing, lithographic

(G-9247)
KALAMAZOO REGALIA INC
728 W Michigan Ave (49007-4538)
PHONE.................................269 344-4299
James Bellinger, President
Terry Squires, Manager
EMP: 14 EST: 1995
SQ FT: 10,000
SALES (est): 837.4K Privately Held
WEB: www.freemasonsusa.com
SIC: 2389 2396 Regalia; automotive & apparel trimmings

(G-9248)
KALAMAZOO SPORTSWEAR INC
728 W Michigan Ave (49007-4538)
PHONE.................................269 344-4242
Jim Bellinger, President
EMP: 21 EST: 1986
SQ FT: 10,000
SALES (est): 2.3MM Privately Held
WEB: www.wmuonline.com
SIC: 2759 Screen printing

(G-9249)
KALAMAZOO STILLHOUSE
618 E Michigan Ave (49007-4914)
PHONE.................................269 352-0250
EMP: 4 EST: 2016
SALES (est): 221.6K Privately Held
WEB: www.kalamazoostillhouse.com
SIC: 2085 Distilled & blended liquors

(G-9250)
KALSEC INC (HQ)
3713 W Main St (49006-2842)
P.O. Box 50511 (49005-0511)
PHONE.................................269 349-9711
Scott M Nykaza, President
Phil Schlein, Managing Dir
James Smith, Managing Dir
Scott Hunter, Vice Pres
Joanne Martz, Vice Pres
◆ EMP: 4 EST: 1958
SQ FT: 80,000

SALES (est): 128MM Privately Held
WEB: www.kalsec.com
SIC: 2099 2087 Spices, including grinding; flavoring extracts & syrups
PA: Kalamazoo Holdings Inc
    3713 W Main St
    Kalamazoo MI 49006
    269 349-9711

(G-9251)
KAMPS INC
1122 E Crosstown Pkwy (49001-2512)
PHONE.................................269 342-8113
Daniel De Verries, Principal
EMP: 23
SALES (corp-wide): 1.7B Privately Held
WEB: www.kampspallets.com
SIC: 2448 Pallets, wood
HQ: Kamps, Inc.
    2900 Peach Ridge Ave Nw
    Grand Rapids MI 49534
    616 453-9676

(G-9252)
KB PROPERTY HOLDINGS LLC ✪
5955 W D Ave (49009-9012)
PHONE.................................269 344-0870
Henry Kalkman
EMP: 20 EST: 2021
SALES (est): 1MM Privately Held
SIC: 3999 Manufacturing industries

(G-9253)
KENNEDY GAME CALLS LLC
8375 W C Ave (49009-8825)
PHONE.................................269 870-5001
Mike Pelletier, Principal
EMP: 4 EST: 2011
SALES (est): 68.5K Privately Held
WEB: www.kennedygamecalls.com
SIC: 3949 Game calls

(G-9254)
KEYSTONE MANUFACTURING LLC
6387 Technology Ave Ste B (49009-8193)
PHONE.................................269 343-4108
Jason Barr, General Mgr
Michael Meinke, Engineer
Len Stoehr, Project Engr
Kathy Hambright, Finance
Jim Medsker,
▲ EMP: 16 EST: 2007
SALES (est): 3.1MM Privately Held
WEB: www.keystone-pd.com
SIC: 3841 Surgical & medical instruments

(G-9255)
KOTOCORP (USA) INC (DH)
5981 E Cork St (49048-9609)
PHONE.................................269 349-1521
Mike Amemiya, President
◆ EMP: 1 EST: 1997
SALES (est): 18.6MM Privately Held
WEB: www.kotobuki-seating.co.jp
SIC: 2531 Stadium seating

(G-9256)
KRAFTBRAU BREWERY INC
402 E Kalamazoo Ave (49007-3810)
PHONE.................................269 384-0288
James Quinn, President
EMP: 6 EST: 1996
SALES (est): 347.3K Privately Held
SIC: 2082 Malt beverages

(G-9257)
LAKE MICHIGAN MAILERS INC (PA)
Also Called: Marana Group
3777 Sky King Blvd (49009-6953)
P.O. Box 19157 (49019-0157)
PHONE.................................269 383-9333
Robert J Rhoa, CEO
Karen Rhoa, Ch of Bd
David Rhoa, President
Marti Lillie, Vice Pres
Marti Veld, Plant Mgr
EMP: 54 EST: 1975
SQ FT: 23,800

SALES (est): 8.5MM Privately Held
WEB: www.barcodemail.com
SIC: 7331 4783 2752 7336 Mailing service; packing goods for shipping; commercial printing, lithographic; promotional printing, lithographic; commercial art & graphic design

(G-9258)
LAPINE METAL PRODUCTS INC
5232 Azo Ct (49048-8560)
P.O. Box 68439, Grand Rapids (49516-8439)
PHONE.................................269 388-5900
Craig Lapine, President
Nathaniel P Burkett, Vice Pres
EMP: 15
SQ FT: 40,000
SALES (est): 1.9MM Privately Held
WEB: www.lapinemetalproducts.com
SIC: 3498 Coils, pipe: fabricated from purchased pipe

(G-9259)
LAWTON RIDGE WINERY LLC
8456 Stadium Dr (49009-9481)
PHONE.................................269 372-9463
Haltom Crick, Owner
Haltom Cricks, Owner
EMP: 4 EST: 2008
SALES (est): 267.6K Privately Held
WEB: www.lawtonridgewinery.com
SIC: 2084 Wines

(G-9260)
LEE-COBB COMPANY
415 W Maple St (49001-3642)
PHONE.................................269 553-0873
Willie Cobb, Partner
Sang Ae Lee-Cobb, Partner
▲ EMP: 4 EST: 1996
SQ FT: 7,000
SALES (est): 374.5K Privately Held
WEB: www.leecobbleathercoat.com
SIC: 2386 Coats & jackets, leather & sheep-lined; hats & caps, leather; garments, leather; pants, leather

(G-9261)
LMM GROUP INC
443 E D Ave (49009-6312)
PHONE.................................269 276-9909
Michael Laughlin, Principal
EMP: 7 EST: 1999
SQ FT: 10,000
SALES (est): 738.9K Privately Held
WEB: www.lmmgroupinc.com
SIC: 3599 Machine shop, jobbing & repair

(G-9262)
M & A MACHINING INC
1523 N Burdick St (49007-2597)
PHONE.................................269 342-0026
Alexander Pinto, President
EMP: 13 EST: 1974
SQ FT: 7,000
SALES (est): 553.3K Privately Held
SIC: 3599 Machine shop, jobbing & repair

(G-9263)
MACKENZIES BAKERY (PA)
1319 Grand Ave (49006-3265)
PHONE.................................269 343-8440
EMP: 40
SALES (est): 3.1MM Privately Held
SIC: 5461 2051 Retail Bakery Mfg Bread/Related Products

(G-9264)
MALL CITY ALUMINUM INC
850 E Crosstown Pkwy (49001-2506)
PHONE.................................269 349-5088
Robert Grosser, President
Maxine Grosser, Vice Pres
EMP: 7 EST: 1987
SQ FT: 15,000
SALES (est): 588.1K Privately Held
WEB: www.starcitymall.com
SIC: 3365 Aluminum & aluminum-based alloy castings

(G-9265)
MANN + HUMMEL USA INC
3411 Ctr Park Plz (49048)
PHONE.................................248 857-8501
Michael Ternes, Vice Pres

(PA)=Parent Co (HQ)=Headquarters (DH)=Div Headquarters
✪ = New Business established in last 2 years

2022 Harris Michigan Industrial Directory

Kalamazoo - Kalamazoo County (G-9266) GEOGRAPHIC SECTION

EMP: 30
SALES (corp-wide): 4.6B **Privately Held**
SIC: 3089 3714 Injection molding of plastics; motor vehicle parts & accessories
HQ: Mann + Hummel Usa, Inc.
6400 S Sprinkle Rd
Portage MI 49002
269 329-3900

(G-9266)
MC NALLY ELEVATOR COMPANY (PA)
223 W Ransom St (49007-3635)
PHONE.....................269 381-1860
Joseph Mc Nally, *President*
Mary C Mc Nally, *Corp Secy*
Ryan McNally, *Vice Pres*
EMP: 18 EST: 1955
SQ FT: 10,000
SALES (est): 2.7MM **Privately Held**
WEB: www.mcnallyelevator.com
SIC: 1796 7699 3534 Elevator installation & conversion; elevators: inspection, service & repair; elevators & equipment

(G-9267)
MCC KALAMAZOO INC (HQ)
Also Called: Mall City Containers, Inc.
2710 N Pitcher St (49004-3490)
P.O. Box 69 (49004-0069)
PHONE.....................269 381-2706
Gary Koster, *President*
Jeff Corstange, *Production*
EMP: 49 EST: 1974
SQ FT: 120,000
SALES (est): 15.2MM
SALES (corp-wide): 24.2MM **Privately Held**
WEB: www.mccpkg.com
SIC: 2653 Boxes, corrugated: made from purchased materials; pads, corrugated: made from purchased materials; display items, corrugated: made from purchased materials; hampers, corrugated: made from purchased materials
PA: Opus Packaging Group, Inc.
6995 Southbelt Dr Se
Caledonia MI 49316
616 871-5200

(G-9268)
MEGEE PRINTING INC
Also Called: Megee Print Document Solutions
509 Mills St (49001-2530)
PHONE.....................269 344-3226
Roger Megee, *President*
EMP: 13 EST: 1985
SQ FT: 15,000
SALES (est): 608.9K **Privately Held**
SIC: 2752 7334 Commercial printing, offset; photocopying & duplicating services

(G-9269)
MICHIGAN BIODIESEL LLC
2813 W Main St (49006-2901)
PHONE.....................269 427-0804
John Oakley,
EMP: 8 EST: 2007
SALES (est): 651.7K **Privately Held**
WEB: www.mibiodiesel.com
SIC: 2079 Soybean oil, refined: not made in soybean oil mills

(G-9270)
MICRO PRECISION MOLDS INC
3915 Ravine Rd (49006-1452)
PHONE.....................269 344-2044
William Longjohn, *President*
Tom Berglund Jr, *President*
Jack Buck, *Vice Pres*
EMP: 22 EST: 1994
SQ FT: 7,000
SALES (est): 796.7K **Privately Held**
SIC: 3544 Industrial molds

(G-9271)
MIDWEST CUSTOM EMBROIDERY CO
621 E North St (49007-3536)
PHONE.....................269 381-7660
Marshall Pallett, *President*
David Davies, *Treasurer*
EMP: 8 EST: 1974
SQ FT: 2,400
SALES (est): 1.1MM **Privately Held**
WEB: www.midwest-embroidery.com
SIC: 2395 Embroidery products, except schiffli machine; embroidery & art needlework

(G-9272)
MILLER ENERGY INC
277 S Rose St Ste 3300 (49007-4722)
P.O. Box 632, Traverse City (49685-0632)
PHONE.....................269 352-5960
C John Miller, *CEO*
Michael J Miller, *President*
Jim Carl, *Corp Secy*
Bret Friend, *VP Opers*
Drew Martin, *Finance*
EMP: 15 EST: 1984
SALES (est): 1.9MM **Privately Held**
WEB: www.miller-energy.com
SIC: 1382 Oil & gas exploration services

(G-9273)
MITTEN FRUIT COMPANY LLC
Also Called: Mitten Fruit Company, The
3680 Stadium Pkwy (49009-9743)
PHONE.....................269 585-8541
Daniel C Hinkle,
EMP: 4 EST: 2014
SALES (est): 348.4K **Privately Held**
SIC: 2033 Fruit juices: fresh

(G-9274)
MODERN NEON SIGN CO INC
1219 E Vine St (49001-3197)
PHONE.....................269 349-8636
Oliver Laclair, *President*
Oliver La Clair, *President*
Mary Ann La Clair, *Vice Pres*
Pamela De Young, *Admin Sec*
EMP: 11 EST: 1946
SQ FT: 10,000
SALES (est): 511.1K **Privately Held**
WEB: www.signshowworld.com
SIC: 1799 3993 Sign installation & maintenance; neon signs

(G-9275)
MOORE INGREDIENTS LTD
1717 Douglas Ave (49007-1600)
PHONE.....................513 881-7144
EMP: 5 EST: 2014
SALES (est): 112.6K **Privately Held**
WEB: www.moorelab.com
SIC: 2087 Flavoring extracts & syrups

(G-9276)
MOPHIE LLC
Also Called: Mstation
6244 Technology Ave (49009-8113)
PHONE.....................269 743-1340
Daniel Huang, *CEO*
▲ EMP: 256 EST: 2006
SALES (est): 37.3MM
SALES (corp-wide): 521.9MM **Privately Held**
WEB: www.zagg.com
SIC: 3692 4812 8999 Primary batteries, dry & wet; cellular telephone services; communication services
HQ: Mophie Inc.
15495 Sand Canyon Ave # 400
Irvine CA 92618
888 866-7443

(G-9277)
MRC INDUSTRIES
1606 S Burdick St (49001-2712)
PHONE.....................269 552-5586
EMP: 7 EST: 2019
SALES (est): 261K **Privately Held**
WEB: www.mrcindustries.org
SIC: 3999 Manufacturing industries

(G-9278)
MRC INDUSTRIES INC (PA)
2538 S 26th St (49048-9610)
PHONE.....................269 343-0747
Christine Zeigler, *CEO*
Christine Zeigler, *CEO*
Breanna Kroeg, *Human Resources*
Melanie Meinema, *Case Mgr*
Karen Baldwin, *Director*
EMP: 50 EST: 1950
SQ FT: 21,000
SALES: 3.7MM **Privately Held**
WEB: www.mrcindustries.org
SIC: 8331 2653 2631 Vocational rehabilitation agency; corrugated & solid fiber boxes; paperboard mills

(G-9279)
MY PRINT WORKS MI
509 Mills St (49001-2530)
PHONE.....................269 344-3226
EMP: 6 EST: 2018
SALES (est): 459.8K **Privately Held**
SIC: 2752 Commercial printing, lithographic

(G-9280)
NATIONAL PRODUCT CO
1206 E Crosstown Pkwy (49001-2563)
P.O. Box 2153 (49003-2153)
PHONE.....................269 344-3640
John Polzin, *Principal*
EMP: 16 EST: 2013
SALES (est): 641.7K **Privately Held**
WEB: www.flavorsum.com
SIC: 2087 Extracts, flavoring

(G-9281)
NEWCRAFT CABINETRY
700 1/2 Hatfield Ave (49001-3280)
PHONE.....................269 220-5440
EMP: 6 EST: 2017
SALES (est): 139.9K **Privately Held**
SIC: 2434 Wood kitchen cabinets

(G-9282)
O I K INDUSTRIES INC
7882 Douglas Ave (49009-6327)
P.O. Box 67 (49004-0067)
PHONE.....................269 382-1210
Dennis J Scheffers, *President*
David Scheffers, *Vice Pres*
Tim Scheffers, *Vice Pres*
EMP: 27 EST: 1962
SQ FT: 22,600
SALES (est): 5.1MM **Privately Held**
WEB: www.oikindustries.com
SIC: 3446 Architectural metalwork

(G-9283)
OPUS PACKAGING - KALAMAZOO LLC ◆
2710 N Pitcher St (49004-3490)
PHONE.....................800 643-6721
Louis F Sicilia, *Mng Member*
EMP: 6 EST: 2021
SALES (est): 90.7K **Privately Held**
SIC: 2653 Boxes, corrugated: made from purchased materials

(G-9284)
PACKAGING CORPORATION AMERICA
Also Called: PCA
809 Harrison St (49007-3567)
PHONE.....................269 567-7340
EMP: 5
SALES (corp-wide): 6.6B **Publicly Held**
WEB: www.packagingcorp.com
SIC: 2653 Boxes, corrugated: made from purchased materials
PA: Packaging Corporation Of America
1 N Field Ct
Lake Forest IL 60045
847 482-3000

(G-9285)
PANOPLATE LITHOGRAPHICS INC
101 N Riverview Dr (49004-1397)
PHONE.....................269 343-4644
Bob Cox, *President*
EMP: 5 EST: 1976
SQ FT: 7,800
SALES (est): 328.4K **Privately Held**
WEB: www.panoplate.com
SIC: 2796 3952 Lithographic plates, positives or negatives; lead pencils & art goods

(G-9286)
PARAMONT MACHINE CO LLC
2810 N Burdick St (49004-3637)
PHONE.....................330 339-3489
EMP: 7 EST: 2015
SALES (est): 542K **Privately Held**
WEB: www.pmcplastic.com
SIC: 3599 Machine shop, jobbing & repair

(G-9287)
PARKER HSD
2220 Palmer Ave (49001-4122)
PHONE.....................269 384-3915
Kyle Oberlee, *Principal*
Nicole Obriecht, *Engineer*
David Vanvels, *Engineer*
Darryl Watkins, *Engineer*
Chad Vliek, *Program Mgr*
EMP: 10 EST: 2014
SALES (est): 553.2K **Privately Held**
SIC: 3594 Fluid power pumps & motors

(G-9288)
PARKER-HANNIFIN CORPORATION
Hydraulic Systems Division
2220 Palmer Ave (49001-4122)
PHONE.....................269 384-3459
Nicole Obriecht, *Project Mgr*
Sean Sharkey, *Materials Mgr*
Keith Jensen, *Senior Buyer*
Brent Cravens, *Buyer*
Terri Ferus, *Buyer*
EMP: 450
SALES (corp-wide): 13.7B **Publicly Held**
WEB: www.parker.com
SIC: 3728 3812 3769 3625 Aircraft parts & equipment; search & navigation equipment; guided missile & space vehicle parts & auxiliary equipment; relays & industrial controls; fluid power pumps & motors; fluid power cylinders & actuators
PA: Parker-Hannifin Corporation
6035 Parkland Blvd
Cleveland OH 44124
216 896-3000

(G-9289)
PARKER-HANNIFIN CORPORATION
Parker Abex
2220 Palmer Ave (49001-4122)
PHONE.....................269 384-3400
Kory Thomas, *Program Mgr*
Bill Cartmill, *Manager*
Amy Brailey, *Manager*
Chad Newcomb, *Manager*
EMP: 6
SALES (corp-wide): 13.7B **Publicly Held**
WEB: www.parker.com
SIC: 3728 Aircraft parts & equipment
PA: Parker-Hannifin Corporation
6035 Parkland Blvd
Cleveland OH 44124
216 896-3000

(G-9290)
PAW ENTERPRISES LLC
Also Called: P.A.w Hardwood Flooring & Sups
3308 Covington Rd Ste 1 (49001-1801)
PHONE.....................269 329-1865
Edward R Westfall III, *Principal*
EMP: 10 EST: 2010
SALES (est): 1.3MM **Privately Held**
WEB: www.paw-enterprises.com
SIC: 2426 Flooring, hardwood

(G-9291)
PEPSI-COLA METRO BTLG CO INC
2725 E Kilgore Rd (49001-0840)
PHONE.....................269 226-6400
Jacob Peterson, *Warehouse Mgr*
John Hoffman, *Manager*
Dave Vander, *Manager*
EMP: 6
SALES (corp-wide): 70.3B **Publicly Held**
WEB: www.pepsico.com
SIC: 2086 Carbonated soft drinks, bottled & canned
HQ: Pepsi-Cola Metropolitan Bottling Company, Inc.
1111 Westchester Ave
White Plains NY 10604
914 767-6000

(G-9292)
PFIZER INC
7171 Portage Rd (49001-0100)
PHONE.....................269 833-5143

GEOGRAPHIC SECTION

Kalamazoo - Kalamazoo County (G-9318)

Robert Miller, *Engineer*
Jim Taylor, *Engineer*
Julie Harpenau, *Human Res Dir*
Sandy Cobine, *Branch Mgr*
Caren Madsen, *Manager*
EMP: 4
SALES (corp-wide): 41.9B **Publicly Held**
WEB: www.pfizer.com
SIC: 2834 Pharmaceutical preparations
PA: Pfizer Inc.
235 E 42nd St Rm 107
New York NY 10017
212 733-2323

(G-9293)
PFIZER INC
7000 Portage Rd (49001-0103)
PHONE 269 833-2358
Nancy Walsh-Sayles, *General Mgr*
Lisa Dunne, *Regional Mgr*
Andrew Muratore, *Counsel*
Teresa Griesing, *Vice Pres*
Erik Meader, *Vice Pres*
EMP: 146
SALES (corp-wide): 41.9B **Publicly Held**
WEB: www.pfizer.com
SIC: 2834 Pharmaceutical preparations
PA: Pfizer Inc.
235 E 42nd St Rm 107
New York NY 10017
212 733-2323

(G-9294)
PHARMACIA & UPJOHN COMPANY LLC
7000 Portage Rd (49001-0199)
PHONE 908 901-8000
Philip Carra, *Branch Mgr*
Lidia Fonseca, *Senior Mgr*
EMP: 54
SALES (corp-wide): 41.9B **Publicly Held**
SIC: 8743 2834 2833 Public relations & publicity; pharmaceutical preparations; organic medicinal chemicals: bulk, uncompounded
HQ: Pharmacia & Upjohn Company Llc
100 Rte 206 N
Peapack NJ 07977
908 901-8000

(G-9295)
PICWOOD USA LLC
Also Called: Picwood USA
2002 Charles Ave (49048-2072)
P.O. Box 50762 (49005-0762)
PHONE 844 802-1599
Thomas Dockham, *President*
EMP: 4 **EST:** 2012
SALES (est): 272.4K **Privately Held**
WEB: www.picwoodusa.com
SIC: 2511 Chairs, bentwood

(G-9296)
PINTO PRODUCTS INC
2525 Miller Rd (49001-4141)
PHONE 269 383-0015
Matthew Pinto, *CEO*
David Pinto, *President*
Cathy Pinto, *Technology*
EMP: 7 **EST:** 1994
SQ FT: 24,000
SALES (est): 1.1MM **Privately Held**
WEB: www.pintoproducts.com
SIC: 3829 Aircraft & motor vehicle measurement equipment; gauging instruments, thickness ultrasonic

(G-9297)
PIPE FABRICATORS INC
1018 Staples Ave (49007-2319)
PHONE 269 345-8657
Willard Harroun, *President*
Craig Harroun, *Vice Pres*
EMP: 7 **EST:** 1940
SQ FT: 6,000
SALES (est): 2.3MM
SALES (corp-wide): 4.8MM **Privately Held**
WEB: www.blharroun.com
SIC: 3498 7692 Fabricated pipe & fittings; welding repair
PA: B L Harroun And Son, Inc.
1018 Staples Ave
Kalamazoo MI 49007
269 345-8657

(G-9298)
PORTAGE PAPER CO INC
401 E Alcott St (49001-6170)
P.O. Box 2048 (49003-2048)
PHONE 616 345-7131
Fernand D Fournier, *President*
Michael Brenn, *General Mgr*
Tom Dardares, *Vice Pres*
Yves Lafontaine, *VP Opers*
Julie Decarr, *Controller*
▼ **EMP:** 120 **EST:** 1992
SQ FT: 905,000
SALES (est): 12.4MM **Privately Held**
SIC: 2621 Paper mills; kraft paper

(G-9299)
PRAB INC (HQ)
Also Called: Prab and Hapman
5801 E N Ave (49048-8702)
P.O. Box 2121 (49003-2121)
PHONE 269 382-8200
Edward Thompson, *Ch of Bd*
David B Fisher, *President*
Dale Steinfeld, *Plant Mgr*
Jim Hileski, *Engineer*
Jason Nichols, *Engineer*
▲ **EMP:** 172 **EST:** 1961
SALES (est): 35.9MM
SALES (corp-wide): 44.7MM **Privately Held**
SIC: 3535 5084 Conveyors & conveying equipment; industrial machinery & equipment
PA: Kalamazoo Manufacturing Corporation Global
5944 E N Ave
Kalamazoo MI 49048
269 382-8200

(G-9300)
PRAB INC
5801 E N Ave (49048-8702)
PHONE 269 382-8200
EMP: 7
SALES (corp-wide): 44.7MM **Privately Held**
SIC: 3535 Conveyors & conveying equipment
HQ: Prab, Inc.
5801 E N Ave
Kalamazoo MI 49048
269 382-8200

(G-9301)
PRAB INC
Hapman Conveyors
5944 E N Ave (49048-9776)
P.O. Box 2121 (49003-2121)
PHONE 269 343-1675
Greg Patterson, *Vice Pres*
Bob Anspaugh, *Engineer*
Kim Wood, *Credit Staff*
Allison Wendt, *Human Resources*
Tim Kamrowski, *Cust Mgr*
EMP: 7
SALES (corp-wide): 44.7MM **Privately Held**
SIC: 3535 Conveyors & conveying equipment
HQ: Prab, Inc.
5801 E N Ave
Kalamazoo MI 49048
269 382-8200

(G-9302)
PRECISION DIAL CO
7240 W KI Ave (49009-7993)
P.O. Box 306, Oshtemo (49077-0306)
PHONE 269 375-5601
Myrna Babushka, *President*
Myrna Babuska, *President*
Robert Babuska, *Vice Pres*
EMP: 8
SQ FT: 3,600
SALES (est): 590K **Privately Held**
WEB: www.precisiondial.com
SIC: 2759 Screen printing

(G-9303)
PRECISION HEAT TREATING CO
660 Gull Rd (49007-3565)
P.O. Box 50326 (49005-0326)
PHONE 269 382-4660
Mary Jeanne Juzwiak, *President*
Donald Juzwiak, *Vice Pres*
EMP: 17 **EST:** 1948
SQ FT: 16,000
SALES (est): 1.6MM **Privately Held**
WEB: www.precisionheat.net
SIC: 3398 Metal heat treating

(G-9304)
PRECISION METALS PLUS INC
7574 E Mich Ave Kalamazoo (49048)
P.O. Box 678, Richland (49083-0678)
PHONE 269 342-6330
Jeremy Brooks, *President*
Jerome Brooks, *Manager*
EMP: 8 **EST:** 2003
SQ FT: 9,000
SALES (est): 1.2MM **Privately Held**
WEB: www.precisionmetalsplus.com
SIC: 3441 Fabricated structural metal

(G-9305)
PRECISION POLYMER MFG INC
3915 Ravine Rd (49006-1452)
PHONE 269 344-2044
William Longjohn, *President*
Tom Berglund, *Vice Pres*
Jack Buck, *Vice Pres*
Clyde Lancaster, *QC Mgr*
▲ **EMP:** 40 **EST:** 1987
SALES (est): 8.4MM **Privately Held**
WEB: www.ppmanufacturing.com
SIC: 3089 3429 7692 3229 Injection molding of plastics; aircraft hardware; welding repair; pressed & blown glass

(G-9306)
PREMIERE TOOL & DIE CAST
6146 W Main St Ste C (49009-4047)
PHONE 269 782-3030
EMP: 6 **EST:** 2019
SALES (est): 352K **Privately Held**
SIC: 3369 Nonferrous foundries

(G-9307)
PRESSBURG LLC
6526 N 2nd St (49009-8814)
PHONE 269 873-0775
Veronika Husovska, *President*
EMP: 5 **EST:** 2014
SALES (est): 129.6K **Privately Held**
SIC: 2893 Printing ink

(G-9308)
PRINTMILL INC
4001 Portage St (49001-4912)
PHONE 269 382-0428
William Schley, *President*
Steve Chapman, *President*
EMP: 6 **EST:** 1983
SQ FT: 1,100
SALES (est): 689.5K **Privately Held**
WEB: www.printmill.com
SIC: 2752 Commercial printing, offset

(G-9309)
PURE PULP PRODUCTS INC
600 Plastics Pl (49001-4882)
PHONE 269 385-5050
Richard H Young, *President*
Michael Roader, *Chairman*
Tyler Sheerer, *Admin Sec*
EMP: 1040 **EST:** 2009
SQ FT: 60,000
SALES (est): 3.4MM
SALES (corp-wide): 64.5MM **Privately Held**
SIC: 2621 Wrapping & packaging papers
PA: Two Mitts, Inc.
600 Plastics Pl
Kalamazoo MI 49001
800 888-5054

(G-9310)
QUALITY PRECAST INC
Also Called: Qpi Precast and Supply
7800 Adobe (49009-5002)
PHONE 269 342-0539
Jeff Schierbeek, *President*
Dan Schierbeek, *Vice Pres*
EMP: 20 **EST:** 2004
SALES (est): 1.6MM **Privately Held**
WEB: www.qualityprecastinc.com
SIC: 3272 Precast terrazo or concrete products

(G-9311)
QUALITY PRECAST CON PDTS LLC
3815 N Westnedge Ave (49004-3450)
PHONE 269 342-0539
Jeff Schierbeek, *President*
Dan Schierbeek, *Vice Pres*
Todd Currier,
EMP: 5 **EST:** 1970
SQ FT: 3,300
SALES (est): 920.2K **Privately Held**
WEB: www.qualityprecastinc.com
SIC: 3272 Concrete products, precast

(G-9312)
R CHAMBERLIN WOODWORKING
229 Woodward Ave (49007-3221)
PHONE 269 377-7232
EMP: 5 **EST:** 2018
SALES (est): 54.1K **Privately Held**
WEB: www.rchamberlinwoodworking.com
SIC: 2431 Millwork

(G-9313)
R H & COMPANY INC
Also Called: Spirit Shoppe
4510 W Kl Ave (49006-5725)
PHONE 269 345-7814
Richard Scheffers, *President*
Heather Scheffers, *Treasurer*
EMP: 10 **EST:** 1996
SQ FT: 3,000
SALES (est): 1MM **Privately Held**
WEB: www.kalamazoospiritshoppe.com
SIC: 5699 5947 5136 2396 Sports apparel; gift shop; sportswear, men's & boys'; screen printing on fabric articles; embroidering of advertising on shirts, etc.

(G-9314)
R JS PRINTING INC
1001 2nd St (49001-2537)
PHONE 773 936-7825
EMP: 6 **EST:** 2017
SALES (est): 586.9K **Privately Held**
WEB: www.rjsprinting.com
SIC: 2752 Commercial printing, offset

(G-9315)
RFC WOODWORKS
1003 Jenks Blvd (49006-2195)
PHONE 810 357-9072
Robert Caswell, *Principal*
EMP: 5 **EST:** 2019
SALES (est): 106.5K **Privately Held**
SIC: 2431 Millwork

(G-9316)
RICHARD-ALLAN SCIENTIFIC CO (DH)
4481 Campus Dr (49008-2590)
PHONE 269 544-5600
John Marotta, *CEO*
◆ **EMP:** 100 **EST:** 1995
SQ FT: 120,000
SALES (est): 24.6MM **Publicly Held**
WEB: www.epredia.com
SIC: 3826 Analytical instruments
HQ: Epredia
20 Post Rd
Portsmouth NH 03801
603 431-8410

(G-9317)
RIEDEL USA INC
2625 Emerald Dr (49001-4542)
PHONE 734 595-9820
EMP: 12 **EST:** 2010
SALES (est): 122.2K **Privately Held**
WEB: www.dimplexthermal.com
SIC: 3585 Air conditioning units, complete: domestic or industrial; air conditioning condensers & condensing units; condensers, refrigeration

(G-9318)
RIEDEL USA INC
2315 Cambridge Dr (49001-4536)
PHONE 734 595-9820
Sean O Driscoll, *Ch of Bd*
Bernhard Wieck, *Vice Pres*
Wolftang Todt, *Director*
▲ **EMP:** 4 **EST:** 2003

Kalamazoo - Kalamazoo County (G-9319) GEOGRAPHIC SECTION

SALES (est): 811.2K
SALES (corp-wide): 3.6MM **Privately Held**
WEB: www.dimplexthermal.com
SIC: 3585 Refrigeration & heating equipment
PA: Glen Dimplex Unlimited Company
Old Airport Road
Dublin K67 V
185 234-00

(G-9319)
RITSEMA PRCISION MACHINING INC
3221 Redmond Ave (49001-4828)
PHONE..................................269 344-8882
Joel Ritsema, *President*
Kris Ritsema, *Treasurer*
Fred Ritsema, *Shareholder*
EMP: 4 EST: 1967
SQ FT: 12,000
SALES (est): 392.6K **Privately Held**
SIC: 3599 Machine shop, jobbing & repair

(G-9320)
RIVER RUN PRESS INC
Also Called: Economy Printing
600 Shoppers Ln (49004-1195)
PHONE..................................269 349-7603
Alfred Higdon, *President*
John Arnsman, *Purchasing*
Jennifer Higdon, *Treasurer*
Ed Ramage, *Accounts Mgr*
John Campbell, *Manager*
EMP: 32 EST: 1979
SQ FT: 9,600
SALES (est): 4.5MM **Privately Held**
WEB: www.riverrunpress.com
SIC: 2752 2791 2789 2759 Commercial printing, offset; typesetting; bookbinding & related work; commercial printing

(G-9321)
ROOT SPRING SCRAPER CO
527 W North St (49007-2494)
PHONE..................................269 382-2025
Frederick Root Jr, *President*
William Root, *Corp Secy*
Rodney Root, *Vice Pres*
Mary Root, *CFO*
Tim Rayman, *Manager*
▼ EMP: 37 EST: 1891
SQ FT: 57,000
SALES (est): 2.3MM **Privately Held**
WEB: www.rootsnowplows.com
SIC: 3531 3524 Snow plow attachments; scrapers (construction machinery); lawn & garden equipment

(G-9322)
RUSSELL FARMS INC
5616 N Riverview Dr (49004-1548)
PHONE..................................269 349-6120
Gail Russell, *President*
Rickard Russell, *Vice Pres*
EMP: 4 EST: 1967
SALES (est): 150K **Privately Held**
SIC: 3111 2499 Hides: tanning, currying & finishing; food handling & processing products, wood

(G-9323)
RWL SIGN CO LLC
Also Called: R Wl Sign Co
6185 W Kl Ave (49009-8060)
PHONE..................................269 372-3629
Jason Hadley, *Project Mgr*
Robert Leet, *Mng Member*
EMP: 7 EST: 2004
SALES (est): 1.5MM **Privately Held**
WEB: www.rwlsign.com
SIC: 3993 Electric signs

(G-9324)
RX OPTICAL LABORATORIES INC (PA)
1825 S Park St (49001-2762)
PHONE..................................269 342-5958
Edward J Fletcher, *CEO*
Stephan J Jepson, *President*
David Vandyke, *Opers Staff*
Steve Yonke, *CFO*
Joni Lapointe, *Controller*
EMP: 55 EST: 1947
SQ FT: 12,000
SALES (est): 36.9MM **Privately Held**
WEB: www.rxoptical.com
SIC: 5995 5048 3851 Opticians; ophthalmic goods; ophthalmic goods

(G-9325)
RX OPTICAL LABORATORIES INC
5349 W Main St Ofc (49009-1007)
PHONE..................................269 349-7627
Stacey Parsons, *Manager*
EMP: 4
SALES (corp-wide): 36.9MM **Privately Held**
WEB: www.rxoptical.com
SIC: 5995 3851 Opticians; ophthalmic goods
PA: Rx Optical Laboratories, Inc.
1825 S Park St
Kalamazoo MI 49001
269 342-5958

(G-9326)
S & C INDUSTRIES INC
Also Called: Oakes Carton Company
5575 Collingwood Ave (49004-1598)
PHONE..................................269 381-6022
James L Oakes, *President*
EMP: 37 EST: 1949
SQ FT: 30,000
SALES (est): 3.7MM **Privately Held**
WEB: www.oakescarton.com
SIC: 2653 Boxes, corrugated: made from purchased materials

(G-9327)
SALES DRIVEN LTD LIABILITY CO
Also Called: Raybend
2723 Kersten Ct (49048-9301)
PHONE..................................269 254-8497
Joseph Mauro, *President*
Dagne Clark, *Controller*
Matthew Martz, *Manager*
◆ EMP: 30 EST: 2013
SQ FT: 22,500
SALES (est): 3.8MM **Privately Held**
WEB: www.raybend.com
SIC: 3561 Pumps & pumping equipment

(G-9328)
SALESPAGE TECHNOLOGIES LLC (PA)
600 E Michigan Ave # 103 (49007-4906)
P.O. Box 2707 (49003-2707)
PHONE..................................269 567-7400
Melissa Jobe, *President*
Jason Meyle, *Project Mgr*
Beek Vande, *Project Mgr*
Rick Bailey, *Engineer*
Amy Avis, *Controller*
EMP: 30 EST: 1981
SQ FT: 11,500
SALES (est): 8.4MM **Privately Held**
WEB: www.salespage.com
SIC: 7372 Business oriented computer software

(G-9329)
SCHAWK INC (PA)
2325 N Burdick St (49007-1876)
PHONE..................................269 381-3820
Mike Bartusch, *President*
Gregory Youdell, *Supervisor*
Cindy Campbell, *Admin Dir*
Stephanie Orr, *Account Dir*
EMP: 112 EST: 2014
SALES (est): 1.1MM **Privately Held**
WEB: www.schawk.com
SIC: 2796 Platemaking services

(G-9330)
SELECT PRODUCTS LIMITED
Also Called: Select Hinges
3258 Stadium Dr (49008-1527)
PHONE..................................269 323-4433
Robert Cronk, *Vice Pres*
Ken Loffredi, *Regl Sales Mgr*
Aaron McElrath, *Regl Sales Mgr*
Chris Orme, *Regl Sales Mgr*
Kimberly Payne, *Sales Staff*
EMP: 44 EST: 1990
SALES (est): 5.3MM **Privately Held**
WEB: www.select-hinges.com
SIC: 3429 Door opening & closing devices, except electrical; furniture builders' & other household hardware

(G-9331)
SERENDIPITY WOODS
7175 Vail Dr (49009-3949)
PHONE..................................269 217-8197
Pam Selkirk, *Principal*
EMP: 6 EST: 2015
SALES (est): 276.8K **Privately Held**
WEB: www.serendipitywoods.com
SIC: 2511 Wood household furniture

(G-9332)
SHIELDS & SHIELDS ENTERPRISES
Also Called: Sign Shop, The
4302 S Westnedge Ave (49008-3227)
PHONE..................................269 345-7744
William Shields, *President*
Susan Shields, *President*
Lori Abramson, *Associate*
Andrea Harris-Peguese, *Associate*
EMP: 4 EST: 1989
SALES (est): 487.7K **Privately Held**
WEB: www.thesignshopkalamazoo.com
SIC: 3993 5999 Signs & advertising specialties; banners

(G-9333)
SIGMA MACHINE INC
3358 Center Park Pl (49048-8646)
PHONE..................................269 806-5679
Jim Van Weelden, *President*
Jim L Van Weelden, *Corp Secy*
Kurt Hinkley, *Vice Pres*
Juan Arciniega, *VP Mfg*
Kathryn Fontanilla, *Analyst*
EMP: 100 EST: 1974
SQ FT: 100,000
SALES (est): 16.4MM **Privately Held**
WEB: www.sigmamachine.net
SIC: 3451 Screw machine products

(G-9334)
SIGN ART INC (PA)
5757 E Cork St (49048-9668)
PHONE..................................269 381-3012
Michael P Williams, *President*
EMP: 48 EST: 1971
SQ FT: 47,550
SALES (est): 8.2MM **Privately Held**
WEB: www.signartinc.com
SIC: 3993 Electric signs

(G-9335)
SIGN CENTER OF KALAMAZOO INC
711 Portage St (49001-2566)
PHONE..................................269 381-6869
Robert M Cook, *President*
EMP: 6 EST: 1983
SQ FT: 2,500
SALES (est): 344K **Privately Held**
WEB: www.signcenter.net
SIC: 3993 7336 Signs & advertising specialties; commercial art & graphic design

(G-9336)
SIGN CITY INC
7178 Stadium Dr (49009-9423)
PHONE..................................269 375-1385
Steve Ellis, *President*
EMP: 7 EST: 1982
SQ FT: 6,000 **Privately Held**
SIC: 3993 Signs & advertising specialties

(G-9337)
SIGN IMPRESSIONS INC
3929 Ravine Rd (49006-1452)
PHONE..................................269 382-5152
Paul Havenaar, *President*
Kim Havenaar, *Vice Pres*
Trevor Lehoczky, *Graphic Designe*
EMP: 5 EST: 1985
SQ FT: 5,280
SALES (est): 375K **Privately Held**
WEB: www.signimpressionsinc.com
SIC: 7336 3993 7389 Silk screen design; signs & advertising specialties; lettering service

(G-9338)
SIGN ON INC
Also Called: Sign Center
711 Portage St (49001-2566)
PHONE..................................269 381-6869
Ryan Talcott, *Principal*
EMP: 8 EST: 2011
SALES (est): 879.9K **Privately Held**
WEB: www.signcenter.net
SIC: 3993 Signs & advertising specialties

(G-9339)
SOUTHWEST MICH INNOVATION CTR
4717 Campus Dr Ste 100 (49008-5602)
PHONE..................................269 353-1823
Robert H Dewit, *President*
Doug Morton, *Manager*
Melissa Farley, *Director*
EMP: 4 EST: 2004
SALES: 2.9MM **Privately Held**
SIC: 3821 Incubators, laboratory

(G-9340)
SPECIALTY BUSINESS FORMS INC
Also Called: Sbf Enterprises
815 E Crosstown Pkwy (49001-2505)
P.O. Box 50049 (49005-0049)
PHONE..................................269 345-0828
Daniel Sherman, *President*
Kenneth L Sherman, *President*
Caroline Sherman, *Treasurer*
Sean Gray, *Cust Mgr*
EMP: 4 EST: 1973
SQ FT: 6,600 **Privately Held**
WEB: www.sbfenterprises.com
SIC: 2752 Commercial printing, offset

(G-9341)
SPECILTY ADHESIVES COATING INC
3334 N Pitcher St (49004-3494)
PHONE..................................269 345-3801
Mark Cox, *General Mgr*
EMP: 8
SALES (corp-wide): 49.5MM **Privately Held**
WEB: www.specialtyadhesivesinc.com
SIC: 2891 Adhesives
PA: Specialty Adhesives & Coating, Inc.
3791 Air Park St
Memphis TN 38118
800 728-9171

(G-9342)
SPICER HEAVY AXLE & BRAKE INC
6938 Elm Valley Dr (49009-7436)
P.O. Box 4097 (49003-4097)
PHONE..................................269 567-1000
Doug Rader, *President*
▲ EMP: 1 EST: 1998
SALES (est): 7.2MM **Publicly Held**
SIC: 3714 Motor vehicle parts & accessories
HQ: Dana Commercial Vehicle Products, Llc
3939 Technology Dr
Maumee OH 43537

(G-9343)
SPOTLIGHT MEDIA LLC
1704 Whites Rd (49008-2840)
PHONE..................................269 808-4473
Jeffrey Ryder, *Principal*
EMP: 6 EST: 2016
SALES (est): 102.2K **Privately Held**
WEB: www.spotlightmedia.com
SIC: 3648 Spotlights

(G-9344)
STURAK BROTHERS INC
2450 S Sprinkle Rd (49001-4624)
PHONE..................................269 345-2929
EMP: 8
SALES (est): 677.7K **Privately Held**
SIC: 1382 Oil/Gas Exploration Services

(G-9345)
SUMMIT POLYMERS INC
5858 E N Ave (49048-9776)
PHONE..................................269 324-9330
Daniel Brown, *Manager*
EMP: 275

▲ = Import ▼ = Export
◆ = Import/Export

GEOGRAPHIC SECTION

Kalamazoo - Kalamazoo County (G-9373)

SALES (corp-wide): 590MM **Privately Held**
WEB: www.summitpolymers.com
SIC: 3089 Injection molding of plastics
PA: Summit Polymers, Inc.
6715 S Sprinkle Rd
Portage MI 49002
269 324-9330

(G-9346)
SUNSET ENTERPRISES INC (PA)
Also Called: The Signwriter
633 W Michigan Ave (49007-3715)
PHONE..............................269 373-6440
Mark W Wrench, *President*
Melissa J Wrench, *Vice Pres*
Amy Livingston, *Electrical Engi*
EMP: 10 EST: 1991
SALES (est): 951.1K **Privately Held**
WEB: www.signwriterkzoo.com
SIC: 3993 Signs & advertising specialties

(G-9347)
SUPERIOR EQUIPMENT LLC
7008 E N Ave (49048-9784)
PHONE..............................269 388-2871
Robert E Hammond II, *Principal*
Michelle Hammond,
EMP: 4 EST: 1997
SALES (est): 385K **Privately Held**
WEB: www.superiorequip.net
SIC: 3991 Street sweeping brooms, hand or machine

(G-9348)
SUPERIOR IMAGING SERVICES INC
4001 Portage St (49001-4912)
PHONE..............................269 382-0428
Paul Verschoof, *President*
Derek McElvain, *Business Mgr*
EMP: 7 EST: 1957
SQ FT: 3,360
SALES (est): 600K **Privately Held**
WEB: www.printmill.com
SIC: 2752 Commercial printing, offset

(G-9349)
SUPERIOR TYPESETTING SERVICE
Also Called: Superior Imaging
4001 Portage St (49001-4912)
PHONE..............................269 382-0428
Paul Verschoof, *President*
EMP: 8 EST: 2012
SALES (est): 476.2K **Privately Held**
WEB: www.printmill.com
SIC: 2752 Commercial printing, offset

(G-9350)
SWEET MANUFACTURING INC
3421 S Burdick St (49001-4835)
PHONE..............................269 344-2086
Randall J Sweet, *President*
Joann Roberts, *Admin Asst*
EMP: 29 EST: 1978
SQ FT: 20,000
SALES (est): 4.3MM **Privately Held**
WEB: www.sweetmfg.biz
SIC: 3714 Motor vehicle steering systems & parts

(G-9351)
T - SHIRT PRINTING PLUS INC
8608 W Main St Ste B (49009-8232)
PHONE..............................269 383-3666
Gary Peshl, *President*
Kathryn Peshl, *Vice Pres*
Drew Cooper, *Sales Staff*
Matt Peshl, *Sales Staff*
Mike Willis, *Sales Staff*
EMP: 21 EST: 1988
SALES (est): 2.9MM **Privately Held**
WEB: www.tsprintingplus.com
SIC: 2396 2395 Screen printing on fabric articles; embroidery & art needlework

(G-9352)
TEAM PHARMA
2022 Fulford St (49001-2085)
PHONE..............................269 344-8326
Daniel Torres, *Principal*
EMP: 5 EST: 2009
SALES (est): 482.8K **Privately Held**
WEB: www.teampharmaceutical.com
SIC: 2834 Pharmaceutical preparations

(G-9353)
TEMPO VINO WINERY KALAMAZOO
260 E Michigan Ave (49007-3910)
PHONE..............................269 342-9463
Irene Kokkinos, *Owner*
EMP: 5 EST: 2010
SALES (est): 295.3K **Privately Held**
WEB: www.tempovinowinery.com
SIC: 2084 Wines

(G-9354)
THE MIX
2804 W Michigan Ave (49006-5577)
PHONE..............................269 382-1300
EMP: 6 EST: 2017
SALES (est): 166.6K **Privately Held**
SIC: 3273 Ready-mixed concrete

(G-9355)
THE SPOTT
550 E Cork St (49001-4873)
PHONE..............................269 459-6462
EMP: 7 EST: 2014
SALES (est): 185.4K **Privately Held**
WEB: www.hitthespott.com
SIC: 3999 5812 ; eating places

(G-9356)
THERMO FISHER SCIENTIFIC INC
Also Called: Epredia
4481 Campus Dr (49008-2590)
PHONE..............................269 544-5600
Melissa Russell, *Buyer*
Jeremy Sokolowski, *Accounts Exec*
Jerry Frendburgh, *Manager*
Aime Chidester, *Manager*
Christopher Husiak, *Manager*
EMP: 5
SALES (corp-wide): 32.2B **Publicly Held**
WEB: www.thermofisher.com
SIC: 3826 Analytical instruments
PA: Thermo Fisher Scientific Inc.
168 3rd Ave
Waltham MA 02451
781 622-1000

(G-9357)
TIRE WHOLESALERS COMPANY
3883 Emerald Dr (49001-7919)
PHONE..............................269 349-9401
Andy Tonissen, *Opers Staff*
Ian Person, *Purchasing*
Jasmin Oliva, *Sales Staff*
Joe Krol, *Manager*
Brian Melstead, *Manager*
EMP: 99
SALES (corp-wide): 68.1MM **Privately Held**
WEB: www.twi.tireweb.com
SIC: 3011 5531 Tires & inner tubes; automotive tires
PA: Tire Wholesalers Company
1783 E 14 Mile Rd
Troy MI 48083
248 589-9910

(G-9358)
TOTAL PLASTICS RESOURCES LLC (DH)
Also Called: Total Plastics International
2810 N Burdick St Ste A (49004-3637)
PHONE..............................269 344-0009
Jason Jenkins, *Mng Member*
◆ EMP: 75 EST: 1978
SQ FT: 12,500
SALES (est): 96MM **Privately Held**
WEB: www.totalplastics.com
SIC: 5162 3083 Plastics sheets & rods; laminated plastics plate & sheet; thermoplastic laminates: rods, tubes, plates & sheet
HQ: Port Plastics, Inc.
5800 Campus Circle Dr E # 1
Irving TX 75063
469 299-7000

(G-9359)
TWO MITTS INC (PA)
600 Plastics Pl (49001-4882)
PHONE..............................800 888-5054
Michael Roeder, *President*
Gary Galia, *CFO*
John Kittredge, *Chief Mktg Ofcr*
EMP: 1 EST: 2014
SQ FT: 25,000
SALES (est): 64.5MM **Privately Held**
SIC: 3089 Thermoformed finished plastic products

(G-9360)
ULTRA FORMS PLUS INC
301 Peekstock Rd (49001-4844)
P.O. Box 2528 (49003-2528)
PHONE..............................269 337-6000
Kim Kugler, *President*
Ken Heegeman, *Vice Pres*
EMP: 10 EST: 1992
SALES (est): 1.1MM **Privately Held**
WEB: www.ultraformsplus.com
SIC: 2761 Computer forms, manifold or continuous

(G-9361)
VERSANT MED PHYSICS RDTION SFE
119 N Church St Ste 201 (49007-3744)
PHONE..............................888 316-3644
Marcie Ramsay, *Partner*
Sandy Konerth, *Vice Pres*
Spencer Vanderweele, *Technical Staff*
Nadeem Khan, *Director*
Sandra Konerth, *Director*
EMP: 23 EST: 2013
SALES (est): 7.9MM **Privately Held**
WEB: www.versantphysics.com
SIC: 8099 8748 2835 0742 Medical services organization; safety training service; radioactive diagnostic substances; animal hospital services, pets & other animal specialties

(G-9362)
VIDEKA LLC
4717 Campus Dr Ste 1500 (49008-5608)
PHONE..............................269 353-5536
Rob Caseria, *Mng Member*
EMP: 10 EST: 2019
SALES (est): 27.9K **Privately Held**
SIC: 2047 Dog food

(G-9363)
VINTNERS CELLAR WINERY OF KAL
260 E Michigan Ave (49007-3910)
PHONE..............................269 342-9463
Irene Kokkinor, *Owner*
EMP: 5 EST: 2005
SALES (est): 135.1K **Privately Held**
SIC: 2084 Wines

(G-9364)
VISIONS CAR & TRUCK ACC
8250 Douglas Ave (49009-5255)
PHONE..............................269 342-2962
Mark Cottingham, *Owner*
EMP: 4 EST: 1994
SALES (est): 246.2K **Privately Held**
SIC: 3714 Motor vehicle parts & accessories

(G-9365)
WABER TOOL & ENGINEERING CO
Also Called: Zip Cut
1335 Ravine Rd (49004-3501)
PHONE..............................269 342-0765
Heidi Waber, *President*
Vicky Roy, *Human Res Dir*
EMP: 18
SQ FT: 25,000
SALES (est): 2.5MM **Privately Held**
WEB: www.zip-cut.com
SIC: 3541 3599 3829 3546 Machine tools, metal cutting type; machine shop, jobbing & repair; measuring & controlling devices; power-driven handtools; special dies, tools, jigs & fixtures

(G-9366)
WEST COLONY GRAPHIC INC
Also Called: West Colony Printing
2519 Summerdale Ave (49004-1922)
PHONE..............................269 375-6625
Richard Reynolds, *President*
Michael Kemple, *Vice Pres*
EMP: 5 EST: 1976
SQ FT: 1,900
SALES (est): 321.8K **Privately Held**
SIC: 2752 Commercial printing, offset

(G-9367)
WEST MICH OFF INTERIORS INC
3308 S Westnedge Ave (49008-4925)
PHONE..............................269 344-0768
Chuck Scheap, *Principal*
Nita Maxwell, *Sales Staff*
Brian Parker, *Sales Staff*
EMP: 6
SALES (corp-wide): 9.8MM **Privately Held**
WEB: www.wmoi.com
SIC: 2521 2522 4225 5712 Panel systems & partitions (free-standing), office: wood; panel systems & partitions, office: except wood; general warehousing & storage; furniture stores; furniture
PA: West Michigan Office Interiors, Inc.
300 E 40th St
Holland MI 49423
616 396-7303

(G-9368)
WHITE PINE FURNITURE LLC
2002 Charles Ave (49048-2072)
PHONE..............................269 366-4469
Tom Dockham, *Mng Member*
EMP: 4 EST: 2014
SALES (est): 194.3K **Privately Held**
WEB: www.whitepinefurniture.com
SIC: 2511 Wood household furniture

(G-9369)
WICWAS PRESS
1620 Miller Rd (49001-4514)
PHONE..............................269 344-8027
Lawrence Connor, *Principal*
EMP: 6 EST: 2008
SALES (est): 348.4K **Privately Held**
WEB: www.wicwas.com
SIC: 2741 Miscellaneous publishing

(G-9370)
WILD FLAVORS INC
Also Called: A.M. Todd
1717 Douglas Ave (49007-1600)
PHONE..............................269 216-2603
Reed Lynn, *Manager*
EMP: 50
SALES (corp-wide): 64.3B **Publicly Held**
WEB: www.wildflavors.com
SIC: 2087 2869 Extracts, flavoring; flavors or flavoring materials, synthetic; perfume materials, synthetic
HQ: Wild Flavors, Inc.
1261 Pacific Ave
Erlanger KY 41018

(G-9371)
WINNING PUBLICATIONS
952 Vassar Dr (49001-4436)
PHONE..............................269 342-8547
Pam Carls, *Principal*
EMP: 6 EST: 2008
SALES (est): 132.5K **Privately Held**
WEB: www.carlschiropractic.com
SIC: 2741 Miscellaneous publishing

(G-9372)
WONDER MAKERS ENVIRONMENTAL
2117 Lane Blvd (49001-4102)
P.O. Box 50209 (49005-0209)
PHONE..............................269 382-4154
Michael Pinto, *CEO*
Susan Pinto, *President*
Dave Batts, *Director*
EMP: 18 EST: 1978
SQ FT: 10,000
SALES (est): 1.6MM **Privately Held**
WEB: www.wondermakers.com
SIC: 8742 3589 3463 Industrial hygiene consultant; asbestos removal equipment; aluminum forgings

(G-9373)
WOOD SMITHS INC
1180 S 8th St (49009-9327)
PHONE..............................269 372-6432
Kenneth C Smith, *President*
Robert Angle, *Principal*
Bob Angle, *Controller*
▲ EMP: 16 EST: 1981
SQ FT: 11,500

Kalamazoo - Kalamazoo County (G-9374)

SALES (est): 2.5MM **Privately Held**
WEB: www.the-woodsmiths.com
SIC: **2431** 5211 7699 Millwork; doors, wood or metal, except storm; door & window repair

(G-9374)
WORLD OF CD-ROM
Also Called: World of Cd-Rom, The
4026 S Westnedge Ave D (49008-4135)
PHONE..................269 382-3766
John Turcott, *Owner*
Mike Clapp, *Manager*
Joe Taylor, *Manager*
EMP: 10 EST: 1994
SALES (est): 570K **Privately Held**
WEB: www.worldofcd-rom.com
SIC: **5734** 7372 Computer & software stores; prepackaged software

(G-9375)
ZOETIS LLC
2605 E Kilgore Rd (49001-5505)
PHONE..................888 963-8471
Fouad Sayegh, *Vice Pres*
Joshua Wickey, *Engineer*
Rebecca Kitchen, *Manager*
Jamie Kneeshaw, *Manager*
Lisa Maddux, *Manager*
EMP: 4
SALES (corp-wide): 6.6B **Publicly Held**
WEB: www.zoetisus.com
SIC: **2834** Pharmaceutical preparations
HQ: Zoetis Llc
10 Sylvan Way
Parsippany NJ 07054
973 822-7000

Kaleva
Manistee County

(G-9376)
BOWLING ENTERPRISES INC
Also Called: Bowling Hydroseeding
9091 Chief Rd (49645-9731)
P.O. Box 457, Bear Lake (49614-0457)
PHONE..................231 864-2653
Floyd Bowling, *President*
Patti Bowling, *Admin Sec*
EMP: 4 EST: 1957
SALES (est): 340K **Privately Held**
WEB: www.bowlinghydroseeding.com
SIC: **3449** 0721 Bars, concrete reinforcing; fabricated steel; crop seeding services

(G-9377)
CREAM CUP DAIRY
7377 Feldhak Rd (49645-9653)
PHONE..................231 889-4158
David Miller,
EMP: 4 EST: 2008 **Privately Held**
SIC: **0241** 2026 Dairy farms; milk processing (pasteurizing, homogenizing, bottling)

(G-9378)
FISCHER TANKS LLC
13884 Rengo Ave (49645)
PHONE..................231 362-8265
Dustin Haw,
EMP: 60 EST: 2017
SQ FT: 85,000
SALES (est): 12.8MM
SALES (corp-wide): 41.3MM **Privately Held**
WEB: www.fischertanks.com
SIC: **3443** 7699 Fuel tanks (oil, gas, etc.): metal plate; tank repair
PA: Granby Industries Limited Partnership
98 Rue Des Industries
Cowansville QC J2K 0
450.378-2334

(G-9379)
FRUIT HAVEN NURSERY INC
Also Called: Calvin Lutz Farm
8576 Chief Rd (49645-9607)
PHONE..................231 889-9973
Calvin Lutz II, *President*
Mark Coe, *Principal*
Mike Feliczak, *Principal*
Ralph Smith, *Principal*
Calvin Lutz III, *Vice Pres*
EMP: 8 EST: 1966

SALES (est): 989.9K **Privately Held**
WEB: www.calvinlutzfarms.com
SIC: **0161** 3999 0782 Corn farm, sweet; asparagus farm; Christmas trees, artificial; landscape contractors

(G-9380)
NORTHERN CHAIN SPECIALTIES
7329 Chief Rd (49645-9712)
PHONE..................231 889-3151
James Kelly, *President*
Barry Crawford, *Vice Pres*
Shelley Bishop, *Administration*
EMP: 12 EST: 2001
SQ FT: 20,000
SALES (est): 2.2MM **Privately Held**
WEB: www.northernchainspecialties.com
SIC: **3441** Fabricated structural metal

Kalkaska
Kalkaska County

(G-9381)
1ST CHOICE TRCKG & RENTL INC
1256 Thomas Rd (49646)
P.O. Box 970 (49646-0970)
PHONE..................231 258-0417
Roger Wilkinson, *President*
Brenda Goosman, *Shareholder*
James Vowels, *Shareholder*
Lyle Vowels, *Shareholder*
Joe Waterman, *Admin Sec*
EMP: 9 EST: 1999
SALES (est): 1.3MM **Privately Held**
SIC: **1389** Haulage, oil field

(G-9382)
BARBRON CORPORATION
200 E Dresden St (49646-8589)
PHONE..................586 716-3530
EMP: 30
SQ FT: 8,500
SALES (est): 2.4MM **Privately Held**
SIC: **3569** 3497 3496 3494 Mfg General Indstl Mach Mfg Metal Foil/Leaf Mfg Misc Fab Wire Prdts Mfg Valves/Pipe Fittings

(G-9383)
BEAVER LOG HOMES INC
850 S Cedar St (49646-8031)
P.O. Box 3 (49646-0003)
PHONE..................231 258-5020
Richard Beaver, *President*
EMP: 10 EST: 1984
SQ FT: 864
SALES (est): 943.1K **Privately Held**
WEB: www.beaverloghomesinc.com
SIC: **2452** Log cabins, prefabricated, wood

(G-9384)
BECKMAN PRODUCTION SVCS INC (HQ)
Also Called: Indril
3786 Beebe Rd (49646-8014)
P.O. Box 670 (49646-0670)
PHONE..................231 258-9524
Tom Cyculla, *CEO*
Ed Sarin, *Safety Mgr*
Mark Bishop, *CFO*
EMP: 179 EST: 1970
SALES (est): 163.3MM
SALES (corp-wide): 310.8MM **Publicly Held**
WEB: www.beckmanproduction.com
SIC: **1389** Oil field services
PA: Nine Energy Service, Inc.
2001 Kirby Dr Ste 200
Houston TX 77019
281 730-5100

(G-9385)
CLEAN HARBORS ENVMTL SVCS INC
4030 Columbus Dr Ne (49646-8484)
PHONE..................231 258-8014
EMP: 10
SALES (corp-wide): 3.1B **Publicly Held**
WEB: www.cleanharbors.com
SIC: **3589** Sewage treatment equipment; swimming pool filter & water conditioning systems

HQ: Clean Harbors Environmental Services, Inc.
42 Longwater Dr
Norwell MA 02061
781 792-5000

(G-9386)
D J AND G ENTERPRISE INC
Also Called: Patton Welding
402 E Dresden St (49646-9701)
PHONE..................231 258-9925
Don Patton, *President*
Jenny Patton, *Corp Secy*
EMP: 6 EST: 1994
SQ FT: 6,000 **Privately Held**
WEB: www.pattonwelding.com
SIC: **7692** Welding repair

(G-9387)
EXODUS PRESSURE CONTROL
110 W Park Dr (49646-9702)
P.O. Box 2053 (49646-2053)
PHONE..................231 258-8001
Jeff Bergman, *Partner*
Troy Fisher, *Partner*
EMP: 6 EST: 1997
SALES (est): 602.4K **Privately Held**
SIC: **1389** Oil field services

(G-9388)
FLOWTEK INC
206 E Park Dr (49646-9785)
P.O. Box 1310 (49646-1310)
PHONE..................231 734-3415
Jeffrey Vincent, *President*
EMP: 17 EST: 2008
SALES (est): 2.4MM **Privately Held**
SIC: **3491** Industrial valves

(G-9389)
GREAT LAKES HYDRA CORPORATION
Also Called: Great Lakes Fluid Power
410 E Dresden St (49646-9701)
PHONE..................231 258-4338
David Apkarian, *President*
Larry Laham, *Vice Pres*
David Plants, *Vice Pres*
Shelly Hillis, *Treasurer*
Art Apkarian, *Director*
EMP: 11 EST: 1969
SALES (est): 3.4MM **Privately Held**
SIC: **3566** 7699 5084 3594 Speed changers, drives & gears; hydraulic equipment repair; hydraulic systems equipment & supplies; fluid power pumps & motors; valves & pipe fittings

(G-9390)
ILLINOIS TOOL WORKS INC
ITW Coding Products
111 W Park Dr (49646-9702)
PHONE..................231 258-5521
Mark Thelen, *Exec Dir*
EMP: 80
SQ FT: 14,000
SALES (corp-wide): 12.5B **Publicly Held**
WEB: www.itw.com
SIC: **3497** Metal foil & leaf
PA: Illinois Tool Works Inc.
155 Harlem Ave
Glenview IL 60025
847 724-7500

(G-9391)
JK MANUFACTURING CO
520 E Dresden St (49646-9701)
P.O. Box 8598, Cedar Rapids IA (52408-8598)
PHONE..................231 258-2638
Jody L Keener, *President*
EMP: 10 EST: 2007
SALES (est): 383.1K **Privately Held**
SIC: **3999** Barber & beauty shop equipment

(G-9392)
KALKASKA SCREW PRODUCTS INC
775 Rabourn Rd Ne (49646-8959)
PHONE..................231 258-2560
Tedd H Stewart, *President*
Kier Parrish, *Opers Staff*
Steve Hartzell, *Purch Agent*
Ken O'Brien, *Purchasing*
Tim Eagleton, *QC Mgr*

EMP: 24 EST: 1963
SQ FT: 30,000
SALES (est): 4.8MM **Privately Held**
WEB: www.kalkaskascrew.com
SIC: **3451** Screw machine products

(G-9393)
KEY ENERGY SERVICES INC
4030 Columbus Dr Ne (49646-8484)
PHONE..................231 258-9637
Duke Upaul, *Manager*
EMP: 4
SALES (corp-wide): 413.8MM **Privately Held**
WEB: www.keyenergy.com
SIC: **1381** Drilling oil & gas wells
PA: Key Energy Services, Inc.
1301 Mckinney St Ste 1800
Houston TX 77010
713 651-4300

(G-9394)
KIBBY WELDING LLC
2695 M 66 Se (49646-8608)
P.O. Box 707, Traverse City (49685-0707)
PHONE..................231 258-8838
Louis Kibby,
Taylor Kibby,
EMP: 17 EST: 2009
SALES (est): 2.6MM **Privately Held**
WEB: www.kibbyweldingllc-com.webs.com
SIC: **7692** Welding repair

(G-9395)
MARSH INDUSTRIAL SERVICES INC
Also Called: Marsh Welding
135 E Mile Rd (49646-9485)
P.O. Box 1107 (49646-1107)
PHONE..................231 258-4870
Donald R Marsh, *President*
Debra Marsh, *Corp Secy*
EMP: 19 EST: 1989
SQ FT: 12,000
SALES (est): 3.4MM **Privately Held**
WEB: www.marshind.com
SIC: **3443** 1799 7692 3713 Fabricated plate work (boiler shop); welding on site; welding repair; truck & bus bodies; industrial trucks & tractors; sheet metalwork

(G-9396)
MICHAEL NIEDERPRUEM
Also Called: Print Shop, The
880 Lake Dr Ne (49646-9642)
PHONE..................231 935-0241
Michael Niederpruem, *Owner*
EMP: 4 EST: 1995
SQ FT: 1,100
SALES (est): 166.8K **Privately Held**
SIC: **2759** Commercial printing

(G-9397)
MICHIGAN AGGR SAND/GRAVEL HAUL
765 Rabourn Rd Ne (49646-8959)
PHONE..................231 258-8237
Frank Peters, *President*
Olive Peters, *Vice Pres*
Timothy Peters, *Treasurer*
EMP: 10 EST: 1973
SQ FT: 3,000
SALES (est): 871.7K **Privately Held**
SIC: **1442** Construction sand & gravel

(G-9398)
MIDWEST TOOL AND CUTLERY CO
Also Called: Forge Div Midwest TI & Cutly
222 Seeley Rd Ne (49646-9483)
PHONE..................231 258-2341
Scott Musser, *Branch Mgr*
EMP: 15
SALES (corp-wide): 14.6MM **Privately Held**
WEB: www.midwestsnips.com
SIC: **3421** 3542 Scissors, shears, clippers, snips & similar tools; forging machinery & hammers
PA: Midwest Tool And Cutlery Company
1210 Progress St
Sturgis MI 49091
269 651-2476

GEOGRAPHIC SECTION

(G-9399)
NORTHERN A 1 SERVICES INC
Also Called: Pollution Control Services
3947 Us Highway 131 Ne (49646-8428)
P.O. Box 1030 (49646-1030)
PHONE....................231 258-9961
Gregg Orr, *President*
Mike Ascione, *President*
EMP: 52 **EST:** 1990
SALES (est): 12.3MM **Privately Held**
WEB: www.northerna1.com
SIC: 1389 Servicing oil & gas wells

(G-9400)
NORTHERN DESIGN SERVICES INC
424 E Dresden St (49646-9701)
PHONE....................231 258-9900
Dan Minder, *President*
Leo Dutton, *Treasurer*
EMP: 20 **EST:** 2001
SQ FT: 14,000 **Privately Held**
SIC: 7692 Welding repair

(G-9401)
PATTON WELDING INC
Also Called: Michigan Modular Service
402 E Dresden St (49646-9701)
PHONE....................231 258-9925
Donald Patton, *President*
Barney Hunter, *Manager*
EMP: 14 **EST:** 1983
SALES (est): 300K **Privately Held**
WEB: www.pattonwelding.com
SIC: 3498 Fabricated pipe & fittings

(G-9402)
ROUGH ROAD TRUCKING LLC
775 Prairie Ln Sw (49646-8814)
PHONE....................231 645-3355
Patrick Taylor, *Principal*
Patrick N Taylor, *Manager*
EMP: 5 **EST:** 2013
SALES (est): 131.4K **Privately Held**
SIC: 4212 3531 7519 3792 Local trucking, without storage; snow plow attachments; pop-up camper rental; travel trailers & campers; snow plows (motor vehicles), assembly of

(G-9403)
SEDCO DIRECTIONAL DRILLING
4030 Columbus Dr Ne (49646-8484)
PHONE....................231 258-5318
EMP: 5 **EST:** 2007
SALES (est): 402.3K **Privately Held**
SIC: 1381 Directional drilling oil & gas wells

(G-9404)
SRM CONCRETE LLC
Also Called: L C Redi Mix
500 M 72 (49646-9403)
PHONE....................231 258-8633
Calvin Hutchinson, *Manager*
EMP: 10
SALES (corp-wide): 170.1MM **Privately Held**
WEB: www.smyrnareadymix.com
SIC: 3273 Ready-mixed concrete
PA: Srm Concrete, Llc
1136 2nd Ave N
Nashville TN 37208
615 355-1028

(G-9405)
SUPERIOR INSPECTION SVC
1864 Prough Rd Sw (49646-7809)
P.O. Box 1509 (49646-1509)
PHONE....................231 258-9400
EMP: 9 **EST:** 2002
SALES (est): 1MM **Privately Held**
WEB: www.superiorinspection.net
SIC: 1389 Construction, repair & dismantling services

(G-9406)
TEAM SERVICES LLC
1587 Enterprise Dr (49646-8255)
P.O. Box 1104 (49646-1104)
PHONE....................231 258-9130
Steve Kwapis, *CEO*
EMP: 35 **EST:** 2008

SALES (est): 6.9MM **Privately Held**
WEB: www.goteamservices.com
SIC: 1389 Servicing oil & gas wells

(G-9407)
TEAM SPOOLING SERVICES LLC
Also Called: Team Acquistions
209 E Park Dr (49646-9785)
P.O. Box 1104 (49646-1104)
PHONE....................231 258-9130
Tim Tinker,
EMP: 4 **EST:** 2001
SALES (est): 760.4K **Privately Held**
WEB: www.goteamservices.com
SIC: 1389 Servicing oil & gas wells

(G-9408)
TODDS WELDING SERVICE INC
Also Called: T W S Wldg & Cstm Fabrication
8604 Us 131 N (49646)
P.O. Box 1113 (49646-1113)
PHONE....................231 587-9969
Todd Chwastek, *President*
Renee Chwastek, *Vice Pres*
EMP: 16 **EST:** 1985
SQ FT: 13,000
SALES (est): 3.4MM **Privately Held**
WEB: www.twsweldandfab.com
SIC: 7692 Welding repair

(G-9409)
TREND SERVICES COMPANY
311 Maple St (49646-5101)
P.O. Box 458 (49646-0458)
PHONE....................231 258-9951
Michael E Babcock, *President*
Mike Ponstein, *Sales Staff*
Steve Dipzinski, *Technician*
Josh Hicks, *Technician*
EMP: 7
SQ FT: 8,500
SALES (est): 1MM **Privately Held**
WEB: www.tsinc.cc
SIC: 1389 Construction, repair & dismantling services; measurement of well flow rates, oil & gas

(G-9410)
WAYNE WIRE A BAG CMPONENTS INC
200 E Dresden St (49646-8589)
PHONE....................231 258-9187
Michael G Brown, *President*
▲ **EMP:** 256 **EST:** 1998
SALES (est): 505.7K
SALES (corp-wide): 30.5MM **Privately Held**
WEB: www.waynewire.com
SIC: 3496 Miscellaneous fabricated wire products
PA: Wayne Wire Cloth Products Inc
200 E Dresden St
Kalkaska MI 49646
231 258-9187

(G-9411)
WAYNE WIRE CLOTH PRODUCTS INC (PA)
Also Called: Wayne Wire Airbag Components
200 E Dresden St (49646-8589)
PHONE....................231 258-9187
Michael G Brown, *President*
David Brown, *President*
Steve Brown, *President*
M G Brown, *Chairman*
Steve Waugh, *COO*
EMP: 100 **EST:** 1943
SQ FT: 175,000
SALES (est): 30.5MM **Privately Held**
WEB: www.waynewire.com
SIC: 3496 Miscellaneous fabricated wire products

(G-9412)
WOODLAND CREEK FURNITURE INC (PA)
Also Called: Arhouzz
546 M 72 E (49646-9417)
P.O. Box 2048 (49646-2048)
PHONE....................231 258-2146
Rob Evina, *President*
Wendy Watson, *Manager*
Donna Laster, *Consultant*
▲ **EMP:** 24 **EST:** 2002

SALES (est): 5.2MM **Privately Held**
WEB: www.woodlandcreekfurniture.com
SIC: 2511 5712 Wood household furniture; custom made furniture, except cabinets

Kawkawlin
Bay County

(G-9413)
ACME SEPTIC TANK CO
2888 S Huron Rd (48631-9107)
P.O. Box 336 (48631-0336)
PHONE....................989 684-3852
Brian Marsh, *President*
Audrey Marsh, *Vice Pres*
EMP: 10 **EST:** 1950
SALES (est): 679.2K **Privately Held**
WEB: www.acmeseptictankco.com
SIC: 3272 1711 1389 Septic tanks, concrete; septic system construction; servicing oil & gas wells

(G-9414)
BAILER AND DE SHAW
204 S Old Kawkawlin Rd (48631-2507)
PHONE....................989 684-3610
Douglas I Bailer, *Partner*
Herman J De Shaw, *Partner*
EMP: 7 **EST:** 1962
SQ FT: 240
SALES (est): 1.8MM **Privately Held**
SIC: 1311 Crude petroleum production

(G-9415)
GLENN KNOCHEL
Also Called: Maple Lane Ag-Bag
2152 E Beaver Rd (48631-9422)
PHONE....................989 684-7869
Glenn Knochel, *Owner*
Jeremy Girard, *Production*
Thad Reavill, *Sales Staff*
Tom Ehlers, *Marketing Staff*
Glen Yungbauer, *Info Tech Mgr*
EMP: 4 **EST:** 1980
SALES (est): 759.7K **Privately Held**
WEB: www.mlagbag.com
SIC: 3523 5999 Crop storage bins; farm equipment & supplies

(G-9416)
HOLSINGER MANUFACTURING CORP
2922 S Huron Rd (48631-9177)
P.O. Box 645 (48631-0645)
PHONE....................989 684-3101
Joe Martuch, *President*
Harley Owen Holsinger, *President*
Barb Crews, *Manager*
EMP: 28 **EST:** 1945
SQ FT: 26,000
SALES (est): 1.3MM **Privately Held**
WEB: www.holsingermfg.com
SIC: 2541 2599 Store fixtures, wood; bar fixtures, wood; office fixtures, wood; bar, restaurant & cafeteria furniture

(G-9417)
HUGO BROTHERS PALLET MFG
2474 River Rd (48631-9409)
PHONE....................989 684-5564
Daniel Hugo, *President*
William Hugo, *Corp Secy*
EMP: 8
SQ FT: 6,720
SALES (est): 890.2K **Privately Held**
SIC: 2448 Pallets, wood

(G-9418)
SAGINAW BAY PLASTICS INC
2768 S Huron Rd (48631-9176)
P.O. Box 507 (48631-0507)
PHONE....................989 686-7860
David Burke, *President*
Sabrina Penkala, *Purchasing*
Greg Cook, *Engineer*
▲ **EMP:** 65 **EST:** 1978
SQ FT: 30,000
SALES (est): 8.6MM **Privately Held**
WEB: www.saginawbayplastics.com
SIC: 3089 Injection molding of plastics

(G-9419)
WOODLAND INDUSTRIES
112 S Huron Rd (48631-9127)
P.O. Box 504 (48631-0504)
PHONE....................989 686-6176
Michael Ferguson, *Owner*
EMP: 5 **EST:** 1984
SQ FT: 4,000
SALES (est): 417.5K **Privately Held**
SIC: 3715 5599 Truck trailers; utility trailers

(G-9420)
X L T ENGINEERING INC
2595 S Huron Rd (48631-9170)
P.O. Box 126 (48631-0126)
PHONE....................989 684-4344
Mike Staszak, *President*
Stacie Staszak, *Vice Pres*
EMP: 27 **EST:** 1992
SALES (est): 1.8MM **Privately Held**
SIC: 3599 3544 Machine shop, jobbing & repair; special dies, tools, jigs & fixtures

Keego Harbor
Oakland County

(G-9421)
GRAPHX SHOP
3089 Orchard Lake Rd (48320-1246)
PHONE....................248 678-5432
Rikki Vestuto, *Owner*
EMP: 4 **EST:** 2007
SALES (est): 315K **Privately Held**
WEB: www.graphxshop.com
SIC: 3993 Signs & advertising specialties

(G-9422)
PR39 INDUSTRIES LLC
1681 Maddy Ln (48320-1155)
PHONE....................248 866-1445
EMP: 4 **EST:** 2019
SALES (est): 54.1K **Privately Held**
WEB: www.pr39industries.com
SIC: 3999 Manufacturing industries

Kenockee
St. Clair County

(G-9423)
BOBS WELDING & FABRICATING
Also Called: B W and F Excavating
5375 Kilgore Rd (48006-3229)
PHONE....................810 324-2592
Robert Goolsby, *Owner*
EMP: 10 **EST:** 1985
SALES (est): 258.3K **Privately Held**
SIC: 7692 Welding repair

(G-9424)
TURNER CUSTOM WOODWORKING
4085 Kilgore Rd (48006-4124)
PHONE....................810 324-6254
John B Turner, *Administration*
EMP: 5 **EST:** 2011
SALES (est): 63.8K **Privately Held**
SIC: 2431 Millwork

Kent City
Kent County

(G-9425)
2255SRV LLC
2825 17 Mile Rd Ste A (49330-8921)
PHONE....................616 678-4900
Dale Flanery,
EMP: 12 **EST:** 2003
SALES (est): 417.3K **Privately Held**
SIC: 3089 Injection molded finished plastic products

(G-9426)
ARC ARCHER LLC
380 W Muskegon St (49330-9796)
P.O. Box 232, Sparta (49345-0232)
PHONE....................616 439-3014

Kent City - Kent County (G-9427) GEOGRAPHIC SECTION

David Bloomquist,
EMP: 14 **EST:** 2010
SALES (est): 1.2MM **Privately Held**
WEB: www.arcarcher.com
SIC: 3441 Fabricated structural metal

(G-9427)
BARBER CREEK SAND & GRAVEL
15666 Barber Creek Ave (49330-9734)
P.O. Box 185 (49330-0185)
PHONE 616 675-7619
Daniel C Groenke, *President*
EMP: 24 **EST:** 1976
SQ FT: 3,840
SALES (est): 3.7MM **Privately Held**
SIC: 1442 Gravel mining

(G-9428)
C & T FABRICATION LLC
90 Spring St (49330-9303)
P.O. Box 187, Sparta (49345-0187)
PHONE 616 678-5133
Dan Boyd, *Partner*
▲ **EMP:** 6 **EST:** 2003
SALES (est): 799.4K **Privately Held**
SIC: 1761 3444 Sheet metalwork; sheet metalwork

(G-9429)
COATINGS BY PCD INC
Also Called: Surplus Coatings
2825 17 Mile Rd Ste C (49330-8921)
PHONE 616 952-0032
Dwayne Behrens, *President*
▼ **EMP:** 6 **EST:** 1993 **Privately Held**
WEB: www.surpluscoatings.com
SIC: 2851 Paints & allied products

(G-9430)
COUNTY LINE PALLET
Also Called: Fisk Wood Products
2031 22 Mile Rd (49330-9450)
PHONE 231 834-8416
EMP: 8
SALES (est): 490K **Privately Held**
SIC: 2448 Mfg Wood Pallets/Skids

(G-9431)
G & C CARPORTS
1324 17 Mile Rd (49330-9058)
PHONE 616 678-4308
Narcizo Gutierrez, *Owner*
EMP: 7 **EST:** 2003
SALES (est): 360.4K **Privately Held**
SIC: 3448 Carports: prefabricated metal

(G-9432)
GT PLASTICS & EQUIPMENT LLC
13425 Peach Ridge Ave (49330-9155)
P.O. Box 158 (49330-0158)
PHONE 616 678-7445
Grady Ogle,
EMP: 19 **EST:** 1994
SQ FT: 10,000
SALES (est): 3.6MM **Privately Held**
SIC: 3089 5084 Blow molded finished plastic products; plastic products machinery

(G-9433)
HICKMANS WOODWORKING LLC
2875 18 Mile Rd (49330-9183)
PHONE 616 678-4180
Aaron Hickman, *Principal*
EMP: 5 **EST:** 2013
SALES (est): 63.5K **Privately Held**
SIC: 2431 Millwork

(G-9434)
KALINIAK DESIGN LLC
13984 Eagle Ridge Dr (49330-9086)
PHONE 616 675-3850
Andrew Kaliniak, *President*
Edie Kaliniak, *Opers Mgr*
EMP: 7 **EST:** 1990
SQ FT: 8,000 **Privately Held**
WEB: www.kaliniakdesign.com
SIC: 2511 2434 Wood household furniture; wood kitchen cabinets

(G-9435)
KENT CITY PLASTICS LLC
90 Spring St Ste B (49330-9305)
PHONE 616 678-4900
Michael Tatman, *General Mgr*
Mary Behler, *Office Mgr*
Joseph Pohlen,
EMP: 15 **EST:** 2018
SALES (est): 2.3MM **Privately Held**
WEB: www.kentcityplastics.com
SIC: 3089 Plastic containers, except foam; injection molding of plastics

(G-9436)
SMITH DUMPSTERS
13546 Kenowa Ave (49330-9502)
PHONE 616 675-9399
Ronald R Smith, *Principal*
EMP: 8 **EST:** 2018
SALES (est): 522.1K **Privately Held**
WEB: www.smithdumpsters.com
SIC: 3443 Dumpsters, garbage

(G-9437)
STONEY RIDGE VINEYARDS LLC
2255 Indian Lakes Rd (49330-9722)
PHONE 616 540-4318
Dale A Flannery, *Principal*
EMP: 6 **EST:** 2015
SALES (est): 94.5K **Privately Held**
WEB: www.stoneyridgevineyards.com
SIC: 2084 Wines

(G-9438)
T 4 MANUFACTURING
390 Wynwood (49330-9786)
PHONE 616 952-0020
Glenna Tollon, *Principal*
EMP: 4 **EST:** 2017
SALES (est): 72.4K **Privately Held**
SIC: 3999 Manufacturing industries

Kenton
Ontonagon County

(G-9439)
EAST BRANCH FOREST PRODUCTS
5160 E Hwy 28 (49967)
PHONE 906 852-3315
EMP: 5
SALES (est): 334.9K **Privately Held**
SIC: 2411 Logging

(G-9440)
INTEGRITY FOREST PRODUCTS LLC
844 E M28 (49967-9499)
PHONE 513 871-8988
James Stoehr III, *President*
Patrick Folz, *CFO*
EMP: 7
SALES (est): 285.1K **Privately Held**
SIC: 2421 Sawmills & planing mills, general

Kentwood
Kent County

(G-9441)
ABACO PARTNERS LLC
Also Called: Surefil
4560 Danvers Dr Se (49512-4039)
PHONE 616 532-1700
Andrea Hecker, *Project Mgr*
Douglas Herr, *Mfg Staff*
Chuck Blaauw, *Purch Mgr*
Tim Kauffman, *CFO*
Luisa Shumpert, *Marketing Staff*
▲ **EMP:** 110 **EST:** 2010
SQ FT: 5,000
SALES (est): 19.9MM **Privately Held**
WEB: www.surefil.com
SIC: 2844 2834 2082 Mouthwashes; druggists' preparations (pharmaceuticals); malt beverages

(G-9442)
ANDRONACO INC (PA)
4855 Broadmoor Ave Se (49512-5360)
PHONE 616 554-4600
Ronald V Andronaco, *CEO*
Adam Hanson, *Engineer*
Michael Matz, *Sales Dir*
Ron Porter, *Manager*
Rick Vining, *Master*
EMP: 13 **EST:** 2013
SALES (est): 144.6MM **Privately Held**
WEB: www.andronaco.com
SIC: 3052 Air line or air brake hose, rubber or rubberized fabric

(G-9443)
ARCANUM ALLOYS INC
4460 44th St Se Ste F (49512-4096)
PHONE 312 810-4479
Daniel Bullard, *CEO*
Ravi Oswal, *Vice Pres*
Joseph McDermott, *VP Mfg*
Zachary Detweiler, *Research*
David Keifer, *VP Sales*
EMP: 7 **EST:** 2011
SALES (est): 1.5MM **Privately Held**
SIC: 3325 Alloy steel castings, except investment

(G-9444)
AUTOCAM CORPORATION (HQ)
Also Called: Autocam Prcsion Cmpnents Group
4180 40th St Se (49512-4122)
P.O. Box 42404, Indianapolis IN (46242-0404)
PHONE 616 698-0707
John R Buchan, *COO*
John Buchan, *Exec VP*
Christopher Qualters, *Exec VP*
Christopher J Qualters, *Exec VP*
Ryan Lothian, *Project Mgr*
▲ **EMP:** 325 **EST:** 1987
SQ FT: 190,000
SALES (est): 140.1MM
SALES (corp-wide): 427.5MM **Publicly Held**
WEB: www.autocam.com
SIC: 3572 3841 5084 3714 Computer disk & drum drives & components; surgical & medical instruments; fuel injection systems; motor vehicle brake systems & parts; truck & automobile assembly plant construction
PA: Nn, Inc.
6210 Ardrey Kell Rd # 600
Charlotte NC 28277
980 264-4300

(G-9445)
AUTOCAM CORPORATION
4060 East Paris Ave Se (49512-3909)
PHONE 616 698-0707
EMP: 4
SALES (corp-wide): 427.5MM **Publicly Held**
WEB: www.autocam.com
SIC: 3599 Machine shop, jobbing & repair
HQ: Autocam Corporation
4180 40th St Se
Kentwood MI 49512
616 698-0707

(G-9446)
AUTOCAM CORPORATION
4070 East Paris Ave Se (49512-3963)
PHONE 616 698-0707
Cori Craciunescu, *Opers Staff*
Alex Briggs, *Mfg Staff*
Matthew Deroo, *Buyer*
Dana Barbera, *Engineer*
John Swistak, *Engineer*
EMP: 113
SALES (corp-wide): 427.5MM **Publicly Held**
WEB: www.autocam.com
SIC: 3714 Motor vehicle parts & accessories
HQ: Autocam Corporation
4180 40th St Se
Kentwood MI 49512
616 698-0707

(G-9447)
AUTOCAM MED DVC HOLDINGS LLC (PA)
4152 East Paris Ave Se (49512-3911)
PHONE 616 541-8080
John C Kennedy, *Partner*
Warren A Veltman, *CFO*
EMP: 2 **EST:** 2009
SQ FT: 190,000
SALES (est): 68.3MM **Privately Held**
WEB: www.autocam-medical.com
SIC: 3841 3842 Surgical & medical instruments; implants, surgical

(G-9448)
CHARTER INDS EXTRUSIONS LLC (PA)
3900 S Greenbrooke Dr Se (49512-5326)
PHONE 616 245-3388
Pete Eardley, *President*
Chuck Eardley, *Vice Pres*
Josh Haveman, *Purchasing*
Elizabeth McKee, *Accounting Mgr*
Jeff Hankins, *Sales Staff*
▲ **EMP:** 8 **EST:** 1991
SALES (est): 2.5MM **Privately Held**
WEB: www.charterindustries.com
SIC: 2491 Structural lumber & timber, treated wood

(G-9449)
CORVAC COMPOSITES LLC (HQ)
4450 36th St Se (49512-1917)
PHONE 616 281-4028
James Fitzell, *President*
Rich Jordan, *President*
Randy Emert, *Plant Mgr*
Christine Black, *Controller*
Matt Bordewyk, *Accountant*
◆ **EMP:** 30 **EST:** 2004
SALES (est): 155.3MM
SALES (corp-wide): 190MM **Privately Held**
WEB: www.corvaccomposites.com
SIC: 3559 Automotive related machinery
PA: Humphrey Companies Llc
2851 Prairie St Sw
Grandville MI 49418
616 530-1717

(G-9450)
EBLING & SON INC
Also Called: Ebling & Son Blacksmith
4484 Rger B Chffee Mem Dr (49548-7522)
PHONE 616 532-8400
James Nammensma, *CEO*
Pamela Nammensma, *Corp Secy*
EMP: 8 **EST:** 1896
SQ FT: 13,600
SALES (est): 1.3MM **Privately Held**
WEB: www.eblingandson.com
SIC: 7692 Welding repair

(G-9451)
ETHYLENE LLC
4855 Broadmoor Ave Se (49512-5360)
PHONE 616 554-3464
Ron V Andronaco,
Michael R Sheridan,
▲ **EMP:** 26 **EST:** 1950
SQ FT: 64,000
SALES (est): 8.5MM
SALES (corp-wide): 144.6MM **Privately Held**
WEB: www.ethylene.com
SIC: 3084 3089 3441 Plastics pipe; fittings for pipe, plastic; fabricated structural metal
PA: Andronaco, Inc.
4855 Broadmoor Ave Se
Kentwood MI 49512
616 554-4600

(G-9452)
FERGUSON ENTERPRISES LLC
Also Called: Ferguson Waterworks
3900 44th St Se (49512-3942)
PHONE 616 803-7521
EMP: 5
SALES (corp-wide): 21.8B **Privately Held**
WEB: www.ferguson.com
SIC: 5074 3432 Plumbing fittings & supplies; plumbing fixture fittings & trim
HQ: Ferguson Enterprises, Llc
12500 Jefferson Ave
Newport News VA 23602
757 874-7795

(G-9453)
FJR INDUSTRIAL SALES INC
4282 Brockton Dr Se Ste D (49512-4074)
PHONE 616 427-3776

GEOGRAPHIC SECTION
Kentwood - Kent County (G-9480)

EMP: 10 EST: 2019
SALES (est): 589.1K Privately Held
WEB: www.fjrindustrialsales.com
SIC: 3599 Machine shop, jobbing & repair

(G-9454)
FLOWCOR LLC (PA)
4855 Broadmoor Ave Se (49512-5360)
PHONE..................................616 554-1100
Ronald V Andronaco, Mng Member
EMP: 5 EST: 2017
SALES (est): 7.7MM Privately Held
WEB: www.andronaco.com
SIC: 3592 Valves

(G-9455)
FRESHWATER DIGITAL
4585 40th St Se (49512-4036)
PHONE..................................616 682-5470
Matt Downey, CEO
EMP: 20 EST: 2010
SALES (est): 1.5MM Privately Held
WEB: www.fwdigital.net
SIC: 3993 Signs & advertising specialties

(G-9456)
FRESHWTER DGTAL MDIA PRTNERS L
4585 40th St Se (49512-4036)
PHONE..................................616 446-1771
Zack Rinvelt, Business Mgr
Jon Dodge, COO
Jonathan Dodge, Exec VP
Lauren Benda, Accounts Mgr
Mathew Downey, Mng Member
EMP: 19 EST: 2010
SALES (est): 10MM Privately Held
WEB: www.fwdigital.net
SIC: 3993 7812 7336 Signs & advertising specialties; video production; graphic arts & related design

(G-9457)
HAERTER STAMPING LLC
3840 Model Ct Se (49512-3938)
PHONE..................................616 871-9400
Martin Haerter, Managing Dir
Kathy Wagner, Buyer
Rachel Higuera, Supervisor
Wolfgang Haerter,
◆ EMP: 60 EST: 1964
SQ FT: 80,385
SALES (est): 14.3MM Privately Held
SIC: 3469 Ornamental metal stampings

(G-9458)
HILLS-MCCANNA LLC
4855 Broadmoor Ave Se (49512-5360)
PHONE..................................616 554-9308
Adelcia Rodrigues, General Mgr
Joe Beaumont, Engineer
Paul Tenbrook, CFO
Bob Varela, Sales Dir
Gary Eldridge, Sales Staff
▲ EMP: 90 EST: 2008
SALES (est): 13.3MM
SALES (corp-wide): 144.6MM Privately Held
WEB: www.hills-mccanna.com
SIC: 3491 Industrial valves
PA: Andronaco, Inc.
    4855 Broadmoor Ave Se
    Kentwood MI 49512
    616 554-4600

(G-9459)
KENTWOOD FUEL INC
1980 44th St Se (49508-5049)
PHONE..................................616 455-2387
EMP: 4 EST: 2015
SALES (est): 181.6K Privately Held
SIC: 2869 Mfg Industrial Organic Chemicals

(G-9460)
KHALSA METAL PRODUCTS INC
3142 Broadmoor Ave Se (49512-1845)
PHONE..................................616 791-4794
Manjinder Singh, President
Menganber Singh, Manager
Navdeep Singh, Admin Mgr
EMP: 6 EST: 2003
SALES (est): 412.2K Privately Held
WEB: www.khalsametalproducts.com
SIC: 3545 Precision tools, machinists'

(G-9461)
LACKS EXTERIOR SYSTEMS LLC
4655 Patterson Ave Se (49512-5337)
PHONE..................................616 554-7805
Brian Benedict, Branch Mgr
EMP: 21 Privately Held
WEB: www.lacksenterprises.com
SIC: 3089 Plastic hardware & building products
HQ: Lacks Exterior Systems, Llc
    5460 Cascade Rd Se
    Grand Rapids MI 49546
    616 949-6570

(G-9462)
LACKS EXTERIOR SYSTEMS LLC
Also Called: Lacks Trim Systems
3703 Patterson Ave Se (49512-4024)
PHONE..................................616 554-7180
Ethan Glatz, Engineer
Alexandria Graff, Engineer
Trevor Richardson, Engineer
Bob Busch, Manager
Richard Lacks,
EMP: 12 Privately Held
WEB: www.lacksenterprises.com
SIC: 3465 Body parts, automobile: stamped metal
HQ: Lacks Exterior Systems, Llc
    5460 Cascade Rd Se
    Grand Rapids MI 49546
    616 949-6570

(G-9463)
LACKS INDUSTRIES INC
Also Called: Lacks Wheel Trim Systems
4655 Patterson Ave Se (49512-5337)
PHONE..................................616 554-7135
Bill Mull, Branch Mgr
EMP: 166 Privately Held
WEB: www.lacksenterprises.com
SIC: 3089 Injection molding of plastics; molding primary plastic
HQ: Lacks Industries, Inc.
    5460 Cascade Rd Se
    Grand Rapids MI 49546
    616 949-6570

(G-9464)
M PRINT DANCE COMPANY
3782 29th St Se (49512-1814)
PHONE..................................616 575-9969
EMP: 5 EST: 2015
SALES (est): 70.5K Privately Held
WEB: www.imprintdanceco.com
SIC: 2752 Commercial printing, lithographic

(G-9465)
MICRON HOLDINGS INC
4436 Broadmoor Ave Se (49512-5305)
PHONE..................................616 698-0707
John C Kennedy, President
John R Buchan, COO
Eduardo Renner De Castilho, COO
John F X Daly, Vice Pres
Jack Daly, Vice Pres
EMP: 2612 EST: 2004
SQ FT: 190,000
SALES (est): 39.9MM Privately Held
SIC: 3714 Motor vehicle parts & accessories

(G-9466)
NIL-COR LLC
4855 Broadmoor Ave Se (49512-5360)
PHONE..................................616 554-3100
Ronald Andronaco, CEO
Richard Smith, General Mgr
David Knoop, Purch Dir
Scott Palmitier, CFO
Tony Hinerman, Director
▲ EMP: 200 EST: 1966
SALES (est): 25.7MM
SALES (corp-wide): 144.6MM Privately Held
WEB: www.nilcor.com
SIC: 3491 Industrial valves
PA: Andronaco, Inc.
    4855 Broadmoor Ave Se
    Kentwood MI 49512
    616 554-4600

(G-9467)
NN INC
4180 40th St Se (49512-4122)
PHONE..................................616 698-0707
EMP: 28
SALES (est): 981K Privately Held
SIC: 3542 Machine tools, metal forming type

(G-9468)
OLYMPUS GROUP
1685 Viewpond Dr Se (49508-4906)
PHONE..................................616 965-2671
EMP: 8 EST: 2018
SALES (est): 450.3K Privately Held
WEB: www.olympusgrp.com
SIC: 2399 Fabricated textile products

(G-9469)
PLASTIC MOLD TECHNOLOGY INC (PA)
4201 Broadmoor Ave Se (49512-3934)
PHONE..................................616 698-9810
Gary K Proos, President
Dave Filling, Principal
Gary S Proos - Plant, Manager
▲ EMP: 51
SQ FT: 33,000
SALES (est): 12MM Privately Held
WEB: www.plasticmold.com
SIC: 3089 Injection molding of plastics

(G-9470)
PLASTIC PLATE LLC
5675 Kraft Ave Se (49512-9624)
PHONE..................................616 698-3678
Jeff Cowdrey, Manager
EMP: 80 Privately Held
SIC: 3714 Motor vehicle parts & accessories
HQ: Plastic Plate, Llc
    3500 Raleigh Dr Se
    Grand Rapids MI 49512
    616 455-5240

(G-9471)
PLASTIC PLATE LLC
3505 Kraft Ave Se (49512-2033)
PHONE..................................616 949-6570
EMP: 80 Privately Held
WEB: www.lacksenterprises.com
SIC: 3714 Motor vehicle parts & accessories
HQ: Plastic Plate, Llc
    3500 Raleigh Dr Se
    Grand Rapids MI 49512
    616 455-5240

(G-9472)
POLYVALVE LLC
Also Called: An Andronaco Industries Co
4855 Broadmoor Ave Se (49512-5360)
PHONE..................................616 554-1100
Ronald V Andronaco, President
▲ EMP: 1 EST: 2011
SALES (est): 8.2MM
SALES (corp-wide): 144.6MM Privately Held
WEB: www.polyvalveusa.com
SIC: 3592 Valves
PA: Andronaco, Inc.
    4855 Broadmoor Ave Se
    Kentwood MI 49512
    616 554-4600

(G-9473)
PUREFLEX INC
4855 Broadmoor Ave Se (49512-5360)
PHONE..................................616 554-1100
Ronald V Andronaco, CEO
Dave Knoop, Purchasing
Scott Palmitier, CFO
Joe Beaumont, Accounting Dir
Ron Webster, Human Res Dir
▲ EMP: 200 EST: 1994
SQ FT: 200,000
SALES (est): 46.5MM
SALES (corp-wide): 144.6MM Privately Held
WEB: www.pureflex.com
SIC: 3052 Rubber hose
PA: Andronaco, Inc.
    4855 Broadmoor Ave Se
    Kentwood MI 49512
    616 554-4600

(G-9474)
RAMPARTS LLC
4855 Broadmoor Ave Se (49512-5360)
PHONE..................................616 656-2250
Ronald V Andronaco, CEO
Dan Urquhart, Engineer
Scott Palmitier, CFO
EMP: 200 EST: 2009
SALES (est): 23.2MM
SALES (corp-wide): 144.6MM Privately Held
WEB: www.rampartspumps.com
SIC: 3561 Pumps & pumping equipment
PA: Andronaco, Inc.
    4855 Broadmoor Ave Se
    Kentwood MI 49512
    616 554-4600

(G-9475)
RANIR LLC
4470 44th St Se Ste B (49512-4113)
PHONE..................................616 957-7790
Julie Pearson, Branch Mgr
EMP: 34 Privately Held
WEB: www.ranir.com
SIC: 3843 Dental equipment & supplies
HQ: Ranir, Llc
    4701 East Paris Ave Se
    Grand Rapids MI 49512
    616 698-8880

(G-9476)
RLS INTERVENTIONAL INC
Also Called: Inrad
4375 Donkers Ct Se (49512-4054)
PHONE..................................616 301-7800
Steve Field, CEO
Susan Field, Vice Pres
Mike Keith, Prdtn Mgr
Diane Lambrix, Office Mgr
John Schaftenaar, Manager
EMP: 10 EST: 1997
SQ FT: 2,500
SALES (est): 1.9MM Privately Held
WEB: www.inradinc.com
SIC: 3841 Biopsy instruments & equipment

(G-9477)
ROBERT BOSCH FUEL SYSTEMS LLC
4700 S Broadmoor Ste 100 (49512)
PHONE..................................616 554-6500
Dave Winfree, Senior Engr
Charlie Syrcuse, Mng Member
EMP: 31 EST: 2003
SALES (est): 14.1MM
SALES (corp-wide): 297.8MM Privately Held
WEB: www.bosch.us
SIC: 3714 Fuel systems & parts, motor vehicle
HQ: Robert Bosch Llc
    38000 Hills Tech Dr
    Farmington Hills MI 48331
    248 876-1000

(G-9478)
ROSKAM BAKING COMPANY
5565 Broadmoor Ave Se (49512-5302)
PHONE..................................616 419-1863
EMP: 289
SALES (corp-wide): 453.5MM Privately Held
WEB: www.rothburyfarms.com
SIC: 2051 Bread, cake & related products
PA: Roskam Baking Company
    4880 Corp Exch Blvd Se
    Grand Rapids MI 49512
    616 574-5757

(G-9479)
SC CUSTOM DISPLAY INC
Also Called: Studiocraft
3010 Shaffer Ave Se Ste 1 (49512-1773)
PHONE..................................616 940-0563
EMP: 8
SQ FT: 9,000
SALES (est): 610K Privately Held
SIC: 2542 Mfg Partitions/Fixtures-Nonwood

(G-9480)
SPECTRUM CUBIC INC (PA)
5265 Kellogg Woods Dr Se (49548-5882)
PHONE..................................616 451-0784
Jay Bassett, CEO

(PA)=Parent Co (HQ)=Headquarters (DH)=Div Headquarters
✪ = New Business established in last 2 years

Kentwood - Kent County (G-9481)

Kevin Bassett, *President*
Keith Bassett, *Vice Pres*
Gina Triick, *CFO*
▲ **EMP:** 75 **EST:** 1979
SQ FT: 122,000
SALES (est): 10MM **Privately Held**
WEB: www.spectrumindustries.com
SIC: 3714 Motor vehicle parts & accessories

(G-9481)
THERMOFORMS INC
4374 Donkers Ct Se (49512-4054)
PHONE..................................616 974-0055
Timmothy Zych, *President*
Belinda Dehaven, *Opers Staff*
Pat Murphy, *Manager*
EMP: 19 **EST:** 1994
SQ FT: 27,000
SALES (est): 3.2MM **Privately Held**
WEB: www.thermoformsinc.com
SIC: 3089 Injection molding of plastics

(G-9482)
TMC FURNITURE INC (PA)
4525 Airwest Dr Se (49512-3951)
PHONE..................................734 622-0080
Blake Ratcliffe, *President*
EMP: 6 **EST:** 1998
SQ FT: 25,000
SALES (est): 3.3MM **Privately Held**
WEB: www.tmcfurniture.com
SIC: 2531 School furniture; library furniture

(G-9483)
WOODRUM SERVICES LLC
1762 Rondo St Se (49508-4965)
PHONE..................................616 827-1197
Keith Woodrum, *Principal*
EMP: 4 **EST:** 2016
SALES (est): 41.5K **Privately Held**
SIC: 2499 Wood products

(G-9484)
ZERO HOUR PARTS
3765 Broadmoor Ave Se (49512-3965)
PHONE..................................734 997-0866
EMP: 11 **EST:** 2012
SALES (est): 634.4K **Privately Held**
WEB: www.zerohourparts.com
SIC: 3499 Fabricated metal products

(G-9485)
ZOE HEALTH
5715 Christie Ave Se (49508-6236)
PHONE..................................616 485-1909
Sharon Chase, *Owner*
EMP: 4
SALES (est): 800K **Privately Held**
SIC: 3999 Manufacturing industries

Kewadin
Antrim County

(G-9486)
DUPONT OFFICE AND SELF ST
1710 Birchview Dr (49648-9769)
PHONE..................................206 471-3700
EMP: 4 **EST:** 2016
SALES (est): 95.8K **Privately Held**
SIC: 2879 Agricultural chemicals

(G-9487)
GREAT LAKES PACKING CO
6556 Quarterline Rd (49648-8907)
PHONE..................................231 264-5561
Jon Beliqutte, *President*
Norman Veliquette, *President*
Dean Veliquette, *Vice Pres*
Jon T Veliquette, *Admin Sec*
▼ **EMP:** 20 **EST:** 1972
SQ FT: 30,000
SALES (est): 2.6MM **Privately Held**
WEB: www.greatlakespacking.com
SIC: 0723 2033 Fruit (fresh) packing services; canned fruits & specialties

(G-9488)
IRON HEART CANNING COMPANY LLC
3630 Sutter Ln (49648-9182)
PHONE..................................231 675-1839
Tyler Wille, *Mng Member*
EMP: 12
SALES (corp-wide): 3.3MM **Privately Held**
WEB: www.ironheartcanning.com
SIC: 3221 Bottles for packing, bottling & canning: glass
PA: Iron Heart Canning Company, Llc
  8025 S Willow St Ste 201
  Manchester NH 03103
  603 664-4208

(G-9489)
SMOOTHIES
11937 Stone Circle Dr (49648-8003)
PHONE..................................231 498-2374
Jeffrey C Urbanavage, *Owner*
EMP: 4 **EST:** 2014
SALES (est): 87K **Privately Held**
SIC: 2037 Frozen fruits & vegetables

Keweenaw Bay
Baraga County

(G-9490)
SUPERIOR TOOL & FABG LLC
13529 Old 41 Rd (49908-9022)
PHONE..................................906 353-7588
EMP: 8 **EST:** 2010
SQ FT: 6,000
SALES (est): 500K **Privately Held**
SIC: 3593 Mfg Fluid Power Cylinders

Kimball
St. Clair County

(G-9491)
AUTO QUIP INC
70 Airport Dr (48074-4404)
PHONE..................................810 364-3366
Paul Sossi, *President*
Annemarie Sossi, *Vice Pres*
EMP: 10 **EST:** 1967
SQ FT: 11,100
SALES (est): 987.1K **Privately Held**
WEB: www.autoquipinc.com
SIC: 3291 Abrasive products

(G-9492)
F C SIMPSON LIME CO
1293 Wadhams Rd (48074-3112)
PHONE..................................810 367-3510
R Kurt Simpson, *President*
EMP: 5 **EST:** 1959
SALES (est): 317.1K **Privately Held**
WEB: www.fcsimpsonlime.com
SIC: 0711 2874 4212 Lime spreading services; soil chemical treatment services; calcium meta-phosphate; animal & farm product transportation services

(G-9493)
HAMMARS CONTRACTING LLC
Also Called: Hammar's Welding
1177 Wadhams Rd (48074-3111)
PHONE..................................810 367-3037
Timothy Hammar, *Owner*
Robert Hammar, *Owner*
EMP: 20 **EST:** 1969
SQ FT: 2,500
SALES (est): 1.2MM **Privately Held**
SIC: 7699 3443 Industrial equipment services; dumpsters; garbage

(G-9494)
LEBALAB INC
35 Ash Dr (48074-4401)
PHONE..................................519 542-4236
Walter Duberry, *Manager*
EMP: 8 **EST:** 2011
SALES (est): 106.5K **Privately Held**
WEB: www.lebalab.com
SIC: 3199 Dog furnishings: collars, leashes, muzzles, etc.: leather

(G-9495)
M THREE MANUFACTURING LLC
71 Ash Dr (48074-4401)
PHONE..................................810 824-4734
EMP: 4 **EST:** 2019
SALES (est): 107.6K **Privately Held**
WEB: www.m3manufacturing.net
SIC: 3999 Manufacturing industries

(G-9496)
MPP CORP
Also Called: Massobrio Precision Products
82 Airport Dr (48074-4404)
P.O. Box 275, Marysville (48040-0275)
PHONE..................................810 364-2939
Carlo Massobrio, *President*
Aurelio Massobrio, *Vice Pres*
Lori Sommers, *Office Mgr*
Frank Nothelle, *Manager*
▲ **EMP:** 20 **EST:** 1991
SQ FT: 13,800
SALES (est): 4.5MM **Privately Held**
WEB: www.mppcorp.net
SIC: 3544 Special dies & tools

(G-9497)
PEPSI BOTTLING GROUP
Also Called: Pepsico
2111 Wadhams Rd (48074-1914)
PHONE..................................810 966-8060
Jared Herrmann, *General Mgr*
Ishpinder Sahni, *General Mgr*
Brian Connelly, *Principal*
Robert Kuchar, *Opers Staff*
Benjamin Fridline, *Financial Analy*
EMP: 15 **EST:** 2009
SALES (est): 971.3K **Privately Held**
WEB: www.pepsico.com
SIC: 2086 Soft drinks: packaged in cans, bottles, etc.

(G-9498)
PEPSI-COLA METRO BTLG CO INC
2111 Wadhams Rd (48074-1914)
PHONE..................................810 987-2181
Brian Connelly, *Manager*
EMP: 4
SALES (corp-wide): 70.3B **Publicly Held**
WEB: www.pepsico.com
SIC: 4225 2086 General warehousing & storage; carbonated beverages, nonalcoholic: bottled & canned
HQ: Pepsi-Cola Metropolitan Bottling Company, Inc.
  1111 Westchester Ave
  White Plains NY 10604
  914 767-6000

(G-9499)
PRECISION DIE CAST INC
65 Gaffield Dr (48074-4533)
PHONE..................................586 463-1800
Craig La Pierre, *CEO*
EMP: 8 **EST:** 2001 **Privately Held**
WEB: www.precisiondiecast.com
SIC: 3363 Aluminum die-castings

(G-9500)
PREFERRED INDUSTRIES INC
11 Ash Dr (48074-4401)
PHONE..................................810 364-4090
Charles Kott, *President*
Alex Morton, *General Mgr*
David Shevnock, *Program Mgr*
Katie Lezin, *Technology*
▲ **EMP:** 30 **EST:** 1977
SQ FT: 20,000
SALES (est): 4.1MM **Privately Held**
WEB: www.preferredind.com
SIC: 3544 5051 Special dies & tools; metals service centers & offices

Kincheloe
Chippewa County

(G-9501)
E U P WOODS SHAVINGS
16816 S Hugginin St (49788-1900)
PHONE..................................906 495-1141
Mickey Hoffman, *Principal*
EMP: 7 **EST:** 2013
SALES (est): 481.2K **Privately Held**
WEB: www.upshavings.com
SIC: 2421 Sawdust, shavings & wood chips

(G-9502)
EUP WOOD SHAVINGS INC
Also Called: Eastern Upper Pnsula WD Shvngs
16888 S Hugginin St (49788-1900)
PHONE..................................586 943-7199
Dan Socia, *President*
EMP: 10 **EST:** 2010
SALES (est): 687.3K **Privately Held**
WEB: www.upshavings.com
SIC: 2411 Wooden logs

(G-9503)
FLORIDA COCA-COLA BOTTLING CO
4760 W Curtis St (49788-1584)
PHONE..................................906 495-2261
Julane Underhill, *Manager*
EMP: 403
SALES (corp-wide): 33B **Publicly Held**
WEB: www.coca-cola.com
SIC: 2086 Bottled & canned soft drinks
HQ: Florida Coca-Cola Bottling Company
  521 Lake Kathy Dr
  Brandon FL 33510
  813 569-2600

(G-9504)
KINROSS FAB & MACHINE INC
17422 S Dolan St (49788-1615)
PHONE..................................906 495-1900
Charles Esson, *President*
Tamie Munz, *General Mgr*
EMP: 22 **EST:** 2011
SALES (est): 2.5MM **Privately Held**
WEB: www.kinrossfab.com
SIC: 7692 Welding repair

(G-9505)
SUPERIOR FABRICATION CO LLC
17499 S Dolan St Bldg 434 (49788-1615)
PHONE..................................906 495-5634
John Eckerle, *Purchasing*
Jason Long, *Engineer*
Ryan Berkompas, *Senior Engr*
Angela Fuller, *Accountant*
Ann Davis, *Sales Staff*
▲ **EMP:** 100 **EST:** 1980
SQ FT: 130,000
SALES (est): 13MM **Privately Held**
WEB: www.supfab.com
SIC: 3812 3531 Defense systems & equipment; construction machinery

Kingsford
Dickinson County

(G-9506)
C J GRAPHICS INC
121 S Carpenter Ave (49802-4520)
PHONE..................................906 774-8636
Nicole Lutz, *President*
EMP: 9 **EST:** 1982
SQ FT: 4,600
SALES (est): 1MM **Privately Held**
WEB: www.cjgraphics.net
SIC: 2752 Commercial printing, offset

(G-9507)
COUNTRY SCHOOLHOUSE KINGSFORD
600 East Blvd (49802-4508)
PHONE..................................906 828-1971
EMP: 4 **EST:** 2016
SALES (est): 92K **Privately Held**
SIC: 2861 Charcoal, except activated

(G-9508)
DICKINSON HOMES INC (PA)
1500 W Breitung Ave (49802-5127)
P.O. Box 2245, Iron Mountain (49802-2245)
PHONE..................................906 774-5800
Albert Santoni, *President*
Paul Santoni, *Vice Pres*
Steve Kindness, *Project Mgr*
Mario Santoni, *Project Mgr*
Ryan Spencer, *Project Mgr*
EMP: 45 **EST:** 1970
SQ FT: 80,000

SALES (est): 9.1MM **Privately Held**
WEB: www.dickinsonhomes.com
SIC: 2452 Modular homes, prefabricated, wood

(G-9509)
GREDE LLC
Iron Mountain Foundry
801 S Carpenter Ave (49802-5511)
PHONE..........................906 774-7250
Randy Priem, *VP Opers*
EMP: 500
SALES (corp-wide): 686.1MM **Privately Held**
WEB: www.grede.com
SIC: 3321 3322 Gray iron castings; malleable iron foundries
HQ: Grede Llc
  20750 Civic Center Dr # 100
  Southfield MI 48076

(G-9510)
HARVEY PATTERN WORKS INC
410 North Blvd (49802-4414)
P.O. Box 2024 (49802-2024)
PHONE..........................906 774-4285
Jeff Harvey, *President*
EMP: 10 EST: 1979
SQ FT: 8,000
SALES (est): 909.1K **Privately Held**
SIC: 3543 Foundry patternmaking

(G-9511)
KINGSFORD BROACH & TOOL INC
2200 Maule Dr (49802-5101)
P.O. Box 2277 (49802-2277)
PHONE..........................906 774-4917
Dominic Shultz, *President*
Jack Raney, *Vice Pres*
Keith Baldwin, *Prdtn Mgr*
Tom Johns, *Engineer*
Connie Lapointe, *Office Mgr*
EMP: 42 EST: 1969
SQ FT: 22,000
SALES: 5.3MM **Privately Held**
WEB: www.kingsfordbroach.com
SIC: 3545 7389 Broaches (machine tool accessories); business services

(G-9512)
LAKE SHORE SYSTEMS INC (PA)
2141 Woodward Ave (49802-4206)
PHONE..........................906 774-1500
Jessica Frost, *CEO*
Fritz Wenzel, *Vice Pres*
Shane Trulock, *Facilities Mgr*
Scott Cameron, *Opers Staff*
Karen L Luce, *Senior Buyer*
▲ EMP: 78 EST: 2016
SQ FT: 20,000
SALES (est): 77MM **Privately Held**
WEB: www.lakeshoresys.com
SIC: 3537 3532 3731 Industrial trucks & tractors; mining machinery; shipbuilding & repairing

(G-9513)
LODAL INC
620 N Hooper St (49802-5400)
PHONE..........................906 779-1700
Bernard Leger, *President*
John R Giuliani, *Corp Secy*
◆ EMP: 70 EST: 1946
SQ FT: 360,000
SALES (est): 8.2MM **Privately Held**
WEB: www.lodal.com
SIC: 3713 Truck bodies (motor vehicles)

(G-9514)
NELSON PAINT CO OF MICH INC (PA)
Also Called: Nelson Technologies
1 Nelson Dr (49802-4561)
P.O. Box 2040 (49802-2040)
PHONE..........................906 774-5566
Richard Louys, *President*
Karen Cox, *Vice Pres*
EMP: 3
SQ FT: 20,000

SALES (est): 1.5MM **Privately Held**
WEB: www.nelsonpaint.com
SIC: 2851 5941 3953 Paints, waterproof; sporting goods & bicycle shops; marking devices

(G-9515)
NELSON PAINT COMPANY ALA INC (PA)
1 Nelson Dr (49802-4561)
P.O. Box 2040 (49802-2040)
PHONE..........................906 774-5566
Barbara N Louys, *President*
Richard Louys, *Vice Pres*
Karen Cox, *Admin Sec*
EMP: 3 EST: 1960
SQ FT: 33,000
SALES (est): 2.5MM **Privately Held**
WEB: www.nelsonpaint.com
SIC: 2851 Paints & paint additives

(G-9516)
NORTHWOODS MANUFACTURING INC
850 East Blvd (49802-4436)
P.O. Box 2294 (49802-2294)
PHONE..........................906 779-2370
Jon Pipp, *President*
Mike Paupore, *Purchasing*
▲ EMP: 70 EST: 1994
SQ FT: 100,000
SALES (est): 13MM **Privately Held**
WEB: www.nwmfginc.com
SIC: 3444 3441 3548 5211 Culverts, flumes & pipes; fabricated structural metal for ships; welding & cutting apparatus & accessories; insulation material, building; barber & beauty shop equipment; fire- or burglary-resistive products

(G-9517)
SMITH CASTINGS INCORPORATED
601 N Balsam St (49802-1133)
P.O. Box 2126 (49802-2126)
PHONE..........................906 774-4956
Eric Frantz, *Principal*
Marie Olson, *Planning*
EMP: 11 EST: 2007
SALES (est): 2.6MM **Privately Held**
WEB: www.smithcastings.com
SIC: 3321 Gray iron castings

(G-9518)
STANDARD ELECTRIC COMPANY
701 Valsam St (49802)
PHONE..........................906 774-4455
Mary Brooks, *Branch Mgr*
EMP: 11
SALES (corp-wide): 210.4MM **Privately Held**
WEB: www.standardelectricco.com
SIC: 5063 3825 Electrical supplies; electrical fittings & construction materials; electrical construction materials; frequency meters: electrical, mechanical & electronic
PA: Standard Electric Company
  2650 Trautner Dr
  Saginaw MI 48604
  989 497-2100

(G-9519)
WILBERT BURIAL VAULT WORKS
609 S Carpenter Ave (49802-5521)
P.O. Box 688, Iron Mountain (49801-0688)
PHONE..........................906 786-0261
Alvin Grabowski, *President*
Keith Grabowski, *Vice Pres*
EMP: 8 EST: 1938
SQ FT: 11,520
SALES (est): 869.7K **Privately Held**
WEB: www.wilbert.com
SIC: 3272 7261 Burial vaults, concrete or precast terrazzo; septic tanks, concrete; crematory

Kingsley
Grand Traverse County

(G-9520)
5 STAR DRCTIONAL DRLG SVCS IND
8553 Blackman Rd (49649-9671)
P.O. Box 194 (49649-0194)
PHONE..........................231 263-2050
Trevor Yetter, *President*
Mike Newman, *Vice Pres*
EMP: 4 EST: 2005
SQ FT: 10,000
SALES (est): 900.2K **Privately Held**
WEB: www.5stardrilling.com
SIC: 1381 Directional drilling oil & gas wells

(G-9521)
BACH SERVICES & MFG CO LLC
2777 Lynx Ln (49649-9528)
PHONE..........................231 263-2777
Kent Wood, *Director*
Robin Bach,
Rick Bach,
Sarah Lock, *Assistant*
EMP: 11 EST: 2006
SALES (est): 2.6MM **Privately Held**
WEB: www.bachservices.com
SIC: 1389 Construction, repair & dismantling services

(G-9522)
D&L LOGGING
6703 Summit City Rd (49649-9665)
PHONE..........................231 709-5477
Lorrie Parks, *Principal*
EMP: 4 EST: 2017
SALES (est): 55.9K **Privately Held**
SIC: 2411 Logging

(G-9523)
EM A GIVE BREAK SAFETY
6502 M 37 (49649-9773)
PHONE..........................231 263-6625
Jeff Mac Dermaid, *Manager*
EMP: 4 EST: 2004
SALES (est): 150.2K **Privately Held**
SIC: 8742 3669 Quality assurance consultant; pedestrian traffic control equipment

(G-9524)
KBS WELDING SERVICE
5546 Weaver Rd (49649-9742)
PHONE..........................231 263-7164
Kenneth Belanger, *Principal*
EMP: 4 EST: 2015
SALES (est): 41K **Privately Held**
SIC: 7692 Welding repair

(G-9525)
MICHAEL CHRIS STORMS
Also Called: Fire-Pit Pellets
1401 W Center Rd (49649-9734)
PHONE..........................231 263-7516
Michael Chris Storms, *Owner*
Joy Storms, *Co-Owner*
EMP: 5 EST: 1991
SALES (est): 469.5K **Privately Held**
WEB: www.cherrypitstore.com
SIC: 2448 Wood pallets & skids

Kingston
Tuscola County

(G-9526)
MIDYNACO LLC
Also Called: MI Dynaco
3719 Ross St (48741-9775)
PHONE..........................989 550-8552
Dale Manor,
Dave Gibson,
EMP: 4 EST: 2004
SALES (est): 588.7K
SALES (corp-wide): 1MM **Privately Held**
WEB: www.midynaco.com
SIC: 3442 Metal doors, sash & trim

PA: Memtech, Inc.
  9033 General Dr
  Plymouth MI 48170
  734 455-8550

Kinross
Chippewa County

(G-9527)
NATURAL HLTH ESSNTIAL OILS LLC
6307 W Kallio Rd (49752-9114)
PHONE..........................906 495-5404
Lorene Nicklas, *Principal*
EMP: 4 EST: 2016
SALES (est): 69.1K **Privately Held**
SIC: 2899 Essential oils

La Salle
Monroe County

(G-9528)
MOYER WLDG & FABRICATION LLC
13685 Dunlap Rd (48145-9770)
PHONE..........................734 243-1212
EMP: 4 EST: 2019
SALES (est): 30.3K **Privately Held**
WEB: www.moyerswelding.com
SIC: 7692 Welding repair

(G-9529)
REED YACHT SALES LLC (PA)
11840 Toledo Beach Rd (48145-9455)
PHONE..........................419 304-4405
Cheryl Bogedain,
EMP: 8 EST: 2013
SALES (est): 1MM **Privately Held**
WEB: www.reedyachtsales.com
SIC: 3732 Yachts, building & repairing

(G-9530)
T & K WOODWORKS
1983 W Stein Rd (48145-9712)
PHONE..........................734 868-0028
Kenneth Gerald Larabell, *Owner*
EMP: 4 EST: 2018
SALES (est): 54.1K **Privately Held**
SIC: 2431 Millwork

Lachine
Alpena County

(G-9531)
BURRONE FAMILY VINEYARDS
212 Pinebrook Dr (49753-9728)
PHONE..........................989 379-3786
Charles A Burrone, *Principal*
EMP: 5 EST: 2008
SALES (est): 121K **Privately Held**
SIC: 2084 Wines

(G-9532)
NORTHERN MICH WLDLIFE ART FRAM
Also Called: Northern Promotions
12595 Long Rapids Rd (49753-9630)
PHONE..........................989 340-1272
Kevan R Rogers,
EMP: 10 EST: 2014
SQ FT: 1,500
SALES (est): 1MM **Privately Held**
WEB: www.northernpromotionsart.com
SIC: 3861 7336 Printing frames, photographic; commercial art & illustration

(G-9533)
PATCHWOOD PRODUCTS INC
105 Stagecoach Dr (49753-9610)
PHONE..........................989 742-2605
Patricia Paczkowski, *Branch Mgr*
EMP: 10
SQ FT: 50,000
SALES (corp-wide): 1.6MM **Privately Held**
WEB: www.patchwood.nfshost.com
SIC: 2448 Pallets, wood

PA: Patchwood Products, Inc.
14797 State St
Hillman MI 49746
989 742-2605

(G-9534)
ROBERT CRAWFORD & SON LOGGING
15490 Green Farm Rd (49753-9359)
PHONE................989 379-2712
Robert Crawford, *CEO*
EMP: 4 **EST:** 1999
SALES (est): 452.9K **Privately Held**
SIC: 2411 Logging camps & contractors

(G-9535)
VIA-TECH CORP
11715 M 32 W (49753-9659)
P.O. Box 233, Alpena (49707-0233)
PHONE................989 358-7028
Gregory C Winter, *President*
Deborah J Winter, *Corp Secy*
EMP: 17 **EST:** 1984
SQ FT: 11,000
SALES (est): 2.7MM **Privately Held**
SIC: 3535 Conveyors & conveying equipment

Laingsburg
Shiawassee County

(G-9536)
LAINGSBURG SCREW INC
9805 Round Lake Rd (48848-9404)
PHONE................517 651-2757
Brian Grable, *President*
Leslie Graham, *Treasurer*
EMP: 6 **EST:** 1994
SQ FT: 2,400
SALES (est): 478.6K **Privately Held**
SIC: 3544 Special dies & tools

(G-9537)
METHODS PRTABLE MACHINING WLDG
9607 Price Rd (48848-9514)
PHONE................989 413-5022
EMP: 4 **EST:** 2020
SALES (est): 78.4K **Privately Held**
SIC: 7692 Welding repair

(G-9538)
TOASTMASTERS INTERNATIONAL
6687 Westview Dr (48848-9489)
PHONE................517 651-6507
Johnson Baugh, *Treasurer*
EMP: 7
SALES (corp-wide): 39.8MM **Privately Held**
WEB: www.toastmasters.org
SIC: 8299 2721 Educational service, non-degree granting; continuing educ.; magazines: publishing only, not printed on site
PA: Toastmasters International
9127 S Jamaica St Ste 400
Englewood CO 80112
949 858-8255

Lake Angelus
Oakland County

(G-9539)
ROBBINS PUBLISHING GROUP INC
945 N Lake Angelus Rd (48326-1024)
PHONE................734 260-3258
Philip Robbins, *Principal*
EMP: 5 **EST:** 2014
SALES (est): 78.8K **Privately Held**
SIC: 2741 Miscellaneous publishing

Lake Ann
Benzie County

(G-9540)
A LITE IN NITE
15782 Hooker Rd (49650-9780)
PHONE................231 275-5900
Howe Jane Demovic, *Owner*
EMP: 4 **EST:** 2016
SALES (est): 95.3K **Privately Held**
WEB: www.aliteinthenite.com
SIC: 3648 Lighting equipment

(G-9541)
ALL DEALER INVENTORY LLC
8148 Maple City Hwy (49650-9620)
P.O. Box 32054, Tucson AZ (85751-2054)
PHONE................231 342-9823
Kimberly Deatrick, *Principal*
EMP: 10 **EST:** 2009
SALES (est): 973.1K **Privately Held**
SIC: 7319 7313 2721 Distribution of advertising material or sample services; electronic media advertising representatives; printed media advertising representatives; magazines: publishing only, not printed on site

(G-9542)
NORTHERN MICHIGAN PROP SP LLC
20080 Maple St (49650-9710)
P.O. Box 86 (49650-0086)
PHONE................231 275-7173
Brandon Sarber,
William Schramm,
EMP: 5 **EST:** 2016
SALES (est): 60K **Privately Held**
SIC: 3732 Boat building & repairing

(G-9543)
NORTHERN OUTDOOR WOODWORKS LLC
8581 Bent Pine Dr (49650-9418)
PHONE................231 275-1181
Paul Sturtevant, *Principal*
EMP: 4 **EST:** 2016
SALES (est): 81.9K **Privately Held**
SIC: 2431 Millwork

Lake City
Missaukee County

(G-9544)
BIEWER SAWMILL-LAKE CITY LLC
1560 W Houghton Lake Rd (49651-9672)
P.O. Box 497, Saint Clair (48079-0497)
PHONE................231 839-7646
Stephan Lemay, *Manager*
EMP: 12 **EST:** 2011
SALES (est): 1.3MM **Privately Held**
WEB: www.biewerlumber.com
SIC: 2421 Sawmills & planing mills, general

(G-9545)
BOHNING COMPANY LTD (PA)
7361 N 7 Mile Rd (49651-9293)
PHONE................231 229-4247
Larry Griffith, *President*
Karen Abrahamson, *Vice Pres*
Dale E Voice, *Vice Pres*
Nicole Vander Meulen, *Production*
Tara Carlson, *Buyer*
◆ **EMP:** 37 **EST:** 1946
SQ FT: 31,400
SALES (est): 11.3MM **Privately Held**
WEB: www.bohning.com
SIC: 3949 2899 Archery equipment, general; chemical preparations

(G-9546)
GAGE NUMERICAL INC
Also Called: Inspection Control Company
900 S 7 Mile Rd (49651-8537)
PHONE................231 328-4426
Glen F Corwin, *President*
Phyllis L Corwin, *Vice Pres*
EMP: 5 **EST:** 1981
SQ FT: 5,168
SALES (est): 350K **Privately Held**
WEB: www.iccnumericalgage.com
SIC: 3545 8734 Gauge blocks; calibration & certification

(G-9547)
JOHN A BIEWER LUMBER COMPANY
1560 W Houghton Lake Rd (49651-9672)
PHONE................231 839-7646
Lawrence Markey Jr, *President*
EMP: 48
SALES (corp-wide): 39MM **Privately Held**
WEB: www.biewerlumber.com
SIC: 2421 Sawmills & planing mills, general
PA: John A. Biewer Lumber Company
812 S Riverside Ave
Saint Clair MI 48079
810 329-4789

(G-9548)
LC MANUFACTURING LLC (PA)
Also Called: Lake City Forge
4150 N Wolcott Rd (49651-9126)
PHONE................231 839-7102
Peter Baenen, *CEO*
Scott Stephens, *Plant Mgr*
Doug Crosby, *Purch Agent*
Dennis Ellens, *Engineer*
Derek Farrell, *Maintence Staff*
EMP: 170 **EST:** 1975
SQ FT: 5,200
SALES (est): 30.8MM **Privately Held**
WEB: www.lcforge.com
SIC: 3462 3544 Automotive forgings, ferrous: crankshaft, engine, axle, etc.; special dies & tools

(G-9549)
LONEYS ALPACA JUNCTION
3109 N 7 Mile Rd (49651-9102)
PHONE................231 229-4530
Gina Loney, *Principal*
EMP: 4 **EST:** 2017
SALES (est): 168.1K **Privately Held**
WEB: www.lajalpaca.com
SIC: 2231 Alpacas, mohair: woven

(G-9550)
MARK BEEM
Also Called: Beem Fence
861 N Green Rd (49651-9230)
P.O. Box 685 (49651-0685)
PHONE................231 510-8122
Mark Beem, *Owner*
EMP: 6 **EST:** 1975
SALES (est): 464.4K **Privately Held**
SIC: 1799 2499 7389 Fence construction; fencing, docks & other outdoor wood structural products;

(G-9551)
MID MICHIGAN LOGGING
9620 N Nelson Rd (49651-9742)
PHONE................231 229-4501
Terry Frever, *Partner*
Larry Niebrzydowski, *Partner*
EMP: 17 **EST:** 1974
SALES (est): 1.1MM **Privately Held**
WEB: www.midmichigantimber.com
SIC: 2411 Logging camps & contractors; wood chips, produced in the field

(G-9552)
MISSAUKEE MOLDED RUBBER INC
6400 W Blue Rd (49651-8948)
PHONE................231 839-5309
Jay W Price, *President*
Kathy Price, *Treasurer*
EMP: 16 **EST:** 1989
SQ FT: 3,456
SALES (est): 1.5MM **Privately Held**
WEB: www.mmri-crc.com
SIC: 3069 Molded rubber products

(G-9553)
PHELPS SERVICES
8466 N 7 Mile Rd (49651-9460)
PHONE................231 942-8044
Megan Bridson, *Principal*
EMP: 4 **EST:** 2017
SALES (est): 64.4K **Privately Held**
SIC: 2411 Logging

(G-9554)
RIVERSIDE DEFENSE TRAINING LLC
5360 S Dickerson Rd (49651-8662)
PHONE................231 825-2895
Richard A Bradley, *Principal*
EMP: 5 **EST:** 2017
SALES (est): 112.2K **Privately Held**
SIC: 3812 Defense systems & equipment

(G-9555)
SRM CONCRETE LLC
1317 W Sanborn Rd (49651-7608)
PHONE................231 839-4319
Kenneth Gilde, *Manager*
EMP: 67
SALES (corp-wide): 170.1MM **Privately Held**
WEB: www.smyrnareadymix.com
SIC: 1442 Common sand mining; gravel mining
PA: Srm Concrete, Llc
1136 2nd Ave N
Nashville TN 37208
615 355-1028

(G-9556)
VAN DUINEN FOREST PRODUCTS
4680 E Houghton Lake Rd (49651-9546)
PHONE................231 328-4507
Carmen Van Duinen, *President*
Charles Van Duinen, *Principal*
Ave Van Duinen, *Treasurer*
EMP: 13 **EST:** 1973
SALES (est): 515.8K **Privately Held**
SIC: 2411 Logging

Lake Leelanau
Leelanau County

(G-9557)
45 NORTH VINEYARD & WINERY
8580 E Horn Rd (49653-9645)
PHONE................231 271-1188
Alanna Grossnickle, *General Mgr*
Steve Grossnickle, *Co-Owner*
Lori Grossnickle, *Co-Owner*
Brian Grossnickle, *Manager*
▲ **EMP:** 15 **EST:** 2007
SALES (est): 1.2MM **Privately Held**
WEB: www.fortyfivenorth.com
SIC: 2084 Wines

(G-9558)
AURORA CELLARS 2015 LLC
7788 E Horn Rd (49653-9640)
PHONE................231 994-3188
Joanna Simpson,
Samuel Simpson,
EMP: 10 **EST:** 2015
SALES (est): 897.4K **Privately Held**
WEB: www.auroracellars.com
SIC: 2084 Wine cellars, bonded: engaged in blending wines

(G-9559)
E S I INDUSTRIES
10 S Highland Dr (49653-9413)
PHONE................231 256-9345
Larry Hudson, *President*
Stanley Hudson, *Vice Pres*
Jerry Dykema, *Treasurer*
EMP: 8 **EST:** 1974
SQ FT: 10,000
SALES (est): 247.3K **Privately Held**
SIC: 3291 Paper, abrasive: garnet, emery, aluminum oxide coated

(G-9560)
FONTAINE CHATEAU
2290 S French Rd (49653-9558)
PHONE................231 256-0000
Dan Matthias, *Owner*
EMP: 5 **EST:** 2005
SALES (est): 192.3K **Privately Held**
WEB: www.chateaufontaine.com
SIC: 2084 5921 5182 Wines; wine; wine

(G-9561)
FRENCH ROAD CELLARS LLC
2300 S French Rd (49653-8712)
PHONE................231 256-0680

GEOGRAPHIC SECTION

Lake Orion - Oakland County (G-9590)

◆ **EMP:** 8 **EST:** 2009
SALES (est): 491.6K **Privately Held**
SIC: 2084 Wines

(G-9562)
GOOD HARBOR VINEYARDS WINERY
34 S Manitou Trl (49653-9589)
PHONE..................231 632-0703
Sam Simpson, *General Mgr*
Debbie Simpson, *Manager*
Taylor Simpson, *Director*
EMP: 8 **EST:** 2017
SALES (est): 138.8K **Privately Held**
WEB: www.goodharbor.com
SIC: 2084 Wines

(G-9563)
LEELANAU ENTERPRISE INC
7200 E Duck Lake Rd (49653-9779)
PHONE..................231 256-9827
Alan C Campbell, *President*
EMP: 29 **EST:** 1877
SALES (est): 2.7MM **Privately Held**
WEB: www.leelanaunews.com
SIC: 2711 Newspapers: publishing only, not printed on site

(G-9564)
PLAMONDON OIL CO INC
525 W Main St (49653-9499)
P.O. Box 139 (49653-0139)
PHONE..................231 256-9261
Michele Gipun, *Principal*
EMP: 6 **EST:** 2001
SALES (est): 381.8K **Privately Held**
SIC: 3569 Gas producers, generators & other gas related equipment

(G-9565)
PROVEMONT HILL VINEYARD
150 S French Rd (49653-9733)
PHONE..................231 256-8839
EMP: 4 **EST:** 2013
SALES (est): 85.8K **Privately Held**
SIC: 2084 Wines

Lake Linden
Houghton County

(G-9566)
AUTUMN ENDEAVORS LLC
51019 Paradise Ln (49945-9643)
PHONE..................906 296-0601
Lawrence Evers, *Owner*
EMP: 4 **EST:** 2018
SALES (est): 79.1K **Privately Held**
SIC: 2759 Commercial printing

(G-9567)
BOB JUTILA LOGGING
55658 Traprock Valley Rd (49945-9739)
PHONE..................906 296-0753
Bob Jutila, *Officer*
EMP: 5 **EST:** 2009
SALES (est): 139K **Privately Held**
SIC: 2411 Logging camps & contractors

(G-9568)
CW CHAMPION WELDING ALLOYS LLC
52705 State Highway M26 (49945-1343)
P.O. Box 10 (49945-0010)
PHONE..................906 296-9633
Charlie Kiilunen, *Principal*
EMP: 6 **EST:** 2010
SALES (est): 193.4K **Privately Held**
SIC: 7692 Welding repair

(G-9569)
PENINSULA PRODUCTS INC
54385 Cemetery Rd (49945-1278)
PHONE..................906 296-9801
Larry R Joosten, *President*
Marcia M Joosten, *Corp Secy*
EMP: 4
SQ FT: 2,500 **Privately Held**
SIC: 3272 Burial vaults, concrete or precast terrazzo; septic tanks, concrete

(G-9570)
SKINNY PETES LLC
700 Calumet St (49945-1005)
PHONE..................906 369-1431
Arthur Lyons,
EMP: 6 **EST:** 2019
SALES (est): 283.2K **Privately Held**
SIC: 2051 Bakery: wholesale or wholesale/retail combined

Lake Odessa
Ionia County

(G-9571)
ALLYMADE
1037 4th Ave (48849-1021)
PHONE..................616 813-0591
Allison R Dorr, *Owner*
EMP: 4 **EST:** 2013
SALES (est): 60.3K **Privately Held**
SIC: 3961 5944 Costume jewelry; jewelry stores

(G-9572)
AUTOMATED PROCESS EQUIPMENT (PA)
Also Called: Apec
1201 4th Ave (48849-1301)
PHONE..................616 374-1000
Kendall Wilcox, *CEO*
Garrett Billmire, *Vice Pres*
Terry Stemler, *Vice Pres*
Robert Crosby, *Development*
Keather Winslow, *Human Res Mgr*
▼ **EMP:** 38 **EST:** 1991
SQ FT: 60,000
SALES (est): 10.5MM **Privately Held**
WEB: www.apecusa.com
SIC: 3556 Food products machinery

(G-9573)
CARBON GREEN BIOENERGY LLC
7795 Saddlebag Lake Rd (48849-9319)
PHONE..................616 374-4000
Mitchell Miller, *CEO*
Mike Vantland, *Prdtn Mgr*
Mikel Slater, *Production*
Jason Jerke, *CFO*
Jim Murphy,
EMP: 45 **EST:** 2009
SALES (est): 17MM **Privately Held**
WEB: www.cgbioenergy.com
SIC: 2869 5169 Ethyl alcohol, ethanol; alcohols

(G-9574)
DADDY DZ GRANOLA CO
619 6th Ave (48849-1223)
PHONE..................616 374-0229
Vernon L Dumond, *Administration*
EMP: 4 **EST:** 2014
SALES (est): 64.9K **Privately Held**
SIC: 2043 Granola & muesli, except bars & clusters

(G-9575)
FRANKLIN METAL TRADING CORP
Also Called: Champion Alloys
609 Tupper Lake St (48849-1062)
PHONE..................616 374-7171
William Boorstein, *President*
Laurie Martin, *Controller*
EMP: 28 **EST:** 1971
SQ FT: 150,000
SALES (est): 8.6MM **Privately Held**
WEB: www.franklinmetaltradingcorp.com
SIC: 5093 3341 Ferrous metal scrap & waste; secondary nonferrous metals

(G-9576)
GREAT LAKES SAND & GRAVEL LLC
7940 Woodland Rd (48849-9300)
PHONE..................616 374-3169
Bob Dejong, *Owner*
EMP: 5 **EST:** 1987
SALES (est): 402.4K **Privately Held**
SIC: 3273 Ready-mixed concrete

(G-9577)
MICHIGAN AG SERVICES INC
Also Called: Michigan Glass Lined Storage
3587 W Tupper Lake Rd (48849-9804)
P.O. Box 573 (48849-0573)
PHONE..................616 374-8803
Martinus Koorn, *President*
Laverne Lettinga, *Vice Pres*
▲ **EMP:** 18 **EST:** 1958
SQ FT: 10,000
SALES (est): 3MM **Privately Held**
SIC: 3523 1542 Farm machinery & equipment; silo construction, agricultural

(G-9578)
MICHIGAN DUTCH BARNS INC
9811 Thompson Rd (48849-9713)
PHONE..................616 693-2754
Steve Swartz, *CEO*
April Swartz, *Treasurer*
EMP: 18 **EST:** 1988
SQ FT: 960
SALES (est): 2.4MM **Privately Held**
WEB: www.michigandutchbarns.com
SIC: 2452 Prefabricated buildings, wood

(G-9579)
TWIN CITY FOODS INC
801 Lincoln St (48849-1399)
PHONE..................616 374-4002
Don Leathem, *Division Mgr*
Joshua Weller, *Division Mgr*
Ken Stensen, *Div Sub Head*
Duwane Blendy, *Plant Mgr*
Shane Hansen, *Plant Mgr*
EMP: 86
SQ FT: 120,000
SALES (corp-wide): 225.1MM **Privately Held**
WEB: www.twincityfoods.com
SIC: 2037 2038 2033 2099 Vegetables, quick frozen & cold pack, excl. potato products; frozen specialties; canned fruits & specialties; food preparations
PA: Twin City Foods, Inc.
10120 269th Pl Nw
Stanwood WA 98292
206 515-2400

(G-9580)
WISMER WOOD WORKS
12125 Jordan Lake Rd (48849-8507)
PHONE..................616 262-9444
Alan Wismer, *Principal*
EMP: 6 **EST:** 2009
SALES (est): 164.7K **Privately Held**
WEB: www.wismerwoodworks.com
SIC: 2431 Millwork

Lake Orion
Oakland County

(G-9581)
8TH CANDLE LLC
2577 Huntington Dr (48360-2293)
PHONE..................248 818-7625
Henry Foster, *Principal*
EMP: 4 **EST:** 2017
SALES (est): 68.5K **Privately Held**
SIC: 3999 Candles

(G-9582)
ACCRA TOOL INC
1218 Cottonwood St (48360-1464)
PHONE..................248 680-9936
Donald Mancier, *President*
Joycelyn Mancier, *Vice Pres*
EMP: 4 **EST:** 1986
SALES (est): 337.9K **Privately Held**
SIC: 3541 Machine tool replacement & repair parts, metal cutting types

(G-9583)
ACME MANUFACTURING COMPANY
101 Premier Dr (48359-1882)
PHONE..................248 393-7300
Clark Merriman, *Director*
EMP: 10
SALES (corp-wide): 14.2MM **Privately Held**
WEB: www.acmemfg.com
SIC: 3541 Machine tools, metal cutting type
PA: Acme Manufacturing Company
4240 N Atlantic Blvd
Auburn Hills MI 48326
248 393-7300

(G-9584)
AIMRITE LLC
Also Called: Aim-Rite Hauling
941 Hinford Ave (48362-2647)
P.O. Box 566 (48361-0566)
PHONE..................248 693-8925
David Bressman, *Owner*
EMP: 4 **EST:** 1998
SALES (est): 241.6K **Privately Held**
WEB: www.aimriteusa.com
SIC: 3537 Trucks: freight, baggage, etc.: industrial, except mining

(G-9585)
AMERICAN BATTERY SOLUTIONS INC
3768 S Lapeer Rd (48359-1324)
PHONE..................248 462-6364
Subhash Dhar, *CEO*
Peter Buccilli, *Vice Pres*
Kelly Qussar, *Purchasing*
Josh Payne, *Director*
John Warner, *Officer*
EMP: 140 **EST:** 2019
SALES (est): 22.9MM **Privately Held**
WEB: www.americanbatterysolutions.com
SIC: 3691 Storage batteries; batteries, rechargeable

(G-9586)
AXALTA
3136 Cedar Key Dr (48360-1511)
PHONE..................248 379-6913
Eric Ridenour, *Engineer*
EMP: 9 **EST:** 2019
SALES (est): 305.1K **Privately Held**
WEB: www.axalta.com
SIC: 2834 Pharmaceutical preparations

(G-9587)
BMAX USA LLC
100 Engelwood Dr Ste B (48359-2411)
PHONE..................248 794-4176
Rani Plaut, *CEO*
Shiran Urieli, *Engineer*
EMP: 20 **EST:** 1987
SALES (corp-wide): 257K **Privately Held**
SIC: 3542 Electroforming machines
PA: Ipulse
78 Rue La Condamine
Paris
609 816-406

(G-9588)
BMS GREAT LAKES LLC
4577 S Lapeer Rd Ste G (48359-2413)
PHONE..................248 390-1598
David Hodgson, *Principal*
EMP: 7 **EST:** 2016
SALES (est): 656.3K **Privately Held**
SIC: 3842 Abdominal supporters, braces & trusses

(G-9589)
BRADLEY JACOB PRINTING LLC
1356 Marina Pointe Blvd (48362-3903)
PHONE..................248 953-9010
Bradley Beesley, *Principal*
EMP: 4 **EST:** 2014
SALES (est): 65.8K **Privately Held**
SIC: 2752 Commercial printing, offset

(G-9590)
BROADWAY EMBROIDERY
24 N Broadway St (48362-3100)
PHONE..................248 838-8074
EMP: 8 **EST:** 2019
SALES (est): 614.4K **Privately Held**
WEB: www.broadway-embroidery.com
SIC: 2395 Embroidery & art needlework

Lake Orion - Oakland County (G-9591)

GEOGRAPHIC SECTION

(G-9591)
BRUCE WELD EDWARDS LLC
1520 S Lapeer Rd Ste 211 (48360-1462)
PHONE..................................248 693-6222
Bruce Edwards, *Owner*
EMP: 5 **EST:** 2017
SALES (est): 44.1K **Privately Held**
SIC: 7692 Welding repair

(G-9592)
C & C MACHINE TOOL INC
1584 Oneida Trl (48362-1242)
PHONE..................................248 693-3347
Richard W Cole, *President*
Clayton E Cobb, *Corp Secy*
EMP: 5 **EST:** 1983
SQ FT: 10,800
SALES (est): 310.5K **Privately Held**
SIC: 3599 Machine shop, jobbing & repair

(G-9593)
CARMENS SCREEN PRINTING & EMB
3451 Indianwood Rd (48362-1039)
PHONE..................................248 535-4161
Carmen Togal, *Principal*
EMP: 5 **EST:** 2015
SALES (est): 92.3K **Privately Held**
SIC: 2752 Commercial printing, lithographic

(G-9594)
COBRA TORCHES INC
Also Called: Detroit Torch Company
180 Englewood Dr Ste J (48359-2417)
P.O. Box 169, Clarkston (48347-0169)
PHONE..................................248 499-8122
Mark Scholl, *President*
EMP: 5 **EST:** 2002
SALES (est): 450.4K **Privately Held**
SIC: 7692 Welding repair

(G-9595)
COLE CARBIDE INDUSTRIES INC (PA)
4930 S Lapeer Rd (48359-2412)
PHONE..................................248 276-1278
John M Cole, *President*
Troy Perry, *Division Mgr*
Amy Kranker, *Exec VP*
John Cole, *Vice Pres*
Scott Kelley, *VP Mfg*
EMP: 17
SQ FT: 11,000
SALES (est): 10.2MM **Privately Held**
WEB: www.colecarbide.com
SIC: 3541 Machine tools, metal cutting type

(G-9596)
COLE TOOLING SYSTEMS INC
Also Called: Millstar
4930 S Lapeer Rd (48359-2412)
PHONE..................................586 573-9450
Donald Gleklen, *Principal*
Walter Stuermer, *Executive*
EMP: 46 **EST:** 1999
SALES (est): 4.7MM
SALES (corp-wide): 10.2MM **Privately Held**
WEB: www.coletooling.com
SIC: 3544 Special dies & tools
PA: Cole Carbide Industries, Inc.
 4930 S Lapeer Rd
 Lake Orion MI 48359
 248 276-1278

(G-9597)
COMPLETE AUTO-MATION INC
Also Called: Bbi Group
1776d W Clarkston Rd (48362-2267)
P.O. Box 65 (48361-0065)
PHONE..................................248 693-0500
Kenneth J Matheis Sr, *President*
John H Matheis, *Vice Pres*
John Matheis, *Vice Pres*
Kenneth J Matheis Jr, *Vice Pres*
James Pomerson, *Vice Pres*
EMP: 100 **EST:** 1985
SQ FT: 49,000
SALES (est): 19.9MM **Privately Held**
WEB: www.completeautomationinc.com
SIC: 3823 Industrial flow & liquid measuring instruments

(G-9598)
COMPLETE FILTRATION INC
Also Called: Complete Companies
1776d W Clarkston Rd (48362-2267)
P.O. Box 65 (48361-0065)
PHONE..................................248 693-0500
Kenneth J Matheis Sr, *President*
John H Matheis, *Vice Pres*
Kenneth J Matheis Jr, *Vice Pres*
Ian Chornoby, *Project Mgr*
Jason Farhat, *Project Mgr*
▲ **EMP:** 16 **EST:** 1986
SQ FT: 20,000
SALES (est): 4.5MM **Privately Held**
WEB: www.completeco.com
SIC: 3564 3567 Filters, air: furnaces, air conditioning equipment, etc.; industrial furnaces & ovens

(G-9599)
CUSTOM THREADS AND SPORTS LLC
260 Englewood Dr Ste A (48359-2443)
PHONE..................................248 391-0088
Mark McCord,
Linda McCord,
EMP: 5 **EST:** 2003
SALES (est): 562.8K **Privately Held**
WEB: www.customthreadsandsports.com
SIC: 2759 Screen printing

(G-9600)
CUSTOM WELDING
4175 S Baldwin Rd (48359-2106)
PHONE..................................586 243-6298
Steve Leach, *Principal*
EMP: 11 **EST:** 2009
SALES (est): 73.1K **Privately Held**
WEB: www.customweldinginc.com
SIC: 7692 Welding repair

(G-9601)
DATACOVER INC
1070 W Silverbell Rd (48359-1327)
PHONE..................................248 391-2163
EMP: 13
SALES: 500K **Privately Held**
SIC: 3089 Mfg Plastic Hardware

(G-9602)
DAVES DIAMOND INC
416 S Broadway St (48362-2742)
PHONE..................................248 693-2482
David Schurman, *President*
Cynthia Schurman, *Vice Pres*
EMP: 9 **EST:** 1976
SQ FT: 3,000
SALES (est): 516.6K **Privately Held**
WEB: www.diamonddavesjewelry.com
SIC: 5944 3911 Jewelry, precious stones & precious metals; jewelry apparel

(G-9603)
DIVINO INTL WINE & SPIRIT LLC
2707 Aldrin Dr (48360-1901)
PHONE..................................586 770-9409
Sebi Fishta,
EMP: 4 **EST:** 2017
SALES (est): 95.4K **Privately Held**
SIC: 2084 Wines

(G-9604)
DRUMMOND PRESS INC
143 Northpointe Dr (48359-1864)
PHONE..................................248 834-7007
EMP: 7 **EST:** 2019
SALES (est): 349.9K **Privately Held**
WEB: www.drummond.co
SIC: 2741 Miscellaneous publishing

(G-9605)
GEDIA MICHIGAN LLC (PA) ◆
315 W Silverbell Rd # 180 (48359-1752)
PHONE..................................248 392-9090
Michael Lehmann, *Mng Member*
EMP: 37 **EST:** 2021
SALES (est): 2.6MM **Privately Held**
SIC: 3465 Automotive stampings

(G-9606)
GENENTECH INC
362 Kirksway Ln (48362-2279)
PHONE..................................650 225-1000
Kenny Levitt, *Division Mgr*
Nancy Vitale, *Branch Mgr*
EMP: 173
SALES (corp-wide): 69.8B **Privately Held**
WEB: www.gene.com
SIC: 2834 Pharmaceutical preparations
HQ: Genentech, Inc.
 1 Dna Way
 South San Francisco CA 94080
 650 225-1000

(G-9607)
GM ORION ASSEMBLY
4555 Giddings Rd (48359-1713)
PHONE..................................248 377-5260
Gary Malkus, *Manager*
EMP: 22 **EST:** 2016
SALES (est): 1MM **Privately Held**
SIC: 3711 Motor vehicles & car bodies

(G-9608)
HILITE INDUSTRIES INC
250 Kay Industrial Dr (48359-2402)
PHONE..................................248 475-4580
Arthur Hughes, *Vice Pres*
James Morehead, *Engineer*
Matt Stolzman, *Engineer*
Charles Jackson, *Electrical Engi*
Marvin Koler, *Manager*
EMP: 5 **Privately Held**
WEB: www.hilite.com
SIC: 3495 3469 Clock springs, precision; metal stampings
HQ: Hilite Industries Inc
 1671 S Broadway St
 Carrollton TX 75006
 972 242-2116

(G-9609)
INFINITY CONTROLS & ENGRG INC
3039 Cedar Key Dr (48360-1515)
PHONE..................................248 397-8267
EMP: 8
SALES: 2MM **Privately Held**
SIC: 3625 8711 Mfg Relays/Industrial Controls Engineering Services

(G-9610)
INFONORM INC
4820 Joslyn Rd (48359-2232)
PHONE..................................248 276-9027
Stefan Kubli, *President*
Amy B Kubli, *Managing Prtnr*
EMP: 4 **EST:** 1998
SQ FT: 750 **Privately Held**
WEB: www.infonorm.com
SIC: 5099 3993 Signs, except electric; signs & advertising specialties

(G-9611)
KAY SCREEN PRINTING INC (DH)
Also Called: Kay Automotive Graphics
57 Kay Industrial Dr (48359-1832)
PHONE..................................248 377-4999
Joseph Kowalczyk, *President*
Jodie Monahan, *Purch Dir*
Jeff Holloway, *Purch Agent*
James Ireland, *VP Engrg*
Chris Zyrowski, *Engineer*
▲ **EMP:** 447 **EST:** 1968
SQ FT: 130,000
SALES: 71.8MM
SALES (corp-wide): 693.6MM **Privately Held**
WEB: www.kayautomotive.com
SIC: 2752 2396 Commercial printing, offset; automotive & apparel trimmings
HQ: Orafol International, Inc.
 1100 Oracal Pkwy
 Black Creek GA 31308
 912 851-5000

(G-9612)
KPMF USA INC
67 Kay Industrial Dr (48359-1832)
PHONE..................................248 377-4999
Joseph Kowalczyk, *President*
EMP: 10 **EST:** 2013
SALES (est): 6.8MM
SALES (corp-wide): 693.6MM **Privately Held**
WEB: www.kpmfusa.com
SIC: 2759 Screen printing

(G-9613)
LABORTRIO ELTTROFISICO USA INC
Also Called: Le USA Walker Scientific
40 Englewood Dr Ste H (48362-2419)
PHONE..................................248 340-7040
Bruno Arosio, *President*
William Sun, *Sales Mgr*
Luca Zanon, *Sales Mgr*
Jacob Hohner, *Sales Staff*
Bruce Pittman, *Sales Staff*
EMP: 6 **EST:** 2008
SALES (est): 2.5MM
SALES (corp-wide): 8.8MM **Privately Held**
WEB: www.laboratorio.elettrofisico.com
SIC: 3829 3823 Measuring & controlling devices; industrial instrmnts msrmnt display/control process variable; pressure measurement instruments, industrial
PA: Laboratorio Elettrofisico Engineering Srl
 Via Gaudenzio Ferrari 14
 Nerviano MI 20014
 033 158-9785

(G-9614)
LAKE ORION CONCRETE ORNA PDTS
62 W Scripps Rd (48360-2116)
PHONE..................................248 693-8683
Gerald Marchioni, *Owner*
EMP: 4 **EST:** 1950
SQ FT: 2,000
SALES (est): 274.6K **Privately Held**
WEB: www.lakeorionconcrete.com
SIC: 3272 5261 Concrete products; nurseries & garden centers

(G-9615)
LASER CRAFT LLC
151 Premier Dr (48359-1882)
PHONE..................................248 340-8922
Richard Ortisis,
Tom Griffin,
Terry Grsyb,
Richard Ortisi,
EMP: 36 **EST:** 1995
SQ FT: 20,000
SALES (est): 3.2MM **Privately Held**
WEB: www.lasercraft.us
SIC: 3441 Fabricated structural metal

(G-9616)
MAR COR PURIFICATION INC
180 Englewood Dr Ste D (48359-2417)
PHONE..................................248 373-7844
Gary Youness, *Branch Mgr*
EMP: 29 **Privately Held**
WEB: www.mcpur.com
SIC: 3589 Water treatment equipment, industrial
HQ: Mar Cor Purification, Inc.
 4450 Township Line Rd
 Skippack PA 19474
 800 633-3080

(G-9617)
MAXIMUM MANUFACTURING LLC
4581 S Lapeer Rd Ste E (48359-2415)
PHONE..................................810 272-0804
Gregory Fletcher,
Muhammad Tariq,
EMP: 4 **EST:** 2016
SALES (est): 82.3K **Privately Held**
SIC: 3999 Manufacturing industries

(G-9618)
MAY VENTURE INC
Also Called: Menchies Frozen Yogurt
4713 S Baldwin Rd (48359-2114)
PHONE..................................248 481-3890
Michael May, *Principal*
EMP: 4 **EST:** 2015
SALES (est): 164.1K **Privately Held**
SIC: 2024 Yogurt desserts, frozen

GEOGRAPHIC SECTION

Lakeview - Montcalm County (G-9645)

(G-9619)
MILFAB SYSTEMS LLC
2388 Canoe Circle Dr (48360-1881)
PHONE 248 391-8100
Steven Wandschneider, *Branch Mgr*
Francis Legasse,
EMP: 16
SQ FT: 400
SALES (corp-wide): 87K **Privately Held**
WEB: www.milfabsystems.com
SIC: 3053 3341 3599 Packing, metallic; secondary nonferrous metals; ties, form: metal
PA: Milfab Systems, Llc
  36700 Woodward Ave # 300
  Bloomfield Hills MI

(G-9620)
MINT STEEL FORGE INC
162 Northpointe Dr (48359-1863)
PHONE 248 276-9000
Terry Kohler, *President*
Allen Gohl, *President*
Jane Boyer, *Vice Pres*
R Jane Boyer, *Vice Pres*
▲ **EMP:** 15 **EST:** 1983
SQ FT: 27,500
SALES (est): 3.3MM **Privately Held**
WEB: www.mintsteelforge.com
SIC: 3714 Motor vehicle parts & accessories

(G-9621)
NEON ROEHLER SERVICES LLC
4508 Rohr Rd (48359-1934)
PHONE 248 895-8705
Burkhardt Roehler, *Principal*
EMP: 6 **EST:** 2008
SALES (est): 170K **Privately Held**
SIC: 2813 Neon

(G-9622)
NORMA MICHIGAN INC
Torca Products
325 W Silverbell Rd (48359-1764)
PHONE 248 373-4300
Barry McHone, *Vice Pres*
Sharon Vessels, *Vice Pres*
Liliana Castillo, *Purchasing*
Milana Puhaca, *Purchasing*
Robert Duncan, *QC Mgr*
EMP: 7
SALES (corp-wide): 1.1B **Privately Held**
SIC: 3714 3429 3713 Motor vehicle parts & accessories; manufactured hardware (general); clamps, metal; truck & bus bodies
HQ: Norma Michigan, Inc.
  2430 E Walton Blvd
  Auburn Hills MI 48326
  248 373-4300

(G-9623)
OAKLAND STAMPING LLC
4555 Giddings Rd (48359-1713)
PHONE 248 340-2520
EMP: 4
SALES (corp-wide): 3.1B **Privately Held**
WEB: www.autokiniton.com
SIC: 3469 Stamping metal for the trade
HQ: Oakland Stamping, Llc
  1200 Woodland St
  Detroit MI 48211

(G-9624)
ODYSSEY INDUSTRIES LLC
3020 Indianwood Rd (48362-1113)
PHONE 248 814-8800
Paul Walsh, *President*
Kurt Nanney, *Vice Pres*
Paul Marentette, *QC Mgr*
Glenn Jacovetti, *Manager*
Leonard Zeigler, *Supervisor*
EMP: 219 **EST:** 1982
SQ FT: 210,000
SALES (est): 39.7MM **Privately Held**
WEB: www.ascentaerospace.com
SIC: 3728 Aircraft parts & equipment

(G-9625)
OERLIKON BLZERS CATING USA INC
199 Kay Industrial Dr (48359-1833)
PHONE 248 409-5900
EMP: 35
SALES (corp-wide): 2.4B **Privately Held**
WEB: www.oerlikon.com
SIC: 3479 Coating of metals & formed products
HQ: Oerlikon Balzers Coating Usa Inc.
  1700 E Golf Rd Ste 200
  Schaumburg IL 60173
  847 619-5541

(G-9626)
PLATT MOUNTS - USA INC
100 Engelwood Dr Ste D (48359-2411)
PHONE 586 202-2920
Wilfred Platt, *President*
EMP: 4 **EST:** 2005 **Privately Held**
WEB: www.plattmounts.com
SIC: 3599 Industrial machinery

(G-9627)
PREMIER PLASTIC RESINS INC
189 W Clarkston Rd Ste 14 (48362-2892)
PHONE 248 766-7578
Michelle Cloutier, *Principal*
EMP: 4 **EST:** 2018
SALES (est): 232.4K **Privately Held**
WEB: www.premierplasticresins.com
SIC: 2821 Plastics materials & resins

(G-9628)
ROMA TOOL INC
50 Northpointe Dr (48359-1846)
PHONE 248 218-1889
Mark Bowery, *Principal*
Joe Pavlik, *Vice Pres*
EMP: 7 **EST:** 2013
SALES (est): 166.6K **Privately Held**
WEB: www.romatool.com
SIC: 3599 Machine shop, jobbing & repair

(G-9629)
S AND N PRODUCTS INC
3001 Canada Ct (48360-1507)
PHONE 810 542-9635
Steven Pursley, *Agent*
EMP: 4 **EST:** 2018
SALES (est): 74.4K **Privately Held**
SIC: 2836 Biological products, except diagnostic

(G-9630)
SA INDUSTRIES 2 INC (PA)
1081 Indianwood Rd (48362-1327)
P.O. Box 5 (48361-0005)
PHONE 248 693-9100
Bonnie Schulz, *Principal*
EMP: 89 **EST:** 2009
SALES (est): 430.9K **Privately Held**
WEB: www.saind2.com
SIC: 3452 Screws, metal

(G-9631)
SONIMA CORP
325 W Silverbell Rd # 250 (48359-1764)
PHONE 302 450-6452
EMP: 14 **EST:** 2014
SALES (est): 2MM
SALES (corp-wide): 243.9MM **Privately Held**
WEB: www.sonima.net
SIC: 3674 Modules, solid state
HQ: Sonima Gmbh
  Ruhweg 17
  Gollheim RP 67307
  635 199-9970

(G-9632)
SU-DAN COMPANY (PA)
Also Called: Sudan
190 Northpointe Dr (48359-1863)
P.O. Box 81700, Rochester (48308-1700)
PHONE 248 651-6035
Dennis J Keat, *President*
David Salkowski, *President*
Cindy Keat, *Chairman*
Douglas Braun, *Vice Pres*
▲ **EMP:** 60 **EST:** 1966
SQ FT: 32,000
SALES (est): 26.3MM **Privately Held**
WEB: www.su-dan.com
SIC: 3465 3469 Body parts, automobile: stamped metal; appliance parts, porcelain enameled

(G-9633)
SU-DAN PLASTICS INC (PA)
190 Northpointe Dr (48359-1863)
P.O. Box 81700, Rochester (48308-1700)
PHONE 248 651-6035
Richard G Dryden, *Ch of Bd*
Dennis J Keat, *President*
EMP: 144 **EST:** 1977
SQ FT: 2,500
SALES (est): 22.1MM **Privately Held**
WEB: www.su-dan.com
SIC: 3714 Motor vehicle parts & accessories

(G-9634)
THORESON-MC COSH INC
2600 Regency Dr (48359-1149)
PHONE 248 362-0960
David Klatt, *President*
▼ **EMP:** 30
SALES (est): 5.1MM **Privately Held**
WEB: www.thoresonmccosh.com
SIC: 3559 3634 3567 3537 Plastics working machinery; electric housewares & fans; industrial furnaces & ovens; industrial trucks & tractors; conveyors & conveying equipment; prefabricated metal buildings

(G-9635)
TRU-SYZYGY INC
1151 Sunset Hills Dr (48360-1412)
PHONE 248 622-7211
Donald Dietz, *Principal*
EMP: 6 **EST:** 2015
SALES (est): 256.1K **Privately Held**
WEB: www.trusyzygy.com
SIC: 7371 7372 7373 7374 Computer software systems analysis & design, custom; business oriented computer software; systems software development services; computer processing services; computer related consulting services

(G-9636)
US FARATHANE HOLDINGS CORP
325 W Silverbell Rd # 220 (48359-1764)
PHONE 248 754-7000
Tony Drumm, *General Mgr*
Mark Blair, *Mfg Mgr*
John Lojewski, *Manager*
EMP: 5
SALES (corp-wide): 549.4MM **Privately Held**
WEB: www.usfarathane.com
SIC: 3089 Injection molding of plastics
PA: U.S. Farathane Holdings Corp.
  2700 High Meadow Cir
  Auburn Hills MI 48326
  248 754-7000

(G-9637)
WEBER SAND AND GRAVEL INC (PA)
1401 E Silverbell Rd (48360-2342)
PHONE 248 373-0900
Everett Jack Weber, *President*
Geraldine Weber, *Corp Secy*
EMP: 10 **EST:** 1950
SALES (est): 2.5MM **Privately Held**
SIC: 1442 Gravel mining

(G-9638)
WESTERN ENGINEERED PRODUCTS
540 N Lapeer Rd Ste 390 (48362-1582)
PHONE 248 371-9259
Donald F Stephanic, *President*
EMP: 7 **EST:** 1997
SQ FT: 7,000
SALES (est): 2MM **Privately Held**
WEB: www.westernep.com
SIC: 3398 3469 3471 Annealing of metal; metal stampings; plating of metals or formed products

Lakeside
Berrien County

(G-9639)
HEARTHWOODS LTD INC
Also Called: Hearthwoods At Home
15310 Red Arrow Hwy (49116-9759)
P.O. Box 30 (49116-0030)
PHONE 269 469-5551
Andrew Brown, *President*
Adrienne Rueske, *Manager*
EMP: 9 **EST:** 1986
SQ FT: 2,000
SALES (est): 753.6K **Privately Held**
WEB: www.hearthwoods.com
SIC: 2511 Wood household furniture; wood lawn & garden furniture; novelty furniture: wood; wood stands & chests, except bedside stands

Lakeview
Montcalm County

(G-9640)
COUNTRY SIDE SAWMILL
7682 N Greenville Rd (48850-9575)
PHONE 989 352-7198
Eli Schrock, *Administration*
EMP: 6 **EST:** 2004
SALES (est): 176.5K **Privately Held**
SIC: 2421 Sawmills & planing mills, general

(G-9641)
GRENELL MANUFACTURING LLC
400 Lake Dr (48850-9333)
PHONE 616 304-1593
Timmy Grenell,
EMP: 4 **EST:** 2019
SALES (est): 77.4K **Privately Held**
SIC: 3052 Air line or air brake hose, rubber or rubberized fabric

(G-9642)
INTREPID PLASTICS MFG INC
7675 Howard Cy Edmore Rd (48850-9116)
PHONE 616 901-5718
Bonnie Knopf, *President*
EMP: 9 **EST:** 2003
SQ FT: 6,000
SALES (est): 484.7K **Privately Held**
SIC: 3089 Injection molding of plastics

(G-9643)
MARKHAM PEAT CORP
9475 Jefferson Rd (48850-9616)
PHONE 800 851-7230
Lee Clemence, *President*
Penny Clemence, *Treasurer*
EMP: 19 **EST:** 1957
SQ FT: 7,500
SALES (est): 1.5MM **Privately Held**
SIC: 1499 2048 2875 Peat mining; bird food, prepared; fertilizers, mixing only

(G-9644)
PARKER FLUID SYST CONNECTORS
8790 Tamarack Rd (48850-9474)
PHONE 989 352-7264
EMP: 4 **EST:** 2019
SALES (est): 88.9K **Privately Held**
SIC: 3446 Architectural metalwork

(G-9645)
PROMOQUIP INC
223 W North St (48850-8707)
P.O. Box 258 (48850-0258)
PHONE 989 287-6211
David Sanderson, *President*
EMP: 5 **EST:** 2010
SALES (est): 590.6K **Privately Held**
WEB: www.promoquip.com
SIC: 3944 Games, toys & children's vehicles

Lakeview - Montcalm County (G-9646)

(G-9646)
STEEPLECHASE TOOL & DIE INC
9307 Howard Cy Edmore Rd (48850-9470)
PHONE.....................989 352-5544
Michael Baird, *President*
Mike Garvey, *Plant Mgr*
Joe Ritter, *Purchasing*
Tim Johnson, *Manager*
EMP: 40 **EST:** 1999
SQ FT: 29,000
SALES (est): 8.9MM **Privately Held**
WEB: www.steeplechasetool.com
SIC: 3544 Special dies & tools

Lakeville
Oakland County

(G-9647)
HIGH POINT GROUP
1284 Rochester Rd (48367-3828)
PHONE.....................810 543-0448
Charles M Hotary, *Administration*
EMP: 4 **EST:** 2012
SALES (est): 64.9K **Privately Held**
WEB: www.highpointwelding.com
SIC: 7692 Welding repair

(G-9648)
KBA DEFENSE
409 Race St (48367-6613)
PHONE.....................586 552-9268
Joseph Bigger, *Principal*
EMP: 5 **EST:** 2017
SALES (est): 98.8K **Privately Held**
SIC: 3812 Defense systems & equipment

(G-9649)
THOR TOOL AND MACHINE LLC
401 E Elmwood (48367-1807)
P.O. Box 786, Leonard (48367-0786)
PHONE.....................248 628-3185
Andrew A Koski,
Axel R Koski,
EMP: 5
SQ FT: 18,800
SALES (est): 268.2K **Privately Held**
WEB: www.thortoolmachine.com
SIC: 3599 Machine shop, jobbing & repair

Lambertville
Monroe County

(G-9650)
BETKO MANUFACTURING LLC
2993 Lennox Ct (48144-8501)
PHONE.....................734 854-1148
Bryan Betkey, *Principal*
EMP: 5 **EST:** 2013
SALES (est): 74.3K **Privately Held**
SIC: 3999 Manufacturing industries

(G-9651)
CUSTER TOOL & MFG LLC
7714 Secor Rd (48144-8672)
PHONE.....................734 854-5943
Lewis Custer, *Manager*
EMP: 4 **EST:** 1972
SALES (est): 446.6K **Privately Held**
SIC: 3544 Special dies & tools

(G-9652)
QUEST - IV INCORPORATED
7116 Summerfield Rd (48144-9415)
PHONE.....................734 847-5487
Donald McCullough Jr, *President*
Randy Mc Cullough, *Vice Pres*
F Bart Fannin, *Treasurer*
EMP: 15 **EST:** 1979
SQ FT: 2,700
SALES (est): 787.9K **Privately Held**
WEB: www.questiv.com
SIC: 7372 Business oriented computer software

(G-9653)
STEVENSON BUILDING AND SUP CO
8197 Secor Rd (48144-8673)
PHONE.....................734 856-3931
Arthur G Stevenson, *President*
Dave Stevenson, *Vice Pres*
EMP: 8 **EST:** 1953
SQ FT: 1,200
SALES (est): 859.5K **Privately Held**
WEB: www.stevensonreadymix.com
SIC: 3273 5211 Ready-mixed concrete; masonry materials & supplies

(G-9654)
TEMPERANCE PRINTING
Also Called: Bedford Press
3363 Hemmingway Ln (48144-9653)
PHONE.....................419 290-6846
Karen Daggett, *Owner*
EMP: 5 **EST:** 1976
SQ FT: 1,500
SALES (est): 290K **Privately Held**
SIC: 2752 7331 Commercial printing, offset; direct mail advertising services

(G-9655)
VX-LLC
8336 Monroe Rd Rm 201 (48144-9340)
P.O. Box 828, Holland OH (43528-0828)
PHONE.....................734 854-8700
EMP: 10 **EST:** 1977
SALES (est): 497K **Privately Held**
WEB: www.vxmachinery.com
SIC: 3321 3351 Rolling mill rolls, cast iron; copper rolling & drawing; brass rolling & drawing

Lanse
Baraga County

(G-9656)
C D C LOGGING
17311 Kent St (49946-8096)
PHONE.....................906 524-6369
Charles D Cavanaugh, *Owner*
EMP: 6 **EST:** 1990
SALES (est): 913.1K **Privately Held**
SIC: 2411 Logging camps & contractors

(G-9657)
CERTAINTEED GYPSUM INC
200 S Main St (49946-1036)
PHONE.....................906 524-6101
Chet Van Aken, *Plant Mgr*
Chet Igan, *Branch Mgr*
EMP: 1366
SALES (corp-wide): 1.8B **Privately Held**
WEB: www.certainteed.com
SIC: 3275 Gypsum products
HQ: Certainteed Gypsum, Inc.
   20 Moores Rd
   Malvern PA 19355

(G-9658)
COLLINS BROTHERS SAWMILL INC
17579 Watters St (49946)
P.O. Box 265 (49946-0265)
PHONE.....................906 524-5511
Tom Collins, *President*
Dave Collins, *Corp Secy*
EMP: 14 **EST:** 1995
SALES (est): 1MM **Privately Held**
SIC: 2421 Sawmills & planing mills, general

(G-9659)
ERICKSON LUMBER & TRUE VALUE
17752 Us Hwy 41 (49946)
P.O. Box 145 (49946-0145)
PHONE.....................906 524-6295
Robert Erickson, *President*
Ann Leclaire, *Corp Secy*
Donna Baxter, *Vice Pres*
Cindy Erickson, *Shareholder*
Jim Erickson, *Shareholder*
EMP: 8 **EST:** 1992
SALES (est): 990.6K **Privately Held**
WEB: www.truevalue.com
SIC: 5251 5211 2426 Hardware; lumber & other building materials; hardwood dimension & flooring mills

(G-9660)
GARY NANKERVIS LOGGING
14210 Bayview Dr (49946-9042)
PHONE.....................906 524-7735
Gary Nankervis, *Principal*
EMP: 5 **EST:** 2010
SALES (est): 124.6K **Privately Held**
SIC: 2411 Logging

(G-9661)
HERMAN HILLBILLIES FARM LLC
Also Called: Herman Hills Sugar Bush
18194 Lahti Rd (49946-8047)
PHONE.....................906 201-0760
James Ballor,
Anita Taisto,
EMP: 6 **EST:** 2014
SQ FT: 1,200
SALES (est): 330.1K **Privately Held**
SIC: 2099 Maple syrup

(G-9662)
JESSE JAMES LOGGING
16938 Dynamite Hill Rd (49946-8085)
P.O. Box 55 (49946-0055)
PHONE.....................906 395-6819
James Lahti, *Principal*
EMP: 6 **EST:** 2011
SALES (est): 232.4K **Privately Held**
SIC: 2411 Logging

(G-9663)
JOHN VUK & SON INC
Vuk Rd (49946)
PHONE.....................906 524-6074
John A Vuk Jr, *President*
John Vuk Sr, *Corp Secy*
EMP: 4
SALES (est): 300K **Privately Held**
SIC: 2411 Logging

(G-9664)
JOHNSON & BERRY MFG INC
15442 Roth Rd (49946-9005)
PHONE.....................906 524-6433
William Johnson, *President*
Cory Frisk, *Corp Secy*
EMP: 7 **EST:** 1980
SQ FT: 2,500
SALES (est): 985.9K **Privately Held**
WEB: www.jbmfginc.com
SIC: 3599 Machine shop, jobbing & repair

(G-9665)
KK LOGGING
16234 Skanee Rd (49946-9017)
PHONE.....................906 524-6047
Ken Ketola, *Principal*
EMP: 5 **EST:** 2010
SALES (est): 92.3K **Privately Held**
SIC: 2411 Logging camps & contractors

(G-9666)
L D J INC
Also Called: L'Anse Sentinel
202 N Main St (49946-1118)
P.O. Box 7 (49946-0007)
PHONE.....................906 524-6194
Edward Danner, *President*
EMP: 10 **EST:** 1881
SQ FT: 5,500
SALES (est): 531.9K **Privately Held**
WEB: www.lansesentinel.net
SIC: 2711 5943 2752 Newspapers, publishing & printing; office forms & supplies; commercial printing, offset

(G-9667)
PATRICK NEWLAND LOGGING LTD
14738 Pequaming Rd (49946-8335)
PHONE.....................906 524-2255
Patrick Newland, *President*
EMP: 6 **EST:** 1998
SALES (est): 574.8K **Privately Held**
SIC: 2411 Logging camps & contractors

(G-9668)
R H HUHTALA AGGREGATES INC
18154 Us Highway 41 (49946-8005)
PHONE.....................906 524-7758
Roland H Huhtala, *Owner*
EMP: 4 **EST:** 1958
SQ FT: 2,940
SALES (est): 315.7K **Privately Held**
SIC: 1442 1611 Construction sand mining; gravel mining; general contractor, highway & street construction

(G-9669)
WEYERHAEUSER COMPANY
15800 Mead Rd (49946-8119)
PHONE.....................906 524-2040
EMP: 6
SALES (corp-wide): 7.5B **Publicly Held**
WEB: www.weyerhaeuser.com
SIC: 0811 2431 2411 0851 Christmas tree farm; millwork; peeler logs; reforestation services
PA: Weyerhaeuser Company
   220 Occidental Ave S
   Seattle WA 98104
   206 539-3000

Lansing
Clinton County

(G-9670)
ADAMS OUTDOOR ADVG LTD PARTNR (PA)
3801 Capitol City Blvd (48906-2109)
PHONE.....................770 333-0399
J Kevin Gleason, *President*
Chris Baughman, *General Mgr*
Carol Floyd, *General Mgr*
Chris Koller, *General Mgr*
Rhonda Lash, *General Mgr*
EMP: 5 **EST:** 1984
SQ FT: 4,000
SALES (est): 43MM **Privately Held**
WEB: www.adamsoutdoor.com
SIC: 7312 3993 Billboard advertising; signs & advertising specialties

(G-9671)
ADAMS OUTDOOR ADVG LTD PARTNR
3801 Capitol City Blvd (48906-2109)
PHONE.....................517 321-2121
Bridgette McCulloch, *Business Mgr*
Margi Moore, *Business Mgr*
Chip Callaham, *Vice Pres*
Craig Acree, *Opers Mgr*
Daniel Martell, *Opers Mgr*
EMP: 50
SALES (corp-wide): 43MM **Privately Held**
WEB: www.adamsoutdoor.com
SIC: 7312 3993 Billboard advertising; signs & advertising specialties
PA: Adams Outdoor Advertising Limited Partnership
   3801 Capitol City Blvd
   Lansing MI 48906
   770 333-0399

(G-9672)
AMERICAN TOOLING CENTER INC
705 E Oakland Ave (48906-5314)
PHONE.....................517 522-8411
John J Basso, *President*
EMP: 9
SALES (corp-wide): 18.5MM **Privately Held**
WEB: www.americantoolingcenter.com
SIC: 3544 Special dies & tools
PA: American Tooling Center, Inc.
   4111 Mount Hope Rd
   Grass Lake MI 49240
   517 522-8411

(G-9673)
ARCOSA SHORING PRODUCTS INC
Pro-Tech Equipment
4837 W Grand River Ave (48906-9122)
PHONE.....................800 292-1225
Ron Wey, *Branch Mgr*
Thomas Marciniak, *Manager*
EMP: 50
SALES (corp-wide): 1.9B **Publicly Held**
WEB: www.gme-shields.com
SIC: 7353 3531 Heavy construction equipment rental; construction machinery

GEOGRAPHIC SECTION

Lansing - Clinton County (G-9698)

HQ: Arcosa Shoring Products, Inc.
8530 M 60
Union City MI 49094
517 741-4300

(G-9674)
BANNASCH WELDING INC
Also Called: Grills To Go At Bannasch Wldg
807 Lake Lansing Rd Ste 1 (48906-4292)
PHONE 517 482-2916
William Bannasch, *President*
Sandy Bannasch, *Vice Pres*
EMP: 16
SQ FT: 14,000
SALES (est): 1.3MM **Privately Held**
WEB: www.lansingwelding.com
SIC: 7692 Welding repair

(G-9675)
BONWRX LTD
924 Terminal Rd (48906-3063)
PHONE 517 481-2924
Erengul Rose Carmichael, *Administration*
EMP: 8 **EST:** 2015
SALES (est): 227.6K **Privately Held**
WEB: www.bonwrx.com
SIC: 3841 Surgical & medical instruments

(G-9676)
CAPITAL CITY BLUE PRINT INC
Also Called: Capital City Reprographics
1110 Center St (48906-5297)
PHONE 517 482-5431
Mark Odeen, *President*
EMP: 8 **EST:** 1928
SQ FT: 11,000
SALES (est): 535.5K **Privately Held**
WEB: www.capcityrepro.com
SIC: 7334 2752 Blueprinting service; commercial printing, lithographic

(G-9677)
CAPITOL BEDDING CO INC
2238 N Grand River Ave (48906-3910)
PHONE 615 370-7000
William J Beuerle, *President*
John Beuerle, *Treasurer*
EMP: 19 **EST:** 1947
SQ FT: 30,000
SALES (est): 2.4MM **Privately Held**
WEB: www.capitolbedding.com
SIC: 2515 Mattresses, innerspring or box spring

(G-9678)
CARRINGTON PRECIOUS METALS LLC
4616 N Grand River Ave # 8 (48906-2576)
PHONE 517 323-9154
Joseph Fata, *Principal*
EMP: 6 **EST:** 2008
SALES (est): 160.6K **Privately Held**
SIC: 3339 Precious metals

(G-9679)
CENTRAL MICHIGAN ENGRAVERS
412 W Gier St (48906-2945)
P.O. Box 15006 (48901-5006)
PHONE 517 485-5865
Fred Root, *President*
EMP: 9 **EST:** 1960
SQ FT: 4,800
SALES (est): 823.5K **Privately Held**
WEB: www.centralmichiganengravers.com
SIC: 3579 Paper handling machines

(G-9680)
CHALLENGE MFG COMPANY
6375 W Grand River Ave (48906)
PHONE 616 735-6500
Douglas Bradley, *Vice Pres*
EMP: 5
SQ FT: 1,000
SALES (corp-wide): 781.8MM **Privately Held**
WEB: www.challenge-mfg.com
SIC: 3449 Miscellaneous metalwork
PA: Challenge Mfg. Company, Llc
3200 Fruit Ridge Ave Nw
Walker MI 49544
616 735-6500

(G-9681)
CHEM STATION
911 Center St (48906-5219)
PHONE 517 371-8068
Stew Coss, *Manager*
EMP: 13 **EST:** 2005
SALES (est): 137.1K **Privately Held**
WEB: www.chemstation.com
SIC: 2841 Soap & other detergents

(G-9682)
COMMUNITY MNTAL HLTH AUTH CLNT
Also Called: Tri-County Diversified Inds
3200 Remy Dr (48906-2759)
PHONE 517 323-9558
Susan Spears, *Director*
EMP: 14
SQ FT: 11,000
SALES (corp-wide): 138MM **Privately Held**
WEB: www.ceicmh.org
SIC: 8621 2759 Health association; promotional printing
PA: Community Mental Health Authority Of Clinton, Eaton & Ingham Counties
812 E Jolly Rd
Lansing MI 48910
517 346-8000

(G-9683)
DAKKOTA INTEGRATED SYSTEMS LLC
16130 Grove Rd (48906-9330)
PHONE 517 321-3064
James Horwarth,
EMP: 7
SALES (corp-wide): 242.2MM **Privately Held**
WEB: www.dakkota.com
SIC: 3711 Automobile assembly, including specialty automobiles
PA: Dakkota Integrated Systems, Llc
123 Brighton Lake Rd # 202
Brighton MI 48116
517 694-6500

(G-9684)
DART CONTAINER CORPORATION
16637 Corporate Avi Dr (48906-9188)
PHONE 517 327-0613
Amy Kelley, *Project Mgr*
Mike Franks, *Buyer*
Kyle Guy, *Accountant*
Brad Burns, *Manager*
Jim Logan, *Director*
EMP: 5 **Privately Held**
WEB: www.dartcontainer.com
SIC: 3089 Plastic containers, except foam
PA: Dart Container Corporation
500 Hogsback Rd
Mason MI 48854

(G-9685)
DELTA PACKAGING INTERNATIONAL
3463 Millwood Rd (48906-2492)
PHONE 517 321-6548
Mario S Diaz, *President*
Dolores J Diaz, *Corp Secy*
▲ **EMP:** 6 **EST:** 1976
SQ FT: 12,000
SALES (est): 750K **Privately Held**
WEB: www.deltapkg.us
SIC: 2448 2449 Pallets, wood; containers, plywood & veneer wood

(G-9686)
DELTA SPORTS SERVICE & EMB
1611 N Grand River Ave # 2 (48906-3995)
PHONE 517 482-6565
Tom Schaberg, *President*
Gerald Schaberg, *Treasurer*
EMP: 8 **EST:** 1988
SQ FT: 5,500
SALES (est): 1.1MM **Privately Held**
WEB: www.deltaembroidery.com
SIC: 5136 5091 2759 2395 Sportswear, men's & boys'; sporting & recreation goods; screen printing; embroidery products, except schiffli machine

(G-9687)
DEMMER CORPORATION (HQ)
4520 N Grand River Ave (48906-2615)
PHONE 517 321-3600
John E Demmer, *Ch of Bd*
William A Demmer, *President*
Heather Shawa De Cook, *CFO*
Duane A Wagner, *CPA*
Chris Butterwick, *Manager*
▲ **EMP:** 114 **EST:** 1951
SALES (est): 31.7MM
SALES (corp-wide): 134.2MM **Privately Held**
WEB: www.demmercorp.com
SIC: 3795 3812 3544 3465 Tanks & tank components; acceleration indicators & systems components, aerospace; special dies, tools, jigs & fixtures; automotive stampings; fabricated structural metal
PA: Loc Performance Products, Llc
13505 N Haggerty Rd
Plymouth MI 48170
734 453-2300

(G-9688)
DEMMER INVESTMENTS INC (PA)
4520 N Grand River Ave (48906-2615)
PHONE 517 321-3600
Stan Sjober, *CEO*
Heather Shawa Decook, *Treasurer*
Edward Demmer, *Shareholder*
Marguerite Demmer, *Shareholder*
William Demmer, *Shareholder*
EMP: 6 **EST:** 2010
SALES (est): 9.4MM **Privately Held**
SIC: 3549 3469 3829 Wiredrawing & fabricating machinery & equipment, ex. die; metal stampings; testing equipment: abrasion, shearing strength, etc.

(G-9689)
DENTAL ART LABORATORIES INC
1721 N Grand River Ave # 1 (48906-3982)
PHONE 517 485-2200
Tom Daulton, *CEO*
Richard Blundy, *President*
Bryan Medler, *Vice Pres*
Michael Mayes, *Sales Staff*
EMP: 69 **EST:** 1950
SALES (est): 3MM
SALES (corp-wide): 195.8MM **Privately Held**
WEB: www.nationaldentex.com
SIC: 8072 8021 3843 Artificial teeth production; crown & bridge production; offices & clinics of dentists; dental equipment & supplies
HQ: National Dentex, Llc
11601 Kew Gardens Ave # 200
Palm Beach Gardens FL 33410
561 537-8300

(G-9690)
EMERGENT BIODEF OPER LNSNG LLC
3500 N Martin Luther King (48906-2933)
PHONE 517 327-1500
Fuad El-Hibri, *Ch of Bd*
Robert Myers, *Exec VP*
Tom Waytes, *Vice Pres*
Chris Marston, *Project Mgr*
Gary Bess, *Buyer*
EMP: 300 **EST:** 1998
SALES (est): 99.2MM
SALES (corp-wide): 1.5B **Publicly Held**
WEB: www.emergentbiosolutions.com
SIC: 2836 2834 Vaccines; pharmaceutical preparations
PA: Emergent Biosolutions Inc.
400 Professional Dr # 400
Gaithersburg MD 20879
240 631-3200

(G-9691)
EMERGENT BIOSOLUTIONS INC
3500 N Mar L King Jr Blvd (48906)
PHONE 517 327-1500
Melissa Ramirez, *Partner*
Julie Rossi, *Counsel*
Aaron Schutzer, *Counsel*
Mark Alley, *Vice Pres*
Sean Kirk, *Vice Pres*
EMP: 9
SALES (corp-wide): 1.5B **Publicly Held**
WEB: www.emergentbiosolutions.com
SIC: 2834 Pharmaceutical preparations
PA: Emergent Biosolutions Inc.
400 Professional Dr # 400
Gaithersburg MD 20879
240 631-3200

(G-9692)
EMS PARTS DIV
16800 Industrial Pkwy (48906-9136)
PHONE 517 319-5306
Carl Vancuren, *Engineer*
EMP: 5 **EST:** 2015
SALES (est): 78.5K **Privately Held**
SIC: 3542 Machine tools, metal forming type

(G-9693)
ENGINEERING GRAPHICS INC
16333 S Us Highway 27 (48906-5633)
PHONE 517 485-5828
Mark Lamond, *President*
Robert Lamond, *President*
Vivian Lamond, *Corp Secy*
EMP: 6 **EST:** 1967
SQ FT: 8,200
SALES (est): 535K **Privately Held**
WEB: www.e-graphicsinc.com
SIC: 7335 3999 Commercial photography; novelties, bric-a-brac & hobby kits

(G-9694)
ENPROTECH INDUSTRIAL TECH LLC
Enprotech Mechanical Svcs
16740 16800 Indus Pkwy (48906)
PHONE 517 372-0950
Pedro Garcia, *President*
Steven Phillipich, *Project Engr*
Laura Fackelman, *Human Res Mgr*
Nate Monroe, *HR Admin*
Ivan Molina, *Sales Engr*
EMP: 122 **Privately Held**
WEB: www.enprotech.com
SIC: 3542 Machine tools, metal forming type
HQ: Enprotech Industrial Technologies, Llc
4259 E 49th St
Cleveland OH 44125
216 883-3220

(G-9695)
ENPROTECH INDUSTRIAL TECH LLC
16800 Industrial Pkwy (48906-9136)
PHONE 216 883-3220
Rick Crosslin, *Regl Sales Mgr*
EMP: 25 **Privately Held**
WEB: www.enprotech.com
SIC: 3547 3599 Rolling mill machinery; custom machinery
HQ: Enprotech Industrial Technologies, Llc
4259 E 49th St
Cleveland OH 44125
216 883-3220

(G-9696)
FAIRFAX PRINTS LTD
Also Called: Frazeli Prints
4918 Delta River Dr (48906-9013)
PHONE 517 321-5590
Gary E Fairfax, *Owner*
EMP: 4 **EST:** 1974
SALES (est): 593.3K **Privately Held**
WEB: www.frazettaprints.com
SIC: 5199 5999 2752 Posters; posters; posters, lithographed

(G-9697)
FAITH PUBLISHING SERVICE
1500 E Saginaw St Ofc C (48906-5517)
PHONE 517 853-7600
Carl Mengeling, *Principal*
EMP: 20 **EST:** 2005
SALES (est): 251.8K **Privately Held**
WEB: www.faithcatholic.com
SIC: 2721 Magazines: publishing & printing

(G-9698)
FLUID-BAG LLC
3463 Millwood Rd (48906-2492)
PHONE 513 310-9550
Mark Evans, *Marketing Staff*
EMP: 12 **EST:** 2015

Lansing - Clinton County (G-9699)

SALES (est): 1.5MM
SALES (corp-wide): 32.1MM **Privately Held**
WEB: www.fluid-bag.com
SIC: 3412 Milk (fluid) shipping containers, metal
HQ: Oy Fluid-Bag Ab
Bottenviksvagen 54
Pietarsaari 68600
207 790-444

(G-9699)
FORESIGHT GROUP INC (PA)
2822 N Mrtn Lther King Jr (48906-2927)
PHONE.................517 485-5700
William K Christofferson, *President*
Denny Hyland, *President*
Scott McPherson, *Vice Pres*
Dan Siwik, *Prdtn Mgr*
Mark Hedden, *Production*
EMP: 36 **EST:** 1978
SQ FT: 24,000
SALES (est): 11.1MM **Privately Held**
WEB: www.foresightgroup.net
SIC: 2759 5199 Screen printing; advertising specialties

(G-9700)
FRANCHINO MOLD & ENGRG CO
5867 W Grand River Ave (48906-9117)
PHONE.................517 321-5609
Robert Franchino, *President*
Mike Hetherington, *Vice Pres*
Todd Phillips, *Vice Pres*
John Kingsley, *QC Mgr*
Thomas Rood, *Engineer*
EMP: 69 **EST:** 1955
SQ FT: 36,000
SALES (est): 19MM **Privately Held**
WEB: www.franchino.com
SIC: 3544 Special dies & tools

(G-9701)
FRIEDLAND INDUSTRIES INC
Also Called: FI
405 E Maple St (48906-5237)
P.O. Box 14180 (48901-4180)
PHONE.................517 482-3000
Lawrence A Bass, *President*
Randolph Rifkin, *Treasurer*
EMP: 40 **EST:** 1987
SQ FT: 6,000
SALES (est): 9.7MM **Privately Held**
WEB: www.friedlandindustries.com
SIC: 5093 4953 3341 2611 Ferrous metal scrap & waste; nonferrous metals scrap; waste paper; recycling, waste materials; secondary nonferrous metals; pulp mills

(G-9702)
H A ECKHART & ASSOCIATES INC
16185 National Pkwy (48906-9114)
PHONE.................517 321-7700
Andrew Storm, *CEO*
Daniel Burseth, *Vice Pres*
Robert Heath, *Mfg Dir*
Joe Berger, *Opers Mgr*
Jacob Garcia, *Technical Mgr*
EMP: 40 **EST:** 1974
SQ FT: 50,000
SALES (est): 18.9MM
SALES (corp-wide): 78MM **Privately Held**
WEB: www.eckhartusa.com
SIC: 3559 Automotive related machinery
HQ: Eckhart Holdings, Inc.
16185 National Pkwy
Lansing MI 48906
517 321-7700

(G-9703)
HEART TRUSS & ENGINEERING CORP
1830 N Grand River Ave (48906-3905)
PHONE.................517 372-0850
Curtis Schaberg, *President*
Joe Butcher, *Vice Pres*
EMP: 102 **EST:** 1963
SQ FT: 20,000
SALES (est): 20.4MM **Privately Held**
WEB: www.hearttruss.net
SIC: 2439 Trusses, wooden roof

(G-9704)
HIGH GRADE MATERIALS COMPANY
1800 Turner St (48906-4049)
PHONE.................517 374-1029
Andy Gibbs, *Branch Mgr*
EMP: 9
SALES (corp-wide): 17.2MM **Privately Held**
WEB: www.highgradematerials.com
SIC: 3273 Ready-mixed concrete
PA: High Grade Materials Company
9266 Snows Lake Rd
Greenville MI 48838
616 754-5545

(G-9705)
INNOVATIVE ENGINEERING MICH
712 Terminal Rd (48906-3059)
PHONE.................517 977-0460
Ryan Cutler, *President*
EMP: 5 **EST:** 1984
SQ FT: 8,000
SALES (est): 497.8K **Privately Held**
WEB: www.innovative-urethane.com
SIC: 2851 5199 3559 3089 Polyurethane coatings; rubber, crude; plastics working machinery; molding primary plastic

(G-9706)
INTER STATE FOODS INC (PA)
Also Called: Paramount Coffee Co.
5133 W Grand River Ave (48906-9117)
P.O. Box 13068 (48901-3068)
PHONE.................517 372-5500
Fax: 517 372-2870
EMP: 10 **EST:** 1935
SQ FT: 40,000
SALES (est): 5MM **Privately Held**
SIC: 2095 Mfg Roasted Coffee

(G-9707)
JIM BENNETT
2607 Lafayette Ave (48906-2748)
PHONE.................517 323-9061
James Bennett, *Owner*
EMP: 4 **EST:** 2015
SALES (est): 49.2K **Privately Held**
SIC: 3999 Manufacturing industries

(G-9708)
JN PRESS
110 E Cesar E Chavez Ave (48906-4847)
PHONE.................517 708-0300
EMP: 4 **EST:** 2016
SALES (est): 56.9K **Privately Held**
SIC: 2741 Miscellaneous publishing

(G-9709)
KANSMACKERS MANUFACTURING CO
Also Called: Source Vending
312 W Willow St (48906-4740)
PHONE.................248 249-6666
Nick Yono, *President*
EMP: 13 **EST:** 1985
SQ FT: 5,000
SALES (est): 646.9K **Privately Held**
WEB: www.kansmackerrecycling.com
SIC: 3559 Recycling machinery

(G-9710)
LANSING ICE AND FUEL COMPANY (PA)
911 Center St (48906-5298)
P.O. Box 20097 (48901-0697)
PHONE.................517 372-3850
Ron Bewersborss, *President*
Ronald Beversdorff, *President*
Floyd Conklin, *Corp Secy*
Robert J Reutter, *Vice Pres*
EMP: 16 **EST:** 1906
SQ FT: 20,000
SALES (est): 4.3MM **Privately Held**
WEB: www.lansingiceandfuel.com
SIC: 5983 5172 2097 Fuel oil dealers; fuel oil; manufactured ice

(G-9711)
LANSING PLATING COMPANY
1303 Case St (48906-4599)
PHONE.................517 485-6915
Dean Vohwinkle, *President*
Lynn Vohwinkle, *Vice Pres*
Andrea Bailey, *Manager*
Jackie Bates, *Manager*
Davis Geanee, *Manager*
EMP: 6 **EST:** 1934
SQ FT: 15,500
SALES (est): 1.2MM **Privately Held**
WEB: www.lansingplatingco.com
SIC: 3471 Electroplating of metals or formed products

(G-9712)
LION LABS LTD
4800 N Grand River Ave (48906-2538)
PHONE.................248 231-0753
Ryan Ratzloff, *President*
EMP: 11 **EST:** 2017
SALES (est): 711.7K **Privately Held**
WEB: www.lionlabsmi.com
SIC: 3999

(G-9713)
LOC PERFORMANCE PRODUCTS LLC
1600 N Larch St (48906-4168)
PHONE.................734 453-2300
Steven Wade, *Buyer*
Teena L Kowalski, *Finance*
Timothy Horner, *Branch Mgr*
Cassandra Wolvin, *Program Mgr*
Andrew Diethrich, *Supervisor*
EMP: 160
SALES (corp-wide): 134.2MM **Privately Held**
WEB: www.locperformance.com
SIC: 3541 Machine tools, metal cutting type
PA: Loc Performance Products, Llc
13505 N Haggerty Rd
Plymouth MI 48170
734 453-2300

(G-9714)
MADAR METAL FABRICATING LLC
3310 Ranger Rd (48906-2725)
P.O. Box 500, Dewitt (48820-0500)
PHONE.................517 267-9610
Greg Madar,
EMP: 11 **EST:** 2003
SALES (est): 1.2MM **Privately Held**
WEB: www.madarmetalfabricating.com
SIC: 3441 Fabricated structural metal

(G-9715)
MARKERBOARD PEOPLE INC
2227 Spikes Ln Unit 1 (48906-3961)
P.O. Box 80560 (48908-0560)
PHONE.................517 372-1666
Harold Spaeth, *President*
Dean Hibler, *General Mgr*
Josh Struble, *Office Mgr*
Chris Zimmerman, *Info Tech Mgr*
▲ **EMP:** 24 **EST:** 1978
SALES (est): 2.7MM **Privately Held**
WEB: www.dryerase.com
SIC: 3952 Boards, drawing, artists'

(G-9716)
MICHALSKI ENTERPRISES INC
Also Called: Tool Craft
16733 Industrial Pkwy (48906-9136)
PHONE.................517 703-0777
Michael Michalski, *President*
William Michalski, *Vice Pres*
Carla Mills, *Office Mgr*
EMP: 22 **EST:** 1966
SQ FT: 6,000
SALES (est): 4.5MM **Privately Held**
WEB: www.toolcraftcorp.com
SIC: 3544 2542 3543 Jigs & fixtures; office & store showcases & display fixtures; industrial patterns

(G-9717)
MPS HOLDCO INC (DH)
Also Called: MPS Holdings
5800 W Grand River Ave (48906-9111)
PHONE.................517 886-2526
Marc Shore, *CEO*
Dennis Kalpman, *President*
Tim Schultz, *Vice Pres*
Dale Baller, *Prdtn Mgr*
Tom Starin, *Safety Mgr*
EMP: 446 **EST:** 2004
SALES (est): 807.5MM
SALES (corp-wide): 17.5B **Publicly Held**
WEB: www.westrock.com
SIC: 2759 Advertising literature: printing

(G-9718)
MPS HRL LLC
Also Called: John Henry
5800 W Grand River Ave (48906-9111)
PHONE.................800 748-0517
EMP: 1 **EST:** 2015
SALES (est): 3.2MM
SALES (corp-wide): 17.5B **Publicly Held**
WEB: www.westrock.com
SIC: 2759 Commercial printing
HQ: Multi Packaging Solutions, Inc.
885 3rd Ave Fl 28
New York NY 10022

(G-9719)
MPS LANSING INC (DH)
5800 W Grand River Ave (48906-9111)
PHONE.................517 323-9000
Marc Shore, *CEO*
Dennis Kaltman, *President*
Michael Klein, *Opers Staff*
Greg Bomers, *Treasurer*
Becky Bush, *Natl Sales Mgr*
◆ **EMP:** 800 **EST:** 1946
SQ FT: 350,000
SALES (est): 250.7MM
SALES (corp-wide): 17.5B **Publicly Held**
SIC: 2759 2731 2761 3089 Commercial printing; screen printing; letterpress printing; tags: printing; books: publishing & printing; continuous forms, office & business; identification cards, plastic; packaging paper & plastics film, coated & laminated

(G-9720)
MPS/IH LLC
5800 W Grand River Ave (48906-9111)
PHONE.................517 323-9001
Dennis Kaltman, *Manager*
EMP: 31 **EST:** 2011
SALES (est): 394.9K **Privately Held**
SIC: 2752 Commercial printing, offset

(G-9721)
MULTI PACKG SOLUTIONS INTL LTD
5800 W Grand River Ave (48906-9111)
PHONE.................517 323-9000
EMP: 640
SALES (corp-wide): 17.5B **Publicly Held**
WEB: www.westrock.com
SIC: 2759 Business forms: printing; letterpress printing; tags: printing
HQ: Multi Packaging Solutions International Limited
885 3rd Ave Fl 28
New York NY 10022
646 885-0005

(G-9722)
NIOWAVE INC
1012 N Walnut St (48906-5061)
PHONE.................517 999-3475
Terry Grimm, *President*
Beth Grimm, *Vice Pres*
Joseph Yancey, *Engineer*
Robert King, *Finance*
Cameron Bott, *Software Dev*
EMP: 2 **EST:** 2005
SALES (est): 2MM **Privately Held**
WEB: www.niowaveinc.com
SIC: 8731 3699 Commercial research laboratory; particle accelerators, high voltage

(G-9723)
PALMER ENGINEERING INC
3525 Capitol City Blvd (48906-2101)
P.O. Box 12030 (48901-2030)
PHONE.................517 321-3600
William Demmer, *President*
Tom Doppke, *QC Mgr*
Tim McKenna, *Executive*
EMP: 25 **EST:** 1947
SQ FT: 15,000
SALES (est): 2.1MM **Privately Held**
WEB: www.palmerenginc.com
SIC: 3469 Stamping metal for the trade

▲ = Import ▼ = Export
◆ = Import/Export

GEOGRAPHIC SECTION — Lansing - Clinton County (G-9749)

(G-9724)
PECKHAM VOCATIONAL INDS INC (PA)
3510 Capitol City Blvd (48906-2102)
PHONE................517 316-4000
Mitchell Tomlinson, *CEO*
Karen Jury, *President*
Stuart Muladore, *President*
Curt Munson, *President*
Marian Blake, *Business Mgr*
EMP: 1000 EST: 1976
SQ FT: 190,000
SALES (est): 212.4MM Privately Held
WEB: www.peckham.org
SIC: 8331 2396 2311 2331 Vocational rehabilitation agency; automotive trimmings, fabric; men's & boys' suits & coats; women's & misses' blouses & shirts; telephone services;

(G-9725)
PECKHAM VOCATIONAL INDS INC
2511 N Mrtn Lthr Kng Jr B (48906-3865)
PHONE................517 316-4478
Patrick Rehmann, *Managing Dir*
Braden Riis, *Managing Dir*
Wayne Parsons, *Principal*
Robert Padgett, *Project Mgr*
Allison Parker, *Materials Mgr*
EMP: 86
SALES (corp-wide): 212.4MM Privately Held
WEB: www.peckham.org
SIC: 8331 2396 2311 2331 Vocational rehabilitation agency; automotive trimmings, fabric; men's & boys' suits & coats; women's & misses' blouses & shirts; motor vehicle parts & accessories
PA: Peckham Vocational Industries, Inc.
    3510 Capitol City Blvd
    Lansing MI 48906
    517 316-4000

(G-9726)
PEPSI-COLA METRO BTLG CO INC
4900 W Grand River Ave (48906-9128)
PHONE................517 321-0231
Paul Hermann, *Manager*
Scott Conant, *Manager*
EMP: 6
SALES (corp-wide): 70.3B Publicly Held
WEB: www.pepsico.com
SIC: 2086 Carbonated soft drinks, bottled & canned
HQ: Pepsi-Cola Metropolitan Bottling Company, Inc.
    1111 Westchester Ave
    White Plains NY 10604
    914 767-6000

(G-9727)
PIERCE ENGINEERS INC
5122 N Grand River Ave # 1 (48906-5810)
PHONE................517 321-5051
John W Pierce, *President*
Johnathan Pierce, *Engineer*
Jim Nordhof, *Manager*
EMP: 4 EST: 1991
SALES (est): 469.8K Privately Held
WEB: www.pierceengineeringltd.com
SIC: 3484 Guns (firearms) or gun parts, 30 mm. & below

(G-9728)
PINE NEEDLE PEOPLE LLC
Also Called: Alien Resources
934 Clark St Ste 4 (48906-5425)
PHONE................517 242-4752
Kevin Karpinski, *CEO*
EMP: 5 EST: 2012
SALES (est): 76.5K Privately Held
SIC: 3559 Robots, molding & forming plastics

(G-9729)
PINSMEDALSCOINS LLC
733 Cleveland St (48906-5529)
PHONE................312 771-2973
Nathan Russell,
EMP: 4 EST: 2017
SALES (est): 39.6K Privately Held
WEB: www.pinsmedalscoins.com
SIC: 3999 Manufacturing industries

(G-9730)
PIZZA CRUST COMPANY INC
728 E Cesar E Chavez Ave (48906-5340)
PHONE................517 482-3368
Keith A Guyer, *President*
Eloy Guyer, *Corp Secy*
EMP: 10 EST: 1961
SQ FT: 1,500
SALES (est): 923K Privately Held
SIC: 2045 Pizza doughs, prepared: from purchased flour; bread & bread type roll mixes: from purchased flour

(G-9731)
PLANNING & ZONING CENTER INC
Also Called: Planning & Zoning News
715 N Cedar St Ste 2 (48906-5275)
PHONE................517 886-0555
Mark A Wyckoff, *President*
Carolyn Freebury, *Vice Pres*
Leslie Hoover, *Treasurer*
EMP: 4 EST: 1982
SALES (est): 301.2K Privately Held
WEB: www.pzcenter.com
SIC: 2721 Magazines: publishing & printing

(G-9732)
PLAS-LABS INCORPORATED
401 E North St Ste 1 (48906-4434)
PHONE................517 372-7178
David L Regan, *President*
Darlene Blinn, *Manager*
Patrick Regan, *Director*
▲ EMP: 20 EST: 1967
SQ FT: 9,000
SALES (est): 3MM Privately Held
WEB: www.plas-labs.com
SIC: 3821 Laboratory equipment: fume hoods, distillation racks, etc.

(G-9733)
PRO-SOIL SITE SERVICES INC
3323 N East St (48906-2037)
P.O. Box 12217 (48901-2217)
PHONE................517 267-8767
Darren Tews, *Vice Pres*
EMP: 10 EST: 2011
SALES (est): 1.6MM Privately Held
WEB: www.prosoil.us
SIC: 3315 1799 5039 Fence gates posts & fittings: steel; construction site cleanup; fence construction; post-disaster renovations; wire fence, gates & accessories

(G-9734)
PURITY CYLINDER GASES INC
1035 Mak Tech Dr Ste A (48906-5618)
PHONE................517 321-9555
Don Grifwald, *Branch Mgr*
Laureen Nelson,
EMP: 9
SALES (corp-wide): 104.1MM Privately Held
WEB: www.puritygas.com
SIC: 5169 3548 5084 Gases, compressed & liquefied; welding apparatus; welding machinery & equipment
HQ: Purity Cylinder Gases, Inc.
    2580 28th St Sw
    Wyoming MI 49519
    616 532-2375

(G-9735)
SAWDUST AND LACE
3532 Delta River Dr (48906-3460)
PHONE................517 331-4535
Joanie Kilchermann, *Principal*
EMP: 4 EST: 2017
SALES (est): 64.1K Privately Held
WEB: www.sawdustandlacellc.com
SIC: 2431 Millwork

(G-9736)
SIGN A RAMA
Also Called: Sign-A-Rama
15851 S Us Highway 27 (48906-5657)
PHONE................517 489-4314
EMP: 5 EST: 2019
SALES (est): 200.1K Privately Held
WEB: www.signarama.com
SIC: 3993 Signs & advertising specialties

(G-9737)
SPARTAN METAL FAB LLC
4905 N Grand River Ave (48906-2541)
PHONE................517 322-9050
Greg Simmer, *Mng Member*
EMP: 4 EST: 2001
SALES (est): 354.1K Privately Held
WEB: www.spartanmetal.net
SIC: 3446 1799 5051 3441 Stairs, staircases, stair treads: prefabricated metal; fence construction; steel; fabricated structural metal

(G-9738)
SPARTAN PRINTING INC
15551 S Us Highway 27 (48906-1409)
PHONE................517 372-6910
Steve Root, *President*
James Fournier, *Accounts Exec*
Dave Schmitt, *Executive*
▲ EMP: 38 EST: 1960
SQ FT: 10,000
SALES (est): 5MM Privately Held
WEB: www.printspartan.com
SIC: 2752 2791 2789 Commercial printing, offset; typesetting; bookbinding & related work

(G-9739)
SPIETH ANDERSON USA LC
Also Called: SA Sport
3327 Ranger Rd (48906-2726)
PHONE................817 536-3366
EMP: 12
SQ FT: 22,000
SALES (est): 1.8MM
SALES (corp-wide): 4.1MM Privately Held
SIC: 3949 Mfg Sporting/Athletic Goods
PA: Spieth-Anderson International Inc
    135 Forestview Rd
    Oro-Medonte ON L3V 0
    705 325-2274

(G-9740)
SPIRIT INDUSTRIES INC
2900 7th Ave (48906-3347)
PHONE................517 371-7840
James Parker Jr, *President*
EMP: 6 EST: 1987
SQ FT: 9,000
SALES (est): 626.9K Privately Held
WEB: www.spiritindustriesinc.net
SIC: 3559 3089 3599 3469 Plastics working machinery; blow molded finished plastic products; machine shop, jobbing & repair; metal stampings

(G-9741)
STAMP-RITE INCORPORATED
Also Called: Stamprite Supersine
2822 N Mrtn Lther King Jr (48906-2927)
PHONE................517 487-5071
Wendell W Parsons, *President*
Scott W Parsons, *Exec VP*
Pam Frei, *Admin Sec*
EMP: 21 EST: 1955
SQ FT: 16,000
SALES (est): 1.7MM Privately Held
WEB: www.foresightgroup.net
SIC: 3993 3953 2752 2759 Signs, not made in custom sign painting shops; embossing seals & hand stamps; commercial printing, offset; labels & seals: printing; platemaking services; packaging paper & plastics film, coated & laminated

(G-9742)
TENNECO AUTOMOTIVE OPER CO INC
4722 Grand Riv (48906)
PHONE................734 243-8000
Marthy Partin, *Branch Mgr*
EMP: 50
SALES (corp-wide): 15.3B Publicly Held
SIC: 3714 3699 Shock absorbers, motor vehicle; electrical equipment & supplies
HQ: Tenneco Automotive Operating Company, Inc.
    500 N Field Dr
    Lake Forest IL 60045
    847 482-5000

(G-9743)
TENNECO CLEAN AIR US INC
4722 N Grand River Ave (48906-2536)
PHONE................517 253-8902
EMP: 18
SALES (corp-wide): 15.3B Publicly Held
WEB: www.tenneco.ufcontent.com
SIC: 3714 Motor vehicle engines & parts
HQ: Tenneco Clean Air Us Inc.
    18765 Seaway Dr
    Lansing MI 48911
    734 384-7867

(G-9744)
TOP SHOP INC
2526 N Grand River Ave (48906-3915)
PHONE................517 323-9085
Vic Toune, *President*
Joseph Sutton, *Vice Pres*
Sam Eyde, *Admin Sec*
EMP: 5 EST: 1971
SQ FT: 7,000
SALES (est): 447.9K Privately Held
WEB: www.thetopshopinc.com
SIC: 2542 Counters or counter display cases: except wood

(G-9745)
TRITON INDUSTRIES INC
Also Called: Manitou Boats
16020 S Lowell Rd (48906-9378)
PHONE................517 322-3822
Steven Van Wagenen, *President*
Thomas Schupbach, *Vice Pres*
Jeff Ohlert, *Finance*
Greg Van Wagenen, *Sales Staff*
Robert Latchaw, *Manager*
EMP: 80 EST: 1985
SQ FT: 50,000
SALES (est): 20.9MM Privately Held
WEB: www.manitoupontoonboats.com
SIC: 3732 Pontoons, except aircraft & inflatable

(G-9746)
UNIQUE EMBROIDERY
4722 W Grand River Ave (48906-9129)
PHONE................517 321-8647
Greg Kwiecien, *Principal*
William Stuart, *Sales Staff*
EMP: 5 EST: 2013
SALES (est): 157.6K Privately Held
WEB: www.uniqueemb.com
SIC: 2759 Screen printing

(G-9747)
VAN-ROB INC
Also Called: Van Rob Lansing
16325 Felton Rd (48906-9144)
PHONE................517 657-2450
Steven Meyer, *Plant Mgr*
EMP: 135
SALES (corp-wide): 1.7B Privately Held
SIC: 3465 5013 Automotive stampings; automotive supplies & parts
HQ: Kirchhoff Automotive Canada Inc
    200 Vandorf Sideroad
    Aurora ON L4G 0
    905 727-8585

(G-9748)
VANERMEN SMITH PRODUCTS INC
319 E North St (48906-4429)
PHONE................517 575-6618
Kevin Vanermen, *President*
Greg Smith, *Admin Sec*
EMP: 10 EST: 2012
SALES (est): 572K Privately Held
WEB: www.vanermensmith.com
SIC: 3449 Bars, concrete reinforcing: fabricated steel

(G-9749)
VERY BEST MOTORS LLC
5131 N Grand River Ave (48906-5811)
PHONE................517 253-0707
Darrell Stanfield,
EMP: 7 EST: 2019
SALES (est): 460K Privately Held
SIC: 3711 Automobile bodies, passenger car, not including engine, etc.

Lansing - Clinton County (G-9750) — GEOGRAPHIC SECTION

(G-9750)
WOLFE WHISTLE
16140 S Lowell Rd (48906-8305)
PHONE..............................517 303-9197
Rebecca Wolfe, *Principal*
EMP: 4 EST: 2011
SALES (est): 103.4K Privately Held
SIC: 3999 Whistles

Lansing
Eaton County

(G-9751)
AIR LIFT COMPANY (PA)
Also Called: Air Lift Performance
2727 Snow Rd (48917-9595)
P.O. Box 80167 (48908-0167)
PHONE..............................517 322-2144
Kevin Mehigh, *President*
Adam Koch, *Plant Mgr*
Kelly Parker, *Engineer*
Al Seger, *Project Engr*
Krista Dejonge, *CFO*
◆ EMP: 49 EST: 1947
SQ FT: 30,000
SALES (est): 10.2MM Privately Held
WEB: www.airliftcompany.com
SIC: 3714 Motor vehicle parts & accessories

(G-9752)
ALLIANCE INTERIORS LLC
4521 W Mount Hope Hwy (48917-9501)
PHONE..............................517 322-0711
Steve Phillips, *CEO*
John Lychos, *Principal*
Anthony Cantin, *Opers Staff*
David Milner, *Production*
John Moreno, *Production*
▲ EMP: 140 EST: 2003
SQ FT: 200,000
SALES (est): 31.6MM Privately Held
WEB: www.allianceinteriors.com
SIC: 3446 Partitions & supports/studs, including accoustical systems
PA: Conform Automotive, Llc
    32500 Telg Rd Ste 207
    Bingham Farms MI 48025

(G-9753)
ALLOY MACHINING LLC
437 N Rosemary St (48917-4915)
PHONE..............................517 204-3306
EMP: 4
SALES (est): 200.1K Privately Held
SIC: 3369 Nonferrous foundries

(G-9754)
ALPINE SIGN AND PRTG SUP INC
Also Called: Michigan Sign Supplies
3105 Sanders Rd (48917-9512)
P.O. Box 504, Portland (48875-0504)
PHONE..............................517 487-1400
Robert Heindel, *President*
EMP: 12 EST: 2005
SQ FT: 6,000
SALES (est): 2.5MM Privately Held
WEB: www.alpinesignsupply.com
SIC: 3555 Printing trades machinery

(G-9755)
ANDROID INDSTRS-DLTA TWNSHIP L
Also Called: Ai-Delta Township
2051 S Canal Rd (48917-8598)
PHONE..............................517 322-0657
Jerry Elson,
▲ EMP: 94 EST: 2005
SALES (est): 6.2MM
SALES (corp-wide): 474.4MM Privately Held
WEB: www.android-ind.com
SIC: 3714 Motor vehicle parts & accessories
PA: Android Industries, L.L.C.
    2155 Executive Hills Dr
    Auburn Hills MI 48326
    248 454-0500

(G-9756)
ART CRAFT DISPLAY INC (PA)
500 Business Centre Dr (48917-3796)
PHONE..............................517 485-2221
Barry Freed, *President*
Dave Beeman, *General Mgr*
Steve Carr, *General Mgr*
Doug Goin, *General Mgr*
Jeanette Kapusto, *Corp Secy*
EMP: 100 EST: 1958
SQ FT: 20,000
SALES (est): 8.9MM Privately Held
WEB: www.artcraftdisplay.com
SIC: 7389 2759 Convention & show services; commercial printing

(G-9757)
CHAIN-SYS CORPORATION (PA)
8530 Ember Glen Pass (48917-8844)
PHONE..............................517 627-1173
Sundaramurugan Rathinam, *President*
Austin Arunasalam, *Vice Pres*
Arun Elangovan, *Project Mgr*
Frank Malangone, *Technical Mgr*
Rachit Gupta, *Software Engr*
EMP: 7 EST: 1998
SQ FT: 6,000
SALES (est): 3.3MM Privately Held
WEB: www.chainsys.com
SIC: 7379 7371 7372 Computer related consulting services; computer software systems analysis & design, custom; prepackaged software

(G-9758)
CONFORM AUTOMOTIVE LLC
Dti Logistics
5421 W Mount Hope Hwy E (48917-8517)
PHONE..............................517 322-0711
Steve Phillips, *Manager*
EMP: 100 Privately Held
WEB: www.conformgroup.com
SIC: 3714 Motor vehicle parts & accessories
PA: Conform Automotive, Llc
    32500 Telg Rd Ste 207
    Bingham Farms MI 48025

(G-9759)
DOUGLAS STEEL FABRICATING CORP
1312 S Waverly Rd (48917-4259)
P.O. Box 27277 (48909-7277)
PHONE..............................517 322-2050
James D Buzzie, *President*
Lawrence F Kruth, *Vice Pres*
Chris Lowe, *Purchasing*
Richard Steffens, *Engineer*
Mike Harris, *CFO*
EMP: 58
SQ FT: 50,000
SALES (est): 17MM Privately Held
WEB: www.douglassteel.com
SIC: 1791 8711 3441 Iron work, structural; sanitary engineers; fabricated structural metal for ships

(G-9760)
FLAVORED GROUP LLC
437 Lentz Ct (48917-3702)
PHONE..............................517 775-4371
Eric Fuentes, *Administration*
EMP: 7 EST: 2011
SALES (est): 242.7K Privately Held
WEB: www.custom.flavoredthreads.com
SIC: 2759 7389 Screen printing; apparel designers, commercial

(G-9761)
GENERAL MOTORS LLC
4400 W Mount Hope Hwy (48917-9501)
PHONE..............................517 885-6669
Dave Larter, *Engineer*
Barb Pohlman, *Manager*
EMP: 14 Publicly Held
WEB: www.gm.com
SIC: 5511 3714 Automobiles, new & used; motor vehicle parts & accessories
HQ: General Motors Llc
    300 Renaissance Ctr L1
    Detroit MI 48243

(G-9762)
GREAT LAKES COCA-COLA DIST LLC
3300 S Creyts Rd (48917-8508)
PHONE..............................517 322-2349
Jamie Fogarty, *Supervisor*
EMP: 12 Privately Held
WEB: www.coca-cola.com
SIC: 2086 2087 5149 Bottled & canned soft drinks; syrups, drink; concentrates, drink; groceries & related products
HQ: Great Lakes Coca-Cola Distribution, Llc
    6250 N River Rd Ste 9000
    Rosemont IL 60018
    847 227-6500

(G-9763)
GRINDMASTER EQP & MCHS USA LLC
6539 Westland Way Ste 13 (48917-9581)
PHONE..............................517 455-3675
Sohail Shaikh, *Opers Staff*
Milind Kelkar,
EMP: 4
SALES (est): 200K Privately Held
WEB: www.grindmaster.com
SIC: 3541 Grinding, polishing, buffing, lapping & honing machines

(G-9764)
HOLDER CORPORATION
2538 W Main St (48917-4341)
PHONE..............................517 484-5453
Kenneth Holz, *President*
Melissa Holz, *Corp Secy*
EMP: 7 EST: 1980
SQ FT: 7,000
SALES (est): 610.5K Privately Held
SIC: 3599 Machine shop, jobbing & repair

(G-9765)
HP INC
7335 Westshire Dr Ste 101 (48917-9703)
PHONE..............................650 857-1501
Earl Smith, *Manager*
EMP: 6
SALES (corp-wide): 56.6B Publicly Held
WEB: www.hp.com
SIC: 3571 Personal computers (microcomputers)
PA: Hp Inc.
    1501 Page Mill Rd
    Palo Alto CA 94304
    650 857-1501

(G-9766)
ICON SIGN & DESIGN INC
3308 W Saint Joseph St (48917-3706)
PHONE..............................517 372-1104
David Finley, *President*
Elaine Slawski, *Vice Pres*
EMP: 7 EST: 1997
SQ FT: 3,000
SALES (est): 539.4K Privately Held
WEB: www.iconsignservice.com
SIC: 3993 Electric signs

(G-9767)
IM A BEER HOUND
602 N Grace St (48917-4912)
PHONE..............................517 331-0528
Chuck Brown, *Owner*
EMP: 5 EST: 2010
SALES (est): 80.7K Privately Held
SIC: 2082 Beer (alcoholic beverage)

(G-9768)
JOB SHOP INK INC
2321 W Main St (48917-4338)
PHONE..............................517 372-3900
Scott McCulloch, *President*
EMP: 5 EST: 1999
SALES (est): 400K Privately Held
WEB: www.jsiapparel.com
SIC: 2752 2759 Commercial printing, offset; commercial printing

(G-9769)
K&H SUPPLY OF LANSING INC (PA)
3503 W Saint Joseph St (48917-3692)
PHONE..............................517 482-7600
Dave Tebben, *President*
EMP: 48 EST: 2003
SALES (est): 402.5K Privately Held
WEB: www.kandhcutting.com
SIC: 3531 Concrete grouting equipment

(G-9770)
KAREMOR INC
Also Called: Auntie Anne's
5242 W Saginaw Hwy (48917-1913)
PHONE..............................517 323-3042
Karen Mory, *President*
EMP: 9 Privately Held
WEB: www.auntieannes.com
SIC: 5461 2052 Pretzels; pretzels
PA: Karemor Inc
    5778 Whisperwood Dr
    Haslett MI 48840

(G-9771)
KENOWA INDUSTRIES INC
2924 Sanders Rd (48917-8570)
PHONE..............................517 322-0311
Gerry Hawkins, *Manager*
EMP: 4
SALES (corp-wide): 5.6MM Privately Held
WEB: www.kenowa.com
SIC: 3449 3441 Miscellaneous metalwork; fabricated structural metal
PA: Kenowa Industries, Inc.
    11405 E Lakewood Blvd
    Holland MI 49424
    616 392-7080

(G-9772)
LANSING ATHLETICS
5572 W Saginaw Hwy (48917-1919)
PHONE..............................517 327-8828
Alfonso Salas, *Owner*
EMP: 5 EST: 1987
SQ FT: 1,000
SALES (est): 280.5K Privately Held
WEB: www.lansingathletics.com
SIC: 5699 5941 2759 2395 Sports apparel; team sports equipment; screen printing; embroidery products, except schiffli machine

(G-9773)
LOUIS PADNOS IRON AND METAL CO
1900 W Willow St (48917-1838)
PHONE..............................517 372-6600
Todd Pastoor, *Branch Mgr*
EMP: 4
SALES (corp-wide): 520.8MM Privately Held
WEB: www.padnos.com
SIC: 5093 3341 4953 Metal scrap & waste materials; ferrous metal scrap & waste; nonferrous metals scrap; secondary nonferrous metals; recycling, waste materials
PA: Louis Padnos Iron And Metal Company
    185 W 8th St
    Holland MI 49423
    800 442-3509

(G-9774)
MELANGE COMPUTER SERVICES INC
808 Century Blvd Ste 100 (48917-8243)
PHONE..............................517 321-8434
Rick White, *President*
Ronald Austin, *Vice Pres*
Rick Bean, *Vice Pres*
Harrold Rappold, *Vice Pres*
EMP: 10 EST: 1989
SQ FT: 11,536
SALES (est): 1.3MM
SALES (corp-wide): 6.1MM Privately Held
WEB: www.planetbingo.com
SIC: 7371 7374 7372 Computer software development; data processing service; prepackaged software
PA: Planet Bingo Llc
    75190 Gerald Ford Dr
    Palm Desert CA 92211
    760 773-0197

(G-9775)
MFR ENTERPRISES INC
623 N Rosemary St (48917-8400)
PHONE..............................517 285-9555
Charles Cascarilla, *President*
EMP: 4 EST: 2016

GEOGRAPHIC SECTION
Lansing - Ingham County (G-9801)

SALES (est): 94.1K **Privately Held**
SIC: 3999 Manufacturing industries

(G-9776)
MID-WEST BEHAVIORAL ASSOCIATES
1148 Runaway Bay Dr 1a (48917-8736)
PHONE................................517 267-5502
David Miner, *Principal*
EMP: 5 **EST:** 2016
SALES (est): 74.4K **Privately Held**
WEB: www.midwestbehavioralcare.com
SIC: 2844 Toilet preparations

(G-9777)
MILLBROOK PRESS WORKS
Also Called: Gladstone Printing
517 S Waverly Rd (48917-3617)
PHONE................................517 323-2111
Travis Millbrook, *Owner*
EMP: 4 **EST:** 1979
SQ FT: 3,000
SALES (est): 380.5K **Privately Held**
WEB: www.gladstoneprinting.com
SIC: 2752 Commercial printing, offset

(G-9778)
MILLIMAN COMMUNICATIONS INC (PA)
4601 W Saginaw Hwy Apt 2 (48917-2756)
PHONE................................517 327-8407
Dirk Milliman, *President*
Teresa Fitzwater, *Vice Pres*
Ann Marie Milliman, *Treasurer*
EMP: 4 **EST:** 1992
SQ FT: 1,000 **Privately Held**
WEB: www.millimancommunications.com
SIC: 2711 Newspapers, publishing & printing

(G-9779)
MONROE SP INC
437 Lentz Ct (48917-3702)
PHONE................................517 374-6544
Steve Monroe, *President*
EMP: 9 **EST:** 1984
SALES (est): 570.9K **Privately Held**
WEB: www.monroescreenprinting.com
SIC: 2759 Screen printing

(G-9780)
MOTOROLA SOLUTIONS INC
6500 Centurion Dr Ste 250 (48917-8240)
PHONE................................517 321-6655
EMP: 8
SALES (corp-wide): 7.4B **Publicly Held**
WEB: www.motorolasolutions.com
SIC: 3663 Radio & TV communications equipment
PA: Motorola Solutions, Inc.
500 W Monroe St Ste 4400
Chicago IL 60661
847 576-5000

(G-9781)
NORPLAS INDUSTRIES INC
Also Called: Dexsys
5589 W Mount Hope Hwy (48917-9559)
PHONE................................517 999-1400
Eric Jorgensen, *Controller*
Doug Garn, *Manager*
EMP: 60
SALES (corp-wide): 32.6B **Privately Held**
WEB: www.norplas.com
SIC: 3714 Bumpers & bumperettes, motor vehicle
HQ: Norplas Industries Inc.
7825 Caple Blvd
Northwood OH 43619
419 662-3317

(G-9782)
OAKWOOD SPORTS INC (PA)
1025 Clark Rd (48917-2129)
PHONE................................517 321-6852
Greg Bria, *President*
Willard Boast, *Vice Pres*
EMP: 5 **EST:** 1998
SQ FT: 8,500
SALES (est): 620.4K **Privately Held**
WEB: www.oakwoodsports.com
SIC: 2499 Decorative wood & woodwork

(G-9783)
PAXTON PRODUCTS INC
Also Called: Paxton Countertops
1340 S Waverly Rd (48917-5206)
P.O. Box 174, Grand Ledge (48837-0174)
PHONE................................517 627-3688
Stephen Paxton, *President*
Rachel Paxton Schroeder, *Principal*
David Paxton, *Vice Pres*
Jane Paxton, *Admin Sec*
EMP: 22 **EST:** 2007
SQ FT: 10,000
SALES (est): 2.6MM **Privately Held**
WEB: www.paxtonsurfaces.com
SIC: 2541 Counter & sink tops

(G-9784)
PIRA TESTING LLC
Also Called: Pira International
6539 Westland Way Ste 24 (48917-9581)
PHONE................................517 574-4297
Rob Peterson, *Senior Engr*
Stephen Frier, *Accounts Mgr*
Michael Dannemiller, *Manager*
Barbara Rojas, *Director*
Michael Kuebler,
EMP: 15 **EST:** 2010
SALES (est): 2.3MM **Privately Held**
WEB: www.smithers.com
SIC: 2869 Industrial organic chemicals

(G-9785)
PRESCOTT INC
2821 W Willow St (48917-1834)
PHONE................................517 515-0007
Tia Prescott, *Principal*
EMP: 5 **EST:** 2018
SALES (est): 79.7K **Privately Held**
SIC: 2711 Newspapers, publishing & printing

(G-9786)
PURINA MILLS LLC
5620 Millett Hwy (48917-8556)
PHONE................................517 322-0200
Lawrence Moorman, *Manager*
EMP: 42
SALES (corp-wide): 2.8B **Privately Held**
WEB: www.purina-mills.com
SIC: 2048 5191 5149 Prepared feeds; animal feeds; groceries & related products
HQ: Purina Mills, Llc
555 Maryvle Univ Dr 200
Saint Louis MO 63141

(G-9787)
ROBERTS SINTO CORPORATION (DH)
Also Called: Shalco Systems
3001 W Main St (48917-4352)
P.O. Box 39, Grand Ledge (48837-0039)
PHONE................................517 371-2460
Richard Stewart, *CEO*
Donald Kvorka, *President*
Michael Halsband, *Exec VP*
Bill Traeger, *Vice Pres*
Keith Brown, *Safety Mgr*
▲ **EMP:** 75 **EST:** 1987
SQ FT: 25,000
SALES (est): 41.4MM **Privately Held**
WEB: www.sintoamerica.com
SIC: 3559 3535 5084 Foundry machinery & equipment; conveyors & conveying equipment; machine tools & metalworking machinery

(G-9788)
ROCKETPLANE GLOBAL INC
3036 W Willow St (48917-1854)
PHONE................................734 476-2888
Charles Lauer, *Owner*
EMP: 5 **EST:** 2017
SALES (est): 88K **Privately Held**
WEB: www.spaceportbarcelona.com
SIC: 3812 Search & navigation equipment

(G-9789)
RYDER INTEGRATED LOGISTICS INC
2901 S Canal Rd (48917-8594)
PHONE................................517 492-4446
Martin Walsh, *Finance Mgr*
Greg Reinke, *Manager*
Thomas Kovarik, *Manager*
David Secord, *Manager*
Joshua Wilson, *Manager*
EMP: 15
SQ FT: 2,760,000
SALES (corp-wide): 2.1B **Publicly Held**
WEB: www.lms.ryder.com
SIC: 4225 3714 General warehousing & storage; motor vehicle parts & accessories
HQ: Ryder Integrated Logistics, Inc.
11690 Nw 105th St
Medley FL 33178
305 500-3726

(G-9790)
SEPHORA INSIDE JCPENNEY
5304 W Saginaw Hwy (48917-1915)
PHONE................................517 323-4000
EMP: 4 **EST:** 2019
SALES (est): 74.4K **Privately Held**
SIC: 2844 Toilet preparations

(G-9791)
SINTO AMERICA INC (HQ)
3001 W Main St (48917-4352)
P.O. Box 40760 (48901-7960)
PHONE................................517 371-2460
James A Donlan, *Ch of Bd*
Mike Toth, *Project Mgr*
Jim Wenson, *Project Mgr*
Pat O 'meara, *Foreman/Supr*
Jim Swanson, *Sales Staff*
▲ **EMP:** 25 **EST:** 1991
SQ FT: 25,000
SALES (est): 59.4MM **Privately Held**
WEB: www.sintoamerica.com
SIC: 3559 3535 5084 3823 Foundry machinery & equipment; conveyors & conveying equipment; industrial machinery & equipment; industrial instrmnts msrmnt display/control process variable

(G-9792)
SUGAR BERRY
5451 W Saginaw Hwy (48917-1982)
PHONE................................517 321-0177
Sarah Pham, *Owner*
EMP: 7 **EST:** 2012
SALES (est): 151.5K **Privately Held**
SIC: 2026 Yogurt

(G-9793)
SUPERIOR MACHINE & TOOL INC
Also Called: Icon Integrated Solutions
1301 Sunset Ave (48917-1807)
PHONE................................800 822-9524
Jason Puuri, *President*
Kortney Puuri, *Program Mgr*
EMP: 10 **EST:** 2013
SALES (est): 1MM **Privately Held**
WEB: www.superiormachinetools.com
SIC: 3599 Machine shop, jobbing & repair

(G-9794)
TUMACS CORPORATION
7619 Northport Dr (48917-9516)
PHONE................................517 816-8141
Kevin McMillan, *Administration*
EMP: 9 **EST:** 2016
SALES (est): 109.1K **Privately Held**
WEB: www.tumacscovers.com
SIC: 2394 Canvas & related products

(G-9795)
UFP LANSING LLC
Also Called: Universal Forest Products
2509 Snow Rd (48917-9506)
PHONE................................517 322-0025
EMP: 5
SALES (est): 506K
SALES (corp-wide): 3.9B **Publicly Held**
SIC: 2491 2499 Wood Preserving Mfg Wood Products
PA: Universal Forest Products, Inc.
2801 E Beltline Ave Ne
Grand Rapids MI 49525
616 364-6161

(G-9796)
XYZ MCHINE TL FABRICATIONS INC
2127 W Willow St (48917-1862)
PHONE................................517 482-3668
John Wieber, *President*
EMP: 8 **EST:** 1994
SQ FT: 6,000

SALES (est): 704.3K **Privately Held**
WEB: www.machinetools.com
SIC: 3842 Surgical appliances & supplies

Lansing
Ingham County

(G-9797)
2 BROTHERS HOLDINGS LLC
Also Called: Tommark Lansing
1115 S Penn Ave Ste B (48912-1658)
PHONE................................517 487-3900
Michael Olds, *Manager*
EMP: 6
SALES (corp-wide): 9.7MM **Privately Held**
SIC: 3829 3494 5075 Measuring & controlling devices; valves & pipe fittings; warm air heating & air conditioning
PA: 2 Brothers Holdings, Llc
7653 Blue Gentian Ct
Dexter MI 48130
517 782-0557

(G-9798)
917 CHITTOCK STREET LLC
Also Called: A Dependable Property MGT
114 Bank St (48910-9159)
PHONE................................866 945-0269
Neil Wright, *Mng Member*
Janell S Wright,
EMP: 10 **EST:** 2002
SQ FT: 2,200
SALES (est): 1MM **Privately Held**
SIC: 8741 6531 1389 Business management; real estate agents & managers; construction, repair & dismantling services

(G-9799)
ACUMEDIA MANUFACTURERS INC
620 Lesher Pl (48912-1509)
PHONE................................517 372-9200
Deb Cook, *Admin Sec*
EMP: 30 **EST:** 2000
SQ FT: 40,000
SALES (est): 21.3MM
SALES (corp-wide): 468.4MM **Publicly Held**
WEB: www.neogen.com
SIC: 2656 Sanitary food containers
PA: Neogen Corporation
620 Lesher Pl
Lansing MI 48912
517 372-9200

(G-9800)
AL FE HEAT TREATING-OHIO INC (PA)
209 W Mount Hope Ave # 1 (48910-9084)
PHONE................................260 747-9422
Kurt H Westman, *President*
Gary P Peatee, *Purch Mgr*
Andy Berg, *Business Anlyst*
Michelle Carver, *Supervisor*
Kathleen K Westman, *Admin Sec*
EMP: 11 **EST:** 1989
SALES (est): 3.8MM **Privately Held**
WEB: www.premierthermal.com
SIC: 3398 Metal heat treating

(G-9801)
AL-FE HEAT TREATING LLC (HQ)
Also Called: Al Fe Corporate Group
209 W Mount Hope Ave # 1 (48910-9084)
PHONE................................260 747-9422
Kurt Westman, *President*
Kathleen K Westman, *Admin Sec*
Frasure Bryan, *Admin Asst*
Kathy Holtsclaw, *Admin Asst*
EMP: 85 **EST:** 1979
SALES (est): 26.7MM
SALES (corp-wide): 74.2MM **Privately Held**
WEB: www.premierthermal.com
SIC: 3398 Metal heat treating
PA: Premier Thermal Solutions, Llc
209 W Mount Hope Ave # 2
Lansing MI 48910
517 485-5090

Lansing - Ingham County (G-9802)
GEOGRAPHIC SECTION

(G-9802)
AL-FE HEAT TREATING LLC
Also Called: Piedmont Heat Treating
209 W Mount Hope Ave # 1 (48910-9084)
PHONE..................888 747-2533
Curt Westman, *President*
EMP: 20
SALES (corp-wide): 74.2MM **Privately Held**
WEB: www.premierthermal.com
SIC: 3398 Metal heat treating
HQ: Al-Fe Heat Treating, Llc
  209 W Mount Hope Ave # 1
  Lansing MI 48910
  260 747-9422

(G-9803)
ALRO STEEL CORPORATION
1800 W Willow St (48915-1430)
PHONE..................517 371-9600
Dave Forquer, *Manager*
EMP: 4
SALES (corp-wide): 1.9B **Privately Held**
WEB: www.alrosteel.com
SIC: 5051 3316 Steel; cold finishing of steel shapes
PA: Alro Steel Corporation
  3100 E High St
  Jackson MI 49203
  517 787-5500

(G-9804)
AMBASSADOR STEEL CORPORATION
Also Called: Harris Rebar
1501 E Jolly Rd (48910-7133)
PHONE..................517 455-7216
William Wear, *Principal*
Jeff Weingarten, *Sales/Mktg Mgr*
Todd Brigham, *Manager*
Melissa Vannortrick, *Administration*
EMP: 23
SALES (corp-wide): 20.1B **Publicly Held**
SIC: 3449 3496 3443 3441 Miscellaneous metalwork; miscellaneous fabricated wire products; fabricated plate work (boiler shop); fabricated structural metal
HQ: Ambassador Steel Corporation
  1340 S Grandstaff Dr
  Auburn IN 46706
  260 925-5440

(G-9805)
APPLICTION SPCLIST KOMPANY INC
Also Called: Application Specialists Co
316 Moores River Dr (48910-1434)
PHONE..................517 676-6633
Dave Paul, *CEO*
Michael Maddocx, *President*
Scott Spalding, *General Mgr*
Michael Brown, *Vice Pres*
Brian Benveniste, *Accounts Mgr*
EMP: 12 EST: 1993
SALES (est): 3MM **Privately Held**
WEB: www.justask.net
SIC: 7371 3577 Computer software writing services; printers & plotters

(G-9806)
ARCTIC GLACIER TEXAS INC
5635 Commerce St Ste B (48911-5347)
PHONE..................517 999-3500
Jim Forsburg, *Regional Mgr*
EMP: 7
SALES (corp-wide): 2.9B **Publicly Held**
SIC: 2097 Block ice
HQ: Arctic Glacier Texas Inc.
  1654 Marthaler Ln
  Saint Paul MN 55118
  806 765-5558

(G-9807)
ASAP PRINTING INC
1110 Keystone Ave (48911-4032)
PHONE..................517 882-3500
Edward Guile, *Branch Mgr*
Lisa Lefler, *Graphic Designe*
EMP: 11 **Privately Held**
WEB: www.asapprinting.net
SIC: 2752 Commercial printing, offset
PA: Asap Printing, Inc.
  2323 Jolly Rd
  Okemos MI 48864

(G-9808)
ATMOSPHERE ANNEALING LLC (HQ)
209 W Mount Hope Ave # 2 (48910-9084)
PHONE..................517 485-5090
Steve Wyatt, *Mng Member*
EMP: 75 EST: 2010
SQ FT: 13,400
SALES (est): 40MM
SALES (corp-wide): 74.2MM **Privately Held**
WEB: www.premierthermal.com
SIC: 3398 Annealing of metal
PA: Premier Thermal Solutions, Llc
  209 W Mount Hope Ave # 2
  Lansing MI 48910
  517 485-5090

(G-9809)
ATMOSPHERE ANNEALING LLC
1801 Bassett St (48915-1597)
PHONE..................517 482-1374
Lew Fortune, *Manager*
EMP: 40
SALES (corp-wide): 74.2MM **Privately Held**
WEB: www.premierthermal.com
SIC: 3398 Annealing of metal
HQ: Atmosphere Annealing, Llc
  209 W Mount Hope Ave # 2
  Lansing MI 48910
  517 485-5090

(G-9810)
AURORA SPCLTY CHEMISTRIES CORP
1520 Lake Lansing Rd (48912-3707)
P.O. Box 227, Lowell (49331-0227)
PHONE..................517 372-9121
Harry J Moyle, *President*
Timothy Pinter, *Vice Pres*
Daron Ross, *Technical Staff*
◆ EMP: 32 EST: 1982
SQ FT: 15,000
SALES (est): 9.9MM **Privately Held**
WEB: www.auroraspecialtychemistries.com
SIC: 2899 8731 Water treating compounds; commercial physical research

(G-9811)
BAKE N CAKES LP
3003 E Kalamazoo St (48912-4614)
PHONE..................517 337-2253
Jeffrey Johnson, *Partner*
Deborah Johnson, *General Ptnr*
Wilford Johnson, *Ltd Ptnr*
EMP: 6 EST: 1983
SQ FT: 2,020
SALES (est): 583.7K **Privately Held**
WEB: www.bakencakes.com
SIC: 2048 5461 Dry pet food (except dog & cat); bakeries

(G-9812)
BARNES GROUP INC
Barnes Aerospace Lansing Div
5300 Aurelius Rd (48911-4116)
P.O. Box 30112, College Station TX (77842-3112)
PHONE..................517 393-5110
Pat Beachnau, *Buyer*
Sevie Jean, *Purchasing*
Sara Gustafson, *Human Res Dir*
Stuart Kale, *Branch Mgr*
EMP: 1434
SALES (corp-wide): 1.4B **Publicly Held**
WEB: www.barnesgroupinc.com
SIC: 3724 Aircraft engines & engine parts
PA: Barnes Group Inc.
  123 Main St
  Bristol CT 06010
  860 583-7070

(G-9813)
BARONS INC
Also Called: Baron's Window Coverings
325 S Washington Sq (48933-2114)
PHONE..................517 484-1366
Donald Baron, *President*
Donald E Baron, *President*
Neil Baron, *Vice Pres*
Ruth Nelson, *Sales Staff*
EMP: 21 EST: 1944
SQ FT: 10,800
SALES (est): 2MM **Privately Held**
WEB: www.baronsblinds.com
SIC: 2391 5714 Curtains, window: made from purchased materials; curtains

(G-9814)
BOOTH NEWSPAPER
108 S Washington Sq Ste 1 (48933-1726)
PHONE..................517 487-8888
Meegan Holland, *Manager*
EMP: 5 EST: 2010
SALES (est): 68.7K **Privately Held**
SIC: 2711 Newspapers, publishing & printing

(G-9815)
BRADFORD PRINTING INC
1020 E Jolly Rd (48910-7123)
PHONE..................517 887-0044
Barry L Bradford, *President*
Pamela A Bradford, *Treasurer*
Nevin Speerbrecker, *Graphic Designe*
EMP: 7 EST: 1990
SQ FT: 4,000
SALES (est): 854.2K **Privately Held**
WEB: www.bradfordprinting.net
SIC: 2752 Commercial printing, offset

(G-9816)
BRD PRINTING INC
912 W Saint Joseph St (48915-1687)
PHONE..................517 372-0268
Donald W Hough, *President*
Julie Brown, *Production*
Pattie Lane, *Controller*
Mark Wells, *Manager*
EMP: 37 EST: 1977
SQ FT: 22,000
SALES (est): 6.2MM **Privately Held**
WEB: www.brdprinting.com
SIC: 2752 2789 Commercial printing, offset; bookbinding & related work

(G-9817)
BRETTON SQUARE INDUSTRIES
812 E Jolly Rd Ste 216 (48910-6839)
PHONE..................517 346-9607
Susan Speers, *Manager*
EMP: 5 EST: 2018
SALES (est): 86.6K **Privately Held**
WEB: www.brettonsquare.com
SIC: 3841 Surgical & medical instruments

(G-9818)
BRETTS PRINTING SERVICE
2435 S Rundle Ave 39 (48910-2746)
PHONE..................517 482-2256
Pauline Brethauder, *Owner*
EMP: 5 EST: 1950
SQ FT: 2,500
SALES (est): 80K **Privately Held**
SIC: 2752 Commercial printing, offset

(G-9819)
BRUCE INC
Also Called: Insty-Prints
108 S Washington Sq (48933-1726)
PHONE..................517 371-5205
Michael S Bruce, *President*
Annette Bruce, *Treasurer*
EMP: 5 EST: 1966
SALES (est): 911.2K **Privately Held**
WEB: www.instyprints.com
SIC: 2752 2791 2789 7331 Commercial printing, offset; typesetting; bookbinding & related work; mailing service; poster advertising, outdoor

(G-9820)
CAMERON TOOL CORPORATION
1800 Bassett St (48915-1598)
PHONE..................517 487-3671
Tracy Selden, *President*
Kathy Bracey, *Exec VP*
Bob Breilein, *Project Mgr*
Yvette Simon, *Purchasing*
Carey Oberlin, *Human Res Mgr*
▲ EMP: 60
SQ FT: 72,000
SALES: 18.6MM **Privately Held**
WEB: www.camerontool.com
SIC: 3544 3469 Special dies & tools; jigs & fixtures; metal stampings

(G-9821)
CAMPBELL INC PRESS REPAIR
925 River St (48912-1027)
PHONE..................517 371-1034
Peter Campbell, *President*
▲ EMP: 20 EST: 1973
SQ FT: 35,000
SALES (est): 4MM **Privately Held**
WEB: www.campbellpress.com
SIC: 7692 5084 Welding repair; industrial machinery & equipment

(G-9822)
CAPITAL IMAGING INC
2521 E Michigan Ave (48912-4010)
PHONE..................517 482-2292
Granville Noles, *Principal*
Nia Noles, *Principal*
EMP: 10 EST: 1995
SQ FT: 7,000
SALES (est): 2.5MM **Privately Held**
WEB: www.capital-imaging.com
SIC: 2752 2754 7334 Commercial printing, offset; commercial printing, gravure; blueprinting service

(G-9823)
CENTRAL MICH KNWRTH LNSING LLC
2556 Alamo Dr (48911-6351)
PHONE..................517 394-7000
Jesse CP Berger, *President*
EMP: 5 EST: 2008
SALES (est): 265.3K **Privately Held**
SIC: 3713 4492 Truck bodies & parts; towing & tugboat service

(G-9824)
CHEAP FAST PRINTS LLC
3309 Jerree St (48911-2628)
PHONE..................517 490-0864
Gray Taylor, *Principal*
EMP: 4 EST: 2017
SALES (est): 83.9K **Privately Held**
SIC: 2752 Commercial printing, lithographic

(G-9825)
COMMERCIAL BLUEPRINT INC
3125 Pinetree Rd Ste B (48911-4244)
PHONE..................517 372-8360
Douglas Schmidt, *President*
Pete Dumond, *Vice Pres*
Shagen Chaliyan, *Purchasing*
Stephanie Schmidt, *Treasurer*
Jay Fink, *Sales Executive*
EMP: 24 EST: 1950
SQ FT: 14,000
SALES (est): 3.8MM **Privately Held**
WEB: www.commblue.com
SIC: 5049 7334 2759 Drafting supplies; blueprinting service; commercial printing

(G-9826)
CONSUMERS CONCRETE CORPORATION
1367 Lake Lansing Rd (48912-3737)
PHONE..................517 267-8428
Dave Carlson, *Branch Mgr*
EMP: 12
SALES (corp-wide): 42.6MM **Privately Held**
WEB: www.consumersconcrete.com
SIC: 3273 Ready-mixed concrete
PA: Consumers Concrete Corporation
  3506 Lovers Ln
  Kalamazoo MI 49001
  269 342-0136

(G-9827)
CUSHION LRRY TRPHIES ENGRV LLC
300 N Clippert St Ste 14 (48912-4637)
PHONE..................517 332-1667
Leann Cushion-Groves, *Owner*
EMP: 4 EST: 1957
SALES (est): 297.5K **Privately Held**
WEB: www.larrycushiontrophies.com
SIC: 5999 3479 Trophies & plaques; name plates: engraved, etched, etc.

▲ = Import ▼ = Export
◆ = Import/Export

GEOGRAPHIC SECTION

Lansing - Ingham County (G-9853)

(G-9828)
DART CONTAINER MICHIGAN LLC
3120 Sovereign Dr Ste 4b (48911-4227)
PHONE................................888 327-8001
EMP: 2628 **Privately Held**
WEB: www.dartcontainer.com
SIC: **3086** 2656 Cups & plates, foamed plastic; paper cups, plates, dishes & utensils
HQ: Dart Container Of Michigan Llc
500 Hogsback Rd
Mason MI 48854
800 248-5960

(G-9829)
DATAMATIC PROCESSING INC (PA)
5545 Enterprise Dr (48911-4131)
PHONE................................517 882-4401
Wesley Benzing, *President*
Alan Ross, *Vice Pres*
Weston Benzing, *CFO*
Marsha Benzing, *Admin Sec*
Lori Middleton,
EMP: 25 EST: 1974
SQ FT: 20,000
SALES (est): 3.8MM **Privately Held**
WEB: www.datamatic.net
SIC: **7372** 5045 7374 Business oriented computer software; computers, peripherals & software; data processing service

(G-9830)
DILLION RENEE ENTITIES
600 Baker St (48910-1708)
PHONE................................989 443-0654
Eddie Wells,
EMP: 5 EST: 2011
SALES (est): 504.4K **Privately Held**
SIC: **6794** 2741 Performance rights, publishing & licensing; miscellaneous publishing

(G-9831)
DIOCESE OF LANSING
Also Called: Liturgical Commission
1500 W Saginaw St Ste 2 (48915-1380)
PHONE................................517 484-4449
Mary Jo Gilliland, *Manager*
EMP: 4
SALES (corp-wide): 39.4MM **Privately Held**
WEB: www.stvcc.org
SIC: **8661** 5942 2721 2731 Catholic Church; books, religious; periodicals: publishing & printing; books: publishing & printing; miscellaneous publishing
PA: Diocese Of Lansing
228 N Walnut St
Lansing MI 48933
517 342-2440

(G-9832)
DIVA PUBLICATIONS
4018 Seaway Dr (48911-2551)
PHONE................................517 887-8271
Marneta L Griffin, *Principal*
EMP: 4 EST: 2017
SALES (est): 60.3K **Privately Held**
SIC: **2741** Miscellaneous publishing

(G-9833)
EDWARDS INDUSTRIAL SALES INC
5646 Commerce St Ste D (48911-5335)
PHONE................................517 887-6100
David Salisbury, *Branch Mgr*
EMP: 4
SALES (corp-wide): 12.8MM **Privately Held**
WEB: www.edwardsindustrial.com
SIC: **3621** 5085 5063 Electric motor & generator parts; bearings; motors, electric
PA: Edwards Industrial Sales, Inc.
424 Mills St
Kalamazoo MI 49001
269 349-7737

(G-9834)
ELMET NORTH AMERICA INC
4103 Grand Oak Dr B102 (48911-7404)
P.O. Box 459, Dimondale (48821-0459)
PHONE................................517 664-9011
Tony Hsu, *General Mgr*

Helmut Gaderer, *Principal*
Paul Fattinger, *Sales Staff*
Andreas Angerer, *Manager*
EMP: 8 EST: 2012
SALES (est): 1.1MM **Privately Held**
WEB: www.elmet.com
SIC: **3089** Injection molded finished plastic products

(G-9835)
ELSIE PUBLISHING INSTITUTE (PA)
500 W Ionia St (48933-1013)
P.O. Box 811, East Lansing (48826-0811)
PHONE................................517 371-5257
Penny Gardner, *President*
Denise Gruben, *Vice Pres*
Katie Watkins, *Manager*
Leane Cassady, *Comp Spec*
EMP: 15 EST: 1974
SALES (est): 582.9K **Privately Held**
WEB: www.Iconline.org
SIC: **2721** 7389 Magazines: publishing only, not printed on site;

(G-9836)
FLORHEAT COMPANY
3130 Sovereign Dr (48911-4241)
PHONE................................517 272-4441
Charlie Karupa, *President*
Gary Smith, *Sales Mgr*
EMP: 7 EST: 2003
SALES (est): 660K **Privately Held**
WEB: www.getfloorheat.com
SIC: **3567** Radiant heating systems, industrial process

(G-9837)
FLUID CHILLERS INC (PA)
Also Called: Coolant Chillers
2730 Alpha Access St (48910-3686)
PHONE................................517 484-9190
Timothy Ayres, *President*
Katlyn Kring, *Purchasing*
Amy Vanburen, *Accounting Mgr*
Tim Ayres, *Sales Staff*
Tom P Ayres, *Sales Staff*
▼ EMP: 45 EST: 2007
SALES (est): 12.3MM **Privately Held**
WEB: www.fluidchillers.com
SIC: **3585** Refrigeration & heating equipment

(G-9838)
FMS LANSING LLC (DH)
920 Winter St (48901)
PHONE................................781 699-9000
William Valle, *CEO*
Rebecca Scorse, *Senior Mgr*
EMP: 4 EST: 2011
SALES (est): 403.1K
SALES (corp-wide): 21.1B **Privately Held**
SIC: **3841** Surgical & medical instruments
HQ: Fms Lansing Dialysis Centers, Llc
920 Winter St
Waltham MA 02451
781 699-9000

(G-9839)
FUDGE AND FROSTING
333 S Washington Sq (48933-2114)
PHONE................................517 763-2040
EMP: 4 EST: 2019
SALES (est): 62.3K **Privately Held**
SIC: **2099** Food preparations

(G-9840)
GADGET FACTORY LLC
5157 Aurelius Rd (48911-4115)
PHONE................................517 449-1444
Mike Mosholder,
EMP: 6 EST: 2008
SALES (est): 374.8K **Privately Held**
WEB: www.the-gadget-factory.com
SIC: **3648** Lighting equipment

(G-9841)
GERDAU MCSTEEL ATMSPHERE ANNLI (DH)
209 W Mount Hope Ave # 1 (48910-9084)
PHONE................................517 782-0415
James McWilliams, *President*
Roger Webster, *Manager*
▲ EMP: 16 EST: 1978
SQ FT: 100,000

SALES (est): 24.6MM **Privately Held**
WEB: www.gerdau.com
SIC: **3398** Annealing of metal
HQ: Gerdau Ameristeel Us Inc.
4221 W Boy Scout Blvd # 600
Tampa FL 33607
813 286-8383

(G-9842)
GERDAU MCSTEEL ATMSPHERE ANNLI
1801 Bassett St (48915-1567)
PHONE................................517 482-1374
Jay Murthy, *Branch Mgr*
EMP: 33 **Privately Held**
SIC: **3398** Metal heat treating
HQ: Gerdau Macsteel Atmosphere Annealing
209 W Mount Hope Ave # 1
Lansing MI 48910
517 782-0415

(G-9843)
GONGWER NEWS SERVICE INC
101 S Wash Sq Ste 540 (48933-1733)
PHONE................................517 482-3500
Scott Miller, *Vice Pres*
EMP: 5
SQ FT: 800
SALES (corp-wide): 1.6MM **Privately Held**
WEB: www.gongwer-oh.com
SIC: **2721** Magazines: publishing only, not printed on site
PA: Gongwer News Service Inc
17 S High St Ste 630
Columbus OH 43215
614 221-1992

(G-9844)
GREATER LANSING BUS MONTHLY
221 W Saginaw St (48933-1254)
PHONE................................517 203-0123
J Chris Holman, *President*
EMP: 5 EST: 1988
SALES (est): 577K **Privately Held**
WEB: www.lansingbusinessnews.com
SIC: **2721** Magazines: publishing only, not printed on site

(G-9845)
GREATER LANSING ORTHOTIC CLINI
200 N Homer St Ste A (48912-4741)
PHONE................................517 337-0856
Joseph Springer, *President*
EMP: 6 EST: 1992
SQ FT: 6,000
SALES (est): 394.1K **Privately Held**
WEB: www.greaterlansingorthoticclinic.com
SIC: **3842** 5999 Braces, orthopedic; orthopedic & prosthesis applications

(G-9846)
GREENBROOK TMS NEUROHEALTH CTR
4136 Legacy Pkwy Ste 110 (48911-4293)
PHONE................................855 940-4867
EMP: 6
SALES (corp-wide): 21.9MM **Privately Held**
WEB: www.greenbrooktms.com
SIC: **3312** Blast furnaces & steel mills
PA: Greenbrook Tms Neurohealth Center
8405 Greensboro Dr # 120
Mc Lean VA 22102
703 356-1568

(G-9847)
GREENMARK BIOMEDICAL INC
3815 Tech Blvd Ste 1055 (48910)
PHONE................................517 336-4665
Steven Bloembergen, *Principal*
Joerg Lahann, *Director*
Kenneth Pienta, *Director*
Frank Van Luttikhuizen, *Director*
EMP: 5 EST: 2016
SALES (est): 440.5K **Privately Held**
WEB: www.greenmark.bio
SIC: **2834** 2835 Pharmaceutical preparations; in vitro & in vivo diagnostic substances

(G-9848)
GROUP INFOTECH INC
3101 Tech Blvd Ste E (48910)
PHONE................................517 336-7110
William Ray, *President*
Hector Chabut, *Vice Pres*
Mark Lowenthal, *Rsch/Dvlpt Mgr*
Bil Moore, *Manager*
Reuben Rettke, *Data Proc Dir*
EMP: 23 EST: 1990
SQ FT: 8,700
SALES (est): 846K **Privately Held**
SIC: **7371** 2796 2759 Custom computer programming services; color separations for printing; commercial printing

(G-9849)
GROWGENERATION MICHIGAN CORP (HQ)
Also Called: Superior Growers Supply
5711 Enterprise Dr (48911-4106)
PHONE................................248 473-0450
Michael Salaman, *President*
EMP: 2 EST: 1983
SQ FT: 16,000
SALES (est): 4MM
SALES (corp-wide): 193.3MM **Publicly Held**
WEB: www.growgeneration.com
SIC: **5261** 3423 Garden supplies & tools; garden & farm tools, including shovels
PA: Growgeneration Corp.
930 W 7th Ave Ste A
Denver CO 80204
800 935-8420

(G-9850)
HACKS KEY SHOP INC
1109 River St (48912-1031)
PHONE................................517 485-9488
Diana Engman, *President*
Danielle Engman, *Sales Staff*
EMP: 20 EST: 1953
SALES (est): 1.5MM **Privately Held**
WEB: www.hackskeyshop.com
SIC: **3442** 7699 7382 Metal doors; lock & key services; security systems services

(G-9851)
HANGER PRSTHETCS & ORTHO INC
Also Called: Institute Adv of Prosthetics
4424 S Pennsylvania Ave (48910-7625)
PHONE................................517 394-5850
Lisa Addams, *Manager*
Jerry Vilminot, *Director*
Chris Jonas, *Technician*
EMP: 10
SALES (corp-wide): 1B **Publicly Held**
WEB: www.hangerclinic.com
SIC: **3842** 5999 Prosthetic appliances; orthopedic & prosthesis applications
HQ: Hanger Prosthetics & Orthotics, Inc.
10910 Domain Dr Ste 300
Austin TX 78758
512 777-3800

(G-9852)
HOTWATER WORKS INC (PA)
Also Called: Hot Tubs
2116 E Michigan Ave (48912-3026)
PHONE................................517 364-8827
James McFarland, *President*
▲ EMP: 4 EST: 1978
SQ FT: 10,000
SALES (est): 882K **Privately Held**
WEB: www.hotwaterworks.com
SIC: **5999** 3431 Swimming pools, above ground; bathtubs: enameled iron, cast iron or pressed metal

(G-9853)
HYDRODYNAMICS INTERNATIONAL
5711 Enterprise Dr (48911-4106)
PHONE................................517 887-2007
Jeffrey A Gibson, *President*
▲ EMP: 6 EST: 1998
SALES (est): 1.4MM **Privately Held**
WEB: www.hydrodynamicsintl.com
SIC: **2875** Fertilizers, mixing only

Lansing - Ingham County (G-9854)   GEOGRAPHIC SECTION

(G-9854)
INFOGUYS INC
Also Called: Mirs News
910 W Ottawa St (48915-1742)
PHONE..................................517 482-2125
John T Reurink, *President*
Michelle Reurink, *Treasurer*
Mary Lou Reurink, *Admin Sec*
Jack Spencer, *Analyst*
EMP: 6 **EST:** 1996
SQ FT: 15,000
SALES (est): 480K **Privately Held**
SIC: 2711 2721 Newspapers; periodicals

(G-9855)
J&S HOMEMADE CANDLES
5608 Appleton Ave Apt 31 (48911-3904)
PHONE..................................517 885-1983
Jason Wrick, *Principal*
EMP: 4 **EST:** 2017
SALES (est): 55.1K **Privately Held**
WEB: www.jsscentedcandles.com
SIC: 3999 Candles

(G-9856)
JAMES GORDON MARSH
1714 Lindbergh Dr (48910-1886)
PHONE..................................517 372-8685
James Gordon Marsh, *Principal*
EMP: 5 **EST:** 2008
SALES (est): 98.1K **Privately Held**
SIC: 2431 Millwork

(G-9857)
LANGENBERG MACHINE PDTS INC
1234 S Holmes St (48912-1928)
PHONE..................................517 485-9450
Sigurd C Langenberg, *President*
EMP: 5 **EST:** 1987
SQ FT: 3,000 **Privately Held**
WEB: www.lmpincmi.net
SIC: 3599 Machine shop, jobbing & repair

(G-9858)
LANSING EASTSIDE GATEWAY
615 E Kalamazoo St (48912-1116)
PHONE..................................517 894-6125
Yvonne Lefave, *Agent*
EMP: 7 **EST:** 2018
SALES (est): 117.9K **Privately Held**
WEB: www.lansingcitypulse.com
SIC: 2711 Newspapers, publishing & printing

(G-9859)
LANSING FORGE INC (HQ)
5232 Aurelius Rd (48911-4114)
PHONE..................................517 882-2056
Dennis M Mosholder, *President*
Matt Partin, *General Mgr*
EMP: 10 **EST:** 1957
SQ FT: 16,000
SALES (est): 2.7MM **Privately Held**
WEB: www.lansingforge.com
SIC: 3462 Iron & steel forgings
PA: Lansing Holding Company Inc
 5232 Aurelius Rd
 Lansing MI 48911
 517 882-2056

(G-9860)
LANSING FUEL VENTURES INC
601 W Saginaw St (48933-8023)
PHONE..................................517 371-1198
EMP: 8 **EST:** 2015
SALES (est): 1.4MM **Privately Held**
WEB: www.lansingiceandfuel.com
SIC: 2869 Fuels

(G-9861)
LANSING HOLDING COMPANY INC (PA)
5232 Aurelius Rd (48911-4114)
PHONE..................................517 882-2056
Dennis M Mosholder, *President*
Mike Mosholder, *Vice Pres*
EMP: 2 **EST:** 1978
SQ FT: 16,000
SALES (est): 2.7MM **Privately Held**
SIC: 3462 Iron & steel forgings

(G-9862)
LANSING NWSPPERS IN EDCATN INC
300 S Wash Sq Ste 300 # 300 (48933-2122)
PHONE..................................517 377-1000
Rebecca Poynter, *Principal*
EMP: 9 **EST:** 2000
SALES (est): 97.5K **Privately Held**
WEB: www.lansingstatejournal.com
SIC: 2721 Trade journals: publishing & printing

(G-9863)
LECTRONIX INC (PA)
5858 Enterprise Dr (48911-4107)
PHONE..................................517 492-1900
Allan Dale, *President*
Tom Bayerl, *Senior VP*
Frederick Roth, *Senior VP*
Rick Roth, *Senior VP*
Frank Pellitta, *Vice Pres*
EMP: 40 **EST:** 2002
SQ FT: 80,000
SALES (est): 10.9MM **Privately Held**
WEB: www.lectronixinc.com
SIC: 8711 3679 Electrical or electronic engineering; electronic circuits

(G-9864)
LIGHTNING LITHO INC
Also Called: Allegra Print Imaging-Lansing
5731 Enterprise Dr (48911-4106)
PHONE..................................517 394-2995
Brad Naghtin, *President*
Angie Lewis, *General Mgr*
Shirley Naghtin, *Vice Pres*
EMP: 10 **EST:** 1973
SQ FT: 4,000
SALES (est): 2.5MM **Privately Held**
WEB: www.ally-press.com
SIC: 2752 7334 Commercial printing, offset; photocopying & duplicating services

(G-9865)
LORANN OILS INC
4518 Aurelius Rd (48910-5897)
PHONE..................................517 882-0215
John Grettenberger Jr, *CEO*
Carl Thelen, *COO*
Carl Thalen, *Vice Pres*
Ron Wood, *Opers Staff*
Joseph Lothamer, *Sales Mgr*
▼ **EMP:** 17 **EST:** 1964
SQ FT: 30,000
SALES (est): 16.9MM **Privately Held**
WEB: www.lorannoils.com
SIC: 2087 Flavoring extracts & syrups

(G-9866)
MAGNA POWERTRAIN AMERICA INC
3140 Spanish Oak Dr (48911-4291)
PHONE..................................517 316-1013
Jennifer Cantarella, *Manager*
Steve Lowe, *Manager*
David Anderson, *Prgrmr*
EMP: 4
SALES (corp-wide): 32.6B **Privately Held**
WEB: www.magna.com
SIC: 3714 Motor vehicle parts & accessories
HQ: Magna Powertrain Of America, Inc.
 1870 Technology Dr
 Troy MI 48083

(G-9867)
MBCD INC
1520 E Malcolm X St (48912-2425)
PHONE..................................517 484-4426
Dale Martin, *President*
EMP: 30 **EST:** 1940
SQ FT: 9,000
SALES (est): 625.5K **Privately Held**
SIC: 3271 3296 3272 1442 Brick, concrete; mineral wool; concrete products; construction sand & gravel

(G-9868)
MERRITT PRESS INC
6534 Aurelius Rd (48911-7103)
P.O. Box 27578 (48909-0578)
PHONE..................................517 394-0118
Scott Merritt, *President*
EMP: 12 **EST:** 1985
SQ FT: 7,300
SALES (est): 2.1MM **Privately Held**
WEB: www.merrittpress.com
SIC: 2752 Commercial printing, offset

(G-9869)
MICHIGAN FORGE COMPANY LLC
2807 S Martin L Kng Jr Bl (48910-2653)
PHONE..................................815 758-6400
Don Jones, *President*
Bharat Forge, *Sales Staff*
Amit Kalyani, *Exec Dir*
EMP: 50 **EST:** 2014
SALES (est): 4.6MM **Privately Held**
WEB: www.forgeresourcesgroup.com
SIC: 3462 Iron & steel forgings

(G-9870)
MICHIGAN OIL AND GAS ASSN
124 W Allegan St Ste 1610 (48933-1750)
PHONE..................................517 487-0480
Frank L Mortl, *President*
Daniel Wyohe, *Chairman*
Jennifer Clark, *Opers Staff*
Jim Stark, *Director*
EMP: 4
SQ FT: 1,400
SALES: 786.4K **Privately Held**
WEB: www.michiganoilandgas.org
SIC: 8611 2721 Trade associations; magazines: publishing only, not printed on site

(G-9871)
MICHIGRAIN DISTILLERY
523 E Shiawassee St (48912-1213)
PHONE..................................517 580-8624
EMP: 5 **EST:** 2017
SALES (est): 271.7K **Privately Held**
WEB: www.michigrain.net
SIC: 2085 Distilled & blended liquors

(G-9872)
MPT LANSING LLC
Also Called: Magna Powertrain Lansing
3140 Spanish Oak Dr Ste A (48911-4291)
PHONE..................................517 316-1013
Heather Bickford, *Materials Mgr*
Rick Rinard,
◆ **EMP:** 140 **EST:** 2005
SALES (est): 49.9MM
SALES (corp-wide): 32.6B **Privately Held**
WEB: www.magna.com
SIC: 3714 Motor vehicle engines & parts
HQ: Magna Powertrain Usa, Inc.
 1870 Technology Dr
 Troy MI 48083
 248 680-4900

(G-9873)
NANORETE INC
3815 Tech Blvd Ste 1050 (48910)
PHONE..................................517 336-4680
Linda Chamberlain, *CEO*
EMP: 9 **EST:** 2011
SALES (est): 483.3K **Privately Held**
WEB: www.nanorete.com
SIC: 3825 2835 Instruments to measure electricity; in vitro diagnostics

(G-9874)
NEOGEN CORPORATION (PA)
620 Lesher Pl (48912-1509)
PHONE..................................517 372-9200
John E Adent, *President*
Ron Cook, *General Mgr*
Pierre Belhadj, *Managing Dir*
Joseph A Corbett, *Vice Pres*
Robert S Donofrio, *Vice Pres*
▲ **EMP:** 833 **EST:** 1982
SQ FT: 300,000
SALES: 468.4MM **Publicly Held**
WEB: www.neogen.com
SIC: 3841 2836 2835 Veterinarians' instruments & apparatus; veterinary biological products; veterinary diagnostic substances

(G-9875)
NEWARK MORNING LEDGER CO
217 N Sycamore St (48933-1033)
PHONE..................................517 487-8888
Meegan Holland, *Branch Mgr*
Medra Burdette, *Manager*
EMP: 87
SALES (corp-wide): 100.8MM **Privately Held**
WEB: www.morrisledger.com
SIC: 7383 7313 2711 News reporting services for newspapers & periodicals; newspaper advertising representative; newspapers
PA: Newark Morning Ledger Co.
 1 Gateway Ctr Ste 1100
 Newark NJ 07102
 973 392-4141

(G-9876)
OASYS LLC
5920 Enterprise Dr (48911-4109)
PHONE..................................414 529-3922
Abigail Tanner, *Sales Staff*
Jennifer Lemke, *Office Mgr*
Stacy McCoy, *Consultant*
Marty Suchorski,
Kristin Kranzusch, *Representative*
EMP: 5 **EST:** 1997
SALES (est): 963.1K **Privately Held**
WEB: www.oasys-llc.com
SIC: 7372 Prepackaged software

(G-9877)
OMC ARCHTRIM
810 E Mount Hope Ave (48910-3260)
PHONE..................................517 482-9411
Jack Olsen, *Principal*
Richard Barnes, *CIO*
EMP: 7 **EST:** 2010
SALES (est): 228.7K **Privately Held**
WEB: www.olsenmastermark.com
SIC: 3398 Metal heat treating

(G-9878)
OMNILINK COMMUNICATIONS CORP
3101 Technology Blvd (48910-8546)
PHONE..................................517 336-1800
Franklin Tarquini, *President*
Henry H Graham, *CFO*
Robert Lindmann, *Officer*
EMP: 25 **EST:** 1996
SQ FT: 13,000
SALES (est): 272.4K **Privately Held**
SIC: 3661 Telephone & telegraph apparatus

(G-9879)
PEANUT SHOP INC
117 S Washington Sq Ste 1 (48933-1789)
PHONE..................................517 374-0008
Tamara Melser, *President*
Glenda Osterhouse, *Treasurer*
EMP: 5
SQ FT: 1,000
SALES (est): 348K **Privately Held**
SIC: 3556 Roasting machinery: coffee, peanut, etc.; confectionery machinery

(G-9880)
PHILLIPS BROS SCREW PDTS CO
2909 S Martin Luther King (48910-2655)
PHONE..................................517 882-0279
Donald Phillips, *Owner*
EMP: 5 **EST:** 1944
SQ FT: 7,000 **Privately Held**
SIC: 3451 Screw machine products

(G-9881)
PITNEY BOWES INC
1545 Keystone Ave (48911-4039)
PHONE..................................517 393-4101
EMP: 5
SALES (corp-wide): 3.5B **Publicly Held**
WEB: www.pitneybowes.com
SIC: 3579 Postage meters
PA: Pitney Bowes Inc.
 3001 Summer St
 Stamford CT 06905
 203 356-5000

(G-9882)
PRATT & WHITNEY AUTOAIR INC (HQ)
Also Called: Auto-Air Composites
5640 Enterprise Dr (48911-4103)
PHONE..................................517 393-4040
Toll Free:..................................888 -
Bennett Croswell, *President*
David Cornwell, *Purch Mgr*

GEOGRAPHIC SECTION — Lansing - Ingham County (G-9907)

William Puetz, *Buyer*
Chris Erdman, *Purchasing*
Megan Keane, *Purchasing*
▲ **EMP:** 232 **EST:** 1956
SQ FT: 225,000
SALES (est): 93.1MM
SALES (corp-wide): 56.5B **Publicly Held**
WEB: www.prattwhitney.com
SIC: 3724 3544 Aircraft engines & engine parts; special dies, tools, jigs & fixtures
PA: Raytheon Technologies Corporation
870 Winter St
Waltham MA 02451
781 522-3000

(G-9883)
PREYDE LLC
303 W Saginaw St Ste C-3 (48933-1131)
PHONE.................517 333-1600
EMP: 6 **EST:** 2009
SALES (est): 173.5K **Privately Held**
SIC: 3561 Pumps, oil well & field

(G-9884)
PRINTING KING
735 E Hazel St (48912-1000)
PHONE.................517 367-7066
EMP: 4 **EST:** 2019
SALES (est): 83.9K **Privately Held**
WEB: www.theprintingking.com
SIC: 2752 Commercial printing, lithographic

(G-9885)
QUALITY AWNING SHOPS INC
4512 S Martin Luther King (48910-5297)
PHONE.................517 882-2491
Don Brand, *President*
Judith A Brand, *Corp Secy*
EMP: 6 **EST:** 1911
SQ FT: 12,800
SALES (est): 673.6K **Privately Held**
SIC: 2394 7641 Awnings, fabric: made from purchased materials; cloth, drop (fabric): made from purchased materials; reupholstery

(G-9886)
QUALITY DAIRY COMPANY
Also Called: Qdc Plastics
111 W Mount Hope Ave 3a (48910-9080)
PHONE.................517 319-4302
Stan Martin, *Owner*
EMP: 7
SALES (corp-wide): 62.8MM **Privately Held**
WEB: www.qualitydairy.com
SIC: 2821 Plastics materials & resins
PA: Quality Dairy Company
111 W Mount Hope Ave 3a
Lansing MI 48910
517 319-4100

(G-9887)
QUALITY DAIRY COMPANY
1400 S Washington Ave (48910-1655)
PHONE.................517 367-2400
Joel Schneider, *Warehouse Mgr*
Kenneth Martin, *Manager*
EMP: 46
SQ FT: 2,000
SALES (corp-wide): 62.8MM **Privately Held**
WEB: www.qualitydairy.com
SIC: 2026 2024 Milk processing (pasteurizing, homogenizing, bottling); ice cream & frozen desserts
PA: Quality Dairy Company
111 W Mount Hope Ave 3a
Lansing MI 48910
517 319-4100

(G-9888)
RIVERFRONT CYCLE INC
507 E Shiawassee St (48912-1213)
PHONE.................517 482-8585
David Hanson, *President*
EMP: 5 **EST:** 1988
SQ FT: 3,500
SALES (est): 606.5K **Privately Held**
WEB: www.riverfrontcycle.com
SIC: 5941 7699 3949 7999 Bicycle & bicycle parts; exercise equipment; recreational sporting equipment repair services; bicycle repair shop; exercise equipment; bicycle rental; motorcycles

(G-9889)
S & S DIE CO
2727 Lyons Ave (48910-3338)
PHONE.................517 272-1100
David H Soltow, *President*
Diana G Hurst, *Vice Pres*
EMP: 24 **EST:** 1971
SQ FT: 7,000
SALES (est): 4.6MM **Privately Held**
WEB: www.ssdie.com
SIC: 3544 Special dies & tools

(G-9890)
SALT BREWING COMPANY LLC
519 W Ionia St (48933-1012)
PHONE.................517 446-0375
Steve Kelly,
EMP: 30 **EST:** 2020
SALES (est): 650K **Privately Held**
SIC: 2082 Beer (alcoholic beverage)

(G-9891)
SCHINDLER ELEVATOR CORPORATION
3135 Pinetree Rd Ste 2b (48911-4242)
PHONE.................517 272-1234
Pete Long, *Manager*
EMP: 10
SALES (corp-wide): 753.4MM **Privately Held**
WEB: www.schindler.com
SIC: 1796 5084 3534 Elevator installation & conversion; elevators; dumbwaiters
HQ: Schindler Elevator Corporation
20 Whippany Rd
Morristown NJ 07960
973 397-6500

(G-9892)
SCHNEIDER SHEET METAL SUP INC
6836 Aurelius Rd (48911-7112)
PHONE.................517 694-7661
William Schneider Jr, *President*
Kimberly Schneider, *Vice Pres*
EMP: 6 **EST:** 1972
SQ FT: 19,000
SALES (est): 697.2K **Privately Held**
SIC: 3444 Ducts, sheet metal

(G-9893)
SCW INDUSTRIES LLC
5134 S Pennsylvania Ave (48911-4001)
PHONE.................616 656-5959
EMP: 5 **EST:** 2016
SALES (est): 259.1K **Privately Held**
SIC: 3999 Manufacturing industries

(G-9894)
SEELYE GROUP LTD
Also Called: Fresh Tracks
912 E Michigan Ave (48912-1418)
PHONE.................517 267-2001
Aaron Pouch, *Division Mgr*
Tim Spaulding, *Vice Pres*
EMP: 5
SALES (corp-wide): 3MM **Privately Held**
WEB: www.sglyes.com
SIC: 1752 2273 7349 Carpet laying; carpets & rugs; cleaning service, industrial or commercial
PA: Seelye Group, Ltd.
1411 Lake Lansing Rd
Lansing MI 48912
517 267-2007

(G-9895)
SLICK SHIRTS SCREEN PRINTING
805 Vine St (48912-1525)
PHONE.................517 371-3600
Brian Kavanagh, *President*
Victor Mendenhal, *Corp Secy*
Victor Mendenhall, *Treasurer*
EMP: 17 **EST:** 1989
SQ FT: 12,000
SALES (est): 800K **Privately Held**
WEB: www.slickshirts.com
SIC: 2261 2759 2395 Screen printing of cotton broadwoven fabrics; commercial printing; embroidery products, except schiffli machine

(G-9896)
SPRINGER PRSTHTIC ORTHTIC SVCS (PA)
200 N Homer St (48912-4741)
PHONE.................517 337-0300
Joe Springer, *President*
Michael Springer, *General Mgr*
Patricia Springer, *Vice Pres*
Linda Burcham, *Office Mgr*
EMP: 9 **EST:** 1990
SQ FT: 6,000
SALES (est): 842.2K **Privately Held**
WEB: www.springerprosthetics.com
SIC: 3842 5999 Prosthetic appliances; artificial limbs

(G-9897)
SUITER INDUSTRIES INC
1931 Devonshire Ave (48910-3540)
PHONE.................989 277-1554
Adam Suiter, *Principal*
EMP: 4 **EST:** 2014
SALES (est): 43.6K **Privately Held**
SIC: 3999 Manufacturing industries

(G-9898)
SWAT ENVIRONMENTAL INC (PA)
2607 Eaton Rapids Rd (48911-6310)
PHONE.................517 322-2999
Jamey Gelina, *Principal*
George Booth, *Opers Staff*
Alexis Terry, *Sales Staff*
Diana Cotton, *Director*
EMP: 23 **EST:** 2002
SALES (est): 8.8MM **Privately Held**
WEB: www.swat-radon.com
SIC: 7342 8744 5084 3822 Disinfecting & pest control services; ; pollution control equipment, air (environmental); hardware for environmental regulators

(G-9899)
TECHNOLOGY MGT & BUDGT DEPT
Also Called: Office Services Division
7461 Crowner Dr (48913-0001)
P.O. Box 30026 (48909-7526)
PHONE.................517 322-1897
Kristi Thompson, *Director*
EMP: 6
SALES (corp-wide): 54.6B **Privately Held**
SIC: 2791 9311 2789 2752 Typesetting; ; bookbinding & related work; commercial printing, lithographic; coated & laminated paper
HQ: Management & Budget Department Of Technology
320 S Walnut St
Lansing MI 48933

(G-9900)
TECOMET INC
5212 Aurelius Rd (48911-4114)
PHONE.................517 882-4311
Jennifer Dalling, *Human Res Mgr*
Clint Newman, *Program Mgr*
Chris Thompson, *Program Mgr*
John Helmoth, *Manager*
David Ferreri, *Director*
EMP: 290
SALES (corp-wide): 832.8MM **Privately Held**
WEB: www.tecomet.com
SIC: 3841 Surgical & medical instruments
HQ: Tecomet Inc.
115 Eames St
Wilmington MA 01887
978 642-2400

(G-9901)
VETERANS UTILITY SERVICES LLC
120 N Washington Sq # 300 (48933-1617)
PHONE.................888 878-4191
EMP: 60 **EST:** 2020
SALES (est): 3.2MM **Privately Held**
WEB: www.veteransutilityservices.com
SIC: 1389 1623 Construction, repair & dismantling services; water, sewer & utility lines

(G-9902)
VINEYARD VENTURES LLC
1104 N Fairview Ave (48912-3203)
PHONE.................517 420-4771
Robin Usborne, *Principal*
EMP: 4 **EST:** 2013
SALES (est): 64.1K **Privately Held**
SIC: 2084 Wines

(G-9903)
W S TOWNSEND COMPANY
Also Called: Michigan Kitchen Distributors
5320 S Pennsylvania Ave (48911-4006)
PHONE.................517 393-7300
Chuck Sayers, *Purchasing*
Melissa Monaghan, *Sales Staff*
Mark Voss, *Manager*
Mark Dixon, *Consultant*
Pamela Frederick, *Consultant*
EMP: 8
SALES (corp-wide): 23.1MM **Privately Held**
WEB: www.mkdkitchens.com
SIC: 2434 5211 1799 1521 Wood kitchen cabinets; millwork & lumber; kitchen & bathroom remodeling; single-family home remodeling, additions & repairs
PA: W. S. Townsend Company
106 E Oliver Dr
Marshall MI 49068
269 781-5131

(G-9904)
WONCH BATTERY COMPANY
Also Called: East Penn Manufacturing
1521 Keystone Ave (48911-4079)
PHONE.................517 394-3600
Chris Pruitt, *CFO*
EMP: 32 **EST:** 1921
SQ FT: 14,000
SALES (est): 9MM
SALES (corp-wide): 2.8B **Privately Held**
WEB: www.eastpennmanufacturing.com
SIC: 3691 Storage batteries
PA: East Penn Manufacturing Co.
102 Deka Rd
Lyon Station PA 19536
610 682-6361

(G-9905)
WOODWORKS & DESIGN COMPANY
109 E South St (48910-1622)
PHONE.................517 482-6665
Thaddeus S Vance, *President*
EMP: 7 **EST:** 1992
SQ FT: 6,000
SALES (est): 754.2K **Privately Held**
WEB: www.woodworks-software.com
SIC: 1521 1751 2431 General remodeling, single-family houses; carpentry work; millwork

(G-9906)
WRIGHT & FILIPPIS LLC
1629 E Mich Ave Apt 101 (48912-2817)
PHONE.................517 484-2624
Beth Burke, *Manager*
EMP: 19
SALES (corp-wide): 77.5MM **Privately Held**
WEB: www.firsttoserve.com
SIC: 3842 5999 5047 3999 Surgical appliances & supplies; orthopedic & prosthesis applications; hospital equipment & furniture; wheelchair lifts
PA: Wright & Filippis, Llc
2845 Crooks Rd
Rochester Hills MI 48309
248 829-8292

(G-9907)
XG SCIENCES INC
2100 S Washington Ave (48910-0824)
PHONE.................517 316-2038
Scott Murray, *Vice Pres*
EMP: 32 **Privately Held**
WEB: www.xgsciences.com
SIC: 2821 Plastics materials & resins
PA: Xg Sciences, Inc.
3101 Grand Oak Dr
Lansing MI 48911

Lansing - Ingham County (G-9908)

(G-9908)
XG SCIENCES INC (PA)
3101 Grand Oak Dr (48911-4224)
PHONE..................................517 703-1110
Robert M Blinstrub, *CEO*
Arnold A Allemang, *Ch of Bd*
Scott Murray, *Vice Pres*
Robert Privette, *Vice Pres*
Benjamin Surato, *Maint Spvr*
▼ **EMP:** 9 **EST:** 2004
SQ FT: 25,000
SALES (est): 782.6K **Privately Held**
WEB: www.xgsciences.com
SIC: 2819 8731 Industrial inorganic chemicals; commercial physical research

(G-9909)
YORK ELECTRIC INC
1905 S Washington Ave (48910-9152)
PHONE..................................517 487-6400
EMP: 4
SALES (corp-wide): 15.7MM **Privately Held**
WEB: www.yorkrepair.com
SIC: 3261 7694 Bathroom accessories/fittings, vitreous china or earthenware; electric motor repair
PA: York Electric, Inc.
611 Andre St
Bay City MI 48706
989 684-7460

Lapeer
Lapeer County

(G-9910)
21ST CENTURY NEWSPAPERS INC
1521 Imlay City Rd (48446-3175)
P.O. Box 220 (48446-0220)
PHONE..................................810 664-0811
Frank Shepherd, *Partner*
EMP: 19
SALES (corp-wide): 274.1MM **Privately Held**
WEB: www.21stcenturynewspapers.com
SIC: 2711 Newspapers, publishing & printing
HQ: 21st Century Newspapers, Inc.
6250 Metropolitan Pkwy
Sterling Heights MI 48312
586 469-4510

(G-9911)
ALBAR INDUSTRIES INC
780 Whitney Dr (48446-2570)
PHONE..................................810 667-0150
Edward A May, *President*
Rowland Plutchak, *Corp Secy*
Glenn Curtis, *Vice Pres*
Christopher May, *Vice Pres*
Lawrence May, *Vice Pres*
EMP: 300
SQ FT: 103,000
SALES (est): 89.7MM **Privately Held**
WEB: www.albar.com
SIC: 3089 Injection molding of plastics

(G-9912)
AMERICANA MANUFACTURING CO
1672 Morris Rd (48446-9420)
PHONE..................................248 505-3277
Ben Logan, *Principal*
EMP: 4 **EST:** 2018
SALES (est): 128.9K **Privately Held**
SIC: 3999 Manufacturing industries

(G-9913)
B M INDUSTRIES INC
130 Harsen Rd (48446-2752)
PHONE..................................810 658-0052
EMP: 4
SALES (est): 230.1K **Privately Held**
SIC: 3451 Mfg Screw Machine Products

(G-9914)
BLUE WATER PRINTING CO INC
655 Mccormick Dr Ste B (48446-3925)
P.O. Box 241 (48446-0241)
PHONE..................................810 664-0643
Gene Becker, *President*
EMP: 7 **EST:** 1974
SQ FT: 6,500
SALES (est): 490.1K **Privately Held**
WEB: www.bluewaterprinting.net
SIC: 2752 2759 Commercial printing, offset; commercial printing

(G-9915)
BOOMERANGS GIFT GALLERY
161 W Nepessing St (48446-2102)
PHONE..................................248 228-0314
EMP: 4 **EST:** 2019
SALES (est): 113.7K **Privately Held**
SIC: 3949 Boomerangs

(G-9916)
BULLS-EYE WIRE & CABLE INC
1498 N Saginaw St Ste 4 (48446-1594)
P.O. Box 556, Lake Orion (48361-0556)
PHONE..................................810 245-8600
Kevin C Morrison, *President*
EMP: 7 **EST:** 2001
SQ FT: 2,500
SALES (est): 1.5MM **Privately Held**
WEB: www.bullseyewire.com
SIC: 3357 Nonferrous wiredrawing & insulating

(G-9917)
BYRNES MANUFACTURING CO LLC
870 Whitney Dr (48446-2565)
P.O. Box 40 (48446-0040)
PHONE..................................810 664-3686
Ryan Byrnes, *Principal*
Bruce Byrnes,
EMP: 4 **EST:** 2014
SALES (est): 616.6K **Privately Held**
SIC: 3544 Dies, plastics forming

(G-9918)
BYRNES TOOL CO INC
870 Whitney Dr (48446-2565)
P.O. Box 40 (48446-0040)
PHONE..................................810 664-3686
Bruce Byrnes, *President*
Robert Byrnes Jr, *Corp Secy*
EMP: 7 **EST:** 1962
SQ FT: 10,000 **Privately Held**
SIC: 3544 Industrial molds

(G-9919)
C P I INC
1449 Bowers Rd (48446-3124)
PHONE..................................810 664-8686
Gerald Jasper, *President*
EMP: 4 **EST:** 1955
SQ FT: 5,100
SALES (est): 322.4K **Privately Held**
WEB: www.ceocpip.com
SIC: 3312 Tool & die steel

(G-9920)
CAPNESITY INC
1778 Imlay City Rd (48446-3206)
PHONE..................................317 401-6766
Jeffrey Gibson, *President*
EMP: 4 **EST:** 2017
SALES (est): 167.9K **Privately Held**
WEB: www.capnesity.com
SIC: 3841 Surgical & medical instruments

(G-9921)
CARBONLESS 365
349 Mccormick Dr (48446-2574)
PHONE..................................810 969-4014
Debra Kane, *Principal*
EMP: 5 **EST:** 2012
SALES (est): 103.8K **Privately Held**
SIC: 2752 Commercial printing, lithographic

(G-9922)
CONTOUR MOLD CORPORATION
1830 N Lapeer Rd (48446-7771)
PHONE..................................810 245-4070
EMP: 17 **EST:** 2005
SALES (est): 643.4K **Privately Held**
SIC: 3544 Industrial molds

(G-9923)
CRAIGS SIGNS
1498 N Saginaw St Ste 2 (48446-1594)
PHONE..................................810 667-7446
Craig Turner, *Owner*
EMP: 5 **EST:** 1995
SALES (est): 417.3K **Privately Held**
WEB: www.craigssigns.com
SIC: 3993 Signs, not made in custom sign painting shops

(G-9924)
CYPRESS COMPUTER SYSTEMS INC
Also Called: Robot Space, The
1778 Imlay City Rd (48446-3206)
PHONE..................................810 245-2300
Paul Ahern, *President*
Anthony J Diodato, *Vice Pres*
Elizabeth Lowe, *Marketing Staff*
▲ **EMP:** 11 **EST:** 1983
SQ FT: 10,000
SALES (est): 1.5MM **Privately Held**
WEB: www.cypressintegration.com
SIC: 7373 7371 3571 3699 Computer integrated systems design; computer software systems analysis & design, custom; electronic computers; security devices; security control equipment & systems; security devices, locks

(G-9925)
D T FOWLER MFG CO INC (PA)
101 N Mapleleaf Rd (48446-8003)
P.O. Box 70 (48446-0070)
PHONE..................................810 245-9336
Christina Fowler White, *President*
EMP: 6 **EST:** 1950
SQ FT: 200,000
SALES (est): 11.2MM **Privately Held**
WEB: www.dtfowler.com
SIC: 2448 2653 Pallets, wood; corrugated & solid fiber boxes

(G-9926)
DADS PANELS INC
Also Called: Tool Organisations Service
2142 Imlay City Rd (48446-3260)
P.O. Box 1342 (48446-5342)
PHONE..................................810 245-1871
Charles English, *President*
Tom Fitzgerald, *Manager*
EMP: 5 **EST:** 1990
SALES (est): 740.3K **Privately Held**
WEB: www.toolorg.com
SIC: 2541 2542 2431 Store & office display cases & fixtures; partitions & fixtures, except wood; millwork

(G-9927)
DALES LLC
348 Cty Center St (48446)
PHONE..................................734 444-4620
Dale Tusek,
EMP: 4 **EST:** 2011
SALES (est): 175.9K **Privately Held**
SIC: 2411 Fuel wood harvesting

(G-9928)
DURAKON INDUSTRIES INC (DH)
2101 N Lapeer Rd (48446-8799)
PHONE..................................608 742-5301
Duane Braskamp, *CFO*
▲ **EMP:** 3 **EST:** 1983
SALES (est): 57MM
SALES (corp-wide): 343.1MM **Privately Held**
WEB: www.durakon.com
SIC: 3714 3713 3081 Motor vehicle parts & accessories; truck & bus bodies; unsupported plastics film & sheet

(G-9929)
ESE LLC
3344 John Conley Dr (48446-4301)
PHONE..................................810 538-1000
Steve Brusie, *Design Engr*
Derek Lehr, *Design Engr*
Kyle Smith, *Design Engr*
Eric Smith,
Aaron Oberle,
▲ **EMP:** 4 **EST:** 1999
SQ FT: 10,500
SALES (est): 1.1MM **Privately Held**
WEB: www.esellc.net
SIC: 3714 Instrument board assemblies, motor vehicle

(G-9930)
EVOLUTION TOOL INC
587 Mccormick Dr (48446-2575)
PHONE..................................810 664-5500
Kari Amore, *Administration*
EMP: 12 **EST:** 2013
SALES (est): 2.3MM **Privately Held**
WEB: www.evolutiontool.com
SIC: 3544 Special dies & tools

(G-9931)
GESTAMP ALABAMA LLC
Also Called: Gestamp North America Plant
100 E Fair St (48446-1502)
PHONE..................................810 245-3100
Robert Greene, *Counsel*
Joan Hall, *Buyer*
Richard Beckner, *Controller*
Justin Zoldos, *Asst Controller*
Tammy Bishop, *Financial Analy*
EMP: 93
SALES (corp-wide): 400.4MM **Privately Held**
WEB: www.gestamp.com
SIC: 3469 Stamping metal for the trade
HQ: Gestamp Alabama, Llc
7000 Jefferson Metro Pkwy
Mc Calla AL 35111
205 497-6400

(G-9932)
GRAMMA N STITCHES
1664 Daley Rd (48446-8671)
PHONE..................................810 664-8606
Marilyn Pearson, *Owner*
EMP: 4 **EST:** 2017
SALES (est): 42.6K **Privately Held**
SIC: 2395 Embroidery & art needlework

(G-9933)
HYDRAULIC TUBES & FITTINGS LLC
434 Mccormick Dr (48446-2518)
P.O. Box 219 (48446-0219)
PHONE..................................810 660-8088
David Berney, *General Mgr*
EMP: 49 **EST:** 2004
SQ FT: 95,000
SALES (est): 8.2MM **Privately Held**
WEB: www.htfllc.com
SIC: 3714 Motor vehicle parts & accessories

(G-9934)
INTERNTNAL DEF FABRICATION LLC
1460 Imlay City Rd T4 (48446-3114)
PHONE..................................810 643-1198
Jason Phelps, *Principal*
James Fenslau, *Principal*
Kevin Lucik, *Principal*
Jeffery Weber, *Principal*
EMP: 5 **EST:** 2020
SALES (est): 271.2K **Privately Held**
WEB: www.idfabllc.com
SIC: 3795 Tanks & tank components

(G-9935)
JAMS MEDIA LLC
1521 Imlay City Rd (48446-3175)
P.O. Box 220 (48446-0220)
PHONE..................................810 664-0811
Wes Smith, *President*
Keith Salisbury, *Editor*
Teresa Poppeck, *Sales Staff*
EMP: 17 **EST:** 2009
SALES (est): 3.9MM **Privately Held**
SIC: 2711 Newspapers, publishing & printing

(G-9936)
KAMAX INC
Also Called: Lapeer Div
1805 Bowers Rd (48446-3303)
PHONE..................................810 272-2090
Dane Schafer, *Vice Pres*
Dan Schram, *Foreman/Supr*
Johanna Denzel, *Human Res Mgr*
Jeremy Coupteau, *Manager*
Keith Racknor, *Manager*
EMP: 140

GEOGRAPHIC SECTION

Lapeer - Lapeer County (G-9963)

SALES (corp-wide): 856.3MM **Privately Held**
WEB: www.kamax.com
SIC: 3452 3444 3316 Bolts, metal; screws, metal; studs & joists, sheet metal; cold finishing of steel shapes
HQ: Kamax Inc.
 1606 Star Batt Dr
 Rochester Hills MI 48309
 248 879-0200

(G-9937)
KAMAX INC
1194 Roods Lake Rd (48446-8366)
PHONE 810 664-7741
David Winn, *VP Opers*
Wayne Powell, *Engineer*
Joseph Hoover, *Design Engr*
Amanda Sandusky, *Human Res Mgr*
Jeremy Coupteau, *Branch Mgr*
EMP: 460
SALES (corp-wide): 856.3MM **Privately Held**
WEB: www.kamax.com
SIC: 3452 Bolts, metal
HQ: Kamax Inc.
 1606 Star Batt Dr
 Rochester Hills MI 48309
 248 879-0200

(G-9938)
LAPEER FUEL VENTURES INC
252 S Main St (48446-2425)
PHONE 810 664-8770
Jennifer Schank, *Principal*
EMP: 5 **EST:** 2005
SALES (est): 783.3K **Privately Held**
SIC: 1389 Oil field services

(G-9939)
LAPEER PLATING & PLASTICS INC
395 Demille Rd (48446-3055)
P.O. Box 898 (48446-0898)
PHONE 810 667-4240
Larry Gatt, *CEO*
Susan Sommerfield, *Purchasing*
Dan Brown, *QC Mgr*
Ewald Dana, *Engineer*
Robert Young, *CFO*
EMP: 225 **EST:** 2010
SALES (est): 33.3MM **Privately Held**
WEB: www.lpp-inc.com
SIC: 2431 3089 Moldings & baseboards, ornamental & trim; injection molded finished plastic products

(G-9940)
LESLEY ELIZABETH INC
449 Mccormick Dr (48446-2555)
PHONE 810 667-0706
Lesley Mc Cowen, *President*
Norm Jelsma, *Natl Sales Mgr*
EMP: 7 **Privately Held**
WEB: www.lesleyelizabeth.com
SIC: 2099 Food preparations
PA: Lesley Elizabeth Inc.
 877 Whitney Dr
 Lapeer MI 48446

(G-9941)
LESLEY ELIZABETH INC (PA)
877 Whitney Dr (48446-2565)
PHONE 810 667-0706
Lesley McCowen, *President*
Sally Burrell, *COO*
John Thouron, *Senior VP*
Catherine Moore, *Shareholder*
▲ **EMP:** 1 **EST:** 1991
SQ FT: 8,200
SALES (est): 2.5MM **Privately Held**
WEB: www.lesleyelizabeth.com
SIC: 2099 Seasonings & spices

(G-9942)
LIBERTY SPRING LAPEER INC
3056 Davison Rd (48446-2984)
PHONE 418 248-7781
Mathieu Ouellet, *President*
Jean Dubois, *Treasurer*
EMP: 15 **EST:** 2019
SALES (est): 337.6K **Privately Held**
WEB: www.ci.lapeer.mi.us
SIC: 3714 Motor vehicle engines & parts

(G-9943)
LLC STAHL CROSS
110 N Saginaw St (48446-4600)
PHONE 810 688-2505
John Stahl, *Mng Member*
EMP: 4 **EST:** 2010
SALES (est): 178.7K **Privately Held**
SIC: 3911 Jewelry apparel

(G-9944)
LOC PERFORMANCE PRODUCTS LLC
290 Mccormick Dr (48446-2518)
PHONE 734 453-2300
Louis Burr, *Principal*
Jason Atkinson, *Principal*
Chad Darr, *Principal*
Jackson Richardson, *Principal*
Victor Vojcek, *Principal*
EMP: 45 **EST:** 1976
SALES (est): 2.4MM **Privately Held**
WEB: www.locperformance.com
SIC: 3541 Machine tools, metal cutting type

(G-9945)
LUMBER & TRUSS INC
162 S Saginaw St (48446-2602)
P.O. Box 729 (48446-0729)
PHONE 810 664-7290
Joseph O'Henley, *President*
Kim Brown, *Treasurer*
Thomas Butterfield, *Admin Sec*
▲ **EMP:** 12 **EST:** 1997
SALES (est): 546.3K **Privately Held**
SIC: 1531 5211 5031 2439 Operative builders; lumber products; lumber, plywood & millwork; trusses, wooden roof; agricultural building contractors

(G-9946)
MANUFCTRING PARTNERS GROUP LLC
1639 Horton Lake Rd (48446-7504)
PHONE 517 749-4050
James Krozek, *Principal*
EMP: 4 **EST:** 2018
SALES (est): 61K **Privately Held**
SIC: 3999 Manufacturing industries

(G-9947)
MASCO CORPORATION OF INDIANA
211 Mccormick Dr (48446-2571)
PHONE 810 664-8501
Rob Lyman, *Supervisor*
EMP: 5
SALES (corp-wide): 7.1B **Publicly Held**
WEB: www.masco.com
SIC: 3088 Tubs (bath, shower & laundry), plastic
HQ: Masco Corporation Of Indiana
 55 E 111th St
 Carmel IN 46280
 317 848-1812

(G-9948)
MOLD MASTERS CO
1455 Imlay City Rd (48446-3142)
PHONE 810 245-4100
Hugo Leonardi, *CEO*
Angela Swiatkowski, *Corp Secy*
Cheryl Sump, *Purchasing*
Tony Visnaw, *Maintence Staff*
▲ **EMP:** 150 **EST:** 1973
SQ FT: 250,000
SALES (est): 22.7MM **Privately Held**
WEB: www.mmasters.org
SIC: 3089 Injection molding of plastics

(G-9949)
MOTION MACHINE COMPANY
524 Mccormick Dr (48446-2518)
PHONE 810 664-9901
Danny L Walters, *President*
David Clemens, *Vice Pres*
Thomas Niazy, *Treasurer*
EMP: 13
SQ FT: 14,200
SALES (est): 2.8MM **Privately Held**
WEB: www.motionmach.com
SIC: 3599 3549 3535 Machine shop, jobbing & repair; metalworking machinery; unit handling conveying systems

(G-9950)
NORTHWEST CONFECTIONS MICH LLC
525 S Court St Ste 110 (48446-2552)
P.O. Box 266, Eaton Rapids (48827-0266)
PHONE 971 666-8282
Aaron Morris, *CEO*
Christopher Joseph, *President*
Rene Kaza, *Sales Mgr*
EMP: 50 **EST:** 2018
SQ FT: 7,398
SALES (est): 5.2MM
SALES (corp-wide): 15.4MM **Privately Held**
WEB: www.michigan.gov
SIC: 2064 Candy & other confectionery products
PA: Northwest Commonwealth, Llc
 11791 Se Highway 212 # 400
 Clackamas OR 97015
 971 277-5407

(G-9951)
OGILVIE MANUFACTURING COMPANY
2445 Henry Rd (48446-9037)
PHONE 810 793-6598
Bruce Ogilvie, *President*
Lyle Ogilvie, *Treasurer*
EMP: 4 **EST:** 1962
SALES (est): 250K **Privately Held**
SIC: 3634 Heating units, for electric appliances

(G-9952)
P & P MANUFACTURING CO INC
260 Mccormick Dr (48446-2518)
PHONE 810 667-2712
Jon M Kirsch, *President*
Jacqueline Linklater, *Controller*
Jack Linklater, *Natl Sales Mgr*
EMP: 38 **EST:** 1962
SQ FT: 15,000
SALES (est): 4.9MM **Privately Held**
SIC: 3545 Tools & accessories for machine tools

(G-9953)
PEGASUS INDUSTRIES
2759 Watchhill Dr (48446-8793)
PHONE 810 356-5579
Thomas Ouzinian, *Principal*
EMP: 12 **EST:** 2010
SALES (est): 115.3K **Privately Held**
WEB: www.pegasustcs.com
SIC: 3999 Manufacturing industries

(G-9954)
PENTIER GROUP INC
587 S Court St Ste 300 (48446-2579)
P.O. Box 350 (48446-0350)
PHONE 810 664-7997
Tony Anderson, *President*
George Adams, *Vice Pres*
Melissa Furgerson, *Office Mgr*
Mike McGregor, *Manager*
EMP: 32 **EST:** 1994
SQ FT: 16,400
SALES (est): 3.9MM **Privately Held**
WEB: www.pentier.com
SIC: 3599 Custom machinery

(G-9955)
POLLUMS NATURAL RESOURCES
732 S Elba Rd (48446-2775)
PHONE 810 245-7268
Harry Pollum, *Principal*
EMP: 7 **EST:** 2007
SALES (est): 121.1K **Privately Held**
WEB: www.pollumsnaturalresources.com
SIC: 2421 Sawmills & planing mills, general

(G-9956)
PTL ENGINEERING INC
3333 John Conley Dr # 2 (48446-4308)
PHONE 810 664-2310
Brian Trombley, *President*
Kris Pender, *Prdtn Mgr*
Nathan Kolvek, *Purch Agent*
Jeremy Burger, *Engineer*
Sherry Trombley, *Accounting Mgr*
EMP: 13 **EST:** 1979
SALES (est): 3.8MM **Privately Held**
WEB: www.ptlengineering.com
SIC: 3442 Screen & storm doors & windows

(G-9957)
QUEST INDUSTRIES INC
3309 John Conley Dr (48446-4301)
PHONE 810 245-4535
Dennis Hoover, *Owner*
Sonya Lee Hoover, *Vice Pres*
Matthew Trisch, *Vice Pres*
Henriette Heinz, *Project Mgr*
Kristy Hanchett, *Purch Mgr*
EMP: 50 **EST:** 2001
SQ FT: 42,000
SALES (est): 8.9MM **Privately Held**
WEB: www.questindustries.net
SIC: 3599 Machine shop, jobbing & repair

(G-9958)
REO FAB LLC (PA)
1567 Imlay City Rd Ste A (48446-3196)
PHONE 810 969-4667
Robert E Fischer,
Tamara Fischer,
EMP: 4 **EST:** 2005
SQ FT: 5,000
SALES (est): 749K **Privately Held**
SIC: 3441 Fabricated structural metal

(G-9959)
ROBERT E NELSON & SON
4375 W Oregon Rd (48446-7706)
PHONE 810 664-6091
Dennis Root, *President*
EMP: 5 **EST:** 2017
SALES (est): 252.8K **Privately Held**
SIC: 2421 Sawmills & planing mills, general

(G-9960)
SHAWS ENTERPRISES INC
Also Called: SE Tools
415 Howard St (48446-2556)
PHONE 810 664-2981
Greg Shaw, *President*
Steven Shaw, *Vice Pres*
Gary Curell, *Purchasing*
▲ **EMP:** 20 **EST:** 1930
SQ FT: 25,000
SALES (est): 4.2MM **Privately Held**
WEB: www.setools.com
SIC: 3423 Hand & edge tools

(G-9961)
SOURIS ENTERPRISES INC
Also Called: Lapeer Manufacturing Company
2045 N Lapeer Rd (48446-8628)
P.O. Box 370 (48446-0370)
PHONE 810 664-2964
Bernice L Souris, *President*
Nicholas Souris, *Vice Pres*
Wendy Walker, *Plant Mgr*
Kimberley Souris, *Admin Sec*
Theresa Monks, *Administration*
EMP: 10 **EST:** 1986
SQ FT: 13,000
SALES (est): 2.1MM **Privately Held**
WEB: www.lapeermanufacturing.com
SIC: 3429 Clamps, metal

(G-9962)
STADIUM BLEACHERS LLC
3597 Lippincott Rd (48446-9638)
PHONE 810 245-6258
EMP: 5
SALES (est): 360K **Privately Held**
SIC: 2531 Mfg Public Building Furniture

(G-9963)
URGENT DESIGN AND MFG INC
Also Called: 3 Dimensional Services
2547 Product Dr (48446)
PHONE 810 245-1300
Douglas Peterson, *President*
Mike Baranowski, *General Mgr*
Alan Peterson, *Vice Pres*
David Turner, *Engineer*
Jason Desotell, *Sales Engr*
EMP: 43 **EST:** 1999
SQ FT: 50,000
SALES (est): 16.2MM **Privately Held**
WEB: www.3dimensional.com
SIC: 3599 Machine shop, jobbing & repair

(G-9964)
URGENT DESIGN AND MFG INC
3142 John Conley Dr (48446-2987)
PHONE..............................810 245-1300
EMP: 17 **EST:** 1999
SALES (est): 1.5MM **Privately Held**
SIC: 3559 Special industry machinery

(G-9965)
VIDON PLASTICS INC
3171 John Conley Dr (48446-2987)
P.O. Box 56 (48446-0056)
PHONE..............................810 667-0634
Donald Dube, *President*
Matthew Dube, *Business Mgr*
Dave Barth, *Controller*
Dennis Burke, *Sales Staff*
▼ **EMP:** 75 **EST:** 1987
SQ FT: 75,000
SALES (est): 19.7MM **Privately Held**
WEB: www.vidonplastics.com
SIC: 3089 3084 3083 Extruded finished plastic products; plastics pipe; laminated plastics plate & sheet

(G-9966)
VILLAGE PRINTING & SUPPLY INC
349 Mccormick Dr (48446-2574)
PHONE..............................810 664-2270
Joseph Morey, *President*
Ardith Westendorf, *Admin Sec*
EMP: 6 **EST:** 1968
SQ FT: 2,500
SALES (est): 603.7K **Privately Held**
WEB: www.ezprintsolutions.com
SIC: 2752 2759 5084 Commercial printing, offset; invitation & stationery printing & engraving; printing trades machinery, equipment & supplies

(G-9967)
VILLAGEBEES
1688 Indian Rd (48446-8053)
PHONE..............................810 217-2962
Tom Beaudet, *Principal*
EMP: 4 **EST:** 2017
SALES (est): 141.2K **Privately Held**
WEB: www.villagetees.net
SIC: 2759 Screen printing

(G-9968)
WOLVERINE TOOL CO
2045 N Lapeer Rd (48446-8628)
PHONE..............................810 664-2964
George Grenzke, *Ch of Bd*
Richard Grenzke, *President*
Norman F Grenzke Jr, *Vice Pres*
EMP: 15 **EST:** 1926
SQ FT: 9,600
SALES (est): 144.5K **Privately Held**
WEB: www.lapeermanufacturing.com
SIC: 3545 3544 3599 Tools & accessories for machine tools; special dies & tools; machine shop, jobbing & repair

(G-9969)
ZF CHASSIS COMPONENTS LLC (DH)
3300 John Conley Dr (48446-4301)
PHONE..............................810 245-2000
Kurt Mueller, *Vice Pres*
Bruce Wrenbeck, *Vice Pres*
Craig Meyer, *Engineer*
George Roesner, *Engineer*
Nida Suroor, *Engineer*
◆ **EMP:** 215 **EST:** 1980
SALES (est): 212.5MM
SALES (corp-wide): 216.2K **Privately Held**
WEB: www.zf.com
SIC: 3714 Steering mechanisms, motor vehicle; tie rods, motor vehicle; ball joints, motor vehicle; motor vehicle steering systems & parts
HQ: Zf Friedrichshafen Ag
Lowentaler Str. 20
Friedrichshafen BW 88046
754 177-0

(G-9970)
ZF CHASSIS COMPONENTS LLC
3255 John Conley Dr (48446-2987)
PHONE..............................810 245-2000
Unknown Mamager, *Branch Mgr*
EMP: 30
SALES (corp-wide): 216.2K **Privately Held**
SIC: 3714 Motor vehicle parts & accessories
HQ: Zf Chassis Components, Llc
3300 John Conley Dr
Lapeer MI 48446
810 245-2000

(G-9971)
ZF CHASSIS COMPONENTS LLC
930 S Saginaw St (48446-4601)
PHONE..............................810 245-2000
Bradley Schmuck, *Branch Mgr*
EMP: 30
SALES (corp-wide): 216.2K **Privately Held**
SIC: 3714 Steering mechanisms, motor vehicle
HQ: Zf Chassis Components, Llc
3300 John Conley Dr
Lapeer MI 48446
810 245-2000

(G-9972)
ZF LEMFORDER CORP
3300 John Conley Dr (48446-4301)
PHONE..............................810 245-7136
Kurt Brown, *Controller*
Adam Arntz, *Manager*
EMP: 14 **EST:** 2015
SALES (est): 2.6MM **Privately Held**
SIC: 3714 Motor vehicle parts & accessories

Lathrup Village
Oakland County

(G-9973)
ACTION PALLETS INC
28000 Southfield Rd Fl 2 (48076-2864)
PHONE..............................248 557-9017
Mitchell B Foster, *President*
Greg Van Dorn, *Controller*
EMP: 6
SQ FT: 7,000
SALES (est): 620K **Privately Held**
WEB: www.apallets.com
SIC: 2448 Pallets, wood

(G-9974)
ALL NATURAL BITES LLC
Also Called: B'Bites
27400 Southfield Rd (48076-3412)
PHONE..............................248 470-6252
Billie Jo Delfin,
EMP: 15 **EST:** 2018
SALES (est): 903.1K **Privately Held**
SIC: 2068 Salted & roasted nuts & seeds

(G-9975)
AUTO PALLETS-BOXES INC (PA)
28000 Southfield Rd Fl 2 (48076-2864)
PHONE..............................248 559-7744
Mitchell B Foster, *President*
James B Foster, *Vice Pres*
James Foster, *Vice Pres*
Greg V Dorn, *Finance*
EMP: 15
SQ FT: 7,000
SALES (est): 6MM **Privately Held**
WEB: www.apallets.com
SIC: 2448 2441 Pallets, wood; boxes, wood

(G-9976)
IDEA MIA LLC
18513 San Quentin Dr (48076-7809)
PHONE..............................248 891-8939
Marco Cucco, *Principal*
Angie Cucco, *Vice Pres*
▲ **EMP:** 8 **EST:** 2010
SALES (est): 118.2K **Privately Held**
WEB: www.thejetbag.com
SIC: 2673 Bags: plastic, laminated & coated

(G-9977)
SPROUTING SUNFLOWERS LLC
17530 Rainbow Dr (48076-4628)
PHONE..............................248 982-2406
Amber Merritt,
EMP: 5 **EST:** 2019
SALES (est): 100K **Privately Held**
SIC: 2731 Book publishing

(G-9978)
SUPERSINE COMPANY
27634 Rackham Dr (48076-3303)
PHONE..............................313 892-6200
EMP: 20 **EST:** 1950
SQ FT: 12,500
SALES (est): 1.5MM **Privately Held**
SIC: 3993 Mfg Signs & Sign Parts

Laurium
Houghton County

(G-9979)
DESIGNOTYPE PRINTERS INC
22950 Airpark Blvd (49913-9241)
PHONE..............................906 482-2424
Brian Helminen, *President*
Henry Roeters, *Accounts Exec*
EMP: 4 **EST:** 1988
SALES (est): 394.8K **Privately Held**
WEB: www.designotype.com
SIC: 2752 Commercial printing, offset

Lawrence
Van Buren County

(G-9980)
A & B PACKING EQUIPMENT INC (PA)
732 W Saint Joseph St (49064-9338)
PHONE..............................269 539-4700
Michael Williamson, *CEO*
Teresa Jamieson, *Human Res Mgr*
Terry Jamison, *Human Res Mgr*
Luis Dominguez, *Accounts Mgr*
Erick Turra, *Sales Staff*
▲ **EMP:** 126 **EST:** 2002
SALES (est): 22.7MM **Privately Held**
WEB: www.abpacking.com
SIC: 3523 Farm machinery & equipment

(G-9981)
COUNTRY CUSTOM CABINETS
57440 Butcher Rd (49064-9632)
PHONE..............................937 354-2163
EMP: 4 **EST:** 2019
SALES (est): 104.6K **Privately Held**
WEB: www.mobaca14.mi.biznet-us.com
SIC: 2434 Wood kitchen cabinets

(G-9982)
LANPHEAR TOOL WORKS INC
Also Called: L T W
311 S Paw Paw St (49064-9686)
P.O. Box 680 (49064-0680)
PHONE..............................269 674-8877
John Lanphear, *President*
Mindy R Lanphear, *Vice Pres*
Heather Lanphear, *Marketing Staff*
EMP: 12
SQ FT: 20,000
SALES (est): 1.2MM **Privately Held**
WEB: www.ltw1.com
SIC: 3599 Machine shop, jobbing & repair

(G-9983)
QUALITY ASSURED PLASTICS INC
1200 Crandall Pkwy (49064-8778)
PHONE..............................269 674-3888
Annette Crandall, *President*
Eugene Crandall, *Vice Pres*
Barbara Daniel, *Treasurer*
Steve Barr, *Sales Mgr*
Jeff Hunt, *Sales Engr*
EMP: 40 **EST:** 1986
SQ FT: 28,000
SALES (est): 8.7MM **Privately Held**
WEB: www.qapinc.com
SIC: 3089 Injection molding of plastics

(G-9984)
RHINO PRODUCTS INC
Also Called: Bowditch
57100 48th Ave (49064-9013)
PHONE..............................269 674-8309
James A Mc Gowan, *President*
Susie Mc Gowan, *Admin Sec*
EMP: 5 **EST:** 1990
SALES (est): 195.8K **Privately Held**
WEB: www.rhinoproducts.com
SIC: 3161 2241 Cases, carrying; narrow fabric mills; strapping webs

(G-9985)
SILL FARMS & MARKET INC
50241 Red Arrow Hwy (49064-8781)
PHONE..............................269 674-3755
Bob Ross, *President*
Jean M Sill, *Vice Pres*
Lois Ross, *Treasurer*
EMP: 23 **EST:** 1950
SQ FT: 25,000
SALES (est): 1.2MM **Privately Held**
WEB: www.sillfarms.com
SIC: 2037 Fruits, quick frozen & cold pack (frozen)

(G-9986)
USA QUALITY METAL FINSHG LLC
67131 56th St (49064-8757)
PHONE..............................269 427-9000
Dave Millword,
EMP: 18 **EST:** 2007
SALES (est): 1MM **Privately Held**
WEB: www.usaqmf.com
SIC: 3471 Electroplating of metals or formed products

Lawton
Van Buren County

(G-9987)
AMJS INCORPORATED
Also Called: Byers Manufacturing
828 S Main St (49065-8743)
P.O. Box 386 (49065-0386)
Fax: 269 624-7322
EMP: 6
SALES (est): 923.3K **Privately Held**
SIC: 3444 Sheet Metalwork, Nsk

(G-9988)
DAVES CONCRETE PRODUCTS INC
79811 M 40 (49065-9355)
PHONE..............................269 624-4100
David Flory, *President*
Todd Docekal, *Vice Pres*
Susan Lockhart, *Manager*
EMP: 19 **EST:** 1985
SALES (est): 2.2MM **Privately Held**
WEB: www.davesconcreteinc.net
SIC: 3272 3273 Septic tanks, concrete; silos, prefabricated concrete; ready-mixed concrete

(G-9989)
PACKERS CANNING CO INC
Also Called: Honee Bear Canning Co
72100 M 40 (49065-8444)
P.O. Box 907 (49065-0907)
PHONE..............................269 624-4681
Robert R Packer, *President*
Steven C Packer, *Vice Pres*
Toby Fields, *Plant Mgr*
Kevin Henderson, *Engineer*
Chris Gosdzinski, *Controller*
◆ **EMP:** 55 **EST:** 1943
SQ FT: 200,000
SALES (est): 17.9MM **Privately Held**
WEB: www.honeebear.com
SIC: 2033 Fruits: packaged in cans, jars, etc.; vegetables: packaged in cans, jars, etc.; fruit juices: packaged in cans, jars, etc.; fruit pie mixes & fillings: packaged in cans, jars, etc.

(G-9990)
WELCH FOODS INC A COOPERATIVE
Also Called: Lawton Plant
400 Walker St (49065-9711)
PHONE.....................269 624-4141
Phyllis Gutz, *Vice Pres*
Jill Gee, *Mfg Staff*
Jacob Koech, *Production*
Larry Angell, *Purch Agent*
Andr Belly, *Purchasing*
EMP: 61
SALES (corp-wide): 482.4MM **Privately Held**
WEB: www.welchs.com
SIC: 2033 2037 Fruit juices: packaged in cans, jars, etc.; preserves, including imitation: in cans, jars, etc.; frozen fruits & vegetables
HQ: Welch Foods Inc., A Cooperative
 575 Virginia Rd
 Concord MA 01742
 978 371-1000

(G-9991)
WEST MICHIGAN AERIAL LLC
62422 M 40 (49065-7497)
P.O. Box 738, Mattawan (49071-0738)
PHONE.....................269 998-4455
Domonic Tykoski, *Mng Member*
EMP: 13 **EST:** 2009
SALES (est): 398.7K **Privately Held**
WEB: www.westmichiganaerial.com
SIC: 3531 Aerial work platforms: hydraulic/elec. truck/carrier mounted

Lennon
Genesee County

(G-9992)
BENTLEY MFG LLC
804 Mack Ct (48449-9617)
PHONE.....................810 621-3616
Lyle Bentley, *Mng Member*
EMP: 4 **EST:** 2011
SALES (est): 154.1K **Privately Held**
WEB: www.bentley-mfg.com
SIC: 3599 Machine shop, jobbing & repair

(G-9993)
DUALL DIVISION
1172 S M 13 (48449-9301)
PHONE.....................989 725-8184
Greg C Kimmer, *Vice Pres*
▲ **EMP:** 2 **EST:** 2011
SALES (est): 1.3MM **Publicly Held**
WEB: www.cecoenviro.com
SIC: 2899 Corrosion preventive lubricant
PA: Ceco Environmental Corp.
 14651 Dallas Pkwy Ste 50
 Dallas TX 75254

(G-9994)
GARYS POLISHING
10720 E Lennon Rd (48449-9670)
PHONE.....................810 621-4137
Gary Lintz, *Principal*
EMP: 4 **EST:** 2009
SALES (est): 103.8K **Privately Held**
SIC: 3471 Polishing, metals or formed products

(G-9995)
MET-PRO TECHNOLOGIES LLC
1172 S M 13 (48449-9301)
P.O. Box 459, Owosso (48867)
PHONE.....................989 725-8184
Fax: 989 725-8188
EMP: 68
SQ FT: 34,166
SALES (corp-wide): 417MM **Publicly Held**
SIC: 3564 Mfg Blowers/Fans
HQ: Met-Pro Technologies Llc
 460 E Swedesford Rd # 2030
 Wayne PA 19087
 215 717-7909

(G-9996)
STEINER TRACTOR PARTS INC
1660 S M 13 (48449-9325)
P.O. Box 449 (48449-0449)
PHONE.....................810 621-3000
Daniel P Steiner, *President*
Leslie Steiner, *Corp Secy*
Jenny Bradshaw, *Vice Pres*
Mandy Crawford, *Cust Mgr*
Brandi Erickson, *Sales Staff*
▲ **EMP:** 43 **EST:** 1960
SALES (est): 8.9MM **Privately Held**
WEB: www.steinertractor.com
SIC: 3523 5083 Farm machinery & equipment; agricultural machinery & equipment

Lenox
Macomb County

(G-9997)
ALBERS CABINET COMPANY
65151 Gratiot Ave (48050-2010)
PHONE.....................586 727-9090
George Alber, *Partner*
James Alber, *Partner*
▼ **EMP:** 9 **EST:** 1965
SQ FT: 10,000
SALES (est): 682.4K **Privately Held**
SIC: 2434 Wood kitchen cabinets

(G-9998)
ICT INDUSTRIES
68001 Lowe Plank Rd (48050-1329)
PHONE.....................586 727-2677
F Rieman, *Principal*
EMP: 5 **EST:** 2008
SALES (est): 71.1K **Privately Held**
SIC: 3999 Manufacturing industries

(G-9999)
LENOX INC
Also Called: Lenox Septic Tanks
65601 Gratiot Ave (48050-2012)
PHONE.....................586 727-1488
Alvin J Harms, *President*
Lori Harms, *Treasurer*
Clarence E Harms, *Admin Sec*
EMP: 5 **EST:** 1969
SQ FT: 100
SALES (est): 542.2K **Privately Held**
WEB: www.lenoxcement.com
SIC: 3272 Septic tanks, concrete; burial vaults, concrete or precast terrazzo

(G-10000)
LENOX PHARMACY LLC
36267 26 Mile Rd Ste 1 (48048-3253)
PHONE.....................313 971-5928
Hassan Ghoul, *Principal*
EMP: 8 **EST:** 2016
SALES (est): 414K **Privately Held**
SIC: 3585 Refrigeration & heating equipment

Leonard
Oakland County

(G-10001)
AREA EXTERIORS
4075 Forest St (48367-1911)
PHONE.....................248 544-0706
Richard Stiltner,
EMP: 4 **EST:** 2006
SALES (est): 225.2K **Privately Held**
SIC: 2431 Garage doors, overhead: wood

(G-10002)
NATIONAL CRANE & HOIST SERVICE
1630 Noble Rd (48367-1658)
P.O. Box 88, Troy (48099-0088)
PHONE.....................248 789-4535
Jack Myers, *President*
Deette Myers, *Admin Sec*
EMP: 5 **EST:** 1998
SALES (est): 500K **Privately Held**
SIC: 3625 Crane & hoist controls, including metal mill

(G-10003)
STEENSON ENTERPRISES
4444 Forest St (48367-1932)
P.O. Box 561 (48367-0561)
PHONE.....................248 628-0036
Curt Steenson, *Partner*
Deborah Steenson, *Partner*
EMP: 5 **EST:** 1983
SQ FT: 2,000
SALES (est): 399.6K **Privately Held**
SIC: 3544 Industrial molds

Leroy
Osceola County

(G-10004)
ADVANCED FIBERMOLDING INC
23095 14 Mile Rd (49655-8552)
PHONE.....................231 768-5177
Dennis Webster, *President*
Norma Jean Webster, *Corp Secy*
Rick Dostal, *Production*
EMP: 40 **EST:** 1992
SQ FT: 24,000
SALES (est): 4.4MM **Privately Held**
WEB: www.advancedfibermold.com
SIC: 3089 Plastic containers, except foam

(G-10005)
D J MCQUESTION & SONS INC
17708 18 Mile Rd (49655-8219)
PHONE.....................231 768-4403
Robert McQuestion, *President*
Julie Gugle, *Human Res Mgr*
Craig Todd, *Benefits Mgr*
Brandy Prosch,
Julie Buys, *Clerk*
EMP: 10 **EST:** 1969
SQ FT: 3,000
SALES (est): 2.8MM **Privately Held**
SIC: 3295 1794 1611 Pulverized earth; excavation work; highway & street construction

(G-10006)
DYERS SAWMILL INC
17688 15 Mile Rd (49655-7501)
P.O. Box 20 (49655-0020)
PHONE.....................231 768-4438
Ross Rothig, *President*
EMP: 22 **EST:** 1935
SQ FT: 12,500
SALES (est): 2.7MM **Privately Held**
SIC: 2421 2435 2426 Lumber: rough, sawed or planed; hardwood veneer & plywood; hardwood dimension & flooring mills

(G-10007)
LEROY TOOL & DIE INC
17951 180th Ave (49655-8427)
PHONE.....................231 768-4336
Terry Wanstead, *President*
Judy Wanstead, *Corp Secy*
Nate Cubitt, *Manager*
▲ **EMP:** 70 **EST:** 1988
SQ FT: 8,000
SALES (est): 13.8MM **Privately Held**
WEB: www.leroytool.com
SIC: 3544 Special dies & tools

(G-10008)
NORTHERN PRECISION PDTS INC
4790 Mackinaw Trl (49655-9320)
P.O. Box 202 (49655-0202)
PHONE.....................231 768-4435
Mary Nagengast, *CEO*
Richard Langdon, *Principal*
Bernard Nagengast, *Vice Pres*
Brian Ringler, *Prdtn Mgr*
David Dubuque, *Engineer*
EMP: 40 **EST:** 1983
SQ FT: 23,000
SALES (est): 4.4MM **Privately Held**
WEB: www.northernprecisionproducts.com
SIC: 3599 Machine shop, jobbing & repair

(G-10009)
PIONEER BROACH MIDWEST INC
13957 Pioneer Ave (49655-9402)
PHONE.....................231 768-5800
Gary Izor, *President*
EMP: 10 **EST:** 1998
SQ FT: 35,000
SALES (est): 1.4MM
SALES (corp-wide): 7.8MM **Privately Held**
WEB: www.pmbroach.com
SIC: 3545 3541 Machine tool accessories; machine tools, metal cutting type
PA: Pioneer Broach Company
 6434 Telegraph Rd
 Commerce CA 90040
 323 728-1263

(G-10010)
PIONEER MICHIGAN BROACH CO
13957 Pioneer Ave (49655-9402)
PHONE.....................231 768-5800
Michael Ochs, *President*
Jerry Ezor, *Principal*
EMP: 15 **EST:** 2008
SALES (est): 590.5K **Privately Held**
WEB: www.pmbroach.com
SIC: 7699 3545 3599 Knife, saw & tool sharpening & repair; broaches (machine tool accessories); machine shop, jobbing & repair; electrical discharge machining (EDM)

(G-10011)
RICHTER SAWMILL
20408 18 Mile Rd (49655-8370)
PHONE.....................231 829-3071
Warren Richter, *Owner*
EMP: 4 **EST:** 1985
SALES (est): 249.2K **Privately Held**
SIC: 2421 Sawmills & planing mills, general

(G-10012)
SUPERIOR AUTOMOTIVE EQP INC
18153 150th Ave (49655-8210)
PHONE.....................231 829-9902
Michael Bell, *President*
◆ **EMP:** 4 **EST:** 2003
SALES (est): 732.6K **Privately Held**
WEB: www.saesupply.com
SIC: 3559 Automotive maintenance equipment

Leslie
Ingham County

(G-10013)
AERO INSPECTION & TOOL LLC
856 Ewers Rd (49251-9524)
PHONE.....................517 525-7373
Nona Roe, *Principal*
EMP: 4 **EST:** 2014
SALES (est): 204.2K **Privately Held**
WEB: www.aeroinspectionandtool.com
SIC: 3728 Aircraft parts & equipment

(G-10014)
LOGAN DIESEL INCORPORATED
4567 Churchill Rd (49251-9732)
PHONE.....................517 589-8811
James L Logan, *President*
Sally Logan, *Admin Sec*
EMP: 5 **EST:** 1988
SQ FT: 3,200
SALES (est): 500K **Privately Held**
WEB: www.logandiesel.com
SIC: 3519 3523 Diesel engine rebuilding; fertilizing, spraying, dusting & irrigation machinery

(G-10015)
MODERN FUR DRESSING LLC
801 Rice St (49251-2500)
P.O. Box 93 (49251-0093)
PHONE.....................517 589-5575
Roger G Smith,
EMP: 9
SQ FT: 2,000
SALES (est): 187K **Privately Held**
WEB: www.tannery.thewildlifegallery.com
SIC: 3999 3111 Furs, dressed: bleached, curried, scraped, tanned or dyed; leather tanning & finishing

Levering
Emmet County

(G-10016)
PERRONE VINEYARDS
6715 N Us Highway 31 (49755-9702)
PHONE..................................231 330-1493
Jerry Perrone, *Principal*
EMP: 5 **EST:** 2015
SALES (est): 140.2K **Privately Held**
WEB: www.perronevineyards.com
SIC: 2084 Wines

Lewiston
Montmorency County

(G-10017)
AMI INDUSTRIES INC (PA)
Also Called: Aggressive Mfg Innovations
5093 N Red Oak Rd (49756-8548)
P.O. Box 269 (49756-0269)
PHONE..................................989 786-3755
Jeff Evans, *President*
Todd Morris, *Mfg Spvr*
Kathie Vollmar, *Purch Mgr*
Carla Gordon, *Plant Engr*
Mick Lamagna, *Finance Mgr*
▲ **EMP:** 80 **EST:** 2002
SQ FT: 30,000
SALES (est): 25.3MM **Privately Held**
SIC: 3559 Automotive related machinery

(G-10018)
BEARDED VINYL LLC
4085 Salling Ave (49756-8745)
PHONE..................................989 786-9994
Earl Osburn, *Agent*
EMP: 5 **EST:** 2018
SALES (est): 133.1K **Privately Held**
WEB: www.beardedvinyl.com
SIC: 2752 Commercial printing, lithographic

(G-10019)
FIELD TECH SERVICES INC
3860 County Road 491 (49756-9210)
PHONE..................................989 786-7046
Anthony Lucas, *President*
Mary Lucas, *Treasurer*
EMP: 7 **EST:** 2001
SALES (est): 1.1MM **Privately Held**
WEB: www.fieldtechservicesinc.com
SIC: 1389 Oil field services

(G-10020)
GREAT LAKES COMPRESSION INC
3690 County Road 491 (49756-9310)
P.O. Box 945 (49756-0945)
PHONE..................................989 786-3788
Ron Bingham, *President*
Keith Koronak, *President*
EMP: 6 **EST:** 2001
SALES (est): 3MM
SALES (corp-wide): 68MM **Publicly Held**
WEB: www.ngsgi.com
SIC: 1389 Oil field services
PA: Natural Gas Services Group, Inc.
404 Veterans Airpark Ln
Midland TX 79705
432 262-2700

(G-10021)
HB CARBIDE COMPANY
4210 Doyle (49756-9083)
PHONE..................................989 786-4223
Norman B Lawton, *President*
Bradley L Lawton, *Vice Pres*
Richard Mc Leod, *Vice Pres*
Boyd E Moilanen, *Vice Pres*
Martin Woodhouse, *Vice Pres*
EMP: 100 **EST:** 1978
SQ FT: 50,000
SALES (est): 24.9MM
SALES (corp-wide): 204.2MM **Privately Held**
WEB: www.hbcarbide.com
SIC: 3544 Special dies, tools, jigs & fixtures
PA: Star Cutter Co.
23461 Industrial Park Dr
Farmington Hills MI 48335
248 474-8200

(G-10022)
JACK & SONS WELDING & FABG LLC ◯
Also Called: J&S Fab
4402 Judy Ave (49756-8863)
PHONE..................................248 302-6496
Robert Dines, *Principal*
EMP: 4 **EST:** 2021
SALES (est): 161.3K **Privately Held**
SIC: 3441 Fabricated structural metal

(G-10023)
LEWISTON SAND & GRAVEL INC
5122 County Road 612 (49756-7853)
P.O. Box 162 (49756-0162)
PHONE..................................989 786-2742
Tom May, *President*
EMP: 6 **EST:** 1959
SQ FT: 5,600
SALES (est): 705.2K **Privately Held**
WEB: www.lewistonsandandgravel.com
SIC: 1794 3281 5999 5211 Excavation work; stone, quarrying & processing of own stone products; rock & stone specimens; sand & gravel

(G-10024)
LINN ENERGY
4890 Airport Rd (49756-9041)
PHONE..................................989 786-7592
EMP: 10 **EST:** 2017
SALES (est): 419.7K **Privately Held**
WEB: www.linnenergy.com
SIC: 1382 Oil & gas exploration services

(G-10025)
N G S G I NATURAL GAS SER
3690 County Road 491 (49756-9310)
PHONE..................................989 786-3788
EMP: 11 **EST:** 2013
SALES (est): 741.1K **Privately Held**
WEB: www.ngsgi.com
SIC: 1389 Oil field services

(G-10026)
NORTHWEST HARDWOODS INC
3293 County Road 491 (49756-9227)
P.O. Box 599 (49756-0599)
PHONE..................................989 786-6100
Michael Avery, *Branch Mgr*
EMP: 4 **Privately Held**
WEB: www.northwesthardwoods.com
SIC: 2421 Sawmills & planing mills, general
PA: Northwest Hardwoods, Inc.
1313 Broadway Ste 300
Tacoma WA 98402

Lexington
Sanilac County

(G-10027)
CHARLES PHIPPS AND SONS LTD
6951 Lakeshore Rd (48450-9002)
PHONE..................................810 359-7141
Charles S Phipps Sr, *President*
Charles S Phipps Jr, *Vice Pres*
Stephan C Phipps, *Treasurer*
Andrew C Phipps, *Admin Sec*
EMP: 14 **EST:** 1962
SQ FT: 3,200
SALES (est): 823.9K **Privately Held**
SIC: 2511 Wood household furniture

(G-10028)
GIELOW PICKLES INC (PA)
5260 Main St (48450-9393)
PHONE..................................810 359-7680
Douglas R Gielow, *President*
Craig Gielow, *Vice Pres*
Marc Gielow, *Plant Mgr*
Dale Phipps, *Engineer*
Dave Bembas, *Broker*
◆ **EMP:** 248 **EST:** 1970
SQ FT: 30,000
SALES: 61.7MM **Privately Held**
WEB: www.gielowpickles.com
SIC: 2035 Cucumbers, pickles & pickle salting

(G-10029)
HURON INC (DH)
6554 Lakeshore Rd (48450-9763)
PHONE..................................810 359-5344
Patrick Paige, *President*
Jerry Solar, *President*
Tamara George, *Buyer*
Kyle Grace, *Manager*
Kayla Kinnee, *Personnel Asst*
▲ **EMP:** 31 **EST:** 1984
SQ FT: 122,000
SALES (est): 120MM
SALES (corp-wide): 21.1MM **Privately Held**
WEB: www.huroninc.com
SIC: 3498 3451 Fabricated pipe & fittings; screw machine products
HQ: Hdt Automotive Solutions Llc
38701 7 Mile Rd Ste 2
Livonia MI 48152
810 359-5344

(G-10030)
LAKESHORE GRAPHICS
7047 Lakeshore Rd (48450-8943)
PHONE..................................810 359-2087
Jason Gonzales, *President*
EMP: 4 **EST:** 2020
SALES (est): 307.4K **Privately Held**
WEB: www.lakeshoregraphics.net
SIC: 3993 Signs & advertising specialties

(G-10031)
PATTON TOOL AND DIE INC
Also Called: Mill Creek Industries
7185 Baker Rd (48450-9750)
P.O. Box 142 (48450-0142)
PHONE..................................810 359-5336
EMP: 10
SQ FT: 7,200
SALES (est): 1.6MM **Privately Held**
SIC: 3089 3544 3469 Mfg Plastic Products Mfg Dies/Tools/Jigs/Fixt Mfg Metal Stampings

(G-10032)
SUNRAISE INC
6547 Lakeshore Rd (48450-9761)
P.O. Box 9 (48450-0009)
PHONE..................................810 359-7301
Lindsey Rankin, *President*
Gary Rankin, *Admin Sec*
▲ **EMP:** 17 **EST:** 1978
SQ FT: 18,000
SALES (est): 2.6MM **Privately Held**
WEB: www.sunraise.com
SIC: 3555 Printing presses

Lincoln
Alcona County

(G-10033)
ALCONA TOOL & MACHINE INC
325 N Lake St (48742-9497)
PHONE..................................989 736-8151
Mark Feldhiser, *General Mgr*
EMP: 4
SQ FT: 10,000
SALES (corp-wide): 7.3MM **Privately Held**
WEB: www.alconatool.com
SIC: 3544 Special dies & tools
PA: Alcona Tool & Machine, Inc.
3040 E Carbide Dr
Harrisville MI 48740
989 736-8151

(G-10034)
GREAT NORTHERN LUMBER MICH LLC
507 W Traverse Bay Rd (48742-9313)
PHONE..................................989 736-6192
Joel S Blom, *Opers Mgr*
Joel Blohm, *Mng Member*
EMP: 7 **EST:** 1993
SALES (est): 176.5K **Privately Held**
SIC: 2421 2448 Custom sawmill; pallets, wood

(G-10035)
HURON QUALITY MFG INC
481 State St (48742-9338)
P.O. Box 400 (48742-0400)
PHONE..................................989 736-8121
Joseph James, *Treasurer*
Joseph P James, *Administration*
EMP: 8 **EST:** 2016
SALES (est): 725.4K **Privately Held**
WEB: www.huronquality.com
SIC: 3599 Machine shop, jobbing & repair

(G-10036)
LINCOLN INDUSTRIES (PA)
202 S Second St (48742)
P.O. Box 388 (48742-0388)
PHONE..................................989 736-6421
Gary H Becker, *President*
EMP: 2
SQ FT: 15,000
SALES (est): 1.1MM **Privately Held**
WEB: www.lincolnindustries.com
SIC: 3089 3479 Injection molding of plastics; identification cards, plastic; painting of metal products

(G-10037)
LINCOLN PRECISION CARBIDE INC
600 S 2nd St (48742)
P.O. Box 129 (48742-0129)
PHONE..................................989 736-8113
Howard Stone, *President*
Kirk Sherwood, *Vice Pres*
Richard Weichel, *Vice Pres*
Steve Weichel, *Vice Pres*
EMP: 22 **EST:** 1974
SQ FT: 12,000
SALES (est): 2.2MM **Privately Held**
WEB: www.lincolnprecision.com
SIC: 3541 3545 Machine tools, metal cutting type; machine tool accessories

(G-10038)
NORTHERN INDUSTRIAL WOOD INC
507 State St (48742-9313)
PHONE..................................989 736-6192
Steve Rhone, *President*
EMP: 28 **EST:** 2017
SALES (est): 3.6MM **Privately Held**
SIC: 2421 Lumber: rough, sawed or planed

(G-10039)
NORTHERN PRECISION INC
601 S Lake St (48742-9466)
P.O. Box 189 (48742-0189)
PHONE..................................989 736-6322
Ralph E Diemond, *President*
Rita Kay Diemond, *Corp Secy*
EMP: 15 **EST:** 1979
SQ FT: 4,800
SALES (est): 1.2MM **Privately Held**
WEB: www.npquality.com
SIC: 3544 3545 Special dies & tools; machine tool accessories

(G-10040)
SCHRAMS CUSTOM WOODWORKING
1179 E Ritchie Rd (48742-9703)
PHONE..................................989 335-0847
Jeffery Schram, *Principal*
EMP: 5 **EST:** 2018
SALES (est): 76K **Privately Held**
SIC: 2431 Millwork

(G-10041)
WEISER METAL PRODUCTS INC
3431 E M 72 (48742)
P.O. Box 370 (48742-0370)
PHONE..................................989 736-8151
Terry Lenard, *President*
Joe James, *Corp Secy*
Keith Kruttlin, *Vice Pres*
Ava Budreau, *Admin Sec*
EMP: 5 **EST:** 2000
SALES (est): 485.3K **Privately Held**
WEB: www.weisermetal.com
SIC: 3493 Cold formed springs

Lincoln Park
Wayne County

(G-10042)
ADAMS MANUFACTURING
1586 Detroit Ave (48146-3217)
PHONE..............................313 383-7804
Allan Adams, *Principal*
EMP: 8 **EST:** 2008
SALES (est): 66.6K **Privately Held**
WEB: www.adamsmfg.com
SIC: 3999 Manufacturing industries

(G-10043)
AMERICAN GRINDING MACHINING CO
1415 Dix Hwy (48146-1496)
PHONE..............................313 388-0440
Wilbur C Thomas, *President*
William Northrup, *Manager*
EMP: 10 **EST:** 1955
SQ FT: 10,000
SALES (est): 1MM **Privately Held**
SIC: 3599 Grinding castings for the trade

(G-10044)
CALDER BROS DAIRY INC
1020 Southfield Rd (48146-2604)
PHONE..............................313 381-8858
William Calder, *President*
John Calder, *Vice Pres*
EMP: 28 **EST:** 1950
SQ FT: 1,600
SALES (est): 996K **Privately Held**
WEB: www.calderdairy.com
SIC: 5812 5963 2026 Ice cream stands or dairy bars; milk delivery; fluid milk

(G-10045)
DOWNRIVER BOATWORKS LTD
1428 Rose Ave (48146-3351)
PHONE..............................313 335-4288
Rick Boros, *Principal*
EMP: 7 **EST:** 2004
SALES (est): 14.8K **Privately Held**
WEB: www.downriverboatworks.com
SIC: 3732 Boat building & repairing

(G-10046)
EVER-FLEX INC
1490 John A Papalas Dr (48146-1460)
PHONE..............................313 389-2060
Merel Epstein, *President*
EMP: 22 **EST:** 1987
SQ FT: 13,000
SALES (est): 1MM **Privately Held**
SIC: 3842 Surgical appliances & supplies

(G-10047)
FK FUEL INC
Also Called: Lincoln Park Fuel
1312 Fort St (48146-1815)
PHONE..............................313 383-6005
John Kizy, *Principal*
EMP: 4 **EST:** 2006
SQ FT: 2,000
SALES (est): 737.6K **Privately Held**
SIC: 2869 Fuels

(G-10048)
GRAPHIC GEAR INC
Also Called: Accents Custom Printwear Plus
3018 Fort St (48146-2428)
PHONE..............................734 283-3864
Julie Mascia, *President*
Vito Mascia, *Treasurer*
EMP: 7 **EST:** 1999
SQ FT: 3,000
SALES (est): 584.7K **Privately Held**
WEB: www.accentstees.com
SIC: 2339 2329 Uniforms, athletic: women's, misses' & juniors'; men's & boys' athletic uniforms

(G-10049)
HURRICANE MACHINE INC
1815 Southfield Rd (48146-2298)
PHONE..............................313 383-8614
Robert Murdock, *President*
Faye Murdock, *Corp Secy*
EMP: 8 **EST:** 1964
SQ FT: 8,000
SALES (est): 865.8K **Privately Held**
WEB: www.hurricanemachinein.wix.com
SIC: 3599 Machine shop, jobbing & repair

(G-10050)
INTHEKNOW313 LLC
2165 White Ave (48146-4511)
PHONE..............................248 445-1953
Shontel Jackson,
EMP: 4 **EST:** 2018
SALES (est): 50K **Privately Held**
SIC: 2741

(G-10051)
LAS TORTUGAS PALLET CO
1583 Austin Ave (48146-2101)
PHONE..............................313 283-3279
Carlos Ruiz, *Principal*
EMP: 5 **EST:** 2016
SALES (est): 119.9K **Privately Held**
SIC: 2448 Wood pallets & skids

(G-10052)
NGU INDUSTRIES LLC
918 Dix Hwy (48146-1215)
PHONE..............................313 283-9570
EMP: 7 **EST:** 2015
SALES (est): 502.1K **Privately Held**
SIC: 3999 Manufacturing industries

(G-10053)
PIERINO FROZEN FOODS INC
1695 Southfield Rd (48146-2275)
PHONE..............................313 928-0950
Gianni Guglielmetti, *President*
Brian Saunders, *QA Dir*
Maria Karizat, *Treasurer*
▲ **EMP:** 48 **EST:** 1969
SQ FT: 25,000
SALES (est): 6.1MM **Privately Held**
WEB: www.pierinofrozenfoods.com
SIC: 2038 2099 2098 Frozen specialties; packaged combination products: pasta, rice & potato; macaroni & spaghetti

(G-10054)
R P T CINCINNATI INC
1636 John A Papalas Dr (48146-1462)
PHONE..............................313 382-5880
Tom Stefani, *President*
▲ **EMP:** 9 **EST:** 2001
SQ FT: 7,500
SALES (est): 1.5MM **Privately Held**
SIC: 3541 Machine tool replacement & repair parts, metal cutting types

(G-10055)
RENEGADE CSTM SCREEN PRTG LLC
2091 Thomas St (48146-2526)
PHONE..............................313 475-8489
Bret Luginski, *Principal*
EMP: 5 **EST:** 2012
SALES (est): 93.5K **Privately Held**
SIC: 2752 Commercial printing, lithographic

(G-10056)
SHAFTMASTERS
1668 John A Papalas Dr (48146-1462)
PHONE..............................313 383-6347
Robert A Eppich, *President*
EMP: 4 **EST:** 2004
SALES (est): 439.5K **Privately Held**
WEB: www.shaftmasters.com
SIC: 3714 Drive shafts, motor vehicle

(G-10057)
TREND MILLWORK LLC
1300 John A Papalas Dr (48146-1356)
PHONE..............................313 383-6300
David Muzzatti, *CEO*
Brian Zuccaro, *COO*
Luke Bonanni, *Vice Pres*
Jeffrey Morche, *Project Mgr*
Matt Parent, *Production*
EMP: 20 **EST:** 1965
SQ FT: 15,000
SALES (est): 3.7MM **Privately Held**
WEB: www.trendmillwork.com
SIC: 2431 Millwork

(G-10058)
WRIGHT & FILIPPIS LLC
Also Called: Fordson Health Care
4050 Fort St (48146-4123)
PHONE..............................313 386-3330
Steve Filippis, *Manager*
EMP: 19
SALES (corp-wide): 77.5MM **Privately Held**
WEB: www.firsttoserve.com
SIC: 5999 3842 3841 Orthopedic & prosthesis applications; surgical appliances & supplies; surgical & medical instruments
PA: Wright & Filippis, Llc
2845 Crooks Rd
Rochester Hills MI 48309
248 829-8292

Linden
Genesee County

(G-10059)
ALLEN AND SONS WOODWORKING
401 Tickner St (48451-9003)
PHONE..............................313 492-1382
Lawrence W Allen Jr, *Principal*
EMP: 4 **EST:** 2016
SALES (est): 64.5K **Privately Held**
WEB: www.allenandsonswoodworking.yolasite.com
SIC: 2431 Millwork

(G-10060)
CHAOTIC COTTON COMPANY LLC
16133 Softwater Lake Dr (48451-9702)
PHONE..............................810 624-6153
Brett Rule, *Principal*
EMP: 6 **EST:** 2015
SALES (est): 73.4K **Privately Held**
SIC: 2299 Textile goods

(G-10061)
FARNELL CONTRACTING INC
3355 Lahring Rd (48451-9434)
PHONE..............................810 714-3421
Doug Farnell, *President*
Scott Farnell, *Vice Pres*
Kathleen M Farnell, *Treasurer*
Kathy Farnell, *Treasurer*
Joel Fisher, *Sales Staff*
EMP: 14 **EST:** 1995
SALES (est): 1.8MM **Privately Held**
WEB: www.farnellcontracting.com
SIC: 2521 Cabinets, office: wood

(G-10062)
GRUPO RESILIENT INTL INC (PA)
15091 Poberezny Ct (48451-9161)
PHONE..............................810 410-8177
Gordon Johnson, *President*
Deeanna Looney, *Admin Sec*
EMP: 8 **EST:** 2004
SQ FT: 2,000
SALES (est): 1.9MM **Privately Held**
SIC: 3812 Search & navigation equipment

(G-10063)
HI-TRAC INDUSTRIES INC
5161 Harp Dr (48451-9060)
PHONE..............................810 625-7193
Joseph W Hood, *Vice Pres*
EMP: 4 **EST:** 1981
SQ FT: 15,000
SALES (est): 411.8K **Privately Held**
SIC: 3842 Crutches & walkers; canes, orthopedic

(G-10064)
LUMMI CUSTOMS LC
707 Cherry St (48451-8958)
PHONE..............................702 713-8428
Asja Thomson,
EMP: 4
SALES (est): 50K **Privately Held**
SIC: 3999 Manufacturing industries

(G-10065)
MCINTYRES SOFT WATER SVC LTD
Also Called: Water Treatment
1014 N Bridge St (48451-8821)
P.O. Box 729 (48451-0729)
PHONE..............................810 735-5778
James Mc Intyre, *President*
EMP: 27 **EST:** 1960
SQ FT: 11,000
SALES (est): 1MM **Privately Held**
SIC: 3589 7389 5499 Water filters & softeners, household type; water softener service; water: distilled mineral or spring

(G-10066)
MICHIGAN MOBILE WELDING CO
8173 Silver Lake Rd (48451-8615)
PHONE..............................810 569-0229
Paula Flannery, *Principal*
EMP: 4 **EST:** 2017
SALES (est): 25K **Privately Held**
SIC: 7692 Welding repair

(G-10067)
MICHIGAN SAWMILL SALES LLC
8392 Argentine Rd (48451-9617)
PHONE..............................810 625-3848
Charles Schultz, *Principal*
EMP: 7 **EST:** 2016
SALES (est): 165.1K **Privately Held**
WEB: www.misawmillsales.com
SIC: 2421 Sawmills & planing mills, general

(G-10068)
MID AMERICA COMMODITIES LLC
7420 Majestic Woods Dr (48451-8836)
PHONE..............................810 936-0108
Katarzyna Chapple,
Brad Chapple,
▲ **EMP:** 5 **EST:** 2004
SQ FT: 2,000
SALES (est): 650K **Privately Held**
WEB: www.caldo-freddo.com
SIC: 2038 Dinners, frozen & packaged

(G-10069)
QCQ DESIGN & FAB INC
5887 Deerfield Indus Dr (48451-8303)
P.O. Box 248 (48451-0248)
PHONE..............................810 735-4033
Joseph J Wilson, *CEO*
Doreen Ahern, *Business Mgr*
EMP: 4 **EST:** 2001
SQ FT: 6,000
SALES (est): 500K **Privately Held**
WEB: www.qcqdesign.com
SIC: 3089 Injection molding of plastics

(G-10070)
ROKAN CORP
5929 Deerfield Indus Dr (48451-8303)
PHONE..............................810 735-9170
Rod Kannisto, *President*
EMP: 5 **EST:** 1985
SQ FT: 10,000
SALES (est): 736K **Privately Held**
WEB: www.rokanreels.com
SIC: 2655 Reels (fiber), textile: made from purchased material

(G-10071)
SOFTAIRE DIFFUSERS INC
4198 Neal Ct (48451-8463)
PHONE..............................810 730-1668
Gary Hodges, *President*
Garry Hodges, *Manager*
EMP: 4 **EST:** 1992
SALES (est): 383K **Privately Held**
WEB: www.softairediffusers.com
SIC: 3822 1711 Air flow controllers, air conditioning & refrigeration; plumbing, heating, air-conditioning contractors

(G-10072)
UNITED TESTING SYSTEMS
15105 Restwood Dr (48451-8771)
PHONE..............................989 494-3664
EMP: 6 **EST:** 2019
SALES (est): 97.6K **Privately Held**
WEB: www.industrialphysics.com
SIC: 3829 Measuring & controlling devices

Linwood
Bay County

(G-10073)
ARC RITE WELDING LLC
606 N Elevator Rd (48634-9462)
PHONE..................989 545-8006
Benjamin Priem, *Principal*
EMP: 4 **EST:** 2016
SALES (est): 30.9K **Privately Held**
WEB: www.arcritewelds.com
SIC: 7692 Welding repair

(G-10074)
LINWOOD TOOL CO INC
229 S Huron Rd (48634-9476)
P.O. Box 69 (48634-0069)
PHONE..................989 697-4403
Matt Copus, *President*
Sherry Ralph, *Corp Secy*
EMP: 32 **EST:** 1957
SQ FT: 4,760
SALES (est): 1.1MM **Privately Held**
WEB: www.linwoodtool.com
SIC: 3544 7692 3549 Special dies & tools; jigs & fixtures; welding repair; metalworking machinery

(G-10075)
WILLIAMS CHEESE CO
Also Called: Amish Country Cheese
998 N Huron Rd (48634-9219)
P.O. Box 249 (48634-0249)
PHONE..................989 697-4492
Michael Williams, *CEO*
EMP: 50 **EST:** 1944
SQ FT: 16,000
SALES (est): 22.8MM **Privately Held**
WEB: www.williamscheese.com
SIC: 5143 2022 Cheese; cheese, natural & processed

Litchfield
Hillsdale County

(G-10076)
AMERICAN AXLE & MFG INC
917 Anderson Rd (49252-9776)
PHONE..................517 542-4241
EMP: 7
SALES (corp-wide): 4.7B **Publicly Held**
WEB: www.aam.com
SIC: 3714 Rear axle housings, motor vehicle
HQ: American Axle & Manufacturing, Inc.
1 Dauch Dr
Detroit MI 48211

(G-10077)
FINISHING TOUCH INC
Also Called: F T I
191 Simpson Dr (49252-9601)
PHONE..................517 542-5581
Thomas A Van Auken, *President*
Darlene D Van Auken, *Vice Pres*
Treva McNair, *Purchasing*
Richard Barnes, *CIO*
EMP: 23 **EST:** 1981
SQ FT: 24,000
SALES (est): 2.4MM **Privately Held**
WEB: www.ftipaint.com
SIC: 1721 3471 Industrial painting; finishing, metals or formed products

(G-10078)
HARVARD CLOTHING COMPANY
411 Marshall St (49252-9703)
P.O. Box 330 (49252-0330)
PHONE..................517 542-2986
Richard Barker Jr, *President*
EMP: 17 **EST:** 1926
SQ FT: 24,000
SALES (est): 2.1MM **Privately Held**
WEB: www.harvardclothing.com
SIC: 2329 2339 Men's & boys' sportswear & athletic clothing; jackets (suede, leatherette, etc.), sport: men's & boys'; women's & misses' outerwear; jackets, untailored: women's, misses' & juniors'; jogging & warmup suits: women's, misses' & juniors'

(G-10079)
HI-LEX AMERICA INCORPORATED
152 Simpson Dr (49252-9601)
PHONE..................517 542-2955
Katsuaki Tokuhrio, *Branch Mgr*
EMP: 117 **Privately Held**
SIC: 3496 Miscellaneous fabricated wire products
HQ: Hi-Lex America, Incorporated
5200 Wayne Rd
Battle Creek MI 49037
269 968-0781

(G-10080)
HI-LEX CONTROLS INCORPORATED (DH)
152 Simpson Dr (49252-9601)
PHONE..................517 542-2955
Tom Strickland, *President*
Tomoharu Otane, *COO*
Gavin Carr, *Mfg Spvr*
Jeff Colotti, *Maint Spvr*
Chad Newberry, *Mfg Staff*
▲ **EMP:** 12 **EST:** 1989
SQ FT: 160,000
SALES (est): 70.4MM **Privately Held**
WEB: www.hi-lex.com
SIC: 3714 Motor vehicle electrical equipment
HQ: Tsk Of America, Inc.
152 Simpson Dr
Litchfield MI 49252
517 542-2955

(G-10081)
JEMS OF LITCHFIELD INC
174 Simpson Dr (49252-9601)
P.O. Box 449 (49252-0449)
PHONE..................517 542-5367
Phil Reneau, *President*
Doud Hawkins, *Principal*
David Palmer, *Treasurer*
EMP: 18 **EST:** 1986
SQ FT: 31,000
SALES (est): 1.9MM **Privately Held**
WEB: www.jemsoflitchfield.com
SIC: 3599 3498 3315 3544 Machine & other job shop work; tube fabricating (contract bending & shaping); steel wire & related products; forms (molds), for foundry & plastics working machinery

(G-10082)
JOHAN VAN DE WEERD CO INC
Also Called: Jvdw
916 Anderson Rd (49252-9776)
PHONE..................517 542-3817
Johan Van De Weerd, *CEO*
Philip Wilson, *President*
EMP: 9 **EST:** 1975
SALES (est): 863.7K **Privately Held**
WEB: www.jvdw.com
SIC: 3545 Boring machine attachments (machine tool accessories)

(G-10083)
MICHIGAN REBUILD & AUTOMTN INC
Also Called: M R A
7460 Herring Rd (49252-9745)
PHONE..................517 542-6000
Timothy Galloway, *President*
▼ **EMP:** 16 **EST:** 1999
SQ FT: 17,500
SALES (est): 4.2MM **Privately Held**
WEB: www.mraweb.com
SIC: 3599 7699 Custom machinery; industrial machinery & equipment repair

(G-10084)
NEWCO INDUSTRIES LLC
Also Called: Nex Solutions
900 Anderson Rd (49252-9776)
PHONE..................517 542-0105
Rodney W Norris,
EMP: 45 **EST:** 2004
SALES (est): 7.3MM **Privately Held**
SIC: 3441 Fabricated structural metal

(G-10085)
TENNECO AUTOMOTIVE OPER CO INC
929 Anderson Rd (49252-9776)
PHONE..................517 542-5511
Doud Minix, *Manager*
Cynthia Bouvay, *Manager*
EMP: 204
SQ FT: 132,000
SALES (corp-wide): 15.3B **Publicly Held**
SIC: 3714 Mufflers (exhaust), motor vehicle
HQ: Tenneco Automotive Operating Company, Inc.
500 N Field Dr
Lake Forest IL 60045
847 482-5000

(G-10086)
TSK OF AMERICA INC (HQ)
Also Called: Hi-Lex
152 Simpson Dr (49252-9601)
PHONE..................517 542-2955
Michele Berchulc, *Project Mgr*
Cindy Cummings, *Buyer*
John Steingass, *Engineer*
Brian Wild, *Engineer*
Heather Golen, *Senior Engr*
EMP: 593 **EST:** 2003
SALES (est): 222.7MM **Privately Held**
WEB: www.hi-lex.com
SIC: 3357 Automotive wire & cable, except ignition sets: nonferrous

(G-10087)
WELLS EQUIPMENT SALES INC
534 Homer Rd (49252)
P.O. Box 208 (49252-0208)
PHONE..................517 542-2376
Steven A Wells, *President*
Clifton F Wells, *Vice Pres*
Frances E Wells, *Treasurer*
Karen K Wells, *Admin Sec*
EMP: 19 **EST:** 1952
SQ FT: 16,000
SALES (est): 2.8MM **Privately Held**
WEB: www.wellsequipmentsales.com
SIC: 5999 3524 5511 Farm equipment & supplies; lawn & garden tractors & equipment; trucks, tractors & trailers: new & used

Livonia
Wayne County

(G-10088)
+VANTAGE CORPORATION
12623 Newburgh Rd (48150-1001)
PHONE..................734 432-5055
Timothy M White, *President*
Pete Kjeldsen, *Sales Engr*
Gary Williams, *Sales Engr*
Eric Matchette, *Marketing Staff*
◆ **EMP:** 45 **EST:** 2003
SQ FT: 20,000
SALES (est): 13.5MM **Privately Held**
WEB: www.vantage-corp.com
SIC: 3569 Assembly machines, non-metalworking

(G-10089)
3715-11TH STREET CORP
Also Called: Alpha Group of Companies, The
32741 Glendale St (48150-1611)
PHONE..................734 523-1000
Nicholas Strumbos, *President*
Chuck Dardas, *COO*
Chuck Shimko, *Production*
EMP: 27 **EST:** 1963
SALES (est): 276.5K **Privately Held**
SIC: 3465 Automotive stampings

(G-10090)
4-M INDUSTRIES INCORPORATED
33855 Capitol St (48150-1566)
PHONE..................734 762-7200
Allen Marsh, *Manager*
Roger Wyatt, *Manager*
EMP: 15 **Privately Held**
WEB: www.4mindustries.com
SIC: 3599 Machine shop, jobbing & repair
PA: 4-M Industries, Incorporated
35300 Glendale St
Livonia MI 48150

(G-10091)
4-M INDUSTRIES INCORPORATED (PA)
35300 Glendale St (48150-1243)
PHONE..................734 762-7200
Allen Marsh, *President*
Chris Marsh, *Vice Pres*
Christopher Marsh, *Vice Pres*
Steven Marsh, *Vice Pres*
Sonya H Hensley, *Manager*
EMP: 68 **EST:** 1988
SQ FT: 38,000
SALES (est): 8.3MM **Privately Held**
WEB: www.4mindustries.com
SIC: 3599 Machine shop, jobbing & repair

(G-10092)
A & R PACKING CO INC
34165 Autry St (48150-1333)
PHONE..................734 422-2060
Larry Kornacki, *President*
Ken Schwarz, *Vice Pres*
EMP: 40 **EST:** 1989
SQ FT: 50,000
SALES (est): 5.1MM **Privately Held**
SIC: 2013 2011 Smoked meats from purchased meat; cured meats from meat slaughtered on site

(G-10093)
A B M TOOL & DIE INC
38281 Schoolcraft Rd D (48150-5000)
PHONE..................734 432-6060
EMP: 5
SQ FT: 3,000
SALES: 1.5MM **Privately Held**
SIC: 3544 Mfg Dies/Tools/Jigs/Fixtures

(G-10094)
A&G CORPORATE HOLDINGS LLC
Also Called: Trigon Metal Products
12725 Inkster Rd (48150-2216)
PHONE..................734 513-3488
Stephen Gordon, *President*
EMP: 8 **EST:** 2016
SQ FT: 22,000
SALES (est): 1.2MM **Privately Held**
WEB: www.trigonmp.com
SIC: 3499 Machine bases, metal

(G-10095)
A123 SYSTEMS LLC
28200 Plymouth Rd (48150-2398)
PHONE..................734 466-6521
Mujeeb Ijaz, *Principal*
EMP: 6 **Privately Held**
WEB: www.a123systems.com
SIC: 3691 Batteries, rechargeable
HQ: A123 Systems Llc
27101 Cabaret Dr
Novi MI 48377
248 412-9249

(G-10096)
AACTUS INC
12671 Richfield Ct (48150-1062)
PHONE..................734 425-1212
John Haapala, *President*
Steven Skowronek, *VP Opers*
Rayleen Morgan, *Bookkeeper*
Todd Faulkner, *Sales Mgr*
EMP: 9 **EST:** 1979
SQ FT: 8,000
SALES (est): 2.1MM **Privately Held**
WEB: www.aactus.com
SIC: 5085 5072 5113 5198 Industrial supplies; staples; pressure sensitive tape; closures, paper & disposable plastic; paints, varnishes & supplies; personal safety equipment; container, packaging & boxboard

(G-10097)
ABC ACQUISITION COMPANY LLC
Also Called: Aetna Bearing Company
31778 Enterprise Dr (48150-1960)
PHONE..................734 335-4083
Chris Bilakos, *Business Mgr*
Donald Koziel, *Opers Mgr*
Jim Newman, *Opers Staff*
Jim Gehrke, *Purch Mgr*
Ziyad Kassir, *Engineer*
▲ **EMP:** 50 **EST:** 1988

SALES (est): 10.2MM **Privately Held**
WEB: www.aetnabearing.com
SIC: 3562 Ball bearings & parts

(G-10098)
ACCESS HEATING & COOLING INC
39001 Ann Arbor Trl (48150-4545)
P.O. Box 510681 (48151-6681)
PHONE.................................734 464-0566
Kathen Hans, *President*
Edsel D Sloan Jr, *Treasurer*
Kathleen Sloan, *Admin Sec*
EMP: 1 **EST:** 1982
SALES (est): 11MM **Privately Held**
WEB: www.accessheatingandcooling.com
SIC: 1711 3444 Mechanical contractor; warm air heating & air conditioning contractor; sheet metalwork

(G-10099)
ACCURATE MACHINED SERVICE INC
Also Called: Accurate Machine Service
30948 Industrial Rd (48150-2024)
PHONE.................................734 421-4660
Frank J Kowal, *President*
Andrew Kowal, *Vice Pres*
EMP: 6 **EST:** 1940
SQ FT: 20,000
SALES (est): 500.3K **Privately Held**
SIC: 3541 Grinding machines, metalworking

(G-10100)
ACORN INDUSTRIES INC (PA)
Also Called: Contamination Control
11844 Brookfield St (48150-1701)
PHONE.................................734 261-2940
Philip Austin, *President*
Philip R Austin, *President*
Philip J Austin, *Vice Pres*
Gynell Rock, *Engineer*
Christine Nagy, *Office Mgr*
EMP: 50 **EST:** 1982
SQ FT: 25,000
SALES (est): 12.8MM **Privately Held**
WEB: www.cleanroom-consulting-group.com
SIC: 8742 3471 Industrial hygiene consultant; plating & polishing

(G-10101)
ADVANCED ELASTOMERS CORP
34481 Industrial Rd (48150-1307)
PHONE.................................734 458-4194
Chris Campbell, *President*
James Pruitt, *Vice Pres*
EMP: 8 **EST:** 1997
SQ FT: 5,000
SALES (est): 775K **Privately Held**
WEB: www.advancedelastomers.com
SIC: 2821 Plastics materials & resins

(G-10102)
ADVANCED SYSTEMS & FORMS
27690 Joy Rd (48150-4146)
PHONE.................................734 422-7180
EMP: 7 **EST:** 2019
SALES (est): 278.2K **Privately Held**
WEB: www.advancedmarketingpartners.com
SIC: 2752 Commercial printing, offset

(G-10103)
ADVANTAGE LASER INC
35684 Veronica St (48150-1204)
PHONE.................................734 367-9936
Michael Lubig, *President*
Brenda Brock, *Treasurer*
EMP: 4 **EST:** 1996
SQ FT: 13,600
SALES (est): 498.5K **Privately Held**
WEB: www.advantage-laser.com
SIC: 3444 Sheet metalwork

(G-10104)
AERO SYSTEMS
13475 Wayne Rd (48150-1245)
PHONE.................................253 269-3000
Jennifer Whales, *Chairman*
EMP: 7 **EST:** 2005
SALES (est): 105.4K **Privately Held**
SIC: 3669 Emergency alarms

(G-10105)
AGHOG INC
30629 Puritan St (48154-3294)
PHONE.................................313 277-2037
Dian Sperry, *President*
EMP: 6 **EST:** 1980
SQ FT: 6,000
SALES (est): 398K **Privately Held**
SIC: 1044 Silver ores processing

(G-10106)
AIR FILTER & EQUIPMENT INC
Also Called: Exfil
37007 Industrial Rd (48150-1146)
PHONE.................................734 261-1860
Fred Marshall, *Branch Mgr*
EMP: 5
SALES (corp-wide): 5.5MM **Privately Held**
WEB: www.exfil.com
SIC: 3564 Filters, air: furnaces, air conditioning equipment, etc.
PA: Air Filter & Equipment, Inc
4110 S 9th St
Kalamazoo MI 49009
269 544-2444

(G-10107)
AIRFLOW SCIENCES EQUIPMENT LLC
12190 Hubbard St (48150-1737)
PHONE.................................734 525-0300
Robert Mudry,
EMP: 6 **EST:** 2012
SALES (est): 634.4K **Privately Held**
WEB: www.airflowsciencesequipment.com
SIC: 3823 Flow instruments, industrial process type

(G-10108)
ALL AMERICAN EMBROIDERY INC
Also Called: All American Essentials
31600 Plymouth Rd (48150-1930)
PHONE.................................734 421-9292
Sandeep Narang, *President*
John Bartle, *Sales Staff*
Nishant Batra, *Software Dev*
EMP: 10 **EST:** 1996
SALES (est): 3.6MM **Privately Held**
WEB: www.aaeforever.com
SIC: 3953 3993 3552 Screens, textile printing; signs & advertising specialties; embroidery machines

(G-10109)
ALLIE BROTHERS INC
Also Called: Allie Brothers Men's Wear
20295 Middlebelt Rd (48152-2001)
PHONE.................................248 477-4434
Hassen J Allie, *President*
Robert Allie, *CFO*
EMP: 14 **EST:** 1986
SQ FT: 7,500
SALES (est): 1.9MM **Privately Held**
WEB: www.alliebros.com
SIC: 5699 5611 2311 Uniforms; men's & boys' clothing stores; suits, men's; clothing accessories: men's & boys'; men's & boys' uniforms

(G-10110)
ALPHA COATINGS INC
Also Called: Alpha Group
32711 Glendale St (48150-1611)
PHONE.................................734 523-9000
Nicholas Strumbos, *President*
Shelly McMahon, *Purchasing*
Rick Heys, *Director*
EMP: 18 **EST:** 1993
SALES (est): 833.9K **Privately Held**
WEB: www.alphausa.com
SIC: 3479 Coating of metals & formed products

(G-10111)
ALPHA STEEL TREATING INC
32969 Glendale St (48150-1613)
PHONE.................................734 523-1035
George Strumbos, *Ch of Bd*
Nicholas Strumbos, *President*
Stanley Martinez, *Exec VP*
Catherine Strumbos, *Vice Pres*
EMP: 13 **EST:** 1989
SQ FT: 80,000
SALES (est): 175.4K **Privately Held**
SIC: 3398 Metal heat treating

(G-10112)
ALTA EQUIPMENT HOLDINGS INC (HQ)
13211 Merriman Rd (48150-1826)
PHONE.................................248 449-6700
Steven Greenawalt, *CEO*
Rob Chiles, *President*
Derek Vantichelt, *President*
Latrice Levy, *General Mgr*
Jeremy Cionca, *Vice Pres*
EMP: 26 **EST:** 2010
SALES (est): 142.3MM
SALES (corp-wide): 873.6MM **Publicly Held**
WEB: www.materialhandling.altaequipment.com
SIC: 3537 5084 Industrial trucks & tractors; lift trucks & parts
PA: Alta Equipment Group Inc.
13211 Merriman Rd
Livonia MI 48150
248 449-6700

(G-10113)
AMANDA MANUFACTURING LLC
Also Called: Msd Stamping
34450 Industrial Rd (48150-1308)
PHONE.................................740 385-9380
Robert Grufchow, *Mng Member*
Chris Muliett, *Maintence Staff*
EMP: 50 **EST:** 1957
SQ FT: 35,000
SALES (est): 11.7MM
SALES (corp-wide): 109.1MM **Privately Held**
WEB: www.amandamanufacturing.com
SIC: 3452 Bolts, nuts, rivets & washers
PA: Deshler Group, Inc.
34450 Industrial Rd
Livonia MI 48150
734 525-9100

(G-10114)
AMERICAN HOUSEHOLD INC
Also Called: Sunbeam
33067 Industrial Rd (48150-1619)
P.O. Box 860, Freeport IL (61032-0860)
PHONE.................................601 296-5000
EMP: 5
SALES (corp-wide): 9.3B **Publicly Held**
SIC: 3631 Barbecues, grills & braziers (outdoor cooking)
HQ: American Household, Inc.
2381 Nw Executive Ctr Dr
Boca Raton FL 33431
561 912-4100

(G-10115)
AMERICAN RING MANUFACTURING
Also Called: Artco Mfg
35955 Veronica St (48150-1207)
PHONE.................................734 402-0426
Gary Howell, *President*
Robert H Morissey, *Principal*
Jack Morrissey, *Vice Pres*
EMP: 26 **EST:** 1990
SQ FT: 15,000
SALES (est): 5.1MM **Privately Held**
WEB: www.shop.americanring.com
SIC: 3493 Steel springs, except wire

(G-10116)
AMERICAN ROLL SHUTTER AWNG CO
Also Called: Maygrove Awning Co.
12700 Merriman Rd (48150-1818)
PHONE.................................734 422-7110
Michael Falahee, *President*
▲ **EMP:** 29 **EST:** 1981
SQ FT: 17,000
SALES (est): 2.1MM **Privately Held**
SIC: 2394 3444 3442 5714 Awnings, fabric: made from purchased materials; awnings, sheet metal; metal doors, sash & trim; drapery & upholstery stores

(G-10117)
AMI LIVONIA LLC
36930 Industrial Rd (48150-1135)
PHONE.................................734 428-3120
Vincent Henderson, *CEO*

EMP: 75 **EST:** 2016
SQ FT: 100,000
SALES (est): 7MM
SALES (corp-wide): 21.1MM **Privately Held**
SIC: 3465 Automotive stampings
PA: Gallant Steel, Inc.
17951 W Austin Rd
Manchester MI 48158
734 428-3105

(G-10118)
AMTRADE SYSTEMS INC
12885 Wayne Rd (48150-1244)
PHONE.................................734 522-9500
Joe Glaser, *President*
David McCormack, *Parts Mgr*
Lisa Harlow, *Accountant*
David Mc Cormack, *Office Mgr*
Ryan Skergan, *Technician*
◆ **EMP:** 5 **EST:** 2003
SQ FT: 10,000
SALES (est): 2.9MM **Privately Held**
WEB: www.amtrade-systems.com
SIC: 5063 1796 7692 Generators; installing building equipment; welding repair

(G-10119)
ANDERSEN CORPORATION
37720 Amrhein Rd (48150-1012)
PHONE.................................734 237-1052
Rob Mannooch, *Branch Mgr*
EMP: 5
SALES (corp-wide): 1.7B **Privately Held**
WEB: www.andersenwindows.com
SIC: 2431 Windows, wood; doors, wood
PA: Andersen Corporation
100 4th Ave N
Bayport MN 55003
651 264-5150

(G-10120)
ANTONIOS LEATHER EXPERTS
12409 Stark Rd (48150-1552)
PHONE.................................734 762-5000
Lea Antonios, *Principal*
EMP: 7 **EST:** 2010
SALES (est): 596.3K **Privately Held**
WEB: www.antoniosrepair.com
SIC: 2819 Tanning agents, synthetic inorganic

(G-10121)
AP IMPRESSIONS INC (PA)
Also Called: Personal Tuch By AP Imprssions
17360 N Laurel Park Dr (48152-3916)
PHONE.................................734 464-8009
Paul Ahn, *President*
EMP: 5 **EST:** 1991
SQ FT: 700
SALES (est): 779.6K **Privately Held**
WEB: www.promousa.com
SIC: 2759 5199 2791 2752 Screen printing; general merchandise, non-durable; typesetting; commercial printing, lithographic; automotive & apparel trimmings; pleating & stitching

(G-10122)
APPLIED PROCESS INC (HQ)
Also Called: AP Southridge
12202 Newburgh Rd (48150-1046)
PHONE.................................734 464-8000
Harold Karp, *CEO*
Holly Capehart, *General Mgr*
John Wagner, *Vice Pres*
Gary Flick, *Plant Mgr*
Bob Prusky, *Plant Mgr*
▲ **EMP:** 38 **EST:** 1984
SQ FT: 49,900
SALES (est): 7.2MM **Privately Held**
WEB: www.appliedprocess.com
SIC: 3398 Metal heat treating

(G-10123)
ARGENT LIMITED
11966 Brookfield St (48150-1736)
PHONE.................................734 427-5533
EMP: 7 **EST:** 1977
SQ FT: 15,000
SALES (est): 1.3MM **Privately Held**
SIC: 2992 Mfg Lubricating Oils/Greases

Livonia - Wayne County (G-10124)

(G-10124)
ARGENT TAPE & LABEL INC
37770 Amrhein Rd (48150-1014)
PHONE....................248 588-4600
Joseph Berkowski, *CFO*
EMP: 14 **EST:** 2019
SALES (est): 506.7K **Privately Held**
WEB: www.argent-label.com
SIC: 2759 Labels & seals: printing

(G-10125)
ASAO LLC
Also Called: American Shortening and Oil Co
34115 Industrial Rd (48150-1305)
PHONE....................734 522-6333
Anthony Gavol, *President*
William W Brown, *President*
Ron Manni, *Buyer*
Vivian Brown, *Treasurer*
EMP: 10 **EST:** 1936
SALES (est): 1.4MM **Privately Held**
WEB: www.americanspecialtyoils.com
SIC: 2079 2077 5145 Shortening & other solid edible fats; animal & marine fats & oils; confectionery

(G-10126)
ATEQ CORPORATION (HQ)
Also Called: Ateq Leak Detecting Service
35980 Industrial Rd (48150-1274)
PHONE....................734 838-3100
Guy Dewailly, *President*
George Cherian, *General Mgr*
Brandon Pilon, *Sales Staff*
Heidi Franklin, *Marketing Mgr*
James Burch, *Manager*
▲ **EMP:** 9 **EST:** 1989
SQ FT: 5,200
SALES (est): 10.4MM
SALES (corp-wide): 35.3MM **Privately Held**
WEB: www.atequsa.com
SIC: 3829 Measuring & controlling devices
PA: Ateq
  Zone Industrielle Des Dames
  Les Clayes Sous Bois 78340
  130 801-020

(G-10127)
ATEQ TPMS TOOLS LC
35990 Industrial Rd (48150-1274)
PHONE....................734 838-3104
Guy Dewailly, *President*
Jim Burch, *Sales Mgr*
Carl Hardt, *Sales Engr*
Zak McGraw, *Sales Engr*
Kyle Krist, *Manager*
EMP: 15 **EST:** 2013
SALES (est): 7MM
SALES (corp-wide): 35.3MM **Privately Held**
WEB: www.ateq-tpms.com
SIC: 3823 Pressure measurement instruments, industrial
HQ: Ateq Corporation
  35980 Industrial Rd
  Livonia MI 48150

(G-10128)
ATMORE INDUSTRIES INC
12887 Fairlane St (48150-1328)
PHONE....................734 455-7655
Timothy Yarnell, *Manager*
EMP: 6 **EST:** 2012
SALES (est): 263.4K **Privately Held**
WEB: www.flotecinc.com
SIC: 3999 Manufacturing industries

(G-10129)
ATS ASSEMBLY AND TEST INC
Assembly Technology & Test
12841 Stark Rd (48150-1525)
PHONE....................734 266-4713
Robert Cerant, *Project Mgr*
Paul Chamberlain, *Engineer*
Mark Hodges, *Engineer*
James Lahaie, *Engineer*
John Paulsen, *Engineer*
EMP: 13
SQ FT: 90,000
SALES (corp-wide): 1B **Privately Held**
WEB: www.atsautomation.com
SIC: 8711 3549 3829 3536 Designing: ship, boat, machine & product; metalworking machinery; measuring & controlling devices; hoists, cranes & monorails
HQ: Ats Assembly And Test, Inc.
  1 Ats Dr
  Wixom MI 48393
  937 222-3030

(G-10130)
AZORE SOFTWARE LLC
12190 Hubbard St (48150-1737)
PHONE....................734 525-0300
Robert Mudry, *President*
Andrew Banka, *Vice Pres*
EMP: 25 **EST:** 2017
SALES (est): 1MM **Privately Held**
WEB: www.azorecfd.com
SIC: 7372 Prepackaged software

(G-10131)
BASF CORPORATION
B A S F Colors & Colorants
13000 Levan Rd (48150-1228)
PHONE....................734 591-5560
Frank Pizzo, *General Mgr*
Pirro Cipi, *Engineer*
Bill Depompolo, *Branch Mgr*
Kristen Hall, *Manager*
Karen Hatch, *Manager*
EMP: 4
SQ FT: 20,000
SALES (corp-wide): 69.9B **Privately Held**
WEB: www.basf.com
SIC: 2869 2899 2821 Industrial organic chemicals; chemical preparations; plastics materials & resins
HQ: Basf Corporation
  100 Park Ave
  Florham Park NJ 07932
  859 577-5797

(G-10132)
BEACON BILLBOARDS LLC
11030 Brookfield St (48150-5709)
PHONE....................734 421-7512
Margaret Warren, *Owner*
EMP: 4 **EST:** 2004
SALES (est): 62.9K **Privately Held**
WEB: www.brasscity.com
SIC: 2711 Newspapers

(G-10133)
BEAVER AEROSPACE & DEFENSE INC (HQ)
11850 Mayfield St (48150-1708)
PHONE....................734 853-5003
Frederick Gagne, *President*
Stephane Arsenault, *Principal*
Gilles Labbe, *Vice Pres*
William Michalski, *Vice Pres*
Bill Neaton, *Production*
◆ **EMP:** 105 **EST:** 1952
SQ FT: 82,200
SALES (est): 30MM
SALES (corp-wide): 461.5MM **Privately Held**
WEB: www.herouxdevtek.com
SIC: 3452 3593 3812 3728 Screws, metal; fluid power cylinders & actuators; acceleration indicators & systems components, aerospace; gears, aircraft power transmission; aircraft maintenance & repair services
PA: Heroux-Devtek Inc
  1111 Rue Saint-Charles O Bureau 600
  Longueuil QC J4K 5
  450 679-5450

(G-10134)
BECK & BOYS CUSTOM APPAREL
33650 5 Mile Rd (48154-2866)
PHONE....................734 458-4015
Kitty Beck, *President*
EMP: 5 **EST:** 2002
SALES (est): 579.3K **Privately Held**
SIC: 2395 Embroidery products, except schiffli machine

(G-10135)
BEEBE FUEL SYSTEMS
13191 Wayne Rd (48150-1266)
PHONE....................734 261-3500
Dale Belsley, *Principal*
EMP: 7 **EST:** 2011
SALES (est): 142.4K **Privately Held**
SIC: 2899 Fuel tank or engine cleaning chemicals

(G-10136)
BELL AND HOWELL LLC
Also Called: Sensible Technologies
12794 Currie Ct (48150-1109)
PHONE....................734 421-1727
EMP: 4
SALES (est): 1.4B **Privately Held**
SIC: 7372 Prepackaged Software Services
HQ: Bell And Howell, Llc
  3791 S Alston Ave
  Durham NC 27713

(G-10137)
BIANCO INC
9805 Fairfield St (48150-2774)
P.O. Box 511234 (48151-7234)
PHONE....................313 682-2612
EMP: 4 **EST:** 2016
SALES (est): 101.5K **Privately Held**
SIC: 3172 Personal leather goods

(G-10138)
BODYCOTE THERMAL PROC INC
31889 Industrial Rd (48150-1821)
PHONE....................734 623-3436
Bryan Ames, *Branch Mgr*
EMP: 6
SALES (corp-wide): 795.2MM **Privately Held**
WEB: www.bodycote.com
SIC: 3398 4225 Brazing (hardening) of metal; general warehousing & storage
HQ: Bodycote Thermal Processing, Inc.
  12750 Merit Dr Ste 1400
  Dallas TX 75251
  214 904-2420

(G-10139)
BODYCOTE THERMAL PROC INC
31888 Glendale St (48150-1827)
PHONE....................734 427-6814
Biji George, *Manager*
EMP: 10
SALES (corp-wide): 795.2MM **Privately Held**
WEB: www.bodycote.com
SIC: 3398 Metal heat treating
HQ: Bodycote Thermal Processing, Inc.
  12750 Merit Dr Ste 1400
  Dallas TX 75251
  214 904-2420

(G-10140)
BORGWARNER POWDERED METALS INC (PA)
32059 Schoolcraft Rd (48150-1833)
PHONE....................734 261-5322
Timothy M Manganello, *CEO*
Art Barrows, *Vice Pres*
Dave Hall, *Vice Pres*
Vittal RAO, *Engineer*
Joanne Adamus, *Accounting Mgr*
EMP: 137 **EST:** 1987
SQ FT: 65,000
SALES (est): 26.8MM **Privately Held**
WEB: www.borgwarner.com
SIC: 3714 3568 3463 3462 Motor vehicle transmissions, drive assemblies & parts; power transmission equipment; nonferrous forgings; iron & steel forgings

(G-10141)
BOWER TOOL & MANUFACTURING INC
27481 Schoolcraft Rd (48150-2201)
PHONE....................734 522-0444
Lois Bower, *President*
Robbie Bower, *Corp Secy*
William Bower, *Vice Pres*
EMP: 4 **EST:** 1984
SQ FT: 4,000
SALES (est): 450.7K **Privately Held**
WEB: www.bowertool.com
SIC: 3545 Gauges (machine tool accessories)

(G-10142)
BUCKINGHAM TOOL CORP
11915 Market St (48150-1163)
PHONE....................734 591-2333
Matt Dixon, *President*
Robin Dixon, *Treasurer*
EMP: 30 **EST:** 1941
SQ FT: 10,000
SALES (est): 2.2MM **Privately Held**
WEB: www.buckinghamtool.com
SIC: 3544 Special dies & tools

(G-10143)
C E S INDUSTRIES INC
12751 Inkster Rd (48150-2216)
PHONE....................734 425-0522
Charles E Strong, *President*
Frances Strong, *Vice Pres*
EMP: 10 **EST:** 1965
SQ FT: 6,000
SALES (est): 180.1K **Privately Held**
SIC: 3599 Machine shop, jobbing & repair

(G-10144)
CAPRICE BRANDS LLC
31183 Schoolcraft Rd (48150-2027)
PHONE....................989 745-1286
Janelle Powers, *Manager*
EMP: 4 **EST:** 2014
SALES (est): 195.4K **Privately Held**
SIC: 5182 2084 Wine & distilled beverages; wine coolers (beverages)

(G-10145)
CARBOLINE COMPANY
32820 Capitol St (48150-1706)
PHONE....................734 525-2824
Richard Preston, *Branch Mgr*
EMP: 4
SALES (corp-wide): 6.1B **Publicly Held**
WEB: www.carboline.com
SIC: 2851 Lacquers, varnishes, enamels & other coatings
HQ: Carboline Company
  2150 Schuetz Rd Fl 1
  Saint Louis MO 63146
  314 644-1000

(G-10146)
CARBON TOOL & MANUFACTURING
12735 Inkster Rd (48150-2216)
PHONE....................734 422-0380
Daniel Kochanek, *President*
EMP: 27 **EST:** 1974
SQ FT: 6,000
SALES (est): 629.3K **Privately Held**
SIC: 3599 Machine shop, jobbing & repair

(G-10147)
CARLSON TECHNOLOGY INC
Also Called: Pitstop Engineering
30945 8 Mile Rd (48152-1605)
PHONE....................248 476-0013
Dennis Carlson, *President*
EMP: 4 **EST:** 1978
SQ FT: 1,000
SALES (est): 372K **Privately Held**
WEB: www.jessicanoel.com
SIC: 8731 3842 Medical research, commercial; respiratory protection equipment, personal

(G-10148)
CASE TOOL INC
12589 Farmington Rd (48150-1700)
PHONE....................734 261-2227
Michael Quigley, *President*
EMP: 5 **EST:** 1994
SQ FT: 2,000 **Privately Held**
WEB: www.casetoolinc.com
SIC: 3694 5013 Ignition coils, automotive; automotive supplies & parts

(G-10149)
CDP DIAMOND PRODUCTS INC
Also Called: Construction Diamond Products
11919 Globe St (48150-1133)
P.O. Box 51727 (48151-5727)
PHONE....................734 591-1041
James Dillon, *Vice Pres*
Jim Dillon, *Vice Pres*
Robb Capeling, *Engineer*
Craig Campbell, *Sales Mgr*
John Oconnell, *Sales Staff*
EMP: 22 **EST:** 1962
SQ FT: 14,020
SALES (est): 3.4MM **Privately Held**
WEB: www.cdpdiamond.com
SIC: 3545 3291 Machine tool accessories; abrasive products

GEOGRAPHIC SECTION
Livonia - Wayne County (G-10178)

(G-10150)
CELANO PRECISION MFG INC
30016 Richland St (48150-3051)
P.O. Box 51448 (48151-5448)
PHONE.................................734 748-1744
Peter Celano, *President*
Cindy Celano, *Vice Pres*
EMP: 4 EST: 1987
SALES (est): 283.7K Privately Held
WEB: www.theveryfew.net
SIC: 3599 Machine shop, jobbing & repair

(G-10151)
CENTRAL ADMXTURE PHRM SVCS INC
Also Called: C A P S
37497 Schoolcraft Rd (48150-1007)
PHONE.................................734 953-6760
Lisa Sigal, *Controller*
Thomas Verdin, *Pharmacist*
John Winter, *Pharmacist*
Glenn Pangrazzi, *Manager*
Margaret Byrd, *Manager*
EMP: 7
SALES (corp-wide): 2.6MM Privately Held
WEB: www.capspharmacy.com
SIC: 2834 5122 Pharmaceutical preparations; pharmaceuticals
HQ: Central Admixture Pharmacy Services, Inc.
6430 Oak Cyn Ste 200
Irvine CA 92618

(G-10152)
CENTURY INSTRUMENT COMPANY
11865 Mayfield St (48150-1707)
PHONE.................................734 427-0340
Azeir O Sigurdsson, *President*
Asgeir Sigurdsson, *General Mgr*
Roger Bingham, *Principal*
Franklin Nau, *Principal*
Oscar Sigurdsson, *Human Res Dir*
▲ EMP: 29 EST: 1950
SQ FT: 19,000
SALES (est): 4.2MM Privately Held
WEB: www.centuryinstrument.com
SIC: 3491 3822 Pressure valves & regulators, industrial; temperature controls, automatic

(G-10153)
CENTURY TRUSS
17199 N Laurel Park Dr # 402 (48152-7905)
PHONE.................................248 486-4000
Ronald Bergeron, *Principal*
EMP: 6 EST: 2010
SALES (est): 88K Privately Held
SIC: 2439 Trusses, wooden roof

(G-10154)
CF COMPONENTS INC
16231 Nola Dr (48154-1206)
PHONE.................................248 670-2974
Fred Hendershot, *Vice Pres*
EMP: 6 EST: 2011
SALES (est): 73.3K Privately Held
SIC: 3519 Parts & accessories, internal combustion engines

(G-10155)
CHEAP ELECTRIC CONTRACTORS CO
16999 S Laurel Park Dr (48154-1121)
PHONE.................................734 452-1964
EMP: 4 EST: 2016
SALES (est): 93.7K Privately Held
SIC: 5082 3699 General construction machinery & equipment; electrical equipment & supplies

(G-10156)
CHEESECAKE AND ECETERA LLC
Also Called: Cheesecake Ecetera
12335 Stark Rd (48150-1544)
PHONE.................................734 335-8757
Michael L Bradford, *Principal*
EMP: 4 EST: 2014
SALES (est): 74.4K Privately Held
SIC: 2099 Food preparations

(G-10157)
CHICAGO TRIBUNE COMPANY LLC
19500 Victor Pkwy Ste 100 (48152-7012)
PHONE.................................734 464-6500
Mark Barrons, *Sales/Mktg Mgr*
EMP: 5
SALES (corp-wide): 746.2MM Privately Held
WEB: www.chicagotribune.com
SIC: 2711 Newspapers, publishing & printing
HQ: Chicago Tribune Company, Llc
160 N Stetson Ave
Chicago IL 60601
312 222-3232

(G-10158)
CJG LLC
Also Called: Golden Refrigerant
31800 Industrial Rd (48150-1820)
PHONE.................................734 793-1400
Carl Grolle, *Mng Member*
EMP: 19 EST: 1995
SQ FT: 101,000
SALES (est): 6.1MM Privately Held
WEB: www.goldenrefrigerant.com
SIC: 2869 1799 Freon; antenna installation

(G-10159)
CLASSIC CONTAINER CORPORATION
32432 Capitol St (48150-1703)
PHONE.................................734 853-3000
Craig Beaudoin, *General Mgr*
EMP: 125 EST: 1975
SQ FT: 75,000
SALES (est): 3.1MM Privately Held
WEB: www.prattindustries.com
SIC: 3086 2653 2675 2671 Packaging & shipping materials, foamed plastic; corrugated & solid fiber boxes; die-cut paper & board; packaging paper & plastics film, coated & laminated; paperboard mills; wood containers
PA: Pratt Industries, Inc.
1800 Sarasot Bus Pkwy Ne S
Conyers GA 30013

(G-10160)
COGSDILL TOOL PRODUCTS INC
Also Called: E-Z Burr Tool
11757 Globe St (48150-1133)
P.O. Box 7007, Camden SC (29021-7007)
PHONE.................................734 744-4500
EMP: 9
SALES (corp-wide): 9.5MM Privately Held
WEB: www.cogsdill.com
SIC: 3599 Machine shop, jobbing & repair
PA: Cogsdill Tool Products, Inc.
1001 Guion Dr
Lugoff SC 29078
803 438-4000

(G-10161)
COMPLETE SERVICES LLC
32401 8 Mile Rd (48152-1301)
PHONE.................................248 470-8247
Johnny R Thompson, *Administration*
EMP: 10 EST: 2015
SALES (est): 417.9K Privately Held
SIC: 8742 8331 2731 2741 Management consulting services; job training & vocational rehabilitation services; book publishing; miscellaneous publishing; language school

(G-10162)
CONTINENTAL MIDLAND LLC
33200 Capitol St (48150-1745)
PHONE.................................734 367-7032
Michael Delfin, *VP Sales*
EMP: 4 EST: 2017
SALES (est): 97.2K Privately Held
SIC: 3599 Machine shop, jobbing & repair

(G-10163)
CONTOUR MACHINING INC
11837 Brookfield St (48150-1701)
PHONE.................................734 525-4877
Frank Schlampp, *President*
EMP: 10 EST: 1991
SQ FT: 4,000
SALES (est): 979.1K Privately Held
WEB: www.cmi-cnc.com
SIC: 3599 Machine shop, jobbing & repair

(G-10164)
COOPER-STANDARD AUTOMOTIVE INC
11820 Globe St (48150-1171)
P.O. Box 8034, Novi (48376-8034)
PHONE.................................734 542-6300
Karl Deline, *Manager*
EMP: 93
SALES (corp-wide): 2.3B Publicly Held
WEB: www.cooperstandard.com
SIC: 3714 Motor vehicle parts & accessories
HQ: Cooper-Standard Automotive Inc.
40300 Traditions Dr
Northville MI 48168
248 596-5900

(G-10165)
CORE ENERGY AND AUTOMATION LLC
35245 Schoolcraft Rd (48150-1209)
PHONE.................................248 830-0476
EMP: 4 EST: 2016
SALES (est): 118.1K Privately Held
SIC: 3822 Auto controls regulating residntl & coml environmt & applncs

(G-10166)
CORELED SYSTEMS LLC
31478 Industrial Rd # 400 (48150-1839)
PHONE.................................734 516-2060
Derek Mallory, *Partner*
Cynthia M Mallory, *Manager*
EMP: 4 EST: 2003
SALES (est): 755.8K Privately Held
WEB: www.coreled.com
SIC: 3648 Lighting equipment

(G-10167)
CORRUGATED PRATT
32432 Capitol St (48150-1703)
PHONE.................................734 853-3030
Brian McPheely, *CEO*
EMP: 27 EST: 2010
SALES (est): 1MM Privately Held
WEB: www.prattindustries.com
SIC: 2653 Boxes, corrugated: made from purchased materials

(G-10168)
CREATIVE AUTOMATION SOLUTIONS
34552 Dover Ave (48150-3659)
PHONE.................................313 790-4848
Ahmad Khreis, *Owner*
EMP: 6 EST: 2012
SALES (est): 155K Privately Held
WEB: www.cautomation.com
SIC: 3711 Automobile assembly, including specialty automobiles

(G-10169)
CROWNE GROUP LLC
17199 N Laurel Park Dr # 322 (48152-2679)
PHONE.................................734 855-4512
EMP: 4 EST: 2008
SALES (est): 391.7K Privately Held
SIC: 3714 Motor vehicle parts & accessories

(G-10170)
CURBELL PLASTICS INC
28455 Schoolcraft Rd # 5 (48150-2238)
PHONE.................................734 513-0531
Tim Cassani, *Manager*
EMP: 8
SALES (corp-wide): 245.7MM Privately Held
WEB: www.curbellplastics.com
SIC: 5162 3669 3842 Plastics products; plastics sheets & rods; plastics materials; plastics film; intercommunication systems, electric; surgical appliances & supplies
HQ: Curbell Plastics, Inc.
7 Cobham Dr
Orchard Park NY 14127

(G-10171)
CUSTOM METAL PRODUCTS CORP
12283 Levan Rd (48150-1499)
PHONE.................................734 591-2500
James C Veale, *President*
Charles W Veale, *Vice Pres*
EMP: 7 EST: 1945
SQ FT: 10,000
SALES (est): 840.6K Privately Held
WEB: www.custommetalcorp.com
SIC: 3441 Fabricated structural metal

(G-10172)
CUTEX INC
12496 Globe St (48150-1144)
PHONE.................................734 953-8908
Boguslaw Gierek, *President*
EMP: 6 EST: 1989
SQ FT: 5,600
SALES (est): 926.7K Privately Held
SIC: 3541 Machine tools, metal cutting type

(G-10173)
D MAC INDUSTRIES INC
31492 Glendale St (48150-1834)
PHONE.................................734 536-7754
Dennis Macdonald, *President*
EMP: 10 EST: 2004
SALES (est): 1.2MM Privately Held
SIC: 3463 Automotive forgings, nonferrous

(G-10174)
DAY INTERNATIONAL INC (DH)
17177 N Laurel Park Dr # 30 (48152-2693)
PHONE.................................734 781-4600
William C Ferguson, *Ch of Bd*
Dennis R Wolters, *President*
Dwaine R Brooks, *Vice Pres*
David B Freimuth, *Vice Pres*
Thomas J Koenig, *Vice Pres*
◆ EMP: 30 EST: 1938
SALES (est): 215.3MM
SALES (corp-wide): 53.5B Publicly Held
WEB: www.flintgrp.com
SIC: 3069 Printers' rolls & blankets: rubber or rubberized fabric
HQ: Flint Group Us Llc
17177 N Laurel Park Dr # 30
Livonia MI 48152
734 781-4600

(G-10175)
DB COMMUNICATIONS INC
32922 Brookside Cir (48152-1419)
PHONE.................................800 692-8200
EMP: 11
SQ FT: 2,500
SALES (est): 2MM Privately Held
SIC: 3661 Mfg Telephone/Telegraph Apparatus

(G-10176)
DEARBORN LITHOGRAPH INC
12380 Globe St (48150-1181)
PHONE.................................734 464-4242
Russell Masura, *President*
Judith Masura, *Vice Pres*
EMP: 21 EST: 1948
SQ FT: 17,250
SALES (est): 2.4MM Privately Held
WEB: www.dearbornlithograph.com
SIC: 2752 2796 Commercial printing, offset; platemaking services

(G-10177)
DEBURRING COMPANY
12690 Newburgh Rd (48150-1002)
PHONE.................................734 542-9800
Robert E Van Schoick Jr, *President*
EMP: 20 EST: 1988
SQ FT: 13,000
SALES (est): 1.1MM Privately Held
WEB: www.deburringcompany.com
SIC: 3471 Finishing, metals or formed products

(G-10178)
DELTA 6 LLC
Also Called: Delta Six
20341 Parker St (48152-1363)
PHONE.................................248 778-6414
Nabil Nouman, *Principal*
EMP: 4 EST: 2014

Livonia - Wayne County (G-10179) GEOGRAPHIC SECTION

SALES (est): 154.7K **Privately Held**
WEB: www.trackkbattle.org
SIC: 3949 7389 Camping equipment & supplies; business services

(G-10179)
DELTA GEAR INC
36251 Schoolcraft Rd (48150-1216)
PHONE.................................734 525-8000
Robert Sakuta, *President*
Bryan Barlow, *Vice Pres*
Chris Holmes, *Purch Dir*
Bill Novak, *Purchasing*
Lana Reed, *Office Mgr*
▲ **EMP:** 37 **EST:** 2004
SQ FT: 20,000
SALES (est): 9.7MM **Privately Held**
WEB: www.delrecorp.com
SIC: 3714 Motor vehicle parts & accessories

(G-10180)
DELTA RESEARCH CORPORATION
32971 Capitol St (48150-1705)
PHONE.................................734 261-6400
Robert Sakuta, *President*
Bob Sakuta, *President*
Tony Werschky, *Partner*
Don McHugh, *Vice Pres*
Ken McConnell, *Program Mgr*
▲ **EMP:** 50 **EST:** 1952
SQ FT: 43,000
SALES (est): 12.2MM **Privately Held**
WEB: www.delrecorp.com
SIC: 3714 Motor vehicle parts & accessories

(G-10181)
DESHLER GROUP INC (PA)
34450 Industrial Rd (48150-1308)
PHONE.................................734 525-9100
Robert Gruschow, *President*
Mark Brodie, *Vice Pres*
Wilbur Darst, *Vice Pres*
Gerald A Gentile, *Vice Pres*
Gerald Gentile, *Vice Pres*
EMP: 150 **EST:** 1968
SQ FT: 100,000
SALES (est): 109.1MM **Privately Held**
WEB: www.deshlergroup.com
SIC: 3496 3599 Miscellaneous fabricated wire products; custom machinery

(G-10182)
DETROIT CLB PRTG HSE CRAFTSMEN
9820 Seltzer St (48150-3252)
PHONE.................................734 953-9729
Eric Westberg, *President*
EMP: 4 **EST:** 2017
SALES (est): 64.1K **Privately Held**
SIC: 2752 Commercial printing, lithographic

(G-10183)
DETROIT QULTY BRUSH MFG CO INC
Also Called: Dqb Industries
32165 Schoolcraft Rd (48150-1833)
PHONE.................................734 525-5660
Donald Weinbaum, *President*
Wim Demees, *Safety Mgr*
Lisa Sprow, *Admin Asst*
▲ **EMP:** 81 **EST:** 1919
SQ FT: 100,000
SALES (est): 9.1MM **Privately Held**
SIC: 3991 Brushes, household or industrial; push brooms

(G-10184)
DIAMOND AUTOMATION LTD
32235 Industrial Rd (48150-1836)
PHONE.................................734 838-7138
Jeffrey Bucher, *President*
Andrew Sieczka, *Vice Pres*
◆ **EMP:** 4 **EST:** 1979
SQ FT: 62,000
SALES (est): 400K **Privately Held**
WEB: www.diamondautomation.net
SIC: 3549 3535 Assembly machines, including robotic; conveyors & conveying equipment

(G-10185)
DIGITAL DIE SOLUTIONS INC
13281 Merriman Rd (48150-1815)
PHONE.................................734 542-2222
Frank Barkman, *Director*
EMP: 12 **EST:** 2009
SALES (est): 700K **Privately Held**
SIC: 3542 Die casting & extruding machines

(G-10186)
DIPSOL OF AMERICA INC
Also Called: Dipsol Chemicals
34005 Schoolcraft Rd (48150-1313)
PHONE.................................734 367-0530
Cara Mahlawi, *President*
Harry Willingmyre, *Sales Dir*
Jamie Flesch, *Marketing Staff*
Steven Kokotovich, *Technician*
▲ **EMP:** 26 **EST:** 1987
SQ FT: 26,000
SALES (est): 7.5MM **Privately Held**
WEB: www.dipsolamerica.com
SIC: 3559 8711 Metal finishing equipment for plating, etc.; pollution control engineering
HQ: Dipsol Chemicals Co., Ltd.
  2-7-12, Yaesu
  Chuo-Ku TKY 104-0

(G-10187)
DON DUFF REBUILDING
31130 Industrial Rd (48150-2034)
PHONE.................................734 522-7700
▲ **EMP:** 5
SQ FT: 8,000
SALES (est): 665K **Privately Held**
SIC: 3694 Mfg Engine Electrical Equipment

(G-10188)
E & R BINDERY SERVICE INC
Also Called: Ink On Paper Printing
37477 Schoolcraft Rd (48150-1007)
PHONE.................................734 464-7954
Howard V Bolitho, *President*
Daniel Flavian, *Corp Secy*
Raymond Connell, *Vice Pres*
EMP: 5 **EST:** 1984
SQ FT: 2,700
SALES (est): 300K **Privately Held**
SIC: 2752 Commercial printing, offset

(G-10189)
EATON STEEL CORPORATION
Also Called: Hercules Drawn Steel Div
38901 Amrhein Rd (48150-1042)
PHONE.................................248 398-3434
Dan Fox, *Purch Mgr*
Hayley Quist, *Purch Agent*
Amanda Bryant, *Sales Staff*
Edgar Cruz, *Sales Staff*
Damien Junkulis, *Sales Staff*
EMP: 75
SALES (corp-wide): 88.9MM **Privately Held**
WEB: www.eatonsteel.com
SIC: 5051 3312 Structural shapes, iron or steel; bars & bar shapes, steel, cold-finished: own hot-rolled
PA: Eaton Steel Corporation
  10221 Capital St
  Oak Park MI 48237
  248 398-3434

(G-10190)
ECLIPSE PRINT EMPORIUM INC
32753 8 Mile Rd (48152-1302)
PHONE.................................248 477-8337
Domingo Nieto, *President*
EMP: 4 **EST:** 1984
SALES (est): 421.5K **Privately Held**
WEB: www.eclipsedetroit.com
SIC: 2759 5199 Screen printing; advertising specialties

(G-10191)
EIGHT MILE SIGNS
30845 8 Mile Rd (48152-1600)
PHONE.................................248 762-3889
Daniella Riccardi, *Principal*
EMP: 4 **EST:** 2018
SALES (est): 257.8K **Privately Held**
WEB: www.eightmilesigns.com
SIC: 3993 Signs & advertising specialties

(G-10192)
EIS INC
Also Called: Egeler Industrial Services
31478 Industrial Rd # 100 (48150-1839)
PHONE.................................734 266-6500
Timothy A Westerdale, *President*
P Vernon Links, *Vice Pres*
Zona Faye Davis, *Treasurer*
EMP: 9 **EST:** 1976
SQ FT: 10,000
SALES (est): 258.4K **Privately Held**
SIC: 1381 Drilling oil & gas wells

(G-10193)
ELECTRODYNAMICS INC
31091 Schoolcraft Rd (48150-2029)
PHONE.................................734 422-5420
Andy Low, *President*
▲ **EMP:** 5 **EST:** 1991
SQ FT: 1,700
SALES (est): 611.5K **Privately Held**
WEB: www.electrodynam.com
SIC: 3694 7389 3825 Battery charging generators, automobile & aircraft; design, commercial & industrial; battery testers, electrical

(G-10194)
ELECTRONIC DESIGN & PACKG CO
Also Called: EDP Company
36704 Commerce St (48150-1164)
PHONE.................................734 591-9176
Richard Bezerko, *President*
Margaret M Bezerko, *Vice Pres*
EMP: 18 **EST:** 1979
SQ FT: 19,000
SALES (est): 3.7MM **Privately Held**
WEB: www.edpcompany.com
SIC: 3812 3699 Detection apparatus: electronic/magnetic field, light/heat; electrical equipment & supplies

(G-10195)
ELITE METAL MANUFACTURING LLC
32473 Schoolcraft Rd (48150-4300)
PHONE.................................734 718-0061
EMP: 4 **EST:** 2016
SALES (est): 43.6K **Privately Held**
SIC: 3999 Manufacturing industries

(G-10196)
ELSIE INC
Also Called: Blind Xpress
12752 Stark Rd Ste 1 (48150-1594)
PHONE.................................734 421-8844
Lawrence Carollo, *President*
EMP: 20 **EST:** 1987
SQ FT: 23,000
SALES (est): 3.8MM **Privately Held**
SIC: 5023 2591 Venetian blinds; venetian blinds

(G-10197)
END GRAIN WOODWORK
32819 W Chicago St (48150-3786)
PHONE.................................248 420-3228
Sam Constantine, *Principal*
EMP: 5 **EST:** 2013
SALES (est): 99.4K **Privately Held**
SIC: 2431 Millwork

(G-10198)
EPI PRINTERS INC
13305 Wayne Rd (48150-1245)
PHONE.................................734 261-9400
Patrick Kolodziejczak, *Vice Pres*
Pat Kolodziejczak, *Manager*
EMP: 55
SQ FT: 30,000
SALES (corp-wide): 160.6MM **Privately Held**
WEB: www.epiinc.com
SIC: 2752 3993 2759 2732 Advertising posters, lithographed; periodicals, lithographed; signs & advertising specialties; commercial printing; book printing
PA: Epi Printers, Inc.
  5404 Wayne Rd
  Battle Creek MI 49037
  800 562-9733

(G-10199)
ERICH JAEGER USA INC
17199 N Laurel Park Dr # 10 (48152-2683)
PHONE.................................734 404-5940
Terri Miller, *President*
EMP: 6 **EST:** 2012
SALES (est): 2MM
SALES (corp-wide): 174.5MM **Privately Held**
WEB: www.erich-jaeger.com
SIC: 5531 5013 3799 3643 Trailer hitches, automotive; trailer parts & accessories; trailers & trailer equipment; electric connectors; harness or harness parts
HQ: Erich Jaeger Gmbh + Co.Kg
  StraBheimerstr. 10
  Friedberg (Hessen) HE 61169
  603 179-40

(G-10200)
EXCEL GRAPHICS
31647 8 Mile Rd (48152-4217)
PHONE.................................248 442-9390
Ruth Dober, *Owner*
EMP: 4 **EST:** 1990
SQ FT: 2,400
SALES (est): 250K **Privately Held**
WEB: www.excelgraphics.biz
SIC: 2752 Commercial printing, offset; publication printing, lithographic

(G-10201)
EXCLUSIVE BRANDS LLC
Also Called: Exclusive Provisioning Center
38701 7 Mile Rd Ste 160 (48152-3968)
PHONE.................................734 210-0107
Aram Freij,
EMP: 13 **EST:** 2018
SALES (est): 607.2K **Privately Held**
SIC: 5993 3999 0139 5159 ; ; ;

(G-10202)
F & G TOOL COMPANY
11863 Brookfield St (48150-1701)
PHONE.................................734 261-0022
Finn Gammerath, *President*
Rick Henegar, *Admin Sec*
EMP: 9 **EST:** 1985
SQ FT: 6,000
SALES (est): 871.8K **Privately Held**
SIC: 3599 Machine shop, jobbing & repair

(G-10203)
FABULOUS PRINTING INC
15076 Middlebelt Rd (48154-4033)
PHONE.................................734 422-5555
Kevin Solomon, *President*
EMP: 5 **EST:** 2013
SALES (est): 382.4K **Privately Held**
WEB: www.fabulousprintinginc.com
SIC: 2752 Commercial printing, offset

(G-10204)
FAIRFIELD INVESTMENT CO
Also Called: Lazer Images
32738 Barkley St (48154-3517)
PHONE.................................734 427-4141
David D Berger, *President*
▲ **EMP:** 4 **EST:** 1984
SQ FT: 1,900
SALES (est): 358.1K **Privately Held**
SIC: 3993 Letters for signs, metal

(G-10205)
FARMINGTON CABINET COMPANY
30795 8 Mile Rd (48152-1601)
PHONE.................................248 476-2666
Fax: 248 476-6438
EMP: 17
SQ FT: 11,500
SALES (est): 1.7MM **Privately Held**
SIC: 2434 5712 Mfg & Ret Of Wood Kitchen Cabinets

(G-10206)
FCA US LLC
37200 Amrhein Rd (48150-1108)
PHONE.................................734 422-0557
Joe Goulart, *Branch Mgr*
EMP: 20
SALES (corp-wide): 102.5B **Privately Held**
WEB: www.chrysler.com
SIC: 3711 Motor vehicles & car bodies

GEOGRAPHIC SECTION
Livonia - Wayne County (G-10231)

HQ: Fca Us Llc
1000 Chrysler Dr
Auburn Hills MI 48326

(G-10207)
FL TOOL HOLDERS LLC
36010 Industrial Rd (48150-1200)
PHONE....................734 591-0134
Edward Vella, *President*
EMP: 20 **EST:** 1965
SQ FT: 15,500
SALES (est): 7.9MM
SALES (corp-wide): 988.5K **Privately Held**
WEB: www.fltoolholders.com
SIC: 3545 Tool holders
HQ: Marposs Corporation
3300 Cross Creek Pkwy
Auburn Hills MI 48326
248 370-0404

(G-10208)
FLINT CPS INKS NORTH AMER LLC (DH)
Also Called: Flint Aic
17177 N Laurel Park Dr # 30 (48152-2693)
PHONE....................734 781-4600
Patti Cowart, *Sales Executive*
William B Miller,
Anila Ruseti,
Peter M Schreck,
EMP: 170 **EST:** 2018
SALES (est): 67.4MM
SALES (corp-wide): 53.5B **Publicly Held**
SIC: 2865 2893 Color pigments, organic; printing ink
HQ: Flint Group Packaging Inks North America Corporation
17177 N Laurel Park Dr # 30
Livonia MI 48152
734 781-4600

(G-10209)
FLINT GROUP PCKG INKS N AMER C (DH)
17177 N Laurel Park Dr # 30 (48152-2693)
PHONE....................734 781-4600
Pierre-Marie De Leener, *Chairman*
EMP: 178 **EST:** 2018
SALES (est): 67.4MM
SALES (corp-wide): 53.5B **Publicly Held**
WEB: www.flintgrp.com
SIC: 2396 Printing & embossing on plastics fabric articles
HQ: Flint Group Us Llc
17177 N Laurel Park Dr # 30
Livonia MI 48152
734 781-4600

(G-10210)
FLINT GROUP PCKG INKS N AMER H (PA)
17177 N Laurel Park Dr # 30 (48152-2693)
PHONE....................734 781-4600
Peter M Schreck,
EMP: 0 **EST:** 2018
SALES (est): 2.9MM **Privately Held**
SIC: 6719 2396 Investment holding companies, except banks; printing & embossing on plastics fabric articles

(G-10211)
FLINT GROUP US LLC (DH)
Also Called: Cdr Pigments & Dispersions
17177 N Laurel Park Dr # 30 (48152-2693)
PHONE....................734 781-4600
Michelle Domas, *Vice Pres*
William Bradley, *Transptn Dir*
Frank Gillette, *Site Mgr*
Julie Fulkerson, *Senior Buyer*
Mike Buystedt, *Sales Staff*
◆ **EMP:** 300 **EST:** 1920
SALES (est): 1.9B
SALES (corp-wide): 53.5B **Publicly Held**
WEB: www.flintgrp.com
SIC: 2865 2893 Color pigments, organic; printing ink
HQ: Flint Group Germany Gmbh
Sieglestr. 25
Stuttgart BW 70469
711 981-60

(G-10212)
FLINT INK RECEIVABLES CORP
17177 N Laurel Park Dr # 300 (48152-2693)
PHONE....................734 781-4600
EMP: 6 **EST:** 2006
SALES (est): 171K **Privately Held**
SIC: 2893 Printing ink

(G-10213)
FLUIR CREATIVE LLC
15223 Farmington Rd (48154-5411)
PHONE....................734 494-0308
Tmothy Steckel, *Principal*
EMP: 4 **EST:** 2015
SALES (est): 92.3K **Privately Held**
WEB: www.fluirphoto.com
SIC: 2752 Commercial printing, lithographic

(G-10214)
FORD MOTOR COMPANY
36200 Plymouth Rd (48150-1498)
PHONE....................734 523-3000
Emerson Camargo, *Mfg Staff*
Chris Strzyzewski, *Engineer*
Jesse WEI, *Engineer*
Ronald Hamlin, *Design Engr*
Robert L Adams, *Branch Mgr*
EMP: 14
SQ FT: 3,300,000
SALES (corp-wide): 127.1B **Publicly Held**
WEB: www.ford.com
SIC: 5511 3714 Automobiles, new & used; motor vehicle parts & accessories
PA: Ford Motor Company
1 American Rd
Dearborn MI 48126
313 322-3000

(G-10215)
FORD MOTOR COMPANY
11871 Middlebelt Rd (48150-2310)
PHONE....................734 523-3000
David Wine, *Engineer*
David McTague, *Branch Mgr*
William Mikkelsen, *Manager*
Cathy Radners, *Receptionist*
EMP: 14
SALES (corp-wide): 127.1B **Publicly Held**
WEB: www.ford.com
SIC: 5511 3713 3714 6153 Automobiles, new & used; truck & bus bodies; motor vehicle parts & accessories; financing of dealers by motor vehicle manufacturers organ.; financing: automobiles, furniture, etc., not a deposit bank; passenger car leasing
PA: Ford Motor Company
1 American Rd
Dearborn MI 48126
313 322-3000

(G-10216)
FORTY EIGHT FORTY SOLUTIONS
31750 Enterprise Dr (48150-1946)
PHONE....................713 332-6145
EMP: 15 **EST:** 2019
SALES (est): 375.8K **Privately Held**
SIC: 7372 Prepackaged software

(G-10217)
G M PARIS BAKERY INC
28418 Joy Rd (48150-4133)
PHONE....................734 425-2060
Daniel Domzalski, *President*
Michael Domzalski, *Vice Pres*
EMP: 6 **EST:** 1956
SQ FT: 3,200
SALES (est): 164.6K **Privately Held**
WEB: www.parisbakerylivonia.com
SIC: 5461 2051 Cakes; bread, cake & related products

(G-10218)
GAGS AND GAMES INC (DH)
Also Called: Man Store, The
35901 Veronica St (48150-1207)
PHONE....................734 591-1717
John Mc Intire, *Co-President*
Christopher Bearss, *Co-President*
▲ **EMP:** 35 **EST:** 1977
SQ FT: 34,400
SALES (est): 51.9MM
SALES (corp-wide): 1.8B **Publicly Held**
WEB: www.partycity.com
SIC: 2389 5947 Costumes; party favors
HQ: Party City Holdings Inc.
80 Grasslands Rd
Elmsford NY 10523
914 345-2020

(G-10219)
GALLAGHER FIRE EQUIPMENT CO
30895 8 Mile Rd (48150-1600)
PHONE....................248 477-1540
Alan Ross, *President*
Bebow Roger, *Exec VP*
EMP: 36 **EST:** 1992
SQ FT: 5,000
SALES (est): 6.9MM **Privately Held**
WEB: www.firedot.com
SIC: 7389 5999 7382 1711 Fire extinguisher servicing; fire protection service other than forestry or public; fire extinguishers; safety supplies & equipment; fire alarm maintenance & monitoring; fire sprinkler system installation; sprinkler systems, fire: automatic

(G-10220)
GASBARRE PRODUCTS INC
Also Called: Major Powdered Metal Tech
12953 Farmington Rd (48150-4202)
P.O. Box 1022, Du Bois PA (15801-1022)
PHONE....................734 425-5165
Thomas Gasbarre, *President*
EMP: 8
SQ FT: 15,000
SALES (corp-wide): 40MM **Privately Held**
WEB: www.gasbarre.com
SIC: 3542 Machine tools, metal forming type
PA: Gasbarre Products, Inc.
590 Division St
Du Bois PA 15801
814 371-3015

(G-10221)
GEISLER COMPANY
Also Called: Sherwood Enterprises
30295 Schoolcraft Rd (48150-2006)
PHONE....................313 255-1450
Norm Macritchie, *President*
Michael Nelson, *VP Opers*
Harrie Denboer, *VP Finance*
▲ **EMP:** 15
SQ FT: 20,000
SALES (est): 10.5MM **Privately Held**
WEB: www.geislerco.com
SIC: 3599 Machine shop, jobbing & repair

(G-10222)
GEOLEAN USA LLC
11998 Merriman Rd (48150-1919)
PHONE....................313 859-9780
Luman Temby, *President*
Tim Floyd, *Vice Pres*
Calvin Williams, *Opers Mgr*
Susi Cook, *Sales Engr*
EMP: 15 **EST:** 2016
SALES (est): 3.4MM **Privately Held**
WEB: www.geoleanusa.com
SIC: 8742 3599 Business consultant; custom machinery

(G-10223)
GIL-MAR MANUFACTURING CO
12841 Stark Rd (48150-1525)
PHONE....................734 422-1925
EMP: 7
SALES (corp-wide): 18.9MM **Privately Held**
WEB: www.gil-mar.ch
SIC: 3599 Machine shop, jobbing & repair
PA: Gil-Mar Manufacturing Co.
7925 Ronda Dr
Canton MI 48187
248 640-4303

(G-10224)
GLOBAL CONNECTIONS & MORE LLC
19335 Fitzgerald St (48152-4039)
PHONE....................248 990-2266
James Treadway,
EMP: 7 **EST:** 2017
SALES (est): 60.3K **Privately Held**
SIC: 3641 Ultraviolet lamps

(G-10225)
GLOBAL INFORMATION SYSTEMS INC
17177 N Laurel Park Dr # 446 (48152-2693)
PHONE....................248 223-9800
Sunitha Devabhaktuni, *President*
Prasad Devabhaktuni, *Principal*
Sirisha Pinnamaneni, *Vice Pres*
Satya Pinnamaneni, *Director*
EMP: 102 **EST:** 1996
SALES (est): 5.1MM **Privately Held**
WEB: www.gissite.com
SIC: 7372 Prepackaged software

(G-10226)
GLOBAL STRGC SUP SOLUTIONS LLC
Also Called: Gs3
34450 Industrial Rd (48150-1308)
PHONE....................734 525-9100
Robert Gruschow, *General Mgr*
Lisa Lunsford, *Mng Member*
◆ **EMP:** 100 **EST:** 2010
SQ FT: 140,000
SALES (est): 5.9MM **Privately Held**
WEB: www.gs3global.com
SIC: 8711 3559 3441 3542 Engineering services; automotive related machinery; fabricated structural metal; machine tools, metal forming type

(G-10227)
GRAKON LLC
Also Called: Grakon Michigan
19500 Victor Pkwy Ste 325 (48152-1084)
PHONE....................734 462-1201
Joe Binetti, *Sales Engr*
EMP: 7
SALES (corp-wide): 1B **Publicly Held**
WEB: www.grakon.com
SIC: 3714 Motor vehicle electrical equipment
HQ: Grakon, Llc
1911 S 218th St
Des Moines WA 98198
206 824-6000

(G-10228)
GRANITE CITY INC
31693 8 Mile Rd (48152-4217)
PHONE....................248 478-0033
Jon Williams, *Principal*
EMP: 19 **EST:** 2009
SALES (est): 1.2MM **Privately Held**
WEB: www.granitecitymi.com
SIC: 3281 5032 Curbing, granite or stone; granite, cut & shaped; granite building stone

(G-10229)
GRAPHICOLOR SYSTEMS INC
Also Called: Graphicolor Exhibits
12788 Currie Ct (48150-1109)
PHONE....................248 347-0271
Anita Mitzel, *President*
Rob Marchesotti, *Prdtn Mgr*
Don Mitzel, *Treasurer*
Katie Marsack, *Marketing Mgr*
Samantha Williams, *Mktg Coord*
EMP: 7 **EST:** 1984
SQ FT: 8,000
SALES (est): 1.1MM **Privately Held**
WEB: www.graphicolor.com
SIC: 7389 2759 Promoters of shows & exhibitions; promotional printing

(G-10230)
GREAT LAKES METAL FABRICATION
13500 Wayne Rd (48150-1270)
PHONE....................248 218-0540
EMP: 8 **EST:** 2017
SALES (est): 59.8K **Privately Held**
WEB: www.glmetalfab.com
SIC: 3441 Fabricated structural metal

(G-10231)
GUARDIAN MANUFACTURING CORP
12193 Levan Rd (48150-1403)
PHONE....................734 591-1454

Melvin Stevens, *President*
Sheryl Kudla, *Vice Pres*
Keith M Stevens, *Vice Pres*
Keith Stevens, *Vice Pres*
Charlene Baker, *Purchasing*
EMP: 35 **EST:** 1946
SQ FT: 18,800
SALES (est): 4.4MM **Privately Held**
WEB: www.guardman.com
SIC: 3545 Machine tool accessories

(G-10232)
HAARALA CERAMIC TILE & MARBLE
30765 Westfield St (48150-5912)
PHONE....................734 422-1168
Daniel Haarala, *President*
EMP: 6 **EST:** 1997
SALES (est): 96.6K **Privately Held**
SIC: 3253 Ceramic wall & floor tile

(G-10233)
HAL INTERNATIONAL INC
Also Called: Dynapath Systems Inc.
34155 Industrial Rd (48150-1305)
PHONE....................248 488-0440
Jacob Pien, *President*
Michael Radiwon, *Purchasing*
Nick Pitsillos, *CFO*
▲ **EMP:** 7 **EST:** 2005
SQ FT: 8,000
SALES (est): 1MM **Privately Held**
SIC: 3541 Machine tools, metal cutting type

(G-10234)
HAMILTON ENGINEERING INC
Also Called: Agritemp
34000 Autry St (48150-1333)
PHONE....................734 419-0200
Jeffrey E Deal, *CEO*
Hilary Carter, *General Mgr*
Diana Deal, *Vice Pres*
Brian Donohue, *Engineer*
Shawn Edmonds, *Engineer*
◆ **EMP:** 35 **EST:** 1981
SQ FT: 76,000
SALES (est): 5.8MM **Privately Held**
WEB: www.hamiltonengineering.com
SIC: 3433 5074 Burners, furnaces, boilers & stokers; boilers, hot water heating

(G-10235)
HANLO GAUGES & ENGINEERING CO
34403 Glendale St (48150-1301)
PHONE....................734 422-4224
Barbara A Williams, *CEO*
Rick Williams, *President*
Mike Williams, *Corp Secy*
EMP: 7 **EST:** 1948
SQ FT: 9,820
SALES (est): 1.5MM **Privately Held**
WEB: www.hanlogages.com
SIC: 3545 Gauges (machine tool accessories)

(G-10236)
HARVEY INDUSTRIES LLC
17177 N Laurel Park Dr # 243 (48152-3952)
PHONE....................734 405-2430
John Brawley, *Principal*
EMP: 8 **EST:** 2015
SALES (est): 305.8K **Privately Held**
SIC: 3999 Manufacturing industries

(G-10237)
HDT AUTOMOTIVE SOLUTIONS LLC (HQ)
38707 7 Mile Rd Ste 2 (48152-1091)
PHONE....................810 359-5344
Patrick Paige, *President*
Rick Cook, *President*
EMP: 8 **EST:** 2017
SALES (est): 120MM
SALES (corp-wide): 21.1MM **Privately Held**
WEB: www.ardian.com
SIC: 3714 Motor vehicle parts & accessories
PA: Ardian Holding
  20 Place Vendome
  Paris 75001
  141 719-200

(G-10238)
HEAR USA
31160 5 Mile Rd (48154-3642)
PHONE....................734 525-3900
Leslie Schwesing, *Manager*
EMP: 7 **EST:** 2012
SALES (est): 151K **Privately Held**
WEB: www.hearusa.com
SIC: 3842 Hearing aids

(G-10239)
HIGH TECH INSULATORS INC
34483 Glendale St (48150-1301)
PHONE....................734 525-9030
James D Allen, *President*
EMP: 17 **EST:** 1989
SALES (est): 6MM **Privately Held**
WEB: www.hightechinsulators.com
SIC: 3086 Insulation or cushioning material, foamed plastic

(G-10240)
HIROSE ELECTRIC USA INC
37727 Prof Ctr Dr Ste 100 (48154)
PHONE....................734 542-9963
Nick Shukuya, *Manager*
EMP: 9 **EST:** 2005
SALES (est): 198.1K **Privately Held**
SIC: 3699 Electron beam metal cutting, forming or welding machines

(G-10241)
HOLBROOK RACING ENGINES
31831 Schoolcraft Rd (48150-1825)
PHONE....................734 762-4315
Chris Holbrook, *General Mgr*
Donald M Soenen,
EMP: 10 **EST:** 1999
SQ FT: 9,000
SALES (est): 1.1MM **Privately Held**
WEB: www.holbrookracingengines.com
SIC: 3711 3519 Motor vehicles & car bodies; internal combustion engines

(G-10242)
HOLO-SOURCE CORPORATION
11700 Belden Ct (48150-1428)
PHONE....................734 427-1530
Robert H Levy, *CEO*
Craig Pomish, *Admin Sec*
◆ **EMP:** 4 **EST:** 1986
SALES (est): 1.6MM **Privately Held**
WEB: www.holo-source.com
SIC: 2671 Packaging paper & plastics film, coated & laminated

(G-10243)
HUEBNER E W & SON MFG CO INC
12871 Farmington Rd (48150-1607)
PHONE....................734 427-2600
Max Riehl, *President*
EMP: 6 **EST:** 1952
SQ FT: 5,000
SALES (est): 509.6K **Privately Held**
SIC: 3548 Electrodes, electric welding

(G-10244)
HUGHES ELECTRONICS PDTS CORP (PA)
34467 Industrial Rd (48150-1305)
PHONE....................734 427-8310
Richard L Smith Jr, *President*
Rick Smith, *General Mgr*
Christopher Thomas, *Vice Pres*
Pauline Smith, *Treasurer*
Michael Gaines, *VP Finance*
EMP: 20 **EST:** 1982
SQ FT: 7,000
SALES (est): 6.1MM **Privately Held**
WEB: www.hugheselectronics.com
SIC: 3672 Circuit boards, television & radio printed

(G-10245)
IDEAL FABRICATORS INC
30579 Schoolcraft Rd (48150-2008)
PHONE....................734 422-5320
John P Fisher, *President*
Mark Logan, *Vice Pres*
EMP: 35 **EST:** 1984
SQ FT: 22,000
SALES (est): 8.8MM **Privately Held**
WEB: www.idealfab.com
SIC: 3443 Tanks, standard or custom fabricated: metal plate

(G-10246)
IMMUNO CONCEPTS NA LTD
17199 N Laurel Park Dr # 320 (48152-7904)
PHONE....................734 464-0701
EMP: 40
SALES (est): 4.1MM **Privately Held**
SIC: 2836 Mfg Biological Products

(G-10247)
IMS/CHINATOOL JV LLC (PA)
Also Called: CT Automotive
17199 N Laurel Park Dr # 412 (48152-2683)
PHONE....................734 466-5151
Robert Schaffer,
◆ **EMP:** 10 **EST:** 2007
SALES (est): 3.3MM **Privately Held**
SIC: 3559 3089 Automotive related machinery; automotive parts, plastic

(G-10248)
INATEG LLC ✪
34081 La Moyne St (48154-2619)
PHONE....................734 276-3899
Robert Pohutski,
EMP: 4 **EST:** 2021
SALES (est): 139.1K **Privately Held**
SIC: 3599 Industrial machinery

(G-10249)
INFUSION TANNING PRODUCTS LLC
Also Called: Infusion Cosmetics
30969 5 Mile Rd (48154-3600)
PHONE....................734 422-9826
Troy Leece, *Mng Member*
EMP: 8 **EST:** 2011
SALES (est): 246.4K **Privately Held**
WEB: www.infusiontanning.com
SIC: 3648 Sun tanning equipment, incl. tanning beds

(G-10250)
INTERNTNAL HRVEST VENTURES LLC
30936 Industrial Rd (48150-2024)
PHONE....................248 387-9944
Sammy Salem,
EMP: 5 **EST:** 2019
SALES (est): 500K **Privately Held**
WEB: www.internationalharvest.com
SIC: 2834 Pharmaceutical preparations

(G-10251)
IPS ASSEMBLY CORP
12077 Merriman Rd (48150-1912)
PHONE....................734 391-0080
Ishvar Sutariya, *President*
Perry Sutariya, *Vice Pres*
EMP: 16 **EST:** 2014
SQ FT: 6,000
SALES (est): 2.2MM **Privately Held**
WEB: www.ipsassembly.com
SIC: 3672 Circuit boards, television & radio printed

(G-10252)
J & J UNITED INDUSTRIES LLC
Also Called: United Fabrications
39111 6 Mile Rd (48152-3926)
P.O. Box 1104, New Boston (48164-1104)
PHONE....................734 443-3737
John Pierce,
EMP: 11 **EST:** 2005
SALES (est): 2.2MM **Privately Held**
WEB: www.fab-united.com
SIC: 3441 Fabricated structural metal

(G-10253)
J & S LIVONIA INC
Also Called: Jaimes Industries
12658 Richfield Ct (48150-1062)
PHONE....................734 793-9000
Ghassan Yonan, *President*
EMP: 8 **EST:** 2010
SALES (est): 2.8MM **Privately Held**
SIC: 3441 Building components, structural steel

(G-10254)
J C GIBBONS MFG INC
35055 Glendale St (48150-1230)
PHONE....................734 266-5544
Jerry Gibbons, *President*
Jeff Gibbons, *Vice Pres*
Jeffery Gibbons, *VP Opers*
Dan Gibbons, *QC Mgr*
EMP: 20 **EST:** 1959
SQ FT: 22,000
SALES (est): 3.1MM **Privately Held**
WEB: www.jcgibbons.com
SIC: 3451 Screw machine products

(G-10255)
JACOBSEN INDUSTRIES INC
12173 Market St (48150-1166)
PHONE....................734 591-6111
Lee S Jacobsen, *President*
Karen Jacobsen, *Manager*
▲ **EMP:** 70 **EST:** 1946
SQ FT: 20,000
SALES (est): 11.4MM **Privately Held**
WEB: www.jacobsenindustries.com
SIC: 2675 3544 3053 Die-cut paper & board; dies, steel rule; gaskets, packing & sealing devices

(G-10256)
JADE PHARMACEUTICALS ENTP LLC
32229 Schoolcraft Rd (48150-4302)
PHONE....................248 716-8333
Sam Alawieh, *Mng Member*
Abraham Alaouie,
EMP: 4 **EST:** 2017
SQ FT: 15,600
SALES (est): 491.4K **Privately Held**
SIC: 2834 Pharmaceutical preparations

(G-10257)
JAIMES TRUSSES AND WALL PANELS
12658 Richfield Ct (48150-1062)
PHONE....................734 462-6100
Samer Sinawi, *Principal*
EMP: 8 **EST:** 2013
SALES (est): 94.7K **Privately Held**
WEB: www.jaimesind.com
SIC: 2411 Wooden bolts, hewn

(G-10258)
JB AUTOTECH LLC
32235 Industrial Rd (48150-1836)
PHONE....................734 838-3963
Jeff Bucher, *General Mgr*
Jon Carlisle, *Project Mgr*
Dave Dixon, *CFO*
EMP: 40 **EST:** 1999
SQ FT: 30,000
SALES (est): 8MM **Privately Held**
WEB: www.jbautotech.com
SIC: 8711 3559 Mechanical engineering; automotive related machinery

(G-10259)
JGS MANUFACTURING LLC
20300 Farmington Rd (48152-1416)
PHONE....................248 376-1659
Johnny Subu, *President*
EMP: 5 **EST:** 2017
SALES (est): 107.4K **Privately Held**
SIC: 3999 Manufacturing industries

(G-10260)
JOES TRAILER MANUFACTURING
13374 Farmington Rd Ste A (48150-4206)
P.O. Box 51908 (48151-5908)
PHONE....................734 261-0050
Douglas J Vandenberg, *President*
Marilynne G Vandenberg, *Corp Secy*
EMP: 5 **EST:** 1976
SQ FT: 18,000
SALES (est): 578.9K **Privately Held**
WEB: www.joes-trailer-mfg.shoplightspeed.com
SIC: 3715 5531 Truck trailers; truck equipment & parts

(G-10261)
JS PRINTING
30777 Schoolcraft Rd (48150-2010)
PHONE....................734 266-3350
Greg Leidhiser, *Owner*

EMP: 6 **EST:** 2007
SALES (est): 359.3K **Privately Held**
WEB: www.jiffysigns.com
SIC: 2752 Commercial printing, offset

(G-10262)
JUST PRESS PLAY
19175 Auburndale St (48152-1526)
PHONE 248 470-7797
Michael Johnson Jr, *Administration*
EMP: 6 **EST:** 2014
SALES (est): 106.2K **Privately Held**
WEB: www.justpressplay.com
SIC: 2741 Miscellaneous publishing

(G-10263)
JUST WEAR IT
33650 5 Mile Rd (48154-2866)
PHONE 734 458-4015
EMP: 4 **EST:** 2019
SALES (est): 39.8K **Privately Held**
SIC: 2395 Embroidery products, except schiffli machine

(G-10264)
KELLER TOOL LTD (PA)
Also Called: O. Keller Tool Engineering Co.
12701 Inkster Rd (48150-2216)
PHONE 734 425-4500
Barry W La Chance, *CEO*
Brian Van Norman, *President*
Paul Krenek, *Prgrmr*
Amy Alstermark, *Receptionist*
EMP: 15 **EST:** 1996
SQ FT: 30,000
SALES (est): 14.5MM **Privately Held**
WEB: www.okeller.com
SIC: 3544 3545 3537 Jigs & fixtures; gauges (machine tool accessories); pallets, metal

(G-10265)
KERRY J MCNEELY
Also Called: Kerry's Pallets
15810 Harrison St (48154-3410)
PHONE 734 776-1928
Kerry J McNeely, *Principal*
EMP: 4 **EST:** 2012
SALES (est): 119.7K **Privately Held**
SIC: 2448 Pallets, wood & wood with metal

(G-10266)
KITTY CONDO LLC
17197 N Laurel Park Dr # 40 (48152-2680)
PHONE 419 690-9063
Michael L Stewart,
Jack L Berry,
Harry Shallop,
Harvy Solway,
EMP: 6 **EST:** 1988
SQ FT: 20,000
SALES (est): 219.9K **Privately Held**
SIC: 3999 Pet supplies

(G-10267)
KPL CUSTOM WOODWORKING LLC
31040 Industrial Rd (48150-2033)
PHONE 313 530-5507
EMP: 4 **EST:** 2019
SALES (est): 84.1K **Privately Held**
SIC: 2431 Millwork

(G-10268)
KRUPP INDUSTRIES LLC
Also Called: Universal Sprial Air
37050 Plymouth Rd (48150-1132)
PHONE 734 261-0410
David C Krupp,
EMP: 20
SALES (corp-wide): 17.1MM **Privately Held**
WEB: www.usaduct.com
SIC: 3444 Ducts, sheet metal
PA: Krupp Industries Llc
2735 West River Dr Nw
Walker MI 49544
616 475-5905

(G-10269)
KTX AMERICA INC
31651 Schoolcraft Rd (48150-1823)
PHONE 734 737-0100
Yasunori Noda, *President*
Jeffery Shimizu, *Vice Pres*
Greg Foreman, *Technician*

▲ **EMP:** 1 **EST:** 2002
SALES (est): 1.1MM **Privately Held**
WEB: www.ktx-america.com
SIC: 3544 Special dies & tools
HQ: Ktx Corporation
51, Jizo, Yasuracho
Konan AIC 483-8

(G-10270)
KURTIS MFG & DISTRG CORP (PA)
Also Called: Kurtis Kitchen & Bath Centers
12500 Merriman Rd (48150-1928)
PHONE 734 522-7600
Howard Kuretzky, *Principal*
Steve Edelman, *Vice Pres*
Wayne Weintraub, *Vice Pres*
Jillian Pickett, *Wholesale*
Adrian Aninos, *Manager*
EMP: 50
SQ FT: 83,000
SALES (est): 38.1MM **Privately Held**
WEB: www.kurtiskitchen.com
SIC: 5021 5211 5031 5712 Household furniture; counter tops; kitchen cabinets; cabinet work, custom; wood kitchen cabinets; wood partitions & fixtures

(G-10271)
KYUNGSHIN CABLE INTL CORP
19500 Victor Pkwy Ste 120 (48152-7012)
PHONE 248 679-7578
Seungkwan Lee, *President*
Min Yong Park, *Admin Sec*
EMP: 15 **EST:** 2013
SALES (est): 93MM **Privately Held**
SIC: 3315 Wire & fabricated wire products

(G-10272)
L I S MANUFACTURING INC
15223 Farmington Rd Ste 8 (48154-5411)
PHONE 734 525-3070
Michael G Jeffery, *President*
EMP: 10 **EST:** 1984
SQ FT: 700
SALES (est): 600.3K **Privately Held**
SIC: 2841 Soap & other detergents

(G-10273)
LAM INDUSTRIES
12985 Wayne Rd (48150-1269)
PHONE 734 266-1404
Larry Lam, *President*
EMP: 5 **EST:** 2004
SALES (est): 393.4K **Privately Held**
WEB: www.lamindustries.com
SIC: 3599 Machine shop, jobbing & repair

(G-10274)
LAMAY WOODWORKING
36713 Richland St (48150-2509)
PHONE 734 421-6032
Donald Lamay, *Principal*
EMP: 5 **EST:** 2008
SALES (est): 66.6K **Privately Held**
SIC: 2431 Millwork

(G-10275)
LEAPERS INC (PA)
32700 Capitol St (48150-1742)
PHONE 734 542-1500
Tina Ding, *President*
Tom Zhu, *General Mgr*
David Ding, *Vice Pres*
Bill Yang, *Engineer*
Andy Chen, *Sales Staff*
▲ **EMP:** 76 **EST:** 1992
SQ FT: 150,000
SALES (est): 38.7MM **Privately Held**
WEB: www.leapers.com
SIC: 5091 3827 Sporting & recreation goods; gun sights, optical

(G-10276)
LETTERING INC
13324 Farmington Rd (48150-4203)
PHONE 248 223-9700
EMP: 7 **EST:** 1939
SALES (est): 294.3K **Privately Held**
WEB: www.letteringinc.com
SIC: 3993 Signs & advertising specialties

(G-10277)
LETTERING INC OF MICHIGAN
13324 Farmington Rd (48150-4203)
PHONE 248 223-9700

Karin Krumpelbeck, *President*
Russell Mull, *General Mgr*
Russell Hall, *Manager*
John Krumpelbeck, *Admin Sec*
EMP: 10 **EST:** 1954
SQ FT: 25,000
SALES (corp-wide): 2MM **Privately Held**
WEB: www.letteringinc.com
SIC: 3993 Signs & advertising specialties
PA: Lettering Inc Of New York
255 Mill Rd
Stamford CT 06903
203 329-7759

(G-10278)
LINAMAR HOLDING NEVADA INC (HQ)
Also Called: McLaren Engineering
32233 8 Mile Rd (48152-1361)
PHONE 248 477-6240
Linda Hasenfratz, *CEO*
Jim Jarrell, *President*
Mike Vandieren, *Vice Pres*
Doug Spencer, *Project Mgr*
Mitch Holland, *Engineer*
EMP: 75 **EST:** 1998
SQ FT: 77,622
SALES (est): 112MM
SALES (corp-wide): 4.4B **Privately Held**
WEB: www.linamar.com
SIC: 3545 Precision measuring tools
PA: Linamar Corporation
287 Speedvale Ave W
Guelph ON N1H 1
519 836-7550

(G-10279)
LINCOLN SERVICE LLC (PA)
11862 Brookfield St (48150-1701)
PHONE 734 793-0083
Mark Lippincott,
EMP: 7 **EST:** 2000
SALES (est): 2.1MM **Privately Held**
WEB: www.lincolnservicecenter.com
SIC: 5063 7694 Motors, electric; motor repair services

(G-10280)
LINE-X OF LIVONIA
35043 Plymouth Rd (48150-1422)
PHONE 734 237-3115
EMP: 8 **EST:** 2018
SALES (est): 104.2K **Privately Held**
WEB: www.linex.com
SIC: 7539 2821 Automotive repair shops; plastics materials & resins

(G-10281)
LINEAR MOLD & ENGINEERING LLC
34435 Glendale St (48150-1301)
PHONE 734 744-4548
Everett Sollars, *Engineer*
John Tenbusch, *Branch Mgr*
EMP: 46
SALES (corp-wide): 18.8MM **Privately Held**
WEB: www.linearams.com
SIC: 3462 Iron & steel forgings
PA: Linear Mold & Engineering, Llc
12163 Globe St
Livonia MI 48150
734 422-6060

(G-10282)
LINEAR MOLD & ENGINEERING LLC (PA)
Also Called: Linear AMS
12163 Globe St (48150-1142)
PHONE 734 422-6060
Lou Young, *President*
Brian Garvey, *Business Mgr*
David Myers, *Business Mgr*
John Tenbusch, *Vice Pres*
Jim Koing, *Controller*
▲ **EMP:** 15
SQ FT: 13,000
SALES (est): 18.8MM **Privately Held**
WEB: www.linearams.com
SIC: 3462 Automotive & internal combustion engine forgings

(G-10283)
LINEAR MOLD & ENGINEERING LLC
Also Called: Linear AMS
35450 Industrial Rd (48150-1223)
PHONE 734 422-6060
EMP: 14
SALES (corp-wide): 18.8MM **Privately Held**
SIC: 3089 Plastics Products, Nec, Nsk
PA: Linear Mold & Engineering, Llc
12163 Globe St
Livonia MI 48150
734 422-6060

(G-10284)
LINK MECHANICAL SOLUTIONS LLC
11970 Mayfield St (48150-1710)
PHONE 734 744-5616
Sean Koneff, *President*
Dave Lively, *Engineer*
EMP: 14 **EST:** 2010
SALES (est): 2.3MM **Privately Held**
WEB: www.link-mechanical.com
SIC: 3599 Custom machinery

(G-10285)
LISI AUTOMOTIVE HI VOL INC
11813 Hubbard St (48150-1732)
PHONE 734 266-6958
Randy Hinz, *Vice Pres*
EMP: 10
SALES (corp-wide): 177.9K **Privately Held**
WEB: www.lisi-automotive.com
SIC: 5084 3399 Fuel injection systems; metal fasteners
HQ: Lisi Automotive Hi Vol Inc.
12955 Inkster Rd
Livonia MI 48150
734 266-6900

(G-10286)
LISI AUTOMOTIVE HI VOL INC (DH)
12955 Inkster Rd (48150-2212)
PHONE 734 266-6900
Christian Darville, *President*
Randy Hinz, *Vice Pres*
Jeff Lederer, *Finance*
David Bennett, *Sales Staff*
Tauras Barauskas, *Manager*
EMP: 120 **EST:** 1951
SQ FT: 60,000
SALES (est): 23.1MM
SALES (corp-wide): 177.9K **Privately Held**
WEB: www.lisi-automotive.com
SIC: 3462 Iron & steel forgings
HQ: Lisi Automotive
2 Rue Juvenal Viellard
Grandvillars 90600
384 586-300

(G-10287)
LIVONIA AUTOMATIC INCORPORATED
12650 Newburgh Rd (48150-1002)
PHONE 734 591-0321
Gerald L Crespi, *President*
Robert J Crespi, *Vice Pres*
EMP: 5 **EST:** 1976
SQ FT: 5,000
SALES (est): 649.5K **Privately Held**
WEB: www.livoniaautomatic.com
SIC: 3451 Screw machine products

(G-10288)
LIVONIA OBSERVER
8928 Virginia St (48150-3643)
PHONE 734 525-4657
Norene Hanchett, *Principal*
EMP: 6 **EST:** 2010
SALES (est): 78.9K **Privately Held**
SIC: 2711 Newspapers, publishing & printing

(G-10289)
LIVONIA TROPHY & SCREEN PRTG
38065 Ann Arbor Rd (48150-3499)
PHONE 734 464-9191
Scott Wilson, *President*

Livonia - Wayne County (G-10290)   GEOGRAPHIC SECTION

EMP: 7 EST: 1976
SQ FT: 2,400
SALES (est): 851.2K Privately Held
WEB: www.livoniatrophy.com
SIC: 5999 2759 Trophies & plaques; screen printing

(G-10290)
LLC HELTON BROTHERS
30958 Industrial Rd Ste A (48150-2058)
PHONE.....................517 927-6941
EMP: 4 EST: 2016
SALES (est): 55.7K Privately Held
SIC: 3993 Signs & advertising specialties

(G-10291)
LLOYD WATERS & ASSOCIATES (PA)
33180 Industrial Rd Ste A (48150-4200)
PHONE.....................734 525-2777
Robert T Waters, President
W Lloyd Waters, Treasurer
EMP: 5 EST: 1957
SQ FT: 2,400
SALES (est): 1.5MM Privately Held
WEB: www.lloydwaters.com
SIC: 7389 7336 2752 Printing broker; graphic arts & related design; commercial printing, offset

(G-10292)
LOONEY BAKER OF LIVONIA INC
13931 Farmington Rd (48154-5403)
PHONE.....................734 425-8569
John N Strauch, President
EMP: 10 EST: 1986
SQ FT: 2,500
SALES (est): 556.7K Privately Held
WEB: www.livoniahockey.org
SIC: 5461 2051 Cookies; doughnuts; bread, cake & related products

(G-10293)
LOVE MACHINERY INC
36232 Lawrence Dr (48150-2506)
PHONE.....................734 427-0824
William J Love, President
Francis Love, Corp Secy
EMP: 5
SQ FT: 4,500
SALES (est): 499.8K Privately Held
SIC: 3541 Machine tools, metal cutting type

(G-10294)
M & J GRAPHICS ENTERPRISES INC
Also Called: Reprographics One
36060 Industrial Rd (48150-1200)
PHONE.....................734 542-8800
Marianne Lewis, CEO
Joseph Kapp, President
EMP: 18 EST: 2002
SQ FT: 22,000
SALES (est): 794.3K Privately Held
WEB: www.reprographicsone.com
SIC: 2759 5734 Commercial printing; printers & plotters; computers

(G-10295)
M M R LLC
31831 Schoolcraft Rd (48150-1825)
PHONE.....................734 502-5239
Mike McManman, Owner
EMP: 8 EST: 2018
SALES (est): 673.5K Privately Held
SIC: 5531 3711 Automotive & home supply stores; motor vehicles & car bodies

(G-10296)
M PRINT
33707 Pondview Cir (48152-1472)
PHONE.....................248 550-4405
Margina Cohen, Principal
EMP: 4 EST: 2018
SALES (est): 74K Privately Held
SIC: 2752 Commercial printing, lithographic

(G-10297)
MACLEAN MASTER LLC
Also Called: Master Automatic
12271 Globe St (48150-1142)
PHONE.....................734 414-0500
Thomas Dennis, Engineer
EMP: 50
SALES (corp-wide): 1.1B Privately Held
WEB: www.macleanfoggcs.com
SIC: 3599 Machine shop, jobbing & repair
HQ: Maclean Master, L.L.C.
40485 Schoolcraft Rd
Plymouth MI 48170
734 414-0500

(G-10298)
MANUFACTURERS / MCH BLDRS SVCS
Also Called: Mmbs
13035 Wayne Rd (48150-1268)
PHONE.....................734 748-3706
Chanya Neal, President
Glen Neal, Principal
Patrick Bomia, Admin Sec
EMP: 4 EST: 2002
SQ FT: 10,400
SALES (est): 450K Privately Held
WEB: www.mmbscorp.com
SIC: 3549 Metalworking machinery

(G-10299)
MANUFACTURING ASSOCIATES INC
39201 Amrhein Rd (48150-5018)
PHONE.....................248 421-4943
Mark Ashworth, President
EMP: 6 EST: 2004
SQ FT: 10,000
SALES (est): 469.5K Privately Held
SIC: 3541 Milling machines; lathes; numerically controlled metal cutting machine tools

(G-10300)
MARIE MINNIE BAKERS INC
Also Called: Awrey Bakeries
12301 Farmington Rd (48150-1747)
PHONE.....................734 522-1100
Ronald Beebe, Ch of Bd
Diane Lynch, Vice Pres
Amanda Sevcik, Manager
Shawn Walker, Technology
EMP: 120 EST: 2013
SALES (est): 25.7MM Privately Held
WEB: www.awrey.com
SIC: 2053 2051 Frozen bakery products, except bread; bread, cake & related products

(G-10301)
MASCO BUILDING PRODUCTS CORP (HQ)
17450 College Pkwy (48152-2300)
PHONE.....................313 274-7400
Allan Barry, President
Raj Parikh, Counsel
Yvette Vanriper, Counsel
Kellie Campbell, Vice Pres
Paul Dambroso, Vice Pres
EMP: 8 EST: 1985
SALES (est): 2.1B
SALES (corp-wide): 7.1B Publicly Held
WEB: www.masco.com
SIC: 3429 3639 3644 Door locks, bolts & checks; major kitchen appliances, except refrigerators & stoves; outlet boxes (electric wiring devices)
PA: Masco Corporation
17450 College Pkwy
Livonia MI 48152
313 274-7400

(G-10302)
MASCO CORPORATION (PA)
17450 College Pkwy (48152-2300)
PHONE.....................313 274-7400
J Michael Losh, Ch of Bd
Keith J Allman, President
Richard A O'Reagan, President
Jai Shah, President
Kenneth G Cole, Vice Pres
◆ EMP: 559 EST: 1929
SALES (est): 7.1B Publicly Held
WEB: www.masco.com
SIC: 3432 3088 3429 1742 Faucets & spigots, metal & plastic; plumbers' brass goods: drain cocks, faucets, spigots, etc.; plastic plumbing fixture fittings, assembly; plastics plumbing fixtures; tubs (bath, shower & laundry), plastic; bathroom fixtures, plastic; hot tubs, plastic or fiberglass; builders' hardware; locks or lock sets; acoustical & insulation work; vanities, bathroom: wood

(G-10303)
MASCO SERVICES INC
17450 College Pkwy (48152-2300)
PHONE.....................313 274-7400
Eugene A Gargaro Jr, Principal
EMP: 36 EST: 1996
SALES (est): 2.1MM
SALES (corp-wide): 7.1B Publicly Held
WEB: www.masco.com
SIC: 2434 Wood kitchen cabinets
PA: Masco Corporation
17450 College Pkwy
Livonia MI 48152
313 274-7400

(G-10304)
MAZZELLA LIFTING TECH INC
12671 Richfield Ct (48150-1062)
PHONE.....................734 953-7300
EMP: 6 Privately Held
SIC: 3496 Manufactures Hoisting And Lifting Devices
HQ: Mazzella Lifting Technologies, Inc.
21000 Aerospace Pkwy
Cleveland OH 44142
440 239-7000

(G-10305)
MCDONALD ENTERPRISES INC
36650 Plymouth Rd (48150-1129)
PHONE.....................734 464-4664
Richard Larance, President
EMP: 10 EST: 1970
SQ FT: 11,000
SALES (est): 1.5MM Privately Held
WEB: www.mcdonaldent.net
SIC: 3599 Machine shop, jobbing & repair

(G-10306)
MCGEAN-ROHCO INC
38521 Schoolcraft Rd (48150-1031)
PHONE.....................216 441-4900
Gliozzi Mara Furth, Business Mgr
Robert Phillips, Plant Engr
Bryan Miller, Accounts Mgr
Michael Velotta, Marketing Mgr
Jim Rector, Manager
EMP: 33
SALES (corp-wide): 41.2MM Privately Held
WEB: www.mcgean.com
SIC: 2899 2819 3471 2842 Chemical preparations; industrial inorganic chemicals; plating & polishing; specialty cleaning, polishes & sanitation goods
PA: Mcgean-Rohco, Inc.
2910 Harvard Ave
Newburgh Heights OH 44105
216 441-4900

(G-10307)
MCKAE GROUP LLC
Also Called: Detroit's Own
15356 Middlebelt Rd (48154-3806)
PHONE.....................313 564-5100
Matthew McKae, CEO
Danny McKae, Vice Pres
Daniel McKae,
EMP: 30 EST: 2015
SALES (est): 2.6MM Privately Held
WEB: www.mydoapparel.com
SIC: 3949 Sporting & athletic goods

(G-10308)
MCKESSON CORPORATION
Also Called: McEsson Drug Company
38220 Plymouth Rd (48150-1050)
PHONE.....................734 953-2523
Craig Vanderburg, Manager
Lori Baronet, IT/INT Sup
Michael Zepke, Director
EMP: 6
SALES (corp-wide): 238.2B Publicly Held
WEB: www.mckesson.com
SIC: 5122 2834 Pharmaceuticals; pharmaceutical preparations
PA: Mckesson Corporation
6555 State Highway 161
Irving TX 75039
972 446-4800

(G-10309)
MCKESSON PHARMACY SYSTEMS LLC
30933 Schoolcraft Rd (48150-2037)
PHONE.....................800 521-1758
Emilie Ray, President
Brian Grobbel, President
EMP: 679 EST: 2008
SALES (est): 116.4MM
SALES (corp-wide): 238.2B Publicly Held
WEB: www.mckesson.com
SIC: 7372 5122 Prepackaged software; pharmaceuticals
PA: Mckesson Corporation
6555 State Highway 161
Irving TX 75039
972 446-4800

(G-10310)
MELODY FARMS LLC
31770 Enterprise Dr (48150-1960)
PHONE.....................734 261-7980
Jerry Shannon,
EMP: 11 EST: 1998
SQ FT: 15,000
SALES (est): 427K Privately Held
SIC: 2026 Fluid milk

(G-10311)
METALCRAFT IMPRESSION DIE CO
Also Called: Metal Craft Impression Die
11914 Brookfield St (48150-1736)
PHONE.....................734 513-8058
Bryan Stenman, President
EMP: 6 EST: 1989
SQ FT: 5,000
SALES (est): 864.9K Privately Held
WEB: www.metalcraftdie.com
SIC: 3462 Iron & steel forgings

(G-10312)
METRO DETROIT PRINTING LLC
12892 Farmington Rd (48150-1603)
PHONE.....................734 469-7174
EMP: 7 EST: 2019
SALES (est): 565K Privately Held
WEB: www.metrodetroitprinting.com
SIC: 3993 Signs & advertising specialties

(G-10313)
METRO MEDICAL EQP MFG INC
38415 Schoolcraft Rd (48150-1031)
PHONE.....................734 522-8400
Paul Mocur, President
Sylvia Mocur, Corp Secy
EMP: 33 EST: 1986
SQ FT: 10,000
SALES (est): 901.5K Privately Held
SIC: 7352 5999 3842 Medical equipment rental; hospital equipment & supplies; prosthetic appliances

(G-10314)
METTES PRINTERY INC
27454 Plymouth Rd (48150-2317)
PHONE.....................734 261-6262
Bruce C Mette, President
Toni Mette, Corp Secy
EMP: 7 EST: 1977
SQ FT: 4,000
SALES (est): 676.7K Privately Held
WEB: www.mettesprinting.com
SIC: 2752 Commercial printing, offset

(G-10315)
MICHAEL JOHN LLC
9840 Mayfield St (48150-5718)
PHONE.....................734 560-9268
Ouidia Marca, Principal
EMP: 5 EST: 2011
SALES (est): 201.9K Privately Held
SIC: 3799 Transportation equipment

GEOGRAPHIC SECTION
Livonia - Wayne County (G-10344)

(G-10316)
MID-WEST SCREW PRODUCTS CO
Also Called: Unco Automotive Products
11975 Globe St (48150-1133)
PHONE 734 591-1800
Kevin Johnson, *President*
Christina Rowland, *Controller*
EMP: 12 **EST:** 1953
SQ FT: 11,000
SALES (est): 2MM **Privately Held**
SIC: 3451 Screw machine products

(G-10317)
MIDWEST STAINLESS FABRICATING
32433 8 Mile Rd (48152-1301)
PHONE 248 476-4502
James Day, *President*
Mark Hall, *Vice Pres*
EMP: 8 **EST:** 1968
SQ FT: 7,500
SALES (est): 741K **Privately Held**
SIC: 3589 Commercial cooking & food-warming equipment

(G-10318)
MILLENNIUM SCREW MACHINE INC
13311 Stark Rd (48150-1548)
PHONE 734 525-5235
Frederick D Mercaldo, *President*
John Baughman, *Vice Pres*
Jerome Genders, *Vice Pres*
Virginia Mercaldo, *Admin Sec*
EMP: 5 **EST:** 1999
SQ FT: 11,000
SALES (est): 316.8K **Privately Held**
WEB: www.sjwcd.org
SIC: 3541 Machine tools, metal cutting type

(G-10319)
MJ CREATIVE PRINTING LLC
19566 Hardy St (48152-1587)
PHONE 248 891-1117
Marianne Groth, *Principal*
EMP: 4 **EST:** 2010
SALES (est): 165.1K **Privately Held**
WEB: www.mjcreativeprinting.com
SIC: 2752 Commercial printing, offset

(G-10320)
MOBILITYTRANS LLC
12633 Inkster Rd (48150-2216)
PHONE 734 262-3760
David Brown, *President*
Geralyn Brown, *Principal*
Nicholas Brown, *Principal*
Brian Beebe, *Sales Engr*
EMP: 49 **EST:** 1992
SALES (est): 30.3MM **Privately Held**
WEB: www.mobilitytrans.com
SIC: 7532 3713 Van conversion; van bodies

(G-10321)
MOHECO PRODUCTS COMPANY
34410 Rosati Ave (48150-1429)
PHONE 734 855-4194
Gerald Herrmann, *President*
EMP: 5 **EST:** 1953
SQ FT: 16,000 **Privately Held**
WEB: www.moheco.com
SIC: 3356 3429 Nonferrous rolling & drawing; furniture hardware

(G-10322)
MORSTAR INC
12868 Farmington Rd (48150-1603)
PHONE 248 605-3291
Qiumin Su, *President*
William Guo, *Vice Pres*
EMP: 12 **EST:** 2009
SALES (est): 1MM **Privately Held**
WEB: www.morstarlighting.com
SIC: 3699 3315 Grids, electric; wire & fabricated wire products

(G-10323)
MOTOR CITY QUICK LUBE ONE INC
11900 Middlebelt Rd Ste A (48150-2300)
PHONE 734 367-6457
Emad Bazzi, *Principal*

EMP: 8 **EST:** 2005
SALES (est): 212.9K **Privately Held**
SIC: 2911 Oils, fuel; oils, lubricating; fuel additives

(G-10324)
MOTOR TOOL MANUFACTURING CO
14710 Flamingo St (48154-3610)
PHONE 734 425-3300
Jack D Kastelic, *President*
Julius Konosky, *Vice Pres*
EMP: 4 **EST:** 1937
SQ FT: 5,600
SALES (est): 318.2K **Privately Held**
SIC: 3545 Cutting tools for machine tools

(G-10325)
MP-TEC INC
32920 Capitol St (48150-1743)
PHONE 734 367-1284
Toshiro Yamagata, *Principal*
EMP: 17 **EST:** 2007
SALES (est): 1.2MM **Privately Held**
WEB: www.mptecinc.com
SIC: 2295 Resin or plastic coated fabrics

(G-10326)
MR PEEL INC
33975 Autry St (48150-1323)
PHONE 734 266-2022
El Roma, *Owner*
EMP: 5 **EST:** 2004
SALES (est): 317.7K **Privately Held**
WEB: www.mrpeel.com
SIC: 2064 Fruit & fruit peel confections

(G-10327)
MULTI STEEL SERVICES
17159 Loveland St (48152-3217)
PHONE 734 261-6201
Richard J Hayward, *Principal*
EMP: 5 **EST:** 2012
SALES (est): 183.7K **Privately Held**
SIC: 3499 Fabricated metal products

(G-10328)
N A ACTUAPLAST INC
31690 Glendale St (48150-1827)
PHONE 734 744-4010
Ronan Perennou, *CEO*
Virginie Tymen, *Admin Mgr*
▲ **EMP:** 10 **EST:** 2014
SALES (est): 2.6MM
SALES (corp-wide): 6.6MM **Privately Held**
WEB: www.actuaplast.fr
SIC: 3089 Blow molded finished plastic products
PA: Actuaplast Group
Lieu Dit La Grande Halte
La Foret Fouesnant 29940
298 569-462

(G-10329)
NAFA PRINTING LLC
37000 Industrial Rd (48150-1135)
PHONE 734 338-2103
EMP: 4 **EST:** 2019
SALES (est): 107.5K **Privately Held**
SIC: 2752 Commercial printing, lithographic

(G-10330)
NAGLE PAVING COMPANY
36780 Amrhein Rd (48150-1104)
PHONE 734 591-1484
Steve Santi, *Branch Mgr*
EMP: 124
SALES (corp-wide): 23.1MM **Privately Held**
WEB: www.naglepaving.com
SIC: 1771 2951 Blacktop (asphalt) work; asphalt paving mixtures & blocks
PA: Nagle Paving Company
39525 W 13 Mile Rd # 300
Novi MI 48377
248 553-0600

(G-10331)
NANOMAG LLC
13753 Otterson Ct (48150-1220)
PHONE 734 261-2800
Stephen Lebeau,
EMP: 7 **EST:** 2005

SALES (est): 1.1MM **Privately Held**
WEB: www.nanomag.us
SIC: 3356 Magnesium

(G-10332)
NATIONAL INSTRUMENTS CORP
20255 Victor Pkwy Ste 195 (48152-7021)
PHONE 734 464-2310
EMP: 338
SALES (corp-wide): 1.2B **Publicly Held**
SIC: 7372 Provides Prepackaged Computer Software
PA: National Instruments Corporation
11500 N Mopac Expy
Austin TX 78759
512 338-9119

(G-10333)
NATIONAL TOOL & DIE WELDING
13340 Merriman Rd (48150-1830)
PHONE 734 522-0072
Stephan Skrobot, *President*
Jeff Skrobot, *Vice Pres*
EMP: 10 **EST:** 1969
SQ FT: 13,000
SALES (est): 557.5K **Privately Held**
SIC: 7692 Welding repair

(G-10334)
NCI MFG INC
12665 Richfield Ct (48150-1062)
PHONE 248 380-4151
Koji Iwata, *Branch Mgr*
EMP: 10 **Privately Held**
WEB: www.ncimfg.com
SIC: 5531 3053 1711 Automotive parts; gaskets, packing & sealing devices; plumbing, heating, air-conditioning contractors
PA: Nci Mfg, Inc.
209 Lnnie E Crawford Blvd
Scottsboro AL 35769

(G-10335)
NEXT IN LINE PUBLISHING LLC
14063 Harrison St (48154-4619)
PHONE 248 954-1280
EMP: 4 **EST:** 2019
SALES (est): 41.3K **Privately Held**
SIC: 2741 Miscellaneous publishing

(G-10336)
NORTHAMERICAN REPRODUCTION
34943 6 Mile Rd (48152-2991)
PHONE 734 421-6800
Taras A Filas, *President*
Cheryl Evenson, *General Mgr*
EMP: 5 **EST:** 1977
SQ FT: 3,000
SALES (est): 210.3K **Privately Held**
SIC: 2752 Commercial printing, offset

(G-10337)
NORTHROP GRMMN SPCE & MSSN SYS
12025 Tech Center Dr (48150-2122)
PHONE 734 266-2600
EMP: 900 **Publicly Held**
SIC: 3714 Mfg Vehicle Brakes Systems & Parts
HQ: Northrop Grumman Space & Mission Systems Corp.
6377 San Ignacio Ave
San Jose CA 95119
703 280-2900

(G-10338)
NOVARES CORPORATION US INC (DH)
19575 Victor Pkwy Ste 400 (48152-7026)
PHONE 248 449-6100
Terry Gohl, *CEO*
EMP: 108 **EST:** 2007
SALES (est): 445.5MM
SALES (corp-wide): 113.4MM **Privately Held**
SIC: 3089 7389 Automotive parts, plastic; design services
HQ: Novares Group
361 Avenue Du General De Gaulle
Clamart
155 955-560

(G-10339)
NOVARES US LLC (DH)
Also Called: Novares Group
19575 Victor Pkwy Ste 400 (48152-7026)
PHONE 248 449-6100
Fernando Duarte, *Vice Pres*
Dean Froney, *Vice Pres*
Thomas Hagan, *Vice Pres*
Dean Proney, *Vice Pres*
David McLaughlin-Smit, *Mfg Spvr*
▲ **EMP:** 64 **EST:** 1996
SQ FT: 24,500
SALES (est): 445.5MM
SALES (corp-wide): 113.4MM **Privately Held**
WEB: www.novaresteam.com
SIC: 3089 Injection molding of plastics
HQ: Novares Corporation Us Inc.
19575 Victor Pkwy Ste 400
Livonia MI 48152
248 449-6100

(G-10340)
NOVASTAR SOLUTIONSCOM LLC
35200 Plymouth Rd (48150-1456)
PHONE 734 453-8003
Matthew Nolff, *Warehouse Mgr*
Michael Gangler, *QC Mgr*
Jacqueline Gangler, *Human Res Mgr*
Josiah Klaus, *Accounts Mgr*
Tim Sturzenegger, *Accounts Exec*
EMP: 74 **EST:** 1998
SQ FT: 23,000
SALES (est): 13.7MM **Privately Held**
WEB: www.novastar.net
SIC: 7378 5045 5734 7379 Computer maintenance & repair; computers, peripherals & software; computer & software stores; computer related consulting services; computers, digital, analog or hybrid

(G-10341)
NU CON CORPORATION
34100 Industrial Rd (48150-1335)
PHONE 734 525-0770
David Stormont, *President*
David L Bernhardt, *Exec VP*
M Robert Barnes, *Treasurer*
Bill Gresham, *Marketing Staff*
Allen Stevens, *Shareholder*
EMP: 32 **EST:** 1973
SQ FT: 5,000 **Privately Held**
WEB: www.nuconcorp.com
SIC: 3511 3728 3724 3714 Turbines & turbine generator sets; aircraft parts & equipment; aircraft engines & engine parts; motor vehicle parts & accessories

(G-10342)
NUKO PRECISION LLC
35455 Schoolcraft Rd (48150-1222)
PHONE 734 464-6856
▲ **EMP:** 17
SQ FT: 17,000
SALES (est): 1.1MM **Privately Held**
SIC: 3451 Mfg Screw Machine Products

(G-10343)
NYX LLC (PA)
Also Called: Nyx Technologies
36111 Schoolcraft Rd (48150-1216)
PHONE 734 462-2385
Dan Taylor, *General Mgr*
James Waldo, *Vice Pres*
Walter Mathews, *Production*
Sarbnoor Gill, *Buyer*
Sunny Singh, *Purchasing*
▲ **EMP:** 225 **EST:** 1978
SQ FT: 45,000
SALES (est): 556.1MM **Privately Held**
WEB: www.nyxinc.com
SIC: 3089 3714 3565 2671 Injection molding of plastics; motor vehicle parts & accessories; packaging machinery; packaging paper & plastics film, coated & laminated

(G-10344)
NYX LLC
Nyx Livonia Plant I
28100 Plymouth Rd (48150-2328)
PHONE 734 261-4324
Muddu Krishna, *Branch Mgr*
EMP: 89

Livonia - Wayne County (G-10345)

SALES (corp-wide): 556.1MM **Privately Held**
WEB: www.nyxinc.com
SIC: **3714** Motor vehicle parts & accessories
PA: Nyx, Llc
36111 Schoolcraft Rd
Livonia MI 48150
734 462-2385

(G-10345)
NYX LLC
30111 Schoolcraft Rd (48150-2006)
PHONE..................................734 421-3850
Chain S Sandhu, *CEO*
Daniel Thornton, *Warehouse Mgr*
Jeannine Laible, *Human Res Dir*
EMP: 63
SALES (corp-wide): 556.1MM **Privately Held**
WEB: www.nyxinc.com
SIC: **3089** Injection molding of plastics
PA: Nyx, Llc
36111 Schoolcraft Rd
Livonia MI 48150
734 462-2385

(G-10346)
NYX LLC
Also Called: Nyx Plymouth
38700 Plymouth Rd (48150-1055)
PHONE..................................734 464-0800
Suresh Gadiyaram, *Vice Pres*
Prabhjit Singh, *Opers Mgr*
Dennis Fuchs, *Maint Spvr*
Joe Kerekes, *Opers Staff*
Vick Bhullar, *Production*
EMP: 76
SALES (corp-wide): 556.1MM **Privately Held**
WEB: www.nyxinc.com
SIC: **3559** 3643 3537 Automotive related machinery; current-carrying wiring devices; industrial trucks & tractors
PA: Nyx, Llc
36111 Schoolcraft Rd
Livonia MI 48150
734 462-2385

(G-10347)
NYX LLC
Also Called: Nyx Livonia Plant II
28350 Plymouth Rd (48150-2790)
PHONE..................................734 261-7535
Aman Deol, *QC Mgr*
Dan Taylor, *Branch Mgr*
EMP: 89
SALES (corp-wide): 556.1MM **Privately Held**
WEB: www.nyxinc.com
SIC: **3714** 3089 3565 2671 Motor vehicle parts & accessories; injection molding of plastics; packaging machinery; packaging paper & plastics film, coated & laminated
PA: Nyx, Llc
36111 Schoolcraft Rd
Livonia MI 48150
734 462-2385

(G-10348)
NYX LLC ◆
Also Called: Nyx Newburgh
36930 Industrial Rd (48150-1135)
PHONE..................................734 462-2385
Jeannine Laible, *Mng Member*
EMP: 100 EST: 2021
SALES (est): 10MM **Privately Held**
SIC: **3711** 8711 Automobile assembly, including specialty automobiles; engineering services

(G-10349)
O KELLER TOOL ENGRG CO LLC
12701 Inkster Rd (48150-2216)
P.O. Box 510327 (48151-6327)
PHONE..................................734 425-4500
Barry W La Chance, *CEO*
Brian W Van Norman, *President*
Daniel Grayson, *COO*
Ryan Lachance, *Plant Mgr*
Danny Kovacs, *Project Mgr*
EMP: 55 EST: 1943
SQ FT: 30,000
SALES (est): 14.5MM **Privately Held**
WEB: www.okeller.com
SIC: **3545** 3544 3537 Gauges (machine tool accessories); jigs & fixtures; pallets, metal
PA: Keller Tool Ltd
12701 Inkster Rd
Livonia MI 48150
734 425-4500

(G-10350)
OAKLAND AUTOMATION LLC
13017 Newburgh Rd (48150-5009)
PHONE..................................248 589-3350
Greg Harvey, *CEO*
Tim Miller, *Business Mgr*
Dan Bickersteth,
Bryan Tolles,
EMP: 40 EST: 2016
SALES (est): 4MM **Privately Held**
WEB: www.oaklandautomation.com
SIC: **3599** 8711 Custom machinery; engineering services

(G-10351)
OBR CONTROL SYSTEMS INC
32233 8 Mile Rd (48152-1361)
PHONE..................................248 672-3339
Ole Buhl, *Principal*
EMP: 6 EST: 2019
SALES (est): 510.8K **Privately Held**
WEB: www.obrcontrolsystems.com
SIC: **3714** Motor vehicle parts & accessories

(G-10352)
ODYSSEY ELECTRONICS INC
12886 Fairlane St (48150-1327)
PHONE..................................734 421-8340
Ernest V Flamont, *President*
Mark Estes, *Vice Pres*
Jen Bartels, *Purchasing*
Traci Cauchi, *QC Mgr*
Mike Burley, *Engineer*
▲ EMP: 70 EST: 1989
SQ FT: 18,420
SALES (est): 22.9MM **Privately Held**
WEB: www.odyssey-oei.com
SIC: **3672** 5065 Printed circuit boards; electronic parts & equipment

(G-10353)
ONE-WAY TOOL & DIE INC
32845 8 Mile Rd (48152-1337)
PHONE..................................248 477-2964
Adam Bowser, *President*
EMP: 5 EST: 1978
SQ FT: 1,800
SALES (est): 400K **Privately Held**
SIC: **3544** Special dies & tools

(G-10354)
OVERSEAS AUTO PARTS INC
32400 Plymouth Rd (48150-1712)
PHONE..................................734 427-4840
John Demrovsky, *President*
Andrew Demrovsky, *President*
Helen Demrovsky, *Treasurer*
Sam Demrovsky, *Admin Sec*
Samuel Demrovsky, *Admin Sec*
EMP: 24 EST: 1958
SQ FT: 20,000
SALES (est): 3MM **Privately Held**
WEB: www.overseasautoparts.com
SIC: **5013** 3694 Motor vehicle supplies & new parts; automotive electrical equipment

(G-10355)
OXBOW MACHINE PRODUCTS INC (PA)
12743 Merriman Rd (48150-1800)
PHONE..................................734 422-7730
John R Tiano, *CEO*
Robert C Tiano, *President*
Michael J Tiano, *Vice Pres*
EMP: 30 EST: 1935
SQ FT: 27,800
SALES (est): 7.7MM **Privately Held**
WEB: www.oxbow-machine.com
SIC: **3544** Special dies & tools

(G-10356)
P M Z TECHNOLOGY INC
Also Called: Video Service Center
33302 7 Mile Rd (48152-1369)
PHONE..................................248 471-0447
Paul Zsenyuk, *President*
Steve Zsenyuk, *Treasurer*
Mariann Zsenyuk, *Admin Sec*
EMP: 4 EST: 1984
SQ FT: 1,200
SALES (est): 300K **Privately Held**
SIC: **3672** Printed circuit boards

(G-10357)
PA PRODUCTS INC
Also Called: P A Products
33709 Schoolcraft Rd (48150-1505)
PHONE..................................734 421-1060
Tim Pilzner, *President*
Timothy Pilzner, *President*
Ellen Pilzner, *Corp Secy*
▲ EMP: 7 EST: 1995
SQ FT: 13,500
SALES (est): 1.2MM **Privately Held**
WEB: www.paprod.com
SIC: **3496** 5072 5046 Screening, woven wire: made from purchased wire; cutlery; restaurant equipment & supplies

(G-10358)
PACKAGING CORPORATION AMERICA
Also Called: PCA
28330 Plymouth Rd (48150-2790)
PHONE..................................734 266-1877
EMP: 5
SALES (corp-wide): 6.6B **Publicly Held**
WEB: www.packagingcorp.com
SIC: **2653** Boxes, corrugated: made from purchased materials
PA: Packaging Corporation Of America
1 N Field Ct
Lake Forest IL 60045
847 482-3000

(G-10359)
PANEL PRO LLC
16809 Ryan Rd (48154-6232)
PHONE..................................734 427-1691
Thomas Lee, *Principal*
EMP: 4 EST: 2004
SALES (est): 225.6K **Privately Held**
WEB: www.panelpro.com
SIC: **3643** Electric switches

(G-10360)
PARKWAY DRAPERY & UPHL CO INC
Also Called: Parkway Contract Group
12784 Currie Ct (48150-1109)
PHONE..................................734 779-1300
Robert Zaguroli, *President*
EMP: 9 EST: 1968
SQ FT: 4,000
SALES (est): 1.6MM **Privately Held**
WEB: www.parkwaycontractgroup.com
SIC: **2591** 2391 7641 5023 Window blinds; blinds vertical; draperies, plastic & textile: from purchased materials; reupholstery; carpets; drapery material, woven; millwork

(G-10361)
PAVCO MCR
38521 Schoolcraft Rd (48150-1031)
PHONE..................................734 464-2220
▲ EMP: 9 EST: 2009
SALES (est): 80.7K **Privately Held**
WEB: www.pavco.com
SIC: **3599** Machine shop, jobbing & repair

(G-10362)
PEPPERIDGE FARM INCORPORATED
Also Called: Pepperidge Farm Thrift Store
29115 8 Mile Rd (48152-2009)
PHONE..................................734 953-6729
Pamela Baker, *Manager*
EMP: 6
SALES (corp-wide): 8.4B **Publicly Held**
WEB: www.pepperidgefarm.com
SIC: **5461** 2052 2099 2053 Bakeries; cookies; bread crumbs, not made in bakeries; frozen bakery products, except bread
HQ: Pepperidge Farm, Incorporated
595 Westport Ave
Norwalk CT 06851
203 846-7000

(G-10363)
PERFORMNCE ASSMBLY SLTIONS LLC
28190 Plymouth Rd (48150-2398)
PHONE..................................734 466-6380
Facundo Bravo, *President*
▲ EMP: 24 EST: 1999
SQ FT: 29,000
SALES (est): 8.8MM **Privately Held**
WEB: www.performanceas.com
SIC: **3714** Motor vehicle parts & accessories

(G-10364)
PHIBER PRINTING LLC
19437 Bainbridge Ave (48152-1790)
PHONE..................................248 471-9435
Alicia Nagel, *Principal*
EMP: 5 EST: 2015
SALES (est): 123.2K **Privately Held**
SIC: **2752** Commercial printing, offset

(G-10365)
PHOENIX IMAGING INC (PA)
Also Called: Phoenix Imaging Machine Vision
29865 6 Mile Rd (48152-3673)
PHONE..................................248 476-4200
Gerald Budd, *President*
Lauren Krawec, *Treasurer*
Jeanie Cox, *Office Admin*
John A Cook, *Admin Sec*
▼ EMP: 12 EST: 1985
SQ FT: 3,400
SALES (est): 3.3MM **Privately Held**
WEB: www.phoeniximaging.com
SIC: **3827** 3648 Optical test & inspection equipment; lighting equipment

(G-10366)
PLASTOMER CORPORATION
37819 Schoolcraft Rd (48150-1096)
PHONE..................................734 464-0700
Walter Baughman III, *President*
David Baughman, *Exec VP*
Scott Gibson, *QC Mgr*
Waler G Baughman, *Technical Mgr*
Roger Baughman, *Treasurer*
▲ EMP: 200
SQ FT: 175,000
SALES (est): 30.8MM **Privately Held**
WEB: www.plastomer.com
SIC: **3089** Injection molding of plastics

(G-10367)
PLYMOUTH GARAGE LLC
33943 Plymouth Rd (48150-1564)
PHONE..................................734 459-3667
EMP: 6 EST: 2019
SALES (est): 366.6K **Privately Held**
WEB: www.theplymouthgarage.com
SIC: **3442** Garage doors, overhead: metal

(G-10368)
POWER CAPES
34029 Schoolcraft Rd (48150-1313)
PHONE..................................313 454-1492
Justin Draplin, *President*
EMP: 5 EST: 2014
SALES (est): 65.9K **Privately Held**
SIC: **2389** Apparel & accessories

(G-10369)
POWER-BRITE OF MICHIGAN INC
12053 Levan Rd (48150-1449)
PHONE..................................734 591-7911
Spence P Babcock, *President*
Dorothy Babcock, *Corp Secy*
T Fred Moseley, *Vice Pres*
EMP: 18 EST: 1978
SQ FT: 10,000
SALES (est): 1.5MM **Privately Held**
SIC: **3589** Car washing machinery

(G-10370)
POWERTHRU INC
11825 Mayfield St (48150-1707)
PHONE..................................734 583-5004
EMP: 8 EST: 2012

GEOGRAPHIC SECTION
Livonia - Wayne County (G-10396)

SALES (est): 710K
SALES (corp-wide): 37.9MM **Privately Held**
SIC: 3621 Mfg Motors/Generators
PA: Phillips Service Industries, Inc.
  11878 Hubbard St
  Livonia MI 48105
  734 853-5000

(G-10371)
POWERTHRU INC
11825 Mayfield St (48150-1707)
P.O. Box 3313 (48151-3313)
PHONE..................734 853-5004
William S Phillips, *CEO*
Lawrence E Perlin, *CFO*
EMP: 12 EST: 2012
SALES (est): 3MM
SALES (corp-wide): 461.5MM **Privately Held**
WEB: www.power-thru.com
SIC: 3621 Motors & generators
HQ: Beaver Aerospace & Defense, Inc.
  11850 Mayfield St
  Livonia MI 48150
  734 853-5003

(G-10372)
PRATT CLASSIC CONTAINER INC
32432 Capitol St (48150-1703)
PHONE..................734 525-0410
Brian McPheely, *President*
EMP: 33 EST: 2004
SALES (est): 642.3K **Privately Held**
WEB: www.prattindustries.com
SIC: 3086 Plastics foam products

(G-10373)
PRATT INDUSTRIES INC
32432 Capitol St (48150-1703)
PHONE..................734 853-3000
Craig Beaudoin, *General Mgr*
Stuart Baskin, *Sales Staff*
Darren Pepple, *Sales Staff*
Hanna Beaudoin, *Executive*
EMP: 5 **Privately Held**
WEB: www.prattindustries.com
SIC: 2653 Boxes, corrugated: made from purchased materials
PA: Pratt Industries, Inc.
  1800 Sarasot Bus Pkwy Ne S
  Conyers GA 30013

(G-10374)
PREMIER PANEL COMPANY
12300 Merriman Rd (48150-1917)
PHONE..................734 427-1700
Tim Oliver, *President*
Jeff Crampton, *President*
Melvin Guthery, *Principal*
William Gutherie, *Admin Sec*
EMP: 17 EST: 2001
SQ FT: 16,000
SALES (est): 392.9K **Privately Held**
WEB: www.premierpanel.net
SIC: 2452 Prefabricated wood buildings

(G-10375)
PSI REPAIR SERVICES INC (HQ)
Also Called: PSI Semicon Services
11900 Mayfield St (48150-1785)
P.O. Box 3313 (48151-3313)
PHONE..................734 853-5000
Scott Phillips, *CEO*
William S Phillips, *President*
William T Phillips, *Chairman*
Bob Phillips, *Vice Pres*
Aaron Lawson, *Project Mgr*
EMP: 200 EST: 1979
SQ FT: 5,800
SALES (est): 27.9MM
SALES (corp-wide): 54.3MM **Privately Held**
WEB: www.psisemiconservices.com
SIC: 7699 7694 7629 Pumps & pumping equipment repair; valve repair, industrial; electric motor repair; circuit board repair
PA: Phillips Service Industries, Inc.
  1800 Landsdowne Rd
  Ann Arbor MI 48105
  734 853-5000

(G-10376)
QUAKER HOUGHTON PA INC
17177 N Laurel Park Dr # 21 (48152-2693)
PHONE..................248 641-3231
EMP: 4
SALES (corp-wide): 1.4B **Publicly Held**
WEB: www.home.quakerhoughton.com
SIC: 2869 Industrial organic chemicals
HQ: Quaker Houghton Pa, Inc.
  901 E Hector St
  Conshohocken PA 19428
  610 832-4000

(G-10377)
QUALITY METALCRAFT INC (HQ)
28101 Schoolcraft Rd (48150-2239)
PHONE..................734 261-6700
Kurt Saldana, *CEO*
Ken Lerg, *COO*
Brian Papke, *Vice Pres*
Louie Ajini, *QC Mgr*
Jim Bowdler, *QC Mgr*
▲ EMP: 234 EST: 1964
SALES (est): 88.8MM
SALES (corp-wide): 160MM **Privately Held**
WEB: www.qmc-emi.com
SIC: 3544 3465 3469 3444 Special dies & tools; automotive stampings; metal stampings; sheet metalwork
PA: Watermill-Qmc Holdings, Corp.
  750 Marrett Rd Ste 401
  Lexington MA 02421
  781 891-6660

(G-10378)
QUALITY METALCRAFT INC
12001 Farmington Rd (48150-1725)
PHONE..................734 261-6700
Alexander Chetcuti, *Ch of Bd*
Julie Ellsworth, *Manager*
EMP: 249
SALES (corp-wide): 160MM **Privately Held**
WEB: www.qmc-emi.com
SIC: 3544 Special dies & tools
HQ: Quality Metalcraft, Inc.
  28101 Schoolcraft Rd
  Livonia MI 48150
  734 261-6700

(G-10379)
QUANTUM CHEMICAL LLC
Also Called: Chemsol
12944 Farmington Rd (48150-4201)
PHONE..................734 429-0033
Robert Skandalaris, *President*
Krista Korte, *Cust Mgr*
EMP: 9 EST: 1994
SQ FT: 8,000
SALES (est): 2.1MM **Privately Held**
WEB: www.chemsol.com
SIC: 2851 5085 5169 Paints & paint additives; undercoatings, paint; polyurethane coatings; abrasives & adhesives; adhesives & sealants; industrial chemicals

(G-10380)
R & B INDUSTRIES INC
12055 Globe St (48150-1142)
PHONE..................734 462-9478
Mark Schloff, *President*
Facundo Bravo, *Principal*
▼ EMP: 20 EST: 1985
SQ FT: 40,000
SALES (est): 623K **Privately Held**
SIC: 3599 3545 Machine shop, jobbing & repair; machine tool accessories

(G-10381)
R CUSHMAN & ASSOCIATES INC
Also Called: Fabco Automotive
12623 Newburgh Rd (48150-1001)
PHONE..................248 477-9900
Richard Cushman, *President*
Marcel Bosca, *Engineer*
JB Derderian, *Director*
Jim Carney, *Planning*
▲ EMP: 1292 EST: 1966
SQ FT: 60,000
SALES (est): 30.9MM **Publicly Held**
WEB: www.rcushman.com
SIC: 3714 8711 Transmissions, motor vehicle; industrial engineers
HQ: Meritor Specialty Products Llc
  2135 W Maple Rd
  Troy MI 48084
  248 435-1000

(G-10382)
R L SCHMITT COMPANY INC
34506 Glendale St (48150-1304)
PHONE..................734 525-9310
Paul L Schmitt, *President*
Bruce J Schmitt, *President*
EMP: 24 EST: 1947
SQ FT: 12,000
SALES (est): 2.5MM **Privately Held**
WEB: www.rlschmitt.com
SIC: 3545 2819 Cutting tools for machine tools; industrial inorganic chemicals

(G-10383)
RC CABINETRY
11140 Karen St (48150-3145)
PHONE..................734 513-2677
Ronald Cuip, *Principal*
EMP: 5 EST: 2003
SALES (est): 153.7K **Privately Held**
SIC: 2434 Wood kitchen cabinets

(G-10384)
REEMCO INCORPORATED
11801 Belden Ct (48150-1460)
PHONE..................734 522-8988
Hanna M Ackall, *President*
Richard C Schultz, *Partner*
EMP: 6 EST: 1991
SQ FT: 10,000
SALES (est): 654.1K **Privately Held**
SIC: 3599 Machine shop, jobbing & repair

(G-10385)
REP INNOVATIONS INC
Also Called: T-Tool Company
34435 Glendale St (48150-1301)
PHONE..................734 744-6968
EMP: 10 EST: 2017
SALES (est): 670.5K **Privately Held**
SIC: 3599 Machine shop, jobbing & repair

(G-10386)
REPLACEMENT WEST GLASS
32401 8 Mile Rd (48152-1301)
PHONE..................248 974-4635
EMP: 4 EST: 2018
SALES (est): 223.7K **Privately Held**
WEB: www.west-glass-replacement.com
SIC: 3442 Metal doors, sash & trim

(G-10387)
RICH-WALL CUSTOM CABINE
28243 Plymouth Rd (48150-5300)
PHONE..................734 237-4934
EMP: 5 EST: 2019
SALES (est): 233.1K **Privately Held**
WEB: www.richwallcabinets.com
SIC: 2434 Wood kitchen cabinets

(G-10388)
RK BORING INC
35425 Schoolcraft Rd (48150-1222)
PHONE..................734 542-7920
Kevin Stevens, *President*
EMP: 7 EST: 1989
SQ FT: 3,300
SALES (est): 982.3K **Privately Held**
SIC: 3544 Special dies & tools

(G-10389)
ROBICCON INC
27521 Schoolcraft Rd (48150-2217)
PHONE..................734 425-7080
John Cottos, *Agent*
EMP: 11 EST: 2020
SALES (est): 607.9K **Privately Held**
WEB: www.robiccon.com
SIC: 3578 Calculating & accounting equipment

(G-10390)
ROLLS-ROYCE SOLUTIONS AMER INC
30946 Industrial Rd (48150-2054)
PHONE..................734 261-0309
EMP: 5
SALES (corp-wide): 15.7B **Privately Held**
WEB: www.mtuamericacareers.com
SIC: 3519 Diesel engine rebuilding
HQ: Rolls-Royce Solutions America Inc.
  39525 Mackenzie Dr
  Novi MI 48377
  248 560-8000

(G-10391)
ROUSH ENTERPRISES INC
12447 Levan Rd (48150-1405)
PHONE..................734 779-7006
EMP: 646 **Privately Held**
WEB: www.roush.com
SIC: 3714 Motor vehicle parts & accessories
PA: Roush Enterprises, Inc.
  34300 W 9 Mile Rd
  Farmington MI 48335

(G-10392)
ROUSH INDUSTRIES INC
36580 Commerce St (48150-1121)
PHONE..................734 779-7016
Jeff Johnston, *Vice Pres*
EMP: 4 **Privately Held**
WEB: www.roush.com
SIC: 8711 3714 8734 7948 Engineering services; motor vehicle parts & accessories; testing laboratories; racing, including track operation
HQ: Roush Industries, Inc.
  12447 Levan Rd
  Livonia MI 48150
  734 779-7006

(G-10393)
ROUSH INDUSTRIES INC
11874 Market St (48150-1123)
PHONE..................734 779-7013
Tom Topper, *Branch Mgr*
EMP: 4 **Privately Held**
WEB: www.roush.com
SIC: 8711 3714 8734 Engineering services; motor vehicle engines & parts; motor vehicle transmissions, drive assemblies & parts; automobile proving & testing ground
HQ: Roush Industries, Inc.
  12447 Levan Rd
  Livonia MI 48150
  734 779-7006

(G-10394)
ROUSH INDUSTRIES INC
12447 Levan Rd Bldg 6 (48150-1405)
PHONE..................734 779-7000
Doug Smith, *Branch Mgr*
EMP: 4 **Privately Held**
WEB: www.roush.com
SIC: 3599 Machine & other job shop work
HQ: Roush Industries, Inc.
  12447 Levan Rd
  Livonia MI 48150
  734 779-7006

(G-10395)
ROUSH MANUFACTURING INC (HQ)
12447 Levan Rd (48150-1405)
PHONE..................734 779-7006
Evan Lyall, *CEO*
Jeff Johnston, *Exec VP*
Dean Massab, *Exec VP*
Steve Sciatto, *Vice Pres*
▲ EMP: 130 EST: 2003
SALES (est): 47.7MM **Privately Held**
WEB: www.roush.com
SIC: 3714 8711 Motor vehicle parts & accessories; engineering services

(G-10396)
S & C TOOL & MANUFACTURING
30954 Industrial Rd Ste A (48150-2061)
PHONE..................313 378-1003
John L Spiteri, *President*
Sandra K Spiteri, *Admin Sec*
EMP: 4 EST: 1980
SQ FT: 2,000
SALES (est): 356.3K **Privately Held**
SIC: 3599 Machine shop, jobbing & repair

Livonia - Wayne County (G-10397)

(G-10397)
S & L TOOL INC
11833 Brookfield St (48150-1701)
PHONE 734 464-4200
EMP: 7
SALES (est): 940.1K Privately Held
SIC: 3541 3542 Machine Tools, Metal Cutting Type

(G-10398)
SALES & ENGINEERING INC
32920 Industrial Rd (48150-1617)
PHONE 734 525-9030
James D Allen, *President*
Cynthia Allen, *Vice Pres*
EMP: 50 EST: 1971
SQ FT: 31,000
SALES (est): 8MM Privately Held
WEB: www.sales-eng.com
SIC: 3465 3498 3441 Body parts, automobile: stamped metal; tube fabricating (contract bending & shaping); fabricated structural metal

(G-10399)
SAMPLING BAG TECHNOLOGIES LLC
27491 Schoolcraft Rd (48150-2201)
PHONE 734 525-8600
George Smith, *General Mgr*
Arthur Coleman, *Mng Member*
EMP: 6 EST: 2006 Privately Held
WEB: www.samplingbagtech.com
SIC: 3634 Blankets, electric

(G-10400)
SB INVESTMENTS LLC
Also Called: Reinhart Industries
12055 Globe St (48150-1142)
PHONE 734 462-9478
Chris Goulet, *Engineer*
Mark J Schloff, *Mng Member*
EMP: 22 EST: 2005
SQ FT: 28,000
SALES (est): 15MM Privately Held
SIC: 3549 3545 Marking machines, metalworking; arbors (machine tool accessories)

(G-10401)
SCHEELS CONCRETE INC
33146 Grennada St (48154-4171)
PHONE 734 782-1464
EMP: 8 EST: 1919
SQ FT: 20,000
SALES (est): 1MM Privately Held
SIC: 3273 Mfg Ready-Mixed Concrete

(G-10402)
SCRAPPY CHIC
33523 8 Mile Rd Ste C1 (48152-4104)
PHONE 248 426-9020
Chris Nicholson, *Executive Asst*
EMP: 4 EST: 2006
SALES (est): 236.7K Privately Held
WEB: www.scrappychiclivonia.com
SIC: 2782 Scrapbooks

(G-10403)
SECURITY COUNTERMEASURES TECH
37637 5 Mile Rd (48154-1543)
PHONE 248 237-6263
William Tisaby, *Principal*
Vivian Allen, *COO*
EMP: 7 EST: 2010
SALES (est): 444.3K Privately Held
SIC: 3131 Counters

(G-10404)
SENSCOMP INC
36704 Commerce St (48150-1164)
PHONE 734 953-4783
Richard Berzerko, *President*
EMP: 7 EST: 2002
SALES (est): 517.5K Privately Held
WEB: www.senscomp.com
SIC: 3829 Measuring & controlling devices

(G-10405)
SHINWON USA INC
12147 Globe St (48150-1142)
PHONE 734 469-2550
EMP: 25 EST: 2019
SALES (est): 2.6MM Privately Held
WEB: www.shinwon-usa.business.site
SIC: 3089 Molding primary plastic

(G-10406)
SIEMENS INDUSTRY SOFTWARE INC
38695 7 Mile Rd Ste 300 (48152-7097)
PHONE 734 953-2700
Lovquist George, *Branch Mgr*
Mary Charnley, *Manager*
Bryan Carr, *Consultant*
Tanya Wogaman, *Consultant*
EMP: 8
SALES (corp-wide): 67.4B Privately Held
WEB: www.siemens.com
SIC: 8249 3699 8331 Business training services; electronic training devices; skill training center
HQ: Siemens Industry Software Inc.
5800 Granite Pkwy Ste 600
Plano TX 75024
972 987-3000

(G-10407)
SIGMA DIAGNOSTICS INC
Also Called: Immunospec
14155 Farmington Rd Ste D (48154-5422)
PHONE 734 744-4846
Mojeeb Shahbain, *Principal*
▲ EMP: 8 EST: 2014
SALES (est): 83.9K Privately Held
SIC: 2835 In vitro & in vivo diagnostic substances

(G-10408)
SIGMA INTERNATIONAL INC (PA)
36800 Plymouth Rd (48150-1136)
PHONE 248 230-9681
Christopher J Naidoo, *CEO*
Patty Jones, *Engineer*
Erik Goerke, *CFO*
April Duncan, *Supervisor*
◆ EMP: 18 EST: 2007
SQ FT: 8,150
SALES (est): 3.9MM Privately Held
WEB: www.sigmaintl.com
SIC: 2396 2821 3471 Fabric printing & stamping; plastics materials & resins; electroplating & plating

(G-10409)
SIGN STUFF INC
13604 Merriman Rd (48150-1814)
PHONE 734 458-1055
William J Buyers IV, *President*
Leann Decker, *Sales Staff*
Danny Desjardin, *Manager*
EMP: 5 EST: 2000
SQ FT: 3,100
SALES (est): 514.2K Privately Held
WEB: www.signstuff.com
SIC: 3993 Signs & advertising specialties

(G-10410)
SIGNS BY TOMORROW
33611 Plymouth Rd (48150-1563)
PHONE 734 522-8440
Gary Phillips, *Owner*
Steve Kade, *Manager*
EMP: 8 EST: 2011
SALES (est): 326.6K Privately Held
WEB: www.signsbytomorrow.com
SIC: 3993 Signs & advertising specialties

(G-10411)
SL WHEELS INC
Also Called: Speedline
38701 7 Mile Rd Ste 155 (48152-3970)
PHONE 734 744-8500
Michele Mazzucconi, *President*
▲ EMP: 5 EST: 1997
SALES (est): 1.3MM
SALES (corp-wide): 1.4B Privately Held
WEB: www.ronalgroup.com
SIC: 3312 Wheels
HQ: Speedline Srl
Via Emilio Salgari 6
Santa Maria Di Sala VE 30036
041 572-5820

(G-10412)
SLOTTING INGRAM & MACHINE
32175 Industrial Rd (48150-1836)
PHONE 248 478-2430
David Ingram, *President*
EMP: 10 EST: 1973
SQ FT: 6,300
SALES (est): 1.1MM Privately Held
SIC: 3599 Machine shop, jobbing & repair; custom machinery

(G-10413)
SOL-I-COR INDUSTRIES
Also Called: Corian By Solicor Industries
30795 8 Mile Rd (48150-1601)
PHONE 248 476-0670
Gary Bohr, *Owner*
EMP: 7 EST: 1997
SALES (est): 134.8K Privately Held
SIC: 3441 Fabricated structural metal

(G-10414)
SOUTH / WIN LLC
11800 Sears St (48150-2107)
PHONE 734 525-9000
Fred Greco, *Branch Mgr*
EMP: 6
SALES (corp-wide): 836.6MM Privately Held
WEB: www.southwinltd.com
SIC: 2841 5169 Soap & other detergents; chemicals & allied products
HQ: South / Win, Llc
112 Maxfield Rd
Greensboro NC 27405

(G-10415)
SPARE DIE INC
30948 Industrial Rd (48150-2024)
PHONE 734 522-2508
Ron Clymer, *President*
EMP: 4 EST: 2002
SALES (est): 322.1K Privately Held
SIC: 3544 Special dies & tools

(G-10416)
SPECTRUM AUTOMATION COMPANY
34447 Schoolcraft Rd (48150-1316)
PHONE 734 522-2160
Richard D Zimmerman, *President*
Thomas Zimmerman, *Corp Secy*
EMP: 25 EST: 1969
SQ FT: 26,000
SALES (est): 3.2MM Privately Held
WEB: www.spectrumautomation.com
SIC: 3535 Unit handling conveying systems

(G-10417)
STANDARD DIE INTERNATIONAL INC (PA)
12980 Wayne Rd (48150-1259)
PHONE 800 838-5464
Douglas C Menzies, *President*
Tim Plymale, *COO*
Alan R Menzies, *Vice Pres*
David Waldeck, *Vice Pres*
Gregory Gagner, *Purch Mgr*
EMP: 50
SQ FT: 30,000
SALES (est): 13.1MM Privately Held
WEB: www.standarddie.com
SIC: 3544 3469 Special dies & tools; stamping metal for the trade

(G-10418)
STANDFAST INDUSTRIES INC
13570 Wayne Rd (48150-1270)
PHONE 248 380-3223
Brian D O'Connor, *President*
Gary T Riddell, *Corp Secy*
Laurette Walsh, *Vice Pres*
EMP: 16 EST: 1988
SQ FT: 27,500
SALES (est): 2.6MM Privately Held
WEB: www.standfastnitrogencylinders.com
SIC: 3561 Cylinders, pump

(G-10419)
STAR DESIGN METRO DETROIT LLC
32401 8 Mile Rd Ste 1-1 (48152-1301)
PHONE 734 740-0189
Ali Ayesh,
EMP: 41 EST: 2012
SQ FT: 1,000
SALES (est): 1.6MM Privately Held
SIC: 7336 7819 2741 3993 Commercial art & graphic design; developing & printing of commercial motion picture film; posters: publishing & printing; electric signs

(G-10420)
STEELCRAFT TOOL CO INC
12930 Wayne Rd (48150-1272)
PHONE 734 522-7130
James P Glaser, *President*
Nancy G Marr, *Vice Pres*
EMP: 18 EST: 1943
SQ FT: 13,000
SALES (est): 1.3MM Privately Held
WEB: www.steelcrafttool.com
SIC: 3545 3423 Cutting tools for machine tools; hand & edge tools

(G-10421)
STEINER ASSOCIATES
15735 Norwich St (48154-2839)
PHONE 734 422-5188
Marvin Steiner, *Owner*
EMP: 6 EST: 1998
SALES (est): 216.3K Privately Held
WEB: www.steiner-associates.com
SIC: 1389 Oil & gas field services

(G-10422)
STORCH PRODUCTS COMPANY INC
Also Called: Storch Magnetics
11827 Globe St (48150-1188)
PHONE 734 591-2200
Marjorie A Storch, *President*
Thomas Papora, *Vice Pres*
Todd Papora, *Vice Pres*
Crystal West, *Production*
Robert Mount, *Engineer*
◆ EMP: 17 EST: 1952
SQ FT: 25,500
SALES (est): 3.7MM Privately Held
WEB: www.storchmagnetics.com
SIC: 3695 3535 Magnetic & optical recording media; conveyors & conveying equipment

(G-10423)
SUGRU INC
38120 Amrhein Rd (48150-5016)
PHONE 877 990-9888
EMP: 20 EST: 2010
SALES (est): 3.3MM
SALES (corp-wide): 12B Privately Held
WEB: www.sugru.com
SIC: 2891 Glue
HQ: Formformform Ltd
Unit 2
London E9 7S

(G-10424)
SUPERIOR INFORMATION TECH LLC
Also Called: Anantics
38701 7 Mile Rd Ste 285 (48152-4123)
PHONE 734 666-9963
Anurag Kulshrestha, *President*
Prashant Rai, *Security Dir*
EMP: 10 EST: 2009
SQ FT: 2,500
SALES (est): 1MM Privately Held
WEB: www.superiorinfotech.com
SIC: 7371 7372 7373 7389 Computer software development; application computer software; utility computer software; systems engineering, computer related; turnkey vendors, computer systems; photogrammatic mapping

(G-10425)
SWEED DREAMS LLC
27552 Schoolcraft Rd (48150-2203)
PHONE 313 704-6694
Tonya Mora, *CEO*
EMP: 4 EST: 2015
SALES (est): 14.6K Privately Held
WEB: www.sweeddreams.com
SIC: 2844 7231 5149 3634 Toilet preparations; beauty shops; natural & organic foods; massage machines, electric, except for beauty/barber shops

GEOGRAPHIC SECTION
Livonia - Wayne County (G-10450)

(G-10426)
SWIRLBERRY
17382 Haggerty Rd (48152-2608)
PHONE......................734 779-0830
EMP: 4 **EST:** 2010
SALES (est): 248.8K **Privately Held**
SIC: 2024 Mfg Ice Cream/Frozen Desert

(G-10427)
SYNCON INC
31001 Schoolcraft Rd (48150-2029)
P.O. Box 23042, Dearborn (48123-2867)
PHONE......................313 914-4481
Ryan Klacking, *President*
Chris Klacking, *Vice Pres*
Renee Ferguson, *Treasurer*
Belle Runyon, *Manager*
EMP: 48 **EST:** 2008
SALES (est): 6.1MM **Privately Held**
WEB: www.synconinc.com
SIC: 3531 Surfacers, concrete grinding

(G-10428)
SYSTEM CONTROLS INC
35245 Schoolcraft Rd (48150-1209)
PHONE......................734 427-0440
Donald Rende, *President*
EMP: 39 **EST:** 2003
SALES (est): 2.8MM **Privately Held**
WEB: www.systemcontrols.com
SIC: 3822 Appliance regulators

(G-10429)
TARA INDUSTRIES INC (PA)
30105 8 Mile Rd (48152-1811)
PHONE......................248 477-6520
Ravi K Tandon, *CEO*
Adam Tandon, *President*
Selma Cimsit, *Treasurer*
EMP: 9 **EST:** 1984
SQ FT: 8,800
SALES (est): 935.8K **Privately Held**
SIC: 3444 3612 3613 Metal housings, enclosures, casings & other containers; lighting transformers, fluorescent; switchboards & parts, power

(G-10430)
TECHNI CAM AND MANUFACTURING
30633 Schoolcraft Rd A (48150-2047)
PHONE......................734 261-6477
Chris Meadows, *President*
Greg Meadows, *Vice Pres*
EMP: 10 **EST:** 1986
SQ FT: 10,000
SALES (est): 999.2K **Privately Held**
WEB: www.technicam.com
SIC: 3545 3599 7538 Cams (machine tool accessories); machine shop, jobbing & repair; general automotive repair shops

(G-10431)
TESTRON INCORPORATED
34153 Industrial Rd (48150-1305)
PHONE......................734 513-6820
Brian E Dombrowsky, *President*
EMP: 16 **EST:** 1970
SQ FT: 8,500
SALES (est): 1.8MM **Privately Held**
WEB: www.testron-corp.com
SIC: 3829 3825 3823 3643 Physical property testing equipment; instruments to measure electricity; industrial instrmnts msrmnt display/control process variable; current-carrying wiring devices

(G-10432)
THERMAL SOLUTIONS MFG (PA)
35255 Glendale St (48150-1254)
PHONE......................734 655-7145
EMP: 66 **EST:** 2018
SALES (est): 1MM **Privately Held**
WEB: www.thermalsolutionsmfg.com
SIC: 3714 Motor vehicle parts & accessories

(G-10433)
TOOLING & EQUIPMENT INTL CORP
12550 Tech Center Dr (48150-2192)
PHONE......................734 522-1422
Oliver Johnson, *President*
Anthony D'Agostini, *Project Mgr*
Anthony D 'agostini, *Sales Staff*

Robert Showalter, *Sales Staff*
Tom Lehman, *Program Mgr*
EMP: 100 **EST:** 1983
SQ FT: 80,000
SALES (est): 24.4MM **Privately Held**
WEB: www.teintl.com
SIC: 3365 Aluminum & aluminum-based alloy castings

(G-10434)
TOWER ACQUISITION CO II LLC
17672 N Laurel Park Dr (48152-3984)
PHONE......................248 675-6000
EMP: 50 **EST:** 2011
SALES (est): 10.2MM
SALES (corp-wide): 3.1B **Privately Held**
WEB: www.autokiniton.com
SIC: 3465 Body parts, automobile: stamped metal
HQ: Tower International, Inc.
  17672 N Laurel Park Dr 400e
  Livonia MI 48152

(G-10435)
TOWER ATMTIVE OPRTONS USA II L (DH)
17672 N Laurel Park Dr 400e (48152-3984)
PHONE......................248 675-6000
Mark Malcolm, *President*
Seth Gardner, *Vice Pres*
Kevin Stephens, *Opers Mgr*
Terry Koopman, *Engineer*
Jeffrey L Lomasky, *Treasurer*
▲ **EMP:** 3 **EST:** 2007
SALES (est): 141.5MM
SALES (corp-wide): 3.1B **Privately Held**
WEB: www.autokiniton.com
SIC: 3465 Automotive stampings

(G-10436)
TOWER ATMTIVE OPRTONS USA III (DH)
17672 N Laurel Park Dr (48152-3984)
PHONE......................248 675-6000
Mark Malcolm, *President*
EMP: 100 **EST:** 2007
SALES (est): 11.7MM
SALES (corp-wide): 3.1B **Privately Held**
WEB: www.autokiniton.com
SIC: 3465 Automotive stampings

(G-10437)
TOWER AUTO HOLDINGS II A LLC
17672 N Laurel Park Dr 400e (48152-3984)
PHONE......................248 675-6000
Mark Malcolm, *Principal*
Seth Gardner, *Principal*
Jeffrey L Lomasky, *Principal*
EMP: 182 **EST:** 2007
SALES (est): 27.9MM
SALES (corp-wide): 3.1B **Privately Held**
WEB: www.autokiniton.com
SIC: 3465 Automotive stampings
HQ: Tower International, Inc.
  17672 N Laurel Park Dr 400e
  Livonia MI 48152

(G-10438)
TOWER AUTO HOLDINGS USA LLC (DH)
Also Called: Tower International
17672 N Laurel Park Dr # 40 (48152-3984)
PHONE......................248 675-6000
Ken Kundrick, *President*
Mark Malcolm, *Mng Member*
Seth Gardner,
James Gouin,
Jeffrey L Lomasky,
▲ **EMP:** 110 **EST:** 2007
SALES (est): 897.5MM
SALES (corp-wide): 3.1B **Privately Held**
WEB: www.autokiniton.com
SIC: 3465 Automotive stampings

(G-10439)
TOWER DEFENSE & AEROSPACE LLC
Also Called: W Industries
17672 N Laurel Park Dr (48152-3984)
PHONE......................248 675-6000
Michael Rajkovic, *Mng Member*
Ron Lecronier,

▲ **EMP:** 48 **EST:** 2011
SALES (est): 34.5MM
SALES (corp-wide): 3.1B **Privately Held**
WEB: www.autokiniton.com
SIC: 3465 3365 3443 Automotive stampings; aerospace castings, aluminum; metal parts
HQ: Tower International, Inc.
  17672 N Laurel Park Dr 400e
  Livonia MI 48152

(G-10440)
TOWER INTERNATIONAL INC (HQ)
17672 N Laurel Park Dr 400e (48152-3984)
PHONE......................248 675-6000
George Thanopoulos, *President*
Kurtis Fournier, *President*
Paul Tiburcio, *President*
Derek Fiebig, *Vice Pres*
Dennis Pike, *Vice Pres*
▲ **EMP:** 300 **EST:** 1993
SQ FT: 76,000
SALES: 1.5B
SALES (corp-wide): 3.1B **Privately Held**
WEB: www.autokiniton.com
SIC: 3465 Body parts, automobile: stamped metal
PA: Autokiniton Us Holdings, Inc.
  17757 Woodland Dr
  New Boston MI 48164
  734 397-6300

(G-10441)
TRANE US INC
33725 Schoolcraft Rd (48150-1505)
PHONE......................734 367-0700
Darren Manees, *Technician*
EMP: 7 **Privately Held**
WEB: www.trane.com
SIC: 3585 Refrigeration & heating equipment
HQ: Trane U.S. Inc.
  3600 Pammel Creek Rd
  La Crosse WI 54601
  608 787-2000

(G-10442)
TRANE US INC
37001 Industrial Rd (48150-1146)
PHONE......................734 452-2000
Mark Wagner, *Branch Mgr*
EMP: 100 **Privately Held**
WEB: www.trane.com
SIC: 3585 Refrigeration & heating equipment
HQ: Trane U.S. Inc.
  3600 Pammel Creek Rd
  La Crosse WI 54601
  608 787-2000

(G-10443)
TRI VECTOR PRINTING
14792 Hubbard St (48154-3525)
PHONE......................734 748-7006
Brandon Hauser, *Principal*
EMP: 4 **EST:** 2018
SALES (est): 83.9K **Privately Held**
SIC: 2752 Commercial printing, lithographic

(G-10444)
TRIGON METAL PRODUCTS INC
12725 Inkster Rd (48150-2216)
PHONE......................734 513-3488
John F Stankey, *President*
Johanna E Stankey, *Corp Secy*
Traci Krohn, *Purchasing*
EMP: 8 **EST:** 1974
SQ FT: 22,000
SALES (est): 1.3MM **Privately Held**
WEB: www.trigonmp.com
SIC: 3444 Sheet metal specialties, not stamped; metal housings, enclosures, casings & other containers

(G-10445)
TRU-LINE SCREW PRODUCTS INC (PA)
Also Called: Tru-Line Metal Products Co
15223 Farmington Rd Ste 5 (48154-5411)
P.O. Box 510323 (48151-6323)
PHONE......................734 261-8780
Thomas E Gresham, *President*
Gary H Burton, *Vice Pres*

EMP: 14 **EST:** 1950
SQ FT: 6,600
SALES (est): 1.9MM **Privately Held**
WEB: www.trulinescrew.com
SIC: 3451 Screw machine products

(G-10446)
TRW ATOMOTIVE HOLDG MEXICO LLC
12001 Tech Center Dr (48150-2122)
PHONE......................734 855-2600
John Plant, *CEO*
EMP: 87 **EST:** 1988
SALES (est): 2.6MM
SALES (corp-wide): 216.2K **Privately Held**
WEB: www.zf.com
SIC: 3714 Motor vehicle parts & accessories
HQ: Zf Trw Automotive Holdings Corp.
  12001 Tech Center Dr
  Livonia MI 48150
  734 855-2600

(G-10447)
TRW AUTOMOTIVE (LV) CORP (DH)
12001 Tech Center Dr (48150-2122)
PHONE......................734 855-2600
John C Plant, *President*
EMP: 1 **EST:** 2002
SALES (est): 6.8MM
SALES (corp-wide): 216.2K **Privately Held**
WEB: www.zf.com
SIC: 3714 Hydraulic fluid power pumps for auto steering mechanism
HQ: Zf Trw Automotive Holdings Corp.
  12001 Tech Center Dr
  Livonia MI 48150
  734 855-2600

(G-10448)
TRW EAST INC
12001 Tech Center Dr (48150-2122)
PHONE......................734 855-2600
EMP: 57 **EST:** 1996
SALES (est): 2.6MM
SALES (corp-wide): 216.2K **Privately Held**
WEB: www.zf.com
SIC: 3714 Motor vehicle parts & accessories
HQ: Zf Trw Automotive Holdings Corp.
  12001 Tech Center Dr
  Livonia MI 48150
  734 855-2600

(G-10449)
TRW ODYSSEY MEXICO LLC
12001 Tech Center Dr (48150-2122)
PHONE......................734 855-2600
Tom Wells, *President*
EMP: 53 **EST:** 1995
SALES (est): 3.1MM
SALES (corp-wide): 216.2K **Privately Held**
WEB: www.zf.com
SIC: 3714 Motor vehicle parts & accessories
HQ: Zf Trw Automotive Holdings Corp.
  12001 Tech Center Dr
  Livonia MI 48150
  734 855-2600

(G-10450)
TRW SAFETY SYSTEMS MEXICO LLC
12001 Tech Center Dr (48150-2122)
PHONE......................734 855-2600
John Plant,
EMP: 1 **EST:** 1993
SALES (est): 4.4MM
SALES (corp-wide): 216.2K **Privately Held**
WEB: www.zf.com
SIC: 3714 3711 Motor vehicle parts & accessories; motor vehicles & car bodies; chassis, motor vehicle
HQ: Zf Trw Automotive Holdings Corp.
  12001 Tech Center Dr
  Livonia MI 48150
  734 855-2600

(PA)=Parent Co (HQ)=Headquarters (DH)=Div Headquarters
✿ = New Business established in last 2 years

Livonia - Wayne County (G-10451)

(G-10451)
TURBINE TOOL & GAGE INC
11901 Brookfield St (48150-1736)
P.O. Box 3334 (48151-3334)
PHONE...............................734 427-2270
Audrey Murtland, *President*
Gregory Murtland, *Vice Pres*
Gregory H Murtland, *Treasurer*
Bruce Rossler, *Supervisor*
EMP: 20 **EST:** 1966
SQ FT: 9,000
SALES (est): 1.2MM **Privately Held**
WEB: www.turbinetoolandgage.com
SIC: 3545 3544 3823 Gauges (machine tool accessories); jigs & fixtures; draft gauges, industrial process type

(G-10452)
U S FABRICATION & DESIGN LLC
32890 Capitol St (48150-1706)
PHONE...............................248 919-2910
Mark Perry,
Robert Provow,
EMP: 12 **EST:** 2009
SQ FT: 25,000
SALES (est): 2.4MM **Privately Held**
WEB: www.usfabinc.com
SIC: 3441 Fabricated structural metal

(G-10453)
UIS INDUSTRIES LLC
39111 6 Mile Rd (48152-3926)
PHONE...............................734 443-3737
John Pierce,
EMP: 4
SALES (est): 132.5K **Privately Held**
SIC: 3999 Manufacturing industries

(G-10454)
US GREEN ENERGY SOLUTIONS LLC
9532 Harrison St (48150-3130)
PHONE...............................810 955-2992
Patrick Smith,
Cassandra Smith,
Edgar Smith,
Peiyi Yao,
EMP: 5
SALES (est): 271.4K **Privately Held**
SIC: 3612 7389 Transformers, except electric; business services

(G-10455)
VALASSIS COMMUNICATIONS INC (DH)
19975 Victor Pkwy (48152-7001)
PHONE...............................734 591-3000
Cali Tran, *President*
Nicholas Freeman, *President*
Bryan Schultz, *President*
Kristin Wilmes, *Partner*
Alan F Schultz, *Chairman*
▲ **EMP:** 1556 **EST:** 1970
SALES (est): 2B **Publicly Held**
WEB: www.valassis.com
SIC: 7319 7331 7372 Distribution of advertising material or sample services; direct mail advertising services; business oriented computer software
HQ: Vericast Corp.
    15955 La Cantera Pkwy
    San Antonio TX 78256
    210 697-8888

(G-10456)
VALASSIS COMMUNICATIONS INC
38905 6 Mile Rd (48152-3933)
PHONE...............................734 432-8000
Bridget Brimm, *Vice Pres*
Ruth Libbey, *Branch Mgr*
EMP: 5 **Publicly Held**
WEB: www.valassis.com
SIC: 7319 7331 7372 Distribution of advertising material or sample services; direct mail advertising services; business oriented computer software
HQ: Valassis Communications, Inc.
    19975 Victor Pkwy
    Livonia MI 48152

(G-10457)
VALASSIS INTERNATIONAL INC (DH)
19975 Victor Pkwy (48152-7001)
PHONE...............................734 591-3000
Ron Goolsby, *CEO*
Rob Mason, *President*
Jim Parkinson, *Exec VP*
Robert L Recchia, *Exec VP*
Todd Wiseley, *Exec VP*
EMP: 350 **EST:** 1994
SQ FT: 85,000
SALES (est): 108.5MM **Publicly Held**
WEB: www.valassis.com
SIC: 8743 3993 2759 2752 Promotion service; sales promotion; signs & advertising specialties; commercial printing; commercial printing, lithographic

(G-10458)
VARN INTERNATIONAL INC
17177 N Laurel Park Dr # 300 (48152-2693)
PHONE...............................734 781-4600
William B Miller, *President*
EMP: 13 **EST:** 2010
SALES (est): 1.7MM **Privately Held**
SIC: 2899 3555 Chemical preparations; type & type making machinery & equipment

(G-10459)
VERBIO NORTH AMERICA CORP (PA)
17199 N Laurel Park Dr # 409 (48152-7911)
PHONE...............................866 306-4777
Greg Northrup, *CEO*
Rand Dueweke, *Vice Pres*
Alicia Webber, *CFO*
EMP: 20 **EST:** 2018
SALES (est): 9.3MM **Privately Held**
WEB: www.verbio.us
SIC: 1389 Cementing oil & gas well casings

(G-10460)
VERTICAL MACHINING SERVICES
37637 Schoolcraft Rd D (48150-5031)
PHONE...............................734 462-1800
EMP: 6
SQ FT: 4,300
SALES (est): 936K **Privately Held**
SIC: 3541 Mfg Machine Tools-Cutting

(G-10461)
VOILA PRINT INC
37000 Industrial Rd (48150-1135)
PHONE...............................866 942-1677
Fatima Ahmed, *President*
EMP: 3 **EST:** 2014
SALES (est): 1MM
SALES (corp-wide): 2.8MM **Privately Held**
WEB: www.voilaprint.com
SIC: 2752 Commercial printing, offset
PA: Instant Printing And Graphics, Inc.
    31373 Industrial Rd
    Livonia MI 48150
    516 300-1234

(G-10462)
VSR TECHNOLOGIES INC
12270 Belden Ct (48150-1459)
PHONE...............................734 425-7172
John Vella, *President*
John A Vella, *Vice Pres*
EMP: 10 **EST:** 1997
SQ FT: 6,000
SALES (est): 6.5MM **Privately Held**
WEB: www.vsrtech.com
SIC: 3825 Test equipment for electronic & electric measurement

(G-10463)
VTEC GRAPHICS INC (PA)
12487 Globe St (48150-1134)
PHONE...............................734 953-9729
Steven Smith, *President*
Mark Mazur, *Vice Pres*
Eric Westberg, *Prdtn Mgr*
EMP: 7 **EST:** 1989
SQ FT: 7,500
SALES (est): 2MM **Privately Held**
WEB: www.vtecprint.com
SIC: 2752 7336 Commercial printing, offset; graphic arts & related design

(G-10464)
WALLIN BROTHERS INC
35270 Glendale St Ste 1 (48150-1264)
PHONE...............................734 525-7750
Ernest Johnson, *President*
Marlene Johnson, *Vice Pres*
EMP: 6 **EST:** 1946
SQ FT: 13,000
SALES (est): 1MM **Privately Held**
SIC: 3544 3469 Special dies & tools; metal stampings

(G-10465)
WAMU FUEL LLC
17151 Middlebelt Rd (48152-3609)
PHONE...............................313 386-8700
Wassef Zahr, *Principal*
EMP: 6 **EST:** 2010
SALES (est): 498.4K **Privately Held**
SIC: 2869 Fuels

(G-10466)
WARREN SCREW WORKS INC
Also Called: Warren Autometric Fasteners
13360 Wayne Rd (48150-1246)
PHONE...............................734 525-2920
Andrew Wojcik, *General Mgr*
EMP: 5 **EST:** 1987
SQ FT: 10,000
SALES (est): 491.8K **Privately Held**
WEB: www.warrenfasteners.com
SIC: 3452 5072 Dowel pins, metal; miscellaneous fasteners; bolts; nuts (hardware)

(G-10467)
WASHERS INCORPORATED (PA)
Also Called: Alphausa
33375 Glendale St (48150-1615)
PHONE...............................734 523-1000
George Strumbos, *Ch of Bd*
Nicholas Strumbos, *President*
Andrew Palushaj, *Buyer*
Glenn Goodsmith, *Design Engr*
Veronica Cruz, *Human Resources*
EMP: 129 **EST:** 1957
SQ FT: 100,000
SALES (est): 26.9MM **Privately Held**
WEB: www.alphausa.com
SIC: 3452 3465 Washers, metal; automotive stampings

(G-10468)
WAYNE-CRAFT INC
Also Called: Wayne Craft
13525 Wayne Rd (48150-1245)
PHONE...............................734 421-8800
Steven McFall, *President*
Steven Mc Fall, *President*
Kathleen Mc Fall, *Controller*
EMP: 18 **EST:** 1946
SQ FT: 35,000
SALES (est): 5.3MM **Privately Held**
WEB: www.waynecraft.com
SIC: 5039 2431 3334 5051 Awnings; awnings, wood; primary aluminum; aluminum bars, rods, ingots, sheets, pipes, plates, etc.

(G-10469)
WELDCRAFT INC
11881 Belden Ct (48150-1460)
PHONE...............................734 779-1303
Chris Novack, *President*
EMP: 5 **EST:** 1976
SQ FT: 3,000
SALES (est): 388.2K **Privately Held**
WEB: www.weldcraftwheels.com
SIC: 7692 Welding repair

(G-10470)
WELK-KO FABRICATORS INC (PA)
11885 Mayfield St (48150-1707)
PHONE...............................734 425-6840
Ronald S Karaisz II, *President*
Timothy P Karaisz, *Vice Pres*
EMP: 10 **EST:** 1967
SALES (est): 2.5MM **Privately Held**
WEB: www.welk-ko.com
SIC: 3444 3699 Sheet metal specialties, not stamped; electrical equipment & supplies

(G-10471)
WELKER CABINETRY & MILLWORK
12338 Stark Rd (48150-1558)
PHONE...............................248 477-6600
EMP: 11 **EST:** 2018
SALES (est): 852.5K **Privately Held**
WEB: www.welkerkb.com
SIC: 2434 Wood kitchen cabinets

(G-10472)
WELLINGTON FRAGRANCE
33306 Glendale St (48150-1616)
PHONE...............................734 261-5531
William Waack, *Principal*
◆ **EMP:** 4 **EST:** 2009
SALES (est): 543.8K **Privately Held**
WEB: www.wellingtonfragrance.com
SIC: 2844 Perfumes & colognes

(G-10473)
WELZ TOOL MCH & BORING CO INC
11952 Hubbard St (48150-1733)
PHONE...............................734 425-3920
Zef Vuljevic, *President*
EMP: 30 **EST:** 1978
SQ FT: 20,000
SALES (est): 856.3K **Privately Held**
WEB: www.welztool.com
SIC: 3599 Machine shop, jobbing & repair

(G-10474)
WESTCO METALCRAFT INC
31846 Glendale St (48150-1827)
PHONE...............................734 425-0900
Penny Johnson, *President*
Matt Johnson, *Vice Pres*
George Sharpe, *Vice Pres*
Patricia Westergaard, *Treasurer*
Harry Keolian, *Admin Sec*
EMP: 10 **EST:** 1953
SQ FT: 11,000
SALES (est): 1MM **Privately Held**
WEB: www.westcometalcraft.com
SIC: 3444 Sheet metal specialties, not stamped

(G-10475)
WILLIAMS DIVERSIFIED INC
13170 Merriman Rd (48150-1816)
PHONE...............................734 421-6100
George Hieronymus, *President*
EMP: 34 **EST:** 1962
SQ FT: 19,000
SALES (est): 1.4MM **Privately Held**
WEB: www.williamsfinishing.com
SIC: 3471 3999 Plating of metals or formed products; custom pulverizing & grinding of plastic materials

(G-10476)
WILLIAMS FINISHING INC
13170 Merriman Rd (48150-1816)
PHONE...............................734 421-6100
George Williams, *Owner*
Ted Williams, *Foreman/Supr*
EMP: 18 **EST:** 2015
SALES (est): 1MM **Privately Held**
WEB: www.williamsfinishing.com
SIC: 3471 Electroplating of metals or formed products

(G-10477)
WIRED TECHNOLOGIES LLC
31099 Schoolcraft Rd (48150-2029)
PHONE...............................313 800-1611
Muhannad Saleh, *Mng Member*
EMP: 7 **EST:** 2017
SALES (est): 500K **Privately Held**
WEB: www.wired-tech.net
SIC: 3625 Control circuit relays, industrial

(G-10478)
WORKFORCE SOFTWARE LLC (PA)
38705 7 Mile Rd Ste 300 (48152-3979)
PHONE...............................734 542-4100
Mike Morini, *CEO*

▲ = Import ▼=Export
◆ =Import/Export

GEOGRAPHIC SECTION

Lowell - Kent County (G-10498)

David Farquhar, *COO*
Shannah Albert, *Vice Pres*
Jose Bordetas, *Vice Pres*
Kathy Cannon, *Vice Pres*
EMP: 160 **EST:** 1999
SQ FT: 10,500
SALES (est): 219.4MM **Privately Held**
WEB: www.workforcesoftware.com
SIC: 7372 7371 Business oriented computer software; custom computer programming services

(G-10479)
ZF ACTIVE SAFETY & ELEC US LLC
12025 Tech Center Dr (48150-2122)
PHONE 586 843-2100
Eric Weiss, *Manager*
Andy Casali, *Analyst*
EMP: 84
SALES (corp-wide): 216.2K **Privately Held**
WEB: www.zf.com
SIC: 3714 Motor vehicle parts & accessories
HQ: Zf Active Safety & Electronics Us Llc
12001 Tech Center Dr
Livonia MI 48150
734 855-2600

(G-10480)
ZF ACTIVE SAFETY & ELEC US LLC
12075 Tech Center Dr (48150-6103)
P.O. Box 51970 (48151-5970)
PHONE 734 855-3631
Mike Andrews, *Chief Engr*
EMP: 36
SALES (corp-wide): 216.2K **Privately Held**
WEB: www.zf.com
SIC: 3469 Metal stampings
HQ: Zf Active Safety & Electronics Us Llc
12001 Tech Center Dr
Livonia MI 48150
734 855-2600

(G-10481)
ZF ACTIVE SAFETY & ELEC US LLC (DH)
Also Called: Active and Passive Safety
12001 Tech Center Dr (48150-2122)
PHONE 734 855-2600
Carsten Maziul, *Project Mgr*
Galo Leon, *Opers Mgr*
John Butler, *Purchasing*
Jerome Dorlack, *Purchasing*
Michael Silvasi, *Chief Engr*
◆ **EMP:** 200 **EST:** 2002
SALES (est): 1.1B
SALES (corp-wide): 216.2K **Privately Held**
WEB: www.zf.com
SIC: 3679 3469 3089 Electronic switches; metal stampings; plastic processing
HQ: Zf Trw Automotive Holdings Corp.
12001 Tech Center Dr
Livonia MI 48150
734 855-2600

(G-10482)
ZF ACTIVE SAFETY US INC (DH)
12025 Tech Center Dr (48150-2122)
P.O. Box 51970 (48151-5970)
PHONE 734 812-6979
Edward Carpenter, *CEO*
Dale Chon, *Vice Pres*
Eliseo Rozas, *Vice Pres*
◆ **EMP:** 14 **EST:** 1986
SALES (est): 388.5MM
SALES (corp-wide): 216.2K **Privately Held**
WEB: www.zf.com
SIC: 3714 Motor vehicle engines & parts
HQ: Zf Trw Automotive Holdings Corp.
12001 Tech Center Dr
Livonia MI 48150
734 855-2600

(G-10483)
ZF ACTIVE SAFETY US INC
12200 Tech Center Dr (48150-2177)
PHONE 734 855-2470
Mike Wong, *Manager*
EMP: 7
SALES (corp-wide): 216.2K **Privately Held**
WEB: www.zf.com
SIC: 3714 Connecting rods, motor vehicle engine
HQ: Zf Active Safety Us Inc.
12025 Tech Center Dr
Livonia MI 48150
734 812-6979

(G-10484)
ZF AUTO HOLDINGS US INC (DH)
12001 Tech Center Dr (48150-2122)
PHONE 734 855-2600
Dr Franz Kleiner, *President*
Brian A Paton, *Counsel*
Ramiro Gutierrez, *Vice Pres*
John Butler, *Purchasing*
Scott Garcia, *Purchasing*
EMP: 1 **EST:** 2002
SALES (est): 18MM
SALES (corp-wide): 216.2K **Privately Held**
WEB: www.zf.com
SIC: 3714 Motor vehicle parts & accessories
HQ: Zf Friedrichshafen Ag
Lowentaler Str. 20
Friedrichshafen BW 88046
754 177-0

(G-10485)
ZF AUTOMOTIVE JV US LLC (DH)
12001 Tech Center Dr (48150-2122)
PHONE 734 855-2787
John Plant,
EMP: 677 **EST:** 2003
SALES (est): 8.9MM
SALES (corp-wide): 216.2K **Privately Held**
WEB: www.zf.com
SIC: 3714 Connecting rods, motor vehicle engine
HQ: Zf Trw Automotive Holdings Corp.
12001 Tech Center Dr
Livonia MI 48150
734 855-2600

(G-10486)
ZF AUTOMOTIVE US INC (DH)
12001 Tech Center Dr (48150-2122)
PHONE 734 855-2600
John C Plant, *President*
Tim Englerth, *Principal*
David Swain, *Principal*
Yong Choe, *Business Mgr*
Natalia Medley, *Counsel*
▲ **EMP:** 500 **EST:** 2002
SALES (est): 1.6B
SALES (corp-wide): 216.2K **Privately Held**
WEB: www.trwauto.com
SIC: 3714 Connecting rods, motor vehicle engine; steering mechanisms, motor vehicle; brake drums, motor vehicle; hydraulic fluid power pumps for auto steering mechanism
HQ: Zf Friedrichshafen Ag
Lowentaler Str. 20
Friedrichshafen BW 88046
754 177-0

(G-10487)
ZF FRIEDRICHSHAFEN AG
Active and Passive Safety Tech
12001 Tech Center Dr (48150-2122)
PHONE 734 855-2600
Mark Chaney, *Vice Pres*
Sarah Kirkwood, *Vice Pres*
Connie Rightmer, *Vice Pres*
Keith Davis, *Materials Dir*
Simon Yang, *Project Mgr*
EMP: 7
SALES (corp-wide): 216.2K **Privately Held**
WEB: www.zf.com
SIC: 3714 Connecting rods, motor vehicle engine; steering mechanisms, motor vehicle; brake drums, motor vehicle; hydraulic fluid power pumps for auto steering mechanism

(G-10488)
ZF PASSIVE SAFETY S AFRICA INC
12001 Tech Center Dr (48150-2122)
PHONE 734 855-2600
EMP: 29 **EST:** 2013
SALES (est): 1.3MM
SALES (corp-wide): 216.2K **Privately Held**
WEB: www.zf.com
SIC: 3714 Motor vehicle parts & accessories
HQ: Zf Auto Holdings Us Inc.
12001 Tech Center Dr
Livonia MI 48150
734 855-2600

(G-10489)
ZF PASSIVE SAFETY US INC (DH)
12001 Tech Center Dr (48150-2122)
PHONE 734 855-2600
Wolf-Henning Scheider, *CEO*
John Harju, *Exec VP*
Dr Peter Holdmann, *Exec VP*
Peter Lake, *Exec VP*
Christophe Marnat, *CFO*
▲ **EMP:** 256 **EST:** 2012
SALES (est): 389.8MM
SALES (corp-wide): 216.2K **Privately Held**
WEB: www.zf.com
SIC: 3714 Motor vehicle parts & accessories
HQ: Zf Trw Automotive Holdings Corp.
12001 Tech Center Dr
Livonia MI 48150
734 855-2600

(G-10490)
ZF PASSIVE SFETY SYSTEMS US IN (DH)
12001 Tech Center Dr (48150-2122)
PHONE 586 232-7200
Joe Gaus, *President*
Peter Holdmann, *Exec VP*
Dale Chon, *Vice Pres*
Holger Huss, *Vice Pres*
Stephanie Zagacki, *Purchasing*
▲ **EMP:** 1473 **EST:** 1987
SALES (est): 1.5B
SALES (corp-wide): 216.2K **Privately Held**
WEB: www.zf.com
SIC: 3714 Motor vehicle parts & accessories
HQ: Zf Trw Automotive Holdings Corp.
12001 Tech Center Dr
Livonia MI 48150
734 855-2600

(G-10491)
ZF STRING ACTIVE SAFETY US INC (DH)
Also Called: TRW Odyssey Inc.
12001 Tech Center Dr (48150-2122)
PHONE 734 855-2600
John Plant, *President*
Joseph Cantie, *CFO*
Mark Oswald, *Director*
▲ **EMP:** 5 **EST:** 2012
SALES (est): 18.3MM
SALES (corp-wide): 216.2K **Privately Held**
WEB: www.zf.com
SIC: 3714 Motor vehicle parts & accessories
HQ: Zf Trw Automotive Holdings Corp.
12001 Tech Center Dr
Livonia MI 48150
734 855-2600

(G-10492)
ZF TRW AUTO HOLDINGS CORP (DH)
12001 Tech Center Dr (48150-2122)
PHONE 734 855-2600
Wolf-Henning Scheider, *CEO*
Franz Kleiner, *President*
John Plant, *Co-CEO*
Peter Holdmann, *Exec VP*
Peter Lake, *Exec VP*
◆ **EMP:** 800 **EST:** 1904
SALES (est): 20.9B
SALES (corp-wide): 216.2K **Privately Held**
WEB: www.zf.com
SIC: 3714 3711 Motor vehicle parts & accessories; motor vehicles & car bodies; chassis, motor vehicle
HQ: Zf North America, Inc.
15811 Centennial Dr
Northville MI 48168
734 416-6200

Lowell
Kent County

(G-10493)
ABILITY WEAVERS LLC
215 W Main St (49331-1607)
PHONE 616 929-0211
EMP: 5 **EST:** 2017
SALES (est): 142.2K **Privately Held**
WEB: www.abilityweavers.com
SIC: 2273 Carpets & rugs

(G-10494)
ADVANCED METAL FABRICATORS
12958 Christopher Dr (49331-9420)
PHONE 616 570-4847
Michael Perdok, *Principal*
EMP: 7 **EST:** 2009
SALES (est): 1.1MM **Privately Held**
SIC: 3499 Fabricated metal products

(G-10495)
ATTWOOD CORPORATION (HQ)
1016 N Monroe St (49331-1197)
PHONE 616 897-2301
James B Fox, *President*
Randy Gray, *Vice Pres*
Thomas Powell, *Vice Pres*
Peter D Zimmer, *Vice Pres*
Jordan Sinclair, *Opers Staff*
◆ **EMP:** 150 **EST:** 1905
SQ FT: 432,000
SALES (est): 64.3MM
SALES (corp-wide): 4.3B **Publicly Held**
WEB: www.brunswick.com
SIC: 3429 Marine hardware
PA: Brunswick Corporation
26125 N Riverwoods Blvd # 500
Mettawa IL 60045
847 735-4700

(G-10496)
BLOUGH INC
9885 Centerline Rd (49331-9224)
PHONE 616 897-8407
Arthur Blough, *President*
EMP: 90 **EST:** 1963
SQ FT: 50,000
SALES (est): 5.9MM **Privately Held**
WEB: www.bloughinc.com
SIC: 3471 Finishing, metals or formed products

(G-10497)
BUYERS GUIDE
Also Called: Lowell Litho
105 N Broadway St (49331-1085)
P.O. Box 128 (49331-0128)
PHONE 616 897-9261
Roger Brown, *Owner*
Terese Brown, *Co-Owner*
EMP: 7 **EST:** 1954
SQ FT: 1,500
SALES (est): 283.2K **Privately Held**
WEB: www.thelowellledger.com
SIC: 2741 2711 Shopping news: publishing only, not printed on site; newspapers

(G-10498)
COMPOSITECH
683 Lincoln Lake Ave Se (49331-9416)
PHONE 269 908-7846
David Kensington, *Manager*
EMP: 8 **EST:** 2017
SALES (est): 140.8K **Privately Held**
WEB: www.isginc.us
SIC: 3999 Manufacturing industries

Lowell - Kent County (G-10499)

(G-10499)
CONVERGENT SOLUTIONS LLC
4343 S Montcalm Ave (49331-8722)
PHONE..................................616 490-8747
Florian Robert, *Principal*
EMP: 5 **EST:** 2016
SALES (est): 130K **Privately Held**
SIC: 3674 Semiconductors & related devices

(G-10500)
ENVISION ENGINEERING LLC
12650 Envision Dr Se (49331-1902)
PHONE..................................616 897-0599
Ryan Baas, *Opers Mgr*
Michael Vanderwilp, *Engineer*
Dave Vanderwilp, *Manager*
Scott Roerig,
Mike Vanderwilt,
▲ **EMP:** 5 **EST:** 1999
SALES (est): 1.3MM **Privately Held**
WEB: www.envisionengineering.us
SIC: 3444 5049 Sheet metalwork; scientific & engineering equipment & supplies

(G-10501)
FLOR TEC INC
4475 Causeway Dr Ne (49331-9412)
PHONE..................................616 897-3122
Freeman L Billock, *President*
EMP: 7 **EST:** 2000 **Privately Held**
SIC: 3996 1542 Hard surface floor coverings; commercial & office buildings, renovation & repair

(G-10502)
HAPPY BUMS
201 Montcalm Ave Se (49331-9101)
PHONE..................................616 987-3159
Cheryl Pratt, *Owner*
EMP: 4 **EST:** 2011
SALES (est): 83.2K **Privately Held**
WEB: www.happybums.org
SIC: 2676 Infant & baby paper products

(G-10503)
HD HUDSON MANUFACTURING CO (PA)
1000 Foreman St (49331-1074)
PHONE..................................800 977-8661
Robert C Hudson Jr, *Ch of Bd*
R C Hudson III, *President*
W A Hudson, *President*
John Romans, *Vice Pres*
Robert Kosinski, *CFO*
◆ **EMP:** 70 **EST:** 1929
SQ FT: 13,639
SALES (est): 22.3K **Privately Held**
WEB: www.hdhudson.com
SIC: 3523 Sprayers & spraying machines, agricultural

(G-10504)
HOOPER PRINTING LLC
2125 Bowes Rd (49331-9562)
P.O. Box 182 (49331-0182)
PHONE..................................616 897-6719
Michael Clark, *Treasurer*
Mike Clark, *Treasurer*
Barb Williams, *Bookkeeper*
Mike Hooper, *Mng Member*
Tina Hooper, *Mng Member*
EMP: 5 **EST:** 1991
SQ FT: 4,000
SALES (est): 505.9K **Privately Held**
WEB: www.hooperprinting.com
SIC: 2752 Commercial printing, offset

(G-10505)
IEQ INDUSTRIES
730 Lincoln Lake Ave Se (49331-9421)
PHONE..................................616 902-1865
Scot Vansolkema, *Officer*
Luanne Wisniewski, *Receptionist*
EMP: 6 **EST:** 2014
SALES (est): 139.2K **Privately Held**
SIC: 3999 Manufacturing industries

(G-10506)
INDUSTRIAL SERVICES GROUP
683 Lincoln Lake Ave Se (49331-9416)
PHONE..................................269 945-5391
David Kensington, *Principal*
EMP: 19 **EST:** 2008

SALES (est): 659.6K **Privately Held**
WEB: www.isginc.us
SIC: 3999 Manufacturing industries

(G-10507)
J & T MACHINING INC
681 Lincoln Lake Ave Se (49331-9416)
PHONE..................................616 897-6744
John Thomas, *President*
Pat Thomas, *Vice Pres*
Robert Thomas, *Vice Pres*
EMP: 8 **EST:** 1964
SQ FT: 4,800
SALES (est): 866.9K **Privately Held**
WEB: www.jtmach.com
SIC: 3599 Machine shop, jobbing & repair

(G-10508)
KING MILLING COMPANY
115 S Broadway St (49331-1666)
PHONE..................................616 897-9264
Brian Doyle, *President*
James M Doyle, *Senior VP*
Stephen Doyle, *Vice Pres*
Patrick Doyle, *Project Mgr*
Julie Cantrell, *Officer*
◆ **EMP:** 55 **EST:** 1890
SALES (est): 9.1MM **Privately Held**
WEB: www.kingflour.com
SIC: 2041 Wheat flour

(G-10509)
LITEHOUSE INC
1400 Foreman St (49331-1076)
P.O. Box 287 (49331-0287)
PHONE..................................616 897-5911
Susan Serne, *Plant Mgr*
Peter Martin, *Opers Spvr*
Tyler Standley, *Mfg Staff*
Rhonda Anderson, *Purch Agent*
Charles Manning, *Controller*
EMP: 140
SALES (corp-wide): 323.8MM **Privately Held**
WEB: www.litehousefoods.com
SIC: 2035 2099 2022 Dressings, salad: raw & cooked (except dry mixes); food preparations; cheese, natural & processed
PA: Litehouse, Inc.
    100 Litehouse Dr
    Sandpoint ID 83864
    208 920-2000

(G-10510)
LYONNAIS INC
3760 Snow Ave Se (49331-8921)
PHONE..................................616 868-6625
EMP: 1
SALES: 1MM **Privately Held**
SIC: 3531 Mfg Construction Machinery

(G-10511)
METRIC MANUFACTURING CO INC
1001 Foreman St (49331-1094)
P.O. Box 226 (49331-0226)
PHONE..................................616 897-5959
Charles S Thomas, *President*
Pat Gilbert, *Vice Pres*
Greg Thomas, *Vice Pres*
Tom Bezinque, *Controller*
Bruce Kraft, *Exec Dir*
EMP: 115 **EST:** 1978
SQ FT: 55,000
SALES (est): 12.9MM **Privately Held**
WEB: www.metricmfg.com
SIC: 3599 Machine shop, jobbing & repair

(G-10512)
OBSOLETE LLC
Also Called: Noisefighters
11901 Fulton St E Ste 1 (49331-8613)
PHONE..................................616 843-0351
Neal Brace,
EMP: 5 **EST:** 2016
SALES (est): 222.3K **Privately Held**
SIC: 3842 Surgical appliances & supplies

(G-10513)
OPTEC INC
199 Smith St (49331-1399)
PHONE..................................616 897-9351
Jeff Dickerman, *President*
Tina Dickerman, *Treasurer*
EMP: 10 **EST:** 1979

SQ FT: 3,700
SALES (est): 1.7MM **Privately Held**
WEB: www.optecinc.com
SIC: 3827 Optical instruments & lenses

(G-10514)
PURFORMS INC
615 Chatham St Ste 1 (49331-1387)
PHONE..................................616 897-3000
Richard A Raimer, *President*
Alan Raimer, *Opers Staff*
Lori Raimer, *Human Res Mgr*
Kenda Haines, *Office Mgr*
Richard Raimer, *Manager*
▼ **EMP:** 24 **EST:** 1995
SQ FT: 66,000
SALES (est): 5MM **Privately Held**
WEB: www.purforms.com
SIC: 3089 Injection molding of plastics

(G-10515)
ROOT-LOWELL MANUFACTURING CO
Also Called: Rl Flo-Master
1000 Foreman St (49331-1074)
PHONE..................................616 897-9211
Tony Asselta, *President*
David Longfield, *Business Mgr*
Lisa Lahr, *Purch Agent*
Tony Barry, *Sales Staff*
Sally Meyer, *Manager*
◆ **EMP:** 100 **EST:** 1914
SQ FT: 100,000
SALES (est): 16.3MM **Privately Held**
WEB: www.hdhudson.com
SIC: 3523 Sprayers & spraying machines, agricultural

(G-10516)
SPRAYERUSA INC
13495 Crestwood Dr (49331-1109)
PHONE..................................800 253-4642
Michael Tummino, *Manager*
EMP: 5 **EST:** 2012
SALES (est): 125.2K **Privately Held**
SIC: 3523 Farm machinery & equipment

(G-10517)
STANDARD REGISTER
43 Kendra Ct (49331-9129)
PHONE..................................616 987-3128
EMP: 4 **EST:** 2009
SALES (est): 55.4K **Privately Held**
SIC: 2741 Miscellaneous publishing

(G-10518)
SUPERIOR WASHING AND PAIN
1033 Lincoln Lk (49331-1015)
PHONE..................................616 293-5347
Ryan Kried, *Principal*
EMP: 5 **EST:** 2010
SALES (est): 71.6K **Privately Held**
WEB: www.superiorpressurewashing.net
SIC: 3589 High pressure cleaning equipment

(G-10519)
SWEET MELLISAS CUPCAKES
4413 Causeway Dr Ne (49331-9412)
PHONE..................................616 889-3998
Mellisa Verstrate, *Principal*
EMP: 4 **EST:** 2012
SALES (est): 60.6K **Privately Held**
SIC: 2051 Bread, cake & related products

(G-10520)
SWIVL - EZE MARINE
1016 N Monroe St (49331-1167)
PHONE..................................616 897-9241
Brunswick Corporation, *Partner*
Perry Kirkland, *Principal*
▲ **EMP:** 30 **EST:** 1998
SALES (est): 2.3MM
SALES (corp-wide): 4.3B **Publicly Held**
WEB: www.brunswick.com
SIC: 3732 Boat building & repairing
PA: Brunswick Corporation
    26125 N Riverwoods Blvd # 500
    Mettawa IL 60045
    847 735-4700

(G-10521)
WADE PRINTING & PUBLISHING LLC
2984 Gulliford Trl (49331-9572)
PHONE..................................616 894-6350
Bradley Wade, *Principal*
EMP: 5 **EST:** 2016
SALES (est): 41.3K **Privately Held**
SIC: 2741 Miscellaneous publishing

(G-10522)
WHITES BRIDGE TOOLING INC
1395 Bowes Rd (49331-8882)
P.O. Box 8 (49331-0008)
PHONE..................................616 897-4151
Peter Odland, *President*
William Dulyea, *Vice Pres*
EMP: 32 **EST:** 1974
SQ FT: 8,400
SALES (est): 5.8MM **Privately Held**
WEB: www.wbtooling.com
SIC: 3569 7692 3535 Assembly machines, non-metalworking; welding repair; conveyors & conveying equipment

(G-10523)
WHITES INDUSTRIAL SERVICE
5010 Abraham Dr Ne (49331-9733)
PHONE..................................616 291-3706
Michael White, *President*
EMP: 5 **EST:** 1995 **Privately Held**
WEB: www.ensler.com
SIC: 1752 3479 Floor laying & floor work; painting, coating & hot dipping

---

Ludington
Mason County

(G-10524)
751 PARTS COMPANY INC
Also Called: NAPA
3351 W Us Highway 10 (49431-9309)
PHONE..................................231 845-1221
Michael William Wedding, *CEO*
Pamela William Wedding, *CFO*
Cody William Wedding, *Admin Sec*
EMP: 12 **EST:** 2019
SALES (est): 1.6MM **Privately Held**
WEB: www.napaonline.com
SIC: 3714 5531 Motor vehicle parts & accessories; automotive parts

(G-10525)
AMERICAN CLASSICS CORP
3750 W Hansen Rd (49431-8604)
P.O. Box 310 (49431-0310)
PHONE..................................231 843-0523
David Gwiazdowski, *Principal*
EMP: 6 **EST:** 2007
SALES (est): 287.5K **Privately Held**
SIC: 2099 Food preparations

(G-10526)
ANDREW J REISTERER D D S PLLC
902 E Ludington Ave (49431-2438)
PHONE..................................231 845-8989
John Piopelle, *Principal*
EMP: 4 **EST:** 2007
SALES (est): 445.2K **Privately Held**
WEB: www.ludingtondentistry.com
SIC: 3843 Enamels, dentists

(G-10527)
ARDY INC
Also Called: True Value
2999 S Palmer Blvd (49431-9763)
PHONE..................................231 845-7318
Rick S Deering, *Administration*
EMP: 8 **EST:** 2001
SALES (est): 90.1K **Privately Held**
WEB: www.truevalue.com
SIC: 3429 5013 5251 Manufactured hardware (general); automotive hardware; hardware

(G-10528)
BRILL COMPANY INC
715 S James St (49431-2362)
PHONE..................................231 843-2430
David Field, *President*
Ken Gibbs, *Vice Pres*
Bill Shaub, *Vice Pres*

GEOGRAPHIC SECTION
Ludington - Mason County (G-10552)

Paul Lange, *Site Mgr*
Bill Sniegowski, *Purch Mgr*
▲ **EMP:** 40 **EST:** 1946
SQ FT: 84,000
SALES (est): 4.7MM **Privately Held**
WEB: www.brillcompany.com
SIC: 2531 2599 Public building & related furniture; restaurant furniture, wood or metal

(G-10529)
CAL-CHLOR CORP
5379 W 6th St (49431-9322)
P.O. Box 622 (49431-0622)
PHONE..................................231 843-1147
Wayne Wagner, *Manager*
Mike Scelsa, *Hlthcr Dir*
EMP: 52
SALES (corp-wide): 75.2MM **Privately Held**
WEB: www.cal-chlor.com
SIC: 4783 2819 Packing goods for shipping; industrial inorganic chemicals
PA: Cal-Chlor Corp.
627 Jefferson St
Lafayette LA 70501
337 264-1449

(G-10530)
CAROM L EMBROIDERY
612 N Lakeshore Dr (49431-1328)
PHONE..................................231 690-0571
EMP: 4 **EST:** 2017
SALES (est): 70.5K **Privately Held**
WEB: www.carrom.com
SIC: 2395 Embroidery & art needlework

(G-10531)
CHANGE PARTS INCORPORATED
185 S Jebavy Dr (49431-2460)
PHONE..................................231 845-5107
Ronald Sarto, *CEO*
Eric Latala, *Design Engr*
Gregory Simsa, *CFO*
Butch Hall, *Regl Sales Mgr*
Chuck Poljanac, *Regl Sales Mgr*
EMP: 40
SQ FT: 40,000
SALES (est): 4.5MM **Privately Held**
WEB: www.changeparts.com
SIC: 3569 3565 3535 Assembly machines, non-metalworking; packaging machinery; conveyors & conveying equipment

(G-10532)
CHANGEOVER INTEGRATION LLC
787 S Pere Marquette Hwy (49431-2662)
PHONE..................................231 845-5320
Dan Sarto, *President*
Eric Latala, *Design Engr*
EMP: 15 **EST:** 2007
SALES (est): 1.2MM **Privately Held**
WEB: www.changeoverintegration.com
SIC: 3471 3479 3541 Anodizing (plating) of metals or formed products; etching & engraving; buffing & polishing machines

(G-10533)
DEBBINK AND SONS INC
1010 Conrad Industrial Dr (49431-2677)
P.O. Box 868 (49431-0868)
PHONE..................................231 845-6421
Craig Debbink, *President*
EMP: 5 **EST:** 1984
SALES (est): 2MM **Privately Held**
SIC: 2521 2512 1521 Cabinets, office: wood; upholstered household furniture; single-family housing construction

(G-10534)
DOW CHEMICAL COMPANY
1600 S Madison St (49431-2597)
PHONE..................................231 845-4285
John Hockstra, *Branch Mgr*
EMP: 4
SALES (corp-wide): 38.5B **Publicly Held**
WEB: www.dow.com
SIC: 2821 Thermoplastic materials
HQ: The Dow Chemical Company
2211 H H Dow Way
Midland MI 48642
989 636-1000

(G-10535)
DREAMWEAVER LURE COMPANY INC
5712 Brookwood Pl (49431-1972)
PHONE..................................231 843-3652
Roger Bogner, *Principal*
Shane Rupoyianes, *Vice Pres*
▲ **EMP:** 10 **EST:** 1995
SQ FT: 7,000
SALES (est): 771.6K **Privately Held**
WEB: www.dreamweaverlures.com
SIC: 3949 Fishing equipment

(G-10536)
FLORACRAFT CORPORATION (PA)
1 Longfellow Pl (49431-1591)
P.O. Box 400 (49431-0400)
PHONE..................................231 845-5127
James V Scatena, *CEO*
Russell Lee Schoenherr, *Ch of Bd*
Victor Burwell, *Exec VP*
Conny Bax, *Vice Pres*
Bill Hellwarth, *Vice Pres*
◆ **EMP:** 125 **EST:** 1946
SQ FT: 350,000
SALES (est): 34.2MM **Privately Held**
WEB: www.floracraft.com
SIC: 3086 2211 Plastics foam products; chenilles, tufted textile

(G-10537)
GOLD COAST ICE MAKERS LLC
Also Called: Gold Coast Icemakers
3785 W Us Highway 10 (49431-9601)
PHONE..................................231 845-2745
Rose Lennox, *President*
EMP: 5 **EST:** 1999
SALES (est): 315.3K **Privately Held**
SIC: 2097 Manufactured ice

(G-10538)
GREAT LAKES CASTINGS LLC (HQ)
800 N Washington Ave (49431-1500)
PHONE..................................231 843-2501
Robert Killips, *President*
Bob Ellis, *Safety Mgr*
Robert Ellis, *Safety Mgr*
David Scott, *Maint Spvr*
Lisa Giammalva, *Production*
EMP: 160 **EST:** 1945
SQ FT: 150,000
SALES (est): 36MM **Privately Held**
WEB: www.greatlakescastings.com
SIC: 3321 Gray & ductile iron foundries

(G-10539)
HOBE INC
Also Called: Ludington Concrete Products
292 N Stiles Rd (49431-9102)
PHONE..................................231 845-5196
Sandra Holcombe, *President*
Tim Martin, *Sales Mgr*
EMP: 4 **EST:** 1995 **Privately Held**
SIC: 3271 Blocks, concrete or cinder: standard

(G-10540)
HOUSE OF FLAVORS INC (HQ)
110 N William St (49431-2092)
PHONE..................................231 845-7369
Whit Gallagher, *President*
Pat Calder, *COO*
Tim Nieboer, *Vice Pres*
Sarah Holmes, *CFO*
Sarah R Holmes, *Controller*
▼ **EMP:** 150 **EST:** 1937
SQ FT: 17,000
SALES (est): 646.7K
SALES (corp-wide): 653.9K **Privately Held**
WEB: www.houseofflavors.com
SIC: 2024 Ice cream, packaged: molded, on sticks, etc.
PA: Protein Holdings Inc.
10 Moulton St Ste 5
Portland ME 04101
207 771-0965

(G-10541)
INDIAN SUMMER COOPERATIVE INC (PA)
3958 W Chauvez Rd Ste 1 (49431-8200)
PHONE..................................231 845-6248
Roy D Hackert, *President*
Doyle Fenner, *Opers Mgr*
Kelly Crocker, *Opers Staff*
Steven Hull, *Treasurer*
Vince Higgs, *Natl Sales Mgr*
◆ **EMP:** 250 **EST:** 1973
SQ FT: 15,000
SALES (est): 74.8MM **Privately Held**
SIC: 2033 0723 4213 2035 Apple sauce: packaged in cans, jars, etc.; fruit (fresh) packing services; trucking, except local; pickles, sauces & salad dressings

(G-10542)
JACKSON PANDROL INC
200 S Jackson Rd (49431-2409)
PHONE..................................231 843-3431
Bruce Bradshaw, *Vice Pres*
Roy J Orrow, *CFO*
EMP: 42 **EST:** 1923
SQ FT: 150,000
SALES (est): 2.5MM
SALES (corp-wide): 2.6MM **Privately Held**
WEB: www.pandrol.com
SIC: 3531 4789 Railroad related equipment; railroad maintenance & repair services
HQ: Pandrol International Limited
Osprey House, 63 Station Road
Addlestone KT15
193 283-4500

(G-10543)
LUDINGTON DAILY NEWS INC
Also Called: Shoreline Media
202 N Rath Ave (49431-1663)
P.O. Box 340 (49431-0340)
PHONE..................................231 845-5181
David R Jackson, *President*
Ray McGrew, *President*
Linda Farley, *Sales Staff*
Jeffrey Evans, *Asst Sec*
EMP: 45 **EST:** 1933
SQ FT: 20,000
SALES (est): 2.9MM **Privately Held**
WEB: www.shorelinemedia.net
SIC: 2711 2741 Commercial printing & newspaper publishing combined; directories, telephone: publishing & printing; shopping news: publishing & printing

(G-10544)
MERDEL GAME MANUFACTURING CO
Also Called: Carrom Company
218 E Dowland St (49431-2309)
P.O. Box 649 (49431-0649)
PHONE..................................231 845-1263
Norman Rosen, *President*
Janice Laplante, *Finance Dir*
Nicole Thaler, *Marketing Staff*
▲ **EMP:** 7 **EST:** 1961
SQ FT: 70,000
SALES (est): 1.6MM **Privately Held**
WEB: www.carrom.com
SIC: 3944 2511 Games, toys & children's vehicles; wood household furniture
PA: The Lightning Group Inc
722 N Market St
Duncannon PA 17020
717 834-3031

(G-10545)
MET INC
640 S Pere Marquette Hwy (49431-2661)
PHONE..................................231 845-1737
Dennis G Eggert, *President*
John Babbin, *Principal*
Mark Todd, *Shareholder*
EMP: 8 **EST:** 1988
SQ FT: 18,000
SALES (est): 799.3K **Privately Held**
WEB: www.metmichigan.net
SIC: 2421 Furniture dimension stock, softwood; kiln drying of lumber

(G-10546)
METALWORKS INC (PA)
Also Called: Great Openings
902 4th St (49431-2693)
PHONE..................................231 845-5136
G William Paine, *Ch of Bd*
Thomas W Paine, *President*
Scott Lakari, *Mfg Staff*
Martin McGraw, *Purch Mgr*
Marcia Schulte, *Buyer*
EMP: 218 **EST:** 1969
SQ FT: 125,000
SALES (est): 39.9MM **Privately Held**
WEB: www.metalworks1.com
SIC: 3499 3444 Furniture parts, metal; sheet metalwork

(G-10547)
NORTH WOODS SIGN SHOP
5111 W Us Highway 10 # 4 (49431-8686)
PHONE..................................231 843-3956
Diana Bondeson, *Partner*
EMP: 6 **EST:** 2010 **Privately Held**
WEB: www.northwoodssignshop.com
SIC: 3993 Signs & advertising specialties

(G-10548)
NORTHWOOD SIGNS INC
5111 W Us Highway 10 # 4 (49431-8686)
PHONE..................................231 843-3956
Dianna Bondeson, *President*
Linwood Bondeson, *Vice Pres*
EMP: 8 **EST:** 1981
SQ FT: 9,500
SALES (est): 554.9K **Privately Held**
SIC: 3993 Signs, not made in custom sign painting shops

(G-10549)
OMIMEX ENERGY INC
4854 W Angling Rd (49431)
PHONE..................................231 845-7358
Ken Prior, *Manager*
EMP: 4
SALES (corp-wide): 33.6MM **Privately Held**
SIC: 1311 Crude petroleum production; natural gas production
HQ: Omimex Energy, Inc.
7950 John T White Rd
Fort Worth TX 76120

(G-10550)
SIGNA GROUP INC
Also Called: Whitehall Industries
5175 W 6th St (49431-9322)
PHONE..................................231 845-5101
Bobbi Areklet, *Engineer*
Wendy Merkey,
EMP: 338
SALES (corp-wide): 37.3MM **Privately Held**
WEB: www.whitehallindustries.com
SIC: 3441 Building components, structural steel
PA: Signa Group, Inc.
540 W Frontage Rd # 2105
Northfield IL 60093
847 386-7639

(G-10551)
STRAITS STEEL AND WIRE COMPANY (HQ)
902 N Rowe St Ste 100 (49431-1495)
P.O. Box 589 (49431-0589)
PHONE..................................231 843-3416
Paul Kara, *President*
Sam J Flocks, *CFO*
◆ **EMP:** 85 **EST:** 1946
SQ FT: 95,000
SALES (est): 5.1MM
SALES (corp-wide): 380.4MM **Privately Held**
WEB: www.sswtechnologies.com
SIC: 3479 3496 4212 3315 Painting, coating & hot dipping; miscellaneous fabricated wire products; local trucking, without storage; steel wire & related products
PA: Ssw Advanced Technologies, Llc
3501 Tulsa St
Fort Smith AR 72903
479 646-1651

(G-10552)
SURFACE EXPRESSIONS LLC
904 1st St (49431-2435)
PHONE..................................231 843-8282
Tim Husted,
EMP: 6 **EST:** 2002
SALES (est): 640.5K **Privately Held**
WEB: www.ludingtongranite.com
SIC: 1799 2434 Kitchen & bathroom remodeling; wood kitchen cabinets

Ludington - Mason County (G-10553)

GEOGRAPHIC SECTION

(G-10553)
TYES INC
Also Called: Safety Decals
5236 W 1st St (49431-9349)
PHONE.........................888 219-6301
Nicholas Tykoski, *CEO*
EMP: 10 **EST:** 2009
SQ FT: 8,400
SALES (est): 900K **Privately Held**
WEB: www.safetydecals.com
SIC: 3993 Signs & advertising specialties

(G-10554)
UACJ AUTO WHITEHALL INDS INC
801 S Madison St (49431-2529)
PHONE.........................231 845-5101
Andy Fritts, *QC Mgr*
Roger Perez, *Engineer*
Drew Pehrson, *Manager*
EMP: 72 **Privately Held**
WEB: www.whitehallindustries.com
SIC: 3354 Aluminum extruded products
HQ: Uacj Automotive Whitehall Industries, Inc.
5175 W 6th St
Ludington MI 49431
231 845-5101

(G-10555)
VANDERVEST ELECTRIC MTR & FABG
5635 W Dewey Rd (49431-9599)
PHONE.........................231 843-6196
Brian Vandervest, *Owner*
EMP: 4 **EST:** 1998
SQ FT: 4,800
SALES (est): 524.9K **Privately Held**
SIC: 3621 Motors, electric

(G-10556)
WEST MICHIGAN WIRE CO
Also Called: Kaines West Michigan Co
211 E Dowland St (49431-2308)
P.O. Box 603 (49431-0603)
PHONE.........................231 845-1281
Les Kaines, *CEO*
John L Kaines, *President*
John Applegarth, *Purch Dir*
Kevin Marcoux, *Manager*
Jim Negele, *Manager*
▲ **EMP:** 85 **EST:** 1965
SQ FT: 48,000 **Privately Held**
WEB: www.kwmco.com
SIC: 3496 3315 Miscellaneous fabricated wire products; steel wire & related products

(G-10557)
WESTERN LAND SERVICES INC (PA)
1100 Conrad Industrial Dr (49431-2679)
PHONE.........................231 843-8878
John K Wilson, *President*
Todd Stowe, *Vice Pres*
Jim Aksamit, *Project Mgr*
Dan Stevenson, *Project Mgr*
Greg Tracy, *Project Mgr*
EMP: 75 **EST:** 1990
SQ FT: 21,000
SALES (est): 70.7MM **Privately Held**
WEB: www.westernls.com
SIC: 1382 Oil & gas exploration services

(G-10558)
WORTEN COPY CENTER INC
Also Called: Kwik Print Plus
601 N Washington Ave (49431-1503)
PHONE.........................231 845-7030
Timothy A Alley, *President*
Debra H Alley, *Treasurer*
EMP: 6 **EST:** 1977
SQ FT: 1,600
SALES (est): 843.4K **Privately Held**
WEB: www.kwikprintplus.com
SIC: 2752 2791 Commercial printing, offset; typesetting

Lum
Lapeer County

(G-10559)
LUMCO MANUFACTURING COMPANY
2027 Mitchell Lake Rd (48412-9243)
PHONE.........................810 724-0582
Patrick J Gleason, *President*
Margaret Gleason, *Corp Secy*
John T Gleason, *Vice Pres*
Gary Skellenger, *Engineer*
EMP: 10 **EST:** 1968
SQ FT: 30,000
SALES (est): 2.7MM **Privately Held**
WEB: www.lumco.com
SIC: 3545 Machine tool accessories

Luna Pier
Monroe County

(G-10560)
DUSCHA MANAGEMENT LLC
4614 N 2nd St (48157-9700)
PHONE.........................352 247-2113
Cher Matthews, *CEO*
EMP: 10 **EST:** 2014
SALES (est): 351.2K **Privately Held**
WEB: www.duschamgt.com
SIC: 2731 8748 8742 Book publishing; business consulting; communications consulting; management consulting services; human resource consulting services

Lupton
Ogemaw County

(G-10561)
BRINDLEY LUMBER & PALLET CO
Also Called: Brindley Pallets
1971 State Rd (48635-9762)
PHONE.........................989 345-3497
James Brindley, *President*
Richard Brindley, *Vice Pres*
EMP: 8 **EST:** 1967
SQ FT: 15,000
SALES (est): 500K **Privately Held**
SIC: 2448 Pallets, wood

(G-10562)
MARK A NELSON
332 Oneil Rd (48635-9759)
PHONE.........................989 305-5769
Mark A Nelson, *Principal*
EMP: 7 **EST:** 2012
SALES (est): 175.6K **Privately Held**
SIC: 2411 Logging

Luther
Lake County

(G-10563)
JEFFERY LUCAS
10975 E Old M 63 (49656-9384)
PHONE.........................231 797-5152
Jeffrey Lucas, *Principal*
EMP: 6 **EST:** 2009
SALES (est): 243.9K **Privately Held**
SIC: 2411 Logging camps & contractors

Lyons
Ionia County

(G-10564)
MID MICHIGAN WOOD SPECIALITES
1370 Divine Hwy (48851-8718)
PHONE.........................989 855-3667
James Smith, *Owner*
EMP: 10 **EST:** 2014
SALES (est): 475.6K **Privately Held**
WEB: www.midmichiganwood.com
SIC: 2434 Wood kitchen cabinets

(G-10565)
PREMIUM MACHINE & TOOL INC
207 Water St (48851-5105)
P.O. Box 286 (48851-0286)
PHONE.........................989 855-3326
Mark L Schneider, *President*
EMP: 12 **EST:** 1993
SQ FT: 10,000
SALES (est): 1MM **Privately Held**
WEB: www.premiummachine.com
SIC: 2514 2522 Metal household furniture; office furniture, except wood

Macatawa
Ottawa County

(G-10566)
ELDEAN COMPANY
Also Called: Eldean Shipyard & Yacht Sales
2223 S Shore Dr (49434-9800)
P.O. Box 6 (49434-0006)
PHONE.........................616 335-5843
Herbert Eldean, *President*
Michael Chesser, *Office Mgr*
Matt Eldean, *Manager*
EMP: 35 **EST:** 1973
SQ FT: 180,000
SALES (est): 3.1MM **Privately Held**
WEB: www.eldean.com
SIC: 4493 3732 Boat yards, storage & incidental repair; boat building & repairing

Mackinac Island
Mackinac County

(G-10567)
ORIGINAL MURDICKS FUDGE CO (PA)
Also Called: Murdick's Fudge Kitchen
7363 Main St (49757)
P.O. Box 481 (49757-0481)
PHONE.........................906 847-3530
Robert J Benser, *President*
EMP: 7 **EST:** 1955
SQ FT: 1,250
SALES (est): 3MM **Privately Held**
WEB: www.originalmurdicksfudge.com
SIC: 5441 2064 5812 2066 Candy; fudge (candy); ice cream stands or dairy bars; chocolate & cocoa products

Mackinaw City
Cheboygan County

(G-10568)
MARSHALLS TRAIL INC
Also Called: Marshall's Fudge
308 E Central Ave (49701-9801)
P.O. Box 639 (49701-0639)
PHONE.........................231 436-5082
Joseph D Scheerens, *President*
Bruce T Thrasher, *Vice Pres*
Michael J Thrasher, *Vice Pres*
Mary J Scheerens, *Treasurer*
EMP: 15 **EST:** 1921
SQ FT: 5,000
SALES (est): 862.5K **Privately Held**
WEB: www.marshallsfudge.com
SIC: 5441 5812 5947 2099 Confectionery produced for direct sale on the premises; delicatessen (eating places); gift shop; food preparations; chocolate & cocoa products; candy & other confectionery products

(G-10569)
SIGN OF THE LOON GIFTS INC
311 W Central Ave (49701-9701)
P.O. Box 309 (49701-0309)
PHONE.........................231 436-5155
Jeffrey Alexander, *President*
Ethyl Alexander, *Vice Pres*
EMP: 4 **EST:** 1989
SALES (est): 266.7K **Privately Held**
WEB: www.signoftheloon.com
SIC: 5947 2261 Gift shop; screen printing of cotton broadwoven fabrics

Macomb
Macomb County

(G-10570)
AARONS FABRICTIONS-TUBE STEEL
50220 Shenandoah Dr (48044-1348)
PHONE.........................586 883-0652
Sue Bursteinowicz, *General Mgr*
EMP: 11 **EST:** 2018
SALES (est): 543.1K **Privately Held**
WEB: www.aaronsfabrication.net
SIC: 3441 Fabricated structural metal

(G-10571)
ADMORE INC
Also Called: Colorworx
24707 Wood Ct (48042-5378)
PHONE.........................586 949-8200
Keith Walters, *CEO*
Paul Brancaleone, *Prdtn Mgr*
Mark Young, *Plant Engr*
Brian Doppke, *Sales Staff*
Jane Hook, *Sales Staff*
EMP: 130 **EST:** 1947
SQ FT: 57,500
SALES (est): 20.3MM
SALES (corp-wide): 357.9MM **Publicly Held**
WEB: www.admorefolders.com
SIC: 2752 Commercial printing, offset
PA: Ennis, Inc.
2441 Presidential Pkwy
Midlothian TX 76065
972 775-9801

(G-10572)
ADVANCED SYSTEMS & CONTRLS INC
15773 Leone Dr (48042-4006)
PHONE.........................586 992-9684
Andrew Zundel, *President*
Kevin P Pray, *Vice Pres*
EMP: 34 **EST:** 1990
SQ FT: 7,100
SALES (est): 6.5MM **Privately Held**
WEB: www.advancedsyst.com
SIC: 3829 3825 Aircraft & motor vehicle measurement equipment; testing equipment: abrasion, shearing strength, etc.; instruments to measure electricity

(G-10573)
ALL AMERICAN CONTAINER CORP
24600 Wood Ct (48042-5919)
PHONE.........................586 949-0000
Harold B Berquist, *CEO*
Dale E Cartwright, *President*
Amanda Garon, *Accounts Mgr*
EMP: 15 **EST:** 1980
SQ FT: 54,000
SALES (est): 6MM **Privately Held**
WEB: www.allamericancontainer.com
SIC: 5113 2448 Corrugated & solid fiber boxes; pallets, wood

(G-10574)
ALLIANCE INDUSTRIES INC
51820 Regency Center Dr (48042-4133)
PHONE.........................248 656-3473
Todd Sangster, *President*
Thomas A Fournier, *Admin Sec*
EMP: 30 **EST:** 1994
SQ FT: 11,000
SALES (est): 2.6MM **Privately Held**
WEB: www.alliance-ind-inc.com
SIC: 3544 Industrial molds

(G-10575)
ALLIED PHOTOCHEMICAL INC
Also Called: Allied Photopolymers
16024 Angelo Dr (48042-4073)
P.O. Box 328, Marysville (48040-0328)
PHONE.........................810 364-6910
Michael Kelly, *President*
Dan Sweetwood, *Vice Pres*
Robert Linders, *Sales Staff*
Norm Beauchamp, *Director*
Chris Kurzweil, *Director*
EMP: 10 **EST:** 1996
SQ FT: 14,000

▲ = Import ▼ =Export
◆ =Import/Export

GEOGRAPHIC SECTION

Macomb - Macomb County (G-10605)

SALES (est): 1.7MM **Privately Held**
WEB: www.alliedphotochemical.com
SIC: 2851 Paints & allied products

(G-10576)
AMERICANLUBRICATIONCOM
45790 Meadows Cir W (48044-3910)
PHONE..................................586 219-9119
Corey Ellis, *President*
EMP: 7 EST: 2007
SALES (est): 123.5K **Privately Held**
WEB: www.americanlubrication.com
SIC: 2911 Oils, lubricating

(G-10577)
ANDRETTA & ASSOCIATES INC
48945 Austrian Pine Dr (48044-6126)
PHONE..................................586 557-6226
Sandro Andretta, *President*
▲ EMP: 10 EST: 2005
SALES (est): 1MM **Privately Held**
SIC: 2084 Wines

(G-10578)
ASCENT AEROSPACE LLC
16445 23 Mile Rd (48042-4005)
PHONE..................................586 726-0500
Paul Walsh, *COO*
Steve Littauer, *CFO*
Andy Jones, *Mng Member*
Graham Mitchell, *Program Mgr*
Nutting Jeremy, *Info Tech Dir*
EMP: 715 EST: 2013
SALES (est): 94.4MM
SALES (corp-wide): 223.8MM **Privately Held**
WEB: www.ascentaerospace.com
SIC: 3812 Acceleration indicators & systems components, aerospace
PA: Ascent Aerospace Holdings Llc
16445 23 Mile Rd
Macomb MI 48042
586 726-0500

(G-10579)
ASCENT AEROSPACE HOLDINGS LLC (PA)
Also Called: American Industrial Partners
16445 23 Mile Rd (48042-4005)
PHONE..................................212 916-8142
Michael Mahfet, *CEO*
Nick Boyd, *Mfg Spvr*
Ryan Saling, *Opers Staff*
Dawn Steele, *Buyer*
Jonathon Levine, *CFO*
▲ EMP: 4
SQ FT: 20,000
SALES (est): 223.8MM **Privately Held**
WEB: www.ascentaerospace.com
SIC: 6799 3721 Investors; aircraft

(G-10580)
ASCENT INTEGRATED PLATFORMS
Also Called: Aip Aerospace
16445 23 Mile Rd (48042-4005)
PHONE..................................586 726-0500
Ray Kauffman, *Mng Member*
EMP: 16 EST: 2014
SALES (est): 1MM **Privately Held**
SIC: 3369 Nonferrous foundries

(G-10581)
BLUE WATER BORING LLC
46522 Erb Dr (48042-5915)
PHONE..................................586 421-2100
Sandra Vezina, *Mng Member*
Michele Vezina,
EMP: 4 EST: 1984
SQ FT: 4,000
SALES (est): 293.8K **Privately Held**
SIC: 3599 Machine shop, jobbing & repair

(G-10582)
CALIGIRLBOOKS LLC
45841 Heather Ridge Dr (48044-4075)
PHONE..................................415 361-1533
Tianna Jones, *Mng Member*
EMP: 4
SALES (est): 65K **Privately Held**
SIC: 7389 2731 ; book music: publishing & printing

(G-10583)
CARROLL TOOL AND DIE CO
46650 Erb Dr (48042-5348)
PHONE..................................586 949-7670
Thomas J Plotzke, *President*
Tony Plotzke, *Vice Pres*
Melvin Sova, *Plant Mgr*
Catherine Plotzke, *Admin Sec*
EMP: 40 EST: 1983
SQ FT: 20,000
SALES (est): 2.6MM **Privately Held**
WEB: www.carrolltool.com
SIC: 3544 Special dies & tools

(G-10584)
CENTURY PLASTICS LLC
51102 Quadrate Dr (48042-4055)
PHONE..................................586 697-5752
Bob Stafford, *Manager*
EMP: 16
SALES (corp-wide): 146.6MM **Privately Held**
WEB: www.cieautomotive.com
SIC: 3089 Injection molding of plastics
HQ: Century Plastics, Llc
15030 23 Mile Rd
Shelby Township MI 48315
586 566-3900

(G-10585)
CONFORM AUTOMOTIVE LLC
Also Called: Dti Plastic Products
51258 Quadrate Dr (48042-4055)
PHONE..................................248 647-0400
Gary Stanus, *Manager*
EMP: 189 **Privately Held**
WEB: www.conformgroup.com
SIC: 3714 Motor vehicle parts & accessories
PA: Conform Automotive, Llc
32500 Telg Rd Ste 207
Bingham Farms MI 48025

(G-10586)
CREATIVE REPAIR SOLUTIONS LLC
51821 Industrial Dr (48042-4027)
PHONE..................................586 615-1517
EMP: 7 EST: 2017
SALES (est): 26K **Privately Held**
WEB: www.creativerepairsolutions.com
SIC: 7699 3089 Repair services; automotive parts, plastic

(G-10587)
DETROIT CYCLE PUB LLC
16089 Diamante Dr (48044-1183)
PHONE..................................231 286-5257
Nicholas Blaszczyk, *Principal*
EMP: 9 EST: 2016
SALES (est): 569.2K **Privately Held**
WEB: www.detroitrollingpub.com
SIC: 2082 Malt beverages

(G-10588)
DISPLAY CSES BY GRNDPAS CBNETS
55750 Danube Ave (48042-2361)
PHONE..................................586 506-2222
Ronald Baluch, *Principal*
EMP: 6 EST: 2007
SALES (est): 152.4K **Privately Held**
SIC: 2434 Wood kitchen cabinets

(G-10589)
DSE INDUSTRIES LLC
51315 Regency Center Dr (48042-4131)
PHONE..................................313 530-6668
Ronald Scott, *CFO*
Ron Scott, *Business Dir*
EMP: 5 EST: 2015
SQ FT: 15,000
SALES (est): 809.3K **Privately Held**
WEB: www.dse-industries.com
SIC: 3672 8711 7389 3714 Printed circuit boards; engineering services; ; motor vehicle parts & accessories; injection molding of plastics

(G-10590)
DYNASTY FAB LLC
51195 Regency Center Dr (48042-4130)
PHONE..................................586 623-0227
Eric Reno,
EMP: 12 EST: 2018
SALES (est): 471.8K **Privately Held**
WEB: www.dynastyfab.com
SIC: 7692 Welding repair

(G-10591)
EPTECH INC
51483 Quadrate Dr Ste C (48042-4061)
PHONE..................................586 254-2722
EMP: 4 EST: 2019
SALES (est): 151K **Privately Held**
SIC: 3599 Industrial machinery

(G-10592)
ESIRPAL INC
55549 Danube Ave (48042-2362)
PHONE..................................586 337-7848
Vincent Laprise, *President*
EMP: 7 EST: 1982
SALES (est): 848.3K **Privately Held**
SIC: 3825 3569 Semiconductor test equipment; assembly machines, non-metalworking

(G-10593)
EXPERIMAC MACOMB
15715 Hall Rd (48044-3887)
PHONE..................................586 884-6292
EMP: 5 EST: 2009
SALES (est): 81.8K **Privately Held**
WEB: www.experimax.com
SIC: 3571 Electronic computers

(G-10594)
FABTRONIC INC
51685 Industrial Dr (48042-4027)
PHONE..................................586 786-6114
Howard G Baisch, *President*
Douglas Clark, *General Mgr*
Jeremy Baisch, *Vice Pres*
Victoria Baisch, *Vice Pres*
Frank Frankin, *QC Mgr*
EMP: 50 EST: 1982
SQ FT: 16,000
SALES (est): 6.4MM **Privately Held**
WEB: www.fabtronic-inc.com
SIC: 3312 Tool & die steel & alloys

(G-10595)
FIVE STAR INDUSTRIES INC
51550 Hayes Rd (48042-4008)
PHONE..................................586 786-0500
Shirley Tomayko, *President*
Randal Tomayko, *Vice Pres*
Ron Tomayko, *Plant Mgr*
EMP: 30 EST: 1981
SQ FT: 21,225
SALES (est): 2.2MM **Privately Held**
WEB: www.fivestarindustries.com
SIC: 3545 3544 3541 Comparators (machinists' precision tools); special dies, tools, jigs & fixtures; machine tools, metal cutting type

(G-10596)
FOAM FACTORY INCORPORATED
17500 23 Mile Rd Ste A (48044-1165)
PHONE..................................586 739-7449
Salvatore Badalamenti, *President*
Sicilia Badalamenti, *Vice Pres*
◆ EMP: 35 EST: 1993
SQ FT: 100,000
SALES (est): 5.9MM **Privately Held**
WEB: www.foambymail.com
SIC: 3086 Plastics foam products

(G-10597)
FUN LEARNING COMPANY LLC
21341 Fairfield Dr (48044-2966)
PHONE..................................269 362-0651
Cathy Joyce, *Mng Member*
EMP: 9 EST: 2013
SALES (est): 493.3K **Privately Held**
SIC: 3999 Education aids, devices & supplies

(G-10598)
G T GUNDRILLING INC
51195 Regency Center Dr (48042-4130)
PHONE..................................586 992-3301
Richard Thibault, *President*
EMP: 6 EST: 1995
SQ FT: 10,500
SALES (est): 688.1K **Privately Held**
SIC: 3429 Manufactured hardware (general)

(G-10599)
GLOBAL TOOLING SYSTEMS LLC
Also Called: Ascent Aerospace
16445 23 Mile Rd (48042-4005)
PHONE..................................586 726-0500
Paul Walsh, *President*
Karl Bumgarner, *Vice Pres*
Tracy Grabman, *QC Mgr*
Eugene Darlak, *Engineer*
Dan Nowicki, *CFO*
▼ EMP: 265 EST: 1999
SQ FT: 215,000
SALES (est): 43.6MM **Privately Held**
WEB: www.ascentaerospace.com
SIC: 3545 3569 Cutting tools for machine tools; gas producers, generators & other gas related equipment

(G-10600)
GRAHAM MEDICAL TECH LLC
Also Called: Gramedica
16137 Leone Dr (48042-4063)
PHONE..................................586 677-9600
Christie Bolda, *Opers Staff*
A Evans, *Finance*
Angela Recchia, *Manager*
Michael Graham,
EMP: 9 EST: 2003
SQ FT: 3,600
SALES (est): 1.4MM **Privately Held**
WEB: www.gramedica.com
SIC: 3841 Surgical & medical instruments

(G-10601)
HARRYS STEERING GEAR REPAIR
52197 Sawmill Creek Dr (48042-5698)
PHONE..................................586 677-5580
Harry Nowak, *President*
Josephine Nowak, *Corp Secy*
EMP: 7 EST: 1986 **Privately Held**
WEB: www.steeringgearrebuilders.com
SIC: 7538 3714 General automotive repair shops; motor vehicle parts & accessories

(G-10602)
HICKS PLASTICS COMPANY INC (HQ)
51308 Industrial Dr (48042-4025)
PHONE..................................586 786-5640
Tim Hicks, *President*
Jeff Ward, *General Mgr*
Gail P Hicks, *Exec VP*
Theresa Teller, *Purchasing*
Sherry McCleary, *QC Mgr*
EMP: 94 EST: 1989
SQ FT: 70,000
SALES (est): 23.6MM **Privately Held**
WEB: www.hicksplastics.com
SIC: 3089 Injection molding of plastics

(G-10603)
HURON GLASS BLOCK
46562 Erb Dr (48042-5916)
PHONE..................................586 598-6900
EMP: 5 EST: 2019
SALES (est): 100.9K **Privately Held**
SIC: 3299 Nonmetallic mineral products

(G-10604)
HYDRA-TECH INC
1483 Quadrate Dr Ste C (48042)
PHONE..................................586 232-4479
Eugene Nelson, *President*
Mark Crowell, *Engineer*
Larry Bryan, *Sales Mgr*
Jo Ann Nelson, *Admin Sec*
EMP: 8 EST: 1983
SQ FT: 6,000
SALES (est): 3.6MM **Privately Held**
WEB: www.hydra-techinc.com
SIC: 3561 5084 Industrial pumps & parts; hydraulic systems equipment & supplies

(G-10605)
INDUSTRIAL PLANT SVCS NAT LLC
51410 Milano Dr Ste 110 (48042-4015)
PHONE..................................586 221-9017
Mark Reynolds, *Mng Member*
EMP: 20 EST: 2013
SQ FT: 10,000

Macomb - Macomb County (G-10606) GEOGRAPHIC SECTION

SALES (est): 3MM **Privately Held**
WEB: www.i-p-services.com
SIC: 3822 Building services monitoring controls, automatic

(G-10606)
INOVATECH AUTOMATION INC
16105 Leone Dr (48042-4063)
PHONE..................586 210-9010
Mark Rathbone, *Principal*
Megan Toth, *Accountant*
EMP: 16 **EST:** 2016
SALES (est): 3.3MM **Privately Held**
WEB: www.inovatech.com
SIC: 3569 Liquid automation machinery & equipment

(G-10607)
JASONS APPLE SERVICE & SLS LLC
48858 Park Place Dr (48044-2241)
PHONE..................586 530-4908
Jason Benson, *Principal*
EMP: 4 **EST:** 2014
SALES (est): 92.8K **Privately Held**
SIC: 3571 Electronic computers

(G-10608)
JOINT PRODUCTION TECH INC (PA)
Also Called: Jpt
15381 Hallmark Ct (48042-4016)
PHONE..................586 786-0080
Robert B Peuterbaugh, *President*
David A Gifford, *Vice Pres*
Ronald Peuterbaugh, *Plant Mgr*
Brian Sitek, *Engineer*
John Wirtanen, *Sales Engr*
EMP: 26 **EST:** 1971
SQ FT: 24,000
SALES (est): 2.8MM **Privately Held**
WEB: www.jptonline.com
SIC: 3545 Cutting tools for machine tools

(G-10609)
KIMBERLY-CLARK CORPORATION
21346 Summerfield Dr (48044-2967)
PHONE..................586 949-1649
EMP: 5
SALES (corp-wide): 19.1B **Publicly Held**
WEB: www.kimberly-clark.com
SIC: 2621 2676 Sanitary tissue paper; infant & baby paper products
PA: Kimberly-Clark Corporation
   351 Phelps Dr
   Irving TX 75038
   972 281-1200

(G-10610)
MACOMB PRODUCTS LLC
20103 Ballantrae Dr (48044-5906)
PHONE..................586 855-0223
Brian Szalewicz, *Principal*
EMP: 5 **EST:** 2016
SALES (est): 86.4K **Privately Held**
WEB: www.miscproducts.com
SIC: 3496 Miscellaneous fabricated wire products

(G-10611)
MACOMB SIGNS & GRAPHICS
46566 Erb Dr (48042-5916)
PHONE..................586 350-9789
Frederick Dudek, *Principal*
EMP: 5 **EST:** 2015
SALES (est): 173.3K **Privately Held**
WEB: www.macombsigns.com
SIC: 3993 Signs & advertising specialties

(G-10612)
MAJESTIC INDUSTRIES INC
15378 Hallmark Ct (48042-4017)
PHONE..................586 786-9100
James Butler, *President*
Eric Sherman, *CFO*
Alan Janiszewski, *Treasurer*
▲ **EMP:** 77 **EST:** 1981
SQ FT: 65,000
SALES (est): 24.3MM **Privately Held**
WEB: www.toolingtechgroup.com
SIC: 3544 Special dies & tools
HQ: Tooling Technology Holdings, Llc
   100 Enterprise Dr
   Fort Loramie OH 45845
   937 295-3672

(G-10613)
MAMEMARQUEES LLC
55711 Broughton Rd (48042-1829)
PHONE..................586 322-2215
EMP: 6 **EST:** 2010
SALES (est): 96.2K **Privately Held**
WEB: www.gameongrafix.com
SIC: 3993 Signs & advertising specialties

(G-10614)
MATERIAL DIFFERENCE TECH LLC
51195 Regency Center Dr (48042-4130)
PHONE..................888 818-1283
Lori Cerqua, *Accountant*
Matt Fields, *Sales Staff*
Jacob Love, *Manager*
Kevin Phillips,
EMP: 10
SALES (corp-wide): 47MM **Privately Held**
WEB: www.materialdifferencetechnologies.com
SIC: 5162 3087 Plastics materials & basic shapes; custom compound purchased resins
PA: Material Difference Technologies Llc
   1501 Sarasota Center Blvd
   Sarasota FL 34240
   888 818-1283

(G-10615)
MATRIX MTLCRAFT LLP A LTD PRTN
15721 Leone Dr (48042-4006)
PHONE..................586 469-9611
Nicholas A Salvatore, *Partner*
Michael Buscaino, *Purch Mgr*
EMP: 25
SALES (corp-wide): 5MM **Privately Held**
WEB: www.tecinternational.com
SIC: 3444 Sheet metalwork
PA: Matrix Metalcraft, Llp, A Limited Partnership
   68 S Squirrel Rd
   Auburn Hills MI 48326
   248 724-1800

(G-10616)
MICHIGAN PROD MACHINING INC (PA)
Also Called: Mpm
16700 23 Mile Rd (48044-1100)
PHONE..................586 228-9700
Tony Anderson, *General Mgr*
Mary Jane West, *Corp Secy*
Kevin West, *Vice Pres*
Leroy Seiber, *Engineer*
Dan Myers, *CFO*
▲ **EMP:** 294 **EST:** 1973
SQ FT: 108,000
SALES (est): 52.6MM **Privately Held**
WEB: www.michpro.com
SIC: 3599 Machine shop, jobbing & repair

(G-10617)
MISC PRODUCTS
16730 Enterprise Dr (48044-1006)
PHONE..................586 263-3300
William Corbit, *President*
Cathy First, *Manager*
Ann Bara,
▼ **EMP:** 63 **EST:** 1970
SQ FT: 28,080
SALES (est): 9.5MM **Privately Held**
WEB: www.miscproducts.com
SIC: 3714 Motor vehicle parts & accessories

(G-10618)
MLS SIGNS INC
50617 Plaza Dr (48042-4634)
PHONE..................586 948-0200
Bill Siewert, *President*
Mordechai Schwimmer, *Representative*
EMP: 10 **EST:** 1992
SALES (est): 733.9K **Privately Held**
WEB: www.mlssigns.com
SIC: 3993 Signs, not made in custom sign painting shops

(G-10619)
MOLLERTECH LLC
51280 Regency Center Dr (48042-4130)
PHONE..................586 615-9154
Steve Jordan, *President*
Kristine Nowowiecki, *Vice Pres*
Eric Strunk, *VP Opers*
Chuck Gietzen, *Opers Mgr*
Chris Morgan, *Prdtn Mgr*
▲ **EMP:** 60 **EST:** 1998
SQ FT: 80,000
SALES (est): 19.3MM
SALES (corp-wide): 257.2K **Privately Held**
WEB: www.moellergroup.com
SIC: 2396 Automotive trimmings, fabric
HQ: Moller Group North America, Inc.
   13877 Teresa Dr
   Shelby Township MI 48315
   586 532-0860

(G-10620)
MPI PLASTICS
51315 Regency Center Dr (48042-4131)
PHONE..................201 502-1534
EMP: 5 **EST:** 2017
SALES (est): 191K **Privately Held**
SIC: 3089 Injection molding of plastics

(G-10621)
MULTI-FORM PLASTICS INC
51315 Regency Center Dr (48042-4131)
PHONE..................586 786-4229
Jenny Travis, *President*
Lorenzo Borbolla, *Vice Pres*
EMP: 10 **EST:** 1990
SQ FT: 8,275
SALES (est): 1.5MM **Privately Held**
SIC: 3089 Injection molding of plastics

(G-10622)
NETWAVE
20539 Country Side Dr (48044-3589)
PHONE..................586 263-4469
Randy Hyduk, *President*
April Hyduk, *Technology*
EMP: 9 **EST:** 1994
SALES (est): 782.9K **Privately Held**
SIC: 3825 Network analyzers

(G-10623)
NYLOK LLC (PA)
15260 Hallmark Ct (48042-4007)
PHONE..................586 786-0100
Tadashi Camey, *General Mgr*
Greg Rawlings, *General Mgr*
John Lumetta, *QC Mgr*
Lauren Doser, *Controller*
Courtney Jenkins, *Controller*
EMP: 112 **EST:** 2009
SALES (est): 32.2MM **Privately Held**
WEB: www.nylok.com
SIC: 3399 Metal fasteners

(G-10624)
OTR PERFORMANCE INC
51619 Industrial Dr (48042-4027)
PHONE..................586 799-4375
Jason Chise, *Principal*
David Melinte, *Cust Mgr*
Raul Ghiurau, *Mktg Coord*
EMP: 8 **EST:** 2012
SALES (est): 935.4K **Privately Held**
WEB: www.otrperformance.com
SIC: 7538 3089 General automotive repair shops; automotive parts, plastic

(G-10625)
P2R METAL FABRICATION INC
49620 Hayes Rd (48044-1509)
PHONE..................586 606-5266
Patrick McAleer, *President*
Ryan Novak, *Treasurer*
Jessica Guseila, *Admin Sec*
EMP: 10 **EST:** 2019
SALES (est): 868.8K **Privately Held**
WEB: www.p2rfab.com
SIC: 3599 3799 3711 3721 Machine & other job shop work; trailers & trailer equipment; military motor vehicle assembly; aircraft; engineering services

(G-10626)
PPG INDUSTRIES INC
54197 Myrica Dr (48042-2223)
PHONE..................248 640-4174
Keith Larson, *Principal*
EMP: 4
SALES (corp-wide): 15.1B **Publicly Held**
WEB: www.ppg.com
SIC: 2851 Paints & allied products
PA: Ppg Industries, Inc.
   1 Ppg Pl
   Pittsburgh PA 15272
   412 434-3131

(G-10627)
PRAET TOOL & ENGINEERING INC
51214 Industrial Dr (48042-4025)
PHONE..................586 677-3800
Alan Praet, *President*
Dennis Praet, *Vice Pres*
Glenn Praet, *Mfg Staff*
Sam Struth, *Design Engr*
George Buchholz, *Associate*
EMP: 37 **EST:** 1983
SQ FT: 30,000
SALES (est): 3.8MM **Privately Held**
WEB: www.praettool.com
SIC: 3544 3599 8711 Special dies & tools; machine shop, jobbing & repair; engineering services

(G-10628)
PRECISION CASTPARTS CORP
46192 Rocker Dr (48044-3751)
PHONE..................586 690-8659
EMP: 7
SALES (corp-wide): 245.5B **Publicly Held**
WEB: www.precast.com
SIC: 3324 Aerospace investment castings, ferrous
HQ: Precision Castparts Corp.
   4650 Sw Mcdam Ave Ste 300
   Portland OR 97239
   503 946-4800

(G-10629)
PRISM PRINTING
51168 Milano Dr (48042-4018)
PHONE..................586 786-1250
Rick Medwith, *Owner*
EMP: 6 **EST:** 1990
SALES (est): 392.6K **Privately Held**
SIC: 2752 Commercial printing, offset

(G-10630)
PRONTO PRINTING
46755 Partridge Creek Dr (48044-3257)
PHONE..................586 215-9670
Sokol Lumaj, *Administration*
EMP: 5 **EST:** 2013
SALES (est): 119.3K **Privately Held**
SIC: 2752 Commercial printing, lithographic

(G-10631)
PTI ENGINEERED PLASTICS INC
50900 Corporate Dr (48044-1008)
PHONE..................586 263-5100
Mark Rathbone, *CEO*
Kurt Nerva, *President*
Chris Behring, *Opers Mgr*
Kerry Carrizal, *Engineer*
Steve Vanderkooi, *Engineer*
▲ **EMP:** 300 **EST:** 1984
SQ FT: 150,000
SALES (est): 84.7MM **Privately Held**
WEB: www.teampti.com
SIC: 3089 3544 Injection molded finished plastic products; forms (molds), for foundry & plastics working machinery

(G-10632)
RIDGE POINTE PUBLISHING LLC
23962 Pointe Dr (48042-5909)
PHONE..................586 948-4660
Paul Stanley, *Principal*
EMP: 4 **EST:** 2014
SALES (est): 55.6K **Privately Held**
SIC: 2741 Miscellaneous publishing

(G-10633)
SEEKING
18518 Country Club Dr (48042-6218)
PHONE..................586 489-2524
Kristy Ostrander, *Principal*
EMP: 8 **EST:** 2014

GEOGRAPHIC SECTION
Madison Heights - Oakland County (G-10662)

SALES (est): 96.7K **Privately Held**
SIC: 3643 Current-carrying wiring devices

(G-10634)
SHEER MADNESS DRAP & BLINDS
21014 Vesper Dr (48044-1368)
PHONE.................................248 379-2145
EMP: 4 EST: 2018
SALES (est): 125.2K **Privately Held**
SIC: 2591 Window blinds

(G-10635)
SIMCO AUTOMOTIVE TRIM
51362 Quadrate Dr (48042-4055)
PHONE.................................800 372-3172
EMP: 60
SQ FT: 32,000
SALES (est): 3.8MM
SALES (corp-wide): 190.4MM **Publicly Held**
SIC: 2211 Broadwoven Fabric Mills, Cotton
PA: Ufp Technologies, Inc.
100 Hale St
Newburyport MA 01950
978 352-2200

(G-10636)
SLIK METAL FABRICATION LLC
55390 Rhine Ave (48042-6190)
PHONE.................................586 344-5621
Scott Kraemer, *Principal*
EMP: 5 EST: 2011
SALES (est): 145.2K **Privately Held**
SIC: 3499 Fabricated metal products

(G-10637)
STERLING DIE & ENGINEERING INC
15767 Claire Ct (48042-4024)
PHONE.................................586 677-0707
Chet Wisniewski, *President*
Donna Wisniewski, *President*
Lori Getz, *Controller*
EMP: 35 EST: 1984
SALES (est): 5.6MM **Privately Held**
WEB: www.sterlingdieandengineering.com
SIC: 3465 3496 3544 3469 Automotive stampings; miscellaneous fabricated wire products; special dies, tools, jigs & fixtures; metal stampings; manufactured hardware (general)

(G-10638)
SUPERIOR USA LLC
16089 Leone Dr (48042-4063)
PHONE.................................586 786-4261
Rob Vargo, *CEO*
Terry Smith, *President*
EMP: 4
SALES (est): 359.3K **Privately Held**
WEB: www.superiorusa.com
SIC: 3542 Machine tools, metal forming type

(G-10639)
SURFACE INDUCTION TECH
51200 Milano Dr Ste C (48042-4012)
PHONE.................................248 881-2481
Charles Snooks, *Principal*
EMP: 6 EST: 2017
SALES (est): 148.5K **Privately Held**
WEB: www.surfindtech.com
SIC: 3599 Machine shop, jobbing & repair

(G-10640)
SWISS PRECISION MACHINING INC
54370 Oconee Dr (48042-6123)
PHONE.................................586 677-7558
Roger Kappeli, *President*
Linda Kappeli, *Vice Pres*
Rolf Kappeli, *Treasurer*
Evelyn Kappeli, *Admin Sec*
EMP: 17 EST: 1959
SQ FT: 7,850
SALES (est): 144.1K **Privately Held**
WEB: www.spmswiss.com
SIC: 3599 3812 Machine shop, jobbing & repair; search & navigation equipment

(G-10641)
TECH ELECTRIC CO LLC
16177 Leone Dr (48042-4063)
PHONE.................................586 697-5095

EMP: 4
SALES (est): 475K **Privately Held**
SIC: 3699 1731 Mfg Electrical Equipment/Supplies Electrical Contractor

(G-10642)
TITANIUM BUILDING CO INC
53355 Fairchild Rd (48042-3334)
PHONE.................................586 634-8580
Denise Kakos, *Principal*
EMP: 6 EST: 2007
SALES (est): 106.4K **Privately Held**
SIC: 3356 Titanium

(G-10643)
TOOLING TECHNOLOGY LLC (PA)
Also Called: Tooling Tech Group
51223 Quadrate Dr (48042-4053)
P.O. Box 319, Fort Loramie OH (45845-0319)
PHONE.................................937 381-9211
Anthony Seger, *CEO*
Gary Peppelman, *President*
Jeff Bradshaw, *Engineer*
Jeff Johnson, *CFO*
Todd Wodzinski, *Ch Credit Ofcr*
EMP: 80 EST: 2006
SQ FT: 42,000
SALES (est): 49.5MM **Privately Held**
WEB: www.toolingtechgroup.com
SIC: 3544 3363 3365 3322 Industrial molds; aluminum die-castings; aluminum foundries; malleable iron foundries

(G-10644)
TRIUMPH GEAR SYSTEMS - MCOMB I
15375 23 Mile Rd (48042-4000)
PHONE.................................586 781-2800
Dan Hennen, *President*
Dennis Blitz, *CFO*
David J Pastori, *Treasurer*
Joseph D Hennen, *VP Sales*
Richard Skokna, *Manager*
◆ **EMP: 198 EST: 1977**
SQ FT: 85,000
SALES (est): 47.9MM **Publicly Held**
WEB: www.triumphgroup.com
SIC: 3728 3599 3462 3444 Gears, aircraft power transmission; machine shop, jobbing & repair; iron & steel forgings; sheet metalwork; gray & ductile iron foundries
PA: Triumph Group, Inc.
899 Cassatt Rd Ste 210
Berwyn PA 19312

(G-10645)
UNDER STAIRS
53715 Sprnghill Madows Dr (48042)
PHONE.................................586 781-6202
Shelly Brothers, *Principal*
EMP: 4 EST: 2015
SALES (est): 94.6K **Privately Held**
SIC: 3446 Stairs, staircases, stair treads: prefabricated metal

(G-10646)
UNITED MACHINING INC
51362 Quadrate Dr (48042-4055)
PHONE.................................586 323-4300
Lou Sabel, *General Mgr*
EMP: 5 Privately Held
WEB: www.wescast.com
SIC: 3714 Motor vehicle parts & accessories
HQ: United Machining Inc.
6300 18 1/2 Mile Rd
Sterling Heights MI 48314
586 323-4300

(G-10647)
UNIVERSAL INDUSTRIES INCO
16115 Violet Dr (48042-5746)
PHONE.................................248 259-2674
Joseph Cavataio, *Principal*
EMP: 5 EST: 2010
SALES (est): 83.8K **Privately Held**
SIC: 3999 Manufacturing industries

(G-10648)
VAIVE WOOD PRODUCTS CO
24935 21 Mile Rd (48042-5114)
PHONE.................................586 949-4900
Richard Vaive, *President*

Allan R Scroggs, *Vice Pres*
Constance Vaive, *Admin Sec*
EMP: 32 EST: 1961
SQ FT: 16,800
SALES (est): 2.5MM **Privately Held**
SIC: 2448 2441 Pallets, wood & metal combination; shipping cases, wood: nailed or lock corner

(G-10649)
VISION GLOBAL INDUSTRIES
16041 Leone Dr (48042-4063)
PHONE.................................248 390-5805
Deborah Paterra, *President*
Mike Locke, *Vice Pres*
EMP: 54 EST: 2011
SALES (est): 603.4K **Privately Held**
WEB: www.visionglobalind.com
SIC: 8711 3544 3999 Professional engineer; industrial molds; atomizers, toiletry

(G-10650)
VOLOS TUBE FORM INC
50395 Corporate Dr (48044-1007)
PHONE.................................586 416-3600
Stanley Volos, *President*
EMP: 20 EST: 1979
SQ FT: 42,600
SALES (est): 4.9MM **Privately Held**
WEB: www.volostubeform.com
SIC: 3498 3569 Tube fabricating (contract bending & shaping); assembly machines, non-metalworking

(G-10651)
WOOD LOVE SIGNS
21448 Sienna Dr (48044-6407)
PHONE.................................586 322-6400
Allan Kamijo, *Principal*
EMP: 4 EST: 2016
SALES (est): 72.6K **Privately Held**
SIC: 3993 Signs & advertising specialties

(G-10652)
YOUR SIGN LADY LLC
50322 Margaret Ave (48044-6340)
PHONE.................................586 741-8585
Jamie Souliotis, *Principal*
EMP: 4 EST: 2018
SALES (est): 46K **Privately Held**
SIC: 3993 Signs & advertising specialties

(G-10653)
ZALCO PRODUCTS LLC
23156 Hidden Creek Dr (48042-5024)
PHONE.................................586 354-0227
Beverly Hickman, *Principal*
EMP: 6 EST: 2010
SALES (est): 85.5K **Privately Held**
SIC: 3599 Machine shop, jobbing & repair

Madison Heights
Oakland County

(G-10654)
A C STEEL RULE DIES INC
324 E Mandoline Ave (48071-4738)
PHONE.................................248 588-5600
Randy Genord, *President*
EMP: 9 EST: 1964
SQ FT: 5,600
SALES (est): 936.7K **Privately Held**
WEB: www.acsteelrule.com
SIC: 3544 3555 Dies, steel rule; printing trades machinery

(G-10655)
AACTRON INC
29306 Stephenson Hwy (48071-2317)
PHONE.................................248 543-6740
Erik M Kafarski, *President*
Mitchell I Kafarski, *Chairman*
Roman J Kafarski, *Vice Pres*
Ron Wroblewski, *Plant Mgr*
Pattie Benoit, *Office Mgr*
EMP: 31 EST: 1965
SQ FT: 25,000
SALES (est): 1.2MM **Privately Held**
WEB: www.aactron.com
SIC: 3479 Coating of metals & formed products

(G-10656)
ABI INTERNATIONAL
Also Called: Inland Craft Products
32052 Edward Ave (48071-1420)
PHONE.................................248 583-7150
Sharon Meadows, *Vice Pres*
EMP: 10 EST: 1997
SALES (est): 1MM **Privately Held**
SIC: 3531 Grinders, stone: portable

(G-10657)
ABRASIVE DIAMOND TOOL COMPANY
Also Called: Adtco
30231 Stephenson Hwy (48071-1661)
P.O. Box 71278 (48071-0278)
PHONE.................................248 588-4800
Ellen Lucas, *Ch of Bd*
Thomas M Lucas, *President*
Dave Plosky, *Vice Pres*
EMP: 25 EST: 1935
SQ FT: 15,000
SALES (est): 2MM **Privately Held**
WEB: www.abrasivediamondtool.com
SIC: 3545 3599 3291 Dressers, abrasive wheel: diamond point or other; diamond cutting tools for turning, boring, burnishing, etc.; machine shop, jobbing & repair; abrasive products

(G-10658)
ACRYLIC SPECIALTIES
32336 Edward Ave (48071-1432)
PHONE.................................248 588-4390
Kathy Jerue, *President*
EMP: 9 EST: 2004
SALES (est): 569.1K **Privately Held**
SIC: 3089 Injection molding of plastics

(G-10659)
ADAM ELECTRONICS INCORPORATED
32020 Edward Ave (48071-1420)
PHONE.................................248 583-2000
Dan Kayganich, *CEO*
Davian Larente, *COO*
Daria Gomez, *Treasurer*
EMP: 20 EST: 1985
SALES (est): 3.8MM **Privately Held**
WEB: www.adamelectronics.com
SIC: 3629 7389 Electronic generation equipment; design services

(G-10660)
ADIENT US LLC
Also Called: Adient Madison Heights
1451 E Lincoln Ave (48071-4136)
PHONE.................................510 771-2300
EMP: 7 Privately Held
WEB: www.adient.com
SIC: 3714 Motor vehicle parts & accessories
HQ: Adient Us Llc
49200 Halyard Dr
Plymouth MI 48170
734 254-5000

(G-10661)
ADVANCED AUTOMATION GROUP LLC
580 Ajax Dr (48071-2428)
PHONE.................................248 299-8100
Shaotang Chen,
▲ **EMP: 5 EST: 2007**
SALES (est): 1.1MM **Privately Held**
WEB: www.advancedautomationgroup.com
SIC: 3625 Motor controls & accessories

(G-10662)
ADVANCED PRINTWEAR INC
31171 Stephenson Hwy (48071-1632)
PHONE.................................248 585-4412
Dale Wrubel, *President*
EMP: 8 EST: 1983
SQ FT: 8,800
SALES (est): 765.8K **Privately Held**
WEB: www.advancedprintwear.com
SIC: 2395 2261 Embroidery & art needlework; screen printing of cotton broadwoven fabrics

Madison Heights - Oakland County (G-10663)

(G-10663)
AERO FILTER INC
Also Called: Air Filter Sales & Service
1604 E Avis Dr (48071-1501)
PHONE..................248 837-4100
Gerald V Festian, *President*
Chuck Dankanics, *Vice Pres*
Jeff Williams, *Vice Pres*
Pam Festian, *Treasurer*
David Polens, *Sales Mgr*
EMP: 28 **EST:** 1978
SQ FT: 30,905
SALES (est): 6.7MM **Privately Held**
WEB: www.aerofilter.com
SIC: 3564 5075 Filters, air: furnaces, air conditioning equipment, etc.; air filters

(G-10664)
AJAX SPRING AND MFG CO
700 Ajax Dr (48071-2488)
PHONE..................248 588-5700
Werner Boelstler, *President*
Shawn Jyawook, *COO*
Nicole Boelstler, *Vice Pres*
▲ **EMP:** 29 **EST:** 1952
SQ FT: 20,000
SALES (est): 2.5MM **Privately Held**
WEB: www.ajaxspring.com
SIC: 3469 3496 3493 3465 Stamping metal for the trade; miscellaneous fabricated wire products; steel springs, except wire; automotive stampings; bolts, nuts, rivets & washers

(G-10665)
ALLPRINTS PLUS LLC
27749 Dequindre Rd (48071-3477)
PHONE..................248 906-2977
Allen Selim, *Principal*
EMP: 5 **EST:** 2015
SALES (est): 76.2K **Privately Held**
WEB: www.allprintsplus.com
SIC: 2752 Commercial printing, lithographic

(G-10666)
AMERICAN ARROW CORP INC
1609 Englewood Ave (48071-1020)
PHONE..................248 435-6115
Donald W Sommer, *President*
Jessica Rand, *Personnel*
EMP: 8 **EST:** 1964
SALES (est): 964.4K **Privately Held**
WEB: www.americanarrowcorp.com
SIC: 3429 Motor vehicle hardware

(G-10667)
AMERICAN SCREW PRODUCTS INC
29866 John R Rd (48071-5408)
PHONE..................248 543-0991
Sekhar Chinasigari, *President*
EMP: 5
SQ FT: 5,100
SALES (est): 380.8K **Privately Held**
SIC: 3451 Screw machine products

(G-10668)
AMERICAN THERMOGRAPHERS
291 E 12 Mile Rd (48071-2557)
PHONE..................248 398-3810
Kerry J Welborn, *Owner*
EMP: 12 **EST:** 1983
SQ FT: 2,300
SALES (est): 389.5K **Privately Held**
WEB: www.amthermo.com
SIC: 2759 Thermography

(G-10669)
ANDERSON BRAZING CO INC
1544 E 11 Mile Rd (48071-3810)
PHONE..................248 399-5155
Robert Stewart, *President*
EMP: 4 **EST:** 1943
SQ FT: 3,000
SALES (est): 278.4K **Privately Held**
WEB: www.andersonbrazing.com
SIC: 7692 Brazing

(G-10670)
APMS INCORPORATED
Also Called: Associated Print & Marketing
31211 Stvnson Hwy Ste 100 (48071)
PHONE..................248 268-1477
Thomas David Elle, *President*
Cameron Elle, *Vice Pres*
Heather Elle, *Treasurer*
EMP: 5 **EST:** 2012
SALES (est): 1.5MM **Privately Held**
SIC: 2752 Commercial printing, lithographic

(G-10671)
AQUA TOOL LLC
32360 Edward Ave Ste 100 (48071-1445)
PHONE..................248 307-1984
Keith Reiber, *Marketing Staff*
Stephen Kamp,
Gary Reiber,
EMP: 16 **EST:** 2003
SQ FT: 9,875
SALES (est): 1.3MM **Privately Held**
WEB: www.aquatool.biz
SIC: 3599 Machine shop, jobbing & repair

(G-10672)
ARGON TOOL INC
Also Called: Argon & Tool Manufacturing Co
32309 Milton Ave (48071-5601)
PHONE..................248 583-1605
Ted Wright, *General Mgr*
▲ **EMP:** 19 **EST:** 1954
SQ FT: 25,000
SALES (est): 941.4K **Privately Held**
WEB: www.argontool.com
SIC: 3953 Marking devices

(G-10673)
ARTECH PRINTING INC
26346 John R Rd (48071-3610)
PHONE..................248 545-0088
Thomas Brien, *Director*
EMP: 7 **EST:** 1996
SQ FT: 2,200
SALES (est): 954.3K **Privately Held**
WEB: www.artechprinting.com
SIC: 2752 Commercial printing, offset

(G-10674)
ASSOCIATED PRINT MARKETING
32350 Howard Ave (48071-1429)
PHONE..................248 268-2726
Tom Elle, *President*
EMP: 6 **EST:** 2013
SALES (est): 197.4K **Privately Held**
WEB: www.apmdetroit.com
SIC: 2752 Commercial printing, offset

(G-10675)
ATLAS GEAR COMPANY
32801 Edward Ave (48071-1450)
PHONE..................248 583-2964
Robert A Bouren, *President*
John Mock, *Manager*
▲ **EMP:** 14 **EST:** 1946
SQ FT: 15,000
SALES (est): 3.3MM **Privately Held**
WEB: www.atlasgear.com
SIC: 3566 3714 Gears, power transmission, except automotive; gears, motor vehicle

(G-10676)
AUTHORITY CUSTOMWEAR LTD
Also Called: Skyline Screen Printing & EMB
32046 Edward Ave (48071-1420)
PHONE..................248 588-8075
Steven Khalil, *President*
David Khalil, *Corp Secy*
EMP: 40 **EST:** 1997
SQ FT: 18,000
SALES (est): 1.8MM **Privately Held**
WEB: www.skylinemi.com
SIC: 7389 7336 2396 2395 Embroidering of advertising on shirts, etc.; silk screen design; automotive & apparel trimmings; pleating & stitching

(G-10677)
BAND-AYD SYSTEMS INTL INC
355 E Whitcomb Ave (48071-4571)
PHONE..................586 294-8851
Susan De Benedetti, *President*
Brenda Vanderheyden, *Vice Pres*
EMP: 10 **EST:** 1989
SQ FT: 20,000
SALES (est): 1.2MM **Privately Held**
WEB: www.band-ayd.com
SIC: 7389 3699 1731 7359 Advertising, promotional & trade show services; convention & show services; trade show arrangement; electric sound equipment; lighting contractor; sound equipment specialization; sound & lighting equipment rental; audio-visual equipment & supply rental; party supplies rental services

(G-10678)
BARNES INDUSTRIES INC
1161 E 11 Mile Rd (48071-3801)
P.O. Box 71543 (48071-0543)
PHONE..................248 541-2333
Glen R Barnes, *President*
Eric Miller, *Sales Engr*
Robert Blanton, *Marketing Staff*
Lori Brown, *Office Mgr*
Joe Voytush, *Admin Asst*
EMP: 50 **EST:** 1969
SQ FT: 62,500
SALES (est): 9.6MM **Privately Held**
WEB: www.barnesballscrew.com
SIC: 3568 Power transmission equipment

(G-10679)
BARON ACQUISITION LLC (PA)
Also Called: Baron Industries
999 E Mandoline Ave (48071-1436)
PHONE..................248 585-0444
Jaime Hartom, *QC Mgr*
John Taylor, *Maintence Staff*
John O'brien,
EMP: 46 **EST:** 2016
SALES (est): 5.6MM **Privately Held**
SIC: 3479 Etching & engraving

(G-10680)
BEACON SIGN CO (PA)
1280 Kempar Ave (48071-1424)
PHONE..................313 368-3410
Salim Haddad, *President*
David Haddad, *CFO*
Daniel Papais, *Sales Staff*
Laura Haddad, *Admin Sec*
EMP: 1 **EST:** 1978
SALES (est): 1MM **Privately Held**
WEB: www.beaconsigncompany.com
SIC: 3993 Signs, not made in custom sign painting shops

(G-10681)
BESPRO PATTERN INC
31301 Mally Dr (48071-1629)
PHONE..................586 268-6970
John J Basso, *President*
Sonjia A Basso, *Vice Pres*
Kris Chernos, *Office Mgr*
Todd Hayden, *Manager*
EMP: 28 **EST:** 1959
SQ FT: 15,000
SALES (est): 2.8MM **Privately Held**
WEB: www.bespropattern.com
SIC: 3543 3553 3086 Industrial patterns; pattern makers' machinery, woodworking; plastics foam products

(G-10682)
BLACK & DECKER CORPORATION
30475 Stephenson Hwy (48071-1615)
PHONE..................248 597-5000
Bill Webb, *Manager*
EMP: 10
SALES (corp-wide): 14.5B **Publicly Held**
WEB: www.blackanddecker.com
SIC: 3546 Power-driven handtools
HQ: The Black & Decker Corporation
701 E Joppa Rd
Towson MD 21286
410 716-3900

(G-10683)
BORITE MANUFACTURING CORP
31711 Sherman Ave (48071-1428)
PHONE..................248 588-7260
Andrew Lankin, *President*
Sheila Emmons, *Manager*
EMP: 8 **EST:** 1960
SQ FT: 8,100
SALES (est): 900.8K **Privately Held**
WEB: www.boritemanufacturing.com
SIC: 3545 Boring machine attachments (machine tool accessories); headstocks, lathe (machine tool accessories)

(G-10684)
BRASCO INTERNATIONAL INC
32400 Industrial Dr (48071-1527)
PHONE..................313 393-0393
William Noecker, *President*
Tom Richmond, *General Mgr*
Douglas N Pew, *COO*
Vanessa Bagwell, *Project Mgr*
James Hunter, *Foreman/Supr*
◆ **EMP:** 60 **EST:** 1993
SQ FT: 57,000
SALES (est): 14.1MM **Privately Held**
WEB: www.brasco.com
SIC: 3448 Buildings, portable: prefabricated metal

(G-10685)
CENTRAL GEAR INC
Also Called: Machining Specialties
540 Ajax Dr (48071-2494)
PHONE..................800 589-1602
Herschel Breazeale, *President*
Richard Moores, *Vice Pres*
Lorraine Breazeale, *Admin Sec*
EMP: 20
SALES (est): 1.1MM **Privately Held**
WEB: www.centralgear.com
SIC: 3599 Machine shop, jobbing & repair

(G-10686)
CG CABINETS WHOLESALE
30776 John R Rd (48071-2129)
PHONE..................248 583-9666
EMP: 4 **EST:** 2019
SALES (est): 168.5K **Privately Held**
WEB: www.cgcabinet.com
SIC: 2434 Wood kitchen cabinets

(G-10687)
CHEMICAL PROCESS INDS LLC
25428 John R Rd (48071-4012)
PHONE..................248 547-5200
Bruce Kafarski, *President*
EMP: 10 **EST:** 2010
SALES (est): 989K **Privately Held**
SIC: 3471 Plating of metals or formed products

(G-10688)
CHEMICAL PROCESSING INC
25428 John R Rd (48071-4012)
PHONE..................313 925-3400
Bruce J Kafarski, *President*
EMP: 23 **EST:** 1950
SQ FT: 57,000
SALES (est): 504.8K **Privately Held**
SIC: 3479 3471 Rust proofing (hot dipping) of metals & formed products; enameling, including porcelain, of metal products; coating of metals & formed products; electroplating of metals or formed products

(G-10689)
CLEARY DEVELOPMENTS INC (PA)
Also Called: Belmont Equipment Company
32055 Edward Ave (48071-1419)
P.O. Box 71013 (48071-0013)
PHONE..................248 588-7011
Lawrence J Ianitelli, *Ch of Bd*
Robert J Ianitelli, *President*
Tony Tyll, *General Mgr*
Jeff Monroe, *Engineer*
Vanessa Vogler, *Accounting Mgr*
▲ **EMP:** 45 **EST:** 1964
SQ FT: 22,000
SALES (est): 25.7MM **Privately Held**
WEB: www.belmont4edm.com
SIC: 5084 5085 3599 3541 Machine tools & accessories; industrial supplies; electrical discharge machining (EDM); machine tools, metal cutting type

(G-10690)
CLEARY DEVELOPMENTS INC
Primeway Tool & Engrg Co Div
32033 Edward Ave (48071-1419)
PHONE..................248 588-6614
Larry Ianitelli, *President*

Madison Heights - Oakland County (G-10715)

Don Ligrow, *Manager*
EMP: 13
SALES (corp-wide): 25.7MM **Privately Held**
WEB: www.belmont4edm.com
SIC: 3599 3544 Machine shop, jobbing & repair; special dies, tools, jigs & fixtures
PA: Cleary Developments Incorporated
  32055 Edward Ave
  Madison Heights MI 48071
  248 588-7011

(G-10691)
CNI ENTERPRISES INC
Also Called: Futuris Automotive
29333 Stephenson Hwy (48071-2307)
PHONE 248 581-0200
Merv Dunn, *CEO*
Ray Bomya, *COO*
William K Peterson, *CFO*
Paul Williams, *Sales Staff*
▲ **EMP:** 50 **EST:** 1984
SQ FT: 5,000
SALES (est): 11.5MM **Privately Held**
WEB: www.cniinc.cc
SIC: 2396 Automotive trimmings, fabric
HQ: Futuris Automotive (Us) Inc.
  14925 W 11 Mile Rd
  Oak Park MI 48237
  248 439-7800

(G-10692)
CNI-OWOSSO LLC
Also Called: Futuris Automotive
1451 E Lincoln Ave (48071-4136)
PHONE 248 586-3300
▲ **EMP:** 1
SQ FT: 35,000
SALES (est): 6.4MM **Privately Held**
SIC: 2396 Automotive And Apparel Trimmings
HQ: Cni Enterprises, Inc.
  1451 E Lincoln Ave
  Madison Heights MI 48071
  248 586-3300

(G-10693)
COBRA ENTERPRISES INC
32303 Howard Ave (48071-1427)
PHONE 248 588-2669
Eric Myers, *President*
Derek Myers, *Vice Pres*
EMP: 10 **EST:** 1990
SQ FT: 7,000
SALES (est): 894.5K **Privately Held**
WEB: www.cobrapatterns.com
SIC: 3599 Machine shop, jobbing & repair

(G-10694)
COBRA PATTERNS & MODELS INC
Also Called: Cobra Enterprises
32303 Howard Ave (48071-1427)
PHONE 248 588-2669
Eric Myers, *President*
Derek Myers, *Admin Sec*
EMP: 27 **EST:** 1989
SQ FT: 7,000
SALES (est): 1MM **Privately Held**
WEB: www.cobrapatterns.com
SIC: 3543 3364 Industrial patterns; non-ferrous die-castings except aluminum

(G-10695)
COLOR COAT PLATING COMPANY
355 W Girard Ave (48071-1841)
PHONE 248 744-0445
Jeffery Swanson, *President*
EMP: 20 **EST:** 1999
SQ FT: 6,500
SALES (est): 2.7MM **Privately Held**
WEB: www.colorcoatplating.com
SIC: 3471 Electroplating of metals or formed products

(G-10696)
COMMERCIAL STEEL TREATING CORP (PA)
31440 Stephenson Hwy (48071-1693)
P.O. Box 908, Troy (48099-0908)
PHONE 248 588-3300
Ralph Hoensheid, *Principal*
Victor Demark, *Production*
Jack Howard, *Treasurer*
▲ **EMP:** 124 **EST:** 1927
SQ FT: 140,000
SALES (est): 46.5MM **Privately Held**
WEB: www.curtismetal.com
SIC: 3479 3398 Coating of metals & formed products; tempering of metal

(G-10697)
COMPUTERIZED SEC SYSTEMS INC (DH)
Also Called: Saflok
31750 Sherman Ave (48071-1453)
PHONE 248 837-3700
Riet Cadonau, *CEO*
Frank Belflower, *President*
▲ **EMP:** 135 **EST:** 1983
SQ FT: 29,000
SALES (est): 30.5MM
SALES (corp-wide): 2.6B **Privately Held**
WEB: www.ilco.us
SIC: 3699 Door opening & closing devices, electrical
HQ: Kaba Ilco Corp.
  400 Jeffreys Rd
  Rocky Mount NC 27804
  252 446-3321

(G-10698)
CREATIVE CONTROLS INC
Also Called: Creative Cntrls Hndcpped Drvin
32217 Stephenson Hwy (48071-5519)
PHONE 248 577-9800
Thomas R Stowers, *President*
▲ **EMP:** 25 **EST:** 1975
SQ FT: 6,500
SALES (est): 1.4MM **Privately Held**
WEB: www.creativecontrolsinc.net
SIC: 3714 Motor vehicle parts & accessories

(G-10699)
CTA ACOUSTICS INC (DH)
25211 Dequindre Rd (48071-4211)
PHONE 248 544-2580
James J Pike, *Ch of Bd*
Thomas Brown, *President*
Barry Gaines, *Vice Pres*
Laura Laisure, *Production*
William Young, *Production*
◆ **EMP:** 50 **EST:** 1973
SQ FT: 400,000
SALES (est): 100.3MM
SALES (corp-wide): 355.8K **Privately Held**
WEB: www.ctaacoustics.com
SIC: 3714 Motor vehicle body components & frame
HQ: Treves Sas
  Treves
  Paris 75008
  144 353-030

(G-10700)
CTMI GROUP INC
Also Called: King Centerless Grinding Co
29800 Stephenson Hwy (48071-2341)
PHONE 248 542-1615
Joel Dean, *President*
EMP: 24 **EST:** 2013
SALES (est): 410.5K **Privately Held**
SIC: 3599 Machine shop, jobbing & repair

(G-10701)
CURTIS METAL FINISHING CO
31440 Stephenson Hwy (48071-1621)
PHONE 248 588-3300
Scott Hoensheid, *President*
EMP: 17 **EST:** 2017
SALES (est): 2.6MM **Privately Held**
WEB: www.curtismetal.com
SIC: 3398 Metal heat treating

(G-10702)
CUSTOM VALVE CONCEPTS INC
Also Called: W.A. Kates Company, The
31651 Research Park Dr (48071-4626)
PHONE 248 597-8999
John D Taube, *President*
Tom McHenry, *General Mgr*
John Taube, *Vice Pres*
Brian Liveoak, *Mfg Staff*
Ryan Boyle, *Project Engr*
◆ **EMP:** 25 **EST:** 1946
SQ FT: 13,000
SALES (est): 4.6MM **Privately Held**
WEB: www.customvalveconcepts.com
SIC: 3823 5084 Flow instruments, industrial process type; industrial machinery & equipment

(G-10703)
D2 PRINT INC
31211 Stephenson Hwy # 10 (48071-1637)
PHONE 248 229-7633
Donald C Dale, *CEO*
EMP: 5 **EST:** 2018
SALES (est): 93.3K **Privately Held**
SIC: 2752 Commercial printing, lithographic

(G-10704)
DATA MAIL SERVICES INC
Also Called: Intelligent Document Solutions
747 E Whitcomb Ave (48071-1409)
PHONE 248 588-2415
William P Hayden, *President*
Bill Hayden, *Owner*
EMP: 50 **EST:** 1992
SQ FT: 26,000
SALES (est): 24.8MM
SALES (corp-wide): 64.6MM **Privately Held**
WEB: www.doxim.com
SIC: 2759 7331 Commercial printing; mailing service
HQ: Intelligent Document Solutions, Inc.
  747 E Whitcomb Ave
  Madison Heights MI 48071

(G-10705)
DESIGN FABRICATIONS INC
Also Called: D Fab
1100 E Mandoline Ave A (48071-1426)
PHONE 248 597-0988
Gregory Geralds, *President*
Bruce Dych, *Chairman*
Nadine Geering, *Vice Pres*
Jeremy Grech, *VP Opers*
James Donohue, *Project Mgr*
▲ **EMP:** 100 **EST:** 1973
SQ FT: 100,000
SALES (est): 13.1MM **Privately Held**
WEB: www.dfabdesign.com
SIC: 7389 2541 3993 Design, commercial & industrial; wood partitions & fixtures; signs & advertising specialties

(G-10706)
DETROIT WIRE ROPE SPLCING CORP
31623 Stephenson Hwy (48071-1646)
PHONE 248 585-1063
Charles W Richards, *President*
Kent Richards, *Vice Pres*
EMP: 8 **EST:** 1971
SQ FT: 12,000
SALES (est): 609K **Privately Held**
SIC: 5084 3496 Materials handling machinery; cable, uninsulated wire: made from purchased wire; slings: made from purchased wire

(G-10707)
DIVERSIFIED E D M INC
1019 E 10 Mile Rd (48071-4226)
PHONE 248 547-2320
Billie Huffman, *President*
Larry Huffman, *Vice Pres*
EMP: 5 **EST:** 1988
SQ FT: 1,200
SALES (est): 404.8K **Privately Held**
SIC: 3599 Electrical discharge machining (EDM)

(G-10708)
DIVERSIFIED TOOLING GROUP INC
31240 Stephenson Hwy (48071-1620)
PHONE 248 837-5828
James Curtin, *Vice Pres*
Jay Warner, *Vice Pres*
Brooks McLaughlin, *Engineer*
Gary Gizinski, *Treasurer*
Rob Hiddings, *Controller*
EMP: 30 **EST:** 2002
SALES (est): 2.1MM **Privately Held**
WEB: www.diversifiedtoolinggroup.com
SIC: 3443 Liners, industrial: metal plate

(G-10709)
DME COMPANY LLC (DH)
29111 Stephenson Hwy (48071-2383)
PHONE 248 398-6000
Gordie Davis, *Warehouse Mgr*
Lynn King, *Purchasing*
Robert Salhaney, *Engineer*
Lisa Close, *Financial Analy*
Nykita Berry, *Sales Staff*
▲ **EMP:** 263 **EST:** 2009
SALES (est): 58.5MM **Publicly Held**
WEB: www.dme.net
SIC: 3544 3545 Industrial molds; precision measuring tools

(G-10710)
DOUGLAS DYNAMICS LLC
531 Ajax Dr (48071-2429)
PHONE 414 362-3890
EMP: 17 **EST:** 2017
SALES (est): 1.4MM **Privately Held**
WEB: www.douglasdynamics.com
SIC: 3531 Construction machinery

(G-10711)
DOUGLAS STAMPING COMPANY
25531 Dequindre Rd (48071-4236)
PHONE 248 542-3940
Nick Maylen, *President*
Matthew Maylen, *Vice Pres*
Mike Petersimes, *Opers Mgr*
David Maylen III, *Admin Sec*
EMP: 12 **EST:** 1947
SQ FT: 6,900
SALES (est): 2.2MM **Privately Held**
WEB: www.dougstampco.com
SIC: 3465 3469 Automotive stampings; stamping metal for the trade

(G-10712)
DRS C3 & AVIATION COMPANY
Also Called: Drs Technical Services
900 E Whitcomb Ave (48071-5612)
PHONE 248 588-0365
Hugh McLeod, *Principal*
EMP: 37
SALES (corp-wide): 10.2B **Privately Held**
WEB: www.leonardodrs.com
SIC: 3812 Search & navigation equipment
HQ: Drs C3 & Aviation Company
  1 Milestone Center Ct
  Germantown MD 20876

(G-10713)
DUNHAMS ATHLEISURE CORPORATION
32101 John R Rd (48071-4722)
PHONE 248 658-1382
Jeremy Miller, *Branch Mgr*
EMP: 9
SALES (corp-wide): 537.6MM **Privately Held**
WEB: www.dunhamssports.com
SIC: 5941 5699 5091 3949 Specialty sport supplies; sports apparel; sporting & recreation goods; sporting & athletic goods
HQ: Dunham's Athleisure Corporation
  5607 New King Dr Ste 125
  Troy MI 48098
  248 530-6700

(G-10714)
DURA THREAD GAGE INC
971 E 10 Mile Rd (48071-4288)
PHONE 248 545-2890
Mary Oliveto, *President*
John Oliveto, *Vice Pres*
Sam Oliveto, *Admin Sec*
EMP: 10 **EST:** 1963
SQ FT: 7,400
SALES (est): 779.1K **Privately Held**
WEB: www.durathreadgage.com
SIC: 3544 3823 3545 Special dies, tools, jigs & fixtures; industrial instrmnts msrmnt display/control process variable; gauges (machine tool accessories)

(G-10715)
EAST - LIND HEAT TREAT INC
32045 Dequindre Rd (48071-1521)
PHONE 248 585-1415
Robert L Easterbrook Sr, *President*
Sue Cardillo, *Vice Pres*
EMP: 36 **EST:** 1976
SQ FT: 27,149

Madison Heights - Oakland County (G-10716)

SALES (est): 5.5MM **Privately Held**
WEB: www.eastlind.com
SIC: 3398 Metal heat treating

(G-10716)
ECOLO-TECH INC
1743 E 10 Mile Rd (48071-4229)
PHONE.................................248 541-1100
Roy Costello, *President*
Roy E Costello, *President*
Thomas Costello, *Vice Pres*
EMP: 22 **EST:** 1967
SQ FT: 4,500
SALES (est): 1.9MM **Privately Held**
WEB: www.ecolo-techinc.com
SIC: 3444 Ducts, sheet metal

(G-10717)
EFD INDUCTION INC
Also Called: E F D
31511 Dequindre Rd (48071-1537)
PHONE.................................248 658-0700
Tom Crocker, *President*
Johan Larsen, *Vice Pres*
Ken Steele, *Purchasing*
Jeremy Mommerency, *Engineer*
Abhilash Saksena, *Engineer*
▲ **EMP:** 17 **EST:** 1989
SQ FT: 16,000
SALES (est): 8.6MM
SALES (corp-wide): 405.4MM **Privately Held**
WEB: www.efd-induction.com
SIC: 3567 Industrial furnaces & ovens
HQ: Efd Induction As
  Bolevegen 10
  Skien 3724
  355 060-00

(G-10718)
EGT PRINTING SOLUTIONS LLC
32031 Townley St (48071-1320)
PHONE.................................248 583-2500
Mike Gillette, *President*
Sherif Azer, *General Mgr*
Michael Gonte, *Vice Pres*
Timothy Beall, *Mfg Mgr*
Sean McInerney, *Purch Mgr*
▲ **EMP:** 104 **EST:** 1975
SQ FT: 75,000
SALES (est): 26.7MM
SALES (corp-wide): 4.7B **Publicly Held**
WEB: www.rrd.com
SIC: 2752 Commercial printing, offset
HQ: Consolidated Graphics, Inc.
  5858 Westheimer Rd # 200
  Houston TX 77057
  713 787-0977

(G-10719)
ELECTRO-PLATING SERVICE INC
945 E 10 Mile Rd (48071-4290)
PHONE.................................248 541-0035
EMP: 15
SQ FT: 11,500
SALES (est): 1.6MM **Privately Held**
SIC: 3471 Plating / Polishing Service

(G-10720)
ELECTROCOM MIDWEST SALES INC (PA)
32500 Concord Dr Ste 298 (48071-1100)
PHONE.................................248 449-2643
Steve Blank, *President*
Brian Blank, *Treasurer*
EMP: 6 **EST:** 1994
SQ FT: 1,300
SALES (est): 1MM **Privately Held**
SIC: 3643 Current-carrying wiring devices

(G-10721)
ELEVEN MILE TRCK FRAME AXLE IN
Also Called: Eleven Mile Truck Collision Co
1750 E 11 Mile Rd (48071-3814)
PHONE.................................248 399-7536
Milan S Krstich, *President*
Ken Krstich, *General Mgr*
Lois Krstich, *Vice Pres*
Rick Krstich, *Admin Sec*
EMP: 26 **EST:** 1972
SQ FT: 32,000
SALES (est): 1MM **Privately Held**
WEB: www.11miletruck.com
SIC: 7538 7532 3713 General truck repair; collision shops, automotive; truck & bus bodies

(G-10722)
ENERGY PRODUCTS INC (PA)
1551 E Lincoln Ave # 101 (48071-4159)
PHONE.................................248 545-7700
Kurt H Smith, *CEO*
Jim Davis, *CFO*
Karen Harrison, *Sales Staff*
Michelle Jack, *Sales Staff*
John Gazdecki, *Manager*
◆ **EMP:** 50 **EST:** 1977
SQ FT: 100,000
SALES (est): 60MM **Privately Held**
WEB: www.energyprod.com
SIC: 7699 5084 7539 3625 Battery service & repair; industrial machinery & equipment; automotive repair shops; relays & industrial controls; storage batteries, industrial

(G-10723)
ENGINEERED HEAT TREAT INC
31271 Stephenson Hwy (48071-1682)
PHONE.................................248 588-5141
Phillip D Pilibosian, *Chairman*
Keith Pilibosian, *Vice Pres*
Jane Bush, *QC Mgr*
Ronald Pilibosian, *Treasurer*
Charlie Caldwell, *Manager*
◆ **EMP:** 35 **EST:** 1959
SQ FT: 47,000
SALES (est): 3.9MM **Privately Held**
WEB: www.ehtinc.com
SIC: 3398 Metal heat treating

(G-10724)
EUREKA WELDING ALLOYS INC
2000 E Avis Dr (48071-1551)
PHONE.................................248 588-0001
Tom Webb, *General Mgr*
Ralph Lameti, *Chairman*
John Kerchkof, *Vice Pres*
Rachael Kamen, *Controller*
Kathleen Nataline, *Human Res Mgr*
◆ **EMP:** 38 **EST:** 1926
SQ FT: 58,000
SALES (est): 4.9MM **Privately Held**
WEB: www.eurekaweldingalloys.com
SIC: 3548 3356 5084 5085 Electrodes, electric welding; welding rods; welding machinery & equipment; welding supplies

(G-10725)
F J MANUFACTURING CO
32329 Milton Ave (48071-5601)
PHONE.................................248 583-4777
Gary Parlove, *President*
Marion Brown, *Purchasing*
EMP: 32 **EST:** 1957
SQ FT: 11,700
SALES (est): 1.5MM **Privately Held**
SIC: 3599 Machine shop, jobbing & repair

(G-10726)
FANTASTIC SAMS HAIR SALON
29341 John R Rd (48071-5405)
PHONE.................................713 861-2500
Fathi Ashley, *Owner*
EMP: 5 **EST:** 2017
SALES (est): 84.3K **Privately Held**
SIC: 3585 Refrigeration & heating equipment

(G-10727)
FICOSA NORTH AMERICA CORP (DH)
30890 Stephenson Hwy (48071-1614)
PHONE.................................248 307-2230
Javier Pujol, *President*
Fred Zicard, *Exec VP*
Marcelo Calache, *Plant Mgr*
Xochitl Gonzalez, *Project Mgr*
Howard Gorter, *Purchasing*
▲ **EMP:** 30 **EST:** 1995
SALES (est): 425.5MM **Privately Held**
WEB: www.ficosa.com
SIC: 3711 Motor vehicles & car bodies
HQ: Ficosa International, Sa
  Calle Gran Via Carles Iii, 98 - 5o Planta
  Barcelona 08028
  933 391-814

(G-10728)
FIRST OPTOMETRY LAB
195 Ajax Dr (48071-2425)
PHONE.................................248 546-1300
EMP: 9 **EST:** 1997
SALES (est): 850K **Privately Held**
SIC: 3827 Mfg Optical Instruments/Lenses

(G-10729)
GAGE PATTERN & MODEL INC
32070 Townley St (48071-1304)
PHONE.................................248 361-6609
Werner Schulte, *President*
Eric Schulte, *Corp Secy*
Ilse Schulte, *Vice Pres*
Lori Vuljaj, *CFO*
Lori M Vuljaj, *CFO*
EMP: 52 **EST:** 1971
SQ FT: 12,000
SALES (est): 4.6MM **Privately Held**
WEB: www.gpminc.com
SIC: 3543 3544 3714 Industrial patterns; jigs & fixtures; motor vehicle parts & accessories

(G-10730)
GALCO INDUSTRIAL ELEC INC
1001 Lincoln St (48071)
PHONE.................................248 542-9090
Paul Kochan, *General Mgr*
Taylor Demees, *Purch Agent*
Steve Giles, *Technical Mgr*
Sejla Jakupovic, *Credit Mgr*
Holly Barber, *Human Resources*
EMP: 13
SALES (corp-wide): 82.4MM **Privately Held**
WEB: www.galco.com
SIC: 5065 7629 3625 Electronic parts; rectifiers, electronic; capacitors, electronic; electronic equipment repair; relays & industrial controls
PA: Galco Industrial Electronics, Inc.
  26010 Pinehurst Dr
  Madison Heights MI 48071
  248 542-9090

(G-10731)
GHI ELECTRONICS LLC
501 E Whitcomb Ave (48071-1408)
PHONE.................................248 397-8856
Ghassan Issa, *Principal*
Gary Beaver, *Opers Staff*
◆ **EMP:** 22 **EST:** 2004
SQ FT: 18,000
SALES (est): 5.5MM **Privately Held**
WEB: www.ghielectronics.com
SIC: 5999 3672 5065 Electronic parts & equipment; printed circuit boards; electronic parts

(G-10732)
GRAPHIC ENTERPRISES INC
1200 E Avis Dr (48071-1507)
PHONE.................................248 616-4900
EMP: 85
SALES (est): 4.6MM **Privately Held**
SIC: 7336 2752 7335 2796 Coml Art/Graphic Design Lithographic Coml Print Commercial Photography Platemaking Services Commercial Printing

(G-10733)
GRAPHITE PRODUCTS CORP
1797 E 10 Mile Rd (48071-4229)
PHONE.................................248 548-7800
Gilbert Liske, *President*
Douglas Wolf, *Vice Pres*
Doug Wolf, *Sales Staff*
▲ **EMP:** 7 **EST:** 1965
SQ FT: 9,000
SALES (est): 680K **Privately Held**
WEB: www.graphiteproductscorp.com
SIC: 3599 Machine shop, jobbing & repair

(G-10734)
GREAT LAKES FOOD CENTER LLC
Also Called: Royal Food Foods
32102 Howard Ave (48071-1451)
PHONE.................................248 397-8166
Ronnie Ayar,
◆ **EMP:** 8 **EST:** 2016
SQ FT: 310,000
SALES (est): 376.7K **Privately Held**
SIC: 2035 Seasonings & sauces, except tomato & dry

(G-10735)
GREAT LAKES LASER SERVICES
147 E 10 Mile Rd (48071-4203)
P.O. Box 868, Royal Oak (48068-0868)
PHONE.................................248 584-1828
Carl R Hildebrand, *CEO*
Carl J Hildebrand, *President*
Bath Buccarielli, *Vice Pres*
Gary Johns, *Manager*
EMP: 6 **EST:** 1980
SQ FT: 1,600
SALES (est): 445K **Privately Held**
WEB: www.greatlakeslaser.com
SIC: 3599 3548 Machine shop, jobbing & repair; resistance welders, electric

(G-10736)
H & L TOOL COMPANY INC
32701 Dequindre Rd (48071-1595)
PHONE.................................248 585-7474
Michael Bourg, *President*
Tony Langlois, *Plant Mgr*
Susan Bireescu, *Controller*
Ed Zwiesele, *Data Proc Staff*
Kimberly A Kirhofer, *Admin Sec*
EMP: 20 **EST:** 1946
SQ FT: 95,000
SALES (est): 2.7MM
SALES (corp-wide): 27.5MM **Publicly Held**
WEB: www.hltool.com
SIC: 3451 3452 3316 Screw machine products; rivets, metal; bolts, metal; cold finishing of steel shapes
PA: Chicago Rivet & Machine Co.
  901 Frontenac Rd
  Naperville IL 60563
  630 357-8500

(G-10737)
H P P
1200 E Avis Dr (48071-1507)
PHONE.................................248 307-4263
Gordon Heidacker, *Owner*
EMP: 7 **EST:** 2018
SALES (est): 375.3K **Privately Held**
SIC: 3052 Rubber & plastics hose & beltings

(G-10738)
HENKEL SURFACE TECHNOLOGIES
31200 Stephenson Hwy (48071-1620)
PHONE.................................248 307-0240
Fax: 248 589-4806
▲ **EMP:** 6
SALES (est): 1.4MM **Privately Held**
SIC: 2842 Mfg Polish/Sanitation Goods

(G-10739)
HENKEL US OPERATIONS CORP
Also Called: Henkel Surface Technologies
32100 Stephenson Hwy (48071-5514)
P.O. Box 27950, Scottsdale AZ (85255-0149)
PHONE.................................248 588-1082
Mark Zahradnik, *General Mgr*
Rick Worthington, *Regional Mgr*
Patrick Apsey, *Business Mgr*
Greg Barrier, *Business Mgr*
John Dudiak, *Business Mgr*
EMP: 300
SQ FT: 250,000
SALES (corp-wide): 22.7B **Privately Held**
WEB: www.henkel.com
SIC: 2899 2869 2819 3823 Corrosion preventive lubricant; industrial organic chemicals; industrial inorganic chemicals; industrial process control instruments

HQ: Henkel Us Operations Corporation
 1 Henkel Way
 Rocky Hill CT 06067
 860 571-5100

(G-10740)
HIGHLAND MANUFACTURING INC
339 E Whitcomb Ave (48071-4754)
PHONE..................................248 585-8040
Hilarion Bibicoff, *President*
Hilarion Larry Bibicoff, *President*
Hilarion Bibicoff VI, *Vice Pres*
EMP: 23 **EST:** 1965
SQ FT: 11,600
SALES (est): 788.7K **Privately Held**
SIC: 3599 3714 Machine shop, jobbing & repair; oil pump, motor vehicle

(G-10741)
HOSMER
90 W Guthrie Ave (48071-3930)
PHONE..................................248 541-9829
Jennifer Hosmer, *Principal*
EMP: 6 **EST:** 2010
SALES (est): 78.2K **Privately Held**
SIC: 3842 Surgical appliances & supplies

(G-10742)
HOWARD FINISHING LLC (PA)
Also Called: Hf
32565 Dequindre Rd (48071-1520)
PHONE..................................248 588-9050
James E Grimes, *President*
Darrell Knuckles, *Supervisor*
William Aikens,
EMP: 120 **EST:** 1947
SQ FT: 150,000
SALES (est): 24.5MM **Privately Held**
WEB: www.howardfinishing.com
SIC: 3449 Miscellaneous metalwork

(G-10743)
HR TECHNOLOGIES INC
32500 N Avis Dr (48071-1558)
PHONE..................................248 284-1170
Tushar Patel, *President*
▲ **EMP:** 144 **EST:** 1996
SQ FT: 111,000
SALES (est): 23.9MM **Privately Held**
WEB: www.hrtechinc.com
SIC: 2273 Mats & matting

(G-10744)
I E & E INDUSTRIES INC (PA)
111 E 10 Mile Rd (48071-4203)
PHONE..................................248 544-8181
Ron Webber, *President*
Judith Miles, *Vice Pres*
Judy Miles, *Vice Pres*
EMP: 19 **EST:** 1957
SQ FT: 10,000
SALES (est): 3MM **Privately Held**
WEB: www.ie-e.com
SIC: 3544 Jigs & fixtures

(G-10745)
IDENTIFY INC
25163 Dequindre Rd (48071-4240)
PHONE..................................313 802-2015
Robert Suszynski, *President*
Gerald Alfred, *Vice Pres*
Thomas Mezza, *Treasurer*
Mike Simmons, *Manager*
EMP: 22 **EST:** 2010
SALES (est): 3.8MM **Privately Held**
WEB: www.chooseid.com
SIC: 3699 1731 Security devices; closed circuit television installation

(G-10746)
INLAND DIAMOND PRODUCTS CO
32051 Howard Ave (48071-1473)
PHONE..................................248 585-1762
Ronald K Wiand, *President*
Dennis Raffaelli, *COO*
Bruce Baker, *Vice Pres*
Kevin Emery, *VP Opers*
Irene Shotkin, *CFO*
▲ **EMP:** 50 **EST:** 1976
SQ FT: 20,000
SALES (est): 8.2MM **Privately Held**
WEB: www.inlanddiamond.com
SIC: 3291 3851 Wheels, abrasive; ophthalmic goods

(G-10747)
INTERNATIONAL NOODLE CO INC
32811 Groveland St (48071-1330)
PHONE..................................248 583-2479
Bob Ip, *Owner*
EMP: 8 **EST:** 1981
SQ FT: 700
SALES (est): 863.1K **Privately Held**
WEB: www.internationalnoodle.com
SIC: 2098 Noodles (e.g. egg, plain & water), dry

(G-10748)
IONBOND LLC (DH)
1823 E Whitcomb Ave (48071-1413)
PHONE..................................248 398-9100
Joe Haggerty, *CEO*
Ton Hurkmans, *President*
Nancy Blendl, *Partner*
Iain Smith, *COO*
Sanjay Brahmankar, *Opers Staff*
▲ **EMP:** 60 **EST:** 1994
SQ FT: 36,767
SALES (est): 101.8MM **Privately Held**
WEB: www.ionbond.com
SIC: 3398 3479 Metal heat treating; bonderizing of metal or metal products
HQ: Ihi Ionbond Ag
 Industriestrasse 9
 Dulliken SO 4657
 625 534-200

(G-10749)
J E WOOD CO
395 W Girard Ave (48071-1841)
PHONE..................................248 585-5711
James E Wood, *Ch of Bd*
Brian Fish, *President*
John Kistela, *Vice Pres*
EMP: 10 **EST:** 1958
SQ FT: 10,000
SALES (est): 110.9K **Privately Held**
SIC: 3545 Cutting tools for machine tools

(G-10750)
J H P INC (PA)
Also Called: Royal Design
32401 Stephenson Hwy (48071-5521)
PHONE..................................248 588-0110
Rodney D Paulick, *Ch of Bd*
Patrick Eveland, *President*
Kurt Frohriep, *Engineer*
EMP: 2 **EST:** 1951
SQ FT: 16,000
SALES (est): 8MM **Privately Held**
WEB: www.variset.com
SIC: 3559 7372 2542 Automotive related machinery; operating systems computer software; racks, merchandise display or storage: except wood

(G-10751)
J J PATTERN & CASTINGS INC (PA)
1780 E 11 Mile Rd (48071-3816)
PHONE..................................248 543-7119
Martin Steudle, *President*
Eric Steudle, *Vice Pres*
EMP: 6 **EST:** 1970
SQ FT: 7,000
SALES (est): 1.6MM **Privately Held**
WEB: www.jjpattern.com
SIC: 3543 5051 Industrial patterns; castings, rough: iron or steel

(G-10752)
JAMES STEEL & TUBE COMPANY (HQ)
29774 Stephenson Hwy (48071-2340)
PHONE..................................248 547-4200
Jim Petkus, *President*
EMP: 19 **EST:** 1946
SQ FT: 106,000
SALES (est): 8.5MM
SALES (corp-wide): 474.5MM **Privately Held**
WEB: www.jamessteel.com
SIC: 3317 Tubes, wrought: welded or lock joint
PA: Avis Industrial Corporation
 1909 S Main St
 Upland IN 46989
 765 998-8100

(G-10753)
JD PLATING COMPANY INC (PA)
25428 John R Rd (48071-4098)
PHONE..................................248 547-5200
George E Wines, *Ch of Bd*
▲ **EMP:** 30 **EST:** 1947
SQ FT: 15,000
SALES (est): 2.5MM **Privately Held**
SIC: 3471 3479 Electroplating of metals or formed products; coating of metals & formed products

(G-10754)
JO-AD INDUSTRIES INC
31465 Stephenson Hwy (48071-1683)
PHONE..................................248 588-4810
Patrick Wagner, *President*
David Gilbert, *Vice Pres*
Jim Davis, *Safety Mgr*
Paul Hacker, *Info Tech Mgr*
Amy Kaip, *Executive*
EMP: 35 **EST:** 1957
SQ FT: 50,000
SALES (est): 4MM **Privately Held**
WEB: www.jo-ad.com
SIC: 3544 Special dies & tools; forms (molds), for foundry & plastics working machinery; jigs & fixtures

(G-10755)
JSP INTERNATIONAL LLC
1443 E 12 Mile Rd (48071-2653)
PHONE..................................248 397-3200
Kevin J Brophy, *Director*
EMP: 5 **Privately Held**
WEB: www.jsp.com
SIC: 3081 Polyethylene film; polypropylene film & sheet
HQ: Jsp International Llc
 1285 Drummers Ln Ste 301
 Wayne PA 19087

(G-10756)
JUST WING IT INC
Also Called: Savers Wholesale Printing
31681 Dequindre Rd (48071-1522)
PHONE..................................248 549-9338
Doreen Wing, *Principal*
EMP: 6 **EST:** 2017
SALES (est): 507.7K **Privately Held**
WEB: www.saversprinting.com
SIC: 2759 Commercial printing

(G-10757)
KA-WOOD GEAR & MACHINE CO
32500 Industrial Dr (48071-5003)
PHONE..................................248 585-8870
Joseph J Kloka III, *President*
Don Carlson, *Vice Pres*
Marge Kloka, *Vice Pres*
Tanya Carlson, *Treasurer*
EMP: 33 **EST:** 1920
SALES (est): 4.6MM **Privately Held**
WEB: www.kawoodgear.com
SIC: 3599 Machine shop, jobbing & repair; catapults

(G-10758)
KAR NUT PRODUCTS COMPANY LLC
Also Called: Kar's Nuts
1200 E 14 Mile Rd Ste A (48071-1421)
PHONE..................................248 588-1903
Victor Mehren, *CEO*
Nick Nicolay, *Chairman*
William P Elam, *Vice Pres*
Eric Martin, *Production*
Julie Rochowiak, *QC Mgr*
EMP: 140 **EST:** 1933
SQ FT: 131,000
SALES: 114.8MM
SALES (corp-wide): 176.8MM **Privately Held**
WEB: www.karsnuts.com
SIC: 5145 2068 Nuts, salted or roasted; nuts: dried, dehydrated, salted or roasted
PA: Knpc Holdco, Llc
 1200 E 14 Mile Rd
 Madison Heights MI 48071
 248 588-1903

(G-10759)
KASPER MACHINE CO (HQ)
29275 Stephenson Hwy (48071-2379)
PHONE..................................248 547-3150
▲ **EMP:** 14
SQ FT: 46,000
SALES (est): 2.3MM
SALES (corp-wide): 735.1MM **Privately Held**
SIC: 3541 3545 Mfg Machine Tools-Cutting Mfg Machine Tool Accessories
PA: Samson Ag
 Weismullerstr. 3
 Frankfurt Am Main 60314
 694 009-0

(G-10760)
KAUTEX INC
32201 N Avis Dr (48071-1502)
PHONE..................................248 616-0327
Dave Zimba, *Branch Mgr*
EMP: 1290
SALES (corp-wide): 11.6B **Publicly Held**
WEB: www.kautex.com
SIC: 3089 Injection molding of plastics
HQ: Kautex Inc
 800 Tower Dr Ste 200
 Troy MI 48098
 248 616-5100

(G-10761)
KERR SCREW PRODUCTS CO INC
32069 Milton Ave (48071-1407)
PHONE..................................248 589-2200
Frank B Kerr, *President*
Patricia Kerr, *Corp Secy*
W Rex Keller, *Vice Pres*
Debbie Keller, *Sales Mgr*
EMP: 9 **EST:** 1959
SQ FT: 12,000
SALES (est): 1MM **Privately Held**
WEB: www.kerrscrew.com
SIC: 3451 Screw machine products

(G-10762)
KEYS PLUS IN 15 MINUTE
27050 John R Rd (48071-3326)
PHONE..................................248 581-0112
EMP: 5 **EST:** 2012
SALES (est): 83.1K **Privately Held**
SIC: 3429 Keys, locks & related hardware

(G-10763)
KNICKERBOCKER BAKING INC
26040 Pinehurst Dr (48071-4139)
PHONE..................................248 541-2110
Steven Corinatis, *President*
Daniel Rubino, *Vice Pres*
Patricia Corinatis, *Treasurer*
EMP: 52 **EST:** 1996
SQ FT: 7,000
SALES (est): 2.6MM **Privately Held**
WEB: www.knickerbockerbaking.com
SIC: 2051 Bread, all types (white, wheat, rye, etc): fresh or frozen; rolls, bread type: fresh or frozen; bagels, fresh or frozen

(G-10764)
KNPC HOLDCO LLC (PA)
1200 E 14 Mile Rd (48071-1421)
PHONE..................................248 588-1903
Vic Mehren, *CEO*
Ernest L Nicolay III, *President*
Herman Brons, *CFO*
Kristin Ropke, *Sales Staff*
EMP: 7 **EST:** 2017
SALES (est): 176.8MM **Privately Held**
SIC: 2068 6719 Nuts: dried, dehydrated, salted or roasted; investment holding companies, except banks

(G-10765)
KS LIQUIDATING LLC
Also Called: Korstone
32031 Howard Ave (48071-1430)
PHONE..................................248 577-8220
James Agley, *Principal*
Timothy Price,
EMP: 7 **EST:** 1996
SQ FT: 18,000
SALES (est): 225.7K **Privately Held**
SIC: 2541 Counter & sink tops

Madison Heights - Oakland County (G-10766)

(G-10766)
LAB LINK TESTING LLC
711 W 13 Mile Rd (48071-1873)
PHONE...............................419 283-6387
Christopher Karrumi,
EMP: 7 **EST:** 2019
SALES (est): 445.1K Privately Held
SIC: 2869 Laboratory chemicals, organic

(G-10767)
LANCE INDUSTRIES LLC
1260 Kempar Ave (48071-1424)
PHONE...............................248 549-1968
Michelle Pfaendtner, Sales Staff
John Witt, Mng Member
EMP: 5 **EST:** 1971
SQ FT: 5,000
SALES (est): 817.4K Privately Held
WEB: www.lancetools.com
SIC: 3544 Special dies & tools

(G-10768)
LAND ENTERPRISES INC
26641 Townley St (48071-3619)
P.O. Box 71730 (48071-0730)
PHONE...............................248 398-7276
Shelley Vasseur, President
EMP: 8 **EST:** 2001
SALES (est): 619.5K Privately Held
SIC: 3446 Open flooring & grating for construction

(G-10769)
LASERTEC INC
Also Called: Intelligent Document Solutions
747 E Whitcomb Ave (48071-1409)
PHONE...............................586 274-4500
Wendy Lokken, President
Wendy Schulte, President
Ben Danielak, Production
Kathleen Lazzarino, Supervisor
William Hayden, Admin Sec
EMP: 26 **EST:** 1983
SQ FT: 28,950
SALES (est): 6.1MM
SALES (corp-wide): 64.6MM Privately Held
WEB: www.lasertecinc.com
SIC: 2759 2791 Laser printing; typesetting
HQ: Intelligent Document Solutions, Inc.
747 E Whitcomb Ave
Madison Heights MI 48071

(G-10770)
LINKED LIVE INC
30550 Brush St (48071-1876)
PHONE...............................248 345-5993
Gheorghe Herdean, CEO
John Herdean, Finance Mgr
EMP: 8 **EST:** 2012
SALES (est): 244K Privately Held
SIC: 7372 Prepackaged software

(G-10771)
LUBO INC
32250 Howard Ave (48071-1452)
PHONE...............................248 632-1185
Young Seok Kim, CEO
EMP: 5 **EST:** 2017
SALES (est): 319.8K Privately Held
SIC: 3364 Brass & bronze die-castings

(G-10772)
LUBO USA INC
32250 Howard Ave (48071-1452)
PHONE...............................810 244-5826
Young Seok Kim, CEO
Yeoung Weon Kim, Corp Secy
Ilyeob Choi, Director
Haejong Lim, Director
▲ **EMP:** 5 **EST:** 2011
SQ FT: 15,000
SALES (est): 927K Privately Held
WEB: www.vdrs.com
SIC: 3364 Brass & bronze die-castings

(G-10773)
MACHINING SPECI
1619 Donna Ave (48071-2063)
PHONE...............................248 589-4070
John Wallace, President
EMP: 5 **EST:** 2018
SALES (est): 89.4K Privately Held
SIC: 3599 Machine shop, jobbing & repair

(G-10774)
MANUFACTURING DYNAMICS CO
1642 E 11 Mile Rd (48071-3812)
PHONE...............................248 670-0264
Jonathon Tamm, General Mgr
Derrick Tamm, Director
EMP: 7 **EST:** 2016
SALES (est): 535.4K Privately Held
SIC: 2431 Floor baseboards, wood

(G-10775)
MAPLE PRESS LLC
31211 Stephenson Hwy # 10 (48071-1637)
PHONE...............................248 733-9669
James Alexander,
EMP: 21 **EST:** 2004
SQ FT: 12,000
SALES (est): 5.5MM Privately Held
WEB: www.maplepressprinting.com
SIC: 2752 Commercial printing, offset

(G-10776)
MARTIN FLUID POWER COMPANY (PA)
Also Called: Enhanced MSC
900 E Whitcomb Ave (48071-5612)
PHONE...............................248 585-8170
Wayne Michael King, CEO
Ryan King, President
Vince Lopez, Vice Pres
Joseph Bailey, VP Mfg
Michael Geddes, Purch Mgr
◆ **EMP:** 13 **EST:** 1977
SQ FT: 10,000
SALES (est): 27.5MM Privately Held
WEB: www.mfpseals.com
SIC: 5085 3053 Seals, industrial; gaskets & sealing devices

(G-10777)
MASTERS MILLWORK LLC
30700 Stephenson Hwy (48071-1607)
PHONE...............................248 987-4511
Rick Rot, Vice Pres
Andy Kubiak, Mng Member
EMP: 10 **EST:** 2013
SQ FT: 8,000
SALES (est): 1.5MM Privately Held
WEB: www.mastersmillwork.com
SIC: 2431 Millwork

(G-10778)
MAZZELLA LIFTING TECH INC
31623 Stephenson Hwy (48071-1646)
PHONE...............................248 585-1063
Mark Shubel, Vice Pres
Jim Humphries, Project Mgr
EMP: 9 Privately Held
WEB: www.mazzellacompanies.com
SIC: 3496 Miscellaneous fabricated wire products
HQ: Mazzella Lifting Technologies, Inc.
21000 Aerospace Pkwy
Cleveland OH 44142
440 239-7000

(G-10779)
MCNAUGHTON-MCKAY ELECTRIC CO (PA)
1357 E Lincoln Ave (48071-4126)
PHONE...............................248 399-7500
Donald D Slominski, CEO
Mark Borin, President
Walt Reynolds, COO
J Christopher Majni, Exec VP
Carol A Hoefler, Vice Pres
EMP: 270 **EST:** 1910
SQ FT: 200,000
SALES: 1.3B Privately Held
WEB: www.mc-mc.com
SIC: 5065 5063 1389 Electronic parts & equipment; electrical apparatus & equipment; oil field services

(G-10780)
MEMORIES XPRESS
29777 Stephenson Hwy (48071-2334)
PHONE...............................248 582-1836
EMP: 5 **EST:** 2016
SALES (est): 110.5K Privately Held
WEB: www.publishingxpress.com
SIC: 2759 Commercial printing

(G-10781)
MICHIGAN AUTO BENDING CORP
Also Called: Mabco
1700 E 14 Mile Rd (48071-1543)
PHONE...............................248 528-1150
Louis St Laurent, President
Robert Shaw, Principal
Keith Macneil, Supervisor
EMP: 23 **EST:** 1976
SQ FT: 20,000
SALES (est): 2.5MM Privately Held
WEB: www.entauto.com
SIC: 3544 7538 Special dies & tools; general automotive repair shops

(G-10782)
MICHIGAN DIVERSFD HOLDINGS INC
Also Called: Sutherland Felt Co
700 E Whitcomb Ave (48071-1416)
PHONE...............................248 280-0450
Thomas Shoan, CEO
Sue Toth, General Mgr
Michele Shoan, Corp Secy
James Dunn, Plant Mgr
Brian Borski, Research
EMP: 13 **EST:** 1902
SQ FT: 10,000
SALES (est): 5.2MM Privately Held
WEB: www.sutherlandfelt.com
SIC: 5199 3111 Felt; die-cutting of leather

(G-10783)
MIDWEST CABINET COUNTERS
650 E Mandoline Ave (48071-1455)
PHONE...............................248 586-4260
Jeff Valenti, Principal
EMP: 6 **EST:** 2010
SALES (est): 1MM Privately Held
WEB: www.midwestcab.net
SIC: 3131 Counters

(G-10784)
MP ACQUISITION LLC (PA)
Also Called: Mopec
800 Tech Row (48071-4678)
PHONE...............................800 362-8491
Jay Troger, CEO
Sally Brandtneris, Principal
Joyce Dejong, Principal
Jeff Pemberton, Vice Pres
Michael Keller, Engineer
EMP: 71 **EST:** 2012
SALES (est): 21MM Privately Held
WEB: www.mopec.com
SIC: 3914 5087 Stainless steel ware; funeral directors' equipment & supplies

(G-10785)
MSI MACHINE TOOL PARTS INC
1619 Donna Ave (48071-2063)
PHONE...............................248 589-0515
John Wallace, President
EMP: 10 **EST:** 2006
SALES (est): 801.8K Privately Held
WEB: www.bullardparts.com
SIC: 3599 Machine shop, jobbing & repair

(G-10786)
MSX INTERNATIONAL INC
30031 Stephenson Hwy (48071-1605)
PHONE...............................248 585-6654
Dennis Groesbeck, Manager
EMP: 135
SALES (corp-wide): 1.8MM Publicly Held
SIC: 7363 3544 Help supply services; special dies, tools, jigs & fixtures
HQ: Msx International, Inc.
500 Woodward Ave Ste 2150
Detroit MI 48226
248 829-6300

(G-10787)
NANO MAGIC HOLDINGS INC (PA)
Also Called: Pen
31601 Research Park Dr (48071-4626)
PHONE...............................844 273-6462
Scott E Rickert, Ch of Bd
Tom J Berman, President
Leandro Vera, CFO
Lynn Lilly, Corp Comm Staff
Jeanne M Rickert,
EMP: 5 **EST:** 1987
SALES (est): 4.7MM Publicly Held
WEB: www.pen-technology.com
SIC: 2842 Specialty cleaning, polishes & sanitation goods

(G-10788)
NATIONAL MILLWORK INC
32350 Howard Ave (48071-1429)
PHONE...............................248 307-1299
Dennis T Figiel, President
Michael K Figiel, Treasurer
EMP: 36 **EST:** 1984
SQ FT: 13,000
SALES (est): 4MM Privately Held
WEB: www.nationalmillwork.us.com
SIC: 2541 Store & office display cases & fixtures; store fixtures, wood

(G-10789)
NAVISTAR DEFENSE LLC
1675 E Whitcomb Ave (48071-1411)
PHONE...............................248 680-7505
Michael Lyons, Manager
James Jezak, Manager
EMP: 8
SALES (corp-wide): 263.5B Privately Held
WEB: www.navistardefense.com
SIC: 3812 Defense systems & equipment
HQ: Navistar Defense Llc
2601 Navistar Dr Bldg 1
Lisle IL 60532
708 617-4500

(G-10790)
NOVELTY HOUSE
1400 E Avis Dr Ste B (48071-9700)
PHONE...............................248 583-9900
EMP: 8 **EST:** 2017
SALES (est): 1.2MM Privately Held
WEB: www.smalltoys.com
SIC: 5199 3999 Gifts & novelties; manufacturing industries

(G-10791)
OGURA CORPORATION
631 Ajax Dr (48071-2415)
PHONE...............................586 749-1900
EMP: 7 **EST:** 2018
SALES (est): 276.6K Privately Held
WEB: www.oguracorp.com
SIC: 3714 Motor vehicle parts & accessories

(G-10792)
ONEIRIC SYSTEMS INC (PA)
31711 Sherman Ave (48071-1428)
PHONE...............................248 554-3090
Everett Hall, President
Jennifer Brown, Opers Mgr
EMP: 5 **EST:** 2010
SALES (est): 765.5K Privately Held
WEB: www.oneiricsystems.com
SIC: 3559 Degreasing machines, automotive & industrial

(G-10793)
OSTRANDER COMPANY INC
Also Called: John Ostrander Company
1200 W 12 Mile Rd (48071-4439)
PHONE...............................248 646-6680
John Ostrander, President
Robin Denby, Office Mgr
Steve Beechler,
EMP: 2 **EST:** 1995
SALES (est): 3MM Privately Held
WEB: www.ostranderco.com
SIC: 3585 Refrigeration & heating equipment

(G-10794)
P X TOOL CO
Also Called: Peerless Tooling Components
32354 Edward Ave (48071-1432)
PHONE...............................248 585-9330
Edmund M Nowak, President
Dawn Wagner, Manager
EMP: 6 **EST:** 1966
SQ FT: 6,000
SALES (est): 709.2K Privately Held
WEB: www.pxtool.com
SIC: 3544 Special dies & tools

GEOGRAPHIC SECTION
Madison Heights - Oakland County (G-10821)

(G-10795)
PARRY PRECISION INC
845 E Mandoline Ave (48071-1472)
PHONE.....................248 585-1234
Donald Payne, *President*
Leon Parry, *President*
Mike Parry, *President*
EMP: 21 EST: 1973
SQ FT: 8,000
SALES (est): 2MM **Privately Held**
WEB: www.parryprecision.com
SIC: 3544 Jigs & fixtures

(G-10796)
PENKA TOOL CORPORATION
Also Called: Penka Cutter Grinding
1717 E 10 Mile Rd (48071-4229)
PHONE.....................248 543-3940
Paul Marinello, *President*
Sharon Marinello, *Vice Pres*
EMP: 8 EST: 1985
SQ FT: 4,500
SALES (est): 801.6K **Privately Held**
WEB: www.pikespeaknapaautocare.com
SIC: 3544 Special dies & tools

(G-10797)
PETERSON SPRING
679 E Mandoline Ave (48071-1442)
PHONE.....................248 799-5400
Spring Peterson, *Principal*
Santosh Gudagunti, *Engineer*
Michael Parker, *Technical Staff*
EMP: 8 EST: 2019
SALES (est): 1.3MM **Privately Held**
WEB: www.pspring.com
SIC: 3495 Wire springs

(G-10798)
PEZCO INDUSTRIES INC
380 E Mandoline Ave (48071-4738)
PHONE.....................248 589-1140
Thomas J Pesamoska, *President*
Barbara J Pesamoska, *Vice Pres*
EMP: 6 EST: 1976
SQ FT: 2,800
SALES (est): 481.8K **Privately Held**
WEB: www.jiggrinding.us
SIC: 3599 Machine shop, jobbing & repair

(G-10799)
PILLAR INDUCTION
30100 Stephenson Hwy (48071-1630)
PHONE.....................586 254-8470
Mike Felvey, *President*
EMP: 17 EST: 2009
SALES (est): 4MM
SALES (corp-wide): 1.3B **Publicly Held**
WEB: www.pillar.com
SIC: 3567 Induction heating equipment
HQ: Ajax Tocco Magnethermic Corporation
1745 Overland Ave Ne
Warren OH 44483
330 372-8511

(G-10800)
PIONEER MACHINE AND TECH INC
1167 E 10 Mile Rd (48071-4207)
P.O. Box 184, Hazel Park (48030-0184)
PHONE.....................248 546-4451
Jeffrey Harris, *President*
Steven Harrris, *Vice Pres*
Chanel Harris, *Treasurer*
EMP: 9 EST: 1998
SQ FT: 5,500
SALES (est): 1MM **Privately Held**
WEB: www.pioneermachinetech.com
SIC: 3599 3441 Machine shop, jobbing & repair; fabricated structural metal

(G-10801)
PLASON SCRAPING CO INC
32825 Dequindre Rd (48071-1519)
PHONE.....................248 588-7280
James Sultana, *President*
Mark Hickerson, *Vice Pres*
Tim Hickerson, *Vice Pres*
EMP: 9 EST: 1959
SQ FT: 3,500
SALES (est): 1MM **Privately Held**
WEB: www.plasonscraping.com
SIC: 3541 7699 Machine tools, metal cutting type; industrial machinery & equipment repair

(G-10802)
PLATING SPECIALTIES INC (PA)
1625 E 10 Mile Rd (48071-4219)
PHONE.....................248 547-8660
Thomas Baker, *President*
Derek Baker, *QC Mgr*
Bill Karpuk, *QC Mgr*
Genna Quick, *Office Mgr*
EMP: 10 EST: 1972
SQ FT: 15,000
SALES (est): 1.1MM **Privately Held**
WEB: www.platspec.com
SIC: 3471 Electroplating of metals or formed products

(G-10803)
PLATING SPECIALTIES INC
1675 E 10 Mile Rd (48071-4294)
PHONE.....................248 547-8660
Thomas Baker, *President*
EMP: 5
SALES (corp-wide): 1.1MM **Privately Held**
WEB: www.platspec.com
SIC: 3471 Electroplating of metals or formed products
PA: Plating Specialties, Inc
1625 E 10 Mile Rd
Madison Heights MI 48071
248 547-8660

(G-10804)
POLY TECH INDUSTRIES INC
395 W Lincoln Ave Ste B (48071-3967)
PHONE.....................248 589-9950
Douglas Dick, *President*
Jeremy Dick, *Prgrmr*
EMP: 8 EST: 1960
SALES (est): 524.2K **Privately Held**
WEB: www.polytechgraphics.com
SIC: 2791 Typesetting, computer controlled

(G-10805)
POPCORN PRESS INC
32400 Edward Ave Ste A (48071-1447)
PHONE.....................248 588-4444
Al Glasby, *President*
EMP: 11 EST: 1993
SQ FT: 8,000
SALES (est): 747.4K **Privately Held**
SIC: 2752 Commercial printing, offset

(G-10806)
POWERTRAIN INTEGRATION LLC
Also Called: Power Solutions International
32505 Industrial Dr (48071-5004)
PHONE.....................248 577-0010
Ed Garda, *Engineer*
Brad Shantry, *Chief Mktg Ofcr*
Robert Pachla,
Ron Meganck,
▲ EMP: 22 EST: 2004
SQ FT: 47,000
SALES (est): 3.7MM **Privately Held**
WEB: www.powertrainintegration.com
SIC: 3568 3519 Power transmission equipment; gasoline engines

(G-10807)
PRESTIGE ADVANCED INC
30031 Stephenson Hwy (48071-1605)
PHONE.....................586 868-4000
William G Fritts, *President*
Satbir Singh, *COO*
Dennis Groesbeck, *Vice Pres*
Amy Peltz, *Controller*
Steve Horne, *Sales Staff*
EMP: 18 EST: 2008
SQ FT: 5,400
SALES (est): 3.7MM **Privately Held**
WEB: www.prestige-grp.com
SIC: 3465 Automotive stampings

(G-10808)
PRESTIGE ENGRG RSRCES TECH INC
Also Called: Prestige Advance
30031 Stephenson Hwy (48071-1605)
PHONE.....................586 573-3070
Dennis M Groesbeck, *Administration*
EMP: 8
SALES (corp-wide): 8MM **Privately Held**
WEB: www.prestige-grp.com
SIC: 3599 3714 Amusement park equipment; motor vehicle engines & parts
PA: Prestige Engineering Resources & Technologies Inc.
24700 Capital Blvd
Clinton Township MI 48036
586 868-4000

(G-10809)
PRIMARY TOOL & CUTTER GRINDING
32388 Edward Ave (48071-1432)
PHONE.....................248 588-1530
Paul Borthwick, *President*
Joe Paupert, *Vice Pres*
Gary Dassatt, *Treasurer*
EMP: 21 EST: 1997
SQ FT: 7,200
SALES (est): 1.2MM **Privately Held**
WEB: www.primarytool.com
SIC: 3545 Cutting tools for machine tools

(G-10810)
PRINT MASTERS INC
Also Called: Print Masters Printing Co
26039 Dequindre Rd (48071-3820)
PHONE.....................248 548-7100
James Gerds, *President*
Laura Carlin, *Vice Pres*
EMP: 13 EST: 1984
SQ FT: 6,000
SALES (est): 2.2MM **Privately Held**
WEB: www.printmasters.com
SIC: 2752 7336 7331 2791 Commercial printing, offset; commercial art & graphic design; direct mail advertising services; typesetting

(G-10811)
PUBLISHING XPRESS
29777 Stephenson Hwy (48071-2334)
PHONE.....................248 582-1834
Salmaan Ahmad, *President*
EMP: 4 EST: 2016
SALES (est): 80.6K **Privately Held**
WEB: www.publishingxpress.com
SIC: 2759 2731 2721 Promotional printing; book publishing; comic books: publishing only, not printed on site

(G-10812)
PYRO SERVICE COMPANY
25812 John R Rd (48071-4020)
PHONE.....................248 547-2552
Gerry Hambright, *President*
▲ EMP: 5 EST: 1951
SQ FT: 6,000
SALES (est): **Privately Held**
WEB: www.pyroservice.com
SIC: 3823 3822 Pyrometers, industrial process type; thermocouples, vacuum: glass

(G-10813)
QC TECH LLC
Also Called: Qcr Tech
1605 E Avis Dr (48071-1514)
PHONE.....................248 597-3984
William Young, *President*
Sean Foster, *General Mgr*
Michael Withee, *CFO*
Mike Withee, *Controller*
Patricia Haggard, *Office Mgr*
EMP: 55
SQ FT: 20,000
SALES (est): 9.1MM **Privately Held**
WEB: www.qcrtech.com
SIC: 3544 3399 Industrial molds; nails: aluminum, brass or other nonferrous metal or wire

(G-10814)
QMI GROUP INC
1645 E Avis Dr (48071-1514)
PHONE.....................248 589-0505
James J Shereda, *President*
Barbara A Shereda, *President*
Mary Schumacher, *Sales Staff*
Joann Streebing, *Manager*
EMP: 25 EST: 1975
SQ FT: 15,000
SALES (est): 5.1MM **Privately Held**
WEB: www.qmigroupinc.com
SIC: 3555 5999 3993 3471 Printing trades machinery; trophies & plaques; signs & advertising specialties; plating & polishing; automotive & apparel trimmings

(G-10815)
QUALITY STAINLESS MFG CO
1150 E 11 Mile Rd (48071-3802)
PHONE.....................248 546-4141
Diana Rudzewicz, *President*
Dan Jankowski, *Vice Pres*
EMP: 10 EST: 1970
SQ FT: 8,500
SALES (est): 1MM **Privately Held**
WEB: www.qualitystainlessmfg.com
SIC: 3444 1711 Restaurant sheet metalwork; mechanical contractor

(G-10816)
R R DONNELLEY & SONS COMPANY
32031 Townley St (48071-1320)
PHONE.....................248 583-2500
Daniel Knotts, *President*
EMP: 7 EST: 2018
SALES (est): 264.7K **Privately Held**
SIC: 2759 Commercial printing

(G-10817)
RB&W DETROIT
30100 Stephenson Hwy (48071-1630)
PHONE.....................234 380-8544
Charlie Wilkinson, *Manager*
Tricia Combe, *Business Dir*
Don Bowersox, *Administration*
EMP: 8 EST: 2015
SALES (est): 132.3K **Privately Held**
SIC: 3599 Machine shop, jobbing & repair

(G-10818)
ROBAL TECH LLC ✪
415 W 11 Mile Rd (48071-3219)
PHONE.....................248 436-8105
Courtney M Hofmann,
EMP: 4 EST: 2021
SALES (est): 171.9K **Privately Held**
SIC: 7372 Application computer software

(G-10819)
ROTARY MULTIFORMS INC
Also Called: R M I
1340 E 11 Mile Rd (48071-3806)
P.O. Box 641009, Detroit (48264-1009)
PHONE.....................586 558-7960
William R Condon, *President*
Jeff Flynn, *Administration*
Rachel Seng, *Graphic Designe*
Kim Causley, *Representative*
Randal Rodriguez, *Representative*
EMP: 9 EST: 1982
SALES (est): 1.6MM **Privately Held**
WEB: www.rmi-printing.com
SIC: 2761 Continuous forms, office & business; strip forms (manifold business forms)

(G-10820)
ROYAL ARC INC
520 Sheffield Dr (48071-2206)
PHONE.....................586 758-0718
Joseph P Lonero, *President*
Joseph Lonero, *Owner*
Nancy Lonero, *Admin Sec*
EMP: 5 EST: 1955
SQ FT: 5,600
SALES (est): 437.1K **Privately Held**
WEB: www.royalarc.com
SIC: 3544 Special dies & tools

(G-10821)
ROYAL DESIGN & MANUFACTURING
32401 Stephenson Hwy (48071-1093)
PHONE.....................248 588-0110
Rodney D Paulick, *Chairman*
Patrick J Eveland, *Vice Pres*
Craig Jones, *Opers Mgr*
▼ EMP: 65 EST: 1951
SQ FT: 16,000

Madison Heights - Oakland County (G-10822)

SALES (est): 8MM **Privately Held**
WEB: www.variset.com
SIC: 3559 2542 3824 3545 Automotive related machinery; racks, merchandise display or storage; except wood; fluid meters & counting devices; machine tool accessories; metal cans
PA: J H P Inc
32401 Stephenson Hwy
Madison Heights MI 48071
248 588-0110

(G-10822)
RR DONNELLEY
32021 Edward Ave (48071-1419)
PHONE.................................248 588-2941
EMP: 9 **EST:** 2015
SALES (est): 183.4K **Privately Held**
SIC: 2759 Commercial printing

(G-10823)
S & L MACHINE PRODUCTS INC
30250 Stephenson Hwy (48071-1612)
PHONE.................................248 543-6633
John Backer, *President*
Ted Purdy, *Manager*
EMP: 15 **EST:** 1982
SQ FT: 15,000
SALES (est): 2.4MM **Privately Held**
SIC: 3599 Machine shop, jobbing & repair

(G-10824)
SANTANNA TOOL & DESIGN LLC
Also Called: Bulldog Factory Service
25880 Commerce Dr (48071-4151)
PHONE.................................248 541-3500
Joe D Newton, *General Mgr*
Gary Newton, *Opers Mgr*
Kathy Celani, *Office Mgr*
Jamilee Newton, *Mng Member*
Tracy Hutchinson, *Officer*
EMP: 70 **EST:** 1937
SQ FT: 50,000
SALES (est): 30MM **Privately Held**
WEB: www.santannatool.com
SIC: 3535 3548 Conveyors & conveying equipment; welding apparatus

(G-10825)
SCOTT & ITOH MACHINE COMPANY
31690 Stephenson Hwy (48071-1642)
PHONE.................................248 585-5385
Jeffrey Scott, *President*
Rebecca Scott, *CFO*
EMP: 21 **EST:** 1991
SQ FT: 36,000
SALES (est): 4.6MM
SALES (corp-wide): 10MM **Privately Held**
WEB: www.scott-itoh.com
SIC: 3599 Machine shop, jobbing & repair
PA: Allan Tool & Machine Co., Inc.
1822 E Maple Rd
Troy MI 48083
248 585-2910

(G-10826)
SHANNON PRECISION FASTENER LLC
Also Called: Shannon Distribution Center
800 E 14 Mile Rd (48071-1425)
PHONE.................................248 658-3015
Scott Mayer, *Plant Mgr*
Jerry Iwanski, *Branch Mgr*
Bob Allison, *Manager*
Philip Menzies, *Manager*
Kyle Marchetti, *Supervisor*
EMP: 100
SALES (corp-wide): 125MM **Privately Held**
WEB: www.shannonpf.com
SIC: 3542 3452 Machine tools, metal forming type; bolts, nuts, rivets & washers
PA: Shannon Precision Fastener, Llc
31600 Stephenson Hwy
Madison Heights MI 48071
248 589-9670

(G-10827)
SHANNON PRECISION FASTENER LLC (PA)
Also Called: Shannon Distribution Center
31600 Stephenson Hwy (48071-1642)
PHONE.................................248 589-9670
Tim Geyer, *Vice Pres*
Glenn Purvin, *Vice Pres*
Robb Thompson, *Vice Pres*
Gerry Iwanski, *Plant Mgr*
John Varani, *Maint Spvr*
▲ **EMP:** 75
SQ FT: 83,000
SALES (est): 125MM **Privately Held**
WEB: www.shannonpf.com
SIC: 3452 Bolts, nuts, rivets & washers

(G-10828)
SIKA AUTO EATON RAPIDS INC (DH)
Also Called: Sika Advanced Resins US
30800 Stephenson Hwy (48071-1614)
PHONE.................................248 588-2270
Marty Poljan, *President*
Jayne Thomas, *Controller*
▲ **EMP:** 10 **EST:** 1979
SALES (est): 20.5MM
SALES (corp-wide): 8.6B **Privately Held**
WEB: www.usa.sika.com
SIC: 7389 3999 2821 Building scale models; models, except toy; elastomers, non-vulcanizable (plastics)
HQ: Sika Corporation
201 Polito Ave
Lyndhurst NJ 07071
201 933-8800

(G-10829)
SIKA CORPORATION
Also Called: Sika Industry
30800 Stephenson Hwy (48071-1614)
PHONE.................................248 577-0020
Thomas Labelle, *Managing Dir*
Lauren Cassidy, *Regional Mgr*
Chuck Steiner, *Regional Mgr*
Jim Bluse, *District Mgr*
Herbert Zwartkruis, *Exec VP*
EMP: 100
SALES (corp-wide): 8.6B **Privately Held**
WEB: www.usa.sika.com
SIC: 3721 8742 8731 2899 Aircraft; management consulting services; commercial physical research; chemical preparations; adhesives & sealants
HQ: Sika Corporation
201 Polito Ave
Lyndhurst NJ 07071
201 933-8800

(G-10830)
SKYAPPLE LLC
Also Called: Allied Bindery
32501 Dequindre Rd (48071-1520)
PHONE.................................248 588-5990
Aditi Chavannavar, *CEO*
EMP: 31 **EST:** 2018
SQ FT: 48,000
SALES (est): 2.6MM **Privately Held**
SIC: 2789 7389 Binding only: books, pamphlets, magazines, etc.; mailing & messenger services

(G-10831)
SOURCE ONE DIST SVCS INC
900 Tech Row (48071-4624)
PHONE.................................248 399-5060
Joseph Gurak Sr, *President*
Joe Gurak, *Vice Pres*
Joseph Gurak Jr, *Vice Pres*
Chris Gurak, *Manager*
EMP: 10 **EST:** 1991
SQ FT: 19,800
SALES (est): 1.9MM **Privately Held**
WEB: www.sourceone-dist.com
SIC: 2759 7331 Laser printing; mailing service

(G-10832)
SPECIAL DRILL AND REAMER CORP
408 E 14 Mile Rd (48071-1458)
P.O. Box 71105 (48071-0105)
PHONE.................................248 588-5333
Michael Obloy, *President*
Phyllis Hudeck, *Vice Pres*
EMP: 37 **EST:** 1958
SQ FT: 26,000
SALES (est): 1.3MM **Privately Held**
SIC: 3545 Drilling machine attachments & accessories; reamers, machine tool

(G-10833)
SPECIAL FABRICATORS INC
31649 Stephenson Hwy (48071-1684)
PHONE.................................248 588-6717
Richard Tieman, *President*
EMP: 7 **EST:** 1938
SQ FT: 10,000 **Privately Held**
WEB: www.specialfabricators.com
SIC: 3441 Fabricated structural metal

(G-10834)
SPECTRUM NEON COMPANY
1280 Kempar Ave (48071-1424)
PHONE.................................313 366-7333
John Haddad, *President*
EMP: 6 **EST:** 1981
SALES (est): 1MM **Privately Held**
WEB: www.spectrumneon.com
SIC: 3993 Neon signs

(G-10835)
STANDARD COATING INC
32565 Dequindre Rd (48071-1520)
PHONE.................................248 297-6650
Michael Mitchell, *President*
Jeff Mertz, *Exec Dir*
EMP: 75 **EST:** 2018
SALES (est): 5.5MM **Privately Held**
SIC: 3449 Miscellaneous metalwork

(G-10836)
STAR TEXTILE INC
1000 Tech Row (48071-4679)
PHONE.................................888 527-5700
Noha Mikhail, *Owner*
▲ **EMP:** 50 **EST:** 1999
SALES (est): 7.1MM **Privately Held**
WEB: www.startextile.com
SIC: 2392 2259 Blankets, comforters & beddings; curtains & bedding, knit

(G-10837)
STEC USA INC (PA)
31900 Sherman Ave (48071-5605)
PHONE.................................248 307-1440
Shuo Wang, *President*
Christopher Shaffer, *Director*
EMP: 10
SQ FT: 30,500
SALES (est): 1.6MM **Privately Held**
WEB: www.stecus.com
SIC: 3559 Automotive maintenance equipment

(G-10838)
SULFO-TECHNOLOGIES LLC
32300 Howard Ave (48071-1429)
PHONE.................................248 307-9150
Larry Gladchun,
Samuel Greenawalt,
Richard Kaspers,
▲ **EMP:** 8 **EST:** 1999
SQ FT: 3,600
SALES (est): 1.2MM **Privately Held**
WEB: www.sulfotech.com
SIC: 2821 Plasticizer/additive based plastic materials

(G-10839)
SUPERIOR CAM INC
31240 Stephenson Hwy (48071-1620)
PHONE.................................248 588-1100
John J Basso, *President*
Donn Helfer, *Superintendent*
Gary Hix, *Superintendent*
Frank Delkov, *Plant Mgr*
Mike Austin, *Mfg Staff*
EMP: 100 **EST:** 1973
SQ FT: 67,000
SALES (est): 19.4MM **Privately Held**
WEB: www.diversifiedtoolinggroup.com
SIC: 3465 Body parts, automobile: stamped metal; fenders, automobile: stamped or pressed metal

(G-10840)
SUPPLEMENT GROUP INC
32787 Stephenson Hwy (48071-5527)
PHONE.................................248 588-2055
EMP: 15

SQ FT: 11,500
SALES (est): 3.5MM **Privately Held**
SIC: 2834 Mfg Pharmaceutical Preparations

(G-10841)
TEXTRON INC
25225 Dequindre Rd (48071-4211)
PHONE.................................248 545-2035
EMP: 4
SALES (corp-wide): 14.2B **Publicly Held**
SIC: 3721 Mfg Aviation Aircrafts
PA: Textron Inc.
40 Westminster St
Providence RI 02903
401 421-2800

(G-10842)
THE SIGN CHAP INC
31211 Stephenson Hwy # 100 (48071-1637)
PHONE.................................248 585-6880
Robert Chapa III, *Principal*
EMP: 5 **EST:** 2005
SALES (est): 75.1K **Privately Held**
SIC: 3993 Signs & advertising specialties

(G-10843)
THERMAL WAVE IMAGING INC
25175 Dequindre Rd (48071-4240)
PHONE.................................248 414-3730
Steven M Shepard, *Owner*
Nicole Wilson-Tejero, *General Mgr*
Bharat Chaudhry, *Managing Dir*
Tasdiq Ahmed, *Research*
Yulin Hou, *Electrical Engi*
▼ **EMP:** 15 **EST:** 1992
SQ FT: 11,500 **Privately Held**
WEB: www.thermalwave.com
SIC: 8734 3829 Testing laboratories; testing equipment: abrasion, shearing strength, etc.

(G-10844)
TOOLING SOLUTIONS GROUP LLC
Also Called: Bokum Tool Company
32301 Dequindre Rd (48071-1594)
PHONE.................................248 585-0222
John Stewart, *Vice Pres*
Fritz Heuser, *Mng Member*
EMP: 9 **EST:** 2019
SALES (est): 739.2K **Privately Held**
WEB: www.bokum.com
SIC: 3545 5084 Cutting tools for machine tools; industrial machinery & equipment

(G-10845)
TOTAL BUSINESS SYSTEMS INC (PA)
Also Called: Deluxe Data Printers
30800 Montpelier Dr (48071-5108)
PHONE.................................248 307-1076
Robert G Finnerty, *President*
Tom Lustig, *Plant Supt*
Justus J Austin Jr, *Treasurer*
EMP: 18 **EST:** 1981
SQ FT: 9,000
SALES (est): 27.6MM **Privately Held**
WEB: www.tbsddp.com
SIC: 2761 2752 Manifold business forms; business forms, lithographed

(G-10846)
TRANE TECHNOLOGIES COMPANY LLC
Ingersoll-Rand
29555 Stephenson Hwy (48071-2332)
PHONE.................................248 398-6200
Jeff Jay, *Sales Staff*
Lisa O'Dell, *Manager*
EMP: 30 **Privately Held**
WEB: www.ingersollrand.com
SIC: 3432 Plumbing fixture fittings & trim
HQ: Trane Technologies Company Llc
800 Beaty St
Davidson NC 28036
704 655-4000

(G-10847)
TRIAD MANUFACTURING CO INC
32020 Edward Ave (48071-1420)
P.O. Box 71591 (48071-0591)
PHONE.................................248 583-9636

Hartmut Rothacker, *President*
EMP: 9 **EST:** 1958
SQ FT: 12,000
SALES (est): 249.5K **Privately Held**
SIC: 3599 Machine shop, jobbing & repair

(G-10848)
TRYNEX INTERNATIONAL LLC
531 Ajax Dr (48071-2429)
PHONE 248 586-3500
James Janik, *CEO*
Larry Ursell, *Controller*
Donna Owiesny, *Accountant*
Jordan Santos, *Human Res Mgr*
William Tomich, *Accounts Mgr*
▲ **EMP:** 15 **EST:** 1992
SQ FT: 14,500
SALES (est): 5.5MM **Publicly Held**
WEB: www.douglasdynamics.com
SIC: 3711 5082 Snow plows (motor vehicles), assembly of; blades for graders, scrapers, dozers & snow plows
PA: Douglas Dynamics, Inc.
7777 N 73rd St
Milwaukee WI 53223

(G-10849)
ULTRA STITCH EMBROIDERY
32475 Stephenson Hwy (48071-5521)
PHONE 586 498-5600
Marilyn Jolet, *Owner*
Robert Jolet, *Owner*
EMP: 10 **EST:** 1994
SALES (est): 542.5K **Privately Held**
SIC: 2395 Embroidery & art needlework

(G-10850)
UMLAUT PRODUCT SOLUTIONS INC
1225 Spartan St (48071-3829)
PHONE 248 703-7724
Colin Goldsmith, *President*
Wu Chau, *Officer*
Samit Ghosh, *Officer*
EMP: 18 **EST:** 2019
SALES (est): 4.8MM **Privately Held**
WEB: www.umlaut.com
SIC: 3714 Motor vehicle electrical equipment
HQ: Umlaut, Inc.
1225 Spartan St
Madison Heights MI 48071

(G-10851)
UNCLE RONS WOODWORKING
611 W Girard Ave (48071-5104)
PHONE 248 585-7837
Ronald Gilbert, *Principal*
EMP: 5 **EST:** 2012
SALES (est): 65K **Privately Held**
SIC: 2431 Millwork

(G-10852)
UNIQUE U MAGAZINE LLC
1221 Christine Ter (48071-3868)
PHONE 586 696-1839
Marsha Williams, *Mng Member*
EMP: 5 **EST:** 2017
SALES (est): 76.2K **Privately Held**
SIC: 2721 Magazines: publishing only, not printed on site

(G-10853)
UNIVERSAL FABRICATORS INC
25855 Commerce Dr (48071-4152)
PHONE 248 399-7565
Anthony F Usakoski Jr, *President*
Bonnie S Usakoski, *Treasurer*
Marylu Guida, *Manager*
EMP: 18 **EST:** 1972
SQ FT: 4,500
SALES (est): 1.1MM **Privately Held**
SIC: 3444 Sheet metalwork

(G-10854)
USI INC
Also Called: Ultimate Systems
31302 Stephenson Hwy A (48071-1634)
PHONE 248 583-9337
Sheryl Chinn, *President*
Angela Ridgeway, *Accounts Exec*
Deanna Gilbert, *Manager*
Ketelnn Rose, *Manager*
Conner Tung, *Analyst*
EMP: 10 **EST:** 2004

SALES (est): 1.6MM **Privately Held**
SIC: 3594 Motors: hydraulic, fluid power or air

(G-10855)
VIGEL NORTH AMERICA INC (DH)
32375 Howard Ave (48071-1433)
PHONE 734 947-9900
Ron Scariol, *President*
Giuseppe Stabile, *Supervisor*
EMP: 7 **EST:** 2005
SALES (est): 5.1MM
SALES (corp-wide): 297.2M **Privately Held**
WEB: www.vigel.com
SIC: 3545 Machine tool accessories
HQ: Vigel Spa
Via Mappano 15/A
Borgaro Torinese TO 10071
011 470-4104

(G-10856)
VIKING TECHNOLOGIES INC
25169 Dequindre Rd (48071-4240)
PHONE 586 914-0819
Leif Goran Lowback, *President*
Ann Lowback, *Vice Pres*
Papa Peterson, *Technology*
Ida Lowback, *Admin Sec*
▼ **EMP:** 7 **EST:** 2009
SQ FT: 4,200
SALES (est): 1.1MM **Privately Held**
WEB: www.viking-technologies.com
SIC: 3674 5065 Memories, solid state; modems, computer

(G-10857)
VISUAL PRECISION INC
111 E 10 Mile Rd (48071-4203)
PHONE 248 546-7984
Ron Webber, *President*
Judy Miles, *Administration*
EMP: 5 **EST:** 1988
SQ FT: 5,000
SALES (est): 568.9K **Privately Held**
WEB: www.vpcharts.com
SIC: 3827 Optical comparators

(G-10858)
W INTERNATIONAL LLC (PA)
31720 Stephenson Hwy (48071-1643)
PHONE 248 577-0364
Edward Walker, *CEO*
John Klausmeier, *COO*
Pat Herta, *Vice Pres*
Todd Miller, *Vice Pres*
Kurt Kilby, *CFO*
EMP: 100 **EST:** 2011
SQ FT: 65,000
SALES: 20.3MM **Privately Held**
WEB: www.w-international.com
SIC: 3499 Welding tips, heat resistant: metal

(G-10859)
WALL CO INCORPORATED (PA)
101 W Girard Ave (48071-1880)
PHONE 248 585-6400
William P Clark Jr, *President*
Ohannes Mangoyan, *General Mgr*
Joseph A Drobot Jr, *Corp Secy*
Joseph M Maria, *Vice Pres*
Paul Whe, *QC Mgr*
◆ **EMP:** 30 **EST:** 1986
SQ FT: 15,000
SALES (est): 115.3MM **Privately Held**
WEB: www.wallcolmonoy.com
SIC: 3399 3398 Powder, metal; brazing (hardening) of metal

(G-10860)
WALL COLMONOY CORPORATION (HQ)
101 W Girard Ave (48071-1880)
PHONE 248 585-6400
William P Clark, *President*
Chelsea Wall, *District Mgr*
Matthew Ranville, *COO*
Robert Heminger, *Vice Pres*
Brian Brasel, *Project Mgr*
◆ **EMP:** 20 **EST:** 1953
SQ FT: 9,000
SALES (est): 115.3MM **Privately Held**
WEB: www.wallcolmonoy.com
SIC: 2891 Adhesives & sealants

PA: Wall Co., Incorporated
101 W Girard Ave
Madison Heights MI 48071
248 585-6400

(G-10861)
WENTZEL ENERGY PARTNERS LLC
999 Tech Row (48071-4619)
PHONE 817 713-3283
EMP: 5 **EST:** 2019
SALES (est): 167.7K **Privately Held**
WEB: www.wentzelenergypartners.com
SIC: 1389 Oil & gas field services

(G-10862)
WHITLOCK BUSINESS SYSTEMS INC
275 E 12 Mile Rd (48071-2557)
PHONE 248 548-1040
Curtis Bledsoe, *Vice Pres*
Kenneth Noonan, *Treasurer*
Linda Foran, *Sales Staff*
Mary Klosinski, *Sales Staff*
Richard Barnes, *CIO*
EMP: 30 **EST:** 1982
SQ FT: 16,000
SALES (est): 10.4MM **Privately Held**
WEB: www.wbsusa.com
SIC: 5112 2761 Business forms; manifold business forms

(G-10863)
WHITLOCK DISTRIBUTION SVCS LLC
275 E 12 Mile Rd (48071-2557)
PHONE 248 548-1040
Kenneth Noonan, *Mng Member*
EMP: 16 **EST:** 2012
SQ FT: 5,000
SALES (est): 967.8K **Privately Held**
WEB: www.wbsusa.com
SIC: 2759 Commercial printing

(G-10864)
WORKHORSE CUSTOM CHASSIS LLC (DH)
1675 E Whitcomb Ave (48071-1411)
PHONE 248 588-5300
Dennis Huffmon, *Vice Pres*
▲ **EMP:** 105 **EST:** 1998
SQ FT: 220,000
SALES (est): 12.4MM
SALES (corp-wide): 263.5B **Privately Held**
WEB: www.internationaltrucks.com
SIC: 3711 Chassis, motor vehicle
HQ: Navistar, Inc.
2701 Navistar Dr
Lisle IL 60532
331 332-5000

Mancelona
Antrim County

(G-10865)
ADVANCE TOOL CO
407 Rose St (49659-8305)
P.O. Box 588 (49659-0588)
PHONE 231 587-5286
William R McGillivray, *Owner*
EMP: 9 **EST:** 1953
SALES (est): 204K **Privately Held**
WEB: www.advancetoolcompany.com
SIC: 3544 Special dies, tools, jigs & fixtures

(G-10866)
ANTRIM MACHINE PRODUCTS INC
9142 Johnson Rd (49659-7964)
P.O. Box 379 (49659-0379)
PHONE 231 587-9114
Gerald Witowski, *President*
Jacob Kelly, *Plant Mgr*
EMP: 25 **EST:** 1971 **Privately Held**
WEB: www.antrimmachine.com
SIC: 3599 3812 Machine shop, jobbing & repair; defense systems & equipment; acceleration indicators & systems components, aerospace

(G-10867)
BUCK-N-HAM MACHINES INC (HQ)
413 Dale Ave (49659-9328)
PHONE 231 587-5322
Rodney Lapointe, *President*
Charles Lapointe, *Vice Pres*
Charles A Lapointe, *Engineer*
Charles La Pointe, *Controller*
EMP: 4 **EST:** 1985
SQ FT: 7,500
SALES (est): 598.7K **Privately Held**
WEB: www.bnhmachines.com
SIC: 3599 Machine shop, jobbing & repair

(G-10868)
BURT MOEKE & SON HARDWOODS
2509 Valley Rd (49659-9344)
P.O. Box 500 (49659-0500)
PHONE 231 587-5385
Fax: 231 587-0550
EMP: 50
SQ FT: 7,000
SALES (est): 5.6MM **Privately Held**
SIC: 2421 2426 Sawmill/Planing Mill Hardwood Dimension/Floor Mill

(G-10869)
EL PASO LLC
8616 Anr Storage Rd Ne (49659-8205)
PHONE 231 587-0704
Bill Brown, *Manager*
EMP: 4 **Publicly Held**
WEB: www.kindermorgan.com
SIC: 1389 Gas field services
HQ: El Paso Llc
1001 Louisiana St
Houston TX 77002
713 420-2600

(G-10870)
FAHL FOREST PRODUCTS INC
2509 Valley Rd (49659-9344)
P.O. Box 500 (49659-0500)
PHONE 231 587-5388
Sam Fahl, *Owner*
EMP: 15 **EST:** 1980
SALES (est): 1.2MM **Privately Held**
WEB: www.fahlforest.com
SIC: 2411 Logging camps & contractors

(G-10871)
FLANNERY MACHINE & TOOL INC
8420 S Us Highway 131 (49659-9789)
PHONE 231 587-5076
Kenneth W Flannery, *President*
Darryl A Antcliff, *Sales Staff*
Julia Flannery, *Admin Sec*
EMP: 30 **EST:** 1991
SQ FT: 9,600
SALES (est): 6MM **Privately Held**
WEB: www.flannerymachine.com
SIC: 3544 Special dies & tools

(G-10872)
HAK INC (PA)
413 Dale Ave (49659-9328)
PHONE 231 587-5322
Henry J Lapointe, *President*
EMP: 6 **EST:** 1988
SQ FT: 4,700
SALES (est): 1.3MM **Privately Held**
SIC: 3549 Metalworking machinery

(G-10873)
LANZEN INCORPORATED
Also Called: Lanzen-Mancelona
611 N East Limits St (49659-7600)
PHONE 231 587-8200
Terry K Lanzen, *President*
Dan Lantis, *Manager*
EMP: 32
SALES (corp-wide): 13.7MM **Privately Held**
WEB: www.lanzen.com
SIC: 3599 Machine shop, jobbing & repair
PA: Lanzen, Incorporated
100 Peyerk Ct
Bruce Twp MI 48065
586 771-7070

Manselona - Antrim County (G-10874)

GEOGRAPHIC SECTION

(G-10874)
MEEDERS DIM & LBR PDTS CO
7810 S M 88 Hwy (49659-8753)
PHONE..................................231 587-8611
Tim Meeder, *CEO*
Shannon Meeder, *President*
D Mitchell Meeder, *Vice Pres*
EMP: 6 **EST:** 1963
SQ FT: 10,000
SALES (est): 464.1K **Privately Held**
SIC: 2426 2511 Furniture dimension stock, hardwood; wood household furniture

(G-10875)
MEEDERS LUMBER CO
7810 S M 88 Hwy (49659-8753)
PHONE..................................231 587-8611
Shannon Meeder, *CEO*
EMP: 8
SQ FT: 12,400
SALES (est): 704.6K **Privately Held**
SIC: 2421 Lumber: rough, sawed or planed

(G-10876)
MERRITT RACEWAY LLC
7300 N Maple Valley Rd Ne (49659-7940)
PHONE..................................231 590-4431
Ricky Ancel, *Principal*
EMP: 4 **EST:** 2011
SALES (est): 82K **Privately Held**
WEB: www.merrittraceway.com
SIC: 3644 Raceways

(G-10877)
MODERNE SLATE INC
8333 County Road 571 Ne (49659-9501)
PHONE..................................231 584-3499
Sylvia Leonard, *President*
EMP: 4 **EST:** 2010
SALES (est): 359.4K **Privately Held**
WEB: www.moderneslate.com
SIC: 3281 Slate products

(G-10878)
REDTAIL SOFTWARE
1414 Plum Valley Rd Ne (49659-9589)
PHONE..................................231 587-0720
Robert Baldwin, *Principal*
EMP: 5 **EST:** 2008
SALES (est): 359.2K **Privately Held**
WEB: www.redtailsoftware.com
SIC: 7372 Prepackaged software

(G-10879)
STEEL TANK & FABRICATING CO
9517 Lake St (49659-7968)
PHONE..................................231 587-8412
Katie Bruce, *Comms Mgr*
Charles Harding, *Manager*
EMP: 75
SALES (corp-wide): 9.5MM **Privately Held**
SIC: 3443 Fabricated plate work (boiler shop)
PA: Steel Tank & Fabricating Co.
4701 White Lake Rd
Clarkston MI 48346
248 625-8700

Manchester
Washtenaw County

(G-10880)
AMCOR RIGID PACKAGING USA LLC (DH)
10521 S M 52 (48158-7333)
PHONE..................................734 428-9741
Michael Schmitt, *President*
Michael Lane, *Principal*
Eric Hernandez, *Business Mgr*
Brian Carvill, *Vice Pres*
Art Castro, *Vice Pres*
♦ **EMP:** 58 **EST:** 1997
SALES (est): 535.3MM
SALES (corp-wide): 12.4B **Privately Held**
WEB: www.amcor.com
SIC: 3089 Plastic containers, except foam

(G-10881)
AMERICAN ENGNRED CMPONENTS INC (PA)
Also Called: His Stamping Division
17951 W Austin Rd (48158-8668)
P.O. Box 338 (48158-0338)
PHONE..................................734 428-8301
John Morrison, *Ch of Bd*
Frederick W Schoen, *President*
William F McGregor, *VP Mfg*
Charles L Dardas, *CFO*
EMP: 139 **EST:** 1992
SQ FT: 108,000
SALES (est): 32MM **Privately Held**
SIC: 3469 Metal stampings

(G-10882)
CEI COMPOSITE MATERIALS LLC
Also Called: Cei
800 E Duncan St (48158-9425)
PHONE..................................734 212-3006
Jeff Henry, *COO*
Garrett Harris, *Project Mgr*
Rob Napper, *Project Mgr*
Dave Renda, *Project Mgr*
Lindsey Skocelas, *Project Mgr*
EMP: 20 **EST:** 2008
SQ FT: 16,000
SALES (est): 7.2MM **Privately Held**
WEB: www.ceicomposites.com
SIC: 3446 Architectural metalwork

(G-10883)
ENKON LLC
Also Called: Broadway
10521 Mi State Road 52 (48158-9474)
PHONE..................................937 890-5678
Kelly Ferguson, *President*
Debra L Doyle,
EMP: 46 **EST:** 2001
SALES (est): 432.7K
SALES (corp-wide): 17.1MM **Privately Held**
WEB: www.broadwayco.com
SIC: 3089 3544 3599 8711 Injection molding of plastics; molding primary plastic; dies, plastics forming; machine & other job shop work; machine tool design; steel wool
PA: The Eco-Groupe Inc
6161 Ventnor Ave
Dayton OH 45414
937 898-2603

(G-10884)
FASTENER ADVANCE PDT CO LTD
750 Hogan Rd (48158-9590)
P.O. Box 728 (48158-0728)
PHONE..................................734 428-8070
Jang-Chon Wang, *President*
Kirstin Wright, *Accountant*
Nicolas Epperson, *Sales Mgr*
Casey Kozlowski, *Manager*
▲ **EMP:** 15 **EST:** 2006
SQ FT: 20,000
SALES (est): 1.4MM **Privately Held**
WEB: www.fasteneradvance.com
SIC: 3452 Bolts, nuts, rivets & washers

(G-10885)
MAC ENTERPRISES INC (PA)
11940 Hieber Rd (48158-9438)
PHONE..................................313 846-4567
Sylvia McCaffery, *President*
Lila D McCaffery, *President*
Mary Ann Nye, *General Mgr*
Paula S McCaffery, *Corp Secy*
▲ **EMP:** 15 **EST:** 1951
SALES (est): 2.4MM **Privately Held**
SIC: 3944 5092 Craft & hobby kits & sets; arts & crafts equipment & supplies; lead pencils & art goods

(G-10886)
MARTINREA INDUSTRIES INC (HQ)
10501 Mi State Road 52 (48158-9432)
PHONE..................................734 428-2400
Morris Rowlett, *CEO*
Robert Wildeboer, *Ch of Bd*
Fred Jaekel, *President*
Joel Altman, *General Mgr*
Brad Graves, *General Mgr*
▲ **EMP:** 25 **EST:** 2002
SALES (est): 582.5MM
SALES (corp-wide): 2.5B **Privately Held**
WEB: www.martinrea.com
SIC: 3714 3317 3089 3544 Motor vehicle parts & accessories; steel pipe & tubes; plastic containers, except foam; special dies, tools, jigs & fixtures
PA: Martinrea International Inc
3210 Langstaff Rd
Vaughan ON
416 749-0314

(G-10887)
OBERTRON ELECTRONIC MFG INC
10098 Mi State Road 52 (48158-9743)
PHONE..................................734 428-0722
Bradley Oberleiter, *President*
▲ **EMP:** 10 **EST:** 1986
SQ FT: 10,000
SALES (est): 1.8MM **Privately Held**
WEB: www.obertron.com
SIC: 3672 Printed circuit boards

(G-10888)
PINNACLE ENGINEERING CO INC
18700 English Rd (48158-9757)
PHONE..................................734 428-7039
Murray Smith, *President*
Gertrude Smith, *Corp Secy*
Gary Smith, *Vice Pres*
EMP: 27 **EST:** 1969
SALES (est): 1MM **Privately Held**
WEB: www.pineng2004.com
SIC: 3544 3541 7692 Special dies & tools; industrial molds; machine tools, metal cutting type; welding repair

(G-10889)
POST PRODUCTION SOLUTIONS LLC
110 Division St Ste 1 (48158-8803)
PHONE..................................734 428-7000
Pete Berger, *General Mgr*
Richard Berger, *Mng Member*
EMP: 10 **EST:** 2002
SALES (est): 1.8MM **Privately Held**
WEB: www.postproductionusa.com
SIC: 3599 Machine shop, jobbing & repair

(G-10890)
TEIJIN AUTO TECH MNCHESTER LLC
Also Called: Continntal Strl Plas Mnchster
17951 W Austin Rd (48158-8668)
PHONE..................................734 428-8301
Steve Rooney, *CEO*
Kevin McKenna, *Mng Member*
▲ **EMP:** 85 **EST:** 2004
SQ FT: 89,000
SALES (est): 21.1MM **Privately Held**
WEB: www.teijinautomotive.com
SIC: 3089 Injection molding of plastics
HQ: Csp Holding Corp.
255 Rex Blvd
Auburn Hills MI 48326
248 237-7800

(G-10891)
TIDY MRO ENTERPRISES LLC
520 Wolverine St (48158-9567)
PHONE..................................734 649-1122
Daniel Alber, *Principal*
EMP: 7 **EST:** 2016
SALES (est): 390.1K **Privately Held**
SIC: 3724 Aircraft engines & engine parts

(G-10892)
WHITE DOVE WOODWORKS
705 E Main St (48158-8539)
PHONE..................................734 717-6042
EMP: 4 **EST:** 2013
SALES (est): 62.5K **Privately Held**
SIC: 2431 Millwork

Manistee
Manistee County

(G-10893)
AMOR SIGN STUDIOS INC
Also Called: Amor Imagepro
443 Water St (49660-1550)
P.O. Box 433 (49660-0433)
PHONE..................................231 723-8361
Thomas E Amor, *President*
Thomas H Amor, *Vice Pres*
Tom Amor, *Sales Mgr*
Myles Amor, *Sales Staff*
Kristina Bajtka, *Sales Staff*
EMP: 44 **EST:** 1946
SQ FT: 9,000
SALES (est): 3.7MM **Privately Held**
WEB: www.amazingmiracles.com
SIC: 7359 7389 3993 Sign rental; lettering & sign painting services; electric signs

(G-10894)
AMPTECH INC (HQ)
201 Glocheski Dr (49660-2640)
PHONE..................................231 464-5492
Lee R Wyatt, *President*
Richard Barnes, *Opers Mgr*
Todd Grover, *Opers Mgr*
Tammy Jans, *Purch Mgr*
Paul Zajac, *Design Engr*
▲ **EMP:** 1 **EST:** 1986
SQ FT: 53,000
SALES (est): 6.9MM **Privately Held**
WEB: www.amptechinc.com
SIC: 3679 Electronic circuits

(G-10895)
BOS MANUFACTURING LLC (PA)
237 Renaissance Dr (49660-9380)
PHONE..................................231 398-3328
David Boothe, *President*
Tim Stone, *Managing Prtnr*
Tonya Guinan, *Accounting Mgr*
Brian Boothe,
♦ **EMP:** 16
SALES (est): 4.9MM **Privately Held**
WEB: www.bosmfg.com
SIC: 3535 Conveyors & conveying equipment

(G-10896)
CONINE PUBLISHING INC (DH)
75 Maple St (49660-1554)
P.O. Box 317 (49660-0317)
PHONE..................................231 723-3592
John A Batdorff, *President*
EMP: 30
SQ FT: 8,000
SALES (est): 18.3MM
SALES (corp-wide): 4.2B **Privately Held**
WEB: www.theheraldreview.com
SIC: 2711 2741 Commercial printing & newspaper publishing combined; miscellaneous publishing
HQ: Pgi Holdings, Inc.
115 N Michigan Ave
Big Rapids MI 49307
231 796-4831

(G-10897)
DYNAMIC DEVELOPMENT INC
314 W Parkdale Ave (49660-1132)
P.O. Box 336 (49660-0336)
PHONE..................................231 723-8318
Gerald Hamilton, *President*
Joseph A Pienta, *Vice Pres*
EMP: 5 **EST:** 1982
SQ FT: 2,000
SALES (est): 584.1K **Privately Held**
WEB: www.dynamicdevco.com
SIC: 1382 Oil & gas exploration services

(G-10898)
DYNAMIC EXPLORATION INC
314 E Parkdale Ave (49660)
P.O. Box 336 (49660-0336)
PHONE..................................231 723-7879
Joseph A Pienta, *President*
Cynthia Luomala, *Treasurer*
EMP: 6 **EST:** 2019
SALES (est): 332K **Privately Held**
SIC: 1389 Oil & gas field services

Manitou Beach - Lenawee County (G-10926)

(G-10899)
FAB-LITE INC
330 Washington St (49660-1260)
P.O. Box 353 (49660-0353)
PHONE..................231 398-8280
Stephen Paine, *President*
Scott Lakari, *Vice Pres*
Brian Maxey, *Prdtn Mgr*
Tina Kelley, *Mfg Mgr*
Pete Anderson, *Manager*
EMP: 26 **EST:** 1995
SQ FT: 40,000
SALES (est): 6.9MM Privately Held
WEB: www.fablite.com
SIC: 3441 Fabricated structural metal

(G-10900)
FORBES SANITATION & EXCAVATION
1878 E Parkdale Ave (49660-9359)
PHONE..................231 723-2311
Don Forbes, *President*
EMP: 10 **EST:** 1957
SALES (est): 925.5K Privately Held
WEB: www.forbessanitation.com
SIC: 1711 1794 3272 7699 Septic system construction; excavation & grading, building construction; septic tanks, concrete; septic tank cleaning service; water, sewer & utility lines

(G-10901)
GOLDEN APPLE
336 River St (49660-2708)
PHONE..................231 477-5366
EMP: 4 **EST:** 2019
SALES (est): 61.9K Privately Held
SIC: 5943 3951 3579 Stationery stores; pens & mechanical pencils; office machines

(G-10902)
JACK BATDORSS
Also Called: Pioneer Group, The
75 Maple St (49660-1554)
PHONE..................231 723-3592
Jessica McHugh, *Sales Mgr*
Jack Batdorff, *Branch Mgr*
John A Batdorff, *Branch Mgr*
Donald Watters, *Manager*
Ken Grabowski, *Assoc Editor*
EMP: 10
SALES (corp-wide): 3.8MM Privately Held
SIC: 2759 7311 Commercial printing; advertising agencies
PA: Jack Batdorss
  22405 18 Mile Rd
  Big Rapids MI 49307
  231 796-4831

(G-10903)
JACKPINE PRESS INCORPORATED (PA)
Also Called: Jackpine Business Center
76 Filer St (49660-2717)
PHONE..................231 723-8344
Jeff Trucks, *President*
Lee Trucks, *Vice Pres*
Sally Koon, *Admin Sec*
Jim Dumas, *Technician*
EMP: 15 **EST:** 1977
SQ FT: 12,000
SALES (est): 3.1MM Privately Held
WEB: www.jackpine.com
SIC: 5943 5999 2752 Office forms & supplies; business machines & equipment; commercial printing, offset

(G-10904)
LIQUID DUSTLAYER INC
3320 Grant Hwy (49660-9477)
PHONE..................231 723-3750
Richard C Rademaker, *President*
Tina Rademaker, *Admin Sec*
EMP: 6 **EST:** 1941
SQ FT: 10,000
SALES (est): 813.2K Privately Held
WEB: www.liquiddustlayer.com
SIC: 2819 Calcium chloride & hypochlorite

(G-10905)
MANISTEE NEWS ADVOCATE
75 Maple St (49660-1554)
PHONE..................231 723-3592
EMP: 16 **EST:** 2007
SALES (est): 675.7K Privately Held
SIC: 2741 Misc Publishing

(G-10906)
MANISTEE WLDG & PIPING SVC INC (PA)
325 Oak Grove St (49660-1121)
PHONE..................231 723-2551
George Edmondson, *President*
Reta Racine, *Corp Secy*
EMP: 7 **EST:** 1952
SQ FT: 3,500
SALES (est): 1.6MM Privately Held
SIC: 1541 7692 3498 3441 Renovation, remodeling & repairs: industrial buildings; welding repair; fabricated pipe & fittings; fabricated structural metal; blast furnaces & steel mills

(G-10907)
MARTIN MRETTA MAGNESIA SPC LLC
1800 E Lake Rd (49660-9394)
P.O. Box 398 (49660-0398)
PHONE..................231 723-2577
Matt Rosenthal, *Vice Pres*
Tim Tritten, *Project Engr*
Jim Reithel, *Branch Mgr*
Kurt Preibisch, *Manager*
John Feliczak, *Technical Staff*
EMP: 22 Publicly Held
WEB: www.magnesiaspecialties.com
SIC: 3297 Cement, magnesia
HQ: Martin Marietta Magnesia Specialties, Llc
  755 Lime Rd
  Woodville OH 43469
  419 849-4223

(G-10908)
MERRITT ENERGY
4000 Fisk Rd (49660-9750)
PHONE..................231 723-6587
Bill Loney, *Manager*
EMP: 6 **EST:** 2017
SALES (est): 90.7K Privately Held
WEB: www.meritenergy.com
SIC: 2911 Petroleum refining

(G-10909)
MI FROZEN FOOD LLC
Also Called: Michigan Farm To Freezer
33 Lake St (49660-1437)
P.O. Box 7069, Detroit (48207-0069)
PHONE..................231 357-4334
Brandon Seng, *Mng Member*
EMP: 7 **EST:** 2016
SQ FT: 100
SALES (est): 600K Privately Held
WEB: www.mifarmtofreezer.com
SIC: 2037 Frozen fruits & vegetables

(G-10910)
MORTON SALT INC
180 6th St (49660-3000)
PHONE..................231 398-0758
Michael Ganger, *QC Mgr*
Candace Owens, *Human Res Mgr*
Phil Carlton, *Branch Mgr*
Dave Slivka, *Executive Asst*
Robert Kinney, *Maintence Staff*
EMP: 5
SALES (corp-wide): 701.2MM Privately Held
WEB: www.mortonsalt.com
SIC: 2899 Salt
HQ: Morton Salt, Inc.
  444 W Lake St Ste 3000
  Chicago IL 60606

(G-10911)
PERFECT SIGNS
338 4th St (49660-2932)
PHONE..................231 233-3721
Bruce Schaub, *Owner*
Jeneva Schaub, *Co-Owner*
EMP: 7 **EST:** 2010
SALES (est): 207.6K Privately Held
SIC: 3993 Signs & advertising specialties

(G-10912)
ROBERT GENTZ FOREST PDTS INC (PA)
9644 Guenthardt Rd (49660-9362)
PHONE..................231 398-9194
Robert Gentz, *President*
David Gentz, *Vice Pres*
Duane Gentz, *Vice Pres*
Paula Gentz, *Vice Pres*
EMP: 17 **EST:** 1990
SALES (est): 2MM Privately Held
SIC: 2411 Saw logs; pulpwood contractors engaged in cutting; wood chips, produced in the field

(G-10913)
SPORTS INK SCREEN PRTG EMB LLC
316 W Parkdale Ave (49660-1132)
PHONE..................231 723-5696
Sharon Monnot, *Owner*
EMP: 4 **EST:** 2005
SALES (est): 280.5K Privately Held
WEB: www.sportsinkmanistee.com
SIC: 2752 5699 Commercial printing, lithographic; designers, apparel

(G-10914)
UBLY BEAN KNIFE MFG INC
1388 Hill Rd (49660-1021)
PHONE..................231 723-3244
John E Misico, *President*
EMP: 4 **EST:** 1986 Privately Held
WEB: www.ublybean.com
SIC: 3523 Farm machinery & equipment

(G-10915)
WAUB AJIJAAK PRESS
281 1st Ave (49660-2675)
PHONE..................248 802-8630
Lapointe R Cecelia, *Owner*
EMP: 5 **EST:** 2016
SALES (est): 69.2K Privately Held
WEB: www.waubajijaak.org
SIC: 2741 Miscellaneous publishing

Manistique
Schoolcraft County

(G-10916)
ADVISOR INC
311 Oak St (49854-1409)
P.O. Box 99 (49854-0099)
PHONE..................906 341-2424
John J Ozanich, *President*
EMP: 6 **EST:** 1948
SALES (est): 4.5MM Privately Held
WEB: www.greatnorthernconn.com
SIC: 2721 Periodicals

(G-10917)
BOSANIC LWRNCE SONS TMBER PDTS
1840n W Kendall Rd (49854-9159)
PHONE..................906 341-5609
Lawrence Bosanic, *Owner*
Greg Bosanic, *Manager*
Greggguy Bosanic, *Manager*
Steave Bosanic, *Manager*
EMP: 8 **EST:** 1975
SALES (est): 600K Privately Held
SIC: 2411 Logging camps & contractors

(G-10918)
FOUR SEASONS PUBLISHING INC
Also Called: Manistique Pioneer Tribune
212 Walnut St (49854-1445)
PHONE..................906 341-5200
Richard Demers, *Principal*
EMP: 7 **EST:** 1998
SALES (est): 500.6K Privately Held
SIC: 2711 Commercial printing & newspaper publishing combined

(G-10919)
JOE BOSANIC FOREST PRODUCTS
1808 Nw Kendall Rd (49854)
PHONE..................906 341-2037
Joseph Bosanic, *Owner*
EMP: 7 **EST:** 1993

SALES (est): 460.6K Privately Held
SIC: 2411 Skidding logs

(G-10920)
JOSEPH LAKOSKY LOGGING
Also Called: Excavation
10502w Government Rd (49854-9383)
PHONE..................906 573-2783
Joseph Lakosky, *Owner*
EMP: 7 **EST:** 1978
SALES (est): 781.3K Privately Held
SIC: 2411 Logging camps & contractors; veneer logs

(G-10921)
MANISTIQUE RENTALS INC
415 Chippewa Ave (49854-1350)
PHONE..................906 341-6955
Elizabeth Slining, *Corp Secy*
George James Slining Jr, *Vice Pres*
David Slining, *Foreman/Supr*
Debbie Musgrave, *Persnl Mgr*
EMP: 5 **EST:** 1966
SQ FT: 18,000
SALES (est): 1MM Privately Held
SIC: 3273 4953 Ready-mixed concrete; refuse collection & disposal services

(G-10922)
NORTHFORK READI MIX INC
5665w Us Highway 2 (49854-9211)
PHONE..................906 341-3445
Brian Skok, *President*
EMP: 6 **EST:** 2006
SALES (est): 669.9K Privately Held
WEB: www.northforkconstruction.com
SIC: 3273 Ready-mixed concrete

(G-10923)
ONLINE ENGINEERING INC
400 N Cedar St (49854-1250)
PHONE..................906 341-0090
James Gardener, *President*
Renae Kennedy, *Business Mgr*
Marilyn Gardener, *Vice Pres*
EMP: 19 **EST:** 1986
SQ FT: 11,000
SALES (est): 2.5MM Privately Held
WEB: www.online-engineering.com
SIC: 3823 3559 Industrial instrmnts msrmnt display/control process variable; screening equipment, electric

(G-10924)
U P FABRICATING CO INC
Manistique Machine
342 Elm St (49854-1247)
PHONE..................906 341-2868
Mike Mahoney, *Engineer*
Leah Rourke, *Payroll Mgr*
Scott Carey, *Manager*
EMP: 5
SALES (corp-wide): 6.7MM Privately Held
WEB: www.upfab.com
SIC: 3599 Machine shop, jobbing & repair
PA: U. P. Fabricating Co. Inc.
  120 Us Highway 41 E Ste A
  Negaunee MI 49866
  906 475-4400

Manitou Beach
Lenawee County

(G-10925)
24 CANVAS
4335 Geneva Hwy (49253-9815)
PHONE..................517 902-5870
EMP: 4 **EST:** 2013
SALES (est): 63.5K Privately Held
SIC: 2211 Canvas

(G-10926)
AFFORDABLE HEAT LLC
2068 Marsh Dr (49253-9750)
PHONE..................517 673-0404
Kraig Cole, *Principal*
EMP: 6
SALES (est): 312K Privately Held
SIC: 3639 Household appliances

Manitou Beach - Lenawee County

(G-10927)
HARDY-REED TOOL & DIE CO INC
Also Called: Kbd Properties
16269 Manitou Beach Rd (49253-9649)
PHONE................................517 547-7107
Scott Strodtman, *President*
Debbie Isenhower, *Office Mgr*
Debra Isenhower, *Office Mgr*
EMP: 20 **EST:** 1960
SQ FT: 13,800
SALES (est): 1.2MM Privately Held
WEB: www.hardyreedtool.com
SIC: 3544 3599 3545 Die sets for metal stamping (presses); custom machinery; tools & accessories for machine tools

(G-10928)
STRIKER TOOLS LLC
210 Park St (49253-9123)
P.O. Box 206 (49253-0206)
PHONE................................248 990-7767
Kelly Nielsen, *CEO*
Margaret Cunningham, *President*
Jami Miller, *CFO*
EMP: 6 **EST:** 2012
SALES (est): 421.3K Privately Held
WEB: www.strikertool.com
SIC: 3546 7389 Hammers, portable: electric or pneumatic, chipping, etc.; business services

Manton
Wexford County

(G-10929)
ALLEN WHITEHOUSE
Also Called: Whitehouse Logging & Hardwood
1270 E 16 1/2 Rd (49663-9721)
PHONE................................231 824-3000
Allen Whitehouse, *Owner*
EMP: 5 **EST:** 2001
SALES (est): 232.4K Privately Held
SIC: 2411 Logging camps & contractors

(G-10930)
BRASS KINGS INC
11725 N Hilbrand Rd (49663-9358)
PHONE................................248 674-1860
Mike Collins, *President*
EMP: 5 **EST:** 1976
SALES (est): 125.2K Privately Held
WEB: www.brass-kings-inc.clarkston.mi.ammunition.tel.com
SIC: 3482 Small arms ammunition

(G-10931)
DANNY K BUNDY
2630 E 16 1/2 Rd (49663-9719)
PHONE................................231 590-6924
Danny K Bundy, *Principal*
EMP: 5 **EST:** 2010
SALES (est): 110.4K Privately Held
SIC: 2411 Logging camps & contractors

(G-10932)
DARREN MCCAFFERY STUCCO
10329 E 20 Rd (49663-9535)
PHONE................................321 303-0988
Darren McCaffery, *Principal*
EMP: 9 **EST:** 2008
SALES (est): 791.5K Privately Held
SIC: 3299 Stucco

(G-10933)
DJL LOGGING INC
5905 N Brown Rd (49663-9090)
PHONE................................231 590-2012
Dustin Lutke, *Principal*
EMP: 5 **EST:** 2013
SALES (est): 316.6K Privately Held
SIC: 2411 Logging

(G-10934)
JASON LUTKE
Also Called: Lutke Forest Products
615 Rw Harris Dr (49663)
PHONE................................231 824-6655
Jason Lutke, *Owner*
EMP: 50 **EST:** 1997
SALES (est): 8.2MM Privately Held
WEB: www.lutkeequipment.com
SIC: 2411 Logging camps & contractors

(G-10935)
LUTKE HYDRAULICS
606 R W Harris Dr (49663-9775)
PHONE................................231 824-9505
James Sutterfield, *Owner*
EMP: 5 **EST:** 2008
SALES (est): 261.9K Privately Held
WEB: www.lutkehydraulics.com
SIC: 3511 Turbines & turbine generator sets

(G-10936)
LUTKE WELDING LLC
7419 N 45 Rd (49663-8554)
PHONE................................231 590-6565
Jayme Lutke, *Mng Member*
EMP: 7 **EST:** 2005
SALES (est): 275.4K Privately Held
SIC: 7692 Welding repair

(G-10937)
MINI STORAGE OF MANTON
656 R W Harris Dr (49663-9775)
P.O. Box 535 (49663-0535)
PHONE................................231 645-6727
EMP: 4 **EST:** 2019
SALES (est): 279.2K Privately Held
WEB: www.ministorageofmanton.com
SIC: 3448 Prefabricated metal buildings

(G-10938)
MOVING & SHIPPING SOLUTIONS
3485 N Brown Rd (49663-9304)
PHONE................................231 824-4190
Cynthia Sisson, *Principal*
EMP: 6 **EST:** 2016
SALES (est): 90.7K Privately Held
SIC: 2656 Sanitary food containers

(G-10939)
WILDCAT BUILDINGS INC
656 Rw Hrris Indus Prk Dr (49663)
PHONE................................231 824-6406
Janet M Triplett, *President*
Tim Loving, *Vice Pres*
Taylor Ulrich, *Vice Pres*
Lisa Kimbel, *Admin Sec*
EMP: 15 **EST:** 1980
SQ FT: 4,000
SALES (est): 3.3MM Privately Held
WEB: www.wildcatbuildings.com
SIC: 3448 Buildings, portable: prefabricated metal

Maple City
Leelanau County

(G-10940)
BINSFELD ENGINEERING INC
4571 Mcfarlane Rd (49664-9673)
PHONE................................231 334-4383
Stephen B Tarsa, *CEO*
Michael W Binsfeld, *President*
Dan Daigger, *Mfg Staff*
Randy Pattison, *Production*
Yvonne Mead, *Accounting Mgr*
EMP: 8 **EST:** 1971
SQ FT: 4,000 Privately Held
WEB: www.binsfeld.com
SIC: 3823 8711 Industrial process measurement equipment; consulting engineer

(G-10941)
ENCORE MUSIC PUBLISHERS
399 W Harbour Ridge Ct (49664-8799)
PHONE................................231 432-8322
EMP: 4 **EST:** 2019
SALES (est): 51.7K Privately Held
WEB: www.encoremupub.com
SIC: 2741 Miscellaneous publishing

(G-10942)
KASSON SAND & GRAVEL CO INC
10282 S Pierce Rd (49664-9742)
P.O. Box 210 (49664-0210)
PHONE................................231 228-5455
Robert W Noonan, *President*
EMP: 18 **EST:** 1959
SQ FT: 2,800
SALES (est): 2.1MM Privately Held
SIC: 1442 Construction sand mining; gravel mining

(G-10943)
LEELANAU REDI-MIX INC
Also Called: Leelanau Redi-Mix & Gravel
12488 S Newman Rd (49664-9734)
PHONE................................231 228-5005
Marilyn Flaska, *President*
Charles Flaska, *Chairman*
Elizabeth Warnes, *Treasurer*
Jerry Flaska, *Manager*
EMP: 41 **EST:** 1950
SQ FT: 4,000
SALES (est): 4.3MM Privately Held
WEB: www.leelanau-redi-mix-inc.business.site
SIC: 3273 3272 1771 Ready-mixed concrete; tanks, concrete; flooring contractor

(G-10944)
MAPLE VALLEY PALLET CO
9285 S Nash Rd (49664-9746)
P.O. Box 134 (49664-0134)
PHONE................................231 228-6641
Everett Lautner, *Partner*
Janice Lautner, *Partner*
EMP: 10 **EST:** 1980
SQ FT: 13,800
SALES (est): 116.2K Privately Held
SIC: 2448 Pallets, wood

Maple Rapids
Clinton County

(G-10945)
KYMORA KANDLES LLC
Also Called: Kandle Shack, The
306 E Union St (48853-5004)
PHONE................................517 667-6067
EMP: 6 **EST:** 2017
SALES (est): 164.5K Privately Held
WEB: www.kymorakandles.com
SIC: 3999 Candles

Marcellus
Cass County

(G-10946)
CB MARCELLUS METALCASTERS INC
214 E Read St (49067-9582)
PHONE................................269 646-0202
Caitlin McMahan, *Principal*
Brad Ade, *Principal*
EMP: 13 **EST:** 2019
SALES (est): 534.1K Privately Held
SIC: 3322 Malleable iron foundries

(G-10947)
FAB MASTERS COMPANY INC
51787 M 40 (49067-8718)
P.O. Box 278 (49067-0278)
PHONE................................269 646-5315
Ronald L Troxell, *President*
Gail Klein, *Corp Secy*
Brian Phillips, *Prdtn Mgr*
Kim Fox, *Manager*
Kimberly Huskey, *Manager*
EMP: 100 **EST:** 1984
SQ FT: 59,000
SALES (est): 18.7MM Privately Held
WEB: www.fabmasters.net
SIC: 3441 Fabricated structural metal

(G-10948)
FAITH PLASTICS LLC
239 E Main St (49067-5103)
P.O. Box 217 (49067-0217)
PHONE................................269 646-2294
Joe Occhipiniti, *President*
Laura Occhipiniti, *Vice Pres*
EMP: 30 **EST:** 2000
SQ FT: 14,000
SALES (est): 5.3MM Privately Held
SALES (corp-wide): 73.8MM Privately Held
WEB: www.faithplastics.com
SIC: 3089 Injection molding of plastics
PA: Gdc, Inc.
815 Logan St
Goshen IN 46528
574 533-3128

(G-10949)
MARCELLUS METALCASTERS INC
214 E Read St (49067-9582)
P.O. Box 182 (49067-0182)
PHONE................................269 646-0202
Andrew Abrams, *President*
Angela Townley, *Office Mgr*
Sally Abrams, *Admin Sec*
EMP: 10 **EST:** 1997
SQ FT: 11,000
SALES (est): 1.1MM Privately Held
WEB: www.marcellus-metalcasters.com
SIC: 3366 Castings (except die)

(G-10950)
PLASTICS BY DESIGN INC
13300 Shannon St (49067-9800)
P.O. Box 220 (49067-0220)
PHONE................................269 646-3388
Ronald E Kish, *Owner*
EMP: 5 **EST:** 2006
SALES (est): 340K Privately Held
WEB: www.plasticsbydesigninc.com
SIC: 3089 Injection molding of plastics

(G-10951)
POWCO INC
56165 Moorlag Rd (49067-9525)
PHONE................................269 646-5385
L Judson Brown, *President*
EMP: 10 **EST:** 1978
SQ FT: 30,000
SALES (est): 748.5K Privately Held
SIC: 3479 Coating of metals & formed products

(G-10952)
SPEED CINCH INC
22724 96th Ave (49067-9700)
P.O. Box 739 (49067-0739)
PHONE................................269 646-2016
James R Bainbridge, *President*
Cindy Peague, *General Mgr*
▼ **EMP:** 4 **EST:** 2013
SQ FT: 4,000
SALES (est): 500K Privately Held
SIC: 3089 Injection molding of plastics

(G-10953)
TRI-STAR MOLDING INC
51540 M 40 (49067-7717)
PHONE................................269 646-0062
Nick Dekoning, *Co-Owner*
David McMorrow, *Co-Owner*
Tim Dekoning, *Purchasing*
EMP: 46 **EST:** 1995
SQ FT: 33,000
SALES (est): 10.3MM Privately Held
WEB: www.tristarmolding.com
SIC: 3089 Injection molding of plastics

Marine City
St. Clair County

(G-10954)
AMERICAN INDUS MCHINERY-MC LLC
2026 S Parker St (48039-2340)
PHONE................................810 420-0949
Gary Corrigan, *Mng Member*
EMP: 7 **EST:** 2020
SALES (est): 616.1K Privately Held
WEB: www.aimmachinery.com
SIC: 3499 Fabricated metal products

(G-10955)
B ERICKSON MANUFACTURING LTD
6317 King Rd (48039-1428)
P.O. Box 934, New Baltimore (48047-0934)
PHONE................................810 765-1144
Brent Erickson, *President*

GEOGRAPHIC SECTION

Marlette - Sanilac County (G-10982)

Constance Erickson, *Corp Secy*
▲ **EMP:** 10 **EST:** 1989
SQ FT: 100
SALES (est): 2MM **Privately Held**
WEB: www.ericksonmfg.com
SIC: 2241 Strapping webs

(G-10956)
BUTLER PLASTICS COMPANY
766 Degurse Ave (48039-1526)
P.O. Box 100 (48039-0100)
PHONE..................................810 765-8811
Kelly Drummond, *President*
Kevin Drummond, *Vice Pres*
Kristy Domerese, *Engineer*
▼ **EMP:** 29 **EST:** 1962
SQ FT: 15,000
SALES (est): 2.8MM **Privately Held**
WEB: www.butlerplastics.com
SIC: 3089 Injection molding of plastics

(G-10957)
CUSTOM METAL WORKS INC
316 S Belle River Ave # 11 (48039-3562)
PHONE..................................810 420-0390
Robert B Peterson, *President*
Kitty Emery, *Office Mgr*
EMP: 4 **EST:** 1960
SQ FT: 10,000
SALES (est): 319.2K **Privately Held**
SIC: 3444 Booths, spray: prefabricated sheet metal; sheet metal specialties, not stamped

(G-10958)
FISHER-BAKER CORPORATION
420 S Water St (48039-1690)
P.O. Box 248 (48039-0248)
PHONE..................................810 765-3548
Virginia Ladensack, *President*
Robert J Baker, *Vice Pres*
▲ **EMP:** 6 **EST:** 1973
SALES (est): 1.2MM **Privately Held**
WEB: www.fisherbaker.com
SIC: 5084 3647 Industrial machinery & equipment; automotive lighting fixtures

(G-10959)
INTELLICHEM LLC
887 Chartier (48039-2324)
PHONE..................................810 765-4075
Jamey Westrick, *Purch Agent*
Mike Westrick,
Michael Westrick,
EMP: 10 **EST:** 2012
SALES (est): 1MM **Privately Held**
WEB: www.intelli-chem.com
SIC: 3569 Lubrication equipment, industrial

(G-10960)
ISLAND MACHINE AND ENGRG LLC
847 Degurse Ave (48039-1532)
P.O. Box 247 (48039-0247)
PHONE..................................810 765-8228
Tony Skudrna, *Mng Member*
EMP: 8 **EST:** 1993
SQ FT: 5,000
SALES (est): 998.2K **Privately Held**
WEB: www.island-machine.com
SIC: 8711 7699 3599 Engineering services; industrial equipment services; machine shop, jobbing & repair

(G-10961)
KLINGLER CONSULTING & MFG
Also Called: Rockford Carving Co
837 Degurse Ave (48039-1532)
PHONE..................................810 765-3700
Robert Klingler, *President*
Sara Klinger, *Admin Sec*
▲ **EMP:** 12 **EST:** 1984
SQ FT: 50,000
SALES (est): 1.5MM **Privately Held**
WEB: www.rockfordcarving.com
SIC: 3931 Saxophones & parts

(G-10962)
MECHANICAL FABRICATORS INC
770 Degurse Ave (48039-1526)
PHONE..................................810 765-8853
Jeff Colman, *President*
Carl Colman, *Vice Pres*
EMP: 25 **EST:** 1961
SQ FT: 10,000

SALES (est): 2.9MM **Privately Held**
SIC: 3441 Building components, structural steel

(G-10963)
MIDWEST FBRGLAS FBRICATORS INC
1796 S Parker St (48039-2337)
PHONE..................................810 765-7445
Anthony Simon, *President*
Anne Costello, *Vice Pres*
EMP: 10 **EST:** 1930
SQ FT: 30,000
SALES (est): 990.5K **Privately Held**
WEB: www.midwestfiberglas.com
SIC: 3053 3296 Gaskets, packing & sealing devices; fiberglass insulation

(G-10964)
PRO RELEASE INC
420 S Water St 275 (48039-1690)
PHONE..................................810 512-4120
Gary J Todd, *President*
▲ **EMP:** 5 **EST:** 1981
SQ FT: 8,000
SALES (est): 441.7K **Privately Held**
WEB: www.prorelease.com
SIC: 3949 Archery equipment, general; bows, archery

(G-10965)
RIVERSIDE SPLINE & GEAR INC
1390 S Parker St (48039-2334)
P.O. Box 340 (48039-0340)
PHONE..................................810 765-8302
Wayne Forest, *President*
Aaron Forest, *Vice Pres*
Valerie Forest, *Vice Pres*
Jeff Krause, *Mfg Mgr*
Jamie Kaatz, *Opers Staff*
EMP: 35 **EST:** 1964
SQ FT: 20,700
SALES (est): 4.4MM **Privately Held**
WEB: www.splineandgear.com
SIC: 3462 3568 3541 3545 Gear & chain forgings; power transmission equipment; machine tools, metal cutting type; machine tool accessories; paints & allied products

(G-10966)
SELECTIVE INDUSTRIES INC
6100 King Rd (48039-1401)
PHONE..................................810 765-4666
John Osterman, *CEO*
Michael Osterman, *President*
Brian Burns, *General Mgr*
David Soboleski, *Production*
Don Tatum, *Engineer*
EMP: 85 **EST:** 1972
SQ FT: 24,000
SALES (est): 9.8MM **Privately Held**
WEB: www.selectiveinc.com
SIC: 3469 Stamping metal for the trade

(G-10967)
THEUT PRODUCTS INC
1910 S Parker St (48039-2339)
PHONE..................................810 765-9321
David Theut, *Branch Mgr*
EMP: 7
SALES (corp-wide): 15.7MM **Privately Held**
WEB: www.theutproductsinc.com
SIC: 3273 Ready-mixed concrete
PA: Theut Products, Inc.
73408 Van Dyke Rd
Bruce Twp MI 48065
586 752-4541

(G-10968)
USMATS INC
Also Called: Woodcraft Industries
6347 King Rd (48039-1428)
P.O. Box 455, Algonac (48001-0455)
PHONE..................................810 765-4545
Dale Nevison, *President*
Anna Nevison, *Treasurer*
EMP: 8 **EST:** 1941
SQ FT: 10,000
SALES (est): 644K **Privately Held**
WEB: www.usmats.com
SIC: 2273 Carpets & rugs

(G-10969)
WM KLOEFFLER INDUSTRIES INC
Also Called: Kloeffler, Wm Industries
6033 King Rd (48039-1403)
PHONE..................................810 765-4068
William H Kloeffler Jr, *President*
Gail Kloeffler, *Admin Sec*
EMP: 8 **EST:** 1966
SQ FT: 18,000
SALES (est): 659.4K **Privately Held**
SIC: 7692 3441 2599 3444 Welding repair; fabricated structural metal; stools, factory; sheet metalwork

(G-10970)
WORSWICK MOLD & TOOL INC
6232 King Rd (48039-1400)
P.O. Box 308 (48039-0308)
PHONE..................................810 765-1700
Stanley Worswick, *President*
Sharon Worswick, *Vice Pres*
Dawn Prowse, *Treasurer*
EMP: 10 **EST:** 1974
SQ FT: 22,000
SALES (est): 917.8K **Privately Held**
WEB: www.worswickmold.com
SIC: 3089 3544 Injection molded finished plastic products; special dies & tools

Marion
Osceola County

(G-10971)
CENTRAL WOOD AND STRAPPING
7300 18 Mile Rd (49665-8330)
PHONE..................................231 743-2800
EMP: 5 **EST:** 2020
SALES (est): 65.4K **Privately Held**
SIC: 2493 Reconstituted wood products

(G-10972)
LAYLINE OIL AND GAS LLC
135 E Main St (49665-9642)
P.O. Box 310 (49665-0310)
PHONE..................................231 743-2452
Christopher Lewis, *Principal*
EMP: 16 **EST:** 2019
SALES (est): 5.1MM **Privately Held**
SIC: 1389 Oil & gas field services

(G-10973)
LOCK AND LOAD CORP
3390 16 Mile Rd (49665-8414)
PHONE..................................800 975-9658
EMP: 4
SALES (est): 330K **Privately Held**
SIC: 2448 3537 3499 Mfg Wood Pallets/Skids Mfg Industrial Trucks/Tractors Mfg Misc Fabricated Metal Products

(G-10974)
MARION PALLET
7414 20 Mile Rd (49665-8440)
PHONE..................................231 743-6124
Daniel Beachy, *Principal*
EMP: 5 **EST:** 2008
SALES (est): 78.5K **Privately Held**
SIC: 2448 Pallets, wood & wood with metal

(G-10975)
NIVERS SAND GRAVEL
19937 M 115 (49665-8078)
PHONE..................................231 743-6126
Don Nivers, *Owner*
EMP: 5 **EST:** 1996
SALES (est): 117K **Privately Held**
SIC: 1442 Construction sand & gravel

(G-10976)
POLLINGTON MACHINE TOOL INC
Also Called: Buck Pole Archery Deerranch
20669 30th Ave (49665-8305)
PHONE..................................231 743-2003
Claude S Pollington, *President*
Ross Richards, *Treasurer*
Penny Miller, *Admin Sec*
▲ **EMP:** 30 **EST:** 1967
SQ FT: 20,000

SALES (est): 6.3MM **Privately Held**
WEB: www.pollingtonmachinetool.com
SIC: 3599 3544 Custom machinery; special dies, tools, jigs & fixtures

Marlette
Sanilac County

(G-10977)
B&T LOGGING
4619 Frenchline Rd (48453-8784)
PHONE..................................810 417-6167
Tyler Hobson, *Principal*
EMP: 5 **EST:** 2019
SALES (est): 89.8K **Privately Held**
SIC: 2411 Logging camps & contractors

(G-10978)
BARTLETT MANUFACTURING CO LLC
Also Called: Bartlett Arborist Sup & Mfrs
7876 S Van Dyke Rd Ste 10 (48453-9207)
PHONE..................................989 635-8900
EMP: 6
SQ FT: 20,000
SALES (est): 1.2MM **Privately Held**
SIC: 3423 Mfg Tree Trimming Hand Tools

(G-10979)
BEAGIOS FRANCHISES INC
Also Called: Beagio's 1
3013 Main St (48453-1232)
PHONE..................................989 635-7173
Edward G Herron, *President*
Janice Herron, *Vice Pres*
Johnna Parker, *Treasurer*
William Herron, *Admin Sec*
EMP: 6 **EST:** 1984
SALES (est): 275.7K **Privately Held**
SIC: 5812 2038 Pizza restaurants; delicatessen (eating places); pizza, frozen

(G-10980)
DGP INC
3260 Fenner St (48453-1229)
P.O. Box 155 (48453-0155)
PHONE..................................989 635-7531
Steve Quade, *President*
Chris Clark Jr, *Vice Pres*
Christopher G Clark, *Marketing Staff*
EMP: 21 **EST:** 1982
SQ FT: 26,000
SALES (est): 5.8MM **Privately Held**
WEB: www.dgpincorporated.com
SIC: 3296 4131 Fiberglass insulation; intercity & rural bus transportation

(G-10981)
EXPERNCED PRCSION MCHINING INC
2720 Lamotte St (48453-1034)
PHONE..................................989 635-2299
Keith P Mexico, *President*
Glenn Mexico, *Vice Pres*
Jim Mexico, *Vice Pres*
Betty Mexico, *Treasurer*
EMP: 6 **EST:** 1994
SALES (est): 836.1K **Privately Held**
SIC: 3714 3724 3599 Motor vehicle parts & accessories; aircraft engines & engine parts; machine shop, jobbing & repair

(G-10982)
GRUPO ANTOLIN MICHIGAN INC (DH)
6300 Euclid St (48453-1424)
PHONE..................................989 635-5055
Jesus Pascual Santos, *CEO*
Jesus Santos, *COO*
David Russell, *Safety Mgr*
Benjamin Chevallier, *Engineer*
Maria Victoria Hidalgo Castao, *CFO*
▲ **EMP:** 160 **EST:** 2003
SQ FT: 180,000
SALES (est): 75.5MM
SALES (corp-wide): 2.6MM **Privately Held**
WEB: www.grupoantolin.com
SIC: 3714 Motor vehicle body components & frame

HQ: Grupo Antolin North America, Inc.
1700 Atlantic Blvd
Auburn Hills MI 48326
248 373-1749

(G-10983)
LUPA R A AND SONS REPAIR
3580 Willis Rd (48453-9323)
PHONE..................810 346-3579
Roger A Lupa, *Owner*
EMP: 6 **EST:** 1988
SQ FT: 2,100
SALES (est): 423.4K **Privately Held**
SIC: 3715 7539 7538 Truck trailers; trailer repair; general truck repair

(G-10984)
M & B WELDING INC
6411 Euclid St (48453-1402)
P.O. Box 162 (48453-0162)
PHONE..................989 635-8017
Matthew Blatt, *President*
EMP: 6 **EST:** 1990
SQ FT: 10,000
SALES (est): 477K **Privately Held**
WEB: www.blattsteel.com
SIC: 7692 Welding repair

(G-10985)
MARINE INDUSTRIES INC
2900 Boyne Rd (48453-9773)
P.O. Box 368 (48453-0368)
PHONE..................989 635-3644
Lowell Driver, *President*
EMP: 18 **EST:** 1957
SQ FT: 34,000
SALES (est): 2.2MM **Privately Held**
WEB: www.marineind.net
SIC: 3429 Marine hardware

(G-10986)
MEN OF STEEL INC
2920 Municipal Dr (48453-1378)
P.O. Box 308 (48453-0308)
PHONE..................989 635-4866
Brian Vanderpool, *President*
Brian K Vanderpool, *President*
Lori A Vanderpool, *Treasurer*
EMP: 15 **EST:** 1996
SQ FT: 4,800
SALES (est): 1MM **Privately Held**
SIC: 1791 3441 Structural steel erection; fabricated structural metal

(G-10987)
SANILAC STEEL INC
2487 S Van Dyke Rd (48453-9781)
P.O. Box 185 (48453-0185)
PHONE..................989 635-2992
James O'Morrow, *President*
David Christensen, *Vice Pres*
James O'Morrow Jr, *Vice Pres*
EMP: 15 **EST:** 1967
SQ FT: 6,300
SALES (est): 2.8MM **Privately Held**
WEB: www.sanilacsteel.com
SIC: 3441 Fabricated structural metal

Marne
Ottawa County

(G-10988)
2 E FABRICATING
1202 Comstock St (49435-8750)
PHONE..................616 498-7036
EMP: 7 **EST:** 2013
SALES (est): 291.2K **Privately Held**
SIC: 3599 Machine shop, jobbing & repair

(G-10989)
AXIS ENTERPRISES INC
15300 8th Ave (49435-9610)
PHONE..................616 677-5281
Jon Dewys, *President*
C T Martin, *Vice Pres*
EMP: 9 **EST:** 1981
SALES (est): 188.3K **Privately Held**
SIC: 3965 Eyelets, metal: clothing, fabrics, boots or shoes

(G-10990)
BORGIA DIE & ENGINEERING INC
14750 Raymer Cir (49435)
P.O. Box 65 (49435-0065)
PHONE..................616 677-3595
Frank Borgia, *President*
Frank Borgia Sr, *Vice Pres*
James Marckini, *Admin Sec*
EMP: 11 **EST:** 1991
SQ FT: 7,000
SALES (est): 735.1K **Privately Held**
WEB: www.borgiacnc.com
SIC: 3544 Special dies & tools

(G-10991)
DEWYS MANUFACTURING INC (PA)
Also Called: American Grow Rack
15300 8th Ave (49435-9600)
PHONE..................616 677-5281
Jon Dewys, *CEO*
C T Martin, *President*
Mark Schoenborn, *COO*
Mike Chatterson, *Production*
Mike Stream, *Engineer*
▲ **EMP:** 169 **EST:** 1977
SQ FT: 90,000
SALES (est): 29.5MM **Privately Held**
WEB: www.dewysmfg.com
SIC: 3444 Sheet metalwork

(G-10992)
DIE-VERSE SOLUTIONS LLC
1174 Comstock St (49435-8801)
PHONE..................616 914-9427
EMP: 7 **EST:** 2013
SALES (est): 242.7K **Privately Held**
WEB: www.die-verse.com
SIC: 3544 Special dies & tools

(G-10993)
HATFIELD ENTERPRISES
15627 24th Ave (49435-8767)
PHONE..................616 677-5215
Dennis Hatfield, *Owner*
EMP: 6 **EST:** 2007
SALES (est): 80.5K **Privately Held**
SIC: 2048 Fish food

(G-10994)
JE MACHINING LLC
1045 Comstock St (49435-9603)
PHONE..................616 340-1786
EMP: 6 **EST:** 2015
SALES (est): 260.6K **Privately Held**
SIC: 3599 Machine shop, jobbing & repair

(G-10995)
LOG JAM FOREST PRODUCTS INC
Also Called: Lj Disposal
15342 24th Ave (49435-8766)
P.O. Box 98 (49435-0098)
PHONE..................616 677-2560
Richard Mellema, *President*
EMP: 5 **EST:** 1987
SALES (est): 477.3K **Privately Held**
WEB: www.logjamforestproducts.com
SIC: 3433 Logs, gas fireplace

(G-10996)
PARADIGM CONVEYOR LLC
15342 24th Ave (49435-8766)
P.O. Box 21 (49435-0021)
PHONE..................616 667-4040
Kenneth Alkema, *Mng Member*
EMP: 10 **EST:** 2012
SALES (est): 450K **Privately Held**
WEB: www.pdmconveyor.com
SIC: 3535 Conveyors & conveying equipment

(G-10997)
PARAMOUNT TOOL AND DIE INC
1245 Comstock St (49435-8750)
P.O. Box 120 (49435-0120)
PHONE..................616 677-0000
Robert Burnett, *President*
Todd Van Loon, *Vice Pres*
Cindee Nowicki, *Office Mgr*
EMP: 14 **EST:** 1997
SQ FT: 20,000
SALES (est): 2MM **Privately Held**
WEB: www.paratool.com
SIC: 3544 Industrial molds; special dies & tools

(G-10998)
R ANDREWS PALLET CO INC
1035 Comstock St (49435-9603)
PHONE..................616 677-3270
EMP: 10 **EST:** 1987
SQ FT: 12,000
SALES (est): 1.2MM **Privately Held**
SIC: 2448 5031 Mfg Wood Pallets/Skids Whol Lumber/Plywood/Millwork

(G-10999)
SOLAIRE MEDICAL STORAGE LLC
1239 Comstock St (49435-8750)
P.O. Box 2808, Grand Rapids (49501-2808)
PHONE..................888 435-2256
Benjamin Barber, *Principal*
Christopher Barber, *Principal*
Daniel Schroeder, *Vice Pres*
John Hanna, *Manager*
Jack Rub, *Manager*
EMP: 60 **EST:** 2011
SALES (est): 5.9MM **Privately Held**
WEB: www.innerspacehealthcare.com
SIC: 2426 5047 Turnings, furniture: wood; medical equipment & supplies

(G-11000)
UNDER PRESSURE PWR WASHERS LLC
885 Meyer Ln (49435-8637)
PHONE..................616 292-4289
Les Williamson, *Owner*
EMP: 4 **EST:** 2009
SALES (est): 65.7K **Privately Held**
SIC: 3452 Washers

(G-11001)
VAN RON STEEL SERVICES LLC
1100 Comstock St (49435-8753)
PHONE..................616 813-6907
Mark Vanportfliet,
EMP: 10 **EST:** 2003
SALES (est): 1.5MM **Privately Held**
SIC: 3315 Steel wire & related products

(G-11002)
VANS PATTERN CORP
11970 24th Ave (49435-9681)
PHONE..................616 364-9483
Daniel E Vandermolen, *CEO*
EMP: 19 **EST:** 1960
SALES (est): 1.5MM **Privately Held**
WEB: www.vanspattern.com
SIC: 3543 Industrial patterns

Marquette
Marquette County

(G-11003)
AL BECK
105 Poplar Trl (49855-9038)
PHONE..................906 249-1645
Al Beck, *CEO*
EMP: 5 **EST:** 2016
SALES (est): 61.9K **Privately Held**
SIC: 2252 Hosiery

(G-11004)
AMERICAN BLDRS CONTRS SUP INC
Also Called: ABC Supply 693
908 W Baraga Ave (49855-4029)
PHONE..................906 226-9665
Brian Russell, *Branch Mgr*
EMP: 8
SALES (corp-wide): 1.8B **Privately Held**
SIC: 2431 5031 Windows & window parts & trim, wood; lumber, plywood & millwork
HQ: American Builders & Contractors Supply Co., Inc.
1 Abc Pkwy
Beloit WI 53511
608 362-7777

(G-11005)
ASSRA
Also Called: Single Shot Rifle Journal
625 Pine St (49855-3723)
PHONE..................906 225-1828
John Merz, *President*
Dale McGee, *Vice Pres*
Richard Eeesley, *Treasurer*
Charles Persons, *Director*
Laurie Gapko, *Admin Sec*
EMP: 10 **EST:** 1948
SALES (est): 470.1K **Privately Held**
WEB: www.assra.com
SIC: 3949 Targets, archery & rifle shooting

(G-11006)
AUGUST LILIA FAMLY MEMORL FUND
1502 W Washington St (49855-3118)
PHONE..................906 228-6088
EMP: 4
SALES (est): 18.4K **Privately Held**
SIC: 2435 Hardwood veneer & plywood

(G-11007)
BINGHAM BOAT WORKS LTD
58 Middle Island Point Rd (49855-9726)
PHONE..................906 225-0050
Joe Bingham, *President*
EMP: 5 **EST:** 1930
SALES (est): 350K **Privately Held**
WEB: www.binghamboatworks.com
SIC: 3732 7699 Boat building & repairing; boat repair

(G-11008)
BLACKROCKS BREWERY LLC
950 W Washington St (49855-4019)
PHONE..................906 273-1333
EMP: 6 **Privately Held**
WEB: www.blackrocksbrewery.com
SIC: 2082 5813 Beer (alcoholic beverage); bars & lounges
PA: Blackrocks Brewery, Llc
424 N 3rd St
Marquette MI 49855

(G-11009)
BLACKROCKS BREWERY LLC (PA)
424 N 3rd St (49855-3555)
PHONE..................906 360-6674
David Manson, *Mng Member*
EMP: 6 **EST:** 2010
SQ FT: 2,000
SALES (est): 846.9K **Privately Held**
WEB: www.blackrocksbrewery.com
SIC: 5813 2082 Bars & lounges; beer (alcoholic beverage)

(G-11010)
BOOMERANG RETRO & RELICS
100 W Washington St (49855-4320)
PHONE..................906 362-7876
EMP: 6 **EST:** 2017
SALES (est): 47K **Privately Held**
WEB: www.boomerangretro.com
SIC: 3949 Boomerangs

(G-11011)
CABELL PUBLISHING LLC
467 Lakewood Ln (49855-9513)
PHONE..................906 361-6828
Brian Cabell, *Principal*
EMP: 5 **EST:** 2017
SALES (est): 72.5K **Privately Held**
WEB: www.wotsmqt.com
SIC: 2741 Miscellaneous publishing

(G-11012)
CHICAGO BLOW PIPE COMPANY
405 Lakewood Ln (49855-9510)
PHONE..................773 533-6100
EMP: 16 **EST:** 1919
SQ FT: 30,000
SALES (est): 3.9MM **Privately Held**
SIC: 3444 3714 3564 3443 Mfg Sheet Metalwork Mfg Motor Vehicle Parts Mfg Blowers/Fans Mfg Fabricated Plate Wrk Structural Metal Fabrctn

GEOGRAPHIC SECTION

Marquette - Marquette County (G-11042)

(G-11013)
CLAIR SAWYER
Also Called: Marquette Machining & Fabg
1225 W Washington St (49855-3111)
PHONE..................................906 228-8242
Clair Sawyer, *Owner*
EMP: 7 EST: 1962
SQ FT: 5,000
SALES (est): 535.1K **Privately Held**
SIC: 3599 7692 3441 Machine shop, jobbing & repair; welding repair; fabricated structural metal

(G-11014)
COMPUDYNE INC
925 W Washington St # 104 (49855-4061)
PHONE..................................906 360-9081
Adam Simonsen, *Sales Staff*
Thomas F Vidovic, *Branch Mgr*
EMP: 14 **Privately Held**
WEB: www.compudyne.com
SIC: 3571 Personal computers (microcomputers)
PA: Compudyne, Inc.
1524 E 37th St
Hibbing MN 55746

(G-11015)
DUQUAINE INCORPORATED
Also Called: Honeywell Authorized Dealer
1744 Presque Isle Ave (49855-2197)
PHONE..................................906 228-7290
Mark Duquaine, *President*
Karen Duquaine, *Admin Sec*
EMP: 9 EST: 1959
SQ FT: 5,800
SALES (est): 1.7MM **Privately Held**
WEB: www.duquaineinc.com
SIC: 1711 3469 Refrigeration contractor; kitchen fixtures & equipment: metal, except cast aluminum

(G-11016)
EASTSIDE SPOT INC
129 E Hewitt Ave (49855-3707)
PHONE..................................906 226-9431
Rich Pascoe, *President*
EMP: 5 EST: 2010
SALES (est): 157.4K **Privately Held**
WEB: www.g-mmarketing.com
SIC: 2082 Beer (alcoholic beverage)

(G-11017)
EMBROIDERY WEARHOUSE
2112 Us Highway 41 W # 3 (49855-2480)
PHONE..................................906 228-5818
Barbara Oneiol, *Owner*
EMP: 4 EST: 2006
SALES (est): 236.2K **Privately Held**
WEB: www.embwh.com
SIC: 2395 Embroidery products, except schiffli machine; embroidery & art needlework

(G-11018)
F & A ENTERPRISES OF MICHIGAN
Also Called: Fred's Rubber Stamp Shop
519 N Lakeshore Blvd (49855-3819)
PHONE..................................906 228-3222
Frederick M Warren, *President*
Audrey Warren, *Vice Pres*
EMP: 4 EST: 1977
SQ FT: 2,500
SALES (est): 256.3K **Privately Held**
WEB: www.fredsrubberstamp.com
SIC: 3953 2759 7389 2796 Marking devices; commercial printing; laminating service; platemaking services

(G-11019)
FRONTIER RNWABLE RESOURCES LLC (PA)
210 N Front St Ste 1 (49855-4200)
PHONE..................................906 228-7960
William J Brady, *CEO*
Stephen Hicks, *CFO*
Bruce Jamerson,
EMP: 4 EST: 2008
SALES (est): 566.6K **Privately Held**
SIC: 2869 Fuels

(G-11020)
HEIDTMAN LOGGING INC
748 County Road 550 (49855-9741)
PHONE..................................906 249-3914
John L Heidtman, *President*
John B Heidtman, *Director*
Gary A Heidtman, *Admin Sec*
EMP: 7 EST: 1970
SALES (est): 800K **Privately Held**
SIC: 2411 Logging camps & contractors

(G-11021)
INN SETTLE & SUITES
1275 Us Highway 41 W (49855-4053)
PHONE..................................214 606-3531
EMP: 5 EST: 2019
SALES (est): 42.5K **Privately Held**
SIC: 2371 Fur goods

(G-11022)
J AND W DOLPHIN LLC
385 Bishop Woods Rd (49855-8606)
PHONE..................................267 686-3713
Jill Leonard, *Agent*
EMP: 4 EST: 1980
SALES (est): 45.8K **Privately Held**
WEB: www.sshatco.com
SIC: 2353 Hats, caps & millinery

(G-11023)
J M LONGYEAR HEIRS INC (PA)
210 N Front St Ste 1 (49855-4200)
PHONE..................................906 228-7960
Rhonda Williams, *Manager*
Ralph M Roberts,
Rusell Bennett,
Charlotte Burton,
Catherine Springer,
EMP: 5 EST: 1964
SQ FT: 18,000
SALES (est): 2.6MM **Privately Held**
WEB: www.jmlongyear.com
SIC: 6519 1499 Real property lessors; precious stones mining

(G-11024)
JANDRON II
605 Couty Rd Hq (49855)
PHONE..................................906 225-9600
Neil Jandron, *Owner*
Kathie Jandron, *Co-Owner*
EMP: 9 EST: 2002
SALES (est): 677.6K **Privately Held**
SIC: 3479 Engraving jewelry silverware, or metal

(G-11025)
JG DISTRIBUTING INC
120 Morgan Meadows Rd (49855-8683)
PHONE..................................906 225-0882
John Manchester, *CEO*
EMP: 5 EST: 2003
SALES (est): 279.3K **Privately Held**
SIC: 3531 Snow plow attachments

(G-11026)
JM LONGYEAR LLC
210 N Front St Ste 1 (49855-4200)
PHONE..................................906 228-7960
Stephen J Hicks, *Vice Pres*
Dennis Cannoot, *Opers Spvr*
Karen D Anderson, *Asst Treas*
Marc Blom, *Finance*
Karen Anderson, *Manager*
EMP: 2 EST: 2005
SALES (est): 1.4MM **Privately Held**
WEB: www.jmlongyear.com
SIC: 2411 Timber, cut at logging camp

(G-11027)
LAKE SUPERIOR PRESS INC
802 S Lake St (49855-5224)
P.O. Box 308 (49855-0308)
PHONE..................................906 228-7450
Thomas E Dubow, *President*
EMP: 10 EST: 1973
SQ FT: 5,000
SALES (est): 654.8K **Privately Held**
WEB: www.lakesuperiorpress.net
SIC: 2752 Commercial printing, offset

(G-11028)
LANDERS DRAFTING INC
Also Called: Sign Solutions
105 Garfield Ave (49855-4013)
PHONE..................................906 228-8690
Dan Landers, *President*
Matt Landers, *Executive*
EMP: 5 EST: 1936
SQ FT: 2,000
SALES (est): 945.2K **Privately Held**
SIC: 7389 3993 Sign painting & lettering shop; electric signs

(G-11029)
LEUTZ ENTERPRISE INC
1200 Wright St Ste 4 (49855-1837)
PHONE..................................906 228-5887
Leutz Scott, *Administration*
EMP: 4 EST: 2014
SALES (est): 102.2K **Privately Held**
SIC: 3993 Signs & advertising specialties

(G-11030)
LEVI OHMAN MICAH
Also Called: Marquette Maple Company
320 W College Ave Apt 1 (49855-3055)
PHONE..................................612 251-1293
Micah Ohman, *Owner*
Garfield Bowen, *Publisher*
Kathy Christian, *Publisher*
Natasja Curtin, *Publisher*
Dawn Derossett, *Publisher*
EMP: 12 EST: 2014
SALES (est): 76.6K **Privately Held**
SIC: 2099 Maple syrup

(G-11031)
LIFESAFER
730 W Washington St (49855-4138)
PHONE..................................888 294-7002
EMP: 5 EST: 2017
SALES (est): 107.6K **Privately Held**
WEB: www.lifesafer.com
SIC: 3829 Measuring & controlling devices

(G-11032)
MAQUET MONTHLY
810 N 3rd St (49855-3502)
PHONE..................................906 226-6500
Patricia Ryan Oday, *President*
EMP: 5 EST: 1992
SALES (est): 389.8K **Privately Held**
WEB: www.marquettemonthly.com
SIC: 7313 2711 Newspaper advertising representative; newspapers

(G-11033)
MARQUETTE DISTILLERY
844 W Bluff St (49855-4122)
PHONE..................................906 869-4933
Chris Gale, *Principal*
EMP: 4 EST: 2015
SALES (est): 90.2K **Privately Held**
SIC: 2082 Malt beverages

(G-11034)
MARQUETTE FENCE COMPANY INC
1446 State Highway M28 E (49855-9562)
PHONE..................................906 249-8000
Robert L Northrup, *President*
Sam Garrow, *Manager*
EMP: 5 EST: 1978
SQ FT: 4,000
SALES (est): 784.3K **Privately Held**
WEB: www.marquettefence.com
SIC: 1799 3446 Fence construction; fences, gates, posts & flagpoles

(G-11035)
MATRIX CONSTRUCTION PDTS LLC
1760 Harbour View Dr (49855-5068)
P.O. Box 1211, Englewood CO (80150-1211)
PHONE..................................720 961-5454
John H Berry, *Principal*
EMP: 3
SALES (est): 2.1MM **Privately Held**
WEB: www.matrixcp.com
SIC: 2911 Fuel additives

(G-11036)
MINING JRNL BSNESS OFFC-DTRIAL
249 W Washington St (49855-4387)
P.O. Box 430 (49855-0430)
PHONE..................................906 228-2500
Fax: 906 228-2617
EMP: 20
SALES (est): 1.4MM **Privately Held**
SIC: 2711 Newspapers-Publishing/Printing

(G-11037)
MORRIS KALL INCORPORATED
2005 Wetton Ave (49855-1826)
PHONE..................................815 528-8665
Austin Morris, *CEO*
Troy Morris, *COO*
Adam Kall, *CFO*
EMP: 6 EST: 2019
SALES (est): 356K **Privately Held**
WEB: www.kallmorris.com
SIC: 3761 Guided missiles & space vehicles, research & development

(G-11038)
OGDEN NEWSPAPERS VIRGINIA LLC
Also Called: Action Shopper
249 W Washington St (49855-4321)
P.O. Box 430 (49855-0430)
PHONE..................................906 228-8920
Richard Havican, *Manager*
EMP: 11 **Privately Held**
WEB: www.ogdennews.com
SIC: 2711 Newspapers: publishing only, not printed on site
HQ: Ogden Newspapers Of Virginia, Llc
1500 Main St
Wheeling WV 26003
304 233-0100

(G-11039)
ORE DOCK BREWING COMPANY LLC
114 W Spring St (49855-4608)
PHONE..................................906 228-8888
Wes Pernsteiner, *Marketing Staff*
Weston Pernsteiner, *Mng Member*
EMP: 18 EST: 2011
SALES (est): 612.7K **Privately Held**
WEB: www.ore-dock.com
SIC: 5813 2082 Bars & lounges; beer (alcoholic beverage)

(G-11040)
PETERSON PUBLISHING INC
Also Called: Algen County Shopper
339 Alger St (49855-3310)
PHONE..................................906 387-3282
Willie J Peterson, *President*
EMP: 8 EST: 1945
SALES (est): 468.5K **Privately Held**
SIC: 2711 5943 Job printing & newspaper publishing combined; office forms & supplies

(G-11041)
PIONEER SURGICAL TECH INC (DH)
Also Called: Rti Surgical
375 River Park Cir (49855-1781)
PHONE..................................906 226-9909
Jeffery W Millin, *President*
M Shane Ray, *General Mgr*
Fred J Taccolini, *Principal*
Eric Baldwin, *COO*
Kelly Herriman, *Vice Pres*
EMP: 170 EST: 1992
SQ FT: 28,000
SALES (est): 112.8MM
SALES (corp-wide): 101.7MM **Publicly Held**
WEB: www.rtix.com
SIC: 3841 Surgical & medical instruments
HQ: Surgalign Spine Technologies, Inc.
520 Lake Cook Rd Ste 315
Deerfield IL 60015
630 227-3809

(G-11042)
PRIDE PRINTING INC
2847 Us Highway 41 W (49855-2252)
PHONE..................................906 228-8182
Richard Wester, *President*
EMP: 6 EST: 1985
SQ FT: 3,200
SALES (est): 479.2K **Privately Held**
WEB: www.prideprinting.ink
SIC: 2752 5199 Commercial printing, offset; advertising specialties

Marquette - Marquette County (G-11043)

(G-11043)
QUICKTROPHY LLC
446 E Crescent St (49855-3621)
PHONE..................906 228-2604
Terrence Dehring, *Mng Member*
▼ EMP: 15 EST: 2000
SQ FT: 14,000
SALES (est): 1.7MM **Privately Held**
WEB: www.quicktrophy.com
SIC: 3914 3993 5999 Trophies; signs & advertising specialties; trophies & plaques

(G-11044)
SUPERIOR ELC MTR SLS & SVC INC
Also Called: Superior Elc Mtr Sls & Svc
1740 Presque Isle Ave (49855-2196)
PHONE..................906 226-9051
Franklin Michael Smith, *President*
EMP: 7 EST: 1950
SQ FT: 4,940
SALES (est): 728.6K **Privately Held**
WEB: www.powerintheup.com
SIC: 7694 5063 Electric motor repair; rewinding stators; motors, electric

(G-11045)
SUPERIOR HOCKEY LLC (PA)
401 E Fair Ave (49855-2951)
PHONE..................906 225-9008
EMP: 15 EST: 2013
SALES (est): 419.9K **Privately Held**
WEB: www.superiorhockeymqt.com
SIC: 3949 Hockey equipment & supplies, general

(G-11046)
UP CATHOLIC NEWSPAPER
347 Rock St (49855-4725)
P.O. Box 1000 (49855-1000)
PHONE..................906 226-8821
Fax: 906 226-6941
EMP: 5 EST: 1946
SALES (est): 170K **Privately Held**
SIC: 2711 Newspapers-Publishing/Printing

(G-11047)
UP LURE COMPANY LLC
209 Jean St (49855-9242)
PHONE..................906 249-3526
Jacob Patterson, *Agent*
EMP: 5 EST: 2016
SALES (est): 68.1K **Privately Held**
SIC: 3949 Winter sports equipment

(G-11048)
UPPER PNNSULA PBLS ATHORS ASSN
126 Ridgewood Dr (49855-9336)
PHONE..................906 226-1543
EMP: 5 EST: 2019
SALES (est): 41.3K **Privately Held**
WEB: www.uppaa.org
SIC: 2741 Miscellaneous publishing

(G-11049)
WATTSSON & WATTSSON JEWELERS
Also Called: Dockside Imports
118 W Washington St # 100 (49855-4353)
PHONE..................906 228-5775
Ron Wattsson, *CEO*
Linda Wilson, *Vice Pres*
EMP: 7 EST: 1985
SQ FT: 18,000
SALES (est): 672.4K **Privately Held**
WEB: www.wandwjewelers.com
SIC: 5944 3911 7631 Jewelry, precious stones & precious metals; jewelry apparel; jewelry repair services

(G-11050)
WESTWOOD LANDS INC
220 W Washington St # 220 (49855-4345)
PHONE..................906 475-9544
Peter E Odovero, *President*
EMP: 10 EST: 2017
SALES (est): 321.5K **Privately Held**
SIC: 3312 Blast furnaces & steel mills

(G-11051)
YOOPER SHIRTS MQT
503 N 3rd St (49855-3517)
PHONE..................906 273-1837
EMP: 7 EST: 2017
SALES (est): 609.3K **Privately Held**
WEB: www.yoopershirts.com
SIC: 2759 Screen printing

Marshall
Calhoun County

(G-11052)
AUTOCAM CORPORATION
1511 George Brown Dr (49068-9596)
PHONE..................269 789-4000
Brian Simon, *Plant Mgr*
Stephen Mertel, *Engineer*
Mike Peters, *Engineer*
Jeff Goodman, *Manager*
EMP: 7
SALES (corp-wide): 427.5MM **Publicly Held**
WEB: www.autocam.com
SIC: 3714 Motor vehicle engines & parts
HQ: Autocam Corporation
 4180 40th St Se
 Kentwood MI 49512
 616 698-0707

(G-11053)
BORGWARNER THERMAL SYSTEMS INC (HQ)
Also Called: Borgwarner Automotive
1507 S Kalamazoo Ave (49068-8310)
PHONE..................269 781-1228
James R Verrier, *CEO*
Timothy M Manganello, *Chairman*
Robin J Adams, *Exec VP*
Jamal M Farhat, *Vice Pres*
Anthony D Hensel, *Vice Pres*
▲ EMP: 105 EST: 1999
SALES (est): 212.4MM
SALES (corp-wide): 10.1B **Publicly Held**
WEB: www.borgwarner.com
SIC: 3714 Motor vehicle parts & accessories
PA: Borgwarner Inc.
 3850 Hamlin Rd
 Auburn Hills MI 48326
 248 754-9200

(G-11054)
BOSTIK INC
205 W Oliver Dr (49068-9543)
PHONE..................269 781-8246
EMP: 9
SALES (corp-wide): 117MM **Privately Held**
WEB: www.bostik.com
SIC: 2992 2891 1731 Lubricating oils & greases; adhesives & sealants; electrical work
HQ: Bostik, Inc.
 11320 W Watertwn Plnk Rd
 Wauwatosa WI 53226
 414 774-2250

(G-11055)
CHELSEA MILLING COMPANY
C & S Carton Division
310 W Oliver Dr (49068-9506)
P.O. Box 70 (49068-0070)
PHONE..................269 781-2823
Donald Stephan, *Manager*
EMP: 14
SALES (corp-wide): 86.6MM **Privately Held**
WEB: www.site.jiffymix.com
SIC: 2652 5113 Boxes, newsboard, metal edged: made from purchased materials; bags, paper & disposable plastic
PA: Chelsea Milling Company
 201 W North St
 Chelsea MI 48118
 734 475-1361

(G-11056)
EATON CORPORATION
19218 B Dr S (49068-8600)
PHONE..................269 781-0200
Jeff Romig, *Vice Pres*
Clayton Ferguson, *Vice Pres*
Stacey Drumm, *Buyer*
Timothy Waxler, *Buyer*
Randy Graves, *Chief Engr*
EMP: 300 **Privately Held**
WEB: www.eatonelectrical.com
SIC: 3724 8734 Research & development on aircraft engines & parts; testing laboratories
HQ: Eaton Corporation
 1000 Eaton Blvd
 Cleveland OH 44122
 440 523-5000

(G-11057)
FABRILASER MFG LLC
1308 S Kalamazoo Ave (49068-1971)
PHONE..................269 789-9490
Mary L Dowding-Harris, *Vice Pres*
Ekaterina Harris, *Controller*
Joey Morales, *Sales Mgr*
Jerry Heisler, *Sales Staff*
Gregory Harris,
EMP: 20 EST: 2009
SALES (est): 2.5MM **Privately Held**
WEB: www.fabrilaser.com
SIC: 3699 3443 3444 5084 Laser systems & equipment; metal parts; forming machine work, sheet metal; welding machinery & equipment; metal cutting services

(G-11058)
FUG INC
315 Woolley Dr (49068-9500)
P.O. Box 305, Tekonsha (49092-0305)
PHONE..................269 781-8036
Donald Kujawa, *President*
EMP: 8 EST: 2012
SALES (est): 790K **Privately Held**
WEB: www.fugonline.com
SIC: 3993 2759 Signs & advertising specialties; screen printing

(G-11059)
GREAT LAKES METAL WORKS
819 Industrial Rd (49068-1744)
PHONE..................269 789-2342
Myron Katz, *President*
William Howard, *Vice Pres*
EMP: 5 EST: 1998
SALES (est): 409.2K **Privately Held**
WEB: www.greatlakesmetalarts.com
SIC: 3441 Fabricated structural metal

(G-11060)
HAZELTREE WOODWORKING
16191 N Dr S (49068-9275)
PHONE..................517 320-2954
Nathan Grabowski, *Principal*
EMP: 5 EST: 2014
SALES (est): 54.1K **Privately Held**
WEB: www.hazeltreewoodworking.com
SIC: 2431 Millwork

(G-11061)
J & L MANUFACTURING CO INC (PA)
1507 George Brown Dr (49068-9596)
P.O. Box 189 (49068-0189)
PHONE..................269 789-1507
Jim Dominique, *President*
Neal Harris, *Engineer*
Kristin Longyear, *Office Mgr*
▲ EMP: 35 EST: 1985
SQ FT: 1,000
SALES (est): 8MM **Privately Held**
SIC: 3498 Tube fabricating (contract bending & shaping)

(G-11062)
J-AD GRAPHICS INC
Community Ad-Visor
514 S Kalamazoo Ave (49068-1702)
P.O. Box 111 (49068-0111)
PHONE..................269 945-9554
John Jacobs, *President*
EMP: 8
SQ FT: 1,000
SALES (corp-wide): 15.1MM **Privately Held**
WEB: www.hastingsprintshop.com
SIC: 2741 2711 Guides: publishing & printing; commercial printing & newspaper publishing combined
PA: J-Ad Graphics, Inc.
 1351 N M 43 Hwy
 Hastings MI 49058
 800 870-7085

(G-11063)
JON MORRIS
914 Jones St (49068-1933)
PHONE..................269 967-2862
Jon Morris, *Principal*
EMP: 6 EST: 2010
SALES (est): 63.6K **Privately Held**
WEB: www.jmorrisvolleyballcamp.com
SIC: 3949 Nets: badminton, volleyball, tennis, etc.

(G-11064)
MARSHALL BLDG COMPONENTS CORP
1605 Brooks Dr (49068-9587)
P.O. Box 724 (49068-0724)
PHONE..................269 781-4236
Leigh Iobe, *President*
EMP: 38 EST: 1967
SQ FT: 13,000
SALES (est): 3.1MM **Privately Held**
SIC: 2439 Trusses, except roof: laminated lumber; trusses, wooden roof

(G-11065)
MARSHALL EXCELSIOR CO (HQ)
1506 George Brown Dr (49068-9596)
PHONE..................269 789-6700
Jeff Begg, *President*
Allen Begg, *Admin Sec*
◆ EMP: 48 EST: 1974
SQ FT: 25,000
SALES (est): 23.8MM
SALES (corp-wide): 1.2B **Privately Held**
WEB: www.marshallexcelsior.com
SIC: 3433 3599 3498 3494 Heating equipment, except electric; machine shop, jobbing & repair; fabricated pipe & fittings; valves & pipe fittings; gaskets, packing & sealing devices
PA: Harbour Group Ltd.
 7733 Forsyth Blvd Fl 23
 Saint Louis MO 63105
 314 727-5550

(G-11066)
MARSHALL GAS CONTROLS INC
450 Leggitt Rd (49068-9555)
PHONE..................269 781-3901
Don C Leggitt Sr, *Ch of Bd*
Don C Leggitt Jr, *President*
Jean T Clearman, *Corp Secy*
Dorothy Mc Redmond, *Asst Treas*
Donald J Brewer, *Asst Sec*
EMP: 5 EST: 1979
SQ FT: 75,000
SALES (est): 1.1MM
SALES (corp-wide): 29.3MM **Privately Held**
WEB: www.marshallexcelsior.com
SIC: 3491 Automatic regulating & control valves
PA: S. H. Leggitt Company
 1000 Civic Center Loop
 San Marcos TX 78666
 956 504-6440

(G-11067)
MARSHALL METAL PRODUCTS INC
1006 E Michigan Ave (49068-9301)
PHONE..................269 781-3924
Dan Stulberg, *President*
Ron Holcomb, *Manager*
EMP: 6 EST: 1956
SQ FT: 14,000
SALES (est): 800K **Privately Held**
WEB: www.marshallmetalproducts.com
SIC: 3469 Stamping metal for the trade

(G-11068)
MAVERICK MACHINE TOOL
101 E Oliver Dr (49068-9505)
P.O. Box 647 (49068-0647)
PHONE..................269 789-1617
Wanda Martin, *Partner*
Jim Dominique, *Partner*
Neil Martin, *Partner*
EMP: 14 EST: 1995
SQ FT: 12,000
SALES (est): 729.7K **Privately Held**
SIC: 3599 Machine shop, jobbing & repair

GEOGRAPHIC SECTION

Marysville - St. Clair County (G-11093)

(G-11069)
MCELROY METAL MILL INC
311 W Oliver Dr (49068-9574)
P.O. Box 527 (49068-0527)
PHONE 269 781-8313
Mark Brotherton, *Branch Mgr*
EMP: 62
SALES (corp-wide): 362MM **Privately Held**
WEB: www.mcelroymetal.com
SIC: 3448 3444 2952 Prefabricated metal buildings; sheet metalwork; asphalt felts & coatings
PA: Mcelroy Metal Mill, Inc.
1500 Hamilton Rd
Bossier City LA 71111
318 747-8000

(G-11070)
MEDALIST
117 E Michigan Ave (49068-1543)
PHONE 269 789-4653
Bill Newcomb, *General Mgr*
EMP: 9 **EST:** 2010
SALES (est): 86.3K **Privately Held**
WEB: www.themedalist.com
SIC: 3949 Shafts, golf club

(G-11071)
MOR-DALL ENTERPRISES INC
Also Called: Darkhorse Brewing Company, The
511 S Kalamazoo Ave (49068-1718)
PHONE 269 558-4915
Erin Moore, *President*
Jim Anderson, *Shareholder*
▲ **EMP:** 6 **EST:** 2000
SQ FT: 2,100
SALES (est): 1.1MM **Privately Held**
WEB: www.darkhorsebrewery.com
SIC: 2082 Beer (alcoholic beverage)

(G-11072)
PROGRESSIVE DYNAMICS INC
507 Industrial Rd (49068-1750)
PHONE 269 781-4241
Ralph McGee, *President*
Delores Schoenborn, *General Mgr*
Tom Phlipo, *Exec VP*
Mike Walters, *Vice Pres*
Jeff Cornell, *Engineer*
▲ **EMP:** 90
SQ FT: 157,000
SALES (est): 19MM **Privately Held**
WEB: www.progressivedyn.com
SIC: 3679 3647 3841 Static power supply converters for electronic applications; vehicular lighting equipment; surgical & medical instruments

(G-11073)
S H LEGGITT COMPANY
Also Called: Marshall Brass Co
450 Leggitt Rd (49068-9555)
PHONE 269 781-3901
Don C Leggitt Sr, *Branch Mgr*
EMP: 317
SALES (corp-wide): 29.3MM **Privately Held**
WEB: www.shleggitt.com
SIC: 3451 3714 3612 3494 Screw machine products; motor vehicle parts & accessories; transformers, except electric; valves & pipe fittings; industrial valves; plumbing fixture fittings & trim
PA: S. H. Leggitt Company
1000 Civic Center Loop
San Marcos TX 78666
956 504-6440

(G-11074)
SPRAY METAL MOLD TECHNOLOGY
200 Woolley Dr (49068-9588)
PHONE 269 781-7151
Mark Warner, *President*
EMP: 5 **EST:** 1990
SQ FT: 2,000
SALES (est): 432.9K **Privately Held**
WEB: www.metal-molds.com
SIC: 3544 Industrial molds

(G-11075)
TENNECO AUTOMOTIVE OPER CO INC
904 Industrial Rd (49068-1741)
PHONE 269 781-1350
Kevin Douglas, *Exec VP*
Renee Briggs, *QC Mgr*
Fred Baumgartner, *Engineer*
Tim Landstoffer, *Engineer*
Randy Rial, *Manager*
EMP: 204
SALES (corp-wide): 15.3B **Publicly Held**
SIC: 3714 Mufflers (exhaust), motor vehicle
HQ: Tenneco Automotive Operating Company, Inc.
500 N Field Dr
Lake Forest IL 60045
847 482-5000

(G-11076)
TRIBAL MANUFACTURING INC (PA)
450 Leggitt Rd (49068-9555)
PHONE 269 781-3901
Joseph N Ismert, *CEO*
John Tracy, *Vice Pres*
Skip Nelson, *Plant Mgr*
Abby Roberts, *Purch Agent*
Ginger Phillips, *Buyer*
▲ **EMP:** 62 **EST:** 2008
SALES (est): 14.5MM **Privately Held**
WEB: www.tribalmfg.com
SIC: 3494 3451 3599 Valves & pipe fittings; screw machine products; machine shop, jobbing & repair

(G-11077)
W L HAMILTON & CO
325 Cherry St (49068-1489)
P.O. Box 766 (49068-0766)
PHONE 269 781-6941
Jeffery A Begg, *President*
▲ **EMP:** 10 **EST:** 1961
SALES (est): 870.6K **Privately Held**
WEB: www.wlhamiltonco.com
SIC: 3494 Sprinkler systems, field

(G-11078)
W S TOWNSEND COMPANY (PA)
Also Called: Michigan Kitchen Distributors
106 E Oliver Dr (49068-9505)
PHONE 269 781-5131
Jack W Townsend, *CEO*
Steve Townsend, *President*
Gregory L Nyenhuis, *Corp Secy*
Katie Frantom, *Accountant*
Marty Fitch, *VP Sales*
EMP: 120 **EST:** 1950
SQ FT: 54,000
SALES (est): 23.1MM **Privately Held**
WEB: www.mkdkitchens.com
SIC: 1799 5031 1751 2434 Closet organizers, installation & design; millwork; carpentry work; wood kitchen cabinets; wood partitions & fixtures

Martin
Allegan County

(G-11079)
ASH INDUSTRIES INC
362 116th Ave (49070-8702)
P.O. Box 147 (49070-0147)
PHONE 269 672-9630
Gordon Ash, *President*
Mary Jo Ash, *Corp Secy*
EMP: 42 **EST:** 1985
SALES (est): 1.9MM **Privately Held**
WEB: www.ashindustries.com
SIC: 3599 Machine shop, jobbing & repair

(G-11080)
MPF ACQUISITIONS INC
Also Called: Marshall Plastic Film
904 E Allegan St (49070-9797)
P.O. Box 125 (49070-0125)
PHONE 269 672-5511
John Roggow, *President*
Ann Jameson, *CFO*
▲ **EMP:** 49 **EST:** 1973
SQ FT: 40,000
SALES (est): 16.6MM
SALES (corp-wide): 290.2MM **Privately Held**
WEB: www.marshallplastic.com
SIC: 3081 Plastic film & sheet
PA: Transcendia, Inc.
9201 Belmont Ave Ste 100a
Franklin Park IL 60131
847 678-1800

Marysville
St. Clair County

(G-11081)
AMERICAN METAL RESTORATION
Also Called: Wilkie Brothers
1765 Michigan Ave Ste 2 (48040-2046)
P.O. Box 219 (48040-0219)
PHONE 810 364-4820
Robert B Wilkie, *President*
Paul Naz, *Vice Pres*
Donald Wilkie, *Vice Pres*
◆ **EMP:** 6 **EST:** 1980
SQ FT: 3,000
SALES (est): 341.2K **Privately Held**
WEB: www.wilkiebros.com
SIC: 7349 3471 Cleaning service, industrial or commercial; plating & polishing

(G-11082)
BLUE WATER MANUFACTURING INC
1765 Michigan Ave (48040-2046)
P.O. Box 219 (48040-0219)
PHONE 810 364-6170
Paul Naz, *President*
◆ **EMP:** 23 **EST:** 1985
SQ FT: 20,000
SALES (est): 3.1MM **Privately Held**
WEB: www.bluewatermfg.com
SIC: 3535 Conveyors & conveying equipment

(G-11083)
CAMPBELL & SHAW STEEL INC
1705 Michigan Ave (48040-1805)
PHONE 810 364-5100
Karen Lietke, *President*
Mike Kepsel, *General Mgr*
Mark Lietke, *Vice Pres*
Kevin Shaw, *Vice Pres*
Karen Shaw, *Admin Sec*
EMP: 14 **EST:** 2011
SALES (est): 6.1MM **Privately Held**
WEB: www.campbellshawsteel.com
SIC: 5051 1791 3441 3449 Steel; structural steel erection; fabricated structural metal; miscellaneous metalwork; fire- or burglary-resistive products

(G-11084)
CONFORMANCE COATINGS PROTOTYPE
2321 Busha Hwy (48040-1946)
PHONE 810 364-4333
Allan Fahner, *President*
Bruce Douglass, *Corp Secy*
Robert Marchione, *Vice Pres*
EMP: 17 **EST:** 1984
SQ FT: 12,700
SALES (est): 1.9MM **Privately Held**
WEB: www.ccproto.com
SIC: 3479 Coating of metals & formed products

(G-11085)
DARRELL R HANSON
579 Michigan Ave (48040-1111)
PHONE 810 364-7892
Darrell Hanson, *President*
EMP: 5 **EST:** 2007
SALES (est): 94.1K **Privately Held**
SIC: 3599 Industrial machinery

(G-11086)
DCP MIDSTREAM LLC
2510 Busha Hwy (48040-1904)
PHONE 936 615-5189
EMP: 7
SALES (corp-wide): 1.9B **Privately Held**
WEB: www.dcpmidstream.com
SIC: 1311 Crude petroleum production

PA: Dcp Midstream, Llc
370 17th St Ste 2500
Denver CO 80202
303 633-2900

(G-11087)
FLOW GAS MISTURE SOLUTIONS INC
Also Called: Fgm Solutions
110 Huron Blvd Ste A (48040-1477)
PHONE 810 488-1492
Timothy Storm, *Director*
Tim Storm, *Director*
EMP: 5 **EST:** 2015
SQ FT: 400
SALES (est): 750K **Privately Held**
WEB: www.flowgasandmoisture.com
SIC: 3632 Household refrigerators & freezers

(G-11088)
HEARTLAND STEEL PRODUCTS LLC (PA)
Also Called: Spacerak
2420 Wills St (48040-1978)
PHONE 810 364-7421
Pat Peplowski, *CEO*
Donny Allen, *Production*
Rich Eastman, *Engineer*
Joseph T Lendo, *CFO*
Melissa Spano, *Accountant*
EMP: 31 **EST:** 2010
SALES (est): 13.9MM **Privately Held**
WEB: www.heartlandsteel.com
SIC: 3441 Fabricated structural metal

(G-11089)
JONES & HOLLANDS INC
Also Called: Jones Equipment Rental
1777 Busha Hwy (48040-1815)
PHONE 810 364-6400
Derek Fleury, *Manager*
EMP: 5 **Privately Held**
WEB: www.jones-equipment.com
SIC: 7353 3546 7359 5083 Heavy construction equipment rental; saws & sawing equipment; equipment rental & leasing; farm & garden machinery
PA: Jones & Hollands, Inc.
4600 24th Ave
Fort Gratiot MI 48059

(G-11090)
MARYSVILLE HYDROCARBONS LLC (DH)
2510 Busha Hwy (48040-1904)
PHONE 586 445-2300
Rai Bhargava, *President*
EMP: 35 **EST:** 1989
SQ FT: 3,000
SALES (est): 7.3MM **Publicly Held**
SIC: 2911 Fractionation products of crude petroleum, hydrocarbons

(G-11091)
METER USA LLC
1765 Michigan Ave (48040-2046)
PHONE 810 388-9373
▲ **EMP:** 15
SALES (est): 1MM **Privately Held**
SIC: 3499 Mfg Misc Fabricated Metal Products

(G-11092)
MODERN TECH MACHINING LLC
808 Gratiot Blvd (48040-1127)
PHONE 810 531-7992
Rob Budgell, *President*
EMP: 5 **EST:** 2013
SALES (est): 442.9K **Privately Held**
WEB: www.mtmmichigan.com
SIC: 3451 Screw machine products

(G-11093)
MUELLER IMPACTS COMPANY INC
2409 Wills St (48040-1979)
PHONE 810 364-3700
James H Rourke, *President*
Jody Weitzel, *Manager*
▼ **EMP:** 125 **EST:** 1991
SQ FT: 140,000

(PA)=Parent Co (HQ)=Headquarters (DH)=Div Headquarters
✺ = New Business established in last 2 years

2022 Harris Michigan Industrial Directory

Marysville - St. Clair County (G-11094)

SALES (est): 24.5MM Publicly Held
WEB: www.muellerindustries.com
SIC: 3469 3354 3463 Metal stampings; aluminum extruded products; nonferrous forgings
HQ: Mueller Brass Co.
2199 Lapeer Ave
Port Huron MI 48060
810 987-7770

(G-11094)
ONE STOP SIGN SERVICES
3731 Ravenswood Rd (48040-1194)
PHONE.................................810 358-1962
Vicki Baakko, *Principal*
EMP: 4 **EST:** 2014
SALES (est): 70.2K Privately Held
SIC: 3993 Signs & advertising specialties

(G-11095)
ONTARIO DIE COMPANY AMERICA (HQ)
1671 5th St (48040-2542)
PHONE.................................810 987-5060
Gary Levene, *President*
▲ **EMP:** 60 **EST:** 1974
SALES (est): 13.1MM
SALES (corp-wide): 1.6MM Privately Held
WEB: www.ontariodie.com
SIC: 3544 3423 Special dies & tools; knives, agricultural or industrial
PA: Ontario Die International Inc
235 Gage Ave
Kitchener ON N2M 2
519 745-1002

(G-11096)
PAUMAC TUBING LLC (PA)
315 Cuttle Rd (48040-1804)
PHONE.................................810 985-9400
Kelly Russell, *Purchasing*
Mary Sanctorum, *Purchasing*
Sue Miller, *Human Res Mgr*
Norman McDonald, *Mng Member*
Alexandra Houston, *Administration*
EMP: 90
SQ FT: 65
SALES (est): 16MM Privately Held
WEB: www.paumactubing.com
SIC: 3498 Tube fabricating (contract bending & shaping)

(G-11097)
PUNCH TECH
2701 Busha Hwy (48040-1905)
PHONE.................................810 364-4811
EMP: 33
SQ FT: 14,400
SALES (est): 2.1MM Privately Held
SIC: 3541 3965 3544 Mfg Machine Tools-Cutting Mfg Fasteners/Buttons/Pins Mfg Dies/Tools/Jigs/Fixtures

(G-11098)
RAK-O-NIZER LLC
Also Called: E Tech Plastics
1718 Colorado St (48040-1646)
PHONE.................................810 444-9807
EMP: 9 **EST:** 2018
SALES (est): 372.3K Privately Held
SIC: 3089 Injection molding of plastics

(G-11099)
SIGNAL MEDICAL CORPORATION (PA)
400 Pyramid Dr Ste 2 (48040-2463)
PHONE.................................810 364-7070
Drleo Whiteside, *President*
Leo Whiteside, *President*
Steve Thueme, *Plant Mgr*
EMP: 10 **EST:** 1996
SALES (est): 1.7MM Privately Held
WEB: www.signalortho.com
SIC: 3842 5999 Surgical appliances & supplies; medical apparatus & supplies

(G-11100)
SMR ATMTIVE MRROR INTL USA INC (DH)
1855 Busha Hwy (48040-1892)
PHONE.................................810 364-4141
Char Zawadzinski, *President*
Dom Stancombe, *Accounts Mgr*
▲ **EMP:** 402 **EST:** 1990

SALES (est): 510MM Privately Held
WEB: www.smr-automotive.com
SIC: 3231 Products of purchased glass
HQ: Smr Automotive Technology Holdings Usa Partners Llp
1855 Busha Hwy
Marysville MI 48040
810 364-4141

(G-11101)
SMR ATMTIVE TECH HLDNGS USA PR (DH)
1855 Busha Hwy (48040-1892)
PHONE.................................810 364-4141
Michael Lady, *Exec VP*
Dean Charron, *Project Engr*
Jeff Kenzie, *Accounts Mgr*
Bogdan Maghiar, *Manager*
Char Zawadzinski,
▲ **EMP:** 100 **EST:** 2000
SALES (est): 571.7MM Privately Held
WEB: www.smr-automotive.com
SIC: 3231 Products of purchased glass
HQ: Smr Automotive Mirror Parts And Holdings Uk Limited
Portchester 2
Fareham HANTS PO16
239 221-0022

(G-11102)
SMR AUTOMOTIVE SYSTEMS USA INC (DH)
Also Called: Samvardhana Mtherson Reflectec
1855 Busha Hwy (48040-1892)
PHONE.................................810 364-4141
Char Zawadzinski, *President*
John Jesionowski, *Corp Secy*
Gary Sinelli, *Vice Pres*
SAI Tatineni, *Vice Pres*
Anthony D 'andrea, *Project Mgr*
▲ **EMP:** 1000 **EST:** 1989
SQ FT: 175,000
SALES (est): 269MM Privately Held
WEB: www.smr-automotive.com
SIC: 3231 Mirrors, truck & automobile: made from purchased glass
HQ: Smr Automotive Mirror International Usa Inc.
1855 Busha Hwy
Marysville MI 48040
810 364-4141

(G-11103)
SOUTH PARK WELDING SUPS LLC (PA)
50 Gratiot Blvd (48040-1199)
PHONE.................................810 364-6521
Judy Darczy,
Lou Darczy,
EMP: 11 **EST:** 1920
SQ FT: 3,500
SALES (est): 2.6MM Privately Held
WEB: www.praxairusa.com
SIC: 2813 5084 Industrial gases; welding machinery & equipment

(G-11104)
ST CLAIR PACKAGING INC
Also Called: St. Clair Paper & Supply
2121 Busha Hwy (48040-1943)
PHONE.................................810 364-4230
David Miotke, *CEO*
Todd Lawson, *President*
Mark St Pierre, *Opers Mgr*
Cindy Harmer, *Buyer*
Richard Ball, *Supervisor*
▲ **EMP:** 35 **EST:** 1980
SQ FT: 100,000
SALES (est): 12.1MM Privately Held
WEB: www.stclairpackaging.com
SIC: 5113 2653 Corrugated & solid fiber boxes; boxes, corrugated: made from purchased materials

(G-11105)
TARPON INDUSTRIES INC
2420 Wills St (48040-1978)
PHONE.................................810 364-7421
James W Bradshaw, *Ch of Bd*
Patrick J Hook, *President*
Pat Peplowski, *Exec VP*
Patrick G Peplowski, *Exec VP*
Joseph T Lendo, *CFO*
EMP: 43 **EST:** 2002
SQ FT: 200,000

SALES (est): 1.1MM Privately Held
SIC: 3317 2542 Tubes, wrought: welded or lock joint; racks, merchandise display or storage: except wood

(G-11106)
THEUT PRODUCTS INC
1444 Gratiot Blvd (48040-1179)
PHONE.................................810 364-7132
Jim Roberts, *Sales/Mktg Mgr*
EMP: 7
SALES (corp-wide): 15.7MM Privately Held
WEB: www.theutproductsinc.com
SIC: 3273 Ready-mixed concrete
PA: Theut Products, Inc.
73408 Van Dyke Rd
Bruce Twp MI 48065
586 752-4541

(G-11107)
THORPE PRINTING SERVICES INC
Also Called: Studio 626
604 Busha Hwy (48040-1310)
PHONE.................................810 364-6222
Lance Thorpe, *President*
Stacie Thorpe, *Exec VP*
Darin Magneson, *Graphic Designe*
EMP: 7 **EST:** 1966
SQ FT: 6,550
SALES (est): 898.1K Privately Held
WEB: www.thorpeprinting.com
SIC: 2752 2399 7336 2791 Commercial printing, offset; banners, pennants & flags; graphic arts & related design; typesetting, computer controlled; bookbinding & related work; commercial printing

(G-11108)
TI GROUP AUTO SYSTEMS LLC
Also Called: Fluid Systems Division
184 Gratiot Blvd (48040-1147)
PHONE.................................810 364-3277
Dawn Hayes, *Materials Mgr*
Tom Miller, *Materials Mgr*
Larry Freeman, *Purch Dir*
Bill Learman, *Engineer*
Pat Lintner, *Marketing Staff*
EMP: 7
SQ FT: 30,000
SALES (corp-wide): 3.3B Privately Held
WEB: www.tifluidsystems.com
SIC: 3714 3089 Motor vehicle parts & accessories; plastic processing
HQ: Ti Group Automotive Systems, Llc
2020 Taylor Rd
Auburn Hills MI 48326
248 296-8000

(G-11109)
TOPS-IN-QUALITY INC
148 Huron Blvd (48040-1422)
P.O. Box 148 (48040-0148)
PHONE.................................810 364-7150
Norman Van Natter, *President*
Cindy Van Natter, *Vice Pres*
EMP: 9 **EST:** 1962
SQ FT: 23,000
SALES (est): 526K Privately Held
WEB: www.whitewatermarineinc.com
SIC: 3444 3429 Sheet metalwork; marine hardware

(G-11110)
TP LOGOS LLC
707 Lomasney Ln (48040-2212)
PHONE.................................810 956-9484
Phil Proctor, *Principal*
Jamie Lamay, *Project Mgr*
Jon Wright, *Sales Staff*
Stephanie Bellman, *Services*
EMP: 6 **EST:** 2011
SQ FT: 1,200
SALES (est): 191.3K Privately Held
WEB: www.tplogos.com
SIC: 2395 2759 7336 Embroidery & art needlework; screen printing; commercial art & graphic design

(G-11111)
VAN KEHRBERG VERN
Also Called: Copy Cat Sign & Print
914 Gratiot Blvd Ste 3 (48040-1141)
PHONE.................................810 364-1066
Vern Van Kehrberg, *Owner*

EMP: 4 **EST:** 1998
SQ FT: 8,500
SALES (est): 165K Privately Held
SIC: 2759 3993 Commercial printing; signs, not made in custom sign painting shops

(G-11112)
VISIOCORP HOLDING USA LLP
1855 Busha Hwy (48040-1892)
PHONE.................................810 388-2403
EMP: 8 **EST:** 2019
SALES (est): 517K Privately Held
WEB: www.visiocorp.com
SIC: 3714 Motor vehicle parts & accessories

(G-11113)
WILKIE BROS CONVEYORS INC
1765 Michigan Ave Ste 2 (48040-2046)
P.O. Box 219 (48040-0219)
PHONE.................................810 364-4820
Donald Wilkie, *President*
Robert B Wilkie, *President*
▼ **EMP:** 50 **EST:** 1974
SQ FT: 120,000
SALES (est): 7.8MM Privately Held
WEB: www.wilkiebros.com
SIC: 3535 3568 3566 3462 Overhead conveyor systems; power transmission equipment; speed changers, drives & gears; iron & steel forgings

(G-11114)
ZF AXLE DRIVES MARYSVILLE LLC
Also Called: Division P
2900 Busha Hwy (48040-2439)
PHONE.................................810 989-8702
Christie Handlon, *Production*
Daniel Waskiewicz, *Production*
Carrie Smith, *Engineer*
David White, *Sales Mgr*
Eric Vaneenoo, *Manager*
▲ **EMP:** 340 **EST:** 2008
SALES (est): 64.1MM
SALES (corp-wide): 216.2K Privately Held
WEB: www.zf.com
SIC: 3714 Motor vehicle parts & accessories
HQ: Zf North America, Inc.
15811 Centennial Dr
Northville MI 48168
734 416-6200

Mason
Ingham County

(G-11115)
A R C WELDING & REPAIR
5261 Bunker Rd (48854-9795)
PHONE.................................517 628-2475
Andrew Hudson, *Partner*
Douglas Hudson, *Partner*
EMP: 6 **EST:** 1999
SALES (est): 131.8K Privately Held
SIC: 7692 Welding repair

(G-11116)
ARCOSA EPI LLC
Also Called: Efficiency Production
685 Hull Rd (48854-9271)
PHONE.................................517 676-8800
EMP: 32 **EST:** 2017
SALES (est): 1.3MM Privately Held
WEB: www.efficiencyproduction.com
SIC: 3531 Construction machinery

(G-11117)
AUTUMN RIDGE WOODWORKS
2020 Kelly Rd (48854-9626)
PHONE.................................517 420-8185
Corey House, *Principal*
EMP: 4 **EST:** 2018
SALES (est): 54.1K Privately Held
SIC: 2431 Millwork

(G-11118)
BAYER CROP SCIENCE
1440 Okemos Rd (48854-9314)
PHONE.................................517 676-3586
John Carew, *Engineer*
Kelby Williams, *Technician*

GEOGRAPHIC SECTION
Mason - Ingham County (G-11143)

EMP: 7 **EST:** 2019
SALES (est): 891K Privately Held
WEB: www.cropscience.bayer.com
SIC: 2879 Agricultural chemicals

(G-11119)
CONCENTRIC LABS INC
715 Hall Blvd (48854-1705)
P.O. Box 164 (48854-0164)
PHONE..................................517 969-3038
Joshua Woodland, *President*
EMP: 6 **EST:** 2014
SALES (est): 239.2K Privately Held
WEB: www.concentric-labs.com
SIC: 3625 Electric controls & control accessories, industrial

(G-11120)
CONTECH ENGNERED SOLUTIONS LLC
661 Jerico Dr (48854-9384)
PHONE..................................517 676-3000
Paul Depuy, *Manager*
EMP: 5 Privately Held
WEB: www.conteches.com
SIC: 3443 Fabricated plate work (boiler shop)
HQ: Contech Engineered Solutions Llc
9025 Centre Pointe Dr # 400
West Chester OH 45069
513 645-7000

(G-11121)
DART CONTAINER CORP CALIFORNIA
500 Hogsback Rd (48854-9547)
PHONE..................................517 244-6408
EMP: 55
SALES (corp-wide): 51.4MM Privately Held
WEB: www.dartcontainer.com
SIC: 3086 Plastics foam products
PA: Dart Container Corporation Of California
150 S Maple Ctr
Corona CA 92880
951 735-8115

(G-11122)
DART CONTAINER CORP FLORIDA (PA)
500 Hogsback Rd (48854-9547)
PHONE..................................800 248-5960
Robert C Dart, *CEO*
Claire T Dart, *President*
William Oberrender, *Safety Dir*
Connie Castillo, *QC Dir*
Kevin Fox, *Treasurer*
EMP: 3 **EST:** 1992
SALES (est): 68.2MM Privately Held
WEB: www.dartcontainer.com
SIC: 3086 Plastics foam products

(G-11123)
DART CONTAINER CORP GEORGIA (PA)
500 Hogsback Rd (48854-9547)
PHONE..................................517 676-3800
Robert C Dart, *President*
Randy Lamie, *Engineer*
Kevin Fox, *Treasurer*
James D Lammers, *Admin Sec*
◆ **EMP:** 300
SQ FT: 50,000
SALES (est): 139.7MM Privately Held
WEB: www.dartcontainer.com
SIC: 3086 Plastics foam products

(G-11124)
DART CONTAINER CORP KENTUCKY (PA)
Also Called: Dart Polymers
500 Hogsback Rd (48854-9547)
PHONE..................................517 676-3800
Robert C Dart, *CEO*
Kevin Fox, *Treasurer*
◆ **EMP:** 13 **EST:** 1960
SALES (est): 31.6MM Privately Held
WEB: www.dartcontainer.com
SIC: 2821 3086 Plastics materials & resins; cups & plates, foamed plastic

(G-11125)
DART CONTAINER CORPORATION
710 Hogsback Rd Bldg 9 (48854-9541)
PHONE..................................517 676-3800
EMP: 6 **EST:** 2006
SALES (est): 190.9K Privately Held
SIC: 3089 Plastic containers, except foam

(G-11126)
DART CONTAINER CORPORATION (PA)
500 Hogsback Rd (48854-9547)
PHONE..................................517 676-3800
Robert C Dart, *President*
Tom Jewell, *Exec VP*
Robert Novak, *Exec VP*
Beston S Chitala, *Vice Pres*
James D Lammers, *Vice Pres*
◆ **EMP:** 780 **EST:** 1937
SALES (est): 2B Privately Held
WEB: www.dartcontainer.com
SIC: 3086 Plastics foam products

(G-11127)
DART CONTAINER MICHIGAN LLC
3120 W Howell Rd (48854-8344)
PHONE..................................517 244-6249
Julie Turner, *Opers Staff*
Ken Turner, *Mfg Staff*
Katie Laatsch, *Production*
Al Turkovich, *Engineer*
Jackie Libera, *Human Res Mgr*
EMP: 2628 Privately Held
WEB: www.dartcontainer.com
SIC: 3086 Plastics foam products
HQ: Dart Container Of Michigan Llc
500 Hogsback Rd
Mason MI 48854
800 248-5960

(G-11128)
DART CONTAINER MICHIGAN LLC (HQ)
500 Hogsback Rd (48854-9547)
P.O. Box 6 (48854-0006)
PHONE..................................800 248-5960
Robert C Dart, *CEO*
Kenneth Dart, *President*
Joseph Obrien, *Counsel*
William A Dart, *Vice Pres*
Timothy Hickey, *Vice Pres*
◆ **EMP:** 1500 **EST:** 2003
SQ FT: 50,000
SALES (est): 670.7MM Privately Held
WEB: www.dartcontainer.com
SIC: 2656 3086 Paper cups, plates, dishes & utensils; cups & plates, foamed plastic

(G-11129)
DART CONTAINER MICHIGAN LLC
432 Hogsback Rd (48854-9548)
PHONE..................................517 676-3803
Peter Matysiak, *Engineer*
Diane Mauk, *Engineer*
Matt Turner, *Project Engr*
Chad Becker, *Sales Staff*
Jeff Watling, *Prgrmr*
EMP: 2628 Privately Held
WEB: www.dartcontainer.com
SIC: 3086 Cups & plates, foamed plastic
HQ: Dart Container Of Michigan Llc
500 Hogsback Rd
Mason MI 48854
800 248-5960

(G-11130)
DIGITAL SUCCESS NETWORK
Also Called: D S N Satellites
205 S Cedar St (48854-1432)
P.O. Box 265 (48854-0265)
PHONE..................................517 244-0771
Bruce Ware, *President*
Amber Wyman, *Manager*
EMP: 20 **EST:** 1998
SQ FT: 5,200
SALES (est): 2.3MM Privately Held
SIC: 4841 2741 Satellite master antenna systems services (SMATV);

(G-11131)
ESL SUPPLIES LLC
600 N College Rd (48854-9544)
PHONE..................................517 525-7877
Rebecca Schwartz,
EMP: 6 **EST:** 2019
SALES (est): 172.5K Privately Held
WEB: www.eslsupplies.com
SIC: 3999 5961 5999 8748 Education aids, devices & supplies; educational supplies & equipment, mail order; education aids, devices & supplies; educational consultant

(G-11132)
FAMILYGRADEGRAVEL YAHOOCOM
924 Chickasaw Dr (48854-9610)
PHONE..................................517 202-4121
Lori Manyen, *Principal*
EMP: 7 **EST:** 2015
SALES (est): 320K Privately Held
WEB: www.familygradegravel.com
SIC: 1442 Construction sand & gravel

(G-11133)
FW SHORING COMPANY (PA)
Also Called: Efficiency Shoring and Supply
685 Hull Rd (48854-9271)
PHONE..................................517 676-8800
Kenneth Forsberg, *President*
Gary Bushong, *Vice Pres*
James McRay, *Marketing Staff*
Becky Valdez, *Manager*
Michael West, *Admin Sec*
EMP: 75 **EST:** 1971
SQ FT: 79,000
SALES (est): 23.4MM Privately Held
WEB: www.efficiencyproduction.com
SIC: 3531 Construction machinery

(G-11134)
GENESIS INTERNATIONAL LLC
Also Called: Genesis Casket Company
200 E Kipp Rd (48854-9291)
PHONE..................................317 777-6700
Wm Anthony Colson, *CEO*
Judy Rossom, *Mng Member*
Denny Knigga,
Adrian Lee,
Billingsley Scott,
◆ **EMP:** 25 **EST:** 2011
SALES (est): 2.6MM Privately Held
SIC: 3995 Burial caskets

(G-11135)
GESTAMP MASON LLC
200 E Kipp Rd (48854-9291)
PHONE..................................517 244-8800
Jeffrey Wilson, *CEO*
John Craig, *President*
Katie Jensen, *Engineer*
James Barry, *CFO*
Sergio Parla, *Controller*
◆ **EMP:** 489 **EST:** 2004
SQ FT: 230,000
SALES (est): 120.4MM
SALES (corp-wide): 400.4MM Privately Held
WEB: www.gestamp.com
SIC: 3398 5013 3714 3711 Metal heat treating; motor vehicle supplies & new parts; motor vehicle parts & accessories; motor vehicles & car bodies; automotive stampings
HQ: Gestamp North America, Inc.
2701 Troy Center Dr # 150
Troy MI 48084

(G-11136)
H & H WELDING & REPAIR LLC
700 Acme Dr (48854)
P.O. Box 371 (48854-0371)
PHONE..................................517 676-1800
Dale Good, *Engineer*
Steven McGeorge, *Manager*
Scott Summerville,
Kris Cook,
EMP: 54 **EST:** 1997
SQ FT: 27,000
SALES (est): 6.1MM Privately Held
WEB: www.hhwelding.com
SIC: 7692 Welding repair

(G-11137)
HEARTLAND MACHINE & ENGRG LLC
4200 Legion Dr (48854-1053)
PHONE..................................616 437-1641
Elliott Parmer, *Marketing Mgr*
David Pachulski, *Branch Mgr*
Terry Kasper, *Manager*
Kyle Garrity, *CIO*
EMP: 5
SALES (corp-wide): 10.9MM Privately Held
WEB: www.heartlandme.com
SIC: 3541 8711 Machine tools, metal cutting type; engineering services
PA: Heartland Machine & Engineering, Llc
2848 N Graham Rd
Franklin IN 46131
317 346-0463

(G-11138)
HOLT PRODUCTS COMPANY
4200 Legion Dr (48854-1053)
P.O. Box 98 (48854-0098)
PHONE..................................517 927-4198
Donald Phillips, *President*
Todd E Hunt, *Corp Secy*
Phyllis Ann Hunt, *Shareholder*
EMP: 35 **EST:** 1939
SQ FT: 10,000
SALES (est): 5.7MM Privately Held
WEB: www.holtproducts.com
SIC: 3451 Screw machine products

(G-11139)
ITS YOURS
306 S Cedar St (48854-1435)
PHONE..................................517 676-7003
EMP: 4 **EST:** 2019
SALES (est): 138.3K Privately Held
WEB: www.itsyoursapparel.com
SIC: 3993 Signs & advertising specialties

(G-11140)
JUSTINSCSTMGATESANDWOOD WORKING
5381 Bunker Rd (48854-9768)
PHONE..................................906 748-1999
Justin Swain, *Principal*
EMP: 4 **EST:** 2018
SALES (est): 66.4K Privately Held
SIC: 2431 Millwork

(G-11141)
LEAR CORPORATION
Also Called: GM Division Plant
454 North St (48854-1588)
PHONE..................................248 447-1500
Bret Badertscher, *Manager*
EMP: 6
SALES (corp-wide): 17B Publicly Held
WEB: www.lear.com
SIC: 2396 2531 Automotive & apparel trimmings; public building & related furniture
PA: Lear Corporation
21557 Telegraph Rd
Southfield MI 48033
248 447-1500

(G-11142)
MASON FORGE & DIE INC
Also Called: Mason Specialty Forge
841 Hull Rd (48854-9273)
P.O. Box 321 (48854-0321)
PHONE..................................517 676-2992
EMP: 10
SQ FT: 17,500
SALES (est): 1.3MM Privately Held
SIC: 3714 3462 Mfg Steering Components And Steel Forgings

(G-11143)
MEECH ROAD LTD
367 E South St (48854-1941)
PHONE..................................734 255-9119
Roberta Gubbins, *Principal*
EMP: 5 **EST:** 2010
SALES (est): 103.7K Privately Held
SIC: 2741 Miscellaneous publishing

Mason - Ingham County (G-11144)

(G-11144)
MICHIGAN PACKAGING COMPANY (DH)
Also Called: Southeastern Packaging
700 Eden Rd (48854-9277)
PHONE..................517 676-8700
Geoffrey A Jollay, *CEO*
John Klein, *General Mgr*
Chris Zimmerman, *Prdtn Mgr*
Jody Stewart, *Purchasing*
John Lauterbach, *CIO*
▲ **EMP:** 100 **EST:** 1967
SQ FT: 210,000
SALES (est): 37.1MM
SALES (corp-wide): 4.5B **Publicly Held**
WEB: www.corrchoice.com
SIC: 2653 Boxes, corrugated: made from purchased materials
HQ: Corrchoice, Inc.
  777 3rd St Nw
  Massillon OH 44647
  330 833-5705

(G-11145)
MICHIGAN WOODWORK
1234 Christian Way (48854)
PHONE..................517 204-4394
Matthew Gustafson, *Owner*
Johnny Barkley, *Opers Staff*
EMP: 6 **EST:** 2013
SALES (est): 260.1K **Privately Held**
WEB: www.miwoodwork.com
SIC: 2431 Millwork

(G-11146)
N2 PUBLICATIONS
Also Called: Belocal
77 Lake Ridge Dr (48854-8327)
PHONE..................517 488-2607
EMP: 4 **EST:** 2017
SALES (est): 41.3K **Privately Held**
WEB: www.n2pub.com
SIC: 2741 Miscellaneous publishing

(G-11147)
NITREX INC (DH)
822 Kim Dr (48854-9366)
P.O. Box 155 (48854-0155)
PHONE..................517 676-6370
Chris Morawski, *President*
▲ **EMP:** 25 **EST:** 1995
SQ FT: 20,000
SALES (est): 12.7MM
SALES (corp-wide): 419.3K **Privately Held**
WEB: www.nitrex.com
SIC: 3398 3714 Metal heat treating; motor vehicle parts & accessories
HQ: Nitrex Metal Inc
  3474 Boul Poirier
  Saint-Laurent QC H4R 2
  514 335-7191

(G-11148)
OMIMEX ENERGY INC
3505 W Barnes Rd (48854-8720)
P.O. Box 258 (48854-0258)
PHONE..................517 628-2820
Kem Pryor, *Manager*
EMP: 6
SALES (corp-wide): 33.6MM **Privately Held**
SIC: 1311 Crude petroleum production
HQ: Omimex Energy, Inc.
  7950 John T White Rd
  Fort Worth TX 76120

(G-11149)
ORCHID ORTHOPEDIC SOLUTIONS
1365 N Cedar Rd (48854-9586)
PHONE..................517 694-2300
Mark Owen, *Engineer*
EMP: 18 **EST:** 2015
SALES (est): 2.5MM **Privately Held**
WEB: www.orchid-ortho.com
SIC: 3841 Surgical & medical instruments

(G-11150)
PR SOLO CUP INC
500 Hogsback Rd (48854-8523)
PHONE..................517 244-2837
EMP: 6 **EST:** 2018
SALES (est): 967.6K **Privately Held**
WEB: www.solocup.com
SIC: 3089 Plastics products

(G-11151)
S G PUBLICATIONS INC (PA)
Also Called: The Shopping Guide
140 E Ash St (48854-2603)
PHONE..................517 676-5100
George Raymund, *President*
George Raymund, *President*
John Raymond, *Corp Secy*
EMP: 15 **EST:** 1935
SQ FT: 1,800
SALES (est): 2.1MM **Privately Held**
SIC: 2741 Shopping news: publishing & printing

(G-11152)
SCHUNK OIL FIELD SERVICE INC
4161 Legion Dr (48854-2547)
P.O. Box 382 (48854-0382)
PHONE..................517 676-8900
Jeff Schunk, *President*
EMP: 6 **EST:** 1992
SQ FT: 200 **Privately Held**
SIC: 1389 Oil field services

(G-11153)
SCIC LLC (PA)
500 Hogsback Rd (48854-8523)
PHONE..................800 248-5960
Robert C Dart, *CEO*
Ronald Whaley, *Principal*
Mike Lonsway, *Exec VP*
Robert Novak, *Exec VP*
Dan Cummins, *Mfg Mgr*
▼ **EMP:** 83 **EST:** 2004
SALES (est): 869.2MM **Privately Held**
WEB: www.solocup.com
SIC: 3089 2656 Cups, plastic, except foam; paper cups, plates, dishes & utensils

(G-11154)
SF HOLDINGS GROUP INC (DH)
Also Called: Solo Cup
500 Hogsback Rd (48854-8523)
PHONE..................800 248-5960
Robert C Dart, *CEO*
Linda Ridgley, *Vice Pres*
◆ **EMP:** 100 **EST:** 1997
SALES (est): 706.7MM
SALES (corp-wide): 869.2MM **Privately Held**
WEB: www.dartcontainer.com
SIC: 2656 Plates, paper: made from purchased material

(G-11155)
SOLO CUP COMPANY LLC (HQ)
500 Hogsback Rd (48854-8523)
PHONE..................800 248-5960
Robert C Dart, *CEO*
Jan Stern Reed, *Vice Pres*
Mike Northington, *Warehouse Mgr*
Mike Edgett, *Production*
Amanda Leksche, *Production*
▲ **EMP:** 150
SQ FT: 133,218
SALES (est): 869.2MM **Privately Held**
WEB: www.solocup.com
SIC: 3089 2656 Cups, plastic, except foam; plates, plastic; plastic containers, except foam; straws, drinking: made from purchased material
PA: Scic Llc
  500 Hogsback Rd
  Mason MI 48854
  800 248-5960

(G-11156)
SOLO CUP OPERATING CORPORATION (DH)
500 Hogsback Rd (48854-8523)
PHONE..................800 248-5960
Robert C Dart, *President*
John Mc Gregor, *Director*
F Purdum, *Admin Asst*
◆ **EMP:** 60 **EST:** 1981
SALES (est): 434MM
SALES (corp-wide): 869.2MM **Privately Held**
WEB: www.solocup.com
SIC: 3089 2656 Plastic kitchenware, tableware & housewear; paper cups, plates, dishes & utensils
HQ: Sf Holdings Group, Inc.
  500 Hogsback Rd
  Mason MI 48854
  800 248-5960

(G-11157)
SPECIAL PROJECTS ENGINEERING
2072 Tomlinson Rd (48854-9203)
P.O. Box 413 (48854-0413)
PHONE..................517 676-8525
Edward Goodman, *President*
Sarah J Goodman, *Vice Pres*
▲ **EMP:** 8 **EST:** 1998
SQ FT: 7,000
SALES (est): 600K **Privately Held**
WEB: www.specialprojectsengineeringinc.wordpress.com
SIC: 3086 Plastics foam products

(G-11158)
SPORTS STOP
Also Called: Sports Stop Sportswear
124 W Ash St (48854-1648)
PHONE..................517 676-2199
Rick L Washburn, *Owner*
EMP: 5 **EST:** 1983
SQ FT: 1,800
SALES (est): 505.7K **Privately Held**
WEB: www.sportsstop.net
SIC: 5699 2396 2395 Sports apparel; screen printing on fabric articles; emblems, embroidered

(G-11159)
SURREY USA LLC
500 Hogsback Rd (48854-8523)
PHONE..................800 248-5960
Jim Lammers, *Mng Member*
EMP: 1 **EST:** 2018
SALES (est): 1.1MM
SALES (corp-wide): 51.4MM **Privately Held**
WEB: www.dartcontainer.com
SIC: 3086 Plastics foam products
PA: Dart Container Corporation Of California
  150 S Maple Ctr
  Corona CA 92880
  951 735-8115

(G-11160)
SWEETHEART CORP
500 Hogsback Rd (48854-8523)
PHONE..................847 405-2100
EMP: 7 **EST:** 2019
SALES (est): 254.2K **Privately Held**
WEB: www.dartcontainer.com
SIC: 3086 Plastics foam products

Mass City
Ontonagon County

(G-11161)
DEHAAN FOREST PRODUCTS INC
25367 Mud Creek Rd (49948-9530)
PHONE..................906 883-3417
Richard Dehaan, *President*
Martin Dehaan, *Vice Pres*
Sharon Dehaan, *Treasurer*
EMP: 10 **EST:** 1996
SALES (est): 3.5MM **Privately Held**
SIC: 2411 0191 Logging; general farms, primarily crop

Mattawan
Van Buren County

(G-11162)
BASF CORPORATION
23930 Concord Ave (49071-9566)
PHONE..................269 668-3371
Larry Labelle, *Manager*
Becky Duclo, *Associate*
EMP: 5
SALES (corp-wide): 69.9B **Privately Held**
WEB: www.basf.com
SIC: 2899 2851 Concrete curing & hardening compounds; paints & allied products
HQ: Basf Corporation
  100 Park Ave
  Florham Park NJ 07932
  859 577-5797

(G-11163)
BOOMERANG ENTERPRISES INC
49759 Wentworth Dr (49071-8889)
P.O. Box 185 (49071-0185)
PHONE..................269 547-9715
Matthew Anderson, *Principal*
EMP: 5 **EST:** 2019
SALES (est): 195.4K **Privately Held**
SIC: 3949 Boomerangs

(G-11164)
CODY KRESTA VINEYARD & WINERY
45727 27th St (49071-9736)
PHONE..................269 668-3800
Cody Kresta, *Executive*
EMP: 4 **EST:** 2010
SALES (est): 361K **Privately Held**
WEB: www.codykrestawinery.com
SIC: 2084 Wines

(G-11165)
MOL-SON INC
Also Called: Western Diversified
53196 N Main St (49071-8305)
PHONE..................269 668-3377
Ronald A Molitor, *President*
Carl Shinabargar, *Engineer*
Shawn Hansen, *Design Engr*
Susan Fritzer, *CFO*
Bill Carbary, *Controller*
EMP: 100 **EST:** 1984
SQ FT: 12,000
SALES (est): 37.6MM **Privately Held**
WEB: www.mol-son.com
SIC: 3544 Special dies & tools

(G-11166)
PRODUCTION TOOLING INC
23650 French Rd (49071-9331)
P.O. Box 399 (49071-0399)
PHONE..................269 668-6789
Thomas Henry, *President*
Karen Henry, *Corp Secy*
EMP: 9 **EST:** 1972
SQ FT: 5,000
SALES (est): 771.9K **Privately Held**
WEB: www.productiontooling.net
SIC: 3599 Machine shop, jobbing & repair

(G-11167)
PUSHARD WELDING LLC
25222 Red Arrow Hwy (49071-9767)
PHONE..................269 760-9611
Chris Pushard,
EMP: 6 **EST:** 1991
SALES (est): 502.3K **Privately Held**
WEB: www.pushardwelding.com
SIC: 7692 Welding repair

(G-11168)
TRI-MATION INDUSTRIES INC
24778 Cole Ave (49071-9333)
P.O. Box 249 (49071-0249)
PHONE..................269 668-4333
Blaine Borkowski, *President*
Dave Beukelman, *Design Engr*
EMP: 44 **EST:** 1996
SALES (est): 6MM **Privately Held**
WEB: www.tri-mation.com
SIC: 3549 3544 Metalworking machinery; special dies, tools, jigs & fixtures

(G-11169)
WESTERN DIVERSIFIED PLAS LLC (PA)
53150 N Main St (49071-8305)
PHONE..................269 668-3393
Gene Crandall, *Mfg Mgr*
Primo Garcia, *Engineer*
Matt Kievit, *Engineer*

GEOGRAPHIC SECTION   Mecosta - Mecosta County (G-11194)

Brenda Lewman, *Engineer*
Richard Schau, *Engineer*
EMP: 1 **EST:** 2005
SALES (est): 6.9MM **Privately Held**
WEB: www.westerndp.com
SIC: 3089 Injection molding of plastics

Maybee
Monroe County

(G-11170)
MIDWEST GRINDING
14222 Cone Rd (48159-9741)
PHONE.................................734 395-1033
Ronald Butts, *Owner*
EMP: 7 **EST:** 2016
SALES (est): 108K **Privately Held**
WEB: www.midwestgrindinginc.com
SIC: 3999 Custom pulverizing & grinding of plastic materials

(G-11171)
RUFF LOVE PET LLC ✪
10914 Grams Rd (48159-9799)
PHONE.................................734 351-6289
Carlotta Rhodes,
EMP: 4 **EST:** 2021
SALES (est): 100K **Privately Held**
SIC: 2399 Pet collars, leashes, etc.: non-leather

(G-11172)
STONECO INC
6837 Scofield Rd (48159-9706)
PHONE.................................734 587-7125
Mark Parron, *Manager*
EMP: 32
SALES (corp-wide): 27.5B **Privately Held**
WEB: www.shellyco.com
SIC: 1611 1422 General contractor, highway & street construction; crushed & broken limestone
HQ: Stoneco, Inc.
   1700 Fostoria Ave Ste 200
   Findlay OH 45840
   419 422-8854

(G-11173)
STUFF A PAL
14401 Cone Rd (48159-9741)
PHONE.................................734 646-3775
Anne Herlocher, *Principal*
EMP: 6 **EST:** 2010
SALES (est): 133.6K **Privately Held**
SIC: 3523 Clippers, for animal use: hand or electric

Mayville
Tuscola County

(G-11174)
WILKINSON CHEMICAL CORPORATION
8290 Lapeer Rd (48744-9305)
PHONE.................................989 843-6163
Irene Wilkinson, *President*
EMP: 15 **EST:** 1948
SQ FT: 5,400
SALES (est): 580.8K **Privately Held**
WEB: www.thewilkinsoncorporation.com
SIC: 2819 Calcium chloride & hypochlorite; magnesium compounds or salts, inorganic

(G-11175)
WILKINSON CORPORATION
8290 Lapeer Rd (48744-9305)
P.O. Box 407 (48744-0407)
PHONE.................................989 843-6163
Irene Walker Wilkinson, *President*
Irene Walkerwilkinson, *Vice Pres*
Arlene E Frank, *Vice Pres*
Donald Wilkinson, *Shareholder*
Shawna Neastman, *Admin Sec*
EMP: 5 **EST:** 1948
SALES (est): 965.3K **Privately Held**
WEB: www.thewilkinsoncorporation.com
SIC: 2819 Industrial inorganic chemicals

Mc Bain
Missaukee County

(G-11176)
BD CLASSIC SEWING
1890 E Stoney Corners Rd (49657-9515)
PHONE.................................231 825-2628
Betty Randall, *Partner*
Deanna Lucas, *Partner*
EMP: 5 **EST:** 1992 **Privately Held**
SIC: 2395 Embroidery products, except schiffli machine

(G-11177)
BIEWER FOREST MANAGEMENT LLC
6400 W Gerwoude Dr (49657-9113)
PHONE.................................231 825-2855
Shane Britt, *Manager*
Wes Windover, *Info Tech Mgr*
Timothy Biewer,
EMP: 5 **EST:** 2011
SALES (est): 378.2K **Privately Held**
WEB: www.biewerlumber.com
SIC: 2421 Specialty sawmill products

(G-11178)
BIEWER SAWMILL INC
6251 W Gerwoude Dr (49657-9105)
P.O. Box 497, Saint Clair (48079-0497)
PHONE.................................231 825-2855
Richard N Biewer, *President*
Brian B Biewer, *Vice Pres*
Sam Bacon, *Purchasing*
Dennis Melczarczyk, *Sales Staff*
Matt Schott, *Sales Staff*
EMP: 30 **EST:** 1984
SQ FT: 2,500
SALES (est): 8.1MM
SALES (corp-wide): 92.1MM **Privately Held**
WEB: www.biewerlumber.com
SIC: 2491 2429 Structural lumber & timber, treated wood; barrels & barrel parts
PA: Biewer Lumber, Llc
   812 S Riverside Ave
   Saint Clair MI 48079
   810 326-3930

(G-11179)
BRINKS FAMILY CREAMERY LLC
3560 E Mulder Rd (49657-9441)
PHONE.................................231 826-0099
Ron Brinks, *Principal*
Barb Brinks, *Principal*
Kathy Lucas, *Principal*
Kenda Rivera, *Principal*
EMP: 5 **EST:** 2018
SALES (est): 60K **Privately Held**
SIC: 2021 Creamery butter

(G-11180)
HIGHLAND HILLS MAPLE SYRUP LLC
10380 S Dickerson Rd (49657-9416)
PHONE.................................231 920-1589
Shari Benthem,
EMP: 4 **EST:** 2015
SALES (est): 116.1K **Privately Held**
SIC: 2099 Maple syrup

(G-11181)
HYDROLAKE INC (HQ)
6151 W Gerwoude Dr (49657-9110)
PHONE.................................231 825-2233
Franklin C Wheatlake, *President*
Roland L Lyons, *Vice Pres*
EMP: 2 **EST:** 1965
SALES (est): 3.2MM **Privately Held**
WEB: www.hydrolake.com
SIC: 2499 Poles, wood

(G-11182)
HYDROLAKE INC
Also Called: Hydrolake Leasing
6151 W Gerwoude Dr (49657-9110)
PHONE.................................231 825-2233
Thomas Jennett, *General Mgr*
EMP: 7 **Privately Held**
WEB: www.hydrolake.com
SIC: 2631 2491 2411 Coated & treated board; wood preserving; logging

HQ: Hydrolake, Inc
   6151 W Gerwoude Dr
   Mc Bain MI 49657
   231 825-2233

(G-11183)
JOHN A BIEWER LUMBER COMPANY
Also Called: Biewer Sawmill
6251 W Gerwoude Dr (49657-9105)
PHONE.................................231 825-2855
Dan Bowen, *General Mgr*
Leo Colantuono, *General Mgr*
Bob McClellan, *General Mgr*
Jason Otto, *Plant Mgr*
Genny Helland, *Controller*
EMP: 48
SALES (corp-wide): 39MM **Privately Held**
WEB: www.biewerlumber.com
SIC: 2491 2426 2421 Structural lumber & timber, treated wood; hardwood dimension & flooring mills; sawmills & planing mills, general
PA: John A. Biewer Lumber Company
   812 S Riverside Ave
   Saint Clair MI 48079
   810 329-4789

(G-11184)
LEE HAMILTON GARY JR
Also Called: Hamilton Ranch Trucking
10695 W Geers Rd (49657-9727)
PHONE.................................231 884-9600
Gary Lee Hamilton Jr, *Owner*
EMP: 6 **EST:** 2005
SALES (est): 581.2K **Privately Held**
SIC: 3537 Trucks: freight, baggage, etc.: industrial, except mining

(G-11185)
MAIN STREET SPECTACLES LLC
310 E Euclid St (49657-9798)
PHONE.................................231 429-7234
Tiffany Ziegler, *CEO*
EMP: 5 **EST:** 2017
SALES (est): 219.4K **Privately Held**
SIC: 3851 Spectacles

(G-11186)
QUALITY PALLETS LLC
9773 S Burkett Rd (49657-9788)
PHONE.................................231 825-8361
Kenneth Otto, *Mng Member*
EMP: 13 **EST:** 2001
SQ FT: 30,000
SALES (est): 995.8K **Privately Held**
SIC: 2448 Pallets, wood

(G-11187)
ROGER BAZUIN & SONS INC
8750 W Stoney Corners Rd (49657-9414)
PHONE.................................231 825-2889
Roger Bazuin, *President*
Mae Bazuin, *Corp Secy*
Jerry Bazuin, *Vice Pres*
Robert Bazuin, *Director*
EMP: 27 **EST:** 1978
SQ FT: 20,000
SALES (est): 3.4MM **Privately Held**
WEB: www.rogerbazuinandsons.com
SIC: 2411 Logging camps & contractors

Mc Millan
Luce County

(G-11188)
GRACE CONTRACTING SERVICES LLC
25688 County Road 98 (49853-9360)
PHONE.................................906 630-4680
Raymond Plesscher, *Mng Member*
EMP: 4 **EST:** 2015
SALES (est): 309.6K **Privately Held**
SIC: 1791 1799 1389 1795 Precast concrete structural framing or panels, placing of; erection & dismantling of forms for poured concrete; grading oil & gas well foundations; demolition, buildings & other structures;

Mears
Oceana County

(G-11189)
CHASSIS SHOP PRFMCE PDTS INC
1931 N 24th Ave (49436-9687)
PHONE.................................231 873-3640
Stuart Spears, *President*
EMP: 7 **EST:** 1986
SQ FT: 10,000
SALES (est): 1MM **Privately Held**
WEB: www.secure.chassisshop.com
SIC: 3799 Recreational vehicles

Mecosta
Mecosta County

(G-11190)
CHROUCH COMMUNICATIONS INC
Also Called: CCI
6644 9 Mile Rd (49332-9703)
PHONE.................................231 972-0339
Kevin Courtnay, *Manager*
Mark Wrubel, *Manager*
EMP: 4
SALES (corp-wide): 1.9MM **Privately Held**
WEB: www.chrouch.com
SIC: 3679 5731 Headphones, radio; electronic circuits; radios, receiver type; radios, two-way, citizens' band, weather, short-wave, etc.
PA: Chrouch Communications, Inc.
   7860 Morrison Lake Rd
   Saranac MI 48881
   616 642-3881

(G-11191)
LUTCO INC
8800 Midstate Dr (49332-9538)
P.O. Box 107 (49332-0107)
PHONE.................................231 972-5566
Janet L Luttman, *Administration*
EMP: 8 **EST:** 2009
SALES (est): 662.3K **Privately Held**
WEB: www.lutco.com
SIC: 3546 3544 Power-driven handtools; special dies, tools, jigs & fixtures

(G-11192)
MANNIX RE HOLDINGS LLC
8965 Midstate Dr (49332-9538)
PHONE.................................231 972-0088
Douglas Shelby, *Office Mgr*
Mike Alvey,
EMP: 5 **EST:** 2004
SALES (est): 835.8K **Privately Held**
WEB: www.mannixllc.com
SIC: 3325 Steel foundries

(G-11193)
MAXS CONCRETE INC
15323 75th Ave (49332-9609)
PHONE.................................231 972-7558
Max Goltz, *President*
Mike Goltz, *Vice Pres*
Marjorie Story, *Treasurer*
Brian Bakos, *Admin Sec*
EMP: 9 **EST:** 1976
SALES (est): 1MM **Privately Held**
SIC: 3273 3272 Ready-mixed concrete; septic tanks, concrete

(G-11194)
WINERY AT YOUNG FARMS LLC
8396 70th Ave (49332-9721)
PHONE.................................989 506-5142
Mark Young, *Owner*
EMP: 10 **EST:** 2016
SALES (est): 452.9K **Privately Held**
WEB: www.thewineryatyoungfarms.com
SIC: 2084 5813 5921 Wines; wine bar; wine

(PA)=Parent Co (HQ)=Headquarters (DH)=Div Headquarters
✪ = New Business established in last 2 years

Melvin
Sanilac County

(G-11195)
MARK GRIESSEL
7068 Jordan Rd (48454-9750)
PHONE..................810 378-6060
Mark Griessel, *Principal*
EMP: 4 **EST:** 2002
SALES (est): 207.2K **Privately Held**
SIC: 3679 Rheostats, for electronic end products

Melvindale
Wayne County

(G-11196)
ACCULIFT INC
17516 Dix Rd (48122-1316)
PHONE..................313 382-5121
William Szekesy, *President*
EMP: 4 **EST:** 1992
SALES (est): 811.7K **Privately Held**
WEB: www.qmigroup.com
SIC: 3625 Actuators, industrial

(G-11197)
COMPRESSOR INDUSTRIES LLC
17162 Francis St (48122-2316)
PHONE..................313 389-2800
Paul Linares,
EMP: 14
SALES (est): 2MM **Privately Held**
SIC: 3585 Compressors for refrigeration & air conditioning equipment

(G-11198)
CORE ELECTRIC COMPANY INC (PA)
Also Called: Michigan Pump
25125 Outer Dr (48122-1955)
PHONE..................313 382-7140
Daniel Goodman, *President*
John Goodman, *Treasurer*
Jeanne Tritt, *Persnl Mgr*
Don Fisher, *Sales Staff*
Leona Goodman, *Admin Sec*
EMP: 14 **EST:** 1976
SQ FT: 40,000
SALES (est): 4.7MM **Privately Held**
WEB: www.coreelectric.net
SIC: 7694 7699 5063 3451 Electric motor repair; coil winding service; pumps & pumping equipment repair; motors, electric; screw machine products

(G-11199)
DRYE CUSTOM PALLETS INC
19400 Allen Rd (48122-2204)
PHONE..................313 381-2681
Michael A Kostrzewa, *President*
Eric Anderson, *Vice Pres*
David Radcliffe, *Vice Pres*
EMP: 24 **EST:** 1990
SQ FT: 33,000
SALES (est): 722.6K **Privately Held**
SIC: 2448 Pallets, wood

(G-11200)
EBONEX CORPORATION (PA)
Also Called: Keystone Universal
18400 Rialto St (48122-1946)
P.O. Box 3247 (48122-0247)
PHONE..................313 388-0063
Michelle Toennids, *President*
Michael F Szczepanik, *President*
Shelly Toenniges, *Manager*
▲ **EMP:** 7 **EST:** 1960
SQ FT: 30,000
SALES (est): 1.1MM **Privately Held**
WEB: www.ebonex.com
SIC: 2816 5169 Bone black; chemicals & allied products

(G-11201)
HEMINGWAY SCREW PRODUCTS INC
17840 Dix Rd (48122-1320)
PHONE..................313 383-7300
Randy Stojanovich, *President*
EMP: 4 **EST:** 1948
SQ FT: 9,500
SALES (est): 330K **Privately Held**
WEB: www.hemingwaysp.com
SIC: 3451 3599 Screw machine products; machine shop, jobbing & repair

(G-11202)
J I B PROPERTIES LLC
17100 Francis St (48122-2316)
P.O. Box 3245 (48122-0245)
PHONE..................313 382-3234
Fax: 313 382-5530
EMP: 8
SQ FT: 37,500
SALES (est): 530K **Privately Held**
SIC: 7699 1796 3599 Repairs Rebuilds Services & Installs Steel Processing Equipment

(G-11203)
LEPAGES 2000 INC
Also Called: Conros
18765 Seaway Dr (48122-1954)
PHONE..................416 357-0041
Sunir Chandaria, *President*
Ajay RAO, *CFO*
Shernee Chandaria, *Treasurer*
Michael Powell, *Manager*
Sheena Chandaria, *Admin Sec*
▲ **EMP:** 6 **EST:** 1985
SQ FT: 3,300
SALES (est): 24.7MM
SALES (corp-wide): 22.7B **Privately Held**
WEB: www.lepages.com
SIC: 5112 2653 2672 Business forms; corrugated & solid fiber boxes; adhesive papers, labels or tapes: from purchased material
HQ: Henkel Canada Corporation
2515 Meadowpine Blvd Unit 1
Mississauga ON L5N 6
905 814-6511

(G-11204)
MFG UNITED LLC
17025 Clarann St (48122-1301)
PHONE..................313 928-1802
Muthana Fadhl Gubran, *Principal*
EMP: 4 **EST:** 2016
SALES (est): 64.8K **Privately Held**
SIC: 3999 Manufacturing industries

(G-11205)
MIRACLE SIGN
2526 Oakwood Blvd (48122-1349)
PHONE..................313 663-0145
Mike Saraj, *Owner*
EMP: 5 **EST:** 2008
SALES (est): 167.8K **Privately Held**
WEB: www.miraclesigns.wix.com
SIC: 3993 Signs & advertising specialties

(G-11206)
MONARCH ELECTRIC SERVICE CO
Also Called: Monarch Electric Apparatus Svc
18800 Meginnity St (48122-1931)
PHONE..................313 388-7800
Dennis Boik, *Branch Mgr*
EMP: 4
SALES (corp-wide): 655.1MM **Privately Held**
WEB: www.monarch-electric.com
SIC: 7699 5063 7694 3621 Industrial machinery & equipment repair; electrical apparatus & equipment; armature rewinding shops; motors & generators
HQ: Monarch Electric Service Company
5325 W 130th St
Cleveland OH 44130
216 433-7800

(G-11207)
MOTOR CONTROL INCORPORATED
17100 Francis St (48122-2316)
PHONE..................313 389-4000
Corbett R Crider Sr, *President*
EMP: 5 **EST:** 1994
SALES (est): 434.7K **Privately Held**
SIC: 3625 5063 Control equipment, electric; motors, electric

(G-11208)
ONODI TOOL & ENGINEERING CO
19150 Meginnity St (48122-1934)
PHONE..................313 386-6682
John Onodi, *President*
Sandy Onodi, *Vice Pres*
▲ **EMP:** 40
SQ FT: 100,000
SALES: 11.3MM **Privately Held**
WEB: www.onoditool.com
SIC: 3711 3365 3369 3324 Military motor vehicle assembly; aerospace castings, aluminum; aerospace castings, nonferrous: except aluminum; aerospace investment castings, ferrous

(G-11209)
PIPING COMPONENTS INC
Also Called: PCI
4205 Oakwood Blvd (48122-1409)
PHONE..................313 382-6400
Neil Matthews, *President*
Neil R Matthews, *President*
Chris Joyce Powell, *CFO*
▲ **EMP:** 6 **EST:** 1984
SQ FT: 10,000
SALES (est): 3.2MM **Privately Held**
WEB: www.pipingcomponents.com
SIC: 5051 8711 3823 Pipe & tubing, steel; consulting engineer; flow instruments, industrial process type

(G-11210)
STANDARD PLAQUE INCORPORATED
17271 Francis St (48122-1338)
PHONE..................313 383-7233
Nick Tarcia, *President*
Robert S Tarcia, *Vice Pres*
EMP: 10 **EST:** 1983
SQ FT: 6,000
SALES (est): 1MM **Privately Held**
WEB: www.standardplaqueinc.com
SIC: 3089 Plastic hardware & building products

(G-11211)
VISIONARY VITAMIN CO
3205 Mckitrick St (48122-1112)
PHONE..................734 788-5934
Marino Apollinari, *President*
EMP: 4
SALES (est): 228.9K **Privately Held**
SIC: 2833 Vitamins, natural or synthetic: bulk, uncompounded

Memphis
St. Clair County

(G-11212)
G5 OUTDOORS LLC (PA)
34775 Potter St (48041-4613)
PHONE..................866 456-8836
Mike Collins, *Sales Mgr*
Brian Anderson, *Accounts Mgr*
Joel Harris, *Marketing Mgr*
Tim Checkeroski, *Marketing Staff*
Christine Graham, *Manager*
▲ **EMP:** 3 **EST:** 2001
SALES (est): 1.1MM **Privately Held**
WEB: www.g5outdoors.com
SIC: 3949 Archery equipment, general

(G-11213)
GRACE ENGINEERING CORP (PA)
34775 Potter St (48041-4613)
P.O. Box 202 (48041-0202)
PHONE..................810 392-2181
Matt Grace, *President*
Matthew Grace, *Vice Pres*
Steve Seneker, *CFO*
Sara Walsh, *Manager*
Courtney Checkeroski, *Technology*
▲ **EMP:** 65
SQ FT: 65,000
SALES (est): 9.4MM **Privately Held**
WEB: www.graceeng.com
SIC: 3451 3841 Screw machine products; surgical & medical instruments

(G-11214)
TIMOTHY MICHAEL GOODWIN
80080 Robert St (48041-4688)
PHONE..................586 322-3312
Angela Goodwin, *Principal*
EMP: 5 **EST:** 2017
SALES (est): 105.8K **Privately Held**
SIC: 3993 Signs & advertising specialties

Mendon
St. Joseph County

(G-11215)
AFFINITY CUSTOM MOLDING INC
21198 M 60 (49072-8757)
P.O. Box 9 (49072-0009)
PHONE..................269 496-8423
David Cook, *President*
Jim Batten, *Trustee*
Don Miller, *Vice Pres*
Todd Cook, *Treasurer*
Kathy Brueck, *Manager*
▲ **EMP:** 43 **EST:** 1994
SQ FT: 40,000
SALES (est): 8.7MM **Privately Held**
WEB: www.affinitycustommolding.com
SIC: 3089 3544 Injection molding of plastics; forms (molds), for foundry & plastics working machinery; industrial molds

(G-11216)
CIRCLE C MOLD & PLAS GROUP INC
55664 Parkville Rd (49072-9748)
PHONE..................269 496-5515
F Earl Carr Jr, *President*
Linda Carr, *Vice Pres*
EMP: 10 **EST:** 1990
SQ FT: 15,000
SALES (est): 1.4MM **Privately Held**
SIC: 3544 Industrial molds

(G-11217)
JASON BRENEMAN & SON LOGGING
26940 Kirby Rd (49072-9641)
PHONE..................269 432-1378
Michelle Breneman, *Principal*
EMP: 4 **EST:** 2016
SALES (est): 81.7K **Privately Held**
SIC: 2411 Logging

(G-11218)
JONATHAN SHOWALTER
Also Called: Bee Line Apiaries & Woodenware
20960 M 60 (49072-8724)
PHONE..................269 496-7001
Jonathan Showalter, *Owner*
EMP: 4 **EST:** 2003
SALES (est): 354.4K **Privately Held**
WEB: www.beelinewoodenware.com
SIC: 0279 2499 Apiary (bee & honey farm); beekeeping supplies, wood

(G-11219)
MANCHESTER INDUSTRIES INC VA
26920 M 60 (49072-9654)
PHONE..................269 496-2715
Mark Schuppel, *Vice Pres*
Ranse McKinney, *Branch Mgr*
EMP: 33 **Publicly Held**
WEB: www.manind.com
SIC: 2679 Paperboard products, converted
HQ: Manchester Industries Inc. Of Virginia
200 Orleans St
Richmond VA 23231
804 226-4250

(G-11220)
PENTAGON MOLD CO
21015 M 60 (49072-8739)
PHONE..................269 496-7072
Jay Crabtree, *President*
Todd Batten, *Vice Pres*
EMP: 4 **EST:** 1983
SQ FT: 4,600 **Privately Held**
SIC: 3544 Industrial molds

GEOGRAPHIC SECTION

Menominee - Menominee County (G-11244)

(G-11221)
SANDERSON INSULATION
840 Avery Dr (49072-9667)
PHONE.....................269 496-7660
Marvin J Sanderson, *Owner*
Gloria Sanderson, *Principal*
EMP: 5 **EST:** 1976
SALES (est): 360K **Privately Held**
SIC: 3357 1761 Nonferrous wiredrawing & insulating; siding contractor; roofing contractor

(G-11222)
TH PLASTICS INC (PA)
106 E Main St (49072-9650)
P.O. Box 188 (49072-0188)
PHONE.....................269 496-8495
Patrick J Haas, *CEO*
Chris Haas, *President*
Michael McCaw, *Vice Pres*
Elizabeth Mitchell, *Vice Pres*
Scott Mitchell, *Vice Pres*
▲ **EMP:** 108
SQ FT: 210,000
SALES (est): 94.9MM **Privately Held**
WEB: www.thplastics.com
SIC: 3089 Injection molding of plastics

(G-11223)
TH PLASTICS INC
Also Called: Plant 2
106 E Main St (49072-9650)
P.O. Box 188 (49072-0188)
PHONE.....................269 496-8495
Scott Mitchell, *Manager*
EMP: 77
SALES (corp-wide): 94.9MM **Privately Held**
WEB: www.thplastics.com
SIC: 3089 3714 Plastic containers, except foam; motor vehicle parts & accessories
PA: Th Plastics, Inc.
106 E Main St
Mendon MI 49072
269 496-8495

Menominee
Menominee County

(G-11224)
ADVANCED BLNDING SOLUTIONS LLC
Also Called: ABS
949 1st St (49858-3265)
P.O. Box 37, Wallace (49893-0037)
PHONE.....................906 914-4180
Brent Berquist, *Vice Pres*
Daniel Haas, *Vice Pres*
Joe Gardon, *Project Mgr*
Janet Kolaszewski, *Purch Agent*
Keith Coroneos, *Engineer*
▲ **EMP:** 17 **EST:** 2009
SQ FT: 12,000
SALES (est): 5MM **Privately Held**
WEB: www.adv-blend.com
SIC: 3634 7629 Blenders, electric; electrical household appliance repair

(G-11225)
ANCHOR COUPLING INC (HQ)
5520 13th St (49858-1014)
PHONE.....................906 863-2672
Bonnie Fetch, *President*
Dave Bozeman, *Principal*
Rick Brown, *Vice Pres*
John Pressler, *Vice Pres*
Dan V Avond, *Maint Spvr*
◆ **EMP:** 225 **EST:** 1992
SQ FT: 88,000
SALES (est): 95.1MM
SALES (corp-wide): 41.7B **Publicly Held**
WEB: www.anchorcoupling.com
SIC: 3429 Clamps & couplings, hose
PA: Caterpillar Inc.
510 Lake Cook Rd Ste 100
Deerfield IL 60015
224 551-4000

(G-11226)
ANDERSON MANUFACTURING CO INC (PA)
Also Called: Ultimate Bed
5300 13th St (49858-1044)
PHONE.....................906 863-8223
Robert F Anderson, *President*
Deb Carley, *Treasurer*
Lois A Anderson, *Admin Sec*
EMP: 11 **EST:** 1962
SQ FT: 50,000
SALES (est): 1.4MM **Privately Held**
SIC: 2511 Dressers, household: wood

(G-11227)
AQUILA RESOURCES INC (PA)
414 10th Ave Ste 1 (49858-3066)
PHONE.....................906 352-4024
Thomas Quigley, *Principal*
Michael McCurry, *Editor*
Jennifer Cortez, *Sales Mgr*
Dan Blondeau, *Corp Comm Staff*
EMP: 8 **EST:** 2011
SALES (est): 594.2K **Privately Held**
WEB: www.aquilaresources.com
SIC: 6211 1481 Oil & gas lease brokers; nonmetallic mineral services

(G-11228)
BEAVER CREEK WOOD PRODUCTS LLC
993 26th St (49858-2212)
P.O. Box 456, Marinette WI (54143-0456)
PHONE.....................920 680-9663
David Koertge, *Mng Member*
EMP: 7 **EST:** 2006
SALES (est): 546.3K **Privately Held**
WEB: www.beavercreekwoodproducts.com
SIC: 2499 Mulch, wood & bark

(G-11229)
COLEMAN MACHINE INC (PA)
Also Called: Coleman Racing Products
N1597 Us Highway 41 (49858-9692)
PHONE.....................906 863-1113
Gene Coleman, *President*
Donna Coleman, *Vice Pres*
▲ **EMP:** 30 **EST:** 1965
SQ FT: 10,000
SALES (est): 4MM **Privately Held**
WEB: www.colemanracing.com
SIC: 3599 3549 Machine shop, jobbing & repair; metalworking machinery

(G-11230)
COMPONENT SOLUTIONS LLC
2219 10th Ave (49858-2301)
P.O. Box 1074, Marinette WI (54143-6074)
PHONE.....................906 863-2682
Kari Jo Bunting, *Owner*
EMP: 45 **EST:** 2003
SALES (est): 11.8MM **Privately Held**
WEB: www.componentsolutions.us
SIC: 5031 2426 Lumber: rough, dressed & finished; lumber, hardwood dimension

(G-11231)
DUFF BRUSH LLC
630 7th St (49858-3159)
PHONE.....................906 863-3319
Matthew Duffrin,
EMP: 8 **EST:** 1998
SALES (est): 148.4K **Privately Held**
WEB: www.duffbrush.com
SIC: 3991 Brooms & brushes

(G-11232)
DUNN PAPER INC
144 1st St (49858-3343)
PHONE.....................810 984-5521
EMP: 5
SALES (corp-wide): 109.5MM **Privately Held**
WEB: www.dunnpaper.com
SIC: 2671 2672 Paper coated or laminated for packaging; coated & laminated paper
HQ: Dunn Paper, Inc.
218 Riverview St
Port Huron MI 48060
810 984-5521

(G-11233)
ENSTROM HELICOPTER CORPORATION
2209 22nd St (49858-3515)
PHONE.....................906 863-1200
Matthew Francour, *CEO*
Gong WEI, *Ch of Bd*
Guo Huaqiang, *Principal*
Kris Brooks, *Safety Mgr*
Lori Okrasinski, *Purch Mgr*
◆ **EMP:** 220 **EST:** 1959
SQ FT: 88,000
SALES (est): 34.5MM **Privately Held**
WEB: www.enstromhelicopter.com
SIC: 3728 Aircraft parts & equipment
PA: Chongqing General Aviation Industry Group Co., Ltd.
No.19,Yinlong Rd.,Longxing Town,Yubei District
Chongqing 40113

(G-11234)
EVEN WEIGHT BRUSH LLC
603 6th St (49858-3163)
P.O. Box 34 (49858-0034)
PHONE.....................906 863-3319
EMP: 4
SALES (est): 300K **Privately Held**
SIC: 3991 Mfg Brooms/Brushes

(G-11235)
FIBREK INC
Also Called: Resolute Forest Products
701 4th Ave (49858-3353)
P.O. Box 277 (49858-0277)
PHONE.....................906 864-9125
Robert Garland, *President*
Todd Clausen, *General Mgr*
Michael Klumb, *Engineer*
Bill Malloy, *Engineer*
Sue Keer, *Controller*
EMP: 146 **EST:** 1998
SALES (est): 5.2MM
SALES (corp-wide): 2.9B **Privately Held**
WEB: www.pfresolu.com
SIC: 2611 Pulp mills
PA: Resolute Forest Products Inc
111 Boul Robert-Bourassa Bureau 5000
Montreal QC H3C 2
514 875-2160

(G-11236)
FIBREK RECYCLING US INC (HQ)
Also Called: Great Lakes Pulp & Fibre
701 4th Ave (49858-3353)
P.O. Box 277 (49858-0277)
PHONE.....................906 863-8137
Richard Garneau, *President*
Alain Boivin, *Vice Pres*
Peter Staiger, *Treasurer*
Jacques Vachon, *Admin Sec*
◆ **EMP:** 100 **EST:** 2006
SQ FT: 5,000
SALES (est): 27.6MM
SALES (corp-wide): 2.9B **Privately Held**
WEB: www.glpf.com
SIC: 2611 Pulp mills, chemical & semi-chemical processing
PA: Resolute Forest Products Inc
111 Boul Robert-Bourassa Bureau 5000
Montreal QC H3C 2
514 875-2160

(G-11237)
FIBREK US INC
701 4th Ave (49858-3353)
PHONE.....................906 864-9125
Richard Garneau, *President*
EMP: 16 **EST:** 2014
SALES (est): 1.9MM
SALES (corp-wide): 2.9B **Privately Held**
WEB: www.pfresolu.com
SIC: 2611 Pulp mills
PA: Resolute Forest Products Inc
111 Boul Robert-Bourassa Bureau 5000
Montreal QC H3C 2
514 875-2160

(G-11238)
FLANDERS INDUSTRIES INC
Also Called: Lloyd Flanders Industries
3010 10th St (49858-1704)
P.O. Box 550 (49858-0550)
PHONE.....................906 863-4491
Dudley K Flanders, *President*
Jeffrey H Starks, *Corp Secy*
Eugene B Davenport, *Exec VP*
Norman Rosebrock, *Senior VP*
Mary Carlson, *Vice Pres*
◆ **EMP:** 110 **EST:** 1929
SALES (est): 1.2MM **Privately Held**
WEB: www.lloydflanders.com
SIC: 2519 2514 Wicker furniture: padded or plain; metal lawn & garden furniture; lawn furniture: metal

(G-11239)
GREAT LAKES EXPLORATION INC
414 10th Ave Ste 1 (49858-3066)
PHONE.....................906 352-4024
Karl Stump, *Principal*
EMP: 9 **EST:** 2001
SALES (est): 233.6K **Privately Held**
WEB: www.glexploration.com
SIC: 7335 3531 4512 8713 Aerial photography, except mapmaking; aerial work platforms: hydraulic/elec. truck/carrier mounted; helicopter carrier, scheduled; surveying services

(G-11240)
JK OUTDOORS LLC
N1180 Country Side Ln P 2 (49858-9223)
PHONE.....................906 863-2932
Jeremy Sallgreen, *Principal*
EMP: 4 **EST:** 2013
SALES (est): 116.1K **Privately Held**
SIC: 2048 Buttermilk emulsion for animal food

(G-11241)
JP SKIDMORE LLC
W5634 Evergreen Road No 3 (49858-9604)
PHONE.....................906 424-4127
EMP: 9 **EST:** 2015
SALES (est): 685.6K **Privately Held**
WEB: www.jpskidmorellc.com
SIC: 3531 Forestry related equipment

(G-11242)
L E JONES COMPANY
1200 34th Ave (49858-1695)
PHONE.....................906 863-1043
David Doll, *CEO*
Peter Vennema, *Ch of Bd*
Douglas Dooley, *Vice Pres*
Todd Trudeau, *Senior Engr*
John Schmitz, *Controller*
▲ **EMP:** 390 **EST:** 1946
SQ FT: 110,000
SALES (est): 49.9MM **Privately Held**
WEB: www.lejones.com
SIC: 3592 3545 Valves, engine; machine tool accessories

(G-11243)
LUMBER JACK HARDWOODS INC (PA)
N2509 O1 Dr (49858-9674)
P.O. Box 397 (49858-0397)
PHONE.....................906 863-7090
John Fleetwood, *President*
Candace Fleetwood, *Corp Secy*
Nathan Fleetwood, *Vice Pres*
EMP: 14 **EST:** 1976
SALES (est): 3.4MM **Privately Held**
SIC: 2426 2421 Hardwood dimension & flooring mills; kiln drying of lumber

(G-11244)
MARSHALL MIDDLEBY HOLDING LLC
Also Called: Nu-Vu Food Service Systems
5600 13th St (49858-1029)
PHONE.....................906 863-4401
◆ **EMP:** 63 **EST:** 2004
SALES (est): 16.5MM
SALES (corp-wide): 2.5B **Publicly Held**
WEB: www.nu-vu.com
SIC: 3556 Food products machinery

Menominee - Menominee County (G-11245)

PA: The Middleby Corporation
1400 Toastmaster Dr
Elgin IL 60120
847 741-3300

(G-11245)
MARTIN SAW & TOOL INC (PA)
1212 19th Ave (49858-2718)
PHONE....................906 863-6812
William W Martin, *President*
Jeffrey Martin, *Vice Pres*
Randy Martin, *Vice Pres*
Phyllis Martin, *Treasurer*
EMP: 6 **EST:** 1960
SQ FT: 21,260
SALES (est): 500K **Privately Held**
SIC: 3599 3425 Machine shop, jobbing & repair; saw blades & handsaws

(G-11246)
MENOMINEE ACQUISITION CORP
Also Called: Clearwater Paper - Menominee
144 1st St (49858-3302)
PHONE....................906 863-5595
Russell Taylor, *President*
Tom Moore, *Vice Pres*
Dianne Scheu, *CFO*
Hugo Vivero, *VP Sales*
▼ **EMP:** 125 **EST:** 1900
SALES (est): 22.6MM
SALES (corp-wide): 109.5MM **Privately Held**
WEB: www.dunnpaper.com
SIC: 2621 Paper mills
HQ: Dunn Paper, Inc.
218 Riverview St
Port Huron MI 48060
810 984-5521

(G-11247)
MENOMINEE CITY OF MICHIGAN
Also Called: Waste Water Treatment
1301 5th Ave (49858)
P.O. Box 453 (49858-0453)
PHONE....................906 863-3050
Mike Thorsen, *Manager*
EMP: 4 **Privately Held**
WEB: www.menominee.us
SIC: 3589 Water treatment equipment, industrial
PA: Menominee City Of Michigan
2511 10th St
Menominee MI 49858
906 863-2656

(G-11248)
MENOMINEE SAW AND SUPPLY CO (PA)
Also Called: Menominee Carbide Cutting Tls
900 16th St (49858-2600)
P.O. Box 515 (49858-0515)
PHONE....................906 863-2609
Felix Ben Mroz, *President*
John Brock, *COO*
Marilyn K Mroz, *Treasurer*
▼ **EMP:** 27 **EST:** 1950
SQ FT: 11,000
SALES (est): 3.4MM **Privately Held**
WEB: www.menomineesaw.com
SIC: 7699 5084 3546 3541 Knife, saw & tool sharpening & repair; sawmill machinery & equipment; power-driven handtools; machine tools, metal cutting type; saw blades & handsaws

(G-11249)
MENOMINEE SAW AND SUPPLY CO
2134 13th St (49858-2104)
PHONE....................906 863-8998
Terry Champeau, *Manager*
EMP: 4
SALES (corp-wide): 3.4MM **Privately Held**
WEB: www.menomineesaw.com
SIC: 7692 Welding repair
PA: Saw Menominee And Supply Company
900 16th St
Menominee MI 49858
906 863-2609

(G-11250)
MENOMNEE RVER LBR DMNSIONS LLC
2219 10th Ave (49858-2301)
P.O. Box 1074, Marinette WI (54143-6074)
PHONE....................906 863-2682
Kari Bunting, *President*
Dave Geier, *Vice Pres*
▲ **EMP:** 7 **EST:** 1996
SQ FT: 60,000
SALES (est): 1MM **Privately Held**
WEB: www.componentsolutions.us
SIC: 5211 2426 Planing mill products & lumber; dimension, hardwood

(G-11251)
MIDDLEBY CORPORATION
Nu-Vu Food Service Systems
5600 13th St (49858-1029)
PHONE....................906 863-4401
Gary Hahn, *Branch Mgr*
EMP: 103
SALES (corp-wide): 2.5B **Publicly Held**
WEB: www.middleby.com
SIC: 3556 Ovens, bakery
PA: The Middleby Corporation
1400 Toastmaster Dr
Elgin IL 60120
847 741-3300

(G-11252)
MINERALS PROCESSING CORP
414 10th Ave (49858-3066)
PHONE....................906 352-4024
EMP: 6 **EST:** 2013
SALES (est): 581.7K **Privately Held**
WEB: www.mpclaboratory.com
SIC: 1081 Metal mining exploration & development services

(G-11253)
N PACK SHIP CENTER
1045 10th St (49858-3025)
PHONE....................906 863-4095
April Davis, *Owner*
EMP: 5 **EST:** 2001
SALES (est): 422.7K **Privately Held**
SIC: 3086 4731 Packaging & shipping materials, foamed plastic; agents, shipping

(G-11254)
NORTHERN COATINGS & CHEM CO
705 6th Ave (49858-3115)
PHONE....................906 863-2641
Larry Melgary, *President*
Susan Ellie, *Vice Pres*
Mark Lavalley, *Vice Pres*
Dustin Kurath, *Technical Staff*
▼ **EMP:** 37 **EST:** 1971
SQ FT: 100,000
SALES (est): 7MM **Privately Held**
WEB: www.northern-coatings.com
SIC: 2851 2899 2869 Paints & paint additives; chemical preparations; industrial organic chemicals

(G-11255)
NORTHERN FAB & MACHINE LLC
5601 13th St (49858-1045)
PHONE....................906 863-8506
Melisa Johnson, *Controller*
Daniel Drifka,
EMP: 12 **EST:** 2000
SALES (est): 2.2MM **Privately Held**
WEB: www.northernfab.net
SIC: 3599 3443 Hose, flexible metallic; weldments

(G-11256)
PLUTCHAK FAB
Also Called: Krane
N1715 Us Highway 41 (49858-9607)
PHONE....................906 864-4650
Chris Plutchak, *Vice Pres*
Tim Plutchak,
EMP: 8 **EST:** 1985
SQ FT: 20,000
SALES (est): 5MM **Privately Held**
WEB: www.plutchakfab.com
SIC: 5084 3441 Cranes, industrial; fabricated structural metal

(G-11257)
R W FERNSTRUM & COMPANY
1716 11th Ave (49858-2500)
P.O. Box 97 (49858-0097)
PHONE....................906 863-5553
Paul W Fernstrum, *President*
Dave Peura, *Engineer*
Jean Granum, *CFO*
Todd Fernstrum, *Treasurer*
Bruce Neece, *Sales Staff*
▲ **EMP:** 35 **EST:** 1943
SQ FT: 34,300
SALES (est): 8.9MM **Privately Held**
WEB: www.fernstrum.com
SIC: 3443 3429 Fabricated plate work (boiler shop); manufactured hardware (general)

(G-11258)
RESOLUTE FP US INC
701 4th Ave (49858-3353)
PHONE....................877 547-2737
Dave Nielsen, *Director*
EMP: 5
SALES (corp-wide): 2.9B **Privately Held**
WEB: www.resolutefp.com
SIC: 2621 Newsprint paper; uncoated paper
HQ: Resolute Fp Us Inc.
5300 Cureton Ferry Rd
Catawba SC 29704
803 981-8000

(G-11259)
SCHULTZ LOGGING
4109 14th St (49858-1117)
PHONE....................906 863-5719
Richard Schultz, *Principal*
EMP: 5 **EST:** 2001
SALES (est): 142.3K **Privately Held**
SIC: 2411 Logging camps & contractors

(G-11260)
STRIDER SOFTWARE INC
1605 7th St (49858-2815)
P.O. Box 513, Marinette WI (54143-0513)
PHONE....................906 863-7798
Kenneth Stillman, *President*
EMP: 6 **EST:** 1987
SALES (est): 473.8K **Privately Held**
WEB: www.typestyler.com
SIC: 7372 Application computer software

(G-11261)
SUPERIOR ATTACHMENT INC
N3522 Us Highway 41 (49858-9653)
PHONE....................906 864-1708
Rich Linsmeier, *Principal*
EMP: 4 **EST:** 2007
SALES (est): 411.8K **Privately Held**
WEB: www.superiorattachments.com
SIC: 3523 Farm machinery & equipment

(G-11262)
YOOPER WINERY LLC
817 48th Ave (49858-1234)
PHONE....................906 361-0318
John R Lucas,
EMP: 5 **EST:** 2017
SALES (est): 112.1K **Privately Held**
WEB: www.yooperwinery.com
SIC: 2084 Wines

Merrill
Saginaw County

(G-11263)
MERRILL TECHNOLOGIES GROUP INC
Also Called: Merrill Tool & Machine
21659 Gratiot Rd (48637-8717)
PHONE....................989 643-7981
Robert Yackel, *CEO*
EMP: 123
SALES (corp-wide): 191.1MM **Privately Held**
WEB: www.merrilltg.com
SIC: 3599 Machine shop, jobbing & repair
PA: Merrill Technologies Group, Inc.
400 Florence St
Saginaw MI 48602
989 791-6676

(G-11264)
SILER PRECISION MACHINE INC
136 E Saginaw St (48637-2528)
P.O. Box 37 (48637-0037)
PHONE....................989 643-7793
Steven J Siler, *President*
George Siler, *Treasurer*
EMP: 4 **EST:** 1994
SQ FT: 14,000
SALES (est): 698.5K **Privately Held**
WEB: www.silermachine.com
SIC: 3599 Machine shop, jobbing & repair

(G-11265)
SUPERIOR VAULT CO
345 E Mahoney (48637-9337)
P.O. Box 118 (48637-0118)
PHONE....................989 643-4200
John Hutchinson, *Owner*
EMP: 4 **EST:** 2001
SALES (est): 410.2K **Privately Held**
WEB: www.superiorvault.com
SIC: 3272 5087 Burial vaults, concrete or precast terrazzo; concrete burial vaults & boxes

Merritt
Missaukee County

(G-11266)
HOWEY TREE BALER CORPORATION
6069 E Gaukel Rd (49667-9738)
PHONE....................231 328-4321
Stephen Howey Jr, *President*
Darleana Howey, *Corp Secy*
Gary Howey, *Vice Pres*
Greg Howey, *Vice Pres*
Stephen Howey Sr, *Vice Pres*
EMP: 5 **EST:** 1967
SQ FT: 8,000
SALES (est): 866.6K **Privately Held**
WEB: www.howeytreebaler.com
SIC: 3523 Balers, farm: hay, straw, cotton, etc.; elevators, farm

(G-11267)
LONEYS WELDING & EXCVTG INC
6735 E Houghton Lake Rd (49667-9743)
PHONE....................231 328-4408
Michael Loney, *President*
Lesia Loney, *Admin Sec*
EMP: 5 **EST:** 1978
SALES (est): 934K **Privately Held**
SIC: 1382 7692 Oil & gas exploration services; welding repair

(G-11268)
TRONOX INCORPORATED
4176 N Dorr Rd (49667-9774)
PHONE....................231 328-4986
Steve Walker, *Branch Mgr*
EMP: 5
SALES (corp-wide): 651.9MM **Privately Held**
WEB: www.tronox.com
SIC: 1311 1321 Crude petroleum production; natural gas liquids
HQ: Tronox Incorporated
263 Tresser Blvd Ste 1100
Stamford CT 06901
203 705-3800

Mesick
Wexford County

(G-11269)
BLUEWATER TECH GROUP INC
6305 W 115 (49668)
PHONE....................231 885-2600
Dennis Whitener, *Exec VP*
Justin Hutchison, *Project Engr*
Mack Truax, *Branch Mgr*
EMP: 5

GEOGRAPHIC SECTION   Michigan Center - Jackson County (G-11296)

SALES (corp-wide): 78.5MM **Privately Held**
WEB: www.bluewatertech.com
SIC: **3651** 5064 7622 7359 Household audio & video equipment; electrical appliances, television & radio; radio & television repair; equipment rental & leasing
HQ: Bluewater Technologies Group, Inc.
  30303 Beck Rd
  Wixom MI 48393
  248 356-4399

(G-11270)
CASSELMAN LOGGING
23400 13 Mile Rd (49668-9604)
PHONE.................................231 885-1040
James A Casselman, *Partner*
Patty Casselman, *Partner*
EMP: 6 EST: 1986
SALES (est): 625.1K **Privately Held**
SIC: **2411** 2421 Pulpwood contractors engaged in cutting; sawmills & planing mills, general

(G-11271)
DART ENERGY CORPORATION
23862 13 Mile Rd (49668-9604)
PHONE.................................231 885-1665
Danny Cagel, *Branch Mgr*
EMP: 14 **Privately Held**
SIC: **1311** 1382 Crude Petroleum And Natural Gas, Nsk

(G-11272)
HOUSLER SAWMILL INC
222 E 16 Rd (49668-9726)
PHONE.................................231 824-6353
Leslie Housler, *President*
Wayl D Housler, *Vice Pres*
EMP: 19 EST: 1942
SALES (est): 1.5MM **Privately Held**
WEB: www.houslerlumber.com
SIC: **2421** Sawmills & planing mills, general

(G-11273)
MESICK MOLD CO
4901 Industrial Dr (49668-9525)
PHONE.................................231 885-1304
Chancey Spencer, *President*
David Spencer, *Vice Pres*
Jon Slabaugh, *Engineer*
Mark Giberson, *Design Engr*
Gertrude Spencer, *Treasurer*
EMP: 28 EST: 1967
SQ FT: 6,000
SALES (est): 2.6MM **Privately Held**
WEB: www.mesickmold.com
SIC: **3544** Forms (molds), for foundry & plastics working machinery; industrial molds

(G-11274)
MY METAL MEDIUM
5774 N M 37 (49668-9123)
PHONE.................................231 590-4051
Matthew Macpherson, *Principal*
EMP: 4 EST: 2016
SALES (est): 89.3K **Privately Held**
WEB: www.mymetalmedium.com
SIC: **3499** Fabricated metal products

(G-11275)
VISUAL PRODUCTIONS INC
6305 W M 115 (49668-9767)
PHONE.................................248 356-4399
Tom Battaglia, *President*
Jeff Dancz, *Project Mgr*
EMP: 75 EST: 1991
SALES (est): 1.2MM
SALES (corp-wide): 78.5MM **Privately Held**
WEB: www.visual.productions
SIC: **8748** 7359 3993 Business consulting; equipment rental & leasing; signs & advertising specialties
PA: M10 Group Holding Company
  24050 Northwestern Hwy
  Southfield MI 48075
  248 356-4399

Metamora
Lapeer County

(G-11276)
AURORA CAD CAM INC
Also Called: Cad CAM
1643 E Brocker Rd (48455-9789)
PHONE.................................810 678-2128
Ron Jovanovitz, *President*
EMP: 10 EST: 1984
SALES (est): 879.2K **Privately Held**
WEB: www.auroracadcaminc.com
SIC: **3543** Industrial patterns

(G-11277)
BELLA BLEU EMBROIDERY LLC
3423 Wynns Mill Rd (48455-9628)
PHONE.................................810 797-2286
Corena Lipkowit, *Principal*
EMP: 4 EST: 2014
SALES (est): 122.1K **Privately Held**
WEB: www.bellableuembroidery.com
SIC: **2395** Embroidery & art needlework

(G-11278)
CROSS COUNTRY OILFLD SVCS INC
4833 Linda Ln (48455-8935)
PHONE.................................337 366-3840
Sherri Dupuis, *President*
EMP: 4 EST: 2014
SALES (est): 174.9K **Privately Held**
SIC: **1389** Oil field services

(G-11279)
GRAPHITE MACHINING INC
4141 S Oak St (48455-9240)
PHONE.................................810 678-2227
Paige Bearss, *Finance Mgr*
Tim Bears, *Manager*
Kathleen Schoch, *Admin Sec*
EMP: 10
SALES (corp-wide): 18.1MM **Privately Held**
WEB: www.graphitemachininginc.com
SIC: **3599** 3624 3295 Machine shop, jobbing & repair; carbon & graphite products; graphite, natural: ground, pulverized, refined or blended
PA: Graphite Machining, Inc.
  240 N Main St
  Topton PA 19562
  610 682-0080

(G-11280)
GREAT LAKES GAGES LLC
3689 Hadley Rd (48455-9111)
PHONE.................................810 797-8300
Joel Bialek,
EMP: 6 EST: 2020
SALES (est): 279.1K **Privately Held**
WEB: www.usa.ral-shop.com
SIC: **3829** Testing equipment: abrasion, shearing strength, etc.

(G-11281)
INDOCOMP SYSTEMS INC
3383 S Lapeer Rd (48455-8968)
PHONE.................................810 678-3990
Mike Keerl, *President*
Brian Daye, *President*
Thomas Foley, *COO*
EMP: 12 EST: 1998
SALES (est): 445.2K **Privately Held**
WEB: www.indocomp.com
SIC: **3571** 7373 Electronic computers; systems integration services

(G-11282)
JOHN R SAND & GRAVEL CO INC
1717 E Dryden Rd (48455-9308)
PHONE.................................810 678-3715
Edward R Evatz Jr, *President*
EMP: 4 EST: 1930
SALES (est): 645.5K **Privately Held**
SIC: **1442** Common sand mining; gravel mining

(G-11283)
L & J ENTERPRISES INC
Also Called: Lady Jane Gourmet Seed Co.
3181 Wynns Mill Ct (48455-8956)
PHONE.................................586 995-4153
Laura Noble, *President*
Joe Noble, *Vice Pres*
EMP: 4 EST: 1997
SALES (est): 303.9K **Privately Held**
WEB: www.ljseedco.com
SIC: **2099** Food preparations

(G-11284)
OXFORD BIOMEDICAL RESEARCH INC (PA)
4600 Gardner Rd (48455-9108)
P.O. Box 522, Oxford (48371-0522)
PHONE.................................248 852-8815
Denis M Callewaert, *President*
Richard McGowen, *Opers Dir*
Karen Callewaert, *Treasurer*
EMP: 2 EST: 1984
SQ FT: 4,000
SALES (est): 2.6MM **Privately Held**
WEB: www.oxfordbiomed.com
SIC: **5122** 8731 2836 Biologicals & allied products; biological research; biological products, except diagnostic

(G-11285)
QUALITY STAINLESS MGF
2820 Island Point Dr (48455-9726)
PHONE.................................248 866-6219
EMP: 4 EST: 2010
SALES (est): 131.4K **Privately Held**
SIC: **3999** Manufacturing industries

(G-11286)
SHADOWOOD TECHNOLOGY INC
4221 Meadow Pond Ln (48455-9751)
P.O. Box 284, Hadley (48440-0284)
PHONE.................................810 358-2569
Todd Hemingway, *President*
Wendy K Hemingway, *CFO*
EMP: 8 EST: 2009
SQ FT: 10,000
SALES (est): 630.1K **Privately Held**
SIC: **3519** Diesel, semi-diesel or duel-fuel engines, including marine; diesel engine rebuilding; engines, diesel & semi-diesel or dual-fuel; governors, pump, for diesel engines

(G-11287)
SUPERIOR DESIGN & MFG
4180 Pleasant St (48455-9403)
P.O. Box 204 (48455-0204)
PHONE.................................810 678-3950
Patrick Clouse, *President*
David Denise, *Treasurer*
EMP: 10 EST: 1992
SQ FT: 4,500
SALES (est): 1.2MM **Privately Held**
SIC: **3545** 3569 3599 Machine tool accessories; assembly machines, non-metalworking; machine shop, jobbing & repair

(G-11288)
SURFACE COATINGS CO
3695 Merritt Lake Dr (48455-8981)
PHONE.................................248 977-9478
EMP: 8 EST: 2019
SALES (est): 164K **Privately Held**
WEB: www.gemsealproducts.com
SIC: **2951** Asphalt paving mixtures & blocks

(G-11289)
TEC-3 PROTOTYPES INC
4321 Blood Rd (48455-9243)
PHONE.................................810 678-8909
EMP: 20
SQ FT: 9,200
SALES (est): 2.7MM **Privately Held**
SIC: **3465** 3496 3495 3444 Mfg Automotive Stampings Mfg Misc Fab Wire Prdts Mfg Wire Springs Mfg Sheet Metalwork Mfg Hardware

Michigan Center
Jackson County

(G-11290)
ADCO PRODUCTS LLC
Also Called: Adco Products, Inc.
4401 Page Ave (49254-1037)
P.O. Box 457 (49254-0457)
PHONE.................................517 841-7238
John Knox, *CEO*
Glenn Frommer, *President*
Kent Lowry, *Materials Mgr*
Sam Ward, *Engineer*
Eric Weidner, *Project Engr*
EMP: 220 EST: 1999
SQ FT: 200,000
SALES (est): 45.2MM
SALES (corp-wide): 2.7B **Publicly Held**
WEB: www.hbfuller.com
SIC: **2891** Adhesives & sealants
HQ: Adco Global, Inc.
  100 Tri State Intl Ste 13
  Lincolnshire IL 60069
  847 282-3485

(G-11291)
CENTER MACHINE & TOOL LLC
150 Factory Rd (49254-1010)
PHONE.................................517 748-2500
Craig Ahrens,
EMP: 7 EST: 2003
SQ FT: 8,000
SALES (est): 977.9K **Privately Held**
WEB: www.scottsimmonds.com
SIC: **3599** Machine shop, jobbing & repair

(G-11292)
ETERNABOND INC
4401 Page Ave (49254-1037)
PHONE.................................847 540-0600
Christopher Margarites, *President*
Gail Margarites, *Vice Pres*
▲ EMP: 7 EST: 1999
SQ FT: 5,000
SALES (est): 866.1K **Privately Held**
WEB: www.eternabond.com
SIC: **2891** Adhesives

(G-11293)
FELEO MFG STRATEGIES LLC
Also Called: Peregrine Manufacturing
4115 Felters Rd (49254-1067)
PHONE.................................517 795-1193
Allison Ireton, *Mng Member*
EMP: 11 EST: 2018
SALES (est): 375.8K **Privately Held**
SIC: **3999**

(G-11294)
MILLENNIUM ADHESIVE PRODUCTS (PA)
4401 Page Ave (49254-1037)
PHONE.................................800 248-4010
EMP: 5 EST: 2011
SALES (est): 293.6K **Privately Held**
WEB: www.millenniumadhesives.com
SIC: **2891** Adhesives

(G-11295)
PRECISION GUIDES LLC
151 Factory Rd (49254-1009)
PHONE.................................517 536-7234
Lee Cole, *Mfg Staff*
Kurt Cole,
Scott Cole,
EMP: 5 EST: 2011
SQ FT: 2,500
SALES (est): 400K **Privately Held**
SIC: **3541** Machine tools, metal cutting type

(G-11296)
SYNCHRONOUS MANUFACTURING INC
4050 Page Ave (49254-1030)
PHONE.................................517 764-6930
Michael Thorrez, *President*
Albert A Thorrez, *Treasurer*
▲ EMP: 16 EST: 1990
SALES (est): 1MM **Privately Held**
SIC: **3499** 3625 3714 Fire- or burglary-resistive products; relays & industrial controls; motor vehicle parts & accessories

Michigan Center - Jackson County (G-11297) — GEOGRAPHIC SECTION

(G-11297)
UNISORB INC (HQ)
Also Called: Unisorb Installation Tech
4117 Felters Rd Ste A (49254-1076)
P.O. Box 1000, Jackson (49204-1000)
PHONE....................517 764-6060
Michael A Considine, *Ch of Bd*
Peter M Moore, *President*
John Richter, *Vice Pres*
Wayne H Whittaker, *Vice Pres*
Neal Lewis, *Project Mgr*
▲ **EMP:** 29 **EST:** 1917
SQ FT: 64,000
SALES (est): 10.4MM **Privately Held**
WEB: www.unisorb.com
SIC: 3499 Machine bases, metal
PA: Considine Financial Corporation
  101 N Indian Hill Blvd
  Claremont CA 91711
  626 793-1000

Middleton
Gratiot County

(G-11298)
MEYERS JOHN
Also Called: Johnny Meyers Trucking
5752 Cleveland Rd (48856-9703)
PHONE....................989 236-5400
John Meyers, *Owner*
EMP: 4 **EST:** 1989
SQ FT: 30,000
SALES (est): 240K **Privately Held**
SIC: 3711 Truck & tractor truck assembly

(G-11299)
MID MCHGAN FEED INGRDIENTS LLC
4585 5 Garfield Rd (48856)
PHONE....................989 236-5014
Kris D Duflo,
EMP: 5 **EST:** 2012
SALES (est): 134.7K **Privately Held**
SIC: 2048 Prepared feeds

(G-11300)
SHADY NOOK FARMS (PA)
Also Called: M.R. Village Pizzeria
129 S Newton St (48856-9788)
PHONE....................989 236-7240
Richard Schaffer, *President*
Don Schaffer, *Vice Pres*
EMP: 4 **EST:** 1940
SALES (est): 853.3K **Privately Held**
SIC: 2099 4225 Pizza, refrigerated: except frozen; miniwarehouse, warehousing

Middleville
Barry County

(G-11301)
ACCURATE MACHINE & TL USA LTD
987 Grand Rapids St (49333-9498)
PHONE....................269 205-2610
Steve Zawacki, *Manager*
EMP: 4
SALES (corp-wide): 5.1MM **Privately Held**
WEB: www.accuratemachineandtool.com
SIC: 3599 Machine shop, jobbing & repair
PA: Accurate Machine & Tool Limited
  1844 Wilson Ave
  North York ON M9M 1
  416 742-8301

(G-11302)
ALLIANCE SHEET METAL INC
6262 N Moe Rd (49333-8749)
PHONE....................269 795-2954
Tim Flohe, *President*
EMP: 17 **EST:** 1995
SQ FT: 44,000
SALES (est): 1.6MM **Privately Held**
SIC: 3444 Sheet metalwork

(G-11303)
BRADFORD-WHITE CORPORATION
200 Lafayette St (49333-7048)
PHONE....................269 795-3364
Nicholas J Giuffre, *CEO*
Eric Lannes, *Senior VP*
Jennifer Russomanno, *Project Mgr*
R Hermenitt, *Prdtn Mgr*
Robbie McCain, *Maint Spvr*
EMP: 900
SQ FT: 300,000
SALES (corp-wide): 171.2MM **Privately Held**
WEB: www.bradfordwhite.com
SIC: 3639 Hot water heaters, household
PA: Bradford White Corporation
  725 Talamore Dr
  Ambler PA 19002
  215 641-9400

(G-11304)
COMMERCIAL WORKS
200 Lafayette St (49333-9492)
PHONE....................269 795-2060
Bradford-White Corporation, *Partner*
Eugene West, *Opers Mgr*
Dan Leedy, *Info Tech Dir*
EMP: 15 **EST:** 1992
SQ FT: 70,000
SALES (est): 381.8K **Privately Held**
SIC: 3433 Heating equipment, except electric

(G-11305)
CROWN MANUFACTURING LLC
6262 N Moe Rd (49333-8749)
PHONE....................616 295-7018
EMP: 11 **EST:** 2010
SALES (est): 139.5K **Privately Held**
WEB: www.crown.com
SIC: 3999 Manufacturing industries

(G-11306)
FORZZA CORPORATION
915 Grand Rapids St (49333-9498)
PHONE....................616 884-6121
EMP: 20
SALES (corp-wide): 410.8K **Privately Held**
SIC: 3585 Parts for heating, cooling & refrigerating equipment
PA: Forzza Corporation
  222 N Lake St
  Madison OH 44057
  440 998-6300

(G-11307)
GREAT LAKES JIG & FIXTURE
11610 Bowens Mill Rd (49333-9758)
PHONE....................269 795-4349
Scott Palazzolo, *Owner*
Dan Friedl, *General Mgr*
Chad Reil, *Foreman/Supr*
Phil Sidor, *QC Mgr*
Steve Wiersma, *Engineer*
EMP: 7 **EST:** 1999
SQ FT: 2,200
SALES (est): 705.8K **Privately Held**
WEB: www.gljf.us
SIC: 3544 Special dies, tools, jigs & fixtures

(G-11308)
H & L MANUFACTURING CO
900 E Main St (49333-9417)
PHONE....................269 795-5000
Steve Sawdy, *CEO*
Roger Van Dyke, *Manager*
Tanya Sawdy, *Admin Sec*
EMP: 130 **EST:** 1964
SQ FT: 28,000
SALES (est): 22.7MM **Privately Held**
WEB: www.hlmanufacturing.com
SIC: 3714 3694 Motor vehicle parts & accessories; engine electrical equipment

(G-11309)
MIDDLEVILLE TOOL & DIE CO INC
1900 Patterson Rd (49333-8410)
PHONE....................269 795-3646
Gary Middleton, *CEO*
Ross Martin, *President*
Mike Cornell, *VP Mfg*
Kris Shyne, *Prdtn Mgr*
Rick Cain, *QC Mgr*
EMP: 70
SQ FT: 53,000
SALES (est): 24.1MM **Privately Held**
WEB: www.mtd-inc.com
SIC: 3469 3544 3465 Stamping metal for the trade; special dies & tools; automotive stampings

(G-11310)
NOBLE INDUSTRIES
6850 N Solomon Rd (49333-9473)
PHONE....................616 245-7400
Lisa Cortese, *Principal*
EMP: 4 **EST:** 2016
SALES (est): 98.2K **Privately Held**
WEB: www.nobleindustries.com
SIC: 3999 Manufacturing industries

(G-11311)
R5 CONSTRUXTION INC
4695 N M 37 Hwy Ste C (49333-8276)
PHONE....................855 480-7663
EMP: 12 **EST:** 2018
SALES (est): 1.1MM **Privately Held**
WEB: www.r5construxtion.weebly.com
SIC: 1521 3069 3295 1761 Single-family housing construction; roofing, membrane rubber; roofing granules; roofing, siding & sheet metal work

(G-11312)
REURINK ROOF MAINT & COATING
12795 Jackson Rd (49333-8596)
PHONE....................269 795-2337
Richard H Reurink, *President*
James Reurink, *Treasurer*
Mary Reurink, *Admin Sec*
EMP: 4
SALES (est): 400K **Privately Held**
SIC: 1761 2952 Roofing contractor; roofing felts, cements or coatings

(G-11313)
ROGUE WELDING SERVICE LLC
5787 Hilltop Dr (49333-8089)
PHONE....................616 648-9723
Adam Plummer, *Principal*
EMP: 4 **EST:** 2017
SALES (est): 72.7K **Privately Held**
SIC: 7692 Welding repair

(G-11314)
STICKMANN BAECKEREI
11332 W M 179 Hwy (49333-8429)
PHONE....................269 205-2444
Rebecca Denney, *Principal*
EMP: 6 **EST:** 2015
SALES (est): 198.8K **Privately Held**
SIC: 2095 Roasted coffee

(G-11315)
TILLERMAN JFP LLC (PA)
10451 W Garbow Rd (49333-8557)
PHONE....................616 443-8346
Remos Lenio, *Mng Member*
EMP: 1 **EST:** 2016
SALES (est): 4.9MM **Privately Held**
SIC: 3069 Molded rubber products

(G-11316)
U S BAIRD CORPORATION
J M Systems Div
8121 108th St Se (49333-9302)
PHONE....................616 826-5013
John Mitteer, *General Mgr*
EMP: 10
SALES (corp-wide): 5.5MM **Privately Held**
SIC: 3542 Spinning, spline rolling & winding machines
PA: The U S Baird Corporation
  1700 Stratford Ave
  Stratford CT
  203 375-3361

Midland
Midland County

(G-11317)
ADMIRAL
1801 S Saginaw Rd (48640-6807)
PHONE....................989 835-9160
Amanda Huntley, *Manager*
EMP: 7 **EST:** 2017
SALES (est): 138K **Privately Held**
SIC: 2911 Petroleum refining

(G-11318)
AGRIGENETICS INC
2030 Dow Ctr (48674-1500)
PHONE....................317 337-3000
Robert M Isackson, *Principal*
EMP: 52 **EST:** 1994
SALES (est): 15.2MM
SALES (corp-wide): 38.5B **Publicly Held**
WEB: www.dow.com
SIC: 2873 Fertilizers: natural (organic), except compost
HQ: The Dow Chemical Company
  2211 H H Dow Way
  Midland MI 48642
  989 636-1000

(G-11319)
ALLOY CONSTRUCTION SERVICE INC (PA)
3500 Contractors Dr (48642-6962)
PHONE....................989 486-6960
Ronnie J Neumann, *President*
Michael Laundra, *Vice Pres*
EMP: 25 **EST:** 1981
SQ FT: 13,000
SALES (est): 8MM **Privately Held**
WEB: www.alloyconstruction.com
SIC: 3441 Fabricated structural metal

(G-11320)
AMERCHOL CORPORATION
2030 Dow Ctr (48674-1500)
PHONE....................989 636-2441
Jamie Howl, *Principal*
▼ **EMP:** 1 **EST:** 1977
SALES (est): 3.8MM
SALES (corp-wide): 38.5B **Publicly Held**
WEB: www.dow.com
SIC: 2869 Laboratory chemicals, organic
HQ: The Dow Chemical Company
  2211 H H Dow Way
  Midland MI 48642
  989 636-1000

(G-11321)
AMPM INC
7403 W Wackerly St (48642-7409)
P.O. Box 1887 (48641-1887)
PHONE....................989 837-8800
Mark Bush, *President*
William Trethaway, *Chairman*
Angela Harrington, *Prdtn Mgr*
Hugo Cruz, *Site Mgr*
Julie Battle, *Director*
EMP: 29 **EST:** 1969
SQ FT: 6,400
SALES (est): 4MM **Privately Held**
WEB: www.ampminc.com
SIC: 7311 3577 8732 Advertising consultant; graphic displays, except graphic terminals; market analysis or research

(G-11322)
APTARGROUP INC
Also Called: LMS
2202 Ridgewood Dr (48642-5841)
PHONE....................989 631-8030
James Manning, *President*
Sandy Murphy, *Human Res Dir*
Keith Heal, *Manager*
Stephen Butterfield, *Business Dir*
Darcy Wright, *Business Dir*
EMP: 5 **Publicly Held**
WEB: www.aptar.com
SIC: 3069 4225 2822 Molded rubber products; general warehousing; synthetic rubber
PA: Aptargroup, Inc.
  265 Exchange Dr Ste 100
  Crystal Lake IL 60014

▲ = Import ▼ = Export
◆ = Import/Export

GEOGRAPHIC SECTION
Midland - Midland County (G-11348)

(G-11323)
BLUE CUBE HOLDING LLC (DH)
2030 Dow Ctr (48674-1500)
PHONE.................................989 636-1000
Thomas Macphee, *President*
Duncan Stuart, *Vice Pres*
Ignacio Molina, *Treasurer*
Daniel Dub, *Admin Sec*
EMP: 143 **EST:** 2013
SALES (est): 24MM
SALES (corp-wide): 5.7B **Publicly Held**
SIC: 2819 Industrial inorganic chemicals
HQ: Blue Cube Spinco Inc.
190 Carondelet Plz # 1530
Saint Louis MO 63105
314 480-1400

(G-11324)
BOSTONTEC INC (PA)
2700 James Savage Rd (48642-6529)
P.O. Box 2044 (48641-2044)
PHONE.................................989 496-9510
Richard Vander Velle, *President*
Dave Clark, *Exec VP*
Pat Perez, *Production*
Mike Chapman, *Design Engr*
Bob Doucette, *Natl Sales Mgr*
▼ **EMP:** 9 **EST:** 2003
SQ FT: 180,000
SALES (est): 1.5MM **Privately Held**
WEB: www.bostontec.com
SIC: 2522 Office furniture, except wood

(G-11325)
BUCKEYS CONTRACTING & SERVICE
707 Jefferson Ave (48640-5391)
PHONE.................................989 835-9512
Richard Buckey, *President*
Janet K Buckey, *Vice Pres*
EMP: 7 **EST:** 1975
SQ FT: 4,800
SALES (est): 1.4MM **Privately Held**
SIC: 1542 7692 Nonresidential construction; welding repair

(G-11326)
BURCH TANK & TRUCK INC
Also Called: Burch Truck and Trailer Parts
4200 James Savage Rd (48642-6522)
PHONE.................................989 495-0342
Tony Near, *Business Mgr*
EMP: 4 **Privately Held**
WEB: www.burchtank.com
SIC: 3795 5088 Tanks & tank components; tanks & tank components
PA: Burch Tank & Truck, Inc.
2113 Enterprise Dr
Mount Pleasant MI 48858

(G-11327)
CASE SYSTEMS INC
2700 James Savage Rd (48642-6529)
P.O. Box 2044 (48641-2044)
PHONE.................................989 496-9510
Robert W Bowden, *Ch of Bd*
Richard W Vanderweele, *President*
David L Clark, *General Mgr*
Dave Clark, *COO*
Kelly Wehner, *Vice Pres*
EMP: 190 **EST:** 1993
SQ FT: 160,000
SALES (est): 36.9MM **Privately Held**
WEB: www.casesystems.com
SIC: 2521 3821 2434 Cabinets, office: wood; filing cabinets (boxes), office: wood; laboratory apparatus & furniture; wood kitchen cabinets

(G-11328)
CENTEN AG LLC (DH)
Also Called: Centen AG Inc
2030 Dow Ctr (48674-1500)
PHONE.................................989 636-1000
Mark A Bachman, *President*
EMP: 326 **EST:** 1997
SALES (est): 50.2MM
SALES (corp-wide): 38.5B **Publicly Held**
WEB: www.dow.com
SIC: 2879 Agricultural chemicals
HQ: The Dow Chemical Company
2211 H H Dow Way
Midland MI 48642
989 636-1000

(G-11329)
CIRCLE K SERVICE CORPORATION
4300 James Savage Rd (48642-6523)
PHONE.................................989 496-0511
Rodney Kloha, *President*
EMP: 36 **EST:** 1986
SQ FT: 15,000
SALES (est): 1MM **Privately Held**
WEB: www.circlekservice.com
SIC: 7538 3537 General truck repair; industrial trucks & tractors

(G-11330)
COBBLESTONE PRESS
4516 Washington St (48642-3583)
PHONE.................................989 832-0166
Harvey Hirsch, *Owner*
EMP: 5 **EST:** 2003
SALES (est): 168.7K **Privately Held**
SIC: 2741 Miscellaneous publishing

(G-11331)
CQ SIMPLE LLC
5103 Eastman Ave Ste 125 (48640-6724)
PHONE.................................989 492-7068
Kim Warmbier, *Opers Staff*
Elaine Blodgett, *Sales Staff*
Dave Root,
EMP: 7 **EST:** 2013
SALES (est): 968.3K **Privately Held**
WEB: www.cqsimple.com
SIC: 7372 Business oriented computer software

(G-11332)
DAILY BILL
610 W Saint Andrews Rd (48640-3354)
PHONE.................................989 631-2068
Bill Daily, *Principal*
EMP: 5 **EST:** 2011
SALES (est): 54.3K **Privately Held**
SIC: 2711 Newspapers, publishing & printing

(G-11333)
DDP SPCLTY ELCTRNIC MTLS US 9
2200 W Salzburg Rd (48686-0001)
PHONE.................................989 496-6000
EMP: 21 **EST:** 2017
SALES (est): 4.9MM
SALES (corp-wide): 20.4B **Publicly Held**
WEB: www.dupont.com
SIC: 3357 Nonferrous wiredrawing & insulating
PA: Dupont De Nemours, Inc.
974 Centre Rd Bldg 730
Wilmington DE 19805
302 774-3034

(G-11334)
DDP SPCLTY ELCTRNIC MTLS US IN
Also Called: Ddp Saginaw Shipping
3800 S Saginaw Rd Gate177 (48640)
PHONE.................................989 708-6737
EMP: 84
SALES (corp-wide): 20.4B **Publicly Held**
SIC: 2821 Thermoplastic materials; thermosetting materials; plasticizer/additive based plastic materials; molding compounds, plastics
HQ: Ddp Specialty Electronic Materials Us, Llc
974 Centre Rd
Wilmington DE 19805
610 244-6000

(G-11335)
DDP SPCLTY ELCTRNIC MTLS US LL
Also Called: Midland Glass Bonding Facility
3400 S Saginaw Rd (48640-5608)
PHONE.................................989 636-9953
EMP: 84
SALES (corp-wide): 20.4B **Publicly Held**
WEB: www.dupont.com
SIC: 2821 Thermoplastic materials; thermosetting materials; plasticizer/additive based plastic materials; molding compounds, plastics
HQ: Ddp Specialty Electronic Materials Us, Llc
974 Centre Rd
Wilmington DE 19805
610 244-6000

(G-11336)
DEBI DESIGNS
2801 Saint Marys Dr (48640-2493)
P.O. Box 1345 (48641-1345)
PHONE.................................989 832-9598
Deborah Campbell, *Executive*
EMP: 5 **EST:** 2016
SALES (est): 65.4K **Privately Held**
SIC: 3579 Office machines

(G-11337)
DENDRITECH INC
3110 Schuette Rd (48642-6944)
PHONE.................................989 496-1152
S Emery Scheibert, *President*
Mark Kaiser, *Manager*
EMP: 6 **EST:** 1992
SQ FT: 6,540
SALES (est): 1.3MM **Privately Held**
WEB: www.dendritech.com
SIC: 2822 Ethylene-propylene rubbers, EPDM polymers

(G-11338)
DENDRITIC NANOTECHNOLOGIES INC
1515 Commerce Dr Ste C (48642-8531)
PHONE.................................989 774-3096
Robert Berry, *CEO*
EMP: 9 **EST:** 2003
SALES (est): 592.9K **Privately Held**
SIC: 3089 Plastic processing

(G-11339)
DIAZEM CORP
1406 E Pine St (48640-5323)
PHONE.................................989 832-3612
EMP: 8
SQ FT: 25,000
SALES (est): 847.1K **Privately Held**
SIC: 2819 Manufactures Chemicals

(G-11340)
DOW AGROSCIENCES LLC
433 Bldg (48674-0001)
P.O. Box 2009 (48641-2009)
PHONE.................................989 636-4400
David Duepre, *Branch Mgr*
Bryon Bootman, *Sr Project Mgr*
Bryan Kriz, *Senior Mgr*
EMP: 35
SALES (corp-wide): 14.2B **Publicly Held**
WEB: www.corteva.us
SIC: 2879 Trace elements (agricultural chemicals)
HQ: Corteva Agriscience Llc
9330 Zionsville Rd
Indianapolis IN 46268

(G-11341)
DOW CHEMICAL COMPANY (HQ)
2211 H H Dow Way (48642-4815)
PHONE.................................989 636-1000
James R Fitterling, *CEO*
Howard Ungerleider, *President*
Shelley Thelen, *Counsel*
Darryl Frickey, *Counsel*
Steve Kennedy, *Counsel*
◆ **EMP:** 7245 **EST:** 1897
SALES: 38.5B **Publicly Held**
WEB: www.dow.com
SIC: 2821 3081 3086 2812 Thermoplastic materials; thermosetting materials; plasticizer/additive based plastic materials; molding compounds, plastics; plastic film & sheet; plastics foam products; insulation or cushioning material, foamed plastic; alkalies & chlorine; fungicides, herbicides; insecticides, agricultural or household; pesticides, agricultural or household
PA: Dow Inc.
2211 H H Dow Way
Midland MI 48642
989 636-1000

(G-11342)
DOW CHEMICAL COMPANY
2511 S Saginaw Rd (48640-5688)
PHONE.................................989 636-1000
Deb Plaver, *Branch Mgr*
Olivia Zwetzig, *Manager*
Richelle Yott, *Technician*
EMP: 75
SALES (corp-wide): 38.5B **Publicly Held**
WEB: www.dow.com
SIC: 2821 Thermoplastic materials
HQ: The Dow Chemical Company
2211 H H Dow Way
Midland MI 48642
989 636-1000

(G-11343)
DOW CHEMICAL COMPANY
1801 Larkin Center Dr (48642-8605)
PHONE.................................989 636-4406
EMP: 150
SALES (corp-wide): 38.5B **Publicly Held**
SIC: 3081 3086 2879 0181 Specialty Chemicals & Agricultural Products
HQ: The Dow Chemical Company
2211 H H Dow Way
Midland MI 48642
989 636-1000

(G-11344)
DOW CHEMICAL COMPANY
2511 E Patrick Rd (48642)
PHONE.................................989 636-1000
EMP: 4
SALES (corp-wide): 38.5B **Publicly Held**
WEB: www.dow.com
SIC: 2821 Thermoplastic materials
HQ: The Dow Chemical Company
2211 H H Dow Way
Midland MI 48642
989 636-1000

(G-11345)
DOW CHEMICAL COMPANY
S Saginaw Bldg 304 (48667-0001)
PHONE.................................989 636-1000
EMP: 4
SALES (corp-wide): 38.5B **Publicly Held**
WEB: www.dow.com
SIC: 2821 3081 Plastics materials & resins; tile, unsupported plastic
HQ: The Dow Chemical Company
2211 H H Dow Way
Midland MI 48642
989 636-1000

(G-11346)
DOW CHEMICAL COMPANY
2050 Abbott Rd (48674-0001)
PHONE.................................989 636-5430
David Wassick, *Research*
Mohamed Saadany, *Finance*
Catherine M Baase, *Manager*
David Asiala, *Technology*
Ian Carlson, *Technology*
EMP: 68
SALES (corp-wide): 38.5B **Publicly Held**
WEB: www.dow.com
SIC: 2821 Plastics materials & resins
HQ: The Dow Chemical Company
2211 H H Dow Way
Midland MI 48642
989 636-1000

(G-11347)
DOW CHEMICAL COMPANY
2030 Willard H Dow Center (48674-0001)
PHONE.................................989 636-1000
Brenda Harris, *Vice Pres*
Heather Lau Turner, *Mktg Dir*
EMP: 4
SALES (corp-wide): 38.5B **Publicly Held**
WEB: www.dow.com
SIC: 2821 Thermoplastic materials
HQ: The Dow Chemical Company
2211 H H Dow Way
Midland MI 48642
989 636-1000

(G-11348)
DOW CHEMICAL COMPANY
2040 Dow Ctr (48674-1500)
P.O. Box 6004 (48641-6004)
PHONE.................................989 832-1000
William Davis, *Manager*
EMP: 150
SALES (corp-wide): 38.5B **Publicly Held**
WEB: www.dow.com
SIC: 2821 5169 Thermoplastic materials; chemicals & allied products

Midland - Midland County (G-11349)

HQ: The Dow Chemical Company
2211 H H Dow Way
Midland MI 48642
989 636-1000

(G-11349)
DOW CHEMICAL COMPANY
1320 Waldo Ave Ste 300 (48642-5868)
PHONE.................................989 636-0540
Anne Mitchell, *Branch Mgr*
EMP: 4
SALES (corp-wide): 38.5B **Publicly Held**
WEB: www.dow.com
SIC: 2821 3081 3086 2879 Plastics materials & resins; unsupported plastics film & sheet; plastics foam products; agricultural chemicals; ornamental nursery products
HQ: The Dow Chemical Company
2211 H H Dow Way
Midland MI 48642
989 636-1000

(G-11350)
DOW CHEMICAL COMPANY
Gpc Building (48667-0001)
P.O. Box 2047 (48641-2047)
PHONE.................................989 638-6441
Andrea David, *District Mgr*
Steve Anderson, *Manager*
Ashutosh Singh, *Consultant*
Ann Mitchell, *Admin Sec*
EMP: 20
SALES (corp-wide): 38.5B **Publicly Held**
WEB: www.dow.com
SIC: 2869 Industrial organic chemicals
HQ: The Dow Chemical Company
2211 H H Dow Way
Midland MI 48642
989 636-1000

(G-11351)
DOW CHEMICAL COMPANY
2030 Dow Ctr (48674-1500)
P.O. Box 1886 (48641-1886)
PHONE.................................925 432-5000
EMP: 4
SALES (corp-wide): 38.5B **Publicly Held**
WEB: www.dow.com
SIC: 2869 Industrial organic chemicals
HQ: The Dow Chemical Company
2211 H H Dow Way
Midland MI 48642
989 636-1000

(G-11352)
DOW CHEMICAL COMPANY
3700 James Savage Rd (48642-6517)
P.O. Box 2560 (48641-2560)
PHONE.................................989 636-5409
EMP: 75
SALES (corp-wide): 38.5B **Publicly Held**
WEB: www.dow.com
SIC: 2821 3081 3086 2812 Thermoplastic materials; thermosetting materials; plasticizer/additive based plastic materials; molding compounds, plastics; plastic film & sheet; plastics foam products; insulation or cushioning material, foamed plastic; alkalies & chlorine; fungicides, herbicides; insecticides, agricultural or household; pesticides, agricultural or household
HQ: The Dow Chemical Company
2211 H H Dow Way
Midland MI 48642
989 636-1000

(G-11353)
DOW CORNING CORPORATION
1404 Peppermill Cir (48642-3066)
PHONE.................................989 839-2808
Jim Fitterling, *CEO*
Howard Ungerleider, *CFO*
Michael Altes, *Manager*
EMP: 12 **EST:** 1943
SALES (est): 1.8MM **Privately Held**
SIC: 2869 2822 Silicones; silicone rubbers

(G-11354)
DOW INC (PA)
2211 H H Dow Way (48642-4815)
PHONE.................................989 636-1000
James R Fitterling, *Ch of Bd*
Jack Broodo, *President*
Diego Donoso, *President*
Mauro Gregorio, *President*
Howard I Ungerleider, *President*
EMP: 1031 **EST:** 2018
SALES (est): 38.5B **Publicly Held**
WEB: www.corporate.dow.com
SIC: 2821 3081 3086 Thermoplastic materials; thermosetting materials; plasticizer/additive based plastic materials; molding compounds, plastics; plastic film & sheet; plastics foam products; insulation or cushioning material, foamed plastic

(G-11355)
DOW INTERNATIONAL HOLDINGS CO (DH)
2030 Dow Ctr (48674-1500)
PHONE.................................989 636-1000
Andrew N Liveris, *Ch of Bd*
EMP: 1 **EST:** 2001
SALES (est): 63.6MM
SALES (corp-wide): 38.5B **Publicly Held**
WEB: www.dow.com
SIC: 2821 Thermoplastic materials
HQ: The Dow Chemical Company
2211 H H Dow Way
Midland MI 48642
989 636-1000

(G-11356)
DOWAKSA USA LLC (PA)
Also Called: Dowaksa Carbon Wrap
3720 James Savage Rd (48642-6517)
PHONE.................................989 600-8610
Douglas Parks, *CEO*
EMP: 5 **EST:** 2013
SALES (est): 919.1K **Privately Held**
WEB: www.dowaksa.com.tr
SIC: 3624 Carbon & graphite products

(G-11357)
DUNKIN DONUTS & BASKIN-ROBBINS
5000 Foxcroft Dr (48642-3299)
PHONE.................................989 835-8412
Gale Letcher, *Owner*
EMP: 11 **EST:** 1996
SALES (est): 109.3K **Privately Held**
WEB: www.dunkindonuts.com
SIC: 5461 2051 5812 Doughnuts; doughnuts, except frozen; ice cream, soft drink & soda fountain stands

(G-11358)
DUPONT
3100 James Savage Rd (48642-6532)
PHONE.................................651 767-2527
Todd Pangburn, *Principal*
Christina Kaiser, *Research*
Laura Gallindo, *Manager*
EMP: 24 **EST:** 2019
SALES (est): 6.8MM **Privately Held**
WEB: www.dupont.com
SIC: 2879 Agricultural chemicals

(G-11359)
EAGLEBURGMANN INDUSTRIES LP
1821 Austin St (48642-6955)
PHONE.................................989 486-1571
Pat McCann, *Manager*
EMP: 5
SALES (corp-wide): 10.4B **Privately Held**
WEB: www.eagleburgmann.us
SIC: 3999 Atomizers, toiletry
HQ: Eagleburgmann Industries Lp
10035 Brookriver Dr
Houston TX 77040
713 939-9515

(G-11360)
ECO BIO PLASTICS MIDLAND INC
4037 S Saginaw Rd (48640-8501)
PHONE.................................989 496-1934
Fukuji Saotome, *CEO*
Jim Plonka, *CEO*
Takamichi Matsushita, *Chairman*
Kenichi Toguchi, *COO*
Greg Dostal, *Plant Engr Mgr*
▲ **EMP:** 10 **EST:** 2011
SQ FT: 38,000
SALES (est): 4.4MM **Privately Held**
WEB: www.ecobioplastics.com
SIC: 3087 Custom compound purchased resins
PA: Eco Research Institute Ltd.
16-29, Nampeidaicho
Shibuya-Ku TKY

(G-11361)
EDGE FITNES TRAINING HDQTR LLC
1403 Washington St # 26 (48640-5676)
PHONE.................................989 486-9870
EMP: 4 **EST:** 2018
SALES (est): 45.6K **Privately Held**
WEB: www.edgefitnessandtraining.com
SIC: 7991 7372 Physical fitness facilities; application computer software

(G-11362)
FALCON ROAD MAINT EQP LLC
Also Called: Falcon Rme
2000 Austin St (48642-5980)
PHONE.................................989 495-9332
Mark Groulx, *President*
Brenda Martin, *Controller*
Nick Vachon, *Accountant*
Brian Thornton, *Regl Sales Mgr*
EMP: 14 **EST:** 2014
SALES (est): 4.4MM **Privately Held**
WEB: www.falconrme.com
SIC: 3531 Construction machinery

(G-11363)
FISHER SAND AND GRAVEL COMPANY
Also Called: Allied Concrete Products
3403 Contractors Dr (48642-6946)
P.O. Box 1703 (48641-1703)
PHONE.................................989 835-7187
James O Fisher, *President*
Ralph Fisher Jr, *Corp Secy*
John Fischer, *Vice Pres*
EMP: 25 **EST:** 1918
SALES (est): 4.4MM **Privately Held**
WEB: www.fishersand.com
SIC: 3273 5032 5211 Ready-mixed concrete; concrete & cinder block; concrete & cinder block

(G-11364)
FLOWSERVE US INC
2420 Schuette Rd (48642-5974)
PHONE.................................989 496-3897
Joseph Kalich, *Research*
Jody Kotecki, *Engineer*
Brad Harrelson, *Manager*
Linda Heinlein, *Manager*
EMP: 5
SALES (corp-wide): 3.7B **Publicly Held**
WEB: www.flowserve.com
SIC: 3561 Pumps & pumping equipment
HQ: Flowserve Us Inc.
5215 N Ocnnor Blvd Ste 23 Connor
Irving TX 75039
972 443-6500

(G-11365)
FOUR LKES SPCIAL ASSSSMENT DST
233 E Larkin St Ste 2 (48640-5110)
PHONE.................................989 941-3005
David Kepler, *President*
Kayla Stryker, *Admin Sec*
EMP: 4 **EST:** 2020
SALES (est): 155.8K **Privately Held**
WEB: www.four-lakes-taskforce-mi.com
SIC: 2531 Public building & related furniture

(G-11366)
FREUDNBERG BTRY PWR SYSTEMS LL ●
2700 S Saginaw Rd (48640-6845)
PHONE.................................989 698-3329
Jeff Michalski, *Mng Member*
EMP: 50 **EST:** 2021
SALES (est): 8.5MM
SALES (corp-wide): 10.4B **Privately Held**
SIC: 3694 Battery charging generators, automobile & aircraft
HQ: Xalt Energy, Llc
2700 S Saginaw Rd
Midland MI 48640

(G-11367)
GANTEC INC
777 E Isabella Rd (48640-8333)
PHONE.................................989 631-9300
Richard Olson, *President*
Lanny Robins, *Principal*
Joe Affholter, *Chairman*
Joseph Affholter, *Chairman*
Clint Yerkes, *Vice Pres*
EMP: 7 **EST:** 2005
SALES (est): 2MM **Privately Held**
WEB: www.gantecinc.com
SIC: 2879 2873 Pesticides, agricultural or household; fertilizers: natural (organic), except compost

(G-11368)
GCI WATER SOLUTIONS LLC
5202 Dale St (48642-3289)
PHONE.................................312 928-9992
Michael Schuette, *Principal*
EMP: 6 **EST:** 2017
SALES (est): 518.6K **Privately Held**
WEB: www.gci-water.com
SIC: 3589 Water treatment equipment, industrial

(G-11369)
GLAXOSMITHKLINE LLC
2518 Abbott Rd Apt V11 (48642-5010)
PHONE.................................989 280-1225
EMP: 4
SALES (corp-wide): 45.3B **Privately Held**
WEB: www.us.gsk.com
SIC: 2834 Pharmaceutical preparations
HQ: Glaxosmithkline Llc
5 Crescent Dr
Philadelphia PA 19119
215 751-4000

(G-11370)
HAMPSHIRE CHEMICAL CORP
2211 H H Dow Way (48642-4815)
PHONE.................................989 636-1000
EMP: 44
SALES (corp-wide): 38.5B **Publicly Held**
SIC: 2869 Alcohols, non-beverage
HQ: Hampshire Chemical Corp
2 E Spit Brook Rd
Nashua NH 03060

(G-11371)
HARRIS SHEET METAL CO
3313 S Saginaw Rd (48640-5697)
PHONE.................................989 496-3080
Mark E Harris, *President*
Mark Harris, *President*
EMP: 23 **EST:** 1982
SQ FT: 9,600
SALES (est): 605.9K **Privately Held**
WEB: www.harrissheetmetal.com
SIC: 3444 1761 Ducts, sheet metal; sheet metalwork

(G-11372)
HEALTH ENHANCEMENT SYSTEMS INC (PA)
800 Cambridge St Ste 101 (48642-7600)
P.O. Box 1035 (48641-1035)
PHONE.................................989 839-0852
Dean Witherspoon, *President*
Kaitlyn Baase, *Accounts Mgr*
Alanna Hartley, *Accounts Mgr*
Caroline Repollet, *Office Mgr*
Lisa Cochran, *Manager*
EMP: 6 **EST:** 1992
SQ FT: 3,000
SALES (est): 2.3MM **Privately Held**
WEB: www.hesonline.com
SIC: 2741 Miscellaneous publishing

(G-11373)
INGERSOLL CM SYSTEMS LLC
3505 Centennial Dr (48642-6940)
PHONE.................................989 495-5000
Chuck Rozewski, *Materials Mgr*
Brian Kennedy, *Opers Staff*
Donald Christensen, *Engineer*
Charlie Shepard, *Engineer*
Mark St Pierre, *Engineer*
◆ **EMP:** 57 **EST:** 2003
SALES (est): 14.1MM **Privately Held**
WEB: www.teamicms.com
SIC: 3541 Machine tools, metal cutting type

▲ = Import ▼ = Export
◆ = Import/Export

Midland - Midland County (G-11400)

(G-11374)
INTERACT WEBSITES INC
Also Called: Interactrv
3526 E Curtis Rd (48642-8432)
P.O. Box 2291 (48641-2291)
PHONE 800 515-9672
Kevin Wallenbeck, *President*
Ron Cheney, *Vice Pres*
Jennifer Ouderkirk, *Opers Staff*
Joyce Dillingham, *Marketing Staff*
Nicolette Matt, *Marketing Staff*
EMP: 18 **EST:** 2004
SALES (est): 1MM **Privately Held**
WEB: www.interactrv.com
SIC: 7372 Prepackaged software

(G-11375)
INTERNATIONAL BUS MCHS CORP
Also Called: IBM
2125 Ridgewood Dr (48642-5836)
PHONE 989 832-6000
EMP: 25
SALES (corp-wide): 79.1B **Publicly Held**
SIC: 3571 Mfg Electronic Computers
PA: International Business Machines Corporation
1 New Orchard Rd Ste 1 # 1
Armonk NY 10504
914 499-1900

(G-11376)
INTERNATIONAL ISOCYANATE INST
1232 Holyrood St (48640-6313)
PHONE 989 878-0336
EMP: 5 **EST:** 2016
SALES (est): 74.4K **Privately Held**
WEB: www.diisocyanates.org
SIC: 2865 Isocyanates

(G-11377)
JLM ELEC
1854 Smith Ct (48640-8946)
PHONE 989 486-3788
Michael Gravis, *Principal*
EMP: 4 **EST:** 2007
SALES (est): 243.8K **Privately Held**
SIC: 3621 Generators & sets, electric

(G-11378)
JOHN CRANE INC
3300 Centennial Dr (48642-5958)
PHONE 989 496-9292
Jerry Smith, *Manager*
EMP: 10
SALES (corp-wide): 3.3B **Privately Held**
WEB: www.johncrane.com
SIC: 3053 Oil seals, rubber; packing: steam engines, pipe joints, air compressors, etc.
HQ: John Crane Inc.
6400 Oakton St
Morton Grove IL 60053
312 605-7800

(G-11379)
JONES RAY WELL SERVICING INC
172 N 11 Mile Rd (48640-9118)
PHONE 989 832-8071
Jeanne Yost, *President*
David Yost, *Vice Pres*
EMP: 15 **EST:** 1940
SALES (est): 451.5K **Privately Held**
SIC: 1389 Servicing oil & gas wells

(G-11380)
JUMPIN JOHNNYS INC
1309 W Reardon St Apt 2 (48640-4817)
PHONE 989 832-0160
John Klein, *President*
Michael Kangas, *Chairman*
EMP: 5 **EST:** 2003
SQ FT: 3,000
SALES (est): 301.2K **Privately Held**
SIC: 2086 Bottled & canned soft drinks

(G-11381)
KAWKAWLIN MANUFACTURING CO (PA)
Also Called: Kawkawlin Church Furn Mfg Co
2707 Highbrook Dr (48642-3923)
P.O. Box 368, Kawkawlin (48631-0368)
PHONE 989 684-5470
Frank King Jr, *President*
Janelle Adamczyk, *Admin Sec*
EMP: 6 **EST:** 1940
SALES (est): 871.9K **Privately Held**
SIC: 2531 Pews, church; church furniture; benches for public buildings

(G-11382)
KINETIC WAVE POWER LLC
2861 N Tupelo Dr (48642-8829)
PHONE 989 839-9757
Joseph Blackmore,
EMP: 5 **EST:** 2007
SALES (est): 228.8K **Privately Held**
WEB: www.kineticwavepower.com
SIC: 3511 Turbines & turbine generator sets

(G-11383)
LAMONS
807 Pershing St (48640-5611)
PHONE 989 488-4580
Terry Allen, *Manager*
EMP: 4 **EST:** 2013
SALES (est): 217.8K **Privately Held**
WEB: www.lamons.com
SIC: 3053 Gaskets, all materials

(G-11384)
LIVING WORD INTERNATIONAL INC
Also Called: Mark Barclay Ministries
2010 N Stark Rd (48642-9439)
PHONE 989 832-7547
Mark Barclay, *President*
Josh Barclay, *Vice Pres*
Bethany Bedtelyon, *Publications*
Jonathan Dolan, *Info Tech Mgr*
William Bailey, *Admin Sec*
EMP: 26 **EST:** 1980
SQ FT: 18,000
SALES (est): 3.4MM **Privately Held**
WEB: www.marktbarclay.com
SIC: 8661 2731 2721 Covenant & Evangelical Church; book publishing; periodicals

(G-11385)
LUBRIZOL CORPORATION
CPI Fluid Engineering
2300 James Savage Rd (48642-6535)
PHONE 989 496-3780
Leslie Hahn, *Vice Pres*
Doug Peake, *Plant Mgr*
Jeff Lyons, *Controller*
Saleem Al-Ahmad, *Sales Staff*
EMP: 5
SALES (corp-wide): 245.5B **Publicly Held**
WEB: www.lubrizol.com
SIC: 2899 8711 Chemical preparations; consulting engineer
HQ: The Lubrizol Corporation
29400 Lakeland Blvd
Wickliffe OH 44092
440 943-4200

(G-11386)
MANUFACTURING OPTIONS
455 E Bradford Rd (48640-9578)
PHONE 989 430-6770
EMP: 4 **EST:** 2019
SALES (est): 79.4K **Privately Held**
SIC: 3999 Manufacturing industries

(G-11387)
MCKAY PRESS INC
7600 W Wackerly St (48642-7405)
P.O. Box 2749 (48641-2749)
PHONE 989 631-2360
Corey Christiansen, *President*
Jim Nigro, *Vice Pres*
Dan Lorenz, *Project Mgr*
Ron Charb, *Purch Mgr*
Bob Smith, *Controller*
EMP: 135 **EST:** 1994
SQ FT: 93,000
SALES (est): 36.6MM
SALES (corp-wide): 4.7B **Publicly Held**
WEB: www.rrd.com
SIC: 2752 Commercial printing, offset
PA: R. R. Donnelley & Sons Company
35 W Wacker Dr
Chicago IL 60601
312 326-8000

(G-11388)
MHR INVESTMENTS INC
Also Called: Mc Creadie Sales
601 S Saginaw Rd (48640-4610)
PHONE 989 832-5395
Richard McCreadie, *President*
Richard Mc Creadie, *President*
EMP: 15 **EST:** 1958
SQ FT: 5,500
SALES (est): 683K **Privately Held**
WEB: www.mccreadiesales.com
SIC: 5699 5812 3993 Shirts, custom made; T-shirts, custom printed; fast-food restaurant, independent; signs & advertising specialties

(G-11389)
MICHIGAN GYPSUM CO
6105 Jefferson Ave (48640-2935)
PHONE 989 792-8734
Francesanna Sargent, *President*
Thomas Webber, *Vice Pres*
EMP: 19 **EST:** 1953
SQ FT: 18,000
SALES (est): 1.7MM **Privately Held**
WEB: www.michigangypsum.com
SIC: 1499 Gypsum mining

(G-11390)
MID MICHIGAN REPAIR SERVICE
3344 N Sturgeon Rd (48642-8323)
PHONE 989 835-6014
Ruhl R Hoover, *President*
EMP: 8 **EST:** 1982
SALES (est): 411.5K **Privately Held**
SIC: 7699 5084 7692 3548 Welding equipment repair; welding machinery & equipment; welding repair; welding apparatus

(G-11391)
MIDLAND BREWING CO LLC
Also Called: Brewing Company
5011 N Saginaw Rd (48642)
PHONE 989 259-7210
Evan Westervelt, *Sales Staff*
Keith Lawrence,
EMP: 7 **EST:** 2010
SALES (est): 802.4K **Privately Held**
WEB: www.midlandbrewing.com
SIC: 5813 2082 Bars & lounges; malt beverage products

(G-11392)
MIDLAND CMPNDING CNSULTING INC
3802 James Savage Rd (48642-6518)
PHONE 989 495-9367
Thayer Brown, *President*
EMP: 7
SQ FT: 24,000
SALES (est): 1.9MM **Privately Held**
WEB: www.midlandcompounding.com
SIC: 2899 2611 Insulating compounds; pulp mills, mechanical & recycling processing

(G-11393)
MIDLAND IRON WORKS INC
57 W Chippewa River Rd (48640-9039)
PHONE 989 832-3041
Stephen D Dent, *President*
Dixie Dent, *Admin Sec*
EMP: 10 **EST:** 1882
SQ FT: 1,600
SALES (est): 784.7K **Privately Held**
SIC: 3321 Gray iron castings; ductile iron castings

(G-11394)
MIDLAND PUBLISHING COMPANY
Also Called: Midland Daily News
124 S Mcdonald St (48640-5161)
PHONE 989 835-7171
Jenny Anderson, *President*
Pam Shauger, *Advt Staff*
Carol Vansluyters, *Manager*
EMP: 105 **EST:** 1858
SQ FT: 27,000
SALES (est): 15.2MM
SALES (corp-wide): 4.2B **Privately Held**
WEB: www.ourmidland.com
SIC: 2711 2752 Newspapers: publishing only, not printed on site; commercial printing, lithographic
PA: The Hearst Corporation
300 W 57th St Fl 42
New York NY 10019
212 649-2000

(G-11395)
MITCHART INC
2611 Schuette Rd Ste A (48642-6965)
PHONE 989 835-3964
Krista Mc Donald, *Principal*
Jamie M McDonald, *COO*
Krista McDonald, *Vice Pres*
EMP: 6 **EST:** 2002
SALES (est): 413.4K **Privately Held**
WEB: www.mitchartinc.com
SIC: 3993 Signs & advertising specialties

(G-11396)
MODERN METALCRAFT INC
2033 Roxbury Ct (48642-8002)
PHONE 989 835-3716
John Mc Peak, *President*
Tamara Schuman, *Controller*
EMP: 18 **EST:** 1941
SQ FT: 29,000
SALES (est): 1MM **Privately Held**
WEB: www.modernmetalcraft.com
SIC: 3444 3599 Sheet metal specialties, not stamped; machine shop, jobbing & repair

(G-11397)
N F P INC
Also Called: Wysong
7550 Eastman Ave (48642-7809)
PHONE 989 631-0009
Jill Barton, *Principal*
Kimberly Wysong, *Treasurer*
Joe Tittle, *Technician*
EMP: 4 **Privately Held**
WEB: www.wysong.net
SIC: 8721 5499 2834 2099 Billing & bookkeeping service; health & dietetic food stores; pharmaceutical preparations; food preparations; prepared feeds
PA: N F P Inc
N5475 Crossman Rd
Lake Mills WI 53551

(G-11398)
NUVOSUN INC
2040 Abbott Rd (48674-1000)
PHONE 408 514-6200
Kirk Thompson, *President*
Bruce Hachtmann, *Vice Pres*
Tom Valeri, *Vice Pres*
Art Wall, *Vice Pres*
▲ **EMP:** 62 **EST:** 2008
SQ FT: 102,000
SALES (est): 11.5MM
SALES (corp-wide): 38.5B **Publicly Held**
WEB: www.dow.com
SIC: 3674 Photovoltaic devices, solid state
HQ: The Dow Chemical Company
2211 H H Dow Way
Midland MI 48642
989 636-1000

(G-11399)
OIL CITY VENTURE INC
Also Called: G & H Producers
172 N 11 Mile Rd (48640-9118)
PHONE 989 832-8071
David Yost, *President*
Jeanne Yost, *Vice Pres*
EMP: 4
SALES (est): 211.1K **Privately Held**
SIC: 1311 Crude petroleum & natural gas

(G-11400)
ORACLE AMERICA INC
2200 Salzburg St (48640-8531)
PHONE 989 495-0465
EMP: 4
SALES (corp-wide): 40.4B **Publicly Held**
WEB: www.oracle.com
SIC: 7372 Prepackaged software

Midland - Midland County (G-11401)

GEOGRAPHIC SECTION

HQ: Oracle America, Inc.
500 Oracle Pkwy
Redwood City CA 94065
650 506-7000

(G-11401)
OWENS BUILDING CO INC
Also Called: Owens Cabinet & Trim
1928 N Stark Rd (48642-9438)
PHONE...................989 835-1293
Ricky Owens, *President*
Nick Smith, *Personnel*
EMP: 25 **EST:** 1978
SQ FT: 21,000
SALES (est): 2.5MM Privately Held
SIC: 2431 2541 5211 1799 Millwork; wood partitions & fixtures; cabinets, kitchen; counter top installation; cabinet & finish carpentry; vanities, bathroom: wood

(G-11402)
PAROUSIA PLASTICS INC
2412 Judith Ct (48642-4751)
PHONE...................989 832-4054
Robert Yore, *President*
EMP: 5 **EST:** 2006
SALES (est): 89.7K Privately Held
SIC: 3089 Injection molding of plastics

(G-11403)
PRECISION TORQUE CONTROL INC
220 Arrow Cv (48642-6950)
PHONE...................989 495-9330
Michael Scott, *President*
Amber Myersturley, *Office Mgr*
Mike Degraw, *Manager*
Angela Licht, *Admin Mgr*
▲ **EMP:** 10 **EST:** 1995
SALES (est): 1.3MM Privately Held
WEB: www.precisiontork.com
SIC: 3714 3568 Clutches, motor vehicle; power transmission equipment

(G-11404)
QG LLC
Also Called: Worldcolor Midland
1700 James Savage Rd (48642-5812)
PHONE...................989 496-3333
Jim Houvener, *Branch Mgr*
EMP: 62
SALES (corp-wide): 2.9B Publicly Held
SIC: 2752 Commercial printing, offset
HQ: Qg, Llc
N61w23044 Harrys Way
Sussex WI 53089

(G-11405)
QRP INC (PA)
Also Called: Quick and Reliable Printing
94 Ashman Cir (48640-4627)
PHONE...................989 496-2955
Robert A Anderson, *President*
Nancy Anderson, *Vice Pres*
Jim Haring, *Sales Executive*
Harold Grunwell, *Technology*
EMP: 7
SQ FT: 3,600
SALES (est): 6.4MM Privately Held
WEB: www.qrp.ink
SIC: 2752 5999 2796 2791 Commercial printing, offset; banners, flags, decals & posters; platemaking services; typesetting; bookbinding & related work; coated & laminated paper

(G-11406)
QRP INC
Also Called: Quick Reliable Printing
3000 James Savage Rd (48642-6533)
PHONE...................989 496-2955
Bob Anderson, *President*
Laurie Casselman, *COO*
Joy Stewart, *Accounts Mgr*
Ken Trethaway, *Accounts Exec*
Jenny Schaefer, *Department Mgr*
EMP: 38
SALES (corp-wide): 6.4MM Privately Held
WEB: www.qrp.ink
SIC: 2752 2791 2789 2759 Commercial printing, offset; typesetting; bookbinding & related work; commercial printing

PA: Qrp, Inc.
94 Ashman Cir
Midland MI 48640
989 496-2955

(G-11407)
R L CANVAS
3429 Rivercrest Ct (48640-6442)
PHONE...................989 837-6352
Robin L Bebeau, *President*
EMP: 4 **EST:** 2015
SALES (est): 88.7K Privately Held
WEB: www.randlcanvas.com
SIC: 2394 Canvas boat seats

(G-11408)
RIDER TYPE & DESIGN
3600 E Mary Jane Dr (48642-9758)
PHONE...................989 839-0015
Robert Rider, *President*
EMP: 4 **EST:** 1986
SALES (est): 400K Privately Held
WEB: www.ridertypedesign.com
SIC: 2791 2752 Typesetting; commercial printing, lithographic

(G-11409)
ROHM HAAS DNMARK INVSTMNTS LLC
2030 Dow Ctr (48674-1500)
PHONE...................989 636-1463
EMP: 12 **EST:** 2015
SALES (est): 6.9MM
SALES (corp-wide): 38.5B Publicly Held
WEB: www.dow.com
SIC: 2821 Plastics materials & resins
HQ: The Dow Chemical Company
2211 H H Dow Way
Midland MI 48642
989 636-1000

(G-11410)
RUSH PRINT AND PACK
1515 Commerce Dr Ste D (48642-8531)
PHONE...................989 835-5161
Michael S Rush, *President*
Dione L Rush, *Vice Pres*
EMP: 4 **EST:** 1945
SQ FT: 1,900
SALES (est): 275.3K Privately Held
WEB: www.rushprintnpack.net
SIC: 2752 Commercial printing, lithographic

(G-11411)
S A TRINSEO
Also Called: TRINSEO S.A.
3700 James Savage Rd (48642-6517)
PHONE...................989 636-5409
EMP: 5 Publicly Held
WEB: www.trinseo.com
SIC: 2821 Plastics materials & resins
PA: Trinseo Plc
1000 Chesterbrook Blvd
Berwyn PA 19312

(G-11412)
S AND P DRCTNAL BORING SVC LLC
Also Called: L L C
801 W Meadowbrook Dr (48640-6023)
PHONE...................989 832-7716
Patrick Zilfki,
▲ **EMP:** 4 **EST:** 2000
SALES (est): 370.9K Privately Held
SIC: 1381 Directional drilling oil & gas wells

(G-11413)
SAGINAW VALLEY INST MTLS INC
4800 James Savage Rd (48642-6528)
PHONE...................989 496-2307
Rebecca Cox, *President*
Theodore Selby, *President*
Jean Selby, *Treasurer*
EMP: 4 **EST:** 1983
SALES (est): 476.3K Privately Held
WEB: www.instituteofmaterials.com
SIC: 1389 8734 Oil field services; testing laboratories

(G-11414)
SARGENT SAND CO
6105 Jefferson Ave (48640-2935)
PHONE...................989 792-8734
Francesanna Sargent, *President*
EMP: 3 **EST:** 1923
SALES (est): 1.5MM Privately Held
WEB: www.sargentsand.com
SIC: 1446 Foundry sand mining

(G-11415)
SECURECOM INC
3079 E Commercial Dr (48642-7840)
PHONE...................989 837-4005
Kevin L Wray, *Principal*
EMP: 7 **EST:** 2010
SALES (est): 169.1K Privately Held
SIC: 3699 Security control equipment & systems

(G-11416)
SERENUS JOHNSON PORTABLES LLC
1928 N Stark Rd (48642-9438)
PHONE...................800 605-0693
Aaron Johnson, *President*
Diane Johnson, *General Mgr*
Phil Blaisdell, *Manager*
EMP: 15 **EST:** 2006 Privately Held
SALES (est): 57.3K Privately Held
WEB: www.goserenus.com
SIC: 3448 Prefabricated metal buildings

(G-11417)
SIGNATURE WALL SOLUTIONS INC
Also Called: Swiftwall Solutions
1928 N Stark Rd (48642-9438)
P.O. Box 1601 (48641-1601)
PHONE...................616 366-4242
Joe Asiala, *CEO*
Joe Afiala, *CEO*
Rick Brouwer, *Co-Founder*
Eli Rytlewsky, *Director*
EMP: 10 **EST:** 2016
SQ FT: 30,000
SALES (est): 1.9MM Privately Held
WEB: www.swiftwall.com
SIC: 1791 3499 2542 Exterior wall system installation; barricades, metal; partitions & fixtures, except wood

(G-11418)
SNOW MACHINES INCORPORATED (PA)
Also Called: SMI Evaporative Systems
1512 Rockwell Dr (48642-9318)
PHONE...................989 631-6091
Joseph M Vanderkelen, *President*
Pat Kotewa, *Mfg Staff*
Kevin Brayman, *Purch Dir*
Bob Abraham, *Design Engr*
Eric Haapala, *Sales Staff*
▲ **EMP:** 23 **EST:** 1974
SQ FT: 9,000
SALES (est): 5.6MM Privately Held
WEB: www.snowmakers.com
SIC: 3585 3821 Snowmaking machinery; evaporation apparatus, laboratory type

(G-11419)
SOURCE POINT PRESS
3603 Orchard Dr (48640-2676)
PHONE...................269 501-3690
Travis Macintire, *Administration*
EMP: 9 **EST:** 2015
SALES (est): 1.1MM Privately Held
WEB: www.sourcepointpress.blogspot.com
SIC: 2741 Miscellaneous publishing

(G-11420)
UNION TANK CAR COMPANY
146 Building Dow Chemical (48667-0001)
PHONE...................989 615-3054
EMP: 6
SALES (corp-wide): 245.5B Publicly Held
WEB: www.utlx.com
SIC: 3743 Train cars & equipment, freight or passenger
HQ: Union Tank Car Company
175 W Jackson Blvd # 2100
Chicago IL 60604
312 431-3111

(G-11421)
W & W TOOL AND DIE INC
1508 E Grove St (48640-5299)
PHONE...................989 835-5522
Dennis Duford, *President*
Kenneth Friedle, *Corp Secy*
EMP: 9 **EST:** 1946
SQ FT: 4,100
SALES (est): 706.8K Privately Held
SIC: 3544 Special dies & tools

(G-11422)
WEATHER TIGHT
4521 Hamilton Dr (48642-5879)
PHONE...................989 817-2149
Ken Small, *Principal*
EMP: 5 **EST:** 2017
SALES (est): 70.8K Privately Held
WEB: www.weather.gov
SIC: 3444 Sheet metalwork

(G-11423)
WILLIAMS WELDING CUSTOM METAL
2819 N Eastman Rd (48642-7857)
PHONE...................989 941-2901
Michael Williams, *Principal*
EMP: 4 **EST:** 2016
SALES (est): 57.3K Privately Held
WEB: www.williamswelding-cmw.com
SIC: 7692 Welding repair

(G-11424)
WYSONG MEDICAL CORPORATION
7550 Eastman Ave (48642-7809)
PHONE...................989 631-0009
Randy L Wysong, *President*
EMP: 15 **EST:** 1976
SQ FT: 16,050
SALES (est): 363.3K Privately Held
WEB: www.wysong.net
SIC: 2048 2047 2099 3841 Feeds, specialty: mice, guinea pig, etc.; dog food; food preparations; surgical & medical instruments

(G-11425)
XAERUS PERFORMANCE FLUIDS LLC
2825 Schuette Rd (48642-6945)
PHONE...................989 631-7871
EMP: 118 Privately Held
WEB: www.xaerusfluids.com
SIC: 2899 Corrosion preventive lubricant
PA: Xaerus Performance Fluids, L.L.C.
1605 Ashman St
Midland MI 48640

(G-11426)
XALT ENERGY LLC (HQ)
2700 S Saginaw Rd (48640-6845)
PHONE...................989 486-8501
Jeff Michalski, *President*
Lisa McKenzie, *Senior VP*
Martin Klein, *Vice Pres*
Alicia Jung, *Buyer*
Camden Pricing, *Buyer*
▲ **EMP:** 15 **EST:** 2009
SQ FT: 17,500
SALES (est): 52.3MM
SALES (corp-wide): 10.4B Privately Held
WEB: www.xaltenergy.com
SIC: 3691 Storage batteries
PA: Freudenberg & Co. Kg
Hohnerweg 2-4
Weinheim BW 69469
620 180-0

(G-11427)
XALT ENERGY LLC
2700 S Saginaw Rd (48640-6845)
PHONE...................816 525-1153
EMP: 5
SALES (corp-wide): 29.9MM Privately Held
SIC: 3629 Mfg Electrical Industrial Apparatus
HQ: Xalt Energy, Llc
2700 S Saginaw Rd
Midland MI 48640

▲ = Import ▼ = Export
◆ = Import/Export

GEOGRAPHIC SECTION

(G-11428)
XALT ENERGY MI LLC
2700 S Saginaw Rd (48640-6845)
PHONE 989 486-8501
Subhash Dhar, *CEO*
Richard Cundiff, *Vice Chairman*
Isaac Keen, *Engineer*
Matt Hanson, *CFO*
Jim Szymanski, *Manager*
◆ **EMP:** 60 **EST:** 2009
SALES (est): 19MM
SALES (corp-wide): 10.4B **Privately Held**
WEB: www.xaltenergy.com
SIC: 3691 Storage batteries
PA: Freudenberg & Co. Kg
   Hohnerweg 2-4
   Weinheim BW 69469
   620 180-0

Milan
Monroe County

(G-11429)
A & JS EMBROIDERY
8666 Acorne Ave (48160-9742)
PHONE 734 417-3694
EMP: 5 **EST:** 2007
SALES (est): 97.7K **Privately Held**
SIC: 2395 Embroidery & art needlework

(G-11430)
AMEX MFG & DISTRG CO INC
640 Ash St (48160-1074)
PHONE 734 439-8560
Phil Varnhagen, *Manager*
EMP: 5 **EST:** 2003
SALES (est): 479.9K **Privately Held**
WEB: www.amexmfg.com
SIC: 3541 Screw machines, automatic

(G-11431)
ARBOR FABRICATING LLC
14030 Tuttlehill Rd (48160-9174)
PHONE 734 626-5864
Chad Derrick Beauchamp, *Administration*
EMP: 7 **EST:** 2013
SALES (est): 617.6K **Privately Held**
SIC: 3569 Filters

(G-11432)
CHEMTOOL INCORPORATED
415 Squires Dr (48160-1253)
PHONE 734 439-7010
Fax: 734 439-7509
EMP: 7
SALES (corp-wide): 210.8B **Publicly Held**
SIC: 2992 3412 Mfg Lubricating Oils/Greases Mfg Metal Barrels/Pails
HQ: Chemtool Incorporated
   801 W Rockton Rd
   Rockton IL 61072
   815 957-4140

(G-11433)
CLARK PERFORATING COMPANY INC
15875 Allen Rd (48160-9278)
P.O. Box 179 (48160-0179)
PHONE 734 439-1170
Sally Clark Freeman, *President*
Ken Clark, *Vice Pres*
Wade Freeman, *Sales Mgr*
EMP: 11
SQ FT: 20,000
SALES (est): 2.2MM **Privately Held**
WEB: www.clarkperforating.com
SIC: 3469 Steel

(G-11434)
CREATION HIGHWAY
160 Canfield St (48160-1618)
PHONE 307 220-7309
Holly Forbis, *Principal*
EMP: 5 **EST:** 2010
SALES (est): 111.1K **Privately Held**
SIC: 2759 Commercial printing

(G-11435)
FINCH SAND & GRAVEL LLC
10980 N Platt Rd (48160-9619)
P.O. Box 269 (48160-0269)
PHONE 734 439-1044
EMP: 6
SALES (est): 360K **Privately Held**
SIC: 1442 Construction Sand/Gravel

(G-11436)
GEORGIA-PACIFIC LLC
951 County St (48160-9785)
PHONE 734 439-2441
Dennis Guenther, *Manager*
EMP: 5
SQ FT: 200,000
SALES (corp-wide): 36.9B **Privately Held**
WEB: www.gp.com
SIC: 2653 3412 Boxes, corrugated: made from purchased materials; metal barrels, drums & pails
HQ: Georgia-Pacific Llc
   133 Peachtree St Nw
   Atlanta GA 30303
   404 652-4000

(G-11437)
GOTTS TRANSIT MIX INC
605 S Platt Rd (48160-9304)
P.O. Box 240 (48160-0240)
PHONE 734 439-1528
Tom Gotts, *President*
Gary Brown, *Vice Pres*
Paul Raetzel, *Dispersing Agnt*
EMP: 12 **EST:** 1957
SQ FT: 5,000
SALES (est): 5.5MM **Privately Held**
WEB: www.gottstransitmix.com
SIC: 5032 3273 Concrete mixtures; ready-mixed concrete

(G-11438)
INNOVATIVE FLUIDS LLC
415 Squires Dr (48160-1253)
PHONE 734 241-5699
Kevin Jaworski, *Opers Staff*
John Lott, *Accounts Mgr*
Geoff Huston, *Sales Staff*
Steven Peters, *Mng Member*
Todd McClead, *Manager*
EMP: 16 **EST:** 2000
SQ FT: 19,000
SALES (est): 4MM **Privately Held**
WEB: www.innovativefluids.com
SIC: 2842 Cleaning or polishing preparations

(G-11439)
JAYTEC LLC
620 S Platt Rd (48160-9305)
PHONE 734 713-4500
Josh Forquer, *Manager*
EMP: 10
SALES (corp-wide): 3.1B **Privately Held**
WEB: www.autokiniton.com
SIC: 3465 Automotive stampings
HQ: Jaytec, Llc
   17757 Woodland Dr
   New Boston MI 48164
   517 451-8272

(G-11440)
LIBERTY RESEARCH CO INC
291 Squires Dr (48160-1253)
P.O. Box 160 (48160-0160)
PHONE 734 508-6237
Derrick Perkins, *Branch Mgr*
EMP: 5
SALES (corp-wide): 5.3MM **Privately Held**
WEB: www.libertyturnedcomponents.com
SIC: 3451 Screw machine products
PA: Liberty Research Co, Inc.
   7 Nadeau Dr
   Rochester NH 03867
   603 332-2730

(G-11441)
LIBERTY TURNED COMPONENTS LLC (PA)
Also Called: Ltc
291 Squires Dr (48160-1253)
P.O. Box 160 (48160-0160)
PHONE 734 508-6237
Derrick Perkins, *CEO*
Michele Perkins, *President*
EMP: 44 **EST:** 2013
SQ FT: 5,400
SALES (est): 5MM **Privately Held**
WEB: www.libertyturnedcomponents.com
SIC: 3451 Screw machine products

(G-11442)
LILLIAN FUEL INC
1200 Dexter St (48160-1100)
PHONE 734 439-8505
EMP: 4 **EST:** 2011
SALES (est): 360.6K **Privately Held**
SIC: 2869 Mfg Industrial Organic Chemicals

(G-11443)
MANAGEMENT TRAINING INN
555 S Platt Rd (48160-9303)
PHONE 734 439-1546
EMP: 4 **EST:** 2019
SALES (est): 91.7K **Privately Held**
SIC: 3499 Fabricated metal products

(G-11444)
MILAN BURIAL VAULT INC
Also Called: Milan Vault
10475 N Ann Arbor Rd (48160-9275)
PHONE 734 439-1538
Daniel C Wagner, *President*
Sam Wagner, *Vice Pres*
Linda J Wagner, *Treasurer*
EMP: 36 **EST:** 1941
SQ FT: 10,000
SALES (est): 1.2MM **Privately Held**
WEB: www.milanvault.com
SIC: 3272 Burial vaults, concrete or precast terrazzo; septic tanks, concrete; concrete products, precast

(G-11445)
MILAN CAST METAL CORPORATION
13905 N Sanford Rd (48160-8809)
P.O. Box 206 (48160-0206)
PHONE 734 439-0510
Donald Kondor, *President*
Steve Coburn, *General Mgr*
David Kondor, *Vice Pres*
Shelly Coburn, *Admin Sec*
EMP: 37 **EST:** 1946
SQ FT: 32,000
SALES (est): 6.6MM **Privately Held**
WEB: www.milancastmetal.com
SIC: 3366 Copper foundries

(G-11446)
MILAN METAL SYSTEMS LLC
555 S Platt Rd (48160-9303)
PHONE 734 439-1546
Mark Turk, *Maint Spvr*
Craig Barnhart, *CFO*
Jeff Carter,
Christine Hunter, *Analyst*
▲ **EMP:** 145 **EST:** 2005
SQ FT: 15,000
SALES (est): 40.5MM **Privately Held**
WEB: www.duraauto.com
SIC: 3714 Motor vehicle parts & accessories
PA: Global Automotive Systems, Llc
   1780 Pond Run
   Auburn Hills MI 48326

(G-11447)
MILAN SCREW PRODUCTS INC
291 Squires Dr (48160-1253)
P.O. Box 180 (48160-0180)
PHONE 734 439-2431
Charles Tellas, *President*
Lorena Tellas, *Vice Pres*
EMP: 19 **EST:** 1950
SQ FT: 37,000
SALES (est): 265.1K **Privately Held**
SIC: 3451 3568 3429 Screw machine products; power transmission equipment; manufactured hardware (general)

(G-11448)
PEPSI CO WIXOM
Also Called: Pepsico
625 E Main St (48160-1552)
PHONE 248 305-3500
Jo Monaghan, *Admin Asst*
EMP: 11 **EST:** 2018
SALES (est): 1.8MM **Privately Held**
WEB: www.pepsico.com
SIC: 2086 Carbonated soft drinks, bottled & canned

(G-11449)
PRECISION DEVICES INC
606 County St (48160-9606)
P.O. Box 220 (48160-0220)
PHONE 734 439-2462
Thomas L Preston, *President*
Kevin Schuler, *Plant Mgr*
Joseph M Kormos, *Treasurer*
EMP: 49 **EST:** 1971
SQ FT: 31,550
SALES (est): 9.2MM **Privately Held**
WEB: www.predev.com
SIC: 3829 3545 Physical property testing equipment; precision tools, machinists'

(G-11450)
STEVEN J DEVLIN
268 S Platt St (48160-1246)
PHONE 734 439-1325
Steven J Devlin, *Principal*
EMP: 4
SALES (est): 203.3K **Privately Held**
SIC: 3724 Research & development on aircraft engines & parts

(G-11451)
WASEM FRUIT FARM
6580 Judd Rd (48160-9734)
PHONE 734 482-2342
Bruce Upston, *Finance Mgr*
Janet Upstom,
Bruce Upstom,
EMP: 5 **EST:** 1942
SALES (est): 331.7K **Privately Held**
WEB: www.wasemfruitfarm.com
SIC: 0175 0191 2086 2033 Apple orchard; peach orchard; general farms, primarily crop; bottled & canned soft drinks; canned fruits & specialties

---

Milford
Oakland County

(G-11452)
4D BUILDING INC
Also Called: McDonald Modular Solutions
54500 Pontiac Trl (48381-4345)
PHONE 248 799-7384
William Duffield, *President*
Brett Holler, *Opers Staff*
Joe Livingway, *Sales Mgr*
Marilynn Kushner, *Sales Staff*
Lisa McNally, *Sales Executive*
EMP: 18 **EST:** 2013
SQ FT: 11,000
SALES (est): 3MM **Privately Held**
WEB: www.mcdonaldmodular.com
SIC: 2452 7359 Prefabricated wood buildings; equipment rental & leasing; shipping container leasing

(G-11453)
A & F ENTERPRISES INC
Also Called: Armstrong Graphics
1203 N Milford Rd (48381-1033)
PHONE 248 714-6529
Dave Armstrong, *President*
EMP: 10 **EST:** 1988
SALES (est): 950K **Privately Held**
SIC: 2721 Magazines: publishing only, not printed on site

(G-11454)
B F S PRINTING AND PROMOT
786 Knolls Landing Dr (48381-1888)
PHONE 248 685-2456
EMP: 4 **EST:** 2009
SALES (est): 85.5K **Privately Held**
SIC: 2759 Screen printing

(G-11455)
BISCAYNE AND ASSOCIATES INC
2515 Charms Rd (48381-3001)
PHONE 248 304-0600
Keven Smith, *President*
Mike Dallaire, *Software Dev*
Melissa Kozicki, *Director*
Catherine Beall, *Loan*
EMP: 36 **EST:** 2002
SALES (est): 2MM **Privately Held**
WEB: www.kevenandkaren.com
SIC: 7372 Prepackaged software

Milford - Oakland County (G-11456)

(G-11456)
BREESPORT HOLDINGS INC
Also Called: Cft Company
1235 Holden Ave (48381-3137)
PHONE................248 685-9500
Robert E Dalton, *President*
James Heller, *Corp Secy*
Peter K Rosenkrands, *Vice Pres*
Stephanie Hartsoe, *Production*
Jason Barnhart, *Engineer*
▼ EMP: 120 EST: 1946
SQ FT: 52,000
SALES (est): 10.6MM **Privately Held**
WEB: www.nogheller.com
SIC: 3599 3545 Machine shop, jobbing & repair; cutting tools for machine tools

(G-11457)
BURNERS INC
4901 Mccarthy Dr (48381-3947)
P.O. Box 735 (48381-0735)
PHONE................248 676-9141
W Michael Bockelman, *President*
Robert Bockelman, *Vice Pres*
Scott Bockelman, *Vice Pres*
Pamela Osinski, *Vice Pres*
Rob Bockelman, *Technician*
▲ EMP: 9 EST: 1962
SQ FT: 12,000
SALES (est): 1MM **Privately Held**
WEB: www.burnersinc.com
SIC: 3433 3625 Gas burners, industrial; control equipment, electric

(G-11458)
CLASSIC DESIGN CONCEPTS LLC
53194 Pontiac Trl (48381-4331)
PHONE................248 504-5202
George Huisman, *Branch Mgr*
Lori Huisman,
▼ EMP: 1 EST: 1990
SQ FT: 10,000
SALES (est): 5.9MM **Privately Held**
WEB: www.classicdesignconcepts.com
SIC: 3714 Exhaust systems & parts, motor vehicle; motor vehicle body components & frame
HQ: Tecstar, Lp
3033 Excelsior Blvd # 300
Minneapolis MN

(G-11459)
CLOUD WHITE PUBLISHING INC
262 Noble St (48381-2059)
PHONE................248 684-6460
EMP: 4 EST: 2011
SALES (est): 58.2K **Privately Held**
SIC: 2741 Miscellaneous publishing

(G-11460)
DAG R&D
1677 Melody Ln (48380-2145)
PHONE................248 444-0575
Eric McBride, *Owner*
EMP: 5 EST: 2008
SALES (est): 177.4K **Privately Held**
SIC: 3499 Fabricated metal products

(G-11461)
DENLIN INDUSTRIES INC
371 Mill Pond Ln (48381-1035)
PHONE................586 303-5209
David C Peck, *President*
EMP: 5 EST: 2007
SALES (est): 401.9K **Privately Held**
SIC: 3444 Sheet metalwork

(G-11462)
DIMITRI MANSOUR
Also Called: Blue Grill Foods
426 N Main St (48381-1958)
PHONE................248 684-4545
Dimitri Mansour, *Owner*
EMP: 5 EST: 2017
SQ FT: 1,100
SALES (est): 199.4K **Privately Held**
WEB: www.thebluegrill.com
SIC: 2035 Pickles, sauces & salad dressings

(G-11463)
EIDEMLLER PRCSION MCHINING INC
Also Called: Kyowa-Dmller Prcsion Machining
4998 Mccarthy Dr (48381-3945)
PHONE................248 669-2660
Martin Eidemiller, *President*
Renee Lagrow, *Purchasing*
Jennifer Dominick, *Personnel*
EMP: 20 EST: 1979
SALES (est): 3.8MM **Privately Held**
WEB: www.epmachining.com
SIC: 3599 Machine shop, jobbing & repair
PA: Kyowa Industrial Co., Ltd.
890, Shimanomachi
Takasaki GNM 370-0

(G-11464)
GM DEFENSE LLC
3300 General Motors Rd # 32 (48380-3726)
PHONE................586 359-8880
John Bryant, *CFO*
EMP: 25 **Publicly Held**
SIC: 3711 3714 Motor vehicles & car bodies; motor vehicle parts & accessories
HQ: Gm Defense Llc
300 Renaissance Ctr Fl 24
Detroit MI 48243
313 462-8782

(G-11465)
GREAT LAKES POST LLC
12466 Scenic View Ct (48380-2861)
PHONE................248 941-1349
Stefan Kogler,
Jennifer Kogler,
EMP: 5
SALES (est): 117.9K **Privately Held**
SIC: 2711 Newspapers, publishing & printing

(G-11466)
HONEYBEES CUSTOM TEES
334 Union St (48381-1966)
PHONE................248 421-0817
Kathleen Jacobs, *Principal*
EMP: 4 EST: 2017
SALES (est): 65K **Privately Held**
SIC: 2759 Screen printing

(G-11467)
INDUSTRIAL FABG SYSTEMS INC
4965 Technical Dr (48381-3952)
PHONE................248 685-7373
Michael P Quin Jr, *President*
Cheryl M Quin, *Vice Pres*
EMP: 20 EST: 1983
SQ FT: 11,000
SALES (est): 4.2MM **Privately Held**
WEB: www.stickybusinessllc.com
SIC: 3443 Industrial vessels, tanks & containers; metal parts

(G-11468)
KLEIN BROS FENCE & STAKES LLC
2400 E Buno Rd (48381-3658)
PHONE................248 684-6919
David Klein Jr, *Mng Member*
EMP: 5 EST: 1957
SQ FT: 1,800
SALES (est): 435.7K **Privately Held**
WEB: www.klein-brothers.business.site
SIC: 2499 Surveyors' stakes, wood

(G-11469)
MARCELLA MANIFOLDS
4625 S Milford Rd (48381-3736)
PHONE................248 259-6696
John Marcella, *Principal*
EMP: 11 EST: 2013
SALES (est): 146.6K **Privately Held**
WEB: www.marcellamanifoldsinc.com
SIC: 3714 Motor vehicle parts & accessories

(G-11470)
MICHIGAN SCIENTIFIC CORP (PA)
321 E Huron St (48381-2352)
PHONE................248 685-3939
Hugh W Larsen, *President*
Michael Castiglione, *Vice Pres*
Andrew Cook, *Vice Pres*
Richard Wurst, *Vice Pres*
Ray Collins, *Project Engr*
◆ EMP: 40 EST: 1960
SALES: 16.7MM **Privately Held**
WEB: www.michsci.com
SIC: 3829 8711 Testing equipment: abrasion, shearing strength, etc.; engineering services

(G-11471)
MILFORD JEWELERS INC
441 N Main St (48381-1960)
PHONE................248 676-0721
Pamar Chopjin, *Principal*
Jen Hill, *Comms Mgr*
Jenny Cullen, *Admin Asst*
EMP: 4 EST: 2002
SQ FT: 4,286
SALES (est): 373.7K **Privately Held**
WEB: www.motifjewelry.com
SIC: 5944 3911 Jewelry, precious stones & precious metals; jewelry, precious metal

(G-11472)
MILFORD REDI-MIX COMPANY
800 Concrete Dr (48381-1511)
PHONE................248 684-1465
Keith Shorr, *President*
Charles Shorr, *Vice Pres*
EMP: 32 EST: 1946
SQ FT: 5,000
SALES (est): 4.2MM **Privately Held**
WEB: www.milfordredimix.com
SIC: 3273 5032 Ready-mixed concrete; concrete building products

(G-11473)
MILLWORK DESIGN GROUP LLC
414 Union St Apt 202 (48381-1988)
PHONE................248 472-2178
Gerald A Rauschenberger,
EMP: 5 EST: 1984
SALES (est): 4.8MM **Privately Held**
SIC: 2434 5211 Wood kitchen cabinets; cabinets, kitchen

(G-11474)
MW MINERALS
3157 Loss Trl (48380-2940)
PHONE................517 294-6709
Walter R Kellogg, *Administration*
EMP: 4 EST: 2018
SALES (est): 87.2K **Privately Held**
WEB: www.mwminerals.com
SIC: 3295 Minerals, ground or treated

(G-11475)
NANO MATERIALS & PROCESSES INC
659 Heritage Dr (48381-2739)
PHONE................248 529-3873
Andrey Factor, *Vice Pres*
Sarah Weingarden, *Accounts Mgr*
Marshall Weingarden, *Administration*
EMP: 4 EST: 2014
SALES (est): 385K **Privately Held**
WEB: www.nanompi.com
SIC: 5169 2911 3479 2821 Oil additives; fuel additives; metal coating & allied service; painting, coating & hot dipping; epoxy resins; plasticizer/additive based plastic materials; custom compound purchased resins

(G-11476)
NATURAL AGGREGATES CORPORATION (PA)
3362 Muir Rd (48380-2947)
P.O. Box 2183, Brighton (48116-5983)
PHONE................248 685-1502
Daniel N Pevos, *President*
Harold Lipsitz, *Vice Pres*
EMP: 13 EST: 1964
SQ FT: 800
SALES (est): 2.4MM **Privately Held**
WEB: www.naturalagg.com
SIC: 1442 Construction sand mining; gravel mining

(G-11477)
NITELIGHTS OF SE MICHIGAN
2675 Fini Dr (48380-3960)
PHONE................248 684-4664
Terry Ryba, *Principal*
EMP: 4 EST: 2004
SALES (est): 75.5K **Privately Held**
SIC: 3645 Garden, patio, walkway & yard lighting fixtures: electric

(G-11478)
NOIR LASER COMPANY LLC
Also Called: Laser Shield
4975 Technical Dr (48381-3952)
P.O. Box 159, South Lyon (48178-0159)
PHONE................800 521-9746
Jamie Hodges, *Regl Sales Mgr*
Mark Gleichert, *Mng Member*
Mike Smiglewski, *Manager*
Gloria Hao, *Technology*
A Brooks Gleicher,
EMP: 25 EST: 1996
SQ FT: 4,000
SALES (est): 1.7MM **Privately Held**
WEB: www.noirlaser.com
SIC: 3851 Protectors, eye

(G-11479)
NOIR MEDICAL TECHNOLOGIES LLC (PA)
Also Called: Noir Manufacturing Co
4975 Technical Dr (48381-3952)
P.O. Box 159, South Lyon (48178-0159)
PHONE................734 769-5565
Arthur B Gleichert,
Rodney Pate, *Technician*
David Bothner,
Marc Gleicher,
Linda Gleichert,
EMP: 11 EST: 1973 **Privately Held**
WEB: www.noirmedical.com
SIC: 3851 Glasses, sun or glare

(G-11480)
PICPATCH LLC
2488 Pearson Rd (48380-4322)
P.O. Box 779 (48381-0779)
PHONE................248 670-2681
David Mamo, *Mng Member*
▼ EMP: 5 EST: 2008
SQ FT: 2,000 **Privately Held**
WEB: www.picpatchlabel.com
SIC: 3699 Security devices

(G-11481)
PRECISION EMBROIDERY
12632 Fleetwood Ct (48380-2654)
PHONE................248 684-1359
Gerald Turnbull, *Principal*
EMP: 5 EST: 2015
SALES (est): 49.3K **Privately Held**
SIC: 2395 Pleating & stitching

(G-11482)
PRECISION MACHINING
4998 Mccarthy Dr (48381-3945)
PHONE................248 669-2660
Martin Eidelmiller, *President*
EMP: 1 EST: 1979
SQ FT: 22,000
SALES (est): 1.1MM
SALES (corp-wide): 718MM **Privately Held**
WEB: www.epmachining.com
SIC: 3599 Machine shop, jobbing & repair
HQ: Elopak-Americas, Inc.
46962 Liberty Dr
Wixom MI 48393

(G-11483)
QUALITY CRAFT WOODWORKING
1711 Pinewood (48381-1341)
PHONE................248 343-6358
EMP: 4 EST: 2014
SALES (est): 93.8K **Privately Held**
SIC: 2431 Millwork

(G-11484)
QUALITY STEEL PRODUCTS INC
4978 Technical Dr (48381-3950)
PHONE................248 684-0555
Joesph Schwegman, *President*
Paul Dolan, *Exec VP*
Matthew Nowak, *Manager*
Marion Purdy, *Admin Sec*
EMP: 45 EST: 1980
SQ FT: 60,000

GEOGRAPHIC SECTION

Mio - Oscoda County (G-11511)

SALES (est): 9.1MM **Privately Held**
WEB: www.qualitysteelforgings.com
SIC: 3462 3714 3568 Automotive forgings, ferrous: crankshaft, engine, axle, etc.; chains, forged steel; motor vehicle parts & accessories; power transmission equipment

(G-11485)
RADIUS LLC
4922 Technical Dr (48381-3950)
PHONE 248 685-0773
Angela Durocher, *Admin Mgr*
Steve Kozerski,
Bill Romero,
EMP: 4 **EST:** 1997
SALES (est): 482.9K **Privately Held**
WEB: www.radius-eng.com
SIC: 3625 Actuators, industrial

(G-11486)
RPD MANUFACTURING LLC
3171 Rolling Green Ct (48380-4472)
PHONE 248 760-4796
EMP: 8 **EST:** 2012
SALES (est): 179.7K **Privately Held**
WEB: www.rpdengineering.com
SIC: 3999 Manufacturing industries

(G-11487)
SCHAEFFLER GROUP USA INC
4574 Windswept Dr (48380-2776)
PHONE 810 360-0294
EMP: 237
SALES (corp-wide): 66.3B **Privately Held**
WEB: www.schaeffler.us
SIC: 3562 Roller bearings & parts
HQ: Schaeffler Group Usa Inc.
  308 Springhill Farm Rd
  Fort Mill SC 29715
  803 548-8500

(G-11488)
SILVER SLATE LLC
4964 Technical Dr (48381-3950)
PHONE 248 486-3989
Ray Merlo, *Mng Member*
Pamela Merlo
EMP: 13 **EST:** 2009
SALES (est): 851.5K **Privately Held**
SIC: 1221 Bituminous coal & lignite-surface mining

(G-11489)
SMJ INC
1151 Stone Barn (48380-1417)
PHONE 248 343-6244
EMP: 7 **EST:** 2019
SALES (est): 537.9K **Privately Held**
SIC: 3599 Machine shop, jobbing & repair

(G-11490)
SOUTH HILL SAND AND GRAVEL
4303 S Hill Rd (48381-3807)
PHONE 248 685-7020
Tom Powell, *Manager*
EMP: 5 **Privately Held**
SIC: 1442 Gravel mining
PA: South Hill Sand And Gravel, Inc
  5877 Livernois Rd Ste 103
  Troy MI 48098

(G-11491)
STERLING PERFORMANCE INC
54420 Pontiac Trl (48381-4344)
PHONE 248 685-7811
Michael J D'Anniballe, *President*
Jeff Burrill, *COO*
▲ **EMP:** 25 **EST:** 1989
SQ FT: 8,000
SALES (est): 2.5MM **Privately Held**
WEB: www.sterlingperformance.org
SIC: 3714 3732 Motor vehicle engines & parts; motorboats, inboard or outboard: building & repairing

(G-11492)
TECHNOLOGY & MANUFACTURING INC
3190 Pine Cone Ct (48381-3398)
PHONE 248 755-1444
Paul Diaz, *CEO*
▲ **EMP:** 7 **EST:** 2003

SALES (est): 729.8K **Privately Held**
SIC: 3559 Automotive related machinery

(G-11493)
TRIAD PROCESS EQUIPMENT INC
4922 Technical Dr (48381-3950)
PHONE 248 685-9938
Steve Kozerski, *President*
Krissy Boyd, *General Mgr*
William Romero, *Vice Pres*
Todd Puchalsky, *Sales Staff*
▲ **EMP:** 9 **EST:** 1994
SQ FT: 1,000
SALES (est): 1MM **Privately Held**
WEB: www.triadprocess.com
SIC: 3491 5085 Industrial valves; industrial supplies

(G-11494)
TRUDEX ONE INC
2300 Old Plank Rd (48381-3251)
PHONE 248 392-2036
Gus Dabringhaus, *Principal*
EMP: 8 **EST:** 2012
SALES (est): 102.2K **Privately Held**
WEB: www.trudexone.com
SIC: 3545 Machine tool accessories

(G-11495)
TWINS STUDIO
2435 Childs Lake Rd (48381-3020)
PHONE 248 676-8157
EMP: 4 **EST:** 2001
SALES (est): 126.3K **Privately Held**
SIC: 3229 Tubing, glass

(G-11496)
VERTEX STEEL INC
2175 Fyke Dr (48381-3687)
PHONE 248 684-4177
Mike Dimet, *President*
Sandy Richardson, *Manager*
EMP: 30 **EST:** 1990
SQ FT: 14,000
SALES (est): 6.8MM **Privately Held**
WEB: www.vertexsteel.com
SIC: 3441 Fabricated structural metal

Millersburg
Presque Isle County

(G-11497)
CEDAR LOG LBR MILLERSBURG INC
6019 Millersburg Rd (49759-8726)
PHONE 989 733-2676
Tyler Tollini, *President*
Rita Tollini, *Vice Pres*
EMP: 10 **EST:** 2011
SALES (est): 1.6MM **Privately Held**
WEB: www.cedarloglumber.com
SIC: 5211 5031 2431 Lumber products; lumber, plywood & millwork; woodwork, interior & ornamental

Millington
Tuscola County

(G-11498)
ADS US INC
Also Called: Advanced Decorative Systems
4705 Industrial Dr (48746-9300)
PHONE 989 871-4550
Robert Morris, *CEO*
John Allard, *President*
Terry Aymer, *President*
James Conaty, *President*
Jaime Sanchez, *Managing Dir*
▲ **EMP:** 85 **EST:** 2009
SQ FT: 52,000
SALES: 14.6MM **Privately Held**
WEB: www.advanceddecorative.com
SIC: 3714 3429 Motor vehicle parts & accessories; manufactured hardware (general)

(G-11499)
DYNA SALES & SERVICE LLC
Also Called: Dynas Products
8440 State Rd (48746-9445)
PHONE 231 734-4433
Nathan Miller, *Principal*
Omer Miller,
Stephen Miller,
EMP: 9 **EST:** 1998
SALES (est): 1.2MM **Privately Held**
WEB: www.dyna-products.com
SIC: 3599 Machine shop, jobbing & repair

(G-11500)
FAMILY TRADITION WDWKG PLANS
8728 State Rd (48746-9665)
P.O. Box 148 (48746-0148)
PHONE 989 871-6688
Buck Coleman, *Owner*
EMP: 5 **EST:** 2005
SALES (est): 83.9K **Privately Held**
WEB: www.familytraditionwwp.com
SIC: 2431 Millwork

(G-11501)
HOME STYLE CO
Also Called: Up To Date Painting
8400 Caine Rd (48746-9132)
PHONE 989 871-3654
Donna J Dipzinski, *Owner*
EMP: 5 **EST:** 1975
SALES (est): 194.3K **Privately Held**
SIC: 7389 1721 2499 Interior designer; painting & paper hanging; handles, wood

(G-11502)
LOUDON STEEL INC
8208 Ellis Rd (48746-9402)
P.O. Box 312 (48746-0312)
PHONE 989 871-9353
Gregg Loudon, *President*
EMP: 40 **EST:** 1984
SQ FT: 26,000
SALES (est): 5.1MM **Privately Held**
WEB: www.loudonsteel.com
SIC: 3441 3535 3537 3496 Fabricated structural metal; conveyors & conveying equipment; industrial trucks & tractors; miscellaneous fabricated wire products; partitions & fixtures, except wood

(G-11503)
STEMCO PRODUCTS INC
Also Called: Stemco Kaiser
4641 Industrial Dr (48746-9300)
PHONE 888 854-6474
EMP: 4
SALES (corp-wide): 1B **Publicly Held**
SIC: 3714 3465 Mfg Motor Vehicle Parts/Accessories Mfg Automotive Stampings
HQ: Stemco Products, Inc.
  300 Industrial Dr
  Longview TX 75602

(G-11504)
WEBERS WOODWORK LLC
6316 Barnes Rd (48746-9553)
PHONE 989 798-7210
Andrew Weber, *Principal*
EMP: 4 **EST:** 2016
SALES (est): 58K **Privately Held**
SIC: 2431 Millwork

(G-11505)
WOOD BURN LLC
8106 Vassar Rd (48746-9479)
PHONE 810 614-4204
Joseph Payne, *Mng Member*
EMP: 9 **EST:** 2006
SALES (est): 197.4K **Privately Held**
WEB: www.outdoorlogfurnace.com
SIC: 3433 Burners, furnaces, boilers & stokers

Minden City
Sanilac County

(G-11506)
SURFACE MAUSOLEUM COMPANY INC
1799 Main St (48456-9301)
P.O. Box 27 (48456-0027)
PHONE 989 864-3460
Phillip G Moses, *President*
Jane Moses, *Corp Secy*
EMP: 6 **EST:** 1932
SQ FT: 8,800
SALES (est): 657.8K **Privately Held**
SIC: 3272 Burial vaults, concrete or precast terrazzo; septic tanks, concrete

Mio
Oscoda County

(G-11507)
GILCHRIST PREMIUM LUMBER PDTS (PA)
Also Called: Woodhaven Log & Lumber
1284 Mapes Rd (48647-9516)
P.O. Box 964 (48647-0964)
PHONE 989 826-8300
Richard Bills, *President*
Anita Bills, *Vice Pres*
EMP: 13 **EST:** 1987
SQ FT: 240
SALES (est): 2.5MM **Privately Held**
WEB: www.woodhavenlog.com
SIC: 2421 Lumber: rough, sawed or planed; siding (dressed lumber)

(G-11508)
GYMS SAWMILL
931 W Kittle Rd (48647-9713)
PHONE 989 826-8299
Michael Gingerich, *Partner*
Nate Hochstetler, *Partner*
Titus Lambright, *Partner*
Ivan Miller, *Partner*
EMP: 4 **EST:** 2005
SALES (est): 800K **Privately Held**
SIC: 2421 Sawmills & planing mills, general

(G-11509)
JIC METALWORKS
1442 W Kittle Rd (48647-9738)
PHONE 989 390-2077
Bryan Wieezorek, *Owner*
EMP: 5 **EST:** 2010
SALES (est): 98K **Privately Held**
WEB: www.metalworks1.com
SIC: 3441 Fabricated structural metal

(G-11510)
METALFAB MANUFACTURING INC
378 Booth Rd (48647-9771)
PHONE 989 826-2301
Joel Yoder, *President*
Jim Weaver, *Plant Mgr*
Jerry Anderson, *Sales Mgr*
Michelle Yoder, *Admin Sec*
Karl Cooper, *Technician*
EMP: 20 **EST:** 2003
SALES (est): 4MM **Privately Held**
WEB: www.metalfabmanufacturing.com
SIC: 3441 Fabricated structural metal

(G-11511)
METALFAB TOOL & MACHINE INC
Also Called: Metal Fab Tool & Machine
55 W Kittle Rd (48647-9704)
PHONE 989 826-6044
Thomas Holzwarth, *President*
Richard Stewart, *Sales Staff*
Elizabeth Holzwarth, *Manager*
EMP: 6 **EST:** 1991
SQ FT: 4,320
SALES (est): 674.8K **Privately Held**
WEB: www.metalfabtool.com
SIC: 3544 Special dies & tools; jigs & fixtures

Mio – Oscoda County (G-11512)

(G-11512)
MORSE CONCRETE & EXCAVATING
106 S Vine St (48647-9459)
P.O. Box 518 (48647-0518)
PHONE..................989 826-3975
Dennis Morse, *President*
Audrey Reghi, *General Mgr*
EMP: 10 **EST:** 1957
SQ FT: 1,200
SALES (est): 974.5K Privately Held
SIC: 3273 1794 1711 1795 Ready-mixed concrete; excavation work; septic system construction; demolition, buildings & other structures

(G-11513)
NORTHWOOD LUMBER
937 W Kittle Rd (48647-9713)
PHONE..................989 826-1751
Neil Bontrager, *Partner*
Leon Hershberger, *Partner*
Nathan Ponpreger, *Partner*
EMP: 5 **EST:** 2001
SALES (est): 445.8K Privately Held
SIC: 2421 Sawmills & planing mills, general

(G-11514)
PERRY CREEK WOODWORKING INC
211 E Kneeland Rd (48647-9707)
PHONE..................989 848-2125
Patrick Holberton, *President*
Amanda Holberton, *Admin Sec*
EMP: 5 **EST:** 2002
SALES (est): 402.7K Privately Held
SIC: 2434 Wood kitchen cabinets

(G-11515)
R & N LUMBER
1388 Caldwell Rd (48647-8738)
PHONE..................989 848-5553
John Miller, *Managing Prtnr*
Samuel Beachy, *Partner*
David Yoder, *Partner*
EMP: 6 **EST:** 1993
SALES (est): 491.8K Privately Held
SIC: 2421 Lumber: rough, sawed or planed

(G-11516)
SPECIALTY TUBE SOLUTIONS
Also Called: STS
339 E Miller Rd (48647-9660)
PHONE..................989 848-0880
Cortney L Sears, *Administration*
EMP: 6 **EST:** 2014
SALES (est): 848.3K Privately Held
WEB: www.specialtytubesolutions.com
SIC: 3317 Pipes, wrought: welded, lock joint or heavy riveted

Mohawk
Keweenaw County

(G-11517)
BIRDS-EYE CREATIONS INC
86 Staton Ave (49950)
P.O. Box 336 (49950-0336)
PHONE..................906 337-5095
Sharon Arntsen, *President*
EMP: 6 **EST:** 1994
SALES (est): 427.2K Privately Held
WEB: www.birdseyecreations.com
SIC: 2431 Millwork

Moline
Allegan County

(G-11518)
GLD HOLDINGS INC
4560 Division (49335)
P.O. Box 337 (49335-0337)
PHONE..................616 877-4288
Gary L De Young, *President*
Matt McCauley, *Vice Pres*
EMP: 24 **EST:** 1979
SQ FT: 15,000
SALES (est): 1.9MM Privately Held
SIC: 5511 3443 7699 Trucks, tractors & trailers: new & used; tanks, lined: metal plate; tank repair

(G-11519)
JONES MFG & SUP CO INC
1177 Electric Ave (49335)
P.O. Box 343 (49335-0343)
PHONE..................616 877-4442
Gary Jones, *President*
Jason Kelly, *Vice Pres*
Jill Kelly, *Treasurer*
EMP: 20 **EST:** 1974
SQ FT: 25,000
SALES (est): 3.9MM Privately Held
WEB: www.jones-metal.com
SIC: 3444 Sheet metal specialties, not stamped

Monroe
Monroe County

(G-11520)
ACTUATOR SERVICES LLC
Also Called: Actuator Specialties
1620 Rose St (48162-5699)
PHONE..................734 242-5456
Mallory Setzler, *CEO*
Wendy Wright, *Treasurer*
Corey Setzler, *Manager*
Randy Wright, *Consultant*
Gwendolyn Wright,
EMP: 5 **EST:** 2015
SQ FT: 11,000
SALES (est): 965.8K Privately Held
WEB: www.actuatorspecialties.com
SIC: 3999 Education aids, devices & supplies

(G-11521)
ADVANCED HEAT TREAT CORP
1625 Rose St (48162-5607)
PHONE..................734 243-0063
Gary Sharp, *President*
Tim Garner, *Plant Mgr*
Chad Brandenburg, *Project Mgr*
Jennifer Lassen, *Hum Res Coord*
Gayla Hoppenworth, *Human Resources*
EMP: 16
SALES (corp-wide): 12.5MM Privately Held
WEB: www.ahtcorp.com
SIC: 3398 Metal heat treating
PA: Advanced Heat Treat Corp.
   2825 Midport Blvd
   Waterloo IA 50703
   319 232-5221

(G-11522)
ADVANCED PUMPS INTL LLC
800 Ternes Dr (48162-5010)
PHONE..................734 230-5013
Eli Oklejas Jr, *Mng Member*
EMP: 4 **EST:** 2012
SALES (est): 86K Privately Held
WEB: www.advanced-pumps.com
SIC: 3561 Pumps & pumping equipment

(G-11523)
AJ AIRCRAFT
2410 N Monroe St (48162-4216)
PHONE..................734 244-4015
EMP: 4 **EST:** 2017
SALES (est): 220.7K Privately Held
WEB: www.aj-aircraft.com
SIC: 3728 Aircraft parts & equipment

(G-11524)
ARC ON MOBILE WELDING LLC
7875 Forrestway Dr (48161-4707)
PHONE..................734 344-7128
Justin Johnson, *Principal*
EMP: 4 **EST:** 2015
SALES (est): 33.4K Privately Held
SIC: 7692 Welding repair

(G-11525)
BACKYARD PLAY SYSTEMS LLC
1000 Ternes Dr (48162-5224)
PHONE..................734 242-6900
Thomas Van Der Meulen, *CEO*
▲ **EMP:** 1 **EST:** 2006
SALES (est): 1.4MM Privately Held
WEB: www.backyardbuildings.com
SIC: 2511 Play pens, children's: wood
PA: Backyard Products, Llc
   1000 Ternes Dr
   Monroe MI 48162

(G-11526)
BACKYARD PRODUCTS LLC (PA)
Also Called: Handy Home
1000 Ternes Dr (48162-5224)
PHONE..................734 242-6900
Larry Peters, *General Mgr*
Selina Flowers, *Regional Mgr*
Nick Nagy, *COO*
Evan Faltys, *Opers Mgr*
Greg Martin, *Opers Staff*
▲ **EMP:** 6 **EST:** 2009
SQ FT: 250,000
SALES (est): 206.6MM Privately Held
WEB: www.backyardproducts.com
SIC: 2452 2511 Prefabricated wood buildings; play pens, children's: wood

(G-11527)
BACKYARD SERVICES LLC
1000 Ternes Dr (48162-5224)
PHONE..................734 242-6900
Daniel R Dalach, *CFO*
Daniel Dalach, *CFO*
Duane Daniels, *Controller*
Thomas Van Der Meulen,
EMP: 1 **EST:** 2005
SALES (est): 3.9MM Privately Held
WEB: www.backyardbuildings.com
SIC: 2511 Storage chests, household: wood; children's wood furniture
PA: Backyard Products, Llc
   1000 Ternes Dr
   Monroe MI 48162

(G-11528)
BALL HARD MUSIC GROUP LLC (PA)
330 E Elm Ave (48162-2655)
PHONE..................833 246-4552
Quentine Turnage, *CEO*
Berlon Watson, *Vice Pres*
EMP: 4 **EST:** 2015
SALES (est): 361.7K Privately Held
WEB: www.ballhardmusicgroup.com
SIC: 7389 7929 2741 Music recording producer; ; entertainment service; miscellaneous publishing

(G-11529)
BAR PROCESSING CORPORATION
550 Ternes Dr (48162-5000)
PHONE..................734 243-8937
Jack Starkey, *Marketing Staff*
John Wilson, *Manager*
EMP: 13
SALES (corp-wide): 39.9MM Privately Held
WEB: www.barprocessingcorp.com
SIC: 3471 Finishing, metals or formed products; polishing, metals or formed products
HQ: Bar Processing Corporation
   26601 W Huron River Dr
   Flat Rock MI 48134
   734 782-4454

(G-11530)
BAY CORRUGATED CONTAINER INC
1655 W 7th St (48161-1688)
P.O. Box 667 (48161-0667)
PHONE..................734 243-5400
Connie Reuther, *CEO*
John Reuther, *President*
Dick Tangeman, *Exec VP*
Phillip Dress, *Vice Pres*
James Goiins, *Vice Pres*
▲ **EMP:** 215 **EST:** 1964
SQ FT: 400,000
SALES (est): 34.4MM Privately Held
WEB: www.baycorr.com
SIC: 2653 Boxes, corrugated; made from purchased materials

(G-11531)
BEKTROM FOODS INC
15610 S Telegraph Rd (48161-4095)
PHONE..................734 241-3796
Kellie Michalak, *VP Finance*
Tom Barbela, *Branch Mgr*
Carrie Puckett, *Manager*
Richard Renaud, *Consultant*
EMP: 4
SALES (corp-wide): 14.7MM Privately Held
WEB: www.bektrom.com
SIC: 2045 Prepared flour mixes & doughs
PA: Bektrom Foods, Inc.
   6800 Jericho Tpke 207w
   Syosset NY 11791
   516 802-3800

(G-11532)
BENESH CORPORATION (PA)
1910 N Telegraph Rd (48162-8900)
P.O. Box 906 (48161-0906)
PHONE..................734 244-4143
Peter Benesh, *President*
Edward Benesh, *Manager*
Kathryn Benesh, *Admin Sec*
EMP: 15 **EST:** 1943
SQ FT: 18,000
SALES (est): 1.2MM Privately Held
SIC: 3465 3535 3829 3845 Body parts, automobile: stamped metal; conveyors & conveying equipment; measuring & controlling devices; electromedical equipment; instruments to measure electricity; switchgear & switchboard apparatus

(G-11533)
CANDLES BY COTTONWOOD
3567 Bluebush Rd (48162-9449)
PHONE..................734 344-2339
Kellie Ziehm, *Principal*
EMP: 4 **EST:** 2018
SALES (est): 39.6K Privately Held
WEB: www.candlesbycottonwood.com
SIC: 3999 Candles

(G-11534)
COMPLETE PACKAGING INC
633 Detroit Ave (48162-2587)
P.O. Box 735 (48161-0735)
PHONE..................734 241-2794
Robert Maul, *President*
Gregg Reau, *Mktg Dir*
EMP: 56 **EST:** 1979
SQ FT: 60,000
SALES (est): 5.4MM Privately Held
WEB: www.completepkg.com
SIC: 2441 2653 2657 2448 Boxes, wood; corrugated & solid fiber boxes; folding paperboard boxes; wood pallets & skids

(G-11535)
D S C SERVICES INC (PA)
1510 E 1st St (48161-1915)
PHONE..................734 241-9500
Mark Berryman, *Principal*
Tammy Aldrich, *Marketing Mgr*
EMP: 6 **EST:** 2006
SALES (est): 36.9MM Privately Held
SIC: 3433 Stokers, mechanical: domestic or industrial

(G-11536)
DD PARKER ENTERPRISES INC
Also Called: Monroe Mold
1402 W 7th St (48161-1681)
PHONE..................734 241-6898
James Ghesquire, *President*
John Kwiechen, *President*
EMP: 16 **EST:** 1977
SQ FT: 4,000
SALES (est): 505K Privately Held
SIC: 3599 3544 Machine shop, jobbing & repair; special dies, tools, jigs & fixtures

(G-11537)
DETROIT STOKER COMPANY
1510 E 1st St (48161-1915)
PHONE..................734 241-9500
Gary K Ludwig, *CEO*
Rich Clasby, *Business Mgr*
Michael Dimonte, *Vice Pres*
John Murray, *Vice Pres*
Tom Rosen, *Plant Mgr*
▲ **EMP:** 225 **EST:** 1898
SQ FT: 300,000

GEOGRAPHIC SECTION

Monroe - Monroe County (G-11562)

SALES (est): 36.9MM **Privately Held**
WEB: www.detroitstoker.com
SIC: 3433 Stokers, mechanical: domestic or industrial
PA: D S C Services Inc
1510 E 1st St
Monroe MI 48161

(G-11538)
ECHO ENGRG & PROD SUPS INC
Also Called: Ammex Plastics
725 Ternes Dr (48162-5005)
PHONE.................................734 241-9622
David Ayala, *General Mgr*
Mitchell Baker, *Engineer*
Chris Wells, *Manager*
EMP: 54
SALES (corp-wide): 26.9MM **Privately Held**
WEB: www.echosupply.com
SIC: 3089 Plastic processing
PA: Echo Engineering & Production Supplies Inc.
7150 Winton Dr Ste 300
Indianapolis IN 46268
317 876-8848

(G-11539)
EVENING NEWS
20 W 1st St (48161-2333)
PHONE.................................734 242-1100
Lonnie Peppler-Moyer, *Principal*
EMP: 6 EST: 2008
SALES (est): 341.2K **Privately Held**
WEB: www.monroenews.com
SIC: 2711 Newspapers, publishing & printing

(G-11540)
FINISHERS UNLIMITED MONROE INC
757 S Telegraph Rd (48161-1674)
PHONE.................................734 243-3502
Eric Kuehnlein, *President*
Jim Mackin, *Vice Pres*
Jackie Nocella, *Sales Associate*
EMP: 20 EST: 1993
SQ FT: 15,000
SALES (est): 2.8MM **Privately Held**
WEB: www.finishersunlimited.com
SIC: 3479 Painting of metal products

(G-11541)
FORD MOTOR COMPANY
3200 E Elm Ave (48162-1970)
PHONE.................................734 241-2498
Sean Towsend, *Warehouse Mgr*
EMP: 7
SALES (corp-wide): 127.1B **Publicly Held**
WEB: www.ford.com
SIC: 3711 Automobile assembly, including specialty automobiles
PA: Ford Motor Company
1 American Rd
Dearborn MI 48126
313 322-3000

(G-11542)
GERDAU MACSTEEL INC
Also Called: Gerdau Special Steel N Amer
3000 E Front St (48161-1973)
P.O. Box 1200 (48161-6200)
PHONE.................................734 243-2446
Jaime Lay, *Production*
Darrel Moore, *Branch Mgr*
Randy Musch, *Technical Staff*
EMP: 536 **Privately Held**
WEB: www.gerdau-macsteel.com
SIC: 3312 Bars & bar shapes, steel, hot-rolled
HQ: Gerdau Macsteel, Inc.
5591 Morrill Rd
Jackson MI 49201

(G-11543)
GERDAU MACSTEEL INC
Also Called: Macsteel Monroe
3000 E Front St (48161-1973)
P.O. Box 1200 (48161-6200)
PHONE.................................734 243-2446
Dominick Castiglione, *Purchasing*
John Finlayson, *Branch Mgr*
Stan McLane, *Manager*
Craig Metzger, *Manager*
Paul Ness, *Supervisor*
EMP: 380
SQ FT: 552 **Privately Held**
WEB: www.gerdau-macsteel.com
SIC: 3312 3316 Bars & bar shapes, steel, cold-finished: own hot-rolled; cold finishing of steel shapes
HQ: Gerdau Macsteel, Inc.
5591 Morrill Rd
Jackson MI 49201

(G-11544)
GLOBAL DIGITAL PRINTING
20 W 1st St (48161-2333)
PHONE.................................734 244-5010
EMP: 5 EST: 2015
SALES (est): 101.5K **Privately Held**
SIC: 2752 Commercial printing, lithographic

(G-11545)
GREAT LAKES TOWERS LLC
Also Called: Ventower Industries
111 Borchert Park Dr (48161-1986)
P.O. Box 589 (48161-0589)
PHONE.................................734 682-4000
Christy Follbaum, *Sales Staff*
Gregory Adanin,
Christopher Marmion, *Technician*
Scott Viciana,
▲ EMP: 180 EST: 2008
SQ FT: 115,000
SALES (est): 34.7MM **Privately Held**
WEB: www.ventower.com
SIC: 3441 Fabricated structural metal

(G-11546)
HANWHA ADVANCED MTLS AMER LLC
Also Called: Hanwha L&C Alabama
1530 E Front St (48161-2456)
PHONE.................................810 629-2496
Larry Rood, *Branch Mgr*
Shelby Marietta, *Admin Asst*
EMP: 15 **Privately Held**
WEB: www.hanwhaus.com
SIC: 3714 Motor vehicle parts & accessories
HQ: Hanwha Advanced Materials America Llc
4400 N Park Dr
Opelika AL 36801
334 741-7725

(G-11547)
HILGRAEVE INC
115 E Elm Ave (48162-2833)
P.O. Box 941 (48161-0941)
PHONE.................................734 243-0576
Patty Thompson, *President*
Emerson Williams, *Info Tech Mgr*
Robert Everett,
John Hile,
Jan Groves, *Clerk*
EMP: 5 EST: 1980
SALES (est): 707.2K **Privately Held**
WEB: www.hilgraeve.com
SIC: 7372 Prepackaged software

(G-11548)
HOPPENJANS INC
Also Called: Fastsigns - 381501
1339 N Telegraph Rd (48162-3374)
PHONE.................................734 344-5304
John Hoppenjans II, *President*
EMP: 15 EST: 2017
SALES (est): 536.2K **Privately Held**
WEB: www.fastsigns.com
SIC: 3993 Signs & advertising specialties

(G-11549)
HYDROCHEM LLC
Also Called: Hydrochempsc
987 W Hurd Rd (48162-9401)
PHONE.................................313 841-5800
Odell Doss, *Warehouse Mgr*
Tim Gaudet, *Human Res Dir*
Gary Noto, *Branch Mgr*
Chaz Perry, *Supervisor*
EMP: 11
SALES (corp-wide): 468MM **Privately Held**
WEB: www.hydrochempsc.com
SIC: 3589 Vacuum cleaners & sweepers, electric: industrial
HQ: Hydrochem Llc
900 Georgia Ave
Deer Park TX 77536
713 393-5600

(G-11550)
INDEPENDENT DAIRY INC (PA)
126 N Telegraph Rd (48162-3299)
PHONE.................................734 241-6016
Michael Cheney, *President*
Jeffery Hutchinson, *Treasurer*
Sherry Walker, *Admin Asst*
EMP: 20 EST: 1934
SALES (est): 3.8MM **Privately Held**
WEB: www.mercuryfs.com
SIC: 2024 5143 5411 Ice cream, bulk; ice cream, packaged: molded, on sticks, etc.; milk & cream, fluid; ice cream & ices; convenience stores, chain

(G-11551)
INTER-PACK CORPORATION (PA)
399 Detroit Ave (48162-2538)
P.O. Box 691 (48161-0691)
PHONE.................................734 242-7755
J Benjiman Watson, *President*
Douglas Southworth, *Shareholder*
EMP: 20 EST: 1967
SQ FT: 80,000
SALES (est): 2MM **Privately Held**
SIC: 2653 3086 7389 Boxes, corrugated: made from purchased materials; plastics foam products; packaging & labeling services

(G-11552)
JERRYS PALLETS
232 E Hurd Rd (48162-9213)
PHONE.................................734 242-1577
EMP: 4 EST: 2009
SALES (est): 190K **Privately Held**
SIC: 2448 Mfg Wood Pallets/Skids

(G-11553)
JORDAN BARNETT
2549 Reinhardt Rd (48162-9225)
PHONE.................................734 243-9565
Jordan Barnett, *Principal*
EMP: 5 EST: 2017
SALES (est): 68K **Privately Held**
SIC: 2721 Periodicals

(G-11554)
KUHLMAN CORPORATION
Also Called: Kuhlman Concrete
15370 S Dixie Hwy (48161-3773)
PHONE.................................734 241-8692
Stan Radabaugh, *Manager*
EMP: 7
SALES (corp-wide): 54.9MM **Privately Held**
WEB: www.kuhlman-corp.com
SIC: 3273 Ready-mixed concrete
PA: Kuhlman Corporation
1845 Indian Wood Cir
Maumee OH 43537
419 897-6000

(G-11555)
LA-Z-BOY CASEGOODS INC (HQ)
Also Called: La-Z-Boy Greensboro, Inc.
1 Lazboy Dr (48162-5138)
PHONE.................................734 242-1444
Kurt L Darrow, *CEO*
Steven M Kincaid, *Principal*
Louis M Riccio, *Vice Pres*
James P Klarr, *Admin Sec*
▲ EMP: 20 EST: 2000
SALES (est): 34.1MM
SALES (corp-wide): 1.7B **Publicly Held**
WEB: www.la-z-boy.com
SIC: 2511 5714 Wood household furniture; upholstery materials
PA: La-Z-Boy Incorporated
1 Lazboy Dr
Monroe MI 48162
734 242-1444

(G-11556)
LA-Z-BOY GLOBAL LIMITED
1 Lazboy Dr (48162-5138)
PHONE.................................734 241-2438
Kurt Droow, *Principal*
EMP: 6 EST: 2014
SALES (est): 992.2K
SALES (corp-wide): 1.7B **Publicly Held**
WEB: www.la-z-boy.com
SIC: 2512 Chairs: upholstered on wood frames
PA: La-Z-Boy Incorporated
1 Lazboy Dr
Monroe MI 48162
734 242-1444

(G-11557)
LA-Z-BOY INCORPORATED (PA)
1 Lazboy Dr (48162-5138)
PHONE.................................734 242-1444
Kurt L Darrow, *Ch of Bd*
Melinda D Whittington, *President*
Darrell D Edwards, *COO*
Otis S Sawyer, *Senior VP*
Darrell Edwards, *Vice Pres*
◆ EMP: 550 EST: 1927
SALES: 1.7B **Publicly Held**
WEB: www.la-z-boy.com
SIC: 2512 2511 5712 Chairs: upholstered on wood frames; couches, sofas & davenports: upholstered on wood frames; recliners: upholstered on wood frames; rockers: upholstered on wood frames; wood household furniture; furniture stores

(G-11558)
LAMOUR PRINTING CO
123 E Front St (48161-2198)
PHONE.................................734 241-6006
Robert Lamour, *Partner*
John Lamour, *Partner*
EMP: 4 EST: 1922
SQ FT: 2,000
SALES (est): 250K **Privately Held**
WEB: www.lamourprinting.com
SIC: 2759 2752 Letterpress printing; commercial printing, offset

(G-11559)
LZB MANUFACTURING INC (HQ)
Also Called: La-Z-Boy
1 Lazboy Dr (48162-5138)
PHONE.................................734 242-1444
Mark S Bacon Sr, *President*
Lindsay Barnes, *Vice Pres*
R Rand Tucker, *Vice Pres*
Louis M Riccio, *CFO*
Greg A Brinks, *Treasurer*
◆ EMP: 5 EST: 2004
SALES (est): 150.5MM
SALES (corp-wide): 1.7B **Publicly Held**
WEB: www.la-z-boy.com
SIC: 2512 Upholstered household furniture
PA: La-Z-Boy Incorporated
1 Lazboy Dr
Monroe MI 48162
734 242-1444

(G-11560)
MIDWAY PRODUCTS GROUP INC (PA)
1 Lyman E Hoyt Dr (48161)
P.O. Box 737 (48161-0737)
PHONE.................................734 241-7242
James E Hoyt, *President*
Dan Ditto, *Area Mgr*
Lloyd A Miller, *Vice Pres*
Roger Yambasky, *Vice Pres*
Scott Morton, *Project Mgr*
▲ EMP: 120 EST: 1991
SALES (est): 314.8MM **Privately Held**
WEB: www.midwayproducts.com
SIC: 3469 Metal stampings

(G-11561)
MONROE ATELLOS 19
830 S Monroe St (48161-1468)
PHONE.................................734 682-3467
EMP: 6 EST: 2017
SALES (est): 126.3K **Privately Held**
WEB: www.monroenews.com
SIC: 2711 Newspapers, publishing & printing

(G-11562)
MONROE ENVIRONMENTAL CORP
Also Called: Business To Business
810 W Front St (48161-1627)
PHONE.................................734 242-2420
Gary Pashaian, *President*

Monroe - Monroe County (G-11563)   GEOGRAPHIC SECTION

Joseph Dragich, *Purch Mgr*
Larry Deranek, *Engineer*
Jay Kolapalli, *Project Engr*
Adam Pashaian, *Sales Staff*
◆ **EMP:** 55 **EST:** 1969
SQ FT: 40,000
SALES (est): 11.2MM **Privately Held**
WEB: www.monroeenvironmental.com
SIC: 3589 Water treatment equipment, industrial

(G-11563)
MONROE EVENING NEWS
20 W 1st St (48161-2333)
PHONE.................................734 242-1100
Larry D Gray, *Principal*
Barbara Krolak, *Editor*
Vicki Price, *Sales Staff*
Kristi Prater, *Advt Staff*
Kendra Wall, *Advt Staff*
EMP: 17 **EST:** 2010
SALES (est): 558.1K **Privately Held**
WEB: www.monroenews.com
SIC: 2711 Newspapers, publishing & printing

(G-11564)
MONROE MACHININING LLC
300 Detroit Ave (48162-5006)
PHONE.................................734 457-2088
EMP: 5 **EST:** 2017
SALES (est): 436.5K **Privately Held**
WEB: www.monroemachiningllc.net
SIC: 3599 Machine shop, jobbing & repair

(G-11565)
MONROE PUBLISHING COMPANY (HQ)
20 W 1st St (48161-2333)
P.O. Box 1176 (48161-6176)
PHONE.................................734 242-1100
Lonnie L Peppler-Moyer, *President*
Barbara Krolak, *Editor*
Jay Hollon, *Corp Secy*
Jamie West, *Advt Staff*
EMP: 100 **EST:** 1927
SQ FT: 25,000
SALES (est): 14.2MM
SALES (corp-wide): 3.4B **Publicly Held**
WEB: www.monroepublishing.com
SIC: 2759 2711 Commercial printing; newspapers, publishing & printing
PA: Gannett Co., Inc.
  7950 Jones Branch Dr
  Mc Lean VA 22102
  703 854-6000

(G-11566)
MONROE SUCCESS VLC
1000 S Monroe St (48161-3901)
PHONE.................................734 682-3720
EMP: 5 **EST:** 2017
SALES (est): 102.9K **Privately Held**
WEB: www.monroenews.com
SIC: 2711 Newspapers, publishing & printing

(G-11567)
NATIONAL GALVANIZING LP
1500 Telb St (48162-2572)
PHONE.................................734 243-1882
Mike Robinson, *Partner*
Chuck Winters, *Controller*
Becky Riley, *Human Res Mgr*
Tony Konczal, *Cust Mgr*
EMP: 1000 **EST:** 1983
SQ FT: 15,000
SALES (est): 53.4MM
SALES (corp-wide): 230MM **Privately Held**
WEB: www.nationalgalvanizing.com
SIC: 3312 3316 3471 3341 Sheet or strip, steel, hot-rolled; strip steel, cold-rolled: from purchased hot-rolled; plating & polishing; secondary nonferrous metals; metals service centers & offices
HQ: Heidtman Steel Products, Inc.
  2401 Front St
  Toledo OH 43605
  419 691-4646

(G-11568)
PAUL C DOERR
Also Called: Kraus & Co
407 E Front St (48161-2048)
PHONE.................................734 242-2058
Paul C Doerr, *Owner*
EMP: 4 **EST:** 1947
SQ FT: 6,500
SALES (est): 198.4K **Privately Held**
SIC: 2752 2791 2789 Advertising posters, lithographed; typesetting; bookbinding & related work

(G-11569)
PIONEER METAL FINISHING LLC
525 Ternes Dr (48162-5001)
PHONE.................................734 384-9000
Ann Shealer, *Branch Mgr*
EMP: 100
SALES (corp-wide): 93MM **Privately Held**
WEB: www.pioneermetal.com
SIC: 3398 3471 Metal heat treating; plating & polishing
PA: Pioneer Metal Finishing, Llc
  480 Pilgrim Way Ste 1400
  Green Bay WI 54304
  877 721-1100

(G-11570)
PRO-POWERSPORTS
7779 Townway Dr (48161-4725)
PHONE.................................734 457-0829
Chris Danish, *Partner*
EMP: 5 **EST:** 1999
SALES (est): 239.7K **Privately Held**
WEB: www.pro-powersports.com
SIC: 3799 Snowmobiles

(G-11571)
PULLMAN COMPANY (DH)
1 International Dr (48161-9345)
PHONE.................................734 243-8000
Thomas E Evans, *President*
James Gray, *President*
▲ **EMP:** 19 **EST:** 1839
SQ FT: 185,000
SALES (est): 175.7MM
SALES (corp-wide): 15.3B **Publicly Held**
SIC: 3714 3715 3061 Motor vehicle parts & accessories; trailer bodies; automotive rubber goods (mechanical)
HQ: Tenneco Automotive Operating Company, Inc.
  500 N Field Dr
  Lake Forest IL 60045
  847 482-5000

(G-11572)
SIGNMEUPCOM INC
1285 N Telegraph Rd (48162-3368)
PHONE.................................312 343-1263
Todd Bellino, *Principal*
EMP: 5 **EST:** 2009
SALES (est): 126.6K **Privately Held**
SIC: 7372 Prepackaged software

(G-11573)
SOURCE CAPITAL BACKYARD LLC
1000 Ternes Dr (48162-5224)
PHONE.................................734 242-6900
Duane Daniels, *Controller*
Thomas Van Der Meulen, *Mng Member*
EMP: 11 **EST:** 2009
SQ FT: 250,000
SALES (est): 85MM **Privately Held**
SIC: 2511 2452 Play pens, children's: wood; prefabricated wood buildings

(G-11574)
SPARTAN STEEL COATING LLC
3300 Wolverine (48162-9393)
PHONE.................................734 289-5400
Brian Skolnik, *Officer*
Neil Bruss,
Dave Brandau,
EMP: 62 **EST:** 1996
SQ FT: 293,000
SALES (est): 24.8MM
SALES (corp-wide): 3.1B **Publicly Held**
WEB: www.worthingtonindustries.com
SIC: 3479 Galvanizing of iron, steel or end-formed products
PA: Worthington Industries, Inc.
  200 W Wlson Bridge Rd
  Worthington OH 43085
  614 438-3210

(G-11575)
SPILLSON LTD
878 Regents Park Dr (48161-9762)
PHONE.................................734 384-0284
John Spillson, *President*
George Spillson, *Corp Secy*
Sophia Spillson, *Vice Pres*
EMP: 4 **EST:** 1980
SQ FT: 4,000 **Privately Held**
SIC: 2011 Canned meats (except baby food), meat slaughtered on site

(G-11576)
SPIRATEX COMPANY
1916 Frenchtown Ctr Dr (48162-9375)
PHONE.................................734 289-4800
Gary Markel, *Vice Pres*
Garry Markle, *Vice Pres*
Amy Poma, *Purchasing*
Dale Tusek, *Engineer*
Alan Harberson, *Plant Engr*
EMP: 70
SALES (corp-wide): 25MM **Privately Held**
WEB: www.spiratex.com
SIC: 3089 3083 3082 Injection molding of plastics; laminated plastics plate & sheet; unsupported plastics profile shapes
PA: The Spiratex Company
  6333 Cogswell St
  Romulus MI 48174
  734 722-0100

(G-11577)
STEPSCREEN PRINTING
656 Saint Marys Ave (48162-2753)
PHONE.................................734 770-5009
Steve Springer, *Principal*
EMP: 5 **EST:** 2018
SALES (est): 405.5K **Privately Held**
WEB: www.stepsp.com
SIC: 2759 Screen printing

(G-11578)
STONECO OF MICHIGAN INC (PA)
15203 S Telegraph Rd (48161-4072)
PHONE.................................734 241-8966
Dennis Rickard, *President*
Jason Rivard, *Vice Pres*
Megan Kansier, *Comms Mgr*
Mike Rapp, *Manager*
Don Sniegowski, *Manager*
EMP: 72 **EST:** 2007
SALES (est): 10MM **Privately Held**
WEB: www.stoneco.net
SIC: 3531 Construction machinery

(G-11579)
TENNECO AUTOMOTIVE OPER CO INC
13910 Lake Dr (48161-3845)
PHONE.................................734 243-8039
Al Sewell, *Buyer*
Thorne Decarlo, *Manager*
Chris Serement, *CIO*
EMP: 4
SALES (corp-wide): 15.3B **Publicly Held**
SIC: 3714 Motor vehicle engines & parts
HQ: Tenneco Automotive Operating Company, Inc.
  500 N Field Dr
  Lake Forest IL 60045
  847 482-5000

(G-11580)
TENNECO AUTOMOTIVE OPER CO INC
1 International Dr (48161-9386)
PHONE.................................734 243-4615
Jeroen Paenhuysen, *Chief Engr*
Brian Jacobs, *Engineer*
Trudy Whipple, *Finance Mgr*
Matthew Ward, *Accountant*
Clayton Moore, *Business Anlyst*
EMP: 15
SALES (corp-wide): 15.3B **Publicly Held**
SIC: 3714 Motor vehicle parts & accessories
HQ: Tenneco Automotive Operating Company, Inc.
  500 N Field Dr
  Lake Forest IL 60045
  847 482-5000

(G-11581)
TENNECO AUTOMOTIVE OPER CO INC
1 International Dr (48161-9386)
PHONE.................................734 243-8000
Joe Pomaranski, *Manager*
Mike Alzamora, *Senior Mgr*
Bill Dawson, *Exec Dir*
EMP: 7
SALES (corp-wide): 15.3B **Publicly Held**
WEB: www.monroe.com
SIC: 3714 Shock absorbers, motor vehicle
HQ: Tenneco Automotive Operating Company, Inc.
  500 N Field Dr
  Lake Forest IL 60045
  847 482-5000

(G-11582)
THOMAS L SNAREY & ASSOC INC (PA)
Also Called: Premier Industries
513 N Dixie Hwy (48162-2563)
PHONE.................................734 241-8474
Thomas L Snarey, *President*
James Cameron, *Vice Pres*
Mike Bossory, *Sales Engr*
Lee Wilder, *Sales Engr*
Kathleen Vadun, *Admin Sec*
▲ **EMP:** 13 **EST:** 1947
SQ FT: 40,000
SALES (est): 7.3MM **Privately Held**
WEB: www.premierindustriescorp.com
SIC: 3599 Machine shop, jobbing & repair

(G-11583)
TMS INTERNATIONAL LLC
3000 E Front St (48161-1973)
PHONE.................................734 241-3007
Candy Clavier, *Clerk*
EMP: 5 **Privately Held**
WEB: www.tmsinternational.com
SIC: 3312 Blast furnaces & steel mills
HQ: Tms International, Llc
  Southside Wrks Bldg 1 3f
  Pittsburgh PA 15203
  412 678-6141

(G-11584)
TMS INTERNATIONAL LLC
3000 E Front St (48161-1973)
P.O. Box 843 (48161-0843)
PHONE.................................734 241-3007
EMP: 18
SQ FT: 672 **Privately Held**
SIC: 3295 Minerals, Ground Or Treated, Nsk

(G-11585)
TOMAN INDUSTRIES INC
1652 E Hurd Rd (48162-9314)
PHONE.................................734 289-1393
Jeffrey S Toman, *President*
EMP: 2 **EST:** 1990
SALES (est): 1.2MM **Privately Held**
SIC: 3549 Assembly machines, including robotic

(G-11586)
TWB COMPANY LLC (HQ)
1600 Nadeau Rd (48162-9317)
PHONE.................................734 289-6400
Ivan Meltzer, *President*
Jeff Keaton, *Purch Mgr*
Rich Barron, *Engineer*
Robert Kistler, *Engineer*
Warren Kile, *Project Engr*
▲ **EMP:** 220 **EST:** 1992
SQ FT: 178,000
SALES (est): 103.9MM
SALES (corp-wide): 3.1B **Publicly Held**
WEB: www.twbcompany.com
SIC: 3312 3353 Structural shapes & pilings, steel; rods, iron & steel: made in steel mills; aluminum sheet, plate & foil
PA: Worthington Industries, Inc.
  200 W Wlson Bridge Rd
  Worthington OH 43085
  614 438-3210

(G-11587)
TWB OF INDIANA INC
1600 Nadeau Rd (48162-9317)
PHONE.................................734 289-6400
Tom Fant, *President*

Manfred Nagel, *Exec VP*
Mike Lowrey, *Vice Pres*
Ivan Meltzer, *Vice Pres*
EMP: 7 **EST:** 2001
SQ FT: 127,800
SALES (est): 170.9K **Privately Held**
SIC: 3429 Motor vehicle hardware

(G-11588)
VAN DAELES INC
Also Called: Al's Cabinet Shop
8830 Ida Maybee Rd (48162-9112)
PHONE 734 587-7165
Leonard Van Daele, *President*
Shirley Van Daele, *Corp Secy*
Jerry Van Daele, *Vice Pres*
EMP: 9 **EST:** 1965
SQ FT: 7,824
SALES (est): 766.2K **Privately Held**
SIC: 2434 5712 Wood kitchen cabinets; cabinet work, custom

(G-11589)
VIVID PUBLISHING
1519 Stewart Rd (48162-9299)
PHONE 614 282-6479
Lillie David, *Principal*
EMP: 5 **EST:** 2012
SALES (est): 79.8K **Privately Held**
WEB: www.vivid-publishing.mybigcommerce.com
SIC: 2741 Miscellaneous publishing

(G-11590)
WASHINGTON STREET PRINTERS LLC
17 Washington St (48161-2276)
PHONE 734 240-5541
EMP: 8 **EST:** 2010
SALES (est): 257.2K **Privately Held**
SIC: 2752 Commercial printing, offset

(G-11591)
WEST BROTHERS LLC
815 Scarlet Oak Dr (48162-3481)
PHONE 734 457-0083
Charles West, *Mng Member*
Julie West, *Mng Member*
EMP: 4 **EST:** 2005
SALES (est): 100K **Privately Held**
SIC: 2099 Sauces: gravy, dressing & dip mixes

(G-11592)
WORTHINGTON INDUSTRIES INC
3300 Wolverine (48162-9393)
PHONE 734 289-5416
Brian Skolnik, *Branch Mgr*
EMP: 8
SALES (corp-wide): 3.1B **Publicly Held**
WEB: www.worthingtonindustries.com
SIC: 3316 Cold finishing of steel shapes
PA: Worthington Industries, Inc.
200 W Old Wilson Bridge Rd
Worthington OH 43085
614 438-3210

(G-11593)
YANFENG US AUTO INTR SYSTEMS I
1833 Frenchtown Ctr Dr (48162-9375)
PHONE 734 289-4841
Brad Meyers, *Branch Mgr*
EMP: 7 **Privately Held**
WEB: www.yfai.com
SIC: 3714 Motor vehicle parts & accessories
HQ: Yanfeng Us Automotive Interior Systems I Llc
41935 W 12 Mile Rd
Novi MI 48377
248 319-7333

Montague
Muskegon County

(G-11594)
ALUDYNE MONTAGUE LLC
Also Called: Chassix - Dmi Montague
5353 Wilcox St (49437-1566)
PHONE 248 479-6455
Andreas Weller, *CEO*
Jim Alderink, *Opers Staff*
Ranee Parmann, *Purchasing*
Tom Abney, *QC Mgr*
Jonathon Blatt, *Engineer*
▲ **EMP:** 600 **EST:** 1988
SQ FT: 320,000
SALES (est): 141MM
SALES (corp-wide): 1.5B **Privately Held**
WEB: www.aludyne.com
SIC: 3714 Motor vehicle parts & accessories
HQ: Aludyne North America Inc.
300 Galleria Ofcntr Ste 5
Southfield MI 48034

(G-11595)
DIVERSIFIED MACHINE INC
5353 Wilcox St (49437-1599)
PHONE 231 894-9562
EMP: 24 **EST:** 2009
SALES (est): 5.2MM **Privately Held**
WEB: www.aludyne.com
SIC: 3714 Motor vehicle parts & accessories

(G-11596)
FABRICATION PLUS
4300 Fruitvale Rd (49437-9522)
PHONE 231 730-9374
Kevin Schutter, *Owner*
EMP: 8 **EST:** 2015
SALES (est): 415.5K **Privately Held**
SIC: 3441 Fabricated structural metal

(G-11597)
GVB GROUP-LA FIESTA LLC
Also Called: La Fiesta Chip Company
8155 Cook St (49437-1512)
PHONE 231 843-7600
Garrit Brown, *Prdtn Mgr*
EMP: 19 **EST:** 1987
SALES (est): 539.5K **Privately Held**
WEB: www.ilovefiestagrande.com
SIC: 5812 2096 Mexican restaurant; tortilla chips

(G-11598)
INTERNATIONAL MASTER PDTS CORP (PA)
Also Called: Master Tag
9751 Us Hhwy 31 (49437)
PHONE 231 894-5651
Richard K Hughes Jr, *President*
Amanda Bogess, *Project Mgr*
Amanda Boggess, *Project Mgr*
Michelle Turner, *Project Mgr*
Lance Vanderleest, *Mfg Mgr*
EMP: 124 **EST:** 1951
SQ FT: 38,000
SALES (est): 39.1MM **Privately Held**
WEB: www.mastertag.com
SIC: 2752 2759 2671 Tags, lithographed; commercial printing; packaging paper & plastics film, coated & laminated

(G-11599)
MONTAGUE METAL PRODUCTS INC
4101 Fruitvale Rd (49437-9531)
PHONE 231 893-0547
Mary Morris, *President*
Mark Morris, *Vice Pres*
John Morris, *Treasurer*
Tyler Morris, *Admin Sec*
EMP: 25 **EST:** 1991
SQ FT: 14,000
SALES (est): 1.7MM **Privately Held**
SIC: 3363 Aluminum die-castings

(G-11600)
SHELLCAST INC
5230 Industrial Park Rd (49437-1528)
PHONE 231 893-8245
Robert F Johnson, *President*
Bob Johnson, *Purchasing*
Scott Miller, *QC Mgr*
Gregg Nash, *QC Mgr*
Jesse Holman, *Supervisor*
EMP: 30 **EST:** 1961
SQ FT: 35,000
SALES (est): 2.5MM **Privately Held**
WEB: www.shellcastinc.com
SIC: 3369 Castings, except die-castings, precision

(G-11601)
SPECTRUM ILLUMINATION CO INC
5114 Industrial Park Rd (49437-1526)
PHONE 231 894-4590
Naomi Muyskens, *President*
Valerie Muyskens, *Admin Sec*
EMP: 5 **EST:** 2004
SQ FT: 2,400
SALES (est): 883.1K **Privately Held**
WEB: www.spectrumillumination.com
SIC: 3648 Lighting equipment

(G-11602)
TOWER LABORATORIES LTD
8060 Whitbeck Rd (49437-1592)
PHONE 231 893-1472
Melissa Miles, *Buyer*
Rachael Whitbeck, *Sales Dir*
Steve Laninga, *Branch Mgr*
Joan Jones, *Manager*
John Fleener, *Maintence Staff*
EMP: 20
SALES (corp-wide): 47.9MM **Privately Held**
WEB: www.towerlabs.com
SIC: 2834 Pharmaceutical preparations
PA: Tower Laboratories, Ltd.
8 Industrial Park Rd
Centerbrook CT 06409
860 767-2127

(G-11603)
WHITE RIVER
7386 Post Rd (49437-9706)
PHONE 231 894-9216
Mike Cockerill, *Principal*
Deborah Harris, *Treasurer*
Joanne Lehman, *Admin Sec*
EMP: 5 **EST:** 1986
SALES (est): 500.5K **Privately Held**
WEB: www.whiterivertwp.com
SIC: 3674 Hall effect devices

Montgomery
Branch County

(G-11604)
WHITEFEATHER CREEK ALPACAS
8274 Alvord Rd (49255-9743)
PHONE 517 368-5393
EMP: 4 **EST:** 2013
SALES (est): 87.5K **Privately Held**
SIC: 2231 Alpacas, mohair: woven

Montrose
Genesee County

(G-11605)
M-57 AGGREGATE COMPANY
170 W State St (48457-9807)
PHONE 810 639-7516
Shane Powell, *Vice Pres*
EMP: 7 **EST:** 2009
SALES (est): 769.6K **Privately Held**
SIC: 1442 7389 Construction sand & gravel;

(G-11606)
MARSHALLS CROSSING
12050 Trident Blvd (48457-8902)
PHONE 810 639-4740
Wendy Brotherton, *Manager*
EMP: 8 **EST:** 1998
SALES (est): 432.4K **Privately Held**
WEB: www.marshallscrossing.com
SIC: 2452 6552 6531 Modular homes, prefabricated, wood; subdividers & developers; real estate agents & managers

(G-11607)
MONTROSE TRAILERS INC
180 Ruth St (48457-9450)
PHONE 810 639-7431
Gary Palinsky, *President*
Barbara Palinsky, *Corp Secy*
EMP: 8 **EST:** 1971
SQ FT: 8,800
SALES (est): 800K **Privately Held**
WEB: www.montrosetrailers.com
SIC: 3799 3792 3715 3537 Trailers & trailer equipment; travel trailers & campers; truck trailers; industrial trucks & tractors; mobile homes

(G-11608)
TRU-COAT INC
10428 Seymour Rd (48457-9015)
PHONE 810 785-3331
Ronald Loafman, *President*
Phil Wood, *General Mgr*
EMP: 5 **EST:** 1987
SQ FT: 8,000
SALES (est): 441.9K **Privately Held**
WEB: www.trucoatinc.com
SIC: 3471 Plating of metals or formed products

Moran
Mackinac County

(G-11609)
GUSTAFSON SMOKED FISH
Also Called: T & J Uphl Sp & Marathon Svc
W4467 Us 2 (49760-9819)
PHONE 906 292-5424
Thomas Gustafson, *Owner*
EMP: 4 **EST:** 1978
SQ FT: 2,500
SALES (est): 325.5K **Privately Held**
WEB: www.gustafsonssmokedfishinc.com
SIC: 2091 7641 5541 Fish, smoked; re-upholstery; filling stations, gasoline

(G-11610)
SAND PRODUCTS CORPORATION
W5021 Us Hwy 2 (49760)
PHONE 906 292-5432
Robert C Cook, *Manager*
EMP: 5
SALES (corp-wide): 18.4MM **Privately Held**
WEB: www.tylercreekcamp.com
SIC: 1446 Foundry sand mining
PA: Sand Products Corporation
13495 92nd St Se
Alto MI 49302
231 722-6691

Morenci
Lenawee County

(G-11611)
GENERAL BROACH COMPANY (HQ)
307 Salisbury St (49256-1043)
PHONE 517 458-7555
Robert Roseliep, *President*
Larry Stover, *General Mgr*
Doyle Collar, *General Mgr*
Boyd Allen, *Engineer*
Mark Hale, *Engineer*
▲ **EMP:** 54 **EST:** 1991
SQ FT: 62,640
SALES (est): 12.5MM
SALES (corp-wide): 305MM **Privately Held**
WEB: www.generalbroach.com
SIC: 3545 3541 Broaches (machine tool accessories); broaching machines
PA: Utica Enterprises, Inc.
5750 New King Dr Ste 200
Troy MI 48098
586 726-4300

(G-11612)
GENERAL BROACH COMPANY
555 W Main St Ste C (49256-1481)
PHONE 517 458-7555
Kerri Schmitz, *General Mgr*
Colleen Martinez, *Purchasing*
Larry Stover, *Branch Mgr*
EMP: 6
SALES (corp-wide): 305MM **Privately Held**
WEB: www.generalbroach.com
SIC: 3545 Broaches (machine tool accessories)

Morenci - Lenawee County (G-11613)

HQ: General Broach Company
307 Salisbury St
Morenci MI 49256

(G-11613)
GREEN MANUFACTURING INC
9650 Packard Rd (49256-9557)
PHONE..................517 458-1500
Kevin Green, *President*
Brian Holly, *COO*
EMP: 9 **EST:** 1995
SQ FT: 2,500
SALES (est): 4.7MM **Privately Held**
WEB: www.greenteeth.com
SIC: 3545 Tools & accessories for machine tools

(G-11614)
LENAWEE TOOL & AUTOMATION INC
807 Gorham St (49256-9701)
PHONE..................517 458-7222
Michael Dwyer, *President*
EMP: 6 **EST:** 1970
SALES (est): 486.3K **Privately Held**
SIC: 3544 Special dies & tools

(G-11615)
ROTH FABRICATING INC
9600 Skyline Dr (49256-9709)
PHONE..................517 458-7541
Simone Haas, *President*
Jeanie Sarnac, *Vice Pres*
Shane Sarnac, *Admin Sec*
EMP: 25 **EST:** 1980
SQ FT: 22,000
SALES (est): 4.7MM **Privately Held**
WEB: www.rothfabricatinginc.com
SIC: 3441 Fabricated structural metal

(G-11616)
SIMI AIR
120 E Congress St (49256-1208)
PHONE..................517 401-0284
EMP: 5 **EST:** 2008
SALES (est): 68.9K **Privately Held**
WEB: www.simiair.com
SIC: 3993 Signs & advertising specialties

(G-11617)
TRIPLE K FARMS INC
Also Called: Grain and Cattle Farm
13648 Wabash Rd (49256-9724)
PHONE..................517 458-9741
Steven Kutzley, *President*
Terry Kutzley, *Vice Pres*
EMP: 4 **EST:** 1996
SQ FT: 10,000
SALES (est): 663.4K **Privately Held**
WEB: www.triplekirrigation.com
SIC: 0211 0119 3523 Beef cattle feedlots; bean (dry field & seed) farm; irrigation equipment, self-propelled

(G-11618)
TURTLE RACING LLC
625 N East St (49256-1248)
PHONE..................517 918-3444
EMP: 5 **EST:** 2016
SALES (est): 113.1K **Privately Held**
SIC: 3751 Motorcycles & related parts

Morley
Mecosta County

(G-11619)
B & D METAL FAB
10717 Arbogast Rd (49336-9609)
PHONE..................616 255-1796
Bob Barr, *Partner*
EMP: 5 **EST:** 2015
SALES (est): 81.9K **Privately Held**
WEB: www.bdmetalfab.com
SIC: 3441 Fabricated structural metal

(G-11620)
KVA ENGINEERING INC
2161 200th Ave (49336-9256)
PHONE..................616 745-7483
Kenneth Vranish, *Principal*
EMP: 5 **EST:** 1988
SALES (est): 425.2K **Privately Held**
WEB: www.kva-engineering.com
SIC: 3812 Search & navigation equipment

(G-11621)
PEACOCKS ECO LOG & SAWMILL LLC
14823 4 Mile Rd (49336-9509)
PHONE..................231 250-3462
Travis Peacock, *Principal*
EMP: 6 **EST:** 2014
SALES (est): 195.5K **Privately Held**
SIC: 2411 Logging camps & contractors

(G-11622)
RICHARD TEACHWORHT
17270 Kent Ave (49336-9458)
PHONE..................231 527-8227
Amelia Gillespie, *Principal*
EMP: 5 **EST:** 2019
SALES (est): 125.3K **Privately Held**
SIC: 2411 Logging

(G-11623)
SUMMIT TOOLING & MFG INC
451 N Cass St (49336-9575)
PHONE..................231 856-7037
EMP: 6
SQ FT: 15,000
SALES (est): 330K **Privately Held**
SIC: 3423 Mfg Hand & Edge Tools

(G-11624)
TREE CUTTING STUMP GRINDING
2245 Brady Lake Dr (49336-9583)
PHONE..................231 856-9021
Aaron Brooks, *Principal*
EMP: 5 **EST:** 2008
SALES (est): 119.5K **Privately Held**
SIC: 3599 Grinding castings for the trade

Morrice
Shiawassee County

(G-11625)
MEAL AND MORE INCORPORATED
130 W 3rd Ave (48857-2547)
P.O. Box 376 (48857-0376)
PHONE..................517 625-3186
Elizabeth Andrus, *President*
Linda Whipple, *Office Mgr*
Timothy Kline, *Software Engr*
Jack Mc Eowen, *Admin Sec*
EMP: 30
SQ FT: 2,400
SALES (est): 9.6MM **Privately Held**
WEB: www.oxyinfo.com
SIC: 2048 Livestock feeds

Mount Clemens
Macomb County

(G-11626)
A-1 ROLL CO
301 Church St (48043-2180)
PHONE..................586 783-6677
Richard F Florka, *President*
EMP: 17 **EST:** 1980
SQ FT: 25,000
SALES (est): 2.1MM **Privately Held**
WEB: www.a1roll.com
SIC: 3441 Fabricated structural metal

(G-11627)
ARTS CRAFTS HARDWARE
169 Smith St (48043-2345)
PHONE..................586 231-5344
EMP: 10
SALES (est): 1MM **Privately Held**
SIC: 3861 Mfg Photographic Equipment/Supplies

(G-11628)
AUTO-TECH PLASTICS INC
Also Called: Pt Woody
164 Grand Ave (48043-5415)
PHONE..................586 783-0103
Ronald Schuman, *President*
Beverly Schuman, *Principal*
EMP: 4 **EST:** 1989
SALES (est): 469.4K **Privately Held**
WEB: www.autotechplastics.com
SIC: 3714 Motor vehicle parts & accessories

(G-11629)
BAKES & KROPP LTD
154 S Rose St (48043-2176)
PHONE..................888 206-0015
Paul Kropp, *CEO*
Robert Bakes, *President*
EMP: 12 **EST:** 2014
SALES (est): 1.3MM **Privately Held**
WEB: www.bakesandkropp.com
SIC: 2599 Cabinets, factory

(G-11630)
BETTER-BILT CABINET CO
99 Cass Ave (48043-2382)
PHONE..................586 469-0080
Aldo Valitutti, *President*
Angeline Valitutti, *Vice Pres*
Lisa Valitutti, *Vice Pres*
EMP: 5 **EST:** 1974
SQ FT: 4,000
SALES (est): 416.9K **Privately Held**
WEB: www.cabinetsbbb.com
SIC: 2434 2439 Wood kitchen cabinets; structural wood members

(G-11631)
BOATTOWN WOODSHOP
108 S Wilson Blvd (48043-2148)
PHONE..................586 703-0538
David Lukaszewski, *Principal*
EMP: 4 **EST:** 2015
SALES (est): 196.4K **Privately Held**
WEB: www.theboattownwoodshop.com
SIC: 2431 Millwork

(G-11632)
CAN YOU HANDLEBAR LLC
239 Church St (48043-2184)
PHONE..................248 821-2171
Doug Geiger, *Mng Member*
EMP: 10 **EST:** 2016
SALES (est): 1MM **Privately Held**
WEB: www.canyouhandlebar.com
SIC: 2844 Toilet preparations

(G-11633)
CANIFF ELECTRIC SUPPLY
75 S Rose St (48043-2179)
PHONE..................586 221-1663
EMP: 9 **EST:** 2016
SALES (est): 139.1K **Privately Held**
WEB: www.caniff.com
SIC: 5063 3699 Electrical supplies; electrical equipment & supplies

(G-11634)
CONCORD TOOL AND MFG INC
118 N Groesbeck Hwy Ste E (48043-5453)
PHONE..................586 465-6537
Ronald Dichtel, *Ch of Bd*
Mark Dichtel, *President*
Neil Dichtel, *Vice Pres*
Justin Babcock, *Purch Mgr*
Tracie Brockett, *Purch Mgr*
▲ **EMP:** 165
SQ FT: 100,000
SALES (est): 35.5MM **Privately Held**
WEB: www.concordtool.com
SIC: 3465 3544 Body parts, automobile: stamped metal; die sets for metal stamping (presses)

(G-11635)
D-MARK INC
130 N Groesbeck Hwy (48043-1529)
PHONE..................586 949-3610
James W Kasmark Jr, *President*
James Reinke, *Human Res Mgr*
EMP: 30 **EST:** 1970
SQ FT: 19,000
SALES: 5.3MM **Privately Held**
WEB: www.dmarkinc.com
SIC: 3564 Filters, air: furnaces, air conditioning equipment, etc.

(G-11636)
DETROIT CUSTOM SERVICES INC (PA)
Also Called: Vertical Vics
150 N Groesbeck Hwy (48043-1529)
PHONE..................586 465-3631
Mitch Bazinski, *President*
Rebecca Bazinski, *Vice Pres*
EMP: 35 **EST:** 1976
SQ FT: 20,000
SALES (est): 3MM **Privately Held**
WEB: www.verticalvics.com
SIC: 2391 2591 5714 5719 Draperies, plastic & textile: from purchased materials; window blinds; draperies; vertical blinds; drapery track installation; window treatment installation

(G-11637)
DISSRAD INC
195 Grand Ave (48043-5413)
PHONE..................586 463-8722
Werner Thurman, *President*
EMP: 5 **EST:** 2018
SALES (est): 136.8K **Privately Held**
WEB: www.superiorradiator.com
SIC: 3999 Manufacturing industries

(G-11638)
FCA US LLC
151 Lafayette St (48043-1557)
PHONE..................586 468-2891
Michael Lyell, *General Mgr*
EMP: 195
SALES (corp-wide): 102.5B **Privately Held**
WEB: www.chrysler.com
SIC: 3711 Motor vehicles & car bodies
HQ: Fca Us Llc
1000 Chrysler Dr
Auburn Hills MI 48326

(G-11639)
FOURNIER ENTERPRISES INC
17 N Rose St Ste A (48043-5462)
PHONE..................586 323-9160
Ronald J Fournier, *President*
Nicole Fournier, *Vice Pres*
EMP: 5 **EST:** 1991
SQ FT: 2,500
SALES (est): 737.3K **Privately Held**
WEB: www.fournierenterprises.com
SIC: 3499 Furniture parts, metal

(G-11640)
HELICAL LAP & MANUFACTURING CO (HQ)
121 Madison Ave (48043-1624)
PHONE..................586 307-8322
Stephen Griffin, *President*
Ken Werner, *Vice Pres*
Mark Gray, *Treasurer*
Donna Lebeda, *Asst Treas*
EMP: 13 **EST:** 1958
SQ FT: 9,200
SALES (est): 1.8MM
SALES (corp-wide): 54.7MM **Privately Held**
WEB: www.helicallap.com
SIC: 3541 Lapping machines
PA: Engis Corporation
105 W Hintz Rd
Wheeling IL 60090
847 808-9400

(G-11641)
HYDRA-LOCK CORPORATION
25000 Joy Blvd (48043-6021)
PHONE..................586 783-5007
Eugene R Andre Sr, *President*
William M Andre, *Corp Secy*
Eugene R Andre Jr, *Vice Pres*
EMP: 40 **EST:** 1944
SQ FT: 18,000
SALES (est): 5.5MM **Privately Held**
WEB: www.hydralock.com
SIC: 3545 Arbors (machine tool accessories); chucks: drill, lathe or magnetic (machine tool accessories); gauges (machine tool accessories)

GEOGRAPHIC SECTION
Mount Morris - Genesee County (G-11669)

(G-11642)
INDEPENDENT NEWSPAPERS INC (DH)
Also Called: The Daily Tribune
100 Macomb Daily Dr (48043-5802)
PHONE..................586 469-4510
Ronald J Wood, *President*
Jerry Bammel, *Vice Pres*
▲ **EMP:** 125 **EST:** 1992
SALES (est): 39.2MM
SALES (corp-wide): 274.1MM **Privately Held**
WEB: www.21stcenturynewspapers.com
SIC: 2711 Newspapers, publishing & printing
HQ: 21st Century Newspapers, Inc.
6250 Metropolitan Pkwy
Sterling Heights MI 48312
586 469-4510

(G-11643)
INTERNATIONAL ROBOT SUPPORT
56 Macomb Pl (48043-5636)
PHONE..................586 783-8000
David Emlawzo, *CEO*
EMP: 8 **EST:** 2010
SALES (est): 157.9K **Privately Held**
WEB: www.irobotsupport.com
SIC: 3569 Robots, assembly line: industrial & commercial

(G-11644)
J B CUTTING INC
Also Called: MCO
171 Grand Ave (48043-5413)
PHONE..................586 468-4765
Joann Filthaut, *President*
William Filthaut, *Vice Pres*
Melissa Rotarius, *Asst Controller*
EMP: 9 **EST:** 1995
SQ FT: 16,000
SALES (est): 1.7MM **Privately Held**
WEB: www.jbcutting.com
SIC: 2434 Wood kitchen cabinets

(G-11645)
JEX MANUFACTURING INC
41 Eldredge St (48043-5410)
PHONE..................586 463-4274
EMP: 4
SQ FT: 1,800
SALES (est): 379K **Privately Held**
SIC: 3599 Mfg Industrial Machinery

(G-11646)
KROPP WOODWORKING INC
154 S Rose St (48043-2176)
PHONE..................586 463-2300
Paul Kropp, *Principal*
EMP: 14 **EST:** 2010
SALES (est): 1MM **Privately Held**
SIC: 2431 Millwork

(G-11647)
LIQUID DRIVE CORPORATION
Also Called: Easco-Sparcatron
18 1st St (48043-2523)
P.O. Box 207, Holly (48442-0207)
PHONE..................248 634-5382
Robert G Nelson, *President*
Gary Brown, *Vice Pres*
EMP: 37 **EST:** 1945
SQ FT: 28,000
SALES (est): 510.1K **Privately Held**
WEB: www.newjerseyselfemployedinsurnace.com
SIC: 3541 3568 8299 Electron-discharge metal cutting machine tools; couplings, shaft: rigid, flexible, universal joint, etc.; vehicle driving school

(G-11648)
MALL TOOLING & ENGINEERING
150 Grand Ave (48043-5415)
PHONE..................586 463-6520
Gregory P Theokas, *President*
EMP: 2 **EST:** 1964
SQ FT: 12,000
SALES (est): 1.7MM
SALES (corp-wide): 2.3MM **Privately Held**
WEB: www.oepushrods.com
SIC: 3714 Motor vehicle engines & parts

PA: Oe Push Rods Inc
150 Grand Ave
Mount Clemens MI 48043
586 463-6520

(G-11649)
MILJOCO CORP (PA)
200 Elizabeth St (48043-1643)
PHONE..................586 777-4280
Howard O Trerice, *President*
Heath M Trerice, *Vice Pres*
Heath Trerice, *Engineer*
David Vermillion, *Technician*
▲ **EMP:** 31 **EST:** 1979
SQ FT: 45,000
SALES (est): 8.5MM **Privately Held**
WEB: www.miljoco.com
SIC: 3829 Measuring & controlling devices

(G-11650)
P R MACHINING & PROTOTYPE INC
39 N Rose St Ste A (48043-5463)
PHONE..................586 468-7146
EMP: 4 **EST:** 2018
SALES (est): 107.4K **Privately Held**
SIC: 3569 General industrial machinery

(G-11651)
PARKER PATTERN INC
195 Malow St (48043-2114)
P.O. Box 154, New Baltimore (48047-0154)
PHONE..................586 466-5900
Jerry Parker, *President*
Fred Parker, *Vice Pres*
EMP: 10 **EST:** 1990
SQ FT: 9,600
SALES (est): 792.1K **Privately Held**
WEB: www.parkerpattern.org
SIC: 3543 Industrial patterns

(G-11652)
PETSCHKE MANUFACTURING COMPANY
187 Hubbard St (48043-5420)
PHONE..................586 463-0841
James Petschke, *President*
Steven Petschke, *Corp Secy*
Ann Petschke, *Vice Pres*
Steve Petschke, *Sales Mgr*
EMP: 15 **EST:** 1943
SQ FT: 13,000
SALES (est): 943.7K **Privately Held**
WEB: www.petschkemfg.com
SIC: 3496 3354 3451 Miscellaneous fabricated wire products; aluminum rod & bar; aluminum pipe & tube; screw machine products

(G-11653)
POWDER COTE II INC (PA)
50 N Rose St (48043-5405)
P.O. Box 368 (48046-0368)
PHONE..................586 463-7040
Eric Trott, *CEO*
Charlie J Trott, *Vice Pres*
Adrienne Williams, *Opers Staff*
Michael Coon, *Manager*
▲ **EMP:** 185 **EST:** 1980
SQ FT: 43,000
SALES (est): 21MM **Privately Held**
WEB: www.powdercoteii.com
SIC: 3479 Coating of metals & formed products

(G-11654)
POWDER COTE II INC
60 N Rose St (48043-5405)
P.O. Box 368 (48046-0368)
PHONE..................586 463-7040
Michael Coon, *Manager*
EMP: 5
SALES (corp-wide): 21MM **Privately Held**
WEB: www.powdercoteii.com
SIC: 3479 Coating of metals & formed products
PA: Powder Cote Ii, Inc.
50 N Rose St
Mount Clemens MI 48043
586 463-7040

(G-11655)
RB CONSTRUCTION COMPANY (PA)
249 Cass Ave (48043-2118)
PHONE..................586 264-9478
Russell C Beaver, *President*
John Stapleton, *Vice Pres*
EMP: 20 **EST:** 1987
SQ FT: 2,000 **Privately Held**
WEB: www.rb-construction.com
SIC: 1542 3448 Commercial & office building, new construction; commercial & office buildings, renovation & repair; prefabricated metal buildings

(G-11656)
REBECCA EIBEN
Also Called: R&R Tool & Gage
191 Grand Ave (48043-5413)
PHONE..................586 231-0548
Rebecca Eiben, *Owner*
Ronald Eiben, *Principal*
EMP: 5 **EST:** 1995
SQ FT: 3,500 **Privately Held**
WEB: www.randrtoolandgage.com
SIC: 3599 Machine shop, jobbing & repair

(G-11657)
SINGLE VISION SOLUTION INC
118 Cass Ave (48043-2204)
PHONE..................586 464-1522
Kenneth Stann, *President*
EMP: 10 **EST:** 1974
SALES (est): 322.3K **Privately Held**
WEB: www.singlevisionsolution.com
SIC: 3211 Optical glass, flat

(G-11658)
SUPERIOR MATERIALS HOLDINGS
40 Floral Ave (48043-2126)
PHONE..................586 468-3544
EMP: 6 **EST:** 2016
SALES (est): 83.1K **Privately Held**
SIC: 5211 3273 Cement; ready-mixed concrete

(G-11659)
T M SMITH TOOL INTL CORP (PA)
360 Hubbard St (48043-5403)
P.O. Box 1065 (48046-1065)
PHONE..................586 468-1465
D F Smith, *Ch of Bd*
Gerald R Norton, *President*
David F Smith II, *Vice Pres*
Jeff McKown, *Safety Dir*
Allen Krenick, *Engineer*
EMP: 29 **EST:** 1952
SQ FT: 22,000
SALES (est): 2.5MM **Privately Held**
WEB: www.tmsmith.com
SIC: 3545 Tool holders

(G-11660)
TEXTILE FABRICATION & DIST INC
120 Grove Park St (48043-1602)
PHONE..................586 566-9100
Timothy Rose, *President*
EMP: 5 **EST:** 2001
SALES (est): 379.9K **Privately Held**
SIC: 3548 2394 Welding apparatus; tarpaulins, fabric: made from purchased materials

(G-11661)
TRU TECH SYSTEMS LLC (HQ)
24550 N River Rd (48043-1910)
P.O. Box 46965 (48046-6965)
PHONE..................586 469-2700
Steve Smarsh, *President*
Shari Michels, *Vice Pres*
Norman Curtiss, *Production*
Mary Rancilio, *Purchasing*
Nelson Hooks, *Regl Sales Mgr*
EMP: 56 **EST:** 1993
SQ FT: 25,000
SALES (est): 18.3MM **Privately Held**
WEB: www.trutechsystems.com
SIC: 7389 3541 Grinding, precision: commercial or industrial; grinding, polishing, buffing, lapping & honing machines

(G-11662)
WEBER SECURITY GROUP INC
Also Called: East Side Locksmith
95 S Rose St Ste A (48043-2187)
PHONE..................586 582-0000
William D Weber Jr, *President*
Judy Weber, *Controller*
EMP: 6 **EST:** 2001
SQ FT: 10,000
SALES (est): 1.2MM **Privately Held**
WEB: www.webersecurity.com
SIC: 3429 3699 Locks or lock sets; security control equipment & systems

(G-11663)
WICKEDGLOW INDUSTRIES INC
Also Called: Body Faders
248 Nrthbound Gratiot Ave (48043-5749)
PHONE..................586 776-4132
Loretta Monley, *President*
Karl Clayton, *Vice Pres*
EMP: 8 **EST:** 2003
SQ FT: 2,000
SALES (est): 595.9K **Privately Held**
WEB: www.bodyfaders.com
SIC: 3641 2253 Glow lamp bulbs; T-shirts & tops, knit

(G-11664)
WINGS MFG INC
1550 Kingsley St (48043-3016)
PHONE..................585 873-3105
EMP: 6 **EST:** 2017
SALES (est): 54K **Privately Held**
SIC: 3999 Manufacturing industries

Mount Morris
Genesee County

(G-11665)
A GAME APPAREL
4330 W Mount Morris Rd # 1 (48458-9380)
PHONE..................810 564-2600
Don Damonth, *Partner*
EMP: 5 **EST:** 2005
SALES (est): 92.1K **Privately Held**
SIC: 2396 Screen printing on fabric articles

(G-11666)
ADNIC PRODUCTS CO
6261 N Saginaw St (48458-2454)
PHONE..................810 789-0321
EMP: 4
SQ FT: 2,400
SALES (est): 325.9K **Privately Held**
SIC: 3644 Mfg Utility Power Pedestal

(G-11667)
AMERICAN BOTTLING COMPANY
Also Called: 7-Up Flint
7300 Enterprise Pkwy (48458-9356)
PHONE..................810 564-1432
Ron Blair, *General Mgr*
Brian Blossom, *Info Tech Mgr*
EMP: 14 **Publicly Held**
WEB: www.keurigdrpepper.com
SIC: 2086 Soft drinks: packaged in cans, bottles, etc.
HQ: The American Bottling Company
6425 Hall Of Fame Ln
Frisco TX 75034

(G-11668)
BEST BUY BONES INC
7426 N Dort Hwy (48458-2232)
P.O. Box 39 (48458-0039)
PHONE..................810 631-6971
Delbert McCord, *President*
Deldert McCord, *President*
EMP: 6 **EST:** 1984
SALES (est): 852.6K **Privately Held**
WEB: www.bestbuybones.com
SIC: 3999 Pet supplies

(G-11669)
C W A MANUFACTURING CO INC
7406 N Dort Hwy (48458-2232)
P.O. Box 10 (48458-0010)
PHONE..................810 686-3030
Fax: 810 686-2410
EMP: 40 **EST:** 1951
SQ FT: 23,000

Mount Morris - Genesee County (G-11670)

SALES (est): 2.5MM Privately Held
SIC: 7389 3714 Commercial Packaging & Labeling & Small Automotive Component Assembly

(G-11670)
DANIEL WARD
Also Called: Colorized Prints
7352 N Tort Hi W Y Ste 2 (48458)
PHONE..................................810 965-6535
Daniel Ward, *Owner*
EMP: 4 EST: 2010
SALES (est): 84K Privately Held
WEB: www.creativecreationsbyshelly.com
SIC: 2752 7334 Business form & card printing, lithographic; blueprinting service

(G-11671)
HAMMOND PUBLISHING COMPANY
G7166 N Saginaw St (48458)
PHONE..................................810 686-8879
Leo F Flynn, *President*
Ann Flynn, *Treasurer*
EMP: 4 EST: 1898
SQ FT: 6,000
SALES (est): 447.7K Privately Held
SIC: 2741 2493 5192 Miscellaneous publishing; reconstituted wood products; books, periodicals & newspapers

(G-11672)
HOMETOWN AMERICA LLC
2197 E Mount Morris Rd (48458-8709)
PHONE..................................810 686-7020
Matt Whorton, *Administration*
EMP: 6
SALES (corp-wide): 174.6MM Privately Held
WEB: www.hometownamerica.com
SIC: 2451 Mobile homes, personal or private use
PA: Hometown America, L.L.C.
 150 N Wacker Dr Ste 2800
 Chicago IL 60606
 312 604-7500

(G-11673)
KINDER COMPANY INC
Also Called: Rockwell Team Sports
7070 N Saginaw Rd (48458-2141)
PHONE..................................810 240-3065
Daren Kinder, *President*
EMP: 6 EST: 2005
SALES (est): 566.7K Privately Held
WEB: www.kinder.com
SIC: 2329 Vests (suede, leatherette, etc.), sport: men's & boys'

(G-11674)
MICHIGAN CHURCH SUPPLY CO INC (PA)
7166 N Saginaw Rd (48458-2165)
P.O. Box 279 (48458-0279)
PHONE..................................810 686-8877
Leo F Flynn, *President*
Leann Cooper, *Corp Secy*
Ann C Lynn, *Vice Pres*
Michael Malik, *Analyst*
EMP: 16 EST: 1965
SQ FT: 28,000
SALES (est): 3.9MM Privately Held
WEB: www.michiganchurchsupply.com
SIC: 5049 3089 Religious supplies; injection molded finished plastic products

(G-11675)
MICHIGAN MACHINING INC
3322 E Mount Morris Rd (48458-8958)
PHONE..................................810 686-6655
Charles M Wood, *President*
EMP: 6 EST: 1990
SALES (est): 610.6K Privately Held
WEB: www.michiganmachining.com
SIC: 3479 Coating of metals & formed products

(G-11676)
PAW PRINT CREATIONS LLC
7484 Braymont St (48458-2922)
PHONE..................................810 577-0410
Stephen Roth, *Administration*
EMP: 4 EST: 2019

SALES (est): 73.6K Privately Held
WEB: www.pawprintcreations.com
SIC: 2752 Commercial printing, lithographic

(G-11677)
ZODIAC ENTERPRISES LLC
1000 Church St Ste 1 (48458-2084)
PHONE..................................810 640-7146
Charles Harburn, *Sales Staff*
EMP: 6 EST: 2008
SALES (est): 702.5K Privately Held
WEB: www.zodiacenterprises.biz
SIC: 2759 Screen printing

Mount Pleasant
Isabella County

(G-11678)
AMERICAN MITSUBA CORPORATION
Also Called: American Mtsuba Corp Mich Plan
2945 Three Leaves Dr (48858-4596)
PHONE..................................989 773-0377
Mike Goin, *Manager*
EMP: 120 Privately Held
WEB: www.americanmitsuba.com
SIC: 3621 Motors, electric
HQ: American Mitsuba Corporation
 2945 Three Leaves Dr
 Mount Pleasant MI 48858

(G-11679)
AMERICAN MITSUBA CORPORATION (HQ)
2945 Three Leaves Dr (48858-4596)
PHONE..................................989 779-4962
Masayoshi Shirato, *President*
Mishel Ashtary, *Senior VP*
David Stevens, *Senior VP*
Hideaki Fujii, *Vice Pres*
Takashi Ichinokawa, *Vice Pres*
◆ EMP: 365
SALES: 606.5MM Privately Held
WEB: www.americanmitsuba.com
SIC: 3714 Motor vehicle parts & accessories

(G-11680)
APOLLO EXPLORATION DEV INC
1710 E Remus Rd (48858-9009)
PHONE..................................989 773-2854
Bob Perrigo, *President*
EMP: 6 EST: 2013
SALES (est): 859.2K Privately Held
WEB: www.apolloexp.com
SIC: 1382 Oil & gas exploration services

(G-11681)
ASPIRE PHARMACY
121 E Broadway St D (48858-2312)
PHONE..................................989 773-7849
James Horton, *General Mgr*
EMP: 6 EST: 1989
SALES (est): 105.7K Privately Held
SIC: 2834 Pharmaceutical preparations

(G-11682)
B & H CEMENTING SERVICES INC
5580 Venture Way (48858-1149)
PHONE..................................989 773-5975
Steve Bagard, *President*
EMP: 5 EST: 2007
SQ FT: 2,000
SALES (est): 431.4K Privately Held
WEB: www.bigardandhuggarddrilling.com
SIC: 1389 Oil field services

(G-11683)
B & H TRACTOR & TRUCK INC
5580 Venture Way (48858-1149)
PHONE..................................989 773-5975
Steven Bigard, *President*
Ricky Huggard, *Vice Pres*
Tim Burggraf, *Manager*
Jeana Falfetta, *Admin Sec*
EMP: 9 EST: 1998
SQ FT: 5,000

SALES (est): 500K Privately Held
WEB: www.bigardandhuggarddrilling.com
SIC: 1389 Haulage, oil field

(G-11684)
BAKER HGHES OLFLD OPRTIONS LLC
Also Called: Baker Oil Tools
1950 Commercial Dr (48858-8913)
P.O. Box 508 (48804-0508)
PHONE..................................989 772-1600
EMP: 9
SALES (corp-wide): 122B Publicly Held
SIC: 1389 Sales And Gas Services
HQ: Baker Hughes Oilfield Operations Llc
 17021 Aldine Westfield Rd
 Houston TX 77073
 713 879-1000

(G-11685)
BAKER HGHES OLFLD OPRTIONS LLC
Also Called: Baker Atlas
2222 Enterprise Dr (48858-2335)
PHONE..................................989 773-7992
Jason Warrens, *Manager*
EMP: 4
SALES (corp-wide): 20.7B Publicly Held
SIC: 1389 1382 Oil field services; well logging; seismograph surveys
HQ: Baker Hughes Oilfield Operations Llc
 2001 Rankin Rd
 Houston TX 77073

(G-11686)
BAKER HUGHES HOLDINGS LLC
Also Called: Baker Hughes Incorporat...
2222 Enterprise Dr (48858-2335)
PHONE..................................989 506-2167
Clint Vericker, *Accounts Mgr*
Deborah Payne, *Branch Mgr*
Richard Hoisington, *Manager*
EMP: 4
SALES (corp-wide): 20.7B Publicly Held
WEB: www.bakerhughes.com
SIC: 1389 Oil field services
HQ: Baker Hughes Holdings Llc
 17021 Aldine Westfield Rd
 Houston TX 77073
 713 439-8600

(G-11687)
BILLS CUSTOM FAB INC
1836 Gover Pkwy (48858-8166)
PHONE..................................989 772-5817
William T Quakenbush, *President*
Michelle Quakenbush, *Vice Pres*
Melissa Quakenbush, *Manager*
EMP: 15 EST: 1990
SQ FT: 5,200
SALES (est): 1.2MM Privately Held
WEB: www.billscustomfab.com
SIC: 3443 5051 Fabricated plate work (boiler shop); steel

(G-11688)
BURCH TANK & TRUCK INC (PA)
Also Called: Burch Truck and Trailer Parts
2113 Enterprise Dr (48858-2300)
PHONE..................................989 772-6266
Jeffrey Harrison, *President*
Craig Haley, *Opers Mgr*
Jason Harrison, *Engineer*
David Daymon, *Sales Staff*
Al Lamphere, *Manager*
EMP: 75 EST: 1989
SALES (est): 11.4MM Privately Held
WEB: www.burchtank.com
SIC: 3795 5088 Tanks & tank components; tanks & tank components

(G-11689)
C & C ENTERPRISES INC
1106 Packard Rd (48858-5324)
PHONE..................................989 772-5095
Charles Caszatt, *President*
Christopher Holsworth, *Corp Secy*
EMP: 5 EST: 1991
SQ FT: 1,600
SALES (est): 2.1MM Privately Held
WEB: www.candcenterprisesinc.com
SIC: 5084 2396 Safety equipment; screen printing on fabric articles

(G-11690)
CENTRAL ASPHALT INC
900 S Bradley St (48858-3046)
P.O. Box 389 (48804-0389)
PHONE..................................989 772-0720
Vance Johnson, *President*
James O Fisher, *Corp Secy*
Arthur J Fisher, *Vice Pres*
Aaron White, *Vice Pres*
Russ Blake, *Plant Mgr*
EMP: 12 EST: 1982
SQ FT: 4,000
SALES (est): 2.7MM Privately Held
WEB: www.centralasphalt.com
SIC: 1611 2951 1771 Resurfacing contractor; asphalt paving mixtures & blocks; concrete work

(G-11691)
CENTRAL MICHIGAN UNIVERSITY
Also Called: Cmu University Press
160 Combined Svcs Bldg (48859-0001)
PHONE..................................989 774-3216
Rhonda Kohler, *Director*
EMP: 8
SALES (corp-wide): 265.7MM Privately Held
WEB: www.cmich.edu
SIC: 2731 8221 Book publishing; university
PA: Central Michigan University
 1280 E Campus Dr
 Mount Pleasant MI 48859
 989 774-3015

(G-11692)
CMU
802 Industrial Dr (48858-4646)
PHONE..................................989 774-7143
Yoon Auh, *Principal*
EMP: 17 EST: 2008
SALES (est): 3.9MM Privately Held
WEB: www.cmich.edu
SIC: 2711 Newspapers

(G-11693)
COIL DRILLING TECHNOLOGIES INC
2362 Northway Dr (48858-1289)
PHONE..................................989 773-6504
Pat Jarman, *President*
EMP: 8 EST: 2006
SQ FT: 85,000
SALES (est): 1MM Privately Held
SIC: 1389 Oil field services

(G-11694)
DAYCO PRODUCTS LLC
1799 Gover Pkwy (48858-8140)
PHONE..................................989 775-0689
Danielle Case, *Asst Controller*
Mike Byrne, *Branch Mgr*
EMP: 6
SALES (corp-wide): 211.2MM Privately Held
WEB: www.daycoproducts.com
SIC: 3559 3714 Automotive related machinery; motor vehicle parts & accessories
HQ: Dayco Products, Llc
 1650 Research Dr Ste 100
 Troy MI 48083

(G-11695)
DELFIELD COMPANY LLC
980 S Isabella Rd (48858-9200)
PHONE..................................989 773-7981
Graham Tillotson, *Exec VP*
Jay Rivers, *Controller*
Robert Howes, *Credit Mgr*
Jon Lamont, *Sales Engr*
Joseph Steffke, *CTO*
▲ EMP: 875 EST: 1991
SQ FT: 345,000
SALES (est): 183.5MM
SALES (corp-wide): 1.1B Publicly Held
WEB: www.delfield.com
SIC: 3589 Commercial cooking & food-warming equipment
PA: Welbilt, Inc.
 2227 Welbilt Blvd
 Trinity FL 34655
 727 375-7010

GEOGRAPHIC SECTION

Mount Pleasant - Isabella County (G-11724)

(G-11696)
ELMERS CRANE AND DOZER INC
781 N Mission Rd (48858-4678)
PHONE.................................231 943-3443
Nick Broad, *Project Mgr*
Jason Horton, *Project Engr*
Paul Wilcoxen, *Controller*
Dan Beckelic, *Sales Staff*
Jason Housner, *Branch Mgr*
EMP: 10
SALES (corp-wide): 48.8MM **Privately Held**
WEB: www.teamelmers.com
SIC: 3273 Ready-mixed concrete
PA: Elmer's Crane And Dozer, Inc.
3600 Rennie School Rd
Traverse City MI 49685
231 943-3443

(G-11697)
EXPRESS SPORTSWEAR INC
Also Called: C&O Sportswear
1530 S Mission Rd (48858-4212)
PHONE.................................989 773-7515
Timothy Mac Gregor, *President*
EMP: 20 **EST:** 1976
SQ FT: 6,200
SALES (est): 602.8K **Privately Held**
WEB: www.candosportswear.net
SIC: 2759 Screen printing

(G-11698)
FISHER CNSTR AGGREGATES INC
900 S Bradley St (48858-3046)
PHONE.................................989 539-6431
Aaron White, *Principal*
EMP: 13 **EST:** 2015
SALES (est): 1.4MM **Privately Held**
WEB: www.fishercompanies.net
SIC: 3273 Ready-mixed concrete

(G-11699)
FOLTZ SCREEN PRINTING
2094 S Isabella Rd (48858-2016)
PHONE.................................989 772-3947
Joe Foltz, *Owner*
EMP: 5 **EST:** 1980
SQ FT: 5,500
SALES (est): 350K **Privately Held**
WEB: www.foltzscreenprinting.com
SIC: 2759 Screen printing

(G-11700)
GRAPH-ADS PRINTING INC
711 W Pickard St Ste I (48858-1587)
P.O. Box 447 (48804-0447)
PHONE.................................989 779-6000
Al Frattura, *President*
EMP: 62 **EST:** 1938
SQ FT: 20,000
SALES (est): 459K
SALES (corp-wide): 274.1MM **Privately Held**
WEB: www.themorningsun.com
SIC: 2711 Newspapers, publishing & printing
HQ: Morning Star Publishing Company
311 E Superior St Ste C
Alma MI 48801
989 779-6000

(G-11701)
HIGGINS AND ASSOCIATES INC
735 S Mission Rd (48858-8596)
PHONE.................................989 772-8853
Mike Higgins, *President*
Michael Higgins, *Principal*
Traves Mikulenal, *Opers Mgr*
EMP: 15 **EST:** 1994
SQ FT: 400
SALES (est): 2.1MM **Privately Held**
WEB: www.higginscrane.com
SIC: 3559 1794 Recycling machinery; excavation work

(G-11702)
HUBSCHER & SON INC (PA)
1101 N Franklin Ave (48858-4617)
P.O. Box 411 (48804-0411)
PHONE.................................989 773-5369
Paul Hubscher, *President*
G Charles Hubscher, *Vice Pres*
EMP: 1 **EST:** 1933

SQ FT: 1,000
SALES (est): 2.1MM **Privately Held**
SIC: 1442 Gravel mining

(G-11703)
INTEGRTED DATABASE SYSTEMS INC
2625 Denison Dr A (48858-5596)
PHONE.................................989 546-4512
Lance Ferden, *Owner*
Kelly Katelyn, *Managing Dir*
Seth Squires, *Accounts Mgr*
Rachel Phillips, *Marketing Staff*
EMP: 18 **EST:** 2005
SALES (est): 1.2MM **Privately Held**
WEB: www.homecaresoftware.com
SIC: 7372 Application computer software

(G-11704)
J & W MACHINE INC
Also Called: J & W Machine & Tool
315 E Pickard St (48858-1553)
P.O. Box 315 (48804-0315)
PHONE.................................989 773-9951
Vernon L Powis Jr, *President*
Dan Sheahan, *President*
EMP: 5 **EST:** 1978
SALES (est): 885.8K **Privately Held**
WEB: www.jwmachine.com
SIC: 3541 Drilling machine tools (metal cutting); screw & thread machines

(G-11705)
JO WELL SERVICE AND TSTG INC
Also Called: J O Well Service
6825 Lea Pick Dr (48858-8911)
PHONE.................................989 772-4221
Kirk Miller, *President*
Greg Elser, *Vice Pres*
Tim Auker, *Treasurer*
EMP: 4 **EST:** 1969
SQ FT: 2,500
SALES (est): 641.9K **Privately Held**
SIC: 1389 Servicing oil & gas wells; oil field services

(G-11706)
KONWINSKI KABNETS INC
1900 Gover Pkwy (48858-8137)
PHONE.................................989 773-2906
Jerel Konwinski, *President*
EMP: 5 **EST:** 1988
SALES (est): 485.8K **Privately Held**
SIC: 2521 Cabinets, office: wood

(G-11707)
LEASE MANAGEMENT INC (PA)
503 Industrial Dr (48858-4639)
P.O. Box 290 (48804-0290)
PHONE.................................989 773-5948
John R Harkins, *President*
Rudolph J Kler, *Treasurer*
EMP: 8 **EST:** 1959
SQ FT: 4,080
SALES (est): 3.5MM **Privately Held**
SIC: 1389 1311 Servicing oil & gas wells; crude petroleum production; natural gas production

(G-11708)
LJS KITCHENS & INTERIORS LTD
1105 N Mission St (48858-1048)
PHONE.................................989 773-2132
Scott Holmes, *President*
Lynn Holmes, *Vice Pres*
Jerilynn Holmes, *Admin Sec*
EMP: 7 **EST:** 1976
SQ FT: 5,000
SALES (est): 1MM **Privately Held**
WEB: www.ljskitchens.com
SIC: 2434 Wood kitchen cabinets

(G-11709)
MANESS PETROLEUM CORP
1425 S Mission Rd (48858-4665)
P.O. Box 313 (48804-0313)
PHONE.................................989 773-5475
David Maness, *President*
Tim Maness, *Vice Pres*
Lora Beatty, *Office Mgr*
EMP: 6 **EST:** 1985
SQ FT: 1,500

SALES (est): 1.5MM **Privately Held**
WEB: www.manesspetroleum.com
SIC: 1382 8711 Oil & gas exploration services; consulting engineer

(G-11710)
MANITWOC FDSRVICE CMPANIES LLC
980 S Isabella Rd (48858-9256)
PHONE.................................989 773-7981
EMP: 4
SALES (corp-wide): 1.1B **Publicly Held**
WEB: www.welbilt.com
SIC: 3585 Refrigeration & heating equipment
HQ: Manitowoc Foodservice Companies, Llc
2227 Welbilt Blvd
Trinity FL 34655

(G-11711)
MICHAEL ENGINEERING LTD
Also Called: Rook Metering Equipment
5625 Venture Way (48858-1152)
PHONE.................................989 772-4073
Ralph M Prewett, *CEO*
Eric V Prewett, *Vice Pres*
Eric Prewett, *Vice Pres*
Chuck Murrey, *Plant Mgr*
Michael Prewett, *Engineer*
EMP: 20 **EST:** 1971
SQ FT: 20,000
SALES (est): 4.8MM **Privately Held**
WEB: www.michaelengineering.com
SIC: 3829 Measuring & controlling devices

(G-11712)
MICHIGAN WIRELINE SERVICE
4854 E River Rd (48858-9203)
P.O. Box 782 (48804-0782)
PHONE.................................989 772-5075
Dennis McConahy, *President*
Ed Crain, *President*
Brian Sharrar, *Corp Secy*
EMP: 20 **EST:** 1988
SQ FT: 4,500
SALES (est): 3MM **Privately Held**
SIC: 1389 Oil field services

(G-11713)
MICHIWEST ENERGY INC
1425 S Mission Rd Ste 2 (48858-4665)
PHONE.................................989 772-2107
William J Strickler, *President*
EMP: 5 **EST:** 1992
SQ FT: 600
SALES (est): 495.3K **Privately Held**
SIC: 1381 Drilling oil & gas wells

(G-11714)
MID STATE OIL TOOLS INC (PA)
1934 Commercial Dr (48858-8913)
PHONE.................................989 773-4114
John Keathley, *President*
Michael Machuta, *Vice Pres*
Brian Tafts, *Controller*
Matt Menzer, *Supervisor*
EMP: 17 **EST:** 1994
SQ FT: 9,000
SALES (est): 10.5MM **Privately Held**
WEB: www.midstateoiltools.com
SIC: 1389 Oil field services

(G-11715)
MID-MICHIGAN INDUSTRIES INC (PA)
Also Called: MMI OF CENTRAL MICHIGAN
2426 Parkway Dr (48858-4723)
PHONE.................................989 773-6918
Alan J Schilling, *President*
Doug Ouellette, *Chairman*
Jeremy Murphy, *Finance*
Sharon McInnis, *Human Res Dir*
Michelle Reed, *Manager*
EMP: 70 **EST:** 1973
SQ FT: 22,000
SALES (est): 5.1MM **Privately Held**
WEB: www.mmionline.com
SIC: 8331 3471 2396 Vocational training agency; plating & polishing; automotive & apparel trimmings

(G-11716)
MODERN BUILDERS
1534 S Wise Rd (48858-9412)
PHONE.................................989 773-1405

Modern Builders, *Principal*
EMP: 4 **EST:** 2016
SALES (est): 65.5K **Privately Held**
SIC: 3559 Special industry machinery

(G-11717)
MONTCALM AGGREGATES INC
2201 Commerce St Ste 4 (48858-9060)
PHONE.................................989 772-7038
EMP: 4
SALES (est): 764K **Privately Held**
SIC: 3295 Mfg Minerals-Ground/Treated

(G-11718)
MOREYS LOGO
3357 E River Rd (48858-8904)
P.O. Box 1552 (48804-1552)
PHONE.................................989 772-4492
Denise Morey, *Principal*
EMP: 6 **EST:** 2007
SALES (est): 104.1K **Privately Held**
SIC: 3993 5099 Signs & advertising specialties; signs, except electric

(G-11719)
MOUNTAIN TOWN STN BREW PUB LLC
Also Called: Mountain Town Stn Brewing Co &
506 W Broadway St (48858-2441)
PHONE.................................989 775-2337
Jim Holton, *President*
EMP: 51 **EST:** 1996
SQ FT: 8,700
SALES (est): 2.1MM **Privately Held**
WEB: www.mountaintown.com
SIC: 5812 2082 Steak restaurant; beer (alcoholic beverage)

(G-11720)
MT PLEASANT BUYERS GUIDE
711 W Pickard St Ste A (48858-1586)
PHONE.................................989 779-6000
Karen Holton, *Principal*
EMP: 7 **EST:** 2007
SALES (est): 78.7K **Privately Held**
WEB: www.themorningsun.com
SIC: 2711 Newspapers, publishing & printing

(G-11721)
MT PLEASANT CENTL CON PDTS CO
900 S Bradley St Ste A (48858-3046)
P.O. Box 389 (48804-0389)
PHONE.................................989 772-3695
Kyle White, *President*
James O Fisher, *Corp Secy*
Arthur J Fisher, *Vice Pres*
EMP: 2 **EST:** 1938
SALES (est): 1.2MM **Privately Held**
WEB: www.central-concrete.net
SIC: 3273 Ready-mixed concrete

(G-11722)
MTW INDUSTRIES INC
706 W Pickard St (48858-9854)
PHONE.................................989 317-3301
Brent Fisher, *President*
Bob Campbell, *Sales Mgr*
Dean Gluch, *Manager*
EMP: 16 **EST:** 2008
SALES (est): 4.3MM **Privately Held**
WEB: www.mtwindustries.com
SIC: 3441 Fabricated structural metal

(G-11723)
MTW PERFORMANCE & FAB
706 W Pickard St (48858-9854)
PHONE.................................989 317-3301
Kevin Curtiss, *Principal*
EMP: 8 **EST:** 2007
SALES (est): 392.8K **Privately Held**
WEB:
www.mtwperformancefabrication.com
SIC: 3441 Fabricated structural metal

(G-11724)
MUSKEGON DEVELOPMENT COMPANY
1425 S Mission Rd Ste 1 (48858-4696)
PHONE.................................989 772-4900
William Myler Jr, *President*
Thomas Myler, *Vice Pres*
Mike Mesbergen, *Engineer*

Mount Pleasant - Isabella County (G-11725)

Eugene Pety, *Controller*
Cliff Roberts, *Analyst*
EMP: 29 **EST:** 1927
SQ FT: 1,600
SALES (est): 6.8MM **Privately Held**
WEB: www.muskegondevelopment.com
SIC: 1311 Crude petroleum production

(G-11725)
MVM7 LLC
210 W Pickard St (48858-1560)
PHONE..................989 317-3901
Michael Otterbine, *Mng Member*
EMP: 35 **EST:** 2016
SQ FT: 5,100
SALES (est): 5MM **Privately Held**
SIC: 3792 Travel trailers & campers

(G-11726)
NANOSYNTHONS LLC
1200 N Fancher Ave (48858-4608)
PHONE..................989 317-3737
Donald Tomalia, *Partner*
EMP: 5 **EST:** 2010
SALES (est): 415.4K **Privately Held**
WEB: www.nanosynthons.com
SIC: 2835 In vitro & in vivo diagnostic substances

(G-11727)
NAVA SOLAR LLC
504 S Fancher St (48858-2617)
PHONE..................734 707-8260
Sunell Joglekar, *Branch Mgr*
EMP: 10
SALES (corp-wide): 94.4K **Privately Held**
SIC: 3559 Semiconductor manufacturing machinery
PA: Nava Solar, Llc
1514 Gilbert Ct Rm R-13
Ann Arbor MI

(G-11728)
OILPATCH MACHINE TOOL INC
Also Called: Oil Patch Machine & Tool
6773 E Pickard Rd (48858-8907)
PHONE..................989 772-0637
Mark Arends, *President*
Deborah Klunzinger, *Controller*
EMP: 9 **EST:** 1981
SQ FT: 6,000
SALES (est): 1.5MM **Privately Held**
WEB: www.amma-usa.com
SIC: 7539 7692 3498 Machine shop, automotive; welding repair; fabricated pipe & fittings

(G-11729)
ON THE MARK INC
801 Industrial Dr (48858-4645)
PHONE..................989 317-8033
Alexander Hollenbeck, *President*
Martha Hollenbeck, *Treasurer*
Alexander J Hollenbeck, *Shareholder*
EMP: 8 **EST:** 2012
SQ FT: 35,000
SALES (est): 1.4MM **Privately Held**
WEB: www.onthemarkindustries.com
SIC: 3549 3482 Metalworking machinery; small arms ammunition

(G-11730)
PEPSI-COLA METRO BTLG CO INC
919 Industrial Dr (48858-4647)
PHONE..................989 772-3158
Dave Pruitt, *Manager*
EMP: 6
SALES (corp-wide): 70.3B **Publicly Held**
WEB: www.pepsico.com
SIC: 2086 Bottled & canned soft drinks
HQ: Pepsi-Cola Metropolitan Bottling Company, Inc.
1111 Westchester Ave
White Plains NY 10604
914 767-6000

(G-11731)
PINNACLE CABINET COMPANY INC
1121 N Fancher Ave (48858-4605)
PHONE..................989 772-3866
Eric McDonald, *President*
Eric Mc Donald, *President*
Joe Mc Donald, *Corp Secy*
Fred Mc Donald, *Vice Pres*

Deb Mc Donald, *VP Finance*
EMP: 20 **EST:** 1995 **Privately Held**
WEB: www.pinnaclecabinetcompany.com
SIC: 2599 2542 2434 Cabinets, factory; partitions & fixtures, except wood; wood kitchen cabinets

(G-11732)
PIONEER OIL TOOLS INC
5179 W Weidman Rd (48858)
P.O. Box 131 (48804-0131)
PHONE..................989 644-6999
Glenn Smith, *President*
EMP: 7 **EST:** 1995
SQ FT: 6,000
SALES (est): 1.5MM **Privately Held**
WEB: www.pioneeroiltools.com
SIC: 1389 Oil & gas wells: building, repairing & dismantling; oil field services

(G-11733)
PLEASANT GRAPHICS INC
6835 Lea Pick Dr (48858-8911)
PHONE..................989 773-7777
Douglas Neff, *President*
Hans Schwarzkopf, *Consultant*
Cindy McClune, *Graphic Designe*
▲ **EMP:** 12 **EST:** 1985
SQ FT: 7,000
SALES (est): 1.9MM **Privately Held**
WEB: www.pleasantgraphics.com
SIC: 2752 Commercial printing, offset

(G-11734)
PREMIER CASING CREWS INC
5580 Venture Way (48858-1149)
PHONE..................989 775-7436
Steve Bigard, *President*
Ricky Huagard, *Vice Pres*
EMP: 7 **EST:** 1997
SALES (est): 747.7K **Privately Held**
SIC: 1389 Construction, repair & dismantling services; oil field services

(G-11735)
Q SAGE INC
2150 Jbs Trl (48858-8303)
PHONE..................989 775-2424
EMP: 11 **EST:** 2008
SALES (est): 864.8K **Privately Held**
WEB: www.q-sage.com
SIC: 3999 Manufacturing industries

(G-11736)
REFRIGERATION RESEARCH INC
Also Called: Oak Division
2174 Commerce St (48858-9060)
PHONE..................989 773-7540
Mike Cummings, *Principal*
Scott Graenser, *QC Mgr*
Matte Howe, *Engineer*
Ron Spangler, *Controller*
EMP: 5
SALES (corp-wide): 9.5MM **Privately Held**
WEB: www.refresearch.com
SIC: 3585 Refrigeration equipment, complete
PA: Refrigeration Research, Inc.
525 N 5th St
Brighton MI 48116
810 227-1151

(G-11737)
RISE MACHINE COMPANY INC
905 N Kinney Ave (48858-1700)
P.O. Box 321 (48804-0321)
PHONE..................989 772-2151
Kenneth Rise, *President*
Donald J Rise Sr, *President*
EMP: 7 **EST:** 1965
SQ FT: 6,480
SALES (est): 300K **Privately Held**
SIC: 3599 7692 Machine shop, jobbing & repair; welding repair

(G-11738)
SMITH & SONS MEAT PROC INC
5080 E Broadway Rd (48858-8413)
PHONE..................989 772-6048
Russell Smith, *President*
EMP: 8 **EST:** 1936
SQ FT: 10,000

SALES (est): 1MM **Privately Held**
WEB: www.smithandsonsmeatprocessing.com
SIC: 5421 Meat packing plants; meat & fish markets; meat markets, including freezer provisioners

(G-11739)
SMITH - SONS ME
5080 E Broadway Rd (48858-8413)
PHONE..................989 772-6048
Ken Rau, *Principal*
EMP: 8 **EST:** 2017
SALES (est): 121.6K **Privately Held**
WEB: www.smithandsonsmeatprocessing.com
SIC: 2011 Meat packing plants

(G-11740)
SMOKE-FREE KIDS INC
3780 Saint Andrews Dr (48858-8043)
PHONE..................989 772-4063
EMP: 4 **EST:** 2018
SALES (est): 170.3K **Privately Held**
WEB: www.jeffreywigand.com
SIC: 2131 Chewing & smoking tobacco

(G-11741)
SOLAR EZ INC
5340 E Jordan Rd (48858-9220)
PHONE..................989 773-3347
EMP: 15
SALES (est): 666K **Privately Held**
SIC: 1799 3433 Trade Contractor Mfg Heating Equipment-Nonelectric

(G-11742)
STEEL-FAB WILSON & MACHINE
1219 N Mission St (48858-1050)
PHONE..................989 773-6046
David L Wilson, *President*
Matt Grimley, *Prdtn Mgr*
David Doty, *Foreman/Supr*
Noah Smith, *Parts Mgr*
EMP: 6 **EST:** 1945
SQ FT: 4,000
SALES (est): 822.8K **Privately Held**
WEB: www.wilsonsteelfab.com
SIC: 3599 Custom machinery; machine shop, jobbing & repair

(G-11743)
STEELHEAD INDUSTRIES LLC
121 E Broadway St (48858-2312)
PHONE..................989 506-7416
Tim Sponseller,
Greg McCarthy,
EMP: 6 **EST:** 2015
SQ FT: 50,000
SALES (est): 156.9K **Privately Held**
WEB: www.americanbarnwood.com
SIC: 3537 Engine stands & racks, metal

(G-11744)
T L V INC
Also Called: Tumbl Trak
5747 W Isabella Rd (48858-9302)
P.O. Box 289 (48804-0289)
PHONE..................989 773-4362
Doug Davis, *President*
Douglas Davis, *President*
Stacy Finnerty, *Vice Pres*
Bill Duddles, *Opers Mgr*
James Parent, *Research*
▲ **EMP:** 11 **EST:** 1988
SQ FT: 3,600
SALES (est): 3.2MM **Privately Held**
WEB: www.tumbltrak.com
SIC: 3949 5091 Gymnasium equipment; gymnasium equipment

(G-11745)
TOTAL LEE SPORTS INC
714 W Pickard St (48858-9854)
P.O. Box 47 (48804-0047)
PHONE..................989 772-6121
Robert Lee, *President*
Karen Lee, *Corp Secy*
Mary Anne Lee, *Vice Pres*
EMP: 4 **EST:** 1991
SALES (est): 344K **Privately Held**
SIC: 2759 5091 5941 Letterpress & screen printing; sporting & recreation goods; sporting goods & bicycle shops

(G-11746)
WEBER BROS SAWMILL INC
2862 N Winn Rd (48858-9736)
PHONE..................989 644-2206
Ed Weber, *President*
John Weber, *President*
Ben Weber, *Corp Secy*
EMP: 29 **EST:** 1956
SQ FT: 15,500
SALES (est): 1.9MM **Privately Held**
WEB: www.weberssawmill.com
SIC: 2421 2426 Lumber: rough, sawed or planed; hardwood dimension & flooring mills

(G-11747)
YOUR CUSTOM IMAGE
2021 E River Rd (48858-8047)
P.O. Box 478, Edmore (48829-0478)
PHONE..................989 621-2250
Nick Houghton, *Owner*
EMP: 4 **EST:** 2010
SALES (est): 200K **Privately Held**
WEB: www.yciusa.com
SIC: 2711 Newspapers

Mulliken
Eaton County

(G-11748)
ALR PRODUCTS INC
Also Called: Polly Products
12 Charlotte St (48861-9701)
PHONE..................517 649-2243
Steve Ault, *CEO*
EMP: 15 **EST:** 2010 **Privately Held**
WEB: www.pollyproducts.com
SIC: 2531 Public building & related furniture

(G-11749)
KELLOGG COMPANY
235 Potter St (48861-9663)
PHONE..................269 961-9387
Leslie Lauderbaugh, *Principal*
EMP: 4
SALES (corp-wide): 13.7B **Publicly Held**
WEB: www.kelloggcompany.com
SIC: 2043 Cereal breakfast foods
PA: Kellogg Company
1 Kellogg Sq
Battle Creek MI 49017
269 961-2000

(G-11750)
RECYCLETECH PRODUCTS INC
12 Charlotte St (48861-9701)
PHONE..................517 649-2243
Tom Vanderhenst, *President*
EMP: 10 **EST:** 1995
SALES (est): 168.9K **Privately Held**
SIC: 2531 5941 Picnic tables or benches, park; playground equipment

Munger
Bay County

(G-11751)
IKES WELDING SHOP AND MFG
50 N Finn Rd (48747-9780)
PHONE..................989 892-2783
Jefferdon Behmlander, *Partner*
Randy Bowman, *Principal*
Roger Bowman, *Principal*
EMP: 6 **EST:** 1945
SALES (est): 570K **Privately Held**
WEB: www.ikeswelding.com
SIC: 3523 Potato diggers, harvesters & planters; grading, cleaning, sorting machines, fruit, grain, vegetable

Munising
Alger County

(G-11752)
NEENAH PAPER INC
501 E Munising Ave (49862-1490)
PHONE..................906 387-2700
George Mannisto, *Maint Spvr*

Chris Simard, *Mfg Staff*
Thomas Grieves, *Engineer*
Patrick McDonald, *Project Engr*
Jim Pytyck, *Manager*
EMP: 340
SALES (corp-wide): 792.6MM **Publicly Held**
WEB: www.neenah.com
SIC: 2621 Paper mills
PA: Neenah, Inc.
    3460 Preston Ridge Rd # 150
    Alpharetta GA 30005
    678 566-6500

(G-11753)
PONTOON RENTALS
Also Called: Seaberg Pontoon Rentals
1330 Commercial St (49862-1358)
PHONE...........................906 387-2685
Sharon Seaberg, *Principal*
EMP: 4 **EST:** 2001
SALES (est): 262.2K **Privately Held**
WEB: www.superiorpontoonrentals.com
SIC: 3728 7999 Pontoons, aircraft; pleasure boat rental

(G-11754)
S & S FOREST PRODUCTS
905 W Munising Ave (49862-1321)
PHONE...........................906 892-8268
Earl Steinhoff, *President*
Milo Steinhoff, *Partner*
EMP: 5
SALES (est): 370K **Privately Held**
SIC: 2411 Logging

(G-11755)
TIMBER PRODUCTS CO LTD PARTNR
Also Called: Michigan Hrdwood Vneer Lbr Div
Hwy M 28 E (49862)
P.O. Box 378 (49862-0378)
PHONE...........................906 452-6221
David Gonyea, *Vice Pres*
Bruce Strand, *Human Res Mgr*
Millard Larsen, *Manager*
EMP: 250
SALES (corp-wide): 376.2MM **Privately Held**
WEB: www.timberproducts.com
SIC: 2421 2435 Sawmills & planing mills, general; hardwood veneer & plywood
PA: Timber Products Co. Limited Partnership
    305 S 4th St
    Springfield OR 97477
    541 747-4577

(G-11756)
TIMBERLAND FORESTRY
E6971 Wildwood Rd (49862-8836)
PHONE...........................906 387-4350
Tom Nolta, *Owner*
EMP: 6 **EST:** 1987
SALES (est): 295.5K **Privately Held**
SIC: 3531 Forestry related equipment

Munith
Jackson County

(G-11757)
R T C ENVIRO FAB INC
9043 M 106 (49259)
P.O. Box 99, Pleasant Lake (49272-0099)
PHONE...........................517 596-2987
Virginia Bubp, *President*
Ronald Bubp, *General Mgr*
EMP: 30 **EST:** 1946
SQ FT: 12,000
SALES (est): 5.2MM **Privately Held**
SIC: 3443 3441 Tanks, lined: metal plate; fabricated structural metal

Muskegon
Muskegon County

(G-11758)
175 NORTH GREEN CREEK INC
3253 Whitehall Rd (49445-1061)
PHONE...........................231 766-2155
Jim Sweet, *Principal*

▲ **EMP:** 5 **EST:** 1970
SALES (est): 484.2K **Privately Held**
WEB: www.ittgage.com
SIC: 3599 Machine shop, jobbing & repair

(G-11759)
A & B WELDING & FABRICATING
Also Called: A&B Welding
2532 S Getty St (49444-1797)
PHONE...........................231 733-2661
Thomas Baker, *President*
Ted Baker, *Vice Pres*
Timothy Baker, *Vice Pres*
Gary Baker, *Treasurer*
Sandra Zahart, *Admin Sec*
EMP: 6
SQ FT: 12,000
SALES (est): 577.3K **Privately Held**
SIC: 3449 7692 3444 3443 Custom roll formed products; welding repair; sheet metalwork; fabricated plate work (boiler shop)

(G-11760)
A & D RUN OFF INC
Also Called: Wells Index Division
701 W Clay Ave (49440-1064)
PHONE...........................231 759-0950
Rick Robison, *President*
EMP: 6 **EST:** 1987
SQ FT: 16,000
SALES (est): 519.1K **Privately Held**
WEB: www.wells-index.com
SIC: 3541 3545 Electrochemical milling machines; milling machine attachments (machine tool accessories)

(G-11761)
ACCESS WORKS INC
Also Called: Fleet Engineers
1800 E Keating Ave (49442-6121)
PHONE...........................231 777-2537
Wesley K Eklund, *President*
Louis E Eklund, *Treasurer*
EMP: 9 **EST:** 1994
SQ FT: 240,000
SALES (est): 1.7MM **Privately Held**
WEB: www.fleetengineers.com
SIC: 3714 Motor vehicle parts & accessories

(G-11762)
ADAC PLASTICS INC
Also Called: Adac Automotive
2653 Olthoff St (49444-2680)
PHONE...........................231 777-2645
Jacob Rupert, *Manager*
Stacey Henkel, *Exec Dir*
EMP: 42
SALES (corp-wide): 285.6MM **Privately Held**
WEB: www.adacautomotive.com
SIC: 3089 Injection molding of plastics
PA: Adac Plastics, Inc.
    5690 Eagle Dr Se
    Grand Rapids MI 49512
    616 957-0311

(G-11763)
ADAC PLASTICS INC
2050 Port City Blvd (49442-6134)
PHONE...........................616 957-0520
Kimberly Simon, *Purch Agent*
Eric Peterson, *Chief Engr*
Dennis Comstock, *Engineer*
Craig Nedeau, *Senior Engr*
Stacey Henkel, *Branch Mgr*
EMP: 42
SALES (corp-wide): 285.6MM **Privately Held**
WEB: www.adacautomotive.com
SIC: 3089 3714 Injection molding of plastics; motor vehicle parts & accessories
PA: Adac Plastics, Inc.
    5690 Eagle Dr Se
    Grand Rapids MI 49512
    616 957-0311

(G-11764)
ADAC PLASTICS INC
Also Called: Adac Automotive
1801 E Keating Ave (49442-6120)
PHONE...........................616 957-0311
Jeff Taylor, *Mfg Staff*
Shane Crawford, *Engineer*
Dan Zielinski, *Engineer*

Jon Wildern, *Project Engr*
Brad Wingett, *Branch Mgr*
EMP: 42
SALES (corp-wide): 285.6MM **Privately Held**
WEB: www.adacautomotive.com
SIC: 3089 3714 Injection molding of plastics; motor vehicle parts & accessories
PA: Adac Plastics, Inc.
    5690 Eagle Dr Se
    Grand Rapids MI 49512
    616 957-0311

(G-11765)
AERO FOIL INTERNATIONAL INC
Also Called: Afi
1920 Port City Blvd (49442-6132)
PHONE...........................231 773-0200
Stephen Kutches, *President*
Brian Blain, *Engineer*
Trevor McClung, *Engineer*
Terry Teitgen, *Engineer*
Christine Peterson, *Accountant*
▼ **EMP:** 50 **EST:** 2004
SQ FT: 30,000
SALES (est): 2MM **Privately Held**
WEB: www.afiusa.net
SIC: 3544 Special dies & tools

(G-11766)
AGSCAP INC
2651 Hoyt St (49444-2141)
P.O. Box 729 (49443-0729)
PHONE...........................231 733-2101
Kurgt Rosen, *Partner*
Bob Van Rooyen, *Project Mgr*
EMP: 8 **EST:** 1962
SALES (est): 143.7K **Privately Held**
SIC: 2992 7389 Lubricating oils & greases; packaging & labeling services

(G-11767)
ALL SIGNS LLC
1005 W Laketon Ave (49441-2943)
PHONE...........................231 755-5540
Charles Cjatkes, *Owner*
EMP: 5 **EST:** 2015
SALES (est): 287.1K **Privately Held**
WEB: www.allsignsmichigan.com
SIC: 3993 Electric signs

(G-11768)
AMERICAN ATHLETIC
418 W Hackley Ave (49444-1032)
P.O. Box 1881 (49443-1881)
PHONE...........................231 798-7300
Timothy Ehilietart, *Partner*
Mark Scott, *Partner*
Eric Jones, *Consultant*
Marianne White, *Admin Asst*
EMP: 11 **EST:** 2010
SALES (est): 642.5K **Privately Held**
WEB: www.americanathletix.com
SIC: 2531 Bleacher seating, portable

(G-11769)
AMERICAN CHEM SOLUTIONS LLC
2406 Roberts St (49444-1843)
PHONE...........................231 655-5840
Todd J Zahn, *Mng Member*
Scott Fisher, *Maintence Staff*
EMP: 24 **EST:** 2018
SALES (est): 7MM **Privately Held**
SIC: 3559 Chemical machinery & equipment

(G-11770)
AMERICAN PORCELAIN ENAMEL CO
1709 Ruddiman Dr (49445-3041)
PHONE...........................231 744-3013
Robert Long Jr, *President*
Harry E Long, *Treasurer*
EMP: 13 **EST:** 1938
SQ FT: 36,000
SALES (est): 201.1K **Privately Held**
SIC: 3479 Enameling, including porcelain, of metal products

(G-11771)
ANDERSON GLOBAL INC
500 W Sherman Blvd (49444-1315)
PHONE...........................231 733-2164

John R Mc Intyre, *President*
John McIntyre, *President*
Troy Leroux, *Opers Mgr*
Joe Merrill, *Engineer*
Chris Hanks, *Project Engr*
▲ **EMP:** 135 **EST:** 1982
SQ FT: 45,000
SALES (est): 26MM **Privately Held**
WEB: www.andersonglobal.com
SIC: 3543 Foundry patternmaking

(G-11772)
APPARELMASTER-MUSKEGON INC
Also Called: Blue Ribbon Linen and Mat Svcs
341 E Apple Ave (49442-3465)
P.O. Box 5337 (49445-0337)
PHONE...........................231 728-5406
Eric Anderson, *President*
Donald Harakas, *Vice Pres*
Lori Anderson, *Treasurer*
Nancy Anderson, *Admin Sec*
EMP: 22 **EST:** 1976
SQ FT: 11,000
SALES (est): 1.5MM **Privately Held**
SIC: 2273 7213 Mats & matting; uniform supply

(G-11773)
ASPHALT PAVING INC
1000 E Sherman Blvd (49444-1808)
P.O. Box 4190 (49444-0190)
PHONE...........................231 733-1409
Joseph Burns, *President*
Nelson Van Leeuwen, *Principal*
Gary Verplank, *Principal*
L J Verplank, *Principal*
Ken Johnson, *Vice Pres*
EMP: 37 **EST:** 1956
SQ FT: 1,000
SALES (est): 2.8MM **Privately Held**
SIC: 1611 3272 Surfacing & paving; resurfacing contractor; paving materials, prefabricated concrete

(G-11774)
BASF
1740 Whitehall Rd (49445-1354)
PHONE...........................231 719-3019
EMP: 12 **EST:** 2019
SALES (est): 3.4MM **Privately Held**
WEB: www.basf.com
SIC: 2869 Industrial organic chemicals

(G-11775)
BAUER SHEET METAL & FABG INC (PA)
1550 Evanston Ave (49442-5327)
PHONE...........................231 773-3244
Michael Bauer, *President*
Mike Heath, *Project Mgr*
Ron Sejat, *Opers Mgr*
Jeff Nason, *Sales Staff*
Ron Gallop, *Manager*
EMP: 34 **EST:** 1933
SQ FT: 17,000
SALES (est): 7.2MM **Privately Held**
WEB: www.bauersheetmetal.com
SIC: 1761 3441 3444 Sheet metalwork; fabricated structural metal; sheet metalwork

(G-11776)
BAYER CROPSCIENCE LP
Also Called: Muskegon Formulation Plant
1740 Whitehall Rd (49445-1354)
PHONE...........................231 744-4711
Steve Smythe, *Branch Mgr*
David Sova, *Manager*
Bryan Crozier, *Technician*
Debra Deyoung, *Technician*
Claire Delo, *Maintence Staff*
EMP: 14
SQ FT: 4,500
SALES (corp-wide): 69.9B **Privately Held**
WEB: www.backedbybayer.com
SIC: 2879 Agricultural chemicals
HQ: Bayer Cropscience Lp
    800 N Lindbergh Blvd
    Saint Louis MO 63167
    412 777-2375

Muskegon - Muskegon County (G-11777)

(G-11777)
BBP INVESTMENT HOLDINGS LLC (PA)
Also Called: Brunswick Bowling Products
525 W Laketon Ave (49441-2601)
PHONE.................................231 725-4966
Corey Dykstra, *Mng Member*
EMP: 282 **EST:** 2015
SQ FT: 430,000
SALES (est): 58.1MM **Privately Held**
WEB: www.brunswickbowling.com
SIC: 3949 6719 Bowling equipment & supplies; investment holding companies, except banks

(G-11778)
BERT HAZEKAMP & SON INC
Also Called: Hazekamps Wholesale Meat Co
3933 S Brooks Rd (49444-9721)
PHONE.................................231 773-8302
David Hazekamp, *President*
Mike Hazekamp, *Vice Pres*
Keith Crowley, *Production*
Julie Hazekamp, *Admin Sec*
EMP: 110 **EST:** 1905
SQ FT: 85,000
SALES (est): 21.1MM **Privately Held**
SIC: 2013 2011 Sausages & other prepared meats; meat packing plants

(G-11779)
BLUE WATER CABINETRY AMP
4845 Airline Rd Ste 4 (49444-4563)
PHONE.................................231 246-2293
EMP: 4 **EST:** 2018
SALES (est): 53.7K **Privately Held**
SIC: 2434 Wood kitchen cabinets

(G-11780)
BMC/INDUSTRIAL EDUCTL SVCS INC
Also Called: BMC Laboratory Casework
2831 Maffett St (49444-2153)
P.O. Box 4089 (49444-0089)
PHONE.................................231 733-1206
Joel Gauthier, *President*
Brian White, *Mfg Staff*
Barry Kennedy, *Natl Sales Mgr*
Diane Geers, *Cust Mgr*
EMP: 46 **EST:** 1970
SQ FT: 40,000
SALES (est): 10.5MM **Privately Held**
WEB: www.bmclab.com
SIC: 5047 3444 3821 Hospital equipment & supplies; medical laboratory equipment; sheet metalwork; laboratory equipment: fume hoods, distillation racks, etc.

(G-11781)
BOARS BELLY
333 W Western Ave (49440-1266)
PHONE.................................231 722-2627
EMP: 4
SALES (est): 471K **Privately Held**
SIC: 2599 Mfg Furniture/Fixtures

(G-11782)
BOLD COMPANIES INC
Also Called: Bold Furniture
2291 Olthoff St (49444-2643)
PHONE.................................231 773-8026
David Folkert, *CEO*
Todd Folkert, *President*
Nick Milanowski, *Vice Pres*
Tom Buffum, *Plant Supt*
Eric Johnson, *Purch Agent*
EMP: 88 **EST:** 2004
SQ FT: 75,000
SALES (est): 18.8MM **Privately Held**
WEB: www.boldfurniture.com
SIC: 2521 Wood office furniture

(G-11783)
BORGMAN TOOL & ENGINEERING LLC
2912 Hamilton Rd (49445-8318)
PHONE.................................231 733-4133
John Borgin,
EMP: 9 **EST:** 2010
SALES (est): 540.4K **Privately Held**
WEB: www.borgmantool.com
SIC: 3544 Special dies & tools

(G-11784)
BRUNSWICK BOWLING PRODUCTS LLC (HQ)
525 W Laketon Ave (49441-2601)
P.O. Box 329 (49443-0329)
PHONE.................................231 725-4966
Corey J Dykstra, *CEO*
Austin Rothbard, *President*
Tj Kusmierski, *Purch Mgr*
Jeff Skinner, *Senior Buyer*
Troy Recknagel, *Engineer*
◆ **EMP:** 498 **EST:** 1845
SQ FT: 160,000
SALES (est): 58.1MM **Privately Held**
WEB: www.brunswickbowling.com
SIC: 3949 Bowling equipment & supplies
PA: Bbp Investment Holdings, Llc
525 W Laketon Ave
Muskegon MI 49441
231 725-4966

(G-11785)
BRUNSWICK INDOOR RECREATION
525 W Laketon Ave (49441-2601)
PHONE.................................231 725-4764
Dustan E McCoy, *CEO*
Ben Uzarski, *Engineer*
Corey Dykstra, *Controller*
EMP: 23 **EST:** 2007
SALES (est): 2.4MM **Privately Held**
SIC: 3949 Sporting & athletic goods

(G-11786)
BULLSEYE POWER
2134 Northwoods Ave (49442-6850)
PHONE.................................231 788-5209
Mark Fazakerley, *Partner*
David M Hall, *Partner*
Charles D Portera, *Partner*
John Workman,
▲ **EMP:** 9 **EST:** 2003
SALES (est): 1.2MM **Privately Held**
WEB: www.bullseyepower.com
SIC: 3714 Motor vehicle parts & accessories

(G-11787)
BUYERS GUIDE
1781 5th St Ste 1 (49441-2600)
PHONE.................................231 722-3784
Dale Bush, *Owner*
Barb Bary, *Manager*
EMP: 8 **EST:** 1972
SQ FT: 8,000
SALES (est): 385.1K **Privately Held**
SIC: 2741 Shopping news: publishing only, not printed on site

(G-11788)
C W MARSH COMPANY (PA)
1385 Hudson St (49441-1814)
P.O. Box 598 (49443-0598)
PHONE.................................231 722-3781
David Utzinger, *President*
James Bradbury, *Chairman*
Elizabeth Bradbury, *Vice Pres*
Dave Pruitt, *Vice Pres*
EMP: 21 **EST:** 1900
SQ FT: 16,000
SALES (est): 5.5MM **Privately Held**
WEB: www.cwmarsh.com
SIC: 3199 3172 3053 Leather belting & strapping; personal leather goods; gaskets, packing & sealing devices

(G-11789)
CAMCAR PLASTICS INC
1732 Glade St (49441-2313)
PHONE.................................231 726-5000
Courtney Gust III, *President*
Teresa Gust, *Vice Pres*
EMP: 14 **EST:** 2000
SQ FT: 18,000
SALES (est): 2.6MM **Privately Held**
WEB: www.ccplasticparts.com
SIC: 3089 Injection molding of plastics

(G-11790)
CEL PLASTICS INC
Also Called: Port City Custom Plastics
1985 E Laketon Ave (49442-6127)
PHONE.................................231 777-3941
Mark Pickett, *President*
Bruce Essex, *Vice Pres*
John Essex, *Vice Pres*
Mark Petzold, *Plant Mgr*
EMP: 10 **EST:** 1996
SQ FT: 10,000
SALES (est): 5.3MM
SALES (corp-wide): 682.5MM **Privately Held**
WEB: www.paceind.com
SIC: 3089 Injection molded finished plastic products
HQ: Pace Industries, Llc
481 S Shiloh Dr
Fayetteville AR 72704
479 443-1455

(G-11791)
CENTURY FOUNDRY INC
339 W Hovey Ave (49444-1306)
P.O. Box 4438 (49444-0438)
PHONE.................................231 733-1572
Scott Le Roux, *President*
Laura Ellis, *Human Res Dir*
Jim Brickley, *Manager*
EMP: 50
SQ FT: 45,000
SALES (est): 8.7MM **Privately Held**
WEB: www.centuryfoundry.com
SIC: 3366 Copper foundries

(G-11792)
CHEESE LADY LLC
Also Called: Cheese Lady Muskegon, The
808 Terrace St (49440-1123)
PHONE.................................231 728-3000
Shelley Lewis, *Principal*
EMP: 9 **EST:** 2016
SALES (est): 357.7K **Privately Held**
SIC: 2022 Natural cheese

(G-11793)
COLES QUALITY FOODS INC
1188 Lakeshore Dr (49441-1613)
PHONE.................................231 722-1651
Wesley S Devon, *CEO*
EMP: 79
SALES (corp-wide): 52.2MM **Privately Held**
WEB: www.coles.com
SIC: 5149 2051 2038 Specialty food items; bread, cake & related products; frozen specialties
PA: Cole's Quality Foods, Inc.
4079 Park East Ct Se A
Grand Rapids MI 49546
231 722-1651

(G-11794)
COMPETITIVE EDGE WOOD SPC INC
711 E Savidge Spring Mi 4 (49441)
PHONE.................................616 842-1063
EMP: 60
SQ FT: 20,000
SALES (est): 5.5MM **Privately Held**
SIC: 2541 Wood Partitions And Fixtures

(G-11795)
CONSUMERS CONCRETE CORPORATION
4450 Evanston Ave (49442-6525)
PHONE.................................231 777-3981
Fred Statler, *Vice Pres*
Danny Frigo, *Accounts Mgr*
Dick Woodward, *Accounts Mgr*
Mike Gerose, *Exec Dir*
Brad Hiedema, *Administration*
EMP: 12
SALES (corp-wide): 42.6MM **Privately Held**
WEB: www.consumersconcrete.com
SIC: 3273 3271 5032 Ready-mixed concrete; blocks, concrete or cinder: standard; gravel; sand, construction
PA: Consumers Concrete Corporation
3506 Lovers Ln
Kalamazoo MI 49001
269 342-0136

(G-11796)
COUNTY OF MUSKEGON
Also Called: Muskegon Pioneer County Park
1563 Scenic Dr (49445-9612)
PHONE.................................231 744-3580
Jim Wood, *Superintendent*
EMP: 21 **Privately Held**
WEB: www.co.muskegon.mi.us
SIC: 3792 Camping trailers & chassis

PA: County Of Muskegon
990 Terrace St
Muskegon MI 49442
231 724-6520

(G-11797)
CUSTOM SERVICE PRINTERS INC
916 E Keating Ave (49442-5953)
PHONE.................................231 726-3297
Stephen Kamp, *President*
Gregory Kamp, *Vice Pres*
Joseph Rupar, *Vice Pres*
Jojean Hecksel, *VP Sales*
Melissa Ferreura, *Office Mgr*
EMP: 12 **EST:** 1960
SQ FT: 17,500
SALES (est): 2MM **Privately Held**
WEB: www.csp-inc.com
SIC: 2752 Commercial printing, offset

(G-11798)
D & J MFG & MACHINING
507 W Hovey Ave (49444-1361)
PHONE.................................231 830-9522
Joann Perley, *Owner*
EMP: 5 **EST:** 2000
SALES (est): 485.4K **Privately Held**
SIC: 3599 Machine shop, jobbing & repair

(G-11799)
DOBB PRINTING INC
2431 Harvey St (49442-6104)
PHONE.................................231 722-1060
Michael L Dobb, *Owner*
Joe Dobb, *Vice Pres*
Mike Dobb, *Sales Mgr*
Nick Dobb, *Sales Staff*
David Neumann, *Sales Staff*
EMP: 50 **EST:** 1958
SQ FT: 22,000
SALES (est): 5.5MM **Privately Held**
WEB: www.dobbprinting.com
SIC: 2752 2789 2759 Commercial printing, offset; letters, circular or form: lithographed; bookbinding & related work; commercial printing

(G-11800)
DONLEY COMPUTER SERVICES LLC
166 N Causeway St (49445-3302)
PHONE.................................231 750-1774
Steven Donley, *President*
EMP: 4 **EST:** 2013
SALES (est): 200K **Privately Held**
WEB: www.donleycomputers.com
SIC: 3651 Home entertainment equipment, electronic

(G-11801)
DSC LABORATORIES INC
1979 Latimer Dr (49442-6229)
PHONE.................................800 492-5988
Edward Kling, *President*
Sandy Bradshaw, *Office Mgr*
Bailey Thompson, *Assistant*
▲ **EMP:** 40 **EST:** 1969
SALES (est): 9.8MM **Privately Held**
WEB: www.dsclab.com
SIC: 2842 2834 2841 Cleaning or polishing preparations; automobile polish; pharmaceutical preparations; soap & other detergents

(G-11802)
EAGLE ALUM PRMNT MOLD CSTNGS I
2134 Northwoods Ave (49442-6850)
PHONE.................................231 788-4884
EMP: 8 **EST:** 2019
SALES (est): 659.6K **Privately Held**
WEB: www.eaglealuminumcastproducts.com
SIC: 3363 Aluminum die-castings

(G-11803)
EAGLE PRECISION CAST PARTS INC
5112 Evanston Ave (49442-4852)
PHONE.................................231 788-3318
Mark Fazackerley, *President*
Debbie Pipoly, *Vice Pres*
John Workman, *Vice Pres*
Shawn Turner, *Production*

GEOGRAPHIC SECTION
Muskegon - Muskegon County (G-11830)

Dean Buikema, *Accountant*
EMP: 42 **EST:** 1989
SQ FT: 37,500
SALES: 8.7MM **Privately Held**
WEB: www.eagleprecisioncastparts.com
SIC: 3324 Steel investment foundries

(G-11804)
EAGLE T M C TECHNOLOGIES
Also Called: Eagle Cnc Technology
2357 Whitehall Rd (49445-1043)
PHONE..................................231 766-3914
Mark Fazakerley, *President*
John Workman, *Vice Pres*
Eric Fazakerley, *Engineer*
Brian Osborne, *Engineer*
Dennis Chester, *Sales Engr*
EMP: 15 **EST:** 1993
SQ FT: 12,000
SALES (est): 2MM **Privately Held**
WEB: www.eaglecnc.com
SIC: 3599 Machine shop, jobbing & repair

(G-11805)
EARLE PRESS INC
Also Called: Earle Press Printing
2140 Latimer Dr (49442-6234)
P.O. Box 327 (49443-0327)
PHONE..................................231 773-2111
Jerry M Grevel, *President*
Wes Pearcy, *Exec VP*
Whitney Eckert, *CFO*
Amy Grevel, *Manager*
EMP: 32 **EST:** 1920
SQ FT: 24,000
SALES (est): 3.8MM **Privately Held**
WEB: www.earlepress.com
SIC: 2752 5112 2791 2789 Commercial printing, offset; business forms; typesetting; bookbinding & related work; manifold business forms; commercial printing

(G-11806)
EAST MUSKEGON ROOFG SHTMTL CO (PA)
Also Called: Certified Sheet Metal
1665 Holton Rd (49445-1450)
PHONE..................................231 744-2461
Gregory R Kanaar, *President*
Benjamin P Kanaar, *General Mgr*
Joseph Kastl, *General Mgr*
Joseph K Kastl, *General Mgr*
Jesse Adkins, *Superintendent*
EMP: 70 **EST:** 1950
SALES: 16.4MM **Privately Held**
WEB: www.eastmuskegon.com
SIC: 1761 3444 Sheet metalwork; roofing contractor; sheet metalwork

(G-11807)
EAST RIVER MACHINE & TOOL INC
1701 Wierengo Dr (49442-6257)
PHONE..................................231 767-1701
Dan Wemsumius, *President*
Les Furst, *Vice Pres*
Tim Huizenga, *Vice Pres*
EMP: 9 **EST:** 1993
SQ FT: 4,900
SALES (est): 700K **Privately Held**
SIC: 3544 Special dies & tools

(G-11808)
EASY DOCK CORP
3823 W Giles Rd (49445-9685)
PHONE..................................231 750-5052
Patrick Bourdon, *Owner*
EMP: 4 **EST:** 2018
SALES (est): 71.6K **Privately Held**
WEB: www.easydockllc.com
SIC: 2499 Wood products

(G-11809)
ECO BRUSHES AND FIBERS
Also Called: Eco Brushes and Fibers S.A.s
2658 Heights Ravenna Rd (49444-3430)
P.O. Box 193 (49443-0193)
PHONE..................................231 683-9202
Virginia Tawney, *Owner*
EMP: 4 **EST:** 2014
SALES (est): 164.9K **Privately Held**
SIC: 3991 7389 Street sweeping brooms, hand or machine;

(G-11810)
EKLUND HOLDINGS INC (PA)
1800 E Keating Ave (49442-6121)
PHONE..................................231 777-2537
Wesley Eklund, *President*
Steve Antekeier, *Vice Pres*
Cliff Oliver, *Production*
Bruce Medema, *QC Mgr*
Leo Gartland, *Engineer*
◆ **EMP:** 121 **EST:** 1963
SQ FT: 240,000
SALES (est): 24.1MM **Privately Held**
WEB: www.fleetengineers.com
SIC: 3714 Motor vehicle parts & accessories

(G-11811)
EMC WELDING & FABRICATION INC
4966 Evanston Ave (49442-4828)
PHONE..................................231 788-4172
Jerry Locke, *Mng Member*
EMP: 8 **EST:** 1984
SQ FT: 5,700
SALES (est): 1MM **Privately Held**
SIC: 3441 Fabricated structural metal

(G-11812)
EMERGENCY SERVICES LLC
Also Called: Great Lakes Coach
1660 Dodson Dr (49442-6604)
PHONE..................................231 727-7400
Robert George, *President*
Dean Hull,
EMP: 17 **EST:** 2011
SALES (est): 2.8MM **Privately Held**
WEB: www.emergencyservices.org
SIC: 7538 3714 General automotive repair shops; motor vehicle transmissions, drive assemblies & parts

(G-11813)
ESCO CO LTD PARTNERSHIP
2406 Roberts St (49444-1843)
PHONE..................................231 726-3106
Ray Klink, *Vice Pres*
EMP: 10 **EST:** 1977
SALES (est): 625.9K **Privately Held**
WEB: www.escocompany.com
SIC: 2865 Cyclic crudes & intermediates

(G-11814)
EXCELL MACHINE & TOOL CO LLC
1084 E Hackley Ave (49444-1887)
PHONE..................................231 728-1210
Joe Wood, *Mng Member*
EMP: 8 **EST:** 1987
SQ FT: 1,500
SALES (est): 800K **Privately Held**
SIC: 3544 Special dies & tools; jigs & fixtures

(G-11815)
FAIRWAY OPTICAL INC
4490 W Giles Rd (49445-9690)
PHONE..................................231 744-6168
Gerald Prince, *President*
EMP: 4 **EST:** 1982
SALES (est): 300K **Privately Held**
SIC: 3851 5049 Lenses, ophthalmic; optical goods

(G-11816)
FEB INC
Also Called: Muskegon Awning & Fabrication
2333 Henry St (49441-3019)
PHONE..................................231 759-0911
David Bayne, *President*
EMP: 15 **EST:** 2005
SALES (est): 672.3K **Privately Held**
WEB: www.muskegonawning.com
SIC: 2394 Awnings, fabric: made from purchased materials

(G-11817)
FINEEYE COLOR SOLUTIONS INC
1218 Tall Tree Ln (49445-1265)
PHONE..................................616 988-6119
Stephen A Macdonald, *CEO*
Peder W Nelson, *President*
Mike Dicosola, *CTO*
Michael Dicosola, *Admin Sec*
Dawn Nelson, *Administration*
▲ **EMP:** 4 **EST:** 1997
SQ FT: 2,500
SALES (est): 800.9K **Privately Held**
WEB: www.fineeyecolor.com
SIC: 2679 Paper products, converted

(G-11818)
FIVE PEAKS TECHNOLOGY LLC
700 Terrace Point Dr # 200 (49440-1166)
PHONE..................................231 830-8099
Reg Adams, *Mng Member*
Andrea Buntley, *Manager*
Chris Davis, *Manager*
Dave Harris, *Admin Sec*
◆ **EMP:** 11 **EST:** 2001
SALES (est): 931.3K **Privately Held**
WEB: www.satelliteindustries.com
SIC: 3089 Toilets, portable chemical: plastic

(G-11819)
FOMCORE LLC
1770 E Keating Ave (49442-6119)
PHONE..................................231 366-4791
Brian Matiga, *Engineer*
Ron Wallish, *CFO*
Laurie Parmalee, *Accountant*
Dave Diller, *Regl Sales Mgr*
Misty Diller, *Marketing Staff*
EMP: 100 **EST:** 2016
SALES (est): 14.3MM **Privately Held**
WEB: www.fomcore.com
SIC: 3086 Plastics foam products

(G-11820)
FORMING TECHNOLOGIES LLC
1885 E Laketon Ave (49442-6123)
P.O. Box 2246, Brighton (48116-6046)
PHONE..................................231 777-7030
Robin Collins, *Project Dir*
Erin Lehman, *Purchasing*
David M Hembree, *Mng Member*
Larry Lee, *Maintence Staff*
Dean W Miller,
EMP: 60
SQ FT: 25,000
SALES (est): 10.7MM **Privately Held**
WEB: www.formtech.org
SIC: 3089 Thermoformed finished plastic products

(G-11821)
FREEDOM TOOL & MFG CO
Also Called: Tool and Die
1741 S Wolf Lake Rd (49442-4879)
PHONE..................................231 788-2898
Carl Barber, *President*
Cynthia Barber, *Admin Sec*
EMP: 7 **EST:** 1983
SQ FT: 4,800
SALES (est): 700K **Privately Held**
WEB: www.freedomtoolmfg.com
SIC: 3544 Special dies & tools

(G-11822)
FROSTY COVE
2133 Lakeshore Dr (49441-1413)
PHONE..................................231 343-6643
Marcia Dula, *Principal*
EMP: 8 **EST:** 2010
SALES (est): 565.7K **Privately Held**
WEB: www.thefrostycove.com
SIC: 2024 Ice cream, bulk

(G-11823)
GEERPRES INC
1780 Harvey St (49442-5396)
P.O. Box 658 (49443-0658)
PHONE..................................231 773-3211
Scott E Ribbe, *President*
Jason Davies, *Vice Pres*
Rudy Fierros, *Purch Agent*
Eric Daly, *CFO*
Bryan Depree, *CFO*
▲ **EMP:** 20 **EST:** 1935
SQ FT: 85,000
SALES (est): 5MM **Privately Held**
WEB: www.geerpres.com
SIC: 3444 3589 3412 Sheet metalwork; commercial cleaning equipment; mop wringers; janitors' carts; metal barrels, drums & pails

(G-11824)
GLASSICART DECORATIVE GLWR
3128 7th St (49444-2834)
PHONE..................................231 739-5956
Michael Stapleton, *Owner*
EMP: 5 **EST:** 1997
SALES (est): 204.5K **Privately Held**
SIC: 3229 Art, decorative & novelty glassware

(G-11825)
GMI COMPOSITES INC
1355 W Sherman Blvd (49441-3538)
PHONE..................................231 755-1611
Bob Brady, *President*
Charles Brady, *Principal*
Louis Simoncini, *Principal*
Jerry Dykstra, *Corp Secy*
Joni Waller, *Human Res Mgr*
▲ **EMP:** 62 **EST:** 1920
SALES (est): 8.4MM **Privately Held**
SIC: 3089 Molding primary plastic

(G-11826)
GRAND RAPIDS GRAVEL COMPANY
Also Called: Port City Redi-Mix Co
1780 S Sheridan Dr (49442-4404)
P.O. Box 9160, Wyoming (49509-0160)
PHONE..................................231 777-2777
Bobbi Hunt, *Plant Mgr*
Tom Williams, *Manager*
EMP: 27
SALES (corp-wide): 23.9MM **Privately Held**
WEB: www.grgravel.com
SIC: 3273 Ready-mixed concrete
PA: Grand Rapids Gravel Company
2700 28th St Sw
Grand Rapids MI 49519
616 538-9000

(G-11827)
GRAPHICS HOUSE PUBLISHING
Also Called: Graphics House Printing
2632 Peck St (49444-2028)
PHONE..................................231 739-4004
Daniel Mc Kinnon, *CEO*
EMP: 33 **EST:** 1991
SALES (est): 3.6MM **Privately Held**
WEB: www.graphicshouse.net
SIC: 2752 Commercial printing, offset

(G-11828)
GRAPHICS HSE SPT PRMOTIONS INC (PA)
Also Called: Gh Imaging
444 Irwin Ave (49442-5009)
PHONE..................................231 739-4004
Brent McKinnon, *President*
Dan McKinnon, *CFO*
Pete Bush, *Accounts Exec*
EMP: 38 **EST:** 1993
SALES (est): 16.1MM **Privately Held**
WEB: www.ghimaging.com
SIC: 2711 2721 2741 Newspapers; magazines: publishing only, not printed on site; miscellaneous publishing

(G-11829)
GRAPHICS HSE SPT PRMOTIONS INC
United Sign Co.
444 Irwin Ave (49442-5009)
PHONE..................................231 733-1877
Brent McKinnon, *President*
EMP: 5
SALES (corp-wide): 16.1MM **Privately Held**
WEB: www.ghimaging.com
SIC: 3993 Signs & advertising specialties
PA: Graphics House Sports Promotions, Inc.
444 Irwin Ave
Muskegon MI 49442
231 739-4004

(G-11830)
GREAT LAKES FINISHING INC
510 W Hackley Ave (49444-1046)
PHONE..................................231 733-9566
Diana Bench, *CEO*
Bruce Vollmer, *Plant Mgr*
Liza Baldwin, *Office Mgr*

Muskegon - Muskegon County (G-11831)

EMP: 13 EST: 2002
SALES (est): 1.7MM **Privately Held**
WEB: www.greatlakesfinishinginc.com
SIC: 3471 Electroplating of metals or formed products

(G-11831)
GREAT LAKES NURSERY SOILS INC
680 S Maple Island Rd (49442-9407)
PHONE..................................231 788-2770
Eric Pratt, *President*
EMP: 10 EST: 1996
SALES (est): 1.3MM **Privately Held**
WEB: www.glnurserysoils.com
SIC: 2875 Potting soil, mixed

(G-11832)
GREATLAKESPOWERTOOLSCOM
4841 Airline Rd (49444-4503)
PHONE..................................231 733-6200
Kaj Langlois, *Principal*
EMP: 5 EST: 2016
SALES (est): 60.4K **Privately Held**
WEB: www.greatlakespowertools.com
SIC: 3999 Manufacturing industries

(G-11833)
GRIFFON INC
820 S Broton Rd (49442-9488)
P.O. Box 1403 (49443-1403)
PHONE..................................231 788-4630
Craig A Zimmer, *President*
Lorraine Zimmer, *Vice Pres*
Holly Esteban, *Assistant*
▼ EMP: 15 EST: 1980
SQ FT: 10,000
SALES (est): 2.1MM **Privately Held**
WEB: www.thegriffon.com
SIC: 3993 Signs, not made in custom sign painting shops; letters for signs, metal

(G-11834)
HACKLEY HEALTH VENTURES INC (DH)
Also Called: Hackley Hearing Center
1675 Leahy St Ste 101 (49442-5538)
PHONE..................................231 728-5720
Richard Witham, *Ch of Bd*
Robert Hovey, *Vice Ch Bd*
Michael T Baker, *President*
David Gingras, *Corp Secy*
EMP: 5 EST: 1984
SQ FT: 1,000
SALES (est): 575K
SALES (corp-wide): 18.8B **Privately Held**
WEB: www.hackleycommunitycare.org
SIC: 8741 5912 3842 8011 Hospital management; nursing & personal care facility management; drug stores; prosthetic appliances; health maintenance organization; rehabilitation center, outpatient treatment; occupational therapist
HQ: Mercy Health Partners
1675 Leahy St Ste 101
Muskegon MI 49442
231 728-4032

(G-11835)
HARBORFRONT INTERIORS INC
2300 Black Creek Rd (49444-2672)
PHONE..................................231 777-3838
David Rikkers, *President*
James Duncan, *President*
Ruth Duncan, *Treasurer*
Dave Carpenter, *Manager*
Mary Kaiser, *Admin Mgr*
EMP: 5 EST: 1986
SQ FT: 12,000
SALES (est): 1MM **Privately Held**
WEB: www.harborfront.com
SIC: 8711 2599 Designing: ship, boat, machine & product; restaurant furniture, wood or metal

(G-11836)
HERALD NEWSPAPERS COMPANY INC
Also Called: Muskegon Chronicle
379 W Western Ave Ste 100 (49440-1265)
PHONE..................................231 722-3161
Gary Ostrom, *Principal*
EMP: 6

SALES (corp-wide): 2.8B **Privately Held**
WEB: www.advancemediany.com
SIC: 2711 Newspapers, publishing & printing
HQ: The Herald Newspapers Company Inc
220 S Warren St
Syracuse NY 13202
315 470-0011

(G-11837)
IED INC
1938 Sanford St (49441-2517)
PHONE..................................231 728-9154
L Scott McNeill, *President*
EMP: 6 EST: 1987
SQ FT: 14,000
SALES (est): 536.8K **Privately Held**
SIC: 3559 5084 Metal finishing equipment for plating, etc.; metal refining machinery & equipment

(G-11838)
IMC PRODUCTS INC
2743 Henry St 130 (49441-3509)
PHONE..................................231 759-3430
Irmgard M Cooper, *President*
Don Johnson, *Vice Pres*
EMP: 10 EST: 1990
SQ FT: 30,000
SALES (est): 939K **Privately Held**
WEB: www.imc-products.com
SIC: 3714 Motor vehicle parts & accessories

(G-11839)
INNOVATIVE SHEET METALS LLC
1681 S Wolf Lake Rd (49442-4839)
PHONE..................................231 788-5751
Andrew Stevens, *Principal*
EMP: 14 EST: 2016
SALES (est): 2.5MM **Privately Held**
WEB: www.innovativesheetmetals.com
SIC: 3444 Sheet metalwork

(G-11840)
INNOVATIVE WOODWORKING
748 E Bard Rd (49445-9532)
PHONE..................................616 638-1139
Andrew Tufts, *President*
EMP: 4 EST: 2017
SALES (est): 69.4K **Privately Held**
SIC: 2431 Millwork

(G-11841)
INTEGRATED CONVEYOR LTD
301 W Laketon Ave (49441-2629)
PHONE..................................231 747-6430
Dick Perri, *President*
Joe Garzolonie, *Manager*
EMP: 4 EST: 2000
SALES (est): 473.1K **Privately Held**
WEB: www.integratedconveyor.com
SIC: 3535 5084 Conveyors & conveying equipment; industrial machinery & equipment

(G-11842)
ITT GAGE INC
3253 Whitehall Rd (49445-1061)
PHONE..................................231 766-2155
EMP: 11 EST: 2015
SALES (est): 582K **Privately Held**
SIC: 3544 Special dies & tools

(G-11843)
J & J MACHINE LTD
3011 S Milliron Rd (49444-3689)
PHONE..................................231 773-4100
Joseph Hammerle, *President*
John Hammerle, *Vice Pres*
EMP: 10 EST: 1997
SQ FT: 3,300 **Privately Held**
WEB: www.jjmachine99.com
SIC: 3599 Machine shop, jobbing & repair; machine & other job shop work

(G-11844)
JBS SHEET METAL INC
2226 S Getty St (49444-1208)
PHONE..................................231 777-2802
Steven Six, *President*
Bryan Six, *Vice Pres*
EMP: 14 EST: 1990
SALES (est): 480.1K **Privately Held**
SIC: 3444 Ducts, sheet metal

(G-11845)
JET FUEL
Also Called: Muskegon Gas and Fuel
2177 S Mill Iron Rd (49442-6445)
PHONE..................................231 767-9566
M Athar, *Manager*
EMP: 9 EST: 2010
SALES (est): 983.9K **Privately Held**
SIC: 2911 Jet fuels

(G-11846)
JOHNSON TECHNOLOGY INC
Also Called: GE Aviation
2034 Latimer Dr (49442-6232)
PHONE..................................231 777-2685
Kevin J Prindable, *President*
EMP: 1 EST: 1993
SALES (est): 3.9MM
SALES (corp-wide): 79.6B **Publicly Held**
SIC: 3724 Aircraft engines & engine parts
HQ: Johnson Technology, Inc.
2034 Latimer Dr
Muskegon MI 49442

(G-11847)
JOHNSON TECHNOLOGY INC (DH)
Also Called: GE Aviation Muskegon
2034 Latimer Dr (49442-6232)
PHONE..................................231 777-2685
Kevin Prindable, *President*
Cheryl Payne, *Opers Staff*
Brad Buzzell, *Engineer*
Melvin Eacker, *Engineer*
Brandon Hartman, *Engineer*
▲ EMP: 345 EST: 1962
SQ FT: 101,000
SALES (est): 150.2MM
SALES (corp-wide): 79.6B **Publicly Held**
WEB: www.geaviation.com
SIC: 3724 Turbines, aircraft type
HQ: Ge Aircraft Engines Holdings, Inc.
1 Aviation Way
Cincinnati OH 45215
888 999-5103

(G-11848)
JOLMAN & JOLMAN ENTERPRISES
1384 Linden Dr (49445-2524)
PHONE..................................231 744-4500
Daniel Jolman, *Owner*
EMP: 6 EST: 2008
SALES (est): 50K **Privately Held**
SIC: 0782 3531 4971 Lawn care services; snow plow attachments; irrigation systems

(G-11849)
JONES ELECTRIC COMPANY
1965 Sanford St (49441-2516)
P.O. Box 785 (49443-0785)
PHONE..................................231 726-5001
Rodney Dobb, *President*
EMP: 21 EST: 1977
SQ FT: 9,000
SALES (est): 1.8MM **Privately Held**
WEB: www.halljones.us
SIC: 7694 7629 Electric motor repair; electrical repair shops

(G-11850)
KAUTEX INC
CWC Textron
1085 W Sherman Blvd (49441-3500)
PHONE..................................231 739-2704
Jim Heethuis, *Branch Mgr*
EMP: 275
SALES (corp-wide): 11.6B **Publicly Held**
WEB: www.kautex.com
SIC: 3714 Camshafts, motor vehicle
HQ: Kautex Inc.
800 Tower Dr Ste 200
Troy MI 48098
248 616-5100

(G-11851)
KL COMPANIES INC
1790 Sun Dolphin Rd (49444-1800)
PHONE..................................231 332-1700
Robert Farber, *President*
Dave Baun, *Vice Pres*
EMP: 70 EST: 2020

SALES (est): 8.3MM **Privately Held**
SIC: 3732 Boat building & repairing; canoes, building & repairing; kayaks, building & repairing

(G-11852)
KRAUSE WELDING INC
4350 Evanston Ave (49442-6523)
PHONE..................................231 773-4443
Brian Krause, *CEO*
Berl W Krause, *President*
David K Krause, *Vice Pres*
Cheryl K Krause, *Treasurer*
EMP: 10 EST: 1979
SQ FT: 8,000
SALES (est): 621.6K **Privately Held**
SIC: 7692 Automotive welding

(G-11853)
L & L PATTERN INC
2401 Park St (49444-1393)
PHONE..................................231 733-2646
Robert C Oosting, *President*
William K Oosting, *Corp Secy*
EMP: 8 EST: 1944
SQ FT: 4,000
SALES (est): 979.8K **Privately Held**
SIC: 3543 3599 3366 Industrial patterns; machine & other job shop work; castings (except die)

(G-11854)
L & P LLC
Also Called: Fun Foods
2376 Dels Dr (49444-2676)
PHONE..................................231 733-1415
Lisa Kordecki,
Patti Derouin,
EMP: 5 EST: 1988
SQ FT: 3,800
SALES (est): 450.4K **Privately Held**
WEB: www.funfoodsmi.com
SIC: 5199 2099 General merchandise, non-durable; ready-to-eat meals, salads & sandwiches; pizza, refrigerated: except frozen

(G-11855)
LAFARGE NORTH AMERICA INC
1047 7th St (49441-1604)
PHONE..................................231 726-3291
EMP: 4
SALES (corp-wide): 25.3B **Privately Held**
WEB: www.lafarge-na.com
SIC: 3273 3271 1442 2951 Ready-mixed concrete; concrete block & brick; construction sand & gravel; asphalt paving mixtures & blocks; cement, hydraulic
HQ: Lafarge North America Inc.
8700 W Bryn Mawr Ave # 30
Chicago IL 60631
773 372-1000

(G-11856)
LAKE MICHIGAN CANDLES LLC
5282 Bittersweet Dr (49445-8835)
PHONE..................................231 766-0412
Kelly Clark, *Principal*
EMP: 4 EST: 2014
SALES (est): 61.4K **Privately Held**
SIC: 3999 Candles

(G-11857)
LAKESIDE CANVAS & UPHOLSTERY
3200 Lakeshore Dr (49441-1292)
PHONE..................................231 755-2514
Joe Vanlente, *President*
Elizabeth Vanlente, *Vice Pres*
EMP: 4 EST: 1979
SALES (est): 383.1K **Privately Held**
WEB: www.lakesidecanvas1.com
SIC: 7532 2394 Top & body repair & paint shops; canvas & related products

(G-11858)
LAKESIDE SPRING LLC
2615 Temple St (49444-1937)
PHONE..................................616 847-2706
Jacob Veltman Jr,
EMP: 9 EST: 2017
SALES (est): 763.8K **Privately Held**
WEB: www.lakesidespring.com
SIC: 3599 Machine shop, jobbing & repair

GEOGRAPHIC SECTION

Muskegon - Muskegon County (G-11885)

(G-11859)
LEGACY CANVAS & UPHOLSTERY LLC
2066 Poplar Ct (49445-1715)
PHONE..................................231 578-9972
Travis Auger, *Principal*
EMP: 4 **EST:** 2015
SALES (est): 59.4K Privately Held
SIC: 2211 Canvas

(G-11860)
LEVEL 6
1991 Lakeshore Dr Unit B (49441-1644)
PHONE..................................231 755-7000
Joe Lalonde, *Owner*
EMP: 7 **EST:** 2010
SALES (est): 174.6K Privately Held
WEB: www.level6.com
SIC: 3949 Skateboards

(G-11861)
LORIN INDUSTRIES INC (PA)
Also Called: Coil Anodizing
1960 Roberts Dr (49442-6087)
PHONE..................................231 722-1631
Park Kersman, *CEO*
Robert L Kersman, *Ch of Bd*
L Philip Kelly, *Corp Secy*
John Montague, *Vice Pres*
Jason Locke, *Opers Mgr*
◆ **EMP:** 87 **EST:** 1943
SQ FT: 300,000
SALES (est): 30.6MM Privately Held
WEB: www.lorin.com
SIC: 3354 Aluminum extruded products

(G-11862)
LUMBERTOWN PORTABLE SAWMILL
1650 Madison St (49442-5945)
PHONE..................................231 206-4600
EMP: 4 **EST:** 2011
SALES (est): 80K Privately Held
SIC: 3559 Kilns

(G-11863)
M 37 CONCRETE PRODUCTS INC (PA)
Also Called: High Grade Concrete Pdts Co
767 E Sherman Blvd (49444-2254)
PHONE..................................231 733-8247
Thomas J Sturrus, *President*
EMP: 20 **EST:** 1971
SQ FT: 5,000
SALES (est): 5.7MM Privately Held
SIC: 3273 Ready-mixed concrete

(G-11864)
MAHLE INDUSTRIES INCORPORATED
1883 E Laketon Ave (49442-6123)
PHONE..................................248 305-8200
Keiya Kimishima, *Engineer*
Roman Somin, *Sales Staff*
EMP: 151
SALES (corp-wide): 504.6K Privately Held
WEB: www.mahle.com
SIC: 3714 Bearings, motor vehicle
HQ: Mahle Industries, Incorporated
23030 Mahle Dr
Farmington Hills MI 48335

(G-11865)
MEGHAN MARCH LLC
3385 Verna Ave (49442-6417)
PHONE..................................231 740-8114
Angela Smith,
EMP: 4 **EST:** 2018
SALES (est): 85K Privately Held
WEB: www.meghanmarch.com
SIC: 2731 Books: publishing & printing

(G-11866)
MERCY HEALTH PARTNERS (DH)
1675 Leahy St Ste 101 (49442-5538)
PHONE..................................231 728-4032
Richard C Lague, *Ch of Bd*
Gordon A Mudler, *President*
John Stalzer, *Fire Chief*
Toni Pruitt, *Business Mgr*
David Gingras, *Vice Pres*
EMP: 85 **EST:** 1984
SQ FT: 100,000
SALES: 666MM
SALES (corp-wide): 18.8B Privately Held
WEB: www.mercyhealth.com
SIC: 8741 6512 3812 Hospital management; nursing & personal care facility management; nonresidential building operators; compasses & accessories
HQ: Trinity Health-Michigan
20555 Victor Pkwy
Livonia MI 48152
810 985-1500

(G-11867)
MERCY HEALTH PARTNERS
Also Called: Orthotics and Prosthetics
1560 E Sherman Blvd # 145 (49444-1850)
PHONE..................................231 672-4886
Gary Allore, *CFO*
Sharon Christian, *Internal Med*
EMP: 31
SALES (corp-wide): 18.8B Privately Held
WEB: www.mercyhealth.com
SIC: 3842 Surgical appliances & supplies
HQ: Mercy Health Partners
1675 Leahy St Ste 101
Muskegon MI 49442
231 728-4032

(G-11868)
METAL ARC INC
3792 E Ellis Rd (49444-8764)
PHONE..................................231 865-3111
Ray Gerdes, *President*
Eric Weller, *Engineer*
Denise Karel, *Office Mgr*
Shannon Conaty, *Manager*
Gregory Gerdes, *Admin Sec*
▲ **EMP:** 28 **EST:** 1969
SQ FT: 47,000
SALES (est): 4.7MM Privately Held
WEB: www.metalarcinc.com
SIC: 3599 3821 2522 Machine shop, jobbing & repair; laboratory furniture; office furniture, except wood

(G-11869)
METAL FINISHING TECHNOLOGY
2652 Hoyt St (49444-2142)
PHONE..................................231 733-9736
David Bernd, *President*
EMP: 5 **EST:** 1996
SALES (est): 914.7K Privately Held
WEB: www.metalfinishingtec.com
SIC: 3479 3471 Coating of metals & formed products; plating & polishing

(G-11870)
MICHIGAN INDUS MET PDTS INC
1674 S Getty St (49442-5857)
PHONE..................................616 786-3922
Maryann Griffin, *President*
John J Griffin, *General Mgr*
EMP: 16 **EST:** 1985
SALES (est): 775.9K Privately Held
SIC: 3441 1542 Fabricated structural metal; nonresidential construction

(G-11871)
MICHIGAN SPRING & STAMPING LLC (DH)
2700 Wickham Dr (49441-3532)
PHONE..................................231 755-1691
Bir Singh, *President*
Dan Wallington, *President*
Jeff Stewart, *Business Mgr*
Geoff Twietmeyer, *Vice Pres*
Paul Vanderlaan, *VP Opers*
▲ **EMP:** 110 **EST:** 2008
SALES: 37MM
SALES (corp-wide): 694.7M Privately Held
WEB: www.msands.com
SIC: 3495 Mechanical springs, precision
HQ: Kern-Liebers Usa, Inc.
1510 Albon Rd
Holland OH 43528
419 865-2437

(G-11872)
MID-WEST SPRING & STAMPING INC
1935 E Laketon Ave (49442-6125)
PHONE..................................231 777-2707
Jeff Kamp, *General Mgr*
Yvonne Dillon, *Human Res Mgr*
EMP: 73
SQ FT: 50,000
SALES (corp-wide): 31.2MM Privately Held
WEB: www.mwspring.com
SIC: 3495 3496 3493 Wire springs; miscellaneous fabricated wire products; steel springs, except wire
HQ: Spring Mid-West And Stamping Inc
1404 N Joliet Rd Ste C
Romeoville IL 60446
630 739-3800

(G-11873)
MID-WEST SPRING MFG CO
1935 E Laketon Ave (49442-6125)
PHONE..................................231 777-2707
Yvonne Dillon, *Office Mgr*
EMP: 10 **EST:** 2018
SALES (est): 821.9K Privately Held
WEB: www.mwspring.com
SIC: 3495 Wire springs

(G-11874)
MIDWEST PRODUCT SPC INC
2190 Aurora Dr (49442-6295)
PHONE..................................231 767-9942
Michael Snyder, *President*
Michone E Snyder, *Vice Pres*
▲ **EMP:** 6 **EST:** 1994
SALES (est): 667.3K Privately Held
SIC: 3297 Nonclay refractories

(G-11875)
MLIVECOM
981 3rd St (49440-1236)
PHONE..................................231 725-6343
Mike Mattson, *Manager*
EMP: 6 **EST:** 2015
SALES (est): 67.9K Privately Held
SIC: 2711 Newspapers, publishing & printing

(G-11876)
MONARCH WELDING & ENGRG INC
519 W Hackley Ave (49444-1045)
PHONE..................................231 733-7222
Johan Bartels, *Branch Mgr*
EMP: 20
SALES (corp-wide): 15.1MM Privately Held
WEB: www.monarchwelding.com
SIC: 1711 7692 3444 Mechanical contractor; boiler & furnace contractors; welding repair; sheet metalwork
PA: Monarch Welding & Engineering, Inc.
23635 Mound Rd
Warren MI 48091
586 754-5400

(G-11877)
MONROES CUSTOM CAMPERS INC
Also Called: Monroe Truck and Auto ACC
2915 E Apple Ave (49442-4503)
PHONE..................................231 773-0005
Nicholas Monroe, *President*
Michael Monroe, *Vice Pres*
Nick Monroe, *Manager*
EMP: 18 **EST:** 1967
SQ FT: 20,000
SALES (est): 1.4MM Privately Held
WEB: www.monroestore.com
SIC: 3792 5531 Campers, for mounting on trucks; pickup covers, canopies or caps; automotive & home supply stores

(G-11878)
MR AXLE
6336 E Apple Ave (49442-4974)
PHONE..................................231 788-4624
Mike Crowell, *Owner*
EMP: 5 **EST:** 1986
SQ FT: 2,800
SALES (est): 472K Privately Held
WEB: www.mraxleautorepair.com
SIC: 3714 5531 5015 Axles, motor vehicle; automotive parts; automotive parts & supplies, used

(G-11879)
MUSKEGON AWNING & MFG CO
2333 Henry St (49441-3097)
PHONE..................................231 759-0911
David Bayne, *President*
Ruth Luker, *Corp Secy*
Gordon Moen, *Vice Pres*
Jeffrey Lindell, *Sales Staff*
EMP: 25 **EST:** 1898
SQ FT: 14,196
SALES (est): 1.5MM Privately Held
WEB: www.muskegonawning.com
SIC: 2394 3444 2591 Awnings, fabric: made from purchased materials; canvas covers & drop cloths; sheet metalwork; drapery hardware & blinds & shades

(G-11880)
MUSKEGON CHARTER TOWNSHIP FIRE
265 N Mararebecah Ln (49442-1576)
PHONE..................................231 329-3068
Lindsay Theile, *Treasurer*
Juanita Bunker, *Admin Sec*
EMP: 7 **EST:** 2018
SALES (est): 88.3K Privately Held
WEB: www.muskegontwp.org
SIC: 3699 Electrical equipment & supplies

(G-11881)
MUSKEGON INDUSTRIAL FINISHNG
2000 Sanford St (49444-1000)
PHONE..................................231 733-7663
EMP: 5
SALES (est): 436.3K Privately Held
SIC: 3471 Plating/Polishing Service

(G-11882)
MUSKEGON MONUMENT & STONE CO
Also Called: Designs In Stones
1396 Pine St (49442-3599)
PHONE..................................231 722-2730
James Bauer, *President*
EMP: 5 **EST:** 1901
SQ FT: 5,000
SALES (est): 465.1K Privately Held
WEB: www.muskegonmonument.com
SIC: 3281 5999 1743 Monuments, cut stone (not finishing or lettering only); stone, quarrying & processing of own stone products; monuments, finished to custom order; monuments & tombstones; terrazzo, tile, marble, mosaic work

(G-11883)
MUSKEGON TOOLS LLC
5142 Evanston Ave (49442-4852)
PHONE..................................231 788-4633
Mark Fazakerley,
Mike Coffey,
Wayne Jarvis,
John Workman,
EMP: 4
SALES (est): 250K Privately Held
WEB: www.muskegontools.com
SIC: 3423 Wrenches, hand tools

(G-11884)
NEW GLDC LLC
Also Called: Great Lakes Die Cast
1940 Henry St (49441-2940)
PHONE..................................989 879-4009
Robert Wolford,
EMP: 12 **EST:** 2018
SALES (est): 1.8MM Privately Held
SIC: 3599 Machine shop, jobbing & repair

(G-11885)
NEW GLDC LLC
Also Called: Great Lakes Die Cast
701 W Laketon Ave (49441-2925)
PHONE..................................231 726-4002
David Jaeger, *President*
Phil Mumford Sr,
EMP: 70 **EST:** 2018
SQ FT: 105,000
SALES (est): 2.5MM Privately Held
SIC: 3363 3089 Aluminum die-castings; injection molded finished plastic products

Muskegon - Muskegon County (G-11886) — GEOGRAPHIC SECTION

(G-11886)
NU TEK SALES PARTS INC
2051 Harvey St (49442-6102)
PHONE............................616 258-0631
Doug Watkoski, *CEO*
EMP: 10 **EST:** 2010
SALES (est): 977.7K **Privately Held**
WEB: www.nuteksales.com
SIC: 3672 Circuit boards, television & radio printed

(G-11887)
ORION MACHINE INC
392 Irwin Ave (49442-5008)
PHONE............................231 728-1229
George R Zukiewicz, *President*
EMP: 5 **EST:** 1981
SQ FT: 10,800
SALES (est): 471.7K **Privately Held**
SIC: 3599 Machine shop, jobbing & repair

(G-11888)
PACE INDUSTRIES LLC
Also Called: Port City Die Cast
2121 Latimer Dr (49442-6233)
PHONE............................231 777-3941
Mark Pickett, *Branch Mgr*
EMP: 7
SALES (corp-wide): 682.5MM **Privately Held**
WEB: www.paceind.com
SIC: 3363 Aluminum die-castings
HQ: Pace Industries, Llc
   481 S Shiloh Dr
   Fayetteville AR 72704
   479 443-1455

(G-11889)
PACE INDUSTRIES LLC
Also Called: Port City Custom Plastics
1868 Port City Blvd (49442-6130)
PHONE............................231 773-4491
EMP: 7
SALES (corp-wide): 682.5MM **Privately Held**
WEB: www.paceind.com
SIC: 3363 Aluminum die-castings
HQ: Pace Industries, Llc
   481 S Shiloh Dr
   Fayetteville AR 72704
   479 443-1455

(G-11890)
PACE INDUSTRIES LLC
Port City Group
1985 E Laketon Ave (49442-6127)
PHONE............................231 777-3941
Dale Keyser, *VP Finance*
John Essex, *Branch Mgr*
James Granger, *Program Mgr*
Heather Reed, *Director*
EMP: 5
SALES (corp-wide): 682.5MM **Privately Held**
WEB: www.paceind.com
SIC: 3542 3089 Die casting & extruding machines; casting of plastic
HQ: Pace Industries, Llc
   481 S Shiloh Dr
   Fayetteville AR 72704
   479 443-1455

(G-11891)
PACE INDUSTRIES LLC
Also Called: Port City Metal Products
2350 Black Creek Rd (49444-2672)
PHONE............................231 777-5615
Mark Pickett, *Branch Mgr*
EMP: 10
SALES (corp-wide): 682.5MM **Privately Held**
WEB: www.paceind.com
SIC: 3363 Aluminum die-castings
HQ: Pace Industries, Llc
   481 S Shiloh Dr
   Fayetteville AR 72704
   479 443-1455

(G-11892)
PACIFIC STAMEX CLG SYSTEMS INC
2259 S Sheridan Dr (49442-6252)
PHONE............................231 773-1330
Larry W Hines, *CEO*
Dave Nelson, *President*
Grant Cheney, *Vice Pres*
Greg Wiese, *Vice Pres*
Jeff Oberlin, *Opers Dir*
◆ **EMP:** 26 **EST:** 1953
SQ FT: 36,000
SALES (est): 6.5MM
SALES (corp-wide): 177.4MM **Privately Held**
WEB: www.pacificfloorcare.com
SIC: 3589 Floor washing & polishing machines, commercial
PA: Hines Corporation
   1218 E Pontaluna Rd Ste B
   Norton Shores MI 49456
   231 799-6240

(G-11893)
PARK STREET MACHINE INC
2201 Park St (49444-1324)
PHONE............................231 739-9165
Joel Kowalski, *President*
EMP: 19 **EST:** 1983
SQ FT: 50,000
SALES (est): 3.9MM **Privately Held**
WEB: www.parkstreetmachine.com
SIC: 3599 3544 Custom machinery; special dies, tools, jigs & fixtures

(G-11894)
PORT CITY INDUSTRIAL FINISHING
1867 Huizenga St (49442-5900)
PHONE............................231 726-4288
Eric G Fri, *President*
EMP: 41 **EST:** 1951
SQ FT: 40,000
SALES (est): 5.1MM **Privately Held**
SIC: 3471 Finishing, metals or formed products

(G-11895)
PORT CITY PAINTS MFG INC
Also Called: Benjamin Moore Authorized Ret
1250 9th St (49440-1092)
PHONE............................231 726-5911
Jerry Klinger, *President*
Roy Spencer, *Admin Sec*
EMP: 6 **EST:** 1940
SQ FT: 20,000
SALES (est): 540.6K **Privately Held**
WEB: www.benjaminmoore.com
SIC: 5231 2851 Paint; paints: oil or alkyd vehicle or water thinned; varnishes

(G-11896)
PORT CY ARCHTCTRAL SIGNAGE LLC
2350 S Getty St (49444-1702)
PHONE............................231 739-3463
Tim Mills, *Mng Member*
Murdock Mills,
▲ **EMP:** 6 **EST:** 2006
SALES (est): 918K **Privately Held**
WEB: www.portcitysignage.com
SIC: 3993 Signs, not made in custom sign painting shops

(G-11897)
PORTER STEEL & WELDING COMPANY
831 E Hovey Ave (49444-1794)
PHONE............................231 733-4495
Robert L Smith, *President*
EMP: 10 **EST:** 1947
SQ FT: 20,000
SALES (est): 964.6K **Privately Held**
WEB: www.portersteelweld.com
SIC: 3449 7692 Custom roll formed products; welding repair

(G-11898)
PRECISION TOOL COMPANY INC
2839 Henry St (49441-4011)
PHONE............................231 733-0811
David A Reck, *President*
Franklin Zadonick, *Vice Pres*
EMP: 32 **EST:** 1942
SQ FT: 12,200
SALES (est): 4.6MM **Privately Held**
WEB: www.precisiontoolinc.com
SIC: 3545 3544 Cutting tools for machine tools; jigs: inspection, gauging & checking

(G-11899)
PRK HOLDINGS INC
1485 S Getty St (49442-5103)
PHONE............................231 728-1155
EMP: 38
SQ FT: 27,000
SALES (est): 6.5MM **Privately Held**
SIC: 3599 Mfg Industrial Machinery
HQ: Waseyabek Development Company, L.L.C.
   16 Monroe Center St Ne # 200
   Grand Rapids MI 49503
   616 278-0320

(G-11900)
PRODUCTION FABRICATORS INC
Also Called: Profab
1608 Creston St (49442-6012)
PHONE............................231 777-3822
Patrick Bauer, *President*
Michael Bauer, *Corp Secy*
Jordan Hoofman, *Plant Mgr*
Mark Vanappel, *Purch Dir*
Rose Dixon, *Manager*
▲ **EMP:** 30 **EST:** 1987
SQ FT: 30,000
SALES (est): 8.2MM **Privately Held**
WEB: www.profablaser.com
SIC: 3496 3542 3469 3444 Miscellaneous fabricated wire products; machine tools, metal forming type; metal stampings; sheet metalwork; fabricated plate work (boiler shop); fabricated structural metal

(G-11901)
QUALITY PALLET INC
Also Called: Peregrine Wood Products
7220 Hall Rd (49442-9408)
PHONE............................231 788-5161
Corky Williams, *President*
EMP: 4 **EST:** 1968
SALES (est): 789.4K **Privately Held**
SIC: 2448 Pallets, wood

(G-11902)
QUALITY TOOL & STAMPING CO INC
Also Called: Qts
541 E Sherman Blvd (49444-2277)
PHONE............................231 733-2538
Edward Kuznar, *President*
Ed Kuznar, *President*
Dan Kuznar, *Vice Pres*
Mike Kuznar, *Plant Mgr*
Kurt Kastelic, *Engineer*
▲ **EMP:** 112 **EST:** 1957
SQ FT: 80,000
SALES (est): 22.1MM **Privately Held**
WEB: www.qtstamping.com
SIC: 3469 Stamping metal for the trade

(G-11903)
QWIK TOOL & MFG INC
480 W Hume Ave (49444-1386)
PHONE............................231 739-8849
EMP: 4
SALES (est): 350K **Privately Held**
SIC: 3544 Manufactures Special Dies Tools Die Sets Jigs Fixtures Or Molds

(G-11904)
R J WOODWORKING INC
3108 Whitehall Rd (49445-1060)
PHONE............................231 766-2511
Robert J Carter Jr, *President*
Kay L Carter, *Corp Secy*
Tonya Hayes, *Administration*
EMP: 22 **EST:** 1978
SQ FT: 32,000
SALES (est): 1.3MM **Privately Held**
WEB: www.rjwoodworking.com
SIC: 2431 Millwork

(G-11905)
RAVENNA SEALCOATING INC
1120 S Mill Iron Rd (49442-4640)
PHONE............................231 766-0571
EMP: 6 **EST:** 2019
SALES (est): 326.8K **Privately Held**
WEB: www.sealcoatservicesin-muskegonmi.com
SIC: 2952 Asphalt felts & coatings

(G-11906)
REAL STEEL MANUFACTURING LLC
304 W Delano Ave (49444-1003)
PHONE............................231 457-4673
Rick Terpstra, *Owner*
EMP: 10 **EST:** 2015
SALES (est): 623.7K **Privately Held**
WEB: www.realsteelmanufacturing.com
SIC: 3999 Manufacturing industries

(G-11907)
RENK AMERICA LLC ○
Also Called: L-3 Combat Propulsion Systems
76 S Getty St (49442-1242)
PHONE............................231 724-2666
Ted Trzesniowski, *Mng Member*
EMP: 99 **EST:** 2021
SALES (est): 25.9MM
SALES (corp-wide): 166.7K **Privately Held**
WEB: www.renk-group.com
SIC: 3795 Tanks & tank components
HQ: Renk Gmbh
   Gogginger Str. 73
   Augsburg BY 86159
   821 570-00

(G-11908)
REPAIRERS OF THE BRACH MSKEGON
1124 Williams St (49442-3943)
P.O. Box 602 (49443-0602)
PHONE............................231 375-0990
Walter Carr, *CEO*
Charissa Carr, *Principal*
EMP: 10 **EST:** 2017
SALES (est): 546.2K **Privately Held**
SIC: 7379 2326 ; service apparel (baker, barber, lab, etc.), washable: men's

(G-11909)
ROE LLC
Also Called: Women Lifestyle Northshore
1446 Randolph Ave (49441-3133)
PHONE............................231 755-5043
Jenni Naffie, *President*
EMP: 5 **EST:** 2005
SALES (est): 248.6K **Privately Held**
WEB: www.sigstadchiropractic.com
SIC: 2721 Magazines: publishing only, not printed on site

(G-11910)
ROGER D RAPOPORT
Also Called: Rdr Books
1487 Glen Ave (49441-3101)
P.O. Box 1231 (49443-1231)
PHONE............................231 755-6665
Roger Rapoport, *Owner*
EMP: 4
SALES (est): 170.4K **Privately Held**
SIC: 2731 Book publishing

(G-11911)
RSI OF WEST MICHIGAN LLC
1485 S Getty St (49442-5103)
PHONE............................231 728-1155
James A Tenbrink, *President*
EMP: 50 **EST:** 2020
SALES (est): 4.1MM **Privately Held**
SIC: 3599 Industrial machinery

(G-11912)
S & M LOGGING LLC
2131 Debaker Rd (49442-6355)
PHONE............................231 830-7317
Nancy Sundberg, *Principal*
EMP: 4 **EST:** 2016
SALES (est): 65.4K **Privately Held**
SIC: 2411 Logging camps & contractors

(G-11913)
SAF-HOLLAND INC (DH)
Also Called: Saf-Holland USA
1950 Industrial Blvd (49442-6114)
P.O. Box 425 (49443-0425)
PHONE............................231 773-3271
Steffen Schewerda, *President*
Ken Shepherd, *Regional Mgr*
Barbara Debruyn, *Vice Pres*
Jack Gisinger, *Vice Pres*
Bill Kindt, *Plant Mgr*
◆ **EMP:** 580 **EST:** 1921
SQ FT: 18,000

GEOGRAPHIC SECTION
Muskegon - Muskegon County (G-11940)

SALES (est): 157.9MM
SALES (corp-wide): 1.1B **Privately Held**
WEB: www.safholland.us
SIC: **3715** 3568 3537 3452 Truck trailers; power transmission equipment; industrial trucks & tractors; bolts, nuts, rivets & washers; trailer hitches, motor vehicle

(G-11914)
SAFARI SIGNS
771 Access Hwy (49442-1236)
PHONE.................................231 727-9200
EMP: 6 EST: 2008
SALES (est): 106K **Privately Held**
WEB: www.safarisigns.com
SIC: **3993** Signs, not made in custom sign painting shops

(G-11915)
SAFFE FURNITURE CORP
200 Viridian Dr (49440-1141)
PHONE.................................231 329-1790
Brandon Gerard, *CEO*
EMP: 5 EST: 2019
SALES (est): 267.1K **Privately Held**
WEB: www.saffefurniture.com
SIC: **3999** Manufacturing industries

(G-11916)
SCHERDEL SALES & TECH INC (DH)
3440 E Laketon Ave (49442-6438)
PHONE.................................231 777-7774
Sander Schoof, *CEO*
Sander Schoos, *President*
Rolf Shumacher, *President*
Yewei Jiang, *Engineer*
Margaret Alexander, *CFO*
▲ EMP: 153 EST: 1996
SQ FT: 22,500
SALES (est): 41.7MM
SALES (corp-wide): 3MM **Privately Held**
WEB: www.scherdel.com
SIC: **3495** Wire springs
HQ: Scherdel Gmbh
Scherdelstr. 2
Marktredwitz 95615
923 160-30

(G-11917)
SECURITY STEELCRAFT CORP
2636 Sanford St (49444-2007)
P.O. Box 118 (49443-0118)
PHONE.................................231 733-1101
Stanley L Horness, *President*
Beth Hudson, *Admin Sec*
EMP: 16 EST: 1954
SQ FT: 73,000
SALES (est): 665.7K **Privately Held**
SIC: **3821** 3444 Laboratory furniture; laboratory equipment: fume hoods, distillation racks, etc.; sheet metalwork; sheet metal specialties, not stamped; cowls or scoops, air (ship ventilators): sheet metal

(G-11918)
SHOE SHOP
Also Called: West Michigan Pedorthics
3324 Glade St (49444-2708)
PHONE.................................231 739-2174
John Yarrington, *Owner*
EMP: 4 EST: 1995
SQ FT: 8,000
SALES (est): 381.6K **Privately Held**
WEB: www.shoeshopmi.com
SIC: **3143** Orthopedic shoes, men's

(G-11919)
SHORELINE MTAL FABRICATORS INC
1880 Park St (49441-2638)
PHONE.................................231 722-4443
Gary Bird, *President*
Andy Fessenden, *Project Mgr*
Sandy Bird, *Office Mgr*
Gary B Bird, *Manager*
EMP: 30 EST: 1996
SQ FT: 9,000
SALES (est): 4.5MM **Privately Held**
WEB: www.slmfab.com
SIC: **3441** Fabricated structural metal

(G-11920)
SHORELINE RECYCLING & SUPPLY
259 Ottawa St (49442-1008)
PHONE.................................231 722-6081
Jeffrey Padnos, *President*
John Jones, *Vice Pres*
EMP: 22 EST: 1916
SALES (est): 273K **Privately Held**
WEB: www.padnos.com
SIC: **5093** 3341 3312 Ferrous metal scrap & waste; secondary nonferrous metals; blast furnaces & steel mills

(G-11921)
SHORT IRON FABRICATION
2861 S Milliron Rd (49444-3686)
PHONE.................................231 375-8825
EMP: 9 EST: 2019
SALES (est): 2.5MM **Privately Held**
WEB: www.shortironfab.com
SIC: **3441** Fabricated structural metal

(G-11922)
SIGN CABINETS INC
2000 9th St (49444-1081)
PHONE.................................231 725-7187
Georg Michael Abraham, *President*
Mike Abraham, *President*
Patrick Abraham, *Office Mgr*
EMP: 4 EST: 1986
SQ FT: 10,000
SALES (est): 746.7K **Privately Held**
WEB: www.signcabinetsinc.com
SIC: **3354** Shapes, extruded aluminum

(G-11923)
SIGNCRAFTERS INC
2325 Black Creek Rd (49444-2673)
PHONE.................................231 773-3343
Steven Carlson, *President*
Vicki Carlson, *Vice Pres*
EMP: 4 EST: 1986
SQ FT: 5,400
SALES (est): 500K **Privately Held**
WEB: www.signcraftersinc.biz
SIC: **3993** Signs, not made in custom sign painting shops

(G-11924)
SPEC ABRASIVES AND FINISHING
Also Called: Spec Abrassive
543 W Southern Ave (49441-2323)
PHONE.................................231 722-1926
Larry Anderson, *President*
EMP: 14 EST: 1984
SQ FT: 9,500
SALES (est): 1.9MM **Privately Held**
SIC: **3471** Sand blasting of metal parts; finishing, metals or formed products

(G-11925)
SRS FIBERGLASS PRODUCTS LLC
1041 E Keating Ave (49442-5961)
PHONE.................................231 747-6839
Steve Bradish, *Mng Member*
EMP: 60 EST: 2009
SALES (est): 8.7MM **Privately Held**
WEB: www.srsfiberglass.com
SIC: **2221** Fiberglass fabrics

(G-11926)
SUN CHEMICAL CORPORATION
5025 Evanston Ave (49442-4899)
PHONE.................................513 681-5950
Felipe Mellado, *Vice Pres*
Brian Martinez, *Sales Staff*
Steve Ferski, *Branch Mgr*
Clay Pinkett, *Technician*
▲ EMP: 17 **Privately Held**
WEB: www.sunchemical.com
SIC: **2893** Printing ink
HQ: Sun Chemical Corporation
35 Waterview Blvd Ste 100
Parsippany NJ 07054
973 404-6000

(G-11927)
SUN CHEMICAL CORPORATION
Pigments Division
5025 Evanston Ave (49442-4899)
PHONE.................................231 788-2371
Thom Bolen, *Vice Pres*
Bernard Sengimana, *Branch Mgr*
Henry Austhof, *Admin Mgr*
EMP: 125 **Privately Held**
WEB: www.sunchemical.com
SIC: **2816** 2865 Inorganic pigments; cyclic crudes & intermediates
HQ: Sun Chemical Corporation
35 Waterview Blvd Ste 100
Parsippany NJ 07054
973 404-6000

(G-11928)
SUPERIOR MONUMENTS CO (PA)
354 Ottawa St (49442-1033)
PHONE.................................231 728-2211
David Sietsema, *President*
Nancy Sietsema, *Treasurer*
EMP: 7 EST: 1986
SALES (est): 860.3K **Privately Held**
WEB: www.superiormonument.com
SIC: **5999** 3272 3281 Monuments, finished to custom order; monuments & tombstones; monuments & grave markers, except terrazo; cut stone & stone products

(G-11929)
T Q MACHINING INC
450 W Hackley Ave (49442-1032)
PHONE.................................231 726-5914
John Dyer Sr, *President*
Jack Smith, *Vice Pres*
Jason Dyer, *Mfg Staff*
Matt Anderson, *Project Engr*
Lori Burns, *Manager*
EMP: 20 EST: 1991
SQ FT: 48,000
SALES (est): 2.4MM **Privately Held**
WEB: www.tqmachine.com
SIC: **3599** Machine shop, jobbing & repair

(G-11930)
TERRELL MANUFACTURING SVCS INC
7245 Hall Rd (49442-9408)
PHONE.................................231 788-2000
Terry Williams, *CEO*
Logan Weesies, *Engineer*
EMP: 16 EST: 2002
SQ FT: 8,000
SALES (est): 2.5MM **Privately Held**
WEB: www.terrellmanufacturing.com
SIC: **3569** 8711 Liquid automation machinery & equipment; machine tool design; industrial engineers

(G-11931)
TFI INC
Also Called: Thompson Fabrication Inds
2620 Park St (49444-1936)
PHONE.................................231 728-2310
Mark Thompson, *President*
Nathan Fillmore, *Project Mgr*
EMP: 23 EST: 2003
SQ FT: 31,000
SALES (est): 3.9MM **Privately Held**
WEB: www.thompsonfab.net
SIC: **3441** Fabricated structural metal

(G-11932)
TIGER NEUROSCIENCE LLC
200 Viridian Dr (49440-1141)
PHONE.................................872 903-1904
Steve Adams, *Mng Member*
Daniel Kallman, *CTO*
EMP: 6 EST: 2018
SALES (est): 260.6K **Privately Held**
WEB: www.tigerpi.com
SIC: **3841** Surgical & medical instruments

(G-11933)
TISCHCO SIGNS
Also Called: Tischco Signs & Service
2107 Henry St Ste 1 (49441-3087)
PHONE.................................231 755-5529
Matthew Tisch, *President*
Vickie Tisch, *Admin Sec*
EMP: 5 EST: 1997
SALES (est): 415.7K **Privately Held**
WEB: www.tischcosigns.com
SIC: **3993** Signs & advertising specialties

(G-11934)
TOTAL QUALITY MACHINING INC
2620 Park St (49444-1936)
PHONE.................................231 767-1825
Paul Reid, *President*
Susan Hornbeck, *Office Mgr*
EMP: 13 EST: 1995
SALES (est): 3.1MM
SALES (corp-wide): 1.1B **Privately Held**
WEB: www.tqmachining.com
SIC: **3599** Machine shop, jobbing & repair
HQ: Essentra Components Company
3123 Station Rd
Erie PA 16510
800 832-8677

(G-11935)
TOURIST PRINTING
2632 Peck St (49444-2028)
PHONE.................................231 733-5687
EMP: 4 EST: 2017
SALES (est): 134.9K **Privately Held**
WEB: www.touristprinting.com
SIC: **2752** Commercial printing, lithographic

(G-11936)
TRI-STATE ALUMINUM LLC (HQ)
1060 E Keating Ave (49442-5962)
PHONE.................................231 722-7825
Randy Clark, *President*
EMP: 10 EST: 1979
SQ FT: 12,800
SALES (est): 4.7MM
SALES (corp-wide): 18.5MM **Privately Held**
WEB: www.tsacc.com
SIC: **3365** Aluminum & aluminum-based alloy castings
PA: Tri-State Cast Technologies Co, Inc
926 N Lake St
Boyne City MI 49712
231 582-0452

(G-11937)
TRINITY EQUIPMENT CO
3918 Holton Rd (49445-8535)
PHONE.................................231 719-1813
Keith Massey, *President*
Scott Feltner, *Sales Staff*
Shelly Thomas, *Sales Staff*
Jennie Kriger, *Marketing Mgr*
▲ EMP: 5 EST: 2010 **Privately Held**
WEB: www.trinityequipmentco.com
SIC: **3743** Railroad equipment

(G-11938)
TRIPLE C GEOTHERMAL INC
487 W Forest Ave (49441-2463)
PHONE.................................517 282-7249
Joel Soelberg, *President*
EMP: 5 EST: 2018
SALES (est): 396.1K **Privately Held**
SIC: **3089** Injection molded finished plastic products

(G-11939)
TRUSS TECHNOLOGIES INC
Also Called: West Michigan Truss Company
404 S Maple Island Rd (49442-9407)
PHONE.................................231 788-6330
Dan Bekkering, *Manager*
EMP: 90 **Privately Held**
WEB: www.trusstechnologies.com
SIC: **2439** Trusses, wooden roof
PA: Truss Technologies, Inc.
4141 16 Mile Rd Ne
Cedar Springs MI 49319

(G-11940)
VAN KAM INC
Also Called: Vankam Trailer Sales & Mfg
1316 Whitehall Rd (49445-2432)
PHONE.................................231 744-2658
Leona Vanderberg, *President*
Michael Vanderberg, *Vice Pres*
EMP: 10 EST: 1967
SQ FT: 7,000
SALES (est): 1.5MM **Privately Held**
WEB: www.vankams.com
SIC: **3792** Campers, for mounting on trucks; pickup covers, canopies or caps; trailer coaches, automobile

Muskegon - Muskegon County (G-11941) — GEOGRAPHIC SECTION

(G-11941)
VERSATILE FABRICATION CO INC
2708 9th St (49444-1945)
PHONE.................................231 739-7115
Joe Balaskovitz, *President*
Kim Gustafson, *Project Mgr*
Sam Taylor, *Foreman/Supr*
Gwen Henning, *Controller*
Ron Balaskovitz, *Sales Staff*
EMP: 44
SQ FT: 12,000
SALES (est): 11.7MM **Privately Held**
WEB: www.versatile-fabrication.com
SIC: 3537 3444 3441 Industrial trucks & tractors; sheet metalwork; fabricated structural metal

(G-11942)
WEST MICH CMNTY HELP NETWRK
Also Called: WUVS 103.7 THE BEAT
1877 Peck St (49441-2534)
PHONE.................................231 727-5007
EMP: 17 EST: 2010
SALES (est): 240.6K **Privately Held**
WEB: www.1037thebeat.com
SIC: 2741 Miscellaneous publishing

(G-11943)
WESTECH CORP
2357 Whitehall Rd (49445-1043)
P.O. Box 5210 (49445-0210)
PHONE.................................231 766-3914
William Seyferth, *President*
Matt Thomas, *Sales Staff*
Richard Barnes, *CIO*
William Sieninger, *Admin Sec*
EMP: 32 EST: 1984
SQ FT: 36,000
SALES (est): 2.6MM **Privately Held**
WEB: www.eaglecnc.com
SIC: 3599 3545 Machine shop, jobbing & repair; machine tool accessories

(G-11944)
WHEELCHAIR BARN
2300 Barclay St Apt 1 (49441-3559)
PHONE.................................231 730-1647
Ron Zok, *Administration*
EMP: 5 EST: 2016
SALES (est): 86.6K **Privately Held**
SIC: 3842 Wheelchairs

(G-11945)
WHITAKER WELDING AND MECH LLC
69 N Hilton Park Rd (49442-9420)
PHONE.................................855 754-2548
Ty Whitaker,
EMP: 4 EST: 2015
SALES (est): 27.6K **Privately Held**
SIC: 7692 Welding repair

(G-11946)
WILBERT BURIAL VAULT COMPANY (PA)
Also Called: West Michigan Crematory Svc
1510 S Getty St (49442-5164)
PHONE.................................231 773-6631
John King, *President*
William King, *Corp Secy*
Virginia King, *Vice Pres*
EMP: 1 EST: 1949
SQ FT: 8,500
SALES (est): 1MM **Privately Held**
WEB: www.westmichiganburialvault.com
SIC: 3272 5087 7261 Burial vaults, concrete or precast terrazzo; caskets; crematory

(G-11947)
WILBERT BURIAL VAULT COMPANY
1546 S Getty St (49442-5164)
PHONE.................................231 773-6631
John King, *Manager*
EMP: 6
SALES (corp-wide): 1MM **Privately Held**
WEB: www.westmichiganburialvault.com
SIC: 3272 Burial vaults, concrete or precast terrazzo

PA: Wilbert Burial Vault Company Inc
1510 S Getty St
Muskegon MI 49442
231 773-6631

(G-11948)
WILBUR PRODUCTS INC
950 W Broadway Ave (49441-3522)
PHONE.................................231 755-3805
Scott Wilbur, *President*
Kevin Keck, *Manager*
Dick Allen,
Nathan Bohr,
Jonathan Bower,
EMP: 10
SQ FT: 1,500
SALES (corp-wide): 4.6MM **Privately Held**
SIC: 5091 2842 2992 2891 Sharpeners, sporting goods; cleaning or polishing preparations; lubricating oils & greases; adhesives & sealants; chemical preparations
PA: Wilbur Products, Inc.
18570 Trimble Ct
Spring Lake MI 49456
616 850-9868

(G-11949)
WILDE SIGNS
Also Called: Wilde Group
771 Access Hwy (49442-1236)
PHONE.................................231 727-1200
Jim Wilde, *Owner*
Sharon Chopp, *Sales Staff*
Christina Wilde, *Administration*
EMP: 10 EST: 2002
SALES (est): 1.6MM **Privately Held**
WEB: www.wilde-signs.com
SIC: 3993 Signs & advertising specialties

(G-11950)
WM TUBE & WIRE FORMING INC
2724 9th St (49444-1945)
P.O. Box 4589 (49444-0589)
PHONE.................................231 830-9393
Eugene Pease, *President*
Charles Colligan, *Vice Pres*
Chuck E Colligan, *Vice Pres*
Steve Colligan, *Vice Pres*
Steven Colligan, *Vice Pres*
EMP: 19 EST: 1999
SQ FT: 25,000
SALES (est): 3.1MM **Privately Held**
WEB: www.wmtubewire.com
SIC: 3315 3312 Wire, ferrous/iron; pipes & tubes

(G-11951)
WORKMAN PRINTING INC
Also Called: Advanced Printing & Graphics
1261 Holton Rd (49445-2517)
PHONE.................................231 744-5500
Brian Balski, *President*
EMP: 8 EST: 2005
SALES (est): 512.7K **Privately Held**
WEB: www.orderapg.com
SIC: 2752 Commercial printing, offset

(G-11952)
Z & A NEWS
1239 W Giles Rd (49445-1267)
PHONE.................................231 747-6232
EMP: 4 EST: 2012
SALES (est): 61.7K **Privately Held**
SIC: 2711 Newspapers, publishing & printing

Napoleon
Jackson County

(G-11953)
LEGENDS GAME CALL CO
100 North St (49261-9011)
P.O. Box 158 (49261-0158)
PHONE.................................517 499-6962
Steven Boley, *Principal*
EMP: 4 EST: 2014
SALES (est): 80.8K **Privately Held**
SIC: 3949 Game calls

Nashville
Barry County

(G-11954)
GREAT NORTHERN QUIVER CO LLC
8635 Thornapple Lake Rd (49073-9789)
PHONE.................................269 838-5437
Robert B Brumm, *Administration*
EMP: 5 EST: 2012
SALES (est): 182K **Privately Held**
SIC: 3949 Sporting & athletic goods

(G-11955)
I & D MANUFACTURING LLC
6895 Marshall Rd (49073-9407)
PHONE.................................517 852-9215
David C Hagon, *Administration*
EMP: 4 EST: 2015
SALES (est): 97.6K **Privately Held**
SIC: 3999 Manufacturing industries

(G-11956)
LEEP LOGGING INC
8445 Guy Rd (49073-8512)
PHONE.................................517 852-1540
Thomas Leep, *Principal*
EMP: 6 EST: 2007
SALES (est): 441.3K **Privately Held**
WEB: www.leeplogging.com
SIC: 2411 Logging

(G-11957)
MIKE HUGHES
Also Called: Meh Logging Co
6054 Marshall Rd (49073-9537)
PHONE.................................269 377-3578
Mike Hughes, *Owner*
EMP: 4 EST: 2001
SALES (est): 93.4K **Privately Held**
SIC: 2411 Logging camps & contractors

(G-11958)
MOO-VILLE INC
Also Called: Moo-Ville Creamery
5875 S M 66 Hwy (49073-9431)
PHONE.................................517 852-9003
Douglas J Westendorp, *President*
Louisa Westendorp, *Vice Pres*
EMP: 15 EST: 2005
SQ FT: 10,000
SALES (est): 3.1MM **Privately Held**
WEB: www.moo-ville.com
SIC: 2024 2021 5451 Ice cream & frozen desserts; creamery butter; ice cream (packaged)

National City
Iosco County

(G-11959)
GOLD BOND BUILDING PDTS LLC
2375 S National City Rd (48748-9623)
PHONE.................................989 756-2741
EMP: 31
SALES (corp-wide): 63.5MM **Privately Held**
WEB: www.nationalgypsum.com
SIC: 2621 Paper mills
PA: Gold Bond Building Products, Llc
2001 Rexford Rd
Charlotte NC 28211
704 365-7300

(G-11960)
NG OPERATIONS LLC
Also Called: Gold Bond
2375 S National City Rd (48748-9623)
PHONE.................................989 756-2741
Rick Penn, *Branch Mgr*
EMP: 4
SALES (corp-wide): 795.8MM **Privately Held**
WEB: www.proformfinishing.com
SIC: 3275 Gypsum products
HQ: Proform Finishing Products, Llc
2001 Rexford Rd
Charlotte NC 28211

Naubinway
Mackinac County

(G-11961)
PETERS SAND AND GRAVEL INC
W7276 Hiawatha Trl (49762-9714)
P.O. Box 161 (49762-0161)
PHONE.................................906 595-7223
Harold Peters, *Administration*
EMP: 4 EST: 2017
SALES (est): 265.6K **Privately Held**
WEB: www.peterssandandgravel.com
SIC: 1442 Construction sand & gravel

Negaunee
Marquette County

(G-11962)
5 PYN INC
Also Called: Signs Now
363 Us Highway 41 E Ste 1 (49866-9698)
PHONE.................................906 228-2828
Mark B Pynnonen, *President*
EMP: 7 EST: 1998
SQ FT: 4,000
SALES (est): 441.3K **Privately Held**
WEB: www.signsnow.com
SIC: 3993 7336 Signs & advertising specialties; commercial art & graphic design

(G-11963)
ASSOCIATED CONSTRUCTORS LLC
Also Called: Associated Redi Mix and Block
14 Industrial Park Dr (49866-9627)
P.O. Box 970, Marquette (49855-0970)
PHONE.................................906 226-6505
Jake Roberts, *Project Mgr*
Peter O'Dovero, *Mng Member*
Paul O 'dovero, *Officer*
Kristy Gervais, *Admin Asst*
Jim O'Dovero,
EMP: 80 EST: 2000
SALES (est): 21.6MM **Privately Held**
WEB: www.acmqt.com
SIC: 3273 Ready-mixed concrete

(G-11964)
CAIN BROTHERS LOGGING INC
1001 County Road 510 (49866-9746)
PHONE.................................906 345-9252
Kim Cain, *President*
EMP: 4 EST: 1990
SALES (est): 460.3K **Privately Held**
SIC: 2411 Logging camps & contractors

(G-11965)
CUMMINS NPOWER LLC
75 Us Hwy 41 N (49866)
PHONE.................................906 475-8800
Tim Kleikamp, *Branch Mgr*
EMP: 29
SALES (corp-wide): 19.8B **Publicly Held**
WEB: www.cummins.com
SIC: 5084 5063 3519 Engines & parts, diesel; generators; internal combustion engines
HQ: Cummins Npower Llc
1600 Buerkle Rd
White Bear Lake MN 55110
800 642-0085

(G-11966)
GREAT LAKES COCA-COLA DIST LLC
201 Summit St 53 (49866-9581)
PHONE.................................906 475-7003
EMP: 12 **Privately Held**
WEB: www.coca-cola.com
SIC: 2086 Bottled & canned soft drinks
HQ: Great Lakes Coca-Cola Distribution, Llc
6250 N River Rd Ste 9000
Rosemont IL 60018
847 227-6500

GEOGRAPHIC SECTION

(G-11967)
GREAT LAKES WOOD PRODUCTS
434 Us Highway 41 E (49866-9626)
PHONE................................906 228-3737
James Thompson, *Owner*
EMP: 4 **EST:** 1985
SQ FT: 7,200
SALES (est): 419K **Privately Held**
WEB: www.greatlakeswoodproducts.com
SIC: 5251 2511 2431 Tools, power; wood lawn & garden furniture; millwork

(G-11968)
ICON SIGNS INC
250 Us Highway 41 E (49866-9616)
PHONE................................906 401-0162
EMP: 4 **EST:** 2018
SALES (est): 212K **Privately Held**
WEB: www.iconsignsinc.com
SIC: 3993 Signs & advertising specialties

(G-11969)
KENNETH DAVID KENT
521 Cherry St (49866-1411)
PHONE................................906 475-7036
Kenneth Kent, *Principal*
EMP: 5 **EST:** 2010
SALES (est): 66.2K **Privately Held**
SIC: 3482 Small arms ammunition

(G-11970)
MOUNT MFG LLC
200 Echelon Dr Ste C (49866-9589)
PHONE................................231 487-2118
John Sanchez, *Principal*
Eric Lintula, *Principal*
EMP: 6 **EST:** 2017
SALES (est): 264.2K **Privately Held**
WEB: www.mountmfg.com
SIC: 3999 Manufacturing industries

(G-11971)
OAK NORTH MANUFACTURING INC
114 Us Highway 41 E (49866-9682)
PHONE................................906 475-7992
Thomas Mahaney, *President*
Brock Micklew, *Vice Pres*
EMP: 20 **EST:** 1981
SQ FT: 10,000
SALES (est): 979.9K **Privately Held**
WEB: www.northoakmfg.com
SIC: 2434 2431 Wood kitchen cabinets; millwork

(G-11972)
REFRESHMENT PRODUCT SVCS INC
201 Summit St Bldg 53 (49866-9581)
PHONE................................906 475-7003
EMP: 6
SALES (corp-wide): .33B **Publicly Held**
WEB: www.coca-cola.com
SIC: 2086 2087 Soft drinks: packaged in cans, bottles, etc.; concentrates, drink
HQ: Refreshment Product Services, Inc.
  1 Coca Cola Plz Nw
  Atlanta GA 30313
  404 676-2121

(G-11973)
ROBBINS INC
Also Called: Integrity Force Products
844 Highway M 28 (49866)
PHONE................................513 619-5936
Dave Fulton, *CEO*
EMP: 9
SALES (corp-wide): 43.5MM **Privately Held**
WEB: www.robbinsfloor.com
SIC: 2426 Flooring, hardwood
PA: Robbins, Inc.
  4777 Eastern Ave
  Cincinnati OH 45226
  513 871-8988

(G-11974)
RUDY GOUPILLE & SONS INC
Also Called: Redi-Crete
117 Midway Dr (49866-9683)
PHONE................................906 475-9816
Adele Goupille, *President*
EMP: 8 **EST:** 1958

SALES (est): 824K **Privately Held**
SIC: 3272 3273 1794 4212 Septic tanks, concrete; ready-mixed concrete; excavation work; local trucking, without storage

(G-11975)
STEPHEN HAAS
Also Called: Haas Food Services
96 Croix St Apt 6 (49866-1157)
PHONE................................906 475-4826
EMP: 6
SALES (est): 282K **Privately Held**
SIC: 2099 Mfg Food Preparations

(G-11976)
U P FABRICATING CO INC (PA)
Also Called: Manistique Machine
120 Us Highway 41 E Ste A (49866-9703)
PHONE................................906 475-4400
Richard W Kauppila, *President*
EMP: 18 **EST:** 1973
SQ FT: 28,000
SALES (est): 6.7MM **Privately Held**
WEB: www.upfab.com
SIC: 3531 3532 3441 Construction machinery; mining machinery; fabricated structural metal

---

New Baltimore
Macomb County

(G-11977)
ALL POINTE TRUCK & TRAILER SVC
54137 Avondale Dr (48047-1010)
PHONE................................586 504-0364
Christopher Bianchi, *Principal*
EMP: 5 **EST:** 2016
SALES (est): 115.6K **Privately Held**
SIC: 3537 Industrial trucks & tractors

(G-11978)
ANCHOR BAY POWDER COAT LLC
51469 Birch St (48047-1587)
PHONE................................586 725-3255
Robert Thomas, *Principal*
EMP: 10 **EST:** 2014
SALES (est): 825.4K **Privately Held**
WEB: www.anchorbaypowdercoat.com
SIC: 3479 Coating of metals & formed products

(G-11979)
CALIBER METALS INC
36870 Green St (48047-1605)
PHONE................................586 465-7650
William M Harber Sr, *President*
Andrew Ligda, *Corp Secy*
Ned Cavallaro, *Vice Pres*
William Harber, *VP Sales*
EMP: 20 **EST:** 1988
SQ FT: 96,000
SALES (est): 4.3MM **Privately Held**
WEB: www.calibermetals.com
SIC: 5033 3442 Roofing & siding materials; metal doors, sash & trim

(G-11980)
EXPAN INC (PA)
51513 Industrial Dr (48047-4149)
P.O. Box 267 (48047-0267)
PHONE................................586 725-0405
William Mc Cormick, *President*
◆ **EMP:** 49 **EST:** 1990
SQ FT: 26,000
SALES (est): 2.9MM **Privately Held**
SIC: 3469 3339 Perforated metal, stamped; primary nonferrous metals

(G-11981)
GRIMM INDUSTRIES LLC
50661 Jefferson Ave Apt 3 (48047-2317)
PHONE................................810 335-3188
Joseph Memeckay, *Principal*
Bill Callahan, *Prdtn Mgr*
Jim Quadri, *Production*
Matthew Kwiatkowski, *Supervisor*
EMP: 9 **EST:** 2011
SALES (est): 119.8K **Privately Held**
WEB: www.grimmindustries.com
SIC: 3089 Injection molding of plastics

(G-11982)
INDUCTION ENGINEERING INC
51517 Industrial Dr (48047-4149)
PHONE................................586 716-4700
Jack Muller, *President*
EMP: 13 **EST:** 1975
SQ FT: 25,000
SALES (est): 407.9K **Privately Held**
WEB: www.magnuminduction.com
SIC: 3398 3677 3621 Metal heat treating; electronic coils, transformers & other inductors; motors & generators

(G-11983)
INDUSTRIAL KINETICS INC
36661 Haley Dr (48047-6338)
PHONE................................586 212-3894
EMP: 11 **EST:** 2016
SALES (est): 95.5K **Privately Held**
WEB: www.iki.com
SIC: 3535 Conveyors & conveying equipment

(G-11984)
INTERNATIONAL CASTING CORP (PA)
37087 Green St (48047-1609)
PHONE................................586 293-8220
Douglas Smith, *President*
Richard Smith, *Vice Pres*
▲ **EMP:** 16 **EST:** 1968
SQ FT: 30,000
SALES (est): 1.6MM **Privately Held**
WEB: www.internationalcastingcorp.com
SIC: 3325 Steel foundries

(G-11985)
KBE PRECISION PRODUCTS LLC
Also Called: Kbe Hoist
51537 Industrial Dr (48047-4149)
PHONE................................586 725-4200
Dave Cope, *Sales Staff*
David Cope, *Sales Staff*
Jay Baumgarten,
Chuck Baumgarten,
Karen Baumgarten,
EMP: 8 **EST:** 2005
SQ FT: 1,400
SALES (est): 1.3MM **Privately Held**
WEB: www.kbeprecisionproducts.com
SIC: 3541 Machine tools, metal cutting type

(G-11986)
MAGNUM INDUCTION INC
51517 Industrial Dr (48047-4149)
PHONE................................586 716-4700
Jack Muller, *President*
John Muller, *Vice Pres*
EMP: 23 **EST:** 1975
SQ FT: 5,000
SALES (est): 1.1MM **Privately Held**
WEB: www.magnuminduction.com
SIC: 3398 Metal heat treating

(G-11987)
MAGNUM TOOL INC
51620 Birch St (48047-1585)
PHONE................................586 716-8075
Lawrence H Obrzut Jr, *President*
EMP: 10 **EST:** 1994
SQ FT: 6,000
SALES (est): 771K **Privately Held**
WEB: www.magnumtoolinc.com
SIC: 3599 Machine shop, jobbing & repair

(G-11988)
MARK MSA
35632 Hamer St (48047-2463)
PHONE................................586 716-5941
Mark Albright, *Principal*
EMP: 5 **EST:** 2011
SALES (est): 85.4K **Privately Held**
SIC: 3651 Audio electronic systems

(G-11989)
NASS CORPORATION
Also Called: Nass Controls
51509 Birch St (48047-1588)
PHONE................................586 725-6610
Randy Bennett, *President*
K Kirchheim, *Principal*
C Ullrich, *Principal*
Cindy Secondino, *Human Resources*

▲ **EMP:** 10 **EST:** 1988
SQ FT: 12,000
SALES (est): 2.7MM
SALES (corp-wide): 55.8MM **Privately Held**
WEB: www.nasscontrols.com
SIC: 3679 5085 Solenoids for electronic applications; valves & fittings
PA: Holding Kirchheim Gmbh + Co. Kg
  Eckenerstr. 4-6
  Hannover NI 30179
  511 674-60

(G-11990)
NORTH COAST PAPER & PACKG LLC
51514 Industrial Dr (48047-4148)
PHONE................................586 648-7600
Edward J Gudeman,
EMP: 6 **EST:** 2018
SALES (est): 57.5K **Privately Held**
SIC: 2621 Packaging paper

(G-11991)
PURUS CANDLES
36346 Saint Clair Dr (48047-5529)
PHONE................................586 876-7800
Patricia Slone, *Principal*
EMP: 5 **EST:** 2016
SALES (est): 83.6K **Privately Held**
SIC: 3999 Candles

(G-11992)
R & DS MANUFACTURING LLC
51690 Birch St (48047-1585)
PHONE................................586 716-9900
Daniel Q Pfaendtner,
EMP: 4 **EST:** 2010
SALES (est): 491.1K **Privately Held**
SIC: 3444 Sheet metalwork

(G-11993)
S & G PROTOTYPE INC
51540 Industrial Dr (48047-4148)
P.O. Box 129 (48047-0129)
PHONE................................586 716-3600
Scott Grove, *President*
Deanna Grove, *Vice Pres*
Jon Holstine, *Manager*
EMP: 18 **EST:** 1990
SQ FT: 15,000
SALES (est): 2.2MM **Privately Held**
WEB: www.sgprototype.com
SIC: 3465 Automotive stampings

(G-11994)
SER INC
51529 Birch St (48047-1588)
P.O. Box 26 (48047-0026)
PHONE................................586 725-0192
William J McCormick, *President*
Charles McCormick, *COO*
Marc Fulker, *Plant Mgr*
▲ **EMP:** 45 **EST:** 1966
SQ FT: 29,000
SALES (est): 8.6MM **Privately Held**
WEB: www.rseincorporated.com
SIC: 3564 Filters, air: furnaces, air conditioning equipment, etc.

(G-11995)
TOOLPAK SOLUTIONS LLC
53689 Dorner Lake Dr (48051-0006)
PHONE................................586 646-5655
EMP: 4 **EST:** 2018
SALES (est): 105.5K **Privately Held**
WEB: www.toolpaksolutions.com
SIC: 3441 Fabricated structural metal

(G-11996)
TRANSNAV HOLDINGS INC (PA)
35105 Cricklewood Blvd (48047-1530)
PHONE................................586 716-5600
Gerrit A Vreeken, *Principal*
Dale Trumble, *Opers Mgr*
Percy Vreeken, *Treasurer*
Jeff Hartwig, *Director*
Steven Vreeken, *Director*
EMP: 200 **EST:** 1997
SQ FT: 152,000
SALES (est): 110.4MM **Privately Held**
WEB: www.transnav.com
SIC: 3089 3111 Injection molding of plastics; leather processing

New Baltimore - Macomb County (G-11997)   GEOGRAPHIC SECTION

(G-11997)
TRANSNAV TECHNOLOGIES INC (HQ)
35105 Cricklewood Blvd (48047-1530)
PHONE..................888 249-9955
Gerrit A Vreeken, *President*
Paul Blue, *Engineer*
Haishan Yu, *Engineer*
Percy P Vreeken, *Treasurer*
Aaron Prout, *Program Mgr*
▲ **EMP:** 200 **EST:** 1991
SQ FT: 152,000
SALES (est): 56.8MM **Privately Held**
WEB: www.transnav.com
SIC: 3089 Injection molded finished plastic products

New Boston
Wayne County

(G-11998)
AJF INC
37015 Pennsylvania Rd (48164-9372)
P.O. Box 697 (48164-0697)
PHONE..................734 753-4410
Michael O'Leary, *President*
Carol Caccia, *General Mgr*
Michael O'Lear, *Vice Pres*
Dan Kleinow, *Manager*
Danny Kleinow, *Manager*
▲ **EMP:** 29 **EST:** 1976
SALES (est): 5.3MM **Privately Held**
WEB: www.ajfrefractories.com
SIC: 3297 5051 Graphite refractories: carbon bond or ceramic bond; foundry products

(G-11999)
ALL IN PRINTING
24026 Waterview Dr (48164-7804)
PHONE..................567 219-3660
Jimmy Posey, *Principal*
EMP: 4 **EST:** 2017
SALES (est): 91.1K **Privately Held**
SIC: 2752 Commercial printing, lithographic

(G-12000)
ALLBRITE PRINTING & LETTERSHOP
28400 Van Horn Rd (48164-9497)
PHONE..................734 516-2623
Laura Leporowski, *Principal*
EMP: 4 **EST:** 2016
SALES (est): 129.4K **Privately Held**
SIC: 2752 Commercial printing, lithographic

(G-12001)
AUTOKINITON US HOLDINGS INC (PA)
Also Called: Autokiniton Global Group
17757 Woodland Dr (48164-9265)
PHONE..................734 397-6300
Scott Jones, *President*
EMP: 181 **EST:** 2018
SALES (est): 3.1B **Privately Held**
SIC: 3465 Body parts, automobile: stamped metal

(G-12002)
BIO SOURCE NATURALS LLC
26594 Romine Rd Bldg B (48164-9221)
P.O. Box 87081, Canton (48187-0081)
PHONE..................877 577-8223
Lezlie Cebulski, *Mng Member*
Brian Cebulski, *Mng Member*
EMP: 4 **EST:** 2007
SALES (est): 233.1K **Privately Held**
WEB: www.biosourcenaturals.com
SIC: 2844 2899 7389 Cosmetic preparations; essential oils;

(G-12003)
BONSAL AMERICAN INC
Also Called: Bonsan American
36506 Sibley Rd (48164-9290)
PHONE..................734 753-4413
Roger Thomas, *Manager*
EMP: 6

SALES (corp-wide): 27.5B **Privately Held**
SIC: 3272 3273 Building materials, except block or brick: concrete; ready-mixed concrete
HQ: Bonsal American, Inc.
625 Griffith Rd Ste 100
Charlotte NC 28217
704 525-1621

(G-12004)
BROSE NEW BOSTON INC (DH)
23400 Bell Rd (48164-9183)
PHONE..................248 339-4021
Jurgen Otto, *CEO*
Jan Kowal, *President*
Volker Herdin, *Corp Secy*
Sandro Scharlibbe, *Exec VP*
Huy Nguyen, *Production*
▲ **EMP:** 151 **EST:** 2008
SALES (est): 137.6MM
SALES (corp-wide): 1.4B **Privately Held**
WEB: www.brose.com
SIC: 3694 Automotive electrical equipment
HQ: Brose North America, Inc.
3933 Automation Ave
Auburn Hills MI 48326
248 339-4000

(G-12005)
BROSE NORTH AMERICA INC
23400 Bell Rd (48164-9183)
PHONE..................734 753-4902
Jim Drolet, *Purchasing*
▲ **EMP:** 6 **EST:** 2012
SALES (est): 879.7K **Privately Held**
WEB: www.brose.com
SIC: 3714 Motor vehicle parts & accessories

(G-12006)
CHAMPION FOODS LLC
23900 Bell Rd (48164-9226)
PHONE..................734 753-3663
David W Kowal, *President*
Evan Litvak, *Vice Pres*
Bert Geans, *Production*
David Krause, *Engineer*
EMP: 300 **EST:** 2002
SALES (est): 80.2MM **Privately Held**
WEB: www.championfoods.com
SIC: 2099 Pizza, refrigerated: except frozen
PA: Ilitch Holdings, Inc.
2211 Woodward Ave
Detroit MI 48201

(G-12007)
CLEVELAND L&W INC
17757 Woodland Dr (48164-9265)
PHONE..................440 882-5195
EMP: 9 **EST:** 2014
SALES (est): 662.1K **Privately Held**
SIC: 3469 Stamping metal for the trade

(G-12008)
DREAM CLEAN TRUCKING SERVICE
24661 Huron River Dr (48164-9723)
PHONE..................313 285-4029
Deante Q Ball, *President*
EMP: 5 **EST:** 2019
SALES (est): 195.6K **Privately Held**
SIC: 2451 Mobile homes, industrial or commercial use

(G-12009)
HERITAGE WOODWORKING
22272 Bell Rd (48164-9227)
PHONE..................734 753-3368
Gordon Stump, *Principal*
EMP: 5 **EST:** 2008
SALES (est): 78.9K **Privately Held**
SIC: 2431 Millwork

(G-12010)
JAYTEC LLC (DH)
17757 Woodland Dr (48164-9265)
PHONE..................517 451-8272
Wayne Jones, *Mng Member*
Wayne D Jones, *Mng Member*
Loren Brushaber, *Technician*
▲ **EMP:** 10 **EST:** 2001
SALES (est): 53.7MM
SALES (corp-wide): 3.1B **Privately Held**
WEB: www.autokiniton.com
SIC: 3465 Automotive stampings

HQ: L & W, Inc.
17757 Woodland Dr
New Boston MI 48164
734 397-6300

(G-12011)
KURRENT WELDING INC
18488 Wahrman Rd (48164-9509)
PHONE..................734 753-9197
Jeff Komisar, *President*
EMP: 4 **EST:** 1987
SQ FT: 2,800
SALES (est): 222.2K **Privately Held**
SIC: 7692 3443 Welding repair; fabricated plate work (boiler shop)

(G-12012)
L & W INC (HQ)
Also Called: L & W Engineering
17757 Woodland Dr (48164-9265)
PHONE..................734 397-6300
Scott L Jones, *President*
Steven Schafer, *COO*
Kim Casper, *Vice Pres*
Cody Forrest, *Production*
Tammy Randall, *Production*
▲ **EMP:** 100 **EST:** 1973
SQ FT: 30,670
SALES (est): 592MM
SALES (corp-wide): 3.1B **Privately Held**
WEB: www.autokiniton.com
SIC: 3465 3469 3441 3429 Automotive stampings; stamping metal for the trade; fabricated structural metal; manufactured hardware (general)
PA: Autokiniton Us Holdings, Inc.
17757 Woodland Dr
New Boston MI 48164
734 397-6300

(G-12013)
LC MANUFACTURING LLC
Also Called: New Boston Forge
36485 S Huron Rd (48164-9275)
PHONE..................734 753-3990
Bill Heller, *Mfg Staff*
Floyd Simmons, *Branch Mgr*
EMP: 50
SALES (corp-wide): 30.8MM **Privately Held**
WEB: www.lcforge.com
SIC: 3462 Iron & steel forgings
PA: Lc Manufacturing, Llc
4150 N Wolcott Rd
Lake City MI 49651
231 839-7102

(G-12014)
NEW BOSTON CANDLE COMPANY
21941 Merriman Rd (48164-9458)
PHONE..................734 782-5809
Ellen Rees, *President*
Ron Rees, *Admin Sec*
EMP: 7 **EST:** 1997
SQ FT: 2,500
SALES (est): 131.9K **Privately Held**
SIC: 3999 5947 Candles; gift, novelty & souvenir shop

(G-12015)
NEW BOSTON RTM INC
19155 Shook Rd (48164-9288)
P.O. Box 188 (48164-0188)
PHONE..................734 753-9956
Michael Angerer, *President*
EMP: 26 **EST:** 1965
SQ FT: 18,000
SALES (est): 5.4MM **Privately Held**
WEB: www.newbostonrtm.com
SIC: 2821 Plastics materials & resins

(G-12016)
ONLY TOOL CO
26360 Bell Rd (48164-9331)
PHONE..................734 552-8876
Dominic Ruffolo, *Principal*
EMP: 4 **EST:** 2015
SALES (est): 65.4K **Privately Held**
SIC: 3541 Machine tools, metal cutting type

(G-12017)
OS HOLDINGS LLC (HQ)
17757 Woodland Dr (48164-9265)
PHONE..................734 397-6300

Scott Jones, *Mng Member*
EMP: 100 **EST:** 2009
SALES (est): 49.6MM
SALES (corp-wide): 3.1B **Privately Held**
SIC: 3469 Metal stampings
PA: Autokiniton Us Holdings, Inc.
17757 Woodland Dr
New Boston MI 48164
734 397-6300

(G-12018)
PLASTIC OMNIUM AUTO INRGY USA
Also Called: Huron Township Plant
36000 Bruelle Ave (48164-8957)
PHONE..................734 753-1350
John Dunn, *Vice Pres*
EMP: 350
SQ FT: 300,000
SALES (corp-wide): 1.8MM **Privately Held**
WEB: www.plasticomnium.com
SIC: 3714 Fuel systems & parts, motor vehicle
HQ: Plastic Omnium Auto Inergy (Usa) Llc
2710 Bellingham Dr
Troy MI 48083
248 743-5700

(G-12019)
QUALITY PIPE PRODUCTS INC
17275 Huron River Dr (48164-8955)
P.O. Box 667 (48164-0667)
PHONE..................734 606-5100
Roger Melton, *CEO*
Sylvia Melton, *Treasurer*
George Rennie, *Treasurer*
Katherine Klages, *Controller*
Steve Abrams, *VP Sales*
◆ **EMP:** 50 **EST:** 1977
SQ FT: 31,000
SALES (est): 9.7MM **Privately Held**
WEB: www.qualitypipe.com
SIC: 3494 3498 3541 5085 Valves & pipe fittings; pipe sections fabricated from purchased pipe; pipe cutting & threading machines; industrial supplies

(G-12020)
SDROL METALS INC
Also Called: Set Steel - Ford
36211 S Huron Rd (48164-9513)
PHONE..................734 753-3410
Fred Tate, *President*
EMP: 80 **EST:** 2020
SALES (est): 7.7MM **Privately Held**
WEB: www.sdrolmetals.com
SIC: 3469 Metal stampings

(G-12021)
TOWER ATMTIVE OPRTONS USA I LL (HQ)
17757 Woodland Dr (48164-9265)
PHONE..................734 397-6300
Scott Jones, *President*
Bob Oneil, *Sales Staff*
Jill Stevens, *Manager*
Ken Lynch, *Technician*
▲ **EMP:** 100 **EST:** 2007
SALES (est): 849.4MM
SALES (corp-wide): 3.1B **Privately Held**
WEB: www.autokiniton.com
SIC: 3465 Automotive stampings
PA: Autokiniton Us Holdings, Inc.
17757 Woodland Dr
New Boston MI 48164
734 397-6300

New Buffalo
Berrien County

(G-12022)
ADAMS DESIGN & PRINT LLC
18702 Oldfield Rd (49117-8879)
PHONE..................269 612-8613
Cheryl Adams, *Branch Mgr*
EMP: 8
SALES (corp-wide): 83.9K **Privately Held**
SIC: 2752 Commercial printing, lithographic
PA: Adams Design & Print Llc
11892 76th St
South Haven MI

▲ = Import ▼ = Export
◆ = Import/Export

GEOGRAPHIC SECTION

New Hudson - Oakland County (G-12049)

(G-12023)
FUSION DESIGN GROUP LTD
30 N Brton St New Bffalo (49117)
P.O. Box 498 (49117-0498)
PHONE....................................269 469-8226
Tim S Rogers, *President*
EMP: 4 **EST:** 1998 **Privately Held**
WEB: www.fusiondg.com
SIC: 7336 4813 2741 7311 Commercial art & graphic design; ; ; advertising agencies; marketing consulting services

(G-12024)
GHOST ISLAND BREWERY
17656 Us Highway 12 (49117-9714)
P.O. Box 822 (49117-0822)
PHONE....................................219 242-4800
Sima Robert Louis, *Owner*
EMP: 9 **EST:** 2017
SALES (est): 898.2K **Privately Held**
WEB: www.ghostislandbrewery.com
SIC: 2082 Malt beverages

(G-12025)
OZINGA BROS INC
825 S Whittaker St (49117-1771)
PHONE....................................269 469-2515
EMP: 21
SALES (corp-wide): 583.3MM **Privately Held**
WEB: www.ozinga.com
SIC: 3273 Ready-mixed concrete
PA: Ozinga Bros., Inc.
   19001 Old Lagrange Rd # 30
   Mokena IL 60448
   708 326-4200

New ERA
Oceana County

(G-12026)
BURNETTE FOODS INC
4856 1st St (49446-9677)
PHONE....................................231 861-2151
Mike Herzog, *VP Opers*
Joel Smith, *Plant Mgr*
Abe Farias, *Warehouse Mgr*
John Pelizzari, *Branch Mgr*
Ben Sexton, *Executive*
EMP: 107
SALES (corp-wide): 95.5MM **Privately Held**
WEB: www.burnettefoods.com
SIC: 2033 Canned fruits & specialties
PA: Burnette Foods, Inc.
   701 S Us Highway 31
   Elk Rapids MI 49629
   231 264-8116

(G-12027)
COUNTRY DAIRY INC (PA)
3476 S 80th Ave (49446-9776)
PHONE....................................231 861-4636
Wendell Van Gunst, *President*
Robert S Eekhoff, *Vice Pres*
Robert Eekhoff, *Vice Pres*
Paul D Arkema, *Treasurer*
Jeff Swanson, *Marketing Mgr*
EMP: 58 **EST:** 1964
SQ FT: 600
SALES (est): 16.2MM **Privately Held**
WEB: www.countrydairy.com
SIC: 0241 2026 Dairy farms; fluid milk

(G-12028)
DOLLARS FROM SCENTS
5190 S Scenic Dr (49446-8066)
PHONE....................................847 650-0317
Gregory Dowling, *Principal*
EMP: 4 **EST:** 2015
SALES (est): 56K **Privately Held**
SIC: 2844 Toilet preparations

New Haven
Macomb County

(G-12029)
CARGILL AMERICAS INC
31029 Comcast Dr Ste 100 (48048-2784)
PHONE....................................810 989-7689
EMP: 98
SALES (est): 7.4MM **Privately Held**
SIC: 2015 Poultry Processing

(G-12030)
CENTERLESS REBUILDERS INC (PA)
Also Called: C R I
57877 Main St (48048-2664)
P.O. Box 480549 (48048-0549)
PHONE....................................586 749-6529
Gerald A Filipek, *President*
Tim Wamboldt, *Opers Staff*
▲ **EMP:** 30 **EST:** 1989
SQ FT: 42,000
SALES: 7.6MM **Privately Held**
WEB: www.centerlessrebuildersinc.com
SIC: 3542 Rebuilt machine tools, metal forming types

(G-12031)
DOMESTIC FORGE & FORMING INC
57760 Main St Ste 2 (48048-2672)
PHONE....................................586 749-9559
Nancy Conforti, *President*
EMP: 8 **EST:** 2009
SALES (est): 249.8K **Privately Held**
SIC: 3312 Structural shapes & pilings, steel

(G-12032)
HOLLAND TRANSPORT SERVICES LLC
57958 Rosecrest St (48048-3314)
PHONE....................................313 605-3103
Rapheal Holland,
EMP: 6 **EST:** 2020
SALES (est): 95.5K **Privately Held**
SIC: 3537 7389 Trucks, tractors, loaders, carriers & similar equipment; business services

(G-12033)
JMA TOOL COMPANY INC
Also Called: Jma Manufacturing
58233 Gratiot Ave (48048-2777)
PHONE....................................586 270-6706
Christine Arciniaga, *President*
John Anguish, *Vice Pres*
EMP: 16 **EST:** 1992
SALES (est): 1.1MM **Privately Held**
WEB: www.jmamfg.com
SIC: 3089 Injection molded finished plastic products; injection molding of plastics

(G-12034)
LYONS GRAPHICS AND TEES
59860 Cynthia Dr (48048-1816)
PHONE....................................586 770-9630
David Lyon, *Principal*
EMP: 5 **EST:** 2019
SALES (est): 101.6K **Privately Held**
SIC: 2759 Screen printing

(G-12035)
MOTE ENTERPRISES INC
57446 River Oaks Dr (48048-3301)
PHONE....................................248 613-3413
James Mote, *CEO*
EMP: 5 **EST:** 1988
SALES (est): 206K **Privately Held**
SIC: 3999 Manufacturing industries

(G-12036)
ROARING RIVER PRESS
57760 Main St Ste 1 (48048-2672)
PHONE....................................248 342-2281
Linda Curatolo, *Principal*
EMP: 5 **EST:** 2016
SALES (est): 40.3K **Privately Held**
WEB: www.roaringriverpress.com
SIC: 2741 Miscellaneous publishing

(G-12037)
STURDY GRINDING MACHINING INC
58600 Rosell Rd (48048-2649)
PHONE....................................586 463-8880
Ray Blake, *President*
Donna Blake, *Admin Sec*
EMP: 18 **EST:** 1963
SQ FT: 13,600
SALES (est): 2.3MM **Privately Held**
WEB: www.sturdygrinding.com
SIC: 3599 Machine shop, jobbing & repair

(G-12038)
SUPERB MACHINE REPAIR INC (PA)
59180 Havenridge Rd (48048-1908)
P.O. Box 480579 (48048-0579)
PHONE....................................586 749-8800
Robert Vanthomme, *President*
James Leonard, *Vice Pres*
Jon Stanley, *Vice Pres*
EMP: 15 **EST:** 1987
SQ FT: 20,000
SALES (est): 3.4MM **Privately Held**
WEB: www.superbmr.com
SIC: 3599 Air intake filters, internal combustion engine, except auto

(G-12039)
TI FLUID SYSTEMS
30600 Commerce Blvd (48048)
PHONE....................................586 948-6036
Charles Cronenworth, *Managing Dir*
Debra Geier, *Purch Agent*
Jim Harrison, *Engineer*
Barb Isei, *Financial Analy*
Patty Dutkiewycz, *Accounts Mgr*
EMP: 79
SALES (corp-wide): 3.3B **Privately Held**
WEB: www.tifluidsystems.com
SIC: 3714 Motor vehicle parts & accessories
HQ: Ti Fluid Systems L.L.C.
   2020 Taylor Rd
   Auburn Hills MI 48326
   248 494-5000

(G-12040)
TRIANGLE GRINDING COMPANY INC
57877 Main St (48048-2664)
P.O. Box 480549 (48048-0549)
PHONE....................................586 749-6540
Mark Plantrich, *CEO*
Paul Duffy, *Vice Pres*
EMP: 25 **EST:** 1955
SQ FT: 6,400
SALES (est): 563.5K **Privately Held**
WEB: www.trianglegrinding.com
SIC: 3599 Machine shop, jobbing & repair; grinding castings for the trade

New Hudson
Oakland County

(G-12041)
ALTA CONSTRUCTION EQP LLC
56195 Pontiac Trl (48165-9702)
PHONE....................................248 356-5200
Nathan N Collins, *Mktg Coord*
Steve Greenawalt, *Mng Member*
Theodore M Schafer,
EMP: 52 **EST:** 2009
SALES (est): 11.3MM
SALES (corp-wide): 873.6MM **Publicly Held**
WEB: www.materialhandling.altaequipment.com
SIC: 3531 Construction machinery
HQ: Alta Equipment Holdings, Inc.
   13211 Merriman Rd
   Livonia MI 48150

(G-12042)
ANTIQUE BOTL & GL COLLECTR LLC
28465 Coyote Ct (48165-8585)
PHONE....................................248 486-0530
John Pastor, *Principal*
EMP: 5 **EST:** 2010
SALES (est): 250.4K **Privately Held**
WEB: www.americanglassgallery.com
SIC: 3211 Antique glass

(G-12043)
ARCHITECTURAL DOOR & MLLWK INC
Also Called: Adam
30150 S Hill Rd (48165-9706)
PHONE....................................248 442-9222
Michael Wujczyk, *President*
Steven J Lebowski, *Treasurer*
EMP: 32 **EST:** 1990
SQ FT: 10,000
SALES (est): 4.1MM **Privately Held**
WEB: www.adamdoor.com
SIC: 2431 Millwork

(G-12044)
BVA INC
Also Called: BVA OILS
29222 Trident Indus Blvd (48165-8559)
P.O. Box 930301, Wixom (48393-0301)
PHONE....................................248 348-4920
David J Vincent, *President*
◆ **EMP:** 21 **EST:** 1983
SQ FT: 25,000
SALES: 19.1MM **Privately Held**
WEB: www.bvaoils.com
SIC: 5172 2911 Lubricating oils & greases; oils, lubricating

(G-12045)
CB INDUSTRIAL LLC
55397 Lyon Industrial Dr (48165-8545)
PHONE....................................248 264-9800
Jacob Sponsler, *CEO*
EMP: 13 **EST:** 2020
SALES (est): 1.8MM **Privately Held**
SIC: 3541 7699 7629 3531 Grinding machines, metalworking; industrial machinery & equipment repair; electrical repair shops; crushers, grinders & similar equipment

(G-12046)
CONTINENTAL ALUMINUM LLC
29201 Milford Rd (48165-9741)
PHONE....................................248 437-1001
Mark Buchmer, *President*
EMP: 60 **EST:** 1998
SALES (est): 3.4MM **Privately Held**
WEB: www.continentalaluminum.com
SIC: 3365 Aluminum foundries

(G-12047)
CUMMINS BRIDGEWAY GROVE CY LLC
21810 Clessie Ct (48165-8573)
PHONE....................................614 604-6000
Dan Ogg, *Principal*
Rohan Mengale, *Technical Mgr*
Jesus Cruz, *Engineer*
EMP: 104 **EST:** 2006
SALES (est): 9.7MM
SALES (corp-wide): 19.8B **Publicly Held**
WEB: www.cummins.com
SIC: 5084 3519 Engines & parts, diesel; internal combustion engines
PA: Cummins Inc.
   500 Jackson St
   Columbus IN 47201
   812 377-5000

(G-12048)
CUMMINS INC
54250 Grand River Ave (48165-9561)
PHONE....................................248 573-1900
Dave Dunbrach, *Manager*
EMP: 4
SALES (corp-wide): 19.8B **Publicly Held**
WEB: www.cummins.com
SIC: 5084 3519 Engines & parts, diesel; internal combustion engines
PA: Cummins Inc.
   500 Jackson St
   Columbus IN 47201
   812 377-5000

(G-12049)
CUMMINS INC
21810 Clessie Ct (48165-8573)
PHONE....................................248 573-1600
Joseph Bernot, *Vice Pres*
Jack Cunningham, *Opers Mgr*
Richelle Hoobler, *Materials Mgr*
Michael Kosinski, *Opers Staff*
Matt Anderson, *Production*
EMP: 7
SALES (corp-wide): 19.8B **Publicly Held**
WEB: www.cummins.com
SIC: 3714 Motor vehicle parts & accessories
PA: Cummins Inc.
   500 Jackson St
   Columbus IN 47201
   812 377-5000

New Hudson - Oakland County (G-12050)   **GEOGRAPHIC SECTION**

(G-12050)
DEMARIA BUILDING COMPANY INC
Taft Steel Div
53655 Grand River Ave (48165-8523)
PHONE..................248 486-2598
Rick Flynn, *Controller*
Larry Lesniak, *Manager*
EMP: 8
SALES (corp-wide): 19.4MM **Privately Held**
WEB: www.demariabuild.com
SIC: 3441 Fabricated structural metal
PA: Demaria Building Company, Inc.
    45500 Grand River Ave
    Novi MI 48374
    248 348-8710

(G-12051)
DRAUGHT HORSE GROUP LLC
57721 Grand River Ave (48165-8542)
PHONE..................231 631-5218
Brad Tiernan, *Principal*
EMP: 8 **EST:** 2015
SALES (est): 1.6MM **Privately Held**
WEB: www.draughthorsebrewery.com
SIC: 2082 Malt beverages

(G-12052)
DRIVEN FABRICATION
29585 Costello Dr (48165-9358)
PHONE..................248 491-4940
EMP: 6 **EST:** 2018
SALES (est): 175.7K **Privately Held**
WEB: www.driven-fab.com
SIC: 3599 Machine shop, jobbing & repair

(G-12053)
EXOTIC RUBBER & PLASTICS CORP (PA)
Also Called: Exotic Automation & Supply
53500 Grand River Ave (48165-8522)
PHONE..................248 477-2122
Thomas M Marino, *CEO*
Scott Peffer, *General Mgr*
Steve Orlando, *Vice Pres*
Camila Fox, *Buyer*
Camila Lange, *Buyer*
EMP: 100 **EST:** 1962
SQ FT: 130,000
SALES (est): 50MM **Privately Held**
WEB: www.exoticautomation.com
SIC: 3089 3069 5085 5162 Injection molded finished plastic products; molded rubber products; hose, belting & packing; plastics sheets & rods; rubber, crude; synthetic rubber

(G-12054)
GOPHER SCOPE MANUFACTURING
29563 Costello Dr (48165-9358)
PHONE..................248 667-4025
Albert Chen, *Principal*
EMP: 7 **EST:** 2010
SALES (est): 130K **Privately Held**
WEB: www.gopherscopes.com
SIC: 3999 Manufacturing industries

(G-12055)
GREAT LAKES CYLINDERS LLC
57075 Pontiac Trl (48165-9748)
PHONE..................248 437-4141
EMP: 10 **EST:** 2014
SALES (est): 93.4K **Privately Held**
WEB: www.glcylinders.com
SIC: 3999 Manufacturing industries

(G-12056)
HARRELLS LLC
53410 Grand River Ave (48165-8521)
PHONE..................248 446-8070
EMP: 6
SALES (corp-wide): 113.6MM **Privately Held**
SIC: 3524 Mfg Lawn/Garden Equipment
HQ: Harrell's, Llc
    5105 New Tampa Hwy
    Lakeland FL 33815

(G-12057)
HENROB CORPORATION (DH)
30000 S Hill Rd (48165-9828)
PHONE..................248 493-3800
Keith Jones, *CEO*
Tim Finkbeiner, *General Mgr*
Dean Monday, *Business Mgr*
Nick Clew, *Vice Pres*
Todd Starr, *Project Mgr*
◆ **EMP:** 80 **EST:** 2004
SQ FT: 60,000
SALES (est): 51.1MM
SALES (corp-wide): 11.5B **Privately Held**
WEB: www.henrob.com
SIC: 3452 5085 5084 Bolts, nuts, rivets & washers; fasteners, industrial: nuts, bolts, screws, etc.; machine tools & accessories

(G-12058)
IDEAL HEATED KNIVES INC
57007 Pontiac Trl (48165-9748)
P.O. Box 187 (48165-0187)
PHONE..................248 437-1510
John T Sukenik, *President*
Margie Andrews, *Bookkeeper*
EMP: 4 **EST:** 1966
SQ FT: 1,000
SALES (est): 338.7K **Privately Held**
WEB: www.idealheatedknives.com
SIC: 3545 Cutting tools for machine tools

(G-12059)
K & S PROPERTY INC (PA)
Also Called: Cummins Bridgeway
21810 Clessie Ct (48165-8573)
PHONE..................248 573-1600
Gregory Boll, *President*
Tony Satterthwaite, *Vice Chairman*
Mark Smith, *Vice Pres*
Ken Clark, *CFO*
EMP: 70 **EST:** 1971
SQ FT: 14,500
SALES (est): 62.4MM **Privately Held**
SIC: 5084 3519 Engines & parts, diesel; internal combustion engines

(G-12060)
MACDERMID INCORPORATED
Also Called: Allied Kelite
29111 Milford Rd (48165-9741)
PHONE..................248 437-8161
Nicholas Banis, *Vice Pres*
Allan Macdonald, *Vice Pres*
David Crotty, *Research*
Tony Cangelosi, *Research*
Jeremy Hogan, *Research*
EMP: 5
SALES (corp-wide): 1.8B **Publicly Held**
WEB: www.macdermid.com
SIC: 2899 Chemical preparations
HQ: Macdermid, Incorporated
    245 Freight St
    Waterbury CT 06702
    203 575-5700

(G-12061)
MAGNA SERVICES AMERICA INC
Also Called: Cosma Body Assembly Michigan
54725 Grand River Ave (48165-8526)
PHONE..................248 617-3200
Mike Zimmerman, *General Mgr*
Vic Giniotis, *General Mgr*
Brad Myers, *General Mgr*
Mike Pando, *General Mgr*
David Mucciacciaro, *Vice Pres*
EMP: 14
SALES (corp-wide): 32.6B **Privately Held**
WEB: www.magna.com
SIC: 3714 Motor vehicle parts & accessories
HQ: Magna Services Of America Inc.
    750 Tower Dr
    Troy MI 48098
    248 631-1100

(G-12062)
MARADA INDUSTRIES
54725 Grand River Ave (48165-8526)
PHONE..................586 264-4908
EMP: 8 **EST:** 2015
SALES (est): 259.1K **Privately Held**
SIC: 3999 Manufacturing industries

(G-12063)
NETWORKS ENTERPRISES INC
57450 Travis Rd (48165-9753)
P.O. Box 930063, Wixom (48393-0063)
PHONE..................248 446-8590
Douglas J Ross, *President*
Kenneth J Ross, *Vice Pres*
EMP: 5 **EST:** 1994
SALES (est): 572.1K **Privately Held**
SIC: 2298 Cargo nets

(G-12064)
NEW HUDSON CORPORATION (PA)
57077 Pontiac Trl (48165-9748)
PHONE..................248 437-3970
Jon P Duprey, *President*
Van R Sandstrom, *President*
Karen Mattson, *Vice Pres*
Gary Cunningham, *Plant Mgr*
Lawrence Holzinger, *Purchasing*
◆ **EMP:** 23
SQ FT: 35,000
SALES (est): 2.9MM **Privately Held**
WEB: www.newhudson.com
SIC: 3317 3398 Seamless pipes & tubes; metal heat treating

(G-12065)
NOF METAL COATINGS NORTH AMER
55860 Grand River Ave (48165-9717)
PHONE..................248 617-3033
Don Dopierala, *Technical Staff*
EMP: 6 **EST:** 2016
SALES (est): 170.2K **Privately Held**
WEB: www.nofmetalcoatings.us
SIC: 3479 Coating of metals & formed products

(G-12066)
NORTECH LLC
30163 Research Dr (48165-8548)
PHONE..................248 446-7575
Richard Cameron, *Principal*
Paul Meinhart, *Engineer*
Tracy Schichl, *Office Mgr*
Michael Walker, *Mng Member*
Doug Arnett, *Manager*
EMP: 25 **EST:** 1985
SALES (est): 5.7MM **Privately Held**
WEB: www.nortechllc.com
SIC: 3499 Automobile seat frames, metal

(G-12067)
PERFORMANCE SPRINGS INC
57575 Travis Rd (48165-9753)
PHONE..................248 486-3372
Steve Bown, *President*
Shawn Kenney, *Production*
Lawrence Luchi, *Treasurer*
Jeff Sweat, *Manager*
EMP: 15 **EST:** 1996
SQ FT: 14,000
SALES (est): 3.7MM **Privately Held**
WEB: www.psisprings.com
SIC: 3714 Motor vehicle engines & parts

(G-12068)
RICHARD TOOL & DIE CORPORATION
29700 Wk Smith Dr (48165-9488)
PHONE..................248 486-0900
Richard A Heidrich, *President*
Steven S Rowe, *Exec VP*
Robert Heidrich, *Vice Pres*
Joe Janiszewski, *Project Mgr*
▲ **EMP:** 80 **EST:** 1966
SALES (est): 13.9MM **Privately Held**
WEB: www.rtdcorp.com
SIC: 3544 Special dies & tools; jigs & fixtures

(G-12069)
ROY A HUTCHINS COMPANY
57455 Travis Rd (48165-9351)
P.O. Box 340 (48165-1340)
PHONE..................248 437-3470
Harold Thomas, *CEO*
Lincoln Thomas, *President*
Gail Merwin, *Corp Secy*
EMP: 4 **EST:** 1946
SQ FT: 9,000
SALES (est): 679.6K **Privately Held**
SIC: 5084 3452 3541 Industrial machinery & equipment; bolts, nuts, rivets & washers; drilling & boring machines

(G-12070)
SLOAN VALVE COMPANY
Sloan Flushmate
30075 Research Dr (48165-8548)
PHONE..................248 446-5300
Bernard Peters, *President*
Chuck Eden, *COO*
Jim Galidio, *Purch Agent*
Tiffany Bouse, *Engineer*
Jerry Sobolewski, *Engineer*
EMP: 85
SALES (corp-wide): 192.7MM **Privately Held**
WEB: www.sloan.com
SIC: 3494 3443 3431 Valves & pipe fittings; fabricated plate work (boiler shop); metal sanitary ware
PA: Sloan Valve Company
    10500 Seymour Ave
    Franklin Park IL 60131
    847 671-4300

(G-12071)
SUPERIOR MACHINING INC
55378 Lyon Industrial Dr (48165-8544)
PHONE..................248 446-9451
Dennis Roggers, *President*
EMP: 14 **EST:** 1988
SQ FT: 14,000
SALES (est): 1.1MM **Privately Held**
WEB: www.sup-mac.com
SIC: 3465 Automotive stampings

(G-12072)
TEC INDUSTRIES INC
Also Called: Maple Industries
55309 Lyon Industrial Dr (48165-8545)
PHONE..................248 446-9560
Patricia Kuschell, *President*
EMP: 7 **EST:** 1973
SQ FT: 5,000
SALES (est): 775.8K **Privately Held**
WEB: www.maple-ind.com
SIC: 3545 Tool holders

(G-12073)
TICO TITANIUM INC
52900 Grand River Ave (48165-8538)
PHONE..................248 446-0400
Dave Robertson, *Principal*
Jeff Hall, *Manager*
EMP: 5 **EST:** 2013
SALES (est): 417.7K **Privately Held**
WEB: www.ticotitanium.com
SIC: 3356 Titanium

(G-12074)
WELK-KO FABRICATORS INC
53655 Grand River Ave (48165-8523)
PHONE..................248 486-2598
EMP: 6
SALES (corp-wide): 2.5MM **Privately Held**
WEB: www.welk-ko.com
SIC: 3312 3449 Blast furnaces & steel mills; bars, concrete reinforcing: fabricated steel
PA: Welk-Ko Fabricators, Inc.
    11885 Mayfield St
    Livonia MI 48150
    734 425-6840

New Troy
Berrien County

(G-12075)
TRU DIE CAST CORPORATION
13066 California Rd (49119-5112)
P.O. Box 366 (49119-0366)
PHONE..................269 426-3361
Bruno Lehmann, *President*
Lewis Rob, *Vice Pres*
Shiela Rose, *Plant Mgr*
Jeff Daniel, *Mfg Staff*
▲ **EMP:** 20
SQ FT: 60,000
SALES (est): 3.8MM **Privately Held**
WEB: www.trudiecast.com
SIC: 3364 3363 Zinc & zinc-base alloy die-castings; aluminum die-castings

▲ = Import ▼ = Export ◆ = Import/Export

GEOGRAPHIC SECTION

Newport - Monroe County (G-12102)

(G-12076)
VICKERS ENGINEERING INC
3604 Glendora Rd (49119-5108)
P.O. Box 346 (49119-0346)
PHONE.....................269 426-8545
Matthew S Tyler, *President*
Scott Gourlay, *Vice Pres*
Jeff Vickers, *Vice Pres*
Matt Wermund, *Vice Pres*
David York, *Vice Pres*
EMP: 120 **EST**: 1970
SQ FT: 120,000
SALES (est): 37.8MM **Privately Held**
WEB: www.vickerseng.com
SIC: 3599 Machine shop, jobbing & repair

Newaygo
Newaygo County

(G-12077)
ARMSTRONG DISPLAY CONCEPTS INC
480 S Industrial Dr (49337-8940)
P.O. Box 668 (49337-0668)
PHONE.....................231 652-1675
Ronald Armstrong, *President*
Pamala Stevens, *Business Mgr*
Beth Rienstra, *Project Mgr*
Scott Faulkner, *CFO*
Michelle Wood, *Department Mgr*
EMP: 11 **EST**: 1986
SQ FT: 6,000
SALES (est): 2MM **Privately Held**
WEB: www.armstrongdisplay.com
SIC: 2653 3993 2394 Display items, solid fiber: made from purchased materials; signs & advertising specialties; canvas & related products

(G-12078)
BUCHER HYDRAULICS INC
201 Cooperative Center Dr (49337-8957)
PHONE.....................231 652-2773
Jainil Chikani, *Engineer*
Andrew Trombley, *Design Engr*
Dan Vaughan, *Branch Mgr*
EMP: 4
SALES (corp-wide): 3B **Privately Held**
WEB: www.bucherhydraulics.com
SIC: 3594 3593 3592 3537 Pumps, hydraulic power transfer; fluid power cylinders, hydraulic or pneumatic; valves; industrial trucks & tractors; valves & pipe fittings; fluid power valves & hose fittings
HQ: Bucher Hydraulics, Inc.
   1363 Michigan St Ne
   Grand Rapids MI 49503
   616 458-1306

(G-12079)
CREEKSIDE LUMBER
3810 W 72nd St (49337-9784)
PHONE.....................231 924-1934
Irvin Beachy, *Owner*
EMP: 4 **EST**: 1998
SALES (est): 278.3K **Privately Held**
SIC: 2421 Sawmills & planing mills, general

(G-12080)
DONNELLY CORP
700 S Industrial Dr (49337-8956)
PHONE.....................231 652-8425
Roger Donga, *Principal*
▲ **EMP**: 8 **EST**: 2010
SALES (est): 350.5K **Privately Held**
SIC: 3714 Motor vehicle parts & accessories

(G-12081)
G-M WOOD PRODUCTS INC (PA)
Also Called: G-M Graphics
531 S Clay St (49337-8521)
P.O. Box 266 (49337-0266)
PHONE.....................231 652-2201
Mark Micho, *President*
Kevin Dumont, *General Mgr*
Gene Pless, *General Mgr*
Kevin Karrip, *Vice Pres*
J Kevin Kirrip, *Vice Pres*
◆ **EMP**: 73 **EST**: 1987
SQ FT: 150,000
SALES (est): 16.7MM **Privately Held**
WEB: www.gmcompanies.com
SIC: 2431 5199 Windows & window parts & trim, wood; art goods & supplies

(G-12082)
GRAPHICUS SIGNS & DESIGNS
477 S Industrial Dr (49337-8940)
PHONE.....................231 652-9160
Sergio Bassetto, *Owner*
Sandra Bassetto, *Co-Owner*
EMP: 5 **EST**: 1989
SALES (est): 358.3K **Privately Held**
WEB: www.graphicussigns.com
SIC: 3993 Signs & advertising specialties

(G-12083)
KARR UNLIMITED INC
515 S Division St (49337-8858)
P.O. Box 471, Grant (49327-0471)
PHONE.....................231 652-9045
Karen S Berndt, *President*
Robert Berndt, *Corp Secy*
EMP: 7 **EST**: 1997
SQ FT: 5,250
SALES (est): 86.4K **Privately Held**
SIC: 3544 Special dies & tools

(G-12084)
LEGACY TOOL LLC
9023 S Baldwin Ave (49337-9674)
PHONE.....................231 335-8983
Dean A Shue,
EMP: 5 **EST**: 2017
SALES (est): 480.6K **Privately Held**
SIC: 3545 Machine tool accessories

(G-12085)
MAGNA MIRRORS AMERICA INC
Also Called: Magna Mirrors Newaygo Division
579 S Industrial Dr (49337-8994)
PHONE.....................616 942-0163
EMP: 5
SALES (corp-wide): 32.6B **Privately Held**
WEB: www.magna.com
SIC: 3231 3647 3827 Mirrors, truck & automobile: made from purchased glass; windshields, glass: made from purchased glass; dome lights, automotive; automotive lighting fixtures; optical instruments & lenses
HQ: Magna Mirrors Of America, Inc.
   5085 Kraft Ave Se
   Grand Rapids MI 49512
   616 786-7000

(G-12086)
MAGNA MIRRORS AMERICA INC
700 S Industrial Dr (49337-8956)
P.O. Box 618 (49337-0618)
PHONE.....................231 652-4450
Brian Chadwell, *General Mgr*
Zach Cousino, *Buyer*
Cathy Winterhalter, *QC Mgr*
David Hunsberger, *Engineer*
Tony Schafer, *Engineer*
EMP: 350
SALES (corp-wide): 32.6B **Privately Held**
WEB: www.magna.com
SIC: 3231 3699 3429 Mirrors, truck & automobile: made from purchased glass; windshields, glass: made from purchased glass; door opening & closing devices, electrical; door opening & closing devices, except electrical
HQ: Magna Mirrors Of America, Inc.
   5085 Kraft Ave Se
   Grand Rapids MI 49512
   616 786-7000

(G-12087)
MB WOODWORKS AND CO
77 W State Rd (49337-8130)
PHONE.....................231 452-6321
EMP: 4 **EST**: 2017
SALES (est): 55.7K **Privately Held**
SIC: 2431 Millwork

(G-12088)
MICHAEL ANDERSON
Also Called: Anderson Screen Printing
4933 E Croton Dr (49337-9012)
PHONE.....................231 652-5717
Michael Anderson, *Owner*
EMP: 4 **EST**: 1983
SALES (est): 204.8K **Privately Held**
WEB: www.andersonssilkscreening.com
SIC: 2759 5999 2396 Screen printing; trophies & plaques; automotive & apparel trimmings

(G-12089)
PLEXUS CARDS
382 W Barton St (49337-8839)
PHONE.....................231 652-5355
Rachel Eager, *Principal*
EMP: 5 **EST**: 2017
SALES (est): 86.4K **Privately Held**
WEB: www.plexus-cards.com
SIC: 2759 Commercial printing

(G-12090)
TECH-SOURCE INTERNATIONAL INC
1000 S Industrial Dr (49337-8916)
PHONE.....................231 652-9100
Michael N Wilson, *President*
David Hummel, *Corp Secy*
EMP: 14 **EST**: 1998
SQ FT: 17,000
SALES (est): 593.2K **Privately Held**
SIC: 3699 Electrical equipment & supplies

(G-12091)
WISNER WOODWORKING
5015 S Wisner Ave (49337-9743)
PHONE.....................231 924-5711
Harvey Miller, *Owner*
EMP: 4 **EST**: 2012
SALES (est): 126.3K **Privately Held**
WEB: www.wisnercanoes.com
SIC: 2431 Millwork

Newberry
Luce County

(G-12092)
LOUISIANA-PACIFIC CORPORATION
7299 N County Road 403 (49868-8285)
PHONE.....................906 293-3265
EMP: 4
SALES (corp-wide): 2.3B **Publicly Held**
WEB: www.lpcorp.com
SIC: 2493 2436 2435 2421 Strandboard, oriented; particleboard products; fiberboard, other vegetable pulp; hardboard, tempered; panels, softwood plywood; panels, hardwood plywood; veneer stock, hardwood; lumber: rough, sawed or planed; moldings & baseboards, ornamental & trim
PA: Louisiana-Pacific Corporation
   414 Union St Ste 2000
   Nashville TN 37219
   615 986-5600

(G-12093)
MCNAMARA & MCNAMARA
Also Called: Clarence McNamara Logging
13123 State Highway M123 (49868-7625)
PHONE.....................906 293-5281
Clarence E McNamara Jr, *Owner*
EMP: 10 **EST**: 1969
SQ FT: 3,360 **Privately Held**
SIC: 2411 4212 Logging camps & contractors; timber trucking, local

(G-12094)
NEUMANN ENTERPRISES INC
1011 Newberry Ave (49868-1510)
PHONE.....................906 293-8122
Joyce Neumann, *President*
EMP: 6 **EST**: 1972
SQ FT: 1,200
SALES (est): 378.7K **Privately Held**
SIC: 2711 5992 Newspapers, publishing & printing; florists

(G-12095)
NEWBERRY BOTTLING CO INC (PA)
Also Called: Pepsicola
80 N Newberry Ave (49868)
P.O. Box 76 (49868-0076)
PHONE.....................906 293-5189
Michael Maki, *President*
EMP: 5 **EST**: 1938
SQ FT: 30,000
SALES (est): 5MM **Privately Held**
WEB: www.newberrychamber.net
SIC: 2086 Carbonated soft drinks, bottled & canned

(G-12096)
NEWBERRY NEWS INC
316 Newberry Ave (49868-1105)
P.O. Box 46 (49868-0046)
PHONE.....................906 293-8401
Bill Diem, *President*
Jackie Applin, *Admin Sec*
EMP: 6 **EST**: 1886
SALES (est): 539.9K **Privately Held**
WEB: www.newberry-news.com
SIC: 2711 2752 Newspapers: publishing only, not printed on site; commercial printing, offset

(G-12097)
NEWBERRY REDI-MIX INC (PA)
307 E Victory Way (49868)
P.O. Box 404 (49868-0404)
PHONE.....................906 293-5178
William J Burton, *President*
Sandra L Burton, *Admin Sec*
EMP: 8 **EST**: 1962
SQ FT: 3,000
SALES (est): 1.4MM **Privately Held**
WEB: www.newberryconcrete.com
SIC: 3273 5211 3272 Ready-mixed concrete; brick; cement; septic tanks, concrete

(G-12098)
NEWBERRY WOOD ENTERPRISES INC
7300 N County Road 403 (49868-7871)
PHONE.....................906 293-3131
Dave Dismuke, *Manager*
EMP: 8
SALES (corp-wide): 1.8MM **Privately Held**
SIC: 2499 Fencing, wood
PA: Newberry Wood Enterprises Inc
   12223 Prospect Rd
   Strongsville OH 44149
   440 238-6127

(G-12099)
NORTHERN HARDWOODS
6946 County Road 392 (49868-8260)
PHONE.....................906 487-6400
EMP: 8 **EST**: 2008
SALES (est): 536.3K **Privately Held**
WEB: www.bankshardwoods.com
SIC: 5031 2426 Lumber, plywood & millwork; hardwood dimension & flooring mills

(G-12100)
NORTHERN WINGS REPAIR INC (PA)
6679 County Road 392 (49868-8170)
P.O. Box 1070, Brookfield WI (53008-1070)
PHONE.....................906 477-6176
David Goudreau, *President*
Christopher Burger, *Opers Mgr*
Dan Hackman, *Opers Staff*
Jonathan Brown, *Supervisor*
◆ **EMP**: 25 **EST**: 2001
SQ FT: 13,000
SALES (est): 12MM **Privately Held**
WEB: www.northernwings.com
SIC: 4581 3728 Aircraft maintenance & repair services; aircraft parts & equipment

(G-12101)
ROBERT CRAIG LOGGING LLC
210 W Avenue C (49868-1612)
PHONE.....................906 287-0906
EMP: 5 **EST**: 2020
SALES (est): 370.5K **Privately Held**
SIC: 2411 Logging

Newport
Monroe County

(G-12102)
HAMBONES WOOD WORKS
4323 E Newport Rd (48166-9763)
PHONE.....................313 304-5590

Newport - Monroe County (G-12103)

GEOGRAPHIC SECTION

Mark Hamel, *Principal*
EMP: 5 **EST:** 2017
SALES (est): 90.7K **Privately Held**
SIC: 2431 Millwork

(G-12103)
J&D INDUSTRIES LLC
4611 Pointe Aux Peaux (48166-9519)
PHONE.....................734 430-6582
Denise Lockard, *Principal*
EMP: 6 **EST:** 2015
SALES (est): 138.6K **Privately Held**
SIC: 3999 Manufacturing industries

(G-12104)
LEVIATHAN DEFENSE GROUP
7720 N Dixie Hwy (48166-9133)
PHONE.....................419 575-7792
James Jacob, *Principal*
EMP: 5 **EST:** 2017
SALES (est): 108.3K **Privately Held**
WEB: www.leviathangroupllc.com
SIC: 3812 Defense systems & equipment

(G-12105)
NEW PORT FUEL STOP
8733 Swan Creek Rd (48166-9273)
PHONE.....................734 586-1401
Mohamed Hejajj, *Principal*
EMP: 7 **EST:** 2016
SALES (est): 395.2K **Privately Held**
SIC: 2869 Fuels

(G-12106)
ROCKWOOD QUARRY LLC
7500 Reaume Rd (48166-9709)
PHONE.....................734 783-7400
Bill Begley, *General Mgr*
Keith Childress, *QC Mgr*
EMP: 8
SALES (corp-wide): 10MM **Privately Held**
WEB: www.greatlakesagg.com
SIC: 3281 Stone, quarrying & processing of own stone products
PA: Rockwood Quarry, Llc
 5699 Ready Rd
 South Rockwood MI 48179
 734 783-7415

(G-12107)
STONECO OF MICHIGAN INC
7250 Reaume Rd (48166-9709)
PHONE.....................734 236-6538
Dean Vanderveld, *Manager*
EMP: 7 **Privately Held**
WEB: www.stoneco.net
SIC: 3531 Construction machinery
PA: Stoneco Of Michigan Inc
 15203 S Telegraph Rd
 Monroe MI 48161

Niles
Berrien County

(G-12108)
ACCESS MANUFACTURING TECHN
1530 W River Rd (49120-8953)
PHONE.....................224 610-0171
Tom Rissmann, *Principal*
▲ **EMP:** 6 **EST:** 2009
SALES (est): 289.7K **Privately Held**
SIC: 3999 Manufacturing industries

(G-12109)
ACCESS TECHNOLOGIES LLC (PA)
1530 W River Rd (49120-8953)
PHONE.....................574 286-1255
Stefan Savastano,
EMP: 1 **EST:** 2006
SALES (est): 1MM **Privately Held**
SIC: 2819 5169 8748 Industrial inorganic chemicals; industrial chemicals; systems engineering consultant, ex. computer or professional; industrial development planning

(G-12110)
AMERICAN AGGREGATE INC
2041 M 140 (49120-1131)
PHONE.....................269 683-6160

Betty Smith, *President*
EMP: 8 **EST:** 2002
SALES (est): 1.5MM **Privately Held**
SIC: 1429 1442 5032 Sandstone, crushed & broken-quarrying; gravel mining; sand, construction; gravel

(G-12111)
ASTAR INC
71135 Fir Rd (49120-5960)
PHONE.....................574 234-2137
Sidney Moore Jr, *President*
Dorothy Moore, *Corp Secy*
Angela Lambert, *Manager*
EMP: 40 **EST:** 1980
SQ FT: 40,000
SALES (est): 5.2MM **Privately Held**
WEB: www.astarinc.net
SIC: 3089 3544 Injection molding of plastics; forms (molds), for foundry & plastics working machinery

(G-12112)
BAUER SOFT WATER CO
1760 Mayflower Rd (49120-8753)
P.O. Box 72 (49120-0072)
PHONE.....................269 695-7900
Matthew Bauer, *President*
EMP: 6 **EST:** 1949
SQ FT: 10,000
SALES (est): 511.8K **Privately Held**
SIC: 3589 7389 Water filters & softeners, household type; water softener service

(G-12113)
BLOCKMATIC INC
Also Called: Blockmatic Company
2519 S 17th St (49120-4597)
PHONE.....................269 683-1655
Jeffery A Cichos, *President*
Sigmund P Cichos, *Vice Pres*
EMP: 7 **EST:** 1968
SQ FT: 5,000
SALES (est): 553.4K **Privately Held**
SIC: 3559 Concrete products machinery

(G-12114)
BLUE SHAMROCK PUBLISHING INC
2585 Portage Rd (49120-8767)
PHONE.....................269 687-7097
Terrance McNamara, *Principal*
EMP: 5 **EST:** 2015
SALES (est): 68.9K **Privately Held**
SIC: 2711 Newspapers

(G-12115)
BONNELL ALUMINUM (NILES) LLC
2005 Mayflower Rd (49120-8625)
PHONE.....................269 697-6063
Dan Formsma, *President*
Randy Johnson, *Opers Staff*
Carl Holderbaum, *Engineer*
Barry Bundesman, *Project Engr*
Michael Mann, *Finance Mgr*
EMP: 220 **EST:** 1997
SQ FT: 91,000
SALES (est): 63MM **Publicly Held**
WEB: www.bonnellaluminum.com
SIC: 3354 Aluminum extruded products
PA: Tredegar Corporation
 1100 Boulders Pkwy # 200
 North Chesterfield VA 23225

(G-12116)
BUCHANAN GLOBAL INC
2121 W Chicago Rd Ste C (49120-8645)
PHONE.....................269 635-5270
Chris Tapper, *President*
Heather Foster, *Office Mgr*
Richard J Tapper, *Admin Sec*
EMP: 8 **EST:** 2017
SALES (est): 142.6K **Privately Held**
WEB: www.buchananglobalinc.com
SIC: 3544 Dies & die holders for metal cutting, forming, die casting

(G-12117)
C & S MACHINE PRODUCTS INC (PA)
2929 Saratore Dr (49120-8703)
PHONE.....................269 695-6859
Joseph J Saratore, *President*
Dominick Saratore, *President*

Rachel Saratore, *Corp Secy*
Chris Fox, *IT/INT Sup*
Keith Blaske, *Prgrmr*
EMP: 41 **EST:** 1966
SQ FT: 18,000
SALES (est): 10.4MM **Privately Held**
WEB: www.candsmachine.com
SIC: 3599 Machine shop, jobbing & repair

(G-12118)
CNC PRODUCTS LLC
2126 S 11th St (49120-4096)
PHONE.....................269 684-5500
Fritz Knauf, *President*
EMP: 20 **EST:** 1987
SQ FT: 41,000
SALES (est): 4.2MM **Privately Held**
WEB: www.cncproducts-llc.com
SIC: 3444 Sheet metal specialties, not stamped; metal housings, enclosures, casings & other containers

(G-12119)
CNC PRODUCTS ACQUISITION INC
2126 S 11th St (49120-4096)
PHONE.....................269 684-5500
Gerri Davis-Parker, *CEO*
EMP: 15 **EST:** 2019
SALES (est): 1.1MM **Privately Held**
SIC: 3499 Fabricated metal products

(G-12120)
CONSUMERS CONCRETE CORPORATION
1523 Lake St (49120-1235)
PHONE.....................269 684-8760
Matt Tober, *Manager*
EMP: 9
SALES (corp-wide): 42.6MM **Privately Held**
WEB: www.consumersconcrete.com
SIC: 3273 Ready-mixed concrete
PA: Consumers Concrete Corporation
 3506 Lovers Ln
 Kalamazoo MI 49001
 269 342-0136

(G-12121)
CRAFT PRESS PRINTING INC
312 Bell Rd (49120-4063)
PHONE.....................269 683-9694
James Dahlgren, *President*
Gina Dahlgren, *Vice Pres*
EMP: 5 **EST:** 1948
SQ FT: 2,800
SALES (est): 451.6K **Privately Held**
WEB: www.danceville.biz
SIC: 2752 3552 Commercial printing, offset; business form & card printing, lithographic; business forms, lithographed; silk screens for textile industry

(G-12122)
CUSTOM MARINE CARPET
Also Called: CMC
423 N 9th St (49120-2531)
PHONE.....................269 684-1922
John Peterson, *Owner*
▼ **EMP:** 6 **EST:** 2002
SQ FT: 25,000
SALES (est): 750K **Privately Held**
WEB: www.snapincarpet.com
SIC: 2273 Carpets & rugs

(G-12123)
DAUGHTRY NWSPAPERS INVESTMENTS
Also Called: Dowagiac Daily News
217 N 4th St (49120-2301)
PHONE.....................269 683-2100
L P Daughtry, *President*
Les P Daughtry, *President*
Daniel G Dean, *Vice Pres*
Wade J Parker, *Treasurer*
EMP: 9
SQ FT: 6,000
SALES (est): 103.1K **Privately Held**
WEB: www.leaderpub.com
SIC: 2711 5994 Newspapers: publishing only, not printed on site; news dealers & newsstands

(G-12124)
DEHRING MOLD E-D-M
1450 Jerome St (49120-3462)
PHONE.....................269 683-5970
Dennis Dehring, *Owner*
EMP: 7 **EST:** 1976
SQ FT: 16,000
SALES (est): 419.5K **Privately Held**
SIC: 3544 Industrial molds

(G-12125)
DELTA MACHINING INC
2361 Reum Rd (49120-5037)
PHONE.....................269 683-7775
Wannis Parris, *CEO*
Scott Bennett, *Plant Mgr*
Michael Smith, *CFO*
William R Robison, *Treasurer*
Keith Parris, *Sales Mgr*
▲ **EMP:** 70 **EST:** 1978
SQ FT: 100,000
SALES (est): 10MM **Privately Held**
WEB: www.deltamach.com
SIC: 3599 3494 Machine shop, jobbing & repair; valves & pipe fittings

(G-12126)
DSS VALVE PRODUCTS INC
Also Called: Valves D S S
1800 Mayflower Rd (49120-8753)
PHONE.....................269 340-7303
David Bergeron, *COO*
James Pellegrini, *Vice Pres*
Bradley Okeley, *Engineer*
Jennifer Foulks, *Controller*
Sharon Fobes, *Sales Staff*
EMP: 25 **EST:** 2017
SQ FT: 2,500
SALES (est): 3.2MM **Privately Held**
WEB: www.dssvalves.com
SIC: 3491 Industrial valves

(G-12127)
DW-NATIONAL STANDARD-NILES LLC
1631 Lake St (49120-1270)
PHONE.....................269 683-8100
Tim Francis,
Brent Steffen,
▲ **EMP:** 135 **EST:** 2010
SALES (est): 50.8MM **Privately Held**
WEB: www.nationalstandard.com
SIC: 3315 Wire & fabricated wire products
HQ: National-Standard, Llc
 1631 Lake St
 Niles MI 49120
 269 683-9902

(G-12128)
EXPRESS PRESS INC
201 E Main St (49120-2303)
PHONE.....................269 684-2080
Mike Cameron, *Principal*
EMP: 7 **EST:** 2016
SALES (est): 113.1K **Privately Held**
WEB: www.express-press.com
SIC: 2752 Commercial printing, offset

(G-12129)
FONTIJNE GROTNES INC
30257 Redfield St (49120-5958)
PHONE.....................269 262-4700
Mike Walker, *CEO*
Marty Pingel, *Opers Staff*
John Lancione, *Engineer*
Carl Grotnes, *Sales Staff*
▲ **EMP:** 40 **EST:** 2015
SALES (est): 10MM **Privately Held**
WEB: www.grotnes.com
SIC: 3714 3549 3547 3545 Wheel rims, motor vehicle; metalworking machinery; rolling mill machinery; machine tool accessories; machine tools, metal forming type

(G-12130)
FOREVER YOUNG PUBLISHERS
2674 Korn St (49120-9325)
PHONE.....................574 276-1805
Cheri Hallwood, *Author*
EMP: 4 **EST:** 2017
SALES (est): 57.5K **Privately Held**
WEB: www.foreveryoungpublishers.com
SIC: 2741 Miscellaneous publishing

GEOGRAPHIC SECTION
Niles - Berrien County (G-12156)

(G-12131)
FRENCH PAPER COMPANY
100 French St (49120-2854)
P.O. Box 398 (49120-0398)
PHONE.................................269 683-1100
Jerry French, *CEO*
Shane Fenske, *VP Mfg*
Rick Vanwynsberghe, *Sales Staff*
Lee Battin, *Director*
Rob Keller, *Director*
◆ **EMP:** 85 **EST:** 1871
SQ FT: 3,362
SALES (est): 24.9MM
SALES (corp-wide): 101.5MM Privately Held
WEB: www.frenchpaper.com
SIC: 2621 Book paper
PA: Finch Paper Holdings Llc
1 Glen St
Glens Falls NY 12801
800 833-9983

(G-12132)
GAMCO INC
3001 S 11th St (49120-4753)
P.O. Box 272 (49120-0272)
PHONE.................................269 683-4280
Gary E Smith, *President*
Martha Smith, *Vice Pres*
▲ **EMP:** 10 **EST:** 1980
SALES (est): 678.8K Privately Held
WEB: www.gamcoinc.com
SIC: 2392 Household furnishings

(G-12133)
GARDEN CITY PRODUCTS INC
833 Carberry Rd (49120-5012)
P.O. Box 967 (49120-0967)
PHONE.................................269 684-6264
Larry Rechanadter, *President*
Larry Rechanadter, *President*
Lydia Reichanadter, *Vice Pres*
EMP: 36 **EST:** 1985
SQ FT: 6,500
SALES (est): 532.2K Privately Held
WEB: www.gc-products.com
SIC: 3599 7389 7692 3544 Machine shop, jobbing & repair; engraving service; welding repair; special dies, tools, jigs & fixtures

(G-12134)
GREAT LAKES PRECISION MACHINE
Also Called: Great Lakes Metal Fabricating
1760 Foundation Dr (49120-8987)
PHONE.................................269 695-4580
Keith Fulbright, *President*
EMP: 23 **EST:** 1994
SQ FT: 11,000
SALES (est): 1.1MM Privately Held
SIC: 3599 Machine shop, jobbing & repair; machine & other job shop work

(G-12135)
HAMMERHEAD INDUSTRIES
1325 Airport Rd (49120-9381)
PHONE.................................574 277-8911
EMP: 12 **EST:** 2018
SALES (est): 514.2K Privately Held
WEB: www.hammerheadtrenchless.com
SIC: 3999 Manufacturing industries

(G-12136)
HOOSIER TANK AND MANUFACTURING
2190 Industrial Dr (49120-1233)
PHONE.................................269 683-3450
EMP: 8 **EST:** 2018
SALES (est): 351.9K Privately Held
WEB: www.hoosiertank.com
SIC: 3999 Manufacturing industries

(G-12137)
INNOVATION MACHINING CORP
1461 S 3rd St (49120-4024)
PHONE.................................269 683-3343
Charles Lord, *President*
EMP: 12 **EST:** 1981
SQ FT: 9,000
SALES (est): 1MM Privately Held
WEB: www.bithero.com
SIC: 3599 Machine shop, jobbing & repair

(G-12138)
INNOVATIVE PDTS UNLIMITED INC
2120 Industrial Dr (49120-1233)
PHONE.................................269 684-5050
Fritz Heerdt, *President*
Bill Becker, *Vice Pres*
William Becker, *Vice Pres*
Melissa Asmus, *Purch Agent*
Gayle Becker, *Sales Staff*
▲ **EMP:** 35 **EST:** 1984
SQ FT: 10,000
SALES (est): 4.3MM Privately Held
WEB: www.ipu.com
SIC: 2599 2519 Hospital beds; fiberglass & plastic furniture

(G-12139)
INTRA BUSINESS LLC
70600 Batchelor Dr (49120-7624)
PHONE.................................269 262-0863
John Kampars, *Mng Member*
EMP: 5 **EST:** 2009
SALES (est): 445.7K Privately Held
SIC: 5112 7389 2893 Office supplies; ; printing ink

(G-12140)
KAMPS INC
2193 Industrial Dr Ste B (49120-1254)
PHONE.................................269 683-6372
Bob McDonald, *Manager*
EMP: 23
SALES (corp-wide): 1.7B Privately Held
WEB: www.kampspallets.com
SIC: 2448 Pallets, wood
HQ: Kamps, Inc.
2900 Peach Ridge Ave Nw
Grand Rapids MI 49534
616 453-9676

(G-12141)
LEADER PUBLICATIONS LLC (PA)
Also Called: Niles Daily Star
217 N 4th St (49120-2301)
P.O. Box 391 (49120-0391)
PHONE.................................269 683-2100
Rhonda Rauen, *Accounting Mgr*
Lisa Oxender, *Marketing Staff*
Angie Marciniak, *Manager*
Doug Sriver, *Manager*
Jan Griffey,
EMP: 60 **EST:** 1886
SQ FT: 8,000
SALES (est): 5.7MM Privately Held
WEB: www.leaderpub.com
SIC: 2711 2752 2741 Newspapers, publishing & printing; commercial printing, lithographic; miscellaneous publishing

(G-12142)
MASSEE PRODUCTS LTD
2612 N 5th St (49120-1174)
P.O. Box 1240 (49120-8240)
PHONE.................................269 684-8255
Jesse Townsend, *President*
Margaret Townsend, *Corp Secy*
EMP: 5 **EST:** 1986
SQ FT: 11,000
SALES (est): 588.5K Privately Held
WEB: www.masseeproducts.com
SIC: 3069 Foam rubber

(G-12143)
MEGAPRO MARKETING USA INC
2710 S 3rd St (49120-4406)
PHONE.................................866 522-3652
Hermann Fruhm, *President*
Salome Van Heerden, *Assistant*
EMP: 10 **EST:** 2003
SQ FT: 21,000
SALES (est): 6MM Privately Held
WEB: www.megaprotools.com
SIC: 3423 Hand & edge tools

(G-12144)
MICHIANA AGGREGATE INC
3265 W Us Highway 12 (49120-8761)
PHONE.................................269 695-7669
John S Yerington II, *President*
EMP: 9 **EST:** 1991
SQ FT: 600
SALES (est): 1MM Privately Held
SIC: 1442 Sand mining; gravel mining

(G-12145)
MODINEER CO LLC (PA)
2190 Industrial Dr (49120-1233)
P.O. Box 640 (49120-0640)
PHONE.................................269 683-2550
Jonathon Stough, *General Mgr*
Michael J Dreher, *Chairman*
Gary Dreher, *Vice Pres*
Scott Palmer, *Prdtn Mgr*
Robert Yagel, *Materials Mgr*
◆ **EMP:** 130
SQ FT: 96,000
SALES (est): 171.4MM Privately Held
WEB: www.modineer.com
SIC: 3469 3599 3544 Stamping metal for the trade; machine shop, jobbing & repair; special dies & tools

(G-12146)
MODINEER CO LLC
2121 W Chicago Rd (49120-8646)
PHONE.................................269 683-2550
Brad Messersmith, *Branch Mgr*
EMP: 20
SALES (corp-wide): 171.4MM Privately Held
WEB: www.modineer.com
SIC: 3469 3544 3599 Stamping metal for the trade; special dies & tools; machine shop, jobbing & repair
PA: Modineer Co. Llc
2190 Industrial Dr
Niles MI 49120
269 683-2550

(G-12147)
MODINEER CO LLC
1501 S 3rd St (49120-4026)
PHONE.................................269 684-3138
Drew M Jeffrey, *Exec Dir*
EMP: 5
SALES (corp-wide): 171.4MM Privately Held
WEB: www.modineer.com
SIC: 3469 3599 3544 Stamping metal for the trade; machine shop, jobbing & repair; special dies & tools
PA: Modineer Co. Llc
2190 Industrial Dr
Niles MI 49120
269 683-2550

(G-12148)
MODINEER P-K TOOL LLC
2190 Industrial Dr (49120-1233)
PHONE.................................269 683-2550
Edward Hamilton, *Mng Member*
EMP: 24 **EST:** 2019
SALES (est): 3.2MM
SALES (corp-wide): 171.4MM Privately Held
WEB: www.modineer.com
SIC: 3469 3599 3544 Stamping metal for the trade; machine shop, jobbing & repair; special dies & tools
PA: Modineer Co. Llc
2190 Industrial Dr
Niles MI 49120
269 683-2550

(G-12149)
N & K FULBRIGHT LLC
Also Called: Great Lakes X-Cel
1760 Foundation Dr (49120-8987)
PHONE.................................269 695-4580
Keith Fultright,
EMP: 11 **EST:** 2008
SALES (est): 4.3MM Privately Held
WEB: www.greatlakesxcel.com
SIC: 3449 Bars, concrete reinforcing: fabricated steel

(G-12150)
NATES CUSTOM WELDING
1101 Carberry Rd (49120-3900)
PHONE.................................574 303-2254
Nathan A Grenert, *Principal*
EMP: 4 **EST:** 2018
SALES (est): 25K Privately Held
SIC: 7692 Welding repair

(G-12151)
NATIONAL-STANDARD LLC (HQ)
1631 Lake St (49120-1270)
PHONE.................................269 683-9902
Jan Deruytter, *Vice Pres*
Bob Winenger, *Buyer*
Leo Martinez, *Engineer*
Branon Tidwell, *Manager*
Jim Hillebrandt,
▲ **EMP:** 165 **EST:** 2008
SQ FT: 456,000
SALES (est): 121.5MM Privately Held
WEB: www.nationalstandard.com
SIC: 3315 3496 Wire & fabricated wire products; wire, ferrous/iron; wire products, ferrous/iron: made in wiredrawing plants; miscellaneous fabricated wire products; wire cloth & woven wire products

(G-12152)
NCP COATINGS INC (PA)
225 Fort St (49120-3429)
P.O. Box 307 (49120-0307)
PHONE.................................269 683-3377
Neil Hannewyk, *President*
Cornelius M Hannewyk III, *President*
Jennifer Moore, *General Mgr*
M Sherman Drew Jr, *Vice Pres*
Sherman Drew, *Vice Pres*
EMP: 95 **EST:** 1948
SQ FT: 6,300
SALES (est): 20.1MM Privately Held
WEB: www.ncpcoatings.com
SIC: 2851 Paints & paint additives

(G-12153)
NILES ALUMINUM PRODUCTS INC
1434 S 9th St (49120-4208)
P.O. Box 607 (49120-0607)
PHONE.................................269 683-1191
Donald Ort, *President*
Vicki Ort, *Corp Secy*
Cydni Kiggins, *Office Mgr*
Gregg Gleason, *Supervisor*
EMP: 23 **EST:** 1959
SQ FT: 23,000
SALES (est): 1.9MM Privately Held
WEB: www.nilesaluminum.com
SIC: 3441 Fabricated structural metal

(G-12154)
NILES MACHINE & TOOL COMPANY
2124 S 11th St (49120-4061)
PHONE.................................269 684-2594
Richard Robbins, *Owner*
EMP: 5 **EST:** 1988
SQ FT: 6,000
SALES (est): 1.2MM Privately Held
SIC: 3599 Machine shop, jobbing & repair

(G-12155)
NILES PRECISION COMPANY
1308 Fort St (49120-3898)
P.O. Box 548 (49120-0548)
PHONE.................................269 683-0585
Jay C Skalla, *President*
Eric C Vinnedge, *Vice Pres*
Charlie Cagle, *Engineer*
Pat Blanda, *Accountant*
Brandon Krisher, *Technician*
EMP: 168 **EST:** 1950
SQ FT: 60,000
SALES (est): 22MM Privately Held
WEB: www.nilesprecision.com
SIC: 3724 3728 3812 Aircraft engines & engine parts; aircraft parts & equipment; search & navigation equipment

(G-12156)
PADDLETEK LLC
1990 S 11th St Ste 3 (49120-4072)
PHONE.................................269 340-5967
Curtis Smith, *Owner*
Janet Vance, *Office Mgr*
Janeth Vance, *Office Mgr*
EMP: 12 **EST:** 2013
SALES (est): 1.8MM Privately Held
WEB: www.paddletek.com
SIC: 2499 Oars & paddles, wood

Niles - Berrien County (G-12157)

(G-12157)
PARAGON TEMPERED GLASS LLC (HQ)
1830 Terminal Rd (49120-1246)
PHONE.................................269 684-5060
Terry Orourke, *President*
Sandra Hamann, *Human Res Mgr*
Dave Stahl, *Maintence Staff*
EMP: 5 **EST:** 2011
SALES (est): 11.3MM **Privately Held**
WEB: www.paragontemperedglass.com
SIC: 3231 Products of purchased glass

(G-12158)
PERFORMANCE MACHINING INC
Also Called: On Sight Armory
919 Michigan St (49120-3330)
PHONE.................................269 683-4370
Susan Millin, *President*
EMP: 9 **EST:** 2005
SALES (est): 935.3K **Privately Held**
SIC: 3599 Machine shop, jobbing & repair

(G-12159)
PILKINGTON NORTH AMERICA INC
Also Called: Pilkington Glass - Niles
2121 W Chicago Rd Ste E (49120-8647)
PHONE.................................269 687-2100
Peter Carpenter, *Plant Mgr*
Doug Wait, *Branch Mgr*
Brian Kelley, *Maintence Staff*
EMP: 4 **Privately Held**
WEB: www.pilkington.com
SIC: 3211 Construction glass
HQ: Pilkington North America, Inc.
811 Madison Ave Fl 3
Toledo OH 43604
419 247-3731

(G-12160)
R & M MANUFACTURING COMPANY
2424 N 5th St (49120-1193)
PHONE.................................269 683-9550
Timothy Mead, *President*
Roger Larson, *Director*
Diana Mead, *Admin Sec*
EMP: 30 **EST:** 1948
SQ FT: 10,000
SALES (est): 1.8MM **Privately Held**
SIC: 3544 Special dies & tools

(G-12161)
REED FUEL LLC
1445 S 3rd St (49120-4024)
PHONE.................................574 520-3101
Reed Ryan, *Administration*
EMP: 5 **EST:** 2010
SALES (est): 161.3K **Privately Held**
SIC: 2869 Fuels

(G-12162)
RELATIONSHIP EXAMINER
604 S Saint Joseph Ave (49120-2857)
PHONE.................................256 653-7374
EMP: 4 **EST:** 2012
SALES (est): 60.9K **Privately Held**
SIC: 2711 Newspapers, publishing & printing

(G-12163)
REVWIRES LLC
1631 Lake St (49120-1270)
PHONE.................................269 683-8100
Brent Steffen,
EMP: 8 **EST:** 2007
SALES (est): 748.7K **Privately Held**
WEB: www.nationalstandard.com
SIC: 3399 Brads: aluminum, brass or other nonferrous metal or wire

(G-12164)
RTI PRODUCTS LLC
1451 Lake St (49120-1235)
PHONE.................................269 684-9960
Ronald G Witchie, *Mng Member*
Linda L Witchie,
▲ **EMP:** 17 **EST:** 1993
SQ FT: 30,000
SALES (est): 2.9MM **Privately Held**
WEB: www.rti-products.com
SIC: 3661 Telephone & telegraph apparatus

(G-12165)
SCHINDLER SOFTWARE LLC
1415 Stonecreek Dr (49120-8628)
PHONE.................................574 360-9045
Bryan Schindler, *Principal*
EMP: 5 **EST:** 2012
SALES (est): 95.2K **Privately Held**
SIC: 7372 Prepackaged software

(G-12166)
SCHRADER STOVES OF MICHIANA
Also Called: Schrader Steel Fabg Svcs
801 N 8th St (49120-1853)
PHONE.................................269 684-4494
Chris Schrader, *President*
John C Schrader, *Chairman*
Karen Barnett, *Vice Pres*
Beverly J Schrader, *Treasurer*
EMP: 35 **EST:** 1977
SQ FT: 67,000
SALES (est): 3MM **Privately Held**
SIC: 3599 7692 3594 3544 Machine shop, jobbing & repair; welding repair; fluid power pumps & motors; special dies, tools, jigs & fixtures; sheet metalwork; fabricated plate work (boiler shop)

(G-12167)
SHIVELY CORP
Also Called: West River Machine
2604 S 11th St (49120-4418)
PHONE.................................269 683-9503
Don Shively, *President*
Betty Shively, *Vice Pres*
EMP: 10 **EST:** 2002
SALES (est): 873.7K **Privately Held**
SIC: 3599 Machine shop, jobbing & repair

(G-12168)
SOUTHAST BERRIEN CNTY LANDFILL
1540 Mayflower Rd (49120-8729)
P.O. Box 142, Buchanan (49107-0142)
PHONE.................................269 695-2500
Carla Cole, *Ch of Bd*
Richard Simon, *Accounting Mgr*
EMP: 45 **EST:** 1969
SQ FT: 454,400
SALES (est): 9.3MM **Privately Held**
WEB: www.sebclandfill.com
SIC: 4953 2611 4212 Sanitary landfill operation; pulp manufactured from waste or recycled paper; garbage collection & transport, no disposal

(G-12169)
SPARTAN TOOL LLC (DH)
1618 Terminal Rd (49120-1298)
PHONE.................................815 539-7411
Kevin Walsh, *President*
Kevin Dineen, *Project Engr*
Tracy Eaves, *Controller*
Mike Sekach, *Natl Sales Mgr*
Warren Richmond, *Sales Mgr*
▲ **EMP:** 25 **EST:** 1961
SALES (est): 27.2MM
SALES (corp-wide): 1.2B **Privately Held**
WEB: www.spartantool.com
SIC: 3589 Sewer cleaning equipment, power
HQ: Pettibone L.L.C.
27501 Bella Vista Pkwy
Warrenville IL 60555
630 353-5000

(G-12170)
SPECIALTY PDTS & POLYMERS INC
2100 Progressive Dr (49120-1285)
PHONE.................................269 684-5931
Rick Rey, *President*
John Ralston, *Prdtn Mgr*
Enriqueto C Rey, *Admin Sec*
▲ **EMP:** 25 **EST:** 1993
SQ FT: 30,000
SALES (est): 3.3MM **Privately Held**
WEB: www.specialtyproductspolymers.com
SIC: 3069 Custom compounding of rubber materials

(G-12171)
TOEFCO ENGINEERING INC
Also Called: Toefco Engnred Coating Systems
1220 N 14th St (49120-1897)
PHONE.................................269 683-0188
Artie McElwee, *President*
Craig Ponsler, *General Mgr*
Patricia McElwee, *Exec VP*
Kami Gatson, *Manager*
Robert Smith, *Manager*
EMP: 35 **EST:** 1955
SQ FT: 47,000
SALES (est): 7.5MM **Privately Held**
WEB: www.toefco.com
SIC: 3479 Coating of metals & formed products

(G-12172)
TRU BLU INDUSTRIES LLC
1920 Industrial Dr (49120-1229)
PHONE.................................269 684-4989
David Kalling, *Manager*
EMP: 9 **EST:** 2002
SALES (est): 1.2MM **Privately Held**
SIC: 2679 Paperboard products, converted

(G-12173)
WHITE ENGINEERING INC
Also Called: White Tool & Engineering
3000 E Geyer Rd (49120-9066)
PHONE.................................269 695-0825
Rolf Krueger, *President*
Hildegarde Krueger, *Corp Secy*
Kurt Krueger, *Vice Pres*
EMP: 4 **EST:** 1962
SQ FT: 4,000
SALES (est): 355.2K **Privately Held**
WEB: www.whiteeng.com
SIC: 3544 Special dies & tools

(G-12174)
YERINGTON BROTHERS INC
3265 W Us Highway 12 (49120-8761)
PHONE.................................269 695-7669
John Yerington, *President*
John S Yerington II, *Treasurer*
Denise Skala, *Admin Sec*
EMP: 8 **EST:** 1990
SQ FT: 500
SALES (est): 867K **Privately Held**
SIC: 3532 4212 Mining machinery; dump truck haulage

(G-12175)
ZELLCO PRECISION INC
1710 E Main St (49120-3832)
PHONE.................................269 684-1720
Eric Zellmer, *President*
Ingrid Zellmer, *Treasurer*
EMP: 5 **EST:** 1965
SQ FT: 5,000
SALES (est): 423.7K **Privately Held**
WEB: www.planthopeforhearts.net
SIC: 3599 Machine shop, jobbing & repair

North Adams
Hillsdale County

(G-12176)
F & F MOLD INC
5931 Knowles Rd (49262-9708)
PHONE.................................517 287-5866
EMP: 7
SQ FT: 7,500
SALES: 1.2MM **Privately Held**
SIC: 3544 Mfg Dies/Tools/Jigs/Fixtures

North Branch
Lapeer County

(G-12177)
CHAMBERS ENTERPRISES II LLC
6595 Bernie Kohler Dr (48461-8886)
PHONE.................................810 688-3750
Gerald Chambers, *Mng Member*
Betty Rogers, *Manager*
EMP: 10 **EST:** 1997
SALES (est): 237.7K **Privately Held**
SIC: 2241 Spindle banding

(G-12178)
DAVID JENKS
5955 Chapman Rd (48461-9532)
PHONE.................................810 793-7340
David Jenks, *Principal*
EMP: 6 **EST:** 2009
SALES (est): 155K **Privately Held**
SIC: 2411 Logging camps & contractors

(G-12179)
JOHNSON WALKER & ASSOC LLC
Also Called: Imperial Plastics Mfg
4337 Mill St (48461-8727)
PHONE.................................810 688-1600
Charles Snooks, *CFO*
Craig S Johnson, *Mng Member*
Tom Walker, *Mng Member*
EMP: 8 **EST:** 2005
SALES (est): 885.7K **Privately Held**
WEB: www.imperialplasticsmfg.com
SIC: 3089 Injection molding of plastics

(G-12180)
KEIZER-MORRIS INTL INC
Also Called: Km International
6561 Bernie Kohler Dr (48461-8886)
PHONE.................................810 688-1234
Bryan Burke, *CEO*
Clifford Cameron, *President*
Brad London, *Plant Supt*
Kurt Schwartz, *Sales Staff*
Greg Welke, *Manager*
EMP: 32 **EST:** 1985
SQ FT: 37,500
SALES (est): 8MM **Privately Held**
WEB: www.kminternational.com
SIC: 3531 Construction machinery

(G-12181)
MK CHAMBERS COMPANY (PA)
2251 Johnson Mill Rd (48461-9744)
PHONE.................................810 688-3750
Gerald Chambers, *President*
Robert Chambers, *Senior VP*
Merle K Chambers, *Vice Pres*
Sharon Chase, *Vice Pres*
Paul Rogers, *Plant Mgr*
▲ **EMP:** 50 **EST:** 1957
SQ FT: 70,000
SALES (est): 10.1MM **Privately Held**
WEB: www.mkchambers.com
SIC: 3451 Screw machine products

(G-12182)
PRECISION MACHINING COMPANY
6637 Bernie Kohler Dr (48461-6112)
PHONE.................................810 688-8674
Mark Grimem, *President*
Karen Koos, *Manager*
EMP: 27 **EST:** 1986
SQ FT: 10,500
SALES (est): 1.3MM **Privately Held**
WEB: www.precision-machiningco.com
SIC: 3599 Machine shop, jobbing & repair

(G-12183)
PRODUCTION THREADED PARTS CO
Also Called: Orr Lumber
6829 Lincoln St (48461-8440)
P.O. Box 320 (48461-0320)
PHONE.................................810 688-3186
Ralph Deshetsky, *President*
Wilfred Deshetsky, *Vice Pres*
Tracey Delong, *Admin Sec*
Marjorie Deshetsky, *Asst Sec*
EMP: 33 **EST:** 1955
SQ FT: 28,000
SALES (est): 3.6MM **Privately Held**
WEB: www.productionthreadedparts.com
SIC: 3541 Machine tools, metal cutting type

(G-12184)
VANCO STEEL INC
6573 Bernie Kohler Dr (48461-8886)
P.O. Box 178 (48461-0178)
PHONE.................................810 688-4333
John Vanecek, *President*
EMP: 21 **EST:** 1991
SALES (est): 2.1MM **Privately Held**
WEB: www.vancosteel.com
SIC: 3441 Fabricated structural metal

GEOGRAPHIC SECTION

Northville - Wayne County (G-12209)

North Star
Gratiot County

(G-12185)
SMITH CONCRETE PRODUCTS
3282 S Crapo Rd (48862)
P.O. Box 38 (48862-0038)
PHONE..................................989 875-4687
Robert Smith, *Owner*
EMP: 4 **EST:** 1927
SALES (est): 270.3K **Privately Held**
WEB: www.neurolearningdisabilities.com
SIC: 3272 Burial vaults, concrete or precast terrazzo

North Street
St. Clair County

(G-12186)
PROFILE GEAR INC
4777 Brott Rd (48049-2317)
PHONE..................................810 324-2731
Edmond P Cloutier II, *President*
Carol Cloutier, *Vice Pres*
▲ **EMP:** 7 **EST:** 1977
SQ FT: 10,000
SALES (est): 800K **Privately Held**
WEB: www.profilegear.com
SIC: 3599 Machine shop, jobbing & repair

Northport
Leelanau County

(G-12187)
GOOD NEIGHBOR ORGANIC
9825 E Engles Rd (49670-9408)
PHONE..................................231 386-5636
Stanley Silverman, *President*
EMP: 6 **EST:** 2010
SALES (est): 132.5K **Privately Held**
WEB: www.greenbirdcellars.com
SIC: 2084 Wines

(G-12188)
LEELANAU PRINTS
6411 N Overlook Rd (49670-9437)
PHONE..................................231 386-7616
Douglas J Racich, *President*
EMP: 4 **EST:** 2011
SALES (est): 76.7K **Privately Held**
WEB: www.leelanauprints.com
SIC: 2752 Commercial printing, lithographic

(G-12189)
LEELANAU WINE CELLARS LTD (PA)
7161 N West Bay Shore Dr (49670-9328)
P.O. Box 68, Omena (49674-0068)
PHONE..................................231 386-5201
Michael H Jacobson, *President*
Bob Jacobson, *Vice Pres*
▲ **EMP:** 19 **EST:** 1975
SQ FT: 8,000
SALES (est): 2.8MM **Privately Held**
WEB: www.lwc.wine
SIC: 2084 Wines

(G-12190)
MASTER CRAFT EXTRUSION TLS INC
771 N Mill St (49670-9701)
PHONE..................................231 386-5149
Donald Allington, *President*
Diane Allington, *Corp Secy*
Juli Waldrup, *Office Mgr*
EMP: 11 **EST:** 1982
SQ FT: 10,000
SALES (est): 1.6MM **Privately Held**
WEB: www.dieshop.com
SIC: 3544 Special dies & tools

(G-12191)
SHERWOOD MANUFACTURING CORP
922 N Mill St (49670-9779)
P.O. Box 366 (49670-0366)
PHONE..................................231 386-5132
Gerald R Woods, *President*
Raymond Keith Woods, *Vice Pres*
Linda E Woods, *Treasurer*
EMP: 17 **EST:** 1970
SQ FT: 20,000
SALES (est): 1.1MM **Privately Held**
WEB: www.sherwoodmanufacturing.com
SIC: 3441 7692 Fabricated structural metal; welding repair

(G-12192)
SPARTAN FLAG COMPANY INC
323 S Shabwasung St (49670-9604)
PHONE..................................231 386-5150
Cheryl Seipke, *President*
Milton Seipke, *Vice Pres*
EMP: 10 **EST:** 1950
SQ FT: 3,400
SALES (est): 271.4K **Privately Held**
SIC: 2399 Flags, fabric; pennants

(G-12193)
THOMAS AND MILLIKEN MLLWK INC (PA)
931 N Mill St (49670-9779)
P.O. Box 265 (49670-0265)
PHONE..................................231 386-7236
Andrew Thomas, *President*
Todd Huck, *Project Mgr*
Peggy Moore, *Sales Staff*
Kent Strawderman, *Sales Staff*
Kathy Ergardt, *Office Mgr*
EMP: 18 **EST:** 1977
SQ FT: 13,000
SALES (est): 3.7MM **Privately Held**
WEB: www.tmmill.com
SIC: 2431 1751 Millwork; cabinet building & installation

Northville
Wayne County

(G-12194)
A A ANCHOR BOLT INC
7390 Salem Rd (48168-9404)
PHONE..................................248 349-6565
Robert P Horton, *President*
Robert M Horton, *Vice Pres*
Kelly Duffy, *Office Mgr*
Kellie Duffy, *Manager*
Krista Strobel, *Director*
EMP: 15 **EST:** 1982
SQ FT: 15,000
SALES (est): 3.5MM **Privately Held**
WEB: www.aaanchorbolt.com
SIC: 3545 3452 Threading tools (machine tool accessories); bolts, metal

(G-12195)
AISIN HOLDINGS AMERICA INC
15300 Centennial Dr (48168-8687)
PHONE..................................734 453-5551
Jun Mukai, *Branch Mgr*
EMP: 5 **Privately Held**
WEB: www.aisinworld.com
SIC: 2395 2499 Emblems, embroidered; seats, toilet
HQ: Aisin Holdings Of America, Inc.
1665 E 4th Street Rd
Seymour IN 47274
812 524-8144

(G-12196)
AISIN TECHNICAL CTR AMER INC
15300 Centennial Dr (48168-8687)
PHONE..................................734 453-5551
Yoshiaki Kato, *President*
Takashi Araki, *Treasurer*
Douglas Wyatt, *Lab Dir*
◆ **EMP:** 71 **EST:** 2008
SALES (est): 23.8MM **Privately Held**
WEB: www.aisintca.com
SIC: 3559 Automotive related machinery
PA: Aisin Corporation
2-1, Asahimachi
Kariya AIC 448-0

(G-12197)
BELANGER INC
1001 Doheny Dr (48167-1957)
PHONE..................................248 349-7010
Denis Pokrovsky, *Director*
EMP: 59
SALES (corp-wide): 6.6B **Publicly Held**
WEB: www.opwglobal.com
SIC: 3291 Abrasive products
HQ: Belanger, Inc.
9393 Prnceton Glendale Rd
West Chester OH 45011
517 870-3206

(G-12198)
BRENTON CONSULTING LLC
21820 Garfield Rd (48167-9712)
PHONE..................................248 342-6590
Brian Brenton, *President*
EMP: 6 **EST:** 2003
SALES (est): 142.3K **Privately Held**
SIC: 7372 7379 7389 Business oriented computer software; computer related consulting services;

(G-12199)
BROWNDOG CREAMERY LLC
118 E Main St (48167-1620)
PHONE..................................248 361-3759
Paul Gabriel, *Principal*
EMP: 11 **EST:** 2015
SALES (est): 509K **Privately Held**
WEB: www.browndogcreamery.com
SIC: 2021 Creamery butter

(G-12200)
CLOUDFACE LLC
996 Grace St (48167-1138)
PHONE..................................248 756-1688
EMP: 4
SALES (est): 92.6K **Privately Held**
WEB: www.cloudfaceusa.com
SIC: 3572 Computer storage devices

(G-12201)
COMPETITIVE CMPT INFO TECH INC
Also Called: Land and Sea Group
100 Maincentre Ste 1 (48167-1579)
PHONE..................................732 829-9699
Vijey R Seri, *CEO*
Srilaz Mi, *President*
Connie Laessig, *Financial Analy*
EMP: 16 **EST:** 1997
SALES (est): 285.4K **Privately Held**
WEB: www.ccitinc.com
SIC: 7371 7372 7379 Computer software development; prepackaged software; computer related consulting services

(G-12202)
COMPUTER DECISIONS INTL INC
22260 Haggerty Rd Ste 300 (48167-8985)
PHONE..................................248 473-5900
EMP: 4 **EST:** 2017
SALES (est): 71.4K **Privately Held**
WEB: www.empowerbiz.com
SIC: 3578 Calculating & accounting equipment

(G-12203)
COOPER-STANDARD AUTO OH LLC
40300 Traditions Dr (48168-9499)
PHONE..................................248 596-5900
David Larry, *Engineer*
Allen J Campbell, *Engineer*
EMP: 1 **EST:** 2001
SQ FT: 110,165
SALES (est): 4.3MM
SALES (corp-wide): 2.3B **Publicly Held**
WEB: www.cooperstandard.com
SIC: 4111 3714 Local & suburban transit; motor vehicle parts & accessories
PA: Cooper-Standard Holdings Inc.
40300 Traditions Dr
Northville MI 48168
248 596-5900

(G-12204)
COOPER-STANDARD AUTOMOTIVE INC (HQ)
40300 Traditions Dr (48168-9499)
PHONE..................................248 596-5900
Jeffrey S Edwards, *Ch of Bd*
D William Pumphrey Jr, *President*
Christopher E Couch, *Senior VP*
Susan P Kampe, *Senior VP*
Rebecca McCabe, *Vice Pres*
▲ **EMP:** 290 **EST:** 1936
SQ FT: 110,165
SALES (est): 2B
SALES (corp-wide): 2.3B **Publicly Held**
WEB: www.cooperstandard.com
SIC: 3714 Motor vehicle parts & accessories
PA: Cooper-Standard Holdings Inc.
40300 Traditions Dr
Northville MI 48168
248 596-5900

(G-12205)
COOPER-STANDARD FHS LLC
40300 Traditions Dr (48168-9499)
PHONE..................................248 596-5900
Jeffrey S Edwards, *CEO*
Allen J Campbell, *Vice Pres*
Juan Fernando De Miguel, *Vice Pres*
Timothy W Hefferon, *Vice Pres*
Barry V Lanken, *Vice Pres*
▲ **EMP:** 191 **EST:** 1994
SQ FT: 110,165
SALES (est): 23.2MM
SALES (corp-wide): 2.3B **Publicly Held**
WEB: www.cooperstandard.com
SIC: 3714 Motor vehicle parts & accessories
PA: Cooper-Standard Holdings Inc.
40300 Traditions Dr
Northville MI 48168
248 596-5900

(G-12206)
COOPER-STANDARD FOUNDATION INC
40300 Traditions Dr (48168-9499)
PHONE..................................248 596-5900
Jeffrey S Edwards, *Ch of Bd*
EMP: 1 **EST:** 2013
SQ FT: 110,168
SALES (est): 5.8MM
SALES (corp-wide): 2.3B **Publicly Held**
WEB: www.cooperstandard.com
SIC: 3714 Motor vehicle parts & accessories
PA: Cooper-Standard Holdings Inc.
40300 Traditions Dr
Northville MI 48168
248 596-5900

(G-12207)
COOPER-STANDARD HOLDINGS INC (PA)
Also Called: COOPER STANDARD
40300 Traditions Dr (48168-9499)
PHONE..................................248 596-5900
Jeffrey S Edwards, *Ch of Bd*
D William Pumphrey Jr, *President*
Christopher E Couch, *Senior VP*
Susan P Kampe, *Senior VP*
Soma Venkat, *Senior VP*
EMP: 5 **EST:** 1960
SALES (est): 2.3B **Publicly Held**
WEB: www.cooperstandard.com
SIC: 3714 Motor vehicle parts & accessories

(G-12208)
COOPER-STNDARD INDUS SPCLTY GR (HQ)
40300 Traditions Dr (48168-9499)
PHONE..................................330 339-3373
Pumphrey William Jr, *President*
Lisa Huntsman, *Vice Pres*
Don Lyons, *Engineer*
Dylan Menter, *Engineer*
Scott Paazig, *Engineer*
EMP: 14 **EST:** 1994
SALES (est): 23.8MM
SALES (corp-wide): 2.3B **Publicly Held**
WEB: www.cooperstandard.com
SIC: 3069 Molded rubber products
PA: Cooper-Standard Holdings Inc.
40300 Traditions Dr
Northville MI 48168
248 596-5900

(G-12209)
COOPER-STNDARD INDUS SPCLTY GR (HQ)
40300 Traditions Dr (48168-9499)
PHONE..................................248 596-5900
Kevin E Gray,
Dale Foland,

Jim Hummel,
Lisa Huntsman,
Chuck Laney,
▲ EMP: 100 EST: 1994
SALES (est): 65.3MM
SALES (corp-wide): 2.3B Publicly Held
WEB: www.cooperstandard.com
SIC: 3069 3061 Molded rubber products; mechanical rubber goods
PA: Cooper-Standard Holdings Inc.
40300 Traditions Dr
Northville MI 48168
248 596-5900

(G-12210)
CORR PACK IN
9833 5 Mile Rd (48168-9403)
PHONE 248 348-4188
Larry Gutowsky, President
EMP: 7 EST: 1977
SQ FT: 20,000
SALES (est): 949.5K Privately Held
SIC: 2653 Boxes, corrugated: made from purchased materials

(G-12211)
CS INTERMEDIATE HOLDCO 1 LLC
40300 Traditions Dr (48168-9499)
PHONE 248 596-5900
Jeffrey S Edwards, Ch of Bd
EMP: 1 EST: 2014
SQ FT: 110,165
SALES (est): 2.8MM
SALES (corp-wide): 2.3B Publicly Held
WEB: www.cooperstandard.com
SIC: 3714 Motor vehicle parts & accessories
PA: Cooper-Standard Holdings Inc.
40300 Traditions Dr
Northville MI 48168
248 596-5900

(G-12212)
DESIGNER WINDOW FASHIONS
436 N Center St (48167-1224)
PHONE 734 421-1600
Gary Zaguroli, Owner
EMP: 4 EST: 1948
SALES (est): 75.4K Privately Held
SIC: 2391 Curtains & draperies

(G-12213)
DETROIT ORIGINAL WINERY
44464 Larchwood Dr (48168-4372)
PHONE 248 924-2920
Kim Notario, Principal
EMP: 4 EST: 2017
SALES (est): 85.4K Privately Held
SIC: 2084 Wines

(G-12214)
DEUWAVE LLC
200 S Wing St (48167-1854)
PHONE 888 238-9283
Alvar Sushma, Administration
Sushma Alvar,
EMP: 4
SALES (est): 247.3K Privately Held
SIC: 3841 Diagnostic apparatus, medical

(G-12215)
ENTRON COMPUTER SYSTEMS INC
44554 Chedworth Ct (48167-8934)
PHONE 248 349-8898
Tim Evans, President
Harry Rodgers, Marketing Staff
EMP: 5 EST: 1995
SALES (est): 349.4K Privately Held
WEB: www.tjeservices.com
SIC: 3571 Electronic computers

(G-12216)
EYE 2 EYE CONTACT
723 River Park Vlg Blvd (48167-2777)
PHONE 313 378-7883
Willie Taylor, Principal
EMP: 4 EST: 2010
SALES (est): 228.1K Privately Held
WEB: www.eye2eyecontact4u2c.com
SIC: 3827 Optical instruments & lenses

(G-12217)
FIFTH BOX INDUSTRIES LLC
292 Ely Dr N (48167-2705)
PHONE 734 323-6388
Donald A Liamini, Principal
EMP: 6 EST: 2016
SALES (est): 184.8K Privately Held
SIC: 3999 Manufacturing industries

(G-12218)
FLORANCE TURNING COMPANY INC
44862 Aspen Ridge Dr (48168-4435)
PHONE 248 347-0068
Frank L Florance, President
Linda Florance, Admin Sec
EMP: 4
SQ FT: 1,800
SALES (est): 280K Privately Held
SIC: 3544 Special dies, tools, jigs & fixtures

(G-12219)
FONTS ABOUT INC
143 Cadycentre 130 (48167-1119)
PHONE 248 767-7504
Aubrie Ann Glennon, President
EMP: 5 EST: 2003 Privately Held
SIC: 7336 2759 Graphic arts & related design; promotional printing

(G-12220)
FULL OF SCENTS
47845 Milan Ct (48167-9817)
PHONE 734 972-6542
Collette Cook, Principal
EMP: 4 EST: 2010
SALES (est): 103.8K Privately Held
SIC: 2844 Toilet preparations

(G-12221)
FUZEN SOFTWARE INC
22260 Haggerty Rd Ste 285 (48167-8971)
PHONE 248 504-6870
EMP: 5 EST: 2009
SALES (est): 110K Privately Held
WEB: www.fuzensoft.com
SIC: 7372 Prepackaged software

(G-12222)
GAS RECOVERY SYSTEMS LLC
10611 5 Mile Rd (48168-9402)
PHONE 248 305-7774
Carlos Wilson, Regional Mgr
Jay Walkinhood, Manager
EMP: 25
SALES (corp-wide): 183.3MM Privately Held
SIC: 1389 Removal of condensate gasoline from field (gathering) lines
HQ: Gas Recovery Systems, Llc
1 N Lexington Ave Ste 620
White Plains NY 10601
914 421-4903

(G-12223)
GDC WORLDWIDE
9833 5 Mile Rd (48168-9403)
PHONE 248 348-4189
Larry Gutowsky, Owner
EMP: 4 EST: 2018
SALES (est): 89.2K Privately Held
SIC: 2653 Corrugated & solid fiber boxes

(G-12224)
GENTHERM INCORPORATED (PA)
21680 Haggerty Rd Ste 101 (48167-8994)
PHONE 248 504-0500
Ronald Hundzinski, Ch of Bd
Phillip M Eyler, President
Yijing Brentano, Senior VP
Matt Fisch, Senior VP
Wayne Kauffman, Senior VP
▲ EMP: 4148 EST: 1991
SALES (est): 913.1MM Publicly Held
WEB: www.gentherm.com
SIC: 3714 Motor vehicle electrical equipment

(G-12225)
GRAPHIC VISIONS INC
455 E Cady St (48167-1855)
PHONE 248 347-3355
Susan Dillon, President
Mike Dillon, Vice Pres
EMP: 29 EST: 1988
SALES (est): 3.1MM Privately Held
WEB: www.volkcorp.com
SIC: 3993 7336 Signs & advertising specialties; graphic arts & related design

(G-12226)
GREAT LAKES INFOTRONICS INC (PA)
22300 Haggerty Rd 100 (48167-8987)
PHONE 248 476-2500
James Rheinhart, Ch of Bd
Christopher Ciapala, President
Alan Witts, Corp Secy
Tom Deedler, Opers Dir
Vicki Rytel, Opers Staff
EMP: 25 EST: 1979
SQ FT: 19,800
SALES (est): 11.7MM Privately Held
WEB: www.infotronics.com
SIC: 5065 7371 7372 Electronic parts & equipment; custom computer programming services; prepackaged software

(G-12227)
GUERNSEY DAIRY STORES INC
Also Called: Guernsey Farms Dairy
21300 Novi Rd (48167-9701)
PHONE 248 349-1466
Martin McGuire, President
Gregory McGuire, Vice Pres
Matthew McGuire, Vice Pres
Rita Rice, CFO
Karen Kinville, Admin Sec
EMP: 170 EST: 1940
SQ FT: 28,000
SALES (est): 19.3MM Privately Held
WEB: www.guernseyfarmsdairy.com
SIC: 2024 5812 5451 Ice cream & frozen desserts; ice cream, soft drink & soda fountain stands; dairy products stores

(G-12228)
HARVEST INDUS & TRADE CO LLC
455 E Cady St (48167-1855)
PHONE 636 675-6430
Colin Wong, President
EMP: 5 EST: 2012
SALES (est): 251K Privately Held
WEB: www.harvestindustrial.com
SIC: 3993 Signs & advertising specialties

(G-12229)
HPI PRODUCTS INC
Also Called: Allpro Vector Group
640 Griswold St Ste 200 (48167-1691)
PHONE 248 773-7460
William E Garvey, Owner
EMP: 5
SQ FT: 600
SALES (corp-wide): 9.1MM Privately Held
WEB: www.hpiproducts.com
SIC: 2879 5191 Insecticides & pesticides; pesticides
PA: Hpi Products, Inc.
222 Sylvanie St
Saint Joseph MO 64501
816 233-1237

(G-12230)
HULET BODY CO INC
19700 Meadowbrook Rd (48167-9556)
PHONE 313 931-6000
Tom Letvin, CEO
Dee Letvin, Vice Pres
EMP: 12 EST: 1919
SQ FT: 15,000
SALES (est): 686.4K Privately Held
SIC: 3713 3715 7532 7538 Truck bodies (motor vehicles); trailer bodies; body shop, trucks; general automotive repair shops

(G-12231)
INNOVATIVE MACHINE TECHNOLOGY
Also Called: IMT
7591 Chubb Rd (48168-9616)
PHONE 248 348-1630
Bret Smith, President
Brian Slaven, General Mgr
Corine Smith, Corp Secy
EMP: 23 EST: 1982
SQ FT: 6,400
SALES (est): 1.2MM Privately Held
WEB: www.innovativemachinetech.com
SIC: 3599 Machine shop, jobbing & repair

(G-12232)
JAY INDUSTRIES INC
7455 Fox Hill Ln (48168-9544)
PHONE 313 240-7535
Theodore Maged, President
EMP: 6 EST: 1997
SALES (est): 455.2K Privately Held
SIC: 3441 Fabricated structural metal

(G-12233)
JOGUE INC
Also Called: Northville Laboratories
100 Rural Hill St (48167-1538)
PHONE 248 349-1501
Andrew Huber, CFO
EMP: 8
SALES (corp-wide): 14.8MM Privately Held
WEB: www.jogue.com
SIC: 2087 2844 2099 Flavoring extracts & syrups; perfumes & colognes; food preparations
PA: Jogue, Inc.
14731 Helm Ct
Plymouth MI 48170
734 207-0100

(G-12234)
KEMAI (USA) CHEMICAL CO LTD
48948 Freestone Dr (48168-8005)
PHONE 248 924-2225
Lizhi LI, General Mgr
John Zhang, Sales Mgr
▲ EMP: 5 EST: 2009
SQ FT: 2,700
SALES (est): 41MM Privately Held
WEB: www.dualrotary.com
SIC: 2869 Laboratory chemicals, organic

(G-12235)
LEMFORDER CORP
15811 Centennial Dr (48168-9629)
P.O. Box 219, Brewer ME (04412-0219)
PHONE 734 416-6200
EMP: 31 EST: 2012
SALES (est): 285.6K Privately Held
SIC: 3711 Motor vehicles & car bodies

(G-12236)
LYDALL PERFORMANCE MTLS US INC
22260 Haggerty Rd Ste 200 (48167-8969)
PHONE 248 596-2800
Louis Dannibale, Manager
EMP: 5
SALES (corp-wide): 4.4B Privately Held
WEB: www.lydallpm.com
SIC: 2631 Paperboard mills
HQ: Lydall Performance Materials (Us), Inc.
216 Wohlsen Way
Lancaster PA 17603

(G-12237)
LYDALL SEALING SOLUTIONS INC
22260 Haggerty Rd Ste 200 (48167-8969)
PHONE 248 596-2800
Franklin Fox, President
EMP: 100
SALES (corp-wide): 4.4B Privately Held
WEB: www.lydall.com
SIC: 3053 5013 Gaskets, packing & sealing devices; motor vehicle supplies & new parts
HQ: Lydall Sealing Solutions, Inc.
410 S 1st Ave
Marshalltown IA 50158

(G-12238)
MACH II ENTERPRISES INC
Also Called: Mach II Tax Service
200 S Main St Ste A (48167-2680)
PHONE 248 347-8822
EMP: 7
SALES (est): 503.6K Privately Held
SIC: 2395 7291 Embroidery & Income Tax Service

GEOGRAPHIC SECTION
Northville - Wayne County (G-12266)

(G-12239)
MEIDEN AMERICA INC
15800 Centennial Dr (48168-9675)
PHONE...................................734 459-1781
Ko Yamamoto, *President*
Junzo Inamura, *Principal*
Hidefumi Miura, *Principal*
Anirudh Sridharan, *Engineer*
Rodd Yamashita, *Engineer*
▲ **EMP:** 23 **EST:** 2003
SQ FT: 78,000
SALES (est): 6.7MM **Privately Held**
WEB: www.meidensha.com
SIC: 3825 3612 Engine electrical test equipment; distribution transformers, electric
PA: Meidensha Corporation
2-1-1, Osaki
Shinagawa-Ku TKY 141-0

(G-12240)
MITSUBISHI ELC AUTO AMER INC
15603 Centennial Dr (48168-8690)
PHONE...................................734 453-6200
Mike Delano, *President*
Dwayne Gray, *Regional Mgr*
Dan Delallo, *Business Mgr*
Ben Sagan, *Business Mgr*
Katsutoshi Urabe, *Vice Pres*
EMP: 80 **Privately Held**
WEB: www.meaa-mea.com
SIC: 3651 Amplifiers: radio, public address or musical instrument
HQ: Mitsubishi Electric Automotive America, Inc.
4773 Bethany Rd
Mason OH 45040
513 573-6614

(G-12241)
MITSUBISHI ELECTRIC US INC
15603 Centennial Dr (48168-8690)
PHONE...................................734 453-6200
Pokiyoshi Shima, *President*
Art Howell, *General Mgr*
Susan Parzych, *Engineer*
Greg Gall, *Controller*
Kurt Burkett, *Manager*
EMP: 4 **Privately Held**
WEB: www.us.mitsubishielectric.com
SIC: 5045 1796 5065 3534 Computer peripheral equipment; elevator installation & conversion; electronic parts & equipment; escalators, passenger & freight
HQ: Mitsubishi Electric Us, Inc.
5900 Katella Ave Ste C
Cypress CA 90630
714 220-2500

(G-12242)
MOBILITY ACCESSORIES LLC
7610 Salem Woods Dr (48168-9488)
PHONE...................................734 262-3760
Dave Brown,
EMP: 4 **EST:** 2017
SALES (est): 39.6K **Privately Held**
SIC: 3999 Manufacturing industries

(G-12243)
MOSER RACING INC
43641 Serenity Dr (48167-8930)
PHONE...................................248 348-6502
Robert Moser, *Owner*
EMP: 11 **EST:** 2003
SALES (est): 112.7K **Privately Held**
SIC: 3711 Automobile assembly, including specialty automobiles

(G-12244)
NORMAC INCORPORATED
720 Baseline Rd (48167-1266)
P.O. Box 245 (48167-0245)
PHONE...................................248 349-2644
Gil Carlson, *Engineer*
Emmanuel Gauzer, *Product Mgr*
EMP: 14
SQ FT: 7,000
SALES (corp-wide): 9.2MM **Privately Held**
WEB: www.normac.com
SIC: 3541 Machine tool replacement & repair parts, metal cutting types

PA: Normac Incorporated
93 Industrial Dr
Hendersonville NC 28739
828 209-9000

(G-12245)
NORTHVILLE CIDER MILL INC
714 Baseline Rd (48167-1266)
PHONE...................................248 349-3181
Diane Jones, *President*
Cheryl Nelson, *Vice Pres*
Robert Nelson, *Treasurer*
Melvin Jones, *Admin Sec*
EMP: 11 **EST:** 1873
SQ FT: 3,200
SALES (est): 1.1MM **Privately Held**
WEB: www.northvillecider.com
SIC: 5431 5499 5921 2086 Fruit stands or markets; beverage stores; wine; bottled & canned soft drinks; wines, brandy & brandy spirits; canned fruits & specialties

(G-12246)
NORTHVILLE LABORATORIES INC
Also Called: Flavors & Fragrances
100 Rural Hill St (48167-1538)
P.O. Box 190 (48167-0190)
PHONE...................................248 349-1500
Patrick Kilpatrick, *President*
EMP: 11 **EST:** 1929
SQ FT: 48,000
SALES (est): 335.7K **Privately Held**
WEB: www.northville.org
SIC: 2087 Extracts, flavoring

(G-12247)
NORTHVILLE STITCHING POST
Also Called: Mark II Enterprises
200 S Main St Ste A (48167-2680)
PHONE...................................248 347-7622
Nancy Lewis, *Partner*
Bruce Mach, *Partner*
EMP: 5 **EST:** 1990
SQ FT: 1,900
SALES (est): 360K **Privately Held**
WEB: www.northville.org
SIC: 2395 Embroidery products, except schiffli machine

(G-12248)
NORTHVILLE WINERY
630 Baseline Rd (48167-1265)
PHONE...................................248 320-6507
Nelson Carina, *Administration*
EMP: 4 **EST:** 2014
SALES (est): 136.2K **Privately Held**
WEB: www.thenorthvillewinery.com
SIC: 2084 Wines

(G-12249)
ONCOFUSION THERAPEUTICS INC
120 W Main St Ste 300 (48167-1584)
PHONE...................................248 361-3341
Arul M Chinnaiyan, *Principal*
Kenneth Pienta, *Principal*
Shaomeng Wang, *Principal*
EMP: 11 **EST:** 2012
SALES (est): 685.4K **Privately Held**
WEB: www.oncofusion.com
SIC: 3845 Electrotherapeutic apparatus

(G-12250)
OX ENGINEERED PRODUCTS LLC (PA)
22260 Haggerty Rd Ste 365 (48167-8970)
PHONE...................................248 289-9950
Dave Ulmer, *CEO*
Mike Lee, *General Mgr*
Cris Fauline, *COO*
Michael Ryan, *Exec VP*
Kevin Monday, *Vice Pres*
EMP: 12 **EST:** 2012
SALES (est): 25MM **Privately Held**
WEB: www.oxengineeredproducts.com
SIC: 2493 Wall tile, fiberboard

(G-12251)
PEERLESS GAGE
39645 Muirfield Ln (48167-3482)
PHONE...................................734 261-3000
Max Powers, *CEO*
EMP: 4 **EST:** 2010

SALES (est): 149.6K **Privately Held**
WEB: www.gtec.org
SIC: 3544 Special dies, tools, jigs & fixtures

(G-12252)
PERSPECTIVE SOFTWARE
143 Cdycntre 86nrthvl 86 Northville (48167)
PHONE...................................248 308-2418
Kenneth Pletzer, *Principal*
EMP: 5 **EST:** 2010
SALES (est): 73.9K **Privately Held**
SIC: 7372 Prepackaged software

(G-12253)
REJOICE INTERNATIONAL CORP
21800 Haggerty Rd Ste 203 (48167-8981)
PHONE...................................855 345-5575
Rowyda H Mackie, *Principal*
EMP: 7 **EST:** 2013
SALES (est): 463.2K **Privately Held**
WEB: www.rejoice-us.com
SIC: 2844 Toilet preparations

(G-12254)
RHYS WORLD PUBLISHING LLC
18579 Innsbrook Dr Apt 2 (48168-2410)
PHONE...................................248 974-7408
Darlissha Sadler, *Principal*
EMP: 4 **EST:** 2016
SALES (est): 64.4K **Privately Held**
SIC: 2741 Miscellaneous publishing

(G-12255)
ROLL IT UP INC
Also Called: Belanger Industrial Products
19414 Gerald St (48167-2517)
PHONE...................................248 735-8900
Lee Belanger, *President*
Richard Belanger, *Vice Pres*
Ian Beason, *Engineer*
Mark Jablonicky, *Engineer*
Jeff Underhill, *Engineer*
▲ **EMP:** 28 **EST:** 2002
SQ FT: 26,000
SALES (est): 11.4MM
SALES (corp-wide): 717.5MM **Privately Held**
WEB: www.motorcitywashworks.com
SIC: 3291 Abrasive wheels & grindstones, not artificial
HQ: Schaffner Manufacturing Co., Inc
21 Herron Ave
Pittsburgh PA 15202
412 761-9902

(G-12256)
SALEM TOOL COMPANY
7811 Salem Rd (48168-9423)
PHONE...................................248 349-2632
Leonard Bourgoin, *President*
EMP: 4 **EST:** 1993
SQ FT: 2,400 **Privately Held**
WEB: www.salemtool.com
SIC: 3599 Machine shop, jobbing & repair

(G-12257)
SANDBOX SOLUTIONS INC
1001 Doheny Dr (48167-1957)
P.O. Box 5470 (48167-5470)
PHONE...................................248 349-7010
L G Belanger, *CEO*
M J Belanger, *President*
Robert Wentworth, *Vice Pres*
Kathy Vandam, *Opers Staff*
Sue Pankratz, *Controller*
▲ **EMP:** 212 **EST:** 1969
SQ FT: 80,000
SALES (est): 25.4MM **Privately Held**
WEB: www.opwglobal.com
SIC: 3589 3291 1542 6719 Commercial cooking & foodwarming equipment; abrasive products; nonresidential construction; investment holding companies, except banks

(G-12258)
SCHLEGEL
17732 Rolling Woods Cir (48168-1890)
PHONE...................................248 344-0997
Peter Schlegel, *Principal*
EMP: 6 **EST:** 2010

SALES (est): 122.6K **Privately Held**
WEB: www.schlegelgiesse.com
SIC: 3999 Manufacturing industries

(G-12259)
SEPRACOR INC
49928 Parkside Dr (48168-6825)
PHONE...................................508 481-6700
EMP: 4 **EST:** 2018
SALES (est): 89.6K **Privately Held**
SIC: 2834 Pharmaceutical preparations

(G-12260)
SFM LLC
43587 Prestwick Cir S (48168-5016)
PHONE...................................248 719-0212
EMP: 5 **EST:** 2019
SALES (est): 147.2K **Privately Held**
WEB: www.sfmgroupllc.com
SIC: 3621 Motors & generators

(G-12261)
SKYWORKS LLC
Also Called: Artificial Sky
15461 Bay Hill Dr (48168-9643)
PHONE...................................972 284-9093
Jim Poore, *Opers Mgr*
Mark Jenzen, *Mng Member*
EMP: 10 **EST:** 2010
SALES (est): 2MM **Privately Held**
WEB: www.artificialsky.com
SIC: 3646 Ceiling systems, luminous

(G-12262)
SPIDERS SOFTWARE SOLUTIONS LLC
Also Called: Corporate
49831 Parkside Dr (48168-6822)
PHONE...................................248 305-3225
Jagadish Boddapati, *CEO*
Gita Boddapati, *President*
EMP: 7 **EST:** 2006
SALES (est): 392.6K **Privately Held**
SIC: 7379 7372 Computer related consulting services; prepackaged software

(G-12263)
STEEL INDUSTRIES INC
41790 Broquet Dr (48167-2402)
PHONE...................................734 427-8550
Harold Eklnuad, *Owner*
EMP: 4 **EST:** 2015
SALES (est): 97.2K **Privately Held**
SIC: 3599 Industrial machinery

(G-12264)
STOKES AUTOMATION
7478 Fox Hill Ln (48168-8814)
PHONE...................................248 573-5277
Don Stokes, *Principal*
EMP: 5 **EST:** 2015
SALES (est): 92.3K **Privately Held**
WEB: www.lin01.stokesautomation.com
SIC: 3569 General industrial machinery

(G-12265)
TENNECO AUTOMOTIVE OPER CO
15701 Technology Dr (48168)
PHONE...................................248 849-1258
Lynnette Vollink, *Human Resources*
EMP: 300 **EST:** 1977
SALES (est): 50MM
SALES (corp-wide): 15.3B **Publicly Held**
WEB: www.tenneco.com
SIC: 3714 Motor vehicle wheels & parts
PA: Tenneco Inc.
500 N Field Dr
Lake Forest IL 60045
847 482-5000

(G-12266)
TRELLBORG SLING SLTIONS US INC
15701 Centennial Dr (48168-8691)
PHONE...................................734 354-1250
EMP: 5
SALES (corp-wide): 3.8B **Privately Held**
WEB: www.trelleborg.com
SIC: 3089 Plastic processing
HQ: Trelleborg Sealing Solutions Us, Inc.
2531 Bremer Rd
Fort Wayne IN 46803
260 749-9631

Northville - Wayne County (G-12267)

(G-12267)
TS ENTERPRISE ASSOCIATES INC
Also Called: Advanced Technologies Cons
110 W Main St (48167-1521)
P.O. Box 905 (48167-0905)
PHONE..........................248 348-2963
Thomas S Close, *CEO*
Susan Close, *President*
Bob Kelly, *Regl Sales Mgr*
Christine Lollar, *Regl Sales Mgr*
Aaron Paul, *Regl Sales Mgr*
▲ **EMP:** 14 **EST:** 1989
SQ FT: 3,000
SALES (est): 2.7MM **Privately Held**
WEB: www.advancedtechnologies.net
SIC: 3826 Analytical instruments

(G-12268)
UNDERSTATED CORRUGATED LLC
635 Horton St (48167-1209)
PHONE..........................248 880-5767
Paul Roberts, *Principal*
EMP: 4 **EST:** 2010
SALES (est): 104.4K **Privately Held**
WEB: www.mykittyblock.com
SIC: 2653 Corrugated & solid fiber boxes

(G-12269)
VIBRACOUSTIC USA INC
Also Called: Trelleborg Automotive
15701 Centennial Dr (48168-8691)
PHONE..........................734 254-9140
Robert Peacock, *Vice Pres*
Steven Molesworth, *Engineer*
Jenna Maisonville, *Project Engr*
Erich Merrill, *Project Engr*
Tristan Roeda, *Project Engr*
EMP: 5
SALES (corp-wide): 2.4B **Privately Held**
WEB: www.vibracoustic.com
SIC: 3061 Mechanical rubber goods
HQ: Vibracoustic Usa, Inc.
400 Aylworth Ave
South Haven MI 49090

(G-12270)
VOLK CORPORATION
Forbes Company
455 E Cady St (48167-1855)
PHONE..........................616 940-9900
Breck Foster, *Opers-Prdtn-Mfg*
EMP: 6
SALES (corp-wide): 23.9MM **Privately Held**
WEB: www.volkcorp.com
SIC: 5113 3953 Shipping supplies; marking devices
PA: Volk Corporation
23936 Indl Pk Dr
Farmington Hills MI 48335
248 477-6700

(G-12271)
WEBSTER COLD FORGE CO
47652 Pine Creek Ct (48168-8527)
PHONE..........................313 554-4500
Robert Webster, *President*
Jack McGill, *Principal*
EMP: 11 **EST:** 1925
SQ FT: 100,000
SALES (est): 379.6K **Privately Held**
SIC: 3462 3465 3469 Iron & steel forgings; automotive stampings; metal stampings

(G-12272)
ZF NORTH AMERICA INC (DH)
Also Called: Division Z
15811 Centennial Dr (48168-9629)
PHONE..........................734 416-6200
Franz Kleiner, *President*
Carl Barbara, *Principal*
Corey Zaren, *Principal*
Gary Bain, *Business Mgr*
Dirk Adamczyk, *Vice Pres*
◆ **EMP:** 500 **EST:** 1979
SQ FT: 5,000
SALES (est): 21.4B
SALES (corp-wide): 216.2K **Privately Held**
WEB: www.zf.com
SIC: 3714 5013 Motor vehicle parts & accessories; automotive supplies & parts
HQ: Zf Friedrichshafen Ag
Lowentaler Str. 20
Friedrichshafen BW 88046
754 177-0

Norton Shores
Muskegon County

(G-12273)
A K INDUSTRIES
1737 Ritter Dr (49441-4603)
PHONE..........................231 726-0134
Anthony Kaster, *Principal*
EMP: 7 **EST:** 2018
SALES (est): 98.4K **Privately Held**
WEB: www.akindustries.com
SIC: 3999 Manufacturing industries

(G-12274)
AEROVISION AIRCRAFT SVCS LLC
620 E Ellis Rd (49441-5672)
PHONE..........................231 799-9000
Jeffrey Barnes, *President*
Greg Van Boxel,
EMP: 42 **EST:** 2004
SALES (est): 21.4MM
SALES (corp-wide): 11.6B **Publicly Held**
WEB: www.aerovi.com
SIC: 3724 3728 Aircraft engines & engine parts; aircraft parts & equipment
PA: Lkq Corporation
500 W Madison St Ste 2800
Chicago IL 60661
312 621-1950

(G-12275)
AEROVISION INTERNATIONAL LLC
620 E Ellis Rd (49441-5672)
PHONE..........................231 799-9000
Dominick P Zarcone, *President*
EMP: 42 **EST:** 2003
SQ FT: 12,000
SALES (est): 19.2MM
SALES (corp-wide): 11.6B **Publicly Held**
WEB: www.aerovi.com
SIC: 3724 3728 4581 Aircraft engines & engine parts; aircraft parts & equipment; aircraft maintenance & repair services
PA: Lkq Corporation
500 W Madison St Ste 2800
Chicago IL 60661
312 621-1950

(G-12276)
AIR MASTER SYSTEMS CORP
6480 Norton Center Dr (49441-6034)
PHONE..........................231 798-1111
Don Nelson, *CEO*
Greg Cook, *Regional Mgr*
Carly K EXT, *Project Mgr*
Rachelle Papp, *Project Mgr*
Luis Corrales, *Engineer*
EMP: 25 **EST:** 1975
SQ FT: 60,000
SALES (est): 7.8MM **Privately Held**
WEB: www.airmastersystems.com
SIC: 3821 Laboratory equipment: fume hoods, distillation racks, etc.

(G-12277)
AVI INVENTORY SERVICES LLC (PA)
620 E Ellis Rd (49441-5672)
PHONE..........................231 799-9000
Nate Russell, *Counsel*
Rick Cramblet, *Exec VP*
Angela Baker, *Vice Pres*
Pete Gibson, *VP Business*
Natalie Medema, *Sales Staff*
EMP: 40 **EST:** 2009
SALES (est): 5.4MM **Privately Held**
WEB: www.aerovi.com
SIC: 3724 3728 Aircraft engines & engine parts; aircraft parts & equipment

(G-12278)
BENCHMARK MANUFACTURING
856 E Broadway Ave (49444-2328)
PHONE..........................231 375-8172
EMP: 4 **EST:** 2018
SALES (est): 143.6K **Privately Held**
SIC: 3999 Manufacturing industries

(G-12279)
BLACKLINE BEAR LLC
5000 Hakes Dr Ste 200 (49441-5574)
PHONE..........................616 291-1521
EMP: 4 **EST:** 2018
SALES (est): 148.5K **Privately Held**
SIC: 3531 Construction machinery

(G-12280)
BRY MAC INC
Also Called: Dietech
865 E Porter Rd (49441-5972)
PHONE..........................231 799-2211
Brian McCarthy, *President*
Bob Tilden, *Engineer*
EMP: 9 **EST:** 1993
SQ FT: 4,000
SALES (est): 1MM **Privately Held**
WEB: www.dietechusa.com
SIC: 3544 Special dies & tools

(G-12281)
BUSH CONCRETE PRODUCTS INC
3584 Airline Rd (49444-3865)
PHONE..........................231 733-1904
Gerald McGrath, *President*
EMP: 12 **EST:** 1928
SQ FT: 15,000
SALES (est): 1.8MM **Privately Held**
WEB: www.bushconcreteproducts.com
SIC: 3272 Concrete products, precast; tanks, concrete; burial vaults, concrete or precast terrazzo

(G-12282)
CABINET HEADQUARTERS LLC
3522 Airline Rd (49444-3865)
PHONE..........................231 286-3207
Mitchell L May, *Principal*
EMP: 7 **EST:** 2018
SALES (est): 509.5K **Privately Held**
WEB: www.cabinetheadquarters.com
SIC: 2434 Wood kitchen cabinets

(G-12283)
CAKE FLOUR
1811 W Norton Ave (49441-4284)
PHONE..........................231 571-3054
Nicholas Sean Johnson, *Owner*
EMP: 4 **EST:** 2014
SALES (est): 71.1K **Privately Held**
SIC: 2041 Cake flour

(G-12284)
CANNON-MUSKEGON CORPORATION
2875 Lincoln St (49441-3313)
P.O. Box 506, Muskegon (49443-0506)
PHONE..........................231 755-1681
Mark Dunagan, *Ch of Bd*
Douglas Orr, *President*
Erik Gentzkow, *General Mgr*
Matthew Werksma, *Controller*
Michael King, *Marketing Staff*
▲ **EMP:** 158 **EST:** 1952
SQ FT: 130,000
SALES (est): 32.7MM
SALES (corp-wide): 245.5B **Publicly Held**
WEB: www.cannonmuskegon.com
SIC: 3313 3341 3339 3312 Alloys, additive, except copper: not made in blast furnaces; secondary nonferrous metals; primary nonferrous metals; blast furnaces & steel mills
HQ: Sps Technologies, Llc
301 Highland Ave
Jenkintown PA 19046
215 572-3000

(G-12285)
CHALLENGE MACHINERY COMPANY (PA)
6125 Norton Center Dr (49441-6081)
PHONE..........................231 799-8484
Larry J Ritsema, *President*
Edgar Martin, *Chairman*
Lawrence D Schrader, *Treasurer*
Susan Hilliard, *Admin Sec*
▲ **EMP:** 43 **EST:** 1870
SQ FT: 40,000
SALES (est): 12.5MM **Privately Held**
WEB: www.challengemachinery.com
SIC: 3554 Die cutting & stamping machinery, paper converting

(G-12286)
COASTLINE MANUFACTURING LLC
6215 Norton Center Dr (49441-6029)
PHONE..........................231 798-1700
Peter A Van Dyke, *Administration*
EMP: 5 **EST:** 2012
SALES (est): 189.6K **Privately Held**
SIC: 3999 Manufacturing industries

(G-12287)
DAMA TOOL & GAUGE COMPANY
Also Called: Unicor
6175 Norton Center Dr (49441-6081)
PHONE..........................616 842-9631
Cesar Castro, *President*
Mary Castro, *Vice Pres*
EMP: 23 **EST:** 1951
SQ FT: 9,000
SALES (est): 3.7MM **Privately Held**
WEB: www.unicor.net
SIC: 1389 3566 Oil field services; drives, high speed industrial, except hydrostatic

(G-12288)
DYNAMIC CONVEYOR CORPORATION
Also Called: Dyna-Con
5980 Grand Haven Rd (49441-6012)
PHONE..........................231 798-0014
Jill Batka, *General Mgr*
Curtis Chambers, *Chairman*
John Stong, *Sales Mgr*
Mark Aamodt, *Sales Staff*
Jim Mueller, *Sales Staff*
EMP: 20 **EST:** 1991
SQ FT: 48,000
SALES (est): 4.8MM **Privately Held**
WEB: www.dynamicconveyor.com
SIC: 3535 Conveyors & conveying equipment

(G-12289)
EAGLE MACHINE TOOL CORPORATION
6060 Grand Haven Rd (49441-6014)
PHONE..........................231 798-8473
Theodore Fleis, *President*
Mary Lou Fleis, *Corp Secy*
EMP: 8 **EST:** 1991
SQ FT: 5,000
SALES (est): 927.4K **Privately Held**
WEB: www.eaglemachinetool.com
SIC: 3542 Machine tools, metal forming type

(G-12290)
EARTHTRONICS INC
800 E Ellis Rd Ste 574 (49441-5622)
PHONE..........................231 332-1188
Tripp Smith, *Vice Pres*
Diane Pena, *Regl Sales Mgr*
Lesley Budde, *Sales Staff*
Nancie Chandonnet, *Sales Staff*
Jennifer Ferenz, *Mktg Dir*
EMP: 15 **EST:** 2007
SALES (est): 2.6MM **Privately Held**
WEB: www.earthtronics.com
SIC: 3646 Commercial indusl & institutional electric lighting fixtures

(G-12291)
EMERALD TOOL INC
6305 Norton Center Dr (49441-6031)
PHONE..........................231 799-9193
Tom Reidy, *President*
Travis Reidy, *Vice Pres*
EMP: 9 **EST:** 1994
SQ FT: 14,000
SALES (est): 912.2K **Privately Held**
WEB: www.emeraldtool.net
SIC: 3599 Machine shop, jobbing & repair

(G-12292)
EQI LTD
5797 Harvey St (49444-7783)
PHONE..........................616 850-2630
EMP: 6

GEOGRAPHIC SECTION

Norton Shores - Muskegon County (G-12318)

SALES (est): 541K **Privately Held**
SIC: 3321 Gray And Ductile Iron Foundries

(G-12293)
FIRST PLACE MANUFACTURING LLC
6234 Norton Center Dr (49441-6030)
PHONE 231 798-1694
Erik Sportell, *Mng Member*
◆ **EMP:** 4 **EST:** 2007
SQ FT: 5,000
SALES (est): 1MM **Privately Held**
WEB: www.firstplacemfg.com
SIC: 3312 Tool & die steel

(G-12294)
FWI INC
Also Called: Flairwood
6230 Norton Center Dr (49441-6030)
PHONE 231 798-8324
Paul Remondino, *President*
Patricia Remondino, *Corp Secy*
Terry Hill, *Vice Pres*
Greg Lonnee, *Vice Pres*
Dan Turcott, *Engineer*
EMP: 30 **EST:** 1976
SQ FT: 32,000
SALES (est): 2.6MM **Privately Held**
WEB: www.flairwood.com
SIC: 2431 2541 3993 2521 Woodwork, interior & ornamental; showcases, except refrigerated: wood; signs & advertising specialties; wood office furniture; wood household furniture; wood kitchen cabinets

(G-12295)
GRAPHICS UNLIMITED INC
1279 Porter Rd (49441-5789)
PHONE 231 773-2696
Wayne Kamp, *President*
EMP: 5 **EST:** 1983
SALES (est): 369.8K **Privately Held**
WEB: www.trafficgraffix.com
SIC: 2791 2752 5699 7336 Typesetting; commercial printing, lithographic; T-shirts, custom printed; graphic arts & related design

(G-12296)
GREAT LAKES PRTG SOLUTIONS INC
5163 Robert Hunter Dr (49441-6547)
PHONE 231 799-6000
David Anderson, *President*
Paul Sikkenga, *Prdtn Mgr*
Ann Fraser, *Accountant*
George Myler, *Sales Executive*
Jack De Jonge, *Manager*
EMP: 21 **EST:** 1999
SQ FT: 45,000
SALES (est): 2.1MM **Privately Held*
WEB: www.glpsi.com
SIC: 2752 Commercial printing, offset

(G-12297)
HESTIA INC
Also Called: American Panel
650 Airport Pl (49441-6550)
PHONE 616 296-0533
Jeffrey R Kreiser, *President*
Ann Kreiser, *Vice Pres*
Jeff Kreiser, *CFO*
EMP: 8 **EST:** 2007
SQ FT: 22,000
SALES (est): 2MM **Privately Held**
WEB: www.americanpanelhearth.com
SIC: 2298 Insulator pads, cordage

(G-12298)
ID SYSTEMS INC
Also Called: Inter Dyne Systems
676 E Ellis Rd (49441-5672)
PHONE 231 799-8760
Ann Moore, *President*
Jack Andree, *Vice Pres*
Greg Ramey, *Sales Mgr*
EMP: 15 **EST:** 1977
SQ FT: 4,000
SALES (est): 3.6MM **Privately Held**
WEB: www.interdynesystems.com
SIC: 3821 Laboratory equipment: fume hoods, distillation racks, etc.

(G-12299)
ILUMIGREEN CORP
6259 Norton Center Dr (49441-6029)
PHONE 616 318-3087
EMP: 7 **EST:** 2015
SALES (est): 610.9K **Privately Held**
WEB: www.ilumigreen.com
SIC: 3648 Lighting equipment

(G-12300)
INTRICATE GRINDING MCH SPC INC
1081 S Gateway Blvd (49441-6074)
PHONE 231 798-2154
Brenda Amaya, *President*
EMP: 35 **EST:** 1968
SQ FT: 16,000
SALES (est): 1.2MM **Privately Held**
WEB: www.intricategrinding.com
SIC: 3599 Machine shop, jobbing & repair

(G-12301)
IOPERATIONS INC
Also Called: IMS
1269 E Mt Grfeld Rd Ste D (49441)
PHONE 616 607-9751
Aaron Russick, *President*
Gilbert McDonald, *Exec VP*
Mike Hecksel, *Program Mgr*
◆ **EMP:** 19 **EST:** 2008
SALES (est): 5MM
SALES (corp-wide): 3.5B **Publicly Held**
WEB: www.rollon-ims.com
SIC: 3599 Machine shop, jobbing & repair
PA: The Timken Company
4500 Mount Pleasant St Nw
North Canton OH 44720
234 262-3000

(G-12302)
J & M MACHINE PRODUCTS INC
1821 Manor Dr (49441-3498)
PHONE 231 755-1622
Joseph J Rahrig, *President*
Robert Lindstrom, *Vice Pres*
Adam Gannon, *QC Mgr*
Pat Smith, *QC Mgr*
Chris Rahrig, *Treasurer*
▲ **EMP:** 80 **EST:** 1980
SQ FT: 30,000
SALES (est): 10.4MM **Privately Held**
WEB: www.jmmachine.com
SIC: 3599 3365 3441 3325 Machine shop, jobbing & repair; aluminum foundries; fabricated structural metal; steel foundries; sheet metalwork

(G-12303)
J F MCCAUGHIN CO (DH)
2817 Mccracken St (49441-3420)
PHONE 231 759-7304
Pat Mc Caughin, *President*
▲ **EMP:** 29 **EST:** 1960
SQ FT: 20,000
SALES (est): 8.9MM
SALES (corp-wide): 741.2MM **Privately Held**
WEB: www.paramelt.com
SIC: 3999 Candles
HQ: Paramelt Usa, Inc.
2817 Mccracken St
Norton Shores MI 49441
231 759-7304

(G-12304)
JACKIESWOODWORKS
753 Ross Rd (49441-4959)
PHONE 616 914-2961
Jackie Danhof, *Principal*
EMP: 4 **EST:** 2018
SALES (est): 102K **Privately Held**
SIC: 2431 Millwork

(G-12305)
JOHNSON TECHNOLOGY INC
6060 Norton Center Dr (49441-6087)
PHONE 231 777-2685
Joyce Carlyle Swartz, *Manager*
EMP: 459
SALES (corp-wide): 79.6B **Publicly Held**
SIC: 3724 Turbines, aircraft type
HQ: Johnson Technology, Inc.
2034 Latimer Dr
Muskegon MI 49442

(G-12306)
KAYDON CORPORATION
Kaydon Bearings Division
2860 Mccracken St (49441-3495)
P.O. Box 688, Muskegon (49443-0688)
PHONE 231 755-3741
Mark Grauberger, *General Mgr*
Chuck Hacker, *General Mgr*
Daniel Parlagreco, *Vice Pres*
Jim Bandelin, *Opers Staff*
Kenny Fenters, *Purch Mgr*
EMP: 160
SALES (corp-wide): 8.6B **Privately Held**
WEB: www.skf.com
SIC: 3562 5085 3568 8711 Ball & roller bearings; industrial supplies; bearings; power transmission equipment; engineering services
HQ: Kaydon Corporation
2723 S State St Ste 300
Ann Arbor MI 48104
734 747-7025

(G-12307)
KOPPEL TOOL & ENGINEERING LLC
1099 N Gateway Blvd (49441-6092)
PHONE 616 638-2611
Matt Koppel, *General Mgr*
Matthew C Koppel, *President*
EMP: 7 **EST:** 1999
SQ FT: 17,000
SALES (est): 708.6K **Privately Held**
WEB: www.koppelindustries.com
SIC: 3599 Machine shop, jobbing & repair

(G-12308)
LAKETON TRUSS INC
1527 Scranton Dr (49441-5245)
PHONE 231 798-3467
Charles Morton, *Principal*
EMP: 6 **EST:** 2009
SALES (est): 230.7K **Privately Held**
SIC: 2439 Structural wood members

(G-12309)
MAW VENTURES INC
6230 Norton Center Dr (49441-6030)
PHONE 231 798-8324
Wayne Baxter, *CEO*
Joel Pyper, *President*
EMP: 30 **EST:** 2015
SQ FT: 50,000
SALES (est): 1.8MM **Privately Held**
SIC: 2431 2541 3993 Woodwork, interior & ornamental; showcases, except refrigerated: wood; signs & advertising specialties

(G-12310)
MHS CONVEYOR CORP ○
1300 E Mount Garfield Rd (49441-6097)
PHONE 231 798-4547
Scott McReynolds, *CEO*
EMP: 300 **EST:** 2021
SALES (est): 27MM
SALES (corp-wide): 808.1MM **Privately Held**
WEB: www.mhsglobal.com
SIC: 3535 Conveyors & conveying equipment
HQ: Material Handling Systems Inc
131 Griffin Way
Mount Washington KY 40047
502 636-0690

(G-12311)
MICRGRAPHICS PRINTING INC (PA)
Also Called: Lee Printing & Graphics
2637 Emerson Blvd (49441-3503)
PHONE 231 739-6575
Richard Voss, *Owner*
Marcia Banninga, *Vice Pres*
EMP: 19 **EST:** 1973
SALES (est): 1.4MM **Privately Held**
WEB: www.micrgraphics.com
SIC: 2752 2759 2791 2789 Commercial printing, offset; letterpress printing; typesetting; bookbinding & related work; manifold business forms

(G-12312)
MONARCH POWDER COATING INC
5906 Grand Haven Rd (49441-6012)
PHONE 231 798-1422
Steven Johnson, *President*
EMP: 5 **EST:** 1998
SQ FT: 5,000
SALES (est): 456.3K **Privately Held**
WEB: www.monarchpowdercoating.com
SIC: 3479 Coating of metals & formed products

(G-12313)
MUSKEGON BRAKE & DISTRG CO LLC (PA)
Also Called: Muskegon Brake & Parts
848 E Broadway Ave (49444-2328)
PHONE 231 733-0874
Robert Cutler,
EMP: 43 **EST:** 1945
SALES (est): 8.4MM **Privately Held**
WEB: www.muskegonbrake.net
SIC: 5531 5013 3493 7539 Automotive tires; motor vehicle supplies & new parts; steel springs, except wire; automotive repair shops

(G-12314)
MUSKEGON HEIGHTS WATER FILTER
2323 Seminole Rd (49441-4230)
PHONE 231 780-3415
Troy Bell, *City Mgr*
Darryl Van Dyke, *Director*
EMP: 8 **EST:** 1977
SALES (est): 606K **Privately Held**
WEB: www.muskegonheights.us
SIC: 3569 Filters

(G-12315)
NATIONAL AMBUCS INC
Also Called: Ambucs Muskegon Chapter
708 Mapleway Dr (49441-6500)
PHONE 231 798-4244
Kevin Dick, *President*
Robert Kendall, *Treasurer*
EMP: 5 **EST:** 2010
SALES (est): 70.2K **Privately Held**
SIC: 3944 7389 Tricycles;

(G-12316)
NEWS ONE INC
Also Called: Mibiz
4080 Oak Hollow Ct (49441-4565)
PHONE 231 798-4669
William R Lowry, *President*
Renee Looman, *Advt Staff*
Tarah Buchan, *Office Mgr*
EMP: 21 **EST:** 1988
SALES (est): 1.6MM **Privately Held**
WEB: www.mibiz.com
SIC: 2711 Newspapers, publishing & printing

(G-12317)
NMP INC
Also Called: Nowak Machine Products
6170 Norton Center Dr (49441-6080)
PHONE 231 798-8851
Kenneth Nowak, *President*
Mike Orchard, *COO*
Carl Dam, *Engineer*
Ken Nowak, *Engineer*
Mark Nowak, *Engineer*
EMP: 50 **EST:** 1983
SQ FT: 60,000
SALES (est): 7.8MM **Privately Held**
WEB: www.nowakmp.com
SIC: 3599 Machine shop, jobbing & repair

(G-12318)
NON-FERROUS CAST ALLOYS INC
1146 N Gateway Blvd (49441-6083)
PHONE 231 799-0550
Dale Boersema, *President*
Ben Boersema, *Vice Pres*
Amy S Rademaker, *Opers Staff*
Seth Adkins, *QC Mgr*
Adam Gannon, *QC Mgr*
▼ **EMP:** 52 **EST:** 1972
SQ FT: 61,000

Norton Shores - Muskegon County (G-12319)

SALES (est): 9.7MM Privately Held
WEB: www.nfca.com
SIC: 3366 3471 3369 3365 Brass foundry; bronze foundry; plating & polishing; nonferrous foundries; aluminum foundries

(G-12319)
NORTHERN MACHINE TOOL COMPANY
761 Alberta Ave (49441-3002)
PHONE 231 755-1603
Gerhard Olsen, *Ch of Bd*
Stephen Olsen, *President*
Steve Olsen, *General Mgr*
Brian Kieft, *Design Engr*
Dan Olsen, *Treasurer*
EMP: 40 **EST:** 1946
SQ FT: 32,000
SALES (est): 4.8MM Privately Held
WEB: www.nmtdie.com
SIC: 3544 Special dies & tools

(G-12320)
NORTON TOOL & GAGE LLC
4442 Hickory Ln (49441-5643)
PHONE 231 750-9789
Steven Smith, *Administration*
EMP: 5 **EST:** 2017
SQ FT: 6,000
SALES (est): 214.3K Privately Held
SIC: 3599 Machine shop, jobbing & repair

(G-12321)
NU-PAK SOLUTIONS INC
2850 Lincoln St (49441-3314)
PHONE 231 755-1662
Herbert Bevelhymer, *President*
EMP: 10 **EST:** 2000
SQ FT: 50,000
SALES (est): 1.6MM Privately Held
WEB: www.nupaksolutions.com
SIC: 3086 Packaging & shipping materials, foamed plastic

(G-12322)
NUGENT SAND COMPANY INC
2925 Lincoln St (49441-3393)
PHONE 231 755-1686
Robert Chandonnet, *Ch of Bd*
David L Terpsma, *Corp Secy*
John A Nevedal, *Vice Pres*
EMP: 45 **EST:** 1912
SQ FT: 6,000
SALES (est): 10.6MM Privately Held
WEB: www.nugsand.com
SIC: 1442 Construction sand & gravel

(G-12323)
PACE INDUSTRIES LLC
Also Called: Port City Castings
711 E Porter Rd (49441-5978)
PHONE 231 777-3941
Mark Pickett, *Branch Mgr*
EMP: 600
SALES (corp-wide): 682.5MM Privately Held
WEB: www.paceind.com
SIC: 3363 Aluminum die-castings
HQ: Pace Industries, Llc
  481 S Shiloh Dr
  Fayetteville AR 72704
  479 443-1455

(G-12324)
PATTERSON PRECISION MFG INC
Also Called: ACE TOOLING
1188 E Broadway Ave (49444-2356)
PHONE 231 733-1913
John Patterson, *CEO*
EMP: 26 **EST:** 2017
SALES (est): 2.2MM Privately Held
WEB: www.pattersonpmfg.com
SIC: 3599 3312 3365 3369 Machine shop, jobbing & repair; tool & die steel & alloys; aerospace castings, aluminum; aerospace castings, nonferrous: except aluminum

(G-12325)
PEPSI-COLA METRO BTLG CO INC
4900 Paul Ct (49441-5566)
PHONE 231 798-1274
Dave Purple, *Manager*
EMP: 6
SALES (corp-wide): 70.3B Publicly Held
WEB: www.pepsico.com
SIC: 2086 Soft drinks: packaged in cans, bottles, etc.
HQ: Pepsi-Cola Metropolitan Bottling Company, Inc.
  1111 Westchester Ave
  White Plains NY 10604
  914 767-6000

(G-12326)
PREDATOR PRODUCTS COMPANY
4030 Chilton Dr (49441-5016)
PHONE 231 799-8300
Lou Pomadille, *Principal*
EMP: 5 **EST:** 2013
SALES (est): 80.9K Privately Held
SIC: 3949 Sporting & athletic goods

(G-12327)
R & D MACHINE AND TOOL INC
6059 Norton Center Dr (49441-6082)
PHONE 231 798-8500
Dan Wilson, *President*
Robert Smith III, *Exec VP*
EMP: 9 **EST:** 1997
SQ FT: 6,000
SALES (est): 1.7MM Privately Held
WEB: www.addmecorp.com
SIC: 3599 3544 Custom machinery; special dies, tools, jigs & fixtures

(G-12328)
RIVERCITY ROLLFORM INC
1130 E Mount Garfield Rd (49441-6076)
PHONE 231 799-9550
Roy Johnson Jr, *President*
Theran Nordstrom, *Engineer*
EMP: 23 **EST:** 1995
SQ FT: 20,000
SALES (est): 2.7MM Privately Held
WEB: www.mi-pcrg.com
SIC: 3544 Special dies & tools

(G-12329)
SCC PLASTICS INC
Also Called: Seabrook Plastics
1869 Lindberg Dr (49441-3410)
PHONE 231 759-8820
Tom Wallace, *President*
Scott Lamphere, *Purchasing*
Craig Gray, *Controller*
Cirila Phillips, *Administration*
▲ **EMP:** 32 **EST:** 1994
SQ FT: 24,000
SALES (est): 6.4MM Privately Held
WEB: www.seabrookplastics.com
SIC: 3089 Injection molding of plastics
PA: Molding Solutions, Inc.
  1734 Airpark Dr Ste F
  Grand Haven MI 49417

(G-12330)
SILVER CREEK MANUFACTURING INC
696 Airport Pl (49441-6550)
PHONE 231 798-3003
Susan Bush, *President*
Andy Bush, *Vice Pres*
George Morales, *QC Mgr*
Lindy Vallier, *Supervisor*
EMP: 10 **EST:** 1998
SQ FT: 20,000
SALES (est): 1.7MM Privately Held
WEB: www.silvercreekmfg.com
SIC: 3469 Stamping metal for the trade

(G-12331)
SMART VISION LIGHTS LLC
5113 Robert Hunter Dr (49441-6547)
PHONE 231 722-1199
David Spaulding, *President*
Dave Spalding, *President*
Paul Powers, *Vice Pres*
Matt Van Bogart, *Vice Pres*
Matt Pinter, *Design Engr*
EMP: 52 **EST:** 2007
SALES (est): 25MM Privately Held
WEB: www.smartvisionlights.com
SIC: 1531 3646 ; commercial indusl & institutional electric lighting fixtures

(G-12332)
SNOOK INC
6430 Norton Center Dr (49441-6034)
PHONE 231 799-3333
Jack De Horn, *President*
EMP: 12 **EST:** 1976
SQ FT: 1,000
SALES (est): 1.9MM Privately Held
WEB: www.snookinc.com
SIC: 3052 Hose, pneumatic: rubber or rubberized fabric

(G-12333)
SOILS AND STRUCTURES INC
Also Called: Consulting Engineering
6480 Grand Haven Rd (49441-6060)
PHONE 800 933-3959
David Hohmeyer, *President*
Eric Tourre, *Manager*
Jon Veeneman, *Manager*
Stephen Hohmeyer, *Admin Sec*
Wendy Nichols, *Admin Asst*
EMP: 63 **EST:** 1974
SQ FT: 4,000
SALES (est): 4.7MM Privately Held
WEB: www.soilsandstructures.com
SIC: 0711 8711 7389 3541 Soil testing services; engineering services; drafting service, except temporary help; drilling & boring machines

(G-12334)
SOURCE ONE DIGITAL LLC
1137 N Gateway Blvd (49441-6099)
PHONE 231 759-3160
Randy Crow, *CEO*
Steve Crow, *President*
George Atkinson, *Vice Pres*
Jane Savidge, *Vice Pres*
Joe Parmer, *Prdtn Mgr*
EMP: 37 **EST:** 2008
SALES (est): 4.7MM Privately Held
WEB: www.sourceonedigital.com
SIC: 2759 3993 Commercial printing; signs & advertising specialties

(G-12335)
STRUCTURAL CONCEPTS CORP (PA)
888 E Porter Rd (49441-5895)
PHONE 231 798-8888
James Doss, *Ch of Bd*
David P Geerts, *President*
Robert Scroggins, *Principal*
Shelly Clark, *COO*
James Dean, *Exec VP*
◆ **EMP:** 619 **EST:** 1971
SQ FT: 180,000
SALES (est): 131MM Privately Held
WEB: www.structuralconcepts.com
SIC: 2542 Cabinets: show, display or storage: except wood; counters or counter display cases: except wood

(G-12336)
TARGET MOLD CORPORATION
4088 Treeline Dr (49441-4500)
PHONE 231 798-3535
Charles Fishel, *Co-President*
EMP: 10 **EST:** 1984
SALES (est): 525.5K Privately Held
WEB: www.targetmold.net
SIC: 3544 3545 Industrial molds; jigs & fixtures; gauges (machine tool accessories)

(G-12337)
THERM-O-DISC INCORPORATED
851 E Porter Rd (49441-5972)
PHONE 231 799-4100
Marie Pierson, *Branch Mgr*
EMP: 512
SALES (corp-wide): 16.7B Publicly Held
WEB: www.climate.emerson.com
SIC: 3823 Industrial instrmnts msrmnt display/control process variable
HQ: Therm-O-Disc, Incorporated
  1320 S Main St
  Mansfield OH 44907
  419 525-8500

(G-12338)
THERM-O-DISC MIDWEST INC
851 E Porter Rd (49441-5972)
PHONE 231 799-4100
Dave Stebnicki, *General Mgr*
EMP: 18 **EST:** 2004
SALES (est): 581.4K Privately Held
SIC: 3823 Industrial instrmnts msrmnt display/control process variable

(G-12339)
THREAD WEST - MICHIGAN
1701 W Sherman Blvd Ste 4 (49441-3572)
PHONE 231 755-5229
Timothy Wolffis, *Principal*
EMP: 4 **EST:** 2017
SALES (est): 55.9K Privately Held
WEB: www.threadwestmi.com
SIC: 2395 Embroidery products, except schiffli machine

(G-12340)
TITAN TOOL & DIE INC
6435 Schamber Dr (49444-9752)
PHONE 231 799-8680
Fernando Vicente, *President*
Tom Stembaugh, *Sales Mgr*
Mark Timmer, *Manager*
EMP: 7 **EST:** 2001
SALES (est): 873.8K Privately Held
WEB: www.titandie.com
SIC: 3544 Special dies & tools

(G-12341)
TOWER LABORATORIES LTD
5163 Robert Hunter Dr (49441-6547)
P.O. Box 306, Centerbrook CT (06409-0306)
PHONE 860 767-2127
Norman Needleman, *President*
EMP: 8 **EST:** 1979
SALES (est): 74.4K Privately Held
SIC: 2834 Pharmaceutical preparations

(G-12342)
WACKER NEUSON CORPORATION
1300 E Mount Garfield Rd (49441-6097)
PHONE 231 799-4500
EMP: 15
SALES (corp-wide): 1.8B Privately Held
SIC: 3531 Mfg Construction Mach
HQ: Wacker Neuson Corporation
  N92w15000 Anthony Ave
  Menomonee Falls WI 53051
  262 255-0500

(G-12343)
WEST MICHIGAN GRINDING SVC INC
Also Called: Wmgm
1188 E Broadway Ave (49444-2356)
P.O. Box 4471, Muskegon (49444-0471)
PHONE 231 739-4245
Donald A Martines, *President*
Damon Hoeltzel, *Manager*
EMP: 18 **EST:** 1962
SQ FT: 20,000
SALES (est): 3.8MM Privately Held
WEB: www.westmichigangrinding.com
SIC: 7699 7389 3599 Industrial tool grinding; grinding, precision: commercial or industrial; machine & other job shop work

Norton Shores
Ottawa County

(G-12344)
ACEMCO INCORPORATED
Also Called: Acemco Automotive
7297 Enterprise Dr (49456-9695)
PHONE 231 799-8612
Jeffrey Giangrande, *Ch of Bd*
Erik Rasmussen, *Exec VP*
Terry Luce, *Maint Spvr*
David Royce, *Mfg Staff*
Glenn Schneider, *Purch Mgr*
▲ **EMP:** 200 **EST:** 1968
SQ FT: 185,000
SALES (est): 27.3MM Privately Held
WEB: www.acemco.com
SIC: 3465 3469 Automotive stampings; stamping metal for the trade

GEOGRAPHIC SECTION
Novi - Oakland County (G-12369)

(G-12345)
BPC ACQUISITION COMPANY
Also Called: Bennett Pump Company
1218 E Pontaluna Rd (49456-9634)
PHONE 231 798-1310
Thomas A Thompson, *President*
James Collier, *Vice Pres*
Pedro Ruiz, *Vice Pres*
Bill Graybeal, *Regl Sales Mgr*
Renee Wilson, *Mktg Coord*
▼ EMP: 175 EST: 1996
SQ FT: 68,000
SALES: 9MM
SALES (corp-wide): 177.4MM **Privately Held**
WEB: www.bennettpump.com
SIC: 8742 3586 Management consulting services; gasoline pumps, measuring or dispensing
PA: Hines Corporation
 1218 E Pontaluna Rd Ste B
 Norton Shores MI 49456
 231 799-6240

(G-12346)
BURNSIDE ACQUISITION LLC
6830 Grand Haven Rd (49456-9616)
PHONE 231 798-3394
Kevin Mesler, *Branch Mgr*
EMP: 124 **Privately Held**
WEB: www.garichards.com
SIC: 3469 Stamping metal for the trade
PA: Burnside Acquisition, Llc
 1060 Kenosha Indus Dr Se
 Grand Rapids MI 49508

(G-12347)
BURNSIDE INDUSTRIES LLC
Also Called: G.A. Rchrds Indstrial Oprtions
6830 Grand Haven Rd (49456-9616)
PHONE 231 798-3394
Brian Burnside, *Mng Member*
EMP: 1 EST: 1932
SQ FT: 66,000
SALES (est): 6.4MM
SALES (corp-wide): 17.1MM **Privately Held**
WEB: www.garichards.com
SIC: 3469 3496 Machine parts, stamped or pressed metal; miscellaneous fabricated wire products
PA: G. A. Richards Company
 1060 Ken O Sha Ind Pk Dr
 Grand Rapids MI 49508
 616 243-2800

(G-12348)
HINES CORPORATION (PA)
1218 E Pontaluna Rd Ste B (49456-9634)
PHONE 231 799-6240
Larry Hines, *President*
Patrick Philbin, *General Mgr*
Jeannie Torres, *General Mgr*
Michele Buckley, *Vice Pres*
George Lancaster, *Vice Pres*
◆ EMP: 12 EST: 1987
SQ FT: 4,000
SALES (est): 177.4MM **Privately Held**
WEB: www.hinescorp.com
SIC: 3443 3823 3589 3531 Boilers: industrial, power, or marine; fluidic devices, circuits & systems for process control; floor washing & polishing machines, commercial; construction machinery; conveyors & conveying equipment; general construction machinery & equipment

(G-12349)
JAY TITANIUM SPORTS LLC
6692 Grand Haven Rd (49456-9616)
PHONE 616 502-5945
Jason Mathew Sheffield, *Principal*
EMP: 6 EST: 2016
SALES (est): 90.8K **Privately Held**
SIC: 3356 Titanium

(G-12350)
POLYCEM LLC
1271 Judson Rd (49456-9681)
P.O. Box 349, Ferrysburg (49409-0349)
PHONE 231 799-1040
Milton Kuyers,
Davee Wiersma, *Maintence Staff*
EMP: 20 EST: 2005
SALES (est): 1.1MM **Privately Held**
SIC: 3272 Concrete products

(G-12351)
PPG INDUSTRIES INC
1224 E Pontaluna Rd (49456-8611)
PHONE 833 279-7021
EMP: 4
SALES (corp-wide): 15.1B **Publicly Held**
WEB: www.ppg.com
SIC: 2851 Paints & allied products
PA: Ppg Industries, Inc.
 1 Ppg Pl
 Pittsburgh PA 15272
 412 434-3131

(G-12352)
PROGRESS MACHINE & TOOL INC
1155 Judson Rd (49456-9635)
PHONE 231 798-3410
Lance H Norris, *President*
Brad Sprague, *General Mgr*
Inja Norris, *Vice Pres*
Angie Keasey, *Production*
EMP: 35 EST: 1969
SQ FT: 20,000
SALES (est): 3MM **Privately Held**
WEB: www.progressmachine.biz
SIC: 3599 Machine shop, jobbing & repair

Norway
Dickinson County

(G-12353)
LOADMASTER CORPORATION
100 E 9th Ave (49870-1107)
P.O. Box 186 (49870-0186)
PHONE 906 563-9226
David Brisson, *President*
Terry Barnes, *Vice Pres*
Debbie Bryant, *Controller*
John Ortenburger, *Regl Sales Mgr*
Ethan Brisson, *Sales Associate*
◆ EMP: 50 EST: 1932
SQ FT: 45,000
SALES (est): 9.5MM **Privately Held**
WEB: www.loadmaster.org
SIC: 3713 3559 Garbage, refuse truck bodies; recycling machinery

(G-12354)
NICKELS LOGGING
1108 Railroad Ave (49870-1432)
P.O. Box 213 (49870-0213)
PHONE 906 563-5880
Jeffrey Nickels, *Partner*
Robert Nickels, *Partner*
EMP: 5 EST: 1982
SALES (est): 624.5K **Privately Held**
WEB: www.nickelslogging.com
SIC: 2411 4212 Logging camps & contractors; lumber (log) trucking, local

(G-12355)
ORION HUNTING PRODUCTS LLC
N2615 Valley View Rd (49870-2271)
PHONE 906 563-1230
Beau Anderson, *Principal*
EMP: 6 EST: 2016
SALES (est): 168.2K **Privately Held**
WEB: www.huntorion.com
SIC: 3949 Sporting & athletic goods

(G-12356)
RENEWABLE WORLD ENERGIES LLC
1001 Stephenson St Ste C (49870-1173)
PHONE 906 828-0808
William Bill Harris, *President*
EMP: 7 EST: 2012
SALES (est): 334.9K **Privately Held**
WEB: www.renewableworldenergies.com
SIC: 3679 Electronic loads & power supplies

(G-12357)
STEINBRECHER STONE CORP (PA)
Also Called: Norway Granite Marble
N1443 Forest Dr (49870-2007)
P.O. Box 41 (49870-0041)
PHONE 906 563-5852
James Steinbrecher, *President*
Kay Steinbrecher, *Corp Secy*
EMP: 6 EST: 1986
SQ FT: 3,800
SALES (est): 807K **Privately Held**
WEB: www.norwaygraniteandmarble.com
SIC: 3281 5099 5999 Monuments, cut stone (not finishing or lettering only); monuments & grave markers; monuments, finished to custom order

Novi
Oakland County

(G-12358)
7 SEAS SOURCING LLC
43000 W 9 Mile Rd Ste 308 (48375-4129)
PHONE 734 357-8560
EMP: 5 EST: 2018
SALES (est): 292.7K **Privately Held**
WEB: www.7seassourcing.com
SIC: 3999 Manufacturing industries

(G-12359)
A123 SYSTEMS LLC (HQ)
27101 Cabaret Dr (48377-3312)
PHONE 248 412-9249
Peter Cirino, *President*
Susan Butler, *Vice Pres*
Jason Forcier, *Vice Pres*
Lisa Steedman, *Vice Pres*
Joe Palo, *Plant Mgr*
▼ EMP: 493 EST: 2001
SALES (est): 380.6MM **Privately Held**
WEB: www.a123systems.com
SIC: 5063 3691 Batteries; storage batteries

(G-12360)
ACCURATE TECHNOLOGIES INC (PA)
Also Called: ATI
26999 Meadowbrook Rd (48377-3523)
PHONE 248 848-9200
Robert Kasprzyk, *President*
Hans Bornemann, *General Mgr*
Ronald Drexler, *Vice Pres*
Bob Miller, *Mfg Mgr*
Lisa Nwakerendu, *Mfg Staff*
EMP: 61 EST: 1992
SQ FT: 22,000
SALES (est): 13MM **Privately Held**
WEB: www.accuratetechnologies.com
SIC: 3825 Test equipment for electronic & electric measurement

(G-12361)
AKWEL CADILLAC USA INC
Also Called: Avon Auotmotive
39750 Grand River Ave (48375-2106)
PHONE 248 476-8072
EMP: 11 **Privately Held**
SIC: 3061 3089 Mfg Mechanical Rubber Goods Mfg Plastic Products
HQ: Akwel Cadillac Usa, Inc
 603 7th St
 Cadillac MI 49601
 231 775-6571

(G-12362)
ANCHOR PRINTING COMPANY
Also Called: Anchor Flexible Packg & Label
22790 Heslip Dr (48375-4143)
PHONE 248 335-7440
Martin Weitz, *President*
Andrew Weitz, *Vice Pres*
Linda Weitz, *Treasurer*
Michael Dion, *Sales Staff*
▲ EMP: 32 EST: 1949
SQ FT: 15,000
SALES (est): 5.6MM **Privately Held**
WEB: www.anchorprinting.com
SIC: 2759 2752 Flexographic printing; commercial printing, offset

(G-12363)
ANDRITZ METALS USA INC
26800 Meadowbrook Rd (48377-3540)
PHONE 248 305-2969
Peter Winkler, *General Mgr*
EMP: 5
SALES (corp-wide): 7.9B **Privately Held**
WEB: www.andritz.com
SIC: 7692 5999 Welding repair; welding supplies
HQ: Andritz Metals Usa Inc.
 501 W 7th Ave
 Homestead PA 15120

(G-12364)
AR2 ENGINEERING LLC
Also Called: Screen Works
26600 Heyn Dr (48374-1821)
PHONE 248 735-9999
Amit Soman,
EMP: 39 EST: 2015
SALES (est): 3.1MM **Privately Held**
WEB: www.screenworks.graphics
SIC: 7336 2759 3993 Commercial art & graphic design; screen printing; signs & advertising specialties

(G-12365)
ASCO LP
46280 Dylan Dr Ste 100 (48377-4910)
PHONE 248 596-3200
Joe Malloi, *Branch Mgr*
Dana Greenly, *Manager*
EMP: 125
SALES (corp-wide): 16.7B **Publicly Held**
SIC: 3491 Valves, automatic control
HQ: Asco, L.P.
 160 Park Ave
 Florham Park NJ 07932
 800 972-2726

(G-12366)
ASMO DETROIT INC
39575 Lewis Dr Ste 800 (48377-2987)
PHONE 248 359-4440
Hiromi Okugawa, *President*
Yasunori Yamada, *President*
▲ EMP: 8 EST: 1993
SALES (est): 1.3MM **Privately Held**
WEB: www.denso.com
SIC: 3714 Motor vehicle parts & accessories
PA: Denso Corporation
 1-1, Showacho
 Kariya AIC 448-0

(G-12367)
ASSISTIVE TECHNOLOGY MICH INC
Also Called: Assistive Technology Cal
43000 W 9 Mile Rd Ste 113 (48375-4180)
PHONE 248 348-7161
Ghassan Souri, *President*
EMP: 4 EST: 1999
SALES (est): 288.6K **Privately Held**
WEB: www.atofmich.com
SIC: 3842 5047 5999 Technical aids for the handicapped; technical aids for the handicapped; technical aids for the handicapped

(G-12368)
AUTODESK INC
26200 Town Center Dr # 300 (48375-1220)
PHONE 248 347-9650
Steven Dennis, *Senior Engr*
Rosa McDermott, *Sales Staff*
Robert Kross, *Branch Mgr*
Jeffrey Curran, *Manager*
Brian Schanen, *Manager*
EMP: 4
SALES (corp-wide): 3.7B **Publicly Held**
WEB: www.autodesk.com
SIC: 7372 7371 Application computer software; custom computer programming services
PA: Autodesk, Inc.
 111 Mcinnis Pkwy
 San Rafael CA 94903
 415 507-5000

(G-12369)
AUTOMATED CONTROL SYSTEMS INC
25168 Seeley Rd (48375-2044)
PHONE 248 476-9490
James B Mellas, *President*
Ryan Mellas, *Mfg Mgr*
Brynn Rogers, *Electrical Engi*
Keely Braud, *Accounts Exec*
Jonathon Wells, *Sales Staff*
EMP: 8 EST: 1981
SQ FT: 8,000

Novi - Oakland County (G-12370)   **GEOGRAPHIC SECTION**

SALES (est): 3.4MM **Privately Held**
WEB: www.autoconsys.net
SIC: 3625 Electric controls & control accessories, industrial

(G-12370)
AUTOMATIC VALVE CORP
Also Called: Automatic Valve Nuclear
22550 Heslip Dr (48375-4139)
PHONE 248 474-6761
Todd Hutchins, *CEO*
Richard Mackie, *Vice Pres*
Karen Troy, *Design Engr*
▲ **EMP:** 50 **EST:** 1945
SQ FT: 14,600
SALES (est): 4.5MM **Privately Held**
WEB: www.automaticvalve.com
SIC: 3492 3494 5085 3491 Fluid power valves & hose fittings; valves & pipe fittings; valves & fittings; industrial valves

(G-12371)
AUTOMATIC VALVE MFG CO IN
22550 Heslip Dr (48375-4139)
PHONE 248 924-7671
EMP: 4 **EST:** 2018
SALES (est): 101.6K **Privately Held**
WEB: www.automaticvalve.com
SIC: 3999 Manufacturing industries

(G-12372)
AUTONEUM NORTH AMERICA INC (HQ)
29293 Haggerty Rd (48377-5501)
PHONE 248 848-0100
Richard Derr, *President*
Jian Pan, *Principal*
Timothy Judy, *Vice Pres*
Hunter Samec, *Production*
Claudio Alves, *Engineer*
▲ **EMP:** 100 **EST:** 1979
SQ FT: 50,000
SALES (est): 877.1MM
SALES (corp-wide): 1.9B **Privately Held**
WEB: www.autoneum.com
SIC: 3714 Motor vehicle parts & accessories
PA: Autoneum Holding Ag
    Schlosstalstrasse 43
    Winterthur ZH 8406
    522 448-282

(G-12373)
BAKELITE N SUMITOMO AMER INC (HQ)
Also Called: Sbhpp
46840 Magellan Dr Ste C (48377-2454)
PHONE 248 313-7000
Shintaro Ishiwata, *CEO*
EMP: 1 **EST:** 2000
SALES (est): 86MM **Privately Held**
WEB: www.compounds.sbna-inc.com
SIC: 2821 Molding compounds, plastics

(G-12374)
BLOSSOM BERRY
44325 W 12 Mile Rd H-172 (48377-2534)
PHONE 517 775-6978
Toan Kinh Chau, *Principal*
EMP: 4
SALES (est): 199.4K **Privately Held**
SIC: 2024 5143 Ice cream & frozen desserts; frozen dairy desserts; ice cream & ices

(G-12375)
BOROPHARM INC (PA)
39555 Orchard Hill Pl # 600 (48375-5374)
PHONE 248 348-5776
Todd Zahn, *President*
Andrew Cipa, *Business Mgr*
Paul Herrinton, *Vice Pres*
EMP: 3 **EST:** 2003
SQ FT: 30,000
SALES (est): 12MM **Privately Held**
WEB: www.boropharm.com
SIC: 2819 Boron compounds, not from mines

(G-12376)
BRASSCRAFT MANUFACTURING CO (HQ)
Also Called: Brass Craft Mfg Co
39600 Orchard Hill Pl (48375-5331)
PHONE 248 305-6000
Tom Assante, *President*
Thomas Assante, *President*
Wade Henderson, *Senior VP*
Dawn Rowley, *Vice Pres*
Wanda Richardson, *Opers Staff*
▲ **EMP:** 146 **EST:** 1946
SQ FT: 60,000
SALES (est): 217.7MM
SALES (corp-wide): 7.1B **Publicly Held**
WEB: www.brasscraft.com
SIC: 3432 Plumbers' brass goods: drain cocks, faucets, spigots, etc.
PA: Masco Corporation
    17450 College Pkwy
    Livonia MI 48152
    313 274-7400

(G-12377)
BROOKS UTILITY PRODUCTS GROUP (PA)
Also Called: Brooks Meter Devices
43045 W 9 Mile Rd (48375-4116)
PHONE 248 477-0250
Susan Cook, *Principal*
Allen Pruehs, *Senior Engr*
John Bettevy, *Manager*
Rober Kiessling, *Manager*
Mark Martin, *Manager*
◆ **EMP:** 75 **EST:** 2009
SALES (est): 12.1MM **Privately Held**
WEB: www.brooksutility.com
SIC: 3643 3469 Sockets, electric; electronic enclosures, stamped or pressed metal

(G-12378)
CAMBRIC CORPORATION
41050 W 11 Mile Rd (48375-1981)
PHONE 801 415-7300
Timothy Hayes, *President*
Ronald Rainson, *President*
Florin Muntean, *Vice Pres*
Merilee Hunt, *Admin Sec*
EMP: 26 **EST:** 1989
SQ FT: 10,000
SALES (est): 1.6MM **Privately Held**
SIC: 8711 3462 Engineering services; automotive & internal combustion engine forgings
HQ: Tata Technologies, Inc.
    6001 Cass Ave Ste 600
    Detroit MI 48202

(G-12379)
CANTON RENEWABLES LLC
46280 Dylan Dr Ste 200 (48377-4910)
PHONE 248 380-3920
Harrison Clay,
EMP: 6 **EST:** 2010
SALES (est): 1.6MM **Privately Held**
SIC: 2813 Industrial gases

(G-12380)
CASCO PRODUCTS CORPORATION
25921 Meadowbrook Rd (48375-1853)
PHONE 248 957-0400
Ron Zender, *Project Engr*
Clark Couyoumjian, *Manager*
Susan Verellen, *Director*
EMP: 10
SALES (corp-wide): 8.6B **Publicly Held**
WEB: www.cascoauto.com
SIC: 3714 Motor vehicle parts & accessories
HQ: Casco Products Corporation
    1000 Lafayette Blvd # 303
    Bridgeport CT 06604

(G-12381)
CAV TOOL COMPANY
22605 Heslip Dr (48375-4142)
PHONE 248 349-7860
Michael Ciaverilla, *President*
EMP: 12 **EST:** 1990
SQ FT: 4,500
SALES (est): 1.5MM **Privately Held**
WEB: www.cavtool.com
SIC: 3544 Special dies & tools

(G-12382)
CELERITY SYSTEMS N AMER INC
28175 Haggerty Rd (48377-2903)
PHONE 248 994-7696
Michael Hurst, *Vice Pres*
EMP: 5 **EST:** 2014
SALES (est): 610.1K **Privately Held**
WEB: www.celerity-systems.com
SIC: 3621 Rotors, for motors

(G-12383)
CLARK INSTRUMENT INC
46590 Ryan Ct (48377-1730)
PHONE 248 669-3100
Richard Antonick, *President*
EMP: 10 **EST:** 1942
SQ FT: 4,000
SALES (est): 1.2MM
SALES (corp-wide): 3MM **Privately Held**
WEB: www.sunteccorp.com
SIC: 3829 Measuring & controlling devices
PA: Sun-Tec, Corp.
    46590 Ryan Ct
    Novi MI 48377
    248 669-3100

(G-12384)
CLARKSON CONTROLS & EQP CO
Also Called: Maspac International
42572 Cherry Hill Rd (48375-2511)
PHONE 248 380-9915
Don Clarkson, *President*
Kenneth J Clarkson, *Vice Pres*
EMP: 6 **EST:** 1973
SQ FT: 2,000 **Privately Held**
WEB: www.clarksoncontrols.co.uk
SIC: 3823 3564 Industrial instrmnts msrmnt display/control process variable; air cleaning systems

(G-12385)
CREFORM CORPORATION
29795 Hudson Dr (48377-1736)
PHONE 248 926-2555
Mark Grice, *Plant Mgr*
Paul Bradford, *Engineer*
Andy Klco, *Engineer*
Robert Lauzon, *Engineer*
Jason Verlee, *Engineer*
EMP: 31 **Privately Held**
WEB: www.creform.com
SIC: 3312 3449 3494 Pipes & tubes; joists, fabricated bar; pipe fittings
HQ: Creform Corporation
    1628 Poplar Drive Ext
    Greer SC 29651
    864 877-7405

(G-12386)
CRUSHING HEARTS AND BLACK
25515 Hillsdale Dr (48374-2157)
PHONE 224 234-9677
Sarah J Brandon, *Administration*
EMP: 6 **EST:** 2011
SALES (est): 174.7K **Privately Held**
SIC: 2741 Miscellaneous publishing

(G-12387)
CSA SERVICES INC
39550 Orchard Hill Pl (48375-5329)
PHONE 248 596-6184
Scott D Zaret, *Principal*
Ben Atkins, *Sales Staff*
Steve Bell, *Sales Staff*
Turner Lawrence, *Sales Staff*
Phillip Smith, *Sales Staff*
EMP: 9 **EST:** 2009
SALES (est): 273.5K **Privately Held**
WEB: www.I.csa.canon.com
SIC: 4111 3714 Local & suburban transit; motor vehicle parts & accessories

(G-12388)
CSQUARED INNOVATIONS INC
45145 W 12 Mile Rd (48377-2517)
PHONE 734 998-8330
Steve Annear, *CEO*
Pravansu Mohanty, *President*
EMP: 10 **EST:** 2011
SALES (est): 664.1K **Privately Held**
WEB: www.csquaredinnovations.com
SIC: 8731 3479 Biotechnical research, commercial; coating electrodes

(G-12389)
D3W INDUSTRIES INC
22865 Heslip Dr (48375-4146)
PHONE 248 798-0703
EMP: 8 **EST:** 2019
SALES (est): 268.4K **Privately Held**
WEB: www.d3windustries.com
SIC: 3999 Manufacturing industries

(G-12390)
DACO HAND CONTROLLERS INC
24404 Catherine Industria (48375-2456)
PHONE 248 982-3266
Roy Engel, *President*
◆ **EMP:** 10 **EST:** 2010
SQ FT: 3,825
SALES (est): 2.5MM
SALES (corp-wide): 13.2MM **Privately Held**
WEB: www.class3electronics.com
SIC: 3577 Computer peripheral equipment
PA: Daco Scientific Limited
    Unit 1
    Reading BERKS RG7 8
    118 981-7311

(G-12391)
DAIFUKU NORTH AMERICA HOLDG CO (HQ)
30100 Cabot Dr (48377-4000)
PHONE 248 553-1000
Aki Nishimura, *President*
John Doychish, *Vice Pres*
Anthony Diponio, *Project Mgr*
Jim Dilworth, *Engineer*
David Noble, *Engineer*
EMP: 127 **EST:** 2011
SALES (est): 787.1MM **Privately Held**
WEB: www.daifuku.com
SIC: 3535 Conveyors & conveying equipment

(G-12392)
DANA INCORPORATED
27870 Cabot Dr (48377-2920)
PHONE 734 629-1200
EMP: 5 **Publicly Held**
WEB: www.dana.com
SIC: 3089 Automotive parts, plastic
PA: Dana Incorporated
    3939 Technology Dr
    Maumee OH 43537

(G-12393)
DELPHINUS MEDICAL TECHNOLOGIES
45525 Grand River Ave (48374-1308)
PHONE 248 522-9600
Mark Forchette, *CEO*
Francis X Dobscha, *Vice Pres*
Shawn O'Brien, *VP Finance*
Shawn O 'brien, *VP Finance*
EMP: 45 **EST:** 2010
SALES (est): 9.7MM **Privately Held**
WEB: www.delphinsmt.com
SIC: 3841 Surgical & medical instruments

(G-12394)
DETROIT DIAMETERS INC
45380 W Park Dr (48374-1369)
PHONE 248 669-2330
Craig Spitery, *President*
Scott Spitery, *Shareholder*
EMP: 9 **EST:** 1955
SQ FT: 4,800
SALES (est): 903.2K **Privately Held**
WEB: www.detdia.com
SIC: 3599 Machine shop, jobbing & repair

(G-12395)
DETROIT RECYCLED CONCRETE CO (PA)
39525 W 13 Mile Rd # 300 (48377-2361)
PHONE 248 553-0600
Michael Santi, *Principal*
James Oliver, *Principal*
EMP: 7 **EST:** 1966
SALES (est): 1.1MM **Privately Held**
WEB: www.novicrushedconcrete.com
SIC: 3273 Ready-mixed concrete

(G-12396)
DETROIT TESTING MACHINE CO
46590 Ryan Ct (48377-1730)
PHONE 248 669-3100
Richard Antonik, *President*
EMP: 4 **EST:** 2004

▲ = Import   ▼ = Export
◆ = Import/Export

SALES (est): 243.6K **Privately Held**
WEB: www.sunteccorp.com
SIC: 3829 Measuring & controlling devices

(G-12397)
DEXKO GLOBAL INC (HQ)
39555 Orchard Hill Pl (48375-5374)
PHONE...................248 533-0029
Fred Bentley, *CEO*
Adam Dexter, *President*
Ed Meador, *COO*
Matt Griffith, *Vice Pres*
Jeff Richard, *CFO*
EMP: 5 EST: 2012
SALES (est): 1.3B
SALES (corp-wide): 3.4B **Privately Held**
WEB: www.dexko.com
SIC: 3799 Trailers & trailer equipment
PA: Kps Capital Partners, Lp
140 E 45th St Fl 39
New York NY 10017
212 338-5100

(G-12398)
DI SQUARE AMERICA INC
39555 Orchard Hill Pl (48375-5374)
PHONE...................248 374-5051
Minoru Habu, *President*
EMP: 10 EST: 2019
SALES (est): 2.4MM **Privately Held**
WEB: www.di-square.co.jp
SIC: 3731 Shipbuilding & repairing
HQ: Di Square Corp.
2-1-6, Sasazuka
Shibuya-Ku TKY 151-0

(G-12399)
DI-COAT CORPORATION
42900 W 9 Mile Rd (48375-4123)
PHONE...................248 349-1211
Zigmund Grutza, *President*
Alan Davis, *Exec VP*
Jeffery Boudrie, *Opers Staff*
Josh Grutza, *Research*
Sean Veit, *Engineer*
EMP: 47 EST: 1971
SQ FT: 14,000
SALES (est): 6MM **Privately Held**
WEB: www.dicoat.com
SIC: 3545 3841 3531 3291 Diamond cutting tools for turning, boring, burnishing, etc.; surgical & medical instruments; construction machinery; abrasive products

(G-12400)
DIKAR TOOL COMPANY INC
22635 Heslip Dr (48375-4142)
P.O. Box 916 (48376-0916)
PHONE...................248 348-0010
Robert J Forsyth, *President*
Edward E Forsyth, *Vice Pres*
Joann Forsyth, *Admin Sec*
EMP: 25 EST: 1956
SQ FT: 10,000
SALES (est): 2.9MM **Privately Held**
WEB: www.dikartool.com
SIC: 3541 Machine tools, metal cutting type

(G-12401)
DIVERSFIED TCHNCAL SYSTEMS INC
25881 Meadowbrook Rd (48375-1851)
PHONE...................248 513-6050
Steve Moss, *President*
Chris Mauney, *Technician*
EMP: 44
SALES (corp-wide): 269.8MM **Publicly Held**
WEB: www.dtsweb.com
SIC: 3679 Electronic circuits
HQ: Diversified Technical Systems, Inc.
1720 Apollo Ct
Seal Beach CA 90740

(G-12402)
DLN PUBLICATIONS LLC
22041 Shadybrook Dr (48375-5156)
PHONE...................248 410-7337
Dana L Nussio, *Principal*
EMP: 4 EST: 2018
SALES (est): 37.5K **Privately Held**
SIC: 2741 Miscellaneous publishing

(G-12403)
DRAGON ACQUISITION INTERMEDIAT
39555 Orchard Hill Pl # 52 (48375-5374)
PHONE...................248 692-4367
Fred Bentley, *CEO*
EMP: 10 EST: 2017
SALES (est): 849.9K
SALES (corp-wide): 5.8MM **Privately Held**
SIC: 3799 Trailers & trailer equipment
PA: Dragon Acquisition Parent, Inc.
39555 Orchard Hill Pl # 52
Novi MI 48375
248 692-4367

(G-12404)
DRAGON ACQUISITION PARENT INC (PA)
39555 Orchard Hill Pl # 52 (48375-5374)
PHONE...................248 692-4367
Fred Bentley, *CEO*
EMP: 16 EST: 2017
SQ FT: 1,300
SALES (est): 5.8MM **Privately Held**
SIC: 3799 Trailers & trailer equipment

(G-12405)
DURA SILL CORPORATION
22500 Heslip Dr (48375-4139)
PHONE...................248 348-2490
Raymond B Morianti, *President*
EMP: 5 EST: 1983 **Privately Held**
SIC: 3281 Marble, building: cut & shaped

(G-12406)
DUREZ CORPORATION (DH)
46820 Magellan Dr Ste C (48377-2454)
PHONE...................248 313-7000
John W Fisher, *CEO*
David L Faust, *Treasurer*
Kelly Lane, *Sales Staff*
Rizwan Zahoor, *Consultant*
Keiichiro Miyajima, *Admin Sec*
◆ EMP: 109 EST: 2000
SALES (est): 28.6MM **Privately Held**
WEB: www.resins.sbna-inc.com
SIC: 2865 2821 Phenol, alkylated & cumene; molding compounds, plastics

(G-12407)
E D M SPECIALTIES INC
26111 Lannys Rd (48375-1025)
PHONE...................248 344-4080
Douglas Higley, *President*
Erik Higley, *Treasurer*
EMP: 7 EST: 1974
SQ FT: 3,948
SALES (est): 869.9K **Privately Held**
WEB: www.edm-specialties.com
SIC: 3544 Special dies, tools, jigs & fixtures

(G-12408)
EAKAS CORP
40000 Grand River Ave # 4 (48375-2121)
PHONE...................815 488-1879
Kohichi Mori, *Vice Pres*
Nicolina Tieman, *Production*
Dean Perino, *Manager*
Linda Christman, *Supervisor*
Jane Bromenschenkel, *Executive Asst*
EMP: 8 EST: 2017
SALES (est): 273.3K **Privately Held**
WEB: www.eakas.com
SIC: 3089 Injection molding of plastics

(G-12409)
ECCO TOOL CO INC
42525 W 11 Mile Rd (48375-1701)
PHONE...................248 349-0840
Floyd Peterson, *President*
EMP: 7 EST: 1955
SQ FT: 8,000 **Privately Held**
WEB: www.eccotool.com
SIC: 3545 Cutting tools for machine tools

(G-12410)
ECOLAB INC
28550 Cabot Dr Ste 100 (48377-2988)
PHONE...................248 697-0202
David Bourgeois, *Branch Mgr*
Bart Yeager, *Manager*
EMP: 6

SALES (corp-wide): 11.7B **Publicly Held**
WEB: www.ecolab.com
SIC: 2841 Soap & other detergents
PA: Ecolab Inc.
1 Ecolab Pl
Saint Paul MN 55102
800 232-6522

(G-12411)
EDW C LEVY CO
Cadillac Asphalt Paving
27575 Wixom Rd (48374-1127)
PHONE...................248 349-8600
Ron Jones, *Manager*
EMP: 9
SALES (corp-wide): 521.9MM **Privately Held**
WEB: www.edwclevy.com
SIC: 1611 2951 Highway & street paving contractor; asphalt paving mixtures & blocks
PA: Edw. C. Levy Co.
9300 Dix
Dearborn MI 48120
313 429-2200

(G-12412)
EKSTROM INDUSTRIES INC
Also Called: Brooks Utility Products Group
43045 W 9 Mile Rd (48375-4116)
PHONE...................248 477-0040
Jeff Hanft, *President*
▲ EMP: 60 EST: 1954
SQ FT: 38,200
SALES (est): 11.6MM
SALES (corp-wide): 470.6MM **Privately Held**
WEB: www.brooksutility.com
SIC: 3643 3544 Current-carrying wiring devices; special dies & tools; jigs & fixtures
HQ: E.J. Brooks Company
409 Hoosier Dr
Angola IN 46703
800 348-4777

(G-12413)
ENERGY EXPLORATION
40411 Oakwood Dr (48375-4453)
PHONE...................248 579-6531
Richard T Buttery, *Administration*
EMP: 9 EST: 2010
SALES (est): 358.7K **Privately Held**
SIC: 1382 Oil & gas exploration services

(G-12414)
ESPAR INC
43780 Gen Mar Ste 3 (48375-1667)
PHONE...................248 994-7010
Gokcen Tural, *Manager*
EMP: 9 EST: 2020
SALES (est): 1.5MM
SALES (corp-wide): 5.4B **Privately Held**
WEB: www.eberspaecher-na.com
SIC: 3585 Air conditioning, motor vehicle
HQ: Eberspacher Climate Control Systems Gmbh
Eberspacherstr. 24
Esslingen Am Neckar BW 73730
711 939-00

(G-12415)
FACET BUSINESS COMMUNICATIONS
22777 Heslip Dr (48375-4144)
PHONE...................248 912-0800
Christine Ellis, *President*
Elaine Camp, *Office Mgr*
EMP: 15 EST: 2011
SALES (est): 1.4MM **Privately Held**
WEB: www.facetcompany.com
SIC: 8742 7319 2394 Marketing consulting services; display advertising service; air cushions & mattresses, canvas

(G-12416)
FISHKORN PUBLISHING LLC
22811 Braydon Ct (48374-3722)
PHONE...................734 624-2211
Erik Belcarz, *Principal*
EMP: 5 EST: 2018
SALES (est): 37.5K **Privately Held**
SIC: 2741 Miscellaneous publishing

(G-12417)
FREESCALE SEMICONDUCTOR INC
28125 Cabot Dr Ste 100 (48377-2985)
PHONE...................248 324-3260
EMP: 9 EST: 2019
SALES (est): 715.4K **Privately Held**
SIC: 3674 Semiconductors & related devices

(G-12418)
FREMONT COMMUNITY DIGESTER LLC
23955 Novi Rd (48375-3244)
PHONE...................248 735-6684
Anand Gangadharan, *President*
EMP: 13 EST: 2009
SALES (est): 4.2MM **Privately Held**
WEB: www.novienergy.com
SIC: 2813 4911 Industrial gases; electric services

(G-12419)
FROUDE INC
Also Called: Go Power Systems
41123 Jo Dr Ste A (48375-1920)
PHONE...................248 579-4295
John G Harris, *CEO*
Andrew Sadlon, *President*
Mike Brown, *Opers Staff*
Julie Smith, *Controller*
Mariana Esterhuyse, *Accountant*
▲ EMP: 54 EST: 1980
SQ FT: 1,800
SALES (est): 11.8MM
SALES (corp-wide): 1.6MM **Privately Held**
WEB: www.gopowersystems.com
SIC: 3829 Dynamometer instruments
HQ: Wintergreen Management Limited
Unit 15c Blackpole
Worcester WORCS WR3 8

(G-12420)
FTC LLC
27611 Sloan St (48374-1008)
PHONE...................313 622-1583
James Parker, *CEO*
EMP: 11 EST: 2018
SALES (est): 660.4K **Privately Held**
WEB: www.ftc-llc.com
SIC: 8742 6531 1389 Management consulting services; real estate agents & managers; real estate leasing & rentals; construction, repair & dismantling services

(G-12421)
FXI NOVI
28700 Cabot Dr (48377-2943)
PHONE...................248 994-0630
EMP: 5 EST: 2011
SALES (est): 169.3K **Privately Held**
WEB: www.fxi.com
SIC: 3086 Plastics foam products

(G-12422)
GENERAL AIRE
43800 Grand River Ave (48375-1115)
PHONE...................866 476-5101
Carl Redner, *Manager*
EMP: 7 EST: 2017
SALES (est): 255.3K **Privately Held**
SIC: 3564 Blowers & fans

(G-12423)
GENERAL FILTERS INC (PA)
Also Called: Gar-Ber
43800 Grand River Ave (48375-1115)
PHONE...................248 476-5100
Carl R Redner, *President*
Robert P Redner, *Vice Pres*
John Redner, *Human Res Dir*
Paige Freeland, *Marketing Mgr*
J Freeland, *Marketing Staff*
◆ EMP: 49 EST: 1937
SQ FT: 110,000
SALES (est): 13.6MM **Privately Held**
WEB: www.generalfilters.com
SIC: 3585 3564 Humidifying equipment, except portable; filters, air: furnaces, air conditioning equipment, etc.

Novi - Oakland County (G-12424)

(G-12424)
GUHRING INC
Also Called: Guhring-Michigan
24975 Trans X Rd (48375-2435)
PHONE...................262 784-6730
Henry Kenneweg, *Branch Mgr*
EMP: 47
SALES (corp-wide): 1.2B **Privately Held**
WEB: www.guhring.com
SIC: 3545 Cutting tools for machine tools
HQ: Guhring, Inc.
   1445 Commerce Ave
   Brookfield WI 53045
   262 784-6730

(G-12425)
HANON SYSTEMS USA LLC (DH)
39600 Lewis Dr (48377-2953)
PHONE...................248 907-8000
Bob Hickson, *President*
Kwangtaek Hong, *Vice Pres*
Jay Son, *Vice Pres*
Sudesh Appaji, *Purch Mgr*
Ann Perry, *Purch Mgr*
EMP: 279 **EST:** 2012
SALES (est): 169.5MM **Privately Held**
WEB: www.hanonsystems.com
SIC: 3714 3585 3699 Air conditioner parts, motor vehicle; radiators & radiator shells & cores, motor vehicle; heaters, motor vehicle; compressors for refrigeration & air conditioning equipment; heat emission operating apparatus

(G-12426)
HARADA INDUSTRY AMERICA INC (HQ)
22925 Venture Dr (48375-4181)
PHONE...................248 374-2587
Toru Sasaki, *CEO*
Shoji Harada, *Ch of Bd*
Yoichi Hiyama, *President*
Sandy Hammett, *General Mgr*
Israel Cruzado, *Vice Pres*
▲ **EMP:** 75 **EST:** 1976
SQ FT: 12,000
SALES (est): 32.6MM **Privately Held**
WEB: www.harada.com
SIC: 3663 Antennas, transmitting & communications

(G-12427)
HARBROOK TOOL INC
40391 Grand River Ave (48375-2123)
PHONE...................248 477-8040
Kim Bergerson, *President*
William Bergerson, *Vice Pres*
EMP: 31 **EST:** 1967
SQ FT: 6,000
SALES (est): 1.1MM **Privately Held**
SIC: 3544 Special dies & tools

(G-12428)
HARMAN BECKER AUTO SYSTEMS INC
30001 Cabot Dr (48377-2910)
PHONE...................248 703-3010
EMP: 6 **Privately Held**
WEB: www.harman.com
SIC: 3812 Navigational systems & instruments
HQ: Harman Becker Automotive Systems, Inc.
   39001 W 12 Mile Rd
   Farmington Hills MI 48331
   248 785-2361

(G-12429)
HARRYS MEME LLC
41679 Magnolia Ct (48377-4529)
PHONE...................248 977-0168
Hai Gu,
EMP: 7 **EST:** 2017
SALES (est): 298.2K **Privately Held**
SIC: 2322 Men's & boys' underwear & nightwear

(G-12430)
HAYES LEMMERZ INTL IMPORT LLC
39500 Orchard Hill Pl # 50 (48375-5370)
PHONE...................734 737-5000
Don Polk, *President*
Steve Esau, *Vice Pres*
EMP: 1 **EST:** 2013
SQ FT: 30,000
SALES (est): 5.5MM **Privately Held**
WEB: www.maxionwheels.com
SIC: 3714 Wheels, motor vehicle
HQ: Maxion Wheels U.S.A. Llc
   39500 Orchard Hill Pl # 500
   Novi MI 48375
   734 737-5000

(G-12431)
HAYES LMMERZ INTRNTNL-GRGIA LL
39500 Orchard Hill Pl # 50 (48375-5370)
PHONE...................734 737-5000
Fred Bentley, *COO*
John A Salvette, *CFO*
▲ **EMP:** 60 **EST:** 2013
SALES (est): 5.6MM **Privately Held**
WEB: www.maxionwheels.com
SIC: 3312 3714 Wheels, locomotive & car; iron & steel; motor vehicle parts & accessories
HQ: Maxion Wheels U.S.A. Llc
   39500 Orchard Hill Pl # 500
   Novi MI 48375
   734 737-5000

(G-12432)
HEPHAESTUS HOLDINGS LLC (DH)
39475 W 13 Mile Rd # 105 (48377-2359)
PHONE...................248 479-2700
EMP: 1
SALES (est): 318.3MM
SALES (corp-wide): 4.7B **Publicly Held**
SIC: 3462 3463 Mfg Iron/Steel Forgings Mfg Nonferrous Forgings
HQ: Forging Holdings, Llc
   1 Dauch Dr
   Detroit MI 48211
   313 758-2000

(G-12433)
HEXAGON MFG INTELLIGENCE INC
Also Called: Brown & Sharpe Precision Ctr
46444 Hexagon Way (48377-4121)
PHONE...................248 662-1740
Tim Cronyn, *Branch Mgr*
Dan Odale, *Technical Staff*
Ralph Okker, *Technical Staff*
EMP: 5 **Privately Held**
WEB: www.hexagonmi.com
SIC: 3823 Industrial instrmnts msrmnt display/control process variable
HQ: Hexagon Manufacturing Intelligence, Inc.
   250 Circuit Dr
   North Kingstown RI 02852
   401 886-2000

(G-12434)
HEXAGON MFG INTELLIGENCE INC
46444 Hexagon Way (48377-4121)
PHONE...................248 449-9400
EMP: 5 **Privately Held**
WEB: www.hexagonmi.com
SIC: 3545 Precision measuring tools
HQ: Hexagon Manufacturing Intelligence, Inc.
   250 Circuit Dr
   North Kingstown RI 02852
   401 886-2000

(G-12435)
HIGH TOUCH HEALTHCARE LLC
29307 Douglas Dr (48377-2891)
PHONE...................248 513-2425
Bhuvan Doneecudi, *Mng Member*
Ravi Kamepalli,
EMP: 4 **EST:** 2019
SALES (est): 350K **Privately Held**
SIC: 7372 7389 Application computer software; business services

(G-12436)
HOWA USA HOLDINGS INC (DH)
25125 Regency Dr (48375-2155)
PHONE...................248 715-4000
Katsuro Saito, *CEO*
Kay Nakamura, *Sales Mgr*
EMP: 0 **EST:** 2008
SALES (est): 13.1MM **Privately Held**
WEB: www.howausahldgs.com
SIC: 6719 3552 Personal holding companies, except banks; textile machinery

(G-12437)
IHI DETROIT TURBO ENGRG CTR
39575 Lewis Dr Ste 100 (48377-2987)
PHONE...................947 777-4976
EMP: 6 **EST:** 2018
SALES (est): 101.4K **Privately Held**
WEB: www.ihi-turbo.com
SIC: 3714 Motor vehicle parts & accessories

(G-12438)
INTEGRATED SECURITY CORP
46755 Magellan Dr (48377-2453)
PHONE...................248 624-0700
Morton Noveck, *President*
John Plecha, *Project Mgr*
Ed Gill, *Production*
Jean Boujoulian, *Purchasing*
Matthew Kaye, *VP Sales*
▼ **EMP:** 18 **EST:** 2010
SALES (est): 3.4MM **Privately Held**
WEB: www.integratedsecuritycorp.com
SIC: 3699 3823 Security control equipment & systems; industrial instrmnts msrmnt display/control process variable

(G-12439)
INTERNET PUBLISHING INC
42733 Faulkner Dr (48377-2730)
PHONE...................248 438-8192
Richard Witter, *Principal*
EMP: 6 **EST:** 2008
SALES (est): 138.6K **Privately Held**
SIC: 2741 Miscellaneous publishing

(G-12440)
IOCHPE HOLDINGS LLC (DH)
39500 Orchard Hill Pl # 500 (48375-5370)
PHONE...................734 737-5000
Dan Ioschpe, *CEO*
Steve Esau, *Vice Pres*
John Salvette, *Vice Pres*
Eric Moraw, *Treasurer*
Julie Timmer, *Asst Sec*
EMP: 100
SQ FT: 20,000
SALES (est): 1.6B **Privately Held**
WEB: www.maxionwheels.com
SIC: 3714 Motor vehicle parts & accessories

(G-12441)
IPG PHOTONICS CORPORATION
Also Called: Ipg Phtnics - Mdwest Oprations
46695 Magellan Dr (48377-2442)
PHONE...................248 863-5001
Kim Bourgeois, *Purch Mgr*
Christine Isidoro, *Asst Controller*
Ipg Photonics, *Sales Staff*
Mike Klos, *Manager*
EMP: 8
SALES (corp-wide): 1.2B **Publicly Held**
WEB: www.ipgphotonics.com
SIC: 3699 Laser systems & equipment
PA: Ipg Photonics Corporation
   50 Old Webster Rd
   Oxford MA 01540
   508 373-1100

(G-12442)
ISINGULARIS INC
45619 Addington Ln (48374-3785)
PHONE...................248 347-0742
Bhavana Toprani, *Principal*
EMP: 5 **EST:** 2008
SALES (est): 11.1K **Privately Held**
WEB: www.isingularis.com
SIC: 2273 Carpets & rugs

(G-12443)
ITT INDUSTRIES HOLDINGS INC
46785 Magellan Dr (48377-2453)
PHONE...................248 863-2153
EMP: 14 **EST:** 2017
SALES (est): 320.1K **Privately Held**
WEB: www.itt.com
SIC: 3625 Control equipment, electric

(G-12444)
ITT MOTION TECH AMER LLC
Also Called: ITT Koni America, LLC
46785 Magellan Dr (48377-2453)
PHONE...................248 863-2161
Denise L Ramos, *CEO*
▲ **EMP:** 18 **EST:** 2004
SALES (est): 5.1MM
SALES (corp-wide): 2.4B **Publicly Held**
WEB: www.itt.com
SIC: 3751 3446 3625 Brakes, friction clutch & other; bicycle; acoustical suspension systems, metal; control equipment, electric
HQ: Itt Llc
   1133 Westchester Ave N-100
   White Plains NY 10604
   914 641-2000

(G-12445)
ITT MOTION TECHNOLOGIES LLC
46785 Magellan Dr (48377-2453)
PHONE...................248 863-2161
Chris Duda, *Principal*
▲ **EMP:** 10 **EST:** 2010
SALES (est): 3.4MM
SALES (corp-wide): 2.4B **Publicly Held**
WEB: www.itt.com
SIC: 3625 Control equipment, electric
PA: Itt Inc.
   1133 Westchester Ave N-100
   White Plains NY 10604
   914 641-2000

(G-12446)
J H BENNETT AND COMPANY INC (PA)
22975 Venture Dr (48375-4181)
PHONE...................248 596-5100
Bill Vincent, *President*
David Cassel, *Exec VP*
▲ **EMP:** 33
SQ FT: 32,000
SALES (est): 36.6MM **Privately Held**
WEB: www.jhbennett.com
SIC: 3594 5084 Fluid power pumps & motors; hydraulic systems equipment & supplies

(G-12447)
JAAZ MANAGEMENT LLC
Also Called: Supplements Geeks
40440 Grand River Ave C (48375-2873)
P.O. Box 1393 (48376-1393)
PHONE...................248 957-9197
Jimmy Sarwal, *Mng Member*
EMP: 4 **EST:** 2014
SALES (est): 56.7K **Privately Held**
SIC: 2023 Dietary supplements, dairy & non-dairy based

(G-12448)
JD GROUP INC
26600 Heyn Dr (48374-1821)
PHONE...................248 735-9999
Michael Grzych, *President*
Michael Tamm, *Vice Pres*
EMP: 18 **EST:** 1985
SQ FT: 14,000
SALES (est): 850.9K **Privately Held**
SIC: 2759 3993 Screen printing; signs & advertising specialties

(G-12449)
JERVIS B WEBB COMPANY (DH)
30100 Cabot Dr (48377-4000)
PHONE...................248 553-1000
Todd Alderman, *President*
Noel Dehne, *Vice Pres*
Richard Baker, *Foreman/Supr*
Ralph Dingle, *Buyer*
Deon Oley, *Engineer*
◆ **EMP:** 300 **EST:** 2020
SQ FT: 180,000
SALES (est): 195.8MM **Privately Held**
WEB: www.jervisbwebb.com
SIC: 3537 3535 3536 3613 Stacking machines, automatic; tractors, used in plants, docks, terminals, etc.; industrial; overhead conveyor systems; cranes & monorail systems; cranes, industrial plant; monorail systems; control panels, electric; iron & steel forgings; chains, forged steel

▲ = Import ▼ = Export
◆ = Import/Export

HQ: Daifuku North America Holding Company
30100 Cabot Dr
Novi MI 48377
248 553-1000

(G-12450)
KALTEC SCIENTIFIC INC
22425 Heslip Dr (48375-4138)
P.O. Box 762 (48376-0762)
PHONE..................................248 349-8100
Jon T Dean, *President*
▼ EMP: 4 EST: 1969
SQ FT: 8,000
SALES (est): 650K **Privately Held**
WEB: www.kaltecsci.com
SIC: 3823 7699 Viscosimeters, industrial process type; scientific equipment repair service

(G-12451)
KERN INDUSTRIES INC
43000 W 10 Mile Rd Frnt (48375-5443)
PHONE..................................248 349-4866
Patrick Kern, *President*
James Kern, *Vice Pres*
Michael Kern, *Vice Pres*
Thomas Kern, *Treasurer*
EMP: 20 EST: 1966
SQ FT: 14,000
SALES (est): 1.7MM **Privately Held**
WEB: www.kernindustriesinc.com
SIC: 3544 Special dies & tools

(G-12452)
KIDDE SAFETY
39550 W 13 Mile Rd # 101 (48377-2360)
PHONE..................................800 880-6788
EMP: 17 EST: 2009
SALES (est): 1MM **Privately Held**
WEB: www.kidde.com
SIC: 3999 Fire extinguishers, portable

(G-12453)
KISTLER INSTRUMENT CORPORATION (HQ)
30280 Hudson Dr (48377-4115)
PHONE..................................248 668-6900
Nick Wilks, *President*
William Zwolinski, *Vice Pres*
Volker Dostmann, *CFO*
Amanda Konja, *Marketing Mgr*
Tracey Rettig, *Marketing Staff*
▲ EMP: 75 EST: 1959
SQ FT: 33,000
SALES (est): 22.6MM
SALES (corp-wide): 395.4MM **Privately Held**
WEB: www.kistler.com
SIC: 3829 Measuring & controlling devices
PA: Kistler Holding Ag
Eulachstrasse 22
Winterthur ZH 8408
522 241-111

(G-12454)
KONECRANES INC
Also Called: Crane Pro Services
43050 W 10 Mile Rd (48375-3206)
PHONE..................................248 380-2626
Margie Bryant, *Manager*
Rick Colombo, *Manager*
EMP: 20 **Privately Held**
WEB: www.konecranes.com
SIC: 3536 Hoists, cranes & monorails
HQ: Konecranes, Inc.
4401 Gateway Blvd
Springfield OH 45502

(G-12455)
KONGSBERG AUTOMOTIVE INC (HQ)
27275 Haggerty Rd Ste 610 (48377-3635)
PHONE..................................248 468-1300
Hans Peter Havdal, *CEO*
Joachim Magnusson, *Exec VP*
Jarle Nymoen, *Exec VP*
Anders Nystrm, *Exec VP*
Trond Stabekk, *Exec VP*
▲ EMP: 100 EST: 1990
SALES (est): 255.1MM
SALES (corp-wide): 1.1B **Privately Held**
WEB: www.kongsbergautomotive.com
SIC: 3714 Heaters, motor vehicle
PA: Kongsberg Automotive Asa
Dyrmyrgata 48
Kongsberg 3611
327 705-00

(G-12456)
KONGSBERG HOLDING I INC (PA)
27275 Haggerty Rd Ste 610 (48377-3635)
PHONE..................................248 468-1300
EMP: 6 EST: 2008
SALES (est): 743.4K **Privately Held**
SIC: 3714 Motor vehicle parts & accessories

(G-12457)
KONGSBERG HOLDING III INC (HQ)
Also Called: Kongsberg Automotive
27275 Haggerty Rd Ste 610 (48377-3635)
PHONE..................................248 468-1300
Raymond Boyma, *President*
Virginia Grando, *Exec VP*
Norbert Loers, *CFO*
Jon Munthe, *General Counsel*
EMP: 25 EST: 2008
SALES (est): 178.3MM
SALES (corp-wide): 1.1B **Privately Held**
WEB: www.kongsbergautomotive.com
SIC: 3714 Motor vehicle parts & accessories
PA: Kongsberg Automotive Asa
Dyrmyrgata 48
Kongsberg 3611
327 705-00

(G-12458)
KONGSBERG INTR SYSTEMS II LLC (DH)
Also Called: Kongsberg Intr Systems I Inc
27275 Haggerty Rd Ste 610 (48377-3635)
PHONE..................................956 465-4541
Hans Peter Havdal, *CEO*
Raymond Bonya, *President*
Anders Mystron, *Exec VP*
Trond Stabekk, *Exec VP*
▲ EMP: 100 EST: 2007
SQ FT: 137,000
SALES (est): 21.1MM
SALES (corp-wide): 1.1B **Privately Held**
SIC: 3714 Motor vehicle parts & accessories

(G-12459)
KUBICA CORP
Also Called: Prime Technologies
22575 Heslip Dr (48375-4140)
P.O. Box 812, Northville (48167-0812)
PHONE..................................248 344-7750
Dennis Kubica, *CEO*
Jennifer Kubica, *CFO*
Bre Andersen, *Marketing Staff*
Daniel Gorman, *Office Mgr*
Nick Walker, *Comp Spec*
EMP: 14 EST: 1995
SQ FT: 15,800
SALES (est): 4.3MM **Privately Held**
WEB: www.kubicacorp.com
SIC: 8711 7371 3823 Consulting engineer; computer software development & applications; industrial process control instruments

(G-12460)
KYOEI ELECTRONICS AMERICA INC
39555 Orchard Hill Pl # 165 (48375-5524)
PHONE..................................248 773-3690
Hiroyuki Komiya, *President*
EMP: 7 EST: 2012
SALES (est): 793.8K **Privately Held**
WEB: www.kyoei.co.jp
SIC: 3931 String instruments & parts
PA: Kyoei Sangyo Co., Ltd.
2-20-4, Shoto
Shibuya-Ku TKY 150-0

(G-12461)
L N T INC
24300 Catherne Ind Dr # 405 (48375-2457)
PHONE..................................248 347-6006
Richard Fink, *President*
EMP: 4 EST: 1982

SALES (est): 311.6K **Privately Held**
SIC: 3915 Jewelers' castings

(G-12462)
LACKS EXTERIOR SYSTEMS LLC
39500 Mackenzie Dr # 500 (48377-1603)
PHONE..................................248 351-0555
Christopher Thoreson, *Branch Mgr*
EMP: 21 **Privately Held**
WEB: www.lacksenterprises.com
SIC: 3089 Plastic hardware & building products
HQ: Lacks Exterior Systems, Llc
5460 Cascade Rd Se
Grand Rapids MI 49546
616 949-6570

(G-12463)
LACKS WHEEL TRIM SYSTEMS LLC
39500 Mackenzie Dr # 500 (48377-1603)
PHONE..................................248 351-0555
Mark Montone, *Principal*
EMP: 11
SALES (corp-wide): 9.9MM **Privately Held**
WEB: www.lacksenterprises.com
SIC: 3089 Injection molding of plastics
PA: Lacks Wheel Trim Systems, Llc
5460 Cascade Rd Se
Grand Rapids MI 49546
616 949-6570

(G-12464)
LACY TOOL COMPANY INC
40375 Grand River Ave (48375-2123)
PHONE..................................248 476-5250
Evan Lacy, *President*
Thelma Lacy, *Corp Secy*
Kevin Malinowski, *Manager*
EMP: 6 EST: 1954
SQ FT: 12,500
SALES (est): 650.4K **Privately Held**
WEB: www.lacytool.com
SIC: 3465 3469 Automotive stampings; metal stampings

(G-12465)
LASER MECHANISMS INC (PA)
25325 Regency Dr (48375-2159)
PHONE..................................248 474-9480
William G Fredrick, *President*
Greg Stone, *Vice Pres*
Richard Lee, *Mfg Mgr*
John Brower, *Engineer*
Daniel Buckley, *Engineer*
EMP: 67 EST: 1980
SQ FT: 25,000
SALES (est): 17.9MM **Privately Held**
WEB: www.lasermech.com
SIC: 3699 Laser systems & equipment

(G-12466)
LUEBKE & VOGT CORPORATION
25903 Meadowbrook Rd (48375-1853)
PHONE..................................248 449-3232
Oliver Aheimer, *President*
Alexander Porzondek, *Opers Staff*
Karin Demuth, *Admin Asst*
◆ EMP: 4 EST: 2007
SALES (est): 523K **Privately Held**
WEB: www.luebke-vogt.com
SIC: 3069 Molded rubber products

(G-12467)
M-TEK INC
29065 Cabot Dr 300 (48377-2951)
PHONE..................................248 553-1581
EMP: 15
SALES (corp-wide): 1.8B **Privately Held**
SIC: 3714 Mfg Plastic Products
HQ: M-Tek, Inc.
1020 Volunteer Pkwy
Manchester TN 37129
931 728-4122

(G-12468)
MACMICHIGAN INC
43422 W Oaks Dr (48377-3300)
PHONE..................................248 613-6372
EMP: 4 EST: 2016

SALES (est): 332.8K **Privately Held**
WEB: www.macmichigan.com
SIC: 3861 Photographic equipment & supplies

(G-12469)
MAGNA SEATING AMERICA INC (HQ)
Also Called: Intier Automotive Seating
30020 Cabot Dr (48377-2910)
PHONE..................................248 567-4000
Joseph Pittel, *President*
John Oilar, *President*
Judy Witte, *Chairman*
Sherri Love, *COO*
Glen Copeland, *Vice Pres*
▲ EMP: 450 EST: 1985
SQ FT: 300,000
SALES (est): 742.6MM
SALES (corp-wide): 32.6B **Privately Held**
WEB: www.magna.com
SIC: 3714 Motor vehicle parts & accessories
PA: Magna International Inc
337 Magna Dr
Aurora ON L4G 7
905 726-2462

(G-12470)
MARBELITE CORP
22500 Heslip Dr (48375-4139)
PHONE..................................248 348-1900
Larry Morianti, *President*
Steve Sist, *Vice Pres*
EMP: 21 EST: 1972
SQ FT: 16,000
SALES (est): 1.3MM **Privately Held**
WEB: www.carstinbrands.com
SIC: 3281 3431 2434 Bathroom fixtures, cut stone; metal sanitary ware; wood kitchen cabinets

(G-12471)
MARIA DISMONDY INC
Also Called: Cardinal Rule Press
1181 West Lake Dr (48377-1337)
PHONE..................................248 302-1800
Maria Dismondy, *President*
◆ EMP: 6 EST: 2016
SALES (est): 89.9K **Privately Held**
SIC: 2731 Books: publishing only

(G-12472)
MASTERY TECHNOLOGIES INC
41214 Bridge St (48375-1301)
PHONE..................................248 888-8420
William M Marker, *President*
Jeff Holth, *Partner*
Kirk V Berry, *Vice Pres*
Michael Caprara, *Accounts Exec*
Dan Raymond, *Accounts Exec*
EMP: 11 EST: 1977
SQ FT: 3,300
SALES (est): 2.4MM **Privately Held**
WEB: www.masterytech.com
SIC: 7372 Business oriented computer software

(G-12473)
MAXION FUMAGALLI AUTO USA
39500 Orchard Hill Pl (48375-5370)
PHONE..................................734 737-5000
EMP: 75
SALES (est): 5.4MM **Privately Held**
SIC: 3714 Mfg Motor Vehicle Parts/Accessories

(G-12474)
MAXION IMPORT LLC
39500 Orchard Hill Pl # 500 (48375-5370)
PHONE..................................734 737-5000
John Salvette, *Vice Pres*
Steven Esau, *Vice Pres*
William Wardle, *Vice Pres*
Eric Moraw, *Treasurer*
▲ EMP: 10 EST: 1978
SQ FT: 1,000
SALES (est): 7.5MM **Privately Held**
WEB: www.maxionwheels.com
SIC: 3714 Motor vehicle parts & accessories
HQ: Iochpe Holdings Llc
39500 Orchard Hill Pl # 500
Novi MI 48375
734 737-5000

Novi - Oakland County (G-12475)

(G-12475)
MAXION WHEELS AKRON LLC
Also Called: Hayes Lemmerz Intl-Commrcl Hwy
39500 Orchard Hill Pl (48375-5370)
PHONE.................................330 794-2310
Don Polk, *President*
Steven Esau, *Vice Pres*
John A Salvette, *Vice Pres*
Ross Schanzmeyer, *Engineer*
Michael Michalec, *Senior Engr*
▲ EMP: 150 EST: 2003
SALES (est): 47.3MM **Privately Held**
WEB: www.maxionwheels.com
SIC: 3714 Motor vehicle parts & accessories
HQ: Maxion Wheels U.S.A. Llc
    39500 Orchard Hill Pl # 500
    Novi MI 48375
    734 737-7000

(G-12476)
MAXION WHEELS LLC (DH)
Also Called: Hayes Lemmerz International
39500 Orchard Hill Pl # 50 (48375-5370)
PHONE.................................734 737-5000
Pieter Klinkers, *CEO*
Don Polk, *President*
Steve Esau, *Vice Pres*
Steven Esau, *Vice Pres*
Giorgio Mariani, *Vice Pres*
◆ EMP: 100 EST: 2003
SALES (est): 1.5B **Privately Held**
WEB: www.maxionwheels.com
SIC: 3714 Wheels, motor vehicle
HQ: Iochpe Holdings Llc
    39500 Orchard Hill Pl # 500
    Novi MI 48375
    734 737-5000

(G-12477)
MAXION WHEELS USA LLC (DH)
39500 Orchard Hill Pl # 500 (48375-5370)
PHONE.................................734 737-5000
Pieter Klinkers, *CEO*
Steve Esau, *Vice Pres*
John Salvette, *Vice Pres*
Bill Wardle, *Vice Pres*
Roberto Antonello, *Opers Mgr*
EMP: 100 EST: 2003
SQ FT: 20,000
SALES (est): 377.4MM **Privately Held**
WEB: www.maxionwheels.com
SIC: 3714 Wheels, motor vehicle
HQ: Maxion Wheels Llc
    39500 Orchard Hill Pl # 500
    Novi MI 48375
    734 737-5000

(G-12478)
MEDTRONIC USA INC
39555 Orchard Hill Pl # 500 (48375-5374)
PHONE.................................248 449-5027
Greg Burrell, *Branch Mgr*
EMP: 4 **Privately Held**
WEB: www.medtronic.com
SIC: 3841 Surgical & medical instruments
HQ: Medtronic Usa, Inc.
    710 Medtronic Pkwy
    Minneapolis MN 55432
    763 514-4000

(G-12479)
METALSA STRUCTURAL PDTS INC (DH)
29575 Hudson Dr (48377-1733)
PHONE.................................248 669-3704
Polo Cedillo, *CEO*
Jose Jaime Salazar Reyes, *President*
David Altemar Sanchez Hernande, *Vice Pres*
Laura Johnson, *Treasurer*
Fernando Perez Valdes, *Admin Sec*
▲ EMP: 70 EST: 2010
SALES (est): 642.4MM **Privately Held**
WEB: www.metalsa.com
SIC: 3714 Motor vehicle parts & accessories

(G-12480)
MICHIGAN CUSTOM MACHINES INC
Also Called: McM
22750 Heslip Dr (48375-4143)
PHONE.................................248 347-7900
Michael Schena, *President*
Andrew Kunkel, *Project Mgr*
Nissa Rademacher Wise, *Purchasing*
Paul Carlson, *Engineer*
Zachary Coblentz, *Engineer*
EMP: 35 EST: 1994
SQ FT: 35,600
SALES (est): 8.8MM **Privately Held**
WEB: www.michigancustommachines.com
SIC: 3599 Machine shop, jobbing & repair

(G-12481)
MICHIGAN MILK PRODUCERS ASSN (PA)
41310 Bridge St (48375-1302)
P.O. Box 8002 (48376-8002)
PHONE.................................248 474-6672
John Dilland, *CEO*
Kenneth Nobis, *President*
Bob Kran, *Vice Pres*
Colt Johnson, *Plant Mgr*
Kaylan Kennel, *Mfg Staff*
EMP: 40 EST: 1916
SQ FT: 20,000
SALES (est): 75.4MM **Privately Held**
WEB: www.mimilk.com
SIC: 5143 2023 2021 8611 Milk & cream, fluid; dried milk; condensed milk; creamery butter; business associations; fluid milk

(G-12482)
MICROWORLD TECHNOLOGIES INC
39555 Orchard Hill Pl # 60 (48375-5374)
P.O. Box 3013, Farmington Hills (48333-3013)
PHONE.................................248 470-1119
Govind Ramamurthay, *President*
Shweta Thakare, *Vice Pres*
Rohini Sonawane, *Officer*
EMP: 1 EST: 1994
SALES (est): 3MM **Privately Held**
WEB: www.escanav.com
SIC: 7372 Business oriented computer software
PA: Microworld Software Services Private Limited
    Plot No. 80, Road No.15, Midc, Marol,
    Mumbai MH 40009

(G-12483)
MIDORI AUTO LEATHER N AMER INC (PA)
40000 Grand River Ave # 206 (48375-2110)
PHONE.................................248 305-6437
Hirohito Koike, *Senior Mgr*
EMP: 4 EST: 2002
SALES (est): 1MM **Privately Held**
WEB: www.midoriautoleather.mx
SIC: 2399 Seat covers, automobile

(G-12484)
MORRISON INDUSTRIES NORTH
46480 Magellan Dr (48377-2439)
PHONE.................................248 859-4864
EMP: 13 EST: 2017
SALES (est): 1MM **Privately Held**
WEB: www.morrisonindustries.com
SIC: 3441 Fabricated structural metal

(G-12485)
NAGEL PRECISION INC
22025 Arbor Ln (48375-5103)
PHONE.................................248 380-4052
Ken Budesky, *Executive*
EMP: 5 EST: 2018
SALES (est): 94.8K **Privately Held**
SIC: 3541 Machine tools, metal cutting type

(G-12486)
NAGLE PAVING COMPANY (PA)
39525 W 13 Mile Rd # 300 (48377-2361)
PHONE.................................248 553-0700
Michael Santi, *President*
Larry Brennan, *Vice Pres*
Lawrence Brennan, *Vice Pres*
Robert Nagle, *Vice Pres*
James P Oliver, *Vice Pres*
EMP: 11 EST: 1958
SQ FT: 3,240
SALES (est): 23.1MM **Privately Held**
WEB: www.naglepaving.com
SIC: 1611 2951 Surfacing & paving; asphalt & asphaltic paving mixtures (not from refineries)

(G-12487)
NAKAGAWA SPECIAL STL AMER INC
42400 Grand River Ave # 102 (48375-2571)
PHONE.................................248 449-6050
Akihiko Saigo, *Principal*
EMP: 32 EST: 2003
SALES (est): 259.7K **Privately Held**
WEB: www.nssiglb.com
SIC: 3291 Abrasive metal & steel products

(G-12488)
NITS SOLUTIONS INC
40850 Grand River Ave # 100 (48375-5705)
PHONE.................................248 231-2267
Neetu Seth, *President*
Kyle Shernoff, *Marketing Mgr*
Alexander Spiess, *Business Anlyst*
Kim Cygan, *Marketing Staff*
Daniel Higgins, *Manager*
EMP: 15 EST: 2009
SALES (est): 2.1MM **Privately Held**
WEB: www.nitssolutions.com
SIC: 7371 7372 7374 8732 Computer software development; application computer software; calculating service (computer); survey service: marketing, location, etc.; telemarketing services

(G-12489)
NITTO INC
Also Called: Nitto Denko
45880 Dylan Dr (48375-4905)
PHONE.................................248 449-2300
Michael Lazich, *Sales Staff*
EMP: 87 **Privately Held**
WEB: www.nitto.com
SIC: 3714 Motor vehicle parts & accessories
HQ: Nitto, Inc.
    1990 Rutgers Univ Blvd
    Lakewood NJ 08701
    732 901-7905

(G-12490)
NOBILIS PIPE COMPANY
30850 Collingdale Dr (48377-1563)
PHONE.................................248 470-5692
Brian Harroun, *President*
Susan Flory, *Officer*
EMP: 12 EST: 2018
SALES (est): 933.6K **Privately Held**
WEB: www.nobilispipe.com
SIC: 3312 Pipes, iron & steel

(G-12491)
NORTHWEST ORTHOTICS-PROSTHETIC
39830 Grand River Ave B1d (48375-2134)
PHONE.................................248 477-1443
Michael Henry, *President*
EMP: 5 EST: 1990
SQ FT: 2,600
SALES (est): 558.9K **Privately Held**
SIC: 3842 5999 Orthopedic appliances; prosthetic appliances; orthopedic & prosthesis applications

(G-12492)
NOVELIS CORPORATION
39550 W 13 Mile Rd # 150 (48377-2360)
PHONE.................................248 668-5111
EMP: 7 **Privately Held**
WEB: www.novelis.com
SIC: 3353 Foil, aluminum
HQ: Novelis Corporation
    3560 Lenox Rd Ne Ste 2000
    Atlanta GA 30326
    404 760-4000

(G-12493)
NOVI CRUSHED CONCRETE LLC
46900 W 12 Mile Rd (48377-3217)
PHONE.................................248 305-6020
Howard K Copeland, *Principal*
EMP: 4 EST: 1999
SALES (est): 570.1K **Privately Held**
WEB: www.novicrushedconcrete.com
SIC: 3273 Ready-mixed concrete

(G-12494)
NOVI MANUFACTURING CO
25555 Seeley Rd (48375-2053)
PHONE.................................248 476-4350
Henry P Kelly, *President*
EMP: 208 EST: 1963
SALES (est): 4.4MM
SALES (corp-wide): 4.5B **Publicly Held**
WEB: www.amerco.com
SIC: 3713 7513 Truck & bus bodies; truck rental & leasing, no drivers
PA: Amerco
    5555 Kietzke Ln Ste 100
    Reno NV 89511
    775 688-6300

(G-12495)
NUTEK INDUSTRIES LLC
Also Called: Nutek Abrasives, LLC
42900 W 9 Mile Rd (48375-4123)
PHONE.................................800 637-9194
Alan Davis,
EMP: 10 EST: 2017
SALES (est): 430K **Privately Held**
WEB: www.nutekabrasives.com
SIC: 3291 Abrasive products

(G-12496)
OKUNO INTERNATIONAL CORP
40000 Grant Rver Ave Ste (48375)
PHONE.................................248 536-2727
Katuyoshi Okuno, *President*
Takako Yatsuka, *General Mgr*
Naoki Okuno, *Vice Pres*
Dayne Kono, *Admin Sec*
▲ EMP: 5 EST: 2012
SALES (est): 436.3K **Privately Held**
WEB: www.okuno-intl.com
SIC: 3563 Dusting outfits for metals, paints & chemicals

(G-12497)
OMRON AUTOMOTIVE ELECTRONICS
29185 Cabot Dr (48377-2936)
PHONE.................................248 893-0200
EMP: 38
SALES (corp-wide): 7.1B **Publicly Held**
SIC: 3694 Mfg Engine Electrical Equipment
HQ: Omron Automotive Electronics, Inc.
    3709 Ohio Ave
    Saint Charles IL 60174
    630 443-6800

(G-12498)
OPTIMEMS TECHNOLOGY INC
43422 W Oaks Dr Ste 183 (48377-3300)
PHONE.................................248 660-0380
Z Joe Huang, *President*
Diana J Huang, *Treasurer*
Linda Zhang, *Admin Sec*
EMP: 9 EST: 2013
SALES (est): 291.3K **Privately Held**
WEB: www.optimems.com
SIC: 3674 Semiconductors & related devices

(G-12499)
OROTEX CORPORATION
22475 Venture Dr (48375-4177)
PHONE.................................248 773-8630
Kenichi Hiura, *President*
Takuji Iida, *Treasurer*
Ritsuko McCarthy, *Accountant*
▲ EMP: 135 EST: 2001
SQ FT: 60,000
SALES: 25.7MM **Privately Held**
WEB: www.orotex.co.jp
SIC: 3714 Motor vehicle parts & accessories
PA: Iida Industry Co., Ltd.
    759, Ichichowari, Mukuicho
    Inazawa AIC 492-8

(G-12500)
OUR NEXT ENERGY INC
Also Called: One.ai
29050 Cabot Dr (48377-2975)
PHONE.................................408 623-1896
Mujeeb Ijaz, *CEO*
Jonathan Chandrakumar, *Finance*

GEOGRAPHIC SECTION
Novi - Oakland County (G-12527)

EMP: 30 EST: 2020
SALES (est): 4.9MM **Privately Held**
SIC: 3691 Storage batteries

(G-12501)
OXID CORPORATION
25325 Regency Dr (48375-2159)
PHONE.................................248 474-9817
William G Fredrick Jr, *President*
Ann Raske, *Technician*
EMP: 26 EST: 1986
SALES (est): 305.6K **Privately Held**
WEB: www.oxid.com
SIC: 3599 Machine shop, jobbing & repair

(G-12502)
PACIFIC ENGINEERING CORP
Also Called: PEC of America
39555 Orchard Hill Pl (48375-5374)
PHONE.................................248 359-7823
Hirohisa Ogawa, *Ch of Bd*
Takahisa Ogawa, *President*
Norio Io, *Exec VP*
EMP: 8 EST: 1990
SALES (est): 290.3K **Privately Held**
SIC: 3465 8711 Body parts, automobile: stamped metal; engineering services

(G-12503)
PCB PIEZOTRONICS INC
4000 Grand River Blvd (48375)
PHONE.................................888 684-0014
Jeff Case, *Branch Mgr*
EMP: 10
SALES (corp-wide): 8.6B **Publicly Held**
WEB: www.larsondavis.com
SIC: 3829 3679 Measuring & controlling devices; transducers, electrical
HQ: Pcb Piezotronics, Inc.
   3425 Walden Ave
   Depew NY 14043
   716 684-0001

(G-12504)
PEC OF AMERICA CORPORATION (HQ)
39555 Orchard Hill Pl # 220 (48375-5374)
PHONE.................................248 675-3130
Takahisa Ogawa, *CEO*
Koichiro Mabuchi, *CFO*
▲ EMP: 15 EST: 1994
SQ FT: 1,200
SALES (est): 33.9MM **Privately Held**
WEB: www.pecj.co.jp
SIC: 3613 3469 Fuses, electric; machine parts, stamped or pressed metal

(G-12505)
PHOENIX INTERGRATION INC
26200 Town Center Dr # 150 (48375-1218)
PHONE.................................586 484-8196
Julie Cunningham, *Opers Mgr*
Subodh Chaudhari, *Engineer*
EMP: 5 EST: 2016
SALES (est): 127.8K **Privately Held**
SIC: 7372 Prepackaged software

(G-12506)
POLYWORKS USA TRAINING CENTER
41700 Gardenbrook Rd (48375-1324)
PHONE.................................216 226-1617
EMP: 7 EST: 2015
SALES (est): 347.5K **Privately Held**
SIC: 7372 Prepackaged software

(G-12507)
POWER CLEANING SYSTEMS INC
46085 Grand River Ave (48374-1319)
PHONE.................................248 347-7727
Pamela McCarthy, *Vice Pres*
EMP: 6 EST: 1990
SALES (est): 116.2K **Privately Held**
WEB: www.powercleaningsystems.com
SIC: 3569 General industrial machinery

(G-12508)
POWER PROCESS ENGRG CO INC
24300 Catherne Ind Dr # 203 (48375-2457)
PHONE.................................248 473-8450
John Walsh, *President*
Donald J Fichter Jr, *Vice Pres*
EMP: 8
SQ FT: 5,000
SALES (est): 3MM **Privately Held**
WEB: www.powerprocessengineering.com
SIC: 3494 Valves & pipe fittings

(G-12509)
POWERLASE PHOTONICS INC
26800 Meadowbrook Rd # 113 (48377-3540)
PHONE.................................248 305-2963
EMP: 5 EST: 2016
SALES (est): 107.7K **Privately Held**
SIC: 3674 Semiconductors & related devices

(G-12510)
PPG INDUSTRIES INC
Also Called: PPG 5622
40400 Grand River Ave C (48375-2872)
PHONE.................................248 478-1300
Tony Bronvich, *Branch Mgr*
EMP: 4
SALES (corp-wide): 15.1B **Publicly Held**
WEB: www.ppg.com
SIC: 2851 Paints & allied products
PA: Ppg Industries, Inc.
   1 Ppg Pl
   Pittsburgh PA 15272
   412 434-3131

(G-12511)
PREMIER SIGNS PLUS INC
24514 Terra Del Mar Dr (48374-2532)
PHONE.................................248 633-5598
Ernest J Devincent Jr, *Principal*
EMP: 5 EST: 2019
SALES (est): 46K **Privately Held**
WEB: www.premiersignsplus.com
SIC: 3993 Signs & advertising specialties

(G-12512)
PRESTOLITE ELECTRIC LLC (HQ)
30120 Hudson Dr (48377-4115)
PHONE.................................248 313-3807
Peter J Corrigan, *COO*
Aubrey Baker, *Opers Staff*
Penny Henry, *Purch Agent*
Nancy Weber, *Buyer*
Gabor Andrejcsik, *Chief Engr*
▲ EMP: 8 EST: 2004
SALES (est): 182.4MM
SALES (corp-wide): 1.1B **Privately Held**
WEB: www.broad-ocean.com
SIC: 3643 3824 3621 3625 Electric switches; electromechanical counters; motors, electric; electric controls & control accessories, industrial; motors, starting: automotive & aircraft
PA: Zhongshan Broad-Ocean Motor Co.,Ltd
   No.1, Guangfeng Industrial Blvd., Xiqu
   Zhongshan 52840
   760 885-5530

(G-12513)
PRESTOLITE ELECTRIC HOLDING
Also Called: Prestolite International Holdg
30120 Hudson Dr (48377-4115)
PHONE.................................248 313-3807
Michael Shen, *CEO*
Charles Lu, *Ch of Bd*
Tom Hogan, *President*
Frank Cavanaugh, *Engineer*
Kerry Zhang, *CFO*
EMP: 2500 EST: 1911
SQ FT: 25,000
SALES (est): 151.9MM
SALES (corp-wide): 1.1B **Privately Held**
SIC: 3621 3694 Motors, electric; motors, starting: automotive & aircraft
HQ: Prestolite Electric, Llc
   30120 Hudson Dr
   Novi MI 48377
   248 313-3807

(G-12514)
PRESTOLITE ELECTRIC INC (HQ)
30120 Hudson Dr (48377-4115)
PHONE.................................866 463-7078
Tony Wong, *President*
Willis Johnson III, *Plant Mgr*
Rob Pattacciato, *Mfg Mgr*
Natalie Turner, *Opers Staff*
Terri Myers, *Buyer*
▲ EMP: 12 EST: 1991
SQ FT: 50,000
SALES (est): 119.7MM
SALES (corp-wide): 1.1B **Privately Held**
WEB: www.broad-ocean.com
SIC: 3621 3694 Starters, for motors; alternators, automotive
PA: Zhongshan Broad-Ocean Motor Co.,Ltd
   No.1, Guangfeng Industrial Blvd., Xiqu
   Zhongshan 52840
   760 885-5530

(G-12515)
PRINTASTIC LLC
46555 Humboldt Dr Ste 200 (48377-2455)
PHONE.................................248 761-5697
EMP: 10 EST: 2015
SALES (est): 888.3K **Privately Held**
WEB: www.printastic.com
SIC: 3993 Signs & advertising specialties

(G-12516)
PRINTING INDUSTRIES OF MICH
41300 Beacon Rd (48375-5202)
PHONE.................................248 946-5895
Nick Wagner, *President*
David Stress, *Technology*
EMP: 5 EST: 1888
SALES (est): 172.5K **Privately Held**
WEB: www.print.org
SIC: 2752 Commercial printing, offset

(G-12517)
PROGRAMMED PRODUCTS CORP
Also Called: Ppc Design
44311 Grand River Ave (48375-1128)
PHONE.................................248 348-7755
Charles Voydanoff, *President*
John E Zafarana, *Chairman*
▼ EMP: 69 EST: 1970
SQ FT: 75,000
SALES (est): 1.5MM **Privately Held**
WEB: www.ppcretaildesign.com
SIC: 3993 2541 2435 Signs & advertising specialties; wood partitions & fixtures; hardwood veneer & plywood

(G-12518)
PUREM NOVI INC
43700 Gen Mar (48375-1667)
PHONE.................................248 778-5231
Eric Phillips, *Branch Mgr*
EMP: 117
SALES (corp-wide): 5.4B **Privately Held**
SIC: 3714 Motor vehicle parts & accessories
HQ: Purem Novi Inc.
   29101 Haggerty Rd
   Novi MI 48377
   248 994-7010

(G-12519)
PUREM NOVI INC (DH)
Also Called: Catem North America
29101 Haggerty Rd (48377-2913)
PHONE.................................248 994-7010
Uwe Sass, *General Mgr*
Gunter Baumann, *Chairman*
Pete Laplante, *Regional Mgr*
Heinrich Baumann, *COO*
Klaus Beetz, *COO*
▲ EMP: 42 EST: 1999
SALES (est): 214MM
SALES (corp-wide): 5.4B **Privately Held**
WEB: www.eberspaecher.com
SIC: 3714 Exhaust systems & parts, motor vehicle
HQ: Eberspacher Climate Control Systems Gmbh
   Eberspacherstr. 24
   Esslingen Am Neckar BW 73730
   711 939-00

(G-12520)
QNX SOFTWARE SYSTEMS
25849 Meadowbrook Rd (48375-1851)
PHONE.................................248 513-3412
Zhiqin Liu, *Software Dev*
EMP: 7 EST: 2016
SALES (est): 373.8K **Privately Held**
WEB: www.blackberry.qnx.com
SIC: 7372 Prepackaged software

(G-12521)
QUANTUM OPUS LLC
22500 Devron Ct (48374-3779)
PHONE.................................517 680-0011
Tim Rambo, *Principal*
EMP: 4 EST: 2017
SALES (est): 101K **Privately Held**
WEB: www.quantumopus.com
SIC: 3674 Semiconductors & related devices

(G-12522)
R H M RUBBER & MANUFACTURING
203 Bernstadt St (48377-1918)
PHONE.................................248 624-8277
Raymond Hoyer, *President*
Kim Cooley, *Partner*
Cathie Hall, *Office Mgr*
EMP: 4
SQ FT: 7,500
SALES (est): 300K **Privately Held**
SIC: 3069 3061 3053 Molded rubber products; mechanical rubber goods; gaskets, packing & sealing devices

(G-12523)
RADIO ADVERTISING BUREAU INC
28175 Haggerty Rd (48377-2903)
PHONE.................................248 514-7048
EMP: 4 EST: 2019
SALES (est): 350.7K **Privately Held**
WEB: www.rab.com
SIC: 3571 Electronic computers

(G-12524)
REDEEM POWER SERVICES
43422 W Oaks Dr Ste 178 (48377-3300)
PHONE.................................248 679-5277
Anthony Johnson,
Blanca Johnson,
EMP: 5 EST: 2012
SQ FT: 900
SALES (est): 179.9K **Privately Held**
SIC: 3629 3691 Inverters, nonrotating: electrical; storage batteries

(G-12525)
REVERE PLASTICS SYSTEMS LLC (DH)
39555 Orchard Hill Pl # 155 (48375-5407)
PHONE.................................833 300-4043
Rustin Shields, *General Mgr*
Kurt Kosel, *Engineer*
George Dewalt, *Project Engr*
Dar McClelland, *Sales Staff*
David Seufert, *Manager*
▲ EMP: 300 EST: 2005
SALES (est): 165.6MM
SALES (corp-wide): 21.1MM **Privately Held**
WEB: www.revereindustries.com
SIC: 3089 Injection molding of plastics

(G-12526)
REWARDPAL INC
43422 W Oaks Dr (48377-3300)
PHONE.................................800 377-6099
Tom Alkatib, *CEO*
EMP: 4 EST: 2017
SALES (est): 105.6K **Privately Held**
WEB: www.rewardpal.net
SIC: 7372 Prepackaged software

(G-12527)
ROBERT BOSCH LLC
Novi Res Pk 27275 Hggrty (48377)
PHONE.................................248 921-9054
Mindy Galloway, *Engineer*
Pres Lawhon, *Branch Mgr*
EMP: 7
SALES (corp-wide): 297.8MM **Privately Held**
WEB: www.bosch.us
SIC: 3714 3694 5013 5064 Motor vehicle parts & accessories; motors, starting: automotive & aircraft; automotive supplies & parts; radios, motor vehicle; packaging machinery; deburring machines
HQ: Robert Bosch Llc
   38000 Hills Tech Dr
   Farmington Hills MI 48331
   248 876-1000

Novi - Oakland County (G-12528)   GEOGRAPHIC SECTION

(G-12528)
ROLLS-ROYCE SOLUTIONS AMER INC (DH)
Also Called: Rolls Royce Power Systems
39525 Mackenzie Dr (48377-1602)
PHONE 248 560-8000
Koenig Thomas, *President*
Mary Anne Lloyd, *Opers Mgr*
Timothy Wille, *Opers Staff*
Torsten Hofmann, *Senior Buyer*
Thomas Schlegel, *Senior Buyer*
▲ **EMP:** 250 **EST:** 1978
SALES (est): 193.8MM
SALES (corp-wide): 15.7B **Privately Held**
WEB: www.mtuamericacareers.com
SIC: 3519 Diesel, semi-diesel or duel-fuel engines, including marine
HQ: Rolls-Royce Solutions Gmbh
Maybachplatz 1
Friedrichshafen BW 88045
754 190-0

(G-12529)
RSI GLOBAL SOURCING LLC
Also Called: Stable ARC
43630 Wendingo Ct (48375-5432)
PHONE 734 604-2448
Randy S Stevens, *President*
EMP: 8 **EST:** 2007
SQ FT: 1,500
SALES (est): 1MM **Privately Held**
WEB: www.stablearc.com
SIC: 3441 3541 3548 Fabricated structural metal; plasma process metal cutting machines; welding apparatus

(G-12530)
S A R COMPANY LLC ⊙
31074 Seneca Ln (48377-1524)
PHONE 248 979-7590
Sonya Futrell,
EMP: 20 **EST:** 2021
SALES (est): 746.9K **Privately Held**
SIC: 3639 Major kitchen appliances, except refrigerators & stoves

(G-12531)
SANDERS INFORMATION PUBLISHING
41606 Kenilworth Ln (48377-1594)
PHONE 248 669-0991
Maurice Sanders, *Principal*
EMP: 5 **EST:** 2009
SALES (est): 90.3K **Privately Held**
SIC: 2741 Miscellaneous publishing

(G-12532)
SCS EMBEDDED TECH LLC
Also Called: Signal Conditioning Solutions
25893 Meadowbrook Rd (48375-1851)
PHONE 248 615-4441
Rachel Rathsburg, *Mng Member*
EMP: 9 **EST:** 2004
SALES (est): 1.8MM **Privately Held**
WEB: www.scsembeddedtech.com
SIC: 3577 5065 5085 Input/output equipment, computer; electronic parts & equipment; industrial supplies

(G-12533)
SEG AUTOMOTIVE NORTH AMER LLC (DH)
27275 Haggerty Rd Ste 420 (48377-3636)
PHONE 248 465-2602
Jonathan Husby, *CEO*
EMP: 48 **EST:** 2016
SALES (est): 13MM **Privately Held**
WEB: www.seg-automotive.com
SIC: 3542 3714 3694 Press brakes; air brakes, motor vehicle; alternators, automotive; battery charging alternators & generators
HQ: Seg Automotive Germany Gmbh
Lotterbergstr. 30
Stuttgart BW 70499
711 400-9800

(G-12534)
SENSOR MANUFACTURING COMPANY
40750 Grand River Ave (48375-2812)
P.O. Box 955 (48376-0955)
PHONE 248 474-7300
Robert L Byrum, *President*
Robert Byrum Jr, *Vice Pres*
Dawn Jones, *Vice Pres*
Richard S Hamlin, *Admin Sec*
EMP: 14 **EST:** 1977
SQ FT: 9,300
SALES (est): 1.7MM **Privately Held**
WEB: www.sensormfg.com
SIC: 3679 Loads, electronic

(G-12535)
SERVICE DIAMOND TOOL COMPANY
Also Called: Service Physical Testers Div
46590 Ryan Ct (48377-1730)
PHONE 248 669-3100
Richard Antonik, *President*
EMP: 9 **EST:** 1942
SQ FT: 10,000
SALES (est): 618.4K **Privately Held**
WEB: www.sunteccorp.com
SIC: 3545 3829 Diamond cutting tools for turning, boring, burnishing, etc.; hardness testing equipment

(G-12536)
SHYFT GROUP INC (PA)
41280 Bridge St (48375-1301)
PHONE 517 543-6400
James A Sharman, *Ch of Bd*
Daryl M Adams, *President*
Todd Fierro, *President*
Stephen K Guillaume, *President*
John W Slawson, *President*
♦ **EMP:** 570 **EST:** 1975
SQ FT: 12,000
SALES (est): 146.2MM **Publicly Held**
WEB: www.spartanmotors.com
SIC: 3711 3714 7519 Chassis, motor vehicle; fire department vehicles (motor vehicles), assembly of; ambulances (motor vehicles), assembly of; motor vehicle parts & accessories; utility trailer rental

(G-12537)
SIGNS BY TOMORROW
40400 Grand River Ave H (48375-2872)
PHONE 248 478-5600
EMP: 5 **EST:** 2019
SALES (est): 46K **Privately Held**
WEB: www.signsbytomorrow.com
SIC: 3993 Signs & advertising specialties

(G-12538)
SIMERICS INC
39500 Orchard Hill Pl # 190 (48375-5520)
PHONE 248 513-3200
Deming Wang, *Branch Mgr*
EMP: 6 **Privately Held**
WEB: www.simerics.com
SIC: 7372 7379 Application computer software; computer related consulting services
PA: Simerics, Inc.
1750 112th Ave Ne C250
Bellevue WA 98004

(G-12539)
SOLEO HEALTH INC
26800 Meadowbrook Rd # 119 (48377-3540)
PHONE 248 513-8687
Anessa Montville, *Manager*
EMP: 10 **Privately Held**
WEB: www.soleohealth.com
SIC: 2834 5912 Druggists' preparations (pharmaceuticals); drug stores & proprietary stores
HQ: Soleo Health Inc.
950 Calcon Hook Rd Ste 19
Sharon Hill PA 19079
888 244-2340

(G-12540)
SOUTEC DIV OF ANDRITZ BRICMONT
26800 Meadowbrook Rd # 113 (48377-3540)
PHONE 248 305-2955
EMP: 40 **EST:** 2014
SALES (est): 1.1MM **Privately Held**
SIC: 7011 7692 Hostels; welding repair

(G-12541)
SRI DELAWARE HOLDINGS LLC (HQ)
39675 Mackenzie Dr # 400 (48377-1607)
PHONE 248 489-9300
Jonathan B Degaynor, *President*
EMP: 1 **EST:** 2018
SALES (est): 5MM **Publicly Held**
WEB: www.stoneridge.com
SIC: 3714 Motor vehicle electrical equipment

(G-12542)
STARTECH SOFTWARE SYSTEMS INC
Also Called: Fdi Group
39500 High Pointe Blvd # 400 (48375-5505)
PHONE 248 344-2266
Mark Churella, *President*
EMP: 6 **EST:** 1997
SALES (est): 1MM
SALES (corp-wide): 23MM **Privately Held**
WEB: www.startechsoftware.com
SIC: 7372 Prepackaged software
PA: Financial Designs, Inc.
39500 High Pointe Blvd
Novi MI 48375
248 348-8200

(G-12543)
STONERIDGE INC (PA)
39675 Mackenzie Dr # 400 (48377-1607)
PHONE 248 489-9300
Karen Recknagel, *CEO*
William M Lasky, *Ch of Bd*
Jonathan B Degaynor, *President*
Caetano R Ferraiolo, *President*
Robert Willig, *President*
♦ **EMP:** 648 **EST:** 1965
SQ FT: 37,713
SALES (est): 648MM **Publicly Held**
WEB: www.stoneridge.com
SIC: 3714 3679 3625 Motor vehicle electrical equipment; instrument board assemblies, motor vehicle; harness assemblies for electronic use: wire or cable; electronic switches; actuators, industrial

(G-12544)
STONERIDGE INC
Pollak Engineered Pdts Group
39675 Mackenzie Dr # 400 (48377-1607)
PHONE 781 830-0340
Allen Braddock, *Engineer*
Chao Yu, *Electrical Engi*
Mike Seely, *Branch Mgr*
Jeffrey P Draime, *Director*
EMP: 400 **Publicly Held**
WEB: www.stoneridge.com
SIC: 3714 3699 Motor vehicle electrical equipment; electrical equipment & supplies
PA: Stoneridge, Inc.
39675 Mackenzie Dr # 400
Novi MI 48377

(G-12545)
STONERIDGE CONTROL DEVICES INC
39675 Mackenzie Dr # 400 (48377-1607)
PHONE 248 489-9300
Jonathan B Degaynor, *President*
Robert Willig, *Vice Pres*
Majdi Ramahi, *Engineer*
Robert R Krakowiak, *Treasurer*
Kristy Eichar, *Human Res Mgr*
EMP: 5 **EST:** 1999
SALES (est): 2.8MM **Publicly Held**
WEB: www.stoneridge.com
SIC: 3625 Industrial electrical relays & switches
PA: Stoneridge, Inc.
39675 Mackenzie Dr # 400
Novi MI 48377

(G-12546)
STRYKER CORPORATION
27275 Haggerty Rd Ste 680 (48377-3634)
PHONE 248 374-6352
Chris Nadeau, *Sales Staff*
John Hebner, *Branch Mgr*
Misty Speelman, *Manager*
EMP: 4
SALES (corp-wide): 14.3B **Publicly Held**
WEB: www.stryker.com
SIC: 3841 Surgical & medical instruments
PA: Stryker Corporation
2825 Airview Blvd
Portage MI 49002
269 385-2600

(G-12547)
STUARTS OF NOVI
41390 W 10 Mile Rd (48375-3404)
PHONE 248 615-2955
Paul Gabriel, *Manager*
Amy Smith, *CTO*
EMP: 10 **EST:** 2009
SALES (est): 183.9K **Privately Held**
WEB: www.stuartsofnovi.com
SIC: 2024 Yogurt desserts, frozen

(G-12548)
SUMITOMO CHEMICAL AMERICA INC
45525 Grand River Ave # 200 (48374-1308)
PHONE 248 284-4797
David Risetter, *Branch Mgr*
EMP: 5 **Privately Held**
WEB: www.sumitomochemicalamerica.com
SIC: 3089 Plastic processing
HQ: Sumitomo Chemical America, Inc.
150 E 42nd St Rm 701
New York NY 10017
212 572-8200

(G-12549)
SUMITOMO ELECTRIC CARBIDE INC
26800 Meadowbrook Rd # 120 (48377-3540)
PHONE 734 451-0200
Tony Desimone, *Engineer*
Jim Beck, *Sales Engr*
Gary Beeler, *Sales Engr*
Jim Davis, *Sales Engr*
Pete King, *Sales Engr*
EMP: 10 **Privately Held**
WEB: www.sumicarbide.com
SIC: 2819 Carbides
HQ: Sumitomo Electric Carbide Inc
1001 E Business Center Dr
Mount Prospect IL 60056
847 635-0044

(G-12550)
SUN-TEC CORP (PA)
46590 Ryan Ct (48377-1730)
PHONE 248 669-3100
Richard Antonik, *President*
Mark Antonik, *Vice Pres*
George Smolboski, *Exec Dir*
▲ **EMP:** 3 **EST:** 1995
SQ FT: 10,000
SALES (est): 3MM **Privately Held**
WEB: www.sunteccorp.com
SIC: 3829 7699 Physical property testing equipment; professional instrument repair services

(G-12551)
SUPPLY LINE INTERNATIONAL LLC
42350 Grand River Ave (48375-1838)
PHONE 248 242-7140
Joshua Kaplan, *Mng Member*
EMP: 18 **EST:** 2012
SQ FT: 11,000
SALES (est): 4MM **Privately Held**
SIC: 3714 Motor vehicle parts & accessories

(G-12552)
SWAROVSKI
27500 Novi Rd (48377-3418)
PHONE 248 344-2922
EMP: 8 **EST:** 2006
SALES (est): 166.6K **Privately Held**
WEB: www.swarovski.com
SIC: 3423 Jewelers' hand tools

(G-12553)
TA DELAWARE INC (PA)
Also Called: Tower International
17672 N Lrel Pk Dr Ste 40 (48377)
PHONE 248 675-6000

▲ = Import ▼=Export
♦ =Import/Export

Mark Malcom, *President*
Michael Rajkovic, *COO*
James Gouin, *Exec VP*
Jay Gowda, *Vice Pres*
Ken Kundrick, *Vice Pres*
EMP: 424 **EST:** 1993
SALES (est): 35.7MM **Privately Held**
SIC: 3465 Automotive stampings

(G-12554)
TEMPERFORM LLC
25425 Trans X Rd (48375-2445)
P.O. Box 767 (48376-0767)
PHONE.................................248 349-5230
Bruce Boettger, *CEO*
Dan Bickersteth, *Director*
◆ **EMP:** 50 **EST:** 1970
SQ FT: 50,000
SALES (est): 12.5MM
SALES (corp-wide): 75.7MM **Privately Held**
WEB: www.temperform.com
SIC: 3325 Alloy steel castings, except investment
PA: Blackeagle Partners, Llc
6905 Telegraph Rd Ste 119
Bloomfield Hills MI 48301
313 647-5340

(G-12555)
THERMAL DESIGNS & MFG
41069 Vincenti Ct (48375-1923)
PHONE.................................248 476-2978
Harold J Gardynik, *President*
EMP: 30 **EST:** 1992
SQ FT: 26,000
SALES (est): 1.1MM
SALES (corp-wide): 20MM **Privately Held**
WEB: www.commercecontrols.com
SIC: 3567 Infrared ovens, industrial
PA: Commerce Controls, Inc.
41069 Vincenti Ct
Novi MI 48375
248 476-1442

(G-12556)
THIELENHAUS MICROFINISH CORP
42925 W 9 Mile Rd (48375-4115)
PHONE.................................248 349-9450
J Peter Thielenhaus, *President*
Manfred Sieringhaus, *Chairman*
Dale Drabicki, *Project Mgr*
John Sabbadin, *Purch Mgr*
Tom Brake, *Sales Mgr*
▲ **EMP:** 38 **EST:** 1981
SQ FT: 27,000
SALES (est): 8MM
SALES (corp-wide): 562.9K **Privately Held**
WEB: www.thielenhaus.com
SIC: 3541 3829 3549 3545 Machine tools, metal cutting type; measuring & controlling devices; metalworking machinery; machine tool accessories
HQ: Thielenhaus Technologies Gmbh
Schwesterstr. 50
Wuppertal NW 42285
202 481-0

(G-12557)
TOYOTA INDUSTRIES ELCTC SYS N
28700 Cabot Dr Ste 100 (48377-2948)
PHONE.................................248 489-7700
Sadanori Suzuki, *President*
EMP: 4 **EST:** 2013
SALES (est): 2.4MM **Privately Held**
WEB: www.toyota.com
SIC: 3559 Electronic component making machinery
HQ: Toyota Industries North America, Inc.
3030 Barker Dr
Columbus IN 47201
812 341-3810

(G-12558)
TREVES N KOTOBUKIYA AMER INC
Also Called: Ktna
39500 Orchard Hill Pl # 110 (48375-5370)
PHONE.................................248 513-4255
James Gray, *Administration*
EMP: 16 **EST:** 2004

SALES (est): 3.5MM **Privately Held**
SIC: 2273 Carpets & rugs

(G-12559)
TSW TECHNOLOGIES LLC
25909 Meadowbrook Rd (48375-1853)
PHONE.................................248 773-5026
Michael Kondogiani,
Jim Allard,
Christopher Kondogiani,
Jeff Zyburt,
EMP: 4 **EST:** 2019
SALES (est): 197K **Privately Held**
SIC: 2843 Surface active agents

(G-12560)
TVA KANE INC (PA)
45380 W 10 Mile Rd # 100 (48375-3000)
PHONE.................................248 946-4670
James C McCaffrey, *Administration*
EMP: 41 **EST:** 2011
SALES (est): 573.8K **Privately Held**
SIC: 5944 3911 Jewelry, precious stones & precious metals; jewelry, precious metal

(G-12561)
TWIG POWER LLC
40480 Grand River Ave J (48375-2874)
PHONE.................................248 613-9652
Jesse Beeker, *President*
Tom Embrescia,
Scott Finerman,
Sean Hilbert,
Phil McDowell,
EMP: 6 **EST:** 2019
SALES (est): 330.9K **Privately Held**
WEB: www.twigpwr.com
SIC: 8711 3699 Engineering services; electrical equipment & supplies

(G-12562)
UCHIYAMA MKTG & DEV AMER LLC
46805 Magellan Dr (48377-2444)
PHONE.................................248 859-3986
Masatomo Sueki, *CEO*
EMP: 15 **EST:** 2014
SQ FT: 18,212
SALES (est): 2.6MM **Privately Held**
WEB: www.umc-umd.com
SIC: 3061 Automotive rubber goods (mechanical)
PA: Uchiyama Manufacturing Corp.
338, Enami, Naka-Ku
Okayama OKA 702-8

(G-12563)
UNIFILTER INC
Also Called: Unifilter Company
43800 Grand River Ave (48375-1115)
P.O. Box 8025 (48376-8025)
PHONE.................................248 476-5100
Robert R Redner, *President*
John Redner, *President*
Carl Redner, *Vice Pres*
John A Redner, *Treasurer*
Carl R Redner, *Admin Sec*
EMP: 12 **EST:** 1932
SQ FT: 60,000
SALES (est): 266K **Privately Held**
WEB: www.generalfilters.com
SIC: 5013 3714 Filters, air & oil; motor vehicle parts & accessories

(G-12564)
VCONVERTER CORPORATION (PA)
43700 Gen Mar (48375-1667)
PHONE.................................248 388-0549
Mark W Midgley, *CEO*
Don Nowland, *President*
Scott Martin, *Vice Pres*
Keith Cox, *Production*
Tim Priest, *Engineer*
EMP: 118 **EST:** 2003
SALES (est): 17.7MM **Privately Held**
WEB: www.vconverter.com
SIC: 3567 Industrial furnaces & ovens

(G-12565)
VECTOR NORTH AMERICA INC
39500 Orchard Hill Pl (48375-5370)
PHONE.................................248 449-9290
Tony Mascolo, *CEO*
Jeff Rothenberg, *Business Mgr*
Ralf Fritz, *Senior Engr*

Samer White, *Senior Engr*
Yvette Michels, *Treasurer*
EMP: 80 **EST:** 1997
SQ FT: 27,000
SALES (est): 24.1MM
SALES (corp-wide): 632.5K **Privately Held**
WEB: www.vector.com
SIC: 7372 7373 Prepackaged software; computer integrated systems design
HQ: Vector Informatik Gmbh
Ingersheimer Str. 24
Stuttgart 70499
711 806-700

(G-12566)
VENTURE TECHNOLOGY GROUPS INC (PA)
Also Called: Process Technology & Controls
24300 Catherine Industria (48375-2457)
PHONE.................................248 473-8450
Don Fichter, *Vice Pres*
Pam Abdallah, *Accounting Dir*
EMP: 15 **EST:** 1987
SQ FT: 16,000
SALES (est): 21.4MM **Privately Held**
WEB: www.vtgi.com
SIC: 5051 5085 3999 Pipe & tubing, steel; industrial supplies; atomizers, toiletry

(G-12567)
VERITAS USA CORPORATION
39555 Orchard Hill Pl # 600 (48375-5374)
PHONE.................................248 374-5019
EMP: 23 **EST:** 2000
SALES (est): 3.7MM
SALES (corp-wide): 696.6MM **Privately Held**
WEB: www.veritas.ag
SIC: 3714 Fuel systems & parts, motor vehicle
HQ: Veritas Ag
Stettiner Str. 1-9
Gelnhausen HE 63571
605 182-10

(G-12568)
VISOTEK INC
25325 Regency Dr (48375-2159)
PHONE.................................734 427-4800
Sheila Jensen, *President*
Elmer Wang, *Electrical Engi*
EMP: 10 **EST:** 2001
SALES (est): 2.2MM
SALES (corp-wide): 17.9MM **Privately Held**
WEB: www.visotekinc.com
SIC: 3699 3827 Laser welding, drilling & cutting equipment; optical instruments & apparatus
PA: Laser Mechanisms, Inc.
25325 Regency Dr
Novi MI 48375
248 474-9480

(G-12569)
WOCO TECH USA INC
28970 Cabot Dr Ste 300 (48377-2909)
PHONE.................................248 385-2854
Petr Tomecek, *President*
Peter Tomecek, *Vice Pres*
EMP: 19 **EST:** 2009
SQ FT: 400
SALES (est): 5.1MM
SALES (corp-wide): 647.4MM **Privately Held**
WEB: www.wocogroup.com
SIC: 7363 3089 Engineering help service; automotive parts, plastic
HQ: Woco Tech De Mexico, S.A. De C.V.
Av. De Las Fuentes No. 17
El Marques QRO. 76246

(G-12570)
YANFENG US AUTO INTR SYSTEMS I (DH)
41935 W 12 Mile Rd (48377-3135)
P.O. Box 7125 (48376-7125)
PHONE.................................248 319-7333
Johannes Roters, *CEO*
Wenguang Wu, *CEO*
Edgard Prado, *General Mgr*
Brent Immink, *Managing Dir*
Mark Vanbeek, *Managing Dir*
EMP: 111 **EST:** 2014

SALES (est): 719MM **Privately Held**
WEB: www.yfai.com
SIC: 3714 Motor vehicle parts & accessories
HQ: Yanfeng International Automotive Technology Hungary Korlatolt Felelossegu Tarsasag
Juhar Utca 17.
Papa 8500
895 117-00

(G-12571)
YANFENG US AUTO INTR SYSTEMS I (DH)
41935 W 12 Mile Rd (48377-3135)
P.O. Box 7125 (48376-7125)
PHONE.................................248 319-7333
EMP: 100 **EST:** 2014
SALES (est): 178.9MM **Privately Held**
WEB: www.yfai.com
SIC: 3714 Motor vehicle parts & accessories
HQ: Yanfeng International Automotive Technology Hungary Korlatolt Felelossegu Tarsasag
Juhar Utca 17.
Papa 8500
895 117-00

(G-12572)
YANFENG US AUTOMOTIVE
41935 W 12 Mile Rd (48377-3135)
PHONE.................................517 721-0179
EMP: 13 **Privately Held**
SIC: 3089 Plastics Products, Nec, Nsk
HQ: Yanfeng Us Automotive Interior Systems Ii Llc
5757 N Green Bay Ave
Milwaukee WI 48377
205 477-4225

(G-12573)
YEUNGS LOTUS EXPRESS
27500 Novi Rd (48377-3418)
PHONE.................................248 380-3820
Dawn Ship, *Principal*
EMP: 8 **EST:** 2006
SALES (est): 191.3K **Privately Held**
SIC: 2741 Miscellaneous publishing

(G-12574)
ZIMMER - LIEFFRING INC (PA)
Also Called: Zimmer Great Lakes
41370 Bridge St (48375-1302)
PHONE.................................734 953-1630
Pete Lieffring, *President*
Mario Locriccchio, *Vice Pres*
Mike Venne, *Sales Staff*
EMP: 15 **EST:** 1983
SALES (est): 4.1MM **Privately Held**
WEB: www.zimmerbiomet.com
SIC: 3842 Orthopedic appliances

Nunica
Ottawa County

(G-12575)
ADVANCED RECOVERY TECH CORP
16684 130th Ave (49448-9445)
PHONE.................................231 788-2911
Dewie D Jordan, *President*
Nancy Jordan, *Vice Pres*
EMP: 9 **EST:** 1989
SQ FT: 8,000
SALES (est): 1.5MM **Privately Held**
WEB: www.advancedrecoverytech.com
SIC: 3569 1796 7389 Filters; pollution control equipment installation; air pollution measuring service

(G-12576)
ALPHA TRAN ENGINEERING CO
12575 Cleveland St (49448-9617)
PHONE.................................616 837-7341
Allen Lemieux, *President*
Richard Pearce, *Vice Pres*
EMP: 32 **EST:** 1967
SQ FT: 10,000
SALES (est): 3.4MM **Privately Held**
WEB: www.alpha-tran.com
SIC: 3613 Control panels, electric

Nunica - Ottawa County (G-12577)

(G-12577)
C-PLASTICS INC
12463 Cleveland St (49448-9617)
PHONE..................................616 837-7396
Chris Kostecki, *President*
Bob Wurn, *Engineer*
EMP: 40 **EST:** 1975
SQ FT: 27,000
SALES (est): 4.6MM **Privately Held**
WEB: www.cplasticsinc.com
SIC: 3089 Injection molding of plastics; plastic processing

(G-12578)
DENNISON AUTOMATICS LLC
12301 Cleveland St Ste A (49448-8602)
PHONE..................................616 837-7063
Norman Anderson,
EMP: 9 **EST:** 1994
SALES (est): 850K **Privately Held**
WEB: www.dennisonllc.com
SIC: 3451 Screw machine products

(G-12579)
DOLTEK ENTERPRISES INC
Also Called: Wood Dowel & Dimension
11335 Apple Dr (49448-9346)
P.O. Box 158 (49448-0158)
PHONE..................................616 837-7828
Mark Schroeder, *President*
Jason Taylor, *Production*
Corinne Schroeder, *VP Sales*
Jackson Schroeder, *Sales Staff*
Andrew Watson, *Sales Staff*
EMP: 25 **EST:** 1949
SQ FT: 50,000
SALES (est): 6.3MM **Privately Held**
WEB: www.versatileus.com
SIC: 2499 2431 2426 Dowels, wood; moldings, wood: unfinished & prefinished; furniture stock & parts, hardwood

(G-12580)
J&S TECHNOLOGIES INC
16952 Woodlane (49448-9644)
PHONE..................................616 837-7080
Leon Sluis, *President*
Debra Sluis, *Vice Pres*
EMP: 4 **EST:** 1998
SQ FT: 6,000
SALES (est): 700K **Privately Held**
WEB: www.jstmachine.com
SIC: 3599 Machine shop, jobbing & repair

(G-12581)
JRM INDUSTRIES INC
Also Called: Integrity Trailers
12409 Cleveland St (49448-9617)
PHONE..................................616 837-9758
John Missimer, *President*
EMP: 5 **EST:** 1978
SALES (est): 488.7K **Privately Held**
WEB: www.integrity-trailers.com
SIC: 3799 Trailers & trailer equipment; boat trailers

(G-12582)
LAKESHORE FABRICATION LLC
8435 Sternberg Rd (49448-9508)
PHONE..................................231 740-5861
David Brady, *Principal*
EMP: 4 **EST:** 2017
SALES (est): 73.7K **Privately Held**
WEB: www.lakeshorefab.com
SIC: 3599 Machine shop, jobbing & repair

(G-12583)
LAKESIDE AGGREGATE LLC (PA)
16861 120th Ave (49448-9618)
PHONE..................................616 837-5858
Dave Meekhof, *President*
EMP: 52 **EST:** 2013
SALES (est): 3.6MM **Privately Held**
SIC: 1442 Construction sand & gravel

(G-12584)
LIVEROOF LLC
14109 Cleveland St (49448-9739)
P.O. Box 533, Spring Lake (49456-0533)
PHONE..................................616 842-1392
Sarah Brown, *General Mgr*
Adam Pierce, *Prdtn Mgr*
Ben Lucas, *CIO*
David McKenzie,
EMP: 30 **EST:** 2006
SALES (est): 7.2MM
SALES (corp-wide): 9.3MM **Privately Held**
WEB: www.liveroof.com
SIC: 2952 8611 Asphalt felts & coatings; growers' associations
PA: Hortech, Inc.
14109 Cleveland St
Nunica MI 49448
616 842-1392

(G-12585)
RIDGEVIEW INDUSTRIES INC
16933 144th Ave (49448-9667)
PHONE..................................616 414-6500
Tom Robbins, *Branch Mgr*
EMP: 90
SALES (corp-wide): 87.6MM **Privately Held**
WEB: www.ridgeviewindustries.com
SIC: 3469 Stamping metal for the trade
PA: Ridgeview Industries, Inc.
3093 Northridge Dr Nw
Grand Rapids MI 49544
616 453-8636

(G-12586)
STEWART GENERAL INCORPORATED
16991 Birchview Dr (49448-9360)
PHONE..................................616 318-4971
Brenda Cook, *Principal*
EMP: 7 **EST:** 2017
SALES (est): 236.3K **Privately Held**
SIC: 3999 Manufacturing industries

(G-12587)
TABS FLOOR COVERING LLC
17370 Woodland Ln (49448-9765)
PHONE..................................616 846-1684
EMP: 4 **EST:** 2018
SALES (est): 73.1K **Privately Held**
SIC: 2721 Periodicals

(G-12588)
TAKE-A-LABEL INC
16900 Power Dr (49448-9465)
PHONE..................................616 837-9300
Gary Systma, *President*
Carol Sytsma, *Vice Pres*
Carol Systma, *Vice Pres*
EMP: 11 **EST:** 2000
SQ FT: 10,000
SALES (est): 2.2MM **Privately Held**
WEB: www.take-a-label.com
SIC: 3565 Labeling machines, industrial

(G-12589)
VARNEYS FAB & WELD LLC
5967 Maple Island Rd (49448-9511)
PHONE..................................231 865-6856
Tina Varney, *Office Mgr*
Scott Varney, *Mng Member*
EMP: 5 **EST:** 1995
SQ FT: 740
SALES (est): 250K **Privately Held**
WEB: www.varneysfabandweld.com
SIC: 3441 1799 Fabricated structural metal; welding on site

(G-12590)
WEST MICHIGAN WELDING LLC
19195 112th Ave (49448-9419)
PHONE..................................231 578-3593
Sheila Romberger, *Principal*
EMP: 4 **EST:** 2016
SALES (est): 27.6K **Privately Held**
SIC: 7692 Welding repair

Oak Park
Oakland County

(G-12591)
APOLLO HEAT TREATING PROC LLC
10400 Capital St (48237-3132)
PHONE..................................248 398-3434
Jeff Goodman, *Mng Member*
EMP: 13 **EST:** 2011
SALES (est): 534.2K **Privately Held**
WEB: www.eatonsteel.com
SIC: 3398 Metal heat treating

(G-12592)
ATLAS CUT STONE INC
12920 Northend Ave (48237-3404)
PHONE..................................248 545-5100
Carol Potrykus, *CEO*
William A Potrykus, *President*
Thelma Potrykus, *Corp Secy*
EMP: 4 **EST:** 1934
SQ FT: 4,800
SALES (est): 431K **Privately Held**
WEB: www.atlascutstone.com
SIC: 3272 5032 Steps, prefabricated concrete; door frames, concrete; window sills, cast stone; limestone

(G-12593)
AUCTION MASTERS
8700 Capital St (48237-2360)
PHONE..................................586 576-7777
EMP: 8 **EST:** 2014
SALES (est): 161.4K **Privately Held**
WEB: www.theauctionmasters.com
SIC: 7389 3585 7699 5046 Auctioneers, fee basis; soda fountain & beverage dispensing equipment & parts; cold drink dispensing equipment (not coin-operated); restaurant equipment repair; restaurant equipment & supplies; retail trade consultant

(G-12594)
AUTO METAL CRAFT INC
Also Called: Auto Chem Craft
12741 Capital St (48237-3175)
PHONE..................................248 398-2240
Patrick N Woody, *Chairman*
Kevin Woody, *Exec VP*
Kent Woody, *Vice Pres*
Kim Woody, *Purch Agent*
Chuck Ball, *Program Mgr*
EMP: 45 **EST:** 1948
SQ FT: 22,000
SALES (est): 7.6MM **Privately Held**
WEB: www.autometal.com
SIC: 3465 3544 Automotive stampings; jigs & fixtures

(G-12595)
BORDRIN MOTOR CORPORATION INC
14925 W 11 Mile Rd (48237-1013)
P.O. Box 3297, Farmington Hills (48333-3297)
PHONE..................................877 507-3267
Yehia Harajli, *Vice Pres*
Jinhuan Kuang, *Engineer*
Karan Sharma, *Engineer*
Jerry Lavine, *CTO*
EMP: 18 **EST:** 2016
SALES (est): 2.2MM **Privately Held**
WEB: www.bordrin.com
SIC: 3711 Automobile bodies, passenger car, not including engine, etc.

(G-12596)
BRILAR LLC
13200 Northend Ave (48237-3213)
PHONE..................................248 547-6439
Randy Hija, *Controller*
Jason Pease, *Accounts Mgr*
Larry Yaffa, *Mng Member*
Bernadette Fletcher, *Manager*
Matt Gerich, *Director*
EMP: 100 **EST:** 2010
SALES (est): 24.4MM **Privately Held**
WEB: www.brilar.net
SIC: 3523 Grounds mowing equipment

(G-12597)
CANDLE KNIGHT LIGHT
10332 W 9 Mile Rd (48237-2913)
PHONE..................................248 291-5483
Ron Hammer, *Owner*
EMP: 4 **EST:** 2015
SALES (est): 90.1K **Privately Held**
WEB: www.knightlightcandle.com
SIC: 3999 Candles

(G-12598)
CORNBELT BEEF CORPORATION
14150 Ludlow Pl (48237-1355)
PHONE..................................313 237-0087
Samuel Flatt, *President*
EMP: 6 **EST:** 1978
SQ FT: 50,000
SALES (est): 244K **Privately Held**
SIC: 5147 2011 Meats, fresh; meat packing plants

(G-12599)
CREATIVE VISIONS PUBLISHING CO
14280 Elgin St (48237-1164)
PHONE..................................248 545-3528
Gail Freid, *Principal*
EMP: 5 **EST:** 2010
SALES (est): 109.1K **Privately Held**
SIC: 2741 Miscellaneous publishing

(G-12600)
CRESCENT CASTING INC
8720 Northend Ave (48237-2363)
PHONE..................................248 541-1052
Brian Lambert, *Principal*
EMP: 16 **EST:** 2014
SALES (est): 583K **Privately Held**
SIC: 3553 Pattern makers' machinery, woodworking

(G-12601)
CRESCENT MACHINING INC
8720 Northend Ave (48237-2363)
PHONE..................................248 541-7010
Greg Summer, *Principal*
EMP: 8 **EST:** 2005
SALES (est): 867.6K **Privately Held**
SIC: 3089 Automotive parts, plastic

(G-12602)
CRESCENT PATTERN COMPANY
8720 Northend Ave (48237-2363)
PHONE..................................248 541-1052
Greg Sommer, *President*
EMP: 33 **EST:** 1945
SQ FT: 3,200
SALES (est): 1.2MM **Privately Held**
WEB: www.crescentpattern.com
SIC: 3543 Industrial patterns

(G-12603)
CUSTOM VERTICALS UNLIMITED
14621 Ludlow St (48237-4112)
PHONE..................................734 522-1615
Martin Vittes, *President*
Howard Vittes, *Vice Pres*
Brian Vittes, *Treasurer*
EMP: 8 **EST:** 1989
SALES (est): 556.1K **Privately Held**
SIC: 2591 5023 Blinds vertical; venetian blinds

(G-12604)
DEPENDABLE GAGE & TOOL CO
15321 W 11 Mile Rd (48237-1076)
PHONE..................................248 545-2100
Leigh P Smith Jr, *President*
Wayne Slowik, *Dept Chairman*
Jeff Smith, *Vice Pres*
Mike Rainney, *Foreman/Supr*
Leigh Smith, *Purchasing*
EMP: 42 **EST:** 1939
SQ FT: 7,200
SALES (est): 2.7MM **Privately Held**
WEB: www.dependablegage.net
SIC: 3545 Precision tools, machinists'; gauges (machine tool accessories)

(G-12605)
DESIGN METAL INC
10841 Capital St (48237-3147)
PHONE..................................248 547-4170
Carmelo Dimaggio, *President*
Sherri Dimaggio, *Vice Pres*
EMP: 19 **EST:** 1982
SQ FT: 15,000
SALES (est): 2.3MM **Privately Held**
WEB: www.designmetalinc.com
SIC: 3444 3465 Sheet metal specialties, not stamped; automotive stampings

(G-12606)
DTOWN GRILLZ LLC
21700 Greenfield Rd # 348 (48237-2581)
PHONE..................................734 624-9657
Russell Moore,
EMP: 9 **EST:** 2007

GEOGRAPHIC SECTION

Oak Park - Oakland County (G-12632)

SALES (est): 301.3K Privately Held
SIC: 3915 5094 5944 Jewelers' castings; jewelers' findings; jewelry stores

(G-12607)
DYNAMIC ENERGY TECH LLC
22181 Morton St (48237-2931)
PHONE..................248 212-5904
David Hochberg, *Branch Mgr*
EMP: 8
SALES (corp-wide): 48.7K Privately Held
WEB: www.dynamicenergy.com
SIC: 3511 Turbines & turbine generator sets
PA: Dynamic Energy Technologies Llc
  156 Sandy Ln Ste 156w
  Walled Lake MI

(G-12608)
E-ZEE SET WOOD PRODUCTS INC
21650 Coolidge Hwy (48237-3109)
PHONE..................248 398-0090
Jeff Lorenz, *President*
Karen Lorenz, *Vice Pres*
▲ EMP: 9 EST: 1969
SQ FT: 13,625
SALES (est): 1.5MM Privately Held
WEB: www.ezeeset.com
SIC: 2431 3442 Doors, wood; louver doors, wood; louvers, shutters, jalousies & similar items

(G-12609)
EATON STEEL CORPORATION (PA)
Also Called: Eaton Steel Bar Company
10221 Capital St (48237-3103)
PHONE..................248 398-3434
Mark Goodman, *President*
Mark Candy, *Vice Pres*
Gary Goodman, *Vice Pres*
Prachi Vesikar, *Engineer*
Antoinette Caldwell, *Accountant*
◆ EMP: 60 EST: 1953
SQ FT: 188,000
SALES (est): 88.9MM Privately Held
WEB: www.eatonsteel.com
SIC: 5051 3312 Structural shapes, iron or steel; bars & bar shapes, steel, cold-finished: own hot-rolled

(G-12610)
EJ USA INC
Also Called: E J I W
13001 Northend Ave (48237-3408)
P.O. Box 439, East Jordan (49727-0439)
PHONE..................248 546-2004
Frank Tainna, *Sales/Mktg Mgr*
EMP: 7
SQ FT: 3,296 Privately Held
WEB: www.eastjordancity.org
SIC: 3321 Manhole covers, metal
HQ: Ej Usa, Inc.
  301 Spring St
  East Jordan MI 49727
  800 874-4100

(G-12611)
ENGINEERED RESOURCES INC
Also Called: Dale Prentice
26511 Harding St (48237-1002)
PHONE..................248 399-5500
Larry Prentice, *President*
Michael Prentice, *Vice Pres*
Mark Schwartz, *Technology*
EMP: 6 EST: 1996
SQ FT: 3,500
SALES (est): 1.8MM Privately Held
WEB: www.prenticeco.com
SIC: 3599 Custom machinery

(G-12612)
FOREWARD LOGISTICS LLC
25900 Grnfeld Rd Ste 326 (48237)
PHONE..................877 488-9724
Tresa Fore, *President*
EMP: 4 EST: 2016
SALES (est): 300K Privately Held
SIC: 4731 2393 5094 Truck transportation brokers; canvas bags; clocks, watches & parts

(G-12613)
FRESH BAKED PRINTS
13807 W 9 Mile Rd (48237-2775)
PHONE..................888 327-4137
EMP: 6 EST: 2015
SALES (est): 532.4K Privately Held
WEB: www.fbprints.com
SIC: 2752 Commercial printing, lithographic

(G-12614)
FUTURIS AUTOMOTIVE (US) INC (DH)
14925 W 11 Mile Rd (48237-1013)
PHONE..................248 439-7800
Merv Dunn, *CEO*
▲ EMP: 50 EST: 2005
SALES (est): 320.3MM Privately Held
SIC: 2396 Automotive trimmings, fabric
HQ: Futuris Global Holdings, Llc
  14925 W 11 Mile Rd
  Oak Park MI 48237
  248 439-7800

(G-12615)
FUTURIS GLOBAL HOLDINGS LLC (HQ)
Also Called: Futuris Automotive
14925 W 11 Mile Rd (48237-1013)
PHONE..................248 439-7800
Merv Dunn, *CEO*
John Colville, *Buyer*
James Glassford, *Sales Mgr*
Bill Starnes, *Program Mgr*
John Brydell, *Manager*
EMP: 100 EST: 2013
SQ FT: 90,000
SALES (est): 500MM Privately Held
WEB: www.adient.com
SIC: 2396 Automotive trimmings, fabric

(G-12616)
H O TRERICE CO INC
12950 W 8 Mile Rd (48237-3214)
PHONE..................248 399-8000
Richard Picut, *President*
Randy Buoy, *CFO*
Debbie N Mackie, *Human Res Dir*
Adam Blaney, *Sales Staff*
Eric Lennon, *Sales Staff*
▲ EMP: 50 EST: 1923
SQ FT: 40,000
SALES (est): 13.1MM Privately Held
WEB: www.trerice.com
SIC: 3823 Temperature measurement instruments, industrial
PA: Picut Industries Inc.
  140 Mount Bethel Rd
  Warren NJ 07059

(G-12617)
HOPEFUL HARVEST FOODS INC
21800 Greenfield Rd (48237-2507)
PHONE..................248 967-1500
EMP: 4
SQ FT: 5,000
SALES (est): 173K Privately Held
SIC: 2033 2035 0723 Mfg Canned Fruits/Vegetables Mfg Pickles/Sauces/Dressing Crop Preparation For Market

(G-12618)
INNOVATIVE TOOL AND DESIGN INC
10725 Capital St (48237-3143)
PHONE..................248 542-1831
Marvin Quezada, *CEO*
◆ EMP: 50 EST: 1997
SQ FT: 35,000
SALES (est): 6.2MM Privately Held
WEB: www.innovativetoolanddesign.com
SIC: 3469 Stamping metal for the trade

(G-12619)
JUST RIGHT DUPLICATIONS LLC
Also Called: Jrd
25900 Greenfield Rd # 258 (48237-1292)
PHONE..................313 655-3555
Leslie Coleman, *Owner*
EMP: 10 EST: 2009
SQ FT: 1,000

SALES (est): 615.1K Privately Held
SIC: 7389 2389 2326 3555 ; ; men's miscellaneous accessories; men's & boys' work clothing; printing trade parts & attachments; printing & embossing on plastics fabric articles; commercial printing, lithographic; business form & card printing, lithographic

(G-12620)
KD ESSENTIALS LLC
23551 Geneva St (48237-2198)
PHONE..................248 632-7180
Kim Stinnett,
EMP: 5 EST: 2020
SALES (est): 74.4K Privately Held
SIC: 2844 7389 Cosmetic preparations;

(G-12621)
KERR PUMP AND SUPPLY INC
12880 Cloverdale St (48237-3206)
P.O. Box 37160 (48237-0160)
PHONE..................248 543-3880
Thomas Gross, *President*
Robert Kalfs, *Vice Pres*
Patrick Wing, *Vice Pres*
Glenn Kline, *Chief Engr*
Darick Husken, *Engineer*
EMP: 48 EST: 1905
SQ FT: 24,000
SALES (est): 20.6MM Privately Held
WEB: www.kerrpump.com
SIC: 5084 3443 3561 Water pumps (industrial); compressors, except air conditioning; heat exchangers, condensers & components; pumps & pumping equipment

(G-12622)
LADUKE CORPORATION
Also Called: Laduke Roofing
10311 Capital St (48237-3139)
PHONE..................248 414-6600
Roger Laduke, *President*
Roger La Duke, *President*
Mike Puzan, *Project Mgr*
Kathleen Laduke, *CFO*
EMP: 40 EST: 1991
SQ FT: 18,000
SALES (est): 5.4MM Privately Held
WEB: www.ladukeroofing.com
SIC: 1761 3441 Roofing contractor; sheet metalwork; fabricated structural metal

(G-12623)
M BESHARA INC
10020 Capital St (48237-3104)
PHONE..................248 542-9220
John Beshara, *President*
Marc Beshara, *Vice Pres*
Joe B Beshara, *Purch Mgr*
EMP: 8 EST: 1968
SALES (est): 797.3K Privately Held
WEB: www.mbesharaprinting.com
SIC: 2752 7336 Commercial printing, offset; graphic arts & related design

(G-12624)
MAGIC TREATZ LLC
24245 Coolidge Hwy (48237-1656)
PHONE..................248 989-9956
Ronda Adams,
EMP: 6 EST: 2019
SALES (est): 50K Privately Held
SIC: 2051 Cakes, bakery: except frozen

(G-12625)
MARBLECAST OF MICHIGAN INC
Also Called: Marblecast Kitchens & Baths
14831 W 11 Mile Rd (48237-1012)
PHONE..................248 398-0600
Walter Olejniczak, *President*
Janet Olejniczak, *Vice Pres*
EMP: 19 EST: 1997
SQ FT: 8,000
SALES (est): 3.4MM Privately Held
WEB: www.marblecastofmichigan.com
SIC: 3281 Bathroom fixtures, cut stone

(G-12626)
MATTRESS WHOLESALE
14510 W 8 Mile Rd (48237-3046)
PHONE..................248 968-2200
Ree Garmo, *Owner*
EMP: 7 EST: 2005

SALES (est): 591.7K Privately Held
WEB: www.mattress-wholesale.com
SIC: 2515 5021 Mattresses & bedsprings; mattresses

(G-12627)
MEHRING BOOKS INC
25900 Greenfield Rd # 258 (48237-1292)
P.O. Box 48377 (48237-5977)
PHONE..................248 967-2924
Helen Halyard, *President*
Heather Jowsey, *Administration*
EMP: 5 EST: 1998
SALES (est): 492.2K Privately Held
WEB: www.mehring.com
SIC: 2731 Books: publishing only

(G-12628)
MICHIGAN DESSERT CORPORATION
Also Called: Midas Foods International
10750 Capital St (48237-3134)
PHONE..................248 544-4574
Richard Elias, *President*
Gary Freeman, *Vice Pres*
Lynn Madsen, *Vice Pres*
Jill May, *Research*
Michael Jacobs, *IT/INT Sup*
EMP: 35 EST: 1980
SQ FT: 45,000
SALES (est): 13MM Privately Held
WEB: www.midasfoods.com
SIC: 2099 Desserts, ready-to-mix

(G-12629)
MURRAYS WORLDWIDE INC
21841 Wyoming St Ste 1 (48237-3126)
PHONE..................248 691-9156
Arthur E Berlin, *President*
Jeffrey Berlin, *Vice Pres*
Jim Berlin, *Vice Pres*
Dan Medow, *Manager*
Gerald Berlin, *Admin Sec*
◆ EMP: 13 EST: 1989
SQ FT: 15,000
SALES (est): 3MM Privately Held
WEB: www.murrayspomade.com
SIC: 2844 Hair preparations, including shampoos

(G-12630)
NATIONAL INNOVATION CENTER
26431 Raine St (48237-1025)
PHONE..................248 414-3913
Miron Shamban, *President*
EMP: 12 EST: 2007
SALES (est): 725.2K Privately Held
SIC: 3499 Shims, metal

(G-12631)
NATIONAL TIME AND SIGNAL CORP
21800 Wyoming St (48237-3117)
PHONE..................248 291-5867
Karson Claussen, *General Mgr*
Mike Burke, *Engineer*
Andrew Simon, *Engineer*
Nathan Allen, *Sales Engr*
Jonathan Hohauser, *Sales Engr*
EMP: 20
SALES (corp-wide): 7.8MM Privately Held
WEB: www.natsco.net
SIC: 3669 3873 Signaling apparatus, electric; fire alarm apparatus, electric; clocks, except timeclocks
PA: National Time And Signal Corporation
  28045 Oakland Oaks Ct
  Wixom MI 48393
  248 380-6264

(G-12632)
NCOC INC
Also Called: National Chemical & Oil
21251 Meyers Rd (48237-3201)
PHONE..................248 548-5950
Ernest N Stacey Jr, *President*
Jagdeep Singh, *Vice Pres*
Navneet Singh, *Vice Pres*
Timothy Noland, *Sales Engr*
Shawn Daffern, *Sales Staff*
▼ EMP: 27 EST: 1962
SQ FT: 23,000

SALES (est): 5.3MM **Privately Held**
WEB: www.ncocinc.com
SIC: **2899** 3356 2891 2851 Metal treating compounds; frit; nonferrous rolling & drawing; adhesives & sealants; paints & allied products; metal heat treating

(G-12633)
NEW VINTAGE USA INC
21840 Wyoming Pl Ste 1 (48237-3138)
PHONE..................................248 259-4964
Mark Surel, *Partner*
Jennifer Surel, *Vice Pres*
▲ EMP: 12 EST: 2008
SALES (est): 1.1MM **Privately Held**
WEB: www.newvintageusallc.mybigcommerce.com
SIC: **3824** Vehicle instruments

(G-12634)
NOIR SPORTSWEAR CORP
Also Called: Empire Sports
13181 W 10 Mile Rd (48237-4630)
PHONE..................................248 607-3615
Michaelyn Roberson, *President*
Michaelyn Robertson,
EMP: 11 EST: 2018
SALES (est): 672.6K **Privately Held**
SIC: **2253** 3949 5611 5137 Knit outerwear mills; sporting & athletic goods; clothing, sportswear, men's & boys'; uniforms, women's & children's; athletic clothing: women's, misses' & juniors'; uniforms, athletic: women's, misses' & juniors'

(G-12635)
OAK LEAF PUBLISHING INC
24731 Parklawn St (48237-4004)
PHONE..................................248 547-7103
EMP: 4 EST: 2011
SALES (est): 52K **Privately Held**
WEB: www.oakleafpublishing.com
SIC: **2741** Miscellaneous publishing

(G-12636)
PARAMOUNT INDUSTRIAL MACHINING
15255 W 11 Mile Rd (48237-1041)
PHONE..................................248 543-2100
Sheila Rossman, *VP Sls/Mktg*
Maxwell Schwartz, *VP Sales*
EMP: 20 EST: 2016
SALES (est): 2MM **Privately Held**
SIC: **3599** Machine & other job shop work

(G-12637)
PCI INDUSTRIES INC
Also Called: Quiet Concepts
21717 Republic Ave (48237-2365)
PHONE..................................248 542-2570
Michael Pomish, *President*
Michael Droske, *Superintendent*
Martin Mellin, *Vice Pres*
Tina Friedmann, *Controller*
Dawn Sketch, *Bookkeeper*
EMP: 53 EST: 1983
SQ FT: 12,000
SALES (est): 30.6MM **Privately Held**
WEB: www.pcionesource.com
SIC: **1751** 1721 2591 1742 Carpentry work; painting & paper hanging; drapery hardware & blinds & shades; plastering, drywall & insulation; wood partitions & fixtures; floor laying & floor work

(G-12638)
QUINCO TOOL
21000 Hubbell St (48237-3023)
PHONE..................................313 353-1340
Sue Gray, *Executive Asst*
EMP: 6 EST: 2017
SALES (est): 42.5K **Privately Held**
SIC: **3999** Manufacturing industries

(G-12639)
REB RESEARCH & CONSULTING CO
12851 Capital St (48237-3160)
PHONE..................................248 545-0155
Robert Buxbaum, *Owner*
EMP: 4 **Privately Held**
WEB: www.rebresearch.com
SIC: **3569** Filters

PA: Reb Research & Consulting Co
25451 Gardner St
Detroit MI 48237

(G-12640)
ROLSTON HOCKEY ACADEMY LLC
13950 Oak Park Blvd (48237-2077)
PHONE..................................248 450-5300
Brian Rolston, *Principal*
EMP: 5 EST: 2016
SALES (est): 405.9K **Privately Held**
WEB: www.rolstonhockeyacademy.com
SIC: **3949** Hockey equipment & supplies, general

(G-12641)
ROYAL CONTAINER INC
21100 Hubbell St (48237-3024)
PHONE..................................248 967-0910
Justin Mooter, *President*
J Anthony Mooter, *Admin Sec*
EMP: 24 EST: 1981
SQ FT: 50,000
SALES (est): 4.6MM **Privately Held**
WEB: www.packpros.net
SIC: **2653** Boxes, corrugated: made from purchased materials

(G-12642)
ROYAL CREST INC
14851 W 11 Mile Rd (48237-1012)
PHONE..................................248 399-2476
Andrea Jeross, *President*
EMP: 6 EST: 1972
SQ FT: 7,500
SALES (est): 738.5K **Privately Held**
WEB: www.detroit-blinds-shades-shutters.com
SIC: **2591** Window shades; blinds vertical

(G-12643)
RYAN POLISHING CORPORATION
10709 Capital St (48237-3143)
PHONE..................................248 548-6832
Warren Wood, *President*
Nancy Wood, *Vice Pres*
Billie Worden, *Manager*
Charles Holmes, *Executive*
EMP: 28 EST: 1961
SQ FT: 15,000
SALES (est): 1.5MM **Privately Held**
WEB: www.ryanpolishing.com
SIC: **3471** 3451 Buffing for the trade; polishing, metals or formed products; screw machine products

(G-12644)
SAFARI MEATS LLC
24570 Oneida Blvd (48237-1716)
PHONE..................................313 539-3367
Shelley Doggett, *Opers Staff*
Max Doggett,
EMP: 5 EST: 2016
SALES (est): 322.8K **Privately Held**
SIC: **2011** Sausages from meat slaughtered on site

(G-12645)
SALIENT SIGN STUDIO
8720 W 9 Mile Rd (48237-2322)
PHONE..................................248 532-0013
EMP: 6 EST: 2017
SALES (est): 204.1K **Privately Held**
WEB: www.salientsignstudio.com
SIC: **3993** Signs & advertising specialties

(G-12646)
SANI ZEEVI
Also Called: Star Lite International LLC
14131 Ludlow Pl (48237-1354)
P.O. Box 965, Southfield (48037-0965)
PHONE..................................248 546-4489
Sani Zeevi, *Mng Member*
David Benjamin, *IT Specialist*
EMP: 4 EST: 1994
SALES (est): 478.3K **Privately Held**
WEB: www.starlite-intl.com
SIC: **5085** 5065 5064 3812 Industrial tools; electric tools; communication equipment; amateur radio communications equipment; electrical entertainment equipment; search & navigation equipment

(G-12647)
T & W TOOL & DIE CORPORATION
21770 Wyoming Pl (48237-3112)
P.O. Box 36667, Grosse Pointe (48236-0667)
PHONE..................................248 548-5400
Herbert W Trute, *President*
Gary Nowakowski, *Vice Pres*
Carol L Trute, *Treasurer*
EMP: 32 EST: 1983
SQ FT: 48,000
SALES (est): 1.6MM **Privately Held**
SIC: **3544** Special dies & tools

(G-12648)
VGAGE LLC
13250 Northend Ave (48237-3213)
PHONE..................................248 589-7455
David Adaline, *Sales Engr*
John T Malane, *Mng Member*
EMP: 55 EST: 2006
SQ FT: 19,000
SALES (est): 9.1MM **Privately Held**
WEB: www.vgage.com
SIC: **3829** Aircraft & motor vehicle measurement equipment

(G-12649)
VILADON CORPORATION
Also Called: Viladon Laboratories
10411 Capital St (48237-3122)
PHONE..................................248 548-0043
Eliezer Meisler, *President*
Astrid Meisler, *Vice Pres*
EMP: 8 EST: 1975
SQ FT: 12,500
SALES (est): 800K **Privately Held**
SIC: **3999** 2844 Pet supplies; hair preparations, including shampoos

(G-12650)
WALKER PRINTERY INC
13351 Cloverdale St (48237-3275)
PHONE..................................248 548-5100
Lawrence J Traison, *President*
Barbara Traison, *Vice Pres*
Steven Traison, *Vice Pres*
▲ EMP: 19 EST: 1924
SQ FT: 16,000 **Privately Held**
WEB: www.walkerprintery.com
SIC: **2752** Business forms, lithographed

(G-12651)
WEATHERGARD WINDOW COMPANY INC
Also Called: Weathergard Window Factory
14350 W 8 Mile Rd (48237-3050)
PHONE..................................248 967-8822
Albert Ben-Ezra, *President*
Elsy Ben-Ezra, *Vice Pres*
Elsy Baron, *Treasurer*
EMP: 100 EST: 1988
SQ FT: 47,638
SALES (est): 18.7MM **Privately Held**
WEB: www.weathergard.com
SIC: **3089** 5031 5211 Windows, plastic; doors, folding: plastic or plastic coated fabric; doors & windows; windows; doors; door & window products; windows, storm: wood or metal; doors, wood or metal, except storm

Oakland
Oakland County

(G-12652)
DIAMOND STANDARD MCH CO LLC
199 Dogwood Dr (48363-1370)
PHONE..................................248 805-7144
Danielle Ross,
EMP: 4 EST: 2016
SALES (est): 62.7K **Privately Held**
SIC: **3541** Milling machines

Oakland Twp
Oakland County

(G-12653)
OPUS PRODUCTS LLC
120 Londonderry Ln (48306-4669)
PHONE..................................586 202-1870
Jacquelyn Kolpasky, *Principal*
EMP: 4 EST: 2013
SALES (est): 112.6K **Privately Held**
SIC: **2064** 5145 Candy & other confectionery products; candy

Oakley
Saginaw County

(G-12654)
COLOMBO SALES AND ENGRG INC
17108 S Hemlock Rd (48649-8747)
PHONE..................................248 547-2820
EMP: 14 EST: 2019
SALES (est): 6.3MM **Privately Held**
WEB: www.beveragechase.com
SIC: **3535** Conveyors & conveying equipment

Okemos
Ingham County

(G-12655)
AMERICAN PROSTHETIC INSTITUTE
Also Called: Stokosa Prosthetic Clinic
2145 University Park Dr # 100 (48864-3982)
PHONE..................................517 349-3130
Jan Stokosa, *President*
Amber Stokosa, *Marketing Staff*
Katie Powell, *Manager*
EMP: 5 EST: 1988
SQ FT: 3,100
SALES (est): 797.1K **Privately Held**
WEB: www.stokosaclinic.com
SIC: **3842** 5999 Limbs, artificial; orthopedic & prosthesis applications

(G-12656)
AMERICAN TANK FABRICATION LLC
2222 W Grand (48864)
PHONE..................................780 663-3552
Sheila Slesher,
Shane Lazaro,
Joseph Wigington,
EMP: 15
SALES (est): 641.3K **Privately Held**
SIC: **3443** Tanks, standard or custom fabricated: metal plate

(G-12657)
ASAP PRINTING INC (PA)
2323 Jolly Rd (48864-3541)
PHONE..................................517 882-3500
Edward Guile, *President*
Bill Davis, *President*
EMP: 8 EST: 1994
SQ FT: 1,500 **Privately Held**
WEB: www.asapprinting.net
SIC: **2752** 2791 2789 Commercial printing, offset; typesetting; bookbinding & related work

(G-12658)
AVIDHRT INC
2721 Sophiea Pkwy (48864-2855)
PHONE..................................517 214-9041
Chandana Weebadde, *President*
EMP: 5 EST: 2016
SALES (est): 327.5K **Privately Held**
WEB: www.avidhrt.com
SIC: **3829** Medical diagnostic systems, nuclear

(G-12659)
BARYAMES TUX SHOP INC
2421 W Grand River Ave (48864-1448)
PHONE..................................517 349-6555

GEOGRAPHIC SECTION
Okemos - Ingham County (G-12688)

EMP: 6
SALES (corp-wide): 957.5K **Privately Held**
SIC: 7299 2311 Miscellaneous Personal Services, Nec, Nsk
PA: Baryames Tux Shop Inc
3023 W Saginaw St
Lansing MI 48917
517 349-6555

(G-12660)
BIOPLSTIC PLYMERS CMPSITES LLC
4275 Conifer Cir (48864-3259)
PHONE..................517 349-2970
Ramani Narayan, *President*
EMP: 5 EST: 1997
SQ FT: 43,000 **Privately Held**
WEB: www.bioplasticpolymers.com
SIC: 2673 8733 Bags: plastic, laminated & coated; noncommercial research organizations

(G-12661)
COAST TO COAST CABINETS LLC (PA)
2398 Jolly Rd Ste 300 (48864-6914)
P.O. Box 649 (48805-0649)
PHONE..................517 719-0118
Robert D Nedds,
EMP: 6 EST: 2009
SALES (est): 1MM **Privately Held**
WEB: www.coasttocoastcabinets.com
SIC: 2434 Wood kitchen cabinets

(G-12662)
DALTON ARMOND PUBLISHERS INC
2867 Jolly Rd (48864-3547)
PHONE..................517 351-8520
Dalton D Ward, *President*
Irene B Arens, *Exec VP*
Phyllis A Ward, *Exec VP*
Carol Borsum, *Opers Staff*
Tina Hawkins, *Assistant*
EMP: 5 EST: 1981
SALES (est): 470.5K **Privately Held**
WEB: www.armonddalton.com
SIC: 2731 Books: publishing only

(G-12663)
DAVID R LACHARITE LMSW
4747 Okemos Rd (48864-1663)
PHONE..................517 347-0988
David R Lacharite, *Principal*
EMP: 6 EST: 2010
SALES (est): 159.6K **Privately Held**
WEB: www.okemospsychotherapy.com
SIC: 3843 Enamels, dentists'

(G-12664)
DIGILINK TECHNOLOGY INC
Also Called: DIGILIANT
5100 Marsh Rd Ste E3 (48864-1152)
PHONE..................517 381-8888
Ying Liu, *President*
EMP: 12 EST: 1994
SQ FT: 3,000
SALES (est): 3.5MM **Privately Held**
SIC: 3572 7378 5734 Computer storage devices; computer maintenance & repair; personal computers

(G-12665)
ELM INTERNATIONAL INC (PA)
4360 Hagadorn Rd (48864-2413)
P.O. Box 1740, East Lansing (48826-1740)
PHONE..................517 332-4900
Marc Santucci, *President*
Etsuko Barrows, *Treasurer*
Deborah Santucci, *Admin Sec*
▲ EMP: 6 EST: 1987
SQ FT: 1,400
SALES (est): 700K **Privately Held**
WEB: www.elm-intl.com
SIC: 2741 8732 8742 Directories: publishing & printing; market analysis or research; marketing consulting services

(G-12666)
EMERALD BIOAGRICULTURE CORP
4211 Okemos Rd Ste 20 (48864-3287)
PHONE..................517 882-7370
John McIntyre, *CEO*
EMP: 5 EST: 2001
SALES (est): 113.6K **Privately Held**
WEB: www.emeraldbio.com
SIC: 2879 Agricultural chemicals

(G-12667)
FABRICATED CUSTOMS
2767 Carnoustie Dr (48864-3348)
PHONE..................517 488-7273
Simeon Lowe, *Principal*
EMP: 4 EST: 2018
SALES (est): 159.9K **Privately Held**
WEB: www.fabricatedcustoms.com
SIC: 2759 Screen printing

(G-12668)
FRUIT FRO YO
5100 Marsh Rd (48864-1195)
PHONE..................517 580-3967
Mary Cao, *Principal*
EMP: 5 EST: 2012
SALES (est): 137.7K **Privately Held**
SIC: 2026 Yogurt

(G-12669)
GOLF STORE
1492 W Grand River Ave (48864-2307)
PHONE..................517 347-8733
EMP: 6 EST: 2007
SALES (est): 280K **Privately Held**
SIC: 3949 Mfg Sporting/Athletic Goods

(G-12670)
INSTRUMENTED SENSOR TECH INC
Also Called: I.S.T.
4704 Moore St (48864-1722)
PHONE..................517 349-8487
Gregory Hoshal, *President*
Celia Hoshal, *Vice Pres*
Patricia Lee, *Purch Agent*
Hope Jones, *Office Mgr*
EMP: 8 EST: 1987
SQ FT: 8,000 **Privately Held**
WEB: www.isthq.com
SIC: 3829 3825 3812 3674 Measuring & controlling devices; instruments to measure electricity; search & navigation equipment; semiconductors & related devices; scientific instruments

(G-12671)
KEVIN WHEAT & ASSOC LTD
Also Called: Wheat Jewelers
4990 Marsh Rd (48864-1194)
PHONE..................517 349-0101
Kevin Wheat, *President*
Rebecca Liebman, *Sales Associate*
EMP: 8 EST: 1983
SQ FT: 5,000
SALES (est): 951.7K **Privately Held**
WEB: www.wheatjewelers.com
SIC: 3915 5094 5944 7631 Jewelers' materials & lapidary work; jewelry & precious stones; jewelry stores; jewelry repair services

(G-12672)
KISSMAN CONSULTING LLC
Also Called: Kissco Publishing
2109 Hamilton Rd Ste 113 (48864-1700)
P.O. Box 744 (48805-0744)
PHONE..................517 256-1077
Tim Kissman,
EMP: 4 EST: 2008
SALES (est): 201.4K **Privately Held**
WEB: www.healthyandfitmagazine.com
SIC: 7311 2721 Advertising agencies; magazines: publishing & printing

(G-12673)
LUXOTTICA OF AMERICA INC
Also Called: Lenscrafters
1982 W Grand River Ave # 815 (48864-1736)
PHONE..................517 349-0784
Sue Lobsiger, *Branch Mgr*
EMP: 4
SALES (corp-wide): 1.7MM **Privately Held**
WEB: www.luxottica.com
SIC: 5995 3851 Eyeglasses, prescription; ophthalmic goods
HQ: Luxottica Of America Inc.
4000 Luxottica Pl
Mason OH 45040

(G-12674)
MERIDIAN SCREEN PRTG & DESIGN
Also Called: Meridian Screen Prtg & Design
3362 Hulett Rd (48864-4204)
PHONE..................517 351-2525
Felly Taylor, *President*
EMP: 6 EST: 1981
SQ FT: 5,000
SALES (est): 609.1K **Privately Held**
WEB: www.meridianscreen.com
SIC: 2395 7336 2261 Embroidery & art needlework; graphic arts & related design; printing of cotton broadwoven fabrics

(G-12675)
MICHIGAN ACDEMY FMLY PHYSCIANS
2164 Commons Pkwy (48864-3986)
PHONE..................517 347-0098
Karlene Ketola, *CEO*
Peter Scuccimarri, *President*
Fred Van Alstine, *Vice Pres*
Dana Lawrence, *Corp Comm Staff*
EMP: 5
SALES (est): 165K **Privately Held**
WEB: www.mafp.com
SIC: 8621 2741 Health association; miscellaneous publishing

(G-12676)
MINOR CREATIONS INCORPORATED
693 W Grand River Ave (48864-3110)
PHONE..................517 347-2900
Julia Story, *President*
Steve Carpenter, *Vice Pres*
Tom Shipping, *Manager*
▲ EMP: 28 EST: 1980
SQ FT: 10,000
SALES (est): 1.4MM **Privately Held**
WEB: www.minorcreations.com
SIC: 2341 Nightgowns & negligees: women's & children's; chemises, camisoles & teddies: women's & children's

(G-12677)
MOKASOFT LLC
4468 Oakwood Dr (48864-2927)
PHONE..................517 703-0237
Joseph Kattelus,
EMP: 4 EST: 2012
SALES (est): 107.2K **Privately Held**
WEB: www.mokasoft.com
SIC: 7372 Application computer software

(G-12678)
MOTEMBO FINE FOODS LLC
Also Called: Motembo Foods
2853 Jolly Rd Ste 3 (48864-3547)
PHONE..................800 692-4814
David Schnepp, *Administration*
Todd Brannock,
Craig Rappel,
EMP: 7 EST: 2018
SALES (est): 975.6K **Privately Held**
WEB: www.motembofoods.com
SIC: 3556 Food products machinery

(G-12679)
MUHLECK ENTERPRISES INC
Also Called: Allegra Print & Imaging
2863 Jolly Rd (48864-3547)
PHONE..................517 333-0713
David Muhleck, *President*
Michelle Devore, *Marketing Staff*
Selena Guidry, *Analyst*
EMP: 27 EST: 1990
SQ FT: 4,600
SALES (est): 6.5MM **Privately Held**
WEB: www.allegramarketingprint.com
SIC: 2752 7334 Commercial printing, offset; photocopying & duplicating services

(G-12680)
OPTI 02 LLC
2174 Butternut Dr (48864-3203)
PHONE..................517 381-9831
Ruby Ghosh, *Info Tech Mgr*
EMP: 4 EST: 2019
SALES (est): 142.6K **Privately Held**
SIC: 3826 Analytical instruments

(G-12681)
PIVOT MATERIALS LLC
1741 Chief Okemos Cir (48864-2225)
PHONE..................248 982-7970
Kylee Guenther, *CEO*
EMP: 4 EST: 2018
SALES (est): 265.5K **Privately Held**
WEB: www.pivot.eco
SIC: 2821 Plastics materials & resins

(G-12682)
POWER CONTROL SYSTEMS INC
2861 Jolly Rd Ste C (48864-3668)
P.O. Box 679 (48805-0679)
PHONE..................517 339-1442
James Darnell, *President*
EMP: 9 EST: 1986
SALES (est): 1.1MM **Privately Held**
SIC: 3612 Voltage regulating transformers, electric power

(G-12683)
ROYAL ACCOUTREMENTS INC
Also Called: Royal Coffee Maker
172 W Sherwood Rd (48864-1235)
PHONE..................517 347-7983
Maria Maes, *President*
▲ EMP: 4 EST: 1988
SALES (est): 80K **Privately Held**
WEB: www.royalcoffeemaker.com
SIC: 5499 3589 Coffee; coffee brewing equipment

(G-12684)
RVI MANAGEMENT INC
Also Called: Robinson Solutions U.S. , Inc.
2152 Commons Pkwy Ste A (48864-3985)
PHONE..................580 531-5826
Michael Robinson, *President*
Shazia Vasdani, *Treasurer*
EMP: 3 EST: 1997
SQ FT: 3,800
SALES (est): 4.5MM
SALES (corp-wide): 1.2MM **Privately Held**
WEB: www.robinsonsolutions.com
SIC: 8741 3629 Nursing & personal care facility management; blasting machines, electrical
HQ: Robinson Solutions Inc
390 Bay St Suite 1520
Toronto ON M5H 2
416 479-7440

(G-12685)
SCITEX TRICK TITANIUM LLC
4251 Hulett Rd (48864-3252)
PHONE..................517 349-3736
Michael Miller, *Principal*
EMP: 9 EST: 2008
SALES (est): 465.8K **Privately Held**
WEB: www.tricktitanium.com
SIC: 3356 Titanium

(G-12686)
SIGN A RAMA
Also Called: Sign-A-Rama
2189 W Grand River Ave (48864-1666)
PHONE..................517 489-4314
Dale Kohlsmith, *Owner*
EMP: 6 EST: 2014
SALES (est): 119K **Privately Held**
WEB: www.signarama.com
SIC: 3993 Signs & advertising specialties

(G-12687)
SIGNING SAVVY LLC
2025 Central Park Dr # 1009 (48805-5001)
PHONE..................517 455-7663
EMP: 4 EST: 2009
SALES (est): 101.5K **Privately Held**
WEB: www.signingsavvy.com
SIC: 3993 Signs & advertising specialties

(G-12688)
TALETYANO PRESS
4107 Breakwater Dr (48864-4413)
PHONE..................517 381-1960
James E White, *Principal*
EMP: 5 EST: 2004
SALES (est): 92.1K **Privately Held**
WEB: www.taletyano.com
SIC: 2741 Miscellaneous publishing

Okemos - Ingham County (G-12689) GEOGRAPHIC SECTION

(G-12689)
TALLON PRINTING
1715 W Grand River Ave (48864-1803)
PHONE 517 721-1307
EMP: 4 **EST:** 2015
SALES (est): 129.8K **Privately Held**
SIC: 2759 Letterpress printing

(G-12690)
TECHNOVA CORPORATION
3927 Dobie Rd (48864-3705)
PHONE 517 485-1402
Parviz Soroushian, *President*
Farangis Jamzadeh, *Vice Pres*
Maggie Soro, *Admin Sec*
EMP: 7 **EST:** 2001
SQ FT: 30,000
SALES (est): 177.6K **Privately Held**
SIC: 2655 8732 8742 Cans, composite: foil-fiber & other; from purchased fiber; commercial nonphysical research; marketing consulting services

(G-12691)
UMAKANTH CONSULTANTS INC
Also Called: Symbiosis International
3581 Cabaret Trl (48864-4082)
PHONE 517 347-7500
Uma Umakanth, *President*
Govindarajan Murali, *Vice Pres*
Thangavelu Suseela, *Admin Sec*
EMP: 10 **EST:** 1988
SQ FT: 1,100
SALES (est): 332.5K **Privately Held**
WEB: www.gosymbiosis.com
SIC: 7372 Prepackaged software

(G-12692)
VANGUARD PUBLICATIONS INC
2807 Jolly Rd Ste 360 (48864-3675)
PHONE 517 336-1600
Judy Scheidt, *President*
EMP: 4 **EST:** 1982
SALES (est): 900K
SALES (corp-wide): 19.2MM **Privately Held**
WEB: www.corporateboard.com
SIC: 2721 2741 Magazines: publishing & printing; shopping news: publishing only, not printed on site
PA: American Collegiate Marketing, Inc.
4440 Hagadorn Rd
Okemos MI 48864
517 336-1600

Olivet
Eaton County

(G-12693)
FABRICATIONS PLUS INC
7898 Marshall Rd (49076-8613)
PHONE 269 749-3050
Pat Hitchcock, *President*
Greg Shaver, *Principal*
Randy Linn, *Vice Pres*
EMP: 4 **EST:** 1998
SALES (est): 398.6K **Privately Held**
SIC: 3444 Sheet metalwork

(G-12694)
MASTERBILT PRODUCTS CORP
719 N Main St (49076-9458)
P.O. Box 518 (49076-0518)
PHONE 269 749-4841
David Craig Masters, *President*
EMP: 14 **EST:** 1955
SQ FT: 40,000
SALES (est): 1.1MM **Privately Held**
WEB: www.masterbiltproducts.com
SIC: 3498 3728 Tube fabricating (contract bending & shaping); aircraft parts & equipment

(G-12695)
OLIVET MACHINE TOOL ENGRG CO
Also Called: Omteco
423 N Main St (49076-9616)
P.O. Box 337 (49076-0337)
PHONE 269 749-2671
Bob Judd, *President*
Kathleen Judd, *Corp Secy*
Mike Judd, *Vice Pres*

EMP: 17 **EST:** 1946
SQ FT: 5,000
SALES (est): 1MM **Privately Held**
WEB: www.omteco.com
SIC: 3544 7692 3545 Special dies & tools; jigs & fixtures; welding repair; machine tool accessories

Omer
Arenac County

(G-12696)
LUBERDA WOOD PRODUCTS INC
1188 E Huron Rd (48749-9639)
PHONE 989 876-4334
Albert Luberda, *President*
EMP: 8 **EST:** 1974
SALES (est): 815.7K **Privately Held**
SIC: 2448 2449 Wood pallets & skids; wood containers

Onaway
Presque Isle County

(G-12697)
BRUNING FOREST PRODUCTS
Also Called: Big Ridge Forest Products
16854 5 Mile Hwy (49765-9390)
PHONE 989 733-2880
Michael Bruning, *Owner*
▲ **EMP:** 5 **EST:** 1981
SQ FT: 400
SALES (est): 903.7K **Privately Held**
WEB: www.northernevergreen.com
SIC: 5193 2411 0811 Nursery stock; timber, cut at logging camp; Christmas tree farm

(G-12698)
DON SAWMILL INC
17131 Twin School Hwy (49765-8887)
PHONE 989 733-2780
EMP: 7 **EST:** 2010
SALES (est): 467.6K **Privately Held**
SIC: 2421 Sawmills & planing mills, general

(G-12699)
METAL QUEST INC
11739 M68-33 Hwy (49765-8720)
P.O. Box 732 (49765-0732)
PHONE 989 733-2011
Thomas Moran, *CEO*
Rebecca Nash, *CFO*
EMP: 8 **EST:** 2016
SALES (est): 247.8K **Privately Held**
SIC: 3443 Plate work for the nuclear industry

(G-12700)
MORAN IRON WORKS INC
11739 M68-33 Hwy (49765-8720)
P.O. Box 732 (49765-0732)
PHONE 989 733-2011
Thomas J Moran, *President*
Danielle Chapman, *Principal*
David Kronberg, *Principal*
Mike Mroz, *Principal*
Keri Sheer, *Principal*
EMP: 65 **EST:** 1978
SQ FT: 50,000
SALES (est): 13.3MM **Privately Held**
WEB: www.moraniron.com
SIC: 3441 Fabricated structural metal

(G-12701)
NU-WAY STOVE INC
6566 Rainey Lake Rd (49765)
PHONE 989 733-8792
Wayne Berry, *President*
Gary Schroeder, *Corp Secy*
▲ **EMP:** 5 **EST:** 1993
SQ FT: 4,800
SALES (est): 903.9K **Privately Held**
WEB: www.nuwaystove.com
SIC: 5064 3633 Electrical appliances, major; stoves, wood & coal burning

(G-12702)
PRECISION FORESTRY
4285 S County Line Rd (49765-7504)
P.O. Box 741 (49765-0741)
PHONE 989 619-1016
Michael Sturgill, *Owner*
EMP: 14 **EST:** 2007
SALES (est): 699.2K **Privately Held**
SIC: 2411 Logging camps & contractors

Onekama
Manistee County

(G-12703)
PORTAGE WIRE SYSTEMS INC
4853 Joseph Rd (49675-9754)
P.O. Box 567 (49675-0567)
PHONE 231 889-4215
Jerome Showalter, *President*
Andrew Showalter, *Admin Sec*
EMP: 30 **EST:** 1975
SQ FT: 30,000
SALES (est): 7.2MM **Privately Held**
WEB: www.portagewire.com
SIC: 3694 3444 Harness wiring sets, internal combustion engines; sheet metalwork

Onsted
Lenawee County

(G-12704)
AMERICAN GRINDING AND MAC
9562 Sand Lake Hwy (49265-9685)
PHONE 517 467-5399
EMP: 10 **EST:** 2010
SALES (est): 227.4K **Privately Held**
WEB: www.americangrinding.com
SIC: 3599 Machine shop, jobbing & repair

(G-12705)
EDWARD E YATES
8573 M 50 (49265-9612)
PHONE 517 467-4961
Bill Sturgill, *Principal*
EMP: 5 **EST:** 2010
SALES (est): 104.7K **Privately Held**
SIC: 3273 Ready-mixed concrete

(G-12706)
MIDCO 2 INC
11703 Pentecost Hwy (49265-9700)
PHONE 517 467-2222
Tom D Johnson, *President*
Charles Roumell, *Corp Secy*
EMP: 5 **EST:** 2008
SQ FT: 3,000
SALES (est): 600K **Privately Held**
WEB: www.midco-manufacturing.com
SIC: 3441 Building components, structural steel

(G-12707)
NATURAL AMERICAN FOODS LLC (PA)
Also Called: Sweet Harvest Foods
10464 Bryan Hwy (49265-9551)
PHONE 517 467-2065
Ken Stickevers, *CEO*
Prashanth Prabhakar, *VP Opers*
Brian Zellmer, *CFO*
Gloria McMichael, *Human Res Mgr*
John Rzeszut, *VP Mktg*
▲ **EMP:** 45 **EST:** 2013
SQ FT: 20,000
SALES (est): 30.5MM **Privately Held**
WEB: www.sweetharvestfoods.com
SIC: 2099 Honey, strained & bottled

(G-12708)
ZONYA HEALTH INTERNATIONAL
Also Called: Zhi Publishing
7134 Donegal Dr (49265-9586)
PHONE 517 467-6995
EMP: 4
SALES (est): 338.2K **Privately Held**
SIC: 2731 Publisher And Public Health Issues Seima

Ontonagon
Ontonagon County

(G-12709)
JAMES POLLARD LOGGING
37294 Tikka Rd (49953-9364)
PHONE 906 884-6744
James Pollard, *Principal*
EMP: 7 **EST:** 2005
SALES (est): 182.1K **Privately Held**
SIC: 2411 Logging camps & contractors

(G-12710)
JCR FABRICATION LLC
23642 W State Highway M64 (49953-9035)
PHONE 906 235-2683
Jason Pestka, *Principal*
Carl Brees,
Roy Holmstrom,
EMP: 4 **EST:** 2012
SALES (est): 245.4K **Privately Held**
SIC: 3449 Miscellaneous metalwork

(G-12711)
K AND W LANDFILL INC
Also Called: Waste Management
11877 State Highway M38 (49953-9351)
PHONE 906 883-3504
Murry Meyers, *President*
Dave Kempainen, *District Mgr*
EMP: 81 **EST:** 1998
SALES (est): 22.9MM
SALES (corp-wide): 15.2B **Publicly Held**
WEB: www.wm.com
SIC: 3443 4953 Dumpsters, garbage; sanitary landfill operation
PA: Waste Management, Inc.
800 Capitol St Ste 3000
Houston TX 77002
713 512-6200

(G-12712)
KARTTUNEN LOGGING
29015 W State Highway M64 (49953-9078)
PHONE 906 884-4312
Todd A Karttunen, *Owner*
EMP: 4 **EST:** 1993
SALES (est): 231.4K **Privately Held**
SIC: 2411 Logging camps & contractors

(G-12713)
KOSKIS LOG HOMES INC
Also Called: Koski Log Homes
35993 Us Highway 45 (49953-9423)
PHONE 906 884-4937
Jerry Koski, *President*
Linda Koski, *Admin Sec*
EMP: 6 **EST:** 1984
SALES (est): 650K **Privately Held**
SIC: 1521 2452 New construction, single-family houses; log cabins, prefabricated, wood

(G-12714)
ONTONAGON HERALD CO INC
326 River St (49953-1612)
PHONE 906 884-2826
Maureen Guzek, *President*
EMP: 8 **EST:** 1881
SQ FT: 2,000
SALES (est): 340K **Privately Held**
WEB: www.ontonagonherald.com
SIC: 2711 5943 Job printing & newspaper publishing combined; office forms & supplies

Orchard Lake
Oakland County

(G-12715)
3D POLYMERS INC
4084 Commerce Rd (48324-2300)
PHONE 248 588-5562
James A Chota, *President*
EMP: 10 **EST:** 1994
SQ FT: 15,000

▲ = Import ▼ = Export
◆ = Import/Export

SALES (est): 1MM Privately Held
WEB: www.3dpolymers.com
SIC: 3089 3714 3544 Injection molding of plastics; motor vehicle parts & accessories; special dies, tools, jigs & fixtures

(G-12716)
DECOR GROUP INTERNATIONAL INC
3748 Sunset Blvd (48324-2957)
PHONE.................................248 307-2430
Dennis Knoblock, *President*
Kelly Davis, *Managing Prtnr*
EMP: 14 EST: 1995
SALES (est): 1.4MM Privately Held
WEB: www.decorgroup.com
SIC: 3993 Signs & advertising specialties

(G-12717)
ESYNTRK INDUSTRIES LLC
4250 Pine Ln (48323-1647)
PHONE.................................248 730-0640
Jane Harper, *Managing Dir*
Takisha Jane Harper, *Principal*
William Harper, *Principal*
EMP: 8 EST: 2017
SALES (est): 264.3K Privately Held
SIC: 3999 Atomizers, toiletry

(G-12718)
PAICE TECHNOLOGIES LLC
5843 Bravo Ct (48324-2911)
PHONE.................................248 376-1115
Richard Ferguson,
EMP: 5 EST: 2008
SALES (est): 100K Privately Held
WEB: www.paicehybrid.com
SIC: 3519 Internal combustion engines

(G-12719)
RED CARPET CAPITAL INC
3514 Arrowvale Dr (48324-1506)
PHONE.................................248 952-8583
Mitchell Rivet, *President*
EMP: 5 EST: 2009
SALES (est): 96.7K Privately Held
SIC: 7922 1521 1389 1542 Theatrical production services; single-family housing construction; construction, repair & dismantling services; commercial & office building contractors; post office construction

(G-12720)
STROYKO CONSTRUCTION GROUP INC
5879 Seville Cir (48324-2948)
PHONE.................................281 240-3332
EMP: 5 EST: 2018
SALES (est): 74.4K Privately Held
WEB: www.stroykoconstruction.com
SIC: 2834 Pharmaceutical preparations

(G-12721)
SUN DAILY
4226 Cherry Hill Dr (48323-1606)
PHONE.................................248 842-2925
EMP: 5 EST: 2013
SALES (est): 78.9K Privately Held
SIC: 2711 Newspapers, publishing & printing

Orion
Oakland County

(G-12722)
ADCOLE CORPORATION
40 Engelwood Dr Ste G (48359-2419)
PHONE.................................508 485-9100
Chris Skinner, *Sales Engr*
Darren Dawes, *Branch Mgr*
EMP: 5
SALES (corp-wide): 30MM Privately Held
WEB: www.adcole.com
SIC: 3829 Aircraft & motor vehicle measurement equipment
PA: Adcole Llc
  669 Forest St
  Marlborough MA 01752
  508 485-9100

(G-12723)
ADVANCED RESEARCH COMPANY
4140 S Lapeer Rd (48359-1865)
P.O. Box 408, Lake Orion (48361-0408)
PHONE.................................248 475-4770
William Sharp, *President*
Kim Frank, *Director*
EMP: 10 EST: 1984
SQ FT: 18,000
SALES (est): 1MM Privately Held
WEB: www.advresearch.com
SIC: 7389 3699 Design services; electrical equipment & supplies

(G-12724)
BECKER ROBOTIC EQUIPMENT CORP
260 Engelwood Dr Ste E (48359-2443)
PHONE.................................470 249-7880
Johan Broekhuijsen, *CEO*
John P Izzi, *Engineer*
EMP: 4
SALES (corp-wide): 177.9K Privately Held
WEB: www.becker-robotic.com
SIC: 3569 Robots, assembly line: industrial & commercial
HQ: Becker Robotic Equipment Corp.
  6410 Atl Blvd Ste 350
  Peachtree Corners GA 30071
  770 837-0449

(G-12725)
COLE KING LLC
4930 S Lapeer Rd (48359-2412)
PHONE.................................248 276-1278
John Cole, *President*
EMP: 5 EST: 2012
SALES (est): 343.2K Privately Held
SIC: 2819 Carbides

(G-12726)
CORBAN INDUSTRIES INC
4590 Joslyn Rd (48359-2229)
PHONE.................................248 393-2720
Roderic C McIntosh, *President*
EMP: 27 EST: 1981
SQ FT: 52,400
SALES (est): 1.1MM Privately Held
SIC: 3469 3544 7692 3441 Stamping metal for the trade; special dies & tools; welding repair; fabricated structural metal

(G-12727)
CREATIVE TECHNIQUES INC
200 Northpointe Dr (48359-2400)
PHONE.................................248 373-3050
Joeseph Banfield, *President*
David Matthews, *Vice Pres*
Richard Parker, *Vice Pres*
Tim Volke, *Purch Mgr*
Harvey Clement, *Engineer*
EMP: 90 EST: 2006
SQ FT: 62,000
SALES (est): 20.9MM Privately Held
WEB: www.creativetechniques.com
SIC: 3544 3089 Special dies, tools, jigs & fixtures; injection molded finished plastic products

(G-12728)
DARING COMPANY
180 Engelwood Dr Ste B (48359-2417)
PHONE.................................248 340-0741
Judy Soutar, *Office Mgr*
Larry Soutar, *Administration*
EMP: 7 EST: 2010
SALES (est): 648.7K Privately Held
WEB: www.daringcompany.com
SIC: 2891 Adhesives

(G-12729)
FATA ALUMINUM LLC (PA)
260 Engelwood Dr (48359-2443)
PHONE.................................248 802-9853
Martin Wright, *CEO*
▲ EMP: 38 EST: 2008
SQ FT: 46,400
SALES (est): 4.4MM Privately Held
WEB: www.fataaluminum.com
SIC: 3559 5084 Foundry machinery & equipment; industrial machinery & equipment

(G-12730)
GEDIA MICHIGAN LLC
269 Kay Industrial Dr (48359-2403)
PHONE.................................248 392-9090
Karl G Neef, *President*
Paul Sprainitis, *CFO*
EMP: 42 EST: 2016
SALES (est): 9MM
SALES (corp-wide): 741.5MM Privately Held
WEB: www.gedia.com
SIC: 3465 Automotive stampings
HQ: Gedia Gebruder Dingerkus Gmbh
  Rontgenstr. 2-4
  Attendorn 57439
  272 269-10

(G-12731)
GEORGE INSTRUMENT COMPANY (PA)
Also Called: Dave Ray & Associates
220 Engelwood Dr Ste D (48359-2414)
PHONE.................................248 280-1111
Cheri Johnson, *CEO*
Mark Johnson, *President*
Dennis Tucker, *Purch Dir*
John Mack, *Engineer*
Yolanda Wright, *Sales Staff*
EMP: 14 EST: 1947
SQ FT: 8,000
SALES (est): 4.2MM Privately Held
WEB: www.georgeinstrument.com
SIC: 3823 Industrial instrmnts msrmnt display/control process variable

(G-12732)
GREAT LAKES WOODWORKING LLC
3361 Aspen Dr Apt 6304 (48359-2315)
PHONE.................................248 550-1991
Steven Lang, *Branch Mgr*
EMP: 26
SALES (corp-wide): 54.1K Privately Held
SIC: 2431 1521 Millwork; single-family housing construction
PA: Great Lakes Woodworking Llc
  2510 S Telegraph Rd Ste L
  Bloomfield Hills MI

(G-12733)
LOTIS TECHNOLOGIES INC
100 Engelwood Dr Ste F (48359-2411)
PHONE.................................248 340-6065
Paul Dunstan, *President*
EMP: 5 EST: 2005
SALES (est): 494.1K Privately Held
WEB: www.lotistechnologies.com
SIC: 7389 2631 Packaging & labeling services; container, packaging & boxboard

(G-12734)
LYMTAL INTERNATIONAL INC (PA)
4150 S Lapeer Rd (48359-1865)
PHONE.................................248 373-8100
Francis M Lymburner, *President*
Magdy M Talaat, *Vice Pres*
▼ EMP: 22 EST: 1994
SQ FT: 34,000
SALES: 16.4MM Privately Held
WEB: www.lymtal.com
SIC: 2851 2899 2891 Polyurethane coatings; chemical preparations; sealants

(G-12735)
M P D WELDING INC (PA)
Also Called: Mpd Welding Center
4200 S Lapeer Rd (48359-1866)
P.O. Box 99277, Troy (48099-9277)
PHONE.................................248 340-0330
Rollin Bondar, *CEO*
Richard Bondar, *President*
Sue Godlewski, *General Mgr*
Dennis Wilette, *General Mgr*
Jerry Lilly, *Purch Mgr*
EMP: 54 EST: 1974
SQ FT: 14,000
SALES (est): 6.4MM Privately Held
WEB: www.mpdweldinginc.com
SIC: 3544 7692 7699 3398 Special dies, tools, jigs & fixtures; welding repair; industrial machinery & equipment repair; shot peening (treating steel to reduce fatigue)

(G-12736)
NATIVE GREEN LLC
180 Engelwood Dr Ste A (48359-2417)
PHONE.................................248 365-4200
Linda Gcarrillo, *Mng Member*
EMP: 13 EST: 2008
SQ FT: 5,000 Privately Held
WEB: www.nativegreenproducts.com
SIC: 2842 Specialty cleaning preparations

(G-12737)
ORACLE CORPORATION
3216 Hickory Dr (48359-1163)
PHONE.................................248 393-2498
William Rutan, *Branch Mgr*
EMP: 4
SALES (corp-wide): 40.4B Publicly Held
WEB: www.oracle.com
SIC: 7372 Business oriented computer software
PA: Oracle Corporation
  2300 Oracle Way
  Austin TX 78741
  737 867-1000

(G-12738)
PATCO AIR TOOL INC
100 Engelwood Dr Ste G (48359-2411)
PHONE.................................248 648-8830
Jon M Kirsch, *President*
Joseph C Linklater, *General Mgr*
Jacqueline Linklater, *CFO*
EMP: 5 EST: 1980
SQ FT: 15,000
SALES (est): 893.2K Privately Held
WEB: www.patcoairtools.com
SIC: 5085 3423 5072 Tools; hand & edge tools; hardware

(G-12739)
US FARATHANE HOLDINGS CORP
4872 S Lapeer Rd (48359-1877)
PHONE.................................248 754-7000
Mike Sermo, *Branch Mgr*
EMP: 5
SALES (corp-wide): 549.4MM Privately Held
WEB: www.usfarathane.com
SIC: 3089 Injection molding of plastics
PA: U.S. Farathane Holdings Corp.
  2700 High Meadow Cir
  Auburn Hills MI 48326
  248 754-7000

Orleans
Ionia County

(G-12740)
MAPLE LEAF WOODWORKING
8863 Lake View Dr (48865-9107)
PHONE.................................616 262-9754
Richard Rasch, *Owner*
EMP: 6 EST: 2015
SALES (est): 109.9K Privately Held
SIC: 2431 Millwork

Ortonville
Oakland County

(G-12741)
ANGSTROM AUTOMOTIVE GROUP LLC
85 Myron St (48462-8824)
PHONE.................................248 627-2871
Jack Boldt, *Branch Mgr*
EMP: 50 Privately Held
WEB: www.angstrom-usa.com
SIC: 3498 3714 Tube fabricating (contract bending & shaping); motor vehicle parts & accessories
PA: Angstrom Automotive Group, Llc
  2000 Town Ctr Ste 100
  Southfield MI 48075

(G-12742)
BEST RATE DUMPSTER RENTAL INC
256 Marrin (48462)
PHONE.................................248 391-5956

Ortonville - Oakland County (G-12743)

Brian Cummings, *President*
EMP: 8
SALES (est): 507.6K **Privately Held**
WEB: www.dumpsterrentalsinc.com
SIC: 3443 Dumpsters, garbage

(G-12743)
BOONE EXPRESS
3920 S Hadley Rd (48462-9139)
PHONE.................................248 583-7080
M Vince, *Principal*
EMP: 4 **EST:** 2006
SALES (est): 175.4K **Privately Held**
SIC: 2741 Miscellaneous publishing

(G-12744)
CITY PRESS INC
30 Rissman Ln (48462-9004)
PHONE.................................800 867-2626
Jeff Bidoli, *Principal*
EMP: 5 **EST:** 1947
SALES (est): 181.8K **Privately Held**
SIC: 2741 Miscellaneous publishing

(G-12745)
CLARKSTON CARBIDE TOOL & MCH (PA)
1959 Viola Dr (48462-8886)
PHONE.................................248 625-3182
Anthony Palazzola, *President*
Barbara Palazzola, *Corp Secy*
EMP: 6 **EST:** 1976
SALES (est): 682.8K **Privately Held**
WEB: www.clarkstoncarbide.com
SIC: 3599 Machine shop, jobbing & repair

(G-12746)
ETHER LLC
4950 Hummer Lake Rd (48462-9793)
PHONE.................................248 795-8830
Cole Denzler, *Principal*
EMP: 4 **EST:** 2015
SALES (est): 119.8K **Privately Held**
SIC: 2869 Ethers

(G-12747)
GRAVELDINGER GRAPHIX
1360 Merkle St (48462-8458)
PHONE.................................248 535-8074
EMP: 5 **EST:** 2016
SALES (est): 145K **Privately Held**
WEB: www.graveldingergraphix.com
SIC: 2759 Screen printing

(G-12748)
GT PERFORMANCE COATINGS LLC
1342 S Ortonville Rd (48462-8722)
PHONE.................................248 627-5905
George Briston,
EMP: 10 **EST:** 2005
SALES (est): 282.9K **Privately Held**
WEB: www.gtperformancecoatings.com
SIC: 3479 Coating of metals & formed products

(G-12749)
MRJ SIGN COMPANY LLC
256 Narrin St (48462-8718)
PHONE.................................248 521-2431
Mark Johnson, *Vice Pres*
Mark R Johnson, *Mng Member*
Susan J Johnson,
EMP: 6 **EST:** 2010
SALES (est): 524.8K **Privately Held**
WEB: www.mrjsign.com
SIC: 3993 Signs & advertising specialties

(G-12750)
PALFAM INDUSTRIES INC
Also Called: Wit-O-Matic
1959 Viola Dr (48462-8886)
PHONE.................................248 922-0590
Anthony Palazzola Sr, *President*
EMP: 16 **EST:** 1971
SALES (est): 694.3K **Privately Held**
SIC: 3541 Grinding machines, metalworking

(G-12751)
SHERI BOSTON
Also Called: Global Silks Gifts N Crafts
1119 Briar Ridge Ln (48462-9760)
PHONE.................................248 627-9576
Sheri Boston, *Owner*

EMP: 4
SALES (est): 75K **Privately Held**
WEB: www.weddingbouquets.com
SIC: 3999 7299 Artificial flower arrangements;

(G-12752)
SHERMAN PUBLICATIONS INC
Also Called: Citizen Newspaper, The
12 South St (48462-7717)
P.O. Box 595 (48462-0595)
PHONE.................................248 627-4332
Alison Heffmer, *Branch Mgr*
EMP: 6
SALES (corp-wide): 4.1MM **Privately Held**
WEB: www.oxfordleader.com
SIC: 2711 Newspapers, publishing & printing
PA: Sherman Publications Inc
666 S Lapeer Rd
Oxford MI 48371
248 628-4801

Oscoda
Iosco County

(G-12753)
A W B INDUSTRIES INC
Also Called: Aircraft Tool Supply
1000 Ausable Rd (48750-9518)
P.O. Box 370 (48750-0370)
PHONE.................................989 739-1447
Desmond Lynch, *CEO*
Frank Barber, *Shareholder*
◆ **EMP:** 21 **EST:** 1974
SQ FT: 38,000 **Privately Held**
WEB: www.aircraft-tool.com
SIC: 3546 3542 5251 5961 Power-driven handtools; machine tools, metal forming type; hardware; catalog & mail-order houses

(G-12754)
BC WOODWORKS
7015 Woodlea Rd W (48750-8764)
PHONE.................................989 820-7680
Brandon Curley, *Principal*
EMP: 5 **EST:** 2017
SALES (est): 98.2K **Privately Held**
SIC: 2431 Millwork

(G-12755)
COZY CUP COFFEE COMPANY LLC
4083 Denise Ct (48750-1062)
P.O. Box 495 (48750-0495)
PHONE.................................989 984-7619
Brian Colorite, *Mng Member*
Lance Thompson,
EMP: 4
SALES (est): 19K **Privately Held**
WEB: www.cozycupcoffee.com
SIC: 2095 Coffee roasting (except by wholesale grocers)

(G-12756)
DIVERSIFORM LLC
4656 Sunset St (48750-9512)
PHONE.................................989 278-9605
Darren Pickens, *Principal*
EMP: 5 **EST:** 2018
SALES (est): 135.1K **Privately Held**
SIC: 3441 Fabricated structural metal

(G-12757)
E A WOOD INC (PA)
6718 Loud Dr (48750-9676)
PHONE.................................989 739-9118
EMP: 10
SALES (est): 973.1K **Privately Held**
SIC: 3273 Mfg Ready-Mixed Concrete

(G-12758)
ENVIRO-BRITE SOLUTIONS LLC
4150 Arrow St (48750-1561)
PHONE.................................989 387-2758
Thomas York, *Plant Mgr*
Dean Wiltse, *Mng Member*
EMP: 5 **EST:** 2008

SALES (corp-wide): 1.3MM **Privately Held**
WEB: www.enviro-britesolutions.com
SIC: 2842 5087 Cleaning or polishing preparations; cleaning & maintenance equipment & supplies
PA: Wiltse's Restaurant Systems Inc
5606 F 41
Oscoda MI 48750
989 739-2231

(G-12759)
GT PLASTICS INCORPORATED
4681 Industrial Row (48750-8823)
PHONE.................................989 739-7803
Gary Thibault, *President*
Duane Thibault, *Manager*
Paula Thibault, *Admin Sec*
EMP: 27 **EST:** 1990
SQ FT: 37,000
SALES (est): 8MM **Privately Held**
WEB: www.gtplastics.com
SIC: 3089 Injection molding of plastics

(G-12760)
INSTACOAT PREMIUM PRODUCT
5920 N Huron Ave (48750-2259)
PHONE.................................877 552-6724
EMP: 9 **EST:** 2018
SALES (est): 250K **Privately Held**
WEB: www.instacoat.com
SIC: 2851 Paints & allied products

(G-12761)
INSTACOAT PREMIUM PRODUCTS LLC (PA)
5920 N Huron Ave (48750-2259)
PHONE.................................586 770-1773
Merry Hart, *Business Mgr*
Michael Dewald, *Mng Member*
Anthony Miriani,
◆ **EMP:** 6 **EST:** 2010
SALES (est): 1.5MM **Privately Held**
WEB: www.instacoat.com
SIC: 2851 Paints & allied products

(G-12762)
IOSCO NEWS PRESS PUBLISHING CO (HQ)
Also Called: Oscoda Press
311 S State St (48750-1636)
P.O. Box 663 (48750-0663)
PHONE.................................989 739-2054
Larry Berratto, *President*
Wayne Hemstreet, *Executive*
EMP: 9 **EST:** 1940
SQ FT: 2,000
SALES (est): 1.4MM **Privately Held**
WEB: www.iosconews.com
SIC: 2711 Commercial printing & newspaper publishing combined; newspapers, publishing & printing

(G-12763)
LAKESHORE CEMENT PRODUCTS
5251 N Us Highway 23 (48750-9560)
PHONE.................................989 739-9341
Larry Gerhardt, *Owner*
EMP: 4 **EST:** 1975
SALES (est): 380K **Privately Held**
WEB: www.lakeshorecementproducts.com
SIC: 3272 5211 5032 Precast terrazo or concrete products; concrete products, precast; paving materials, prefabricated concrete; masonry materials & supplies; paving stones; brick, stone & related material

(G-12764)
LANGLEY POWDER COATING
4025 Arrow St (48750-2214)
PHONE.................................989 739-5203
David Langley, *Owner*
EMP: 6 **EST:** 2006
SALES (est): 196.8K **Privately Held**
SIC: 3479 Coating of metals & formed products

(G-12765)
MIGATRON PRECISION PRODUCTS (PA)
Also Called: Fine Manufacturing & Tool Co
4296 E River Rd (48750-1027)
P.O. Box 100 (48750-0100)
PHONE.................................989 739-1439
Ronald Edwards, *Vice Pres*
EMP: 13 **EST:** 1979
SQ FT: 6,000
SALES (est): 1.1MM **Privately Held**
WEB: www.migatronprecision.net
SIC: 3541 Machine tools, metal cutting type

(G-12766)
NTF MANUFACTURING USA LLC
Also Called: Ntf Filter
4691 Industrial Row (48750-8823)
PHONE.................................989 739-8560
Cathy Williams, *Marketing Staff*
EMP: 15 **EST:** 2007
SALES (est): 2.8MM **Privately Held**
SIC: 3677 Filtration devices, electronic

(G-12767)
OSCODA PLASTICS INC (PA)
Also Called: Jrb Enterprises
5585 N Huron Ave (48750-1583)
P.O. Box 189 (48750-0189)
PHONE.................................989 739-6900
Tom Saeli, *CEO*
John Burt, *Ch of Bd*
Jim McAlpine, *District Mgr*
Shawn Sny, *Exec VP*
Jason Tunney, *Exec VP*
EMP: 35 **EST:** 1993
SQ FT: 130,000
SALES: 11.7MM **Privately Held**
WEB: www.oscodaplastics.com
SIC: 2821 3089 Polyvinyl chloride resins (PVC); floor coverings, plastic

(G-12768)
P&L DEVELOPMENT & MFG LLC
Also Called: P&L Development and Mfg
4025 Arrow St (48750-2214)
PHONE.................................989 739-5203
Paul Merdzinski, *Manager*
David Langley,
EMP: 75 **EST:** 2007
SALES (est): 9.6MM **Privately Held**
WEB: www.pl-dev.com
SIC: 3545 Machine tool accessories

(G-12769)
PCS OUTDOORS
5911 Mission St (48750-1544)
PHONE.................................989 569-3480
EMP: 4 **EST:** 2017
SALES (est): 194.9K **Privately Held**
WEB: www.pcsoutdoors.com
SIC: 3949 Sporting & athletic goods

(G-12770)
PHOENIX CMPOSITE SOLUTIONS LLC
5911 Mission St (48750-1544)
PHONE.................................989 739-7108
Erick Martin, *Division Mgr*
Erick C Martin, *COO*
Lucas Jaqua, *Plant Mgr*
Ian Spragg, *QC Mgr*
Scott Phillips, *Engineer*
◆ **EMP:** 150 **EST:** 2003
SQ FT: 118,000
SALES (est): 23.1MM **Privately Held**
WEB: www.phoenix-mi.com
SIC: 3728 Aircraft assemblies, subassemblies & parts

(G-12771)
SAGE CONTROL ORDNANCE INC
3455 Kings Corner Rd (48750-9667)
PHONE.................................989 739-2200
John Klein, *President*
▲ **EMP:** 23 **EST:** 1990
SALES (est): 1.2MM **Privately Held**
WEB: www.sageinternationalltd.com
SIC: 3482 Small arms ammunition

GEOGRAPHIC SECTION

Otsego - Allegan County (G-12797)

(G-12772)
SAGE INTERNATIONAL LIMITED
3455 Kings Corner Rd (48750-9667)
PHONE.................................989 739-7000
John M Klein, *President*
Marvin Clark, *General Mgr*
Kristina Millard,
EMP: 15 **EST:** 1973
SQ FT: 20,000 **Privately Held**
WEB: www.sageinternationalltd.com
SIC: 3484 Small arms

(G-12773)
TIP-TOP SCREW MFG INC
4183 Forest St (48750-2335)
P.O. Box 665 (48750-0665)
PHONE.................................989 739-5157
Thomas Saeli, *CEO*
Bob Stewart, *General Mgr*
Tom Hollingsworth, *Exec VP*
Shawn Sny, *Exec VP*
Jason Tunney, *Exec VP*
EMP: 20 **EST:** 1999
SQ FT: 50,000
SALES (est): 6.2MM **Privately Held**
WEB: www.tip-topscrew.com
SIC: 3452 Bolts, nuts, rivets & washers

(G-12774)
YATES FOREST PRODUCTS INC
7110 Woodlea Rd (48750-9722)
PHONE.................................989 739-8412
James Yates III, *President*
Steven Christopher Yates, *Vice Pres*
Faye Yates, *Admin Sec*
EMP: 6 **EST:** 1996
SALES (est): 693K **Privately Held**
SIC: 2411 Logging

Osseo
Hillsdale County

(G-12775)
JOHNS SMALL ENGINE AND OUTDOO
6560 Reading Rd E (49266-9052)
PHONE.................................517 523-1060
Jonnathan T Killman, *Administration*
EMP: 4 **EST:** 2016
SALES (est): 108.6K **Privately Held**
SIC: 3599 Machine shop, jobbing & repair

(G-12776)
R C PLASTICS INC
4790 Hudson Rd (49266-9626)
PHONE.................................517 523-2112
Lewis L Cox, *President*
Greg Cox, *Vice Pres*
Terry Reed, *Supervisor*
Sharon Cox, *Admin Sec*
Terry Cox, *Asst Sec*
◆ **EMP:** 16 **EST:** 1966
SQ FT: 24,000
SALES (est): 2.2MM **Privately Held**
WEB: www.rcplasticsinc.com
SIC: 3089 Injection molded finished plastic products; injection molding of plastics

(G-12777)
SPRINGDALE AUTOMATICS INC
7201 Hudson Rd (49266-9534)
PHONE.................................517 523-2424
Ronald Ball, *President*
Jennifer M Ball, *Corp Secy*
Andrew Ball, *Vice Pres*
Michael Ball, *Vice Pres*
EMP: 9 **EST:** 1997
SALES (est): 922.9K **Privately Held**
WEB: www.springdaleautomatics.com
SIC: 3451 Screw machine products

Ossineke
Alpena County

(G-12778)
OSSINEKE INDUSTRIES INC
10401 Piper Rd (49766-9653)
P.O. Box 82 (49766-0082)
PHONE.................................989 471-2197
Brad Lawton, *President*
Bradley L Lawton, *Exec VP*
Jeffery Lawton, *Vice Pres*
Richard Mc Leod, *Vice Pres*
Boyd E Moilanen, *Vice Pres*
◆ **EMP:** 14 **EST:** 1972
SQ FT: 25,000
SALES (est): 3.6MM
SALES (corp-wide): 204.2MM **Privately Held**
WEB: www.starcutter.com
SIC: 3541 Machine tools, metal cutting type
PA: Star Cutter Co.
23461 Industrial Park Dr
Farmington Hills MI 48335
248 474-8200

(G-12779)
PURE PRODUCTS INTERNATIONAL IN
11925 Us Highway 23 S (49766-9507)
PHONE.................................989 471-1104
Terry Derouin, *Owner*
EMP: 9 **EST:** 2010
SALES (est): 557.9K **Privately Held**
WEB: www.theedenpurestore.com
SIC: 2421 Building & structural materials, wood

(G-12780)
ULTRA TOOL GRIND INC
2616 Gehrke Rd (49766-9708)
PHONE.................................989 471-5169
Thomas F Kensa, *President*
EMP: 7 **EST:** 2002
SALES (est): 99.3K **Privately Held**
SIC: 3599 Grinding castings for the trade

Otisville
Genesee County

(G-12781)
HEAVEN SCENT CANDLE CO & DECOR
10067 N State Rd Unit B (48463-8425)
PHONE.................................810 374-6279
Mariea Clapper, *Principal*
EMP: 4 **EST:** 2018
SALES (est): 73.8K **Privately Held**
WEB: www.heavenscentcandlecoga.square.site
SIC: 3999 Candles

(G-12782)
LARSEN SERVICE INC
11018 Clar Eve Dr (48463-9434)
PHONE.................................810 374-6132
Shawn Larsen, *President*
Dawn Larsen, *Admin Sec*
EMP: 4 **EST:** 2000
SALES (est): 344K **Privately Held**
SIC: 3443 Retorts, industrial: smelting, etc.

(G-12783)
MASON TACKLE COMPANY
11273 Center St (48463-9707)
P.O. Box 56 (48463-0056)
PHONE.................................810 631-4571
Daniel Powell, *Ch of Bd*
Richard A Powell, *President*
Doris M Powell, *Corp Secy*
Jeffrey D Powell, *Vice Pres*
▲ **EMP:** 20 **EST:** 1939
SQ FT: 30,000
SALES (est): 2.2MM **Privately Held**
WEB: www.masontackle.com
SIC: 2298 3089 3949 3496 Fishing lines, nets, seines: made in cordage or twine mills; injection molded finished plastic products; sporting & athletic goods; miscellaneous fabricated wire products

Otsego
Allegan County

(G-12784)
COMMUNITY SHOPPERS GUIDE INC
117 N Farmer St (49078-1147)
P.O. Box 168 (49078-0168)
PHONE.................................269 694-9431
Ron Bennett, *President*
Marty Bennet, *Vice Pres*
Grant Bennett, *Vice Pres*
EMP: 8 **EST:** 1944
SQ FT: 2,500
SALES (est): 655.7K **Privately Held**
WEB: www.communityshoppersguide.net
SIC: 2711 Newspapers, publishing & printing

(G-12785)
ELECTRA-TEC INC
567 W M 89 Hwy (49078)
P.O. Box 17 (49078-0017)
PHONE.................................269 694-6652
Robert J Pawlowski, *President*
▲ **EMP:** 9 **EST:** 1979
SQ FT: 20,000
SALES (est): 1MM **Privately Held**
WEB: www.electratec.com
SIC: 5021 2522 Office furniture; office furniture, except wood

(G-12786)
GEORGE WASHBURN
Also Called: Washburn Woodwork & Cabinet
515 S Wilmott St (49078-1444)
PHONE.................................269 694-2930
George Washburn, *Owner*
EMP: 5 **EST:** 1981
SQ FT: 5,000
SALES (est): 218.4K **Privately Held**
SIC: 2434 2517 2431 Wood kitchen cabinets; wood television & radio cabinets; millwork

(G-12787)
GREEN SIGN MAN
311 S North St (49078-1361)
PHONE.................................269 370-0554
Kristen Basaran, *Principal*
EMP: 5 **EST:** 2008
SALES (est): 61.2K **Privately Held**
SIC: 3993 Signs & advertising specialties

(G-12788)
IMPERT INDUSTRIES INC
Also Called: Electro Tech
557 Lincoln Rd (49078-1080)
P.O. Box 17 (49078-0017)
PHONE.................................269 694-2727
Brian Hoeksema, *President*
EMP: 4 **EST:** 1976
SQ FT: 18,000
SALES (est): 300K **Privately Held**
SIC: 2542 3821 3443 Cabinets: show, display or storage: except wood; laboratory furniture; fabricated plate work (boiler shop)

(G-12789)
JIFFY PRINT
381 W Allegan St Ste C (49078-1089)
PHONE.................................269 692-3128
Jack Lawrence, *Owner*
EMP: 7 **EST:** 1982
SALES (est): 379.4K **Privately Held**
WEB: www.jiffyprintotsego.com
SIC: 2752 Commercial printing, offset

(G-12790)
MC PHERSON PLASTICS INC
1347 E M 89 89 M (49078)
P.O. Box 58 (49078-0058)
PHONE.................................269 694-9487
Timothy J Mc Pherson, *President*
Bernard C Mc Pherson Jr, *Vice Pres*
Hazel Mc Pherson, *Treasurer*
Melinda Kling, *Admin Sec*
EMP: 75 **EST:** 1960
SQ FT: 45,000
SALES (est): 11MM **Privately Held**
WEB: www.mcpherson-plastics.com
SIC: 3089 Injection molding of plastics

(G-12791)
MILL ASSIST SERVICES INC
141 N Farmer St (49078-1165)
PHONE.................................269 692-3211
Denis Gloede, *President*
Bill Land, *Human Res Mgr*
EMP: 26 **EST:** 1997
SQ FT: 20,300
SALES (est): 1.6MM **Privately Held**
WEB: www.millassist.com
SIC: 3547 Primary rolling mill equipment

(G-12792)
OTSEGO CRANE & HOIST LLC ✪
1677 116th Ave (49078-8720)
PHONE.................................269 672-7222
Aaron Wong,
EMP: 8 **EST:** 2021
SALES (est): 461.9K **Privately Held**
SIC: 3536 Cranes, overhead traveling

(G-12793)
OTSEGO PAPER INC
320 N Farmer St (49078-1150)
PHONE.................................269 692-6141
Al Coleman, *Engineer*
EMP: 61 **EST:** 2006
SALES (est): 14.9MM
SALES (corp-wide): 10.7B **Privately Held**
WEB: www.usg.com
SIC: 2621 Paper mills
HQ: Usg Corporation
550 W Adams St
Chicago IL 60661
312 436-4000

(G-12794)
PARKER & ASSOCIATES
338 W Franklin St (49078-1212)
P.O. Box 419 (49078-0419)
PHONE.................................269 694-6709
Charles Parker, *Owner*
▲ **EMP:** 4 **EST:** 1985
SALES (est): 187.9K **Privately Held**
SIC: 2741 Miscellaneous publishing

(G-12795)
PARKER-HANNIFIN CORPORATION
Fluid System Connectors Div
300 Parker Dr (49078-1431)
PHONE.................................269 694-9411
Anthony Vanlerberghe, *Division Mgr*
Robert Moore, *Plant Mgr*
Mike Dewitt, *Prdtn Mgr*
Angela Blaha, *Buyer*
Geoffrey Lindberg, *Engineer*
EMP: 287
SALES (corp-wide): 13.7B **Publicly Held**
WEB: www.parker.com
SIC: 3366 3494 3432 Bushings & bearings, brass (nonmachined); valves & pipe fittings; plumbing fixture fittings & trim
PA: Parker-Hannifin Corporation
6035 Parkland Blvd
Cleveland OH 44124
216 896-3000

(G-12796)
PARKER-HANNIFIN CORPORATION
Also Called: Hydraulic Pump Division
100 Parker Dr (49078-1400)
PHONE ✪.................................269 692-6254
Richard Dusa, *Principal*
Patrick Scott, *Manager*
Kevin Cooney, *Retailers*
EMP: 4
SALES (corp-wide): 13.7B **Publicly Held**
WEB: www.parker.com
SIC: 3594 Fluid power pumps & motors
PA: Parker-Hannifin Corporation
6035 Parkland Blvd
Cleveland OH 44124
216 896-3000

(G-12797)
PARKER-HANNIFIN CORPORATION
Also Called: Schrader Bellows
601 S Wilmott St (49078-1505)
PHONE.................................330 253-5239
Richard Surwicz, *General Mgr*
Geoff Hoare, *Analyst*
EMP: 4
SALES (corp-wide): 13.7B **Publicly Held**
WEB: www.parker.com
SIC: 3593 3492 3569 3053 Fluid power cylinders, hydraulic or pneumatic; control valves, fluid power: hydraulic & pneumatic; filter elements, fluid, hydraulic line; gaskets & sealing devices; aircraft & motor vehicle measurement equipment

PA: Parker-Hannifin Corporation
6035 Parkland Blvd
Cleveland OH 44124
216 896-3000

(G-12798)
PELOTON INC
124 E Allegan St (49078-1102)
P.O. Box 202 (49078-0202)
PHONE.................................269 694-9702
Nathan Hunt, *President*
Brian Ernst, *Project Mgr*
Shane Rickert, *Project Mgr*
Brett Vantilburg, *Info Tech Mgr*
Levi Hunt, *Technician*
EMP: 9 **EST:** 2003
SQ FT: 4,200
SALES (est): 1.6MM **Privately Held**
WEB: www.pelotoninc.com
SIC: 8711 3559 3544 Engineering services; paint making machinery; special dies, tools, jigs & fixtures

(G-12799)
SAFARI CIRCUITS INC (PA)
411 Washington St (49078-1241)
PHONE.................................269 694-9471
Lawrence R Cain, *CEO*
Michael L Kintz Jr, *President*
Eric Bearss, *Maint Spvr*
Debbie Woodstock, *Buyer*
Don Hendrick, *Engineer*
▲ **EMP:** 165 **EST:** 1996
SALES (est): 79.4MM **Privately Held**
WEB: www.safaricircuits.com
SIC: 3679 3661 3625 7812 Antennas, receiving; electronic circuits; fiber optics communications equipment; switches, electronic applications; control equipment, electric; video tape production; audio-visual program production

(G-12800)
TENGAM ENGINEERING INC
545 Washington St (49078-1243)
PHONE.................................269 694-9466
William R Mc Pherson, *President*
Bernard Mc Pherson Jr, *Vice Pres*
Mark M Pherson, *Plant Mgr*
Greg Johnson, *Opers Staff*
Mark Morey, *Purchasing*
▲ **EMP:** 30 **EST:** 1975
SQ FT: 21,000
SALES (est): 3.9MM **Privately Held**
WEB: www.tengam.com
SIC: 3499 3825 3264 Magnets, permanent; metallic; test equipment for electronic & electrical circuits; porcelain electrical supplies

(G-12801)
UNITED STATES GYPSUM COMPANY
Also Called: Otsego Paper
320 N Farmer St (49078-1150)
PHONE.................................269 384-6335
Henry Krell, *Plant Mgr*
Julie Bushee, *Human Res Mgr*
Todd Oldham, *Manager*
EMP: 70
SALES (corp-wide): 10.7B **Privately Held**
WEB: www.usg.com
SIC: 3275 Gypsum products
HQ: United States Gypsum Company
550 W Adams St Ste 1300
Chicago IL 60661
312 606-4000

(G-12802)
VANMEER CORPORATION
Also Called: E & B Machine Co
1754 106th Ave (49078-9763)
PHONE.................................269 694-6090
Douglas Vandermeulen, *President*
Douglas Vander Meulen, *President*
John Vander Meulen, *Vice Pres*
EMP: 10 **EST:** 1954
SQ FT: 14,000
SALES (est): 500.7K **Privately Held**
SIC: 3444 Sheet metal specialties, not stamped

Ottawa Lake
Monroe County

(G-12803)
ASSEMBLTECH INC
7076 Schnipke Dr (49267-9637)
PHONE.................................734 769-2800
Mike McClung, *CEO*
EMP: 50 **EST:** 2017
SALES (est): 2.5MM **Privately Held**
WEB: www.pinnacletec.com
SIC: 3672 Printed circuit boards

(G-12804)
BISCHOFF ENTERPRISES LLC
5732 St Anthony Rd (49267)
PHONE.................................734 856-8490
Scott Bischoff, *Manager*
EMP: 4 **EST:** 1994
SALES (est): 332.9K **Privately Held**
SIC: 3599 Machine shop, jobbing & repair

(G-12805)
CUSTOM INTERIORS OF TOLEDO
Also Called: Custombilt of Toledo
7979 Whiteford Rd (49267-8600)
PHONE.................................419 865-3090
Michael Thornton, *President*
Ted Weemes, *Manager*
EMP: 5 **EST:** 1954
SQ FT: 11,500
SALES (est): 225.6K **Privately Held**
SIC: 7641 2511 Furniture upholstery repair; wood household furniture

(G-12806)
F&B TECHNOLOGIES
Also Called: Erie Technologies
6875 Memorial Hwy (49267-5908)
PHONE.................................734 856-2118
Mark Bauman, *President*
Patrick Flynn, *Vice Pres*
Kristopher Hoag, *Project Mgr*
JD Korepta, *Engineer*
Philip Bauman, *Sales Staff*
EMP: 16
SQ FT: 2,000
SALES (est): 4.3MM **Privately Held**
WEB: www.erie-tech.com
SIC: 3449 7699 3536 Miscellaneous metalwork; industrial equipment services; hoists, cranes & monorails

(G-12807)
LINK MANUFACTURING INC
Also Called: Link Engineering Company
8000 Yankee Rd Ste 105 (49267-9571)
PHONE.................................734 387-1001
Joe Wells, *Branch Mgr*
EMP: 5 **Privately Held**
WEB: www.linkeng.com
SIC: 3829 Physical property testing equipment; testing equipment: abrasion, shearing strength, etc.
HQ: Link Manufacturing, Inc.
43855 Plymouth Oaks Blvd
Plymouth MI 48170
734 453-0800

(G-12808)
MIDWEST II INC
6194 Section Rd (49267-9526)
PHONE.................................734 856-5200
Olin White, *President*
EMP: 130 **EST:** 1960
SALES (est): 19.4MM **Privately Held**
WEB: www.midwestecoat.com
SIC: 3471 Electroplating of metals or formed products

(G-12809)
MIDWEST PRODUCTS FINSHG CO INC
6194 Section Rd (49267-9526)
PHONE.................................734 856-5200
Mike Alcala, *President*
Mark Pawlaczyk, *COO*
EMP: 77 **EST:** 1977
SQ FT: 150,000
SALES (est): 816.8K **Privately Held**
WEB: www.midwestecoat.com
SIC: 3479 Coating of metals & formed products

(G-12810)
PINNACLE TECHNOLOGY GROUP
7076 Schnipke Dr (49267-9637)
PHONE.................................734 568-6600
Richard Wasserman, *President*
Chris Sell, *Sales Staff*
Travis Romines, *Supervisor*
Scott Savage, *Admin Sec*
EMP: 60 **EST:** 1996
SQ FT: 6,500
SALES (est): 26.8MM **Privately Held**
WEB: www.pinnacletec.com
SIC: 3841 3561 Diagnostic apparatus, medical; physiotherapy equipment, electrical; hydrojet marine engine units

(G-12811)
PURE LIBERTY MANUFACTURING LLC
Also Called: Global Builder Supply
7075 Schnipke Dr (49267-9637)
P.O. Box 107 (49267-0107)
PHONE.................................734 224-0333
Tyler Decker,
▲ **EMP:** 6 **EST:** 2005
SALES (est): 985.2K **Privately Held**
WEB: www.purelibertymfg.us
SIC: 3431 Bathroom fixtures, including sinks

(G-12812)
YAKKERTECH LIMITED
Also Called: Eleetus
8000 Yankee Rd Ste 350 (49267-9580)
PHONE.................................734 568-6162
William Bales, *CEO*
Bill Bales, *Sales Executive*
EMP: 8 **EST:** 2015
SQ FT: 3,000
SALES (est): 614.6K **Privately Held**
WEB: www.eleetus.com
SIC: 3699 Flight simulators (training aids), electronic; automotive driving simulators (training aids), electronic

Ovid
Clinton County

(G-12813)
CLINTON MACHINE INC
1300 S Main St (48866-9724)
P.O. Box 617 (48866-0617)
PHONE.................................989 834-2235
Terry Loznak, *President*
George L Burkitt, *Corp Secy*
Tom Domagala, *Vice Pres*
Loren Hall, *Controller*
EMP: 50 **EST:** 1964
SQ FT: 50,000
SALES (est): 9.3MM **Privately Held**
WEB: www.clintonmachine.com
SIC: 3535 Conveyors & conveying equipment

(G-12814)
HOMETOWN PUBLISHING INC
Also Called: Meridian Weekly, The
200 S Main St (48866-9608)
P.O. Box 11 (48866-0011)
PHONE.................................989 834-2264
Deborah Price, *President*
EMP: 5 **EST:** 1991
SALES (est): 321.1K **Privately Held**
WEB: www.meridianweekly.com
SIC: 2711 Newspapers, publishing & printing

(G-12815)
MICHIGAN MILK PRODUCERS ASSN
431 W Williams St (48866-9697)
P.O. Box 47 (48866-0047)
PHONE.................................989 834-2221
Kris Wardin, *Vice Pres*
Dave Davis, *Plant Supt*
Brent Weller, *Production*
Jill Feldpausch, *QC Mgr*

Gasper Calandrino, *Engineer*
EMP: 85
SALES (corp-wide): 75.4MM **Privately Held**
WEB: www.mimilk.com
SIC: 2026 2023 2021 5143 Milk processing (pasteurizing, homogenizing, bottling); dry, condensed, evaporated dairy products; creamery butter; dairy products, except dried or canned
PA: Michigan Milk Producers Association
41310 Bridge St
Novi MI 48375
248 474-6672

(G-12816)
RESEARCH TOOL CORPORATION
1401 S Main St (48866-9720)
P.O. Box 76 (48866-0076)
PHONE.................................989 834-2246
Francis J Todosciuk, *President*
Harry Todosciuk, *Vice Pres*
Jeff Beebe, *Marketing Mgr*
Sandra Fongers, *Admin Sec*
EMP: 28 **EST:** 1959
SQ FT: 19,000
SALES (est): 4.2MM **Privately Held**
WEB: www.researchtoolcorp.com
SIC: 3544 Special dies & tools

(G-12817)
TWO TRACKS BOW CO
8317 Welter Rd (48866-9631)
PHONE.................................989 834-0588
Charles Deshler, *Owner*
EMP: 4 **EST:** 2013
SALES (est): 142.1K **Privately Held**
WEB: www.twotracksoutdoors.com
SIC: 3949 Sporting & athletic goods

Owosso
Shiawassee County

(G-12818)
201 E EXCHANGE
201 E Exchange St (48867-3009)
PHONE.................................989 725-6397
Thomas Campbell, *Owner*
EMP: 5 **EST:** 2016
SALES (est): 62.9K **Privately Held**
WEB: www.fendelmanlaw.com
SIC: 2711 Newspapers

(G-12819)
ADVANCED DRAINAGE SYSTEMS INC
770 S Chestnut St (48867-3314)
PHONE.................................989 723-5208
Rick Lamb, *Plant Mgr*
Dan Must, *Branch Mgr*
EMP: 5
SALES (corp-wide): 1.9B **Publicly Held**
WEB: www.adspipe.com
SIC: 3084 3523 3317 3083 Plastics pipe; farm machinery & equipment; steel pipe & tubes; laminated plastics plate & sheet
PA: Advanced Drainage Systems, Inc.
4640 Trueman Blvd
Hilliard OH 43026
614 658-0050

(G-12820)
AGNEW GRPHICS SIGNS PROMOTIONS
1905 W M 21 A (48867-9317)
PHONE.................................989 723-4621
Mark Agnew, *Owner*
Debi Agnew, *Manager*
EMP: 4 **EST:** 1985
SALES (est): 323.8K **Privately Held**
WEB: www.agnewgraphics.com
SIC: 3993 7336 Signs, not made in custom sign painting shops; commercial art & graphic design

(G-12821)
ALLIANCE HNI LLC
525 S Gould St (48867-3241)
PHONE.................................989 729-2804
Andrew Heyek, *President*
Greg Hedecore, *Vice Pres*
Debbie Athertin, *Manager*

GEOGRAPHIC SECTION
Owosso - Shiawassee County (G-12846)

EMP: 21 EST: 1997
SALES (est): 1MM Privately Held
WEB: www.alliance-hni.com
SIC: 3826 Magnetic resonance imaging apparatus

(G-12822)
ALLIED MOTION TECHNOLOGIES INC
201 S Delaney Rd (48867-9100)
P.O. Box 127 (48867-0127)
PHONE..................989 725-5151
Rob Pumford, President
Ken Laymen, Branch Mgr
EMP: 5
SALES (corp-wide): 366.6MM Publicly Held
WEB: www.alliedmotion.com
SIC: 3621 Motors, electric
PA: Allied Motion Technologies Inc.
  495 Commerce Dr Ste 3
  Amherst NY 14228
  716 242-8634

(G-12823)
AMERICAN SPEEDY PRINTING CTRS
111 S Washington St (48867-2921)
PHONE..................989 723-5196
John G Bennett, Owner
EMP: 4 EST: 1981
SALES (est): 200K Privately Held
WEB: www.americanspeedy.com
SIC: 2752 Commercial printing, offset

(G-12824)
ARGUS PRESS COMPANY
201 E Exchange St (48867-3094)
PHONE..................989 725-5136
Tom E Campbell, President
Richard E Campbell, Vice Pres
EMP: 28 EST: 1894
SQ FT: 10,000
SALES (est): 3.2MM Privately Held
WEB: www.argus-press.com
SIC: 2711 2791 2752 Newspapers: publishing only, not printed on site; typesetting; commercial printing, lithographic

(G-12825)
CARGILL INCORPORATED
1510 Hathaway St (48867-2107)
PHONE..................608 868-5150
Greg Hammond, Plant Mgr
Jillian Green, Consultant
EMP: 13
SALES (corp-wide): 113.4B Privately Held
WEB: www.cargill.com
SIC: 2075 2046 2048 2011 Soybean oil, cake or meal; corn oil, refined; corn oil, meal; gluten meal; high fructose corn syrup (HFCS); prepared feeds; meat packing plants; beef products from beef slaughtered on site; poultry slaughtering & processing; wheat
PA: Cargill, Incorporated
  15407 Mcginty Rd W
  Wayzata MN 55391
  952 742-7575

(G-12826)
CLARK ENGINEERING CO (PA)
1470 Mcmillan Rd (48867-9702)
P.O. Box 166 (48867-0166)
PHONE..................989 723-7930
Paul West, President
Daniel Craig, President
Scott Hewitt, CFO
EMP: 37 EST: 1947
SQ FT: 42,000
SALES (est): 5MM Privately Held
WEB: www.clarkengineering.net
SIC: 3496 Miscellaneous fabricated wire products

(G-12827)
CONSTINE INC
Also Called: Woods & Fields Community
2625 W M 21 (48867-8117)
PHONE..................989 723-6043
Mike Constine, President
Mark Constine, Vice Pres
Rodney Constine, Treasurer
EMP: 23 EST: 1960

SALES (est): 1.3MM Privately Held
WEB: www.owossohomes.net
SIC: 1521 4214 1011 General remodeling, single-family houses; local trucking with storage; underground iron ore mining; iron ore beneficiating

(G-12828)
CREST MARINE LLC
2710 S M 52 (48867-9203)
P.O. Box 190 (48867-0190)
PHONE..................989 725-5188
Scott Luebbert, Purchasing
Tracy McKinney, Engineer
Wendy Strauss, Human Resources
Dava Miller, Sales Staff
Patrick D May, Mng Member
EMP: 50 EST: 2010
SALES (est): 15.5MM
SALES (corp-wide): 525.8MM Publicly Held
WEB: www.crestpontoonboats.com
SIC: 3732 Pontoons, except aircraft & inflatable
PA: Mastercraft Boat Holdings, Inc.
  100 Cherokee Cove Dr
  Vonore TN 37885
  423 884-2221

(G-12829)
CSH INCORPORATED
2151 W M 21 Ste A (48867-8161)
PHONE..................989 723-8985
Dan Turnwall, President
EMP: 6 EST: 2011
SALES (est): 685.3K Privately Held
WEB: www.cshincorporated.com
SIC: 3699 Electrical equipment & supplies

(G-12830)
DANEKS GOODTIME ICE CO INC
210 N Gould St (48867-3238)
PHONE..................989 725-5920
Lora Danek, President
James Patrick Danek, Vice Pres
EMP: 7 EST: 1952
SQ FT: 2,220
SALES (est): 587.6K Privately Held
SIC: 2097 Manufactured ice

(G-12831)
DETROIT ABRASIVES COMPANY
1500 W Oliver St (48867-2138)
P.O. Box 504 (48867-0504)
PHONE..................989 725-2405
Darell Wallace, Manager
EMP: 7
SALES (corp-wide): 1.5MM Privately Held
SIC: 3291 Abrasive products
PA: Detroit Abrasives Company
  11910 Dexter Chelsea Rd
  Chelsea MI 48118
  734 475-1651

(G-12832)
EDWARDS SIGN & SCREEN PRINTING
1585 S M 52 (48867-8915)
P.O. Box 727 (48867-0727)
PHONE..................989 725-2988
Arlington C Edwards, Ch of Bd
Douglas Edwards, President
Sandra K Hall, Corp Secy
EMP: 8 EST: 1947
SQ FT: 4,000
SALES (est): 614.4K Privately Held
WEB: www.edwardssign.com
SIC: 7336 2759 5199 Art design services; screen printing; advertising specialties

(G-12833)
FISHER REDI MIX CONCRETE
599 Oakwood Ave (48867)
P.O. Box 916 (48867-0916)
PHONE..................989 723-1622
James Coldiron, Manager
EMP: 6 EST: 2001
SALES (est): 418.1K Privately Held
SIC: 3273 Ready-mixed concrete

(G-12834)
FUOSS GRAVEL COMPANY
Also Called: Fuoss Bros
777 Busha Rd (48867-8114)
PHONE..................989 725-2084

Michael L Fuoss, President
James Fuoss, Vice Pres
Ronald Fuoss, Treasurer
Jon Fuoss, Admin Sec
EMP: 10 EST: 1948
SQ FT: 3,200
SALES (est): 2MM Privately Held
WEB: www.fuossgravelcompany.com
SIC: 1442 Construction sand mining; gravel mining

(G-12835)
GEORGIA-PACIFIC LLC
465 S Delaney Rd (48867-9114)
P.O. Box 130 (48867-0130)
PHONE..................989 725-5191
John Keyes, Maint Spvr
William Smith, Sales & Mktg St
Joe Brigman, Supervisor
EMP: 5
SALES (est): 36.9B Privately Held
WEB: www.gp.com
SIC: 2653 3412 Boxes, corrugated: made from purchased materials; metal barrels, drums & pails
HQ: Georgia-Pacific Llc
  133 Peachtree St Nw
  Atlanta GA 30303
  404 652-4000

(G-12836)
HANKERDS SPORTSWEAR BASIC TS
116 W Exchange St (48867-2816)
PHONE..................989 725-2979
John Hankerd, Owner
EMP: 4 EST: 1995
SALES (est): 263.6K Privately Held
WEB: www.tshirt22.com
SIC: 2759 Screen printing

(G-12837)
HEARTH-N-HOME INC (PA)
Also Called: Heart-N-Home
6990 W M 21 (48867-9344)
P.O. Box 108, Perry (48872-0108)
PHONE..................517 625-5586
Randy L Whitbeck, President
EMP: 11 EST: 1991
SQ FT: 14,000
SALES (est): 787.6K Privately Held
SIC: 5719 3429 Fireplace equipment & accessories; fireplace equipment, hardware: andirons, grates, screens

(G-12838)
INDEPNDENT ADVSOR NWSPPR GROUP
Also Called: Shiawassee County Independent
1907 W M 21 (48867-9317)
PHONE..................989 723-1118
Michael Flores, President
EMP: 11 EST: 1984
SALES (est): 645.3K Privately Held
WEB: www.owossoindependent.com
SIC: 2711 Newspapers: publishing only, not printed on site

(G-12839)
MACHINE TOOL & GEAR INC
Also Called: Cie Newcor Mtg Owosso
401 S Chestnut St (48867-3307)
PHONE..................989 723-5486
EMP: 153
SALES (corp-wide): 146.6MM Privately Held
SIC: 3599 Machine shop, jobbing & repair
HQ: Machine Tool & Gear, Inc.
  1021 N Shiawassee St
  Corunna MI 48817
  989 743-3936

(G-12840)
MARRS DISCOUNT FURNITURE
1544 E M 21 (48867-9051)
PHONE..................989 720-5436
Richard L Marr, Owner
EMP: 5 EST: 1970
SQ FT: 14,000
SALES (est): 540.4K Privately Held
SIC: 5712 5722 5941 2515 Furniture stores; electric household appliances, major; specialty sport supplies; mattresses & foundations; mattresses, innerspring or box spring

(G-12841)
MAURELL PRODUCTS INC
Also Called: Crest Boats
2710 S M 52 (48867-9203)
P.O. Box 190 (48867-0190)
PHONE..................989 725-5188
Linda Tomczak, President
Patrick May, COO
Scott Luebbert, Purch Mgr
Wendy Strauss, Human Resources
Michael Patrick, Regl Sales Mgr
▲ EMP: 33 EST: 1952
SQ FT: 75,000
SALES (est): 5.4MM Privately Held
WEB: www.crestpontoonboats.com
SIC: 3732 Houseboats, building & repairing

(G-12842)
MCLAREN INC
Also Called: McLaren Plumbing Htg & Coolg
2170 W M 21 (48867-9312)
PHONE..................989 720-4328
Sam McLaren, President
Gregory C Marsh, General Mgr
Jonelle Kowalsky, Sales Staff
EMP: 5 EST: 1976
SQ FT: 22,000
SALES (est): 1.3MM Privately Held
WEB: www.mclarenphc.com
SIC: 1711 5074 5251 3492 Plumbing contractors; boiler maintenance contractor; warm air heating & air conditioning contractor; plumbing & hydronic heating supplies; hardware; control valves, fluid power: hydraulic & pneumatic

(G-12843)
MID-WEST WALTHAM ABRASIVES CO
Also Called: Mwa Company
510 S Washington St (48867-3545)
PHONE..................517 725-7161
Gopal Malkani, President
George L Mercer, Comp Spec
▼ EMP: 30 EST: 1929
SQ FT: 190,000
SALES (est): 2.6MM Privately Held
SIC: 3291 3541 Sandpaper; wheels, abrasive; hones; grinding machines, metalworking; buffing & polishing machines

(G-12844)
MIDWEST BUS CORPORATION (PA)
1940 W Stewart St (48867-4090)
P.O. Box 787 (48867-0787)
PHONE..................989 723-5241
Daniel D Morrill, President
Julie Velasco, Admin Sec
▲ EMP: 75 EST: 1980
SQ FT: 39,000
SALES (est): 11.2MM Privately Held
WEB: www.midwestbus.com
SIC: 7532 5013 3713 Top & body repair & paint shops; motor vehicle supplies & new parts; truck & bus bodies

(G-12845)
MOTOR PRODUCTS CORPORATION (HQ)
201 S Delaney Rd (48867-9100)
P.O. Box 127 (48867-0127)
PHONE..................989 725-5151
Fred Stanuszek, President
▲ EMP: 150 EST: 1972
SQ FT: 86,942
SALES (est): 20.9MM
SALES (corp-wide): 366.6MM Publicly Held
WEB: www.alliedmotion.com
SIC: 3621 Motors, electric
PA: Allied Motion Technologies Inc.
  495 Commerce Dr Ste 3
  Amherst NY 14228
  716 242-8634

(G-12846)
NATIONAL COMPOSITES LLC (PA)
401 S Delaney Rd (48867-9114)
PHONE..................989 723-8997
Adam Fenton, CEO
Paula Montayne, Human Resources
EMP: 43 EST: 2016

Owosso - Shiawassee County (G-12847)

SALES (est): 43.7MM Privately Held
WEB: www.nationalcomposites.com
SIC: 5551 3261 Marine supplies & equipment; bathroom accessories/fittings, vitreous china or earthenware

(G-12847)
OSTER MANUFACTURING COMPANY
1535 N Hickory Rd (48867-9492)
PHONE....................989 729-1160
EMP: 7 EST: 2017
SALES (est): 135.7K Privately Held
WEB: www.ostermfg.com
SIC: 3541 Machine tools, metal cutting type

(G-12848)
OWOSSO COUNTRY CLUB PRO SHOP
4200 N Chipman Rd (48867-9444)
P.O. Box 276 (48867-0276)
PHONE....................989 723-1470
Steve Wakulsky, *Owner*
EMP: 4 EST: 1971
SQ FT: 400
SALES (est): 578.1K Privately Held
WEB: www.owossocountryclub.com
SIC: 3949 5941 Sporting & athletic goods; golf goods & equipment

(G-12849)
OWOSSO GRAPHIC ARTS INC
151 N Delaney Rd (48867-1380)
P.O. Box 276 (48867-0276)
PHONE....................989 725-7112
Craig Ellenberg, *President*
Kathy Wilson, *Exec VP*
Jake Gadd, *Purch Mgr*
Joe Holden, *Technical Staff*
Tia Blue, *Graphic Designe*
▲ EMP: 35 EST: 1965
SQ FT: 45,500
SALES (est): 7.6MM Privately Held
WEB: www.owosso.com
SIC: 2796 3643 3544 2789 Photoengraving plates, linecuts or halftones; current-carrying wiring devices; special dies, tools, jigs & fixtures; bookbinding & related work

(G-12850)
OWOSSO READY MIX CO
441 Cleveland Ave (48867-1369)
P.O. Box 484 (48867-0484)
PHONE....................989 723-1295
L Robert Ardelean, *President*
Arlene Ardelean, *Corp Secy*
EMP: 8 EST: 1948
SQ FT: 16,000
SALES (est): 908.8K Privately Held
SIC: 3273 Ready-mixed concrete

(G-12851)
POLYMER PRODUCTS GROUP INC
3670 N M 52 (48867-1050)
P.O. Box 1084 (48867-6984)
PHONE....................989 723-9510
Daniel Clayton, *President*
Troy Clayton, *Vice Pres*
Vickie Clayton, *Treasurer*
Danielle Clayton, *Admin Sec*
EMP: 7 EST: 1994
SALES (est): 750K Privately Held
WEB: www.polymerproductsgroup.com
SIC: 3089 Injection molding of plastics

(G-12852)
RUESS WINCHESTER INC
Also Called: Rwi Manufacturing
705 Mcmillan Rd (48867-9776)
P.O. Box 847 (48867-0847)
PHONE....................989 725-5809
Bret Russ, *President*
John Pardell, *Vice Pres*
Jesse Mroz, *Agent*
EMP: 11 EST: 2003
SALES (est): 1.7MM Privately Held
WEB: www.rwimfg.com
SIC: 3441 Fabricated structural metal

(G-12853)
RUGGED LINER INC
200 Universal Dr (48867-3539)
PHONE....................989 725-8354
William Reminder, *President*
Kelly Kneifl, *COO*
Al Rogier, *Project Mgr*
Jim Bresingham, *CFO*
Brian Swett, *Controller*
◆ EMP: 25 EST: 1997
SALES (est): 8.2MM
SALES (corp-wide): 623.9MM Privately Held
WEB: www.ruggedliner.com
SIC: 3714 Motor vehicle parts & accessories
HQ: Tectum Holdings, Inc.
5400 Data Ct
Ann Arbor MI 48108
734 677-0444

(G-12854)
SA AUTOMOTIVE LTD LLC
751 S Delaney Rd (48867-9122)
PHONE....................989 723-0425
Mike Lewis, *Branch Mgr*
EMP: 4 Privately Held
WEB: www.saautomotive.com
SIC: 8611 3714 Manufacturers' institute; motor vehicle parts & accessories
PA: Sa Automotive, Ltd.
1307 Highview Dr
Webberville MI 48892

(G-12855)
SAKOR TECHNOLOGIES INC
1900 Krouse Rd (48867-9116)
PHONE....................989 720-2700
Randal Beattie, *President*
Brian Beattie, *COO*
Leonard Morris, *Engineer*
Lori Bartlett, *Office Mgr*
Jamie Horton, *Manager*
EMP: 11 EST: 1987
SQ FT: 12,700
SALES (est): 3.1MM Privately Held
WEB: www.sakor.com
SIC: 3577 Computer peripheral equipment

(G-12856)
SOBAKS PHARMACY INC (PA)
112 W Exchange St (48867-2816)
PHONE....................989 725-2785
EMP: 17
SQ FT: 11,000
SALES (est): 2MM Privately Held
SIC: 3845 5999 5947 Mfg Electromedical Equip Ret Misc Merchandise

(G-12857)
SONOCO PRTECTIVE SOLUTIONS INC
123 N Chipman St (48867-2028)
P.O. Box 627, Dekalb IL (60115-0627)
PHONE....................989 723-3720
Joe Bender, *Branch Mgr*
EMP: 5
SALES (corp-wide): 5.2B Publicly Held
WEB: www.sonoco.com
SIC: 3086 Packaging & shipping materials, foamed plastic
HQ: Sonoco Protective Solutions, Inc.
1 N 2nd St
Hartsville SC 29550
843 383-7000

(G-12858)
SPORTS RESORTS INTERNATIONAL
200 Universal Dr (48867-3539)
PHONE....................989 725-8354
Donald J Williamson, *CEO*
Gregory T Strzynski, *CFO*
EMP: 20 EST: 1993
SQ FT: 240,000
SALES (est): 630.8K Privately Held
SIC: 3714 7948 Pickup truck bed liners; race track operation

(G-12859)
SUPERIOR THREADING INC
Also Called: Oster Pipe Threaders
1535 N Hickory Rd (48867-9492)
P.O. Box 160 (48867-0160)
PHONE....................989 729-1160
Doug Kenyon, *Ch of Bd*
EMP: 14 EST: 1893
SQ FT: 10,000
SALES (est): 1.8MM Privately Held
WEB: www.ostermfg.com
SIC: 3552 Thread making machines, spinning machinery

(G-12860)
SVRC INDUSTRIES INC
Also Called: Shiawssee Rhbilitation Program
2009 Corunna Ave (48867-3952)
PHONE....................989 723-8205
Angela Gwizdala, *Controller*
Ruth Jandik, *Branch Mgr*
EMP: 147
SALES (corp-wide): 9.9MM Privately Held
WEB: www.svrcindustries.com
SIC: 8331 2671 Vocational rehabilitation agency; packaging paper & plastics film, coated & laminated
PA: Svrc Industries, Inc.
203 S Washington Ave
Saginaw MI 48607
989 280-3038

(G-12861)
TED SENK TOOLING INC
1117 E Henderson Rd (48867-9460)
PHONE....................989 725-6067
Larry Senk, *President*
Terri Senk, *Vice Pres*
EMP: 7 EST: 1982
SQ FT: 4,300
SALES (est): 750.8K Privately Held
WEB: www.senktooling.com
SIC: 3599 Machine shop, jobbing & repair

(G-12862)
TRAMM TECH INC
807 S Delaney Rd (48867-9122)
P.O. Box 848 (48867-0848)
PHONE....................989 723-2944
Thomas Walser, *President*
Ruth Ann Carlton, *Vice Pres*
EMP: 7 EST: 1991
SQ FT: 8,000
SALES (est): 500K Privately Held
WEB: www.trammtech.com
SIC: 3599 Machine shop, jobbing & repair

(G-12863)
TRANSIT BUS REBUILDERS INC
Also Called: Owosso Fabrication and Design
500 Smith Ave (48867-3639)
PHONE....................989 277-3645
Scott Sterling, *President*
EMP: 15 EST: 1997
SQ FT: 8,000
SALES (est): 212.9K Privately Held
SIC: 3713 Bus bodies (motor vehicles)

(G-12864)
TUSCARORA INC -VS
123 N Chipman St (48867-2028)
PHONE....................989 729-2780
Rob Cole, *Owner*
EMP: 9 EST: 2011
SALES (est): 320.4K Privately Held
SIC: 3083 Plastic finished products, laminated

(G-12865)
UNIVERSAL HDLG EQP OWOSSO LLC
Also Called: Universal Handling Eqpt
1650 Industrial Dr (48867-8979)
PHONE....................989 720-1650
Lance Hodges, *Mng Member*
EMP: 29 EST: 2014
SALES (est): 7.3MM Privately Held
WEB: www.universalhandling.com
SIC: 3312 Blast furnaces & steel mills

(G-12866)
VIRON INTERNATIONAL CORP (PA)
505 N Hintz Rd (48867-9603)
PHONE....................254 773-9292
Gary J Gregoricka, *President*
Larry M Gregoricka, *Vice Pres*
Terry S Gregoricka, *Vice Pres*
Gary Gregoricka, *Plant Mgr*
Tony Sovey, *Design Engr*
◆ EMP: 75 EST: 1971
SQ FT: 32,000
SALES (est): 17.8MM Privately Held
WEB: www.vironintl.com
SIC: 3564 Air purification equipment

(G-12867)
WILLIAMSTON PRODUCTS INC
615 N Delany Rd (48867)
PHONE....................989 723-0149
EMP: 100 Privately Held
SIC: 3089 Mfg Plastic Products
PA: Williamston Products, Inc.
845 Progress Ct
Williamston MI 48895

(G-12868)
WILLOUGHBY PRESS
1407 Corunna Ave (48867-3853)
P.O. Box 306 (48867-0306)
PHONE....................989 723-3360
Terry J Kemp, *Owner*
EMP: 4 EST: 1923
SQ FT: 1,800
SALES (est): 379.6K Privately Held
WEB: www.willoughbypress.net
SIC: 2752 Commercial printing, offset

(G-12869)
WOODARD—CM LLC
210 S Delaney Rd (48867-9100)
PHONE....................989 725-4265
Louis Zelenka, *Plant Mgr*
Steve Inhulsen, *Prdtn Mgr*
Brian March, *Production*
Reed Stauffer, *Engrg Dir*
Carol Gaskin, *Human Res Mgr*
EMP: 150
SALES (corp-wide): 90.7MM Privately Held
SIC: 2511 2521 2531 2599 Wood household furniture; wood office furniture; public building & related furniture; factory furniture & fixtures
HQ: Woodard—Cm, Llc
650 S Royal Ln Ste 100
Coppell TX 75019
972 393-3800

Oxford
Oakland County

(G-12870)
ACORN STAMPING INC
600 S Glaspie St (48371-5134)
PHONE....................248 628-5216
Bobby T Cox, *President*
Sandra K Cox, *Vice Pres*
Sandy Cox, *Vice Pres*
Jeremy R Cox, *Shareholder*
Terry K St John, *Shareholder*
▲ EMP: 18
SQ FT: 26,400
SALES (est): 4MM Privately Held
WEB: www.acornstamping.com
SIC: 3469 3443 5251 Stamping metal for the trade; heat exchangers: coolers (after, inter), condensers, etc.; door locks & lock sets

(G-12871)
ADVANCED AUTO TRENDS INC (PA)
2230 Metamora Rd (48371-2347)
PHONE....................248 628-6111
Sandra L Cornell, *President*
Richard Koshorek, *QC Mgr*
Rick Koshorek, *QC Mgr*
Patrick Dobson, *Engineer*
Sandra Cornell, *Plant Engr*
▲ EMP: 40 EST: 1980
SQ FT: 22,000
SALES (est): 16.7MM Privately Held
WEB: www.advancedautotrends.com
SIC: 3089 3465 3469 3714 Injection molded finished plastic products; automotive stampings; metal stampings; motor vehicle parts & accessories

(G-12872)
ADVANCED AUTO TRENDS INC
Also Called: Aati
3485 Metamora Rd (48371-1619)
PHONE....................248 628-4850
Charmain Bauerschmidt, *Vice Pres*

▲ = Import ▼ = Export
◆ = Import/Export

GEOGRAPHIC SECTION

Oxford - Oakland County (G-12899)

Jerri Parkins, *Safety Mgr*
Peter Reddish, *Production*
Jay Cornell, *Engineer*
Ron Wilson, *Branch Mgr*
EMP: 30
SALES (corp-wide): 16.7MM **Privately Held**
WEB: www.advancedautotrends.com
SIC: 3089 3465 3714 3544 Injection molded finished plastic products; automotive stampings; motor vehicle parts & accessories; special dies, tools, jigs & fixtures
PA: Advanced Auto Trends, Inc.
2230 Metamora Rd
Oxford MI 48371
248 628-6111

(G-12873)
AMERICAN AXLE OXFORD
2300 Xcelsior Dr Ste 230 (48371-2300)
PHONE 248 361-6044
Richard Taugh, *Owner*
Peter Mooney, *Purchasing*
Michael Kamen, *Engineer*
EMP: 7 **EST:** 2008
SALES (est): 516.9K **Privately Held**
SIC: 3714 Motor vehicle parts & accessories

(G-12874)
APERION INFORMATION TECH INC (PA)
144 S Washington St (48371-4975)
PHONE 248 969-9791
Mark Comins, *President*
Randy Fietsam, *Vice Pres*
Patricia Comins, *Treasurer*
Diane Giovannini, *Accounts Mgr*
Dana N Stefko, *Office Mgr*
EMP: 16 **EST:** 1998
SQ FT: 2,500
SALES (est): 3MM **Privately Held**
WEB: www.aperion.com
SIC: 7379 3572 Computer related consulting services; computer storage devices

(G-12875)
BARRON GROUP INC
215 Plexus Dr (48371-2367)
P.O. Box 138 (48371-0138)
PHONE 248 628-4300
Paul E Barron, *CEO*
Bruce Barron, *President*
Bill Larsen, *Controller*
EMP: 70 **EST:** 1984
SALES (est): 2.3MM **Privately Held**
WEB: www.barron-industries.com
SIC: 8741 3324 3599 3366 Administrative management; steel investment foundries; aerospace investment castings, ferrous; machine shop, jobbing & repair; castings (except die): bronze

(G-12876)
BARRON INDUSTRIES INC (PA)
Also Called: Barron Cast
215 Plexus Dr (48371-2367)
P.O. Box 138 (48371-0138)
PHONE 248 628-4300
Bruce Barron, *President*
Michelle Drolshagen, *Corp Secy*
Greg Barron, *Vice Pres*
Jeff Barron, *Vice Pres*
Terri Frankenstein, *Purch Mgr*
◆ **EMP:** 65 **EST:** 1967
SQ FT: 48,000
SALES (est): 24.1MM **Privately Held**
WEB: www.barron-industries.com
SIC: 3366 3369 3324 Castings (except die): bronze; nonferrous foundries; aerospace investment castings, ferrous

(G-12877)
BARRON INDUSTRIES INC
215 Plexus Dr (48371-2367)
P.O. Box 138 (48371-0138)
PHONE 248 628-4300
Bruce Barron, *Manager*
EMP: 10
SALES (corp-wide): 24.1MM **Privately Held**
WEB: www.barron-industries.com
SIC: 3324 Commercial investment castings, ferrous

PA: Barron Industries, Inc.
215 Plexus Dr
Oxford MI 48371
248 628-4300

(G-12878)
BBG NORTH AMERICA LTD PARTNR
2371 Xcelsior Dr (48371-2301)
PHONE 248 572-6550
Christian Fritz, *Principal*
EMP: 10 **EST:** 2014
SALES (est): 4MM **Privately Held**
SIC: 3312 Tool & die steel

(G-12879)
BEAVER STAIR COMPANY
549 E Lakeville Rd (48371-5147)
P.O. Box 555 (48371-0555)
PHONE 248 628-0441
Robert Carbone, *President*
EMP: 9
SQ FT: 5,500
SALES (est): 639.1K **Privately Held**
WEB: www.beaverstair.com
SIC: 2431 Staircases & stairs, wood; stair railings, wood

(G-12880)
CASEMER TOOL & MACHINE INC
2765 Metamora Rd (48371-2357)
PHONE 248 628-4807
Amy Reed, *President*
Robert E Trottier, *Vice Pres*
Jeanne M Trottier, *Treasurer*
Robert E Trottier Jr, *Admin Sec*
▼ **EMP:** 20 **EST:** 1979
SQ FT: 24,500
SALES (est): 4.9MM **Privately Held**
WEB: www.casemer.com
SIC: 3599 Machine shop, jobbing & repair

(G-12881)
CEDAR RIDGE CUSTOM WDWKG LLC
500 S Glaspie St Ste B (48371-5132)
PHONE 248 425-0185
EMP: 8 **EST:** 2016
SALES (est): 460.5K **Privately Held**
SIC: 2431 Millwork

(G-12882)
DELTA OPTICAL SUPPLY INC
496 Harwood Ct (48371-4428)
PHONE 248 628-3977
Kevin Saulter, *President*
Jeff Laskowsky, *General Mgr*
EMP: 4 **EST:** 1996
SALES (est): 359.2K **Privately Held**
WEB: www.deltaopticalsupply.com
SIC: 3851 7389 Ophthalmic goods;

(G-12883)
DRY COOLERS INC (PA)
575 S Glaspie St (48371-5133)
PHONE 248 969-3400
Brian Russell, *President*
Douglas Kowalski, *COO*
Matt Reed, *Engineer*
Michael Gorman, *Project Engr*
Brie Getsinger-Hylla, *Human Resources*
◆ **EMP:** 38 **EST:** 1985
SQ FT: 20,000
SALES (est): 9.5MM **Privately Held**
WEB: www.drycoolers.com
SIC: 3724 Cooling systems, aircraft engine

(G-12884)
GLAXOSMITHKLINE LLC
875 Island Lake Dr (48371-3721)
PHONE 989 928-6535
EMP: 4
SALES (corp-wide): 45.3B **Privately Held**
WEB: www.us.gsk.com
SIC: 2834 Pharmaceutical preparations
HQ: Glaxosmithkline Llc
5 Crescent Dr
Philadelphia PA 19112
215 751-4000

(G-12885)
GRAVEL CAPITAL BREWING LLC
14 N Washington St (48371-4699)
PHONE 248 895-8399
Theresa Wrobel, *Mng Member*
EMP: 10 **EST:** 2018
SALES (est): 677.6K **Privately Held**
WEB: www.gravcapbrewing.com
SIC: 2082 Beer (alcoholic beverage)

(G-12886)
HAMPTON BLOCK CO
Also Called: Hampton Block & Supply
465 Tanview Dr (48371-4770)
PHONE 248 628-1333
Eugene E Hampton, *President*
Robert E Hampton, *Vice Pres*
EMP: 4
SQ FT: 1,500
SALES (est): 265.6K **Privately Held**
SIC: 3271 Blocks, concrete or cinder: standard

(G-12887)
HOFF ENGINEERING CO INC (PA)
475 S Glaspie St (48371-5131)
PHONE 248 969-8272
Edward M Doyle, *President*
Dan Argue, *Vice Pres*
Mike Doyle, *Vice Pres*
Edward Doyle, *Manager*
EMP: 9 **EST:** 1958
SQ FT: 13,000
SALES (est): 5MM **Privately Held**
WEB: www.hoffengineering.com
SIC: 3569 3714 Filters, general line: industrial; filters: oil, fuel & air, motor vehicle

(G-12888)
ILLINOIS TOOL WORKS INC
2425 N Lapeer Rd (48371-2425)
PHONE 248 969-4248
EMP: 91
SALES (corp-wide): 14.3B **Publicly Held**
SIC: 3089 Mfg Plastic & Metal Components & Fasteners
PA: Illinois Tool Works Inc.
155 Harlem Ave
Glenview IL 60025
847 724-7500

(G-12889)
INDUSTRIAL MACHINE PDTS INC
Also Called: I M P
32 Louck St (48371-4637)
P.O. Box 186 (48371-0186)
PHONE 248 628-3621
Timothy S Twork, *President*
Robert Twork, *Vice Pres*
Deborah Lock, *Accountant*
EMP: 55 **EST:** 1974
SQ FT: 35,000
SALES (est): 7.8MM **Privately Held**
WEB: www.industrialmachineprod.com
SIC: 3469 Metal stampings

(G-12890)
INTEGRITY DESIGN & MFG LLC
3285 Metamora Rd Ste A (48371-1648)
PHONE 248 628-6927
EMP: 4
SQ FT: 4,000
SALES (est): 582K **Privately Held**
SIC: 3541 8711 Engineering Services Mfg Machine Tools-Cutting

(G-12891)
JLM WHLSALE S/VERETT DUKES INC
3095 Mullins Ct (48371-1643)
PHONE 800 522-2940
Dennis Ingamells, *Treasurer*
EMP: 15 **EST:** 2015
SALES (est): 101K **Privately Held**
WEB: www.jlmwholesale.com
SIC: 2431 Door frames, wood

(G-12892)
K & S AUTOMATION LLC
275 S Glaspie St (48371-5190)
PHONE 248 861-2123

Kevin McClellan,
EMP: 7 **EST:** 2020
SALES (est): 743.7K **Privately Held**
WEB: www.knsautomation.com
SIC: 3599 Industrial machinery

(G-12893)
KING STEEL FASTENERS INC
Also Called: King-Hughes Fasteners
1800 Metamora Rd (48371-2418)
P.O. Box 98, Imlay City (48444-0098)
PHONE 810 721-0300
John King, *President*
Jason Hoeft, *QC Mgr*
Mark Filberth, *Sales Mgr*
Sara Herrera, *Supervisor*
▲ **EMP:** 20 **EST:** 1995
SQ FT: 24,000
SALES (est): 3MM **Privately Held**
WEB: www.hogrings.com
SIC: 3496 Wire fasteners

(G-12894)
L & M WOODWORKING LLC
2062 Easy Ct (48370-2447)
PHONE 404 391-3868
EMP: 4 **EST:** 2018
SALES (est): 54.1K **Privately Held**
SIC: 2431 Millwork

(G-12895)
LAKE STATE CLEANING INC
154 East St (48371-4946)
PHONE 314 961-7939
EMP: 5 **EST:** 2018
SALES (est): 64.5K **Privately Held**
WEB: www.lakestatecleaning.com
SIC: 2393 Textile bags

(G-12896)
LIGHTNING TECHNOLOGIES INC (PA)
2171 Xcelsior Dr (48371-2363)
PHONE 248 572-6700
Jeffrey Owen, *CEO*
Lars Wrebo, *Chairman*
Roland Heiberger, *Vice Pres*
Cody Gehrig, *Opers Spvr*
Todd Vanbynen, *CFO*
EMP: 42 **EST:** 2013
SALES (est): 4.3MM **Privately Held**
SIC: 2448 Wood pallets & skids

(G-12897)
M ANTONIK
690 Golf Villa Dr (48371-3695)
PHONE 248 236-0333
Michael Antonik, *Principal*
EMP: 7 **EST:** 2007
SQ FT: 4,800
SALES (est): 364.7K **Privately Held**
WEB: www.m-antonik.com
SIC: 3829 Testing equipment: abrasion, shearing strength, etc.

(G-12898)
M D HUBBARD SPRING CO INC
595 S Lapeer Rd (48371-5035)
P.O. Box 425 (48371-0425)
PHONE 248 628-2528
Charles D Hubbard, *President*
N M Hubbard, *Vice Pres*
Todd Jacobs, *Vice Pres*
Victor Psotka, *Sales Mgr*
Craig Bryce, *Manager*
▼ **EMP:** 30 **EST:** 1905
SQ FT: 25,000
SALES (est): 5.4MM **Privately Held**
WEB: www.hubbardspring.com
SIC: 3496 3493 3495 3469 Miscellaneous fabricated wire products; coiled flat springs; wire springs; metal stampings

(G-12899)
MASTER MFG INC
3287 Metamora Rd (48371-1615)
P.O. Box 573 (48371-0573)
PHONE 248 628-9400
Renee Organek, *President*
Julie Ann Weedon, *Vice Pres*
Pradeep Saxena, *Broker*
EMP: 22 **EST:** 1982
SQ FT: 20,000

Oxford - Oakland County (G-12900)   GEOGRAPHIC SECTION

SALES (est): 2.8MM **Privately Held**
WEB: www.mastermfginc.net
SIC: **3599** 7694 3714 Machine shop, jobbing & repair; armature rewinding shops; motor vehicle parts & accessories

(G-12900)
MCDONALDS
655 N Lapeer Rd (48371-3616)
P.O. Box 464 (48371-0464)
PHONE..................................248 851-7310
EMP: 18 EST: 2019
SALES (est): 174.4K **Privately Held**
WEB: www.mcdonalds.com
SIC: **5813** 5812 5499 2038 Drinking places; eating places; miscellaneous food stores; frozen specialties

(G-12901)
MEDICAL LASER RESOURCES LLC
Also Called: Medical Laser Group
610 Gallagher Ct (48371-4191)
PHONE..................................248 628-8120
Alison Bouck,
▲ EMP: 4 EST: 2007
SALES (est): 306.4K **Privately Held**
WEB: www.medicallaserresources.com
SIC: **3841** Surgical lasers

(G-12902)
MIDWEST FORKLIFT PARTS LLC
456 Sunset Blvd (48371-5186)
PHONE..................................248 830-5982
Sebastian Harris, *Principal*
EMP: 4 EST: 2017
SALES (est): 165.4K **Privately Held**
WEB: www.midwestforkliftparts.com
SIC: **3537** Forklift trucks

(G-12903)
MIKE VAUGHN CUSTOM SPORTS INC
550 S Glaspie St (48371-5132)
PHONE..................................248 969-8956
Michael Vaughn, *President*
Arlene Vaughn, *Vice Pres*
Steve Fowler, *Prdtn Mgr*
▲ EMP: 44 EST: 1986
SQ FT: 29,000
SALES (est): 5.8MM **Privately Held**
SIC: **3949** Pads: football, basketball, soccer, lacrosse, etc.; gloves, sport & athletic: boxing, handball, etc.; protectors: baseball, basketball, hockey, etc.; hockey equipment & supplies, general

(G-12904)
MSP INDUSTRIES CORPORATION
Also Called: Oxford Manufacturing Facility
45 W Oakwood Rd (48371-1631)
PHONE..................................248 628-4150
Micheal North, *President*
Ronald Kramer, *Principal*
▲ EMP: 250 EST: 1999
SQ FT: 72,000
SALES (est): 94.2MM
SALES (corp-wide): 4.7B **Publicly Held**
WEB: www.aam.com
SIC: **3714** Motor vehicle parts & accessories
HQ: American Axle & Manufacturing, Inc.
1 Dauch Dr
Detroit MI 48211

(G-12905)
NIERESCHERS PRINT
411 Nuttal Br (48371-6367)
PHONE..................................248 736-4501
Andrew Nierescher, *Principal*
EMP: 4 EST: 2017
SALES (est): 92.3K **Privately Held**
SIC: **2752** Commercial printing, lithographic

(G-12906)
OXFORD BRANDS LLC
318 N Lapeer Rd Ste A (48371-3705)
PHONE..................................248 408-4020
Coleen Downs, *Sales Staff*
Leslie Thomas,
James Adams,
EMP: 5 EST: 2018
SALES (est): 271.2K **Privately Held**
WEB: www.oxfordbrandsllc.com
SIC: **2844** Toilet preparations

(G-12907)
OXFORD FORGE INC
2300 Xcelsior Dr (48371-2300)
PHONE..................................248 628-1303
Diane Simser, *Principal*
Bryon Stoneburg, *Technician*
EMP: 1 EST: 2007
SALES (est): 2MM
SALES (corp-wide): 4.7B **Publicly Held**
WEB: www.aam.com
SIC: **3714** Motor vehicle parts & accessories
HQ: American Axle & Manufacturing, Inc.
1 Dauch Dr
Detroit MI 48211

(G-12908)
PURITAN MAGNETICS INC
533 S Lapeer Rd Ste C (48371-6512)
PHONE..................................248 628-3808
Al Crawshaw, *President*
Elaine Cantu, *Corp Secy*
Jack Hagen, *Vice Pres*
EMP: 15 EST: 1994
SALES (est): 2.1MM **Privately Held**
WEB: www.puritanmagnetics.com
SIC: **3559** 5084 Separation equipment, magnetic; industrial machinery & equipment

(G-12909)
QUALITY CABLE ASSEMBLY LLC
465 S Glaspie St Ste A (48371-5175)
PHONE..................................248 236-9915
William Connors,
Randy Nettle,
EMP: 17 EST: 2003
SQ FT: 3,000
SALES (est): 2.1MM **Privately Held**
SIC: **3679** Harness assemblies for electronic use: wire or cable

(G-12910)
R L M INDUSTRIES INC
100 Hummer Lake Rd (48371-2304)
P.O. Box 505 (48371-0505)
PHONE..................................248 628-5103
Louis Verville, *President*
Stacy Garcia, *Vice Pres*
Tammy Halsey, *Vice Pres*
Tam Halsey, *Controller*
Rick Meachum, *VP Sales*
▲ EMP: 85
SQ FT: 45,000
SALES (est): 9.6MM **Privately Held**
WEB: www.rlmcastings.com
SIC: **3324** Steel investment foundries

(G-12911)
RAVEN ENGINEERING INC
725 S Glaspie St (48371-5137)
PHONE..................................248 969-9450
Robert Corbin, *President*
Brad Jeffrey, *General Mgr*
Tamie Bluthardt, *Purchasing*
Bruce Schafer, *Technical Mgr*
Jeff Hanft, *Sales Staff*
▲ EMP: 20 EST: 1997
SQ FT: 10,000
SALES (est): 4.7MM **Privately Held**
WEB: www.raven-engineering.com
SIC: **3541** Drilling & boring machines

(G-12912)
RELIABLE SALES CO
660 Lakes Edge Dr (48371-5229)
PHONE..................................248 969-0943
Robert L Moncrieff, *President*
Daniel Moncrieff, *Vice Pres*
EMP: 8 EST: 1975
SQ FT: 1,200
SALES (est): 700K **Privately Held**
SIC: **5084** 3542 Industrial machinery & equipment; rebuilt machine tools, metal forming types

(G-12913)
ROCHESTER WELDING COMPANY INC
2793 Metamora Rd (48371-2357)
P.O. Box 715, Lake Orion (48361-0715)
PHONE..................................248 628-0801
Thomas G Sears, *President*
Diane M Sears, *Corp Secy*
Roe Myung, *COO*
Stephanie Marracco, *Vice Pres*
EMP: 20 EST: 1976
SQ FT: 22,500
SALES (est): 4.5MM **Privately Held**
WEB: www.rochesterwelding.com
SIC: **3441** Fabricated structural metal

(G-12914)
ROYAL OAK INDUSTRIES INC
700 S Glaspie St (48371-5136)
PHONE..................................248 628-2830
Fax: 248 628-2929
EMP: 60
SALES (corp-wide): 197.6MM **Privately Held**
SIC: **3599** Trade Contractor
PA: Oak Royal Industries Inc
39533 Woodward Ave # 175
Bloomfield Hills MI 48304
248 340-9200

(G-12915)
SASHABAW BEAD CO
2730 S Sashabaw Rd (48371-5422)
PHONE..................................248 969-1353
Cynthia Phillips, *Principal*
EMP: 7
SALES (est): 430K **Privately Held**
SIC: **3999** Stringing beads

(G-12916)
SHERMAN PUBLICATIONS INC (PA)
Also Called: Oxford Leader
666 S Lapeer Rd (48371-5034)
P.O. Box 108 (48371-0108)
PHONE..................................248 628-4801
James A Sherman, *President*
Luan Offer, *Treasurer*
Susan Speed, *Admin Sec*
EMP: 50 EST: 1898
SQ FT: 9,000
SALES (est): 4.1MM **Privately Held**
WEB: www.oxfordleader.com
SIC: **2711** Newspapers: publishing only, not printed on site

(G-12917)
SKYWALKER DRONE SOLUTIONS LLC
335 Ridgemont Rd (48370-3043)
PHONE..................................248 342-6747
Robert Walker, *Principal*
EMP: 5 EST: 2016
SALES (est): 129.5K **Privately Held**
SIC: **3721** Motorized aircraft

(G-12918)
SPENCER TOOL
2800 Birch Grove Ct (48370-2248)
PHONE..................................877 956-6868
EMP: 5 EST: 2019
SALES (est): 493.2K **Privately Held**
WEB: www.spencertool.com
SIC: **3827** Optical instruments & lenses

(G-12919)
SPENCER TOOL
3100 Adventure Ln (48371-1637)
PHONE..................................248 628-3677
Jeff Britt, *Owner*
EMP: 11 EST: 1996
SALES (est): 671.6K **Privately Held**
WEB: www.spencertool.com
SIC: **3544** Special dies, tools, jigs & fixtures

(G-12920)
STANISCI DESIGN AND MFG INC
700 S Glaspie St (48371-5136)
PHONE..................................248 572-6880
William Stanisci, *Owner*
Theresa Stanisci, *Vice Pres*
Adam Moore, *Sales Staff*
EMP: 8 EST: 2000
SALES (est): 1.3MM **Privately Held**
WEB: www.wood-hood.com
SIC: **2434** Wood kitchen cabinets

(G-12921)
SUPERIOR ABRASIVE PRODUCTS
Also Called: Electro Diamond Tools
85 S Glaspie St Ste A (48371-5158)
PHONE..................................248 969-4090
Dennis Smornell, *President*
EMP: 11 EST: 2005
SALES (est): 641.8K **Privately Held**
SIC: **3291** Abrasive products

(G-12922)
TEC WELDING SALES INCORPORATED
Also Called: Tws
3202 Adventure Ln (48371-1638)
PHONE..................................248 969-7490
Douglas J Black, *President*
Jeffrey J Black, *Admin Sec*
Jeffrey Black, *Admin Sec*
EMP: 4 EST: 1980
SQ FT: 500
SALES (est): 517.9K **Privately Held**
WEB: www.tecwelding.com
SIC: **7692** Welding repair

(G-12923)
THERMO VAC INC
201 W Oakwood Rd (48371-1635)
PHONE..................................248 969-0300
Walter Peterman, *President*
Stephen Boergert, *General Mgr*
Greg Johnson, *General Mgr*
Dean Struebing, *Purch Mgr*
Kim Johnson, *Purch Agent*
EMP: 52 EST: 1984
SQ FT: 55,000
SALES (est): 15.2MM **Privately Held**
WEB: www.thermovac.com
SIC: **3564** 3532 Blowing fans: industrial or commercial; exhaust fans: industrial or commercial; air purification equipment; crushing, pulverizing & screening equipment

(G-12924)
TOOLTECH MACHINERY INC (PA)
625 S Glaspie St (48371-5135)
P.O. Box 543 (48371-0543)
PHONE..................................248 628-1813
Robert E Trottier, *President*
Steve Trottier, *Vice Pres*
Jeanne Trottier, *Treasurer*
Melanie Trottier, *Manager*
EMP: 8 EST: 1982
SQ FT: 5,000
SALES (est): 1.5MM **Privately Held**
WEB: www.tooltechgunsight.com
SIC: **3545** Tools & accessories for machine tools

(G-12925)
TRISON TOOL AND MACHINE INC
925 S Glaspie St (48371-5141)
PHONE..................................248 628-8770
Robert E Trottier, *President*
Theodore F Trottier, *Vice Pres*
Jeanne Trottier, *Treasurer*
Tamara Lyerla, *Admin Sec*
EMP: 9 EST: 1989
SQ FT: 6,250
SALES (est): 1.5MM **Privately Held**
WEB: www.trisontool.com
SIC: **3599** Machine shop, jobbing & repair

(G-12926)
TURN KEY AUTOMOTIVE LLC
Also Called: Turn Key/Redico
2171 Xcelsior Dr (48371-2363)
PHONE..................................248 628-5556
Lynn Rinke, *Mng Member*
EMP: 14 EST: 2007
SALES (est): 839.8K **Privately Held**
WEB: www.copopartsdirect.com
SIC: **3711** 8711 Automobile assembly, including specialty automobiles; engineering services

GEOGRAPHIC SECTION

(G-12927)
TURN KEY HARNESS & WIRE LLC
2171 Xcelsior Dr (48371-2363)
PHONE.................................248 236-9915
EMP: 20 EST: 2016
SALES (est): 2.2MM Privately Held
WEB: www.tkharness-wire.com
SIC: 3355 3679 Aluminum wire & cable; harness assemblies for electronic use: wire or cable

(G-12928)
ULTRA FAB & MACHINE INC
465 S Glaspie St Ste D (48371-5175)
P.O. Box 747 (48371-0747)
PHONE.................................248 628-7065
Matt Blades, *President*
Amy Reed, *Project Engr*
EMP: 4 EST: 1999
SALES (est): 417.1K Privately Held
WEB: www.ultrafabmachine.com
SIC: 3599 Machine shop, jobbing & repair

(G-12929)
WILDFIRE SIGNS & GRAPHICS
1359 Somerville Dr (48371-5952)
PHONE.................................248 872-1998
Mike Graft, *Owner*
EMP: 4 EST: 2014
SALES (est): 147.9K Privately Held
WEB: www.wildfiregraphics.com
SIC: 3993 Signs & advertising specialties

Palmer
Marquette County

(G-12930)
EMPIRE IRON MINING PARTNERSHIP
Empire Mine Rd (49871)
P.O. Box 38 (49871-0038)
PHONE.................................906 475-3600
David B Blake, *Branch Mgr*
EMP: 627
SALES (corp-wide): 47.3MM Privately Held
SIC: 1011 Iron ores
PA: Empire Iron Mining Partnership
  1100 Superior Ave E Fl 15
  Cleveland OH 44114
  216 694-5700

Paradise
Chippewa County

(G-12931)
ENVIRO INDUSTRIES INC
11874 N Whitefish Pt Rd (49768-9604)
PHONE.................................906 492-3402
Brent Biehl, *President*
EMP: 8 EST: 1991
SQ FT: 25,000
SALES (est): 854.9K Privately Held
SIC: 2499 Mulch or sawdust products, wood

Paris
Mecosta County

(G-12932)
CREATIVE LOOP
21241 Northland Dr (49338-9476)
PHONE.................................231 629-8228
Leif Duddles, *Principal*
EMP: 4 EST: 2012
SALES (est): 293.5K Privately Held
SIC: 2395 Embroidery products, except schiffli machine

(G-12933)
DOYLE FOREST PRODUCTS INC
21364 Meceola Rd (49338-9509)
PHONE.................................231 832-5586
Joseph D Doyle, *President*
EMP: 15 EST: 2009
SALES (est): 1.1MM Privately Held
WEB: www.doyleforestproducts.com
SIC: 2411 Logging

(G-12934)
HOPE NETWORK WEST MICHIGAN
21685 Northland Dr (49338-9794)
P.O. Box 66 (49338-0066)
PHONE.................................231 796-4801
Jill Moerland, *Branch Mgr*
EMP: 20
SALES (corp-wide): 13.1MM Privately Held
WEB: www.hopenetwork.org
SIC: 3469 3714 3479 0182 Metal stampings; motor vehicle parts & accessories; enameling, including porcelain, of metal products; hydroponic crops grown under cover
HQ: Hope Network West Michigan
  795 36th St Se
  Grand Rapids MI 49548
  616 248-5900

(G-12935)
JOHNSON SIGN MINT CNSLTING LLC
5555 E 13 Mile Rd (49338-9629)
PHONE.................................231 796-8880
Loni J Johnson,
EMP: 8 EST: 2006
SALES (est): 381.8K Privately Held
SIC: 3993 Signs & advertising specialties

Parma
Jackson County

(G-12936)
BP GAS/ JB FUEL
107 W Main St (49269-8904)
PHONE.................................517 531-3400
EMP: 4 EST: 2009
SALES (est): 338.5K Privately Held
SIC: 2869 Mfg Industrial Organic Chemicals

(G-12937)
CAMERONS OF JACKSON LLC
Also Called: Fuel of Parma
107 W Main St (49269-8904)
PHONE.................................517 531-3400
Debbie Burnham, *Principal*
EMP: 5 EST: 2010
SALES (est): 259.3K Privately Held
SIC: 2869 Fuels

(G-12938)
MICHIGAN AUTO COMPRSR INC (HQ)
Also Called: Maci
2400 N Dearing Rd (49269-9415)
PHONE.................................517 796-3200
Yuji Ishizaki, *President*
Stephen Sauter, *General Mgr*
Steve Sauter, *General Mgr*
Yoichi Kizukuri, *Vice Pres*
Scott Otsubo, *Vice Pres*
◆ EMP: 575 EST: 1989
SQ FT: 457,000
SALES (est): 110MM Privately Held
WEB: www.michauto.com
SIC: 3585 3714 3568 3563 Air conditioning, motor vehicle; motor vehicle parts & accessories; power transmission equipment; air & gas compressors

(G-12939)
SPRAY FOAM FABRICATION LLC
3627 Pickett Rd (49269-9611)
PHONE.................................517 745-7885
Ryan McCormick,
EMP: 6 EST: 2012
SALES (est): 649K Privately Held
SIC: 3563 Spraying & dusting equipment

(G-12940)
TRIPLE E LLC
8535 E Michigan Ave (49269-9785)
PHONE.................................517 531-4481
William Dobbins,
EMP: 17 EST: 1971
SQ FT: 10,000
SALES (est): 306.9K Privately Held
WEB: www.tripleellc.com
SIC: 3599 Machine shop, jobbing & repair

Paw Paw
Van Buren County

(G-12941)
BEHRENS CUSTOM CABINETRY LLC
200 S Gremps St (49079-1510)
PHONE.................................269 720-4950
Keith M Behrens, *Principal*
EMP: 6 EST: 2011
SALES (est): 100.5K Privately Held
WEB: www.behrenscabinetry.com
SIC: 2434 2521 2541 Wood kitchen cabinets; wood office filing cabinets & bookcases; cabinets, except refrigerated: show, display, etc.: wood

(G-12942)
BELLE FEEDS
34026 M 40 (49079)
PHONE.................................269 628-1231
Steve Stassek, *Partner*
EMP: 4 EST: 1999
SALES (est): 234.4K Privately Held
SIC: 2048 Prepared feeds

(G-12943)
COCA-COLA COMPANY
38279 W Red Arrow Hwy (49079-9384)
P.O. Box 229 (49079-0229)
PHONE.................................269 657-3171
Dirk Lunsford, *Manager*
Kevin Mills, *Consultant*
Kyle Maris, *Technology*
Steve Presser, *Maintence Staff*
EMP: 6
SALES (corp-wide): 33B Publicly Held
WEB: www.coca-colacompany.com
SIC: 2086 Bottled & canned soft drinks
PA: The Coca-Cola Company
  1 Coca Cola Plz Nw
  Atlanta GA 30313
  404 676-2121

(G-12944)
COCA-COLA REFRESHMENTS USA INC
38279 W Red Arrow Hwy (49079-9384)
PHONE.................................269 657-8538
Carol Jackson, *Branch Mgr*
Dana Smallidge, *Manager*
EMP: 6
SALES (corp-wide): 33B Publicly Held
WEB: www.coca-cola.com
SIC: 2086 Bottled & canned soft drinks
HQ: Coca-Cola Refreshments Usa, Inc.
  2500 Windy Ridge Pkwy Se
  Atlanta GA 30339
  770 989-3000

(G-12945)
DAS TECHNOLOGIES INC
138 Ampey Rd (49079-1815)
P.O. Box 186 (49079-0186)
PHONE.................................269 657-0541
Clifton Runkle, *President*
EMP: 6 EST: 2001
SALES (est): 1MM Privately Held
WEB: www.dastechnologies.net
SIC: 3599 Machine shop, jobbing & repair

(G-12946)
DFORTE INC
57440 County Road 671 (49079-9726)
PHONE.................................269 657-6996
Amelio Dacoba, *President*
EMP: 10 EST: 1984
SQ FT: 5,000
SALES (est): 612.9K Privately Held
WEB: www.dforte.en.ecplaza.net
SIC: 2038 3841 2099 2035 Frozen specialties; surgical & medical instruments; food preparations; dressings, salad: raw & cooked (except dry mixes)

(G-12947)
DIE CAST PRESS MFG CO INC (PA)
56480 Kasper Dr (49079-1197)
PHONE.................................269 657-6060
Kasper Smidt III, *President*
Connie Smidt, *Purchasing*
Janine Byler, *Accountant*
Mari Lynn Orosz, *Accountant*
Ken Smith, *Sales Mgr*
EMP: 28 EST: 1977
SQ FT: 12,000
SALES (est): 6.3MM Privately Held
WEB: www.diecastpress.com
SIC: 3542 3452 5084 3429 Die casting machines; presses: hydraulic & pneumatic, mechanical & manual; bolts, nuts, rivets & washers; machine tools & metalworking machinery; manufactured hardware (general); blast furnaces & steel mills

(G-12948)
GLCC CO
39149 W Red Arrow Hwy (49079-9389)
P.O. Box 329 (49079-0329)
PHONE.................................269 657-3167
Jonathan Davis, *President*
Tom Manion, *Sales Mgr*
Samantha Alderman, *Sales Staff*
Thomas Manion, *Sales Staff*
▼ EMP: 20 EST: 1996
SQ FT: 35,000
SALES (est): 3.4MM Privately Held
WEB: www.glccflavors.com
SIC: 2087 Concentrates, drink

(G-12949)
HARLOFF MANUFACTURING CO LLC
828 Duo Tang Rd Unit A (49079-1811)
PHONE.................................269 655-1097
Jason Harloff, *Mng Member*
EMP: 24 EST: 2013
SALES (est): 2.7MM Privately Held
WEB: www.hmcmj.com
SIC: 3599 Machine shop, jobbing & repair

(G-12950)
KNOUSE FOODS COOPERATIVE INC
815 S Kalamazoo St (49079-9230)
PHONE.................................269 657-5524
Merri Beebe, *Purch Agent*
Frederick Jeffers, *Manager*
Bob Woods, *Manager*
Ron Hensley, *Maintence Staff*
Sherry Warrick, *Clerk*
EMP: 111
SQ FT: 111,000
SALES (corp-wide): 281.7MM Privately Held
WEB: www.knouse.com
SIC: 2033 2099 2035 Fruit juices: fresh; apple sauce: packaged in cans, jars, etc.; food preparations; pickles, sauces & salad dressings
PA: Knouse Foods Cooperative, Inc.
  800 Pach Glen Idaville Rd
  Peach Glen PA 17375
  717 677-8181

(G-12951)
LUCKY GIRL BRWING - CROSS RADS
34016 M 43 (49079-8464)
PHONE.................................630 723-4285
Jeffrey Wescott, *Principal*
EMP: 9 EST: 2016
SALES (est): 820.5K Privately Held
SIC: 2082 Malt beverages

(G-12952)
MANNING ENTERPRISES INC
45872 30th St (49079-8004)
PHONE.................................269 657-2346
Steve Manning, *President*
Sheri Manning, *Controller*
EMP: 25 EST: 1993
SQ FT: 10,000
SALES (est): 4.9MM Privately Held
WEB: www.manningmetal.com
SIC: 3444 7692 Sheet metalwork; welding repair

Paw Paw - Van Buren County (G-12953)

(G-12953)
MINUTE MAID CO
38279 W Red Arrow Hwy (49079-9384)
PHONE..................................269 657-3171
Candi Ewert, *Principal*
EMP: 7 **EST:** 2016
SALES (est): 481.5K **Privately Held**
SIC: 2086 Bottled & canned soft drinks

(G-12954)
PAW PAW EVERLAST LABEL COMPANY
37837 Peters Dr (49079-8762)
P.O. Box 93 (49079-0093)
PHONE..................................269 657-4921
Steven Starbuck, *President*
EMP: 10 **EST:** 1963
SALES (est): 1MM **Privately Held**
WEB: www.everlastlabel.com
SIC: 3469 Metal stampings

(G-12955)
PAW PAW FUEL STOP
60902 M 51 (49079-9769)
PHONE..................................269 657-7357
Cheryl Muirhead, *Manager*
EMP: 8 **EST:** 2009
SALES (est): 551.3K **Privately Held**
SIC: 2869 Fuels

(G-12956)
SPORTING IMAGE INC
Also Called: Looksharp Marketing
37174 W Red Arrow Hwy (49079-9311)
P.O. Box 24 (49079-0024)
PHONE..................................269 657-5646
John Tapper III, *President*
Kerry Tapper, *Principal*
Linda Tapper, *Vice Pres*
EMP: 18 **EST:** 1984
SQ FT: 15,000
SALES (est): 1.5MM **Privately Held**
WEB: www.looksharponline.com
SIC: 2396 2395 3993 Screen printing on fabric articles; embroidery products, except schiffli machine; signs, not made in custom sign painting shops

(G-12957)
ST JULIAN WINE COMPANY INC (PA)
716 S Kalamazoo St (49079-1558)
P.O. Box 127 (49079-0127)
PHONE..................................269 657-5568
David Braganini, *President*
David R Braganini, *President*
Phyllis Braganini, *Corp Secy*
David Miller, *Vice Pres*
William Zuiderveen, *Vice Pres*
EMP: 35
SQ FT: 104,000
SALES (est): 13.2MM **Privately Held**
WEB: www.stjulian.com
SIC: 2033 2084 Fruit juices: packaged in cans, jars, etc.; wines

(G-12958)
US SALON SUPPLY LLC
760 S Kalamazoo St (49079-1558)
PHONE..................................616 365-5790
Stan Woodward, *Principal*
▲ **EMP:** 12 **EST:** 2012
SQ FT: 31,500
SALES (est): 1.3MM **Privately Held**
WEB: www.ussalonsupply.com
SIC: 3999 5087 5112 5961 Barber & beauty shop equipment; beauty salon & barber shop equipment & supplies; stationery & office supplies; office supplies; cosmetics & perfumes, mail order

(G-12959)
VINEYARD PRESS INC
Also Called: Paw Paw Flashes
125 E Michigan Ave (49079-1429)
P.O. Box 189, Allegan (49010-0189)
PHONE..................................269 657-5080
Steven Racette, *President*
EMP: 17 **EST:** 1957
SALES (est): 1.5MM **Privately Held**
WEB: www.wilcoxnewspapers.com
SIC: 2741 Shopping news: publishing only, not printed on site; newspapers: publishing only, not printed on site

Peck
Sanilac County

(G-12960)
AMETEK INC
Also Called: Dynotech Driveshafts
6380 Brockway Rd (48466-9506)
PHONE..................................248 362-2777
EMP: 5
SALES (corp-wide): 4.5B **Publicly Held**
WEB: www.ametek.com
SIC: 3823 Industrial instrmnts msrmnt display/control process variable
PA: Ametek, Inc.
1100 Cassatt Rd
Berwyn PA 19312
610 647-2121

(G-12961)
AMETEK INC
Also Called: Ametek Automtn & Process Tech
6380 Brockway Rd (48466-9506)
PHONE..................................248 435-7540
EMP: 5
SALES (corp-wide): 4.5B **Publicly Held**
WEB: www.ametek.com
SIC: 3621 Motors & generators
PA: Ametek, Inc.
1100 Cassatt Rd
Berwyn PA 19312
610 647-2121

(G-12962)
PATRIOT SENSORS & CONTRLS CORP
Also Called: Ametek Patriot Sensors
6380 Brockway Rd (48466-9506)
PHONE..................................810 378-5511
Mark Overstreet, *Branch Mgr*
EMP: 11
SQ FT: 30,000
SALES (corp-wide): 4.5B **Publicly Held**
SIC: 3625 3823 3643 3613 Electric controls & control accessories, industrial; switches, electronic applications; brakes, electromagnetic; controllers for process variables, all types; current-carrying wiring devices; switchgear & switchboard apparatus
HQ: Patriot Sensors & Controls Corporation
6380 Brockway Rd
Peck MI 48466

(G-12963)
PATRIOT SENSORS & CONTRLS CORP (HQ)
Also Called: Ametek-APT
6380 Brockway Rd (48466-9506)
PHONE..................................248 435-0700
Bob Soeder, *Vice Pres*
Jeffrey Bitzner, *Engineer*
Heidemarie Lelowicz, *Train & Dev Mgr*
◆ **EMP:** 95 **EST:** 1987
SALES (est): 45.3MM
SALES (corp-wide): 4.5B **Publicly Held**
WEB: www.ametek.com
SIC: 3823 3829 3643 3621 Controllers for process variables, all types; accelerometers; pressure transducers; current-carrying wiring devices; motors & generators; switchgear & switchboard apparatus; switches, electronic applications
PA: Ametek, Inc.
1100 Cassatt Rd
Berwyn PA 19312
610 647-2121

Pelkie
Houghton County

(G-12964)
KOSTAMO LOGGING
10408 Kostamo Rd (49958-9650)
PHONE..................................906 353-6171
Calvin Kostamo, *Principal*
EMP: 5 **EST:** 2010
SALES (est): 133K **Privately Held**
SIC: 2411 Logging camps & contractors

(G-12965)
TOM CLISCH LOGGING INC
Hwy 134700 (49958)
PHONE..................................906 338-2900
Tom Clisch, *Owner*
EMP: 7 **EST:** 2005
SALES (est): 336.1K **Privately Held**
SIC: 2411 Logging camps & contractors

(G-12966)
TURPEINEN BROS INC
12920 State Highway M38 (49958-9271)
PHONE..................................906 338-2870
Peter R Turpeinen, *President*
EMP: 9 **EST:** 1966
SALES (est): 503.4K **Privately Held**
WEB: www.turpeinen.com
SIC: 2411 Wood chips, produced in the field

Pellston
Emmet County

(G-12967)
DONALD LLL SONS LOGGING
260 Townline Rd (49769-9024)
PHONE..................................231 420-3800
Harvey L Sidell, *Principal*
EMP: 5 **EST:** 2010
SALES (est): 180.5K **Privately Held**
SIC: 2411 Logging

(G-12968)
VTE INC
Also Called: Stella-Maris
5437 Robinson Rd (49769-9398)
P.O. Box 790 (49769-0790)
PHONE..................................231 539-8000
Willem Roelof Van Tielen, *President*
Brian R Hart, *Senior VP*
Mike Ennik, *Vice Pres*
Collin Hart, *Purch Mgr*
Denise Chanda, *Manager*
▲ **EMP:** 27 **EST:** 1982
SQ FT: 37,000
SALES (est): 4.5MM **Privately Held**
WEB: www.vte-europe.com
SIC: 3069 3694 Molded rubber products; battery cable wiring sets for internal combustion engines; automotive electrical equipment

(G-12969)
ZULSKI LUMBER INC
2465 Zulski Rd (49769-9320)
PHONE..................................231 539-8909
Frank Zulski, *President*
Mary Zulski, *Corp Secy*
EMP: 7
SALES (est): 496.3K **Privately Held**
SIC: 2421 Custom sawmill

Pentwater
Oceana County

(G-12970)
AUTHORS COALITION AMERICA LLC
438 6th St (49449-8905)
P.O. Box 929 (49449-0929)
PHONE..................................231 869-2011
Dorien Kelly, *Principal*
EMP: 4 **EST:** 2014
SALES (est): 234.5K **Privately Held**
WEB: www.authorscoalition.org
SIC: 2741 Miscellaneous publishing

(G-12971)
CASE QUALITY UPKEEP LLC
3237 Jefferson Rd (49449-8546)
PHONE..................................231 233-8013
Logan Case, *Principal*
EMP: 5 **EST:** 2017
SALES (est): 219.7K **Privately Held**
SIC: 3523 Farm machinery & equipment

(G-12972)
GRATEFULTHREADEMBROIDER
661 N Wythe St (49449-8564)
PHONE..................................231 855-1340
EMP: 4 **EST:** 2016
SALES (est): 77.1K **Privately Held**
WEB: www.gratefulembroidery.com
SIC: 2395 Embroidery & art needlework

(G-12973)
RANCH PRODUCTION LLC
3908 W Hogan Rd (49449-9451)
PHONE..................................231 869-2050
Lynette Adams, *President*
Jennifer Adams, *Admin Sec*
EMP: 13 **EST:** 1993
SALES (est): 1.2MM **Privately Held**
SIC: 1382 Oil & gas exploration services

(G-12974)
RIVERBEND WOODWORING
1293 W Adams Rd (49449-9473)
PHONE..................................231 869-4965
Karen Williams, *Owner*
EMP: 6 **EST:** 2007
SALES (est): 256.4K **Privately Held**
SIC: 2491 Wood preserving

(G-12975)
WINDY LAKE LLC
Also Called: P W P
474 S Carroll St (49449-8772)
P.O. Box 947 (49449-0947)
PHONE..................................877 869-6911
Lawrence Svabek,
Rick Svabek,
EMP: 100 **EST:** 2011
SQ FT: 75,000
SALES (est): 10.7MM
SALES (corp-wide): 59MM **Privately Held**
SIC: 3496 3993 3537 Shelving, made from purchased wire; signs & advertising specialties; industrial trucks & tractors
PA: Archer Wire International Corp.
7300 S Narragansett Ave
Bedford Park IL 60638
708 563-1700

Perrinton
Gratiot County

(G-12976)
SHOOKS ASPHALT PAVING CO INC (PA)
3588 W Cleveland Rd (48871-9686)
PHONE..................................989 236-7740
Gary C Shook Jr, *President*
Debra Shook, *Vice Pres*
EMP: 6 **EST:** 1966
SALES (est): 1.2MM **Privately Held**
SIC: 1611 2951 Highway & street paving contractor; asphalt paving mixtures & blocks

Perry
Shiawassee County

(G-12977)
FOUNDATIONS PRESS INC
308 N Madison St (48872-8177)
PHONE..................................517 625-3052
Anne Elliott, *Principal*
EMP: 7 **EST:** 2017
SALES (est): 37.5K **Privately Held**
WEB: www.foundationspress.com
SIC: 2741 Miscellaneous publishing

(G-12978)
LIONS PRIDE PRESSURE WSHG LLC
140 W Willow St (48872-8137)
PHONE..................................989 251-5577
Christopher Hoort,
EMP: 4 **EST:** 2017
SALES (est): 63.4K **Privately Held**
SIC: 3589 High pressure cleaning equipment

(G-12979)
MARTIN POWDER COATING
124 W Third St (48872-8164)
PHONE..................................517 625-4220
Wayne Brandon, *Manager*
EMP: 5 **EST:** 2016

▲ = Import ▼=Export
◆ =Import/Export

GEOGRAPHIC SECTION
Petoskey - Emmet County (G-13007)

SALES (est): 27.6K **Privately Held**
SIC: **7692** 3479 Welding repair; galvanizing of iron, steel or end-formed products

(G-12980)
SADIE OIL LLC
12635 Red Pine Ln (48872-9137)
PHONE 517 675-1325
Philip Hoholik, *Owner*
EMP: 7 EST: 2012
SALES (est): 875K **Privately Held**
SIC: **1389** 1731 Oil field services; energy management controls

(G-12981)
SAGE TOOL & ENGINEERING
10980 S M 52 (48872-9705)
PHONE 517 625-7817
Milton Sage, *Owner*
EMP: 4 EST: 2017
SALES (est): 81.4K **Privately Held**
SIC: **3599** Industrial machinery

(G-12982)
X-TREME GRAPHICS N SIGNS LLC
13076 S State Rd (48872-9540)
PHONE 989 277-7517
Robert Noble, *Principal*
EMP: 4 EST: 2013
SALES (est): 73.5K **Privately Held**
SIC: **3993** Signs & advertising specialties

Petersburg
Monroe County

(G-12983)
DTE HANKIN INC
Also Called: Hankins & Assoc
399 E Center St (49270-9702)
P.O. Box 66 (49270-0066)
PHONE 734 279-1831
Geary Hankin, *President*
EMP: 5 EST: 1941
SQ FT: 10,000
SALES (est): 121.8K **Privately Held**
SIC: **8711** 3541 Industrial engineers; milling machines

(G-12984)
MILAN METAL WORX LLC
Also Called: All Wood Log Splitters
16779 Ida West Rd (49270-9563)
PHONE 734 369-7115
Robert J Barta,
EMP: 8 EST: 2013
SALES (est): 603.4K **Privately Held**
WEB: www.allwoodlogsplitters.com
SIC: **3531** 3535 Log splitters; conveyors & conveying equipment

(G-12985)
SUPERIOR ROLL LLC
Also Called: Superior Roll & Turning
399 E Center St (49270-9702)
P.O. Box 5 (49270-0005)
PHONE 734 279-1831
Jeff Johnson,
EMP: 10 EST: 2005
SALES (est): 1.6MM **Privately Held**
WEB: www.superiorroll.com
SIC: **3599** Machine shop, jobbing & repair

(G-12986)
SUPERIOR STITCH
14724 W Dunbar Rd (49270-9515)
PHONE 734 347-1956
Amy Szabo, *Principal*
EMP: 4 EST: 2014
SALES (est): 38.1K **Privately Held**
WEB: www.superiorstitch.net
SIC: **2395** Embroidery & art needlework

Petoskey
Emmet County

(G-12987)
ADEPT DEFENSE LLC
1307 Howard St (49770-3002)
PHONE 231 758-2792
Jason Hitchings, *Principal*
EMP: 4 EST: 2018
SALES (est): 228.7K **Privately Held**
WEB: www.adeptdefensetraining.com
SIC: **3812** Defense systems & equipment

(G-12988)
AMERICAN SPOON FOODS INC (PA)
1668 Clarion Ave (49770-9263)
P.O. Box 566 (49770-0566)
PHONE 231 347-9030
Justin Rashid, *President*
Noah Marshall-Rashid, *Vice Pres*
Jessica Kruskie, *QC Mgr*
Neal Pasciak, *Controller*
Carol Rice, *Manager*
EMP: 40 EST: 1982
SQ FT: 12,000
SALES (est): 9.9MM **Privately Held**
WEB: www.spoon.com
SIC: **2035** 2034 2032 2033 Pickles, sauces & salad dressings; dehydrated fruits, vegetables, soups; canned specialties; preserves, including imitation: in cans, jars, etc.

(G-12989)
BALLY BLOCK CO
1420 Standish Ave (49770-3049)
PHONE 231 347-4170
EMP: 8 EST: 2019
SALES (est): 41.5K **Privately Held**
WEB: www.butcherblock.com
SIC: **2499** Wood products

(G-12990)
BEARCUB OUTFITTERS LLC
321 E Lake St Unit 1 (49770-2479)
PHONE 231 439-9500
Rebecca Philipp-Kranig, *Vice Pres*
Becky Phillip-King, *Mng Member*
Barbara J Shawn,
Lawrence Shawn,
EMP: 10 EST: 1998
SQ FT: 2,400
SALES (est): 1.1MM **Privately Held**
WEB: www.bearcuboutfitters.com
SIC: **5641** 5941 5699 2211 Children's & infants' wear stores; camping & backpacking equipment; sports apparel; apparel & outerwear fabrics, cotton

(G-12991)
BEARDS BREWERY LLC
215 E Lake St (49770-2415)
PHONE 231 753-2221
Kathleen Chimko, *Med Doctor*
Ben Slocum, *Mng Member*
Peter Manthei,
EMP: 40 EST: 2012
SALES (est): 3MM **Privately Held**
WEB: www.beardsbrewery.com
SIC: **2082** Beer (alcoholic beverage)

(G-12992)
CARTERS IMAGEWEAR & AWARDS
300 W Mitchell St (49770-2328)
PHONE 231 881-9324
EMP: 5 EST: 2015
SALES (est): 119K **Privately Held**
SIC: **2759** Screen printing

(G-12993)
CIRCUIT CONTROLS CORPORATION
2277 M 119 (49770-8916)
PHONE 231 347-0760
Tetsu Yamamoto, *President*
Donald W Winn, *Vice Pres*
David Duncan, *Mfg Staff*
Sabura Aihara, *Treasurer*
Shilo Ayotte, *Technical Staff*
▲ EMP: 200 EST: 1986
SQ FT: 80,000
SALES (est): 24.3MM **Privately Held**
WEB: www.circuitcontrols.com
SIC: **3714** Motor vehicle parts & accessories
HQ: Yazaki International Corporation
6801 N Haggerty Rd 4707e
Canton MI 48187

(G-12994)
COMPASS INTERIORS LLC
Also Called: Quiet Moose
300 E Mitchell St (49770-2656)
PHONE 231 348-5353
Mark Jensen,
EMP: 12 EST: 1994
SQ FT: 10,000
SALES (est): 2.4MM **Privately Held**
WEB: www.quietmoose.com
SIC: **0782** 0781 5712 2511 Landscape contractors; landscape planning services; furniture stores; wood household furniture; interior design services

(G-12995)
CROW AND MOSS LLC
Also Called: Crow & Moss Chocolate
1601 Standish Ave Unit 3 (49770-8452)
PHONE 231 838-9875
EMP: 6 EST: 2018
SALES (est): 398.3K **Privately Held**
WEB: www.crowandmoss.com
SIC: **2066** Chocolate & cocoa products

(G-12996)
CYGNUS INC
829 Charlevoix Ave (49770-2255)
P.O. Box 292 (49770-0292)
PHONE 231 347-5404
Robert Waugh, *President*
EMP: 22 EST: 1989
SQ FT: 1,000
SALES (est): 1.5MM **Privately Held**
WEB: www.cygnusincusa.com
SIC: **2521** Cabinets, office: wood

(G-12997)
FLOWING WELL PUBLICATIONS
510 Jennings Ave (49770-3106)
PHONE 231 622-8630
Fred Gray, *Principal*
EMP: 4 EST: 2008
SALES (est): 144.9K **Privately Held**
SIC: **2759** Publication printing

(G-12998)
GREAT NORTH WOODWORKS
1131 Emmet St (49770-2963)
PHONE 231 622-6200
Paul Gauden, *Principal*
EMP: 4 EST: 2016
SALES (est): 74.8K **Privately Held**
SIC: **2431** Millwork

(G-12999)
GREENWELL MACHINE SHOP INC
1048 Emmet St (49770-2930)
PHONE 231 347-3346
Gary Greenwell, *President*
EMP: 7 EST: 1947
SQ FT: 9,000
SALES (est): 1.3MM **Privately Held**
SIC: **5051** 3599 3446 Steel; machine shop, jobbing & repair; stairs, staircases, stair treads: prefabricated metal

(G-13000)
HARBOR SOFTWARE INTL INC
231 State St Ste 5 (49770-2785)
P.O. Box 831 (49770-0831)
PHONE 231 347-8866
Paul Fifer, *President*
EMP: 5 EST: 1995
SALES (est): 458.9K **Privately Held**
WEB: www.harborsoft.com
SIC: **7371** 7372 Computer software development; prepackaged software

(G-13001)
KILWINS QULTY CONFECTIONS INC (PA)
Also Called: Kilwins Chocolate Kitchen
1050 Bay View Rd (49770-9006)
PHONE 231 347-3800
Don McCarty, *President*
EMP: 101 EST: 1995
SALES (est): 10.4MM **Privately Held**
WEB: www.kilwins.com
SIC: **2066** Chocolate bars, solid

(G-13002)
LANZEN-PETOSKEY LLC
126 Fulton St (49770-2932)
PHONE 231 881-9602
Terry Lanzen, *President*
EMP: 21 EST: 2017
SALES (est): 4.1MM
SALES (corp-wide): 13.7MM **Privately Held**
WEB: www.lanzen.com
SIC: **3444** Sheet metalwork
PA: Lanzen, Incorporated
100 Peyerk Ct
Bruce Twp MI 48065
586 771-7070

(G-13003)
MAGNETIC SYSTEMS INTERNATIONAL
3890 Charlevoix Rd (49770-8422)
PHONE 231 582-9600
Michael Markiewicz, *Manager*
EMP: 7 EST: 2004
SALES (est): 374.7K **Privately Held**
WEB: www.msimagnets.com
SIC: **3572** Magnetic storage devices, computer

(G-13004)
MANTHEI INC
Also Called: Manthei Veneer
3996 Charlevoix Rd (49770-8426)
PHONE 231 347-4672
Tom Manthei, *President*
James Manthei, *Vice Pres*
Daniel Manthei, *Treasurer*
Joe Zielinski, *Finance Dir*
Jason Miller, *Sales Dir*
▲ EMP: 150 EST: 1945
SQ FT: 142,000
SALES (est): 21.5MM **Privately Held**
WEB: www.mantheiveneer.com
SIC: **2435** Veneer stock, hardwood

(G-13005)
MANTHEI DEVELOPMENT CORP
Also Called: N D C Contracting
3996 Charlevoix Rd (49770-8426)
PHONE 231 347-6282
Joe Sladek, *Manager*
EMP: 6
SALES (corp-wide): 1.2MM **Privately Held**
WEB: www.mantheiconstruction.com
SIC: **3273** Ready-mixed concrete
PA: Manthei Development Corporation
5481 Us Highway 31 S
Charlevoix MI 49720
231 547-6595

(G-13006)
MICHIGAN MAPLE BLOCK COMPANY
1420 Standish Ave (49770-3049)
P.O. Box 245 (49770-0245)
PHONE 231 347-4170
Joe Bareerheck, *President*
Fredrick J Polhemus, *Corp Secy*
Ann D Conway, *Vice Pres*
Pat Stanley, *Vice Pres*
Jack Palmer, *Engineer*
EMP: 53 EST: 1881
SQ FT: 120,000
SALES (est): 7.5MM
SALES (corp-wide): 15.3MM **Privately Held**
WEB: www.butcherblock.com
SIC: **2541** Wood partitions & fixtures
HQ: Bally Block Company
30 S 7th St
Bally PA 19503
610 845-7511

(G-13007)
MITCHELL GRAPHICS INC (PA)
2363 Mitchell Park Dr (49770-9600)
PHONE 231 347-4635
Gary Fedus, *President*
Richard Dietrick, *Vice Pres*
Jeff Streelman, *Vice Pres*
Walter Lightfoot, *Purch Mgr*
William H Fedus, *Treasurer*
▲ EMP: 34 EST: 1972
SQ FT: 31,000

Petoskey - Emmet County (G-13008)

SALES (est): 8.9MM Privately Held
WEB: www.mitchellgraphics.com
SIC: 2752 2791 2789 Commercial printing, offset; post cards, picture: lithographed; typesetting; bookbinding & related work

(G-13008)
NORTHERN MICH HARDWOODS INC
5151 Manthei Rd (49770-9803)
PHONE................................231 347-4575
Philip Manthei, *President*
Steve Maniaci, *Treasurer*
Carol Manthei, *Admin Sec*
EMP: 17 EST: 1980
SQ FT: 6,000
SALES (est): 2.9MM Privately Held
WEB: www.nmhardwoods.com
SIC: 2421 3442 2435 2431 Lumber: rough, sawed or planed; metal doors, sash & trim; hardwood veneer & plywood; millwork; hardwood dimension & flooring mills

(G-13009)
NORTHERN MICHIGAN REVIEW INC
Also Called: Charlevoix Courier, The
319 State St (49770-2746)
P.O. Box 671, Charlevoix (49720-0671)
PHONE................................231 547-6558
Angela Lasher, *Governor*
Kim Taylor, *Sales Staff*
EMP: 4
SALES (corp-wide): 9MM Privately Held
WEB: www.petoskeynews.com
SIC: 2711 Newspapers: publishing only, not printed on site
PA: Northern Michigan Review, Inc.
2058 S Otsego Ave
Gaylord MI 49735
231 547-6558

(G-13010)
NU-TECH NORTH INC
445 E Mitchell St Ste 6 (49770-2670)
P.O. Box 486 (49770-0486)
PHONE................................231 347-1992
Joe Mullin, *President*
EMP: 7 EST: 1995
SALES (est): 448.8K Privately Held
WEB: www.nu-tech.us
SIC: 2759 Commercial printing

(G-13011)
PAINT YOUR MASTERPIECE
110 Williams St (49770-2546)
PHONE................................231 622-8824
Jennifer Margherita, *Owner*
EMP: 5 EST: 2004
SALES (est): 143.3K Privately Held
SIC: 3269 Pottery products

(G-13012)
PAUL W REED DDS
Also Called: Paul W Reed DDS Ms
414 Petoskey St (49770-2618)
PHONE................................231 347-4145
Paul W Reed, *Owner*
EMP: 9 EST: 1996
SALES (est): 443.1K Privately Held
WEB: www.paulreedortho.com
SIC: 3842 8021 Braces, orthopedic; offices & clinics of dentists

(G-13013)
PERSONAL GRAPHICS
270 Creekside Dr (49770-7606)
PHONE................................231 347-6347
Debra Baker, *Owner*
Jacobe Mooar, *Co-Owner*
Meghan Meyer, *Marketing Staff*
EMP: 4 EST: 2001
SALES (est): 306.2K Privately Held
WEB: www.personalgraphicsonline.com
SIC: 2395 2752 2759 Embroidery products, except schiffli machine; embroidery & art needlework; commercial printing, lithographic; screen printing

(G-13014)
PETOSKEY FRMS VNYRD WINERY LLC
3720 Atkins Rd (49770-8901)
PHONE................................231 290-9463
Tracie Roush,
EMP: 7 EST: 2014
SALES (est): 409.6K Privately Held
WEB: www.petoskeyfarms.com
SIC: 2084 Wines

(G-13015)
PETOSKEY PLASTICS INC (PA)
1 Petoskey St (49770-2480)
PHONE................................231 347-2602
Paul C Keiswetter, *President*
Jason Keiswetter, *Exec VP*
Mike Barto, *Vice Pres*
Doug Stepanian, *Vice Pres*
David Blankenhagen, *Research*
◆ EMP: 30
SQ FT: 11,000
SALES (est): 139MM Privately Held
WEB: www.petoskeyplastics.com
SIC: 3089 Injection molding of plastics

(G-13016)
PETOSKEY PLASTICS INC
4226 Us Hwy 31 (49770)
PHONE................................231 347-2602
Mark Anderson, *Division Mgr*
Gregory Scheidemantel, *Vice Pres*
Doug Stepanian, *Vice Pres*
Jason Withers, *Production*
Denise Degear, *Purchasing*
EMP: 91
SALES (corp-wide): 139MM Privately Held
WEB: www.petoskeyplastics.com
SIC: 3081 Plastic film & sheet
PA: Petoskey Plastics, Inc.
1 Petoskey St
Petoskey MI 49770
231 347-2602

(G-13017)
PRINT ROOM
208 W Mitchell St Ste 1 (49770-4302)
PHONE................................231 489-8181
Lori Lowery, *Principal*
EMP: 4 EST: 2018
SALES (est): 74.4K Privately Held
SIC: 2752 Commercial printing, lithographic

(G-13018)
PRINT SHOP
324 Michigan St (49770-2663)
PHONE................................231 347-2000
Denise Berger, *Owner*
EMP: 7 EST: 1975
SQ FT: 2,000
SALES (est): 455.7K Privately Held
WEB: www.printshoppetoskey.com
SIC: 2752 Commercial printing, offset

(G-13019)
REDI-ROCK INTERNATIONAL LLC
2940 Parkview Dr (49770-8795)
PHONE................................866 222-8400
Cayce Armstrong, *Marketing Staff*
Elizabeth Sherwood, *Manager*
EMP: 10 EST: 2019
SALES (est): 614.8K Privately Held
WEB: www.redi-rock.com
SIC: 3272 Concrete products

(G-13020)
REVIEW DIRECTORIES INC
Also Called: Phone Guide
311 E Mitchell St (49770-2615)
P.O. Box 671, Charlevoix (49720-0671)
PHONE................................231 347-8606
Doug Caldwell, *President*
Kathie Lambert, *Production*
EMP: 10 EST: 1987
SALES (est): 261K Privately Held
SIC: 2741 Telephone & other directory publishing

(G-13021)
ROSENTHAL LOGGING
577 Blanchard Rd (49770-9638)
PHONE................................231 348-8168

Klaus Rosenthal, *Principal*
EMP: 5 EST: 2000
SALES (est): 120.7K Privately Held
SIC: 2411 Logging camps & contractors

(G-13022)
RUFF LIFE LLC
309 Howard St (49770-2413)
PHONE................................231 347-1214
Jary Albert, *Mng Member*
EMP: 4 EST: 2012
SALES (est): 322.1K Privately Held
WEB: www.rufflifepet.com
SIC: 5999 3999 Pet supplies; pet supplies

(G-13023)
SIGN AND DESIGN
427 Creekside Dr (49770-7624)
PHONE................................231 348-9256
Robert Scudder, *Owner*
EMP: 6 EST: 1974
SALES (est): 456.6K Privately Held
WEB: www.proimagedesigninc.net
SIC: 3993 Signs, not made in custom sign painting shops

(G-13024)
SKOP POWDER COATING
2469 N Us Highway 31 (49770-9322)
PHONE................................231 881-9909
EMP: 4 EST: 2019
SALES (est): 128.2K Privately Held
WEB: www.skop-powder-coating.business.site
SIC: 3479 Coating of metals & formed products

(G-13025)
SLUDGEHAMMER GROUP LTD
4772 Us Highway 131 (49770-9220)
PHONE................................231 348-5866
Arthur Jenks, *CEO*
Daniel E Wickham, *President*
Anthony Wiegman, *COO*
Kathy Beer, *Opers Staff*
EMP: 5 EST: 2004 Privately Held
WEB: www.sludgehammer.net
SIC: 3589 Sewage & water treatment equipment

(G-13026)
WALOON LAKE WINERY
2505 Blackbird Rd (49770-9758)
PHONE................................231 622-8645
EMP: 4 EST: 2014
SALES (est): 118.5K Privately Held
WEB: www.walloonlakewinery.com
SIC: 2084 Wines

Pewamo
Ionia County

(G-13027)
DEVEREAUX SAW MILL INC
2872 N Hubbardston Rd (48873-9721)
P.O. Box 67 (48873-0067)
PHONE................................989 593-2552
Bruce Devereaux, *President*
Ann Thelen, *Treasurer*
Craig Devereaux, *VP Sales*
Rob Paradise, *Sales Staff*
Rick Wagar, *Sales Staff*
▼ EMP: 60 EST: 1965
SALES (est): 9.7MM Privately Held
WEB: www.devereauxsawmill.com
SIC: 2421 2426 Lumber: rough, sawed or planed; lumber, hardwood dimension

(G-13028)
GOODRICH BROTHERS INC (PA)
11409 E Blwter Hwy Pewamo (48873)
P.O. Box 362 (48873-0362)
PHONE................................989 593-2104
Jerald Goodrich, *President*
Alfred Goodrich III, *Corp Secy*
Anthony Goodrich, *Vice Pres*
EMP: 20 EST: 1981
SQ FT: 60,000
SALES (est): 4.8MM Privately Held
WEB: www.goodrichbrothers.com
SIC: 5211 2431 Millwork & lumber; door & window products; millwork; moldings, wood: unfinished & prefinished

(G-13029)
WESTENDORFF TRANSIT MIX
Also Called: Westendorff Redi-Mix
3344 N Hubbardston Rd (48873-9614)
PHONE................................989 593-2488
Roy Westendorff, *Owner*
EMP: 6 EST: 1972
SALES (est): 390.6K Privately Held
WEB: www.gottstransitmix.com
SIC: 3273 Ready-mixed concrete

Pickford
Chippewa County

(G-13030)
BEACOM ENTERPRISES INC
Also Called: Beacom's Chipping & Logging
6671 E Rockview Rd (49774-9038)
PHONE................................906 647-3831
William Beacom, *President*
Rhoda Beacom, *Corp Secy*
EMP: 9 EST: 1975 Privately Held
SIC: 2411 Logging camps & contractors

(G-13031)
NORTH ARROW LOG HOMES INC
5943 N 3 Mile Rd (49774-9023)
P.O. Box 645, Cedarville (49719-0645)
PHONE................................906 484-5524
EMP: 6
SALES (est): 785.3K Privately Held
SIC: 2452 1521 Prefabricated Wood Buildings

(G-13032)
WILDERNESS TREASURES
Also Called: Anchor Bay Tackle
101 S M 129 (49774-9274)
P.O. Box 644 (49774-0644)
PHONE................................906 647-4002
Tom Ball, *Owner*
Carley Ball, *Co-Owner*
EMP: 10 EST: 2000
SALES (est): 256.8K Privately Held
WEB: www.wildernesstreasures.net
SIC: 5941 3949 Bait & tackle; sporting & athletic goods

Pierson
Montcalm County

(G-13033)
LUMBERJACK LOGGING LLC
4778 Whitefish Woods Dr (49339-9448)
PHONE................................616 799-4657
Dustin Hiler, *Administration*
EMP: 5 EST: 2015
SALES (est): 161.8K Privately Held
WEB: www.lumberjackloggingllc.com
SIC: 2411 Logging camps & contractors

Pigeon
Huron County

(G-13034)
ACTIVE FEED COMPANY (PA)
Also Called: Farm Crest Foods
7564 Pigeon Rd (48755-9597)
P.O. Box 350 (48755-0350)
PHONE................................989 453-2472
Diane Maust, *President*
Emma Maust, *Vice Pres*
▲ EMP: 53 EST: 1960
SQ FT: 12,000
SALES (est): 24.7MM Privately Held
WEB: www.activefeedco.com
SIC: 5191 0252 2048 Feed; chicken eggs; prepared feeds

(G-13035)
AXIS MACHINING INC
7061 Hartley St (48755-5191)
P.O. Box 170 (48755-0170)
PHONE................................989 453-3943
Leroy Wurst, *President*
Devere Sturm, *Vice Pres*
EMP: 23 EST: 1988
SQ FT: 20,000

SALES (est): 1.1MM Privately Held
WEB: www.axismachining.com
SIC: 3599 Machine shop, jobbing & repair

(G-13036)
BERNE ENTERPRISES INC
7190 Berne Rd (48755-9784)
PHONE..................................989 453-3235
Keith Wurst, *President*
EMP: 16 EST: 1945
SQ FT: 35,000
SALES (est): 2.1MM Privately Held
WEB: www.berneenterprises.com
SIC: 3325 3321 3369 Alloy steel castings, except investment; ductile iron castings; gray iron castings; nonferrous foundries

(G-13037)
GRM CORPORATION (PA)
39 N Caseville Rd (48755-9704)
P.O. Box 689 (48755-0689)
PHONE..................................989 453-2322
Lee Steinman, *CEO*
Sherril L Steinman, *Chairman*
EMP: 45 EST: 1989
SQ FT: 16,000
SALES (est): 5.5MM Privately Held
WEB: www.grmcorporation.com
SIC: 2822 2869 3089 Silicone rubbers; industrial organic chemicals; molding primary plastic

(G-13038)
GRM CORPORATION
7375 Crescent Beach Rd (48755-9602)
PHONE..................................989 453-2322
James Steinman, *Manager*
EMP: 5 Privately Held
WEB: www.grmcorporation.com
SIC: 3053 Gaskets & sealing devices
PA: Grm Corporation
    39 N Caseville Rd
    Pigeon MI 48755

(G-13039)
HURON CASTING INC (PA)
Also Called: Hci
7050 Hartley St (48755-5190)
P.O. Box 679 (48755-0679)
PHONE..................................989 453-3933
Leroy Wurst, *President*
Devere Sturm, *Vice Pres*
Linda Beyer, *Purchasing*
Matt Davis, *CFO*
Timothy Rafalski, *Sales Mgr*
◆ EMP: 393 EST: 1976
SQ FT: 350,000
SALES (est): 94.2MM Privately Held
WEB: www.huroncasting.com
SIC: 3325 3369 Alloy steel castings, except investment; nonferrous foundries

(G-13040)
RICHMONDS STEEL INC
6767 Pigeon Rd (48755-9502)
P.O. Box 290 (48755-0290)
PHONE..................................989 453-7010
Nick Pavlichek, *President*
Chris Pavlichek, *Vice Pres*
EMP: 10 EST: 1990
SQ FT: 22,000
SALES (est): 760.6K Privately Held
SIC: 3441 Fabricated structural metal

(G-13041)
THUMB TRUCK AND TRAILER CO
Also Called: Daryls Use Truck Sales
8305 Geiger Rd (48755-9562)
PHONE..................................989 453-3133
Daryl Elenbaum, *President*
Debra Heilig, *Admin Sec*
EMP: 9 EST: 1963
SQ FT: 3,300
SALES (est): 1.3MM Privately Held
WEB: www.thumbtruckbedliners.com
SIC: 3715 Trailer bodies; semitrailers for truck tractors

(G-13042)
VOLLMER READY-MIX INC (PA)
196 S Caseville Rd 204 (48755-9531)
PHONE..................................989 453-2262
David R Vollmer, *President*
Audrey Vollmer, *Treasurer*
Jenny Vollmer, *Manager*
EMP: 5 EST: 1958
SQ FT: 4,000 Privately Held
WEB: www.vollmerreadymix.weebly.com
SIC: 3273 Ready-mixed concrete

Pinckney
Livingston County

(G-13043)
AKAMAI TECHNOLOGIES INC
9394 Anne St (48169-8933)
PHONE..................................734 424-1142
Thorn Vogel, *Principal*
EMP: 4
SALES (corp-wide): 3.2B Publicly Held
WEB: www.akamai.com
SIC: 7372 Prepackaged software
PA: Akamai Technologies, Inc.
    145 Broadway
    Cambridge MA 02142
    617 444-3000

(G-13044)
CARLEE WOODWORKING
15777 Twin Ponds (48169-9802)
PHONE..................................734 660-0491
EMP: 5 EST: 2015
SALES (est): 175.4K Privately Held
WEB: www.carlee-woodworking.com
SIC: 2431 Millwork

(G-13045)
CRAIN FAMILY BIBLE
11399 Saddlebrook Cir (48169-8029)
PHONE..................................734 673-8620
EMP: 4 EST: 2013
SALES (est): 102.8K Privately Held
SIC: 2741 Miscellaneous publishing

(G-13046)
DAKOTA AEROSPACE LLC
10116 Kress Rd (48169-9373)
PHONE..................................787 403-3564
Francisco Alfonso Lopez,
EMP: 4 EST: 2017
SALES (est): 82.4K Privately Held
SIC: 3721 Aircraft

(G-13047)
ECONO PRINT INC
10312 Dexter Pinckney Rd (48169-8963)
P.O. Box 823 (48169-0823)
PHONE..................................734 878-5806
Ted Stilber, *President*
EMP: 8 EST: 1981
SQ FT: 1,500
SALES (est): 1MM Privately Held
WEB: www.econoprintusa.com
SIC: 2752 7331 2791 2789 Commercial printing, offset; direct mail advertising services; typesetting; bookbinding & related work

(G-13048)
FROYO PINCKNEY LLC
3282 Swarthout Rd (48169-9253)
PHONE..................................248 310-4465
Scott Roller, *Principal*
EMP: 5 EST: 2018
SALES (est): 140.2K Privately Held
SIC: 2024 Yogurt desserts, frozen

(G-13049)
GLOBAL DRAUGHT SERVICE
418 Pearl St (48169-9259)
PHONE..................................810 844-6888
EMP: 4 EST: 2016
SALES (est): 68.9K Privately Held
WEB: www.globaldraught.com
SIC: 2082 Malt beverages

(G-13050)
LEXATRONICS LLC
9768 Cedar Lake Rd (48169-8826)
PHONE..................................734 878-6237
John Lincsay PHD, *President*
EMP: 4 EST: 2005
SALES (est): 215.2K Privately Held
SIC: 3674 Radiation sensors

(G-13051)
MCMACKON MKTG ADM PUBG SVCS LL
8407 Old Mill Dr (48169-8931)
PHONE..................................734 878-3198
Diane Wilson, *Principal*
EMP: 4 EST: 2016
SALES (est): 37.5K Privately Held
SIC: 2741 Miscellaneous publishing

(G-13052)
MIDWEST AQUATICS GROUP INC
Also Called: Portage Yacht Club
8930 Dexter Pinckney Rd (48169-9430)
PHONE..................................734 426-4155
Thomas F Ehman, *President*
Ruth Ehman, *Vice Pres*
EMP: 8 EST: 1962
SQ FT: 13,000
SALES (est): 1MM Privately Held
WEB: www.ms-pyc.com
SIC: 5551 7997 5088 5812 Sailboats & equipment; sailboats, unpowered; marine supplies; boating club, membership; marine crafts & supplies; marine supplies; eating places; marinas; boat building & repairing

(G-13053)
PINCKNEY AUTOMATIC & MFG
6128 Cedar Lake Rd (48169-8807)
P.O. Box 98 (48169-0098)
PHONE..................................734 878-3430
Robert Dudenhoefer, *President*
Barbara J Dudenhoefer, *Corp Secy*
EMP: 9
SQ FT: 3,000
SALES (est): 475.8K Privately Held
WEB: www.pinckneyautorepair.net
SIC: 3451 3492 3452 Screw machine products; fluid power valves & hose fittings; bolts, nuts, rivets & washers

(G-13054)
R GARI SIGN AND DISPLAY INC
10098 Imus Rd (48169-9669)
PHONE..................................810 355-1245
EMP: 6 EST: 2017
SALES (est): 92.2K Privately Held
WEB: www.rgari.com
SIC: 3993 Signs & advertising specialties

(G-13055)
SEMISOURCE CORPORATION
1116 Arthurs Ct (48169-9077)
PHONE..................................734 331-2104
Michael Head, *Principal*
EMP: 7 EST: 1997
SALES (est): 204K Privately Held
WEB: www.motioncontrolshop.com
SIC: 3575 Computer terminals, monitors & components

(G-13056)
SPD AMERICA LLC
Also Called: Vela Sciences
195 E Hamburg St (48169-8053)
PHONE..................................734 709-7624
Tyler J Richardson, *Mng Member*
EMP: 5 EST: 2012
SALES (est): 438.6K Privately Held
SIC: 2721 7389 2732 5961 Trade journals: publishing & printing; subscription fulfillment services: magazine, newspaper, etc.; books: printing & binding; catalog & mail-order houses

(G-13057)
STEP INTO SUCCESS INC
Also Called: Ellsworth, Belinda
9940 Sunrise Dr (48169-9423)
P.O. Box 712, Lakeland (48143-0712)
PHONE..................................734 426-1075
Belinda Ellsworth, *President*
EMP: 8 EST: 1995
SALES (est): 717K Privately Held
WEB: www.stepintosuccess.com
SIC: 8299 8999 2759 Educational services; lecturing services; magazines: printing

(G-13058)
VORTEK
440 S Dexter St (48169-9070)
PHONE..................................248 767-2992
EMP: 8 EST: 2014
SALES (est): 736.1K Privately Held
WEB: www.vortekproducts.com
SIC: 3714 Motor vehicle parts & accessories

Pinconning
Bay County

(G-13059)
BERTHIAUME SLAUGHTER HOUSE
719 Jane St (48650-9404)
PHONE..................................989 879-4921
Robert Berthiaume, *President*
Charlie Berthiaume, *General Mgr*
EMP: 6 EST: 1950
SALES (est): 453.6K Privately Held
SIC: 2011 0751 Meat packing plants; slaughtering: custom livestock services

(G-13060)
CONAIR NORTH AMERICA
Also Called: Iteg
503 S Mercer St (48650-9309)
PHONE..................................814 437-6861
Chris Weinrich, *General Mgr*
Rich Shaffer, *Vice Pres*
EMP: 50 EST: 2013
SALES (est): 3.1MM Privately Held
WEB: www.conairgroup.com
SIC: 3569 General industrial machinery

(G-13061)
LLOYDS CABINET SHOP INC
1947 N Huron Rd (48650-9773)
PHONE..................................989 879-3015
Ken Selle, *President*
EMP: 15 EST: 1961
SQ FT: 24,000
SALES (est): 2.2MM Privately Held
WEB: www.lloydscabinetshop.com
SIC: 2434 5211 Wood kitchen cabinets; cabinets, kitchen

(G-13062)
M AND A CASTINGS LTD
3603 N Huron Rd (48650-9510)
P.O. Box 934 (48650-0934)
PHONE..................................517 879-2222
Ted A Wayman, *President*
EMP: 10 EST: 1955
SQ FT: 25,000
SALES (est): 1MM Privately Held
WEB: www.macastings.com
SIC: 3363 3364 Aluminum die-castings; magnesium & magnesium-base alloy die-castings

(G-13063)
MR CHIPS INC (HQ)
2628 N Huron Rd (48650-9512)
PHONE..................................989 879-3555
Joseph F Janicke, *President*
Randy Hugo, *Vice Pres*
Jay Janicke, *Vice Pres*
Sharon Janicke, *Vice Pres*
▲ EMP: 5 EST: 1969
SALES (est): 2.9MM
SALES (corp-wide): 82.4MM Privately Held
WEB: www.bayviewfoods.com
SIC: 2035 Pickles, sauces & salad dressings
PA: Bay View Food Products Company
    2606 N Huron Rd
    Pinconning MI
    989 879-3555

(G-13064)
PINCONNING METALS INC
1140 E Cody Estey Rd (48650-8485)
P.O. Box 36 (48650-0036)
PHONE..................................989 879-3144
Richard Yaros, *President*
Bonnie Yaros, *Corp Secy*
EMP: 6 EST: 1968
SQ FT: 10,000

Pinconning - Bay County (G-13065)

SALES (est): 878.4K **Privately Held**
WEB: www.pmimetals.com
SIC: **3469** 3465 3089 Stamping metal for the trade; body parts, automobile: stamped metal; molding primary plastic

(G-13065)
TIMS CABINET INC
Also Called: Tim's Cabinet Shop
5309 S Huron Rd (48650-6409)
PHONE.............................989 846-9831
Tim Jasman, *President*
Deborah Jasman, *Vice Pres*
EMP: 7 **EST:** 1976
SQ FT: 5,000
SALES (est): 579.2K **Privately Held**
WEB: www.timscabinet.com
SIC: **1751** 2521 2434 Cabinet building & installation; wood office filing cabinets & bookcases; wood kitchen cabinets

(G-13066)
TUBULAR METAL SYSTEMS LLC (HQ)
401 E 5th St (48650-9321)
PHONE.............................989 879-2611
Craig Barnhart, *CFO*
Dan Mullins,
▲ **EMP:** 149 **EST:** 2005
SQ FT: 225,000
SALES (est): 44.4MM **Privately Held**
WEB: www.duraauto.com
SIC: **3465** Body parts, automobile: stamped metal

Pittsford
Hillsdale County

(G-13067)
BERLIN HOLDINGS LLC
Also Called: Alumi Span
4445 S Pittsford Rd (49271-9864)
P.O. Box 205 (49271-0205)
PHONE.............................517 523-2444
Rex D Hoover, *Ch of Bd*
David Berlin, *Mng Member*
EMP: 8 **EST:** 1957
SQ FT: 3,000 **Privately Held**
WEB: www.alumi-span.com
SIC: **3448** 3999 Docks: prefabricated metal; dock equipment & supplies, industrial

(G-13068)
REEDS EQUIPMENT LLC
Also Called: Franks Performance Development
10815 S Pittsford Rd (49271-9792)
P.O. Box 87 (49271-0087)
PHONE.............................517 567-4415
EMP: 8 **EST:** 2007
SALES (est): 380.8K **Privately Held**
SIC: **3524** Lawn & garden mowers & accessories

Plainwell
Allegan County

(G-13069)
ACRO-TECH MANUFACTURING INC
12229 M 89 (49080-9049)
PHONE.............................269 629-4300
Hans Nikolaas, *President*
Robert Tenhoor, *Vice Pres*
Jan Nikolaas, *Treasurer*
EMP: 15 **EST:** 1989
SALES (est): 651.6K **Privately Held**
SIC: **3599** Machine shop, jobbing & repair

(G-13070)
ANO-KAL COMPANY
734 Jersey St (49080-1668)
PHONE.............................269 685-5743
Richard Kinsey, *Owner*
EMP: 10 **EST:** 2004
SALES (est): 866.1K **Privately Held**
SIC: **3471** Anodizing (plating) of metals or formed products

(G-13071)
CHIPPEWA DEVELOPMENT INC
Also Called: Empire Forest Products Company
960 Industrial Pkwy (49080-1402)
PHONE.............................269 685-2646
William L Adams, *President*
Andra Curtice, *Sales Staff*
▼ **EMP:** 14 **EST:** 1979
SQ FT: 8,000
SALES (est): 547.9K **Privately Held**
WEB: www.proshedbuildings.com
SIC: **2431** Millwork

(G-13072)
CONSUMERS CONCRETE CORPORATION
465 12th St (49080-1901)
PHONE.............................800 643-4235
Jerry Deboer, *Opers Mgr*
Brad Deneau, *Opers-Prdtn-Mfg*
Tom Thomas, *Engineer*
Mike Weber, *Marketing Mgr*
EMP: 6
SALES (corp-wide): 42.6MM **Privately Held**
WEB: www.consumersconcrete.com
SIC: **3273** Ready-mixed concrete
PA: Consumers Concrete Corporation
3506 Lovers Ln
Kalamazoo MI 49001
269 342-0136

(G-13073)
DARBY METAL TREATING INC
892 Wakefield (49080-1425)
PHONE.............................269 204-6504
Tom Darby, *President*
Frank Metelka, *Engineer*
EMP: 17 **EST:** 2012
SALES (est): 2.9MM **Privately Held**
WEB: www.darbymetaltreating.com
SIC: **3398** Metal heat treating

(G-13074)
DATA PRO INC
108 S Main St Ste B (49080-1776)
P.O. Box 457 (49080-0457)
PHONE.............................269 685-9214
Donald Ponozzo, *President*
Scott Willoughby, *CTO*
EMP: 4 **EST:** 1982
SQ FT: 2,000
SALES (est): 586.8K **Privately Held**
WEB: www.data-pro.com
SIC: **7371** 7372 Custom computer programming services; prepackaged software

(G-13075)
DEANS ICE CREAM INC
307 N Sherwood Ave (49080-1330)
PHONE.............................269 685-6641
Gery Bentley, *President*
Gerald Bentley, *President*
EMP: 12 **EST:** 1920
SALES (est): 1.3MM **Privately Held**
WEB: www.deansicecream.com
SIC: **2024** 5812 Ice cream, bulk; drive-in restaurant

(G-13076)
E LEET WOODWORKING
10175 3 Mile Rd (49080-9020)
PHONE.............................269 664-5203
Patrick J Leet, *Owner*
EMP: 5 **EST:** 1986
SALES (est): 450.9K **Privately Held**
WEB: www.eleetwoodworking.com
SIC: **2431** Millwork

(G-13077)
FUSION FLEXO LLC
156 10th St (49080-9746)
P.O. Box 356 (49080-0356)
PHONE.............................269 685-5827
Grayce Lancaster, *Vice Pres*
Brad Boyd, *Vice Pres*
EMP: 30
SALES (corp-wide): 1.3MM **Privately Held**
WEB: www.fusionflexo.com
SIC: **2796** Photoengraving plates, linecuts or halftones

PA: Fusion Flexo, Llc
6330 Canterwood Dr
Richland MI 49083
269 685-5827

(G-13078)
JBS PACKERLAND INC
11 11th St (49080-9711)
P.O. Box 247 (49080-0247)
PHONE.............................269 685-6886
Charlie Gach, *President*
Bob Pennock, *Vice Pres*
EMP: 10 **Publicly Held**
WEB: www.jbsfoodsgroup.com
SIC: **2011** Boxed beef from meat slaughtered on site
HQ: Jbs Packerland, Inc.
1330 Lime Kiln Rd
Green Bay WI 54311
920 468-4000

(G-13079)
JBS PLAINWELL INC
11 11th St (49080-9711)
P.O. Box 247 (49080-0247)
PHONE.............................269 685-6886
Richard Besta, *Ch of Bd*
Paul Murray Jr, *President*
Craig Liegel, *Corp Secy*
Brian Lawson, *Engineer*
Jesse Mortensen, *Human Res Dir*
EMP: 250 **EST:** 1927
SQ FT: 250,000
SALES (est): 32.7MM **Publicly Held**
WEB: www.jbsfoodsgroup.com
SIC: **2011** Boxed beef from meat slaughtered on site
HQ: Jbs Usa Food Company
1770 Promontory Cir
Greeley CO 80634
970 506-8000

(G-13080)
KALAMAZOO METAL MUNCHER INC
3428 E B Ave (49080-8908)
PHONE.............................269 492-0268
Albert Kimball, *President*
John Gay, *Corp Secy*
James Lofts, *Vice Pres*
EMP: 5 **EST:** 2011
SQ FT: 2,000
SALES (est): 357.4K **Privately Held**
WEB: www.kalamazoometalmuncher.com
SIC: **3441** Fabricated structural metal

(G-13081)
LAWRENCE INDUSTRIES INC
329 Highland Ct (49080-9108)
P.O. Box 141 (49080-0141)
PHONE.............................269 664-4614
Ruth Lovelace Murphy, *Administration*
EMP: 4 **EST:** 2015
SALES (est): 138.2K **Privately Held**
WEB: www.lawrenceindustriesinc.com
SIC: **3999** Manufacturing industries

(G-13082)
MAGIERA HOLDINGS INC
Also Called: Hytech Spring and Machine Co
950 Lincoln Pkwy (49080-1438)
PHONE.............................269 685-1768
Andrew Magiera, *President*
Mike Bowman, *Vice Pres*
EMP: 28 **EST:** 1984
SALES (est): 4.5MM **Privately Held**
SIC: **3495** 3599 Wire springs; machine shop, jobbing & repair

(G-13083)
MOTAN INC
320 Acorn St (49080-1412)
PHONE.............................269 685-1050
Mark McKibbin, *President*
Carl Litherland, *Vice Pres*
Steven Watson, *Technical Mgr*
Mark McKibben, *CFO*
Don Deluca, *Controller*
◆ **EMP:** 30 **EST:** 1981
SQ FT: 30,000

SALES (est): 9.9MM
SALES (corp-wide): 115.2MM **Privately Held**
WEB: www.motan-colortronic.com
SIC: **3535** Conveyors & conveying equipment
PA: Motan Holding Gmbh
Stromeyersdorfstr. 12
Konstanz BW 78467
756 276-0

(G-13084)
OPTO SOLUTIONS INC
140 E Bridge St (49080-1718)
PHONE.............................269 254-9716
Todd Reynolds, *President*
Ryan Fisher, *Vice Pres*
EMP: 9 **EST:** 2010
SALES (est): 177.9K **Privately Held**
WEB: www.optosolutions.net
SIC: **3571** Electronic computers

(G-13085)
PERCEPTIVE CONTROLS INC
140 E Bridge St (49080-1718)
PHONE.............................269 685-3040
Todd Reynolds, *President*
Ryan Fisher, *Vice Pres*
Tim McKinnon, *Engineer*
Joseph Wills, *Engineer*
Rod Koning, *Sales Engr*
EMP: 29 **EST:** 2001
SALES (est): 4.5MM **Privately Held**
WEB: www.perceptivecontrols.com
SIC: **3823** Industrial process measurement equipment

(G-13086)
PERCEPTIVE INDUSTRIES INC
951 Industrial Pkwy (49080-1401)
PHONE.............................269 204-6768
Charles Dearman, *President*
Dean Decker, *Vice Pres*
Craig Sanford, *Engineer*
Donald Dickerson, *Project Engr*
Pamela England, *Office Mgr*
EMP: 32 **EST:** 2002
SQ FT: 26,000
SALES (est): 8MM **Privately Held**
WEB: www.perceptiveindustries.com
SIC: **3567** Industrial furnaces & ovens

(G-13087)
PIERCE PERSONAL DEFENSE LLC
12320 Crum Rd (49080-9016)
PHONE.............................269 664-6960
Catherine Pierce, *Principal*
EMP: 4 **EST:** 2016
SALES (est): 77.4K **Privately Held**
SIC: **3812** Defense systems & equipment

(G-13088)
PLAINWELL ICE CREAM CO
621 E Bridge St (49080-1804)
PHONE.............................269 685-8586
Arthur Gaylord, *President*
Judy Gaylord, *Vice Pres*
EMP: 11 **EST:** 1978
SQ FT: 2,100
SALES (est): 1.7MM **Privately Held**
WEB: www.plainwellicecreamco.com
SIC: **2024** Ice cream & frozen desserts

(G-13089)
PLAS-TECH MOLD AND DESIGN INC
946 Industrial Pkwy (49080-1402)
PHONE.............................269 225-1223
David J Williamson, *President*
Scott A Anson, *Vice Pres*
▲ **EMP:** 6 **EST:** 1995
SQ FT: 5,000
SALES (est): 689.3K **Privately Held**
WEB: www.plastechmd.com
SIC: **3544** Industrial molds

(G-13090)
PLASTISNOW LLC
Also Called: Msnow
200 Prince St (49080-1230)
PHONE.............................414 397-1233
Lucas Schrab, *Mng Member*
Adam Schrab,
EMP: 4 **EST:** 2013

▲ = Import ▼=Export
◆ =Import/Export

GEOGRAPHIC SECTION

Plymouth - Wayne County (G-13117)

SALES (est): 433K **Privately Held**
WEB: www.msnow.ski
SIC: 3949 7999 Snow skis; ski instruction

(G-13091)
PREFERRED PLASTICS INC (PA)
800 E Bridge St (49080-1800)
PHONE 269 685-5873
Tracy J Tucker, *CEO*
Daniel Julien, *Plant Mgr*
Greg Mathis, *Safety Mgr*
Neil Mohan, *Purch Mgr*
Fred Castaneda, *Engineer*
EMP: 80 EST: 1993
SQ FT: 160,000
SALES (est): 26.6MM **Privately Held**
WEB: www.preferredplastics.com
SIC: 3089 Automotive parts, plastic

(G-13092)
RECOVERE LLC
3261 E B Ave (49080-8904)
PHONE 269 370-3165
Jay Hoinville,
EMP: 9 EST: 2012
SALES (est): 257K **Privately Held**
WEB: www.recovere.biz
SIC: 1629 3589 Waste water & sewage treatment plant construction; sewage & water treatment equipment

(G-13093)
RIZZO PACKAGING INC
930 Lincoln Pkwy (49080-1438)
P.O. Box 278 (49080-0278)
PHONE 269 685-5808
Paul Rizzo, *President*
Phil Broekhuizen, *General Mgr*
Bart A Rizzo, *Vice Pres*
Mark Kampen, *Plant Mgr*
Bart Rizzo, *Sales Staff*
EMP: 45 EST: 1977
SQ FT: 40,000
SALES (est): 8.8MM **Privately Held**
WEB: www.rizzopackaging.com
SIC: 2631 2675 2621 Paperboard mills; cutouts, cardboard, die-cut: from purchased materials; packaging paper

(G-13094)
ROB ENTERPRISES INC
156 10th St (49080-9746)
P.O. Box 356 (49080-0356)
PHONE 269 685-5827
Brian Anderson, *CEO*
J Lee Murphy, *Admin Sec*
EMP: 11 EST: 1974
SQ FT: 10,000
SALES (est): 512.9K **Privately Held**
SIC: 2796 Photoengraving plates, linecuts or halftones

(G-13095)
SELECT MILLWORK
960 Industrial Pkwy (49080-1402)
PHONE 269 685-2646
EMP: 9 EST: 2019
SALES (est): 367.7K **Privately Held**
WEB: www.selectmillwork.com
SIC: 2431 Millwork

(G-13096)
SPUNKY DUCK PRESS
802 N Main St (49080-1323)
PHONE 269 365-7285
Dok Stevens-Dehring, *Principal*
EMP: 4 EST: 2018
SALES (est): 109.5K **Privately Held**
SIC: 2741 Miscellaneous publishing

(G-13097)
SZYMANOWSKI ELECTRIC LLC
784 105th Ave (49080-9540)
PHONE 612 928-8370
EMP: 4 EST: 2018
SALES (est): 88.9K **Privately Held**
SIC: 3089 Plastics products

(G-13098)
TMD MACHINING INC
751 Wakefield (49080-1499)
P.O. Box 342 (49080-0342)
PHONE 269 685-3091
Tom Darby, *President*
Michelle Heeres, *Purch Agent*
Robert Milham, *Buyer*
Michelle Porte, *Buyer*
Dale Darby, *Engineer*
EMP: 47 EST: 1995
SQ FT: 18,000
SALES (est): 10.5MM **Privately Held**
WEB: www.tmdmach.com
SIC: 3599 Machine shop, jobbing & repair

(G-13099)
TOKUSEN HYTECH INC
Also Called: Hytech Spring and Machine Co.
950 Lincoln Pkwy (49080-1438)
PHONE 269 685-1768
Hiromi Kanai, *Ch of Bd*
Richard Graff, *President*
Michael Bowman, *Vice Pres*
Barbara Magiera, *Vice Pres*
Justin Lagrow, *QC Mgr*
EMP: 125 EST: 2013
SALES (est): 19.4MM **Privately Held**
SIC: 3495 3843 5047 Wire springs; dental metal; medical laboratory equipment; instruments, surgical & medical

(G-13100)
TOKUSEN HYTECH INC
Also Called: Hytech Spring and Machine
950 Lincoln Pkwy (49080-1438)
PHONE 269 658-1768
EMP: 99
SQ FT: 107,000
SALES (est): 8.8MM **Privately Held**
SIC: 3495 Mfg Wire Springs

(G-13101)
TRAVIS CREEK TOOLING
923 Industrial Pkwy (49080-1401)
P.O. Box 116, Kalamazoo (49004-0116)
PHONE 269 685-2000
Ronnie Bickings, *Owner*
EMP: 7 EST: 1996
SQ FT: 4,000
SALES (est): 791.2K **Privately Held**
WEB: www.traviscreektool.com
SIC: 3544 Industrial molds

(G-13102)
UCB ADVERTISING
12047 Oakridge Rd (49080-9273)
PHONE 269 808-2411
Tim Miller, *Vice Pres*
EMP: 4
SALES (est): 174.5K **Privately Held**
SIC: 3993 Electric signs

Pleasant Lake
Jackson County

(G-13103)
LARRYS TAXIDERMY INC
Also Called: Larry's Taxidermy Studio
8640 N Meridian Rd (49272-9752)
PHONE 517 769-6104
Larry W Angus, *President*
EMP: 5 EST: 1967
SALES (est): 70K **Privately Held**
SIC: 7699 3111 Taxidermists; tanneries, leather

(G-13104)
PEAK MANUFACTURING INC
11855 Bunkerhill Rd (49272-9798)
PHONE 517 769-6900
Christopher A Salow, *CEO*
Kyle Messner, *Supervisor*
Dani Manning, *Software Dev*
EMP: 30 EST: 2007
SALES (est): 4.4MM **Privately Held**
WEB: www.peakmfgpro.com
SIC: 1241 7539 Coal mining services; machine shop, automotive

Pleasant Ridge
Oakland County

(G-13105)
HANON PRINTING COMPANY
34 Cambridge Blvd (48069-1103)
PHONE 248 541-9099
C Robert Hanon, *President*
EMP: 4 EST: 1977
SQ FT: 3,400
SALES (est): 256.9K **Privately Held**
SIC: 2752 Commercial printing, offset

(G-13106)
TMC GROUP INC
26 Elm Park Blvd (48069-1105)
PHONE 248 819-6063
Kimberley Hanke, *President*
Jay Zettervall, *Admin Sec*
EMP: 7 EST: 2010
SALES (est): 96.8K **Privately Held**
SIC: 8711 8733 8999 3679 Professional engineer; scientific research agency; technical writing; electronic circuits; storage batteries; oils & greases, blending & compounding

(G-13107)
YOUR PERSONAL MEMOIR LLC
36 Oakdale Blvd (48069-1032)
PHONE 248 629-0697
Susan Carroll, *Founder*
EMP: 4 EST: 2012
SALES (est): 111.6K **Privately Held**
WEB: www.yourpersonalmemoir.com
SIC: 2741 Miscellaneous publishing

Plymouth
Wayne County

(G-13108)
A & D PLASTICS INC
1255 S Mill St (48170-4318)
PHONE 734 455-2255
Gerald A Jagacki, *President*
Jeffery Jagacki, *Manager*
EMP: 44 EST: 1968
SQ FT: 20,000
SALES (est): 2MM **Privately Held**
WEB: www.adplastic.com
SIC: 3089 Injection molding of plastics; plastic containers, except foam

(G-13109)
A2E MANUFACTURING
45209 Helm St (48170-6023)
PHONE 734 622-9800
Glenn Theisen, *Principal*
EMP: 9 EST: 2016
SALES (est): 51.8K **Privately Held**
WEB: www.a2emfg.com
SIC: 3999 Manufacturing industries

(G-13110)
AA ANDERSON & CO INC
Also Called: Anderson Process
41304 Concept Dr (48170-4253)
P.O. Box 324, Farmington Hills (48332-0324)
PHONE 248 476-7782
David Tatro, *Manager*
Craig Maass, *Contractor*
EMP: 39
SALES (corp-wide): 35.6MM **Privately Held**
WEB: www.andersonprocess.com
SIC: 5084 3569 Industrial machinery & equipment; liquid automation machinery & equipment
PA: A.A. Anderson & Co., Inc.
21365 Gateway Ct
Brookfield WI 53045
262 784-3340

(G-13111)
ABSOPURE WATER COMPANY LLC
8835 General Dr (48170-4623)
P.O. Box 701220 (48170-0961)
PHONE 734 459-8000
Arthur Amelotte, *Opers Staff*
Jay McCline, *Production*
Glen Davis, *QC Mgr*
Kimberly Schimmelfennig, *Accountant*
Cara Lupinski, *Cust Mgr*
EMP: 300
SALES (corp-wide): 193MM **Privately Held**
WEB: www.absopure.com
SIC: 2086 Water, pasteurized: packaged in cans, bottles, etc.
PA: Absopure Water Company Llc
8845 General Dr
Plymouth MI 48170
313 898-1200

(G-13112)
ACTION PRINTECH INC
41079 Concept Dr (48170-4252)
PHONE 734 207-6000
Chris Dunlap, *President*
Estelle Dunlap, *Vice Pres*
Linda Dunlap, *Treasurer*
EMP: 16 EST: 1977
SQ FT: 17,000
SALES (est): 2MM **Privately Held**
WEB: www.actionprintech.co
SIC: 2752 7336 Commercial printing, offset; graphic arts & related design

(G-13113)
ADEPT BROACHING CO
6253 Barbara Ln (48170-5000)
PHONE 734 427-9221
Raymond Monticelli, *President*
Linda Monticelli, *Vice Pres*
EMP: 5 EST: 1962
SQ FT: 8,000
SALES (est): 423.1K **Privately Held**
WEB: www.allnaturalgym.com
SIC: 3599 Machine shop, jobbing & repair

(G-13114)
ADIENT INC (DH)
49200 Halyard Dr (48170-2481)
PHONE 734 254-5000
Doug Del Grosso, *CEO*
Nirav Patel, *Counsel*
Neil Marchuk, *Exec VP*
Bruce McDonald, *Exec VP*
Russ Burgei, *Vice Pres*
EMP: 2190 EST: 2015
SALES (est): 628.1MM **Privately Held**
WEB: www.adient.com
SIC: 2531 Seats, automobile

(G-13115)
ADIENT US ENTPS LTD PARTNR
49200 Halyard Dr (48170-2481)
PHONE 734 254-5000
Cathleen Ebacher, *Partner*
Mark A Skonieczny, *General Ptnr*
EMP: 120 EST: 2019
SALES (est): 62MM **Privately Held**
WEB: www.adient.com
SIC: 3714 Motor vehicle parts & accessories
HQ: Adient Global Holdings Ltd
3rd Floor 37 Esplanade
Jersey

(G-13116)
ADIENT US LLC (DH)
49200 Halyard Dr (48170-2481)
P.O. Box 981700, El Paso TX (79998-1700)
PHONE 734 254-5000
Cathleen Ebacher, *President*
Steven Mullen, *Superintendent*
Jennifer Marrocco, *Vice Pres*
Marie Eaton, *Buyer*
David Silva, *Buyer*
◆ EMP: 1100
SQ FT: 70,000
SALES (est): 1B **Privately Held**
WEB: www.adient.com
SIC: 3714 Motor vehicle parts & accessories

(G-13117)
ADIENT US LLC
47700 Halyard Dr (48170-2477)
P.O. Box 8010 (48170-8010)
PHONE 734 254-5000
Linas Polteraitis, *Vice Pres*
Eugen Craciun, *Engineer*
Aditya Doshi, *Engineer*
Alex Kobzar, *Engineer*
Max Reck, *Finance*
EMP: 300 **Privately Held**
WEB: www.adient.com
SIC: 3714 Motor vehicle parts & accessories
HQ: Adient Us Llc
49200 Halyard Dr
Plymouth MI 48170
734 254-5000

Plymouth - Wayne County (G-13118) — GEOGRAPHIC SECTION

(G-13118)
ADIENT US LLC
45000 Helm St (48170-6046)
PHONE 734 414-9215
EMP: 7 Privately Held
WEB: www.adient.com
SIC: 3714 Motor vehicle parts & accessories
HQ: Adient Us Llc
 49200 Halyard Dr
 Plymouth MI 48170
 734 254-5000

(G-13119)
ADVANCED AVIONICS INC
Also Called: Laser Blast
6118 Gotfredson Rd (48170-5073)
PHONE 734 259-5300
Carla Ewald, President
Timothy Ewald, Vice Pres
Mike Ewald, Bd of Directors
EMP: 9 EST: 1992
SQ FT: 2,300
SALES (est): 1.5MM Privately Held
WEB: www.laserblast.com
SIC: 3699 Heat emission operating apparatus

(G-13120)
AFB CORPORATE OPERATIONS LLC
Also Called: American Speedy Printing
47585 Galleon Dr (48170-2466)
PHONE 248 669-1188
Kevin Woodgate, Purchasing
Magda Dudek, Human Resources
Chuck Chupack, Sales Staff
Joanna Gonzales, Marketing Staff
Laura Pierce-Marutz, Mng Member
EMP: 22 EST: 1971
SQ FT: 25,000
SALES (est): 9.1MM
SALES (corp-wide): 47.1MM Privately Held
WEB: www.americanspeedy.com
SIC: 2752 7334 2789 2759 Commercial printing, offset; photocopying & duplicating services; bookbinding & related work; commercial printing
PA: Alliance Franchise Brands Llc
 47585 Galleon Dr
 Plymouth MI 48170
 248 596-8600

(G-13121)
ALLEGION S&S HOLDING CO INC
44704 Helm St (48170-6019)
PHONE 734 680-7429
EMP: 5 Privately Held
WEB: www.allegion.com
SIC: 3429 Locks or lock sets
HQ: Allegion S&S Holding Company Inc.
 11819 N Penn St
 Carmel IN 46032
 317 810-3700

(G-13122)
ALLIANCE FRANCHISE BRANDS LLC (PA)
Also Called: Insty-Prints
47585 Galleon Dr (48170-2466)
PHONE 248 596-8600
Carl Gerhardt, CEO
Julie Ledford, Business Mgr
Joe Haddad, Exec VP
Tom Hutchinson, Vice Pres
George Kummer, Vice Pres
EMP: 19 EST: 2017
SALES (est): 47.1MM Privately Held
WEB: www.alliancefranchisebrands.com
SIC: 2752 6794 Commercial printing, offset; franchises, selling or licensing

(G-13123)
AMERICAN FURUKAWA INC (DH)
Also Called: A F I
47677 Galleon Dr (48170-2466)
PHONE 734 446-2200
Kazuhisa Sakata, CEO
Dave Thomas, Senior VP
Shuichi Takagi, Vice Pres
Toru Umemoto, Vice Pres
Allan Landivar, Engineer
◆ EMP: 42 EST: 1996
SQ FT: 24,000
SALES (est): 55MM Privately Held
WEB: www.americanfurukawa.com
SIC: 3357 3572 5013 5065 Fiber optic cable (insulated); computer disk & drum drives & components; automotive supplies & parts; electronic parts

(G-13124)
ARGENT INTERNATIONAL INC
Also Called: Argent Automotive Systems
41016 Concept Dr (48170-4252)
P.O. Box 701007 (48170-0957)
PHONE 734 582-9800
Fred Perenic, President
James Beesley, Business Mgr
James Rudis, Plant Mgr
Kim Chesney, Accountant
Shirley Atcho, Human Res Mgr
◆ EMP: 128 EST: 1978
SQ FT: 84,000
SALES (est): 32.6MM Privately Held
WEB: www.argent-international.com
SIC: 2891 Adhesives

(G-13125)
ARGENT TAPE & LABEL INC (PA)
41016 Concept Dr Ste A (48170-4252)
P.O. Box 701007 (48170-0957)
PHONE 734 582-9956
Lynn Perenic, President
Deborah Sellis, COO
Cathie Melvin, Accounts Mgr
Melvin Cathie, Manager
Kimberly Schmitt, Analyst
EMP: 6 EST: 1984
SQ FT: 20,000
SALES (est): 2.5MM Privately Held
WEB: www.argent-label.com
SIC: 2672 3714 2671 Adhesive papers, labels or tapes: from purchased material; motor vehicle parts & accessories; packaging paper & plastics film, coated & laminated

(G-13126)
ARTCRAFT PRINTING CORPORATION
Also Called: Elegant Invitations
14919 Maplewood Ln (48170-2655)
PHONE 734 455-8893
John J Zunich, President
EMP: 4 EST: 1975
SALES (est): 300K Privately Held
WEB: www.artcraftprintingdetroit.com
SIC: 2752 Commercial printing, offset

(G-13127)
ATLAS TUBE (PLYMOUTH) INC
13101 Eckles Rd (48170-4245)
PHONE 734 738-5600
Barry M Zekelman, CEO
Dave Seeger, President
David W Seeger, President
Michael E Mechley, Exec VP
Tony Frabotta, Vice Pres
◆ EMP: 60 EST: 1996
SQ FT: 27,000
SALES (est): 26.4MM Privately Held
WEB: www.atlastube.com
SIC: 3317 Steel pipe & tubes
HQ: Atlas Holding Inc.
 1855 E 122nd St
 Chicago IL 60633

(G-13128)
ATRA PLASTICS INC
43938 Plymouth Oaks Blvd (48170-2584)
PHONE 734 237-3393
WEI Wang, President
Robert Say, Vice Pres
Pat Runnels, QC Mgr
David Kunz, Accounts Mgr
EMP: 14 EST: 2004
SALES (est): 4.1MM Privately Held
WEB: www.atrausa.com
SIC: 3089 Injection molding of plastics

(G-13129)
AUTOSYSTEMS AMERICA INC
Also Called: Litetek
46600 Port St (48170-6030)
PHONE 734 582-2300
Jeff Stecher, President
Jennifer Mitton, Controller
Shawn Bentley, Manager
Kristy Florian, Manager
Bradley Young, Technical Staff
EMP: 300 EST: 2003
SQ FT: 150,000
SALES (est): 52.1MM
SALES (corp-wide): 32.6B Privately Held
WEB: www.magna.com
SIC: 3647 Automotive lighting fixtures
PA: Magna International Inc
 337 Magna Dr
 Aurora ON L4G 7
 905 726-2462

(G-13130)
AVL MICHIGAN HOLDING CORP (DH)
47519 Halyard Dr (48170-2438)
PHONE 734 414-9600
Don Manvel, CEO
Helmut O List, CEO
Andreas Loecker, Business Mgr
Marko Dekena, Exec VP
Laura Ramirez, Purchasing
EMP: 100 EST: 1993
SALES (est): 113.2MM
SALES (corp-wide): 242.1K Privately Held
WEB: www.avl.com
SIC: 3823 Industrial instrmnts msrmnt display/control process variable
HQ: Avl List Gmbh
 Hans-List-Platz 1
 Graz 8020
 316 787-0

(G-13131)
AVL NORTH AMER CORP SVCS INC
47603 Halyard Dr (48170-2429)
PHONE 734 414-9600
Chester S Ricker, Principal
Patricia Bess, Opers Staff
Robert Fischer, Engineer
Jennifer Fulton, Accounting Mgr
Joyce Weishaar, Exec Dir
EMP: 609 EST: 2013
SALES (est): 154.4MM
SALES (corp-wide): 242.1K Privately Held
WEB: www.avl.com
SIC: 3569 Liquid automation machinery & equipment
HQ: Avl List Gmbh
 Hans-List-Platz 1
 Graz 8020
 316 787-0

(G-13132)
AVL POWERTRAIN TECHNOLOGIES (PA)
Also Called: A V L Instrumentation Test Sys
47603 Halyard Dr (48170-2429)
PHONE 734 414-9600
Raymond Corbin, President
Don Manvel, Chairman
Stuart Schulman, Treasurer
Tim Vannatter, Accounts Mgr
John Chevalier, Technical Staff
EMP: 4 EST: 1993
SALES (est): 3.4MM Privately Held
WEB: www.avl.com
SIC: 3714 Motor vehicle parts & accessories

(G-13133)
AVL PROPERTIES INC
47603 Halyard Dr (48170-2429)
PHONE 734 414-9600
Eric Green, Engineer
Douglas Fiorani, Sales Mgr
Tim Domin, Manager
Bill Jensen, Manager
Bob Nemeth, Director
EMP: 21 EST: 2015
SALES (est): 14.7MM
SALES (corp-wide): 242.1K Privately Held
WEB: www.avl.com
SIC: 3714 Motor vehicle parts & accessories
HQ: Avl List Gmbh
 Hans-List-Platz 1
 Graz 8020
 316 787-0

(G-13134)
AVL TEST SYSTEMS INC
47603 Halyard Dr (48170-2429)
PHONE 734 414-9600
Don Manvel, CEO
Gregory Hopton, President
Joseph Strelow, President
Thomas Lang, Business Mgr
Josef Maier, Vice Pres
▲ EMP: 121 EST: 1962
SQ FT: 68,500
SALES (est): 52.1MM
SALES (corp-wide): 242.1K Privately Held
WEB: www.avl.com
SIC: 3823 3829 3564 Industrial instrmnts msrmnt display/control process variable; measuring & controlling devices; blowers & fans
HQ: Avl Michigan Holding Corporation
 47519 Halyard Dr
 Plymouth MI 48170

(G-13135)
BERGER LLC
44160 Plymouth Oaks Blvd (48170-2584)
PHONE 734 414-0402
Carla Smith, CIO
Rick Dunkley, Technical Staff
Klaus Niemann,
Kecia Simmons, Cardiology
▲ EMP: 9 EST: 2004
SALES (est): 1.1MM Privately Held
WEB: www.bergergruppe.de
SIC: 3541 Grinding machines, metalworking

(G-13136)
BEST BINDING LLC
41230 Joy Rd (48170-4697)
PHONE 734 459-7785
James Decker,
EMP: 6 EST: 2011
SALES (est): 437.7K Privately Held
SIC: 2732 Books: printing & binding

(G-13137)
BR SAFETY PRODUCTS INC
1255 S Mill St (48170-4318)
PHONE 734 582-4499
Robert Milkowski, CEO
William Williamson, Principal
EMP: 9 EST: 2016
SALES (est): 184.9K Privately Held
WEB: www.brsafetyproducts.com
SIC: 3316 5051 Bars, steel, cold finished, from purchased hot-rolled; bars, metal

(G-13138)
BREMBO NORTH AMERICA INC (DH)
Also Called: Brembo Racing
47765 Halyard Dr (48170-2429)
PHONE 734 416-1275
Daniel Sandberg, President
Chris Husted, Opers Dir
Jason Wolfe, Mfg Staff
Kevin Duda, Purch Mgr
Emily Demeritt, Purch Agent
◆ EMP: 60 EST: 1989
SQ FT: 45,000
SALES (est): 189.2MM Privately Held
WEB: www.siti.com
SIC: 3714 5013 Motor vehicle parts & accessories; motor vehicle supplies & new parts; automotive supplies & parts; automotive supplies
HQ: Brembo Spa
 Viale Europa 2
 Stezzano BG 24040
 035 605-111

(G-13139)
BRUGOLA OEB INDSTRIALE USA INC
45555 Port St (48170-6051)
PHONE 734 468-0009
Egidio Brugola, President
Kim Kuras, Buyer
Massimiliano Ruzzi, Manager
▲ EMP: 13 EST: 1996
SQ FT: 109,000

GEOGRAPHIC SECTION
Plymouth - Wayne County (G-13165)

SALES (est): 11.8MM **Privately Held**
WEB: www.brugola.com
SIC: 3714 Motor vehicle parts & accessories
HQ: Brugola O.E.B. Industriale Spa
Piazza Papa Giovanni Xxiii 36
Lissone MB
039 244-41

(G-13140)
BULLETIN MOON
44315 Plymouth Oaks Blvd (48170-2585)
PHONE 734 453-9985
Ted Boloven, *Owner*
EMP: 9 **EST:** 2000
SALES (est): 651K **Privately Held**
SIC: 2711 Newspapers, publishing & printing

(G-13141)
CARBIDE SAVERS
41960 Joy Rd (48170-4636)
PHONE 248 388-1572
EMP: 5 **EST:** 2017
SALES (est): 331.8K **Privately Held**
WEB: www.carbidesavers.com
SIC: 2819 Carbides

(G-13142)
CARDIAC ASSIST HOLDINGS LLC
Also Called: Hbeat Medical
46701 Commerce Center Dr (48170-2475)
PHONE 781 727-1391
Kurt Dasse,
Allen Kantrowitz,
EMP: 4
SQ FT: 700
SALES (est): 164.1K **Privately Held**
SIC: 3841 Surgical & medical instruments

(G-13143)
CELLAR 849 WINERY
849 Penniman Ave Ste 101 (48170-3776)
PHONE 734 254-0275
John Robert Corsi, *Owner*
EMP: 6 **EST:** 2009
SALES (est): 192.1K **Privately Held**
SIC: 2084 Wines

(G-13144)
CEQUENT UK LTD
Also Called: Horizon Global Americas
47912 Halyard Dr Ste 100 (48170-2796)
PHONE 734 656-3000
EMP: 7
SALES (corp-wide): 661.2MM **Publicly Held**
SIC: 3714 Motor vehicle engines & parts
HQ: Cequent Uk Limited
Drome Road
Deeside

(G-13145)
CHANGAN US RES & DEV CTR INC
Also Called: Changan US R&D Center
47799 Halyard Dr Ste 77 (48170-3771)
PHONE 734 259-6440
Hong Su, *Vice Pres*
Ed Khalil, *Engineer*
Zeljko Medenica, *Engineer*
Jim Robertson, *Engineer*
Haoyu Sun, *Engineer*
▲ **EMP:** 4 **EST:** 2010
SALES (est): 4.9MM **Privately Held**
WEB: www.changanusa.com
SIC: 3069 Rubber automotive products
HQ: Changan Connected Car Technology Co., Ltd.
No.260 ,E(Ast) Jianxin Road,Jiangbei District
Chongqing 40002

(G-13146)
CHRYSAN INDUSTRIES INC (PA)
14707 Keel St (48170-6001)
PHONE 734 451-5411
Glenn Gerhard, *President*
Carolyn Booms, *Purchasing*
Alexander Bennett, *Engineer*
Suk Kyu Koh, *Director*
◆ **EMP:** 23 **EST:** 1977
SQ FT: 25,000
SALES (est): 40.1MM **Privately Held**
WEB: www.chrysanindustries.com
SIC: 2992 2842 Lubricating oils & greases; specialty cleaning preparations

(G-13147)
CLEAN TECH INC (HQ)
41605 Ann Arbor Rd E (48170-4304)
PHONE 734 455-3600
William C Young, *President*
Michael Plotzke, *CFO*
Karl Hatopp, *Sales Staff*
Heather Matheson, *Manager*
Gemma Bradshaw, *Admin Mgr*
▲ **EMP:** 47 **EST:** 1989
SQ FT: 90,000
SALES (est): 44.2MM
SALES (corp-wide): 2.9B **Privately Held**
WEB: www.cleantechrecycling.com
SIC: 3087 4953 Custom compound purchased resins; recycling, waste materials
PA: Plastipak Holdings, Inc.
41605 Ann Arbor Rd E
Plymouth MI 48170
734 455-3600

(G-13148)
COLCHA LINENS INC
14555 Jib St (48170-6011)
PHONE 313 355-8300
Anthony Jacobs, *Branch Mgr*
EMP: 15
SALES (corp-wide): 2MM **Privately Held**
WEB: www.canadabedandbath.com
SIC: 2392 Blankets, comforters & beddings
PA: Colcha Linens Inc
3 Queens Ave Suite 100
Leamington ON N8H 3
519 818-9140

(G-13149)
CONSOLIDATED CLIPS CLAMPS INC
Also Called: Clips & Clamps Industries
15050 Keel St (48170-6006)
PHONE 734 455-0880
Michael A Aznavorian, *President*
Alexandria Dul Mily, *Vice Pres*
Jeff Ross, *Vice Pres*
Kathleen Dul Aznavorian, *Treasurer*
Laura Mullin, *Human Resources*
EMP: 60 **EST:** 1954
SQ FT: 37,600
SALES (est): 11MM **Privately Held**
WEB: www.clipsclamps.com
SIC: 3469 3496 3429 Stamping metal for the trade; miscellaneous fabricated wire products; manufactured hardware (general)

(G-13150)
COOPER GENOMICS
705 S Main St (48170-2089)
PHONE 313 579-9650
EMP: 8 **EST:** 2017
SALES (est): 205.3K **Privately Held**
SIC: 2835 Microbiology & virology diagnostic products

(G-13151)
DADCO INC (PA)
Also Called: Power Components
43850 Plymouth Oaks Blvd (48170-2598)
PHONE 734 207-1100
Michael C Diebolt, *President*
Linda Diebolt, *COO*
Kimberly Wadowski, *Vice Pres*
Bill Brotherton, *Plant Mgr*
Ted Conroy, *Opers Staff*
◆ **EMP:** 95
SQ FT: 125,000
SALES (est): 15.1MM **Privately Held**
WEB: www.dadco.net
SIC: 3593 3492 5084 Fluid power cylinders & actuators; fluid power valves & hose fittings; industrial machinery & equipment

(G-13152)
DARE AUTO INC
Also Called: Fzb Technology
47548 Halyard Dr Ste B. (48170-4284)
PHONE 734 228-6243
Jim Yang, *President*
Yanshuo Wang, *Director*
EMP: 23 **EST:** 2013
SQ FT: 28,500
SALES (est): 5.8MM
SALES (corp-wide): 514.4MM **Privately Held**
WEB: www.dare-auto.us
SIC: 3625 3594 Motor starters & controllers, electric; fluid power pumps & motors
HQ: Southern Dare Co., Ltd.
No.1 Building Zhuyuan Industrial Park #69 Guanlan Blvd Guanlan
Shenzhen 51810
755 335-0053

(G-13153)
DENTON ATD INC
47460 Galleon Dr (48170-2467)
PHONE 734 451-7878
Dave Stein, *Branch Mgr*
EMP: 40 **Privately Held**
SIC: 3999 Mannequins
PA: Denton Atd, Inc.
900 Denton Dr
Huron OH 44839

(G-13154)
DESIGN USA INC
14680 Jib St (48170-6013)
PHONE 734 233-8677
John Mulgrew, *Principal*
Michele Holtzhausen, *Principal*
Bradley Springer, *Office Mgr*
EMP: 3 **EST:** 2017
SALES (est): 1.2MM **Privately Held**
WEB: www.designdesign.us
SIC: 3714 Motor vehicle parts & accessories
PA: Des Group (Pty) Ltd
18 Palmgate Cressoutgate Industrial Park
Kwa-Zulu Natal 4126

(G-13155)
DESIGNSHIRTSCOM INC
Also Called: Versatranz
14777 Keel St (48170-6001)
PHONE 734 414-7604
Francesco Viola, *President*
James Sheridan, *Vice Pres*
EMP: 6 **EST:** 2000
SALES (est): 1MM **Privately Held**
WEB: www.designshirts.com
SIC: 2759 Screen printing

(G-13156)
DHAKE INDUSTRIES INC
15169 Northville Rd (48170-2548)
PHONE 734 420-0101
Bhimashankar G Dhake, *President*
Sapna Dhake, *Vice Pres*
Priyanka Dhake, *Finance Mgr*
Arjun Dhake, *VP Mktg*
Rob Clements, *Manager*
EMP: 24 **EST:** 1978
SQ FT: 30,000
SALES (est): 5.6MM **Privately Held**
WEB: www.dhakeindustries.com
SIC: 2851 Paints & allied products

(G-13157)
DIAMOND TOOL MANUFACTURING INC
14540 Jib St (48170-6013)
P.O. Box 701484 (48170-0965)
PHONE 734 416-1900
Michael McHugh, *President*
Frank Jablonowski, *Mfg Mgr*
Samantha Krall, *Finance*
Rob Chipelewski, *Manager*
Philip Clemens, *Shareholder*
EMP: 32 **EST:** 1986
SQ FT: 10,400
SALES (est): 4.6MM **Privately Held**
WEB: www.diamondtoolmfg.com
SIC: 3545 3471 3291 Diamond cutting tools for turning, boring, burnishing, etc.; plating & polishing; abrasive products

(G-13158)
DIJET INCORPORATED (HQ)
45807 Helm St (48170-6025)
PHONE 734 454-9100
Keiichiro Izumi, *President*
Sandy Szybisty, *Admin Sec*
▲ **EMP:** 8 **EST:** 1983
SQ FT: 18,000
SALES (est): 3.1MM **Privately Held**
WEB: www.dijetusa.com
SIC: 3545 5084 Cutting tools for machine tools; metalworking tools (such as drills, taps, dies, files)

(G-13159)
DNA SOFTWARE INC
46701 Commerce Center Dr (48170-2475)
PHONE 734 222-9080
John Santalucia, *CEO*
Norm Watkins, *COO*
Joseph A Johnson, *Vice Pres*
Rashad Khaddaj, *Marketing Staff*
Lars Anderson, *Software Dev*
EMP: 10 **EST:** 2001
SALES (est): 1.2MM **Privately Held**
WEB: www.dnasoftware.com
SIC: 7372 Business oriented computer software

(G-13160)
DNR INC
45759 Helm St (48170-6025)
PHONE 734 722-4000
Guy Roberts, *Vice Pres*
EMP: 5 **Privately Held**
WEB: www.dnrpartscleaning.com
SIC: 3471 7349 Tumbling (cleaning & polishing) of machine parts; cleaning service, industrial or commercial
PA: D.N.R. Inc.
38475 Webb Dr
Westland MI 48185

(G-13161)
DONALD K STAPPERT
Also Called: Creative Woodworks
6400 Curtis Rd (48170)
PHONE 734 459-0004
Donald Stappert, *Owner*
EMP: 4 **EST:** 1984
SALES (est): 72.8K **Privately Held**
SIC: 2434 Wood kitchen cabinets

(G-13162)
DUO GARD INDUSTRIES INC
1317 Sheridan St (48170-1530)
PHONE 734 459-9166
David Miller, *Principal*
EMP: 5 **EST:** 2017
SALES (est): 97.5K **Privately Held**
WEB: www.duo-gard.com
SIC: 3999 Manufacturing industries

(G-13163)
DVS TECHNOLOGY AMERICA INC
44099 Plymouth Oaks Blvd (48170-6527)
PHONE 734 656-2080
Ralf Georg Eitel, *CEO*
EMP: 5 **EST:** 2015
SQ FT: 4,500
SALES (est): 7MM **Privately Held**
WEB: www.dvs-technology-america-inc.business.site
SIC: 3541 Machine tools, metal cutting type

(G-13164)
E & E MANUFACTURING CO INC (PA)
300 400 Indus Drv Plymouth (48170)
PHONE 734 451-7600
Wes Smith, *President*
Rick Lahood, *Business Mgr*
Marcin Bienasz, *Plant Mgr*
Christopher Damewood, *Plant Mgr*
Tammy Adkins, *Project Mgr*
▲ **EMP:** 220 **EST:** 1962
SQ FT: 250,000
SALES (est): 61.3MM **Privately Held**
WEB: www.eemfg.com
SIC: 3469 Stamping metal for the trade

(G-13165)
E & E MANUFACTURING CO INC
200 Industrial Dr (48170-1804)
PHONE 734 451-7600
Andreas Boehm, *Purchasing*
E Manufacturing, *Branch Mgr*
Arek Gladysz, *Department Mgr*
Ray Miles, *Manager*
Mark Roldan, *IT/INT Sup*
EMP: 10

Plymouth - Wayne County (G-13166) — GEOGRAPHIC SECTION

SALES (corp-wide): 61.3MM **Privately Held**
WEB: www.eemfg.com
SIC: **3465** Automotive stampings
PA: E & E Manufacturing Company, Inc.
300 400 Indus Drv Plymouth
Plymouth MI 48170
734 451-7600

(G-13166)
ELRINGKLINGER NORTH AMER INC
Also Called: (FORMERLY: ELRINGKLINGER SEALING SYSTEMS (USA) INC)
47912 Halyard Dr Ste 111 (48170-2796)
PHONE..................................734 738-1800
Andreas Brandl, *President*
David Beyer, *General Mgr*
Hinrich Hornbostel, *Vice Pres*
Jens Winter, *Vice Pres*
Darko Acoski, *Opers Spvr*
◆ EMP: 63 EST: 1995
SALES (est): 18MM
SALES (corp-wide): 144.1K **Privately Held**
WEB: www.elringklinger.de
SIC: **3465** Automotive stampings
HQ: Elringklinger Ag
Max-Eyth-Str. 2
Dettingen An Der Erms BW 72581
712 372-40

(G-13167)
EMERSON ELECTRIC CO
15024 Robinwood Dr (48170-2677)
PHONE..................................734 420-0832
Roger Craig, *Engineer*
Christophe Somercik, *Branch Mgr*
EMP: 5
SALES (corp-wide): 16.7B **Publicly Held**
WEB: www.emerson.com
SIC: **3823** Industrial instrmnts msrmnt display/control process variable
PA: Emerson Electric Co.
8000 West Florissant Ave
Saint Louis MO 63136
314 553-2000

(G-13168)
ERNEST INDS ACQUISITION LLC
Also Called: Ernest Industries Company
14601 Keel St (48170-6002)
PHONE..................................734 459-8881
EMP: 8
SALES (corp-wide): 7.2MM **Privately Held**
SIC: **3469** Mfg Metal Stampings
PA: Ernest Industries Acquisition, Llc
39133 Webb Dr
Westland MI 48185
734 595-9500

(G-13169)
FREUDENBERG N AMER LTD PARTNR (DH)
47774 W Anchor Ct (48170-2456)
PHONE..................................734 354-5505
Leesa A Smith, *President*
Robert G Evans, *Vice Pres*
Parker Stone, *Project Mgr*
Daniel Lee, *Research*
Christopher Vance, *Marketing Staff*
◆ EMP: 7 EST: 1984
SALES (est): 1.5B
SALES (corp-wide): 10.4B **Privately Held**
WEB: www.fst.com
SIC: **2821** **3714** **3053** **3061** Plastics materials & resins; motor vehicle parts & accessories; gaskets, packing & sealing devices; mechanical rubber goods
HQ: Freudenberg Fst Gmbh
Hohnerweg 2-4
Weinheim BW 69469
620 180-6666

(G-13170)
FREUDENBERG-NOK GENERAL PARTNR (DH)
Also Called: Freudenberg-Nok Sealing Tech
47774 W Anchor Ct (48170-2456)
PHONE..................................734 451-0020
Mohsen M Sohi, *CEO*
Brad Norton, *President*
John Rice, *President*
Martin Wentzler, *Chairman*
Dr Michael Heidingsfelder, *Senior VP*

◆ EMP: 200 EST: 1989
SQ FT: 80,000
SALES (est): 1.3B
SALES (corp-wide): 10.4B **Privately Held**
WEB: www.freudenberg.com
SIC: **2821** **3714** **3053** **3061** Plastics materials & resins; motor vehicle parts & accessories; gaskets, packing & sealing devices; mechanical rubber goods

(G-13171)
FREUDENBERG-NOK GENERAL PARTNR
47805 Galleon Dr (48170-2434)
PHONE..................................734 451-0020
Claus M Hlenkamp, *Branch Mgr*
EMP: 4
SALES (corp-wide): 10.4B **Privately Held**
WEB: www.fst.com
SIC: **2821** Plastics materials & resins
HQ: Freudenberg-Nok General Partnership
47774 W Anchor Ct
Plymouth MI 48170
734 451-0020

(G-13172)
FUTURIS AUTOMOTIVE (CA) LLC
49200 Halyard Dr (48170-2481)
PHONE..................................510 771-2300
Merv Dunn, *CEO*
Marjorie Watson, *Prdtn Mgr*
Rigoberto Ibarra, *Production*
Cherilyn Stoneman, *Buyer*
Gerald Rust, *Technical Mgr*
▲ EMP: 280 EST: 2011
SALES (est): 58.3MM **Privately Held**
SIC: **2396** Automotive trimmings, fabric
HQ: Futuris Automotive (Us) Inc.
14925 W 11 Mile Rd
Oak Park MI 48237
248 439-7800

(G-13173)
GARRETT MOTION INC (PA)
47548 Halyard Dr (48170-3796)
PHONE..................................734 359-5901
Carlos Cardoso, *Ch of Bd*
Olivier Rabillier, *President*
Craig Balis, *Senior VP*
Daniel Deiro, *Senior VP*
Thierry Mabru, *Senior VP*
EMP: 1232 EST: 2018
SALES: 3B **Privately Held**
SIC: **3714** Motor vehicle parts & accessories

(G-13174)
GATCO INCORPORATED
42330 Ann Arbor Rd E (48170-4303)
PHONE..................................734 453-2295
Mark E Sulkowski, *President*
EMP: 15 EST: 1913
SALES (est): 3MM **Privately Held**
WEB: www.gatcobushing.com
SIC: **3549** Metalworking machinery

(G-13175)
GI MILLWORKS INC
14970 Cleat St (48170-6053)
PHONE..................................734 451-1100
John Malcom, *President*
Thomas Rener, *Principal*
EMP: 18 EST: 1995
SALES (est): 1.1MM **Privately Held**
SIC: **2431** Moldings, wood: unfinished & prefinished

(G-13176)
GLASSLINE INCORPORATED
199 W Ann Arbor Trl (48170-1639)
PHONE..................................734 453-2728
Guy R Kenny, *President*
EMP: 16 EST: 1963
SALES (est): 1.6MM **Privately Held**
WEB: www.glassline.us
SIC: **2221** Fiberglass fabrics

(G-13177)
GLOBAL CNC INDUSTRIES LTD
15150 Cleat St (48170-6014)
PHONE..................................734 464-1920
Helen Stassinos, *President*
Catherine Stassinos, *Vice Pres*
Lambros Stassinos, *Treasurer*
Teresa Rupert, *VP Human Res*
Christine Stassinos, *Admin Sec*

▲ EMP: 34 EST: 1983
SQ FT: 23,000
SALES (est): 8.2MM **Privately Held**
WEB: www.globalcnc.com
SIC: **3545** **5084** **3366** Cutting tools for machine tools; industrial machinery & equipment; copper foundries

(G-13178)
GLOBE TECH LLC
Also Called: Globe Tech Manufactured Pdts
40300 Plymouth Rd (48170-4210)
PHONE..................................734 656-2200
Brian Swanson, *General Mgr*
John Meng, *CFO*
Kellean Lych, *Marketing Staff*
Gerry Graham, *Manager*
▲ EMP: 20 EST: 2003
SALES (est): 8.3MM **Privately Held**
WEB: www.globe-tech.biz
SIC: **3469** **3465** **3544** **3542** Metal stampings; automotive stampings; special dies, tools, jigs & fixtures; machine tools, metal forming type; machine tools, metal cutting type

(G-13179)
GRAPH-X SIGNS
45650 Mast St (48170-6007)
PHONE..................................734 420-0906
Tom Lunsford, *Owner*
Dina Calibeo, *Vice Pres*
Don Williams, *Opers Staff*
Glenn Nenninger, *Sales Staff*
Thomas Lunsford, *Manager*
EMP: 5 EST: 1995 **Privately Held**
WEB: www.graphxsigns.com
SIC: **3993** Neon signs

(G-13180)
GREKO PRINT & IMAGING INC
260 Ann Arbor Rd W (48170-4281)
PHONE..................................734 453-0341
Paul Degrazia, *President*
EMP: 14 EST: 2006
SALES (est): 2.2MM **Privately Held**
WEB: www.grekoprinting.com
SIC: **2752** Commercial printing, offset

(G-13181)
GRIP STUDIOS
743 Wing St Rear Bldg (48170-6450)
PHONE..................................248 757-0796
Dale Ryans, *Principal*
EMP: 6 EST: 2012 **Privately Held**
WEB: www.guitargrip.com
SIC: **3931** Guitars & parts, electric & non-electric

(G-13182)
HAIR VAULT LLC
1098 Ann Arbor Rd W Ste 5 (48170-2129)
PHONE..................................586 649-8218
Alexis McCrae,
EMP: 5 EST: 2020
SALES (est): 96K **Privately Held**
WEB: www.thehairvaultatl.com
SIC: **3999** Hair & hair-based products

(G-13183)
HATTERAS INC
Also Called: Focus 1
13200 N Haggerty Rd # 160 (48170-4296)
PHONE..................................734 525-5500
Claudia Nesbitt, *President*
Rebecca McFarlane, *Corp Secy*
Rebecca Zbozen, *Exec VP*
James Nesbitt, *Vice Pres*
Lincoln Puffer, *Regl Sales Mgr*
EMP: 35 EST: 1971
SALES (est): 8.6MM **Privately Held**
WEB: www.focus1data.com
SIC: **2752** **2791** **2789** Commercial printing, offset; typesetting; bookbinding & related work

(G-13184)
HAVIS INC
47099 Five Mile Rd (48170-3765)
PHONE..................................734 414-0699
Joe Bernert, *CEO*
Marcus Mlegette, *Production*
Ian Mark, *Engineer*
Steve Ferarro, *CFO*
Lori Layer, *Human Res Dir*
▲ EMP: 11 EST: 2010

SALES (est): 981.3K **Privately Held**
WEB: www.customers.havis.com
SIC: **3714** Directional signals, motor vehicle

(G-13185)
HAYDEN - MCNEIL LLC
14903 Pilot Dr (48170-3674)
PHONE..................................734 455-7900
Patrick R Olson, *CEO*
Jeff McCarthy, *President*
Moira Baker, *Sales Staff*
Amanda Humphrey, *Supervisor*
Danielle Mohler-Aceves, *Supervisor*
EMP: 30 EST: 1992
SQ FT: 11,500
SALES (est): 5.2MM
SALES (corp-wide): 1.6B **Privately Held**
WEB: www.haydenmcneil.com
SIC: **2731** Textbooks; publishing only, not printed on site
HQ: Macmillan Holdings, Llc
120 Broadway Fl 22
New York NY 10271

(G-13186)
HELM INCORPORATED (HQ)
47911 Halyard Dr (48170-3751)
PHONE..................................734 468-3700
Justin Gusick, *CEO*
Lorne Dubrowsky, *CFO*
▲ EMP: 97 EST: 1932
SQ FT: 155,000
SALES (est): 27.5MM
SALES (corp-wide): 47.6MM **Privately Held**
WEB: www.helm.com
SIC: **7389** **5199** **2741** Packaging & labeling services; advertising specialties; technical manual & paper publishing
PA: Helm Holding Company
47911 Halyard Dr
Detroit MI 48203
800 445-4831

(G-13187)
HERITAGE
1405 Gold Smith (48170-1082)
PHONE..................................734 414-0343
Gary Cummins, *Mng Member*
John Dempfey,
EMP: 5 EST: 1998
SALES (est): 474.4K **Privately Held**
WEB: www.heritagelogoworks.com
SIC: **3999** Embroidery kits

(G-13188)
HITEC SENSOR DEVELOPMENTS INC
47460 Galleon Dr (48170-2467)
PHONE..................................313 506-2460
Terry Theodore, *Principal*
Jeff Boyd, *Sales Staff*
EMP: 6 **Privately Held**
WEB: www.hitec.humaneticsgroup.com
SIC: **3823** Industrial process measurement equipment
PA: Hitec Sensor Developments, Inc.
10 Elizabeth Dr Ste 5
Chelmsford MA 01824

(G-13189)
HONEYWELL INTERNATIONAL INC
47548 Halyard Dr (48170-3796)
PHONE..................................734 392-5501
Roger Bratcher, *Manager*
EMP: 6
SALES (corp-wide): 32.6B **Publicly Held**
WEB: www.honeywell.com
SIC: **3724** Aircraft engines & engine parts
PA: Honeywell International Inc.
855 S Mint St
Charlotte NC 28202
704 627-6200

(G-13190)
HOOVER UNIVERSAL INC (HQ)
Also Called: Johnson Cntrls-Bttle Creek Vnt
49200 Halyard Dr (48170-2481)
PHONE..................................734 454-0994
Keith E Wandell, *President*
Bryan Johnson, *Superintendent*
Amy ACS, *Vice Pres*
James Conklin, *Vice Pres*
Jeffrey S Edwards, *Vice Pres*

GEOGRAPHIC SECTION
Plymouth - Wayne County (G-13214)

▲ **EMP:** 20 **EST:** 1985
SALES (est): 445.9MM **Privately Held**
WEB: www.adient.com
SIC: 2531 Seats, automobile

(G-13191)
HORIZON GLOBAL AMERICAS INC (HQ)
Also Called: Cequent Performance Group
47912 Halyard Dr Ste 100 (48170-2796)
PHONE.................................734 656-3000
John Aleva, *President*
Tom Aepelbacher, *Vice Pres*
Marcie Albright, *Vice Pres*
Paul Caruso, *Vice Pres*
Mike Finos, *Vice Pres*
◆ **EMP:** 200 **EST:** 1855
SALES (est): 550.4MM
SALES (corp-wide): 661.2MM **Publicly Held**
WEB: www.horizonglobal.com
SIC: 3714 3799 Trailer hitches, motor vehicle; trailer hitches
PA: Horizon Global Corporation
47912 Halyard Dr Ste 100
Plymouth MI 48170
734 656-3000

(G-13192)
HORIZON GLOBAL CORPORATION (PA)
47912 Halyard Dr Ste 100 (48170-2796)
PHONE.................................734 656-3000
Terrence G Gohl, *CEO*
Gangaram Gavli, *Managing Dir*
Kyle Luginski, *Regional Mgr*
Matthew Pollick, *COO*
Lee Adelman, *Vice Pres*
EMP: 1317 **EST:** 2015
SALES (est): 661.2MM **Publicly Held**
WEB: www.horizonglobal.com
SIC: 3714 3711 5531 Trailer hitches, motor vehicle; motor vehicle electrical equipment; wreckers (tow truck), assembly of; automobile & truck equipment & parts

(G-13193)
HUMAN SYNERGISTICS INC
39819 Plymouth Rd (48170-4290)
PHONE.................................734 459-1030
Robert A Cooke, *Principal*
Thomas W Cross, *Chairman*
Odile Ambrus, *Finance*
Mary Himmel, *Accounts Mgr*
Meghan Oliver, *Corp Comm Staff*
EMP: 22 **EST:** 1970
SQ FT: 9,000 **Privately Held**
WEB: www.humansynergistics.com
SIC: 2741 8742 Miscellaneous publishing; business consultant

(G-13194)
HYDRO-ABRASIVE PRODUCTS LLC
45507 Denise Dr (48170-3633)
PHONE.................................734 459-1544
James C Boomis, *Principal*
EMP: 5 **EST:** 2015
SALES (est): 101.2K **Privately Held**
SIC: 3291 Abrasive products

(G-13195)
IAC PLYMOUTH LLC
47785 W Anchor Ct (48170-2456)
PHONE.................................734 207-7000
Kathleen Paison, *Supervisor*
EMP: 41 **EST:** 2007
SALES (est): 19MM **Privately Held**
WEB: www.iacgroup.com
SIC: 3089 Automotive parts, plastic
HQ: International Automotive Components Group North America, Inc.
27777 Franklin Rd # 2000
Southfield MI 48034

(G-13196)
ILMOR ENGINEERING INC (PA)
Also Called: Ilmor High Performance Marine
43939 Plymouth Oaks Blvd (48170-2557)
PHONE.................................734 456-3600
Paul Ray, *President*
Julie Bernard, *Vice Pres*
Darren Dowding, *Opers Mgr*
Matthew Magers, *Maint Spvr*

Wayne Bennett, *Opers Staff*
▲ **EMP:** 75 **EST:** 1990
SQ FT: 45,000
SALES (est): 20MM **Privately Held**
WEB: www.ilmor.com
SIC: 3714 Motor vehicle engines & parts

(G-13197)
INSTRUMENT AND VALVE SERVICES
14789 Keel St (48170-6001)
PHONE.................................734 459-0375
EMP: 4
SALES (est): 300K **Privately Held**
SIC: 3491 Mfg Industrial Valves

(G-13198)
INTERNTNAL AUTO CMPNNTS GROUP
47785 W Anchor Ct (48170-2456)
PHONE.................................734 456-2800
EMP: 5 **Privately Held**
WEB: www.iacgroup.com
SIC: 3089 Automotive parts, plastic
HQ: International Automotive Components Group North America, Inc.
27777 Franklin Rd # 2000
Southfield MI 48034

(G-13199)
J L BECKER ACQUISITION LLC
Also Called: J. L. Becker Co.
41150 Joy Rd (48170-4634)
PHONE.................................734 656-2000
Thomas Gasbarre, *CEO*
Benjamin Gasbarre, *President*
Ben Gasbarre, *General Mgr*
Tom Sutter, *Engineer*
Anwelli Okpue, *Project Engr*
EMP: 40 **EST:** 1973
SQ FT: 55,640
SALES (est): 13MM
SALES (corp-wide): 40MM **Privately Held**
WEB: www.gasbarre.com
SIC: 3567 Industrial furnaces & ovens
PA: Gasbarre Products, Inc.
590 Division St
Du Bois PA 15801
814 371-3015

(G-13200)
JACK RIPPER & ASSOCIATES INC
14708 Keel St (48170-6028)
PHONE.................................734 453-7333
John L Ripper, *President*
John E Ripper, *President*
Daniel Ripper, *Vice Pres*
David L Ripper, *Vice Pres*
EMP: 8 **EST:** 1976
SQ FT: 28,000
SALES (est): 1.1MM **Privately Held**
WEB: www.jackripper.com
SIC: 2399 Banners, made from fabric

(G-13201)
JCIM MEXICO HOLDINGS LLC
45000 Helm St Ste 200 (48170-6046)
PHONE.................................734 254-3100
Patrick Flannagan, *Principal*
EMP: 16 **EST:** 2008
SALES (est): 1.2MM **Publicly Held**
WEB: www.johnsoncontrols.com
SIC: 3089 Injection molding of plastics
HQ: Johnson Controls, Inc.
5757 N Green Bay Ave
Glendale WI 53209
800 382-2804

(G-13202)
JIER NORTH AMERICA INC
14975 Cleat St (48170-6015)
PHONE.................................734 404-6683
Zhiqiang Hao, *President*
Sue Morgan, *Controller*
▲ **EMP:** 10 **EST:** 2011
SQ FT: 10,000
SALES (est): 26.5MM **Privately Held**
WEB: www.jier-na.com
SIC: 3542 Machine tools, metal forming type

PA: Jier Machine-Tool Group Co., Ltd.
No.2, Machine Tool No.2 Plant Road,
Huaiyin District
Jinan 25000

(G-13203)
JOGUE INC (PA)
Also Called: Northville Laboratories
14731 Helm Ct (48170-6096)
P.O. Box 190, Northville (48167-0190)
PHONE.................................734 207-0100
Anil Sastry, *President*
Ryan Richards, *Vice Pres*
Dr Dattu Sastry, *Vice Pres*
Pushpa Sastry, *Vice Pres*
Andrew Huber, *CFO*
◆ **EMP:** 27 **EST:** 1984
SQ FT: 48,000
SALES (est): 14.8MM **Privately Held**
WEB: www.jogue.com
SIC: 2087 2844 2099 Extracts, flavoring; perfumes & colognes; food preparations

(G-13204)
JOHNSON CONTROLS INC
49200 Halyard Dr (48170-2465)
PHONE.................................734 254-5000
Robert Schommer, *Principal*
EMP: 7 **Publicly Held**
WEB: www.johnsoncontrols.com
SIC: 3713 2531 Truck bodies & parts; public building & related furniture
HQ: Johnson Controls, Inc.
5757 N Green Bay Ave
Glendale WI 53209
800 382-2804

(G-13205)
JOHNSON CONTROLS INC
47700 Halyard Dr (48170-2477)
PHONE.................................734 254-7200
Jim Keys, *Principal*
EMP: 7 **Publicly Held**
WEB: www.johnsoncontrols.com
SIC: 3714 Motor vehicle parts & accessories
HQ: Johnson Controls, Inc.
5757 N Green Bay Ave
Glendale WI 53209
800 382-2804

(G-13206)
JOHNSON ELECTRIC N AMER INC (DH)
47660 Halyard Dr (48170-2453)
PHONE.................................734 392-5300
Patrick Shui-Chung Wang, *Chairman*
Yue LI, *Vice Pres*
Stephanie Brewer, *Production*
Tom McCarty, *Production*
Penny Calvert, *Buyer*
▲ **EMP:** 100
SQ FT: 5,000
SALES (est): 1.5B **Privately Held**
WEB: www.johnsonelectric.com
SIC: 5063 3625 3674 8711 Motors, electric; solenoid switches (industrial controls); microcircuits, integrated (semiconductor); engineering services

(G-13207)
JRA-SIGN SUPPLIES
14708 Keel St (48170-6004)
PHONE.................................800 447-7365
EMP: 4 **EST:** 2019
SALES (est): 103.4K **Privately Held**
WEB: www.jra-signsupplies.com
SIC: 3993 Signs & advertising specialties

(G-13208)
JTEKT AUTOMOTIVE N AMER INC
47771 Halyard Dr (48170-2479)
PHONE.................................734 454-1500
Yoshio Tsuji, *President*
Charles Brandt, *Vice Pres*
John Jaloszynski, *Vice Pres*
Rikako Demko, *Buyer*
Joshua Behmlander, *Engineer*
EMP: 1000 **EST:** 1988
SALES (est): 151.7MM **Privately Held**
WEB: www.jtekt-na.com
SIC: 3714 Motor vehicle parts & accessories

HQ: Jtekt North America Corporation
7 Research Dr Ste A
Greenville SC 29607
440 835-1000

(G-13209)
K-TOOL CORPORATION MICHIGAN (PA)
Also Called: K-Tool International
45225 Five Mile Rd (48170-2556)
PHONE.................................863 603-0777
Robert E Geisinger, *President*
Bill Driscoll, *Corp Secy*
Andy Dunham, *Sales Staff*
Doreen Morris, *Sales Staff*
Darcy Gignac, *Supervisor*
▲ **EMP:** 60 **EST:** 1981
SQ FT: 104,000
SALES (est): 21.4MM **Privately Held**
WEB: www.ktoolinternational.com
SIC: 5013 5072 3545 3544 Tools & equipment, automotive; hardware; machine tool accessories; special dies, tools, jigs & fixtures; machine tools, metal cutting type

(G-13210)
KARMANN MANUFACTURING LLC
14967 Pilot Dr (48170-3674)
PHONE.................................734 582-5900
EMP: 38
SALES (est): 31.7K
SALES (corp-wide): 4.1B **Privately Held**
SIC: 3999 Manufacturing Industries, Nec, Nsk
HQ: Webasto Convertibles Usa Inc.
14988 Pilot Dr
Plymouth MI 48170

(G-13211)
KEMIN INDUSTRIES INC
Also Called: Algal Scientific
14925 Galleon Ct (48170-6536)
PHONE.................................248 869-3080
EMP: 12
SALES (corp-wide): 333.8MM **Privately Held**
WEB: www.kemin.com
SIC: 4952 2048 8099 Sewerage systems; feed supplements; nutrition services
PA: Kemin Industries, Inc.
1900 Scott Ave
Des Moines IA 50317
515 559-5100

(G-13212)
KEMKRAFT ENGINEERING INC
47650 Clipper St (48170-2469)
PHONE.................................734 414-6500
Edward J Kemski Jr, *President*
Vickie Kemski, *Admin Sec*
EMP: 15 **EST:** 1988
SALES (est): 1.7MM **Privately Held**
WEB: www.kemkraft.com
SIC: 3829 Physical property testing equipment

(G-13213)
KEMNITZ FINE CANDIES
Also Called: Kemnitz Fine Candies & Gifts
896 W Ann Arbor Trl (48170-1602)
PHONE.................................734 453-0480
Cynthia Smith, *Owner*
Merle Hamlin, *Purchasing*
EMP: 8 **EST:** 1951
SQ FT: 1,200
SALES (est): 401.7K **Privately Held**
WEB: www.kemnitzcandies.com
SIC: 5441 2066 Candy; chocolate & cocoa products

(G-13214)
KEY PLASTICS LLC
44191 Plymouth Oaks Blvd (48170-6530)
PHONE.................................248 449-6100
Karen Dahowski, *Materials Mgr*
Tina Mosley, *Personnel Assit*
EMP: 17 **EST:** 2015
SALES (est): 605.8K **Privately Held**
SIC: 3083 5162 Plastic finished products, laminated; plastics materials & basic shapes

Plymouth - Wayne County (G-13215) GEOGRAPHIC SECTION

(G-13215)
KIMPRINT INC
Also Called: Progressive Printing
14875 Galleon Ct (48170-6523)
PHONE..................734 459-2960
Kimberly A Price, *President*
Bruce M Price, *Vice Pres*
Bruce Price, *Vice Pres*
Todd Conte, *Opers Mgr*
Bruce M Price, *CFO*
EMP: 27 **EST:** 1989
SQ FT: 18,500
SALES: 3.8MM **Privately Held**
SIC: 7331 2752 Mailing service; commercial printing, offset

(G-13216)
KINGDOM CARTRIDGE INC
11704 Morgan Ave (48170-4439)
P.O. Box 5478 (48170-5478)
PHONE..................734 564-1590
Dave Kozler, *President*
EMP: 9 **EST:** 2011
SALES (est): 129.2K **Privately Held**
SIC: 3577 Printers, computer

(G-13217)
LARSON-JUHL US LLC
47584 Galleon Dr (48170-2467)
PHONE..................734 416-3302
EMP: 4
SALES (corp-wide): 245.5B **Publicly Held**
WEB: www.larsonjuhl.com
SIC: 2499 Applicators, wood
HQ: Larson-Juhl Us Llc
   1925 Breckinridge Plz # 200
   Duluth GA 30096
   770 279-5200

(G-13218)
LASER MFG INC
Also Called: Sealmaster/Michigan
9965 Lapham Way (48170-5853)
PHONE..................313 292-2299
Michael Laser, *President*
Tony Rutger, *Vice Pres*
EMP: 7 **EST:** 1993
SALES (est): 993.9K **Privately Held**
WEB: www.sealmaster.net
SIC: 2951 Asphalt paving mixtures & blocks

(G-13219)
LASERLINE INC
46025 Port St (48170-6080)
PHONE..................248 826-5041
EMP: 7 **EST:** 2017
SALES (est): 386.1K **Privately Held**
WEB: www.laserline.com
SIC: 3714 Motor vehicle parts & accessories

(G-13220)
LAW ENFORCEMENT DEVELOPMENT CO
Also Called: Ledco-Chargeguard
47801 W Anchor Ct (48170-6018)
PHONE..................734 656-4100
Joe Bernert, *CEO*
Michael J Bernert, *President*
Michael Zani, *COO*
Jay Shaw, *Engrg Dir*
Steve Ferraro, *CFO*
▲ **EMP:** 39 **EST:** 1988
SQ FT: 26,000
SALES (est): 3.3MM
SALES (corp-wide): 52.5MM **Privately Held**
WEB: www.customers.havis.com
SIC: 3577 Computer peripheral equipment
PA: Havis, Inc.
   75 Jacksonville Rd
   Warminster PA 18974
   215 957-0720

(G-13221)
LINDEN ART GLASS
580 Forest Ave Ste 2a (48170-1780)
PHONE..................734 459-5060
EMP: 4 **EST:** 2019
SALES (est): 39.7K **Privately Held**
WEB: www.lindenartglass.com
SIC: 3229 Pressed & blown glass

(G-13222)
LINK GROUP INC (PA)
Also Called: Link Engineering Company
43855 Plymouth Oaks Blvd (48170-2539)
PHONE..................734 453-0800
Roy Link, *CEO*
Derek Stoneburg, *CFO*
▲ **EMP:** 100 **EST:** 2010
SALES (est): 139.1MM **Privately Held**
WEB: www.linkeng.com
SIC: 3829 Measuring & controlling devices

(G-13223)
LINK MANUFACTURING INC (HQ)
Also Called: Link Engineering Company
43855 Plymouth Oaks Blvd (48170-2539)
PHONE..................734 453-0800
Roy Link, *Ch of Bd*
Warren Brown, *Vice Pres*
Timothy Olex, *Vice Pres*
Derek Stoneburg, *CFO*
John Ligerakism, *Sales Mgr*
▲ **EMP:** 100 **EST:** 1953
SQ FT: 73,000
SALES (est): 46.2MM **Privately Held**
WEB: www.linkeng.com
SIC: 3829 Physical property testing equipment; testing equipment: abrasion, shearing strength, etc.

(G-13224)
LOC PERFORMANCE PRODUCTS LLC (PA)
13505 N Haggerty Rd (48170-4251)
PHONE..................734 453-2300
Jason Atkinson, *COO*
James Joo, *Plant Mgr*
Jeff Hanson, *Mfg Staff*
Alex Bibeau, *Purch Agent*
Michael Barker, *Buyer*
◆ **EMP:** 200 **EST:** 1971
SQ FT: 246,000
SALES (est): 134.2MM **Privately Held**
WEB: www.locperformance.com
SIC: 3541 Machine tools, metal cutting type

(G-13225)
LOCHINVAR LLC
45900 Port St (48170-6052)
PHONE..................734 454-4480
Jack Myers, *Vice Pres*
Simon Gaines, *Manager*
Rich Murphy, *Manager*
Dan Walker, *Administration*
EMP: 35
SALES (corp-wide): 2.9B **Publicly Held**
WEB: www.lochinvar.com
SIC: 5074 5091 3443 Water heaters, except electric; swimming pools, equipment & supplies; fabricated plate work (boiler shop)
HQ: Lochinvar Llc
   300 Maddox Simpson Pkwy
   Lebanon TN 37090

(G-13226)
LOCPAC INC
13505 N Haggerty Rd (48170-4251)
PHONE..................734 453-2300
Victor Vojcek, *CEO*
Lou Burr, *President*
Jason Atkinson, *COO*
Paul Hobson, *Purch Agent*
Thomas Horne, *CFO*
EMP: 20 **EST:** 1985
SQ FT: 35,000
SALES (est): 1.5MM
SALES (corp-wide): 134.2MM **Privately Held**
WEB: www.locperformance.com
SIC: 7389 3479 Packaging & labeling services; painting of metal products
PA: Loc Performance Products, Llc
   13505 N Haggerty Rd
   Plymouth MI 48170
   734 453-2300

(G-13227)
LRS INC
9448 Northern Ave (48170-4048)
PHONE..................734 416-5050
Lawrence R Schafer, *Ch of Bd*
John Schafer, *President*
Mary C Schafer, *Corp Secy*
Shawn Snyder, *Marketing Staff*
EMP: 6 **EST:** 1967
SALES (est): 461.7K **Privately Held**
SIC: 3544 Dies & die holders for metal cutting, forming, die casting

(G-13228)
LSR INCORPORATED
11050 N Beck Rd (48170-3327)
PHONE..................734 455-6530
Larry Runnion, *President*
EMP: 10 **EST:** 2000
SALES (est): 500K **Privately Held**
WEB: www.animalcareandsurgicalhospital.com
SIC: 0782 3499 Landscape contractors; giftware, copper goods

(G-13229)
LUKE LEGACY PUBLICATIONS LLC
1098 Ann Arbor Rd W (48170-2129)
PHONE..................313 363-5949
EMP: 4 **EST:** 2019
SALES (est): 229.7K **Privately Held**
WEB: www.legacypublications.com
SIC: 2741 Miscellaneous publishing

(G-13230)
M-52 SAND & GRAVEL LLC
8483 Ann Arbor Rd W (48170-5101)
PHONE..................734 453-3695
Rick Perlongo, *Principal*
EMP: 6 **EST:** 2009
SALES (est): 398.8K **Privately Held**
SIC: 1442 Construction sand & gravel

(G-13231)
MAGNESIUM PRODUCTS AMERICA INC (HQ)
Also Called: Meridian Lightweight Tech
47805 Galleon Dr (48170-2434)
PHONE..................734 416-8600
Erick Showalter, *President*
Andrea Ward, *Superintendent*
Scheurer Joe, *Engineer*
Brian Roes, *Engineer*
Jessica Landon, *CFO*
▲ **EMP:** 359 **EST:** 1992
SQ FT: 160,000
SALES (est): 92.5MM
SALES (corp-wide): 138.8MM **Privately Held**
SIC: 3364 3369 3714 Magnesium & magnesium-base alloy die-castings; nonferrous foundries; motor vehicle parts & accessories
PA: Mlth Holdings Inc
   25 Mcnab St
   Strathroy ON
   519 246-9600

(G-13232)
MAJESKE MACHINE INC
44650 Pinetree Dr (48170-3841)
PHONE..................319 273-8905
Gerald Majeske Jr, *President*
EMP: 7 **EST:** 1995
SALES (est): 218.6K **Privately Held**
SIC: 3545 Precision tools, machinists'

(G-13233)
MANUFACTURING PRODUCTS & SVCS
260 Ann Arbor Rd W (48170-4281)
PHONE..................734 927-1964
Paul Degrazi, *President*
EMP: 10 **EST:** 2008
SALES (est): 911.7K **Privately Held**
SIC: 3465 3711 4225 7389 Automotive stampings; automobile assembly, including specialty automobiles; general warehousing & storage; commodity inspection; industrial & commercial equipment inspection service

(G-13234)
MARIO ANTHONY TABONE
379 Red Ryder Dr (48170-2160)
PHONE..................734 667-2946
Mario Anthony Tabone, *Principal*
EMP: 4 **EST:** 2015
SALES (est): 119.9K **Privately Held**
WEB: www.tabonevineyards.com
SIC: 2084 Wines

(G-13235)
MARJO PLASTICS COMPANY INC
1081 Cherry (48170-1304)
PHONE..................734 455-4130
Fred D Hovorka, *President*
EMP: 4 **EST:** 1948
SQ FT: 3,600
SALES (est): 432.2K **Privately Held**
WEB: www.marjoplastics.com
SIC: 3089 Injection molding of plastics

(G-13236)
MATERIALISE USA LLC
44650 Helm Ct (48170-6061)
PHONE..................734 259-6445
Wilifried Vancrean, *CEO*
Michael Lawrenchuk, *Business Mgr*
Thomas Cullum, *Engineer*
Colleen Flanagan, *Engineer*
Arden McDonough, *Engineer*
EMP: 60 **EST:** 1996
SQ FT: 1,200
SALES (est): 27.6MM
SALES (corp-wide): 131.3MM **Privately Held**
WEB: www.materialise.openfos.com
SIC: 5734 2759 Computer software & accessories; laser printing
PA: Materialise
   Technologielaan 15
   Leuven 3001
   163 966-11

(G-13237)
MC REA CORPORATION
40422 Cove Ct (48170-2684)
PHONE..................734 420-2116
Raymond Fredrickson, *President*
EMP: 6 **EST:** 1967
SQ FT: 10,000
SALES (est): 462.1K **Privately Held**
SIC: 3548 Spot welding apparatus, electric

(G-13238)
MCCOIG MATERIALS LLC
40500 Ann Arbor Rd E # 20 (48170-4483)
P.O. Box 703238 (48170-0994)
PHONE..................734 414-6179
Kathy Hayes, *Controller*
Nancy Skaggs, *Accountant*
EMP: 40 **EST:** 2012
SALES (est): 6.2MM **Privately Held**
WEB: www.smyrnareadymix.com
SIC: 3273 Ready-mixed concrete

(G-13239)
MED MICHIGAN HOLDINGS LLC (PA)
40600 Ann Arbor Rd E (48170-4675)
PHONE..................888 891-1200
Mike Schroeder, *President*
EMP: 0 **EST:** 2019
SALES (est): 1.9MM **Privately Held**
SIC: 6719 3841 Investment holding companies, except banks; surgical & medical instruments

(G-13240)
MEMTECH INC (PA)
9033 General Dr (48170-4680)
PHONE..................734 455-8550
Dale Manor, *President*
Amy Prater-Manor, *Project Engr*
Carl Evans, *Admin Sec*
EMP: 10 **EST:** 1983
SALES (est): 1MM **Privately Held**
WEB: www.memtechbrush.com
SIC: 3053 5085 8711 5033 Gaskets & sealing devices; seals, industrial; engineering services; roofing, siding & insulation; miscellaneous fabricated wire products; metal doors, sash & trim

(G-13241)
MERIDIAN LIGHTWEIGHT TECH INC
47805 Galleon Dr Ste B (48170-2434)
PHONE..................248 663-8100
Eric Showalter, *CEO*
Jeffrey L Moyer, *Vice Pres*

▲ = Import ▼ = Export
◆ = Import/Export

Tony Papa, *Vice Pres*
Mike Pyles, *Maint Spvr*
Kyla Lewis, *Manager*
EMP: 32 **EST:** 2013
SALES (est): 1.1MM **Privately Held**
WEB: www.meridian-mag.com
SIC: 1081 8641 Metal mining services; environmental protection organization
HQ: Meridian Lightweight Technologies Holdings Inc.
25 Mcnab St
Strathroy ON N7G 4
519 246-9600

(G-13242)
MILLER MACHINE INC
41250 Joy Rd (48170-4697)
PHONE 734 455-5333
Raymond Miller, *President*
Gary Robert, *Vice Pres*
EMP: 4 **EST:** 1988
SQ FT: 3,000
SALES (est): 427.7K **Privately Held**
SIC: 3599 Machine shop, jobbing & repair

(G-13243)
MILLER TECHNICAL SERVICES INC
Also Called: M T S
47801 W Anchor Ct (48170-6018)
PHONE 734 207-3159
▲ **EMP:** 15
SQ FT: 35,000
SALES (est): 2.8MM **Privately Held**
SIC: 3842 Mfg Surgical Appliances/Supplies

(G-13244)
MILLER TOOL DIE CO
47801 W Anchor Ct (48170-6018)
PHONE 734 738-1970
Rick Tunstall, *Principal*
EMP: 5 **EST:** 2017
SALES (est): 282.9K **Privately Held**
SIC: 3398 Metal heat treating

(G-13245)
MJ CABINET DESIGNS
9475 Red Maple Dr (48170-3282)
PHONE 734 354-9633
EMP: 6 **EST:** 2014
SALES (est): 235.7K **Privately Held**
WEB: www.mj-kitchens.com
SIC: 2434 Wood kitchen cabinets

(G-13246)
MJS INVESTING LLC
Also Called: Hvac
41170 Joy Rd (48170-4634)
PHONE 734 455-6500
Josh Pennington, *President*
EMP: 50 **EST:** 1977
SALES (est): 5.1MM **Privately Held**
WEB: www.colonialhc.com
SIC: 1711 3585 5074 Ventilation & duct work contractor; warm air heating & air conditioning contractor; air conditioning equipment, complete; plumbing & hydronic heating supplies

(G-13247)
MOLDED MATERIALS
14555 Jib St (48170-6011)
PHONE 734 927-1989
Mark Marra, *Engineer*
Mike Wolf, *Manager*
Anna Gluzman, *Info Tech Mgr*
▲ **EMP:** 16 **EST:** 2010
SALES (est): 300.3K **Privately Held**
WEB: www.mmi-es.com
SIC: 3089 Molding primary plastic

(G-13248)
MOOG INC
Also Called: Moog Fcs
47495 Clipper St (48170-2470)
PHONE 734 738-5862
Drew Steele, *Principal*
Joe Morrill, *Director*
EMP: 4
SALES (corp-wide): 2.8B **Publicly Held**
WEB: www.moog.com
SIC: 7373 3674 Computer integrated systems design; semiconductors & related devices

PA: Moog Inc.
400 Jamison Rd
Elma NY 14059
716 652-2000

(G-13249)
MPG INC (PA)
47659 Halyard Dr (48170-2429)
PHONE 734 207-6200
Thomas V Chambers, *President*
George Thomas, *President*
Witkow Edward, *COO*
Tina Kozak, *COO*
Beverly Mathews, *COO*
▲ **EMP:** 150 **EST:** 1999
SQ FT: 50,000
SALES (est): 127.6MM **Privately Held**
SIC: 3499 Aerosol valves, metal; aquarium accessories, metal; doors, safe & vault: metal

(G-13250)
MPG HOLDCO I INC
47659 Halyard Dr (48170-2429)
PHONE 734 207-6200
EMP: 1 **EST:** 2014
SALES (est): 8.1MM
SALES (corp-wide): 4.7B **Publicly Held**
WEB: www.aam.com
SIC: 3714 Motor vehicle parts & accessories
PA: American Axle & Manufacturing Holdings, Inc.
1 Dauch Dr
Detroit MI 48211
313 758-2000

(G-13251)
MYCRONA INC
14777 Keel St (48170-6001)
PHONE 734 453-9348
EMP: 15
SQ FT: 8,000
SALES (est): 1.3MM **Privately Held**
SIC: 5084 7699 3823 Whol & Services Industrial Measuring Equipment

(G-13252)
NATIONAL WHOLESALE PRTG CORP
41290 Joy Rd (48170-4697)
PHONE 734 416-8400
Brian L Marr, *President*
EMP: 9 **EST:** 1983
SQ FT: 7,500
SALES (est): 927.3K **Privately Held**
WEB: www.nationalprintingmi.com
SIC: 2752 7331 Commercial printing, offset; direct mail advertising services

(G-13253)
NEEDLES N PINS INC
754 S Main St (48170-2047)
PHONE 734 459-0625
Rl Laird, *Owner*
EMP: 6 **EST:** 2001
SALES (est): 514.6K **Privately Held**
SIC: 3552 Embroidery machines

(G-13254)
OILES AMERICA CORPORATION
44099 Plymouth Oaks Blvd (48170-6527)
PHONE 734 414-7400
Terry Wright, *QC Mgr*
Eric Liu, *Engineer*
Alan Qu, *Engineer*
Chris Furgason, *Sales Staff*
Mickey Rosiu, *Branch Mgr*
EMP: 115 **Privately Held**
WEB: www.oilesglobal.com
SIC: 3714 Motor vehicle parts & accessories
HQ: Oiles America Corporation
4510 Enterprise Dr Nw
Concord NC 28027
704 784-4500

(G-13255)
OLD WORLD OLIVE PRESS
467 Forest Ave (48170-1721)
PHONE 734 667-2755
Jack Rabinowitz, *Principal*
EMP: 6 **EST:** 2011
SALES (est): 145.7K **Privately Held**
WEB: www.theoldworldoliveco.com
SIC: 2079 Olive oil

(G-13256)
OPTIMAL ELECTRIC VEHICLES LLC
47802 W Anchor Ct (48170-2459)
PHONE 734 414-7933
Song Ling Young, *CEO*
EMP: 30 **EST:** 2017
SALES (est): 1.1MM **Privately Held**
SIC: 3713 Truck & bus bodies

(G-13257)
OPTRAND INC
46155 Five Mile Rd (48170-2424)
PHONE 734 451-3480
Marek T Wlodarczyk, *President*
EMP: 22 **EST:** 1992
SQ FT: 10,000
SALES (est): 671.6K **Privately Held**
WEB: www.optrand.com
SIC: 3229 Glass fiber products

(G-13258)
ORTHOTOOL LLC (PA)
50325 Ann Arbor Rd W (48170-6333)
PHONE 734 455-8103
John Chiatalas, *CEO*
David Hellar, *COO*
James B Stiehl, *Chief Mktg Ofcr*
EMP: 4 **EST:** 2009
SQ FT: 200
SALES (est): 218.7K **Privately Held**
SIC: 3143 3144 3149 5047 Orthopedic shoes, men's; orthopedic shoes, women's; orthopedic shoes, children's; orthopedic equipment & supplies

(G-13259)
PACKAGING CORPORATION AMERICA
Pca/Plymouth 364
936 N Sheldon Rd (48170-1016)
PHONE 734 453-6262
Joe Pozek, *General Mgr*
Willie Lathon, *Cust Mgr*
Kavanagh Gary, *Executive*
Ernest Foerster,
EMP: 100
SALES (corp-wide): 6.6B **Publicly Held**
WEB: www.packagingcorp.com
SIC: 2653 Boxes, corrugated: made from purchased materials
PA: Packaging Corporation Of America
1 N Field Ct
Lake Forest IL 60045
847 482-3000

(G-13260)
PALIOT SOLUTIONS LLC (PA) ✪
41100 Plymouth Rd (48170-3799)
PHONE 616 648-5939
Paul Barry, *CEO*
EMP: 5 **EST:** 2021
SALES (est): 625.2K **Privately Held**
SIC: 2448 Wood pallets & skids

(G-13261)
PENNISULAR PACKAGING LLC
13505 N Haggerty Rd (48170-4251)
PHONE 313 304-4724
Wesley Charles, *President*
EMP: 4 **EST:** 2015
SQ FT: 5,000
SALES (est): 195.1K **Privately Held**
SIC: 3325 Steel foundries

(G-13262)
PENROSE THERAPEUTIX LLC
46701 Commerce Center Dr (48170-2475)
PHONE 847 370-0303
Maysaa Doughan, *Research*
Umrai Gill, *Mng Member*
Nick Conde, *Director*
James Jaber,
EMP: 5 **EST:** 2016
SQ FT: 1,000
SALES (est): 1.6MM **Privately Held**
WEB: www.penrosetherapeutx.com
SIC: 2834 Proprietary drug products

(G-13263)
PERCEPTRON INC (DH)
47827 Halyard Dr (48170-2461)
PHONE 734 414-6100
Jay W Freeland, *Ch of Bd*
Brad Armstrong, *COO*

Richard J Van Valkenburg, *Vice Pres*
John Barnes, *Project Mgr*
David Guo, *Engineer*
▲ **EMP:** 282 **EST:** 1981
SQ FT: 70,000
SALES: 62.2MM
SALES (corp-wide): 11.5B **Privately Held**
WEB: www.perceptron.com
SIC: 3827 3829 Optical instruments & lenses; measuring & controlling devices

(G-13264)
PINE TECH INC (PA)
14941 Cleat St (48170-6015)
PHONE 989 426-0006
Lawrence H Markey Jr, *President*
Keith A Iverson, *Treasurer*
EMP: 44 **EST:** 1987
SQ FT: 6,000
SALES (est): 3.8MM **Privately Held**
WEB: www.pflumber.com
SIC: 2421 2431 2426 Furniture dimension stock, softwood; kiln drying of lumber; millwork; hardwood dimension & flooring mills

(G-13265)
PIOLAX CORPORATION
47075 Five Mile Rd (48170-3765)
PHONE 734 668-6005
Fred Beauregard, *Manager*
EMP: 73 **Privately Held**
SIC: 5013 3572 Automotive supplies & parts; disk drives, computer
HQ: Piolax Corporation
139 Etowah Industrial Ct
Canton GA 30114
770 479-2227

(G-13266)
PLASTIPAK HOLDINGS INC (PA)
41605 Ann Arbor Rd E (48170-4304)
P.O. Box 701575 (48170-0967)
PHONE 734 455-3600
William C Young, *President*
Sharon Hedgecock, *President*
Joseph Lalik, *COO*
John Hilliard, *Vice Pres*
Pradeep Modi, *Vice Pres*
◆ **EMP:** 15 **EST:** 1998
SQ FT: 37,500
SALES (est): 2.9B **Privately Held**
WEB: www.plastipak.com
SIC: 3089 Blow molded finished plastic products

(G-13267)
PLYMOUTH PLATING WORKS INC
42200 Joy Rd (48170-4636)
PHONE 734 453-1560
Donald E Webb, *President*
Dale E Webb, *Vice Pres*
Paul Pearce, *Director*
EMP: 10 **EST:** 1923
SQ FT: 18,000
SALES (est): 838.3K **Privately Held**
WEB: www.plymouthplating.com
SIC: 3471 Electroplating of metals or formed products

(G-13268)
PLYMOUTH-CANTON CMNTY CRIER (PA)
Also Called: Comma
821 Penniman Ave (48170-1621)
PHONE 734 453-6900
W Edward Wendover, *President*
EMP: 30 **EST:** 1974
SQ FT: 10,000
SALES (est): 2.7MM **Privately Held**
WEB: www.plymouthlibrary.org
SIC: 2711 Newspapers: publishing only, not printed on site

(G-13269)
POWER PROCESS PIPING INC (PA)
45780 Port St (48170-6049)
PHONE 734 451-0130
Graham Williams, *CEO*
Danny Woods, *Superintendent*
Art Espey, *COO*
Jerry L Palmer, *Vice Pres*
Jerryl Palmer, *Vice Pres*

Plymouth - Wayne County (G-13270)   GEOGRAPHIC SECTION

EMP: 35 EST: 1974
SQ FT: 30,000
SALES (est): 29.1MM Privately Held
WEB: www.ppphq.com
SIC: 3498 1711 Fabricated pipe & fittings; plumbing, heating, air-conditioning contractors

(G-13270)
PREMIUM SUND SLUTIONS AMER LLC (PA)
Also Called: Pss
44099 Plymouth Oaks Blvd (48170-6527)
PHONE.............................734 259-6142
Esther Nelson, *Engineer*
Rodney Garman, *Manager*
Christophe Lobelle, *Manager*
Eric Woelkers, *Business Dir*
Erik Roeren,
EMP: 1 EST: 2013
SALES (est): 1.5MM Privately Held
WEB: www.premiumsoundsolutions.com
SIC: 3651 Audio electronic systems

(G-13271)
PSI HYDRAULICS
14492 N Sheldon Rd # 374 (48170-2493)
PHONE.............................734 261-4160
William T Phillips, *President*
Eugene G Lawrie, *COO*
B J De Boe, *Vice Pres*
Mark W Jahnke, *CFO*
Jill Sak, *Executive Asst*
EMP: 28 EST: 1967
SALES (est): 1.7MM
SALES (corp-wide): 54.3MM Privately Held
WEB: www.psi-online.com
SIC: 3452 7629 7699 Bolts, nuts, rivets & washers; electrical repair shops; pumps & pumping equipment repair; valve repair, industrial
PA: Phillips Service Industries, Inc.
  1800 Landsdowne Rd
  Ann Arbor MI 48105
  734 853-5000

(G-13272)
PYXIS TECHNOLOGIES LLC
45911 Port St (48170-6010)
PHONE.............................734 414-0261
Todd Kuehn,
Jeffrey Wickens,
▲ EMP: 43
SQ FT: 51,000
SALES (est): 18MM Privately Held
WEB: www.pyxistechnologies.com
SIC: 3599 Machine shop, jobbing & repair

(G-13273)
QUARTERS LLC
1415 Sheridan St (48170-1532)
PHONE.............................313 510-5555
Leonard Daitch, *Mng Member*
EMP: 4 EST: 2002
SALES (est): 420.8K Privately Held
SIC: 3581 Automatic vending machines

(G-13274)
R & D ENTERPRISES INC
46900 Port St (48170-6035)
PHONE.............................248 349-7077
George Sheriff, *CEO*
Richard D Cox, *CEO*
Diane Cox, *CFO*
Yvonne Cox, *Treasurer*
◆ EMP: 50 EST: 1974
SQ FT: 58,000
SALES (est): 5.5MM Privately Held
SIC: 3443 3519 3429 Heat exchangers: coolers (after, inter), condensers, etc.; parts & accessories, internal combustion engines; manufactured hardware (general)

(G-13275)
RASSINI CHASSIS SYSTEMS LLC
14500 N Beck Rd (48170-3383)
PHONE.............................419 485-1524
Tammy Burroughs, *Human Res Mgr*
Robert Anderson, *Mng Member*
Eugenio Madero, *Director*
Pam Vandermoon,
EMP: 60 EST: 2001

SALES (est): 21.4MM Privately Held
WEB: www.rassini.com
SIC: 3495 Wire springs
HQ: Rassini Suspensiones, S.A. De C.V.
  Monte Pelvoux No. 220, Piso 8
  Ciudad De Mexico CDMX 11000

(G-13276)
RAYCHRIS
9278 General Dr (48170-4689)
PHONE.............................734 404-5485
EMP: 4 EST: 2014
SALES (est): 61.8K Privately Held
SIC: 2741 Miscellaneous publishing

(G-13277)
RB OIL ENTERPRISES LLC
Plymouth Mi (48170)
PHONE.............................734 354-0700
Abe Rababeh, *Mng Member*
Yasseen Rababeh,
EMP: 8 EST: 2009
SALES (est): 468.9K Privately Held
SIC: 3559 7699 Automotive maintenance equipment; miscellaneous automotive repair services

(G-13278)
RBD CREATIVE
705 S Main St Ste 220 (48170-5436)
PHONE.............................313 259-5507
Stan Dickson, *Principal*
EMP: 5 EST: 2012
SALES (est): 100.6K Privately Held
WEB: www.rbdcreative.com
SIC: 2759 Publication printing

(G-13279)
RBT MFG LLC
Also Called: Replacement Brush Tables
9033 General Dr (48170-4680)
PHONE.............................800 691-8204
Jeff Fettig, *Sales Mgr*
Greg Gach,
EMP: 10 EST: 2017
SALES (est): 215.9K Privately Held
WEB: www.brushtables.com
SIC: 3991 Brushes, household or industrial

(G-13280)
RECARDO NORTH AMERICA INC
49200 Halyard Dr (48170-2481)
PHONE.............................248 364-3818
EMP: 61 EST: 2020
SALES (est): 2.5MM Privately Held
SIC: 3714 Motor vehicle parts & accessories
HQ: Adient Setex Holding Llc
  135 S 84th St Ste 200
  Milwaukee WI 53214
  414 524-1200

(G-13281)
REX M TUBBS
Also Called: Engraving Connection
1205 S Main St (48170-2215)
PHONE.............................734 459-3180
Rex M Tubbs, *Owner*
EMP: 5 EST: 1978
SQ FT: 3,500
SALES (est): 368K Privately Held
WEB: www.engravingconnectionstore.com
SIC: 7389 3544 3069 Engraving service; jewelry, precious stones & precious metals; custom compounding of rubber materials

(G-13282)
RIPPER VENTURES LLC
14708 Keel St (48170-6004)
PHONE.............................248 808-2325
Kimberly Ripper, *President*
David Ripper,
EMP: 6 EST: 2012
SALES (est): 355K Privately Held
SIC: 3949 Gymnasium equipment

(G-13283)
RIVIAN AUTOMOTIVE INC (PA)
13250 N Haggerty Rd (48170-4206)
PHONE.............................734 855-4350
Robert Scaringe, *CEO*
Evan Bartley, *Counsel*
Jimmy Knauf, *Exec VP*
Steven Holmes, *Vice Pres*

Anshu Narula, *Vice Pres*
EMP: 1482 EST: 2015
SQ FT: 40,000
SALES (est): 1.3B Privately Held
WEB: www.rivian.com
SIC: 3711 Automobile assembly, including specialty automobiles

(G-13284)
RIVIAN AUTOMOTIVE INC
41100 Plymouth Rd 4ne (48170-3799)
PHONE.............................408 483-1987
EMP: 7
SALES (corp-wide): 1.3B Privately Held
WEB: www.rivian.com
SIC: 3711 Automobile assembly, including specialty automobiles
PA: Rivian Automotive, Inc.
  13250 N Haggerty Rd
  Plymouth MI 48170
  734 855-4350

(G-13285)
RIVIAN AUTOMOTIVE LLC (HQ)
13250 N Haggerty Rd (48170-4206)
PHONE.............................734 855-4350
Robert Scaringe, *CEO*
Laura Schwab, *VP Sls/Mktg*
Amy Taylor, *Controller*
Christopher Brown, *Ch Credit Ofcr*
Neil Sitron, *General Counsel*
◆ EMP: 90 EST: 2009
SQ FT: 40,000
SALES (est): 157MM
SALES (corp-wide): 1.3B Privately Held
WEB: www.rivian.com
SIC: 3711 3714 Motor vehicles & car bodies; motor vehicle parts & accessories
PA: Rivian Automotive, Inc.
  13250 N Haggerty Rd
  Plymouth MI 48170
  734 855-4350

(G-13286)
RMT ACQUISITION COMPANY LLC (PA)
Also Called: Rmt Woodworth
45755 Five Mile Rd (48170-2476)
PHONE.............................248 353-4229
Terry Woodworth, *CEO*
Kelly Block, *Controller*
Rick Woodworth, *Technical Staff*
EMP: 5 EST: 2005
SALES (est): 1MM Privately Held
WEB: www.rmtwoodworth.com
SIC: 3398 Metal heat treating

(G-13287)
ROBERT BOSCH LLC
15000 N Haggerty Rd (48170-3698)
PHONE.............................734 979-3000
Stefan Mischo, *Vice Pres*
Kevin Moore, *Vice Pres*
Richard Volansky, *Vice Pres*
Nicole Howard, *Project Mgr*
John Wills, *Project Mgr*
EMP: 7
SALES (corp-wide): 297.8MM Privately Held
WEB: www.bosch.us
SIC: 3714 3694 5013 5064 Motor vehicle engines & parts; motor vehicle brake systems & parts; motor vehicle electrical equipment; motors, starting: automotive & aircraft; distributors, motor vehicle engine; automotive supplies & parts; automotive engines & engine parts; automotive brakes; radios, motor vehicle; packaging machinery; deburring machines
HQ: Robert Bosch Llc
  38000 Hills Tech Dr
  Farmington Hills MI 48331
  248 876-1000

(G-13288)
ROBERT BOSCH LLC
39775 Five Mile Rd (48170-2708)
PHONE.............................734 979-3412
Kevin Schmaltz, *IT/INT Sup*
EMP: 7
SALES (corp-wide): 297.8MM Privately Held
WEB: www.bosch.us
SIC: 3714 Motor vehicle parts & accessories

HQ: Robert Bosch Llc
  38000 Hills Tech Dr
  Farmington Hills MI 48331
  248 876-1000

(G-13289)
ROCK TOOL & MACHINE CO INC
45145 Five Mile Rd (48170-2596)
PHONE.............................734 455-9840
Robert Oak, *President*
Laura Frehrenvach, *CFO*
Jonathon Plemmons, *CFO*
Glenn Simms, *Treasurer*
Clay Kessler, *Admin Sec*
▲ EMP: 44 EST: 1969
SQ FT: 27,000
SALES (est): 7.8MM Privately Held
WEB: www.rocktool.com
SIC: 3541 3549 3423 Deburring machines; machine tool replacement & repair parts, metal cutting types; assembly machines, including robotic; hand & edge tools

(G-13290)
ROFIN-SINAR TECHNOLOGIES LLC (HQ)
40984 Concept Dr (48170-4252)
PHONE.............................734 416-0206
Noemi Otero Carbon, *Engineer*
Lisa Rice, *Finance Mgr*
EMP: 9 EST: 1996
SQ FT: 52,128
SALES (est): 15.1MM
SALES (corp-wide): 1.2B Publicly Held
WEB: www.coherent.com
SIC: 3699 3845 Laser systems & equipment; electromedical equipment
PA: Coherent, Inc.
  5100 Patrick Henry Dr
  Santa Clara CA 95054
  408 764-4000

(G-13291)
RUBBER STAMPS UNLIMITED INC
334 S Harvey St Ste 1 (48170-2270)
PHONE.............................734 451-7300
Maryellen Lewandowski, *President*
William Lewandowski, *Vice Pres*
Richard Barnes, *CIO*
EMP: 13 EST: 1975
SQ FT: 1,500
SALES (est): 915.8K Privately Held
WEB: www.thestampmaker.com
SIC: 3953 5999 5099 Embossing seals & hand stamps; rubber stamps; rubber stamps

(G-13292)
SAMES KREMLIN INC (DH)
Also Called: Exel Industries Group
45001 Five Mile Rd (48170-2587)
PHONE.............................734 979-0100
Jean Patry, *CEO*
Brent Frederick, *Regional Mgr*
Robert Ryder, *Vice Pres*
Steven Carter, *Opers Mgr*
Michael Mazur, *Mfg Staff*
▲ EMP: 114 EST: 1980
SQ FT: 52,000
SALES (est): 45.5MM
SALES (corp-wide): 3.4K Privately Held
WEB: www.sames-kremlin.com
SIC: 5084 5231 3492 Paint spray equipment, industrial; paint & painting supplies; fluid power valves & hose fittings
HQ: Sames Kremlin
  13 Chemin De Malacher
  Meylan 38240
  476 416-060

(G-13293)
SAMES KREMLIN INC
45001 Five Mile Rd (48170-2587)
PHONE.............................734 979-0100
Matthew Lentz, *Project Mgr*
Rob Pianczk, *Purch Mgr*
Todd O'Neill, *Treasurer*
Pam Ceci, *Asst Controller*
Gary Chrostowski, *Technician*
EMP: 4
SQ FT: 52,000

GEOGRAPHIC SECTION
Plymouth - Wayne County (G-13320)

SALES (corp-wide): 3.4K **Privately Held**
WEB: www.sames-kremlin.com
SIC: 5084 3561 5231 Paint spray equipment, industrial; pumps & pumping equipment; paint & painting supplies
HQ: Sames Kremlin Inc
   45001 Five Mile Rd
   Plymouth MI 48170
   734 979-0100

(G-13294)
SAVANNA INC
Also Called: Rmt Woodworth
45755 Five Mile Rd (48170-2476)
PHONE 734 254-0566
Bob Bosquez, *Plant Mgr*
EMP: 40 **Privately Held**
WEB: www.rmtwoodworth.com
SIC: 3398 Metal heat treating
PA: Savanna, Inc.
   20941 East St
   Southfield MI 48033

(G-13295)
SEALMASTER/MICHIGAN
9965 Lapham Way (48170-5853)
PHONE 313 779-8415
Brenda Laser, *Principal*
EMP: 6 EST: 2018
SALES (est): 99.8K **Privately Held**
WEB: www.sealmaster.net
SIC: 2951 Asphalt paving mixtures & blocks

(G-13296)
SGO CORPORATE CENTER LLC (PA)
Also Called: Image360-Plymouth
47581 Galleon Dr (48170-2466)
PHONE 248 596-8626
Michael Marcantonio,
EMP: 10 EST: 1996
SQ FT: 66,000
SALES (est): 4.2MM **Privately Held**
SIC: 3993 Signs & advertising specialties

(G-13297)
SIGN & GRAPHICS OPERATIONS LLC
Also Called: Signs By Tomorrow
47585 Galleon Dr (48170-2466)
PHONE 248 596-8626
Laura Pierce-Marutz,
EMP: 45 EST: 2011
SQ FT: 60,000
SALES (est): 5.2MM
SALES (corp-wide): 47.1MM **Privately Held**
WEB: www.signsbytomorrow.com
SIC: 3993 Signs & advertising specialties
PA: Alliance Franchise Brands Llc
   47585 Galleon Dr
   Plymouth MI 48170
   248 596-8600

(G-13298)
SIGNALX TECHNOLOGIES LLC
41100 Plymouth Rd Ste 3 (48170-3757)
PHONE 248 935-4237
Garrett Marsh, *Software Engr*
Michael Albright,
Aaron Grzymkowski,
John Niezgoski,
EMP: 20 EST: 2004
SQ FT: 10,000
SALES (est): 3.2MM **Privately Held**
WEB: www.signalxtech.com
SIC: 7379 7372 Computer related consulting services; prepackaged software

(G-13299)
SIMOLEX RUBBER CORPORATION
14505 Keel St (48170-6002)
PHONE 734 453-4500
Bob Dungarani, *President*
EMP: 15 EST: 1994
SQ FT: 15,000
SALES (est): 1.8MM **Privately Held**
WEB: www.simolex.com
SIC: 3069 Molded rubber products

(G-13300)
SKYWAY PRECISION INC (PA)
Also Called: B & D Sales and Service
41225 Plymouth Rd (48170-6123)
PHONE 734 454-3550
Bill Bonnell, *President*
Dennis Dundas, *Mfg Spvr*
Robert Powell, *Purch Agent*
Kelly Sharpe, *Human Res Mgr*
Pamela Bissell, *Manager*
◆ EMP: 137 EST: 1969
SQ FT: 84,000
SALES (est): 43.3MM **Privately Held**
WEB: www.skywayprecision.com
SIC: 3599 Machine shop, jobbing & repair

(G-13301)
SOLUTIONS IN STONE INC
41980 Ann Arbor Rd E (48170-4371)
PHONE 734 453-4444
Michael Doherty, *President*
EMP: 5 EST: 2004
SALES (est): 308.7K **Privately Held**
SIC: 3281 Granite, cut & shaped

(G-13302)
SPECIAL PROJECTS INC
45901 Helm St (48170-6025)
PHONE 734 455-7130
Kenneth E Yanez, *President*
Terry Steller, *Sales Executive*
Kyle Yanez, *Corp Comm Staff*
Scott Pachy, *Program Mgr*
Dave Buyak, *Manager*
EMP: 46 EST: 1983
SALES (est): 5.7MM **Privately Held**
WEB: www.specproj.com
SIC: 3711 3441 Automobile bodies, passenger car, not including engine, etc.; fabricated structural metal

(G-13303)
STARDOCK SYSTEMS INC (PA)
15090 N Beck Rd Ste 300 (48170-4385)
PHONE 734 927-0677
Bradley Wardell, *President*
Derek Paxton, *General Mgr*
Angela Marshall, *COO*
Kris Kwilas, *Vice Pres*
Patrick Shaw, *Production*
EMP: 50 EST: 1993
SQ FT: 30,000
SALES (est): 8.3MM **Privately Held**
WEB: www.stardock.com
SIC: 7372 7371 Prepackaged software; custom computer programming services

(G-13304)
STRATFORD-CAMBRIDGE GROUP CO (PA)
Also Called: Stratford-Cambridge Group, The
801 W Ann Arbor Trl # 235 (48170-1694)
PHONE 734 404-6047
Stephen J Ellis, *President*
EMP: 4 EST: 2015
SALES (est): 9.6MM **Privately Held**
WEB: www.scgequity.com
SIC: 3545 Machine tool attachments & accessories

(G-13305)
SUN PLASTICS COATING COMPANY
Also Called: Sun Coating Co
42105 Postiff Ave (48170-4688)
PHONE 734 453-0822
Joseph Tate, *President*
Mark Tate, *Vice Pres*
Andrew Tate, *Production*
Richard Barnes, *CIO*
Sandy Tate, *Technology*
EMP: 18 EST: 1963
SQ FT: 38,000
SALES (est): 3.1MM **Privately Held**
WEB: www.suncoating.com
SIC: 3479 Coating of metals & formed products

(G-13306)
SUPERIOR CONTROLS INC
Also Called: Redviking
46247 Five Mile Rd (48170-2421)
PHONE 734 454-0500
Randall Brodzik, *President*
Mark Sobkow, *President*
Julie Higgins, *COO*
Ray Boudreau, *Vice Pres*
Josh McNeely, *Vice Pres*
EMP: 195 EST: 1983
SQ FT: 45,000
SALES (est): 20.1MM **Privately Held**
WEB: www.redviking.com
SIC: 3613 3823 8711 3829 Control panels, electric; controllers for process variables, all types; consulting engineer; dynamometer instruments; relays & industrial controls; machine tool accessories

(G-13307)
SYNCHRON LASER SERVICE INC
41303 Concept Dr (48170-4253)
PHONE 248 486-0402
Brett Moon, *President*
EMP: 15 EST: 2010
SALES (est): 650.4K **Privately Held**
WEB: www.synchronlaser.com
SIC: 3599 Machine shop, jobbing & repair

(G-13308)
T & L TRANSPORT INC
13801 Westbrook Rd (48170-2405)
PHONE 313 350-1535
Thomas Marciniak, *Owner*
EMP: 7 EST: 2014
SALES (est): 720.5K **Privately Held**
SIC: 3537 Trucks, tractors, loaders, carriers & similar equipment

(G-13309)
TAYLOR MACHINE PRODUCTS INC
176 S Harvey St (48170-1616)
PHONE 734 287-3550
Charles W Jones, *Ch of Bd*
EMP: 19 EST: 1967
SALES (est): 462.3K **Privately Held**
SIC: 3451 Screw machine products

(G-13310)
TECH TOOL SUPPLY LLC
9060 General Dr (48170-4624)
PHONE 734 207-7700
Amy Hogarty, *Opers Mgr*
Sam Lafata, *Sales Staff*
Brent Hagood, *Mng Member*
EMP: 6 EST: 2005
SALES (est): 1.1MM **Privately Held**
WEB: www.techtoolsupply.com
SIC: 3823 Digital displays of process variables

(G-13311)
TECHNOTRIM INC
49200 Halyard Dr (48170-2481)
PHONE 734 254-5000
Brian Grady, *Ch of Bd*
Kazunori Hashimoto, *President*
Lynda Watters, *Controller*
EMP: 1500 EST: 1986
SALES (est): 103.6MM **Privately Held**
WEB: www.tachi-s.com
SIC: 2399 Seat covers, automobile
HQ: Adient Inc.
   49200 Halyard Dr
   Plymouth MI 48170
   734 254-5000

(G-13312)
TEMPRO INDUSTRIES INC
47808 Galleon Dr (48170-2468)
PHONE 734 451-5900
Sarah M Fedor, *President*
Matthew Fedor, *Treasurer*
EMP: 22 EST: 1980
SQ FT: 13,500
SALES (est): 1.2MM **Privately Held**
WEB: www.temproinc.com
SIC: 2396 3498 Automotive & apparel trimmings; tube fabricating (contract bending & shaping)

(G-13313)
TENNECO INC
44099 Plymouth Oaks Blvd (48170-6527)
PHONE 734 254-1122
Derek Garden, *Manager*
EMP: 7
SALES (corp-wide): 15.3B **Publicly Held**
WEB: www.tenneco.com
SIC: 3714 Motor vehicle parts & accessories
PA: Tenneco Inc.
   500 N Field Dr
   Lake Forest IL 60045
   847 482-5000

(G-13314)
THUNDERDOME MEDIA LLC
Also Called: Functional Hand Strength
6218 Valleyfield Dr (48170-7620)
P.O. Box 4429, Ann Arbor (48106-4429)
PHONE 800 978-0206
John Wood,
EMP: 4 EST: 2007 **Privately Held**
WEB: www.functionalhandstrength.com
SIC: 3949 Sporting & athletic goods

(G-13315)
TITANIUM INDUSTRIES
14555 Jib St (48170-6011)
PHONE 734 335-2808
Jill Lane, *Sales Staff*
EMP: 4 EST: 2019
SALES (est): 74.4K **Privately Held**
SIC: 2816 Inorganic pigments

(G-13316)
TNT-EDM INC
47689 E Anchor Ct (48170-2455)
PHONE 734 459-1700
Tom Mullen, *Principal*
Todd Gardiner, *CFO*
Debbie Reed, *Personnel*
Sam Shegitz, *Prgrmr*
Chris Skinner, *Administration*
EMP: 25 EST: 1979
SQ FT: 76,000
SALES (est): 4.6MM **Privately Held**
WEB: www.tntedm.com
SIC: 3544 Forms (molds), for foundry & plastics working machinery

(G-13317)
TOLEDO MOLDING & DIE INC
Also Called: Development Office
47912 Halyard Dr (48170-2494)
PHONE 734 233-6338
Kurt Kehren, *Sales Staff*
Don Harbaugh, *Branch Mgr*
EMP: 5 **Privately Held**
WEB: www.tmdinc.com
SIC: 3823 5013 Fluidic devices, circuits & systems for process control; automotive supplies & parts
HQ: Toledo Molding & Die, Llc
   1429 Coining Dr
   Toledo OH 43612

(G-13318)
TOMAS PLASTICS INC
9833 Tennyson Dr (48170-3643)
PHONE 734 455-4706
Frank Tomaszycki, *President*
EMP: 8 EST: 1984
SQ FT: 7,200
SALES (est): 145.8K **Privately Held**
WEB: www.thomasplastic.com
SIC: 3089 Injection molding of plastics

(G-13319)
TOOLCO INC
47709 Galleon Dr (48170-2466)
PHONE 734 453-9911
William Tustian, *President*
Terry Decamillo, *Engineer*
EMP: 35 EST: 1982
SQ FT: 16,000
SALES (est): 2.6MM **Privately Held**
WEB: www.toolcoinc.net
SIC: 3544 Special dies & tools; wire drawing & straightening dies

(G-13320)
TOWER ATMTIVE OPRTONS USA I LL
43955 Plymouth Oaks Blvd (48170-2557)
P.O. Box 701580 (48170-0967)
PHONE 734 414-3100
Fred Effinger, *Engineer*
Todd Lee, *Manager*
EMP: 100

Plymouth - Wayne County (G-13321)

SALES (corp-wide): 3.1B **Privately Held**
WEB: www.autokiniton.com
SIC: 3465 Automotive stampings
HQ: Tower Automotive Operations Usa I, Llc
17757 Woodland Dr
New Boston MI 48164

(G-13321)
TRAILER TECH REPAIR INC
Also Called: Trailer Tech One
13101 Eckles Rd (48170-4245)
PHONE.................................734 354-6680
Paul Storey, *President*
EMP: 6 **EST:** 2002
SALES (est): 791.7K **Privately Held**
WEB: www.trailertechone.com
SIC: 3711 Truck tractors for highway use, assembly of

(G-13322)
TRAM INC (HQ)
47200 Port St (48170-6082)
PHONE.................................734 254-8500
Masayuki Morita, *CEO*
Yoshihei Iida, *Ch of Bd*
Yutaka Yamauchi, *President*
Koichi Kihira, *Vice Pres*
Rich Peavler, *Vice Pres*
▲ **EMP:** 135 **EST:** 1986
SQ FT: 50,000
SALES (est): 257.2MM **Privately Held**
WEB: www.tokai-rika-usa.com
SIC: 3714 3643 Motor vehicle electrical equipment; current-carrying wiring devices

(G-13323)
TRI-POWER MANUFACTURING INC
9229 General Dr Ste B (48170-4672)
PHONE.................................734 414-8084
Marilyn Tringali, *CEO*
Nick Tringali, *General Mgr*
EMP: 8 **EST:** 2007
SALES (est): 1MM **Privately Held**
WEB: www.tripowermfg.com
SIC: 3599 Machine shop, jobbing & repair

(G-13324)
TRIN INC
47200 Port St (48170-6082)
PHONE.................................260 587-9282
Jason Barrett, *Business Mgr*
Swati Rathore, *Project Mgr*
Nathan Edwards, *Maint Spvr*
Cindy Wheeler, *Production*
Emily Frederick, *Engineer*
EMP: 45 **Privately Held**
SIC: 3714 Motor vehicle parts & accessories
HQ: Trin, Inc.
803 H L Thompson Jr Dr
Ashley IN 46705
260 587-9282

(G-13325)
TROY DESIGN & MANUFACTURING CO (HQ)
14425 N Sheldon Rd (48170-2407)
PHONE.................................734 738-2300
John L Lowery, *President*
Tim Jagoda, *Vice Pres*
Jim Hartsuff, *Purch Mgr*
Doug Randlett, *Engineer*
Ed Strach, *Comptroller*
▲ **EMP:** 187 **EST:** 1981
SQ FT: 115,000
SALES (est): 130.4MM
SALES (corp-wide): 127.1B **Publicly Held**
WEB: www.troydm.com
SIC: 3465 Automotive stampings
PA: Ford Motor Company
1 American Rd
Dearborn MI 48126
313 322-3000

(G-13326)
TRUANS CANDIES INC (PA)
4251 Fleming Way (48170-6361)
PHONE.................................313 281-0185
Mark A Truan, *President*
EMP: 11 **EST:** 1930
SQ FT: 15,000
SALES (est): 814.2K **Privately Held**
WEB: www.truanscandiesonline.com
SIC: 2064 5441 Candy bars, including chocolate covered bars; chocolate candy, except solid chocolate; candy

(G-13327)
TRUMPF INC
47711 Clipper St (48170-3591)
PHONE.................................734 354-9770
Kevin Domingue, *Vice Pres*
Denise Gentile, *Purchasing*
Diane Tuchmatulin, *Purchasing*
Roland Fix, *QC Mgr*
Tim Morris, *Technical Mgr*
EMP: 50
SALES (corp-wide): 3.8B **Privately Held**
WEB: www.trumpf.com
SIC: 3699 Laser welding, drilling & cutting equipment
HQ: Trumpf, Inc.
111 Hyde Rd
Farmington CT 06032
860 255-6000

(G-13328)
USUI INTERNATIONAL CORPORATION (HQ)
44780 Helm St (48170-6026)
PHONE.................................734 354-3626
Takayoshi Ito, *President*
Brian Burnside, *Project Engr*
Timothy Sircy, *Treasurer*
Monique Taras, *Accounts Mgr*
Ljupce Nastovski, *Manager*
◆ **EMP:** 30 **EST:** 1986
SALES (est): 90.1MM **Privately Held**
WEB: www.usuiusa.com
SIC: 3714 3317 Motor vehicle parts & accessories; steel pipe & tubes

(G-13329)
VARROC LIGHTING SYSTEMS INC (HQ)
Also Called: USA Hq Michigan
47828 Halyard Dr (48170-2454)
PHONE.................................734 446-4400
Christian Paschel, *CEO*
My Simon, *Superintendent*
Jorge Cornejo, *Vice Pres*
Scott Montesi, *Vice Pres*
Enrique Galvan, *Opers Staff*
▲ **EMP:** 100 **EST:** 2010
SALES (est): 544.5MM **Privately Held**
WEB: www.varroclighting.com
SIC: 3751 Motorcycles, bicycles & parts

(G-13330)
VELESCO PHRM SVCS INC (DH)
46701 Commerce Center Dr (48170-2475)
PHONE.................................734 274-9877
David Barnes, *CEO*
Gerry Cox, *COO*
Olivia Cook, *Opers Staff*
Darcy Wargolet, *QC Mgr*
EMP: 7 **EST:** 2007
SQ FT: 2,300
SALES (est): 2.6MM
SALES (corp-wide): 64.8MM **Privately Held**
WEB: www.velescopharma.com
SIC: 3559 2834 Pharmaceutical machinery; druggists' preparations (pharmaceuticals)

(G-13331)
VENTURA INDUSTRIES INC
46301 Port St (48170-6043)
PHONE.................................734 357-0114
Gary Winkler, *President*
Nicholas Mustola, *Engineer*
EMP: 16 **EST:** 1966
SQ FT: 22,000
SALES (est): 355.5K **Privately Held**
SIC: 3728 Aircraft assemblies, subassemblies & parts

(G-13332)
VICO COMPANY
41555 Ann Arbor Rd E (48170-4300)
PHONE.................................734 453-3777
Curt Schultz, *President*
▲ **EMP:** 6 **EST:** 1993
SQ FT: 6,000
SALES (est): 617.4K **Privately Held**
WEB: www.vico.com
SIC: 3299 Sand lime products

(G-13333)
VICO LOUISVILLE LLC
41555 Ann Arbor Rd E (48170-4300)
PHONE.................................502 245-1616
Frank Dietrich, *General Mgr*
Mike Orlandi, *Production*
Dave Beaudoin, *Manager*
Debra Coopman, *Manager*
EMP: 26 **EST:** 1997
SALES (est): 1MM **Privately Held**
WEB: www.vico.com
SIC: 3714 3621 3462 Motor vehicle brake systems & parts; control equipment for electric buses & locomotives; automotive forgings, ferrous: crankshaft, engine, axle, etc.

(G-13334)
VICO PRODUCTS CO (PA)
41555 Ann Arbor Rd E (48170-4397)
PHONE.................................734 453-3777
Curt R Schultz, *President*
Caryn Williams, *Vice Pres*
Joaquin Pasha, *Program Mgr*
◆ **EMP:** 91 **EST:** 1943
SQ FT: 88,000
SALES (est): 22.6MM **Privately Held**
WEB: www.vico.com
SIC: 3452 Bolts, metal

(G-13335)
VORTEX INDUSTRIES INC
739 S Mill St (48170-1821)
PHONE.................................855 867-8399
Terry Saxton, *Principal*
EMP: 13 **EST:** 2011
SALES (est): 1.1MM **Privately Held**
WEB: www.vortexxpressurewashers.com
SIC: 5072 5013 3592 Hardware; pumps, oil & gas; valves

(G-13336)
WEBASTO CONVERTIBLES USA INC (DH)
Also Called: Webasto-Group
14988 Pilot Dr (48170-3672)
PHONE.................................734 582-5900
Mark Denny, *CEO*
Dr Holger Engelmann, *Ch of Bd*
Axel Schulmeyer, *President*
Wisam Aljoher, *Engineer*
Stephen Chesna, *CFO*
▲ **EMP:** 130 **EST:** 2010
SQ FT: 144,000
SALES (est): 110MM
SALES (corp-wide): 3.9B **Privately Held**
WEB: www.webasto-comfort.com
SIC: 3714 Tops, motor vehicle
HQ: Webasto Roof Systems Inc.
2500 Executive Hills Dr
Auburn Hills MI 48326
248 997-5100

(G-13337)
WEBASTO ROOF SYSTEMS INC
14200 N Haggerty Rd (48170-4273)
PHONE.................................248 997-5100
Andre Schoenekaes, *President*
EMP: 257
SALES (corp-wide): 3.9B **Privately Held**
WEB: www.webasto-comfort.com
SIC: 3714 Motor vehicle parts & accessories
HQ: Webasto Roof Systems Inc.
2500 Executive Hills Dr
Auburn Hills MI 48326
248 997-5100

(G-13338)
WESTPORT FUEL SYSTEMS US INC
Also Called: Westport Innovations
14900 Galleon Ct (48170-6536)
PHONE.................................734 233-6850
John Lapetz, *Vice Pres*
Jim Maccallun, *Vice Pres*
▼ **EMP:** 78 **EST:** 1999
SALES (est): 10MM
SALES (corp-wide): 305.3MM **Privately Held**
WEB: www.wfsinc.com
SIC: 1321 Natural gas liquids production
PA: Westport Fuel Systems Inc
1750 75th Ave W Suite 101
Vancouver BC
604 718-2000

(G-13339)
WRKCO INC
11333 General Dr (48170-4374)
PHONE.................................734 453-6700
Jeff Bettelom, *Branch Mgr*
Chris Neagle, *Manager*
EMP: 50
SALES (corp-wide): 17.5B **Publicly Held**
SIC: 2653 Boxes, corrugated: made from purchased materials
HQ: Wrkco Inc.
1000 Abernathy Rd Ste 12
Atlanta GA 30328
770 448-2193

(G-13340)
YALE TOOL & ENGRAVING INC
1471 Gold Smith (48170-1082)
PHONE.................................734 459-7171
Frank A Bauss, *President*
Robert B Zalobsky, *President*
Daniel J Damiani, *Vice Pres*
Janice P Zalobsky, *Admin Sec*
EMP: 8 **EST:** 1982
SQ FT: 5,100
SALES (est): 591.9K **Privately Held**
WEB: www.yaletool.net
SIC: 3599 3479 Machine shop, jobbing & repair; etching & engraving

(G-13341)
YANFENG US AUTO INTR SYSTEMS I
49200 Halyard Dr (48170-2481)
PHONE.................................734 254-5000
Nick Doing, *Engineer*
Yating Chen, *Finance Mgr*
Kevin Sanner, *Sales Staff*
Alan Mumby, *Branch Mgr*
Ilango Govindaswamy, *Program Mgr*
EMP: 7 **Privately Held**
WEB: www.yfai.com
SIC: 3714 Motor vehicle parts & accessories
HQ: Yanfeng Us Automotive Interior Systems I Llc
41935 W 12 Mile Rd
Novi MI 48377
248 319-7333

(G-13342)
ZHONGDING SALING PARTS USA INC (HQ)
48600 Five Mile Rd (48170)
PHONE.................................734 241-8870
Marcio Lima, *CEO*
Steve Seketa, *General Mgr*
Zhi Cheng, *Finance*
Dennis Cruz, *Manager*
▲ **EMP:** 4 **EST:** 1946
SALES (est): 118.3MM
SALES (corp-wide): 1.7B **Privately Held**
WEB: www.zhongdinggroup.com
SIC: 3069 Molded rubber products

Pontiac
Oakland County

(G-13343)
21ST CENTURY NEWSPAPERS INC
Also Called: Homes For Sale
28 W Huron St (48342-2100)
PHONE.................................586 469-4510
Justin Wilcox, *Manager*
EMP: 19
SALES (corp-wide): 274.1MM **Privately Held**
WEB: www.21stcenturynewspapers.com
SIC: 2711 Newspapers, publishing & printing
HQ: 21st Century Newspapers, Inc.
6250 Metropolitan Pkwy
Sterling Heights MI 48312
586 469-4510

GEOGRAPHIC SECTION
Pontiac - Oakland County (G-13370)

(G-13344)
ACCESSORIES WHOLESALE INC
Also Called: Accessories R US
555 Friendly St (48341-2650)
PHONE.................248 755-7465
Claudia Tomina, *President*
Mitch Gappy, *Partner*
Sahir Gappy, *Partner*
Brent Gappy, *Opers Staff*
EMP: 14 **EST:** 2006
SQ FT: 32,000
SALES (est): 1.3MM **Privately Held**
WEB: www.accessoryinc.com
SIC: 3679 Antennas, receiving

(G-13345)
AIRLITE SYNTHETICS MFG INC
342 Irwin Ave (48341-2949)
PHONE.................248 335-8131
Ronald Herman, *President*
Sharon Herman, *Corp Secy*
Eric Herman, *Vice Pres*
EMP: 10 **EST:** 1974
SQ FT: 36,400
SALES (est): 898.5K **Privately Held**
WEB: www.airlitemanufacturing.com
SIC: 2299 Pillow fillings: curled hair, cotton waste, moss, hemp tow; quilt fillings: curled hair, cotton waste, moss, hemp tow

(G-13346)
AKZO NOBEL COATINGS INC
120 Franklin Rd (48341-2220)
P.O. Box 669 (48341)
PHONE.................248 451-6231
Richard Gray, *General Mgr*
Keith Estes, *Managing Dir*
Larry Haack, *Business Mgr*
Marten Booisma, *Vice Pres*
Roger Workman, *Project Mgr*
EMP: 34
SALES (corp-wide): 10B **Privately Held**
SIC: 2851 2869 Paints & allied products; industrial organic chemicals
HQ: Akzo Nobel Coatings Inc.
8220 Mohawk Dr
Strongsville OH 44136
440 297-5100

(G-13347)
AKZO NOBEL COATINGS INC
Also Called: Deco Finishes
117 Brush St (48341-2215)
PHONE.................248 637-0400
Dave Bupler, *Principal*
Cor Degrauw, *Administration*
EMP: 34
SALES (corp-wide): 10B **Privately Held**
SIC: 2851 8731 Wood stains; commercial physical research
HQ: Akzo Nobel Coatings Inc.
8220 Mohawk Dr
Strongsville OH 44136
440 297-5100

(G-13348)
ALLIED SCREEN & GRAPICS LLC
73 W Walton Blvd (48340-1159)
PHONE.................248 499-8204
Diane Bynum, *President*
EMP: 5 **EST:** 2010
SALES (est): 155.9K **Privately Held**
WEB: www.alliedscreen.com
SIC: 3993 Signs & advertising specialties

(G-13349)
ALUMINUM BLANKING CO INC
Also Called: Abco
360 W Sheffield Ave (48340-1879)
PHONE.................248 338-4422
Marvin Hole, *CEO*
Eric Hole, *President*
Bill Sautter, *Engineer*
Enoch Davis, *Technology*
Gary Lecznar, *Business Dir*
▲ **EMP:** 80
SQ FT: 160,000

SALES (est): 21.2MM **Privately Held**
WEB: www.albl.com
SIC: 3469 3446 3444 3353 Metal stampings; architectural metalwork; sheet metalwork; aluminum sheet, plate & foil; copper rolling & drawing; secondary nonferrous metals

(G-13350)
AMERICAN ASSEMBLERS INC
40 W Howard St Ste 222 (48342-1282)
PHONE.................248 334-9777
Gerald Shohan, *President*
Sandy Clemons, *Manager*
EMP: 6 **EST:** 1993
SQ FT: 2,000
SALES (est): 796.5K **Privately Held**
SIC: 3544 Industrial molds

(G-13351)
AUTOLIV ASP INC
Also Called: Autoliv Technical Center-W
856 Featherstone St (48342-1723)
PHONE.................248 761-0081
Kevin Morgan, *Buyer*
Christopher Brenton, *Engineer*
Chad Moore, *Design Engr*
EMP: 239
SALES (corp-wide): 7.4B **Publicly Held**
SIC: 3714 Motor vehicle parts & accessories
HQ: Autoliv Asp, Inc.
3350 Airport Rd
Ogden UT 84405

(G-13352)
CBS ENTERPRISES LLC
938 Featherstone St (48342-1827)
PHONE.................248 335-6702
Denise Schaenzer,
EMP: 6
SALES (est): 220.6K **Privately Held**
SIC: 3999 Manufacturing industries

(G-13353)
CLAMP INDUSTRIES INCORPORATED
342 Irwin Ave (48341-2949)
PHONE.................248 335-8131
Eric Herman, *Principal*
EMP: 8 **EST:** 1995
SQ FT: 35,000
SALES (est): 105.8K **Privately Held**
SIC: 2299 Textile mill waste & remnant processing

(G-13354)
CLYDES FRAME & WHEEL SERVICE
725 Cesar E Chavez Ave (48340-2464)
PHONE.................248 338-0323
Charles Spurgeon, *President*
Charlene Spurgeon, *Treasurer*
EMP: 17 **EST:** 1961
SQ FT: 17,000
SALES (est): 1.2MM **Privately Held**
WEB: www.clydesbigtex.com
SIC: 7539 4959 5012 3715 Automotive repair shops; snowplowing; trailers for trucks, new & used; truck trailers

(G-13355)
CONNEXION INC
Also Called: Tangico
40 W Howard St Ste 404 (48342-1282)
PHONE.................248 453-5177
Susan Kinch, *CEO*
Katie McIntosh, *General Mgr*
Jennifer Garrison, *COO*
EMP: 8 **EST:** 2004
SQ FT: 1,500
SALES (est): 1.2MM **Privately Held**
SIC: 2499 5099 Cork & cork products; cork products, fabricated

(G-13356)
CREATIVE DESIGNS & SIGNS INC
146 Cesar E Chavez Ave (48342-2047)
PHONE.................248 334-5580
Albert F Lalonde, *President*
Jody C La Londe, *Vice Pres*
EMP: 5 **EST:** 1987
SQ FT: 12,000

SALES (est): 476.6K **Privately Held**
WEB: www.creativedesignssigns.com
SIC: 3993 Signs, not made in custom sign painting shops

(G-13357)
DAILY OAKLAND PRESS
58 W Huron St (48342-2103)
PHONE.................248 332-8181
Frank Shepherd, *Owner*
Len Cote, *MIS Dir*
EMP: 300
SALES (corp-wide): 274.1MM **Privately Held**
WEB: www.theoaklandpress.com
SIC: 2711 Newspapers: publishing only, not printed on site
HQ: Daily Oakland Press
38500 Woodward Ave # 100
Bloomfield Hills MI 48304
248 332-8181

(G-13358)
DATACOVER INC
1735 Highwood W (48340-1264)
PHONE.................844 875-4076
Justin Powers, *CEO*
Roberto Loftin, *CEO*
EMP: 4 **EST:** 2015
SQ FT: 6,000
SALES (est): 286K **Privately Held**
SIC: 3089 Boxes, plastic; cases, plastic

(G-13359)
DELL MARKING SYSTEMS
938 Featherstone St (48342-1827)
PHONE.................248 481-2119
EMP: 6 **EST:** 2019
SALES (est): 379.7K **Privately Held**
WEB: www.dellid.com
SIC: 2899 Chemical preparations

(G-13360)
DETROIT SEWN INC
67 N Saginaw St (48342-2154)
PHONE.................248 722-8407
Karen Buscemi, *CEO*
EMP: 25 **EST:** 2015
SALES (est): 1.4MM **Privately Held**
WEB: www.detroitsewn.com
SIC: 2335 2211 Dresses, paper: cut & sewn; damasks, cotton

(G-13361)
DETROIT STEEL TREATING COMPANY
1631 Highwood E (48340-1236)
PHONE.................248 334-7436
Raymond D Fox, *President*
Helene Fox, *Treasurer*
Janet Fox, *Admin Sec*
EMP: 22 **EST:** 1923
SQ FT: 18,000
SALES (est): 1MM **Privately Held**
WEB: www.detroitsteeltreating.com
SIC: 3398 3544 3471 3423 Metal heat treating; special dies, tools, jigs & fixtures; plating & polishing; hand & edge tools; industrial furnaces & ovens

(G-13362)
DONE RIGHT ENGRAVING INC
Also Called: Done Right Enterprises
119 N Saginaw St (48342-2113)
PHONE.................248 332-3133
Kathleen Trombly, *CEO*
Steven C Trombly, *President*
Kevin Ollila, *General Mgr*
Bruce D Trombly, *Vice Pres*
Austin Simat, *Graphic Designe*
EMP: 5 **EST:** 1972
SQ FT: 23,500
SALES (est): 875.2K **Privately Held**
WEB: www.donerightsigns.com
SIC: 7336 3479 Silk screen design; etching & engraving

(G-13363)
E AND K ARTS AND MORE
71 N Saginaw St (48342-2154)
PHONE.................855 285-0320
EMP: 4 **EST:** 2016
SALES (est): 251.8K **Privately Held**
SIC: 3952 Canvas board, artists'

(G-13364)
EASTERN OIL COMPANY (PA)
Also Called: Bipco
590 S Paddock St (48341-3236)
PHONE.................248 333-1333
Mike Skuratovich, *CEO*
Theodore R Plafchan, *President*
Ryan Pawloski, *Division Mgr*
Carol L Plafchan, *Vice Pres*
Tina Nowry, *Supervisor*
EMP: 40 **EST:** 1980
SQ FT: 26,000
SALES (est): 45.3MM **Privately Held**
WEB: www.easternoil.com
SIC: 5172 2992 5087 3471 Lubricating oils & greases; lubricating oils & greases; service establishment equipment; plating & polishing; chemical preparations

(G-13365)
ELAN DESIGNS INC
238 S Telegraph Rd (48341-1933)
PHONE.................248 682-3000
Elan Bauer, *President*
EMP: 4 **EST:** 1989
SQ FT: 2,400
SALES (est): 348.3K **Privately Held**
WEB: www.duncanginine.com
SIC: 2434 2431 Wood kitchen cabinets; millwork

(G-13366)
ELECTROLUX PROFESSIONAL INC
Also Called: Aerus Electrolux
214 S Telegraph Rd (48341-1933)
PHONE.................248 338-4320
EMP: 5
SALES (corp-wide): 13.4B **Privately Held**
WEB: www.beyondbyaerus.com
SIC: 5722 5064 3635 Vacuum cleaners; vacuum cleaners; household vacuum cleaners
HQ: Electrolux Professional, Llc
20445 Emerald Pkwy
Cleveland OH 44135
980 236-2000

(G-13367)
EPIPHANY STUDIOS LTD
770 Orchard Lake Rd (48341-2041)
PHONE.................248 745-3786
April Wagner, *Principal*
April Epiphany, *Exec Dir*
EMP: 4 **EST:** 1995
SQ FT: 3,930
SALES (est): 1.1MM **Privately Held**
WEB: www.epiphanyglass.com
SIC: 3559 Glass making machinery: blowing, molding, forming, etc.

(G-13368)
ERAE AMS AMERICA CORP
2011 Centerpoint Pkwy (48341-3148)
PHONE.................419 386-8876
James Kim, *CEO*
JB Yoon, *CFO*
EMP: 17 **EST:** 2018
SQ FT: 155,000 **Privately Held**
SIC: 6719 3714 Investment holding companies, except banks; drive shafts, motor vehicle

(G-13369)
ERAE AMS USA MANUFACTURING LLC
Also Called: Branch Office
2011 Centerpoint Pkwy (48341-3148)
PHONE.................314 600-3434
James Kim, *President*
Joongbeom Yoon, *CFO*
EMP: 17 **EST:** 2016
SQ FT: 160,000
SALES (est): 2.3MM **Privately Held**
SIC: 3559 Automotive related machinery

(G-13370)
ESYS AUTOMATION LLC
1500 Highwood E (48341-0233)
PHONE.................284 484-9724
Kevin Whaley, *Branch Mgr*
EMP: 30 **Privately Held**
WEB: www.jrautomation.com

Pontiac - Oakland County (G-13371)   GEOGRAPHIC SECTION

SIC: 3549 3599 8711 8742 Assembly machines, including robotic; custom machinery; engineering services; automation & robotics consultant; robotic conveyors
HQ: Esys Automation, Llc
1000 Brown Rd
Auburn Hills MI 48326
248 484-9927

(G-13371)
FREIBORNE INDUSTRIES INC
15 W Silverdome Indus Par (48342-2994)
PHONE 248 333-2490
Kevin Gill, *CEO*
Scott Herkes, *President*
Maureen Gill, *Chairman*
Keith Sturgeon, *Plant Mgr*
Pat Przygoda, *Accounting Mgr*
EMP: 20 **EST:** 1976
SQ FT: 24,000
SALES (est): 4.8MM **Privately Held**
WEB: www.freiborne.com
SIC: 2899 Chemical preparations

(G-13372)
FREQUENCY FINDERS LLC
793 3rd Ave (48340-2013)
PHONE 734 660-3357
Travis Stebelton, *Owner*
EMP: 11 **EST:** 2017
SALES (est): 151K **Privately Held**
WEB: www.thefrequencyfinders.com
SIC: 3825 Instruments to measure electricity

(G-13373)
FULL UPHOLSTERY LLC
900 Cesar E Chavez Ave (48340-2334)
PHONE 248 760-3985
Jaime Saavedra, *Principal*
EMP: 7 **EST:** 2018
SALES (est): 334.8K **Privately Held**
WEB: www.fullupholstery.com
SIC: 2842 Specialty cleaning, polishes & sanitation goods

(G-13374)
GENERAL MOTORS LLC
895 Joslyn Ave (48340-2920)
PHONE 248 874-1737
EMP: 190
SALES (corp-wide): 155.9B **Publicly Held**
SIC: 3711 3714 Mfg Motor Vehicle/Car Bodies Mfg Motor Vehicle Parts/Accessories
HQ: General Motors Llc
300 Renaissance Ctr L1
Detroit MI 48243
313 556-5000

(G-13375)
GENERAL MOTORS LLC
1251 Joslyn Ave (48340-2064)
PHONE 248 857-3500
Stephanie Malave, *Branch Mgr*
EMP: 700 **Publicly Held**
WEB: www.gm.com
SIC: 5511 5012 3711 Automobiles, new & used; automobiles & other motor vehicles; motor vehicles & car bodies
HQ: General Motors Llc
300 Renaissance Ctr L1
Detroit MI 48243

(G-13376)
GVN GROUP CORP (PA)
Also Called: Sharpertek
486 S Opdyke Rd (48341-3119)
PHONE 248 340-0342
Gus Nasrala, *President*
Ghassan Nasrallah, *General Mgr*
Joyce Nasrala, *COO*
Tim Bartlett, *Accounts Mgr*
▲ **EMP:** 29 **EST:** 2004
SQ FT: 33,000
SALES (est): 7.8MM **Privately Held**
WEB: www.sharpertek.com
SIC: 3699 Cleaning equipment, ultrasonic, except medical & dental

(G-13377)
HEAT TREATING SVCS CORP AMER (PA)
217 Central Ave (48341-2924)
P.O. Box 430269 (48343-0269)
PHONE 248 858-2230
Stephen R Hynes, *President*
Tara Kranz, *Corp Secy*
Brad Hynes, *Vice Pres*
Sara Bales, *Engineer*
Jeff Naylor, *Sales Staff*
EMP: 40 **EST:** 1978
SQ FT: 36,000
SALES (est): 26MM **Privately Held**
WEB: www.htsmi.com
SIC: 3398 Metal heat treating

(G-13378)
HEAT TREATING SVCS CORP AMER
915 Cesar E Chavez Ave (48340-2374)
PHONE 248 332-1510
Bob Culbreath, *Principal*
EMP: 6
SALES (corp-wide): 26MM **Privately Held**
WEB: www.htsmi.com
SIC: 3398 Metal heat treating
PA: Heat Treating Services Corporation Of America
217 Central Ave
Pontiac MI 48341
248 858-2230

(G-13379)
HERITAGE NEWSPAPERS
28 W Huron St (48342-2100)
PHONE 586 783-0300
EMP: 10 **EST:** 2015
SALES (est): 145K **Privately Held**
WEB: www.heritagenews.com
SIC: 2711 Newspapers, publishing & printing

(G-13380)
HIGHWOOD DIE & ENGINEERING INC
1353 Highwood Blvd (48340-1925)
PHONE 248 338-1807
Marilyn Miller, *President*
John Marsh, *Opers Staff*
Mike Miller, *Treasurer*
Jodi Sheridan, *Admin Sec*
EMP: 30 **EST:** 1968
SQ FT: 20,000
SALES (est): 8.3MM **Privately Held**
WEB: www.highwooddie.com
SIC: 3469 3544 Stamping metal for the trade; special dies, tools, jigs & fixtures

(G-13381)
INTEGRATED MARKETING SVCS LLC
Also Called: IMS
125 E Columbia Ave (48340-2715)
PHONE 248 625-7444
Robert C Schaffer, *Mng Member*
Robert Schaffer, *Mng Member*
Larry Orlando, *Creative Dir*
Stephanie Dudek,
EMP: 8 **EST:** 1999
SALES (est): 925K **Privately Held**
WEB: www.4ims.net
SIC: 3823 Water quality monitoring & control systems

(G-13382)
IRVIN ACQUISITION LLC (HQ)
2600 Centerpoint Pkwy (48341-3172)
PHONE 248 451-4100
Brian Cooper, *Vice Pres*
Vincent Johnson,
EMP: 381 **EST:** 2015
SALES (est): 1.1B
SALES (corp-wide): 2.3B **Privately Held**
WEB: www.irvinproducts.com
SIC: 2396 Automotive & apparel trimmings
PA: Piston Group, L.L.C.
3000 Town Ctr Ste 3250
Southfield MI 48075
248 226-3976

(G-13383)
IRVIN AUTOMOTIVE PRODUCTS LLC (DH)
2600 Centerpoint Pkwy (48341-3172)
PHONE 248 451-4100
Tim Mann, *Vice Pres*
Justin Szerlong, *Vice Pres*
Ryan Slobodian, *Mfg Staff*
Alexis Ferman, *Buyer*
Bryan Busha, *Engineer*
▲ **EMP:** 150 **EST:** 1995
SQ FT: 70,000
SALES (est):
SALES (corp-wide): 2.3B **Privately Held**
WEB: www.irvinproducts.com
SIC: 2396 Automotive & apparel trimmings
HQ: Irvin Acquisition Llc
2600 Centerpoint Pkwy
Pontiac MI 48341
248 451-4100

(G-13384)
JAC HOLDING CORPORATION (DH)
3937 Campus Dr (48341-3124)
PHONE 248 874-1800
Jack Falcon, *CEO*
Mike Wood, *COO*
Noel Ranka, *Vice Pres*
Mike Vanloon, *CFO*
◆ **EMP:** 5 **EST:** 1994
SALES (est): 270.2MM
SALES (corp-wide): 748.6MM **Privately Held**
WEB: www.jacproducts.com
SIC: 3089 Injection molding of plastics
HQ: Argonaut Private Equity Fund Iii, Lp
7030 S Yale Ave Ste 810
Tulsa OK 74136
918 392-9600

(G-13385)
JAC PRODUCTS INC
3937 Campus Dr (48341-3124)
PHONE 248 874-1800
Don Cline, *Branch Mgr*
EMP: 70
SALES (corp-wide): 748.6MM **Privately Held**
WEB: www.jacproducts.com
SIC: 3089 3714 Injection molding of plastics; motor vehicle parts & accessories
HQ: Jac Products, Inc.
225 S Industrial Dr
Saline MI 48176
734 944-8844

(G-13386)
JOMAR PERFORMANCE PRODUCTS LLC
211 N Cass Ave (48342-1005)
PHONE 248 322-3080
John J Ansteth, *Mng Member*
Geraldine Ansteth,
Jonathan Best,
EMP: 4 **EST:** 1966
SQ FT: 3,600
SALES (est): 611.2K **Privately Held**
WEB: www.jomarperformance.com
SIC: 3714 Motor vehicle parts & accessories

(G-13387)
JON BEE DISTRIBUTION LLC ⊙
247 Ridgemont Dr (48340-3056)
PHONE 248 846-0491
Johnny B Edwards,
EMP: 5 **EST:** 2021
SALES (est): 54.3K **Privately Held**
SIC: 3496 7389 Paper clips, made from purchased wire;

(G-13388)
JOY INDUSTRIES INC
117 Turk St (48341-3068)
PHONE 248 334-4062
Norman Beaubien, *President*
EMP: 10 **EST:** 1996
SALES (est): 870K **Privately Held**
WEB: www.joyindustries.com
SIC: 7692 Automotive welding

(G-13389)
JUNK MAN LLC
111 Vernon Dr (48342-2559)
PHONE 248 459-7359
Jaquan Whittaker,
EMP: 5 **EST:** 2019
SALES (est): 426K **Privately Held**
SIC: 3711 Wreckers (tow truck), assembly of

(G-13390)
JUS KUTZ LLC
1213 Colony Ln (48340-2209)
PHONE 248 882-5462
Lateasha Grinage,
EMP: 4
SALES (est): 15K **Privately Held**
SIC: 3999 Barber & beauty shop equipment

(G-13391)
KAYS GLROUS BKED GDS DIST LLC
5 Lantern Ln (48340-1648)
PHONE 248 830-1717
Marilyn Long, *Manager*
EMP: 4 **EST:** 2019
SALES (est): 195K **Privately Held**
SIC: 2051 Bakery: wholesale or wholesale/retail combined

(G-13392)
KENT UPHOLSTERY INC
Also Called: Great Lkes Finshg Svcs Detroit
408 Auburn Ave (48340-3208)
PHONE 248 332-7260
Nicholas Henbury, *President*
Tracy Henbury, *Treasurer*
▲ **EMP:** 4 **EST:** 1979
SALES (est): 442.4K **Privately Held**
SIC: 7641 5231 5712 7389 Furniture refinishing; reupholstery; furniture upholstery repair; wallpaper; paint; furniture stores; interior decorating; wood household furniture; upholstered household furniture

(G-13393)
KODIAK MANUFACTURING CO INC
51920 Woodward Ave Ste B (48342-5035)
PHONE 248 335-5552
James Warrick, *President*
Julie Ozias, *Manager*
EMP: 9 **EST:** 1979
SALES (est): 915.3K **Privately Held**
WEB: www.kodiakconnector.com
SIC: 3599 Machine shop, jobbing & repair

(G-13394)
LASER RE-NU LLC
239 Voorheis St (48341-1901)
PHONE 248 630-1454
EMP: 6 **EST:** 2015
SALES (est): 324.2K **Privately Held**
WEB: www.pontiacprinterrepairservice.com
SIC: 3572 Computer tape drives & components

(G-13395)
MANTA GROUP LLC
Also Called: Pk Global Logistics
35 W Huron St Ste 10 (48342-2120)
PHONE 248 325-8264
Reginald B Kelley Sr,
EMP: 10 **EST:** 2008
SALES (est): 533.7K **Privately Held**
WEB: www.mantagroup.com
SIC: 3296 Mineral wool

(G-13396)
MAXXLITE LED SIGNS
44731 Woodward Ave (48341-5021)
PHONE 248 397-5769
Haitham Sitto, *CEO*
EMP: 4 **EST:** 2015
SALES (est): 53.7K **Privately Held**
WEB: www.maxxlite.com
SIC: 3993 Signs & advertising specialties

GEOGRAPHIC SECTION
Pontiac - Oakland County (G-13424)

(G-13397)
METALWORKING LUBRICANTS CO (PA)
25 W Silverdome Indus Par (48342-2994)
P.O. Box 214379, Auburn Hills (48321-4379)
PHONE..................248 332-3500
Robert F Tomlinson, *Ch of Bd*
Kim Onnie, *General Mgr*
Adam Bujoll, *Vice Pres*
Dr Nilda Grenier, *Vice Pres*
James P Tomlinson Jr, *Treasurer*
▲ **EMP:** 75 **EST:** 1952
SQ FT: 26,000
SALES (est): 220.3MM **Privately Held**
WEB: www.metalworkinglubricants.com
SIC: 5172 2869 2843 2992 Lubricating oils & greases; phosphoric acid esters; emulsifiers, except food & pharmaceutical; cutting oils, blending: made from purchased materials; rust arresting compounds, animal or vegetable oil base

(G-13398)
MIS ASSOCIATES INC
Also Called: Data Cover .com
1735 Highwood W (48340-1264)
PHONE..................844 225-8156
Roberto Llftin, *President*
Roberto Loftin, *President*
Rob Loftin, *General Mgr*
Justin Powers, *General Mgr*
Joe Ross, *Director*
EMP: 5 **EST:** 1987
SQ FT: 4,000
SALES (est): 829.6K **Privately Held**
WEB: www.inksupply.com
SIC: 5112 2865 5085 Office supplies; color lakes or toners; ink, printers'

(G-13399)
MORNING STAR PUBLISHING CO
Also Called: Northern Star
48 W Huron St (48342-2101)
PHONE..................989 732-5125
Kevin Jones, *Manager*
EMP: 22
SALES (corp-wide): 274.1MM **Privately Held**
WEB: www.themorningsun.com
SIC: 2711 Newspapers, publishing & printing
HQ: Morning Star Publishing Company
311 E Superior St Ste A
Alma MI 48801
989 779-6000

(G-13400)
NAFTA BENCHMARKING CENTER
2500 Centerpoint Pkwy (48341-3115)
PHONE..................248 335-0366
EMP: 5 **EST:** 2015
SALES (est): 109.7K **Privately Held**
SIC: 3714 Motor vehicle parts & accessories

(G-13401)
NEW AGE COATINGS
415 N Cass Ave (48342-1012)
PHONE..................248 217-1842
EMP: 4 **EST:** 2019
SALES (est): 98.1K **Privately Held**
SIC: 3479 Coating of metals & formed products

(G-13402)
NORTHERN STAIRCASE CO INC
630 Cesar E Chavez Ave (48342-1057)
PHONE..................248 836-0652
Patrick Donovan, *President*
James Steinhaus, *Vice Pres*
EMP: 17 **EST:** 1996
SQ FT: 18,000
SALES (est): 1.1MM **Privately Held**
WEB: www.northernstaircase.com
SIC: 2431 Staircases & stairs, wood

(G-13403)
NORTHSTAR METALCRAFT
35 W Silverdome Indus Par (48342-2994)
PHONE..................248 858-8484
Kevin Sherry, *Manager*
EMP: 5 **EST:** 2016

SALES (est): 364.9K **Privately Held**
WEB: www.northstarmetalcraft.com
SIC: 3499 Fabricated metal products

(G-13404)
OAK WAY MANUFACTURING INC
Also Called: Cant Products
556 N Saginaw St (48342-1466)
PHONE..................248 335-9476
Mahlon A Benson III, *President*
Ozzie Jackson, *General Mgr*
Joseph Benson, *Treasurer*
Jack Wood, *Sales Staff*
EMP: 10 **EST:** 1963
SQ FT: 10,000
SALES (est): 981.4K **Privately Held**
SIC: 2952 Roofing materials

(G-13405)
OC TEES
180 N Saginaw St (48342-2054)
PHONE..................248 858-9191
Mark Peters, *Principal*
EMP: 7 **EST:** 2010
SALES (est): 288.1K **Privately Held**
WEB: www.octees.net
SIC: 2759 Screen printing

(G-13406)
PEPSI-COLA METRO BTLG CO INC
960 Featherstone St (48342-1827)
PHONE..................248 335-3528
Jennifer Mayer, *Financial Exec*
Nina Bommarito, *Sales Staff*
Jeff Branam, *Sales Staff*
Jeff Bickerman, *Manager*
Joel Phillips, *Manager*
EMP: 6
SALES (corp-wide): 70.3B **Publicly Held**
WEB: www.pepsico.com
SIC: 2086 Carbonated soft drinks, bottled & canned
HQ: Pepsi-Cola Metropolitan Bottling Company, Inc.
1111 Westchester Ave
White Plains NY 10604
914 767-6000

(G-13407)
PMD AUTOMOTIVE LLC
40 W Pike St (48342-2109)
PHONE..................248 732-7554
Gordon Heidacker, *CEO*
EMP: 7 **EST:** 2018
SALES (est): 635K **Privately Held**
WEB: www.pmdgarage.com
SIC: 8711 3089 8748 3999 Engineering services; automotive parts, plastic; testing services; manufacturing industries

(G-13408)
PONTIAC ELECTRIC MOTOR WORKS
224 W Sheffield Ave (48340-1854)
PHONE..................248 332-4622
Peter A Polk, *President*
Joan E Polk, *Corp Secy*
Anthony Polk, *Vice Pres*
EMP: 5 **EST:** 1930
SQ FT: 2,400
SALES (est): 1.9MM **Privately Held**
WEB: www.pontiacelectricmotors.com
SIC: 5063 7694 Motors, electric; electric motor repair

(G-13409)
PONTIAC PROPERTIES LLC
28 N Saginaw St (48342-2134)
PHONE..................248 639-4360
John K Mullins, *Principal*
EMP: 4
SALES (est): 165.7K **Privately Held**
WEB: www.theoaklandpress.com
SIC: 2711 Newspapers, publishing & printing

(G-13410)
PRESS ROOM EQP SLS & SVC CO
244 W Sheffield Ave (48340-1854)
PHONE..................248 334-1880
Rick Hole, *President*
Scott Hole, *Vice Pres*
EMP: 6 **EST:** 1954

SQ FT: 6,000
SALES (est): 866.3K **Privately Held**
WEB: www.ensightsolutions.us
SIC: 5084 3542 Machine tools & accessories; machine tools, metal forming type

(G-13411)
PRIMO CRAFTS
1304 University Dr (48342-1974)
PHONE..................248 373-3229
Brian F Mc Carthy, *Owner*
EMP: 5 **EST:** 1973
SQ FT: 3,500
SALES (est): 190K **Privately Held**
WEB: www.primocrafts.com
SIC: 2759 Screen printing

(G-13412)
RAQ LLC
392 S Sanford St (48342-3448)
PHONE..................313 473-7271
Jon Sader, *Mng Member*
EMP: 13
SQ FT: 7,500
SALES (est): 104.9K **Privately Held**
WEB: www.solarraq.com
SIC: 3449 Custom roll formed products

(G-13413)
RESOURCE RCOVERY SOLUTIONS INC
100 W Sheffield Ave (48340-1850)
PHONE..................248 454-3442
Andrew Quigley, *President*
EMP: 7 **EST:** 2007
SQ FT: 15,000
SALES (est): 846.5K **Privately Held**
WEB: www.resourcerecoverysolutions.net
SIC: 3339 5093 Primary nonferrous metals; nonferrous metals scrap; metal scrap & waste materials

(G-13414)
SALEEN
777 Enterprise Dr Ste 100 (48341-3169)
PHONE..................248 499-5333
EMP: 8 **EST:** 2019
SALES (est): 278.5K **Privately Held**
WEB: www.saleen.com
SIC: 3711 Motor vehicles & car bodies

(G-13415)
SALK COMMUNICATIONS INC
Also Called: Salk Sound
40 W Howard St Ste 204 (48342-1284)
PHONE..................248 342-7109
Jim Salk, *Owner*
Matthew Wyman, *Manager*
▲ **EMP:** 4 **EST:** 2011
SALES (est): 221.8K **Privately Held**
WEB: www.salksound.com
SIC: 3651 Loudspeakers, electrodynamic or magnetic

(G-13416)
SLC METER LLC
595 Bradford St (48341-3112)
PHONE..................248 625-0667
Ryan Eichbrecht, *Vice Pres*
Rocky Sampson, *Sales Associate*
John F Traynor,
EMP: 15 **EST:** 2010
SALES (est): 6.7MM **Privately Held**
WEB: www.slcmeter.com
SIC: 3824 Water meters

(G-13417)
SOUTHERN AUTO WHOLESALERS INC
597 N Saginaw St (48342-1468)
PHONE..................248 335-5555
Thomas M Tyson, *President*
Jeff Fast, *General Mgr*
▲ **EMP:** 14 **EST:** 1980
SQ FT: 6,800
SALES (est): 3.6MM **Privately Held**
WEB: www.southernautomotive.com
SIC: 3621 3694 3643 3625 Motors, electric; motors, starting: automotive & aircraft; ignition apparatus, alternators, automotive; electric switches; electric controls & control accessories, industrial; electromechanical counters; motor vehicle supplies & new parts

(G-13418)
STITCH KUSTOMS
304 N Johnson St (48341-1026)
PHONE..................248 622-4563
EMP: 4 **EST:** 2018
SALES (est): 71.6K **Privately Held**
SIC: 2395 Embroidery products, except schiffli machine

(G-13419)
TIANHAI ELECTRIC N AMER INC (DH)
70 E Silverdome Indus Par (48342-2986)
PHONE..................248 987-2100
Jun Lan, *President*
John Nye, *Vice Pres*
Stefanie Gotzeff, *Materials Mgr*
Randall Tietz, *Purch Dir*
Michael Kosnik, *Purch Agent*
◆ **EMP:** 86 **EST:** 2009
SQ FT: 30,000
SALES (est): 39.1MM **Privately Held**
WEB: www.te-na.com
SIC: 3714 Motor vehicle parts & accessories

(G-13420)
TRANS TUBE INC
34 W Sheffield Ave (48342-1846)
PHONE..................248 334-5720
Leslie Dale Walter, *President*
Daisy P Walter, *Corp Secy*
EMP: 14 **EST:** 1970
SQ FT: 60,000
SALES (est): 2.1MM **Privately Held**
WEB: www.tsescorts.com
SIC: 3317 Steel pipe & tubes

(G-13421)
UNIQUE FOOD MANAGEMENT INC
Also Called: RANDY'S CATERING
248 S Telegraph Rd (48341-1933)
PHONE..................248 738-9393
Rosa Randolph, *President*
Jim Lang, *Vice Pres*
Lou Hawkins, *Admin Sec*
EMP: 22 **EST:** 1987
SALES (est): 860.2K **Privately Held**
WEB: www.uniquefoodmgt.com
SIC: 2099 Food preparations

(G-13422)
UNITED FBRCNTS STRAINRITE CORP
Also Called: Oakland Engineering Filtration
481 N Saginaw St Ste A (48342-1453)
PHONE..................800 487-3136
William Okay, *Opers Mgr*
Ed Bush, *Sales Mgr*
Alan Roberts, *Sales Staff*
EMP: 39
SALES (corp-wide): 25.2MM **Privately Held**
WEB: www.strainrite.com
SIC: 3569 Filters, general line: industrial
HQ: United Fabricants Strainrite Corporation
65 First Flight Dr
Auburn ME 04210
207 376-1600

(G-13423)
UVSHELTRON INC
1601 Valdosta Cir (48340-1082)
PHONE..................888 877-7946
Saliel D'Souza, *Exec Dir*
EMP: 5 **EST:** 2020
SALES (est): 39.6K **Privately Held**
WEB: www.uvsheltron.com
SIC: 3999 Manufacturing industries

(G-13424)
WENZ & GIBBENS ENTERPRISES
Also Called: City Sign Company
101 E Walton Blvd (48340-1266)
PHONE..................248 333-7938
Gerald Gibbens, *President*
Dave Wenz, *Vice Pres*
EMP: 7 **EST:** 1959
SQ FT: 2,400

Pontiac - Oakland County (G-13425)

SALES (est): 902.1K Privately Held
WEB: www.citysignco.com
SIC: 3993 1799 Electric signs; sign installation & maintenance

(G-13425)
WILLIAMS INTERNATIONAL CO LLC (PA)
Also Called: Willc
2000 Centerpoint Pkwy (48341-3146)
PHONE..................................248 624-5200
Frank Smith, Senior VP
John Becker, Vice Pres
Jim Devlin, Vice Pres
Troy Petrowski, Vice Pres
Cindy Nelson, Opers Staff
▲ EMP: 651 EST: 1955
SALES (est): 379.1MM Privately Held
WEB: www.williams-int.com
SIC: 3724 3764 Turbines, aircraft type; engines & engine parts, guided missile

(G-13426)
WOODWORTH INC (PA)
500 Centerpoint Pkwy N (48341-3171)
PHONE..................................248 481-2354
Terry R Woodworth, President
Dennis Deciechi, General Mgr
Matt Woodworth, Vice Pres
Sean Backer, Plant Mgr
Jeff Hunt, Mfg Staff
EMP: 35 EST: 1990
SQ FT: 380,000
SALES (est): 13.9MM Privately Held
WEB: www.woodworthheattreating.com
SIC: 3398 Metal heat treating

(G-13427)
WOODWORTH RASSINI HOLDING LLC (PA)
500 Centerpoint Pkwy N (48341-3171)
PHONE..................................248 481-2354
Matt Woodworth, Principal
EMP: 53 EST: 2011
SALES (est): 90.8K Privately Held
SIC: 3398 Metal heat treating

Port Austin
Huron County

(G-13428)
PORT AUSTIN LEVEL & TL MFG CO
130 Arthur St (48467-6703)
P.O. Box 365 (48467-0365)
PHONE..................................989 738-5291
Robert Upthegrove, President
Robert B Upthegrove, President
Mary Jaworski, Admin Sec
EMP: 13 EST: 1947
SQ FT: 30,000
SALES (est): 662.5K Privately Held
WEB: www.portaustinlevelandtool.com
SIC: 3423 3829 Hand & edge tools; measuring & controlling devices

Port Hope
Huron County

(G-13429)
LAKEVIEW CABINETRY
5674 Lakeview Dr (48468-9749)
P.O. Box 213 (48468-0213)
PHONE..................................810 650-1420
Bruce Middel, Principal
EMP: 5 EST: 2015
SALES (est): 218K Privately Held
SIC: 2434 Wood kitchen cabinets

Port Huron
St. Clair County

(G-13430)
ABLE SOLUTIONS LLC
2030 10th St (48060-6217)
PHONE..................................810 216-6106
Paul Horn, President
EMP: 8 EST: 2014
SQ FT: 1,608
SALES (est): 718.3K Privately Held
WEB: www.able-solutions.com
SIC: 2842 3089 5169 Specialty cleaning preparations; holders: paper towel, grocery bag, etc.: plastic; specialty cleaning & sanitation preparations

(G-13431)
AFX INDUSTRIES LLC (DH)
Also Called: Afx/Trim
1411 3rd St Ste G (48060-5480)
PHONE..................................810 966-4650
David Sommerville, VP Sls/Mktg
Julie Ainsworth, Manager
Duane Webster, Webmaster
Bill Schroers,
Drew Knight,
▲ EMP: 5 EST: 1998
SQ FT: 91,000
SALES (est): 99.2MM
SALES (corp-wide): 311.7MM Privately Held
WEB: www.afxindustries.com
SIC: 3111 5531 Industrial leather products; automotive parts
HQ: Exco Inc.
    1007 N Orange St
    Wilmington DE 19801
    905 477-3065

(G-13432)
AFX INDUSTRIES LLC
Also Called: Brusarosco
1411 3rd St Ste G (48060-5480)
PHONE..................................810 966-4650
Bill Schroers,
EMP: 7
SALES (corp-wide): 311.7MM Privately Held
WEB: www.afxindustries.com
SIC: 3111 Industrial leather products
HQ: Afx Industries, L.L.C.
    1411 3rd St Ste G
    Port Huron MI 48060
    810 966-4650

(G-13433)
AINSWORTH ELECTRIC INC
3200 Dove Rd Ste A (48060-7489)
PHONE..................................810 984-5768
Richard R Ainsworth, President
Cynthia Ainsworth, Corp Secy
▲ EMP: 20 EST: 1982
SQ FT: 10,000
SALES (est): 5.2MM Privately Held
WEB: www.ainsworthelectric.com
SIC: 1731 7629 3621 5063 General electrical contractor; generator repair; generator sets: gasoline, diesel or dual-fuel; generators

(G-13434)
ALD THERMAL TREATMENT INC
2656 24th St (48060-6419)
PHONE..................................810 357-0693
Jim Kassan, Vice Pres
Hector Ibarra, Vice Pres
Michael Heifner, Production
Julie Mathews, Purch Agent
Orlando Aldape, Engineer
▲ EMP: 174 EST: 2000
SQ FT: 78,424
SALES (est): 38.5MM
SALES (corp-wide): 937.1MM Privately Held
WEB: www.heat-treatment-services.com
SIC: 3398 Metal heat treating
HQ: Metallurg, Inc.
    435 Devon Park Dr Ste 200
    Wayne PA 19087
    610 293-2501

(G-13435)
ALTAGAS MARKETING (US) INC
1411 3rd St Ste A (48060-5480)
PHONE..................................810 887-4105
David M Harris, President
Deborah S Stein, Senior VP
Nicholas Galotti, Vice Pres
Steven W Warsinske, Vice Pres
Shaun Toivanen, Treasurer
EMP: 50 EST: 2001
SALES (est): 3MM
SALES (corp-wide): 4.2MM Privately Held
WEB: www.altagas.ca
SIC: 4923 1321 Gas transmission & distribution; natural gasoline production
PA: Altagas Ltd
    355 4 Ave Sw Suite 1700
    Calgary AB T2P 0
    403 691-7575

(G-13436)
ALTAGAS POWER HOLDINGS US INC (DH)
1411 3rd St Ste A (48060-5480)
PHONE..................................810 887-4105
David M Harris, President
Deborah S Stein, Senior VP
Nicholas Galotti, Vice Pres
Steven W Warsinske, Vice Pres
Shaun Toivanen, Treasurer
EMP: 100 EST: 2012
SALES (est): 43.9MM
SALES (corp-wide): 4.2MM Privately Held
SIC: 1321 4923 Natural gasoline production; gas transmission & distribution

(G-13437)
ALUDYNE EAST MICHIGAN LLC
Also Called: Chassis Co. of Michigan, LLC
2223 Dove St (48060-6738)
PHONE..................................810 987-7633
Sergi Barbero, Vice Pres
Michael Dorah, Vice Pres
Jeff Bellinger, Purchasing
Andreas Weller, Mng Member
Jonnah Bullis, Manager
▲ EMP: 80 EST: 2007
SALES (est): 20.6MM
SALES (corp-wide): 1.5B Privately Held
WEB: www.chassix.com
SIC: 3714 Motor vehicle parts & accessories
HQ: Aludyne International, Inc
    300 Galleria Ofcntr Ste 5
    Southfield MI 48034

(G-13438)
ALUDYNE US LLC
3150 Dove St (48060-6766)
PHONE..................................810 987-1112
Ranee Parmann, Purchasing
Jean Brewer, QC Mgr
Ray Casper, Prgrmr
EMP: 100
SALES (corp-wide): 1.5B Privately Held
WEB: www.aludyne.com
SIC: 3465 3714 3549 Body parts, automobile: stamped metal; motor vehicle parts & accessories; metalworking machinery
HQ: Aludyne Us Llc
    300 Galleria Ofcntr Ste 5
    Southfield MI 48034

(G-13439)
ANCHOR RECYCLING INC
2829 Goulden St (48060-6975)
PHONE..................................810 984-5545
EMP: 9
SALES (est): 980.1K Privately Held
SIC: 2611 4953 Pulp Mill Refuse System

(G-13440)
ARCTIC GLACIER GRAYLING INC
1755 Yeager St (48060-2594)
PHONE..................................810 987-7100
Robert Nagy, President
Keith McMahon, Vice Pres
EMP: 11 EST: 2004
SQ FT: 12,000
SALES (est): 440.4K Privately Held
SIC: 2097 Manufactured ice

(G-13441)
ARCTIC GLACIER INC
1755 Yeager St (48060-2594)
PHONE..................................734 485-0430
David Blind, Vice Pres
Kerry Chamberlin,
▲ EMP: 46 EST: 1926
SALES (est): 8.5MM Privately Held
WEB: www.arcticglacier.com
SIC: 5199 2097 Ice, manufactured or natural; manufactured ice

(G-13442)
ARCTIC GLACIER NEWBURGH INC (DH)
1755 Yeager St (48060-2594)
PHONE..................................845 561-0549
Robert Nagy, President
Keith McMahon, Vice Pres
Hugh Adams, Admin Sec
EMP: 15 EST: 2004
SALES (est): 16.6MM
SALES (corp-wide): 2.9B Publicly Held
WEB: www.arcticglacier.com
SIC: 2097 Manufactured ice
HQ: Agi Ccaa Inc
    625 Henry Ave
    Winnipeg MB R3A 0
    204 772-2473

(G-13443)
ARCTIC GLACIER USA INC
1755 Yeager St (48060-2594)
PHONE..................................215 283-0326
Peter Stack, President
EMP: 12 EST: 1976
SALES (est): 426.7K Privately Held
SIC: 2097 Ice cubes

(G-13444)
ARCTIC GLACIER USA INC
1755 Yeager St (48060-2594)
PHONE..................................204 772-2473
EMP: 37
SALES (corp-wide): 628.1MM Privately Held
WEB: www.arcticglacier.com
SIC: 2097 Manufactured ice
HQ: Arctic Glacier U.S.A., Inc.
    1654 Marthaler Ln
    Saint Paul MN 55118
    204 784-5873

(G-13445)
ARCTIC GLACIER USA INC
1755 Yeager St (48060-2594)
PHONE..................................204 772-2473
EMP: 37
SALES (corp-wide): 628.1MM Privately Held
WEB: www.arcticglacier.com
SIC: 2097 Manufactured ice
HQ: Arctic Glacier U.S.A., Inc.
    1654 Marthaler Ln
    Saint Paul MN 55118
    204 784-5873

(G-13446)
ARCTIC GLACIER USA INC
1755 Yeager St (48060-2594)
PHONE..................................204 772-2473
EMP: 37
SALES (corp-wide): 628.1MM Privately Held
WEB: www.arcticglacier.com
SIC: 2097 Manufactured ice
HQ: Arctic Glacier U.S.A., Inc.
    1654 Marthaler Ln
    Saint Paul MN 55118
    204 784-5873

(G-13447)
ARCTIC GLACIER USA INC
1755 Yeager St (48060-2594)
PHONE..................................204 772-2473
Debra Rodd, Principal
EMP: 37
SALES (corp-wide): 628.1MM Privately Held
WEB: www.arcticglacier.com
SIC: 2097 Block ice
HQ: Arctic Glacier U.S.A., Inc.
    1654 Marthaler Ln
    Saint Paul MN 55118
    204 784-5873

(G-13448)
ARCTIC GLACIER USA INC
1755 Yeager St (48060-2594)
PHONE..................................204 772-2473
Debra Rodd, Manager
EMP: 37

GEOGRAPHIC SECTION
Port Huron - St. Clair County (G-13473)

SALES (corp-wide): 628.1MM **Privately Held**
WEB: www.arcticglacier.com
SIC: 2097 Manufactured ice
HQ: Arctic Glacier U.S.A., Inc.
1654 Marthaler Ln
Saint Paul MN 55118
204 784-5873

(G-13449)
ARCTIC GLACIER USA INC
1755 Yeager St (48060-2594)
PHONE....................204 772-2473
Debra Rodd, *Manager*
EMP: 37
SALES (corp-wide): 628.1MM **Privately Held**
WEB: www.arcticglacier.com
SIC: 2097 Manufactured ice
HQ: Arctic Glacier U.S.A., Inc.
1654 Marthaler Ln
Saint Paul MN 55118
204 784-5873

(G-13450)
ARCTIC GLACIER USA INC
1755 Yeager St (48060-2594)
PHONE....................204 772-2473
EMP: 37
SALES (corp-wide): 628.1MM **Privately Held**
WEB: www.arcticglacier.com
SIC: 2097 Manufactured ice
HQ: Arctic Glacier U.S.A., Inc.
1654 Marthaler Ln
Saint Paul MN 55118
204 784-5873

(G-13451)
ARCTIC GLACIER USA INC
1755 Yeager St (48060-2594)
PHONE....................204 772-2473
EMP: 37
SALES (corp-wide): 628.1MM **Privately Held**
WEB: www.arcticglacier.com
SIC: 2097 Manufactured ice
HQ: Arctic Glacier U.S.A., Inc.
1654 Marthaler Ln
Saint Paul MN 55118
204 784-5873

(G-13452)
ARCTIC GLACIER USA INC
1755 Yeager St (48060-2594)
PHONE....................204 772-2473
EMP: 37
SALES (corp-wide): 628.1MM **Privately Held**
WEB: www.arcticglacier.com
SIC: 2097 Manufactured ice
HQ: Arctic Glacier U.S.A., Inc.
1654 Marthaler Ln
Saint Paul MN 55118
204 784-5873

(G-13453)
ARCTIC GLACIER USA INC
1755 Yeager St (48060-2594)
PHONE....................204 772-2473
EMP: 37
SALES (corp-wide): 628.1MM **Privately Held**
WEB: www.arcticglacier.com
SIC: 2097 Manufactured ice
HQ: Arctic Glacier U.S.A., Inc.
1654 Marthaler Ln
Saint Paul MN 55118
204 784-5873

(G-13454)
ARCTIC GLACIER WISCONSIN INC
1755 Yeager St (48060-2594)
PHONE....................262 345-6999
Tom Leezer, *President*
EMP: 40 **EST:** 2005
SALES (est): 3.9MM **Privately Held**
SIC: 3559 Ice resurfacing machinery

(G-13455)
AUTO ANODICS INC
2407 16th St (48060-6196)
PHONE....................810 984-5600
Max Andrew Wiener, *Vice Pres*
Lisa Wiener, *Vice Pres*
Max Andrew, *Technology*
EMP: 50 **EST:** 1978
SQ FT: 56,000
SALES (est): 4.4MM **Privately Held**
WEB: www.autoanodics.com
SIC: 3471 Plating of metals or formed products; anodizing (plating) of metals or formed products

(G-13456)
B & L INDUSTRIES INC
2121 16th St (48060-6175)
P.O. Box 611011 (48061-1011)
PHONE....................810 987-9121
Richard Foster, *President*
Margaret J Foster, *Vice Pres*
EMP: 23 **EST:** 1971
SQ FT: 10,000
SALES (est): 1.9MM **Privately Held**
SIC: 3444 Sheet metalwork

(G-13457)
BARRY ELECTRIC-ROVILL CO
1431 White St (48060-5736)
PHONE....................810 985-8960
Vicki Smith, *President*
EMP: 5 **EST:** 1950
SQ FT: 1,500
SALES (est): 200K **Privately Held**
SIC: 7694 Electric motor repair

(G-13458)
BIOPRO INC
2929 Lapeer Rd (48060-2558)
PHONE....................810 982-7777
Patrick E Pringle, *President*
Dennis Tickle, *Production*
Michael Gorman, *Engineer*
Mary Burns, *Finance*
Jeffrey Hendrix, *Regl Sales Mgr*
EMP: 27 **EST:** 1999
SQ FT: 26,000
SALES (est): 6.8MM **Privately Held**
WEB: www.bioproimplants.com
SIC: 3842 5999 Prosthetic appliances; orthopedic & prosthesis applications

(G-13459)
BLACK RIVER MANUFACTURING INC (PA)
2625 20th St (48060-6443)
PHONE....................810 982-9812
Jarold Hawks, *President*
Debbie Rabidue, *Finance Mgr*
Jason Keil, *Info Tech Mgr*
EMP: 45 **EST:** 1977
SQ FT: 3,000
SALES (est): 20.6MM **Privately Held**
WEB: www.blackrivermfg.biz
SIC: 3714 3451 3441 3061 Motor vehicle engines & parts; transmission housings or parts, motor vehicle; screw machine products; fabricated structural metal; mechanical rubber goods

(G-13460)
BLACK RIVER MANUFACTURING INC
2401 20th St (48060-6406)
PHONE....................810 982-9812
Kim Matthews, *QC Mgr*
Debbie Keil, *Branch Mgr*
EMP: 100
SALES (corp-wide): 20.6MM **Privately Held**
WEB: www.blackrivermfg.biz
SIC: 3714 Motor vehicle engines & parts
PA: Black River Manufacturing Inc
2625 20th St
Port Huron MI 48060
810 982-9812

(G-13461)
BME INC
3763 Lapeer Rd Ste E (48060-4523)
PHONE....................810 937-2974
Brett May, *President*
EMP: 5 **EST:** 2007
SALES (est): 1.7MM **Privately Held**
SIC: 3569 3531 Assembly machines, non-metalworking; construction machinery

(G-13462)
BOWMAN PRINTING INC
Also Called: Sir Speedy
600 Huron Ave (48060-3702)
PHONE....................810 982-8202
Lisa Bowman, *President*
Cary Bowman, *Vice Pres*
EMP: 4 **EST:** 1965
SQ FT: 3,000
SALES (est): 708.5K **Privately Held**
WEB: www.sirspeedy.com
SIC: 2752 Commercial printing, lithographic

(G-13463)
BRITT MANUFACTURING
2600 20th St (48060-6444)
PHONE....................810 982-9720
EMP: 13 **EST:** 2019
SALES (est): 923K **Privately Held**
WEB: www.brittmfg.com
SIC: 3999 Manufacturing industries

(G-13464)
CIPA USA INC (PA)
Also Called: Auto & Truck Components, Co.
3350 Griswold Rd (48060-4742)
PHONE....................810 982-3555
Rick Leveille, *President*
Paul J Leveille, *Exec VP*
Janet Studaker, *Regl Sales Mgr*
◆ **EMP:** 40 **EST:** 1986
SQ FT: 105,000
SALES (est): 9.9MM **Privately Held**
WEB: www.cipausa.com
SIC: 3714 Motor vehicle parts & accessories

(G-13465)
COOPER & COOPER SALES INC
851 W Pointe (48060-4454)
P.O. Box 611107 (48061-1107)
PHONE....................810 327-6247
Steve G Cooper, *CEO*
Diane M Cooper, *President*
Grant Cooper, *Vice Pres*
EMP: 5 **EST:** 1982
SALES (est): 385.3K **Privately Held**
WEB: www.coopertube.com
SIC: 3441 Fabricated structural metal

(G-13466)
COSNER ICE COMPANY INC
1755 Yeager St (48060-2594)
PHONE....................812 279-8930
Reath Cosner, *President*
Luke Flynn, *Manager*
EMP: 285 **EST:** 1970
SALES (est): 2.5MM
SALES (corp-wide): 628.1MM **Privately Held**
WEB: www.cosnerice.com
SIC: 2097 4215 Manufactured ice; courier services, except by air
HQ: Arctic Glacier U.S.A., Inc.
1654 Marthaler Ln
Saint Paul MN 55118
204 784-5873

(G-13467)
COUNTY OF ST CLAIR
1221 Pine Grove Ave (48060-3511)
PHONE....................810 982-4111
Daniel Spitz, *Branch Mgr*
Chelsea Kendrick, *Clerk*
EMP: 15
SALES (corp-wide): 89MM **Privately Held**
WEB: www.stclaircounty.org
SIC: 2711 Newspapers, publishing & printing
PA: County Of St Clair
200 Grand River Ave Ste 2
Port Huron MI 48060
810 989-6900

(G-13468)
DICKS SIGNS
2560 40th St (48060-2571)
PHONE....................810 987-9002
Dick Darling, *Owner*
EMP: 5 **EST:** 1996
SALES (est): 233.3K **Privately Held**
SIC: 3993 7532 Signs & advertising specialties; truck painting & lettering

(G-13469)
DOMTAR INDUSTRIES LLC
Also Called: Domtar Gypsum
1700 Washington Ave (48060-3400)
P.O. Box 5003 (48061-5003)
PHONE....................810 982-0191
Mark Bessette, *Vice Pres*
Conrad Sternot, *Production*
Michelle L Morris, *Purchasing*
Ed Cook, *Engineer*
Andrew Goulet, *Engineer*
EMP: 93 **EST:** 1971
SALES (est): 15.9MM **Privately Held**
WEB: www.domtar.com
SIC: 2621 Paper mills

(G-13470)
DUNN PAPER INC (HQ)
218 Riverview St (48060-2996)
PHONE....................810 984-5521
Brent Earnshaw, *President*
Wade Kemnitz, *COO*
Greg Howe, *Exec VP*
Gregory Howe, *Exec VP*
Rob Emigh, *Vice Pres*
◆ **EMP:** 10 **EST:** 2003
SQ FT: 165,000
SALES (est): 102.3MM
SALES (corp-wide): 109.5MM **Privately Held**
WEB: www.dunnpaper.com
SIC: 2671 2672 Paper coated or laminated for packaging; coated & laminated paper
PA: Dunn Paper Holdings, Inc.
218 Riverview St
Port Huron MI 48060
810 984-5521

(G-13471)
DUNN PAPER - WIGGINS LLC
218 Riverview St (48060-2976)
PHONE....................810 984-5521
Alain Magnan, *President*
EMP: 1 **EST:** 2011
SALES (est): 1MM
SALES (corp-wide): 109.5MM **Privately Held**
WEB: www.dunnpaper.com
SIC: 2671 Paper coated or laminated for packaging
HQ: Dunn Paper, Inc.
218 Riverview St
Port Huron MI 48060
810 984-5521

(G-13472)
DUNN PAPER HOLDINGS INC (PA)
218 Riverview St (48060-2976)
PHONE....................810 984-5521
Brent Earnshaw, *President*
Richard Voss, *Vice Pres*
Christopher Anderson, *Opers Mgr*
Gerry Konop, *Opers Staff*
Sharon Brown, *Senior Buyer*
EMP: 3 **EST:** 2010
SQ FT: 165,000
SALES (est): 109.5MM **Privately Held**
WEB: www.dunnpaper.com
SIC: 2621 2672 Paper mills; coated & laminated paper

(G-13473)
E B EDDY PAPER INC
Also Called: Domtar Eddy Specialty Papers
1700 Washington Ave (48060-3462)
P.O. Box 5003 (48061-5003)
PHONE....................810 982-0191
John Williams, *CEO*
Gilles Pharand, *Vice Pres*
Charlie Dees, *Director*
Al Martin, *Director*
Tom Wik, *Director*
EMP: 324 **EST:** 1987
SQ FT: 525,000
SALES (est): 99.7MM
SALES (corp-wide): 3.6B **Privately Held**
WEB: www.domtar.com
SIC: 2621 Packaging paper; specialty papers; offset paper; fine paper
HQ: Domtar Inc.
395 Boul De Maisonneuve O Bureau 200
Montreal QC H3A 1
514 848-5555

(PA)=Parent Co (HQ)=Headquarters (DH)=Div Headquarters
✪ = New Business established in last 2 years

Port Huron - St. Clair County (G-13474)

(G-13474)
EISSMANN AUTO PORT HURON LLC (DH)
2440 20th St (48060-6436)
PHONE..............810 216-6300
Brian Tinney, *Co-President*
Joerg Schultz, *Co-President*
Lucas Butterstein, *CFO*
Janna Rippon, *Accounts Mgr*
Manuel Carozzi, *Manager*
▲ **EMP:** 130 **EST:** 2014
SALES (est): 32.8MM
SALES (corp-wide): 451.6MM **Privately Held**
WEB: www.eissmann.com
SIC: 2396 Automotive trimmings, fabric
HQ: Eissmann Automotive North America, Inc.
599 Ed Gardner Dr
Pell City AL 35125
205 338-4044

(G-13475)
ELUCIDATION FABRICATION
3921 32nd St (48060-6950)
PHONE..............586 612-4601
Brent Hencak, *Principal*
EMP: 6 **EST:** 2018
SALES (est): 153K **Privately Held**
WEB: www.elucidationfabrication.com
SIC: 3599 Machine shop, jobbing & repair

(G-13476)
EXCALIBUR CROSSBOW INC
2929 Lapeer Rd (48060-2558)
PHONE..............810 937-5864
EMP: 4 **EST:** 2017
SALES (est): 47K **Privately Held**
WEB: www.excaliburcrossbow.com
SIC: 3949 Crossbows

(G-13477)
EXPERT MACHINE & TOOL INC
2424 Lapeer Rd (48060-2528)
PHONE..............810 984-2323
Micheal J Biga, *President*
EMP: 9 **EST:** 1989
SQ FT: 8,000
SALES (est): 953.4K **Privately Held**
SIC: 3544 Special dies & tools; jigs & fixtures

(G-13478)
FORT GRTIOT CBNETS COUNTER LLC
3390 Ravenswood Rd (48060-4662)
PHONE..............810 364-1924
Jeain Lenn, *Owner*
Jean Lenn,
EMP: 7 **EST:** 2006
SALES (est): 176.1K **Privately Held**
SIC: 2434 Wood kitchen cabinets

(G-13479)
GB DYNAMICS INC
1620 Kearney St (48060-3420)
PHONE..............313 400-3570
Jonathan Granger, *CEO*
Keith Gardner, *CFO*
EMP: 8 **EST:** 2004
SALES (est): 257.1K **Privately Held**
WEB: www.gbdynamicsinc.com
SIC: 4789 2869 Cargo loading & unloading services; fuels

(G-13480)
GEARTEC INC
1105 24th St (48060-4849)
P.O. Box 5006 (48061-5006)
PHONE..............810 987-4700
John O Wirtz, *President*
Bruce Patchel, *Finance*
EMP: 20 **EST:** 2013
SQ FT: 24,000
SALES (est): 1.6MM **Privately Held**
WEB: www.geartec.com
SIC: 3566 7389 Reduction gears & gear units for turbines, except automotive;

(G-13481)
GREENE MANUFACTURING TECH LLC
Also Called: Greene Group Industries
2600 20th St (48060-6444)
PHONE..............810 982-9370
Oscar Dean, *Credit Mgr*
Mark Ward, *Mng Member*
EMP: 110 **EST:** 1996
SALES (est): 14.1MM **Privately Held**
SIC: 3499 3559 Friction material, made from powdered metal; electronic component making machinery

(G-13482)
HOLD-IT INC
2301 16th St (48060-6401)
P.O. Box 611391 (48061-1391)
PHONE..............810 984-4213
Debra Sullivan, *President*
Hope Sexton, *Admin Sec*
Bonnie Steece, *Administration*
EMP: 7 **EST:** 1987
SALES (est): 634.1K **Privately Held**
SIC: 3069 Grips or handles, rubber

(G-13483)
HP PELZER AUTO SYSTEMS INC
Also Called: Adler Pelzer Group
2415 Dove St (48060-6716)
PHONE..............810 987-4444
Tim Hockney, *Branch Mgr*
EMP: 283
SALES (corp-wide): 177.9K **Privately Held**
WEB: www.adlerpelzer.com
SIC: 3559 5013 3714 3429 Automotive related machinery; automotive supplies & parts; motor vehicle parts & accessories; mineral wool
HQ: Hp Pelzer Automotive Systems, Inc.
1175 Crooks Rd
Troy MI 48084

(G-13484)
HP PELZER AUTOMOTIVE SYSTEMS
2630 Dove St (48060-6719)
PHONE..............810 987-0725
Janet Goldsbey, *Principal*
▲ **EMP:** 40 **EST:** 2004
SALES (est): 18.2MM
SALES (corp-wide): 177.9K **Privately Held**
WEB: www.adlerpelzer.com
SIC: 3711 Automobile bodies, passenger car, not including engine, etc.
HQ: Hp Pelzer Automotive Systems, Inc.
1175 Crooks Rd
Troy MI 48084

(G-13485)
HURON INDUSTRIES INC
2301 16th St (48060-6401)
P.O. Box 610104 (48061-0104)
PHONE..............810 984-4213
Verna Boukamp, *President*
Debra Sullivan, *Purchasing*
John W Boukamp, *Treasurer*
▼ **EMP:** 5 **EST:** 1961
SQ FT: 5,000
SALES (est): 471.2K **Privately Held**
SIC: 2992 2891 2911 Lubricating oils; sealants; greases, lubricating

(G-13486)
HURON SOAP CANDLE COMPANY
313 Huron Ave (48060-3823)
PHONE..............810 989-5952
EMP: 5 **EST:** 2015
SALES (est): 118.2K **Privately Held**
SIC: 2841 Soap & other detergents

(G-13487)
IMPRINT HOUSE LLC
1113 Military St (48060-5418)
PHONE..............810 985-8203
Ted Smith, *Owner*
EMP: 4 **EST:** 1989
SALES (est): 322.4K **Privately Held**
WEB: www.theimprinthouse.com
SIC: 5199 2396 2395 2759 Advertising specialties; screen printing on fabric articles; embroidery products, except schiffli machine; business forms; printing

(G-13488)
INTERNTNAL AUTO CMPNNTS GROUP
1905 Beard St (48060-6440)
PHONE..............810 987-8500
Chad Schisler, *Maint Spvr*
Christopher Baranick, *Director*
EMP: 6 **Privately Held**
WEB: www.iacgroup.com
SIC: 2396 3714 3429 Automotive trimmings, fabric; motor vehicle parts & accessories; manufactured hardware (general)
HQ: International Automotive Components Group North America, Inc.
27777 Franklin Rd # 2000
Southfield MI 48034

(G-13489)
JABARS COMPLEMENTS LLC
Also Called: Chefshell Catering
2639 24th St (48060-6418)
PHONE..............810 966-8371
Mark Wrubel, *Managing Prtnr*
Michelle Wrubel, *Managing Prtnr*
EMP: 7 **EST:** 1988
SQ FT: 1,100
SALES (est): 550K **Privately Held**
SIC: 2035 5812 Pickles, sauces & salad dressings; eating places

(G-13490)
JGR PLASTICS LLC
Also Called: Prism
2040 International Way (48060-7471)
PHONE..............810 990-1957
Tom Zobl, *Opers Mgr*
Adam Smith, *Project Engr*
Rhonda Wallace, *Accounts Mgr*
Gerry Phillips, *Mng Member*
Barry Reiser, *Program Mgr*
EMP: 31 **EST:** 1999
SQ FT: 18,000
SALES (est): 8.6MM **Privately Held**
WEB: www.prismplastics.com
SIC: 3089 Injection molding of plastics

(G-13491)
K TWO WELDING
1307 Oak St (48060-6109)
PHONE..............810 858-3072
EMP: 4 **EST:** 2016
SALES (est): 63.6K **Privately Held**
SIC: 7692 Welding repair

(G-13492)
K&G WELDING LLC
2515 Elmwood St (48060-2620)
PHONE..............810 887-0560
Christopher Brennan, *Principal*
EMP: 5 **EST:** 2016
SALES (est): 28.2K **Privately Held**
SIC: 7692 Welding repair

(G-13493)
KEROSENE FRAGRANCES
1613 Court St (48060-5031)
PHONE..............810 292-5772
EMP: 4
SALES (est): 126.4K **Privately Held**
WEB: www.houseofkerosene.com
SIC: 2911 Kerosene

(G-13494)
KIMBERLY-CLARK CORPORATION
2609 Electric Ave Ste C (48060-6589)
PHONE..............810 985-1830
EMP: 5
SALES (corp-wide): 19.1B **Publicly Held**
WEB: www.kimberly-clark.com
SIC: 2621 2676 Sanitary tissue paper; infant & baby paper products
PA: Kimberly-Clark Corporation
351 Phelps Dr
Irving TX 75038
972 281-1200

(G-13495)
KNOWLTON ENTERPRISES INC (PA)
Also Called: Party Time Ice Co
1755 Yeager St (48060-2594)
PHONE..............810 987-7100
Norman F Knowlton, *President*
Charles J Knowlton, *Vice Pres*
EMP: 55 **EST:** 1967
SALES (est): 5.3MM **Privately Held**
SIC: 2097 Block ice; ice cubes

(G-13496)
KTWO WELDING
3390 Ravenswood Rd (48060-4662)
PHONE..............810 216-6087
EMP: 4 **EST:** 2017
SALES (est): 51.1K **Privately Held**
SIC: 7692 Welding repair

(G-13497)
M C WARD INC
4100 Griswold Rd (48060-7495)
PHONE..............810 982-9720
Mark C Ward, *President*
EMP: 17 **EST:** 1988
SALES (est): 688.6K **Privately Held**
SIC: 3544 Industrial molds

(G-13498)
MAG AUTOMOTIVE LLC
2555 20th St (48060-6450)
PHONE..............586 446-7000
EMP: 12 **Privately Held**
WEB: www.service.mag-ias.com
SIC: 3559 Automotive related machinery
HQ: Mag Automotive Llc
6015 Center Dr
Sterling Heights MI 48312
586 446-7000

(G-13499)
MAJOR INDUSTRIES LTD
521 Michigan St (48060-3810)
PHONE..............810 985-9372
Algong Lee, *President*
Todd Goldman, *Vice Pres*
▲ **EMP:** 18 **EST:** 2004
SALES (est): 473.4K **Privately Held**
WEB: www.majorindustriesltd.com
SIC: 3312 Tool & die steel & alloys

(G-13500)
MAPAL INC (HQ)
4032 Dove Rd (48060-7442)
PHONE..............810 364-8020
Dieter Kress, *President*
Paul Abbott, *Prdtn Mgr*
Shawn Andrews, *Mfg Staff*
Kelia McCkarty, *Purchasing*
Frank Duke, *QC Mgr*
◆ **EMP:** 60 **EST:** 1975
SQ FT: 45,000
SALES (est): 25.8MM
SALES (corp-wide): 718.1MM **Privately Held**
WEB: www.mapal.com
SIC: 3545 Cutting tools for machine tools
PA: Mapal Fabrik Fur Prazisionswerkzeuge Dr. Kress Kg
Obere Bahnstr. 13
Aalen BW 73431
736 158-50

(G-13501)
MICHIGAN METAL COATINGS CO
2015 Dove St (48060-6738)
PHONE..............810 966-9240
Yasutaka Hasegawa, *President*
Richard Rumohr, *QC Mgr*
Traci Reitano, *Supervisor*
Steve Hlywa, *Technical Staff*
EMP: 53 **EST:** 1986
SALES (est): 12MM **Privately Held**
WEB: www.michiganmetalcoatings.com
SIC: 3479 Coating of metals & formed products
PA: Mc Systems Inc.
4-1, Tomifunecho, Nakagawa-Ku
Nagoya AIC 454-0

(G-13502)
MILITARY APPAREL CO
2664 Military St (48060-8136)
PHONE..............810 637-1542
Lori Thueme, *Manager*
EMP: 5 **EST:** 2015
SALES (est): 61.2K **Privately Held**
WEB: www.militaryapparelcompany.com
SIC: 3171 Women's handbags & purses

GEOGRAPHIC SECTION
Port Huron - St. Clair County (G-13531)

(G-13503)
MODERN PLASTICS TECHNOLOGY LLC
2043 International Way (48060-7471)
PHONE..................................810 966-3376
Doug Archer, *CFO*
Jim Essad,
▲ **EMP:** 100 **EST:** 1998
SQ FT: 20,000
SALES (est): 8.9MM **Privately Held**
SIC: 3089 Injection molding of plastics

(G-13504)
MUELLER BRASS CO (DH)
Also Called: Mueller Brass Products
2199 Lapeer Ave (48060-4155)
PHONE..................................810 987-7770
Steffen Sigloch, *President*
Kent A McKee, *Treasurer*
◆ **EMP:** 150 **EST:** 1917
SALES (est): 322.2MM **Publicly Held**
WEB: www.muellerindustries.com
SIC: 3463 3354 3494 3351 Nonferrous forgings; plumbing fixture forgings, nonferrous; aluminum extruded products; valves & pipe fittings; plumbing & heating valves; copper pipe

(G-13505)
MUELLER BRASS CO
2199 Lapeer Ave (48060-4155)
P.O. Box 5021 (48061-5021)
PHONE..................................810 987-7770
Doug Westbrook, *Manager*
EMP: 51 **Publicly Held**
WEB: www.muellerindustries.com
SIC: 3366 3351 Brass foundry; pipe, brass & bronze
HQ: Mueller Brass Co.
  2199 Lapeer Ave
  Port Huron MI 48060
  810 987-7770

(G-13506)
MUELLER BRASS FORGING CO INC
2199 Lapeer Ave (48060-4155)
PHONE..................................810 987-7770
James H Rourke, *President*
Kent A Mc Kee, *CFO*
James E Browne, *Asst Sec*
EMP: 90 **EST:** 1991
SQ FT: 60,000
SALES (est): 28.6MM **Publicly Held**
WEB: www.muellerindustries.com
SIC: 3463 Aluminum forgings
HQ: Mueller Brass Co.
  2199 Lapeer Ave
  Port Huron MI 48060
  810 987-7770

(G-13507)
MUELLER INDUSTRIAL REALTY CO
2199 Lapeer Ave (48060-4155)
PHONE..................................810 987-7770
William H Hensley, *VP Legal*
James R Rourke, *Vice Pres*
Karl J Bambas, *Vice Pres*
Kent A McKee, *Treasurer*
Earl W Bunkers, *VP Finance*
EMP: 1 **EST:** 1919
SALES (est): 7.3MM **Publicly Held**
WEB: www.muellerindustries.com
SIC: 3312 Rods, iron & steel: made in steel mills
HQ: Mueller Brass Co.
  2199 Lapeer Ave
  Port Huron MI 48060
  810 987-7770

(G-13508)
MURTECH ENERGY SERVICES LLC
3097 Aberdeen Ct (48060-2348)
PHONE..................................810 653-5681
Clifford Murray, *General Mgr*
Marilyn I Murray,
EMP: 4 **EST:** 2006
SALES (est): 216.1K **Privately Held**
WEB: www.murtechenergyservices.com
SIC: 3564 3585 Blowers & fans; air conditioning equipment, complete

(G-13509)
NORTH COAST GOLF COMPANY LLC
3968 Jack Pine Ln (48060-1578)
PHONE..................................810 547-4900
Matt Fernandez, *Principal*
EMP: 7 **EST:** 2018
SALES (est): 411.1K **Privately Held**
WEB: www.northcoastgolfco.com
SIC: 3949 Golf equipment

(G-13510)
NORTHERN PURE ICE CO L L C
Also Called: Ice Makers
1755 Yeager St (48060-2594)
PHONE..................................989 344-2088
Robert Reutter, *Principal*
Charles J Knowlton, *Principal*
EMP: 19 **EST:** 1977
SALES (est): 305.2K **Privately Held**
SIC: 2097 Ice cubes; block ice

(G-13511)
O E M COMPANY INC
3495 24th St (48060-6809)
PHONE..................................810 985-9070
Larry Fletcher, *President*
Everette Fletcher, *Vice Pres*
EMP: 17 **EST:** 1987
SALES (est): 1MM **Privately Held**
WEB: www.oemcompanyinc.com
SIC: 7692 Automotive welding

(G-13512)
OXMASTER INC (PA)
1105 24th St (48060-4849)
PHONE..................................810 987-7600
John O Wirtz, *CEO*
EMP: 2 **EST:** 1992
SALES (est): 5.6MM **Privately Held**
SIC: 3559 Automotive related machinery

(G-13513)
P AND K GRAPHICS INC
Also Called: Kimball's Brand Source
945 Lapeer Ave (48060-4413)
PHONE..................................810 984-1575
Nick J Bondarek Jr, *Owner*
EMP: 7 **EST:** 1994
SALES (est): 378.5K **Privately Held**
SIC: 3639 5731 Floor waxers & polishers, electric: household; radio, television & electronic stores; video cameras, recorders & accessories

(G-13514)
P J WALLBANK SPRINGS INC
2121 Beard St (48060-6422)
PHONE..................................810 987-2992
Melvyn J Wallbank, *President*
Mary Gilbert, *Opers Staff*
Rob Cronce, *Engineer*
Brad Williamson, *Engineer*
Jana Donaldson, *Controller*
EMP: 85 **EST:** 1980
SQ FT: 66,000
SALES (est): 10.8MM **Privately Held**
WEB: www.pjws.com
SIC: 3493 Steel springs, except wire

(G-13515)
P M R INDUSTRIES INC
2311 16th St (48060-6401)
PHONE..................................810 989-5020
Timothy Colein, *President*
Robert Colein, *Vice Pres*
EMP: 16 **EST:** 1967
SQ FT: 10,000
SALES (est): 1.3MM **Privately Held**
WEB: www.pmrindustries.com
SIC: 3542 3541 3599 Forging machinery & hammers; cutoff machines (metalworking machinery); machine shop, jobbing & repair

(G-13516)
PARKSIDE SPEEDY PRINT INC
1319 Military St (48060-5422)
P.O. Box 610396 (48061-0396)
PHONE..................................810 985-8484
James Paulus, *President*
Donna Paulus, *Vice Pres*
EMP: 6 **EST:** 1969
SQ FT: 1,500
SALES (est): 450.9K **Privately Held**
WEB: www.parksideprintingink.com
SIC: 2752 2791 2789 Lithographing on metal; typesetting; bookbinding & related work

(G-13517)
PLASTIC DRESS-UP SERVICE INC
2735 20th St (48060-6452)
PHONE..................................586 727-7878
Ronald Jacques, *President*
EMP: 13 **EST:** 1989
SALES (est): 3.6MM **Privately Held**
WEB: www.plasticdressup.com
SIC: 3089 Injection molding of plastics

(G-13518)
PLASTIC PLAQUE INC
1635 Poplar St (48060-3329)
P.O. Box 610964 (48061-0964)
PHONE..................................810 982-9591
Charles W Fead, *Ch of Bd*
William C Fead, *President*
EMP: 9 **EST:** 1954
SQ FT: 8,000
SALES (est): 767.6K **Privately Held**
WEB: www.plasticplaqueprod.com
SIC: 3082 Unsupported plastics profile shapes

(G-13519)
PORT HURON BUILDING SUPPLY CO
Also Called: Do It Best
3555 Electric Ave (48060-6621)
PHONE..................................810 987-2666
Fax: 810 987-4531
EMP: 12
SQ FT: 25,000
SALES (est): 1.2MM **Privately Held**
SIC: 5251 3271 3273 3272 Ret Hardware Mfg Concrete Block/Brick Mfg Ready-Mixed Concrete Mfg Concrete Products

(G-13520)
R D M ENTERPRISES CO INC
4045 Griswold Rd (48060-4752)
PHONE..................................810 985-4721
Alvin Rinke, *President*
EMP: 8 **EST:** 1987
SQ FT: 11,000 **Privately Held**
WEB: www.rdmenterprises.net
SIC: 3465 3544 Body parts, automobile: stamped metal; die sets for metal stamping (presses)

(G-13521)
RAE PRECISION PRODUCTS INC
1327 Cedar St (48060-6176)
PHONE..................................810 987-9170
EMP: 5
SALES (est): 167.6K **Privately Held**
SIC: 3599 Mfg Industrial Machinery

(G-13522)
RAY SCOTT INDUSTRIES INC
3921 32nd St (48060-6950)
PHONE..................................248 535-2528
Raymond H Bunton, *President*
EMP: 9 **EST:** 2017
SALES (est): 547K **Privately Held**
SIC: 3089 7389 Injection molded finished plastic products; printers' services: folding, collating

(G-13523)
RESOURCEMFG
203 Huron Ave (48060-3821)
PHONE..................................810 937-5058
EMP: 10 **EST:** 2018
SALES (est): 243.3K **Privately Held**
WEB: www.resourcemfg.com
SIC: 3999 Manufacturing industries

(G-13524)
ROSS PALLET CO
3360 Petit St (48060-4737)
PHONE..................................810 966-4945
John Ross, *Mng Member*
Dennis Ross,
EMP: 8 **EST:** 2003
SALES (est): 490K **Privately Held**
SIC: 2448 Pallets, wood

(G-13525)
SBR PRINTING USA INC
2101 Cypress St (48060-6080)
PHONE..................................810 388-9441
Terry Kraft, *President*
▲ **EMP:** 11 **EST:** 2002
SALES (est): 400.6K **Privately Held**
SIC: 2752 Commercial printing, offset

(G-13526)
SHAWMUT LLC
Also Called: Shawmut Mills
2770 Dove St (48060-6719)
PHONE..................................810 987-2222
Kevin Schmidt, *COO*
Eric Finn, *Plant Mgr*
David Fistner, *Engineer*
Monica Cadarit, *Branch Mgr*
Evans Bennett, *Manager*
EMP: 7
SALES (corp-wide): 178.2MM **Privately Held**
WEB: www.shawmutcorporation.com
SIC: 2295 2672 3083 2671 Laminating of fabrics; coated & laminated paper; laminated plastics plate & sheet; packaging paper & plastics film, coated & laminated
PA: Shawmut Llc
  208 Manley St
  West Bridgewater MA 02379
  508 588-3300

(G-13527)
SIGNS PLUS (PA)
1604 Stone St (48060-3344)
PHONE..................................810 987-7446
Deanna Vanlerberghe, *Owner*
EMP: 9 **EST:** 1989
SALES (est): 746.6K **Privately Held**
WEB: www.mysignsplus.com
SIC: 3993 1799 Signs, not made in custom sign painting shops; sign installation & maintenance

(G-13528)
SMITH MEAT PACKING INC
2043 International Way (48060-7471)
PHONE..................................810 985-5900
Anthony Peters, *President*
EMP: 30
SQ FT: 24,000
SALES: 13.7MM **Privately Held**
WEB: www.smithmeatpacking.com
SIC: 2011 Meat packing plants

(G-13529)
SMR AUTOMOTIVE SYSTEMS USA INC
2611 16th St (48060-6456)
PHONE..................................810 937-2456
Cindy Grimson, *Branch Mgr*
EMP: 10 **Privately Held**
WEB: www.smr-automotive.com
SIC: 3231 Products of purchased glass
HQ: Smr Automotive Systems Usa Inc.
  1855 Busha Hwy
  Marysville MI 48040

(G-13530)
STONE SHOP INC
2920 Wright St (48060-8529)
PHONE..................................248 852-4700
Gary Vermander, *President*
Kenneth Vermander, *Vice Pres*
EMP: 13 **EST:** 1960
SALES (est): 596.6K **Privately Held**
WEB: www.puzzlesprint.com
SIC: 3281 Stone, quarrying & processing of own stone products; marble, building: cut & shaped

(G-13531)
TAPEX AMERICAN CORPORATION
Also Called: Formex International Div
2626 20th St (48060-6444)
P.O. Box 610233 (48061-0233)
PHONE..................................810 987-4722
Norman Catlos, *President*
EMP: 15 **EST:** 1972
SQ FT: 80,000
SALES (est): 2.1MM **Privately Held**
WEB: www.tapex.net
SIC: 2241 3399 Cords, fabric; metal fasteners

Port Huron - St. Clair County (G-13532)

(G-13532)
TIMES HERALD COMPANY (DH)
1411 3rd St Ste E (48060-5458)
P.O. Box 5009 (48061-5009)
PHONE..................................810 985-7171
Timothy Dowd, *President*
Eric Ahrens, *Vice Pres*
EMP: 90 **EST:** 1910
SALES (est): 22.3MM
SALES (corp-wide): 3.4B **Publicly Held**
WEB: www.thetimesherald.com
SIC: 2791 2752 2711 Typesetting; commercial printing, lithographic; newspapers, publishing & printing
HQ: Gannett Media Corp.
7950 Jones Branch Dr
Mc Lean VA 22102
703 854-6000

(G-13533)
TOOLING CNCEPTS DESIGN NOT INC
Also Called: Tooling Solutions Plus
3921 32nd St (48060-6950)
PHONE..................................810 444-9807
Jerry Eschenburg, *Branch Mgr*
EMP: 11 **Privately Held**
WEB: www.jackmitchellins.com
SIC: 3089 5013 Injection molding of plastics; tools & equipment, automotive
PA: Tooling Concepts & Design, Inc (Not Inc)
34357 Jefferson Ave
Harrison Township MI 48045

(G-13534)
TOUGH WELD FABRICATION
1486 Michigan Rd (48060-4668)
PHONE..................................810 937-2038
EMP: 4 **EST:** 2019
SALES (est): 49.8K **Privately Held**
WEB: www.toughweldfabrication.com
SIC: 7692 Welding repair

(G-13535)
TPI INDUSTRIES LLC
2770 Dove St (48060-6719)
PHONE..................................810 987-2222
EMP: 62
SALES (corp-wide): 178.2MM **Privately Held**
SIC: 2295 Laminating of fabrics
HQ: Tpi Industries, Llc
265 Ballard Rd
Middletown NY 10941
845 692-2820

(G-13536)
US FARATHANE HOLDINGS CORP
2133 Petit St (48060-6433)
PHONE..................................248 754-7000
John Lojewski, *Manager*
EMP: 5
SALES (corp-wide): 549.4MM **Privately Held**
WEB: www.usfarathane.com
SIC: 3089 Injection molding of plastics; thermoformed finished plastic products; casting of plastic
PA: U.S. Farathane Holdings Corp.
2700 High Meadow Cir
Auburn Hills MI 48326
248 754-7000

(G-13537)
WARWICK MAS & EQUIPMENT CO
1621 Pine Grove Ave (48060-3325)
PHONE..................................810 966-3431
Garry Warwick, *Owner*
Brian Linne, *Manager*
EMP: 5 **EST:** 2016
SALES (est): 115.3K **Privately Held**
WEB: www.warwickmaskcompany.com
SIC: 3842 Surgical appliances & supplies

(G-13538)
WIRCO MANUFACTURING LLC
2550 20th St (48060-6493)
PHONE..................................810 984-5576
Ronald W Scafe, *President*
▼ **EMP:** 10 **EST:** 2010
SALES (est): 1MM **Privately Held**
WEB: www.wirco.com
SIC: 3465 Automotive stampings

(G-13539)
WIRCO PRODUCTS INC
2550 20th St (48060-6493)
PHONE..................................810 984-5576
Ronald W Scafe, *President*
Joe Piechotte, *COO*
EMP: 21 **EST:** 1978
SQ FT: 20,000
SALES (est): 1.6MM **Privately Held**
WEB: www.wircoproducts.com
SIC: 3465 Body parts, automobile: stamped metal

(G-13540)
WIRTZ MANUFACTURING CO INC (PA)
1105 24th St (48060-4894)
P.O. Box 5006 (48061-5006)
PHONE..................................810 987-7600
John O Wirtz, *President*
Ken Marzka, *Technical Mgr*
Sergiu Nicoara, *Engineer*
Jonmarc Hewett, *Electrical Engi*
Keith Lepla, *Controller*
◆ **EMP:** 95 **EST:** 1932
SALES (est): 22.2MM **Privately Held**
WEB: www.wirtzusa.com
SIC: 3559 Automotive related machinery

(G-13541)
YANFENG US AUTO INTR SYSTEMS I
2133 Petit St (48060-6433)
PHONE..................................810 987-2434
EMP: 7 **Privately Held**
WEB: www.yfai.com
SIC: 3714 Motor vehicle parts & accessories
HQ: Yanfeng Us Automotive Interior Systems I Llc
41935 W 12 Mile Rd
Novi MI 48377
248 319-7333

(G-13542)
YEN GROUP LLC
2340 Dove St (48060-6740)
PHONE..................................810 201-6457
David Yen,
Andrew Cesarski,
Jane Chang,
Benjamin Yen,
EMP: 15 **EST:** 2016
SALES (est): 1.2MM **Privately Held**
WEB: www.yengroup.us
SIC: 3599 Crankshafts & camshafts, machining

Portage
Kalamazoo County

(G-13543)
AMERICA INK AND TECHNOLOGY
8975 Shaver Rd (49024-6156)
PHONE..................................269 345-4657
Brady Garrison, *President*
Andy Nappi, *Manager*
EMP: 6 **EST:** 2005
SALES (est): 1.1MM **Privately Held**
WEB: www.aminks.com
SIC: 2893 Printing ink

(G-13544)
AUSTIN COMPANY
9764 Portage Rd (49002-7251)
PHONE..................................269 329-1181
Brandon Davis, *Vice Pres*
Jeff Deel, *Human Res Dir*
Tamara Zupancic, *Marketing Staff*
Steve Vanwormer, *Manager*
EMP: 19 **EST:** 2013
SALES (est): 11.1MM **Privately Held**
WEB: www.theaustin.com
SIC: 3644 Raceways

(G-13545)
BAKEWELL COMPANY
2725 E Milham Ave (49002-1740)
PHONE..................................269 459-8030
Erin Hill, *Principal*
EMP: 5 **EST:** 2016
SALES (est): 249.7K **Privately Held**
WEB: www.brazilianoven.com
SIC: 2051 Bakery: wholesale or wholesale/retail combined

(G-13546)
BARNES WOOD WORKS
7531 Lake Wood Dr (49002-4337)
PHONE..................................269 599-3479
Jennifer Barnes, *Principal*
EMP: 4 **EST:** 2008
SALES (est): 114.3K **Privately Held**
SIC: 5211 2421 Lumber products; sawmills & planing mills, general

(G-13547)
BOSKAGE COMMERCE PUBLICATIONS
510 E Milham Ave (49002-1439)
PHONE..................................269 673-7242
EMP: 5
SALES (est): 553.9K **Privately Held**
SIC: 2731 4731 Books-Publishing/Printing Freight Transportation Arrangement

(G-13548)
BOWMAN ENTERPRISES INC
Also Called: Great Deals Magazine
1905 Lakeview Dr (49002-6926)
P.O. Box 1862 (49081-1862)
PHONE..................................269 720-1946
John M Bowman, *President*
EMP: 6 **EST:** 2002
SQ FT: 1,000
SALES (est): 1.6MM **Publicly Held**
WEB: www.clippermagazine.com
SIC: 2721 7311 Magazines: publishing & printing; advertising agencies
HQ: Clipper Magazine, Llc
3708 Hempland Rd
Mountville PA 17554
717 569-5100

(G-13549)
BREAK MOLD LLC
1601 W Centre Ave # 104 (49024-5396)
PHONE..................................269 359-0822
John Sweeney, *Principal*
EMP: 4 **EST:** 2015
SALES (est): 262.4K **Privately Held**
WEB: www.breakthemoldkzoo.com
SIC: 3599 Industrial machinery

(G-13550)
BUNTING BEARINGS LLC
4252 E Kilgore Rd (49002-1910)
PHONE..................................269 345-8691
Chris Griffin, *Production*
Jason Mugford, *Controller*
Doug Miller, *Sales Staff*
Jordan Oakman, *Sales Staff*
Doug Smith, *Sales Staff*
EMP: 29 **Privately Held**
WEB: www.buntingbearings.com
SIC: 3568 Power transmission equipment
PA: Bunting Bearings, Llc
1001 Holland Park Blvd
Holland OH 43528

(G-13551)
BUSINESS CARDS PLUS INC
8785 Portage Indus Dr (49024-6148)
P.O. Box 644 (49081-0644)
PHONE..................................269 327-7727
Vaughn Leonard, *President*
Cyndee Garrod,
EMP: 19 **EST:** 1984
SQ FT: 14,000
SALES (est): 3.5MM **Privately Held**
WEB: www.businesscardsplus.com
SIC: 2752 Commercial printing, offset

(G-13552)
CG CABINET WHOLESALE
6033 S Westnedge Ave (49002-2800)
PHONE..................................269 459-6833
EMP: 4 **EST:** 2018
SALES (est): 188.5K **Privately Held**
WEB: www.cgcabinet.com
SIC: 2434 Wood kitchen cabinets

(G-13553)
COLONIAL ENGINEERING INC (PA)
6400 Corporate Ave (49002-9399)
PHONE..................................269 323-2495
Mark F Bainbridge, *President*
Carroll J Haas, *Principal*
Patrick Beebe, *Vice Pres*
◆ **EMP:** 14 **EST:** 1972
SQ FT: 15,000
SALES (est): 6.4MM **Privately Held**
WEB: www.colonialengineering.com
SIC: 3089 5085 3494 Fittings for pipe, plastic; industrial supplies; valves & pipe fittings

(G-13554)
CONCENTRIC MEDICAL INC
2825 Airview Blvd (49002-1802)
PHONE..................................269 385-2600
Kevin A Lobo, *Ch of Bd*
Brett Hale, *CFO*
EMP: 40 **EST:** 1999
SQ FT: 22,000
SALES (est): 6.3MM
SALES (corp-wide): 14.3B **Publicly Held**
WEB: www.stryker.com
SIC: 3841 Surgical & medical instruments
PA: Stryker Corporation
2825 Airview Blvd
Portage MI 49002
269 385-2600

(G-13555)
CUSTOM DESIGN INC
4481 Commercial Ave (49002-9743)
PHONE..................................269 323-8561
Tim Bickings, *President*
Jim Heldt, *General Mgr*
EMP: 40 **EST:** 1981
SQ FT: 30,000
SALES (est): 4.4MM **Privately Held**
WEB: www.customdesignusa.com
SIC: 3544 Forms (molds), for foundry & plastics working machinery

(G-13556)
DYNAMIC AUTO TEST ENGINEERING
Also Called: Datec
1017 W Kilgore Rd (49024-5815)
PHONE..................................269 342-1334
EMP: 5
SQ FT: 7,500
SALES (est): 300K **Privately Held**
SIC: 7549 3825 Automotive Services Mfg Electrical Measuring Instruments

(G-13557)
ELIASON CORPORATION (DH)
Also Called: Doors4
9229 Shaver Rd (49024-6799)
PHONE..................................269 327-7003
Chris Herrick, *Regional Mgr*
Tim St Onge, *VP Opers*
Tom Mack, *Opers Staff*
Mason Deluca, *Production*
Patrick McMullen, *CFO*
◆ **EMP:** 93 **EST:** 1952
SQ FT: 52,000
SALES (est): 21.4MM
SALES (corp-wide): 1.3B **Privately Held**
WEB: www.eliasoncorp.com
SIC: 3442 3089 Metal doors; plastic containers, except foam
HQ: Eliason Holdings Corporation
9229 Shaver Rd
Portage MI 49024
269 327-7003

(G-13558)
ERBSLOEH ALUM SOLUTIONS INC
Also Called: Wkw Extrusion
6565 S Sprinkle Rd (49002-9717)
PHONE..................................269 323-2565
Jon H Bowers, *President*
Meredith Warnicke, *Finance Mgr*
Bryan Farwell, *Manager*
▲ **EMP:** 290 **EST:** 1928
SQ FT: 300,000

GEOGRAPHIC SECTION

Portage - Kalamazoo County (G-13585)

SALES (est): 52.4MM
SALES (corp-wide): 144.1K **Privately Held**
WEB: www.wkw.de
SIC: **3471** 3354 3353 3444 Anodizing (plating) of metals or formed products; aluminum extruded products; aluminum sheet, plate & foil; sheet metalwork
HQ: Wkw North America, Llc
103 Parkway E
Pell City AL 35125
205 338-4242

(G-13559)
EVE SALONSPA
7117 S Westnedge Ave 3b (49002-4201)
PHONE..................................269 327-4811
EMP: 4
SALES (est): 535.1K **Privately Held**
SIC: **2844** Mfg Toilet Preparations

(G-13560)
FEMA CORPORATION OF MICHIGAN
1716 Vanderbilt Ave (49024-6069)
PHONE..................................269 323-1369
Robert T Banfield, *President*
Tony Meeker, *Mfg Spvr*
Allison Wilde, *Engineer*
John Pula, *Controller*
Nate Pursley, *Controller*
EMP: 200 EST: 1976
SQ FT: 49,000
SALES (est): 51.6MM **Privately Held**
WEB: www.fema-corp.com
SIC: **3679** 3728 Solenoids for electronic applications; aircraft parts & equipment

(G-13561)
FRED OSWALTS PINS UNLTD
2610 Hill An Brook Dr (49024-5621)
PHONE..................................269 342-1387
Nancy Olds, *Principal*
EMP: 5 EST: 2004
SALES (est): 71.6K **Privately Held**
SIC: **3452** Pins

(G-13562)
GREAT LAKES CHEMICAL SERVICES
616 W Centre Ave (49024-5308)
PHONE..................................269 372-6886
John Braganini, *President*
Edward Overbeck, *Vice Pres*
Kelly Carr, *Controller*
Charles Holley, *Accounts Exec*
Kristin Schultz, *Accounts Exec*
EMP: 40 EST: 1991
SALES (est): 9.7MM **Privately Held**
WEB: www.glchemical.com
SIC: **2819** Chemicals, high purity: refined from technical grade

(G-13563)
GYS TECH LLC
Also Called: Cardan Robotics
2825 Airview Blvd (49002-1802)
PHONE..................................269 385-2600
Kevin A Lobo, *Ch of Bd*
EMP: 13 EST: 2015
SALES (est): 3.5MM
SALES (corp-wide): 14.3B **Publicly Held**
WEB: www.stryker.com
SIC: **3845** Surgical support systems: heart-lung machine, exc. iron lung
PA: Stryker Corporation
2825 Airview Blvd
Portage MI 49002
269 385-2600

(G-13564)
HARVEST TIME PARTNERS INC
6842 Shallowford Way (49024-1715)
PHONE..................................269 254-8999
EMP: 5 EST: 2019
SALES (est): 62.8K **Privately Held**
WEB: www.harvesttimepartners.com
SIC: **2731** Book publishing

(G-13565)
HIGH PRFMCE MET FINSHG INC
1821 Vanderbilt Ave (49024-6010)
PHONE..................................269 327-8897
Patrick Greene, *President*
Kevin Greene, *Vice Pres*
Bruce E Justin, *Treasurer*
Bruce Justin, *Administration*
EMP: 10 EST: 2007
SQ FT: 30,000
SALES (est): 1MM **Privately Held**
WEB: www.hpmetalfinishing.com
SIC: **3471** Finishing, metals or formed products

(G-13566)
HOWMEDICA OSTEONICS CORP
1901 Romence Road Pkwy (49002-3672)
PHONE..................................269 389-8959
Garren Hammons, *Sales Staff*
EMP: 9
SALES (corp-wide): 14.3B **Publicly Held**
SIC: **3842** Surgical appliances & supplies
HQ: Howmedica Osteonics Corp.
325 Corporate Dr
Mahwah NJ 07430
201 831-5000

(G-13567)
HY-KO PRODUCTS COMPANY LLC
9031 Shaver Rd (49024-6164)
PHONE..................................330 467-7446
Michael Bass, *President*
EMP: 40 EST: 2020
SALES (est): 567.4K
SALES (corp-wide): 68.2MM **Privately Held**
WEB: www.hy-ko.com
SIC: **3993** Signs & advertising specialties
PA: Midwest Fastener Corp.
9031 Shaver Rd
Portage MI 49024
269 327-6917

(G-13568)
INTEGRA MOLD INC
10746 S Westnedge Ave (49002-7353)
PHONE..................................269 327-4337
Alan Blood, *President*
Michael Blood, *Corp Secy*
EMP: 5 EST: 1987
SALES (est): 485K **Privately Held**
WEB: www.integramold.com
SIC: **3089** Injection molding of plastics

(G-13569)
J RETTENMAIER USA LP
1615 Vanderbilt Ave (49024-6008)
PHONE..................................269 323-1588
EMP: 6 EST: 2019
SALES (est): 302.9K **Privately Held**
SIC: **2034** Dehydrated fruits, vegetables, soups

(G-13570)
JUNKLESS FOODS INC
6749 S Westnedge Ave K (49024-3574)
PHONE..................................616 560-7895
Ernest Pang, *CEO*
Laurence Beyer, *Treasurer*
EMP: 11 EST: 2015
SALES (est): 715.4K **Privately Held**
WEB: www.junklessfoods.com
SIC: **2064** Breakfast bars

(G-13571)
KALAMAZOO MACHINE TOOL CO INC
6700 Quality Way (49002-9756)
PHONE..................................269 321-8860
James R Larson, *President*
▲ EMP: 5 EST: 1987
SQ FT: 10,000
SALES (est): 942.3K **Privately Held**
WEB: www.kmtsaw.com
SIC: **3541** Machine tools, metal cutting type

(G-13572)
KALAMAZOO STRIPPING DERUSTING
3921 E Centre Ave (49002-5855)
PHONE..................................269 323-1340
Anthony Pienta, *President*
Kathy Paul, *Opers Mgr*
EMP: 10 EST: 1984
SQ FT: 22,000
SALES (est): 1MM **Privately Held**
WEB: www.kalamazoostripping.com
SIC: **3471** Finishing, metals or formed products

(G-13573)
KAUFMAN ENTERPRISES INC (PA)
Also Called: Allegra Print & Imaging No 38
6054 Lovers Ln (49002-3026)
PHONE..................................269 324-0040
Victor W Kaufman, *President*
Brian Kaufman, *Principal*
EMP: 9 EST: 1988
SQ FT: 3,500
SALES (est): 3.5MM **Privately Held**
WEB: www.allegramarketingprint.com
SIC: **2752** Commercial printing, offset

(G-13574)
KONECRANES INC
865 Lenox Ave Ste A (49024-5410)
PHONE..................................269 323-1222
Tom Barry, *Manager*
EMP: 10 **Privately Held**
WEB: www.konecranes.com
SIC: **3536** Hoists, cranes & monorails
HQ: Konecranes, Inc.
4401 Gateway Blvd
Springfield OH 45502

(G-13575)
LEVANNES INC
8840 Portage Indus Dr (49024-6151)
PHONE..................................269 327-4484
Theodere Stender, *President*
Tony Stender, *Vice Pres*
Dave Vandelaare, *Engineer*
EMP: 27 EST: 1966
SQ FT: 13,000
SALES (est): 3.3MM **Privately Held**
WEB: www.levannes.com
SIC: **3544** Forms (molds), for foundry & plastics working machinery; industrial molds

(G-13576)
LIBERTY MANUFACTURING COMPANY
Also Called: Liberty Molds
8631 Portage Indus Dr (49024-6174)
PHONE..................................269 327-0997
Bill Berghuis, *President*
Pat Stevens, *Principal*
Todd Charlton, *Vice Pres*
Mark Israels, *Engineer*
Patrick Stevens, *Engineer*
▲ EMP: 26 EST: 1986
SALES (est): 5.2MM **Privately Held**
WEB: www.libertymolds.com
SIC: **3544** Industrial molds

(G-13577)
LINK TECHNOLOGY INC
Also Called: Silverglide Surgical Tech,
4100 E Milham Ave (49024-9704)
PHONE..................................269 324-8212
EMP: 10
SQ FT: 500
SALES (est): 780K **Privately Held**
SIC: **3841** Mfg Surgical/Medical Instruments

(G-13578)
LIVBIG LLC
Also Called: Submerge Camera
1821 Vanderbilt Ave Ste A (49024-6010)
PHONE..................................888 519-8290
EMP: 6
SALES (est): 1MM **Privately Held**
SIC: **5946** 7335 5941 3663 Ret Cameras/Photo Supply Commercial Photography Ret Sport Goods/Bicycles Mfg Radio/Tv Comm Equip Photo Portrait Studio

(G-13579)
LLOMEN INC
Also Called: Super Book
5346 Ivanhoe Ct (49002-1555)
P.O. Box 20353, Kalamazoo (49019-1353)
PHONE..................................269 345-3555
Barbera Menlen, *President*
EMP: 8 EST: 1996
SALES (est): 657.5K **Privately Held**
SIC: **2741** Miscellaneous publishing

(G-13580)
LUBE-TECH INC
Also Called: Great Lakes Lube-Tech
3960 Arbutus Trl (49005-1065)
P.O. Box 51301, Kalamazoo (49005-1301)
PHONE..................................269 329-1269
John J Cugnetti, *President*
Sharyn E Cugnetti, *Corp Secy*
EMP: 6 EST: 1982
SALES (est): 419.6K **Privately Held**
WEB: www.lubetech.com
SIC: **2992** 5084 Re-fining lubricating oils & greases; petroleum industry machinery

(G-13581)
MANN + HUMMEL INC (DH)
6400 S Sprinkle Rd (49002-9706)
PHONE..................................269 329-3900
Alfred Weber, *President*
Fua Nipah, *President*
Stefan Tolle, *President*
Marco Nava, *Vice Pres*
Andrew James, *Engineer*
▲ EMP: 1 EST: 1996
SQ FT: 60,000
SALES (est): 626.7MM
SALES (corp-wide): 4.6B **Privately Held**
WEB: www.mann-filter.com
SIC: **3559** 3585 Plastics working machinery; dehumidifiers electric, except portable
HQ: Mann+Hummel Gmbh
Schwieberdinger Str. 126
Ludwigsburg BW 71636
714 198-0

(G-13582)
MANN + HUMMEL USA INC (DH)
Also Called: Mannhummel
6400 S Sprinkle Rd (49002-9706)
PHONE..................................269 329-3900
Alfred Weber, *CEO*
Frank B Jehle, *President*
Emese Weissenbacher, *CFO*
◆ EMP: 19 EST: 1983
SQ FT: 133,000
SALES (est): 893MM
SALES (corp-wide): 4.6B **Privately Held**
WEB: www.mann-hummel.com
SIC: **3089** 3714 Injection molding of plastics; motor vehicle parts & accessories
HQ: Mann + Hummel Holding Gmbh
Schwieberdinger Str. 126
Ludwigsburg BW 71636
714 198-0

(G-13583)
MANUFACTURING HERO
10619 Chancellor St (49002-8413)
PHONE..................................269 271-0031
Mike Orley, *Principal*
EMP: 6 EST: 2016
SALES (est): 39.8K **Privately Held**
WEB: www.manufacturinghero.com
SIC: **8711** 3053 Engineering services; gaskets, packing & sealing devices

(G-13584)
MELTTOOLS LLC
7849 S Sprinkle Rd (49002-9432)
PHONE..................................269 978-0968
Nicole Maturen,
EMP: 2 EST: 2011
SQ FT: 3,000
SALES (est): 1MM **Privately Held**
WEB: www.melttools.com
SIC: **3548** Welding & cutting apparatus & accessories

(G-13585)
METROPOLITAN INDUS LITHOGRAPHY
Also Called: Portage Printing
1116 W Centre Ave (49024-5391)
PHONE..................................269 323-9333
Craig Vestal, *President*
Lorraine Phillips, *Sales Staff*
EMP: 6 EST: 1982
SALES (est): 602.6K **Privately Held**
WEB: www.portageprinting.com
SIC: **2752** 2791 2789 Commercial printing, offset; typesetting; bookbinding & related work

Portage - Kalamazoo County (G-13586) GEOGRAPHIC SECTION

(G-13586)
MV METAL PDTS & SOLUTIONS LLC (PA)
3585 Bellflower Dr (49024-3974)
PHONE..................................269 471-7715
EMP: 7
SALES (est): 136.8MM **Privately Held**
SIC: 3364 Mfg Nonferrous Die-Castings

(G-13587)
NELSON HARDWARE
Also Called: Do It Best
9029 Portage Rd (49002-6419)
PHONE..................................269 327-3583
Bill Rowe, *President*
Jean Rowe Truitt, *Admin Sec*
EMP: 8 EST: 1969
SQ FT: 10,000
SALES (est): 1MM **Privately Held**
WEB: www.galesburghardware.com
SIC: 5251 3498 Hardware; fabricated pipe & fittings

(G-13588)
NORTH AMERICAN COLOR INC
5960 S Sprinkle Rd (49002-9712)
PHONE..................................269 323-0552
Lawrence Leto Jr, *President*
B Jane Leto, *Vice Pres*
Tim Leto, *Plant Mgr*
Kellie Pijaszek, *Graphic Designe*
EMP: 27 EST: 1981
SQ FT: 35,000
SALES (est): 4.9MM **Privately Held**
WEB: www.nac-mi.com
SIC: 2796 2752 Color separations for printing; commercial printing, lithographic

(G-13589)
NOVA INTERNATIONAL LLC
Also Called: Nova Steel
9110 Portage Rd (49002-6422)
P.O. Box 2317, Kalamazoo (49003-2317)
PHONE..................................269 381-6779
Dave Trombley, *General Mgr*
James Dally, *Mng Member*
EMP: 20 EST: 2000
SALES (est): 2.5MM **Privately Held**
SIC: 3441 5051 Building components, structural steel; structural shapes, iron or steel

(G-13590)
PARAGON LEATHER INC USA
10210 Shaver Rd Ste A (49024-7706)
PHONE..................................269 323-9483
Irfanairfan Gill, *Principal*
EMP: 5 EST: 2010
SALES (est): 308.4K **Privately Held**
WEB: www.paragonleather.com
SIC: 3199 Leather goods

(G-13591)
PERSPECTIVE ENTERPRISES INC
7829 S Sprinkle Rd Ste A (49002-9013)
P.O. Box 670 (49081-0670)
PHONE..................................269 327-0869
Norman Root, *President*
Melisa Root, *Vice Pres*
Sharron Root, *Admin Sec*
EMP: 6 EST: 1979
SQ FT: 4,200
SALES (est): 609.6K **Privately Held**
WEB: www.perspectiveenterprises.com
SIC: 3841 3713 Surgical & medical instruments; specialty motor vehicle bodies

(G-13592)
PETERMAN MOBILE CONCRETE INC (PA)
Also Called: Peterman Concrete Co
333 Peterman Ln (49002-5158)
PHONE..................................269 324-1211
Frank Peterman, *President*
Helen Peterman, *Corp Secy*
Jim Peterman, *Vice Pres*
Scott Peterman, *Vice Pres*
EMP: 25 EST: 1982
SALES (est): 3.2MM **Privately Held**
WEB: www.petermanconcrete.com
SIC: 3273 Ready-mixed concrete

(G-13593)
PHADIA US INC (HQ)
4169 Commercial Ave (49002-9701)
PHONE..................................269 492-1940
David Esposito, *President*
James S Palmere, *Corp Secy*
▲ EMP: 250 EST: 2004
SALES (est): 57.9MM
SALES (corp-wide): 32.2B **Publicly Held**
WEB: www.thermofisher.com
SIC: 3826 Analytical instruments
PA: Thermo Fisher Scientific Inc.
168 3rd Ave
Waltham MA 02451
781 622-1000

(G-13594)
PRECISION PRINTER SERVICES INC
9185 Portage Indus Dr (49024-6193)
PHONE..................................269 384-5725
Roy Gooch, *President*
Patricia Gooch, *Principal*
Kathy Buttke, *VP Sales*
Dan Frattura, *Sales Staff*
David Barker, *Technician*
EMP: 29 EST: 1991
SQ FT: 7,000
SALES (est): 7MM **Privately Held**
WEB: www.precisionprinterservices.com
SIC: 3861 5734 7378 Toners, prepared photographic (not made in chemical plants); computer & software stores; printers & plotters: computers; computer maintenance & repair; computer peripheral equipment repair & maintenance

(G-13595)
PRINS BETHESDA LLC
3026 Witters Ct (49024-6656)
PHONE..................................269 903-2237
Rachel Mol, *Principal*
EMP: 5 EST: 2016
SALES (est): 70K **Privately Held**
SIC: 2752 Commercial printing, lithographic

(G-13596)
PRINTING SERVICES
7419 S Sprinkle Rd (49002-9436)
P.O. Box 2646 (49081-2646)
PHONE..................................269 321-9826
EMP: 4
SALES (est): 535.2K **Privately Held**
SIC: 2752 Lithographic Commercial Printing

(G-13597)
QSV PHARMA LLC
3585 Bellflower Dr (49024-3974)
PHONE..................................269 324-2358
EMP: 4
SALES (est): 324.1K **Privately Held**
SIC: 2834 Pharmaceutical Preparations

(G-13598)
R H CROSS ENTERPRISES INC
6080 Corporate Ave (49002-9396)
PHONE..................................269 488-4009
Ronald H Cross, *CEO*
EMP: 4 EST: 1979
SALES (est): 527.5K **Privately Held**
WEB: www.crossenterprises.com
SIC: 3841 Surgical & medical instruments

(G-13599)
RATHCO SAFETY SUPPLY INC
6742 Lovers Ln (49002-3669)
PHONE..................................269 323-0153
Russell Rathburn, *President*
Sally Rathburn, *Corp Secy*
EMP: 25 EST: 1980
SQ FT: 17,000
SALES (est): 1.4MM **Privately Held**
SIC: 3993 5063 Signs, not made in custom sign painting shops; signaling equipment, electrical

(G-13600)
ROLLIE WILLIAMS PAINT SPOT
Also Called: Benjamin Moore Authorized Ret
4570 Commercial Ave (49002-9747)
PHONE..................................269 321-3174
Michael Ellis, *Sales Staff*
Mark Johnson, *Manager*
Kevin Kehrwecker, *Manager*
EMP: 5
SALES (corp-wide): 23.1MM **Privately Held**
WEB: www.rolliewilliams.com
SIC: 2851 Paints & allied products
PA: Rollie Williams Paint Spot Inc
1179 Kent St
Elkhart IN 46514
574 264-3174

(G-13601)
RTA INDUSTRIES LLC
7086 Sandpiper St (49024-7408)
PHONE..................................269 327-2916
Leslie Ashbaugh, *Principal*
EMP: 4 EST: 2010
SALES (est): 63.1K **Privately Held**
SIC: 3999 Manufacturing industries

(G-13602)
RUBBAIR LLC
9229 Shaver Rd (49024-6763)
PHONE..................................269 327-7003
Patrick McMullen, *CFO*
EMP: 20 EST: 2016
SALES (est): 1.2MM
SALES (corp-wide): 1.3B **Privately Held**
WEB: www.chasedoors.com
SIC: 3442 Metal doors, sash & trim
HQ: Chase Industries, Inc.
10021 Commerce Park Dr
West Chester OH 45246
513 860-5565

(G-13603)
S & K TOOL & DIE COMPANY INC
4401 Environmental Dr (49002-9307)
PHONE..................................269 345-2174
Philip Best, *President*
EMP: 22 EST: 1947
SQ FT: 5,500
SALES (est): 1.7MM **Privately Held**
WEB: www.sktool.com
SIC: 3544 Forms (molds), for foundry & plastics working machinery

(G-13604)
S2 GAMES LLC
950 Trade Centre Way # 200 (49002-0487)
PHONE..................................269 344-8020
EMP: 95
SALES (est): 5.2MM **Privately Held**
SIC: 7372 Prepackaged Software

(G-13605)
SANITOR MFG CO
1221 W Centre Ave (49024-5384)
P.O. Box 2433 (49081-2433)
PHONE..................................269 327-3001
David J Dietrich, *President*
Katherine Morris, *Treasurer*
David Dietrich, *Human Res Dir*
Diane Dietrich, *Admin Sec*
▼ EMP: 17 EST: 1931
SQ FT: 24,000
SALES (est): 2.2MM **Privately Held**
WEB: www.sanitorusa.com
SIC: 2621 Toweling tissue, paper; sanitary tissue paper

(G-13606)
SHAMROCK PUBLICATIONS
10711 Portage Rd (49002-7306)
PHONE..................................269 459-1099
Thomas M McKenna, *Principal*
EMP: 4 EST: 2017
SALES (est): 37.6K **Privately Held**
WEB: www.shamrockpublicaations.com
SIC: 2741 Miscellaneous publishing

(G-13607)
SINGH AUTOMATION LLC
7804 S Sprinkle Rd (49002-9429)
PHONE..................................269 267-6078
JAS Kaur, *Mng Member*
Gurdeet Signh, *Mng Member*
EMP: 6 EST: 2014
SALES (est): 500K **Privately Held**
WEB: www.singhautomation.com
SIC: 7373 3625 Computer systems analysis & design; relays & industrial controls

(G-13608)
SKAMP INDUSTRIES INC
5255 Bronson Blvd (49024-5747)
PHONE..................................269 731-2666
Mike Duggan, *Owner*
EMP: 4 EST: 2014
SALES (est): 105.1K **Privately Held**
WEB: www.skamp.us
SIC: 3537 Industrial trucks & tractors

(G-13609)
SOLUTIONSNOWBIZ
8675 Portage Rd Ste 7 (49002-5700)
PHONE..................................269 321-5062
EMP: 4 EST: 2015
SALES (est): 279.6K **Privately Held**
WEB: www.solutionsnow.biz
SIC: 8742 2759 Marketing consulting services; publication printing

(G-13610)
STAINLESS FABG & ENGRG INC
Also Called: SFE
9718 Portage Rd (49002-7251)
P.O. Box 627 (49081-0627)
PHONE..................................269 329-6142
Laura Goff, *President*
Mike Keeler, *Vice Pres*
EMP: 7 EST: 2005
SQ FT: 22,000
SALES (est): 1.3MM **Privately Held**
WEB: www.sfeinc.us
SIC: 3599 Machine shop, jobbing & repair

(G-13611)
STAR CRANE HIST SVC OF KLMAZOO
8722 Portage Indus Dr (49024-6149)
PHONE..................................269 321-8882
Craig Derks, *President*
Scott De Kryger, *Vice Pres*
Larry Derks, *Vice Pres*
EMP: 5 EST: 1996
SALES (est): 206.7K **Privately Held**
SIC: 7699 3536 7389 Industrial machinery & equipment repair; cranes & monorail systems; hoists; crane & aerial lift service

(G-13612)
STRYKER AUSTRALIA LLC (HQ)
2825 Airview Blvd (49002-1802)
PHONE..................................269 385-2600
Kevin A Lobo, *Ch of Bd*
EMP: 236 EST: 2004
SALES (est): 2.9MM
SALES (corp-wide): 14.3B **Publicly Held**
WEB: www.strykermeded.com
SIC: 3841 3842 Surgical instruments & apparatus; saws, surgical; bone drills; suction therapy apparatus; implants, surgical
PA: Stryker Corporation
2825 Airview Blvd
Portage MI 49002
269 385-2600

(G-13613)
STRYKER COMMUNICATIONS INC (HQ)
2825 Airview Blvd (49002-1802)
PHONE..................................972 410-7000
Kevin A Lobo, *Ch of Bd*
Erika Myers, *Project Mgr*
Glorianne Gonzalez, *Research*
Mike Woolever, *Regl Sales Mgr*
Joe Gibson, *Sales Staff*
▲ EMP: 117 EST: 1999
SALES (est): 99.7MM
SALES (corp-wide): 14.3B **Publicly Held**
WEB: www.stryker.com
SIC: 3841 Surgical & medical instruments
PA: Stryker Corporation
2825 Airview Blvd
Portage MI 49002
269 385-2600

(G-13614)
STRYKER CORPORATION
Stryker Instruments
6300 S Sprinkle Rd (49002-9705)
PHONE..................................269 389-3741
Yoshiro Yamamoto, *Technical Mgr*
Tim Waldrop, *Sales Mgr*
Aaron Bowman, *Sales Staff*

GEOGRAPHIC SECTION   Portage - Kalamazoo County (G-13636)

Matthew Burge, *Sales Staff*
Alex Crawford, *Sales Staff*
EMP: 42
SALES (corp-wide): 14.3B **Publicly Held**
WEB: www.stryker.com
SIC: 3842 3841 Personal safety equipment; surgical appliances & supplies; surgical & medical instruments
PA: Stryker Corporation
2825 Airview Blvd
Portage MI 49002
269 385-2600

(G-13615)
STRYKER CORPORATION (PA)
2825 Airview Blvd (49002-1802)
PHONE.................................269 385-2600
Kevin A Lobo, *Ch of Bd*
Viju S Menon, *President*
Timothy J Scannell, *President*
Yin C Becker, *Vice Pres*
William E Berry Jr, *Vice Pres*
EMP: 30 **EST:** 1941
SALES (est): 14.3B **Publicly Held**
WEB: www.stryker.com
SIC: 3841 3842 Surgical & medical instruments; surgical instruments & apparatus; saws, surgical; suction therapy apparatus; surgical appliances & supplies; implants, surgical

(G-13616)
STRYKER CORPORATION
Stryker Corp - Shared Svcs
1901 Romence Road Pkwy (49002-3672)
PHONE.................................269 389-2300
Nic Hillman, *Regional Mgr*
Alexio Casas, *Finance*
Emily Immekus, *Hum Res Coord*
Christopher Dukes, *Human Resources*
Teagan Murillo, *Human Resources*
EMP: 20
SALES (corp-wide): 14.3B **Publicly Held**
WEB: www.stryker.com
SIC: 3841 Surgical instruments & apparatus; medical instruments & equipment, blood & bone work
PA: Stryker Corporation
2825 Airview Blvd
Portage MI 49002
269 385-2600

(G-13617)
STRYKER CUSTOMS BROKERS LLC
1901 Romence Road Pkwy (49002-3672)
PHONE.................................269 389-2300
Kevin A Lobo, *Ch of Bd*
David Furgason,
EMP: 19 **EST:** 2018
SALES (est): 3.8MM
SALES (corp-wide): 14.3B **Publicly Held**
WEB: www.stryker.com
SIC: 3842 Implants, surgical
PA: Stryker Corporation
2825 Airview Blvd
Portage MI 49002
269 385-2600

(G-13618)
STRYKER FAR EAST INC (HQ)
2825 Airview Blvd (49002-1802)
PHONE.................................269 385-2600
Kevin A Lobo, *President*
Yin C Becker, *Vice Pres*
Steven P Benscoter, *Vice Pres*
William R Jellison, *Vice Pres*
Katherine A Owen, *Vice Pres*
EMP: 2695 **EST:** 1986
SALES (est): 35.5MM
SALES (corp-wide): 14.3B **Publicly Held**
WEB: www.stryker.com
SIC: 3841 3842 2599 8049 Surgical instruments & apparatus; saws, surgical; bone drills; suction therapy apparatus; implants, surgical; hospital beds; physical therapist
PA: Stryker Corporation
2825 Airview Blvd
Portage MI 49002
269 385-2600

(G-13619)
STRYKER PRFMCE SOLUTIONS LLC
2825 Airview Blvd (49002-1802)
PHONE.................................269 385-2600
Kevin A Lobo, *CEO*
EMP: 15 **EST:** 2019
SALES (est): 2.2MM
SALES (corp-wide): 14.3B **Publicly Held**
WEB: www.stryker.com
SIC: 3841 Surgical instruments & apparatus
PA: Stryker Corporation
2825 Airview Blvd
Portage MI 49002
269 385-2600

(G-13620)
STRYKER SALES LLC
Stryker Craniomaxillofacial
750 Trade Cntre Way Ste 2 (49002)
PHONE.................................269 324-5346
Ramie Yesh, *Opers Staff*
Arshia Acree, *Credit Staff*
Gil Durfee, *Sales Staff*
Joseph Lewko, *Sales Staff*
Joe Lewko, *Admin Sec*
EMP: 16
SALES (corp-wide): 14.3B **Publicly Held**
WEB: www.stryker.com
SIC: 3841 Surgical & medical instruments
HQ: Stryker Sales, Llc
2825 Airview Blvd
Portage MI 49002

(G-13621)
STRYKER SALES LLC
Also Called: Stryker Instruments
1941 Stryker Way (49002-9711)
PHONE.................................269 323-1027
Daniel Mc Combs, *Engineer*
Michael Mruzek, *Engineer*
Darren Schaaf, *Engineer*
Devin Pavel, *Regl Sales Mgr*
Chris Berg, *Sales Staff*
EMP: 38
SALES (corp-wide): 14.3B **Publicly Held**
WEB: www.stryker.com
SIC: 3842 3841 Personal safety equipment; surgical appliances & supplies; surgical & medical instruments
HQ: Stryker Sales, Llc
2825 Airview Blvd
Portage MI 49002

(G-13622)
SUMMIT POLYMERS INC (PA)
Also Called: Technical Center
6715 S Sprinkle Rd (49002-9707)
PHONE.................................269 324-9330
Andrea Haas, *President*
Dan Brown, *General Mgr*
Jody Flinton, *General Mgr*
Gregory Goodman, *Vice Pres*
Mark Hammer, *Vice Pres*
▲ **EMP:** 185 **EST:** 1972
SQ FT: 70,000
SALES (est): 590MM **Privately Held**
WEB: www.summitpolymers.com
SIC: 3089 Injection molding of plastics

(G-13623)
SUMMIT POLYMERS INC
6615 S Sprinkle Rd (49002-9709)
PHONE.................................269 324-9320
Kay Salyer, *Manager*
EMP: 5
SALES (corp-wide): 590MM **Privately Held**
WEB: www.summitpolymers.com
SIC: 3089 Injection molding of plastics
PA: Summit Polymers, Inc.
6715 S Sprinkle Rd
Portage MI 49002
269 324-9330

(G-13624)
SUMMIT POLYMERS INC
Also Called: Plant 1
4750 Executive Dr (49002-9388)
PHONE.................................269 323-1301
Steve Rizor, *Project Mgr*
Casey Winslow, *Mfg Mgr*
Ted Caulkins, *Buyer*
Sean Duymovic, *Buyer*
Terry Baldwin, *Engineer*

EMP: 300
SALES (corp-wide): 590MM **Privately Held**
WEB: www.summitpolymers.com
SIC: 3089 3083 Injection molding of plastics; laminated plastics plate & sheet
PA: Summit Polymers, Inc.
6715 S Sprinkle Rd
Portage MI 49002
269 324-9330

(G-13625)
THERMO FISHER SCIENTIFIC INC
4169 Commercial Ave (49002-9701)
PHONE.................................800 346-4364
Richard Gibbs, *Analyst*
EMP: 5
SALES (corp-wide): 32.2B **Publicly Held**
WEB: www.thermofisher.com
SIC: 3826 Analytical instruments
PA: Thermo Fisher Scientific Inc.
168 3rd Ave
Waltham MA 02451
781 622-1000

(G-13626)
TINDALL PACKAGING INC
9718 Portage Rd (49002-7251)
PHONE.................................269 649-1163
Marianne Tindall, *President*
EMP: 5 **EST:** 1971
SALES (est): 729.9K **Privately Held**
WEB: www.tindallpackaging.com
SIC: 3565 7699 8742 3523 Packaging machinery; industrial machinery & equipment repair; manufacturing management consultant; farm machinery & equipment

(G-13627)
TRUTH SAND CONTEMPLATIONS
5145 Morningside Dr (49024-5713)
PHONE.................................269 342-0369
Sheryl Lilly, *Principal*
EMP: 6 **EST:** 2015
SALES (est): 139.3K **Privately Held**
SIC: 1442 Construction sand & gravel

(G-13628)
UKC LIQUIDATING INC (PA)
Also Called: United Kennel Club
100 E Kilgore Rd (49002-0506)
PHONE.................................269 343-9020
Wayne Cavanaugh, *President*
Todd Kellam, *Vice Pres*
Mark Threlfaoo, *Vice Pres*
Allen Gingerich, *Opers Staff*
Kirstin Kendall, *Opers Staff*
EMP: 8 **EST:** 1898
SQ FT: 16,500
SALES (est): 3.4MM **Privately Held**
WEB: www.ukcdogs.com
SIC: 2721 0752 7997 Magazines: publishing only, not printed on site; pedigree record services, pet & animal specialties; membership sports & recreation clubs

(G-13629)
UNIFAB CORPORATION
Also Called: Unifab Cages
5260 Lovers Ln (49002-1560)
PHONE.................................269 382-2803
Rob Thayer, *CEO*
Mick Madden, *President*
EMP: 23 **EST:** 1940
SQ FT: 40,000
SALES (est): 8.8MM **Privately Held**
WEB: www.unifabcorporation.com
SIC: 3444 3496 Sheet metalwork; cages, wire

(G-13630)
USA SUMMIT PLAS SILAO 1 LLC
6715 S Sprinkle Rd (49002-9707)
PHONE.................................269 324-9330
Andrea Haas, *President*
James Haas, *President*
John Meyer, *CFO*
Reed Kendell, *Asst Sec*
EMP: 230 **EST:** 2011
SALES (est): 62.1MM
SALES (corp-wide): 590MM **Privately Held**
WEB: www.summitpolymers.com
SIC: 3089 Injection molding of plastics

PA: Summit Polymers, Inc.
6715 S Sprinkle Rd
Portage MI 49002
269 324-9330

(G-13631)
W SOULE & CO (PA)
Also Called: W Soule & Co Service Group
7125 S Sprinkle Rd (49002-9437)
P.O. Box 2169, Kalamazoo (49003-2169)
PHONE.................................269 324-7001
John Soule, *President*
Kevin Waterstradt, *Vice Pres*
Matt Sparks, *Project Mgr*
Brett Walters, *Project Mgr*
Patrick Wolocko, *Safety Mgr*
EMP: 100
SQ FT: 5,100
SALES (est): 81.3MM **Privately Held**
WEB: www.wsoule.com
SIC: 1711 3444 Process piping contractor; sheet metal specialties, not stamped

(G-13632)
WKW ROOF RAIL SYSTEMS LLC
6565 S Sprinkle Rd (49002-9717)
PHONE.................................205 338-4242
Sam Cropsey, *Accounts Mgr*
Deborah Grant,
▲ **EMP:** 1 **EST:** 2013
SALES (est): 3.3MM
SALES (corp-wide): 144.1K **Privately Held**
WEB: www.wkw.de
SIC: 3462 Automotive forgings, ferrous: crankshaft, engine, axle, etc.
HQ: Wkw North America Holding, Inc.
103 Parkway E
Pell City AL 35125

(G-13633)
WL MOLDING OF MICHIGAN LLC
8212 Shaver Rd (49024-5440)
PHONE.................................269 327-3075
Anil Arakkal, *Opers Mgr*
Gary Leverence, *Manager*
Nigam Tripathi,
EMP: 60 **EST:** 1945
SQ FT: 43,000
SALES (est): 10.1MM **Privately Held**
WEB: www.wlmolding.com
SIC: 3089 3069 Injection molding of plastics; floor coverings, rubber

(G-13634)
WMH FLUIDPOWER INC (PA)
Also Called: W M H Fluidpower
6256 American Ave (49002-9302)
PHONE.................................269 327-7011
Dave Gruss, *President*
William Beaupre, *Vice Pres*
Pete Asaro, *Accounts Mgr*
Bill Elhart, *Accounts Mgr*
Kathy Martin, *Sales Staff*
EMP: 13 **EST:** 1968
SALES (est): 7.1MM **Privately Held**
WEB: www.depatie.com
SIC: 5084 3492 3728 3594 Hydraulic systems equipment & supplies; pneumatic tools & equipment; control valves, fluid power: hydraulic & pneumatic; hose & tube fittings & assemblies, hydraulic/pneumatic; aircraft parts & equipment; fluid power pumps & motors; turbines & turbine generator sets

(G-13635)
WOODEN MOON STUDIO
10334 Portage Rd (49002-7279)
PHONE.................................269 329-3229
Brad Johnson, *President*
EMP: 4 **EST:** 2018
SALES (est): 46K **Privately Held**
WEB: www.woodenmoon.com
SIC: 3993 Signs & advertising specialties

(G-13636)
WRAPS N SIGNS
8324 Shaver Rd (49024-5441)
PHONE.................................269 377-8488
Richard Deneve, *Principal*
Macal Deneve, *Office Mgr*
EMP: 9 **EST:** 2014

Portland
Ionia County

(G-13637)
ARCHER-DANIELS-MIDLAND COMPANY
Also Called: ADM
401 E Grand River Ave (48875-1403)
P.O. Box 260 (48875-0260)
PHONE.....................517 647-4155
Tony Kolarik, *Branch Mgr*
EMP: 4
SALES (corp-wide): 64.3B **Publicly Held**
WEB: www.adm.com
SIC: 2041 2047 Flour & other grain mill products; dog & cat food
PA: Archer-Daniels-Midland Company
77 W Wacker Dr Ste 4600
Chicago IL 60601
312 634-8100

(G-13638)
GREAT LAKES PUBLISHING INC
212 Kent St Ste 6 (48875-1480)
P.O. Box 499 (48875-0499)
PHONE.....................517 647-4444
Ken Kramer, *President*
EMP: 9 EST: 1991
SQ FT: 2,000
SALES (est): 793.7K **Privately Held**
WEB: www.greatlakespub.com
SIC: 2741 6531 Telephone & other directory publishing; real estate agents & managers

(G-13639)
MICHIGAN STEEL AND TRIM INC
349 N Water St (48875-1060)
P.O. Box 346 (48875-0346)
PHONE.....................517 647-4555
Jennifer Biddle, *Administration*
EMP: 5 EST: 2014
SALES (est): 705.2K **Privately Held**
WEB: www.michigansteelandtrim.com
SIC: 2952 Roofing materials

(G-13640)
PORTLAND PLASTICS CO
3 Industrial Dr (48875)
P.O. Box 436 (48875-0436)
PHONE.....................517 647-4115
Robert Tait, *President*
Steve Macksoob, *Vice Pres*
▲ EMP: 18 EST: 1981
SQ FT: 57,000
SALES (est): 1.3MM **Privately Held**
SIC: 3087 2891 2851 Custom compound purchased resins; adhesives & sealants; paints & allied products

(G-13641)
ROWE CUSTOM CABINETRY
815 Kent St (48875-1742)
PHONE.....................517 526-1413
John Rowe, *Principal*
EMP: 4 EST: 2015
SALES (est): 81.4K **Privately Held**
WEB: www.rowecustomcabinetry.com
SIC: 2434 Wood kitchen cabinets

(G-13642)
THK RHYTHM AUTO MICH CORP
902 Lyons Rd (48875-1000)
PHONE.....................517 647-4121
Akihiro Teramachi, *President*
Brian Shivley, *QC Mgr*
Lance Goodemoot, *Engineer*
Ryan Irrer, *Engineer*
Lee Schneider, *Engineer*
EMP: 291 EST: 2015
SALES (est): 49.2MM **Privately Held**
WEB: www.thk-rhythm-auto.com
SIC: 3714 Motor vehicle parts & accessories
PA: Thk Co., Ltd.
2-12-10, Shibaura
Minato-Ku TKY 108-0

SALES (est): 866.3K **Privately Held**
WEB: www.autowrapsnsigns.com
SIC: 3993 Signs & advertising specialties

Posen
Presque Isle County

(G-13643)
HINCKA LOGGING LLC
6464 Lake Augusta Hwy (49776-9765)
P.O. Box 218 (49776-0218)
PHONE.....................989 766-8893
Clarence Hincka Sr,
Fernades Clarence, *Admin Sec*
EMP: 5 EST: 2001
SALES (est): 605K **Privately Held**
SIC: 2411 Logging camps & contractors

(G-13644)
MAPLE RIDGE COMPANIES INC
9528 S Bolton Rd (49776-9625)
PHONE.....................989 356-4807
Gerald J Kamysiak, *President*
EMP: 11 EST: 1977
SQ FT: 30,000
SALES (est): 519.1K **Privately Held**
WEB: www.mapleridgesupply.com
SIC: 3999 0811 Novelties, bric-a-brac & hobby kits; Christmas tree farm

Potterville
Eaton County

(G-13645)
21ST CENTURY PLASTICS CORP (PA)
300 Wright Pkwy (48876)
P.O. Box 188 (48876-0188)
PHONE.....................517 645-2695
Greg Dobie, *President*
Craig Wright, *Vice Pres*
Kate Nowicki, *Accounting Dir*
▲ EMP: 65 EST: 1988
SQ FT: 68,000
SALES (est): 10.6MM **Privately Held**
WEB: www.21stcpc.com
SIC: 3089 Injection molding of plastics

(G-13646)
KAMPS INC
4400 Shance Hwy (48876)
PHONE.....................517 645-2800
Tony Sokoloski, *Branch Mgr*
EMP: 23
SALES (corp-wide): 1.7B **Privately Held**
WEB: www.kampspallets.com
SIC: 2448 2449 Pallets, wood; wood containers
HQ: Kamps, Inc.
2900 Peach Ridge Ave Nw
Grand Rapids MI 49534
616 453-9676

(G-13647)
PROFILE INC
345 Wright Indus Pkwy (48876)
PHONE.....................517 224-8012
Peter Roginski, *Sales Mgr*
EMP: 40 EST: 2012
SALES (est): 2.9MM **Privately Held**
WEB: www.profilemetal.com
SIC: 3469 Metal stampings

Powers
Menominee County

(G-13648)
◀◀◀ 702 CEDAR RIVER LBR INC
W4249 Us Highway 2 (49874-9647)
P.O. Box 340 (49874-0340)
PHONE.....................906 497-5365
Donald S Leboeuf, *President*
Donald S Le Boeuf, *President*
Cathy Phelps, *Vice Pres*
Greg Le Boeuf, *Marketing Staff*
EMP: 31 EST: 1979
SQ FT: 3,000
SALES (est): 634.8K **Privately Held**
WEB: www.cedarriverlumber.com
SIC: 2421 2452 2491 Planing mills; custom sawmill; prefabricated wood buildings; wood preserving

(G-13649)
OGDEN NEWSPAPERS INC
Also Called: Powers Printing
W3985 2nd St (49874-9601)
PHONE.....................906 497-5652
Jeff Schwaller, *Principal*
EMP: 4 **Privately Held**
WEB: www.ogdennews.com
SIC: 2711 Newspapers: publishing only, not printed on site
HQ: The Ogden Newspapers Inc
1500 Main St
Wheeling WV 26003
304 233-0100

(G-13650)
U P MACHINE & ENGINEERING CO
Also Called: U.P. Machine
N15930 Main St (49874-9610)
P.O. Box 400 (49874-0400)
PHONE.....................906 497-5278
Cal Land, *President*
Jeff Land, *Vice Pres*
Cindy Meiner, *Office Mgr*
EMP: 25 EST: 1963
SQ FT: 23,000
SALES (est): 3MM **Privately Held**
WEB: www.upmachine.com
SIC: 3599 Machine shop, jobbing & repair

Prescott
Ogemaw County

(G-13651)
IDEAL WHOLESALE INC
Also Called: K & D Wholesale & Embroidery
3430 Henderson Lake Rd (48756-9338)
PHONE.....................989 873-5850
Keith Dupuis, *President*
Darlene Dupuis, *Vice Pres*
EMP: 4 EST: 1992
SALES (est): 706.8K **Privately Held**
SIC: 5199 5092 5136 5137 Gifts & novelties; toys & hobby goods & supplies; men's & boys' sportswear & work clothing; women's & children's sportswear & swimsuits; schiffli machine embroideries; embroidery products, except schiffli machine

(G-13652)
SWANSONS EXCAVATING INC
2733 Greenwood Rd (48756-9143)
PHONE.....................989 873-4419
Richard E Swanson, *President*
EMP: 4 EST: 1945
SQ FT: 5,000
SALES (est): 200K **Privately Held**
SIC: 3273 1794 Ready-mixed concrete; excavation work

Presque Isle
Presque Isle County

(G-13653)
AUSTIN POWDER COMPANY
11351 E Grand Lake Rd (49777-8383)
PHONE.....................989 595-2400
EMP: 12
SALES (corp-wide): 418.2MM **Privately Held**
SIC: 2892 Mfg Explosives
HQ: Austin Powder Company
25800 Science Park Dr # 300
Cleveland OH 44122
216 464-2400

(G-13654)
LAFARGE NORTH AMERICA INC
11351 E Grand Lake Rd (49777-8383)
PHONE.....................989 595-3820
Nicole Heberling, *General Mgr*
Gabe Orban, *Plant Supt*
Dave Nelson, *Branch Mgr*
EMP: 4
SALES (corp-wide): 25.3B **Privately Held**
WEB: www.lafarge-na.com
SIC: 3241 Cement, hydraulic

HQ: Lafarge North America Inc.
8700 W Bryn Mawr Ave # 30
Chicago IL 60631
773 372-1000

Prudenville
Roscommon County

(G-13655)
AMERICAN VAULT SERVICE (PA)
2063 Norway Ln (48651-9506)
PHONE.....................989 366-8657
James W Stender, *Owner*
EMP: 4 EST: 1976
SALES (est): 600K **Privately Held**
WEB: www.autumnvalleycrematory.com
SIC: 5087 3544 7261 Caskets; welding positioners (jigs); crematory

(G-13656)
BILLS WELDING
136 Cottage Dr (48651-9319)
PHONE.....................989 330-1014
EMP: 4 EST: 2008
SALES (est): 47.7K **Privately Held**
SIC: 7692 Welding repair

(G-13657)
COPPER KETTLE DISTILLING CO
939 W Houghton Lake Dr (48651-9694)
P.O. Box 443 (48651-0443)
PHONE.....................989 366-4412
Loretta Czada, *Principal*
EMP: 4 EST: 2018
SALES (est): 188.1K **Privately Held**
WEB: www.copperkettledistilling.com
SIC: 2085 Distilled & blended liquors

(G-13658)
MAPLE VALLEY TRUSS CO
4287 E West Branch Rd (48651-9441)
PHONE.....................989 389-4267
Richard Gurzenda, *President*
EMP: 14 EST: 1987
SQ FT: 11,800
SALES (est): 521.2K **Privately Held**
SIC: 2439 Trusses, except roof: laminated lumber; trusses, wooden roof

(G-13659)
VIKING OIL LLC
Also Called: Performance Plus
55 W Houghton Lake Dr (48651)
PHONE.....................989 366-4772
John Mendynk, *Manager*
EMP: 5
SALES (corp-wide): 50K **Privately Held**
SIC: 3599 Oil filters, internal combustion engine, except automotive
PA: Viking Oil, Llc
6228 Crystal Beach Rd Nw
Rapid City MI

(G-13660)
WILLIAM BARNES
508 Iroquois Ave (48651-9641)
PHONE.....................989 424-1849
William Barnes, *Principal*
EMP: 4 EST: 2012
SALES (est): 110K **Privately Held**
SIC: 7692 Welding repair

Quincy
Branch County

(G-13661)
ALUMIRAMP INC
855 E Chicago Rd (49082-9450)
PHONE.....................517 639-8777
Linda Burke, *President*
Jenifer Bruke, *Vice Pres*
Barbara Anderson, *Art Dir*
EMP: 10 EST: 1986
SALES (est): 1.3MM **Privately Held**
WEB: www.alumiramp.com
SIC: 3448 Ramps: prefabricated metal

GEOGRAPHIC SECTION

(G-13662)
ARCTECH PRECISION WELDING
929 E Chicago Rd (49082-8410)
PHONE...................................517 614-5722
EMP: 5 EST: 2017
SALES (est): 516.3K Privately Held
WEB: www.arctechwelding.net
SIC: 7692 Welding repair

(G-13663)
BAADE FABRICATING & ENGRG
210 S Ray Quincy Rd (49082-9523)
PHONE...................................517 639-4536
Jon R Baade, *President*
Judy Baade, *Treasurer*
EMP: 5 EST: 1967
SQ FT: 12,000
SALES (est): 449.4K Privately Held
SIC: 3599 Machine shop, jobbing & repair

(G-13664)
BRECO LLC
57 Cole St (49082-1031)
P.O. Box 216 (49082-0216)
PHONE...................................517 317-2211
Ken Holroyd, *Principal*
EMP: 15 EST: 2015
SALES (est): 1.5MM Privately Held
WEB: www.brecollc.com
SIC: 3599 Machine & other job shop work; machine shop, jobbing & repair

(G-13665)
CONAGRA BRANDS INC
4551 Squires Rd (49082-9601)
PHONE...................................402 240-8210
John Hennessy, *Branch Mgr*
EMP: 7
SALES (corp-wide): 11.1B Publicly Held
WEB: www.conagrabrands.com
SIC: 2099 Food preparations
PA: Conagra Brands, Inc.
   222 Mdse Mart Plz Ste 1
   Chicago IL 60654
   312 549-5000

(G-13666)
CPS LLC
Also Called: Commercial Painting Services
11 E Chicago St (49082-1101)
PHONE...................................517 639-1464
Ian Bernard,
EMP: 12 EST: 2014
SQ FT: 7,000
SALES (est): 1.2MM Privately Held
WEB: www.commercialpaintingservices.com
SIC: 1721 1761 3531 Industrial painting; commercial painting; roofing contractor; surfacers, concrete grinding

(G-13667)
CREATIVE EYEBALL AGENCY
11 E Chicago St (49082-1101)
PHONE...................................517 398-8008
EMP: 4 EST: 2009
SALES (est): 177.2K Privately Held
WEB: www.creativeeyeball.com
SIC: 2752 Commercial printing, lithographic

(G-13668)
EAB FABRICATION INC
150 S Main St (49082-1223)
PHONE...................................517 639-7080
April Lams, *Branch Mgr*
EMP: 25
SALES (corp-wide): 9.1MM Privately Held
WEB: www.eabfab.com
SIC: 3441 Fabricated structural metal for ships
PA: Eab Fabrication Inc.
   64 Cole St
   Quincy MI 49082
   517 639-7080

(G-13669)
EAB FABRICATION INC (PA)
64 Cole St (49082-1032)
P.O. Box 72 (49082-0072)
PHONE...................................517 639-7080
Edwin A Bowerman, *President*
Thelma Bowerman, *Corp Secy*
Sandy Coffee, *Human Res Mgr*
EMP: 50 EST: 2003
SQ FT: 20,000
SALES (est): 9.1MM Privately Held
WEB: www.eabfab.com
SIC: 3441 Fabricated structural metal

(G-13670)
HART FABRICATION INC
912 Beckwith Shr (49082-1072)
P.O. Box 9 (49082-0009)
PHONE...................................517 924-1109
EMP: 13 EST: 2019
SALES (est): 252.8K Privately Held
WEB: www.hartfab.com
SIC: 3444 Sheet metalwork

(G-13671)
MARSH BROTHERS INC
9800 Youngs Rd (49082-9605)
PHONE...................................517 869-2653
Dan Marsh, *President*
George Calvin Marsh, *Vice Pres*
EMP: 19 EST: 1985
SQ FT: 15,000
SALES (est): 2MM Privately Held
WEB: www.pontoonspecialists.com
SIC: 7699 3732 5551 Marine engine repair; boat building & repairing; outboard motors

(G-13672)
MISS PRINT ROCKS
13 E Chicago St (49082-1101)
PHONE...................................517 639-8785
Jacinda Locke, *Principal*
EMP: 6 EST: 2015
SALES (est): 132.9K Privately Held
WEB: www.missprintapparelanddesigns.com
SIC: 2752 Commercial printing, lithographic

(G-13673)
MUNIMULA INC
548 Squires Rd (49082-8423)
PHONE...................................517 605-5343
Pauline K Munn, *CEO*
Barbara Anderson, *Graphic Designe*
EMP: 11 EST: 2011
SALES (est): 197.4K Privately Held
WEB: www.munimula.com
SIC: 3089 Plastic kitchenware, tableware & houseware

(G-13674)
SPEEDRACK PRODUCTS GROUP LTD
42 Cole St (49082-1032)
PHONE...................................517 639-8781
John Oliveira, *Regional Mgr*
Mike Roney, *Vice Pres*
Corrine Towns, *Branch Mgr*
Bretton Johnson, *Program Mgr*
Greg Dunneback, *Manager*
EMP: 141 Privately Held
WEB: www.speedrack.net
SIC: 3449 Miscellaneous metalwork
PA: Speedrack Products Group, Ltd.
   7903 Venture Ave Nw
   Sparta MI 49345

(G-13675)
SUN GRO HORTICULTURE DIST INC
1150 E Chicago Rd (49082-9585)
PHONE...................................517 639-3115
Daniel Johnson, *Manager*
Rolene Eberts, *Manager*
EMP: 4 Privately Held
WEB: www.sungro.com
SIC: 2875 0781 Potting soil, mixed; horticultural counseling services
PA: Sun Gro Horticulture Distribution Inc.
   770 Silver St
   Agawam MA 01001

Quinnesec
Dickinson County

(G-13676)
PASTY OVEN INC (PA)
W7279 Us Highway 2 (49876-9709)
P.O. Box 100 (49876-0100)
PHONE...................................906 774-2328
Gene Carollo, *President*
▲ EMP: 7 EST: 1997
SQ FT: 2,400 Privately Held
WEB: www.pastys.com
SIC: 2038 Ethnic foods, frozen

(G-13677)
UP TRUCK CENTER INC
4920 Menominee St (49876)
P.O. Box 261 (49876-0261)
PHONE...................................906 774-0098
Thomas Sullivan, *President*
Greg Gendron, *Manager*
Beth Sullivan, *Admin Sec*
◆ EMP: 32 EST: 1985
SQ FT: 26,650
SALES (est): 10.4MM Privately Held
WEB: www.uptruckcenter.com
SIC: 5511 5531 7692 Trucks, tractors & trailers: new & used; truck equipment & parts; automotive welding

(G-13678)
VERSO PAPER HOLDING LLC
W6791 Us Highway 2 (49876-9703)
P.O. Box 211, Norway (49870-0211)
PHONE...................................906 779-3200
Randall Lorenz, *Human Res Dir*
Mike Sussman, *Manager*
Ronn Gregor, *Manager*
Don Davy, *Info Tech Dir*
George Curran, *Executive*
EMP: 10 Publicly Held
SIC: 2671 2611 2621 Paper coated or laminated for packaging; pulp mills; paper mills
HQ: Verso Paper Holding Llc
   8540 Gander Creek Dr
   Miamisburg OH 45342
   877 855-7243

(G-13679)
VERSO QUINNESEC LLC
W6791 Us Highway 2 (49876-9703)
P.O. Box 221, Norway (49870-0221)
PHONE...................................877 447-2737
David J Paterson,
EMP: 8 EST: 2006
SALES (est): 3.4MM Publicly Held
WEB: www.versoco.com
SIC: 2621 Paper mills
PA: Verso Corporation
   8540 Gander Creek Dr
   Miamisburg OH 45342

(G-13680)
VERSO QUINNESEC REP LLC
W6705 Us Highway 2 (49876)
PHONE...................................906 779-3200
John Valas, *Credit Staff*
EMP: 4 Publicly Held
SIC: 2621 Paper mills
HQ: Verso Quinnesec Rep Llc
   8540 Gander Creek Dr
   Miamisburg OH 45342
   901 369-4100

Rapid City
Kalkaska County

(G-13681)
KNUST MASONRY
6092 Aarwood Rd Nw (49676-9483)
PHONE...................................231 322-2587
Rick Knust, *Owner*
EMP: 7 EST: 1985 Privately Held
WEB: www.sundownconstruction.com
SIC: 3241 1741 Masonry cement; masonry & other stonework

Rapid River
Delta County

(G-13682)
CANAM UNDRWTER HOCKEY GEAR LLC
7660 Perkins 30.5 Rd (49878-9319)
PHONE...................................906 399-7857
EMP: 4 EST: 2013
SALES (est): 123.2K Privately Held
WEB: www.canamuwhgear.com
SIC: 3949 Sporting & athletic goods

(G-13683)
CREATIVE COMPOSITES INC
7637 Us Highway 2 (49878-9791)
PHONE...................................906 474-9941
Brad McPhee, *President*
Stepnaie Lockhart, *Office Mgr*
EMP: 30 EST: 1994
SQ FT: 8,500
SALES (est): 4.3MM Privately Held
WEB: www.creativecompositesinc.com
SIC: 3446 8711 Architectural metalwork; engineering services

(G-13684)
DUANE F PROEHL INC
11064 T.65 Rd (49878-9313)
PHONE...................................906 474-6630
Duane F Proehl, *President*
Ruth Proehl, *Admin Sec*
EMP: 5 EST: 1984
SALES (est): 505.1K Privately Held
SIC: 2411 Logging

(G-13685)
POMEROY FOREST PRODUCTS INC
9577 Ee.25 Rd (49878-9103)
PHONE...................................906 474-6780
Mark Pomeroy, *President*
Vicky Pomeroy, *Admin Sec*
EMP: 9 EST: 1977
SALES (est): 1MM Privately Held
WEB: www.pomeroyforest.business.site
SIC: 2411 Logging

(G-13686)
RAPID RIVER RUSTIC INC (PA)
Also Called: Rapid River Loghome
9211 County 511 22 And (49878)
P.O. Box 10 (49878-0010)
PHONE...................................906 474-6404
Ivan R Malnar, *President*
Jodi Malnar, *Corp Secy*
EMP: 40 EST: 1970
SALES (est): 4.1MM Privately Held
WEB: www.rapidriverrustic.com
SIC: 2421 2499 3496 2439 Lumber stacking or sticking; fencing, wood; miscellaneous fabricated wire products; structural wood members; logging

(G-13687)
WILLIAMS MILLING & MOULDING IN
10304 Bay Shore Dr (49878-9796)
PHONE...................................906 474-9222
Gene Williams, *Principal*
EMP: 5 EST: 2008
SALES (est): 330.2K Privately Held
WEB: www.softhouse.com
SIC: 2421 Sawmills & planing mills, general

Ravenna
Muskegon County

(G-13688)
CRYSTAL ICE RESOURCE LLC
6054 S Moorland Rd (49451-9426)
P.O. Box 31, Coopersville (49404-0031)
PHONE...................................616 560-8102
Richard Shinliger, *Mng Member*
EMP: 5 EST: 2011 Privately Held
WEB: www.crystalicresource.com
SIC: 3585 Refrigeration equipment, complete

(G-13689)
GRIPTRAC INC
Also Called: Gilbert & Riplo Company
4865 S Ravenna Rd (49451-9174)
PHONE...................................231 853-2284
Fred Riplo, *President*
▲ EMP: 18 EST: 1943
SQ FT: 10,000

Ravenna - Muskegon County (G-13690)

SALES (est): 6.1MM Privately Held
WEB: www.griptrac.com
SIC: **3523** 3441 7692 Combines (harvester-threshers); fabricated structural metal; welding repair

(G-13690)
JERRYS WELDING INC
11210 Ellis Rd (49451-9443)
PHONE..................................231 853-6494
Jerry Ruch, *President*
Robert Ruch, *Vice Pres*
EMP: 5 EST: 1980
SQ FT: 1,800
SALES (est): 725.3K Privately Held
SIC: **7692** Welding repair

(G-13691)
LIBERTY PRODUCTS INC
Also Called: Stud Boy Traction
3073 Mortimer St (49451-9566)
P.O. Box 338 (49451-0338)
PHONE..................................231 853-2323
Ronald Pattyn, *President*
Robert Baker, *Vice Pres*
▲ EMP: 19 EST: 1990
SQ FT: 12,000
SALES (est): 3.4MM Privately Held
WEB: www.studboytraction.com
SIC: **3799** Snowmobiles

(G-13692)
RAVENNA CASTING CENTER INC
3800 Adams Rd (49451-9450)
P.O. Box 397 (49451-0397)
PHONE..................................231 853-0300
Rick James, *CEO*
Keith Turner, *COO*
EMP: 1 EST: 1999
SALES (est): 3.6MM
SALES (corp-wide): 261.8MM Privately Held
WEB: www.metal-technologies.com
SIC: **3714** 3321 Motor vehicle parts & accessories; ductile iron castings
PA: Metal Technologies Of Indiana Llc
1401 S Grandstaff Dr
Auburn IN 46706
260 925-4717

(G-13693)
RAVENNA PATTERN & MFG
Also Called: Ravenna Hydraulics
13101 Apple Ave (49451-9755)
P.O. Box 219 (49451-0219)
PHONE..................................231 853-2264
Joshua Emery, *President*
Neil Emery, *Vice Pres*
Michael Emery, *Engineer*
Andy Emery, *Manager*
Chad Wenzinger, *Administration*
EMP: 40 EST: 1962
SQ FT: 37,000
SALES (est): 9.4MM Privately Held
WEB: www.ravennapattern.com
SIC: **3544** 3543 Industrial molds; industrial patterns

(G-13694)
ROGERS PRINTING INC
3350 Main St (49451-9400)
P.O. Box 215 (49451-0215)
PHONE..................................231 853-2244
Tom Rogers, *CEO*
Jeff Selk, *Vice Pres*
Jeff Raap, *Mfg Mgr*
Rick Feist, *CFO*
Kristin Duffy, *Cust Mgr*
EMP: 133 EST: 1888
SQ FT: 40,000
SALES (est): 20.8MM Privately Held
WEB: www.rogersprinting.net
SIC: **2752** 2759 2732 Commercial printing, offset; commercial printing; book printing

(G-13695)
SWANSON GRADING & BRINING INC
11561 Heights Ravenna Rd (49451-9243)
P.O. Box 211 (49451-0211)
PHONE..................................231 853-2289
John W Swanson II, *President*
EMP: 13 EST: 2000
SQ FT: 1,000
SALES: 10.4MM Privately Held
SIC: **2035** Pickles, sauces & salad dressings

(G-13696)
SWANSON PICKLE CO INC
11561 Heights Ravenna Rd (49451-9243)
P.O. Box 211 (49451-0211)
PHONE..................................231 853-2289
John Swanson, *President*
Donald Swanson, *Chairman*
Katie Hensley, *Finance*
David Swanson, *Shareholder*
Paul Swanson, *Admin Sec*
EMP: 20 EST: 1936
SQ FT: 6,000
SALES: 4.2MM Privately Held
SIC: **2035** Cucumbers, pickles & pickle salting

Ray
Macomb County

(G-13697)
A-OK PRECISION PROTOTYPE INC
59539 Romeo Plank Rd (48096-3529)
PHONE..................................586 758-3430
Robert D Watson, *President*
Mary Nepper, *Admin Sec*
EMP: 9 EST: 1970
SQ FT: 12,000
SALES (est): 335.6K Privately Held
WEB: www.aokprecision.com
SIC: **3565** Packaging machinery

(G-13698)
D4 APPAREL LLC
60480 Kunstman Rd (48096-3621)
PHONE..................................586 207-1841
Nancy Dodson, *Owner*
EMP: 5 EST: 2013
SALES (est): 125.5K Privately Held
WEB: www.d4apparel.com
SIC: **2759** Screen printing

(G-13699)
GLEASON HOLBROOK MFG CO
22401 28 Mile Rd (48096-3204)
PHONE..................................586 749-5519
Daniel E Gleason, *President*
Thomas Gleason, *Vice Pres*
EMP: 10 EST: 1964
SQ FT: 21,700
SALES (est): 636.3K Privately Held
SIC: **3544** Special dies & tools

(G-13700)
LATITUDE RECYCLING INC
60451 Kunstman Rd (48096-3616)
PHONE..................................586 243-5153
Jason McCallum, *President*
EMP: 5
SALES (est): 207.2K Privately Held
SIC: **3559** 7389 Recycling machinery;

(G-13701)
OMAX TOOL PRODUCTS INC
Also Called: Arrow Adtech Tool Co
68500 Hawkins Ln (48096-1420)
P.O. Box 67, Romeo (48065-0067)
PHONE..................................517 768-0300
Onas Deskins Jr, *President*
Mitchell Deskins, *Admin Sec*
EMP: 10 EST: 1916
SQ FT: 6,600
SALES (est): 277.5K Privately Held
SIC: **3545** 5085 Machine tool accessories; tools

(G-13702)
PARAMOUNT SOLUTIONS INC
59285 Elizabeth Ln (48096-3552)
PHONE..................................586 914-0708
Linda Kuskowski, *Owner*
Danny Kuskowski, *Vice Pres*
Ashley Audain, *Opers Staff*
EMP: 5 EST: 2007
SALES (est): 500K Privately Held
WEB: www.paramountsolutionsinc.com
SIC: **3083** Plastic finished products, laminated

(G-13703)
SCOTCO WOODWORKING
23793 28 Mile Rd (48096-3336)
PHONE..................................586 749-9805
EMP: 4 EST: 2011
SALES (est): 153.4K Privately Held
SIC: **2431** Millwork

Reading
Hillsdale County

(G-13704)
ROLL TECH INC
104 Enterprise St (49274-9587)
P.O. Box 419 (49274-0419)
PHONE..................................517 283-3811
Michael Clark, *President*
EMP: 7 EST: 1994
SALES (est): 578.2K Privately Held
WEB: www.rolleigh.com
SIC: **3544** Special dies, tools, jigs & fixtures

(G-13705)
ROLLEIGH INC
104 Enterprise St (49274-9587)
P.O. Box 419 (49274-0419)
PHONE..................................517 283-3811
Michael L Clark, *President*
William R Clark, *Vice Pres*
Mikec Clark, *Manager*
Derrick Clark, *Supervisor*
Matt Clark Jr, *Shareholder*
EMP: 13 EST: 1988
SQ FT: 8,000
SALES (est): 2.4MM Privately Held
WEB: www.rolleigh.com
SIC: **3544** Dies, steel rule; industrial molds

(G-13706)
STONEY CREEK TMBER QRTER HRSES
810 Lester Rd (49274-9521)
PHONE..................................517 677-9661
EMP: 4 EST: 2009
SALES (est): 54K Privately Held
SIC: **3131** Quarters

(G-13707)
TIMERS ENTERPRISES LLC
871 Brown Rd (49274-9516)
PHONE..................................517 617-3092
Timothy Pearson, *Principal*
EMP: 9
SALES (corp-wide): 94.4K Privately Held
SIC: **3484** Guns (firearms) or gun parts, 30 mm. & below
PA: Timers Enterprises Llc
20 N Main St
Quincy MI

Redford
Wayne County

(G-13708)
87 GRAMS LLC
18226 Dalby (48240-1730)
PHONE..................................248 558-0424
Isaac Nash,
EMP: 10 EST: 2020
SALES (est): 409.5K Privately Held
SIC: **2836** Culture media

(G-13709)
AAA INDUSTRIES INC
24500 Capitol (48239-2446)
PHONE..................................313 255-0420
Mark Yessian, *President*
Charles Torosian, *Vice Pres*
EMP: 32 EST: 1962
SQ FT: 13,600
SALES (est): 2.3MM Privately Held
WEB: www.aaaind.com
SIC: **3451** 3452 3541 Screw machine products; bolts, nuts, rivets & washers; machine tools, metal cutting type

(G-13710)
AC COVERS INC
Also Called: A/C Covers
25544 5 Mile Rd (48239-3229)
PHONE..................................313 541-7770
Constance Kowalczyk, *President*
John A Kowalczyk, *Treasurer*
Kisha Falkner, *Research Analys*
EMP: 10 EST: 1981
SALES (est): 1MM Privately Held
WEB: www.accovers.com
SIC: **3564** Blowers & fans

(G-13711)
ADVERTISING ACCENTS INC
18845 Denby (48240-2040)
PHONE..................................313 937-3890
Tom Krause, *President*
EMP: 7 EST: 1985
SQ FT: 4,000
SALES (est): 756.5K Privately Held
WEB: www.advertisingaccentsinc.com
SIC: **5199** 2261 Advertising specialties; screen printing of cotton broadwoven fabrics

(G-13712)
ALL ABOUT BUS CNSTR AABC LLC
16935 Wakenden (48240-2467)
PHONE..................................248 229-3031
Diona Pickens, *Mng Member*
EMP: 5 EST: 2020
SALES (est): 125.4K Privately Held
SIC: **1389** Construction, repair & dismantling services

(G-13713)
ALPINE POWER SYSTEMS INC (HQ)
24355 Capitol Ste 1 (48239-2466)
PHONE..................................313 531-6600
Paul Hirschberg, *President*
Bob Bildstein, *General Mgr*
Scott Declaire, *Vice Pres*
Eric Light, *Vice Pres*
Darin Jones, *Project Mgr*
▼ EMP: 84 EST: 1966
SQ FT: 25,000
SALES (est): 69.8MM Privately Held
WEB: www.alpinepowersystems.com
SIC: **5063** 7699 3691 Batteries; battery service & repair; storage batteries
PA: Tfi, Inc
24355 Capitol Ste 1
Redford MI 48239
313 531-6600

(G-13714)
ANGELS OF DETROIT LLC ◆
7741 Lamphere (48239-1082)
PHONE..................................248 796-1079
Darius Wilbert, *CEO*
EMP: 4 EST: 2021
SALES (est): 154.9K Privately Held
SIC: **1795** 7389 1081 5087 Wrecking & demolition work; ; metal mining exploration & development services; service establishment equipment; disinfecting services

(G-13715)
APPLY PRSSURE MBL DTAILING LLC
11360 Garfield (48239-2014)
PHONE..................................248 794-7710
Tyron King,
EMP: 7 EST: 2018
SALES (est): 664.4K Privately Held
WEB: www.madisonmobiledetailing.com
SIC: **3714** Cleaners, air, motor vehicle

(G-13716)
ARGUS CORPORATION (PA)
12540 Beech Daly Rd (48239-2469)
PHONE..................................313 937-2900
Fred Ransford, *President*
Gary Mausold, *Manager*
EMP: 36 EST: 1990
SQ FT: 135,000
SALES: 25.1MM Privately Held
WEB: www.arguscorporation.com
SIC: **3544** Special dies & tools

Redford - Wayne County

(G-13717)
ATHLETIC UNIFORM LETTERING
26114 W 6 Mile Rd (48240-2217)
PHONE..............................313 533-9071
Joseph J Copperstone, *President*
EMP: 5 **EST:** 1976
SQ FT: 3,600
SALES (est): 306.6K **Privately Held**
WEB: www.athleticuniformlettering.com
SIC: 2396 Screen printing on fabric articles

(G-13718)
BEIRUT BAKERY INC
25706 Schoolcraft (48239-2631)
PHONE..............................313 533-4422
Alex Wakim, *President*
Iskandar Wakim, *President*
Hala Wakim, *Corp Secy*
Milad Wakim, *Vice Pres*
EMP: 17 **EST:** 1979
SQ FT: 2,500
SALES (est): 1.1MM **Privately Held**
WEB: www.beirutbakery.net
SIC: 2051 5149 Bakery: wholesale or wholesale/retail combined; bakery products

(G-13719)
BEST PRODUCTS INC
14208 Sarasota (48239-2889)
PHONE..............................313 538-7414
Jim Gonzales, *CEO*
EMP: 12 **EST:** 1993
SQ FT: 12,500
SALES (est): 401.1K **Privately Held**
SIC: 3714 3826 Motor vehicle parts & accessories; analytical instruments

(G-13720)
BIG D LLC
26038 Grand River Ave (48240-1439)
PHONE..............................248 787-2724
Vadim Yelizarov, *CEO*
EMP: 4 **EST:** 2017
SALES (est): 250.4K **Privately Held**
SIC: 2759 Screen printing

(G-13721)
BOOMS STONE COMPANY
12275 Dixie (48239-2490)
PHONE..............................313 531-3000
Richard Booms, *President*
Dan Nault, *Associate*
▲ **EMP:** 60 **EST:** 1987
SQ FT: 42,000
SALES (est): 8.3MM **Privately Held**
WEB: www.boomsstone.com
SIC: 3281 Cut stone & stone products

(G-13722)
C R STITCHING
26150 5 Mile Rd 1c (48239-3244)
PHONE..............................313 538-1660
Cynthia Moll, *Owner*
EMP: 4 **EST:** 1984
SQ FT: 1,800
SALES (est): 178.8K **Privately Held**
SIC: 2395 Embroidery products, except schiffli machine

(G-13723)
CHOSEN TEES LLC
25122 Donald (48239-3332)
PHONE..............................313 766-4550
Gregory McDaniel, *Principal*
EMP: 5 **EST:** 2018
SALES (est): 79K **Privately Held**
WEB: www.chosen-tees.net
SIC: 2759 Screen printing

(G-13724)
CKC INDUSTRIES INC
24824 Ross Dr (48239-3380)
PHONE..............................248 667-6286
Leslie Wells, *Principal*
EMP: 5 **EST:** 2015
SALES (est): 172.8K **Privately Held**
SIC: 3999 Manufacturing industries

(G-13725)
CLASSIC PLATING INC
12600 Farley (48239-2643)
PHONE..............................313 531-1440
Susan Barbret, *President*
J R Morgan, *Vice Pres*
Mike Morgan, *Vice Pres*
Steve Morgan, *Vice Pres*
EMP: 8 **EST:** 1985
SQ FT: 17,195
SALES (est): 1.1MM **Privately Held**
WEB: www.classicplatinginc.com
SIC: 3471 Electroplating of metals or formed products

(G-13726)
CMP ACQUISITIONS LLC
Also Called: Detroit Architectural Metal
25501 Glendale (48239-2650)
PHONE..............................888 519-2286
EMP: 13
SALES (est): 2.1MM **Privately Held**
WEB: www.detroitarc.com
SIC: 5047 3821 1761 Medical & hospital equipment; medical laboratory equipment; laboratory apparatus & furniture; architectural sheet metal work

(G-13727)
CREATIVE SOLUTIONS GROUP INC
Also Called: Csg Storage Facility
12285 Dixie (48239-2491)
PHONE..............................734 425-2257
Kristina Valentine, *Accounts Exec*
Don Holms, *Manager*
Jack McCoy, *Manager*
EMP: 4
SALES (corp-wide): 12.3MM **Privately Held**
WEB: www.csgnow.com
SIC: 7389 2542 Advertising, promotional & trade show services; partitions & fixtures, except wood
PA: Creative Solutions Group, Inc.
1250 N Crooks Rd
Clawson MI 48017
248 288-9700

(G-13728)
CUJOGRAPHYX LLC
18812 Glenmore (48240-1741)
PHONE..............................248 318-6407
Gregory McCliment, *Administration*
EMP: 5 **EST:** 2017
SALES (est): 138.1K **Privately Held**
WEB: www.cujographyx.com
SIC: 2759 Screen printing

(G-13729)
DAIMAY NORTH AMERICA AUTO INC (HQ)
24400 Plymouth Rd (48239-1617)
PHONE..............................313 533-9680
Jay Wang, *President*
Allen Reinwasser, *Engineer*
David Yao, *Program Mgr*
Joseph Greco, *Director*
EMP: 50 **EST:** 2009
SQ FT: 2,500
SALES (est): 33MM **Privately Held**
SIC: 3714 Motor vehicle parts & accessories

(G-13730)
DETROIT DIESEL CORPORATION
12200 Telegraph Rd (48239)
PHONE..............................313 592-8256
EMP: 15
SALES (corp-wide): 193.7B **Privately Held**
SIC: 3519 3714 7538 Mfg Intrnl Cmbstn Engine Mfg Motor Vehicle Parts General Auto Repair
HQ: Detroit Diesel Corporation
13400 W Outer Dr
Detroit MI 48239
313 592-5000

(G-13731)
DETROIT TECH INNOVATION LLC
Also Called: Dti
25036 W 6 Mile Rd (48240-2101)
PHONE..............................734 259-4168
Baojian Liao, *General Mgr*
EMP: 8 **EST:** 2013
SQ FT: 2,000
SALES (est): 818.5K **Privately Held**
SIC: 3559 Automotive related machinery

(G-13732)
FAMILY MACHINISTS
20456 Lexington (48240-1149)
PHONE..............................734 340-1848
Darrell Riesenberger, *President*
EMP: 4 **EST:** 2018
SALES (est): 139K **Privately Held**
SIC: 3599 Machine shop, jobbing & repair

(G-13733)
FARBER CONCESSIONS INC
Also Called: Detroit Popcorn Company
14950 Telegraph Rd (48239-3457)
PHONE..............................313 387-1600
David Barber, *President*
Evan Singer, *Vice Pres*
Chris Deneen, *Manager*
EMP: 25 **EST:** 1942
SQ FT: 70,000
SALES (est): 7.2MM **Privately Held**
WEB: www.detroitpopcorn.com
SIC: 5046 7359 2038 2087 Commercial cooking & food service equipment; equipment rental & leasing; snacks, including onion rings, cheese sticks, etc.; beverage bases, concentrates, syrups, powders & mixes; cane sugar refining; frozen fruits & vegetables

(G-13734)
FEDERAL INDUSTRIAL SERVICES
12980 Inkster Rd (48239-3045)
PHONE..............................313 533-9888
Michael Hadwin, *Principal*
EMP: 4 **EST:** 2016
SALES (est): 90.8K **Privately Held**
SIC: 3398 Metal heat treating

(G-13735)
FRANKLIN FASTENER COMPANY
12701 Beech Daly Rd (48239-2472)
PHONE..............................313 537-8900
James M Sampson, *President*
Fred Trott, *General Mgr*
Andrew W Hayes, *Vice Pres*
Norma E Sampson, *Admin Sec*
Stacey Kawsarani, *Analyst*
▼ **EMP:** 31 **EST:** 1953
SQ FT: 26,500
SALES (est): 6.1MM **Privately Held**
WEB: www.franklinfastener.com
SIC: 3496 3469 3429 3452 Miscellaneous fabricated wire products; metal stampings; manufactured hardware (general); bolts, nuts, rivets & washers; automotive stampings

(G-13736)
GC BORING INC
12570 Inkster Rd (48239-2562)
PHONE..............................313 937-2320
Gene Sekutowski, *Owner*
EMP: 5 **EST:** 2007
SALES (est): 93.3K **Privately Held**
SIC: 3599 Machine shop, jobbing & repair

(G-13737)
GEORGE W TRAPP CO (PA)
15000 Fox (48239-2794)
PHONE..............................313 531-7180
Richard E Trapp, *President*
EMP: 25 **EST:** 1930
SQ FT: 36,000
SALES (est): 1.5MM **Privately Held**
WEB: www.gwtrapp.com
SIC: 3442 Sash, door or window: metal

(G-13738)
HART ACQUISITION COMPANY LLC
12700 Marion (48239-2653)
PHONE..............................313 537-0490
Scott Weyandt, *Mng Member*
Keith Thornton,
EMP: 30 **EST:** 2017
SQ FT: 50,000
SALES (est): 2.5MM **Privately Held**
WEB: www.hart-precision.com
SIC: 3444 Casings, sheet metal

(G-13739)
HART PRECISION PRODUCTS INC
12700 Marion (48239-2695)
PHONE..............................313 537-0490
Darlene Hart Weyandt, *President*
Beatrice Hart, *Corp Secy*
EMP: 50 **EST:** 1953
SQ FT: 35,000
SALES (est): 8.3MM **Privately Held**
WEB: www.hart-precision.com
SIC: 3728 3537 Aircraft parts & equipment; tractors, used in plants, docks, terminals, etc.: industrial

(G-13740)
INSTALLATIONS INC
25257 W 8 Mile Rd (48240-1003)
PHONE..............................313 532-9000
Pearl Baltes, *President*
Lawrence S Baltes, *Corp Secy*
Steven Baltes, *VP Sales*
EMP: 15
SQ FT: 10,000
SALES (est): 2.9MM **Privately Held**
WEB: www.installations.org
SIC: 3089 1799 Flat panels, plastic; home/office interiors finishing, furnishing & remodeling

(G-13741)
KINGSTON PRPERTY ADVISERS CORP ✪
25742 Schoolcraft (48239-2631)
PHONE..............................248 825-9657
Marlon Davis Jr, *President*
EMP: 6 **EST:** 2021
SALES (est): 300.2K **Privately Held**
SIC: 6531 1389 Real estate agents & managers; construction, repair & dismantling services

(G-13742)
LPS-2 INC
24755 5 Mile Rd Ste 100 (48239-3665)
PHONE..............................313 538-0181
Michael Dorsey, *President*
EMP: 5 **EST:** 2007
SALES (est): 290.7K **Privately Held**
WEB: www.lps-2.com
SIC: 3955 Print cartridges for laser & other computer printers

(G-13743)
M & R PRINTING INC
26430 W 7 Mile Rd (48240-1917)
PHONE..............................248 543-8080
Ronald Purvey, *President*
Michael Purvey, *Vice Pres*
EMP: 5 **EST:** 1987
SQ FT: 2,500
SALES (est): 490K **Privately Held**
SIC: 2752 Commercial printing, offset

(G-13744)
MCNICHOLS POLSG & ANODIZING (PA)
12139 Woodbine (48239-2417)
PHONE..............................313 538-3470
G Rose Smith, *President*
Diana L Tibbits, *Admin Sec*
EMP: 16
SQ FT: 10,000
SALES (est): 2MM **Privately Held**
WEB: www.mcnicholsanodizing.com
SIC: 3471 Anodizing (plating) of metals or formed products; polishing, metals or formed products; buffing for the trade

(G-13745)
MCNICHOLS POLSG & ANODIZING
12139 Wormer (48239-2422)
PHONE..............................313 538-3470
Diane Tibbits, *Manager*
EMP: 8
SALES (corp-wide): 2MM **Privately Held**
WEB: www.mcnicholsanodizing.com
SIC: 3471 Anodizing (plating) of metals or formed products
PA: Mcnichols Polishing & Anodizing Inc
12139 Woodbine
Redford MI 48239
313 538-3470

Redford - Wayne County (G-13746) — GEOGRAPHIC SECTION

(G-13746)
METRO STAMPING & MFG CO
26955 Fullerton (48239-2592)
PHONE..................................313 538-6464
Robert H Leonard, *President*
Richard M Leonard, *Treasurer*
Carol J Doak, *Shareholder*
EMP: 25 **EST:** 1959
SQ FT: 14,000
SALES (est): 1.4MM **Privately Held**
WEB: www.metrostamp.com
SIC: 3469 Stamping metal for the trade

(G-13747)
MOLDEX CRANK SHAFT INC
12255 Wormer (48239-2424)
PHONE..................................313 561-7676
Joseph Flower, *President*
EMP: 5 **EST:** 1945
SQ FT: 18,000
SALES (est): 410K **Privately Held**
WEB: www.moldexcrankshaft.com
SIC: 3714 Crankshaft assemblies, motor vehicle

(G-13748)
MR EVERYTHING LLC (PA)
15994 Sumner (48239-3855)
PHONE..................................248 301-2580
Andrew Gibson,
EMP: 5 **EST:** 2018
SALES (est): 97K **Privately Held**
SIC: 1389 Construction, repair & dismantling services

(G-13749)
NOVI TOOL & MACHINE COMPANY
Also Called: Novi Matic Valves
12202 Woodbine (48239-2420)
PHONE..................................313 532-0900
David Sumara, *President*
EMP: 15 **EST:** 1950
SQ FT: 4,000
SALES (est): 416.1K **Privately Held**
SIC: 3541 3494 3547 3498 Cutoff machines (metalworking machinery); valves & pipe fittings; rolling mill machinery; fabricated pipe & fittings; fluid power valves & hose fittings; industrial valves

(G-13750)
NUCAST LLC
11745 Woodbine (48239-2415)
PHONE..................................313 532-4610
Marco Rosati, *Mng Member*
EMP: 6 **EST:** 2016
SALES (est): 741.5K **Privately Held**
WEB: www.nucastprecast.com
SIC: 3272 Concrete products, precast

(G-13751)
OMO ENTERPRISES LLC ◯
19646 Brady (48240-1365)
PHONE..................................248 392-6397
Tejaan Tupree Simmons,
EMP: 5 **EST:** 2021
SALES (est): 100K **Privately Held**
SIC: 3845 Medical cleaning equipment, ultrasonic

(G-13752)
ONEIDA TOOL CORPORATION
12700 Inkster Rd (48239-3099)
PHONE..................................313 537-0770
John Darnbrook, *President*
Ed Darnbrook, *Vice Pres*
Anthony Antinozzzi, *Technology*
▲ **EMP:** 20 **EST:** 1966
SQ FT: 12,000
SALES (est): 1MM **Privately Held**
WEB: www.bestdarntoolshop.com
SIC: 3599 3545 Machine shop, jobbing & repair; machine tool accessories

(G-13753)
PECK ENGINEERING INC
12660 Farley (48239-2643)
PHONE..................................313 534-2950
George Thomas, *President*
David Post, *Vice Pres*
Kelly Morrison, *Director*
EMP: 20 **EST:** 1952
SALES (est): 2.1MM **Privately Held**
WEB: www.peckengineeringdivision.com
SIC: 3069 Molded rubber products

(G-13754)
PEGASUS INDUSTRIES INC
12380 Beech Daly Rd (48239-2433)
PHONE..................................313 937-0770
Kenneth P Zecman, *President*
Kris Zecman, *Principal*
Kurt Zecman, *Principal*
EMP: 17 **EST:** 1980
SALES (est): 2.4MM **Privately Held**
WEB: www.pegasustcs.com
SIC: 3544 Special dies & tools

(G-13755)
PET TREATS PLUS
14141 Marion (48239-2843)
PHONE..................................313 533-1701
Fax: 313 533-4031
EMP: 10
SALES (est): 852.8K **Privately Held**
SIC: 2048 Mfg Prepared Feeds

(G-13756)
PISTON AUTOMOTIVE LLC (HQ)
12723 Telegraph Rd Ste 1 (48239-1489)
PHONE..................................313 541-8674
Robert Holloway, *President*
Vincent Johnson, *Chairman*
Amit Singhi, *COO*
David Chon, *Vice Pres*
Frank W Ervin III, *Vice Pres*
◆ **EMP:** 300 **EST:** 1997
SQ FT: 260,000
SALES (est): 1.1B
SALES (corp-wide): 2.3B **Privately Held**
WEB: www.pistongroup.com
SIC: 3714 Motor vehicle parts & accessories
PA: Piston Group, L.L.C.
3000 Town Ctr Ste 3250
Southfield MI 48075
248 226-3976

(G-13757)
PLASTICRAFTS INC
25675 W 8 Mile Rd (48240-1007)
PHONE..................................313 532-1900
Rajni Dhawan, *President*
Anil Dhawan, *Vice Pres*
Angela Hamilton, *Executive*
▲ **EMP:** 5 **EST:** 1980
SQ FT: 14,840
SALES (est): 666.4K **Privately Held**
WEB: www.plasticrafts.com
SIC: 3993 3089 Signs, not made in custom sign painting shops; plastic containers, except foam; kitchenware, plastic; organizers for closets, drawers, etc.: plastic

(G-13758)
POSITIVE TOOL & ENGINEERING CO
26025 W 7 Mile Rd (48240-1846)
PHONE..................................313 532-1674
Robert J Hewitt, *President*
EMP: 4 **EST:** 1960
SQ FT: 3,200
SALES (est): 434.9K **Privately Held**
SIC: 3544 Special dies & tools; jigs & fixtures

(G-13759)
PRINT 4 U PROMOTIONAL PRTG LLC
8211 Chatham (48239-1109)
PHONE..................................313 575-1080
Melissa Stewart, *Principal*
EMP: 5 **EST:** 2009
SALES (est): 127.1K **Privately Held**
WEB: www.stewartpromos.com
SIC: 2752 Commercial printing, lithographic

(G-13760)
QUALITY TOOL & GEAR INC
12693 Marlin Dr (48239-2765)
PHONE..................................734 266-1500
Domenico Pelle, *President*
Angelo Berlase, *Vice Pres*
Fred Pelle, *Vice Pres*
Joe Pelle, *Opers Mgr*
Kathy Diovardi, *Office Mgr*
EMP: 25 **EST:** 1994
SQ FT: 23,000
SALES (est): 4.1MM **Privately Held**
WEB: www.qualitytoolandgear.com
SIC: 3599 Machine shop, jobbing & repair

(G-13761)
RAR GROUP INC
Also Called: Pinnacle Printing & Promotions
19994 Lennane (48240-1023)
PHONE..................................248 353-2266
Richard M Reinman, *President*
Ann Reinman, *Admin Sec*
EMP: 6 **EST:** 1984 **Privately Held**
SIC: 2752 Commercial printing, offset

(G-13762)
RATIO MACHINING INC
12214 Woodbine (48239-2420)
PHONE..................................313 531-5155
EMP: 4
SALES (est): 410K **Privately Held**
SIC: 3599 Mfg Industrial Machinery

(G-13763)
RCD QUALITY COATINGS
15534 Dixie (48239-3602)
PHONE..................................313 575-8125
Richard Davis, *Principal*
EMP: 5 **EST:** 2013
SALES (est): 96.3K **Privately Held**
SIC: 3479 Metal coating & allied service

(G-13764)
REYNOLDS CNTRLESS GRINDING LLC
26730 W Davison (48239-2705)
PHONE..................................313 418-5109
EMP: 5 **EST:** 2018
SALES (est): 151.5K **Privately Held**
SIC: 3999 Custom pulverizing & grinding of plastic materials

(G-13765)
RICH MARS MOBILE SPA LLC
13464 Garfield (48239-4512)
PHONE..................................734 210-2797
Jamar Marshall, *Mng Member*
EMP: 5 **EST:** 2020
SALES (est): 20K **Privately Held**
WEB: www.t-mobile.com
SIC: 3589 Car washing machinery

(G-13766)
ROUSH INDUSTRIES INC
12100 Inkster Rd (48239-2573)
PHONE..................................313 937-8603
EMP: 12 **EST:** 2016
SALES (est): 171.1K **Privately Held**
WEB: www.roush.com
SIC: 3999 Manufacturing industries

(G-13767)
ROYAL CABINETS
15730 Telegraph Rd (48239-3530)
PHONE..................................313 541-1190
Hamze Chehade, *Owner*
EMP: 4 **EST:** 2003
SALES (est): 452.1K **Privately Held**
SIC: 2434 Wood kitchen cabinets

(G-13768)
RTG PRODUCTS INC
15924 Centralia (48239-3821)
PHONE..................................734 323-8916
Thomas Kappler, *Principal*
EMP: 8 **EST:** 2011
SALES (est): 841.1K **Privately Held**
SIC: 3612 Transformers, except electric

(G-13769)
RUSAS PRINTING CO INC
26770 Grand River Ave (48240-1529)
P.O. Box 2609, Detroit (48202-0609)
PHONE..................................313 952-2977
Donald Frank Rusas, *President*
EMP: 8 **EST:** 1993
SQ FT: 20,000
SALES (est): 518.2K **Privately Held**
SIC: 2752 Commercial printing, offset

(G-13770)
SATELLITE CONTROLS
13446 Crosley (48239-4519)
PHONE..................................313 532-6848
Stephen Richards, *Principal*
EMP: 6 **EST:** 2010
SALES (est): 135.5K **Privately Held**
SIC: 3663 Space satellite communications equipment

(G-13771)
SHIPPING CONTAINER CORPORATION
26000 Capitol (48239-2402)
PHONE..................................313 937-2411
Joseph Anton Mooter, *President*
Bob Schuelke, *General Mgr*
Geames Bailey, *Manager*
Robert Walker, *Executive*
EMP: 20 **EST:** 1943
SQ FT: 20,000
SALES (est): 2.7MM **Privately Held**
WEB: www.packpros.net
SIC: 2653 Boxes, corrugated: made from purchased materials

(G-13772)
SMEDE-SON STEEL AND SUP CO INC (PA)
12584 Inkster Rd (48239-2569)
PHONE..................................313 937-8300
Albert A Huyser, *President*
Anthony Huyser, *Vice Pres*
Barbara Huyser, *Admin Sec*
EMP: 55 **EST:** 1954
SQ FT: 6,000
SALES (est): 17MM **Privately Held**
WEB: www.smedeson.com
SIC: 3441 5251 Fabricated structural metal; builders' hardware

(G-13773)
SPRAY BOOTH PRODUCTS INC
26211 W 7 Mile Rd (48240-1850)
PHONE..................................313 766-4400
Kenneth Mikols, *President*
Tami Zellner, *Office Mgr*
EMP: 34 **EST:** 2009
SALES (est): 3.3MM **Privately Held**
WEB: www.sprayboothproducts.net
SIC: 1711 3053 5084 Mechanical contractor; packing: steam engines, pipe joints, air compressors, etc.; industrial machinery & equipment

(G-13774)
STEEL INDUSTRIES INC
12600 Beech Daly Rd (48239-2455)
PHONE..................................313 535-8505
Drew F Baker, *President*
Drew Baker, *Exec VP*
Jim Kuehl, *Vice Pres*
Mark Wejroch, *Vice Pres*
Frank Witte, *Plant Mgr*
◆ **EMP:** 175 **EST:** 1913
SQ FT: 217,000
SALES (est): 37.2MM
SALES (corp-wide): 602MM **Privately Held**
WEB: www.afgholdings.com
SIC: 3398 3312 Metal heat treating; forgings, iron & steel
PA: Ameriforge Group Inc.
19450 State Highway 249 # 5
Houston TX 77070
713 393-4200

(G-13775)
STERLING TRUCK AND WSTN STAR (DH)
Also Called: Sterling Trucking
13400 W Outer Dr (48239-1309)
PHONE..................................313 592-4200
Jim Hebe, *President*
John Merrifield, *Senior VP*
◆ **EMP:** 50 **EST:** 1997
SALES (est): 51.9MM
SALES (corp-wide): 182.4B **Privately Held**
WEB: www.daimler-trucksnorthamerica.com
SIC: 3537 Trucks, tractors, loaders, carriers & similar equipment
HQ: Daimler Trucks North America Llc
4555 N Channel Ave
Portland OR 97217
503 745-8000

▲ = Import ▼ =Export
◆ =Import/Export

GEOGRAPHIC SECTION

Reed City - Osceola County (G-13802)

(G-13776)
SY FUEL INC
27360 Grand River Ave (48240-1609)
PHONE..................................313 531-5894
Jim Hamade, *Principal*
EMP: 8 **EST:** 2009
SALES (est): 343.1K **Privately Held**
SIC: 2869 Fuels

(G-13777)
TALENT INDUSTRIES INC
12950 Inkster Rd (48239-3000)
PHONE..................................313 531-4700
William L Randall, *President*
John Robert, *Corp Secy*
Rick Robert, *Vice Pres*
EMP: 15 **EST:** 1956
SQ FT: 7,500
SALES (est): 1.9MM **Privately Held**
WEB: www.talentindustries.us
SIC: 3544 Special dies & tools

(G-13778)
THERMA-TECH ENGINEERING INC
Also Called: A. R. Lintern Division
24900 Capitol (48239-2449)
PHONE..................................313 537-5330
Benjamin Greenberg, *CEO*
Ron O'Dell, *President*
Maryanne Camp, *Vice Pres*
Terri Boyle, *Buyer*
Doug Riddell, *Sales Mgr*
EMP: 30 **EST:** 2004
SALES (est): 5.2MM **Privately Held**
WEB: www.vehicleclimate.com
SIC: 3714 3585 3822 3564 Defrosters, motor vehicle; heaters, motor vehicle; air conditioner parts, motor vehicle; air conditioning, motor vehicle; refrigeration/air-conditioning defrost controls; air cleaning systems

(G-13779)
TOMMIE INC
24801 5 Mile Rd Ste 26 (48239-3653)
PHONE..................................313 377-2931
EMP: 7 **EST:** 2016
SALES (est): 356.8K **Privately Held**
WEB: www.fiwinc.com
SIC: 3599 Machine shop, jobbing & repair

(G-13780)
TRAMAR INDUSTRIES
12693 Marlin Dr (48239-2765)
PHONE..................................313 387-3600
EMP: 6 **EST:** 2019
SALES (est): 152.9K **Privately Held**
WEB: www.tramarindustries.com
SIC: 3999 Manufacturing industries

(G-13781)
ULTRALIGHT PROSTHETICS INC
24781 5 Mile Rd (48239-3632)
PHONE..................................313 538-8500
Jeffery Giacinto, *President*
Joseph Giacinto, *Treasurer*
EMP: 5 **EST:** 1986
SQ FT: 1,100
SALES (est): 518.3K **Privately Held**
WEB: www.ultralightprosthetics.com
SIC: 3842 Limbs, artificial; prosthetic appliances

(G-13782)
V & S DETROIT GALVANIZING LLC
12600 Arnold (48239-2637)
PHONE..................................313 535-2600
Tim Woll, *Principal*
Tom Bottorff, *Plant Mgr*
Don Houston, *Opers Mgr*
EMP: 28 **EST:** 2006
SALES (est): 2.4MM **Privately Held**
WEB: www.hotdipgalvanizing.com
SIC: 3479 Galvanizing of iron, steel or end-formed products

(G-13783)
VARCO PRECISION PRODUCTS CO
26935 W 7 Mile Rd (48240-2008)
PHONE..................................313 538-4300
Donald A Vartoogian, *President*
Sandra Vartoogian, *Corp Secy*
EMP: 6 **EST:** 1949
SQ FT: 6,000
SALES (est): 548.4K **Privately Held**
WEB: www.varcoprecision.com
SIC: 3544 Special dies & tools

(G-13784)
VOIGT SCHWTZER GALVANIZERS INC
12600 Arnold (48239-2637)
PHONE..................................313 535-2600
Werner Niehaus, *President*
Brian Miller, *Vice Pres*
Maia Johnson, *Admin Sec*
EMP: 1 **EST:** 1985
SQ FT: 50,000
SALES (est): 2.2MM
SALES (corp-wide): 878.3MM **Privately Held**
WEB: www.hotdipgalvanizing.com
SIC: 3479 Hot dip coating of metals or formed products; galvanizing of iron, steel or end-formed products
HQ: Voigt & Schweitzer Llc
987 Buckeye Park Rd
Columbus OH 43207
614 449-8281

(G-13785)
W T & M INC
Also Called: Walker Tool & Manufacturing
12635 Arnold (48239-2636)
PHONE..................................313 533-7888
Donald W Hoyt, *President*
Katherine M Hoyt, *Principal*
Nick Cosentino, *Vice Pres*
Kathy Cosentino, *Admin Sec*
EMP: 8 **EST:** 1960
SQ FT: 17,000
SALES (est): 941.2K **Privately Held**
WEB: www.walkertoolmfg.com
SIC: 3599 Machine shop, jobbing & repair

(G-13786)
WE POP CORN LLC
Also Called: Detroit Popcorn Company
14950 Telegraph Rd (48239-3457)
PHONE..................................313 387-1600
Kenneth Harris,
Reginald Kelley Sr,
EMP: 10 **EST:** 2020
SALES (est): 502K **Privately Held**
WEB: www.detroitpopcorn.com
SIC: 2096 Potato chips & similar snacks

(G-13787)
Z TECHNOLOGIES CORPORATION
26500 Capitol (48239-2506)
PHONE..................................313 937-0710
Ellis L Breskman, *President*
Wayne Hall, *Plant Mgr*
Todd Belcher, *QC Mgr*
Ellis Breskman, *Food Svc Dir*
▲ **EMP:** 25 **EST:** 1996
SQ FT: 60,000
SALES (est): 7.6MM **Privately Held**
WEB: www.ztechcoatings.com
SIC: 2891 3479 2851 Sealants; coating of metals & formed products; paints & paint additives; epoxy coatings

Reed City
Osceola County

(G-13788)
AXLINE ADVANCED INDUSTRIES
229 W North Ave (49677-1030)
PHONE..................................231 679-7907
Joshua Axline, *Principal*
EMP: 4 **EST:** 2015
SALES (est): 98.8K **Privately Held**
SIC: 3999 Manufacturing industries

(G-13789)
BCT-2017 INC (PA)
Also Called: Bentek
710 E Church Ave (49677-9194)
P.O. Box 1117, Big Rapids (49307-0307)
PHONE..................................231 832-3114
Thomas C Benedict, *President*
EMP: 29 **EST:** 1983
SQ FT: 22,000
SALES (est): 2.7MM **Privately Held**
SIC: 3599 Machine shop, jobbing & repair

(G-13790)
GENERAL MILLS INC
128 E Slosson Ave (49677-1229)
PHONE..................................231 832-3285
David Rohdy, *Mfg Staff*
Jim Dawson, *Engineer*
Carol McKernan, *Train & Dev Mgr*
Dan Boerma, *Sales Staff*
David Towner, *Manager*
EMP: 25
SALES (corp-wide): 18.1B **Publicly Held**
WEB: www.generalmills.com
SIC: 2026 2041 Yogurt; flour mixes
PA: General Mills, Inc.
1 General Mills Blvd
Minneapolis MN 55426
763 764-7600

(G-13791)
HYDROLAKE INC
420 S Roth St Ste A (49677-9115)
P.O. Box 88 (49677-0088)
PHONE..................................231 825-2233
Mike Bigford, *Principal*
EMP: 6 **Privately Held**
WEB: www.uscco.com
SIC: 2499 Poles, wood
HQ: Hydrolake, Inc
6151 W Gerwoude Dr
Mc Bain MI 49657
231 825-2233

(G-13792)
JC METAL FABRICATING INC
21831 9 Mile Rd (49677-8466)
PHONE..................................231 629-0425
John Cook, *President*
EMP: 13 **EST:** 2005
SALES (est): 1.9MM **Privately Held**
WEB: www.cookmfg.com
SIC: 3441 Fabricated structural metal

(G-13793)
KRAFTUBE INC
925 E Church Ave (49677-9196)
PHONE..................................231 832-5562
John Kinnally, *President*
Kevin Kinnally, *President*
Mike Kinnally, *Purchasing*
Scott Gray, *Engineer*
Todd Reitzel, *Engineer*
▲ **EMP:** 145 **EST:** 1946
SQ FT: 100,000
SALES (est): 20.3MM **Privately Held**
WEB: www.kraftube.com
SIC: 3444 3441 3585 3544 Furnace casings, sheet metal; fabricated structural metal; refrigeration & heating equipment; die sets for metal stamping (presses)

(G-13794)
KRAUTER FOREST PRODUCTS LLC
21224 Sylvan Rd (49677-7911)
PHONE..................................815 317-6561
Ashley Adams, *Office Mgr*
Thomas D Krauter,
EMP: 15 **EST:** 2010
SQ FT: 18,000
SALES (est): 866.5K **Privately Held**
SIC: 2448 Pallets, wood

(G-13795)
MARTINREA INDUSTRIES INC
Reed City Tool and Die
603 E Church Ave (49677-9102)
PHONE..................................231 832-5504
Ardy Rasmussen, *Purch Agent*
Rod Weck, *Chief Mktg Ofcr*
Kris Raymond, *Office Mgr*
EMP: 22
SQ FT: 85,000
SALES (corp-wide): 2.5B **Privately Held**
WEB: www.martinrea.com
SIC: 3317 3089 3544 3542 Steel pipe & tubes; plastic processing; special dies, tools, jigs & fixtures; machine tools, metal forming type
HQ: Martinrea Industries, Inc.
10501 Mi State Road 52
Manchester MI 48158
734 428-2400

(G-13796)
NABCO INC (DH)
660 Commerce Dr (49677-9300)
PHONE..................................231 832-2001
Lyle Lodholtz, *Division Mgr*
Ron Johnson, *Manager*
EMP: 50 **EST:** 1968
SQ FT: 92,000
SALES (est): 5.6MM
SALES (corp-wide): 10.1B **Publicly Held**
SIC: 5063 5013 3694 3625 Motor controls, starters & relays: electric; alternators; engine electrical equipment; relays & industrial controls

(G-13797)
REED CITY GROUP LLC
603 E Church Ave (49677-9102)
PHONE..................................231 832-7500
John Barnett, *CEO*
Bill Dunlop, *Business Mgr*
Bob Apsey, *Plant Mgr*
Martin Mund, *Opers Staff*
Mike Seay, *Accounts Mgr*
▲ **EMP:** 97 **EST:** 2009
SQ FT: 82,000
SALES (est): 17.4MM **Privately Held**
WEB: www.reedcitygroup.com
SIC: 3089 Injection molding of plastics

(G-13798)
SMART POWER SYSTEMS INC
5000 N Us 131 (49677)
PHONE..................................231 832-5525
Norman Rautiola, *President*
Arvilla H Hepner, *Vice Pres*
Minesh Patel, *Technology*
EMP: 200
SALES (est): 12.9MM **Privately Held**
WEB: www.smartpower.com
SIC: 3621 Generators & sets, electric

(G-13799)
SRM CONCRETE LLC
Also Called: Lc Redi Mix
955 E Church Ave (49677-9196)
PHONE..................................231 832-5460
Denny Daniels, *Manager*
EMP: 9
SALES (corp-wide): 170.1MM **Privately Held**
WEB: www.smyrnareadymix.com
SIC: 3273 Ready-mixed concrete
PA: Srm Concrete, Llc
1136 2nd Ave N
Nashville TN 37208
615 355-1028

(G-13800)
THORN CREEK LUMBER LLC
9676 S Hawkins Rd (49677-8702)
PHONE..................................231 832-1600
David Miller, *President*
John Kaufman,
James Miller,
EMP: 8 **EST:** 1991
SALES (est): 690K **Privately Held**
WEB: www.thorn-creek-lumber-llc-mi-1.hub.biz
SIC: 2421 Sawmills & planing mills, general

(G-13801)
TUBELITE INC
4878 Mackinaw Trl (49677-9186)
PHONE..................................800 866-2227
Ken Werbowy, *President*
Gary R Johnson, *Vice Pres*
Terry Britt, *Client Mgr*
Tom Minnon, *Sales Staff*
Uriah Maczala, *Marketing Staff*
EMP: 53
SALES (corp-wide): 1.2B **Publicly Held**
WEB: www.tubeliteinc.com
SIC: 3449 Miscellaneous metalwork
HQ: Tubelite Inc.
3056 Walker Ridge Dr Nw
Walker MI 49544

(G-13802)
UTILITY SUPPLY AND CNSTR CO (PA)
420 S Roth St Ste A (49677-9115)
PHONE..................................231 832-2297
Michael Bigford, *President*
Franklin C Wheatlake, *Principal*

(PA)=Parent Co (HQ)=Headquarters (DH)=Div Headquarters
✪ = New Business established in last 2 years

Reed City - Osceola County (G-13803)

James Balkonis, *Vice Pres*
Brad Hilliard, *Vice Pres*
Kent Lawrence, *Engineer*
EMP: 3 **EST:** 2007
SALES (est): 218.9MM **Privately Held**
WEB: www.uscco.com
SIC: 2411 2491 2631 5063 Logging; wood preserving; coated & treated board; electrical supplies

(G-13803)
UUSI LLC
Also Called: Nartron
5000 Old Us Highway 131 (49677-7922)
PHONE..................................231 832-5513
Bradley Looy, *Vice Pres*
Norman Rautiola
▲ **EMP:** 75 **EST:** 1968
SQ FT: 210,000
SALES (est): 13.8MM **Privately Held**
SIC: 3674 Semiconductors & related devices

(G-13804)
YOPLAIT USA
128 E Slosson Ave (49677-1229)
P.O. Box 33 (49677-0033)
PHONE..................................231 832-3285
Dave Towner, *President*
EMP: 16 **EST:** 2008
SALES (est): 2.2MM **Privately Held**
WEB: www.yoplait.com
SIC: 2026 Fluid milk

Reese
Tuscola County

(G-13805)
ADVANCED MCRONUTRIENT PDTS INC
Also Called: A M P
2405 W Vassar Rd (48757-9340)
PHONE..................................989 752-2138
Robert Bowen, *President*
John Bowen, *Vice Pres*
Terry Hart, *Plant Mgr*
Mark Whitfield, *CFO*
◆ **EMP:** 30 **EST:** 2014
SALES (est): 5.9MM
SALES (corp-wide): 21.1MM **Privately Held**
WEB: www.cameronchemicals.com
SIC: 2873 Fertilizers: natural (organic), except compost
PA: Cameron Chemicals, Inc.
    4530 Prof Cir Ste 201
    Virginia Beach VA 23455
    757 487-0656

(G-13806)
GREENIA CUSTOM WOODWORKING INC
2380 W Vassar Rd (48757-9300)
PHONE..................................989 868-9790
Thomas Greenia, *President*
Kathleen Greenia, *Vice Pres*
EMP: 21 **EST:** 1979
SQ FT: 60,000
SALES (est): 1.6MM **Privately Held**
WEB: www.carlislelaw.net
SIC: 5211 5031 2434 1751 Millwork & lumber; lumber, plywood & millwork; building materials, exterior; building materials, interior; wood kitchen cabinets; carpentry work

(G-13807)
REIS CUSTOM CABINETS
1398 S Bradford Rd (48757-9541)
PHONE..................................586 791-4925
Randy Reis, *Owner*
Tamala Reis, *Manager*
EMP: 4 **EST:** 1990
SALES (est): 246.5K **Privately Held**
SIC: 2541 5712 5211 Cabinets, lockers & shelving; cabinet work, custom; cabinets, kitchen

(G-13808)
ROHLOFF BUILDERS INC
Also Called: Oak Tree Cabinet & Woodworking
9916 Saginaw St (48757-9401)
P.O. Box 158 (48757-0158)
PHONE..................................989 868-3191
Steve Rohloff, *President*
EMP: 9 **EST:** 1936
SQ FT: 3,840
SALES (est): 277.3K **Privately Held**
WEB: www.oaktreecabinets.com
SIC: 2434 Wood kitchen cabinets

(G-13809)
T & L PRODUCTS
2586 S Bradleyville Rd (48757-9214)
PHONE..................................989 868-4428
Thomas K Kabat, *Owner*
EMP: 6 **EST:** 1990
SALES (est): 564.6K **Privately Held**
WEB: www.tandlproducts.com
SIC: 5088 3429 Marine supplies; marine hardware

(G-13810)
VOORHEIS HAUSBECK EXCAVATING
2695 W Vassar Rd (48757-9352)
P.O. Box 375 (48757-0375)
PHONE..................................989 752-9666
Donald N Voorheis, *President*
Dave Hausbeck, *Owner*
EMP: 25 **EST:** 1972
SQ FT: 2,000
SALES (est): 617K **Privately Held**
WEB: www.dht-inc.com
SIC: 1794 3273 Excavation & grading, building construction; ready-mixed concrete

(G-13811)
WILFRED SWARTZ & SWARTZ G
11465 Holland Rd (48757-9309)
PHONE..................................989 652-6322
Wilfred Swartz, *Manager*
EMP: 4 **EST:** 2000
SALES (est): 146K **Privately Held**
SIC: 3993 Signs & advertising specialties

Remus
Mecosta County

(G-13812)
AIRPLANE FACTORY
6400 W Lake Shore Dr (49340-9643)
PHONE..................................989 561-5381
John Manley, *Principal*
EMP: 4 **EST:** 2005
SALES (est): 134.7K **Privately Held**
SIC: 3999 Airplane models, except toy

(G-13813)
BANDIT INDUSTRIES INC
6750 W Millbrook Rd (49340-9662)
PHONE..................................989 561-2270
Jerry M Morey, *President*
Dianne C Morey, *Vice Pres*
Ben Fox, *Production*
Amelia McCreight, *Production*
Ben Bigelow, *Engineer*
◆ **EMP:** 400 **EST:** 1988
SQ FT: 12,000
SALES (est): 101.6MM **Privately Held**
WEB: www.banditchippers.com
SIC: 3531 5082 Chippers: brush, limb & log; logging & forestry machinery & equipment

(G-13814)
BRIAN A BROOMFIELD
Also Called: B&B Dumpsters
14776 10th Ave (49340-9787)
PHONE..................................989 309-0709
Brian A Broomfield, *Principal*
EMP: 6 **EST:** 2012
SALES (est): 134.7K **Privately Held**
SIC: 3443 Dumpsters, garbage

(G-13815)
LEPRINO FOODS COMPANY
311 N Sheridan Ave (49340-9114)
P.O. Box 208 (49340-0208)
PHONE..................................989 967-3635
Dennis Turgeon, *Maint Spvr*
Marianne Thomsen, *Plt & Fclts Mgr*
Kathryn McLeod, *Manager*
Megan Blamer, *Supervisor*
Neal Smith, *Info Tech Mgr*
EMP: 253
SALES (corp-wide): 1.9B **Privately Held**
WEB: www.leprinofoods.com
SIC: 2022 Natural cheese
PA: Leprino Foods Company
    1830 W 38th Ave
    Denver CO 80211
    303 480-2600

(G-13816)
LOR PRODUCTS INC
2962 16 Mile Rd (49340-9516)
PHONE..................................989 382-9020
Duane Martin, *President*
Christina Martin, *Admin Sec*
EMP: 7 **EST:** 1994
SALES (est): 590.1K **Privately Held**
WEB: www.lorproducts.com
SIC: 3449 Miscellaneous metalwork

(G-13817)
SMORACY LLC
6750 W Millbrook Rd (49340-9662)
PHONE..................................989 561-2270
Craig Davis, *Sales Staff*
Jerry M Morey
EMP: 7 **EST:** 1998
SALES (est): 942.3K **Privately Held**
WEB: www.banditchippers.com
SIC: 3599 Custom machinery

(G-13818)
TRELAN MANUFACTURING
498 8 Mile Rd (49340-9316)
PHONE..................................989 561-2280
Nell Schumacher, *President*
EMP: 18 **EST:** 2000
SQ FT: 45,000
SALES (est): 1.8MM **Privately Held**
WEB: www.trelan.com
SIC: 3531 Chippers: brush, limb & log

Republic
Marquette County

(G-13819)
ANTILLA LOGGING INC
7794 State Highway M95 (49879-9041)
PHONE..................................906 376-2374
Oscar Antilla, *President*
David Antilla, *Corp Secy*
Joan Antilla, *Vice Pres*
EMP: 6 **EST:** 1958
SALES (est): 689K **Privately Held**
WEB: www.grandvillefamilydentalcare.com
SIC: 2411 Logging camps & contractors

(G-13820)
DILLON FOREST PRODUCTS INC
Also Called: Dillon Forest Products
2666 State Highway M95 (49879-9210)
P.O. Box 94 (49879-0094)
PHONE..................................906 869-4671
Timothy Dillon, *President*
Charles Dillon, *President*
EMP: 6 **EST:** 1975
SALES (est): 759.2K **Privately Held**
SIC: 2411 Pulpwood camp not operating a pulp mill at same site

(G-13821)
WILLIAM S WIXTROM
Also Called: Wixtrom Lumber Co
2131 County Road 601 (49879-9167)
PHONE..................................906 376-8247
William S Wixtrom, *Owner*
EMP: 4 **EST:** 1963
SQ FT: 12,000
SALES (est): 385.5K **Privately Held**
SIC: 2421 5031 2431 2426 Sawmills & planing mills, general; lumber: rough, dressed & finished; millwork; hardwood dimension & flooring mills

Rhodes
Gladwin County

(G-13822)
BRADLEY ALLEN INTERIORS INC
6788 N Swede Rd (48652-9613)
PHONE..................................989 689-6770
EMP: 8
SALES (est): 1.2MM **Privately Held**
SIC: 2434 Mfg Wood Kitchen Cabinets

(G-13823)
VALLEY VENTURES MAPPING LLC
2555 Pinconning Rd (48652-9535)
PHONE..................................989 879-5023
Jeramey Valley, *Owner*
EMP: 5 **EST:** 2011
SALES (est): 142.8K **Privately Held**
WEB: www.vvmapping.com
SIC: 3799 All terrain vehicles (ATV)

Richland
Kalamazoo County

(G-13824)
EILEEN SMELTZER
Also Called: Chaubrei Gardens
8227 N 30th St (49083-9743)
PHONE..................................269 629-8056
Eileen Smeltzer, *Owner*
EMP: 5 **EST:** 1986
SALES (est): 249.1K **Privately Held**
SIC: 3999 Artificial flower arrangements

(G-13825)
FUSION FLEXO LLC (PA)
6330 Canterwood Dr (49083-8431)
PHONE..................................269 685-5827
Brian Anderson, *CEO*
Grayce Lancaster, *Vice Pres*
EMP: 6 **EST:** 2014
SALES (est): 1.3MM **Privately Held**
WEB: www.fusionflexo.com
SIC: 2796 Photoengraving plates, linecuts or halftones

(G-13826)
PARKER-HANNIFIN CORPORATION
Pneumatic North America
8676 M 89 (49083-9580)
PHONE..................................269 629-5000
Melissa Dalrymple, *Engineer*
Timothy Miller, *Engineer*
Rick Prather, *Engineer*
Gerald Ebel, *Branch Mgr*
Cheryl Emanuel, *Manager*
EMP: 350
SALES (corp-wide): 13.7B **Publicly Held**
WEB: www.parker.com
SIC: 3494 3613 3612 3593 Valves & pipe fittings; switchgear & switchboard apparatus; transformers, except electric; fluid power cylinders & actuators; blowers & fans; fluid power valves & hose fittings
PA: Parker-Hannifin Corporation
    6035 Parkland Blvd
    Cleveland OH 44124
    216 896-3000

(G-13827)
PRINTEX PRINTING & GRAPHICS
8988 E D Ave (49083-8442)
PHONE..................................269 629-0122
James Berry, *Owner*
Marlene Berry, *Principal*
EMP: 5 **EST:** 1989
SQ FT: 1,400
SALES (est): 260K **Privately Held**
WEB: www.printexfullcolor.com
SIC: 2752 Commercial printing, offset

▲ = Import ▼ = Export
◆ = Import/Export

GEOGRAPHIC SECTION   River Rouge - Wayne County (G-13856)

(G-13828)
RICHLAND MACHINE & PUMP CO
9854 M 89 (49083-9645)
PHONE 269 629-4344
Jerome Bohl Jr, *CEO*
Joseph Bohl, *CFO*
EMP: 9 **EST:** 1984
SQ FT: 13,000
SALES (est): 963K **Privately Held**
SIC: 3599 7699 Machine shop, jobbing & repair; industrial machinery & equipment repair

(G-13829)
SHEPHERD SPECIALITY PAPERS INC (PA)
10211 M 89 Ste 230 (49083-8308)
P.O. Box 346 (49083-0346)
PHONE 269 629-8001
Joel M Shepherd III, *President*
Dina Waddell, *General Mgr*
Rene Ketelsen, *Regl Sales Mgr*
Rene Croskey, *Cust Mgr*
Dina K Waddell, *Admin Sec*
◆ **EMP:** 9 **EST:** 1981
SQ FT: 75,000
SALES (est): 7.2MM **Privately Held**
WEB: www.ssponline.com
SIC: 2679 Paper products, converted

(G-13830)
STEDMAN CORP
10301 M 89 (49083-9347)
PHONE 269 629-5930
William Hannapel, *President*
EMP: 5 **EST:** 1992
SQ FT: 6,000
SALES (est): 541.6K **Privately Held**
WEB: www.stedmanusa.com
SIC: 3651 5736 Microphones; musical instrument stores

Richmond
Macomb County

(G-13831)
ADVANTAGE DESIGN AND TOOL
35800 Big Hand Rd (48062-4204)
PHONE 586 801-7413
Michelle Kerner, *President*
Joseph Torregrossa, *Vice Pres*
EMP: 7 **EST:** 1990
SALES (est): 545.6K **Privately Held**
WEB: www.advantagedesign.com
SIC: 3544 3545 Jigs & fixtures; gauges (machine tool accessories)

(G-13832)
ALLWOOD BUILDING COMPONENTS
35377 Division Rd (48062-1301)
P.O. Box 547 (48062-0547)
PHONE 586 727-2731
Eric O Lundquist, *President*
Irvin Strickstein, *Admin Sec*
EMP: 65 **EST:** 1980
SQ FT: 26,000
SALES (est): 6.3MM **Privately Held**
WEB: www.allwoodbc.com
SIC: 2439 Trusses, except roof: laminated lumber

(G-13833)
B & D PUBLISHING LLC
35688 Diane Ln (48062-1600)
PHONE 586 651-3623
Dietrich Maerz, *Owner*
EMP: 5 **EST:** 2016
SALES (est): 112.6K **Privately Held**
SIC: 2741 Miscellaneous publishing

(G-13834)
B & H PLASTIC CO INC
66725 S Forest Ave (48062)
P.O. Box 117 (48062-0117)
PHONE 586 727-7100
Hiram J S Badia, *President*
Judith Badia, *Vice Pres*
John Badia, *Director*
EMP: 10 **EST:** 1982
SQ FT: 9,000
SALES (est): 834.2K **Privately Held**
SIC: 3089 Injection molding of plastics

(G-13835)
DARK STAR PUBLISHING
34633 Cedar Rdg (48062-5571)
PHONE 810 858-1135
Dayne Edmondson, *Principal*
EMP: 4 **EST:** 2017
SALES (est): 51.8K **Privately Held**
SIC: 2741 Miscellaneous publishing

(G-13836)
DOUGLAS GAGE INC
69681 Lowe Plank Rd (48062-5345)
PHONE 586 727-2089
Kennth Loria, *President*
Douglas Clark, *President*
EMP: 15 **EST:** 1980
SQ FT: 6,000
SALES (est): 1.5MM **Privately Held**
WEB: www.douglasgage.net
SIC: 3545 Gauges (machine tool accessories)

(G-13837)
EMPIRE HARDCHROME
33450 Bordman Rd (48062-2306)
PHONE 810 392-3122
William Hall, *Principal*
EMP: 5 **EST:** 2003
SALES (est): 126.8K **Privately Held**
SIC: 3471 Chromium plating of metals or formed products

(G-13838)
GIOVANNIS APPTZING FD PDTS INC
37775 Division Rd (48062-5422)
P.O. Box 26 (48062-0026)
PHONE 773 960-1945
Philip Ricossa, *President*
Giovanni Ricossa, *Vice Pres*
▲ **EMP:** 5 **EST:** 1933
SQ FT: 1,700
SALES (est): 659.5K **Privately Held**
WEB: www.gioapp.com
SIC: 2099 Food preparations

(G-13839)
GREAT LAKES PHOTO INC
29080 Armada Ridge Rd (48062-4509)
PHONE 586 784-5446
Mark Ezzo, *President*
Victoria Ezzo, *Vice Pres*
Cheryl Ezzo, *Admin Sec*
EMP: 4 **EST:** 1977
SQ FT: 3,300
SALES (est): 300K **Privately Held**
SIC: 7221 2732 School photographer; books: printing & binding

(G-13840)
HOLZ ENTERPRISES INC
37994 Weber Rd (48062-3122)
PHONE 810 392-2840
Mark Holz, *Owner*
EMP: 4 **EST:** 2005
SALES (est): 74.1K **Privately Held**
SIC: 3799 Transportation equipment

(G-13841)
MG WELDING INC
76380 Andrews Rd (48062-3705)
PHONE 586 405-2909
EMP: 4 **EST:** 2016
SALES (est): 25K **Privately Held**
SIC: 7692 Welding repair

(G-13842)
MIRKWOOD PROPERTIES INC
Also Called: Miller Transit Mix
35555 Division Rd (48062-1387)
PHONE 586 727-3363
Terry Miller, *President*
Gayl Miller, *Corp Secy*
Alan Miller, *Vice Pres*
EMP: 5 **EST:** 1923
SQ FT: 2,400
SALES (est): 972.7K **Privately Held**
SIC: 6512 3273 Commercial & industrial building operation; ready-mixed concrete

(G-13843)
NEW IMAGE DENTAL P C
35000 Division Rd Ste 4 (48062-1566)
PHONE 586 727-1100
Daryl Thomas Peraino, *Principal*
EMP: 8 **EST:** 2007
SALES (est): 466.9K **Privately Held**
SIC: 3843 Enamels, dentists'

(G-13844)
PRINT ALL
69347 N Main St (48062-1144)
PHONE 586 430-4383
Eric Gordon, *Principal*
Michelle Aiken, *CFO*
Sarah Roose, *Graphic Designe*
EMP: 6 **EST:** 2015
SALES (est): 268.6K **Privately Held**
WEB: www.miprintall.com
SIC: 2752 Commercial printing, offset

(G-13845)
PROSPER-TECH MACHINE & TL LLC
69160 Skinner Dr (48062-1538)
PHONE 586 727-8800
Heidi Devroy, *Mng Member*
Robert Devroy,
EMP: 11 **EST:** 2007
SALES (est): 1.1MM **Privately Held**
WEB: www.prosper-tech.net
SIC: 3544 3599 Special dies, tools, jigs & fixtures; machine shop, jobbing & repair

(G-13846)
THREADED PRODUCTS CO
68750 Oak St (48062-1267)
P.O. Box 26, Grafton OH (44044-0026)
PHONE 586 727-3435
Kevin Flanigan, *President*
Daneil W Sedor, *Corp Secy*
EMP: 23 **EST:** 1957
SALES (est): 1.4MM **Privately Held**
SIC: 3321 3366 Pressure pipe & fittings, cast iron; bushings & bearings, brass (nonmachined)

(G-13847)
U S PATTERN COMPANY INC
69150 Skinner Dr (48062-1538)
P.O. Box 220 (48062-0220)
PHONE 586 727-2896
Louis M Trautman, *President*
Michael R Trautman, *Vice Pres*
Mary Leonard, *Treasurer*
EMP: 26 **EST:** 1940
SQ FT: 30,000
SALES (est): 3.2MM **Privately Held**
WEB: www.uspattern.com
SIC: 3543 Industrial patterns

Riga
Lenawee County

(G-13848)
DENUDTS PORTABLE WELDING
12152 Wegner Rd (49276-9701)
PHONE 517 605-5154
Michael Denudt, *Owner*
EMP: 4 **EST:** 2018
SALES (est): 25K **Privately Held**
WEB: www.denudtswelding.com
SIC: 7692 Welding repair

Riley
St. Clair County

(G-13849)
DRW SYSTEMS CARBIDE LLC
12618 Masters Rd (48041-2304)
PHONE 810 392-3526
David Rushing, *Principal*
EMP: 8 **EST:** 2005
SALES (est): 592.7K **Privately Held**
SIC: 2819 Carbides

(G-13850)
GRACE ENGINEERING CORP
11501 Lambs Rd (48041-3107)
P.O. Box 202, Memphis (48041-0202)
PHONE 810 392-2181
Louis Grace, *President*
EMP: 25
SALES (corp-wide): 9.4MM **Privately Held**
WEB: www.graceeng.com
SIC: 3544 Special dies, tools, jigs & fixtures
PA: Grace Engineering Corp.
  34775 Potter St
  Memphis MI 48041
  810 392-2181

(G-13851)
JOSEPH D ECKENSWILLER
27759 Bordman Rd (48041-4013)
PHONE 586 784-8542
Joseph D Eckenswiller, *Principal*
EMP: 5 **EST:** 2010
SALES (est): 118.6K **Privately Held**
SIC: 2711 Newspapers, publishing & printing

River Rouge
Wayne County

(G-13852)
BUCKLIN TOWNSHIP CANDLES LLC
111 Walnut St (48218-1545)
PHONE 248 403-0600
Chad Duffie, *Principal*
EMP: 4 **EST:** 2012
SALES (est): 77.7K **Privately Held**
WEB: www.apothe.boutique
SIC: 3999 Candles

(G-13853)
CARMEUSE LIME INC
Also Called: Carmeuse Lime & Stone
25 Marion Ave (48218-1469)
P.O. Box 18118 (48218-0118)
PHONE 313 849-9268
Thomas A Buck, *CEO*
Jeffrey Bittner, *General Mgr*
EMP: 123
SQ FT: 900
SALES (corp-wide): 177.9K **Privately Held**
SIC: 1422 Crushed & broken limestone
HQ: Carmeuse Lime, Inc.
  11 Stanwix St Fl 21
  Pittsburgh PA 15222
  412 995-5500

(G-13854)
FURNACES OVENS & BATHS INC
195 Campbell St (48218-1001)
PHONE 248 625-7400
Jeffrey Hynes, *President*
Jennifer Calhoun, *Vice Pres*
Karen Hynes, *Vice Pres*
EMP: 4 **EST:** 1980
SQ FT: 25,000
SALES (est): 851.7K **Privately Held**
WEB: www.fobinc.com
SIC: 3567 Heating units & devices, industrial: electric

(G-13855)
GOLDEN SATCHEL LLC
402 Palmerston St (48218-1142)
PHONE 248 636-0550
Tijuan Cash, *Principal*
EMP: 4 **EST:** 2016
SALES (est): 77.4K **Privately Held**
SIC: 3161 Satchels

(G-13856)
INTERNTNAL PRCAST SLUTIONS LLC
60 Haltiner St (48218-1259)
PHONE 313 843-0073
Loris Collavino, *CEO*
Don Little, *President*
Anil Mehta, *Vice Pres*
Paul Phillips, *Vice Pres*
Ian Donald, *Project Mgr*
EMP: 100 **EST:** 2008

River Rouge - Wayne County (G-13857)

SALES (est): 23.5MM
SALES (corp-wide): 28.2MM **Privately Held**
WEB: www.theprecaster.com
SIC: 3272 Concrete products, precast
PA: Prestressed Systems Incorporated
4955 Walker Rd
Windsor ON N9A 6
519 737-1216

(G-13857)
KEYSTONE MANUFACTURING
100 E Cicotte St (48218-1653)
PHONE.................................248 796-2546
Varadee Dunaskis, *Owner*
EMP: 7 **EST**: 2017
SALES (est): 98.6K **Privately Held**
WEB: www.keystonehydraulics.com
SIC: 3599 Machine shop, jobbing & repair

(G-13858)
NICHOLSON TERMINAL & DOCK CO (PA)
380 E Great Lakes St (48218-2606)
P.O. Box 18066 (48218-0066)
PHONE.................................313 842-4300
Daniel Deane, *President*
Thomas Deane, *Vice Pres*
Patrick Sutka, *Treasurer*
Brendan Deane, *Asst Sec*
▲ **EMP**: 100 **EST**: 1928
SALES (est): 14.8MM **Privately Held**
WEB: www.nicholson-terminal.com
SIC: 4491 3731 4225 7692 Marine terminals; shipbuilding & repairing; general warehousing; welding repair; sheet metalwork; fabricated plate work (boiler shop)

(G-13859)
PRESTRESSED GROUP
60 Haltiner St (48218-1259)
PHONE.................................313 962-9189
Ken Borman, *Principal*
Gil Gallego, *QC Mgr*
Alex Baker, *Controller*
EMP: 9 **EST**: 2016
SALES (est): 387.6K **Privately Held**
WEB: www.theprecaster.com
SIC: 3272 Concrete products

(G-13860)
SHELL LUBRICANTS
245 Marion Ave (48218-2603)
PHONE.................................313 354-1187
EMP: 7 **EST**: 2019
SALES (est): 494.2K **Privately Held**
WEB: www.shell.us
SIC: 2992 Lubricating oils & greases

(G-13861)
UNITED STATES GYPSUM COMPANY
10090 W Jefferson Ave (48218-1363)
PHONE.................................313 624-4232
Michael Inman, *Engineer*
Kevin Rennie, *Branch Mgr*
EMP: 70
SALES (corp-wide): 10.7B **Privately Held**
WEB: www.usg.com
SIC: 3275 Gypsum products
HQ: United States Gypsum Company
550 W Adams St Ste 1300
Chicago IL 60661
312 606-4000

(G-13862)
US GYPSUM CO
10090 W Jefferson Ave (48218-1363)
PHONE.................................313 842-5800
Jim Sherwin, *Principal*
EMP: 9 **EST**: 2009
SALES (est): 257.2K **Privately Held**
SIC: 3275 Gypsum products

Riverdale
Gratiot County

(G-13863)
DANIEL D SLATER
Also Called: Log Cabin Lumber
10361 W Van Buren Rd (48877-9708)
PHONE.................................989 833-7135
Daniel E Slater, *Owner*

EMP: 4 **EST**: 1982
SQ FT: 5,700
SALES (est): 700K **Privately Held**
WEB: www.trimfromatree.com
SIC: 5031 5211 2431 2421 Lumber: rough, dressed & finished; lumber & other building materials; millwork; sawmills & planing mills, general

Riverside
Berrien County

(G-13864)
MONTE PACKAGE COMPANY LLC
3752 Riverside Rd (49084-5101)
P.O. Box 128 (49084-0128)
PHONE.................................269 849-1722
Anthony Monte, *President*
EMP: 40 **EST**: 2018
SALES (est): 8MM
SALES (corp-wide): 13.4B **Privately Held**
WEB: www.shop.montepkg.com
SIC: 2449 2653 Fruit crates, wood: wirebound; vegetable crates, wood: wirebound; boxes, corrugated: made from purchased materials
PA: Bunzl Public Limited Company
York House
London W1H 7
208 560-1244

(G-13865)
RIVERSIDE ELECTRIC SERVICE INC
3864 Riverside Rd (49084-5100)
P.O. Box 32 (49084-0032)
PHONE.................................269 849-1222
Walter Sewcyck, *President*
Paul T Sewcyck, *Treasurer*
EMP: 8 **EST**: 1946
SQ FT: 3,000
SALES (est): 571K **Privately Held**
WEB: www.reselectricmotors.com
SIC: 7694 5063 Electric motor repair; motors, electric

(G-13866)
TPS LLC
Also Called: Lindberg/Mph
3827 Riverside Rd (49084-5103)
P.O. Box 131 (49084-0131)
PHONE.................................269 849-2700
Tim Perdue, *Partner*
Jeffrey Comitz, *Engineer*
David Gibson, *Engineer*
Donald Kublick, *Engineer*
Dennis Mendler, *Engineer*
EMP: 60
SALES (corp-wide): 101.6MM **Privately Held**
WEB: www.thermalproductsolutions.com
SIC: 3567 Industrial furnaces & ovens
HQ: Tps, Llc
2821 Old Route 15
New Columbia PA 17856
570 538-7200

Riverview
Wayne County

(G-13867)
A A A WIRE ROPE & SPLICING INC
12650 Sibley Rd (48193-4597)
P.O. Box 2153 (48193-1153)
PHONE.................................734 283-1765
Robert Matthews, *President*
Greg Lubaway, *Sales Staff*
Louise Blessing, *Admin Sec*
EMP: 12 **EST**: 1965
SQ FT: 10,000
SALES (est): 3.3MM **Privately Held**
WEB: www.aaawirerope.com
SIC: 3496 Miscellaneous fabricated wire products

(G-13868)
ALL CITY ELECTRIC MOTOR REPAIR
18750 Fort St Apt 15 (48193-7407)
PHONE.................................734 284-2268
Mark Watson, *President*
Kelly Watson, *Vice Pres*
EMP: 4 **EST**: 1988
SQ FT: 5,500
SALES (est): 790K **Privately Held**
WEB: www.allcityelectricmotorrepair.com
SIC: 7694 Electric motor repair

(G-13869)
AMERICAN STEEL WORKS INC
12615 Nixon Ave (48193-4517)
PHONE.................................734 282-0300
Robert P Schneider, *President*
Yvonne Schneider, *Admin Sec*
EMP: 10 **EST**: 1994
SQ FT: 25,000
SALES (est): 861.5K **Privately Held**
SIC: 7699 3441 Industrial equipment services; fabricated structural metal

(G-13870)
DFC INC
Also Called: Denesczuk Firebrick Company
17651 Yorkshire Dr (48193-8166)
PHONE.................................734 285-6749
Gail Denesczuk, *President*
Ted Denesczuk, *Vice Pres*
EMP: 5 **EST**: 1975
SALES (est): 355K **Privately Held**
SIC: 3567 1711 Industrial furnaces & ovens; boiler & furnace contractors

(G-13871)
ELEVATOR CONCEPTS LTD
18720 Krause St (48193-4249)
PHONE.................................734 246-4700
EMP: 5 **EST**: 2019
SALES (est): 107.7K **Privately Held**
SIC: 3534 Elevators & moving stairways

(G-13872)
FAR ASSOCIATES INC
11801 Longsdorf St (48193-4250)
PHONE.................................734 282-1881
Frederick J Rotter, *President*
Randall Gibbs, *Vice Pres*
EMP: 8 **EST**: 1976
SQ FT: 6,300
SALES (est): 1.1MM **Privately Held**
SIC: 3599 Machine shop, jobbing & repair

(G-13873)
FLASHPOINT SIGN LLC
18073 Ray St (48193-7424)
PHONE.................................734 231-3361
EMP: 4 **EST**: 2014
SALES (est): 78.1K **Privately Held**
SIC: 3993 Signs & advertising specialties

(G-13874)
HOMESPUN FURNITURE INC
18540 Fort St (48193-7442)
PHONE.................................734 284-6277
Ronald Snider, *President*
Scott Hamelin, *General Mgr*
Gary Ogden, *Vice Pres*
Angela Rohde, *Project Mgr*
Karen Ogden, *Treasurer*
EMP: 17 **EST**: 1974
SQ FT: 20,000
SALES (est): 5.2MM **Privately Held**
WEB: www.homespunfurniture.com
SIC: 5712 5713 7641 7389 Furniture stores; carpets; reupholstery; interior decorating; upholstered household furniture; floor laying & floor work

(G-13875)
HURON HIGH SCHOOL
12431 Longsdorf St (48193-4202)
PHONE.................................734 782-2441
Julie Sly, *Admin Asst.*
EMP: 10 **EST**: 2017
SALES (est): 87.9K **Privately Held**
WEB: www.riversideindustriesllc.com
SIC: 7692 Welding repair

(G-13876)
J & Z DISTRIBUTION CO LLC
15846 Golfview Dr (48193-8089)
PHONE.................................925 828-6260
EMP: 4 **EST**: 2016
SALES (est): 62.3K **Privately Held**
SIC: 2084 Wines, brandy & brandy spirits

(G-13877)
J&C INDUSTRIES
20129 Coachwood Rd (48193-7875)
PHONE.................................734 479-0069
Joseph Maciolek, *Principal*
EMP: 4 **EST**: 2010
SALES (est): 87K **Privately Held**
WEB: www.oldmasterdrawings.com
SIC: 3999 Manufacturing industries

(G-13878)
JONES CHEMICAL INC
18000 Payne St (48193-4252)
PHONE.................................734 283-0677
Jeff Jones, *President*
EMP: 9 **EST**: 1963
SALES (est): 923.1K **Privately Held**
SIC: 2899 Chemical preparations

(G-13879)
LLC ASH STEVENS (DH)
Also Called: Piramal Pharma Solutions
18655 Krause St (48193-4260)
PHONE.................................734 282-3370
Stephen A Munk, *President*
Dr James M Hamby, *Vice Pres*
EMP: 70 **EST**: 1952
SQ FT: 47,000
SALES: 41.9MM **Privately Held**
WEB: www.piramalpharmasolutions.com
SIC: 2834 Pharmaceutical preparations

(G-13880)
MATERIALS PROCESSING INC
Also Called: M P I Coating
17423 Jefferson (48193-4205)
PHONE.................................734 282-1888
Emmett Windisch III, *President*
Gaylord Sayre, *Vice Pres*
Joanne Frid, *Foreman/Supr*
Scott Boyd, *Maint Spvr*
Tracye Nara, *QC Mgr*
◆ **EMP**: 80 **EST**: 1981
SQ FT: 900,000
SALES (est): 9.6MM **Privately Held**
WEB: www.mpi-usa.com
SIC: 4225 4226 2891 2851 General warehousing & storage; special warehousing & storage; adhesives & sealants; paints & allied products

(G-13881)
NARBURGH & TIDD LLC
Also Called: William F McGraw & Company
18835 Krause St (48193-4248)
PHONE.................................734 281-1959
Keith Tidd,
EMP: 7 **EST**: 1941
SQ FT: 22,000
SALES (est): 637.7K **Privately Held**
SIC: 3089 Injection molding of plastics

(G-13882)
P & A CONVEYOR SALES INC
18999 Quarry St (48193-4552)
P.O. Box 2145 (48193-1145)
PHONE.................................734 285-7970
Donny Joe Strong, *President*
EMP: 6 **EST**: 1971
SQ FT: 27,000
SALES (est): 514.8K **Privately Held**
SIC: 3535 5084 Conveyors & conveying equipment; conveyor systems

(G-13883)
PERRY TOOL COMPANY INC
12329 Hale St (48193-4562)
PHONE.................................734 283-7393
William L Perry, *President*
Donna Perry, *Corp Secy*
EMP: 5 **EST**: 1985
SQ FT: 4,500
SALES (est): 488.6K **Privately Held**
WEB: www.perrytool.com
SIC: 3545 Gauges (machine tool accessories); tools & accessories for machine tools

▲ = Import ▼ = Export
◆ = Import/Export

GEOGRAPHIC SECTION

Rochester - Oakland County (G-13912)

(G-13884)
WSI INDUSTRIAL SERVICES INC (PA)
18555 Fort St (48193-7436)
PHONE.....................................734 942-9300
Philip Rye, *President*
Thomas Redmond, *Exec VP*
Craig Colmer, *Vice Pres*
Jerry Tolstyka, *Treasurer*
EMP: 45 **EST:** 1989
SQ FT: 13,000
SALES (est): 12.7MM **Privately Held**
WEB: www.wsiind.com
SIC: 3471 Cleaning & descaling metal products

Rives Junction
Jackson County

(G-13885)
BLACK BARN VINYRD & WINERY LLC
10605 Churchill Rd (49277-9757)
PHONE.....................................517 569-2164
Lloyd Westers, *Principal*
EMP: 4 **EST:** 2017
SALES (est): 338.7K **Privately Held**
WEB: www.blackbarnvineyardandwinery.com
SIC: 2084 Wines

(G-13886)
HACKER MACHINE INC
Also Called: Hmi
11200 Broughwell Rd (49277-9671)
PHONE.....................................517 569-3348
Charles Hacker, *President*
EMP: 20 **EST:** 1973
SQ FT: 26,000
SALES (est): 1.4MM **Privately Held**
SIC: 3714 3544 Motor vehicle engines & parts; special dies & tools

(G-13887)
METTER FLOORING LLC
Also Called: Metter Flooring and Cnstr
2531 W Territorial Rd (49277-9709)
PHONE.....................................517 914-2004
David Metter,
EMP: 4 **EST:** 2007
SALES (est): 159.7K **Privately Held**
SIC: 2426 3315 1799 1542 Hardwood dimension & flooring mills; chain link fencing; fence construction; commercial & office building, new construction

(G-13888)
RIVES MANUFACTURING INC
4000 Rives Eaton Rd (49277-9650)
P.O. Box 98 (49277-0098)
PHONE.....................................517 569-3380
Richard R Stahl, *President*
Vincent P Stahl, *Vice Pres*
Jason Boisher, *QC Mgr*
Jon Grinstead, *Maintence Staff*
EMP: 34 **EST:** 1992
SQ FT: 50,000
SALES (est): 7.4MM **Privately Held**
WEB: www.rivesmfg.com
SIC: 3496 3441 Miscellaneous fabricated wire products; fabricated structural metal

---

Rochester
Oakland County

(G-13889)
ADVANCED COMPOSITE TECH INC
417 E 2nd St (48307-2007)
PHONE.....................................248 709-9097
EMP: 7
SALES (corp-wide): 1.3MM **Privately Held**
SIC: 3089 2221 2396 Plastics Products, Nec, Nsk
PA: Advanced Composite Technology, Inc.
4200 N Atlantic Blvd
Auburn Hills MI

(G-13890)
ADVERTSING NTWRK SOLUTIONS INC (PA)
Also Called: American Newspaper Solutions
530 Pine St Ste F (48307-1482)
PHONE.....................................248 475-7881
Jerry Bellanger, *CEO*
Doug Marchal, *Vice Pres*
Doug Maxwell, *Opers Staff*
Richard Decook, *CFO*
EMP: 6 **EST:** 2003
SALES (est): 12MM **Privately Held**
SIC: 3993 Advertising novelties

(G-13891)
AMERICAN VINTNERS LLC
Also Called: Vinifera
612 W University Dr # 200 (48307-1895)
PHONE.....................................248 310-0575
Jon Gerstenschlager,
EMP: 13 **EST:** 2015
SALES (est): 2.4MM **Privately Held**
WEB: www.avintners.com
SIC: 2084 Wines

(G-13892)
AURUM DESIGN INC
Also Called: Aurum Design Jewelry
400 S Main St (48307-2031)
PHONE.....................................248 651-9040
Daren Schurman, *Owner*
EMP: 6 **EST:** 1988
SQ FT: 2,043
SALES (est): 565.2K **Privately Held**
WEB: www.aurumdesign.com
SIC: 3911 5944 Jewelry, precious metal; jewelry stores

(G-13893)
BIZCARD XPRESS
229 N Alice Ave (48307-1811)
PHONE.....................................248 288-4800
EMP: 4 **EST:** 2012
SALES (est): 138.9K **Privately Held**
SIC: 2752 Commercial printing, offset

(G-13894)
BRADY WORLDWIDE INC
632 Rewold Dr (48307-2233)
PHONE.....................................248 650-1952
EMP: 4 **EST:** 2019
SALES (est): 157.3K **Privately Held**
SIC: 3999 Identification badges & insignia

(G-13895)
BUSINESS PRESS INC
Also Called: American Speedy Printing
917 N Main St (48307-1436)
PHONE.....................................248 652-8855
William Davies, *President*
EMP: 4 **EST:** 1979
SQ FT: 2,000
SALES (est): 474.1K **Privately Held**
WEB: www.asprochestermi.com
SIC: 2752 2791 2789 2761 Commercial printing, offset; typesetting; bookbinding & related work; manifold business forms

(G-13896)
COSELLA DORKEN PRODUCTS INC
1795 Chase Dr (48307-1799)
PHONE.....................................888 433-5824
EMP: 4 **EST:** 2016
SALES (est): 127.9K **Privately Held**
SIC: 3272 Concrete products

(G-13897)
CPR III INC
Also Called: Preferred Engineering
380 South St (48307-2240)
P.O. Box B1458 (48308-1458)
PHONE.....................................248 652-2900
Charles P Ring III, *President*
Paul Kidwell, *Vice Pres*
EMP: 48 **EST:** 1987
SQ FT: 10,000
SALES (est): 3.9MM **Privately Held**
SIC: 3825 Test equipment for electronic & electrical circuits

(G-13898)
DAVID KIMBERLY DOOR COMPANY
394 South St Ste B (48307-2240)
P.O. Box 81090 (48308-1090)
PHONE.....................................248 652-8833
Leonard R Sikkelee, *President*
Karon L Sikkelee, *Vice Pres*
Len S Sikkelee, *Manager*
EMP: 15 **EST:** 1980
SQ FT: 14,000
SALES (est): 1.8MM **Privately Held**
WEB: www.davidkimberly.com
SIC: 3429 Manufactured hardware (general)

(G-13899)
EVENTS TO ENVY
113 E University Dr Ste 5 (48307-6719)
PHONE.....................................248 841-8400
Gayle Mundt, *Principal*
EMP: 5 **EST:** 2012
SALES (est): 69.8K **Privately Held**
SIC: 3953 Stationery embossers, personal

(G-13900)
FEDEX OFFICE & PRINT SVCS INC
133 S Main St (48307-2032)
PHONE.....................................248 651-2679
EMP: 6
SALES (corp-wide): 83.9B **Publicly Held**
SIC: 7334 2711 Photocopying & duplicating services; commercial printing & newspaper publishing combined
HQ: Fedex Office And Print Services, Inc.
7900 Legacy Dr
Plano TX 75024
800 463-3339

(G-13901)
FIELDSTONE HARD CIDER
388 South St (48307-2240)
PHONE.....................................248 923-1742
EMP: 4 **EST:** 2015
SALES (est): 67.3K **Privately Held**
SIC: 2084 Wines

(G-13902)
GORANG INDUSTRIES INC
Also Called: Wheel Truing Brake Shoe Co
305 South St (48307-2241)
P.O. Box 80636 (48308-0636)
PHONE.....................................248 651-9010
Michael Gorang, *President*
Sue Gorang, *Vice Pres*
EMP: 4 **EST:** 1898
SQ FT: 4,600 **Privately Held**
WEB: www.wheeltruing.com
SIC: 3743 Brakes, air & vacuum: railway

(G-13903)
HARMAN CORPORATION (PA)
360 South St (48307-6632)
P.O. Box 80665 (48308-0665)
PHONE.....................................248 651-4477
Jeff Harman, *President*
Ron Harman, *Vice Pres*
John Johnston, *Plant Mgr*
Ted Fisher, *Opers Mgr*
Rachel Wood, *Opers Staff*
▲ **EMP:** 34 **EST:** 1962
SQ FT: 65,500
SALES (est): 10.4MM **Privately Held**
WEB: www.harmancorp.com
SIC: 3089 3643 Blow molded finished plastic products; current-carrying wiring devices

(G-13904)
HOME BAKERY
300 S Main St (48307-2030)
PHONE.....................................248 651-4830
Larry Morevick, *President*
EMP: 8 **EST:** 1956
SQ FT: 3,600
SALES (est): 504.4K **Privately Held**
WEB: www.thehomebakery.com
SIC: 5461 2051 Cakes; bread, cake & related products

(G-13905)
HOUSEART LLC
386 South St (48307-2240)
PHONE.....................................248 651-8124
Mark Finley, *Vice Pres*
Ginger Finley,
▼ **EMP:** 4 **EST:** 2000
SQ FT: 2,000
SALES (est): 397.1K **Privately Held**
WEB: www.houseart.net
SIC: 3612 5251 5063 Doorbell transformers, electric; hardware; lighting fixtures

(G-13906)
IMAGES UNLIMITED LLC
361 South St Ste A (48307-2259)
PHONE.....................................248 608-8685
John Meyer,
EMP: 4 **EST:** 1996
SQ FT: 1,400
SALES (est): 263.9K **Privately Held**
WEB: www.images-unltd.com
SIC: 3993 Signs & advertising specialties

(G-13907)
INKWELL SCREEN PRINTING
289 South St Ste B (48307-6630)
PHONE.....................................586 292-4050
EMP: 4 **EST:** 2010
SALES (est): 139.2K **Privately Held**
WEB: www.inkwellscreenprinting.com
SIC: 2752 Commercial printing, lithographic

(G-13908)
INNOVATIVE WELD SOLUTIONS LLC
1022 Miners Run (48306-4590)
PHONE.....................................937 545-7695
Venkat Ananthanarayanan, *Principal*
EMP: 8 **EST:** 2007
SQ FT: 8,000
SALES (est): 500.1K **Privately Held**
WEB: www.innovativeweldsolutions.com
SIC: 8733 3691 8711 8731 Scientific research agency; storage batteries; engineering services; commercial physical research; business consulting

(G-13909)
INTERPRO TECHNOLOGY INC
722 W University Dr (48307-1851)
PHONE.....................................248 650-8695
Kevin Ouellette, *Owner*
Sandra McGuffie, *Owner*
EMP: 13 **EST:** 1991
SQ FT: 5,800
SALES (est): 1.9MM **Privately Held**
WEB: www.interpro-tech.com
SIC: 7372 Application computer software

(G-13910)
JENDA CONTROLS INC
363 South St Apt B (48307-2274)
PHONE.....................................248 656-0090
David Lewinski, *President*
EMP: 8 **EST:** 1985
SALES (est): 756.7K **Privately Held**
SIC: 3625 Electric controls & control accessories, industrial

(G-13911)
METALMITE CORPORATION
194 S Elizabeth St (48307-2027)
PHONE.....................................248 651-9415
Tom Gendich, *President*
Michael Gendich Jr, *President*
Bob Supernaw, *Foreman/Supr*
Steve Shelton, *Manager*
Ryan Matz, *Supervisor*
EMP: 18 **EST:** 1968
SQ FT: 10,000
SALES (est): 2.9MM **Privately Held**
WEB: www.metalmite.com
SIC: 3599 3544 Machine shop, jobbing & repair; special dies, tools, jigs & fixtures

(G-13912)
MOON RIVER SOAP CO LLC
339 East St Ste 100 (48307-7400)
PHONE.....................................248 930-9467
Elizabeth Aprea, *Mng Member*
Carlos Aprea,
EMP: 5 **EST:** 2009 **Privately Held**
WEB: www.moonriversoap.com
SIC: 2841 Soap & other detergents

Rochester - Oakland County (G-13913)

(G-13913)
NORBORD PANELS USA INC
410 W University Dr # 210 (48307-1938)
PHONE.................................248 608-0387
Peter Wijnbergen, *President*
David Van Maele, *Asst Treas*
EMP: 2000 **EST:** 1987
SALES (est): 600MM
SALES (corp-wide): 3.6B **Privately Held**
WEB: www.westfraser.com
SIC: 2493 Flakeboard
HQ: Norbord Inc
    1 Toronto St Suite 600
    Toronto ON M5C 2
    416 365-0705

(G-13914)
NOVAVAX INC
870 Parkdale Rd (48307-1740)
PHONE.................................248 656-5336
EMP: 4 **Publicly Held**
WEB: www.novavax.com
SIC: 2836 Vaccines & other immunizing products
PA: Novavax, Inc.
    21 Firstfield Rd
    Gaithersburg MD 20878

(G-13915)
OAKLAND SAIL INC
Also Called: OAKLAND POST
61 Oakland Ctr (48309-4409)
PHONE.................................248 370-4268
Holly Gilbert, *President*
EMP: 17 **EST:** 1996
SALES (est): 9.9K **Privately Held**
WEB: www.oakland.edu
SIC: 2711 Newspapers, publishing & printing

(G-13916)
ONESTREAM SOFTWARE CORP
425 S Main St Ste 203 (48307-6729)
P.O. Box 81605 (48308-1605)
PHONE.................................248 841-1356
Thomas Shae, *President*
Jeff Degrieck, *COO*
Craig Colby, *Vice Pres*
Eric Davidson, *Vice Pres*
Ken Hohenstein, *Vice Pres*
EMP: 9 **EST:** 2009
SQ FT: 1,200
SALES (est): 684.3K **Privately Held**
WEB: www.onestreamsoftware.com
SIC: 7372 Business oriented computer software

(G-13917)
ONESTREAM SOFTWARE LLC (PA)
362 South St (48307-2240)
P.O. Box 81605 (48308-1605)
PHONE.................................248 342-1541
Jody Digiovanni, *Partner*
Matthew Dellenger, *Regional Mgr*
Marcus Hartwell, *Business Mgr*
Jim Campbell, *Exec VP*
Bill Lovelace, *Senior VP*
EMP: 5 **EST:** 2012
SQ FT: 2,100
SALES (est): 7.2MM **Privately Held**
WEB: www.onestreamsoftware.com
SIC: 7372 Business oriented computer software

(G-13918)
OPTIMIZERX CORPORATION (PA)
400 Water St Ste 200 (48307-2090)
PHONE.................................248 651-6568
William J Febbo, *CEO*
Gus D Halas, *Ch of Bd*
Miriam J Paramore, *President*
Angelo Campano, *Senior VP*
Terence J Hamilton, *Senior VP*
EMP: 3 **EST:** 2006
SALES (est): 43.3MM **Publicly Held**
WEB: www.optimizerx.com
SIC: 7372 Business oriented computer software

(G-13919)
PALADIN BAKING COMPANY LLC
Also Called: Give Thanks Bakery
225 S Main St (48307-2034)
PHONE.................................248 601-1542
Kathryn Knoer,
EMP: 11 **EST:** 2020
SALES (est): 500K **Privately Held**
WEB: www.dipaolobakingcompany.com
SIC: 2051 Bakery: wholesale or wholesale/retail combined

(G-13920)
PAR STERILE PRODUCTS LLC
Also Called: Par Pharmaceutical
870 Parkdale Rd (48307-1740)
PHONE.................................248 651-9081
Ralph Napolitano, *Vice Pres*
Scott Sims, *Vice Pres*
Paula Del Papa, *Opers Staff*
Jeffrey Eastman, *Opers Staff*
Christopher Thomas, *Opers Staff*
EMP: 314 **Privately Held**
WEB: www.parsterileproducts.com
SIC: 2834 Pharmaceutical preparations
HQ: Par Sterile Products, Llc
    6 Ram Ridge Rd
    Chestnut Ridge NY 10977

(G-13921)
PARKEDALE PHARMACEUTICALS INC
1200 Parkdale Rd (48307-1744)
PHONE.................................248 650-6400
Matthew Lepore, *President*
Brian McMachon, *Treasurer*
Susan Grant, *Admin Sec*
EMP: 78 **EST:** 1997
SALES (est): 17.4MM
SALES (corp-wide): 41.9B **Publicly Held**
WEB: www.pfizer.com
SIC: 2834 Pharmaceutical preparations
PA: Pfizer Inc.
    235 E 42nd St Rm 107
    New York NY 10017
    212 733-2323

(G-13922)
PRACTICAL POWER
202 South St (48307-2238)
PHONE.................................866 385-2961
Mark Bunting, *President*
EMP: 4 **EST:** 2005
SALES (est): 329.4K **Privately Held**
WEB: www.practicalpowerinc.com
SIC: 3679 Power supplies, all types: static

(G-13923)
PROTEIN CHEESECAKE COMPANY
454 Romeo Rd Unit 213 (48307-1670)
PHONE.................................248 495-3258
Jon Lapolla, *Principal*
EMP: 4 **EST:** 2017
SALES (est): 89.8K **Privately Held**
SIC: 2591 Window blinds

(G-13924)
RBM CHEMICAL COMPANY LLC
4108 Oak Tree Cir (48306-4659)
PHONE.................................248 766-1974
Rajinder Minhas,
EMP: 4 **EST:** 2019
SALES (est): 353.3K **Privately Held**
SIC: 2899 Corrosion preventive lubricant

(G-13925)
REMY INTERNATIONAL INC
60558 Pennington Way (48306-2065)
PHONE.................................765 778-6499
Sidney Rard, *Principal*
EMP: 5 **EST:** 2016
SALES (est): 76.1K **Privately Held**
SIC: 3714 Motor vehicle parts & accessories

(G-13926)
SALES DRIVEN SERVICES LLC
Also Called: Raybend
3128 Walt Blvd Ste 216 (48309)
PHONE.................................586 854-9494
Jon Reesman, *President*
Joseph Mauro, *Mng Member*
▲ **EMP:** 5 **EST:** 2010

SQ FT: 15,000
SALES (est): 568.5K **Privately Held**
WEB: www.salesdrivenservices.com
SIC: 3561 5084 Pumps, domestic: water or sump: water pumps (industrial)

(G-13927)
SAMPSON TOOL INCORPORATED
383 South St (48307-2241)
PHONE.................................248 651-3313
William C Reese, *President*
EMP: 5 **EST:** 1976
SQ FT: 4,200
SALES (est): 403.7K **Privately Held**
WEB: www.toolandmachineshop.com
SIC: 3544 Special dies & tools

(G-13928)
SEXTANT ADVISOR GROUP INC
431 6th St (48307-1401)
PHONE.................................248 650-8280
EMP: 6 **EST:** 2015
SALES (est): 84K **Privately Held**
SIC: 3812 Sextants

(G-13929)
SHELFGENIE SOUTHEASTERN MICH
Also Called: Shelf Genie
523 Wilcox St (48307-1443)
PHONE.................................248 805-1834
EMP: 6 **EST:** 2017
SALES (est): 80.3K **Privately Held**
WEB: www.shelfgenie.com
SIC: 2511 Wood household furniture

(G-13930)
STONE FOR YOU
111 W 2nd St Ste A (48307-6738)
PHONE.................................248 651-9940
Costin Dragnea, *President*
EMP: 6 **EST:** 2011
SALES (est): 345.8K **Privately Held**
WEB: www.stone4u.us
SIC: 3441 Fabricated structural metal

(G-13931)
SU-DAN COMPANY
4693 Gallagher Rd (48306-1501)
PHONE.................................248 754-1430
Brian Rambo, *Manager*
EMP: 220
SALES (corp-wide): 26.3MM **Privately Held**
WEB: www.su-dan.com
SIC: 3469 3465 Metal stampings; automotive stampings
PA: The Su-Dan Company
    190 Northpointe Dr
    Lake Orion MI 48359
    248 651-6035

(G-13932)
SU-DAN PLASTICS INC
4693 Gallagher Rd (48306-1501)
PHONE.................................248 651-6035
Mike Brockway, *Manager*
EMP: 156
SALES (corp-wide): 22.1MM **Privately Held**
SIC: 3089 3544 Injection molding of plastics; industrial molds
PA: Su-Dan Plastics, Inc.
    190 Northpointe Dr
    Lake Orion MI 48359
    248 651-6035

(G-13933)
THINK CLUB PUBLICATION
4353 Stonewood Ct (48306-4645)
PHONE.................................248 651-3106
EMP: 4 **EST:** 2014
SALES (est): 76.2K **Privately Held**
SIC: 2741 Miscellaneous publishing

(G-13934)
TRANS INDUSTRIES PLASTICS LLC (PA)
Also Called: KY Holdings
414 East St (48307-2016)
PHONE.................................248 310-0008
William Gruits,
EMP: 20 **EST:** 2005
SQ FT: 60,000

SALES (est): 3.5MM **Privately Held**
SIC: 3089 Injection molding of plastics

(G-13935)
TROY LABORATORIES INC
440 South St (48307-2242)
P.O. Box 80154 (48308-0154)
PHONE.................................248 652-6000
Christopher Tornber, *President*
EMP: 12 **EST:** 1970
SQ FT: 200,000
SALES (est): 342.2K **Privately Held**
WEB: www.troylaboratories.com
SIC: 3471 Finishing, metals or formed products

(G-13936)
US ENERGIA LLC
Also Called: Energy Products & Services
400 Water St Ste 250 (48307-2091)
PHONE.................................248 669-1462
Jeff Moss, *President*
EMP: 9 **EST:** 2006
SALES (est): 726K **Privately Held**
SIC: 8711 3613 Engineering services; control panels, electric

(G-13937)
VERGASON TECHNOLOGY INC
1672 Stony Creek Dr (48307-1783)
PHONE.................................248 568-0120
Kerney Paul, *Principal*
Paul Kerney, *Business Mgr*
EMP: 8 **EST:** 2016
SALES (est): 142.7K **Privately Held**
WEB: www.vergason.com
SIC: 3479 Coating of metals & formed products

Rochester Hills
Oakland County

(G-13938)
A RAYMOND CORP N AMER INC (HQ)
2350 Austin Ave Ste 200 (48309-3679)
PHONE.................................248 853-2500
Earl Brown, *CEO*
Lonnie Jenkins, *Plant Mgr*
Jason Reznar, *Mfg Mgr*
Donald Dunbar, *Safety Mgr*
Philippe Babou, *Chf Purch Ofc*
EMP: 23 **EST:** 2009
SALES (est): 315.6MM
SALES (corp-wide): 177.9K **Privately Held**
WEB: www.araymond.com
SIC: 5085 3469 6719 Fasteners & fastening equipment; metal stampings; investment holding companies, except banks
PA: A Raymond Et Compagnie
    113 Cours Berriat
    Grenoble
    476 210-233

(G-13939)
A RAYMOND TINNERMAN MEXICO
3091 Research Dr (48309-3581)
PHONE.................................248 537-3404
Daniel Dolan,
EMP: 1 **EST:** 2012
SALES (est): 1MM
SALES (corp-wide): 177.9K **Privately Held**
WEB: www.araymond.com
SIC: 3965 Fasteners
HQ: Araymond Manufacturing Center North America, Inc.
    3091 Research Dr
    Rochester Hills MI 48309
    248 260-2121

(G-13940)
ACCURATE GAUGE & MFG INC (PA)
Also Called: A G
2943 Technology Dr (48309-3589)
PHONE.................................248 853-2400
Raymond Velthuysen, *President*
Nancy Cream, *CFO*
Clint Velthuysen, *Technology*
Dennis Brophy, *Director*

GEOGRAPHIC SECTION
Rochester Hills - Oakland County (G-13967)

EMP: 59 EST: 1966
SQ FT: 64,000
SALES (est): 13.4MM **Privately Held**
WEB: www.accurategauge.com
SIC: 3599 3586 3568 Machine shop, jobbing & repair; measuring & dispensing pumps; power transmission equipment

(G-13941)
ADCO CIRCUITS INC (PA)
2868 Bond St (48309-3514)
PHONE.....................248 853-6620
Archie J Damman III, *President*
Marc J Damman, *Vice Pres*
Kevin Barrett, *Opers Spvr*
Jennifer Brown, *Production*
Tracy Sting, *Purch Mgr*
▲ EMP: 145 EST: 1981
SQ FT: 55,000
SALES (est): 38.7MM **Privately Held**
WEB: www.adcocircuits.com
SIC: 3672 Printed circuit boards

(G-13942)
ADDUXI
2791 Research Dr (48309-3575)
PHONE.....................248 564-2000
Xavier Ovize, *CEO*
Stacey Ellenwood, *Office Mgr*
▲ EMP: 20 EST: 2014
SALES (est): 3.4MM **Privately Held**
WEB: www.adduxi.com
SIC: 3089 Automotive parts, plastic

(G-13943)
ADVANCE GRAPHIC SYSTEMS INC
1806 Rochester Indl Dr (48309-3337)
PHONE.....................248 656-8000
James E Hall, *President*
Charles Springer, *Research*
James Hall, *Technology*
Robert Mack, *Technology*
EMP: 50 EST: 1981
SQ FT: 47,800
SALES (est): 8.7MM **Privately Held**
SIC: 2791 2759 2752 2396 Typesetting; commercial printing; commercial printing, lithographic; automotive & apparel trimmings; signs, not made in custom sign painting shops

(G-13944)
ADVANCED VHCL ASSEMBLIES LLC ✪
2917 Waterview Dr (48309-4600)
PHONE.....................248 299-7500
Dave Pettyes, *CEO*
EMP: 1001 EST: 2021
SALES (est): 43.7MM **Privately Held**
SIC: 3714 Motor vehicle parts & accessories

(G-13945)
AG INDUSTRIES
1720 Star Batt Dr (48309-3707)
PHONE.....................248 564-2758
Jeffrey Hearn, *Principal*
EMP: 15 EST: 2017
SALES (est): 149.7K **Privately Held**
WEB: www.agindustries.com
SIC: 3999 Manufacturing industries

(G-13946)
AMERICAN AXLE & MFG INC
Also Called: AAM Technical Center
2965 Technology Dr (48309-3589)
PHONE.....................248 299-2900
Daniel Sagady, *Vice Pres*
Carl Peterson, *Technician*
EMP: 7
SALES (corp-wide): 4.7B **Publicly Held**
WEB: www.aam.com
SIC: 3714 Motor vehicle parts & accessories
HQ: American Axle & Manufacturing, Inc.
1 Dauch Dr
Detroit MI 48211

(G-13947)
AMERIFORM ACQUISITION CO LLC
Also Called: KI Outdoor
2619 Bond St (48309-3510)
PHONE.....................231 733-2725
Tory Ferrier, *Credit Mgr*
Thomas Harris, *Mng Member*
◆ EMP: 300 EST: 2010
SALES (est): 52.2MM **Privately Held**
SIC: 3732 7359 Non-motorized boat, building & repairing; portable toilet rental

(G-13948)
ANIMO GAMES LLC
864 Rambling Dr (48307-2883)
PHONE.....................586 201-9699
Joshua Patton, *Principal*
EMP: 4 EST: 2017
SALES (est): 108.8K **Privately Held**
WEB: www.animocards.com
SIC: 2741 Miscellaneous publishing

(G-13949)
APPLIED AUTOMATION TECH INC
1688 Star Batt Dr (48309-3705)
PHONE.....................248 656-4930
Ray Karadayi, *President*
Benjamin Gembis, *Opers Staff*
Aat PM, *Program Mgr*
▲ EMP: 22 EST: 1987
SQ FT: 9,800
SALES (est): 2MM **Privately Held**
WEB: www.aat3d.com
SIC: 3695 8243 Computer software tape & disks: blank, rigid & floppy; software training, computer

(G-13950)
ARAYMOND MFG CTR N AMER INC
2900 Technology Dr (48309-3588)
PHONE.....................248 537-3147
Don Brown, *Branch Mgr*
EMP: 8
SALES (corp-wide): 177.9K **Privately Held**
SIC: 3312 Rail joints or fastenings
HQ: Araymond Manufacturing Center North America, Inc.
3091 Research Dr
Rochester Hills MI 48309
248 260-2121

(G-13951)
ASC INDUSTRIES INC
3255 W Hamlin Rd (48309-3231)
PHONE.....................586 722-7871
EMP: 7 EST: 2017
SALES (est): 168.7K **Privately Held**
WEB: www.ascindustries.com
SIC: 3999 Manufacturing industries

(G-13952)
ASSEMBLY ALTERNATIVES INC
501 Longford Dr (48309-2416)
PHONE.....................248 362-1616
Herman Walker, *CEO*
Richard F Schafer, *President*
EMP: 7 EST: 1996
SALES (est): 600.9K **Privately Held**
SIC: 3672 Printed circuit boards

(G-13953)
ATLAS DIE LLC
2960 Technology Dr (48309-3588)
PHONE.....................413 289-1276
Colin Macgray, *Opers Staff*
Susan Slagle, *Human Resources*
David Lord, *Branch Mgr*
Lori Salmon, *Prgrmr*
EMP: 38
SALES (corp-wide): 116.4MM **Privately Held**
WEB: www.atlasdie.com
SIC: 3423 3544 Cutting dies, except metal cutting; special dies, tools, jigs & fixtures
HQ: Atlas Die, Llc
2000 Middlebury St
Elkhart IN 46516
574 295-0050

(G-13954)
ATLAS DIE LLC
2960 Technology Dr (48309-3588)
PHONE.....................770 981-6585
Shawn Bragg, *Branch Mgr*
EMP: 38
SALES (corp-wide): 116.4MM **Privately Held**
WEB: www.atlasdie.com
SIC: 3423 3544 Cutting dies, except metal cutting; industrial molds
HQ: Atlas Die, Llc
2000 Middlebury St
Elkhart IN 46516
574 295-0050

(G-13955)
ATLAS DIE INC
2960 Technology Dr (48309-3588)
PHONE.....................574 295-0050
Nick Bragg, *Sales Staff*
Doug Boland, *Manager*
EMP: 21 EST: 1986
SALES (est): 2.8MM **Privately Held**
WEB: www.atlasdie.com
SIC: 3544 Dies, steel rule

(G-13956)
AURORA SOFTWARE
3135 Primrose Dr (48307-5241)
PHONE.....................248 853-2358
James E Tarchinski, *Owner*
EMP: 5 EST: 2014
SALES (est): 91K **Privately Held**
SIC: 7372 Prepackaged software

(G-13957)
AUTOMOTIVE INTERNATIONAL SVCS
774 Snowmass Dr (48309-1327)
PHONE.....................248 808-8112
Keith Leigh-Monstevens, *Principal*
EMP: 4 EST: 2017
SALES (est): 87.2K **Privately Held**
SIC: 3714 Motor vehicle parts & accessories

(G-13958)
AVON BROACH & PROD CO LLC
1089 John R Rd (48309-3207)
P.O. Box 80310, Rochester (48308-0310)
PHONE.....................248 650-8080
George M Buhaj, *President*
▲ EMP: 21 EST: 1950
SQ FT: 30,000
SALES (est): 750.6K **Privately Held**
WEB: www.avonbroach.com
SIC: 3599 3545 Machine shop, jobbing & repair; broaches (machine tool accessories)

(G-13959)
AVON CABINETS ATKINS
2596 Hessel Ave (48307-4824)
PHONE.....................248 237-1103
Brian Gatkins, *Principal*
EMP: 5 EST: 2010
SALES (est): 68K **Privately Held**
SIC: 2434 Wood kitchen cabinets

(G-13960)
AVON PLASTIC PRODUCTS INC
2890 Technology Dr (48309-3586)
PHONE.....................248 852-1000
Edward J Gorski, *President*
EMP: 32 EST: 1978
SQ FT: 24,000
SALES (est): 2.9MM **Privately Held**
SIC: 3089 3714 Injection molding of plastics; motor vehicle parts & accessories

(G-13961)
BARCLAY PHARMACY
75 Barclay Cir Ste 114 (48307-5803)
PHONE.....................248 852-4600
Jignesh Patel, *Owner*
EMP: 5 EST: 2010
SALES (est): 256.3K **Privately Held**
SIC: 2834 Pharmaceutical preparations

(G-13962)
BERKLEY SCREW MACHINE PDTS INC
2100 Royce Haley Dr (48309-3703)
PHONE.....................248 853-0044
Kenneth Haley, *President*
Ken Janik, *General Mgr*
Patricia M Lewis, *Corp Secy*
Royce Haley Jr, *Vice Pres*
Tim Jones, *Mfg Spvr*
EMP: 41 EST: 1961
SQ FT: 30,000
SALES (est): 4.3MM **Privately Held**
WEB: www.berkleyscrew.com
SIC: 3451 3429 Screw machine products; manufactured hardware (general)

(G-13963)
BERMAXX LLC
2960 Technology Dr (48309-3588)
PHONE.....................248 299-3600
Paul Madill, *Principal*
EMP: 7 EST: 2010
SALES (est): 218.3K **Privately Held**
SIC: 3556 Dehydrating equipment, food processing

(G-13964)
BERNAL LLC
Also Called: Cerutti Bernal
2960 Technology Dr (48309-3588)
PHONE.....................248 299-3600
Jerry Mosingo, *CEO*
Kenneth Smott, *CEO*
Frank Penksa, *VP Mfg*
Jerry Bell, *Engineer*
Michael Fazzini, *Engineer*
▲ EMP: 60 EST: 2002
SQ FT: 42,000
SALES (est): 12.4MM
SALES (corp-wide): 116.4MM **Privately Held**
WEB: www.bernalrotarydies.com
SIC: 3544 3554 Special dies & tools; paper industries machinery
PA: Auxo Investment Partners, Llc
146 Monroe Center St Nw # 1125
Grand Rapids MI 49503
616 200-4454

(G-13965)
BOS AUTOMOTIVE PRODUCTS INC (HQ)
2956 Waterview Dr (48309-3484)
PHONE.....................248 289-6072
Stefan Grein, *Ch of Bd*
Ivan Jones, *President*
Dennis Bowles, *Manager*
Bill Pompili, *Manager*
▲ EMP: 40 EST: 1994
SQ FT: 20,000
SALES (est): 23MM
SALES (corp-wide): 933.7MM **Privately Held**
WEB: www.bos.de
SIC: 3714 Motor vehicle parts & accessories
PA: Bos Gmbh & Co. Kg
Ernst-Heinkel-Str. 2
Ostfildern BW 73760
711 936-00

(G-13966)
BUHLER TECHNOLOGIES LLC
1030 W Hamlin Rd (48309-3354)
P.O. Box 70212 (48307-0004)
PHONE.....................248 652-1546
Gerd R Biller, *Principal*
Rick Brown, *COO*
Douglas Prange, *Sales Staff*
Ulrich Zietz, *Manager*
Brian Gilmore, *Technical Staff*
EMP: 23 EST: 2007
SALES (est): 5.2MM
SALES (corp-wide): 32.7MM **Privately Held**
WEB: www.buehler-technologies.com
SIC: 3492 3569 Control valves, fluid power: hydraulic & pneumatic; filters
PA: Buhler Technologies Gmbh
Harkortstr. 29
Ratingen NW
210 249-890

(G-13967)
BURTON PRESS CO INC
2156 Avon Industrial Dr (48309-3610)
PHONE.....................248 853-0212
Edward Lapierre, *President*
EMP: 5
SQ FT: 1,500
SALES (est): 453.7K **Privately Held**
WEB: www.burtonpress.com
SIC: 3542 3549 Presses: hydraulic & pneumatic, mechanical & manual; metalworking machinery

Rochester Hills - Oakland County (G-13968)

GEOGRAPHIC SECTION

(G-13968)
BUSHINGS INC
1967 Rochester Indus Dr (48309-3344)
PHONE..................................248 650-0603
Thomas Jacob, *President*
Rob Wolf, *Vice Pres*
Rodney Wolf, *Vice Pres*
Ken Maust, *Manager*
Kenneth Maust, *Data Proc Exec*
◆ EMP: 15 EST: 1942
SALES (est): 2.4MM **Privately Held**
WEB: www.bushingsinc.com
SIC: 3069 3714 Bushings, rubber; motor vehicle parts & accessories

(G-13969)
BYK USA INC
2932 Waterview Dr (48309-3484)
PHONE..................................203 265-2086
Louis Martin, *Branch Mgr*
EMP: 61
SALES (corp-wide): 3.1B **Privately Held**
WEB: www.byk.com
SIC: 2821 Plastics materials & resins
HQ: Byk Usa Inc.
    524 S Cherry St
    Wallingford CT 06492
    203 265-2086

(G-13970)
CANADIAN AMRCN RSTORATION SUPS (PA)
Also Called: C.A.R.S.
2600 Bond St (48309-3509)
PHONE..................................248 853-8900
Larry Wallie, *President*
Dave Pini, *Vice Pres*
▲ EMP: 28 EST: 1976
SQ FT: 15,000
SALES (est): 8.2MM **Privately Held**
WEB: www.carsinc.com
SIC: 5013 2396 5531 Automotive supplies & parts; automotive trimmings, fabric; automotive parts; automotive accessories

(G-13971)
CANDLELITE PUBLISHING LLC
1438 Oakbrook E (48307-1126)
PHONE..................................248 841-8925
Anita Louise Koch, *Principal*
EMP: 5 EST: 2016
SALES (est): 66.8K **Privately Held**
WEB: www.candle-lite.com
SIC: 2741 Miscellaneous publishing

(G-13972)
CARLSON ENTERPRISES INC
Also Called: Cookie Bouquet
922 S Rochester Rd (48307-2742)
PHONE..................................248 656-1442
Connie Carlson, *President*
Tom Carlson, *Vice Pres*
EMP: 6 EST: 1996
SALES (est): 346.6K **Privately Held**
WEB: www.cupcakebydesign.com
SIC: 5461 5947 2051 Cookies; gift baskets; bread, cake & related products

(G-13973)
CARTER FUEL SYSTEMS LLC
3255 W Hamlin Rd (48309-3231)
PHONE..................................248 371-8392
Rick Rhoades, *Director*
EMP: 33
SALES (corp-wide): 3.3B **Privately Held**
WEB: www.carterengineered.com
SIC: 3714 Fuel pumps, motor vehicle
HQ: Carter Fuel Systems, Llc
    101 E Industrial Blvd
    Logansport IN 46947
    574 722-6141

(G-13974)
CELLULAR CONCEPTS CO INC
Also Called: Cell-Con
3667 Merriweather Ln (48306-3642)
PHONE..................................313 371-4800
George Simon II, *President*
▲ EMP: 5 EST: 1989
SQ FT: 70,000
SALES (est): 832.1K
SALES (corp-wide): 15.6MM **Privately Held**
WEB: www.cellcon.com
SIC: 3541 Numerically controlled metal cutting machine tools
HQ: U. S. Equipment Co.
    3667 Merriweather Ln
    Rochester Hills MI 48306
    313 526-8300

(G-13975)
CLYMER MANUFACTURING COMPANY
1605 W Hamlin Rd (48309-3312)
PHONE..................................248 853-5555
Todd Wilms, *President*
Tammy Wilms, *Office Mgr*
EMP: 7 EST: 1951
SQ FT: 7,700
SALES (est): 687.1K **Privately Held**
WEB: www.clymertool.com
SIC: 3545 Cutting tools for machine tools

(G-13976)
COLE WAGNER CABINETRY
2511 Leach Rd (48309-3556)
PHONE..................................248 852-2406
Cole Wagner,
EMP: 15 EST: 2006
SALES (est): 1.1MM **Privately Held**
WEB: www.cwcabinetry.com
SIC: 2434 Wood kitchen cabinets

(G-13977)
COLOR DETROIT PUBLISHING LLC
321 Lonesome Oak Dr (48306-2836)
PHONE..................................313 974-9000
Christopher M Robinson, *Principal*
EMP: 4 EST: 2016
SALES (est): 37.5K **Privately Held**
SIC: 2741 Miscellaneous publishing

(G-13978)
COLWELL INDUSTRIES INC
1780 N Livernois Rd (48306-3334)
PHONE..................................248 841-1254
Dennis Kotyk, *Principal*
EMP: 7 EST: 2010
SALES (est): 86.1K **Privately Held**
WEB: www.colwellcolour.com
SIC: 3999 Manufacturing industries

(G-13979)
COMBUSTION RESEARCH CORP
2516 Leach Rd (48309-3555)
PHONE..................................248 852-3611
Winifred Johnson, *CEO*
Sharon Demeritt, *President*
Paul Demeritt, *Vice Pres*
Daryl Tincher, *Facilities Mgr*
Vail Demeritt, *Mfg Staff*
◆ EMP: 20
SQ FT: 25,000
SALES (est): 4.6MM **Privately Held**
WEB: www.combustionresearch.com
SIC: 3585 3564 Heating equipment, complete; blowers & fans

(G-13980)
COMMONWEALTH SERVICE SLS CORP
1715 W Hamlin Rd (48309-3368)
PHONE..................................313 581-8050
John S Seraphin, *President*
Victoria Seraphin, *Admin Sec*
EMP: 5 EST: 1936
SALES (est): 390.6K **Privately Held**
WEB: www.commonwealthservice.com
SIC: 7694 5063 Electric motor repair; motors, electric

(G-13981)
COMPUNETICS SYSTEMS INC
3235 Fulham Dr (48309-4388)
P.O. Box 108, Howell (48844-0108)
PHONE..................................248 531-0015
David Gore, *President*
Jeff Drabek, *Vice Pres*
EMP: 6 EST: 1996
SQ FT: 2,700
SALES (est): 617.5K **Privately Held**
WEB: www.compuneticssystems.com
SIC: 3577 Bar code (magnetic ink) printers

(G-13982)
CONCEPT CIRCUITS CORPORATION
Also Called: Phototron
1854 Star Batt Dr (48309-3709)
PHONE..................................248 852-5200
H R Rowley, *President*
EMP: 7 EST: 1993
SALES (est): 567.1K **Privately Held**
WEB: www.photo-tron.com
SIC: 3679 Electronic circuits

(G-13983)
CONNER STEEL PRODUCTS (PA)
2295 Star Ct (48309-3625)
PHONE..................................248 852-5110
David Barnhart, *Partner*
Gunther George, *Partner*
EMP: 19 EST: 1977
SALES (est): 1.4MM **Privately Held**
SIC: 3469 3444 3443 Stamping metal for the trade; sheet metalwork; fabricated plate work (boiler shop)

(G-13984)
CONTEMPORARY AMPEREX TECH USA
Also Called: Catl USA
2114 Austin Ave (48309-3667)
PHONE..................................248 289-6200
Jian Wang, *President*
Qim Wang, *Manager*
EMP: 8 EST: 2018
SQ FT: 3,000
SALES (est): 1.5MM **Privately Held**
SIC: 3691 5013 Storage batteries; automotive batteries

(G-13985)
CRANE TECHNOLOGIES GROUP INC
Also Called: Michigan Crane Parts & Svc Co
1954 Rochester Indus Dr (48309-3343)
PHONE..................................248 652-8700
Charles J Bauss, *Ch of Bd*
Dorothy Bauss, *President*
David Bauss, *Vice Pres*
Tim McCann, *Foreman/Supr*
Steven Minaudo, *Design Engr*
▲ EMP: 33 EST: 1973
SQ FT: 38,000
SALES (est): 6.1MM **Privately Held**
WEB: www.cranetechnologies.com
SIC: 7389 5084 3536 Crane & aerial lift service; cranes, industrial; cranes, industrial plant

(G-13986)
CROSSCON INDUSTRIES LLC
2889 Bond St (48309-3515)
PHONE..................................248 852-5888
Don Shi, *Mng Member*
◆ EMP: 18 EST: 2005
SALES (est): 2.5MM **Privately Held**
WEB: www.crosscon-ind.com.cn
SIC: 3694 Automotive electrical equipment

(G-13987)
CS EXPRESS INC
2181 Siboney Ct (48309-3748)
PHONE..................................248 425-1726
Ann Soos, *President*
EMP: 4 EST: 2005
SALES (est): 161.9K **Privately Held**
SIC: 2741 Miscellaneous publishing

(G-13988)
CUBBIE PUBLICATIONS
590 Lehigh Rd (48307-3743)
PHONE..................................248 852-5297
Dale Gensman, *Principal*
EMP: 5 EST: 2010
SALES (est): 58.5K **Privately Held**
SIC: 2741 Miscellaneous publishing

(G-13989)
DAMICK ENTERPRISES
1801 Rochester Indus Ct (48309-3336)
PHONE..................................248 652-7500
Frank Sikorski, *President*
Mike Janes, *Vice Pres*
Dale Janes, *Treasurer*
EMP: 17 EST: 1979
SQ FT: 8,300
SALES (est): 3MM **Privately Held**
WEB: www.damick.net
SIC: 3599 Electrical discharge machining (EDM)

(G-13990)
DATASPEED INC (PA)
Also Called: Engineering
2736 Research Dr (48309-3574)
PHONE..................................248 243-8889
Paul Fleck, *CEO*
James Fleck, *Engineer*
Mike Norman, *Engineer*
Paul Mc Cown, *CFO*
Hoda Abdalla, *Accounts Mgr*
EMP: 34 EST: 2005
SALES (est): 5MM **Privately Held**
WEB: www.dataspeedinc.com
SIC: 3699 Automotive driving simulators (training aids), electronic

(G-13991)
DELFINGEN US INC (DH)
3985 W Hamlin Rd (48309-3233)
PHONE..................................716 215-0300
Bernard Streit, *President*
Emmanuel Klinklin, *Exec VP*
Marc Lemke, *Vice Pres*
Rouelito Pilario, *Engineer*
Maria Sanchez, *Engineer*
◆ EMP: 25 EST: 1992
SALES (est): 110.7MM
SALES (corp-wide): 3.1MM **Privately Held**
WEB: www.delfingen.com
SIC: 3089 Extruded finished plastic products
HQ: Delfingen Us-Holding, Inc.
    3985 W Hamlin Rd
    Rochester Hills MI 48309
    248 230-3500

(G-13992)
DELFINGEN US-CENTRAL AMER INC
3985 W Hamlin Rd (48309-3233)
PHONE..................................248 230-3500
Gerald Streit, *CEO*
Bernard Streit, *President*
Mark Blanke, *CFO*
Leilani Santos, *Controller*
Emmanuel Klinklin, *Admin Sec*
EMP: 1 EST: 2004
SALES (est): 1.1MM
SALES (corp-wide): 3.1MM **Privately Held**
WEB: www.delfingen.com
SIC: 3089 Extruded finished plastic products
HQ: Delfingen Us-Holding, Inc.
    3985 W Hamlin Rd
    Rochester Hills MI 48309
    248 230-3500

(G-13993)
DELFINGEN US-HOLDING INC (DH)
Also Called: Delfingen Industry
3985 W Hamlin Rd (48309-3233)
PHONE..................................248 230-3500
Bernard Streit, *President*
Mark Blanke, *CFO*
◆ EMP: 1 EST: 1998
SQ FT: 5,000
SALES (est): 150.1MM
SALES (corp-wide): 3.1MM **Privately Held**
WEB: www.delfingen.com
SIC: 3089 Extruded finished plastic products; injection molded finished plastic products

(G-13994)
DELL MARKING SYSTEMS INC
6841 N Rochester Rd # 250 (48306-4375)
PHONE..................................248 547-7750
Michael A Grattan, *President*
Darren Witherspoon, *Sales Staff*
Gabriella Randazzo, *Marketing Staff*
Shannon McKinley, *Manager*
Norton Delidow, *Consultant*
◆ EMP: 9 EST: 1987

GEOGRAPHIC SECTION

Rochester Hills - Oakland County (G-14021)

SQ FT: 7,000
SALES (est): 1.3MM **Privately Held**
WEB: www.dellid.com
SIC: 2899 Ink or writing fluids

(G-13995)
DETROIT TORCH
1555 W Hamlin Rd (48309-3353)
PHONE..................................248 499-8122
EMP: 7 EST: 2017
SALES (est): 252.1K **Privately Held**
WEB: www.detroittorch.com
SIC: 7692 Welding repair

(G-13996)
DL ENGINEERING & TECH INC
Also Called: Rytam Technolgy
1749 W Hamlin Rd (48309-3373)
PHONE..................................248 852-6900
David Lubera, *President*
EMP: 6 EST: 1979
SQ FT: 8,500
SALES (est): 890.7K **Privately Held**
WEB: www.rytamtech.com
SIC: 3089 Injection molding of plastics

(G-13997)
DURA GLOBAL TECHNOLOGIES INC
2791 Research Dr (48309-3575)
PHONE..................................248 299-7500
EMP: 49 EST: 1999
SALES (est): 1.6MM **Privately Held**
WEB: www.duraauto.com
SIC: 3714 Motor vehicle parts & accessories

(G-13998)
DURA SHIFTER LLC
2791 Research Dr (48309-3575)
PHONE..................................248 299-7500
EMP: 13 EST: 2002
SALES (est): 839.3K **Privately Held**
SIC: 3714 Motor vehicle parts & accessories

(G-13999)
ECO PAPER
1150 W Hamlin Rd (48309-3356)
PHONE..................................248 652-3601
EMP: 5
SALES (est): 482.3K **Privately Held**
SIC: 2653 Mfg Corrugated/Solid Fiber Boxes

(G-14000)
EDS INDUSTRIES
1543 W Hamlin Rd (48309-3353)
PHONE..................................989 274-2551
EMP: 5 EST: 2013
SALES (est): 241K **Privately Held**
SIC: 3999 Manufacturing industries

(G-14001)
EID REAL ESTATES LLC
533 Slumber Ln (48307-2885)
PHONE..................................717 471-5996
EMP: 4 EST: 2018
SALES (est): 113.3K **Privately Held**
SIC: 2512 Upholstered household furniture

(G-14002)
EISSMANN AUTO PORT HURON LLC
2655 Product Dr (48309-3808)
PHONE..................................248 829-4990
EMP: 50
SALES (corp-wide): 519.2MM **Privately Held**
SIC: 2396 Mfg Auto/Apparel Trimming
HQ: Eissmann Automotive Port Huron Llc
2440 20th St
Port Huron MI 48060
810 216-6300

(G-14003)
ELITE ENGINEERING INC
Also Called: Eflex Sytems
210 W Tienken Rd (48306-4404)
PHONE..................................517 304-3254
Dan McKiernan, *President*
George Jewell, *Vice Pres*
Jason Bullard, *Sales Engr*
Josh Easterling, *Sales Staff*
Tina Kennedy, *Mktg Dir*
EMP: 39 EST: 1989
SQ FT: 11,000
SALES (est): 2.7MM **Privately Held**
WEB: www.eflexsystems.com
SIC: 8711 7371 3577 Consulting engineer; computer software development; computer peripheral equipment

(G-14004)
ENERGY STEEL & SUPPLY CO
1785 Northfield Dr (48309-3819)
PHONE..................................810 538-4990
James Lines, *CEO*
Joseph Aliasso, *General Mgr*
Bob Paton, *Vice Pres*
Robert J Paton, *Vice Pres*
Will Gardner, *Project Mgr*
▼ EMP: 55 EST: 1982
SALES (est): 17MM
SALES (corp-wide): 97.4MM **Publicly Held**
WEB: www.energysteel.com
SIC: 3317 5051 Steel pipe & tubes; pipe & tubing, steel
PA: The Graham Corporation
20 Florence Ave
Batavia NY 14020
585 343-2216

(G-14005)
ENTREPRENEURIAL PURSUITS
Also Called: Jan Fan
2727 Product Dr (48309-3810)
PHONE..................................248 829-6903
John Hamernik, *President*
Mark Goatley, *Vice Pres*
EMP: 4 EST: 2014
SALES (est): 469.4K **Privately Held**
SIC: 3564 Blowing fans: industrial or commercial

(G-14006)
EWS LEGACY LLC (PA)
2119 Austin Ave (48309-3668)
PHONE..................................248 853-6363
Robert Brzustewicz, *General Mgr*
Tomoji Yamamoto, *Vice Pres*
Dawn Holladay, *Purchasing*
William Stadnikia, *Purchasing*
Thomas Roach, *QC Mgr*
▲ EMP: 144 EST: 1999
SQ FT: 53,000
SALES (est): 46.8MM **Privately Held**
SIC: 3641 3613 3357 3643 Electric lamps; switchgear & switchboard apparatus; nonferrous wiredrawing & insulating; current-carrying wiring devices; electronic computers; noncurrent-carrying wiring services

(G-14007)
EXTRUSION PUNCH & TOOL COMPANY
1977 Rochester Indus Dr (48309-3344)
PHONE..................................248 689-3300
Roger D Michels, *CEO*
Greg Ornazian, *President*
EMP: 25 EST: 1980
SQ FT: 8,000
SALES (est): 1.8MM **Privately Held**
SIC: 3599 3544 3494 Machine shop, jobbing & repair; special dies, tools, jigs & fixtures; valves & pipe fittings

(G-14008)
F I D CORPORATION
Also Called: Epcon
3424 Charlwood Dr (48306-3619)
PHONE..................................248 373-7005
Felix Nedorezov, *President*
Nina Nedorezov, *Vice Pres*
EMP: 8 EST: 1982
SQ FT: 2,000
SALES (est): 1.5MM **Privately Held**
SIC: 3829 8742 Aircraft & motor vehicle measurement equipment; business consultant

(G-14009)
FANUC AMERICA CORPORATION (HQ)
3900 W Hamlin Rd (48309-3253)
PHONE..................................248 377-7000
Richard E Schneider, *Ch of Bd*
Mike Cicco, *President*
Chip Wells, *District Mgr*
Niles Kevin Ostby, *Vice Pres*
Steven Stanko, *Vice Pres*
◆ EMP: 500 EST: 1992
SQ FT: 370,000
SALES (est): 377.1MM **Privately Held**
WEB: www.fanucamerica.com
SIC: 3559 3548 3569 3542 Metal finishing equipment for plating, etc.; electric welding equipment; robots, assembly line: industrial & commercial; robots for metal forming: pressing, extruding, etc.

(G-14010)
FEDERAL HEATH SIGN COMPANY LLC
1806 Rochester Indl Dr (48309-3337)
PHONE..................................248 656-8000
EMP: 42
SALES (corp-wide): 1.8B **Privately Held**
WEB: www.federalheath.com
SIC: 2791 2759 2752 2396 Typesetting; commercial printing; commercial printing, lithographic; automotive & apparel trimmings; signs, not made in custom sign painting shops
HQ: Federal Heath Sign Company, Llc
2300 St Hwy 121
Euless TX 76039

(G-14011)
FIDIA CO
3098 Research Dr (48309-3580)
PHONE..................................248 680-0700
Giuseppe Morfino, *President*
Andy Taylor, *Regl Sales Mgr*
Doug Michael, *Manager*
▲ EMP: 15 EST: 2005
SALES (est): 8.3MM
SALES (corp-wide): 35.6MM **Privately Held**
WEB: www.fidia.it
SIC: 3625 7699 Numerical controls; industrial equipment services
PA: Fidia Spa
Corso Lombardia 11
San Mauro Torinese TO 10099
011 222-7111

(G-14012)
FOAMPARTNER AMERICAS INC
Also Called: Otto Bock
2923 Technology Dr (48309-3589)
PHONE..................................248 243-3100
Olaf Vorwald, *CEO*
Peter Gansen, *President*
Hans Georg Nader, *Vice Pres*
Nancy Feeney, *Controller*
▲ EMP: 7 EST: 1999
SALES (est): 12.4MM
SALES (corp-wide): 143MM **Privately Held**
WEB: www.recticelengineeredfoams.com
SIC: 2821 Plastics materials & resins
HQ: Recticel Engineered Foams Germany Gmbh
Schlaraffiastr. 1-10
Bochum 44867

(G-14013)
FORMFAB LLC
3044 Research Dr (48309-3580)
PHONE..................................248 844-3676
Norman P Caetano, *President*
Cory Radomski, *QC Mgr*
EMP: 50 EST: 1998
SQ FT: 26,000
SALES (est): 8.8MM **Privately Held**
WEB: www.formfabllc.com
SIC: 3317 3498 3714 3544 Steel pipe & tubes; fabricated pipe & fittings; air conditioner parts, motor vehicle; forms (molds), for foundry & plastics working machinery

(G-14014)
FRAM GROUP OPERATIONS LLC (DH)
Also Called: Fram Group Limited
3255 W Hamlin Rd (48309-3231)
P.O. Box 94440, Lubbock TX (79493-4440)
PHONE..................................800 890-2075
Jeffrey Mathis, *Counsel*
Joe Doolan, *Vice Pres*
Mark Farrugia, *Vice Pres*
Scott Felts, *Vice Pres*
Paul Sproles, *Vice Pres*
SALES (est): 27.4MM
SALES (corp-wide): 3.3B **Privately Held**
WEB: www.fram.com
SIC: 3694 3714 Engine electrical equipment; motor vehicle parts & accessories
HQ: Framauto Holdings, Llc
127 Public Sq Ste 5110
Cleveland OH 44114
216 589-0198

(G-14015)
FRASER FAB AND MACHINE INC
1696 Star Batt Dr (48309-3705)
PHONE..................................248 852-9050
David Hartig, *President*
James Hartig, *Treasurer*
EMP: 24 EST: 1967
SQ FT: 13,000
SALES (est): 4.3MM **Privately Held**
WEB: www.fraserfab.com
SIC: 3599 7692 3535 Machine shop, jobbing & repair; welding repair; conveyors & conveying equipment

(G-14016)
FROM PHOTOS TO CANVAS PRINTS
492 Buttercup Dr (48307-5211)
PHONE..................................248 760-4694
EMP: 4 EST: 2017
SALES (est): 83.9K **Privately Held**
SIC: 2752 Commercial printing, lithographic

(G-14017)
FUDGE BUSINESS FORMS INC
2251 Star Ct (48309-3625)
PHONE..................................248 299-3666
William Fudge, *President*
Beverly Fudge, *Corp Secy*
EMP: 8 EST: 1992
SALES (est): 999.6K **Privately Held**
SIC: 2752 Commercial printing, offset

(G-14018)
FUTURISTIC ARTWEAR INC
787 Majestic (48306-3572)
PHONE..................................248 680-0200
Michael Cannon, *President*
EMP: 10 EST: 1978
SQ FT: 16,000
SALES (est): 541.4K **Privately Held**
SIC: 2759 Screen printing

(G-14019)
G P DURA
2791 Research Dr (48309-3575)
PHONE..................................248 299-7500
EMP: 18 EST: 2002
SALES (est): 684.2K **Privately Held**
SIC: 3714 Motor vehicle parts & accessories

(G-14020)
GATES CORPORATION
Also Called: Worldwide Power Transm Div
2975 Waterview Dr (48309-4600)
PHONE..................................248 260-2300
Rick Lesperance, *Production*
JP Rodrigues, *Purch Dir*
Susanne Leblanc, *Buyer*
Gabrielle May, *Engineer*
Richard Billings, *Senior Engr*
EMP: 5
SALES (corp-wide): 2.7B **Publicly Held**
WEB: www.gates.com
SIC: 3052 8731 3568 3714 Rubber belting; commercial physical research; power transmission equipment; motor vehicle parts & accessories; manufactured hardware (general)
HQ: The Gates Corporation
1144 15th St Ste 1400
Denver CO 80202
303 744-1911

(G-14021)
GENERAL DYNAMICS MISSION
2909 Waterview Dr (48309-4600)
PHONE..................................530 271-2500
Gregg Walker, *Engineer*
EMP: 1284

Rochester Hills - Oakland County (G-14022)

SALES (corp-wide): 37.9B **Publicly Held**
WEB: www.gdmissionsystems.com
SIC: 3827 3861 Optical instruments & apparatus; photographic equipment & supplies; aerial cameras
HQ: General Dynamics Mission Systems, Inc.
12450 Fair Lakes Cir
Fairfax VA 22033
877 449-0600

(G-14022)
GENERAL DYNMICS GLOBL IMGING T (DH)
2909 Waterview Dr (48309-4600)
PHONE.............................248 293-2929
Scott Butler, *President*
Mike Clifford, *Design Engr*
Thomas Vettese, *Director*
▲ **EMP:** 597 **EST:** 2012
SALES (est): 217MM
SALES (corp-wide): 37.9B **Publicly Held**
WEB: www.gdmissionsystems.com
SIC: 3827 3861 Optical instruments & apparatus; photographic equipment & supplies; aerial cameras
HQ: General Dynamics Government Systems Corporation
2941 Fairview Park Dr
Falls Church VA 22042
703 876-3000

(G-14023)
GENERAL PLYMERS THRMPLSTIC MTL
6841 N Rochester Rd Stdio1 (48306-4375)
P.O. Box 146, Romeo (48065-0146)
PHONE.............................800 920-8033
Douglas Miner, *Manager*
Gregory Boston,
Mike Kirtley,
EMP: 2 **EST:** 2016
SALES (est): 1MM **Privately Held**
WEB: www.gp-materials.com
SIC: 2821 Plastics materials & resins

(G-14024)
GEORGE KOCH SONS LLC
Also Called: Jessup Systems
2745 Bond St (48309-3513)
PHONE.............................248 237-1100
John Patton, *Manager*
EMP: 40
SALES (corp-wide): 1B **Privately Held**
WEB: www.kochllc.com
SIC: 3559 Metal finishing equipment for plating, etc.
HQ: George Koch Sons, Llc
10 S 11th Ave
Evansville IN 47712
812 465-9600

(G-14025)
GET CUSTOMIZED
3055 Crooks Rd (48309-4148)
PHONE.............................586 909-3881
Michael Goughler, *Principal*
EMP: 5 **EST:** 2014
SALES (est): 396.8K **Privately Held**
WEB: www.getcustomized.com
SIC: 2323 Men's & boys' neckwear

(G-14026)
GOOD PARTS
140 W Hamlin Rd (48307-3831)
PHONE.............................248 656-7643
Joseph Gendich, *Owner*
EMP: 5 **EST:** 2015
SALES (est): 132.7K **Privately Held**
SIC: 3566 Speed changers, drives & gears

(G-14027)
GRANITE PRECISION TOOL CORP
2257 Star Ct (48309-3625)
PHONE.............................248 299-8317
Richard Przybylowicz, *President*
EMP: 9 **EST:** 1995
SQ FT: 1,600
SALES (est): 847.6K **Privately Held**
SIC: 3544 Special dies & tools

(G-14028)
GST AUTOLEATHER HOLDCO CORP
2920 Waterview Dr (48309-3484)
PHONE.............................248 436-2300
Dennis E Hiller, *CEO*
EMP: 12 **EST:** 2008
SALES (est): 195.3K **Privately Held**
WEB: www.gstautoleather.com
SIC: 3199 Equestrian related leather articles

(G-14029)
HAMLIN TOOL & MACHINE CO INC
1671 E Hamlin Rd (48307-3624)
PHONE.............................248 651-6302
Patrick Pihjalic, *President*
Mike Gaskin, *Plant Supt*
Patrick Pihajlic, *Export Mgr*
Stan Damer, *Engineer*
Craig Dobson, *Manager*
EMP: 46 **EST:** 1952
SQ FT: 55,000
SALES (est): 17.9MM **Privately Held**
WEB: www.hamlintool.com
SIC: 3714 3465 Motor vehicle parts & accessories; automotive stampings

(G-14030)
HI-LEX AMERICA INCORPORATED
Also Called: Hi-Lex Automotive Centre
2911 Research Dr (48309-3579)
PHONE.............................248 844-0096
Kimberley Griffiths, *Purchasing*
Hank Ratliff, *Engineer*
Ken Repke, *Engineer*
Ed Lother, *Senior Engr*
Alan Schneider, *Finance Mgr*
EMP: 272 **Privately Held**
SIC: 3714 3496 3643 Motor vehicle parts & accessories; cable, uninsulated wire: made from purchased wire; current-carrying wiring devices
HQ: Hi-Lex America, Incorporated
5200 Wayne Rd
Battle Creek MI 49037
269 968-0781

(G-14031)
HI-TECH MOLD & ENGINEERING INC
1758 Northfield Dr (48309-3818)
PHONE.............................248 844-0722
EMP: 20
SALES (corp-wide): 58.8MM **Privately Held**
SIC: 3544 Mfg Plastic Injection Molds & Dies
PA: Hi-Tech Mold & Engineering, Inc.
2775 Commerce Dr
Rochester Hills MI 48309
248 852-6600

(G-14032)
HI-TECH MOLD & ENGINEERING INC (PA)
2775 Commerce Dr (48309-3815)
PHONE.............................248 852-6600
Robert Schulte, *President*
Siegfried Schulte, *Chairman*
Paul Glowicki, *COO*
Edwin Berrios, *Vice Pres*
Klaus Bohn, *Vice Pres*
▲ **EMP:** 37 **EST:** 1982
SQ FT: 140,000
SALES (est): 56.1MM **Privately Held**
WEB: www.hitechmold.com
SIC: 3544 Forms (molds), for foundry & plastics working machinery; dies, plastics forming

(G-14033)
HIRSCHMANN AUTO N AMER LLC
2927 Waterview Dr (48309-4600)
PHONE.............................248 495-2677
Angelo Holzknecht, *Mng Member*
EMP: 3 **EST:** 2014
SALES (est): 1.6MM
SALES (corp-wide): 2.6MM **Privately Held**
WEB: www.hirschmann-automotive.com
SIC: 3678 Electronic connectors
HQ: Hirschmann Automotive Gmbh
Oberer Paspelsweg 6-8
Rankweil 6830
552 230-70

(G-14034)
HOT MELT TECHNOLOGIES INC
Also Called: H M T
1723 W Hamlin Rd (48309-3368)
P.O. Box 80067, Rochester (48308-0067)
PHONE.............................248 853-2011
Bryan J Tanury, *President*
Ester C Tanury, *Vice Pres*
Rosalyn Wilson, *Production*
Gary Bessey, *Regl Sales Mgr*
Scott Jarvis, *Sales Staff*
▼ **EMP:** 30 **EST:** 1981
SQ FT: 18,000
SALES (est): 5MM **Privately Held**
WEB: www.hotmelt-tech.com
SIC: 3565 5084 3569 Packaging machinery; industrial machinery & equipment; packaging machinery & equipment; assembly machines, non-metalworking

(G-14035)
HS INC
Also Called: H S Express
1720 Star Batt Dr (48309-3707)
PHONE.............................248 373-4048
John Centers, *Purchasing*
Jeffrey Hearn, *Manager*
EMP: 4
SALES (corp-wide): 50MM **Privately Held**
WEB: www.hsinc.us
SIC: 3442 Molding, trim & stripping; window & door frames
PA: H.S. Inc.
O-215 Lake Michigan Dr Nw
Grand Rapids MI 49534
616 453-5451

(G-14036)
HYDRAULIC SYSTEMS TECHNOLOGY
1156 Whispering Knoll Ln (48306-4176)
PHONE.............................248 656-5810
Perry Decuir, *President*
EMP: 5 **EST:** 1993
SALES (est): 529.4K **Privately Held**
WEB: www.hstpress.com
SIC: 5013 5065 3625 8734 Motor vehicle supplies & new parts; electronic parts & equipment; motor controls & accessories; product testing laboratories

(G-14037)
HYDRO-CRAFT INC
1821 Rochester Indus Ct (48309-3336)
PHONE.............................248 652-8100
Peter Blumbergs, *Branch Mgr*
EMP: 9
SALES (corp-wide): 2.2MM **Privately Held**
WEB: www.hydro-craft.com
SIC: 3429 3541 3714 3594 Manufactured hardware (general); machine tools, metal cutting type; motor vehicle parts & accessories; fluid power pumps & motors; fabricated plate work (boiler shop); machine tool attachments & accessories
PA: Hydro-Craft, Inc.
410 E Paradise Hills Dr
Henderson NV 89002
702 566-8798

(G-14038)
ILLUMINATION MACHINES LLC
Also Called: Im
2830 Steamboat Springs Dr (48309-1385)
PHONE.............................856 685-7403
Edward Bailey,
EMP: 5 **EST:** 2010
SALES (est): 359.5K **Privately Held**
SIC: 3646 3647 3648 3641 Commercial indusl & institutional electric lighting fixtures; headlights (fixtures), vehicular; reflectors for lighting equipment: metal; electric lamps & parts for specialized applications; consulting engineer

(G-14039)
INDUSTRIAL AUTOMATION LLC (PA)
2968 Waterview Dr (48309-3484)
PHONE.............................248 598-5900
Jeff Kotila, *General Mgr*
Craig Walters, *Business Mgr*
Adrienne Young, *Purch Mgr*
Katelynn Haas, *Accountant*
Amelia Hariton, *Human Res Mgr*
◆ **EMP:** 68 **EST:** 1992
SQ FT: 15,000
SALES (est): 17.6MM **Privately Held**
WEB: www.industrialautomationllc.com
SIC: 3549 5084 Metalworking machinery; industrial machinery & equipment

(G-14040)
INOVISION INC
2610 Bond St (48309-3509)
PHONE.............................248 299-1915
Chad Fares, *Project Engr*
Zhipeng Liang, *Software Engr*
EMP: 29 **Privately Held**
SIC: 7372 Prepackaged software
PA: Inovision Software Solutions, Inc.
50561 Chesterfield Rd
Chesterfield MI 48051

(G-14041)
INZI CONTROLS DETROIT LLC
2950 Technology Dr (48309-3588)
PHONE.............................334 282-4237
Gyuwan Kim, *President*
▲ **EMP:** 3 **EST:** 2014
SALES (est): 6.7MM **Privately Held**
SIC: 3714 Motor vehicle parts & accessories
HQ: Inzi Controls Alabama, Inc.
375 Alabama Highway 203
Elba AL 36323

(G-14042)
JAMES W LIESS CO INC
3410 Baroque Ct (48306-3704)
PHONE.............................248 547-9160
EMP: 4
SALES (corp-wide): 469.7K **Privately Held**
SIC: 3536 Man/Ret Gantries
PA: James W Liess Co Inc
3628 Thornwood Dr
Auburn Hills MI 48326
248 373-1510

(G-14043)
JENOPTIK AUTOMOTIVE N AMER LLC
Also Called: Hommel Movomatic
1500 W Hamlin Rd (48309-3365)
PHONE.............................248 853-5888
Steve Green, *President*
Martin Kuhnhen, *Chairman*
Andy Dine, *Regional Mgr*
Dawn Laslie, *Vice Pres*
Linda Brownie, *Purchasing*
◆ **EMP:** 142 **EST:** 1970
SQ FT: 100,000
SALES (est): 31.4MM
SALES (corp-wide): 907.3MM **Privately Held**
WEB: www.jenoptik.us
SIC: 3827 Optical instruments & lenses
HQ: Jenoptik North America, Inc.
16490 Innovation Dr
Jupiter FL 33478

(G-14044)
KAMAX INC (HQ)
1606 Star Batt Dr (48309-3705)
PHONE.............................248 879-0200
Mark Hilfinger, *President*
Joachim Lang, *General Mgr*
Tushar Mulherkar, *Vice Pres*
David Winn, *Vice Pres*
Chris Zandi, *Plant Mgr*
◆ **EMP:** 40 **EST:** 1935
SQ FT: 162,000
SALES (est): 147.9MM
SALES (corp-wide): 856.3MM **Privately Held**
WEB: www.kamax.com
SIC: 3452 Bolts, metal

GEOGRAPHIC SECTION
Rochester Hills - Oakland County (G-14072)

PA: Karnax Holding Gmbh & Co. Kg
Dr.-Rudolf-Kellermann-Str. 2
Homberg (Ohm) HE 35315
663 379-0

(G-14045)
KEYS N MORE
2985 Crooks Rd (48309-3663)
PHONE....................248 260-1967
EMP: 5 **EST:** 2014
SALES (est): 97.9K **Privately Held**
SIC: 3429 Keys, locks & related hardware

(G-14046)
KORENS
1685 W Hamlin Rd (48309-3312)
PHONE....................248 817-5188
Tae Jin Kim, *Administration*
EMP: 5 **EST:** 2013
SALES (est): 456.8K **Privately Held**
WEB: www.korens.com
SIC: 3069 Rubber automotive products

(G-14047)
KOSTAL KONTAKT SYSTEME INC
Also Called: Kostal Group
1350 W Hamlin Rd (48309-3361)
PHONE....................248 284-7600
Holger Lettmann, *CEO*
David Delgado, *Vice Pres*
Derrick Busch, *Project Mgr*
Mark Lee, *Mfg Staff*
Douglas Marcellino, *Engineer*
▲ **EMP:** 200 **EST:** 2010
SALES (est): 62.5MM
SALES (corp-wide): 1.1MM **Privately Held**
WEB: www.kostal.com
SIC: 3678 Electronic connectors
HQ: Kostal Automobil Elektrik Gmbh & Co. Kg
An Der Bellmerei 10
Ludenscheid NW 58513
235 116-0

(G-14048)
LANE TOOL
1940 S Livernois Rd (48307-3368)
PHONE....................248 528-1606
Justin Garrido, *Purchasing*
EMP: 8 **EST:** 1967
SALES (est): 398.5K **Privately Held**
WEB: www.lanetool.net
SIC: 3544 Special dies & tools

(G-14049)
LANE TOOL AND MFG CORP
1940 S Livernois Rd (48307-3368)
PHONE....................248 528-1606
Kevin Harper, *President*
Chris Harper, *Treasurer*
Michael Harper, *Manager*
Scott Harper, *Admin Sec*
EMP: 9 **EST:** 1968
SQ FT: 6,000
SALES (est): 1MM **Privately Held**
WEB: www.lanetoolmichigan.com
SIC: 3544 Jigs & fixtures; dies, steel rule

(G-14050)
LEAR CORPORATION
3000 Research Dr (48309-3580)
PHONE....................248 299-7100
Greg Laporte, *Engineer*
Bret Eadertsher, *Branch Mgr*
EMP: 7
SALES (corp-wide): 17B **Publicly Held**
WEB: www.lear.com
SIC: 3714 Motor vehicle parts & accessories
PA: Lear Corporation
21557 Telegraph Rd
Southfield MI 48033
248 447-1500

(G-14051)
LEAR CORPORATION
Also Called: Rochester Hills Facility
2930 W Auburn Rd (48309-3505)
PHONE....................248 853-3122
Adarsha Madhu, *Engineer*
Brian Corbett, *Corp Comm Staff*
EMP: 7
SALES (corp-wide): 17B **Publicly Held**
WEB: www.lear.com
SIC: 3111 Leather tanning & finishing
PA: Lear Corporation
21557 Telegraph Rd
Southfield MI 48033
248 447-1500

(G-14052)
LEGACY DESIGN STUDIO LLC
1010 W Hamlin Rd (48309-3354)
PHONE....................248 710-3219
EMP: 5 **EST:** 2018
SALES (est): 88.6K **Privately Held**
SIC: 2759 Screen printing

(G-14053)
LETICA CORPORATION (DH)
52585 Dequindre Rd (48307-2321)
P.O. Box 5005, Rochester (48308-5005)
PHONE....................248 652-0557
Anton Letica, *CEO*
Thaddeus F Kaczorowski, *Principal*
Edward Doyle, *District Mgr*
Neal Craig, *Business Mgr*
Ed Doyle, *Business Mgr*
◆ **EMP:** 150 **EST:** 1968
SQ FT: 92,584
SALES (est): 450MM **Publicly Held**
WEB: www.letica.com
SIC: 2656 3089 Sanitary food containers; plastic containers, except foam

(G-14054)
LUMEN NORTH AMERICA INC
2850 Commerce Dr (48309-3816)
PHONE....................248 289-6100
Jonathan Evans, *President*
Michael Waterson, *Vice Pres*
EMP: 15 **EST:** 2013
SALES (est): 2.4MM **Privately Held**
WEB: www.lumen.com.au
SIC: 3357 3694 Automotive wire & cable, except ignition sets: nonferrous; automotive electrical equipment

(G-14055)
LXR BIOTECH LLC
2983 Waterview Dr (48309-4600)
PHONE....................248 860-4246
Andrew Krause, *Branch Mgr*
EMP: 25 **Privately Held**
WEB: www.lxrbiotech.com
SIC: 2834 Pharmaceutical preparations
PA: Lxr Biotech, Llc
4225 N Atlantic Blvd
Auburn Hills MI 48326

(G-14056)
M P I INTERNATIONAL INC (PA)
2129 Austin Ave (48309-3668)
PHONE....................608 764-5416
Mike Bryant, *CEO*
Robert Kuth, *Vice Pres*
Michael Niemiec, *CFO*
Esmeralda Arias, *Finance Mgr*
Craig Riess, *Manager*
EMP: 500 **EST:** 1969
SALES (est): 82.7MM **Privately Held**
SIC: 3462 3714 3469 Automotive forgings, ferrous: crankshaft, engine, axle, etc.; motor vehicle transmissions, drive assemblies & parts; metal stampings

(G-14057)
MAGNA CAR TOP SYSTEMS AMER INC (HQ)
456 Wimpole Dr (48309-2152)
PHONE....................248 836-4500
Shawn Bentley, *General Mgr*
Timothy Dawson, *Engineer*
Ray Zeller, *Engineer*
Ruth Kell, *Finance Dir*
▲ **EMP:** 225 **EST:** 1999
SALES (est): 108MM
SALES (corp-wide): 32.6B **Privately Held**
WEB: www.magna.com
SIC: 2394 Convertible tops, canvas or boat: from purchased materials
PA: Magna International Inc
337 Magna Dr
Aurora ON L4G 7
905 726-2462

(G-14058)
MANUFACTURING CTRL SYSTEMS INC
1928 Star Batt Dr Ste C (48309-3722)
PHONE....................248 853-7400
Joseph L Steimel, *President*
Nancy Steimel, *Vice Pres*
EMP: 7 **EST:** 1979
SALES (est): 2.3MM **Privately Held**
WEB: www.mfgcontrolservice.com
SIC: 3625 8711 Industrial controls: push button, selector switches, pilot; electrical or electronic engineering

(G-14059)
MATHEW PARMELEE
Also Called: Parma Diversified Technologies
707 W Hamlin Rd (48307-3434)
PHONE....................248 894-5955
Mathew Parmelee, *Partner*
Ken Schafer, *Partner*
EMP: 4 **EST:** 1999
SALES (est): 160.1K **Privately Held**
WEB: www.parmeleemusicstudios.com
SIC: 8299 3599 Musical instrument lessons; machine shop, jobbing & repair

(G-14060)
MAXUM LLC
600 Oliver Dr (48309)
P.O. Box 70025, Rochester (48307-0001)
PHONE....................248 726-7110
James Pamey,
EMP: 6 **EST:** 2010
SALES (est): 504.2K **Privately Held**
WEB: www.maxumair.com
SIC: 3599 Industrial machinery

(G-14061)
MCKENNA ENTERPRISES INC
3128 Walton Blvd (48309-1265)
PHONE....................248 375-3388
Kevin McKenna, *Manager*
EMP: 7 **EST:** 2004
SALES (est): 139.7K **Privately Held**
SIC: 2674 Shipping & shopping bags or sacks

(G-14062)
METAL MERCHANTS OF MICHIGAN
2691 Leach Rd (48309-3558)
PHONE....................248 293-0621
Robert Allen, *CEO*
EMP: 13 **EST:** 1973
SALES (est): 387K **Privately Held**
WEB: www.allenbrothersinc.com
SIC: 3444 Concrete forms, sheet metal

(G-14063)
MID-WEST WIRE PRODUCTS INC
1109 Brompton Rd (48309-4384)
PHONE....................248 548-3200
Richard Geralds, *CEO*
William Klein, *President*
George Buchanan, *Vice Pres*
Christopher Wozniacki, *Vice Pres*
▼ **EMP:** 44 **EST:** 1927
SQ FT: 80,000
SALES (est): 2.2MM **Privately Held**
WEB: www.midwestwire.com
SIC: 3496 Miscellaneous fabricated wire products

(G-14064)
MIS CONTROLS INC
2890 Technology Dr (48309-3586)
PHONE....................586 339-3900
Naji Gebara, *President*
EMP: 25 **EST:** 2014
SALES (est): 1.2MM **Privately Held**
WEB: www.miscontrols.com
SIC: 3281 Switchboard panels, slate

(G-14065)
MOTOR PARTS INC OF MICHIGAN
2751 Commerce Dr (48309-3815)
PHONE....................248 852-1522
Earl Moede, *President*
EMP: 21 **EST:** 1967
SQ FT: 18,600
SALES (est): 2.7MM **Privately Held**
SIC: 3714 Motor vehicle engines & parts

(G-14066)
MPI PRODUCTS HOLDINGS LLC (DH)
2129 Austin Ave (48309-3668)
PHONE....................248 237-3007
Steven Crain, *President*
Thomas Janson, *Engineer*
Mike Putz, *CFO*
EMP: 100 **EST:** 2012
SALES (est): 266.8MM
SALES (corp-wide): 486.7MM **Privately Held**
WEB: www.mpiproducts.com
SIC: 3448 Prefabricated metal components
HQ: Mpi Global Holdings Corp.
2129 Austin Ave
Rochester Hills MI 48309
248 237-3007

(G-14067)
MPI PRODUCTS LLC
2129 Austin Ave (48309-3668)
PHONE....................248 237-3007
Frans Boos, *Vice Pres*
Carlos Luca, *Mfg Staff*
Steve Fitzgerald, *Engineer*
David Crisp, *VP Sales*
Trevor Meyers, *Mng Member*
EMP: 73 **EST:** 1969
SALES (est): 2.6MM **Privately Held**
SIC: 3365 Machinery castings, aluminum

(G-14068)
NATIONAL PACKAGING CORPORATION
1150 W Hamlin Rd (48309-3356)
PHONE....................248 652-3600
William Icikson, *President*
Ester Icikson, *Vice Pres*
EMP: 11 **EST:** 1978
SQ FT: 40,000
SALES (est): 305K **Privately Held**
SIC: 5113 2653 Corrugated & solid fiber boxes; corrugated & solid fiber boxes

(G-14069)
NEXIQ TECHNOLOGIES INC
2950 Waterview Dr (48309-4601)
PHONE....................248 293-8200
Jack Michael, *President*
David Shock, *Manager*
EMP: 13 **EST:** 2008
SALES (est): 508.6K **Privately Held**
WEB: www.nexiq.com
SIC: 7372 Application computer software

(G-14070)
NORGREN AUTOMTN SOLUTIONS LLC
2871 Bond St (48309-3515)
PHONE....................586 463-3000
Timothy Key, *President*
EMP: 17
SALES (corp-wide): 2.4B **Privately Held**
SIC: 3549 Metalworking machinery
HQ: Norgren Automation Solutions, Llc
1325 Woodland Dr
Saline MI 48176
734 429-4989

(G-14071)
NORTHBOUND INDUSTRIES LLC
469 Arms Ct (48307-3176)
PHONE....................661 510-8537
Bryan Buckler, *Principal*
EMP: 5 **EST:** 2018
SALES (est): 102.8K **Privately Held**
SIC: 3999 Barber & beauty shop equipment

(G-14072)
NORTHERN STAMPINGS INC (PA)
Also Called: Nsi
1853 Rochester Indus Ct (48309-3336)
PHONE....................586 598-6969
Charles Johnson, *President*
Austin Fletcher, *Opers Mgr*
EMP: 10 **EST:** 2002
SQ FT: 5,000
SALES (est): 2.7MM **Privately Held**
WEB: www.northernstampings.com
SIC: 3469 Stamping metal for the trade

Rochester Hills - Oakland County (G-14073)

(G-14073)
NORTHVILLE CIRCUITS INC
Also Called: N. C. I.
1679 W Hamlin Rd (48309-3312)
PHONE..................248 853-3232
Frederick P Freeland, *President*
EMP: 8 **EST:** 1979
SALES (est): 614.5K **Privately Held**
WEB: www.tribalrealty.com
SIC: 3672 8711 3824 Printed circuit boards; engineering services; fluid meters & counting devices

(G-14074)
NYLUBE PRODUCTS COMPANY LLC (PA)
Also Called: Nylube Products Div
2299 Star Ct (48309-3625)
PHONE..................248 852-6500
Shirley Edwards, *Treasurer*
Frank R Edwards,
Frank M Edwards,
▲ **EMP:** 19 **EST:** 1936
SQ FT: 30,000
SALES (est): 3.4MM **Privately Held**
WEB: www.nylube.com
SIC: 3646 3534 Commercial indusl & institutional electric lighting fixtures; elevators & equipment

(G-14075)
ONYX MANUFACTURING INC
1663 Star Batt Dr (48309-3706)
PHONE..................248 687-8611
Raymond Wisniewski, *President*
Stephen Roach III, *Vice Pres*
EMP: 7 **EST:** 2013
SALES (est): 687.5K **Privately Held**
WEB: www.onyxmfg.com
SIC: 7373 3569 3711 8711 Computer-aided manufacturing (CAM) systems service; computer-aided design (CAD) systems service; robots, assembly line: industrial & commercial; automobile assembly, including specialty automobiles; machine tool design;

(G-14076)
ORACLE SYSTEMS CORPORATION
1365 N Fairview Ln (48306-4133)
PHONE..................248 614-5139
Thomas Robb, *Branch Mgr*
EMP: 4
SALES (corp-wide): 40.4B **Publicly Held**
SIC: 7372 Prepackaged software
HQ: Oracle Systems Corporation
500 Oracle Pkwy
Redwood City CA 94065

(G-14077)
OSCO INC
2937 Waterview Dr (48309-4600)
PHONE..................248 852-7310
Jane L Johnson, *President*
Peter Rebholz, *Vice Pres*
Charles Gilliland, *Sales Staff*
EMP: 25
SQ FT: 30,000
SALES (est): 6.6MM **Privately Held**
WEB: www.oscosystems.com
SIC: 3089 Plastic containers, except foam

(G-14078)
PANGEA MADE INC (PA)
2920 Waterview Dr (48309-3484)
PHONE..................248 436-2300
Randy Johnson, *CEO*
Timothy Brennan, *President*
Eric Evans, *President*
Francisco Escapite, *Vice Pres*
Tony Kmeid, *Vice Pres*
EMP: 4379 **EST:** 2018
SALES (est): 500MM **Privately Held**
WEB: www.gstautoleather.com
SIC: 2396 Automotive trimmings, fabric

(G-14079)
PARSON ADHESIVES INC (PA)
3345 W Auburn Rd Ste 107 (48309-5501)
PHONE..................248 299-5585
Pete Shah, *Vice Pres*
Chuck Parekh,
▲ **EMP:** 7 **EST:** 2002
SALES (est): 11.9MM **Privately Held**
WEB: www.parsonadhesives.com
SIC: 2891 Adhesives

(G-14080)
PATENT LCNSING CLRINGHOUSE LLC
2791 Research Dr (48309-3575)
PHONE..................248 299-7500
EMP: 13 **EST:** 2005
SALES (est): 806.1K **Privately Held**
SIC: 3714 Motor vehicle parts & accessories

(G-14081)
PEPPERLEE PAPER COMPANY
722 Glen Cir (48307-2913)
PHONE..................313 949-5917
Latrese Loftin, *Principal*
EMP: 4 **EST:** 2016
SALES (est): 62.9K **Privately Held**
SIC: 2711 Newspapers

(G-14082)
PGF TECHNOLOGY GROUP INC
2993 Technology Dr (48309-3589)
PHONE..................248 852-2800
Naji Gebara, *CEO*
Ghassan Gebara, *President*
Tim Nieman, *Plant Mgr*
Kathy Ardner, *Buyer*
EMP: 35 **EST:** 1970
SQ FT: 38,000
SALES (est): 5.1MM **Privately Held**
WEB: www.pgftech.com
SIC: 3672 3714 Printed circuit boards; automotive wiring harness sets

(G-14083)
PHOTO-TRON CORP
1854 Star Batt Dr (48309-3709)
PHONE..................248 852-5200
Roger Rowley, *President*
EMP: 6 **EST:** 1978
SQ FT: 3,000 **Privately Held**
WEB: www.photo-tron.com
SIC: 3679 Electronic circuits

(G-14084)
PITTSBURGH GLASS WORKS LLC
Also Called: Pgw
3255 W Hamlin Rd (48309-3231)
PHONE..................248 371-1700
Joe Stas, *President*
Patricia Philiph, *Branch Mgr*
EMP: 200 **Privately Held**
WEB: www.pgwglass.com
SIC: 3211 2851 2893 2821 Flat glass; paints & allied products; printing ink; plastics materials & resins; alkalies & chlorine; motor vehicle supplies & new parts
HQ: Pittsburgh Glass Works, Llc
323 N Shore Dr Ste 600
Pittsburgh PA 15212

(G-14085)
PLAS-TEC INC
1926 Northfield Dr (48309-3823)
PHONE..................248 853-7777
Daniel Loscher, *President*
Nelly Loscher, *Corp Secy*
Paul Loscher, *Vice Pres*
EMP: 8 **EST:** 1987
SQ FT: 15,000
SALES (est): 1.2MM **Privately Held**
WEB: www.plas-tec-inc.com
SIC: 3544 Special dies & tools; jigs & fixtures

(G-14086)
PLYMOUTH TECHNOLOGY INC
2700 Bond St (48309-3512)
PHONE..................248 537-0081
Amanda Christides, *President*
Steven Buday, *Vice Pres*
Angela McConachie, *Controller*
Stacey Danna, *Human Res Dir*
Joseph Kelm, *Sales Staff*
▲ **EMP:** 13 **EST:** 1991
SQ FT: 3,000
SALES (est): 10MM **Privately Held**
WEB: www.plymouthtechnology.com
SIC: 5074 1629 3589 Water softeners; railroad & subway construction; water filters & softeners, household type

(G-14087)
PRECISION MASTERS INC (PA)
Also Called: Maple Mold Technologies
1985 Northfield Dr (48309-3824)
PHONE..................248 853-0308
Doug Bachan, *President*
Chris Bethune, *Engineer*
Suzanne Howard, *Accountant*
Kristy Francis, *Human Res Mgr*
Frank Nothelle, *Program Mgr*
▲ **EMP:** 30 **EST:** 1969
SQ FT: 16,000
SALES (est): 12.3MM **Privately Held**
WEB: www.maplemoldtechnologies.com
SIC: 3544 Industrial molds

(G-14088)
PRECISION PARTS HOLDINGS INC
2129 Austin Ave (48309-3668)
PHONE..................248 853-9010
John Lutsi, *Ch of Bd*
Michael Bryant, *President*
Michael Niemic, *Treasurer*
Karen Tuleta, *Admin Sec*
EMP: 1163 **EST:** 2003
SALES (est): 223.4MM **Privately Held**
WEB: www.firstatlanticcapital.com
SIC: 3465 3469 3544 Automotive stampings; metal stampings; die sets for metal stamping (presses)
PA: First Atlantic Capital, Ltd.
477 Madison Ave Ste 330
New York NY 10022

(G-14089)
PRECISION PRINT LABEL
2140 Avon Industrial Dr (48309-3610)
PHONE..................248 853-9007
Martin Testasecca, *President*
EMP: 7 **EST:** 2014
SALES (est): 118.1K **Privately Held**
WEB: www.styleritelabel.com
SIC: 2752 Commercial printing, offset

(G-14090)
PREMIER KITCHEN CABINETRY INC
587 Castlebar Dr (48309-2406)
PHONE..................248 375-0124
Marc Dybowski, *Administration*
EMP: 7 **EST:** 2010
SALES (est): 273.5K **Privately Held**
SIC: 2434 Wood kitchen cabinets

(G-14091)
PROCOLRCOPY A DIV PRCLOR GROUP
1581 W Hamlin Rd (48309-3335)
PHONE..................248 458-2040
EMP: 5 **EST:** 2019
SALES (est): 181.6K **Privately Held**
SIC: 2752 Commercial printing, offset

(G-14092)
PUBLISHING SYSTEMS INC
3740 Warwick Dr (48309-4715)
PHONE..................248 852-0185
Mark F Cykowski, *Principal*
Mark Cykowski, *Officer*
EMP: 5 **EST:** 2010
SALES (est): 97.5K **Privately Held**
SIC: 2741 Miscellaneous publishing

(G-14093)
QUAD PRECISION TOOL CO INC
1763 W Hamlin Rd (48309-3373)
PHONE..................248 608-2400
Robert Klein, *President*
Joseph Smyles, *President*
Chris Sneary, *Vice Pres*
William Bedeski, *Treasurer*
EMP: 13 **EST:** 1992
SQ FT: 15,000
SALES (est): 1MM **Privately Held**
WEB: www.quadprecisiontool.com
SIC: 3544 Special dies & tools

(G-14094)
QUALITY BUSINESS ENGRAVING
Also Called: Q B E
2167 1/2 W Avon Rd (48309-2461)
PHONE..................248 852-5123
Michael Neely, *CEO*

EMP: 7 **EST:** 1989
SALES (est): 792K **Privately Held**
WEB: www.qbetags.com
SIC: 3479 3993 3613 Name plates: engraved, etched, etc.; name plates: except engraved, etched, etc.: metal; signs, not made in custom sign painting shops; control panels, electric

(G-14095)
QUANTUM DATA ANALYTICS INC
1411 Pembroke Dr (48307-5729)
PHONE..................248 894-7442
Carol Biernat, *Administration*
EMP: 4 **EST:** 2015
SALES (est): 95.4K **Privately Held**
SIC: 3572 Computer storage devices

(G-14096)
QUASAR INDUSTRIES INC (PA)
1911 Northfield Dr (48309-3824)
PHONE..................248 844-7190
Denise Higgins, *President*
L Ann Peterson, *Corp Secy*
EMP: 85 **EST:** 1967
SQ FT: 40,000
SALES (est): 11.9MM **Privately Held**
WEB: www.quasar.com
SIC: 3544 3599 Forms (molds), for foundry & plastics working machinery; machine shop, jobbing & repair

(G-14097)
QUASAR INDUSTRIES INC
2687 Commerce Dr (48309-3813)
PHONE..................248 852-0300
Wayne Miller, *Manager*
EMP: 35
SALES (corp-wide): 11.9MM **Privately Held**
WEB: www.quasar.com
SIC: 3599 3544 Machine shop, jobbing & repair; electrical discharge machining (EDM); forms (molds), for foundry & plastics working machinery
PA: Quasar Industries, Inc.
1911 Northfield Dr
Rochester Hills MI 48309
248 844-7190

(G-14098)
R E R SOFTWARE INC
345 Diversion St Ste 206 (48307-6617)
PHONE..................586 744-0881
Roger Bassous, *President*
Ed Bassous, *Consultant*
EMP: 7 **EST:** 2016
SALES (est): 75.2K **Privately Held**
WEB: www.rersoftware.com
SIC: 7372 Prepackaged software

(G-14099)
RAVAL USA INC
1939 Northfield Dr (48309-3824)
PHONE..................248 260-4050
AVI Livne, *President*
Denise Chodzko, *Plant Mgr*
Dennis Rainwater, *Engineer*
▲ **EMP:** 16 **EST:** 2007
SQ FT: 30,000
SALES (est): 9.8MM **Privately Held**
WEB: www.raval.co.il
SIC: 3714 Gas tanks, motor vehicle
PA: Raval A.C.S. Ltd
11 Hakotzer
Beer Sheva 84889

(G-14100)
RAYCONNECT INC
2350 Austin Ave Ste 100 (48309-3679)
PHONE..................248 265-4000
Earl Brown, *President*
Gary Warren, *Plant Mgr*
Christine Saglimbene, *Buyer*
Mick Benedict, *Engineer*
Audra Guzick, *Engineer*
▲ **EMP:** 60 **EST:** 2003
SQ FT: 64,000
SALES (est): 14.6MM
SALES (corp-wide): 177.9K **Privately Held**
WEB: www.catalog.araymond-automotive.com
SIC: 3999 Atomizers, toiletry

HQ: Araymond France
Fixation Fr Agrafe Fr 113 Et 115
Grenoble 38000
476 210-233

(G-14101)
ROCHESTER FUDGE COMPANY LLC
1101 Hickory Hill Dr (48309-1706)
PHONE..................................248 402-3444
Shane Kaszyca, *Principal*
EMP: 4 **EST:** 2018
SALES (est): 77.7K **Privately Held**
WEB: www.rochesterfudge.com
SIC: 2064 Fudge (candy)

(G-14102)
ROCHESTER PALLET
2641 W Auburn Rd (48309-4014)
PHONE..................................248 266-1094
James Lee Miles, *Principal*
EMP: 4 **EST:** 2013
SALES (est): 207.9K **Privately Held**
SIC: 2448 Pallets, wood

(G-14103)
ROCHESTER SPORTS LLC
Also Called: Soccer World's
1900 S Rochester Rd (48307-3534)
PHONE..................................248 608-6000
Terry Sana, *Owner*
EMP: 10 **EST:** 2004
SALES (est): 1.2MM **Privately Held**
WEB: www.generalsportsworldwide.com
SIC: 3949 Sporting & athletic goods

(G-14104)
S & J INC
Also Called: Aria Furniture
1860 Star Batt Dr (48309-3709)
PHONE..................................248 299-0822
Steven Scott, *President*
Jennifer Scott, *Vice Pres*
EMP: 7 **EST:** 1989
SQ FT: 8,000
SALES (est): 831.1K **Privately Held**
WEB: www.ariafurniture.com
SIC: 2521 Wood office furniture

(G-14105)
SAARSTEEL INCORPORATED
445 S Livernois Rd # 222 (48307-2576)
PHONE..................................248 608-0849
Frank Hartgers, *Principal*
▼ **EMP:** 4 **EST:** 2013
SALES (est): 699.9K **Privately Held**
SIC: 3325 Steel foundries

(G-14106)
SANDE-WELLS COMPANY
1554 Charter Oak Dr (48309-2702)
PHONE..................................248 276-9313
Mary Beth Wells, *Principal*
EMP: 5 **EST:** 2008
SALES (est): 100K **Privately Held**
SIC: 2732 Books: printing & binding

(G-14107)
SANDKEY PUBLISHING LLC
2060 Hickory Trail Dr (48309-4506)
PHONE..................................248 475-3662
James Stathakios, *Principal*
EMP: 4 **EST:** 2010
SALES (est): 82.2K **Privately Held**
SIC: 2741 Miscellaneous publishing

(G-14108)
SANYO MACHINE AMERICA CORP
950 S Rochester Rd (48307-2742)
PHONE..................................248 651-5911
Masatake Horiba, *President*
Frank Kramarczyk, *President*
James Gorski, *Plant Mgr*
Rick Wood, *Facilities Mgr*
Atsushi Matsuoka, *Controller*
▲ **EMP:** 75 **EST:** 1986
SQ FT: 164,000
SALES (est): 9.6MM **Privately Held**
WEB: www.sanyo-machine.com
SIC: 3548 3569 Spot welding apparatus, electric; assembly machines, non-metalworking

(G-14109)
SCHAENZLE TOOL AND DIE INC
1785 E Hamlin Rd (48307-3625)
PHONE..................................248 656-0596
Horst W Schaenzle, *President*
Elizabeth Schaenzle, *Vice Pres*
EMP: 5 **EST:** 1972
SQ FT: 7,000
SALES (est): 486.8K **Privately Held**
SIC: 3544 Special dies & tools

(G-14110)
SCIEMETRIC INC (HQ)
1670 Star Batt Dr (48309-3705)
PHONE..................................248 509-2209
Nathan Sheaff, *CEO*
Don Silverman, *CFO*
Cyndi Gould, *Controller*
Greg Len, *Sales Mgr*
EMP: 11 **EST:** 1997
SQ FT: 4,000
SALES (est): 5.5MM
SALES (corp-wide): 4.3MM **Privately Held**
WEB: www.sciemetric.com
SIC: 3825 7371 Instruments to measure electricity; computer software development
PA: Sciemetric Instruments Inc
359 Terry Fox Dr Suite 100
Kanata ON K2K 2
613 254-7054

(G-14111)
SIGNS BY TMRROW - RCHSTER HLLS
1976 Star Batt Dr (48309-3711)
PHONE..................................248 299-9229
EMP: 5 **EST:** 2018
SALES (est): 99.2K **Privately Held**
WEB: www.signsbytomorrow.com
SIC: 3993 Signs & advertising specialties

(G-14112)
SIMIRON INC
Also Called: Epoxi-Pro
3000 Research Dr (48309-3580)
PHONE..................................248 585-7500
Simon Palushi, *President*
Cindy Hay, *Purchasing*
Barry Bundy, *Controller*
Jim Hay, *Natl Sales Mgr*
Kristopher Felice, *Sales Staff*
▲ **EMP:** 30 **EST:** 1994
SALES (est): 9.9MM **Privately Held**
WEB: www.simiron.com
SIC: 2851 Epoxy coatings

(G-14113)
SLW AUTOMOTIVE INC (DH)
Also Called: Slpt Global Pump Group
1955 W Hamlin Rd (48309-3338)
PHONE..................................248 464-6200
Dean Luo, *President*
Dennis Koenig, *Chief Engr*
Andrew Volker, *Design Engr*
Christine Morr, *Manager*
◆ **EMP:** 100 **EST:** 2009
SQ FT: 10,000
SALES (est): 49.2M **Privately Held**
WEB: www.slpt.com
SIC: 3714 Fuel pumps, motor vehicle

(G-14114)
SMART AUTOMATION SYSTEMS INC (PA)
950 S Rochester Rd (48307-2742)
PHONE..................................248 651-5911
Takeshi Horiba, *Ch of Bd*
Masatake Horiba, *President*
Bev Baron, *Human Resources*
Kazuyoshi Hara, *Director*
▲ **EMP:** 6 **EST:** 1992
SQ FT: 68,000
SALES (est): 3.8MM **Privately Held**
WEB: www.sanyo-machine.com
SIC: 3711 Automobile assembly, including specialty automobiles

(G-14115)
SMARTEYE CORPORATION
2637 Bond St (48309-3510)
PHONE..................................248 853-4495
James L De Lange, *President*
Julie Amrhein, *COO*
Curtis Clary, *Project Engr*
Ronny Arndt, *Manager*
Michael Baxter, *Manager*
EMP: 20 **EST:** 1981
SALES (est): 2.7MM **Privately Held**
WEB: www.smarteyecorporation.com
SIC: 3823 Computer interface equipment for industrial process control

(G-14116)
SPECIAL MOLD ENGINEERING INC (PA)
Also Called: Rochester Grinding
1900 Production Dr (48309-3352)
PHONE..................................248 652-6600
Marta Macdonald, *President*
Dina J De Weese, *Corp Secy*
Darin Macdonald, *Vice Pres*
David Macdonald, *Vice Pres*
G Keith Macdonald, *Vice Pres*
EMP: 20 **EST:** 1973
SQ FT: 40,000
SALES (est): 8.9MM **Privately Held**
WEB: www.specialmold.com
SIC: 3544 3443 3089 5122 Industrial molds; fabricated plate work (boiler shop); injection molded finished plastic products; pharmaceuticals

(G-14117)
SSB HOLDINGS INC
Also Called: Comtrex
2619 Bond St (48309-3510)
PHONE..................................586 755-1660
Chain S Sandhu, *President*
Jatinder-Bir S Sandhu, *CFO*
EMP: 31 **EST:** 1968
SQ FT: 120,000
SALES (est): 2.4MM **Privately Held**
SIC: 3089 3087 Extruded finished plastic products; custom compound purchased resins

(G-14118)
STANDARD AUTOMATION LLC
3939 W Hamlin Rd (48309-3233)
PHONE..................................248 227-6964
Anthony Marino,
EMP: 21 **EST:** 2019
SALES (est): 1.3MM **Privately Held**
WEB: www.standard-automation.com
SIC: 3549 Assembly machines, including robotic

(G-14119)
STANT USA CORP
1955 Enterprise Dr (48309-3804)
PHONE..................................765 827-8104
Rick Willis, *Manager*
EMP: 209
SALES (corp-wide): 5.7B **Privately Held**
WEB: www.stant.com
SIC: 3714 Motor vehicle parts & accessories
HQ: Stant Usa Corp.
1620 Columbia Ave
Connersville IN 47331

(G-14120)
STYLERITE LABEL CORPORATION (PA)
2140 Avon Industrial Dr (48309-3610)
PHONE..................................248 853-7977
Andrea Pescijones, *President*
Dick Pesci, *Principal*
Coleen Platz, *Plant Mgr*
Dan Jones, *QC Mgr*
EMP: 34 **EST:** 1988
SQ FT: 26,000
SALES (est): 3.4MM **Privately Held**
WEB: www.styleritelabel.com
SIC: 2759 Labels & seals: printing

(G-14121)
SU-DAN PLASTICS INC
1949 Rochester Indus Dr (48309-3344)
PHONE..................................248 651-6035
EMP: 12
SQ FT: 26,000
SALES (est): 1.7MM **Privately Held**
SIC: 3089 3544 Mfg Plastic Products Mfg Dies/Tools/Jigs/Fixtures

(G-14122)
SU-TEC INC
Also Called: Alpha Engineered Refrigeration
1852 Star Batt Dr (48309-3705)
PHONE..................................248 852-4711
Howard Dibble, *Principal*
EMP: 18 **EST:** 2001
SQ FT: 17,000
SALES (est): 384.5K **Privately Held**
SIC: 3585 Refrigeration equipment, complete

(G-14123)
TA SYSTEMS INC
1842 Rochester Indus Dr (48309-3337)
PHONE..................................248 656-5150
Tim Gale, *President*
Hendrik Stoltz, *COO*
Patrick Burke, *Vice Pres*
James Barclay, *Purch Mgr*
Mike Sadler, *Engineer*
EMP: 90
SQ FT: 45,000
SALES (est): 23.3MM **Privately Held**
WEB: www.ta-systems.com
SIC: 3549 Assembly machines, including robotic

(G-14124)
TESCA USA INC
2638 Bond St (48309-3509)
PHONE..................................586 991-0744
Christopher Glinka, *General Mgr*
Gregory Harrison, *Opers Staff*
Christopher Schad, *Purchasing*
Chris Glinka, *Marketing Staff*
Thomas Leffler, *Manager*
EMP: 43 **EST:** 2004
SQ FT: 34,300
SALES (est): 8MM **Privately Held**
SIC: 2396 3089 3465 3714 Automotive trimmings, fabric; injection molding of plastics; automotive stampings; automotive wiring harness sets

(G-14125)
THREE-DIMENSIONAL SERVICES INC
Also Called: 3-Dimensional Services
2547 Product Dr (48309-3806)
PHONE..................................248 852-1333
Douglas Peterson, *President*
Alan R Peterson, *Vice Pres*
Andy Barnowsky, *Plant Mgr*
Brenda Sylver, *Opers Mgr*
Kristina Underwood, *Sales Engr*
EMP: 200 **EST:** 1992
SQ FT: 54,000
SALES (est): 34.6MM **Privately Held**
WEB: www.3dimensional.com
SIC: 7539 8711 3545 Machine shop, automotive; engineering services; machine tool accessories

(G-14126)
THUNDER TECHNOLOGIES LLC
1618 Star Batt Dr (48309-3705)
PHONE..................................248 844-4875
Dan Hollenkamp, *Sales Mgr*
Andrew Kalinowski, *Sales Staff*
Marc Kalinowski,
EMP: 12 **EST:** 2009
SALES (est): 2.5MM **Privately Held**
WEB: www.thundertechllc.com
SIC: 3069 3599 3052 Sheets, hard rubber; flexible metal hose, tubing & bellows; rubber & plastics hose & beltings

(G-14127)
TOMS SIGN SERVICE
Also Called: Tom's Sign
2926 Grant Rd (48309-3623)
PHONE..................................248 852-3550
Tom Tioran, *Owner*
EMP: 9 **EST:** 1952
SALES (est): 291.6K **Privately Held**
SIC: 3993 Signs & advertising specialties

(G-14128)
TORSION CONTROL PRODUCTS INC
1900 Northfield Dr (48309-3823)
PHONE..................................248 537-1900
Timothy A Thane, *President*
Michael Mackool, *Vice Pres*

Rochester Hills - Oakland County (G-14129)

Michael Youngerman, *Vice Pres*
EMP: 19 **EST:** 1987
SQ FT: 11,300
SALES (est): 20MM
SALES (corp-wide): 3.5B **Publicly Held**
WEB: www.torsioncontrol.com
SIC: 3714 8711 Transmission housings or parts, motor vehicle; engineering services
PA: The Timken Company
4500 Mount Pleasant St Nw
North Canton OH 44720
234 262-3000

(G-14129)
TOTAL PLASTICS RESOURCES LLC
1661 Northfield Dr (48309-3825)
PHONE 248 299-9500
Vince R BR, *Manager*
EMP: 10 **Privately Held**
WEB: www.totalplastics.com
SIC: 5162 3089 Plastics sheets & rods; plastic processing
HQ: Total Plastics Resources Llc
2810 N Burdick St Ste A
Kalamazoo MI 49004
269 344-0009

(G-14130)
TOWING & EQUIPMENT MAGAZINE
1700 W Hamlin Rd Ste 100 (48309-3346)
PHONE 248 601-1385
Jim McNeely, *President*
Kristofer Petruska, *Marketing Staff*
EMP: 8 **EST:** 1985
SALES (est): 713.2K **Privately Held**
WEB: www.towequip.com
SIC: 2721 Magazines: publishing only, not printed on site

(G-14131)
TRICO GROUP INC
3255 W Hamlin Rd (48309-3231)
PHONE 800 388-7426
Michael McKee, *Exec VP*
Thomas Dugan, *Vice Pres*
Greg Galvin, *Vice Pres*
Kevin O 'dowd, *Vice Pres*
Regnier Tempels, *Vice Pres*
EMP: 2 **EST:** 1997
SALES (est): 1.1MM **Privately Held**
WEB: www.tricoproducts.com
SIC: 3714 Wipers, windshield, motor vehicle

(G-14132)
TRICO PRODUCTS CORPORATION (DH)
3255 W Hamlin Rd (48309-3231)
PHONE 248 371-1700
Patrick James, *President*
Michael McKee, *Exec VP*
Michael Defao, *Vice Pres*
Richard Obenauer, *Materials Mgr*
Frank Arellano, *Transportation*
◆ **EMP:** 150 **EST:** 1920
SQ FT: 75,000
SALES (est): 525.1MM
SALES (corp-wide): 3.3B **Privately Held**
WEB: www.tricoproducts.com
SIC: 3069 3082 8734 8731 Tubing, rubber; tubes, unsupported plastic; testing laboratories; commercial physical research; windshield wiper systems, motor vehicle
HQ: Ktri Holdings, Inc.
127 Public Sq Ste 5110
Cleveland OH 44114
216 371-1700

(G-14133)
TROY MILLWORK INC
1841 Northfield Dr (48309-3822)
PHONE 248 852-8383
Terrence T Cruice, *President*
Terrence T Cruice, *President*
EMP: 8 **EST:** 1979
SQ FT: 5,600
SALES (est): 734K **Privately Held**
WEB: www.troymillwork.com
SIC: 2431 Millwork

(G-14134)
U S EQUIPMENT CO (HQ)
Also Called: Roto Flo
3667 Merriweather Ln (48306-3642)
PHONE 313 526-8300
Paul Simon, *Ch of Bd*
George Simon II, *President*
April Simon, *Vice Pres*
▲ **EMP:** 25 **EST:** 1946
SALES (est): 4.3MM
SALES (corp-wide): 15.6MM **Privately Held**
WEB: www.usequipment.com
SIC: 3541 5084 7629 Numerically controlled metal cutting machine tools; industrial machinery & equipment; electrical repair shops
PA: U. S. Group, Inc.
3667 Merriweather Ln
Rochester Hills MI 48306
313 372-7900

(G-14135)
U S GROUP INC (PA)
3667 Merriweather Ln (48306-3642)
PHONE 313 372-7900
Paul Simon, *Chairman*
George Simon, *Vice Pres*
▼ **EMP:** 3 **EST:** 1981
SQ FT: 70,000
SALES (est): 15.6MM **Privately Held**
SIC: 5084 3599 Machine tools & accessories; machine shop, jobbing & repair

(G-14136)
UNIQUE FABRICATING NA INC
2817 Bond St (48309-3515)
PHONE 248 853-2333
Douglas Stahl, *President*
Tim Packer, *Plant Mgr*
Mark Altovilla, *QC Mgr*
Marc Pearlman, *Manager*
Michael Rucker, *Manager*
EMP: 5
SQ FT: 22,000
SALES (corp-wide): 120.2MM **Publicly Held**
WEB: www.uniquefab.com
SIC: 3053 3086 Gaskets, all materials; plastics foam products
HQ: Unique Fabricating Na, Inc.
800 Standard Pkwy
Auburn Hills MI 48326
248 853-2333

(G-14137)
UNIVERSAL TUBE INC
2607 Bond St (48309-3510)
PHONE 248 853-5100
Karl Konen, *Exec VP*
Robert Hammond, *Vice Pres*
Michael Smith, *Engineer*
Rebecca Tyszkowski, *Human Res Mgr*
Bernie N Wathen, *Human Res Mgr*
▲ **EMP:** 160 **EST:** 1980
SQ FT: 75,200
SALES (est): 20MM **Privately Held**
WEB: www.universaltube.com
SIC: 3498 Tube fabricating (contract bending & shaping)

(G-14138)
URGENT PLASTIC SERVICES INC (PA)
2777 Product Dr (48309-3810)
PHONE 248 852-8999
Douglas Peterson, *President*
Jeffrey Peterson, *General Mgr*
Alan R Peterson, *Vice Pres*
Alan Peteson, *Vice Pres*
Jerry Eversole, *Opers Staff*
EMP: 3 **EST:** 1995
SQ FT: 54,000
SALES (est): 10.2MM **Privately Held**
WEB: www.3dimensional.com
SIC: 3089 Injection molded finished plastic products

(G-14139)
VALIANT SPECIALTIES INC
301 Hacker St Unit 3 (48307-2636)
PHONE 248 656-1001
James Riley, *President*
EMP: 4 **EST:** 1984
SQ FT: 1,500

SALES (est): 60K **Privately Held**
WEB: www.valiantspecialties.com
SIC: 7692 Welding repair

(G-14140)
VETERAN LIQUIDS LLC
318 Bourbon Ct (48307-3802)
PHONE 586 698-2100
Amanda Cesnick,
EMP: 5 **EST:** 2017
SALES (est): 214K **Privately Held**
SIC: 2141 Tobacco stemming & redrying

(G-14141)
WARA CONSTRUCTION COMPANY LLC
2927 Waterview Dr (48309-4600)
PHONE 248 299-2410
EMP: 99
SQ FT: 7,500
SALES (est): 1.9MM **Privately Held**
SIC: 1382 1389 4212 8711 Oil/Gas Exploration Svcs Oil/Gas Field Services Oil/Gas Field Services Local Trucking Operator Engineering Services

(G-14142)
WEB LITHO INC
560 John R Rd (48307-2349)
PHONE 586 803-9000
Fax: 586 268-5046
EMP: 8
SQ FT: 12,000
SALES (est): 1.6MM **Privately Held**
SIC: 2752 Lithographic Commercial Printing

(G-14143)
WEBASTO CONVERTIBLES USA INC
2817 Bond St (48309-3515)
PHONE 734 582-5900
Mark Denny, *Branch Mgr*
EMP: 45
SALES (corp-wide): 3.9B **Privately Held**
WEB: www.webasto-comfort.com
SIC: 3559 Automotive related machinery
HQ: Webasto Convertibles Usa Inc.
14988 Pilot Dr
Plymouth MI 48170

(G-14144)
WEBASTO ROOF SYSTEMS INC
Also Called: Webasto Sunroofs
2700 Product Dr (48309-3809)
PHONE 248 299-2000
Fred Olson, *President*
Craig Marx, *Engineer*
Ed Hennessey, *Manager*
EMP: 257
SQ FT: 74,000
SALES (corp-wide): 3.9B **Privately Held**
WEB: www.webasto-comfort.com
SIC: 3714 Motor vehicle parts & accessories
HQ: Webasto Roof Systems Inc.
2500 Executive Hills Dr
Auburn Hills MI 48326
248 997-5100

(G-14145)
WEBASTO ROOF SYSTEMS INC
Also Called: Webasto Assembly
2700 Product Dr (48309-3809)
PHONE 248 997-5100
Michelle Mitchel, *Manager*
EMP: 110
SALES (corp-wide): 3.9B **Privately Held**
WEB: www.webasto-comfort.com
SIC: 3469 3714 3441 Metal stampings; motor vehicle parts & accessories; fabricated structural metal
HQ: Webasto Roof Systems Inc.
2500 Executive Hills Dr
Auburn Hills MI 48326
248 997-5100

(G-14146)
WEC GROUP LLC
1850 Northfield Dr (48309-3821)
PHONE 248 260-4252
Greg Wolf, *Mng Member*
EMP: 20 **EST:** 2006
SALES (est): 2.4MM **Privately Held**
WEB: www.wecgroupllc.com
SIC: 2396 Automotive & apparel trimmings

(G-14147)
WIRIC CORPORATION
2781 Bond St (48309-3513)
PHONE 248 598-5297
Philip H Warburton, *President*
Phil Warburton, *General Mgr*
Curt Powers, *Sales Mgr*
◆ **EMP:** 36 **EST:** 2004
SQ FT: 18,000
SALES (est): 9.4MM **Privately Held**
WEB: www.wiric.com
SIC: 3714 3694 Automotive wiring harness sets; automotive electrical equipment

(G-14148)
YASKAWA AMERICA INC
2050 Austin Ave (48309-3665)
PHONE 248 668-8800
EMP: 6
SALES (corp-wide): 3.3B **Privately Held**
SIC: 3569 Mfg Robotic Assembly Systems
HQ: Yaskawa America, Inc.
2121 Norman Dr
Waukegan IL 60085
847 887-7000

(G-14149)
YATES CIDER MILL INC
1990 E Avon Rd (48307-6815)
PHONE 248 651-8300
Leslie J Posey, *President*
Karen Posey, *Admin Sec*
EMP: 7 **EST:** 1863
SQ FT: 9,800
SALES (est): 1.4MM **Privately Held**
WEB: www.yatescidermill.com
SIC: 2099 0175 5431 5441 Cider, nonalcoholic; apple orchard; fruit stands or markets; candy, nut & confectionery stores; doughnuts

Rock
Delta County

(G-14150)
KANERVA FOREST PRODUCTS INC
15096 Autumn Ln (49880-9525)
P.O. Box 55 (49880-0055)
PHONE 906 356-6061
Terry Kanerva, *President*
EMP: 8 **EST:** 1981
SALES (est): 744.2K **Privately Held**
WEB: www.mimlc.com
SIC: 2411 Logging camps & contractors

Rockford
Kent County

(G-14151)
AC DESIGN LLC
Also Called: Signs With Design
8550 Young Ave Ne (49341-9342)
PHONE 616 874-9007
Lexy Ader, *President*
EMP: 7 **EST:** 2000
SALES (est): 336.1K **Privately Held**
WEB: www.signswithdesign.net
SIC: 3993 Signs & advertising specialties

(G-14152)
ACCRA-WIRE CONTROLS INC (PA)
Also Called: A W C
10891 Northland Dr Ne A (49341-8887)
PHONE 616 866-3434
Johnnie Jones, *President*
EMP: 9 **EST:** 1975
SQ FT: 34,668
SALES (est): 1MM **Privately Held**
WEB: www.accrainc.com
SIC: 3496 Miscellaneous fabricated wire products

(G-14153)
ALL-STAR EQUIPMENT LLC
7205 10 Mile Rd Ne (49341-9337)
P.O. Box 475 (49341-0475)
PHONE 855 273-8265
EMP: 11 **EST:** 2001

▲ = Import ▼ = Export
◆ = Import/Export

GEOGRAPHIC SECTION

Rockford - Kent County (G-14181)

SALES (est): 649K **Privately Held**
WEB: www.asetanks.com
SIC: 3715 Truck trailers

(G-14154)
ALLOY EXCHANGE INC (PA)
300 Rockford Park Dr Ne (49341-7818)
PHONE..................616 863-0640
Robert W Corl III, *President*
Greg Thebo, *VP Opers*
Becky Mitchell, *Controller*
Blaine Gorby, *Sales Staff*
EMP: 14 **EST:** 1980
SQ FT: 56,000
SALES (est): 3.7MM **Privately Held**
WEB: www.alloyexchangeinc.com
SIC: 3082 Unsupported plastics profile shapes

(G-14155)
ASHLEY ROSE
11080 Angel Pond Dr Ne (49341-8770)
PHONE..................616 634-4919
Ashley Rose, *Principal*
EMP: 4 **EST:** 2008
SALES (est): 69.9K **Privately Held**
WEB: www.theashleyrose.com
SIC: 2335 Wedding gowns & dresses

(G-14156)
AXIS MOLD WORKS INC
8005 Childsdale Ave Ne (49341-8588)
PHONE..................616 866-2222
Dan Adams, *President*
John Liefferrs, *Vice Pres*
EMP: 15 **EST:** 2005
SALES (est): 1.4MM **Privately Held**
WEB: www.axismoldworks.com
SIC: 3544 Industrial molds

(G-14157)
BIER DISTILLERY COMPANY
6263 Egypt Valley Ave Ne (49341-8209)
PHONE..................616 633-8601
EMP: 5 **EST:** 2019
SALES (est): 95.7K **Privately Held**
WEB: www.bierdistillery.com
SIC: 2085 Distilled & blended liquors

(G-14158)
BOLD AMMO & GUNS INC
Also Called: Bold Services
5083 Natchez Ct Ne (49341-9308)
PHONE..................616 826-0913
Terrance Debold, *Principal*
Willam Baker, *Opers Staff*
Sheri Plakos-Debold, *Admin Sec*
EMP: 5 **EST:** 2015
SQ FT: 400
SALES (est): 309.1K **Privately Held**
SIC: 3482 0781 3544 0783 Small arms ammunition; landscape services; special dies, tools, jigs & fixtures; removal services, bush & tree

(G-14159)
BYRNE ELEC SPECIALISTS INC (PA)
320 Byrne Industrial Dr (49341-1083)
PHONE..................616 866-3461
Norman R Byrne, *President*
Richard Meng, *General Mgr*
Rosemary Byrne, *Vice Pres*
John Willcox, *Vice Pres*
William Van Os, *Opers Staff*
▲ **EMP:** 523 **EST:** 1970
SQ FT: 52,000
SALES (est): 38.4MM **Privately Held**
WEB: www.byrne.com
SIC: 3679 Harness assemblies for electronic use: wire or cable

(G-14160)
BYRNE ELEC SPECIALISTS INC
725 Byrne Industrial Dr (49341-1089)
PHONE..................616 866-3461
Norman R Byrne, *Branch Mgr*
EMP: 29
SALES (corp-wide): 38.4MM **Privately Held**
WEB: www.byrne.com
SIC: 3679 Harness assemblies for electronic use: wire or cable
PA: Byrne Electrical Specialists, Inc.
320 Byrne Industrial Dr
Rockford MI 49341
616 866-3461

(G-14161)
BYRNE TOOL & DIE INC
316 Byrne Industrial Dr (49341-1083)
PHONE..................616 866-4479
Norman R Byrne, *CEO*
EMP: 24 **EST:** 1974
SQ FT: 10,000
SALES (est): 5.5MM **Privately Held**
WEB: www.byrne-tool.com
SIC: 3599 3544 Machine shop, jobbing & repair; special dies, tools, jigs & fixtures

(G-14162)
CANNONSBURG WOOD PRODUCTS INC
10251 Northland Dr Ne (49341-9730)
P.O. Box 678 (49341-0678)
PHONE..................616 866-4459
Dave Powers Sr, *President*
EMP: 24 **EST:** 1975
SQ FT: 5,000
SALES (est): 1.4MM **Privately Held**
WEB: www.cannonsburgwoodproducts.com
SIC: 2448 Pallets, wood

(G-14163)
CTC ACQUISITION COMPANY LLC
Also Called: Grand Rapids Controls Company
825 Northland Dr Ne (49341-7655)
PHONE..................616 884-7100
Lily Wang, *General Mgr*
Rob Binns, *Mfg Mgr*
Scott Todd, *Warehouse Mgr*
Emily Foster, *Engineer*
Eric Pierman, *Engineer*
▲ **EMP:** 175 **EST:** 2004
SQ FT: 82,000
SALES (est): 29.1MM **Privately Held**
WEB: www.grcontrols.com
SIC: 3625 3679 Actuators, industrial; harness assemblies for electronic use: wire or cable
PA: C. T. Charlton & Associates, Inc.
24000 Greater Mack Ave
Saint Clair Shores MI 48080
586 775-2900

(G-14164)
DERBY FABG SOLUTIONS LLC
Also Called: Aftech
687 Byrne Industrial Dr (49341-1085)
PHONE..................616 866-1650
EMP: 80
SALES (corp-wide): 49.8MM **Privately Held**
WEB: www.derbyfab.com
SIC: 3089 3086 2499 3069 Injection molding of plastics; plastics foam products; cork & cork products; rubber hardware; gaskets, all materials
PA: Derby Fabricating Solutions, Llc
4500 Produce Rd
Louisville KY 40218
502 964-9135

(G-14165)
DISTINCTIVE MACHINE CORP
300 Byrne Industrial Dr B (49341-1423)
PHONE..................616 433-4111
Gary Berkenpas, *President*
Jeff Tait, *Vice Pres*
EMP: 21 **EST:** 1991
SQ FT: 8,300
SALES (est): 2.6MM **Privately Held**
WEB: www.distinctive-machine.com
SIC: 3599 Machine shop, jobbing & repair

(G-14166)
EXTRACT
7303 Cuesta Way Dr Ne (49341-9496)
PHONE..................269 362-4879
Victoria Hansen, *Principal*
EMP: 4 **EST:** 2018
SALES (est): 94.8K **Privately Held**
SIC: 2836 Extracts

(G-14167)
EZ VENT LLC
8235 Belding Rd Ne (49341-9628)
PHONE..................616 874-2787
Nichole Nelson, *Opers Mgr*
Robert Fortin, *Mng Member*
EMP: 6 **EST:** 2000
SALES (est): 876.3K **Privately Held**
WEB: www.ezventwindows.com
SIC: 2741 5031 Directories: publishing & printing; windows

(G-14168)
FOREST ELDERS PRODUCTS INC
10367 Northland Dr Ne (49341-9730)
P.O. Box 557, Cedar Springs (49319-0557)
PHONE..................616 866-9317
Jerry Elder, *President*
Chad Elder, *Vice Pres*
EMP: 20 **EST:** 1981
SQ FT: 6,000
SALES (est): 2.4MM **Privately Held**
WEB: www.eldersforestproducts.com
SIC: 2421 2426 Lumber: rough, sawed or planed; hardwood dimension & flooring mills

(G-14169)
HERMANS BOY
220 Northland Dr Ne (49341-1042)
PHONE..................616 866-2900
Floyd Havemeier, *Owner*
EMP: 7 **EST:** 1979
SQ FT: 4,500
SALES (est): 384K **Privately Held**
WEB: www.hermansboy.com
SIC: 5441 5499 5149 2095 Candy, nut & confectionery stores; coffee; coffee, green or roasted; coffee roasting (except by wholesale grocers)

(G-14170)
HY-TEST INC
9341 Courtland Dr Ne (49351-1002)
PHONE..................616 866-5500
Blake Krueger, *President*
EMP: 5 **EST:** 1903
SALES (est): 1.3MM
SALES (corp-wide): 1.7B **Publicly Held**
WEB: www.hytest.com
SIC: 3143 Boots, dress or casual: men's
PA: Wolverine World Wide, Inc.
9341 Courtland Dr Ne
Rockford MI 49351
616 866-5500

(G-14171)
IRONWOOD CONSULTING LLC
507 Rock Hollow Dr Ne (49341-7571)
PHONE..................616 916-9111
Jesse Adams, *Principal*
EMP: 5 **EST:** 2014
SALES (est): 50.2K **Privately Held**
WEB: www.ironwoodbio.com
SIC: 2499 Wood products

(G-14172)
ITW DAHTI SEATING
206 Byrne Industrial Dr (49341-1075)
PHONE..................616 866-1323
Ryan Wolters, *Buyer*
Rob Bratty, *Engineer*
Penny Smith, *Engineer*
Rick Vandekopple, *Project Engr*
Michelle Coleman, *Controller*
▼ **EMP:** 34 **EST:** 2009
SALES (est): 17.3MM **Privately Held**
WEB: www.itw-dahti.com
SIC: 2531 Public building & related furniture

(G-14173)
K & T TOOL AND DIE INC
7805 Childsdale Ave Ne (49341-7487)
PHONE..................616 884-5900
Witt Kurtz, *President*
Rick Kurtz, *President*
EMP: 11 **EST:** 1992
SQ FT: 24,000 **Privately Held**
WEB: www.kttooldie.com
SIC: 3544 Special dies & tools; jigs & fixtures

(G-14174)
KNAPE INDUSTRIES INC
10701 Northland Dr Ne (49341-8008)
PHONE..................616 866-1651
William Knape, *President*
Herbert F Knape, *Chairman*
◆ **EMP:** 20 **EST:** 1965
SQ FT: 34,000 **Privately Held**
WEB: www.knapeinc.com
SIC: 3479 Painting of metal products

(G-14175)
LOCAL BSKET CASE LLC - RCKFORD
65 Courtland St (49341-1055)
PHONE..................616 884-0749
EMP: 7 **EST:** 2019
SALES (est): 54.5K **Privately Held**
SIC: 3523 Farm machinery & equipment

(G-14176)
MAHER GROUP LLC
575 Byrne Industrial Dr (49341-1085)
PHONE..................616 863-6046
Owen Maher, *Principal*
John Schenk, *Sales Mgr*
Andrew May, *Manager*
Varney Kim, *Exec Dir*
EMP: 9 **EST:** 2009
SALES (est): 489.2K **Privately Held**
WEB: www.themahergroup.com
SIC: 2295 Resin or plastic coated fabrics

(G-14177)
MARREL CORPORATION
4750 14 Mile Rd Ne (49341-8427)
PHONE..................616 863-9155
Jerome Semay, *CEO*
Vincent Revol, *President*
▲ **EMP:** 5 **EST:** 1986
SQ FT: 20,000
SALES (est): 4.3MM
SALES (corp-wide): 1.2MM **Privately Held**
WEB: www.amplirollusa.com
SIC: 5084 3711 Hydraulic systems equipment & supplies; motor vehicles & car bodies
HQ: Marrel
42 Avenue De Saint Etienne
Andrezieux Boutheon 42160
477 362-961

(G-14178)
MATERIALS GROUP LLC
Also Called: Tmg
575 Byrne Industrial Dr (49341-1085)
PHONE..................616 863-6046
Amy Stephen, *Engineer*
Derek Reed, *Sales Staff*
Owen R Maher,
Sara Macconnachie,
▲ **EMP:** 16 **EST:** 2001
SQ FT: 75,000
SALES (est): 4.4MM **Privately Held**
WEB: www.thematerialsgroup.com
SIC: 2821 Plastics materials & resins

(G-14179)
MIDWEST TOOL & DIE INC
7970 Childsdale Ave Ne (49341-8392)
PHONE..................616 863-8187
Dave O'Keefe, *President*
Mark O'Keefe, *Vice Pres*
Greg Usher, *Treasurer*
EMP: 12 **EST:** 1998
SQ FT: 18,000
SALES (est): 1.5MM **Privately Held**
WEB: www.midwestdieinc.com
SIC: 3544 Special dies & tools

(G-14180)
MOTOR CITY AEROSPACE
10500 Harvard Ave Ne (49341-8471)
PHONE..................616 916-5473
Russell Golemba, *Owner*
EMP: 6 **EST:** 2010
SALES (est): 65K **Privately Held**
SIC: 3728 Aircraft parts & equipment

(G-14181)
NEWKIRK AND ASSOCIATES INC
Also Called: Whiteboard Depot
9767 Shaw Creek Ct Ne (49341-9777)
PHONE..................616 863-9899

Rockford - Kent County (G-14182)

Chris Newkirk, *President*
EMP: 5 **EST:** 1996
SALES (est): 293.1K **Privately Held**
WEB: www.whiteboarddepot.com
SIC: 2599 Boards: planning, display, notice

(G-14182)
NORTHLAND TOOL & DIE INC
10399 Northland Dr Ne (49341-9730)
PHONE.................................616 866-4451
Richard Cossin, *President*
David Cossin, *Vice Pres*
Perri Cossin, *Vice Pres*
EMP: 25 **EST:** 1983
SQ FT: 18,500
SALES (est): 5.4MM **Privately Held**
WEB: www.ntdusa.com
SIC: 3544 Special dies & tools

(G-14183)
PETERSON JIG & FIXTURE INC (PA)
Also Called: Precision Jig & Fixture
301 Rockford Park Dr Ne (49341-7817)
PHONE.................................616 866-8296
David Schuiling, *President*
Dan Ketelaar, *Vice Pres*
Anthony Calain, *QC Mgr*
Scott Hansen, *QC Mgr*
Gene Burley, *VP Bus Dvlpt*
EMP: 45 **EST:** 1995
SQ FT: 20,000
SALES (est): 8.9MM **Privately Held**
WEB: www.pjfinc.com
SIC: 3544 Special dies & tools; jigs: inspection, gauging & checking

(G-14184)
PLAY WRIGHT LLC
8162 Rockford Pnes Ne (49341-7731)
PHONE.................................616 784-5437
EMP: 5 **EST:** 2012
SALES (est): 205.1K **Privately Held**
SIC: 3949 Playground equipment

(G-14185)
QUEST PRECISION LLC
7462 Las Palmas Dr Ne (49341-9581)
PHONE.................................616 288-6101
James Neihof, *Principal*
EMP: 6 **EST:** 2016
SALES (est): 106.6K **Privately Held**
WEB: www.quest-precision.com
SIC: 3599 Machine shop, jobbing & repair

(G-14186)
RACE FUEL CANDLES LLC
10455 Country Aire Dr Ne (49341-8759)
PHONE.................................616 889-1674
Kory Jannereth, *Principal*
EMP: 4 **EST:** 2015
SALES (est): 88.7K **Privately Held**
WEB: www.racefuelcandles.com
SIC: 3999 Candles

(G-14187)
RIVERVIEW PRODUCTS INC
201 Byrne Industrial Dr (49341-1078)
PHONE.................................616 866-1305
Christopher J Martin, *President*
Tucker Martin, *Project Mgr*
Margaret Osuler, *Production*
Brad Vorel, *Manager*
EMP: 5 **EST:** 1989
SQ FT: 10,000
SALES (est): 1.1MM **Privately Held**
WEB: www.riverview-products.squarespace.com
SIC: 3496 Miscellaneous fabricated wire products

(G-14188)
ROCKFORD CONTRACT MFG
Also Called: Wizard Electronics
198 Rollingwood Dr (49341-1192)
P.O. Box 207 (49341-0207)
PHONE.................................616 304-3837
Paul Michael Magnan, *President*
EMP: 5 **EST:** 2001
SQ FT: 5,200
SALES (est): 492.9K **Privately Held**
SIC: 3679 Electronic circuits

(G-14189)
ROCKFORD MOLDING & TRIM
8317 Woodcrest Dr Ne (49341-8507)
PHONE.................................616 874-8997
Richard Kirchhoff, *President*
EMP: 6 **EST:** 2008
SALES (est): 189.3K **Privately Held**
SIC: 3089 Molding primary plastic

(G-14190)
ST JULIAN WINERY
4425 14 Mile Rd Ne (49341-7453)
PHONE.................................616 263-9087
EMP: 5 **EST:** 2019
SALES (est): 80.5K **Privately Held**
WEB: www.stjulian.com
SIC: 2084 Wines

(G-14191)
TRENDWELL ENERGY CORPORATION
10 E Bridge St Ste 200 (49341-1431)
P.O. Box 560 (49341-0560)
PHONE.................................616 866-5024
Thomas H Mall, *CEO*
Todd R Mall, *President*
Angela Adams, *Vice Pres*
Kyle Patterson, *Vice Pres*
David Heinz, *Executive*
EMP: 15 **EST:** 1978
SQ FT: 2,000
SALES (est): 10MM **Privately Held**
WEB: www.trendwellenergy.com
SIC: 1311 Crude petroleum production; natural gas production

(G-14192)
UNIVERSAL PRODUCTS INC
210 Rockford Park Dr Ne (49341-7827)
P.O. Box 369, Howard City (49329-0369)
PHONE.................................231 937-5555
Kenneth Koster, *President*
Dale Cederquist, *Vice Pres*
William Herberg, *Vice Pres*
Christine Olson, *Purchasing*
▲ **EMP:** 41 **EST:** 1991
SQ FT: 26,500
SALES (est): 10.2MM **Privately Held**
WEB: www.upimi.com
SIC: 3089 Injection molding of plastics

(G-14193)
WESTERN ADHESIVE INC
6768 Kitson Dr Ne (49341-9423)
PHONE.................................616 874-5869
David Trebilcock, *President*
EMP: 10 **EST:** 1995
SALES (est): 500K **Privately Held**
SIC: 2891 Adhesives

(G-14194)
WOLVERINE PROCUREMENT INC
Also Called: Wolverine Worldwide
175 S Main St (49341-1221)
PHONE.................................616 866-9521
Pgskin Leather, *Vice Pres*
Jeff Swaney, *Opers Staff*
Jim Falcinelii, *Marketing Mgr*
EMP: 185
SALES (corp-wide): 1.7B **Publicly Held**
WEB: www.wolverineworldwide.com
SIC: 3143 3144 3131 Men's footwear, except athletic; women's footwear, except athletic; footwear cut stock
HQ: Wolverine Procurement, Inc.
9341 Ne Courland Dr
Rockford MI 49341

(G-14195)
WOLVERINE PROCUREMENT INC (HQ)
9341 Ne Courland Dr (49341)
PHONE.................................616 866-5500
Gordon Baird, *President*
Kate Rosa, *Manager*
▲ **EMP:** 10 **EST:** 1989
SALES: 94.5MM
SALES (corp-wide): 1.7B **Publicly Held**
WEB: www.wolverineworldwide.com
SIC: 3143 3021 Men's footwear, except athletic; rubber & plastics footwear
PA: Wolverine World Wide, Inc.
9341 Courtland Dr Ne
Rockford MI 49351
616 866-5500

(G-14196)
WOLVERINE SLIPPER GROUP INC (HQ)
9341 Courtland Dr Ne Hb1141 (49351-1002)
PHONE.................................616 866-5500
Blake W Krueger, *President*
John Estes, *Vice Pres*
Cherrelle Jones, *Admin Asst*
Brenda Vugteveen, *Administration*
EMP: 283 **EST:** 1998
SALES (est): 1MM
SALES (corp-wide): 1.7B **Publicly Held**
WEB: www.wolverineworldwide.com
SIC: 3142 House slippers
PA: Wolverine World Wide, Inc.
9341 Courtland Dr Ne
Rockford MI 49351
616 866-5500

(G-14197)
WOLVERINE WORLD WIDE INC (PA)
9341 Courtland Dr Ne (49351-0001)
PHONE.................................616 866-5500
Blake W Krueger, *Ch of Bd*
Matt Blonder, *President*
Brendan L Hoffman, *President*
Isabel Soriano, *President*
Jim Zwiers, *President*
◆ **EMP:** 1888 **EST:** 1883
SQ FT: 225,000
SALES: 1.7B **Publicly Held**
WEB: www.wolverineworldwide.com
SIC: 3143 3149 3144 3111 Men's footwear, except athletic; athletic shoes, except rubber or plastic; women's footwear, except athletic; leather tanning & finishing

Rockwood
Wayne County

(G-14198)
CUSTOM PRO PRODUCTS INC
31550 Gossett Dr Ste B (48173-7413)
PHONE.................................734 558-2070
Dan Vanderheiden, *President*
EMP: 6 **EST:** 2004
SALES (est): 96.1K **Privately Held**
SIC: 3714 Motor vehicle parts & accessories

(G-14199)
H & J PRINTING
22411 Silver Creek Ln (48173-1038)
PHONE.................................734 344-9447
EMP: 4 **EST:** 2013
SALES (est): 135.6K **Privately Held**
SIC: 2752 Commercial printing, lithographic

(G-14200)
INSTANTWHIP DETROIT INC
31607 Gossett Dr (48173-9700)
PHONE.................................734 379-9474
EMP: 4 **EST:** 2019
SALES (est): 86.3K **Privately Held**
SIC: 2026 Fluid milk

(G-14201)
LAFRONTERA TORTILLAS INC
32845 Cleveland St (48173-9602)
PHONE.................................734 231-1701
Orfanidia Garza, *President*
EMP: 4 **EST:** 2005
SALES (est): 437.7K **Privately Held**
WEB: www.lafronteratortillas.com
SIC: 2099 Tortillas, fresh or refrigerated

(G-14202)
LET LOVE RULE
21391 Russell St (48173-9749)
PHONE.................................734 749-7435
EMP: 4 **EST:** 2015
SALES (est): 202.7K **Privately Held**
WEB: www.letloverule.com
SIC: 2759 Screen printing

(G-14203)
PENSTONE INC
31605 Gossett Dr (48173-9700)
PHONE.................................734 379-3160
EMP: 20
SQ FT: 57,640
SALES (est): 2.2MM
SALES (corp-wide): 355.2MM **Privately Held**
SIC: 3231 3429 Mfg Products-Purchased Glass Mfg Hardware
PA: Ishizaki Honten Co.,Ltd.
1-2-15, Yanoshimmachi, Aki-Ku
Hiroshima HIR 736-0
828 201-600

(G-14204)
REBORN WEAR
31967 Groat Blvd (48173-8635)
PHONE.................................313 680-6806
Chad Dohring, *Owner*
EMP: 5 **EST:** 2015
SALES (est): 138K **Privately Held**
SIC: 2759 Screen printing

(G-14205)
SUEZ WATER INDIANA LLC
34001 W Jefferson Ave (48173-9639)
PHONE.................................734 379-3855
David Dupuis, *Branch Mgr*
EMP: 35
SALES (corp-wide): 117.1MM **Privately Held**
SIC: 2899 Water treating compounds
HQ: Suez Water Indiana Llc
461 From Rd Ste F
Paramus NJ 07652
201 767-9300

Rodney
Mecosta County

(G-14206)
CHIPPEWA STONE & GRAVEL INC
15240 110th Ave (49342-9757)
PHONE.................................231 867-5757
Walter Hazen, *President*
Deb Wiersma, *Office Mgr*
EMP: 4 **EST:** 1988
SQ FT: 400
SALES (est): 631.3K **Privately Held**
SIC: 1442 Gravel mining

(G-14207)
RAINBOW HOLLOW PRESS
16695 115th Ave (49342-9727)
PHONE.................................231 825-2962
Samuel Chupp, *Principal*
EMP: 5 **EST:** 2010
SALES (est): 51.7K **Privately Held**
SIC: 2741 Miscellaneous publishing

Rogers City
Presque Isle County

(G-14208)
CADILLAC PRODUCTS INC
Rogers City Plant
4858 Williams Rd (49779-9606)
PHONE.................................989 766-2294
Kenneth Ritzema, *Sales Staff*
Steven Harris, *Branch Mgr*
Art Ditullio, *Info Tech Dir*
Neil Young, *Maintence Staff*
EMP: 17
SALES (corp-wide): 74.4MM **Privately Held**
WEB: www.cadprod.com
SIC: 3089 2621 2673 5199 Automotive parts, plastic; paper mills; bags: plastic, laminated & coated; fabrics, yarns & knit goods; motor vehicle parts & accessories; unsupported plastics film & sheet
PA: Cadillac Products, Inc.
5800 Crooks Rd Ste 100
Troy MI 48098
248 813-8200

▲ = Import ▼ =Export
◆ =Import/Export

GEOGRAPHIC SECTION

Romeo - Macomb County (G-14235)

(G-14209)
E H TULGESTKA & SONS INC
1160 Hwy F 21 S (49779)
P.O. Box 169 (49779-0169)
PHONE 989 734-2129
Erhardt Tulgestka Sr, *President*
Christopher Tulgestka, *Treasurer*
Nancy Tulgestka, *Admin Sec*
EMP: 15 **EST:** 1963
SQ FT: 1,000
SALES (est): 2.2MM **Privately Held**
SIC: 2411 2421 4213 Logging camps & contractors; sawmills & planing mills, general; trucking, except local

(G-14210)
ESSENTIAL PHOTO GEAR
5782 Church Hwy (49779-9718)
PHONE 502 244-2888
Travis Peltz, *CEO*
EMP: 4 **EST:** 2017
SALES (est): 77.4K **Privately Held**
WEB: www.essentialphotogear.com
SIC: 3861 Photographic equipment & supplies

(G-14211)
LEES READY MIX INC
3232 Birchwood Dr (49779-1551)
PHONE 989 734-7666
EMP: 4 **EST:** 1985
SQ FT: 3,000
SALES: 500K **Privately Held**
SIC: 3273 Mfg Ready-Mixed Concrete

(G-14212)
LINDAS WOODCRAFTS & CABINETS
3350 W Heythaler Hwy (49779-9748)
PHONE 989 734-2903
Linda K Kuznicki, *Owner*
EMP: 5 **EST:** 2013
SALES (est): 92K **Privately Held**
SIC: 2434 Wood kitchen cabinets

(G-14213)
NORTHERN PROCESSING
286 W Huron Ave (49779-1338)
PHONE 989 734-9007
Christine Augsburger, *Owner*
EMP: 4 **EST:** 2014
SALES (est): 69.9K **Privately Held**
SIC: 2011 Meat packing plants

(G-14214)
O-N MINERALS MICHIGAN COMPANY
Also Called: Carmeuse Lime & Stone
1035 Calcite Rd (49779-1900)
PHONE 989 734-2131
EMP: 152
SALES (corp-wide): 177.9K **Privately Held**
SIC: 1422 Crushed & broken limestone
HQ: O-N Minerals (Michigan) Company
 11 Stanwix St Fl 21
 Pittsburgh PA 15222
 412 995-5500

(G-14215)
O-N MINERALS MICHIGAN COMPANY (PA)
Also Called: Division Oglebay Norton Co
1035 Calcite Rd (49779-1900)
PHONE 989 734-2131
Michelle Harris, *President*
Joe Chevreaux, *Plant Mgr*
Darryl Hubble, *Buyer*
Dean Roof, *Project Engr*
Michael McCannon, *CFO*
EMP: 200 **EST:** 1998
SQ FT: 2,000
SALES (est): 33.1MM **Privately Held**
SIC: 1411 1422 5032 Limestone, dimension-quarrying; dolomite, dimension-quarrying; crushed & broken limestone; limestone

(G-14216)
PERSONS INC
285 S Bradley Hwy Ste 2 (49779-2141)
PHONE 989 734-3835
Richard M Lewandowski, *Principal*
EMP: 4 **EST:** 2010

SALES (est): 245.1K **Privately Held**
SIC: 2992 Oils & greases, blending & compounding

(G-14217)
PRESQUE ISLE NEWSPAPERS INC
Also Called: Advance
104 S 3rd St (49779-1710)
P.O. Box 50 (49779-0050)
PHONE 989 734-2105
Richard Lamb, *President*
Cella Bade, *Adv Mgr*
EMP: 10 **EST:** 1878
SQ FT: 3,250
SALES (est): 897.1K **Privately Held**
WEB: www.piadvance.com
SIC: 2711 2741 Job printing & newspaper publishing combined; shopping news: publishing only, not printed on site

(G-14218)
SCHLEBEN FOREST PRODUCTS INC
Also Called: Schleben Rhinold Forest Pdts
3302 S Ward Branch Rd (49779-9678)
PHONE 989 734-2858
EMP: 4
SALES (est): 520K **Privately Held**
SIC: 5099 2421 5031 Whol Durable Goods Sawmill/Planing Mill Whol Lumber/Plywood/Millwork

Romeo
Macomb County

(G-14219)
ALCO PLASTICS INC (PA)
160 E Pond Dr (48065-4902)
PHONE 586 752-4527
Daniel J Conway, *President*
Joshua Hautamaki, *General Mgr*
Cathy Conway, *Vice Pres*
Darren Oreilly, *Opers Staff*
Derrick Miller, *QC Mgr*
EMP: 100 **EST:** 1976
SQ FT: 66,000
SALES (est): 18.4MM **Privately Held**
WEB: www.alcoplastics.com
SIC: 3089 Injection molding of plastics

(G-14220)
AWCCO USA INCORPORATED
171 Shafer Dr (48065-4913)
PHONE 586 336-9135
Arthur Capon, *President*
Perry Kloska, *General Mgr*
Miriam Capon, *CFO*
EMP: 6 **EST:** 2011
SQ FT: 14,000
SALES (est): 589.6K **Privately Held**
WEB: www.awcco.com
SIC: 3321 7373 3369 Gray iron castings; computer-aided design (CAD) systems service; computer-aided manufacturing (CAM) systems service; nonferrous foundries

(G-14221)
CALIBER INDUSTRIES LLC
Also Called: Pneumatic Feed Service
100 Shafer Dr (48065-4907)
PHONE 586 774-6775
Eric Werner, *President*
EMP: 15 **EST:** 2016
SALES (est): 4.1MM **Privately Held**
WEB: www.minster.com
SIC: 3535 Conveyors & conveying equipment
HQ: Nidec Minster Corporation
 240 W 5th St
 Minster OH 45865
 419 628-2331

(G-14222)
CAMMAND MACHINING LLC
101 Shafer Dr (48065-4913)
PHONE 586 752-0366
Clarence A Meltzer Jr,
Jeff Bond,
Clarence Meltzer,
EMP: 23 **EST:** 2002
SQ FT: 7,500

SALES (est): 3.4MM **Privately Held**
WEB: www.cammand.com
SIC: 3544 Special dies & tools

(G-14223)
D & N BENDING CORP (PA)
Also Called: D & N Casting
150 Shafer Dr (48065-4907)
PHONE 586 752-5511
Brian Murray, *President*
Steve Murray, *Vice Pres*
Mark Filer, *Manager*
▲ **EMP:** 34 **EST:** 1980
SQ FT: 12,000
SALES (est): 25.7MM **Privately Held**
WEB: www.dnbending.com
SIC: 3465 Moldings or trim, automobile: stamped metal

(G-14224)
D & N GAGE INC
161 E Pond Dr (48065-4903)
PHONE 586 336-2110
Dan Schweiger, *President*
EMP: 10 **EST:** 2001
SALES (est): 1.7MM **Privately Held**
WEB: www.dngage.com
SIC: 3829 Gauges, motor vehicle: oil pressure, water temperature; instrument board gauges, automotive: computerized

(G-14225)
ENGINRED PLSTIC COMPONENTS INC
187 E Pond Dr (48065-4903)
PHONE 586 336-9500
EMP: 260 **Privately Held**
WEB: www.epcmfg.com
SIC: 3089 Injection molded finished plastic products
PA: Engineered Plastic Components, Inc.
 4500 Westown Pkwy Ste 277
 West Des Moines IA 50266

(G-14226)
I S P COATINGS CORP
130 E Pond Dr (48065-4902)
PHONE 586 752-5020
John Malinich, *President*
EMP: 19 **EST:** 1975
SQ FT: 15,000
SALES (est): 1.4MM **Privately Held**
WEB: www.ispcoatingscorp.com
SIC: 3479 Coating of metals & formed products; painting, coating & hot dipping

(G-14227)
KRIEWALL ENTERPRISES INC
140 Shafer Dr (48065-4907)
PHONE 586 336-0600
Edwin C Kriewall, *CEO*
Theresa Chase, *President*
Sandra Kriewall, *Vice Pres*
EMP: 50 **EST:** 1970
SQ FT: 10,000
SALES (est): 3.4MM **Privately Held**
WEB: www.keiprototype.com
SIC: 3599 3444 3469 3999 Machine shop, jobbing & repair; sheet metalwork; metal stampings; barber & beauty shop equipment; manufactured hardware (general); fabricated structural metal

(G-14228)
LITTLE BUILDINGS INC
161 Shafer Dr (48065-4913)
PHONE 586 752-7100
James B Sudomier, *President*
Linda Sudomier, *Vice Pres*
Nicole Fitch, *Admin Asst*
EMP: 6 **EST:** 1997
SQ FT: 8,800
SALES (est): 1MM **Privately Held**
WEB: www.littlebuildingsinc.com
SIC: 3448 2452 Buildings, portable: prefabricated metal; prefabricated wood buildings

(G-14229)
MC PHERSON INDUSTRIAL CORP
Also Called: Quality Chaser Co Div
120 E Pond Dr (48065-4902)
P.O. Box 496 (48065-0496)
PHONE 586 752-5555
Keith Mc Pherson, *President*

Ursla Mc Pherson, *Corp Secy*
EMP: 22 **EST:** 1944
SQ FT: 8,000
SALES (est): 1.1MM **Privately Held**
SIC: 3545 3541 Thread cutting dies; machine tools, metal cutting type

(G-14230)
NIDEC CHS LLC
Also Called: Metal Stmping Spport Group LLC
100 Shafer Dr (48065-4907)
PHONE 586 777-7440
Eric Werner, *Mng Member*
Sherry Barkatt,
James Hewines,
EMP: 11 **EST:** 2002
SALES (est): 5.3MM **Privately Held**
WEB: www.chsautomation.com
SIC: 3469 3549 Machine parts, stamped or pressed metal; metalworking machinery
HQ: Nidec Minster Corporation
 240 W 5th St
 Minster OH 45865
 419 628-2331

(G-14231)
P & K TECHNOLOGIES INC
111 Shafer Dr (48065-4913)
PHONE 586 336-9545
Paul Kasper, *President*
EMP: 6 **EST:** 1988
SQ FT: 3,200
SALES (est): 528.6K **Privately Held**
WEB: www.pk-technologies.com
SIC: 3089 Injection molding of plastics

(G-14232)
PETROLEUM RESOURCES INC (PA)
134 W Saint Clair St (48065-4656)
P.O. Box 466 (48065-0466)
PHONE 586 752-7856
Ernest G Moeller Jr, *President*
Stanley N Masoner, *Principal*
Michael E Moeller, *Principal*
Charles A Brennecker Jr, *Vice Pres*
EMP: 6 **EST:** 1962
SALES (est): 6.4MM **Privately Held**
SIC: 1311 Crude petroleum production

(G-14233)
RAMTEC CORP
409 E Saint Clair St (48065-5270)
PHONE 586 752-9270
Mark Nichols, *President*
Joshua Phelps, *Prgrmr*
EMP: 10 **EST:** 1999
SALES (est): 1MM **Privately Held**
WEB: www.ramtecco.net
SIC: 3599 7389 Electrical discharge machining (EDM); grinding, precision: commercial or industrial

(G-14234)
ROMEO PRINTING COMPANY INC
225 N Main St (48065-4617)
PHONE 586 752-9003
Jon Malzahn, *President*
Randall Seidel, *Vice Chairman*
Christine Malzahn, *Vice Pres*
EMP: 4 **EST:** 1983
SQ FT: 2,360
SALES (est): 349.1K **Privately Held**
WEB: www.romeoprinting.com
SIC: 2752 2759 Commercial printing, offset; letterpress printing

(G-14235)
SEAL SUPPORT SYSTEMS INC (DH)
141 Shafer Dr (48065-4913)
PHONE 918 258-6484
Juan Johnson, *President*
EMP: 30 **EST:** 1990
SQ FT: 7,250
SALES (est): 10.8MM
SALES (corp-wide): 10.4B **Privately Held**
WEB: www.eagleburgmann.us
SIC: 3443 2891 Heat exchangers, condensers & components; adhesives & sealants

Romeo - Macomb County (G-14236) — GEOGRAPHIC SECTION

HQ: Eagleburgmann Industries Lp
10035 Brookriver Dr
Houston TX 77040
713 939-9515

(G-14236)
T/D VILLAGE WINERY LLC
134 W Saint Clair St (48065-4656)
PHONE.....................586 752-5510
Anthony Hafner, *Principal*
EMP: 5 **EST:** 2010
SALES (est): 101.6K **Privately Held**
WEB: www.villagewineryromeomi.com
SIC: 2084 Wines

(G-14237)
THREE ROSES WOODWORK
439 N Main St (48065-4625)
PHONE.....................248 763-1837
EMP: 4 **EST:** 2018
SALES (est): 112.2K **Privately Held**
SIC: 2431 Millwork

(G-14238)
TK MOLD & ENGINEERING INC
131 Shafer Dr (48065-4913)
PHONE.....................586 752-5840
Thomas W Barr, *Principal*
Tom Barr, *Manager*
Sam Viviano, *Manager*
◆ **EMP:** 23
SALES: 3.5MM **Privately Held**
WEB: www.tkmoldeng.com
SIC: 3089 Injection molding of plastics

(G-14239)
WHITCOMB AND SONS SIGN CO INC
Also Called: Whitcomb Sign
315 E Lafayette St (48065-5239)
PHONE.....................586 752-3576
Lawrence Whitcomb, *President*
Leslie Whitcomb, *Vice Pres*
Larry Whitcomb, *Plt & Fclts Mgr*
EMP: 5 **EST:** 1957
SQ FT: 5,500
SALES (est): 456K **Privately Held**
WEB: www.whitcombsign.com
SIC: 7336 3993 Graphic arts & related design; electric signs

(G-14240)
WRANOSKY & SONS INC
105 S Main St (48065-5125)
PHONE.....................586 336-9761
Gary John Wranosky, *Principal*
EMP: 8 **EST:** 2007
SALES (est): 503.1K **Privately Held**
WEB: www.leonardwranoskyandsonscarpentry.com
SIC: 3423 Carpenters' hand tools, except saws: levels, chisels, etc.

(G-14241)
ZF PASSIVE SFETY SYSTEMS US IN
Also Called: TRW Oss
14761 E32 Mile Rd (48065)
PHONE.....................586 752-1409
Julieta Santacruz, *Branch Mgr*
EMP: 7
SALES (corp-wide): 216.2K **Privately Held**
WEB: www.zf.com
SIC: 3714 Motor vehicle parts & accessories
HQ: Zf Passive Safety Systems Us Inc.
12001 Tech Center Dr
Livonia MI 48150

Romulus
Wayne County

(G-14242)
A S AUTO LIGHTS INC
15326 Oakwood Dr (48174-3610)
PHONE.....................734 941-1164
EMP: 7 **EST:** 2015
SALES (est): 123.3K **Privately Held**
WEB: www.allstarautolights.com
SIC: 3647 Motor vehicle lighting equipment

(G-14243)
A123 SYSTEMS LLC
Also Called: A123 Systems Rmulus Operations
38100 Ecorse Rd (48174-5306)
PHONE.....................734 772-0600
William Zhao, *Exec VP*
Jim Paye, *Vice Pres*
John Patel, *CFO*
Bing Sun, *CFO*
Michael O'Kronley, *Exec Dir*
EMP: 6 **Privately Held**
WEB: www.a123systems.com
SIC: 3691 Storage batteries
HQ: A123 Systems Llc
27101 Cabaret Dr
Novi MI 48377
248 412-9249

(G-14244)
ABRASIVE SERVICES INCORPORATED
29040 Northline Rd (48174-2836)
PHONE.....................734 941-2144
Steve Belinc, *Owner*
EMP: 5 **EST:** 2007
SALES (est): 395.2K **Privately Held**
WEB: www.polishingserviceromulus.com
SIC: 3471 3541 4812 4813 Plating of metals or formed products; buffing & polishing machines; cellular telephone services; data telephone communications

(G-14245)
ACTIA ELECTRONICS INC
15385 Pine (48174-3659)
PHONE.....................574 264-2373
Adam Ramouni, *CEO*
Gary Cooper, *Human Resources*
EMP: 1 **EST:** 2018
SALES (est): 12.6MM
SALES (corp-wide): 2.7MM **Privately Held**
WEB: www.actiaus.com
SIC: 3629 3612 3677 Electronic generation equipment; transformers, except electric; transformers power supply, electronic type
HQ: Actia Corporation
2809 Bridger Ct
Elkhart IN 46514

(G-14246)
AE GROUP LLC
Also Called: Aerostar Manufacturing
28275 Northline Rd (48174-2829)
PHONE.....................734 942-0615
Gaurav Aggarwal, *Business Mgr*
Ken Krasnodemski, *Vice Pres*
Kaustubh Zinjarde, *Project Mgr*
Melvin Koslowski, *Mfg Mgr*
Troy Carney, *Engineer*
▲ **EMP:** 150 **EST:** 1994
SQ FT: 50,000
SALES (est): 35.7MM **Privately Held**
WEB: www.aerostarmfg.com
SIC: 3599 Machine shop, jobbing & repair

(G-14247)
AIR CONDITIONING PRODUCTS CO (PA)
30350 Ecorse Rd (48174-3595)
PHONE.....................734 326-0050
Philip K Mebus Jr, *President*
Christopher Mebus, *President*
Ed Kirstein, *Engineer*
Chrisopher Mebus, *Treasurer*
Tim Fleitz, *Sales Mgr*
▲ **EMP:** 50 **EST:** 1945
SQ FT: 110,000
SALES (est): 9MM **Privately Held**
WEB: www.acpshutters.com
SIC: 3444 3354 2431 Ventilators, sheet metal; aluminum extruded products; millwork

(G-14248)
AMERIPAVE
5931 Panam St (48174-2353)
PHONE.....................843 509-5502
EMP: 5 **EST:** 2017
SALES (est): 120.7K **Privately Held**
SIC: 2952 Asphalt felts & coatings

(G-14249)
AMSCO CHAMPION LLC
6775 Brandt St (48174-3507)
PHONE.....................734 728-8500
EMP: 5 **EST:** 2019
SALES (est): 116.7K **Privately Held**
SIC: 3599 Machine shop, jobbing & repair

(G-14250)
APPROVED AIRCRAFT ACCESSORIES
Also Called: Aero Test
29300 Goddard Rd (48174-2704)
P.O. Box 666, Taylor (48180-0666)
PHONE.....................734 946-9000
Gail A Yancheck, *President*
Jerry Helgeson, *Vice Pres*
Jerry Wicker, *Mfg Staff*
EMP: 9 **EST:** 1957
SQ FT: 7,500
SALES (est): 992.8K **Privately Held**
SIC: 3724 4581 Aircraft engines & engine parts; airports, flying fields & services

(G-14251)
APS COMPOUNDING LLC
30735 Cypress Rd Ste 400 (48174-3541)
PHONE.....................734 710-6702
Huarng Jyh-Chiang,
EMP: 10 **EST:** 2016
SALES (est): 82.5K **Privately Held**
SIC: 2821 Molding compounds, plastics

(G-14252)
AWESOME MUSICAL INSTRS LLC
16646 Mary Grace Ln (48174-3316)
PHONE.....................734 941-2927
EMP: 4 **EST:** 2018
SALES (est): 41K **Privately Held**
SIC: 3931 Musical instruments

(G-14253)
AZTEC MANUFACTURING CORP
15378 Oakwood Dr (48174-3653)
PHONE.....................734 942-7433
Francis Lopez, *President*
Rick Johnson, *Corp Secy*
Ken Johnson, *Engineer*
Mike Warner, *Engineer*
Richard Johnson, *Treasurer*
◆ **EMP:** 130 **EST:** 1983
SQ FT: 73,300
SALES (est): 16.8MM **Privately Held**
WEB: www.aztecmfgcorp.com
SIC: 3599 Machine shop, jobbing & repair

(G-14254)
B & K BUFFING INC
29040 Northline Rd (48174-2836)
PHONE.....................734 941-2144
Steve Belinc, *President*
Gerald Krohn, *Vice Pres*
EMP: 6 **EST:** 1969
SQ FT: 3,200
SALES (est): 312K **Privately Held**
SIC: 3471 Buffing for the trade; finishing, metals or formed products; polishing, metals or formed products

(G-14255)
BARRETT PAVING MATERIALS INC
13501 S Huron River Dr (48174-3663)
PHONE.....................734 941-0200
Rock Frazier, *Manager*
EMP: 4
SALES (corp-wide): 271.8MM **Privately Held**
WEB: www.barrettpaving.com
SIC: 2951 Asphalt paving mixtures & blocks
HQ: Barrett Paving Materials Inc.
3 Becker Farm Rd Ste 307
Roseland NJ 07068
973 533-1001

(G-14256)
BAWDEN INDUSTRIES INC
29909 Beverly Rd (48174-2031)
PHONE.....................734 721-6414
John Bawden, *President*
EMP: 16 **EST:** 1960
SQ FT: 4,500
SALES (est): 1MM **Privately Held**
SIC: 3544 Dies & die holders for metal cutting, forming, die casting

(G-14257)
BENLEE INC (PA)
30383 Ecorse Rd (48174-3521)
PHONE.....................586 791-1830
Gregory Brown, *CEO*
William B Wolok, *President*
Ron Ostrowski, *Opers Staff*
David Gibb, *CFO*
Used Lugger, *Sales Staff*
EMP: 34 **EST:** 2004
SALES (est): 6.8MM **Privately Held**
WEB: www.benlee.com
SIC: 3715 7538 5511 7539 Truck trailers; general truck repair; trucks, tractors & trailers: new & used; automotive repair shops

(G-14258)
BIOBEST USA INC (DH)
11700 Mtr Arpt Ctr Dr # 110 (48174-1410)
PHONE.....................734 626-5693
Richard Ward, *CEO*
EMP: 1 **EST:** 1997
SALES (est): 2.9MM
SALES (corp-wide): 16.9MM **Privately Held**
WEB: www.biobestgroup.com
SIC: 2879 Pesticides, agricultural or household
HQ: Biobest Group
Ilse Velden 18
Westerlo 2260
142 579-80

(G-14259)
BIRCLAR ELECTRIC AND ELEC LLC
12060 Wayne Rd (48174-3776)
PHONE.....................734 941-7400
Tim Martindale, *CEO*
James Fitzwater, *Division Mgr*
Kim Marion, *Sales Staff*
Helen Lafreniere, *Marketing Staff*
Jim Bunker, *Supervisor*
EMP: 18 **EST:** 1987
SALES (est): 3.4MM **Privately Held**
SIC: 7694 Electric motor repair

(G-14260)
CARTEX CORPORATION
Also Called: Dynaflex
15573 Oakwood Dr (48174-3656)
PHONE.....................734 857-5961
Stephen Murphy, *Branch Mgr*
EMP: 82
SQ FT: 41,000
SALES (corp-wide): 157.8MM **Privately Held**
SIC: 7532 2821 Top & body repair & paint shops; plastics materials & resins
HQ: Cartex Corporation
1515 Equity Dr 100
Troy MI 48084
610 759-1650

(G-14261)
CASTINO CORPORATION (PA)
16777 Wahrman St (48174-3633)
PHONE.....................734 941-7200
Robert L Castino Jr, *President*
Jim Nash, *Sales Mgr*
EMP: 35 **EST:** 1981
SQ FT: 25,000
SALES (est): 5.3MM **Privately Held**
WEB: www.castinocorp.com
SIC: 3089 Injection molding of plastics

(G-14262)
COLFRAN INDUSTRIAL SALES INC
38127 Ecorse Rd (48174-1349)
PHONE.....................734 595-8920
Carl Stevens, *President*
EMP: 9 **EST:** 1982
SALES (est): 261.2K **Privately Held**
SIC: 5169 3341 Industrial chemicals; secondary nonferrous metals

(G-14263)
CONTROL ELECTRONICS
29231 Northline Rd (48174-2835)
PHONE.....................734 941-5008

▲ = Import ▼ = Export
◆ = Import/Export

John Mayor, *President*
EMP: 5 EST: 1981
SALES (est): 104K Privately Held
SIC: 3679 Electronic components

(G-14264)
COUNTRY FRESH LLC
Also Called: Embest
28795 Goddard Rd Ste 204 (48174-2866)
PHONE.................................734 261-7980
Bruce Evans, *Manager*
EMP: 473 Publicly Held
WEB: www.deanfoods.com
SIC: 2026 Fluid milk
HQ: Country Fresh, Llc
 2711 N Haskell Ave # 3400
 Dallas TX 75204
 616 243-0173

(G-14265)
CRYSTAL CUT TOOL INC
10360 Harrison (48174-2635)
PHONE.................................734 946-0099
Wayne Robinson, *President*
Wesley Wiley, *Corp Secy*
EMP: 7 EST: 1989
SQ FT: 6,000
SALES (est): 617K Privately Held
WEB: www.crystalcuttools.com
SIC: 3545 Diamond cutting tools for turning, boring, burnishing, etc.

(G-14266)
CURTISS-WRIGHT SURFACE TECH
30100 Cypress Rd (48174-3591)
PHONE.................................734 728-8600
EMP: 7 EST: 2019
SALES (est): 132.1K Privately Held
WEB: www.cwst.com
SIC: 3398 Metal heat treating

(G-14267)
DETROIT TARPAULIN REPR SP INC
6760 Metro Plex Dr (48174-2012)
PHONE.................................734 955-8200
Guy Sullins, *President*
Lou Stephenson, *Principal*
Roy Sullins, *Principal*
Thomas Stephenson, *Vice Pres*
Donald Sullins, *Vice Pres*
▲ EMP: 24 EST: 1945
SQ FT: 32,000
SALES (est): 4.8MM Privately Held
WEB: www.detroittarp.com
SIC: 2394 5013 Tarpaulins, fabric: made from purchased materials; automotive trim

(G-14268)
DST INDUSTRIES INC (HQ)
Also Called: Diversified Services Tech
34364 Goddard Rd (48174-3451)
PHONE.................................734 941-0300
Brenda Lewo, *President*
Joe Lewo, *Principal*
Don Snell, *COO*
Dianna Andrikos, *Controller*
▲ EMP: 225 EST: 1955
SQ FT: 125,000
SALES (est): 30.5MM Privately Held
WEB: www.dstindustries.com
SIC: 3465 Fenders, automobile: stamped or pressed metal

(G-14269)
EAGLE RIDGE PAPER LTD
15355 Oakwood Dr (48174-3611)
PHONE.................................248 376-9503
EMP: 17
SALES (corp-wide): 22.6MM Privately Held
WEB: www.eagleridgepaper.com
SIC: 2621 Printing paper
HQ: Eagle Ridge Paper Ltd.
 100 S Anaheim Blvd # 250
 Anaheim CA 92805
 714 780-1799

(G-14270)
ELEMENT FACILITY SERVICES
6094 2nd St (48174-1868)
PHONE.................................734 895-8716
EMP: 7 EST: 2018
SALES (est): 164.6K Privately Held
WEB: www.element.com
SIC: 2819 Industrial inorganic chemicals

(G-14271)
ELKINS MACHINE & TOOL CO INC (PA)
27510 Northline Rd (48174-2826)
PHONE.................................734 941-0266
Tim Swoish, *President*
Rick Sollars, *Vice Pres*
Jerry Verhoven, *Opers Mgr*
Ryan Parker, *Administration*
EMP: 33 EST: 1978
SQ FT: 11,500
SALES (est): 5MM Privately Held
WEB: www.elkinsmachine.net
SIC: 3599 3451 3469 Machine shop, jobbing & repair; screw machine products; metal stampings

(G-14272)
EQ RESOURCE RECOVERY INC (DH)
36345 Van Born Rd (48174-4057)
PHONE.................................734 727-5500
Jeffrey R Feeler, *President*
Simon Bell, *Vice Pres*
Eric Gerratt, *Treasurer*
Wayne Ipsen, *Admin Sec*
EMP: 3 EST: 1971
SQ FT: 15,000
SALES (est): 6MM
SALES (corp-wide): 933.8MM Publicly Held
WEB: www.usecology.com
SIC: 2869 Solvents, organic
HQ: Us Ecology Holdings, Inc.
 101 S Capitol Blvd # 1000
 Boise ID 83702
 208 331-8400

(G-14273)
EUCLID MACHINE & MFG CO
29030 Northline Rd (48174-2836)
PHONE.................................734 941-1080
Robert Kluba, *President*
Brian Kluba, *Vice Pres*
Dolores Kluba, *Admin Sec*
EMP: 23 EST: 1978
SQ FT: 7,200
SALES (est): 951.6K Privately Held
WEB: www.euclidgages.com
SIC: 3599 Machine shop, jobbing & repair

(G-14274)
FEDERAL SCREW WORKS (PA)
34846 Goddard Rd (48174-3400)
PHONE.................................734 941-4211
Thomas Zurschmiede, *CEO*
W T Zurschmiede Jr, *Ch of Bd*
Robert F Zurschmiede, *Exec VP*
Jeffrey M Harness, *Vice Pres*
Jeffrey Harness, *Vice Pres*
▲ EMP: 15 EST: 1919
SQ FT: 12,000
SALES (est): 78.9MM Privately Held
WEB: www.federalscrewworks.com
SIC: 3444 3592 3452 Studs & joists, sheet metal; pistons & piston rings; bolts, metal

(G-14275)
FEDERAL SCREW WORKS
Also Called: Romulus Nut Division
34846 Goddard Rd (48174-3400)
PHONE.................................734 941-4211
R F Zurschmiede, *President*
EMP: 203
SALES (corp-wide): 78.9MM Privately Held
WEB: www.federalscrewworks.com
SIC: 3357 3452 Building wire & cable, nonferrous; nuts, metal
PA: Federal Screw Works
 34846 Goddard Rd
 Romulus MI 48174
 734 941-4211

(G-14276)
FINTEX LLC
8900 Inkster Rd (48174-2695)
PHONE.................................734 946-3100
Linda Born, *Sales Staff*
David Purcell, *Manager*
Renee Yustick, *Manager*
Mike Rapp, *Executive*
Kent M Desjardins,
▲ EMP: 31 EST: 1999
SALES (est): 3.4MM Privately Held
WEB: www.fintex.net
SIC: 3471 Electroplating of metals or formed products

(G-14277)
FUTURE TOOL AND MACHINE INC
28900 Goddard Rd (48174-2700)
PHONE.................................734 946-2100
Leslee Franzel, *CEO*
Larry Franzel, *President*
Gregory Dickie, *Plant Mgr*
Kris Surcek, *Opers Mgr*
Tony Konopka, *Purch Agent*
EMP: 45 EST: 1986
SQ FT: 50,000
SALES (est): 9.5MM Privately Held
WEB: www.futuretool.com
SIC: 3599 Machine shop, jobbing & repair

(G-14278)
GLOBAL AUTOMOTIVE PRODUCTS INC
Also Called: Gap
38100 Jay Kay Dr (48174-4000)
P.O. Box 891, Melville NY (11747-0891)
PHONE.................................734 589-6179
Paul Foertsch, *COO*
▲ EMP: 10 EST: 2013
SQ FT: 72,000
SALES (est): 403K Privately Held
WEB: www.falconsteering.com
SIC: 3089 Automotive parts, plastic

(G-14279)
GM POWERTRAIN-ROMULUS ENGINE
36880 Ecorse Rd (48174-1395)
PHONE.................................734 595-5203
Ralph Pierce, *Manager*
EMP: 5 EST: 2010
SALES (est): 1.3MM Publicly Held
WEB: www.gm.com
SIC: 3519 Internal combustion engines
PA: General Motors Company
 300 Renaissance Ctr L1
 Detroit MI 48243

(G-14280)
GMA INDUSTRIES INC
38127 Ecorse Rd (48174-1349)
PHONE.................................734 595-7300
Carl Stevens, *President*
Coleen Stevens, *Corp Secy*
Erin Jameson, *Opers Staff*
Larry Friesen, *Regl Sales Mgr*
Tyson Baird, *Supervisor*
▲ EMP: 20 EST: 1982
SQ FT: 26,000
SALES (est): 6.8MM Privately Held
WEB: www.gmaind.com
SIC: 3291 Steel shot abrasive; grit, steel; aluminum oxide (fused) abrasives

(G-14281)
GROUP B INDUSTRIES II INC
15399 Oakwood Dr (48174-3655)
PHONE.................................734 941-6640
Bonnie Burry, *President*
EMP: 4 EST: 2005
SQ FT: 9,600
SALES (est): 644K Privately Held
WEB: www.groupbind.com
SIC: 3544 Special dies & tools

(G-14282)
H & J MFG CONSULTING SVCS CORP
15771 S Huron River Dr (48174-3668)
PHONE.................................734 941-8314
Bill Junge, *President*
EMP: 7 EST: 1980
SQ FT: 28,000
SALES (est): 1.2MM Privately Held
SIC: 3479 2842 Painting of metal products; specialty cleaning, polishes & sanitation goods

(G-14283)
HOME CITY ICE COMPANY
15475 Oakwood Dr (48174-3655)
PHONE.................................734 955-9094
Greg Hug, *Branch Mgr*
EMP: 43
SALES (corp-wide): 99.1MM Privately Held
WEB: www.homecityice.com
SIC: 2097 Ice cubes
PA: The Home City Ice Company
 6045 Bridgetown Rd Ste 1
 Cincinnati OH 45248
 513 574-1800

(G-14284)
HUYS INDUSTRIES
28421 Highland Rd (48174-2506)
PHONE.................................734 895-3067
EMP: 7 EST: 2019
SALES (est): 251.3K Privately Held
WEB: www.huysindustries.com
SIC: 3999 Manufacturing industries

(G-14285)
IMPRESSIVE AUTO CARE LLC
8428 Wahrman St (48174-4162)
PHONE.................................734 306-4880
Tonise Jones, *President*
EMP: 10 EST: 2015
SALES (est): 438.6K Privately Held
WEB: www.impressiveautoservice.com
SIC: 3589 Car washing machinery

(G-14286)
INTERNATIONAL PAINT STRIPPING (PA)
15300 Oakwood Dr (48174-3610)
PHONE.................................734 942-0500
Joseph Kochanoski, *President*
Mark Kochanoski, *Vice Pres*
Carol Kochanoski, *Treasurer*
Rudy Castle, *Info Tech Mgr*
EMP: 12 EST: 1982
SQ FT: 21,200
SALES (est): 1.4MM Privately Held
WEB: www.internationalpaintstripping.com
SIC: 3471 Cleaning & descaling metal products

(G-14287)
INTERNATIONAL PAINT STRIPPING
15326 Oakwood Dr (48174-3610)
PHONE.................................734 942-0500
Joseph Kochananoski, *President*
EMP: 6
SALES (corp-wide): 1.4MM Privately Held
WEB: www.internationalpaintstripping.com
SIC: 3471 Cleaning & descaling metal products
PA: International Paint Stripping Inc
 15300 Oakwood Dr
 Romulus MI 48174
 734 942-0500

(G-14288)
J L INTERNATIONAL INC (PA)
Also Called: Pft Industries
34364 Goddard Rd (48174-3451)
PHONE.................................734 941-0300
Brenda Lewo, *President*
EMP: 200 EST: 1991
SQ FT: 125,000
SALES (est): 31.8MM Privately Held
SIC: 3714 5065 Motor vehicle parts & accessories; telephone equipment

(G-14289)
JADE MFG INC
36535 Grant St (48174-1443)
P.O. Box 864, Dearborn (48121-0864)
PHONE.................................734 942-1462
James M Egyed, *President*
Diane B Egyed, *Corp Secy*
EMP: 6 EST: 2000
SQ FT: 3,500
SALES (est): 961.4K Privately Held
WEB: www.jademfg.com
SIC: 3495 Wire springs

Romulus - Wayne County (G-14290) — GEOGRAPHIC SECTION

(G-14290)
JLR PRINTING INC
Also Called: American Speedy Printing
7559 Merriman Rd (48174-1919)
PHONE.................................734 728-0250
Jeff Reynolds, *General Mgr*
EMP: 7 **EST:** 1992
SALES (est): 96.4K Privately Held
WEB: www.americanspeedy.com
SIC: 2752 Commercial printing, offset

(G-14291)
JOHN JOHNSON COMPANY
Also Called: Detroit Cover
15500 Oakwood Dr (48174-3670)
PHONE.................................313 496-0600
Richard H Dancy Jr, *President*
Robert B Dancy, *Vice Pres*
▲ **EMP:** 90 **EST:** 1800
SALES (est): 9.6MM Privately Held
WEB: www.johnjohnsonco.com
SIC: 2221 Upholstery, tapestry & wall covering fabrics

(G-14292)
JOINT CLUTCH & GEAR SVC INC (PA)
30200 Cypress Rd (48174-3538)
PHONE.................................734 641-7575
Gary R Scherz, *Exec VP*
Jason Sierocki, *Vice Pres*
James Quarles, *Vice Pres*
David L Scherz, *Vice Pres*
Stanley C Drabik, *CFO*
EMP: 25
SQ FT: 20,000
SALES (est): 5.5MM Privately Held
WEB: www.jointclutchandgear.com
SIC: 5013 5531 3714 Truck parts & accessories; automobile & truck equipment & parts; motor vehicle parts & accessories

(G-14293)
JUST COVER IT UP
34754 Lynn Dr (48174-1565)
PHONE.................................734 247-4729
Ann McCauley, *Principal*
EMP: 4 **EST:** 2007
SALES (est): 259.9K Privately Held
WEB: www.justcoveritup.com
SIC: 2448 Cargo containers, wood & wood with metal

(G-14294)
KERR CORPORATION
Also Called: Kerr Manufacturing
28200 Wick Rd (48174-2600)
PHONE.................................734 946-7800
Tony Molitor, *District Mgr*
Allen Schwager, *District Mgr*
Rob Starcher, *Vice Pres*
Sam Chung, *Finance Dir*
Jonathan Gegerson, *Sales Mgr*
EMP: 286
SALES (corp-wide): 22.2B Publicly Held
WEB: www.kerrdental.com
SIC: 3843 Dental materials; dental laboratory equipment; impression material, dental; dental hand instruments
HQ: Kerr Corporation
1717 W Collins Ave
Orange CA 92867
714 516-7400

(G-14295)
KIRMIN DIE & TOOL INC
36360 Ecorse Rd (48174-4159)
PHONE.................................734 722-9210
Tom Mulanka, *President*
Casimira Buraczewski, *Corp Secy*
EMP: 30 **EST:** 1969
SQ FT: 21,000
SALES (est): 4.2MM Privately Held
WEB: www.kirminind.com
SIC: 3465 3544 Automotive stampings; special dies & tools

(G-14296)
KRMC LLC
Also Called: Kut-Rite Manufacturing Company
27456 Northline Rd (48174-2826)
P.O. Box 1417, Taylor (48180-5817)
PHONE.................................734 955-9311
Cathy Lisowski, *Supervisor*
Ralph O Neri,
Joyce Chenoweth, *Nurse*
Patricia Bosserman,
Lauri Stevens,
▲ **EMP:** 9 **EST:** 1947
SQ FT: 65,000
SALES (est): 1.8MM Privately Held
SIC: 3291 3545 3541 Wheels, abrasive; machine tool accessories; machine tools, metal cutting type

(G-14297)
LABELED LUCKY BRAND INC ◆
38701 Valley View Dr (48174-4746)
PHONE.................................517 962-1729
William Gilbert, *CEO*
EMP: 6 **EST:** 2021
SALES (est): 329.7K Privately Held
SIC: 2311 Men's & boys' suits & coats

(G-14298)
LEWKOWICZ CORPORATION
Also Called: Landis Machine Shop
36425 Grant St (48174-1112)
PHONE.................................734 941-0411
Mark Lewkowicz, *President*
Candace Lewkowicz, *Vice Pres*
Kristen Andrews, *Purchasing*
EMP: 10 **EST:** 1928
SQ FT: 7,200 Privately Held
SIC: 3599 3366 Machine shop, jobbing & repair; castings (except die): brass

(G-14299)
LINCOLN PARK BORING CO
28089 Wick Rd (48174-2622)
PHONE.................................734 946-8300
Richard N Yesue, *President*
Gary C Yesue, *Vice Pres*
Gary Yesue, *Vice Pres*
Nancy M Yesue, *Treasurer*
Nancy Jesue, *Executive*
▲ **EMP:** 30 **EST:** 1956
SQ FT: 60,000
SALES (est): 8MM Privately Held
WEB: www.lincolnparkboring.com
SIC: 3599 Machine shop, jobbing & repair

(G-14300)
MAGNUM TOOLSCOM LLC
30690 Cypress Rd (48174-3599)
PHONE.................................734 595-4600
Sean Green, *Sales Dir*
Daniel B Martin,
Ashley Riopelle,
▲ **EMP:** 11 **EST:** 2006
SQ FT: 96,000
SALES (est): 3.2MM Privately Held
WEB: www.magnumtools.com
SIC: 5082 3531 Construction & mining machinery; construction machinery

(G-14301)
MBM FABRICATORS CO INC
36333 Northline Rd (48174-3645)
PHONE.................................734 941-0100
Donald A Makins, *President*
Joe Leslie, *General Mgr*
Ernie Peterson, *Plant Mgr*
Piper Myers, *Office Mgr*
EMP: 215 **EST:** 1962
SQ FT: 38,619
SALES (est): 23.4MM Privately Held
WEB: www.mbmfab.com
SIC: 1791 3441 Structural steel erection; fabricated structural metal

(G-14302)
METAL IMPROVEMENT COMPANY LLC
30100 Cypress Rd (48174-3591)
PHONE.................................734 728-8600
Perry Celsi, *Manager*
Byron Beattie, *Manager*
EMP: 55
SALES (corp-wide): 2.3B Publicly Held
WEB: www.cwst.com
SIC: 3398 Shot peening (treating steel to reduce fatigue)
HQ: Metal Improvement Company, Llc
80 E Rte 4 Ste 310
Paramus NJ 07652
201 843-7800

(G-14303)
METREX RESEARCH LLC
28210 Wick Rd (48174-2639)
PHONE.................................734 947-6700
Tobin Johnson, *Manager*
EMP: 75
SALES (corp-wide): 22.2B Publicly Held
WEB: www.metrex.com
SIC: 2819 3845 8731 Industrial inorganic chemicals; electromedical equipment; commercial physical research
HQ: Metrex Research, Llc
1717 W Collins Ave
Orange CA 92867
800 841-1428

(G-14304)
METRO MACHINE WORKS INC
11977 Harrison (48174-2799)
PHONE.................................734 941-4571
Eric Beckeman, *President*
Timothy R Zink, *President*
Roger Stewart, *Vice Pres*
Thomas Szymanski, *QC Mgr*
Laura Beckeman, *Controller*
EMP: 60 **EST:** 1919
SQ FT: 27,000
SALES (est): 9.8MM Privately Held
WEB: www.metromachineworks.net
SIC: 3724 7692 3545 3511 Turbines, aircraft type; welding repair; machine tool accessories; turbines & turbine generator sets; metal heat treating

(G-14305)
MICHIGAN ATF HOLDINGS LLC (HQ)
Also Called: Header Products
11850 Wayne Rd (48174-1447)
PHONE.................................734 941-2220
Michael Brennan, *Purchasing*
Kimberly Bottenhorn, *Director*
John J Glazier Jr,
▲ **EMP:** 100 **EST:** 2012
SALES (est): 55MM
SALES (corp-wide): 108MM Privately Held
WEB: www.atf-inc.com
SIC: 3965 Buckles & buckle parts
PA: Atf Inc.
3550 W Pratt Ave
Lincolnwood IL 60712
847 677-1300

(G-14306)
MILLENNIUM TECHNOLOGY II INC
Also Called: Damar Tool Manufacturing
28888 Goddard Rd Ste 200 (48174-2752)
PHONE.................................734 479-4440
EMP: 14
SQ FT: 12,000
SALES (est): 3MM Privately Held
SIC: 3545 Mfg Machine Tool Accessories

(G-14307)
MULTI MCHNING CAPABILITIES INC
27482 Northline Rd # 100 (48174-2826)
PHONE.................................734 955-5592
Richard Sollars Jr, *President*
Tim Swoish, *Vice Pres*
Dave Camilleri, *Plant Mgr*
Steve Lupinski, *Plant Mgr*
Jerry Verhoven, *Sales Staff*
EMP: 5 **EST:** 1998
SALES (est): 626.2K Privately Held
WEB: www.mmc-cnc.com
SIC: 3599 Machine shop, jobbing & repair

(G-14308)
NATIONAL METAL SALES INC
27400 Northline Rd (48174-2826)
PHONE.................................734 942-3000
William Molnar Jr, *CEO*
Robert Molnar, *President*
EMP: 9 **EST:** 2011
SALES (est): 1.2MM Privately Held
WEB: www.nationalmetalsales.com
SIC: 3441 Fabricated structural metal

(G-14309)
NELMS TECHNOLOGIES INC
15385 Pine (48174-3659)
PHONE.................................734 955-6500
Edwin Nelms, *Ch of Bd*
Mark Nelms, *Vice Pres*
EMP: 21 **EST:** 1995
SALES (est): 582.1K Privately Held
SIC: 3592 3451 Valves; screw machine products

(G-14310)
NITTO INC
36663 Van Born Rd Ste 360 (48174-4160)
PHONE.................................732 276-1039
EMP: 87 Privately Held
WEB: www.nitto.com
SIC: 3714 Motor vehicle parts & accessories
HQ: Nitto, Inc.
1990 Rutgers Univ Blvd
Lakewood NJ 08701
732 901-7905

(G-14311)
NITTO INC
Also Called: Nitto Denko Automotive
36663 Van Born Rd Ste 360 (48174-4160)
PHONE.................................734 729-7800
Denny Pedri, *Vice Pres*
Myrna Cerwinski, *Sales Staff*
EMP: 14 Privately Held
WEB: www.nitto.com
SIC: 3714 Motor vehicle parts & accessories
HQ: Nitto, Inc.
1990 Rutgers Univ Blvd
Lakewood NJ 08701
732 901-7905

(G-14312)
NOR-DIC TOOL COMPANY INC
6577 Beverly Plz (48174-3513)
PHONE.................................734 326-3610
Edward Christie, *President*
Lisa Swinton, *Corp Secy*
Kurt Christie, *Vice Pres*
EMP: 16 **EST:** 1968
SQ FT: 52,000
SALES (est): 1.1MM Privately Held
WEB: www.nordictool.com
SIC: 3469 1799 Stamping metal for the trade; welding on site

(G-14313)
OAK MOUNTAIN INDUSTRIES
14770 5 M Center Dr (48174-2869)
PHONE.................................734 941-7000
Mike Lafferty, *General Mgr*
Cindy Bevluvko, *Manager*
EMP: 7 **EST:** 2009
SALES (est): 260.2K Privately Held
SIC: 3999 Manufacturing industries

(G-14314)
OSBORNE CONCRETE CO
37500 Northline Rd (48174-1180)
PHONE.................................734 941-3008
John D Osborne Sr, *President*
EMP: 6 **EST:** 1965
SQ FT: 17,000
SALES (est): 1.2MM Privately Held
WEB: www.osborne-inc.com
SIC: 3273 Ready-mixed concrete

(G-14315)
PACKAGING SPECIALTIES INC (HQ)
Also Called: Manhattan Container
8111 Middlebelt Rd (48174-2134)
PHONE.................................586 473-6703
Kurt Tabor, *President*
Claredine Tabor, *Treasurer*
▲ **EMP:** 30 **EST:** 1964
SALES (est): 11.3MM
SALES (corp-wide): 457.7MM Privately Held
WEB: www.welchpkg.com
SIC: 2653 2652 2671 2657 Boxes, corrugated: made from purchased materials; partitions, corrugated: made from purchased materials; sheets, corrugated: made from purchased materials; setup paperboard boxes; packaging paper & plastics film, coated & laminated; folding paperboard boxes; paperboard mills; nailed wood boxes & shook

▲ = Import ▼ = Export ◆ = Import/Export

PA: Welch Packaging Group, Inc.
1020 Herman St
Elkhart IN 46516
574 295-2460

(G-14316)
PARAGON TOOL COMPANY
36130 Ecorse Rd (48174-4103)
PHONE.....................734 326-1702
Raymond F Wasielewski, *President*
Raymond A Wasielewski, *President*
EMP: 7 **EST:** 1953
SQ FT: 3,500
SALES (est): 450K **Privately Held**
SIC: 3541 Machine tools, metal cutting: exotic (explosive, etc.)

(G-14317)
PENN AUTOMOTIVE INC
Also Called: Romulus Division
7845 Middlebelt Rd # 200 (48174-2174)
PHONE.....................734 595-3000
Robert Wiese, *Admin Sec*
EMP: 136 **Privately Held**
SIC: 3429 Manufactured hardware (general)
HQ: Penn Automotive, Inc.
5331 Dixie Hwy
Waterford MI 48329
248 599-3700

(G-14318)
PENN SIGN
10160 Miriam St (48174-3942)
PHONE.....................814 932-7181
Chris Johnson, *Principal*
EMP: 5 **EST:** 2019
SALES (est): 217K **Privately Held**
WEB: www.pennsign.com
SIC: 3993 Signs & advertising specialties

(G-14319)
PENTEL TOOL & DIE INC
26531 King Rd (48174-9430)
PHONE.....................734 782-9500
EMP: 6
SQ FT: 7,200
SALES: 786.3K **Privately Held**
SIC: 3544 Mfg Dies Tools Jigs & Fixtures

(G-14320)
PLASTIPAK PACKAGING INC
36445 Van Born Rd Ste 200 (48174-4051)
PHONE.....................734 467-7519
Fax: 734 467-7547
▲ **EMP:** 14 **EST:** 2001
SALES (est): 986.6K **Privately Held**
SIC: 3085 Mfg Plastic Bottles

(G-14321)
PLUM BROTHERS LLC
Also Called: Klassic Tool Crib
9350 Harrison (48174-2503)
PHONE.....................734 947-8100
Paul Brotz, *Info Tech Mgr*
Tom Brotz,
EMP: 6 **EST:** 2007
SALES (est): 600K **Privately Held**
WEB: www.klassictoolcrib.com
SIC: 3546 Power-driven handtools

(G-14322)
PRECISION MTL HDLG EQP LLC
36663 Van Born Rd Ste 350 (48174-4160)
PHONE.....................734 351-7350
Shaun Kastarek, *Branch Mgr*
EMP: 56
SALES (corp-wide): 20.3MM **Privately Held**
SIC: 3441 Fabricated structural metal
HQ: Precision Material Handling Equipment, Llc
26700 Princeton St
Inkster MI 48141
313 789-8101

(G-14323)
R & L MACHINE PRODUCTS INC
15995 S Huron River Dr (48174-3668)
PHONE.....................734 992-2574
Robert Fitzpatrick, *President*
EMP: 5 **EST:** 1986
SQ FT: 6,500
SALES (est): 461.9K **Privately Held**
WEB: www.randlmachine.com
SIC: 3599 Machine shop, jobbing & repair

(G-14324)
RAINBOW TAPE & LABEL INC
11600 Wayne Rd (48174-1462)
P.O. Box 74453 (48174-0453)
PHONE.....................734 941-6090
Richard Walters, *President*
Thelma Walters, *Corp Secy*
David R Walters, *Systems Staff*
EMP: 16 **EST:** 1964
SQ FT: 14,000
SALES (est): 903.3K **Privately Held**
WEB: www.2rtl.com
SIC: 2759 Labels & seals: printing

(G-14325)
RITE WAY PRINTING
5821 Essex St (48174-1839)
PHONE.....................734 721-2746
Arthur Tabbs, *Principal*
EMP: 4
SALES (est): 223.1K **Privately Held**
SIC: 2752 Commercial printing, offset

(G-14326)
RM MACHINE & MOLD
30399 Ecorse Rd (48174-3521)
P.O. Box 278, Taylor (48180-0278)
PHONE.....................734 721-8800
EMP: 7
SALES (est): 996.1K **Privately Held**
SIC: 3544 Mfg Dies/Tools/Jigs/Fixtures

(G-14327)
SATURN ELECTRONICS CORP
28450 Northline Rd (48174-2832)
PHONE.....................734 941-8100
Nagji Sutariya, *President*
Raj Sutariya, *Vice Pres*
Yash Sutariya, *Vice Pres*
Sean Haggerty, *Natl Sales Mgr*
John Goci, *Marketing Mgr*
▲ **EMP:** 200 **EST:** 1985
SQ FT: 89,000
SALES (est): 32.8MM **Privately Held**
WEB: www.saturnelectronics.com
SIC: 3672 Circuit boards, television & radio printed

(G-14328)
SATURN FLEX SYSTEMS INC
27642 Northline Rd (48174-2826)
PHONE.....................734 532-4093
Sutariya Yash, *President*
Frank Reed, *Vice Pres*
EMP: 10 **EST:** 2010
SALES (est): 934.3K **Privately Held**
WEB: www.saturnflex.com
SIC: 3672 Printed circuit boards

(G-14329)
SOUTH POINTE RADIATOR
30026 Beverly Rd (48174-2030)
PHONE.....................734 941-1460
Adam Purdy, *Executive*
EMP: 5 **EST:** 2019
SALES (est): 177K **Privately Held**
WEB: www.southpointeradiator.com
SIC: 3511 Turbines & turbine generator sets

(G-14330)
SPARTAN BARRICADING
27730 Ecorse Rd (48174-2429)
PHONE.....................313 292-2488
Fax: 313 292-2366
EMP: 4
SALES (est): 260K **Privately Held**
SIC: 1799 3499 Trade Contractor Mfg Misc Fabricated Metal Products

(G-14331)
SPECIALTY ENGINE COMPONENTS
15385 Pine (48174-3659)
PHONE.....................734 955-6500
Mark Nelms, *Manager*
EMP: 13 **EST:** 2003
SALES (est): 296.1K **Privately Held**
WEB: www.wathomas.com
SIC: 3599 Machine shop, jobbing & repair

(G-14332)
SUPERIOR MATERIALS LLC
39001 W Huron River Dr (48174-1104)
PHONE.....................734 941-2479
EMP: 26
SALES (corp-wide): 8.5MM **Privately Held**
WEB: www.superiormaterialsllc.com
SIC: 5211 3273 Cement; ready-mixed concrete
PA: Superior Materials, Llc
30701 W 10 Mile Rd
Farmington Hills MI 48336
248 788-8000

(G-14333)
SYBRON DENTAL SPECIALTI
28210 Wick Rd (48174-2639)
PHONE.....................734 947-6927
EMP: 5 **EST:** 2019
SALES (est): 95.6K **Privately Held**
SIC: 3841 Surgical & medical instruments

(G-14334)
UNITED BRASS MANUFACTURERS INC (PA)
Also Called: Daca Div
35030 Goddard Rd (48174-3444)
P.O. Box 74095 (48174-0095)
PHONE.....................734 941-0700
James R Donahey, *President*
Raymond Frisbie, *Corp Secy*
EMP: 35 **EST:** 1950
SQ FT: 120,000
SALES (est): 5MM **Privately Held**
WEB: www.unitedbrass.com
SIC: 3432 3463 Plumbers' brass goods: drain cocks, faucets, spigots, etc.; nonferrous forgings

(G-14335)
UNITED BRASS MANUFACTURERS INC
Also Called: Machine Division
39000 W Huron River Dr (48174-1105)
PHONE.....................734 942-9224
Charles Droullard, *Manager*
EMP: 17
SALES (corp-wide): 5MM **Privately Held**
WEB: www.unitedbrass.com
SIC: 3463 3432 Nonferrous forgings; plumbers' brass goods: drain cocks, faucets, spigots, etc.
PA: United Brass Manufacturers, Inc.
35030 Goddard Rd
Romulus MI 48174
734 941-0700

(G-14336)
VACUUM ORNA METAL COMPANY INC
11380 Harrison (48174-2722)
PHONE.....................734 941-9100
Jan Reydon, *Vice Pres*
EMP: 21 **EST:** 1954
SQ FT: 40,000
SALES (est): 2.5MM **Privately Held**
WEB: www.vacuumorna-metal.com
SIC: 3089 3471 3429 Injection molding of plastics; electroplating & plating; manufactured hardware (general)

(G-14337)
WESTSIDE POWDER COAT LLC
35777 Genron Ct (48174-3654)
PHONE.....................734 729-1667
Joseph Seror,
EMP: 8 **EST:** 2012
SALES (est): 594K **Privately Held**
WEB: www.westsideprocoat.com
SIC: 3479 Coating of metals & formed products

(G-14338)
WHITE AUTOMATION & TOOL CO
28888 Goddard Rd Ste 100 (48174-2752)
PHONE.....................734 947-9822
Gary White, *President*
Donna Nemeth, *Corp Secy*
Allen White, *Vice Pres*
EMP: 14 **EST:** 1984
SQ FT: 7,200
SALES (est): 776.7K **Privately Held**
SIC: 3544 Special dies & tools

(G-14339)
WOLVERINE CRANE & SERVICE INC
30777 Beverly Rd Ste 150 (48174-2052)
PHONE.....................734 467-9066
Rich Kelps, *President*
Chrissy Musk, *Office Mgr*
Jerry Nastale, *Manager*
EMP: 10 **Privately Held**
WEB: www.wolverinecrane.com
SIC: 3536 7699 Cranes, overhead traveling; industrial equipment services
PA: Wolverine Crane & Service Inc
2557 Thornwood St Sw
Grand Rapids MI 49519

(G-14340)
WORLDTEK INDUSTRIES LLC
36310 Eureka Rd (48174-3652)
PHONE.....................734 494-5204
Michael Crooks, *CEO*
Emily Taylor, *COO*
Rob Jenkins, *QC Mgr*
Sharon Thibodeau, *Officer*
Deanna Crooks,
EMP: 130 **EST:** 2010
SQ FT: 100,000
SALES (est): 19.1MM **Privately Held**
WEB: www.worldtek-ind.com
SIC: 3441 Fabricated structural metal

(G-14341)
WRITERS BIBLE LLC
6037 4th St (48174-1859)
PHONE.....................734 286-7793
Casheena Parker, *CEO*
EMP: 5 **EST:** 2020
SALES (est): 84.2K **Privately Held**
SIC: 2741 8999 7371 ; commercial & literary writings; author; writing for publication; computer software writing services; computer software development & applications

(G-14342)
YANFENG US AUTO INTR SYSTEMS I
9800 Inkster Rd (48174-2616)
PHONE.....................734 946-0600
EMP: 5 **Privately Held**
SIC: 3089 Plastic containers, except foam
HQ: Yanfeng Us Automotive Interior Systems Ii Llc
41935 W 12 Mile Rd
Novi MI 48377
248 319-7333

(G-14343)
YAPP USA AUTO SYSTEMS INC
36320 Eureka Rd (48174-3652)
PHONE.....................248 404-8696
Jack McKarns, *Engineer*
Erik Grant, *Director*
EMP: 9 **Privately Held**
WEB: www.yappusa.com
SIC: 3089 3714 Automotive parts, plastic; fuel systems & parts, motor vehicle
HQ: Yapp Usa Automotive Systems, Inc.
300 Abc Blvd
Gallatin TN 37066

(G-14344)
Z&G AUTO CARRIERS LLC
34260 Pinewoods Cir # 203 (48174-8213)
PHONE.....................586 819-1809
Antonio Madden,
EMP: 5 **EST:** 2020
SALES (est): 86K **Privately Held**
SIC: 3799 7389 Transportation equipment;

(G-14345)
ZYNP INTERNATIONAL CORP
Also Called: Zyongyuan International
27501 Hldbrndt Rd Ste 300 (48174)
PHONE.....................734 947-1000
Frank Yang, *CEO*
◆ **EMP:** 25 **EST:** 2005
SALES (est): 8.3MM **Privately Held**
WEB: www.zynpusa.com
SIC: 3714 Motor vehicle parts & accessories
PA: Zynp Corporation
No.69, Huaihe Avenue, Chanye Jiju District
Mengzhou 45475

Roscommon
Roscommon County

(G-14346)
ACE CONSULTING & MGT INC
Also Called: Northline Express
10386 S Leline Rd (48653-9782)
PHONE.....................989 821-7040
Robert Cochran, *President*
Joe Cochran, *Vice Pres*
▲ **EMP:** 23 **EST:** 1994
SQ FT: 24,000
SALES (est): 719.5K **Privately Held**
WEB: www.aceplusconsulting.com
SIC: 3317 Steel pipe & tubes

(G-14347)
C & S SECURITY INC
138 Argus Ct (48653-8905)
PHONE.....................989 821-5759
Jamie Cullip, *President*
EMP: 4 **EST:** 1971
SALES (est): 425.4K **Privately Held**
WEB: www.candssecurity.com
SIC: 3429 Handcuffs & leg irons

(G-14348)
DM VAULT FORMS
10713 Johnson Rd (48653-9162)
PHONE.....................989 275-4797
Dwaine Jefferson Moore, *President*
EMP: 6 **EST:** 2013
SALES (est): 380.1K **Privately Held**
WEB: www.dmvaultforms.com
SIC: 5087 3272 Concrete burial vaults & boxes; burial vaults, concrete or precast terrazzo

(G-14349)
FINN DIRECTIONAL INC
6775 W Pine Dr (48653-7169)
PHONE.....................231 944-0923
Christopher J Finn, *Principal*
Julie Cunningham, *Administration*
EMP: 7 **EST:** 2014
SALES (est): 246.9K **Privately Held**
SIC: 1381 Directional drilling oil & gas wells

(G-14350)
HIGGINS CORP
219 Old Stage Rd (48653-7711)
PHONE.....................269 365-7744
Ethan Brand, *Principal*
EMP: 5 **EST:** 2010
SALES (est): 248K **Privately Held**
WEB: www.brandelectronics.com
SIC: 3825 Instruments to measure electricity

(G-14351)
LEAR CORPORATION
10161 N Roscommon Rd (48653-9296)
P.O. Box 488 (48653-0488)
PHONE.....................989 275-5794
EMP: 200
SALES (corp-wide): 20.4B **Publicly Held**
SIC: 3714 Mfg Motor Vehicle Parts/Accessories
PA: Lear Corporation
21557 Telegraph Rd
Southfield MI 48033
248 447-1500

(G-14352)
NAVIGATOR WIRELINE SERVICE INC
609 S 5th St (48653-2504)
P.O. Box 950 (48653-0950)
PHONE.....................989 275-9112
Susan Jock, *President*
Carl Jock, *Treasurer*
EMP: 16 **EST:** 2002
SALES (est): 2.5MM **Privately Held**
WEB: www.navigatorwirelineservice.com
SIC: 1389 1381 Oil field services; directional drilling oil & gas wells

(G-14353)
NEARS LOGGING
11391 Billman Rd (48653-9778)
PHONE.....................989 390-4951
EMP: 4 **EST:** 2019
SALES (est): 121.2K **Privately Held**
SIC: 2411 Logging camps & contractors

(G-14354)
NORTH CENTRAL WELDING CO
Also Called: Nucraft Metal Products
402 Southline Rd (48653-7652)
PHONE.....................989 275-8054
Lee Wiltse, *President*
Dale Wiltse, *Vice Pres*
Ronald Wiltse, *Vice Pres*
EMP: 26 **EST:** 1979
SQ FT: 20,000
SALES (est): 3.1MM **Privately Held**
WEB: www.nucraftonline.com
SIC: 3443 3536 Fabricated plate work (boiler shop); hoists, cranes & monorails

(G-14355)
NORTHERN MICH ENDOCRINE PLLC
103 Misty Meadow Ct (48653-7676)
PHONE.....................989 281-1125
Bashar Kiami, *Principal*
EMP: 4 **EST:** 2014
SALES (est): 104.9K **Privately Held**
SIC: 2435 Hardwood veneer & plywood

(G-14356)
SCOTTS ENTERPRISES INC
Also Called: Scott's Wood Products
554 W Federal Hwy (48653-9700)
P.O. Box 739 (48653-0739)
PHONE.....................989 275-5011
Mark Scott, *President*
EMP: 16 **EST:** 1973
SQ FT: 5,000
SALES (est): 506.8K **Privately Held**
WEB: www.scottsent.com
SIC: 2449 2448 2653 2441 Rectangular boxes & crates, wood; pallets, wood; corrugated & solid fiber boxes; nailed wood boxes & shook

(G-14357)
TRAVEL INFORMATION SERVICES
101 E Federal Hwy (48653-9318)
PHONE.....................989 275-8042
Charles E Mires, *President*
Charles Scott Mires, *Vice Pres*
Linda S Mires, *Vice Pres*
EMP: 13 **EST:** 1981
SALES (est): 40K **Privately Held**
WEB: www.travelbrochure.com
SIC: 4724 2759 5199 Tourist agency arranging transport, lodging & car rental; commercial printing; general merchandise, non-durable

Rose City
Ogemaw County

(G-14358)
ADMIN INDUSTRIES LLC
3049 Beechwood Rd (48654-9562)
PHONE.....................989 685-3438
Eric Carlson, *Mng Member*
Stephanie Carlson,
EMP: 10 **EST:** 1971
SQ FT: 5,600
SALES (est): 862.3K **Privately Held**
SIC: 3999 3443 3444 3441 Dock equipment & supplies, industrial; fabricated plate work (boiler shop); sheet metalwork; fabricated structural metal

(G-14359)
AMERICAN PLASTIC TOYS INC
3059 Beechwood Rd (48654-9562)
PHONE.....................989 685-2455
Ken Hebert, *Branch Mgr*
EMP: 63
SALES (corp-wide): 44.6MM **Privately Held**
WEB: www.americanplastictoys.com
SIC: 3944 5092 Games, toys & children's vehicles; toys
PA: American Plastic Toys, Inc.
799 Ladd Rd
Walled Lake MI 48390
248 624-4881

(G-14360)
AMERICAN PLEASURE PRODUCTS INC
2823 E Industrial Dr (48654-9478)
PHONE.....................989 685-8484
Robert Brodie, *President*
Michael Gilligan, *Corp Secy*
EMP: 9 **EST:** 1967
SALES (est): 804.5K **Privately Held**
WEB: www.aquacycleusa.com
SIC: 3732 Pontoons, except aircraft & inflatable

(G-14361)
ASSEMBLY CONCEPTS INC
Also Called: Aci
2651 S M 33 (48654)
P.O. Box 589 (48654-0589)
PHONE.....................989 685-2603
Michael Quigley, *President*
Patti Quigley, *Vice Pres*
EMP: 10 **EST:** 1982
SQ FT: 5,000
SALES (est): 195.5K **Privately Held**
SIC: 3544 3599 Special dies, tools, jigs & fixtures; machine shop, jobbing & repair

(G-14362)
ATF INC
Also Called: Header Products
285 Casemaster Dr (48654-9676)
P.O. Box 366 (48654-0366)
PHONE.....................989 685-2468
Duane Lawrence, *Project Engr*
Steve Simison, *Human Res Mgr*
Leslie Quigley, *Manager*
Laurie Patton, *Manager*
Richard Grzegorczyk, *Agent*
EMP: 45
SALES (corp-wide): 108MM **Privately Held**
WEB: www.atf-inc.com
SIC: 3499 3714 3451 Stabilizing bars (cargo), metal; motor vehicle parts & accessories; screw machine products
HQ: Michigan Atf Holdings, Llc
11850 Wayne Rd
Romulus MI 48174

(G-14363)
FORGE TECH INC
464 E Industrial Dr (48654-9457)
PHONE.....................989 685-3443
EMP: 5 **EST:** 2014
SALES (est): 42.3K **Privately Held**
SIC: 7692 Welding repair

(G-14364)
LITES ALTERNATIVE INC
Also Called: Litesalternative
2643 S M 33 (48654)
PHONE.....................989 685-3476
Michael Quigly, *President*
EMP: 10 **EST:** 1996
SQ FT: 7,000
SALES (est): 934.4K **Privately Held**
SIC: 3089 Windows, plastic

(G-14365)
MASONS LUMBER & HARDWARE INC
Also Called: Do It Best
2493 S M 33 (48654)
PHONE.....................989 685-3999
Gloria Neubecker, *President*
Randy Mason, *Treasurer*
EMP: 7 **EST:** 1992
SQ FT: 16,000
SALES (est): 1MM **Privately Held**
WEB: www.masons.doitbest.com
SIC: 5251 5211 2452 Hardware; lumber & other building materials; log cabins, prefabricated, wood

Rosebush
Isabella County

(G-14366)
AR-TEE ENTERPRISES LLC
4131 E Rosebush Rd (48878-9772)
PHONE.....................989 433-5546
Roberta Tarlton, *Principal*
EMP: 4 **EST:** 2016
SALES (est): 59.5K **Privately Held**
SIC: 2759 Screen printing

(G-14367)
SUMMIT-REED CITY INC
4147 E Monroe St (48878-5008)
P.O. Box 365, Mount Pleasant (48804-0365)
PHONE.....................989 433-5716
Jeff Wilson, *Manager*
EMP: 37
SALES (corp-wide): 10.5MM **Privately Held**
SIC: 4225 1311 General warehousing; crude petroleum & natural gas
PA: Summit-Reed City, Inc.
1315 S Mission Rd
Mount Pleasant MI 48858
989 772-2028

Roseville
Macomb County

(G-14368)
ACAL UNIVERSAL GRINDING CO
Also Called: Acal Precision Products
20200 Cornillie Dr (48066-1746)
PHONE.....................586 296-3900
Joseph Elsesser, *President*
Gregg Blind, *Sales Staff*
Thomas Elsesser, *Executive*
EMP: 39 **EST:** 1945
SQ FT: 15,400
SALES (est): 1.8MM **Privately Held**
WEB: www.acalprecision.com
SIC: 3599 Machine shop, jobbing & repair

(G-14369)
ADVANCE PRECISION GRINDING CO
29739 Groesbeck Hwy (48066-1940)
PHONE.....................586 773-1330
William A Kemp, *President*
William Kemp Jr, *Vice Pres*
EMP: 6 **EST:** 1974
SQ FT: 16,000
SALES (est): 490.3K **Privately Held**
WEB: www.advance-precision-grinding-co.roseville.mi.amfibi.company
SIC: 3599 Machine shop, jobbing & repair

(G-14370)
AERO BOX COMPANY
20101 Cornillie Dr (48066-1766)
PHONE.....................586 415-0000
Gary Corte, *Manager*
EMP: 4 **EST:** 1986
SALES (est): 540.1K **Privately Held**
WEB: www.aeroboxllc.com
SIC: 2653 Boxes, corrugated: made from purchased materials

(G-14371)
AERO GRINDING INC (PA)
Also Called: Centerless Grinder Repair Div
28300 Groesbeck Hwy (48066-2382)
PHONE.....................586 774-6450
William Magee, *Vice Pres*
EMP: 60 **EST:** 1954
SQ FT: 30,000
SALES (est): 15MM **Privately Held**
WEB: www.aerogrinding.com
SIC: 5084 3599 7629 Machine tools & metalworking machinery; machine shop, jobbing & repair; electrical repair shops

(G-14372)
AERO GRINDING INC
Also Called: Grind Repair
28240 Groesbeck Hwy (48066-2389)
PHONE.....................586 774-6450
Roland Di Mattia, *Owner*
EMP: 4
SALES (corp-wide): 15MM **Privately Held**
WEB: www.aerogrinding.com
SIC: 3599 5084 Machine shop, jobbing & repair; industrial machinery & equipment
PA: Aero Grinding, Inc.
28300 Groesbeck Hwy
Roseville MI 48066
586 774-6450

GEOGRAPHIC SECTION

Roseville - Macomb County (G-14400)

(G-14373)
AMERICAN BEVERAGE EQUIPMENT CO
27560 Groesbeck Hwy (48066-2759)
PHONE....................................586 773-0094
James Testori, *President*
Andrew Holt, *Vice Pres*
Lawrence Marchorni, *Vice Pres*
Christopher Pochmara, *Vice Pres*
Josephine Testori, *Vice Pres*
▲ **EMP:** 20 **EST:** 1930
SQ FT: 12,000
SALES (est): 2.6MM **Privately Held**
WEB: www.americanbeverageequipment.com
SIC: 3432 5074 Faucets & spigots, metal & plastic; plumbers' brass goods & fittings

(G-14374)
APOLLO PLATING INC
15765 Sturgeon St (48066-1879)
PHONE....................................586 777-0070
James E Grimes, *CEO*
EMP: 153 **EST:** 1970
SQ FT: 50,000
SALES (est): 8.6MM **Privately Held**
WEB: www.apolloplatinginc.com
SIC: 3471 Electroplating of metals or formed products; polishing, metals or formed products

(G-14375)
ARIN INC
29139 Calahan Rd (48066-1850)
PHONE....................................586 779-3410
Carol Gee-Romanoski, *President*
Carol Gee-Romanoski, *President*
Geraldine Kipke, *Vice Pres*
Elizabeth Mewton, *Safety Mgr*
Nicholas Cebulski, *Manager*
EMP: 19 **EST:** 1959
SQ FT: 24,000
SALES (est): 2.6MM **Privately Held**
WEB: www.arininc.com
SIC: 3699 Laser welding, drilling & cutting equipment

(G-14376)
ARMARTIS MANUFACTURING INC
20815 Kraft Blvd (48066-2232)
PHONE....................................248 308-9622
Christof Traidl, *Principal*
EMP: 50 **EST:** 2017
SQ FT: 34,000
SALES (est): 1.6MM **Privately Held**
SIC: 3711 Universal carriers, military, assembly of

(G-14377)
AUTOMATION ENTERPRISES INC
29970 Parkway (48066-1961)
PHONE....................................586 774-0280
Gene Jarvis, *President*
EMP: 8 **EST:** 1984
SQ FT: 5,000
SALES (est): 749.7K **Privately Held**
WEB: www.bgautomation.com
SIC: 1799 3613 Hydraulic equipment, installation & service; control panels, electric

(G-14378)
AVO DENTAL SUPPLIES LLC
Also Called: Goldendent
27251 Gratiot Ave (48066-2967)
PHONE....................................586 585-1210
Jacquelyn Golden, *CEO*
Jackie Golden, *Managing Prtnr*
Curt Lawler, *Mng Member*
EMP: 6 **EST:** 2011
SALES (est): 403.1K **Privately Held**
WEB: www.physicsforceps.com
SIC: 3843 Dental equipment & supplies

(G-14379)
BAY ELECTRONICS INC
20805 Kraft Blvd (48066-2232)
P.O. Box 397 (48066-0397)
PHONE....................................586 296-0900
Daniel J Olsen, *President*
Dan Olsen, *Safety Mgr*
Jane Gerds, *Production*
Ed Relyea, *Info Tech Mgr*

EMP: 49 **EST:** 1972
SQ FT: 11,000
SALES (est): 8.6MM **Privately Held**
WEB: www.bayelectronics.net
SIC: 3625 3679 Industrial electrical relays & switches; harness assemblies for electronic use: wire or cable

(G-14380)
BEACON PARK FINISHING LLC
15765 Sturgeon St (48066-1816)
PHONE....................................248 318-4286
Inga Brown, *Controller*
EMP: 17 **EST:** 2017
SALES (est): 1.9MM **Privately Held**
WEB: www.beaconparkfinishing.com
SIC: 3471 Plating & polishing

(G-14381)
BRECKERS ABC TOOL COMPANY INC
15919 E 12 Mile Rd (48066-1846)
PHONE....................................586 779-1122
George Buhler Jr, *President*
Ramona Iafrate,
EMP: 32 **EST:** 1953
SQ FT: 7,200
SALES (est): 4.3MM **Privately Held**
WEB: www.breckers.com
SIC: 3545 Cutting tools for machine tools

(G-14382)
CADILLAC PRODUCTS INC
Also Called: Cadillac Products Auto Co
29784 Little Mack Ave (48066-2239)
PHONE....................................586 774-1700
Eric Ebenhoeh, *General Mgr*
Mike Terrill, *Plant Mgr*
Richard Fabirkiewicz, *Buyer*
Dana Irwin, *Purchasing*
Todd Luczak, *Program Mgr*
EMP: 24
SALES (corp-wide): 74.4MM **Privately Held**
WEB: www.cadprod.com
SIC: 3714 2673 3081 Motor vehicle parts & accessories; plastic bags: made from purchased materials; polyethylene film
PA: Cadillac Products, Inc.
5800 Crooks Rd Ste 100
Troy MI 48098
248 813-8200

(G-14383)
CDP ENVIRONMENTAL INC
Also Called: Curbs and Dampers
16517 Eastland St (48066-2032)
PHONE....................................586 776-7890
John Gabridge, *President*
Frank Brunell, *Vice Pres*
EMP: 29 **EST:** 1982
SQ FT: 8,000
SALES (est): 1.2MM **Privately Held**
WEB: www.curbsanddampers.com
SIC: 3444 Sheet metalwork

(G-14384)
CLANCY EXCAVATING CO
Also Called: Clancy Crushed Concrete
29950 Little Mack Ave (48066-2272)
PHONE....................................586 294-2900
Robert J Clancy, *President*
Gerald Clancy, *Vice Pres*
EMP: 9 **EST:** 1963
SQ FT: 2,000
SALES (est): 1.1MM **Privately Held**
SIC: 1611 3272 1794 Highway & street paving contractor; concrete products; excavation & grading, building construction

(G-14385)
CMN FABRICATION INC
32580 Kelly Rd (48066-1059)
PHONE....................................586 294-1941
Nick Saliga, *President*
Leslie Saliga, *Vice Pres*
EMP: 7 **EST:** 2003
SALES (est): 479.3K **Privately Held**
SIC: 3444 Sheet metal specialties, not stamped

(G-14386)
COLORTECH GRAPHICS INC
28700 Hayes Rd (48066-2316)
PHONE....................................586 779-7800
Alleyne Kelly, *President*

Daniel P Kelly, *Vice Pres*
Audrene Apostolos, *Purchasing*
Dan P Kelly, *Sales Staff*
Tom Lafontaine, *Sales Staff*
EMP: 65 **EST:** 1986
SQ FT: 31,000
SALES (est): 8.5MM **Privately Held**
WEB: www.colortechgraphics.com
SIC: 2752 Commercial printing, offset

(G-14387)
COMFORT MATTRESS CO
Also Called: King Coil
30450 Little Mack Ave (48066-1707)
PHONE....................................586 293-4000
Pete Hage, *President*
▲ **EMP:** 75 **EST:** 1981
SQ FT: 65,000
SALES (est): 9.4MM **Privately Held**
SIC: 2515 Mattresses, innerspring or box spring

(G-14388)
CONCRETE MANUFACTURING INC
29100 Groesbeck Hwy (48066-1922)
PHONE....................................586 777-3320
Elvira M Bizzocchi, *President*
EMP: 5 **EST:** 1983
SALES (est): 456.6K **Privately Held**
SIC: 2891 3272 Cement, except linoleum & tile; concrete products

(G-14389)
CONWAY DETROIT CORPORATION
Also Called: National Bronze Mfg Co
28070 Hayes Rd (48066-5049)
PHONE....................................586 552-8413
Frederick Conway, *President*
William Austerberry, *Vice Pres*
Sophie Maes, *Sales Staff*
▲ **EMP:** 20 **EST:** 1911
SQ FT: 26,000
SALES (est): 10.5MM **Privately Held**
WEB: www.nationalbronze.com
SIC: 5051 3366 Metals service centers & offices; machinery castings: copper or copper-base alloy

(G-14390)
COPYRITE PRINTING INC
30503 Gratiot Ave (48066-1775)
PHONE....................................586 774-0006
Bernard Palo, *President*
Bob Clinton, *Sales Staff*
EMP: 5 **EST:** 1985
SALES (est): 466.3K **Privately Held**
WEB: www.copyriteprinting.net
SIC: 2752 Commercial printing, offset

(G-14391)
CROWN BORING INDUSTRIES LLC
15985 Sturgeon St (48066-1818)
PHONE....................................586 447-3900
EMP: 20 **EST:** 2018
SALES (est): 569.9K **Privately Held**
WEB: www.crownboringsamco.com
SIC: 3541 Machine tools, metal cutting type

(G-14392)
CURBS & DAMPER PRODUCTS INC
16525 Eastland St (48066-2032)
PHONE....................................586 776-7890
John W Gabridge, *President*
Frank Brunell, *Vice Pres*
Jason Gabridge, *Vice Pres*
EMP: 16 **EST:** 1982
SQ FT: 10,000
SALES (est): 1.8MM **Privately Held**
WEB: www.curbsanddampers.com
SIC: 3444 3442 Hoods, range: sheet metal; metal doors, sash & trim

(G-14393)
DAYCO PRODUCTS LLC
16000 Common Rd (48066-1822)
PHONE....................................248 404-6537
Wendy Spencer, *Human Res Mgr*
Brent Charles, *Branch Mgr*
Anthony Archambault, *Manager*
Gary Baruth, *Manager*

EMP: 5
SALES (corp-wide): 211.2MM **Privately Held**
WEB: www.daycoproducts.com
SIC: 3052 Rubber hose; plastic hose; rubber belting; plastic belting
HQ: Dayco Products, Llc
1650 Research Dr Ste 100
Troy MI 48083

(G-14394)
DAYCO PRODUCTS LLC
16000 Common Rd (48066-1822)
PHONE....................................248 404-6500
Joel Wiegert, *CEO*
Laura Kowalchik, *CFO*
EMP: 5
SALES (est): 75.6K **Privately Held**
SIC: 3999 Manufacturing industries

(G-14395)
DECCA PATTERN CO INC
29778 Little Mack Ave (48066-2239)
PHONE....................................586 775-8450
Frederick Stemmler Jr, *President*
Carmen J Neaton, *Treasurer*
EMP: 4 **EST:** 1949
SQ FT: 6,400
SALES (est): 359.5K **Privately Held**
SIC: 3543 Industrial patterns

(G-14396)
DESIGNS N SIGNS LLC
28020 Groesbeck Hwy (48066-2345)
PHONE....................................248 789-8797
Joshua D Yiatras, *Administration*
EMP: 6 **EST:** 2016
SALES (est): 499.1K **Privately Held**
WEB: www.designsnsigns.net
SIC: 3993 Signs & advertising specialties

(G-14397)
DETROIT EDGE TOOL COMPANY
Michigan Flame Hardening
28370 Groesbeck Hwy (48066-2384)
PHONE....................................586 776-3727
Ken Hoffman, *Manager*
EMP: 4
SALES (corp-wide): 18.9MM **Privately Held**
WEB: www.detroitedge.com
SIC: 3398 Metal heat treating
PA: Detroit Edge Tool Company
6570 E Nevada St
Detroit MI 48234
313 366-4120

(G-14398)
DETROIT EDGE TOOL COMPANY
Also Called: Kirby Grinding
28370 Groesbeck Hwy (48066-2384)
PHONE....................................586 776-1598
Pat Ebbing, *Sales Mgr*
Samuel Olarte, *Manager*
EMP: 59
SALES (corp-wide): 18.9MM **Privately Held**
WEB: www.detroitedge.com
SIC: 3545 3599 3541 Machine knives, metalworking; machine & other job shop work; machine tools, metal cutting type
PA: Detroit Edge Tool Company
6570 E Nevada St
Detroit MI 48234
313 366-4120

(G-14399)
DIETECH NORTH AMERICA LLC
Also Called: Dietech NA
16630 Eastland St (48066-2087)
PHONE....................................586 771-8580
J Christopher Kantgias,
Dennis M Alderson,
David A Pascoe,
EMP: 100 **EST:** 1976
SQ FT: 72,009
SALES (est): 16.2MM **Privately Held**
WEB: www.dietechna.com
SIC: 3544 Dies & die holders for metal cutting, forming, die casting

(G-14400)
DJD MFG LLC
29970 Calahan Rd (48066-1889)
PHONE....................................586 359-2090
John Michajlyszyn,

Roseville - Macomb County (G-14401)

EMP: 8 EST: 2004
SALES (est): 648.7K Privately Held
SIC: 3441 Building components, structural steel

(G-14401)
DNL FABRICATION LLC
28514 Hayes Rd (48066-2314)
PHONE..............................586 872-2656
Kevin Verkest, *Engineer*
Lyn M Classy,
EMP: 24 EST: 2011
SALES (est): 2.7MM Privately Held
WEB: www.dnlfabco.com
SIC: 3549 Wiredrawing & fabricating machinery & equipment, ex. die

(G-14402)
DOMINION TECH GROUP INC
Also Called: Sturgeon Controls
15736 Sturgeon St (48066-1817)
PHONE..............................586 773-3303
Edward Lashier Jr, *President*
David Denhart, *Project Mgr*
Kristin Leinweber, *Project Mgr*
Scott Carney, *Engineer*
Bill Devaul, *Engineer*
◆ EMP: 185 EST: 1965
SQ FT: 203,000
SALES (est): 58.7MM Privately Held
WEB: www.dominiontec.com
SIC: 3549 Assembly machines, including robotic

(G-14403)
DYEMUREX INC
26670 Belleair St (48066-3578)
PHONE..............................586 447-2509
Karl Clayton, *Principal*
EMP: 6 EST: 2014
SALES (est): 178.8K Privately Held
WEB: www.dyemurex.com
SIC: 2759 Commercial printing

(G-14404)
EASY SCRUB LLC
16629 Bettmar St (48066-3225)
PHONE..............................586 565-1777
Glen Moore, *President*
EMP: 4 EST: 2016
SALES (est): 171.6K Privately Held
SIC: 3589 Commercial cleaning equipment

(G-14405)
END PRODUCT RESULTS LLC
Also Called: Golden Dental Solutions
27115 Gratiot Ave Ste B (48066-2900)
PHONE..............................586 585-1210
Jackie Golden, *Mng Member*
Rebecca Tyler, *Graphic Designe*
EMP: 10 EST: 2006
SALES (est): 580.9K Privately Held
SIC: 3843 Dental equipment & supplies

(G-14406)
EUROPEAN CABINET MFG CO
30665 Groesbeck Hwy (48066-1546)
PHONE..............................586 445-8909
Giulio Zaccagnini, *President*
Ben Lograsso, *Vice Pres*
Carlo Zaccagnini, *Treasurer*
▲ EMP: 38 EST: 1976
SQ FT: 14,000
SALES (est): 4MM Privately Held
SIC: 3469 2511 2434 2541 Metal stampings; wood household furniture; wood kitchen cabinets; wood partitions & fixtures; wood television & radio cabinets

(G-14407)
FLAT IRON LLC (PA)
27251 Gratiot Ave (48066-2967)
PHONE..............................248 268-1668
Ryan Wargner, *President*
EMP: 16 EST: 2015
SALES (est): 1.5MM Privately Held
SIC: 2869 Casing fluids for curing fruits, spices, tobacco, etc.

(G-14408)
G & G WOOD & SUPPLY INC
29920 Little Mack Ave (48066-2272)
PHONE..............................586 293-0450
Mario Grillo, *President*
EMP: 24 EST: 1968
SQ FT: 8,000
SALES (est): 1MM Privately Held
SIC: 2439 5712 6512 2541 Trusses, except roof: laminated lumber; cabinet work, custom; commercial & industrial building operation; wood partitions & fixtures; wood kitchen cabinets

(G-14409)
G & L POWERUP INC
Also Called: Batteries Plus
31044 Gratiot Ave (48066-4510)
PHONE..............................586 200-2169
Gregory Beltowski, *Principal*
EMP: 4 EST: 2013
SALES (est): 430K Privately Held
WEB: www.batteriesplus.com
SIC: 5531 3691 5063 3641 Batteries, automotive & truck; batteries, rechargeable; light bulbs & related supplies; electric light bulbs, complete; primary batteries, dry & wet

(G-14410)
GATHERALL BINDERY INC
15085 E 11 Mile Rd (48066-2703)
PHONE..............................248 669-6850
Mark A Culley, *President*
Brian C Johnson, *Treasurer*
EMP: 9 EST: 1993
SQ FT: 3,000
SALES (est): 1MM Privately Held
WEB: www.gatherall.net
SIC: 2789 Binding only: books, pamphlets, magazines, etc.

(G-14411)
GATHERALL BINDERY INC
15085 E 11 Mile Rd (48066-2703)
PHONE..............................248 669-6850
EMP: 4
SALES (est): 61.8K Privately Held
SIC: 2789 Bookbinding/Related Work

(G-14412)
GFM LLC (DH)
29685 Calahan Rd (48066-1807)
PHONE..............................586 859-4587
Senthil Kumar, *CEO*
Dave Papak, *President*
Alina Kozlowski, *Purch Mgr*
Paula Speller, *Human Res Mgr*
EMP: 48
SQ FT: 60,000
SALES (est): 15MM Privately Held
WEB: www.gfmcorp.com
SIC: 3465 Automotive stampings
HQ: Lgb Usa Inc.
15585 Sturgeon St
Roseville MI 48066
586 777-4542

(G-14413)
GLOBAL ROLLFORMING SYSTEMS LLC
Also Called: Global Automotive Systems
15500 E 12 Mile Rd (48066-1804)
PHONE..............................586 218-5100
Lynne Tillman,
Craig Barnhart,
Torben V Staden,
EMP: 5 EST: 2006
SALES (est): 8.4MM Privately Held
WEB: www.duraauto.com
SIC: 3714 Motor vehicle parts & accessories
PA: Global Automotive Systems, Llc
1780 Pond Run
Auburn Hills MI 48326

(G-14414)
GORDINIER ELECTRONICS CORP
16380 E 13 Mile Rd (48066-1557)
PHONE..............................586 778-0426
James A Gordinier, *President*
Ann Patricia Gordinier, *Vice Pres*
EMP: 5 EST: 1975
SQ FT: 10,000
SALES (est): 350K Privately Held
WEB: www.gordinier.com
SIC: 3823 Industrial instrmnts msrmnt display/control process variable

(G-14415)
GRAPHICS EAST INC
16005 Sturgeon St (48066-1827)
PHONE..............................586 598-1500
Michael J Easthope, *President*
John Griffin, *CFO*
Tom Tennant, *Accounts Exec*
Yvonne Busby-Dean, *Sales Staff*
EMP: 35 EST: 1977
SQ FT: 28,000
SALES (est): 7MM Privately Held
WEB: www.graphicseast.com
SIC: 2752 Commercial printing, offset

(G-14416)
GREAT LAKES PAPER STOCK CORP
Also Called: Glr
30835 Groesbeck Hwy (48066-1510)
PHONE..............................586 779-1310
Sandy Rosen, *CEO*
Michael Bassirpour, *President*
Ilene Rosen Bischer, *Vice Pres*
Michael Mione, *CFO*
Shannon Semik, *Controller*
EMP: 80
SQ FT: 100,000
SALES (est): 42.2MM Privately Held
WEB: www.glradvanced.com
SIC: 5093 3341 2611 Waste paper; secondary nonferrous metals; pulp mills

(G-14417)
GREIF INC
20101 Cornillie Dr (48066-1766)
PHONE..............................586 415-0000
Kathryn Bommarito, *Human Res Dir*
George Petzelt, *Branch Mgr*
Doug Duda, *Executive*
EMP: 5
SALES (corp-wide): 4.5B Publicly Held
WEB: www.greif.com
SIC: 2655 Fiber cans, drums & similar products
PA: Greif, Inc.
425 Winter Rd
Delaware OH 43015
740 549-6000

(G-14418)
GRIPPE MACHINING AND MFG CO
15642 Common Rd (48066-1826)
PHONE..............................586 778-3150
Salvatore Militello, *President*
Angeline Militello, *Vice Pres*
EMP: 31 EST: 1954
SQ FT: 17,500
SALES (est): 1.8MM Privately Held
SIC: 3599 Machine shop, jobbing & repair

(G-14419)
H & M MACHINING INC
29625 Parkway (48066-1927)
PHONE..............................586 778-5028
David Glaza, *President*
EMP: 19 EST: 1979
SQ FT: 18,000
SALES (est): 1.7MM Privately Held
SIC: 3544 7692 Jigs & fixtures; welding repair

(G-14420)
HAULIN OATS INC
18090 Buckhannon St (48066-4923)
PHONE..............................248 225-1672
Donald R Riddle, *Principal*
EMP: 4 EST: 2010
SALES (est): 88.8K Privately Held
SIC: 5153 2051 7389 Oats; bread, all types (white, wheat, rye, etc): fresh or frozen;

(G-14421)
HUSKY LLC
Also Called: Husky Precision
28100 Hayes Rd (48066-5049)
PHONE..............................586 774-6148
Richard Seleno,
Glen Schleicher,
EMP: 12 EST: 1997
SQ FT: 10,500
SALES (est): 979K Privately Held
WEB: www.huskymachine.com
SIC: 3599 Machine shop, jobbing & repair

(G-14422)
INDUSTRIAL DUCT SYSTEMS INC
Also Called: IDS
30015 Groesbeck Hwy (48066-1508)
PHONE..............................586 498-3993
Glen Croft, *President*
Miechelle Croft, *Vice Pres*
Marilyn Rogers, *Manager*
EMP: 5 EST: 1999
SALES (est): 869.1K Privately Held
WEB: www.industduct.com
SIC: 3444 Sheet metalwork

(G-14423)
INDUSTRIAL STAMPING & MFG CO
16590 E 13 Mile Rd (48066-1507)
PHONE..............................586 772-8430
Marvin J Tomlan, *President*
Kristine Morse, *Purchasing*
EMP: 20 EST: 1956
SQ FT: 45,000
SALES (est): 2.6MM Privately Held
WEB: www.industrialstamping.com
SIC: 3469 Stamping metal for the trade

(G-14424)
INTERNATIONAL ABRASIVES INC
27980 Groesbeck Hwy (48066-2757)
PHONE..............................586 778-8490
George F Barnett, *President*
Gloria Barnett, *Manager*
◆ EMP: 4 EST: 2003
SQ FT: 7,500
SALES (est): 488.5K Privately Held
WEB: www.intabrasives.com
SIC: 3291 Abrasive products

(G-14425)
INTERNATIONAL CASTING CORP
28178 Hayes Rd (48066-2346)
PHONE..............................586 293-8220
Doug Smith, *Branch Mgr*
EMP: 4
SALES (corp-wide): 1.6MM Privately Held
WEB: www.internationalcastingcorp.com
SIC: 3325 3322 Steel foundries; malleable iron foundries
PA: International Casting Corporation
37087 Green St
New Baltimore MI 48047
586 293-8220

(G-14426)
IRON FETISH METALWORKS INC
Also Called: Ifm
30233 Groesbeck Hwy (48066-1548)
PHONE..............................586 776-8311
Karen Arondoski, *President*
Jeffrey Maxwell, *Exec VP*
EMP: 15 EST: 2002
SQ FT: 14,110
SALES (est): 600K Privately Held
WEB: www.ifmetalworks.com
SIC: 7692 3441 3446 Welding repair; fabricated structural metal; architectural metalwork

(G-14427)
J & E MANUFACTURING COMPANY
16470 E 13 Mile Rd (48066-1501)
PHONE..............................586 777-5614
John Babiarz, *President*
Evelyn Babiarz, *Corp Secy*
EMP: 7 EST: 1988
SQ FT: 3,000
SALES (est): 628.8K Privately Held
SIC: 3599 Machine shop, jobbing & repair

(G-14428)
JOSEPH M HOFFMAN INC (PA)
16560 Industrial St (48066-1944)
PHONE..............................586 774-8500
Joseph M Hoffman, *President*
Fred C Pike, *Corp Secy*
EMP: 17
SQ FT: 8,000

GEOGRAPHIC SECTION

Roseville - Macomb County (G-14457)

SALES (est): 1.4MM **Privately Held**
SIC: **3479** Name plates: engraved, etched, etc.

(G-14429)
K AND J LIGHTING
28041 Ginley St (48066-2634)
PHONE....................586 625-2001
William Hawkins, *Principal*
EMP: 6 EST: 2012
SALES (est): 90.8K **Privately Held**
SIC: **3648** Lighting equipment

(G-14430)
KOLENE CORPORATION
Also Called: Upton Furnace Division
30435 Groesbeck Hwy (48066-1592)
PHONE....................586 771-1200
Scott Shiiling, *Branch Mgr*
EMP: 17
SALES (corp-wide): 13.5MM **Privately Held**
SIC: **3567** 3559 Industrial furnaces & ovens; metal finishing equipment for plating, etc.
PA: Kolene Corporation
  12890 Westwood St
  Detroit MI 48223
  313 273-9220

(G-14431)
KOMARNICKI TOOL & DIE COMPANY
29650 Parkway (48066-1928)
PHONE....................586 776-9300
Joseph R Komarnicki, *President*
EMP: 11 EST: 1984
SQ FT: 11,000
SALES (est): 842.5K **Privately Held**
SIC: **3544** Special dies & tools

(G-14432)
LGB USA INC (HQ)
15585 Sturgeon St (48066-1816)
PHONE....................586 777-4542
EMP: 3 EST: 2012
SALES (est): 15MM **Privately Held**
WEB: www.lgb.co.in
SIC: **3465** Automotive stampings

(G-14433)
LITHO-GRAPHICS PRINTING PDTS
19361 E 10 Mile Rd (48066-3904)
P.O. Box 66202 (48066-6202)
PHONE....................586 775-1670
Kenneth R La Forest, *Owner*
EMP: 5 EST: 1999
SQ FT: 3,000
SALES (est): 480.5K **Privately Held**
WEB: www.litho-graphics.net
SIC: **2752** 2759 Commercial printing, offset; letterpress printing

(G-14434)
MACHINING & FABRICATING INC
30546 Groesbeck Hwy (48066-1567)
PHONE....................586 773-9288
Robert C Gielghem, *President*
Sarah Shields, *Admin Sec*
EMP: 32 EST: 1975
SQ FT: 9,600
SALES (est): 2.5MM **Privately Held**
SIC: **3545** Tools & accessories for machine tools

(G-14435)
MARSACK SAND & GRAVEL INC
20900 E 14 Mile Rd (48066-1169)
PHONE....................586 293-4414
Thomas Marsack, *President*
Gary Marsack, *Vice Pres*
Ken Marsack, *Treasurer*
Edward Marsack, *Admin Sec*
EMP: 9 EST: 1928
SQ FT: 2,650
SALES (est): 607.8K **Privately Held**
SIC: **1442** Construction sand & gravel

(G-14436)
MARTIN TOOL & MACHINE INC
29739 Groesbeck Hwy (48066-1940)
PHONE....................586 775-1800
Edward Kunnath, *President*
William A Kemp, *Admin Sec*

EMP: 5 EST: 1960
SQ FT: 7,200 **Privately Held**
WEB: www.martintoolmachine.com
SIC: **3544** Special dies & tools

(G-14437)
MATHESON
26415 Gratiot Ave (48066-5108)
PHONE....................586 498-8315
Robert Wayne, *Manager*
EMP: 6 EST: 2015
SALES (est): 340.7K **Privately Held**
SIC: **2813** Industrial gases

(G-14438)
MCKECHNIE VHCL CMPNNTS USA INC
Also Called: McKechnie Tooling and Engrg
27087 Gratiot Ave 2 (48066-2947)
PHONE....................218 894-1218
Jeanie Johnson, *Principal*
David Kolstad, *Principal*
Steve Palmer, *Principal*
Brent Fischmann, *Manager*
EMP: 309 **Privately Held**
SIC: **3089** 3544 3083 2821 Molding primary plastic; thermoformed finished plastic products; special dies, tools, jigs & fixtures; laminated plastics plate & sheet; plastics materials & resins
HQ: Mckechnie Vehicle Components Usa, Inc.
  27087 Gratiot Ave Fl 2
  Roseville MI 48066
  586 491-2600

(G-14439)
MCKECHNIE VHCL CMPNNTS USA INC (HQ)
Also Called: Mvc
27087 Gratiot Ave Fl 2 (48066-2947)
PHONE....................586 491-2600
Mike Torakis, *CEO*
Linda Torakis, *President*
Mike Auten, *Vice Pres*
Tim Coots, *Vice Pres*
Shaun Raney, *Plant Mgr*
EMP: 14 EST: 1988
SQ FT: 10,000
SALES (est): 56.1MM **Privately Held**
SIC: **3089** Automotive parts, plastic; plastic processing

(G-14440)
MERCURY METAL FORMING TECH LLC
Also Called: M.M.F.T.
29440 Calahan Rd (48066-1852)
PHONE....................586 778-4444
Randell Stark,
EMP: 16 EST: 2009
SALES (est): 2.3MM **Privately Held**
SIC: **3469** Automobile license tags, stamped metal

(G-14441)
MICROPHOTO INCORPORATED
30499 Edison Dr (48066-1577)
PHONE....................586 772-1999
Richard Wade, *President*
Brian Wade, *Vice Pres*
Craig Ban Mill, *Director*
EMP: 20 EST: 1965
SQ FT: 17,000
SALES (est): 3.4MM **Privately Held**
WEB: www.microphoto.net
SIC: **3569** Filters & strainers, pipeline

(G-14442)
MIDWEST GEAR & TOOL INC
15700 Common Rd (48066-1893)
PHONE....................586 779-1300
Craig Ross, *President*
EMP: 48 EST: 1980
SQ FT: 5,000
SALES (est): 3.6MM **Privately Held**
WEB: www.ceoattglobal.com
SIC: **3462** Gears, forged steel

(G-14443)
MIDWEST MOLD SERVICES INC
29900 Hayes Rd (48066-1820)
PHONE....................586 888-8800
John Hill, *President*
Kevin Taverner, *Engineer*

Gary Verrier, *Engineer*
▲ EMP: 26 EST: 1994
SQ FT: 37,000
SALES (est): 7.2MM **Privately Held**
WEB: www.midwestmold.com
SIC: **3544** Industrial molds

(G-14444)
MIDWEST RESIN INC
15320 Common Rd (48066-1802)
PHONE....................586 803-3417
William Hughes, *President*
Michael Ouimet, *Vice Pres*
Robert Limeright, *Treasurer*
Chris Ouimet, *Accounts Mgr*
Steve Mueller, *Manager*
EMP: 5
SQ FT: 10,000
SALES (est): 1.2MM **Privately Held**
WEB: www.midwestresins.com
SIC: **2821** Plastics materials & resins

(G-14445)
MJ INDUSTRIES LLC
28540 Utica Rd (48066-2568)
PHONE....................586 200-3903
EMP: 4 EST: 2016
SALES (est): 69.5K **Privately Held**
SIC: **3999** Manufacturing industries

(G-14446)
MOON ROOF CORPORATION AMERICA (PA)
Also Called: MRC Manufacturing
28117 Groesbeck Hwy (48066-2344)
PHONE....................586 772-8730
Quirino D Alessandro, *CEO*
William Schauffer, *President*
Paul Torres, *COO*
Stan Droomer, *Plant Mgr*
EMP: 23 EST: 1975
SQ FT: 62,000
SALES (est): 11.4MM **Privately Held**
WEB: www.mrcmanufacturing.com
SIC: **3089** Automotive parts, plastic

(G-14447)
MOON ROOF CORPORATION AMERICA
30750 Edison Dr (48066-1554)
PHONE....................586 552-1901
Mike Spencer, *Branch Mgr*
EMP: 50
SALES (corp-wide): 11.4MM **Privately Held**
WEB: www.mrcmanufacturing.com
SIC: **3089** Injection molding of plastics
PA: Moon Roof Corporation Of America
  28117 Groesbeck Hwy
  Roseville MI 48066
  586 772-8730

(G-14448)
MP TOOL & ENGINEERING COMPANY
15850 Common Rd (48066-1895)
PHONE....................586 772-7730
Longine V Morawski, *President*
Lukas Morawski, *General Mgr*
Lawrence Marawski, *Vice Pres*
Lawrence Morawski, *Vice Pres*
EMP: 30 EST: 1946
SQ FT: 24,000
SALES (est): 6MM **Privately Held**
WEB: www.mptool.com
SIC: **3545** 3559 Tools & accessories for machine tools; gauges (machine tool accessories); metal finishing equipment for plating, etc.

(G-14449)
MRC INDSUTRIES
30700 Edison Dr (48066-1554)
PHONE....................586 204-5241
EMP: 5 EST: 2016
SALES (est): 265.9K **Privately Held**
SIC: **3999** Manufacturing industries

(G-14450)
MVC HOLDINGS LLC (PA)
27087 Gratiot Ave Fl 2 (48066-2947)
PHONE....................586 491-2600
Michael Torakis, *CEO*
Linda Torakis, *President*
Vickie Thompson, *Principal*

Timothy Coots, *Mfg Staff*
Jeffrey Palazzolo, *Treasurer*
EMP: 14 EST: 2008
SALES (est): 56.1MM **Privately Held**
SIC: **3714** 3465 3429 3471 Motor vehicle wheels & parts; automotive stampings; manufactured hardware (general); plating & polishing

(G-14451)
NATIONAL CONEY ISLAND CHILI CO
Also Called: National Chili
27947 Groesbeck Hwy (48066-5221)
PHONE....................313 365-5611
James Giftos, *President*
Paul Neiman, *General Mgr*
John Dallas, *Vice Pres*
EMP: 15 EST: 1963
SQ FT: 16,000
SALES (est): 2.2MM **Privately Held**
WEB: www.nationalchili.com
SIC: **2032** Chili with or without meat: packaged in cans, jars, etc.

(G-14452)
NBC TRUCK EQUIPMENT INC (PA)
Also Called: Fleet Truck Service
28130 Groesbeck Hwy (48066-2389)
PHONE....................586 774-4900
E William Roland Jr, *President*
Daniel A Sabedra Jr, *Vice Pres*
George Wimbrow, *Vice Pres*
Michael Roland, *Sales Staff*
David Petit, *Marketing Staff*
EMP: 49 EST: 1968
SQ FT: 34,000
SALES (est): 15MM **Privately Held**
WEB: www.nbctruckequip.com
SIC: **5013** 5012 3713 3441 Truck parts & accessories; truck bodies; truck & bus bodies; fabricated structural metal

(G-14453)
NEW CONCEPTS SOFTWARE INC
28490 Bohn St (48066-2487)
P.O. Box 688 (48066-0688)
PHONE....................586 776-2855
Julius M Boleyn, *President*
Deborah L Boleyn, *Treasurer*
EMP: 4 EST: 1987
SALES (est): 100K **Privately Held**
WEB: www.ncsoftware.com
SIC: **7372** 7371 Prepackaged software; custom computer programming services

(G-14454)
NEW DIMENSION LASER INC
29540 Calahan Rd (48066-1853)
PHONE....................586 415-6041
EMP: 4
SALES (est): 557.9K **Privately Held**
SIC: **3541** Mfg Electrical Equipment/Supplies

(G-14455)
NORTH COAST STUDIOS INC
29181 Calahan Rd (48066-1850)
PHONE....................586 359-6630
Steven J Burns, *President*
EMP: 10 EST: 1998
SQ FT: 12,000 **Privately Held**
WEB: www.northcoaststudiosinc.com
SIC: **3999** Stage hardware & equipment, except lighting

(G-14456)
ODEN SANITATION LLC ✪
25666 Carl St (48066-3810)
PHONE....................248 513-5763
Raymond Conley, *Mng Member*
EMP: 7 EST: 2021
SALES (est): 245.3K **Privately Held**
SIC: **2842** Sanitation preparations

(G-14457)
OWL WINERIES
28087 Gratiot Ave (48066-4204)
PHONE....................586 229-7217
Brooke Goodnough, *Administration*
EMP: 6 EST: 2014
SALES (est): 217.3K **Privately Held**
SIC: **2084** Wines

Roseville - Macomb County (G-14458)

(G-14458)
PARADIGM ENGINEERING INC
Also Called: Detail Standard Company
16470 E 13 Mile Rd (48066-1501)
PHONE..................................586 776-5910
Peter Manetta, *President*
EMP: 6 **EST:** 1996
SALES (est): 200K **Privately Held**
WEB: www.detailstandard.com
SIC: 5084 3469 Industrial machine parts; machine parts, stamped or pressed metal

(G-14459)
PARAMOUNT BAKING COMPANY
29790 Little Mack Ave (48066-2256)
PHONE..................................313 690-4844
Joseph Hanna, *President*
EMP: 16 **EST:** 1965
SQ FT: 9,859
SALES (est): 3.4MM **Privately Held**
SIC: 2051 Breads, rolls & buns

(G-14460)
PAUL MURPHY PLASTICS CO (PA)
Also Called: Murphy Software Company
15301 E 11 Mile Rd (48066-2780)
PHONE..................................586 774-4880
J Murphy, *President*
Paul Murphy, *Treasurer*
Julianne Murphy, *Admin Sec*
EMP: 32 **EST:** 1963
SQ FT: 31,000
SALES (est): 5MM **Privately Held**
WEB: www.paulmurphyplastics.com
SIC: 3089 3442 3272 3131 Plastic processing; metal doors, sash & trim; concrete products; footwear cut stock; laminated plastics plate & sheet

(G-14461)
PENINSULAR INC
Also Called: Peninsular Cylinder Company
27650 Groesbeck Hwy (48066-2759)
PHONE..................................586 775-7211
Brent Paterson, *President*
Keith Ford, *Regl Sales Mgr*
Sharon Garnett, *Sales Engr*
Dave Bucek, *Sales Staff*
Jim Dean, *Sales Staff*
EMP: 50 **EST:** 1949
SQ FT: 20,000
SALES (est): 10.1MM **Privately Held**
WEB: www.peninsularcylinders.com
SIC: 3443 3593 3537 3429 Cylinders, pressure: metal plate; fluid power cylinders & actuators; industrial trucks & tractors; manufactured hardware (general)

(G-14462)
PENTECH INDUSTRIES INC
15645 Sturgeon St (48066-1816)
PHONE..................................586 445-1070
David Vernier, *President*
Jeff Vernier, *Office Mgr*
EMP: 35 **EST:** 2001
SQ FT: 9,400
SALES (est): 2.5MM **Privately Held**
WEB: www.pentechind.com
SIC: 3541 Machine tools, metal cutting type

(G-14463)
PIPER INDUSTRIES INC
15930 Common Rd (48066-1812)
P.O. Box 41 (48066-0041)
PHONE..................................586 771-5100
Walter A Wosik, *President*
▲ **EMP:** 100 **EST:** 1946
SQ FT: 40,000
SALES (est): 8.9MM **Privately Held**
WEB: www.piperindustries.com
SIC: 3494 3594 3492 Pipe fittings; fluid power pumps & motors; fluid power valves & hose fittings

(G-14464)
PRECISION HONING
16627 Eastland St (48066-2089)
PHONE..................................586 757-0304
John Canning, *President*
EMP: 4 **EST:** 1998

SALES (est): 369.8K **Privately Held**
WEB: www.precisionhoningcorp.com
SIC: 3541 Machine tool replacement & repair parts, metal cutting types

(G-14465)
PRF MANUFACTURING USA INC
15232 Common Rd (48066-1810)
PHONE..................................586 218-3055
EMP: 7 **EST:** 2019
SALES (est): 42.8K **Privately Held**
WEB: www.prfmfg.com
SIC: 3999 Manufacturing industries

(G-14466)
PROPHOTONIX LIMITED
Also Called: Stilson Die-Draulic
15935 Sturgeon St (48066-1818)
PHONE..................................586 778-1100
Tom Graskewicz, *Manager*
EMP: 5
SQ FT: 50,000
SALES (corp-wide): 21.1MM **Publicly Held**
WEB: www.prophotonix.com
SIC: 3542 3594 3544 3537 Machine tools, metal forming type; fluid power pumps & motors; special dies, tools, jigs & fixtures; industrial trucks & tractors
PA: Prophotonix Limited
13 Red Roof Ln Ste 200
Salem NH 03079
603 893-8778

(G-14467)
PROTO-TEK MANUFACTURING INC
16094 Common Rd (48066-1814)
PHONE..................................586 772-2663
Thomas Strubbe, *President*
Richard Hansen, *President*
EMP: 20 **EST:** 1988
SQ FT: 12,800
SALES (est): 2.1MM **Privately Held**
WEB: www.proto-tekmfg.net
SIC: 3544 3599 Jigs & fixtures; machine shop, jobbing & repair

(G-14468)
R & T TOOLING
26725 Groveland St (48066-3339)
PHONE..................................586 218-7644
Roger Rennie, *Principal*
EMP: 4 **EST:** 2016
SALES (est): 58.6K **Privately Held**
SIC: 3541 Machine tools, metal cutting type

(G-14469)
RCO AEROSPACE PRODUCTS LLC
15725 E 12 Mile Rd (48066-1844)
PHONE..................................586 774-8400
Michael Carollo, *CEO*
EMP: 55 **EST:** 2014
SALES (est): 7.9MM
SALES (corp-wide): 102.8MM **Privately Held**
WEB: www.rcoeng.com
SIC: 3769 Guided missile & space vehicle parts & aux eqpt, rsch & dev
PA: Rco Engineering, Inc.
29200 Calahan Rd
Roseville MI 48066
586 774-0100

(G-14470)
RESKA SPLINE GAGE INC
29171 Calahan Rd (48066-1850)
PHONE..................................586 778-4000
David Sinclair, *President*
◆ **EMP:** 9 **EST:** 2010
SQ FT: 11,000
SALES (est): 912.2K **Privately Held**
WEB: www.reskasplinegauge.com
SIC: 3545 Machine tool accessories

(G-14471)
ROBERT & SON BLACK OX SPECIAL
30665 Edison Dr (48066-1583)
PHONE..................................586 778-7633
Tim Roberts, *President*
Matt Roberts, *Manager*
EMP: 8 **EST:** 1988

SQ FT: 8,000
SALES (est): 906.6K **Privately Held**
WEB: www.blackoxidespecialist.com
SIC: 3471 Electroplating of metals or formed products

(G-14472)
ROCKSTEADY MANUFACTURING LLC
Also Called: H & M Machining
29625 Parkway (48066-1927)
PHONE..................................586 778-5028
EMP: 13 **EST:** 2018
SALES (est): 917.5K **Privately Held**
SIC: 3441 3449 3443 3599 Fabricated structural metal; miscellaneous metalwork; fabricated plate work (boiler shop); weldments; machine & other job shop work

(G-14473)
ROYAL OAK NAME PLATE COMPANY
16560 Industrial St (48066-1997)
PHONE..................................586 774-8500
Joseph M Hoffman, *President*
Linda Hoffman, *Vice Pres*
Fred C Pike, *Treasurer*
EMP: 8 **EST:** 1955
SQ FT: 14,500
SALES (est): 1.1MM
SALES (corp-wide): 1.4MM **Privately Held**
WEB: www.ronp.com
SIC: 3479 3993 Name plates: engraved, etched, etc.; signs & advertising specialties
PA: Joseph M Hoffman Inc
16560 Industrial St
Roseville MI 48066
586 774-8500

(G-14474)
RPS TOOL AND ENGINEERING INC (PA)
16149 Common Rd (48066-1813)
PHONE..................................586 298-6590
Richard May, *President*
Scott Constantine, *Vice Pres*
Adam Hudson, *Design Engr Mgr*
Ryan Furtah, *Program Mgr*
April Smith, *Executive*
EMP: 35 **EST:** 2011
SALES (est): 5.6MM **Privately Held**
WEB: www.rpstooleng.com
SIC: 3089 8711 Injection molding of plastics; engineering services

(G-14475)
SALINE MANUFACTURING INC
15890 Sturgeon Ct (48066-1823)
PHONE..................................586 294-4701
Bruce Steffens, *President*
Debbie Makowski, *Manager*
EMP: 15 **EST:** 2007
SQ FT: 15,000
SALES (est): 2.3MM **Privately Held**
WEB: www.salinemanufacturing.com
SIC: 3443 Trash racks, metal plate

(G-14476)
SAMCO INDUSTRIES LLC
15985 Sturgeon St (48066-1818)
PHONE..................................586 447-3900
Sam Munaco,
EMP: 19 **EST:** 2010
SALES (est): 412.8K **Privately Held**
WEB: www.crownboringsamco.com
SIC: 3914 Silverware & plated ware

(G-14477)
SKIP PRINTING AND DUP CO
Also Called: Skip Printing Co.
28032 Groesbeck Hwy (48066-2345)
PHONE..................................586 779-2640
Robert Sauers III, *President*
Gail S Sauers, *Treasurer*
EMP: 8 **EST:** 1978
SQ FT: 2,010
SALES (est): 1MM **Privately Held**
WEB: www.skipprinting.com
SIC: 2752 7336 2791 Commercial printing, offset; graphic arts & related design; typesetting, computer controlled

(G-14478)
SODECIA AUTO DETROIT CORP
Also Called: AZ Automotive
15260 Common Rd (48066-1810)
PHONE..................................586 759-2200
Damien Pica, *Plant Mgr*
Damian Pica, *Project Mgr*
Rick Rhoades, *Purchasing*
Rodney Boskovich, *Engineer*
Ervin Facic, *Engineer*
EMP: 300
SQ FT: 28,400
SALES (corp-wide): 225.3K **Privately Held**
WEB: www.sodecia.com
SIC: 3465 Body parts, automobile: stamped metal
HQ: Sodecia Automotive Detroit Corp.
24331 Sherwood
Center Line MI 48015
586 759-2200

(G-14479)
SPARTAN GRINDING INC
28186 Hayes Rd (48066-2390)
PHONE..................................586 774-1970
Richard Smith, *President*
EMP: 5 **EST:** 1914
SQ FT: 5,000
SALES (est): 830.6K
SALES (corp-wide): 16.3MM **Privately Held**
WEB: www.spartangrinding.com
SIC: 3599 Machine shop, jobbing & repair
PA: Wolverine Bronze Company
28178 Hayes Rd
Roseville MI 48066
586 776-8180

(G-14480)
STATE WIDE GRINDING CO
27980 Groesbeck Hwy (48066-2757)
PHONE..................................586 778-5700
George H Barnett, *President*
EMP: 9 **EST:** 1977
SQ FT: 10,000 **Privately Held**
SIC: 3599 Machine shop, jobbing & repair

(G-14481)
STILSON PRODUCTS LLC
28400 Groesbeck Hwy (48066-2329)
PHONE..................................586 778-1100
Jeff Smith,
EMP: 18 **EST:** 2001
SALES (est): 1.1MM **Privately Held**
WEB: www.stilsonproducts.com
SIC: 3542 Machine tools, metal forming type

(G-14482)
T E C BORING
15645 Sturgeon St (48066-1816)
PHONE..................................586 443-5437
Michael Crusoe, *Administration*
EMP: 4 **EST:** 2012
SALES (est): 406.9K **Privately Held**
SIC: 3541 Drilling & boring machines

(G-14483)
TBL FABRICATIONS INC
28178 Hayes Rd (48066-2346)
PHONE..................................586 294-2087
Douglas Smith, *President*
Richard Smith, *Vice Pres*
Dennis Mascioli, *Treasurer*
EMP: 5 **EST:** 1985
SQ FT: 30,000
SALES (est): 1MM
SALES (corp-wide): 16.3MM **Privately Held**
WEB: www.wolverinebronze.com
SIC: 3441 Building components, structural steel
PA: Wolverine Bronze Company
28178 Hayes Rd
Roseville MI 48066
586 776-8180

(G-14484)
THERMAL DESIGNS & MANUFACTURNG
16660 E 13 Mile Rd (48066-1556)
PHONE..................................586 773-5231
L Garnick, *Owner*
Tim Scheid, *Sales Engr*
EMP: 13 **EST:** 2002

SALES (est): 566.1K Privately Held
SIC: 1761 7692 3567 3444 Sheet metalwork; welding repair; industrial furnaces & ovens; sheet metalwork

(G-14485)
TRI-WAY MANUFACTURING INC
Also Called: Tri-Way Mold & Engineering
15363 E 12 Mile Rd (48066-1834)
PHONE................................586 776-0700
John J Burke, *President*
Robert Zerrafa, *Vice Pres*
Tammy Leonard, *Admin Sec*
▲ **EMP:** 30
SQ FT: 20,800
SALES: 6.6MM Privately Held
WEB: www.tri-waymold.com
SIC: 3599 3089 3544 Electrical discharge machining (EDM); injection molded finished plastic products; special dies, tools, jigs & fixtures

(G-14486)
TRIANGLE PRINTING INC
30520 Gratiot Ave (48066-1728)
PHONE................................586 293-7530
Jeff Lawson, *President*
Cathy Lawson, *Vice Pres*
EMP: 6 **EST:** 1982
SQ FT: 1,500
SALES (est): 826K Privately Held
WEB: www.triangleprintinginc.com
SIC: 2752 Commercial printing, offset

(G-14487)
TRUE INDUSTRIAL CORPORATION (PA)
Also Called: True Industries
15300 E 12 Mile Rd (48066-1835)
PHONE................................586 771-3500
Gregory L Kiesgen, *CEO*
Gary A Kiesgen, *President*
Rob Paulson, *Foreman/Supr*
Emil Cook, *Purch Agent*
Jill Pickering, *Buyer*
▲ **EMP:** 57 **EST:** 1951
SQ FT: 42,300
SALES: 6.7MM Privately Held
SIC: 3544 Die sets for metal stamping (presses)

(G-14488)
TURRIS ITALIAN FOODS INC (PA)
16695 Common Rd (48066-1901)
PHONE................................586 773-6010
Anthony P Turri Jr, *President*
John Sadowsky, *General Mgr*
Mary Derlicki, *Corp Secy*
John Turri, *COO*
Thomas Turri, *Vice Pres*
▲ **EMP:** 80 **EST:** 1950
SQ FT: 24,000
SALES (est): 18MM Privately Held
WEB: www.turrisitalianfoods.com
SIC: 2038 2098 Ethnic foods, frozen; macaroni & spaghetti

(G-14489)
ULTIMATION INDUSTRIES LLC
15935 Sturgeon St (48066-1818)
PHONE................................586 771-1881
Jacqueline Canny, *CEO*
Dawn Milot, *Purch Mgr*
Carol Barker, *Accounting Mgr*
EMP: 45 **EST:** 2011
SALES (est): 8.5MM Privately Held
WEB: www.ultimationinc.com
SIC: 3535 Conveyors & conveying equipment

(G-14490)
VERSI-TECH INCORPORATED
Also Called: Versa Tech Technologies
29901 Calahan Rd (48066-1892)
PHONE................................586 944-2330
Ron Schroeder, *Principal*
EMP: 10 **EST:** 1973
SQ FT: 16,500
SALES (est): 2.1MM
SALES (corp-wide): 54.7MM Privately Held
WEB: www.versatechmi.com
SIC: 3599 Machine shop, jobbing & repair

PA: Mid-West Forge Corporation
2778 S M Ctr Rd Ste 200
Willoughby OH 44094
216 481-3030

(G-14491)
VIKING LASER LLC (PA)
29900 Parkway (48066-1961)
PHONE................................586 200-5369
Robert Robson, *Mng Member*
EMP: 4 **EST:** 2014
SQ FT: 7,000
SALES (est): 521.6K Privately Held
WEB: www.vikinglaser.com
SIC: 3714 Motor vehicle body components & frame

(G-14492)
VIRTEC MANUFACTURING LLC
28302 Hayes Rd (48066-2317)
PHONE................................313 590-2367
Charles Palms, *Mng Member*
Kevin Kosciolek, *Mng Member*
Jeff Miller, *Mng Member*
EMP: 10 **EST:** 2009
SQ FT: 14,200
SALES (est): 938K Privately Held
WEB: www.virtecmanufacturing.com
SIC: 7692 7389 Automotive welding; metal cutting services

(G-14493)
WESTGOOD MANUFACTURING CO (PA)
15211 E 11 Mile Rd (48066-2789)
PHONE................................586 771-3970
Edna Westerman, *President*
Lisa Spear, *Treasurer*
EMP: 15 **EST:** 1957
SQ FT: 11,000
SALES (est): 1.3MM Privately Held
SIC: 3544 3451 Special dies & tools; screw machine products

(G-14494)
WINTERSET WOODWORKS LLC
28310 Hayes Rd (48066-2317)
PHONE................................248 207-8795
EMP: 7 **EST:** 2017
SALES (est): 898.5K Privately Held
SIC: 2431 Millwork

(G-14495)
WOLVERINE BRONZE COMPANY (PA)
Also Called: Wb
28178 Hayes Rd (48066-2391)
PHONE................................586 776-8180
Richard A Smith, *President*
Bill Smith Jr, *General Mgr*
Dennis Mascioli, *Corp Secy*
Douglas Smith, *Vice Pres*
William P Smith, *VP Mfg*
EMP: 60
SQ FT: 90,000
SALES (est): 16.3MM Privately Held
WEB: www.wolverinebronze.com
SIC: 3365 3364 3322 Aluminum & aluminum-based alloy castings; brass & bronze die-castings; malleable iron foundries

(G-14496)
WOLVERINE PLATING CORPORATION
29456 Groesbeck Hwy (48066-1969)
PHONE................................586 771-5000
Rick Keith, *President*
Tim Slater, *COO*
Richard Sorensen, *Acting CFO*
Ken Wrobel, *Vice Pres*
Kenneth Wrobel, *Vice Pres*
▲ **EMP:** 50 **EST:** 1956
SALES (est): 14MM Privately Held
WEB: www.wolverineplating.com
SIC: 3471 Electroplating of metals or formed products

(G-14497)
ZUCKERO & SONS INC
27450 Groesbeck Ave (48066-2715)
PHONE................................586 772-3377
David Zuckero, *President*
Michael Zuckero, *Vice Pres*
Sarah Zuckero, *VP Finance*

Sue Zuckero, *Executive Asst*
EMP: 40 **EST:** 1980
SQ FT: 15,000
SALES (est): 6.5MM Privately Held
WEB: www.zuckero.com
SIC: 2541 Cabinets, except refrigerated: show, display, etc.: wood

Rothbury
Oceana County

(G-14498)
S & N MACHINE & FABRICATING
Also Called: S&N Fabricating
7989 S Michigan Ave (49452-7949)
PHONE................................231 894-2658
Steven Putnam, *President*
Nancy Putnam, *Treasurer*
EMP: 22 **EST:** 1984
SALES (est): 1.9MM Privately Held
SIC: 3449 3444 3441 Miscellaneous metalwork; sheet metalwork; fabricated structural metal

(G-14499)
WELLMASTER CONSULTING INC
2658 W Winston Rd (49452-9777)
PHONE................................231 893-9266
EMP: 13
SQ FT: 19,000
SALES (est): 1.9MM Privately Held
SIC: 1389 Oil/Gas Field Services

Royal Oak
Oakland County

(G-14500)
360OFME INC
225 S Main St Ste 200 (48067-2656)
P.O. Box 4449, Traverse City (49685-4449)
PHONE................................844 360-6363
EMP: 6
SQ FT: 1,850
SALES (est): 148.8K Privately Held
SIC: 7372 Prepackaged Software Services

(G-14501)
AAM PWDER METAL COMPONENTS INC
Also Called: Cloyes-Renold
2727 W 14 Mile Rd (48073-1712)
PHONE................................248 597-3800
David Schaefer, *Manager*
EMP: 7
SALES (corp-wide): 4.7B Publicly Held
SIC: 3714 Motor vehicle parts & accessories
HQ: Aam Powder Metal Components, Inc.
615 W Walnut St
Paris AR 72855
479 963-2105

(G-14502)
AAM ROYAL OAK MFG
2727 W 14 Mile Rd (48073-1712)
PHONE................................248 597-3800
EMP: 8 **EST:** 2019
SALES (est): 681.2K Privately Held
SIC: 3999 Manufacturing industries

(G-14503)
ABRETEC GROUP LLC (PA)
Also Called: Rpb Safety
2807 Samoset Rd (48073-1726)
PHONE................................248 591-4000
Philip Ivory,
▲ **EMP:** 40 **EST:** 2012
SALES (est): 53.4MM Privately Held
SIC: 5084 1731 3842 Safety equipment; safety & security specialization; respiratory protection equipment, personal

(G-14504)
ADVANTAGE BLNDS SHDS SHTTERS L
815 Maplegrove Ave (48067-1692)
PHONE................................248 399-2154
EMP: 10 **EST:** 2019
SALES (est): 919.3K Privately Held
SIC: 2591 Window blinds

(G-14505)
ALLMET INDUSTRIES INC
5030 Leafdale Blvd (48073-1011)
PHONE................................248 280-4600
Rodney R Floyd, *President*
Sheralyn M Floyd, *Vice Pres*
EMP: 5 **EST:** 1983
SQ FT: 4,500
SALES (est): 389K Privately Held
WEB: www.allmetindustries.com
SIC: 3599 Machine shop, jobbing & repair

(G-14506)
ALTA VISTA TECHNOLOGY LLC
26622 Woodward Ave # 105 (48067-0955)
PHONE................................855 913-3228
Jeremy Maurer, *Accounts Exec*
Scott Jackson, *Mng Member*
Hollie Murray,
David Valade,
EMP: 19 **EST:** 2014
SALES (est): 1.6MM Privately Held
WEB: www.altavistatech.com
SIC: 7372 7371 Application computer software; computer software development

(G-14507)
AMERICAN INDUSTRIAL GAUGE INC
Also Called: Standard Spring
4839 Leafdale Blvd (48073-1008)
PHONE................................248 280-0048
John M Payne, *President*
EMP: 5 **EST:** 1966
SQ FT: 2,800
SALES (est): 461.1K Privately Held
SIC: 3545 Gauges (machine tool accessories); tools & accessories for machine tools

(G-14508)
ANGLER STRATEGIES LLC
2815 Benjamin Ave (48073-3088)
PHONE................................248 439-1420
Sean Dunlop, *Principal*
EMP: 4 **EST:** 2014
SALES (est): 66.7K Privately Held
SIC: 2711 Newspapers

(G-14509)
APIS NORTH AMERICA LLC
938 N Washington Ave (48067-1740)
PHONE................................800 470-8970
Lynn Johnson, *President*
EMP: 3 **EST:** 2016
SALES (est): 1.3MM Privately Held
WEB: www.apis-iq.com
SIC: 7372 8243 8748 Application computer software; software training, computer; systems analysis & engineering consulting services
PA: Dr Holding Gmbh
Gewerbepark A 13
Worth A.D.Donau BY 93086

(G-14510)
ARBOR PRESS LLC
Also Called: Arboroakland Group
4303 Normandy Ct (48073-2266)
PHONE................................248 549-0150
Niels Winther, *CEO*
Ken Dause, *Partner*
Paul Cartwright, *Vice Pres*
Jim Duprey, *Vice Pres*
Michael Penkala, *Purchasing*
EMP: 58 **EST:** 2005
SQ FT: 30,000
SALES (est): 10.2MM Privately Held
WEB: www.arboroakland.com
SIC: 2752 8742 8299 Commercial printing, offset; marketing consulting services; educational services

(G-14511)
ARCHITECTURAL PRODUCTS INC
4850 Coolidge Hwy Unit B (48073-1022)
PHONE................................248 585-8272
Ronald Crossley, *President*
EMP: 5 **EST:** 1967
SALES (est): 870K Privately Held
WEB: www.apicustom.com
SIC: 2431 Millwork

Royal Oak - Oakland County (G-14512) GEOGRAPHIC SECTION

(G-14512)
ARROWHEAD MANUFACTURING
1406 Woodsboro Dr (48067-1182)
PHONE..................................248 688-8939
Craig T Gossett, *Administration*
EMP: 4 **EST:** 2010
SALES (est): 125.1K **Privately Held**
SIC: 3999 Manufacturing industries

(G-14513)
ASP HHI HOLDINGS INC
2727 W 14 Mile Rd (48073-1712)
PHONE..................................248 597-3800
Mike Johnson, *CFO*
EMP: 3000 **EST:** 2012
SALES (est): 638MM
SALES (corp-wide): 4.7B **Publicly Held**
SIC: 3714 Motor vehicle parts & accessories
HQ: Mpg Holdco I Inc.
299 Park Ave Fl 34
New York NY

(G-14514)
ASPN WOOD CONSTRUCTION LLC
418 N Main St (48067-1813)
PHONE..................................810 246-8044
Charles Johnson,
EMP: 10 **EST:** 2020
SALES (est): 326.7K **Privately Held**
SIC: 1389 Construction, repair & dismantling services

(G-14515)
ASTRO DUMPSTER RENTAL LLC
922 Forestdale Rd (48067-1646)
PHONE..................................313 444-7905
Cole Giles,
EMP: 7 **EST:** 2019
SALES (est): 88.9K **Privately Held**
SIC: 3443 Dumpsters, garbage

(G-14516)
BERLINE GROUP INC
423 N Main St Ste 300 (48067-1884)
PHONE..................................248 203-0492
James Berline, *CEO*
Michelle Horowitz, *President*
EMP: 30 **EST:** 1982
SQ FT: 10,000
SALES (est): 5.7MM **Privately Held**
WEB: www.berline.com
SIC: 7311 3993 Advertising consultant; signs & advertising specialties

(G-14517)
BLUE DE-SIGNS LLC
4605 Briarwood Ave (48073-1734)
PHONE..................................248 808-2583
Sasha Nedelkoski, *Mng Member*
EMP: 5 **EST:** 2007 **Privately Held**
WEB: www.bluedesignsusa.com
SIC: 3993 Signs & advertising specialties

(G-14518)
BONAL INTERNATIONAL INC (PA)
1300 N Campbell Rd Ste A (48067-1573)
PHONE..................................248 582-0900
Paul Y Hebel, *Vice Ch Bd*
Thomas E Hebel, *President*
Harold Hebel, *CFO*
Brian F York, *Treasurer*
Gregory Merritt, *VP Sales*
EMP: 15 **EST:** 1984
SQ FT: 13,500 **Privately Held**
WEB: www.bonal.com
SIC: 3829 Stress, strain & flaw detecting/measuring equipment

(G-14519)
BONAL TECHNOLOGIES INC
1300 N Campbell Rd (48067-1573)
PHONE..................................248 582-0900
Thomas E Hebel, *Ch of Bd*
A George Hebel III, *Ch of Bd*
Greg Merritt, *Vice Pres*
Brian F York, *Treasurer*
Daniel Kazmierski, *Accounts Exec*
EMP: 14 **EST:** 1984
SQ FT: 11,600

SALES (est): 897.7K **Privately Held**
WEB: www.bonal.com
SIC: 3829 3544 Stress, strain & flaw detecting/measuring equipment; special dies, tools, jigs & fixtures
PA: Bonal International, Inc.
1300 N Campbell Rd Ste A
Royal Oak MI 48067
248 582-0900

(G-14520)
BOSTON BIOSCIENCE INC
2710 Oliver Rd (48073-3184)
PHONE..................................617 515-5336
James Dixon, *President*
EMP: 4 **EST:** 1993
SALES (est): 346.5K **Privately Held**
WEB: www.bostonbioscience.com
SIC: 2816 Inorganic pigments

(G-14521)
BROLLYTIME INC
306 S Washington Ave # 400 (48067-3845)
PHONE..................................312 854-7606
Greg Edson, *President*
EMP: 10 **EST:** 2011
SALES (est): 400.4K **Privately Held**
WEB: www.brollytime.com
SIC: 3991 3999 2399 Brushes, household or industrial; umbrellas, canes & parts; pet collars, leashes, etc.: non-leather

(G-14522)
C S L INC
Also Called: Sir Speedy
1323 E 11 Mile Rd (48067-2051)
P.O. Box 7648, Libertyville IL (60048-7648)
PHONE..................................248 549-4434
Cynthia K Leigh, *President*
Scott Leigh, *Vice Pres*
Kristine Alexy, *Graphic Designe*
EMP: 7 **EST:** 1989
SQ FT: 5,000
SALES (est): 740.7K **Privately Held**
WEB: www.sirspeedy.com
SIC: 2752 Commercial printing, lithographic

(G-14523)
C&E WELDING
920 Cloverdale Dr (48067-1258)
PHONE..................................248 990-3191
EMP: 4 **EST:** 2012
SALES (est): 60.3K **Privately Held**
WEB: www.keystonestripping.net
SIC: 7692 Welding repair

(G-14524)
CANYOUHANDLEBAR LLC
3031 Glenview Ave (48073-3118)
PHONE..................................313 354-5851
EMP: 5
SALES (est): 186.6K **Privately Held**
WEB: www.canyouhandlebar.com
SIC: 2844 Toilet preparations

(G-14525)
CHANGE DYNAMIX INC
4327 Delemere Ct (48073-1809)
PHONE..................................248 671-6700
Robert Capinjola, *CEO*
Steve Akers, *CTO*
EMP: 7 **EST:** 2015
SQ FT: 4,000
SALES (est): 800K **Privately Held**
WEB: www.changedynamix.io
SIC: 7372 Application computer software

(G-14526)
CHELSEA GRINDING COMPANY
2417 Vinsetta Blvd (48073-3337)
PHONE..................................517 796-0343
EMP: 41 **EST:** 1953
SQ FT: 11,500
SALES (est): 3.5MM **Privately Held**
SIC: 3599 Machine Shop
PA: Das Group, Inc.
2417 Vinsetta Blvd
Royal Oak MI 48073
248 670-2718

(G-14527)
CRAWFORD ASSOCIATES INC
Also Called: Creative Graphic Concepts
4526 Fernlee Ave (48073-1782)
PHONE..................................248 549-9494

Gregg Kaitner, *President*
Chris Kaitner, *Corp Secy*
EMP: 6 **EST:** 1976
SQ FT: 3,200
SALES (est): 354K **Privately Held**
SIC: 2396 Screen printing on fabric articles

(G-14528)
CULVER J MANUFACTURING COMPANY
520 Forest Ave (48067-1958)
PHONE..................................248 541-0297
Norman C Dell, *Principal*
EMP: 4 **EST:** 2015
SALES (est): 78.7K **Privately Held**
SIC: 3999 Manufacturing industries

(G-14529)
DAS GROUP INC
2417 Vinsetta Blvd (48073-3337)
PHONE..................................248 670-2718
Doug Steward, *President*
EMP: 17 **EST:** 1999
SQ FT: 25,000
SALES (est): 367K **Privately Held**
SIC: 3599 3549 Machine shop, jobbing & repair; assembly machines, including robotic

(G-14530)
DETROIT STEEL GROUP INC
916 S Washington Ave (48067-3216)
PHONE..................................248 298-2900
Terry Boyette, *President*
EMP: 6 **EST:** 2004
SQ FT: 2,000
SALES (est): 2.3MM **Privately Held**
WEB: www.dsgsteel.com
SIC: 5051 3312 Steel; blast furnaces & steel mills

(G-14531)
DIXON & RYAN CORPORATION
4343 Normandy Ct Ste A (48073-2201)
PHONE..................................248 549-4000
Mark D Ryan, *President*
Richard Dixon, *Vice Pres*
EMP: 10 **EST:** 1929
SQ FT: 6,500
SALES (est): 1.9MM **Privately Held**
WEB: www.dixonryan.com
SIC: 7699 3545 3544 Professional instrument repair services; machine tool accessories; special dies, tools, jigs & fixtures

(G-14532)
EMATRIX ENERGY SYSTEMS INC
4425 Fernlee Ave (48073-1722)
PHONE..................................248 629-9111
Idan Kovent, *President*
Matthew Griffith, *Admin Sec*
EMP: 4 **EST:** 2017
SQ FT: 2,900
SALES (est): 288.9K **Privately Held**
WEB: www.ematrixenergy.com
SIC: 3691 Batteries, rechargeable

(G-14533)
EMMA SOGOIAN INC
4336 Normandy Ct (48073-2265)
PHONE..................................248 549-8690
Emma Sogoian, *President*
Kal P Sogoian, *Vice Pres*
Alexander J Jemal Jr, *Admin Sec*
EMP: 33 **EST:** 1951
SQ FT: 20,000
SALES (est): 1MM **Privately Held**
SIC: 3599 3714 Machine shop, jobbing & repair; motor vehicle parts & accessories

(G-14534)
ENGINERED COMBUSTN SYSTEMS LLC
4240 Delemere Ct (48073-1808)
PHONE..................................248 549-1703
David Beebe,
Bart Tinsley,
EMP: 7 **EST:** 2003
SQ FT: 5,000
SALES (est): 1.7MM **Privately Held**
WEB: www.ecsystems-usa.com
SIC: 3823 Combustion control instruments

(G-14535)
EPATH LOGIC INC
418 N Main St 200 (48067-1813)
PHONE..................................313 375-5375
Michael Germain, *President*
EMP: 6 **EST:** 2012
SALES (est): 265.8K **Privately Held**
WEB: www.epathlogic.com
SIC: 7372 Application computer software

(G-14536)
EXCLUSIVE IMAGERY INC
1505 E 11 Mile Rd (48067-2027)
PHONE..................................248 436-2999
Ceaser Yaldo, *Co-Owner*
EMP: 7 **EST:** 2007
SQ FT: 10,000
SALES (est): 534.9K **Privately Held**
WEB: www.eisigns.com
SIC: 2752 7336 3479 2396 Commercial printing, offset; poster & decal printing, lithographic; commercial art & graphic design; etching & engraving; screen printing on fabric articles

(G-14537)
FORERUNNER PRESS LLC
29300 Woodward Ave # 101 (48073-0959)
PHONE..................................248 677-3272
PHD Margaret Dwyer, *Principal*
EMP: 4 **EST:** 2016
SALES (est): 39.7K **Privately Held**
SIC: 2741 Miscellaneous publishing

(G-14538)
FORMTECH INDS HOLDINGS LLC
2727 W 14 Mile Rd (48073-1712)
PHONE..................................248 597-3800
Charles W Moore, *CFO*
EMP: 5 **EST:** 2009
SALES (est): 677.3K **Privately Held**
SIC: 3714 Motor vehicle parts & accessories

(G-14539)
GAYLES CHOCOLATES LIMITED
417 S Washington Ave (48067-3823)
P.O. Box 1873, Sedona AZ (86339-1873)
PHONE..................................248 398-0001
▲ **EMP:** 23
SQ FT: 5,000
SALES (est): 1.8MM **Privately Held**
SIC: 5441 2064 2066 Mfg Candy/Confectionery Ret Candy/Confectionery Mfg Chocolate/Cocoa Prdt

(G-14540)
GIFTS ENGRAVED INC
1526 Butternut Ave (48073-3210)
PHONE..................................248 321-8900
Harel Dotan, *Principal*
EMP: 4 **EST:** 2016
SALES (est): 92.6K **Privately Held**
WEB: www.shopgiftsengraved.com
SIC: 2759 Commercial printing

(G-14541)
GOODYEAR TIRE & RUBBER COMPANY
29444 Woodward Ave (48073-0903)
PHONE..................................248 336-0135
EMP: 4
SALES (corp-wide): 12.3B **Publicly Held**
WEB: www.goodyear.com
SIC: 5531 3011 Automotive tires; inner tubes, all types
PA: The Goodyear Tire & Rubber Company
200 E Innovation Way
Akron OH 44316
330 796-2121

(G-14542)
H A KING CO INC (PA)
5038 Leafdale Blvd (48073-1011)
PHONE..................................248 280-0006
Alfred W Rich, *President*
EMP: 6 **EST:** 1927
SQ FT: 3,500
SALES (est): 2.2MM **Privately Held**
WEB: www.ha-king.com
SIC: 3069 Molded rubber products

Royal Oak - Oakland County (G-14572)

(G-14543)
HAWTHORNE METAL PRODUCTS CO
4336 Coolidge Hwy (48073-1694)
PHONE...................248 549-1375
Del Stanley, *President*
Gary Grieme, *Vice Pres*
Wayne C Inman, *Vice Pres*
David Woodward, *CFO*
Vicki Earnest, *Controller*
▼ **EMP:** 350 **EST:** 1936
SQ FT: 225,000
SALES (est): 70MM Privately Held
SIC: 3465 Automotive stampings

(G-14544)
HHI FORGING LLC (DH)
2727 W 14 Mile Rd (48073-1712)
PHONE...................248 284-2900
EMP: 31
SALES (est): 298.2MM
SALES (corp-wide): 4.7B Publicly Held
SIC: 3462 Mfg Iron/Steel Forgings

(G-14545)
HHI FORMTECH LLC
2727 W 14 Mile Rd (48073-1712)
PHONE...................248 597-3800
George Thanopoulos, *Mng Member*
Matt Nosewicz,
▲ **EMP:** 500 **EST:** 2009
SALES (est): 102.9MM
SALES (corp-wide): 4.7B Publicly Held
WEB: www.aam.com
SIC: 3462 Automotive & internal combustion engine forgings
PA: American Axle & Manufacturing Holdings, Inc.
    1 Dauch Dr
    Detroit MI 48211
    313 758-2000

(G-14546)
HHI FORMTECH INDUSTRIES LLC
2727 W 14 Mile Rd (48073-1712)
PHONE...................248 597-3800
R Harris, *COO*
Richard J Larkin, *Exec VP*
Charles Moore, *CFO*
▼ **EMP:** 66 **EST:** 2006
SALES (est): 12.4MM Privately Held
SIC: 3714 Motor vehicle parts & accessories

(G-14547)
HOEGANAES CORPORATION
304 Mount Vernon Blvd (48073-5103)
PHONE...................248 435-6764
Eric Boreczky, *Manager*
EMP: 97
SALES (corp-wide): 11.6B Privately Held
WEB: www.gknpm.com
SIC: 3399 Metal powders, pastes & flakes
HQ: Hoeganaes Corporation
    1001 Taylors Ln
    Cinnaminson NJ 08077
    856 303-0366

(G-14548)
HOGGE CROCHET
200 W 2nd St Unit 951 (48068-7041)
PHONE...................313 808-1302
Yolanda Taylor, *Principal*
EMP: 4 **EST:** 2016
SALES (est): 50.1K Privately Held
SIC: 2399 Hand woven & crocheted products

(G-14549)
IMAGE PRINTING INC
1902 Crooks Rd (48073-4048)
PHONE...................248 585-4080
Donald F Edgerly, *President*
Sandra Edgerly, *Admin Sec*
EMP: 4 **EST:** 1978
SQ FT: 4,200
SALES (est): 532.4K Privately Held
WEB: www.imageprintingroyaloak.com
SIC: 2752 Commercial printing, offset; letters, circular or form: lithographed

(G-14550)
INSTYLE CABINETS LLC
4300 Rochester Rd (48073-2040)
PHONE...................248 589-0300
EMP: 6 **EST:** 2017
SALES (est): 162.9K Privately Held
WEB: www.instylekitchenandbath.com
SIC: 2434 Wood kitchen cabinets

(G-14551)
JD HEMP INC
Also Called: Signs By Tomorrow
31930 Woodward Ave (48073-0939)
PHONE...................248 549-0095
Diana Hemp, *President*
Jack Hemp, *Vice Pres*
EMP: 5 **EST:** 1993
SQ FT: 2,000
SALES (est): 520K Privately Held
WEB: www.signsbytomorrow.com
SIC: 3993 Signs & advertising specialties

(G-14552)
JONES PRECISION JIG GRINDING
4520 Fernlee Ave (48073-1782)
PHONE...................248 549-4866
Jimmy Jones, *President*
EMP: 4 **EST:** 1990
SQ FT: 4,000
SALES (est): 401.9K Privately Held
SIC: 3599 Machine shop, jobbing & repair

(G-14553)
KLEIBERIT ADHESIVES USA INC
4305 Beverly Ct (48073-6349)
PHONE...................248 709-9308
EMP: 5 **EST:** 2017
SALES (est): 90.3K Privately Held
WEB: www.kleiberit.com
SIC: 2891 Adhesives

(G-14554)
KTD PRINT
120 E Hudson Ave (48067-3784)
PHONE...................248 670-4200
Sean Dunlop, *Corp Comm Staff*
EMP: 5 **EST:** 2019
SALES (est): 155.1K Privately Held
WEB: www.ktdprint.com
SIC: 2752 Commercial printing, lithographic

(G-14555)
KYRIE ENTERPRISES LLC
Also Called: Kp Sogoian
4336 Normandy Ct (48073-2265)
PHONE...................248 549-8690
Kevin Colvin Jr, *Web Dvlpr*
Kevin L Colvin,
Michelle Colvin,
EMP: 11 **EST:** 2010
SALES (est): 1.2MM Privately Held
WEB: www.kyriellc.com
SIC: 3089 7538 Automotive parts, plastic; engine repair

(G-14556)
LESSON ROOMS
309 N Main St (48067-1810)
PHONE...................248 677-1341
Sonya Mastick, *Administration*
EMP: 6 **EST:** 2012
SALES (est): 111K Privately Held
WEB: www.thelessonrooms.com
SIC: 3931 Musical instruments

(G-14557)
LMI TECHNOLOGIES INC
29488 Woodward Ave # 331 (48073-0903)
PHONE...................248 298-2839
Mike Snow, *Business Mgr*
Len Chamberlain, *Vice Pres*
Doug Hope, *Project Mgr*
Waleed Sarwar, *Accountant*
Glenn Hennin, *Branch Mgr*
EMP: 13
SALES (corp-wide): 1.5B Privately Held
WEB: www.lmi3d.com
SIC: 3577 Magnetic ink & optical scanning devices
HQ: Lmi Technologies, Inc
    29488 Woodward Ave # 331
    Royal Oak MI 48073
    248 298-2839

(G-14558)
MAC LEAN-FOGG COMPANY
Also Called: Mac Lean Fasteners
3200 W 14 Mile Rd (48073-1609)
PHONE...................248 280-0880
Greg Rizzo, *General Mgr*
Laura Burgi, *Business Mgr*
Mark Leeser, *Project Mgr*
Ryan Heslin, *Materials Mgr*
Mark Serazin, *Materials Mgr*
EMP: 150
SQ FT: 78,607
SALES (corp-wide): 1.1B Privately Held
WEB: www.macleanfogg.com
SIC: 3678 3452 3714 Electronic connectors; bolts, nuts, rivets & washers; motor vehicle parts & accessories
PA: Mac Lean-Fogg Company
    1000 Allanson Rd
    Mundelein IL 60060
    847 566-0010

(G-14559)
MANUFCTURING ASSEMBLY INTL LLC (PA)
Also Called: International Mfg & Assembly
2521 Torquay Ave (48073-1014)
PHONE...................248 549-4700
Gilles Teste, *Executive*
▲ **EMP:** 14 **EST:** 2002
SQ FT: 51,000
SALES (est): 5.1MM Privately Held
WEB: www.intmnfg.com
SIC: 3465 Body parts, automobile: stamped metal

(G-14560)
MARQUETTE CASTINGS LLC
123 W 5th St (48067-2527)
PHONE...................248 798-8035
K Steckling, *Principal*
EMP: 5 **EST:** 2016
SALES (est): 115.3K Privately Held
WEB: www.marquettecastings.com
SIC: 3272 Concrete products

(G-14561)
MAYO WELDING & FABRICATING CO
5061 Delemere Ave (48073-1004)
PHONE...................248 435-2730
James Suratt, *President*
EMP: 7 **EST:** 1938
SQ FT: 6,200
SALES (est): 500K Privately Held
WEB: www.bumsteerbbq.com
SIC: 3599 3446 3444 3443 Welding repair; architectural metalwork; sheet metalwork; fabricated plate work (boiler shop); fabricated structural metal

(G-14562)
MCCLURES PICKLES LLC
212 Royal Ave (48073-5118)
PHONE...................248 837-9323
EMP: 4
SALES (est): 290K Privately Held
SIC: 2035 Mfg Pickles/Sauces/Dressing

(G-14563)
MICHIGAN SOY PRODUCTS COMPANY
1213 N Main St (48067-1364)
PHONE...................248 544-7742
EMP: 6
SQ FT: 1,600
SALES (est): 586.9K Privately Held
SIC: 2099 Mfg Food Preparations

(G-14564)
MYCO ENTERPRISES INC (PA)
3608 Dukeshire Hwy (48073-6426)
P.O. Box 113, Northville (48167-0113)
PHONE...................248 348-3806
Frank Firek Jr, *President*
Frank Firek Sr, *Owner*
Diana Cataldo, *Controller*
◆ **EMP:** 6 **EST:** 1994
SALES (est): 959.7K Privately Held
WEB: www.mycoent.com
SIC: 3498 Pipe sections fabricated from purchased pipe; tube fabricating (contract bending & shaping)

(G-14565)
NATIONAL SOAP COMPANY INC
1911 Bellaire Ave (48067-1514)
PHONE...................248 545-8180
Gerald Carafelly, *President*
Carol Carafelly, *Corp Secy*
EMP: 4
SQ FT: 5,000
SALES (est): 861.5K Privately Held
SIC: 5087 2841 Janitors' supplies; soap: granulated, liquid, cake, flaked or chip; detergents, synthetic organic or inorganic alkaline

(G-14566)
NUBILL CORPORATION
4815 Delemere Ave (48073-1002)
PHONE...................248 246-7640
EMP: 12 **EST:** 2015
SALES (est): 102.2K Privately Held
WEB: www.nubill.com
SIC: 7372 Prepackaged software

(G-14567)
PETNET SOLUTIONS INC
3601 W 13 Mile Rd (48073-6712)
PHONE...................865 218-2000
Eric Bishop, *Branch Mgr*
EMP: 4
SALES (corp-wide): 67.4B Privately Held
WEB: www.siemens.com
SIC: 2835 Radioactive diagnostic substances
HQ: Petnet Solutions, Inc.
    810 Innovation Dr
    Knoxville TN 37932
    865 218-2000

(G-14568)
PILKINGTON NORTH AMERICA INC
1920 Bellaire Ave (48073-1515)
PHONE...................248 542-8300
EMP: 15 Privately Held
SIC: 3211 Mfg Flat Glass
HQ: Pilkington North America, Inc.
    811 Madison Ave Fl 1
    Toledo OH 43604
    419 247-4955

(G-14569)
PRIMEWAY INC
4250 Normandy Ct (48073-2263)
PHONE...................248 583-6922
Kevin Walby, *President*
Nof Mistretta, *Accounts Exec*
EMP: 12 **EST:** 1990
SQ FT: 12,000
SALES (est): 2.1MM Privately Held
WEB: www.primewayinc.com
SIC: 2521 Wood office furniture

(G-14570)
PRIORAT IMPORTERS CORPORATION
815 Baldwin Ave (48067-4207)
PHONE...................248 217-4608
Craig Bell,
EMP: 5 **EST:** 2018
SALES (est): 126.9K Privately Held
SIC: 2079 2099 Olive oil; honey, strained & bottled

(G-14571)
RALEIGH & RON CORPORATION (PA)
Also Called: Oakridge Supermarket
2560 Crooks Rd (48073-3352)
P.O. Box 71028, Madison Heights (48071-0028)
PHONE...................248 280-2820
Ron Kohler, *President*
Raleigh Wilburn, *Vice Pres*
EMP: 100 **EST:** 1977
SQ FT: 15,500
SALES (est): 25.5MM Privately Held
WEB: www.oakridgemarkets.com
SIC: 5411 2051 Grocery stores, independent; bread, cake & related products

(G-14572)
RAM METER INC (HQ)
1815 Bellaire Ave Ste B (48067-1578)
PHONE...................248 362-0990
Jerry Marsoupian, *CEO*

Royal Oak - Oakland County (G-14573)

EMP: 13 EST: 1936
SQ FT: 25,000
SALES (est): 4MM
SALES (corp-wide): 26.8MM **Privately Held**
WEB: www.rammeter.com
SIC: **5065** 3825 3829 Electronic parts & equipment; instruments to measure electricity; measuring & controlling devices
PA: Hughes Corporation
16900 Foltz Pkwy
Strongsville OH 44149
440 238-2550

(G-14573)
RAYS ICE CREAM CO INC
4233 Coolidge Hwy (48073-1696)
PHONE..................248 549-5256
Dale B Stevens, *President*
Thomas Stevens, *President*
EMP: 14 EST: 1958
SQ FT: 4,300
SALES (est): 1.5MM **Privately Held**
WEB: www.raysicecream.com
SIC: **2024** 5812 2099 2038 Ice cream, bulk; ice cream stands or dairy bars; food preparations; frozen specialties

(G-14574)
RECYCLING RIZZO SERVICES LLC
Also Called: Royal Oak Recycling
414 E Hudson Ave (48067-3740)
PHONE..................248 541-4020
Charles Rizzo Jr, *CEO*
Wade Stevenson, *CFO*
EMP: 7 EST: 2013
SALES (est): 6.7MM
SALES (corp-wide): 12.4MM **Privately Held**
WEB: www.royaloakrecycling.com
SIC: **4953** 2611 Recycling, waste materials; pulp mills, mechanical & recycling processing
PA: Gfl Environmental Real Property Inc
26999 Central Park Blvd # 200
Southfield MI 48076
888 877-4996

(G-14575)
RED FALCON PRESS
123 W Sunnybrook Dr (48073-2531)
PHONE..................248 439-0432
David Trimboli, *Principal*
EMP: 4 EST: 2018
SALES (est): 70.2K **Privately Held**
SIC: **2741** Miscellaneous publishing

(G-14576)
REVOLUTIONS SIGNS DESIGNS LLC
2429 N Connecticut Ave (48073-4214)
PHONE..................248 439-0727
Mark Mulcahy, *Mng Member*
EMP: 5 EST: 2009
SQ FT: 800
SALES (est): 160.4K **Privately Held**
SIC: **3993** Signs & advertising specialties

(G-14577)
ROCKET COPY PRINT SHIP INC
605 S Washington Ave (48067-3827)
PHONE..................248 336-3636
Vaughn Masropian, *Principal*
EMP: 9 EST: 2006
SALES (est): 702.2K **Privately Held**
SIC: **2752** Commercial printing, offset

(G-14578)
ROYAL OAK & BIRMINGHAM TENT (PA)
Also Called: Birmingham Royal Oak Tent Awng
2625 W 14 Mile Rd (48073-1710)
PHONE..................248 542-5552
Carol Genereau,
EMP: 15
SQ FT: 2,100
SALES (est): 1.8MM **Privately Held**
WEB: www.royaloakandbirminghamawning.com
SIC: **2394** 1799 Awnings, fabric: made from purchased materials; awning installation

(G-14579)
SEE OUR DESIGNS
924 E 12 Mile Rd (48073-4230)
PHONE..................866 431-0025
EMP: 4 EST: 2013
SALES (est): 155.8K **Privately Held**
WEB: www.digitizer.com
SIC: **3949** Sporting & athletic goods

(G-14580)
SET ENTERPRISES INC (PA)
29488 Woodward Ave 296 (48073-0903)
PHONE..................586 573-3600
Sidney Taylor, *President*
Jody Nielsen, *General Mgr*
Michael Sindelar, *General Mgr*
Stephen Studdard, *General Mgr*
Adam Myers, *COO*
EMP: 20 EST: 1989
SALES (est): 67.6MM **Privately Held**
WEB: www.setenterprises.com
SIC: **7389** 3465 3544 3312 Metal cutting services; automotive stampings; special dies, tools, jigs & fixtures; blast furnaces & steel mills

(G-14581)
SODIUS CORPORATION
418 N Main St Ste 200 (48067-1813)
PHONE..................248 270-2950
Jean-Philippe Lerat, *Vice Pres*
EMP: 3 EST: 2003
SALES (est): 1.6MM
SALES (corp-wide): 2.6MM **Privately Held**
WEB: www.sodiuswillert.com
SIC: **7372** Application computer software
PA: Sodius
34 Boulevard Marechal Alphonse Juin
Nantes 44100
228 236-060

(G-14582)
SPARKS EXHBITS ENVRNMENTS CORP
600 E 11 Mile Rd (48067-1998)
PHONE..................248 291-0007
John Ballard, *Opers Staff*
James Sabourin, *Engrg Dir*
Mee Ryan, *Manager*
EMP: 5 **Privately Held**
WEB: www.wearesparks.com
SIC: **3999** 7389 Advertising display products; trade show arrangement
HQ: Sparks Exhibits & Environments Pa Llc
2828 Charter Rd
Philadelphia PA 19154
215 676-1100

(G-14583)
SWEET EARTH
313 S Main St (48067-2613)
PHONE..................248 850-8031
Ryan Robertson, *Owner*
EMP: 7 EST: 2012
SALES (est): 149.2K **Privately Held**
SIC: **2026** Yogurt

(G-14584)
TEE - THE EXTRA EFFORT LLC
333 E Parent Ave Unit 42 (48067-3763)
PHONE..................734 891-4789
Linda Taliaferro, *Principal*
EMP: 4 EST: 2017
SALES (est): 114.5K **Privately Held**
WEB: www.lindataliaferro.com
SIC: **2759** Screen printing

(G-14585)
TREE TECH
820 S Washington Ave (48067-3286)
PHONE..................248 543-2166
Charles Seidel, *Partner*
Chuck Seidel, *Partner*
James Seidel, *Partner*
EMP: 4 EST: 1995
SALES (est): 208.5K **Privately Held**
WEB: www.treetechinc.com
SIC: **2499** Kitchen, bathroom & household ware: wood

(G-14586)
TRI-MASTER INC
1616 W Houstonia Ave (48073-3992)
PHONE..................248 541-1864
William G Staubach, *Principal*
EMP: 7 EST: 2002
SALES (est): 177K **Privately Held**
WEB: www.precinmac.com
SIC: **3599** Machine shop, jobbing & repair

(G-14587)
UNITED RESIN INC (PA)
4359 Normandy Ct (48073-2266)
PHONE..................800 521-4757
Jane Wyer, *President*
John B Los, *Vice Pres*
EMP: 21 EST: 1970
SQ FT: 20,000
SALES (est): 5.9MM **Privately Held**
WEB: www.unitedresin.com
SIC: **2821** Epoxy resins

(G-14588)
V & M CORPORATION (PA)
Also Called: Royal Oak Recycling
313 E Hudson Ave (48067-3712)
PHONE..................248 591-6580
Habib Mamou, *President*
Ed Mamou, *Vice Pres*
Diane White, *Treasurer*
Kristy Allen, *Controller*
Evan Barrett, *Sales Mgr*
EMP: 39 EST: 1935
SQ FT: 70,000
SALES (est): 20.8MM **Privately Held**
SIC: **5093** 4953 3341 2611 Waste paper; refuse systems; secondary nonferrous metals; pulp mills

(G-14589)
VERSICOR LLC
333 W 7th St (48067-2513)
PHONE..................734 306-9137
Christina Coplen, *President*
EMP: 10 EST: 2013
SQ FT: 1,400
SALES (est): 796.1K **Privately Held**
WEB: www.goversicor.com
SIC: **3829** Measuring & controlling devices

(G-14590)
WALL PRO PAINTING
912 E 12 Mile Rd (48073-4230)
PHONE..................248 632-8525
Steve Wall, *Principal*
EMP: 4 EST: 2016
SALES (est): 150.9K **Privately Held**
WEB: www.wallpropainting.net
SIC: **5198** 2851 Paints, varnishes & supplies; wood fillers or sealers

(G-14591)
WEALTH CLUB NATION LLC
418 N Main St Ste 200 (48067-1813)
PHONE..................323 695-1636
Darius Ellis, *Mng Member*
EMP: 7 EST: 2020
SALES (est): 299.4K **Privately Held**
SIC: **2326** Men's & boys' work clothing

(G-14592)
WESLOPE INDUSTRIES INC
4822 Leafdale Blvd (48073-1009)
PHONE..................248 320-7007
Andrew F Colburn, *Administration*
EMP: 5 EST: 2014
SALES (est): 44.6K **Privately Held**
WEB: www.westslopeindustries.com
SIC: **3999** Manufacturing industries

(G-14593)
Y SQUARED INC (PA)
5050b Leafdale Blvd (48073-1011)
PHONE..................248 435-0301
John W Youngerman, *President*
EMP: 4 EST: 1995
SQ FT: 6,000
SALES (est): 583.8K **Privately Held**
WEB: www.ysquared-inc.com
SIC: **3679** Harness assemblies for electronic use: wire or cable

Rudyard
Chippewa County

(G-14594)
POSTMA BROTHERS MAPLE SYRUP
10702 W Ploegstra Rd (49780-9345)
PHONE..................906 478-3051
Greg Postma, *Principal*
EMP: 6 EST: 2011
SALES (est): 207.1K **Privately Held**
WEB: www.postmabrosmaple.com
SIC: **2099** Maple syrup

(G-14595)
RMG FAMILY SUGAR BUSH INC
11866 W Thompson Rd (49780-9372)
PHONE..................906 478-3038
Joy Ross, *President*
Mike Ross, *Vice Pres*
EMP: 4 EST: 1995
SALES (est): 329.2K **Privately Held**
WEB: www.rmgmaple.com
SIC: **2099** Maple syrup

(G-14596)
RMG MAPLE PRODUCTS INC
11866 W Thompson Rd (49780-9372)
PHONE..................906 478-3038
Mike Ross, *President*
EMP: 8 EST: 2013
SALES (est): 902.8K **Privately Held**
SIC: **5145** 2099 Syrups, fountain; maple syrup

Ruth
Huron County

(G-14597)
D & M CABINET SHOP INC
5230 Purdy Rd (48470-9769)
PHONE..................989 479-9271
Douglas Klee, *President*
Marilyn Klee, *Corp Secy*
EMP: 6 EST: 1980
SQ FT: 8,000
SALES (est): 440.4K **Privately Held**
WEB: www.dandmcabinet.com
SIC: **2434** 2521 5211 Wood kitchen cabinets; wood office furniture; cabinets, kitchen

(G-14598)
RUTH DRAIN TILE INC
4551 Ruth Rd (48470-9780)
PHONE..................989 864-3406
Margaret D Goniwiecha, *President*
John Goniwiecha, *Vice Pres*
EMP: 5 EST: 1958
SQ FT: 2,000
SALES (est): 472.1K **Privately Held**
SIC: **3273** 3272 Ready-mixed concrete; precast terrazo or concrete products

Saginaw
Saginaw County

(G-14599)
3DFX INTERACTIVE INC
1813 Mackinaw St (48602-3031)
PHONE..................918 938-8967
Deanna Nixon, *CEO*
Jackson Nixon, *CEO*
Zachary Nixon,
David Weiner,
EMP: 4 EST: 2012
SALES (est): 80.1K **Privately Held**
SIC: **7373** 7372 7371 3511 Turnkey vendors, computer systems; operating systems computer software; computer software systems analysis & design, custom; computer software development & applications; turbines & turbine generator set units, complete; windmills, electric generating; personal computers (microcomputers)

▲ = Import ▼=Export
◆ =Import/Export

GEOGRAPHIC SECTION
Saginaw - Saginaw County (G-14627)

(G-14600)
ACCURATE CARBIDE TOOL CO INC
5655 N Westervelt Rd (48604-1200)
PHONE.....................989 755-0429
Marshall J Longtain, *President*
EMP: 26 **EST:** 1947
SQ FT: 7,200
SALES (est): 1.2MM **Privately Held**
WEB: www.activmfg.com
SIC: 3545 Cutting tools for machine tools; machine tool attachments & accessories

(G-14601)
ADVANCE TECH SOLUTIONS LLC
Also Called: Remote Tank Monitors
1348 Delta Dr (48638-4610)
PHONE.....................989 928-1806
Peter Giles,
Jerry Ruthruff,
EMP: 6 **EST:** 2004
SQ FT: 10,000
SALES (est): 800K **Privately Held**
SIC: 3824 Liquid meters

(G-14602)
AIRTIFICIAL INTELLIGENT ROBOTS
3175 Christy Way S Ste 5 (48603-2210)
PHONE.....................989 799-6669
Jaine Calaramunt, *President*
Salvabor Montaner, *Vice Pres*
EMP: 6 **EST:** 2003
SQ FT: 3,000
SALES: 1MM
SALES (corp-wide): 5.4MM **Privately Held**
WEB: www.airtificial.com
SIC: 3569 Assembly machines, non-metalworking
HQ: Airitificial Intelligent Robots Sau
Calle La Coma (Pol. Ind. Pla De Santa Anna), 15 - 17
Sant Fruitos De Bages 08272

(G-14603)
AL-FE HEAT TREATING LLC
1300 Leon Scott Ct (48601-1204)
PHONE.....................989 752-2819
Matt Jones, *Manager*
EMP: 20
SALES (corp-wide): 74.2MM **Privately Held**
WEB: www.premierthermal.com
SIC: 3398 Metal heat treating
HQ: Al-Fe Heat Treating, Llc
209 W Mount Hope Ave # 1
Lansing MI 48910
260 747-9422

(G-14604)
ALLIED TOOL AND MACHINE CO
3545 Janes Ave (48601-6369)
P.O. Box 1407 (48605-1407)
PHONE.....................989 755-5384
Bruce Dankert, *President*
Thomas Shabluk, *Vice Pres*
Scott Slominski, *Vice Pres*
Carrie Stedry, *Treasurer*
EMP: 23 **EST:** 1945
SQ FT: 20,000
SALES (est): 5MM **Privately Held**
WEB: www.atamc.com
SIC: 3549 3544 Assembly machines, including robotic; special dies & tools

(G-14605)
ARTISANS CSTM MMORY MATTRESSES
Also Called: Artisans Mattresses
2200 S Hamilton St Ste 3 (48602-1377)
PHONE.....................989 793-3208
Dale Humbert, *President*
EMP: 14 **EST:** 1999
SQ FT: 5,000
SALES (est): 951.2K **Privately Held**
WEB: www.artisansmattress.com
SIC: 2515 5712 3732 3714 Mattresses & foundations; furniture stores; boat building & repairing; motor vehicle parts & accessories

(G-14606)
B K CORPORATION
5675 Dixie Hwy (48601-5828)
PHONE.....................989 777-2111
Robert Webber, *President*
Jeff Maslin, *Partner*
EMP: 10 **EST:** 2015
SALES (est): 2.1MM **Privately Held**
WEB: www.kuka-at.com
SIC: 3829 Measuring & controlling devices

(G-14607)
B&P LITTLEFORD DAY LLC
1000 Hess Ave (48601-3729)
PHONE.....................989 757-1300
EMP: 80
SALES (est): 8.9MM **Privately Held**
SIC: 3552 3559 3554 3556 Mfg Special Industrial Machinery For Process Industries Including Food Chemical Plastics Pharmaceuticals Textile & Paper

(G-14608)
B&P LITTLEFORD LLC (PA)
Also Called: B&P Process Eqp & Systems
1000 Hess Ave (48601-3729)
PHONE.....................989 757-1300
Laurence S Slovin, *President*
Robert Lytkowski, *Vice Pres*
Steve Burk, *Buyer*
Jamie Curtis, *Buyer*
Joni Harshman, *Buyer*
◆ **EMP:** 40 **EST:** 1959
SQ FT: 80,000
SALES (est): 19.1MM **Privately Held**
WEB: www.bplittleford.com
SIC: 3559 3542 3531 Chemical machinery & equipment; machine tools, metal forming type; construction machinery

(G-14609)
BANNER ENGINEERING & SALES INC
Also Called: BANNER-DAY
1840 N Michigan Ave Ste 1 (48602-5567)
PHONE.....................989 755-0584
J Michael Day, *Owner*
Margie Patterson,
EMP: 18 **EST:** 1949
SQ FT: 12,000
SALES (est): 3.6MM **Privately Held**
SIC: 3556 5074 3823 3433 Bakery machinery; gas burners; oil burners; boilers, hot water heating; industrial process control instruments; heating equipment, except electric

(G-14610)
BARNEYS WELDING AND FABG
965 Shattuck Rd (48604-2359)
PHONE.....................989 753-4892
EMP: 4 **EST:** 2019
SALES (est): 201.8K **Privately Held**
WEB: www.barneyswelding.com
SIC: 7692 Welding repair

(G-14611)
BARRETT SIGNS
321 Lyon St (48602-1522)
PHONE.....................989 792-7446
Steve Jordan, *Owner*
EMP: 5 **EST:** 2009
SALES (est): 950K **Privately Held**
WEB: www.barrettsign.net
SIC: 3993 Signs & advertising specialties

(G-14612)
BECKERT & HIESTER INC
2025 Carman Dr (48602-2915)
P.O. Box 1885 (48605-1885)
PHONE.....................989 793-2420
Bruce A Beckert, *President*
O Wendell Hiester, *Vice Pres*
EMP: 4 **EST:** 1921
SQ FT: 2,000
SALES (est): 364.2K **Privately Held**
WEB: www.bhdustcollectors.com
SIC: 3564 5075 Dust or fume collecting equipment, industrial; dust collecting equipment

(G-14613)
BELL ENGINEERING INC
735 S Outer Dr (48601-6598)
PHONE.....................989 753-3127
Richard L Bell, *President*
Dottie M Bell, *Vice Pres*
Bruce Lupcke, *Prgrmr*
EMP: 18 **EST:** 1964
SQ FT: 25,000
SALES (est): 1.8MM **Privately Held**
WEB: www.bell-engineering.com
SIC: 3599 Machine shop, jobbing & repair

(G-14614)
BELL ENGINEERING LLC
735 S Outer Dr (48601-6598)
PHONE.....................989 753-3127
Kenneth Bess, *President*
EMP: 7 **EST:** 2016
SALES (est): 499.8K **Privately Held**
WEB: www.bell-engineering.com
SIC: 3599 Machine shop, jobbing & repair

(G-14615)
BERNIER CAST METALS INC
2626 Hess Ave (48601-7498)
PHONE.....................989 754-7571
Joshua Bernier, *President*
Richard Barnes, *CIO*
EMP: 8 **EST:** 1945
SQ FT: 20,800
SALES (est): 1.5MM **Privately Held**
WEB: www.bernierinc.com
SIC: 3365 3321 3366 Aluminum & aluminum-based alloy castings; gray & ductile iron foundries; castings (except die): brass; castings (except die): bronze; castings (except die): copper & copper-base alloy

(G-14616)
BIERI HEARING INSTRUMENTS INC (PA)
Also Called: Bieri Digital Hearing Center
2650 Mccarty Rd (48603-2554)
PHONE.....................989 793-2701
Catherine Bieri Ryan, *President*
Marie Bieri, *Vice Pres*
EMP: 6 **EST:** 1952
SALES (est): 1.2MM **Privately Held**
WEB: www.bierihearing.com
SIC: 5999 3845 Hearing aids; audiological equipment, electromedical

(G-14617)
BLUE THUMB DISTRIBUTING INC
Also Called: Eponds.com
2650 Schust Rd (48603-1302)
PHONE.....................989 921-3474
Kip Northrup, *President*
Nicole Northrup, *Vice Pres*
Jason Erickson, *Sales Staff*
Chris McDonald, *Supervisor*
Penny Murday,
▲ **EMP:** 30 **EST:** 2000
SALES (est): 3.6MM **Privately Held**
WEB: www.bluethumbponds.com
SIC: 5261 5191 5083 3089 Garden supplies & tools; garden supplies; landscaping equipment; aquarium accessories, plastic

(G-14618)
BLUEWATER THERMAL SOLUTIONS
Also Called: Saginaw
2240 Veterans Mem Pkwy (48601-1268)
PHONE.....................989 753-7770
Michael Wellham, *President*
Ben Crawford, *COO*
Keith Beasley, *CFO*
EMP: 8 **EST:** 2004
SALES (est): 1.4MM **Privately Held**
WEB: www.bluewaterthermal.com
SIC: 3398 Metal heat treating
HQ: Bwt Llc
201 Brookfield Pkwy
Greenville SC 29607

(G-14619)
BODY LANGUAGE SCENTED CANDLES
1303 S Center Rd (48638-6323)
PHONE.....................989 906-0354
Anthony Barnett Lee, *Principal*
EMP: 4 **EST:** 2019
SALES (est): 55K **Privately Held**
SIC: 3999 Candles

(G-14620)
BREMER PROSTHETICS LLC
3995 Fashion Square Blvd # 1 (48603-1291)
PHONE.....................989 249-9400
Scott Baranek,
EMP: 8 **EST:** 1998
SALES (est): 524.1K **Privately Held**
WEB: www.bremerprosthetics.com
SIC: 3842 Prosthetic appliances

(G-14621)
CARPENTERS CABINETS
5066 Dixie Hwy (48601-5454)
PHONE.....................989 777-1070
Matt Johnson, *Owner*
EMP: 4 **EST:** 1946
SQ FT: 7,000
SALES (est): 337.6K **Privately Held**
WEB: www.carpenterscabinetsllc.com
SIC: 2541 Table or counter tops, plastic laminated; cabinets, lockers & shelving

(G-14622)
CARROLLTON CONCRETE MIX INC
2924 Carrollton Rd (48604-2397)
PHONE.....................989 753-7737
Hans Langschwager, *President*
Fred Langschwager, *Corp Secy*
EMP: 4 **EST:** 1923
SALES (est): 487K **Privately Held**
SIC: 3273 Ready-mixed concrete

(G-14623)
CARROLLTON PAVING CO
2924 Carrollton Rd (48604-2305)
PHONE.....................989 752-7139
Hans Langschwager, *Partner*
Fred P Lanschwager, *Treasurer*
John H Lanschwager, *Admin Sec*
EMP: 10 **EST:** 1923
SQ FT: 20,000
SALES (est): 584.2K **Privately Held**
WEB: www.carrolltontwp.com
SIC: 1771 3273 1446 Blacktop (asphalt) work; driveway contractor; curb construction; ready-mixed concrete; industrial sand

(G-14624)
CENTENNIAL TECHNOLOGIES INC
1335 Agricola Dr (48604-9247)
PHONE.....................989 752-6167
James F Hammis, *President*
Carolyn Hammis, *Corp Secy*
Angie Bluem, *Marketing Staff*
Linda Jackson, *Clerk*
EMP: 25 **EST:** 1976
SQ FT: 24,000
SALES (est): 3.8MM **Privately Held**
WEB: www.centennialtech.com
SIC: 3544 3559 Extrusion dies; foundry machinery & equipment

(G-14625)
CENTRAL MICH KNWRTH SGINAW LLC
3046 Commerce Centre Dr (48601-9697)
PHONE.....................989 754-4500
Jesse Berger, *President*
EMP: 9 **EST:** 2010
SALES (est): 1.2MM **Privately Held**
SIC: 3713 4492 Truck bodies & parts; towing & tugboat service

(G-14626)
CESERE ENTERPRISES INC
Also Called: Napolitano Bakery
2614 State St (48602-3994)
PHONE.....................989 799-3350
Leo A Cesere, *President*
Ann S Cesere, *Vice Pres*
EMP: 24 **EST:** 1915
SQ FT: 3,100
SALES (est): 1.1MM **Privately Held**
SIC: 2051 Breads, rolls & buns; bakery; wholesale or wholesale/retail combined

(G-14627)
CHARLES LANGE
Also Called: Cignys Bridgeport
5763 Dixie Hwy (48601-5916)
PHONE.....................989 777-0110

Saginaw - Saginaw County (G-14628) GEOGRAPHIC SECTION

Charles Lange, *Owner*
Kirk Peterson, *Vice Pres*
Ron Weidenmiller, *Purchasing*
Bill Lee, *Engineer*
Jeff Shelagowski, *Engineer*
EMP: 15 **EST:** 2010
SALES (est): 1.6MM **Privately Held**
SIC: 3537 Industrial trucks & tractors

(G-14628)
CHR W LLC
Also Called: Mid-Michigan Truss Components
2795 Harrison St (48604-2314)
P.O. Box 407, Carrollton (48724-0407)
PHONE 989 755-4000
Jeff Ross,
EMP: 19 **EST:** 2010
SALES (est): 3.5MM **Privately Held**
WEB: www.midmichigantruss.com
SIC: 2499 Decorative wood & woodwork

(G-14629)
CIGNYS INC
68 Williamson St (48601-3246)
PHONE 989 753-1411
Don Mastromatteo, *Vice Pres*
◆ **EMP:** 3 **EST:** 2001
SALES (est): 1.1MM
SALES (corp-wide): 23.9MM **Privately Held**
WEB: www.cignys.com
SIC: 3535 Conveyors & conveying equipment
PA: Saginaw Products Corporation
68 Williamson St
Saginaw MI 48601
989 753-1411

(G-14630)
CITY OF SAGINAW
Also Called: Traffic Engineering
1741 S Jefferson Ave (48601-2849)
PHONE 989 759-1670
Randy Chesney, *Manager*
EMP: 9 **Privately Held**
WEB: www.japaneseculturalcenter.org
SIC: 3669 Traffic signals, electric
PA: City Of Saginaw
1315 S Washington Ave
Saginaw MI 48601
989 759-1400

(G-14631)
CLICK CARE LLC
2650 Mcleod Dr N (48604-2850)
PHONE 989 792-1544
William Richter,
Derrick Richardson,
Michelle Richter,
EMP: 4 **EST:** 2013
SALES (est): 172.9K **Privately Held**
SIC: 7372 7373 Utility computer software; systems software development services

(G-14632)
COUNTRY REGISTER OF MICH INC
3790 Manistee St (48603-3143)
PHONE 989 793-4211
William Howell, *President*
Marlene Howell, *Vice Pres*
EMP: 7 **EST:** 1989
SALES (est): 410.2K **Privately Held**
WEB: www.countryregister.com
SIC: 2741 Miscellaneous publishing

(G-14633)
CUMMINS INC
722 N Outer Dr (48601-6236)
PHONE 989 752-5200
Thomas Lidletei, *Manager*
EMP: 4
SALES (corp-wide): 19.8B **Publicly Held**
WEB: www.cummins.com
SIC: 5084 7538 3519 Engines & parts, diesel; diesel engine repair; automotive; internal combustion engines
PA: Cummins Inc.
500 Jackson St
Columbus IN 47201
812 377-5000

(G-14634)
CUSTOM FOODS INC
634 Kendrick St (48602-1237)
PHONE 989 249-8061

John J Hausbeck, *President*
Mary Hausbeck, *Vice Pres*
EMP: 12 **EST:** 1997
SQ FT: 2,000
SALES (est): 459K **Privately Held**
SIC: 2035 2099 Pickles, vinegar; food preparations

(G-14635)
DALER INC
1115 W Genesee Ave (48602-5450)
PHONE 989 752-1582
Daler Singh, *Principal*
EMP: 7 **EST:** 2009
SALES (est): 133.2K **Privately Held**
SIC: 3578 Automatic teller machines (ATM)

(G-14636)
DAVES PRINTING
2600 State St (48602-3994)
PHONE 989 355-1204
David W Martin, *Principal*
EMP: 5 **EST:** 2013
SALES (est): 127.3K **Privately Held**
SIC: 2752 Commercial printing, offset

(G-14637)
DELTA STEEL INC
1410 Webber St (48601-3438)
P.O. Box 3231 (48605-3231)
PHONE 989 752-5129
Elizabeth Maczik, *President*
Arlene Maczik, *Vice Pres*
Erica Meisel, *Project Mgr*
Ron Markey, *Production*
EMP: 7
SQ FT: 7,000
SALES (est): 1.2MM **Privately Held**
WEB: www.deltasteelinc.com
SIC: 3441 Fabricated structural metal

(G-14638)
DETROIT NEWSPAPER PARTNR LP
Also Called: Detroit Free Press
2654 N Outer Dr Ste 4 (48601-6012)
PHONE 989 752-3023
EMP: 6
SALES (corp-wide): 6B **Publicly Held**
SIC: 2711 Newspapers-Publishing/Printing
HQ: Detroit Newspaper Partnership, L.P.
160 W Fort St
Detroit MI 48226
313 222-2300

(G-14639)
DIAL TENT & AWNING CO
5330 Davis Rd (48604-9497)
PHONE 989 793-0741
Mark Rieffel, *President*
EMP: 13 **EST:** 1936
SQ FT: 14,000
SALES (est): 1MM **Privately Held**
WEB: www.dialtentandawning.com
SIC: 7359 2394 Tent & tarpaulin rental; awnings, fabric: made from purchased materials; liners & covers, fabric: made from purchased materials

(G-14640)
DUPERON CORPORATION
1200 Leon Scott Ct (48601-1273)
PHONE 800 383-8479
Tammy L Bernier, *President*
Terry L Duperon, *Chairman*
Tammy Cavenaugh, *Project Mgr*
Brandon Dayton, *Project Mgr*
Jodi Jaskiewicz, *Project Mgr*
▲ **EMP:** 60 **EST:** 1985
SQ FT: 72,000
SALES (est): 16.4MM **Privately Held**
WEB: www.duperon.com
SIC: 3569 Filters

(G-14641)
DURO-LAST INC (PA)
Also Called: Duro-Last Roofing
525 E Morley Dr (48601)
PHONE 800 248-0280
Tom Saeli, *CEO*
Troy Jenison, *Regional Mgr*
Scott Shockey, *Regional Mgr*
Charles Smith, *Regional Mgr*
Tom Lawler, *COO*
▼ **EMP:** 280 **EST:** 1981
SQ FT: 74,480

SALES (est): 228.3MM **Privately Held**
WEB: www.duro-last.com
SIC: 2295 Resin or plastic coated fabrics

(G-14642)
DURO-LAST INC
525 W Morley Dr (48601-9485)
P.O. Box 3301 (48605-3301)
PHONE 800 248-0280
Tom Hollingworth, *President*
EMP: 21
SALES (corp-wide): 228.3MM **Privately Held**
WEB: www.duro-last.com
SIC: 2295 Resin or plastic coated fabrics
PA: Duro-Last, Inc.
525 E Morley Dr
Saginaw MI 48601
800 248-0280

(G-14643)
ELDERBERRY STEAM ENGINES
5215 Pheasant Run Dr # 5 (48638-6349)
PHONE 989 245-0652
EMP: 4 **EST:** 2016
SALES (est): 130.5K **Privately Held**
SIC: 3511 Steam engines

(G-14644)
ERIE MARKING INC
Also Called: Erie Custom Signs
1017 S Wheeler St (48602-1112)
PHONE 989 754-8360
Lisa R Shabluk, *President*
Michael R Sahbluk, *Treasurer*
EMP: 14 **EST:** 2009
SQ FT: 12,000
SALES (est): 1.3MM **Privately Held**
WEB: www.eriecustomsigns.com
SIC: 3993 5099 Signs, not made in custom sign painting shops; signs, except electric

(G-14645)
FERGUSON ENTERPRISES LLC
Also Called: Johnson Contrls Authorized Dlr
3944 Fortune Blvd (48603-2253)
PHONE 989 790-2220
Casey Bradley, *Branch Mgr*
EMP: 5
SALES (corp-wide): 21.8B **Publicly Held**
WEB: www.ferguson.com
SIC: 5074 5085 5051 3498 Plumbing fittings & supplies; valves & fittings; pipe & tubing, steel; pipe fittings, fabricated from purchased pipe
HQ: Ferguson Enterprises, Llc
12500 Jefferson Ave
Newport News VA 23602
757 874-7795

(G-14646)
FRANKENMUTH WELDING & FABG
4765 E Holland Rd (48601-9463)
PHONE 989 754-9457
Micheal Schreiber, *President*
Daniel Vesterfelt, *President*
EMP: 7 **EST:** 1981
SALES (est): 974.4K **Privately Held**
WEB: www.frankenmuthwelding.com
SIC: 3449 3444 7692 Miscellaneous metalwork; sheet metalwork; welding repair

(G-14647)
FRITO-LAY NORTH AMERICA INC
100 S Outer Dr (48601-6330)
PHONE 989 754-0435
Robert Licht, *Manager*
EMP: 6
SALES (corp-wide): 70.3B **Publicly Held**
WEB: www.fritolay.com
SIC: 5145 2052 Snack foods; pretzels
HQ: Frito-Lay North America, Inc.
7701 Legacy Dr
Plano TX 75024

(G-14648)
FULLERTON TOOL COMPANY INC (PA)
121 Perry St (48602-1496)
P.O. Box 2008 (48605-2008)
PHONE 989 799-4550
Morgan L Curry Jr, *CEO*

Patrick Curry, *President*
Richard Curry, *Vice Pres*
Gary Bruff, *Mfg Staff*
Michael Fischer, *Engineer*
EMP: 106 **EST:** 1942
SQ FT: 27,000
SALES (est): 23.3MM **Privately Held**
WEB: www.fullertontool.com
SIC: 3545 Files, machine tool; milling machine attachments (machine tool accessories); reamers, machine tool

(G-14649)
GENERAL MACHINE SERVICE INC
494 E Morley Dr (48601-9402)
PHONE 989 752-5161
Stephen G Slachta, *President*
Meredith Wilkinson, *VP Finance*
EMP: 34 **EST:** 1979
SQ FT: 25,000
SALES (est): 1.4MM **Privately Held**
WEB: www.genmachine.com
SIC: 3599 Machine shop, jobbing & repair

(G-14650)
GENERAL MOTORS COMPANY
1629 N Washington Ave (48601-1211)
PHONE 989 757-1576
Craig Jablonski, *Engineer*
Cameron Morford, *Engineer*
Kai Spande, *Engineer*
John Lancaster, *Branch Mgr*
EMP: 7 **Publicly Held**
WEB: www.gm.com
SIC: 3325 Steel foundries
PA: General Motors Company
300 Renaissance Ctr L1
Detroit MI 48243

(G-14651)
GENERAL MOTORS LLC
3900 N Towerline Rd (48601-9242)
PHONE 989 757-0528
Howard Wachner, *Fire Chief*
Travis Hester, *Vice Pres*
Ray Wright, *Manager*
EMP: 7 **Publicly Held**
WEB: www.gm.com
SIC: 3321 3325 3334 Gray & ductile iron foundries; steel foundries; primary aluminum
HQ: General Motors Llc
300 Renaissance Ctr L1
Detroit MI 48243

(G-14652)
GLASTENDER INC (PA)
5400 N Michigan Rd (48604-9700)
PHONE 989 752-4275
Jon D Hall Sr, *President*
Todd Hall, *Principal*
Mark Norris, *Vice Pres*
Alejandra Bohorquez, *Purch Mgr*
Amy Rouech, *Purchasing*
◆ **EMP:** 360
SQ FT: 187,000
SALES (est): 71.9MM **Privately Held**
WEB: www.glastender.com
SIC: 3589 2542 3585 Dishwashing machines, commercial; bar fixtures, except wood; refrigeration & heating equipment

(G-14653)
GLS DIOCESAN REPORTS (PA)
Also Called: Catholic Weekly
1520 Court St (48602-4067)
PHONE 989 793-7661
Mark Myczkowiak, *President*
Christine Brass, *Corp Secy*
Elaine Raymond, *Director*
Sister Elaine Raymond, *Director*
EMP: 6 **EST:** 1942
SQ FT: 2,000
SALES: 291K **Privately Held**
SIC: 2711 Newspapers: publishing only, not printed on site

(G-14654)
GODFREY & WING INC
2240 Veterans Mem Pkwy (48601-1268)
PHONE 330 562-1440
Nick Chapman, *Manager*
EMP: 8

GEOGRAPHIC SECTION

Saginaw - Saginaw County (G-14681)

SALES (corp-wide): 19.3MM **Privately Held**
WEB: www.godfreywing.com
SIC: 3479 Coating of metals with plastic or resins
PA: Godfrey & Wing Inc.
220 Campus Dr
Aurora OH 44202
330 562-1440

(G-14655)
GOMBAR CORP
Also Called: Print Shop, The
5645 State St Ste B (48603-3691)
P.O. Box 6893 (48608-6893)
PHONE................................989 793-9427
Ben Gombar, *President*
Linda Gombar, *Vice Pres*
Dan Samolewski, *Graphic Designe*
EMP: 8 EST: 1975
SQ FT: 2,000
SALES (est): 970.1K **Privately Held**
WEB: www.printshopsaginaw.com
SIC: 2752 2791 2789 Commercial printing, offset; typesetting; bookbinding & related work

(G-14656)
GOSEN TOOL & MACHINE INC
2054 Brettrager Dr (48601-9790)
PHONE................................989 777-6493
Jeff Gosen, *President*
Steve Gosen, *Vice Pres*
Bill Gosen, *Treasurer*
EMP: 16 EST: 1993
SQ FT: 8,000
SALES (est): 1.1MM **Privately Held**
WEB: www.gosentoolandmachine.com
SIC: 3599 3441 Machine shop, jobbing & repair; fabricated structural metal

(G-14657)
GOWER CORPORATION
2840 Universal Dr (48603-2411)
PHONE................................989 249-5938
EMP: 6
SQ FT: 2,400
SALES (est): 430K **Privately Held**
SIC: 7694 5063 Armature Rewinding Whol Electrical Equip

(G-14658)
GRAMINEX LLC (PA)
95 Midland Rd (48638-5770)
PHONE................................989 797-5502
Harold Baldauf, *Mng Member*
Alexander Grantz, *Security Dir*
Cynthia May,
EMP: 5 EST: 1997
SALES (est): 3.3MM **Privately Held**
WEB: www.graminex.com
SIC: 3559 Pharmaceutical machinery

(G-14659)
GREGORY M BOESE
Also Called: Boese Equipment Co
2929 River St (48601-4343)
PHONE................................989 754-2990
Gregory M Boese, *Owner*
EMP: 12 EST: 1996
SQ FT: 30,000
SALES (est): 7MM **Privately Held**
WEB: www.boeseharvester.com
SIC: 5083 5084 3599 Harvesting machinery & equipment; hydraulic systems equipment & supplies; custom machinery

(G-14660)
HAMILTON ELECTRIC CO
3175 Pierce Rd (48604-9755)
PHONE................................989 799-6291
Mark Doyle, *President*
Candice Lagan, *General Mgr*
Sherry Raymond, *Admin Sec*
EMP: 16 EST: 1974
SQ FT: 1,700
SALES (est): 3.3MM **Privately Held**
WEB: www.hamiltonelec.com
SIC: 7694 5063 Electric motor repair; motors, electric

(G-14661)
HAUSBECK PICKLE COMPANY (PA)
1626 Hess Ave (48601-3970)
PHONE................................989 754-4721
Tim Hausbeck, *CEO*
Timothy Hausbeck, *President*
John Joseph Hausbeck, *Vice Pres*
Matthew Turner, *Prdtn Mgr*
Joshua Hernandez, *Production*
◆ EMP: 60 EST: 1926
SQ FT: 60,000
SALES (est): 27.3MM **Privately Held**
WEB: www.hausbeck.com
SIC: 2035 Pickled fruits & vegetables; cucumbers, pickles & pickle salting

(G-14662)
HAWK DESIGN INC
Also Called: Print Express Office Products
7760 Gratiot Rd (48609-5043)
PHONE................................989 781-1152
Michael Slasinski, *President*
Leanne Slasinski, *Principal*
Steve Slasinski, *Vice Pres*
EMP: 4 EST: 1993
SQ FT: 2,750
SALES (est): 543.7K **Privately Held**
WEB: www.printexpressmi.com
SIC: 8711 5943 2752 Engineering services; office forms & supplies; commercial printing, offset

(G-14663)
HI-TECH OPTICAL INC
3139 Christy Way S (48603-2226)
P.O. Box 1443 (48605-1443)
PHONE................................989 799-9390
Tom Ryan, *President*
Denise Cieslinski, *Production*
Dean Sheehan, *Regl Sales Mgr*
Josh Brown, *Manager*
Brian Schneider, *Manager*
EMP: 25
SQ FT: 4,000
SALES (est): 5.3MM **Privately Held**
WEB: www.hi-techoptical.com
SIC: 5048 3851 5661 5699 Frames, ophthalmic; lenses, ophthalmic; lens coating, ophthalmic; shoe stores; customized clothing & apparel; surgical appliances & supplies; optical goods

(G-14664)
HI-TECH STEEL TREATING INC
2720 Roberts St (48603-3197)
PHONE................................800 835-8294
James A Stone, *President*
George Clauss, *Vice Pres*
Tom McGrandy, *Vice Pres*
Charles Parsell, *Treasurer*
Kevin Stone, *Sales Staff*
EMP: 55 EST: 1983
SQ FT: 50,000
SALES (est): 6.2MM **Privately Held**
WEB: www.hitechsteel.com
SIC: 3398 Metal heat treating

(G-14665)
HIGHER IMAGE SIGNS & WRAPS LLC
2905 Mccarty Rd (48603-2444)
PHONE................................989 964-0443
Shad Sprague, *Owner*
EMP: 7 EST: 2010
SALES (est): 611.9K **Privately Held**
WEB: www.higherimage.net
SIC: 3993 Signs & advertising specialties

(G-14666)
HMG AGENCY
4352 Bay Rd Ste 131 (48603-1206)
PHONE................................989 443-3819
Loreal Hartwell,
EMP: 15 EST: 2018
SALES (est): 377.9K **Privately Held**
SIC: 2741

(G-14667)
HOLCIM (US) INC
900 N Adams St (48604-1248)
PHONE................................989 755-7515
Filiberto Ruiz, *President*
EMP: 4
SALES (corp-wide): 25.3B **Privately Held**
WEB: www.lafargeholcim.us
SIC: 3241 5032 Portland cement; cement
HQ: Holcim (Us) Inc.
8700 W Bryn Mawr Ave
Chicago IL 60631

(G-14668)
HOMESTEAD ELEMENTS LLC
3984 Cabaret Trl W (48603-2270)
PHONE................................248 560-7122
Tanya McDonald, *Mng Member*
Eric McDonald,
EMP: 8 EST: 2016
SALES (est): 561.5K **Privately Held**
WEB: www.homesteadelements.com
SIC: 2299 5021 Batting, wadding, padding & fillings; household furniture

(G-14669)
HONEYWELL INTERNATIONAL INC
5153 Hampton Pl (48604-9576)
PHONE................................989 792-8707
Eric Starke, *Project Mgr*
Shelly Crannell, *Administration*
EMP: 6
SALES (corp-wide): 32.6B **Publicly Held**
WEB: www.honeywell.com
SIC: 3724 Aircraft engines & engine parts
PA: Honeywell International Inc.
855 S Mint St
Charlotte NC 28202
704 627-6200

(G-14670)
HOWARD STRUCTURAL STEEL INC
807 Veterans Mem Pkwy (48601-1498)
PHONE................................989 752-3000
Kenneth Hioward Westlund Jr, *President*
James Englehardt, *Vice Pres*
Sharon K Westlund, *Admin Sec*
EMP: 25 EST: 1974
SQ FT: 20,000
SALES (est): 6.6MM **Privately Held**
WEB: www.howard-steel.com
SIC: 3441 1791 3535 5033 Building components, structural steel; structural steel erection; conveyors & conveying equipment; roofing, asphalt & sheet metal

(G-14671)
INNOVATIVE APPAREL PRINTING
1921 Wood St (48602-1190)
PHONE................................989 395-1204
EMP: 4 EST: 2015
SALES (est): 114.4K **Privately Held**
WEB: www.iaprinting.com
SIC: 2752 Commercial printing, lithographic

(G-14672)
J & B PRODUCTS LTD
Also Called: Ultra Derm Systems
2201 S Michigan Ave (48602-1293)
PHONE................................989 792-6119
Joseph Bommarito, *CEO*
Linda Bommarito, *President*
▼ EMP: 15 EST: 1979
SQ FT: 22,000
SALES (est): 1.9MM **Privately Held**
SIC: 3648 Lighting equipment

(G-14673)
JCP LLC
Also Called: Johnson Carbide Products
1422 S 25th St (48601-6601)
PHONE................................989 754-7496
James Foulds, *Mng Member*
◆ EMP: 28 EST: 2009 **Privately Held**
WEB: www.johnsoncarbide.com
SIC: 3823 Industrial instrmnts msrmnt display/control process variable

(G-14674)
JORDAN ADVERTISING INC
Also Called: Barrett Advertising
321 Lyon St (48602-1522)
PHONE................................989 792-7446
Steven D Jordan, *President*
EMP: 7 EST: 1930
SQ FT: 10,000
SALES (est): 333.7K **Privately Held**
WEB: www.barrettsign.net
SIC: 3993 Signs & advertising specialties

(G-14675)
K2 STONEWORKS LLC
5195 Dixie Hwy (48601-5569)
PHONE................................989 790-3250
Jeff Koski, *Owner*
EMP: 15 EST: 2014
SALES (est): 681.3K **Privately Held**
WEB: www.k2stoneworks.com
SIC: 3281 Marble, building: cut & shaped; granite, cut & shaped; limestone, cut & shaped

(G-14676)
KAPEX MANUFACTURING LLC
3130 Christy Way N Ste 3 (48603-2258)
P.O. Box 5589 (48603-0589)
PHONE................................989 928-4993
Timothy Tapert,
James Kowalczyk,
EMP: 7 EST: 1964
SQ FT: 10,000 **Privately Held**
WEB: www.kapexmanf.com
SIC: 3544 3549 3559 Special dies & tools; metalworking machinery; plastics working machinery

(G-14677)
KERNEL BURNER
6171 Tittabawassee Rd (48603-9627)
PHONE................................989 792-2808
Gerald Savage, *Principal*
EMP: 5 EST: 2007
SALES (est): 234.8K **Privately Held**
WEB: www.thekernelburner.com
SIC: 3567 Electrical furnaces, ovens & heating devices, exc. induction

(G-14678)
KLC ENTERPRISES INC
4765 E Holland Rd (48601-9463)
P.O. Box 42, Birch Run (48415-0042)
PHONE................................989 753-0496
Scott Counts, *President*
Susan Auernhammer, *Corp Secy*
Donald S Counts, *VP Mfg*
Donald Counts, *VP Mfg*
Kathy Tucker, *Buyer*
EMP: 23 EST: 1969
SQ FT: 10,000
SALES (est): 2.4MM **Privately Held**
SIC: 3829 Measuring & controlling devices

(G-14679)
KLOPP GROUP LLC
Also Called: B.K. Vending
3535 Bay Rd Ste 3 (48603-2464)
PHONE................................877 256-4528
Brian Klopp, *Mng Member*
EMP: 6
SALES (est): 650K **Privately Held**
SIC: 2064 Candy & other confectionery products

(G-14680)
KUKA ASSEMBLY AND TEST CORP (DH)
5675 Dixie Hwy (48601-5828)
P.O. Box 1968 (48605-1968)
PHONE................................989 220-3088
Scott Orendach, *President*
Richard Boaz, *Project Mgr*
Brian Hoy, *Mfg Mgr*
Scott Green, *Engineer*
Michael Grusnick, *Engineer*
▲ EMP: 160 EST: 1948
SQ FT: 120,000
SALES (est): 74.5MM **Privately Held**
WEB: www.kuka-at.com
SIC: 3829 3549 Testing equipment: abrasion, shearing strength, etc.; assembly machines, including robotic
HQ: Kuka Ag
Zugspitzstr. 140
Augsburg BY 86165
821 797-50

(G-14681)
KUREK TOOL INC
4735 Dixie Hwy (48601-4259)
PHONE................................989 777-5300
Joann Kurek, *President*
EMP: 11 EST: 1965
SQ FT: 7,000
SALES (est): 1.6MM **Privately Held**
WEB: www.kurektool.com
SIC: 3544 3545 Special dies & tools; machine tool accessories

Saginaw - Saginaw County (G-14682)

(G-14682)
LAFARGE NORTH AMERICA INC
1701 N 1st St (48601-1063)
PHONE..................989 399-1005
Frances Sargent, *Branch Mgr*
EMP: 4
SALES (corp-wide): 25.3B **Privately Held**
WEB: www.lafarge-na.com
SIC: 3241 Cement, hydraulic
HQ: Lafarge North America Inc.
8700 W Bryn Mawr Ave # 30
Chicago IL 60631
773 372-1000

(G-14683)
LINEAR MOTION LLC
Also Called: Thomson Aerospace & Defense
628 N Hamilton St (48602-4301)
PHONE..................989 759-8300
Nathan Hendrix, *President*
Craig Palmer, *President*
▲ EMP: 170 EST: 2002
SALES (est): 49.7MM **Privately Held**
WEB: www.umbragroup.com
SIC: 3728 Aircraft parts & equipment
HQ: Umbragroup Spa
Via Valter Baldaccini 1
Foligno PG 06034
074 232-1168

(G-14684)
LOGGERS BREWING CO
1215 S River Rd (48609-5208)
PHONE..................989 401-3085
EMP: 5 EST: 2015
SALES (est): 106.6K **Privately Held**
WEB: www.loggersbrewingcompany.com
SIC: 2082 5084 Beer (alcoholic beverage); brewery products manufacturing machinery, commercial

(G-14685)
M CURRY CORPORATION
Also Called: Endurance Carbide
4475 Marlea Dr (48601-7203)
P.O. Box 269, Bridgeport (48722-0269)
PHONE..................989 777-7950
Patrick H Curry, *President*
Brian Hammond, *Vice Pres*
Mark Springer, *Prdtn Mgr*
Ted Cymbal, *Purchasing*
Mark Porath, *Sales Executive*
EMP: 26 EST: 1961
SQ FT: 18,000
SALES (est): 3.8MM **Privately Held**
WEB: www.endurancecarbide.com
SIC: 3545 3544 Drill bushings (drilling jig); gauges (machine tool accessories); punches, forming & stamping; special dies & tools

(G-14686)
MARKETING VI GROUP INC
Also Called: Sir Speedy
4414 Bay Rd Ste 1 (48603-5222)
PHONE..................989 793-3933
Carol Henthorn, *President*
EMP: 7 EST: 1988
SQ FT: 2,500
SALES (est): 492.2K **Privately Held**
WEB: www.sirspeedy.com
SIC: 2752 2796 2791 Commercial printing, lithographic; platemaking services; typesetting

(G-14687)
MARSHALL TOOL SERVICE INC
2700 Iowa Ave (48601-5459)
P.O. Box 480, Bridgeport (48722-0480)
PHONE..................989 777-3137
EMP: 9
SALES (est): 997.1K **Privately Held**
SIC: 3599 5251 Mfg Industrial Machinery Ret Hardware

(G-14688)
MASTERS TOOL & DIE INC
4485 Marlea Dr (48601-7203)
PHONE..................989 777-2450
Charles Smith, *President*
EMP: 6 EST: 1965
SQ FT: 5,000
SALES (est): 951.5K **Privately Held**
SIC: 3544 Jigs & fixtures

(G-14689)
MCCRAY PRESS
2710 State St (48602-3736)
PHONE..................989 792-8681
Robert D Mc Cray, *Partner*
Flora E McCray, *Partner*
EMP: 13 EST: 1956
SALES (est): 169.1K **Privately Held**
SIC: 3089 2672 Laminating of plastic; coated & laminated paper

(G-14690)
MEAN ERECTORS INC
1928 Wilson Ave (48638-6704)
PHONE..................989 737-3285
Todd B Culver, *President*
EMP: 12 EST: 2001
SALES (est): 310.2K **Privately Held**
WEB: www.meanerectors.com
SIC: 1791 3312 Iron work, structural; structural shapes & pilings, steel

(G-14691)
MEANS INDUSTRIES INC (HQ)
3715 E Washington Rd (48601-9623)
PHONE..................989 754-1433
Jeremy Holt, *President*
Ed Shemanski, *Vice Pres*
Edward Shemanski, *Vice Pres*
Amy Moore, *Senior Buyer*
Ellen Erway, *Purch Agent*
◆ EMP: 175 EST: 1922
SQ FT: 40,000
SALES (est): 153.7MM
SALES (corp-wide): 2.4B **Privately Held**
WEB: www.meansindustries.com
SIC: 3714 3465 Transmission housings or parts, motor vehicle; automotive stampings
PA: Amsted Industries Incorporated
180 N Stetson Ave # 1800
Chicago IL 60601
312 645-1700

(G-14692)
MEANS INDUSTRIES INC
1811 S Jefferson Ave (48601-2825)
PHONE..................989 754-0312
EMP: 14
SALES (corp-wide): 2.4B **Privately Held**
WEB: www.meansindustries.com
SIC: 3714 3465 Transmission housings or parts, motor vehicle; automotive stampings
HQ: Means Industries, Inc.
3715 E Washington Rd
Saginaw MI 48601
989 754-1433

(G-14693)
MEANS INDUSTRIES INC
1860 S Jefferson Ave (48601-2824)
PHONE..................989 754-3300
Paul Barghahn, *Business Mgr*
Tom Meier, *Vice Pres*
Jim Schroeder, *Project Mgr*
Steve Wynn, *Maint Spvr*
Dave Faulmann, *Production*
EMP: 6
SALES (corp-wide): 2.4B **Privately Held**
WEB: www.meansindustries.com
SIC: 3465 3469 Body parts, automobile: stamped metal; metal stampings
HQ: Means Industries, Inc.
3715 E Washington Rd
Saginaw MI 48601
989 754-1433

(G-14694)
MEGGITT
628 N Hamilton St (48602-4301)
PHONE..................989 759-8327
EMP: 5
SALES (est): 496.4K **Privately Held**
SIC: 3728 Mfg Aircraft Parts/Equipment

(G-14695)
MENU PULSE INC
1901 Kollen St (48602-2730)
PHONE..................989 708-1207
Andrew Lay, *President*
EMP: 7 EST: 2016
SALES (est): 290.6K **Privately Held**
WEB: www.menupulse.com
SIC: 8742 7372 Marketing consulting services; application computer software
PA: Lay Enterprises, Inc
1901 Kollen St
Saginaw MI
989 708-1207

(G-14696)
MERRILL TECHNOLOGIES GROUP
Also Called: Merrill Aviation & Defense
1023 S Wheeler St (48602-1112)
PHONE..................989 921-1490
Tony Monk, *Teacher*
EMP: 20
SALES (corp-wide): 191.1MM **Privately Held**
WEB: www.merrilltg.com
SIC: 3724 3728 8734 Aircraft engines & engine parts; aircraft parts & equipment; testing laboratories; product certification, safety or performance
PA: Merrill Technologies Group, Inc.
400 Florence St
Saginaw MI 48602
989 791-6676

(G-14697)
MERRILL TECHNOLOGIES GROUP INC (PA)
Also Called: Merrill Tool Holding Company
400 Florence St (48602-1203)
PHONE..................989 791-6676
Robert Yackel, *President*
Gary Yackel, *Chairman*
Rob Schmaltz, *Business Mgr*
Robin Schmaltz, *Business Mgr*
Mary K Yackel, *Corp Secy*
▲ EMP: 70 EST: 1969
SQ FT: 100,000
SALES (est): 191.1MM **Privately Held**
WEB: www.merrilltg.com
SIC: 3443 3599 8734 8711 Fabricated plate work (boiler shop); machine & other job shop work; testing laboratories; engineering services; aircraft engines & engine parts

(G-14698)
MICHIGAN SATELLITE
Also Called: Future Vision
3215 Christy Way S (48603-2245)
PHONE..................989 792-6666
John Dawson, *President*
EMP: 19 EST: 2001
SALES (est): 1.1MM **Privately Held**
WEB: www.primestar1.com
SIC: 3663 1731 Space satellite communications equipment; electrical work

(G-14699)
MICRON PRECISION MACHINING INC (PA)
225 E Morley Dr (48601-9482)
PHONE..................989 759-1030
Darrin Krogman, *President*
Matt Doherty, *Foreman/Supr*
Heidi McNoy, *Opers Staff*
Dan Rytlewski, *Sales Mgr*
Thomas Steudle, *Prgrmr*
EMP: 37 EST: 2000
SQ FT: 4,000
SALES (est): 6.1MM **Privately Held**
WEB: www.micronpm.com
SIC: 3599 Machine shop, jobbing & repair

(G-14700)
MIDWEST MARKETING INC
Also Called: Sweney-Kern Manufacturing
105 Lyon St (48602-1565)
P.O. Box 6858 (48608-6858)
PHONE..................989 793-9393
Randy Kern, *President*
Diane Sweney, *Vice Pres*
EMP: 7 EST: 1994
SQ FT: 21,000
SALES (est): 1.3MM **Privately Held**
SIC: 2048 Bird food, prepared

(G-14701)
MISTEQUAY GROUP LTD
1212 N Niagara St (48602-4742)
PHONE..................989 752-7700
Ryan West, *Engineer*
Ken Jones, *Branch Mgr*
EMP: 29 **Privately Held**
WEB: www.mistequaygroup.com
SIC: 3544 Special dies & tools
PA: Mistequay Group Ltd.
1156 N Niagara St
Saginaw MI 48602

(G-14702)
MISTEQUAY GROUP LTD (PA)
Also Called: Mistequay NDT Center
1156 N Niagara St (48602-4741)
PHONE..................989 752-7700
James Paas, *President*
Wayne Bamberg, *Mfg Spvr*
Craig Cory, *Engineer*
Darwin Eschenbacher, *Engineer*
Gary Steele, *CFO*
▲ EMP: 13 EST: 1978
SQ FT: 22,500
SALES (est): 21.9MM **Privately Held**
WEB: www.mistequaygroup.com
SIC: 3544 3714 3812 3545 Special dies, tools, jigs & fixtures; motor vehicle parts & accessories; search & navigation equipment; machine tool accessories

(G-14703)
MKR FABRICATING INC
Also Called: Companions' Cuisine
810 N Towerline Rd (48601-9466)
PHONE..................989 753-8100
Rob Webb, *President*
Jennifer Eaton, *Principal*
Jake Mattes, *Principal*
Meghann Webb, *Principal*
Robert Hickey, *Vice Pres*
EMP: 18 EST: 1987
SALES (est): 4.5MM **Privately Held**
WEB: www.mkrfab.com
SIC: 3441 Fabricated structural metal

(G-14704)
MORNING STAR
306 E Remington St (48601-2508)
PHONE..................989 755-2660
Charles Bird, *Owner*
EMP: 4 EST: 2007
SALES (est): 270.8K **Privately Held**
WEB: www.morningstardetail.com
SIC: 2741 2711 Miscellaneous publishing; newspapers, publishing & printing

(G-14705)
MOTION INDUSTRIES INC
D.P. Brown of Detroit
1646 Champagne Dr N (48604-9202)
PHONE..................989 771-0200
Chuck Mort, *Branch Mgr*
Carol Plaza, *Manager*
EMP: 9
SALES (corp-wide): 16.5B **Publicly Held**
WEB: www.motionindustries.com
SIC: 5063 5085 3535 Power transmission equipment, electric; industrial supplies; conveyors & conveying equipment
HQ: Motion Industries, Inc.
1605 Alton Rd
Birmingham AL 35210
205 956-1122

(G-14706)
NATIONAL PATTERN INC
5900 Sherman Rd (48604-1199)
PHONE..................989 755-6274
C Gregory Larson, *President*
Debbie Fisher, *Purchasing*
Greg Larson, *CFO*
Erdeen Frank, *Human Res Mgr*
▲ EMP: 22 EST: 1978
SQ FT: 25,000
SALES (est): 946.1K **Privately Held**
WEB: www.nationalpattern.com
SIC: 3543 Industrial patterns

(G-14707)
NATIONAL ROOFG & SHTMTL CO INC
200 Lee St (48602-1443)
PHONE..................989 964-0557
Brian Ora, *Branch Mgr*
EMP: 80
SALES (corp-wide): 16.8MM **Privately Held**
WEB: www.nr-sm.com
SIC: 1761 3444 Roofing contractor; sheet metal specialties, not stamped

GEOGRAPHIC SECTION

Saginaw - Saginaw County (G-14733)

PA: National Roofing And Sheet Metal Co., Inc.
4130 Flint Asphalt Dr
Burton MI 48529
810 742-7373

(G-14708)
NATIONWIDE NETWORK INC (PA)
Also Called: Nationwide Intelligence
3401 Peale Dr (48602-3472)
P.O. Box 1922 (48605-1922)
PHONE..................989 793-0123
David Oppermann, *President*
EMP: 3 **EST:** 1974
SALES (est): 1.1MM **Privately Held**
SIC: 7389 4724 7929 2721 Convention & show services; travel agencies; entertainment service; periodicals: publishing only

(G-14709)
NESTLE USA INC
222 E Morley Dr (48601)
PHONE..................989 755-7940
EMP: 208
SALES (corp-wide): 92.3B **Privately Held**
WEB: www.nestleusa.com
SIC: 2023 Dry, condensed, evaporated dairy products
HQ: Nestle Usa, Inc.
1812 N Moore St Ste 118
Rosslyn VA 22209
440 264-7249

(G-14710)
NEXTEER AUTOMOTIVE CORPORATION
Also Called: Nexteer Saginaw
3900 E Holland Rd (48601-9494)
PHONE..................989 757-5000
Tammy Lounsberry, *Business Mgr*
Andrew Stewart, *Plant Mgr*
Jason Hatfield, *Opers Mgr*
Mike Kettler, *Opers Mgr*
Jim Winiarski, *Mfg Staff*
EMP: 300 **Privately Held**
WEB: www.nexteer.com
SIC: 5531 3711 3545 3714 Automobile & truck equipment & parts; motor vehicles & car bodies; tools & accessories for machine tools; steering mechanisms, motor vehicle
HQ: Nexteer Automotive Corporation
1272 Doris Rd
Auburn Hills MI 48326

(G-14711)
NEXTEER AUTOMOTIVE CORPORATION
Nexteer Saginaw Prototype Ctr
2975 Nodular Dr (48601-9264)
PHONE..................989 754-1920
Robert Remenar, *Branch Mgr*
EMP: 252 **Privately Held**
WEB: www.nexteer.com
SIC: 3714 Motor vehicle parts & accessories
HQ: Nexteer Automotive Corporation
1272 Doris Rd
Auburn Hills MI 48326

(G-14712)
NEXTEER AUTOMOTIVE CORPORATION
Also Called: Nexteer - Saginaw Plant 7
3900 E Holland Rd (48601-9494)
PHONE..................989 757-5000
Robert Remenar, *Branch Mgr*
Joshua Schuler, *Software Dev*
EMP: 252 **Privately Held**
WEB: www.nexteer.com
SIC: 3714 Gears, motor vehicle
HQ: Nexteer Automotive Corporation
1272 Doris Rd
Auburn Hills MI 48326

(G-14713)
NEXTEER AUTOMOTIVE CORPORATION
Also Called: Nexteer - Saginaw Plant 5
3900 E Holland Rd (48601-9494)
PHONE..................989 757-5000
Robert Remenar, *Branch Mgr*
EMP: 252 **Privately Held**
WEB: www.nexteer.com

SIC: 3714 Axles, motor vehicle
HQ: Nexteer Automotive Corporation
1272 Doris Rd
Auburn Hills MI 48326

(G-14714)
NEXTEER AUTOMOTIVE CORPORATION
Also Called: Nexteer - Plant 6
3900 E Holland Rd (48601-9494)
PHONE..................989 757-5000
Roger Johnson, *Engineer*
Andrew Stewart, *Branch Mgr*
EMP: 252 **Privately Held**
WEB: www.nexteer.com
SIC: 3714 Motor vehicle parts & accessories
HQ: Nexteer Automotive Corporation
1272 Doris Rd
Auburn Hills MI 48326

(G-14715)
NEXTEER AUTOMOTIVE CORPORATION
Also Called: Nexteer - Saginaw Plant 4
3900 E Holland Rd (48601-9494)
PHONE..................989 757-5000
Robert Remenar, *Branch Mgr*
EMP: 252 **Privately Held**
WEB: www.nexteer.com
SIC: 3714 Axles, motor vehicle
HQ: Nexteer Automotive Corporation
1272 Doris Rd
Auburn Hills MI 48326

(G-14716)
NEXTEER AUTOMOTIVE CORPORATION
Also Called: Nexteer - Saginaw Plant 3
3900 E Holland Rd (48601-9494)
PHONE..................989 757-5000
Dragi Kuzmanovski, *Opers Mgr*
EMP: 252 **Privately Held**
WEB: www.nexteer.com
SIC: 3714 Motor vehicle parts & accessories
HQ: Nexteer Automotive Corporation
1272 Doris Rd
Auburn Hills MI 48326

(G-14717)
NEXTEER AUTOMOTIVE CORPORATION
Nexteer Plant 8
3900 E Holland Rd (48601-9494)
PHONE..................989 757-5000
Todd Banning, *Plant Mgr*
EMP: 100 **Privately Held**
WEB: www.nexteer.com
SIC: 3714 Motor vehicle parts & accessories
HQ: Nexteer Automotive Corporation
1272 Doris Rd
Auburn Hills MI 48326

(G-14718)
NEXTEER AUTOMOTIVE CORPORATION
Also Called: Nexteer - Plant 6 E-Bike
3900 E Holland Rd (48601-9494)
PHONE..................989 757-5000
John Riester, *Director*
EMP: 50 **Privately Held**
WEB: www.nexteer.com
SIC: 3714 Motor vehicle parts & accessories
HQ: Nexteer Automotive Corporation
1272 Doris Rd
Auburn Hills MI 48326

(G-14719)
NEXTEER AUTOMOTIVE CORPORATION
Also Called: Nexteer - Saginaw Plant 1
3900 E Holland Rd (48601-9494)
PHONE..................989 757-5000
Robert Remenar, *Branch Mgr*
EMP: 252 **Privately Held**
WEB: www.nexteer.com
SIC: 3714 Power steering equipment, motor vehicle
HQ: Nexteer Automotive Corporation
1272 Doris Rd
Auburn Hills MI 48326

(G-14720)
NEXTEER AUTOMOTIVE CORPORATION
Nexteer - Saginaw Plant 18
5153 Hess Rd (48601)
PHONE..................989 757-5000
Robert Remenar, *Branch Mgr*
EMP: 252 **Privately Held**
WEB: www.nexteer.com
SIC: 3714 Motor vehicle steering systems & parts
HQ: Nexteer Automotive Corporation
1272 Doris Rd
Auburn Hills MI 48326

(G-14721)
NEXTEER AUTOMOTIVE GROUP LTD
3900 E Holland Rd (48601-9494)
PHONE..................989 757-5000
Zhao Guibin, *CEO*
Bresson Laurent Robert, *President*
Perkins Joseph Michael, *Vice Pres*
Joshua Golimbieski, *Engineer*
Venkata Kotta, *Engineer*
EMP: 5179 **EST:** 2014
SALES (est): 30.7MM **Privately Held**
WEB: www.nexteer.com
SIC: 3714 Motor vehicle steering systems & parts
HQ: Nexteer Automotive Corporation
1272 Doris Rd
Auburn Hills MI 48326

(G-14722)
NORTHERN SIERRA CORPORATION
5450 East Rd (48601-9748)
PHONE..................989 777-4784
Ross A Lake, *President*
EMP: 5 **EST:** 2003
SQ FT: 10,500
SALES (est): 734.3K **Privately Held**
SIC: 3543 Industrial patterns

(G-14723)
OSCODA PLASTICS INC
525 W Morley Dr (48601-9485)
PHONE..................989 739-6900
Tom Saeli, *CEO*
EMP: 7 **Privately Held**
WEB: www.oscodaplastics.com
SIC: 2821 Plastics materials & resins
PA: Oscoda Plastics, Inc.
5585 N Huron Ave
Oscoda MI 48750

(G-14724)
PAPER MACHINE SERVICE INDS (PA)
3075 Shattuck Rd Ste 801 (48603-3299)
PHONE..................989 695-2646
Mark R Baluha, *Owner*
EMP: 12 **EST:** 1987
SQ FT: 15,000
SALES (est): 2MM **Privately Held**
WEB: www.papermachine.com
SIC: 3554 Paper industries machinery

(G-14725)
PARAMOUNT TECHNOLOGIES INC (PA)
3636 Christy Way W (48601-7200)
PHONE..................248 960-0909
Salim A Khalife, *CEO*
Beth Brademeyer, *Partner*
Beth Wobbema, *Partner*
Barry Thompson, *VP Sales*
Joe Pelegrino, *Sales Staff*
EMP: 25 **EST:** 1995
SALES (est): 3.8MM **Privately Held**
WEB: www.paramountworkplace.com
SIC: 7372 Business oriented computer software

(G-14726)
PEPSI BEVERAGES CO
100 S Outer Dr (48601-6330)
PHONE..................989 754-0435
Mike Fraser, *Principal*
EMP: 5 **EST:** 2016

SALES (est): 96.2K **Privately Held**
WEB: www.pepsico.com
SIC: 2086 Carbonated soft drinks, bottled & canned

(G-14727)
PEPSI-COLA METRO BTLG CO INC
736 N Outer Dr (48601-6236)
PHONE..................989 755-1020
Matt Chapelain, *Branch Mgr*
EMP: 6
SALES (corp-wide): 70.3B **Publicly Held**
WEB: www.pepsico.com
SIC: 2086 5078 Carbonated soft drinks, bottled & canned; beverage coolers
HQ: Pepsi-Cola Metropolitan Bottling Company, Inc.
1111 Westchester Ave
White Plains NY 10604
914 767-6000

(G-14728)
PILKINGTON NORTH AMERICA INC
1400 Weiss St (48602-5278)
PHONE..................989 754-2956
Dan Corl, *Manager*
EMP: 4 **Privately Held**
WEB: www.pilkington.com
SIC: 3211 Flat glass
HQ: Pilkington North America, Inc.
811 Madison Ave Fl 3
Toledo OH 43604
419 247-3731

(G-14729)
PLASTATECH ENGINEERING LTD (PA)
725 E Morley Dr (48601)
PHONE..................989 754-6500
John C Burt, *Ch of Bd*
Tom Saeli, *President*
Laura Storey, *Business Mgr*
Shawn Sny, *Exec VP*
Jason Tunney, *Exec VP*
EMP: 80 **EST:** 1987
SQ FT: 125,000
SALES (est): 15.5MM **Privately Held**
WEB: www.plastatech.com
SIC: 2295 Laminating of fabrics

(G-14730)
POOR BOY WOODWORKS INC
3075 Shattuck Rd (48603-3299)
PHONE..................989 799-9440
EMP: 17 **EST:** 2017
SALES (est): 347K **Privately Held**
WEB: www.poorboywoodworks.com
SIC: 2431 Millwork

(G-14731)
PSI MARINE INC
Also Called: Tideslide Mooring Products
5690 Hackett Rd (48603-9612)
PHONE..................989 695-2646
Renee Baluha, *CEO*
▼ **EMP:** 14 **EST:** 2000
SQ FT: 5,000
SALES (est): 1MM **Privately Held**
WEB: www.tideslide.com
SIC: 3441 3531 4491 Fabricated structural metal for ships; marine related equipment; docks, piers & terminals

(G-14732)
R & R READY-MIX INC (PA)
6050 Melbourne Rd (48604-9710)
PHONE..................989 753-3862
Russell A Willett, *President*
Richard Willett, *Corp Secy*
EMP: 10 **EST:** 1958
SALES (est): 2.5MM **Privately Held**
WEB: www.rrreadymix.com
SIC: 3273 Ready-mixed concrete

(G-14733)
R & S CUTTER GRIND INC
2870 Universal Dr (48603-2411)
PHONE..................989 791-3100
Richard Terry, *President*
Alan McNalley, *Manager*
EMP: 6 **EST:** 1979
SQ FT: 3,700

Saginaw - Saginaw County (G-14734) — GEOGRAPHIC SECTION

SALES (est): 984.5K **Privately Held**
WEB: www.rscuttergrind.com
SIC: 3599 7699 Grinding castings for the trade; industrial tool grinding

(G-14734)
R A TOWNSEND COMPANY
2845 Mccarty Rd (48603-2442)
PHONE..........989 498-7000
Therese M Muszynski, *Branch Mgr*
Gwen Siler, *Consultant*
EMP: 7
SALES (corp-wide): 24.2MM **Privately Held**
WEB: www.ratownsend.com
SIC: 3088 Plastics plumbing fixtures
PA: R. A. Townsend Company
1100 N Bagley St
Alpena MI 49707
989 354-3105

(G-14735)
RANGER TOOL & DIE CO
317 S Westervelt Rd (48604-1330)
PHONE..........989 754-1403
John Kuhnle, *President*
Tom Schick, *Vice Pres*
Brian Keidel, *Director*
EMP: 19 EST: 1954
SQ FT: 16,000
SALES (est): 1.8MM **Privately Held**
WEB: www.ranger-tool.com
SIC: 3544 7692 3469 Special dies & tools; welding repair; metal stampings

(G-14736)
REIMOLD PRINTING CORPORATION
Also Called: Cuadvantage Mktg Solutions
5171 Blackbeak Dr (48604-9704)
PHONE..........989 799-0784
Ronald Reimold, *President*
Michael White, *Owner*
Mary Reimold, *Corp Secy*
Brittney Coney, *Administration*
Mike Hatfield, *Representative*
EMP: 9 EST: 1964
SQ FT: 5,000
SALES (est): 1.4MM **Privately Held**
WEB: www.reimoldprinting.com
SIC: 2752 Commercial printing, offset

(G-14737)
RHINEVAULT OLSEN MACHINE & TL
2533 Carrollton Rd (48604-2455)
PHONE..........989 753-4363
Glen Olsen, *President*
Michael Olsen, *Vice Pres*
EMP: 6 EST: 1932
SQ FT: 5,000
SALES (est): 480K **Privately Held**
WEB: www.olsentool.tripod.com
SIC: 3545 Tools & accessories for machine tools

(G-14738)
ROBBIE DS LLC
3175 Shattuck Arms Blvd (48603-6822)
PHONE..........989 992-0153
Robbie Delgado, *Mng Member*
EMP: 4 EST: 2018
SALES (est): 57.1K **Privately Held**
SIC: 2599 Food wagons, restaurant

(G-14739)
ROCK REDI MIX LLC
Also Called: Rock Products
5606 N Westervelt Rd (48604-1238)
PHONE..........989 754-5861
William Webber, *Principal*
EMP: 7 EST: 2011
SALES (est): 623.3K **Privately Held**
SIC: 3273 5999 Ready-mixed concrete; safety supplies & equipment; concrete products, pre-cast

(G-14740)
ROSE LAILA
420 Hancock St (48602-4221)
PHONE..........989 598-0950
Jacqueline Carrington, *Principal*
EMP: 4 EST: 2015
SALES (est): 76.7K **Privately Held**
WEB: www.lailarose.com
SIC: 3171 Handbags, women's

(G-14741)
RPC COMPANY
Also Called: A H Webster
1708 N Michigan Ave (48602-5343)
P.O. Box 1944 (48605-1944)
PHONE..........989 752-3618
George Roe, *President*
Holly Duncan, *Recruiter*
EMP: 10 EST: 1935
SQ FT: 8,000
SALES (est): 2.5MM **Privately Held**
WEB: www.workwearstore.com
SIC: 5136 5699 2759 2284 Sportswear, men's & boys'; work clothing, men's & boys'; work clothing; commercial printing; embroidery thread

(G-14742)
S F S CARBIDE TOOL
Also Called: Service File Sharpening
4480 Marlea Dr (48601-7203)
P.O. Box 394, Clawson (48017-0394)
PHONE..........989 777-3890
Robert White, *Owner*
EMP: 5 EST: 1960
SALES (est): 416.7K **Privately Held**
WEB: www.sfscarbide.com
SIC: 3545 7699 5251 Cutting tools for machine tools; knife, saw & tool sharpening & repair; tools

(G-14743)
SAFETY-KLEEN SYSTEMS INC
3899 Wolf Rd (48601-9256)
PHONE..........989 753-3261
Steve Tratt, *Branch Mgr*
Andrew Ontiveros, *Manager*
EMP: 4
SALES (corp-wide): 3.1B **Publicly Held**
WEB: www.safety-kleen.com
SIC: 7359 3559 Equipment rental & leasing; degreasing machines, automotive & industrial
HQ: Safety-Kleen Systems, Inc.
42 Longwater Dr
Norwell MA 02061
972 265-2000

(G-14744)
SAGINAW BEARING COMPANY
1400 Agricola Dr (48604-9771)
PHONE..........989 752-3169
Robert L Pieschke Sr, *President*
Curtis J Olsen, *Vice Pres*
EMP: 10 EST: 1920
SQ FT: 18,000
SALES (est): 1.6MM **Privately Held**
WEB: www.saginawbearing.com
SIC: 3568 Bearings, bushings & blocks

(G-14745)
SAGINAW CONTROL & ENGRG INC (PA)
Also Called: SCE
95 Midland Rd (48638-5791)
PHONE..........989 799-6871
Harold C Baldauf, *Ch of Bd*
Frederick H May Jr, *President*
John Garner, *Prdtn Mgr*
David Baldauf, *Treasurer*
Janet Baldauf, *Admin Sec*
▲ EMP: 300 EST: 1963
SALES (est): 88.7MM **Privately Held**
WEB: www.saginawcontrol.com
SIC: 3699 3444 Electrical equipment & supplies; sheet metalwork

(G-14746)
SAGINAW INDUSTRIES LLC
1622 Champagne Dr N (48604-9202)
PHONE..........989 752-5514
James Kruske, *President*
Harold Boehler, *Vice Pres*
Chad Daenzer, *Project Engr*
EMP: 16 EST: 1998
SQ FT: 4,800
SALES (est): 2.3MM **Privately Held**
WEB: www.saginwindustries.com
SIC: 3553 Pattern makers' machinery, woodworking

(G-14747)
SAGINAW MACHINE SYSTEMS INC
Also Called: SMS
800 N Hamilton St (48602-4354)
PHONE..........989 753-8465
James Buckley, *President*
Theodore D Birkmeier, *Vice Pres*
Pamela K Baran, *CFO*
Gary Rottman, *Manager*
Raymond Beebe, *Director*
▲ EMP: 40 EST: 1854
SQ FT: 70,000
SALES (est): 11.9MM **Privately Held**
WEB: www.mag-sms.com
SIC: 3829 3548 3541 Measuring & controlling devices; arc welders, transformer-rectifier; resistance welders, electric; welding & cutting apparatus & accessories; drilling & boring machines
PA: Sms Holding Co., Inc
800 N Hamilton St
Saginaw MI 48602
989 753-8465

(G-14748)
SAGINAW PRODUCTS CORPORATION (PA)
Also Called: Cignys-Shields
68 Williamson St (48601-3246)
PHONE..........989 753-1411
James Kendall, *President*
Elaine D Rapanos, *Owner*
Dan Rutkowski, *Vice Pres*
Jeff Adams, *Engineer*
Jacob Bowden, *Engineer*
▲ EMP: 38 EST: 1920
SQ FT: 70,000
SALES (est): 23.9MM **Privately Held**
WEB: www.cignys.com
SIC: 3535 3423 Conveyors & conveying equipment; jacks; lifting, screw or ratchet (hand tools)

(G-14749)
SAGINAW PRODUCTS CORPORATION
5763 Dixie Hwy (48601-5916)
PHONE..........989 753-1411
EMP: 39
SALES (corp-wide): 23.9MM **Privately Held**
WEB: www.cignys.com
SIC: 3599 Machine shop, jobbing & repair
PA: Saginaw Products Corporation
68 Williamson St
Saginaw MI 48601
989 753-1411

(G-14750)
SAGINAW PRODUCTS CORPORATION
Also Called: Cignys
1320 S Graham Rd (48609-8832)
PHONE..........989 753-1411
Matthew Ware, *Manager*
EMP: 39
SALES (corp-wide): 23.9MM **Privately Held**
WEB: www.cignys.com
SIC: 3599 Machine shop, jobbing & repair
PA: Saginaw Products Corporation
68 Williamson St
Saginaw MI 48601
989 753-1411

(G-14751)
SAGINAW ROCK PRODUCTS CO
5606 N Westervelt Rd (48604-1238)
P.O. Box 39, Carrollton (48724-0039)
PHONE..........989 754-6589
Frances A Sargent, *President*
Marc Short, *General Mgr*
William Webber, *Admin Sec*
◆ EMP: 17 EST: 1946
SALES (est): 1.7MM **Privately Held**
WEB: www.1rockproducts.com
SIC: 3273 5032 1442 Ready-mixed concrete; aggregate; sand, construction; gravel; stone, crushed or broken; construction sand & gravel

(G-14752)
SANDLOT SPORTS
2900 Universal Dr (48603-2414)
PHONE..........989 835-9696
Adam McCauley, *Branch Mgr*
EMP: 11
SALES (corp-wide): 1.3MM **Privately Held**
WEB: www.sandlotsports301.com
SIC: 5949 2759 Sewing & needlework; screen printing
PA: Sandlot Sports
600 N Euclid Ave
Bay City MI 48706
989 391-9684

(G-14753)
SEVERANCE TOOL INDUSTRIES INC (PA)
3790 Orange St (48601-5549)
P.O. Box 1866 (48605-1866)
PHONE..........989 777-5500
Robert Severence Jr, *Ch of Bd*
John Pease, *President*
Helen McLaughlin, *Human Res Mgr*
Paul De Wyse, *Sales Executive*
EMP: 20 EST: 1930
SQ FT: 43,148
SALES (est): 2.6MM **Privately Held**
WEB: www.severancetools.com
SIC: 3545 Cutting tools for machine tools

(G-14754)
SEVERANCE TOOL INDUSTRIES INC
2150 Iowa Ave (48601-5521)
PHONE..........989 777-5500
Robert Severance, *President*
EMP: 4
SALES (corp-wide): 2.6MM **Privately Held**
WEB: www.severancetools.com
SIC: 3545 Cutting tools for machine tools
PA: Severance Tool Industries Inc.
3790 Orange St
Saginaw MI 48601
989 777-5500

(G-14755)
SHAY WATER CO INC
320 W Bristol St (48602-4610)
P.O. Box 1926 (48605-1926)
PHONE..........989 755-3221
James Shay, *President*
EMP: 22 EST: 1929
SQ FT: 10,000
SALES (est): 3.2MM **Privately Held**
WEB: www.shaywater.com
SIC: 2899 7389 Distilled water; coffee service

(G-14756)
SIGN IMAGE INC
8155 Gratiot Rd (48609-4876)
PHONE..........989 781-5229
John Eggers, *President*
EMP: 10 EST: 2001
SALES (est): 771.7K **Privately Held**
WEB: www.signimage1.com
SIC: 3993 7319 Electric signs; display advertising service

(G-14757)
SIGN PAL
2301 N Michigan Ave (48602-5817)
PHONE..........989 755-7773
Paul Labrenz, *Principal*
EMP: 7 EST: 2014
SALES (est): 260.5K **Privately Held**
SIC: 3993 Signs & advertising specialties

(G-14758)
SKORIC HEARING AID CENTER LLC
5462 State St (48603-3678)
P.O. Box 6131 (48608-6131)
PHONE..........248 961-4329
Boro Skoric, *Principal*
EMP: 5 EST: 2018
SALES (est): 301K **Privately Held**
WEB: www.beltoneskorichearing.com
SIC: 3842 Hearing aids

▲ = Import ▼ = Export
◆ = Import/Export

GEOGRAPHIC SECTION

Saginaw - Saginaw County (G-14786)

(G-14759)
SMS HOLDING CO INC (PA)
Also Called: SMS Group
800 N Hamilton St (48602-4354)
PHONE...................989 753-8465
Paul Chen, *President*
James Buckley, *President*
David Jay Albert, *Vice Pres*
William Spievak, *Vice Pres*
Pamela Baran, *CFO*
EMP: 150 **EST:** 1981
SQ FT: 100,000
SALES (est): 11.9MM **Privately Held**
SIC: 3541 Drilling & boring machines

(G-14760)
SPATZ BAKERY INC
1120 State St (48602-5438)
P.O. Box 6303 (48608-6303)
PHONE...................989 755-5551
Joseph Spatz, *President*
EMP: 12 **EST:** 1912
SQ FT: 4,000
SALES (est): 840.3K **Privately Held**
WEB: www.utrmichigan.com
SIC: 2051 Bakery: wholesale or wholesale/retail combined

(G-14761)
SPAULDING MACHINE CO INC
5366 East Rd (48601-9748)
PHONE...................989 777-0694
Lucile Brettrager, *Corp Secy*
Cindy Cherry, *Parts Mgr*
EMP: 26 **EST:** 1968
SQ FT: 5,600
SALES (est): 645.2K **Privately Held**
SIC: 3599 7692 Machine shop, jobbing & repair; welding repair

(G-14762)
SPAULDING MFG INC
5366 East Rd (48601-9748)
PHONE...................989 777-4550
Edward Brettrager, *President*
Michelle Desonia, *Principal*
Lucile Brettrager, *Corp Secy*
EMP: 25 **EST:** 1982
SALES (est): 3.6MM **Privately Held**
WEB: www.spauldingmfg.com
SIC: 3531 Road construction & maintenance machinery

(G-14763)
SPECIALTY MANUFACTURING INC
2210 Midland Rd (48603-3440)
PHONE...................989 790-9011
Kathleen Thompson, *President*
Amanda Schiedner, *Vice Pres*
Kristi Wiechmann, *Vice Pres*
Tony Rowe, *Plant Mgr*
Jordan Cooper, *Engineer*
EMP: 45
SQ FT: 25,000
SALES (est): 10MM **Privately Held**
WEB: www.smimfg.com
SIC: 3089 Injection molding of plastics

(G-14764)
SPITTING IMAGE PBLICATIONS LLC
1902 Ottawa St (48602-2743)
PHONE...................989 498-9459
Alfreda L Randle, *CEO*
EMP: 5 **EST:** 2018
SALES (est): 361.7K **Privately Held**
SIC: 2741 Miscellaneous publishing

(G-14765)
SPORTS JUNCTION (PA)
5605 State St (48603-3682)
PHONE...................989 791-5900
Arthur W Tolfree Jr, *Partner*
David A Bedford, *Partner*
EMP: 7 **EST:** 1987
SQ FT: 3,000
SALES (est): 785.5K **Privately Held**
WEB: www.sandlotsports301.com
SIC: 5699 5941 2759 2395 Sports apparel; team sports equipment; baseball equipment; basketball equipment; football equipment; screen printing; embroidery products, except schiffli machine

(G-14766)
STANDING COMPANY
Also Called: Standing Wheelchair Company
5848 Dixie Hwy (48601-5967)
PHONE...................989 746-9100
David J Maczik, *President*
Dawn Devereaux, *Human Resources*
Eddie Cox, *Mktg Coord*
EMP: 14 **EST:** 1990
SQ FT: 4,800
SALES (est): 2.1MM **Privately Held**
WEB: www.thestandingcompany.com
SIC: 3842 Wheelchairs

(G-14767)
STEERING SOLUTIONS - PLANT 3
3900 E Holland Rd (48601-9494)
PHONE...................989 757-5000
EMP: 12 **EST:** 2010
SALES (est): 1.9MM **Privately Held**
SIC: 3714 Motor vehicle parts & accessories

(G-14768)
SVRC INDUSTRIES INC (PA)
Also Called: Saginaw Vly Rehabilitation Ctr
203 S Washington Ave (48607-1208)
PHONE...................989 280-3038
Dean Emerson, *President*
Rose Jurek, *Vice Pres*
Matthew Muempfer, *Vice Pres*
Deborah Snyder, *Vice Pres*
Eve Flynn, *Plant Mgr*
EMP: 50 **EST:** 1962
SQ FT: 42,000
SALES (est): 9.9MM **Privately Held**
WEB: www.svrcindustries.com
SIC: 8331 7349 8299 3089 Vocational rehabilitation agency; building & office cleaning services; educational services; automotive parts, plastic

(G-14769)
SWEENEY METALWORKING LLC
4450 Marlea Dr (48601-7203)
P.O. Box 605, Bridgeport (48722-0605)
PHONE...................989 401-6531
Doug Sweeney, *Mng Member*
EMP: 12 **EST:** 2011
SQ FT: 13,000
SALES (est): 1.2MM **Privately Held**
WEB: www.sweeneymetalworking.com
SIC: 3544 Special dies, tools, jigs & fixtures

(G-14770)
SWEET CREATIONS
1375 Lathrup Ave (48638-4736)
PHONE...................989 327-1157
Ronald Stanley, *Principal*
EMP: 6 **EST:** 2011
SALES (est): 229.5K **Privately Held**
WEB: www.sweetcreationsmi.com
SIC: 2053 Cakes, bakery: frozen

(G-14771)
SWS - TRIMAC INC
Also Called: Special Welding Services
5225 Davis Rd (48604-9419)
PHONE...................989 791-4595
Gordon McIntosh, *President*
Ryan Stewart, *QC Mgr*
EMP: 33 **EST:** 1984
SQ FT: 20,000
SALES (est): 5.9MM **Privately Held**
WEB: www.sws-trimac.com
SIC: 8711 7692 3599 Engineering services; welding repair; machine shop, jobbing & repair

(G-14772)
T & M HOMES
1018 Lindsay Dr (48602-2933)
PHONE...................989 239-4699
Tim Ellithorpe, *Principal*
EMP: 4 **EST:** 2016
SALES (est): 86.7K **Privately Held**
WEB: www.tmloghomes.com
SIC: 2452 Prefabricated wood buildings

(G-14773)
TEAMTECH MOTORSPORTS SAFETY
6285 Bay Rd Ste 7 (48604-8798)
P.O. Box 5586 (48603-0586)
PHONE...................989 792-4880
Curt Tucker, *President*
EMP: 8 **EST:** 1988
SQ FT: 4,000
SALES (est): 968.5K **Privately Held**
WEB: www.teamtechmotorsports.com
SIC: 2399 3714 3728 3429 Seat belts, automobile & aircraft; motor vehicle parts & accessories; aircraft parts & equipment; aircraft hardware; marine hardware; scientific research agency; motor vehicle supplies & new parts

(G-14774)
THERMAGLAS CORPORATION
1930 S 23rd St (48601-2451)
P.O. Box 1426 (48605-1426)
PHONE...................517 754-7461
Julius Ott, *Ch of Bd*
Larry G Ott, *President*
Carol Kuhl, *President*
Ronald Aldrich, *Vice Pres*
EMP: 60 **EST:** 1961
SQ FT: 100,000
SALES (est): 3.6MM **Privately Held**
SIC: 3231 Insulating units, multiple-glazed: made from purchased glass

(G-14775)
THREADS BY BB
6285 Bay Rd Ste 4 (48604-8798)
PHONE...................989 401-7525
EMP: 5 **EST:** 2013
SALES (est): 55.7K **Privately Held**
WEB: www.bnbthreads.com
SIC: 2395 Embroidery products, except schiffli machine

(G-14776)
TIP TOP SCREW MANUFACTURI
725 W Morley Dr (48601-8405)
P.O. Box 2491 (48605-2491)
PHONE...................989 739-5157
EMP: 7 **EST:** 2014
SALES (est): 419K **Privately Held**
SIC: 3999 Manufacturing industries

(G-14777)
TOW-LINE TRAILERS
Also Called: Tow-Line Trailer Sales
4854 E Holland Rd (48601-9463)
PHONE...................989 752-0055
Freda Hewitt, *Owner*
EMP: 7 **EST:** 1984
SQ FT: 2,400
SALES (est): 1MM **Privately Held**
WEB: www.towlinetrailers.com
SIC: 5599 3715 5511 Utility trailers; truck trailers; trucks, tractors & trailers: new & used

(G-14778)
TREIB INC (PA)
Also Called: Central Metalizing & Machine
850 S Outer Dr (48604-6504)
PHONE...................989 752-4821
Kenneth Treib, *President*
David Treib, *Corp Secy*
Robert Treib, *Vice Pres*
EMP: 14 **EST:** 1955
SQ FT: 2,500
SALES (est): 7.1MM **Privately Held**
WEB: www.centralmetallizing.com
SIC: 3599 7542 5541 Machine shop, jobbing & repair; carwash, automatic; filling stations, gasoline

(G-14779)
TRI-CITY VINYL INC
640 E Morley Dr (48601-9401)
P.O. Box 3301 (48605-3301)
PHONE...................989 401-7992
John C Burt, *Ch of Bd*
Kathy Allen, *Vice Pres*
Mark Irwin, *Plant Mgr*
Robert Wood, *Manager*
EMP: 15 **EST:** 1975
SQ FT: 35,000
SALES (est): 1.9MM **Privately Held**
WEB: www.tricityvinyl.com
SIC: 2295 Resin or plastic coated fabrics

(G-14780)
TSUNAMI INC
Also Called: Easy Printing Center
6235 Gratiot Rd (48638-5987)
PHONE...................989 497-5200
Robert C Hansens, *President*
Richard M Welzein, *President*
EMP: 6 **EST:** 1972
SQ FT: 4,000
SALES (est): 630K **Privately Held**
WEB: www.easyprintingcenter.com
SIC: 2752 Commercial printing, offset

(G-14781)
TUPES OF SAGINAW INC
845 Windrush Ct Unit 15 (48609-6753)
P.O. Box 5989 (48603-0989)
PHONE...................989 799-1550
James R Kaylor, *President*
Sharon A Kaylor, *Admin Sec*
EMP: 13 **EST:** 1933
SALES (est): 1.8MM **Privately Held**
WEB: www.tupesinc.com
SIC: 5084 5169 5083 7692 Welding machinery & equipment; safety equipment; oxygen; acetylene; farm equipment parts & supplies; welding repair; welding apparatus

(G-14782)
TURNER BUSINESS FORMS INC (PA)
Also Called: Tbf Graphics
19 Slatestone Dr (48603-2890)
PHONE...................989 752-5540
Gregory J Turner, *President*
Gregory S Turner, *COO*
EMP: 25
SQ FT: 18,000
SALES: 2.9MM **Privately Held**
SIC: 2752 5112 2791 2789 Commercial printing, offset; business forms; typesetting; bookbinding & related work; commercial printing

(G-14783)
U S GRAPHITE INC (PA)
1620 E Holland Ave (48601-2999)
PHONE...................989 755-0441
Richard Gledhill, *President*
Rodger New, *Vice Pres*
Russ Homan, *Production*
Sarah Witgen, *Human Res Dir*
Victor Monroe, *Director*
▲ **EMP:** 44 **EST:** 1896
SQ FT: 290,000
SALES (est): 9.1MM **Privately Held**
WEB: www.usggledco.co.uk
SIC: 3624 3568 3053 Carbon & graphite products; power transmission equipment; gaskets, packing & sealing devices

(G-14784)
UNIVERSAL / DEVLIEG INC
1270 Agricola Dr (48604-9702)
PHONE...................989 752-3077
Sherry Carpenter, *President*
EMP: 10 **EST:** 2014
SQ FT: 10,000
SALES (est): 858.5K **Privately Held**
WEB: www.universaldevlieg.com
SIC: 3545 Cutting tools for machine tools

(G-14785)
UNIVERSAL/DEVLIEG LLC
1270 Agricola Dr (48604-9702)
PHONE...................989 752-7700
Sherry Carpenter, *Info Tech Mgr*
R James Paas,
Sherry R Carpenter,
James Shinners,
▲ **EMP:** 10 **EST:** 2005
SQ FT: 22,500
SALES (est): 2.5MM **Privately Held**
WEB: www.universaldevlieg.com
SIC: 3545 Tool holders

(G-14786)
VALLEY GLASS CO INC
2424 Midland Rd (48603-3444)
PHONE...................989 790-9342
Thomas J Witkowski, *President*
EMP: 8 **EST:** 1980
SQ FT: 5,600

Saginaw - Saginaw County (G-14787)   GEOGRAPHIC SECTION

SALES (est): 954.1K Privately Held
WEB: www.valleyglass.co
SIC: 1793 5231 3231 3211 Glass & glazing work; glass; products of purchased glass; flat glass

(G-14787)
VALLEY GROUP OF COMPANIES
Also Called: Valley Services
548 Shattuck Rd Ste B (48604-2468)
PHONE..................989 799-9669
EMP: 11
SQ FT: 7,000
SALES (est): 1.1MM Privately Held
SIC: 1799 1742 3625 Trade Contractor Drywall/Insulating Contractor Mfg Relays/Industrial Controls

(G-14788)
VALLEY STEEL COMPANY
1322 King St (48602-1403)
P.O. Box 1386 (48605-1386)
PHONE..................989 799-2600
Tom Maczik, *President*
Lois Maczik, *Vice Pres*
Gary E Maczik, *Admin Sec*
EMP: 28 EST: 1982
SQ FT: 20,000
SALES (est): 4.7MM Privately Held
SIC: 3441 Fabricated structural metal

(G-14789)
VARGAS & SONS
125 S Park Ave (48607-1547)
PHONE..................989 754-4636
Albert Vargas Jr, *Owner*
Mike Vargas, *VP Mktg*
EMP: 10 EST: 1947
SALES (est): 559.2K Privately Held
WEB: www.vargastortillas.com
SIC: 2051 Bread, cake & related products

(G-14790)
VERDONI PRODUCTIONS INC
Also Called: Hispanic Visions
5090 Overhill Dr (48603-1750)
PHONE..................989 790-0845
Ricardo Verdoni, *President*
Clarillen Verdoni, *Treasurer*
EMP: 5 EST: 1977
SQ FT: 7,000
SALES (est): 223.2K Privately Held
SIC: 7812 8742 2741 2721 Audio-visual program production; video tape production; management consulting services; marketing consulting services; newsletter publishing; technical manuals: publishing only, not printed on site; magazines: publishing only, not printed on site

(G-14791)
WALKER TELECOMMUNICATIONS
1375 S Center Rd (48638-6321)
PHONE..................989 274-7384
Roy Walker, *Owner*
EMP: 5 EST: 2001
SALES (est): 256.5K Privately Held
SIC: 3699 1731 Electrical equipment & supplies; voice, data & video wiring contractor

(G-14792)
WEIGHMAN ENTERPRISES INC
Also Called: Dornbos Printing Impressions
1131 E Genesee Ave (48607-1746)
PHONE..................989 755-2116
Ron Weighman, *President*
EMP: 6 EST: 2004
SQ FT: 8,600
SALES (est): 853.8K Privately Held
SIC: 2752 2796 2759 Commercial printing, offset; letterpress plates, preparation of; commercial printing

(G-14793)
WENDLING SHEET METAL INC
2633 Carrollton Rd (48604-2401)
PHONE..................989 753-5286
Kevin Wendling, *President*
Stephanie Patrzik, *Principal*
Chad Wojciecho, *Vice Pres*
EMP: 35 EST: 2004
SQ FT: 25,600
SALES (est): 4.6MM Privately Held
SIC: 3444 Sheet metalwork

(G-14794)
WILBERT SAGINAW VAULT CORP (PA)
2810 Hess Ave (48601-7416)
P.O. Box 1346 (48605-1346)
PHONE..................989 753-3065
Jack Swihart, *President*
Lori J Davis, *COO*
Cynthia Swihart, *Vice Pres*
Lianne Kossick, *Office Mgr*
EMP: 3 EST: 1929
SQ FT: 25,000
SALES (est): 2.5MM Privately Held
SIC: 3272 7261 Burial vaults, concrete or precast terrazzo; crematory

(G-14795)
WRIGHT-K TECHNOLOGY INC
Also Called: Wright-K Spare Parts and Svcs
2025 E Genesee Ave (48601-2499)
PHONE..................989 752-2588
Constance Kostrzewa, *Ch of Bd*
John Sivey, *President*
Tom Greenwood, *Mfg Mgr*
Colin Hubbard, *Purchasing*
Christie Coombe, *Controller*
EMP: 35 EST: 1920
SQ FT: 65,180
SALES (est): 8MM Privately Held
WEB: www.wright-k.com
SIC: 8711 3549 3541 Designing: ship, boat, machine & product; assembly machines, including robotic; drilling machine tools (metal cutting)

(G-14796)
WRIGHTS WOODWORKS
11735 Swan Creek Rd (48609-9767)
PHONE..................989 295-7456
Thomas Wright, *Principal*
EMP: 4 EST: 2018
SALES (est): 80.4K Privately Held
SIC: 2431 Millwork

(G-14797)
ZF ACTIVE SAFETY US INC
2828 E Genesee Ave (48601)
PHONE..................248 863-2412
EMP: 7
SALES (corp-wide): 216.2K Privately Held
WEB: www.zf.com
SIC: 3714 Motor vehicle parts & accessories; motor vehicle engines & parts; motor vehicle body components & frame; motor vehicle electrical equipment
HQ: Zf Active Safety Us Inc.
   12025 Tech Center Dr
   Livonia MI 48150
   734 812-6979

Sagola
Dickinson County

(G-14798)
MINERICK LOGGING INC
N10670 State Highway M95 (49881-9730)
P.O. Box 99 (49881-0099)
PHONE..................906 542-3583
Robert Minerick, *President*
Margaret Minerick, *Corp Secy*
Phillip Minerick, *Vice Pres*
EMP: 15 EST: 1970
SQ FT: 10,000
SALES (est): 1.2MM Privately Held
WEB: www.minericklogging.com
SIC: 2411 Logging camps & contractors

(G-14799)
SAGOLA HARDWOODS INC
N10640 State Highway M95 (49881-9730)
P.O. Box 99 (49881-0099)
PHONE..................906 542-7200
Margaret Minerick, *President*
Robert Minerick, *Vice Pres*
Kim Olson, *Office Mgr*
EMP: 56 EST: 1997
SALES (est): 5.8MM Privately Held
WEB: www.minericklogging.com
SIC: 2421 Sawmills & planing mills, general

Saint Charles
Saginaw County

(G-14800)
ABLE WELDING INC
5265 S Graham Rd (48655-8523)
PHONE..................989 865-9611
Bernard Schultz Sr, *President*
EMP: 5 EST: 1977
SQ FT: 5,200
SALES (est): 350K Privately Held
WEB: www.ablewelding.com
SIC: 7692 3471 Welding repair; plating & polishing

(G-14801)
BLACKLEDGE TOOL INC
305 Entrepreneur Dr (48655-8644)
P.O. Box 117 (48655-0117)
PHONE..................989 865-8393
Clark Blackledge, *President*
Kay Blackledge, *Bookkeeper*
EMP: 5 EST: 1995
SALES (est): 431.1K Privately Held
SIC: 3544 3599 Special dies & tools; machine shop, jobbing & repair

(G-14802)
EAGLE CREEK MFG & SALES
6753 S Steel Rd (48655-9732)
PHONE..................989 643-7521
Roger Miller, *Owner*
Sharon Miller, *Co-Owner*
EMP: 7 EST: 1980
SQ FT: 4,000
SALES (est): 422.3K Privately Held
SIC: 3451 Screw machine products

(G-14803)
JUNGNITSCH BROS LOGGING
15250 W Townline Rd (48655-9760)
PHONE..................989 233-8091
Scott Jungnitsch, *Principal*
EMP: 6 EST: 2009
SALES (est): 170.5K Privately Held
SIC: 2411 Logging

(G-14804)
M J MECHANICAL INC
Also Called: Mj Mechanical Services
11787 Prior Rd (48655-9559)
PHONE..................989 865-9633
Matthew Berent, *President*
EMP: 20 EST: 2002
SALES (est): 2MM Privately Held
SIC: 3444 Sheet metalwork

(G-14805)
MICHIGAN PALLET INC (PA)
Also Called: Lewiston Forest Products
1225 N Saginaw St (48655-1024)
P.O. Box 97 (48655-0097)
PHONE..................989 865-9915
Paul Kamps, *President*
Nick Engelsma, *Sales Staff*
EMP: 15 EST: 1983
SQ FT: 13,000
SALES (est): 2.4MM Privately Held
WEB: www.mipallet.com
SIC: 2448 Pallets, wood

(G-14806)
MTI PRECISION MACHINING INC
Also Called: Method Tool
11980 Beaver Rd (48655-9687)
P.O. Box 205 (48655-0205)
PHONE..................989 865-9880
Stuart Yntema, *President*
Robert Milbrandt, *Supervisor*
EMP: 38 EST: 1999
SALES (est): 2.1MM
SALES (corp-wide): 9.7MM Privately Held
WEB: www.tpipm.com
SIC: 3599 Machine shop, jobbing & repair
PA: Tpi Powder Metallurgy, Inc.
   12030 Beaver Rd
   Saint Charles MI 48655
   989 865-9921

(G-14807)
POREX TECHNOLOGIES CORP
Also Called: Filtrona Porous Technologies
5301 S Graham Rd (48655-8522)
PHONE..................989 865-8200
Julie Hill, *Manager*
EMP: 25
SALES (corp-wide): 1B Privately Held
WEB: www.porex.com
SIC: 3842 3082 Surgical appliances & supplies; unsupported plastics profile shapes
HQ: Porex Technologies Corp.
   1625 Ashton Park Dr Ste A
   South Chesterfield VA 23834
   804 524-4983

(G-14808)
PRECISION JIG GRINDING INC
165 Entrepreneur Dr (48655-9600)
P.O. Box 208 (48655-0208)
PHONE..................989 865-7953
John Sievert, *President*
Dawn Sievert, *Treasurer*
EMP: 5 EST: 1993
SQ FT: 3,000
SALES (est): 407.5K Privately Held
WEB: www.s-b-jiggrinding.com
SIC: 3541 Machine tools, metal cutting type

(G-14809)
ST CHARLES HARDWOOD MICHIGAN
10500 Mckeighan Rd (48655-8637)
P.O. Box 96 (48655-0096)
PHONE..................989 865-9299
Gary Tarr, *President*
Lorraine Lewenberger, *Corp Secy*
Linda Tarr, *Vice Pres*
EMP: 10 EST: 1964
SALES (est): 222.3K Privately Held
SIC: 2421 1629 Sawmills & planing mills, general; land clearing contractor

(G-14810)
TK ENTERPRISES INC
1225 N Saginaw St (48655-1024)
PHONE..................989 865-9915
Paul M Kamps, *President*
EMP: 12 EST: 1967
SQ FT: 70,000
SALES (est): 327K Privately Held
SIC: 2448 2449 Pallets, wood; skids, wood; fruit crates, wood: wirebound; vegetable crates, wood: wirebound

(G-14811)
TPI POWDER METALLURGY INC (PA)
12030 Beaver Rd (48655-8639)
P.O. Box 69 (48655-0069)
PHONE..................989 865-9921
Stuart H Yntema Jr, *President*
Stuart Yntema Jr, *President*
Stu Yntema, *Controller*
Steven B Yntema, *Admin Sec*
EMP: 20 EST: 1967
SQ FT: 20,000
SALES (est): 9.7MM Privately Held
WEB: www.tpipm.com
SIC: 3399 Powder, metal

(G-14812)
ULTIMATE GRAPHIC AND SIGN LLC
8071 S Iva Rd (48655-8754)
PHONE..................989 865-5200
Greg Armstrong, *Principal*
Gregory S Armstrong,
EMP: 5 EST: 2008
SALES (est): 195.9K Privately Held
WEB: www.ultimategraphicandsign.com
SIC: 3993 2759 2396 2397 Signs & advertising specialties; screen printing; poster & decal printing & engraving; decals: printing; fabric printing & stamping; schiffli machine embroideries

Saint Clair
St. Clair County

(G-14813)
AURIA ST CLAIR LLC
2001 Christian B Haas Dr (48079-4297)
PHONE 810 329-8400
Brian Pour, *CEO*
Dennis Hillman, *Engineer*
EMP: 197 **EST:** 2007
SALES (est): 50MM
SALES (corp-wide): 17.3MM **Privately Held**
WEB: www.auriasolutions.com
SIC: 3714 Motor vehicle parts & accessories
HQ: Auria Solutions Usa Inc.
26999 Cntrl Pk Blvd # 300
Southfield MI 48076
248 728-8000

(G-14814)
BIEWER OF LANSING LLC
812 S Riverside Ave (48079-5393)
P.O. Box 497 (48079-0497)
PHONE 810 326-3930
Gary Olmstead, *CFO*
Kerry McIntyre, *Manager*
Richard N Biewer,
EMP: 40
SQ FT: 5,000
SALES (est): 4.4MM **Privately Held**
WEB: www.biewerlumber.com
SIC: 2491 Structural lumber & timber, treated wood

(G-14815)
BIEWER SAWMILL WINONA INC
812 S Riverside Ave (48079-5393)
PHONE 810 329-4789
Timothy Biewer, *CEO*
EMP: 125 **EST:** 2020
SALES (est): 10.1MM **Privately Held**
WEB: www.biewerlumber.com
SIC: 2421 Sawmills & planing mills, general

(G-14816)
CARGILL INCORPORATED
916 S Riverside Ave (48079-5335)
PHONE 810 329-2736
John Armstrong, *Production*
Leland Widger, *Research*
Ike Venker, *Manager*
EMP: 284
SALES (corp-wide): 113.4B **Privately Held**
WEB: www.cargill.com
SIC: 2899 5169 Salt; salts, industrial
PA: Cargill, Incorporated
15407 Mcginty Rd W
Wayzata MN 55391
952 742-7575

(G-14817)
CASTING INDUSTRIES INC
315 Whiting St (48079-4981)
P.O. Box 668, Saint Clair Shores (48080-0668)
PHONE 586 776-5700
Fred E Kilgus, *President*
EMP: 19 **EST:** 1974
SQ FT: 3,500
SALES (est): 421.7K **Privately Held**
SIC: 3321 3365 Gray iron castings; aluminum & aluminum-based alloy castings

(G-14818)
CENTRACORE LLC
315 Whiting St (48079-4981)
P.O. Box 668, Saint Clair Shores (48080-0668)
PHONE 586 776-5700
Gary Ray, *Engineer*
Tim Wehner, *Sales Engr*
Frederick E Kilgus, *Mng Member*
Scott Chadwick, *Manager*
Cyndi Stahl, *Clerk*
▲ **EMP:** 12 **EST:** 2003
SALES (est): 4.2MM **Privately Held**
WEB: www.centracore.com
SIC: 3365 3559 Aerospace castings, aluminum; automotive related machinery

(G-14819)
CENTRACORE DE MEXICO LLC
315 Whiting St (48079-4981)
PHONE 586 776-5700
Todd Kilgus, *Principal*
EMP: 20 **EST:** 2017
SALES (est): 2.2MM **Privately Held**
WEB: www.centracore.com
SIC: 3363 Aluminum die-castings

(G-14820)
CORSON FABRICATING LLC
1701 Sinclair St Ste B (48079-5906)
PHONE 810 326-0532
Gary Corrigan, *Partner*
Jennifer Tope, *Executive Asst*
Michael Gibson,
EMP: 25 **EST:** 1999
SALES (est): 2.6MM **Privately Held**
WEB: www.corsonfab.com
SIC: 1791 3449 Structural steel erection; bars, concrete reinforcing: fabricated steel

(G-14821)
CRAIG ASSEMBLY INC
1111 Fred W Moore Hwy (48079-4967)
PHONE 810 326-1374
Werner Deggim, *CEO*
Thomas Geiser, *President*
Russel Hutchins, *Vice Pres*
Tom Geiser, *Plant Mgr*
David Searle, *Project Mgr*
▲ **EMP:** 150 **EST:** 1982
SQ FT: 30,000
SALES (est): 32.1MM
SALES (corp-wide): 1.1B **Privately Held**
WEB: www.normagroup.com
SIC: 3492 3089 5013 Fluid power valves & hose fittings; injection molded finished plastic products; seat belts
PA: Norma Group Se
Edisonstr. 4
Maintal HE 63477
618 140-30

(G-14822)
DANA LIMITED
Also Called: Thermal Products
2020 Christian B Haas Dr (48079-5701)
PHONE 810 329-2500
John Geddes, *Asst Treas*
Vic Avram, *Sales Staff*
Bob Albrecht, *Branch Mgr*
Tim Williams, *Program Mgr*
Jason Hammond, *Supervisor*
EMP: 7 **Publicly Held**
WEB: www.dana.com
SIC: 3714 Motor vehicle parts & accessories
HQ: Dana Limited
3939 Technology Dr
Maumee OH 43537

(G-14823)
DANA THERMAL PRODUCTS LLC
Power Technologies Group
2020 Christian B Haas Dr (48079-5701)
PHONE 810 329-2500
David Dumas, *Production*
EMP: 29 **Publicly Held**
WEB: www.dana.com
SIC: 3714 Motor vehicle parts & accessories
HQ: Dana Thermal Products, Llc
3939 Technology Dr
Maumee OH 43537

(G-14824)
DANA THERMAL PRODUCTS LLC
Also Called: Long Manufacturing
2020 Christian B Haas Dr (48079-5701)
PHONE 810 329-2500
Tim Cajac, *Manager*
EMP: 29 **Publicly Held**
WEB: www.dana.com
SIC: 3714 Motor vehicle parts & accessories
HQ: Dana Thermal Products, Llc
3939 Technology Dr
Maumee OH 43537

(G-14825)
DECKER GEAR INC (PA)
1500 Glendale St (48079-5100)
PHONE 810 388-1500
Louise Decker, *President*
Rick Decker, *President*
EMP: 12 **EST:** 1995
SQ FT: 5,400
SALES (est): 2.5MM **Privately Held**
SIC: 3566 3599 3462 Gears, power transmission, except automotive; machine shop, jobbing & repair; gear & chain forgings

(G-14826)
ENGINRED PLSTIC COMPONENTS INC
Also Called: EPC Columbia
2015 S Range Rd (48079-4120)
PHONE 810 326-1650
Reza Kargarzadeh, *Branch Mgr*
EMP: 5 **Privately Held**
WEB: www.epcmfg.com
SIC: 3089 Injection molding of plastics
PA: Engineered Plastic Components, Inc.
4500 Westown Pkwy Ste 277
West Des Moines IA 50266

(G-14827)
ENGINRED PLSTIC COMPONENTS INC
2000 Christian B Haas Dr (48079-5701)
PHONE 810 326-1650
Miky Hartman, *Manager*
EMP: 5 **Privately Held**
WEB: www.epcmfg.com
SIC: 3089 Injection molding of plastics
PA: Engineered Plastic Components, Inc.
4500 Westown Pkwy Ste 277
West Des Moines IA 50266

(G-14828)
ENGINRED PLSTIC COMPONENTS INC
2015 S Range Rd (48079-4120)
PHONE 810 326-3010
Stuart Duncan, *Branch Mgr*
EMP: 5 **Privately Held**
WEB: www.epcmfg.com
SIC: 3089 Injection molding of plastics
PA: Engineered Plastic Components, Inc.
4500 Westown Pkwy Ste 277
West Des Moines IA 50266

(G-14829)
EPC-COLUMBIA INC
2000 Christian B Haas Dr (48079-5701)
PHONE 810 326-1650
Reza Kargarzadeh, *President*
EMP: 80 **EST:** 2007
SALES (est): 15MM **Privately Held**
WEB: www.epcmfg.com
SIC: 3089 Injection molding of plastics
PA: Engineered Plastic Components, Inc.
4500 Westown Pkwy Ste 277
West Des Moines IA 50266

(G-14830)
FLIGHT MOLD & ENGINEERING INC
1940 Fred W Moore Hwy (48079-4701)
PHONE 810 329-2900
Robert A Ward, *President*
EMP: 30
SQ FT: 17,500
SALES (est): 5.6MM **Privately Held**
WEB: www.flightmoldeng.com
SIC: 3089 Injection molding of plastics

(G-14831)
HODGES & IRVINE INC
1900 Sinclair St (48079-5513)
P.O. Box 197 (48079-0197)
PHONE 810 329-4787
Roger Powers, *President*
Valeria Shatzel, *Systems Dir*
John Jeffrey Hodges, *Director*
EMP: 11 **EST:** 1940
SQ FT: 4,000
SALES (est): 612K **Privately Held**
WEB: www.hodgesandirvine.com
SIC: 2754 2789 2759 2752 Job printing, gravure; bookbinding & related work; commercial printing; commercial printing, lithographic

(G-14832)
JGS MACHINING LLC
4455 Davis Rd (48079-2807)
PHONE 810 329-4210
John Sams, *Mng Member*
EMP: 5 **EST:** 1999
SQ FT: 3,500
SALES (est): 425.7K **Privately Held**
SIC: 3829 Testing equipment: abrasion, shearing strength, etc.

(G-14833)
JOHN A BIEWER CO OF ILLINOIS
812 S Riverside Ave (48079-5393)
P.O. Box 497 (48079-0497)
PHONE 810 326-3930
Richard N Biewer, *President*
Brian B Biewer, *Corp Secy*
Timothy Biewer, *Vice Pres*
EMP: 105 **EST:** 1982
SQ FT: 5,000
SALES (est): 2.3MM
SALES (corp-wide): 92.1MM **Privately Held**
WEB: www.biewerlumber.com
SIC: 2491 Structural lumber & timber, treated wood
PA: Biewer Lumber, Llc
812 S Riverside Ave
Saint Clair MI 48079
810 326-3930

(G-14834)
JOHN A BIEWER LUMBER COMPANY (PA)
812 S Riverside Ave (48079-5393)
P.O. Box 497 (48079-0497)
PHONE 810 329-4789
Richard Biewer, *President*
Richard N Biewer, *President*
Brian B Biewer, *Corp Secy*
Timothy Biewer, *Vice Pres*
▲ **EMP:** 30 **EST:** 1961
SQ FT: 5,000
SALES (est): 39MM **Privately Held**
WEB: www.biewerlumber.com
SIC: 2491 Structural lumber & timber, treated wood; pilings, treated wood

(G-14835)
MAGNA SERVICES AMERICA INC
Also Called: Magna Elc Vhcl Strctres - Mich
1811 S Range Rd (48079-3408)
PHONE 816 602-5872
Christopher Hinman, *Branch Mgr*
EMP: 75
SALES (corp-wide): 32.6B **Privately Held**
WEB: www.magna.com
SIC: 3714 Motor vehicle parts & accessories
HQ: Magna Services Of America Inc.
750 Tower Dr
Troy MI 48098
248 631-1100

(G-14836)
MEMORIES MANOR
5011 Davis Rd (48079-2010)
PHONE 810 329-2800
Janine Zimmer, *Principal*
EMP: 4 **EST:** 2008
SALES (est): 303.4K **Privately Held**
WEB: www.memoriesmanor.com
SIC: 2782 Scrapbooks

(G-14837)
MICHIGAN PRCSION SWISS PRTS IN
Also Called: MPS
2145 Wadhams Rd (48079-3808)
P.O. Box 376 (48079-0376)
PHONE 810 329-2270
David D Murphy, *CEO*
Cheryl Pryor, *CFO*
Gerald D Meldrum, *Treasurer*
EMP: 45 **EST:** 1966
SQ FT: 38,000
SALES (est): 7.3MM **Privately Held**
WEB: www.mpswiss.com
SIC: 3451 Screw machine products

Saint Clair - St. Clair County

(G-14838)
NORMA GROUP CRAIG ASSEMBLY
1219 Fred Moore Hwy (48079)
PHONE..................810 326-1374
EMP: 4 EST: 2015
SALES (est): 85.1K **Privately Held**
SIC: 3678 Electronic connectors

(G-14839)
PIER ONE POLYMERS INCORPORATED
Also Called: Bh Polymers
2011 Christian B Haas Dr (48079-4297)
PHONE..................810 326-1456
Michael D Pier, *President*
Shawna Brasty, *Exec VP*
Jason Macuga, *CFO*
Cathy Pier, *Treasurer*
▲ EMP: 11 EST: 1999
SQ FT: 7,800
SALES (est): 5MM **Privately Held**
WEB: www.pieronepolymers.com
SIC: 2821 Plastics materials & resins

(G-14840)
PRECISION DIE AND MACHINE CO
1400 S Carney Dr (48079-5549)
PHONE..................810 329-2861
Garnet W Lozon, *President*
Mary Jo Lozon, *Corp Secy*
Robert Lozon, *Manager*
EMP: 12 EST: 1958
SALES (est): 1.6MM **Privately Held**
WEB: www.precisiondmco.com
SIC: 3544 Forms (molds), for foundry & plastics working machinery

(G-14841)
REELING SYSTEMS LLC
Also Called: Dirkes Industries
5323 Gratiot Ave (48079-1426)
P.O. Box 265, Marysville (48040-0265)
PHONE..................810 364-3900
Chris Graham,
EMP: 9 EST: 1980
SQ FT: 16,000
SALES (est): 2.4MM **Privately Held**
WEB: www.reelingsystems-gi.com
SIC: 3357 3563 Nonferrous wiredrawing & insulating; spraying outfits: metals, paints & chemicals (compressor)

(G-14842)
RIVERSIDE TANK & MFG CORP
1230 Clinton Ave (48079-4958)
P.O. Box 67 (48079-0067)
PHONE..................810 329-7143
Fred Cartwright, *President*
Vicki Cartwright, *Admin Sec*
▼ EMP: 25 EST: 1944
SQ FT: 20,000
SALES (est): 4.9MM **Privately Held**
WEB: www.riversidetank.com
SIC: 3443 3714 Tanks for tank trucks, metal plate; motor vehicle parts & accessories

(G-14843)
SEW SAINTLY
2245 Wadhams Rd (48079-3810)
PHONE..................586 773-8480
Mary Cefarek, *Owner*
EMP: 4 EST: 1990
SALES (est): 56.7K **Privately Held**
WEB: www.sewsaintly.com
SIC: 2395 Embroidery & art needlework

(G-14844)
WACHTEL TOOL & BROACH INC
6676 Fred W Moore Hwy (48079-4401)
PHONE..................586 758-0110
Klaus Wachtel, *President*
Susan Wachtel, *Admin Sec*
EMP: 9 EST: 1978
SQ FT: 2,500
SALES (est): 603.2K **Privately Held**
SIC: 3545 Broaches (machine tool accessories)

(G-14845)
WRIGHT PLASTIC PRODUCTS CO LLC
2021 Christian B Haas Dr (48079-4297)
PHONE..................810 326-3000
Matt Phillips, *Prdtn Mgr*
Colleen Kirk, *Production*
Aboudi Saoud, *Engineer*
Skip Hines, *Accounts Mgr*
Tom Arquette, *Branch Mgr*
EMP: 8
SALES (corp-wide): 14.3MM **Privately Held**
WEB: www.wppllc.com
SIC: 3089 3544 5162 Injection molded finished plastic products; forms (molds), for foundry & plastics working machinery; plastics products
PA: Wright Plastic Products Co L.L.C.
201 E Condensery Rd
Sheridan MI 48884
989 291-3211

Saint Clair Shores
Macomb County

(G-14846)
ACP TECHNOLOGIES LLC
20527 Stephens St (48080-1048)
PHONE..................586 322-3511
Thomas Holcombe, *CEO*
Dennis Wend, *President*
D Chris Boyer, *Shareholder*
Donald P Malone, *Shareholder*
EMP: 6 EST: 2017
SALES (est): 251.5K **Privately Held**
WEB: www.acp-technologies.net
SIC: 3624 2821 Fibers, carbon & graphite; molding compounds, plastics

(G-14847)
ALLIANCE TOOL AND MACHINE CO
21418 Timberidge St (48082-2257)
PHONE..................586 427-6411
EMP: 10 EST: 1944
SQ FT: 4,200
SALES (est): 1.1MM **Privately Held**
SIC: 3544 Mfg Dies/Tools/Jigs/Fixtures

(G-14848)
AMERICAN GRAPHICS INC
Also Called: American Speedy Printing
27413 Harper Ave (48081-1921)
PHONE..................586 774-8880
Donald Girodat, *President*
Sandra Girodat, *Vice Pres*
EMP: 8 EST: 1981
SQ FT: 2,500
SALES (est): 722.1K **Privately Held**
WEB: www.americanspeedy.com
SIC: 2752 Commercial printing, offset

(G-14849)
BRAKE TEAM
19803 E 9 Mile Rd (48080-1774)
PHONE..................313 914-6000
Patrick Walby, *Principal*
EMP: 4 EST: 2019
SALES (est): 132.4K **Privately Held**
WEB: www.braketeam-stclairshores.com
SIC: 3714 Motor vehicle parts & accessories

(G-14850)
BRIGHTER SIGN AGE
22700 Stephens St (48080-4302)
PHONE..................248 719-5389
Michael Bauman, *Principal*
EMP: 4 EST: 2017
SALES (est): 46K **Privately Held**
WEB: www.brightersignage.com
SIC: 3993 Signs & advertising specialties

(G-14851)
C H M GRAPHICS & LITHO INC
23519 Little Mack Ave (48080-1145)
PHONE..................586 777-4550
Kathleen Campbell, *President*
Philip Mousseau, *Vice Pres*
EMP: 4 EST: 1984
SALES (est): 315.9K **Privately Held**
WEB: www.chmgraphics.com
SIC: 2752 Commercial printing, offset

(G-14852)
C T MACHINING INC
23108 Edgewater St (48082-2036)
PHONE..................586 772-0320
Charles T Corder, *President*
EMP: 6 EST: 1989
SALES (est): 485.7K **Privately Held**
SIC: 3599 Machine shop, jobbing & repair

(G-14853)
CAL CHEMICAL MANUFACTURING CO
605 Shore Club Dr (48080-1559)
PHONE..................586 778-7006
EMP: 5 EST: 1962
SQ FT: 2,250
SALES (est): 150K **Privately Held**
SIC: 2842 Mfg Cleaning Compounds

(G-14854)
CTC DISTRIBUTION INC (PA)
Also Called: Drano
20200 E 9 Mile Rd (48080-1791)
PHONE..................313 486-2225
Christopher T Charlton, *President*
Rob Tiede, *Senior VP*
▲ EMP: 5 EST: 1989
SQ FT: 20,000
SALES (est): 1.4MM **Privately Held**
WEB: www.ctcdistribution.com
SIC: 3714 5051 Motor vehicle body components & frame; aluminum bars, rods, ingots, sheets, pipes, plates, etc.

(G-14855)
EASTSIDE COATINGS
25614 Jefferson Ave (48081-2311)
PHONE..................313 936-1000
Michele Duross, *Administration*
EMP: 7 EST: 2016
SALES (est): 442.7K **Privately Held**
SIC: 3479 Metal coating & allied service

(G-14856)
ELITE WOODWORKING LLC
Also Called: Detroit Woodworking
22960 W Industrial Dr (48080-1182)
PHONE..................586 204-5882
Amy Lee, *Office Mgr*
Daniel J Connell, *Mng Member*
EMP: 50 EST: 2011
SALES (est): 3.4MM **Privately Held**
SIC: 2431 Millwork

(G-14857)
EMBROIDERY & MUCH MORE LLC
27419 Harper Ave (48081-1921)
PHONE..................586 771-3832
Linda Bologna,
EMP: 10 EST: 2002
SALES (est): 816.8K **Privately Held**
WEB: www.embroiderymore.com
SIC: 2395 5699 Embroidery products, except schiffli machine; pleating & tucking, for the trade; sports apparel

(G-14858)
FISHER & COMPANY INCORPORATED (PA)
Also Called: Fisher Dynamics
33300 Fisher Dr (48082)
PHONE..................586 746-2000
Peter Mealing, *General Mgr*
Alfred J Fisher III, *Chairman*
Alfred J Fisher III, *Chairman*
James Babiasz, *Vice Pres*
Joseph E Blake, *Vice Pres*
▲ EMP: 450 EST: 1800
SQ FT: 135,000
SALES (est): 448.1MM **Privately Held**
WEB: www.fisherco.com
SIC: 2531 Seats, automobile

(G-14859)
FISHER & COMPANY INCORPORATED
Also Called: Fisher Safety Structures
33200 Fisher Dr (48082-1071)
PHONE..................586 746-2280
Scott Wax, *Principal*
SALES (est): 315.9K **Privately Held**
WEB: www.chmgraphics.com
SIC: 2752 Commercial printing, offset
Alfred J Fisher IV, *Division Pres*
Gary Farmer, *VP Mfg*
Rey Calvillo, *QC Mgr*
Sandra Kenney, *Manager*
EMP: 11
SALES (corp-wide): 448.1MM **Privately Held**
WEB: www.fisherco.com
SIC: 3714 Motor vehicle parts & accessories
PA: Fisher & Company, Incorporated
33300 Fisher Dr
Saint Clair Shores MI 48082
586 746-2000

(G-14860)
FISHER DYNAMICS CORPORATION
33300 Fisher Dr (48082)
PHONE..................586 746-2000
Michael Lauhoff, *Purchasing*
EMP: 190 EST: 2014
SALES (est): 4MM
SALES (corp-wide): 448.1MM **Privately Held**
WEB: www.fisherco.com
SIC: 3714 Motor vehicle parts & accessories
PA: Fisher & Company, Incorporated
33300 Fisher Dr
Saint Clair Shores MI 48082
586 746-2000

(G-14861)
FOURTH SEACOAST PUBLISHING CO
Also Called: Quick Caller, The
25300 Little Mack Ave (48081-3369)
P.O. Box 145 (48080-0145)
PHONE..................586 779-5570
Thomas Buysse, *President*
Sharon Roman, *Sales Staff*
EMP: 7 EST: 1960
SQ FT: 1,300
SALES (est): 822.9K **Privately Held**
WEB: www.quickcalleronline.com
SIC: 2741 4731 Directories: publishing only, not printed on site; freight transportation arrangement

(G-14862)
GENERAL MEDIA LLC
Also Called: Used Car News
24114 Harper Ave (48080-1234)
P.O. Box 80800 (48080-5800)
PHONE..................586 541-0075
Lynda Thomas, *Mng Member*
EMP: 21 EST: 1994
SALES (est): 2.7MM **Privately Held**
WEB: www.usedcarnews.com
SIC: 2711 Newspapers, publishing & printing

(G-14863)
GREENLIGHT HOME INSPECTION SVC
23340 Westbury St (48080-2540)
PHONE..................313 885-5616
Philip Hutchings, *Principal*
EMP: 5 EST: 2004
SALES (est): 212.6K **Privately Held**
SIC: 1389 Construction, repair & dismantling services

(G-14864)
HARDY & SONS SIGN SERVICE INC
22340 Harper Ave (48080-1818)
PHONE..................586 779-8018
Carolyn Hardy, *President*
David Hardy, *Treasurer*
EMP: 5 EST: 1953
SALES (est): 317.9K **Privately Held**
SIC: 3993 Electric signs

(G-14865)
HOMEWORKS
28024 Nieman St (48081-2937)
PHONE..................810 533-2030
EMP: 5 EST: 2018
SALES (est): 235K **Privately Held**
WEB: www.homeworkspainting.net
SIC: 2431 Millwork

GEOGRAPHIC SECTION

Saint Ignace - Mackinac County (G-14894)

(G-14866)
K&K STAMPING COMPANY
23015 W Industrial Dr (48080-1187)
PHONE..........................586 443-7900
Joseph J Koch, *President*
Richard N Koch, *Vice Pres*
▲ **EMP:** 50 **EST:** 1969
SQ FT: 45,000
SALES (est): 6.7MM **Privately Held**
WEB: www.kandkcorp.com
SIC: 3465 3544 3469 Body parts, automobile: stamped metal; special dies & tools; metal stampings

(G-14867)
LAKEVIEW PUBLISHING COMPANY
26824 Koerber St (48081-2448)
PHONE..........................586 443-5913
Mary Clancey, *Principal*
EMP: 5 **EST:** 2018
SALES (est): 71.4K **Privately Held**
SIC: 2741 Miscellaneous publishing

(G-14868)
LANDRA PRSTHTICS ORTHOTICS INC
29840 Harper Ave (48082-2608)
PHONE..........................586 294-7188
Steven Landra, *Branch Mgr*
EMP: 5 **Privately Held**
SIC: 3842 5047 8082 8099 Prosthetic appliances; medical & hospital equipment; home health care services; medical services organization
PA: Landra Prosthetics And Orthotics, Inc.
14725 Northline Rd
Southgate MI 48195

(G-14869)
MARK FOUR CAM INC
22926 W Industrial Dr (48080-1131)
PHONE..........................586 204-5906
Edward A Gieche, *President*
Ronald Dooley, *Treasurer*
Alan Imboden, *Admin Sec*
EMP: 8 **EST:** 1989
SQ FT: 9,500
SALES (est): 830.8K **Privately Held**
WEB: www.markfourcaminc.com
SIC: 3544 Industrial molds

(G-14870)
METALS PRESERVATION GROUP LLC
23010 E Industrial Dr (48080-1177)
PHONE..........................586 944-2720
Joseph Louisell, *President*
EMP: 17 **EST:** 2013 **Privately Held**
WEB: www.mpgrustsolutions.com
SIC: 5199 2842 Packaging materials; rust removers

(G-14871)
MICHIGAN FOR VACCINE CHOICE
22615 Francis St (48082-1791)
PHONE..........................586 294-3074
Suzanne Waltman, *Administration*
EMP: 4 **EST:** 2014
SALES (est): 77.7K **Privately Held**
WEB: www.michiganvaccinechoice.org
SIC: 2836 Vaccines

(G-14872)
MICROFORM TOOL COMPANY INC
20601 Stephens St (48080-1047)
PHONE..........................586 776-4840
Thomas Alschbach, *President*
Margaret Alschbach, *Admin Sec*
EMP: 4 **EST:** 1961
SQ FT: 4,000
SALES (est): 386.5K **Privately Held**
WEB: www.microformtool.com
SIC: 3541 Machine tools, metal cutting type

(G-14873)
MOTOR CITY CARBURETOR
19907 Maxine St (48080-3793)
PHONE..........................586 443-8048
Bruce Beattie, *Agent*
EMP: 3 **EST:** 2017
SALES (est): 77.7K **Privately Held**
SIC: 3592 Carburetors

(G-14874)
NORTH SAILS GROUP LLC
Also Called: North Sails-Detroit
22600 Greater Mack Ave (48080-2015)
PHONE..........................586 776-1330
Fax: 586 776-2762
EMP: 4 **Privately Held**
SIC: 2394 Mfg Canvas/Related Products
HQ: North Sails Group, Llc
125 Old Gate Ln Ste 7
Milford CT 06607
203 874-7548

(G-14875)
O2TOTES LLC
20315 E 9 Mile Rd (48080-1757)
PHONE..........................734 730-4472
▲ **EMP:** 10 **EST:** 2013
SALES (est): 680.2K **Privately Held**
WEB: www.o2totes.com
SIC: 3949 Sporting & athletic goods

(G-14876)
OPENSYSTEMS PUBLISHING LLC (PA)
Also Called: Compact PCI Systems
30233 Jefferson Ave (48082-1787)
PHONE..........................586 415-6500
Micheal Hopper, *President*
John McHale, *Exec VP*
Richard Nass, *Exec VP*
Arthur Swift, *Vice Pres*
Rosemary Kristoff, *CFO*
EMP: 13 **EST:** 1985
SQ FT: 1,200
SALES (est): 3.3MM **Privately Held**
WEB: www.opensysmedia.com
SIC: 2721 Magazines: publishing only, not printed on site

(G-14877)
PORTABLE FACTORY
20600 Stephens St (48080-1084)
PHONE..........................586 883-6843
Sorin Coman, *President*
Chris Wolfe, *CFO*
EMP: 10 **EST:** 2011
SALES (est): 2.2MM **Privately Held**
WEB: www.theportablefactory.com
SIC: 3694 8711 Automotive electrical equipment; engineering services

(G-14878)
PRINT PLUS INC
Also Called: Reproductions Resource
28324 Elmdale St (48081-1483)
PHONE..........................586 888-8000
John Blumline, *President*
EMP: 4 **EST:** 1987
SALES (est): 294.3K **Privately Held**
WEB: www.printplusmi.com
SIC: 2752 Commercial printing, offset

(G-14879)
PRINTING BUYING SERVICE
Also Called: Printing Buying Services
28108 Roy St (48081-1632)
PHONE..........................586 907-2011
Mike Mandell, *Owner*
EMP: 4 **EST:** 1980
SALES (est): 215.3K **Privately Held**
SIC: 2752 Commercial printing, lithographic

(G-14880)
RADICAL PLANTS LLC
25967 Little Mack Ave (48081-3378)
PHONE..........................586 243-8128
Melissa Heath, *Principal*
EMP: 6 **EST:** 2016
SALES (est): 280.5K **Privately Held**
WEB: www.radicalplants.com
SIC: 2099 Dips, except cheese & sour cream based

(G-14881)
ROBERT ANDERSON
31384 Harper Ave (48082-2450)
PHONE..........................586 552-5648
EMP: 4 **EST:** 2019
SALES (est): 56.4K **Privately Held**
SIC: 3449 Miscellaneous metalwork

(G-14882)
ROHM AND MONSANTO PLC
31408 Harper Ave (48082-2451)
PHONE..........................313 886-1966
EMP: 4 **EST:** 2018
SALES (est): 176.8K **Privately Held**
SIC: 2879 Agricultural chemicals

(G-14883)
SHOCK-TEK LLC
23336 Robert John St (48080-2611)
PHONE..........................313 886-0530
Arthur Porter, *Principal*
Valk Estate, *Mng Member*
A Spitzer Glvoe,
EMP: 5 **EST:** 1995
SALES (est): 228.1K **Privately Held**
WEB: www.shocktek.com
SIC: 3842 Bandages & dressings

(G-14884)
SIGMA LUMINOUS LLC
23000 W Industrial Dr B (48080-1185)
PHONE..........................866 755-3563
Jessica Sorbo, *VP Bus Dvlpt*
Richard Saxby, *Sales Staff*
Allen Middleton, *Mng Member*
▲ **EMP:** 7
SQ FT: 10,000
SALES (est): 1.8MM **Privately Held**
WEB: www.sigmaluminous.com
SIC: 3674 Light emitting diodes

(G-14885)
SOUTH BAY SUPPLY LLC
Also Called: South Bay Superabrasives
21250 Harper Ave Ste 1 (48080-2221)
PHONE..........................313 882-8090
Charles T Stormes, *Mng Member*
EMP: 8 **EST:** 2006
SALES (est): 68.8K **Privately Held**
SIC: 3291 Abrasive products

(G-14886)
SPECTRUM WIRELESS (USA) INC
27601 Little Mack Ave (48080-1833)
P.O. Box 538 (48080-0538)
PHONE..........................586 693-7525
Gordon Mayhew, *President*
EMP: 4 **EST:** 2015
SQ FT: 2,000
SALES (est): 765K **Privately Held**
WEB: www.spectrum-communications.us
SIC: 3663 Radio & TV communications equipment

(G-14887)
STAHLS INC (PA)
Also Called: Groupe Stahl
25901 Jefferson Ave (48081-2333)
P.O. Box 628 (48080-0628)
PHONE..........................800 478-2457
Ted Stahl, *CEO*
Brett Stahl, *General Mgr*
Rich Ellsworth, *Vice Pres*
Greg Peirce, *Vice Pres*
Daniel Robinson, *Opers Mgr*
◆ **EMP:** 34 **EST:** 1932
SALES (est): 76.9MM **Privately Held**
WEB: www.stahls.com
SIC: 2891 5045 3585 2399 Adhesives; computers, peripherals & software; computer software; evaporative condensers, heat transfer equipment; emblems, badges & insignia: from purchased materials; pleating & stitching; finishing plants, manmade fiber & silk fabrics

(G-14888)
TECHNOLOGY NETWORK SVCS INC (PA)
Also Called: Tech Enterprises
31375 Harper Ave (48082-2453)
PHONE..........................586 294-7771
Sam Agosta, *President*
EMP: 11 **EST:** 1985
SQ FT: 2,400
SALES (est): 1MM **Privately Held**
WEB: www.techenterprise.com
SIC: 5045 5065 5044 5087 Computers; facsimile equipment; photocopy machines; shredders, industrial & commercial; business oriented computer software; custom computer programming services

(G-14889)
TRIN-MAC COMPANY INC
24825 Little Mack Ave (48080-3224)
PHONE..........................586 774-1900
Dan Mc Closkey, *President*
EMP: 4 **EST:** 1973
SQ FT: 4,000
SALES (est): 374K **Privately Held**
SIC: 1799 3369 Sandblasting of building exteriors; nonferrous foundries

(G-14890)
VINYL GRAPHIX INC
24731 Harper Ave (48080-1256)
PHONE..........................586 774-1188
Charles Bird, *President*
Diane Bird, *Admin Sec*
EMP: 5 **EST:** 1987
SALES (est): 407.8K **Privately Held**
WEB: www.vinylgraphix.com
SIC: 7336 3993 Art design services; signs & advertising specialties

(G-14891)
WARTIAN LOCK COMPANY
20525 E 9 Mile Rd (48080-1798)
PHONE..........................586 777-2244
George Wartian, *President*
Loretta Banek, *Treasurer*
▲ **EMP:** 9 **EST:** 1948
SQ FT: 36,000
SALES (est): 1.2MM **Privately Held**
WEB: www.wartianlock.com
SIC: 3429 3462 Door locks, bolts & checks; keys & key blanks; door opening & closing devices, except electrical; keys, locks & related hardware; iron & steel forgings

(G-14892)
YATES INDUSTRIES INC (PA)
Also Called: Yates Cylinders
23050 E Industrial Dr (48080-1177)
PHONE..........................586 778-7680
William H Yates III, *President*
Bill Yates III, *General Mgr*
Crystal Brock, *Vice Pres*
Mark Cook, *Vice Pres*
Scott Malik, *Purch Mgr*
▲ **EMP:** 56 **EST:** 1972
SQ FT: 100,000
SALES (est): 15.8MM **Privately Held**
WEB: www.yatesind.com
SIC: 3593 7699 3594 3053 Fluid power cylinders, hydraulic or pneumatic; hydraulic equipment repair; fluid power pumps & motors; gaskets, packing & sealing devices; engineering services

Saint Helen
Roscommon County

(G-14893)
ADVANCED METAL RECYCLERS
2360 S Maple Valley Rd (48656-9670)
PHONE..........................989 389-7708
David Moore, *Owner*
EMP: 4 **EST:** 2016
SALES (est): 43.2K **Privately Held**
SIC: 7692 Welding repair

Saint Ignace
Mackinac County

(G-14894)
ARROW SIGNS
N975 Martin Lake Rd (49781-9834)
PHONE..........................989 350-4357
EMP: 4 **EST:** 2013
SALES (est): 61.5K **Privately Held**
WEB: www.mystreetsigns.com
SIC: 3993 Signs & advertising specialties

Saint Ignace - Mackinac County (G-14895)

(G-14895)
ST IGNACE NEWS
Also Called: Town Crier
359 Reagon St (49781-1144)
P.O. Box 277 (49781-0277)
PHONE..................906 643-9150
Wesley Maurer Jr, *Owner*
EMP: 14 EST: 1975
SQ FT: 4,500
SALES (est): 1.2MM **Privately Held**
SIC: 2711 Commercial printing & newspaper publishing combined

(G-14896)
STICKERCHEF LLC
141 Joseph St (49781-1413)
PHONE..................231 622-9900
Robert Vanheuvelen, *Principal*
EMP: 4 EST: 2017
SALES (est): 87.2K **Privately Held**
WEB: www.stickerchef.com
SIC: 3993 Signs & advertising specialties

Saint Johns
Clinton County

(G-14897)
COG MARKETERS LTD
Also Called: Agriculture Liqiud Fertilizers
3026 W M 21 (48879-8746)
PHONE..................989 224-4117
Galynn Beer, *Sales Mgr*
Jeff Luiken, *Branch Mgr*
Troy Bancroft, *Manager*
EMP: 18
SALES (corp-wide): 37.7MM **Privately Held**
WEB: www.agroliquid.com
SIC: 2874 Phosphatic fertilizers
PA: Cog Marketers, Ltd.
3055 W M 21
Saint Johns MI 48879
989 227-3827

(G-14898)
COG MARKETERS LTD
Also Called: Argo Liquid
3055 W M 21 (48879-8745)
PHONE..................989 224-4117
EMP: 18
SALES (corp-wide): 37.7MM **Privately Held**
WEB: www.agroliquid.com
SIC: 2875 Fertilizers, mixing only
PA: Cog Marketers, Ltd.
3055 W M 21
Saint Johns MI 48879
989 227-3827

(G-14899)
CUSTOM EMBROIDERY PLUS LLC (PA)
304 N Lansing St (48879-1424)
PHONE..................989 227-9432
Cory Gartside,
Kirk Gartside,
EMP: 5 EST: 2001
SALES (est): 675K **Privately Held**
WEB: www.ceplusonline.com
SIC: 2395 Embroidery & art needlework

(G-14900)
GOODRICH BROTHERS INC
3060 County Farm Rd (48879-9278)
PHONE..................989 224-4944
EMP: 9
SALES (corp-wide): 7.2MM **Privately Held**
SIC: 2431 Mfg Millwork
PA: Goodrich Brothers, Inc.
11409 E Bluewater Hwy
Pewamo MI 48873
989 593-2104

(G-14901)
HOT PRINTS INC
103 N Clinton Ave (48879-1501)
PHONE..................989 627-6463
Rebecca Whitaker, *Principal*
EMP: 5 EST: 2018
SALES (est): 321.5K **Privately Held**
SIC: 2752 Commercial printing, lithographic

(G-14902)
INNOVATIVE POLYMERS INC
Also Called: Innovtive Polymers Rampf Group
208 Kuntz St (48879-1172)
PHONE..................989 224-9500
Mike Molitor, *President*
Matt Buckland, *Mfg Mgr*
◆ EMP: 11 EST: 1994
SQ FT: 12,000
SALES (est): 9.5MM
SALES (corp-wide): 711.6K **Privately Held**
WEB: www.innovative-polymers.com
SIC: 2821 2851 Polyurethane resins; polyurethane coatings
HQ: Rampf Group, Inc.
49037 Wixom Tech Dr
Wixom MI 48393
248 295-0223

(G-14903)
JET SPEED PRINTING COMPANY
313 N Clinton Ave (48879-1505)
PHONE..................989 224-6475
James Pratl, *President*
EMP: 6 EST: 1986
SQ FT: 2,800
SALES (est): 708.7K **Privately Held**
WEB: www.jetspeedprinting.com
SIC: 2752 Commercial printing, offset

(G-14904)
LUPAUL INDUSTRIES INC (PA)
Also Called: Mercury Stamping Div
310 E Steel St (48879-1302)
PHONE..................517 783-3223
J Michael Smith, *President*
Jim Drake, *Corp Secy*
M Jank, *Vice Pres*
M Moran, *Vice Pres*
EMP: 15 EST: 1940
SQ FT: 23,000
SALES (est): 5MM **Privately Held**
WEB: www.lupaul.com
SIC: 3544 3469 3496 Special dies & tools; metal stampings; miscellaneous fabricated wire products

(G-14905)
MACO TOOL & ENGINEERING INC
210 Spring St (48879-1534)
PHONE..................989 224-6723
Mark Hoover, *President*
Gary Criner, *Purch Agent*
Mary Walker, *Treasurer*
EMP: 30 EST: 1971
SQ FT: 23,000
SALES (est): 4MM **Privately Held**
WEB: www.macotool.com
SIC: 3544 Special dies & tools

(G-14906)
MAHLE AFTERMARKET INC
Also Called: Mahle Service Solutions
916 W State St Ste B (48879-1404)
PHONE..................717 840-0678
EMP: 7
SALES (corp-wide): 504.6K **Privately Held**
WEB: www.mahle-aftermarket.com
SIC: 3714 Motor vehicle parts & accessories
HQ: Mahle Aftermarket Inc.
23030 Mahle Dr
Farmington MI 48335

(G-14907)
MAHLE ENG COMPONENTS USA INC (DH)
916 W State St (48879-1404)
PHONE..................989 224-2384
Michael Best, *Controller*
EMP: 78 EST: 2004
SALES (est): 2.7MM
SALES (corp-wide): 504.6K **Privately Held**
WEB: www.mahle.com
SIC: 3714 Motor vehicle parts & accessories
HQ: Mahle Gmbh
Pragstr. 26-46
Stuttgart BW 70376
711 501-0

(G-14908)
MICHIGAN GRAPHICS & SIGNS
1110 E Steel Rd (48879-1185)
PHONE..................989 224-1936
Bruce Delong, *Owner*
Conne Delong, *Co-Owner*
EMP: 4 EST: 2002
SALES (est): 169.4K **Privately Held**
WEB: www.migsigns.com
SIC: 3993 5999 Signs, not made in custom sign painting shops; banners, flags, decals & posters

(G-14909)
MICHIGAN POLYMER RECLAIM INC
Also Called: Mpr, Visitmpr
107 E Walker Rd (48879-8526)
PHONE..................989 227-0497
John C Stehlik, *President*
Paul Marsh, *Engineer*
EMP: 12 EST: 1991
SQ FT: 30,000
SALES (est): 2.4MM **Privately Held**
WEB: www.visitmpr.com
SIC: 2821 Plastics materials & resins

(G-14910)
MWC (MICHIGAN) LLC
1640 Technical Dr (48879-9801)
PHONE..................575 791-9559
Thomas Tench,
Philomena Brigid Walsh,
EMP: 5 EST: 2018
SALES (est): 2.8MM **Privately Held**
SIC: 2022 Natural cheese

(G-14911)
OLYMPIAN TOOL LLC
604 N Us Highway 27 (48879-1125)
P.O. Box 416 (48879-0416)
PHONE..................989 224-4817
Todd Deitrich, *President*
Michelle Geller, *Sales Staff*
Robert Frostick, *Officer*
EMP: 25
SQ FT: 20,000
SALES (est): 4.9MM **Privately Held**
WEB: www.olympiantool.com
SIC: 3544 3545 Special dies & tools; machine tool accessories

(G-14912)
OMNI TECHNICAL SERVICES INC
Also Called: Omni Ergonomics
203 E Tolles Dr (48879-1166)
P.O. Box 37, Owosso (48867-0037)
PHONE..................989 227-8900
John Schafer, *CEO*
Jack Roth, *Vice Pres*
EMP: 11 EST: 1978
SQ FT: 45,000
SALES (est): 245.1K **Privately Held**
SIC: 8711 3496 Mechanical engineering; conveyor belts

(G-14913)
QUEST SOFTWARE LLC
Also Called: Q S I
106 W Tolles Dr (48879-9800)
P.O. Box 166 (48879-0166)
PHONE..................800 541-2593
Ronee Zyzelewski, *President*
Jean Zyzelewski, *Corp Secy*
Matt Peterson, *COO*
Terance Miller, *Vice Pres*
Jane Coblentz, *Human Resources*
EMP: 300 EST: 1983
SQ FT: 10,000
SALES (est): 45.3MM **Privately Held**
WEB: www.quest.com
SIC: 7372 Prepackaged software

(G-14914)
SAYLOR-BEALL MANUFACTURING CO
400 N Kibbee St (48879-1602)
PHONE..................989 224-2371
Bruce C Mc Fee, *President*
Mary George, *Purchasing*
▲ EMP: 254 EST: 1915
SQ FT: 52,500
SALES (est): 30.3MM **Privately Held**
WEB: www.saylor-beall.com
SIC: 3563 Air & gas compressors including vacuum pumps

(G-14915)
SEARLES CONSTRUCTION INC (PA)
1213 N Us 127 (48879)
PHONE..................989 224-3297
Lillian Searles, *Ch of Bd*
Leon Searles, *President*
▲ EMP: 4 EST: 1951
SQ FT: 1,000
SALES (est): 4.9MM **Privately Held**
SIC: 1442 1794 Construction sand & gravel; excavation & grading, building construction

(G-14916)
ST JOHNS COMPUTER MACHINING
Also Called: Saint Johns Computer Machining
501 E Steel St (48879-1171)
PHONE..................989 224-7664
Michael J Jorae, *President*
Renee Jorae, *Admin Sec*
EMP: 6 EST: 1985
SQ FT: 2,400
SALES (est): 483.6K **Privately Held**
WEB: www.sjfloristandgreenhouse.com
SIC: 3312 3599 Tool & die steel & alloys; machine shop, jobbing & repair

(G-14917)
STONY CREEK ESSENTIAL OILS
6718 W Centerline Rd (48879-9572)
PHONE..................989 227-5500
Thomas Irrer, *Principal*
EMP: 6 EST: 2005
SALES (est): 902.3K **Privately Held**
WEB: www.sceoinc.com
SIC: 2899 5169 Oils & essential oils; oil additives

(G-14918)
TOPDUCK PRODUCTS LLC
203 E Tolles Dr (48879-1166)
PHONE..................517 322-3202
Donald Kettles, *President*
EMP: 10 EST: 2004
SALES (est): 1MM **Privately Held**
WEB: www.superzilla.us
SIC: 2899 Corrosion preventive lubricant

(G-14919)
UNCLE JOHNS CIDER MILL INC
8614 N Us Highway 27 (48879-9425)
PHONE..................989 224-3686
John Beck, *CEO*
Michael John Beck, *President*
Carolyn Beck, *Vice Pres*
EMP: 24
SQ FT: 4,900
SALES (est): 1.9MM **Privately Held**
WEB: www.ujcidermill.com
SIC: 0175 5431 2099 2051 Apple orchard; fruit stands or markets; cider, non-alcoholic; bread, cake & related products; canned fruits & specialties; groceries & related products

(G-14920)
UNIFIED SCRNING CRSHING - MI L
305 E Walker Rd (48879-8574)
PHONE..................888 464-9473
Tom Lencsch, *Mng Member*
Chrell Hoffman, *Manager*
EMP: 15 EST: 1996
SQ FT: 17,000
SALES (est): 10.7MM
SALES (corp-wide): 15.6MM **Privately Held**
WEB: www.unifiedscreening.com
SIC: 3496 3535 Miscellaneous fabricated wire products; conveyors & conveying equipment
PA: Unified Screening & Crushing - Mn, Inc.
3350 Highway 149
Eagan MN 55121
651 454-8835

Saint Joseph
Berrien County

(G-14921)
AAA1 BOX DIVISION CONTAINER
233 Hawthorne Ave (49085-2613)
PHONE.................................269 983-1563
Thomas Van Lierop, *Manager*
EMP: 6 **EST**: 2018
SALES (est): 99.8K **Privately Held**
SIC: 2653 Boxes, corrugated: made from purchased materials

(G-14922)
AMERICAN SOC AG BLGCAL ENGNERS
2950 Niles Rd (49085-8607)
PHONE.................................269 429-0300
Darrin Drollinger, *President*
Mark Zielke, *CFO*
Donna Hull, *Pub Rel Staff*
Joann McQuone, *Executive Asst*
Beth Settles, *Administration*
EMP: 24 **EST**: 1907
SQ FT: 17,000
SALES (est): 2.7MM **Privately Held**
WEB: www.asabe.org
SIC: 8621 2731 Engineering association; book publishing

(G-14923)
AMERICAN TRIM
1010 Main St (49085-2058)
PHONE.................................269 281-0651
EMP: 8 **EST**: 2017
SALES (est): 104.8K **Privately Held**
WEB: www.amtrim.com
SIC: 3469 Metal stampings

(G-14924)
COLSON CASTERS
2024 Hawthorne Ave (49085-2618)
PHONE.................................269 944-6063
Darrell Metzger, *Director*
EMP: 12
SALES (est): 1.1MM **Privately Held**
WEB: www.colsoncaster.com
SIC: 3499 Fabricated metal products

(G-14925)
CUSTOM PRODUCTS INC
Also Called: Custometal Products
180 Kerth St (49085-2630)
P.O. Box 950 (49085-0950)
PHONE.................................269 983-9500
Dan Kirksey, *President*
Ronald Bowman, *Admin Sec*
EMP: 17 **EST**: 1964
SQ FT: 45,000
SALES (est): 1.2MM **Privately Held**
WEB: www.custometalproducts.com
SIC: 3444 Sheet metal specialties, not stamped; machine guards, sheet metal; metal housings, enclosures, casings & other containers

(G-14926)
DESIGNERS SHEET METAL INC
205 Palladium Dr (49085-9552)
PHONE.................................269 429-4133
Bruce E Ringer, *President*
Jeanne Grabowski, *Manager*
EMP: 5 **EST**: 1991
SQ FT: 6,000
SALES (est): 418.4K **Privately Held**
SIC: 1761 3444 Sheet metalwork; sheet metalwork

(G-14927)
DRIVEN-4 LLC
3515 Lakeshore Dr Ste 1 (49085-2952)
PHONE.................................269 281-7567
Alfredo Bellio, *Managing Prtnr*
Fred Bellio, *Managing Prtnr*
Bala Shetty, *Mfg Staff*
James Danforth, *Mng Member*
Carl Wendtland, *Mng Member*
EMP: 4 **EST**: 2016
SALES (est): 553.4K **Privately Held**
WEB: www.driven-4.com
SIC: 7372 7373 7371 Prepackaged software; computer integrated systems design; computer software systems analysis & design, custom

(G-14928)
EL SOL CUSTOM LIGHTING
3909 Stonegate Park (49085-9130)
PHONE.................................269 281-0435
Willie Tovar, *Vice Pres*
▲ **EMP**: 15 **EST**: 2009
SALES (est): 2.1MM **Privately Held**
WEB: www.elsolcustomlighting.com
SIC: 3646 Chandeliers, commercial

(G-14929)
EMPIRE MACHINE COMPANY
350 Palladium Dr (49085-9128)
PHONE.................................269 684-3713
Lazell Davis, *President*
EMP: 15 **EST**: 1967
SQ FT: 21,000
SALES (est): 882.3K **Privately Held**
SIC: 3544 Special dies & tools

(G-14930)
F P ROSBACK CO
125 Hawthorne Ave (49085-2636)
PHONE.................................269 983-2582
Lawrence H Fish, *Ch of Bd*
Larry Bowman, *President*
Ronald Bowman, *Vice Pres*
Tim Eversole, *Plant Mgr*
Sandy Bowman, *Purch Mgr*
▲ **EMP**: 25 **EST**: 1881
SQ FT: 124,256
SALES (est): 2.1MM **Privately Held**
WEB: www.rosbackcompany.com
SIC: 3555 Bookbinding machinery

(G-14931)
FUZZYBUTZ
306 State St Ste A (49085-2292)
PHONE.................................269 983-9663
Rick Schaut, *Principal*
EMP: 6 **EST**: 2010
SALES (est): 320.7K **Privately Held**
WEB: www.fuzzybutzpetbakery.com
SIC: 2253 T-shirts & tops, knit

(G-14932)
GREAT LAKES ELECTRIC LLC
Also Called: Gle Solar Energy
1776 Hilltop Rd (49085-2305)
PHONE.................................269 408-8276
Zheng Zhang, *Mng Member*
EMP: 6 **EST**: 2008
SALES (est): 50K **Privately Held**
WEB: www.gl-electric.com
SIC: 3625 3433 Motor controls & accessories; solar heaters & collectors

(G-14933)
HANSON COLD STORAGE LLC (DH)
Also Called: Hanson Logistics
440 Renaissance Dr (49085-2176)
PHONE.................................269 982-1390
Ken Hanson, *President*
Greg Hanson, *Vice Chairman*
Gregory Hanson, *Vice Chairman*
Blake Larkin, *Senior VP*
Daniel Bernson, *Vice Pres*
▲ **EMP**: 16 **EST**: 1954
SALES (est): 39.8MM **Privately Held**
WEB: www.hansonlogistics.com
SIC: 4222 4225 2097 Storage, frozen or refrigerated goods; warehousing, cold storage or refrigerated; general warehousing & storage; manufactured ice
HQ: Lineage Logistics, Llc
  46500 Humboldt Dr
  Novi MI 48377
  248 863-4400

(G-14934)
HANSON INTERNATIONAL INC (PA)
Also Called: Hanson Mold Division
440 Renaissance Dr (49085-2176)
PHONE.................................269 429-5555
Merlin Hanson, *Ch of Bd*
Daniel Bernson, *President*
Ken Patzkowski, *Vice Pres*
Gene Stemm, *Vice Pres*
Gene N Stemm, *Vice Pres*
EMP: 3 **EST**: 1978
SALES (est): 10.1MM **Privately Held**
WEB: www.hansonmold.com
SIC: 3544 Special dies & tools

(G-14935)
HANSON INTERNATIONAL INC
Hanson Mold
3500 Hollywood Rd (49085-9581)
PHONE.................................269 429-5555
Gene Stemm, *Vice Pres*
Ken Patzkowsky, *Plant Mgr*
Elmer Rudlaff, *Mfg Spvr*
Mark Graham, *Purch Agent*
Tom Reule, *Engineer*
EMP: 107
SALES (corp-wide): 10.1MM **Privately Held**
WEB: www.hansonmold.com
SIC: 3363 3549 3544 Aluminum die-castings; marking machines, metalworking; special dies, tools, jigs & fixtures
PA: Hanson International, Inc.
  440 Renaissance Dr
  Saint Joseph MI 49085
  269 429-5555

(G-14936)
HOFFMANN DIE CAST LLC
229 Kerth St (49085-2623)
PHONE.................................269 983-1102
Michael Oros, *President*
Jim Selmer, *Vice Pres*
Tom Redding, *Chief Engr*
William E Criswell, *Finance Dir*
William Criswell, *Finance*
EMP: 108
SQ FT: 100,000
SALES (est): 4.5MM **Privately Held**
WEB: www.hoffmanndc.com
SIC: 3363 3364 3369 3365 Aluminum die-castings; zinc & zinc-base alloy die-castings; nonferrous foundries; aluminum foundries

(G-14937)
INDUSTRIAL FABRIC PRODUCTS INC
Also Called: Tarps Now
4133 M 139 (49085-8689)
P.O. Box 667, Stevensville (49127-0667)
PHONE.................................269 932-4440
Mike Dill, *CEO*
◆ **EMP**: 18 **EST**: 2010
SQ FT: 46,000
SALES (est): 6.6MM **Privately Held**
SIC: 2394 Canvas awnings & canopies; canvas covers & drop cloths; shades, canvas: made from purchased materials

(G-14938)
JOURNAL DISPOSITION CORP
Also Called: IPC Communication Services
2180 Maiden Ln (49085-9596)
PHONE.................................269 428-2054
Richard Butterworth, *Principal*
EMP: 89
SALES (corp-wide): 296.6MM **Privately Held**
SIC: 2752 Periodicals, lithographed
HQ: Journal Disposition Corporation
  2180 Maiden Ln
  Saint Joseph MI 49085
  888 563-3220

(G-14939)
JUANITA L SIGNS
1101 Wedgewood Rd (49085-3258)
PHONE.................................269 429-7248
Juanita L Signs, *Principal*
EMP: 4 **EST**: 2009
SALES (est): 172.1K **Privately Held**
SIC: 3993 Signs & advertising specialties

(G-14940)
KATTS CANDLES & MORE
2666 Lincoln Ave (49085-3305)
PHONE.................................269 281-6805
Kathryn Grigereit, *Principal*
EMP: 4 **EST**: 2019
SALES (est): 58.5K **Privately Held**
SIC: 3999 Candles

(G-14941)
KAY MANUFACTURING COMPANY
3491 S Lakeshore Dr (49085-8289)
PHONE.................................269 408-8344
Scott Dekker, *Vice Pres*
Jason Kope, *Engineer*
EMP: 33 **EST**: 2013
SALES (est): 1.3MM **Privately Held**
WEB: www.kaymfg.com
SIC: 3714 Motor vehicle parts & accessories

(G-14942)
KISMET STRATEGIC SOURCING PART
717 Sint Jseph Dr Ste 270 (49085)
PHONE.................................269 932-4990
Orlando Malone, *Opers Staff*
Scott Lange,
EMP: 5 **EST**: 2008
SALES (est): 232.6K **Privately Held**
WEB: www.kismetssp.com
SIC: 3571 Personal computers (microcomputers)

(G-14943)
KVA INC
2095 Niles Rd (49085-2473)
PHONE.................................269 982-2888
Lydia Demski, *CEO*
EMP: 17 **EST**: 2008
SALES (est): 1MM **Privately Held**
WEB: www.scope-services.com
SIC: 3822 Energy cutoff controls, residential or commercial types

(G-14944)
LAFARGE NORTH AMERICA INC
200 Upton Dr (49085-1148)
PHONE.................................269 983-6333
Rick Moore, *Manager*
EMP: 5
SALES (corp-wide): 25.3B **Privately Held**
WEB: www.lafarge-na.com
SIC: 3241 Cement, hydraulic
HQ: Lafarge North America Inc.
  8700 W Bryn Mawr Ave # 30
  Chicago IL 60631
  773 372-1000

(G-14945)
LAZY BALLERINA WINERY LLC (PA)
315 State St (49085-1247)
PHONE.................................269 363-6218
Melanie Owen,
Lauren Kniebes,
EMP: 11 **EST**: 2016
SALES (est): 581.9K **Privately Held**
WEB: www.lazyballerinawinery.com
SIC: 2084 Wines

(G-14946)
LECO CORPORATION (PA)
Also Called: Tem-Press Division
3000 Lakeview Ave (49085-2319)
PHONE.................................269 983-5531
Carl S Warren, *President*
B John Hawkins, *President*
Larry S O'Brien, *President*
Elizabeth S Warren, *President*
Larry O 'brien, *General Mgr*
◆ **EMP**: 500
SQ FT: 300,000
SALES (est): 137.6MM **Privately Held**
WEB: www.leco.com
SIC: 3821 3826 3825 3823 Laboratory apparatus, except heating & measuring; chemical laboratory apparatus; analytical instruments; instruments to measure electricity; industrial instrmnts msrmnt display/control process variable; porcelain electrical supplies

(G-14947)
LECO CORPORATION
Hilltop Rd (49085)
PHONE.................................269 985-5496
EMP: 5
SALES (corp-wide): 137.6MM **Privately Held**
WEB: www.leco.com
SIC: 3821 Laboratory apparatus & furniture

Saint Joseph - Berrien County (G-14948)

PA: Leco Corporation
3000 Lakeview Ave
Saint Joseph MI 49085
269 983-5531

(G-14948)
LIBERTY STEEL FABRICATING INC
Also Called: Liberty 3d Technologies
350 Palladium Dr (49085-9128)
PHONE..................................269 556-9792
Andrew Gantenbein, President
James Parmer, Prdtn Mgr
David Coard, Opers Staff
John Bournay, Finance Mgr
Pete Ciula, Sales Engr
EMP: 40 EST: 1998
SALES (est): 8MM Privately Held
WEB: www.libsteel.com
SIC: 3541 3444 3443 7699 Machine tool replacement & repair parts, metal cutting types; sheet metalwork; fabricated plate work (boiler shop); metal reshaping & re-plating services

(G-14949)
MASTER WOODWORKS
2916 Veronica Ct (49085-2373)
PHONE..................................269 240-3262
John Ott, Owner
EMP: 5 EST: 2015
SALES (est): 89K Privately Held
SIC: 2421 Sawmills & planing mills, general

(G-14950)
NELSON SPECIALTIES COMPANY
1389 Norman Rd (49085-9778)
PHONE..................................269 983-1878
Keith Nelson, CEO
Mike Nelson, President
Lisa Eyerly, Corp Secy
Dorwin Nelson, Vice Pres
Kathy Heine, Senior Buyer
EMP: 17 EST: 1994
SALES (est): 2.1MM Privately Held
WEB: www.circuitboards.com
SIC: 3679 Electronic circuits

(G-14951)
NEOGEN CORPORATION
Also Called: Steven Schadler
2620 S Cleveland Ave # 100 (49085-3021)
PHONE..................................800 327-5487
Tina German, Research
Jeanne Strine, Manager
Cornelia Schafer, Administration
EMP: 4
SALES (corp-wide): 468.4MM Publicly Held
WEB: www.neogen.com
SIC: 2835 In vitro & in vivo diagnostic substances
PA: Neogen Corporation
620 Lesher Pl
Lansing MI 48912
517 372-9200

(G-14952)
NORTH PIER BREWING COMPANY LLC
3266 Estates Dr (49085-3428)
PHONE..................................312 545-0446
Jeff Fettig, Principal
EMP: 5 EST: 2015
SALES (est): 75.4K Privately Held
SIC: 2082 Malt beverages

(G-14953)
PAXTON MEDIA GROUP LLC
Also Called: Herald Palladium, The
3450 Hollywood Rd (49085-9155)
P.O. Box 128 (49085-0128)
PHONE..................................269 429-2400
David Holgate, Branch Mgr
EMP: 100
SALES (corp-wide): 243.1MM Privately Held
WEB: www.paducahsun.com
SIC: 2711 4833 Newspapers, publishing & printing; television broadcasting stations
PA: Paxton Media Group, Llc
100 Television Ln
Paducah KY 42003
270 575-8630

(G-14954)
PEERLESS CANVAS PRODUCTS INC
2355 Niles Rd (49085-2813)
PHONE..................................269 429-0600
Paul Kosachuk, Principal
EMP: 4 EST: 1962
SQ FT: 3,200
SALES (est): 372.1K Privately Held
SIC: 2394 Convertible tops, canvas or boat: from purchased materials; awnings, fabric: made from purchased materials

(G-14955)
PRINTEK INC (PA)
3515 Lakeshore Dr Ste 1 (49085-2952)
PHONE..................................269 925-3200
Thomas C Yeager, President
Julie Payovich, Exec VP
Daniel Davin, Vice Pres
Jennifer Reynolds, Sales Staff
Chris Yeager, Marketing Staff
EMP: 80 EST: 1980
SQ FT: 70,000
SALES (est): 13MM Privately Held
WEB: www.printek.com
SIC: 3577 Printers, computer; printers & plotters

(G-14956)
RESISTNCE WLDG MCH ACCSSORY LL
255 Palladium Dr (49085-9552)
PHONE..................................269 428-4770
Clifton Adams, President
Gene Hays, Mfg Staff
Tim Duer, Sales Engr
▲ EMP: 19 EST: 1992
SQ FT: 6,000
SALES (est): 2.7MM Privately Held
WEB: www.resweld.com
SIC: 3463 3544 3548 Nonferrous forgings; special dies & tools; spot welding apparatus, electric

(G-14957)
ROBERT BOSCH LLC
Also Called: Bosch Chassis St Joseph Plant
3737 Red Arrow Hwy (49085-9208)
PHONE..................................269 429-3221
Steve Pear, Opers Mgr
Christine Gerlach, Controller
Ricardo Tanaka, Sales Mgr
Ron Lumfden, Manager
Heidi Mucci, Manager
EMP: 7
SALES (corp-wide): 297.8MM Privately Held
WEB: www.bosch.us
SIC: 3714 3594 3321 3322 Motor vehicle brake systems & parts; fluid power pumps & motors; gray & ductile iron foundries; malleable iron foundries
HQ: Robert Bosch Llc
38000 Hills Tech Dr
Farmington Hills MI 48331
248 876-1000

(G-14958)
ROI RICH OLES INDUSTRIES LLC
4464 Lincoln Ave (49085-9737)
PHONE..................................616 610-7050
EMP: 4 EST: 2016
SALES (est): 67.6K Privately Held
SIC: 3999 Manufacturing industries

(G-14959)
ROYAL ENTERPRIZES
1394 Linden Dr (49085-9695)
PHONE..................................269 429-5878
EMP: 4 EST: 2019
SALES (est): 78.5K Privately Held
WEB: www.royalenterprizes.com
SIC: 2431 Millwork

(G-14960)
SEWPHISTICATED STITCHING
1349 Nelson Rd (49085-9499)
PHONE..................................269 428-4402
Bekki Sue Lund, Principal
EMP: 4 EST: 2011
SALES (est): 74.9K Privately Held
SIC: 2395 Embroidery & art needlework

(G-14961)
SONOCO PRODUCTS COMPANY
500 Renaissance Dr 102d (49085-2175)
PHONE..................................269 408-0182
EMP: 5
SALES (corp-wide): 5.2B Publicly Held
WEB: www.sonoco.com
SIC: 2631 Paperboard mills
PA: Sonoco Products Company
1 N 2nd St
Hartsville SC 29550
843 383-7000

(G-14962)
SOPER MANUFACTURING COMPANY
3638 Bacon School Rd (49085-9634)
PHONE..................................269 429-5245
John Soper IV, President
John Globensky, Admin Sec
EMP: 14 EST: 1946
SQ FT: 35,000
SALES (est): 300.6K Privately Held
SIC: 3369 3544 3363 Zinc & zinc-base alloy castings, except die-castings; special dies, tools, jigs & fixtures; aluminum die-castings

(G-14963)
STAR SHADE CUTTER CO
2028 Washington Ave (49085-2421)
PHONE..................................269 983-2403
Michael Gast, President
Albert K Gast, Vice Pres
EMP: 4 EST: 1907
SQ FT: 2,800 Privately Held
WEB: www.starshade.com
SIC: 3552 Textile machinery

(G-14964)
STEELE SUPPLY CO
3413 Hill St (49085-2621)
PHONE..................................269 983-0920
Thomas D Steele, President
EMP: 8 EST: 1998
SALES (est): 1.4MM Privately Held
WEB: www.steeles.com
SIC: 5047 3841 3842 Diagnostic equipment, medical; surgical & medical instruments; surgical appliances & supplies

(G-14965)
TERRACE HILL VINEYARDS
1464 Silverbrook Ln (49085-9720)
PHONE..................................269 428-2168
Thomas J Zabadal, Principal
EMP: 4 EST: 2010
SALES (est): 13.6K Privately Held
SIC: 2084 Wines, brandy & brandy spirits

(G-14966)
TUTEUR INC
Also Called: Oscar's Printing
1721 Lakeshore Dr (49085-1637)
PHONE..................................269 983-1246
Edwin Stubelt, President
EMP: 8 EST: 1973
SQ FT: 1,400
SALES (est): 1MM Privately Held
WEB: www.oscarsprinting.com
SIC: 2752 Commercial printing, offset

(G-14967)
TWIN CITIES ORTHOTIC & PROSTHE
3538 Magnolia Ln (49085-8265)
PHONE..................................269 428-2910
EMP: 4
SQ FT: 1,500
SALES (est): 389.6K Privately Held
SIC: 3842 Mfg Braces & Artificial Limbs

(G-14968)
TWIN CITY ENGRAVING COMPANY
Also Called: Premier Promotions
2024 Washington Ave Ste 3 (49085-2422)
P.O. Box 85 (49085-0085)
PHONE..................................269 983-0601
Jeffrey Jones, President
Jerold Jones, Vice Pres
EMP: 8 EST: 1938
SALES (est): 1MM Privately Held
WEB: www.premierpromos.espwebsite.com
SIC: 7389 5199 4225 2796 Engraving service; embroidering of advertising on shirts, etc.; advertising, promotional & trade show services; advertising specialties; general warehousing; platemaking services; automotive & apparel trimmings; pleating & stitching

(G-14969)
UNITED FOR SRVVAL ST JSPHS RCY
2215 Wilson Ct (49085-1833)
PHONE..................................269 983-3820
Tim Schroeder, President
Gale Cutler, Vice Pres
Jackie Taglia, Treasurer
John Tielemeier, Director
EMP: 9 EST: 1965
SALES (est): 127.7K Privately Held
SIC: 2611 Pulp mills, mechanical & recycling processing

(G-14970)
UNIVERSAL INDUCTION INC
207 Hawthorne Ave Ste 2 (49085-2670)
PHONE..................................269 983-5543
EMP: 5 EST: 2019
SALES (est): 92.9K Privately Held
SIC: 3441 Fabricated structural metal

(G-14971)
VENTURE MANUFACTURING INC
3542 Crestview Rd (49085-8902)
PHONE..................................269 429-6337
William Warren, President
Donald Warren, Vice Pres
EMP: 7 EST: 1986
SALES (est): 564.7K Privately Held
SIC: 3544 Special dies & tools

(G-14972)
VERSATILE STAIR SYSTEM
1111 Orchard Ave (49085-2113)
PHONE..................................269 983-5437
Edward Hunt, Principal
EMP: 6 EST: 2016
SALES (est): 160.7K Privately Held
WEB: www.versatilestairsystem.com
SIC: 3446 Stairs, staircases, stair treads: prefabricated metal

(G-14973)
WALSWORTH PUBLISHING CO INC
Also Called: Walsworth Print Group
2180 Maiden Ln (49085-9596)
PHONE..................................269 428-2054
Patti Robbins, Accounts Mgr
Jeffrey Morris, Sales Staff
Mike Wells, Manager
EMP: 31
SALES (corp-wide): 296.6MM Privately Held
WEB: www.walsworth.com
SIC: 2741 Yearbooks: publishing & printing
PA: Walsworth Publishing Company, Inc.
306 N Kansas Ave
Marceline MO 64658
660 376-3543

(G-14974)
WEB PRINTING & MKTG CONCEPTS
Also Called: Xpress Printing
4086 Red Arrow Hwy (49085-9209)
PHONE..................................269 983-4646
Walter Buesing, President
Joanne Buesing, Admin Sec
EMP: 8 EST: 1980
SQ FT: 6,400
SALES (est): 878.6K Privately Held
WEB: www.xpressprinting.net
SIC: 2752 5112 5199 Commercial printing, offset; business forms; advertising specialties

Saline - Washtenaw County (G-15000)

(G-14975)
WENDY WILLIAMSON
Also Called: Agapy Publishing
1608 Sun Prairie Dr (49085-9431)
PHONE..................321 345-8297
Wendy Williamson, *Principal*
EMP: 4 **EST:** 2010
SALES (est): 62.1K **Privately Held**
WEB: www.agapy.com
SIC: 2741 Miscellaneous publishing

(G-14976)
WHIRLPOOL CORPORATION
500 Renaissance Dr # 102 (49085-2174)
PHONE..................269 923-7441
Gary Bormann, *Counsel*
Karen Schiltz, *Buyer*
Michael Embury, *Engineer*
Raymond Smith, *Senior Engr*
Robert Mink, *Branch Mgr*
EMP: 5
SALES (corp-wide): 19.4B **Publicly Held**
WEB: www.whirlpoolcorp.com
SIC: 3633 Household laundry machines, including coin-operated
PA: Whirlpool Corporation
2000 N M 63
Benton Harbor MI 49022
269 923-5000

(G-14977)
WHIRLPOOL CORPORATION
2901 Lakeshore Dr (49085-2376)
PHONE..................404 547-3194
Robert English, *General Mgr*
Jason Hudock, *Engineer*
EMP: 5
SALES (corp-wide): 19.4B **Publicly Held**
WEB: www.whirlpoolcorp.com
SIC: 3633 Household laundry equipment
PA: Whirlpool Corporation
2000 N M 63
Benton Harbor MI 49022
269 923-5000

(G-14978)
WHIRLPOOL CORPORATION
303 Upton Dr (49085-1149)
PHONE..................269 923-6057
Michael Goslee, *Engineer*
Vernen Labelle, *Engineer*
Patrick McCann, *Engineer*
Dean Peppel, *Engineer*
Richard Wrege, *Engineer*
EMP: 5
SALES (corp-wide): 19.4B **Publicly Held**
WEB: www.whirlpoolcorp.com
SIC: 3633 Household laundry equipment
PA: Whirlpool Corporation
2000 N M 63
Benton Harbor MI 49022
269 923-5000

(G-14979)
WHITE PINE WINERY
317 State St (49085-1247)
PHONE..................269 281-0098
David Miller, *Owner*
EMP: 5 **EST:** 2011
SALES (est): 236.3K **Privately Held**
WEB: www.whitepinewinery.com
SIC: 2084 Wines

(G-14980)
WOLVERINE METAL STAMPING INC (PA)
3600 Tennis Ct (49085-9502)
PHONE..................269 429-6600
Eric Jackson, *President*
Greg Matthews, *Plant Supt*
Robert Hornbuckle, *Opers Staff*
Richard Frederick, *Purch Mgr*
Joseph Glinka, *QA Dir*
▲ **EMP:** 89 **EST:** 1967
SQ FT: 104,000
SALES (est): 13.5MM **Privately Held**
WEB: www.wolverinecorp.com
SIC: 3469 3443 Stamping metal for the trade; fabricated plate work (boiler shop)

(G-14981)
WORLDWIDE MARKETING SVCS INC
Also Called: Owens Classic International
1776 Hilltop Rd (49085-2305)
PHONE..................269 556-2000
Peter J Marr, *President*
Tracy Marr, *Vice Pres*
Bobbi Jo Hahm, *Controller*
◆ **EMP:** 14 **EST:** 1990
SQ FT: 6,000
SALES (est): 3.3MM **Privately Held**
SIC: 5013 3713 Automotive supplies & parts; truck bodies & parts; truck tops

(G-14982)
Y M C A FAMILY CENTER
Also Called: YMCA
3665 Hollywood Rd (49085-9581)
PHONE..................269 428-9622
Nicole Weber, *Exec Dir*
Daniel Astyn, *Director*
Mike Ahearn, *Director*
EMP: 4 **EST:** 1997
SALES (est): 2.1MM **Privately Held**
SIC: 7999 3949 Recreation center; exercise equipment

Saint Louis
Gratiot County

(G-14983)
4 SEASONS GYM LLC
Also Called: Extreme Fitness Gym
116 N Mill St (48880-1521)
P.O. Box 24 (48880-0024)
PHONE..................989 681-8175
EMP: 5 **EST:** 2017
SALES (est): 176K **Privately Held**
WEB: www.4seasonsgym.com
SIC: 8099 2759 Nutrition services; screen printing

(G-14984)
AMERICAN SOFT TRIM INC
Also Called: Owosso Soft Trim
300 Woodside Dr (48880-1148)
PHONE..................989 681-0037
Mark Dupuie, *President*
EMP: 8 **EST:** 1988
SQ FT: 15,000
SALES (est): 233.5K **Privately Held**
WEB: www.americansofttrim.com
SIC: 2211 Upholstery fabrics, cotton

(G-14985)
AMERICAST LLC
107 Enterprize Dr (48880-1059)
PHONE..................989 681-4800
Dan Bishop,
EMP: 6 **EST:** 2002
SQ FT: 12,000
SALES (est): 400K **Privately Held**
WEB: www.americastllc.com
SIC: 3261 Bathroom accessories/fittings, vitreous china or earthenware

(G-14986)
APEX MARINE INC
300 Woodside Dr (48880-1148)
PHONE..................989 681-4300
Mark Dupuie, *President*
Ed Eldred, *Purchasing*
Kyle Acker, *Engineer*
Brad Dupuie, *Engineer*
Terry Glover, *Regl Sales Mgr*
▼ **EMP:** 65 **EST:** 2003
SQ FT: 25,000
SALES (est): 13.8MM **Privately Held**
WEB: www.apexmarineinc.com
SIC: 3069 Pontoons, rubber

(G-14987)
BEAR CREEK SAND & GRAVEL LLC
10907 Riverside Dr (48880-9455)
PHONE..................989 681-3641
Matthew D Mikek, *Administration*
EMP: 7 **EST:** 2015
SALES (est): 401.9K **Privately Held**
SIC: 1442 Construction sand & gravel

(G-14988)
BEAR TRUSS - US LBM LLC
721 E Washington St (48880-1986)
PHONE..................989 681-5774
EMP: 19 **EST:** 2015
SALES (est): 246K **Privately Held**
WEB: www.beartruss.net
SIC: 2439 Trusses, wooden roof; trusses, except roof: laminated lumber

(G-14989)
CENTRAL MICHIGAN TANK RENTAL
9701 Gruett Rd (48880-9732)
PHONE..................989 681-5963
EMP: 4
SQ FT: 3,600
SALES (est): 270K **Privately Held**
SIC: 1389 Oil/Gas Field Services

(G-14990)
CRIPPEN MANUFACTURING COMPANY
400 Woodside Dr (48880-1057)
P.O. Box 128, Alma (48801-0128)
PHONE..................989 681-4323
Jim Gascho, *President*
Jeff Gascho, *Sales Staff*
Mark Wilk, *Director*
Kevin Vogt, *Executive*
▼ **EMP:** 25 **EST:** 1988
SALES (est): 3.6MM **Privately Held**
WEB: www.crippenmfg.com
SIC: 3523 3841 3829 3535 Cleaning machines for fruits, grains & vegetables; surgical & medical instruments; measuring & controlling devices; conveyors & conveying equipment; abrasive products

(G-14991)
JER-DEN PLASTICS INC (PA)
750 Woodside Dr (48880-1051)
P.O. Box 240 (48880-0240)
PHONE..................989 681-4303
Dennis J Howe, *President*
Jerry Sprague Sr, *Vice Pres*
EMP: 38 **EST:** 1995
SQ FT: 35,000
SALES (est): 7.2MM **Privately Held**
WEB: www.jer-denplastics.com
SIC: 3089 Injection molding of plastics; plastic processing

(G-14992)
KEN LUNEACK CONSTRUCTION INC (PA)
Also Called: Bear Truss & Components
721 E Washington St (48880-1986)
P.O. Box 239 (48880-0239)
PHONE..................989 681-5774
Paul B Luneack, *President*
Pam Luneack, *CFO*
EMP: 168 **EST:** 1976
SQ FT: 60,000
SALES (est): 19.7MM **Privately Held**
WEB: www.beartruss.net
SIC: 2439 Trusses, wooden roof; trusses, except roof: laminated lumber

(G-14993)
MOMENTUM INDUSTRIES INC
100 Woodside Dr (48880-1144)
PHONE..................989 681-5735
Dean Sharick, *President*
EMP: 18 **EST:** 1987
SQ FT: 15,000
SALES (est): 2.2MM **Privately Held**
WEB: www.momentumind.com
SIC: 3544 7389 3599 Special dies & tools; grinding, precision: commercial or industrial; custom machinery

(G-14994)
NORTH STATE SALES
6298 N State Rd (48880-9207)
PHONE..................989 681-2806
Roger Anna, *Owner*
EMP: 8 **EST:** 2000
SALES (est): 500K **Privately Held**
WEB: www.northstatesalesonline.com
SIC: 2434 Wood kitchen cabinets

(G-14995)
PLASTI - PAINT INC (PA)
801 Woodside Dr (48880-1054)
P.O. Box 280 (48880-0280)
PHONE..................989 285-2280
David D Roslund, *President*
Chris Bonner, *QC Mgr*
Megan Burgess, *Human Resources*
Adam Krebs, *Manager*
Terri Rhoades, *Manager*
EMP: 30 **EST:** 1989
SALES (est): 18.3MM **Privately Held**
WEB: www.plastipaint.com
SIC: 3479 Coating of metals & formed products; painting, coating & hot dipping

(G-14996)
POWELL FABRICATION & MFG LLC
740 E Monroe Rd (48880-9200)
PHONE..................989 681-2158
Duane Powell,
Norman L Winterstein,
▼ **EMP:** 34 **EST:** 1964
SQ FT: 33,000
SALES (est): 10.7MM **Privately Held**
WEB: www.powellsolutions.com
SIC: 3559 3441 Chemical machinery & equipment; fabricated structural metal

Saline
Washtenaw County

(G-14997)
ACADIA GROUP LLC
Also Called: Allegra Print & Imaging
1283 Industrial Dr (48176-9434)
PHONE..................734 944-1404
Patrick M Mahoney, *Corp Secy*
Jason McLean, *Accounts Mgr*
Francis Olegario, *Accounts Mgr*
Deare Mahoney,
EMP: 20 **EST:** 1973
SQ FT: 27,000
SALES (est): 1MM **Privately Held**
WEB: www.allegramarketingprint.com
SIC: 2752 7334 Commercial printing, offset; photocopying & duplicating services

(G-14998)
ACCU PRODUCTS INTERNATIONAL
7836 Bethel Church Rd (48176-9732)
PHONE..................734 429-9571
John M Kosmalski, *President*
Patricia Kosmalski, *Vice Pres*
▲ **EMP:** 5 **EST:** 1982
SALES (est): 375.2K **Privately Held**
WEB: www.accuproducts.com
SIC: 3545 5961 Precision measuring tools; tools & hardware, mail order

(G-14999)
AKERVALL TECHNOLOGIES INC
Also Called: Sisu Mouthguards
1512 Woodland Dr (48176-1632)
PHONE..................800 444-0570
Liz Akervall, *CEO*
Jan Akervall, *Corp Secy*
Kathy Capelli, *COO*
Mark Ish, *Exec VP*
Ben Bloomfield, *Project Mgr*
EMP: 12 **EST:** 2008
SALES (est): 2.1MM **Privately Held**
WEB: www.sisuguard.com
SIC: 3843 Dental equipment & supplies

(G-15000)
AMERICAN FARM PRODUCTS INC
1382 Industrial Dr Ste 4 (48176-9487)
PHONE..................734 484-4180
William R Absalom, *President*
Brigitte Grobbel, *Manager*
Howard Jensen, *Manager*
Larry Jones, *Manager*
Arlin Koglin, *Manager*
EMP: 10 **EST:** 1982
SQ FT: 2,000
SALES (est): 1.7MM **Privately Held**
WEB: www.afpltd.net
SIC: 2869 Enzymes

Saline - Washtenaw County (G-15001) — GEOGRAPHIC SECTION

(G-15001)
AMERICAN SOY PRODUCTS INC
Also Called: A S P
1474 Woodland Dr (48176-1282)
PHONE................................734 429-2310
Hiroyasu Iwatsuki, *CEO*
Ron Roller, *President*
James Fox, *VP Opers*
Sue Denison, *Purchasing*
Cassandra Stephenson, *Purchasing*
▲ **EMP:** 70 **EST:** 1985
SQ FT: 65,000
SALES (est): 19.1MM **Privately Held**
WEB: www.americansoy.com
SIC: 2099 Food preparations

(G-15002)
ANN ARBOR JOURNAL
106 W Michigan Ave (48176-1325)
PHONE................................734 429-7380
Michelle Rogers, *Manager*
EMP: 4 **EST:** 2017
SALES (est): 73.8K **Privately Held**
SIC: 2711 Newspapers, publishing & printing

(G-15003)
ANN ARBOR PLASTICS INC
Also Called: American Plastic Solutions
815 Woodland Dr (48176-1259)
PHONE................................734 944-0800
K Anthony Glinke, *President*
Lori Stefanski, *Office Mgr*
EMP: 8 **EST:** 1969
SQ FT: 18,000
SALES (est): 987.9K **Privately Held**
WEB: www.americanplasticsolutions.com
SIC: 3089 5162 Injection molding of plastics; blow molded finished plastic products; plastics sheets & rods

(G-15004)
ARCON VERNOVA INC
271 Old Creek Dr (48176-1686)
PHONE................................734 904-1895
Thomas M Curran, *President*
Thomas Curran, *General Mgr*
EMP: 5 **EST:** 2008
SALES (est): 271.4K **Privately Held**
WEB: www.fcesoftware.com
SIC: 3559 Special industry machinery

(G-15005)
B C & A CO
1270 Barnes Ct (48176-9589)
PHONE................................734 429-3129
Bruce D Clyde, *President*
David Clyde, *Vice Pres*
Connie Petrinovic, *Opers Mgr*
John Cameron, *Engineer*
EMP: 27 **EST:** 1986
SQ FT: 28,000
SALES (est): 1MM **Privately Held**
SIC: 3089 Injection molding of plastics

(G-15006)
C & M TOOL LLC
1235 Industrial Dr Ste 7 (48176-1742)
PHONE................................734 944-3355
Richard Leonte, *Office Mgr*
Pavel Leonte, *Mng Member*
Carmen Leonte,
EMP: 7 **EST:** 1994
SQ FT: 3,000
SALES (est): 750K **Privately Held**
SIC: 3544 Special dies & tools

(G-15007)
CANDLES BY LORI LLC
390 E Castlebury Cir (48176-1477)
PHONE................................734 474-6314
Lori Debling, *Principal*
EMP: 4 **EST:** 2017
SALES (est): 57.8K **Privately Held**
WEB: www.candlesbylori.com
SIC: 3999 Candles

(G-15008)
COBREX LTD
5880 Braun Rd (48176-8903)
PHONE................................734 429-9758
Rex Smith, *President*
Judith Smith, *Corp Secy*
EMP: 4

SALES (est): 416.1K **Privately Held**
SIC: 2759 3993 Screen printing; signs & advertising specialties

(G-15009)
CONDAT CORPORATION
250 S Industrial Dr (48176-9397)
PHONE................................734 944-4994
Brad Sulkey, *CEO*
Roberto Castillo, *Regl Sales Mgr*
◆ **EMP:** 30 **EST:** 1854
SALES (est): 15.5MM
SALES (corp-wide): 127.7MM **Privately Held**
WEB: www.condatcorp.com
SIC: 2992 5169 5172 Oils & greases, blending & compounding; rustproofing chemicals; lubricating oils & greases
PA: Condat Sa
  Condat
  Chasse Sur Rhone 38670
  478 738-641

(G-15010)
CRESCIVE DIE AND TOOL INC
Also Called: MTI-Saline
905 Woodland Dr (48176-1625)
P.O. Box 70 (48176-0070)
PHONE................................734 482-0303
Joe Ponteri, *CEO*
Mike Wilson, *CFO*
EMP: 17 **EST:** 1998
SALES (est): 883.2K **Privately Held**
SIC: 3465 Automotive stampings

(G-15011)
DAVCO MANUFACTURING LLC
1600 Woodland Dr (48176-1629)
PHONE................................734 429-5665
Kevin Rucinski, *COO*
Steven Emery, *Project Mgr*
EMP: 9 **EST:** 1995
SALES (est): 1.9MM **Privately Held**
WEB: www.davco.com
SIC: 5013 3714 3443 Motor vehicle supplies & new parts; motor vehicle parts & accessories; fabricated plate work (boiler shop)

(G-15012)
DAVCO TECHNOLOGY LLC
1600 Woodland Dr (48176-1629)
PHONE................................734 429-5665
Mark Bera, *President*
◆ **EMP:** 52 **EST:** 1976
SQ FT: 54,000
SALES (est): 11.6MM
SALES (corp-wide): 5.1B **Privately Held**
WEB: www.davco.com
SIC: 3714 Fuel systems & parts, motor vehicle
PA: Penske Corporation
  2555 S Telegraph Rd
  Bloomfield Hills MI 48302
  248 648-2000

(G-15013)
DTM INC
1283 Industrial Dr (48176-9434)
PHONE................................734 944-1109
Patrick Ahoney, *Treasurer*
EMP: 6 **EST:** 2017
SALES (est): 304.8K **Privately Held**
SIC: 2752 Commercial printing, lithographic

(G-15014)
ELECTROCRAFT MICHIGAN INC
1705 Woodland Dr (48176-1606)
P.O. Box 7746, Ann Arbor (48107-7746)
PHONE................................603 516-1297
Jim Elsmer, *President*
EMP: 22 **EST:** 2009
SQ FT: 8,000
SALES (est): 4.2MM **Privately Held**
WEB: www.electrocraft.com
SIC: 3625 Motor starters & controllers, electric

(G-15015)
ELEGANT GLASSWORKS
8636 Roundhill Ct (48176-9458)
PHONE................................734 845-1901
Deborah Brodie, *Principal*
EMP: 5 **EST:** 2017

SALES (est): 70.1K **Privately Held**
SIC: 3231 Products of purchased glass

(G-15016)
F AND R ASSOCIATES
745 Woodland Dr (48176-1771)
PHONE................................734 316-7763
EMP: 4 **EST:** 2017
SALES (est): 84.5K **Privately Held**
SIC: 3312 Blast furnaces & steel mills

(G-15017)
FAURECIA INTR SYSTEMS SLINE LL
7700 E Michigan Ave (48176-1721)
PHONE................................734 429-0030
Stuart Weiss,
▲ **EMP:** 1 **EST:** 2011
SALES (est): 17.5MM
SALES (corp-wide): 41.2MM **Privately Held**
SIC: 3714 Motor vehicle parts & accessories
HQ: Faurecia Interior Systems, Inc.
  2800 High Meadow Cir
  Auburn Hills MI 48326
  248 724-5100

(G-15018)
GANNONS GENERAL CONTRACT
9216 Yorkshire Dr (48176-9442)
PHONE................................734 429-5859
Thomas Gannon, *Owner*
EMP: 5 **EST:** 2001
SALES (est): 63.5K **Privately Held**
SIC: 3479 Painting, coating & hot dipping

(G-15019)
GENTILE PACKAGING MACHINERY CO
8300 Boettner Rd (48176-9828)
PHONE................................734 429-1177
Aliseo Gentile, *President*
Cathy Gentile, *Corp Secy*
Rob Wilkerson, *Plant Mgr*
Jody Oconnor, *Sales Staff*
EMP: 5 **EST:** 1969
SQ FT: 1,500
SALES (est): 596.9K **Privately Held**
WEB: www.gentilemachinery.com
SIC: 3565 Packaging machinery

(G-15020)
HEAR CLEAR INC
311 Castlebury Dr (48176-1473)
PHONE................................734 525-8467
David R Wizgird, *Principal*
EMP: 6 **EST:** 2005
SALES (est): 65.9K **Privately Held**
SIC: 3613 Regulators, power

(G-15021)
INVERTECH INC
1404 Industrial Dr Ste 1 (48176-9495)
PHONE................................734 944-4400
Lance Ennis, *COO*
Lori Kill, *Prdtn Mgr*
EMP: 8 **EST:** 2006
SALES (est): 681.3K **Privately Held**
WEB: www.invertech.com
SIC: 3829 Gas detectors

(G-15022)
JAC PRODUCTS INC
151 S Industrial Dr (48176-9182)
PHONE................................734 944-8844
EMP: 5
SALES (corp-wide): 748.6MM **Privately Held**
WEB: www.jacproducts.com
SIC: 3089 Injection molding of plastics
HQ: Jac Products, Inc.
  225 S Industrial Dr
  Saline MI 48176
  734 944-8844

(G-15023)
KYOCERA UNIMERCO TOOLING INC
Also Called: Unimerco Group A/S
6620 State Rd (48176-9274)
PHONE................................734 944-4433
Jeremy Parrish, *President*
▲ **EMP:** 48 **EST:** 1995

SQ FT: 50,000
SALES (est): 12.9MM **Privately Held**
WEB: www.kyocera-unimerco.us
SIC: 7699 3545 5084 Knife, saw & tool sharpening & repair; cutting tools for machine tools; machine tools & accessories
HQ: Kyocera Unimerco A/S
  Drejervej 2
  Sunds 7451
  962 923-00

(G-15024)
LIEBHERR AEROSPACE SALINE INC
1465 Woodland Dr (48176-1627)
PHONE................................734 429-7225
Alex Vlielander, *President*
Steven Fracassa, *Engineer*
Derek Hampel, *Manager*
James Will, *Manager*
Jim Will, *Manager*
▲ **EMP:** 145 **EST:** 2004
SQ FT: 100,000
SALES (est): 41.4MM
SALES (corp-wide): 12.8B **Privately Held**
WEB: www.liebherr.com
SIC: 4581 7699 3728 Aircraft servicing & repairing; aircraft & heavy equipment repair services; alighting (landing gear) assemblies, aircraft
PA: Liebherr-International Ag
  Rue Hans-Liebherr 7
  Bulle FR 1630
  269 133-111

(G-15025)
MCNAUGHTON & GUNN INC (PA)
960 Woodland Dr (48176-1634)
P.O. Box 10 (48176-0010)
PHONE................................734 429-5411
Julie McFarland, *President*
Julie Mc Farland, *President*
Robert L Mc Naughton, *President*
Jim Clark, *Vice Pres*
Ruth Spaulding, *Production*
▼ **EMP:** 123 **EST:** 1975
SQ FT: 82,000
SALES (est): 32.5MM **Privately Held**
WEB: www.mcnaughton-gunn.com
SIC: 2732 2789 Books: printing & binding; bookbinding & related work

(G-15026)
MECTRON ENGINEERING CO INC
400 S Industrial Dr (48176-9497)
PHONE................................734 944-8777
James L Hanna, *President*
Mark L Hanna, *COO*
Carol A Hanna, *Vice Pres*
Andrew Hanna, *Engineer*
Kathy Gram, *Controller*
▲ **EMP:** 38 **EST:** 1968
SQ FT: 39,000
SALES (est): 4.7MM **Privately Held**
WEB: www.mectroninspection.com
SIC: 3826 Analytical instruments

(G-15027)
MIKAN CORPORATION
Also Called: Akki Products
1271 Industrial Dr Ste 3 (48176-8400)
P.O. Box 381 (48176-0381)
PHONE................................734 944-9447
Margaret G Stevens, *President*
Michael G Stevens, *Vice Pres*
EMP: 10
SQ FT: 7,800
SALES: 1.6MM **Privately Held**
WEB: www.mikancorp.com
SIC: 3955 7378 5045 5112 Print cartridges for laser & other computer printers; computer peripheral equipment repair & maintenance; computers, peripherals & software; printers, computer; stationery & office supplies

(G-15028)
MMI ENGINEERED SOLUTIONS INC (HQ)
Also Called: Drayton Plains Tool Company
1715 Woodland Dr (48176-1614)
PHONE................................734 429-4664
Doug Callahan, *President*

Andrew Valade, *Business Mgr*
Bev Gengler, *Production*
Edgar Hernandez, *Engineer*
Kurtis Mallory, *Engineer*
▲ **EMP**: 79 **EST**: 1983
SQ FT: 80,000
SALES (est): 24.3MM **Privately Held**
WEB: www.mmi-es.com
SIC: 3089 8711 Injection molding of plastics; engineering services

(G-15029)
MOGULTECH LLC
1454 Judd Rd (48176-8819)
PHONE.................................734 944-5053
Jeff Stockwell, *Info Tech Mgr*
Lori Stockwell,
EMP: 5 **EST**: 1998
SALES (est): 479.4K **Privately Held**
WEB: www.mogultechmachining.com
SIC: 3599 Machine shop, jobbing & repair

(G-15030)
NORGREN AUTOMTN SOLUTIONS LLC (DH)
Also Called: I.S.I. Automation Products
1325 Woodland Dr (48176-1626)
PHONE.................................734 429-4989
Tim Key, *President*
Frank Alex, *CFO*
▲ **EMP**: 200 **EST**: 1996
SQ FT: 90,000
SALES (est): 43MM
SALES (corp-wide): 2.4B **Privately Held**
WEB: www.norgren.com
SIC: 3549 Assembly machines, including robotic
HQ: Norgren Llc
  5400 S Delaware St
  Littleton CO 80120
  303 794-5000

(G-15031)
PLASTECHS OF MICHIGAN LLC
1270 Barnes Ct (48176-9589)
PHONE.................................734 429-3129
Connie Petrinovic, *Opers Mgr*
Nigam Tripathi,
EMP: 26 **EST**: 2015
SALES (est): 3.6MM **Privately Held**
WEB: www.plastesllc.com
SIC: 3089 Injection molding of plastics

(G-15032)
PRINTING SERVICES INC
Also Called: Allegra Printing & Imaging
1283 Industrial Dr (48176-9434)
PHONE.................................734 944-1404
Patrick Mahoney, *President*
Deare Mahoney, *Corp Secy*
EMP: 17 **EST**: 1963
SALES (est): 600.3K **Privately Held**
WEB: www.allegramarketingprint.com
SIC: 2752 Commercial printing, offset

(G-15033)
PRS JUDD
1035 Judd Rd (48176-8823)
PHONE.................................734 470-6162
EMP: 4 **EST**: 2009
SALES (est): 62.2K **Privately Held**
SIC: 2741 Miscellaneous publishing

(G-15034)
R & B PLASTICS MACHINERY LLC
1605 Woodland Dr (48176-1638)
PHONE.................................734 429-9421
Fred Piercy, *General Mgr*
Tom Redies, *Vice Pres*
Al Hodge, *Vice Pres*
Thomas Redies, *Vice Pres*
Paul Smith, *Plant Mgr*
▲ **EMP**: 38 **EST**: 2002
SQ FT: 80,000
SALES (est): 8.3MM **Privately Held**
WEB: www.rbplasticsmachinery.com
SIC: 3559 3544 Plastics working machinery; industrial molds

(G-15035)
RALRUBE INC
8423 Boettner Rd (48176-9829)
PHONE.................................734 429-0033
Robert Skandalaris, *President*
EMP: 6

SQ FT: 8,000
SALES (est): 785.8K **Privately Held**
SIC: 2899 Chemical preparations

(G-15036)
REPORTER PAPERS INC
106 W Michigan Ave (48176-1325)
PHONE.................................734 429-5428
Jim Williams, *President*
EMP: 8 **EST**: 1951
SALES (est): 123.1K **Privately Held**
SIC: 2711 Newspapers, publishing & printing

(G-15037)
SALINE LECTRONICS INC
710 N Maple Rd (48176-1294)
PHONE.................................734 944-2120
Victor Giglio, *CEO*
Steven Telgen, *President*
Dana Zickafoose, *Purchasing*
Lance Bowley, *QC Mgr*
Brittany Macneil, *Accounts Mgr*
▲ **EMP**: 122 **EST**: 2002
SQ FT: 110,000
SALES (est): 64.2MM
SALES (corp-wide): 84.8MM **Privately Held**
WEB: www.lectronics.net
SIC: 3672 Printed circuit boards
PA: Megatronics Us Ultimate Holdco Llc
  32 Northwestern Dr
  Salem NH 03079
  603 499-4300

(G-15038)
SGS WOOD WORKS LLC
3702 Meadow Ln (48176-9060)
PHONE.................................239 564-8449
John Federici, *Principal*
EMP: 5 **EST**: 2016
SALES (est): 69K **Privately Held**
SIC: 2431 Millwork

(G-15039)
SHIELDS CLASSIC TOYS
Also Called: Puzzleman Toys, The
1400 E Michigan Ave Ste F (48176-1733)
P.O. Box 187, Chesaning (48616-0187)
PHONE.................................888 806-2632
Roy Shields, *CEO*
Charles H W Hall, *Owner*
Charles Hall, *Finance*
EMP: 4 **EST**: 2019
SQ FT: 3,900
SALES (est): 318.2K **Privately Held**
WEB: www.shieldschildcaresupplies.com
SIC: 3993 3544 3172 2511 Signs & advertising specialties; special dies, tools, jigs & fixtures; personal leather goods; wood household furniture; nailed wood boxes & shook; games, toys & children's vehicles

(G-15040)
SHIFT ROASTING COMPANY LLC
9304 Warner Rd (48176-9374)
PHONE.................................734 915-3666
EMP: 4 **EST**: 2020
SALES (est): 62.3K **Privately Held**
SIC: 2095 Roasted coffee

(G-15041)
STONY LAKE CORPORATION
5115 Saline Waterworks Rd (48176-9703)
P.O. Box 771 (48176-0771)
PHONE.................................734 944-9426
Gerald Tubbs, *Principal*
EMP: 5 **EST**: 2014
SALES (est): 71.6K **Privately Held**
WEB: www.stonylakebrewing.com
SIC: 2082 Beer (alcoholic beverage)

(G-15042)
SVN INC
Also Called: Lookingbus
6763 Heatheridge Dr (48176-9230)
PHONE.................................734 707-7131
Nirit Glazer, *CEO*
Zvi Zuler, *Principal*
EMP: 4 **EST**: 2008
SALES (est): 285K **Privately Held**
WEB: www.svn.com
SIC: 2899 Food contamination testing or screening kits

(G-15043)
VERTIGEE CORPORATION
1722 Wildwood Trl (48176-1655)
PHONE.................................313 999-1020
Stephen Farr, *CEO*
Jean Fideler, *Admin Sec*
EMP: 7 **EST**: 2016
SALES (est): 280.4K **Privately Held**
SIC: 7372 Prepackaged software

(G-15044)
WELLWOOD SOLUTIONS LLC
2198 Windmill Way (48176-8022)
PHONE.................................734 368-0368
James Woods, *Principal*
EMP: 4 **EST**: 2015
SALES (est): 61.3K **Privately Held**
SIC: 2499 Wood products

(G-15045)
WINDSOR MOLD INC
Also Called: Precision Plastic
1294 Beach Ct (48176-9185)
P.O. Box 32523, Detroit (48232-0523)
PHONE.................................734 944-5080
EMP: 5
SALES (corp-wide): 796K **Privately Held**
WEB: www.windsormoldgroup.com
SIC: 3089 Injection molding of plastics
HQ: Windsor Mold Inc
  4035 Malden Rd
  Windsor ON N9C 2
  519 972-9032

(G-15046)
WINDSOR MOLD USA INC
Also Called: Windsor Mold Saline
1294 Beach Ct (48176-9185)
P.O. Box 32523, Detroit (48232-0523)
PHONE.................................734 944-5080
Keith Henry, *President*
Greg Mahoney, *Corp Secy*
EMP: 50 **EST**: 2013
SQ FT: 73,000
SALES (est): 9.9MM
SALES (corp-wide): 796K **Privately Held**
WEB: www.windsormoldgroup.com
SIC: 3089 Injection molding of plastics
PA: 873740 Ontario Inc
  4035 Malden Rd
  Windsor ON N9C 2
  519 972-9032

(G-15047)
YOUNG CABINETRY INC
1400 E Michigan Ave (48176-1733)
P.O. Box 782 (48176-0782)
PHONE.................................734 316-2896
EMP: 5 **EST**: 2017
SALES (est): 65K **Privately Held**
WEB: www.youngcabinetry.com
SIC: 2434 Wood kitchen cabinets

Sand Lake
Kent County

(G-15048)
HIGH GRADE MATERIALS COMPANY
16180 Northland Dr (49343-8856)
PHONE.................................616 696-9540
Casey Chatman, *Parts Mgr*
James Sturris, *Manager*
EMP: 9
SALES (corp-wide): 17.2MM **Privately Held**
WEB: www.highgradematerials.com
SIC: 3273 Ready-mixed concrete
PA: High Grade Materials Company
  9266 Snows Lake Rd
  Greenville MI 48838
  616 754-5545

(G-15049)
MELLEMAS CUT STONE
16610 Findley Dr (49343-9256)
PHONE.................................616 984-2493
Greg Mellema, *Principal*
EMP: 6 **EST**: 2010
SALES (est): 425.7K **Privately Held**
SIC: 3281 Cut stone & stone products

(G-15050)
NORTH KENT BASE LLC
109 N 3rd St (49343-5114)
P.O. Box 32 (49343-0032)
PHONE.................................616 636-4300
John Todd, *Principal*
Dan Myslenski, *Plant Mgr*
EMP: 8 **EST**: 2007
SALES (est): 207.6K **Privately Held**
WEB: www.northkentbase.com
SIC: 3599 Machine & other job shop work

(G-15051)
R & C REDI-MIX INC
Also Called: Ensley Sand & Gravel
11991 Elm St (49343)
P.O. Box 185, Grant (49327-0185)
PHONE.................................616 636-5650
Raymond Oppenhuizen Jr, *President*
EMP: 9 **EST**: 1989
SQ FT: 2,800
SALES (est): 770.6K **Privately Held**
WEB: www.rcredimix.com
SIC: 3273 Ready-mixed concrete

(G-15052)
R & S PROPELLER INC
Also Called: R & S Propeller Repair
212 S 3rd St (49343-9203)
PHONE.................................616 636-8202
Judith A Rowland, *President*
EMP: 10 **EST**: 2001
SALES (est): 787.4K **Privately Held**
SIC: 3449 Miscellaneous metalwork

(G-15053)
RC METAL PRODUCTS INC
4365 21 Mile Rd (49343-9473)
P.O. Box 129, Grandville (49468-0129)
PHONE.................................616 696-1694
Richard Crooks, *President*
EMP: 9 **EST**: 1989
SQ FT: 7,000
SALES (est): 562.5K **Privately Held**
SIC: 3443 Metal parts

Sandusky
Sanilac County

(G-15054)
ASCO LP
Also Called: Numatics
360 Thelma St (48471-1415)
PHONE.................................810 648-9141
EMP: 195
SALES (corp-wide): 16.7B **Publicly Held**
SIC: 3491 Industrial valves
HQ: Asco, L.P.
  160 Park Ave
  Florham Park NJ 07932
  800 972-2726

(G-15055)
BADER & CO
Also Called: Tri-County Equip-Sandusky
989 W Sanilac Rd (48471-9789)
PHONE.................................810 648-2404
Dan Wadsworth, *President*
EMP: 19 **EST**: 2008
SALES (est): 1.5MM **Privately Held**
WEB: www.tricountyequipment.net
SIC: 3523 7699 5261 Farm machinery & equipment; lawn mower repair shop; lawnmowers & tractors

(G-15056)
BAY-HOUSTON TOWING COMPANY
Also Called: Michigan Peak Company
875 E Sanilac Rd (48471-8790)
P.O. Box 312 (48471-0312)
PHONE.................................810 648-2210
David Newman, *Vice Pres*
Kevin Wormwood, *Plant Mgr*
Doug Landrith, *Maintence Staff*
EMP: 19
SALES (corp-wide): 15.5MM **Privately Held**
WEB: www.bayhouston.com
SIC: 4212 1499 2875 5083 Local trucking, without storage; peat grinding; fertilizers, mixing only; landscaping equipment; hand & edge tools

Sandusky - Sanilac County (G-15057)

PA: Bay-Houston Towing Company
2243 Milford St
Houston TX 77098
713 529-3755

(G-15057)
CINNABAR ENGINEERING INC
116 Orval St (48471-1411)
PHONE..................................810 648-2444
R Weston Caughlan, *President*
EMP: 17 **EST:** 1993
SQ FT: 15,000
SALES (est): 1MM **Privately Held**
WEB: www.gmcmotorhomepeople.com
SIC: 3714 5013 Motor vehicle parts & accessories; automotive supplies & parts

(G-15058)
ELDON PUBLISHING LLC
Also Called: Tribune Recorder
43 S Elk St (48471-1353)
PHONE..................................810 648-5282
William Dixon,
EMP: 4 **EST:** 2010
SQ FT: 800
SALES (est): 227.2K **Privately Held**
WEB: www.sanduskytribune.com
SIC: 2711 Newspapers, publishing & printing

(G-15059)
GREAT NORTHERN PUBLISHING INC
Also Called: Buyers Guide
356 E Sanilac Rd (48471-1151)
P.O. Box 72 (48471-0072)
PHONE..................................810 648-4000
Jane Vanderpoel, *President*
EMP: 66 **EST:** 1969
SALES (est): 1.4MM
SALES (corp-wide): 274.1MM **Privately Held**
WEB: www.21stcenturynewspapers.com
SIC: 2741 Shopping news: publishing & printing
HQ: 21st Century Newspapers, Inc.
6250 Metropolitan Pkwy
Sterling Heights MI 48312
586 469-4510

(G-15060)
INDUSTRIAL ATOMATED DESIGN LLC
245 S Stoutenburg Rd (48471-8649)
PHONE..................................810 648-9200
Brian Park, *Administration*
Vance Upper,
EMP: 14 **EST:** 1999
SQ FT: 11,005
SALES (est): 665.3K **Privately Held**
WEB: www.iadesigns.net
SIC: 3569 Robots, assembly line: industrial & commercial

(G-15061)
J R C INC (PA)
Also Called: Bargain Hunter
356 E Sanilac Rd (48471-1151)
P.O. Box 72 (48471-0072)
PHONE..................................810 648-4000
Eric Levine, *Advt Staff*
Jane Vanderpoel, *Manager*
EMP: 14 **EST:** 1973
SQ FT: 10,000
SALES (est): 1.1MM **Privately Held**
SIC: 2711 2752 Newspapers, publishing & printing; commercial printing, offset

(G-15062)
JENSEN BRIDGE & SUPPLY COMPANY (PA)
400 Stoney Creek Dr (48471-1043)
P.O. Box 151 (48471-0151)
PHONE..................................810 648-3000
Roger A Loding, *President*
Edward D Giroux, *Vice Pres*
Scott Anger, *Human Resources*
Kevin Simmons, *Representative*
EMP: 25 **EST:** 1923
SQ FT: 52,000
SALES (est): 8.2MM **Privately Held**
WEB: www.jensenbridge.com
SIC: 3444 5039 5211 Culverts; sheet metal; prefabricated structures; lumber & other building materials

(G-15063)
NELSON MANUFACTURING INC
1240 W Sanilac Rd Ste A (48471-9654)
PHONE..................................810 648-0065
Brian Nelson, *President*
Debra Nelson, *Vice Pres*
EMP: 7 **EST:** 1993
SALES (est): 620.6K **Privately Held**
SIC: 3469 3312 Machine parts, stamped or pressed metal; structural shapes & pilings, steel

(G-15064)
NICHOLAS E KAPPEL
1335 W Frenchline Rd (48471-9798)
PHONE..................................810 404-9486
Nick Kappel, *Principal*
EMP: 6 **EST:** 2010
SALES (est): 131.3K **Privately Held**
SIC: 2511 Wood household furniture

(G-15065)
PRODUCTION DEV SYSTEMS LLC
245 Campbell Rd (48471-1427)
PHONE..................................810 648-2111
EMP: 15 **EST:** 2014
SALES (est): 2.9MM **Privately Held**
SIC: 3599 Mfg Industrial Machinery

(G-15066)
SANDUSKY CONCRETE & SUPPLY
376 E Sanilac Rd (48471-1158)
PHONE..................................810 648-2627
William Burgess Jr, *President*
John Bungart, *Vice Pres*
Curt Backus, *Treasurer*
Jeff Walkup, *Office Mgr*
Alex Galligan, *Admin Sec*
EMP: 4 **EST:** 1946
SQ FT: 2,500
SALES (est): 824K **Privately Held**
WEB: www.sanduskychamber.us
SIC: 5032 5211 3171 3272 Concrete mixtures; sand, construction; gravel; concrete & cinder block; sand & gravel; cement; purses, women's; septic tanks, concrete

(G-15067)
SANILAC DRAIN AND TILE CO
61 Orval St (48471-1410)
PHONE..................................810 648-4100
Robert Hall, *President*
Deanna Stone, *Admin Sec*
EMP: 6 **EST:** 1952
SQ FT: 5,000
SALES (est): 600K **Privately Held**
WEB: www.crimsonquartet.com
SIC: 3272 Concrete products used to facilitate drainage

(G-15068)
STOUTENBURG INC
Also Called: Breiten Lumber
121 Campbell Rd (48471-1412)
PHONE..................................810 648-4400
Clinton A Stoutenburg, *President*
Gary Bright, *Plant Mgr*
EMP: 25 **EST:** 2007
SQ FT: 300,000
SALES (est): 569.7K **Privately Held**
WEB: www.breitenlumber.com
SIC: 2448 Pallets, wood

(G-15069)
THUMB BIOENERGY LLC
155 Orval St (48471-1491)
PHONE..................................810 404-2466
James Hastings, *Principal*
Alex Ritter, *Prdtn Mgr*
EMP: 10 **EST:** 2010
SALES (est): 3MM **Privately Held**
WEB: www.thumbbioenergy.com
SIC: 2869 High purity grade chemicals, organic

(G-15070)
VIBRACOUSTIC USA INC
Also Called: Trelleborg Automotive
180 Dawson St (48471-1034)
PHONE..................................810 648-2100
Hakan Cirag, *Vice Pres*
Larry Cloos, *Vice Pres*
Jason Booms, *Prdtn Mgr*
Bill Tobin, *Branch Mgr*
Mark Wheeler, *Manager*
EMP: 300
SQ FT: 280,000
SALES (corp-wide): 2.4B **Privately Held**
WEB: www.vibracoustic.com
SIC: 3061 Automotive rubber goods (mechanical)
HQ: Vibracoustic Usa, Inc.
400 Aylworth Ave
South Haven MI 49090

(G-15071)
VIBRACOUSTIC USA INC
370 Industrial St (48471-1493)
PHONE..................................810 648-2100
Bill Tobin, *Branch Mgr*
EMP: 6
SALES (corp-wide): 2.4B **Privately Held**
WEB: www.vibracoustic.com
SIC: 3061 Mechanical rubber goods
HQ: Vibracoustic Usa, Inc.
400 Aylworth Ave
South Haven MI 49090

Sanford
Midland County

(G-15072)
BRIGGS CONTRACTING
62 E Saginaw Rd (48657-9250)
P.O. Box 319 (48657-0319)
PHONE..................................989 687-7331
Gary L Briggs, *Owner*
Anne Briggs, *Corp Secy*
EMP: 7 **EST:** 1966
SQ FT: 3,200
SALES (est): 1.1MM **Privately Held**
WEB: www.briggslandscapesupply.com
SIC: 1442 Construction sand & gravel

(G-15073)
MARK MOLD AND ENGINEERING
773 W Beamish Rd (48657-9489)
P.O. Box 407 (48657-0407)
PHONE..................................989 687-9786
Mark Reynaert, *Owner*
EMP: 10 **EST:** 1994
SQ FT: 3,500
SALES (est): 740.4K **Privately Held**
WEB: www.markmold.com
SIC: 3544 Special dies & tools

(G-15074)
NATIONAL INDUS SP COATINGS LLC
2600 N West River Rd (48657-9457)
PHONE..................................989 894-8538
Roger Griffin,
EMP: 15 **EST:** 2019
SALES (est): 1MM **Privately Held**
WEB: www.niscoatings.com
SIC: 3479 Coating of metals & formed products

Saranac
Ionia County

(G-15075)
ADAC PLASTICS INC
Also Called: Adac Automotive
6138 Riverside Dr (48881-8778)
PHONE..................................616 642-0109
Richard Burns, *General Mgr*
Linda Marquez, *Director*
EMP: 58
SALES (corp-wide): 285.6MM **Privately Held**
WEB: www.adacautomotive.com
SIC: 3714 Acceleration equipment, motor vehicle
PA: Adac Plastics, Inc.
5690 Eagle Dr Se
Grand Rapids MI 49512
616 957-0311

(G-15076)
ADVERTISER PUBLISHING CO INC
Also Called: Ionia County Shoppers Guide
13 N Bridge St (48881-5122)
P.O. Box 46 (48881-0046)
PHONE..................................616 642-9411
John Brown, *President*
Carol Benjamin, *Admin Sec*
EMP: 6
SQ FT: 2,800
SALES (est): 665K **Privately Held**
WEB: www.ioniacountyshoppersguide.com
SIC: 2741 Guides: publishing only, not printed on site

(G-15077)
DYNAMIC WOOD PRODUCTS INC
9385 Potters Rd (48881-9661)
PHONE..................................616 897-8114
Donald Braam, *President*
Jeffrey Braam, *Vice Pres*
Jeff Braam, *Plant Mgr*
David Thornton, *Purch Agent*
Craig Braam, *Treasurer*
EMP: 4 **EST:** 1991
SALES (est): 1.2MM **Privately Held**
WEB: www.dwpinc.net
SIC: 2521 Wood office furniture

(G-15078)
IMPACT OPERATIONS LLC
8808 Grand River Ave (48881-9820)
PHONE..................................616 642-9570
EMP: 12
SALES (est): 1.3MM **Privately Held**
SIC: 3471 Finishing, metals or formed products

(G-15079)
JOE S HANDYMAN SERVICE
8194 Morrison Lake Gdns (48881-8787)
PHONE..................................616 642-6038
Joeseph P Lipinski, *Owner*
EMP: 4 **EST:** 1996
SALES (est): 145.8K **Privately Held**
SIC: 3432 Plumbing fixture fittings & trim

(G-15080)
PINKNEY HILL MEAT CO
3577 Pinckney Rd (48881-9429)
PHONE..................................616 897-4921
Phil Husche, *President*
EMP: 4 **EST:** 2000
SALES (est): 246.1K **Privately Held**
SIC: 2011 Meat packing plants

(G-15081)
SARANAC TANK INC
100 W Main St (48881-5117)
P.O. Box 26 (48881-0026)
PHONE..................................616 642-9481
Gregory Grieves, *President*
Vickey Grieves, *Corp Secy*
EMP: 7 **EST:** 1974
SQ FT: 5,000
SALES (est): 693.3K **Privately Held**
SIC: 3443 7699 Tanks, standard or custom fabricated: metal plate; tank repair

(G-15082)
UNITED SIGN CO
6983 Bluewater Hwy (48881-9535)
PHONE..................................616 642-0200
Gage Mitchell, *CEO*
EMP: 7 **EST:** 2014
SALES (est): 283.7K **Privately Held**
WEB: www.unitedsignco.com
SIC: 3993 Signs & advertising specialties

Saugatuck
Allegan County

(G-15083)
ENAGON LLC
3381 Blue Star Hwy (49453-9724)
PHONE..................................269 455-5110
Brian Ryckbost, *VP Business*
Terry Ebels, *Mng Member*
EMP: 7 **EST:** 2016

GEOGRAPHIC SECTION

SALES (est): 2MM **Privately Held**
WEB: www.enagonllc.com
SIC: 3541 Milling machines

(G-15084)
N D R ENTERPRISES INC
Also Called: Macatawa Bay Boat Works
297 S Maple St (49453-9795)
PHONE.................................269 857-4556
Jonathan Reuf, *President*
EMP: 6 **EST:** 1982
SQ FT: 8,000
SALES (est): 531.9K **Privately Held**
WEB: www.mbbw.com
SIC: 3732 Boat building & repairing

(G-15085)
SISTERS IN INC
3467 Blue Star Hwy (49453-9400)
PHONE.................................269 857-4085
Trudi Engelbrecht, *Owner*
EMP: 6 **EST:** 2007
SALES (est): 188.4K **Privately Held**
WEB: www.sistersinink.com
SIC: 2759 Screen printing

Sault Sainte Marie
Chippewa County

(G-15086)
AMI INDUSTRIES INC
1351 Industrial Park Dr (49783-1453)
PHONE.................................989 786-3755
Ryan Thorpe, *General Mgr*
Stephen Macdonald, *Plant Mgr*
Jeff Evans, *Branch Mgr*
John Mack, *Technology*
EMP: 5
SALES (corp-wide): 25.3MM **Privately Held**
PA: Ami Industries, Inc.
5093 N Red Oak Rd
Lewiston MI 49756
989 786-3755
SIC: 3559 Automotive related machinery

(G-15087)
BELTONE SKORIC HEARNG AID CNTR
240 W Portage Ave (49783-1922)
PHONE.................................906 379-0606
EMP: 5 **EST:** 2015
SALES (est): 94.1K **Privately Held**
WEB: www.beltoneskorichearing.com
SIC: 7629 3842 Lamp repair & mounting; absorbent cotton, sterilized

(G-15088)
CANUSA LLC
Also Called: Quarter To 5
2510 Ashmun St (49783-3745)
PHONE.................................906 259-0800
Kristina Thibault, *Principal*
Eric Thibault, *Principal*
EMP: 14 **EST:** 2019
SALES (est): 654K **Privately Held**
SIC: 3131 Quarters

(G-15089)
DENNCO LLC
Also Called: Printing Lounge The
418 Ashmun St Ste E (49783-2993)
PHONE.................................866 977-4467
Lori Henderson-Bayn, *Mng Member*
EMP: 5 **EST:** 2020
SALES (est): 156.9K **Privately Held**
SIC: 2759 Commercial printing

(G-15090)
GENE BROW & SONS INC
2754 W 20th St (49783-9459)
PHONE.................................906 635-0859
EMP: 10
SALES (est): 1MM **Privately Held**
SIC: 3273 Mfg Ready-Mixed Concrete

(G-15091)
GREAT LAKES FINE CABINETRY
844 E 3 Mile Rd (49783-9305)
PHONE.................................906 493-5780
Philip Winkel, *President*
Rick Bouwma, *Vice Pres*
EMP: 5 **EST:** 1989
SQ FT: 5,000
SALES (est): 407.5K **Privately Held**
WEB: www.228859.com
SIC: 2434 1751 Wood kitchen cabinets; cabinet & finish carpentry

(G-15092)
J A S VENEER & LUMBER INC
1300 W 12th St (49783-1356)
PHONE.................................906 635-0710
Jack A Schikofsky, *President*
Mike Schikofsky, *Vice Pres*
EMP: 20 **EST:** 1978
SQ FT: 33,000
SALES (est): 3.9MM **Privately Held**
SIC: 2435 Veneer stock, hardwood

(G-15093)
K & K RACING LLC
Also Called: K & K Motorsports
1877 Timber Wolf Ln (49783-9442)
PHONE.................................906 322-1276
Walt Komarnizki, *Owner*
Walter Komarnizki, *Owner*
Rebecca Komarnizki, *Corp Secy*
EMP: 15
SALES (est): 250K **Privately Held**
SIC: 3799 Recreational vehicles

(G-15094)
LSJD PUBLICATIONS LLC
324 E Spruce St (49783-2151)
PHONE.................................843 576-9040
EMP: 4 **EST:** 2016
SALES (est): 40K **Privately Held**
WEB: www.empoweringkidswithjoy.com
SIC: 2741 Miscellaneous publishing

(G-15095)
MALEPORTS SAULT PRTG CO INC
314 Osborn Blvd (49783-1820)
P.O. Box 323 (49783-0323)
PHONE.................................906 632-3369
Ronald T Maleport, *President*
Cindy Albon, *Corp Secy*
Michael Maleport, *Vice Pres*
EMP: 20 **EST:** 1969
SQ FT: 12,500
SALES (est): 5.8MM **Privately Held**
WEB: www.saultprinting.com
SIC: 5112 5044 5021 2752 Office supplies; office equipment; office furniture; commercial printing, offset; bookbinding & related work; commercial printing

(G-15096)
PRECISION EDGE SRGCAL PDTS LLC (PA)
415 W 12th Ave (49783-2607)
PHONE.................................906 632-5600
John Truckey, *President*
Todd Fewins, *Opers Mgr*
Scott Nagy, *Opers Mgr*
Ryan Nichols, *Engineer*
Patt Blanchard, *Human Res Mgr*
EMP: 169 **EST:** 1994
SQ FT: 35,000
SALES (est): 24.7MM **Privately Held**
WEB: www.precisionedge.com
SIC: 3841 Surgical & medical instruments

(G-15097)
R & B ELECTRONICS INC (PA)
1520 Industrial Park Dr (49783-1474)
PHONE.................................906 632-1542
Debra Rogers, *President*
James Cloudman, *Engineer*
Jim Cloudman, *Engineer*
Wayne Olsen, *CFO*
EMP: 51 **EST:** 1985
SQ FT: 12,160
SALES (est): 8.1MM **Privately Held**
WEB: www.randbelectronics.com
SIC: 3728 Aircraft assemblies, subassemblies & parts

(G-15098)
ROGERS BEEF FARMS
6917 S Nicolet Rd (49783-9609)
PHONE.................................906 632-1584
Dan Rogers, *Principal*
EMP: 6 **EST:** 2004
SALES (est): 353.5K **Privately Held**
SIC: 2011 Beef products from beef slaughtered on site

(G-15099)
SAULT TRIBE NEWS
Also Called: Communications Dept
531 Ashmun St (49783-1926)
PHONE.................................906 632-6398
Aaron Payment, *Chairman*
Allan Kamuda, *Director*
Cory Wilson, *Deputy Dir*
Genevieve Maloney, *Family Practiti*
Lindsey Hill, *Assistant*
EMP: 15 **EST:** 1979
SALES (est): 322.6K **Privately Held**
WEB: www.saulttribe.com
SIC: 2711 Newspapers, publishing & printing

(G-15100)
SOO WELDING INC
934 E Portage Ave (49783-2444)
P.O. Box 1583 (49783-7583)
PHONE.................................906 632-8241
Charles M Fabry, *President*
Jody Fabry, *Admin Sec*
EMP: 9 **EST:** 1927
SQ FT: 3,000
SALES (est): 1MM **Privately Held**
WEB: www.soowelding.com
SIC: 5051 7692 3599 5085 Steel; pipe & tubing, steel; welding repair; machine shop, jobbing & repair; welding supplies

(G-15101)
SUPERIOR MAR & ENVMTL SVCS LLC
3779 S Riverside Dr (49783-9505)
PHONE.................................906 253-9448
Christina Sams, *Partner*
Thomas L Farnquist, *Partner*
Jenny Oliver, *Principal*
Sandra Sawyer, *Principal*
Kenny Wagner, *Principal*
EMP: 4 **EST:** 2012
SALES (est): 204.5K **Privately Held**
SIC: 4493 4492 1389 7389 Marine basins; marine towing services; running, cutting & pulling casings, tubes & rods; divers, commercial; marine reporting

(G-15102)
VAN SLOTEN ENTERPRISES INC (PA)
Also Called: Northern Sand & Gravel
1320 W 3 Mile Rd (49783-9251)
P.O. Box 365 (49783-0365)
PHONE.................................906 635-5151
Raymond Van Sloten, *President*
Gerald Van Sloten, *Vice Pres*
Allan Van Sloten, *Treasurer*
Gladys Norris, *Admin Sec*
EMP: 17 **EST:** 1963
SQ FT: 1,800 **Privately Held**
WEB: www.northernsand.com
SIC: 3273 1442 3272 Ready-mixed concrete; common sand mining; gravel mining; concrete products

(G-15103)
WALLIS DIESEL WELDING
479 W M 80 (49783-8531)
PHONE.................................906 647-3245
EMP: 5 **EST:** 1998
SALES (est): 216K **Privately Held**
SIC: 7692 Welding repair

(G-15104)
WENDRICKS TRUSS INC
6142 S Mackinac Trl (49783-8974)
P.O. Box 463 (49783-0463)
PHONE.................................906 635-8822
Steve Hagan, *Manager*
EMP: 10
SALES (corp-wide): 8.3MM **Privately Held**
WEB: www.wendrickstruss.com
SIC: 2439 Trusses, wooden roof
PA: Wendricks Truss, Inc.
W5728 Old Us 2 Road No 43
Hermansville MI 49847
906 498-7709

(G-15105)
YOOPER WD WRKS RESTORATION LLC
Also Called: Yooper Wood Works & Designs
312 Barbeau St (49783-2404)
PHONE.................................906 203-0056
Walter Komarnizk, *Mng Member*
EMP: 4 **EST:** 2019
SALES (est): 124.6K **Privately Held**
SIC: 2491 2426 Wood preserving; carvings, furniture: wood

Sawyer
Berrien County

(G-15106)
ARLINGTON METALS CORPORATION
13100 Arlington Dr (49125-9376)
P.O. Box 284 (49125-0284)
PHONE.................................269 426-3371
Ron Sowizrol, *Plant Mgr*
Rob Woredehoff, *Opers-Prdtn-Mfg*
Ted Orlowski, *Mktg Dir*
Lisa Gagliano, *Manager*
Geri Slattery, *Manager*
EMP: 27
SALES (corp-wide): 26.5MM **Privately Held**
WEB: www.arlingtonmetals.com
SIC: 7389 3312 5051 Metal cutting services; blast furnaces & steel mills; metals service centers & offices
PA: Arlington Metals Corporation
11355 Franklin Ave
Franklin Park IL 60131
847 451-9100

(G-15107)
BURKHOLDER EXCAVATING INC
4898 Weechik Rd (49125-9255)
PHONE.................................269 426-4227
Scott Burkholder, *CEO*
EMP: 6 **EST:** 1991
SALES (est): 540K **Privately Held**
SIC: 1389 Excavating slush pits & cellars

(G-15108)
CC INDUSTRIES LLC
Also Called: Corvette Central
13550 Three Oaks Rd (49125-9328)
P.O. Box 16 (49125-0016)
PHONE.................................269 426-3342
Scott Kohen, *Sales Executive*
Linda Svoboda, *Supervisor*
Gerald E Kohn,
Marcia Dinges, *Admin Asst*
▲ **EMP:** 100 **EST:** 1974
SQ FT: 40,000
SALES (est): 18.9MM **Privately Held**
WEB: www.corvettecentral.com
SIC: 5013 5531 3714 Automotive supplies & parts; automobile & truck equipment & parts; motor vehicle parts & accessories

(G-15109)
INFUSCO COFFEE ROASTERS LLC
5846 Sawyer Rd (49125-9387)
PHONE.................................269 213-5282
Richard Siri,
EMP: 8 **EST:** 2011
SQ FT: 1,800
SALES (est): 632.4K **Privately Held**
WEB: www.infuscocoffee.com
SIC: 2095 3556 Roasted coffee; roasting machinery: coffee, peanut, etc.

(G-15110)
KEY CASTING COMPANY INC (PA)
13145 Red Arrow Hwy (49125-9175)
P.O. Box 246 (49125-0246)
PHONE.................................269 426-3800
Dale R Ender, *President*
Joyce Ender, *Corp Secy*
EMP: 4 **EST:** 1956
SQ FT: 12,000

Sawyer - Berrien County (G-15111)
GEOGRAPHIC SECTION

SALES (est): 610.9K **Privately Held**
SIC: 3363 3364 3544 Aluminum die-castings; zinc & zinc-base alloy die-castings; special dies & tools

(G-15111)
QUALI TONE CORPORATION
Also Called: Quali Tone Pwdr Cating Sndblst
13092 Red Arrow Hwy (49125-9174)
PHONE 269 426-3664
Anthony Pitone, *President*
Joseph Pitone, *Vice Pres*
EMP: 15 **EST:** 1991
SQ FT: 23,000
SALES (est): 2.2MM **Privately Held**
WEB: www.qualitonecorp.com
SIC: 3479 3471 Coating of metals & formed products; plating & polishing

Schoolcraft
Kalamazoo County

(G-15112)
C2DX INC
555 E Eliza St Ste A (49087-8831)
PHONE 269 409-0068
Kevin McLeod, *CEO*
Chad Olson, *Vice Pres*
Amy Papranec, *Vice Pres*
Jennifer Brant, *CFO*
Ian Bund, *Director*
EMP: 10 **EST:** 2018
SALES (est): 1.6MM **Privately Held**
SIC: 5047 3841 Medical equipment & supplies; surgical & medical instruments

(G-15113)
CANADIAN HARVEST LP (DH)
16369 Us Highway 131 S (49087-9150)
PHONE 952 835-6429
Scott Gordon, *General Mgr*
Nathan French, *CFO*
EMP: 6 **EST:** 2014
SALES (est): 16.5MM
SALES (corp-wide): 355.8K **Privately Held**
WEB: www.jrs.de
SIC: 2099 Food preparations
HQ: J. Rettenmaier & Sohne Gmbh + Co. Kg
Holzmuhle 1
Rosenberg BW 73494
796 715-20

(G-15114)
CHEM LINK INC
353 E Lyons St (49087-9478)
P.O. Box 9 (49087-0009)
PHONE 269 679-4440
John E Thomas, *President*
Randy Copeland, *Division Mgr*
Rocky Stroud, *Division Mgr*
Ted McGee, *Regional Mgr*
Don Webb, *Plant Mgr*
EMP: 70 **EST:** 1990
SQ FT: 50,000
SALES (est): 53.3MM
SALES (corp-wide): 12.3MM **Privately Held**
WEB: www.chemlink.com
SIC: 2891 Adhesives
HQ: Soprema, Inc.
310 Quadral Dr
Wadsworth OH 44281

(G-15115)
COMMAND ELECTRONICS INC
15670 Morris Indus Dr (49087-9628)
PHONE 269 679-4011
Cary Campagna, *President*
Chris Campagna, *Vice Pres*
Beth Campagna-Kindle, *Sales Mgr*
▲ **EMP:** 48 **EST:** 1969
SQ FT: 26,000
SALES (est): 9.2MM **Privately Held**
WEB: www.commandelectronics.com
SIC: 3646 3613 Commercial indusl & institutional electric lighting fixtures; control panels, electric

(G-15116)
CONCEPT MOLDS INC
12273 N Us Highway 131 (49087-8902)
PHONE 269 679-2100
Chris Williams, *President*
Lane Smous, *COO*
Dan Northup, *Vice Pres*
Daniel Northup, *Vice Pres*
Joseph Dutka, *Design Engr*
EMP: 18 **EST:** 1992
SQ FT: 25,000
SALES (est): 3.7MM **Privately Held**
WEB: www.conceptmolds.com
SIC: 3544 Industrial molds

(G-15117)
CRAFT PRECISION INC
610 E Eliza St (49087-8740)
PHONE 269 679-5121
Steve Sutton, *President*
Michael Rochholz, *QC Mgr*
EMP: 40 **EST:** 1990
SQ FT: 10,000
SALES (est): 2.7MM **Privately Held**
WEB: www.craftprecision.com
SIC: 3599 Machine shop, jobbing & repair

(G-15118)
INTERFIBE CORPORATION (PA)
16369 Us Highway 131 S (49087-9150)
PHONE 269 327-6141
John Karnemaat, *President*
Christopher Sullivan, *Corp Secy*
Terry L Mleczewski, *Vice Pres*
EMP: 15 **EST:** 1982
SQ FT: 80,000
SALES (est): 2.2MM **Privately Held**
WEB: www.interfibe.com
SIC: 2821 Plastics materials & resins

(G-15119)
J L MILLING INC
15262 Industrial Dr (49087-9612)
PHONE 269 679-5769
Linda Schuring, *President*
Jerry Schuring, *Corp Secy*
EMP: 10 **EST:** 1990
SQ FT: 10,000
SALES (est): 2.2MM **Privately Held**
WEB: www.fenderskirts.com
SIC: 2951 Asphalt paving mixtures & blocks

(G-15120)
J RETTENMAIER USA LP (DH)
16369 Us Highway 131 S (49087-9150)
PHONE 269 679-2340
Thorsten Willmann, *Partner*
Aaron Hart, *Business Mgr*
Dia Panzer, *Vice Pres*
Lee Rockstead, *Plant Mgr*
Elaine Thomas, *Plant Mgr*
◆ **EMP:** 129 **EST:** 1997
SQ FT: 250,000
SALES (est): 79.9MM
SALES (corp-wide): 355.8K **Privately Held**
WEB: www.jrs.eu
SIC: 2823 Cellulosic manmade fibers
HQ: J. Rettenmaier & Sohne Gmbh + Co. Kg
Holzmuhle 1
Rosenberg BW 73494
796 715-20

(G-15121)
JAC MFG INC
12611 N Us Highway 131 (49087-8901)
PHONE 269 679-3301
James Garside, *Principal*
EMP: 4 **EST:** 2016
SALES (est): 51.6K **Privately Held**
SIC: 3999 Manufacturing industries

(G-15122)
KALAMAZOO CHUCK MFG SVC CTR CO
11825 S Shaver Rd (49087-9403)
PHONE 269 679-2325
Duane Burnham, *President*
EMP: 10 **EST:** 1998
SALES (est): 977.6K **Privately Held**
WEB: www.kzoochuck.com
SIC: 3545 Chucks: drill, lathe or magnetic (machine tool accessories)

(G-15123)
LIBERTY ADVISORS INC
11811 S Shaver Rd (49087-9403)
PHONE 269 679-3281
EMP: 5 **EST:** 2015
SALES (est): 134K **Privately Held**
WEB: www.liftsladdersanddocks.com
SIC: 3999 Manufacturing industries

(G-15124)
METAL MECHANICS INC
350 S 14th St (49087)
P.O. Box 447 (49087-0447)
PHONE 269 679-2525
Thomas Dailey, *President*
Barbara Dailey, *Principal*
James Dailey, *Principal*
Elizabeth Delisle, *Vice Pres*
Jim Delisle, *Prdtn Mgr*
EMP: 14 **EST:** 1950
SQ FT: 10,000
SALES (est): 2.4MM **Privately Held**
WEB: www.metalmechanics.com
SIC: 3599 3542 Machine shop, jobbing & repair; presses: hydraulic & pneumatic, mechanical & manual

(G-15125)
NEW CONCEPT PRODUCTS INC
Also Called: Hole Chief
277 E Lyons St (49087-9772)
PHONE 269 679-5970
Kelly Molenaar, *Principal*
EMP: 8 **EST:** 1985
SALES (est): 1MM **Privately Held**
SIC: 3599 7539 Machine shop, jobbing & repair; machine shop, automotive

(G-15126)
OUTERWEARS INC
12611 N Us Highway 131 (49087-8901)
PHONE 269 679-3301
James Garside, *President*
Steve Giebel, *Marketing Mgr*
EMP: 21 **EST:** 1979
SQ FT: 14,000
SALES (est): 1.9MM **Privately Held**
WEB: www.outerwears.com
SIC: 2399 Belting & belt products

(G-15127)
PREMIER CUSTOM TRAILERS LLC
12394 N Us Highway 131 (49087-8465)
PHONE 877 327-0888
Chris Campbell, *Sales Staff*
Rusty Davis, *Sales Staff*
Brandon Eshuis, *Sales Staff*
Brian Davis, *Mng Member*
EMP: 10 **EST:** 2010
SQ FT: 5,520
SALES (est): 1.2MM **Privately Held**
WEB: www.premiercustomtrailers.com
SIC: 5599 3799 7519 7549 Utility trailers; trailers & trailer equipment; trailer rental; trailer maintenance; trailers for passenger vehicles

(G-15128)
ST MARYS CEMENT INC (US)
640 South St (49087-9166)
PHONE 269 679-5253
Fax: 269 679-5254
EMP: 4 **Privately Held**
SIC: 3271 5032 Mfg Concrete Block/Brick Whol Brick/Stone Material
HQ: St. Marys Cement Inc. (U.S.)
9333 Dearborn St
Detroit MI 48209
313 842-4600

(G-15129)
SUNOPTA INGREDIENTS INC
16369 Us Highway 131 S (49087-9150)
PHONE 502 587-7999
Fax: 502 587-8999
EMP: 26
SALES (corp-wide): 1.2B **Privately Held**
SIC: 8731 2099 2087 Commercial Physical Research Mfg Food Preparations Mfg Flavor Extracts/Syrup
HQ: Sunopta Ingredients Inc.
7301 Ohms Ln Ste 600
Edina MN 55439
831 685-6506

Scotts
Kalamazoo County

(G-15130)
CHIP SYSTEMS INTERNATIONAL
10953 Norscott St (49088-5107)
P.O. Box 68 (49088-0068)
PHONE 269 626-8000
Jeff Dudley, *President*
Michael Dudley, *Corp Secy*
Jill Wilson, *Vice Pres*
▲ **EMP:** 10 **EST:** 1990
SQ FT: 30,000
SALES (est): 1MM **Privately Held**
WEB: www.chipsystemsintl.com
SIC: 3589 3569 3535 Shredders, industrial & commercial; centrifuges, industrial; belt conveyor systems, general industrial use

(G-15131)
COLE CARTER INC
Also Called: Pease Packing
8713 38th St S (49088-9338)
PHONE 269 626-8891
David Pease, *President*
EMP: 9 **EST:** 1940
SQ FT: 11,250
SALES (est): 850.2K **Privately Held**
SIC: 2011 0291 Meat packing plants; livestock farm, general

(G-15132)
KRISTUS INC
Also Called: Airpower America
8370 Greenfield Shores Dr (49088-8727)
PHONE 269 321-3330
Barry Kearns, *President*
Ben Ipema, *Vice Pres*
▲ **EMP:** 10 **EST:** 1999
SQ FT: 10,000
SALES (est): 1MM **Privately Held**
WEB: www.airpoweramerica.com
SIC: 3561 Pumps & pumping equipment

(G-15133)
ROBERTS MOVABLE WALLS INC
9611 32nd St S (49088-9751)
PHONE 269 626-0227
Lane Mottor, *President*
EMP: 7 **EST:** 2005
SALES (est): 257.5K **Privately Held**
WEB: www.robertsinstallationandrepair.com
SIC: 2653 Corrugated boxes, partitions, display items, sheets & pad

(G-15134)
TLR COATINGS
6275 26th St S (49088-9717)
PHONE 269 870-3083
EMP: 4 **EST:** 2019
SALES (est): 91.7K **Privately Held**
WEB: www.tlrcoatings.com
SIC: 3479 Coating of metals & formed products

Scottville
Mason County

(G-15135)
KELDER LLC
979 W 1st St (49454-8520)
P.O. Box 83 (49454-0083)
PHONE 231 757-3000
Jeff Barnett, *President*
EMP: 12 **EST:** 2000
SALES (est): 644.6K **Privately Held**
SIC: 3272 Concrete stuctural support & building material

(G-15136)
PADDLESPORTS WAREHOUSE INC
467 W Us Highway 10 31 (49454-9301)
PHONE 231 757-9051
Edward Spyker, *President*
Aleshia Smith,
▲ **EMP:** 7 **EST:** 2003

▲ = Import ▼ = Export
◆ = Import/Export

GEOGRAPHIC SECTION

Shelby - Oceana County (G-15160)

SALES (est): 1.5MM Privately Held
WEB: www.paddlesportswarehouse.com
SIC: 5091 2499 5551 Canoes; oars & paddles, wood; canoe & kayak dealers

Sears
Osceola County

(G-15137)
MORGAN COMPOSTING INC (PA)
Also Called: Dairy Doo
4353 Us Highway 10 (49679-8706)
PHONE................................231 734-2451
Brad Morgan, *President*
Caitlin Marsh, *Principal*
Jeremie Morgan, *Principal*
Diane Sprague, *Principal*
Justin Morgan, *Vice Pres*
EMP: 2 EST: 1995
SALES (est): 9.5MM Privately Held
WEB: www.dairydoo.com
SIC: 2875 Compost

(G-15138)
MORGAN COMPOSTING INC
Also Called: Morgan Farm and Gardens
4281 Us Highway 10 (49679-8706)
PHONE................................231 734-2790
Brad Morgan, *President*
Luke Orth, *Representative*
EMP: 37
SALES (corp-wide): 9.5MM Privately Held
WEB: www.dairydoo.com
SIC: 2875 Compost; potting soil, mixed
PA: Morgan Composting, Inc.
    4353 Us Highway 10
    Sears MI 49679
    231 734-2451

Sebewaing
Huron County

(G-15139)
DARWIN SNELLER
8677 Kilmanagh Rd (48759-9725)
PHONE................................989 977-3718
Darwin Sneller, *Owner*
Roger Gremel, *Owner*
EMP: 4 EST: 1983
SALES (est): 236.4K Privately Held
SIC: 2046 2063 2051 2048 Wet corn milling; granulated sugar from sugar beets; bread, all types (white, wheat, rye, etc); fresh or frozen; alfalfa or alfalfa meal, prepared as animal feed; soybeans

(G-15140)
GREAT LAKES PALLET INC
714 N Beck St (48759-1120)
P.O. Box 537 (48759-0537)
PHONE................................989 883-9220
Renda Joworski, *President*
EMP: 5 EST: 1991
SQ FT: 4,000 Privately Held
SIC: 2448 Pallets, wood

(G-15141)
MICHIGAN SUGAR COMPANY
763 N Beck St (48759-1119)
P.O. Box 626 (48759-0626)
PHONE................................989 883-3200
Jim Ruhlman, *Exec VP*
Linda Orndorff, *Warehouse Mgr*
Kerry Grifka, *Engineer*
Elizabeth Taylor, *VP Sls/Mktg*
Rob Clark, *Corp Comm Staff*
EMP: 165
SQ FT: 375,000
SALES (corp-wide): 189.4MM Privately Held
WEB: www.michigansugar.com
SIC: 2063 2061 Beet sugar; raw cane sugar
PA: Michigan Sugar Company
    122 Uptown Dr Unit 300
    Bay City MI 48708
    989 686-0161

(G-15142)
NITZ VALVE HARDWARE INC
8610 Unionville Rd (48759-9568)
P.O. Box 654 (48759-0654)
PHONE................................989 883-9500
Vincent Nitz, *President*
James Leppek, *Design Engr*
EMP: 15 EST: 1983
SQ FT: 3,500
SALES (est): 703.1K Privately Held
WEB: www.nitzvalve.com
SIC: 3599 Machine shop, jobbing & repair

(G-15143)
SEBEWAING CONCRETE PDTS INC
8552 Unionville Rd (48759-9568)
PHONE................................989 883-3860
Terry Wissner, *President*
Christina Wissner, *Corp Secy*
Scott Wissner, *Vice Pres*
EMP: 21 EST: 1927
SQ FT: 3,500
SALES (est): 858.6K Privately Held
WEB: www.rrreadymix.com
SIC: 3273 Ready-mixed concrete

(G-15144)
SEBEWAING TOOL AND ENGRG CO
Also Called: Sebewaing Flow Control
415 Union St (48759-1054)
P.O. Box 685 (48759-0685)
PHONE................................989 883-2000
Shawn Marshall, *President*
Daniel Healey, *Mfg Mgr*
Dan Healey, *Mfg Staff*
Ural Lupton, *Project Engr*
Richard Barnes, *CIO*
◆ EMP: 40 EST: 1937
SQ FT: 40,000
SALES (est): 4.9MM Privately Held
WEB: www.sebewaingtool.com
SIC: 3599 Machine shop, jobbing & repair

(G-15145)
TRUCKSFORSALECOM
Also Called: Ellenbaum Truck Sales
8440 Unionville Rd (48759-9567)
PHONE................................989 883-3382
John Elenbaum, *President*
John Ellenbaum, *Owner*
Rhonda Ellenbaum, *Vice Pres*
▼ EMP: 8 EST: 1999
SALES (est): 691.8K Privately Held
WEB: www.trucksforsale.com
SIC: 3596 5521 Truck (motor vehicle) scales; used car dealers

(G-15146)
VENTURE TOOL & METALIZING
42 E Main St (48759-1555)
PHONE................................989 883-9121
John F Sigmund, *Owner*
EMP: 5 EST: 1984
SQ FT: 15,000
SALES (est): 150K Privately Held
WEB: www.venturetoolandmetalizing.com
SIC: 3599 Machine shop, jobbing & repair

Selfridge Angb
Macomb County

(G-15147)
DHS/CBP
41130 Castle Ave (48045-4962)
PHONE................................586 954-2214
EMP: 7 EST: 2018
SALES (est): 217.4K Privately Held
SIC: 3728 Military aircraft equipment & armament

Shelby
Oceana County

(G-15148)
BECKMAN BROTHERS INC
3455 W Baker Rd (49455-9708)
P.O. Box 268 (49455-0268)
PHONE................................231 861-2031
Robert Beckman, *President*
EMP: 28 EST: 1946
SALES (est): 6.3MM Privately Held
SIC: 3273 Ready-mixed concrete

(G-15149)
CHERRY CENTRAL COOPERATIVE INC
Also Called: Oceana Foods
168 Lincoln St (49455-1277)
P.O. Box 156 (49455-0156)
PHONE................................231 861-2141
Doyle Fenner, *Vice Pres*
William Smilie, *Maint Spvr*
Mark McAuliffe, *Buyer*
Carl Schuchardt, *QC Mgr*
Brent Tackett, *Natl Sales Mgr*
EMP: 28
SALES (corp-wide): 47.5MM Privately Held
WEB: www.cherrycentral.com
SIC: 2033 2034 Fruits: packaged in cans, jars, etc.; fruit pie mixes & fillings: packaged in cans, jars, etc.; fruit juices: packaged in cans, jars, etc.; dehydrated fruits, vegetables, soups
PA: Cherry Central Cooperative, Inc.
    1771 N Us Highway 31 S
    Traverse City MI 49685
    231 946-1860

(G-15150)
JARVIS SAW MILL INC
Also Called: Jarvis Sawmill
1570 S 112th Ave (49455-9782)
PHONE................................231 861-2078
Robert Mayo, *President*
EMP: 8 EST: 1960
SQ FT: 2,000
SALES (est): 821.1K Privately Held
WEB: www.jarvissawmill.com
SIC: 2448 2426 Pallets, wood; furniture stock & parts, hardwood

(G-15151)
JERSHON INC
980 Industrial Park Dr (49455-8234)
P.O. Box 337 (49455-0337)
PHONE................................231 861-2900
Rodney Kurzer, *President*
EMP: 7 EST: 1990
SALES (est): 868K Privately Held
WEB: www.jershon.com
SIC: 3499 Ladder assemblies, combination workstand: metal

(G-15152)
KASZA SUGAR BUSH ✪
2500 W Buchanan Rd (49455-9246)
PHONE................................231 742-1930
Samuel Kasza, *Partner*
EMP: 6 EST: 2021
SALES (est): 80K Privately Held
SIC: 2099 Maple syrup

(G-15153)
KELLEY LABORATORIES INC
Also Called: Beechem Labs
617 Industrial Park Dr (49455-9584)
P.O. Box 188 (49455-0188)
PHONE................................231 861-6257
Larry P Kelley, *President*
EMP: 11 EST: 1939
SQ FT: 3,900
SALES (est): 614.7K Privately Held
WEB: www.beechemlayoutfluid.com
SIC: 2869 2851 Solvents, organic; lacquers, varnishes, enamels & other coatings

(G-15154)
KELLEY MACHINING INC
647 Industrial Park Dr (49455-9584)
P.O. Box 309 (49455-0309)
PHONE................................231 861-0951
Art Kelley, *President*
Chad Kelley, *Vice Pres*
Rick Hartley,
EMP: 8 EST: 1995
SQ FT: 6,000
SALES (est): 599K Privately Held
WEB: www.kelleymachining.com
SIC: 3599 Machine shop, jobbing & repair

(G-15155)
KOTZIAN TOOL INC
6971 W Shelby Rd (49455-9385)
PHONE................................231 861-5377
Brett Kotzian, *President*
Joyce Kotzian, *Corp Secy*
Mike Usiak, *Vice Pres*
EMP: 10 EST: 1970
SQ FT: 5,000 Privately Held
WEB: www.kotziantool.com
SIC: 3599 Custom machinery

(G-15156)
LAKEWOOD ORGANICS LLC (PA)
3104 W Baseline Rd (49455-9633)
PHONE................................231 861-6333
Aaron L Peterson,
EMP: 50 EST: 2020
SALES (est): 15.3MM Privately Held
SIC: 2033 Fruit juices: fresh

(G-15157)
OCEANA FOODS INC
168 Lincoln St (49455-1277)
P.O. Box 156 (49455-0156)
PHONE................................231 861-2141
Jeff Tucker, *General Mgr*
Richard Bogard, *President*
William Smilie, *Maint Spvr*
Mark McAuliffe, *Buyer*
Vince Higgs, *Natl Sales Mgr*
▲ EMP: 125 EST: 1989
SALES (est): 4.8MM
SALES (corp-wide): 47.5MM Privately Held
WEB: www.cherrycentral.com
SIC: 2033 Fruits: packaged in cans, jars, etc.
PA: Cherry Central Cooperative, Inc.
    1771 N Us Highway 31 S
    Traverse City MI 49685
    231 946-1860

(G-15158)
OCEANA FOREST PRODUCTS INC
2033 Loop Rd (49455-9751)
PHONE................................231 861-6115
Steven Aslakson, *President*
EMP: 7 EST: 1985
SALES (est): 500K Privately Held
SIC: 2421 Sawmills & planing mills, general

(G-15159)
PETERSON FARMS INC
3104 W Baseline Rd (49455-9633)
P.O. Box 115 (49455-0115)
PHONE................................231 861-6333
Aaron L Peterson, *CEO*
Earl L Peterson, *Ch of Bd*
Lorraine Odle Dp, *President*
Linda A Peterson, *Corp Secy*
Sarah M Peterson-Schlkebir, *Vice Pres*
◆ EMP: 400
SQ FT: 800,000
SALES (est): 159.9MM Privately Held
WEB: www.petersonfarmsinc.com
SIC: 2037 0723 2033 Fruits, quick frozen & cold pack (frozen); fruit (fresh) packing services; fruit juices: fresh

(G-15160)
SILVER STREET INCORPORATED
Also Called: Mediatechnologies
892 Industrial Park Dr (49455-8235)
P.O. Box 159 (49455-0159)
PHONE................................231 861-2194
Craig Hardy, *President*
Randy Seaver, *Corp Secy*
Jason Pochyla, *Prdtn Mgr*
Robert English, *Purch Agent*
Jamie Ritter, *Marketing Staff*
▲ EMP: 45 EST: 1979
SQ FT: 30,000
SALES (est): 8.5MM Privately Held
WEB: www.mediatechnologies.com
SIC: 2499 2521 Decorative wood & woodwork; wood office furniture

Shelby Township
Macomb County

(G-15161)
ACCU-RITE INDUSTRIES LLC
51047 Oro Dr (48315-2912)
PHONE.....................586 247-0060
Kirko Mickovski, *President*
John Loudon, *Vice Pres*
Megan Chevalier, *Purchasing*
Craig Hawkins, *Program Mgr*
Ray Vanlith, *Program Mgr*
EMP: 30 **EST:** 1993
SQ FT: 8,500
SALES (est): 6.1MM **Privately Held**
WEB: www.accu-rite.com
SIC: 3549 Metalworking machinery

(G-15162)
ACCU-TECH MANUFACTURING INC
51210 Oro Dr (48315-2903)
PHONE.....................586 532-4000
Louis Rahhal, *President*
Christy Mc Keogh, *Vice Pres*
Theodore Wiley, *Treasurer*
EMP: 24 **EST:** 1994
SALES (est): 747.8K **Privately Held**
WEB: www.atmfg.com
SIC: 3599 Machine shop, jobbing & repair

(G-15163)
ACE & 1 LOGISTICS LLC
2076 Jonathan Cir (48317-3823)
PHONE.....................601 335-3625
EMP: 6 **EST:** 2020
SALES (est): 262.9K **Privately Held**
SIC: 3549 7389 Assembly machines, including robotic; business services

(G-15164)
ACG SERVICES INC
51512 Schoenherr Rd (48315-2754)
PHONE.....................586 232-4698
Nancy Marsack, *Principal*
EMP: 4 **EST:** 2011
SALES (est): 462K **Privately Held**
SIC: 3545 3544 Collets (machine tool accessories); subpresses, metalworking

(G-15165)
ACUMEN TECHNOLOGIES INC
51445 Celeste (48315-2905)
PHONE.....................586 566-8600
Clifford S Willner, *President*
Cliff Willner, *President*
Russell Dibbel, *Vice Pres*
EMP: 12 **EST:** 1997
SQ FT: 11,000
SALES (est): 2.4MM **Privately Held**
WEB: www.acumen-tech.com
SIC: 3569 5085 Lubrication equipment, industrial; industrial supplies

(G-15166)
ACUTE FIXTURE & TOOLING INC
13313 W Star Dr (48315-2701)
PHONE.....................586 323-4132
Kenneth Powell, *Principal*
EMP: 6 **EST:** 2018
SALES (est): 476.7K **Privately Held**
SIC: 3599 Machine shop, jobbing & repair

(G-15167)
AHD LLC
50649 Central Indus Dr (48315-3119)
PHONE.....................586 922-6511
Vishal Bhagat,
EMP: 6 **EST:** 2015
SALES (est): 511.2K **Privately Held**
WEB: www.ahd-llc.com
SIC: 3511 Hydraulic turbine generator set units, complete

(G-15168)
ALL SEASON ENCLOSURES
2760 Marissa Way (48316-1297)
PHONE.....................248 650-8020
Robert John Pelzel, *Executive Asst*
EMP: 8 **EST:** 2008
SALES (est): 661.5K **Privately Held**
SIC: 3448 Screen enclosures

(G-15169)
AMERICAN WOOD MOLDINGS LLC
52976 Van Dyke Ave (48316-3548)
PHONE.....................586 726-9050
EMP: 9 **EST:** 2019
SALES (est): 370.6K **Privately Held**
WEB: www.americanwoodmoldings.com
SIC: 2431 Millwork

(G-15170)
ANDROID INDUSTRIES-WIXOM LLC
50150 Ryan Rd (48317-1035)
PHONE.....................248 255-5434
Greg Nichols, *Branch Mgr*
EMP: 10
SALES (corp-wide): 474.4MM **Privately Held**
SIC: 3714 Motor vehicle parts & accessories
HQ: Android Industries-Wixom Llc
4444 W Maple Dr
Auburn Hills MI 48326
248 732-0000

(G-15171)
ARCHITECTURAL TRIM & WDWRK LLC
15003 Totten Pl (48315-2147)
PHONE.....................586 321-1860
Ronald Ragon Baker, *Principal*
EMP: 5 **EST:** 2009
SALES (est): 124.9K **Privately Held**
SIC: 2431 Millwork

(G-15172)
ARISTO-COTE INC
11655 Park Ct (48315-3109)
PHONE.....................586 447-9049
EMP: 70 **Privately Held**
WEB: www.aristoind.com
SIC: 3479 Painting, coating & hot dipping
PA: Aristo-Cote, Inc.
24951 Henry B Joy Blvd
Harrison Township MI 48045

(G-15173)
ATLANTIC PRECISION PDTS INC
51745 Filomena Dr (48315-2948)
PHONE.....................586 532-9420
Ron Kris, *Executive*
EMP: 6 **EST:** 2004
SALES (est): 138.4K **Privately Held**
SIC: 3089 Plastics products

(G-15174)
ATLANTIC PRECISION PDTS INC
51234 Filomena Dr (48315-2942)
PHONE.....................586 532-9420
Rosa Slongo, *President*
Norma Gorski, *Vice Pres*
Christoba Prieto, *Production*
Jennifer Kurtzhals, *QC Mgr*
Jennifer Morris, *QC Mgr*
EMP: 15 **EST:** 2004
SALES (est): 6.2MM **Privately Held**
WEB: www.atlanticpp.com
SIC: 3089 1446 3021 Molding primary plastic; molding sand mining; shoes, rubber or plastic molded to fabric

(G-15175)
AVON MACHINING LLC
Also Called: Avon Gear
11968 Investment Dr (48315-1794)
PHONE.....................586 884-2200
Chad Fietsam, *CEO*
Richard Kitchen, *Engineer*
▲ **EMP:** 100 **EST:** 1974
SQ FT: 110,000
SALES (est): 22MM
SALES (corp-wide): 179.2MM **Privately Held**
WEB: www.avonmachining.com
SIC: 3462 3011 3465 Gears, forged steel; truck or bus inner tubes; body parts, automobile: stamped metal
PA: Speyside Equity Fund I Lp
430 E 86th St
New York NY 10028
212 994-0308

(G-15176)
AVON MACHINING HOLDINGS INC
11968 Investment Dr (48315-1794)
PHONE.....................586 884-2200
Chad Fietsam, *CEO*
Matt Korth, *President*
EMP: 125
SQ FT: 100,000
SALES (est): 35MM
SALES (corp-wide): 179.2MM **Privately Held**
WEB: www.avonmachining.com
SIC: 6719 3462 3011 3465 Investment holding companies, except banks; gears, forged steel; truck or bus inner tubes; body parts, automobile: stamped metal
PA: Speyside Equity Fund I Lp
430 E 86th St
New York NY 10028
212 994-0308

(G-15177)
B T I INDUSTRIES
49820 Oakland Dr (48315-3943)
PHONE.....................586 532-8411
Edward Bohmier, *Principal*
Samantha Bohmier, *Accounts Mgr*
Jesse McDonald, *Manager*
EMP: 13 **EST:** 2010
SALES (est): 321K **Privately Held**
WEB: www.btiindustries.com
SIC: 3999 Barber & beauty shop equipment

(G-15178)
BOOMERANG AMUSEMENTS
46600 Vineyard Ave (48317-3937)
PHONE.....................586 323-3327
Matthew Mark, *Owner*
Dereck Scheppelman, *Co-Owner*
EMP: 10 **EST:** 2004
SALES (est): 180K **Privately Held**
SIC: 3599 Amusement park equipment

(G-15179)
BROWN-CAMPBELL COMPANY (PA)
Also Called: Brown-Campbell Steel
11800 Investment Dr (48315-1794)
PHONE.....................586 884-2180
John D Campbell Sr, *Ch of Bd*
Murdoch Campbell, *President*
Tracy Garrett, *Purch Mgr*
Dawn Krause, *Controller*
Dan Shaffern, *Accounts Mgr*
◆ **EMP:** 10
SALES (est): 61.5MM **Privately Held**
WEB: www.brown-campbell.com
SIC: 5051 3446 Steel; stairs, staircases, stair treads: prefabricated metal

(G-15180)
C H INDUSTRIES INC
Also Called: C.H. Industries
50699 Central Indus Dr (48315-3119)
PHONE.....................586 997-1717
Ryan Haas, *Mng Member*
Sue Hibberd,
EMP: 10 **EST:** 1988
SQ FT: 18,000
SALES (est): 1.3MM **Privately Held**
SIC: 3721 Aircraft

(G-15181)
CARLO JOHN INC
Also Called: National Asphalt Products
12345 23 Mile Rd (48315-2619)
PHONE.....................586 254-3800
Brian Stlouis, *Branch Mgr*
EMP: 47
SALES (corp-wide): 24.3MM **Privately Held**
WEB: www.johncarlo.com
SIC: 2951 Asphalt paving mixtures & blocks
PA: Carlo John Inc
20848 Hall Rd
Clinton Township MI 48038

(G-15182)
CBS TOOL INC
51601 Oro Dr (48315-2934)
PHONE.....................586 566-5945
Bruce Dettloff, *President*
Robert Legato, *Vice Pres*
EMP: 10 **EST:** 1998
SQ FT: 10,000
SALES (est): 1.8MM **Privately Held**
WEB: www.cbs-tool.com
SIC: 3541 3544 Machine tools, metal cutting type; special dies, tools, jigs & fixtures

(G-15183)
CENTER FOR QLTY TRNING INTL LL
50485 Utica Dr (48315-3211)
PHONE.....................586 212-9524
Albert Dustan II,
EMP: 4 **EST:** 2019
SALES (est): 303.5K **Privately Held**
SIC: 3812 Defense systems & equipment

(G-15184)
CENTURY PLASTICS LLC (DH)
Also Called: Cie USA
15030 23 Mile Rd (48315-3010)
PHONE.....................586 566-3900
Joe Carroll, *President*
Mark Simon, *COO*
Brian Enjaian, *CFO*
▲ **EMP:** 205 **EST:** 1985
SQ FT: 14,000
SALES (est): 107.7MM
SALES (corp-wide): 146.6MM **Privately Held**
WEB: www.cieautomotive.com
SIC: 3089 Injection molding of plastics

(G-15185)
CG LIQUIDATION INCORPORATED
Also Called: Crown Group, The
12020 Shelby Tech Dr (48315-1789)
PHONE.....................586 803-1000
Glen Ford, *Manager*
EMP: 82
SALES (corp-wide): 15.1B **Publicly Held**
SIC: 3479 Coating of metals & formed products
HQ: Cg Liquidation, Incorporated
2111 Walter P Reuther Dr
Warren MI 48091
586 575-9800

(G-15186)
CHAMPION LABORATORIES INC
51180 Celeste (48315-2938)
PHONE.....................586 247-9044
John Evans, *President*
Angela Brys, *Office Mgr*
EMP: 7
SALES (corp-wide): 1.4B **Privately Held**
WEB: www.champlabs.com
SIC: 3714 Filters: oil, fuel & air, motor vehicle
HQ: Champion Laboratories, Inc.
200 S 4th St
Albion IL 62806
618 445-6011

(G-15187)
CIE AUTOMOTIVE USA INC (HQ)
15030 23 Mile Rd (48315-3010)
PHONE.....................734 793-5320
Jesus Herrera, *CEO*
Jaime Aguirre, *Principal*
Patrick Specci, *Materials Mgr*
EMP: 60
SALES (est): 14.4MM
SALES (corp-wide): 146.6MM **Privately Held**
WEB: www.cieautomotive.com
SIC: 3089 Automotive parts, plastic
PA: Cie Automotive, Sa
Alameda Mazarredo, 69 - Piso 8o
Bilbao 48009
946 054-835

(G-15188)
CINCINNATI TYROLIT INC
4636 Regency Dr (48316-1533)
PHONE.....................513 458-8121
Fritz Corradi, *President*
▲ **EMP:** 190 **EST:** 2004
SQ FT: 225,000

GEOGRAPHIC SECTION
Shelby Township - Macomb County (G-15218)

SALES (est): 36.8MM
SALES (corp-wide): 778.5MM **Privately Held**
WEB: www.tyrolit.at
SIC: 3291 Wheels, grinding: artificial
PA: Tyrolit - Schleifmittelwerke Swarovski K.G.
SwarovskistraBe 33
Schwaz 6130
524 260-60

(G-15189)
CIRKO LLC
54080 Birchfield Dr E (48316-1351)
PHONE..................................586 504-1313
Nebojsa Atanasovski, *Principal*
EMP: 4 **EST:** 2012
SALES (est): 74.6K **Privately Held**
SIC: 3999 Manufacturing industries

(G-15190)
CLARK BROTHERS INSTRUMENT CO
56680 Mound Rd (48316-4906)
PHONE..................................586 781-7000
Thomas F Wright Sr, *President*
Thomas F Wright Jr, *Vice Pres*
Daria Johnson, *Opers Mgr*
Mark Sokez, *Engineer*
Mary Patrick, *Technology*
▲ **EMP:** 18 **EST:** 1959
SQ FT: 17,600
SALES (est): 4.3MM **Privately Held**
WEB: www.clarkbrothers.net
SIC: 3824 Vehicle instruments

(G-15191)
COLONIAL PLASTICS INCORPORATED
Also Called: Colonial Group
51734 Filomena Dr (48315-2948)
PHONE..................................586 469-4944
Cathy Roberts, *President*
Bill Mead, *Sales Staff*
EMP: 36 **EST:** 1985
SQ FT: 46,000
SALES (est): 11.4MM **Privately Held**
WEB: www.colgrp.com
SIC: 3089 Injection molding of plastics

(G-15192)
COMPLETE HM ADVG MDIA PRMTNAL
Also Called: Rabaut Printing Co
15018 Technology Dr (48315-3950)
PHONE..................................586 254-9555
Mark B Rabaut, *President*
Claudia Rabaut, *Corp Secy*
EMP: 5 **EST:** 1981
SQ FT: 4,000
SALES (est): 388.1K **Privately Held**
SIC: 2752 Commercial printing, offset

(G-15193)
CONLEY MANUFACTURING INC
51559 Oro Dr (48315-2932)
PHONE..................................586 262-4484
John Jones, *President*
Shana Miller, *Officer*
EMP: 7 **EST:** 2017
SALES (est): 828.9K **Privately Held**
WEB: www.conleymanufacturing.com
SIC: 3544 Jigs & fixtures

(G-15194)
CONNECT WITH US LLC
4311 Kingmont Dr (48317-1139)
PHONE..................................586 262-4359
Greg Newman, *CEO*
Robert Santoro, *Partner*
EMP: 9 **EST:** 2012
SALES (est): 818.8K **Privately Held**
WEB: www.connect-wu.com
SIC: 3679 Harness assemblies for electronic use: wire or cable

(G-15195)
CONTINENTAL PLASTICS CO
50900 Birch Rd (48315-3205)
PHONE..................................586 294-4600
Joan Luckino, *Ch of Bd*
Anthony Catenacci, *President*
Russell Thomas, *COO*
Frances Luckino Catenacci, *Admin Sec*
◆ **EMP:** 520 **EST:** 1957

SQ FT: 206,000
SALES (est): 48.9MM **Privately Held**
SIC: 3089 Injection molding of plastics

(G-15196)
COOK SIGN PLUS
48534 Van Dyke Ave (48317-3266)
PHONE..................................586 254-7000
Dan Cook, *President*
EMP: 5 **EST:** 2004
SALES (est): 300K **Privately Held**
WEB: www.cookssignsplus.com
SIC: 3993 Signs, not made in custom sign painting shops

(G-15197)
CRAFT INDUSTRIES INC
13231 23 Mile Rd (48315-2713)
PHONE..................................586 726-4300
Thomas J Carter, *President*
Stefan Wanczyk, *Vice Pres*
EMP: 373 **EST:** 1971
SQ FT: 62,640
SALES (est): 8.6MM
SALES (corp-wide): 305MM **Privately Held**
WEB: www.uticaenterprises.com
SIC: 3548 3569 3544 3541 Resistance welders, electric; assembly machines, non-metalworking; special dies, tools, jigs & fixtures; machine tools, metal cutting type
PA: Utica Enterprises, Inc.
5750 New King Dr Ste 200
Troy MI 48098
586 726-4300

(G-15198)
CREATIVITEES STUDIO
54470 Aurora Park (48316-6011)
PHONE..................................586 565-2213
Helena Toutant, *Principal*
EMP: 4 **EST:** 2018
SALES (est): 197.6K **Privately Held**
SIC: 2759 Screen printing

(G-15199)
CRYSTAL LK APRTMNTS FMLY LTD P (PA)
2001 Crystal Lake Dr (48316-2818)
PHONE..................................586 731-3500
Antonio Lo Chirco, *Partner*
Michael Lo Chirco, *General Ptnr*
▲ **EMP:** 25 **EST:** 1974
SQ FT: 1,200
SALES (est): 3.5MM **Privately Held**
SIC: 2434 Vanities, bathroom: wood

(G-15200)
CUT-RITE EDM SERVICES LLC
51445 Oro Dr (48315-2932)
PHONE..................................586 566-0100
Craig Sizemore, *President*
EMP: 13 **EST:** 1992
SQ FT: 8,300
SALES (est): 1.1MM **Privately Held**
WEB: www.cutriteedm.com
SIC: 3599 Electrical discharge machining (EDM); machine shop, jobbing & repair

(G-15201)
DDKS INDUSTRIES LLC
14954 Technology Dr (48315-3949)
PHONE..................................586 323-5909
Kimberly S Kelley, *Mng Member*
David Kelley,
▲ **EMP:** 6 **EST:** 2008
SQ FT: 5,500
SALES (est): 565.2K **Privately Held**
WEB: www.ddksindustries.com
SIC: 3594 3599 Fluid power pumps & motors; crankshafts & camshafts, machining

(G-15202)
DELAND MANUFACTURING INC
50674 Central Indus Dr (48315-3116)
PHONE..................................586 323-2350
Dennis L Wygocki, *President*
Diane J Wygocki, *Treasurer*
EMP: 20 **EST:** 1966
SQ FT: 35,500
SALES (est): 3.2MM **Privately Held**
WEB: www.delandcorp.com
SIC: 3599 3544 Machine shop, jobbing & repair; special dies, tools, jigs & fixtures

(G-15203)
DELAWARE DYNAMICS MICHIGAN LLC
50590 Central Indus Dr (48315-3119)
PHONE..................................586 997-1717
Ryan Haas,
EMP: 15 **EST:** 2020
SALES (est): 1.1MM **Privately Held**
WEB: www.delawaredynamicsmi.com
SIC: 3312 Tool & die steel & alloys

(G-15204)
DENALI LIGHTING LLC
Also Called: Lighting One
50178 Van Dyke Ave (48317-1351)
PHONE..................................586 731-0399
James Plutter, *President*
Liz Gamble, *Office Mgr*
EMP: 7 **EST:** 2006
SQ FT: 8,000
SALES (est): 1.2MM **Privately Held**
WEB: www.lighting-one.com
SIC: 3648 Lighting fixtures, except electric: residential

(G-15205)
DIESEL PERFORMANCE PRODUCTS
Also Called: K A L Enterprises
7459 Flickinger Dr (48316-2333)
PHONE..................................586 726-7478
Keith Long, *President*
Mary Long, *Vice Pres*
EMP: 8 **EST:** 2000
SALES (est): 664K **Privately Held**
WEB:
www.dieselperformanceproducts.com
SIC: 3714 Motor vehicle parts & accessories

(G-15206)
DIGITAL PRINTING & GRAPHICS
50711 Wing Dr (48315-3269)
PHONE..................................586 566-9499
Sheldon Wildeman, *Owner*
EMP: 4 **EST:** 1976
SQ FT: 5,000
SALES (est): 244.4K **Privately Held**
WEB: www.dpgprinting.com
SIC: 2752 Commercial printing, offset

(G-15207)
DIGITAL PRINTING SOLUTIONS LLC
48688 Eagle Butte Ct (48315-4268)
PHONE..................................586 566-4910
Larry Schehr Sr, *Principal*
EMP: 5 **EST:** 2011
SALES (est): 88.4K **Privately Held**
SIC: 2752 Commercial printing, offset

(G-15208)
DIRKSEN SCREW PRODUCTS CO (PA)
14490 23 Mile Rd (48315-2916)
PHONE..................................586 247-5400
Clifford S Dirksen, *CEO*
Mike Potter, *Plant Mgr*
Joe Oss, *Purchasing*
Peter Cicci, *Engineer*
Richard G Dirksen Sr, *Treasurer*
▲ **EMP:** 50 **EST:** 1939
SQ FT: 80,000
SALES (est): 13MM **Privately Held**
WEB: www.dirksenscrew.com
SIC: 3452 3451 3356 Bolts, nuts, rivets & washers; screw machine products; non-ferrous rolling & drawing

(G-15209)
DJC PRODUCTS INC
56700 Mound Rd (48316-4942)
PHONE..................................586 992-1352
EMP: 5 **EST:** 2017
SALES (est): 311.8K **Privately Held**
SIC: 3599 Amusement park equipment

(G-15210)
DRIP THERAPI LLC ✪
14202 Lakeside Blvd N 1a (48315-6073)
PHONE..................................586 488-1256
Irving Fleming,
EMP: 4 **EST:** 2021
SALES (est): 156.7K **Privately Held**
SIC: 2834 Intravenous solutions

(G-15211)
DUBETSKY K9 ACADEMY LLC
50699 Central Indus Dr (48315-3119)
PHONE..................................586 997-1717
Dan T Moore,
Bryan Dubetsky,
EMP: 11 **EST:** 2018
SALES (est): 482.9K **Privately Held**
SIC: 3544 Special dies, tools, jigs & fixtures

(G-15212)
DUGGAN MANUFACTURING LLC
50150 Ryan Rd (48317-1028)
PHONE..................................586 254-7400
Tony Pinho, *President*
Terry Silkowski, *Purchasing*
Chris Matt, *Engineer*
Jared Sperry, *Sales Engr*
Mike Arndt, *Sales Staff*
▼ **EMP:** 150 **EST:** 2004
SQ FT: 70,000
SALES (est): 22.3MM **Privately Held**
WEB: www.dugganmfg.com
SIC: 3599 Machine shop, jobbing & repair

(G-15213)
DUGGANS LIMITED LLC
50150 Ryan Rd Ste 15 (48317-1035)
PHONE..................................586 254-7400
Kevin Justice, *Program Mgr*
Jared Thompson, *Program Mgr*
Ramona Kellner, *Manager*
Rusty Pawley, *Manager*
Anthony Pinho,
EMP: 20 **EST:** 2000
SQ FT: 7,000
SALES (est): 279.8K **Privately Held**
WEB: www.dugganmfg.com
SIC: 3469 Metal stampings

(G-15214)
DUO ROBOTIC SOLUTIONS INC
50570 Wing Dr (48315-3289)
PHONE..................................586 883-7559
Dominique Girard, *President*
EMP: 12 **EST:** 2017
SQ FT: 12,660
SALES (est): 3.5MM **Privately Held**
WEB: www.duorobot.com
SIC: 3549 Assembly machines, including robotic
HQ: Duo Machinery Equipment(Shanghai)Co., Ltd.
No.66 Fulian 3th Rd, Baoshan Dist
Shanghai 20043
215 048-1965

(G-15215)
DURAFLEX COATINGS LLC
8589 Mary Ann Ave (48317-3209)
PHONE..................................586 855-1087
EMP: 5 **EST:** 2014
SALES (est): 128.9K **Privately Held**
SIC: 3479 Metal coating & allied service

(G-15216)
DYNAMITE MACHINING INC
51149 Filomena Dr (48315-2940)
PHONE..................................586 247-8230
Scott R Laskowski, *President*
EMP: 8 **EST:** 1999
SQ FT: 10,000
SALES (est): 973.5K **Privately Held**
WEB: www.dynamitemachining.com
SIC: 3599 Machine shop, jobbing & repair

(G-15217)
E M SMOKERS INC
14052 Patterson Dr (48315-4263)
PHONE..................................586 207-1172
El Haddad, *Owner*
EMP: 5 **EST:** 2008
SALES (est): 154K **Privately Held**
SIC: 3999 Cigarette & cigar products & accessories

(G-15218)
EAGLE MANUFACTURING CORP
Also Called: Eaglematic
52113 Shelby Pkwy (48315-1778)
PHONE..................................586 323-0303
Brent Short, *President*
EMP: 18 **EST:** 1960

Shelby Township - Macomb County (G-15219)

SQ FT: 30,000
SALES (est): 3.7MM Privately Held
WEB: www.eaglematic.com
SIC: 3089 Injection molding of plastics

(G-15219)
ELITE MOLD & ENGINEERING INC
Also Called: Elite Medical Molding
51548 Filomena Dr (48315-2946)
PHONE..................586 314-4000
Joseph Mandeville, *President*
Daniel Mandeville, *Marketing Staff*
Kristen Chase, *Office Mgr*
Mark Fletcher, *Manager*
Eugene McCaffrey, *Manager*
EMP: 25 EST: 1982
SQ FT: 17,400
SALES (est): 5.7MM Privately Held
WEB: www.teameliteonline.com
SIC: 3544 Dies, plastics forming; industrial molds

(G-15220)
ELITE PLASTIC PRODUCTS INC
51354 Filomena Dr (48315-2944)
PHONE..................586 247-5800
Robert Mandeville, *President*
Mary Sutter, *General Mgr*
Joseph Mandeville, *Vice Pres*
Scott Downey, *Purch Agent*
Jeff Hutchinson, *QC Mgr*
EMP: 30 EST: 1995
SQ FT: 24,000
SALES (est): 7.7MM Privately Held
WEB: www.elitecplasticproducts.com
SIC: 3089 3714 Injection molding of plastics; motor vehicle parts & accessories

(G-15221)
ENGRAVED MEMORIES
54989 Sherwood Ln (48315-1551)
PHONE..................586 703-7983
Robert Lemmon, *Manager*
EMP: 4 EST: 2007
SALES (est): 94.7K Privately Held
WEB: www.engravedmemoriesstore.com
SIC: 2899 Plastic wood

(G-15222)
ENTERPRISE PLASTICS LLC
51354 Filomena Dr (48315-2944)
PHONE..................586 665-1030
Michael Flores, *CEO*
Salvatore Cassisi, *President*
EMP: 7 EST: 1999
SQ FT: 36,000
SALES (est): 95.1K Privately Held
SIC: 3089 Injection molded finished plastic products

(G-15223)
EPIC EQUIPMENT & ENGRG INC
52301 Shelby Pkwy (48315-1778)
PHONE..................586 314-0020
Mark Milewicz, *President*
Steve Wilkins, *Vice Pres*
Eric Szlachtowicz, *Plant Mgr*
Ken Herzog, *Design Engr*
David Gardiner, *Controller*
EMP: 85 EST: 1997
SQ FT: 50,000
SALES (est): 23.3MM
SALES (corp-wide): 32.7MM Privately Held
WEB: www.epicequipment.com
SIC: 3599 Custom machinery
PA: Bpg International Finance Co Llc
4760 Fulton St E Ste 201
Ada MI 49301
616 855-1480

(G-15224)
FABRICATIONS UNLIMITED INC (PA)
45757 Cornwall St (48317-4709)
PHONE..................313 567-9616
Lee Perrell, *President*
Fred Martin, *Vice Pres*
Patricia Perrell, *Admin Sec*
EMP: 2 EST: 1985
SALES (est): 1.1MM Privately Held
WEB: www.fabrications-unlimited.com
SIC: 3443 Tanks, standard or custom fabricated: metal plate

(G-15225)
FEC INC
Also Called: FEC Automation Systems
51341 Celeste (48315-2943)
PHONE..................586 580-2622
Ronald Jaeger, *President*
Mark Ishikawa, *Managing Dir*
Benny La Rocca, *Managing Dir*
Tom Caruso, *Mfg Staff*
Paul Gomez, *Engineer*
▲ EMP: 15 EST: 1983
SQ FT: 43,000
SALES (est): 4.3MM Privately Held
WEB: www.fec-usa.com
SIC: 3569 Assembly machines, non-metal-working

(G-15226)
FIRST WILSON INC ◐
54036 Birchfield Dr W (48316-1393)
PHONE..................586 935-2687
Kenneth Wilson, *President*
EMP: 9 EST: 2021
SALES (est): 402K Privately Held
SIC: 2741

(G-15227)
FLEX-N-GATE SHELBY LLC
52674 Shelby Pkwy (48315-1778)
PHONE..................586 251-2300
Steve Wachowski, *Accounts Mgr*
David Ekblad, *Mng Member*
EMP: 200 EST: 2016
SQ FT: 125,000
SALES (est): 28.4MM
SALES (corp-wide): 1.5B Privately Held
WEB: www.flex-n-gate.com
SIC: 3089 Automotive parts, plastic
PA: Flex-N-Gate Llc
1306 E University Ave
Urbana IL 61802
217 384-6600

(G-15228)
FLUE SENTINEL LLC
8123 Janis St (48317-5315)
PHONE..................586 739-4373
EMP: 6
SALES (est): 527.7K
SALES (corp-wide): 1.2B Privately Held
SIC: 3429 Mfg Electric Fireplace Damper
HQ: Field Controls, L.L.C.
2630 Airport Rd
Kinston NC 28504
252 208-7300

(G-15229)
G&G INDUSTRIES INC
50665 Corporate Dr (48315-3100)
PHONE..................586 726-6000
Bruce M Gantner, *President*
Craig Gantner, *Vice Pres*
Richard Flavell, *Plant Mgr*
Michelle Hanchett, *Materials Mgr*
George Opi, *Purchasing*
▲ EMP: 47 EST: 1992
SQ FT: 18,000
SALES (est): 10MM Privately Held
WEB: www.gandgindustries.com
SIC: 7532 3545 3429 Upholstery & trim shop, automotive; precision measuring tools; manufactured hardware (general)

(G-15230)
GLOBAL ENGINEERING INC
50685 Rizzo Dr (48315-3227)
PHONE..................586 566-0423
Mark Koerner, *President*
Bernd Koerner, *Vice Pres*
Barry York, *Vice Pres*
Mardie James, *Office Mgr*
EMP: 23 EST: 1987
SQ FT: 23,000
SALES (est): 5.2MM Privately Held
WEB: www.globaleng.com
SIC: 3545 3544 Machine tool accessories; special dies, tools, jigs & fixtures

(G-15231)
GREAT HARVEST BREAD CO
48923 Hayes Rd (48315-4400)
PHONE..................586 566-9500
Steve Troszak, *Owner*
EMP: 10 EST: 2006
SALES (est): 206K Privately Held
WEB: www.greatharvest.com
SIC: 5461 2051 Bread; bread, cake & related products

(G-15232)
HARRISON STEEL LLC
50390 Utica Dr (48315-3290)
PHONE..................586 247-1230
John Chirakas,
Mark Jacobs,
Rick Nicolay,
EMP: 6 EST: 1999
SQ FT: 75,000
SALES (est): 658.4K Privately Held
WEB: www.harrisonsteel.net
SIC: 3312 5051 Slabs, steel; steel

(G-15233)
HB MANUFACTURING LLC
49333 Mackinaw Ct (48315-3955)
PHONE..................586 703-5269
Eugene Height, *Principal*
EMP: 4 EST: 2014
SALES (est): 121.3K Privately Held
WEB: www.hbmanufacturing.com
SIC: 3999 Manufacturing industries

(G-15234)
HELIAN TECHNOLOGIES LLC
5974 Windemere Ln (48316-5375)
PHONE..................248 535-6545
Gustavo Gonzalez,
EMP: 5 EST: 2017
SALES (est): 78.1K Privately Held
SIC: 3674 Solar cells

(G-15235)
HI-TECH FURNACE SYSTEMS INC
13179 W Star Dr (48315-2736)
PHONE..................586 566-0600
Robert Kornfeld, *President*
Richard Mueller, *Vice Pres*
Rick Hazard, *Plant Mgr*
▲ EMP: 13 EST: 1990
SQ FT: 11,000
SALES (est): 3.7MM Privately Held
WEB: www.hi-techfurnace.com
SIC: 3567 8711 Heating units & devices, industrial: electric; engineering services

(G-15236)
HUNTLER INDUSTRIES INC
Also Called: Visionary Landscaping
51532 Schoenherr Rd (48315-2727)
PHONE..................586 566-7684
Kipp Rammler, *President*
Steve Dhondt, *Vice Pres*
EMP: 10 EST: 2002
SQ FT: 4,500
SALES (est): 625.5K Privately Held
SIC: 2891 Sealants

(G-15237)
HYDRAULIC PRESS SERVICE
4175 22 Mile Rd (48317-1503)
PHONE..................586 859-7099
EMP: 6 EST: 2015
SALES (est): 117.7K Privately Held
SIC: 2711 Newspapers

(G-15238)
IANNA FAB INC
5575 22 Mile Rd (48317-1531)
PHONE..................586 739-2410
Daniel D Iannamico, *President*
John Iannamico, *Admin Sec*
EMP: 6 EST: 1976
SQ FT: 4,800
SALES (est): 400K Privately Held
WEB: www.iannafab.com
SIC: 7692 Automotive welding

(G-15239)
INTERGRTED DSPNSE SLUTIONS LLC
Also Called: IDS
14310 Industrial Ctr Dr (48315-3292)
PHONE..................586 554-7404
Dave Ritchie, *General Mgr*
Doug Holsbeke, *Opers Mgr*
Brendan Ritchie, *Marketing Mgr*
Jan Pitzer, *Mng Member*
Thomas Murray, *Mng Member*
EMP: 10 EST: 2014
SQ FT: 12,000
SALES (est): 2.7MM
SALES (corp-wide): 9.2MM Privately Held
WEB: www.carlisleft.com
SIC: 3728 Countermeasure dispensers, aircraft
PA: Hosco, Inc
28026 Oakland Oaks Ct
Wixom MI 48393
248 912-1750

(G-15240)
ITALIAN TRIBUNE
45445 Mound Rd (48317-5178)
PHONE..................586 783-3260
Marilyn Borner, *Principal*
EMP: 14 EST: 2010
SALES (est): 317.7K Privately Held
WEB: www.italian-tribune.com
SIC: 2711 Commercial printing & newspaper publishing combined

(G-15241)
J & J SPRING CO INC
14100 23 Mile Rd (48315-2910)
PHONE..................586 566-7600
Richard E McGuire, *President*
Cheryl McGuire, *Vice Pres*
EMP: 15 EST: 1952
SQ FT: 14,500
SALES (est): 1.6MM Privately Held
WEB: www.jandjspring.com
SIC: 3493 3495 3465 Torsion bar springs; coiled flat springs; flat springs, sheet or strip stock; wire springs; automotive stampings

(G-15242)
J & J SPRING ENTERPRISES LLC
14100 23 Mile Rd (48315-2910)
PHONE..................586 566-7600
Joseph Kattula,
EMP: 8 EST: 2009
SALES (est): 1.1MM Privately Held
WEB: www.jandjspring.com
SIC: 3495 Wire springs

(G-15243)
JAC PRODUCTS INC
12000 Shelby Tech Dr (48315-1789)
PHONE..................586 254-1534
Mark Jakson, *General Mgr*
EMP: 8
SALES (corp-wide): 748.6MM Privately Held
WEB: www.jacproducts.com
SIC: 3714 Motor vehicle parts & accessories
HQ: Jac Products, Inc.
225 S Industrial Dr
Saline MI 48176
734 944-8844

(G-15244)
JBL SYSTEMS INC
51935 Filomena Dr (48315-2950)
PHONE..................586 802-6700
James Bogaski, *President*
Cori Fiscelli, *Technology*
EMP: 7 EST: 1985
SQ FT: 5,000
SALES (est): 690.6K Privately Held
WEB: www.jblsys.com
SIC: 3544 Die sets for metal stamping (presses)

(G-15245)
JOLICO/J-B TOOL INC
4325 22 Mile Rd (48317-1507)
PHONE..................586 739-5555
Patricia Wieland, *President*
Todd Galerneau, *Plant Mgr*
Robin Crise, *Purch Agent*
W Michael Wieland, *Admin Sec*
EMP: 42 EST: 1962
SQ FT: 55,000
SALES (est): 4.6MM Privately Held
WEB: www.jolico.com
SIC: 3544 3599 Special dies & tools; jigs & fixtures; machine shop, jobbing & repair

Shelby Township - Macomb County (G-15272)

(G-15246)
JOLICOR MANUFACTURING SERVICES
13357 W Star Dr (48315-2701)
PHONE.................................586 323-5090
John Livingstone, *President*
Elizabeth Livingstone, *Vice Pres*
EMP: 23 EST: 1994
SQ FT: 10,500
SALES (est): 1.2MM **Privately Held**
SIC: 4953 3089 Recycling, waste materials; plastic processing

(G-15247)
JSS - MACOMB LLC
11858 Forest Glen Ln (48315-1722)
PHONE.................................586 709-6305
Patrick Jones,
EMP: 10 EST: 2014
SQ FT: 1,450
SALES (est): 638.7K **Privately Held**
SIC: 2711 Newspapers, publishing & printing

(G-15248)
JVIS - USA LLC (PA)
Also Called: Jvis Masonic
52048 Shelby Pkwy (48315-1787)
PHONE.................................586 884-5700
Arthur Hariskos, *President*
Nicole Kafoury, *General Mgr*
Jack Furey, *Vice Pres*
Richard Schaut, *Production*
Mark Morrow, *Engineer*
EMP: 18 EST: 2006
SQ FT: 100,000
SALES (est): 226.2MM **Privately Held**
WEB: www.jvis.us
SIC: 3089 3711 Automotive parts, plastic; automobile assembly, including specialty automobiles

(G-15249)
JVIS INTERNATIONAL LLC (HQ)
Also Called: Jvis - USA
52048 Shelby Pkwy (48315-1787)
PHONE.................................586 739-9542
Jason Murar, *CEO*
Tim Bradley,
▲ EMP: 234 EST: 1997
SQ FT: 650,000
SALES (est): 172.1MM
SALES (corp-wide): 226.2MM **Privately Held**
WEB: www.jvis.us
SIC: 3089 Injection molding of plastics
PA: Jvis - Usa, Llc
    52048 Shelby Pkwy
    Shelby Township MI 48315
    586 884-5700

(G-15250)
KUKA ROBOTICS CORPORATION
Also Called: Kuka Omnimove
51870 Shelby Pkwy (48315-1787)
PHONE.................................586 795-2000
Leroy Rodgers, *President*
EMP: 45 EST: 1997
SALES (est): 16MM **Privately Held**
WEB: www.kuka.com
SIC: 3549 Metalworking machinery
HQ: Kuka Systems North America Llc
    6600 Center Dr
    Sterling Heights MI 48312
    586 795-2000

(G-15251)
KUKA SYSTEMS NORTH AMERICA LLC
13231 23 Mile Rd (48315-2713)
PHONE.................................586 726-4300
Lawrence Drake, *President*
EMP: 5 **Privately Held**
WEB: www.kuka.com
SIC: 3549 Assembly machines, including robotic
HQ: Kuka Systems North America Llc
    6600 Center Dr
    Sterling Heights MI 48312
    586 795-2000

(G-15252)
L & H DIVERSIFIED MFG USA LLC
51559 Oro Dr (48315-2932)
P.O. Box 183667 (48318-3667)
PHONE.................................586 615-4873
Marcus Murray, *Mng Member*
Mark Shows,
Conston Taylor,
EMP: 4
SALES (est): 310K **Privately Held**
SIC: 3549 Assembly machines, including robotic

(G-15253)
L T C SOLUTIONS INC
50150 Shelby Rd (48317-1569)
PHONE.................................586 323-2071
EMP: 5 EST: 2018
SALES (est): 81.4K **Privately Held**
WEB: www.ltc-solutions.com
SIC: 3599 Industrial machinery

(G-15254)
LABEL TECH INC
51322 Oro Dr (48315-2928)
P.O. Box 94048, Washington (48094-4048)
PHONE.................................586 247-6444
Barbara Schemanske, *President*
EMP: 10 EST: 1985
SQ FT: 10,000
SALES (est): 734.4K **Privately Held**
WEB: www.labeltechinc.com
SIC: 2759 5112 5045 Labels & seals: printing; inked ribbons; office supplies; computer software

(G-15255)
LAFATA CABINET SHOP (PA)
Also Called: La Fata Cabinets
50905 Hayes Rd (48315-3237)
PHONE.................................586 247-6536
Peter La Fata, *President*
Giovanni Lafata, *Vice Pres*
Colleen Maher, *Sales Mgr*
Brian Beckeman, *Sales Staff*
EMP: 92 EST: 1962
SQ FT: 35,000
SALES (est): 16.8MM **Privately Held**
WEB: www.lafata.com
SIC: 5211 2434 2541 Cabinets, kitchen; wood kitchen cabinets; cabinets, except refrigerated: show, display, etc.: wood

(G-15256)
LAKEPOINT ELEC
56812 Mound Rd (48316-4943)
PHONE.................................586 983-2510
Paul Olivieri, *Owner*
EMP: 7 EST: 2007
SALES (est): 893K **Privately Held**
WEB: www.mylakepointeelectric.com
SIC: 3699 Electrical equipment & supplies

(G-15257)
LAPEER INDUSTRIES INC (PA)
14100 23 Mile Rd (48315-2910)
PHONE.................................810 538-0589
Daniel Schreiber, *President*
Bryan Deblois, *President*
Daniel C Schreiber, *Chairman*
Chris Erickson, *Vice Pres*
Matt Jones, *Vice Pres*
▲ EMP: 162 EST: 1974
SALES (est): 34.9MM **Privately Held**
WEB: www.lapeerind.com
SIC: 3728 3544 Military aircraft equipment & armament; turrets & turret drives, aircraft; turret test fixtures, aircraft; special dies & tools

(G-15258)
LASTEK INDUSTRIES LLC
50515 Corporate Dr (48315-3103)
PHONE.................................586 739-6666
Christopher Krystek,
Janusz Lachowski,
EMP: 5 EST: 2002
SQ FT: 9,000 **Privately Held**
SIC: 3699 Welding machines & equipment, ultrasonic

(G-15259)
LDB PLASTICS INC
50845 Rizzo Dr (48315-3249)
PHONE.................................586 566-9698
Renae A Syrowik, *President*
Daniel J Syrowik, *Exec VP*
Daniel Syrowik, *Exec VP*
Billy L Duncan, *Vice Pres*
▼ EMP: 7 EST: 1999
SQ FT: 9,200
SALES (est): 732K **Privately Held**
WEB: www.ldbplastics.com
SIC: 3089 Injection molding of plastics

(G-15260)
LEADER CORPORATION (PA)
51644 Filomena Dr (48315-2947)
PHONE.................................586 566-7114
Michael Arcari, *President*
Brenda Arcari, *Vice Pres*
Gary Spencer, *QC Mgr*
Justin Arcari, *Engineer*
EMP: 26 EST: 1958
SQ FT: 14,500
SALES (est): 5.7MM **Privately Held**
WEB: www.leader-corp.com
SIC: 3545 3541 3823 Gauges (machine tool accessories); jig boring & grinding machines; industrial instrmnts msrmnt display/control process variable

(G-15261)
LEADING EDGE ENGINEERING INC
14498 Oakwood Dr (48315-1526)
PHONE.................................586 786-0382
Anthony J Solomon, *President*
EMP: 10 EST: 1992
SQ FT: 10,000
SALES (est): 1MM **Privately Held**
WEB: www.leadingedgeengineering.com
SIC: 3599 8711 Custom machinery; industrial engineers

(G-15262)
LEWMAR CUSTOM DESIGNS INC
56588 Scotland Blvd (48316-5045)
P.O. Box 70674, Rochester Hills (48307-0013)
PHONE.................................586 677-5135
EMP: 4
SALES: 35K **Privately Held**
SIC: 2389 Mfg Apparel/Accessories

(G-15263)
LIBERTY TRANSIT MIX LLC
7520 23 Mile Rd (48316-4422)
PHONE.................................586 254-2212
Cheryl A Menlen, *President*
EMP: 12 EST: 1979
SALES (est): 787.8K **Privately Held**
WEB: www.libertytransitmix.com
SIC: 3272 Concrete structural support & building material

(G-15264)
LUBE - POWER INC
50146 Utica Dr (48315-3293)
PHONE.................................586 247-6500
Dale McNeill, *President*
Brian Lightcap, *Vice Pres*
Jim Thorpe, *Prdtn Mgr*
Leah-Marie Couwlier, *Buyer*
Cathy Schomer, *Buyer*
▲ EMP: 83
SQ FT: 70,784
SALES (est): 32.9MM **Privately Held**
WEB: www.lubepower.com
SIC: 3569 5084 8711 Lubrication equipment, industrial; hydraulic systems equipment & supplies; consulting engineer

(G-15265)
LUMASMART TECHNOLOGY INTL INC
Also Called: Lst Lighting
51560 Celeste (48315-2924)
PHONE.................................586 232-4125
Antonio Zucca, *President*
Kimberly Cosens, *Treasurer*
Lindsey Yaklin, *Marketing Staff*
Dennis Dobosz, *Director*
Wayne Forman, *Director*
▲ EMP: 61 EST: 2006
SQ FT: 37,355
SALES (est): 19.8MM **Privately Held**
WEB: www.lumasmart.com
SIC: 3674 Light emitting diodes

(G-15266)
MACOMB NORTH CLINTON ADVISOR
Also Called: Advisor The
48075 Van Dyke Ave (48317-3258)
PHONE.................................586 731-1000
Frank Sheaper, *Owner*
Wayne Oehmke, *Principal*
EMP: 5 EST: 1993
SALES (est): 77.7K **Privately Held**
SIC: 2711 Newspapers, publishing & printing

(G-15267)
MACOMB STAIRS INC
51032 Oro Dr (48315-2966)
PHONE.................................586 226-2800
Tom Vitale, *President*
Vince E Vitale, *Vice Pres*
Vince Vitale, *Vice Pres*
Rhonda Yaroch, *Director*
James A Vitale, *Admin Sec*
EMP: 18 EST: 1993
SQ FT: 16,000
SALES: 3.4MM **Privately Held**
WEB: www.macombstairs.com
SIC: 2431 Staircases & stairs, wood; moldings & baseboards, ornamental & trim

(G-15268)
MAGNA SEATING AMERICA INC
Also Called: Shelby Foam Systems
6200 26 Mile Rd (48316-5000)
PHONE.................................586 816-1400
Brian Bartkowiak, *Manager*
EMP: 5
SALES (corp-wide): 32.6B **Privately Held**
WEB: www.magna.com
SIC: 3714 Motor vehicle parts & accessories
HQ: Magna Seating Of America, Inc.
    30020 Cabot Dr
    Novi MI 48377

(G-15269)
MARK SCHWAGER INC
13170 W Star Dr (48315-2736)
PHONE.................................248 275-1978
Mark Schwager, *President*
▲ EMP: 14 EST: 2005 **Privately Held**
WEB: www.msi-mold.com
SIC: 5162 3089 Plastics materials & basic shapes; injection molded finished plastic products; injection molding of plastics

(G-15270)
MASTER MODEL & FIXTURE INC
51731 Oro Dr (48315-2934)
PHONE.................................586 532-1153
Brian Grasso, *President*
EMP: 10 EST: 1994
SQ FT: 12,000
SALES (est): 907.4K **Privately Held**
WEB: www.mastermodelandfixtures.com
SIC: 3544 Special dies & tools

(G-15271)
MAYA PLASTICS INC
13179 W Star Dr (48315-2736)
P.O. Box 183817, Utica (48318-3817)
PHONE.................................586 997-6000
EMP: 40
SQ FT: 10,800
SALES (est): 4.6MM **Privately Held**
SIC: 3089 Mfg Injection Molding Of Plastics

(G-15272)
MEGA PRECAST INC
14670 23 Mile Rd (48315-3000)
PHONE.................................586 477-5959
Amedeo Piccinini, *President*
Sam Eid, *Vice Pres*
EMP: 11 EST: 2011
SALES (est): 1.9MM **Privately Held**
WEB: www.nationalprecast.com
SIC: 3272 Concrete products

Shelby Township - Macomb County (G-15273) — GEOGRAPHIC SECTION

(G-15273)
METAL FORMING & COINING CORP
51810 Danview Tech Ct (48315)
PHONE.....................586 731-2003
Dave Huber, *Manager*
Erik Piper, *Manager*
EMP: 4
SALES (corp-wide): 22.1MM **Privately Held**
WEB: www.mfccorp.com
SIC: 3462 Iron & steel forgings
PA: Metal Forming & Coining Corp
  1007 Illinois Ave
  Maumee OH 43537
  419 897-9530

(G-15274)
METALFORM INDUSTRIES LLC
52830 Tuscany Grv (48315-2081)
PHONE.....................248 462-0056
Craig Scott,
EMP: 5 **EST:** 2011
SALES (est): 332.9K **Privately Held**
SIC: 8711 8742 3569 3544 Machine tool design; management engineering; assembly machines, non-metalworking; special dies, tools, jigs & fixtures

(G-15275)
METRIC HYDRULIC COMPONENTS LLC
13870 Cavaliere Dr (48315-2961)
PHONE.....................586 786-6990
Jerry Pizzimenti, *Principal*
EMP: 10 **EST:** 2006
SALES (est): 972.1K **Privately Held**
WEB: www.metrichydraulics.com
SIC: 3823 Fluidic devices, circuits & systems for process control

(G-15276)
METRO DETROIT SCREEN PRTG LLC
14416 Towering Oaks Dr (48315-1965)
PHONE.....................586 337-5167
Scott Dawda, *Principal*
EMP: 4 **EST:** 2013
SALES (est): 170.3K **Privately Held**
WEB: www.metrodetroitscreenprinting.com
SIC: 2759 Screen printing

(G-15277)
MFC NETFORM INC
51810 Danview Tech Ct (48315)
PHONE.....................586 731-2003
Tim Cripsey, *President*
Dan Januszek, *General Mgr*
Scott Breil, *Plant Mgr*
Tim Beckwith, *Engineer*
Erik Piper, *Engineer*
EMP: 18 **EST:** 2000
SALES (est): 6.5MM **Privately Held**
WEB: www.mfcnetform.com
SIC: 3462 Iron & steel forgings

(G-15278)
MJB STAIRS LLC
56728 Mound Rd (48316-4942)
PHONE.....................586 822-9559
EMP: 6 **EST:** 2008
SALES (est): 139K **Privately Held**
WEB: www.mjbstairsllc.com
SIC: 3423 2431 Carpenters' hand tools, except saws: levels, chisels, etc.; staircases & stairs, wood

(G-15279)
MLC WINDOW CO INC (PA)
Also Called: Mlcwindows & Doors
2001 Crystal Lake Dr (48316-2818)
PHONE.....................586 731-3500
Michael Lochirco, *President*
▲ **EMP:** 23 **EST:** 1991
SQ FT: 1,000
SALES (est): 5MM **Privately Held**
WEB: www.mlcwindows.com
SIC: 2431 Storm windows, wood

(G-15280)
MOBILITY INNOVATIONS LLC
51277 Celeste (48315-2941)
PHONE.....................586 843-3816
James Morrison, *CEO*
EMP: 5 **EST:** 2018
SALES (est): 470.3K **Privately Held**
WEB: www.mobilityinnovators.com
SIC: 3711 Motor vehicles & car bodies

(G-15281)
MODELS & TOOLS INC
51400 Bellestri Ct (48315-2749)
PHONE.....................586 580-6900
Randal Bellestri, *CEO*
Philip Neale, *President*
Richard Querro, *Engineer*
Rick Faubert, *CFO*
Bill Urbanowicz, *Program Mgr*
EMP: 180 **EST:** 1974
SQ FT: 115,000
SALES (est): 24.8MM **Privately Held**
WEB: www.modelsandtools.com
SIC: 3544 Special dies & tools

(G-15282)
MODULAR DATA SYSTEMS INC
53089 Bellamine Dr (48316-2101)
PHONE.....................586 739-5870
Gerald J Wolschlager, *President*
Robert Luxa, *Vice Pres*
Judy Wolschlager, *Admin Sec*
EMP: 10 **EST:** 1970
SALES (est): 750K **Privately Held**
WEB: www.modulardata.com
SIC: 3824 Electromechanical counters

(G-15283)
MOLD SPECIALTIES INC
51232 Oro Dr (48315-2903)
PHONE.....................586 247-4660
Reiner Buchholtz, *President*
EMP: 8 **EST:** 1988
SQ FT: 3,000
SALES (est): 993.7K **Privately Held**
SIC: 3544 Industrial molds

(G-15284)
MOLLER GROUP NORTH AMERICA INC (DH)
Also Called: Megaplast North America
13877 Teresa Dr (48315-2929)
PHONE.....................586 532-0860
Peter Von Moller, *President*
▲ **EMP:** 100 **EST:** 1998
SALES (est): 94.4MM
SALES (corp-wide): 257.2K **Privately Held**
WEB: www.moellergroup.com
SIC: 3089 Injection molding of plastics
HQ: Mollertech International Gmbh
  Kupferhammer
  Bielefeld 33649
  521 447-70

(G-15285)
MOORE SIGNS INVESTMENTS INC
5220 Rail View Ct Apt 245 (48316-5703)
P.O. Box 836, Mount Clemens (48046-0836)
PHONE.....................586 783-9339
Frank Declerck, *President*
EMP: 13 **EST:** 1919
SQ FT: 12,000
SALES (est): 219.5K **Privately Held**
WEB: www.realestatesignsite.com
SIC: 3993 Signs & advertising specialties

(G-15286)
MSINC
50463 Wing Dr (48315-3261)
P.O. Box 183335, Utica (48318-3335)
PHONE.....................248 275-1978
Mark Schwager, *Principal*
▲ **EMP:** 13 **EST:** 2011
SALES (est): 919.9K **Privately Held**
SIC: 3089 Injection molding of plastics

(G-15287)
NATIONAL CASE CORP
13220 W Star Dr (48315-2745)
PHONE.....................586 803-3245
Michael Klenner, *Principal*
EMP: 5 **EST:** 2012
SALES (est): 73.7K **Privately Held**
SIC: 3523 Farm machinery & equipment

(G-15288)
NATIONAL PRECAST STRL INC
14670 23 Mile Rd (48315-3000)
PHONE.....................586 294-6430
John Ciulus, *President*
Gino Piccinini, *Vice Pres*
▲ **EMP:** 14 **EST:** 2002
SALES (est): 458K **Privately Held**
SIC: 3272 Precast terrazo or concrete products

(G-15289)
NEW LINE INC
Also Called: New Line Laminate Design
15164 Commercial Dr (48315-3982)
PHONE.....................586 228-4820
Giovanni Ferrazzo, *President*
EMP: 8 **EST:** 1987
SQ FT: 6,000
SALES (est): 500K **Privately Held**
SIC: 2434 3469 2519 Wood kitchen cabinets; kitchen fixtures & equipment, porcelain enameled; fiberglass & plastic furniture

(G-15290)
NORTH AMERICAN CONTROLS INC
13955 Teresa Dr (48315-2930)
PHONE.....................586 532-7140
Antonio Sciacca, *President*
Adam Stumpf, *Production*
Zachary Flint, *Buyer*
Sean Steiner, *Engineer*
Edward E Page III, *CFO*
▼ **EMP:** 37 **EST:** 1990
SQ FT: 17,000
SALES (est): 5.8MM **Privately Held**
WEB: www.nacontrols.com
SIC: 3829 Measuring & controlling devices

(G-15291)
NORTH AMERICAN MCH & ENGRG CO
Also Called: North American Machine & Engrg
13290 W Star Dr (48315-2741)
PHONE.....................586 726-6700
James R Howes, *President*
EMP: 5 **EST:** 1981
SQ FT: 6,000
SALES (est): 151.2K **Privately Held**
SIC: 7699 5084 3599 Industrial machinery & equipment repair; industrial machinery & equipment; machine shop, jobbing & repair

(G-15292)
NORTHERN METALCRAFT INC
50490 Corporate Dr (48315-3104)
PHONE.....................586 997-9630
Joseph Toepfner, *President*
Nikolaus Kolling, *Vice Pres*
Elisabeth Hammer, *Treasurer*
Karin Schwalbe, *Persnl Dir*
Bob Hammer, *IT/INT Sup*
EMP: 15 **EST:** 1975
SQ FT: 26,000
SALES (est): 1.5MM **Privately Held**
WEB: www.northernmetalcraft.com
SIC: 3465 Automotive stampings

(G-15293)
NT FABRICATING INC
15061 Technology Dr (48315-3952)
PHONE.....................586 566-7280
Jeffrey M Reid, *Principal*
EMP: 11 **EST:** 2005
SALES (est): 699.3K **Privately Held**
SIC: 3441 Fabricated structural metal

(G-15294)
ORTHOTIC SHOP INC
14200 Industrial Ctr Dr (48315-3259)
PHONE.....................800 309-0412
Matthew Behnke, *President*
Shelby Orlando, *Sales Staff*
EMP: 3 **EST:** 2007
SALES (est): 1.1MM **Privately Held**
WEB: www.orthoticshop.com
SIC: 3842 Orthopedic appliances

(G-15295)
PARAGON READY MIX INC (PA)
48000 Hixson Ave (48317-2731)
P.O. Box 81430, Rochester (48308-1430)
PHONE.....................586 731-8000
Steve Simpson, *President*
EMP: 27 **EST:** 2010
SALES (est): 4.6MM **Privately Held**
WEB: www.paragonreadymix.com
SIC: 3273 Ready-mixed concrete

(G-15296)
PASLIN COMPANY
52550 Shelby Pkwy (48315-1778)
PHONE.....................248 953-8419
Richard Stathakis, *Superintendent*
EMP: 200 **Privately Held**
WEB: www.paslin.com
SIC: 3548 3544 3535 Electric welding equipment; jigs & fixtures; conveyors & conveying equipment
HQ: The Paslin Company
  25303 Ryan Rd
  Warren MI 48091
  586 758-0200

(G-15297)
PEAKE ASPHALT INC
48181 Ryan Rd (48317-2882)
PHONE.....................586 254-4567
Mariah Peake, *Manager*
EMP: 15 **EST:** 2017
SALES (est): 30MM **Privately Held**
WEB: www.peakeasphalt.com
SIC: 2951 Asphalt paving mixtures & blocks

(G-15298)
PEG-MASTER BUSINESS FORMS INC
Also Called: Michigan Printing Impressions
15018 Technology Dr (48315-3950)
PHONE.....................586 566-8694
Linda Ianni, *President*
EMP: 9 **EST:** 1964
SALES (est): 773.1K **Privately Held**
WEB: www.pegmasterprinting.com
SIC: 2752 2791 2761 2759 Commercial printing, offset; typesetting; manifold business forms; commercial printing

(G-15299)
PERMAN INDUSTRIES LLC
51523 Celeste (48315-2923)
PHONE.....................586 991-5600
EMP: 15
SALES (est): 241.5K **Privately Held**
SIC: 3599 Mfg Industrial Machinery

(G-15300)
PERSICO USA INC
50450 Wing Dr (48315-3288)
PHONE.....................248 299-5100
Pierino Persico, *President*
Raffaella Baschenis, *Buyer*
Alison Traver, *Purchasing*
Martino Kinaya, *Manager*
◆ **EMP:** 68 **EST:** 1997
SALES (est): 10.5MM **Privately Held**
WEB: www.persico.com
SIC: 3423 Soldering tools

(G-15301)
PHILLIPS ENTERPRISES INC
Also Called: Banner Sign Specialties
51245 Filomena (48315-2942)
PHONE.....................586 615-6208
Mark Phillips, *President*
Dianna Phillips, *Vice Pres*
Justina Brede, *Manager*
Mark Ryan, *Executive*
Bill Day, *Admin Sec*
EMP: 46 **EST:** 1987
SQ FT: 6,000
SALES (est): 10.6MM **Privately Held**
SIC: 3993 Signs & advertising specialties

(G-15302)
PINK PIN LADY LLC
47768 Barclay Ct (48317-3678)
PHONE.....................586 731-1532
Jacqueline Nash, *Principal*
EMP: 5 **EST:** 2007
SALES (est): 73.1K **Privately Held**
SIC: 3452 Pins

(G-15303)
PLASTIC TRENDS INC
Also Called: Royal Building Products
56400 Mound Rd (48316-4904)
PHONE.................................586 232-4167
Jon Houghton, *President*
Judith Peddle, *Buyer*
◆ EMP: 95 EST: 1968
SQ FT: 265,000
SALES (est): 22.5MM **Publicly Held**
WEB: www.axiall.com
SIC: 3089 Injection molding of plastics
HQ: Axiall Corporation
2801 Post Oak Blvd # 600
Houston TX 77056
304 455-2200

(G-15304)
POLYMER PROCESS DEV LLC
11969 Shelby Tech Dr (48315-1788)
PHONE.................................586 464-6400
Perry Giese, *President*
Robert Brisley, *Vice Pres*
Bret Bailey, *VP Opers*
Jeff Matthews, *Project Mgr*
Tyler Nault, *Engineer*
EMP: 72 EST: 1996
SALES (est): 15.4MM **Privately Held**
WEB: www.ppdllc.com
SIC: 3089 3231 Injection molding of plastics; products of purchased glass

(G-15305)
POND BIOLOGICS LLC
56828 Mound Rd (48316-4943)
PHONE.................................800 527-9420
Nicholas A Salvatore, *Owner*
EMP: 10 EST: 2012
SALES (est): 523.6K **Privately Held**
WEB: www.pondbiologics.com
SIC: 2086 4941 Mineral water, carbonated: packaged in cans, bottles, etc.; water supply

(G-15306)
POPPED KERNEL
14107 Silent Woods Dr (48315-6806)
PHONE.................................586 295-4977
Gerlyn Aprile, *Principal*
EMP: 5 EST: 2015
SALES (est): 128.5K **Privately Held**
WEB: www.thepoppedkernelco.com
SIC: 2064 Candy & other confectionery products

(G-15307)
PPG INDUSTRIES INC
Also Called: PPG 5624
13651 23 Mile Rd (48315-2906)
PHONE.................................586 566-3789
EMP: 4
SALES (corp-wide): 15.1B **Publicly Held**
WEB: www.ppg.com
SIC: 2851 Paints & allied products
PA: Ppg Industries, Inc.
1 Ppg Pl
Pittsburgh PA 15272
412 434-3131

(G-15308)
PRISM PLASTICS INC
50581 Sabrina Dr (48315-2963)
PHONE.................................810 292-6300
Stan Nosakowski, *Branch Mgr*
EMP: 25
SALES (corp-wide): 245.5B **Publicly Held**
WEB: www.prismplastics.com
SIC: 3089 Injection molding of plastics
HQ: Prism Plastics, Inc.
52111 Sierra Dr
Chesterfield MI 48047
810 292-6300

(G-15309)
PROGRESSIVE CUTTER GRINDING CO
14207 Rick Dr (48315-2935)
PHONE.................................586 580-2367
Jorgo Villa, *President*
EMP: 7 EST: 2006
SALES (est): 837.4K **Privately Held**
SIC: 3479 Coating of metals & formed products

(G-15310)
PROTODESIGN INC
50495 Corporate Dr Ste 10 (48315-3132)
PHONE.................................586 739-4340
Tony Sajkowski, *President*
John Zimmer, *Mfg Spvr*
Linda Labarbera, *Purchasing*
Ryan Sajkowski, *Electrical Engi*
Amy Campbell, *Manager*
EMP: 20 EST: 1992
SQ FT: 10,000
SALES (est): 5MM **Privately Held**
WEB: www.teampdi.com
SIC: 3672 Printed circuit boards

(G-15311)
PROTOTYPE CAST MFG INC (PA)
Also Called: Pcmi Manufacturing Integration
51752 Danview Tech Ct (48315)
PHONE.................................586 739-0180
William Edney, *CEO*
Bill Edney, *Vice Pres*
Hai Zheng, *Engineer*
Harry Zheng, *Engineer*
Kristina Edney, *Finance*
▲ EMP: 8 EST: 2003
SQ FT: 25,410
SALES (est): 2.5MM **Privately Held**
WEB: www.pcmi-mfg.com
SIC: 3363 3599 Aluminum die-castings; machine & other job shop work

(G-15312)
QUANTUM GRAPHICS INC
50720 Corporate Dr (48315-3105)
PHONE.................................586 566-5656
Michael Burton, *President*
Gerard Buczek, *Vice Pres*
Steve Burton, *Vice Pres*
EMP: 24 EST: 1992
SQ FT: 26,380
SALES (est): 3.2MM **Privately Held**
WEB: www.quantumgraphics.com
SIC: 2752 Commercial printing, offset

(G-15313)
R S C PRODUCTIONS
Also Called: Contemporary Bride
7811 24 Mile Rd (48316-2509)
PHONE.................................586 532-9200
Riccardo Coletti, *President*
EMP: 6 EST: 1988
SALES (est): 484.2K **Privately Held**
WEB: www.rscproductions.com
SIC: 7389 2741 Advertising, promotional & trade show services; miscellaneous publishing

(G-15314)
RANKAM METAL PRODUCTS
48582 Van Dyke Ave (48317-3269)
PHONE.................................586 799-4259
Sam Gatto, *Vice Pres*
EMP: 5 EST: 2018
SALES (est): 54.3K **Privately Held**
WEB: www.rankam.com
SIC: 3499 Fabricated metal products

(G-15315)
RASSEY INDUSTRIES INC
50375 Central Indus Dr (48315-3114)
PHONE.................................586 803-9500
Louis N Rassey, *President*
Edward A Rassey, *Vice Pres*
Edward Rassey, *VP Prdtn*
Adam Besso, *QC Mgr*
Abhishek Pathri, *Engineer*
▲ EMP: 22 EST: 1970
SQ FT: 36,000
SALES (est): 3MM **Privately Held**
WEB: www.rassey.com
SIC: 3714 3599 Motor vehicle parts & accessories; machine shop, jobbing & repair

(G-15316)
REW INDUSTRIES INC
51572 Danview Tech Ct (48315)
PHONE.................................586 803-1150
Russell Willauer, *President*
Holly Kobe, *Office Mgr*
EMP: 29 EST: 1995
SQ FT: 12,000
SALES (est): 3.2MM **Privately Held**
WEB: www.rewindustries.com
SIC: 3469 Stamping metal for the trade

(G-15317)
ROSS CABINETS II INC
50169 Hayes Rd (48315-3229)
PHONE.................................586 752-7750
Antonio Verelli, *President*
Anthony Verelli, *President*
EMP: 18 EST: 1981
SALES (est): 1.2MM **Privately Held**
SIC: 2541 2517 2434 Cabinets, lockers & shelving; wood television & radio cabinets; wood kitchen cabinets

(G-15318)
RSI
14026 Simone Dr (48315-3235)
PHONE.................................586 566-7716
Dan Hickey, *Principal*
EMP: 5 EST: 2014
SALES (est): 92.3K **Privately Held**
SIC: 3441 Fabricated structural metal

(G-15319)
RSLS CORP
51084 Filomena Dr (48315-2937)
PHONE.................................248 726-0675
Russell Carter, *President*
EMP: 5 EST: 2012
SALES (est): 440.5K **Privately Held**
SIC: 2396 3993 Screen printing on fabric articles; letters for signs, metal

(G-15320)
S N D STEEL FABRICATION INC
11611 Park Ct (48315-3109)
PHONE.................................586 997-1500
Milivoje Djordjevic, *President*
Zoran Djordjevic, *Vice Pres*
EMP: 17 EST: 1979
SQ FT: 24,000
SALES (est): 2.5MM **Privately Held**
WEB: www.sndsteel.com
SIC: 3441 Fabricated structural metal

(G-15321)
SAINT-GOBAIN PRFMCE PLAS CORP
51424 Van Dyke Ave (48316-4406)
PHONE.................................586 884-9237
EMP: 4
SALES (corp-wide): 2.1B **Privately Held**
WEB: www.plastics.saint-gobain.com
SIC: 2821 Plastics materials & resins
HQ: Saint-Gobain Performance Plastics Corporation
31500 Solon Rd
Solon OH 44139
440 836-6900

(G-15322)
SAPA TRANSMISSION INC
51901 Shelby Pkwy (48315-1787)
PHONE.................................954 608-0125
Deniz Balta, *Director*
Kelly Balta, *Administration*
EMP: 10 EST: 2003
SALES (est): 1MM **Privately Held**
WEB: www.sapatransmission.com
SIC: 3714 Transmissions, motor vehicle

(G-15323)
SBTI COMPANY
Also Called: Smith Bros. Tool Company
50600 Corporate Dr (48315-3107)
PHONE.................................586 726-5756
Hodges Tennyson Smith, *President*
Jere Rush, *President*
EMP: 55 EST: 1981
SQ FT: 130,000
SALES (est): 4.8MM **Privately Held**
WEB: www.smithbrostool.com
SIC: 3543 3544 3545 Industrial patterns; special dies, tools, jigs & fixtures; machine tool accessories

(G-15324)
SCENARIO SYSTEMS LTD
50466 Rizzo Dr (48315-3275)
PHONE.................................586 532-1320
Edward Strehl, *President*
Gary Pizzimenti, *Vice Pres*
EMP: 7 EST: 1993
SQ FT: 36,000
SALES (est): 630.9K **Privately Held**
WEB: www.scenariosystems.com
SIC: 3499 Welding tips, heat resistant: metal

(G-15325)
SCHWAB INDUSTRIES INC
Also Called: Plant 2
50750 Rizzo Dr (48315-3274)
PHONE.................................586 566-8090
Brian Gibson, *Manager*
EMP: 10
SQ FT: 70,000
SALES (corp-wide): 22.7MM **Privately Held**
WEB: www.schwabind.com
SIC: 3714 Motor vehicle parts & accessories
PA: Schwab Industries, Inc.
50850 Rizzo Dr
Shelby Township MI 48315
586 566-8090

(G-15326)
SCHWAB INDUSTRIES INC (PA)
50850 Rizzo Dr (48315-3248)
PHONE.................................586 566-8090
Reiner Koerner, *President*
Craig Harrison, *Project Mgr*
Shane Serra, *Program Mgr*
Tami Morin, *Manager*
Jeffrey Harris, *Prgrmr*
EMP: 25 EST: 1984
SQ FT: 110,000
SALES (est): 22.7MM **Privately Held**
WEB: www.schwabind.com
SIC: 3544 3469 3465 3291 Die sets for metal stamping (presses); ornamental metal stampings; fenders, automobile: stamped or pressed metal; steel wool

(G-15327)
SENSORDATA TECHNOLOGIES INC
50207 Hayes Rd (48315-3230)
PHONE.................................586 739-4254
Sherif Gindy, *President*
Michael Parker, *Vice Pres*
Sharif Gindy, *Chief Engr*
Mike Parker, *Regl Sales Mgr*
EMP: 15 EST: 1992
SQ FT: 2,000 **Privately Held**
WEB: www.sensordata-burster.com
SIC: 3829 Measuring & controlling devices

(G-15328)
SGL TECHNIC LLC
Also Called: Sgl Carbon Group
2156 Willow Cir (48316-1054)
PHONE.................................248 540-9508
William J Raven, *Manager*
Dan Gillig, *Technical Staff*
EMP: 4
SALES (corp-wide): 1B **Privately Held**
WEB: www.sglcarbon.com
SIC: 3295 Graphite, natural: ground, pulverized, refined or blended
HQ: Sgl Technic Llc
28176 Avenue Stanford
Valencia CA 91355
661 257-0500

(G-15329)
SHAYN ALLEN MARQUETRY
14009 Simone Dr (48315-3234)
PHONE.................................586 991-0445
Shayn Smith, *Partner*
EMP: 4 EST: 2015
SALES (est): 300K **Privately Held**
SIC: 2431 2434 Floor baseboards, wood; wood kitchen cabinets

(G-15330)
SHELBY ANTOLIN INC
52888 Shelby Pkwy (48315-1778)
PHONE.................................734 395-0328
Joseph McCluskey, *General Mgr*
Amy Sargeant, *Opers Staff*
EMP: 12 EST: 2017
SQ FT: 350,000
SALES (est): 209K
SALES (corp-wide): 2.6MM **Privately Held**
WEB: www.grupoantolin.com
SIC: 3714 Motor vehicle body components & frame

Shelby Township - Macomb County (G-15331)

HQ: Grupo Antolin North America, Inc.
1700 Atlantic Blvd
Auburn Hills MI 48326
248 373-1749

(G-15331)
SHELBY INDUSTRIES INC
15002 Technology Dr (48315-3950)
PHONE................586 884-4421
EMP: 6 EST: 2018
SALES (est): 391.4K Privately Held
SIC: 3999 Manufacturing industries

(G-15332)
SHELBY SIGNARAMA TOWNSHIP
51053 Celeste (48315-2921)
PHONE................586 843-3702
Russell Carter, President
EMP: 4 EST: 2012 Privately Held
SIC: 3993 7336 Signs & advertising specialties; commercial art & graphic design

(G-15333)
SIGNS365COM LLC
51245 Filomena Dr (48315-2942)
PHONE................800 265-8830
Emily Valin, Sales Staff
Lyle Mueller, Supervisor
Alexander Stewart, Supervisor
Dianna Phillips, Administration
EMP: 6 EST: 2011
SALES (est): 1.1MM Privately Held
WEB: www.signs365.com
SIC: 2759 5131 3993 Screen printing; flags & banners; signs & advertising specialties

(G-15334)
SM ANDIA SEALCOATING LLC
52711 Brenton (48316-3025)
PHONE................586 997-9752
Steve Mandia, Principal
EMP: 5 EST: 2018
SALES (est): 96.3K Privately Held
SIC: 2952 Asphalt felts & coatings

(G-15335)
SMITH BROTHERS TOOL COMPANY
50600 Corporate Dr (48315-3107)
PHONE................586 726-5756
Karl Lapeer, Ch of Bd
Jere Rush, Vice Pres
Carl Russo, Vice Pres
Christopher Gessner, Admin Sec
EMP: 53 EST: 2012
SQ FT: 36,984
SALES (est): 7.6MM Privately Held
WEB: www.smithbrostool.com
SIC: 3544 Special dies & tools

(G-15336)
SMS ELOTHERM NORTH AMERICA LLC
13129 23 Mile Rd (48315-2711)
PHONE................586 469-8324
Matthew Aulph, Sales Staff
Lou Bianchi, Department Mgr
Johann Rinnhofer,
Martin Schulteis,
EMP: 15 EST: 2011
SALES (est): 8.5MM Privately Held
WEB: www.sms-elotherm.com
SIC: 3567 Induction heating equipment

(G-15337)
SNYDER CORPORATION
13231 23 Mile Rd (48315-2713)
PHONE................586 726-4300
Thomas J Carter, Ch of Bd
Stefan Wanczyk, President
EMP: 133 EST: 1987
SQ FT: 62,640
SALES (est): 3.4MM
SALES (corp-wide): 305MM Privately Held
WEB: www.uticaenterprises.com
SIC: 3541 Machine tools, metal cutting type
PA: Utica Enterprises, Inc.
5750 New King Dr Ste 200
Troy MI 48098
586 726-4300

(G-15338)
SOLUTION STEEL TREATING LLC
51689 Oro Dr (48315-2934)
PHONE................586 247-9250
Steve Hawkins,
Jeff Flannery,
Edward Lowmaster,
Stephen Spohn,
EMP: 15 EST: 2000
SQ FT: 8,300
SALES (est): 1MM Privately Held
SIC: 3398 Metal heat treating

(G-15339)
SOS WELL SERVICES LLC
51330 Oro Dr (48315-2928)
PHONE................586 580-2576
Robet Schmid,
EMP: 55 EST: 2000
SALES (est): 5.9MM Privately Held
WEB: www.soswellservices.com
SIC: 1389 Oil field services

(G-15340)
SPEC TECHNOLOGIES INC
Also Called: Spec Check
51455 Schoenherr Rd (48315-2734)
PHONE................586 726-0000
Rick Schneider, President
Wayne Russell, Vice Pres
Amy Schmelzer, Vice Pres
Amy Schneider, Vice Pres
Robert O'Neill, CFO
EMP: 60 EST: 1987
SQ FT: 40,000
SALES (est): 8MM Privately Held
WEB: www.spectech-us.com
SIC: 3599 7549 Machine shop, jobbing & repair; inspection & diagnostic service, automotive

(G-15341)
SPI LLC
Also Called: Sterling
51370 Celeste (48315-2902)
PHONE................586 566-5870
Crystal Chackman, Purchasing
Pat King, QC Mgr
Werner Kleinert,
Donald Barnhart,
Michael Kleinert,
EMP: 30 EST: 1996
SQ FT: 30,000
SALES (est): 5.5MM Privately Held
WEB: www.spillc.com
SIC: 3089 Injection molded finished plastic products

(G-15342)
SPRING DESIGN AND MFG INC
14105 Industrial Ctr Dr D (48315-3260)
PHONE................586 566-9741
John Gehart, President
Ryan Kelley, Business Mgr
CJ Martens, Engineer
EMP: 50 EST: 1996
SALES (est): 7.1MM Privately Held
WEB: www.springdesignmfg.com
SIC: 3495 Wire springs

(G-15343)
SRA INDUSTRIES
14938 Technology Dr (48315-3949)
PHONE................586 251-2000
EMP: 7 EST: 2017
SALES (est): 465.1K Privately Held
SIC: 3999 Manufacturing industries

(G-15344)
SUMMIT PLASTIC MOLDING INC
51340 Celeste (48315-2902)
PHONE................586 262-4500
Raymond Kalinowski, President
Mark Tuscany, CFO
Brian Kowalski, Controller
Gina Depasquale, Supervisor
▲ EMP: 45 EST: 1986
SQ FT: 15,000
SALES (est): 9.7MM Privately Held
WEB: www.summitplasticmolding.com
SIC: 3089 Injection molding of plastics; injection molded finished plastic products

(G-15345)
SUMMIT PLASTIC MOLDING II INC (PA)
51340 Celeste (48315-2902)
PHONE................586 262-4500
Raymond Kalinowski, President
▲ EMP: 1 EST: 1992
SQ FT: 15,000
SALES (est): 3.6MM Privately Held
WEB: www.summitplasticmolding.com
SIC: 3089 Injection molding of plastics; injection molded finished plastic products

(G-15346)
SUMMIT SERVICES INC
51340 Celeste (48315-2902)
PHONE................586 977-8300
Raymond Kalinowski, President
EMP: 21 EST: 1982
SQ FT: 18,000
SALES (est): 906.4K Privately Held
WEB: www.nolancg.com
SIC: 3544 Industrial molds

(G-15347)
SUPERIOR CUTTER GRINDING INC
54631 Franklin Dr (48316-1622)
PHONE................586 781-2365
Gene L Ursu, President
EMP: 6 EST: 1962
SQ FT: 3,000
SALES (est): 476.1K Privately Held
SIC: 3599 Grinding castings for the trade

(G-15348)
T K INDUSTRIES INC
53586 Applewood Dr (48315-1341)
PHONE................586 242-5969
EMP: 4 EST: 2018
SALES (est): 199.4K Privately Held
SIC: 3999 Manufacturing industries

(G-15349)
TAKE US-4-GRANITE INC
13000 23 Mile Rd (48315-2702)
PHONE................586 803-1305
Matthew S Anderson, President
Michael Naiorano, Corp Secy
EMP: 7 EST: 2008
SALES (est): 600K Privately Held
WEB: www.exotic-granite.com
SIC: 1411 Granite dimension stone

(G-15350)
TELSONIC ULTRASONICS INC (DH)
14120 Industrial Ctr Dr (48315-3276)
PHONE................586 802-0033
Jochen Bacher, President
Gustavo Garcia-Cota, Managing Dir
Nicole Bacher, Accounting Mgr
James Kimley, Sales Engr
Andrew Lange, Info Tech Dir
▲ EMP: 19 EST: 2005
SQ FT: 20,000
SALES (est): 9.2MM
SALES (corp-wide): 333.5K Privately Held
WEB: www.telsonic.com
SIC: 3541 3699 Ultrasonic metal cutting machine tools; cleaning equipment, ultrasonic, except medical & dental
HQ: Telsonic Ag
Industriestrasse 6b
Bronschhofen SG 9552
719 139-888

(G-15351)
TI-COATING INC
50500 Corporate Dr (48315-3102)
PHONE................586 726-1900
Charles Zichichi, Ch of Bd
Rosemarie Zichichi, Ch of Bd
William C Zichichi, President
Keith Metzinger, Sales Mgr
Leonard Jankowski, Marketing Staff
EMP: 47 EST: 1975
SQ FT: 32,000
SALES (est): 10.1MM Privately Held
WEB: www.ticoating.com
SIC: 3479 3559 Coating of metals & formed products; chemical machinery & equipment

(G-15352)
TITAN PHARMACEUTICAL MCHY INC
50649 Central Indus Dr (48315-3119)
PHONE................248 220-7421
EMP: 5 EST: 2018
SALES (est): 422.5K Privately Held
SIC: 3559 Pharmaceutical machinery

(G-15353)
TNJ MANUFACTURING LLC
Also Called: Jvis-Teresa
13877 Teresa Dr (48315-2929)
P.O. Box 530, Mount Clemens (48046-0530)
PHONE................586 251-1900
Michael Alexander, Vice Pres
Jason Murar,
Tim Bradley,
EMP: 22 EST: 2020
SALES (est): 4.8MM
SALES (corp-wide): 226.2MM Privately Held
WEB: www.jvis.us
SIC: 3089 Automotive parts, plastic
PA: Jvis - Usa, Llc
52048 Shelby Pkwy
Shelby Township MI 48315
586 884-5700

(G-15354)
TOP DECK SYSTEMS INC
48247 Milonas Dr (48315-4926)
PHONE................586 263-1550
Robert Jankowski, President
Magda O'Hanlon, Vice Pres
Joe Guastella, Marketing Staff
Magda Ohanlon, Programmer Anys
▲ EMP: 8 EST: 1990
SALES (est): 1MM Privately Held
WEB: www.alusett.com
SIC: 3993 Displays & cutouts, window & lobby

(G-15355)
TRANSFORM AUTOMOTIVE LLC
52400 Shelby Pkwy (48315-1778)
PHONE................586 826-8500
Shannon Schneider, QC Mgr
Karl Yates, Manager
EMP: 7
SALES (corp-wide): 2.4B Privately Held
SIC: 3714 Motor vehicle parts & accessories
HQ: Transform Automotive, Llc
7026 Sterling Ponds Ct
Sterling Heights MI 48312
586 826-8500

(G-15356)
TRI COUNTY OIL & GAS CO INC
54739 Pelican Ln (48315-1381)
P.O. Box 700385, Plymouth (48170-0947)
PHONE................248 390-0682
EMP: 6 EST: 2010
SALES (est): 652.5K Privately Held
SIC: 1382 Oil & gas exploration services

(G-15357)
TROY INDUSTRIES INC
13300 W Star Dr (48315-2700)
PHONE................586 739-7760
Stojan Stojanovski, President
Christopher Amidon, IT/INT Sup
EMP: 10 EST: 1977
SQ FT: 7,000
SALES (est): 744.8K Privately Held
WEB: www.troytools.com
SIC: 3541 Machine tools, metal cutting type

(G-15358)
TURBOSOCKS PERFORMANCE
50765 Cedargrove Rd (48317-1105)
PHONE................586 864-3252
Nate Poole, Principal
EMP: 5 EST: 2015
SALES (est): 184.4K Privately Held
WEB: www.turbosocks.com
SIC: 2252 Socks

▲ = Import ▼ = Export
◆ = Import/Export

GEOGRAPHIC SECTION

(G-15359)
TWIN MOLD AND ENGINEERING LLC
51738 Filomena Dr (48315-2948)
PHONE..................................586 532-8558
Jason Van Laere, *Mng Member*
EMP: 29 EST: 2005
SQ FT: 10,000
SALES (est): 4.7MM **Privately Held**
WEB: www.twinmold.com
SIC: 3544 Industrial molds

(G-15360)
US FARATHANE HOLDINGS CORP
11650 Park Ct Bldg B (48315-3108)
PHONE..................................248 754-7000
EMP: 5
SALES (corp-wide): 549.4MM **Privately Held**
WEB: www.usfarathane.com
SIC: 3089 Automotive parts, plastic
PA: U.S. Farathane Holdings Corp.
2700 High Meadow Cir
Auburn Hills MI 48326
248 754-7000

(G-15361)
US FARATHANE HOLDINGS CORP
11650 Park Ct (48315-3108)
PHONE..................................586 726-1200
Steve Maczko, *General Mgr*
EMP: 5
SALES (corp-wide): 549.4MM **Privately Held**
WEB: www.usfarathane.com
SIC: 3089 Injection molding of plastics
PA: U.S. Farathane Holdings Corp.
2700 High Meadow Cir
Auburn Hills MI 48326
248 754-7000

(G-15362)
UVA MARE INC
12489 24 Mile Rd (48315-1719)
PHONE..................................858 848-4440
Stefano Caruso, *President*
EMP: 6 EST: 2015
SALES (est): 116.3K **Privately Held**
SIC: 2084 Wines

(G-15363)
VAN LOON INDUSTRIES INC
51583 Filomena Dr (48315-2946)
PHONE..................................586 532-8530
Thomas J V Loon, *President*
Diana V Loon, *Vice Pres*
Christine Dixson, *Admin Sec*
Paul Van Loon, *Technician*
EMP: 25 EST: 1948
SQ FT: 12,000
SALES (est): 4.7MM **Privately Held**
WEB: www.vligroup.com
SIC: 3469 3444 3443 Metal stampings; sheet metalwork; fabricated plate work (boiler shop)

(G-15364)
VEIGEL NORTH AMERICA LLC
Also Called: Mobility Products and Design
51277 Celeste (48315-2941)
P.O. Box 182160 (48318-2160)
PHONE..................................586 843-3816
James Morrison, *Partner*
Kirk Dearhamer, *Opers Mgr*
Brandy Spear, *Sales Mgr*
EMP: 10 EST: 2009
SQ FT: 11,000
SALES (est): 1.3MM **Privately Held**
WEB: www.mobilityinnovators.com
SIC: 3711 Automobile assembly, including specialty automobiles

(G-15365)
VENETIAN CABINETS
14293 23 Mile Rd (48315-2925)
PHONE..................................586 580-3288
EMP: 8 EST: 2018
SALES (est): 300.7K **Privately Held**
WEB: www.venetiancabinets.com
SIC: 2434 Wood kitchen cabinets

(G-15366)
VISION FUELS LLC
51969 Van Dyke Ave (48316-4455)
PHONE..................................586 997-3286
EMP: 6 EST: 2008
SALES (est): 456.3K **Privately Held**
SIC: 2869 Fuels

(G-15367)
WEBER ELECTRIC MFG CO
Also Called: Wemco
2465 23 Mile Rd (48316-3805)
PHONE..................................586 323-9000
Salvatore P Munaco, *President*
▲ EMP: 35 EST: 1957
SQ FT: 20,000
SALES (est): 3.7MM **Privately Held**
WEB: www.wemco-usa.com
SIC: 3549 Wiredrawing & fabricating machinery & equipment, ex. die

(G-15368)
WHATS YOUR MIX MENCHIES LLC
2168 Scarboro Ct (48316-1266)
PHONE..................................248 840-1668
Louis Messina, *Principal*
EMP: 8 EST: 2012
SALES (est): 236K **Privately Held**
SIC: 3273 Ready-mixed concrete

(G-15369)
WIKID VINYL
49862 Newark Dr (48315-3781)
PHONE..................................313 585-7814
Gerald Lajiness, *Principal*
EMP: 4 EST: 2017
SALES (est): 59.3K **Privately Held**
SIC: 3993 Signs & advertising specialties

(G-15370)
WORLD CLASS EQUIPMENT COMPANY
Also Called: Wcec
51515 Celeste (48315-2923)
PHONE..................................586 331-2121
Mark Matheson, *President*
Jeff Hinsperger, *Vice Pres*
Jerry Stein, *Buyer*
Joe Phillips, *Sales Engr*
EMP: 11 EST: 2012
SALES (est): 2.5MM **Privately Held**
SIC: 3599 8711 Machine shop, jobbing & repair; machine tool design

(G-15371)
XPRESS PACKAGING SOLUTIONS LLC
11655 Park Ct (48315-3109)
PHONE..................................231 629-0463
Matt Murray, *CEO*
EMP: 4 EST: 2015
SALES (est): 499.6K **Privately Held**
SIC: 2655 Fiber shipping & mailing containers

(G-15372)
YELL SWEETS LLC
14142 Lakeside Blvd N (48315-6072)
PHONE..................................586 799-4560
Danielle Jackson, *Mng Member*
EMP: 5 EST: 2017
SALES (est): 257.9K **Privately Held**
WEB: www.yellsweetsllc.business.site
SIC: 2051 Bakery, for home service delivery

(G-15373)
ZINK
5429 Vincent Trl (48316-5257)
PHONE..................................586 781-5314
Maryann Zink, *Principal*
EMP: 5 EST: 2010
SALES (est): 142.6K **Privately Held**
SIC: 2311 Men's & boys' suits & coats

Shelbyville
Allegan County

(G-15374)
STRAIT ASTRID
4139 1/2 W Joy Rd (49344-9604)
PHONE..................................269 672-4110
Todd Strait, *Principal*
EMP: 4 EST: 2018
SALES (est): 147K **Privately Held**
SIC: 2759 Screen printing

(G-15375)
TECH WORLD LLC
2515 5th St (49344-9737)
PHONE..................................616 901-2611
Garth Felton,
EMP: 6 EST: 2015
SALES (est): 335.4K **Privately Held**
WEB: www.techworldllc.net
SIC: 3999 Dock equipment & supplies, industrial

Shepherd
Isabella County

(G-15376)
CONTOUR ENGINEERING INC
2305 E Coe Rd (48883-9575)
PHONE..................................989 828-6526
Kurt Willoughby, *President*
Craig Davis, *Engineer*
Janelle Snyder, *Admin Sec*
EMP: 10 EST: 1996
SQ FT: 12,000
SALES (est): 914.7K **Privately Held**
WEB: www.contourengineering.com
SIC: 3089 3469 Thermoformed finished plastic products; patterns on metal

(G-15377)
PATRICK D DUFFY
306 N 4th St (48883-9022)
PHONE..................................989 828-5467
EMP: 4 EST: 1998
SALES (est): 51.8K **Privately Held**
SIC: 7692 Welding repair

(G-15378)
PAUL JEFFREY KENNY
Also Called: Kenny Machining
1345 E Pleasant Valley Rd (48883-9528)
PHONE..................................989 828-6109
Paul Jeffrey Kenny, *Owner*
EMP: 8 EST: 1986
SQ FT: 4,000
SALES (est): **Privately Held**
SIC: 3599 Machine shop, jobbing & repair

(G-15379)
TOTAL CHIPS COMPANY INC
11285 S Winn Rd (48883-9544)
PHONE..................................989 866-2610
Ben C Nestle, *President*
Edward Morey, *Vice Pres*
EMP: 10 EST: 1972
SQ FT: 6,000
SALES (est): 744K **Privately Held**
WEB: www.stars1stcars.com
SIC: 2411 2421 Logging; sawmills & planing mills, general

Sheridan
Montcalm County

(G-15380)
BARNES WELDING & FAB LLC
8200 S Holland Rd (48884-9396)
PHONE..................................989 287-0161
Jason Barnes, *Principal*
EMP: 4 EST: 2018
SALES (est): 42.8K **Privately Held**
SIC: 7692 Welding repair

(G-15381)
BUSY BEES EMB & GIFTS LLC
3018 Log Cabin Trl (48884-9417)
PHONE..................................989 261-7446
Jodie Litwiller, *Principal*
EMP: 5 EST: 2019
SALES (est): 487.3K **Privately Held**
WEB: www.cvsdbusybees.com
SIC: 2759 Screen printing

(G-15382)
PATRIOT PYROTECHNICS
5735 S Townhall Rd B (48884-9630)
PHONE..................................989 831-7788
Bill Collins, *Owner*
EMP: 4 EST: 1994
SALES (est): 207.6K **Privately Held**
SIC: 2899 Fireworks

(G-15383)
PRECISION TOOL & MACHINE INC
154 E Condensery Rd (48884-9647)
PHONE..................................989 291-3365
John Roy, *President*
Heather Hardy, *Manager*
EMP: 5 EST: 1981
SQ FT: 4,500
SALES (est): **Privately Held**
SIC: 3599 Machine shop, jobbing & repair

(G-15384)
TOMMY JOE REED
Also Called: A & J Pallets
6551 S Townhall Rd (48884-9757)
PHONE..................................989 291-5768
Tommy J Reed, *Owner*
Joseph Reed, *Owner*
EMP: 5 EST: 1990
SQ FT: 1,536
SALES (est): 259.3K **Privately Held**
SIC: 2448 Pallets, wood

(G-15385)
VICKERYVILLE LUMBER CO LLC
7042 S Vickeryville Rd (48884-9727)
PHONE..................................989 261-3100
Leonard S Schrock, *President*
EMP: 7 EST: 2019
SALES (est): 86.7K **Privately Held**
SIC: 2421 Lumber: rough, sawed or planed

(G-15386)
WRIGHT PLASTIC PRODUCTS CO LLC (PA)
201 E Condensery Rd (48884-9654)
PHONE..................................989 291-3211
Robert W Luce, *Sales Staff*
Bob Luce, *Mng Member*
Jodi Halliwill, *Manager*
Dina Calcagno Masek,
Timothy Masek,
▲ EMP: 67
SQ FT: 79,000
SALES (est): 14.3MM **Privately Held**
WEB: www.wppllc.com
SIC: 3089 Injection molding of plastics

Sherwood
Branch County

(G-15387)
WOODCRAFTERS
Also Called: Woodcrafters Custom Furniture
855 Athens Rd (49089-9701)
PHONE..................................517 741-7423
Bill Shoop, *Partner*
Cal Shoop, *Partner*
EMP: 4 EST: 1962
SQ FT: 10,000
SALES (est): **Privately Held**
SIC: 2431 2511 Staircases, stairs & railings; wood household furniture

Six Lakes
Montcalm County

(G-15388)
HIGH GRADE MATERIALS COMPANY
3261 W Fleck Rd (48886-9738)
PHONE..................................989 365-3010
Ben Reynolds, *Manager*
EMP: 9

Snover - Sanilac County (G-15389) — GEOGRAPHIC SECTION

SALES (corp-wide): 17.2MM Privately Held
WEB: www.highgradematerials.com
SIC: 3273 Ready-mixed concrete
PA: High Grade Materials Company
   9266 Snows Lake Rd
   Greenville MI 48838
   616 754-5545

Snover
Sanilac County

(G-15389)
ADVANCED AUTO TRENDS INC
3279 Washington St (48472-9601)
PHONE..................810 672-9203
Ron Wilson, *Plant Mgr*
Shirley Hogan, *Production*
Crystal Rundell, *Purchasing*
Pete Koprowski, *Branch Mgr*
EMP: 30
SALES (corp-wide): 16.7MM Privately Held
WEB: www.advancedautotrends.com
SIC: 3089 Injection molding of plastics
PA: Advanced Auto Trends, Inc.
   2230 Metamora Rd
   Oxford MI 48371
   248 628-6111

(G-15390)
ALBRECHT SAND & GRAVEL CO
3790 W Sanilac Rd (48472-9703)
PHONE..................810 672-9272
Robert G Albrecht, *President*
Karen Downing, *Corp Secy*
EMP: 30 EST: 1954
SQ FT: 1,000
SALES (est): 12.2MM Privately Held
SIC: 1442 Gravel mining

(G-15391)
B&M WELDING INC
2635 Wheeler Rd (48472-9759)
PHONE..................810 837-0742
EMP: 4 EST: 2019
SALES (est): 267.2K Privately Held
SIC: 7692 Welding repair

Sodus
Berrien County

(G-15392)
ANCAST INC
3194 Townline Rd (49126-9715)
PHONE..................269 927-1985
Robert Idzi, *President*
EMP: 27 EST: 1971
SQ FT: 42,000
SALES (est): 2.4MM Privately Held
WEB: www.ancast.com
SIC: 3325 3369 Alloy steel castings, except investment; nonferrous foundries

(G-15393)
CLOSSONS MANUFACTURING LLC
3783 S Pipestone Rd (49126-9712)
PHONE..................269 363-4261
EMP: 5 EST: 2017
SALES (est): 39.6K Privately Held
WEB: www.clossons3dtruckrepair.com
SIC: 3999 Manufacturing industries

(G-15394)
SODUS HARD CHROME INC
3085 Yore Ave (49126-9761)
PHONE..................269 925-2077
Edward Thomas Sosnowski, *President*
Sally Sosnowski, *Vice Pres*
EMP: 15 EST: 1971
SQ FT: 40,800
SALES (est): 620.6K Privately Held
WEB: www.sodushardchromeinc.com
SIC: 7389 3471 Grinding, precision: commercial or industrial; chromium plating of metals or formed products

South Boardman
Kalkaska County

(G-15395)
ADVANCED ENERGY SERVICES LLC
Also Called: Advanced Energy Svc
5894 Puffer Rd Sw (49680-9723)
P.O. Box 5549, Traverse City (49696-5549)
PHONE..................231 369-2602
Gary Provins, *President*
Jeff Welch, *Vice Pres*
Jeffery Welch, *Vice Pres*
Chris Diepenhorst, *CFO*
Randall Parsons,
EMP: 60 EST: 2000
SQ FT: 50,000
SALES (est): 10.3MM Privately Held
WEB: www.aenergy.net
SIC: 1381 Drilling oil & gas wells

South Branch
Ogemaw County

(G-15396)
MATTHEWS MILL INC
6400 E County Line Rd (48761-9637)
P.O. Box 282 (48761-0282)
PHONE..................989 257-3271
George Matthews Sr, *President*
George Matthews Jr, *Vice Pres*
Leroy Matthews, *Vice Pres*
Lisa Matthews, *Admin Sec*
EMP: 10 EST: 1973
SALES (est): 1MM Privately Held
SIC: 2421 2448 Sawmills & planing mills, general; wood pallets & skids

(G-15397)
QUIGLEY LUMBER INC
5874 Heath Rd (48761-9515)
P.O. Box 141 (48761-0141)
PHONE..................989 257-5116
James F Quigley, *President*
EMP: 9 EST: 1955
SQ FT: 2,160
SALES (est): 1.5MM Privately Held
SIC: 2421 2426 Lumber: rough, sawed or planed; hardwood dimension & flooring mills

South Haven
Van Buren County

(G-15398)
AMERICAN TWISTING COMPANY (PA)
Also Called: AM Twist
1675 Stieve Dr (49090-9167)
P.O. Box 391 (49090-0391)
PHONE..................269 637-8581
Thomas F Phelps Sr, *President*
Jeanne Phelps, *Vice Pres*
Thomas E Phelps Jr, *Treasurer*
Mark Rydecki, *Sales Mgr*
Toni Phelps Gohn, *Admin Sec*
▲ EMP: 26 EST: 1955
SQ FT: 104,000
SALES (est): 4.9MM Privately Held
WEB: www.americantwisting.com
SIC: 2298 2621 2396 Twine, cord & cordage; cord, braided; cable, fiber; paper mills; automotive & apparel trimmings

(G-15399)
ANDERSEN BOAT WORKS
815 Wells St (49090-8643)
P.O. Box 856, Saugatuck (49453-0856)
PHONE..................616 836-2502
Dave Andersen, *President*
EMP: 6 EST: 1981
SALES (est): 545.1K Privately Held
WEB: www.askiff.com
SIC: 3732 Boat building & repairing

(G-15400)
AUTUMN DESIGNS LLC
225 Broadway St Ste 11 (49090-2402)
PHONE..................269 455-0490
Julie Roy, *Mng Member*
EMP: 5 EST: 2016
SALES (est): 268.9K Privately Held
WEB: www.autumndesigns.org
SIC: 2434 Wood kitchen cabinets

(G-15401)
B & K MACHINE PRODUCTS INC
100 Aylworth Ave (49090-1637)
P.O. Box 187 (49090-0187)
PHONE..................269 637-3001
Gary Plankenhorn, *President*
Rich Ransom, *Vice Pres*
Paula Plankenhorn, *Treasurer*
EMP: 16 EST: 1951
SALES (est): 1MM Privately Held
WEB: www.bandkmachineproducts.com
SIC: 3599 Machine shop, jobbing & repair

(G-15402)
COASTAL CONCIERGE
1210 Phoenix St Ste 9 (49090-7914)
PHONE..................269 639-1515
Julie Vincent, *Owner*
EMP: 4 EST: 2005
SALES (est): 479K Privately Held
WEB: www.coastalclean.net
SIC: 2842 Cleaning or polishing preparations

(G-15403)
DAWSON MFG CO MORGANFIELD
400 Aylworth Ave (49090-1707)
PHONE..................269 639-4229
Bob Trivedi, *CEO*
▲ EMP: 14 EST: 2013
SALES (est): 178.8K Privately Held
WEB: www.dawsonmfg.com
SIC: 3999 Manufacturing industries

(G-15404)
DO-IT CORPORATION
1201 Blue Star Mem Hwy (49090)
P.O. Box 592 (49090-0592)
PHONE..................269 637-1121
Mark T Mc Clendon, *President*
Aubrey Fairley, *Business Mgr*
Mark Haskin, *Opers Staff*
Jeff Wilson, *Mfg Staff*
Bonnie Lobdell, *Production*
◆ EMP: 65 EST: 1985
SQ FT: 50,000
SALES (est): 16.3MM Privately Held
WEB: www.do-it.com
SIC: 3089 Clothes hangers, plastic

(G-15405)
FOODTOOLS CONSOLIDATED INC
190 Veterans Blvd (49090-8630)
PHONE..................269 637-9969
David Thompson, *Opers Staff*
Rebecca Hillman, *Purchasing*
Todd Schubert, *Regl Sales Mgr*
Neil Johnson, *Sales Staff*
Michael Zhen, *Sales Staff*
EMP: 28
SALES (corp-wide): 11.2MM Privately Held
WEB: www.foodtools.com
SIC: 3556 Slicers, commercial, food
PA: Foodtools Consolidated, Inc.
   315 Laguna St
   Santa Barbara CA 93101
   805 962-8383

(G-15406)
GAC
1301 M 43 (49090-7506)
PHONE..................269 639-3010
Bill Pater, *Owner*
▲ EMP: 9 EST: 2010
SALES (est): 611.4K Privately Held
SIC: 3713 Truck bodies & parts

(G-15407)
GRAND STRATEGY LLC
15038 73rd St (49090-8976)
PHONE..................269 637-8330
Gregory L Fones, *President*
John Jackoboice,
Jeffrey G Muth,
Edward Perdue,
EMP: 4 EST: 2008
SQ FT: 1,500 Privately Held
WEB: www.grandstrategyllc.com
SIC: 2211 Towels, dishcloths & washcloths: cotton

(G-15408)
LITTLE MAN WINERY
7143 107th Ave (49090-9678)
PHONE..................269 637-2229
Ron Edwards, *Principal*
EMP: 6 EST: 2014
SALES (est): 121.9K Privately Held
SIC: 2084 Wines

(G-15409)
LOOPE ENTERPRISES INC
Also Called: South Haven Packaging
73475 8th Ave (49090-9769)
PHONE..................269 639-1567
Brian Loope, *President*
EMP: 7 EST: 2012
SQ FT: 55,000
SALES (est): 250.6K Privately Held
SIC: 2653 Boxes, corrugated: made from purchased materials

(G-15410)
NATIONAL APPLIANCE PARTS CO
Also Called: Napco
900 Indiana Ave (49090)
P.O. Box 474 (49090-0474)
PHONE..................269 639-1469
Sandra Keathley, *Vice Pres*
▲ EMP: 20 EST: 1993
SALES (est): 497.3K Privately Held
SIC: 3567 Heating units & devices, industrial: electric

(G-15411)
PETTER INVESTMENTS INC
Also Called: Riveer Environmental, The
233 Veterans Blvd (49090-8632)
PHONE..................269 637-1997
Mathew Petter, *President*
Doug Petter, *Vice Pres*
Mike Todd, *Purchasing*
Andy Litts, *Engineer*
Jeff Rowan, *Sales Engr*
▲ EMP: 15 EST: 1983
SQ FT: 7,000
SALES (est): 5MM Privately Held
WEB: www.riveer.com
SIC: 3569 3531 5082 Filters; construction machinery; pavers

(G-15412)
SOUTH HAVEN COIL INC (HQ)
05585 Blue Star Mem Hwy (49090-8189)
P.O. Box 2008, Kalamazoo (49003-2008)
PHONE..................269 637-5201
Randall M Webber, *Ch of Bd*
EMP: 30 EST: 1957
SQ FT: 18,000
SALES (est): 22.7MM
SALES (corp-wide): 34MM Privately Held
WEB: www.southhavencoil.com
SIC: 3677 Coil windings, electronic
PA: Humphrey Products Company
   5070 E N Ave
   Kalamazoo MI 49048
   269 381-5500

(G-15413)
SOUTH HAVEN FINISHING INC
1610 Stieve Dr (49090-9167)
PHONE..................269 637-2047
Eric Ellison, *President*
EMP: 21 EST: 1986
SQ FT: 12,000
SALES (est): 616.5K Privately Held
WEB: www.southhavenfinishing.com
SIC: 3471 3398 Finishing, metals or formed products; polishing, metals or formed products; buffing for the trade; cleaning, polishing & finishing; metal heat treating

(G-15414)
SOUTH HAVEN PACKAGING INC
73475 8th Ave (49090-9769)
PHONE..................269 639-1567
Randy Mohler, *President*
EMP: 149 EST: 1994
SQ FT: 31,000

▲ = Import ▼ = Export
◆ = Import/Export

SALES (est): 15.4MM **Privately Held**
WEB: www.southhaven.org
SIC: 2653 Boxes, corrugated: made from purchased materials
PA: Kindlon Enterprises, Inc
2300 Raddant Rd Ste B
Aurora IL 60502

(G-15415)
SOUTH HAVEN TRIBUNE
308 Kalamazoo St (49090-1308)
P.O. Box 128, Saint Joseph (49085-0128)
PHONE..................................269 637-1104
Becky Burkert, *General Mgr*
Jim Pezzuto, *Superintendent*
EMP: 4 **EST:** 1900
SALES (est): 346.6K **Privately Held**
WEB: www.heraldpalladium.com
SIC: 2711 Newspapers: publishing only, not printed on site

(G-15416)
SPENCER MANUFACTURING INC
165 Veterans Dr (49090-8650)
PHONE..................................269 637-9459
Brian Spencer, *President*
Peggy Spencer, *Treasurer*
Garrett Spencer, *Marketing Staff*
Ken Wattrick, *Manager*
Amy Dannenberg, *Technology*
EMP: 15 **EST:** 1984
SQ FT: 26,000
SALES (est): 4.3MM **Privately Held**
WEB: www.spencerfiretrucks.com
SIC: 3711 Fire department vehicles (motor vehicles), assembly of

(G-15417)
SYSTEM COMPONENTS INC
1635 Stieve Dr (49090-9167)
PHONE..................................269 637-2191
Eugen Gawreliuk, *President*
Mary Gawreliuk, *Vice Pres*
Candace Olivier, *Sales Mgr*
▲ **EMP:** 40 **EST:** 1965
SQ FT: 40,000
SALES (est): 5.2MM **Privately Held**
WEB: www.sci-couplings.com
SIC: 3568 Couplings, shaft: rigid, flexible, universal joint, etc.

(G-15418)
TAYLOR CONTROLS INC
10529 Blue Star Mem Hwy (49090-9401)
P.O. Box 362 (49090-0362)
PHONE..................................269 637-8521
Terry L Taylor, *President*
EMP: 14 **EST:** 1981
SQ FT: 5,400
SALES: 691.2K **Privately Held**
SIC: 3297 3822 3823 3443 Cement: high temperature, refractory (nonclay); thermostats & other environmental sensors; industrial instrmnts msrmnt display/control process variable; fabricated plate work (boiler shop)

(G-15419)
TRELLEBORG CORPORATION (HQ)
200 Veterans Blvd Ste 3 (49090-8663)
PHONE..................................269 639-9891
Torgney Astrom, *President*
Ydo Doornbos, *Managing Dir*
Martin Hignett, *Managing Dir*
Ranjan Sen, *Managing Dir*
Richard Hodgson, *Vice Pres*
◆ **EMP:** 1 **EST:** 1988
SALES (est): 1.6B
SALES (corp-wide): 3.8B **Privately Held**
WEB: www.trelleborg.com
SIC: 3341 1021 1044 1031 Secondary precious metals; copper ore mining & preparation; silver ores mining; zinc ores mining; liquid storage; gold ores mining
PA: Trelleborg Ab
Johan Kocksgatan 10
Trelleborg 231 4
410 670-00

(G-15420)
US TARP INC
1425 Kalamazoo St (49090-1945)
P.O. Box 935 (49090-0935)
PHONE..................................269 639-3010
Thomas Bronz, *CEO*
William Peter, *President*
Ashley Hanko, *Sales Staff*
Fred Stark, *Sales Staff*
EMP: 70 **EST:** 2008
SALES (est): 7.9MM **Privately Held**
WEB: www.ustarp.com
SIC: 2394 3537 Tarpaulins, fabric: made from purchased materials; industrial trucks & tractors

(G-15421)
VIBRACOUSTIC NORTH AMERICA LP (HQ)
400 Aylworth Ave (49090-1707)
PHONE..................................269 637-2116
Mehdi Ilkhani, *President*
Jeff Jones, *General Mgr*
Robert G Evans, *General Ptnr*
Ronald S Guest, *General Ptnr*
Leesa Smith, *General Ptnr*
◆ **EMP:** 20 **EST:** 2004
SALES (est): 106.1MM
SALES (corp-wide): 2.4B **Privately Held**
WEB: www.vibracoustic.com
SIC: 2821 3061 3053 3714 Plastics materials & resins; mechanical rubber goods; gaskets, packing & sealing devices; motor vehicle parts & accessories
PA: Vibracoustic Se
Europaplatz 4
Darmstadt HE 64293
615 139-640

(G-15422)
VIBRACOUSTIC USA INC (HQ)
Also Called: Trelleborg Automotive
400 Aylworth Ave (49090-1707)
PHONE..................................269 637-2116
Kelly Reynolds, *President*
Eric Finn, *General Mgr*
Bob Prostko, *Managing Dir*
Casey Caplea, *Vice Pres*
Evelyn Wu, *Purch Mgr*
▲ **EMP:** 165 **EST:** 1955
SQ FT: 60,000
SALES (est): 294.5MM
SALES (corp-wide): 2.4B **Privately Held**
WEB: www.vibracoustic.com
SIC: 3061 3625 Automotive rubber goods (mechanical); noise control equipment
PA: Vibracoustic Se
Europaplatz 4
Darmstadt HE 64293
615 139-640

(G-15423)
VOCHASKA ENGINEERING
66935 County Road 388 (49090-9320)
PHONE..................................269 637-5670
Vern A Vochaska, *Owner*
EMP: 4 **EST:** 1984
SQ FT: 6,656
SALES (est): 365.5K **Privately Held**
SIC: 7539 3441 7692 Machine shop, automotive; fabricated structural metal; welding repair

(G-15424)
W R GRACE & CO-CONN
1421 Kalamazoo St (49090-1945)
PHONE..................................410 531-4000
Hudson La Force, *General Mgr*
Mike Helms, *Safety Mgr*
David Bennett, *Engineer*
Cornell Burton, *Auditor*
Janice Rissley, *Sales Executive*
EMP: 134
SALES (corp-wide): 4.4B **Privately Held**
WEB: www.grace.com
SIC: 2819 Industrial inorganic chemicals
HQ: W. R. Grace & Co.-Conn.
7500 Grace Dr
Columbia MD 21044

(G-15425)
WEST MICHIGAN FABRICATION
860 68th St (49090-9666)
PHONE..................................269 637-2415
EMP: 4 **EST:** 2019
SALES (est): 142.9K **Privately Held**
SIC: 3441 Fabricated structural metal

(G-15426)
WHITE KNIGHT INDUSTRIES
972 68th St (49090-9665)
PHONE..................................269 823-4207
Jessup Joseph, *Owner*
EMP: 6 **EST:** 2012
SALES (est): 99.7K **Privately Held**
WEB: www.awhiteknight.com
SIC: 3999 Manufacturing industries

South Lyon
Oakland County

(G-15427)
BEEBE FUEL SYSTEMS INC
6351 Wilderness Dr (48178-7038)
PHONE..................................248 437-3322
Dale Belsley, *Principal*
EMP: 4 **EST:** 2010
SALES (est): 94.4K **Privately Held**
SIC: 2869 Fuels

(G-15428)
BROWNIE SIGNS LLC
8791 Earhart Rd (48178-7015)
PHONE..................................248 437-0800
Brad Braun,
EMP: 4 **EST:** 1954
SALES (est): 274.9K **Privately Held**
WEB: www.browniesigns.net
SIC: 3993 Neon signs

(G-15429)
CAMBRIDGE SHARPE INC
8325 N Rushton Rd (48178-9119)
PHONE..................................248 613-5562
Richard E Sharpe, *President*
EMP: 11 **EST:** 2006
SQ FT: 100,000
SALES (est): 247.4K **Privately Held**
SIC: 2096 3714 Potato chips & similar snacks; motor vehicle parts & accessories

(G-15430)
CHANGSTAR INDUSTRIES LLC
12364 Nantucket Dr (48178-8517)
PHONE..................................248 446-1811
Barbara Changas, *Principal*
EMP: 4 **EST:** 2004
SALES (est): 6.8K **Privately Held**
SIC: 3999 Manufacturing industries

(G-15431)
CLIPS COUPONS OF ANN ARBO
9477 Silverside (48178-8809)
PHONE..................................248 437-9294
William Bunn, *Owner*
EMP: 4 **EST:** 1996
SALES (est): 215.9K **Privately Held**
WEB: www.clipscouponsusa.com
SIC: 3993 Signs & advertising specialties

(G-15432)
CYTK CORP
111 S Lafayette St # 880 (48178-9924)
P.O. Box 683, San Anselmo CA (94979-0683)
PHONE..................................313 288-9360
Bryan Levenson, *CEO*
Kate Schneider, *CTO*
EMP: 12 **EST:** 2018
SALES (est): 764.1K **Privately Held**
WEB: www.cytk.io
SIC: 7372 Application computer software

(G-15433)
DOT BRIDGE INC
25905 Cobblers Ln (48178-1573)
PHONE..................................248 921-7363
Jeff Allain, *Vice Pres*
EMP: 4 **EST:** 2019
SALES (est): 62.4K **Privately Held**
WEB: www.dotbridge.com
SIC: 3861 Photographic equipment & supplies

(G-15434)
EMERY DESIGN & WOODWORK LLC
8277 Tower Rd (48178-9683)
PHONE..................................734 709-1687
Jacquelyn Emery, *Principal*
EMP: 7 **EST:** 2010
SALES (est): 227.7K **Privately Held**
WEB: www.emerywoodwork.com
SIC: 2431 Millwork

(G-15435)
EXACT FABRICATION
8990 Pontiac Trl (48178-9601)
PHONE..................................248 240-4506
Christopher James Olson, *Administration*
EMP: 5 **EST:** 2015
SALES (est): 112.9K **Privately Held**
WEB: www.exactfabrication.com
SIC: 7692 Welding repair

(G-15436)
EXPRESS CARE OF SOUTH LYON
501 S Lafayette St (48178-1490)
PHONE..................................248 437-6919
Travis Curry, *Owner*
EMP: 4 **EST:** 2004
SALES (est): 227.8K **Privately Held**
SIC: 1382 Oil & gas exploration services

(G-15437)
HARRY & ASSOC LLC
Also Called: Market Place Pet Supplies
11432 Hammerstone Dr (48178-8535)
PHONE..................................248 446-8820
David Pasek, *Principal*
EMP: 4 **EST:** 2011
SALES (est): 198.3K **Privately Held**
SIC: 3999 Pet supplies

(G-15438)
INDUSTRIES INDY BEAR
883 Hidden Creek Dr (48178-2526)
PHONE..................................248 446-1435
Carrie Jones, *Principal*
EMP: 10 **EST:** 2015
SALES (est): 61K **Privately Held**
SIC: 3999 Manufacturing industries

(G-15439)
INTEGRATED PRACTICE SERVICE
111 S Lafayette St # 609 (48178-9924)
PHONE..................................248 646-7009
Jeff Burton, *Principal*
EMP: 5 **EST:** 2017
SALES (est): 232.3K **Privately Held**
SIC: 7372 Prepackaged software

(G-15440)
INTERNATIONAL MACHINING SVC
Also Called: Imservice
12622 10 Mile Rd (48178-9141)
P.O. Box 142 (48178-0142)
PHONE..................................248 486-3600
Fred Smith, *President*
EMP: 4 **EST:** 2000
SALES (est): 320K **Privately Held**
SIC: 3599 7371 Machine shop, jobbing & repair; custom computer programming services

(G-15441)
KILLER PAINT BALL
509 S Lafayette St (48178-1490)
PHONE..................................248 491-0088
EMP: 7 **EST:** 2000
SALES (est): 416.3K **Privately Held**
SIC: 3949 Mfg Sporting/Athletic Goods

(G-15442)
KOLCO INDUSTRIES INC
10078 Colonial Indus Dr (48178-9154)
PHONE..................................248 486-1690
Chris Koltz, *President*
EMP: 6 **EST:** 1993
SALES (est): 564.3K **Privately Held**
SIC: 3559 Automotive related machinery

(G-15443)
LGA RETAIL INC
22770 Spy Glass Hill Dr (48178-9433)
PHONE..................................248 910-1918
EMP: 5
SALES (corp-wide): 1.1MM **Privately Held**
SIC: 3571 Personal computers (microcomputers)

South Lyon - Oakland County (G-15444) — GEOGRAPHIC SECTION

PA: Lga Retail, Inc.
37560 Enterprise Ct
Farmington Hills MI 48331
248 760-1312

(G-15444)
M K EATON SERVICES LLC
11036 Woodland Ridge Ct (48178-6606)
PHONE..................608 852-3118
Michael Eaton, *Principal*
EMP: 5 EST: 2013
SALES (est): 103.9K Privately Held
SIC: 3625 Relays & industrial controls

(G-15445)
MACS MARINA MOTORSPORTS
546 Mcmunn St (48178-1331)
PHONE..................248 486-8300
Sam Iaquinto, *President*
EMP: 11 EST: 2016
SALES (est): 104.6K Privately Held
WEB: www.macsmarina.com
SIC: 4493 3732 Marinas; non-motorized boat, building & repairing

(G-15446)
MASK MAKERS LLC
23769 Point O Woods Ct (48178-9069)
PHONE..................313 790-1784
Ryan Gusick,
EMP: 7 EST: 2020
SALES (est): 500K Privately Held
SIC: 3842 Personal safety equipment

(G-15447)
MULTIFORM STUDIOS LLC
12012 Doane Rd (48178-8801)
PHONE..................248 437-5964
James Leacock, *Principal*
EMP: 5 EST: 1982
SQ FT: 4,000
SALES (est): 338.9K Privately Held
WEB: www.multiformstudios.com
SIC: 2531 Public building & related furniture

(G-15448)
MYKIN INC
Also Called: Midnight Scoop
10056 Colonial Indus Dr (48178-9154)
PHONE..................248 667-8030
Michael Chou, *President*
Jennifer Recchione, *Accounts Mgr*
◆ EMP: 12 EST: 2005
SALES (est): 1.1MM Privately Held
WEB: www.mykin.com
SIC: 3069 2822 5122 Custom compounding of rubber materials; rubber automotive products; synthetic rubber; butadiene-acrylonitrile, nitrile rubbers, NBR; medical rubber goods

(G-15449)
NIMS PRECISION MACHINING INC
9493 Pontiac Trl (48178-7020)
PHONE..................248 446-1053
Joann Nims, *President*
Myrom Nims, *Vice Pres*
EMP: 4 EST: 1984 Privately Held
WEB: www.nims-precision.com
SIC: 3599 Machine shop, jobbing & repair

(G-15450)
NOIR MEDICAL TECHNOLOGIES LLC
Also Called: Noir Manufacturing
10125 Colonial Indus Dr (48178-9151)
PHONE..................248 486-3760
A Brooks Gleichert, *Partner*
Michael Smiglewski, *Mfg Staff*
Marc Gleichert, *Purch Dir*
EMP: 16 Privately Held
WEB: www.noirlaser.com
SIC: 3851 3842 Glasses, sun or glare; surgical appliances & supplies
PA: Noir Medical Technologies Llc
4975 Technical Dr
Milford MI 48381
734 769-5565

(G-15451)
NOPRAS TECHNOLOGIES INC
13513 Windmoor Dr (48178-8145)
PHONE..................248 486-6684
EMP: 6 EST: 2017
SALES (est): 84.6K Privately Held
WEB: www.nopras-tech.com
SIC: 5912 5122 2834 Drug stores & proprietary stores; toothbrushes, except electric; pharmaceutical preparations

(G-15452)
PERRAS HOLSTER SALES LLC
57680 Deere Ct (48178-8616)
PHONE..................248 467-4254
Jason Perras, *Principal*
EMP: 5 EST: 2016
SALES (est): 109.5K Privately Held
SIC: 3199 Holsters, leather

(G-15453)
PHOENIX INDUCTION CORPORATION
10132 Colonial Indus Dr (48178-9150)
PHONE..................248 486-7377
Marc Senters, *President*
Robert Van Aken, *Vice Pres*
Robert Vanaken, *Vice Pres*
EMP: 10 EST: 2000
SQ FT: 6,000
SALES (est): 1.9MM Privately Held
WEB: www.phoenixinduction.com
SIC: 3567 5075 Induction heating equipment; furnaces, heating: electric; fans, heating & ventilation equipment

(G-15454)
PITNEY BOWES INC
23594 Prescott Ln W (48178-8240)
PHONE..................203 356-5000
David Appicelli, *Principal*
EMP: 5
SALES (corp-wide): 3.5B Publicly Held
WEB: www.pitneybowes.com
SIC: 3579 Postage meters
PA: Pitney Bowes Inc.
3001 Summer St
Stamford CT 06905
203 356-5000

(G-15455)
PIXEL RUSH PRINTING
264 Gibson St (48178-1105)
PHONE..................248 231-4642
Scott Wightman, *Principal*
EMP: 5 EST: 2015
SALES (est): 81.9K Privately Held
SIC: 2752 Commercial printing, lithographic

(G-15456)
SERENITY WOODWORKING LLC
61155 Serene Ct (48178-9227)
PHONE..................734 812-5429
Christina Cooper, *Principal*
EMP: 5 EST: 2016
SALES (est): 65.4K Privately Held
SIC: 2431 Millwork

(G-15457)
SERVICE IRON WORKS INC
245 S Mill St (48178-1813)
PHONE..................248 446-9750
Kerry Holmes, *President*
Cindee Ahn, *Principal*
Bob Harteg, *Principal*
Claudia Needham, *Principal*
Stan Zasuwa, *Principal*
EMP: 25 EST: 1930
SQ FT: 60,000
SALES (est): 4.7MM Privately Held
WEB: www.serviceiron.com
SIC: 3441 3312 Fabricated structural metal; blast furnaces & steel mills

(G-15458)
SOUTH LYON BB INC
21775 Pontiac Trl (48178-9408)
PHONE..................248 437-8000
Sam Saleh, *Owner*
EMP: 9 EST: 2010
SALES (est): 675.7K Privately Held
WEB: www.southlyonmi.org
SIC: 3663 Receivers, radio communications

(G-15459)
SUN STEEL TREATING INC
550 N Mill St (48178-1263)
P.O. Box 759 (48178-0759)
PHONE..................877 471-0844
William Niedzwiecki, *Principal*
Chris Baer, *Buyer*
EMP: 67 EST: 1958
SQ FT: 40,000
SALES (est): 10MM Privately Held
WEB: www.sunsteeltreating.com
SIC: 3398 Annealing of metal

(G-15460)
TRIUNFAR INDUSTRIES INC
10813 Bouldercrest Dr (48178-8200)
PHONE..................313 790-5592
Anthony Morales II, *CEO*
EMP: 4 EST: 2017
SALES (est): 170.4K Privately Held
SIC: 3999 Manufacturing industries

South Range
Houghton County

(G-15461)
NORTHERN HARDWOODS OPER CO LLC
45807 Hwy M 26 (49963)
PHONE..................860 632-3505
Theodore P Rossi, *Mng Member*
Andrew E Becker,
EMP: 70 EST: 2010
SQ FT: 4,500
SALES (est): 7.1MM Privately Held
WEB: www.northernhdwds.com
SIC: 2421 5031 Sawmills & planing mills, general; lumber, plywood & millwork

(G-15462)
SOUTH RANGE BOTTLING WORKS INC
23 Champion St (49963-5108)
P.O. Box 9 (49963-0009)
PHONE..................906 370-2295
Margaret Hayrynen, *President*
Scott Hayrynen, *Trustee*
Randall Hayrynen, *Vice Pres*
EMP: 3 EST: 1963
SQ FT: 5,000
SALES (est): 1.9MM Privately Held
WEB: www.southrange.com
SIC: 5149 2086 Soft drinks; bottled & canned soft drinks

South Rockwood
Monroe County

(G-15463)
BRADYS FENCE COMPANY INC
11093 Armstrong Rd (48179-9762)
PHONE..................313 492-8804
Mark Brady, *President*
EMP: 4 EST: 2005
SALES (est): 959.3K Privately Held
WEB: www.bradysfence.com
SIC: 1799 3089 3446 5039 Fence construction; fences, gates & accessories: plastic; fences or posts, ornamental iron or steel; wire fence, gates & accessories

(G-15464)
GREAT LAKES AGGREGATES LLC (PA)
Also Called: Sylvania Minerals
5699 Ready Rd (48179-9592)
PHONE..................734 379-0311
Chris Kinney, *President*
Mike Parsons, *Sales Mgr*
Tom Downs, *Manager*
Daniel Clark,
James M Friel,
EMP: 107 EST: 2003
SALES (est): 23.9MM Privately Held
WEB: www.greatlakesagg.net
SIC: 3273 Ready-mixed concrete

(G-15465)
ROCKWOOD QUARRY LLC (PA)
5699 Ready Rd (48179-9592)
P.O. Box 406 (48179-0406)
PHONE..................734 783-7415
Jim Friel, *Mng Member*
Jamie Jacobs,
Chris Peyerk,
EMP: 121 EST: 2003
SALES (est): 10MM Privately Held
WEB: www.greatlakesagg.com
SIC: 3281 Stone, quarrying & processing of own stone products

(G-15466)
WAYNES PORTABLE WELDING SVC
5751 Labo Rd (48179-9773)
PHONE..................734 777-9888
Wayne M Reaume, *Owner*
EMP: 7 EST: 1996
SALES (est): 212.8K Privately Held
SIC: 7692 Welding repair

Southfield
Oakland County

(G-15467)
313 INDUSTRIES
21686 Berg Rd (48033-6620)
PHONE..................313 969-8570
Dan Kendall, *Principal*
EMP: 7 EST: 2017
SALES (est): 192.4K Privately Held
WEB: www.313industriesinc.com
SIC: 3999 Manufacturing industries

(G-15468)
AAK FABRICATION & PLASTICS INC
26140 W 9 Mile Rd (48033-6509)
PHONE..................734 525-1391
Andre Knight, *President*
EMP: 4 EST: 1996
SALES (est): 455.8K Privately Held
WEB: www.aakfabrplastics.com
SIC: 3089 Injection molding of plastics

(G-15469)
AAM CASTING
26533 Evergreen Rd Ste 13 (48076-4234)
PHONE..................313 758-5968
EMP: 5 EST: 2019
SALES (est): 97.8K Privately Held
WEB: www.aam.com
SIC: 3714 Motor vehicle parts & accessories

(G-15470)
ABC GROUP HOLDINGS INC (DH)
Also Called: ABC Group Sale & Marketing
24133 Northwestern Hwy (48075-2568)
PHONE..................248 352-3706
Mike Schmidt, *President*
James Augustine, *Treasurer*
Keith Bourasaw, *Manager*
◆ EMP: 1 EST: 2001
SALES (est): 312.7MM Publicly Held
WEB: www.abctechnologies.com
SIC: 3089 Blow molded finished plastic products; injection molded finished plastic products
HQ: Abc Group Limited
2 Norelco Dr
North York ON M9L 2
416 246-1782

(G-15471)
AFTON CHEMICAL CORPORATION
Also Called: Ethyl
2000 Town Ctr Ste 1160 (48075-1259)
PHONE..................248 350-0640
Tom Mc Donnell, *Director*
EMP: 4
SALES (corp-wide): 2B Publicly Held
WEB: www.aftonchemical.com
SIC: 2899 Chemical preparations

HQ: Afton Chemical Corporation
500 Spring St
Richmond VA 23219
804 788-5800

(G-15472)
AIN PLASTICS
23235 Telegraph Rd (48033-4127)
P.O. Box 5116 (48086-5116)
PHONE.....................................248 356-4000
Michael Dantonio, *President*
Kathy Baxter, *Purch Agent*
EMP: 13 **EST:** 2010
SALES (est): 1.7MM **Privately Held**
SIC: 3089 Injection molding of plastics

(G-15473)
AIR-MATIC PRODUCTS COMPANY INC (PA)
22218 Telegraph Rd (48033-4263)
PHONE.....................................248 356-4200
Jeffrey W Smolek, *President*
EMP: 25 **EST:** 1950
SQ FT: 44,000
SALES (est): 3.6MM **Privately Held**
WEB: www.air-matic.com
SIC: 3451 Screw machine products

(G-15474)
AKTIS ENGRG SOLUTIONS INC
17340 W 12 Mile Rd Ste 20 (48076-2122)
PHONE.....................................313 450-2420
Sandeep Nair, *President*
Shuvendu Mishra, *Manager*
EMP: 2 **EST:** 2011
SQ FT: 350
SALES (est): 2MM **Privately Held**
WEB: www.aktisengineering.com
SIC: 3089 8711 Automotive parts, plastic; designing; ship, boat, machine & product
PA: Aktis Engineering Solutions Private Limited
I Floor Jnr Plaza
Bengaluru KA 56006

(G-15475)
ALLEGRA PRINT & IMAGING
28810 Northwestern Hwy (48034-1831)
PHONE.....................................248 354-1313
Gerald Christensen, *Principal*
EMP: 8 **EST:** 2011
SALES (est): 959.4K **Privately Held**
WEB: www.allegramarketingprint.com
SIC: 2752 Commercial printing, offset

(G-15476)
ALPHA 21 LLC
22400 Telegraph Rd Ste A (48033-6800)
PHONE.....................................248 352-7330
Walter Hutchinson, *Mng Member*
Arnold Weingart,
EMP: 4 **EST:** 1975
SQ FT: 2,700
SALES (est): 318.8K **Privately Held**
WEB: www.alpha21.com
SIC: 2796 7336 Color separations for printing; art design services

(G-15477)
ALTA DISTRIBUTION LLC
21650 W 11 Mile Rd (48076-3715)
PHONE.....................................313 363-1682
Kenneth Allen,
EMP: 10 **EST:** 2017
SALES (est): 994.1K **Privately Held**
WEB: www.altadistribution.com
SIC: 3999 5047 Manufacturing industries; medical & hospital equipment

(G-15478)
ALUDYNE INC (HQ)
300 Galleria Ofcntr # 501 (48034-8460)
PHONE.....................................248 728-8700
Andreas Weller, *President*
Julie Samson, *President*
Jenifer Zbiegien, *Vice Pres*
Bob Cook, *Plant Mgr*
Steve McKenzie, *Opers Staff*
EMP: 200 **EST:** 2012
SQ FT: 28,000
SALES (est): 1.5B **Privately Held**
WEB: www.aludyne.com
SIC: 3714 Motor vehicle parts & accessories
PA: Uc Holdings, Inc.
300 Galleria Officentre
Southfield MI 48034
248 728-8642

(G-15479)
ALUDYNE INTERNATIONAL INC (DH)
300 Galleria Ofcntr Ste 5 (48034-4700)
PHONE.....................................248 728-8642
Andreas Weller, *CEO*
Pierre L Dubeauclard, *Vice Pres*
Julie Samson, *Vice Pres*
Mitzy Gordon, *Human Res Mgr*
EMP: 1 **EST:** 1987
SQ FT: 28,000
SALES (est): 125.2MM
SALES (corp-wide): 1.5B **Privately Held**
WEB: www.aludyne.com
SIC: 3714 Motor vehicle parts & accessories
HQ: Aludyne, Inc.
300 Galleria Ofcntr # 501
Southfield MI 48034
248 728-8700

(G-15480)
ALUDYNE MEXICO LLC (DH)
Also Called: Dmi Edon, LLC
300 Gllria Ofc Ctr Ste 50 (48034)
PHONE.....................................248 728-8642
Stephen M Bay, *COO*
Shankar Kiru, *CFO*
Chris Connely,
▲ **EMP:** 106 **EST:** 2009
SALES (est): 2.3BB
SALES (corp-wide): 1.5B **Privately Held**
WEB: www.aludyne.com
SIC: 3714 Motor vehicle parts & accessories

(G-15481)
ALUDYNE NORTH AMERICA INC (DH)
300 Galleria Ofcntr Ste 5 (48034-4700)
PHONE.....................................248 728-8642
Andreas Weller, *CEO*
Eric Rouchy, *Vice Pres*
Julie Samson, *Vice Pres*
Brent Campbell, *Plant Mgr*
Joseph Headley, *Maint Spvr*
▲ **EMP:** 5 **EST:** 1988
SQ FT: 28,000
SALES (est): 280.2MM
SALES (corp-wide): 1.5B **Privately Held**
WEB: www.aludyne.com
SIC: 3714 Motor vehicle parts & accessories
HQ: Aludyne, Inc.
300 Galleria Ofcntr # 501
Southfield MI 48034
248 728-8700

(G-15482)
ALUDYNE NORTH AMERICA LLC (DH)
300 Galleria Ofcntr Ste 5 (48034-4700)
PHONE.....................................248 728-8700
Andreas Weller, *Mng Member*
EMP: 100 **EST:** 2020
SALES (est): 221.2MM
SALES (corp-wide): 1.5B **Privately Held**
WEB: www.aludyne.com
SIC: 3714 Motor vehicle parts & accessories
HQ: Aludyne, Inc.
300 Galleria Ofcntr # 501
Southfield MI 48034
248 728-8700

(G-15483)
ALUDYNE US LLC (DH)
300 Galleria Ofcntr Ste 5 (48034-4700)
PHONE.....................................248 728-8700
Andreas Weller, *President*
Michael Dorah, *Vice Pres*
Eric Rouchy, *Vice Pres*
Vicki Mitchell, *Purch Agent*
Guillaume Ruelle, *Engineer*
▲ **EMP:** 100 **EST:** 1996
SQ FT: 85,000
SALES (est): 55.8MM
SALES (corp-wide): 1.5B **Privately Held**
WEB: www.aludyne.com
SIC: 3714 Motor vehicle parts & accessories

(G-15484)
AMBERS ESSENTIALS
25504 Shiawassee Rd # 45 (48033-3721)
PHONE.....................................313 282-4615
Amber Barnette, *CEO*
EMP: 4
SALES (est): 156.7K **Privately Held**
SIC: 2899 Essential oils

(G-15485)
AMERICAN AXLE & MFG INC
20750 Civic Center Dr (48076-4152)
PHONE.....................................248 353-2155
Allen Beasley, *Manager*
Jason Fenech, *Manager*
Zeena Shina, *Analyst*
Jeff Dean, *Associate*
EMP: 9
SALES (corp-wide): 4.7B **Publicly Held**
WEB: www.aam.com
SIC: 3714 Motor vehicle parts & accessories
HQ: American Axle & Manufacturing, Inc.
1 Dauch Dr
Detroit MI 48211

(G-15486)
AMERICAN WLDG & PRESS REPR INC
26500 W 8 Mile Rd (48033-5924)
PHONE.....................................248 358-2050
William A Sheffer, *President*
EMP: 10 **EST:** 1960
SQ FT: 18,000
SALES (est): 1.9MM **Privately Held**
WEB: www.americanpressrepair.com
SIC: 7699 7692 7629 3542 Industrial machinery & equipment repair; welding repair; electrical repair shops; machine tools, metal forming type

(G-15487)
ANGSTROM AUTOMOTIVE GROUP LLC (PA)
2000 Town Ctr Ste 100 (48075-1303)
PHONE.....................................734 756-1164
Nagesh Palakurthi, *CEO*
Raj Banga, *Vice Pres*
EMP: 20 **EST:** 2010
SALES (est): 85.5MM **Privately Held**
WEB: www.angstrom-usa.com
SIC: 3714 7389 7692 Axle housings & shafts, motor vehicle; ball joints, motor vehicle; drive shafts, motor vehicle; cloth cutting, bolting or winding; automotive welding

(G-15488)
ANGSTROM USA LLC (HQ)
2000 Town Ctr Ste 1100 (48075-1251)
PHONE.....................................313 295-0100
Nagesh Palakurthi, *CEO*
Rajenesh Banga, *Vice Pres*
Jayanth Karnam, *Plant Mgr*
Lalitha Dadiraju, *Controller*
Sandra Bradford, *Ch Credit Ofcr*
◆ **EMP:** 25 **EST:** 2003
SALES (est): 59MM **Privately Held**
WEB: www.angstrom-usa.com
SIC: 5531 3317 Automotive parts; tubes, seamless steel

(G-15489)
ANSO PRODUCTS
21380 Telegraph Rd (48033-4217)
PHONE.....................................248 357-2300
Tom Timmins, *President*
EMP: 5 **EST:** 2005
SALES (est): 358.9K **Privately Held**
WEB: www.ansoofficefurniture.com
SIC: 2522 5021 5932 Office furniture, except wood; office & public building furniture; office furniture & store fixtures, secondhand

(G-15490)
ARETE INDUSTRIES INC
24001 Southfield Rd (48075-2816)
PHONE.....................................248 352-7205
Jerry Bazinski, *Principal*
EMP: 6 **EST:** 2016
SALES (est): 39.6K **Privately Held**
WEB: www.areteindustries.us
SIC: 3999 Manufacturing industries

(G-15491)
ARTISTIC PRINTING INC
26040 W 12 Mile Rd (48034-1783)
PHONE.....................................248 356-1004
Roy Swinea Jr, *President*
EMP: 4 **EST:** 1985
SQ FT: 1,500
SALES (est): 450K **Privately Held**
SIC: 2752 2759 Commercial printing, offset; laser printing

(G-15492)
ASIMCO INTERNATIONAL INC (DH)
1000 Town Ctr Ste 1050 (48075-1261)
PHONE.....................................248 213-5200
Gary W Riley, *President*
▲ **EMP:** 8 **EST:** 1997
SQ FT: 7,000
SALES (est): 2.8MM **Privately Held**
WEB: www.asimco.com
SIC: 5013 3679 Automotive supplies & parts; recording & playback apparatus, including phonograph
HQ: Asimco Technologies, Inc.
1000 Town Ctr Ste 1050
Southfield MI 48075
248 213-5200

(G-15493)
ASP GREDE ACQUISITIONCO LLC (PA)
20750 Civic Center Dr # 100 (48076-4152)
PHONE.....................................248 440-9515
Cary Wood, *CEO*
Paul Suber, *COO*
Mike Lobbia, *CFO*
EMP: 41 **EST:** 2014
SQ FT: 13,312
SALES (est): 686.1MM **Privately Held**
SIC: 3714 3711 Motor vehicle parts & accessories; motor vehicles & car bodies

(G-15494)
ATLAS INDUSTRIES
26100 American Dr Ste 600 (48034-6185)
PHONE.....................................310 694-7457
EMP: 6 **EST:** 2016
SALES (est): 161.6K **Privately Held**
WEB: www.atlasindustries.tv
SIC: 3999 Manufacturing industries

(G-15495)
AURIA ALBEMARLE LLC (DH)
26999 Centrl Pk Blvd # 30 (48076-4174)
PHONE.....................................248 728-8000
Brian Pour, *President*
Richard Zeff, *Vice Pres*
Wade Garrett, *Production*
Cindy Freeman, *Finance*
Chris Harwood, *Technology*
EMP: 100 **EST:** 2014
SALES (est): 58.8MM
SALES (corp-wide): 17.3MM **Privately Held**
WEB: www.auriasolutions.com
SIC: 3714 Motor vehicle parts & accessories
HQ: Auria Solutions Usa Inc.
26999 Centrl Pk Blvd # 300
Southfield MI 48076
248 728-8000

(G-15496)
AURIA SOLUTIONS INTL INC
26999 Centrl Pk Blvd # 30 (48076-4174)
PHONE.....................................734 456-2800
Brian Pour, *President*
EMP: 1 **EST:** 2017
SALES (est): 2.8MM
SALES (corp-wide): 17.3MM **Privately Held**
WEB: www.auriasolutions.com
SIC: 3714 Motor vehicle parts & accessories
HQ: Auria Solutions Usa Inc.
26999 Centrl Pk Blvd # 300
Southfield MI 48076
248 728-8000

(G-15497)
AURIA SOLUTIONS USA INC (DH)
26999 Centrl Pk Blvd # 300 (48076-4178)
PHONE.....................................248 728-8000

Southfield - Oakland County (G-15498)

GEOGRAPHIC SECTION

Brian Pour, *President*
Maurice Sessel, *COO*
Tom Allard, *Vice Pres*
Marcos Tonndorf, *Vice Pres*
Michael Bowman, *Plant Supt*
EMP: 1085 **EST:** 2017
SALES (est): 475.7MM
SALES (corp-wide): 17.3MM Privately Held
WEB: www.auriasolutions.com
SIC: 3714 Motor vehicle parts & accessories
HQ: Auria Solutions Uk I Ltd.
 C/O Iac Group
 Birmingham W MIDLANDS
 167 546-4999

(G-15498)
AUTO ELECTRIC INTERNATIONAL
22211 Telegraph Rd (48033-4221)
PHONE.................................248 354-2082
Eugene Neugebohr, *President*
Regina Neugebohr, *Treasurer*
▲ **EMP:** 26 **EST:** 1981
SQ FT: 5,000
SALES (est): 4.5MM Privately Held
WEB: www.aeimich.com
SIC: 3694 Motors, starting: automotive & aircraft; alternators, automotive; generators, automotive & aircraft

(G-15499)
AUTOMOTIVE LLC
300 Galleria Office Ctr (48034)
PHONE.................................248 712-1175
Pierre Dubeauclard, *President*
Alberto Rosales, *Project Mgr*
Steven Witcher, *Finance*
Pam Williams, *Sales Staff*
SRI Boyina, *Manager*
◆ **EMP:** 140 **EST:** 1999
SQ FT: 147,000
SALES (est): 55.8MM
SALES (corp-wide): 1.5B Privately Held
WEB: www.aludyne.com
SIC: 3714 Motor vehicle parts & accessories
HQ: Aludyne Us Llc
 300 Galleria Ofcntr Ste 5
 Southfield MI 48034

(G-15500)
B & B PRETZELS INC (PA)
Also Called: Auntie Anne's
19155 Addison Dr (48075-2404)
PHONE.................................248 358-1655
Ernest Boyce, *President*
Carol Ann Boyce, *Vice Pres*
EMP: 12 **EST:** 1998
SQ FT: 1,040
SALES (est): 1.1MM Privately Held
WEB: www.auntieannes.com
SIC: 5461 2099 Pretzels; food preparations

(G-15501)
BAKE STATION BAKERIES MICH INC
26000 W 8 Mile Rd (48033-5916)
PHONE.................................248 352-9000
Steven Katz, *CEO*
EMP: 18 **EST:** 2007
SALES (est): 1.2MM Privately Held
WEB: www.bakestation.com
SIC: 5461 2051 Bakeries; bakery: wholesale or wholesale/retail combined

(G-15502)
BARCROFT TECHNOLOGY LLC
29193 Nw Hwy St 715 (48034)
PHONE.................................313 378-0133
Christopher Conroy, *President*
Jon Conroy, *President*
EMP: 4 **EST:** 2006
SALES (est): 129.2K Privately Held
WEB: www.barcrofttech.com
SIC: 7371 2678 Computer software systems analysis & design, custom; stationery products

(G-15503)
BASF CORPORATION
Coatings & Refinish Division
26701 Telegraph Rd (48033-2442)
PHONE.................................248 827-4670

Mike Imwalle, *Project Mgr*
Thomas M Lynch, *Opers Mgr*
Bill Dolan, *Research*
Roddie L Metz, *Engineer*
Tom Morrison, *Engineer*
EMP: 101
SALES (corp-wide): 69.9B Privately Held
WEB: www.basf.com
SIC: 2869 Industrial organic chemicals
HQ: Basf Corporation
 100 Park Ave
 Florham Park NJ 07932
 859 577-5797

(G-15504)
BBJ GRAPHICS INC
Also Called: Southfield Signs & Lighting
18940 W 8 Mile Rd (48075-5701)
PHONE.................................248 450-3149
Muhannad Zaitouna, *President*
EMP: 6 **EST:** 2017
SALES (est): 249.2K Privately Held
SIC: 3993 7389 Signs & advertising specialties; interior design services; sign painting & lettering shop

(G-15505)
BEHRMANN PRINTING COMPANY INC
21063 Bridge St (48033-4088)
PHONE.................................248 799-7771
Ivan Behrmann, *President*
Steve Behrmann, *Corp Secy*
Scott Behrmann, *Vice Pres*
Jim Behrman, *Sales Staff*
EMP: 15 **EST:** 1968
SQ FT: 20,000
SALES (est): 1.7MM Privately Held
WEB: www.behrmannprinting.com
SIC: 2752 2759 2796 Commercial printing, offset; commercial printing; embossing on paper; platemaking services

(G-15506)
BERCI PRINTING SERVICES INC
22400 Telegraph Rd Ste B (48033-6800)
PHONE.................................248 350-0206
John Berci, *President*
EMP: 4 **EST:** 1981
SQ FT: 6,300
SALES (est): 336.9K Privately Held
SIC: 2752 2759 Commercial printing, offset; letterpress printing

(G-15507)
BIG BOY RESTAURANTS INTL LLC (PA)
Also Called: Big Boy Restaurant Management
26300 Telg Rd Ste 101 (48033)
PHONE.................................586 759-6000
Keith E Sirois, *CEO*
Kelly Murphy, *Opers Staff*
Jennifer Nicosia, *Opers Staff*
Linda Grady, *Bookkeeper*
Kelly Osegueda, *Marketing Staff*
EMP: 200 **EST:** 2001
SALES (est): 49.4MM Privately Held
WEB: www.bigboy.com
SIC: 5812 2099 Restaurant, family: chain; food preparations

(G-15508)
BIO-VAC INC
21316 Bridge St (48033-4900)
PHONE.................................248 350-2150
Lee Allen Stouse, *President*
Anthony Crivella, *Vice Pres*
Winchester Rice, *Supervisor*
Charles Crivella, *Admin Sec*
EMP: 33 **EST:** 1984
SQ FT: 16,000
SALES (est): 560.9K Privately Held
WEB: www.orchid-ortho.com
SIC: 3479 3841 Coating of metals & formed products; surgical instruments & apparatus

(G-15509)
BLAACK&CO LLC
Also Called: Blaaco
17312 Alta Vista Dr (48075-1987)
PHONE.................................313 971-1857
Semaj Williams, *CEO*
EMP: 20 **EST:** 2020

SALES (est): 773.2K Privately Held
SIC: 2211 Apparel & outerwear fabrics, cotton

(G-15510)
BRADLEY-THOMPSON TOOL COMPANY
Also Called: BT Aerospace
22108 W 8 Mile Rd (48033-4494)
PHONE.................................248 352-1466
Jeff Sutter, *President*
Michael D Huard, *President*
Arthur Watson III, *President*
Sherry Hamilton, *Purch Agent*
Brent Ottenbacher, *Purchasing*
EMP: 25 **EST:** 1952
SQ FT: 19,000
SALES (est): 5.4MM Privately Held
WEB: www.bradleythompsontool.com
SIC: 3544 3728 Special dies & tools; jigs & fixtures; aircraft assemblies, subassemblies & parts

(G-15511)
BRIANS FOODS LLC
21444 Bridge St (48033-4031)
PHONE.................................248 739-5280
Steve Katz, *Mng Member*
Brian Jacobs, *Mng Member*
EMP: 8 **EST:** 2013
SALES (est): 418.7K Privately Held
WEB: www.briansfoods.com
SIC: 2099 Food preparations

(G-15512)
BUDD MAGNETIC PRODUCTS INC
22525 Telegraph Rd (48033-4106)
PHONE.................................248 353-2533
Robert W Budd, *President*
Gladys Budd, *Corp Secy*
Vincent Gilles, *Vice Pres*
EMP: 6
SQ FT: 6,000
SALES (est): 654.7K Privately Held
SIC: 3537 Trucks, tractors, loaders, carriers & similar equipment

(G-15513)
BUSCHE SOUTHFIELD INC
Also Called: Busche Performance Group
26290 W 8 Mile Rd (48033-3650)
PHONE.................................248 357-5180
Joseph Perkins, *CEO*
Erica Bell, *Ch Credit Ofcr*
Patricia Longo, *Manager*
Tom Brush, *Exec Dir*
▲ **EMP:** 150 **EST:** 2006
SQ FT: 136,000
SALES (est): 33.6MM
SALES (corp-wide): 332.2MM Privately Held
WEB: www.mobexglobal.com
SIC: 7539 3559 Machine shop, automotive; automotive maintenance equipment
PA: Shipston Group U.S., Inc.
 22122 Telegraph Rd
 Southfield MI 48033
 248 372-9018

(G-15514)
BUSINESS DESIGN SOLUTIONS INC (PA)
Also Called: American Cmmnities Media Group
17360 W 12 Mile Rd # 201 (48076-2117)
PHONE.................................248 672-8007
Dimitri Lebedinskiy, *President*
EMP: 6 **EST:** 2002
SALES (est): 474.9K Privately Held
WEB: www.bdsus.com
SIC: 2752 Catalogs, lithographed; business form & card printing, lithographic

(G-15515)
CAMRYN INDUSTRIES LLC (HQ)
21624 Melrose Ave (48075-7905)
PHONE.................................248 663-5850
Jim Comer,
▲ **EMP:** 150 **EST:** 2006
SALES (est): 33.7K Privately Held
WEB: www.comerholdings.com
SIC: 2821 Molding compounds, plastics

(G-15516)
CAPITAL ASSETS RESOURCES LLC
17253 Magnolia Pkwy (48075-4221)
PHONE.................................248 252-7854
EMP: 4 **EST:** 2018
SALES (est): 81.9K Privately Held
SIC: 1382 Oil & gas exploration services

(G-15517)
CARR ENGINEERING
21557 Telegraph Rd (48033-4248)
PHONE.................................248 447-4109
EMP: 5 **EST:** 2016
SALES (est): 192.9K Privately Held
SIC: 3714 Motor vehicle parts & accessories

(G-15518)
CDM MACHINE CO
23009 Lake Ravines Dr (48033-3453)
PHONE.................................313 538-9100
Calvin Davidson, *President*
EMP: 9 **EST:** 1979
SALES (est): 441.3K Privately Held
WEB: www.cdm-machine.com
SIC: 3599 Machine shop, jobbing & repair

(G-15519)
CHARIDIMOS INC
Also Called: Athena Foods
23100 Telegraph Rd (48033-4155)
PHONE.................................248 827-7733
Charidimos A Sitaras, *President*
Jim Sitaras, *Manager*
EMP: 8 **EST:** 1990
SQ FT: 3,600
SALES (est): 976.9K Privately Held
WEB: www.athena-foods.com
SIC: 2099 Food preparations

(G-15520)
CHASSIX HOLDINGS INC
300 Galleria Ofc Ctr (48034-4700)
PHONE.................................248 728-8700
Mark Allan, *CEO*
Safi Hamid, *Vice Pres*
Eric Rouchy, *Vice Pres*
Mike Bolles, *Plant Mgr*
Calvin White, *Production*
EMP: 35 **EST:** 2015
SALES (est): 1.9MM Privately Held
WEB: www.aludyne.com
SIC: 3711 3365 Chassis, motor vehicle; machinery castings, aluminum

(G-15521)
CHEMICO SYSTEMS INC (PA)
Also Called: Chemico Mays
25200 Telg Rd Ste 120 (48034)
PHONE.................................248 723-3263
Leon C Richardson, *President*
David Macleod, *Vice Pres*
Harry Seifert, *Vice Pres*
Paul Sinko, *Treasurer*
Bob Luzac, *Program Mgr*
EMP: 20 **EST:** 1989
SALES (est): 19.5MM Privately Held
WEB: www.thechemicogroup.com
SIC: 7699 2819 Industrial equipment cleaning; chemicals, high purity: refined from technical grade

(G-15522)
CHRIS BROWN INDUSTRIES LLC
21415 Civic Center Dr # 300 (48076-3909)
PHONE.................................734 323-5651
Chris Brown, *Principal*
EMP: 8 **EST:** 2014
SALES (est): 143.4K Privately Held
WEB: www.brownindustrial.com
SIC: 3999 Manufacturing industries

(G-15523)
CITATION CAMDEN CAST CTR LLC
20750 Civic Center Dr # 100 (48076-4152)
PHONE.................................248 727-1800
John E Utley, *Ch of Bd*
Steven M Palm, *President*
William T Kirk, *Engineer*
Ben Sherard, *Controller*
Nancy Roberts, *Finance*
EMP: 348 **EST:** 1973
SQ FT: 150,000

SALES (est): 2.5MM
SALES (corp-wide): 686.1MM **Privately Held**
WEB: www.grede.com
SIC: 3714 Motor vehicle parts & accessories
HQ: Grede Ii Llc
   20750 Civic Center Dr # 100
   Southfield MI 48076
   248 440-9500

(G-15524)
CLAIRE ALDIN PUBLICATIONS
20813 Wkfield Way Apt 203 (48076)
PHONE.................................313 702-4028
De'andrea Matthews, *Principal*
EMP: 4 EST: 2017
SALES (est): 62.6K **Privately Held**
WEB: www.clairealdin.com
SIC: 2741 Miscellaneous publishing

(G-15525)
CLARIENCE TECHNOLOGIES LLC (HQ)
20600 Civic Center Dr (48076-4110)
PHONE.................................716 665-6214
Brian Kupchella, *CEO*
Robert Willing, *CFO*
EMP: 100 EST: 2011
SALES (est): 557.5MM **Privately Held**
WEB: www.gencap.com
SIC: 3647 Vehicular lighting equipment

(G-15526)
CLARITY COMM ADVISORS INC
Also Called: Clarity Voice
2 Corporate Dr Ste 250 (48076-3716)
PHONE.................................248 327-4390
Gary A Goerke, *President*
Melissa Fisher, *COO*
Rosemary Perras, *Vice Pres*
Heather Spangler, *Vice Pres*
Elizabeth Rutherford, *Human Resources*
EMP: 24 EST: 2008
SALES (est): 4.4MM **Privately Held**
WEB: www.clarityvoice.com
SIC: 3661 Telegraph or telephone carrier & repeater equipment

(G-15527)
COLOR CONNECTION
29487 Northwestern Hwy (48034)
PHONE.................................248 351-0920
Albert Scaglione, *President*
Amelia Scaglione, *Admin Sec*
EMP: 6
SALES (est): 457.6K **Privately Held**
SIC: 2752 2791 2789 Commercial printing, offset; typesetting; bookbinding & related work

(G-15528)
COLORS & EFFECTS USA LLC (DH)
3000 Town Ctr Ste 2400 (48075-1154)
PHONE.................................973 245-6000
Alexander Haunschild, *Senior VP*
EMP: 100 EST: 2016
SALES (est): 50.6MM **Privately Held**
WEB: www.basf.com
SIC: 2844 Toilet preparations; cosmetic preparations
HQ: Sun Chemical Corporation
   35 Waterview Blvd Ste 100
   Parsippany NJ 07054
   973 404-6000

(G-15529)
COLORS & EFFECTS USA LLC
24710 W 11 Mile Rd (48034-2494)
PHONE.................................248 304-5753
EMP: 31 **Privately Held**
SIC: 2869 Industrial organic chemicals
HQ: Colors & Effects Usa Llc
   3000 Town Ctr Ste 2400
   Southfield MI 48075
   973 245-6000

(G-15530)
COMAU LLC (DH)
Also Called: Comau Pico
21000 Telegraph Rd (48033-4280)
PHONE.................................248 353-8888
Eric Waller, *CEO*
Brendan Blenner-Hassett, *President*
Brian Larabell, *General Mgr*

Lisa Zaffina, *General Mgr*
Andrew Lloyd, *COO*
◆ EMP: 400 EST: 2015
SQ FT: 198,000
SALES (est): 414.4MM
SALES (corp-wide): 102.5B **Privately Held**
WEB: www.comau.com
SIC: 3548 3829 3545 3339 Resistance welders, electric; testing equipment: abrasion, shearing strength, etc.; gauges (machine tool accessories); tools & accessories for machine tools; primary nonferrous metals; engineering services
HQ: Comau Spa
   Via Rivalta 30
   Grugliasco TO 10095
   011 004-9111

(G-15531)
COMAU LLC
Also Called: Pico
21175 Telegraph Rd (48033-4200)
PHONE.................................248 219-0756
Lisa Zaffina, *General Mgr*
Fabrizio Mina, *Vice Pres*
Ilaria Polinetti, *Vice Pres*
Patrice Coat, *Plant Mgr*
Larry Gietzen, *Project Mgr*
EMP: 65
SALES (corp-wide): 102.5B **Privately Held**
WEB: www.comau.com
SIC: 3569 7373 8742 Liquid automation machinery & equipment; office computer automation systems integration; automation & robotics consultant
HQ: Comau Llc
   21000 Telegraph Rd
   Southfield MI 48033
   248 353-8888

(G-15532)
CONTRACT PEOPLE CORPORATION
29444 Northwestern Hwy (48034-1029)
P.O. Box 3112 (48037-3112)
PHONE.................................248 304-9900
Terry A Wallace, *President*
EMP: 10 EST: 1981
SQ FT: 1,200
SALES (est): 749.1K **Privately Held**
SIC: 7363 3679 8731 8711 Employee leasing service; electronic circuits; commercial physical research; engineering services

(G-15533)
COVISINT CORPORATION (HQ)
26533 Evergreen Rd # 500 (48076-4234)
PHONE.................................248 483-2000
Mark J Barrenechea, *CEO*
Muhi Majzoub, *Exec VP*
Douglas M Parker, *Senior VP*
Nicholas Iconos, *Assistant VP*
Pooja Mishra, *Assistant VP*
EMP: 353 EST: 2000
SQ FT: 33,786
SALES: 70.2MM
SALES (corp-wide): 3.1B **Privately Held**
WEB: www.cn.covisint.com
SIC: 7374 7372 Data processing service; prepackaged software
PA: Open Text Corporation
   275 Frank Tompa Dr
   Waterloo ON N2L 0
   519 888-7111

(G-15534)
CUSTOM GIANT LLC
22721 Nottingham Ln (48033-3365)
PHONE.................................313 799-2085
Darnell Wilson, *Owner*
EMP: 4 EST: 2011
SALES (est): 339.3K **Privately Held**
SIC: 5651 2329 Unisex clothing stores; riding clothes., men's, youths' & boys'

(G-15535)
D&E INCORPORATED
20542 Oldham Rd (48076-4026)
PHONE.................................313 673-3283
Damious Eason, *President*
EMP: 4 EST: 2012
SALES (est): 270.5K **Privately Held**
SIC: 2211 7389 Osnaburgs;

(G-15536)
DAGHER SIGNS
22476 Telegraph Rd (48033-6819)
PHONE.................................313 729-9555
Kal Dagher, *Principal*
EMP: 6 EST: 2017
SALES (est): 294.8K **Privately Held**
SIC: 3993 Signs & advertising specialties

(G-15537)
DAVIDS HEATING & COOLING INC
17000 Cedarcroft Pl (48076-4757)
PHONE.................................586 601-5108
David Gal, *Owner*
EMP: 4 EST: 2019
SALES (est): 107.4K **Privately Held**
WEB: www.davidsheatingandcooling.com
SIC: 3567 Industrial furnaces & ovens

(G-15538)
DENSO INTERNATIONAL AMER INC (HQ)
24777 Denso Dr (48033-5244)
PHONE.................................248 350-7500
Kenichiro Ito, *President*
Kazumasa Kimura, *COO*
Masahiko Miyaki, *Exec VP*
Atsuhiko Shimmura, *Exec VP*
Tom Esser, *Vice Pres*
◆ EMP: 700 EST: 1949
SQ FT: 43,000
SALES (est): 2.1B **Privately Held**
WEB: www.denso.com
SIC: 3714 Motor vehicle engines & parts

(G-15539)
DETROIT COUTURE
17390 W 8 Mile Rd (48075-4301)
PHONE.................................734 237-6826
June Eaton, *CEO*
EMP: 4 EST: 2018
SALES (est): 331.2K **Privately Held**
WEB: www.detroitcouture.com
SIC: 5099 8742 3161 Durable goods; retail trade consultant; clothing & apparel carrying cases

(G-15540)
DIVERSIFIED TUBE LLC
21056 Bridge St (48033-4087)
PHONE.................................313 790-7348
Cassaundra Bing, *Mng Member*
EMP: 10 EST: 2010
SALES (est): 709K **Privately Held**
SIC: 3317 Steel pipe & tubes

(G-15541)
DLHBOWLES INC
20755 Greenfield Rd # 806 (48075-5403)
PHONE.................................248 569-0652
Jamie Yates, *Engineer*
Dan McNary, *VP Sales*
EMP: 10
SALES (corp-wide): 136.7MM **Privately Held**
WEB: www.dlh-inc.com
SIC: 8711 3089 3082 Engineering services; injection molding of plastics; tubes, unsupported plastic
PA: Dlhbowles, Inc.
   2422 Leo Ave Sw
   Canton OH 44706
   330 478-2503

(G-15542)
DMP SIGN COMPANY
20732 Negaunee St (48033-3526)
PHONE.................................248 996-9281
EMP: 7 EST: 2016
SALES (est): 297.3K **Privately Held**
WEB: www.dmpsignco.com
SIC: 3993 Signs & advertising specialties

(G-15543)
DUNNS WELDING INC
22930 Lahser Rd (48033-4408)
PHONE.................................248 356-3866
Thomas P Dunn, *President*
Peter Dunn, *Vice Pres*
Margaret Dunn, *Treasurer*
Judee Dunn, *Manager*
EMP: 6 EST: 1965
SQ FT: 9,600
SALES (est): 107K **Privately Held**
WEB: www.dunnswelding.com

SIC: 3441 1799 7692 Fabricated structural metal; welding on site; welding repair

(G-15544)
DURR INC (HQ)
26801 Northwestern Hwy (48033-6251)
PHONE.................................734 459-6800
Bruno Welsch, *President*
Gary Wolinski, *Business Mgr*
Norbert Klapper, *Vice Pres*
Olaf Remmers, *Vice Pres*
Oliver Gary, *Plant Mgr*
▲ EMP: 1 EST: 1991
SQ FT: 270,000
SALES (est): 843MM
SALES (corp-wide): 3.9B **Privately Held**
WEB: www.durr.com
SIC: 3559 3567 Metal finishing equipment for plating, etc.; incinerators, metal: domestic or commercial
PA: Durr Ag
   Carl-Benz-Str. 34
   Bietigheim-Bissingen BW 74321
   714 278-0

(G-15545)
DURR SYSTEMS INC (DH)
Also Called: Pfs - Pnt Fnal Assmbly Systems
26801 Northwestern Hwy (48033-6251)
P.O. Box 5030, De Pere WI (54115-5030)
PHONE.................................248 450-2000
Ralf W Dieter, *CEO*
Varun Gupta, *General Mgr*
Jacob Wert, *Editor*
Martin Schrter, *Business Mgr*
Dave Ciuffoletti, *Vice Pres*
◆ EMP: 300 EST: 1970
SQ FT: 270,000
SALES (est): 131.5MM
SALES (corp-wide): 3.9B **Privately Held**
WEB: www.durrsystems.com
SIC: 3559 3567 Metal finishing equipment for plating, etc.; incinerators, metal: domestic or commercial

(G-15546)
DURR SYSTEMS INC
Also Called: APT Division
26801 Northwestern Hwy (48033-6251)
PHONE.................................248 745-8500
Werner Baumgartner, *Principal*
David Jackson, *Principal Engr*
John Cassidy, *Branch Mgr*
Brolan Conkey, *Manager*
David Seraphinoff, *Senior Mgr*
EMP: 18
SALES (corp-wide): 3.9B **Privately Held**
WEB: www.durrsystems.com
SIC: 3559 Metal finishing equipment for plating, etc.
HQ: Durr Systems, Inc
   26801 Northwestern Hwy
   Southfield MI 48033
   248 450-2000

(G-15547)
EATON CORPORATION
Eaton Fuel Vapor Systems Div
26201 Northwestern Hwy (48076-3926)
PHONE.................................248 226-6347
Michael Stefaniak, *Business Mgr*
Chuck Molnar, *Vice Pres*
Kaylah Berndt, *Engineer*
Ricardo Collaco, *Engineer*
Erik Dykes, *Engineer*
EMP: 5 **Privately Held**
WEB: www.eatonelectrical.com
SIC: 5993 3566 3822 Tobacco stores & stands; speed changers, drives & gears; auto controls regulating residntl & coml environmt & applncs
HQ: Eaton Corporation
   1000 Eaton Blvd
   Cleveland OH 44122
   440 523-5000

(G-15548)
EATON CORPORATION
Also Called: Vehicles
26101 Northwestern Hwy (48076-3925)
PHONE.................................248 226-6200
Brian O'Neil, *Engineer*
Cindy Shane, *Manager*
Scott Adams, *Exec Dir*
EMP: 7 **Privately Held**
WEB: www.eatonelectrical.com

Southfield - Oakland County (G-15549) — GEOGRAPHIC SECTION

SIC: 3714 Motor vehicle parts & accessories
HQ: Eaton Corporation
1000 Eaton Blvd
Cleveland OH 44122
440 523-5000

(G-15549)
EATON INOAC COMPANY (DH)
26101 Northwestern Hwy (48076-3925)
PHONE.................................248 226-6200
Gustavo M Decruz, *Partner*
▲ EMP: 20 EST: 1988
SQ FT: 7,650
SALES (est): 3.9MM **Privately Held**
WEB: www.eatonelectrical.com
SIC: 3089 Blow molded finished plastic products; injection molding of plastics
HQ: Eaton Corporation
1000 Eaton Blvd
Cleveland OH 44122
440 523-5000

(G-15550)
ECJ PROCESSING
17379 Park Ln (48076-7716)
PHONE.................................248 540-2336
EMP: 4 EST: 2017
SALES (est): 139.7K **Privately Held**
SIC: 3471 Electroplating of metals or formed products

(G-15551)
ECO TAX GROUP INC
24901 Northwestern Hwy # 409 (48075-2214)
PHONE.................................313 422-1300
Seanita Armstrong, *Partner*
EMP: 8 EST: 2014
SQ FT: 2,200
SALES (est): 309.4K **Privately Held**
WEB: www.ecotaxshop.com
SIC: 7372 Business oriented computer software

(G-15552)
ECOCLEAN INC (HQ)
26801 Northwestern Hwy (48033-6251)
PHONE.................................248 450-2000
Andreas Reger, *President*
James Clarke, *Project Mgr*
Ken Banack, *Opers Staff*
Brett Sigurdson, *Purchasing*
Steve Heinrich, *CFO*
▲ EMP: 149 EST: 1998
SQ FT: 45,000
SALES (est): 44.1MM **Privately Held**
WEB: www.ecoclean-group.net
SIC: 3452 3677 Washers; filtration devices, electronic

(G-15553)
ELITE DOG AND PET SUPPLY LLC
24100 Sthfeld Rd Ste 110c (48075)
PHONE.................................947 900-1101
Curtis Ellison,
EMP: 10 EST: 2016
SALES (est): 283.4K **Privately Held**
SIC: 2048 Dry pet food (except dog & cat)

(G-15554)
ELRINGKLINGER AUTO MFG INC (DH)
Also Called: Elringklinger North Amer Inc
23300 Northwestern Hwy (48075-3350)
PHONE.................................248 727-6600
Stefan Wolf, *CEO*
Stephan Maier, *General Mgr*
Reiner Drews, *COO*
Thomas Jessulat, *CFO*
Theo Becker, *CTO*
▲ EMP: 20 EST: 1945
SQ FT: 27,000
SALES (est): 14.6MM
SALES (corp-wide): 144.1K **Privately Held**
WEB: www.elringklinger.de
SIC: 3498 Tube fabricating (contract bending & shaping)
HQ: Elringklinger Ag
Max-Eyth-Str. 2
Dettingen An Der Erms BW 72581
712 372-40

(G-15555)
ELRINGKLINGER AUTO MFG INC
23300 Northwestern Hwy (48075-3350)
PHONE.................................248 727-6600
EMP: 27
SALES (corp-wide): 144.1K **Privately Held**
SIC: 3498 Tube fabricating (contract bending & shaping)
HQ: Elringklinger Automotive Manufacturing, Inc.
23300 Northwestern Hwy
Southfield MI 48075
248 727-6600

(G-15556)
EMATRIX ENERGY SYSTEMS INC
21520 Bridge St (48033-4073)
PHONE.................................248 797-2149
Emma Dusenbury, *Sales Associate*
EMP: 14 EST: 2018
SALES (est): 2.6MM **Privately Held**
WEB: www.ematrixenergy.com
SIC: 3691 Storage batteries

(G-15557)
ENGINEERING SERVICE OF AMERICA
Also Called: Engineering Systems Intl
21556 Telegraph Rd (48033-6815)
P.O. Box 7 (48037-0007)
PHONE.................................248 357-3800
James A Karchon, *President*
Richard Scott, *Vice Pres*
Dennis M Karchon, *Asst Sec*
EMP: 55 EST: 1941
SQ FT: 22,600
SALES (est): 744.1K **Privately Held**
WEB: www.ietintl.com
SIC: 8711 3714 Designing: ship, boat, machine & product; motor vehicle parts & accessories

(G-15558)
FASTSIGNS
22554 Telegraph Rd (48033-4107)
PHONE.................................248 372-9554
EMP: 4 EST: 2018
SALES (est): 116.8K **Privately Held**
WEB: www.fastsigns.com
SIC: 3993 Signs & advertising specialties

(G-15559)
FEDERAL GROUP USA INC
Also Called: Federal Group, The
21126 Bridge St (48033-4032)
PHONE.................................248 545-5000
Robert Levy, *President*
Melinda McGill, *Manager*
▲ EMP: 11 EST: 1980
SALES (est): 6MM **Privately Held**
WEB: www.tfgusa.com
SIC: 5072 3321 3324 3363 Bolts; nuts (hardware); screws; gray iron castings; commercial investment castings, ferrous; aluminum die-castings; castings, except die-castings, precision

(G-15560)
FEDERAL-MOGUL CHASSIS LLC (HQ)
Also Called: Federal-Mogul Motorparts
27300 W 11 Mile Rd # 100 (48034-6193)
PHONE.................................248 354-7700
Brad Norton, *CEO*
Rainer Jueckstock, *Co-CEO*
Michelle E Taigman, *Senior VP*
Jerome Rouquet, *CFO*
Marco Desanto, *Ch Credit Ofcr*
EMP: 14 EST: 2013
SALES (est): 7.9MM
SALES (corp-wide): 15.3B **Publicly Held**
WEB: www.tenneco.com
SIC: 3714 Motor vehicle parts & accessories
PA: Tenneco Inc.
500 N Field Dr
Lake Forest IL 60045
847 482-5000

(G-15561)
FEDERAL-MOGUL CORPORATION (DH)
Also Called: Federal Mgul Wrldwide Aftrmrke
26555 Northwestern Hwy (48033-2199)
P.O. Box 21787, Tulsa OK (74121-1787)
PHONE.................................248 354-7700
Steve Miller, *CEO*
Joe Felicelli, *President*
▲ EMP: 44 EST: 2006
SALES (est): 18.5MM
SALES (corp-wide): 15.3B **Publicly Held**
SIC: 3714 Motor vehicle parts & accessories

(G-15562)
FEDERAL-MOGUL IGNITION LLC (DH)
26555 Northwestern Hwy (48033-2199)
PHONE.................................248 354-7700
David A Bozynski, *President*
▲ EMP: 100 EST: 1938
SQ FT: 400,000
SALES (est): 34.8MM
SALES (corp-wide): 15.3B **Publicly Held**
WEB: www.championautoparts.com
SIC: 3714 Motor vehicle parts & accessories

(G-15563)
FEDERAL-MOGUL MOTORPARTS LLC (HQ)
27300 W 11 Mile Rd # 100 (48034-6193)
P.O. Box 981469, El Paso TX (79998-1469)
PHONE.................................248 354-7700
Brad Norton, *CEO*
John Kleinschmidt, *Project Mgr*
Tim Meadors, *Materials Mgr*
Tyler Common, *Buyer*
Derek Schonhoff, *Buyer*
EMP: 100 EST: 2012
SALES (est): 140.6MM
SALES (corp-wide): 15.3B **Publicly Held**
WEB: www.drivparts.com
SIC: 3714 Motor vehicle parts & accessories
PA: Tenneco Inc.
500 N Field Dr
Lake Forest IL 60045
847 482-5000

(G-15564)
FEDERAL-MOGUL PISTON RINGS INC (HQ)
26555 Northwestern Hwy (48033-2199)
PHONE.................................248 354-7700
David Krohn, *President*
Rainer Jueckstock, *Exec VP*
William Sarver, *Plant Mgr*
Christopher Sutherland, *Plant Mgr*
Randy Whitt, *Plant Mgr*
▲ EMP: 15 EST: 1978
SALES (est): 300.6MM
SALES (corp-wide): 15.3B **Publicly Held**
WEB: www.ceofmo.com
SIC: 3592 3053 3369 Pistons & piston rings; gaskets & sealing devices; gaskets, all materials; nonferrous foundries
PA: Tenneco Inc.
500 N Field Dr
Lake Forest IL 60045
847 482-5000

(G-15565)
FEDERAL-MOGUL POWERTRAIN LLC (HQ)
27300 W 11 Mile Rd # 100 (48034-6193)
PHONE.................................248 354-7700
Rainer Jueckstock, *CEO*
David Bozynski, *President*
Robert Katz, *Vice Pres*
Robert Rozycki, *Vice Pres*
Scott Fischer, *Mfg Staff*
▲ EMP: 8 EST: 1986
SALES (est): 452.3MM
SALES (corp-wide): 15.3B **Publicly Held**
WEB: www.tenneco.com
SIC: 3366 Bushings & bearings
PA: Tenneco Inc.
500 N Field Dr
Lake Forest IL 60045
847 482-5000

(G-15566)
FEDERAL-MOGUL PRODUCTS US LLC (HQ)
26555 Northwestern Hwy (48033-2199)
PHONE.................................248 354-7700
David A Bozynski, *President*
Alice Hutchens, *Purchasing*
Tony Ertz, *Engineer*
Lori Galle, *Controller*
Sergio Hinokuma, *Supervisor*
▲ EMP: 2600 EST: 1977
SQ FT: 500,000
SALES (est): 254.5MM
SALES (corp-wide): 15.3B **Publicly Held**
WEB: www.tenneco.com
SIC: 3714 Ball joints, motor vehicle
PA: Tenneco Inc.
500 N Field Dr
Lake Forest IL 60045
847 482-5000

(G-15567)
FEDERAL-MOGUL VALVE TRAIN INTE (HQ)
27300 W 11 Mile Rd (48034-6147)
PHONE.................................248 354-7700
Daniel Ninivaggi, *Co-CEO*
Rainer Jueckstock, *Co-CEO*
Rajesh Shah, *CFO*
EMP: 75 EST: 2014
SALES (est): 105.4MM
SALES (corp-wide): 15.3B **Publicly Held**
WEB: www.tenneco.com
SIC: 3592 Valves, engine
PA: Tenneco Inc.
500 N Field Dr
Lake Forest IL 60045
847 482-5000

(G-15568)
FEDERAL-MOGUL WORLD WIDE INC (HQ)
26555 Northwestern Hwy (48033-2199)
PHONE.................................248 354-7700
Richard Snell, *President*
EMP: 100 EST: 1991
SALES (est): 105.8MM
SALES (corp-wide): 15.3B **Publicly Held**
WEB: www.tenneco.com
SIC: 3714 Motor vehicle parts & accessories
PA: Tenneco Inc.
500 N Field Dr
Lake Forest IL 60045
847 482-5000

(G-15569)
FEDERL-MGUL DUTCH HOLDINGS INC
26555 Northwestern Hwy (48033-2146)
PHONE.................................248 354-7700
Brian J Kesseler, *CEO*
EMP: 85 EST: 1998
SALES (est): 24.6MM
SALES (corp-wide): 15.3B **Publicly Held**
WEB: www.tenneco.com
SIC: 3053 Gaskets, packing & sealing devices
PA: Tenneco Inc.
500 N Field Dr
Lake Forest IL 60045
847 482-5000

(G-15570)
FM INTERNATIONAL LLC (HQ)
26555 Northwestern Hwy (48033-2146)
PHONE.................................248 354-7700
David Bozynski, *President*
Lori Boyer, *Manager*
EMP: 1 EST: 2000
SALES (est): 3.9MM
SALES (corp-wide): 15.3B **Publicly Held**
WEB: www.tenneco.com
SIC: 3053 Gaskets & sealing devices
PA: Tenneco Inc.
500 N Field Dr
Lake Forest IL 60045
847 482-5000

(G-15571)
FUTURE REPRODUCTIONS INC
21477 Bridge St Ste L (48033-4079)
PHONE.................................248 350-2060
Kathryn Warras, *President*
Steve Warras, *Vice Pres*

GEOGRAPHIC SECTION   **Southfield - Oakland County (G-15598)**

EMP: 12 EST: 1976
SQ FT: 13,500
SALES (est): 1.5MM **Privately Held**
WEB: www.futurereproductions.com
SIC: 2752 2791 2789 Commercial printing, offset; typesetting; bookbinding & related work

(G-15572)
GARAGE GRUS FDRL-MGUL MTRPARTS
24477 W 10 Mile Rd (48033-2931)
PHONE.................................800 325-8886
EMP: 11 EST: 2019
SALES (est): 288.1K **Privately Held**
SIC: 3714 Motor vehicle parts & accessories

(G-15573)
GASKET HOLDINGS INC
26555 Northwestern Hwy (48033-2146)
PHONE.................................248 354-7700
Brian J Kesseler, *CEO*
EMP: 5 EST: 1992
SALES (est): 1.1MM
SALES (corp-wide): 15.3B **Publicly Held**
WEB: www.tenneco.com
SIC: 3714 Motor vehicle parts & accessories
PA: Tenneco Inc.
    500 N Field Dr
    Lake Forest IL 60045
    847 482-5000

(G-15574)
GEORGE BROWN LEGACY GROUP ✪
Also Called: Gbl Group The
23375 Riverside Dr (48033-3364)
PHONE.................................313 770-9928
Deanna M Brown,
EMP: 5 EST: 2021
SALES (est): 227.5K **Privately Held**
SIC: 3799 7389 Transportation equipment;

(G-15575)
GFL ENVRONMENTAL REAL PROPERTY (PA)
Also Called: Rizzo Environmental Services
26999 Central Park Blvd # 200 (48076-4174)
PHONE.................................888 877-4996
Wade Stevenson, *CFO*
Jim Queen, *Manager*
Charles Rizzo Jr,
EMP: 42 EST: 2013
SALES (est): 12.4MM **Privately Held**
SIC: 2611 Pulp mills, mechanical & recycling processing

(G-15576)
GLOBAL FLEET SALES LLC
24255 W 12 Mile Rd # 114 (48034-8345)
PHONE.................................248 327-6483
Kevin R Whitcraft, *President*
Carol Grakul, *Vice Pres*
Alexander Brenneisen, *CFO*
Mark I Whitcraft, *Treasurer*
▼ EMP: 8 EST: 2004
SQ FT: 1,350
SALES (est): 2.4MM **Privately Held**
WEB: www.ford.globalfleetsales.com
SIC: 5012 8711 3621 Automobiles & other motor vehicles; engineering services; generators & sets, electric

(G-15577)
GLOBAL INDUSTRIES INC
25925 Telg Rd Ste 145 (48033)
PHONE.................................248 357-7211
Lynette Poole, *Principal*
EMP: 4 EST: 2017
SALES (est): 49.1K **Privately Held**
SIC: 3999 Manufacturing industries

(G-15578)
GOGETTAZ CLOTHING COMPANY LLC
17314 Bonstelle Ave (48075-3415)
PHONE.................................630 800-3279
Curtis Watson,
EMP: 85 EST: 2014
SALES (est): 2.8MM **Privately Held**
SIC: 2211 Apparel & outerwear fabrics, cotton

(G-15579)
GREDE HOLDINGS LLC (HQ)
20750 Civic Center Dr # 100 (48076-4129)
PHONE.................................248 440-9500
Cary Wood, *CEO*
Toney Lovell, *President*
Paul Suber, *COO*
Mike Lobbia, *CFO*
EMP: 25 EST: 2010
SQ FT: 24,000
SALES (est): 656.1MM
SALES (corp-wide): 686.1MM **Privately Held**
WEB: www.grede.com
SIC: 3321 Gray iron castings; ductile iron castings
PA: Asp Grede Acquisitionco Llc
    20750 Civic Center Dr # 100
    Southfield MI 48076
    248 440-9515

(G-15580)
GREDE II LLC (DH)
20750 Civic Center Dr # 100 (48076-4152)
PHONE.................................248 440-9500
Cary Wood, *CEO*
Toney Lovell, *President*
Paul Suber, *COO*
Mike Lobbia, *CFO*
▲ EMP: 35 EST: 1994
SQ FT: 24,000
SALES (est): 323.8MM
SALES (corp-wide): 686.1MM **Privately Held**
WEB: www.grede.com
SIC: 3321 Ductile iron castings; gray iron castings

(G-15581)
GREDE LLC (DH)
20750 Civic Center Dr # 100 (48076-4129)
PHONE.................................248 440-9500
Cary Wood, *CEO*
Toney Lovell, *President*
Paul Suber, *COO*
Mike Lobbia, *CFO*
▲ EMP: 365 EST: 2010
SQ FT: 23,000
SALES (est): 194.1MM
SALES (corp-wide): 686.1MM **Privately Held**
WEB: www.grede.com
SIC: 3321 Gray iron castings; ductile iron castings

(G-15582)
GREDE OMAHA LLC
Also Called: Omaha Plant
20750 Civic Center Dr # 100 (48076-4152)
PHONE.................................248 727-1800
David C Dauch, *Ch of Bd*
EMP: 170 EST: 2011
SALES (est): 1.8MM
SALES (corp-wide): 686.1MM **Privately Held**
WEB: www.grede.com
SIC: 3714 3711 Motor vehicle parts & accessories; motor vehicles & car bodies
HQ: Grede Ii Llc
    20750 Civic Center Dr # 100
    Southfield MI 48076
    248 440-9500

(G-15583)
GREDE WSCNSIN SUBSIDIARIES LLC (DH)
Also Called: Citation Berlin
20750 Civic Center Dr # 100 (48076-4152)
PHONE.................................248 727-1800
Mike Dowling, *President*
Douglas J Grimm, *Chairman*
Todd Heavin, *Senior VP*
Todd A Heavin, *Senior VP*
Louis Lavorata, *Senior VP*
▼ EMP: 163 EST: 1920
SQ FT: 229,864
SALES (est): 96.3MM
SALES (corp-wide): 686.1MM **Privately Held**
WEB: www.grede.com
SIC: 3321 Gray iron castings

(G-15584)
GREENGLOW PRODUCTS LLC
21170 Bridge St (48033-4032)
P.O. Box 760164, Lathrup Village (48076-0164)
PHONE.................................248 827-1451
Barry Fleischer, *Mng Member*
EMP: 6
SALES (est): 729.3K **Privately Held**
SIC: 2851 Paints & allied products

(G-15585)
GRIGG GRAPHIC SERVICES INC
Also Called: Bridge Street Design & Mktg
20982 Bridge St (48033-4033)
PHONE.................................248 356-5005
Stuart W Grigg, *President*
Chris Trombley, *Project Mgr*
Ed Owen, *Opers Staff*
Bob Engel, *Manager*
Dawn Sinclair, *Manager*
EMP: 27 EST: 1953
SQ FT: 7,500
SALES (est): 5MM **Privately Held**
WEB: www.grigg.com
SIC: 2752 7336 Commercial printing, offset; graphic arts & related design

(G-15586)
GSC RIII - GREDE LLC
20750 Civic Center Dr # 100 (48076-4152)
PHONE.................................248 440-9500
Cary Wood, *President*
Debbie Klemm, *Finance*
EMP: 1 EST: 2010
SALES (est): 3.5MM
SALES (corp-wide): 686.1MM **Privately Held**
SIC: 3321 Gray & ductile iron foundries
PA: Asp Grede Acquisitionco Llc
    20750 Civic Center Dr # 100
    Southfield MI 48076
    248 440-9515

(G-15587)
GUARDHAT INC
20300 Civic Center Dr # 1103 (48076-4169)
PHONE.................................248 281-6089
Saikat Dey, *CEO*
Gerrit Reepmeyer, *COO*
Steven Friedman, *Vice Pres*
Greg Harrington, *Engineer*
Mikhail Zhavoronkov, *CFO*
EMP: 6 EST: 2015
SALES (est): 1.3MM **Privately Held**
WEB: www.guardhat.com
SIC: 7372 Application computer software

(G-15588)
GUILFORD PERFORMANCE TEXTILES
21557 Telegraph Rd (48033-4248)
PHONE.................................910 794-5810
EMP: 14 EST: 2019
SALES (est): 1.7MM **Privately Held**
WEB: www.lear.com
SIC: 2211 Tapestry fabrics, cotton

(G-15589)
GUYOUNG TECH USA INC (HQ)
26555 Evergreen Rd # 1515 (48076-4206)
PHONE.................................248 746-4261
Moo Chan Lee, *President*
▲ EMP: 100 EST: 2004
SALES (est): 66.1MM **Privately Held**
WEB: www.guyoungtech.com
SIC: 3465 Automotive stampings

(G-15590)
HBM INC
26555 Evergreen Rd # 700 (48076-4206)
PHONE.................................248 350-8300
Michael Singer, *CEO*
EMP: 2 EST: 2013
SALES (est): 1MM **Privately Held**
WEB: www.ncode.com
SIC: 3829 Measuring & controlling devices

(G-15591)
HEALS & HERBS LLC
29255 Franklin Hills Dr (48034-1150)
PHONE.................................888 604-1474
Sherita Griffith, *President*
John Coleman Jr, *Principal*

Jessica Cousins, *Principal*
Ebony Gibbs, *Principal*
Tryrina Gibbs, *Principal*
EMP: 5 EST: 2020
SALES (est): 738.2K **Privately Held**
SIC: 2833 Medicinals & botanicals

(G-15592)
HELPING HANDS THERAPY
23999 Northwestern Hwy (48075-2578)
PHONE.................................313 492-6007
Tina Williams,
EMP: 5 EST: 2013
SALES (est): 392K **Privately Held**
WEB: www.helpinghands-therapy.com
SIC: 3845 Electromedical equipment

(G-15593)
HOUSEY PHRM RES LABS LLC
16800 W 12 Mile Rd (48076-2108)
PHONE.................................248 663-7000
Gerard Housey, *President*
EMP: 7 EST: 2005
SALES (est): 1.2MM **Privately Held**
WEB: www.housey.com
SIC: 2834 Pharmaceutical preparations

(G-15594)
HUGHES NETWORK SYSTEMS LLC
24000 Northwestern Hwy (48075-2567)
PHONE.................................301 428-5500
Doug Mamley, *Manager*
EMP: 6 **Publicly Held**
WEB: www.echostar.com
SIC: 3663 Radio & TV communications equipment
HQ: Hughes Network Systems, Llc
    11717 Exploration Ln
    Germantown MD 20876
    301 428-5500

(G-15595)
HUXL DENIM
16500 N Park Dr Apt 1914 (48075-4771)
PHONE.................................248 595-8480
Derrick Jones, *Principal*
EMP: 4 EST: 2017
SALES (est): 58.2K **Privately Held**
SIC: 2211 Denims

(G-15596)
HYDRO KING INCORPORATED
Also Called: Detroit Recker Sales
21384 Mcclung Ave (48075-3297)
PHONE.................................313 835-8700
Rick Farrell, *President*
Betty Farrell, *Vice Pres*
EMP: 10 EST: 1986
SALES (est): 567K **Privately Held**
SIC: 3799 Towing bars & systems

(G-15597)
IAC CREATIVE LLC
Also Called: Interntnal Auto Cmpnnts Group
27777 Franklin Rd # 2000 (48034-2337)
PHONE.................................248 455-7000
Tanya Geffrard, *Business Mgr*
Melissa Krajniak, *Business Mgr*
Dennis E Richardville, *Exec VP*
Janis N Acosta, *Exec VP*
Mark Schneider, *Vice Pres*
EMP: 494 EST: 2012
SALES (est): 29.6MM **Privately Held**
WEB: www.iacgroup.com
SIC: 2759 Commercial printing
HQ: International Automotive Components Group North America, Inc.
    27777 Franklin Rd # 2000
    Southfield MI 48034

(G-15598)
IAC MEXICO HOLDINGS INC (DH)
27777 Franklin Rd # 2000 (48034-2337)
PHONE.................................248 455-7000
Manfred Gingl, *CEO*
Robert Cook, *General Mgr*
David Heseltine, *General Mgr*
Joe Goudzward, *Opers Mgr*
Marcus Martin, *Opers Mgr*
EMP: 2194 EST: 2007
SALES (est): 13.7MM **Privately Held**
WEB: www.iacgroup.com
SIC: 3089 Automotive parts, plastic

Southfield - Oakland County (G-15599) — GEOGRAPHIC SECTION

(G-15599)
IDEMITSU CHEMICALS USA CORP
3000 Town Ctr Ste 2820 (48075-1203)
PHONE..................248 355-0666
Kazuto Hasaimoto, *President*
▲ **EMP:** 8 **EST:** 1986
SQ FT: 3,600
SALES (est): 15MM **Privately Held**
WEB: www.idemitsu-chemicals.de
SIC: 3082 5169 5162 Unsupported plastics profile shapes; chemicals & allied products; plastics materials & basic shapes
PA: Idemitsu Kosan Co..Ltd.
1-2-1, Otemachi
Chiyoda-Ku TKY 100-0

(G-15600)
IDEMITSU LUBRICANTS AMER CORP
3000 Town Ctr Ste 2820 (48075-1203)
PHONE..................248 355-0666
Mike Grimes, *Division Mgr*
Michael Park, *Division Mgr*
Masanori Enomoto, *Principal*
Jason Couch, *Prdtn Mgr*
Scott Rajala, *Chief Engr*
EMP: 22 **Privately Held**
WEB: www.ilacorp.com
SIC: 2992 5162 Lubricating oils & greases; plastics materials & basic shapes
HQ: Idemitsu Lubricants America Corporation
701 Port Rd
Jeffersonville IN 47130

(G-15601)
IDP INC
21300 W 8 Mile Rd (48075-5638)
PHONE..................248 352-0044
Isaac Benezra, *President*
▲ **EMP:** 21 **EST:** 2006
SALES (est): 2.4MM **Privately Held**
WEB: www.idpframes.com
SIC: 2431 Door frames, wood

(G-15602)
INDEX PRINTS
25901 W 10 Mile Rd (48033-2857)
PHONE..................248 327-6621
EMP: 5 **EST:** 2017
SALES (est): 252.6K **Privately Held**
WEB: www.indexprints.com
SIC: 2752 Commercial printing, lithographic

(G-15603)
INDUSTRIAL BAG & SPC INC
17800 Northland Park Ct # 107 (48075-4304)
PHONE..................248 559-5550
Kenneth M Borin, *President*
Phillip Quartana, *Vice Pres*
EMP: 19 **EST:** 1936
SQ FT: 3,500
SALES (est): 784.5K **Privately Held**
WEB: www.industrialbag.com
SIC: 2393 2394 Bags & containers, except sleeping bags: textile; duffle bags, canvas: made from purchased materials; liners & covers, fabric: made from purchased materials

(G-15604)
INDUSTRIAL EXPRMENTAL TECH LLC
Also Called: Iet
21556 Telegraph Rd (48033-4247)
PHONE..................248 948-1100
James Karchon, *Mng Member*
EMP: 30 **EST:** 2018
SALES (est): 1.4MM **Privately Held**
WEB: www.ietintl.com
SIC: 3599 Machine shop, jobbing & repair

(G-15605)
INFORMA BUSINESS MEDIA INC
Also Called: Wards Automotive International
3000 Town Ctr Ste 2750 (48075-1245)
PHONE..................248 357-0800
EMP: 48
SALES (corp-wide): 3.7B **Privately Held**
SIC: 2721 Publishes Automotive Magazine
HQ: Informa Business Media, Inc.
605 3rd Ave Fl 22
New York NY 10158
212 204-4200

(G-15606)
INTERNTNAL AUTO CMPNNTS GROUP (DH)
Also Called: IAC Group
27777 Franklin Rd # 2000 (48034-2337)
PHONE..................248 455-7000
David Prystash, *CEO*
Manfred Gingl, *President*
Ted Rickabus, *President*
Prayag Thakkar, *General Mgr*
Janis Acosta, *Exec VP*
◆ **EMP:** 800 **EST:** 2006
SALES (est): 1.2B **Privately Held**
WEB: www.iacgroup.com
SIC: 3714 Motor vehicle parts & accessories
HQ: International Automotive Components Group, S.A.
Avenue Charles De Gaulle 2
Sandweiler
267 504-22

(G-15607)
INVEST POSITIVE LLC
26213 Summerdale Dr (48033-6138)
PHONE..................313 205-9815
Tiauna West,
EMP: 5
SALES (est): 156.9K **Privately Held**
SIC: 2759 Screen printing

(G-15608)
IPP LOGISTIC LLC
29155 Northwestern Hwy (48034-1011)
PHONE..................248 330-5379
William H Winbush,
EMP: 8 **EST:** 2020
SALES (est): 800K **Privately Held**
SIC: 3537 Trucks: freight, baggage, etc.: industrial, except mining

(G-15609)
ITAC SOFTWARE INC
26801 Northwestern Hwy (48033-6251)
PHONE..................248 450-2446
EMP: 33 **EST:** 2005
SALES (est): 1MM
SALES (corp-wide): 3.9B **Privately Held**
WEB: www.itacsoftware.com
SIC: 3559 Special industry machinery
PA: Durr Ag
Carl-Benz-Str. 34
Bietigheim-Bissingen BW 74321
714 278-0

(G-15610)
JAIMES LIQUIDATION INC
19270 W 8 Mile Rd (48075-5722)
PHONE..................248 356-8600
Rudolph Taylor, *President*
Michael Redding, *Data Proc Dir*
Bill Barr, *Admin Sec*
EMP: 28 **EST:** 1979
SALES (est): 753.4K **Privately Held**
SIC: 3441 Joists, open web steel: long-span series

(G-15611)
JANESVILLE LLC (DH)
Also Called: Janesville Acoustics
29200 Northwestern Hwy # 400 (48034-1068)
PHONE..................248 948-1811
Alex Hamilton, *Asst Controller*
Shannon White, *Mng Member*
EMP: 54 **EST:** 2018
SALES (est): 57.9MM
SALES (corp-wide): 316MM **Privately Held**
WEB: www.janesvillesolutions.com
SIC: 3086 Insulation or cushioning material, foamed plastic
HQ: Motus Llc
88 E 48th St
Holland MI 49423
616 422-7557

(G-15612)
JERRYS QUALITY QUICK PRINT
Also Called: American Speedy Printing
28810 Northwestern Hwy (48034-1831)
PHONE..................248 354-1313
Gerald Christensen, *President*
EMP: 7 **EST:** 1981
SQ FT: 2,800
SALES (est): 501K **Privately Held**
WEB: www.americanspeedy.com
SIC: 2752 Commercial printing, offset

(G-15613)
JIT
21145 Virginia St (48076-6003)
PHONE..................248 799-9210
Joseph Nwabueze, *Owner*
EMP: 7 **EST:** 1995
SALES (est): 468.5K **Privately Held**
WEB: www.jitmasters.com
SIC: 2211 Apparel & outerwear fabrics, cotton

(G-15614)
JUST-IN TIME AUTO DTAILING LLC
17356 W 12 Mile Rd Ste 20 (48076-2128)
PHONE..................248 590-0085
Justin Mason, *Mng Member*
EMP: 6
SALES (est): 200K **Privately Held**
SIC: 3589 Car washing machinery

(G-15615)
JUVENEX INC
26222 Telegraph Rd (48033-5318)
PHONE..................248 436-2866
▲ **EMP:** 10
SALES (est): 796.3K **Privately Held**
SIC: 2037 Mfg Frozen Fruits/Vegetables

(G-15616)
KEVIAR CANDLES
16400 N Park Dr Apt 306 (48075-4726)
PHONE..................248 325-4087
Tamika Malloy, *Principal*
EMP: 4 **EST:** 2017
SALES (est): 66.6K **Privately Held**
SIC: 3999 Candles

(G-15617)
KIRK ENTERPRISES INC
20905 Telegraph Rd (48033-6816)
PHONE..................248 357-5070
Fax: 248 357-1430
EMP: 6 **EST:** 1971
SQ FT: 7,500
SALES: 720K **Privately Held**
SIC: 3613 Mfg Electric Control Panels

(G-15618)
KNIGHT TONYA
Also Called: Knights Glass Block Windows
17390 W 8 Mile Rd (48075-4301)
PHONE..................313 255-3434
Tonya Knight, *Owner*
EMP: 6 **EST:** 2004
SQ FT: 2,732
SALES (est): 458.3K **Privately Held**
WEB: www.knightsglassblockwindows.com
SIC: 1793 3231 5231 Glass & glazing work; products of purchased glass; glass

(G-15619)
KRONOS INC
20750 Civic Center Dr 380 (48076-4171)
PHONE..................248 357-5604
EMP: 9 **EST:** 2019
SALES (est): 226.6K **Privately Held**
WEB: www.kronos.com
SIC: 7372 Business oriented computer software

(G-15620)
KRYSAK INDUSTRIES LLC
30515 Fairfax St (48076-1588)
PHONE..................312 848-1952
EMP: 4 **EST:** 2018
SALES (est): 78.5K **Privately Held**
WEB: www.krysakindustries.com
SIC: 3999 Manufacturing industries

(G-15621)
KSR INDUSTRIAL CORPORATION
26261 Evergreen Rd # 415 (48076-4447)
PHONE..................248 213-7208
Geoffrey De Liberato, *Administration*
EMP: 6 **EST:** 2015
SALES (est): 251.2K **Privately Held**
SIC: 3714 Motor vehicle parts & accessories

(G-15622)
KTR DENTAL LAB & PDTS LLC
17040 W 12 Mile Rd # 150 (48076-2131)
PHONE..................248 224-9158
Robert Stern,
Sylvan Stern, *Advisor*
EMP: 10 **EST:** 2009
SQ FT: 2,000
SALES (est): 726.3K **Privately Held**
WEB: www.ktrdental.com
SIC: 3843 8072 Dental equipment & supplies; dental laboratories

(G-15623)
LACHMAN ENTERPRISES INC
Also Called: Lachman & Company
20955 Telegraph Rd (48033-4240)
PHONE..................248 948-9944
Carrie Lachman, *President*
EMP: 6 **EST:** 1893
SQ FT: 6,000
SALES (est): 1MM **Privately Held**
WEB: www.lachmanandco.com
SIC: 5094 5947 5999 7389 Trophies; gift, novelty & souvenir shop; novelties & giftware, including trophies; balloons, novelty & toy

(G-15624)
LAVANWAY SIGN CO INC
22124 Telegraph Rd (48033-4213)
PHONE..................248 356-1600
Lawrence K Lavanway Jr, *President*
Michael Kean, *Project Mgr*
Brett Laslett, *Graphic Designe*
EMP: 8 **EST:** 1974
SQ FT: 11,000
SALES (est): 957.1K **Privately Held**
WEB: www.lavanwaysigns.com
SIC: 3993 Signs, not made in custom sign painting shops

(G-15625)
LEAR CORP EEDS AND INTERIORS (DH)
21557 Telegraph Rd (48033-4248)
PHONE..................248 447-1500
Robert Rossiter, *President*
Sherry Burgess, *Treasurer*
▼ **EMP:** 8 **EST:** 1982
SALES (est): 51.1MM
SALES (corp-wide): 17B **Publicly Held**
WEB: www.lear.com
SIC: 3714 Motor vehicle parts & accessories

(G-15626)
LEAR CORPORATION
21557 Telg Rd Ste 300 (48033)
PHONE..................313 852-7800
Tony Tucker, *Branch Mgr*
EMP: 7
SALES (corp-wide): 17B **Publicly Held**
WEB: www.lear.com
SIC: 3714 Motor vehicle parts & accessories
PA: Lear Corporation
21557 Telegraph Rd
Southfield MI 48033
248 447-1500

(G-15627)
LEAR CORPORATION
21700 Telegraph Rd (48033-4249)
PHONE..................248 447-1500
EMP: 7
SALES (corp-wide): 17B **Publicly Held**
WEB: www.lear.com
SIC: 3714 Motor vehicle parts & accessories
PA: Lear Corporation
21557 Telegraph Rd
Southfield MI 48033
248 447-1500

GEOGRAPHIC SECTION

Southfield - Oakland County (G-15652)

(G-15628)
LEAR CORPORATION (PA)
21557 Telegraph Rd (48033-4248)
PHONE..................................248 447-1500
Gregory C Smith, *Ch of Bd*
Raymond E Scott, *President*
Carl A Esposito, *President*
Frank C Orsini, *President*
Ajmal Ansari, *Principal*
◆ **EMP:** 281 **EST:** 1917
SALES (est): 17B **Publicly Held**
WEB: www.lear.com
SIC: 3714 2531 2396 3643 Motor vehicle electrical equipment; instrument board assemblies, motor vehicle; automotive wiring harness sets; motor vehicle body components & frame; seats, automobile; automotive & apparel trimmings; current-carrying wiring devices

(G-15629)
LEAR EUROPEAN OPERATIONS CORP
21557 Telegraph Rd (48033-4248)
PHONE..................................248 447-1500
Robert E Rossiter, *Ch of Bd*
EMP: 5 **EST:** 2006
SALES (est): 4.4MM
SALES (corp-wide): 17B **Publicly Held**
WEB: www.lear.com
SIC: 2531 3714 Seats, automobile; motor vehicle electrical equipment; instrument board assemblies, motor vehicle; automotive wiring harness sets; motor vehicle body components & frame
PA: Lear Corporation
    21557 Telegraph Rd
    Southfield MI 48033
    248 447-1500

(G-15630)
LEAR GLOBAL TECHNOLOGY CORP UK (HQ)
21557 Telegraph Rd (48033-4248)
PHONE..................................248 447-1500
EMP: 15 **EST:** 2020
SALES (est): 1.1MM
SALES (corp-wide): 17B **Publicly Held**
WEB: www.lear.com
SIC: 3714 Motor vehicle electrical equipment
PA: Lear Corporation
    21557 Telegraph Rd
    Southfield MI 48033
    248 447-1500

(G-15631)
LEAR MEXICAN SEATING CORP (HQ)
21557 Telegraph Rd (48033-4248)
PHONE..................................248 447-1500
Matthew J Simoncini, *CEO*
Jeffrey H Vanneste, *President*
▲ **EMP:** 1 **EST:** 1997
SALES (est): 23.7MM
SALES (corp-wide): 17B **Publicly Held**
WEB: www.lear.com
SIC: 3714 Motor vehicle parts & accessories
PA: Lear Corporation
    21557 Telegraph Rd
    Southfield MI 48033
    248 447-1500

(G-15632)
LEAR OPERATIONS CORPORATION (HQ)
21557 Telegraph Rd (48033-4248)
P.O. Box 5008 (48086-5008)
PHONE..................................248 447-1500
Robert Rossiter, *President*
Sherri Burgess, *Treasurer*
◆ **EMP:** 1 **EST:** 1995
SALES (est): 434.5MM
SALES (corp-wide): 17B **Publicly Held**
WEB: www.lear.com
SIC: 3089 Plastic processing
PA: Lear Corporation
    21557 Telegraph Rd
    Southfield MI 48033
    248 447-1500

(G-15633)
LEAR TRIM LP (PA)
21557 Telegraph Rd (48033-4248)
PHONE..................................248 447-1500
Conrad Mallett, *Director*
EMP: 239 **EST:** 1997
SALES (est): 50.3MM **Privately Held**
WEB: www.lear.com
SIC: 3714 Motor vehicle parts & accessories

(G-15634)
LEJANAE DESIGNS LLC ✿
26747 Stanford Dr E (48033-6128)
PHONE..................................248 621-3677
Leslie Cooper,
EMP: 5 **EST:** 2021
SALES (est): 41K **Privately Held**
SIC: 3944 Craft & hobby kits & sets

(G-15635)
LEXMARK INTERNATIONAL INC
2 Towne Sq Ste 150 (48076-3762)
PHONE..................................248 352-0616
EMP: 14
SALES (corp-wide): 2.5B **Privately Held**
SIC: 3577 Mfg Computer Peripheral Equipment
PA: Lexmark International, Inc.
    740 W New Circle Rd
    Lexington KY 40511
    859 232-2000

(G-15636)
LINDE GAS & EQUIPMENT INC
Also Called: Linde Gas North America
21421 Hilltop St Ste 1 (48033-4009)
PHONE..................................630 857-6460
Kirk Phelps, *Area Mgr*
EMP: 5 **Privately Held**
WEB: www.lindeus.com
SIC: 2813 Oxygen, compressed or liquefied; nitrogen; argon; hydrogen
HQ: Linde Gas & Equipment Inc.
    10 Riverview Dr
    Danbury CT 06810
    203 837-2000

(G-15637)
LITTLE SPOKE BIG WHEEL PUBG
20880 Duns Scotus St (48075-3206)
PHONE..................................313 779-9327
Keith Watkins, *Principal*
EMP: 4 **EST:** 2015
SALES (est): 42.1K **Privately Held**
SIC: 2741 Miscellaneous publishing

(G-15638)
M A S INFORMATION AGE TECH
23132 Lake Ravines Dr (48033-6531)
PHONE..................................248 352-0162
Michael Steele, *President*
EMP: 5 **EST:** 1996
SQ FT: 1,200
SALES (est): 333.9K **Privately Held**
WEB: www.masbnr.com
SIC: 3651 Home entertainment equipment, electronic

(G-15639)
M10 GROUP HOLDING COMPANY (PA)
24050 Northwestern Hwy (48075-2567)
PHONE..................................248 356-4399
Suzanne Schoeneberger, *President*
EMP: 5 **EST:** 2016
SALES (est): 78.5MM **Privately Held**
SIC: 3651 5064 7622 7359 Household audio & video equipment; electrical appliances, television & radio; radio & television repair; equipment rental & leasing; investment holding companies, except banks

(G-15640)
MAGNETI MARELLI TENNESSEE LLC
26555 Northwestern Hwy (48033-2146)
PHONE..................................248 418-3000
EMP: 12 **EST:** 2009
SALES (est): 256.1K **Privately Held**
SIC: 3714 Motor vehicle parts & accessories

(G-15641)
MALACH GROUP PLUTONIUM PAINT
21170 Bridge St (48033-4032)
P.O. Box 760164, Lathrup Village (48076-0164)
PHONE..................................248 827-4844
EMP: 4
SALES (est): 531.3K **Privately Held**
WEB: www.plutoniumpaint.com
SIC: 2851 Paints & allied products

(G-15642)
MARELLI AUTOMOTIVE LTG LLC (DH)
Also Called: Automotive Lighting North Amer
26555 Northwestern Hwy (48033-2146)
PHONE..................................248 418-3000
Sylvain Dubois, *CEO*
John Bono, *Buyer*
Alberto Berrino, *Engineer*
Eduardo Escalera, *Engineer*
Mark Waggoner, *Engineer*
◆ **EMP:** 40 **EST:** 1998
SALES (est): 553.4MM **Publicly Held**
WEB: www.al.world
SIC: 8711 3647 Engineering services; headlights (fixtures), vehicular
HQ: Marelli Europe Spa
    Viale Aldo Borletti 61/63
    Corbetta MI 20011
    029 722-71

(G-15643)
MARELLI HOLDING USA LLC (DH)
Also Called: Magneti Marelli
26555 Northwestern Hwy (48033-2146)
PHONE..................................248 418-3000
E Razelli, *Ch of Bd*
Eugenio Razelli, *Ch of Bd*
James Rosseau, *President*
Gene Spektor, *Vice Pres*
Jose Galetto, *Plant Mgr*
EMP: 31220 **EST:** 2004
SALES (est): 1B **Publicly Held**
WEB: www.marelli.com
SIC: 3714 Motor vehicle parts & accessories
HQ: Marelli Europe Spa
    Viale Aldo Borletti 61/63
    Corbetta MI 20011
    029 722-71

(G-15644)
MARELLI NORTH AMERICA INC (DH)
Also Called: Ckna
26555 Northwestern Hwy (48033-2146)
PHONE..................................931 684-4490
Shingo Yamamoto, *CEO*
Seiichi Kakizawa, *President*
Kiyoto Shinohra, *President*
Eric Huch, *COO*
Bharat Vennapusa, *COO*
◆ **EMP:** 697 **EST:** 1983
SALES (est): 1.4B **Publicly Held**
WEB: www.calsonic.com
SIC: 3585 3714 Air conditioning, motor vehicle; acceleration equipment, motor vehicle

(G-15645)
MARELLI NORTH AMERICA INC
26555 Northwestern Hwy (48033-2146)
PHONE..................................248 403-2033
Dave Keeney, *Branch Mgr*
Romi Shah, *Director*
EMP: 4 **Publicly Held**
WEB: www.calsonic.com
SIC: 3585 8734 8711 5162 Air conditioning, motor vehicle; testing laboratories; engineering services; plastics materials & basic shapes; warm air heating & air conditioning
HQ: Marelli North America, Inc.
    26555 Northwestern Hwy
    Southfield MI 48033
    931 684-4490

(G-15646)
MARELLI TENNESSEE USA LLC
26555 Northwestern Hwy (48033-2146)
PHONE..................................248 418-3000
Mario Corsi, *Branch Mgr*
EMP: 4 **Publicly Held**
SIC: 3714 Shock absorbers, motor vehicle
HQ: Marelli Tennessee Usa Llc
    181 Bennett Dr
    Pulaski TN 38478

(G-15647)
MARSHALL-GRUBER COMPANY LLC (HQ)
Also Called: Gruber Supplies & Accessories
26776 W 12 Mile Rd Ste 20 (48034-7807)
PHONE..................................248 353-4100
◆ **EMP:** 10 **EST:** 2014
SALES (est): 12.8MM
SALES (corp-wide): 20MM **Privately Held**
WEB: www.rjmarshall.com
SIC: 3545 5085 3255 Machine tool attachments & accessories; industrial supplies; industrial tools; clay refractories
PA: The R J Marshall Company
    26776 W 12 Mile Rd # 201
    Southfield MI 48034
    248 353-4100

(G-15648)
MAXITROL COMPANY (PA)
23555 Telegraph Rd (48033-4176)
P.O. Box 2230 (48037-2230)
PHONE..................................248 356-1400
Bonnie Kern-Koskela, *Ch of Bd*
Larry Koskela, *COO*
Rodney Broder, *Vice Pres*
Doug Danziger, *Vice Pres*
Dennis Hartmann, *Vice Pres*
▲ **EMP:** 75 **EST:** 1946
SQ FT: 45,000
SALES (est): 57MM **Privately Held**
WEB: www.mertik.net
SIC: 3625 3823 3494 3612 Relays & industrial controls; temperature instruments: industrial process type; valves & pipe fittings; transformers, except electric; temperature controls, automatic

(G-15649)
MAYNE MCKENNEY
26300 Northwestern Hwy # 300 (48076-3747)
PHONE..................................248 709-5250
Shawn Zhu, *Cust Mgr*
Richard Leonard, *Manager*
Gunho Park, *CIO*
EMP: 6 **EST:** 2018
SALES (est): 1.5MM **Privately Held**
WEB: www.mayne-mckenney.com
SIC: 3714 Motor vehicle parts & accessories

(G-15650)
MC DONALD COMPUTER CORPORATION
21411 Civic Center Dr # 100 (48076-3910)
PHONE..................................248 350-9290
James B Mc Donald, *President*
Neil Stevenson, *Vice Pres*
Mary Hassell, *Office Mgr*
EMP: 20 **EST:** 1976
SQ FT: 5,200
SALES (est): 745.8K **Privately Held**
WEB: www.mcdonaldcomputer.com
SIC: 7374 7372 Data processing service; business oriented computer software

(G-15651)
MCNICHOLS CONVEYOR COMPANY
21411 Civic Center Dr # 204 (48076-3950)
PHONE..................................248 357-6077
Robert Iwrey, *President*
EMP: 10 **EST:** 1926
SALES (est): 990.7K **Privately Held**
WEB: www.mcnicholsconveyor.com
SIC: 3535 Conveyors & conveying equipment

(G-15652)
MEANS INDUSTRIES INC
Also Called: Means Inds - Southfield MI Off
Oakland Cmmons Ii 20750 C (48034)
PHONE..................................989 754-1433
Jeremy Holt, *President*
EMP: 14

SALES (corp-wide): 2.4B Privately Held
WEB: www.meansindustries.com
SIC: 3714 Motor vehicle parts & accessories
HQ: Means Industries, Inc.
3715 E Washington Rd
Saginaw MI 48601
989 754-1433

(G-15653)
MEJENTA SYSTEMS INC
Also Called: Npo Synergy Donor Management
30233 Southfield Rd # 113 (48076-1304)
PHONE..................................248 434-2583
Nirmaia Nallabhantu, President
Sreekrishna Vinjamoori, Vice Pres
Santosh Bojanki, Manager
EMP: 20 EST: 2003
SQ FT: 1,300
SALES (est): 1.2MM Privately Held
WEB: www.mejenta.com
SIC: 7374 7372 7373 7371 Data processing & preparation; educational computer software; application computer software; systems software development services; computer systems analysis & design, custom; computer software development & applications; consulting engineer

(G-15654)
METALDYNE PRFMCE GROUP INC (HQ)
Also Called: Mpg
1 Towne Sq Ste 550 (48076-3710)
PHONE..................................248 727-1800
Kevin Penn, Ch of Bd
Michael K Simonte, President
Douglas Grimm, COO
Russell Bradley, Exec VP
Thomas M Dono Jr, Exec VP
EMP: 708 EST: 2005
SQ FT: 25,000
SALES: 2.7B
SALES (corp-wide): 4.7B Publicly Held
WEB: www.aam.com
SIC: 3714 Motor vehicle transmissions, drive assemblies & parts
PA: American Axle & Manufacturing Holdings, Inc.
1 Dauch Dr
Detroit MI 48211
313 758-2000

(G-15655)
METALDYNE TBLAR COMPONENTS LLC (DH)
1 Towne Sq Ste 550 (48076-3710)
P.O. Box 185, Hamburg (48139-0185)
PHONE..................................248 727-1800
Joseph Nowak, President
Scott Ferriman, Vice Pres
Bob Kirkendall, Vice Pres
Timothy Wadhams, Treasurer
Pat Senak, Controller
EMP: 61 EST: 1945
SQ FT: 60,000
SALES (est): 25.5MM
SALES (corp-wide): 4.7B Publicly Held
WEB: www.flexiblemetal.com
SIC: 3714 3498 3441 Manifolds, motor vehicle; fabricated pipe & fittings; fabricated structural metal
HQ: Metaldyne Powertrain Components, Inc.
1 Dauch Dr
Detroit MI 48211
313 758-2000

(G-15656)
MEXICAN FOOD SPECIALTIES INC
Also Called: Don Marcos Tortillas
21084 Bridge St (48033-4087)
PHONE..................................734 779-2370
Mark A Gutierrez, President
Daniel Gutierrez, Vice Pres
Deya Gutierrez, Treasurer
EMP: 5 EST: 1985
SQ FT: 4,000
SALES (est): 545K Privately Held
WEB: www.don-marcos.com
SIC: 2099 5141 Tortillas, fresh or refrigerated; food brokers

(G-15657)
MICHIGAN METALS AND MFG INC
29100 Northwestern Hwy (48034-1046)
P.O. Box 252684, West Bloomfield (48325-2684)
PHONE..................................248 910-7674
Isaac Lakritz, President
Richard Freedland, Vice Pres
Larry A Berry, VP Finance
EMP: 4 EST: 2007
SALES (est): 524.9K Privately Held
WEB: www.michmm.com
SIC: 3295 Minerals, ground or treated

(G-15658)
MICRO FOCUS SOFTWARE INC
Also Called: Novell
26677 W 12 Mile Rd Ste 1 (48034-1514)
PHONE..................................248 353-8010
Mark Conley, Branch Mgr
Brent Beachem, Software Dev
EMP: 4 Privately Held
WEB: www.microfocus.com
SIC: 7372 Prepackaged software
HQ: Micro Focus Software Inc.
1800 Novell Pl
Provo UT 84606
801 861-7000

(G-15659)
MINERAL COSMETICS INC
Also Called: European Skin Care & Cosmetics
21314 Hilltop St (48033-4063)
PHONE..................................248 542-7733
Robert S Glancz, President
Lucy Selezer, Vice Pres
EMP: 6 EST: 1977
SALES (est): 480.7K Privately Held
SIC: 2844 Cosmetic preparations

(G-15660)
MKP ENTERPRISES INC
Also Called: Alternatives In Advertising
19785 W 12 Mile Rd 338 (48076-2584)
PHONE..................................248 809-2525
Madelyn Phillips, President
Mike Phillips, Vice Pres
EMP: 4 EST: 2006
SALES (est): 365.8K Privately Held
SIC: 7389 7319 2752 Advertising, promotional & trade show services; distribution of advertising material or sample services; commercial printing, offset

(G-15661)
MOBIMOGUL INC
29193 Northwestern Hwy (48034-1011)
PHONE..................................313 575-2795
Marcus Huddleston, CEO
Gary Curry, CFO
EMP: 4 EST: 2008
SQ FT: 1,000
SALES (est): 318.6K Privately Held
SIC: 3663 Radio & TV communications equipment

(G-15662)
MORRIS ASSOCIATES INC
Also Called: Milliken and Company
24007 Telegraph Rd (48033-3031)
PHONE..................................248 355-9055
Zeno R Windley, President
Chris Allen, Regional Mgr
Brad Smith, Vice Pres
Donald Hooper, Sales Dir
Peter Dow, Manager
EMP: 32 EST: 1939
SQ FT: 17,000
SALES (est): 3.6MM Privately Held
WEB: www.morris-coolideas.com
SIC: 3711 5131 Automobile assembly, including specialty automobiles; piece goods & notions

(G-15663)
MY DREAM DRESS BRDAL SALON LLC
19471 W 10 Mile Rd (48075-2461)
PHONE..................................248 327-6049
June Eaton, CEO
EMP: 6 EST: 2012

SALES (est): 919.4K Privately Held
SIC: 5021 8742 2335 Dressers; retail trade consultant; wedding gowns & dresses

(G-15664)
NEMAK INTERNATIONAL INC
2 Towne Sq Ste 300 (48076-3761)
PHONE..................................248 350-3999
Clifford Munson, President
Kurt Krzewinski, Director
Lyle Wolberg, Advisor
EMP: 32 EST: 2000
SALES (est): 17.7MM Privately Held
WEB: www.nemak.com
SIC: 3334 Primary aluminum
HQ: Nemak Mexico, S.A.
Libramiento Arco Vial Km. 3.8
Garcia N.L. 66000

(G-15665)
NEMO CAPITAL PARTNERS LLC
28819 Franklin Rd Ste 130 (48034-1656)
PHONE..................................855 944-2995
Ali Safiedine, CEO
Nick Gerasimidis, COO
Jeff Frederick, Exec VP
John Leardi, Exec VP
Faisal Ghazi, Vice Pres
EMP: 70 EST: 2014
SALES (est): 7.7MM Privately Held
WEB: www.nemohealth.com
SIC: 7372 Operating systems computer software

(G-15666)
NEXT LEVEL MEDIA INC
Also Called: Azon Elite Summaries
15989 Addison St (48075-6902)
PHONE..................................248 762-7043
Kalon Willis, CEO
EMP: 5
SALES (est): 193.9K Privately Held
SIC: 2731 Textbooks: publishing only, not printed on site

(G-15667)
NOVARES US ENG COMPONENTS INC
29200 Northwestern Hwy (48034-1013)
PHONE..................................248 799-8949
Russ Bush, General Mgr
Brad Viles, Production
Nathan Amend, Engineer
Joseph Belmonte, Engineer
Dennis Yakes, Senior Engr
EMP: 5
SALES (corp-wide): 113.4MM Privately Held
SIC: 3089 Injection molded finished plastic products
HQ: Novares Us Engine Components, Inc.
100 Wisconsin St
Walworth WI 53184
262 275-5791

(G-15668)
NV LABS INC
Also Called: Reforma
20777 East St (48033-3603)
PHONE..................................248 358-9022
Vesna Deljosevic, CEO
Suzana Margilaj, Manager
EMP: 52
SQ FT: 20,000
SALES (est): 1MM Privately Held
WEB: www.reformagroup.com
SIC: 2899 Chemical preparations

(G-15669)
ONE STOP EMBROIDERY
29207 Northwestern Hwy (48034-1024)
PHONE..................................248 799-8662
EMP: 5 EST: 2011
SALES (est): 7.7K Privately Held
SIC: 2395 Embroidery & art needlework

(G-15670)
P & O SERVICES INC
Also Called: Novacare Prosthetics Orthotics
24293 Telg Rd Ste 140 (48033)
PHONE..................................248 809-3072
Zia Rahman, President
EMP: 5 EST: 2014
SQ FT: 1,800

SALES (est): 566.9K
SALES (corp-wide): 5B Publicly Held
WEB: www.novacare.com
SIC: 3842 Prosthetic appliances
PA: Select Medical Holdings Corporation
4714 Gettysburg Rd
Mechanicsburg PA 17055
717 972-1100

(G-15671)
P G K ENTERPRISES LLC
23450 Telegraph Rd (48033-4157)
PHONE..................................248 535-4411
Paul Kokx, Administration
EMP: 5 EST: 2012
SALES (est): 365.1K Privately Held
SIC: 2411 Wheelstock, hewn

(G-15672)
PARJANA DISTRIBUTION LLC
21455 Melrose Ave Ste 22 (48075-7980)
PHONE..................................313 915-5418
EMP: 7
SQ FT: 1,200
SALES (est): 1.2MM Privately Held
WEB: www.parjana.com
SIC: 3823 Water quality monitoring & control systems

(G-15673)
PETERSON AMERICAN CORPORATION (DH)
Also Called: Peterson Spring-Tech Pdts Ctr
21200 Telegraph Rd (48033-4243)
PHONE..................................248 799-5400
Mike Putz, President
Travis Bell, General Mgr
Gary Brewer, General Mgr
Craig Gray, General Mgr
Brent Stine, General Mgr
▲ EMP: 50 EST: 1932
SQ FT: 45,000
SALES (est): 235.3MM
SALES (corp-wide): 1.6B Privately Held
WEB: www.pspring.com
SIC: 3495 Wire springs
HQ: Middleground Capital, Llc
201 E Main St Ste 810
Lexington KY 40507
917 698-3754

(G-15674)
PISTON GROUP LLC (PA)
3000 Town Ctr Ste 3250 (48075-1216)
PHONE..................................248 226-3976
Vincent Johnson, CEO
Amit Singhi, COO
Rob Fisher, Vice Pres
EMP: 483 EST: 2017
SALES (est): 2.3B Privately Held
WEB: www.pistongroup.com
SIC: 3714 Motor vehicle parts & accessories

(G-15675)
PLATFORM COMPUTING INC
2000 Town Ctr Ste 1900 (48075-1152)
PHONE..................................248 359-7825
Russ McKee, Branch Mgr
EMP: 4
SALES (corp-wide): 64.8MM Privately Held
SIC: 7372 Prepackaged software
HQ: Platform Computing, Inc.
4400 N 1st St
San Jose CA
408 392-4900

(G-15676)
PLT EXPRESS TRANSPORTATION LLC
17348 W 12 Mile Rd Ste 20 (48076-2120)
PHONE..................................248 809-3241
Ikechukwu Mordi, Mng Member
EMP: 8 EST: 2020
SALES (est): 505.8K Privately Held
SIC: 3799 Transportation equipment

(G-15677)
POLYMER INC (PA)
Also Called: United Paint & Chemical
24671 Telegraph Rd (48033-3035)
PHONE..................................248 353-3035
John G Piceu Jr, CEO
J Geoffrey Piceu, Vice Pres
Michael Gallagher, Purchasing

GEOGRAPHIC SECTION

Southfield - Oakland County (G-15704)

▲ **EMP:** 99 **EST:** 1953
SQ FT: 65,000
SALES (est): 21.1MM **Privately Held**
WEB: www.unitedpaint.com
SIC: 2851 5231 Paints: oil or alkyd vehicle or water thinned; paint

(G-15678)
PPG INDUSTRIES INC
Also Called: PPG 5625
23361 Telegraph Rd (48033-4119)
PHONE..................................248 357-4817
Dan Braurer, *Branch Mgr*
EMP: 4
SALES (corp-wide): 15.1B **Publicly Held**
WEB: www.ppg.com
SIC: 2851 Paints & allied products
PA: Ppg Industries, Inc.
  1 Ppg Pl
  Pittsburgh PA 15272
  412 434-3131

(G-15679)
PPG INDUSTRIES INC
23361 Telegraph Rd (48033-4119)
PHONE..................................734 287-2110
Dan Coski, *Branch Mgr*
EMP: 4
SALES (corp-wide): 15.1B **Publicly Held**
WEB: www.ppg.com
SIC: 2851 Paints & allied products
PA: Ppg Industries, Inc.
  1 Ppg Pl
  Pittsburgh PA 15272
  412 434-3131

(G-15680)
PRESTIGE PET PRODUCTS INC
Also Called: Hacht Sales
30410 Balewood St (48076-1566)
PHONE..................................248 615-1526
James R Hacht, *President*
▲ **EMP:** 5 **EST:** 1995
SALES (est): 508.7K **Privately Held**
WEB: www.prestigeproductseast.com
SIC: 2047 0742 Dog & cat food; veterinary services, specialties

(G-15681)
PRESTOLITE WIRE LLC (DH)
26677 W 12 Mile Rd (48034-1514)
PHONE..................................248 355-4422
Michael Murphy, *VP Bus Dvlpt*
Gregory Ulewicz, *Mng Member*
John Cattell,
Martin Halle,
◆ **EMP:** 25 **EST:** 1895
SALES (est): 108.2MM **Privately Held**
WEB: www.prestolitewire.com
SIC: 3694 Battery cable wiring sets for internal combustion engines

(G-15682)
PRINTING BY MARC
26074 Summerdale Dr (48033-2228)
PHONE..................................248 355-0848
Rose Hechler, *Owner*
Mark Hechler, *Co-Owner*
▲ **EMP:** 4 **EST:** 1991
SALES (est): 212.2K **Privately Held**
WEB: www.tru-visionhomes.com
SIC: 2752 Commercial printing, lithographic

(G-15683)
PRO-TECH GROUP LLC
21555 Melrose Ave Ste 24 (48075-7981)
PHONE..................................888 221-1505
EMP: 14 **EST:** 1999
SALES (est): 498.7K **Privately Held**
SIC: 3799 Transportation equipment

(G-15684)
PROCESS ANALYTICS FACTORY LLC (DH)
Also Called: Pafnow
2000 Town Ctr Ste 1800 (48075-1165)
PHONE..................................929 350-4053
Tobias Rother, *CEO*
Pascal Redaoui, *Exec VP*
EMP: 6 **EST:** 2020
SALES (est): 1.2MM
SALES (corp-wide): 5MM **Privately Held**
WEB: www.pafnow.com
SIC: 7372 Prepackaged software

HQ: Process Analytics Factory GmbH
  Kasinostr. 60
  Darmstadt HE 64293
  615 185-0774

(G-15685)
QP ACQUISITION 2 INC
2000 Town Ctr Ste 2450 (48075-1208)
PHONE..................................248 594-7432
Wallace L Rueckel, *President*
Jason G Runco, *Treasurer*
EMP: 5052 **EST:** 1997
SQ FT: 10,000
SALES (est): 489.9K
SALES (corp-wide): 34.5MM **Privately Held**
SIC: 3714 7532 3465 2711 Sun roofs, motor vehicle; customizing services, non-factory basis; moldings or trim, automobile: stamped metal; newspapers, publishing & printing; motel, franchised; leaf springs: automobile, locomotive, etc.
PA: Questor Partners Fund li, L.P.
  101 Southfield Rd 2
  Birmingham MI 48009
  248 593-1930

(G-15686)
QUANTAM SOLUTIONS LLC
18877 W 10 Mile Rd Ste 10 (48075-2613)
PHONE..................................248 395-2200
Larry Freimark, *President*
EMP: 8 **EST:** 2016
SALES (est): 2.1MM **Privately Held**
WEB: www.iquantam.com
SIC: 3572 Computer storage devices

(G-15687)
R J MARSHALL COMPANY (PA)
26776 W 12 Mile Rd # 201 (48034-7807)
PHONE..................................248 353-4100
Richard Marshall, *CEO*
Guy Borin, *Business Mgr*
Joan E Marshall, *Exec VP*
Daniel Mahlmeister, *Vice Pres*
Tim Price, *Vice Pres*
▲ **EMP:** 19 **EST:** 1979
SQ FT: 6,000
SALES (est): 20MM **Privately Held**
WEB: www.rjmarshall.com
SIC: 3295 5169 Minerals, ground or otherwise treated; chemicals & allied products

(G-15688)
REVSTONE INDUSTRIES LLC
2000 Town Ctr Ste 2100 (48075-1130)
PHONE..................................248 351-8800
S Mitchell, *Office Mgr*
EMP: 4 **Privately Held**
SIC: 2821 Plastics materials & resins
PA: Revstone Industries, Llc
  2008 Cypress St Ste 100
  Paris KY 40361

(G-15689)
RICHARD LARABEE
Also Called: Richard Reproductions
22132 W 9 Mile Rd (48033-6007)
PHONE..................................248 827-7755
Richard Larabee, *Owner*
Marcia Larabee, *Co-Owner*
EMP: 5 **EST:** 1972
SQ FT: 4,000
SALES (est): 417.1K **Privately Held**
WEB: www.richardreproductions.com
SIC: 2752 2791 Commercial printing, offset; typesetting

(G-15690)
ROYAL LUX MAGAZINE
25055 Champlaign Dr (48034-1203)
PHONE..................................248 602-6565
Johnson Shantel, *Principal*
EMP: 4 **EST:** 2015
SALES (est): 59.9K **Privately Held**
SIC: 2711 Newspapers

(G-15691)
SABA SOFTWARE INC
26999 Centrl Pk Blvd # 210 (48076-4174)
PHONE..................................248 228-7300
Sridhar Guduguntla, *Manager*
EMP: 4

SALES (corp-wide): 238.9K **Privately Held**
WEB: www.cornerstoneondemand.com
SIC: 7372 Application computer software
HQ: Saba Software, Inc.
  4120 Dublin Blvd Ste 200
  Dublin CA 94568
  877 722-2101

(G-15692)
SAGE AUTOMOTIVE INTERIORS INC
24007 Telegraph Rd (48033-3031)
PHONE..................................248 355-9055
Steve Morris, *Branch Mgr*
EMP: 6 **EST:** 2013
WEB: www.sageautomotiveinteriors.com
SIC: 2399 Seat covers, automobile
HQ: Sage Automotive Interiors Inc
  3 Research Dr Ste 300
  Greenville SC 29607

(G-15693)
SAMS SUIT FCTRY & ALTERATION
25040 Southfield Rd (48075-1902)
PHONE..................................248 424-8666
Abbas Sarmad, *Managing Prtnr*
EMP: 9 **EST:** 2013
SALES (est): 431.6K **Privately Held**
SIC: 2329 Riding clothes:, men's, youths' & boys'

(G-15694)
SATIN PETALS LLC
15599 Agnew Pl (48075-3103)
PHONE..................................248 905-3866
Tzipora Schwartz, *Administration*
EMP: 4 **EST:** 2019
SALES (est): 49.7K **Privately Held**
SIC: 2221 Satins

(G-15695)
SAVANNA INC (PA)
Also Called: Rmt Woodworth Heat Treating
20941 East St (48033-5934)
PHONE..................................248 353-8180
Terry R Woodworth, *President*
Tom Villerot, *General Mgr*
Rick Woodworth, *COO*
Scott Berry, *Director*
▲ **EMP:** 40 **EST:** 1994
SALES (est): 11.2MM **Privately Held**
SIC: 3398 Metal heat treating

(G-15696)
SELECT STEEL FABRICATORS INC
23281 Telegraph Rd (48033-4127)
PHONE..................................248 945-9582
Philip F Baker, *President*
Melody Baker, *Vice Pres*
EMP: 36 **EST:** 1994
SQ FT: 22,000
SALES (est): 5.3MM **Privately Held**
WEB: www.selectsteelfab.com
SIC: 3541 3545 Machine tools, metal cutting type; machine tool accessories

(G-15697)
SENICA LLC
24293 Telg Rd Ste 218 (48033)
PHONE..................................248 426-2200
Bryan Weinstein, *Administration*
EMP: 4 **EST:** 2016
SALES (est): 100.4K **Privately Held**
SIC: 2844 Toilet preparations

(G-15698)
SHEPHERD JNES PBLCATIONS PRESS
17140 Maryland St (48075-2968)
PHONE..................................313 221-3000
Joyce Jones, *Principal*
EMP: 5 **EST:** 2010
SALES (est): 58.2K **Privately Held**
SIC: 2741 Miscellaneous publishing

(G-15699)
SHIPSTON ALUM TECH INTL INC (DH)
Also Called: Busche Aluminum Technologies
22122 Telegraph Rd (48033-4213)
PHONE..................................317 738-0282
Nick Busche, *CEO*

Joseph Perkins, *President*
Craig Conaty, *President*
Steve Aldridge, *Maint Spvr*
Bruce Weldon, *Engineer*
EMP: 5 **EST:** 2006
SALES (est): 23.4MM
SALES (corp-wide): 332.2MM **Privately Held**
WEB: www.mobexglobal.com
SIC: 3365 Aluminum & aluminum-based alloy castings

(G-15700)
SHIPSTON ALUM TECH INTL LLC (HQ)
Also Called: Mobex Global
22122 Telegraph Rd (48033-4213)
PHONE..................................317 738-0282
Craig Conaty, *CFO*
Erika Bell, *Ch Credit Ofcr*
Joseph Perkins, *Mng Member*
David Ralstin,
EMP: 110 **EST:** 2007
SALES (est): 133.3MM
SALES (corp-wide): 332.2MM **Privately Held**
WEB: www.mobexglobal.com
SIC: 3365 Aluminum & aluminum-based alloy castings
PA: Shipston Group U.S., Inc.
  22122 Telegraph Rd
  Southfield MI 48033
  248 372-9018

(G-15701)
SHIPSTON ALUMINUM TECH IND INC
Also Called: Busche Alum Tchnlgies Franklin
22122 Telegraph Rd (48033-4213)
PHONE..................................317 738-0282
Joseph Perkins, *CEO*
Erica Bell, *General Mgr*
EMP: 65 **EST:** 1992
SALES (est): 15.4MM
SALES (corp-wide): 332.2MM **Privately Held**
WEB: www.mobexglobal.com
SIC: 3365 Aluminum foundries
HQ: Shipston Aluminum Technologies International, Inc.
  22122 Telegraph Rd
  Southfield MI 48033

(G-15702)
SHIPSTON GROUP US INC (PA)
Also Called: Mobex Global
22122 Telegraph Rd (48033-4213)
PHONE..................................248 372-9018
Joseph Perkins, *President*
Paul Kenrick, *COO*
Christopher Lilla, *CFO*
EMP: 24 **EST:** 2014
SALES (est): 332.2MM **Privately Held**
SIC: 2819 3334 3353 5051 Aluminum compounds; primary aluminum; aluminum sheet, plate & foil; aluminum bars, rods, ingots, sheets, pipes, plates, etc.

(G-15703)
SHOP IV SBUSID INV GREDE LLC
20750 Civic Center Dr # 100 (48076-4152)
PHONE..................................248 440-9515
Cary Wood, *President*
EMP: 1 **EST:** 2010
SALES (est): 3.7MM
SALES (corp-wide): 686.1MM **Privately Held**
SIC: 3321 Gray & ductile iron foundries
PA: Asp Grede Acquisitionco Llc
  20750 Civic Center Dr # 100
  Southfield MI 48076
  248 440-9515

(G-15704)
SIMPLY DIVINE BAKING LLC
25162 Coral Gables St (48033-2403)
P.O. Box 225 (48037-0225)
PHONE..................................313 903-2881
Adrienne Smiley, *Principal*
EMP: 4 **EST:** 2008
SALES (est): 240.9K **Privately Held**
SIC: 2051 Bread, cake & related products

Southfield - Oakland County (G-15705)

(G-15705)
SITRONIC NORTH AMERICA CORP
2000 Town Ctr Ste 1800 (48075-1165)
PHONE.................................248 939-5910
EMP: 6 EST: 2019
SALES (est): 140.6K Privately Held
WEB: www.sitronic.us
SIC: 3714 Motor vehicle parts & accessories

(G-15706)
SKOKIE CASTINGS LLC
20750 Civic Center Dr # 100 (48076-4152)
PHONE.................................248 727-1800
EMP: 95 EST: 2010
SALES (est): 4.1MM
SALES (corp-wide): 686.1MM Privately Held
WEB: www.grede.com
SIC: 3714 Motor vehicle parts & accessories
HQ: Grede Ii Llc
    20750 Civic Center Dr # 100
    Southfield MI 48076
    248 440-9500

(G-15707)
SPEYSIDE REAL ESTATE LLC
26555 Northwestern Hwy (48033-2146)
PHONE.................................248 354-7700
Brian J Kesseler, CEO
EMP: 10 EST: 1997
SALES (est): 2.2MM
SALES (corp-wide): 15.3B Publicly Held
WEB: www.tenneco.com
SIC: 3053 Gaskets & sealing devices
PA: Tenneco Inc.
    500 N Field Dr
    Lake Forest IL 60045
    847 482-5000

(G-15708)
STARTECH-SOLUTIONS LLC
26300 Telg Rd Ste 101 (48033)
PHONE.................................248 419-0650
Kevin Williams, Vice Pres
Joe Williams, Vice Pres
Joyce A Williams,
EMP: 6 EST: 2015
SQ FT: 2,000
SALES (est): 556K Privately Held
WEB: www.startechsolutions.net
SIC: 3429 3577 3651 4813 Security cable locking system; data conversion equipment, media-to-media: computer; household audio & video equipment; telephone/video communications; video & audio equipment

(G-15709)
STERLING SECURITY LLC
21700 Northwestern Hwy (48075-4906)
PHONE.................................248 809-9309
Eric Williamson, CEO
EMP: 21 EST: 2010
SALES (est): 2MM Privately Held
WEB: www.sterlingsecurityllc.com
SIC: 7381 7382 Security guard service; building services monitoring controls, automatic; burglar alarm maintenance & monitoring

(G-15710)
STONED LIKE WILLY LLC
26677 W 12 Mile Rd (48034-1514)
PHONE.................................833 378-6633
William Thomas, CEO
EMP: 5 EST: 2017
SALES (est): 57.7K Privately Held
SIC: 3161 Clothing & apparel carrying cases

(G-15711)
SUN COMMUNITIES INC (PA)
27777 Franklin Rd Ste 200 (48034-8205)
PHONE.................................248 208-2500
Gary A Shiffman, Ch of Bd
John B McLaren, President
Caroline Mize, General Mgr
Stacey Ostien, General Mgr
Jeff Wall, General Mgr
EMP: 773 EST: 1975
SALES (est): 1.4B Publicly Held
WEB: www.suncommunities.com
SIC: 6798 2451 Real estate investment trusts; mobile homes

(G-15712)
SUPERIOR INDUSTRIES INTL INC (PA)
26600 Telg Rd Ste 400 (48033)
PHONE.................................248 352-7300
Timothy C McQuay, Ch of Bd
Majdi B Abulaban, President
Michael Dorah, President
Andreas Meyer, President
Martin Rivas, General Mgr
▲ EMP: 250 EST: 1957
SALES (est): 1.1B Publicly Held
WEB: www.supind.com
SIC: 3714 Motor vehicle wheels & parts

(G-15713)
SUPERIOR INDUSTRIES N AMER LLC
26600 Telegraph Rd # 400 (48033-5300)
PHONE.................................248 352-7300
Steven J Borick, Ch of Bd
▲ EMP: 91 EST: 2013
SALES (est): 4.7MM
SALES (corp-wide): 1.1B Publicly Held
WEB: www.supind.com
SIC: 3714 Motor vehicle wheels & parts
HQ: Superior Industries International Holdings, Llc
    7800 Woodley Ave
    Van Nuys CA 91406
    818 781-4973

(G-15714)
SURE-WELD & PLATING RACK CO (PA)
Also Called: Sure-Plating Rack Co
21680 W 8 Mile Rd (48075-5637)
PHONE.................................248 304-9430
EMP: 5 EST: 1947
SQ FT: 25,000
SALES (est): 1.2MM Privately Held
SIC: 3444 3479 Mfg Metal Industrial Material Handling Racks & Stands & Plastic Coating Metal

(G-15715)
SUSE LLC
Also Called: Suse Linux
26677 W 12 Mile Rd Ste 1 (48034-1514)
PHONE.................................248 353-8010
Paul McKeith, Technology
EMP: 13
SALES (corp-wide): 177.9K Privately Held
WEB: www.suse.com
SIC: 7372 Prepackaged software
HQ: Suse Llc
    1800 Novell Pl
    Provo UT 84606
    801 623-1640

(G-15716)
SYNDEVCO INC
24205 Telegraph Rd (48033-7915)
P.O. Box 265 (48037-0265)
PHONE.................................248 356-2839
William M Straith, Ch of Bd
Thomas W Straith, President
Tom Straith, Vice Pres
Ronald M Grobbel, Treasurer
Bryan Murphree, Accounts Mgr
EMP: 16 EST: 1958
SQ FT: 22,000
SALES (est): 3.3MM Privately Held
WEB: www.syndevco.com
SIC: 3612 3643 Transformers, except electric; connectors & terminals for electrical devices

(G-15717)
TAYLOR COMMUNICATIONS INC
24800 Denso Dr Ste 140 (48033-7448)
PHONE.................................248 304-4800
Doug McDougall, Principal
EMP: 10
SALES (corp-wide): 3.6B Privately Held
WEB: www.taylor.com
SIC: 2754 8741 Business forms: gravure printing; management services
HQ: Taylor Communications, Inc.
    1725 Roe Crest Dr
    North Mankato MN 56003
    866 541-0937

(G-15718)
TECNOMA LLC
Also Called: Tecnoma Industries
26400 Lahser Rd Ste 310 (48033-2604)
PHONE.................................248 354-8888
Melody Irish, General Mgr
Leslie Lipski, Finance
Richard W Norton Jr, Mng Member
Heath W Norton,
Richard A Sutton,
▲ EMP: 15 EST: 2003
SQ FT: 3,000
SALES (est): 1.4MM Privately Held
WEB: www.tecnoma.us
SIC: 3089 3713 Automotive parts, plastic; truck bodies & parts

(G-15719)
TEKSID ALUMINUM NORTH AMER INC (HQ)
2 Towne Sq Ste 300 (48076-3761)
PHONE.................................248 304-4001
Massimo Fracchia, President
Keith Farrell, Administration
EMP: 20 EST: 2002
SQ FT: 11,420
SALES (est): 14MM
SALES (corp-wide): 1.7MM Privately Held
SIC: 3714 5013 Motor vehicle parts & accessories; motor vehicle supplies & new parts

(G-15720)
TENNECO INC
26555 Northwestern Hwy (48033-2146)
P.O. Box 77539, Detroit (48277-0539)
PHONE.................................248 354-7700
Rozi Petrovski, Controller
EMP: 7
SALES (corp-wide): 15.3B Publicly Held
WEB: www.tenneco.com
SIC: 3714 Motor vehicle parts & accessories
PA: Tenneco Inc.
    500 N Field Dr
    Lake Forest IL 60045
    847 482-5000

(G-15721)
TEQUIONBROOKINS LLC
21460 Glenmorra St (48076-6013)
PHONE.................................313 290-0303
Tequion Brookins, CEO
EMP: 6 EST: 2018
SALES (est): 20K Privately Held
SIC: 7389 8741 8742 7379 ; administrative management; human resource consulting services; marketing consulting services; ; business oriented computer software

(G-15722)
THYSSENKRUPP MATERIALS NA INC (HQ)
Also Called: Thyssenkrupp Steel Svcs Trdg
22355 W 11 Mile Rd (48033-4735)
P.O. Box 5116 (48086-5116)
PHONE.................................248 233-5600
Christian Dohr, President
Christiane Stuart, President
Armando Figueroa, General Mgr
Joachim Limberg, Chairman
Norbert Goertz, Exec VP
◆ EMP: 200 EST: 1931
SQ FT: 30,000
SALES (est): 1.3B
SALES (corp-wide): 34B Privately Held
WEB: www.thyssenkrupp-materials-na.com
SIC: 3081 3441 Plastic film & sheet; fabricated structural metal
PA: Thyssenkrupp Ag
    Thyssenkrupp Allee 1
    Essen NW 45143
    201 844-0

(G-15723)
TILLMAN MANUFACTURING COM
27067 Lincolnshire Dr (48034-4706)
PHONE.................................248 802-8430
EMP: 9 EST: 2019
SALES (est): 127.4K Privately Held
WEB: www.jtillman.com
SIC: 3999 Manufacturing industries

(G-15724)
TOTAL TOXICOLOGY LABS LLC
24525 Southfield Rd (48075-2740)
PHONE.................................248 352-7171
Martin Bluth, Director
EMP: 8 EST: 2014
SALES (est): 562.6K Privately Held
WEB: www.totaltoxicology.com
SIC: 3821 Time interval measuring equipment, electric (lab type)

(G-15725)
TRACTECH INC (DH)
26201 Northwestern Hwy (48076-3926)
PHONE.................................248 226-6800
Carl Pittner, President
EMP: 45 EST: 1999
SALES (est): 1.6MM Privately Held
WEB: www.eatonelectrical.com
SIC: 3714 3713 3568 Motor vehicle parts & accessories; truck & bus bodies; power transmission equipment
HQ: Eaton Corporation
    1000 Eaton Blvd
    Cleveland OH 44122
    440 523-5000

(G-15726)
TRISTONE FLOWTECH USA INC (DH)
2000 Town Ctr Ste 660 (48075-1199)
PHONE.................................248 560-1724
Jon Hagan, Managing Dir
Kimberly Mohr, Finance
John Edgemon, Exec Dir
EMP: 37 EST: 2013
SQ FT: 215,000
SALES (est): 18.3MM
SALES (corp-wide): 1.7B Privately Held
WEB: www.tristone.com
SIC: 3714 Motor vehicle parts & accessories
HQ: Tristone Flowtech Holding
    Zone Industrielle Nantes Carquefou
    Carquefou 44470
    251 851-818

(G-15727)
TRIUMPH PUBLISHING HOUSE INC
18000 W 9 Mile Rd Ste 520 (48075-4014)
PHONE.................................248 423-1765
EMP: 4 EST: 2019
SALES (est): 99.1K Privately Held
SIC: 2741 Miscellaneous publishing

(G-15728)
TRUARX INC
2000 Town Ctr Ste 2050 (48075-1131)
PHONE.................................248 538-7809
EMP: 15
SQ FT: 2,100
SALES (est): 1MM
SALES (corp-wide): 2.2B Privately Held
SIC: 7372 Prepackaged Software Services
HQ: Anxebusiness, Llc
    2000 Town Ctr Ste 2050
    Southfield MI 48076
    248 263-3400

(G-15729)
TYSON FRESH MEATS INC
I B P Smoked Meat Division
26999 Central Park Blvd (48076-4174)
PHONE.................................248 213-1000
Ron Spangler, Principal
Larry Swafford, Vice Pres
EMP: 6
SALES (corp-wide): 47B Publicly Held
WEB: www.tysonfreshmeats.com
SIC: 2011 Meat packing plants
HQ: Tyson Fresh Meats, Inc.
    800 Stevens Port Dr
    Dakota Dunes SD 57049
    479 290-6397

GEOGRAPHIC SECTION

Southgate - Wayne County (G-15758)

(G-15730)
UC HOLDINGS INC (PA)
300 Galleria Officentre (48034-4700)
PHONE.................................248 728-8642
Andreas Weller, *CEO*
Putian Chen, *Research*
Tasha Collins, *Supervisor*
EMP: 100 **EST:** 2005
SQ FT: 10,000
SALES (est): 1.5B **Privately Held**
WEB: www.aludyne.com
SIC: 6719 3714 Public utility holding companies; motor vehicle engines & parts

(G-15731)
UNIQUE CONNECTION PUBG CO
26282 Summerdale Dr (48033-6136)
PHONE.................................248 304-0030
Mary Johnson Grant, *Principal*
EMP: 4 **EST:** 2018
SALES (est): 37.5K **Privately Held**
SIC: 2741 Miscellaneous publishing

(G-15732)
UNITED PAINT AND CHEMICAL CORP
24671 Telegraph Rd (48033-3035)
PHONE.................................248 353-3035
John G Piceu, *CEO*
EMP: 60 **EST:** 1953
SQ FT: 60,000
SALES (est): 13.6MM
SALES (corp-wide): 21.1MM **Privately Held**
WEB: www.unitedpaint.com
SIC: 2851 Paints: oil or alkyd vehicle or water thinned
PA: Polymer, Inc.
       24671 Telegraph Rd
       Southfield MI 48033
       248 353-3035

(G-15733)
UNIVERSAL WARRANTY CORPOR
300 Galleria Officentre (48034-4700)
PHONE.................................248 263-6900
Rose Soper, *President*
Hj Bolar, *Principal*
EMP: 5 **EST:** 2010
SALES (est): 130.3K **Privately Held**
SIC: 3498 Tube fabricating (contract bending & shaping)

(G-15734)
URBAN SPECIALTY APPAREL INC
29540 Southfield Rd # 102 (48076-2047)
PHONE.................................248 395-9500
Ronald Jones, *President*
EMP: 11 **EST:** 2003
SALES (est): 1.1MM **Privately Held**
SIC: 2834 Pharmaceutical preparations

(G-15735)
US RAC
28995 Telegraph Rd (48034-7509)
PHONE.................................248 505-0413
William McMurray, *Manager*
EMP: 7 **EST:** 2015
SALES (est): 200.1K **Privately Held**
WEB: www.amazingsecurity.life
SIC: 3429 Security cable locking system

(G-15736)
VEONEER INC (PA)
26360 American Dr (48034-6116)
PHONE.................................248 223-0600
Jan Carlson, *Ch of Bd*
Satoru Yamaguchi, *Managing Dir*
Robert Bisciotti, *Exec VP*
Thomas Jonsson, *Exec VP*
Mikael Landberg, *Exec VP*
EMP: 600 **EST:** 2017
SALES (est): 1.3B **Publicly Held**
WEB: www.veoneer.com
SIC: 3694 3714 Automotive electrical equipment; motor vehicle parts & accessories

(G-15737)
VEONEER US INC (HQ)
26360 American Dr (48034-6116)
PHONE.................................248 223-8074
Steve Rode, *CEO*
Eric R Swanson, *President*
Luis Abreu, *Software Engr*
EMP: 312 **EST:** 2017
SALES (est): 267.2MM
SALES (corp-wide): 1.3B **Publicly Held**
WEB: www.veoneer.com
SIC: 3694 3674 Automotive electrical equipment; semiconductors & related devices
PA: Veoneer, Inc.
       26360 American Dr
       Southfield MI 48034
       248 223-0600

(G-15738)
VEONEER US INC
Also Called: Veoneer Southfield
26360 American Dr (48034-6116)
PHONE.................................248 223-0600
Veronica Sheredy, *Buyer*
Amol Shelar, *Associate*
EMP: 496
SALES (corp-wide): 1.3B **Publicly Held**
WEB: www.veoneer.com
SIC: 3694 Automotive electrical equipment
HQ: Veoneer Us, Inc.
       26360 American Dr
       Southfield MI 48034
       248 223-8074

(G-15739)
VIVA BEVERAGES LLC
Also Called: Quick Beverages
27777 Franklin Rd # 1640 (48034-8265)
PHONE.................................248 746-7044
Harry Bigelow, *President*
Robert Nistico, *President*
Gary Shiffman, *Mng Member*
Ron Ferber,
Lon Kufman,
◆ **EMP:** 8 **EST:** 2009
SQ FT: 1,800
SALES (est): 2.8MM **Privately Held**
WEB: www.quickenergy.com
SIC: 5149 2086 Beverages, except coffee & tea; carbonated beverages, nonalcoholic: bottled & canned

(G-15740)
VIVIAN ENTERPRISES LLC
Also Called: Bagel Brothers Cafe
29111 Telegraph Rd (48034-7603)
PHONE.................................248 792-9925
Matthew Shouneyia, *Mng Member*
Johnny Shouneyia,
EMP: 32 **EST:** 2018
SALES (est): 300K **Privately Held**
WEB: www.bagelbrotherscafe.com
SIC: 5812 7372 Cafe; application computer software

(G-15741)
W T BERESFORD CO
26261 Evergreen Rd # 455 (48076-4447)
PHONE.................................248 350-2900
Chris Beresford, *President*
Thomas Beresford, *Vice Pres*
William T Beresford, *Vice Pres*
▲ **EMP:** 11 **EST:** 1975
SALES (est): 1.8MM **Privately Held**
WEB: www.beresfordco.com
SIC: 3089 5045 Identification cards, plastic; computers, peripherals & software

(G-15742)
WALTON WOODWORKING
30680 Pierce St (48076-7616)
PHONE.................................248 730-2017
EMP: 4 **EST:** 2015
SALES (est): 72K **Privately Held**
SIC: 2431 Millwork

(G-15743)
WARREN CHASSIX
300 Galleria Ofcntr Ste 5 (48034-4700)
PHONE.................................248 728-8700
Warren Chassix, *Principal*
Mike Bolles, *Opers Staff*
Robert Schwink, *Engineer*
Jeffrey Vernon, *Controller*
Daphne Haynes, *Supervisor*
EMP: 17 **EST:** 2013
SALES (est): 4.7MM **Privately Held**
WEB: www.aludyne.com
SIC: 3714 Motor vehicle parts & accessories

(G-15744)
X-CEL INDUSTRIES INC
21121 Telegraph Rd (48034-4253)
PHONE.................................248 226-6000
James M Richard Jr, *President*
James Kendall, *General Mgr*
Carl Hawkins, *Plant Mgr*
Ted Hundich, *Human Res Dir*
Raymond Dobring, *Executive*
▲ **EMP:** 110 **EST:** 1994
SQ FT: 110,000
SALES (est): 18.4MM **Privately Held**
WEB: www.xcelpaint.com
SIC: 3479 Coating of metals & formed products

(G-15745)
YOUNG DIVERSIFIED INDUSTRIES
21015 Bridge St (48033-4088)
PHONE.................................248 353-1867
Richard Young, *President*
EMP: 6 **EST:** 1987
SQ FT: 3,500
SALES (est): 717.7K **Privately Held**
WEB: www.ydicorp.com
SIC: 3714 Motor vehicle parts & accessories

(G-15746)
ZIMMERMANN ENGINEERING CO INC
24260 Telegraph Rd (48033-3056)
PHONE.................................248 358-0044
Paul Zimmermann, *President*
Donald Zimmermann, *Treasurer*
EMP: 5 **EST:** 1945
SALES (est): 489.5K **Privately Held**
SIC: 3451 3545 Screw machine products; cutting tools for machine tools

---

Southgate
Wayne County

(G-15747)
ABTECH INSTALLATION & SVC INC
Also Called: Ems Equipment Management Svcs
11900 Reeck Rd Ste 100 (48195-2229)
PHONE.................................800 548-2381
Sorinel Andronic, *President*
Christopher Andronic, *General Mgr*
Tony Andronic, *Vice Pres*
EMP: 28 **EST:** 2004
SQ FT: 18,000
SALES (est): 2.9MM **Privately Held**
SIC: 3825 Semiconductor test equipment; test equipment for electronic & electric measurement; digital test equipment, electronic & electrical circuits

(G-15748)
AZTECNOLOGY LLC
15677 Noecker Way Ste 100 (48195-2272)
PHONE.................................734 857-2045
Ken Jones, *Mng Member*
Pauline Kemke,
EMP: 8 **EST:** 2005
SALES (est): 2MM **Privately Held**
WEB: www.aztecnology.com
SIC: 3679 Electronic circuits

(G-15749)
CHEAP ELECTRIC CONTRACTORS CO
12269 Dix Toledo Rd (48195-1704)
PHONE.................................734 286-9165
EMP: 4 **EST:** 2016
SALES (est): 98K **Privately Held**
SIC: 5082 3699 General construction machinery & equipment; electrical equipment & supplies

(G-15750)
CUNNINGHAM INDUSTRIES LLC
13814 Cameron Ave (48195-3188)
PHONE.................................734 225-1044
Matthew Cunningham, *Principal*
EMP: 4 **EST:** 2017
SALES (est): 103.9K **Privately Held**
SIC: 3999 Manufacturing industries

(G-15751)
KJM SPECIALTY WELDING LLC
15669 Scott St (48195-1321)
PHONE.................................734 626-2442
Kevin Manchizh, *Principal*
EMP: 5 **EST:** 2017
SALES (est): 80K **Privately Held**
SIC: 7692 Welding repair

(G-15752)
L & M HARDWOOD & SKIDS LLC
15361 Goddard Rd (48195-2218)
PHONE.................................734 281-3043
Debra Mosley,
EMP: 4 **EST:** 1973
SQ FT: 5,000
SALES (est): 495.4K **Privately Held**
SIC: 2448 5031 Skids, wood; lumber: rough, dressed & finished

(G-15753)
LANDRA PRSTHTICS ORTHOTICS INC (PA)
14725 Northline Rd (48195-2407)
PHONE.................................734 281-8144
Steve Landra, *CEO*
EMP: 4 **EST:** 2005
SALES (est): 818K **Privately Held**
SIC: 3842 Limbs, artificial; prosthetic appliances

(G-15754)
MICHIGAN VEHICLE SOLUTIONS LLC
16600 Fort St (48195-1440)
PHONE.................................734 720-7649
Richard Oliver, *Principal*
EMP: 8 **EST:** 2013
SALES (est): 129.4K **Privately Held**
WEB: www.mivehiclesolutions.com
SIC: 3465 Body parts, automobile: stamped metal; moldings or trim, automobile: stamped metal

(G-15755)
PEPSICO INC
12862 Reeck Rd (48195-2270)
PHONE.................................734 374-9841
EMP: 10 **EST:** 2017
SALES (est): 646.3K **Privately Held**
WEB: www.pepsicojobs.com
SIC: 2086 Carbonated soft drinks, bottled & canned

(G-15756)
QUALITY METAL DETECTORS
14253 Longtin St (48195-1989)
PHONE.................................734 624-8462
Lisa Gregoria, *Principal*
EMP: 4 **EST:** 2015
SALES (est): 106.9K **Privately Held**
WEB: www.qualitymetaldetectors.net
SIC: 3669 Metal detectors

(G-15757)
STOP & GO NO 10 INC
13785 Allen Rd (48195-3001)
PHONE.................................734 281-7500
Chuck Mayzer, *President*
EMP: 6 **EST:** 2007
SALES (est): 490.6K **Privately Held**
SIC: 3563 Air & gas compressors

(G-15758)
TRADE SPECIFIC SOLUTIONS LLC
13092 Superior St (48195-1204)
PHONE.................................734 752-7124
Greg Boland,
EMP: 4 **EST:** 2013
SALES (est): 20K **Privately Held**
WEB: www.tssllc.net
SIC: 3444 Metal roofing & roof drainage equipment

Spalding
Menominee County

(G-15759)
EARL ST JOHN FOREST PRODUCTS
N16226 Birch St (49886)
P.O. Box 130 (49886-0130)
　PHONE...................................906 497-5667
　Earl St John Jr, *President*
　Edgar A Larche, *Admin Sec*
　EMP: 19 **EST:** 1962
　SQ FT: 10,000
　SALES (est): 1.5MM **Privately Held**
　WEB: www.st-john-forest-products.business.site
　SIC: 2411 Logging

Sparta
Kent County

(G-15760)
BESSEY TOOL & DIE INC
617 10 Mile Rd Nw (49345-9459)
　PHONE...................................616 887-8820
　Steven Bessey, *President*
　Rocky Johnston, *Vice Pres*
　Marlene Bessey, *Treasurer*
　EMP: 18 **EST:** 1988
　SQ FT: 26,000
　SALES (est): 1.9MM **Privately Held**
　SIC: 3544 Special dies & tools

(G-15761)
BUILDERS IRON INC
7770 Venture Ave Nw (49345-8206)
　PHONE...................................616 647-9288
　Tom Hopping, *Owner*
　Tim Hopping, *Vice Pres*
　Kathie Kruizenga, *Vice Pres*
　EMP: 25 **EST:** 1990
　SQ FT: 7,500
　SALES (est): 7.3MM **Privately Held**
　WEB: www.buildersiron.com
　SIC: 3441 Fabricated structural metal

(G-15762)
CASCADE DIE CASTING GROUP INC
Great Lakes Division
9983 Sparta Ave Nw (49345-9786)
　PHONE...................................616 887-1771
　John Koetje, *Principal*
　Art Hamrick, *Regl Sales Mgr*
　Andrew Bodfish, *Manager*
　Jeremy Rochow, *IT/INT Sup*
　EMP: 80
　SALES (corp-wide): 79.1MM **Privately Held**
　WEB: www.cascade-cdc.com
　SIC: 3364 3365 3363 Zinc & zinc-base alloy die-castings; aluminum foundries; aluminum die-castings
　HQ: Cascade Die Casting Group Inc
　　7441 Division Ave S A1
　　Grand Rapids MI 49548
　　616 281-1660

(G-15763)
CELIA CORPORATION (PA)
Also Called: General Formulations
309 S Union St (49345-1529)
P.O. Box 158 (49345-0158)
　PHONE...................................616 887-7387
　Celia Said, *President*
　James Clay, *Vice Pres*
　Jim Pool, *Regl Sales Mgr*
　Don Stevens, *Technical Staff*
　▲ **EMP:** 2 **EST:** 1953
　SQ FT: 200,000
　SALES (est): 54.7MM **Privately Held**
　WEB: www.generalformulations.com
　SIC: 2672 2759 2893 7389 Adhesive backed films, foams & foils; screen printing; printing ink; laminating service

(G-15764)
COACH HOUSE IRON INC
1005 9 Mile Rd Nw Ste 1 (49345-7202)
　PHONE...................................616 785-8967
　Michael Bergstrom, *President*
　Herb Bergstrom, *Vice Pres*
　EMP: 7 **EST:** 1977
　SQ FT: 9,000 **Privately Held**
　SIC: 3312 Blast furnaces & steel mills

(G-15765)
GREAT AMERICAN PUBLISHING CO
75 Applewood Dr Ste A (49345-1741)
P.O. Box 128 (49345-0128)
　PHONE...................................616 887-9008
　Matt Mc Callum, *President*
　Ana Olvera, *Editor*
　Kimberly Baker, *COO*
　Bob Ziltz, *Vice Pres*
　David Fairbourn, *Manager*
　EMP: 36 **EST:** 1962
　SALES (est): 6.2MM **Privately Held**
　WEB: www.greatamericanmediaservices.com
　SIC: 2711 Newspapers, publishing & printing

(G-15766)
HANDY WACKS CORPORATION (PA)
100 E Averill St (49345-1516)
P.O. Box 129 (49345-0129)
　PHONE...................................616 887-8268
　Henry B Fairchild III, *President*
　Michael Moberly, *Site Mgr*
　Marcia Fairchild, *Treasurer*
　Chris Roberts, *Sales Staff*
　Lisa Vanmale, *Manager*
　▲ **EMP:** 40 **EST:** 1935
　SQ FT: 44,000
　SALES (est): 12.8MM **Privately Held**
　WEB: www.handywacks.com
　SIC: 2621 Paper mills

(G-15767)
HANDY WACKS CORPORATION
100 E Averill St (49345-1516)
P.O. Box 129 (49345-0129)
　PHONE...................................616 887-8268
　Paul Steffens, *Production*
　Fran Bryant, *Manager*
　EMP: 8
　SALES (corp-wide): 12.8MM **Privately Held**
　WEB: www.handywacks.com
　SIC: 2631 Coated paperboard
　PA: Handy Wacks Corporation
　　100 E Averill St
　　Sparta MI 49345
　　616 887-8268

(G-15768)
HART ENTERPRISES USA INC
400 Apple Jack Ct (49345-1708)
　PHONE...................................616 887-0400
　Alan Taylor, *President*
　Robert Striebel, *Vice Pres*
　EMP: 78 **EST:** 1976
　SQ FT: 35,000
　SALES (est): 9.4MM **Privately Held**
　WEB: www.hartneedles.com
　SIC: 3841 Surgical & medical instruments

(G-15769)
IMAGES 2 PRINT
486 E Division St (49345-1339)
　PHONE...................................616 383-1121
　EMP: 4 **EST:** 2017
　SALES (est): 101.5K **Privately Held**
　SIC: 2752 Commercial printing, offset

(G-15770)
K & K MFG INC
951 9 Mile Rd Nw (49345-9428)
　PHONE...................................616 784-4286
　Timothy W Kidder, *President*
　Pat Kidder, *Vice Pres*
　Patricia V Kidder, *Vice Pres*
　Patricia Kidder, *Vice Pres*
　Steve Kidder, *Sales Staff*
　▲ **EMP:** 9 **EST:** 1982
　SQ FT: 12,000
　SALES (est): 1.5MM **Privately Held**
　WEB: www.kkmfg.com
　SIC: 5531 5013 3465 Automotive parts; automotive supplies & parts; automotive stampings

(G-15771)
LEGGETT PLATT COMPONENTS INC
Also Called: Moiron Branch 0918
7701 Venture Ave Nw (49345-8369)
　PHONE...................................616 784-7000
　Paul Haverkate, *Manager*
　EMP: 100
　SALES (corp-wide): 4.2B **Publicly Held**
　WEB: www.leggett.com
　SIC: 2515 Mattresses & bedsprings
　HQ: Leggett & Platt Components Company, Inc.
　　115 N Industrial Rd
　　Tupelo MS 38801
　　662 844-4224

(G-15772)
MICHIGAN TOOLING SOLUTIONS LLC
8226 Vinton Ave Nw (49345-9396)
　PHONE...................................616 681-2210
　Joseph Williams, *Principal*
　EMP: 9 **EST:** 2014
　SALES (est): 136.3K **Privately Held**
　WEB: www.michigantoolingsolutions.com
　SIC: 3444 Sheet metalwork

(G-15773)
NORTHERN BLIND CO
1511 Indian Lakes Rd Ne (49345-9590)
　PHONE...................................616 299-9399
　Denis Miller, *Principal*
　EMP: 6 **EST:** 1999
　SALES (est): 227.1K **Privately Held**
　SIC: 2431 Awnings, blinds & shutters, wood

(G-15774)
OLD ORCHARD BRANDS LLC
1991 12 Mile Rd Nw (49345-9757)
P.O. Box 66 (49345-0066)
　PHONE...................................616 887-1745
　Mark Saur, *President*
　Tony Woody, *General Mgr*
　Jeffrey Pochop, *Business Mgr*
　Greg Mangione, *COO*
　Gregory V Mangione, *Vice Pres*
　◆ **EMP:** 95 **EST:** 1994
　SQ FT: 140,000
　SALES (est): 44.5MM
　SALES (corp-wide): 402MM **Privately Held**
　WEB: www.oldorchard.com
　SIC: 2033 2037 Fruit juices: packaged in cans, jars, etc.; frozen fruits & vegetables
　HQ: Lassonde Industries Inc
　　755 Rue Principale
　　Rougemont QC J0L 1
　　450 469-4926

(G-15775)
PRINT METRO INC
98 E Division St (49345-1395)
P.O. Box 268 (49345-0268)
　PHONE...................................616 887-1723
　Tom Kastelz, *Principal*
　EMP: 8 **EST:** 2016
　SALES (est): 598.9K **Privately Held**
　WEB: www.printmetro.net
　SIC: 2752 Commercial printing, offset

(G-15776)
PRO COATINGS INC
233 1/2 Prospect St (49345-1459)
P.O. Box 419 (49345-0419)
　PHONE...................................616 887-8808
　Nathan Ronald Rider, *President*
　EMP: 20 **EST:** 1979
　SQ FT: 10,000
　SALES (est): 2MM **Privately Held**
　SIC: 2851 Paints & paint additives; varnishes

(G-15777)
RIVERIDGE CIDER CO LLC
9000 Fruit Ridge Ave Nw (49345-9724)
　PHONE...................................616 887-6873
　EMP: 7 **EST:** 2017
　SALES (est): 207.4K **Privately Held**
　SIC: 2099 Cider, nonalcoholic

(G-15778)
SPARTA OUTLETS
470 E Division St (49345-1339)
　PHONE...................................616 887-6010
　Ken Miller, *Owner*
　John Foley, *Co-Owner*
　EMP: 4 **EST:** 2005
　SALES (est): 244.8K **Privately Held**
　WEB: www.spartapc.co
　SIC: 3629 Electrical industrial apparatus

(G-15779)
SPARTA WASH & STORAGE LLC
510 S State St (49345-1547)
　PHONE...................................616 887-1034
　Mark Sinkelstein, *CEO*
　Bryan Bailey, *Manager*
　EMP: 6 **EST:** 2018
　SQ FT: 2,170
　SALES (est): 210K **Privately Held**
　WEB: www.aanddministorage.com
　SIC: 3589 4225 Car washing machinery; warehousing, self-storage

(G-15780)
SPARTAN GRAPHICS INC
200 Applewood Dr (49345-1712)
P.O. Box 218 (49345-0218)
　PHONE...................................616 887-1073
　James Clay, *CEO*
　David Clay, *President*
　Krystle King, *Accounts Mgr*
　Adam Baker, *Business Dir*
　EMP: 85 **EST:** 1952
　SQ FT: 50,000
　SALES (est): 18MM **Privately Held**
　WEB: www.spartangraphics.com
　SIC: 2752 2796 2789 2759 Commercial printing, offset; platemaking services; bookbinding & related work; commercial printing

(G-15781)
SPEC TOOL COMPANY (PA)
389 E Div St (49345)
P.O. Box 127 (49345-0127)
　PHONE...................................888 887-1717
　Lee Hiler, *President*
　Rick Diekevers, *Opers Mgr*
　Carol Forward, *Controller*
　Steve Bosch, *Finance Mgr*
　Corey Sikes, *Info Tech Mgr*
　EMP: 92 **EST:** 1970
　SQ FT: 15,000
　SALES (est): 13.8MM **Privately Held**
　WEB: www.spec-tool.com
　SIC: 3599 Machine shop, jobbing & repair

(G-15782)
SPEEDRACK PRODUCTS GROUP LTD (PA)
Also Called: Integrted Systems Group Div of
7903 Venture Ave Nw (49345-9427)
　PHONE...................................616 887-0002
　Ron Ducharme, *CEO*
　Jim Johnson, *President*
　Timothy Bastic, *Vice Pres*
　John Kettman, *Vice Pres*
　Mike Roney, *Vice Pres*
　▼ **EMP:** 35 **EST:** 1989
　SQ FT: 16,820
　SALES (est): 32.8MM **Privately Held**
　WEB: www.speedrack.net
　SIC: 3449 Miscellaneous metalwork

(G-15783)
STORAGE CONTROL SYSTEMS INC (PA)
Also Called: Gas Control Systems
100 Applewood Dr (49345-1711)
P.O. Box 304 (49345-0304)
　PHONE...................................616 887-7994
　Jim Schaefer, *President*
　Andrew Klipa, *Marketing Staff*
　▲ **EMP:** 20 **EST:** 1982
　SQ FT: 34,000
　SALES (est): 8.4MM **Privately Held**
　WEB: www.storagecontrol.com
　SIC: 3829 Measuring & controlling devices

(G-15784)
STRUCTURAL STANDARDS INC
465 Apple Jack Ct (49345-1708)
　PHONE...................................616 813-1798

▲ = Import ▼ = Export
◆ = Import/Export

GEOGRAPHIC SECTION
Spring Lake - Ottawa County (G-15809)

Scott Johnson, *President*
EMP: 25 **EST:** 1986
SQ FT: 4,800
SALES (est): 5MM **Privately Held**
SIC: 3441 Fabricated structural metal

(G-15785)
TESA PLANT SPARTA LLC
324 S Union St (49345-1530)
PHONE..................................616 887-1757
EMP: 7 **EST:** 2017
SALES (est): 1.2MM
SALES (corp-wide): 12B **Privately Held**
WEB: www.testatape.com
SIC: 2672 Tape, pressure sensitive: made from purchased materials
HQ: Tesa Tape, Inc.
 5825 Carnegie Blvd
 Charlotte NC 28209

(G-15786)
TESA TAPE INC
324 S Union St (49345-1530)
PHONE..................................616 887-3107
Deb Szczepanski, *Principal*
Al Tramper, *Opers Mgr*
Michael Kavaky, *Warehouse Mgr*
Kyle Cunningham, *Production*
Ben Walker, *Purchasing*
EMP: 5
SQ FT: 140,000
SALES (corp-wide): 12B **Privately Held**
WEB: www.tesa.com
SIC: 2672 3842 3644 2671 Tape, pressure sensitive: made from purchased materials; surgical appliances & supplies; noncurrent-carrying wiring services; packaging paper & plastics film, coated & laminated
HQ: Tesa Tape, Inc.
 5825 Carnegie Blvd
 Charlotte NC 28209

(G-15787)
TIP TOP DRILLING LLC
8274 Alpine Ave (49345-9413)
PHONE..................................616 291-8006
Aaron Dekubber, *President*
Jessica Dekubber,
EMP: 4 **EST:** 2010
SQ FT: 10,000
SALES (est): 863.6K **Privately Held**
WEB: www.tiptopdrilling.com
SIC: 1381 Directional drilling oil & gas wells

(G-15788)
VEGETABLE GROWERS NEWS
343 S Union St (49345-1531)
P.O. Box 128 (49345-0128)
PHONE..................................616 887-9008
Sally Ostman, *Manager*
EMP: 8 **EST:** 2018
SALES (est): 216.5K **Privately Held**
WEB: www.vegetablegrowersnews.com
SIC: 2711 Newspapers

Spring Arbor
Jackson County

(G-15789)
B & B CUSTOM AND PROD WLDG
10391 Spring Arbor Rd (49283-9621)
PHONE..................................517 524-7121
Bill Burk, *President*
Debbie Burk, *Corp Secy*
EMP: 10 **EST:** 1994
SQ FT: 6,000
SALES (est): 931.6K **Privately Held**
SIC: 1799 3599 Welding on site; machine & other job shop work

(G-15790)
DIVERSIFIED PRECISION PDTS INC
6999 Spring Arbor Rd (49283-9737)
P.O. Box 488 (49283-0488)
PHONE..................................517 750-2310
Stephen J Lazaroff, *President*
Deborah Lazaroff, *Vice Pres*
Phil Vannest, *Mfg Mgr*
Linda Farrow, *Treasurer*

EMP: 35 **EST:** 1969
SQ FT: 18,000
SALES (est): 3.8MM **Privately Held**
WEB: www.diversifiedprecision.com
SIC: 3541 7389 Grinding machines, metalworking; grinding, precision: commercial or industrial

(G-15791)
FABRICATION CONCEPTS LLC
Also Called: Fire Fabrication & Supply
347 E Main St (49283-9617)
P.O. Box 225 (49283-0225)
PHONE..................................517 750-4742
Robert Morse, *General Mgr*
Brian Fletcher, *Controller*
Javier Franco, *Sales Staff*
Yadi Zepeda, *Manager*
Bruce Ulrich, *Executive*
EMP: 14 **EST:** 2000
SQ FT: 30,000
SALES (est): 2.1MM **Privately Held**
WEB: www.firefabsupply.com
SIC: 3569 Sprinkler systems, fire: automatic

(G-15792)
HATCH STAMPING CO
190 W Main St (49283-9669)
PHONE..................................734 475-6507
EMP: 7 **EST:** 2018
SALES (est): 644.6K **Privately Held**
SIC: 3465 Automotive stampings

(G-15793)
LAB TOOL AND ENGINEERING CORP
7755 King Rd (49283-9777)
P.O. Box 400 (49283-0400)
PHONE..................................517 750-4131
Randall Ball, *CEO*
Joan Croad, *Vice Pres*
Phyllis Ball, *Admin Sec*
EMP: 19 **EST:** 1968
SQ FT: 20,000
SALES (est): 793.6K **Privately Held**
WEB: www.lab-tool.com
SIC: 3544 3549 3714 3545 Special dies & tools; assembly machines, including robotic; motor vehicle parts & accessories; machine tool accessories; metal stampings

(G-15794)
LOCAL LOGIC MEDIA
123 Marietta Rd (49283-9679)
PHONE..................................517 914-2486
Kenneth Seneff, *Principal*
EMP: 4 **EST:** 2016
SALES (est): 41.3K **Privately Held**
SIC: 2741 Miscellaneous publishing

(G-15795)
LOMAR MACHINE & TOOL CO
7755 King Rd (49283-9777)
PHONE..................................517 750-4089
EMP: 21
SALES (corp-wide): 24.3MM **Privately Held**
WEB: www.lomar.com
SIC: 3599 Machine shop, jobbing & repair
PA: Lomar Machine & Tool Co.
 135 Main St
 Horton MI 49246
 517 563-8136

(G-15796)
MICRO FORM INC
180 Teft Rd (49283-9688)
P.O. Box 130 (49283-0130)
PHONE..................................517 750-3660
David Kane, *President*
Suzanne Kane, *Vice Pres*
EMP: 4 **EST:** 1970
SQ FT: 7,200
SALES (est): 405.1K **Privately Held**
WEB: www.microforminc.com
SIC: 3545 Precision tools, machinists'; cutting tools for machine tools; gauges (machine tool accessories)

(G-15797)
R J DESIGNERS INC
Also Called: Fritz Advertising Company
8032 Spring Arbor Rd (49283-9764)
P.O. Box 397 (49283-0397)
PHONE..................................517 750-1990
Rhonda Pickrell, *President*
Leslie Johnson, *Corp Comm Staff*
EMP: 8 **EST:** 1949
SQ FT: 4,000
SALES (est): 650K **Privately Held**
WEB: www.fritzsigns.com
SIC: 3993 5039 7312 Electric signs; architectural metalwork; billboard advertising

(G-15798)
WARDCRAFT INDUSTRIES LLC
1 Wardcraft Dr (49283-9757)
PHONE..................................517 750-9100
James Snyder, *President*
Brian Sifers, *Prdtn Mgr*
Aquanita Johnson, *Controller*
EMP: 29 **EST:** 2019
SALES (est): 3.5MM **Privately Held**
WEB: www.wardcraftconveyor.com
SIC: 3544 3535 Special dies, tools, jigs & fixtures; unit handling conveying systems

Spring Lake
Ottawa County

(G-15799)
A & A MANUFACTURING CO
19033 174th Ave (49456-9708)
PHONE..................................616 846-1730
Jim Fairbanks, *CEO*
Alex C Marciniak, *Partner*
Lawrence Marciniak, *Partner*
Gina Fairbanks, *Supervisor*
EMP: 5 **EST:** 1967
SQ FT: 4,400
SALES (est): 723.7K **Privately Held**
WEB: www.aa-mfg.com
SIC: 3711 3469 3544 Chassis, motor vehicle; metal stampings; special dies, tools, jigs & fixtures

(G-15800)
A LASTING IMPRESSION INC
17796 North Shore Dr (49456-9102)
PHONE..................................616 847-2380
David Hegedus, *President*
David J Hegedus, *President*
Gilbert Hegedus, *Vice Pres*
Marilyn Hegedus, *Treasurer*
EMP: 5 **EST:** 1989
SALES (est): 260K **Privately Held**
WEB: www.aliwoodworking.com
SIC: 2541 2511 Cabinets, except refrigerated: show, display, etc.: wood; wood household furniture

(G-15801)
ACTIVE MANUFACTURING CORP
17150 Hickory St (49456-9712)
PHONE..................................616 842-0800
Jeff Braak, *President*
Kurt Krizan, *Purchasing*
Dustin Shrum, *Purchasing*
Pat Fitzgerald, *QC Mgr*
Jeff Berry, *Treasurer*
▲ **EMP:** 30 **EST:** 1986
SQ FT: 44,000
SALES (est): 4.8MM **Privately Held**
WEB: www.activemfg.net
SIC: 3599 Machine shop, jobbing & repair

(G-15802)
ALMOND PRODUCTS INC
17150 148th Ave (49456-9514)
PHONE..................................616 844-1813
John De Maria, *Ch of Bd*
John Somers, *General Mgr*
Joy Ponce, *Vice Pres*
Matt Moore, *Mfg Mgr*
Jason Ponce, *Mfg Staff*
EMP: 85 **EST:** 1981
SQ FT: 33,000

SALES (est): 17MM **Privately Held**
WEB: www.almondproducts.com
SIC: 3479 3471 Painting of metal products; anodizing (plating) of metals or formed products

(G-15803)
AMERICAN FABRICATED PDTS INC
16910 148th Ave (49456-9570)
PHONE..................................616 607-8785
Andy Bush, *President*
Kevin Gagnon, *General Mgr*
EMP: 29 **EST:** 2008
SALES (est): 5.1MM **Privately Held**
WEB: www.american-fab.com
SIC: 3444 3469 3537 3711 Sheet metalwork; metal stampings; containers (metal), air cargo; pallets, metal; military motor vehicle assembly

(G-15804)
AVPI LIMITED
Also Called: Van Pelt Industries
612 W Savidge St (49456-1674)
P.O. Box 541, Grand Haven (49417-0541)
PHONE..................................616 842-1200
Lorraine Van Pelt, *President*
Steven A Van Pelt, *President*
Jayne C Flaska, *Corp Secy*
EMP: 5 **EST:** 1951
SQ FT: 21,000
SALES (est): 300K **Privately Held**
WEB: www.vanpeltindustries.com
SIC: 3498 Tube fabricating (contract bending & shaping)

(G-15805)
BIO CMMUNICATION SOLUTIONS LLC
Also Called: Biocomm.solutions
15526 Linn Ct (49456-1547)
PHONE..................................616 502-0238
Ross E Pope,
EMP: 5 **EST:** 2017
SALES (est): 94.6K **Privately Held**
SIC: 3842 Radiation shielding aprons, gloves, sheeting, etc.

(G-15806)
BIOCOMSOLUTIONS LLC
Also Called: Cell Safe
15526 Linn Ct (49456-1547)
PHONE..................................616 502-0238
Ross E Pope,
EMP: 6 **EST:** 2017
SALES (est): 95.3K **Privately Held**
SIC: 3842 Radiation shielding aprons, gloves, sheeting, etc.

(G-15807)
BT ENGINEERING LLC
223 River St (49456-2050)
PHONE..................................734 417-2218
Stephen Manuel, *Opers Staff*
Blake Little, *Engineer*
Jessica Boria,
Joshua Matthews, *Technician*
Karl Brakora,
EMP: 4 **EST:** 2011 **Privately Held**
WEB: www.btengin.com
SIC: 3699 Electrical equipment & supplies

(G-15808)
CONCEPT METAL PRODUCTS INC (PA)
Also Called: Concept Metals Group
16928 148th Ave (49456-9570)
PHONE..................................231 799-3202
John Walton, *CEO*
Paul Horstman, *President*
Graham Howe, *President*
Scott Wemple, *Opers Staff*
Brian Campbell, *Engineer*
EMP: 70 **EST:** 1983
SALES (est): 18.3MM **Privately Held**
WEB: www.conceptmetalsgroup.com
SIC: 3441 Fabricated structural metal

(G-15809)
CRAFT STEEL PRODUCTS INC
16885 148th Ave (49456-8861)
PHONE..................................616 935-7575
Chris Kieffer, *Principal*
EMP: 8 **EST:** 1980

Spring Lake - Ottawa County (G-15810)

SQ FT: 17,500
SALES (est): 590.3K **Privately Held**
SIC: 3568 3469 Bearings, plain; metal stampings

(G-15810)
CUSTOM CRAFTSMEN WOODWORKING
17915 Mohawk Dr (49456-9121)
PHONE..................616 638-4768
EMP: 4 **EST:** 2009
SALES (est): 119K **Privately Held**
SIC: 2431 Millwork

(G-15811)
DYNAMIC WOOD SOLUTIONS
18518 Trimble Ct (49456-9725)
PHONE..................616 935-7727
Gary Moody, *President*
Ryan Gardner, *Partner*
Chris Abbott, *Opers Mgr*
EMP: 8 **EST:** 2010
SALES (est): 751.8K **Privately Held**
WEB: www.dynamicwoodsolutions.net
SIC: 2499 Decorative wood & woodwork

(G-15812)
EAGLE QUEST INTERNATIONAL LTD
Also Called: Eqi, Ltd.
17863 170th Ave Ste 201 (49456-1243)
PHONE..................616 850-2630
Blake Phillips, *President*
Ben Jiang, *Vice Pres*
David Redeker, *Vice Pres*
Jim Brown, *QC Mgr*
Mike Rederstorf, *Engineer*
◆ **EMP:** 11 **EST:** 2004
SQ FT: 1,800
SALES (est): 2.6MM **Privately Held**
WEB: www.eqiltd.com
SIC: 3321 5084 Gray & ductile iron foundries; industrial machine parts

(G-15813)
FALCON CORPORATION
Also Called: Falcon Tool & Die
14510 Cleveland St (49456-9151)
PHONE..................616 842-7071
Gerald J Johnston, *President*
David L Peppin, *President*
Pam Burdick, *Purchasing*
Jeremy Johnston, *Manager*
EMP: 57 **EST:** 1964
SQ FT: 11,000
SALES (est): 7.4MM **Privately Held**
WEB: www.falconcorporation.net
SIC: 3544 Special dies & tools; jigs & fixtures

(G-15814)
FOCAL POINT METAL FAB LLC
17354 Teunis Dr (49456-9727)
PHONE..................616 844-7670
Matt Campau, *Mng Member*
EMP: 12 **EST:** 2006
SALES (est): 1.6MM **Privately Held**
SIC: 3441 Fabricated structural metal

(G-15815)
G A RICHARDS COMPANY
701 E Savidge St (49456-2430)
PHONE..................616 850-8528
Derek Huizinga, *Assistant VP*
Todd Bathrick, *Prdtn Mgr*
Tim Hartzell, *Prdtn Mgr*
Mary Bruce, *Production*
Tim May, *Project Engr*
EMP: 4
SALES (corp-wide): 17.1MM **Privately Held**
WEB: www.garichards.com
SIC: 3444 Sheet metalwork
PA: G. A. Richards Company
1060 Ken O Sha Ind Pk Dr
Grand Rapids MI 49508
616 243-2800

(G-15816)
GAZELLE PROTOTYPE LLC
18683 Trimble Ct (49456-8822)
PHONE..................616 844-1820
Willard Van Harn,
Roma Van Harn,
EMP: 5 **EST:** 1995
SALES (est): 409.6K **Privately Held**
WEB: www.gazelleprototype.com
SIC: 3082 Unsupported plastics profile shapes

(G-15817)
GIVING PRESS
324 E Exchange St (49456-2023)
PHONE..................702 302-2039
Benjamin Zimmerman, *Agent*
EMP: 4 **EST:** 2018
SALES (est): 80.9K **Privately Held**
SIC: 2741 Miscellaneous publishing

(G-15818)
GRAND RIVER POLISHING CO CORP
19191 174th Ave (49456-9700)
PHONE..................616 846-1420
Larry R Scott, *President*
EMP: 23 **EST:** 1985
SQ FT: 7,500
SALES (est): 5.8MM
SALES (corp-wide): 4.2B **Publicly Held**
WEB: www.lpworkfurniture.com
SIC: 3471 Polishing, metals or formed products
PA: Leggett & Platt, Incorporated
1 Leggett Rd
Carthage MO 64836
417 358-8131

(G-15819)
GREAT LAKES CORDAGE INC
Also Called: Great Lakes American
17045 148th Ave (49456-9580)
PHONE..................616 842-4455
Jeffrey S Bovid, *President*
▲ **EMP:** 14 **EST:** 1993
SALES (est): 2.1MM **Privately Held**
WEB: www.greatlakescordage.com
SIC: 2298 Cordage & twine

(G-15820)
GREAT LAKES TOLL SERVICES
17354 Teunis Dr Ste D (49456-9727)
PHONE..................616 847-1868
John Memmott, *President*
▲ **EMP:** 4 **EST:** 1997
SQ FT: 8,600
SALES (est): 566.4K **Privately Held**
WEB: www.greatlakestoll.com
SIC: 2893 Printing ink

(G-15821)
HART CONCRETE LLC
540 Maple St (49456-9070)
PHONE..................231 873-2183
Steven Freed,
EMP: 8
SQ FT: 3,000
SALES (est): 1.2MM **Privately Held**
WEB: www.highgradematerials.com
SIC: 3273 Ready-mixed concrete

(G-15822)
HIGH GRADE CONCRETE PDTS CO
540 Maple St (49456-9070)
PHONE..................616 842-8630
Thomas J Sturrus, *President*
EMP: 10 **EST:** 2017
SALES (est): 386.1K **Privately Held**
WEB: www.highgradematerials.com
SIC: 3273 Ready-mixed concrete

(G-15823)
HOLIDAY RMBLER RECRTL VHCL CLB
18134 N Fruitport Rd (49456-1572)
PHONE..................616 847-0582
H McCann, *Principal*
EMP: 4 **EST:** 2019
SALES (est): 79.6K **Privately Held**
SIC: 3799 Recreational vehicles

(G-15824)
INDUSTRIAL MTAL IDNTFCTION INC
Also Called: I M I
17796 North Shore Dr (49456-9102)
PHONE..................616 847-0060
David Engel, *President*
EMP: 5 **EST:** 1983 **Privately Held**
WEB: www.imisignshop.com
SIC: 3999 2759 Identification tags, except paper; screen printing

(G-15825)
INTEGRATED METAL TECH INC
17155 Van Wagoner Rd (49456-9793)
P.O. Box 302, Zeeland (49464-0302)
PHONE..................616 844-3032
Phil Pool, *President*
Raymond Muscat, *Vice Pres*
EMP: 104 **EST:** 1959
SQ FT: 220,000
SALES (est): 6.7MM
SALES (corp-wide): 2.4B **Publicly Held**
WEB: www.hermanmiller.com
SIC: 3444 2522 Sheet metalwork; filing boxes, cabinets & cases: except wood
PA: Millerknoll, Inc.
855 E Main Ave
Zeeland MI 49464
616 654-3000

(G-15826)
INTEGRICOAT INC
16928 148th Ave (49456-9570)
PHONE..................616 935-7878
Graham Howe, *President*
Phil Spahr, *Business Mgr*
Will Crane, *Controller*
EMP: 20 **EST:** 2000
SQ FT: 22,000
SALES (est): 2.2MM **Privately Held**
WEB: www.integricoat.com
SIC: 3479 Coating of metals & formed products

(G-15827)
INTERIOR CONCEPTS CORPORATION
18525 Trimble Ct (49456-9794)
PHONE..................616 842-5550
Donald Ott, *Ch of Bd*
Russell Nagel, *COO*
Norbert Borzak, *Vice Pres*
Susan Bush, *Vice Pres*
Jan M Doughty, *Vice Pres*
▼ **EMP:** 43 **EST:** 1992
SQ FT: 72,000
SALES (est): 13MM **Privately Held**
WEB: www.interiorconcepts.com
SIC: 2522 2521 Office furniture, except wood; wood office furniture

(G-15828)
JSJ CORPORATION
Also Called: Counter Point Furniture Pdts
17237 Van Wagoner Rd (49456-9702)
PHONE..................616 847-7000
EMP: 159
SALES (corp-wide): 596.1MM **Privately Held**
SIC: 2521 Mfg Wood Office Furniture
PA: Jsj Corporation
700 Robbins Rd
Grand Haven MI 49417
616 842-6350

(G-15829)
LAKESHORE PUBLISHING
109 S Buchanan St (49456-2011)
PHONE..................616 846-0620
EMP: 5 **EST:** 2017
SALES (est): 60.4K **Privately Held**
WEB: www.lakeshorepublishing.com
SIC: 2741 Miscellaneous publishing

(G-15830)
LUDVANWALL INC
Also Called: Vander Wall Bros
19156 174th Ave (49456-9722)
P.O. Box 473 (49456-0473)
PHONE..................616 842-4500
Dale Vanderwall, *President*
Dale Vander Wall, *President*
Paul Vander Wall, *Vice Pres*
EMP: 20 **EST:** 1946
SQ FT: 20,000
SALES (est): 2.4MM **Privately Held**
WEB: www.vanderwallbros.com
SIC: 3271 5211 Blocks, concrete or cinder: standard; brick

(G-15831)
LUMENFLOW CORP
15346 Leonard Rd (49456-9100)
P.O. Box 216, Caledonia (49316-0216)
PHONE..................269 795-9007
Paul Bourget, *President*
Brian Zatzke, *Corp Secy*
Harold Brunt, *Vice Pres*
Brian Post, *Vice Pres*
EMP: 6 **EST:** 2000
SALES (est): 520.4K **Privately Held**
WEB: www.lumenflow.com
SIC: 3827 Optical instruments & lenses

(G-15832)
MARQUIS INDUSTRIES INC
Also Called: Michigan Brass Division
17310 Teunis Dr (49456-9727)
PHONE..................616 842-2810
Douglas L Pimm, *President*
Jake Pimm, *Opers Staff*
Carla Hower, *VP Finance*
Jeremy Hower, *Manager*
Kari Vannatter, *Master*
▲ **EMP:** 32
SQ FT: 9,000
SALES (est): 7.4MM **Privately Held**
SIC: 3432 5074 Plumbers' brass goods: drain cocks, faucets, spigots, etc.; plumbing & hydronic heating supplies

(G-15833)
MEDALLION INSTRMNTTION SYSTEMS
17150 Hickory St (49456-9712)
PHONE..................616 847-3700
Nick Hoiles, *Managing Dir*
Martin Payne, *Principal*
Joseph Celestin, *Opers Staff*
Sandra Pope, *Purch Agent*
Mike Debat, *Engineer*
▲ **EMP:** 135 **EST:** 2003
SQ FT: 80,000
SALES (est): 49.1MM **Privately Held**
WEB: www.medallionis.com
SIC: 3714 3824 Motor vehicle parts & accessories; fluid meters & counting devices

(G-15834)
META TOOL TECHNOLOGIES LLC ✪
Also Called: Manufacturing
17024 Taft Rd (49456-9705)
PHONE..................616 295-2115
Peter Klahorst, *Principal*
EMP: 10 **EST:** 2021
SALES (est): 550.9K **Privately Held**
SIC: 3544 Special dies, tools, jigs & fixtures

(G-15835)
MICHIGAN SHIPPERS SUPPLY INC (PA)
17369 Taft Rd (49456-9711)
P.O. Box 315, Ferrysburg (49409-0315)
PHONE..................616 935-6680
Stephen D Wooldridge, *President*
EMP: 12 **EST:** 1959
SALES (est): 2MM **Privately Held**
WEB: www.michiganshippers.com
SIC: 5084 2672 3953 Industrial machinery & equipment; adhesive papers, labels or tapes: from purchased material; marking devices

(G-15836)
MLC MANUFACTURING
18784 174th Ave (49456-9760)
PHONE..................616 846-6990
EMP: 20 **EST:** 2014
SALES (est): 1MM **Privately Held**
WEB: www.mlcmfg.com
SIC: 3999 Manufacturing industries

(G-15837)
MLP MFG INC
18630 Trimble Ct (49456-8822)
P.O. Box 231 (49456-0231)
PHONE..................616 842-8767
Michael L Palkowski, *CEO*
Kirk Palkowski, *President*
EMP: 16 **EST:** 1987
SQ FT: 31,000

▲ = Import ▼ = Export
◆ = Import/Export

GEOGRAPHIC SECTION
Springfield - Calhoun County (G-15865)

SALES (est): 1.2MM **Privately Held**
WEB: www.mlpmfg.com
SIC: 3444 Sheet metal specialties, not stamped

(G-15838)
MULTI-LAB LLC
Also Called: Keur Industries Acquisition Co
18784 174th Ave (49456-9760)
PHONE...................................616 846-6990
Mike Keur, *Vice Pres*
Mark Deal, *Mng Member*
EMP: 18 EST: 1974
SQ FT: 20,000
SALES (est): 3.2MM **Privately Held**
WEB: www.multilab.net
SIC: 3821 Autoclaves, laboratory

(G-15839)
NEW RULES MARKETING INC
Also Called: Duratran Company, The
540 Oak St (49456-9157)
PHONE...................................800 962-3119
Casey Ford, *President*
Nick Ford, *Principal*
Jennifer Krampe, *Principal*
Lacey Riggs, *Principal*
Amy Vitto, *Business Mgr*
EMP: 25 EST: 2000
SALES (est): 2.5MM **Privately Held**
WEB: www.40visuals.com
SIC: 8742 3993 Marketing consulting services; signs & advertising specialties

(G-15840)
NORTH SHORE MACHINE WORKS INC
595 W 2nd (49456-8836)
PHONE...................................616 842-8360
Michael Olthof, *President*
Donald Olthof, *President*
Roger Olthof, *Vice Pres*
Annel Olthof, *Executive*
EMP: 22 EST: 1945
SALES (est): 1.5MM **Privately Held**
SIC: 3451 3599 Screw machine products; machine shop, jobbing & repair

(G-15841)
OLECO INC (PA)
Also Called: Global Technologies
18683 Trimble Ct (49456-8822)
PHONE...................................616 842-6790
Jeff Olds, *CEO*
Stanley Richentstien Jr, *Vice Pres*
Kevin Wood, *Engineer*
EMP: 47 EST: 1968
SQ FT: 20,000
SALES (est): 12MM **Privately Held**
WEB: www.globaltec.com
SIC: 3699 Electrical equipment & supplies

(G-15842)
PHOENIX FIXTURES LLC (AZ)
16910 148th Ave (49456-9570)
PHONE...................................616 847-0895
EMP: 2
SALES (est): 1.2MM **Privately Held**
SIC: 2542 Mfg Office & Store Fixtures

(G-15843)
PLIANT PLASTICS CORP (PA)
17000 Taft Rd (49456-9705)
PHONE...................................616 844-0300
Jeff McMartin, *President*
Owen Moynihan, *Principal*
Dawn Noyes, *Buyer*
Brooke Vanderwel, *Engineer*
Michael Dowker, *Human Res Mgr*
▲ EMP: 53 EST: 1967
SALES (est): 24MM **Privately Held**
WEB: www.pliantplastics.com
SIC: 3089 Injection molding of plastics

(G-15844)
PLIANT PLASTICS CORP
17024 Taft Rd (49456-9705)
PHONE...................................616 844-3215
Daniel Bloom, *Branch Mgr*
EMP: 10
SALES (corp-wide): 24MM **Privately Held**
WEB: www.pliantplastics.com
SIC: 3089 Injection molding of plastics

PA: Pliant Plastics Corp.
17000 Taft Rd
Spring Lake MI 49456
616 844-0300

(G-15845)
PROCORE DRONES LLC
19091 W Spring Lake Rd (49456-1047)
PHONE...................................850 774-0604
Michael Fett, *Principal*
EMP: 5 EST: 2017
SALES (est): 98.3K **Privately Held**
WEB: www.procoredrones.com
SIC: 3721 Motorized aircraft

(G-15846)
REYERS COMPANY INC
Also Called: Reyers Advertising
700 E Savidge St (49456-1959)
PHONE...................................616 414-5530
Harlan Reyers, *President*
Sharon Reyers, *Corp Secy*
EMP: 10 EST: 1956
SQ FT: 12,000
SALES (est): 721.7K **Privately Held**
SIC: 2771 2789 5021 5044 Greeting cards; bookbinding & related work; office & public building furniture; office equipment; shopping center, property operation only

(G-15847)
ROOMS OF GRAND RAPIDS LLC
17971 N Fruitport Rd (49456-1569)
PHONE...................................616 260-1452
Katherine M Cather, *Mng Member*
EMP: 9 EST: 2013
SALES (est): 79.9K **Privately Held**
SIC: 7021 2211 2511 Furnished room rental; furniture denim; wood bedroom furniture

(G-15848)
SABO CREATIVE
16402 Lannin Ln (49456-2139)
PHONE...................................616 842-7226
John Sabo, *Principal*
EMP: 4 EST: 2014
SALES (est): 96.9K **Privately Held**
SIC: 2842 Specialty cleaning, polishes & sanitation goods

(G-15849)
SAC PLASTICS INC
17259 Hickory St (49456-9703)
PHONE...................................616 846-0820
Richard Lattin, *President*
Mike Lawton, *General Mgr*
Beverly Lattin, *Vice Pres*
EMP: 9 EST: 1985
SQ FT: 25,400
SALES (est): 1.6MM **Privately Held**
WEB: www.sacplastics.com
SIC: 3089 Injection molding of plastics

(G-15850)
SCHAP SPECIALTY MACHINE INC (PA)
17309 Taft Rd Ste A (49456-8809)
PHONE...................................616 846-6530
William Schap, *President*
John Deppe, *Project Mgr*
Mark Yoder, *Opers Mgr*
Brian Corcoran, *Mfg Staff*
Wanda Martin, *Office Mgr*
EMP: 19 EST: 1991
SQ FT: 16,000
SALES (est): 6.1MM **Privately Held**
WEB: www.schapmachine.com
SIC: 3829 3569 Aircraft & motor vehicle measurement equipment; assembly machines, non-metalworking

(G-15851)
SHAPE CORP
17155 Van Wagoner Rd (49456-9793)
PHONE...................................616 846-8700
Robert Currier, *President*
EMP: 7
SALES (corp-wide): 597.1MM **Privately Held**
WEB: www.shapecorp.com
SIC: 3449 Custom roll formed products

PA: Shape Corp.
1900 Hayes St
Grand Haven MI 49417
616 846-8700

(G-15852)
SINTEL INC
18437 171st Ave (49456-9731)
PHONE...................................616 842-6960
Nicholas Kulkarni, *CEO*
Jeff Falzone, *QC Mgr*
Nicholas Lardo, *CFO*
Kari Wymer, *Human Resources*
Russ Andreas, *Sales Engr*
EMP: 105
SQ FT: 120,000
SALES (est): 26.8MM **Privately Held**
WEB: www.sintelinc.com
SIC: 3444 3469 Sheet metal specialties, not stamped; stamping metal for the trade

(G-15853)
STRAIGHT LINE DESIGN
18055 174th Ave (49456-9767)
PHONE...................................616 296-0920
Randy Ruter, *Mng Member*
EMP: 4 EST: 2011
SALES (est): 1MM **Privately Held**
WEB: www.straightlinekitchens.com
SIC: 2434 7389 Wood kitchen cabinets; design services

(G-15854)
SUPREME DOMESTIC INTL SLS CORP
18686 172nd Ave (49456-9720)
PHONE...................................616 842-6550
Gregory Olson, *President*
EMP: 19 EST: 2012
SALES (est): 306.9K **Privately Held**
WEB: www.supreme1.com
SIC: 3451 Screw machine products

(G-15855)
SUPREME MACHINED PDTS CO INC (PA)
18686 172nd Ave (49456-9720)
PHONE...................................616 842-6550
Gregory Olson, *President*
Bruce Rice, *General Mgr*
Andrea Jackson, *Plant Mgr*
Mike Workman, *Purch Mgr*
Joshua Datte, *QC Mgr*
▲ EMP: 138 EST: 1965
SALES (est): 28.4MM **Privately Held**
WEB: www.supreme1.com
SIC: 3451 Screw machine products

(G-15856)
TELCO TOOLS
510 Elm St (49456-7900)
PHONE...................................616 296-0253
Richard Beaudreault, *Vice Pres*
▲ EMP: 10 EST: 2007
SALES (est): 944.5K **Privately Held**
WEB: www.telcotoolsinc.com
SIC: 3544 3546 Special dies & tools; power-driven handtools

(G-15857)
TIMBER COAST WOODWORKS
17501 Reitsma Ln (49456-9516)
PHONE...................................231 287-3042
Dustin Langlois, *Principal*
EMP: 4 EST: 2019
SALES (est): 72.7K **Privately Held**
SIC: 2431 Millwork

(G-15858)
WEBER PRECISION GRINDING INC
18438 171st Ave (49456-9717)
P.O. Box 484 (49456-0484)
PHONE...................................616 842-1634
Michael J Bonevelle, *President*
Pamela J Bonevelle, *Admin Sec*
EMP: 6 EST: 1943
SQ FT: 3,700
SALES (est): 300K **Privately Held**
SIC: 7699 3545 Knife, saw & tool sharpening & repair; machine tool accessories

Springfield
Calhoun County

(G-15859)
AMERICAN PUBLIC WORKS ASSN
601 Avenue A (49037-7774)
PHONE...................................816 472-6100
Kris Vogel, *Manager*
EMP: 4 EST: 2018
SALES (est): 76K **Privately Held**
SIC: 2721 Periodicals

(G-15860)
BACK MACHINE SHOP LLC
1300 W Dickman Rd (49037-4843)
PHONE...................................269 963-7061
Dan Back, *Mng Member*
EMP: 7 EST: 1995
SALES (est): 727.9K **Privately Held**
WEB: www.back-machine-shop.com
SIC: 3599 7699 Machine shop, jobbing & repair; industrial equipment services

(G-15861)
BEECH & RICH INC
525 20th St N (49037-7897)
PHONE...................................269 968-8012
James E Beech, *President*
Kadra Parker, *Business Mgr*
Scott Lowery, *Opers Staff*
Glenn Lussier, *Sales Dir*
Kim Combs, *Office Mgr*
EMP: 25 EST: 1924
SQ FT: 50,000
SALES (est): 1.7MM **Privately Held**
WEB: www.beechandrich.com
SIC: 1721 3471 3479 Industrial painting; sand blasting of metal parts; coating of metals & formed products

(G-15862)
BOWERS ALUMINUM
1401 Shiga Dr (49037-5605)
PHONE...................................269 251-8625
EMP: 9 EST: 2018
SALES (est): 1.1MM **Privately Held**
WEB: www.bowersaluminumco.com
SIC: 3471 Anodizing (plating) of metals or formed products

(G-15863)
CHRISTMAN SCREENPRINT INC
2851 W Dickman Rd (49037-7962)
PHONE...................................800 962-9330
David Christman, *President*
Michael Christman, *Vice Pres*
Mike Christman, *Vice Pres*
Dana Christman, *Treasurer*
Dana L Christman, *Treasurer*
EMP: 20 EST: 1917
SALES (est): 1.7MM **Privately Held**
WEB: www.christmanscreenprint.com
SIC: 2752 5699 Commercial printing, offset; T-shirts, custom printed

(G-15864)
DARE PRODUCTS INC
860 Betterly Rd (49037-8392)
P.O. Box 157, Battle Creek (49016-0157)
PHONE...................................269 965-2307
Robert M Wilson Jr, *President*
Steven A Wilson, *Vice Pres*
Sheri Johnson, *Manager*
▲ EMP: 35 EST: 1946
SALES (est): 7.1MM **Privately Held**
WEB: www.dareproducts.com
SIC: 3644 3229 3699 3089 Insulators & insulation materials, electrical; pressed & blown glass; electrical equipment & supplies; injection molded finished plastic products; miscellaneous fabricated wire products

(G-15865)
GAGE COMPANY
Also Called: Gage Printing
4550 Wayne Rd (49037-7347)
PHONE...................................269 965-4279
Michael Fatt, *President*
Linda Fatt, *Corp Secy*
EMP: 7 EST: 1967
SQ FT: 5,500

Springfield - Calhoun County (G-15866)

SALES (est): 173.2K **Privately Held**
WEB: www.proconnections.us
SIC: 2752 Commercial printing, offset

(G-15866)
GHF CORP
2813 Wilbur St (49037-7990)
PHONE.................269 968-3351
Carolyn Torres, *Manager*
EMP: 4 **EST:** 2014
SALES (est): 73.4K **Privately Held**
SIC: 3931 Strings, musical instrument

(G-15867)
GHS CORPORATION
Also Called: Ghs Strings
2813 Wilbur St (49037-7990)
PHONE.................269 968-3351
Russell S McFee, *President*
Paul Jenkins, *Engineer*
Robert D McFee, *Admin Sec*
◆ **EMP:** 25 **EST:** 1981
SQ FT: 25,000
SALES (est): 3.4MM **Privately Held**
WEB: www.ghsstrings.com
SIC: 3931 3679 Guitars & parts, electric & nonelectric; electronic circuits

(G-15868)
GHS CORPORATION (PA)
Also Called: D'Angelico Strings
2813 Wilbur St (49037-7990)
PHONE.................800 388-4447
Russell S McFee, *President*
Constance McFee, *Marketing Staff*
Paula McQuern, *Manager*
Elizabeth Randall, *Manager*
Robert D McFee, *Admin Sec*
EMP: 62 **EST:** 1964
SALES (est): 56.9MM **Privately Held**
WEB: www.ghsstrings.com
SIC: 3931 Strings, musical instrument

(G-15869)
JB WHISKEY CREEK
3905 W Dickman Rd (49037-7592)
PHONE.................269 965-4052
EMP: 5 **EST:** 2016
SALES (est): 119.2K **Privately Held**
WEB: www.jbswhiskey.com
SIC: 2084 Wines, brandy & brandy spirits

(G-15870)
JN NEWMAN CONSTRUCTION LLC
Also Called: Newman Construction
2869 W Dickman Rd (49037-7962)
PHONE.................269 968-1290
Joseph Newman,
Patricia Newman,
EMP: 8 **EST:** 1992
SQ FT: 3,500
SALES (est): 3.1MM **Privately Held**
WEB: www.newmanconstruction.com
SIC: 1522 1521 1389 1542 Residential construction; single-family housing construction; new construction, single-family houses; construction, repair & dismantling services; nonresidential construction

(G-15871)
KEYES-DAVIS COMPANY
74 14th St N (49037-8216)
P.O. Box 1557, Battle Creek (49016-1557)
PHONE.................269 962-7505
Robert Barker, *President*
Mardell Barker, *Treasurer*
EMP: 20 **EST:** 1901
SQ FT: 28,500
SALES (est): 1.2MM **Privately Held**
WEB: www.keyesdavis.com
SIC: 3999 3469 Identification plates; identification tags, except paper; metal stampings

(G-15872)
MARKETPLUS SOFTWARE INC (PA)
Also Called: Owl Leasing
2821 Wilbur St (49037-7953)
P.O. Box 2422, Battle Creek (49016-2422)
PHONE.................269 968-4240
Russell Mc Fee, *President*
Constance Mc Fee, *Principal*
EMP: 8 **EST:** 1990

SALES (est): 1MM **Privately Held**
WEB: www.mcfeetech.com
SIC: 7372 7359 Prepackaged software; equipment rental & leasing

(G-15873)
PALLET MAN
555 Upton Ave (49037-8383)
PHONE.................269 274-8825
Byron Jones, *Principal*
EMP: 4
SALES (est): 223K **Privately Held**
SIC: 2448 Pallets, wood

(G-15874)
PERFORMCOAT OF MICHIGAN LLC
319 Mcintyre Ln (49037-7686)
PHONE.................269 282-7030
Christian Kunz,
EMP: 10 **EST:** 2011
SALES (est): 917.3K **Privately Held**
WEB: www.performcoat.com
SIC: 3479 Coating of metals & formed products

(G-15875)
SPRINGFIELD MACHINE AND TL INC
257 30th St N (49037-7911)
PHONE.................269 968-8223
Cheryl Thornton, *President*
Glen Thornton, *Vice Pres*
Allan Thornton, *Treasurer*
EMP: 8 **EST:** 2002
SALES (est): 926.7K **Privately Held**
WEB: www.springfieldmachine.com
SIC: 3599 Machine shop, jobbing & repair

(G-15876)
TRAFFIC SIGNS INC
341 Helmer Rd N (49037-7777)
PHONE.................269 964-7511
Cristy Merkle, *President*
Robert Wolfe, *President*
Jake Hooper, *Vice Pres*
Tracy Clough-Champion, *Admin Sec*
EMP: 8 **EST:** 2000
SQ FT: 16,000
SALES (est): 930.7K **Privately Held**
WEB: www.trafficsignsinc.com
SIC: 3993 Electric signs

(G-15877)
TRI K CYLINDER SERVICE INC
4539 Wayne St (49037-7348)
PHONE.................269 965-3981
Kurk Sparks, *President*
EMP: 4 **EST:** 1982 **Privately Held**
WEB: www.leeberner.com
SIC: 3471 Plating of metals or formed products

(G-15878)
TSC GROUP INC
226 N 28th St (49037-7968)
PHONE.................269 544-9966
EMP: 6 **EST:** 2009
SALES (est): 355.6K **Privately Held**
WEB: www.tscgroupusa.com
SIC: 3841 Surgical & medical instruments

Springport
Jackson County

(G-15879)
COCHRAN CORPORATION
120 Mill St (49284-9534)
P.O. Box 219 (49284-0219)
PHONE.................517 857-2211
Anthony Cochran, *President*
Andy Cochran, *Manager*
EMP: 22 **EST:** 1994
SQ FT: 45,000
SALES (est): 2.1MM **Privately Held**
SIC: 3599 7699 Machine shop, jobbing & repair; industrial machinery & equipment repair

(G-15880)
DOWDING TOOL PRODUCTS LLC
8950 Narrow Lake Rd (49284-9311)
PHONE.................517 541-2795
Maurice Dowding,
EMP: 15 **EST:** 2011
SALES (est): 2.3MM **Privately Held**
WEB: www.dowdingtoolproducts.com
SIC: 3444 Sheet metalwork

(G-15881)
ELDER CREEK SIGN DESIGN
28354 W Dr N (49284-9445)
PHONE.................517 857-4252
Kathy Heisler, *Owner*
EMP: 4 **EST:** 1998
SALES (est): 75.9K **Privately Held**
WEB: www.ecsigndesign.com
SIC: 3993 Signs & advertising specialties

(G-15882)
JP CASTINGS INC
Also Called: Specialty Castings
211 Mill St (49284-9479)
P.O. Box 129 (49284-0129)
PHONE.................517 857-3660
EMP: 27
SALES (est): 3.6MM **Privately Held**
SIC: 3321 Gray/Ductile Iron Foundry

(G-15883)
MASSIVE MINERAL MIX LLC
21110 29 1/2 Mile Rd (49284-9403)
PHONE.................517 857-4544
Jack Hadley, *Principal*
EMP: 7 **EST:** 2010
SALES (est): 302.8K **Privately Held**
SIC: 3273 Ready-mixed concrete

(G-15884)
TROJAN SAND AND GRAVEL LLC
1771 Charlotte Landing Rd (49284-9423)
PHONE.................517 712-5086
EMP: 6 **EST:** 2017
SALES (est): 1.8MM **Privately Held**
SIC: 1442 Construction sand & gravel

Spruce
Alcona County

(G-15885)
CHIPPEWA FARM SUPPLY LLC
6701 N Us Highway 23 (48762-9706)
PHONE.................989 471-5523
Myron Martin, *President*
EMP: 8 **EST:** 2016
SQ FT: 25,000
SALES (est): 1.1MM **Privately Held**
SIC: 0723 2048 5191 Feed milling custom services; poultry feeds; stock feeds, dry; fertilizers & agricultural chemicals

Standish
Arenac County

(G-15886)
AIRPARK PLASTICS LLC
Also Called: Vantage Plastics
1415 W Cedar St (48658-9527)
PHONE.................989 846-1029
Paul Aultman, *President*
George Aultman,
EMP: 15 **EST:** 1996
SALES (est): 3.6MM **Privately Held**
WEB: www.vantageplastics.com
SIC: 3089 Thermoformed finished plastic products
PA: P.R.A. Company
1415 W Cedar St
Standish MI 48658

(G-15887)
ARQUETTE CONCRETE & SUPPLY (PA)
4374 Airpark Dr (48658-9447)
P.O. Box 178 (48658-0178)
PHONE.................989 846-4131
Norman Willett, *President*

EMP: 5 **EST:** 1945
SALES (est): 997K **Privately Held**
WEB: www.rrreadymix.com
SIC: 3273 5231 5211 Ready-mixed concrete; paint; brick; cement; concrete & cinder block

(G-15888)
GLOBE TECHNOLOGIES CORPORATION
1109 W Cedar St (48658-9535)
P.O. Box 1070 (48658-1070)
PHONE.................989 846-9591
Norman N Van Wormer Sr, *Ch of Bd*
▲ **EMP:** 35 **EST:** 1976
SQ FT: 45,000
SALES (est): 6.9MM **Privately Held**
WEB: www.globetechnologies.com
SIC: 3469 Spinning metal for the trade

(G-15889)
JOES TABLES LLC
2700 W Huron Rd (48658-9169)
PHONE.................989 846-4970
Joseph R Guoan,
EMP: 6 **EST:** 1983
SQ FT: 18,000
SALES (est): 466.9K **Privately Held**
WEB: www.joestables.com
SIC: 2531 Picnic tables or benches, park

(G-15890)
MAGLINE INC (PA)
1205 W Cedar St (48658-9563)
PHONE.................800 624-5463
D Brian Law, *CEO*
Sam Cina, *President*
Michael A Kirby, *President*
George Lehnerer, *Treasurer*
Matt Laplant, *Info Tech Mgr*
◆ **EMP:** 110 **EST:** 1945
SQ FT: 110,000
SALES (est): 32.7MM **Privately Held**
WEB: www.magliner.com
SIC: 3537 Trucks, tractors, loaders, carriers & similar equipment; dollies (hand or power trucks), industrial except mining

(G-15891)
MAGLINE INC
Also Called: Standish Magline
1205 W Cedar St (48658-9563)
PHONE.................800 624-5463
Mike Kirby, *Branch Mgr*
EMP: 6
SQ FT: 40,000
SALES (corp-wide): 32.7MM **Privately Held**
WEB: www.magliner.com
SIC: 3537 3535 Trucks, tractors, loaders, carriers & similar equipment; conveyors & conveying equipment
PA: Magline, Inc.
1205 W Cedar St
Standish MI 48658
800 624-5463

(G-15892)
MAGLINE INTERNATIONAL LLC
1205 W Cedar St (48658-9563)
PHONE.................989 512-1000
Charlotte Bennett, *Purch Mgr*
Karen Perry, *Manager*
D Brian Law,
Bruce W Law,
EMP: 7 **EST:** 2001
SQ FT: 1,500
SALES (est): 754.2K **Privately Held**
SIC: 3537 Trucks, tractors, loaders, carriers & similar equipment; dollies (hand or power trucks), industrial except mining

(G-15893)
MISTEQUAY GROUP LTD
1015 W Cedar St (48658-9421)
PHONE.................989 846-1000
Ken Jones, *Plant Mgr*
Laura Littleton, *Sales Staff*
Kevin Harvey, *Manager*
Carrie C Gasta, *Director*
EMP: 29 **Privately Held**
WEB: www.mistequaygroup.com
SIC: 6159 3769 3714 Machinery & equipment finance leasing; guided missile & space vehicle parts & auxiliary equipment; motor vehicle parts & accessories

PA: Mistequay Group Ltd.
1156 N Niagara St
Saginaw MI 48602

(G-15894)
POOLES MEAT PROCESSING
3084 Grove Street Rd (48658-9215)
P.O. Box 867 (48658-0867)
PHONE.................................989 846-6348
Gary L Poole, *President*
Kathleen Poole, *Vice Pres*
EMP: 4
SQ FT: 50,000
SALES (est): 276.1K **Privately Held**
SIC: 2011 0751 Meat packing plants; slaughtering: custom livestock services

(G-15895)
PRA COMPANY (PA)
Also Called: Vantage Plastics
1415 W Cedar St (48658-9527)
PHONE.................................989 846-1029
Paul Aultman, *President*
Scott Zietz, *Plant Mgr*
Buck Myre, *Engineer*
Megan Osier, *Engineer*
Nathan Ostroski, *Project Engr*
EMP: 88 EST: 1994
SQ FT: 77,000
SALES (est): 68.5MM **Privately Held**
WEB: www.vantageplastics.com
SIC: 3089 3069 Thermoformed finished plastic products; rubberized fabrics

(G-15896)
SPARTAN VILLAGE LLC ✪
5742 Bordeau Rd (48658-9566)
PHONE.................................661 724-6438
Nicholas Schmidt,
EMP: 4 EST: 2021
SALES (est): 100K **Privately Held**
WEB: www.spartan-village.com
SIC: 2399 Military insignia, textile

(G-15897)
TECHNICAL MANUFACTURERS INC
4767 S Huron Rd (48658-9552)
P.O. Box 146 (48658-0146)
PHONE.................................989 846-6885
Kenneth J Kruchowski, *President*
▲ EMP: 5 EST: 1988
SQ FT: 6,000
SALES (est): 462.7K **Privately Held**
SIC: 3544 Special dies & tools

Stanton
Montcalm County

(G-15898)
AFFORDABLE OEM AUTOLIGHTING
3068 W Klees Rd (48888-9717)
PHONE.................................989 400-6106
Keith Howard, *Principal*
EMP: 5 EST: 2014
SALES (est): 163.3K **Privately Held**
SIC: 3648 Lighting equipment

(G-15899)
BUCK STOP LURE COMPANY INC
3600 N Grow Rd (48888-9648)
P.O. Box 636 (48888-0636)
PHONE.................................989 762-5091
Dawn Phenix, *President*
EMP: 4 EST: 1952
SQ FT: 20,000
SALES (est): 438.7K **Privately Held**
WEB: www.buckstopscents.com
SIC: 3949 Hunting equipment

(G-15900)
DOUBLE SIX SPORTS COMPLEX
4860 N Sheridan Rd (48888)
PHONE.................................989 762-5342
EMP: 10
SALES (est): 449.6K **Privately Held**
SIC: 3949 Mfg Sporting/Athletic Goods

(G-15901)
FULLER PRINTING
2688 E Stanton Rd (48888-9542)
PHONE.................................989 304-0230
Lewis Fuller, *Principal*
EMP: 5 EST: 2010
SALES (est): 59.5K **Privately Held**
WEB: www.fullersprinting.com
SIC: 2752 Commercial printing, lithographic

Stanwood
Mecosta County

(G-15902)
AVIAN CONTROL TECHNOLOGIES LLC
6800 Mayfair Dr (49346-9600)
PHONE.................................231 349-9050
Bruce Vergote,
EMP: 5 EST: 2009
SALES (est): 220.4K **Privately Held**
WEB: www.aviancontrolinc.com
SIC: 3499 Barricades, metal

(G-15903)
BRYAN K SERGENT
19383 10 Mile Rd (49346-8861)
PHONE.................................231 670-2106
Bryan Sergent, *Principal*
EMP: 6 EST: 2013
SALES (est): 192.7K **Privately Held**
SIC: 2411 Logging

(G-15904)
JRJ ENERGY SERVICES LLC
7302 Northland Dr (49346-8742)
P.O. Box 338 (49346-0338)
PHONE.................................231 823-2171
John R Johnson, *General Mgr*
EMP: 13 EST: 2006
SALES (est): 2.3MM **Privately Held**
WEB: www.jrjenergyservices.com
SIC: 1389 Construction, repair & dismantling services

(G-15905)
KUSTOM WELDING LLC
9770 185th Ave (49346-9575)
PHONE.................................231 823-2912
Troy Koepke, *Principal*
EMP: 4 EST: 2016
SALES (est): 47.9K **Privately Held**
SIC: 7692 Welding repair

Stephenson
Menominee County

(G-15906)
B AND C LOGGING
N8759 P 1 Rd (49887-8556)
PHONE.................................906 753-2425
Bruce Baumler, *President*
EMP: 4 EST: 2017
SALES (est): 78K **Privately Held**
SIC: 2411 Logging camps & contractors

(G-15907)
FORTE INDUSTRIES MILL INC
N8076 Us Highway 41 (49887-9008)
P.O. Box 279 (49887-0279)
PHONE.................................906 753-6256
Charles Duffrin, *President*
Richard Duffrin, *Vice Pres*
◆ EMP: 20 EST: 1982
SQ FT: 8,000
SALES (est): 1.6MM **Privately Held**
WEB: www.forteind.com
SIC: 2421 2436 2435 2426 Sawmills & planing mills, general; softwood veneer & plywood; hardwood veneer & plywood; hardwood dimension & flooring mills

(G-15908)
KELLS SAWMILL INC
N8780 County Road 577 (49887-8333)
PHONE.................................906 753-2778
Allen Majkrzak, *President*
Laurel Majkrzak, *Corp Secy*
EMP: 6 EST: 1956
SALES (est): 178K **Privately Held**
SIC: 2499 2421 2411 Surveyors' stakes, wood; sawmills & planing mills, general; logging

(G-15909)
MENOMINEE CNTY JURNL PRINT SP
S322 Menominee St (49887-5106)
P.O. Box 247 (49887-0247)
PHONE.................................906 753-2296
Gilbert G Grinsteiner, *Owner*
EMP: 10 EST: 1956
SALES (est): 416K **Privately Held**
WEB: www.menomineecountyjournal.com
SIC: 2711 2752 Commercial printing and newspaper publishing combined; commercial printing, lithographic

(G-15910)
ROSARY WORKSHOP
5209 W 16 5 Ln (49887)
PHONE.................................906 788-4846
Margot Blair, *Owner*
EMP: 5 EST: 1997
SALES (est): 160.6K **Privately Held**
WEB: www.rosaryworkshop.com
SIC: 8661 3961 Religious organizations; rosaries & small religious articles, except precious metal

(G-15911)
RULEAU BROTHERS INC (PA)
Also Called: Door County White Fish
W521 Stephenson S Dr (49887)
P.O. Box 337 (49887-0337)
PHONE.................................906 753-4767
Robert Ruleau, *President*
Kathleen Ruleau, *Corp Secy*
▼ EMP: 30 EST: 1957
SALES (est): 2MM **Privately Held**
SIC: 0912 2092 2091 Finfish; fresh or frozen packaged fish; fish, salted; fish, smoked

(G-15912)
TERRY HEIDEN
Also Called: Heiden Lumber & Fencing
N8745 Us Highway 41 (49887-8512)
PHONE.................................906 753-6248
Terry Heiden, *Owner*
EMP: 4 EST: 1982
SQ FT: 7,700
SALES (est): 372.6K **Privately Held**
SIC: 2421 Sawmills & planing mills, general

Sterling
Arenac County

(G-15913)
MAPLE RIDGE HARDWOODS INC
Also Called: East Michigan Lumber
2270 Dobler Rd (48659-9442)
PHONE.................................989 873-5305
Douglas Devereaux, *President*
Tom Barbier, *Principal*
Todd Southworth, *Principal*
Peter Barbier, *Corp Secy*
EMP: 50 EST: 1967 **Privately Held**
WEB: www.mapleridgehardwoodsinc.com
SIC: 2421 2426 Lumber: rough, sawed or planed; hardwood dimension & flooring mills

(G-15914)
U P NORTH STRUCTURES
6300 Ward Rd (48659-9716)
PHONE.................................989 654-2350
Judy Fenske, *Owner*
EMP: 5 EST: 2001
SALES (est): 231.8K **Privately Held**
SIC: 2452 Log cabins, prefabricated, wood

Sterling Heights
Macomb County

(G-15915)
21ST CENTURY NEWSPAPERS INC (HQ)
Also Called: Macomb Daily
6250 Metropolitan Pkwy (48312-1022)
PHONE.................................586 469-4510
Bob Jelenic, *CEO*
Robert M Jelenic, *Principal*
Scott Wright, *Senior VP*
Jameson Cook, *Relations*
EMP: 200 EST: 1995
SALES (est): 129.4MM
SALES (corp-wide): 274.1MM **Privately Held**
WEB: www.21stcenturynewspapers.com
SIC: 2711 Newspapers, publishing & printing
PA: Journal Register Company
5 Hanover Sq Fl 25
New York NY 10004
212 257-7212

(G-15916)
420 GROUP
38300 Van Dyke Ave (48312-1123)
PHONE.................................586 978-0420
Richard Arden, *Principal*
EMP: 6 EST: 2011
SALES (est): 87K **Privately Held**
SIC: 3999 Hydroponic equipment

(G-15917)
A & R TOOL & MFG CO
36760 Metro Ct (48312-1010)
PHONE.................................586 553-9623
Alan Ligda, *Principal*
EMP: 5 EST: 2016
SALES (est): 68.2K **Privately Held**
SIC: 3999 Manufacturing industries

(G-15918)
A G SIMPSON (USA) INC
6700 18 1/2 Mile Rd (48314-3206)
PHONE.................................586 268-4817
Paul Sobocan, *Branch Mgr*
EMP: 9
SALES (corp-wide): 365.5MM **Privately Held**
SIC: 3465 Body parts, automobile: stamped metal
HQ: A. G. Simpson (Usa), Inc.
6640 Sterling Dr S
Sterling Heights MI 48312

(G-15919)
A G SIMPSON (USA) INC
6700 18 1/2 (48314)
PHONE.................................586 268-4817
Paul Sobocan, *Branch Mgr*
EMP: 10
SALES (corp-wide): 365.5MM **Privately Held**
SIC: 3465 Body parts, automobile: stamped metal
HQ: A. G. Simpson (Usa), Inc.
6640 Sterling Dr S
Sterling Heights MI 48312

(G-15920)
A G SIMPSON (USA) INC (HQ)
6640 Sterling Dr S (48312-5845)
PHONE.................................586 268-5844
Joe Loparco, *President*
Joe Leon, *Vice Pres*
Rob Dinatale, *Exec Dir*
Adele Leandro, *Admin Sec*
EMP: 30 EST: 1993
SQ FT: 126,000
SALES (est): 24.2MM
SALES (corp-wide): 365.5MM **Privately Held**
SIC: 3465 Body parts, automobile: stamped metal
PA: J2 Management Corp
200 Yorkland Blvd Suite 800
Toronto ON
416 438-6650

Sterling Heights - Macomb County (G-15921)

(G-15921)
ABSOLUTE LSER WLDG SLTIONS LLC
6545 19 Mile Rd (48314-2116)
PHONE...................................586 932-2597
David Gall, *Principal*
David L Gall, *Principal*
EMP: 9 **EST:** 2013
SALES (est): 1.2MM **Privately Held**
WEB: www.alwsllc.com
SIC: 7692 Welding repair

(G-15922)
ACCUTEK MOLD & ENGINEERING
35815 Stanley Dr (48312-2663)
PHONE...................................586 978-1335
Luciano Pierobon, *President*
Marco Pierobon, *Vice Pres*
EMP: 38 **EST:** 1976
SALES (est): 1MM **Privately Held**
WEB: www.luckmarrplastics.com
SIC: 3312 Tool & die steel

(G-15923)
ACME SIGN CO
42732 Merrill Rd (48314-3244)
PHONE...................................248 930-9718
Sam Kizy, *Principal*
EMP: 7 **EST:** 2016
SALES (est): 155K **Privately Held**
WEB: www.acmesignco.com
SIC: 3993 Signs & advertising specialties

(G-15924)
ACUMENT GLOBAL TECH INC (DH)
6125 18 Mile Rd (48314-4205)
PHONE...................................586 254-3900
Patrick Paige, *President*
Lynn Stanton, *Business Mgr*
John Clark, *Exec VP*
Daniel Di Sebastian, *VP Opers*
Mike Cunningham, *Plant Mgr*
▲ **EMP:** 45 **EST:** 2006
SQ FT: 10,000
SALES (est): 1.7B **Privately Held**
WEB: www.acument.com
SIC: 3965 5072 Fasteners; hardware
HQ: Fontana America Incorporated
 6125 18 Mile Rd
 Sterling Heights MI 48314
 586 997-5600

(G-15925)
AERO EMBEDDED TECHNOLOGIES INC
Also Called: In-Tronics
6580 Cotter Ave (48314-2148)
PHONE...................................586 251-2980
Peter G Vanheusden, *President*
Raymond Taraski, *Mfg Mgr*
Causha Hale, *Technician*
EMP: 4 **EST:** 1984
SALES (est): 1.1MM **Privately Held**
WEB: www.aeroembedded.com
SIC: 3672 Printed circuit boards

(G-15926)
AG DAVIS GAGE & ENGRG CO (PA)
Also Called: AG Davis
6533 Sims Dr (48313-3724)
PHONE...................................586 977-9000
Michelle A C Beckman, *President*
Greg Chapman, *Vice Pres*
Gregory Chapman, *Vice Pres*
Michelle Beckman, *CFO*
James Sobol, *Sales Mgr*
EMP: 30 **EST:** 1951
SQ FT: 20,000
SALES (est): 7.1MM **Privately Held**
WEB: www.agdavis.com
SIC: 3545 5084 3825 3823 Gauges (machine tool accessories); industrial machinery & equipment; instruments to measure electricity; industrial instrmnts msrmnt display/control process variable; laboratory apparatus & furniture; relays & industrial controls

(G-15927)
ALIS CUSTOM EMBROIDERY
3031 Juanita Dr (48310-3647)
PHONE...................................586 744-9442
Asim Ali, *Principal*
EMP: 5 **EST:** 2016
SALES (est): 66.6K **Privately Held**
SIC: 2395 Embroidery & art needlework

(G-15928)
ALLSTATE HM LEISURE STRLNG HTS
44605 Schoenherr Rd (48313-1135)
PHONE...................................734 838-6500
Brian Hayner, *Store Mgr*
EMP: 7 **EST:** 2020
SALES (est): 202.9K **Privately Held**
WEB: www.homeleisure.com
SIC: 5719 5712 5261 2519 Miscellaneous home furnishings; furniture stores; nurseries & garden centers; household furniture

(G-15929)
AM SPECIALTIES INC
5985 Wall St (48312-1074)
PHONE...................................586 795-9000
Alan G Klinger, *President*
Tabitha Lupi, *Office Admin*
Brian Jeffers, *Supervisor*
EMP: 19 **EST:** 1982
SQ FT: 11,000
SALES (est): 2.8MM **Privately Held**
WEB: www.am-specialtiesinc.com
SIC: 3714 Radiators & radiator shells & cores, motor vehicle

(G-15930)
AMERICAN RHNMTALL VEHICLES LLC
33844 Sterling Ponds Blvd (48312-5808)
PHONE...................................586 942-0139
Matthew Warnick, *Mng Member*
EMP: 15 **EST:** 2019
SALES (est): 3.4MM
SALES (corp-wide): 6.9B **Privately Held**
WEB: www.rheinmetall-defence.com
SIC: 3795 Tanks & tank components
PA: Rheinmetall Ag
 Rheinmetall-Platz 1
 Dusseldorf NW 40476
 211 473-01

(G-15931)
AMPLAS COMPOUNDING LLC
6675 Sterling Dr N (48312-4559)
PHONE...................................586 795-2555
Geraldine Beaupre, *President*
Darin Beaupre, *Exec VP*
EMP: 15 **EST:** 1986
SQ FT: 63,000
SALES (est): 4.2MM
SALES (corp-wide): 5.4MM **Privately Held**
WEB: www.deltapoly.com
SIC: 3089 2821 3087 Plastic processing; plastics materials & resins; custom compound purchased resins
PA: Delta Polymers Co.
 6685 Sterling Dr N
 Sterling Heights MI 48312
 586 795-2900

(G-15932)
AMX CORP
38780 Hartwell Dr (48312-1327)
P.O. Box 759, Novi (48376-0759)
PHONE...................................469 624-8000
Dave Hill, *Principal*
EMP: 11 **EST:** 2016
SALES (est): 2.1MM **Privately Held**
WEB: www.amx.com
SIC: 3625 Relays & industrial controls

(G-15933)
APHASE II INC (PA)
6120 Center Dr (48312-2614)
PHONE...................................586 977-0790
Edward Bluthardt, *President*
Steve Klager, *General Mgr*
Rob Bluthardt, *Vice Pres*
Tigi Lukose, *Controller*
Jim McAndrews, *Accounts Mgr*
EMP: 92 **EST:** 1984
SQ FT: 36,771
SALES (est): 15.7MM **Privately Held**
WEB: www.aphaseii.com
SIC: 8711 3465 Engineering services; automotive stampings

(G-15934)
ASMUS SEASONING INC
36625 Metro Ct Ste A (48312-1060)
PHONE...................................586 939-4505
Marvin Asmus Jr, *President*
Tom Fritz, *Vice Pres*
EMP: 11 **EST:** 2008
SALES (est): 2.4MM **Privately Held**
WEB: www.asmusseas.info
SIC: 2099 5149 Seasonings & spices; spices & seasonings

(G-15935)
ASTRA ASSOCIATES INC
Also Called: Mid-West Instrument Company
6500 Dobry Dr (48314-1424)
PHONE...................................586 254-6500
Michael A Lueck, *President*
Ellen I Lueck, *Corp Secy*
James F Lueck, *Vice Pres*
Mike Lueck, *Research*
Brandon Wilson, *Engineer*
EMP: 40 **EST:** 1958
SQ FT: 35,000
SALES (est): 12MM **Privately Held**
WEB: www.midwestinstrument.com
SIC: 3823 3829 3822 3643 Differential pressure instruments, industrial process type; measuring & controlling devices; auto controls regulating residntl & coml environmt & applncs; current-carrying wiring devices

(G-15936)
ATOTECH USA LLC
Also Called: Chemprotect
35840 Beattie Dr (48312-2620)
PHONE...................................586 939-3040
Scott McEuen, *Business Mgr*
Daniel Wan, *Vice Pres*
Bill Krenz, *Regl Sales Mgr*
Robert D Nelson, *Branch Mgr*
EMP: 13
SALES (corp-wide): 2.9B **Publicly Held**
WEB: www.atotech.com
SIC: 2899 Chemical preparations
HQ: Atotech Usa, Llc
 1750 Overview Dr
 Rock Hill SC 29730

(G-15937)
AUTOMOTIVE COMPONENT MFG (PA)
Also Called: Acm
36155 Mound Rd (48310-4736)
PHONE...................................705 549-7406
Robert Hall, *President*
Doug Ewen, *Vice Pres*
EMP: 3 **EST:** 2010
SALES (est): 25.1MM **Privately Held**
SIC: 3559 Automotive related machinery

(G-15938)
AUTOMOTIVE TECHNOLOGY LLC
6015 Center Dr (48312-2667)
PHONE...................................586 446-7000
Brian Prina, *President*
Robert Dudek, *Treasurer*
EMP: 221 **EST:** 2012
SALES (est): 49.2MM **Privately Held**
SIC: 3559 Automotive related machinery
HQ: M-Sko las Holdings, Inc.
 1395 Brickell Ave Ste 800
 Miami FL 33131
 786 871-2904

(G-15939)
AW CARBIDE FABRICATORS INC
35434 Mound Rd (48310-4721)
PHONE...................................586 294-1850
Dennis A Wegner, *President*
James T Wegner, *Vice Pres*
EMP: 25 **EST:** 1961
SALES (est): 1MM **Privately Held**
WEB: www.awcarbide.com
SIC: 3545 3544 3541 Cutting tools for machine tools; special dies, tools, jigs & fixtures; machine tools, metal cutting type

(G-15940)
B & B HOLDINGS GROESBECK LLC
Also Called: Krh Industries, LLC
42450 R Mancini Dr (48314-3265)
PHONE...................................586 554-7600
Stephanie Serra-Bartolotta,
EMP: 12 **EST:** 2016
SALES (est): 1MM **Privately Held**
SIC: 1799 7389 3542 Welding on site; metal cutting services; punching, shearing & bending machines

(G-15941)
BADGER TOOL LLC
35425 Beattie Dr (48312-2613)
PHONE...................................586 246-1810
Scott Bellow, *Administration*
EMP: 4 **EST:** 2012
SALES (est): 244.7K **Privately Held**
WEB: www.badgertoolbelts.com
SIC: 3544 Special dies & tools

(G-15942)
BAE SYSTEMS LAND ARMAMENTS LP
34201 Van Dyke Ave (48312-4648)
PHONE...................................586 596-4123
Cheryl Sienkiewicz, *Editor*
Scott Witting, *Opers Staff*
Joe Hoffman, *Buyer*
Luna Fakhouri, *Engineer*
Neil Gavrich, *Engineer*
EMP: 541
SALES (corp-wide): 25.6B **Privately Held**
WEB: www.baesystems.com
SIC: 3812 Search & navigation equipment
HQ: Bae Systems Land & Armaments L.P.
 2941 Frview Pk Dr Ste 100
 Falls Church VA 22042
 571 461-6000

(G-15943)
BAIRD INVESTMENTS LLC (PA)
Also Called: Jaan Technolgies
43333 Westview Dr (48313-2170)
PHONE...................................586 665-0154
Jacqueline Baird, *Mng Member*
Steven Baird, *Program Mgr*
EMP: 6 **EST:** 2009
SALES (est): 1.3MM **Privately Held**
SIC: 3569 Assembly machines, non-metalworking

(G-15944)
BARTEC USA LLC
44231 Phoenix Dr (48314-1466)
PHONE...................................586 685-1300
Scot Holloway, *CEO*
Jeannie Cayetano-Bryja, *Sales Staff*
Barb Winters, *Sales Staff*
Diane Hubbard, *Office Mgr*
Scot Halloway, *Manager*
▲ **EMP:** 22 **EST:** 2004
SQ FT: 25,000
SALES (est): 4.9MM **Privately Held**
WEB: www.bartecusa.com
SIC: 3714 Motor vehicle parts & accessories

(G-15945)
BESTOP INC
5555 Gatewood Dr (48310-2227)
PHONE...................................586 268-0602
EMP: 10
SALES (corp-wide): 83.1MM **Privately Held**
WEB: www.bestop.com
SIC: 2394 3714 Convertible tops, canvas or boat: from purchased materials; motor vehicle parts & accessories
PA: Bestop, Inc.
 333 Centennial Pkwy Ste B
 Louisville CO 80027
 303 464-2548

(G-15946)
BIRMINGHAM JEWELRY INC
34756 Dequindre Rd (48310-5279)
PHONE...................................586 939-5100
Gregory Pilibosian, *President*
Reba Pilibosian, *Vice Pres*
EMP: 5 **EST:** 1973
SQ FT: 5,000

GEOGRAPHIC SECTION
Sterling Heights - Macomb County (G-15973)

SALES (est): 497.6K **Privately Held**
WEB: www.birminghamjewelry.com
SIC: 3911 5992 Jewelry, precious metal; flowers, fresh

(G-15947)
BOLMAN DIE SERVICES INC
7523 19 Mile Rd (48314-3222)
PHONE 810 919-2262
Scott Bolman, *President*
EMP: 10 **EST:** 2008
SALES (est): 767.8K **Privately Held**
WEB: www.bolmanservices.com
SIC: 3544 Special dies & tools; punches, forming & stamping

(G-15948)
BRANSON ULTRASONICS CORP
6590 Sims Dr (48313-3751)
PHONE 586 276-0150
Ryan McEntee, *Manager*
EMP: 8
SALES (corp-wide): 16.7B **Publicly Held**
WEB: www.bransonultrasonics.com
SIC: 3699 Cleaning equipment, ultrasonic, except medical & dental
HQ: Branson Ultrasonics Corporation
120 Park Ridge Rd
Brookfield CT 06804
203 796-0400

(G-15949)
C & C MANUFACTURING INC
35605 Stanley Dr (48312-2659)
PHONE 586 268-3650
Joseph Colella, *President*
Paul Cusmasno, *Vice Pres*
Joseph Alnaraie, *Project Mgr*
Andy Simonds, *Opers Mgr*
Jennifer Wither, *Cust Mgr*
EMP: 11 **EST:** 2004
SQ FT: 6,500
SALES (est): 2MM **Privately Held**
WEB: www.ccmfg.net
SIC: 3441 Fabricated structural metal

(G-15950)
CAMCAR LLC (DH)
6125 18 Mile Rd (48314-4205)
PHONE 586 254-3900
Richard Dauch, *President*
David Harlow, *Vice Pres*
Keith Kim, *Vice Pres*
Mary Sigler, *Vice Pres*
Michael Claassen, *VP Engrg*
EMP: 100 **EST:** 2005
SALES (est): 130.8MM **Privately Held**
WEB: www.acument.com
SIC: 3452 5072 Bolts, nuts, rivets & washers; bolts, nuts & screws
HQ: Acument Global Technologies, Inc.
6125 18 Mile Rd
Sterling Heights MI 48314
586 254-3900

(G-15951)
CAPITAL INDUCTION INC
6505 Diplomat Dr (48314-1421)
PHONE 586 322-1444
Larry Misner, *President*
Claire Tomlinson, *Admin Sec*
▼ **EMP:** 10 **EST:** 1983
SQ FT: 13,000
SALES (est): 1.4MM **Privately Held**
WEB: www.capitalinduction.com
SIC: 3567 Induction heating equipment

(G-15952)
CAPLER MFG
6664 Sterling Dr N (48312-4558)
PHONE 586 264-7851
Tomas Capler, *Manager*
EMP: 8 **EST:** 2005
SALES (est): 401.1K **Privately Held**
SIC: 3999 Manufacturing industries

(G-15953)
CASADEI STRUCTURAL STEEL INC
Also Called: Casadei Steel
40675 Mound Rd (48310-2263)
P.O. Box 70 (48311-0070)
PHONE 586 698-2898
Bruno Casadei, *President*
Robert Casadei, *Vice Pres*
Casadei Robert, *Vice Pres*
Tony Babcock, *Project Mgr*
Marc Steinhobel, *VP Engrg*
EMP: 35
SQ FT: 150,000
SALES (est): 18MM **Privately Held**
WEB: www.casadeisteel.com
SIC: 3441 Fabricated structural metal

(G-15954)
CENTRAL ON LINE DATA SYSTEMS
34200 Mound Rd (48310-6613)
PHONE 586 939-7000
F V McBrien, *President*
Ronald Lech, *Vice Pres*
Agnes A Moroun, *Admin Sec*
EMP: 6 **EST:** 1973
SQ FT: 42,600
SALES (est): 987.3K
SALES (corp-wide): 1.1B **Privately Held**
WEB: www.centraltransportint.com
SIC: 3661 7622 Telephone & telegraph apparatus; communication equipment repair
PA: Centra Inc.
12225 Stephens Rd
Warren MI 48089
586 939-7000

(G-15955)
CERTIFIED REDUCER RBLDRS INC
6480 Sims Dr (48313-3700)
PHONE 248 585-0883
Michael P Ruger, *President*
Robert L Wenzel, *Corp Secy*
EMP: 15 **EST:** 1979
SQ FT: 6,000
SALES (est): 1.9MM **Privately Held**
WEB: www.certifiedreducer.net
SIC: 7699 3566 Industrial machinery & equipment repair; speed changers, drives & gears

(G-15956)
CHALKER TOOL & GAUGE INC
35425 Beattie Dr (48312-2613)
PHONE 586 977-8660
Patrick Chalker, *President*
Dwain Chalker, *Manager*
Bonnie Chalker, *Shareholder*
EMP: 11 **EST:** 1987
SQ FT: 7,920
SALES (est): 2MM **Privately Held**
SIC: 3544 Special dies & tools

(G-15957)
CHARDAM GEAR COMPANY INC
40805 Mound Rd (48310-2258)
PHONE 586 795-8900
Mike Brzoska, *President*
Miike Brzoska, *President*
Eric Schmidt, *Superintendent*
Kay Becker, *Vice Pres*
Dough Perzyk, *Vice Pres*
EMP: 170 **EST:** 1946
SQ FT: 12,000
SALES (est): 28.8MM **Privately Held**
WEB: www.chardam.com
SIC: 3462 3728 Iron & steel forgings; aircraft parts & equipment

(G-15958)
CHRYSLER GROUP LLC
Also Called: Chrysler Sterling Test Center
7150 Metropolitan Pkwy (48312-1040)
PHONE 586 977-4900
Fax: 586 977-4913
EMP: 100
SALES (corp-wide): 90.3MM **Privately Held**
SIC: 3711 Mfg Motor Vehicle/Car Bodies
HQ: Chrysler Group Llc
1000 Chrysler Dr
Auburn Hills MI 48326
248 512-2950

(G-15959)
CIRCLE ENGINEERING INC
5495 Gatewood Dr (48310-2226)
PHONE 586 978-8120
EMP: 9
SQ FT: 10,500
SALES (est): 1.4MM **Privately Held**
SIC: 3544 Mfg Dies/Tools/Jigs/Fixtures

(G-15960)
CLASSIC STITCH
42450 Van Dyke Ave (48314-3322)
PHONE 586 737-7767
Hajrie Kasa, *Principal*
EMP: 4 **EST:** 2016
SALES (est): 93.9K **Privately Held**
SIC: 2395 Embroidery & art needlework

(G-15961)
CLASSIC TOOL & BORING INC
5970 Wall St (48312-1069)
PHONE 586 795-8967
Lou Gavrilovski, *President*
EMP: 9 **EST:** 1988
SQ FT: 11,000
SALES (est): 790K **Privately Held**
WEB: www.classictb.com
SIC: 3599 Machine shop, jobbing & repair

(G-15962)
CLOUD 9 PIPE TOBACCO INC
Also Called: Galaxy Pipe Tobacco
33878 Dequindre Rd (48310-5881)
PHONE 313 522-1957
Jafar Alsheen, *President*
EMP: 13 **EST:** 2010
SALES (est): 443.9K **Privately Held**
SIC: 2111 Cigarettes

(G-15963)
COLD FORMING TECHNOLOGY INC
44476 Phoenix Dr (48314-1467)
PHONE 586 254-4600
John T Donnelly, *Ch of Bd*
James A Ferrett, *Vice Pres*
Suren B RAO, *Vice Pres*
▲ **EMP:** 19 **EST:** 1992
SQ FT: 7,200
SALES (est): 3MM **Privately Held**
WEB: www.coldformingtechnology.com
SIC: 3541 Machine tools, metal cutting type

(G-15964)
COLE TOOLING SYSTEMS INC
34841 Mound Rd Ste 224 (48310-5723)
PHONE 586 558-9450
John Cole, *Principal*
EMP: 9 **EST:** 2005
SALES (est): 87.2K **Privately Held**
WEB: www.indexa-v.com
SIC: 3599 Machine shop, jobbing & repair

(G-15965)
COMMERCIAL GRAPHICS INC
42704 Mound Rd (48314-3254)
PHONE 586 726-8150
Tracy Simmons, *President*
EMP: 8 **EST:** 1985
SALES (est): 914.7K **Privately Held**
WEB: www.comgraphicinc.com
SIC: 2752 Commercial printing, offset

(G-15966)
COMPUTER MAIL SERVICES INC (PA)
44648 Mound Rd (48314-1322)
PHONE 248 352-6700
Lih-Tah Wong, *President*
Daniel J Deward, *Vice Pres*
Alan Sitek, *Vice Pres*
Richard Wongsonegoro, *Vice Pres*
EMP: 11 **EST:** 1982
SQ FT: 4,000
SALES (est): 1.7MM **Privately Held**
WEB: www.praetor.net
SIC: 7372 4822 7371 Business oriented computer software; electronic mail; computer software development

(G-15967)
COMPUTER SCIENCES CORPORATION
6000 17 Mile Rd (48313-4541)
PHONE 586 825-5043
Mark Dieterle, *Branch Mgr*
EMP: 4
SALES (corp-wide): 17.7B **Publicly Held**
WEB: www.dxc.com
SIC: 7373 7372 Systems integration services; prepackaged software
HQ: Computer Sciences Corporation
1775 Tysons Blvd Fl 8
Tysons VA 22102
855 716-0853

(G-15968)
CONTEUR PUBLISHING LLC
37382 Catherine Marie Dr (48312-2020)
PHONE 248 602-9749
Jason Davis, *Principal*
EMP: 4 **EST:** 2018
SALES (est): 37.5K **Privately Held**
SIC: 2741 Miscellaneous publishing

(G-15969)
CONTROL ONE INC
6460 Sims Dr Ste A (48313-3721)
PHONE 586 979-6106
Fax: 586 979-6109
EMP: 9
SQ FT: 10,000
SALES (est): 780K **Privately Held**
SIC: 3625 1731 1799 Mfg Relays/Industrial Controls Electrical Contractor Trade Contractor

(G-15970)
CONTROL TECHNIQUE INCORPORATED
Also Called: C T I
41200 Technology Park Dr (48314-4102)
PHONE 586 997-3200
Richard C Mueller, *President*
Jim Shereda, *Vice Pres*
Martin R Shereda, *Vice Pres*
Mike Duerden, *Engineer*
Angie Mueller, *Shareholder*
EMP: 75 **EST:** 1983
SQ FT: 40,000
SALES (est): 12.8MM **Privately Held**
WEB: www.c-t-i-usa.com
SIC: 3613 Control panels, electric

(G-15971)
CONVEX MOLD INC
35360 Beattie Dr (48312-2610)
PHONE 586 978-0808
Joseph Bolton, *President*
EMP: 7 **EST:** 1967
SQ FT: 7,600
SALES (est): 1.1MM
SALES (corp-wide): 5.2B **Publicly Held**
SIC: 3544 7699 Industrial molds; tool repair services
HQ: Sebro Plastics, Inc.
29200 Wall St
Wixom MI 48393
248 348-4121

(G-15972)
COPLAS INC
Also Called: Coplas-Tiercon
6700 18 1/2 Mile Rd (48314-3206)
PHONE 586 739-8940
Joseph P Leon, *CEO*
Kermit Welch, *Manager*
EMP: 9 **EST:** 2005
SALES (est): 3.1MM
SALES (corp-wide): 365.5MM **Privately Held**
SIC: 2821 Molding compounds, plastics
HQ: A. G. Simpson (Usa), Inc.
6640 Sterling Dr S
Sterling Heights MI 48312

(G-15973)
COTSON FABRICATING INC
5971 Product Dr (48312-4561)
PHONE 248 589-2758
Joan Cotsonika, *President*
Philip Calvert, *General Mgr*
Cindy Calvert, *Vice Pres*
Doug Courter, *Info Tech Mgr*
EMP: 32 **EST:** 2006
SQ FT: 11,500
SALES (est): 5.2MM **Privately Held**
WEB: www.cont-usa.com
SIC: 3449 Bars, concrete reinforcing: fabricated steel

Sterling Heights - Macomb County (G-15974)

(G-15974)
CREATIVE IMAGE & PRINTING LLC
34841 Mound Rd Ste 291 (48310-5723)
PHONE..................586 222-4288
EMP: 5 **EST:** 2016
SALES (est): 92.3K **Privately Held**
WEB: www.creativeimageprinting.com
SIC: 2752 Commercial printing, lithographic

(G-15975)
C S X PRESS INC
5621 Toronto Dr (48314-4107)
PHONE..................586 864-3360
EMP: 4 **EST:** 2016
SALES (est): 106.7K **Privately Held**
SIC: 2741 Miscellaneous publishing

(G-15976)
CYPRIUM INDUCTION LLC
42770 Mound Rd (48314-3254)
PHONE..................586 884-4982
James Link,
Christina Liccardello,
EMP: 5 **EST:** 2014
SALES (est): 763.3K **Privately Held**
WEB: www.cypriuminduction.com
SIC: 3398 3567 Annealing of metal; induction heating equipment

(G-15977)
D & F CORPORATION
42455 Merrill Rd (48314-3268)
PHONE..................586 254-5300
William Y Gard, *Ch of Bd*
Paul Gard, *President*
Paul D Gard, *President*
Van Smith, *Vice Pres*
Tammy Szymanski, *Human Res Mgr*
EMP: 60 **EST:** 1953
SQ FT: 83,000
SALES (est): 10.5MM **Privately Held**
WEB: www.d-f.com
SIC: 3544 3559 3999 3545 Jigs: inspection, gauging & checking; forms (molds), for foundry & plastics working machinery; automotive related machinery; models, general, except toy; machine tool accessories

(G-15978)
D M TOOL & FAB INC
6101 18 1/2 Mile Rd (48314-3116)
PHONE..................586 726-8390
Americo Valente, *President*
Theresa Rinker, *Office Mgr*
EMP: 70
SQ FT: 10,000
SALES (est): 14MM **Privately Held**
WEB: www.dmtoolfab.com
SIC: 3544 3542 Industrial molds; machine tools, metal forming type

(G-15979)
DAG LTD LLC
34400 Mound Rd (48310-5757)
PHONE..................586 276-9310
Dale Hadel, *Mng Member*
▲ **EMP:** 15 **EST:** 2004
SALES (est): 1.3MM **Privately Held**
SIC: 3479 2399 Name plates: engraved, etched, etc.; emblems, badges & insignia

(G-15980)
DELTA POLYMERS CO (PA)
6685 Sterling Dr N (48312-4559)
PHONE..................586 795-2900
Delmer Beaupre, *President*
Brian Beaupre, *President*
Darin Beaupre, *Vice Pres*
Michele Johns, *Plant Mgr*
▲ **EMP:** 25 **EST:** 1977
SQ FT: 96,000
SALES (est): 5.4MM **Privately Held**
WEB: www.deltapoly.com
SIC: 2821 Molding compounds, plastics

(G-15981)
DETROIT BORING & MCH CO LLC
42818 Mound Rd (48314-3256)
PHONE..................586 604-6506
William E Noll,
EMP: 4 **EST:** 2010

SALES (est): 250K **Privately Held**
SIC: 3541 Machine tools, metal cutting type

(G-15982)
DETROIT HOIST & CRANE CO L L C
Also Called: Brandnburg Tech Div Dtroit His
6650 Sterling Dr N (48312-4558)
PHONE..................586 268-2600
Ulrich Vorpahl, *President*
Greg Kanasty, *Sales Mgr*
Gregory Kanasty, *Sales Mgr*
Chelsea Hurttgam, *Sales Staff*
Piyush Parikh, *Admin Sec*
▲ **EMP:** 35 **EST:** 1905
SQ FT: 60,000
SALES (est): 9.4MM **Privately Held**
WEB: www.detroithoist.com
SIC: 3536 Hoists

(G-15983)
DETROIT NEWS INC
Also Called: Detroit News, The
6200 Metropolitan Pkwy (48312-1022)
P.O. Box 8001 (48311-8001)
PHONE..................313 222-6400
Michael Quinn, *Vice Pres*
EMP: 4
SQ FT: 360,000
SALES (corp-wide): 1.8B **Privately Held**
WEB: www.detroitnews.com
SIC: 2711 2752 Newspapers, publishing & printing; commercial printing, lithographic
HQ: Detroit Free Press, Inc.
  160 W Fort St Fl 1
  Detroit MI 48226
  313 222-2300

(G-15984)
DETROIT NEWSPAPER PARTNR LP
6200 Metropolitan Pkwy (48312-1022)
PHONE..................586 826-7187
Dave Eschmann, *Division Mgr*
Keith Pierce, *Vice Pres*
Karen Brioc, *Sales Staff*
EMP: 668
SALES (corp-wide): 3.4B **Publicly Held**
WEB: www.michigan.com
SIC: 2711 2752 Commercial printing & newspaper publishing combined; advertising posters, lithographed
HQ: Detroit Newspaper Partnership, L.P.
  160 W Fort St
  Detroit MI 48226

(G-15985)
DETRONIC INDUSTRIES INC (PA)
35800 Beattie Dr (48312-2620)
P.O. Box 608 (48311-0608)
PHONE..................586 977-5660
James D Carne, *President*
Marilyn A Carne, *Corp Secy*
Ryan M Carne, *Vice Pres*
Bill Birta, *Purch Agent*
Mike Mallegg, *Purchasing*
EMP: 78 **EST:** 1958
SQ FT: 55,510
SALES (est): 13MM **Privately Held**
WEB: www.detronic.com
SIC: 3444 Sheet metal specialties, not stamped

(G-15986)
DIAGNOSTIC INSTRUMENTS INC
Also Called: Spot Imaging Solutions
6540 Burroughs Ave (48314-2133)
PHONE..................586 731-6000
Patrick Merlo, *President*
Phil Merlo, *Vice Pres*
Philip Merlo, *Vice Pres*
Phillip Merlo, *Vice Pres*
Michael Szymula, *Production*
EMP: 26 **EST:** 1967
SQ FT: 13,000
SALES (est): 6.1MM **Privately Held**
WEB: www.spotimaging.com
SIC: 3827 3851 Optical instruments & lenses; ophthalmic goods

(G-15987)
DIHYDRO SERVICES INC
40833 Brentwood Dr (48310-2215)
PHONE..................586 978-0900
Dann Hutchins, *President*
Denel Tuszynski, *Manager*
EMP: 23 **EST:** 1948
SQ FT: 6,000
SALES (est): 3.4MM **Privately Held**
WEB: www.dihydro.com
SIC: 3589 Water treatment equipment, industrial

(G-15988)
DIVERSIFIED MFG & ASSEMBLY LLC (PA)
Also Called: Dma
5545 Bridgewood Dr (48310-2219)
PHONE..................586 272-2431
Tommy Longest, *President*
Michael Minard, *Program Mgr*
EMP: 9 **EST:** 2013
SALES (est): 1.7MM **Privately Held**
WEB: www.diversifiedmanufacturingassembly.com
SIC: 3714 Rear axle housings, motor vehicle

(G-15989)
DK CONCEPTS LLC
13943 Amanda Dr (48313-3505)
PHONE..................586 222-5255
David Kennedy,
EMP: 5 **EST:** 2017
SALES (est): 54.9K **Privately Held**
SIC: 7692 Welding repair

(G-15990)
DOBDAY MANUFACTURING CO INC
42750 Merrill Rd (48314-3244)
PHONE..................586 254-6777
Desmond I Dobday, *President*
EMP: 18 **EST:** 1965
SQ FT: 8,000
SALES (est): 400.6K **Privately Held**
WEB: www.gewp.com
SIC: 3599 3545 Machine shop, jobbing & repair; machine tool accessories

(G-15991)
DU VAL INDUSTRIES LLC
6410 19 Mile Rd (48314-2109)
PHONE..................586 737-2710
Theodore Elward,
Kimberly Elward,
Brett Kurily,
EMP: 21 **EST:** 1983
SQ FT: 11,600
SALES (est): 3.4MM **Privately Held**
WEB: www.du-val.com
SIC: 3544 Industrial molds
PA: Pacific Tool & Engineering Ltd.
  6410 19 Mile Rd
  Sterling Heights MI 48314
  586 737-2710

(G-15992)
DUPLICAST CORPORATION
44648 Mound Rd 202 (48314-1322)
PHONE..................586 756-5900
Thomas Doyle, *President*
EMP: 7 **EST:** 1959 **Privately Held**
WEB: www.duplicast.com
SIC: 3366 Copper foundries

(G-15993)
DURA HOG INC
Also Called: Fitzpatrick Manufacturing
33637 Sterling Ponds Blvd (48312-5810)
PHONE..................586 825-0066
Michael Fitzpatrick, *President*
Barbara Fitzpatrick, *Admin Sec*
EMP: 4 **EST:** 1993
SALES (est): 505.6K **Privately Held**
WEB: www.fitzpatrickmfgco.com
SIC: 3599 Machine shop, jobbing & repair

(G-15994)
DYNAMIC PRINT & IMAGING
2107 Koper Dr (48310-5229)
PHONE..................586 738-4367
EMP: 4 **EST:** 2012

SALES (est): 167.5K **Privately Held**
SIC: 2752 Commercial printing, lithographic

(G-15995)
E Q R 2 INC
Also Called: Imagamerica
44479 Phoenix Dr (48314-1468)
PHONE..................586 731-3383
Mike Resnick, *President*
Bev Resnick, *Vice Pres*
Matt Resnick, *Admin Sec*
EMP: 5 **EST:** 1993
SQ FT: 1,600 **Privately Held**
SIC: 2395 2396 Embroidery products, except schiffli machine; automotive & apparel trimmings

(G-15996)
E&S SALES LLC
36252 Tindell Dr (48312-3372)
PHONE..................586 212-6018
Eric Groffo,
EMP: 6
SALES (est): 182.4K **Privately Held**
SIC: 2396 Furniture trimmings, fabric

(G-15997)
EAGLE MACHINE PRODUCTS COMPANY
35440 Stanley Dr (48312-2656)
PHONE..................586 268-2460
Vasel Nicaj, *President*
EMP: 5 **EST:** 1985
SQ FT: 10,000
SALES (est): 534.3K **Privately Held**
WEB: www.eaglemachineproducts.com
SIC: 3599 Machine shop, jobbing & repair

(G-15998)
EAGLE MASKING FABRICATION INC
6633 Diplomat Dr (48314-1423)
PHONE..................586 992-3080
Christopher J Sinicki, *President*
Timothy C Hicks, *Corp Secy*
EMP: 6 **EST:** 2003
SALES (est): 500K **Privately Held**
WEB: www.eaglemasking.com
SIC: 3544 Industrial molds

(G-15999)
EAGLE THREAD VERIFIER LLC
40631 Firesteel Dr (48313-4219)
PHONE..................586 764-8218
Gordon Taylor,
EMP: 8 **EST:** 1990
SALES (est): 582.2K **Privately Held**
WEB: www.eaglethreadverifier.com
SIC: 3714 5013 Motor vehicle parts & accessories; automotive supplies & parts

(G-16000)
EAGLE TOOL GROUP LLC
42724 Mound Rd (48314-3254)
P.O. Box 143, Bloomfield Hills (48303-0143)
PHONE..................586 997-0800
EMP: 10
SALES (est): 699.1K **Privately Held**
SIC: 3423 Mfg Hand Tools

(G-16001)
EAST PENN MANUFACTURING CO
Also Called: Deka Batteries & Cables
6023 Progress Dr (48312-2621)
PHONE..................586 979-5300
Jeff Pruett, *Principal*
Michael Gilmour, *Sales Staff*
Ajay Shah, *Sales Staff*
EMP: 6
SALES (corp-wide): 2.8B **Privately Held**
WEB: www.eastpennmanufacturing.com
SIC: 3691 Storage batteries
PA: East Penn Manufacturing Co.
  102 Deka Rd
  Lyon Station PA 19536
  610 682-6361

(G-16002)
ELMHIRST INDUSTRIES INC
7630 19 Mile Rd (48314-3221)
PHONE..................586 731-8663
John Elmhirst, *President*

Jennifer Howard, *Vice Pres*
Dahood Ali, *Sales Mgr*
Sephora White, *Manager*
EMP: 45 **EST:** 1994
SQ FT: 28,500
SALES (est): 6MM **Privately Held**
WEB: www.elmhirst.net
SIC: 3545   3543   3469   Machine tool accessories; industrial patterns; metal stampings

(G-16003)
EMERSON ELECTRIC CO
6590 Sims Dr (48313-3751)
PHONE...................586 268-3104
EMP: 5
SALES (corp-wide): 16.7B **Publicly Held**
WEB: www.emerson.com
SIC: 3823   Industrial instrmnts msrmnt display/control process variable
PA: Emerson Electric Co.
8000 West Florissant Ave
Saint Louis MO 63136
314 553-2000

(G-16004)
EMITTED ENERGY INC (PA)
6559 Diplomat Dr (48314-1421)
PHONE...................855 752-3347
Gordon Pesola, *President*
David Kember, *Vice Pres*
Roy Ray, *Vice Pres*
Adam Bierl, *Natl Sales Mgr*
Richard Peach, *Mktg Coord*
EMP: 11 **EST:** 2010
SALES (est): 2.1MM **Privately Held**
WEB: www.emittedenergy.com
SIC: 3641   3823   Electric lamps & parts for specialized applications; industrial process control instruments

(G-16005)
ESYS AUTOMATION LLC
6701 Center Dr (48312-2627)
PHONE...................248 484-9702
Todd Thelen, *Branch Mgr*
EMP: 40   **Privately Held**
WEB: www.jrautomation.com
SIC: 3549   3599   8711   8742   Assembly machines, including robotic; custom machinery; engineering services; automation & robotics consultant; robotic conveyors
HQ: Esys Automation, Llc
1000 Brown Rd
Auburn Hills MI 48326
248 484-9927

(G-16006)
ETHNIC ARTWORK INC
Also Called: E.a Graphics
42111 Van Ave (48314)
P.O. Box 595 (48311-0595)
PHONE...................586 726-1400
Robert W Artymovich, *President*
Elaine Artymovich, *Treasurer*
Elaine Arymovich, *Accounts Exec*
EMP: 18 **EST:** 1978
SQ FT: 18,000
SALES (est): 2.8MM **Privately Held**
WEB: www.eagraphics.com
SIC: 2396   Screen printing on fabric articles

(G-16007)
EURO-CRAFT INTERIORS INC
6611 Diplomat Dr (48314-1423)
PHONE...................586 254-9130
Gaspare Vitale, *President*
Vince Vitale, *Vice Pres*
Maria Vitale, *Treasurer*
EMP: 18 **EST:** 1987
SQ FT: 6,000
SALES (est): 2.6MM **Privately Held**
WEB: www.eurocraftinteriors.com
SIC: 2434   Wood kitchen cabinets

(G-16008)
EXCEPTIONAL PRODUCT SALES LLC
13425 19 Mile Rd Ste 300 (48313-1991)
PHONE...................586 286-3240
Elliott Brackett, *Vice Pres*
Michael Kovacs, *Mng Member*
Wendy Herb, *Manager*
Brent Solek,
EMP: 10 **EST:** 2004

SALES (est): 327.6K **Privately Held**
SIC: 3317   Steel pipe & tubes

(G-16009)
EXPERI-METAL INC
6385 Wall St (48312-1079)
PHONE...................586 977-7800
Valiena A Allison, *President*
James Beindit, *Dept Chairman*
Dan Paterson, *Dept Chairman*
Bernard McConnell, *Production*
Gary Sears, *Draft/Design*
EMP: 144 **EST:** 1959
SQ FT: 285,000
SALES (est): 42.4MM **Privately Held**
WEB: www.qmc-emi.com
SIC: 3544   3444   3469   Special dies, tools, jigs & fixtures; sheet metalwork; stamping metal for the trade

(G-16010)
FAUCHER INDUSTRIES
5971 Product Dr (48312-4561)
PHONE...................586 434-5115
EMP: 4 **EST:** 2017
SALES (est): 47.3K **Privately Held**
WEB: www.faucher.ca
SIC: 3999   Manufacturing industries

(G-16011)
FCA US LLC
Also Called: Chrysler International Sales
38111 Van Dyke Ave (48312-1138)
PHONE...................586 978-0067
James Bauer, *Manager*
EMP: 14
SALES (corp-wide): 102.5B **Privately Held**
WEB: www.chrysler.com
SIC: 5511   3711   Automobiles, new & used; motor vehicles & car bodies
HQ: Fca Us Llc
1000 Chrysler Dr
Auburn Hills MI 48326

(G-16012)
FENIXX TECHNOLOGIES LLC
6633 Diplomat Dr (48314-1423)
PHONE...................586 254-6000
Sylwia Okruta, *Executive*
Lawrence J Schaller,
EMP: 7 **EST:** 2008
SQ FT: 36,000
SALES (est): 1MM **Privately Held**
WEB: www.fenixxtech.com
SIC: 3444   Sheet metalwork

(G-16013)
FETTES MANUFACTURING CO
35855 Stanley Dr (48312-2663)
PHONE...................586 939-8500
James E McKown, *President*
Tony Schodowski, *Purchasing*
Greg Davies, *QC Mgr*
Kimberly Martin, *Accounting Mgr*
Jean Camilletti, *Manager*
EMP: 44 **EST:** 1955
SQ FT: 25,000
SALES (est): 9.6MM **Privately Held**
WEB: www.pcmfettes.com
SIC: 3451   Screw machine products

(G-16014)
FIBRO LAEPPLE TECHNOLOGY INC
33286 Sterling Ponds Blvd (48312-5978)
PHONE...................248 591-4494
Guido Setzkorn, *Principal*
Zivko Nikolic, *Vice Pres*
EMP: 4 **EST:** 2014
SQ FT: 16,500
SALES (est): 1.3MM
SALES (corp-wide): 572.2MM **Privately Held**
WEB: www.flt-us.com
SIC: 3535   Robotic conveyors
HQ: Fibro Lapple Technology Gmbh
August-Lapple-Weg
HaBmersheim BW 74585
626 673-0

(G-16015)
FIRE FLY
35837 Deville Dr (48312-3918)
PHONE...................586 601-8792
Jeffrey Johnson, *Principal*

EMP: 4 **EST:** 2014
SALES (est): 86.5K **Privately Held**
SIC: 3993   Signs & advertising specialties

(G-16016)
FISHER & COMPANY INCORPORATED
Also Called: Fisher Dynamics Metal Forming
6550 Progress Dr (48312-2618)
PHONE...................586 746-2000
Wayne Ferris, *Plant Mgr*
Ryan Barney, *Opers Staff*
Katelin Hammond, *Buyer*
Stacy Glezman, *Purchasing*
Michael Rumel, *Purchasing*
EMP: 11
SALES (corp-wide): 448.1MM **Privately Held**
WEB: www.fisherco.com
SIC: 3714   Motor vehicle parts & accessories
PA: Fisher & Company, Incorporated
33300 Fisher Dr
Saint Clair Shores MI 48082
586 746-2000

(G-16017)
FLEX BUILDING SYSTEMS LLC
42400 Merrill Rd (48314-3238)
P.O. Box 180149, Utica (48318-0149)
PHONE...................586 803-6000
Matthew Winget, *President*
Allen Grajek, *CFO*
EMP: 5 **EST:** 2014
SQ FT: 150,000
SALES (est): 748.8K **Privately Held**
WEB: www.flexbuildingsystems.com
SIC: 2451   Mobile buildings: for commercial use

(G-16018)
FORMAX PRECISION GEAR INC
6047 18 Mile Rd (48314-4264)
PHONE...................586 323-9067
Thomas Rosa, *President*
Jack Higgins, *Vice Pres*
EMP: 11 **EST:** 1980
SALES (est): 561.3K **Privately Held**
WEB: www.formax-precision-gear.sterling-heights.mi.amfibi.company
SIC: 3462   Gear & chain forgings

(G-16019)
FORMS TRAC ENTERPRISES INC
37827 Brookwood Dr (48312-1915)
PHONE...................248 524-0006
Harold Hoover, *Owner*
EMP: 4 **EST:** 1979
SALES (est): 309.9K **Privately Held**
SIC: 2761   Manifold business forms

(G-16020)
FOUR STAR TOOLING & ENGRG INC
40550 Brentwood Dr (48310-2208)
PHONE...................586 264-4090
Stan Bilek, *President*
Grace Dzierzanowski, *Vice Pres*
Peter Bilek, *Plant Mgr*
Mark Bilek, *QC Mgr*
John Bilek, *Admin Sec*
EMP: 8 **EST:** 1990
SQ FT: 36,000
SALES (est): 1.5MM **Privately Held**
WEB: www.fste.us
SIC: 3469   3544   Stamping metal for the trade; special dies & tools

(G-16021)
FRA-WOD COMPANY INC
44035 Phoenix Dr (48314-1464)
PHONE...................586 254-4450
Christopher Snarski, *President*
Joseph S Jamrus, *Treasurer*
Danielle Provo, *Office Mgr*
EMP: 7 **EST:** 1952
SALES (est): 530K **Privately Held**
SIC: 3544   Industrial molds

(G-16022)
FREE RNGE NTRALS DOG TRATS INC
44648 Mound Rd (48314-1322)
PHONE...................586 737-0797

EMP: 9 **EST:** 2010
SALES (est): 671.1K **Privately Held**
SIC: 2047   Dog food

(G-16023)
FRICIA ENTERPRISES INC
Also Called: Industrial Metal Coating Co
6070 18 Mile Rd (48314-4202)
PHONE...................586 977-1900
Philip A Oliver, *President*
Philip Oliver, *Programmer Anys*
Concetta Oliver, *Admin Sec*
EMP: 9 **EST:** 1994
SALES (est): 1.6MM **Privately Held**
SIC: 3479   Coating of metals & formed products

(G-16024)
FRIENDSHIP INDUSTRIES INC (PA)
6520 Arrow Dr (48314-1412)
PHONE...................586 323-0033
Herman Spiess, *President*
Ben Suenaga, *Editor*
Cynthia Spiess, *Vice Pres*
EMP: 20 **EST:** 1986
SQ FT: 18,000
SALES (est): 2.1MM **Privately Held**
WEB: www.friendshipind.com
SIC: 3549   3499   Metalworking machinery; stabilizing bars (cargo), metal

(G-16025)
FRIENDSHIP INDUSTRIES INC
6521 Arrow Dr (48314-1413)
PHONE...................586 997-1325
Blake Francis, *Manager*
EMP: 10
SALES (corp-wide): 2.1MM **Privately Held**
WEB: www.friendshipind.com
SIC: 3549   Metalworking machinery
PA: Friendship Industries, Inc.
6520 Arrow Dr
Sterling Heights MI 48314
586 323-0033

(G-16026)
G TECH SALES LLC
6601 Burroughs Ave (48314-2132)
PHONE...................586 803-9393
Lawrence Gniatczyk,
EMP: 4 **EST:** 2002
SALES (est): 367K **Privately Held**
WEB: www.gtechsales.net
SIC: 3711   5012   Motor vehicles & car bodies; automobile auction

(G-16027)
GENERAL MOTORS LLC
6200 19 Mile Rd (48314-2103)
PHONE...................586 342-2728
Joseph Moraschinelli, *Branch Mgr*
EMP: 14   **Publicly Held**
WEB: www.gm.com
SIC: 5511   3714   Automobiles, new & used; motor vehicle parts & accessories
HQ: General Motors Llc
300 Renaissance Ctr L1
Detroit MI 48243

(G-16028)
GENERAL TACTICAL VEHICLES LLC
38500 Mound Rd (48310-3260)
PHONE...................586 825-7242
Janet Chybar, *Principal*
Don Howe, *Exec Dir*
Maryann Essary,
EMP: 5
SALES (est): 282.9K **Privately Held**
SIC: 3795   Tanks & tank components

(G-16029)
GENIX LLC (PA)
Also Called: G P Technologies
43665 Utica Rd (48314-2359)
PHONE...................248 419-0231
Edward Kim, *Mng Member*
Marc Santucci,
EMP: 10
SQ FT: 10,000
SALES (est): 6.7MM **Privately Held**
SIC: 3559   3599   Automotive related machinery; custom machinery

Sterling Heights - Macomb County (G-16030)

(G-16030)
GLOBAL WHOLESALE & MARKETING
Also Called: Polsorb Sales
6566 Burroughs Ave (48314-2133)
PHONE...............................248 910-8302
EMP: 4
SQ FT: 1,100
SALES: 50K Privately Held
SIC: 2842 Mfg Polish/Sanitation Goods

(G-16031)
GM GDLS DEFENSE GROUP LLC (DH)
38500 Mound Rd (48310-3260)
PHONE...............................586 825-4000
J Keith Zerebecki, President
Mark Roulet, Vice Pres
Geo Zarins, Plant Mgr
Julie Farina Percy,
▲ EMP: 100 EST: 1999
SALES (est): 4.7MM
SALES (corp-wide): 37.9B Publicly Held
WEB: www.gdls.com
SIC: 3711 8711 Motor vehicles & car bodies; consulting engineer
HQ: General Dynamics Land Systems Inc.
38500 Mound Rd
Sterling Heights MI 48310
586 825-4000

(G-16032)
GMR STONE PRODUCTS LLC
Also Called: Gmr Quality Stone
36955 Metro Ct (48312-1015)
PHONE...............................586 739-2700
Mike Povraznik, Office Mgr
Craig Griffin,
▲ EMP: 12 EST: 2003
SALES (est): 2.1MM Privately Held
WEB: www.gmrqualitystoneproducts.com
SIC: 3281 Cut stone & stone products

(G-16033)
GREAT LKES INDUS FRNC SVCS INC
6780 19 1/2 Mile Rd (48314-1403)
PHONE...............................586 323-9200
Charles Hatala, President
Tammy Hatala, Vice Pres
EMP: 15 EST: 1993
SQ FT: 4,000
SALES (est): 3.2MM Privately Held
WEB: www.glifs.com
SIC: 3567 7699 Heating units & devices, industrial; electric; industrial equipment services

(G-16034)
HART INDUSTRIES LLC
43718 Utica Rd (48314-2361)
PHONE...............................313 588-1837
Lisa Brown,
Paul Hartigan,
EMP: 10 EST: 2012
SALES (est): 303.4K Privately Held
WEB: www.hart-ind.com
SIC: 3599 Machine & other job shop work

(G-16035)
HAWKSHADOW PUBLISHING COMPANY
34481 Heartsworth Ln (48312-5738)
PHONE...............................586 979-5046
Steven Gibbs, Manager
EMP: 4 EST: 2012
SALES (est): 5.6K Privately Held
SIC: 2741 Miscellaneous publishing

(G-16036)
HAWTAL WHITING
41155 Technology Park Dr (48314-4155)
PHONE...............................248 262-2020
Robert Valcke, Partner
EMP: 5 EST: 2010
SALES (est): 118.1K Privately Held
WEB: www.hawtalwhiting.com
SIC: 3812 Search & navigation equipment

(G-16037)
HEADQRTER STRLNG HTS OPRATIONS
6125 18 Mile Rd (48314-4205)
PHONE...............................765 654-0477
EMP: 9 EST: 2018
SALES (est): 179.8K Privately Held
WEB: www.acument.com
SIC: 3452 Bolts, nuts, rivets & washers

(G-16038)
HEGENSCHEIDT-MFD CORPORATION
6255 Center Dr (48312-2667)
PHONE...............................586 274-4900
David Phillips, Vice Pres
Rock Smith, Purch Mgr
Martin Pielach, Engineer
Debbie Osaer, Controller
Sue Gonzales, Administration
▲ EMP: 21 EST: 1966
SQ FT: 30,000
SALES (est): 6MM
SALES (corp-wide): 212.8K Privately Held
WEB: www.hegenscheidt-mfd.com
SIC: 3541 Machine tools, metal cutting type
HQ: Hegenscheidt-Mfd Gmbh
Hegenscheidt-Platz
Erkelenz NW 41812
243 186-0

(G-16039)
HERMIZ PUBLISHING IN
3567 Du Pon Dr (48310-2549)
PHONE...............................586 212-4490
EMP: 4 EST: 2018
SALES (est): 87K Privately Held
SIC: 2741 Miscellaneous publishing

(G-16040)
HIGH END SIGNS SVC & LIGHTING
40213 Tonabee Ct (48313-4177)
PHONE...............................248 596-9301
Henry Nivelt, Principal
EMP: 4 EST: 2008
SALES (est): 88.3K Privately Held
SIC: 3993 Signs & advertising specialties

(G-16041)
HORSTMAN INC
Also Called: Milair
44215 Phoenix Dr (48314-1466)
PHONE...............................586 737-2100
Larry Humphrey, President
Steve Gaspard, President
Drew Lippert, General Mgr
James Kuhns, Vice Pres
Andy Godshaw, Engineer
EMP: 32 EST: 2010
SQ FT: 13,000
SALES (est): 9.5MM
SALES (corp-wide): 166.7K Privately Held
WEB: www.horstmangroup.com
SIC: 3714 3795 3711 Axle housings & shafts, motor vehicle; tanks & tank components; ambulances (motor vehicles), assembly of
HQ: Horstman Defence Systems Limited
Locksbrook Road
Bath

(G-16042)
HTI CYBERNETICS
40033 Mitchell Dr (48313-4507)
PHONE...............................586 826-8346
Danny Shea, Engineer
Roz Ryniak, Manager
EMP: 8 EST: 2020
SALES (est): 233.6K Privately Held
WEB: www.hticybernetics.com
SIC: 3542 Machine tools, metal forming type

(G-16043)
HTI CYBERNETICS INC (PA)
40033 Mitchell Dr (48313-4507)
PHONE...............................586 826-8346
Arno Rabin, CEO
Dennis Dawes, Vice Pres
Dennis Sims, Vice Pres
LI Weng, Vice Pres
Brian Elms, Project Mgr
EMP: 43 EST: 1983
SQ FT: 48,750
SALES (est): 10.1MM Privately Held
WEB: www.hticybernetics.com
SIC: 3542 3548 3549 3545 Bending machines; resistance welders, electric; metalworking machinery; machine tool accessories; special dies, tools, jigs & fixtures; automotive related machinery

(G-16044)
HUDSON INDUSTRIES INC
Also Called: Xtol
34543 Sandpebble Dr (48310-5561)
PHONE...............................313 777-5622
Bryan Hudson, CEO
EMP: 5 EST: 2016
SQ FT: 1,500
SALES (est): 251.1K Privately Held
SIC: 3229 3714 3599 7349 Lenses, lantern, flashlight, headlight, etc.; glass; windshield wiper systems, motor vehicle; oil filters, internal combustion engine, except automotive; janitorial service, contract basis

(G-16045)
I PALLET LLC
3187 Kilborne Dr (48310-6030)
PHONE...............................586 625-2238
Manhal Jerjosa,
EMP: 4 EST: 2017
SALES (est): 76.1K Privately Held
SIC: 2448 Wood pallets & skids

(G-16046)
IMPEL INDUSTRIES INC
44494 Phoenix Dr (48314-1467)
PHONE...............................586 254-5800
Tom Patzer, President
Ed Bohmier, Vice Pres
Steve Lloyd, Purchasing
Suzan Patzer, Treasurer
Stephanie Harris, Manager
EMP: 45 EST: 2000
SQ FT: 18,000
SALES (est): 5.5MM Privately Held
WEB: www.impelind.com
SIC: 3542 Sheet metalworking machines

(G-16047)
INDICON LLC (PA)
6125 Center Dr (48312-2667)
PHONE...............................586 274-0505
Paul Duhaime, CEO
Andrew T Conti, Corp Secy
Jeff Angus, Controller
Leonard Grawburg, Manager
EMP: 218 EST: 1993
SQ FT: 52,500
SALES (est): 61.5MM Privately Held
WEB: www.indicon.com
SIC: 3613 3625 Control panels, electric; relays & industrial controls

(G-16048)
INDUSTRIAL FRNC INTERIORS INC
Also Called: I F I
35160 Stanley Dr (48312-2650)
PHONE...............................586 977-9600
Clyde Bennett, President
Clyde J Bennett, President
EMP: 5 EST: 1982
SQ FT: 8,000
SALES (est): 855.8K Privately Held
WEB: www.ifi-inc.com
SIC: 3567 Heating units & devices, industrial; electric

(G-16049)
INNOVTIVE DESIGN SOLUTIONS INC
Also Called: IDS
6801 15 Mile Rd (48312-4517)
PHONE...............................248 583-1010
Robert Ford, President
Shawn Haley, Vice Pres
▲ EMP: 120 EST: 1992
SALES (est): 29.9MM
SALES (corp-wide): 2.8B Publicly Held
WEB: www.lci1.com
SIC: 3571 Electronic computers
HQ: Lippert Components, Inc.
3501 County Road 6 E
Elkhart IN 46514
574 535-1125

(G-16050)
INTEC AUTOMATED CONTROLS INC
44440 Phoenix Dr (48314-1467)
PHONE...............................586 532-8881
Jeff Spada, President
Ronald Bellestri, General Mgr
Scott Krueger, Vice Pres
Greg Spada, Mfg Mgr
Jim Hude, Engineer
EMP: 50 EST: 1996
SQ FT: 3,600 Privately Held
WEB: www.intecautomated.com
SIC: 3613 Control panels, electric

(G-16051)
INTERNTNAL AUTO CMPNNTS GROUP
6600 15 Mile Rd (48312-4512)
PHONE...............................586 795-7800
EMP: 5 Privately Held
WEB: www.iacgroup.com
SIC: 3089 Automotive parts, plastic
HQ: International Automotive Components Group North America, Inc.
27777 Franklin Rd # 2000
Southfield MI 48034

(G-16052)
J G KERN ENTERPRISES INC
44044 Merrill Rd (48314-1440)
PHONE...............................586 531-9472
Joseph G Kern, Ch of Bd
Brian Kern, President
Alan Kern, Vice Pres
Lester Castillo, Plant Mgr
Geoff Pitts, Plant Mgr
▲ EMP: 62 EST: 1967
SQ FT: 152,000
SALES (est): 14.2MM Privately Held
WEB: www.jgkern.com
SIC: 3714 3566 Motor vehicle parts & accessories; gears, power transmission, except automotive

(G-16053)
J W FROEHLICH INC
7305 19 Mile Rd (48314-3217)
PHONE...............................586 580-0025
Andrew Laurie, General Mgr
▲ EMP: 5 EST: 2006
SQ FT: 4,000
SALES (est): 1.7MM
SALES (corp-wide): 73MM Privately Held
WEB: www.jwfroehlich.com
SIC: 3549 Assembly machines, including robotic
HQ: Jw Froehlich Maschinenfabrik Gmbh
Kohlhammerstr. 18-24
Leinfelden-Echterdingen BW 70771
711 797-660

(G-16054)
JBR ASSOCIATES
36950 Dequindre Rd (48310-4255)
PHONE...............................586 693-5666
EMP: 4 EST: 2019
SALES (est): 100.2K Privately Held
SIC: 2893 Printing ink

(G-16055)
JBR JUNK REMOVAL LLC
34841 Mound Rd Ste 314 (48310-5723)
PHONE...............................248 818-3471
Chris Nierman,
EMP: 5 EST: 2019
SALES (est): 790K Privately Held
WEB: www.jbrjunk.com
SIC: 2851 Removers & cleaners

(G-16056)
JOE DAVIS CRUSHING INC
42101 Bobjean St (48314-3126)
PHONE...............................586 757-3612
Joe Davis, President
Bonnie Davis, Corp Secy
EMP: 6 EST: 1952
SQ FT: 3,000
SALES (est): 482.4K Privately Held
SIC: 3241 Cement, hydraulic

GEOGRAPHIC SECTION

Sterling Heights - Macomb County (G-16083)

(G-16057)
JOHNSON CONTROLS INC
6111 Sterling Dr N (48312-4549)
PHONE.............................586 826-8845
Alfred Loosvelt, *President*
EMP: 7 **Publicly Held**
WEB: www.johnsoncontrols.com
SIC: 3714 Motor vehicle body components & frame
HQ: Johnson Controls, Inc.
  5757 N Green Bay Ave
  Glendale WI 53209
  800 382-2804

(G-16058)
JVRF UNIFIED INC
13854 Lakeside Cir 503-O (48313-1443)
PHONE.............................248 973-2006
Daniel Lewis, *CEO*
Chanel Lewis, *President*
EMP: 8 **EST:** 2010
SALES (est): 1.1MM **Privately Held**
WEB: www.jvrfunifieddigitalsigns.com
SIC: 3993 Electric signs

(G-16059)
K & K DIE INC
40700 Enterprise Dr (48314-3760)
PHONE.............................586 268-8812
Manfred Kunath, *President*
Christian Kunath, *Vice Pres*
Steve Schucker, *QC Mgr*
D 'anna Hood, *Controller*
Mike Scavone, *Program Mgr*
EMP: 50 **EST:** 1974
SQ FT: 56,000
SALES (est): 9.1MM **Privately Held**
WEB: www.kandkdie.com
SIC: 3469 Stamping metal for the trade

(G-16060)
K-B TOOL CORPORATION
5985 Wall St (48312-1074)
PHONE.............................586 795-9003
Alan G Klinger, *President*
EMP: 9 **EST:** 1978
SQ FT: 11,000
SALES (est): 804.5K **Privately Held**
WEB: www.kbtoolanddie.com
SIC: 3544 Special dies & tools; jigs & fixtures

(G-16061)
KATH KHEMICALS LLC
6050 19 Mile Rd (48312-2101)
PHONE.............................586 275-2646
Emmett Jones, *President*
Rita K Holston, *Vice Pres*
▲ **EMP:** 11 **EST:** 1985
SALES (est): 736.7K **Privately Held**
SIC: 2842 Specialty cleaning, polishes & sanitation goods

(G-16062)
KAYLER MOLD & ENGINEERING INC
35620 Beattie Dr (48312-2616)
PHONE.............................586 739-0699
Candee B Boschman, *President*
Theodore Boschman, *Business Mgr*
EMP: 5 **EST:** 1999
SALES (est): 877.5K **Privately Held**
WEB: www.kaylermold.com
SIC: 2821 Plastics materials & resins

(G-16063)
KINDER PRODUCTS UNLIMITED LLC
6471 Metro Pkwy (48312-1027)
PHONE.............................586 557-3453
Andrew Blake,
Paul Blake,
Peter Blake,
Gino Roncelli,
EMP: 5 **EST:** 2019
SALES (est): 375.5K **Privately Held**
WEB: www.kinder.com
SIC: 2833 Vitamins, natural or synthetic: bulk, uncompounded

(G-16064)
KROPP WOODWORKING INC
6812 19 1/2 Mile Rd (48314-1304)
PHONE.............................586 997-3000
Paul Kropp, *Principal*

EMP: 5 **EST:** 2004
SALES (est): 435.8K **Privately Held**
SIC: 2431 Millwork

(G-16065)
KUKA SYSTEMS NORTH AMERICA LLC
7408 Metropolitan Pkwy (48312-1046)
PHONE.............................586 795-2000
Jim Gouin, *Engineer*
Rohit Kantharaju, *Engineer*
Detlev Ziesel, *Manager*
Dan Coulter, *Supervisor*
Sam Clark, *Prgrmr*
EMP: 12 **EST:** 2014
SALES (est): 669.3K **Privately Held**
WEB: www.kuka.com
SIC: 3549 Metalworking machinery

(G-16066)
KUKA SYSTEMS NORTH AMERICA LLC (DH)
Also Called: Kuka Aerospace
6600 Center Dr (48312-2666)
PHONE.............................586 795-2000
Lawrence A Drake, *President*
Ron Bochniak, *Project Mgr*
Tim Carlson, *Project Mgr*
Saeed Malik, *Project Mgr*
Charlie Pierce, *Project Mgr*
▲ **EMP:** 400 **EST:** 1935
SQ FT: 320,000
SALES (est): 471.9MM **Privately Held**
WEB: www.kuka.com
SIC: 3549 Assembly machines, including robotic
HQ: Kuka Systems Gmbh
  Blucherstr. 144
  Augsburg BY 86165
  821 797-0

(G-16067)
KUKA US HOLDINGS COMPANY LLC (DH)
Also Called: Kuka Robotics
6600 Center Dr (48312-2666)
PHONE.............................586 795-2000
Robert Giaier, *Vice Pres*
James Marshall, *Project Mgr*
Andrea Kovacic, *Buyer*
Matt Beyer, *Engineer*
Darrel Calcaterra, *Engineer*
▲ **EMP:** 89 **EST:** 2004
SALES (est): 48.3MM **Privately Held**
WEB: www.kuka.com
SIC: 5084 3549 Industrial machinery & equipment; assembly machines, including robotic
HQ: Kuka Deutschland Gmbh
  Zugspitzstr. 140
  Augsburg BY 86165
  821 797-4000

(G-16068)
KUSTOM CREATIONS INC
6665 Burroughs Ave (48314-2132)
PHONE.............................586 997-4141
Harvey Ledesma, *President*
EMP: 7 **EST:** 2007
SALES (est): 876.5K **Privately Held**
WEB: www.kustomcreations.net
SIC: 7539 3449 Automotive repair shops; miscellaneous metalwork

(G-16069)
LEADERSHIP GROUP LLC
14225 Southgate Dr (48313-5640)
PHONE.............................586 251-2090
Ted Amsden, *Owner*
EMP: 5 **EST:** 2017
SALES (est): 109.4K **Privately Held**
SIC: 3531 Construction machinery

(G-16070)
LED SOURCE DETROIT
6095 15 Mile Rd (48312-4501)
PHONE.............................586 983-9905
Marcel Fairbairn, *CEO*
Gavin Cooper, *President*
Dean Ernst, *Vice Pres*
Dan Ocasio, *Vice Pres*
EMP: 5 **EST:** 2015

SALES (est): 125.9K **Privately Held**
WEB: www.ledsource.com
SIC: 5063 3641 Lighting fixtures; electric lamps

(G-16071)
LESNAU PRINTING COMPANY
6025 Wall St (48312-1075)
PHONE.............................586 795-9200
Robert A Lesnau, *President*
Paul Lesnau, *Vice Pres*
Michael Lesnau, *Treasurer*
EMP: 23 **EST:** 1948
SQ FT: 45,000
SALES (est): 1MM **Privately Held**
WEB: www.lesnauprinting.com
SIC: 2752 2759 Commercial printing, offset; letterpress printing

(G-16072)
LETNAN INDUSTRIES INC
Also Called: Rh Spies Group
6520 Arrow Dr (48314-1412)
PHONE.............................586 726-1155
Cynthia Spiess, *CEO*
Erica Francis, *President*
Herman Spiess, *President*
Christina Vloch, *President*
Michelle Thorndyke, *Purchasing*
◆ **EMP:** 37 **EST:** 1964
SQ FT: 19,000
SALES (est): 4.3MM **Privately Held**
WEB: www.letnanind.com
SIC: 3549 Assembly machines, including robotic

(G-16073)
LIBERTY TOOL INC
44404 Phoenix Dr (48314-1467)
PHONE.............................586 726-2449
Chris Maier, *President*
Shannon Maier, *COO*
Shannon Cimini, *Vice Pres*
Richard McNaughton, *Opers Mgr*
Shannon Maler, *Purchasing*
EMP: 22 **EST:** 1995
SQ FT: 11,000
SALES (est): 3.8MM **Privately Held**
WEB: www.liberty-tool.com
SIC: 3541 3599 3544 3728 Machine tools, metal cutting type; machine shop, jobbing & repair; special dies, tools, jigs & fixtures; aircraft parts & equipment

(G-16074)
LIGHTHOUSE ELEC PROTECTION LLC
7314 19 Mile Rd (48314-3214)
PHONE.............................586 932-2690
Scott Lowes, *Mng Member*
Scott Riesfield,
EMP: 8 **EST:** 2005
SQ FT: 6,500
SALES (est): 1.2MM **Privately Held**
SIC: 3699 Electrical equipment & supplies

(G-16075)
LIPPERT COMPONENTS INC
6801 15 Mile Rd (48312-4517)
PHONE.............................586 275-2107
Joyce Schofield, *Vice Pres*
Stefan Hjertsson, *Production*
Michael Steinmann, *Engineer*
Donald Moore, *Technician*
EMP: 7
SALES (corp-wide): 2.8B **Publicly Held**
WEB: www.lci1.com
SIC: 3714 Motor vehicle parts & accessories
HQ: Lippert Components, Inc.
  3501 County Road 6 E
  Elkhart IN 46514
  574 535-1125

(G-16076)
LOC PERFORMANCE PRODUCTS INC
33852 Sterling Ponds Blvd (48312-5808)
PHONE.............................734 453-2300
Anthony Militello, *Manager*
EMP: 5
SALES (corp-wide): 129.7MM **Privately Held**
WEB: www.locperformance.com
SIC: 3541 Machine tools, metal cutting type

PA: Loc Performance Products, Inc.
  13505 N Haggerty Rd
  Plymouth MI 48170
  734 453-2300

(G-16077)
LUCKMARR PLASTICS INC
Also Called: L M Group
35735 Stanley Dr (48312-2661)
PHONE.............................586 978-8498
Luciano Pierobon, *President*
Kurt Hahn, *General Mgr*
Virgil Nicaise, *General Mgr*
Marco Pierobon, *Vice Pres*
Andy Miller, *Plant Mgr*
EMP: 65 **EST:** 1983
SQ FT: 36,000
SALES (est): 10MM **Privately Held**
WEB: www.luckmarrplastics.com
SIC: 3089 3544 3469 Injection molding of plastics; special dies, tools, jigs & fixtures; metal stampings

(G-16078)
M & M MACHINING INC
42876 Mound Rd (48314-3256)
P.O. Box 191 (48311-0191)
PHONE.............................586 997-9910
Marco Lachapelle, *President*
Michelle Lachapelle, *Vice Pres*
EMP: 5 **EST:** 1996
SQ FT: 2,450
SALES (est): 445.5K **Privately Held**
WEB: www.mmjobshop.com
SIC: 3599 Machine shop, jobbing & repair

(G-16079)
M & M THREAD & ASSEMBLY INC
42716 Mound Rd (48314-3254)
PHONE.............................248 583-9696
James Milonoff, *President*
Eugene Wojtowicz, *Vice Pres*
Kandis Milonoff, *Treasurer*
EMP: 8 **EST:** 1961
SQ FT: 22,000
SALES (est): 246.5K **Privately Held**
SIC: 3545 Thread cutting dies

(G-16080)
MADAIN POSTAL SERVICES LLC
43755 Saint Julian Ct (48314-1804)
PHONE.............................586 323-3573
Hanna Alhindi, *Principal*
EMP: 4 **EST:** 2015
SALES (est): 62.1K **Privately Held**
SIC: 2752 Commercial printing, lithographic

(G-16081)
MAG AUTOMOTIVE LLC (DH)
6015 Center Dr (48312-2667)
PHONE.............................586 446-7000
Brian Prina,
Paul Chen,
Robert Dudek,
EMP: 209 **EST:** 2013
SALES: 183.2MM **Privately Held**
WEB: www.service.mag-ias.com
SIC: 3559 Automotive related machinery
HQ: Mag Us Holding Inc.
  6015 Center Dr
  Sterling Heights MI 48312
  586 446-7000

(G-16082)
MAG-POWERTRAIN
6015 Center Dr (48312-2667)
PHONE.............................586 446-7000
Bob Dudek, *Principal*
Ronald Quaile, *Marketing Staff*
William Thee, *Corp Counsel*
Debbie Lueker, *Admin Sec*
Shauna Chaityn, *Administration*
▲ **EMP:** 15 **EST:** 2008
SALES (est): 562K **Privately Held**
WEB: www.service.mag-ias.com
SIC: 3541 Drilling & boring machines

(G-16083)
MAN U TEC INC
Also Called: Manutec
6522 Diplomat Dr (48314-1420)
PHONE.............................586 262-4085
James Kaleniecki, *President*
Jeremy Kaleniecki, *Manager*

Sterling Heights - Macomb County (G-16084) GEOGRAPHIC SECTION

Stacey Castillo, *Admin Sec*
EMP: 8 **EST:** 1988
SQ FT: 4,000
SALES (est): 1.2MM **Privately Held**
WEB: www.manutec-bci.com
SIC: 3599 Machine shop, jobbing & repair

(G-16084)
MANNINO TILE & MARBLE INC
Also Called: Tile Installation
38790 Hartwell Dr (48312-1327)
PHONE.................586 978-3390
Rodney J Mannino, *President*
Kenzie Mannino, *Admin Sec*
EMP: 5 **EST:** 1990
SALES (est): 92.6K **Privately Held**
SIC: 3253 Ceramic wall & floor tile

(G-16085)
MASTER PRECISION TOOL CORP
7362 19 Mile Rd (48314-3214)
PHONE.................586 739-3240
Douglas De Wolfe, *President*
Chuck Busuisto, *Vice Pres*
EMP: 15 **EST:** 1978
SQ FT: 7,800
SALES (est): 961.7K **Privately Held**
WEB: www.masterpneumatic.com
SIC: 3544 Special dies & tools

(G-16086)
MASTERS PUBLISHING
42126 Bobjean St (48314-3121)
PHONE.................586 323-2723
Darleen Urbanek, *Principal*
EMP: 4 **EST:** 2008
SALES (est): 56.6K **Privately Held**
SIC: 2741 Miscellaneous publishing

(G-16087)
MAYCO INTERNATIONAL LLC (PA)
Also Called: Njt Enterprises LLC
42400 Merrill Rd (48314-3238)
P.O. Box 180149, Utica (48318-0149)
PHONE.................586 803-6000
Tom Eckhout, *Exec VP*
Delia Nikprelevic, *Buyer*
Jason Tignanelli, *Purchasing*
Dennis Marion, *Plant Engr Mgr*
Kris Cabanilla, *Engineer*
▲ **EMP:** 750 **EST:** 2006
SQ FT: 700,000
SALES (est): 350MM **Privately Held**
WEB: www.maycointernational.com
SIC: 3089 Injection molding of plastics

(G-16088)
MB AEROSPACE HOLDINGS III CORP
38111 Commerce Dr (48312-1007)
PHONE.................586 977-9200
EMP: 10
SALES (est): 628.5K **Privately Held**
WEB: www.mbaerospace.com
SIC: 3599 Machine shop, jobbing & repair

(G-16089)
MB AEROSPACE STERLING HTS INC
38111 Commerce Dr (48312-1007)
PHONE.................586 977-9200
Craig Gallagher, *CEO*
Kevin Johnston, *President*
Tim Zak, *Facilities Mgr*
Ken Brubaker, *Human Res Mgr*
George Adams, *Officer*
▲ **EMP:** 75 **EST:** 1969
SQ FT: 30,000
SALES (est): 15.5MM
SALES (corp-wide): 55.5MM **Privately Held**
WEB: www.mbaerospace.com
SIC: 3599 Machine shop, jobbing & repair
PA: Mb Aerospace Acp Holdings Iii Corp.
  2711 Centerville Rd # 400
  Wilmington DE 19808
  586 772-2500

(G-16090)
MEANS INDUSTRIES INC
Also Called: Means Trnsform Pdts - Strlng H
7026 Sterling Ponds Ct (48312-5809)
PHONE.................586 826-8500
Jeremy Holt, *President*
EMP: 14
SALES (corp-wide): 2.4B **Privately Held**
WEB: www.meansindustries.com
SIC: 3714 Motor vehicle parts & accessories
HQ: Means Industries, Inc.
  3715 E Washington Rd
  Saginaw MI 48601
  989 754-1433

(G-16091)
MERRIFIELD MCHY SOLUTIONS INC
5430 Gatewood Dr (48310-2224)
PHONE.................248 494-7335
Nicholas Merrifield, *President*
Richard Rohn, *Exec VP*
Paul Sienkiewicz, *Purchasing*
Fred Gravelle, *Finance Mgr*
Barbara Lewis, *Sales Staff*
EMP: 34
SALES (est): 4.8MM **Privately Held**
WEB: www.merrifieldmachinery.com
SIC: 3545 5084 Machine tool accessories; industrial machinery & equipment

(G-16092)
METALSA STRUCTURAL PDTS INC
Also Called: Metalsa SA De Cv
40117 Mitchell Dr (48313-4507)
PHONE.................248 669-3704
EMP: 583 **Privately Held**
WEB: www.metalsa.com
SIC: 3714 Motor vehicle parts & accessories
HQ: Metalsa Structural Products, Inc.
  29575 Hudson Dr
  Novi MI 48377

(G-16093)
METRO PRINTS INC
5580 Gatewood Dr Ste 103 (48310-2228)
PHONE.................586 979-9690
Terry Hillker, *Principal*
EMP: 10 **EST:** 2007
SALES (est): 530.7K **Privately Held**
SIC: 2752 Commercial printing, offset

(G-16094)
METROASTYLING
5400 18 Mile Rd (48314-4104)
PHONE.................586 991-6854
Chris Anawky, *Principal*
EMP: 6 **EST:** 2011
SALES (est): 129.2K **Privately Held**
WEB: www.metrorestyling.com
SIC: 2759 Commercial printing

(G-16095)
METTLE CRAFT MANUFACTURING LLC
3223 15 Mile Rd (48310-5348)
PHONE.................586 306-8962
Katie Bigelow, *Principal*
Kathryn Bigelow, *Principal*
Danielle Deshard, *Principal*
Heidi Devroy, *Principal*
EMP: 5 **EST:** 2019
SALES (est): 251.6K **Privately Held**
WEB: www.mettleops.com
SIC: 3999 Manufacturing industries

(G-16096)
MGR MOLDS INC
6450 Cotter Ave (48314-2146)
PHONE.................586 254-6020
Robert Walter, *President*
Renae Walter, *Administration*
◆ **EMP:** 15 **EST:** 1980
SQ FT: 12,822
SALES (est): 3.5MM **Privately Held**
WEB: www.mgrmold.com
SIC: 3544 3089 Industrial molds; injection molded finished plastic products

(G-16097)
MIBA HYDRAMECHANICA CORP
6625 Cobb Dr (48312-2625)
PHONE.................586 264-3094
Werner Kollment, *President*
Rick Huston, *Vice Pres*
Volker Reulein, *Vice Pres*
Sebastian Seiter, *Project Mgr*
Bruce Rigard, *Opers Mgr*
◆ **EMP:** 58 **EST:** 1985
SQ FT: 26,080
SALES (est): 21.6MM
SALES (corp-wide): 637.8K **Privately Held**
WEB: www.mibahmc.com
SIC: 3499 Friction material, made from powdered metal
HQ: Miba Aktiengesellschaft
  Dr. Mitterbauer-StraBe 3
  Laakirchen 4663
  761 325-410

(G-16098)
MICROPRECISION CLEANING
6145 Wall St (48312-1058)
PHONE.................586 997-6960
Larry Roads, *President*
Dave Baumgarten, *General Mgr*
EMP: 13 **EST:** 1971
SALES (est): 156.5K **Privately Held**
SIC: 3541 Deburring machines

(G-16099)
MIDWAY GROUP LLC
Also Called: Protocon Rm
6227 Metropolitan Pkwy (48312-1023)
PHONE.................586 264-5380
Edward C Levy Jr, *President*
Gary Lowell, *President*
Robert Scholz, *Vice Pres*
S E Weiner, *Vice Pres*
EMP: 18 **EST:** 2014
SALES (est): 4.1MM
SALES (corp-wide): 521.9MM **Privately Held**
WEB: www.protoconrm.com
SIC: 3273 Ready-mixed concrete
PA: Edw. C. Levy Co.
  9300 Dix
  Dearborn MI 48120
  313 429-2200

(G-16100)
MIDWEST TUBE FABRICATORS INC
36845 Metro Ct (48312-1013)
PHONE.................586 264-9898
James Mc Carthy, *President*
Debi Cavanaugh, *General Mgr*
Victoria Mc Carthy, *Vice Pres*
Kim Mills, *Office Mgr*
Grace Butler, *Manager*
▲ **EMP:** 24 **EST:** 1980
SQ FT: 5,500
SALES (est): 6.1MM **Privately Held**
WEB: www.midwesttubefab.com
SIC: 3498 Tube fabricating (contract bending & shaping)

(G-16101)
MILLIKEN MILLWORK INC (HQ)
Also Called: Mmi Door
6361 Sterling Dr N (48312-4553)
PHONE.................586 264-0950
Mark Beck, *President*
David Marion, *Project Mgr*
Ethan Kabler, *Opers Mgr*
Edwina Infante, *Purch Mgr*
Ryan Wiltfang, *Purchasing*
▲ **EMP:** 280
SQ FT: 220,000
SALES (est): 82.5MM **Publicly Held**
WEB: www.mmidoor.com
SIC: 2431 Millwork

(G-16102)
MITCHS SLOTS
41751 Marold Dr (48314-4139)
PHONE.................586 739-5157
Mitch Bialczak, *Principal*
EMP: 5 **EST:** 2010
SALES (est): 228K **Privately Held**
WEB: www.slotmachinerepairmacombmi.com
SIC: 3824 Mechanical & electromechanical counters & devices

(G-16103)
MOLDING CONCEPTS INC
6700 Sims Dr (48313-3727)
PHONE.................586 264-6990
Mark Mies, *President*
EMP: 23 **EST:** 1987
SQ FT: 10,000
SALES (est): 2.5MM **Privately Held**
WEB: www.moldingconcepts.com
SIC: 3089 Injection molding of plastics

(G-16104)
MR ES EATERY LLC
33742 Elford Dr (48312-5913)
PHONE.................313 502-9256
William Evans,
EMP: 4 **EST:** 2020
SALES (est): 90K **Privately Held**
SIC: 2599 Food wagons, restaurant

(G-16105)
MS INTERNATIONAL HOLDINGS LLC ✪
7205 Sterling Ponds Ct (48312-5813)
PHONE.................443 210-1446
Michael Wagner, *Principal*
EMP: 5 **EST:** 2021
SALES (est): 122.6K **Privately Held**
SIC: 1499 Gemstone & industrial diamond mining

(G-16106)
MSE
40809 Brentwood Dr (48310-2215)
PHONE.................586 264-4120
Steven Wiebe, *President*
EMP: 4 **EST:** 2017
SALES (est): 39.6K **Privately Held**
SIC: 3999 Manufacturing industries

(G-16107)
MSE FABRICATION LLC
6624 Burroughs Ave (48314-2135)
PHONE.................586 991-6138
Neil Wiebe,
Margaret Wiebe,
EMP: 13 **EST:** 2001
SQ FT: 130,000
SALES (est): 826.1K **Privately Held**
SIC: 3444 Sheet metalwork

(G-16108)
MTM MACHINE INC
35310 Stanley Dr (48312-2654)
PHONE.................586 443-5703
Glenn Middler, *President*
Peter Middler, *Vice Pres*
EMP: 8 **EST:** 2004
SQ FT: 8,300
SALES (est): 1MM **Privately Held**
SIC: 3599 7539 Machine shop, jobbing & repair; machine shop, automotive

(G-16109)
MULTIFORM PLASTICS INC
6594 Diplomat Dr (48314-1420)
PHONE.................586 726-2688
EMP: 11 **EST:** 2018
SALES (est): 88.9K **Privately Held**
WEB: www.multiformplasticsinc.com
SIC: 3089 Jars, plastic

(G-16110)
MYCDBDMK SERVICES LLC ✪
Also Called: Mj Global Services
35251 Malibu Dr (48312-4047)
PHONE.................586 994-7910
Michael Jordan, *CEO*
EMP: 5 **EST:** 2021
SALES (est): 150K **Privately Held**
SIC: 3452 Bolts, nuts, rivets & washers

(G-16111)
N/C PRODUCTION & GRINDING INC
43758 Merrill Rd (48314-2172)
PHONE.................586 731-2150
Scott Carter, *President*
EMP: 4 **EST:** 1988
SQ FT: 5,600
SALES (est): 333.1K **Privately Held**
WEB: www.ncproductionandgrinding.com
SIC: 3599 Machine shop, jobbing & repair

(G-16112)
NATIONAL CASE CORPORATION
42710 Mound Rd (48314-3254)
PHONE.................586 726-1710
EMP: 5
SQ FT: 3,000

▲ = Import ▼ = Export
◆ = Import/Export

GEOGRAPHIC SECTION

Sterling Heights - Macomb County (G-16142)

SALES (est): 430K Privately Held
SIC: 2542 3089 2441 2394 Designer Manufacturer Distributors Of Shipping And/Or Carrying Cases / Industrial Sewing

(G-16113)
NATIONWIDE DESIGN INC
6605 Burroughs Ave (48314-2132)
P.O. Box 385, Howell (48844-0385)
PHONE...................586 254-5493
EMP: 16
SQ FT: 14,000
SALES (est): 225K Privately Held
SIC: 3714 3711 Mfg Automotive Parts & Body Prototypes

(G-16114)
NEW ELECTRIC
34000 Mound Rd (48310-6609)
PHONE...................586 580-2405
Brett Glover, *Project Mgr*
Tim Perry, *Branch Mgr*
EMP: 12 EST: 2011
SALES (est): 6.4MM Privately Held
WEB: www.sparkpowercorp.com
SIC: 3699 Electrical equipment & supplies

(G-16115)
NIDEC INDL AUTOMATION USA
41200 Technology Park Dr (48314-4102)
PHONE...................203 735-6367
EMP: 4 EST: 2019
SALES (est): 87.2K Privately Held
SIC: 3541 Machine tools, metal cutting type

(G-16116)
NIKOLIC INDUSTRIES INC
43252 Merrill Rd (48314-2162)
PHONE...................586 254-4810
Martha Nikolic, *President*
Veliko Nikolic, *Vice Pres*
EMP: 20 EST: 1977
SQ FT: 12,000
SALES (est): 3MM Privately Held
WEB: www.nikolicind.com
SIC: 3599 Machine shop, jobbing & repair

(G-16117)
NISSHINBO AUTOMOTIVE MFG INC
6100 19 Mile Rd (48314-2102)
PHONE...................586 997-1000
Yukhiko Konno, *President*
Keith Davis, *Engineer*
Andy Ozburn, *Engineer*
Chris Barrett, *Human Resources*
EMP: 33 Privately Held
WEB: www.nisshinboauto.com
SIC: 3714 3441 Motor vehicle brake systems & parts; fabricated structural metal
HQ: Nisshinbo Automotive Manufacturing Inc.
    14187 Nisshinbo Dr
    Covington GA 30014
    770 787-2002

(G-16118)
NORTHERN PLASTICS INC
6137 Product Dr (48312-4565)
PHONE...................586 979-7737
Philip K Truscott, *President*
EMP: 30 EST: 1984
SALES (est): 4.1MM Privately Held
WEB: www.northernplasticsusa.com
SIC: 3089 Injection molding of plastics

(G-16119)
NPWORLD CO
14235 Valusek Dr (48312-6667)
PHONE...................586 826-9702
Paul Sowinski, *Principal*
EMP: 4 EST: 2004
SALES (est): 128.8K Privately Held
SIC: 2899 Ink or writing fluids

(G-16120)
OLIVER INDUSTRIES INC
Also Called: Industrial Metal Finishing Co
6070 18 Mile Rd (48314-4202)
PHONE...................586 977-7350
Concetta F Oliver, *President*
Philip A Oliver, *Vice Pres*
EMP: 21 EST: 1984
SQ FT: 50,000
SALES (est): 1.1MM Privately Held
WEB: www.industrialmetalfinishing.com
SIC: 3471 Finishing, metals or formed products

(G-16121)
P & G TECHNOLOGIES INC
6503 19 1/2 Mile Rd (48314-1407)
PHONE...................248 399-3135
Gary Bowden, *President*
Adam Bowden, *Vice Pres*
EMP: 8 EST: 2000
SALES (est): 1.1MM Privately Held
WEB: www.pgtech.org
SIC: 3599 Machine shop, jobbing & repair

(G-16122)
PACIFIC TOOL & ENGINEERING LTD (PA)
6410 19 Mile Rd (48314-2109)
PHONE...................586 737-2710
Ted Elward II, *President*
Kim Elward, *Shareholder*
EMP: 4 EST: 1993
SQ FT: 11,600
SALES (est): 3.4MM Privately Held
WEB: www.pte-usa.com
SIC: 3544 Industrial molds

(G-16123)
PALM SWEETS LLC
Also Called: Palm Sweets Bakery & Cafe
3605 15 Mile Rd (48310-5356)
PHONE...................586 554-7979
Suha Toma, *Principal*
Nuha Toma, *Administration*
EMP: 8 EST: 2016
SALES (est): 1.1MM Privately Held
WEB: www.palmsweets.com
SIC: 2051 Cakes, bakery: except frozen

(G-16124)
PEPSICO INC
6600 17 Mile Rd (48313-4501)
PHONE...................586 276-4102
Erica Young, *Admin Asst*
EMP: 8 EST: 2017
SALES (est): 149.6K Privately Held
WEB: www.pepsico.com
SIC: 2086 Carbonated soft drinks, bottled & canned

(G-16125)
PERFORMANCE MACHINERY LLC
5430 Gatewood Dr (48310-2224)
PHONE...................586 698-2508
EMP: 12 EST: 2015
SALES (est): 962.6K Privately Held
WEB: www.merrifieldmachinery.com
SIC: 3599 Machine shop, jobbing & repair

(G-16126)
PHOTOGRAPHIC SUPPORT INC
Also Called: PSI Automotive Support Group
6210 Product Dr (48314-4566)
PHONE...................586 264-9957
William F Beaudin Jr, *President*
Mark Linz, *Vice Pres*
Lymm Beaudin, *Admin Sec*
EMP: 5 EST: 1993
SQ FT: 25,000 Privately Held
WEB: www.psiautomotive.com
SIC: 3599 Machine shop, jobbing & repair

(G-16127)
PIONEER AUTOMOTIVE INC
6425 19 Mile Rd (48314-2115)
PHONE...................586 758-7730
James E Williams, *CEO*
EMP: 13 EST: 1992
SQ FT: 18,000
SALES (est): 176K Privately Held
SIC: 3089 8748 8742 7376 Pallets, plastic; business consulting; management consulting services; computer facilities management; prepackaged software

(G-16128)
PIONEER PLASTICS INC
35871 Mound Rd 201 (48310-4777)
PHONE...................586 262-0159
Darin Steven Morisette, *Principal*
EMP: 16 Privately Held
WEB: www.pioneermolding.com
SIC: 2295 Resin or plastic coated fabrics
PA: Pioneer Plastics, Inc.
    2295 Bart Ave
    Warren MI 48091
    586 262-0159

(G-16129)
PLASTIC MOLDING DEVELOPMENT
42400 Yearego Dr (48314-3262)
PHONE...................586 739-4500
Gary Kitts, *President*
Albie Kitts, *Vice Pres*
EMP: 4 EST: 1985
SQ FT: 25,000
SALES (est): 811.6K Privately Held
WEB: www.plasticmoldingdevelopment.com
SIC: 3089 Injection molding of plastics

(G-16130)
POWER PRECISION INDUSTRIES INC
43545 Utica Rd (48314-2358)
PHONE...................586 997-0600
Gary Churchill, *President*
Clarence Churchill, *Vice Pres*
Martha Churchill, *Admin Sec*
Benjamin Churchill, *Admin Asst*
EMP: 7 EST: 1985
SQ FT: 28,000
SALES (est): 699.5K Privately Held
WEB: www.powerprecision.us
SIC: 3599 Machine shop, jobbing & repair

(G-16131)
PRECISION LASER & MFG LLC
Also Called: Iza Design and Manufacturing
5690 18 Mile Rd (48314-4108)
PHONE...................519 733-8422
Peter Friesen, *CEO*
EMP: 4
SALES (corp-wide): 12.4MM Privately Held
WEB: www.prelas.com
SIC: 3713 8748 Truck beds; systems analysis & engineering consulting services
HQ: Precision Laser & Mfg Llc
    80 Motivation Dr
    Lawrenceburg TN 38464

(G-16132)
PREMIER PROTOTYPE INC
7775 18 1/2 Mile Rd (48314-3675)
PHONE...................586 323-6114
Jim Elmhirst, *President*
Emily Meza, *General Mgr*
Betty Elmhirst, *Vice Pres*
EMP: 24 EST: 1994
SQ FT: 26,500
SALES (est): 2.9MM Privately Held
WEB: www.premierprototype.co
SIC: 3469 3441 Metal stampings; fabricated structural metal for bridges

(G-16133)
PRESTIGE COATING SOLUTIONS
4955 Cromwell Rd (48310-2088)
PHONE...................248 402-3732
Joseph Vucaj, *Principal*
EMP: 4 EST: 2017
SALES (est): 76.9K Privately Held
SIC: 3479 Coating of metals & formed products

(G-16134)
PRO PRECISION INC
14178 Randall Dr (48313-3557)
PHONE...................586 247-6160
Robert M Proszkowski, *President*
EMP: 8 EST: 1986
SQ FT: 10,000
SALES (est): 783.2K Privately Held
SIC: 3541 Numerically controlled metal cutting machine tools

(G-16135)
PROFICIENT PRODUCTS INC
6283 Millett Ave (48312-2645)
PHONE...................586 977-8630
Joe Robinson, *President*
John Robinson, *Corp Secy*
EMP: 5 EST: 1977
SQ FT: 8,900
SALES (est): 481K Privately Held
WEB: www.proficientproducts.com
SIC: 3544 Forms (molds), for foundry & plastics working machinery

(G-16136)
PROTO GAGE INC
Also Called: Manufacturing Center
5972 Product Dr (48312-4560)
PHONE...................586 978-2783
Michael Stanton, *President*
Jim Quinn, *Production*
EMP: 45
SALES (corp-wide): 7.8MM Privately Held
WEB: www.protogage.com
SIC: 3544 Special dies & tools
PA: Proto Gage, Inc.
    35320 Beattie Dr
    Sterling Heights MI 48312
    586 979-1172

(G-16137)
PROTOTYPE CAST MFG INC
42872 Mound Rd (48314-3256)
PHONE...................586 615-8524
William Edney, *Branch Mgr*
EMP: 5
SALES (corp-wide): 2.5MM Privately Held
WEB: www.pcmi-mfg.com
SIC: 3363 Aluminum die-castings
PA: Prototype Cast Manufacturing, Inc.
    51752 Danview Tech Ct
    Shelby Township MI 48315
    586 739-0180

(G-16138)
PULL-BUOY INC
6515 Cotter Ave (48314-2149)
PHONE...................586 997-0900
Kurt Carbonero, *President*
Fred L Carbonero, *Admin Sec*
▲ EMP: 8 EST: 1964
SQ FT: 15,000
SALES (est): 604.2K Privately Held
WEB: www.pullbuoy.com
SIC: 3949 Gymnasium equipment

(G-16139)
PURE HERBS LTD
33410 Sterling Ponds Blvd (48312-5808)
PHONE...................586 446-8200
Eugene Watkins, *President*
EMP: 16 EST: 1982
SQ FT: 16,000
SALES (est): 2.6MM Privately Held
WEB: www.pureherbs.com
SIC: 2087 Extracts, flavoring

(G-16140)
QUALITY INSPECTIONS INC
7563 19 Mile Rd (48314-3222)
PHONE...................586 323-6135
Norman Soeder, *President*
Jim Lama, *Vice Pres*
EMP: 4 EST: 2004
SALES (est): 495K Privately Held
SIC: 3711 Automobile bodies, passenger car, not including engine, etc.

(G-16141)
QUANTUM MOLD & ENGINEERING LLC
6300 Sterling Dr N (48312-4552)
PHONE...................586 276-0100
Jason B Bojan, *Owner*
James Apolzan, *Project Mgr*
Matt Tarnowsky, *Accounts Mgr*
Eric Plati, *Technician*
Tony Andren,
EMP: 11 EST: 1996
SALES (est): 2.8MM Privately Held
WEB: www.quantummold.com
SIC: 3559 3544 Plastics working machinery; special dies, tools, jigs & fixtures

(G-16142)
RAPID COATING SOLUTIONS LLC
6559 Diplomat Dr (48314-1421)
PHONE...................586 255-7142
EMP: 7 EST: 2015

Sterling Heights - Macomb County (G-16143)

SALES (est): 276.8K **Privately Held**
WEB: www.rapidcoatingsolutions.com
SIC: 3479 Coating of metals & formed products

(G-16143)
RAVE COMPUTER ASSOCIATION INC
7171 Sterling Ponds Ct (48312-5813)
PHONE 586 939-8230
Frederick Darter, *CEO*
Sara Blackmer, *President*
Tony Scicluna, *Vice Pres*
Sarah Scott, *Accounts Mgr*
Rosalinda Knop, *Sales Staff*
EMP: 25 **EST:** 1988
SQ FT: 35,000
SALES (est): 29.5MM **Privately Held**
WEB: www.rave.com
SIC: 5045 5065 3571 3572 Computers; electronic parts; electronic computers; computer storage devices

(G-16144)
RAYCO MANUFACTURING INC
5520 Bridgewood Dr (48310-2217)
PHONE 586 795-2884
Douglas Cole, *President*
Dennis Szymanski, *Sales Staff*
EMP: 14 **EST:** 1978
SQ FT: 6,400
SALES (est): 2.8MM **Privately Held**
WEB: www.raycofixture.com
SIC: 3545 3829 Precision tools, machinists'; measuring & controlling devices

(G-16145)
REKLEIN PLASTICS INCORPORATED
Also Called: Resin Services
42130 Mound Rd (48314-3152)
PHONE 586 739-8850
Americo Valente, *President*
Joe Frank, *Engineer*
EMP: 8 **EST:** 1975
SQ FT: 14,750
SALES (est): 1.5MM **Privately Held**
WEB: www.rekleinplastics.com
SIC: 3089 3086 2821 Panels, building: plastic; plastics foam products; plastics materials & resins

(G-16146)
RELIANT INDUSTRIES INC
6119 15 Mile Rd (48312-4503)
PHONE 586 275-0479
Donald Zack, *President*
David Winfield, *Vice Pres*
Stephanie Tessman, *Office Mgr*
EMP: 20 **EST:** 2000
SQ FT: 18,000
SALES (est): 2.4MM **Privately Held**
WEB: www.reliantindustries.com
SIC: 3469 3465 Stamping metal for the trade; automotive stampings

(G-16147)
RESIN SERVICES INC
5959 18 1/2 Mile Rd (48314-3114)
PHONE 586 254-6770
Americo Valente, *President*
EMP: 10 **EST:** 1976
SQ FT: 12,000
SALES (est): 2MM **Privately Held**
WEB: www.resinservices.com
SIC: 2821 Epoxy resins

(G-16148)
RESPONSE WELDING INC
40785 Brentwood Dr (48310-2214)
PHONE 586 795-8090
Robert Shepherd, *President*
EMP: 6 **EST:** 1985 **Privately Held**
WEB: www.responsewelding.com
SIC: 7692 Automotive welding

(G-16149)
RICARDO DEFENSE INC
35860 Beattie Dr (48312-2620)
PHONE 805 882-1884
EMP: 8
SALES (corp-wide): 498MM **Privately Held**
WEB: www.control-pt.com
SIC: 8711 3714 Engineering services; motor vehicle brake systems & parts

HQ: Ricardo Defense, Inc.
175 Cremona Dr Ste 140
Goleta CA 93117
805 882-1884

(G-16150)
RICHCOAT LLC
40573 Brentwood Dr (48310-2210)
PHONE 586 978-1311
Timothy Richardson,
Jeffery M Scott,
EMP: 12 **EST:** 1984
SQ FT: 14,000
SALES (est): 971.8K **Privately Held**
WEB: www.richcoat.com
SIC: 3479 3471 Coating of metals & formed products; plating & polishing

(G-16151)
RICHELIEU AMERICA LTD (HQ)
Also Called: Chair City Supply
7021 Sterling Ponds Ct (48312-5809)
PHONE 586 264-1240
Richard Lord, *President*
Marion Kloibhofer, *General Mgr*
John Statton, *General Mgr*
Joselin Proteau, *Chairman*
Marjolaine Plante, *Vice Pres*
◆ **EMP:** 35 **EST:** 1998
SALES (est): 1B
SALES (corp-wide): 797.8MM **Privately Held**
WEB: www.richelieu.com
SIC: 5072 5031 2435 Builders' hardware; kitchen cabinets; panels, hardwood plywood
PA: Richelieu Hardware Ltd
7900 Boul Henri-Bourassa O Bureau 200
Saint-Laurent QC H4S 1
514 336-4144

(G-16152)
RING SCREW LLC (DH)
6125 18 Mile Rd (48314-4205)
PHONE 586 997-5600
Patrick Paige, *Mng Member*
▲ **EMP:** 75 **EST:** 2006
SALES (est): 152.7MM **Privately Held**
WEB: www.acument.com
SIC: 3532 3452 Stamping mill machinery (mining machinery); bolts, nuts, rivets & washers
HQ: Acument Global Technologies, Inc.
6125 18 Mile Rd
Sterling Heights MI 48314
586 254-3900

(G-16153)
RITE TOOL COMPANY INC
36740 Metro Ct (48312-1010)
PHONE 586 264-1900
Steven Berger, *President*
EMP: 9 **EST:** 1985
SALES (est): 1MM **Privately Held**
WEB: www.ritetoolinc.com
SIC: 3599 Machine shop, jobbing & repair

(G-16154)
RITE WAY ASPHALT INC
Also Called: Patch Master Services
6699 16 Mile Rd Ste B (48312-1004)
PHONE 586 264-1020
EMP: 5 **EST:** 1987
SALES: 500K **Privately Held**
SIC: 2951 Mfg Asphalt Mixtures/Blocks

(G-16155)
RIVAS INC (PA)
12146 Monsbrook Dr (48312-1343)
PHONE 586 566-0326
Evangelina Young, *CEO*
Bill Young, *President*
Peer Larson, *Vice Pres*
Randy Meder, *Vice Pres*
Yvette Young, *Treasurer*
▲ **EMP:** 59 **EST:** 1998
SQ FT: 32,000
SALES (est): 10MM **Privately Held**
SIC: 3714 Motor vehicle parts & accessories

(G-16156)
RJ ACQUISITION CORP RJ USA
5585 Gatewood Dr (48310-2227)
PHONE 586 268-2300

Giacomo Iuculano, *CEO*
Roco Vella, *General Mgr*
▲ **EMP:** 23 **EST:** 1955
SQ FT: 17,500
SALES (est): 4MM
SALES (corp-wide): 43.3MM **Privately Held**
WEB: www.rj-group.it
SIC: 3469 Machine parts, stamped or pressed metal
PA: R.J. Srl
Via Per Caluso 31
San Giorgio Canavese TO 10090
012 445-211

(G-16157)
ROBOVENT PRODUCTS GROUP INC (HQ)
37900 Mound Rd (48310-4132)
PHONE 586 698-1800
John Reid, *President*
Chris Duda, *Exec VP*
Steve McCallum, *VP Opers*
Mike Szandzik, *Project Dir*
Mark Shalawylo, *Project Mgr*
◆ **EMP:** 33 **EST:** 1989
SQ FT: 50,000
SALES (est): 16MM
SALES (corp-wide): 38.9MM **Privately Held**
WEB: www.robovent.com
SIC: 3564 5075 Air cleaning systems; air pollution control equipment & supplies
PA: Air Filtration Holdings, Llc
900 N Michigan Ave # 1800
Chicago IL 60611
312 649-5666

(G-16158)
ROCKSTAR DIGITAL INC
Also Called: Rockstar Group
6520 Cotter Ave (48314-2148)
PHONE 888 808-5868
Robinder Dhillon, *President*
Shubhpreet Dhillon, *Shareholder*
EMP: 12 **EST:** 2013
SQ FT: 8,000
SALES (est): 1MM **Privately Held**
WEB: www.rockstar4u.com
SIC: 3993 3672 Signs & advertising specialties; printed circuit boards

(G-16159)
RONAL INDUSTRIES INC
6615 19 Mile Rd (48314-2117)
PHONE 248 616-9691
Dolores Fishman, *CEO*
Joe Busch, *President*
Mike Harned, *Vice Pres*
Cheryl Kimack, *Purchasing*
Michael Boggess, *QC Mgr*
EMP: 15
SQ FT: 17,200
SALES (est): 5.3MM **Privately Held**
WEB: www.ronalind.com
SIC: 3795 3564 3599 Specialized tank components, military; blowers & fans; air intake filters, internal combustion engine, except auto

(G-16160)
ROTTMAN MANUFACTURING GROUP
35566 Mound Rd (48310-4722)
PHONE 586 693-5676
Raymond Rottmann, *Principal*
EMP: 8 **EST:** 2014
SALES (est): 346.2K **Privately Held**
SIC: 3999 Manufacturing industries

(G-16161)
RUCCI FORGED WHEELS INC (PA)
Also Called: Forgetek
2003 E 14 Mile Rd (48310-5905)
PHONE 248 577-3500
Andy Franko, *CEO*
Nick Abouna, *President*
EMP: 3 **EST:** 2013
SQ FT: 10,000
SALES (est): 1.2MM **Privately Held**
WEB: www.rucciwheels.com
SIC: 3312 Wheels

(G-16162)
SAMHITA PRESS
33803 Bartola Dr (48312-5794)
PHONE 248 747-7792
Anna Milashevych, *Principal*
EMP: 4 **EST:** 2015
SALES (est): 37.5K **Privately Held**
WEB: www.samhitapress.com
SIC: 2741 Miscellaneous publishing

(G-16163)
SANKUER COMPOSITE TECH INC
36850 Metro Ct (48312-1012)
PHONE 586 264-1880
Patrick Sankuer, *Owner*
Andrew Nadeau, *Manager*
Timothy Doty II, *Director*
EMP: 22 **EST:** 2012
SALES (est): 5.1MM **Privately Held**
WEB: www.sankuercompositetech.com
SIC: 3624 Fibers, carbon & graphite

(G-16164)
SAS AUTOMOTIVE USA INC (DH)
Also Called: Sas Automotive Systems
42555 Merrill Rd (48314-3241)
PHONE 248 606-1152
Steve Demuro, *CEO*
Francisco Alcalde, *CFO*
John Smith, *Finance*
▲ **EMP:** 40 **EST:** 2005
SQ FT: 110,000
SALES (est): 15MM
SALES (corp-wide): 41.2MM **Privately Held**
WEB: www.sas-automotive.com
SIC: 3714 3711 Motor vehicle parts & accessories; automobile assembly, including specialty automobiles
HQ: Sas Autosystemtechnik GmbH
Siemensallee 84
Karlsruhe BW 76187
721 350-550

(G-16165)
SAVE ON PRINTING
38062 Douglas Dr (48312-2828)
PHONE 586 202-4469
Jerry Jorolan, *Principal*
EMP: 5 **EST:** 2012
SALES (est): 183.2K **Privately Held**
SIC: 2752 Commercial printing, lithographic

(G-16166)
SCHROTH ENTERPRISES INC
40736 Brentwood Dr (48310-2212)
PHONE 586 939-0770
James L Schroth, *Manager*
EMP: 10
SALES (corp-wide): 11.6MM **Privately Held**
SIC: 3496 Woven wire products
PA: Schroth Enterprises Inc
95 Tonnacour Pl
Grosse Pointe Farms MI 48236
586 759-4240

(G-16167)
SCOTTS COMPANY LLC
6575 Arrow Dr (48314-1413)
PHONE 586 254-6849
Mike Brelinski, *Branch Mgr*
EMP: 4
SALES (corp-wide): 4.1B **Publicly Held**
WEB: www.scotts.com
SIC: 2873 Fertilizers: natural (organic), except compost
HQ: The Scotts Company Llc
14111 Scottslawn Rd
Marysville OH 43040
937 644-0011

(G-16168)
SELECTOR SPLINE PRODUCTS CO
6576 Diplomat Dr (48314-1420)
PHONE 586 254-4020
Thomas P Tabaka, *President*
Gregory J Shalagan, *Treasurer*
EMP: 10 **EST:** 1941
SQ FT: 5,000

▲ = Import ▼ = Export
◆ = Import/Export

GEOGRAPHIC SECTION

Sterling Heights - Macomb County (G-16195)

SALES (est): 1.1MM **Privately Held**
WEB: www.selectorspline.com
SIC: **3545** Precision tools, machinists'; gauges (machine tool accessories)

(G-16169)
SENSUAL SCENTS
11242 Saar Dr (48314-3547)
PHONE 586 306-4233
EMP: 4 EST: 2012
SALES (est): 63.9K **Privately Held**
SIC: **2844** Toilet preparations

(G-16170)
SEOUL INTERNATIONAL INC
40622 Mound Rd (48310-2240)
PHONE 586 275-2494
Anthony Chang, *President*
EMP: 4 EST: 1998
SALES (est): 371.9K **Privately Held**
WEB: www.seoulstone.com
SIC: **3911** Jewelry, precious metal

(G-16171)
SERAPID INC
Also Called: Serapid Scenic Technologies
34100 Mound Rd (48310-6612)
PHONE 586 274-0774
Said Lounis, *President*
Bruce Downer, *Project Mgr*
Denis Pronin, *Project Mgr*
Eric Mackey, *Materials Mgr*
Ben Gregory, *Foreman/Supr*
▲ EMP: 18 EST: 1991
SQ FT: 13,000
SALES (est): 6.2MM **Privately Held**
WEB: www.serapid.com
SIC: **3625** 5072 Actuators, industrial; chains

(G-16172)
SERRA SPRING & MFG LLC
7515 19 Mile Rd (48314-3222)
PHONE 586 932-2202
Sarah Balkisson, *CEO*
EMP: 5 EST: 2013
SQ FT: 17,000 **Privately Held**
WEB: www.serraspring.com
SIC: **3495** 5051 5719 Mechanical springs, precision; stampings, metal; lighting, lamps & accessories

(G-16173)
SESCO PRODUCTS GROUP INC
40549 Brentwood Dr (48310-2210)
PHONE 586 979-4400
John C Coe, *President*
EMP: 11 EST: 1999
SQ FT: 20,000
SALES (est): 2MM
SALES (corp-wide): 20.6MM **Privately Held**
WEB: www.cpec.com
SIC: **3545** Machine tool attachments & accessories
PA: Coe Press Equipment Corporation
40549 Brentwood Dr
Sterling Heights MI 48310
586 979-4400

(G-16174)
SET ENTERPRISES OF MI INC (HQ)
38600 Van Dyke Ave # 325 (48312-1170)
PHONE 586 573-3600
Sid Etaylor, *Chairman*
Ken Pachla, *CFO*
EMP: 100 EST: 1991
SQ FT: 4,000
SALES (est): 24.5MM **Privately Held**
WEB: www.setenterprises.com
SIC: **3444** 3544 7692 3469 Metal housings, enclosures, casings & other containers; special dies, tools, jigs & fixtures; welding repair; metal stampings

(G-16175)
SHELBY AUTO TRIM INC
Also Called: Shelby Trim Auto Uphl Cnvrtibl
40430 Mound Rd (48310-2243)
PHONE 586 939-9090
Daniel A Kreucher, *President*
Teresa Kreucher, *Corp Secy*
EMP: 20 EST: 1979
SQ FT: 10,000

SALES (est): 781.6K **Privately Held**
WEB: www.shelbytrim.com
SIC: **7532** 2394 Upholstery & trim shop, automotive; tops (canvas or plastic), installation or repair: automotive; convertible tops, canvas or boat: from purchased materials

(G-16176)
SHELER CORPORATION
37885 Commerce Dr (48312-1001)
PHONE 586 979-8560
Gary L Burnash, *President*
Eddie Raffoul, *Sales Staff*
EMP: 22 EST: 1960
SQ FT: 8,000
SALES (est): 2.3MM **Privately Held**
WEB: www.shelercorp.com
SIC: **3567** Induction heating equipment

(G-16177)
SIGN & VINYL GRAPHIX EXPRESS
34423 Richard O Dr (48310-6129)
PHONE 586 838-4741
Christopher Ankawi, *Principal*
EMP: 5 EST: 2010
SALES (est): 110K **Privately Held**
SIC: **3993** Signs & advertising specialties

(G-16178)
SINK RITE DIE COMPANY
6170 Wall St (48312-1071)
PHONE 586 268-0000
Alfred C Harris, *President*
Sandra Harris, *Corp Secy*
Kirk Harris, *Vice Pres*
EMP: 16 EST: 1979
SQ FT: 16,000
SALES (est): 2.2MM **Privately Held**
SIC: **3544** Special dies & tools

(G-16179)
SME HOLDINGS LLC
Also Called: Sterling Manufacturing & Engrg
6750 19 Mile Rd (48314-2112)
PHONE 586 254-5310
William Davis, *Manager*
Rick Tate, *Supervisor*
Kenneth Orlowski, *Info Tech Mgr*
Bill Davis,
Caron Hall, *Administration*
EMP: 28 EST: 2015
SALES (est): 2.7MM **Privately Held**
WEB: www.sterling-gages.com
SIC: **3545** Precision measuring tools

(G-16180)
SMEKO INC
6750 19 Mile Rd (48314-2112)
PHONE 586 254-5310
EMP: 25
SQ FT: 18,000
SALES (est): 5.9MM **Privately Held**
SIC: **3545** 3544 Mfg Machine Tool Accessories Mfg Dies/Tools/Jigs/Fixtures

(G-16181)
SOFTWARE ADVANTAGE CONSULTING
8814 Pemberton Dr (48312-1967)
PHONE 586 264-5632
David P Miller, *President*
EMP: 4 EST: 1986 **Privately Held**
WEB: www.sacc.com
SIC: **7379** 7372 Computer related consulting services; application computer software

(G-16182)
SONOCO PRODUCTS COMPANY
35360 Beattie Dr (48312-2610)
PHONE 586 978-0808
EMP: 5
SALES (corp-wide): 5.2B **Publicly Held**
WEB: www.sonoco.com
SIC: **2631** Paperboard mills
PA: Sonoco Products Company
1 N 2nd St
Hartsville SC 29550
843 383-7000

(G-16183)
SPARTAN TOOL SALES INC
13715 Heritage Rd (48312-6531)
PHONE 586 268-1556
Bill Ozinian, *President*
Judy Ozinlan, *Vice Pres*
EMP: 8 EST: 1967
SALES (est): 671.5K **Privately Held**
WEB: www.spartantoolsales.com
SIC: **3545** Gauges (machine tool accessories)

(G-16184)
SPLINE SPECIALIST INC
7346 19 Mile Rd (48314-3214)
PHONE 586 731-4569
Thomas Kassin, *President*
EMP: 4 EST: 1994
SALES (est): 477.3K **Privately Held**
WEB: www.splinespecialist.net
SIC: **3542** Spline rolling machines

(G-16185)
SQUARE M LLC
42150 Mound Rd (48314-3152)
PHONE 720 988-5836
Madhu Natarajan, *Mng Member*
EMP: 15 EST: 2020
SALES (est): 5MM **Privately Held**
SIC: **2844** Lotions, shaving

(G-16186)
SRG GLOBAL AUTOMOTIVE LLC
Also Called: Automotive Moulding
35555 Mound Rd (48310-4724)
PHONE 586 757-7800
Chris Harrison, *Manager*
EMP: 492
SQ FT: 67,000
SALES (corp-wide): 36.9B **Privately Held**
WEB: www.guardian.com
SIC: **3465** 3442 3429 Moldings or trim, automobile: stamped metal; metal doors, sash & trim; manufactured hardware (general)
HQ: Srg Global Automotive, Llc
23751 Amber Ave
Warren MI 48089
586 757-7800

(G-16187)
SS STRIPPING
36870 Metro Ct (48312-1012)
PHONE 586 268-5799
Marvin Asmus, *President*
EMP: 4 EST: 2015
SALES (est): 145.2K **Privately Held**
WEB: www.ssstripping.co
SIC: **3471** Plating & polishing

(G-16188)
SSI TECHNOLOGY INC
35715 Stanley Dr (48312-2661)
PHONE 248 582-0600
Robert A Bloom, *President*
Gary Kippe, *President*
Lou Zagone, *Mfg Staff*
EMP: 55 EST: 1972
SQ FT: 12,500
SALES (est): 15.4MM **Privately Held**
WEB: www.ssi-tek.com
SIC: **3829** 3629 3823 3625 Aircraft & motor vehicle measurement equipment; gauges, motor vehicle: oil pressure, water temperature; power conversion units, a.c. to d.c.: static-electric; industrial instrmnts msrmnt display/control process variable; relays & industrial controls

(G-16189)
STANDARD COMPONENTS LLC
Also Called: SCI Consulting
44208 Phoenix Dr (48314-1465)
PHONE 586 323-9700
Joseph Luncent, *President*
Michael Gottschling, *General Mgr*
David Jackson, *Vice Pres*
Joe Lucent, *Vice Pres*
John Kalist, *Plant Supt*
▼ EMP: 48 EST: 2001
SQ FT: 35,000
SALES (est): 11.7MM **Privately Held**
WEB: www.scigage.com
SIC: **3544** Special dies & tools

(G-16190)
STECHSCHULTE/WEGERLY AG LLC
Also Called: Endura Coatings
42250 Yearego Dr (48314-3260)
PHONE 586 739-0101
David Lawson, *Business Mgr*
Michael Stechschulte, *Vice Pres*
Terise Padilla, *Controller*
Kevin Stechschulte, *Sales Mgr*
Adrian Kniahynycky, *Program Mgr*
EMP: 56 EST: 1971
SQ FT: 10,000
SALES (est): 8.8MM **Privately Held**
WEB: www.enduracoatings.com
SIC: **3479** Coating of metals & formed products

(G-16191)
STERLING CREATIVE TEAM INC
Also Called: Fastsigns
34238 Van Dyke Ave Ste A (48312-4615)
PHONE 586 978-0100
Andy Batti, *President*
Allen Chika, *President*
EMP: 4 EST: 2020
SALES (est): 250.4K **Privately Held**
WEB: www.fastsigns.com
SIC: **3993** Signs & advertising specialties

(G-16192)
STERLING DIAGNOSTICS INC
36645 Metro Ct (48312-1009)
P.O. Box 817 (48311-0817)
PHONE 586 979-2141
Eli Santa Maria, *President*
Lou Maria, *Vice Pres*
Lou Icasas, *Project Mgr*
Dave Callender, *CFO*
EMP: 18 EST: 1984
SQ FT: 5,000
SALES (est): 596.2K **Privately Held**
WEB: www.sterlingdiagnostics.com
SIC: **2819** Inorganic acids, except nitric & phosphoric; lithium compounds, inorganic

(G-16193)
STERLING METAL WORKS LLC
Also Called: Liberty Cast Products
35705 Beattie Dr (48312-2619)
PHONE 586 977-9577
Amy Jeric, *Office Mgr*
Rajiv Pithadia, *Mng Member*
EMP: 5 EST: 2005
SQ FT: 11,200 **Privately Held**
WEB: www.libertycastproducts.com
SIC: **3365** 3366 Aluminum & aluminum-based alloy castings; copper foundries

(G-16194)
STERLING PRMEASURE SYSTEMS INC
6750 19 Mile Rd (48314-2112)
PHONE 586 254-5310
Mark Stapleton, *President*
EMP: 20 EST: 1988
SQ FT: 26,000
SALES (est): 1.8MM **Privately Held**
WEB: www.sterling-gages.com
SIC: **3829** Aircraft & motor vehicle measurement equipment

(G-16195)
STONEBRIDGE INDUSTRIES INC
Also Called: Mayco Plastics
42400 Merrill Rd (48314-3238)
PHONE 586 323-0348
Ed Wright, *President*
Robert Roberts, *COO*
Mark Blaufuss, *CFO*
▲ EMP: 318 EST: 1996
SALES (est): 12MM **Privately Held**
WEB: www.maycointernational.com
SIC: **3496** 3462 3451 Miscellaneous fabricated wire products; iron & steel forgings; screw machine products
PA: Kirtland Capital Partners L.P.
3201 Entp Pkwy Ste 200
Beachwood OH 44122

Sterling Heights - Macomb County (G-16196)

(G-16196)
STRIVE ORTHTICS PRSTHETICS LLC
Also Called: Strive O&P
41400 Dequindre Rd # 105 (48314-3763)
PHONE..................................586 803-4325
Matthew McEwin, *Principal*
EMP: 7 **EST:** 2017
SALES (est): 534.9K **Privately Held**
WEB: www.striveop.com
SIC: 3842 Orthopedic appliances

(G-16197)
SUPERIOR MOLD SERVICES INC
6100 15 Mile Rd (48312-4502)
PHONE..................................586 264-9570
Gordon Bishop, *President*
Cheyrl Conn, *Controller*
EMP: 17 **EST:** 1994
SQ FT: 13,000
SALES (est): 2.6MM **Privately Held**
WEB: www.superiorairflow.com
SIC: 3544 Forms (molds), for foundry & plastics working machinery

(G-16198)
SWEET & SWEETER INC
Also Called: Sweet & Sweeter By Linda
4059 17 Mile Rd (48310-6837)
PHONE..................................586 977-9338
Fouad Juka, *President*
EMP: 4 **EST:** 2006
SALES (est): 179.8K **Privately Held**
WEB: www.sweetandsweetercakes.com
SIC: 5461 2051 Cakes; cakes, pies & pastries

(G-16199)
T J K INC
Also Called: Sir Speedy
39370 Bella Vista Dr (48313-5214)
PHONE..................................586 731-9639
Timothy J Knapps, *President*
Bob Richardson, *Telecomm Dir*
Barbara Knapps, *Admin Sec*
EMP: 5 **EST:** 1984
SQ FT: 2,400
SALES (est): 364.8K **Privately Held**
WEB: www.sirspeedy.com
SIC: 2752 2791 2789 2759 Commercial printing, lithographic; typesetting; bookbinding & related work; commercial printing; secretarial & court reporting

(G-16200)
TAPESTRY INC
14000 Lakeside Cir (48313-1320)
PHONE..................................631 724-8066
Michelle Carte, *Branch Mgr*
EMP: 7 **Publicly Held**
WEB: www.tapestry.com
SIC: 3171 Handbags, women's
PA: Tapestry, Inc.
10 Hudson Yards Fl 18
New York NY 10001

(G-16201)
TARUS PRODUCTS INC (PA)
38100 Commerce Dr (48312-1006)
PHONE..................................586 977-1400
Douglas J Greig, *President*
Carolyn Greig, *Vice Pres*
Doug Greig, *Safety Mgr*
Steve Ponke, *Purch Agent*
Chris Morton, *Engineer*
▲ **EMP:** 83 **EST:** 1970
SQ FT: 98,000
SALES (est): 9.9MM **Privately Held**
WEB: www.tarus.com
SIC: 3541 Machine tools, metal cutting type

(G-16202)
TD INDUSTRIAL COVERINGS INC
Also Called: T D I C
6220 18 1/2 Mile Rd (48314-3111)
PHONE..................................586 731-2080
Tommaso Dandreta, *CEO*
Mark Dandreta, *President*
Nichole Chevalier, *General Mgr*
Phillipa Dandreta, *Corp Secy*
Sharon D'andretta-wal, *Vice Pres*
▲ **EMP:** 85 **EST:** 1981
SQ FT: 34,000
SALES (est): 10.2MM **Privately Held**
WEB: www.tdic.com
SIC: 2394 Canvas covers & drop cloths

(G-16203)
TENNESSEE FABRICATORS LLC
35900 Mound Rd (48310-4730)
PHONE..................................615 793-4444
Brian Jardine, *Mng Member*
Lanny Jardine,
Nicholas Jardine,
Nancy Wade,
EMP: 8 **EST:** 2013
SALES (est): 714.9K **Privately Held**
SIC: 3449 Bars, concrete reinforcing; fabricated steel

(G-16204)
TEST PRODUCTS INCORPORATED
41255 Technology Park Dr (48314-4102)
PHONE..................................586 997-9600
David Bruszewski, *President*
Ken Jankowski, *Division Mgr*
Richard Gillies, *Vice Pres*
Dave Coatney, *Safety Mgr*
Angie Bauman, *Production*
EMP: 30 **EST:** 1989
SQ FT: 18,000
SALES (est): 7.9MM **Privately Held**
WEB: www.testprod.com
SIC: 3825 Test equipment for electronic & electric measurement

(G-16205)
THREAD-CRAFT INC
43643 Utica Rd (48312-2359)
P.O. Box 220 (48311-0220)
PHONE..................................586 323-1116
Dennis Johnson, *President*
Scott Mailloux, *Purch Mgr*
John Fauer, *Purchasing*
Celeste Johnson, *CFO*
▲ **EMP:** 70 **EST:** 1958
SQ FT: 27,000
SALES: 8.5MM **Privately Held**
WEB: www.threadcraft.com
SIC: 3599 3545 Machine shop, jobbing & repair; machine tool accessories

(G-16206)
TOOL-CRAFT INDUSTRIES INC
6101 Product Dr (48312-4565)
PHONE..................................248 549-0077
Chester A Wilson Jr, *President*
Teri Wilson, *Sales Staff*
EMP: 33 **EST:** 1954
SQ FT: 8,160
SALES (est): 2.8MM **Privately Held**
WEB: www.tool-craft.com
SIC: 3545 5084 Cutting tools for machine tools; industrial machinery & equipment

(G-16207)
TRANSFORM AUTOMOTIVE LLC
33596 Sterling Ponds Blvd (48312-5808)
PHONE..................................586 826-8500
Haizhou LI, *Engineer*
EMP: 7
SALES (corp-wide): 2.4B **Privately Held**
SIC: 3714 Motor vehicle parts & accessories
HQ: Transform Automotive, Llc
7026 Sterling Ponds Ct
Sterling Heights MI 48312
586 826-8500

(G-16208)
TRANSFORM AUTOMOTIVE LLC (DH)
7026 Sterling Ponds Ct (48312-5809)
PHONE..................................586 826-8500
Teds Ens, *President*
Thomas Meier, *Vice Pres*
Almir Grahovic, *Production*
Jeff Graffa, *Director*
James Pastori,
▲ **EMP:** 121 **EST:** 1996
SQ FT: 75,000
SALES (est): 44.3MM
SALES (corp-wide): 2.4B **Privately Held**
WEB: www.meansindustries.com
SIC: 3714 Motor vehicle transmissions, drive assemblies & parts; motor vehicle engines & parts
HQ: Means Industries, Inc.
3715 E Washington Rd
Saginaw MI 48601
989 754-1433

(G-16209)
TRANSPAK INC
Also Called: GP Strategies C/O Transpak
34400 Mound Rd (48310-5757)
PHONE..................................586 264-2064
Fax: 586 795-2126
EMP: 40
SQ FT: 25,000
SALES (est): 3.4MM **Privately Held**
SIC: 4225 5013 3714 3086 General Warehse/Storage Whol Auto Parts/Supplies Mfg Motor Vehicle Parts Mfg Plastic Foam Prdts

(G-16210)
TRI-STAR TOOLING LLC
Also Called: Tri-Star Engineering
35640 Beattie Dr (48312-2616)
PHONE..................................586 978-0435
Richard Ignagni, *Mng Member*
William Butler, *Analyst*
EMP: 32 **EST:** 1979
SQ FT: 11,300
SALES (est): 1.2MM **Privately Held**
WEB: www.tristarengineering.com
SIC: 3544 3543 7389 Industrial molds; industrial patterns; inspection & testing services

(G-16211)
TRIPLE TOOL
40715 Brentwood Dr (48310-2214)
PHONE..................................586 795-1785
Ursula Czachor, *Owner*
EMP: 9 **EST:** 2009
SALES (est): 778.7K **Privately Held**
SIC: 5251 3542 Tools; machine tools, metal forming type

(G-16212)
TUNKERS INC
Also Called: Tunkers-Mastech
36200 Mound Rd (48310-4737)
PHONE..................................734 744-5990
Olaf Tuenkers, *President*
Gary Gavioli, *Vice Pres*
Christian Heyer, *Vice Pres*
George Owens, *Opers Mgr*
Steve Lorenz, *Accounts Mgr*
▲ **EMP:** 25 **EST:** 1997
SALES (est): 8.7MM
SALES (corp-wide): 177.9K **Privately Held**
WEB: www.tuenkers.de
SIC: 3711 Automobile assembly, including specialty automobiles
HQ: Tunkers Maschinenbau Gmbh
Am Rosenkothen 4-12
Ratingen 40880
210 245-170

(G-16213)
TWEDDLE LITHO INC
34000 Mound Rd (48310-6609)
PHONE..................................586 795-0515
Paul Wilbur, *President*
EMP: 7 **EST:** 2014
SALES (est): 241K **Privately Held**
WEB: www.tweddle.com
SIC: 2752 Commercial printing, offset

(G-16214)
UMIX DISSOULTION CORP
6050 15 Mile Rd (48312-4500)
PHONE..................................586 446-9950
Tak Mimura, *President*
▲ **EMP:** 15 **EST:** 2006
SALES (est): 767.7K **Privately Held**
WEB: www.umix.co.jp
SIC: 3423 7389 Hand & edge tools; hand tool designers
PA: Umix Co., Ltd.
2-37-1, Kasugakitamachi
Hirakata OSK 573-0

(G-16215)
UNIQUE HOOKA AND TOBACCO
4086 17 Mile Rd (48310-6836)
PHONE..................................586 883-7674
Marie Lukosdich, *Principal*
EMP: 5 **EST:** 2013
SALES (est): 156.5K **Privately Held**
WEB: www.uniquehookah.com
SIC: 2111 Cigarettes

(G-16216)
UNITED MACHINING INC (DH)
6300 18 1/2 Mile Rd (48314-3112)
PHONE..................................586 323-4300
Edward G Frackowiak, *CEO*
◆ **EMP:** 180 **EST:** 1998
SQ FT: 62,000
SALES (est): 46.3MM **Privately Held**
WEB: www.wescast.com
SIC: 3714 Motor vehicle parts & accessories
HQ: Wescast Industries Inc
200 Water St
Wingham ON N0G 2
519 357-3450

(G-16217)
UNIVERSAL TL EQP & CONTRLS INC
Also Called: Utec
42409 Van Dyke Ave (48314-3200)
PHONE..................................586 268-4380
Stephanie Serra-Bartolotta, *President*
Bill Bartolotta, *Vice Pres*
EMP: 98 **EST:** 2009
SQ FT: 200,000
SALES (est): 21.2MM **Privately Held**
WEB: www.universaltecinc.com
SIC: 3569 Robots, assembly line: industrial & commercial

(G-16218)
US FARATHANE HOLDINGS CORP
38000 Mound Rd (48310-3461)
PHONE..................................586 726-1200
Steve Macdko, *Principal*
EMP: 5
SALES (corp-wide): 549.4MM **Privately Held**
WEB: www.usfarathane.com
SIC: 3089 Injection molding of plastics
PA: U.S. Farathane Holdings Corp.
2700 High Meadow Cir
Auburn Hills MI 48326
248 754-7000

(G-16219)
US FARATHANE HOLDINGS CORP
6543 Arrow Dr (48314-1413)
PHONE..................................586 991-6922
Karl Brunsman, *Principal*
EMP: 30
SALES (corp-wide): 549.4MM **Privately Held**
WEB: www.usfarathane.com
SIC: 3714 Motor vehicle parts & accessories
PA: U.S. Farathane Holdings Corp.
2700 High Meadow Cir
Auburn Hills MI 48326
248 754-7000

(G-16220)
US FARATHANE HOLDINGS CORP
Also Called: US Farathane Merrill Plant
42155 Merrill Rd (48314-3233)
PHONE..................................586 685-4000
John Lojewski, *Principal*
Jim Curtis, *Safety Mgr*
Kevin Baxter, *Info Tech Mgr*
EMP: 5
SALES (corp-wide): 549.4MM **Privately Held**
WEB: www.usfarathane.com
SIC: 3089 Injection molding of plastics
PA: U.S. Farathane Holdings Corp.
2700 High Meadow Cir
Auburn Hills MI 48326
248 754-7000

▲ = Import ▼ = Export
◆ = Import/Export

GEOGRAPHIC SECTION

Stevensville - Berrien County (G-16248)

(G-16221)
VAN PELT CORPORATION (PA)
Also Called: Service Steel Company
36155 Mound Rd (48310-4736)
PHONE.................................313 365-3600
Roger Van Pelt, *CEO*
A Joyce Pelt, *Chairman*
Charles Debeau, *Vice Pres*
Scott Streeter, *Maint Spvr*
Darren Thompson, *Opers Staff*
▲ **EMP:** 8
SQ FT: 83,000
SALES (est): 29.1MM **Privately Held**
WEB: www.servicesteel.com
SIC: 3441 5051 Fabricated structural metal; metals service centers & offices

(G-16222)
VERSA HANDLING CO (PA)
Also Called: Cleveland Tramrail Systems
35700 Stanley Dr (48312-2660)
PHONE.................................313 491-0500
James K McKean, *President*
Lisa McKean, *Principal*
Diane Kula, *Sales Staff*
EMP: 7 **EST:** 1985
SALES (est): 1.6MM **Privately Held**
WEB: www.versahandling.com
SIC: 3535 3536 3312 Conveyors & conveying equipment; cranes, overhead traveling; rails, steel or iron

(G-16223)
VILLAGE CABINET SHOPPE INC
37975 Commerce Dr (48312-1003)
PHONE.................................586 264-6464
Richard Breitenbeck, *President*
Kelly Breitenbeck, *Admin Sec*
EMP: 9 **EST:** 1971
SQ FT: 5,000
SALES (est): 1.1MM **Privately Held**
WEB: www.villagecabinetshoppe.com
SIC: 1751 2434 2541 Cabinet building & installation; wood kitchen cabinets; counter & sink tops

(G-16224)
VINCE KRSTEVSKI
Also Called: Vancho Tool and Engineering
43450 Merrill Rd (48314-2166)
PHONE.................................586 739-7600
Vince Krstevski, *Owner*
EMP: 4 **EST:** 1986
SQ FT: 7,100
SALES (est): 300K **Privately Held**
WEB: www.vanchotool.com
SIC: 3599 Machine shop, jobbing & repair

(G-16225)
VISOR FRAMES LLC
6400 Sterling Dr N Ste B (48312-4514)
PHONE.................................586 864-6058
EMP: 10 **EST:** 2011
SALES (est): 650.5K **Privately Held**
WEB: www.visorframes.com
SIC: 3465 Body parts, automobile: stamped metal

(G-16226)
VOICE COMMUNICATIONS CORP (PA)
Also Called: Voice Newspapers, The
6250 Metropolitan Pkwy (48312-1022)
PHONE.................................586 716-8100
Debbie Loggins, *General Mgr*
Jim McCormick, *Principal*
EMP: 25 **EST:** 1982
SALES (est): 2.7MM **Privately Held**
WEB: www.voicenews.com
SIC: 2711 Newspapers: publishing only, not printed on site

(G-16227)
WALKER WIRE (ISPAT) INC
42744 Mound Rd (48314-3254)
PHONE.................................248 399-4800
EMP: 4
SALES (est): 370.1K **Privately Held**
SIC: 3398 Metal Heat Treating

(G-16228)
WAPC HOLDINGS INC
Also Called: Weave Alloy Products Company
40736 Brentwood Dr (48310-2212)
PHONE.................................586 939-0770
Timothy Brownfield, *President*
EMP: 10 **EST:** 1954
SQ FT: 12,000
SALES (est): 2MM **Privately Held**
WEB: www.weavealloy.com
SIC: 3315 Wire, ferrous/iron

(G-16229)
WARREN BROACH & MACHINE CORP
6541 Diplomat Dr (48314-1421)
PHONE.................................586 254-7080
James McMahon, *President*
Donald Mc Mahon, *President*
Bill Foth, *General Mgr*
William Foth, *General Mgr*
Michael Beaudoin, *Site Mgr*
EMP: 18 **EST:** 1967
SQ FT: 14,000
SALES (est): 1.8MM **Privately Held**
WEB: www.warrenbroach.com
SIC: 3545 3541 Broaches (machine tool accessories); machine tools, metal cutting type

(G-16230)
WEIR FABRICATION LLC
35480 Mound Rd (48310-4721)
PHONE.................................248 953-8363
Douglas J Weir, *Mng Member*
EMP: 6 **EST:** 2015
SALES (est): 270.1K **Privately Held**
SIC: 3441 Fabricated structural metal

(G-16231)
WINES PRINTING CO
41516 Schoenherr Rd (48313-3442)
PHONE.................................586 924-6229
Alfonse Falsone, *Principal*
EMP: 4 **EST:** 2015
SALES (est): 101.5K **Privately Held**
SIC: 2752 Commercial printing, lithographic

(G-16232)
WING PATTERN INC
42200 Mound Rd (48314-3145)
PHONE.................................248 588-1121
Thomas Booser, *President*
James Booser, *Vice Pres*
EMP: 5 **EST:** 1968
SALES (est): 484.6K **Privately Held**
WEB: www.wingpattern.com
SIC: 3553 3543 Pattern makers' machinery, woodworking; industrial patterns

(G-16233)
WYATT SERVICES INC
6425 Sims Dr (48313-3722)
PHONE.................................586 264-8000
Jean M Wyatt, *President*
Billy C Wyatt Jr, *Vice Pres*
Debbie Andrews, *Finance*
Debbie L Andrews, *Admin Sec*
EMP: 18 **EST:** 1969
SQ FT: 18,000
SALES (est): 2.4MM **Privately Held**
WEB: www.wyattservices.net
SIC: 3398 Metal heat treating

(G-16234)
ZF ACTIVE SAFETY US INC
42315 R Mancini Dr (48314-3265)
PHONE.................................586 899-2807
Mike Obrien, *Manager*
EMP: 7
SALES (corp-wide): 216.2K **Privately Held**
WEB: www.zf.com
SIC: 3714 Motor vehicle engines & parts
HQ: Zf Active Safety Us Inc.
  12025 Tech Center Dr
  Livonia MI 48150
  734 812-6979

Sterling Hts
Macomb County

(G-16235)
ARROW SIGN CO
13335 15 Mile Rd (48312-4210)
PHONE.................................586 939-9966
Gaetano Nicosia, *Principal*
Joseph Menzel, *Marketing Staff*
Dan Jetke, *Sr Project Mgr*
Oscar Chavez, *Manager*
Tina Mowdy, *Manager*
EMP: 12 **EST:** 2011
SALES (est): 280.1K **Privately Held**
WEB: www.arrowsigncompany.com
SIC: 3993 Electric signs

(G-16236)
INTL GIUSEPPES OILS & VINEGARS
38033 Opatik Ct (48312-1408)
PHONE.................................586 698-2754
Joseph Cucinello, *Principal*
EMP: 5 **EST:** 2010
SALES (est): 71.4K **Privately Held**
SIC: 2099 Vinegar

Stevensville
Berrien County

(G-16237)
ACCU DIE & MOLD INC
7473 Red Arrow Hwy (49127-9248)
PHONE.................................269 465-4020
Daniel Reifschneider, *President*
Will Reifschneider, *QC Mgr*
Mark Payne, *Prgrmr*
EMP: 39 **EST:** 1990
SALES (est): 5.6MM **Privately Held**
WEB: www.accu-die.com
SIC: 3544 Special dies & tools; industrial molds

(G-16238)
ACCUSPEC GRINDING INC (PA)
2660 Lawrence St (49127-1252)
P.O. Box 121 (49127-0121)
PHONE.................................269 556-1410
Joseph Ondraka, *CEO*
Jeffery J Ondraka, *President*
Anette Ondraka, *Exec VP*
EMP: 23 **EST:** 1992
SQ FT: 35,000
SALES (est): 2.5MM **Privately Held**
SIC: 3451 Screw machine products

(G-16239)
ALPHA RESOURCES LLC
3090 Johnson Rd (49127-1270)
P.O. Box 199 (49127-0199)
PHONE.................................269 465-5559
Philip T Lunsford, *President*
Joyce Lunsford, *Corp Secy*
Lloyd Goslin, *Finance*
◆ **EMP:** 43 **EST:** 1978
SQ FT: 70,000
SALES (est): 13.3MM **Privately Held**
WEB: www.alpharesources.com
SIC: 5049 3255 3821 3313 Laboratory equipment, except medical or dental; clay refractories; laboratory apparatus & furniture; electrometallurgical products

(G-16240)
ALUDYNE WEST MICHIGAN LLC
2800 Yasdick Dr (49127-1241)
PHONE.................................248 728-8642
Pierre Dubeauclard,
Michael Beyer,
▲ **EMP:** 134 **EST:** 2003
SALES (est): 32.3MM
SALES (corp-wide): 1.5B **Privately Held**
WEB: www.aludyne.com
SIC: 3714 Motor vehicle parts & accessories
HQ: Aludyne International, Inc
  300 Galleria Ofcntr Ste 5
  Southfield MI 48034

(G-16241)
BRIDGVILLE PLASTICS INC
7380 Jericho Rd (49127-9209)
PHONE.................................269 465-6516
Thomas Moneta, *President*
Angela Meltinos, *General Mgr*
Carol Moneta, *Vice Pres*
Angie Meltinos, *Admin Asst*
EMP: 16 **EST:** 1987
SQ FT: 10,000
SALES (est): 4.1MM **Privately Held**
WEB: www.bridgville.com
SIC: 3089 Injection molding of plastics

(G-16242)
CARSON WOOD SPECIALTIES INC
7526 Jericho Rd (49127-9723)
PHONE.................................269 465-6091
Thomas Carson, *President*
Charlene Carson, *Co-Owner*
EMP: 5 **EST:** 1997
SALES (est): 716.9K **Privately Held**
WEB: www.carsonwoodspecialties.com
SIC: 5031 5211 2431 2434 Lumber, plywood & millwork; lumber products; doors & door parts & trim, wood; wood kitchen cabinets; chairs, table & arm

(G-16243)
CUSTOM TOOL AND DIE CO
Also Called: Trim Die Manufacturer
7059 Red Arrow Hwy (49127-9681)
PHONE.................................269 465-9130
EMP: 30
SQ FT: 13,350
SALES (est): 6.3MM **Privately Held**
SIC: 3544 Special Dies,Tools,Jigs,And Fixtures, Nsk

(G-16244)
D M P E
5790 Saint Joseph Ave (49127-1237)
PHONE.................................269 428-5070
EMP: 8 **EST:** 2013
SALES (est): 1.1MM **Privately Held**
SIC: 3714 Motor vehicle engines & parts

(G-16245)
DANE SYSTEMS LLC
Also Called: Jr Automation Technologies
7275 Red Arrow Hwy (49127-9734)
PHONE.................................269 465-3263
Bryan Jones, *Principal*
Scot Lindemann, *Co-CEO*
Barry Kohn, *CFO*
Bryan V Dorpowski, *Controller*
Allen Shuler, *Training Super*
▲ **EMP:** 87 **EST:** 2004
SQ FT: 45,000
SALES (est): 20.4MM **Privately Held**
WEB: www.jrautomation.com
SIC: 3549 Assembly machines, including robotic
HQ: Jr Technology Group, Llc
  13365 Tyler St
  Holland MI 49424
  616 399-2168

(G-16246)
DEE-BLAST CORPORATION (PA)
Also Called: Air Source
5992 Oelke Park St (49127-1233)
P.O. Box 983, Coloma (49038-0983)
PHONE.................................269 428-2400
Michael A Johnson, *President*
David Tompkins, *Chairman*
Allan Johnson, *Vice Pres*
Justin Hopkins, *Opers Mgr*
Todd Patterson, *Sales Mgr*
EMP: 10 **EST:** 1967
SQ FT: 24,000
SALES (est): 5MM **Privately Held**
WEB: www.dee-blast.com
SIC: 3569 5084 3469 2542 Blast cleaning equipment, dustless; industrial machinery & equipment; metal stampings; partitions & fixtures, except wood

(G-16247)
DISCOVERY GOLD CORP
4472 Winding Ln (49127-9330)
PHONE.................................269 429-7002
Steve Flechner, *Owner*
EMP: 4 **EST:** 2015
SALES (est): 93.9K **Privately Held**
SIC: 1499 Miscellaneous nonmetallic minerals

(G-16248)
DURA MOLD INC
3390 W Linco Rd (49127-9725)
PHONE.................................269 465-3301
Franz Bock, *President*
▲ **EMP:** 70 **EST:** 2004
SQ FT: 22,000
SALES (est): 15MM **Privately Held**
WEB: www.duramold.net
SIC: 3544 Special dies & tools

Stevensville - Berrien County (G-16249)

(G-16249)
ESMIES CABINET
1565 N Teakwood Dr (49127-9622)
PHONE.................................269 921-1578
EMP: 4 EST: 2013
SALES (est): 63.2K Privately Held
WEB: www.esmiescabinet.com
SIC: 2434 Wood kitchen cabinets

(G-16250)
FALCON LAKESIDE MFG INC
4999 Advance Way (49127-9544)
PHONE.................................269 429-6193
Francis Sant, *Principal*
Jennifer Sill, *Principal*
Dennis Whitaker, *Opers Mgr*
Nikki Blumka, *Production*
Darren Mackey, *Engineer*
EMP: 24 EST: 2011
SALES (est): 2.5MM Privately Held
WEB: www.falconlakeside.com
SIC: 3544 Dies & die holders for metal cutting, forming, die casting

(G-16251)
GREAT LAKES DRONE COMPANY LLC
2618 W John Beers Rd (49127-1213)
PHONE.................................317 430-5291
Matthew Quinn, *Principal*
EMP: 7 EST: 2016
SALES (est): 260K Privately Held
WEB: www.greatlakesdronecompany.com
SIC: 3721 Motorized aircraft

(G-16252)
GRIFFIN TOOL INC
2951 Johnson Rd (49127-1216)
P.O. Box 528 (49127-0528)
PHONE.................................269 429-4077
Greg Griffin, *President*
Griffin Christol, *Vice Pres*
Steven Scudder, *Draft/Design*
Rod McGilvra, *Design Engr*
Greg Davis, *Sales Staff*
EMP: 25 EST: 1988
SQ FT: 11,000
SALES (est): 5.7MM Privately Held
WEB: www.griffintool.com
SIC: 3544 Special dies & tools

(G-16253)
HARBOR ISLE PLASTICS LLC
2337 W Marquette Woods Rd (49127-9587)
PHONE.................................269 465-6004
Ewald Lehmann,
Peter Bartschke,
Mark Lehmann,
▲ EMP: 18 EST: 2002
SQ FT: 110,000
SALES (est): 3MM Privately Held
SIC: 3089 Injection molding of plastics

(G-16254)
JOE BEAM WOODWORKING
6000 Red Arrow Hwy (49127-1165)
PHONE.................................269 873-0160
EMP: 4 EST: 2015
SALES (est): 62.9K Privately Held
SIC: 2431 Millwork

(G-16255)
JOHN LAMANTIA CORPORATION
Also Called: Lamantia Machine Company
4825 Roosevelt Rd (49127-9522)
P.O. Box 320 (49127-0320)
PHONE.................................269 428-8100
Anthony Lamantia, *President*
EMP: 6 EST: 1978
SQ FT: 5,500
SALES (est): 750K Privately Held
SIC: 3469 3544 8711 Metal stampings; special dies & tools; consulting engineer

(G-16256)
KLAUS NIXDORF
Also Called: Flour Shop Bakery & Pizza, The
1727 W John Beers Rd (49127-9403)
PHONE.................................269 429-3259
Klaus Nixdorf, *Owner*
EMP: 6 EST: 1989
SQ FT: 2,700
SALES (est): 198.8K Privately Held
WEB: www.flourshopbakeryandpizza.com
SIC: 5461 5812 2051 Cakes; pizzeria, independent; bread, cake & related products

(G-16257)
LAKESHORE MARBLE COMPANY INC
4410 N Roosevelt Rd (49127-9100)
P.O. Box 132 (49127-0132)
PHONE.................................269 429-8241
James Chartrand, *President*
Thad Chartrand, *Vice Pres*
Matthew Chartrand, *Treasurer*
EMP: 13 EST: 1971
SQ FT: 20,000
SALES (est): 686.3K Privately Held
SIC: 3281 3431 2434 3088 Marble, building: cut & shaped; building stone products; metal sanitary ware; wood kitchen cabinets; plastics plumbing fixtures; plastics materials & resins

(G-16258)
LAKESHORE MOLD AND DIE LLC
2355 W Marquette Woods Rd (49127-9587)
PHONE.................................269 429-6764
Todd Nitz, *Mng Member*
Sherri Nitz,
EMP: 5 EST: 1995
SQ FT: 12,000
SALES (est): 632.1K Privately Held
WEB: www.lakeshoremoldanddie.com
SIC: 3544 Industrial molds; forms (molds), for foundry & plastics working machinery

(G-16259)
LAKESIDE MANUFACTURING CO
4999 Advance Way (49127-9544)
PHONE.................................269 429-6193
Lawrence Holben, *President*
Alvin Ziebart, *Vice Pres*
Larry Holben, *Consultant*
Henry Kraklau Jr, *Director*
EMP: 42 EST: 1967
SQ FT: 34,000
SALES (est): 1MM Privately Held
WEB: www.falconlakeside.com
SIC: 3599 3544 Machine shop, jobbing & repair; special dies & tools

(G-16260)
MEIJER INC
5019 Red Arrow Hwy (49127-1013)
PHONE.................................269 556-2400
Rob Vassar, *Principal*
EMP: 83
SALES (corp-wide): 1.1B Privately Held
WEB: www.spectrumhealth.org
SIC: 3421 Table & food cutlery, including butchers'
HQ: Meijer, Inc.
2929 Walker Ave Nw
Grand Rapids MI 49544
616 453-6711

(G-16261)
MEMCON NORTH AMERICA LLC
6000 Red Arrow Hwy Unit I (49127-1166)
PHONE.................................269 281-0478
Martin Gilbert, *President*
Simon Blackwell, *Administration*
EMP: 10 EST: 2013
SALES (est): 650.8K Privately Held
WEB: www.memcon.eu
SIC: 3613 5063 Switchgear & switchboard apparatus; switchboards

(G-16262)
ON THE LEVEL WOODWORKING
4712 Jamestown Dr (49127-9516)
PHONE.................................269 429-4570
Ned Wollenslegel, *Principal*
EMP: 4 EST: 2009
SALES (est): 82.9K Privately Held
SIC: 2431 Millwork

(G-16263)
R J FLOOD PROFESSIONAL CO
2691 Orchard Ln (49127-9382)
PHONE.................................269 930-3608
Robert Flood, *Principal*
EMP: 4 EST: 2008
SALES (est): 194K Privately Held
SIC: 3553 Cabinet makers' machinery

(G-16264)
SCIENTIFIC NOTEBOOK COMPANY
3295 W Linco Rd (49127-9240)
P.O. Box 238 (49127-0238)
PHONE.................................269 429-8285
Ben Gallup, *President*
Penny Mengel, *General Mgr*
Patrick Gallup, *Vice Pres*
EMP: 14 EST: 1960
SQ FT: 25,000
SALES (est): 2MM Privately Held
WEB: www.snco.com
SIC: 2678 Notebooks: made from purchased paper

(G-16265)
SLAUGHTER INSTRUMENT COMPANY
4356 N Roosevelt Rd (49127-9527)
PHONE.................................269 428-7471
Charles Eversole, *President*
EMP: 12 EST: 1925
SQ FT: 8,100
SALES (est): 641.2K Privately Held
WEB: www.slaughtercoinc.com
SIC: 3841 Surgical instruments & apparatus

(G-16266)
STANDARD TOOL & DIE INC
2950 Johnson Rd (49127-1217)
P.O. Box 608 (49127-0608)
PHONE.................................269 465-6004
Peter Bartschke, *CEO*
Mark Lehmann, *President*
James Fogelsonger, *VP Mfg*
Layne Brower, *Sales Mgr*
Dennis Matthews, *Info Tech Mgr*
▲ EMP: 43 EST: 1983
SQ FT: 54,000
SALES (est): 9.2MM Privately Held
WEB: www.standardtool.net
SIC: 3544 Dies & die holders for metal cutting, forming, die casting; forms (molds), for foundry & plastics working machinery; industrial molds

(G-16267)
SUPREME CASTING INC
3389 W Linco Rd (49127-9725)
PHONE.................................269 465-5757
William Bancroft, *President*
Elizabeth Kohn, *Corp Secy*
Robert Kohn, *Engineer*
Carrie Aleman, *Office Mgr*
Robert Bancroft, *Shareholder*
EMP: 60
SQ FT: 56,000
SALES (est): 17.2MM Privately Held
WEB: www.supremecasting.com
SIC: 3363 3365 Aluminum die-castings; aluminum foundries

(G-16268)
TOGREENCLEANCOM
4791 S Cedar Trl (49127-9546)
PHONE.................................269 428-4812
Janice Bussone, *Principal*
EMP: 6 EST: 2008
SALES (est): 99.1K Privately Held
WEB: www.togreenclean.com
SIC: 3471 Cleaning & descaling metal products

(G-16269)
TRI-M-MOLD INC
3390 W Linco Rd (49127-9725)
PHONE.................................269 465-3301
Manfred Moneta, *President*
Carol Moneta, *Vice Pres*
Tom Moneta, *Vice Pres*
EMP: 24 EST: 1969
SQ FT: 22,000
SALES (est): 916.4K Privately Held
SIC: 3544 Special dies & tools

(G-16270)
Z-BRITE METAL FINISHING INC
6979 Stvnsville Baroda Rd (49127-9781)
PHONE.................................269 422-2191
Gary F Zavoral Sr, *President*
Gary Zavoral, *President*
Patricia Zoral, *Principal*
EMP: 14 EST: 1992
SALES (est): 677.7K Privately Held
SIC: 3559 Metal finishing equipment for plating, etc.

(G-16271)
ZAV-TECH METAL FINISHING
6979 Stvnsville Baroda Rd (49127-9781)
P.O. Box 576 (49127-0576)
PHONE.................................269 422-2559
Chad Zavoral, *Partner*
EMP: 6 EST: 1996
SALES (est): 414.8K Privately Held
SIC: 3471 Electroplating of metals or formed products

Stockbridge
Ingham County

(G-16272)
BRANDT MANUFACTURING INC
4974 Bird Dr (49285-9476)
PHONE.................................517 851-7000
Brandt Andreas, *Principal*
EMP: 9 EST: 2010
SALES (est): 270.5K Privately Held
WEB: www.brandt-mfg.com
SIC: 3999 Barber & beauty shop equipment

(G-16273)
DAVID GAUSS LOGGING
4635 Cooper Rd (49285-9752)
PHONE.................................517 851-8102
Mary Gauss, *Principal*
EMP: 4 EST: 2012
SALES (est): 135K Privately Held
SIC: 2411 Logging

(G-16274)
FOLK SIGN STUDIO LLC
5215 Moechel Rd (49285-9539)
PHONE.................................734 883-8259
Kendra S Becklehamer, *Principal*
EMP: 4 EST: 2015
SALES (est): 66.8K Privately Held
WEB: www.folksignstudio.com
SIC: 3993 Signs & advertising specialties

(G-16275)
GRAF ACRES LLC
4230 Swan Rd (49285-9748)
PHONE.................................517 851-8693
Glenn Graf, *President*
Fred Graf, *Partner*
EMP: 5 EST: 1970 Privately Held
SIC: 3556 0213 Dairy & milk machinery; hogs

(G-16276)
LINCOLN WELDING COMPANY
4445 Brogan Rd (49285-9467)
PHONE.................................313 292-2299
Richard Aquino, *President*
Donna Aquino, *Admin Sec*
EMP: 4 EST: 1943
SQ FT: 9,550
SALES (est): 379.4K Privately Held
SIC: 3441 Fabricated structural metal

(G-16277)
PRO POLYMERS INC
4974 Bird Dr (49285-9476)
PHONE.................................734 222-8820
Peter Unger, *CEO*
▲ EMP: 8 EST: 1996
SQ FT: 22,000
SALES (est): 969.4K Privately Held
WEB: www.propolymers.com
SIC: 2821 Plastics materials & resins

(G-16278)
STOCKBRIDGE MANUFACTURING CO
4859 E Main St (49285-9153)
P.O. Box 189 (49285-0189)
PHONE.................................517 851-7865
Camiel Thorrez, *President*
EMP: 1 EST: 1948
SQ FT: 27,000

SALES (est): 1.3MM
SALES (corp-wide): 28.3MM **Privately Held**
WEB: www.brandt-mfg.com
SIC: 3451 Screw machine products
PA: C. Thorrez Industries, Inc.
 4909 W Michigan Ave
 Jackson MI 49201
 517 750-3160

Sturgis
St. Joseph County

(G-16279)
ABBOTT LABORATORIES
Abbott Nutrition
901 N Centerville Rd (49091-9302)
PHONE..................................269 651-0600
Terry Cressman, *Engineer*
Steve Vanmol, *Manager*
Kary Williams, *Supervisor*
EMP: 420
SALES (corp-wide): 34.6B **Publicly Held**
WEB: www.abbott.com
SIC: 2834 Druggists' preparations (pharmaceuticals)
PA: Abbott Laboratories
 100 Abbott Park Rd
 Abbott Park IL 60064
 224 667-6100

(G-16280)
ACM PLASTIC PRODUCTS INC
507 Saint Joseph St (49091-1345)
P.O. Box 580 (49091-0580)
PHONE..................................269 651-7888
Maurice K Walters, *President*
Chuck Walters, *Vice Pres*
▲ EMP: 64 EST: 1977
SQ FT: 70,000
SALES (est): 5MM **Privately Held**
WEB: www.acmplastic.com
SIC: 3089 Blow molded finished plastic products; injection molding of plastics

(G-16281)
BOGEN CONCRETE INC
26959 Bogen Rd (49091-8713)
PHONE..................................269 651-6751
Mark R Bogen, *President*
Dennis French, *Opers Mgr*
EMP: 7 EST: 1983
SALES (est): 747.8K **Privately Held**
WEB: www.bogenconcrete.com
SIC: 3273 Ready-mixed concrete

(G-16282)
BURR OAK TOOL INC (PA)
Also Called: Burr Oak Tool
405 W South St (49091-2192)
PHONE..................................269 651-9393
Brian McConell, *President*
Newell Franks, *Chairman*
David Clark, *Vice Pres*
Andy Boes, *Production*
Stacie Ogg, *Senior Buyer*
◆ EMP: 294 EST: 1944
SQ FT: 250,000
SALES (est): 54MM **Privately Held**
WEB: www.burroak.com
SIC: 3999 3443 3317 Atomizers, toiletry; finned tubes, for heat transfer; tubes, seamless steel

(G-16283)
CLASSIC MFG
21900 Us Highway 12 (49091-9295)
PHONE..................................616 651-2921
EMP: 4 EST: 2019
SALES (est): 118.3K **Privately Held**
SIC: 3999 Manufacturing industries

(G-16284)
COLLIER ENTERPRISE III
Also Called: Tough Coatings
1510 Sunnyfield Rd (49091-9761)
P.O. Box 1056, Paradise CA (95967-1056)
PHONE..................................269 503-3402
EMP: 5
SALES (est): 261.3K **Privately Held**
SIC: 1752 3953 7389 Floor Laying And Floor Work, Nec

(G-16285)
CON-DE MANUFACTURING INC
Also Called: Midwest Fire Protection
26436 Us Highway 12 (49091-9705)
P.O. Box 366 (49091-0366)
PHONE..................................269 651-3756
Jim Reilly, *President*
Dave Yunker, *Corp Secy*
EMP: 5 EST: 1961
SQ FT: 6,500
SALES (est): 497.1K **Privately Held**
SIC: 3448 3499 1799 5999 Docks: prefabricated metal; ladders, portable: metal; dock equipment installation, industrial; fire extinguishers; safety supplies & equipment

(G-16286)
CUSTOM MOLDS
1325 Rolling Ridge Ln (49091-8701)
PHONE..................................574 326-7576
Jack McHenry, *Principal*
EMP: 12 EST: 2015
SALES (est): 112.7K **Privately Held**
SIC: 3599 Industrial machinery

(G-16287)
DAVE BRAND
Also Called: Red Rose Flooring Shop
26541 Us 12 (49091-9703)
PHONE..................................269 651-4693
Dave Brand, *Owner*
EMP: 5 EST: 1986
SQ FT: 2,500
SALES (est): 250K **Privately Held**
WEB: www.redrosefloor.com
SIC: 5713 2591 7217 Carpets; window blinds; carpet & upholstery cleaning

(G-16288)
GATEHOUSE MEDIA LLC
Sturgis Journal
209 John St (49091-1459)
P.O. Box 287, Hillsdale (49242-0287)
PHONE..................................269 651-5407
Dennis Volkert, *Editor*
Candice Phelps, *Regional Mgr*
Shelly Fox, *Sales Staff*
Dan Tolleson, *Manager*
EMP: 25
SALES (corp-wide): 3.4B **Publicly Held**
WEB: www.gannett.com
SIC: 2711 Newspapers, publishing & printing
HQ: Gatehouse Media, Llc
 175 Sullys Trl Fl 3
 Pittsford NY 14534
 585 598-0030

(G-16289)
GRAPHIC PACKAGING INTL LLC
305 W South St (49091-2149)
P.O. Box 570 (49091-0570)
PHONE..................................269 651-2365
Eric Hansen, *General Mgr*
Daniel Barnell, *Manager*
Sandy Dudley,
EMP: 70 **Publicly Held**
WEB: www.americraft.com
SIC: 2657 Folding paperboard boxes
HQ: Graphic Packaging International, Llc
 1500 Riveredge Pkwy # 100
 Atlanta GA 30328

(G-16290)
GRAV CO LLC
400 Norwood St (49091-2132)
P.O. Box 599 (49091-0599)
PHONE..................................269 651-5467
Brent Sheehan,
EMP: 10 EST: 1948
SQ FT: 35,000
SALES (est): 1MM **Privately Held**
WEB: www.gravcollc.com
SIC: 2842 3559 Specialty cleaning preparations; metal finishing equipment for plating, etc.

(G-16291)
GRAVEL FLOW INC (PA)
400 Norwood St (49091-2179)
P.O. Box 2168, Kalamazoo (49003-2168)
PHONE..................................269 651-5467
R Scott Davidson, *President*
EMP: 4 EST: 1978
SQ FT: 10,000
SALES (est): 1.3MM **Privately Held**
SIC: 5085 3559 Industrial supplies; metal finishing equipment for plating, etc.

(G-16292)
HAMILTON HARLEY-DAVIDSON
68951 White School Rd Us-12 (49091-9799)
PHONE..................................269 651-3424
EMP: 5
SALES (est): 54.6K **Privately Held**
WEB: www.hamitonhd.com
SIC: 3751 Motorcycles, bicycles & parts

(G-16293)
ICEBERG ENTERPRISES LLC
1505 W Chicago Rd (49091)
P.O. Box 7039 (49091-7039)
PHONE..................................269 651-9488
Howard Green, *CEO*
John Carter, *Vice Pres*
Richard Fox, *Vice Pres*
Mark Rudy, *Engineer*
Jamie Robinson, *Manager*
EMP: 120
SALES (est): 22MM **Privately Held**
WEB: www.icebergenterprises.com
SIC: 3089 Plastics products

(G-16294)
INDUSTRIAL CONTROL SYSTEMS LLC
70380 M 66 (49091-9433)
P.O. Box 718 (49091-0718)
PHONE..................................269 689-3241
Thomas Tison, *Mng Member*
EMP: 5 EST: 2010
SALES (est): 500.5K **Privately Held**
WEB: www.controls-ics.com
SIC: 1381 Drilling oil & gas wells

(G-16295)
JIM DETWEILER
64177 Rommel Rd (49091-9363)
PHONE..................................269 467-7728
James Detweiler, *Principal*
EMP: 6 EST: 2008
SALES (est): 248.3K **Privately Held**
SIC: 2411 Logging

(G-16296)
JOHNSON PRECISION MOLD & ENGRG
1001 Haines Blvd (49091-9685)
PHONE..................................269 651-2553
Randal Lee Johnson, *President*
Mark Bingaman, *Prgrmr*
Shirley Johnson, *Admin Sec*
EMP: 9 EST: 1990
SALES (est): 1.2MM **Privately Held**
WEB: www.johnsonmold.com
SIC: 3544 3599 Industrial molds; forms (molds), for foundry & plastics working machinery; machine & other job shop work

(G-16297)
KRONTZ GENERAL MACHINE & TOOL
412 W Congress St (49091-1617)
PHONE..................................269 651-5882
Roger Krontz, *President*
William Krontz, *Vice Pres*
EMP: 4 EST: 1978
SQ FT: 29,000
SALES (est): 396.3K **Privately Held**
SIC: 3599 Machine shop, jobbing & repair

(G-16298)
LAKE FABRICATORS INC
Also Called: Unique Truck Accessories
1000 N Clay St (49091-1011)
P.O. Box 7067 (49091-7067)
PHONE..................................269 651-1935
Stanley Lake, *President*
Greg Chamberlain, *Vice Pres*
Chris Rosenberg, *Natl Sales Mgr*
EMP: 25 EST: 1993
SQ FT: 20,000
SALES (est): 4.5MM **Privately Held**
WEB: www.uniquetruckaccessories.com
SIC: 3469 Boxes: tool, lunch, mail, etc.: stamped metal

(G-16299)
LAKESIDE CSTM CBINETS BLDG LLC
24088 Findley Rd (49091-9370)
PHONE..................................269 718-7960
Randy Troyer, *Principal*
EMP: 4 EST: 2017
SALES (est): 71K **Privately Held**
WEB: www.lakesidecabinets.com
SIC: 2434 Wood kitchen cabinets

(G-16300)
LAVERN BEECHY
65022 Balk Rd (49091-9311)
PHONE..................................269 651-5095
Laverne Beechy, *Owner*
EMP: 4 EST: 2015
SALES (est): 145.1K **Privately Held**
WEB: www.indianawoodcrafters.com
SIC: 2431 Millwork

(G-16301)
LCA MOLD & ENGINEERING INC
1200 W Lafayette St (49091-1093)
PHONE..................................269 651-1193
William Luttmann, *President*
Doug Cossairt, *Treasurer*
Bob Anderson, *Admin Sec*
EMP: 8 EST: 1999
SQ FT: 3,000
SALES (est): 664.7K **Privately Held**
SIC: 3544 Special dies & tools

(G-16302)
LITHO PRINTERS INC
620 N Centerville Rd (49091-9602)
PHONE..................................269 651-7309
Mark Wentzel, *President*
Jill Wentzel, *Vice Pres*
EMP: 10 EST: 1964
SQ FT: 5,500
SALES (est): 1MM **Privately Held**
SIC: 2752 Commercial printing, offset

(G-16303)
LUTTMANN PRECISION MOLD INC
1200 W Lafayette St (49091-1093)
PHONE..................................269 651-1193
William R Luttmann, *President*
EMP: 21 EST: 1981
SQ FT: 18,000
SALES (est): 2.8MM **Privately Held**
WEB: www.luttmannprecisionmold.com
SIC: 3544 Special dies & tools

(G-16304)
MARTIN PRODUCTS COMPANY INC
66635 M 66 N (49091)
P.O. Box 269 (49091-0269)
PHONE..................................269 651-1721
Daniel Martin, *President*
EMP: 7 EST: 1979
SQ FT: 16,000
SALES (est): 278.5K **Privately Held**
WEB: www.martin-products.com
SIC: 2499 3479 Picture & mirror frames, wood; painting, coating & hot dipping

(G-16305)
MAYER TOOL & ENGINEERING INC
1404 N Centerville Rd (49091-9699)
P.O. Box 8 (49091-0008)
PHONE..................................269 651-1428
John Mayer, *President*
Patrick Rouffey, *President*
Caralee A Mayer, *Treasurer*
Deborah Mayer, *Admin Asst*
▲ EMP: 37 EST: 1975
SALES (est): 6.2MM **Privately Held**
WEB: www.mayertool.com
SIC: 3544 Forms (molds), for foundry & plastics working machinery; industrial molds

(G-16306)
MICHIANA CORRUGATED PDTS CO
110 N Franks Ave (49091-1582)
P.O. Box 790 (49091-0790)
PHONE..................................269 651-5225
Eric Jones, *President*
Chris Fayling, *Sales Mgr*

Sturgis - St. Joseph County (G-16307)

Tim Farwig, *Sales Staff*
Jeff Holtz, *Manager*
EMP: 24 **EST:** 1990
SQ FT: 53,000
SALES (est): 3.7MM **Privately Held**
WEB: www.michianacorrugated.com
SIC: 2653 Boxes, corrugated; made from purchased materials

(G-16307)
MICHIGAN ROLLER INC
1113 N Clay St (49091-1012)
PHONE.................................269 651-2304
Jesse Fogleman, *President*
Mary Fogleman, *Corp Secy*
EMP: 5 **EST:** 1974
SQ FT: 6,000
SALES (est): 414.6K **Privately Held**
WEB: www.michiganroller.com
SIC: 3069 5084 Printers' rolls & blankets: rubber or rubberized fabric; printing trades machinery, equipment & supplies

(G-16308)
MICHIGAN TOOL WORKS LLC
618 N Centerville Rd (49091-9602)
P.O. Box 158 (49091-0158)
PHONE.................................269 651-5139
Robert Morgan,
Peter Stemen,
EMP: 20 **EST:** 2006
SALES (est): 1.8MM **Privately Held**
WEB: www.michigantoolworks.com
SIC: 3599 Machine shop, jobbing & repair

(G-16309)
MIDWEST PLASTIC ENGINEERING
1501 Progress St (49091-8301)
P.O. Box 320 (49091-0320)
PHONE.................................269 651-5223
Dennis E Baker, *President*
Judith A Baker, *Corp Secy*
▲ **EMP:** 100
SALES (est): 20.8MM **Privately Held**
WEB: www.midwestplastic.com
SIC: 3089 3544 Injection molded finished plastic products; forms (molds), for foundry & plastics working machinery

(G-16310)
MIDWEST TOOL AND CUTLERY CO (PA)
1210 Progress St (49091-9386)
P.O. Box 160 (49091-0160)
PHONE.................................269 651-2476
Stephen Deter, *President*
David Schmick, *Vice Pres*
Scott Musser, *Engineer*
Timothy S Eagan, *Treasurer*
Becky Worth, *Controller*
▼ **EMP:** 80 **EST:** 1960
SQ FT: 26,000
SALES (est): 14.6MM **Privately Held**
WEB: www.midwestsnips.com
SIC: 3545 3421 Machine tool accessories; scissors, shears, clippers, snips & similar tools

(G-16311)
MORGAN OLSON LLC (HQ)
1801 S Nottawa St (49091-8723)
PHONE.................................269 659-0200
Michael Ownbey, *President*
Dan Desrochers, *Exec VP*
David Halladay, *Vice Pres*
Rich Tremmel, *Vice Pres*
Harold Baldridge, *Plant Mgr*
◆ **EMP:** 700 **EST:** 2003
SQ FT: 384,000
SALES (est): 270.2MM
SALES (corp-wide): 1.3B **Privately Held**
WEB: www.morganolson.com
SIC: 3713 Truck bodies (motor vehicles)
PA: J. B. Poindexter & Co., Inc.
600 Travis St Ste 200
Houston TX 77002
713 655-9800

(G-16312)
N & S CUSTOMS
66315 Austrian Ln (49091-9106)
PHONE.................................269 651-8237
Dan Napier, *Principal*
EMP: 4 **EST:** 2016
SALES (est): 82.2K **Privately Held**
WEB: www.nnscustoms.com
SIC: 7692 Welding repair

(G-16313)
NEO MANUFACTURING INC
Also Called: Neo Trailers
21900 Us Highway 12 (49091-9295)
PHONE.................................269 503-7630
Serena Corder, *Office Mgr*
Grant Wolf, *Director*
Wade Wolf,
EMP: 18 **EST:** 2009
SQ FT: 40,000
SALES (est): 3.6MM **Privately Held**
WEB: www.neotrailers.com
SIC: 3715 Truck trailers

(G-16314)
OAK PRESS SOLUTIONS INC
504 Wade Rd (49091-9765)
PHONE.................................269 651-8513
Newell A Franks II, *Ch of Bd*
David L Franks, *President*
Brian P McConnell, *Vice Pres*
◆ **EMP:** 50 **EST:** 1965
SQ FT: 136,000
SALES (est): 9.9MM **Privately Held**
WEB: www.oakpresses.com
SIC: 3542 Presses: forming, stamping, punching, sizing (machine tools)

(G-16315)
OWENS PRODUCTS INC
1107 Progress St (49091-9375)
P.O. Box 670 (49091-0670)
PHONE.................................269 651-2300
Gary Kirtley, *CEO*
Jill Schmidt, *Controller*
Susan Ford, *Bookkeeper*
▼ **EMP:** 40 **EST:** 1992
SQ FT: 35,000
SALES (est): 7MM
SALES (corp-wide): 7.3MM **Privately Held**
WEB: www.owens-pro.com
SIC: 3714 Motor vehicle body components & frame
PA: Owens-Classic Inc
1000 Progress St
Sturgis MI 49091
269 651-2300

(G-16316)
PARMA TUBE CORP
1008 Progress St (49091-9375)
PHONE.................................269 651-2351
Mark A Roberts, *President*
Russ Ahrens, *Plant Mgr*
Steve Toner, *Sales Engr*
Bill Wetzel, *Supervisor*
EMP: 48 **EST:** 1964
SQ FT: 60,000
SALES (est): 7MM **Privately Held**
WEB: www.parmatube.com
SIC: 3317 7692 3498 Steel pipe & tubes; welding repair; fabricated pipe & fittings

(G-16317)
PDC (PA)
69701 White St (49091-2187)
PHONE.................................269 651-9975
Rick Pennzoni, *President*
Rick Savage, *Vice Pres*
▲ **EMP:** 13 **EST:** 1992
SQ FT: 6,000
SALES (est): 1.5MM **Privately Held**
WEB: www.prosperportland.us
SIC: 2541 Display fixtures, wood; showcases, except refrigerated: wood

(G-16318)
PENGUIN LLC
Also Called: Penguin-Iceberg Enterprises
1855 W Chicago Rd (49091-8736)
P.O. Box 7039 (49091-7039)
PHONE.................................269 651-9488
Christine Parker, *Safety Mgr*
George Oliva, *CFO*
Jamie O'dell, *Manager*
John Carter, *Exec Dir*
Tracy Bernstein, *Senior Editor*
▲ **EMP:** 110 **EST:** 2002
SQ FT: 100,000
SALES (est): 19.5MM
SALES (corp-wide): 35MM **Privately Held**
WEB: www.icebergenterprises.com
SIC: 3089 Blow molded finished plastic products; injection molding of plastics
PA: Iceberg Enterprises, Llc
2700 S River Rd Ste 303
Des Plaines IL 60018
847 685-9500

(G-16319)
PRAIRIE WOOD PRODUCTS INC
506 Prairie St (49091-2180)
PHONE.................................269 659-1163
Mike Melvin, *President*
Carolyn Melvin, *Corp Secy*
EMP: 15 **EST:** 2000
SALES (est): 540.6K **Privately Held**
WEB: www.prairiewoodproducts.com
SIC: 2448 Pallets, wood

(G-16320)
PRECISION SPEED EQUIPMENT INC
1400 W Lafayette St (49091-8905)
P.O. Box 7036 (49091-7036)
PHONE.................................269 651-4303
Robert Griffioen, *President*
Josephine Griffioen, *Vice Pres*
Tom Beal, *Engineer*
Matt Kleine, *Engineer*
▲ **EMP:** 125 **EST:** 1967
SQ FT: 22,000
SALES (est): 22MM **Privately Held**
WEB: www.pse-usa.com
SIC: 3822 Appliance controls except air-conditioning & refrigeration; flame safety controls for furnaces & boilers; ignition controls for gas appliances & furnaces, automatic; gas burner, automatic controls

(G-16321)
REHAU INCORPORATED
1110 N Clay St (49091-1013)
PHONE.................................269 651-7845
Bruce Claridge, *Manager*
EMP: 5
SALES (corp-wide): 392.5K **Privately Held**
WEB: www.rehau.com
SIC: 3069 3543 3083 Molded rubber products; industrial patterns; laminated plastics plate & sheet
HQ: Rehau Incorporated
1501 Edwards Ferry Rd Ne
Leesburg VA 20176

(G-16322)
SE-KURE DOMES & MIRRORS INC
1139 Haines Blvd (49091-9619)
PHONE.................................269 651-9351
Roger Leyden, *Principal*
Melody Curtis, *Assistant*
EMP: 19 **EST:** 1999
SALES (est): 1.5MM **Privately Held**
WEB: www.domesandmirrors.com
SIC: 7382 3231 Security systems services; mirrored glass

(G-16323)
STURGIS ELECTRIC MOTOR SERVICE
703 N Centerville Rd (49091-9603)
P.O. Box 255 (49091-0255)
PHONE.................................269 651-2955
Allen White, *Owner*
EMP: 4 **EST:** 1952
SQ FT: 4,500
SALES (est): 486.3K **Privately Held**
WEB: www.sturgiselectricmotor.com
SIC: 7694 Electric motor repair

(G-16324)
STURGIS MOLDED PRODUCTS CO
Also Called: Smp
70343 Clark Rd (49091-9755)
PHONE.................................269 651-9381
Mark D Weishaar, *President*
Bud Clark, *Senior VP*
Chris Emery, *Vice Pres*
Paul G Feaman, *Vice Pres*
Jason Harloff, *Vice Pres*
EMP: 200 **EST:** 1966
SQ FT: 145,000
SALES (est): 45.5MM **Privately Held**
WEB: www.smpco.com
SIC: 3089 3544 Injection molding of plastics; special dies, tools, jigs & fixtures

(G-16325)
STURGIS TOOL AND DIE INC
817 Broadus St (49091-1373)
P.O. Box 368 (49091-0368)
PHONE.................................269 651-5435
Robert M Zimmerman, *President*
Ronald S Zimmerman, *Vice Pres*
Steve Zimmerman, *VP Sales*
EMP: 25 **EST:** 1966
SQ FT: 26,000
SALES (est): 4.2MM **Privately Held**
WEB: www.sturgistool.com
SIC: 3544 Dies & die holders for metal cutting, forming, die casting; special dies & tools

(G-16326)
SUMMIT POLYMERS INC
Also Called: Syntech Plant
1211 Progress St (49091-9386)
PHONE.................................269 651-1643
Kay Salyer, *Purch Agent*
Brent Yager, *Manager*
Michael Schuller, *Manager*
EMP: 293
SALES (corp-wide): 590MM **Privately Held**
WEB: www.summitpolymers.com
SIC: 3089 3083 Thermoformed finished plastic products; laminated plastics plate & sheet
PA: Summit Polymers, Inc.
6715 S Sprinkle Rd
Portage MI 49002
269 324-9330

(G-16327)
TJ PANT LLC
25993 Us Highway 12 (49091-9712)
PHONE.................................419 215-8434
Thomas Pant, *Principal*
EMP: 8 **EST:** 2017
SALES (est): 513.9K **Privately Held**
WEB: www.tjpantllc.com
SIC: 3993 Signs & advertising specialties

(G-16328)
VCI INC (PA)
Also Called: Basin Material Handling
1500 Progress St (49091-8301)
P.O. Box 7034 (49091-7034)
PHONE.................................269 659-3676
Eugene R Harrison, *President*
Rusty Smith, *Vice Pres*
Al Stimson, *Sales Staff*
▲ **EMP:** 90 **EST:** 1998
SQ FT: 100,000
SALES (est): 17.7MM **Privately Held**
SIC: 3537 3441 Platforms, stands, tables, pallets & similar equipment; building components, structural steel

(G-16329)
WEIDERMAN MOTORSPORTS
28386 Witt Lake Rd (49091-8805)
PHONE.................................269 689-0264
Matt Weiderman, *Principal*
EMP: 6 **EST:** 2010
SALES (est): 149.1K **Privately Held**
WEB: www.weidermanmotorsports.com
SIC: 3713 Car carrier bodies

(G-16330)
WINGS OF STURGIS LLC
71005 Miller Rd (49091-9405)
P.O. Box 7156 (49091-7156)
PHONE.................................269 689-9326
EMP: 5 **EST:** 2015
SALES (est): 140.6K **Privately Held**
WEB: www.sturgisjournal.com
SIC: 2711 Newspapers, publishing & printing

Sumner
Gratiot County

(G-16331)
HAYDEN NEITZKE LLC
Also Called: Saia Fabricating
2035 S Warner Rd (48889-9725)
PHONE...................989 875-2440
Hayden Neitzke, *Mng Member*
EMP: 4 **EST:** 2016
SALES (est): 506.3K **Privately Held**
SIC: 5051 3441 Steel; fabricated structural metal

(G-16332)
HUBSCHER & SON INC
8189 W Washington Rd (48889-8716)
PHONE...................989 875-2151
Oscar Rulapaugh, *Manager*
EMP: 6
SALES (corp-wide): 2.1MM **Privately Held**
SIC: 1442 Gravel mining
PA: Hubscher & Son Inc
1101 N Franklin Ave
Mount Pleasant MI 48858
989 773-5369

Sunfield
Eaton County

(G-16333)
AUTOMOTIVE MANUFACTURING
101 Main St (48890)
P.O. Box 148 (48890-0148)
PHONE...................517 566-8174
Michael Frey, *Owner*
EMP: 5 **EST:** 1987
SALES (est): 300K **Privately Held**
SIC: 3089 7389 Injection molding of plastics; design services

(G-16334)
EAST JORDAN IRONWORKS INC
7300 W Grand Ledge Hwy (48890-9776)
PHONE...................517 566-7211
Tom Teske, *Principal*
EMP: 8 **EST:** 2015
SALES (est): 289.6K **Privately Held**
SIC: 1791 3321 Iron work, structural; manhole covers, metal

(G-16335)
GREAT LAKES TREATMENT CORP
5630 E Eaton Hwy (48890-9730)
PHONE...................517 566-8008
Kerry J Haynor, *President*
Rodney Haynor, *General Mgr*
Janice Powell, *Office Mgr*
EMP: 4 **EST:** 1988
SALES (est): 511.4K **Privately Held**
SIC: 2899 Water treating compounds

Superior Township
Washtenaw County

(G-16336)
EFESTO LLC
3400 Woodhill Cir (48198-9650)
PHONE...................734 913-0428
EMP: 3
SALES: 3MM **Privately Held**
SIC: 3599 Mfg Industrial Machinery

(G-16337)
LONGSON INTERNATIONAL CORP
3336 Woodhill Cir (48198-9650)
PHONE...................734 657-8719
Ye MA, *Administration*
▲ **EMP:** 5 **EST:** 2010
SALES (est): 217.6K **Privately Held**
SIC: 3714 Motor vehicle parts & accessories

Suttons Bay
Leelanau County

(G-16338)
BIG LTTLE WINES TRAVERSE CY MI
4519 S Elm Valley Rd (49682-9473)
PHONE...................231 714-4854
EMP: 5 **EST:** 2017
SALES (est): 74.5K **Privately Held**
WEB: www.biglittlewines.com
SIC: 2084 Wines

(G-16339)
BLACK STAR FARMS LLC (PA)
Also Called: Suttons Bay Tasting Room
10844 E Revold Rd (49682-9703)
PHONE...................231 271-4970
Chris Lopez, *General Mgr*
Michael Lahti, *CFO*
John Schoelles, *Controller*
Sherri Fenton, *Comms Dir*
Grace Malley, *Manager*
▲ **EMP:** 15 **EST:** 1998
SALES (est): 3.4MM **Privately Held**
WEB: www.blackstarfarms.com
SIC: 2084 7011 0752 Wines; brandy; bed & breakfast inn; boarding services, horses: racing & non-racing; training services, horses (except racing horses)

(G-16340)
HANG ON EXPRESS
316 N Saint Joseph St (49682-5104)
P.O. Box 907 (49682-0907)
PHONE...................231 271-0202
Hang Vang, *Owner*
Maika Hang, *Co-Owner*
EMP: 4 **EST:** 2007
SALES (est): 150K **Privately Held**
SIC: 2741 Miscellaneous publishing

(G-16341)
HEARTH & VINE
10844 E Revold Rd (49682-9703)
PHONE...................231 944-1297
Valerie Micham, *President*
EMP: 8 **EST:** 2014
SALES (est): 91.6K **Privately Held**
WEB: www.blackstarfarms.com
SIC: 2084 Wines

(G-16342)
SHADY LANE ORCHARDS INC
Also Called: Shady Lane Cellars
9580 E Shady Ln (49682-9440)
PHONE...................231 935-1620
Adam Atchwell, *General Mgr*
Andrew Fles, *Manager*
Tyler Parks, *Manager*
▲ **EMP:** 10 **EST:** 2000
SALES (est): 1.4MM **Privately Held**
WEB: www.shadylanecellars.com
SIC: 5921 2084 Wine; wines

(G-16343)
SUTTONS BAY CIDERS
10530 E Hilltop Rd (49682-9420)
PHONE...................734 646-3196
Madelynn Korzon, *Principal*
EMP: 6 **EST:** 2015
SALES (est): 397.8K **Privately Held**
WEB: www.suttonsbayciders.com
SIC: 2084 Wines

(G-16344)
TANDEM CIDERS INC
2055 N Setterbo Rd (49682-9393)
PHONE...................231 271-0050
Sarah Hoskins, *Principal*
EMP: 4 **EST:** 2008
SALES (est): 370.5K **Privately Held**
WEB: www.tandemciders.com
SIC: 2084 Wines

(G-16345)
THREE FIRES WINE
5046 S West Bay Shore Dr (49682-9721)
P.O. Box 277, West Olive (49460-0277)
PHONE...................231 620-9463
EMP: 6 **EST:** 2019
SALES (est): 197.6K **Privately Held**
WEB: www.threefireswine.com
SIC: 2084 Wines, brandy & brandy spirits

(G-16346)
TILCO INC
Also Called: Med-Tek
1719 S Apple Ct (49682-9545)
PHONE...................248 644-0901
Stephen R Tille, *President*
Melissa Tille, *Admin Sec*
EMP: 9 **EST:** 1997
SALES (est): 438.8K **Privately Held**
SIC: 3841 5199 Surgical & medical instruments; advertising specialties

(G-16347)
WILLOW VINEYARDS INC
10702 E Hilltop Rd (49682-9419)
PHONE...................231 271-4810
Joe Crampton, *Vice Pres*
John Crampton, *Vice Pres*
EMP: 8 **EST:** 1996
SALES (est): 297.1K **Privately Held**
WEB: www.willowvineyardwine.com
SIC: 2084 Wines

Swartz Creek
Genesee County

(G-16348)
AHLUSION LLC
5118 Morrish Rd (48473-1327)
PHONE...................888 277-0001
Alyssa Foo,
EMP: 9 **EST:** 2011
SALES (est): 1.2MM **Privately Held**
WEB: www.ahlusion.us
SIC: 2869 Perfumes, flavorings & food additives

(G-16349)
ALCO PRODUCTS
5217 Seymour Rd (48473-1029)
PHONE...................715 346-3174
Johanna Green, *Principal*
EMP: 7 **EST:** 2008
SALES (est): 69.1K **Privately Held**
SIC: 3599 Machine shop, jobbing & repair

(G-16350)
ASSENMACHER LIGHTWEIGHT CYCLES (PA)
Also Called: Assenmachers Hill Road Cyclery
8053 Miller Rd (48473-1333)
P.O. Box 97 (48473-0097)
PHONE...................810 635-7844
Matthew Assenmacher, *Owner*
Barbara Assenmacher, *Co-Owner*
EMP: 5 **EST:** 1974
SQ FT: 6,000
SALES (est): 993.2K **Privately Held**
WEB: www.assenmachers.com
SIC: 5941 3751 Bicycle & bicycle parts; frames, motorcycle & bicycle; bicycles & related parts

(G-16351)
BILL DAUP SIGNS INC
7389 Ponderosa Dr (48473-9453)
PHONE...................810 235-4080
EMP: 4
SQ FT: 3,000
SALES: 390K **Privately Held**
SIC: 3993 1799 Mfg And Maintenance Of Signs

(G-16352)
D O W ASPHALT PAVING LLC
10421 Calkins Rd (48473-9757)
PHONE...................810 743-2633
James Weisberg, *President*
Robert Ward,
EMP: 8 **EST:** 1982
SALES (est): 376K **Privately Held**
SIC: 1771 2951 1611 Blacktop (asphalt) work; asphalt paving mixtures & blocks; surfacing & paving

(G-16353)
FIRESIDE COFFEE COMPANY INC
3239 S Elms Rd (48473-7928)
PHONE...................810 635-9196
Carol Davis, *President*
Mike Davis, *Vice Pres*
Ruthi Spillane, *Warehouse Mgr*
EMP: 18 **EST:** 1992
SQ FT: 4,800
SALES (est): 1MM **Privately Held**
WEB: www.firesidecoffee.com
SIC: 2095 5149 Instant coffee; groceries & related products

(G-16354)
GENERAL MOTORS LLC
6060 W Bristol Rd (48473)
PHONE...................810 635-5281
EMP: 7 **Publicly Held**
WEB: www.gm.com
SIC: 3714 Motor vehicle parts & accessories
HQ: General Motors Llc
300 Renaissance Ctr L1
Detroit MI 48243

(G-16355)
HOUGEN MANUFACTURING INC
3001 Hougen Dr (48473-7935)
P.O. Box 2005, Flint (48501-2005)
PHONE...................810 635-7111
Randall Hougen, *CEO*
Gregory Phillips, *President*
Mary Chrastek, *General Mgr*
Victor Hougen, *Vice Pres*
Greg Phillips, *Vice Pres*
◆ **EMP:** 130 **EST:** 1959
SQ FT: 80,000
SALES (est): 29.1MM **Privately Held**
WEB: www.hougen.com
SIC: 5084 3545 3546 3541 Machine tools & metalworking machinery; drill bits, metalworking; broaches (machine tool accessories); power-driven handtools; machine tools, metal cutting type

(G-16356)
KHARON INDUSTRIES
7445 Grove St (48473-1411)
PHONE...................810 630-6355
EMP: 4 **EST:** 2012
SALES (est): 79K **Privately Held**
SIC: 3999 Manufacturing industries

(G-16357)
NAGEL PAPER INC
Also Called: Abzac - US
6437 Lennon Rd (48473-7916)
PHONE...................810 644-7043
Marcus J Baker, *President*
James L Baker, *CFO*
Linda Elaine Baker, *Admin Sec*
▲ **EMP:** 20 **EST:** 1924
SQ FT: 35,000
SALES (est): 5.8MM **Privately Held**
WEB: www.nagelpaper.com
SIC: 2655 Tubes, fiber or paper: made from purchased material

(G-16358)
SHIRT TRAVELER
6005 Miller Rd Ste 7 (48473-1535)
PHONE...................800 403-4117
Autumn Jesme, *CEO*
EMP: 5 **EST:** 2016
SALES (est): 356.1K **Privately Held**
WEB: www.shirttraveler.com
SIC: 2759 5999 Screen printing; alcoholic beverage making equipment & supplies

Sylvan Lake
Oakland County

(G-16359)
AVIAN ENTERPRISES LLC (PA)
Also Called: Avian Control
2000 Pontiac Dr (48320-1758)
PHONE...................888 366-0709
Jon Stone, *President*
Steven Stone, *Exec VP*
Kenneth Stone, *Vice Pres*
EMP: 20 **EST:** 2013

Sylvan Lake - Oakland County (G-16360)

SQ FT: 100,000
SALES (est): 2.6MM **Privately Held**
WEB: www.aviancontrolinc.com
SIC: 2879 Agricultural chemicals

(G-16360)
DEAN RICHARD WOODWORKING
2655 Orchard Lake Rd (48320-1571)
PHONE..................586 764-6586
EMP: 6 **EST:** 2019
SALES (est): 967.2K **Privately Held**
SIC: 2431 Millwork

(G-16361)
HYGIENE OF SWEDEN USA LLC
2681 Orchard Lake Rd E (48320-1572)
PHONE..................248 760-3241
Nicolas Andreasson,
EMP: 5
SALES (est): 500K **Privately Held**
WEB: www.hygieneofsweden.com
SIC: 2842 Sanitation preparations, disinfectants & deodorants

(G-16362)
STONE SOAP COMPANY INC
2000 Pontiac Dr (48320-1758)
PHONE..................248 706-1000
Kenneth Stone, *Ch of Bd*
Steven Stone, *Exec VP*
Jackie Elchemmas, *Plant Mgr*
Jon Stone, *Controller*
Donna Designs, *Marketing Staff*
▲ **EMP:** 50 **EST:** 1932
SQ FT: 150,000
SALES (est): 9.9MM **Privately Held**
WEB: www.stonesoap.com
SIC: 2841 2844 Soap & other detergents; cosmetic preparations

(G-16363)
WORLD WIDE CABINETS INC
2655 Orchard Lake Rd # 101 (48320-1571)
PHONE..................248 683-2680
Ralph Campbell, *President*
EMP: 10 **EST:** 1990
SQ FT: 4,000
SALES (est): 870K **Privately Held**
WEB: www.worldwidecabinets.com
SIC: 2434 Wood kitchen cabinets

Tawas City
Iosco County

(G-16364)
ADVANCE MACHINE CORP
612 9th Ave (48763-9532)
P.O. Box 789 (48764-0789)
PHONE..................989 362-9192
Gary Schulman, *President*
Daniel Chomin, *QC Mgr*
Kellee Chomin, *Manager*
EMP: 5 **EST:** 1980
SQ FT: 9,000
SALES (est): 434.6K **Privately Held**
WEB: www.advancemachinecorp.com
SIC: 3599 Machine shop, jobbing & repair

(G-16365)
PLASTIC TRIM INC
905 Cedar St (48763-9200)
PHONE..................937 429-1100
Bill Carroll, *President*
▲ **EMP:** 13 **EST:** 1990
SALES (est): 478.7K **Privately Held**
SIC: 3089 Extruded finished plastic products; injection molding of plastics

(G-16366)
PLASTIC TRIM INTERNATIONAL INC
905 Cedar St (48763-9200)
PHONE..................989 362-4419
Howard Boyer, *CEO*
Jessica Collins, *Asst Controller*
EMP: 44
SQ FT: 84,000 **Privately Held**
SIC: 3089 Extruded finished plastic products

HQ: Plastic Trim International, Inc.
935 Aulerich Rd
East Tawas MI 48730
248 259-7468

(G-16367)
R E GLANCY INC (PA)
124 W M 55 (48763-9251)
P.O. Box 418 (48764-0418)
PHONE..................989 362-0997
Michael Glancy, *President*
Rhoda Moelter, *Corp Secy*
Robert E Glancy Jr, *Vice Pres*
EMP: 5 **EST:** 1963
SALES (est): 2.3MM **Privately Held**
SIC: 1422 Limestones, ground

(G-16368)
STRAITS CORPORATION (PA)
616 Oak St (48763-9338)
PHONE..................989 684-5088
Michael D Seward, *CEO*
Charles A Pinkerton III, *President*
Michael J Biber, *Treasurer*
Katie Look, *Controller*
William F Bartlett, *Manager*
EMP: 12 **EST:** 1953
SQ FT: 15,200
SALES (est): 21.7MM **Privately Held**
WEB: www.straitsopsprops.com
SIC: 4011 0211 2491 5712 Railroads, line-haul operating; beef cattle feedlots; wood preserving; furniture stores

(G-16369)
STRAITS OPERATIONS COMPANY
616 Oak St (48763-9338)
PHONE..................989 684-5088
Charles A Pinkerton III, *President*
Michael Biber, *Treasurer*
EMP: 9 **EST:** 2006
SALES (est): 2MM
SALES (corp-wide): 21.7MM **Privately Held**
WEB: www.straitsopsprops.com
SIC: 2491 Wood preserving
PA: The Straits Corporation
616 Oak St
Tawas City MI 48763
989 684-5088

(G-16370)
STRAITS SERVICE CORPORATION
616 Oak St (48763-9338)
PHONE..................989 684-5088
Charles A Pinkerton III, *President*
EMP: 1 **EST:** 1976
SQ FT: 14,000
SALES (est): 2.1MM
SALES (corp-wide): 21.7MM **Privately Held**
WEB: www.straitsopsprops.com
SIC: 2491 Wood preserving
PA: The Straits Corporation
616 Oak St
Tawas City MI 48763
989 684-5088

(G-16371)
STRAITS WOOD TREATING INC (HQ)
616 Oak St (48763-9338)
PHONE..................989 684-5088
Charles A Pinkerton III, *President*
James P Pitz, *Vice Pres*
EMP: 1
SALES: 4.7MM
SALES (corp-wide): 21.7MM **Privately Held**
WEB: www.straitsopsprops.com
SIC: 2491 Wood preserving
PA: The Straits Corporation
616 Oak St
Tawas City MI 48763
989 684-5088

(G-16372)
TAWAS PLATING COMPANY
510 Industrial Ave (48763-9110)
P.O. Box 419 (48764-0419)
PHONE..................989 362-2011
Kevin T Jungquist, *President*
Deborah K Jungquist, *Corp Secy*

Diane Knight, *Vice Pres*
Harold J Knight, *Vice Pres*
Lynette Knight, *Vice Pres*
EMP: 35 **EST:** 1954
SQ FT: 30,000
SALES (est): 3MM **Privately Held**
WEB: www.tawasplating.com
SIC: 3471 Plating of metals or formed products

(G-16373)
TAWAS POWDER COATING INC
510 Industrial Ave (48763-9110)
P.O. Box 419 (48764-0419)
PHONE..................989 362-2011
Harold Knight, *President*
Gene Freehling, *Manager*
EMP: 20 **EST:** 1989
SQ FT: 18,000
SALES (est): 829.8K **Privately Held**
SIC: 3479 Coating of metals & formed products

Taylor
Wayne County

(G-16374)
AEROSTAR MANUFACTURING
24340 Northline Rd (48180-4586)
PHONE..................734 947-2558
EMP: 7 **EST:** 2014
SALES (est): 267.4K **Privately Held**
SIC: 3999 Manufacturing industries

(G-16375)
AJM PACKAGING CORPORATION
Also Called: Roblaw Industries
21130 Trolley Indus Dr (48180-1871)
PHONE..................313 291-6500
Keith Stillson, *Administration*
EMP: 93
SALES (corp-wide): 419.9MM **Privately Held**
WEB: www.ajmpack.com
SIC: 2674 2679 Paper bags: made from purchased materials; plates, pressed & molded pulp: from purchased material
PA: A.J.M. Packaging Corporation
E-4111 Andover Rd
Bloomfield Hills MI 48302
248 901-0040

(G-16376)
AMERICAN SPEEDY PRINTING CTRS
20320 Ecorse Rd (48180-1953)
PHONE..................313 928-5820
Jeff Reynolds, *Owner*
EMP: 6 **EST:** 1990
SALES (est): 518K **Privately Held**
WEB: www.americanspeedy.com
SIC: 2752 Commercial printing, offset

(G-16377)
AMERICAN TOOL & GAGE INC
26312 Susan St (48180-3023)
PHONE..................313 587-7923
Ted A Schiebold, *Administration*
EMP: 5 **EST:** 2011
SALES (est): 170K **Privately Held**
WEB: www.atggages.com
SIC: 3799 Trailers & trailer equipment

(G-16378)
ANDEX LASER INC
12222 Universal Dr (48180-4074)
PHONE..................734 947-9840
Robert Anderson, *President*
Kevin Dexter, *Vice Pres*
EMP: 5 **EST:** 2004
SALES (est): 676.7K **Privately Held**
WEB: www.andexlaser.com
SIC: 3699 Laser welding, drilling & cutting equipment; laser systems & equipment

(G-16379)
ANH ENTERPRISES LLC (PA)
Also Called: Midas Muffler
21538 Goddard Rd (48180-4246)
PHONE..................313 887-0800
Nasser Halwani, *President*
Amer Halwani, *President*

EMP: 10 **EST:** 2013
SALES (est): 1.5MM **Privately Held**
WEB: www.midas.com
SIC: 3011 7539 Automobile tires, pneumatic; automotive repair shops

(G-16380)
ANNALUX CANDLES LLC
1546 Park Village Blvd (48180)
PHONE..................313 566-3289
Cierra Betts, *Mng Member*
EMP: 4 **EST:** 2019
SALES (est): 250K **Privately Held**
SIC: 3999 Candles

(G-16381)
APEX POWDER COATING LLC
27258 Wick Rd (48180-3017)
PHONE..................734 921-3177
Amber Boggess,
EMP: 4 **EST:** 2019
SALES (est): 65K **Privately Held**
WEB: www.apexqualitycoatings.com
SIC: 3479 Coating of metals & formed products

(G-16382)
AUTOMOTIVE TRIM TECHNOLOGIES
12400 Universal Dr (48180-6837)
P.O. Box 726 (48180-0726)
PHONE..................734 947-0344
Gino Martino, *CEO*
Carina Navarro, *Prdtn Mgr*
Diane Goodreau, *Engineer*
Carron Kochoian, *Human Resources*
▲ **EMP:** 20 **EST:** 2006
SQ FT: 5,000
SALES (est): 2MM **Privately Held**
WEB: www.attproto.com
SIC: 2396 Automotive trimmings, fabric

(G-16383)
AVANTI PRESS INC
22701 Trolley Industrial (48180-1895)
PHONE..................313 961-0022
EMP: 30
SALES (corp-wide): 18.5MM **Privately Held**
WEB: www.avantipress.com
SIC: 2771 Greeting cards
PA: Avanti Press, Inc.
155 W Congress St Ste 200
Detroit MI 48226
800 228-2684

(G-16384)
B & D THREAD ROLLING INC
Also Called: B & D Cold Heading
25000 Brest (48180-4042)
PHONE..................734 728-7070
Dennis Doyle, *President*
Tom Glinski, *Vice Pres*
Andy Sanderson, *CFO*
Scott Sanderson, *CFO*
Lucy Doyle, *Treasurer*
▲ **EMP:** 62
SQ FT: 110,000
SALES (est): 25.3MM **Privately Held**
WEB: www.bdcoldheadedproducts.com
SIC: 3444 3452 Studs & joists, sheet metal; bolts, metal

(G-16385)
B AND R OIL COMPANY INC
24501 Ecorse Rd (48180-1641)
PHONE..................313 292-5500
Sam Simon, *Owner*
EMP: 1 **EST:** 2009
SALES (est): 1.1MM **Privately Held**
WEB: www.atlasoil.com
SIC: 2999 Coke
PA: Atlas Oil Holding Company
24501 Ecorse Rd
Taylor MI 48180

(G-16386)
B G INDUSTRIES INC
6835 Monroe Blvd (48180-1815)
PHONE..................313 292-5355
Gerald Cummings, *President*
EMP: 15 **EST:** 1950
SQ FT: 50,000
SALES (est): 201.6K **Privately Held**
SIC: 3599 Machine shop, jobbing & repair

GEOGRAPHIC SECTION

(G-16387)
BALOGH
14102 Jackson St (48180-5349)
PHONE..................................734 283-3972
Timothy Balogh, *Principal*
EMP: 6 **EST:** 2010
SALES (est): 147.7K **Privately Held**
WEB: www.tagmaster.com
SIC: 3661 Telephone & telegraph apparatus

(G-16388)
C L RIECKHOFF COMPANY INC (PA)
26265 Northline Rd (48180-4412)
PHONE..................................734 946-8220
Charles Rieckhoff, *President*
Dan Rieckhoff, *Project Mgr*
David Lange, *Engineer*
Paul Rieckhoff, *Engineer*
Tim Smith, *Treasurer*
▲ **EMP:** 120
SQ FT: 60,000
SALES (est): 21.1MM **Privately Held**
WEB: www.rieckhoff.com
SIC: 3444 1761 Sheet metalwork; siding contractor

(G-16389)
C&C FORKLIFT
15060 Michael St (48180-5013)
PHONE..................................313 729-2850
Jay Newby, *Principal*
EMP: 4 **EST:** 2017
SALES (est): 143.9K **Privately Held**
SIC: 3537 Forklift trucks

(G-16390)
CAMPBELL SOUP COMPANY
21740 Trlley Indus Dr D (48180-1874)
PHONE..................................313 295-6884
Gordon McCarty, *Branch Mgr*
EMP: 6
SALES (corp-wide): 8.4B **Publicly Held**
WEB: www.campbellsoupcompany.com
SIC: 5461 2038 2033 2052 Bakeries; frozen specialties; canned fruits & specialties; cookies & crackers; bread, cake & related products; potato chips & similar snacks
PA: Campbell Soup Company
  1 Campbell Pl
  Camden NJ 08103
  856 342-4800

(G-16391)
CATTLEMANS MEAT COMPANY
Also Called: Cattlemans Fresh Mt & Fish Mkt
11400 Telegraph Rd (48180-4078)
PHONE..................................734 287-8260
David S Rohtbart, *President*
Benjamin D Govaere, *Senior VP*
Markus Rohtbart, *Treasurer*
EMP: 275 **EST:** 1972
SQ FT: 56,500 **Privately Held**
WEB: www.cattlemansmeats.com
SIC: 2013 5421 Prepared beef products from purchased beef; meat markets, including freezer provisioners

(G-16392)
CFH INC
Also Called: Specialty Fabrication
12550 Universal Dr (48180-6838)
PHONE..................................734 947-9574
Steve Smith, *President*
Kathy Rose, *Marketing Staff*
EMP: 20 **EST:** 2000
SALES (est): 1.9MM **Privately Held**
SIC: 3544 Special dies, tools, jigs & fixtures

(G-16393)
CO-PIPE PRODUCTS INC
20501 Goddard Rd (48180-4352)
PHONE..................................734 287-1000
Jenny Coco, *CEO*
Rocky Coco, *President*
Nina Coco, *Manager*
Monica Marshall, *Manager*
EMP: 40 **EST:** 1930
SALES (est): 7.9MM **Privately Held**
WEB: www.copipe.com
SIC: 3272 Sewer pipe, concrete

(G-16394)
COLONIAL TOOL SALES & SVC LLC
Also Called: Advanced Cutting Tool Systems
12344 Delta St (48180-6832)
PHONE..................................734 946-2733
Sam Verduce, *Sales Mgr*
Paul Thrasher,
Lori Kozodoy, *Administration*
Brett Froats,
▲ **EMP:** 10 **EST:** 1998
SQ FT: 28,000
SALES (est): 1.6MM **Privately Held**
WEB: www.colonialtool.com
SIC: 3545 Machine tool accessories

(G-16395)
COMMERCIAL GROUP INC (PA)
Also Called: Commercial Group Lifting Pdts
12801 Universal Dr (48180-6844)
PHONE..................................313 931-6100
Garland Knight, *President*
Scottie Knight, *COO*
Tony Zomparelli, *Vice Pres*
Matt Glynn, *Foreman/Supr*
Sonja Chumura, *Purch Agent*
▼ **EMP:** 47 **EST:** 1956
SQ FT: 220,000
SALES (est): 47.8MM **Privately Held**
SIC: 5085 5051 3496 3537 Industrial supplies; rope, wire (not insulated); cable, uninsulated wire: made from purchased wire; industrial trucks & tractors; elevators & moving stairways

(G-16396)
COMMUNITY PUBLISHING & MKTG
Also Called: Waterford Today
26955 Northline Rd (48180-4408)
PHONE..................................866 822-0101
Paul Borg, *Principal*
Dan Zahn, *Accounts Exec*
Shannon Esper, *Graphic Designe*
EMP: 7 **EST:** 2012
SALES (est): 741.5K **Privately Held**
WEB: www.communitypublishing.com
SIC: 5192 2721 Magazines; magazines: publishing & printing

(G-16397)
CUSTOM COATING TECH INC
24341 Brest (48180-6848)
P.O. Box 1090, Flat Rock (48134-2090)
PHONE..................................734 442-4074
James Anderson, *President*
EMP: 7 **EST:** 2017
SALES (est): 119.1K **Privately Held**
WEB: www.customcoatingtech.com
SIC: 3479 Coating of metals & formed products

(G-16398)
CUT ALL WATER JET CUTTING INC
25944 Northline Rd (48180-4413)
PHONE..................................734 946-7880
Patrick Spence, *President*
EMP: 8 **EST:** 1995
SQ FT: 6,000
SALES (est): 884.6K **Privately Held**
WEB: www.cut-all.com
SIC: 3599 Machine shop, jobbing & repair

(G-16399)
D SHARP MASONRY
6360 Mcguire St (48180-1133)
PHONE..................................313 292-2375
EMP: 4 **EST:** 2018
SALES (est): 55.8K **Privately Held**
SIC: 2024 Yogurt desserts, frozen

(G-16400)
DEARBORN MID-WEST COMPANY LLC (PA)
20334 Superior Rd (48180-6301)
PHONE..................................734 288-4400
Jeff Homenik, *President*
Ryan Langnes, *Superintendent*
C Bagierek, *Vice Pres*
Steve Dorchak, *Vice Pres*
Marius Vlad, *Project Mgr*
▲ **EMP:** 53 **EST:** 2014
SALES (est): 176.4MM **Privately Held**
WEB: www.dmwcc.com
SIC: 3535 Conveyors & conveying equipment

(G-16401)
DETROIT RADIATOR CORPORATION
26111 Northline Rd (48180-4412)
PHONE..................................800 525-0011
Robert Deblander, *Vice Pres*
Edward M Griffin, *CFO*
Robert J Duquet, *Executive*
EMP: 110 **EST:** 1997
SALES (est): 10.7MM **Privately Held**
WEB: www.detroitradiatorcorp.com
SIC: 3714 7539 Radiators & radiator shells & cores, motor vehicle; automotive repair shops; radiator repair shop, automotive; automotive air conditioning repair

(G-16402)
DOC POPCORN
23000 Eureka Rd (48180-6039)
PHONE..................................734 250-8133
EMP: 4 **EST:** 2017
SALES (est): 90.8K **Privately Held**
WEB: www.docpopcorn.com
SIC: 5145 2096 Syrups, fountain; potato sticks

(G-16403)
DOLPHIN MANUFACTURING INC
12650 Universal Dr (48180-6839)
PHONE..................................734 946-6322
Alvin R Fritz, *President*
Teresa Fritz, *Treasurer*
EMP: 25 **EST:** 1982
SQ FT: 33,000
SALES (est): 4.1MM **Privately Held**
WEB: www.dolphinmanufacturing.com
SIC: 3714 3728 3544 3429 Motor vehicle engines & parts; aircraft parts & equipment; special dies, tools, jigs & fixtures; manufactured hardware (general)

(G-16404)
DONGAH AMERICA INC
Also Called: DTR Logistics
24500 Northline Rd (48180-5292)
PHONE..................................734 946-7940
S H Kim, *President*
Jae Kim, *Engineer*
Rose Lloyd, *Manager*
Rose Lloyd-Rose, *Manager*
Duck Hwang, *Director*
◆ **EMP:** 40 **EST:** 2001
SALES (est): 13.1MM **Privately Held**
WEB: www.x-probattery.co.kr
SIC: 3465 Body parts, automobile: stamped metal
PA: Dtr Automotive Corporation
  12 Cheoyongsaneop 2-Gil, Onsan-Eup, Ulju-Gun
  Ulsan 44993

(G-16405)
DOWNRIVER CRUSHED CONCRETE
20538 Pennsylvania Rd (48180-5331)
PHONE..................................734 283-1833
Larry Roy, *Owner*
EMP: 8 **EST:** 1988
SALES (est): 449.4K **Privately Held**
SIC: 3273 1442 Ready-mixed concrete; construction sand & gravel

(G-16406)
DOWNRIVER DEBURRING INC
20248 Lorne St (48180-1970)
PHONE..................................313 388-2640
Bryan Neely, *President*
EMP: 4 **EST:** 1955
SQ FT: 4,600
SALES (est): 250K **Privately Held**
WEB: www.downriverdeburring.com
SIC: 3471 Finishing, metals or formed products

(G-16407)
DUKE DE JONG LLC
12680 Delta St (48180-6833)
PHONE..................................734 403-1708
Hillary Carter, *Plant Mgr*
Michael De Jong, *Opers Staff*
Janice Gruenberg, *Purch Agent*
Maurtis De Jong, *Sales Staff*
William Duprey, *Sales Staff*
▲ **EMP:** 5 **EST:** 2008
SQ FT: 20,000
SALES (est): 6MM
SALES (corp-wide): 183.7K **Privately Held**
WEB: www.dejongduke.us
SIC: 3556 Roasting machinery: coffee, peanut, etc.
HQ: J.M. De Jong Duke Automatenfabriek B.V.
  Marisstraat 2
  Sliedrecht 3364
  184 496-769

(G-16408)
DURA-PACK INC
Also Called: Dura Pack
7641 Holland Rd (48180-1450)
PHONE..................................313 299-9600
Tim Harrison, *President*
Linda Harrison, *Corp Secy*
Kevin Yang, *Engineer*
▲ **EMP:** 20 **EST:** 1976
SQ FT: 25,000
SALES (est): 6.3MM **Privately Held**
WEB: www.dura-pack.com
SIC: 3565 5046 Packaging machinery; scales, except laboratory

(G-16409)
EDGEWELL PERSONAL CARE COMPANY
12103 Delta St (48180-4082)
PHONE..................................866 462-8669
Alan Hoskins, *Branch Mgr*
EMP: 5
SALES (corp-wide): 1.9B **Publicly Held**
WEB: www.schick.com
SIC: 3421 Razor blades & razors
PA: Edgewell Personal Care Company
  6 Research Dr Ste 400
  Shelton CT 06484
  203 944-5500

(G-16410)
EFTEC NORTH AMERICA LLC (DH)
20219 Northline Rd (48180-4786)
PHONE..................................248 585-2200
Denny Pedri, *Vice Pres*
Mark Brown, *Prdtn Mgr*
Qavi Anjum, *Research*
Abul Molla, *Research*
Nicole Cumbo, *Human Resources*
▲ **EMP:** 90 **EST:** 1997
SQ FT: 50,000
SALES (est): 90.8MM
SALES (corp-wide): 355.8K **Privately Held**
WEB: www.ems-group.com
SIC: 2891 8731 3296 2899 Adhesives & sealants; commercial physical research; mineral wool; chemical preparations; paints & allied products
HQ: Ems-Chemie Holding Ag
  C/O Ems-Chemie Ag
  Domat/Ems GR 7013
  449 157-000

(G-16411)
ELDEN CYLINDER TESTING INC
9465 Inkster Rd (48180-3044)
PHONE..................................734 946-6900
Denis J Hurley III, *President*
Brian Hurley, *General Mgr*
EMP: 7 **EST:** 2001
SALES (est): 220.5K **Privately Held**
WEB: www.eldencylindertesting.com
SIC: 3443 Cylinders, pressure: metal plate

(G-16412)
ELDEN INDUSTRIES CORP
9465 Inkster Rd (48180-3044)
PHONE..................................734 946-6900
Dennis J Hurley III, *President*
Brian Hurley, *General Mgr*
Lorie Ouellette, *Office Mgr*
EMP: 13 **EST:** 1979
SQ FT: 13,000

Taylor - Wayne County (G-16413) — GEOGRAPHIC SECTION

SALES (est): 518.8K **Privately Held**
WEB: www.eldenindustries.com
SIC: **7692** 8734 3369 2295 Cracked casting repair; testing laboratories; non-ferrous foundries; coated fabrics, not rubberized

(G-16413)
EMESA FOODS COMPANY LLC
13430 Huron St (48180-6333)
PHONE.................248 982-3908
Rakan Chabaan, *CEO*
EMP: 5 EST: 2016
SALES (est): 66.1K **Privately Held**
WEB: www.emesafoods.com
SIC: **5499** 5141 2051 5149 Gourmet food stores; groceries, general line; bread, all types (white, wheat, rye, etc); fresh or frozen; specialty food items; bakery products; candy & other confectionery products

(G-16414)
EPIC FINE ARTS COMPANY INC (HQ)
21001 Van Born Rd (48180-1340)
PHONE.................313 274-7400
Eugene Gargaro, *President*
EMP: 5 EST: 1992
SALES (est): 71.9MM
SALES (corp-wide): 7.1B **Publicly Held**
WEB: www.masco.com
SIC: **3993** 3432 Advertising artwork; faucets & spigots, metal & plastic
PA: Masco Corporation
  17450 College Pkwy
  Livonia MI 48152
  313 274-7400

(G-16415)
F & M GAS
22422 Wick Rd (48180-3519)
PHONE.................313 292-2519
Fay Hashem, *Administration*
EMP: 5 EST: 2011
SALES (est): 592.8K **Privately Held**
SIC: **1389** Oil & gas field services

(G-16416)
F F INDUSTRIES
7620 Telegraph Rd (48180-2237)
PHONE.................313 291-7600
Eric Joseph Gonda, *Administration*
EMP: 9 EST: 2012
SALES (est): 762K **Privately Held**
SIC: **2542** Pallet racks: except wood

(G-16417)
FASTIME RACING ENGINES & PARTS
12254 Universal Dr (48180-4074)
PHONE.................734 947-1600
Christine Smith, *Owner*
Clayton Smith, *Principal*
EMP: 4 EST: 2010
SALES (est): 368.3K **Privately Held**
WEB: www.fastimeracing.com
SIC: **3714** Motor vehicle parts & accessories

(G-16418)
FAURECIA EMSSONS CTRL TECH USA
24850 Northline Rd (48180-4594)
PHONE.................734 947-1688
Richard Belcher, *Branch Mgr*
EMP: 443
SALES (corp-wide): 41.2MM **Privately Held**
SIC: **3714** Motor vehicle parts & accessories
HQ: Faurecia Emissions Control Technologies Usa, Llc
  2800 High Meadow Cir
  Auburn Hills MI 48326

(G-16419)
FORD MOTOR COMPANY
21001 Van Born Rd (48180-1340)
PHONE.................910 381-7998
Darra White, *Project Mgr*
Gerald Kolynuk, *Manager*
Cheryl Kitze, *Supervisor*
EMP: 14
SALES (corp-wide): 127.1B **Publicly Held**
WEB: www.ford.com
SIC: **5511** 3713 Automobiles, new & used; truck & bus bodies
PA: Ford Motor Company
  1 American Rd
  Dearborn MI 48126
  313 322-3000

(G-16420)
G & R MACHINE TOOL INC
20410 Superior Rd (48180-5362)
PHONE.................734 641-6560
Alejandro Kornijenko, *President*
Jorge Kornijenko, *Vice Pres*
Ralph Sulek, *Vice Pres*
Lucy Sulek, *Treasurer*
EMP: 9 EST: 1996
SALES (est): 2.7MM **Privately Held**
WEB: www.gnrmachinetool.com
SIC: **3599** Machine shop, jobbing & repair

(G-16421)
GENERAL DYNAMICS CORPORATION
Also Called: Wireless Svcs Div Navy A Force
25435 Brest (48180-6811)
PHONE.................615 427-5768
Steve Baier, *Manager*
EMP: 6
SALES (corp-wide): 37.9B **Publicly Held**
WEB: www.gd.com
SIC: **3812** Aircraft/aerospace flight instruments & guidance systems
PA: General Dynamics Corporation
  11011 Sunset Hills Rd
  Reston VA 20190
  703 876-3000

(G-16422)
GREAT FRESH FOODS CO LLC
Also Called: Clean Planet Foods
21740 Trolley Industrial (48180-1875)
PHONE.................734 904-0731
Jack Aronson, *Ch of Bd*
Shawn Spencer, *President*
Nicholas Frederick, *Controller*
Dan Aronson, *Sales Mgr*
David Koslosky, *Director*
EMP: 35 EST: 2012
SALES (est): 2.5MM **Privately Held**
SIC: **2013** Cooked meats from purchased meat

(G-16423)
GREENSEED LLC
26980 Trolley Indus Dr (48180-1424)
PHONE.................313 295-0100
EMP: 5 EST: 2008
SQ FT: 30,000
SALES (est): 390K **Privately Held**
SIC: **3463** Nonferrous Forgings

(G-16424)
HANCOCK ENTERPRISES INC
Also Called: Corky's Bar and Restaurant
20655 Northline Rd (48180-4797)
PHONE.................734 287-8840
John Hancock, *CEO*
Bob Joly, *President*
Pam Hancock, *CFO*
Cindy Joly, *Treasurer*
Robert Joly, *Manager*
▲ EMP: 65 EST: 1939
SQ FT: 80,000
SALES (est): 8.1MM **Privately Held**
WEB: www.hancockent.com
SIC: **3444** 3354 Metal roofing & roof drainage equipment; aluminum extruded products

(G-16425)
HB FULLER CO
20219 Northline Rd (48180-4786)
PHONE.................248 585-2200
Ted Zbizek, *Facilities Mgr*
EMP: 7 EST: 2017
SALES (est): 136.3K **Privately Held**
WEB: www.hbfuller.com
SIC: **3479** Metal coating & allied service

(G-16426)
HEAVY DUTY RADIATOR LLC
Also Called: Detroit Radiator
26111 Northline Rd (48180-4412)
PHONE.................800 525-0011
David Bitel, *General Mgr*
Mary Richards, *CFO*
Amanda Bingham, *Human Res Mgr*
Bryan Idzior, *Executive*
Bill Baker,
EMP: 34 EST: 2016
SALES (est): 3.3MM **Privately Held**
WEB: www.detroitradiatorcorp.com
SIC: **3714** Motor vehicle parts & accessories

(G-16427)
IMPRESSIONS PROMOTIONAL GROUP
20449 Ecorse Rd (48180-1913)
PHONE.................313 299-3140
Louise Leveque, *Executive*
EMP: 4 EST: 2018
SALES (est): 42.5K **Privately Held**
SIC: **2389** Apparel & accessories

(G-16428)
ISCUPLT LLC ◆
9440 Oak St (48180-3495)
PHONE.................313 728-7982
Jasmine Jones,
EMP: 5 EST: 2021
SALES (est): 88.3K **Privately Held**
SIC: **3634** Massage machines, electric, except for beauty/barber shops

(G-16429)
IXL GRAPHICS
6000 Pardee Rd (48180-1316)
PHONE.................313 350-2800
August Grebinski, *Owner*
EMP: 7 EST: 2016
SALES (est): 160.8K **Privately Held**
SIC: **2759** Commercial printing

(G-16430)
J & B PRECISION INC
5886 Pelham Rd (48180-1391)
PHONE.................313 565-3431
Beverly Bartoszek, *President*
Stanley Bartoszek, *Chairman*
EMP: 6 EST: 1975
SQ FT: 5,000
SALES (est): 506.6K **Privately Held**
SIC: **3599** Machine shop, jobbing & repair

(G-16431)
JAMISON INDUSTRIES INC
12669 Delta St (48180-6835)
PHONE.................734 946-3088
Eugene Jamison Jr, *President*
Matt J Jamison, *General Mgr*
Sharon Jamison, *Corp Secy*
Gene Jamison, *Prdtn Mgr*
EMP: 32 EST: 1981
SQ FT: 10,000
SALES (est): 2.4MM **Privately Held**
WEB: www.jamisonind.com
SIC: **3599** Machine shop, jobbing & repair

(G-16432)
JOHNSON MATTHEY NORTH AMER INC
12600 Universal Dr (48180-6839)
PHONE.................734 946-9856
Robert Bullen-Smith, *General Mgr*
Danielle Blevins, *Principal*
Jeffery Hoshaw, *Principal*
Carlisle S Martin, *Principal*
Tim Stevenson, *Chairman*
EMP: 1 EST: 1985
SALES (est): 18.1MM
SALES (corp-wide): 22B **Privately Held**
WEB: www.matthey.com
SIC: **3341** Gold smelting & refining (secondary)
HQ: Johnson Matthey Holdings, Inc.
  435 Devon Park Dr Ste 600
  Wayne PA 19087
  610 971-3000

(G-16433)
KAMPS INC
20310 Pennsylvania Rd (48180-6370)
PHONE.................734 281-3300
Kim Collura, *Manager*
EMP: 23
SALES (corp-wide): 1.7B **Privately Held**
WEB: www.kampspallets.com
SIC: **2448** Pallets, wood
HQ: Kamps, Inc.
  2900 Peach Ridge Ave Nw
  Grand Rapids MI 49534
  616 453-9676

(G-16434)
KRUSH INDUSTRIES INC
12729 Universal Dr (48180-6843)
PHONE.................248 238-2296
Kyle T Rushing, *President*
EMP: 4 EST: 2010
SQ FT: 3,600
SALES (est): 250K **Privately Held**
SIC: **3569** Robots, assembly line: industrial & commercial

(G-16435)
LEONARD & RANDY INC
20555 Northline Rd (48180-4779)
PHONE.................734 287-9500
Randy Sides, *President*
Leonard Sides, *Vice Pres*
Crystal Bryant, *Admin Sec*
EMP: 8 EST: 2001
SALES (est): 769.9K **Privately Held**
SIC: **3715** 4212 Semitrailers for truck tractors; steel hauling, local

(G-16436)
LITHO PHOTO ENTERPRISES LLC
6000 Pardee Rd (48180-1316)
PHONE.................313 717-6615
EMP: 4 EST: 2019
SALES (est): 145.4K **Privately Held**
WEB: www.lithophoto.com
SIC: **2752** Commercial printing, offset

(G-16437)
MA MA LA ROSA FOODS INC
12100 Universal Dr (48180-4000)
PHONE.................734 946-7878
James D Larosa, *President*
Michael Franchi, *Vice Pres*
Kevin Zevchak, *Sales Mgr*
Sandy Cherry, *Executive*
EMP: 24 EST: 1982
SQ FT: 15,000
SALES (est): 1.1MM **Privately Held**
WEB: www.mamalarosafoods.com
SIC: **2045** Pizza doughs, prepared: from purchased flour

(G-16438)
MARFOOD USA
21655 Trolley Indus Dr (48180-1811)
PHONE.................313 292-4100
EMP: 9 EST: 2019
SALES (est): 620.6K **Privately Held**
WEB: www.marfoodusa.com
SIC: **2099** Food preparations

(G-16439)
MASCO DE PUERTO RICO INC
21001 Van Born Rd (48180-1340)
PHONE.................313 274-7400
Richard Manoogian, *CEO*
EMP: 35 EST: 1996
SALES (est): 4.3MM
SALES (corp-wide): 7.1B **Publicly Held**
WEB: www.masco.com
SIC: **3432** Plumbing fixture fittings & trim
PA: Masco Corporation
  17450 College Pkwy
  Livonia MI 48152
  313 274-7400

(G-16440)
MEL PRINTING CO INC
Also Called: Mel Media Group
6000 Pardee Rd (48180-1316)
PHONE.................313 928-5440
Michael Filkovich, *President*
August Grebinski, *Vice Pres*
Joyce Hunter, *Vice Pres*
Michelle Martinez, *Prdtn Mgr*
Alison Cave, *Manager*
EMP: 26 EST: 1961
SQ FT: 10,000

▲ = Import ▼ = Export
◆ = Import/Export

SALES (est): 9.2MM **Privately Held**
WEB: www.mel.company
SIC: 2752 2796 2789 2732 Commercial printing, offset; platemaking services; bookbinding & related work; book printing

(G-16441)
MESSENGER PRINTING SERVICE INC
20136 Ecorse Rd (48180-1957)
PHONE..............................313 381-0300
Robert Herriman, *President*
EMP: 15 EST: 1987
SQ FT: 4,200
SALES (est): 1.6MM **Privately Held**
WEB: www.messengerprinting.com
SIC: 2752 Commercial printing, offset

(G-16442)
METRIC PRECISION TOOL LLC
12222 Universal Dr (48180-4074)
PHONE..............................734 946-8114
Pat D'Ambrosio, *Mng Member*
EMP: 16 EST: 1973
SQ FT: 12,000
SALES (est): 330.3K **Privately Held**
SIC: 3544 Special dies & tools

(G-16443)
METRIE INC
27025 Trolley Indus Dr (48180-1423)
PHONE..............................313 299-1860
Larry Boldt, *Opers Staff*
Sherry Andrews, *Info Tech Mgr*
EMP: 28
SALES (corp-wide): 183.4MM **Privately Held**
WEB: www.metrie.com
SIC: 2431 Millwork
HQ: Metrie Inc.
 2200 140th Ave E Ste 600
 Sumner WA 98390
 253 470-5050

(G-16444)
MI CUSTOM SIGNS LLC
20109 Northline Rd (48180-4726)
PHONE..............................734 946-7446
Jon Mundy, *Sales Staff*
Ken Moreno, *Marketing Staff*
Rene R Pare, *Mng Member*
EMP: 10 EST: 2011
SALES (est): 1MM **Privately Held**
WEB: www.micustomsigns.com
SIC: 3993 Signs, not made in custom sign painting shops

(G-16445)
MICHIGAN INDUSTRIAL TRIM INC (PA)
12400 Universal Dr (48180-6837)
P.O. Box 726 (48180-0726)
PHONE..............................734 947-0344
Gino Martino, *CEO*
Renee Perez, *Controller*
EMP: 16 EST: 2000
SQ FT: 12,000
SALES (est): 1MM **Privately Held**
WEB: www.attproto.com
SIC: 2399 Automotive covers, except seat & tire covers

(G-16446)
MICRO FIXTURES INC
Also Called: Elco Machine Enterprises
20448 Lorne St (48180-1968)
PHONE..............................313 382-9781
Martin D Malloy, *President*
EMP: 5 EST: 1993
SQ FT: 4,000
SALES (est): 432.3K **Privately Held**
WEB: www.microfixtures.com
SIC: 3599 Machine shop, jobbing & repair

(G-16447)
MIDWEST FABRICATING INC
26465 Northline Rd (48180-4479)
PHONE..............................734 921-3914
Joyce Smith, *CEO*
Steve Smith, *President*
EMP: 5 EST: 2014
SQ FT: 8,000
SALES (est): 500K **Privately Held**
SIC: 3441 7539 7692 Fabricated structural metal; machine shop, automotive; automotive welding

(G-16448)
MODERN CAM AND TOOL CO
27272 Wick Rd (48180-3097)
PHONE..............................734 946-9800
Scott A Bitters, *President*
EMP: 8 EST: 1928
SQ FT: 6,750
SALES (est): 702.7K **Privately Held**
WEB: www.moderncam.com
SIC: 3545 Machine tool accessories

(G-16449)
MONOGRAMS & MORE INC
Also Called: Impressions Specialty Advg
20449 Ecorse Rd (48180-1913)
PHONE..............................313 299-3140
Louise A Leveque, *President*
Marlene Zerkel, *Vice Pres*
EMP: 31 EST: 1982
SALES (est): 2.3MM **Privately Held**
WEB: www.impressionsco.com
SIC: 2395 2759 5199 Embroidery products, except schiffli machine; screen printing; advertising specialties

(G-16450)
MOTOR CITY METAL FAB INC
24340 Northline Rd (48180-4586)
PHONE..............................734 345-1001
Sheri Zimmerman, *Principal*
▼ EMP: 20 EST: 2017
SALES (est): 1.8MM **Privately Held**
WEB: www.motorcitymetalfab.com
SIC: 3479 Coating of metals & formed products

(G-16451)
MOTOWN HARLEY-DAVIDSON INC
Also Called: Biker Bobs Hrly-Dvidson Motown
14100 Telegraph Rd (48180-8208)
PHONE..............................734 947-4647
Robert A Demattia, *President*
A Jason Breckenridge, *Vice Pres*
Steven Chapin, *Vice Pres*
Paul Rzepka, *CFO*
Vanessa Turner, *Controller*
EMP: 68 EST: 1997
SQ FT: 55,000
SALES (est): 14.7MM **Privately Held**
WEB: www.motownhog.com
SIC: 5571 7694 Motorcycles; motor repair services

(G-16452)
NEWELL BRANDS INC
20033 Eureka Rd (48180-5372)
PHONE..............................734 284-2528
Tim Hollingsworth, *Branch Mgr*
EMP: 4
SALES (corp-wide): 9.3B **Publicly Held**
WEB: www.newellbrands.com
SIC: 3911 Jewelry, precious metal
PA: Newell Brands Inc.
 6655 Pachtree Dunwoody Rd
 Atlanta GA 30328
 770 418-7000

(G-16453)
OAKWOOD ENERGY MANAGEMENT INC (HQ)
Also Called: Oakwood Expansion
9755 Inkster Rd (48180-3048)
PHONE..............................734 947-7700
Richard Audi, *President*
Anthony Dipaolo, *Accounts Mgr*
Jonathan Black, *Program Mgr*
Frank Bowlin, *Info Tech Mgr*
▲ EMP: 19 EST: 1990
SQ FT: 41,000
SALES (est): 23.3MM
SALES (corp-wide): 89.6MM **Privately Held**
WEB: www.theoakwoodgroup.com
SIC: 3479 3544 3441 3089 Coating of metals & formed products; special dies & tools; fabricated structural metal; injection molded finished plastic products
PA: Oakwood Metal Fabricating Co.
 1100 Oakwood Blvd
 Dearborn MI 48124
 313 561-7740

(G-16454)
OAKWOOD METAL FABRICATING CO
Oakwood Plastic Division
9755 Inkster Rd (48180-3048)
PHONE..............................734 947-7740
Tony Shackelford, *QC Mgr*
Joe Maisano, *Accounts Mgr*
Stan Keennarv, *Manager*
Sharon Harper, *Administration*
EMP: 30
SALES (corp-wide): 89.6MM **Privately Held**
WEB: www.theoakwoodgroup.com
SIC: 3465 Automotive stampings
PA: Oakwood Metal Fabricating Co.
 1100 Oakwood Blvd
 Dearborn MI 48124
 313 561-7740

(G-16455)
OLDCASTLE BUILDINGENVELOPE INC
26471 Nrthline Cmmerce Dr (48180-7951)
PHONE..............................734 947-9670
EMP: 19
SALES (corp-wide): 23.7B **Privately Held**
SIC: 3231 5231 Mfg Products-Purchased Glass Ret Paint/Glass/Wallpaper
HQ: Oldcastle Buildingenvelope, Inc.
 5005 Lbj Fwy Ste 1050
 Dallas TX 75244
 214 273-3400

(G-16456)
PERFECT DISH LLC
21867 Kings Pte Blvd (48180)
P.O. Box 84 (48180-0084)
PHONE..............................734 272-9871
Antionette Arnold,
EMP: 5 EST: 2018
SQ FT: 1,800
SALES (est): 240K **Privately Held**
SIC: 2599 Food wagons, restaurant

(G-16457)
PGP CORP (PA)
Also Called: Voss Steel
7925 Beech Daly Rd (48180-2033)
PHONE..............................313 291-7500
Paul M Voss, *President*
Tim Bilkey, *Managing Dir*
Cynthia Squiers, *Vice Pres*
▲ EMP: 90
SQ FT: 200,000
SALES (est): 82.4MM **Privately Held**
WEB: www.vossindustries.com
SIC: 5051 3559 7389 Steel; metal pickling equipment; metal slitting & shearing

(G-16458)
PRECISION FRAMING SYSTEMS INC
Also Called: Pfs
21001 Van Born Rd (48180-1340)
PHONE..............................704 588-6680
EMP: 50
SALES (est): 4.9MM
SALES (corp-wide): 7.6B **Publicly Held**
SIC: 2439 2435 Mfg Wood House Frames Wood Trusses
PA: Masco Corporation
 17450 College Pkwy
 Livonia MI 48152
 313 274-7400

(G-16459)
PREFERRED PACKG SOLUTIONS INC
27000 Wick Rd (48180-3015)
P.O. Box 2018 (48180-8918)
PHONE..............................734 844-9092
Craig Vanriper, *President*
Dan Hoppe, *Vice Pres*
EMP: 3 EST: 2010
SALES (est): 1.3MM **Privately Held**
WEB: www.preferredpkg.com
SIC: 5199 2653 Packaging materials; boxes, corrugated: made from purchased materials

(G-16460)
PRIME INDUSTRIES INC
12350 Universal Dr (48180-4070)
P.O. Box 1890 (48180-5990)
PHONE..............................734 946-8588
EMP: 20
SQ FT: 8,000
SALES (est): 1.8MM **Privately Held**
SIC: 3541 3545 3544 Mfg Machine Tools-Cutting Mfg Machine Tool Accessories Mfg Dies/Tools/Jigs/Fixtures

(G-16461)
PRINTING SYSTEMS INC
12005 Beech Daly Rd (48180-3936)
PHONE..............................734 946-5111
Edwin G Stevens, *President*
Mark Stevens, *Vice Pres*
Ronda Wilson, *Director*
EMP: 6 EST: 1970
SALES (est): 1.5MM **Privately Held**
WEB: www.printingsystems.us
SIC: 2752 Commercial printing, offset

(G-16462)
PRINTWELL ACQUISITION CO INC
Also Called: Printwell Printing
26975 Northline Rd (48180-4408)
PHONE..............................734 941-6300
Paul Borg, *Ch of Bd*
Jerry Leasure, *Project Mgr*
Nicholas McNamara, *Prdtn Mgr*
Kevin R Donley, *VP Sls/Mktg*
Shawn Borg, *CFO*
▲ EMP: 97 EST: 1983
SQ FT: 18,000
SALES (est): 19.4MM **Privately Held**
WEB: www.printwell.com
SIC: 2789 7331 2759 Bookbinding & related work; direct mail advertising services; commercial printing

(G-16463)
PROTO MANUFACTURING INC
12350 Universal Dr (48180-4070)
PHONE..............................734 946-0974
Michael Brauss, *President*
Daniel Gorzen, *Vice Pres*
Scott Teall, *Production*
Fred Downey, *Sales Staff*
Thomas Baker, *Supervisor*
EMP: 25 EST: 2005
SQ FT: 20,000
SALES (est): 4.6MM **Privately Held**
WEB: www.protoxrd.com
SIC: 3826 Analytical instruments

(G-16464)
QUANTA CONTAINERS LLC (PA)
15801 Huron St (48180-5281)
PHONE..............................734 282-3044
Vincent Concessi, *Mng Member*
EMP: 6 EST: 2010
SALES (est): 5MM **Privately Held**
WEB: www.quantacontainers.com
SIC: 2655 Fiber cans, drums & containers

(G-16465)
RAINBOW PIZZA INC
Also Called: New Delray Baking Co
14702 Allen Rd (48180-5383)
PHONE..............................734 246-4250
Fax: 734 753-5867
EMP: 8
SALES (est): 666K **Privately Held**
SIC: 2051 5461 Bakery & Ret Bakery Goods

(G-16466)
REVAK PRECISION GRINDING INC
20188 Lorne St (48180-1941)
PHONE..............................313 388-2626
Steve Hernandez, *President*
EMP: 4
SQ FT: 1,500
SALES (est): 281.4K **Privately Held**
WEB: www.revakprecisiongrinding.com
SIC: 3599 Machine shop, jobbing & repair

(G-16467)
RHINO STRAPPING PRODUCTS INC
24341 Brest (48180-6848)
PHONE.................................734 442-4040
Gary Galliers, *President*
EMP: 12 **EST:** 1977
SQ FT: 30,000
SALES (est): 3MM **Privately Held**
WEB: www.rhinostrappingproducts.com
SIC: 3053 3493 3965 Gaskets & sealing devices; flat springs, sheet or strip stock; buckles & buckle parts

(G-16468)
ROUTE 66 PENNZOIL
20121 Ecorse Rd (48180-1958)
PHONE.................................313 382-8888
EMP: 4 **EST:** 2019
SALES (est): 267.5K **Privately Held**
WEB: www.route66quicklube.com
SIC: 1311 Crude petroleum & natural gas

(G-16469)
RUDYS SOCK DRIVE
7615 Weddel St (48180-2660)
P.O. Box 1401, Belleville (48112-1401)
PHONE.................................313 409-1778
S Lewis-Washington, *Principal*
EMP: 4 **EST:** 2018
SALES (est): 89.3K **Privately Held**
SIC: 2252 Socks

(G-16470)
SB TOOLS LLC
9827 Sil St (48180-3088)
PHONE.................................313 729-2759
Steven Burmeister, *Principal*
EMP: 6 **EST:** 2015
SALES (est): 324.4K **Privately Held**
SIC: 3599 Industrial machinery

(G-16471)
SERVOTECH INDUSTRIES INC (PA)
25580 Brest (48180-4065)
PHONE.................................734 697-5555
Hamid Servati, *President*
EMP: 9 **EST:** 1994
SQ FT: 10,000
SALES (est): 1.1MM **Privately Held**
WEB: www.servotechco.com
SIC: 3599 3714 3444 3441 Machine shop, jobbing & repair; motor vehicle parts & accessories; sheet metalwork; fabricated structural metal

(G-16472)
SFS LLC
Also Called: Specialty Fabrication Services
12621 Universal Dr (48180-6842)
PHONE.................................734 947-4377
Kathy Rose, *General Mgr*
EMP: 5 **EST:** 2013
SQ FT: 8,000
SALES (est): 432.4K **Privately Held**
WEB: www.sfsfabrication.com
SIC: 3599 Machine shop, jobbing & repair

(G-16473)
SILK REFLECTIONS
22018 Haig St (48180-3652)
PHONE.................................313 292-1150
Susan Ann Gray, *Partner*
Fred Gray, *Partner*
EMP: 4 **EST:** 1982
SALES (est): 185.9K **Privately Held**
SIC: 2399 Hand woven & crocheted products

(G-16474)
SMI AMERICAN INC
6835 Monroe Blvd (48180-1815)
PHONE.................................313 438-0096
Vince Schiller, *Principal*
EMP: 5 **EST:** 2013
SALES (est): 217.1K **Privately Held**
WEB: www.tangerinecleaningny.com
SIC: 3441 Fabricated structural metal

(G-16475)
SMS GROUP INC
Also Called: Acutus Gladwin Industries
15200 Huron St (48180-6032)
PHONE.................................734 246-8230
Greg Merta, *General Mgr*
Daniel De Shetler, *Production*
Mike Helms, *Accounts Mgr*
EMP: 89
SALES (corp-wide): 144.1K **Privately Held**
WEB: www.sms-group.us
SIC: 3569 Assembly machines, non-metalworking
HQ: Sms Group Inc.
    100 Sandusky St
    Pittsburgh PA 15212
    412 231-1200

(G-16476)
SMW MFG INC
25575 Brest (48180-6846)
PHONE.................................517 596-3300
Bob Danford, *Manager*
EMP: 36
SALES (corp-wide): 2.4B **Privately Held**
WEB: www.smw-mfg.com
SIC: 3599 Machine shop, jobbing & repair
HQ: Smw Mfg, Inc.
    8707 Samuel Barton Dr
    Van Buren Twp MI 48111
    517 596-3300

(G-16477)
SPECIALTY ENG COMPONENTS LLC (PA)
Also Called: Johnson Lifters
25940 Northline Rd (48180-4413)
PHONE.................................734 955-6500
Mike Akowitz, *Plant Mgr*
Mark E Nelms, *Mng Member*
Charles Pipis,
▲ **EMP:** 78 **EST:** 1946
SQ FT: 60,000
SALES (est): 7.5MM **Privately Held**
WEB: www.wathomas.com
SIC: 3714 Motor vehicle engines & parts

(G-16478)
SPOTLIGHT COUTURE LLC
23663 Irving St (48180-2304)
PHONE.................................313 768-5305
Brian McGriff, *Agent*
EMP: 4 **EST:** 2016
SALES (est): 88.3K **Privately Held**
SIC: 3648 Spotlights

(G-16479)
SRG GLOBAL INC
12620 Delta St (48180-6833)
PHONE.................................586 757-7800
Kyle Wolfe, *Mfg Staff*
Shamieka Williams, *Production*
Carla Dew, *Engineer*
Shamus Mulvihill, *Engineer*
Joe Nevel, *Human Res Mgr*
EMP: 6
SALES (corp-wide): 36.9B **Privately Held**
WEB: www.srgglobal.com
SIC: 2396 Automotive & apparel trimmings
HQ: Srg Global, Llc
    800 Stephenson Hwy
    Troy MI 48083

(G-16480)
SUN COAST COVERINGS LLC
26395 Northline Commrc Dr (48180-7947)
PHONE.................................734 947-1230
EMP: 11 **EST:** 2015
SALES (est): 176.7K **Privately Held**
WEB: www.suncoastcoverings.com
SIC: 3999 Manufacturing industries

(G-16481)
SUPERIOR FLUID SYSTEMS
7804 Beech Daly Rd (48180-1533)
PHONE.................................734 246-4550
Duane Brow, *Mng Member*
EMP: 11 **EST:** 2006
SALES (est): 645.4K **Privately Held**
SIC: 3498 Piping systems for pulp paper & chemical industries

(G-16482)
SUPERIOR SPINDLE SERVICES LLC
25377 Brest (48180-4054)
PHONE.................................734 946-4646
Kenneth Kirchner, *CEO*
Ray Baldwin, *President*
Pamela Egnatowski, *Purch Mgr*
Ronald Jaeger, *CFO*
EMP: 14 **EST:** 2005
SALES (est): 3MM **Privately Held**
WEB: www.superiorspindle.com
SIC: 2241 Spindle banding

(G-16483)
TAPOOS LLC
21813 Hunter Cir S (48180-6362)
PHONE.................................619 319-4872
Fahad Aslam,
EMP: 5
SALES (est): 130.5K **Privately Held**
SIC: 2741

(G-16484)
TAYLOR HILLS COMPOST FACILITY
16300 Racho Blvd (48180-5209)
PHONE.................................734 991-3902
Jason Mach, *Owner*
EMP: 5 **EST:** 2014
SALES (est): 81.5K **Privately Held**
WEB: www.cityoftaylor.com
SIC: 2875 Compost

(G-16485)
TOP FABRICATORS
6390 Pelham Rd (48180-1356)
PHONE.................................313 563-7126
Dave Brown, *Principal*
EMP: 9 **EST:** 2013
SALES (est): 340.7K **Privately Held**
WEB: www.topfabricatorsllc.net
SIC: 2434 Wood kitchen cabinets

(G-16486)
VINEWOOD METALCRAFT INC
9501 Inkster Rd (48180-3044)
P.O. Box 186 (48180-0186)
PHONE.................................734 946-8733
Claud M Mick Jr, *President*
Fred Mick, *President*
Jim Gietl, *Partner*
Mark Caudell, *Engineer*
Mike Simonds, *Sales Staff*
EMP: 35 **EST:** 1944
SQ FT: 23,000
SALES (est): 4.3MM **Privately Held**
WEB: www.vinewoodmetalcraft.com
SIC: 3469 Stamping metal for the trade

(G-16487)
W A THOMAS COMPANY
25940 Northline Rd (48180-4413)
PHONE.................................734 955-6500
Micheal Akowitz, *Principal*
Mark Nelms, *Principal*
EMP: 9 **EST:** 2007
SALES (est): 133.5K **Privately Held**
WEB: www.wathomas.com
SIC: 2273 3471 3312 Carpets & rugs; plating of metals or formed products; tool & die steel & alloys

(G-16488)
W B MASON CO INC
25299 Brest (48180-6850)
PHONE.................................734 947-6370
EMP: 30
SALES (corp-wide): 1B **Privately Held**
WEB: www.wbmason.com
SIC: 5943 5712 2752 Office forms & supplies; office furniture; commercial printing, lithographic
PA: W. B. Mason Co., Inc.
    59 Ctr St
    Brockton MA 02301
    508 586-3434

(G-16489)
WALLSIDE INC
Also Called: Wallside Window Factory
27000 Trolley Indus Dr (48180-1422)
PHONE.................................313 292-4400
Stanford Blanck, *President*
Donell Bradford, *Production*
Stuart Blanck, *Treasurer*
Katy Cook, *Human Res Mgr*
Chuck Rockov, *Manager*
EMP: 10 **EST:** 1944
SQ FT: 75,000
SALES (est): 4.9MM **Privately Held**
WEB: www.wallsidewindows.com
SIC: 1751 3442 Window & door (prefabricated) installation; metal doors, sash & trim

(G-16490)
WORTHINGTON STEEL OF MICHIGAN (HQ)
11700 Worthington Dr (48180-4390)
PHONE.................................734 374-3260
John Christie, *President*
David Nickelson, *Production*
Dale T Brinkman, *Admin Sec*
Dave Freeman, *Maintence Staff*
▲ **EMP:** 168 **EST:** 1986
SQ FT: 361,000
SALES (est): 328.8MM
SALES (corp-wide): 3.1B **Publicly Held**
WEB: www.worthingtonindustries.com
SIC: 3316 3312 Cold finishing of steel shapes; blast furnaces & steel mills
PA: Worthington Industries, Inc.
    200 W Wlson Bridge Rd
    Worthington OH 43085
    614 438-3210

Tecumseh
Lenawee County

(G-16491)
CLASSIC CABINETS INTERIORS LLC (PA)
118 W Chicago Blvd (49286-1553)
PHONE.................................517 423-2600
Charles Barnes, *Ch of Bd*
Joyce Holden, *Office Mgr*
Amie Pelham, *Mng Member*
Josh Kohler, *Products*
EMP: 4 **EST:** 2008
SALES (est): 2.5MM **Privately Held**
WEB: www.classiccabinetsandinteriors.com
SIC: 2434 Wood kitchen cabinets

(G-16492)
CME PLASTICS
903 Industrial Dr (49286-9701)
PHONE.................................517 456-7722
Helmut Linsgeseder, *Owner*
EMP: 10 **EST:** 1981
SALES (est): 97.8K **Privately Held**
WEB: www.cmeplastics.com
SIC: 3089 Plastics products

(G-16493)
COMSTAR AUTOMOTIVE USA LLC
900 Industrial Dr (49286-9701)
PHONE.................................517 266-2445
Praveen Chakrapani, *Vice Pres*
▲ **EMP:** 10 **EST:** 2012
SQ FT: 12,500
SALES (est): 23.2MM **Privately Held**
SIC: 3711 Automobile assembly, including specialty automobiles

(G-16494)
CONWAY PUBLICATIONS
9390 Newburg Ct (49286-9755)
PHONE.................................517 424-1614
EMP: 4 **EST:** 2018
SALES (est): 37.5K **Privately Held**
WEB: www.conway-publications.com
SIC: 2741 Miscellaneous publishing

(G-16495)
DCD IDID ENTERPRISE LLC
Also Called: Ididit, LLC
610 S Maumee St (49286-2051)
PHONE.................................517 424-0577
E Craig Moore, *Mng Member*
EMP: 46 **EST:** 2015
SALES (est): 3.3MM **Privately Held**
SIC: 3714 Motor vehicle parts & accessories

(G-16496)
DIGGYPOD INC
301 Industrial Dr (49286-9788)
PHONE.................................734 429-3307
Tim Simpson, *President*
EMP: 7 **EST:** 1988
SQ FT: 1,250

GEOGRAPHIC SECTION

Tecumseh - Lenawee County (G-16521)

SALES (est): 582K **Privately Held**
WEB: www.diggypod.com
SIC: **2741** Miscellaneous publishing

(G-16497)
DIVERSE MANUFACTURING SOLTION
805 S Maumee St (49286-2053)
P.O. Box 400 (49286-0400)
PHONE.................................517 423-6691
EMP: 5 EST: 2017
SALES (est): 276.2K **Privately Held**
SIC: **3999** Manufacturing industries

(G-16498)
DMS MNUFACTURING SOLUTIONS INC
800 S Maumee St (49286-2061)
P.O. Box 400 (49286-0400)
PHONE.................................517 423-6691
James Roberts, *President*
EMP: 8 EST: 2013
SALES (est): 996.3K **Privately Held**
SIC: **3053** Packing: steam engines, pipe joints, air compressors, etc.

(G-16499)
DPRINTER INC
Also Called: D' Printer Inc-Shop
6197 N Adrian Hwy (49286-9797)
PHONE.................................517 423-6554
David Hawkins, *President*
Jaina R Brown, *Vice Pres*
Jaina Brown, *Vice Pres*
Cherie Hawkins, *Office Mgr*
EMP: 4 EST: 1993
SQ FT: 2,800
SALES (est): 350K **Privately Held**
WEB: www.dprinter.net
SIC: **2752** 2791 2789 Commercial printing, offset; typesetting; bookbinding & related work

(G-16500)
ERVIN INDUSTRIES INC
Also Called: Ervin Development Center
200 Industrial Dr (49286-9787)
PHONE.................................517 423-5477
Tim Mostowy, *Engineer*
Ron Bates, *Manager*
EMP: 30
SALES (corp-wide): 200MM **Privately Held**
WEB: www.ervinindustries.com
SIC: **8731** 3291 Commercial physical research; abrasive products
PA: Ervin Industries, Inc.
   3893 Research Park Dr
   Ann Arbor MI 48108
   734 769-4600

(G-16501)
EXTRUNET AMERICA INC
903 Industrial Dr (49286-9701)
PHONE.................................517 301-4504
Helmut Linsgeseder, *President*
Thomas Stadlhuber, *Managing Dir*
Thomas Fehringer, *Production*
Kami Linsgeseder, *Human Resources*
Ferdinand Bagin, *Sales Staff*
▲ EMP: 9 EST: 2014
SQ FT: 12,000
SALES (est): 1.8MM **Privately Held**
WEB: www.extrunet.com
SIC: **3355** Extrusion ingot, aluminum: made in rolling mills

(G-16502)
GLOV ENTERPRISES LLC
412 S Maumee St (49286-2055)
PHONE.................................517 423-9700
Mike Cunningham, *Controller*
Louis Farkas, *Mng Member*
Cheryl Fanning, *Supervisor*
Moritz Vonmoeller,
EMP: 74 EST: 2010
SALES (est): 12MM **Privately Held**
WEB: www.glovellc.com
SIC: **3089** 8711 7389 Injection molding of plastics; engineering services; design services;

(G-16503)
GLYCON CORP
Also Called: Great Lakes Feedscrews
912 Industrial Dr (49286-9701)
PHONE.................................517 423-8356
Jeffrey A Kuhman, *President*
Jonathon L Kuhman, *President*
John M Phelan, *Vice Pres*
Jeff Howard, *Plant Mgr*
John Phelan, *Sales Mgr*
EMP: 30 EST: 1976
SQ FT: 22,000
SALES (est): 5.9MM **Privately Held**
WEB: www.glycon.com
SIC: **3559** 3544 3452 3443 Plastics working machinery; special dies, tools, jigs & fixtures; bolts, nuts, rivets & washers; fabricated plate work (boiler shop)

(G-16504)
HERALD PUBLISHING COMPANY
Also Called: Tecumseh Herald
110 E Logan St (49286-1559)
P.O. Box 218 (49286-0218)
PHONE.................................517 423-2174
James C Lincoln, *President*
Dorothy Lincoln, *Vice Pres*
Sharon Baxter, *Bookkeeper*
Koda Woodward, *Graphic Designe*
EMP: 29 EST: 1957
SQ FT: 9,000
SALES (est): 2.9MM **Privately Held**
WEB: www.tecumsehherald.com
SIC: **2752** 2711 Commercial printing, lithographic; newspapers

(G-16505)
HOT ROD HOLDINGS INC
Also Called: Ididit
610 S Maumee St (49286-2051)
PHONE.................................517 424-0577
Ken Callison, *CEO*
Jane Callison, *President*
Ted W Keating, *General Mgr*
Ted Keating, *General Mgr*
Scott Callison, *Vice Pres*
EMP: 38 EST: 1986
SQ FT: 32,000
SALES (est): 7.7MM **Privately Held**
WEB: www.ididitinc.com
SIC: **3714** 5531 5013 Motor vehicle steering systems & parts; automotive parts; automotive supplies & parts

(G-16506)
KIRCHHOFF AUTO TECUMSEH INC (DH)
1200 E Chicago Blvd (49286-9674)
PHONE.................................517 423-2400
Allan Power, *President*
Joshua Cox, *Production*
James Zywica, *Production*
Ana Lugo, *QC Mgr*
Richard Fleschner, *Engineer*
▲ EMP: 329 EST: 1987
SQ FT: 300,000
SALES (est): 73.3MM
SALES (corp-wide): 1.7B **Privately Held**
WEB: www.tecumsehherald.com
SIC: **3465** Body parts, automobile: stamped metal
HQ: Kirchhoff Automotive Gmbh
   Stefanstr. 2
   Iserlohn NW 58638
   237 182-000

(G-16507)
LIBRA PRECISION MACHINING INC
Also Called: Libra Manufacturing
5353 N Rogers Hwy (49286-9535)
PHONE.................................517 423-1365
Fax: 517 423-2531
EMP: 12
SQ FT: 11,500
SALES: 1MM **Privately Held**
SIC: **3599** Mfg Industrial Machinery

(G-16508)
MILACRON LLC
5550 S Occidental Rd (49286-8749)
PHONE.................................517 424-8981
EMP: 5 **Publicly Held**
WEB: www.milacron.com
SIC: **3549** Metalworking machinery
HQ: Milacron Llc
   4165 Half Acre Rd
   Batavia OH 45103

(G-16509)
NATIONAL AIRCRAFT SERVICE INC
9133 Tecumseh Clinton Hwy (49286-1128)
PHONE.................................517 423-7589
Wesley M Plattner, *President*
Rod Guth, *Vice Pres*
EMP: 24 EST: 1977
SQ FT: 8,000
SALES (est): 2.1MM **Privately Held**
SIC: **3728** 3585 Aircraft parts & equipment; refrigeration & heating equipment

(G-16510)
PEGASUS MOLD & DIE INC
415 E Russell Rd (49286-7502)
PHONE.................................517 423-2009
Deborah Loveland, *President*
EMP: 6 EST: 1979
SQ FT: 5,100
SALES (est): 694.6K **Privately Held**
WEB: www.pegasusmold-die.com
SIC: **3544** Special dies & tools

(G-16511)
PENTAMERE WINERY
131 E Chicago Blvd Ste 1 (49286-1570)
P.O. Box 96 (49286-0096)
PHONE.................................517 423-9000
Edward Gerten, *Managing Prtnr*
Daniel Measel, *Partner*
Ed Gerten, *Opers Mgr*
EMP: 10 EST: 2002
SALES (est): 783.1K **Privately Held**
WEB: www.pentamerewinery.com
SIC: **2084** Wines

(G-16512)
RARE TOOL INC
300 E Russell Rd (49286-2058)
PHONE.................................517 423-5000
Jack Reeck, *President*
Gary Anderson, *Corp Secy*
EMP: 17 EST: 1995
SQ FT: 10,000
SALES (est): 2.1MM **Privately Held**
WEB: www.raretoolinc.com
SIC: **3544** Special dies & tools

(G-16513)
ROBERTS TOOL COMPANY
800 S Maumee St (49286-2061)
P.O. Box 400 (49286-0400)
PHONE.................................517 423-6691
Allen Roberts, *President*
James D Roberts, *Vice Pres*
EMP: 10
SQ FT: 2,500
SALES (est): 1.7MM **Privately Held**
WEB: www.robertstoolco.com
SIC: **3599** Machine shop, jobbing & repair

(G-16514)
ROESCH MAUFACTURING CO LLC
Also Called: Roesch Manufacturing
904 Industrial Dr (49286-9701)
PHONE.................................517 424-6300
George Edward Roesch,
Candice Roesch,
Karalyn Roesch,
Ross Roesch,
EMP: 7 EST: 1936
SQ FT: 8,000 **Privately Held**
WEB: www.roeschmfg.com
SIC: **3545** 5084 3546 3423 Machine tool accessories; industrial machinery & equipment; power-driven handtools; hand & edge tools

(G-16515)
SCHAFER HARDWOOD FLOORING CO
Also Called: Schaffer Woodworks
10695 Macon Hwy (49286-9624)
PHONE.................................989 732-8800
Scott F Schafer, *President*
Rob Robinson, *Manager*
EMP: 45 EST: 1997
SALES (est): 1.7MM **Privately Held**
SIC: **2426** Flooring, hardwood

(G-16516)
SOUTHWESTERN INDUSTRIES INC
3124 Cobblestone Rdg (49286-7787)
PHONE.................................517 667-0466
David Barr, *Executive*
EMP: 4 EST: 2018
SALES (est): 69.3K **Privately Held**
WEB: www.southwesternindustries.com
SIC: **3999** Manufacturing industries

(G-16517)
SPECTRUM PRINTERS INC
400 E Russell Rd Ste 1 (49286-7501)
PHONE.................................517 423-5735
Andy Van Staveren, *President*
Rick Nadeau, *Vice Pres*
Gale Shaver, *Accounts Exec*
Cindy Dumeyer, *Manager*
Diane Ketola, *Supervisor*
EMP: 33 EST: 1986
SQ FT: 24,000
SALES (est): 4.7MM **Privately Held**
WEB: www.spectrumprinters.com
SIC: **2752** 2791 2789 Commercial printing, offset; typesetting; bookbinding & related work

(G-16518)
TECUMSEH PACKG SOLUTIONS INC (PA)
Also Called: Tecumseh Division
707 S Evans St (49286-1919)
P.O. Box 427 (49286-0427)
PHONE.................................517 423-2126
William C Akers II, *President*
Michael Akey II, *Vice Pres*
James F Akers, *Admin Sec*
EMP: 50 EST: 2006
SQ FT: 100,000
SALES (est): 11.6MM **Privately Held**
WEB: www.akers-pkg.com
SIC: **2653** Boxes, corrugated: made from purchased materials

(G-16519)
TOTAL MOLDING SOLUTIONS INC
416 E Cummins St (49286-2063)
PHONE.................................517 424-5900
Rajiv Naik, *President*
EMP: 21 EST: 2001
SQ FT: 45,000
SALES (est): 1.3MM **Privately Held**
WEB: www.totalmoldingsolutions.com
SIC: **3089** Injection molding of plastics

(G-16520)
UNILOY INC (PA)
5550 S Occidental Rd B (49286-8749)
PHONE.................................514 424-8900
Brian Marston, *CEO*
Tom McDonald, *Vice Pres*
Richard Darm, *Facilities Mgr*
Michael Kippnick, *Technical Mgr*
Mike Allshouse, *Engineer*
EMP: 56 EST: 2015
SALES (est): 21.3MM **Privately Held**
WEB: www.uniloy.com
SIC: **3089** Injection molding of plastics

(G-16521)
VAN-ROB USA HOLDINGS (HQ)
Also Called: Kirchhoff Automotive Companies
1200 E Chicago Blvd (49286-9674)
PHONE.................................517 423-2400
Darik Chapman, *Buyer*
Les Marz, *CIO*
EMP: 35 EST: 2018
SALES (est): 16.4MM
SALES (corp-wide): 1.7B **Privately Held**
WEB: www.kirchhoff-group.com
SIC: **3559** Automotive related machinery
PA: Kirchhoff Automotive Holding Gmbh & Co. Kg
   Stefanstr. 2
   Iserlohn NW 58638
   237 182-000

Tekonsha - Calhoun County (G-16522) — GEOGRAPHIC SECTION

Tekonsha
Calhoun County

(G-16522)
DOUGLAS CORP
103 S Main St (49092-9480)
P.O. Box 310 (49092-0310)
 PHONE.................517 767-4112
Terry T Hampton, *President*
Rob Zimmermann, *Sales Staff*
EMP: 20
SQ FT: 20,000
SALES (est): 1.6MM **Privately Held**
WEB: www.douglasflamespraying.com
SIC: 7699 3479 7629 2851 Pumps & pumping equipment repair; painting, coating & hot dipping; electrical repair shops; paints & allied products; inorganic pigments

(G-16523)
MARKING MACHINE CO
286 Spires Pkwy (49092-9347)
P.O. Box 159 (49092-0159)
 PHONE.................517 767-4155
Dan Kempton, *President*
Carol Kimball, *Corp Secy*
EMP: 10 **EST:** 1950
SQ FT: 20,000
SALES (est): 747.8K **Privately Held**
WEB: www.markingmachine.com
SIC: 2759 3549 Engraving; marking machines, metalworking

(G-16524)
RANDALL FOODS INC
401 S Main St (49092-9255)
 PHONE.................517 767-3247
Denise Maurer, *Human Res Mgr*
Randy Waltz, *Manager*
EMP: 13
SALES (corp-wide): 3.1MM **Privately Held**
WEB: www.randallbeans.com
SIC: 5411 2033 2032 Grocery stores; canned fruits & specialties; beans, baked with meat: packaged in cans, jars, etc.
PA: Randall Foods Inc.
 312 Walnut St Ste 1600
 Cincinnati OH 45202
 513 793-6525

Temperance
Monroe County

(G-16525)
ACCUWORX LLC (PA)
7156 Sulier Dr (48182-9510)
 PHONE.................734 847-6115
Angela Lehmann, *Accountant*
Jeff Loch, *Mng Member*
Rachel Lienemann, *Program Mgr*
Mark Pucel, *Manager*
Larry Carter,
EMP: 32 **EST:** 2008
SALES (est): 4.6MM **Privately Held**
WEB: www.accuworx.net
SIC: 3599 Custom machinery

(G-16526)
ALLEN TOOL AND DIE LLC
7355 Sulier Dr (48182-9510)
 PHONE.................734 224-7900
Tim Allen,
EMP: 5 **EST:** 2005
SALES (est): 470.6K **Privately Held**
SIC: 3544 Special dies & tools

(G-16527)
ALLIED MASK & TOOLING
7507 Willow Pointe Dr (48182-7500)
 PHONE.................419 470-2555
Mike Murray, *President*
EMP: 5 **EST:** 1998
SALES (est): 93.3K **Privately Held**
SIC: 3423 Hand & edge tools

(G-16528)
BEL-KUR INC
Also Called: Ttg Automation
7297 Express Rd (48182-9592)
 PHONE.................734 847-0651
Jeffery J Kuhr, *President*
Pat Kuhr, *Vice Pres*
Kevin Kuhr, *Purch Dir*
EMP: 40 **EST:** 1985
SQ FT: 12,000
SALES (est): 11.7MM
SALES (corp-wide): 49.5MM **Privately Held**
WEB: www.toolingtechgroup.com
SIC: 3544 3549 7692 8711 Special dies & tools; industrial molds; metalworking machinery; welding repair; engineering services
PA: Tooling Technology, Llc
 51223 Quadrate Dr
 Macomb MI 48042
 937 381-9211

(G-16529)
BURROW INDUSTRIES INC
7380 Express Rd (48182-9597)
P.O. Box 359 (48182-0359)
 PHONE.................734 847-1842
Oliver F Burrow, *President*
Mark Burrow, *Vice Pres*
Dean Portratz, *Sales Staff*
Sue Dunlap, *Manager*
▼ **EMP:** 23 **EST:** 1977
SQ FT: 12,400
SALES (est): 4MM **Privately Held**
WEB: www.burrowindustries.com
SIC: 3599 Machine shop, jobbing & repair

(G-16530)
FISCHER TOOL & DIE CORP (PA)
7155 Industrial Dr Ste A (48182-9172)
 PHONE.................734 847-4788
Joe Hembree, *President*
Sean Ball, *Manager*
◆ **EMP:** 44 **EST:** 1987
SQ FT: 45,000
SALES (est): 9.6MM **Privately Held**
WEB: www.fischertool.com
SIC: 3544 Special dies & tools

(G-16531)
FOREST VIEW LANES LLC
2345 W Dean Rd (48182-9400)
P.O. Box 279 (48182-0279)
 PHONE.................734 847-4915
Richard Allen Kenny, *CEO*
EMP: 50 **EST:** 1962
SQ FT: 16,900
SALES: 2.7MM **Privately Held**
WEB: www.forestviewlanes.com
SIC: 7933 7997 5812 3949 Ten pin center; membership sports & recreation clubs; eating places; nets: badminton, volleyball, tennis, etc.; banquet hall facilities

(G-16532)
FUSION MFG SOLUTIONS LLC
7193 Sulier Dr (48182-9510)
 PHONE.................734 224-7216
Mark Mallory, *Mfg Mgr*
Lee Myers, *Opers Staff*
EMP: 12 **EST:** 2010
SALES (est): 2.5MM **Privately Held**
WEB: www.fusionmanufacturingsolutions.com
SIC: 3599 Machine shop, jobbing & repair

(G-16533)
H E L P PRINTERS INC
9673 Lewis Ave (48182-9358)
 PHONE.................734 847-0554
Carol R Lutman, *President*
Wayne Gamble, *Vice Pres*
EMP: 4 **EST:** 1980
SALES (est): 350K **Privately Held**
WEB: www.helpprinters.com
SIC: 2752 2759 Commercial printing, offset; promotional printing

(G-16534)
HI TECH MECHANICAL SVCS LLC
Also Called: Honeywell Authorized Dealer
7070 Crabb Rd (48182-9552)
 PHONE.................734 847-1831
William Murry,
EMP: 6 **EST:** 2002
SALES (est): 805.1K **Privately Held**
WEB: www.hitechmechanicalllc.com
SIC: 3599 1731 1711 Machine shop, jobbing & repair; electrical work; plumbing, heating, air-conditioning contractors

(G-16535)
I D PRO EMBROIDERY LLC
1287 W Sterns Rd (48182-1504)
 PHONE.................734 847-6650
EMP: 4
SQ FT: 2,000
SALES (est): 326.6K **Privately Held**
SIC: 2395 Custom Embroidery / Screen Printing

(G-16536)
LAKE ERIE MED SURGICAL SUP INC (PA)
7560 Lewis Ave (48182-9539)
P.O. Box 1267, Holland OH (43528-1267)
 PHONE.................734 847-3847
Michael W Holmes, *President*
Joeseph Braker, *Principal*
Robert Holmes, *Vice Pres*
Jeannie Sieren, *Treasurer*
Adrianne Holmes, *Accounting Mgr*
EMP: 22 **EST:** 1978
SQ FT: 13,000
SALES (est): 13.3MM **Privately Held**
SIC: 5047 3826 3841 Medical equipment & supplies; analytical instruments; surgical & medical instruments

(G-16537)
LOONAR STN TWO THE 2 OR 2ND
6656 Lewis Ave Ste 5 (48182-1201)
 PHONE.................419 720-1222
EMP: 4 **EST:** 2010
SALES (est): 399.2K **Privately Held**
WEB: www.loonarstation.com
SIC: 5051 2221 3999 Pipe & tubing, steel; upholstery, tapestry & wall covering fabrics; tobacco pipes, pipestems & bits

(G-16538)
M & N CONTROLS INC
7180 Sulier Dr (48182-9510)
 PHONE.................734 850-2127
Michael J Nagy, *President*
EMP: 20 **EST:** 1974
SQ FT: 2,000
SALES (est): 2.5MM **Privately Held**
WEB: www.mncontrols.com
SIC: 3613 Control panels, electric

(G-16539)
MATRIX NORTH AMERCN CNSTR INC
6945 Crabb Rd (48182-9547)
 PHONE.................734 847-4605
Eric Foster, *Branch Mgr*
EMP: 99
SALES (corp-wide): 673.4MM **Publicly Held**
SIC: 7699 3443 3441 Tank repair & cleaning services; fabricated plate work (boiler shop); fabricated structural metal
HQ: Matrix North American Construction, Inc.
 5100 E Skelly Dr Ste 100
 Tulsa OK 74135

(G-16540)
MET-L-TEC LLC (PA)
7310 Express Rd (48182-9514)
 PHONE.................734 847-7004
Aaron Soldenwagner, *Engineer*
Paul Schmitz, *Sales Mgr*
Paul Schmidt, *Mng Member*
Paul J Schmitz III,
EMP: 20 **EST:** 1971
SQ FT: 15,000
SALES (est): 9.3MM **Privately Held**
WEB: www.met-l-tec.com
SIC: 3544 3559 Special dies & tools; forms (molds), for foundry & plastics working machinery; metal finishing equipment for plating, etc.

(G-16541)
MICHIGAN TUBE SWGERS FBRCTORS (PA)
Also Called: MTS Seating
7100 Industrial Dr (48182-9105)
 PHONE.................734 847-3875
Paul Swy, *President*
Barton Kulish, *President*
John Menas, *Vice Pres*
Peter Swy, *Vice Pres*
Matt Smart, *Prdtn Mgr*
◆ **EMP:** 370 **EST:** 1955
SQ FT: 218,000
SALES (est): 80.1MM **Privately Held**
WEB: www.mtsseating.com
SIC: 2521 Wood office furniture

(G-16542)
MTS BURGESS LLC
1244 W Dean Rd (48182-3800)
P.O. Box 489 (48182-0416)
 PHONE.................734 847-2937
Ken Auger, *General Mgr*
Aaron Gretka, *Engineer*
Jim Griffith, *Engineer*
Joe Restivo, *Treasurer*
Peter Swy, *Treasurer*
▼ **EMP:** 100 **EST:** 2000
SALES (est): 11.4MM
SALES (corp-wide): 80.1MM **Privately Held**
WEB: www.mtsseating.com
SIC: 2514 Chairs, household: metal
PA: Michigan Tube Swagers And Fabricators, Inc.
 7100 Industrial Dr
 Temperance MI 48182
 734 847-3875

(G-16543)
NATURE PATCH SOAPS
2300 W Dean Rd (48182-9400)
 PHONE.................734 847-3759
Sherry Young, *Principal*
EMP: 6 **EST:** 2002
SALES (est): 84.4K **Privately Held**
WEB: www.naturepatchsoaps.com
SIC: 2841 Soap & other detergents

(G-16544)
PANTLESS JAMS LLC
6937 Maplewood Dr (48182-1326)
 PHONE.................419 283-8470
Jessica Hopkins, *Principal*
EMP: 5 **EST:** 2017
SALES (est): 116.3K **Privately Held**
WEB: www.pantlessjams.com
SIC: 2033 Jams, jellies & preserves: packaged in cans, jars, etc.

(G-16545)
PRO LINEZ OF ANN ARBOR
10236 Gilcyn St (48182-9711)
 PHONE.................734 755-7309
EMP: 5 **EST:** 2011
SALES (est): 176.4K **Privately Held**
WEB: www.prolinez.com
SIC: 3993 Signs & advertising specialties

(G-16546)
QUALITY CARE PRODUCTS LLC
7560 Lewis Ave (48182-9539)
 PHONE.................734 847-3847
Michael W Holmes, *CEO*
Pat Earl, *Vice Pres*
Brandon Holmes, *Vice Pres*
EMP: 12 **EST:** 2001
SALES (est): 261.2K **Privately Held**
WEB: www.qcprx.com
SIC: 2834 Pharmaceutical preparations

(G-16547)
ROLLED ALLOYS INC (PA)
125 W Sterns Rd (48182-9567)
 PHONE.................734 847-0561
Thomas Nichol, *President*
Normand Levesque, *General Mgr*
James Lilly, *General Mgr*
Gerard Macdonald, *General Mgr*
John Sappington, *General Mgr*
◆ **EMP:** 92
SQ FT: 83,000

▲ = Import ▼=Export
◆ =Import/Export

SALES (est): 212.6MM **Privately Held**
WEB: www.rolledalloys.com
SIC: 5051 3369 3341 3317 Steel; nonferrous foundries; secondary nonferrous metals; steel pipe & tubes; chemical preparations; paints & allied products

(G-16548)
ROYAL STEWART ENTERPRISES
Also Called: Kustom Kaps
7355 Lewis Ave Ste B (48182-1465)
P.O. Box 273 (48182-0273)
PHONE 734 224-7994
Richard Stewart, *Partner*
Tim Stewart, *Partner*
▲ **EMP:** 5 **EST:** 1992
SQ FT: 2,400
SALES (est): 508.1K **Privately Held**
SIC: 2395 2759 Embroidery products, except schiffli machine; emblems, embroidered; screen printing

(G-16549)
SPECIALTY HARDWOOD MOLDINGS
1244 W Dean Rd (48182-3800)
PHONE 734 847-3997
EMP: 10
SALES (est): 1MM **Privately Held**
SIC: 2431 Mfg Millwork

(G-16550)
TEMPERANCE DISTILLING COMPANY
Also Called: Zippers
177 Reed Dr (48182-8900)
PHONE 734 847-5262
John Buckey, *CEO*
Zachary Owen, *Vice Pres*
Cindy Jechura, *Accountant*
EMP: 15 **EST:** 1998
SQ FT: 2,200
SALES (est): 5.3MM **Privately Held**
WEB: www.usatdc.com
SIC: 2085 Distilled & blended liquors

(G-16551)
UNIQUE TOOL & MFG CO INC
100 Reed Dr (48182-8900)
PHONE 336 498-2614
Daniel J Althaus, *President*
David H Althaus, *Exec VP*
Bill Jones, *Manager*
EMP: 27 **EST:** 1962
SQ FT: 72,000
SALES (est): 2.8MM **Privately Held**
WEB: www.uniquetool.com
SIC: 3465 3544 3469 Automotive stampings; special dies, tools, jigs & fixtures; metal stampings

(G-16552)
WESTOOL CORPORATION
7383 Sulier Dr (48182-9510)
PHONE 734 847-2520
Greg West, *President*
▲ **EMP:** 23 **EST:** 1997
SQ FT: 25,000
SALES (est): 4.7MM **Privately Held**
WEB: www.westools.com
SIC: 3544 Special dies & tools

Thompsonville
Benzie County

(G-16553)
CRYSTAL VISTA VINEYARD LLC
10911 Heuser Hwy (49683-9462)
PHONE 231 269-4165
Michael Joseph Heuser, *Principal*
EMP: 4 **EST:** 2017
SALES (est): 70.4K **Privately Held**
SIC: 2084 Wines

Three Oaks
Berrien County

(G-16554)
C & K HARDWOODS LLC
7325 Elm Valley Rd (49128-8503)
PHONE 269 231-0048
Greg Kerigan, *Ch of Bd*
Thomas Carson, *President*
Jennifer Hickory, *Treasurer*
Charlene Carson, *Admin Sec*
EMP: 7
SQ FT: 15,000
SALES (est): 300K **Privately Held**
SIC: 2431 Millwork

(G-16555)
CENTER OF WORLD WOODSHOP INC
4102 Hanover Rd (49128-9529)
P.O. Box 354, New Troy (49119-0354)
PHONE 269 469-5687
Terry Hanover, *President*
Rebecca Gloe, *Corp Secy*
EMP: 9 **EST:** 1985 **Privately Held**
WEB: www.centerofworld.net
SIC: 2511 Wood household furniture

(G-16556)
H & K MACHINE COMPANY INC
7451 Us Highway 12 (49128-9166)
PHONE 269 756-7339
Fax: 269 756-7501
EMP: 5
SQ FT: 10,000
SALES: 500K **Privately Held**
SIC: 3451 Mfg Screw Machine Products

(G-16557)
JOURNEYMAN DISTILLERY LLC
109 Generation Dr (49128-1064)
PHONE 269 820-2050
Robert Krass, *VP Sales*
Chelsey Erickson, *Marketing Mgr*
Sandi Weindling, *Marketing Mgr*
Torie Jaques, *Manager*
Michelle Kennedy, *Manager*
EMP: 7 **EST:** 2012 **Privately Held**
WEB: www.journeymandistillery.com
SIC: 2085 Distilled & blended liquors

(G-16558)
SHEPHERD HARDWARE PRODUCTS INC
6961 Us Highway 12 (49128-9556)
P.O. Box 394 (49128-0394)
PHONE 269 756-3830
Marvin W Ross, *President*
R C Gluth, *Treasurer*
Joe Margol, *Technology*
Robert W Webb, *Admin Sec*
▲ **EMP:** 95 **EST:** 1990
SQ FT: 200,000
SALES (est): 9.6MM **Privately Held**
WEB: www.shepherdhardware.com
SIC: 3429 5072 Manufactured hardware (general); casters & glides

(G-16559)
THREE OAKS ENGRAVING & ENGRG
14381 Three Oaks Rd (49128-9716)
PHONE 269 469-2124
John Schmidt, *President*
EMP: 5 **EST:** 1946
SALES (est): 291.2K **Privately Held**
WEB: www.threeoaksengineering.com
SIC: 3479 Engraving jewelry silverware, or metal

(G-16560)
TO WILLOW HARBOR VINEYARD
3223 Kaiser Rd (49128-8543)
PHONE 269 369-3900
Kristie Kelleher, *Principal*
EMP: 6 **EST:** 2005
SALES (est): 77.1K **Privately Held**
WEB: www.willowharborvineyards.com
SIC: 2084 Wines

(G-16561)
VICKERS ENGINEERING INC
16860 Three Oaks Rd (49128-8581)
P.O. Box 346, New Troy (49119-0346)
PHONE 269 756-9133
Dan Reiter, *COO*
James Vickers, *Executive*
EMP: 14 **EST:** 1970
SALES (est): 289.9K **Privately Held**
WEB: www.vickerseng.com
SIC: 3599 Machine shop, jobbing & repair

Three Rivers
St. Joseph County

(G-16562)
AMERICAN AXLE & MFG INC
Also Called: Three Rivers Driveline Fcilty
1 Manufacturing Dr (49093-8907)
PHONE 269 278-0211
Miranda Minton, *Partner*
Shannon Curry, *Vice Pres*
Pat Brosnan, *Maint Spvr*
Nathan Stiemke, *Production*
Lawrence Lesinski, *Buyer*
EMP: 600
SALES (corp-wide): 4.7B **Publicly Held**
WEB: www.aam.com
SIC: 3714 Axles, motor vehicle
HQ: American Axle & Manufacturing, Inc.
1 Dauch Dr
Detroit MI 48211

(G-16563)
AMERICAN METAL FAB INC
Also Called: A M F
55515 Franklin Dr (49093-9692)
PHONE 269 279-5108
John Crowell, *President*
Jason Crowell, *Vice Pres*
Gerald S Eplee, *Vice Pres*
Dane Hoover, *Plant Mgr*
Kelley Crowell, *Treasurer*
EMP: 60 **EST:** 1975
SQ FT: 100,000
SALES (est): 10.1MM **Privately Held**
WEB: www.americanmetalfab.us
SIC: 3444 3469 2531 3443 Sheet metal specialties, not stamped; metal stampings; seats, automobile; fabricated plate work (boiler shop)

(G-16564)
AQUATIC CO
Lasco Bathware
888 W Broadway St (49093-1900)
PHONE 269 279-7461
Jim Dreher, *Branch Mgr*
EMP: 240
SALES (corp-wide): 640.9MM **Privately Held**
WEB: www.aquaticbath.com
SIC: 3088 Hot tubs, plastic or fiberglass; shower stalls, fiberglass & plastic
HQ: Aquatic Co.
665 Industrial Rd
Savannah TN 38372

(G-16565)
ARMSTRONG FLUID HANDLING INC
221 Armstrong Blvd (49093-2374)
PHONE 269 279-3600
David Armstrong, *President*
Steve Gibson, *Treasurer*
Tom Morris, *Admin Sec*
▲ **EMP:** 67 **EST:** 1996
SQ FT: 6,000
SALES (est): 4.9MM
SALES (corp-wide): 455MM **Privately Held**
WEB: www.armstronginternational.com
SIC: 3594 Fluid power pumps
PA: Armstrong International, Inc.
816 Maple St
Three Rivers MI 49093
269 273-1415

(G-16566)
ARMSTRONG HOT WATER INC
221 Armstrong Blvd (49093-2374)
PHONE 269 278-1413
Larry Daugherty, *President*

Stephen Gibson, *Treasurer*
Mandy Armstrong, *Marketing Staff*
Thomas J Morris, *Admin Sec*
▲ **EMP:** 45 **EST:** 1997
SALES (est): 10.3MM
SALES (corp-wide): 455MM **Privately Held**
WEB: www.armstronginternational.com
SIC: 3433 5074 Boilers, low-pressure heating: steam or hot water; sanitary ware, china or enameled iron
PA: Armstrong International, Inc.
816 Maple St
Three Rivers MI 49093
269 273-1415

(G-16567)
ARMSTRONG INTERNATIONAL INC (PA)
816 Maple St (49093-2345)
PHONE 269 273-1415
Douglas Bloss, *CEO*
Patrick Armstrong, *Ch of Bd*
Rex Cummings, *General Mgr*
Higginbotham Kyle, *Superintendent*
Daniel Lane, *Counsel*
▲ **EMP:** 220 **EST:** 1895
SQ FT: 149,000
SALES (est): 455MM **Privately Held**
WEB: www.armstronginternational.com
SIC: 3491 Steam traps; pressure valves & regulators, industrial; regulators (steam fittings)

(G-16568)
CALM WELDING
18388 M 86 (49093-9320)
PHONE 417 358-8131
Corey Wickey, *Principal*
EMP: 4 **EST:** 2016
SALES (est): 86.7K **Privately Held**
SIC: 7692 Welding repair

(G-16569)
CELIA DEBOER
14791 Hoffman Rd (49093-9703)
PHONE 269 279-9102
Celia Deboer, *Owner*
EMP: 10
SALES (est): 714.9K **Privately Held**
SIC: 2951 Asphalt paving mixtures & blocks

(G-16570)
DENNY GRICE INC
Also Called: R & H Machine Products
702 Webber Ave (49093-8911)
P.O. Box 32, Marcellus (49067-0032)
PHONE 269 279-6113
Denny Grice, *President*
EMP: 20 **EST:** 1967
SQ FT: 10,000
SALES (est): 1.4MM **Privately Held**
WEB: www.rh-machine.net
SIC: 3451 Screw machine products

(G-16571)
DOCK FOUNDRY COMPANY
429 4th St (49093-1697)
PHONE 269 278-1765
Douglas Monroe, *President*
EMP: 2 **EST:** 1940
SQ FT: 110,000
SALES (est): 1.2MM
SALES (corp-wide): 261.8MM **Privately Held**
WEB: www.afsinc.org
SIC: 3321 Gray iron castings
PA: Metal Technologies Of Indiana Llc
1401 S Grandstaff Dr
Auburn IN 46706
260 925-4717

(G-16572)
FASTENER COATINGS INC
1111 River St (49093-1151)
PHONE 269 279-5134
Douglas Garvey, *CEO*
Joy Garvey, *President*
Beverly Garvey, *Corp Secy*
EMP: 19 **EST:** 1968
SQ FT: 10,000
SALES (est): 1.6MM **Privately Held**
WEB: www.fastenercoatings.com
SIC: 3479 Coating of metals & formed products

Three Rivers - St. Joseph County (G-16573)

(G-16573)
FIGMENT SCREEN PRINTING
307 West St (49093-2221)
PHONE.............................269 858-9998
Levi Nerad, *Principal*
EMP: 4 EST: 2018
SALES (est): 90.4K Privately Held
SIC: 2759 Screen printing

(G-16574)
GAR-V MANUFACTURING INC
1111 River St (49093-1199)
PHONE.............................269 279-5134
Joy Garvey, *President*
EMP: 7 EST: 1967
SQ FT: 20,000
SALES (est): 789.1K Privately Held
WEB: www.gar-v.com
SIC: 3469 Stamping metal for the trade

(G-16575)
H B D M INC
1149 Millard St (49093-9567)
P.O. Box 15 (49093-0015)
PHONE.............................269 273-1976
Ford Brewder, *Manager*
EMP: 12
SALES (corp-wide): 834K Privately Held
SIC: 3544 Special dies & tools
PA: H B D M Inc
 207 Portage Ave
 Three Rivers MI 49093
 269 273-1976

(G-16576)
INTERNATIONAL PAPER COMPANY
1321 3rd St (49093-2726)
PHONE.............................269 273-8461
John Pavletic, *Sales Staff*
Scott Dillon, *Manager*
EMP: 5
SQ FT: 260,000
SALES (corp-wide): 20.5B Publicly Held
WEB: www.internationalpaper.com
SIC: 2621 Paper mills
PA: International Paper Company
 6400 Poplar Ave
 Memphis TN 38197
 901 419-7000

(G-16577)
KADANT JOHNSON LLC (HQ)
805 Wood St (49093-1053)
PHONE.............................269 278-1715
Greg Wedel, *President*
Dan Snyder, *Mfg Dir*
Chad Minger, *Engineer*
Danielle Rohrer, *Marketing Staff*
Jeff Fruehauf, *Manager*
◆ EMP: 150
SQ FT: 130,000
SALES (est): 210.9MM Publicly Held
WEB: www.kadant.com
SIC: 3494 8711 1389 3052 Steam fittings & specialties; construction & civil engineering; construction, repair & dismantling services; rubber hose

(G-16578)
KDF FLUID TREATMENT INC
1500 Kdf Dr (49093-9287)
PHONE.............................269 273-3300
Issa Al-Kahrusy, *CEO*
John B Heskett, *President*
Dorothy M Heskett, *Chairman*
Denise Al-Kahrusy, *Vice Pres*
Donna Smith, *Treasurer*
EMP: 10 EST: 1984
SQ FT: 5,000
SALES (est): 1.6MM Privately Held
WEB: www.kdfft.com
SIC: 3569 Filters; filter elements, fluid, hydraulic line; filters, general line: industrial

(G-16579)
MORTON BUILDINGS INC
59924 S Us Highway 131 (49093-8579)
PHONE.............................616 696-4737
Mike Martin, *Principal*
EMP: 5
SALES (corp-wide): 247.1MM Privately Held
WEB: www.mortonbuildings.com
SIC: 3448 5039 1796 Prefabricated metal buildings; prefabricated structures; installing building equipment
PA: Morton Buildings, Inc.
 252 W Adams St
 Morton IL 61550
 800 447-7436

(G-16580)
PETERSON AMERICAN CORPORATION
Also Called: Peterson Spring Cima
16805 Heimbach Rd (49093-9622)
PHONE.............................269 279-7421
Mark Jozwiski, *Branch Mgr*
Bill Platko, *Manager*
Gregory Tibbetts, *Supervisor*
EMP: 60
SQ FT: 12,000
SALES (corp-wide): 1.6B Privately Held
WEB: www.pspring.com
SIC: 3429 3495 Clamps & couplings, hose; wire springs
HQ: Peterson American Corporation
 21200 Telegraph Rd
 Southfield MI 48033
 248 799-5400

(G-16581)
PRECISION WIRE FORMS INC (PA)
1100 W Broadway St (49093-8701)
P.O. Box 29 (49093-0029)
PHONE.............................269 279-0053
Francoise Beuter, *President*
▲ EMP: 36 EST: 1997
SQ FT: 34,000
SALES (est): 6.8MM Privately Held
WEB: www.wire-forms.com
SIC: 3496 Miscellaneous fabricated wire products

(G-16582)
PROGRESSIVE PAPER CORP
Also Called: Castel Leasing
1111 3rd St (49093-1926)
P.O. Box 308 (49093-0308)
PHONE.............................269 279-6320
EMP: 8
SQ FT: 250,000
SALES (est): 1.6MM Privately Held
SIC: 2679 Mfg Custom Paper Converters

(G-16583)
REPUBLIC ROLLER CORPORATION
205 S Us Highway 131 (49093-9295)
P.O. Box 330 (49093-0330)
PHONE.............................269 273-9591
Daniel Meeth, *President*
Rohit Shah, *Vice Pres*
Sherrie Holden, *Treasurer*
Gene Lempert, *Analyst*
EMP: 34 EST: 1981
SQ FT: 80,000
SALES (est): 4.4MM Privately Held
WEB: www.republicroller.com
SIC: 3069 Rubber rolls & roll coverings

(G-16584)
SIMPSONS ENTERPRISES INC
55255 Franklin Dr (49093-9685)
P.O. Box 351 (49093-0351)
PHONE.............................269 279-7237
James W Simpson, *President*
Gerald A Simpson, *Treasurer*
EMP: 12 EST: 1975
SQ FT: 40,000
SALES (est): 630.5K Privately Held
WEB: www.simpsonsent.com
SIC: 3544 3543 Industrial molds; forms (molds), for foundry & plastics working machinery; industrial patterns

(G-16585)
SS CUSTOM MARKET
405 S Constantine St (49093-2503)
PHONE.............................269 816-1311
Shawn Rhodes, *Principal*
EMP: 5 EST: 2009
SALES (est): 49.3K Privately Held
SIC: 2431 Millwork

(G-16586)
TAMARA TOOL INC
1234 William R Monroe Blv (49093-8626)
PHONE.............................269 273-1463
Robert L Hempel Jr, *President*
Kathryn Hempel, *Vice Pres*
EMP: 10 EST: 1989
SQ FT: 12,000
SALES (est): 771.3K Privately Held
WEB: www.tamara-tool.tripod.com
SIC: 3544 Special dies & tools

(G-16587)
TEXTISS USA
61245 S Us Highway 131 (49093-9288)
PHONE.............................310 909-6062
EMP: 4 EST: 2019
SALES (est): 204.5K Privately Held
SIC: 2711 Newspapers, publishing & printing

(G-16588)
THREE RIVERS COMMERCIAL NEWS
Also Called: Penny Saver
124 N Main St (49093-1559)
P.O. Box 130 (49093-0130)
PHONE.............................269 279-7488
Richard Milliman II, *President*
Penelope Faber Milliman, *Vice Pres*
Ann M Milliman, *Treasurer*
David Allen, *Advt Staff*
Arteria Taylor, *Advt Staff*
EMP: 20 EST: 1895
SQ FT: 15,500
SALES (est): 2.6MM Privately Held
WEB: www.threeriversnews.com
SIC: 2711 Newspapers, publishing & printing
PA: Milliman Communications Inc
 4601 W Saginaw Hwy Apt 2
 Lansing MI 48917
 517 327-8407

(G-16589)
TRIM PAC INC
315 7th Ave (49093-1132)
P.O. Box 118 (49093-0118)
PHONE.............................269 279-9498
Dan Fuller, *President*
Greg Ellis, *Vice Pres*
EMP: 5
SQ FT: 6,000
SALES (est): 800K Privately Held
WEB: www.trim-pac.com
SIC: 2679 2675 2631 Paper products, converted; die-cut paper & board; chip board

(G-16590)
X-L MACHINE CO INC
20481 M 60 (49093-8000)
PHONE.............................269 279-5128
James King, *President*
Bob Hendrixson, *Opers Staff*
Linda Finch, *Manager*
Darren King, *Prgrmr*
▲ EMP: 47 EST: 1977
SQ FT: 8,000
SALES (est): 10.1MM
SALES (corp-wide): 104.3MM Privately Held
WEB: www.xlmachine.com
SIC: 3599 Machine shop, jobbing & repair
PA: Burke E. Porter Machinery Company
 730 Plymouth Ave Ne
 Grand Rapids MI 49505
 616 234-1200

Tipton
Lenawee County

(G-16591)
MICHIGAN CHESE PRTEIN PDTS LLC
10015 Wisner Hwy (49287-9704)
PHONE.............................517 403-5247
Gregg Hardy, *CEO*
EMP: 7 EST: 2014
SQ FT: 265,000
SALES (est): 307.9K Privately Held
SIC: 2022 Cheese, natural & processed

Toivola
Houghton County

(G-16592)
SAURS CUSTOM WOODWORKING
7400 Autumn Blaze Trl (49965-9418)
PHONE.............................906 288-3202
Jim Saur, *Principal*
EMP: 4 EST: 2011
SALES (est): 164.2K Privately Held
SIC: 2431 Millwork

(G-16593)
THOMAS CHEAL
Also Called: Cheal Woodworking
40240 Aspen Rd (49965-9393)
PHONE.............................906 288-3487
Thomas Cheal, *Owner*
EMP: 4 EST: 1998
SALES (est): 170K Privately Held
WEB: www.chealwoodworking.com
SIC: 2431 Moldings & baseboards, ornamental & trim

Traverse City
Grand Traverse County

(G-16594)
5 BY 5 LLC
333 W Grandview Pkwy # 404 (49684-2291)
PHONE.............................855 369-6757
Troy Hill, *President*
Rishon Kimber, *President*
Travis McDougall, *Vice Pres*
EMP: 10 EST: 2018
SALES (est): 10MM Privately Held
WEB: www.5by5.services
SIC: 1389 Pipe testing, oil field service

(G-16595)
ACE WELDING & MACHINE INC
1505 Premier St (49686-4391)
P.O. Box 2059 (49685-2059)
PHONE.............................231 941-9664
Terry Walters, *President*
Beth Walters, *Manager*
EMP: 12 EST: 1950
SQ FT: 6,000
SALES (est): 400K Privately Held
WEB: www.aceweldingtc.com
SIC: 7692 3441 3444 Welding repair; fabricated structural metal; forming machine work, sheet metal

(G-16596)
ACOUSTIC TAP ROOM
119 N Maple St (49684-2238)
PHONE.............................231 714-5028
EMP: 6 EST: 2016
SALES (est): 59.4K Privately Held
SIC: 5813 2082 Beer garden (drinking places); malt beverages

(G-16597)
ACTRON STEEL INC
2341 Molon Dr (49684-9101)
P.O. Box 966 (49685-0966)
PHONE.............................231 947-3981
Ronald Watson, *President*
Brian Moore, *Vice Pres*
EMP: 23 EST: 1977
SQ FT: 43,450
SALES (est): 16.7MM Privately Held
WEB: www.actronsteel.com
SIC: 5051 3441 3469 3412 Steel; fabricated structural metal; metal stampings; metal barrels, drums & pails; dumpsters, garbage

(G-16598)
ALCOTEC WIRE CORPORATION (DH)
2750 Aero Park Dr (49686-9263)
PHONE.............................800 228-0750
Tom Svaboda, *President*
Thomas Pfaller, *Engineer*
George Townsend, *CFO*
Ron Stahura, *Sales Staff*
Bill Ferguson, *Supervisor*

▲ EMP: 85 EST: 1983
SQ FT: 180,000
SALES (est): 42.1MM
SALES (corp-wide): 3B Publicly Held
WEB: www.alcotec.com
SIC: 3355 8711 3548 Aluminum wire & cable; engineering services; welding apparatus
HQ: The Esab Group Inc
2800 Airport Rd
Denton TX 76207
800 372-2123

(G-16599)
ALFIE EMBROIDERY INC
2425 Switch Dr Ste A (49684-4342)
PHONE.................................231 935-1488
Bonnie Alfonso, President
Marty Beaudoin, Vice Pres
Tricia Bowden, Purchasing
Mike Alfonso, Treasurer
Amber Rogers, Sales Staff
EMP: 12 EST: 1990
SALES (est): 1.1MM Privately Held
WEB: www.goalfie.com
SIC: 2395 Embroidery products, except schiffli machine

(G-16600)
ALLESK ENTERPRISES INC (PA)
Also Called: Allegra Printing
1224 Centre St (49686-3406)
PHONE.................................231 941-5770
Roger Leask, President
EMP: 6 EST: 1984
SQ FT: 1,860
SALES (est): 977.4K Privately Held
WEB: www.allegramarketingprint.com
SIC: 2752 2759 Commercial printing, offset; commercial printing

(G-16601)
AMERICAN WIRELINE SERVICES INC
820 Duell Rd (49686-4801)
PHONE.................................231 218-6849
Scott K Norris, President
EMP: 9 EST: 2009
SALES (est): 719K Privately Held
WEB: www.americanwireline.com
SIC: 1382 Oil & gas exploration services

(G-16602)
ARBOR OPERATING LLC
333 W Grandview Pkwy # 401 (49684-2298)
PHONE.................................231 941-2237
Terry L Beia, Mng Member
James Eichstadt,
EMP: 5 EST: 2005
SALES (est): 782.7K Privately Held
SIC: 1382 Oil & gas exploration services

(G-16603)
ASHER BRANDON INDUSTRIES
425 W Twelfth St (49684-4005)
PHONE.................................231 313-3513
Brandon Asher, Owner
EMP: 4 EST: 2013
SALES (est): 82.7K Privately Held
SIC: 3999 Manufacturing industries

(G-16604)
ASTRO BUILDING PRODUCTS INC (HQ)
221 W South Airport Rd (49686-4876)
PHONE.................................231 941-0324
Fred C Deschler, President
Michael Deschler, Vice Pres
John Everest, Vice Pres
Merry McCray, Treasurer
Scott Schoech, Admin Sec
EMP: 5 EST: 1977
SQ FT: 19,000
SALES (est): 3.5MM
SALES (corp-wide): 27.5B Privately Held
WEB: www.astrobuildingproducts.com
SIC: 5211 3442 5033 5031 Siding; metal doors, sash & trim; siding, except wood; lumber, plywood & millwork
PA: Crh Public Limited Company
Stonemasons Way
Dublin D16 K
140 410-00

(G-16605)
ATI MARKETING
506 N Spruce St (49684-1442)
P.O. Box 1859 (49685-1859)
PHONE.................................231 590-9600
Michelle Corteggiano, Principal
EMP: 4 EST: 2016
SALES (est): 75.7K Privately Held
WEB: www.atimarketing.com
SIC: 3312 Stainless steel

(G-16606)
ATTITUDE & EXPERIENCE INC
Also Called: A & E Sign
1230 S M 37 (49685-8506)
PHONE.................................231 946-7446
Jason Orton, President
Jeffrey Orton, Vice Pres
EMP: 15 EST: 2004
SQ FT: 3,600
SALES (est): 839.2K Privately Held
WEB: www.attitudeandexperience.com
SIC: 5099 3993 Signs, except electric; signs & advertising specialties

(G-16607)
ATWATER FOODS LLC
10850 E Traverse Hwy # 4001 (49684-1317)
PHONE.................................231 941-4336
Colleen House, Partner
EMP: 6 EST: 2011
SALES (est): 207.8K Privately Held
SIC: 3556 Food products machinery

(G-16608)
AUXIER & ASSOCIATES LLC
Also Called: Signs Now
1702 Barlow St Ste A (49684-4723)
PHONE.................................231 486-0641
Jeff Dufort, Project Mgr
Dan Reed, Project Mgr
Elis Auxier,
EMP: 5 EST: 1994
SALES (est): 281.6K Privately Held
WEB: www.signsnow.com
SIC: 3993 Signs & advertising specialties

(G-16609)
AUXIER & ASSOCIATES LLC
741 Woodmere Ave (49686-3348)
PHONE.................................231 933-7446
William Auxier, President
EMP: 8 EST: 1995
SQ FT: 1,500
SALES (est): 925.9K Privately Held
SIC: 3993 Signs, not made in custom sign painting shops

(G-16610)
BAG STITCHERY
536 Woodland Dr (49686-3550)
PHONE.................................231 276-3163
Mary Jo Berger, Principal
EMP: 4 EST: 2017
SALES (est): 45K Privately Held
SIC: 2395 Embroidery & art needlework

(G-16611)
BAKER HGHES OLFLD OPRTIONS LLC
2397 Traversefield Dr (49686-9266)
PHONE.................................231 342-9408
EMP: 4 EST: 2020
SALES (est): 306.1K Privately Held
SIC: 1389 Oil & gas field services

(G-16612)
BANNERGALAXYCOM LLC
2322 Cass Rd (49684-9147)
PHONE.................................231 941-8200
Paul Britten,
▲ EMP: 12 EST: 2000
SALES (est): 264.1K Privately Held
WEB: www.onlinebanners.brittenbanners.com
SIC: 2399 5999 Banners, made from fabric; banners

(G-16613)
BAY AREA TOOL LLC
466 Hughes Dr (49696-8255)
PHONE.................................231 946-3500
John Bergman, Partner
Mike Doriot, Partner
EMP: 4 EST: 1986
SQ FT: 8,000
SALES (est): 419.3K Privately Held
SIC: 3544 Special dies & tools

(G-16614)
BAY BREAD CO
601 Randolph St (49684-2246)
PHONE.................................231 922-8022
Stacey Wilcox, President
Steven Wilcox, Vice Pres
Edna Angel, Manager
EMP: 9 EST: 1998
SALES (est): 1.1MM Privately Held
WEB: www.baybreadco.com
SIC: 2051 5812 Bread, all types (white, wheat, rye, etc): fresh or frozen; lunchrooms & cafeterias

(G-16615)
BAY MOTOR PRODUCTS INC
3100 Cass Rd Ste 1 (49684-6963)
P.O. Box 982 (49685-0982)
PHONE.................................231 941-0411
Andrew Robitshek, President
Dave Bleich, Opers Mgr
Brian Roubal, QC Mgr
Greg Hill, Engineer
Andy Robitshek, Products
EMP: 33 EST: 2014
SQ FT: 18,500
SALES (est): 5.4MM Privately Held
WEB: www.baymotorproducts.com
SIC: 3621 Motors, electric

(G-16616)
BAY SUPPLY & MARKETING INC
520 Us Highway 31 S (49685-8018)
PHONE.................................231 943-3249
Charles Benson, President
Andrew Benson, Marketing Staff
EMP: 7 EST: 1979
SQ FT: 10,000
SALES (est): 2.2MM Privately Held
WEB: www.baysupplyinc.com
SIC: 5199 2399 2395 2396 Advertising specialties; flags, fabric; banners, made from fabric; embroidery products, except schiffli machine; screen printing on fabric articles

(G-16617)
BAYGEO INC
Also Called: Bay Geophysical
528 Hughes Dr (49696-8255)
PHONE.................................231 941-7660
Phil Vanhollebeke, President
Ronald Carr, Vice Pres
Pam Hornak, Treasurer
EMP: 25 EST: 2005
SALES (est): 2.6MM Privately Held
WEB: www.baygeo.com
SIC: 8748 8999 1382 Environmental consultant; earth science services; oil & gas exploration services; geological exploration, oil & gas field; geophysical exploration, oil & gas field; seismograph surveys

(G-16618)
BAYSIDE INDUSTRIES
921 Mitchell St (49684-3619)
PHONE.................................231 632-2222
EMP: 5 EST: 2016
SALES (est): 126.6K Privately Held
WEB: www.baysideindustries.com
SIC: 3999 Manufacturing industries

(G-16619)
BBB INDUSTRIES
10515 S Monaco Way (49684-6817)
PHONE.................................231 735-6060
EMP: 4 EST: 2018
SALES (est): 68.9K Privately Held
SIC: 3999 Manufacturing industries

(G-16620)
BIG DIPPER DOUGH CO INC
5109 Heritage Way (49685-8958)
PHONE.................................231 883-6035
Austin Groesser, CEO
EMP: 7
SQ FT: 2,000
SALES (est): 1.8MM Privately Held
WEB: www.bigdipperdough.com
SIC: 2045 Doughs, frozen or refrigerated: from purchased flour

(G-16621)
BIG MAPLE PRESS
3933 Blue Water Rd (49686-8586)
PHONE.................................231 313-4059
Jerry Dennis, Administration
EMP: 5 EST: 2015
SALES (est): 59.2K Privately Held
WEB: www.bigmaplepress.com
SIC: 2741 Miscellaneous publishing

(G-16622)
BLOOM INDUSTRIES LLC
726 Hastings St Ste A (49686-3461)
PHONE.................................616 890-8029
EMP: 11
SALES (corp-wide): 280.4K Privately Held
SIC: 3999 Barber & beauty shop equipment
PA: Bloom Industries Llc
2218 Ashcreek Ct Nw
Grand Rapids MI 49534
616 453-2946

(G-16623)
BODY EXOTICS
6649 Boone Rd Ste 207 (49685-8187)
PHONE.................................231 753-8590
Julie Weber, CEO
EMP: 12 EST: 2008
SALES (est): 521K Privately Held
SIC: 2844 Perfumes & colognes

(G-16624)
BOSTWICK ENTERPRISES INC (PA)
Also Called: Wilbert Burial Vault Co
3575 Veterans Dr (49684-4512)
PHONE.................................231 946-8613
Alan Bostwick, President
EMP: 6 EST: 1978
SALES (est): 1.7MM Privately Held
SIC: 3272 Burial vaults, concrete or precast terrazzo

(G-16625)
BOTSG INC
Also Called: Boride Engineered Abrasives
2615 Aero Park Dr (49684-9101)
PHONE.................................231 929-2121
Larry Tiefenbach, President
Kenneth Osborne, Vice Pres
Annette Thompson, Project Mgr
John Sak, VP Sales
▲ EMP: 54 EST: 1993
SQ FT: 22,000
SALES (est): 8.4MM Privately Held
WEB: www.borideabrasives.com
SIC: 3291 3281 Abrasive products; cut stone & stone products

(G-16626)
BOWERS HARBOR VINYRD & WINERY
Also Called: 45th Parallel
2896 Bowers Harbor Rd (49686-9735)
PHONE.................................231 223-7615
Spencer Stegenga, President
Linda Stegenga, Corp Secy
Kristy McClellan, Opers Mgr
Justin Leshinsky, Sales Staff
EMP: 8 EST: 1991
SALES (est): 1.2MM Privately Held
WEB: www.bowersharbor.com
SIC: 2084 5812 Wines; eating places

(G-16627)
BRITTEN INC
2322 Cass Rd (49684-9147)
PHONE.................................231 941-8200
Paul Britten, President
Carmen Hayes, General Mgr
Cole Swinehart, Vice Pres
Kim Jordan, Project Mgr
Patty Schmerge, Project Mgr
EMP: 240 EST: 2018

Traverse City - Grand Traverse County (G-16628)   GEOGRAPHIC SECTION

SALES (est): 25.7MM **Privately Held**
WEB: www.britteninc.com
SIC: **2399** 3993 2796 2396 Banners, pennants & flags; banners, made from fabric; signs & advertising specialties; platemaking services; automotive & apparel trimmings; architectural metalwork; sheet metalwork

(G-16628)
BRITTEN BANNERS LLC
Also Called: Sideline Signatures
2322 Cass Rd (49684-9147)
PHONE.................................231 941-8200
Paul Britten, *President*
Rylan Ash, *Project Mgr*
Mike Dudek, *Design Engr*
Casey Gelow, *Accounts Exec*
Courtney Look, *Accounts Exec*
◆ EMP: 165 EST: 1985
SQ FT: 50,000
SALES (est): 33MM **Privately Held**
WEB: www.britteninc.com
SIC: **2399** 3993 2796 2396 Banners, pennants & flags; banners, made from fabric; signs & advertising specialties; platemaking services; automotive & apparel trimmings

(G-16629)
BRITTEN METALWORKS LLC
1661 Northern Star Dr (49696-9243)
PHONE.................................231 421-1615
Aul Briten, *President*
Mark A Augustine,
EMP: 9 EST: 2008
SQ FT: 11,000
SALES (est): 723.8K **Privately Held**
WEB: www.brittenmetalworks.com
SIC: **7692** 3465 Automotive welding; automotive stampings

(G-16630)
BRITTEN WOODWORKS INC
2322 Cass Rd (49684-9147)
PHONE.................................231 275-5457
Paul Britten, *President*
Michael Bean, *Vice Pres*
EMP: 17 EST: 2015
SALES (est): 2MM **Privately Held**
WEB: www.brittenwoodworks.com
SIC: **2431** Interior & ornamental woodwork & trim

(G-16631)
BRYS WINERY LC
3309 Blue Water Rd (49686-8561)
PHONE.................................231 223-8446
Erick Outcalt, *Sales Mgr*
Aileen Brys, *Mng Member*
EMP: 7 EST: 2001
SALES (est): 990.9K **Privately Held**
WEB: www.brysestate.com
SIC: **2084** Wines

(G-16632)
BUILDERS PLBG SUP TRAVERSE CY
1610 W South Airport Rd (49686-4793)
PHONE.................................800 466-5160
EMP: 6 EST: 2016
SALES (est): 89.9K **Privately Held**
WEB: www.wittock.com
SIC: **3432** Plumbing fixture fittings & trim

(G-16633)
BURNETTE FOODS INC
2955 Kroupa Rd (49686-9731)
PHONE.................................231 223-4282
Jim Horton, *President*
Donald Shea, *Vice Pres*
Clint Warren, *Manager*
EMP: 15 EST: 1952
SQ FT: 28,000
SALES (est): 2.8MM **Privately Held**
SIC: **5148** 4222 0723 2099 Fruits, fresh; warehousing, cold storage or refrigerated; fruit crops market preparation services; food preparations

(G-16634)
BUSINESS NEWS
Also Called: Eyes Media
129 E Front St Unit 200 (49684-2659)
PHONE.................................231 929-7919
Luke Haase, *President*
Gayle Neu, *Editor*
EMP: 4 EST: 1996 **Privately Held**
WEB: www.tcbusinessnews.com
SIC: **2711** Newspapers, publishing & printing

(G-16635)
C R T & ASSOCIATES INC
806 Hastings St Ste H (49686-3400)
PHONE.................................231 946-1680
Doug Hamar, *Principal*
Karen Milatz, *Vice Pres*
EMP: 5 EST: 1999
SALES (est): 381.5K **Privately Held**
WEB: www.crt-a.com
SIC: **7372** Prepackaged software

(G-16636)
CABINETS BY ROBERT INC
Also Called: Cbr Industries
2774 Garfield Rd N Ste C (49686-5090)
PHONE.................................231 947-3261
Gary Godziebiewski, *President*
Chuck Goudey, *Foreman/Supr*
Robert Godziebiewski, *Shareholder*
EMP: 10 EST: 1978
SQ FT: 3,600
SALES (est): 1.9MM **Privately Held**
WEB: www.cabinetsbyrobert.com
SIC: **2434** Wood kitchen cabinets

(G-16637)
CAKE CONNECTION TC LLC
5730 Cherry Blossom Dr (49685-8369)
PHONE.................................231 943-3531
Sherry Keech, *Principal*
EMP: 5 EST: 2016
SALES (est): 111.1K **Privately Held**
WEB: www.cakeconnectiontc.com
SIC: **5461** 2051 Cakes; cakes, bakery: except frozen

(G-16638)
CANDLE FACTORY GRAND TRAVERSE
Also Called: Home Elements
301 W Grandview Pkwy (49684-2365)
P.O. Box 807 (49685-0807)
PHONE.................................231 946-2280
John Teichman, *Owner*
EMP: 6 EST: 1971
SALES (est): 566.9K **Privately Held**
WEB: www.candles.net
SIC: **5719** 3999 Housewares; candles

(G-16639)
CARBON IMPACT INC
2628 Garfield Rd N Ste 38 (49686-5089)
PHONE.................................231 929-8152
Pierre Pujos, *President*
EMP: 7 EST: 1994
SQ FT: 2,000
SALES (est): 533.5K **Privately Held**
WEB: www.carbonimpact.com
SIC: **3949** Arrows, archery

(G-16640)
CBBN RESTORATION LLC
967 E Commerce Dr Bldg 1 (49685-9371)
PHONE.................................231 220-9892
Barry Newton, *Mng Member*
EMP: 6 EST: 2020
SALES (est): 750K **Privately Held**
SIC: **1389** Construction, repair & dismantling services

(G-16641)
CENTURY INC (PA)
Also Called: Century-Sun Metal Treating
2410 W Aero Park Ct (49686-9102)
PHONE.................................231 947-6400
William G Janis, *President*
Charlie Janis, *General Mgr*
Keith Ford, *COO*
Chelsea Malinoff, *Project Mgr*
Pat Lott, *Opers Mgr*
◆ EMP: 170 EST: 1966
SQ FT: 76,000
SALES (est): 34.7MM **Privately Held**
WEB: www.centinc.com
SIC: **3544** 3398 3399 3559 Special dies, tools, jigs & fixtures; metal heat treating; powder, metal; plastics working machinery; machine tools, metal forming type

(G-16642)
CENTURY INC
Century Rollforming
2410 W Aero Park Ct (49686-9102)
PHONE.................................231 946-7500
Daniel Olsen, *Engineer*
Chris Darelston, *Branch Mgr*
EMP: 8
SALES (corp-wide): 34.7MM **Privately Held**
WEB: www.century-sun.com
SIC: **3544** 3545 Special dies, tools, jigs & fixtures; tools & accessories for machine tools
PA: Century, Inc.
2410 W Aero Park Ct
Traverse City MI 49686
231 947-6400

(G-16643)
CERNY INDUSTRIES LLC
Also Called: Strata Design
1645 Park Dr (49686-4701)
P.O. Box 6250 (49696-6250)
PHONE.................................231 929-2140
David Hill, *Manager*
Tyler Cerny,
EMP: 25 EST: 1988
SQ FT: 32,000
SALES (est): 3.6MM **Privately Held**
SIC: **2522** Cabinets, office: except wood

(G-16644)
CF MANUFACTURING LLC
3028 Keystone Rd N (49686-8104)
PHONE.................................231 409-9468
Rick Flees, *Principal*
EMP: 4 EST: 2016
SALES (est): 197.5K **Privately Held**
WEB: www.cfmfgtc.com
SIC: **3999** Manufacturing industries

(G-16645)
CHARLES A SPECIALTIES LLC
2694 Garfield Rd N Ste 28 (49686-5177)
PHONE.................................231 946-3389
Charles Svec, *Principal*
EMP: 6 EST: 2014
SALES (est): 129.9K **Privately Held**
SIC: **2431** Millwork

(G-16646)
CHATEAU GRAND TRAVERS LTD
Also Called: Grand Traverse Vineyards
12239 Center Rd (49686-8558)
PHONE.................................231 223-7355
Edward L O'Keefe Jr, *CEO*
Edward L O'Keefe III, *President*
Tom Simmonds, *Supervisor*
EMP: 4 EST: 1975
SQ FT: 10,000
SALES (est): 662.3K
SALES (corp-wide): 2.5MM **Privately Held**
SIC: **2084** Wines
PA: O'keefe Centre, Ltd.
12239 Center Rd
Traverse City MI 49686
231 223-7355

(G-16647)
CHATEAU OPERATIONS LTD
Also Called: Chateau Chantal
15900 Rue De Vin (49686-9379)
PHONE.................................231 223-4110
Robert Begin, *CEO*
Terrie McClelland, *Controller*
Sarah West, *Accounting Mgr*
Christine Raymond, *Marketing Mgr*
Kyle Brownley, *Marketing Staff*
▲ EMP: 34 EST: 1991
SQ FT: 11,000
SALES (est): 4.8MM **Privately Held**
WEB: www.chateauchantal.com
SIC: **0172** 2084 5921 7011 Grapes; wines; wine; bed & breakfast inn

(G-16648)
CHERRY CENTRAL COOPERATIVE INC (PA)
1771 N Us Highway 31 S (49685-8748)
P.O. Box 988 (49685-0988)
PHONE.................................231 946-1860
Melanie Laperriere, *President*
George Wright, *Corp Secy*
Rick Luther, *COO*
Roy Hackert, *Vice Pres*
Shawn Walter, *Opers Mgr*
◆ EMP: 30 EST: 1973
SQ FT: 15,000
SALES (est): 47.5MM **Privately Held**
WEB: www.cherrycentral.com
SIC: **2033** Canned fruits & specialties

(G-16649)
CHERRY CONE LLC
240 E Front St (49684-2526)
PHONE.................................231 944-1036
Joe Welsh,
EMP: 5 EST: 2014
SQ FT: 1,965
SALES (est): 399.7K **Privately Held**
SIC: **2052** Cones, ice cream

(G-16650)
CHERRY GROWERS INC
Also Called: Cherry Growers Plant 2
9440 S Center Hwy (49684-9557)
PHONE.................................231 947-2502
EMP: 5
SALES (est): 250.3K
SALES (corp-wide): 24MM **Privately Held**
SIC: **2037** 2033 Freezer Plant
PA: Cherry Growers, Inc.
6331 Us Highway 31
Grawn MI 48009
231 276-9241

(G-16651)
CHERRYFLEX INC
2811 Cass Rd Ste C1 (49684-6954)
PHONE.................................888 947-4047
EMP: 7
SALES (est): 314.1K **Privately Held**
SIC: **2023** Mfg Dry/Evaporated Dairy Products

(G-16652)
CIMA ENERGY LP
125 S Park St Ste 450 (49684-3605)
PHONE.................................231 941-0633
Stephen Trippe, *Manager*
EMP: 4 **Privately Held**
WEB: www.cima-energy.com
SIC: **1311** Crude petroleum & natural gas
HQ: Cima Energy, Lp
1221 Mckinney St Ste 3700
Houston TX 77010

(G-16653)
CLARK MANUFACTURING COMPANY
2485 Aero Park Dr (49686-9119)
PHONE.................................231 946-5110
Robert Milliron, *President*
Cameron Fuller, *Vice Pres*
Brian Walter, *Vice Pres*
Wendy Gauthier, *Accountant*
Sandy Goodman, *Office Mgr*
EMP: 100
SQ FT: 60,000
SALES (est): 16.7MM **Privately Held**
WEB: www.clarkmfg.com
SIC: **3599** Machine shop, jobbing & repair

(G-16654)
CLOVER INDUSTRIES INC
1424 International Dr (49686-8751)
PHONE.................................231 929-1660
Brian J Molloy Jr, *Principal*
EMP: 6 EST: 1994
SALES (est): 58.9K **Privately Held**
SIC: **3999** Atomizers, toiletry

(G-16655)
COCA-COLA REFRESHMENTS USA INC
1031 Hastings St (49686-3444)
PHONE.................................231 947-4150
Charlie Raymond, *Manager*
EMP: 6
SALES (corp-wide): 33B **Publicly Held**
WEB: www.coca-cola.com
SIC: **2086** Bottled & canned soft drinks
HQ: Coca-Cola Refreshments Usa, Inc.
2500 Windy Ridge Pkwy Se
Atlanta GA 30339
770 989-3000

GEOGRAPHIC SECTION

Traverse City - Grand Traverse County (G-16682)

(G-16656)
COGNISYS INC
459 Hughes Dr (49696-8255)
PHONE..................................231 943-2425
Paul Dezeeuw, *President*
Matt Cardwell, *Admin Sec*
EMP: 5 **EST:** 2008
SALES (est): 719.2K **Privately Held**
WEB: www.cognisys-inc.com
SIC: 3861 5963 Photographic instruments, electronic; direct selling establishments

(G-16657)
COMET ENERGY SERVICES LLC
Also Called: Oil Field Investments Limited
954 Business Park Dr (49686-8763)
PHONE..................................231 933-3600
T D Provins, *Mng Member*
EMP: 5 **EST:** 1999
SQ FT: 1,000
SALES (est): 962.1K **Privately Held**
SIC: 1381 Drilling oil & gas wells

(G-16658)
CONE DRIVE OPERATIONS INC (HQ)
Also Called: Cone Drive Gearing Solutions
240 E Twelfth St (49684-3269)
P.O. Box 272 (49685-0272)
PHONE..................................231 946-8410
Kurt Gamelin, *CEO*
Vicki Lardie, *General Mgr*
Michael King, *Vice Pres*
Tom Peters, *Opers Staff*
Shayne Gatzke, *Mfg Staff*
◆ **EMP:** 150 **EST:** 1986
SQ FT: 135,000
SALES (est): 70.7MM
SALES (corp-wide): 3.5B **Publicly Held**
WEB: www.timken.com
SIC: 3566 Speed changers (power transmission equipment), except auto
PA: The Timken Company
4500 Mount Pleasant St Nw
North Canton OH 44720
234 262-3000

(G-16659)
COOPER PUBLISHING GROUP LLC
251 Knollwood Dr (49686-1856)
PHONE..................................231 933-9958
Joanne Cooper,
Irving Butch Cooper,
EMP: 5 **EST:** 1985
SQ FT: 3,000
SALES (est): 320K **Privately Held**
WEB: www.cooperpublishinggroup.com
SIC: 2731 Textbooks: publishing only, not printed on site

(G-16660)
COPY CENTRAL INC
Also Called: Printing Place, The
314 E Eighth St (49684-2540)
PHONE..................................231 941-2298
Mark Bonter, *President*
Rhonda Carlson, *Manager*
Mark Lemley, *Manager*
Pam Bonter, *Admin Sec*
EMP: 7 **EST:** 1989
SQ FT: 4,000
SALES (est): 530.1K **Privately Held**
WEB: www.copycentraltc.com
SIC: 7334 7374 2752 3993 Blueprinting service; computer processing services; offset & photolithographic printing; signs & advertising specialties; typesetting; bookbinding & related work

(G-16661)
CORE ENERGY LLC
1011 Noteware Dr (49686-8184)
PHONE..................................231 946-2419
Robert Mannes, *CEO*
Allen Modroo, *Partner*
Brian Dorr, *COO*
Rick Pardini, *Vice Pres*
Randy Odell, *Foreman/Supr*
EMP: 6 **EST:** 2002
SALES (est): 1.4MM **Privately Held**
SIC: 1382 Oil & gas exploration services

(G-16662)
COX MACHINE LLC
2823 Cass Rd Ste F1 (49684-7139)
PHONE..................................269 953-5446
Nathan Cox, *Principal*
EMP: 14 **EST:** 2016
SALES (est): 1MM **Privately Held**
WEB: www.coxmach.com
SIC: 3599 Machine shop, jobbing & repair; machine & other job shop work; electrical discharge machining (EDM)

(G-16663)
CPM ACQUISITION CORP
2412 W Aero Park Ct (49686-9102)
PHONE..................................231 947-6400
EMP: 9
SALES (corp-wide): 215MM **Privately Held**
WEB: www.cpmroskamp.com
SIC: 3523 3355 Farm machinery & equipment; extrusion ingot, aluminum: made in rolling mills
HQ: Cpm Acquisition Corp.
2975 Airline Cir
Waterloo IA 50703
319 232-8444

(G-16664)
CPM ACQUISITION CORP
Also Called: CPM Century Extrusion
2412 W Aero Park Ct (49686-9102)
PHONE..................................231 947-6400
Cliff Anderson, *President*
Butch Cook, *Senior Buyer*
Tom Urban, *Regl Sales Mgr*
Bill Goehman, *Manager*
▲ **EMP:** 85 **EST:** 2006
SALES (est): 8.4MM **Privately Held**
SIC: 3451 Screw machine products

(G-16665)
CRM INC
495 W South Airport Rd (49686-4842)
PHONE..................................231 947-0304
Clare Ray, *President*
Mark Ray, *Vice Pres*
Fred Belles, *Manager*
EMP: 90 **EST:** 1984
SQ FT: 42,000
SALES (est): 6MM **Privately Held**
WEB: www.crminctc.com
SIC: 3479 Coating of metals & formed products

(G-16666)
CROWN EQUIPMENT CORPORATION
Also Called: Crown Lift Trucks
903 Lynch Dr Ste 103 (49686-4800)
PHONE..................................616 530-3000
Eric McNutt, *Manager*
EMP: 6
SALES (corp-wide): 3.6B **Privately Held**
WEB: www.crown.com
SIC: 3537 Lift trucks, industrial: fork, platform, straddle, etc.
PA: Crown Equipment Corporation
44 S Washington St
New Bremen OH 45869
419 629-2311

(G-16667)
DANIEL SNDERSON CSTM CABINETRY
5148 Stonefield Dr (49684-9725)
PHONE..................................231 421-5743
Daniel L Sanderson, *Administration*
EMP: 5 **EST:** 2010
SALES (est): 61.1K **Privately Held**
SIC: 2434 Wood kitchen cabinets

(G-16668)
DIAMONDBCK-DRECTIONAL DRLG LLC
Also Called: Directional Drilling Contrs
2122 S M 37 (49685-8061)
P.O. Box 6156 (49696-6156)
PHONE..................................231 943-3000
EMP: 15
SALES (est): 2MM **Privately Held**
SIC: 1381 Oil/Gas Well Drilling

(G-16669)
DISCOVERY MAP
958 Shamrock Ln (49696-8743)
PHONE..................................231 421-1466
Rob Wallace, *Principal*
EMP: 5 **EST:** 2016
SALES (est): 46.3K **Privately Held**
WEB: www.discoverymap.com
SIC: 2741 Maps: publishing & printing

(G-16670)
DOUG MURDICKS FUDGE INC
4500 N Us Highway 31 N (49686-3761)
PHONE..................................231 938-2330
Doug Murdick, *Owner*
EMP: 6
SALES (corp-wide): 856.4K **Privately Held**
WEB: www.murdicksfudge.com
SIC: 2064 5441 Fudge (candy); candy
PA: Doug Murdick's Fudge Inc
116 E Front St
Traverse City MI 49684
231 947-4841

(G-16671)
DRINK BRANDERS LLC
1015 Noteware Dr (49686-8109)
PHONE..................................231 668-4121
Stephen Thompson, *Principal*
EMP: 16 **EST:** 2017
SALES (est): 1.9MM **Privately Held**
WEB: www.drinkbranders.com
SIC: 2759 Screen printing

(G-16672)
DTE GAS & OIL COMPANY
Also Called: MCN Oil & Gas
10691 E Carter Rd Ste 201 (49684-5499)
PHONE..................................231 995-4000
Richard Redmond, *President*
EMP: 10 **EST:** 1992
SQ FT: 15,000
SALES (est): 311.6K **Privately Held**
SIC: 1382 Oil & gas exploration services

(G-16673)
DUNLOP DREAMS CANDLES
1112 Rose St (49686-4235)
PHONE..................................231 633-4064
Jamie Dunlop, *Principal*
EMP: 4 **EST:** 2017
SALES (est): 39.6K **Privately Held**
SIC: 3999 Candles

(G-16674)
DYNATECT MANUFACTURING IN
2101 Precision Dr (49686-9239)
PHONE..................................231 947-4124
EMP: 12 **EST:** 2017
SALES (est): 273.3K **Privately Held**
WEB: www.dynatect.com
SIC: 3999 Manufacturing industries

(G-16675)
ELECTRO-OPTICS TECHNOLOGY INC (PA)
Also Called: Eot
3340 Parkland Ct (49686-8723)
P.O. Box 987 (49685-0987)
PHONE..................................231 935-4044
David Scerbak, *President*
Ben Nelson, *Vice Pres*
Michael Torrance, *Vice Pres*
Lisa S Long, *Purchases*
Lisa Long, *Purchasing*
▲ **EMP:** 69 **EST:** 1980
SQ FT: 15,000
SALES (est): 12.1MM **Privately Held**
WEB: www.eotech.com
SIC: 3827 Optical instruments & lenses

(G-16676)
ELMERS CRANE AND DOZER INC (PA)
Also Called: Elmers Construction Engrg
3600 Rennie School Rd (49685-9170)
P.O. Box 6150 (49686-6150)
PHONE..................................231 943-3443
Russell L Broad, *President*
Gary Holcombe, *Corp Secy*
Tanya Broad, *Vice Pres*
Todd Broad, *Vice Pres*
Troy Broad, *Vice Pres*
EMP: 119 **EST:** 1977

SQ FT: 12,000
SALES (est): 48.8MM **Privately Held**
WEB: www.teamelmers.com
SIC: 1771 1794 1611 3273 Driveway, parking lot & blacktop contractors; excavation work; highway & street paving contractor; ready-mixed concrete; asphalt paving mixtures & blocks; construction sand & gravel

(G-16677)
EMERSON GEOPHYSICAL LLC
3819 4 Mile Rd N (49686-9344)
PHONE..................................231 943-1400
Mitchell Pasinski, *Mng Member*
EMP: 20 **EST:** 2012
SALES (est): 1.1MM **Privately Held**
WEB: www.emersongeophysical.com
SIC: 1382 Seismograph surveys

(G-16678)
ENSIGN EMBLEM LTD (PA)
Also Called: Ensign Technical Services
1746 Keane Dr (49696-8257)
PHONE..................................231 946-7703
Gayle M Zreliak, *President*
John Matthews, *COO*
Toni Butkovich, *Opers Mgr*
EMP: 85 **EST:** 1974
SQ FT: 20,000
SALES (est): 13.4MM **Privately Held**
WEB: www.ensignemblem.com
SIC: 2395 Embroidery products, except schiffli machine

(G-16679)
EXPRESS PUBLICATIONS INC
Also Called: Northern Express Publications
135 W State St (49684-2403)
P.O. Box 4020 (49685-4020)
PHONE..................................231 947-8787
Robert Downes, *President*
Katy McCain, *Sales Staff*
Jamie Kauffold, *Manager*
EMP: 10 **EST:** 1991
SALES (est): 619.1K **Privately Held**
SIC: 2711 Newspapers, publishing & printing

(G-16680)
FASTSIGNS INTERNATIONAL INC
1420 Trade Center Dr (49696-8917)
PHONE..................................231 941-0300
Omar Rahaman, *Partner*
Matt Harris, *General Mgr*
Jason Haviland, *General Mgr*
Shishir Mehta, *General Mgr*
Rhonda Pullis, *General Mgr*
EMP: 4
SALES (corp-wide): 36.8MM **Privately Held**
WEB: www.fastsigns.com
SIC: 3993 Signs & advertising specialties
PA: Fastsigns International, Inc.
2542 Highlander Way
Carrollton TX 75006
888 285-5935

(G-16681)
FEDERAL SCREW WORKS
2270 Traversefield Dr (49686-9251)
PHONE..................................231 922-9500
W T Zurschiede Jr, *Chairman*
Katie Groesbeck, *Controller*
Scott Rozema, *Accountant*
EMP: 8
SALES (corp-wide): 78.9MM **Privately Held**
WEB: www.federalscrewworks.com
SIC: 3452 3325 Bolts, metal; steel foundries
PA: Federal Screw Works
34846 Goddard Rd
Romulus MI 48174
734 941-4211

(G-16682)
FINISHING TOUCHES BY ODELL
7138 Lake Leelanau Dr (49684-9536)
PHONE..................................231 947-3080
Dan O'Dell, *Owner*
EMP: 6 **EST:** 2016

Traverse City - Grand Traverse County (G-16683) GEOGRAPHIC SECTION

SALES (est): 120.9K Privately Held
WEB: www.tubworks.net
SIC: 3732 Non-motorized boat, building & repairing

(G-16683)
FLOODWELL PRINT STUDIO
903 Woodmere Ave (49686-4244)
PHONE................................231 943-2930
Chad Bailey, *Principal*
EMP: 4 EST: 2016
SALES (est): 147.8K Privately Held
WEB: www.floodwell.com
SIC: 2752 Commercial printing, lithographic

(G-16684)
FOOD FOR THOUGHT INC
7738 N Long Lake Rd (49685-8226)
PHONE................................231 326-5444
Gregory Young, *President*
Lesley Sly, *Manager*
EMP: 20 EST: 1995
SALES (est): 4.3MM Privately Held
WEB: www.foodforthought.net
SIC: 2033 Fruits & fruit products in cans, jars, etc.

(G-16685)
FOREWORD MAGAZINE INC
425 Boardman Ave (49684-2687)
PHONE................................231 933-3699
Victoria Sutherland, *CEO*
Matt Sutherland, *Manager*
Allyce Amidon, *Assoc Editor*
EMP: 10 EST: 1998
SALES (est): 1.3MM Privately Held
WEB: www.forewordreviews.com
SIC: 2721 2731 Magazines: publishing only, not printed on site; book publishing

(G-16686)
FOREWORD MAGAZINE INC
413 E Eighth St (49686-2626)
PHONE................................231 933-3699
EMP: 6 EST: 2019
SALES (est): 325.1K Privately Held
WEB: www.forewordreviews.com
SIC: 2741 Miscellaneous publishing

(G-16687)
FOREWORD REVIEWS
425 Boardman Ave (49684-2687)
PHONE................................231 933-5397
Stacy Price, *Executive*
EMP: 5 EST: 2016
SALES (est): 100.3K Privately Held
WEB: www.forewordreviews.com
SIC: 2741 Miscellaneous publishing

(G-16688)
FORKARDT INC
Also Called: Forkardt North America
2155 Traversefield Dr (49686-8699)
PHONE................................231 995-8300
Richard L Simons, *President*
Glen Scarbrough, *Engineer*
Philipp Lopane, *Sales Mgr*
Brian Braden, *Regl Sales Mgr*
Bob Holtz, *Sales Staff*
EMP: 30 EST: 1969
SALES (est): 8.8MM Privately Held
WEB: www.forkardt.com
SIC: 3545 Machine tool accessories

(G-16689)
FORWARD INKING DESIGN & PRINT
404 Hughes Dr (49696-8244)
PHONE................................231 714-8646
EMP: 5 EST: 2014
SALES (est): 124.2K Privately Held
WEB: www.forwardinking.com
SIC: 2752 Commercial printing, lithographic

(G-16690)
FULTZ MANUFACTURING INC
1631 Park Dr Ste A (49686-4772)
PHONE................................231 947-5801
Charles Fultz, *President*
Dennis Bartlett, *Manager*
Jacqueline Fultz, *Admin Sec*
EMP: 7 EST: 1973
SQ FT: 19,000
SALES (est): 931.5K Privately Held
WEB: www.fultzmfg.com
SIC: 2493 Reconstituted wood products

(G-16691)
G F INC
Also Called: Glynn, Mark, Builder
1032 Woodmere Ave Ste B (49686-4265)
PHONE................................231 946-5330
Angela Glynn, *President*
Jim Swartout, *Vice Pres*
EMP: 7 EST: 1991
SQ FT: 8,000
SALES (est): 270.6K Privately Held
SIC: 2431 Millwork

(G-16692)
GARY CORK INCORPORATED (PA)
Also Called: Snap Quickprint
806 S Garfield Ave Ste B (49686-3430)
PHONE................................231 946-1061
Gary Cork, *President*
EMP: 5 EST: 1979
SQ FT: 1,200
SALES (est): 534.5K Privately Held
SIC: 2752 7334 Commercial printing, offset; photocopying & duplicating services

(G-16693)
GEOMEMBRANE RESEARCH
1567 W South Airport Rd (49686-4702)
PHONE................................231 943-2266
Daniel S Rohe, *Principal*
EMP: 11 EST: 2015
SALES (est): 201.3K Privately Held
SIC: 2821 Plastics materials & resins

(G-16694)
GET IN GAME MARKETING LLC
Also Called: Threads
2322 Cass Rd (49684-9147)
PHONE................................231 846-1976
Joshua Ludka, *Mng Member*
EMP: 8 EST: 2012
SALES (est): 602.1K Privately Held
WEB: www.getinthegamemarketing.com
SIC: 2399 Banners, pennants & flags

(G-16695)
GODIN TOOL INC
466 Hughes Dr (49696-8255)
P.O. Box 6246 (49696-6246)
PHONE................................231 946-2210
Allen F Godin, *President*
EMP: 7 EST: 1988
SALES (est): 566.4K Privately Held
WEB: www.godintool.com
SIC: 3541 Machine tools, metal cutting type

(G-16696)
GOODWILL INDS NTHRN MICH INC
Also Called: Goodwill Inn
1329 S Division St (49684-4427)
PHONE................................231 922-4890
Lois Lannin, *Branch Mgr*
EMP: 9
SALES (corp-wide): 15.5MM Privately Held
WEB: www.goodwillnmi.org
SIC: 5932 8331 2431 8322 Used merchandise stores; sheltered workshop; millwork; meal delivery program; settlement house
PA: Goodwill Industries Of Northern Michigan, Inc.
2279 S Airport Rd W
Traverse City MI 49684
231 922-4805

(G-16697)
GRAND TRAVERSE CANVAS WORKS
3975 3 Mile Rd N (49686-9164)
PHONE................................231 947-3140
Mary Wodzien, *President*
Larry Wodzien, *Vice Pres*
EMP: 12 EST: 1982
SQ FT: 6,000
SALES (est): 652.3K Privately Held
WEB: www.gtcanvas.com
SIC: 2394 7641 Awnings, fabric: made from purchased materials; convertible tops, canvas or boat: from purchased materials; reupholstery

(G-16698)
GRAND TRAVERSE CONTINUOUS INC
1661 Park Dr (49686-4701)
PHONE................................231 941-5400
Walter Gallagher, *President*
Daryl Richardson, *IT/INT Sup*
Ross Hazelton, *Representative*
EMP: 22 EST: 1980
SQ FT: 10,000
SALES (est): 2MM Privately Held
WEB: www.gtcontinuous.com
SIC: 2761 2759 2752 Manifold business forms; commercial printing; commercial printing, lithographic

(G-16699)
GRAND TRAVERSE MACHINE CO
1247 Boon St (49686-4349)
PHONE................................231 946-8006
Mike Alfonso, *President*
Dave Rahe, *Vice Pres*
Scott Larigan, *Business Anlyst*
Richard Barnes, *CIO*
Chris Laundry, *Prgrmr*
EMP: 65 EST: 1966
SQ FT: 21,400
SALES (est): 9.1MM Privately Held
WEB: www.gtmachine.com
SIC: 3599 Machine shop, jobbing & repair

(G-16700)
GRAND TRAVERSE REELS INC
Also Called: Grand Traverse Container
1050 Business Park Dr (49686-8372)
PHONE................................231 946-1057
Brian Blain, *General Mgr*
Thomas Schofield, *Principal*
Mike Chereskin, *Vice Pres*
Karyn Oncu, *Vice Pres*
Tanya Flores, *CFO*
EMP: 104 EST: 1995
SQ FT: 80,000
SALES (est): 16.5MM Privately Held
WEB: www.gtcontainer.com
SIC: 2653 Boxes, corrugated: made from purchased materials

(G-16701)
GRAND TRAVERSE STAMPING CO
1677 Park Dr (49686-4750)
PHONE................................231 929-4215
Fred Militz, *President*
Kenneth A Batterbee, *Principal*
Robert J Fair Jr, *Principal*
Richard J Lauer, *Principal*
John J Murray, *Corp Secy*
EMP: 28 EST: 1986
SALES (est): 747.6K Privately Held
WEB: www.aeesinc.com
SIC: 3469 Stamping metal for the trade

(G-16702)
GRAND TRAVERSE TOOL INC
396 Hughes Dr (49696-8255)
PHONE................................231 929-4743
Jeff Gothrup, *President*
EMP: 5 EST: 1995
SQ FT: 2,000
SALES (est): 119.8K Privately Held
WEB: www.grandtraversetool.com
SIC: 2821 Molding compounds, plastics

(G-16703)
GREAT LAKES BATH & BODY INC
110 E Front St (49684-2509)
P.O. Box 924 (49685-0924)
PHONE................................231 421-9160
Lynn Rodenroth, *Principal*
EMP: 4 EST: 2012
SALES (est): 286.4K Privately Held
WEB: www.greatlakesbathandbody.com
SIC: 7532 2841 Body shop, automotive; detergents, synthetic organic or inorganic alkaline

(G-16704)
GREAT LAKES FORGE INC
Also Called: Grand Traverse Forging & Steel
2465 N Aero Park Ct (49686-9262)
PHONE................................231 947-4931
Peter Jones, *President*
Greg Behrens, *Vice Pres*
Sherry Steffen-Detwile, *Office Mgr*
Helen Zakrzewski, *Manager*
▲ EMP: 9
SQ FT: 22,000
SALES (est): 2.5MM Privately Held
WEB: www.glforge.com
SIC: 3462 Iron & steel forgings

(G-16705)
GREAT LAKES STAINLESS INC
1305 Stepke Ct (49685-9331)
PHONE................................231 943-7648
Terry Berden, *CEO*
Michael De Bruyn, *President*
Rayma Berden, *Corp Secy*
Peter Berden, *Vice Pres*
Todd Sears, *Design Engr*
EMP: 30 EST: 1996
SQ FT: 50,000
SALES (est): 8.2MM Privately Held
WEB: www.greatlakesstainless.com
SIC: 3441 Fabricated structural metal

(G-16706)
GREAT LAKES WELD LLC
889 S East Silver Lake Rd (49685-9340)
PHONE................................231 943-4180
Shawn Boyd, *Mng Member*
EMP: 5 EST: 1998
SALES (est): 299.6K Privately Held
WEB: www.greatlakesweld.com
SIC: 7692 7699 Welding repair; cash register repair

(G-16707)
GUEST PUBLICATIONS LLC
3804 Morningside Dr (49684-2913)
PHONE................................231 651-9281
EMP: 4 EST: 2016
SALES (est): 37.5K Privately Held
SIC: 2741 Miscellaneous publishing

(G-16708)
H AND M LUBE DBA JLUBE
529 W Fourteenth St (49684-4042)
PHONE................................231 929-1197
Moses Nasser, *Managing Prtnr*
EMP: 4 EST: 2013
SALES (est): 435.7K Privately Held
WEB: www.jlubeservices.com
SIC: 2992 Lubricating oils & greases

(G-16709)
H M DAY SIGNS INC
233 E Twelfth St (49684-3215)
PHONE................................231 946-7132
Harry M Day Jr, *President*
Patricia Day, *Treasurer*
EMP: 6 EST: 1919
SALES (est): 600K Privately Held
WEB: www.daysignstc.com
SIC: 7374 3993 1799 Computer graphics service; signs & advertising specialties; neon signs; sign installation & maintenance

(G-16710)
HARBOR KITCHEN & BATH LLC
987 S Forestlane Dr (49686-4345)
PHONE................................231 624-8060
EMP: 4 EST: 2018
SALES (est): 91.2K Privately Held
SIC: 2434 Wood kitchen cabinets

(G-16711)
HILLSHIRE BRANDS COMPANY
2314 Sybrant Rd (49684-9151)
PHONE................................231 947-2100
Paul Clark, *Plant Mgr*
Randy Tucker, *Branch Mgr*
James Taber, *Supervisor*
EMP: 7
SALES (corp-wide): 47B Publicly Held
WEB: www.tysonfoods.com
SIC: 2013 Sausages & other prepared meats

HQ: The Hillshire Brands Company
400 S Jefferson St Ste 1n
Chicago IL 60607
312 614-6000

(G-16712)
HOBART BROTHERS LLC
Also Called: Maxal Hobart Brothers
1631 International Dr (49686-8964)
PHONE..................................231 933-1234
Sundaran Magarajan, *President*
EMP: 5
SALES (corp-wide): 12.5B **Publicly Held**
WEB: www.hobartbrothers.com
SIC: 3548 3537 Welding apparatus; industrial trucks & tractors
HQ: Hobart Brothers Llc
101 Trade Sq E
Troy OH 45373
937 332-5439

(G-16713)
HOMES BRACELET
516 E Eighth St (49686-2629)
PHONE..................................231 499-9402
Erik Akerley, *Principal*
EMP: 4 **EST:** 2018
SALES (est): 86.3K **Privately Held**
WEB: www.homesbracelets.com
SIC: 3961 Bracelets, except precious metal

(G-16714)
HOMES BRACELET LLC
807 Airport Access Rd Ste (49686)
PHONE..................................231 463-9808
EMP: 5 **EST:** 2019
SALES (est): 339.9K **Privately Held**
WEB: www.homesbracelets.com
SIC: 3961 Bracelets, except precious metal

(G-16715)
HORIZONTAL LIFT TECHNOLOGIES
1503 Garfield Rd N (49696-1111)
PHONE..................................231 421-9696
Bill Quinlan, *President*
EMP: 6 **EST:** 2018
SALES (est): 230.7K **Privately Held**
WEB: www.horizontallifttechnologies.com
SIC: 1382 Oil & gas exploration services

(G-16716)
HOWARD ENERGY CO INC (PA)
125 S Park St Ste 250 (49684-3601)
P.O. Box 949 (49685-0949)
PHONE..................................231 995-7850
Richard Newell, *Admin Sec*
Jeanie Northern, *Executive Asst*
EMP: 28 **EST:** 1983
SQ FT: 12,000
SALES (est): 2.8MM **Privately Held**
WEB: www.howardenergy.com
SIC: 1382 4924 4922 Oil & gas exploration services; natural gas distribution; storage, natural gas

(G-16717)
HSS INDUSTRIES INC
2464 Cass Rd (49684-9148)
P.O. Box 2060 (49685-2060)
PHONE..................................231 946-6101
Herman Hinsenkamp, *President*
Darren Hinsenkamp, *Vice Pres*
▲ **EMP:** 20 **EST:** 1982
SQ FT: 16,000
SALES (est): 2.7MM **Privately Held**
WEB: www.hsspostal.com
SIC: 2542 Locker boxes, postal service: except wood; cabinets: show, display or storage: except wood

(G-16718)
IDEL LLC
1315 Woodmere Ave (49686-4308)
PHONE..................................231 929-3195
Leonard Korson,
EMP: 7 **EST:** 1994
SQ FT: 7,500
SALES (est): 633.4K **Privately Held**
WEB: www.idelllc.com
SIC: 3544 Special dies & tools

(G-16719)
ILLINOIS TOOL WORKS INC
Also Called: I T W Workholding
2155 Traversefield Dr (49686-8699)
P.O. Box 547 (49685-0547)
PHONE..................................231 947-5755
Chuck Delonghi, *Manager*
EMP: 5
SALES (corp-wide): 12.5B **Publicly Held**
WEB: www.itw.com
SIC: 3545 Machine tool accessories
PA: Illinois Tool Works Inc.
155 Harlem Ave
Glenview IL 60025
847 724-7500

(G-16720)
ILLINOIS TOOL WORKS INC
Forkardt North America
2155 Traversefield Dr (49686-8699)
PHONE..................................231 947-5755
EMP: 6
SALES (corp-wide): 14.3B **Publicly Held**
SIC: 3545 Mfg Machine Tool Accessories
PA: Illinois Tool Works Inc.
155 Harlem Ave
Glenview IL 60025
847 724-7500

(G-16721)
IN THE STARS CANDLES
226 E Eleventh St (49684-3212)
PHONE..................................231 590-7407
Heather Halt, *Principal*
EMP: 4 **EST:** 2016
SALES (est): 89.2K **Privately Held**
SIC: 3999 Candles

(G-16722)
INSTANT CAR CREDIT INC
3650 N Us Highway 31 S (49684-4441)
PHONE..................................231 922-8180
Benton Jacobson, *Principal*
EMP: 7 **EST:** 2007
SALES (est): 221.9K **Privately Held**
WEB: www.northpointmotors.com
SIC: 2752 Commercial printing, lithographic

(G-16723)
INSTANT FRAMER
322 S Union St (49684-2535)
PHONE..................................231 947-8908
Ken Meyer, *Owner*
EMP: 4 **EST:** 1988
SALES (est): 288.5K **Privately Held**
SIC: 2752 Commercial printing, lithographic

(G-16724)
INTEGRITY SPRAY FOAM LLC
3601 Bluff Rd (49686)
PHONE..................................231 631-6084
EMP: 4 **EST:** 2019
SALES (est): 90.3K **Privately Held**
WEB: www.integrityspray.com
SIC: 3086 Insulation or cushioning material, foamed plastic

(G-16725)
INTERACTIVE AERIAL INC
2662 Cass Rd Ste B (49684-9150)
PHONE..................................231 645-6007
Christian Smith, *CEO*
Pierce Thomas, *COO*
Christopher Schmidt, *Chief Engr*
Justin Bensten, *Development*
Justin Bentsen, *CIO*
EMP: 5 **EST:** 2016
SQ FT: 2,000
SALES (est): 613.3K **Privately Held**
WEB: www.interactiveaerial.com
SIC: 3812 Aircraft/aerospace flight instruments & guidance systems

(G-16726)
JADE TOOL INC
891 Duell Rd (49686-4859)
PHONE..................................231 946-7710
John A Korson, *President*
Dora Korson, *Corp Secy*
Don Dowker, *Engineer*
Jason Kent, *Engineer*
EMP: 20 **EST:** 1982
SQ FT: 6,150

SALES (est): 1.1MM **Privately Held**
WEB: www.jadetool.com
SIC: 3545 Tool holders; boring machine attachments (machine tool accessories); tools & accessories for machine tools

(G-16727)
JANTEC INCORPORATED
1777 Northern Star Dr (49696-4339)
PHONE..................................231 941-4339
Ronald Sommerfield, *President*
Robert Leusby, *Vice Pres*
EMP: 20 **EST:** 1979
SQ FT: 20,000
SALES (est): 2.2MM **Privately Held**
WEB: www.jantec.com
SIC: 3535 Conveyors & conveying equipment

(G-16728)
JENKINS GROUP INC
Also Called: Axiom Business Book Awards
1129 Woodmere Ave Ste B (49686-4275)
PHONE..................................231 933-4954
Jerrold Jenkins, *CEO*
Jim Kalajian, *President*
Rachel Jones, *Marketing Staff*
▲ **EMP:** 9 **EST:** 1993
SQ FT: 2,400
SALES (est): 2MM **Privately Held**
WEB: www.jenkinsgroupinc.com
SIC: 2731 2732 Book publishing; book printing

(G-16729)
JENTEES CUSTOM SCREEN PRTG LLC
Also Called: Jentees Custom Logo Gear
515 Wellington St (49686-2660)
PHONE..................................231 929-3610
Mark Jensen,
EMP: 10 **EST:** 1991
SQ FT: 4,000
SALES (est): 859.9K **Privately Held**
WEB: www.jentees.com
SIC: 2759 Screen printing

(G-16730)
JOHNSON-CLARK PRINTERS INC
Also Called: Prepress Services
1224 Centre St (49686-3491)
PHONE..................................231 947-6898
Sandy Henschell, *President*
Wayne Miller, *Vice Pres*
EMP: 10 **EST:** 1949
SQ FT: 9,000
SALES (est): 711.8K **Privately Held**
SIC: 2752 2759 Commercial printing, offset; letterpress printing

(G-16731)
JORDAN EXPLORATION CO LLC
1503 Garfield Rd N (49696-1111)
PHONE..................................231 935-4220
Bill Quinlan, *Vice Pres*
Tom Robb, *Opers Mgr*
Benjamin Brower, *VP Bus Dvlpt*
Bob Boeve, *CFO*
Jessica Fellows, *Accountant*
EMP: 42 **EST:** 1996
SALES (est): 8MM **Privately Held**
WEB: www.jordanex.com
SIC: 1311 Crude petroleum production

(G-16732)
KELLY OIL & GAS INC
303 S Union St Ofc C (49684-5775)
PHONE..................................231 929-0591
Robert K Robinson, *President*
Colleen Heron, *Corp Secy*
Madeline Robinson, *Vice Pres*
EMP: 8 **EST:** 1985
SQ FT: 1,200
SALES (est): 969.1K **Privately Held**
WEB: www.kellyoilandgas.com
SIC: 1311 Crude petroleum production

(G-16733)
KENNAMETAL INC
2879 Aero Park Dr (49686-8494)
PHONE..................................231 946-2100
Keith Kopriva, *Plant Mgr*
Doug Grove, *Mfg Mgr*
Kelly Stachnik, *Materials Mgr*
Sue Acha, *Purchasing*

Susan G Acha, *Purchasing*
EMP: 5
SALES (corp-wide): 1.8B **Publicly Held**
WEB: www.kennametal.com
SIC: 3545 Cutting tools for machine tools
PA: Kennametal Inc.
525 William Penn Pl # 3300
Pittsburgh PA 15219
412 248-8000

(G-16734)
KTC INDUSTRIES LLC
100 N Park St (49684-5700)
PHONE..................................989 838-0388
Wesley Crumby, *Principal*
EMP: 5 **EST:** 2018
SALES (est): 397.9K **Privately Held**
SIC: 3999 Manufacturing industries

(G-16735)
KWIKIE INC
Also Called: Traverse City Print & Copy
700 Boon St (49686-4301)
PHONE..................................231 946-9942
Anthony Casciani, *President*
Kathleen Casciani, *Vice Pres*
Carmen Casciani, *Treasurer*
EMP: 6 **EST:** 1996
SQ FT: 1,800
SALES (est): 325K **Privately Held**
WEB: www.tcprint-copy.com
SIC: 2752 7334 Commercial printing, offset; photocopying & duplicating services

(G-16736)
L & C ENTERPRISES INC
Also Called: Grand Traverse Crane
3876 Blair Townhall Rd (49685-9196)
PHONE..................................231 943-7787
Craig Derks, *President*
Nathan Derks, *Business Mgr*
Scott Dekryger, *Corp Secy*
Larry Derks, *Vice Pres*
EMP: 4 **EST:** 1964
SQ FT: 23,000
SALES (est): 346.3K **Privately Held**
SIC: 7699 3536 Industrial machinery & equipment repair; cranes, overhead traveling; hoists

(G-16737)
LACO INC
1561 Laitner Dr (49696-8878)
PHONE..................................231 929-3300
▲ **EMP:** 30 **EST:** 1855
SQ FT: 42,000
SALES (est): 2.8MM **Privately Held**
SIC: 3991 Mfg Brooms/Brushes

(G-16738)
LANDMAN
602 W Tenth St (49684-3139)
PHONE..................................231 946-4678
Dwayne Vick, *Principal*
EMP: 4 **EST:** 2018
SALES (est): 81.9K **Privately Held**
SIC: 1311 Crude petroleum & natural gas

(G-16739)
LASER PRINTER TECHNOLOGIES INC
1379 Trade Center Dr (49696-8913)
PHONE..................................231 941-5273
Ross Clement, *President*
Jeremy Defrance, *General Mgr*
Mike Deering, *Technician*
EMP: 6 **EST:** 1994
SQ FT: 4,400
SALES (est): 909K **Privately Held**
WEB: www.gettonernow.com
SIC: 2752 Commercial printing, offset

(G-16740)
LEAD SCREWS INTERNATIONAL INC
2101 Precision Dr (49686-9239)
PHONE..................................262 786-1500
David L Busch, *President*
▼ **EMP:** 75 **EST:** 1985
SQ FT: 45,000
SALES (est): 9.7MM
SALES (corp-wide): 1.2B **Privately Held**
WEB: www.dynatect.com
SIC: 3545 Precision tools, machinists'

Traverse City - Grand Traverse County (G-16741)

HQ: Dynatect Manufacturing, Inc.
2300 S Calhoun Rd
New Berlin WI 53151
262 786-1500

(G-16741)
LEAR CORPORATION
710 Carver St (49686-3202)
PHONE....................231 947-0160
Thomas Didonato, *Senior VP*
Oscar Dominguez, *Vice Pres*
Elie Ghazal, *Vice Pres*
Jeff Huston, *Vice Pres*
David McNulty, *Vice Pres*
EMP: 7
SALES (corp-wide): 17B **Publicly Held**
WEB: www.lear.com
SIC: 3714 Motor vehicle parts & accessories
PA: Lear Corporation
21557 Telegraph Rd
Southfield MI 48033
248 447-1500

(G-16742)
LEELANAU INDUSTRIES INC
6052 E Traverse Hwy (49684-7949)
P.O. Box 4120 (49685-4120)
PHONE....................231 947-0372
Tonya Otten, *President*
Thomas L Fraser, *Purchasing*
Rob Krinnock, *QC Mgr*
Tom Fraser, *Engineer*
Tom Van Fossen, *Engineer*
EMP: 31 **EST:** 1980
SQ FT: 40,000
SALES (est): 5.3MM **Privately Held**
WEB: www.leeindinc.com
SIC: 3599 Machine shop, jobbing & repair

(G-16743)
LEELANAU WOODWORKING
9995 E Lincoln Rd (49684-7692)
PHONE....................231 946-4437
EMP: 4 **EST:** 2017
SALES (est): 54.1K **Privately Held**
SIC: 2431 Millwork

(G-16744)
LEFT FOOT CHARLEY
806 Reads Run (49685-8982)
PHONE....................231 995-0500
Ryan Olbrick, *Owner*
Bryan Ulbrich, *General Mgr*
Melissa Fischer, *Sales Staff*
EMP: 7 **EST:** 2007
SALES (est): 479.1K **Privately Held**
WEB: www.leftfootcharley.com
SIC: 2084 Wine cellars, bonded: engaged in blending wines; wines

(G-16745)
LEGACY DISTILLERS INC
10691 E Carter Rd Ste 101 (49684-5499)
PHONE....................231 933-0631
Derek Weeks,
Christine Skibowski,
David Skibowski,
Carolyn Weeks,
EMP: 15 **EST:** 2020
SALES (est): 924.4K **Privately Held**
SIC: 2085 Distilled & blended liquors

(G-16746)
LOBO SIGNS INC
Also Called: Nu Art Designs Sign Fabg
322 E Welch Ct (49686-4873)
PHONE....................231 941-7739
Carla Chappell, *CEO*
Chad Albaugh, *President*
Michael J Albaugh, *Vice Pres*
Todd Ritzer, *Project Mgr*
EMP: 21 **EST:** 1986
SQ FT: 2,000
SALES (est): 2.3MM **Privately Held**
SIC: 3993 Signs & advertising specialties

(G-16747)
LOG HOME SPECIALTY
903 Hammond Pl S (49686-8009)
PHONE....................231 943-9410
Kenneth Shurkey, *Principal*
EMP: 4 **EST:** 2002
SALES (est): 80.3K **Privately Held**
SIC: 2452 Log cabins, prefabricated, wood

(G-16748)
LOUIES MEATS INC
2040 Cass Rd (49685-8839)
PHONE....................231 946-4811
Anthony Alpers, *President*
EMP: 26
SALES (est): 2.2MM **Privately Held**
WEB: www.louiesmeats.com
SIC: 2013 Sausages & related products, from purchased meat

(G-16749)
LYLE JAMIESON WOOD TURNING
285 Lauri Wil Ln (49696-9477)
PHONE....................231 947-2348
Lyle Jamieson, *Principal*
EMP: 7 **EST:** 2002
SALES (est): 171.8K **Privately Held**
WEB: www.lylejamieson.com
SIC: 2499 Carved & turned wood

(G-16750)
M-22 CHALLENGE
121 E Front St Ste 104 (49684-2570)
PHONE....................231 392-2212
Matt Wiesen, *Principal*
Charlie Socks,
EMP: 6 **EST:** 2011
SALES (est): 321.4K **Privately Held**
WEB: www.m22.com
SIC: 3949 Sporting & athletic goods

(G-16751)
MACK OIL CORPORATION
7721 Outer Dr S (49685-9029)
PHONE....................231 590-5903
John W Mack, *President*
Michael Mack, *Vice Pres*
Robert Mack, *Admin Sec*
EMP: 5 **EST:** 1961
SQ FT: 1,300
SALES (est): 506.1K **Privately Held**
SIC: 1311 Crude petroleum production; natural gas production

(G-16752)
MANUFAX INC
1324 Barlow St Ste D (49686-4396)
PHONE....................231 929-3226
Kurt Hansemann, *President*
Randy L Shaw, *Vice Pres*
Randy Shaw, *Vice Pres*
EMP: 6 **EST:** 1988
SQ FT: 4,000
SALES (est): 562.2K **Privately Held**
WEB: www.manufax.us
SIC: 3544 Industrial molds

(G-16753)
MARI VILLA VINEYARDS
8175 Center Rd (49686-1669)
PHONE....................231 935-4513
Alex Lagina, *General Mgr*
Karen Derlatka, *Manager*
EMP: 12 **EST:** 2011
SALES (est): 1MM **Privately Held**
WEB: www.marivineyards.com
SIC: 0172 2084 Grapes; wines

(G-16754)
MARTEC LAND SERVICES INC
3335 S Arprt Rd W Ste A5 (49684)
PHONE....................231 929-3971
Randy Marshall, *President*
EMP: 10 **EST:** 2006
SALES (est): 342.3K **Privately Held**
WEB: www.martecland.com
SIC: 1382 Oil & gas exploration services

(G-16755)
MAVERICK EXPLORATION PROD INC
3301 Veterans Dr Ste 107 (49684-4564)
PHONE....................231 929-3923
Dwight Gookin, *President*
Rita Gookin, *Admin Sec*
EMP: 4 **EST:** 1981
SQ FT: 700
SALES (est): 552.5K **Privately Held**
SIC: 1382 Oil & gas exploration services

(G-16756)
MICHIGAN WINE TRAIL
2561 East Crown Dr (49685-7211)
PHONE....................231 944-5220
Lorri Hathaway, *Principal*
Matt Moersch, *Vice Pres*
Brian Lesperance, *Admin Sec*
EMP: 5 **EST:** 2017
SALES (est): 118.9K **Privately Held**
WEB: www.michigancraftbeverage.com
SIC: 2084 Wines

(G-16757)
MIDWEST AIR PRODUCTS CO INC
281 Hughes Dr (49696-8255)
P.O. Box 5319 (49696-5319)
PHONE....................231 941-5865
Rick Whiteherse, *Owner*
Jamie M Shellenbarger, *Manager*
▼ **EMP:** 20 **EST:** 1979
SQ FT: 21,100
SALES (est): 1.9MM **Privately Held**
WEB: www.midwestair.com
SIC: 3564 Air purification equipment

(G-16758)
MILLER EXPLORATION COMPANY (PA)
3104 Logan Valley Rd (49684-4772)
P.O. Box 348 (49685-0348)
PHONE....................231 941-0004
John W Elias, *President*
Kelly E Miller, *President*
Deanna L Cannon, *CFO*
Lew P Murray, *Executive*
EMP: 10 **EST:** 1986
SQ FT: 10,500
SALES (est): 1.4MM **Privately Held**
SIC: 1311 2911 Crude petroleum & natural gas; crude petroleum production; natural gas production; petroleum refining

(G-16759)
MILLER INVESTMENT COMPANY LLC
10850 E Traverse Hwy # 5595 (49684-1325)
P.O. Box 348 (49685-0348)
PHONE....................231 933-3233
Kelly E Miller, *CEO*
Adam W Miller, *Managing Prtnr*
Adam Miller, *Managing Prtnr*
Curtiss R Yeite, *CFO*
EMP: 13 **EST:** 2013
SALES (est): 1MM **Privately Held**
WEB: www.millerinvestmentcompany.com
SIC: 6531 1389 Real estate listing services; cementing oil & gas well casings

(G-16760)
MIRACLE PETROLEUM LLC
2780 Garfield Rd N (49685-6004)
P.O. Box 6320 (49696-6320)
PHONE....................231 946-8090
Sally Somsel, *Manager*
Gene Farber,
Edward Gage,
EMP: 6 **EST:** 1996
SALES (est): 120K **Privately Held**
SIC: 1382 Oil & gas exploration services

(G-16761)
MISSION POINT PRESS
2554 Chandler Rd (49696-8139)
PHONE....................231 421-9513
EMP: 5 **EST:** 2017
SALES (est): 37.5K **Privately Held**
WEB: www.chandlerlakebooks.com
SIC: 2741 Miscellaneous publishing

(G-16762)
MOLD MATTER
1650 Barlow St (49686-4721)
PHONE....................231 933-6653
EMP: 5
SALES (est): 616.4K **Privately Held**
SIC: 3544 Mfg Dies/Tools/Jigs/Fixtures

(G-16763)
MOOMERS HOMEMADE ICE CREAM LLC
7263 N Long Lake Rd (49685-7495)
PHONE....................231 941-4122
Nancy Plummer, *CEO*
John Plummer, *Mng Member*
Becky Plummer,
Robert Plummer,
EMP: 12 **EST:** 1998
SQ FT: 1,700
SALES (est): 1.2MM **Privately Held**
WEB: www.moomers.com
SIC: 2024 5812 5143 Ice cream & ice milk; ice cream stands or dairy bars; ice cream & ices

(G-16764)
MOPEGA LLC
Also Called: Flea
238 E Front St (49684-2526)
P.O. Box 7047 (49696-7047)
PHONE....................231 631-2580
Pierre Pujoy, *Mng Member*
EMP: 5 **EST:** 2015
SQ FT: 2,000
SALES (est): 346.6K **Privately Held**
SIC: 5651 2389 Unisex clothing stores; disposable garments & accessories

(G-16765)
MP6 LLC
2488 Cass Rd (49684-9148)
PHONE....................231 409-7530
Vicki Paulus, *Principal*
Fred Sorensen, *Business Dir*
Rick Flees,
EMP: 6 **EST:** 2010
SALES (est): 392.4K **Privately Held**
WEB: www.mp6llc.com
SIC: 3089 Injection molding of plastics

(G-16766)
NATHANIEL ROSE WINE
10417 E Bingham Rd (49684-7412)
PHONE....................989 302-3297
EMP: 5 **EST:** 2019
SALES (est): 119.8K **Privately Held**
WEB: www.lpwines.com
SIC: 2084 Wines

(G-16767)
NATURAL GAS CMPRSSION SYSTEMS (PA)
2480 Aero Park Dr (49684-9180)
PHONE....................231 941-0107
A J Yuncker, *President*
Mark Riitola, *VP Opers*
Mark Ritola, *VP Opers*
Jim Stricker, *Opers Staff*
Annette Jacobson, *Sales Staff*
EMP: 25 **EST:** 2001
SALES (est): 12.6MM **Privately Held**
WEB: www.natgascomp.com
SIC: 1389 Oil field services

(G-16768)
NEPTUNE CANDLES LLC
6360 Herkner Rd (49685-8210)
PHONE....................231 947-0554
Donald Sheehan, *Principal*
EMP: 4 **EST:** 2017
SALES (est): 39.6K **Privately Held**
SIC: 3999 Candles

(G-16769)
NOMAD CIDERY LLC
2500 Kroupa Rd (49686-9731)
PHONE....................231 313-8627
John Kroupa, *Administration*
EMP: 5 **EST:** 2016
SALES (est): 262.8K **Privately Held**
WEB: www.nomadcidery.com
SIC: 2084 Wines

(G-16770)
NOORA HEALTH
18833 Whispering Trl (49686-8720)
PHONE....................402 981-0421
Edith Elliott, *CEO*
Shahed Alam, *President*
Catherine Ashe, *COO*
EMP: 8 **EST:** 2014
SALES (est): 465.4K **Privately Held**
WEB: www.noorahealth.org
SIC: 7372 Educational computer software

(G-16771)
NORMIC INDUSTRIES INC
1733 Park Dr (49686-4788)
PHONE....................231 947-8860
George Kausler, *President*

▲ = Import ▼ = Export
◆ = Import/Export

Robert Kausler, *Vice Pres*
Jeffry Palisin, *Vice Pres*
Dennis Runwick, *Chief Mktg Ofcr*
Stacey Pezzetti, *Shareholder*
EMP: 44 **EST:** 1969
SQ FT: 14,000
SALES (est): 2.4MM **Privately Held**
WEB: www.normicind.com
SIC: 3479 3993 Etching & engraving; name plates: engraved, etched, etc.; signs & advertising specialties

(G-16772)
NORTHERN MICH SUPPORTIVE HSING
250 E Front St (49684-3602)
PHONE..................................231 929-1309
EMP: 5
SALES (est): 605.9K **Privately Held**
SIC: 2435 Mfg Hardwood Veneer/Plywood

(G-16773)
NORTHERN MICHIGAN GLASS LLC
1101 Hammond Rd W (49686-9241)
PHONE..................................231 941-0050
Jeff Fogo, *Mng Member*
Linda Mc Daniel, *Manager*
Michael Braden,
EMP: 20 **EST:** 2001
SQ FT: 13,000
SALES (est): 3.3MM **Privately Held**
WEB: www.northernmichiganglass.com
SIC: 1793 1761 3449 1542 Glass & glazing work; skylight installation; curtain wall, metal; curtain walls for buildings, steel; store front construction

(G-16774)
NORTHERN MICHIGAN PUBLISHING
2438 Potter Rd E (49696-8599)
PHONE..................................231 946-7878
Joshua Mitchell, *Owner*
James Mitchell, *Principal*
EMP: 4
SALES (est): 154.9K **Privately Held**
WEB: www.northernmichiganpublishing.com
SIC: 2741 Miscellaneous publishing

(G-16775)
NORTHWEST PAINT PROS
1620 Andrew Pl (49686-4957)
PHONE..................................231 944-3446
Brandon Schropp, *Principal*
EMP: 5 **EST:** 2017
SALES (est): 62.1K **Privately Held**
WEB: www.northwestpaintpros.com
SIC: 1721 2851 Residential painting; exterior residential painting contractor; commercial painting; epoxy coatings

(G-16776)
NPI WIRELESS (PA)
3054 Cass Rd (49684-8800)
P.O. Box 879 (49685-0879)
PHONE..................................231 922-9273
Frank Noverr, *President*
EMP: 44 **EST:** 1972
SQ FT: 8,000
SALES (est): 4.7MM **Privately Held**
WEB: www.npiwireless.com
SIC: 2711 2741 2752 5999 Newspapers, publishing & printing; directories, telephone: publishing & printing; catalogs, lithographed; telephone equipment & systems; radio, television & electronic stores

(G-16777)
OIL ENERGY CORP (PA)
954 Businemi Pk Dr Ste 5 (49686)
PHONE..................................231 933-3600
T D Provins, *CEO*
EMP: 10 **EST:** 1982
SALES (est): 1.7MM **Privately Held**
SIC: 1382 Oil & gas exploration services

(G-16778)
OILGEAR COMPANY (DH)
1424 International Dr (49686-8751)
PHONE..................................231 929-1660
Craig Lafave, *President*
Alan Circo, *General Mgr*
Chris Howie, *Vice Pres*
Marc Langs, *CFO*
Vin Comeau, *Manager*
▲ **EMP:** 70 **EST:** 1921
SALES (est): 50MM
SALES (corp-wide): 336.9MM **Privately Held**
WEB: www.oilgear.com
SIC: 3594 3492 Fluid power pumps; motors: hydraulic, fluid power or air; control valves, fluid power: hydraulic & pneumatic
HQ: Texas Hydraulics, Inc.
3410 Range Rd
Temple TX 76504
254 778-4701

(G-16779)
OKEEFE CENTRE LTD (PA)
Also Called: Chateau Grand Traverse
12239 Center Rd (49686-8558)
PHONE..................................231 223-7355
Edward Okeefe, *CEO*
Edward O'Keefe The Third,
▲ **EMP:** 3 **EST:** 1971
SQ FT: 15,000
SALES (est): 2.5MM **Privately Held**
SIC: 2084 Wines

(G-16780)
OLD MISSION GAZETTE
12875 Bluff Rd (49686-8447)
PHONE..................................231 590-4715
Jane Boursaw, *Principal*
EMP: 6 **EST:** 2017
SALES (est): 139.1K **Privately Held**
WEB: www.oldmission.net
SIC: 2711 Newspapers, publishing & printing

(G-16781)
OLD MISSION MULTIGRAIN LLC
1515 Chimney Ridge Dr (49686-9233)
PHONE..................................231 366-4121
Pearl Brown,
Peter Brown,
EMP: 9 **EST:** 2016
SQ FT: 2,000
SALES (est): 480.5K **Privately Held**
WEB: www.oldmissionmultigrain.com
SIC: 2051 Bakery: wholesale or wholesale/retail combined

(G-16782)
ONCOURSE INC
10660 E Carter Rd (49684-5437)
PHONE..................................231 946-1259
Bridget Fowler, *Project Mgr*
Suzette Lopez, *Project Mgr*
Brian Ronsayro, *Opers Staff*
Tom Marinucci, *Administration*
EMP: 10 **EST:** 2009
SALES (est): 465.4K **Privately Held**
WEB: www.oncourseinc.com
SIC: 1389 Oil field services

(G-16783)
OPTI TEMP INC
1500 International Dr (49686-8752)
P.O. Box 5246 (49696-5246)
PHONE..................................231 946-2931
Dan Dorn, *CEO*
James A Childs, *President*
Dennis Curtice, *Engineer*
Tyson Shink, *Engineer*
Steven Szot, *Regl Sales Mgr*
EMP: 45 **EST:** 1990
SQ FT: 22,500
SALES (est): 7.8MM **Privately Held**
WEB: www.optitemp.com
SIC: 3585 Refrigeration & heating equipment

(G-16784)
OPTION ENERGY LLC
102 E River Rd (49696-8222)
PHONE..................................269 329-4317
Jon Rockwood, *Mng Member*
EMP: 7 **EST:** 2008
SQ FT: 15,000
SALES (est): 819.7K **Privately Held**
SIC: 4924 1311 4931 1711 Natural gas distribution; natural gas production; ; solar energy contractor

(G-16785)
OXFORD WOODWORKS
9536 S West Bay Shore Dr (49684-9213)
PHONE..................................248 736-3090
EMP: 4 **EST:** 2015
SALES (est): 65.4K **Privately Held**
WEB: www.oxfordwoodworks.com
SIC: 2431 Millwork

(G-16786)
PDM INDUSTRIES INC
1124 Stepke Ct (49685-9331)
PHONE..................................231 943-9601
Roger Werly, *President*
Rod Werly, *Vice Pres*
EMP: 24 **EST:** 1975
SALES (est): 766.3K **Privately Held**
WEB: www.pdmind.com
SIC: 3479 3089 Coating of metals with plastic or resins; coating of metals & formed products; molding primary plastic

(G-16787)
PENINSULA CELLARS
Also Called: Grape Harbor
2464 Kroupa Rd (49686-9731)
PHONE..................................231 223-4050
Dave Kroupa, *CEO*
John Owner, *President*
EMP: 10 **EST:** 2001
SALES (est): 675.6K **Privately Held**
WEB: www.peninsulacellars.com
SIC: 2084 Wines

(G-16788)
PEPSI-COLA METRO BTLG CO INC
4248 Cherri Pepsi Way (49685-7204)
PHONE..................................231 946-0452
Magaret Addis, *Branch Mgr*
Mark Darrow, *Manager*
Chris McManus, *Manager*
EMP: 6
SALES (corp-wide): 70.3B **Publicly Held**
WEB: www.pepsico.com
SIC: 2086 Carbonated soft drinks, bottled & canned
HQ: Pepsi-Cola Metropolitan Bottling Company, Inc.
1111 Westchester Ave
White Plains NY 10604
914 767-6000

(G-16789)
PERFECT SYNC INC
1902 Penbroke Dr (49696-8314)
PHONE..................................231 947-9300
Eric Pearson, *Administration*
EMP: 4 **EST:** 2018
SALES (est): 72.9K **Privately Held**
SIC: 7372 Prepackaged software

(G-16790)
PHOENIX TECHNOLOGY SVCS USA
Also Called: Nevis Energy
327 E Welch Ct Ste A (49686-5449)
PHONE..................................231 995-0100
EMP: 16
SALES (corp-wide): 67.5MM **Privately Held**
SIC: 1381 Drilling Oil And Gas Wells, Nsk
HQ: Phoenix Technology Services Usa Inc
12329 Cutten Rd
Houston TX 77043
713 337-0600

(G-16791)
PHOTODON LLC
1517 Nthrn Star Dr Ste A (49696)
PHONE..................................847 377-1185
Donald Basch, *CEO*
Mandy Peterson, *Principal*
Jo Paige, *Sales Staff*
▲ **EMP:** 10 **EST:** 2000
SALES (est): 1.1MM **Privately Held**
WEB: www.photodon.com
SIC: 5734 3575 5999 Computer peripheral equipment; computer terminals, monitors & components; cleaning equipment & supplies

(G-16792)
PICKLE PRINT & MARKETING LLC
525 W Fourteenth St D (49684-4061)
PHONE..................................231 668-4148
Marcus Christian, *Principal*
EMP: 7 **EST:** 2008
SALES (est): 345.8K **Privately Held**
WEB: www.pickleprint.net
SIC: 2752 Commercial printing, lithographic

(G-16793)
PIPING PLOVER PRINTS
817 Parsons Rd (49686-3645)
PHONE..................................231 929-0261
Kirt Susan, *Owner*
EMP: 4 **EST:** 2015
SALES (est): 60.2K **Privately Held**
SIC: 2752 Commercial printing, lithographic

(G-16794)
PLAMONDONS WELDING/FAB LLC
10200 E Cherry Bend Rd (49684-5294)
PHONE..................................231 632-0406
Travis Plamondon, *Principal*
EMP: 4 **EST:** 2019
SALES (est): 40.6K **Privately Held**
WEB: www.plamondons-weldingfab-llc.business.site
SIC: 7692 Welding repair

(G-16795)
PLASCON
250 E Front St Ste 317 (49684-2552)
PHONE..................................231 421-3119
Nancy Hodges, *Marketing Mgr*
EMP: 6 **EST:** 2018
SALES (est): 103.2K **Privately Held**
WEB: www.plascongroup.com
SIC: 3599 Machine shop, jobbing & repair

(G-16796)
PLASCON INC
2375 Traversefield Dr (49686-9266)
P.O. Box 6231 (49696-6231)
PHONE..................................231 935-1580
David Peterson, *President*
Brett Milliman, *COO*
Todd Cote, *QA Dir*
Jeff Klug, *CFO*
Bill Hendry, *Human Res Dir*
▲ **EMP:** 43 **EST:** 2000
SALES (est): 8.3MM **Privately Held**
WEB: www.plascongroup.com
SIC: 2821 Plastics materials & resins

(G-16797)
PLASCON FILMS INC
2375 Traversefield Dr (49686-9266)
P.O. Box 6231 (49696-6231)
PHONE..................................231 935-1580
David Peterson, *President*
EMP: 21 **EST:** 2009
SALES (est): 950K **Privately Held**
WEB: www.plascongroup.com
SIC: 2821 Plastics materials & resins

(G-16798)
PLASPORT INC
2375 Traversefield Dr (49686-9266)
P.O. Box 6231 (49696-6231)
PHONE..................................231 935-1580
David E Peterson, *President*
▲ **EMP:** 20 **EST:** 2006
SALES (est): 497.2K **Privately Held**
WEB: www.plascongroup.com
SIC: 2673 Bags: plastic, laminated & coated

(G-16799)
PLASTIC SOLUTIONS LLC
1300 Stepke Ct (49685-9331)
PHONE..................................231 824-7350
Dan C McGrew, *Agent*
Dan McGrew, *Agent*
EMP: 5 **EST:** 2000
SALES (est): 363.3K **Privately Held**
SIC: 3089 Injection molding of plastics

Traverse City - Grand Traverse County (G-16800) — GEOGRAPHIC SECTION

(G-16800)
PRESS ON JUICE
305 Knollwood Dr (49686-1858)
PHONE..................................231 409-9971
Kristin Rockwood, *Principal*
EMP: 7 **EST:** 2014
SALES (est): 112.6K **Privately Held**
WEB: www.pressonjuice.com
SIC: 2741 Miscellaneous publishing

(G-16801)
PRESS PLAY
3134 Voss Dr (49685-7873)
PHONE..................................231 753-2841
Samantha Ehle, *Owner*
EMP: 4 **EST:** 2017
SALES (est): 59.4K **Privately Held**
SIC: 2741 Miscellaneous publishing

(G-16802)
PRISM PUBLICATIONS INC
Also Called: Traverse Nthrn Michigans Mag
125 S Park St Ste 155 (49684-3601)
PHONE..................................231 941-8174
Deborah Wyatt Fellows, *President*
Theresa Baehr, *Prdtn Dir*
Ann Gatrell, *Accounts Exec*
Rob Diclemente, *Manager*
Roger Lamb, *Web Dvlpr*
EMP: 25 **EST:** 1981
SQ FT: 3,000
SALES (est): 4MM **Privately Held**
SIC: 2721 Magazines: publishing only, not printed on site

(G-16803)
PRO IMAGE DESIGN
331 W South Airport Rd (49686-4841)
PHONE..................................231 322-8052
Alan Hubbard, *Owner*
Tara Hubbard, *Co-Owner*
EMP: 4 **EST:** 1998
SALES (est): 528.9K **Privately Held**
WEB: www.proimagedesigninc.net
SIC: 3993 Electric signs

(G-16804)
PRODUCTION INDUSTRIES II INC
3535 Rennie School Rd (49685-9171)
PHONE..................................231 352-7500
Charles C Frost, *President*
EMP: 8 **EST:** 2004
SALES (est): 7.1MM **Privately Held**
WEB: www.prodind.com
SIC: 3568 Belting, chain
PA: Frost Links
2020 Bristol Ave Nw
Grand Rapids MI 49504
616 785-9030

(G-16805)
PROGRESS PRINTERS INC
1445 Woodmere Ave (49686-4309)
PHONE..................................231 947-5311
James M Novak, *President*
EMP: 7 **EST:** 1949
SQ FT: 7,000
SALES (est): 429K
SALES (corp-wide): 8.9MM **Privately Held**
WEB: www.progress-printers.com
SIC: 2752 Commercial printing, offset
PA: Mitchell Graphics, Inc.
2363 Mitchell Park Dr
Petoskey MI 49770
231 347-4635

(G-16806)
PROMETHIENT INC
2382 Cass Rd (49684-9147)
PHONE..................................231 525-0500
William Myers, *CEO*
Bill Myers, *Bd of Directors*
EMP: 7 **EST:** 2017
SALES (est): 1MM **Privately Held**
WEB: www.thermavance.com
SIC: 3674 Semiconductors & related devices

(G-16807)
PYRINAS LLC
10574 Waterford Rd (49684-6235)
PHONE..................................810 422-7535
Nathan Bildeaux,
▲ **EMP:** 4 **EST:** 2016
SQ FT: 1,000
SALES (est): 250K **Privately Held**
SIC: 3433 8711 Solar heaters & collectors; engineering services

(G-16808)
QSDG MANUFACTURING LLC
1576 International Dr (49686-8752)
PHONE..................................231 941-1222
Frederick E Reynolds, *President*
EMP: 13 **EST:** 2008
SALES (est): 1MM **Privately Held**
SIC: 3999 Barber & beauty shop equipment

(G-16809)
QUALITY DIAL INC
404 Hughes Dr (49696-8244)
PHONE..................................231 947-1071
Mike Wallace, *President*
EMP: 7 **EST:** 2013
SALES (est): 96.3K **Privately Held**
WEB: www.qualitytc.com
SIC: 3599 Machine shop, jobbing & repair

(G-16810)
QUALITY TIME COMPONENTS
343 Hughes Dr (49696-8255)
PHONE..................................231 947-1071
Mike Wallace, *President*
Keith Hart, *General Mgr*
EMP: 15 **EST:** 1985
SQ FT: 15,000
SALES (est): 2MM **Privately Held**
WEB: www.qualitytc.com
SIC: 3873 Watches, clocks, watchcases & parts

(G-16811)
QUANTUM SAILS DESIGN GROUP LLC (PA)
1576 International Dr (49686-8752)
PHONE..................................231 941-1222
Frederick Reynolds, *President*
▼ **EMP:** 43 **EST:** 2008
SALES (est): 6.3MM **Privately Held**
WEB: www.quantumsails.com
SIC: 3732 Sailboats, building & repairing

(G-16812)
R M YOUNG COMPANY
2801 Aero Park Dr (49686-9171)
PHONE..................................231 946-3980
Thomas Young, *President*
Robert Young, *Chairman*
Michael Young, *Vice Pres*
EMP: 34 **EST:** 1964
SQ FT: 19,200
SALES (est): 4.3MM **Privately Held**
WEB: www.youngusa.com
SIC: 3829 Meteorological instruments

(G-16813)
R W SUMMERS CO
90 E River Rd (49696-8222)
PHONE..................................231 946-7923
Robert Summers, *Principal*
EMP: 5 **EST:** 2008
SALES (est): 128.1K **Privately Held**
WEB: www.rwsummers.com
SIC: 3949 Sporting & athletic goods

(G-16814)
RAINBOW SEAMLESS SYSTEMS INC (PA)
4107 Manor Wood Dr S (49685-8768)
PHONE..................................231 933-8888
Michael Collins, *President*
Matthew Collins, *Principal*
Patrick Collins, *Principal*
Skye Vedrode, *Office Mgr*
Billy Woods, *Consultant*
EMP: 9 **EST:** 1988
SQ FT: 1,500 **Privately Held**
WEB: www.rainbowseamless.com
SIC: 3444 1761 Gutters, sheet metal; gutter & downspout contractor

(G-16815)
RAMPANT MEDIA LLC
206 E Ninth St (49684-3204)
PHONE..................................231 218-0401
Chris Simpson,
EMP: 7 **EST:** 2020
SALES (est): 201.6K **Privately Held**
WEB: www.rampant-media.com
SIC: 2399 Banners, pennants & flags

(G-16816)
RANDYS SEAL COAT
7182 Cherry Ln (49685-8305)
PHONE..................................231 342-8031
Randall Wilson, *Principal*
EMP: 6 **EST:** 2018
SALES (est): 90.7K **Privately Held**
SIC: 2952 Asphalt felts & coatings

(G-16817)
RARE EARTH HARDWOODS INC
Also Called: Extreem Laser Dynamics
5800 Denali Dr (49684-8445)
PHONE..................................231 946-0043
Richard Paid, *President*
Deborah Paid, *Vice Pres*
▲ **EMP:** 16 **EST:** 1982
SALES (est): 2.3MM **Privately Held**
WEB: www.rare-earth-hardwoods.com
SIC: 2426 5031 5211 Flooring, hardwood; lumber: rough, dressed & finished; millwork & lumber

(G-16818)
RAVENWOOD
503 Devonshire Ct (49686-5408)
PHONE..................................231 421-5682
Lisa Berry, *President*
EMP: 4 **EST:** 1983 **Privately Held**
SIC: 2844 Cosmetic preparations

(G-16819)
REILCHZ INC
Also Called: Cheese Lady The
600 W Front St (49684-2210)
PHONE..................................231 421-9600
Christina Zinn, *President*
EMP: 5 **EST:** 2015
SALES (est): 390K **Privately Held**
SIC: 5149 5451 7213 3269 Specialty food items; cheese; linen supply; cookware: stoneware, coarse earthenware & pottery

(G-16820)
RIGHT BRAIN BREWERY
1837 Carlisle Rd (49696-9156)
PHONE..................................231 922-9662
Russ Springsteen, *President*
EMP: 6 **EST:** 2001
SALES (est): 82.4K **Privately Held**
WEB: www.rightbrainbrewery.com
SIC: 2041 Corn grits & flakes, for brewers' use

(G-16821)
RIVERSIDE ENERGY MICHIGAN LLC
10691 E Carter Rd Ste 201 (49684-5499)
PHONE..................................231 995-4000
Rob Gerhard, *CEO*
Rob Symons, *CFO*
Brady Defeyter, *Technician*
Chad Piehl, *Technician*
EMP: 30 **EST:** 2016
SQ FT: 15,000
SALES (est): 6.7MM **Privately Held**
WEB: www.riversideenergygroup.com
SIC: 1389 Gas compressing (natural gas) at the fields

(G-16822)
RJG TECHNOLOGIES INC (PA)
3111 Park Dr (49686-4713)
PHONE..................................231 947-3111
Matt Groleau, *CEO*
Andrew Pawlowicz, *General Mgr*
Michael Groleau, *Vice Pres*
Rodney Groleau, *Treasurer*
Amanda Oneil, *Accounts Exec*
EMP: 99 **EST:** 1989
SQ FT: 21,000
SALES (est): 20.8MM **Privately Held**
WEB: www.rjginc.com
SIC: 3823 3625 Industrial instrmnts msrmnt display/control process variable; relays & industrial controls

(G-16823)
ROBE AEROSPACE
895 N Keystone Rd (49696-8109)
PHONE..................................231 933-9355
Edward Borstel, *Owner*
EMP: 6 **EST:** 2006
SALES (est): 78.4K **Privately Held**
SIC: 3324 Aerospace investment castings, ferrous

(G-16824)
SAVOY EXPLORATION INC
Also Called: Savoy Energy
920 Hastings St Ste A (49686-3443)
P.O. Box 1560 (49685-1560)
PHONE..................................231 941-9552
Thomas C Pangborn, *CEO*
Cheryl A De Young, *Corp Secy*
EMP: 7 **EST:** 1995
SQ FT: 3,200
SALES (est): 1.2MM **Privately Held**
WEB: www.savoyexp.com
SIC: 1382 Oil & gas exploration services

(G-16825)
SCHELDE ENTERPRISES INC
Also Called: North Peak Brewing Company
400 W Front St (49684-2800)
PHONE..................................231 941-7325
Michael Lloyd, *General Mgr*
EMP: 4
SALES (corp-wide): 12.8MM **Privately Held**
SIC: 2082 5813 5812 Beer (alcoholic beverage); drinking places; eating places
PA: Schelde Enterprises Inc
741 Kenmoor Ave Se Ste B
Grand Rapids MI

(G-16826)
SCHMUDE OIL INC
2150 Ste B S Airport Rd W (49684)
P.O. Box 1008 (49685-1008)
PHONE..................................231 947-4410
Dennis Schmude, *President*
Mary Jo Schmude, *Admin Sec*
EMP: 4 **EST:** 1983
SQ FT: 1,560
SALES (est): 857.3K **Privately Held**
WEB: www.schmudeoil.com
SIC: 1382 Oil & gas exploration services

(G-16827)
SDS LLC
537 W Fourteenth St (49684-4042)
PHONE..................................231 492-5996
EMP: 4 **EST:** 2015
SALES (est): 86.6K **Privately Held**
WEB: www.vesastuff.com
SIC: 3999 Manufacturing industries

(G-16828)
SELESTIAL SOAP LLC
Also Called: MY GREEN FEELS
345 W Airport Rd (49686)
P.O. Box 5117 (49696-5117)
PHONE..................................231 944-1978
Stevens Ezell, *CEO*
Gary Poynter, *Controller*
Gary Poyntr, *Controller*
Eric Wistrand, *Software Dev*
Craig Wesley, *Director*
EMP: 50
SALES (est): 1MM **Privately Held**
WEB: www.mygreenfills.com
SIC: 5087 5169 2841 Detergents; soap & other detergents; alarm & safety equipment stores

(G-16829)
SENECA ENTERPRISES LLC
Also Called: Rf System Lab
1745 Barlow St (49686-4722)
PHONE..................................231 943-1171
Joel Green, *General Mgr*
Sean Oconnor, *General Mgr*
Joel Greene, *Sales Staff*
Steven Swaney, *Marketing Staff*
Sean O'Connor,
EMP: 9 **EST:** 2008
SALES (est): 1.6MM **Privately Held**
WEB: www.viewtech.com
SIC: 3825 3827 Instruments to measure electricity; optical instruments & lenses

Traverse City - Grand Traverse County (G-16858)

(G-16830)
SHEET METAL WORKERS LOCAL
3912 Blair Townhall Rd (49685-9197)
PHONE.....................231 590-1112
EMP: 6 EST: 2019
SALES (est): 94.5K **Privately Held**
WEB: www.sheetmetal7.org
SIC: 3444 Sheet metalwork

(G-16831)
SHEREN PLUMBING & HEATING INC
3801 Rennie School Rd (49685-8245)
PHONE.....................231 943-7916
Jerry Sheren, *President*
EMP: 40 EST: 2009
SQ FT: 5,500
SALES (est): 4.1MM
SALES (corp-wide): 2.8B **Publicly Held**
WEB: www.sheren.tc
SIC: 1711 3444 Plumbing contractors; warm air heating & air conditioning contractor; ventilation & duct work contractor; sheet metalwork
PA: Comfort Systems Usa, Inc.
  675 Bering Dr Ste 400
  Houston TX 77057
  713 830-9600

(G-16832)
SIGNPLICITY SIGN SYSTEMS INC
1555 S M 37 (49685-8505)
P.O. Box 168 (49685-0168)
PHONE.....................231 943-3800
Simon Wolf, *President*
EMP: 5 EST: 2002
SALES (est): 631.5K **Privately Held**
WEB: www.signplicity.com
SIC: 3993 Signs, not made in custom sign painting shops

(G-16833)
SILIKIDS INC
153 1/2 E Front St Ste B (49684-2508)
P.O. Box 2443 (49685-2443)
PHONE.....................866 789-7454
Hilary Abbott, *Corp Comm Staff*
▲ EMP: 5 EST: 2014
SALES (est): 372K **Privately Held**
WEB: www.gosili.com
SIC: 3089 Plastics products

(G-16834)
SKILLED MANUFACTURING INC (PA)
Also Called: SMI Automotive
3680 Cass Rd (49684-9153)
PHONE.....................231 941-0290
Dodd Russell, *President*
Richard Watson, *General Mgr*
Brent Mitchell, *Exec VP*
Jerry A Carlson, *Vice Pres*
Thomas Lawson, *Vice Pres*
▲ EMP: 123 EST: 1980
SQ FT: 100,000
SALES (est): 100.9MM **Privately Held**
WEB: www.skilledmfg.com
SIC: 3714 Motor vehicle parts & accessories

(G-16835)
SLOTBROKERS LLC
1625 Lake Dr (49685-8918)
PHONE.....................231 929-7568
EMP: 5 EST: 2010
SALES (est): 242.3K **Privately Held**
WEB: www.slotbroker.com
SIC: 3999 Coin-operated amusement machines

(G-16836)
SOCKS & ASSOCIATES DEVELOPMENT
516 Hidden Ridge Dr (49686-1867)
PHONE.....................231 421-5150
John R Socks, *Principal*
EMP: 6 EST: 2009
SALES (est): 111.1K **Privately Held**
SIC: 2252 Socks

(G-16837)
SOMOCO INC
13685 S West Bay Shore Dr (49684-6200)
PHONE.....................231 946-0200
Robert E Tucker Jr, *President*
Gary L Gottschalk, *Vice Pres*
David Rataj, *Treasurer*
Cynthia Buit, *Admin Sec*
EMP: 9 EST: 1984
SQ FT: 2,700
SALES (est): 302.3K **Privately Held**
SIC: 1311 Crude petroleum production; natural gas production

(G-16838)
SPIRIT PUBLISHING LLC
7977 S Shoreside Dr (49684-9569)
PHONE.....................231 399-1538
Terrance Swejkoski, *Principal*
EMP: 5 EST: 2015
SALES (est): 105.4K **Privately Held**
WEB: www.spiritpublishingllc.com
SIC: 2741 Miscellaneous publishing

(G-16839)
SRM CONCRETE LLC
Also Called: Lake City Redi Mix
3165 S M 37 (49685-8718)
PHONE.....................231 943-4818
Josh Gilde, *Branch Mgr*
EMP: 53
SALES (corp-wide): 170.1MM **Privately Held**
WEB: www.smyrnareadymix.com
SIC: 3273 Ready-mixed concrete
PA: Srm Concrete, Llc
  1136 2nd Ave N
  Nashville TN 37208
  615 355-1028

(G-16840)
SRW INC
10691 E Carter Rd Ste 201 (49684-5499)
PHONE.....................989 732-8884
EMP: 15
SALES (corp-wide): 2.9MM **Privately Held**
SIC: 1381 1389 Gas Production/Distribution
PA: Srw, Inc.
  175 Thompson Rd Ste A
  Bad Axe MI 48413
  989 269-8528

(G-16841)
STONE HOUSE BREAD LLC (PA)
4200 Us Highway 31 S (49685-9301)
PHONE.....................231 933-8864
Jeffery McMullen,
EMP: 30 EST: 2004
SQ FT: 5,000
SALES (est): 4.5MM **Privately Held**
WEB: www.stonehousebread.com
SIC: 2051 5461 Bakery: wholesale or wholesale/retail combined; bread

(G-16842)
STONE HOUSE BREAD INC
4200 Us Highway 31 S (49685-9301)
PHONE.....................231 933-8864
Robert Pisor, *President*
Ellen Pisor, *Corp Secy*
EMP: 20
SQ FT: 1,700
SALES (est): 500K **Privately Held**
WEB: www.stonehousebread.com
SIC: 2051 2052 5461 5149 Breads, rolls & buns; cookies & crackers; bakeries; groceries & related products

(G-16843)
STROMBERG-CARLSON PRODUCTS INC
2323 Traversefield Dr (49686-9266)
P.O. Box 266 (49685-0266)
PHONE.....................231 947-8600
Robert C Brammer Jr, *President*
Charles Brammer, *Vice Pres*
Kim Mendrea, *Controller*
▲ EMP: 15 EST: 1959
SQ FT: 35,000
SALES (est): 5.4MM **Privately Held**
WEB: www.strombergcarlson.com
SIC: 3429 5561 3714 Manufactured hardware (general); recreational vehicle dealers; motor vehicle parts & accessories

(G-16844)
SUGAR KISSED CUPCAKES LLC
127 E Front St (49684-2508)
PHONE.....................231 421-9156
Christina Burke, *Mng Member*
EMP: 5 EST: 2012
SALES (est): 349.2K **Privately Held**
SIC: 2024 Non-dairy based frozen desserts

(G-16845)
SUMMIT PETROLEUM COMPANY LLC
Also Called: Miller Energy Company
102 W Front St Ste 200 (49684-1200)
P.O. Box 632 (49685-0632)
PHONE.....................231 942-8134
EMP: 10 EST: 2018
SALES (est): 2.7MM **Privately Held**
SIC: 1382 Oil & gas exploration services

(G-16846)
SUPERIOR COLLISION INC
9419 Westwood Dr (49685-8814)
PHONE.....................231 946-4983
EMP: 6
SALES (est): 658.5K **Privately Held**
SIC: 7532 3479 Collision Service & Rust Proofing

(G-16847)
SYMPHONY CABINETRY LLC
811 S Garfield Ave (49686-3429)
PHONE.....................231 421-5421
EMP: 4 EST: 2016
SALES (est): 135.3K **Privately Held**
SIC: 2434 Wood kitchen cabinets

(G-16848)
SYSCOM TECHNOLOGIES INC
3124 Logan Valley Rd (49684-4772)
PHONE.....................231 946-1411
Gary D Popovits, *Principal*
EMP: 9 EST: 2013
SALES (est): 493.5K **Privately Held**
WEB: www.syscombusiness.com
SIC: 3825 Network analyzers

(G-16849)
T E TECHNOLOGY INC
1590 Keane Dr (49696-8257)
PHONE.....................231 929-3966
Richard J Buist, *President*
Paul G Lau, *Vice Pres*
Michael J Nagy, *Vice Pres*
Kristina Hendrickson, *Assistant*
◆ EMP: 36 EST: 1989
SQ FT: 11,600
SALES (est): 8.7MM **Privately Held**
WEB: www.tetech.com
SIC: 3674 3829 3822 8711 Thermoelectric devices, solid state; measuring & controlling devices; auto controls regulating residntl & coml environmt & applncs; consulting engineer

(G-16850)
TABONE VINEYARDS LLC
14916 Peninsula Dr (49686-9733)
PHONE.....................734 354-7271
Mario Tabone, *Principal*
Mario A Tabone, *Principal*
EMP: 8 EST: 2013
SQ FT: 3,000
SALES (est): 433.3K **Privately Held**
WEB: www.tabonevineyards.com
SIC: 2084 Wines

(G-16851)
TC OFFICE EXPRESS
3311 S Airport Rd W (49684-7879)
PHONE.....................231 929-3549
EMP: 6 EST: 2015
SALES (est): 199.4K **Privately Held**
SIC: 2759 Commercial printing

(G-16852)
TCWC LLC (HQ)
201 E Fourteenth St (49684-3222)
PHONE.....................231 922-8292
Christopher Fredrickson, *President*
Jared Rapp, *Mng Member*
EMP: 34 EST: 2011
SQ FT: 12,500
SALES (est): 4.5MM **Privately Held**
WEB: www.tcwhiskey.com
SIC: 5813 2087 2085 Drinking places; cocktail mixes, nonalcoholic; distilled & blended liquors

(G-16853)
TELLUREX CORPORATION (PA)
1462 International Dr (49686-8751)
P.O. Box 1439, Boulder CO (80306-1439)
PHONE.....................231 947-0110
Clyde E McKenzie, *CEO*
Craig Tremp, *COO*
Gregory P Smith, *Vice Pres*
Catherine Collins, *Treasurer*
Catherine S Collins, *Director*
▲ EMP: 20 EST: 1986
SQ FT: 7,500
SALES (est): 5.3MM **Privately Held**
WEB: www.tellurex.com
SIC: 3674 Semiconductors & related devices

(G-16854)
TENTCRAFT LLC
2662 Cass Rd (49684-9150)
PHONE.....................800 950-4553
Matt Bulloch, *President*
Chris Bush, *General Mgr*
Tj Shimek, *Vice Pres*
Brent Whitten, *Vice Pres*
Josie Shink, *Project Mgr*
◆ EMP: 70 EST: 2009
SALES (est): 9.2MM **Privately Held**
WEB: www.tentcraft.com
SIC: 2754 3993 Commercial printing, gravure; signs & advertising specialties

(G-16855)
TETRADYN LTD
9833 E Cherry Bend Rd (49684-7607)
PHONE.....................202 415-7295
Martin Dudziak, *Principal*
EMP: 8 EST: 2011
SALES (est): 441.1K **Privately Held**
SIC: 3674 3812 8731 Radiation sensors; detection apparatus: electronic/magnetic field, light/heat; biotechnical research, commercial

(G-16856)
THERMO FISHER SCIENTIFIC INC
6270 S West Bay Shore Dr (49684-9209)
PHONE.....................231 932-0242
Bob Walton, *Branch Mgr*
EMP: 5
SALES (corp-wide): 32.2B **Publicly Held**
WEB: www.thermofisher.com
SIC: 3826 Analytical instruments
PA: Thermo Fisher Scientific Inc.
  168 3rd Ave
  Waltham MA 02451
  781 622-1000

(G-16857)
THOMPSON SURGICAL INSTRS INC
10170 E Cherry Bend Rd (49684-6843)
PHONE.....................231 922-0177
Daniel K Farley, *President*
Stephanie Myers, *Research*
Travis Witulski, *Design Engr*
Eric Grost, *CFO*
Colleen Farran, *Accounts Mgr*
EMP: 20 EST: 1947
SALES (est): 6.9MM **Privately Held**
WEB: www.thompsonsurgical.com
SIC: 3841 8011 Surgical & medical instruments; offices & clinics of medical doctors

(G-16858)
THOMPSON SURGICAL INSTRS INC
10341 E Cherry Bend Rd (49684-5241)
PHONE.....................231 922-5169
Chelsea Dennis, *Marketing Staff*
EMP: 6 EST: 2018
SALES (est): 338.5K **Privately Held**
WEB: www.thompsonsurgical.com
SIC: 3841 Surgical & medical instruments

Traverse City - Grand Traverse County (G-16859)

(G-16859)
THOMPSON SURGICAL INSTRS INC
10321 E Cherry Bend Rd (49684-5241)
PHONE.................................231 922-5169
EMP: 5 EST: 2019
SALES (est): 86.6K Privately Held
WEB: www.thompsonsurgical.com
SIC: 3841 Surgical & medical instruments

(G-16860)
TILE CRAFT INC (PA)
1430 Trade Center Dr (49696-8917)
P.O. Box 2004 (49685-2004)
PHONE.................................231 929-7207
Dale Censer, *President*
▲ EMP: 19 EST: 1986
SQ FT: 3,500
SALES (est): 2MM Privately Held
WEB: www.tilecrafttc.com
SIC: 1743 3281 Tile installation, ceramic; marble, building: cut & shaped

(G-16861)
TOOL NORTH INC
2475 N Aero Park Ct (49686-9262)
PHONE.................................231 941-1150
Kenneth G Berg, *President*
Gary H Barg, *Vice Pres*
Timothy G Berg, *Vice Pres*
Jon Lejeune, *Vice Pres*
Grant Woods, *Project Mgr*
EMP: 24 EST: 1978
SQ FT: 34,000
SALES (est): 4.7MM Privately Held
WEB: www.toolnorth.com
SIC: 3569 3544 Assembly machines, nonmetalworking; special dies, tools, jigs & fixtures

(G-16862)
TOP SHELF EMBROIDERY LLC
1567 W South Arprt Rd # 3 (49686-4702)
P.O. Box 705 (49685-0705)
PHONE.................................231 932-0688
Michael Pascarelli, *Principal*
EMP: 5 EST: 2013
SALES (est): 49K Privately Held
SIC: 2395 Embroidery & art needlework

(G-16863)
TOP SHELLS EMBROIDERY LLC
Also Called: Embroid ME
1525 S Div St Ste 106 (49684)
PHONE.................................231 932-0688
Michael Pascarelli,
EMP: 4 EST: 2005
SALES (est): 300.2K Privately Held
SIC: 2395 Embroidery & art needlework

(G-16864)
TRAVERSE CITY PIE COMPANY LLC
2911 Garfield Rd N (49686-5007)
PHONE.................................231 929-7437
Mike Busley,
Tim Rice,
EMP: 10 EST: 2008
SQ FT: 4,500
SALES (est): 750K Privately Held
WEB: www.gtpie.com
SIC: 2051 Cakes, pies & pastries

(G-16865)
TRAVERSE CITY PRODUCTS LLC
501 Hughes Dr (49696-8255)
PHONE.................................231 946-4414
Herman J Thomas Jr, *President*
Martin B Cotanche, *Treasurer*
Doug Lucas, *Manager*
Jay Langler, *Supervisor*
EMP: 90 EST: 1982
SQ FT: 35,000
SALES (est): 10.8MM Privately Held
WEB: www.tcproducts.net
SIC: 3465 3356 Automotive stampings; nonferrous rolling & drawing

(G-16866)
TRAVERSE CY RECORD- EAGLE INC
Also Called: Traverse City Record-Eagle
120 W Front St (49684-2202)
P.O. Box 632 (49685-0632)
PHONE.................................231 946-2000
Ann Reed, *President*
EMP: 5 EST: 2001
SALES (est): 2.7MM
SALES (corp-wide): 26.3B Privately Held
WEB: www.record-eagle.com
SIC: 2711 2752 Newspapers: publishing only, not printed on site; commercial printing, lithographic
HQ: Community Newspaper Group, Llc
3500 Colonnade Pkwy # 600
Birmingham AL 35243

(G-16867)
TRIMET INDUSTRIES INC
829 Duell Rd (49686-4859)
PHONE.................................231 929-9100
Daniel Mello, *CEO*
Robert Leppo, *Principal*
Mark Ludwig, *Principal*
Kirk Schuch, *Principal*
Nadine Dolan, *Purch Mgr*
EMP: 20 EST: 1995
SQ FT: 9,000
SALES (est): 4MM Privately Held
WEB: www.trimetindustries.com
SIC: 3441 Fabricated structural metal

(G-16868)
TRULY FREE LLC (PA)
3175 Continental Dr (49686-4878)
PHONE.................................231 252-4571
Gary Pointer, *Controller*
Stephen Ezell, *Mng Member*
EMP: 29 EST: 2020
SALES (est): 1.1MM Privately Held
SIC: 5961 5999 3589 ; cleaning equipment & supplies; commercial cleaning equipment

(G-16869)
TWIN BAY DOCK AND PRODUCTS
982 E Commerce Dr Ste B (49685-6956)
PHONE.................................231 943-8420
Robert Serschen, *President*
Walter Drabek, *Vice Pres*
Tom Drabek, *Vice Pres*
Joyce Serschen, *Admin Sec*
EMP: 6 EST: 1989
SALES (est): 794.5K Privately Held
WEB: www.twinbaydockproducts.com
SIC: 3448 Docks: prefabricated metal

(G-16870)
TYSON FOODS INC
2314 Sybrant Rd (49684-9151)
PHONE.................................231 922-3214
EMP: 6
SALES (corp-wide): 47B Publicly Held
WEB: www.tysonfoods.com
SIC: 2011 Meat packing plants
PA: Tyson Foods, Inc.
2200 W Don Tyson Pkwy
Springdale AR 72762
479 290-4000

(G-16871)
TYSON FOODS INC
845 Bertina Ln (49696-8629)
PHONE.................................231 929-2456
EMP: 6
SALES (corp-wide): 47B Publicly Held
WEB: www.tysonfoods.com
SIC: 2011 Meat packing plants
PA: Tyson Foods, Inc.
2200 W Don Tyson Pkwy
Springdale AR 72762
479 290-4000

(G-16872)
UNITED ENGINEERED TOOLING
Also Called: United Tool
1974 Cass Hartman Ct (49685-9133)
PHONE.................................231 947-3650
Dietrich Heyde, *President*
Shawn McClellan, *General Mgr*
EMP: 24 EST: 1978
SQ FT: 7,800
SALES (est): 3.8MM Privately Held
WEB: www.unitedengtech.com
SIC: 3599 Machine shop, jobbing & repair

(G-16873)
UNITED SHIELD INTL LLC
1462 International Dr (49686-8751)
PHONE.................................231 933-1179
Paul Banducci, *President*
Terry Hand, *Managing Dir*
▲ EMP: 40 EST: 2005 Privately Held
WEB: www.unitedshield.net
SIC: 3949 Protective sporting equipment

(G-16874)
VILLAGE PRESS INC
Also Called: Vp Demand Creation Services
2779 Aero Park Dr (49686-9100)
P.O. Box 968 (49685-0968)
PHONE.................................231 946-3712
Robert Goff, *President*
Neil Knopf, *Editor*
Katie Rollert, *Business Mgr*
McKenzie Decker, *Vice Pres*
Mike Revard, *Opers Mgr*
EMP: 9 EST: 2011
SALES (est): 2.4MM Privately Held
WEB: www.vpdcs.com
SIC: 2741 Miscellaneous publishing

(G-16875)
VILLAGE SHOP INC
2779 Aero Park Dr (49686-9101)
P.O. Box 968 (49685-0968)
PHONE.................................231 946-3712
Robert Goff, *President*
Neil Knopf, *Editor*
Gretchen Christensen, *Advt Staff*
Ken Kingsley, *Manager*
Heather Farago, *Supervisor*
▲ EMP: 37 EST: 1969
SQ FT: 35,000
SALES (est): 4.3MM Privately Held
WEB: www.vpdcs.com
SIC: 2721 2752 2791 2789 Magazines: publishing & printing; commercial printing, offset; typesetting; bookbinding & related work

(G-16876)
W BAY CUPCAKES
524 W Thirteenth St (49684-4014)
PHONE.................................231 632-2010
Breanna Thomas, *Principal*
EMP: 4 EST: 2013
SALES (est): 173.4K Privately Held
SIC: 2051 Bread, cake & related products

(G-16877)
WEST BAY EXPLORATION COMPANY (PA)
13685 S West Bay Shore Dr (49684-1399)
PHONE.................................231 946-3529
Robert E Tucker Jr, *President*
Tim Baker, *Vice Pres*
Patrick Gibson, *Vice Pres*
Gary L Gottschalk, *Vice Pres*
Harry Graham, *Vice Pres*
EMP: 15 EST: 1981
SALES (est): 8MM Privately Held
WEB: www.westbayexploration.com
SIC: 1311 Crude petroleum production; natural gas production

(G-16878)
WEST BAY GEOPHYSICAL INC
13685 S West Bay Shore Dr (49684-6200)
PHONE.................................231 946-3529
Robert E Tucker Jr, *President*
Gary Gottschalk, *Vice Pres*
David Rataj, *Treasurer*
Layton Boebe, *Manager*
Cynthia Buit, *Admin Sec*
EMP: 3 EST: 1990
SQ FT: 286
SALES (est): 7.7MM
SALES (corp-wide): 8MM Privately Held
WEB: www.westbayexploration.com
SIC: 1382 Seismograph surveys
PA: West Bay Exploration Company
13685 S West Bay Shore Dr
Traverse City MI 49684
231 946-3529

(G-16879)
WHEELOCK & SON WELDING SHOP
Also Called: Wheelock & Sons Welding
9954 N Long Lake Rd (49685-9635)
PHONE.................................231 947-6557
Addison Wheelock Jr, *Owner*
Randolph Wheelock, *Co-Owner*
Bonny Wheelock, *Manager*
Jamie Wheelock, *Manager*
EMP: 8 EST: 1947
SQ FT: 6,900
SALES (est): 1.2MM Privately Held
WEB: www.wheelockandsons.com
SIC: 3448 7692 Docks: prefabricated metal; welding repair

(G-16880)
WILLIAM SHAW INC
Also Called: Sky Electric Northern Michigan
402 Wadsworth St (49684-3116)
PHONE.................................231 536-3569
William Rodney Shaw, *President*
Daniel A Bruce, *Admin Sec*
EMP: 8 EST: 1991
SQ FT: 3,000
SALES (est): 291.5K Privately Held
SIC: 3569 Filters & strainers, pipeline

(G-16881)
WOOD PLUS CLOTH
144 Hall St Ste 101 (49684-2282)
PHONE.................................231 421-8710
EMP: 4 EST: 2015
SALES (est): 85.8K Privately Held
WEB: www.woodandcloth.com
SIC: 2499 Wood products

(G-16882)
WORLD MAGNETICS COMPANY LLC
810 Hastings St (49686-3497)
PHONE.................................231 946-3800
Jeff Kramer, *Managing Dir*
Steve McLintock, *Engineer*
Martin Paul, *Engineer*
John Siddall, *Engineer*
Janice Blackburn, *CFO*
▲ EMP: 27 EST: 1962
SQ FT: 15,100
SALES (est): 5.6MM Privately Held
SIC: 3829 3679 Pressure & vacuum indicators, aircraft engine; recording & playback heads, magnetic

Trenary
Alger County

(G-16883)
ANYWHERE WELDING
N3550 Et Rd (49891-9572)
PHONE.................................906 250-7217
Kelsey McMaster, *Principal*
EMP: 8
SALES (est): 88.7K Privately Held
SIC: 7692 Welding repair

(G-16884)
FM RESEARCH MANAGEMENT LLC
1958 Eben Trenary Rd (49891)
PHONE.................................906 360-5833
Jeffery Millin, *CEO*
EMP: 4
SALES (est): 172.3K Privately Held
SIC: 2821 Plastics materials & resins

(G-16885)
HOLMQUIST FEED MILL
Also Called: Trenary Wood Products
232 N Main St (49891)
P.O. Box 208 (49891-0208)
PHONE.................................906 446-3325
Sharon Boyer, *Owner*
EMP: 7
SQ FT: 3,171
SALES (est): 640.9K Privately Held
WEB: www.trenarywoodproducts.com
SIC: 2048 5191 2429 Livestock feeds; animal feeds; shingles, wood: sawed or hand split

GEOGRAPHIC SECTION

Trenton
Wayne County

(G-16886)
AUTOSPORT DEVELOPMENT LLC
2331 Toledo St (48183-4715)
PHONE.................................734 675-1620
David Moxlow, *President*
Jim Schiesel,
EMP: 8 **EST:** 1999
SALES (est): 734.1K **Privately Held**
WEB: www.autosportdevelopment.com
SIC: 3599 Amusement park equipment

(G-16887)
DEWSBURY MANUFACTURING COMPANY
3022 Strohm Ave (48183-1887)
P.O. Box 627 (48183-0627)
PHONE.................................734 839-6376
EMP: 7 **EST:** 2012
SALES (est): 213.8K **Privately Held**
WEB: www.dewsco.com
SIC: 3999 Manufacturing industries

(G-16888)
FRITZ ENTERPRISES (HQ)
Also Called: Fritz Products Inc
1650 W Jefferson Ave (48183-2136)
PHONE.................................734 283-7272
Leonard Fritz, *President*
Eric Fritz, *Admin Sec*
EMP: 28 **EST:** 1986
SALES (est): 6.2MM
SALES (corp-wide): 35.7MM **Privately Held**
WEB: www.fritzinc.com
SIC: 3312 3295 1442 Hot-rolled iron & steel products; minerals, ground or treated; construction sand & gravel
PA: Fritz Enterprises, Inc.
 1650 W Jefferson Ave
 Trenton MI 48183
 734 692-4231

(G-16889)
HURON VALLEY STEEL CORPORATION (PA)
1650 W Jefferson Ave (48183-2136)
PHONE.................................734 479-3500
Eric R Fritz, *President*
Ronald Dalton, *President*
David Wallace, *Senior VP*
Ron Dalton, *Vice Pres*
Mark Gaffney, *Vice Pres*
◆ **EMP:** 110 **EST:** 1961
SQ FT: 7,000
SALES (est): 61.9MM **Privately Held**
WEB: www.hvsc.net
SIC: 5093 3341 3559 Nonferrous metals scrap; zinc smelting & refining (secondary); recycling machinery

(G-16890)
PFIZER INC
3495 Margarette Dr (48183-2309)
PHONE.................................734 671-9315
Robert Camilleri, *Branch Mgr*
EMP: 5
SALES (corp-wide): 41.9B **Publicly Held**
WEB: www.pfizer.com
SIC: 2834 Pharmaceutical preparations
PA: Pfizer Inc.
 235 E 42nd St Rm 107
 New York NY 10017
 212 733-2323

(G-16891)
RICK WYKLE LLC
Also Called: Dewsbury Manufactruing Company
3022 Strohm Ave (48183-1887)
P.O. Box 627 (48183-0627)
PHONE.................................734 839-6376
Rick Wykle, *Owner*
EMP: 5 **EST:** 1986 **Privately Held**
SIC: 5065 3444 3625 Electronic parts & equipment; metal housings, enclosures, casings & other containers; relays & industrial controls

(G-16892)
SOLUTIA INC
5100 W Jefferson Ave (48183-4729)
PHONE.................................734 676-4400
Gary Williams, *Branch Mgr*
EMP: 4 **Publicly Held**
WEB: www.eastman.com
SIC: 2821 2824 3231 2819 Plastics materials & resins; organic fibers, noncellulosic; products of purchased glass; industrial inorganic chemicals
HQ: Solutia Inc.
 575 Maryville Centre Dr
 Saint Louis MO 63141
 423 229-2000

(G-16893)
STEELWORKS INC
2335 Toledo St (48183-4715)
P.O. Box 390 (48183-0390)
PHONE.................................734 692-3020
Charles W Teichart Jr, *President*
Jan L Macnamara, *Treasurer*
Esther C Teichart, *Admin Sec*
EMP: 10 **EST:** 1993
SQ FT: 13,000
SALES (est): 1.8MM **Privately Held**
SIC: 3398 Metal burning

(G-16894)
STYROLOUTION
4906 Jackson St (48183-4595)
PHONE.................................734 676-3616
Keith McLellan, *Manager*
EMP: 5 **EST:** 2018
SALES (est): 94.7K **Privately Held**
SIC: 3089 Plastics products

(G-16895)
TRENTON FORGING COMPANY
5523 Hoover St (48183-4791)
PHONE.................................734 675-1620
David M Moxlow, *President*
Renee Moxlow, *Treasurer*
Jim Schiesel, *Controller*
Greg Fink, *Manager*
David Montiy, *Manager*
EMP: 92
SQ FT: 35,000
SALES (est): 29.7MM **Privately Held**
WEB: www.trentonforging.com
SIC: 3462 Iron & steel forgings

(G-16896)
TRENTON JEWELERS LTD
2355 West Rd (48183-3617)
PHONE.................................734 676-0188
Wayne H McDermitt, *President*
Wayne McDwight, *President*
Jenea McDermitt, *Manager*
EMP: 7 **EST:** 1936
SQ FT: 2,400
SALES (est): 790.5K **Privately Held**
WEB: www.trenton-jewelers.com
SIC: 5944 3915 7631 Jewelry, precious stones & precious metals; watches; jewelers' findings & materials; jewelry repair services; watch repair

Trout Creek
Ontonagon County

(G-16897)
CALDERWOOD WD PDTS & SVCS LLC
Also Called: Calderwood Enterprises
9968 Calderwood Rd (49967-5106)
P.O. Box 131 (49967-0131)
PHONE.................................906 852-3232
Fred Sliger,
EMP: 5 **EST:** 2005 **Privately Held**
SIC: 2439 Structural wood members

Troy
Oakland County

(G-16898)
1732 BRENTWOOD LLC
4909 Somerton Dr (48085-4739)
PHONE.................................248 457-9695
Firdosh Chinoy, *Principal*
EMP: 7 **EST:** 2016
SALES (est): 224.3K **Privately Held**
SIC: 2499 Wood products

(G-16899)
A & D DISTRIBUTION INC
2701 Troy Center Dr # 100 (48084-4753)
PHONE.................................248 378-1418
Brandon Billingslea, *President*
EMP: 11 **EST:** 2016
SALES (est): 501.6K **Privately Held**
SIC: 2051 Bakery: wholesale or wholesale/retail combined

(G-16900)
A ME VERTICAL INCORPORATED
675 E Big Beaver Rd (48083-1418)
PHONE.................................248 720-0245
Jeanne Vautaw, *General Mgr*
David Easterbrook, *Principal*
Bryan Talaga, *VP Sales*
EMP: 9 **EST:** 2010
SALES (est): 459.3K **Privately Held**
WEB: www.amecompanies.com
SIC: 2591 Blinds vertical

(G-16901)
AAM MTAL FRMING TROY MFG FCLTY
690 W Maple Rd (48084-5437)
PHONE.................................248 362-8500
EMP: 6 **EST:** 2018
SALES (est): 318.6K **Privately Held**
SIC: 3999 Manufacturing industries

(G-16902)
ACCELERATED PRESS INC
1337 Piedmont Dr (48083-1918)
PHONE.................................248 524-1850
Gaylord Vince, *President*
EMP: 7
SQ FT: 3,800
SALES (est): 750.8K **Privately Held**
WEB: www.acceleratedpress.com
SIC: 2752 7334 Commercial printing, offset; photocopying & duplicating services

(G-16903)
ACE CANVAS & TENT CO
465 Stephenson Hwy (48083-1130)
PHONE.................................313 842-3011
Michael A Caruso, *President*
EMP: 10 **EST:** 1974
SQ FT: 8,000
SALES (est): 786.5K **Privately Held**
WEB: www.acecanvasandtent.com
SIC: 7359 2394 7699 Tent & tarpaulin rental; tents: made from purchased materials; tent repair shop

(G-16904)
ACE ELECTRONICS LLC MICHIGAN
401 Minnesota Dr (48083-4698)
PHONE.................................443 327-6100
Amanda Burgos, *Marketing Staff*
Nick Pugliese, *Business Dir*
Nish Patel,
EMP: 6 **EST:** 2011 **Privately Held**
WEB: www.aceelectronics.com
SIC: 3679 Electronic components

(G-16905)
ACTALENT SERVICES LLC
Also Called: Easi
340 E Big Beaver Rd (48083-1218)
PHONE.................................248 712-2750
Sandeep Agarwal, *Project Mgr*
Jill Spangler, *Project Mgr*
Connor Mark, *Design Engr*
Hushedar Mehta, *Branch Mgr*
Denise Myslicki, *Technical Staff*
EMP: 33
SALES (corp-wide): 12.2B **Privately Held**
WEB: www.actalentservices.com
SIC: 3822 Energy cutoff controls, residential or commercial types
HQ: Actalent Services, Llc
 7320 Parkway Dr
 Hanover MD 21076
 717 553-7700

(G-16906)
ADS LLC
Also Called: A D S Environmental Srvs
1100 Owendale Dr Ste K (48183-1914)
PHONE.................................248 740-9593
Larry Greene, *Manager*
EMP: 6
SALES (corp-wide): 2.3B **Publicly Held**
WEB: www.adsenv.com
SIC: 3823 8748 8711 Flow instruments, industrial process type; business consulting; engineering services
HQ: Ads Llc
 340 The Bridge St Ste 204
 Huntsville AL 35806
 256 430-3366

(G-16907)
ADVANCED BORING AND TOOL CO
5750 New King Dr Ste 200 (48098-2611)
PHONE.................................586 598-9300
Thomas J Carter, *Ch of Bd*
Stefan Wanczyk, *President*
EMP: 80 **EST:** 1994
SALES (est): 12MM
SALES (corp-wide): 305MM **Privately Held**
WEB: www.advancedboringandtool.com
SIC: 3599 Machine shop, jobbing & repair
PA: Utica Enterprises, Inc.
 5750 New King Dr Ste 200
 Troy MI 48098
 586 726-4300

(G-16908)
ADVANCED FEEDLINES LLC
Also Called: Dallas Industries
103 Park Dr (48083-2770)
PHONE.................................248 583-9400
Willie Chacko, *CEO*
Joseph A Gentilia, *President*
Dave Laws, *Sales Mgr*
Warren Gideon, *Regl Sales Mgr*
John Heuring, *Regl Sales Mgr*
EMP: 47 **EST:** 1959
SALES (est): 7.5MM **Privately Held**
WEB: www.dallasindustries.com
SIC: 3542 5084 3549 3545 Machine tools, metal forming type; industrial machinery & equipment; metalworking machinery; machine tool accessories

(G-16909)
ADVANCED-CABLE LLC
1179 Chicago Rd (48083-4239)
PHONE.................................586 491-3073
Deanna J Zwiesele, *Manager*
Deanna Zwiesele,
EMP: 10
SALES (est): 1.5MM **Privately Held**
WEB: www.advanced-cable.com
SIC: 5065 3669 Electronic parts; visual communication systems

(G-16910)
AFFILIATED TROY DERMATOLOGIST
4600 Investment Dr (48098-6365)
PHONE.................................248 267-5020
Marcia Cardelli, *Partner*
Snehal Desai, *Med Doctor*
EMP: 18 **EST:** 2000
SALES (est): 2.7MM **Privately Held**
WEB: www.myatderm.com
SIC: 2834 8011 Dermatologicals; offices & clinics of medical doctors

(G-16911)
AIP GROUP INC
2041 E Square Lake Rd # 100 (48085-3897)
PHONE.................................248 828-4400
Meiling Ngai, *Chairman*
Adrian Donev, *VP Opers*
Maggie Flood, *Technology*
Nanci Murphy, *Assistant*
EMP: 6 **EST:** 2001
SALES (est): 887.1K **Privately Held**
WEB: www.aipma.com
SIC: 2754 Business forms: gravure printing

Troy - Oakland County (G-16912)

(G-16912)
AJAX MATERIALS CORPORATION (DH)
Also Called: Detroit Asphalt Paving Company
1957 Crooks Rd A (48084-5504)
P.O. Box 7058 (48084)
PHONE..................248 244-3300
James A Jacob, *President*
Jim Price, *Project Mgr*
EMP: 4 **EST:** 1962
SQ FT: 10,000
SALES (est): 7.2MM **Privately Held**
WEB: www.ajaxpaving.com
SIC: 2951 Asphalt & asphaltic paving mixtures (not from refineries)
HQ: Ajax Paving Industries, Inc.
1957 Crooks Rd A
Troy MI 48084
248 244-3300

(G-16913)
AJAX PAVING INDUSTRIES INC (HQ)
1957 Crooks Rd A (48084-5504)
P.O. Box 7058 (48007-7058)
PHONE..................248 244-3300
Herbert H Jacob, *Ch of Bd*
James A Jacob, *President*
Christie Alvaro, *General Mgr*
Dale G Hauer, *Vice Pres*
Jim Price, *Project Mgr*
EMP: 200 **EST:** 1951
SQ FT: 10,000
SALES (est): 287.5MM **Privately Held**
WEB: www.ajaxpaving.com
SIC: 1611 2951 3273 3272 Highway & street paving contractor; concrete construction: roads, highways, sidewalks, etc.; resurfacing contractor; asphalt & asphaltic paving mixtures (not from refineries); ready-mixed concrete; concrete products

(G-16914)
AKZO NOBEL COATINGS INC
1845 Maxwell Dr Ste 100 (48084-4506)
PHONE..................248 637-0400
EMP: 34
SALES (corp-wide): 10B **Privately Held**
SIC: 2851 Paints & allied products
HQ: Akzo Nobel Coatings Inc.
8220 Mohawk Dr
Strongsville OH 44136
440 297-5100

(G-16915)
AKZO NOBEL COATINGS INC
27 Brush St (48084)
PHONE..................248 451-6231
John Lindeman, *Manager*
EMP: 34
SALES (corp-wide): 10B **Privately Held**
SIC: 2851 Paints & allied products
HQ: Akzo Nobel Coatings Inc.
8220 Mohawk Dr
Strongsville OH 44136
440 297-5100

(G-16916)
AKZO NOBEL COATINGS INC
2373 John R Rd Ste A (48083-2567)
PHONE..................248 528-0715
Kevin Hales, *Manager*
EMP: 8
SALES (corp-wide): 10B **Privately Held**
SIC: 2851 Paints & allied products
HQ: Akzo Nobel Coatings Inc.
8220 Mohawk Dr
Strongsville OH 44136
440 297-5100

(G-16917)
AKZONOBEL SIGN FINISHES
1845 Maxwell Dr (48084-4506)
PHONE..................770 317-6361
EMP: 1 **EST:** 2017
SALES (est): 17MM **Privately Held**
WEB: www.grip-gard.com
SIC: 3993 Signs & advertising specialties

(G-16918)
AL-CRAFT DESIGN & ENGRG INC (PA)
Also Called: Al-Craft Industries
710 Minnesota Dr (48083-6204)
PHONE..................248 589-3827
John Graham, *CEO*
Jane Nido, *President*
Lisa Schroeder, *Accounting Mgr*
EMP: 5 **EST:** 1965
SQ FT: 32,000
SALES (est): 3.6MM **Privately Held**
WEB: www.al-craft.com
SIC: 3544 3543 Special dies & tools; industrial patterns

(G-16919)
ALEX DELVECCHIO ENTPS INC
1343 Piedmont Dr (48083-1918)
P.O. Box 1256 (48099-1256)
PHONE..................248 619-9600
Alex J Delvecchio Jr, *President*
Gail Ryder, *Sales Executive*
EMP: 14 **EST:** 1986
SQ FT: 5,000
SALES (est): 1.6MM **Privately Held**
WEB: www.theimprintshop.com
SIC: 5199 3993 Advertising specialties; signs, not made in custom sign painting shops; name plates: except engraved, etched, etc.: metal

(G-16920)
ALEXANDER J BONGIORNO INC
101 W Big Beavr Rd # 135 (48084-5353)
PHONE..................248 689-7766
Alexander J Bongiorno, *President*
David Anthony Bongiorno, *Office Mgr*
EMP: 5
SQ FT: 1,565
SALES (est): 633.2K **Privately Held**
WEB: www.bongiornojewelers.com
SIC: 3911 5944 Jewelry, precious metal; jewelry stores

(G-16921)
ALFMEIER FRIEDRICHS & RATH LLC
340 E Big Beaver Rd # 135 (48083-1218)
PHONE..................248 526-1650
Derek Loader, *Principal*
Omar Garcia, *Engineer*
Adrian Kerrigan, *Engineer*
Andrea Corley, *Human Res Mgr*
David Eisenbacher, *Sales Staff*
EMP: 6
SALES (corp-wide): 20.7K **Privately Held**
WEB: www.afrna.com
SIC: 3714 Fuel systems & parts, motor vehicle
HQ: Alfmeier Friedrichs & Rath Llc
120 Elcon Dr
Greenville SC 29605

(G-16922)
ALHERN-MARTIN INDUS FRNC CO
2155 Austin Dr (48083-2237)
PHONE..................248 689-6363
James J Van Etten, *President*
Scott Jones, *Vice Pres*
EMP: 20 **EST:** 1932
SQ FT: 10,000
SALES (est): 4.9MM **Privately Held**
WEB: www.alhern-martin.com
SIC: 5074 3567 3433 Heating equipment (hydronic); heating units & devices, industrial: electric; heating equipment, except electric

(G-16923)
ALL ACCESS NAME TAGS
1435 Rochester Rd (48083-6016)
PHONE..................866 955-8247
Timothy Hourigan, *Principal*
Erin Dawkins, *Marketing Staff*
EMP: 9 **EST:** 2010
SQ FT: 4,000
SALES (est): 573.9K **Privately Held**
WEB: www.allaccesstags.com
SIC: 2759 Tags: printing

(G-16924)
ALL WELDING AND FABG CO INC
1882 Woodslee Dr (48083-2207)
PHONE..................248 689-0986
Thomas Cameron, *President*
EMP: 12 **EST:** 1981
SQ FT: 18,000
SALES (est): 1.5MM **Privately Held**
WEB: www.allweldfab.com
SIC: 7692 Welding repair

(G-16925)
ALLAN TOOL & MACHINE CO INC (PA)
1822 E Maple Rd (48083-4240)
PHONE..................248 585-2910
Jeffrey M Scott, *President*
Ron Boehmer, *Manager*
Bob Boyce, *Manager*
Don Prucha, *Info Tech Dir*
Marian Neumann, *Admin Sec*
▲ **EMP:** 85 **EST:** 1955
SQ FT: 45,000
SALES (est): 10MM **Privately Held**
WEB: www.allantool.com
SIC: 3451 3471 Screw machine products; anodizing (plating) of metals or formed products

(G-16926)
ALLEGRA MARKETING PRINT MAIL
1307 E Maple Rd Ste E (48083-6023)
PHONE..................248 602-0545
EMP: 7 **EST:** 2018
SALES (est): 183.8K **Privately Held**
WEB: www.allegramarketingprint.com
SIC: 2752 Commercial printing, offset

(G-16927)
ALLOYING SURFACES INC
Also Called: Surfalloy
1346 Wheaton Dr (48083-1989)
PHONE..................248 524-9200
William H Bagley, *President*
Janet E Bagley, *Vice Pres*
EMP: 4 **EST:** 1972
SQ FT: 5,000
SALES (est): 1MM **Privately Held**
WEB: www.surfalloy.com
SIC: 3325 3313 3341 2851 Alloy steel castings, except investment; alloys, additive, except copper: not made in blast furnaces; secondary nonferrous metals; paints & allied products; inorganic pigments

(G-16928)
ALTAIR ENGINEERING INC (PA)
1820 E Big Beaver Rd (48083-2031)
PHONE..................248 614-2400
James Scapa, *CEO*
James R Scapa, *Ch of Bd*
Brett Chouinard, *President*
Scott Suchyta, *Partner*
Tony Gray, *Principal*
EMP: 200 **EST:** 1985
SQ FT: 132,900
SALES (est): 469.9MM **Publicly Held**
WEB: www.altair.com
SIC: 7372 8711 Prepackaged software; engineering services

(G-16929)
ALUMALIGHT LLC
1307 E Maple Rd Ste E (48083-6023)
P.O. Box 944, Birmingham (48012-0944)
PHONE..................248 457-9302
Bill Tocco, *General Mgr*
Michael Stenback, *Mng Member*
Gary Dillon,
EMP: 8 **EST:** 2007
SQ FT: 10,000
SALES (est): 893.3K **Privately Held**
WEB: www.alumalight.com
SIC: 3646 Commercial indusl & institutional electric lighting fixtures

(G-16930)
AMALGAMATIONS LTD
6181 Elmoor Dr (48098-1896)
P.O. Box 127 (48099-0127)
PHONE..................248 879-7345
Sharon Meyer, *President*
EMP: 5 **EST:** 1983
SALES (est): 339.1K **Privately Held**
SIC: 3961 3911 Costume jewelry, ex. precious metal & semiprecious stones; jewelry, precious metal

(G-16931)
AMERI-SERV GROUP
2855 Coolidge Hwy Ste 112 (48084-3215)
PHONE..................734 426-9700
EMP: 13 **EST:** 1999
SALES (est): 1.8MM **Privately Held**
SIC: 3565 7629 Air Vac Machinery Service And Repair

(G-16932)
AMERICAN MSC INC
2451 Elliott Dr (48083-4503)
PHONE..................248 589-7770
John Behler, *Manager*
EMP: 10 **Privately Held**
WEB: www.americanmsc.com
SIC: 3493 Automobile springs
HQ: American Msc Inc.
2401 Elliott Dr
Troy MI 48083
248 589-7770

(G-16933)
AMERICAN MSC INC (HQ)
2401 Elliott Dr (48083-4503)
PHONE..................248 589-7770
Ichiro Murata, *Ch of Bd*
Norimoto Usui, *Exec VP*
Brian Peters, *Info Tech Mgr*
▲ **EMP:** 50 **EST:** 1987
SQ FT: 50,000
SALES (est): 11.4MM **Privately Held**
WEB: www.americanmsc.com
SIC: 3493 3999 Automobile springs; atomizers, toiletry

(G-16934)
AMERICAN PRINTING SERVICES INC
6931 Killarney Dr (48098-2190)
PHONE..................248 568-5543
Linda Saylor, *Administration*
EMP: 4 **EST:** 2014
SALES (est): 118K **Privately Held**
SIC: 2752 Commercial printing, offset

(G-16935)
AMS CO LTD
Also Called: AMS America
3221 W Big Beaver Rd # 117 (48084-2803)
PHONE..................248 712-4435
Jin Chae Lee, *Office Mgr*
Jason Rupkey, *Program Mgr*
EMP: 4 **Privately Held**
SIC: 8711 3699 Engineering services; automotive driving simulators (training aids), electronic
PA: Ams Co., Ltd
5/F Dukam Bldg.
Seoul 05831

(G-16936)
ANCOR INFORMATION MGT LLC (PA)
Also Called: Utilitec
1911 Woodslee Dr (48083-2236)
PHONE..................248 740-8866
Tom Schneider, *Vice Pres*
Mary Franzoni, *Project Mgr*
Heather Regier, *Project Mgr*
Erin Romo, *Project Mgr*
Randall Kolodziejski, *Opers Mgr*
EMP: 100 **EST:** 1993
SALES (est): 24.7MM **Privately Held**
WEB: www.ancorinfo.com
SIC: 7374 7371 2759 7331 Data processing service; custom computer programming services; laser printing; direct mail advertising services

(G-16937)
ANDERTON EQUITY LLC (PA)
3001 W Big Beaver Rd # 310 (48084-3101)
PHONE..................248 430-6650
EMP: 0 **EST:** 2013

SALES (est): 62.4MM **Privately Held**
WEB: www.andertonindustries.com
SIC: **6719** 3465 Investment holding companies, except banks; body parts, automobile: stamped metal

(G-16938)
ANTOLIN INTERIORS USA INC
600 Wilshire Dr (48084-1625)
PHONE.................................248 567-4000
Ajit Khatra, *Engineer*
Peter Littkemann, *Engineer*
Jeff Jermyn, *Branch Mgr*
Ashutosh Chaudhary, *Program Mgr*
Renee Wester, *Administration*
EMP: 51
SALES (corp-wide): 2.6MM **Privately Held**
SIC: 3714 Motor vehicle parts & accessories
HQ: Antolin Interiors Usa, Inc.
  1700 Atlantic Blvd
  Auburn Hills MI 48326
  248 373-1749

(G-16939)
APB INC
Also Called: Allegra Print & Imaging
3334 Rochester Rd (48083-5426)
PHONE.................................248 528-2990
Stuart Glasier, *President*
Gerald Savalle, *Opers Mgr*
James Myers, *Director*
EMP: 7 **EST:** 1985
SQ FT: 1,300
SALES (est): 1.2MM **Privately Held**
WEB: www.allegramarketingprint.com
SIC: **2752** 2791 2789 2759 Commercial printing, offset; typesetting; bookbinding & related work; commercial printing

(G-16940)
APOLLO TRICK TITANIUM INC
321 Elmwood Dr (48083-2754)
P.O. Box 428, Holt (48842-0428)
PHONE.................................517 694-7449
Regis A Gully, *President*
EMP: 29 **EST:** 1969
SQ FT: 9,000
SALES (est): 450.7K **Privately Held**
WEB: www.tricktitanium.com
SIC: **3369** Titanium castings, except die-casting

(G-16941)
APROTECH POWERTRAIN LLC (PA)
2150 Butterfield Dr (48084-3427)
PHONE.................................248 649-9200
Danny Nichols, *Mng Member*
▼ **EMP:** 21 **EST:** 2007
SALES (est): 7.6MM **Privately Held**
WEB: www.aprotechgroup.com
SIC: **3612** Vibrators, interrupter

(G-16942)
APTIV CORPORATION (HQ)
5725 Innovation Dr (48098-2852)
PHONE.................................248 813-2000
Rodney O'Neal, *CEO*
Jeffrey Florek, *Principal*
Ryan Houde, *Principal*
Douglas Vande Lune, *Principal*
Douglas McMahan, *Principal*
◆ **EMP:** 1433 **EST:** 1998
SQ FT: 264,000
SALES (est): 444.2MM
SALES (corp-wide): 14.3B **Privately Held**
WEB: www.borgwarner.com
SIC: 3714 Motor vehicle parts & accessories
PA: Aptiv Plc
  Queensway House Hilgrove Street
  Jersey JE1 1
  163 422-4000

(G-16943)
APTIV CORPORATION (HQ)
5820 Innovation Dr (48098-2824)
PHONE.................................248 813-3005
Rodney O'Neal, *President*
Timothy Seitz, *Vice Pres*
Jackeline Rousseau, *Project Mgr*
Duane Swanson, *Project Mgr*
Kyle Cooper, *Engineer*
EMP: 600 **EST:** 2009

SALES (est): 2B
SALES (corp-wide): 14.3B **Privately Held**
WEB: www.aptiv.com
SIC: 3714 Motor vehicle parts & accessories
PA: Aptiv Plc
  Queensway House Hilgrove Street
  Jersey JE1 1
  163 422-4000

(G-16944)
APTIV INTL SVCS CO LLC
5820 Innovation Dr (48098-2824)
P.O. Box 5086 (48007-5086)
PHONE.................................248 813-2000
Rodney O'Neal, *President*
EMP: 1 **EST:** 2009
SALES (est): 3MM
SALES (corp-wide): 14.3B **Privately Held**
WEB: www.borgwarner.com
SIC: 3714 Motor vehicle parts & accessories
PA: Aptiv Plc
  Queensway House Hilgrove Street
  Jersey JE1 1
  163 422-4000

(G-16945)
APTIV MEXICAN HOLDINGS US LLC (HQ)
5820 Innovation Dr (48098-2824)
PHONE.................................248 813-2000
EMP: 241 **EST:** 2000
SALES (est): 8.5MM
SALES (corp-wide): 14.3B **Privately Held**
WEB: www.borgwarner.com
SIC: 3714 Motor vehicle parts & accessories
PA: Aptiv Plc
  Queensway House Hilgrove Street
  Jersey JE1 1
  163 422-4000

(G-16946)
APTIV SERVICES 3 (US) LLC
Also Called: Delphi
5725 Innovation Dr (48098-2852)
PHONE.................................248 813-2000
Jeffrey Boring, *Mfg Staff*
Christopher Cass, *Engineer*
Arquimedes Godoy, *Engineer*
Leopoldo Hernandez, *Engineer*
Donald Johnson, *Engineer*
◆ **EMP:** 1 **EST:** 2009
SALES (est): 4.7MM **Privately Held**
SIC: 3714 Motor vehicle parts & accessories

(G-16947)
APTIV SERVICES 5 US LLC
5820 Innovation Dr (48098-2824)
P.O. Box 5082 (48007-5082)
PHONE.................................248 813-2000
Jeff Anderson,
EMP: 1 **EST:** 1998
SALES (est): 4MM
SALES (corp-wide): 14.3B **Privately Held**
WEB: www.borgwarner.com
SIC: 3714 Motor vehicle parts & accessories
PA: Aptiv Plc
  Queensway House Hilgrove Street
  Jersey JE1 1
  163 422-4000

(G-16948)
APTIV SERVICES US LLC
Also Called: Delphi
5820 Innovation Dr (48098-2824)
PHONE.................................330 373-7666
Steve Duca, *Branch Mgr*
EMP: 7
SALES (corp-wide): 14.3B **Privately Held**
SIC: 3714 Motor vehicle parts & accessories
HQ: Aptiv Services Us, Llc
  5725 Innovation Dr
  Troy MI 48098

(G-16949)
APTIV SERVICES US LLC
Delphi
5725 Innovation Dr (48098-2852)
PHONE.................................248 813-2000
Theresa Lindley, *Project Mgr*
Kevin Campbell, *Engineer*

David Stevens, *Financial Analy*
Julie Carmany, *Manager*
William Goetze, *Software Engr*
EMP: 7
SALES (corp-wide): 14.3B **Privately Held**
SIC: 3714 Motor vehicle parts & accessories
HQ: Aptiv Services Us, Llc
  5725 Innovation Dr
  Troy MI 48098

(G-16950)
APTIV TRADE MGT SVCS US LLC
5820 Innovation Dr (48098-2824)
PHONE.................................248 813-2000
EMP: 21 **EST:** 2009
SALES (est): 1MM
SALES (corp-wide): 14.3B **Privately Held**
WEB: www.aptiv.com
SIC: 3714 Motor vehicle parts & accessories
PA: Aptiv Plc
  Queensway House Hilgrove Street
  Jersey JE1 1
  163 422-4000

(G-16951)
ARAS CORP
3290 W Big Beaver Rd # 315 (48084-2910)
PHONE.................................248 385-5293
EMP: 15 **EST:** 2014
SALES (est): 258.4K **Privately Held**
WEB: www.aras.com
SIC: 7372 Prepackaged software

(G-16952)
ARPLAS USA LLC
1030 Chicago Rd (48083-4203)
PHONE.................................888 527-5553
Karel Pieterman, *Mng Member*
EMP: 4 **EST:** 2006
SALES (est): 674.7K **Privately Held**
WEB: www.arplassystems.com
SIC: 3548 Resistance welders, electric

(G-16953)
ART OF CUSTOM FRAMING INC
3863 Rochester Rd (48083-5245)
PHONE.................................248 435-3726
Denise Bashi, *President*
Art Bashi, *Vice Pres*
EMP: 8 **EST:** 2011
SALES (est): 1MM **Privately Held**
WEB: www.framingart.net
SIC: **2499** 8412 Picture & mirror frames, wood; art gallery

(G-16954)
ART OF SHAVING - FL LLC
2800 W Big Beavr Rd Fl 2 (48084-3206)
PHONE.................................248 649-5872
Moira Gallo, *Branch Mgr*
EMP: 4
SALES (corp-wide): 76.1B **Publicly Held**
WEB: www.theartofshaving.com
SIC: **5999** 2844 3421 5122 Hair care products; toilet preparations; razor blades & razors; razor blades
HQ: The Art Of Shaving - Fl Llc
  1 Gillette Park
  Boston MA 02127

(G-16955)
ARTIC TECHNOLOGIES INTL
3456 Rochester Rd (48083-5210)
PHONE.................................248 689-9884
Tim A Gargagliano, *President*
Kathryn L Gargagliano, *VP Opers*
EMP: 6 **EST:** 1984
SQ FT: 6,000
SALES (est): 402.9K **Privately Held**
SIC: **7373** 3577 Systems software development services; computer peripheral equipment

(G-16956)
ARTICULATE SIGNS
1923 Ring Dr (48083-4229)
PHONE.................................248 577-1860
Jeff Young, *Owner*
EMP: 4 **EST:** 2017
SALES (est): 74.5K **Privately Held**
WEB: www.sobernotstuck.com
SIC: 3993 Signs & advertising specialties

(G-16957)
ARVINMERITOR OE LLC (HQ)
2135 W Maple Rd (48084-7121)
PHONE.................................248 435-1000
Carmen De Stefano, *Business Mgr*
Charles G McClure Jr, *Mng Member*
▲ **EMP:** 1 **EST:** 1997
SALES (est): 238.3MM **Publicly Held**
WEB: www.meritor.com
SIC: 3714 Motor vehicle parts & accessories

(G-16958)
ASCO POWER TECHNOLOGIES LP
1975 Technology Dr Ste B (48083-4247)
PHONE.................................248 957-9050
Kevin Chmielewski, *Engineer*
Kevin Chmielewskri, *Manager*
EMP: 8
SALES (corp-wide): 177.9K **Privately Held**
WEB: www.ascopower.com
SIC: 3699 Electrical equipment & supplies
HQ: Asco Power Technologies, L.P.
  160 Park Ave
  Florham Park NJ 07932

(G-16959)
ASPEN DOOR SUPPLY LLC
1195 Rochester Rd Ste P (48083-6027)
PHONE.................................248 291-5303
Phillip Hall, *President*
EMP: 7 **EST:** 2012
SALES (est): 127.7K **Privately Held**
WEB: www.aspendoorsupply.com
SIC: **2431** 5211 Door frames, wood; door & window products

(G-16960)
ASSEMBLY TECHNOLOGIES INTL INC
Also Called: American Beauty Tools
1937 Barrett Dr (48084-5372)
PHONE.................................248 280-2810
Eric Soderlund, *President*
Joanna Soderlund, *General Mgr*
Brad Ditomaso, *VP Opers*
◆ **EMP:** 14 **EST:** 1995
SQ FT: 13,000
SALES (est): 3.6MM **Privately Held**
WEB: www.americanbeautytools.com
SIC: **5084** 3423 7699 3548 Welding machinery & equipment; soldering irons or coppers; welding equipment repair; welding apparatus

(G-16961)
ASSET HEALTH INC
2250 Butterfield Dr # 100 (48084-3404)
PHONE.................................248 822-2870
David Wilson, *CEO*
Mike Creal, *Vice Pres*
Daniel Parke, *Sales Dir*
Kennyle Jones, *Accounts Mgr*
Robert Wilson, *Marketing Staff*
EMP: 53 **EST:** 2005
SALES (est): 6.4MM **Privately Held**
WEB: www.assethealth.com
SIC: 7372 Application computer software

(G-16962)
ATLAS WELDING ACCESSORIES INC
501 Stephenson Hwy (48083-1166)
P.O. Box 969 (48099-0969)
PHONE.................................248 588-4666
Betty Honhart, *President*
Keith Honhart, *Vice Pres*
John Honhart, *Treasurer*
Anne Honhart, *Software Engr*
EMP: 52 **EST:** 1939
SQ FT: 44,000
SALES (est): 4.6MM **Privately Held**
WEB: www.shop.atlaswelding.com
SIC: **3423** 3548 5084 Hand & edge tools; welding & cutting apparatus & accessories; welding machinery & equipment; safety tools

(G-16963)
ATMO-SEAL INC
Also Called: Atmo-Seal Enginering
1091 Wheaton Dr (48083-1928)
PHONE.................................248 528-9640

Troy - Oakland County (G-16964)

Everett O Carter, *President*
Tammy Jenkins, *Production*
EMP: 8 **EST:** 1999
SALES (est): 973.5K **Privately Held**
WEB: www.atmoseal.com
SIC: 3823 8711 Industrial process measurement equipment; analyzers, industrial process type; annunciators, relay & solid state types; infrared instruments, industrial process type; engineering services

(G-16964)
ATOS SYNTEL INC (HQ)
525 E Big Beaver Rd # 300 (48083-1367)
PHONE 248 619-2800
Rakesh Khanna, *President*
Ramakumar Singampalli, *Senior VP*
Satchi Sarangi, *Vice Pres*
Venkatramana Acharya, *Project Mgr*
Ayyaril Babu, *Project Mgr*
EMP: 18657 **EST:** 1980
SQ FT: 6,430
SALES: 923.8MM
SALES (corp-wide): 146.7MM **Privately Held**
WEB: www.atos-syntel.net
SIC: 7372 8748 7371 Prepackaged software; systems analysis & engineering consulting services; computer software development
PA: Atos Se
  Immeuble River Ouest
  Bezons 95870
  964 450-614

(G-16965)
AUTOMATE INDUSTRIES INC
1906 Brinston Dr (48083-2217)
PHONE 248 740-7022
Gerard Ouellette, *President*
EMP: 8 **EST:** 1991
SQ FT: 3,200
SALES (est): 825.9K **Privately Held**
WEB: www.automateindustries.com
SIC: 3599 Machine shop, jobbing & repair

(G-16966)
AUTOMOTIVE MEDIA LLC
Also Called: I.M. Branded
500 W Long Lake Rd (48098-4540)
PHONE 248 537-8500
Jim Whitehead, *President*
Kathleen Borschke, *Vice Pres*
Steve Ripplinger, *Vice Pres*
Robin Ellis, *Project Mgr*
Ruth Roosen, *Project Mgr*
EMP: 125 **EST:** 2001
SALES (est): 30MM **Privately Held**
WEB: www.imbranded.com
SIC: 2752 Commercial printing, lithographic

(G-16967)
AVALON TOOLS INC
1910 Barrett Dr (48084-5371)
PHONE 248 269-0001
Robert Beatty, *President*
Sheryl Beatty, *Vice Pres*
EMP: 5 **EST:** 1998
SQ FT: 2,000
SALES (est): 562.8K **Privately Held**
WEB: www.avalontoolsinc.com
SIC: 3546 Power-driven handtools

(G-16968)
BARRON LLC
247 Minnesota Dr (48083-4674)
PHONE 248 879-6203
Diane Dettloff, *Principal*
EMP: 5 **EST:** 2012
SALES (est): 99.3K **Privately Held**
SIC: 3541 Machine tools, metal cutting type

(G-16969)
BECKER OREGON INC
635 Executive Dr (48083-4576)
PHONE 248 588-7480
Kyle Scott, *CEO*
EMP: 28 **EST:** 1990
SQ FT: 16,000
SALES (est): 302.6K **Privately Held**
WEB: www.beckerorthopedic.com
SIC: 3842 Braces, orthopedic

(G-16970)
BECKER ORTHOPEDIC APPLIANCE CO (PA)
635 Executive Dr (48083-4576)
PHONE 248 588-7480
Rudolf Becker, *Ch of Bd*
Timothy Piggott, *Business Mgr*
Ingrid Becker, *Corp Secy*
Rudy Becker, *Vice Pres*
John Lesner, *Plant Mgr*
▲ **EMP:** 65 **EST:** 1934
SQ FT: 36,000
SALES (est): 31MM **Privately Held**
WEB: www.beckerorthopedic.com
SIC: 3842 5999 Limbs, artificial; orthopedic & prosthesis applications

(G-16971)
BEET INC
1742 Crooks Rd (48084-5501)
PHONE 248 432-0052
Joseph Brady, *Engineer*
Dylan McClure, *Engineer*
David Wang, *Mng Member*
Kusmady Susanto, *Prgrmr*
Lance Lehmann, *Director*
▼ **EMP:** 10 **EST:** 2010
SQ FT: 5,000
SALES (est): 1.5MM **Privately Held**
WEB: www.beet.com
SIC: 7371 3823 3829 8748 Computer software systems analysis & design, custom; primary elements for process flow measurement; aircraft & motor vehicle measurement equipment; systems analysis & engineering consulting services

(G-16972)
BELL METALS
1107 Wheaton Dr (48083-6701)
PHONE 248 227-0407
EMP: 5 **EST:** 2018
SALES (est): 102.8K **Privately Held**
SIC: 3441 Fabricated structural metal

(G-16973)
BERG MARKETING GROUP
560 Kirts Blvd Ste 114 (48084-4141)
PHONE 314 457-9400
EMP: 4 **EST:** 2019
SALES (est): 108.8K **Privately Held**
WEB: www.bergmg.com
SIC: 3799 Transportation equipment

(G-16974)
BERGHOF GROUP NORTH AMER INC
1500 W Big Beavr Rd 2nd (48084-3522)
PHONE 313 720-6884
William Doell, *Director*
EMP: 10 **EST:** 2016
SALES (est): 1.6MM
SALES (corp-wide): 3.3MM **Privately Held**
WEB: www.berghof.com
SIC: 3559 Automotive maintenance equipment
PA: Berghof Gmbh
  Arbachtalstr. 26
  Eningen Unter Achalm 72800
  712 189-40

(G-16975)
BERMAR ASSOCIATES INC
433 Minnesota Dr (48083-4698)
P.O. Box 99430 (48099-9430)
PHONE 248 589-2460
Janet Roncelli, *President*
Dan Gorney, *Vice Pres*
EMP: 10 **EST:** 1969
SQ FT: 10,900
SALES (est): 1.5MM **Privately Held**
WEB: www.bermarassociates.com
SIC: 3089 Injection molded finished plastic products; injection molding of plastics

(G-16976)
BESWICK CORPORATION
2591 Elliott Dr (48083-4605)
PHONE 248 589-0562
Keith Banish, *President*
Arlene Beswick, *Vice Pres*
▲ **EMP:** 10 **EST:** 1965
SQ FT: 10,000
SALES (est): 1.6MM **Privately Held**
WEB: www.beswickcorp.com
SIC: 3444 3569 Sheet metalwork; filters & strainers, pipeline

(G-16977)
BLACK BOX CORPORATION
1287 Rankin Dr (48083-6007)
PHONE 248 743-1320
Rick Gannon, *President*
Ken Mage, *Business Mgr*
Dan Costanzo, *Opers Mgr*
EMP: 5
SALES (corp-wide): 573.9MM **Privately Held**
WEB: www.blackbox.com
SIC: 3577 4899 Computer peripheral equipment; data communication services
HQ: Black Box Corporation
  1000 Park Dr
  Lawrence PA 15055
  724 746-5500

(G-16978)
BNP MEDIA INC (PA)
2401 W Big Beavr Rd # 700 (48084-3333)
P.O. Box 2600 (48007-2600)
PHONE 248 362-3700
Harper Henderson, *President*
Jill Bloom, *Publisher*
Tom Fowler, *Publisher*
Glen Gudino, *Publisher*
Pamela Hugill, *Publisher*
EMP: 202 **EST:** 1926
SQ FT: 45,000
SALES (est): 97.2MM **Privately Held**
WEB: www.bnpmedia.com
SIC: 2721 Trade journals: publishing only, not printed on site

(G-16979)
BOLLHOFF
820 Kirts Blvd Spc 500 (48084-4898)
PHONE 313 506-0150
EMP: 8 **EST:** 2018
SALES (est): 1MM **Privately Held**
WEB: www.boellhoff.com
SIC: 3452 Bolts, nuts, rivets & washers

(G-16980)
BOLLHOFF RIVNUT
800 Kirts Blvd Ste 500 (48084-4879)
PHONE 248 269-0475
Mariko Custer, *General Mgr*
Shane La Rocca, *Project Mgr*
Erik Zavicar, *Engineer*
Kip Reynolds, *Accounts Exec*
Cindy Husk, *Manager*
EMP: 7 **EST:** 2009
SALES (est): 136.3K **Privately Held**
WEB: www.boellhoff.com
SIC: 3452 Bolts, nuts, rivets & washers

(G-16981)
BOMARK INDUSTRIES LLC
1803 Smallbrook Dr (48085-1423)
PHONE 248 879-9577
Bohdan Fedorak, *Administration*
EMP: 4 **EST:** 2019
SALES (est): 145.9K **Privately Held**
SIC: 3999 Manufacturing industries

(G-16982)
BONTAZ CENTRE USA INC
1099 Chicago Rd (48083-4204)
PHONE 248 588-8113
Yves Bontaz, *CEO*
Joseph Butkovich, *Opers Staff*
Christopher Bontaz, *Treasurer*
Donna Swagert, *Human Res Dir*
Abigail Brueckner, *Manager*
▲ **EMP:** 15 **EST:** 2001
SQ FT: 40,000
SALES (est): 6.9MM
SALES (corp-wide): 3MM **Privately Held**
WEB: www.bontaz.com
SIC: 3694 Engine electrical equipment
HQ: Bontaz Centre
  Zone Industrielle Des Valignons
  Marnaz 74460
  450 960-025

(G-16983)
BORGWARNER PDS ANDERSON LLC
5455 Corporate Dr Ste 116 (48098-2620)
PHONE 248 641-3045
EMP: 4
SALES (corp-wide): 9.8B **Publicly Held**
SIC: 3714 Mfg Motor Vehicle Parts/Accessories
HQ: Borgwarner Pds (Anderson), L.L.C.
  13975 Borgwarner Dr
  Noblesville IN 46060

(G-16984)
BORGWRNER PRPLSION SYSTEMS LLC
Delphi
5725 Innovation Dr (48098-2852)
PHONE 248 813-2000
Ray Divasta, *Engineer*
Leopoldo Hernandez, *Engineer*
Guy Hachey, *Manager*
David Boleyn, *Manager*
Martin Sykes, *Manager*
EMP: 209
SALES (corp-wide): 10.1B **Publicly Held**
WEB: www.borgwarner.com
SIC: 3714 Motor vehicle parts & accessories
HQ: Borgwarner Propulsion Systems Llc
  3000 University Dr
  Auburn Hills MI 48326
  248 707-5224

(G-16985)
BRINSTON ACQUISITION LLC
Also Called: New World Systems
840 W Long Lake Rd (48098-6356)
PHONE 248 269-1000
Bryan Proctor, *President*
Jennifer Korsak, *Partner*
Brian Leary, *Vice Pres*
Craig Nelson, *Vice Pres*
Rob Simonds, *Vice Pres*
EMP: 70 **EST:** 2015
SALES (est): 10.4MM
SALES (corp-wide): 1B **Publicly Held**
WEB: www.tylertech.com
SIC: 7372 Prepackaged software
PA: Tyler Technologies, Inc.
  5101 Tennyson Pkwy
  Plano TX 75024
  972 713-3700

(G-16986)
BRISTOL-MYERS SQUIBB COMPANY
2460 Waltham Dr (48085-3550)
PHONE 248 528-2476
Tanya Edwards, *Sales Staff*
EMP: 4
SALES (corp-wide): 42.5B **Publicly Held**
WEB: www.bms.com
SIC: 2834 Pharmaceutical preparations
PA: Bristol-Myers Squibb Company
  430 E 29th St Fl 14
  New York NY 10016
  212 546-4000

(G-16987)
BULLETSAFE BULLETPROOF VESTS
352 Oliver Dr (48084-5401)
PHONE 248 457-6877
EMP: 7 **EST:** 2017
SALES (est): 195.4K **Privately Held**
WEB: www.bulletsafe.com
SIC: 3842 Bulletproof vests

(G-16988)
BUSINESS NEWS PUBLISHING
2401 W Big Beavr Rd # 70 (48084-3306)
PHONE 248 362-3700
Taggart Henderson, *CEO*
Scott Coleman, *Partner*
Sean Bogle, *Natl Sales Mgr*
EMP: 12 **EST:** 2006
SALES (est): 2.5MM **Privately Held**
WEB: www.bnpmedia.com
SIC: 2721 Magazines: publishing only, not printed on site

GEOGRAPHIC SECTION

Troy - Oakland County (G-17015)

(G-16989)
C I I LTD
354 Indusco Ct (48083-4643)
PHONE..................................248 585-9905
Shrikant Mehta, *President*
Neena Metha, *Vice Pres*
EMP: 6 **EST:** 1991
SALES (est): 391.9K **Privately Held**
SIC: 3911 Jewelry, precious metal

(G-16990)
C2 IMAGING LLC
Also Called: Tepel Brothers
1725 John R Rd (48083-2512)
PHONE..................................248 743-2903
Jim Tepel, *President*
EMP: 105
SALES (corp-wide): 258MM **Privately Held**
WEB: www.c2imaging.com
SIC: 2759 Commercial printing
HQ: C2 Imaging, Llc
    201 Plaza Two
    Jersey City NJ 07311

(G-16991)
CABIN-N-WOODS LLC
657 Trinway Dr (48085-3121)
PHONE..................................248 828-4138
Christine Mulka, *Principal*
EMP: 5 **EST:** 2016
SALES (est): 41.5K **Privately Held**
SIC: 2499 Wood products

(G-16992)
CADILLAC PRODUCTS INC (PA)
5800 Crooks Rd Ste 100 (48098-2830)
PHONE..................................248 813-8200
Robert J Williams Sr, *Ch of Bd*
Michael P Williams II, *President*
Robert J Williams Jr, *President*
Eric Ebenhoeh, *Plant Mgr*
Steven Lee, *Engineer*
▲ **EMP:** 450 **EST:** 1942
SQ FT: 25,000
SALES (est): 74.4MM **Privately Held**
WEB: www.cadprodauto.com
SIC: 3714 3081 2673 3089 Motor vehicle parts & accessories; polyethylene film; plastic bags: made from purchased materials; thermoformed finished plastic products

(G-16993)
CADILLAC PRODUCTS PACKAGING CO (PA)
5800 Crooks Rd (48098-2830)
PHONE..................................248 879-5000
Robert Williams Jr, *CEO*
Roger Williams, *Treasurer*
Edna Wellborn, *Accountant*
Casey Turner, *Marketing Staff*
Michael Williams II, *Director*
EMP: 205 **EST:** 1999
SALES (est): 52.6MM **Privately Held**
WEB: www.cadprod.com
SIC: 3081 2671 Packing materials, plastic sheet; plastic film, coated or laminated for packaging

(G-16994)
CADILLAC PRSENTATION SOLUTIONS
1195 Equity Dr (48084-7108)
PHONE..................................248 288-9777
Kurt Streng, *President*
Chris Delusky, *Opers Dir*
Saad Nouman, *Production*
Kristen Streng, *Treasurer*
Tom Krebaum, *Sales Staff*
▲ **EMP:** 43 **EST:** 1951
SQ FT: 45,000
SALES (est): 5.7MM **Privately Held**
WEB: www.cadpres.com
SIC: 2782 2759 2675 2396 Looseleaf binders & devices; commercial printing; die-cut paper & board; automotive & apparel trimmings

(G-16995)
CAMBRIDGE FINANCIAL SERVICES
5435 Corporate Dr Ste 250 (48098-2631)
PHONE..................................248 840-6350
Kim Stine, *Founder*
EMP: 5 **EST:** 2016
SALES (est): 86.2K **Privately Held**
SIC: 2752 Commercial printing, lithographic

(G-16996)
CAMDEX INC
2330 Alger Dr (48083-2001)
PHONE..................................248 528-2300
Robert A Leich, *President*
Eugene Leich, *Vice Pres*
EMP: 15 **EST:** 1966
SQ FT: 5,000
SALES (est): 537.1K **Privately Held**
WEB: www.camdexloader.com
SIC: 3489 Ordnance & accessories

(G-16997)
CAPCO AUTOMOVITE
82 Park Dr (48083-2723)
PHONE..................................248 616-8888
Anthony Candella, *Principal*
EMP: 8 **EST:** 2011
SALES (est): 1.4MM **Privately Held**
WEB: www.capcoauto.com
SIC: 3465 Hub caps, automobile: stamped metal

(G-16998)
CAR PAK
1250 Allen Dr (48083-4011)
PHONE..................................248 280-1401
Jerold Levine, *Vice Pres*
EMP: 4 **EST:** 2018
SALES (est): 54.1K **Privately Held**
WEB: www.car-pak.com
SIC: 3541 Machine tools, metal cutting type

(G-16999)
CAR PAK MANUFACTURING CO
1401 Axtell Dr (48084-7002)
P.O. Box 421 (48099-0421)
PHONE..................................480 625-3655
EMP: 6 **EST:** 2018
SALES (est): 96.2K **Privately Held**
WEB: www.carpak.com
SIC: 3999 Manufacturing industries

(G-17000)
CARLEX GLASS AMERICA LLC
1209 E Big Beaver Rd (48083-1905)
PHONE..................................248 824-8800
Linda Leonard, *Marketing Staff*
EMP: 600 **Privately Held**
WEB: www.carlex.com
SIC: 3231 Products of purchased glass
HQ: Carlex Glass America, Llc
    7200 Centennial Blvd
    Nashville TN 37209

(G-17001)
CARLSON
1950 Austin Dr (48083-2205)
PHONE..................................248 824-7600
Susan Walton, *President*
EMP: 27 **EST:** 2006
SALES (est): 206.3K **Privately Held**
WEB: www.carlsonmetal.com
SIC: 3444 Sheet metalwork

(G-17002)
CARLSON METAL PRODUCTS INC
2335 Alger Dr (48083-2052)
PHONE..................................248 528-1931
John Martin, *President*
Julie Martin, *Treasurer*
Paul Stoll, *Prgrmr*
EMP: 30 **EST:** 1971
SQ FT: 17,000
SALES (est): 4.8MM **Privately Held**
WEB: www.carlsonmetal.com
SIC: 3444 Sheet metal specialties, not stamped

(G-17003)
CARO CARBIDE CORPORATION
553 Robbins Dr (48083-4559)
PHONE..................................248 588-4252
Richard Cieszkowski, *President*
EMP: 16 **EST:** 1972
SQ FT: 10,000
SALES (est): 1MM **Privately Held**
WEB: www.caro-carbide.com
SIC: 3545 Cutting tools for machine tools

(G-17004)
CARPATHIANS MANUFACTURING
1250 Rankin Dr Ste B (48083-2844)
PHONE..................................248 291-6232
Julie Dotan, *President*
EMP: 5 **EST:** 2013
SALES (est): 77.2K **Privately Held**
SIC: 3999 Manufacturing industries

(G-17005)
CARTEX CORPORATION (DH)
1515 Equity Dr 100 (48084-7129)
PHONE..................................610 759-1650
Hugh W Sloan Jr, *President*
Robert Magee, *Exec VP*
Carol Dickson, *Vice Pres*
Richard Jocsak, *Treasurer*
Marie Claude Manseau, *Admin Sec*
EMP: 7 **EST:** 1949
SQ FT: 108,000
SALES (est): 36.7MM
SALES (corp-wide): 157.8MM **Privately Held**
WEB: www.woodbridgegroup.com
SIC: 3069 Foam rubber
HQ: Woodbridge Holdings Inc.
    1515 Equity Dr Ste 100
    Troy MI 48084
    248 288-0100

(G-17006)
CENTRAL SCREW PRODUCTS COMPANY
Also Called: CSP Truck
1070 Maplelawn Dr (48084-5332)
PHONE..................................313 893-9100
Arnot B Heller II, *President*
Paul Atwood, *Vice Pres*
Eric Harman, *Engineer*
Julie Bonilla, *Human Resources*
Elizabeth Feldt, *Info Tech Mgr*
▲ **EMP:** 15 **EST:** 1924
SQ FT: 12,000
SALES (est): 4.7MM **Privately Held**
WEB: www.centralscrewproducts.com
SIC: 3451 Screw machine products

(G-17007)
CHAMPION HOME BUILDERS INC (HQ)
755 W Big Beavr Rd # 1000 (48084-4908)
PHONE..................................248 614-8200
John N Lawless, *CEO*
Kevin Bouvia, *General Mgr*
Pat Cross, *General Mgr*
Ken Hodson, *General Mgr*
Lj Lewis, *General Mgr*
EMP: 75 **EST:** 1953
SQ FT: 16,000
SALES (est): 1.1B
SALES (corp-wide): 1.4B **Publicly Held**
WEB: www.championhomes.com
SIC: 1521 2451 New construction, single-family houses; mobile homes, except recreational
PA: Skyline Champion Corporation
    755 W Big Beavr Rd # 100
    Troy MI 48084
    248 614-8211

(G-17008)
CHECK TECHNOLOGY SOLUTIONS LLC
1800 Stephenson Hwy (48083-2148)
PHONE..................................248 680-2323
Robert Check, *CEO*
Shulan Yu, *Engineer*
Manushi Sheth, *Design Engr*
Brian Champa, *Sales Mgr*
Tom Stuef, *Sales Mgr*
▲ **EMP:** 50 **EST:** 1992
SQ FT: 40,000
SALES (est): 12.3MM **Privately Held**
WEB: www.checkcorp.com
SIC: 3585 3714 Heating equipment, complete; motor vehicle parts & accessories

(G-17009)
CHELSEA-MEGAN HOLDING INC
Also Called: Compound Technology
1121 Rochester Rd (48083-6012)
PHONE..................................248 307-9160
Willis Engle, *President*
EMP: 15 **EST:** 2005
SQ FT: 38,000
SALES (est): 4MM **Privately Held**
WEB: www.compoundtech.com
SIC: 2821 Plastics materials & resins

(G-17010)
CHICL LLC
Also Called: Chicago Miniature Optoelectron
1708 Northwood Dr (48084-5521)
PHONE..................................859 294-5590
Steve Imgham, *CEO*
William Drexles, *CFO*
▲ **EMP:** 1399 **EST:** 2000
SQ FT: 15,000
SALES (est): 176.9MM **Privately Held**
SIC: 3641 Electric lamps
PA: Revstone Industries, Llc
    2008 Cypress St Ste 100
    Paris KY 40361

(G-17011)
CHOR INDUSTRIES INC
500 Robbins Dr (48083-4514)
PHONE..................................248 585-3323
David M Chor, *President*
Ellen Chor, *Vice Pres*
EMP: 23 **EST:** 1995
SQ FT: 19,000
SALES (est): 2.8MM **Privately Held**
WEB: www.chorindustries.com
SIC: 3471 Finishing, metals or formed products; electroplating of metals or formed products

(G-17012)
CITY ANIMATION CO (PA)
Also Called: Neway Manufacturing
57 Park Dr (48083-2753)
PHONE..................................248 589-0600
Eric Schultz, *CEO*
Brian Cybul, *CFO*
Mary Eickholt, *Admin Sec*
EMP: 50 **EST:** 1960
SQ FT: 22,000
SALES (est): 11.2MM **Privately Held**
WEB: www.cityeventsgroup.com
SIC: 5099 3993 7359 7812 Video & audio equipment; signs & advertising specialties; audio-visual equipment & supply rental; video tape production; machine tools, metal cutting type

(G-17013)
CKD USA CORPORATION
675 E Big Beaver Rd (48083-1418)
PHONE..................................248 740-7004
EMP: 4 **Privately Held**
WEB: www.ckdusa.com
SIC: 3592 Valves
HQ: Ckd Usa Corporation
    1605 N Penny Ln
    Schaumburg IL 60173
    847 368-0539

(G-17014)
CLASSIC STONE MBL & GRAN INC
2340 Alger Dr (48083-2001)
PHONE..................................248 588-1599
Adrian Bejan, *Administration*
EMP: 11 **EST:** 2004
SALES (est): 1MM **Privately Held**
WEB: www.newsurfaces.com
SIC: 1799 3281 5032 Counter top installation; granite, cut & shaped; marble building stone

(G-17015)
CLASSIC SYSTEMS LLC
Also Called: Classic Design
2400 Stephenson Hwy (48083-2171)
PHONE..................................248 588-2738
Jeff Eckerle, *General Mgr*
John Edwards, *Managing Dir*
Richard H Baird, *Principal*
Pamela Polvere, *Principal*
Doug Sanders, *Exec VP*
EMP: 110 **EST:** 2011
SALES (est): 29.8MM **Privately Held**
WEB: www.classic-co.com
SIC: 8711 3569 Consulting engineer; robots, assembly line: industrial & commercial

Troy - Oakland County (G-17016)

PA: Mba Tech, Inc.
1100 Piedmont Dr
Troy MI 48083

(G-17016)
CNC PROTOTYPE OF MICHIGAN
101 W Big Beavr Rd # 1400 (48084-5295)
PHONE..................586 218-3291
EMP: 5 EST: 2018
SALES (est): 148.6K Privately Held
SIC: 3599 Machine shop, jobbing & repair

(G-17017)
COBRA MAUFACTURING
1147 Rankin Dr (48083-6006)
PHONE..................248 585-1606
Wayne Pabisz, Owner
EMP: 10 EST: 1997
SQ FT: 3,760
SALES (est): 1.6MM Privately Held
SIC: 3423 Hand & edge tools

(G-17018)
COLOR SOURCE GRAPHICS INC
Also Called: Woodward Printing Co
1925 W Maple Rd Ste A (48084-7116)
PHONE..................248 458-2040
Craig Sobolewski, President
EMP: 4 EST: 1975
SQ FT: 5,000
SALES (est): 394.5K Privately Held
WEB: www.procolorcopy.com
SIC: 2752 Commercial printing, offset

(G-17019)
COMBINE INTERNATIONAL INC (PA)
Also Called: Artistic
354 Indusco Ct (48083-4643)
PHONE..................248 585-9900
Shrikant C Mehta, President
Sanjay Rami, Vice Pres
Roger D Parsons, CFO
Cyril Valimattom, CFO
Sudesh Rami, Controller
◆ EMP: 172 EST: 1977
SQ FT: 35,000
SALES (est): 25.2MM Privately Held
WEB: www.mail.cigportal.com
SIC: 3911 5094 Jewelry, precious metal; pearls

(G-17020)
COMMANDO LOCK COMPANY LLC
395 Elmwood Dr (48083-2754)
PHONE..................248 709-7901
Kim Marsh,
Patrick Smith,
▲ EMP: 10 EST: 2013
SALES (est): 2MM Privately Held
WEB: www.commandolock.com
SIC: 3429 Locks or lock sets

(G-17021)
COMPLETE DATA PRODUCTS INC (PA)
5755 New King Dr Ste 210 (48098-2649)
P.O. Box 7169, Bloomfield Hills (48302-7169)
PHONE..................248 651-8602
Tom Carswell, President
Neal Doshi, Partner
Nirav Doshi, Partner
EMP: 14 EST: 1986
SALES (est): 3.5MM Privately Held
WEB: www.securecdp.com
SIC: 5112 7372 7371 7373 Business forms; computer & photocopying supplies; application computer software; business oriented computer software; computer software development; systems software development services

(G-17022)
COMPUNETICS INCORPORATED
2500 Rochester Ct (48083-5200)
PHONE..................248 524-6376
Donald R Bernier, President
Don Bernier, Vice Pres
Bruce R Shaw, Vice Pres
Barry Blake, Sales Dir
Bob Gosliak, Executive
EMP: 20 EST: 1971
SQ FT: 21,000
SALES (est): 4.2MM Privately Held
WEB: www.compuneticsinc.com
SIC: 8711 3674 Engineering services; microprocessors

(G-17023)
CONTINENTAL AUTO SYSTEMS INC
Siemens VDO North America
4685 Investment Dr (48098-6335)
PHONE..................248 267-9408
Craig Love, Accounts Mgr
Keith Robinson, Branch Mgr
EMP: 7
SALES (corp-wide): 44.6B Privately Held
WEB: www.continental-automotive.com
SIC: 3714 5013 3621 Motor vehicle parts & accessories; motor vehicle supplies & new parts; motors & generators
HQ: Continental Automotive Systems, Inc.
1 Continental Dr
Auburn Hills MI 48326

(G-17024)
CONTINNTAL AUTO SYSTEMS US INC
4685 Investment Dr (48098-6335)
PHONE..................248 764-6400
Jennifer Wahnschaff, Vice Pres
Javier Mayo, Engineer
EMP: 57 EST: 1994
SALES (est): 908.1K Privately Held
SIC: 3714 Motor vehicle parts & accessories

(G-17025)
CONTOUR METROLOGICAL & MFG INC (PA)
Also Called: Cmm Optic
488 Oliver Dr (48084-5426)
PHONE..................248 273-1111
Kevin McMahon, President
Joshua Valascho, Engineer
Joseph Robillard, Manager
Janet Soller, Administration
EMP: 8 EST: 1989
SQ FT: 15,000
SALES (est): 3.3MM Privately Held
WEB: www.cmmoptic.com
SIC: 3827 Optical instruments & lenses

(G-17026)
CONTROL POWER-RELIANCE LLC (HQ)
Also Called: C P R
310 Executive Dr 314 (48083-4532)
PHONE..................248 583-1020
J Edgar Myles, President
Scott Myles,
EMP: 8 EST: 1994
SALES (est): 2.5MM
SALES (corp-wide): 11.3MM Privately Held
WEB: www.cp-r.com
SIC: 3829 Measuring & controlling devices
PA: J. E. Myles Inc.
310 Executive Dr
Troy MI 48083
248 583-1020

(G-17027)
CONTROLLED POWER COMPANY (PA)
1955 Stephenson Hwy Ste G (48083-2183)
PHONE..................248 528-3700
Christian Tazzia, President
Chuck Wiesman, Regional Mgr
Dave Gerds, Vice Pres
Mark Hunt, Vice Pres
Frank Loria, Vice Pres
▼ EMP: 113 EST: 1968
SQ FT: 90,000
SALES: 17.3MM Privately Held
WEB: www.controlledpwr.com
SIC: 3612 3629 3677 8711 Rectifier transformers; power conversion units, a.c. to d.c.; static-electric; electronic coils, transformers & other inductors; engineering services

(G-17028)
COPELAND-GIBSON PRODUCTS CORP
1025 E Maple Rd (48083-2814)
PHONE..................248 740-4400
Raymond E Howard, President
Dave Barrett, Vice Pres
Nancy Howard, Vice Pres
Charles Howard, Treasurer
Ann Howard, Admin Sec
EMP: 25 EST: 1934
SQ FT: 6,500
SALES (est): 1.1MM Privately Held
WEB: www.copeland-gibson.com
SIC: 7389 3053 Metal cutting services; gaskets & sealing devices

(G-17029)
CORNING INCORPORATED
50 W Big Beavr Rd Ste 225 (48084-5203)
PHONE..................248 680-4701
Jeffrey S King, Research
Ron Rogers, Manager
EMP: 4
SALES (corp-wide): 11.3B Publicly Held
WEB: www.corning.com
SIC: 3229 Pressed & blown glass
PA: Corning Incorporated
1 Riverfront Plz
Corning NY 14831
607 974-9000

(G-17030)
CORPORATE ELECTRONIC STY INC
Also Called: Colorpoint Print.com
2708 American Dr (48084-4625)
PHONE..................248 583-7070
Bonnie Mc Donald, President
James W Mc Donald II, Vice Pres
Scott Wolkhamer, Vice Pres
Stephanie Lucas, Credit Mgr
Kelley McDonald, Mktg Dir
EMP: 75 EST: 1981
SQ FT: 17,940
SALES (est): 11.2MM Privately Held
WEB: www.colorpointprint.com
SIC: 2759 2791 2752 Thermography; typesetting; commercial printing, lithographic

(G-17031)
COSMA INTERNATIONAL AMER INC (HQ)
Also Called: Cosma Engineering
750 Tower Dr (48098-2863)
PHONE..................248 631-1100
Don Walker, CEO
Eric J Wilds, Exec VP
Elizabeth Maccabe, Vice Pres
Matt Blanford, Purchasing
Rachel Mack, Cust Mgr
▲ EMP: 300 EST: 1978
SALES (est): 1.1B
SALES (corp-wide): 32.6B Privately Held
WEB: www.magna.com
SIC: 3714 Motor vehicle parts & accessories
PA: Magna International Inc
337 Magna Dr
Aurora ON L4G 7
905 726-2462

(G-17032)
CREATIVE PERFORMANCE RACG LLC
Also Called: Cpr Racing
120 Birchwood Dr (48083-1711)
PHONE..................248 250-6187
Goran Bogdanovic,
EMP: 6 EST: 1997
SQ FT: 4,000
SALES (est): 300K Privately Held
WEB: www.cprracing.com
SIC: 3714 3559 Automotive wiring harness sets; automotive related machinery

(G-17033)
CREATIVE PRINT CREW LLC
1119 Rochester Rd (48083-6013)
PHONE..................248 629-9404
Joseph Gatt, Owner
EMP: 4 EST: 2010
SALES (est): 356.5K Privately Held
WEB: www.creativeprintcrew.net
SIC: 2752 Commercial printing, offset

(G-17034)
CREWBOTIQ LLC
755 W Big Beaver Rd # 2020 (48084-4925)
PHONE..................248 939-4229
Michelle Mopkins, President
EMP: 20 EST: 2017
SALES (est): 1MM Privately Held
SIC: 3822 Auto controls regulating residntl & coml environmt & applncs

(G-17035)
CROWN GROUP CO (HQ)
Also Called: PPG Coatings Services
5875 New King Ct (48098-2692)
PHONE..................586 575-9800
Eric Vermillion, General Mgr
Jim Keena, COO
Frank Knoth, Vice Pres
Chris Wypych, QC Mgr
Wayne Oliver, CFO
EMP: 442 EST: 2013
SQ FT: 14,000
SALES (est): 216.6MM
SALES (corp-wide): 15.1B Publicly Held
WEB: www.ppgcoatingsservices.com
SIC: 3479 Coating of metals & formed products
PA: Ppg Industries, Inc.
1 Ppg Pl
Pittsburgh PA 15272
412 434-3131

(G-17036)
CRUUX LLC
4897 River Bank Ct (48085-4896)
PHONE..................248 515-8411
In Seok OH,
MI Jeong OH,
EMP: 4 EST: 2009
SALES (est): 20K Privately Held
SIC: 3499 7389 Magnetic shields, metal;

(G-17037)
CUCINA MODA - BIRMINGHAM LLC (PA)
Also Called: Scavolini By Cucina Moda
1700 Stutz Dr Ste 37 (48084-4503)
PHONE..................248 792-2285
Nicole Schrag, Principal
EMP: 12 EST: 2009
SALES (est): 545.1K Privately Held
WEB: www.cucinamoda.com
SIC: 1799 5031 3261 Kitchen & bathroom remodeling; kitchen cabinets; bathroom accessories/fittings, vitreous china or earthenware

(G-17038)
CUSTOM ENGINEERING & DESIGN
3448 Rowland Ct (48083-5677)
PHONE..................248 680-1435
Dennis Nowicki, President
EMP: 6 EST: 1990
SQ FT: 3,200
SALES (est): 481.9K Privately Held
SIC: 3625 Relays & industrial controls

(G-17039)
CUSTOM PRINTING
1659 Rochester Rd (48083-1829)
PHONE..................248 509-7134
EMP: 6 EST: 2017
SALES (est): 272.7K Privately Held
SIC: 2752 Commercial printing, lithographic

(G-17040)
CUSTOM PRINTING OF MICHIGAN
1659 Rochester Rd (48083-1829)
PHONE..................248 585-9222
Mark Grimske, President
EMP: 11 EST: 1987
SQ FT: 7,000
SALES (est): 847K Privately Held
SIC: 2752 Commercial printing, offset

▲ = Import ▼ = Export
◆ = Import/Export

GEOGRAPHIC SECTION
Troy - Oakland County (G-17065)

(G-17041)
CYBERLOGIC TECHNOLOGIES INC
755 W Big Beavr Rd # 2020 (48084-4925)
PHONE..................................248 631-2200
Kemal Turedi, *Ch of Bd*
Pawel T Mikulski, *President*
Alex Mikulski, *Business Mgr*
EMP: 21 **EST:** 1992
SALES (est): 2.2MM **Privately Held**
WEB: www.cyberlogic.com
SIC: 7372 Prepackaged software

(G-17042)
D & M TRUCK TOP CO INC
2354 Dorchester Dr N # 108 (48084-3722)
PHONE..................................248 792-7972
Aaron Greenspon, *President*
Cynthia Greenspon, *Admin Sec*
EMP: 8 **EST:** 1944
SQ FT: 15,800
SALES (est): 647.9K **Privately Held**
SIC: 3714 Tops, motor vehicle

(G-17043)
D FIND CORPORATION
1955 Rolling Woods Dr (48098-6606)
P.O. Box 1715 (48099-1715)
PHONE..................................248 641-2858
Varsha Baxi, *President*
Indra Baxi, *Vice Pres*
▲ **EMP:** 4 **EST:** 1998
SQ FT: 4,500 **Privately Held**
WEB: www.finddcorp.com
SIC: 1731 3089 8742 Access control systems specialization; injection molded finished plastic products; marketing consulting services

(G-17044)
DAIEK PRODUCTS INC
Also Called: Daiek Door Sytem
1725 Blaney Dr (48084-4620)
PHONE..................................248 816-1360
David E Daiek, *President*
▲ **EMP:** 12 **EST:** 1963
SQ FT: 8,400
SALES (est): 2.5MM **Privately Held**
WEB: www.daiek.com
SIC: 3442 5031 3089 Metal doors; doors & windows; fiberglass doors

(G-17045)
DAYCO LLC (PA)
1650 Research Dr Ste 100 (48083-2143)
PHONE..................................248 404-6500
Joel E Wiegert, *CEO*
Steve McWilliams, *Business Mgr*
Wouter Nijenhuis, *Exec VP*
Yann Taurel, *Vice Pres*
Richard Coppinger, *Maint Spvr*
EMP: 30 **EST:** 2014
SALES (est): 211.2MM **Privately Held**
SIC: 3568 Power transmission equipment

(G-17046)
DAYCO INCORPORATED (HQ)
1650 Research Dr Ste 100 (48083-2143)
PHONE..................................248 404-6500
Joel E Wiegert, *CEO*
Jeremy Coles, *Production*
David Courville, *Program Mgr*
Kyle Strube, *Manager*
Debra Dewetter, *IT/INT Sup*
EMP: 100 **EST:** 1970
SALES (est): 194.3MM
SALES (corp-wide): 211.2MM **Privately Held**
SIC: 3465 Body parts, automobile: stamped metal
PA: Dayco, Llc
1650 Research Dr Ste 100
Troy MI 48083
248 404-6500

(G-17047)
DAYCO PRODUCTS LLC
Also Called: Mark 4 Automotive
1650 Research Dr Ste 100 (48083-2143)
PHONE..................................248 404-6506
Jim Orchard, *Principal*
EMP: 5
SALES (corp-wide): 211.2MM **Privately Held**
WEB: www.daycoproducts.com
SIC: 3052 8711 Automobile hose, plastic; automobile hose, rubber; plastic belting; rubber belting; engineering services
HQ: Dayco Products, Llc
1650 Research Dr Ste 100
Troy MI 48083

(G-17048)
DAYCO PRODUCTS LLC (DH)
1650 Research Dr Ste 100 (48083-2143)
PHONE..................................248 404-6500
John T Bohenick, *CEO*
Doug Bowen, *President*
John Kinnick, *President*
Al Devore, *Vice Pres*
Dan Engler, *Vice Pres*
EMP: 86 **EST:** 1986
SALES (est): 194.3MM
SALES (corp-wide): 211.2MM **Privately Held**
WEB: www.daycoproducts.com
SIC: 3568 Power transmission equipment

(G-17049)
DBUSINESS
5750 New King Dr Ste 100 (48098-2696)
PHONE..................................313 929-0090
Rj King, *Editor*
Emma Klug, *Assoc Editor*
EMP: 16 **EST:** 2017
SALES (est): 544.5K **Privately Held**
WEB: www.dbusiness.com
SIC: 2721 Magazines: publishing only, not printed on site

(G-17050)
DEBRON INDUSTRIAL ELEC LLC
591 Executive Dr (48083-4507)
PHONE..................................248 588-7220
Peter J Stouffer, *CEO*
Matthew McIntosh, *CEO*
Heather Crim, *Materials Mgr*
David Koslosky, *CFO*
Bill Csernits, *Accounts Mgr*
EMP: 75 **EST:** 2020
SALES (est): 8.1MM **Privately Held**
WEB: www.debron-electronics.com
SIC: 3679 8711 3672 3825 Electronic circuits; electrical or electronic engineering; printed circuit boards; test equipment for electronic & electric measurement; electrodes used in industrial process measurement; motor vehicle parts & accessories

(G-17051)
DELCO ELEC OVERSEAS CORP (HQ)
5820 Innovation Dr (48098-2824)
PHONE..................................248 813-2000
William Ramseyer, *Project Engr*
EMP: 216 **EST:** 2005
SALES (est): 1MM
SALES (corp-wide): 14.3B **Privately Held**
WEB: www.borgwarner.com
SIC: 3714 Motor vehicle parts & accessories
PA: Aptiv Plc
Queensway House Hilgrove Street
Jersey JE1 1
163 422-4000

(G-17052)
DELPHI
5725 Innovation Dr (48098-2852)
PHONE..................................248 813-2000
Luiz R Corrallo, *President*
Kevin P Clark, *COO*
Majdi B Abulaban, *Senior VP*
Jessica L Holscott, *Vice Pres*
Dan Hamilton, *Engineer*
EMP: 30 **EST:** 2015
SALES (est): 781.7K **Privately Held**
WEB: www.borgwarner.com
SIC: 3714 Motor vehicle parts & accessories

(G-17053)
DELPHI AUTOMOTIVE SYSTEMS
5820 Innovation Dr (48098-2824)
PHONE..................................248 813-2000
Diane Kaye, *Principal*
EMP: 58 **EST:** 1996
SALES (est): 2MM
SALES (corp-wide): 14.3B **Privately Held**
WEB: www.borgwarner.com
SIC: 3714 Motor vehicle parts & accessories
PA: Aptiv Plc
Queensway House Hilgrove Street
Jersey JE1 1
163 422-4000

(G-17054)
DELPHI PWRTRAIN TECH GEN PRTNR
5820 Innovation Dr (48098-2824)
PHONE..................................248 813-2000
Walter Piock, *Chief Engr*
Alex Ashmore, *Executive*
EMP: 33 **EST:** 2017
SALES (est): 9.1MM
SALES (corp-wide): 10.1B **Publicly Held**
WEB: www.borgwarner.com
SIC: 3714 Motor vehicle parts & accessories
HQ: Borgwarner Technologies Limited
13 Castle Street St Helier
Jersey JE1 1
163 423-4422

(G-17055)
DELPHI WORLD HEADQUARTERS
5725 Innovation Dr (48098-2852)
PHONE..................................248 813-3045
EMP: 4 **EST:** 2018
SALES (est): 185.5K **Privately Held**
WEB: www.borgwarner.com
SIC: 3714 Motor vehicle parts & accessories

(G-17056)
DEPOR INDUSTRIES INC (HQ)
Also Called: Magnicote
1902 Northwood Dr (48084-5523)
PHONE..................................248 362-3900
David E Berry, *Ch of Bd*
James W Cooper, *Vice Pres*
Dan McAllister, *Facilities Mgr*
James Pool, *Maint Spvr*
Amelia Bradford, *Production*
▲ **EMP:** 3 **EST:** 1972
SALES (est): 11MM
SALES (corp-wide): 72.9MM **Privately Held**
WEB: www.deporindustries.net
SIC: 3479 Coating, rust preventive
PA: The Magni Group Inc
390 Park St Ste 300
Birmingham MI 48009
248 647-4500

(G-17057)
DETROIT LEGAL NEWS PUBG LLC
1409 Allen Dr Ste B (48083-4003)
PHONE..................................248 577-6100
Tom Kirvan, *Chief*
Brad Thompson, *Mng Member*
Cynthia Price, *Director*
Suzanne Favaley,
Chad T Parks,
EMP: 31 **EST:** 1930
SALES (est): 5.7MM **Privately Held**
WEB: www.detroitlegalnewspublishing.com
SIC: 2711 8111 2791 Newspapers, publishing & printing; legal services; typesetting

(G-17058)
DGA PRINTING INC
Also Called: Sterling Printing & Graphics
567 Robbins Dr (48083-4515)
PHONE..................................586 979-2244
Deborah Majchrzak, *President*
Gary Majchrzak, *Vice Pres*
EMP: 4 **EST:** 1988
SQ FT: 2,000
SALES (est): 398.9K **Privately Held**
SIC: 2752 Commercial printing, offset

(G-17059)
DIANAMIC ABRASIVE PRODUCTS
2566 Industrial Row Dr (48084-7035)
PHONE..................................248 280-1185
George Collins, *President*
Steven Vafeas, *Vice Pres*
Vasiliki Collins, *Admin Sec*
EMP: 14 **EST:** 1985
SQ FT: 13,500
SALES (est): 1.8MM **Privately Held**
WEB: www.dianamic.com
SIC: 3291 Abrasive products; wheels, abrasive

(G-17060)
DICK AND JANE BAKING CO LLC
755 W Big Beaver Rd # 2020 (48084-4925)
PHONE..................................248 519-2418
Richard Held, *Mng Member*
Robert Fell,
Mike Lukas,
EMP: 4 **EST:** 2008
SALES (est): 1MM **Privately Held**
WEB: www.educationalsnacks.us
SIC: 5149 2052 Bakery products; cookies & crackers

(G-17061)
DIEOMATIC INCORPORATED (DH)
Also Called: Benco Manufacturing
750 Twer Dr Mail Code 700 (48098)
PHONE..................................319 668-2031
John Farrell, *President*
Brian Duivesteyn, *Principal*
Michele Baccellieri, *Treasurer*
Tommy Skudutis, *Director*
Rabih Abou El Assal, *Admin Sec*
EMP: 100 **EST:** 1972
SALES (est): 846MM
SALES (corp-wide): 32.6B **Privately Held**
SIC: 3714 Motor vehicle parts & accessories
HQ: Cosma International Of America, Inc.
750 Tower Dr
Troy MI 48098
248 631-1100

(G-17062)
DIGITAL PERFORMANCE TECH
3221 W Big Beaver Rd (48084-2803)
PHONE..................................877 983-4230
Lisa Klein, *CEO*
EMP: 11 **EST:** 2018
SALES (est): 723.6K **Privately Held**
SIC: 8742 3823 Maintenance management consultant; data loggers, industrial process type

(G-17063)
DIGITALEO CORPORATION
755 W Big Beaver Rd (48084-4900)
PHONE..................................248 250-9205
Jocelyn Denis, *Founder*
EMP: 5 **EST:** 2010
SALES (est): 167.4K **Privately Held**
SIC: 3829 Thermometers, including digital: clinical

(G-17064)
DOUGLAS INNOVATION LLC
1389 Wheaton Dr Ste 300 (48083-1929)
PHONE..................................586 596-3641
Timothy Gornall, *General Mgr*
Mitchel Davis, *Principal*
EMP: 7 **EST:** 2018
SALES (est): 424K **Privately Held**
SIC: 3999 Manufacturing industries

(G-17065)
DPH LLC
Also Called: Delphi
5820 Innovation Dr (48098-2824)
PHONE..................................248 813-2000
Robert Brust,
Lynne Isaacs, *Analyst*
◆ **EMP:** 1000 **EST:** 2002
SALES (est): 111.7MM
SALES (corp-wide): 14.3B **Privately Held**
WEB: www.borgwarner.com
SIC: 3714 Motor vehicle parts & accessories
PA: Aptiv Plc
Queensway House Hilgrove Street
Jersey JE1 1
163 422-4000

Troy - Oakland County (G-17066)

(G-17066)
DPH-DAS GLOBAL (HOLDINGS) LLC
5820 Innovation Dr (48098-2824)
PHONE..................................248 813-2000
Bette Walker, *Principal*
Lindsey Williams, *Pub Rel Mgr*
Luis Herrera, *Mng Member*
▲ **EMP:** 249 **EST:** 1998
SALES (est): 11.3MM
SALES (corp-wide): 14.3B **Privately Held**
WEB: www.borgwarner.com
SIC: 3714 Motor vehicle parts & accessories
PA: Aptiv Plc
  Queensway House Hilgrove Street
  Jersey JE1 1
  163 422-4000

(G-17067)
DPH-DAS LLC
5820 Innovation Dr (48098-2824)
PHONE..................................248 813-2000
Richard Hu, *Vice Pres*
J T Battenberg III,
◆ **EMP:** 177 **EST:** 1998
SALES (est): 20.2MM
SALES (corp-wide): 14.3B **Privately Held**
WEB: www.borgwarner.com
SIC: 3714 Motor vehicle parts & accessories
PA: Aptiv Plc
  Queensway House Hilgrove Street
  Jersey JE1 1
  163 422-4000

(G-17068)
DRACO MFG INC
629 Minnesota Dr (48083-6202)
PHONE..................................248 585-0320
Michael McArthur, *President*
James McArthur, *President*
Deborah Amundson, *Treasurer*
▼ **EMP:** 7 **EST:** 1986
SQ FT: 7,200
SALES (est): 852.3K **Privately Held**
WEB: www.dracomfg.com
SIC: 3599 Machine shop, jobbing & repair

(G-17069)
DREAL INC
5820 Innovation Dr (48098-2824)
PHONE..................................248 813-2000
EMP: 14 **EST:** 2009
SALES (est): 816.5K
SALES (corp-wide): 14.3B **Privately Held**
WEB: www.borgwarner.com
SIC: 3714 Motor vehicle parts & accessories
PA: Aptiv Plc
  Queensway House Hilgrove Street
  Jersey JE1 1
  163 422-4000

(G-17070)
DSM ENGINEERING PLASTICS INC
203 W Big Beaver Rd (48084-5201)
PHONE..................................608 477-0157
Fran Marchand, *Marketing Staff*
Matt Marnell, *Manager*
Juliana Bernalostos-Boy, *Director*
EMP: 6
SALES (corp-wide): 9.9B **Privately Held**
WEB: www.dsm.com
SIC: 2821 Plastics materials & resins
HQ: Dsm Engineering Materials, Inc.
  2267 W Mill Rd
  Evansville IN 47720

(G-17071)
DUN MOR EMBROIDERY & DESIGNS
Also Called: Dun Mor Design
360 E Maple Rd Ste O (48083-2707)
PHONE..................................248 577-1155
Linda Dunmore, *President*
Rich Dunmore, *Vice Pres*
EMP: 10 **EST:** 1990
SQ FT: 5,000
SALES (est): 470.2K **Privately Held**
WEB: www.dunmordesign.com
SIC: 2395 Emblems, embroidered

(G-17072)
DYNAMIC JIG GRINDING CORP
Also Called: Dynamic Precision Tool & Mfg
985 Troy Ct (48083-2728)
PHONE..................................248 589-3110
John A Eckhout, *President*
Sue Eckhout, *Officer*
EMP: 20 **EST:** 1982
SQ FT: 15,000
SALES (est): 2.1MM **Privately Held**
WEB: www.dynamicprecision.net
SIC: 3599 3545 3544 Machine shop, jobbing & repair; machine tool accessories; special dies, tools, jigs & fixtures

(G-17073)
DYNETICS INC
1100 Owendale Dr (48083-1914)
PHONE..................................248 619-1681
Alix Reinhalter, *Branch Mgr*
EMP: 4 **Publicly Held**
WEB: www.dynetics.com
SIC: 3465 Body parts, automobile: stamped metal
HQ: Dynetics, Inc.
  1002 Explorer Blvd Nw
  Huntsville AL 35806
  256 964-4000

(G-17074)
DYSON SERVICE CENTER
1969 W Maple Rd (48084-7109)
PHONE..................................248 808-6952
EMP: 5 **EST:** 2018
SALES (est): 111.9K **Privately Held**
WEB: www.dyson.com
SIC: 3635 Household vacuum cleaners

(G-17075)
E & C MANUFACTURING LLC
2125 Butterfield Dr # 200 (48084-3410)
PHONE..................................248 330-0400
Barry Connelly, *Mng Member*
Stephen J Paver Jr,
EMP: 10 **EST:** 2007
SALES (est): 1.9MM **Privately Held**
WEB: www.e-cmfg.com
SIC: 5047 3599 Hospital equipment & furniture; machine & other job shop work

(G-17076)
EAGLE FASTENERS INC
Also Called: Efi Custom Injection Molding
185 Park Dr (48083-2770)
PHONE..................................248 577-1441
Theresa C Srock, *President*
James P Srock, *Vice Pres*
Joseph C Srock, *Vice Pres*
▲ **EMP:** 12 **EST:** 1976
SQ FT: 23,000
SALES (est): 2.8MM **Privately Held**
WEB: www.eficustominjectionmolding.com
SIC: 3089 Injection molding of plastics

(G-17077)
EDM INC
1900 Stephenson Hwy # 100 (48083-2133)
PHONE..................................586 933-3187
EMP: 4 **EST:** 2018
SALES (est): 179.9K **Privately Held**
WEB:
www.electricaldischargemachining.com
SIC: 2759 Commercial printing

(G-17078)
EDON CONTROLS INC
2891 Industrial Row Dr (48084-7041)
PHONE..................................248 280-0420
Norman N Fender, *President*
Christine Fender, *Vice Pres*
EMP: 7 **EST:** 1999
SQ FT: 10,000
SALES (est): 860.1K **Privately Held**
WEB: www.edoncontrols.com
SIC: 3625 Industrial electrical relays & switches

(G-17079)
EHC INC (PA)
Also Called: Evans Holding Company
3150 Livernois Rd Ste 170 (48083-5058)
PHONE..................................313 259-2266
Robert B Evans Jr, *Ch of Bd*
▲ **EMP:** 8 **EST:** 1982
SALES (est): 39.4MM **Privately Held**
SIC: 3366 3365 3519 3621 Brass foundry; aluminum foundries; marine engines; motors & generators; injection molded finished plastic products; hard rubber & molded rubber products

(G-17080)
EIKOS HOLDINGS INC
2613 Industrial Row Dr (48084-7038)
PHONE..................................248 280-0300
Nicholas Stavropoulos, *President*
Gus Stavropoulos, *President*
Mark Stavropoulos, *Vice Pres*
Arthur Keysaer, *Plant Supt*
James Nelson, *Plant Mgr*
EMP: 38 **EST:** 1965
SQ FT: 30,000
SALES (est): 3MM **Privately Held**
SIC: 3599 3541 3544 3316 Electrical discharge machining (EDM); machine tools, metal cutting type; grinding machines, metalworking; special dies & tools; cold finishing of steel shapes

(G-17081)
ELBA INC
Also Called: ELBA LABORATORIES
1925 W Maple Rd Ste B (48084-7116)
PHONE..................................248 288-6098
Michael Froehlich, *CEO*
Patette Jarema,
▲ **EMP:** 50 **EST:** 1982
SQ FT: 22,000
SALES (est): 12.1MM **Privately Held**
WEB: www.elba-labs.com
SIC: 2834 Pharmaceutical preparations

(G-17082)
ELDOR AUTOMOTIVE N AMER INC
100 W Big Beavr Rd # 200 (48084-5206)
PHONE..................................248 878-9193
EMP: 35 **EST:** 2015
SALES (est): 5.3MM **Privately Held**
WEB: www.eldorgroup.com
SIC: 3694 Ignition coils, automotive
HQ: Eldor Corporation Spa
  Via Don Paolo Berra 18
  Orsenigo CO 22030
  031 636-111

(G-17083)
ELECTRIC LAST MILE INC
Also Called: Electric Last Mile Solutions
1055 W Square Lake Rd (48098-2523)
PHONE..................................888 825-9111
Benjamin F Wu, *Chairman*
Praveen Cherian, *Vice Pres*
Georgette Borrego Dulworth, *VP Human Res*
Eric Keipper, *Exec Dir*
EMP: 2 **EST:** 2020
SALES (est): 4.6MM **Publicly Held**
SIC: 3711 Cars, electric, assembly of
PA: Electric Last Mile Solutions, Inc.
  1055 W Square Lake Rd
  Troy MI 48098
  888 825-9111

(G-17084)
ELECTRICAL PRODUCT SALES INC
2611 Elliott Dr (48083-4637)
PHONE..................................248 583-6100
Richard Stone, *President*
EMP: 25 **EST:** 1985
SQ FT: 10,000
SALES (est): 143.2K **Privately Held**
WEB: www.epp-1.com
SIC: 3643 Current-carrying wiring devices

(G-17085)
ELSA ENTERPRISES INC
Also Called: Rocky Mountain Chocolate
2800 W Big Beaver Rd # 124 (48084-3206)
PHONE..................................248 816-1454
Alan Rosen, *President*
EMP: 6 **EST:** 1997 **Privately Held**
WEB: www.rmcf.com
SIC: 5441 2064 Candy; chocolate candy, except solid chocolate

(G-17086)
ELUMIGEN LLC
820 Kirts Blvd Ste 300 (48084-4836)
PHONE..................................855 912-0477
Alfred Laspina, *CEO*
Gerry Fedele, *President*
Mounir El-Mourad, *Financial Analy*
EMP: 8 **EST:** 2010
SALES (est): 797.9K **Privately Held**
WEB: www.elumigen.com
SIC: 3641 3646 Electric light bulbs, complete; commercial indusl & institutional electric lighting fixtures

(G-17087)
EMHART TEKNOLOGIES LLC
Also Called: STANLEY ENGINEERED FASTENING
2500 Meijer Dr (48084-7146)
PHONE..................................248 677-9693
◆ **EMP:** 100
SALES (est): 10.2MM
SALES (corp-wide): 11.1B **Publicly Held**
SIC: 3999 1541 8742 Mfg Misc Products Industrial Building Construction Management Consulting Services
PA: Stanley Black & Decker, Inc.
  1000 Stanley Dr
  New Britain CT 06053
  860 225-5111

(G-17088)
EMHART TEKNOLOGIES LLC
Also Called: Stanley Engineered Fastening
2400 Meijer Dr Bldg 2 (48084-7110)
PHONE..................................800 783-6427
James Puscas, *VP Sales*
EMP: 5
SALES (corp-wide): 14.5B **Publicly Held**
SIC: 3541 Machine tools, metal cutting type
HQ: Emhart Teknologies Llc
  4 Shelter Rock Ln
  Danbury CT 06810
  800 783-6427

(G-17089)
EMHART TEKNOLOGIES LLC
Stanley Engineered Fastening
2500 Meijer Dr (48084-7146)
PHONE..................................800 783-6427
EMP: 5
SALES (corp-wide): 14.5B **Publicly Held**
SIC: 3541 Machine tools, metal cutting type
HQ: Emhart Teknologies Llc
  4 Shelter Rock Ln
  Danbury CT 06810
  800 783-6427

(G-17090)
ENERGY PRODUCTS INC
Also Called: Energy Products Service Dept
315 Indusco Ct (48083-4646)
PHONE..................................248 866-5622
Dave Budde, *Branch Mgr*
EMP: 9 **Privately Held**
WEB: www.energyprod.com
SIC: 5063 5084 7699 3625 Storage batteries, industrial; industrial machinery & equipment; battery service & repair; relays & industrial controls; motors & generators
PA: Energy Products, Inc.
  1551 E Lincoln Ave # 101
  Madison Heights MI 48071

(G-17091)
ENGINEERING TECH ASSOC INC (PA)
Also Called: E T A
5445 Corporate Dr Ste 300 (48098-2629)
PHONE..................................248 729-3010
Abraham N Keisoglou, *President*
Jeremy Swick, *Counsel*
Arthur Tang, *Vice Pres*
Hui Ouyang, *Engineer*
Srivatsa Pradeep, *Project Engr*
EMP: 60 **EST:** 1983
SALES (est): 18MM **Privately Held**
WEB: www.eta.com
SIC: 7371 8711 7372 Computer software development; engineering services; prepackaged software

GEOGRAPHIC SECTION
Troy - Oakland County (G-17118)

(G-17092)
ENGINRED PLSTIC COMPONENTS INC
Also Called: Wilbert Plastic Services
100 W Big Beavr Rd # 200 (48084-5206)
PHONE..................248 825-4508
EMP: 5 Privately Held
WEB: www.epcmfg.com
SIC: 3089 Injection molding of plastics
PA: Engineered Plastic Components, Inc.
4500 Westown Pkwy Ste 277
West Des Moines IA 50266

(G-17093)
ENTERTAINMENT PUBLICATIONS INC
1401 Crooks Rd Ste 150 (48084-7106)
PHONE..................248 404-1000
Kimberly Bohn, President
Helen Wallace, President
Nancy McCabe, Principal
Robert Stevens, Principal
Garrett Mullins, Exec VP
EMP: 73 EST: 1962
SALES (est): 4.6MM Privately Held
WEB: www.entertainment.com
SIC: 2731 Book publishing

(G-17094)
ENVIROLITE LLC (PA)
1700 W Big Beavr Rd # 150 (48084-3550)
PHONE..................248 792-3184
Vatche Tazian, President
Brad Patterson, Mfg Staff
Carol Schaff, Accountant
Tara Clayfield, Accounts Mgr
Max Kelmigian, Accounts Mgr
▲ EMP: 15 EST: 2008
SQ FT: 7,000
SALES (est): 16.9MM Privately Held
WEB: www.envirolite.com
SIC: 5199 5999 3086 Foams & rubber; foam & foam products; plastics foam products

(G-17095)
ENVIRONMENTAL CATALYSTS LLC
5820 Innovation Dr (48098-2824)
PHONE..................248 813-2000
EMP: 14 EST: 2009
SALES (est): 849.3K
SALES (corp-wide): 14.3B Privately Held
WEB: www.borgwarner.com
SIC: 3714 Motor vehicle parts & accessories
PA: Aptiv Plc
Queensway House Hilgrove Street
Jersey JE1 1
163 422-4000

(G-17096)
EQUITABLE ENGINEERING CO INC
1840 Austin Dr (48083-2204)
P.O. Box 1159 (48099-1159)
PHONE..................248 689-9700
Randy J Pasko, Vice Pres
Glenn R Pasko, CFO
Steven Pyke, Manager
EMP: 20 EST: 1951
SQ FT: 21,000 Privately Held
WEB: www.equitable-eng.com
SIC: 3462 7699 3829 3812 Gears, forged steel; industrial equipment services; measuring & controlling devices; search & navigation equipment; power transmission equipment; machine tool accessories

(G-17097)
ETHNICEMEDIA LLC
Also Called: Ethnicemeida
338 Thistle Ln (48098-4644)
PHONE..................248 762-8904
Saravanan Govindaraj,
EMP: 4 EST: 2014
SALES (est): 50K Privately Held
SIC: 2741 7371 7389 Directories: publishing & printing; software programming applications; business services

(G-17098)
EURIDIUM SOLUTIONS LLC
55 E Long Lake Rd Ste 243 (48085-4738)
P.O. Box 99610 (48099-9610)
PHONE..................248 535-7005
Lee A Holly, Mng Member
EMP: 6 EST: 2000
SQ FT: 2,000 Privately Held
WEB: www.euridium.com
SIC: 3312 Coated or plated products

(G-17099)
EVANS COATINGS LLC
1330 Souter Dr (48083-2839)
PHONE..................248 583-9890
David Evans, Mng Member
Mike Evans,
EMP: 9 EST: 2008 Privately Held
WEB: www.evanscoatings.com
SIC: 3479 Coating of metals & formed products

(G-17100)
EVANS INDUSTRIES INC (HQ)
Also Called: Great Lakes Plastics Division
3150 Livernois Rd Ste 170 (48083-5058)
PHONE..................313 259-2266
Robert Beverly Evans, Ch of Bd
Jeff Johnson, Vice Pres
William Martin, Director
▲ EMP: 3 EST: 1971
SALES (est): 21.5MM
SALES (corp-wide): 39.4MM Privately Held
SIC: 6726 3363 3364 3089 Investment offices; aluminum die-castings; brass & bronze die-castings; injection molding of plastics; rubber automotive products
PA: Ehc, Inc.
3150 Livernois Rd Ste 170
Troy MI 48083
313 259-2266

(G-17101)
EXO-S US LLC
1500 W Big Beaver Rd 101c (48084-3522)
PHONE..................248 614-9707
EMP: 5
SALES (corp-wide): 49.5MM Privately Held
SIC: 3089 Mfg Plastic Products
HQ: Exo-S Us Llc
6505 N State Road 9
Howe IN 46746
260 562-4100

(G-17102)
EXONE AMERICAS LLC (HQ)
2341 Alger Dr (48083-2052)
PHONE..................248 740-1580
John H Gemmill, CFO
Terry Senish, Manager
▲ EMP: 6 EST: 2008
SALES (est): 1.2MM
SALES (est): 59.2MM Publicly Held
WEB: www.exone.com
SIC: 2754 Job printing, gravure
PA: The Exone Company
127 Industry Blvd
North Huntingdon PA 15642
724 863-9663

(G-17103)
FAB-ALL MANUFACTURING INC
645 Executive Dr (48083-4536)
PHONE..................248 585-6700
Josef F Hubert, President
EMP: 100 EST: 1978
SQ FT: 36,000
SALES (est): 11.2MM Privately Held
SIC: 3465 Automotive stampings

(G-17104)
FAIR INDUSTRIES LLC
3260 Talbot Dr (48083-5092)
PHONE..................248 740-7841
Michael J Kuron, President
Edward J Apfel, Vice Pres
EMP: 16 EST: 1979
SALES (est): 50MM Privately Held
WEB: www.fairindustries.com
SIC: 3548 3541 3544 Resistance welders, electric; spot welding apparatus, electric; arc welders, transformer-rectifier; boring mills; milling machines; special dies, tools, jigs & fixtures

(G-17105)
FALCON NETWORK SERVICES INC
200 E Big Beaver Rd (48083-1208)
PHONE..................248 726-0577
Alan Winkel, Principal
Kenneth Bostic, Manager
EMP: 8 EST: 2016
SALES (est): 1.5MM Privately Held
WEB: www.fns1.com
SIC: 7372 Prepackaged software

(G-17106)
FALLEN OAKS CABINET SHOP INC
302 Robbins Dr (48083-4558)
PHONE..................586 463-4454
William Kerner, President
Hope Kerner, Admin Sec
EMP: 5 EST: 1978
SALES (est): 369.5K Privately Held
WEB: www.frankring.com
SIC: 2434 Wood kitchen cabinets

(G-17107)
FAUCHER INDUSTRIES
1005 Troy Ct (48083-2784)
PHONE..................248 515-4772
EMP: 4 EST: 2011
SALES (est): 101.4K Privately Held
SIC: 3999 Manufacturing industries

(G-17108)
FISHER & COMPANY INCORPORATED
1625 W Maple Rd (48084-7118)
PHONE..................248 280-0808
Samantha Stark, Project Engr
Mark Waggener, VP Finance
Christina Moreno, Marketing Staff
Faiz Jergees, Branch Mgr
EMP: 6
SALES (corp-wide): 448.1MM Privately Held
WEB: www.fisherco.com
SIC: 3714 Motor vehicle parts & accessories
PA: Fisher & Company, Incorporated
33300 Fisher Dr
Saint Clair Shores MI 48082
586 746-2000

(G-17109)
FISHER & COMPANY INCORPORATED
1625 W Maple Rd (48084-7118)
PHONE..................248 280-0808
Jeff Thompson, Branch Mgr
EMP: 5
SALES (corp-wide): 448.1MM Privately Held
WEB: www.fisherco.com
SIC: 3465 3469 Automotive stampings; metal stampings
PA: Fisher & Company, Incorporated
33300 Fisher Dr
Saint Clair Shores MI 48082
586 746-2000

(G-17110)
FISHER & COMPANY INCORPORATED
1625 W Marble Rd (48084)
PHONE..................586 746-2101
Joe Conway, Buyer
Samantha Stark, Project Engr
Jeff Thompson, Branch Mgr
EMP: 11
SALES (corp-wide): 448.1MM Privately Held
WEB: www.fisherco.com
SIC: 3714 Motor vehicle parts & accessories
PA: Fisher & Company, Incorporated
33300 Fisher Dr
Saint Clair Shores MI 48082
586 746-2000

(G-17111)
FISLL MEDIA LLC
2950 W Square Lake Rd (48098-5725)
PHONE..................646 492-8533
Allan Houston, Mng Member
David Huie,
EMP: 8 EST: 2016
SALES (est): 1.1MM Privately Held
WEB: www.fisll.com
SIC: 5136 5137 2329 2339 Men's & boys' clothing; women's & children's clothing; men's & boys' sportswear & athletic clothing; women's & misses' athletic clothing & sportswear; women's handbags & purses

(G-17112)
FITZ MANUFACTURING INC
324 Robbins Dr (48083-4558)
PHONE..................248 589-1780
Patrick J Fitzpatrick, President
Bobbie Fitzpatrick, Treasurer
Clayton Burnett, Sales Staff
Robert Laskos, Sales Staff
Stephanie Fitzpatrick, Manager
EMP: 15 EST: 1977
SQ FT: 18,000
SALES (est): 1.8MM Privately Held
WEB: www.fitzmanufacturing.com
SIC: 3599 Machine shop, jobbing & repair

(G-17113)
FITZ-RITE PRODUCTS INC
1122 Naughton Dr (48083-1930)
PHONE..................248 528-8440
W Dean Fitzpatrick, President
Peter Petrash, Marketing Staff
EMP: 20 EST: 1979
SQ FT: 15,500
SALES (est): 2.9MM Privately Held
WEB: www.fitzrite.com
SIC: 3625 5084 3545 3544 Numerical controls; industrial machinery & equipment; machine tool accessories; special dies, tools, jigs & fixtures

(G-17114)
FLEX-N-GATE TROY LLC
1400 Rochester Rd (48083-6014)
PHONE..................586 759-8900
Bill Beistline,
EMP: 21 EST: 2019
SALES (est): 2.8MM Privately Held
SIC: 3465 Automotive stampings

(G-17115)
FLIPSNACK LLC
2701 Troy Center Dr # 255 (48084-4753)
PHONE..................650 741-1328
Gabriel Ciordas,
EMP: 36
SALES (est): 900K Privately Held
WEB: www.flipsnack.com
SIC: 2741 Miscellaneous publishing

(G-17116)
FLORIDA PRODUCTION ENGRG INC
Also Called: Fpe
550 Stephenson Hwy # 360 (48083-1109)
PHONE..................248 588-4870
EMP: 10
SALES (corp-wide): 307.3MM Privately Held
SIC: 2821 Mfg Plastic Materials/Resins
HQ: Florida Production Engineering, Inc.
2 E Tower Cir
Ormond Beach FL 32174
386 677-2566

(G-17117)
FORKLIFT PARTS GROUP
2601 Fox Chase Dr (48098-2329)
PHONE..................248 792-7132
Gregory Neilson, Principal
EMP: 4 EST: 2016
SALES (est): 126.7K Privately Held
SIC: 3537 Forklift trucks

(G-17118)
FORM G TECH CO
1291 Rochester Rd (48083-2879)
PHONE..................248 583-3610
Shkelqim Lumani, President
▲ EMP: 53 EST: 1998

Troy - Oakland County (G-17119)

SQ FT: 32,000
SALES (est): 100K **Privately Held**
WEB: www.formgtech.com
SIC: **3599** Machine shop, jobbing & repair

(G-17119)
FORTIS ENERGY SERVICES INC (PA)
3001 W Big Beaver Rd # 525 (48084-3101)
PHONE..........................248 283-7100
George Molski, *President*
Warren Jensen, *Opers Mgr*
Randy Martinez, *Opers Mgr*
Susan Censoni, *CFO*
Meghan Berg, *VP Human Res*
EMP: 79 **EST**: 2004
SALES (est): 41MM **Privately Held**
WEB: www.fortisenergyservices.com
SIC: **1381** 3625 3621 Drilling oil & gas wells; noise control equipment; motors & generators

(G-17120)
FOSTERS VENTURES LLC
Also Called: Signs & More
1371 Souter Dr (48083-2840)
PHONE..........................248 519-7446
Larry Foster,
Molly Smith,
EMP: 10 **EST**: 2001
SALES (est): 1.1MM **Privately Held**
WEB: www.signsandmoremi.com
SIC: **3993** Signs & advertising specialties

(G-17121)
FOUR-WAY TOOL AND DIE INC (PA)
239 Indusco Ct (48083-4679)
PHONE..........................248 585-8255
Lawrence Erickson, *President*
Helen Erickson, *Corp Secy*
David Erickson, *Asst Treas*
EMP: 27
SQ FT: 17,000
SALES (est): 2.7MM **Privately Held**
SIC: **3544** 3643 Special dies & tools; current-carrying wiring devices

(G-17122)
FRACO PRODUCTS LTD
5225 Renshaw Dr (48085-4071)
PHONE..........................248 667-9260
Scott Guilbault, *Manager*
EMP: 4
SALES (corp-wide): 950K **Privately Held**
WEB: www.fraco.com
SIC: **3272** Concrete products
HQ: Fraco Products Ltd
91 Ch Des Patriotes
Saint-Mathias-Sur-Richelieu QC
514 990-7750

(G-17123)
FSP INC
Also Called: Five Star Products
1270 Rankin Dr Ste B (48083-2843)
PHONE..........................248 585-0760
Charles E Wallace, *President*
Neil Wallace, *Corp Secy*
Richard Holmes, *Executive*
EMP: 20 **EST**: 1949
SQ FT: 10,000
SALES (est): 517.4K **Privately Held**
SIC: **3545** Cutting tools for machine tools; tool holders

(G-17124)
G T JERSEYS LLC
997 Rochester Rd Ste C (48083-6025)
PHONE..........................248 588-3231
Virginia Thackaberry, *Mng Member*
EMP: 10 **EST**: 1976
SQ FT: 2,800
SALES (est): 650K **Privately Held**
WEB: www.gtjerseys.com
SIC: **7336** 7299 2211 Silk screen design; chart & graph design; stitching, custom; chenilles; tufted textile; uniforms

(G-17125)
GAGE RITE PRODUCTS INC
Also Called: Royal Oak Products Company
356 Executive Dr (48083-4532)
PHONE..........................248 588-7796
Art Jadach, *President*

EMP: 12 **EST**: 1989
SQ FT: 10,300
SALES (est): 2.1MM **Privately Held**
WEB: www.gagerite.com
SIC: **3599** Machine shop, jobbing & repair

(G-17126)
GALLAGHER-KAISER CORPORATION (PA)
777 Chicago Rd Ste 1 (48083-4234)
PHONE..........................313 368-3100
Robert S Kaiser, *CEO*
Tracy E Roberts, *COO*
Nick O'Connor, *Engineer*
Nathan Tokarz, *Engineer*
Kenneth M Krause, *CFO*
◆ EMP: 75 **EST**: 1952
SQ FT: 100,000
SALES (est): 114.4MM **Privately Held**
WEB: www.gkcorp.com
SIC: **3444** 1761 3567 3564 Booths, spray: prefabricated sheet metal; sheet metalwork; paint baking & drying ovens; air purification equipment

(G-17127)
GARDNER SIGNS INC
1087 Naughton Dr (48083-1911)
PHONE..........................248 689-9100
Scott Gardner, *Manager*
Bryan Witt, *Manager*
EMP: 10
SALES (corp-wide): 2.7MM **Privately Held**
WEB: www.gardnersigns.com
SIC: **3993** Electric signs; neon signs
PA: Gardner Signs, Inc.
3800 Airport Hwy
Toledo OH 43615
419 385-6669

(G-17128)
GAZETTE NEWSPAPERS INC
Also Called: Troy Somerset Gazette
6966 Crooks Rd Ste 22 (48098-1798)
P.O. Box 482 (48099-0482)
PHONE..........................248 524-4868
Claire Weber, *President*
Mark Nicholson, *Publisher*
Cynthia K Mett, *Editor*
EMP: 6 **EST**: 1980
SQ FT: 1,800
SALES (est): 750K **Privately Held**
WEB: www.getyourgazette.com
SIC: **2711** 2791 Newspapers: publishing only, not printed on site; typesetting

(G-17129)
GENERAL BROACH & ENGRG INC
5750 New King Dr Ste 200 (48098-2611)
PHONE..........................586 726-4300
Stefan Wandzyk, *President*
Sharon Van Doren, *Production*
EMP: 137 **EST**: 1991
SQ FT: 62,640
SALES (est): 2.7MM
SALES (corp-wide): 305MM **Privately Held**
WEB: www.uticaenterprises.com
SIC: **3541** 3545 3599 Broaching machines; broaches (machine tool accessories); machine shop, jobbing & repair
PA: Utica Enterprises, Inc.
5750 New King Dr Ste 200
Troy MI 48098
586 726-4300

(G-17130)
GESTAMP NORTH AMERICA INC (HQ)
2701 Troy Center Dr # 150 (48084-4753)
PHONE..........................248 743-3400
Jeffrey Wilson, *President*
Kevin Stobbs, *General Mgr*
Robert Greene, *Counsel*
John Craig, *Vice Pres*
Aritz Iturbe, *Vice Pres*
▲ EMP: 213 **EST**: 2004
SALES (est): 981.5MM
SALES (corp-wide): 400.4MM **Privately Held**
WEB: www.corporaciongestamp.com
SIC: **3714** Motor vehicle parts & accessories

PA: Acek Desarrollo Y Gestion Industrial Sl.
Calle Alfonso Xii 16
Madrid
913 791-999

(G-17131)
GOODPACK
2820 W Maple Rd Ste 128 (48084-7047)
PHONE..........................248 458-0041
EMP: 4
SALES (est): 270K **Privately Held**
SIC: **2655** Mfg Fiber Cans/Drums

(G-17132)
GRAPHIC RESOURCE GROUP INC
Also Called: Grg
528 Robbins Dr (48083-4514)
PHONE..........................248 588-6100
Deborah Pyc, *CEO*
Chester Allen Pyc, *President*
Karen Delaney, *CFO*
Shane Collom, *Accounts Exec*
Ronald Carson, *Sales Staff*
▲ EMP: 21 **EST**: 1990
SQ FT: 11,500
SALES (est): 8.7MM **Privately Held**
WEB: www.graphicresource.com
SIC: **7336** 7312 3577 5199 Graphic arts & related design; outdoor advertising services; poster advertising, outdoor; graphic displays, except graphic terminals; gifts & novelties; advertising specialties; marketing consulting services

(G-17133)
GREAT LAKES DIAGNOSTICS INC
1713 Larchwood Dr Ste B (48083-2233)
PHONE..........................248 307-9494
Nicholas Toben, *President*
Suzanne Toben, *President*
Howard Toben, *Admin Sec*
EMP: 4 **EST**: 1989
SQ FT: 3,000
SALES (est): 598.9K **Privately Held**
SIC: **5047** 2835 Diagnostic equipment, medical; in vitro & in vivo diagnostic substances

(G-17134)
GREG LINSKA SALES INC
2987 Hill Dr (48085-3715)
PHONE..........................248 765-6354
Greg Linska, *President*
EMP: 2
SQ FT: 1,250
SALES (est): 1.6MM **Privately Held**
SIC: **3089** Identification cards, plastic

(G-17135)
HA AUTOMOTIVE SYSTEMS INC (HQ)
1300 Coolidge Hwy (48084-7018)
PHONE..........................248 781-0001
William Chen, *President*
EMP: 14 **EST**: 2014
SALES (est): 7.9MM **Privately Held**
SIC: **3647** Motor vehicle lighting equipment

(G-17136)
HALTERMANN CARLESS US INC
901 Wilshire Dr Ste 570 (48084-1665)
PHONE..........................248 422-6548
Daniel Haamann, *Principal*
EMP: 23 **EST**: 2007
SALES (est): 2.6MM **Privately Held**
WEB: www.haltermann-carless.com
SIC: **2899** Chemical preparations
HQ: Haltermann Carless Deutschland Gmbh
Schlengendeich 17
Hamburg HH 21107
403 331-80

(G-17137)
HANHO AMERICA CO LTD
Also Called: Hha
100 E Big Beaver Rd # 845 (48083-1204)
PHONE..........................248 422-6921
Hyun Dong Lee, *Administration*
EMP: 9 **EST**: 2016

SALES (est): 663.7K **Privately Held**
WEB: www.hanhoamerica.com
SIC: **3714** Motor vehicle parts & accessories
PA: Hanho Industry Co.,Ltd.
148-32 Guil-Gil, Naenam-Myeon
Gyeongju 38195

(G-17138)
HBPO NORTH AMERICA INC
Also Called: Mahale
700 Tower Dr (48098-2808)
PHONE..........................248 823-7076
Tibor Wesseling, *President*
Gary Poole, *General Mgr*
Brendan Donnelly, *Maint Spvr*
Simon Plant, *QC Mgr*
Guido Opperbeck, *Research*
EMP: 125 **EST**: 1999
SALES (est): 56.5MM
SALES (corp-wide): 1.8MM **Privately Held**
WEB: www.hbpogroup.com
SIC: **3465** 8711 Body parts, automobile: stamped metal; engineering services
HQ: Hbpo Gmbh
Rixbecker Str. 111
Lippstadt NW 59557
294 128-380

(G-17139)
HEAD OVER HEELS
164 E Maple Rd Ste G (48083-2700)
PHONE..........................248 435-2954
Sarah Hyland, *Owner*
EMP: 7 **EST**: 2006
SALES (est): 251.3K **Privately Held**
SIC: **3999** Hair curlers, designed for beauty parlors

(G-17140)
HELLER INC
1225 Equity Dr (48084-7107)
PHONE..........................248 288-5000
Rolf Klenk, *President*
Karen Muchitsch, *Principal*
Manfred Maier, *COO*
Stephen Pegram, *Vice Pres*
Steve Pegram, *Vice Pres*
EMP: 32 **EST**: 1982
SQ FT: 32,000
SALES (est): 2MM **Privately Held**
WEB: www.heller.biz
SIC: **3541** Machine tools, metal cutting type

(G-17141)
HENZE STAMPING & MFG CO (PA)
Also Called: Henze Industries
754 W Maple Rd (48084-5315)
PHONE..........................248 588-5620
Judith A Canning, *President*
William D Canning, *Corp Secy*
EMP: 2 **EST**: 1979
SQ FT: 24,000
SALES (est): 5.4MM **Privately Held**
SIC: **3544** 3469 3465 Special dies & tools; metal stampings; automotive stampings

(G-17142)
HEXAGON ENTERPRISES INC
256 Minnesota Dr (48083-4667)
P.O. Box 1320 (48099-1320)
PHONE..........................248 583-0550
Lou Cudin, *President*
Patrick O Berry, *Vice Pres*
Kaitlin Williams, *Warehouse Mgr*
EMP: 17 **EST**: 1982
SQ FT: 8,000
SALES (est): 604.1K **Privately Held**
WEB: www.midwestacornnut.com
SIC: **3452** 5085 Nuts, metal; fasteners, industrial: nuts, bolts, screws, etc.

(G-17143)
HHJ HOLDINGS LIMITED (PA)
1957 Crooks Rd A (48084-5504)
PHONE..........................248 652-9716
James Friel, *Controller*
Rodney Cyrowski,
EMP: 10 **EST**: 1998
SQ FT: 10,000

GEOGRAPHIC SECTION

Troy - Oakland County (G-17169)

SALES (est): 308MM Privately Held
SIC: 1611 2951 Highway & street paving contractor; asphalt & asphaltic paving mixtures (not from refineries)

(G-17144)
HIRZEL CANNING COMPANY
6363 Livernois Rd (48098-1568)
PHONE.................................419 360-3220
EMP: 7 EST: 2015
SALES (est): 106K Privately Held
SIC: 2033 Canned fruits & specialties

(G-17145)
HMS MFG CO (PA)
1230 E Big Beaver Rd (48083-1904)
PHONE.................................248 689-3232
Janet Sofy, *President*
Brian Wood, *General Mgr*
Michelle Strawska, *Business Mgr*
David Sofy, *Corp Secy*
Nancy Negohosian, *Vice Pres*
▲ EMP: 60 EST: 1987
SQ FT: 6,000
SALES (est): 33.8MM Privately Held
WEB: www.hmsmfg.com
SIC: 3089 Injection molded finished plastic products

(G-17146)
HMS PRODUCTS CO
1200 E Big Beaver Rd (48083-1982)
PHONE.................................248 689-8120
David Sofy, *President*
David A Sofy, *President*
Nancy A Negohosian, *Vice Pres*
Kevin Vandenbrouck, *Engineer*
Richard Wodnicki, *Project Engr*
▲ EMP: 80
SQ FT: 39,000
SALES (est): 19.1MM Privately Held
WEB: www.hmsproducts.com
SIC: 3535 3549 3542 Conveyors & conveying equipment; metalworking machinery; machine tools, metal forming type

(G-17147)
HONEYWELL
234 E Maple Rd (48083-2716)
PHONE.................................248 362-7154
EMP: 21 EST: 2019
SALES (est): 467.3K Privately Held
WEB: www.honeywell.com
SIC: 3724 Aircraft engines & engine parts

(G-17148)
HONHART MID-NITE BLACK CO
501 Stephenson Hwy (48083-1134)
PHONE.................................248 588-1515
Betty Honhart, *President*
Keith Honhart, *Vice Pres*
John Honhart, *Treasurer*
EMP: 18 EST: 1962
SQ FT: 8,000
SALES (est): 620.5K Privately Held
WEB: www.detroitsteeltreating.com
SIC: 3471 6512 Plating of metals or formed products; commercial & industrial building operation

(G-17149)
HORIBA AUTOMOTIVE TEST SYSTEMS
2890 John R Rd (48083-2353)
PHONE.................................248 689-9000
Atsushi Horiba, *CEO*
EMP: 33 EST: 2013
SALES (est): 10.1MM Privately Held
WEB: www.horiba.com
SIC: 3826 Analytical instruments

(G-17150)
HORIBA INSTRUMENTS INC
2890 John R Rd (48083-2353)
PHONE.................................248 689-9000
Ken Mitira, *Office Mgr*
EMP: 5 Privately Held
WEB: www.horiba.com
SIC: 3823 Industrial process measurement equipment; analyzers, industrial process type; controllers for process variables, all types
HQ: Horiba Instruments Incorporated
9755 Research Dr
Irvine CA 92618
949 250-4811

(G-17151)
HORN CORPORATION
Also Called: Eclipse Tanning
1263 Rochester Rd (48083-2879)
PHONE.................................248 583-7789
Matthew Horn, *President*
Timothy Horn, *Corp Secy*
Jamie Horn, *Vice Pres*
EMP: 14 EST: 1990
SQ FT: 5,200
SALES (est): 1.4MM Privately Held
SIC: 2752 5943 Commercial printing, offset; stationery stores

(G-17152)
HOUR MEDIA LLC (PA)
Also Called: Hour Detroit Magazine
5750 New King Dr Ste 100 (48098-2696)
PHONE.................................248 691-1800
David Christensen, *Partner*
Ed Peabody, *General Mgr*
Danielle Szatkowski, *Editor*
Lakshmi Varanasi, *Editor*
Mike Muszall, *Vice Pres*
EMP: 50 EST: 1996
SQ FT: 4,000
SALES (est): 37.6MM Privately Held
WEB: www.hourdetroit.com
SIC: 2721 Magazines: publishing only, not printed on site

(G-17153)
HOUR MEDIA GROUP LLC
5750 New King Dr Ste 100 (48098-2696)
PHONE.................................248 691-1800
John Balardo,
EMP: 1 EST: 2016
SALES (est): 1.2MM Privately Held
WEB: www.hourdetroit.com
SIC: 2721 Magazines: publishing only, not printed on site
PA: Hour Media, L.L.C.
5750 New King Dr Ste 100
Troy MI 48098

(G-17154)
HP INC
560 Kirts Blvd Ste 120 (48084-4141)
PHONE.................................248 614-6600
Adam T Schwerin, *Principal*
Phil Madis, *Manager*
EMP: 5
SALES (corp-wide): 56.6B Publicly Held
WEB: www.hp.com
SIC: 3571 Personal computers (microcomputers)
PA: Hp Inc.
1501 Page Mill Rd
Palo Alto CA 94304
650 857-1501

(G-17155)
HP PELZER AUTO SYSTEMS INC (DH)
Also Called: Adler Pelzer Group
1175 Crooks Rd (48084-7136)
PHONE.................................248 280-1010
Aberto Buniato, *President*
Pietro Lardini, *COO*
Daniel Benenati, *Plant Mgr*
Lori Post, *Materials Mgr*
Tracy Parker, *QC Mgr*
▲ EMP: 45 EST: 1995
SALES (est): 289MM
SALES (corp-wide): 177.9K Privately Held
WEB: www.adlerpelzer.com
SIC: 3061 2273 Automotive rubber goods (mechanical); carpets & rugs

(G-17156)
HSP EPI ACQUISITION LLC (PA)
Also Called: Entertainment
1401 Crooks Rd Ste 150 (48084-7106)
PHONE.................................248 404-1520
Tania Baez, *Accounts Exec*
Sylvia Douglas, *Sales Staff*
Chris Smith, *Sales Staff*
Veronica Archer, *Sales Executive*
Lowell Potiker, *Mng Member*
EMP: 135 EST: 2013
SQ FT: 81,000
SALES (est): 21.2MM Privately Held
WEB: www.entertainment.com
SIC: 2731 Books: publishing only

(G-17157)
I-9 ADVANTAGE
101 W Big Beaver Rd 14 (48084-5253)
PHONE.................................800 724-8546
Kelly Thompson, *Project Mgr*
Melissa Prentice, *Manager*
Rose Bruce, *Administration*
EMP: 13 EST: 2015
SALES (est): 340.7K Privately Held
WEB: www.i9advantage.com
SIC: 7372 Prepackaged software

(G-17158)
IDEAL MACHINE TOOL TECH LLC
Also Called: Imtt
675 E Big Beaver Rd # 105 (48083-1427)
PHONE.................................248 320-4729
Lauren Hylton,
EMP: 4 EST: 2010
SALES (est): 202.7K Privately Held
WEB: www.idealmachinetools.com
SIC: 3599 Machine shop, jobbing & repair

(G-17159)
IES-SYNERGY INC
330 E Maple Rd Ste U (48083-2706)
PHONE.................................586 206-4410
EMP: 6 EST: 2008
SALES (est): 113.9K Privately Held
WEB: www.ies-synergy.com
SIC: 3621 Storage battery chargers, motor & engine generator type

(G-17160)
IKEA CHIP LLC
2609 Crooks Rd Ste 235 (48084-4714)
PHONE.................................877 218-9931
Hao Ivy,
EMP: 9 EST: 2017
SALES (est): 769.9K Privately Held
SIC: 1542 8748 2426 Custom builders, non-residential; business consulting; carvings, furniture: wood

(G-17161)
ILLINOIS TOOL WORKS INC
ITW Deltar Fastener
100 Kirts Blvd (48084-5217)
PHONE.................................248 589-2500
Steven Bonnell, *Principal*
Mike Omastiak, *Plant Mgr*
Rick Spiegel, *Technical Mgr*
Aimee Balyeat, *Engineer*
Paul Jelonek, *Engineer*
EMP: 5
SALES (corp-wide): 12.5B Publicly Held
WEB: www.itw.com
SIC: 3089 5013 3544 3711 Automotive parts, plastic; automotive engines & engine parts; dies & die holders for metal cutting, forming, die casting; dies, plastics forming; automobile assembly, including specialty automobiles; automotive stampings; tapping machines
PA: Illinois Tool Works Inc.
155 Harlem Ave
Glenview IL 60025
847 724-7500

(G-17162)
IMPRESSION CENTER CO
224 Minnesota Dr (48083-4667)
PHONE.................................248 989-8080
Daniel Goehmann, *President*
Jenifer Goehmann, *Admin Sec*
EMP: 4 EST: 1987
SQ FT: 2,000
SALES (est): 200K Privately Held
WEB: www.impressioncenter.com
SIC: 2759 Screen printing

(G-17163)
INDEPNDNCE TLING SOLUTIONS LLC
1200 Rochester Rd (48083-2833)
PHONE.................................586 274-2300
Beth McReynolds, *Vice Pres*
Tony Parete, *Vice Pres*
Lloyd Brown, *Mng Member*
EMP: 23 EST: 2015
SQ FT: 16,400
SALES (est): 2.8MM Privately Held
WEB: www.indytooling.com
SIC: 3545 Tools & accessories for machine tools
PA: Waltonen Engineering, Inc.
31330 Mound Rd
Warren MI 48092

(G-17164)
INDIANA NEWSPAPERS LLC
Also Called: Gannett National Newspaper Sls
340 E Big Beaver Rd Ste 1 (48083-1218)
PHONE.................................248 680-9905
Jim Chauvin, *Branch Mgr*
EMP: 69
SALES (corp-wide): 3.4B Publicly Held
WEB: www.indystar.com
SIC: 2711 Newspapers, publishing & printing
HQ: Indiana Newspapers Llc
130 S Meridian St
Indianapolis IN 46225
317 444-4000

(G-17165)
INDRATECH LLC (PA)
1212 E Maple Rd (48083-2817)
PHONE.................................248 377-1877
Surendre Khambete,
EMP: 20 EST: 2003
SALES (est): 11.5MM Privately Held
WEB: www.indratech.com
SIC: 2515 Mattresses & foundations

(G-17166)
INFORMATION BUILDERS INC
Also Called: I Way Software
1301 W Long Lake Rd # 150 (48098-6336)
PHONE.................................248 641-8820
Sharon Kohler, *Opers Mgr*
Robert Szczerba, *Engineer*
Kimball Cole, *Senior Engr*
Bill Dykema, *Senior Engr*
Mark Zimmerman, *Senior Engr*
EMP: 4
SALES (corp-wide): 885.6MM Privately Held
WEB: www.ibi.com
SIC: 7372 Prepackaged software
HQ: Information Builders, Inc.
11 Penn Plz Fl 8
New York NY 10001
212 736-4433

(G-17167)
INGERSOLL PROD SYSTEMS LLC
1000 John R Rd Ste 108 (48083-4317)
PHONE.................................248 585-9130
William Kalp, *Manager*
EMP: 8 Privately Held
WEB: www.ingersollprodsys.com
SIC: 3541 Machine tools, metal cutting type
HQ: Ingersoll Production Systems Llc
1301 Eddy Ave
Rockford IL 61103
815 637-8500

(G-17168)
INNOVATIVE SUPPORT SVCS INC
Also Called: ISS
1270 Souter Dr (48083-2837)
PHONE.................................248 585-3600
William Herndon, *President*
EMP: 13 EST: 1987
SQ FT: 3,500
SALES (est): 577.3K Privately Held
WEB: www.vegacnc.com
SIC: 7629 3625 3823 3577 Electronic equipment repair; motor controls & accessories; industrial instrmnts msrmnt display/control process variable; computer peripheral equipment

(G-17169)
INOAC USA INC (DH)
1515 Equity Dr Ste 200 (48084-7129)
PHONE.................................248 619-7031
Toyohiko Okina, *CEO*
Charles Little, *President*
Carl D Malz, *President*
Soichi Inoue, *Chairman*
Andrew Dargavell, *Vice Pres*
▲ EMP: 31 EST: 1926

Troy - Oakland County (G-17170)

SALES (est): 501.6MM **Privately Held**
WEB: www.inoacusa.com
SIC: 3085 3714 Plastics bottles; motor vehicle parts & accessories

(G-17170)
INTELLITECH SYSTEMS INC
303 Evaline Dr (48085-5510)
PHONE..................586 219-3737
Chadi Shaya, *President*
EMP: 6 EST: 2011 **Privately Held**
WEB: www.intellitech-systems.com
SIC: 7929 3651 Entertainment service; home entertainment equipment, electronic

(G-17171)
INTERNATIONAL AUTO COMPONENTS
750 Chicago Rd (48083-4222)
PHONE..................248 755-3928
Chris Griggs, *Senior Engr*
Lennard Harris, *Supervisor*
EMP: 14 EST: 2015
SALES (est): 879.3K **Privately Held**
SIC: 3714 Motor vehicle parts & accessories

(G-17172)
INTERNATIONAL MACHINERY
225 Elmwood Dr (48083-4801)
PHONE..................248 619-9999
EMP: 5 EST: 2019
SALES (est): 102.2K **Privately Held**
WEB: www.internationalmachine.net
SIC: 3542 Machine tools, metal forming type

(G-17173)
INTEVA PRODUCTS LLC
Also Called: Inteva - Troy Engineering Ctr
2305 Crooks Rd (48084)
PHONE..................248 655-8886
Joe Long, *Branch Mgr*
EMP: 7
SALES (corp-wide): 3.2B **Privately Held**
WEB: www.intevaproducts.com
SIC: 3714 Motor vehicle parts & accessories
HQ: Inteva Products, Llc
    1401 Crooks Rd
    Troy MI 48084

(G-17174)
INTEVA PRODUCTS LLC (HQ)
1401 Crooks Rd (48084-7106)
PHONE..................248 655-8886
Gerard Roose, *President*
Michelle Brown, *Principal*
Steven Galle, *Principal*
Dennis Hodges, *Principal*
Carolyn Bohlken, *Regional Mgr*
◆ EMP: 400 EST: 2007
SQ FT: 200,000
SALES (est): 821.3MM
SALES (corp-wide): 3.2B **Privately Held**
WEB: www.intevaproducts.com
SIC: 3714 5085 5013 Motor vehicle parts & accessories; industrial supplies; motor vehicle supplies & new parts
PA: The Renco Group Inc
    1 Rockefeller Plz Fl 29
    New York NY 10020
    212 541-6000

(G-17175)
INTEVA PRODUCTS USA LLC
1401 Crooks Rd (48084-7106)
PHONE..................248 655-8886
Lon Offenbacher, *President*
William Dircks, *Exec VP*
Steven Galle, *Vice Pres*
Jan Griffiths, *Vice Pres*
Thomas Munley, *Vice Pres*
EMP: 127 EST: 2010
SALES (est): 20.9MM
SALES (corp-wide): 3.2B **Privately Held**
WEB: www.intevaproducts.com
SIC: 3714 Motor vehicle parts & accessories
HQ: Inteva Products, Llc
    1401 Crooks Rd
    Troy MI 48084

(G-17176)
IWIS ENGINE SYSTEMS LP
340 E Big Beaver Rd # 155 (48083-1269)
PHONE..................248 247-3178
Johannes Winklhoser, *Mng Member*
Scott E Tarter,
▲ EMP: 5 EST: 2010
SALES (est): 1.6MM **Privately Held**
WEB: www.iwis.com
SIC: 3462 Automotive forgings, ferrous: crankshaft, engine, axle, etc.
PA: Iwis Se & Co. Kg
    Albert-RoBhaupter-Str. 53
    Munchen BY 81369

(G-17177)
J DAVID INC
2626 Elliott Dr A (48083-4633)
PHONE..................888 274-0669
David J Yousif, *Administration*
EMP: 7 EST: 2011
SALES (est): 374.1K **Privately Held**
SIC: 2211 2258 2299 Table cover fabrics, cotton; covers, lace: chair, dresser, piano & table; curtains & curtain fabrics, lace; linen fabrics

(G-17178)
J E MYLES INC (PA)
Also Called: Myles Group
310 Executive Dr (48083-4587)
PHONE..................248 583-1020
J Edgar Myles, *President*
J Scott Myles, *Vice Pres*
EMP: 23 EST: 1957
SQ FT: 24,700
SALES (est): 11.3MM **Privately Held**
WEB: www.jemyles.com
SIC: 5085 8734 3829 Pistons & valves; product testing laboratory, safety or performance; measuring & controlling devices

(G-17179)
J NAYLOR LLC
4072 Greensboro Dr (48085-3615)
PHONE..................248 227-8250
Joe Naylor, *Administration*
Joseph Naylor, *Administration*
EMP: 5 EST: 2012
SALES (est): 140.2K **Privately Held**
SIC: 3931 Musical instruments

(G-17180)
J2 LICENSING INC (PA)
351 Executive Dr (48083-4533)
PHONE..................586 307-3400
John P Debay, *President*
Jon Rose, *Director*
▲ EMP: 3 EST: 1987
SQ FT: 4,500
SALES (est): 1.7MM **Privately Held**
WEB: www.j2licensing.com
SIC: 2759 2396 2395 Letterpress & screen printing; automotive & apparel trimmings; pleating & stitching

(G-17181)
JASLIN ASSEMBLY INC
4537 Harold Dr (48085-5703)
PHONE..................248 528-3024
EMP: 6
SALES (est): 473.9K **Privately Held**
SIC: 3496 Electronic Cable Assembly

(G-17182)
JAY/ENN CORPORATION
Also Called: Jay Enn
33943 Dequindre Rd (48083-4632)
PHONE..................248 588-2393
Burton J Kirsten, *President*
Nathan Jakey, *Corp Secy*
Jeffrey Baroli, *Vice Pres*
Jim Harris, *Plant Mgr*
Ben Dekiere, *Opers Staff*
EMP: 65 EST: 1970
SQ FT: 38,000
SALES (est): 9.2MM **Privately Held**
WEB: www.jayenn.com
SIC: 3543 3823 8711 3544 Industrial patterns; industrial instrmnts msrmnt display/control process variable; designing: ship, boat, machine & product; special dies, tools, jigs & fixtures

(G-17183)
JB PRODUCTS INC
143 Indusco Ct (48083-4644)
PHONE..................248 549-1900
Larry Brown, *President*
▲ EMP: 8 EST: 1974
SQ FT: 14,500
SALES (est): 1.4MM **Privately Held**
WEB: www.jbproductsinc.com
SIC: 2821 Plastics materials & resins

(G-17184)
JEMMS-CASCADE INC
238 Executive Dr (48083-4530)
PHONE..................248 526-8100
Donald E Galat, *President*
Amber Mattox, *Administration*
EMP: 11 EST: 1988
SQ FT: 5,000
SALES (est): 1.5MM **Privately Held**
WEB: www.jemms-cascade.com
SIC: 3546 Power-driven handtools

(G-17185)
JET BOX CO INC
1822 Thunderbird (48084-5479)
PHONE..................248 362-1260
Kathryn L Woch, *President*
Lynda K Zardus, *Principal*
Robert Louis Zardus, *Vice Pres*
EMP: 18 EST: 1967
SQ FT: 23,000
SALES (est): 4.4MM **Privately Held**
WEB: www.jetboxco.com
SIC: 2653 Boxes, corrugated: made from purchased materials

(G-17186)
JETPACK INDUSTRIES LLC
3848 Darleen Ct (48084-1756)
PHONE..................248 689-5083
Daniel Dennis, *Principal*
EMP: 4 EST: 2013
SALES (est): 53.6K **Privately Held**
SIC: 3999 Manufacturing industries

(G-17187)
JL GEISLER SIGN COMPANY
1017 Naughton Dr (48083-1911)
PHONE..................586 574-1800
Jane Geisler, *President*
Gary Geisler, *Vice Pres*
Tammy Kelly, *Vice Pres*
Corinne Skawski, *Project Mgr*
EMP: 13 EST: 1966
SQ FT: 8,000
SALES (est): 1.5MM **Privately Held**
WEB: www.michigansignshops.com
SIC: 3993 3953 5112 Signs, not made in custom sign painting shops; marking devices; office supplies

(G-17188)
JO-MAR INDUSTRIES INC
2876 Elliott Dr (48083-4635)
PHONE..................248 588-9625
Richard J Roth, *President*
Christine Forster, *Manager*
▼ EMP: 23 EST: 1985
SQ FT: 12,400
SALES (est): 1.2MM **Privately Held**
WEB: www.jomarindustries.com
SIC: 3544 Special dies & tools

(G-17189)
JOMESA NORTH AMERICA INC
2095 E Big Beaver Rd (48083-2356)
PHONE..................248 457-0023
Polly Hongisto, *Principal*
EMP: 14 EST: 2013
SALES (est): 2.7MM **Privately Held**
WEB: www.jomesa.com
SIC: 3569 Filters, general line: industrial

(G-17190)
JUST GIRLS LLC
Also Called: Justgirls Boutique
6907 Orchard Lake Rd (48098)
PHONE..................248 952-1967
Jill Oleski, *Mng Member*
EMP: 6 EST: 2010
SALES (est): 370.4K **Privately Held**
WEB: www.justgirlsboutique.com
SIC: 2369 Children's culottes & shorts; coat & legging sets: girls' & children's; pantsuits: girls', children's & infants'

(G-17191)
K-VALUE INSULATION LLC
4956 Butler Dr (48085-3526)
P.O. Box 4481 (48099-4481)
PHONE..................248 688-5816
Anthony Noel,
EMP: 4 EST: 2010
SALES (est): 315.6K **Privately Held**
SIC: 3292 Pipe covering (heat insulating material), except felt

(G-17192)
KARJO TRUCKING INC
1890 E Maple Rd (48083-4240)
PHONE..................248 597-3700
Mike Karjo, *President*
▲ EMP: 10 EST: 1993
SALES (est): 651.6K **Privately Held**
WEB: www.karjotrucking.com
SIC: 2448 Cargo containers, wood & metal combination

(G-17193)
KAUTEX INC (HQ)
800 Tower Dr Ste 200 (48098-2843)
PHONE..................248 616-5100
Vicente Perez-Lucerga, *President*
Hanno Neizer, *COO*
Klaus Konig, *Exec VP*
John H Bracken, *Vice Pres*
Mira Eigler, *Vice Pres*
▲ EMP: 900 EST: 1996
SALES (est): 1.4B
SALES (corp-wide): 11.6B **Publicly Held**
WEB: www.kautex.com
SIC: 3714 Instrument board assemblies, motor vehicle
PA: Textron Inc.
    40 Westminster St
    Providence RI 02903
    401 421-2800

(G-17194)
KIRCHHOFF AUTOMOTIVE USA INC
2600 Bellingham Dr # 400 (48083-2014)
PHONE..................248 247-3740
Josh Forquer, *Vice Pres*
Kevin Kelly, *Sales Mgr*
William Van Sickle, *Sales Staff*
Carlos Perez-Galicia, *Program Mgr*
Berneda Dodd, *Senior Mgr*
EMP: 10 EST: 2019
SALES (est): 2.5MM
SALES (corp-wide): 1.7B **Privately Held**
WEB: www.kirchhoff-automotive.com
SIC: 7538 3465 General automotive repair shops; body parts, automobile: stamped metal
PA: Kirchhoff Automotive Holding Gmbh & Co. Kg
    Stefanstr. 2
    Iserlohn NW 58638
    237 182-000

(G-17195)
KM AND I
3155 W Big Beaver Rd # 111 (48084-3006)
PHONE..................248 792-2782
William Cantwell, *President*
EMP: 6 EST: 2011
SALES (est): 100.3K **Privately Held**
SIC: 3089 Plastic processing

(G-17196)
KORCAST PRODUCTS INCORPORATED (PA)
Also Called: Kor-Cast Products
1725 Larchwood Dr (48083-2224)
PHONE..................248 740-2340
Larry Bremner, *President*
EMP: 4 EST: 1965
SQ FT: 4,500
SALES (est): 1.3MM **Privately Held**
SIC: 2541 1799 Cabinets, except refrigerated: show, display, etc.: wood; counters or counter display cases, wood; counter top installation

(G-17197)
KORCAST PRODUCTS INCORPORATED
Also Called: Modern Kitchen & Bath
1725 Larchwood Dr (48083-2224)
PHONE..................248 740-2340

Larry Bremner, *Branch Mgr*
EMP: 9
SALES (corp-wide): 1.3MM **Privately Held**
SIC: 2541 1799 3281 Cabinets, except refrigerated: show, display, etc.: wood; kitchen & bathroom remodeling; cut stone & stone products
PA: Korcast Products Incorporated
1725 Larchwood Dr
Troy MI 48083
248 740-2340

(G-17198)
KOSTAL OF AMERICA INC
Also Called: Kostal North America
350 Stephenson Hwy (48083-1119)
PHONE....................248 284-6500
Andreas Kostal, *Chairman*
Brendan Walsh, *Mfg Staff*
Tim Oconnor, *Purch Mgr*
Juan Serrano, *Purch Mgr*
Rhonda Miller, *Purch Agent*
▲ **EMP:** 237 **EST:** 1987
SQ FT: 78,000
SALES (est): 65.5MM
SALES (corp-wide): 1.1MM **Privately Held**
WEB: www.kostal.us
SIC: 3714 Motor vehicle parts & accessories
HQ: Kostal Beteiligungsges. Mbh
Wiesenstr. 47
Ludenscheid NW 58507
235 116-0

(G-17199)
KRAMER INTERNATIONAL INC
5750 New King Dr Ste 200 (48098-2611)
PHONE....................586 726-4300
Paul Rhodes, *Vice Pres*
EMP: 12 **EST:** 2011
SALES (est): 363.2K **Privately Held**
SIC: 3322 Malleable iron foundries

(G-17200)
KUNSTSTOFF TCHNIK SCHRER TRIER
3150 Livernois Rd Ste 275 (48083-5034)
PHONE....................734 944-5080
Tom Kozyra, *President*
▲ **EMP:** 27 **EST:** 2004
SQ FT: 75,000
SALES (est): 3.3MM **Privately Held**
SIC: 3089 Plastic processing

(G-17201)
L PERRIGO COMPANY
101 W Big Beaver Rd (48084-5253)
PHONE....................248 687-1036
EMP: 4 **Privately Held**
WEB: www.perrigo.com
SIC: 2834 Analgesics
HQ: L. Perrigo Company
515 Eastern Ave
Allegan MI 49010
269 673-8451

(G-17202)
L S MACHINING INC
1250 Rankin Dr Ste E (48083-2844)
PHONE....................248 583-7277
Lyle A Stuemke, *President*
Guyann Stuemke, *Vice Pres*
EMP: 5 **EST:** 1978
SQ FT: 4,800
SALES (est): 426.2K **Privately Held**
SIC: 3599 3544 Machine shop, jobbing & repair; special dies, tools, jigs & fixtures

(G-17203)
LAFORCE LLC
289 Robbins Dr (48083-4513)
PHONE....................248 588-5601
Kevin Letto, *Branch Mgr*
Dan Sproull, *Manager*
EMP: 9
SALES (corp-wide): 132MM **Privately Held**
WEB: www.laforceinc.com
SIC: 3442 5031 5072 Metal doors, sash & trim; lumber, plywood & millwork; hardware
PA: Laforce, Llc
1060 W Mason St
Green Bay WI 54303
920 497-7100

(G-17204)
LAMACS INC
360 E Maple Rd Ste I (48083-2707)
PHONE....................248 643-9210
William L Haines Jr, *President*
Peggy Donnelly, *Vice Pres*
EMP: 4 **EST:** 1970
SALES (est): 386.3K **Privately Held**
WEB: www.lamacsembroidery.com
SIC: 2399 5136 Emblems, badges & insignia: from purchased materials; uniforms, men's & boys'

(G-17205)
LAVALIER CORP
Also Called: Tapemaster
900 Rochester Rd (48083-6009)
PHONE....................248 616-8880
Thomas Laviolette, *Principal*
EMP: 24 **EST:** 2018
SALES (est): 1.1MM **Privately Held**
SIC: 3555 8711 Plates, metal: engravers'; mechanical engineering

(G-17206)
LAWRENCE SURFACE TECH INC
1895 Crooks Rd (48084-5382)
PHONE....................248 609-9001
Bret Evans, *President*
EMP: 2 **EST:** 2012
SQ FT: 2,500
SALES (est): 15MM **Privately Held**
WEB: www.huaxianginternational.com
SIC: 3471 Decorative plating & finishing of formed products
PA: Ningbo Huaxiang Import & Export Co., Ltd.
Zhen'an Road, Xizhou Town, Xiangshan County
Ningbo 31501

(G-17207)
LEGENDARY MILLWORK INC
2655 Elliott Dr (48083-4637)
PHONE....................248 588-6663
Doug Massey, *President*
Matthew Snarski, *Vice Pres*
EMP: 4 **EST:** 1998
SQ FT: 10,000 **Privately Held**
WEB: www.legendarymillwork.com
SIC: 2431 Millwork

(G-17208)
LEONI WIRING SYSTEMS INC
Also Called: Lws - Design Center Detroit
2800 Livernois Rd Ste 600 (48083-1215)
PHONE....................586 782-4444
EMP: 10
SALES (corp-wide): 4.8B **Privately Held**
WEB: www.leoni.com
SIC: 3679 Electronic circuits
HQ: Leoni Wiring Systems, Inc.
3100 N Campbell Ave # 101
Tucson AZ 85719

(G-17209)
LG ELECTRONICS USA INC
1835 Technology Dr (48083-4244)
PHONE....................248 268-5100
Chip Howard, *General Mgr*
Stephan Bruner, *Regional Mgr*
Richsan Hindman, *Regional Mgr*
Jason Thompson, *Regional Mgr*
James Dale, *Business Mgr*
EMP: 140 **Privately Held**
WEB: www.lg.com
SIC: 3651 5064 Household audio & video equipment; electrical appliances, major
HQ: Lg Electronics U.S.A., Inc.
111 Sylvan Ave
Englewood Cliffs NJ 07632
201 816-2000

(G-17210)
LG ELECTRONICS VEHICLE COMPONE
1835 Technology Dr Bldg E (48083-4244)
PHONE....................248 268-5851
Kenneth Cheng, *President*
EMP: 190 **Privately Held**
SIC: 3694 Automotive electrical equipment
HQ: Lg Electronics Vehicle Components U.S.A., Llc
1400 E 10 Mile Rd Ste 100
Hazel Park MI 48030
248 268-5851

(G-17211)
LG ENERGY SOLUTION MICH INC
3221 W Big Beaver Rd (48084-2803)
PHONE....................248 291-2385
EMP: 179 **Privately Held**
WEB: www.lgenergymi.com
SIC: 3691 Storage batteries
HQ: Lg Energy Solution Michigan, Inc.
1 Lg Way
Holland MI 49423

(G-17212)
LG ENERGY SOLUTION MICH INC
Also Called: Lg Chem Michigan Inc Tech Ctr
1857 Technology Dr (48083-4244)
PHONE....................248 307-1800
Denise Gray, *Branch Mgr*
EMP: 179 **Privately Held**
WEB: www.lgenergymi.com
SIC: 3691 Storage batteries
HQ: Lg Energy Solution Michigan, Inc.
1 Lg Way
Holland MI 49423

(G-17213)
LIVE EDGE DETROIT
241 Park Dr (48083-2726)
PHONE....................248 909-2259
Jennifer Barger, *Principal*
EMP: 7 **EST:** 2019
SALES (est): 442.5K **Privately Held**
WEB: www.liveedgedetroit.com
SIC: 2431 Millwork

(G-17214)
LIVERMORE SOFTWARE TECH LLC
1740 W Big Beavr Rd # 100 (48084-3507)
PHONE....................925 449-2500
EMP: 14
SALES (corp-wide): 1.6B **Publicly Held**
WEB: www.ansys.com
SIC: 7372 Prepackaged software
HQ: Livermore Software Technology, Llc
7374 Las Positas Rd
Livermore CA 94551
925 449-2500

(G-17215)
LONERO ENGINEERING CO INC
2050 Stephenson Hwy (48083-2151)
P.O. Box 935 (48099-0935)
PHONE....................248 689-9120
Vincent J Lonero, *President*
Tod F Lonero, *Vice Pres*
Scott Galer, *Senior Engr*
Phillip Varvatos, *CFO*
Tod Lonero, *Treasurer*
EMP: 30 **EST:** 1951
SQ FT: 18,000
SALES (est): 4.1MM **Privately Held**
WEB: www.deeprolling.com
SIC: 3544 Jigs & fixtures; dies & die holders for metal cutting, forming, die casting

(G-17216)
M & M SERVICES INC
1844 Woodslee Dr (48083-2207)
PHONE....................248 619-9861
Marion J Kras, *President*
Pam Givens, *Officer*
EMP: 9 **EST:** 1983
SQ FT: 7,000
SALES (est): 750K **Privately Held**
WEB: www.mmgrinding.com
SIC: 3544 3599 Special dies & tools; machine & other job shop work

(G-17217)
MAC-TECH TOOLING CORPORATION
1874 Larchwood Dr (48083-2225)
PHONE....................248 743-1400
William Macinnis, *President*
Curtis Macinnis, *President*
Amy McCaffrey, *Vice Pres*
EMP: 9 **EST:** 1993
SQ FT: 5,500
SALES (est): 647.9K **Privately Held**
WEB: www.mactechtooling.com
SIC: 7699 3545 Tool repair services; cutting tools for machine tools

(G-17218)
MACAUTO USA INC
2654 Elliott Dr (48083-4633)
PHONE....................248 556-5256
Wu Miller, *Branch Mgr*
EMP: 20 **Privately Held**
WEB: www.macauto-usa.com
SIC: 3089 Automotive parts, plastic
HQ: Macauto Usa, Inc.
80 Excel Dr
Rochester NY 14621
585 342-2060

(G-17219)
MAGNA ELECTRONICS INC
1465 Combermere Dr (48083-2745)
PHONE....................810 606-0444
Yvonne Nerswick, *Buyer*
Ross Parpart, *Design Engr*
Stewart Wu, *Electrical Engi*
Rajeev Joshi, *Branch Mgr*
Andrea Medrano, *Manager*
EMP: 57
SALES (corp-wide): 32.6B **Privately Held**
WEB: www.magna.com
SIC: 3699 Electrical equipment & supplies
HQ: Magna Electronics Inc.
2050 Auburn Rd
Auburn Hills MI 48326

(G-17220)
MAGNA EXTERIORS AMERICA INC (HQ)
Also Called: Decoma Admark
750 Tower Dr (48098-2863)
PHONE....................248 631-1100
Donald J Walker, *CEO*
Guenther Apfalter, *President*
Tom J Skudutis, *COO*
Marc Neeb, *Exec VP*
William Frederiksen, *Vice Pres*
◆ **EMP:** 800 **EST:** 1987
SALES (est): 929.2MM
SALES (corp-wide): 32.6B **Privately Held**
WEB: www.magna.com
SIC: 3714 3544 8711 Motor vehicle body components & frame; forms (molds), for foundry & plastics working machinery; engineering services
PA: Magna International Inc
337 Magna Dr
Aurora ON L4G 7
905 726-2462

(G-17221)
MAGNA EXTRORS INTRORS AMER INC
750 Tower Dr (48098-2863)
PHONE....................248 729-2400
Laurie Curran, *General Mgr*
Tony Dingman, *Business Mgr*
Randy Koenigsknecht, *Vice Pres*
Sandi Macdonald, *Vice Pres*
John Wyskiel, *Vice Pres*
EMP: 185
SALES (corp-wide): 32.6B **Privately Held**
WEB: www.magna.com
SIC: 3714 Motor vehicle parts & accessories
HQ: Magna Exteriors Of America, Inc.
750 Tower Dr
Troy MI 48098
248 631-1100

(G-17222)
MAGNA INTERNATIONAL AMER INC (HQ)
750 Twer Dr Mail Code 700 (48084)
PHONE....................248 729-2400
Donald Walker, *President*
Marc Neeb, *President*
John Hackett, *General Mgr*
Andy Hrasky, *General Mgr*
Sabrina Griffin, *District Mgr*
EMP: 468 **EST:** 1988
SALES (est): 1.5B
SALES (corp-wide): 32.6B **Privately Held**
WEB: www.magna.com
SIC: 3714 Motor vehicle parts & accessories

Troy - Oakland County (G-17223) — GEOGRAPHIC SECTION

PA: Magna International Inc
337 Magna Dr
Aurora ON L4G 7
905 726-2462

(G-17223)
MAGNA POWERTRAIN AMERICA INC (HQ)
1870 Technology Dr (48083-4232)
PHONE..................248 597-7811
Donald J Walker, *CEO*
Diba Ilunga, *General Mgr*
Tom More, *Vice Pres*
Mike McLean, *Project Mgr*
Dave Sage, *Facilities Mgr*
▲ EMP: 150 EST: 1992
SALES (est): 116.6MM
SALES (corp-wide): 32.6B Privately Held
WEB: www.magna.com
SIC: 3714 Motor vehicle parts & accessories
PA: Magna International Inc
337 Magna Dr
Aurora ON L4G 7
905 726-2462

(G-17224)
MAGNA POWERTRAIN USA INC (HQ)
1870 Technology Dr (48083-4232)
PHONE..................248 680-4900
Donald J Walker, *CEO*
Kim Sikorski, *Human Res Mgr*
Joe Mueller, *Mktg Dir*
Robert Dubois, *Manager*
▲ EMP: 94 EST: 2004
SQ FT: 31,000
SALES (est): 912.3MM
SALES (corp-wide): 32.6B Privately Held
WEB: www.magna.com
SIC: 3714 Motor vehicle engines & parts
PA: Magna International Inc
337 Magna Dr
Aurora ON L4G 7
905 726-2462

(G-17225)
MAGNA POWERTRAIN USA INC
1875 Research Dr (48083-2191)
PHONE..................248 524-1397
Graciela Alarcon, *Human Resources*
EMP: 44
SALES (corp-wide): 32.6B Privately Held
WEB: www.magna.com
SIC: 3714 Motor vehicle engines & parts
HQ: Magna Powertrain Usa, Inc.
1870 Technology Dr
Troy MI 48083
248 680-4900

(G-17226)
MAGNA POWERTRAIN USA INC
1870 Technology Dr (48083-4232)
P.O. Box 78305, Detroit (48278-8305)
PHONE..................248 680-4900
Mike Hinterleitner, *Buyer*
Kristin Lamar, *Buyer*
Manfred Hartmann, *Purchasing*
Juan Ceballos, *Accounts Mgr*
Nick Morgan, *Sales Staff*
EMP: 44
SALES (corp-wide): 32.6B Privately Held
WEB: www.magna.com
SIC: 3714 Motor vehicle parts & accessories
HQ: Magna Powertrain Usa, Inc.
1870 Technology Dr
Troy MI 48083
248 680-4900

(G-17227)
MAGNA STEYR LLC
Also Called: Magna Steyr North America
1965 Research Dr Ste 100 (48083-2175)
PHONE..................248 740-0214
Dimitra Marantidis, *Manager*
Ian R Simmons, *Exec Dir*
August Hofbauer,
Mark Lukasiak,
Michael J Scott,
▲ EMP: 252 EST: 2000
SQ FT: 10,400
SALES (est): 22MM
SALES (corp-wide): 32.6B Privately Held
WEB: www.magna.com
SIC: 3711 Motor vehicles & car bodies

PA: Magna International Inc
337 Magna Dr
Aurora ON L4G 7
905 726-2462

(G-17228)
MAGNETOOL INC
505 Elmwood Dr (48083-2755)
PHONE..................248 588-5400
Albert T Churchill, *President*
▲ EMP: 31 EST: 1951
SQ FT: 30,000
SALES (est): 3MM Privately Held
WEB: www.magnetoolinc.com
SIC: 3542 Magnetic forming machines

(G-17229)
MAHINDRA N AMERCN TECHNICAL
1322 Rankin Dr (48083-2826)
PHONE..................248 268-6600
EMP: 6 EST: 2016
SALES (est): 88.7K Privately Held
SIC: 3711 Motor vehicles & car bodies

(G-17230)
MAHLE BEHR DAYTON LLC
2700 Daley Dr (48083-1949)
PHONE..................937 369-2900
Ryan Laros, *Mng Member*
EMP: 102 EST: 2002
SALES (est): 4.6MM
SALES (corp-wide): 504.6K Privately Held
WEB: www.mahle.com
SIC: 3714 Radiators & radiator shells & cores, motor vehicle; motor vehicle engines & parts; air conditioner parts, motor vehicle
HQ: Mahle Behr Usa Inc.
2700 Daley Dr
Troy MI 48083

(G-17231)
MAHLE BEHR MFG MGT INC
2700 Daley Dr (48083-1949)
PHONE..................248 735-3623
Wilm Uhlenbecker, *Vice Pres*
EMP: 26 EST: 2015
SALES (est): 23.3MM
SALES (corp-wide): 504.6K Privately Held
WEB: www.mahle-stiftung.de
SIC: 5013 3714 Automotive supplies & parts; air conditioner parts, motor vehicle
PA: M A H L E - S T I F T U N G
Gesellschaft Mit Beschrankter Haftung
Leibnizstr. 35
Stuttgart BW 70193
711 656-6169

(G-17232)
MAHLE BEHR USA INC (DH)
Also Called: Behr Climate Systems
2700 Daley Dr (48083-1949)
PHONE..................248 743-3700
Hans Lange, *President*
Jeremiah Scott, *Manager*
▲ EMP: 150 EST: 1969
SQ FT: 115,800
SALES (est): 140.9MM
SALES (corp-wide): 504.6K Privately Held
WEB: www.mahle.com
SIC: 3585 3714 Air conditioning, motor vehicle; radiators & radiator shells & cores, motor vehicle

(G-17233)
MAHLE BEHR USA INC
5820 Innovation Dr (48098-2824)
PHONE..................248 735-3623
EMP: 68
SALES (corp-wide): 504.6K Privately Held
SIC: 3714 Motor vehicle parts & accessories
HQ: Mahle Behr Usa Inc.
2700 Daley Dr
Troy MI 48083
248 743-3700

(G-17234)
MAHLE BEHR USA INC (DH)
2700 Daley Dr (48083-1949)
PHONE..................248 743-3700
Wilm Uhlenbecker, *President*
Dean Arneson, *Vice Pres*
Kara Leroy, *Purch Mgr*
Dawn Jasenas, *Buyer*
Randy Pierre, *Purchasing*
▲ EMP: 500 EST: 1990
SQ FT: 10,000
SALES (est): 1.3B
SALES (corp-wide): 504.6K Privately Held
WEB: www.mahle.com
SIC: 3714 Radiators & radiator shells & cores, motor vehicle
HQ: Mahle Gmbh
Pragstr. 26-46
Stuttgart BW 70376
711 501-0

(G-17235)
MAKS INCORPORATED
Also Called: Multi Tech Systems
1150 Rankin Dr (48083-6003)
PHONE..................248 733-9771
Mohamed Khalil, *President*
Sanaa Khalil, *Vice Pres*
Isaac Eiler, *Project Mgr*
Nabil Sater, *Marketing Staff*
EMP: 45 EST: 1992
SQ FT: 17,500
SALES (est): 9.7MM Privately Held
WEB: www.maksinc.net
SIC: 8711 3679 Electrical or electronic engineering; electronic circuits

(G-17236)
MARELLI TENNESSEE USA LLC
Also Called: Magneti Mrlli Cfap Suspensions
1389 Wheaton Dr (48083-1933)
PHONE..................248 680-8872
Donna Kjeldsen, *Buyer*
Carlos Rosado, *Buyer*
Andrea Zani, *Buyer*
Leonardo Ortuso, *Purchasing*
Gabriele Curcuruto, *Engineer*
EMP: 2270 EST: 2009
SALES (est): 1.4MM Publicly Held
WEB: www.marelli.com
SIC: 3714 Shock absorbers, motor vehicle
HQ: Marelli Holding Usa Llc
26555 Northwestern Hwy
Southfield MI 48033

(G-17237)
MARIAH INDUSTRIES INC (PA)
1407 Allen Dr Ste E (48083-4009)
PHONE..................248 237-0404
Samone Delagarza, *President*
Maria Christina Sammon, *Bd of Directors*
◆ EMP: 23 EST: 1972
SQ FT: 42,000
SALES (est): 8MM Privately Held
SIC: 3714 Motor vehicle parts & accessories

(G-17238)
MARK CARBIDE CO
1830 Brinston Dr (48083-2215)
PHONE..................248 545-0606
William Blanc, *President*
EMP: 7 EST: 1952
SALES (est): 540.2K Privately Held
WEB: www.markcarbide.com
SIC: 3544 Special dies & tools

(G-17239)
MARSHAL E HYMAN AND ASSOCIATES
3250 W Big Beavr Rd # 529 (48084-2902)
PHONE..................248 643-0642
Marshal Hyman, *President*
EMP: 9 EST: 2001
SALES (est): 625.5K Privately Held
WEB: www.marshalhyman.com
SIC: 3942 8111 Dolls, except stuffed toy animals; legal services

(G-17240)
MASTER MACHINING INC
1960 Thunderbird (48084-5466)
PHONE..................248 509-7185
James Armstrong, *President*
Denise Armstrong, *Treasurer*
EMP: 10 EST: 1986
SQ FT: 6,000
SALES (est): 650.6K Privately Held
WEB: www.mastermachining.net
SIC: 3599 Machine shop, jobbing & repair

(G-17241)
MATHSON GROUP INC
1737 Thunderbird (48084-5465)
PHONE..................248 821-5478
Boney Mathew, *Principal*
EMP: 7 EST: 2009
SALES (est): 75.5K Privately Held
SIC: 3089 Automotive parts, plastic

(G-17242)
MDLA INC
Also Called: Somerset Cleaners
2862 W Maple Rd (48084-7001)
PHONE..................248 643-0807
Marjana Kik, *Principal*
EMP: 10 EST: 2009
SALES (est): 737.7K Privately Held
WEB: www.somersetcleaners.com
SIC: 5087 3589 2842 Laundry & dry cleaning equipment & supplies; servicing machines, except dry cleaning, laundry: coin-oper.; laundry cleaning preparations

(G-17243)
MED-KAS HYDRAULICS INC
1805 Brinston Dr (48083-2216)
P.O. Box 1163 (48099-1163)
PHONE..................248 585-3220
Thomas Medici, *President*
Terry Medici, *Vice Pres*
EMP: 15 EST: 1964
SALES (est): 3.4MM Privately Held
WEB: www.med-kas.com
SIC: 3714 3594 Hydraulic fluid power pumps for auto steering mechanism; fluid power pumps & motors

(G-17244)
MEDWIN PUBLISHERS LLC
2609 Crooks Rd Ste 229 (48084-4714)
PHONE..................248 247-6042
Charlotte Kristine, *Manager*
Shravan Yeluvaka, *Administration*
EMP: 6 EST: 2019
SALES (est): 167.3K Privately Held
WEB: www.medwinpublishers.com
SIC: 2741 Miscellaneous publishing

(G-17245)
MERIDIAN INDUSTRIES
2500 Rochester Ct (48083-1873)
PHONE..................248 526-0444
Dan Surdell, *Principal*
EMP: 9 EST: 2006
SALES (est): 124.1K Privately Held
WEB: www.meridiancus.com
SIC: 3999 Manufacturing industries

(G-17246)
MERITOR INC (PA)
2135 W Maple Rd (48084-7121)
PHONE..................248 435-1000
Jeffrey A Craig, *Ch of Bd*
Chris Villavarayan, *President*
John Nelligan, *President*
Ben Bradley, *District Mgr*
Pierre Perron, *District Mgr*
◆ EMP: 250 EST: 1909
SALES (est): 3B Publicly Held
WEB: www.meritor.com
SIC: 3714 3493 3625 3465 Drive shafts, motor vehicle; automobile springs; actuators, industrial; automotive stampings

(G-17247)
MERITOR HEAVY VHCL SYSTEMS LLC (HQ)
2135 W Maple Rd (48084-7121)
PHONE..................248 435-1000
Jeffrey Craig, *CEO*
Carl Anderson, *Vice Pres*
Lee French, *Technical Mgr*
Patrick McNally, *Engineer*
Kevin Nowlan, *CFO*
▲ EMP: 1177 EST: 1997
SALES (est): 27.1MM Publicly Held
WEB: www.meritor.com
SIC: 3711 Military motor vehicle assembly

GEOGRAPHIC SECTION
Troy - Oakland County (G-17276)

(G-17248)
MERITOR INDUSTRIAL PDTS LLC (HQ)
2135 W Maple Rd (48084-7121)
PHONE...................888 725-9355
Jeffrey A Craig, *President*
Theresa Skotak, *Vice Pres*
Daniel Ruiz, *Prdtn Mgr*
Lora Daviston, *Production*
Rich Hunt, *Production*
▲ **EMP:** 5 **EST:** 2002
SQ FT: 16,000
SALES (est): 24.6MM **Publicly Held**
WEB: www.meritor.com
SIC: 3714 Motor vehicle parts & accessories

(G-17249)
MERITOR INTL HOLDINGS LLC (HQ)
2135 W Maple Rd (48084-7121)
PHONE...................248 435-1000
EMP: 1 **EST:** 2017
SALES (est): 11.7MM **Publicly Held**
WEB: www.meritor.com
SIC: 3714 Motor vehicle parts & accessories

(G-17250)
MERITOR SPECIALTY PRODUCTS LLC (HQ)
2135 W Maple Rd (48084-7121)
PHONE...................248 435-1000
Dan Ursu, *Engineer*
Carl D Anderson II,
Brett L Ellander,
▲ **EMP:** 1128 **EST:** 1987
SALES (est): 334.6MM **Publicly Held**
WEB: www.meritor.com
SIC: 3714 Axles, motor vehicle; gears, motor vehicle; transmission housings or parts, motor vehicle; transmissions, motor vehicle

(G-17251)
METAVATION LLC (HQ)
900 Wilshire Dr Ste 270 (48084-1600)
PHONE...................248 351-1000
John M Hrit, *Mng Member*
◆ **EMP:** 40 **EST:** 2006
SALES (est): 127.8MM **Privately Held**
WEB: www.metavationllc.com
SIC: 3714 Motor vehicle parts & accessories

(G-17252)
METHODICA TECHNOLOGIES LLC (PA)
100 W Big Beavr Rd # 200 (48084-5206)
PHONE...................312 622-7697
Ritu Anand, *Business Mgr*
Vikram Verma,
Natasha Verma,
EMP: 25 **EST:** 2015
SQ FT: 2,000
SALES: 2.9MM **Privately Held**
WEB: www.methodicatech.com
SIC: 8711 7372 7371 Engineering services; application computer software; software programming applications

(G-17253)
METRO PRINTING SERVICE INC
Also Called: Metro Promotional Specialties
1950 Barrett Dr (48084-5371)
PHONE...................248 545-4444
William J Brown, *CEO*
William R Brown, *President*
Mindy L Brown, *Admin Sec*
◆ **EMP:** 7 **EST:** 1977
SALES (est): 2.5MM **Privately Held**
WEB: www.metronbranding.com
SIC: 5199 2752 Advertising specialties; commercial printing, offset

(G-17254)
METRO TECHNOLOGIES LTD
1462 E Big Beaver Rd (48083-1950)
PHONE...................248 528-9240
Alfred J Hook, *President*
Patricia Hook, *Treasurer*
EMP: 60 **EST:** 1984
SQ FT: 20,000
SALES (est): 8.2MM **Privately Held**
WEB: www.mtl-troy.com
SIC: 3543 3544 Industrial patterns; special dies, tools, jigs & fixtures

(G-17255)
MFR ENTERPRISES LLC
1223 Chicago Rd (48083-4231)
PHONE...................248 965-3220
EMP: 5 **EST:** 2017
SALES (est): 194K **Privately Held**
SIC: 3999 Manufacturing industries

(G-17256)
MICHAEL-STEPHENS COMPANY
1206 E Maple Rd (48083-2817)
PHONE...................248 583-7767
Michael King, *President*
Chris Wymer, *Sales Staff*
EMP: 8 **EST:** 1976
SALES (est): 550.4K **Privately Held**
WEB: www.sealkits.com
SIC: 3053 Gaskets, packing & sealing devices

(G-17257)
MICHIGAN CARBIDE COMPANY INC
1263 Souter Dr (48083-2838)
PHONE...................586 264-8780
Rick Kosky, *President*
EMP: 14 **EST:** 1976
SQ FT: 10,000
SALES (est): 1.3MM **Privately Held**
WEB: www.michigancarbide.com
SIC: 3291 Tungsten carbide abrasive

(G-17258)
MICROCIDE INC
2209 Niagara Dr (48083-5933)
PHONE...................248 526-9663
John Lopes, *President*
Kathy Bolio, *Consultant*
EMP: 5 **EST:** 1990 **Privately Held**
WEB: www.microcide.com
SIC: 2844 2869 Mouthwashes; industrial organic chemicals

(G-17259)
MICRODENTAL LABORATORIES INC (PA)
500 Stephenson Hwy (48083-1118)
PHONE...................877 711-8778
Marjorie Coll, *Principal*
Wayne Coll, *Principal*
Trisha Hoofard, *Office Mgr*
Susan Paris, *Med Doctor*
EMP: 7 **EST:** 2016
SALES (est): 6.7MM **Privately Held**
WEB: www.microdental.com
SIC: 3843 Dental equipment & supplies

(G-17260)
MICROSOFT CORPORATION
2800 W Big Beaver Rd (48084-3206)
PHONE...................248 205-5990
EMP: 4
SALES (corp-wide): 168B **Publicly Held**
WEB: www.microsoft.com
SIC: 7372 Prepackaged software
PA: Microsoft Corporation
  1 Microsoft Way
  Redmond WA 98052
  425 882-8080

(G-17261)
MIDWEST ACORN NUT COMPANY (PA)
256 Minnesota Dr (48083-4671)
PHONE...................800 422-6887
Monica E Kopsch, *President*
Brian Smith, *Vice Pres*
Kathy Murphy, *Controller*
Mary Cudin, *Sales Staff*
Jim Towley, *Sales Staff*
EMP: 20
SQ FT: 10,000
SALES (est): 3.5MM **Privately Held**
WEB: www.midwestacornnut.com
SIC: 3452 Nuts, metal

(G-17262)
MITSUBISHI STEEL MFG CO LTD
Mssc
2040 Crooks Rd Ste A (48084-5520)
PHONE...................248 502-8000
Anita Turner, *Branch Mgr*
EMP: 7 **Privately Held**
WEB: www.mitsubishisteel.co.jp
SIC: 3714 Motor vehicle engines & parts
PA: Mitsubishi Steel Mfg. Co., Ltd.
  4-16-13, Tsukishima
  Chuo-Ku TKY 104-0

(G-17263)
MMI COMPANIES LLC
1094 Naughton Dr (48083-1910)
PHONE...................248 528-1680
Thomas Rickel, *Mng Member*
Tom Rickel, *Mng Member*
Mark Rickel, *Program Mgr*
Joseph Kosmolski,
EMP: 21 **EST:** 2010
SQ FT: 21,000
SALES (est): 3.9MM **Privately Held**
WEB: www.mmi-companies.com
SIC: 3089 Injection molding of plastics

(G-17264)
MODEL-MATIC INC
1094 Naughton Dr (48083-1910)
PHONE...................248 528-1680
Stanley M Kosmalski, *President*
Joseph Kosmalski, *Vice Pres*
Wilma Kosmalski, *Admin Sec*
EMP: 10 **EST:** 1969
SQ FT: 28,000
SALES (est): 854.7K **Privately Held**
SIC: 3544 3714 Industrial molds; motor vehicle parts & accessories

(G-17265)
MORE SIGNATURE CAKES LLC
Also Called: Thomas Cake Shop
5065 Livernois Rd (48098-3201)
PHONE...................248 266-0504
EMP: 4 **EST:** 2018
SALES (est): 300.8K **Privately Held**
WEB: www.moresignaturecakes.com
SIC: 2051 Cakes, bakery: except frozen; cakes, pies & pastries

(G-17266)
MOUND STEEL & SUPPLY INC
1450 Rochester Rd (48083-6014)
PHONE...................248 852-6630
David Simko, *President*
Frank Ianelli, *Admin Sec*
EMP: 19 **EST:** 1964
SQ FT: 4,000
SALES (est): 2.3MM **Privately Held**
SIC: 5211 3441 Lumber & other building materials; fabricated structural metal

(G-17267)
MPI ENGINEERED TECH LLC
901 Tower Dr Ste 315 (48098-2817)
PHONE...................248 237-3007
EMP: 13 **EST:** 2019
SALES (est): 2.2MM **Privately Held**
SIC: 3469 Machine parts, stamped or pressed metal

(G-17268)
MPT DRIVELINE SYSTEMS
1870 Technology Dr (48083-4232)
PHONE...................248 680-3786
EMP: 18 **EST:** 2013
SALES (est): 812.1K **Privately Held**
SIC: 3714 Motor vehicle parts & accessories

(G-17269)
MSCSOFTWARE CORPORATION
50 W Big Beavr Rd Ste 430 (48084-5204)
PHONE...................734 994-3800
EMP: 4
SALES (corp-wide): 4.5B **Privately Held**
WEB: www.mscsoftware.com
SIC: 7372 Business oriented computer software
HQ: Msc.Software Corporation
  5161 California Ave # 200
  Irvine CA 92617
  714 540-8900

(G-17270)
MSSC INC (HQ)
2040 Crooks Rd Ste A (48084-5520)
PHONE...................248 502-8000
Gerald Anderson, *President*
Murray Moffatt, *Mfg Mgr*
Thomas Lacy, *Purch Agent*
John Bessen, *Buyer*
Shannon Waring, *Buyer*
▲ **EMP:** 148 **EST:** 1986
SQ FT: 8,000
SALES (est): 23.7MM **Privately Held**
WEB: www.msscna.com
SIC: 3714 Motor vehicle body components & frame

(G-17271)
MUSTANG AERONAUTICS INC
1990 Heide Dr (48084-5314)
PHONE...................248 649-6818
Christopher Tieman, *President*
EMP: 5 **EST:** 1989
SQ FT: 8,000
SALES (est): 691.2K **Privately Held**
WEB: www.mustangaero.com
SIC: 3721 Aircraft

(G-17272)
N S INTERNATIONAL LTD (HQ)
600 Wilshire Dr (48084-1625)
PHONE...................248 251-1600
Teruyuki Matsui, *CEO*
Patrick Nadeau, *Managing Dir*
Joe Bleau, *Facilities Mgr*
Therissa Allen, *Purchasing*
Adam Cooley, *QC Mgr*
▲ **EMP:** 170 **EST:** 1972
SALES (est): 70.8MM **Privately Held**
WEB: www.nsusa.com
SIC: 5013 3672 3812 Automotive supplies & parts; printed circuit boards; detection apparatus: electronic/magnetic field, light/heat

(G-17273)
NATIONAL INDUSTRIAL SUP CO INC
Also Called: N I S
1201 Rochester Rd (48083-2834)
PHONE...................248 588-1828
Kathreen Harper, *President*
Charles W Brett, *Corp Secy*
Kevin Brett, *Vice Pres*
Mary Dingman, *Vice Pres*
Garry Breen, *Foreman/Supr*
EMP: 12 **EST:** 1982
SQ FT: 10,000
SALES (est): 4.2MM **Privately Held**
WEB: www.nischain.com
SIC: 3496 5085 Woven wire products; industrial fittings

(G-17274)
NESTLE PURINA PETCARE COMPANY
600 Executive Dr (48083-4537)
P.O. Box 7027 (48083)
PHONE...................888 202-4554
EMP: 27
SALES (corp-wide): 92.3B **Privately Held**
WEB: www.purina.com
SIC: 2047 Dog & cat food
HQ: Nestle Purina Petcare Company
  800 Chouteau Ave
  Saint Louis MO 63102
  314 982-1000

(G-17275)
NEW LAYER CUSTOMS LLC
330 E Maple Rd Ste A (48083-2706)
PHONE...................313 358-3629
Serhiy Yakobchak,
EMP: 5 **EST:** 2017
SALES (est): 116.6K **Privately Held**
WEB: www.newlayercustoms.com
SIC: 2851 Coating, air curing

(G-17276)
NIAGARA CUTTER LLC
2805 Bellingham Dr (48083-2046)
PHONE...................248 528-5220
EMP: 7 **EST:** 2016

Troy - Oakland County (G-17277)

SALES (est): 281.7K Privately Held
WEB: www.niagaracutter.com
SIC: 3541 Machine tools, metal cutting type

(G-17277)
NIHIL ULTRA CORPORATION
55 E Long Lake Rd (48085-4738)
PHONE..............................413 723-3218
Saikat Ghosh, *Principal*
EMP: 4 EST: 2010
SALES (est): 180.8K Privately Held
WEB: www.nihilultra.com
SIC: 3674 Light emitting diodes

(G-17278)
NIPPON PAINT AUTO AMERICAS INC
901 Wilshire Dr 105 (48084-1665)
PHONE..............................248 365-1100
Maureen Ison, *Buyer*
Calvin Dunn, *Engineer*
Michael Dwyer, *Engineer*
Stephen Fitzgerald, *Engineer*
Chris Kusper, *Engineer*
EMP: 9 Privately Held
WEB: www.nipponpaintamericas.com
SIC: 2851 Paints & allied products
HQ: Nippon Paint Automotive Americas, Inc.
    2701 E 170th St
    Lansing IL 60438
    800 323-3224

(G-17279)
NITTO SEIKO CO LTD
1301 Rankin Dr (48083-6008)
PHONE..............................248 588-0133
Masami Zaiki, *President*
▲ EMP: 7 Privately Held
WEB: www.nittoseiko.co.jp
SIC: 3399 Metal fasteners
PA: Nitto Seiko Co.,Ltd.
    20, Umegahata, Inokuracho
    Ayabe KYO 623-0

(G-17280)
NOACK VENTURES LLC
Also Called: Alba Plastics
1407 Allen Dr Ste G (48083-4009)
PHONE..............................248 583-0311
Mike Daley, *Principal*
EMP: 4 EST: 2004
SALES (est): 410.2K Privately Held
WEB: www.albaplastics.com
SIC: 3089 Injection molding of plastics

(G-17281)
NORTHSTAR SOURCING LLC
1399 Combermere Dr (48083)
PHONE..............................313 782-4749
John Koussa, *Mng Member*
Mike Bayoff,
EMP: 7 EST: 2017
SQ FT: 40,000
SALES (est): 1.5MM Privately Held
WEB: www.northstarsourcing.com
SIC: 2621 Paper mills

(G-17282)
NTVB MEDIA INC (PA)
Also Called: National Television Book Co
213 Park Dr (48083-2726)
PHONE..............................248 583-4190
Andrew V De Angelis, *President*
Tom Comi, *Partner*
Gary Kleinman, *Partner*
Barb Oates, *Editor*
Rick Gables, *Vice Pres*
EMP: 50 EST: 1981
SQ FT: 22,000
SALES (est): 57MM Privately Held
WEB: www.ntvbmedia.com
SIC: 2752 Commercial printing, offset

(G-17283)
NUBREED NUTRITION INC
318 John R Rd Ste 310 (48083-4542)
PHONE..............................734 272-7395
John Kazmar, *President*
EMP: 16 EST: 2013
SALES (est): 597.4K Privately Held
WEB: www.nubreednutrition.com
SIC: 8049 2075 Nutrition specialist; soybean protein concentrates & isolates

(G-17284)
NVENT THERMAL LLC
900 Wilshire Dr Ste 150 (48084-1600)
PHONE..............................248 273-3359
Dwight Hansell, *Manager*
EMP: 50 Privately Held
WEB: www.raychem.nvent.com
SIC: 3678 Electronic connectors
HQ: Nvent Thermal Llc
    899 Broadway St
    Redwood City CA 94063
    650 474-7414

(G-17285)
OAKWOOD VENEER COMPANY
1830 Stephenson Hwy Ste A (48083-2173)
PHONE..............................248 720-0288
Peter Rodgers, *President*
Jay White, *Warehouse Mgr*
◆ EMP: 18 EST: 1988
SQ FT: 44,000
SALES (est): 2.8MM Privately Held
WEB: www.oakwoodveneer.com
SIC: 2499 Veneer work, inlaid

(G-17286)
ODIN DEFENSE INDUSTRIES INC
2145 Crooks Rd Ste 210 (48084-5539)
PHONE..............................248 434-5072
Joseph Caradonna, *Principal*
EMP: 5 EST: 2018
SALES (est): 335.1K Privately Held
SIC: 3999 Manufacturing industries

(G-17287)
OERLIKON METCO (US) INC
1972 Meijer Dr (48084-7143)
PHONE..............................248 288-0027
Sofya Dadiomova, *Engineer*
Kevin Luer, *Manager*
Fortuna Deni, *Manager*
Frank Geyer, *Manager*
Penny Stack, *Admin Asst*
EMP: 50
SALES (corp-wide): 2.4B Privately Held
WEB: www.oerlikon.com
SIC: 5084 3356 3341 2819 Textile machinery & equipment; nonferrous rolling & drawing; secondary nonferrous metals; industrial inorganic chemicals; inorganic pigments
HQ: Oerlikon Metco (Us) Inc.
    1101 Prospect Ave
    Westbury NY 11590
    516 334-1500

(G-17288)
OFFICE EXPRESS INC
Also Called: Oex
1280 E Big Beaver Rd A (48083-1946)
PHONE..............................248 307-1850
Anna Sinagra, *CEO*
Jeff Eusebio, *President*
Kevin Monreal, *Accountant*
Steve Victory, *Sales Mgr*
Mike Carr, *Accounts Mgr*
EMP: 22 EST: 1957
SQ FT: 10,000
SALES (est): 24.3MM Privately Held
WEB: www.oexusa.com
SIC: 5112 2752 5943 Stationery & office supplies; commercial printing, offset; stationery stores

(G-17289)
ONLINE PUBLICATIONS INC
55 E Long Lake Rd (48085-4738)
PHONE..............................248 879-2133
EMP: 6 EST: 2016
SALES (est): 45.4K Privately Held
WEB: www.nieonline.com
SIC: 2741 Miscellaneous publishing

(G-17290)
ORACLE SYSTEMS CORPORATION
3290 W Big Beavr Rd # 30 (48084-2903)
PHONE..............................248 816-8050
Ric Ginsberg, *Vice Pres*
Douglas Bacon, *Sales Staff*
Mike Messina, *Sales Staff*
Richard Lawshaw, *Manager*
Victor Capton, *Info Tech Mgr*
EMP: 4
SALES (corp-wide): 40.4B Publicly Held
SIC: 7372 Prepackaged software
HQ: Oracle Systems Corporation
    500 Oracle Pkwy
    Redwood City CA 94065

(G-17291)
ORBIS CORPORATION
999 Chicago Rd (48083-4227)
PHONE..............................248 616-3232
Dan Roovers, *Exec VP*
Mike Naseef, *Project Mgr*
Jack Fillmore, *Branch Mgr*
Krystal Roye Dobbins, *Director*
EMP: 5
SALES (corp-wide): 1.9B Privately Held
WEB: www.orbiscorporation.com
SIC: 3089 Synthetic resin finished products
HQ: Orbis Corporation
    1055 Corporate Center Dr
    Oconomowoc WI 53066
    262 560-5000

(G-17292)
ORTHO-CLINICAL DIAGNOSTICS INC
2128 Lancer Dr (48084-1308)
PHONE..............................248 797-8087
EMP: 4
SALES (corp-wide): 705.7MM Privately Held
WEB: www.orthoclinicaldiagnostics.com
SIC: 2835 Blood derivative diagnostic agents
PA: Ortho-Clinical Diagnostics, Inc.
    1001 Route 202
    Raritan NJ 08869
    908 218-8000

(G-17293)
OTB ENTERPRISES LLC
Also Called: Chunk Nibbles
1407 Allen Dr Ste A (48083-4009)
PHONE..............................248 266-5568
Brad Cocklin, *CEO*
EMP: 5 EST: 2018
SALES (est): 147.3K Privately Held
SIC: 2052 Biscuits, dry

(G-17294)
P G S INC
Also Called: Precision Global Systems
1600 E Big Beaver Rd (48083-2002)
PHONE..............................248 526-3800
Stephanie Najarian, *CEO*
Richard T Najarian, *President*
Nick Vieaux, *Plant Mgr*
Mary Ann Mackay, *Controller*
EMP: 185 EST: 1983
SQ FT: 175,000
SALES (est): 24.4MM Privately Held
WEB: www.pgsinc.net
SIC: 7389 7549 5013 3714 Inspection & testing services; inspection & diagnostic service, automotive; motor vehicle supplies & new parts; differentials & parts, motor vehicle; motor vehicle transmissions, drive assemblies & parts; axle housings & shafts, motor vehicle

(G-17295)
PALMER PAINT PRODUCTS INC
1291 Rochester Rd (48083-2879)
P.O. Box 1058 (48099-1058)
PHONE..............................248 588-4500
Beverly A Geisler, *President*
Garrett J Hess, *Vice Pres*
Garrett Hess, *Marketing Staff*
▲ EMP: 55 EST: 1932
SQ FT: 54,000
SALES (est): 1.3MM Privately Held
SIC: 2851 Paints: oil or alkyd vehicle or water thinned; lacquers, varnishes, enamels & other coatings

(G-17296)
PELZER
2878 Roundtree Dr (48083-2344)
PHONE..............................248 250-6161
C Pelzer, *Principal*
EMP: 4 EST: 2010
SALES (est): 69.8K Privately Held
WEB: www.adlerpelzer.com
SIC: 3714 Motor vehicle parts & accessories

(G-17297)
PERFORMANCE FUELS SYSTEMS INC
3108 Newport Ct (48084-1323)
PHONE..............................248 202-1789
Al Petrulis, *Administration*
EMP: 5 EST: 2011
SALES (est): 313.2K Privately Held
WEB: www.performancefuelsystems.com
SIC: 2869 Fuels

(G-17298)
PERSPECTIVES CUSTOM CABINETRY
Also Called: Perspectives Cabinetry
1401 Axtell Dr (48084-7002)
PHONE..............................248 288-4100
John A Morgan, *Partner*
EMP: 29 EST: 1986
SQ FT: 22,000
SALES (est): 4.5MM Privately Held
WEB: www.perspectivescabinetry.com
SIC: 2511 2434 Wood household furniture; vanities, bathroom: wood

(G-17299)
PETER-LACKE USA LLC (DH)
865 Stephenson Hwy (48083-1142)
PHONE..............................248 588-9400
John Bilson, *COO*
Susan Bork, *Purchasing*
David Peter, *Mng Member*
Jim Devereux, *Technical Staff*
▲ EMP: 9 EST: 2014
SQ FT: 21,000
SALES (est): 48.7MM
SALES (corp-wide): 107.1MM Privately Held
WEB: www.peter-lacke.de
SIC: 2851 Paints & paint additives
HQ: Peter-Lacke Holding Gmbh
    Herforder Str. 80
    Hiddenhausen 32120
    522 196-250

(G-17300)
PHOENIX PRESS INCORPORATED
Also Called: Phoenix Innovate
1775 Bellingham Dr (48083-2056)
PHONE..............................248 435-8040
Geoffrey Vercnocke, *President*
Kirk Vercnocke, *Corp Secy*
Trish Dewald, *Exec VP*
Paul King, *Exec VP*
Mark Gaskill, *Vice Pres*
EMP: 35 EST: 1987
SQ FT: 14,000
SALES (est): 9.6MM Privately Held
WEB: www.phoenixinnvnovate.com
SIC: 2752 8742 Commercial printing, offset; marketing consulting services

(G-17301)
PHOENIX WIRE CLOTH INC
Also Called: Phoenix Safety Systems
585 Stephenson Hwy (48083-1134)
P.O. Box 610 (48099-0610)
PHONE..............................248 585-6350
Toll Free:..............................877
Richard J Holmes, *President*
John D Holmes, *Chairman*
William D Holmes, *Vice Pres*
Chuck Thomas, *Sales Engr*
▲ EMP: 30 EST: 1885
SQ FT: 60,000
SALES (est): 6.7MM Privately Held
WEB: www.phoenixwirecloth.com
SIC: 3496 3446 5051 Mesh, made from purchased wire; architectural metalwork; wire

(G-17302)
PIPELINE PACKAGING
1421 Piedmont Dr (48083-1952)
PHONE..............................248 743-0248
EMP: 4
SALES (est): 338K Privately Held
SIC: 3053 Mfg Gaskets/Packing/Sealing Devices

(G-17303)
PITSS AMERICA LLC
570 Kirts Blvd Ste 207 (48084-4112)
PHONE..............................248 740-0935

▲ = Import ▼ = Export
◆ = Import/Export

Anna Daugherty, *Marketing Staff*
Ashwani Braj, *Software Dev*
Jeremy Stahl, *Software Dev*
Martin Disterheft,
EMP: 21 **EST:** 2007
SALES (est): 2.1MM **Privately Held**
WEB: www.pitss.com
SIC: 7372 Prepackaged software

(G-17304)
PLASTIC OMNIUM INC
2710 Bellingham Dr # 400 (48083-2045)
PHONE...................................248 458-0772
Adeline Mickeler, *Exec VP*
Danica Bailey, *Purch Mgr*
Ange Chay, *Purchasing*
Bradley Gainey, *Engineer*
Roberto Mesnik, *Engineer*
EMP: 5 **EST:** 1991
SALES (est): 5.2MM **Privately Held**
WEB: www.plasticomnium.com
SIC: 3011 Tires & inner tubes

(G-17305)
PLASTIC OMNIUM AUTO INRGY USA
2585 W Maple Rd (48084-7114)
PHONE...................................248 743-5700
Larry Boeberitz, *Engineer*
Dino Ferhatovic, *Engineer*
Bill Starrs, *Manager*
Kim Kuzak, *Manager*
EMP: 7
SALES (corp-wide): 1.8MM **Privately Held**
WEB: www.plasticomnium.com
SIC: 3714 Motor vehicle parts & accessories
HQ: Plastic Omnium Auto Inergy (Usa) Llc
2710 Bellingham Dr
Troy MI 48083
248 743-5700

(G-17306)
PLASTIC OMNIUM AUTO INRGY USA (DH)
2710 Bellingham Dr (48083-2045)
PHONE...................................248 743-5700
Mark Sullivan, *Mng Member*
Sandra Taylor, *Director*
▲ **EMP:** 468 **EST:** 2000
SALES (est): 550MM
SALES (corp-wide): 1.8MM **Privately Held**
WEB: www.plasticomnium.com
SIC: 3714 Fuel systems & parts, motor vehicle
HQ: Plastic Omnium Auto Exteriors
19 Boulevard Jules Carteret
Lyon 69007
140 876-400

(G-17307)
PLEAD ARMS LLC
1093 Badder Dr Ste A (48083-2836)
PHONE...................................248 563-1822
Matthew Poe, *Principal*
EMP: 4 **EST:** 2010
SALES (est): 140.9K **Privately Held**
WEB: www.michigansilencercompany.com
SIC: 3489 Guns or gun parts, over 30 mm.

(G-17308)
PORITE USA CO LTD
1295 Combermere Dr (48083-2734)
PHONE...................................248 597-9988
Chui Lung Chu, *President*
▲ **EMP:** 5 **EST:** 2006
SALES (est): 1.3MM **Privately Held**
WEB: www.porite-usa.com
SIC: 3566 Gears, power transmission, except automotive
PA: Porite Corporation
2-121, Nisshincho, Kita-Ku
Saitama STM 331-0

(G-17309)
PPG INDUSTRIES INC
5875 New King Ct (48098-2692)
PHONE...................................248 641-2000
Ken Laberdee, *Prdtn Mgr*
Steve Hamay, *Production*
Debra Grice, *Purchasing*
Gordie Shafer, *Marketing Mgr*
Rebecca Liebert, *Branch Mgr*
EMP: 19

SALES (corp-wide): 15.1B **Publicly Held**
WEB: www.ppg.com
SIC: 3211 3231 3229 2812 Flat glass; strengthened or reinforced glass; windshields, glass: made from purchased glass; glass fiber products; fiber optics strands; alkalies & chlorine; chlorine, compressed or liquefied; caustic soda, sodium hydroxide; plastics materials & resins; paints & paint additives
PA: Ppg Industries, Inc.
1 Ppg Pl
Pittsburgh PA 15272
412 434-3131

(G-17310)
PRECISION COMPONENTS
324 Robbins Dr (48083-4558)
PHONE...................................248 588-5650
Bobbie Fitzgerald, *Owner*
Robert Haas, *Sales Mgr*
EMP: 18 **EST:** 1985
SQ FT: 18,000
SALES (est): 294K **Privately Held**
WEB: www.pctooling.com
SIC: 3545 Machine tool accessories

(G-17311)
PRECISION EXTRACTION CORP
Also Called: Precision Extraction Solutions
2468 Industrial Row Dr (48084-7005)
PHONE...................................855 420-0020
Nic Shafer, *Vice Pres*
Sean Elliott, *Plant Mgr*
Andrew Jaboro, *Project Mgr*
Sean Urbin, *Project Mgr*
Brian Towns, *Opers Staff*
EMP: 16 **EST:** 2015
SALES (est): 5.1MM **Privately Held**
WEB: www.precisionextraction.com
SIC: 3556 Juice extractors, fruit & vegetable: commercial type

(G-17312)
PREMIUM AIR SYSTEMS INC
1051 Naughton Dr (48083-1911)
PHONE...................................248 680-8800
Leonard A Framalin, *President*
Elsie Stewart, *Mfg Staff*
Jack Chechlowski, *Manager*
Mark Findora, *Manager*
EMP: 43 **EST:** 1980
SQ FT: 15,000
SALES (est): 3.5MM **Privately Held**
WEB: www.premiumair.net
SIC: 1711 3312 Warm air heating & air conditioning contractor; refrigeration contractor; blast furnaces & steel mills

(G-17313)
PRESTIGE MACHINING
5651 Houghten Dr (48098-2942)
PHONE...................................248 879-1028
Eugene Alessandro, *CEO*
EMP: 5 **EST:** 2002
SALES (est): 98K **Privately Held**
WEB: www.prestige-grp.com
SIC: 3599 Machine shop, jobbing & repair

(G-17314)
PRICELESS DTILS AUTO CNCRGE LL
1093 Foxboro (48083-5460)
PHONE...................................313 701-6851
Eboni Darnell Lucas,
EMP: 4 **EST:** 2020
SALES (est): 225.2K **Privately Held**
WEB: www.autoconcierge.net
SIC: 3589 Car washing machinery

(G-17315)
PRINTING XPRESS AMP PROMO
1755 Livernois Rd (48083-1735)
PHONE...................................586 915-9043
EMP: 4 **EST:** 2018
SALES (est): 83.9K **Privately Held**
SIC: 2752 Commercial printing, lithographic

(G-17316)
PROBUS TECHNICAL SERVICES INC
2424 Crooks Rd Apt 21 (48084-5337)
PHONE...................................876 255-6692
EMP: 10

SALES (est): 226.8K **Privately Held**
SIC: 8742 3999 Management Consulting Services

(G-17317)
PRODUCT ASSEMBLY GROUP LLC
1080 Naughton Dr (48083-1910)
PHONE...................................586 549-8601
Douglass Goad, *President*
Jonathan Paquin,
EMP: 6 **EST:** 2013
SQ FT: 4,000
SALES (est): 781.3K **Privately Held**
SIC: 3714 Motor vehicle parts & accessories

(G-17318)
PRODUCTION SPRING LLC
1151 Allen Dr (48083-4002)
PHONE...................................248 583-0036
Roderick Frazier, *Owner*
Jenny Evans, *Manager*
Zachary Savas,
EMP: 40 **EST:** 1980
SQ FT: 31,000
SALES (est): 7.4MM **Privately Held**
WEB: www.production-spring.com
SIC: 3469 Stamping metal for the trade

(G-17319)
PROMAC NORTH AMERICA CORP
1395 Wheaton Dr Ste 200 (48083-1967)
PHONE...................................248 817-2346
EMP: 5 **EST:** 2015
SALES (est): 352.9K **Privately Held**
WEB: www.promac.eu
SIC: 3541 Machine tools, metal cutting type

(G-17320)
PURE & SIMPLE SOLUTIONS LLC
Also Called: Casa D'Oro
1187 Souter Dr (48083-2821)
PHONE...................................248 398-4600
Douglas P Blunden,
▲ **EMP:** 9 **EST:** 2001
SQ FT: 12,500
SALES (est): 440.8K **Privately Held**
WEB: www.italiangoldcharms.com
SIC: 3911 5094 Bracelets, precious metal; jewelry

(G-17321)
PX2 HOLDINGS LLC
2468 Industrial Row Dr (48084-7005)
PHONE...................................855 420-0020
Marc Beginin, *CEO*
EMP: 60 **EST:** 2011
SALES (est): 2.6MM **Privately Held**
SIC: 3999 Manufacturing industries

(G-17322)
QFC
1134 E Big Beaver Rd (48083-1934)
PHONE...................................248 786-0272
Jeff Desandre, *Principal*
EMP: 44 **EST:** 2010
SALES (est): 846K **Privately Held**
WEB: www.qfc.com
SIC: 2131 Smoking tobacco

(G-17323)
QUAD ELECTRONICS INC (DH)
Also Called: Cablcon
359 Robbins Dr (48083-4561)
PHONE...................................800 969-9220
Bryan Kadrich, *CEO*
Clay Pace, *President*
Gerald Demski, *Vice Pres*
Mary Jenuwine, *Accounting Mgr*
Murl Watts, *Accounts Mgr*
▲ **EMP:** 128 **EST:** 2006
SQ FT: 29,000
SALES (est): 39.1MM
SALES (corp-wide): 160.7MM **Privately Held**
WEB: www.cablcon.com
SIC: 3357 5063 Nonferrous wiredrawing & insulating; electrical apparatus & equipment

HQ: Iewc Corp.
5001 S Towne Dr
New Berlin WI 53151
262 782-2255

(G-17324)
QUAD/GRAPHICS INC
3250 W Big Beavr Rd # 12 (48084-2900)
PHONE...................................248 637-9950
John Stano, *Manager*
EMP: 4
SALES (corp-wide): 2.9B **Publicly Held**
WEB: www.quad.com
SIC: 2752 Commercial printing, offset
PA: Quad/Graphics Inc.
N61w23044 Harrys Way
Sussex WI 53089
414 566-6000

(G-17325)
QUAKER HOUGHTON PA INC
5750 New King Dr 350 (48098-2605)
PHONE...................................248 265-7745
Dan Logan, *Manager*
Steven Abelman, *Manager*
EMP: 20
SALES (corp-wide): 1.4B **Publicly Held**
WEB: www.home.quakerhoughton.com
SIC: 2869 2992 2899 2842 Hydraulic fluids, synthetic base; re-refining lubricating oils & greases; rust arresting compounds, animal or vegetable oil base; cutting oils, blending: made from purchased materials; heat treating salts; cleaning or polishing preparations; processing assistants
HQ: Quaker Houghton Pa, Inc.
901 E Hector St
Conshohocken PA 19428
610 832-4000

(G-17326)
QUIRKROBERTS PUBLISHING LTD
Also Called: Young Ideas Enterprises
6219 Seminole Dr (48085-1127)
P.O. Box 71 (48099-0071)
PHONE...................................248 879-2598
Linda Hodgdon, *President*
EMP: 8 **EST:** 1985
SALES (est): 885.1K **Privately Held**
WEB: www.quirkroberts.com
SIC: 2731 8748 Books: publishing only; educational consultant

(G-17327)
R H K TECHNOLOGY INC
Also Called: Sonic Alert
1233 Chicago Rd (48083-4231)
PHONE...................................248 577-5426
Adam Kollin, *President*
Laura Rae, *Controller*
Allen G Vallei, *Marketing Staff*
▲ **EMP:** 42 **EST:** 1978
SALES (est): 9MM **Privately Held**
WEB: www.rhk-tech.com
SIC: 3826 3669 Analytical instruments; signaling apparatus, electric

(G-17328)
RAFALSKI CPA
1607 E Big Beaver Rd # 103 (48083-2028)
PHONE...................................248 689-1685
David Rafalski, *Principal*
EMP: 4 **EST:** 2010
SALES (est): 128.5K **Privately Held**
SIC: 1381 8721 Drilling oil & gas wells; accounting, auditing & bookkeeping

(G-17329)
REKEY LUXURY HOMES LLC
637 E Big Beaver Rd # 103 (48083-1423)
PHONE...................................586 747-0342
Roy Eaton, *Principal*
EMP: 6 **EST:** 2015
SALES (est): 583.8K **Privately Held**
SIC: 3625 Motor controls & accessories

(G-17330)
REPUBLIC DRILL/APT CORP
Also Called: Michigan Drill
1863 Larchwood Dr (48083-2243)
PHONE...................................248 689-5050
Randy Tucker, *Opers Mgr*
Mark Linari, *Sales Staff*
Hyman Ash, *Branch Mgr*
Kim Jackson, *Executive*

Troy - Oakland County (G-17331)   GEOGRAPHIC SECTION

EMP: 120
SALES (corp-wide): 21.4MM **Privately Held**
WEB: www.michigandrill.com
SIC: 3545 3544 Machine tool accessories; special dies, tools, jigs & fixtures
PA: Republic Drill/Apt, Corp.
7840 Nw 62nd St
Miami FL 33166
305 592-7777

(G-17331)
REVSTONE INDUSTRIES LLC
900 Wilshire Dr Ste 270 (48084-1600)
P.O. Box 1720, Birmingham (48012-1720)
PHONE.................................248 351-1000
Scott Hofmeister, *Branch Mgr*
EMP: 4 **Privately Held**
SIC: 2821 3086 3341 Plastics materials & resins; plastics foam products; secondary nonferrous metals
PA: Revstone Industries, Llc
2008 Cypress St Ste 100
Paris KY 40361

(G-17332)
REXAIR HOLDINGS INC
2600 W Big Beavr Rd # 555 (48084-3337)
PHONE.................................248 643-7222
F Philip Handy, *CEO*
◆ **EMP:** 22 **EST:** 1987
SALES (est): 5.2MM
SALES (corp-wide): 9.3B **Publicly Held**
WEB: www.rainbowsystem.com
SIC: 3635 Household vacuum cleaners
HQ: Jarden Llc
221 River St
Hoboken NJ 07030

(G-17333)
RINGMASTER SOFTWARE CORP
631 E Big Beaver Rd # 109 (48083-1419)
PHONE.................................802 383-1050
Susan Dorn, *President*
Michael Rooney, *Exec VP*
EMP: 10 **EST:** 2004
SALES (est): 441.4K **Privately Held**
WEB: www.ringmastersw.com
SIC: 7372 Prepackaged software

(G-17334)
RIVORE METALS LLC (PA)
850 Stephenson Hwy # 308 (48083-1152)
PHONE.................................800 248-1250
Reanna Peyton, *Vice Pres*
Kosta Marselis,
EMP: 3 **EST:** 2012
SALES (est): 4.1MM **Privately Held**
WEB: www.rivore.com
SIC: 3914 5051 Carving sets, stainless steel; copper

(G-17335)
ROCKWELL AUTOMATION INC
1441 W Long Lake Rd # 150 (48098-4403)
PHONE.................................248 696-1200
Eric Hopp, *Safety Dir*
Harry Valdes, *Project Mgr*
Kim Bergman, *Opers Staff*
Beth Glaspie, *Engineer*
Julia Gilbert, *Sales Staff*
EMP: 5 **Publicly Held**
WEB: www.rockwellautomation.com
SIC: 3625 7389 Relays & industrial controls; personal service agents, brokers & bureaus
PA: Rockwell Automation, Inc.
1201 S 2nd St
Milwaukee WI 53204

(G-17336)
ROCKWELL AUTOMATION INC
2135 W Maple Rd (48084-7121)
PHONE.................................248 435-2574
Nate Ustick, *Branch Mgr*
Larry Yost, *Manager*
EMP: 45
SQ FT: 8,100 **Publicly Held**
WEB: www.rockwellautomation.com
SIC: 3625 Relays & industrial controls
PA: Rockwell Automation, Inc.
1201 S 2nd St
Milwaukee WI 53204

(G-17337)
ROSS DECCO COMPANY
Also Called: Detroit Coil
1250 Stephenson Hwy (48083-1115)
PHONE.................................248 764-1845
Don Jamisom, *President*
Jay Dalal, *Vice Pres*
Don Swanson, *Vice Pres*
Kevin Browning, *Materials Mgr*
Scott Hilt, *Marketing Staff*
▲ **EMP:** 46 **EST:** 2011
SALES (est): 14MM
SALES (corp-wide): 54.8MM **Privately Held**
WEB: www.rossdecco.com
SIC: 3625 Relays & industrial controls
PA: Ross Operating Valve Company
1250 Stephenson Hwy
Troy MI 48083
248 764-1800

(G-17338)
RUSH MACHINING INC
256 Minnesota Dr (48083-4667)
PHONE.................................248 583-0550
Brian Smith, *Vice Pres*
Patrick O Berry, *Vice Pres*
Colleen Gagnon, *Treasurer*
EMP: 20 **EST:** 1984
SQ FT: 8,000
SALES (est): 726.8K **Privately Held**
SIC: 3452 5085 Nuts, metal; fasteners, industrial: nuts, bolts, screws, etc.

(G-17339)
S C JOHNSON & SON INC
Also Called: S C Johnson Wax
3001 W Big Beavr Rd # 40 (48084-3101)
PHONE.................................248 822-2174
Calvin Comeau, *Manager*
EMP: 6
SALES (corp-wide): 1.1B **Privately Held**
WEB: www.scjohnson.com
SIC: 2842 2844 Floor waxes; shampoos, rinses, conditioners: hair
PA: S. C. Johnson & Son, Inc.
1525 Howe St
Racine WI 53403
262 260-2000

(G-17340)
SADIA ENTERPRISES INC
Also Called: Prairie Pride Carrier
3373 Rochester Rd (48083-5427)
PHONE.................................248 854-4666
EMP: 10 **EST:** 2010
SALES (est): 1.5MM **Privately Held**
SIC: 3537 4789 Lift trucks, industrial: fork, platform, straddle, etc.; pipeline terminal facilities, independently operated

(G-17341)
SAINT JULIAN WINERY
506 W 14 Mile Rd (48083-4205)
PHONE.................................248 951-2113
EMP: 5 **EST:** 2018
SALES (est): 74.4K **Privately Held**
WEB: www.stjulian.com
SIC: 2084 Wines

(G-17342)
SALEEN SPECIAL VEHICLES INC
1225 E Maple Rd (48083-2818)
PHONE.................................909 978-6700
▲ **EMP:** 297
SQ FT: 184,000
SALES (est): 38.1MM **Privately Held**
SIC: 3711 Mfg Motor Vehicle/Car Bodies

(G-17343)
SANDMAN INC
5877 Livernois Rd Ste 103 (48098-3100)
PHONE.................................248 652-3432
Joel Garrett, *President*
Thomas Powell, *Treasurer*
EMP: 6
SALES (est): 1MM **Privately Held**
SIC: 1442 Construction sand mining

(G-17344)
SARGAM INTERNATIONAL INC
Also Called: Agent 18
3751 Finch Dr (48084-1613)
PHONE.................................310 855-9694
Sargam Patel, *President*
▲ **EMP:** 12 **EST:** 2004
SALES (est): 914.5K **Privately Held**
WEB: www.agent18.com
SIC: 3651 Audio electronic systems

(G-17345)
SAVE ON EVERYTHING LLC (PA)
1000 W Maple Rd Ste 200 (48084-5368)
PHONE.................................248 362-9119
Michael Gauthier, *President*
Heather Uballe, *COO*
Eric Birtch, *Vice Pres*
Bill Davis, *Vice Pres*
Emilea Weaver, *Finance*
EMP: 55 **EST:** 1987
SQ FT: 24,000
SALES (est): 17.6MM **Privately Held**
WEB: www.saveon.com
SIC: 2759 Coupons: printing

(G-17346)
SBZ CORPORATION
3001 W Big Beaver Rd # 402 (48084-3101)
PHONE.................................248 649-1166
Laurence Holder, *President*
Wendy Wood, *Business Mgr*
Sungseung Yun,
EMP: 4 **EST:** 2006
SALES (est): 452.1K **Privately Held**
WEB: www.sbzcorporation.com
SIC: 2819 Industrial inorganic chemicals

(G-17347)
SECO HOLDING CO INC
2805 Bellingham Dr (48083-2046)
PHONE.................................248 528-5200
Bruce E Belden, *President*
Michael L Neel, *Corp Secy*
David Ladzick, *Manager*
Anders Ericsson, *Exec Dir*
▲ **EMP:** 66 **EST:** 1928
SQ FT: 650,000
SALES (est): 2MM
SALES (corp-wide): 9.9B **Privately Held**
WEB: www.secotools.com
SIC: 3545 Cutting tools for machine tools
HQ: Seco Tools Ab
Bjornbacksvagen 10
Fagersta 737 3
223 400-00

(G-17348)
SHADKO ENTERPRISES INC
1701 Lexington Dr (48084-5711)
P.O. Box 36806, Grosse Pointe (48236-0806)
PHONE.................................248 816-1712
Leposava Shadko, *President*
EMP: 4 **EST:** 1952
SALES (est): 381.2K **Privately Held**
SIC: 3462 Chains, forged steel

(G-17349)
SHELTON TECHNOLOGY LLC
4201 Frostwood Ct (48098-4240)
PHONE.................................248 816-1585
Shaotang Chen, *CEO*
EMP: 3 **EST:** 2016
SALES (est): 3MM **Privately Held**
WEB: www.shelton.com
SIC: 3625 3647 Motor controls & accessories; motor vehicle lighting equipment

(G-17350)
SIEMENS INDUSTRY INC
777 Chicago Rd (48083-4234)
PHONE.................................248 307-3400
Andrew Fylak, *Manager*
EMP: 8
SALES (corp-wide): 67.4B **Privately Held**
WEB: www.new.siemens.com
SIC: 3674 1711 Semiconductors & related devices; plumbing, heating, air-conditioning contractors
HQ: Siemens Industry, Inc.
1000 Deerfield Pkwy
Buffalo Grove IL 60089
847 215-1000

(G-17351)
SIGN CONCEPTS CORPORATION
Also Called: Asi Signage Innovation
1119 Wheaton Dr (48083-6701)
PHONE.................................248 680-8970
Craig Breeden, *President*
Philip Miller, *Corp Secy*
John Watkins, *Vice Pres*
Allison Emerson, *Project Mgr*
Jeff Podina, *Manager*
EMP: 18 **EST:** 1980
SQ FT: 15,000
SALES (est): 2.1MM **Privately Held**
WEB: www.asisignage.com
SIC: 3993 Signs, not made in custom sign painting shops

(G-17352)
SIGNPROCO INC
Also Called: Signarama Troy Metro Detroit
1017 Naughton Dr (48083-1911)
PHONE.................................248 585-6880
Robert Chapa, *President*
Matthew R Godwin, *COO*
EMP: 15 **EST:** 1998
SQ FT: 2,500
SALES (est): 3.3MM **Privately Held**
WEB: www.michigansignshops.com
SIC: 3993 Signs, not made in custom sign painting shops

(G-17353)
SIGNS & LASER ENGRAVING
1221 E 14 Mile Rd (48083-4656)
PHONE.................................248 577-6191
Elton Topalli, *Owner*
EMP: 5 **EST:** 2007
SALES (est): 416.1K **Privately Held**
WEB: www.signsmh.com
SIC: 3993 Signs & advertising specialties

(G-17354)
SILKROUTE GLOBAL INC
950 Stephenson Hwy (48083-1113)
PHONE.................................248 854-3409
Amjad Hussain, *President*
Tammy Stark, *Vice Pres*
Adam Moy, *CTO*
Katie Williams, *Software Engr*
Williams Katherine, *Sr Software Eng*
EMP: 50 **EST:** 2008
SQ FT: 67,000
SALES (est): 7.3MM **Privately Held**
WEB: www.silkrouteglobal.com
SIC: 7371 7372 Computer software development; prepackaged software; application computer software; business oriented computer software

(G-17355)
SIZMEK DSP INC
Also Called: Rocket Fuel
101 W Big Beaver Rd (48084-5253)
PHONE.................................313 516-4482
EMP: 25 **Privately Held**
SIC: 3999 Advertising display products
HQ: Sizmek Dsp, Inc.
2000 Seaport Blvd Ste 400
Redwood City CA 94063

(G-17356)
SKYLINE CHAMPION CORPORATION (PA)
755 W Big Beavr Rd # 100 (48084-4900)
PHONE.................................248 614-8211
Keith Anderson, *CEO*
Timothy Bernlohr, *Ch of Bd*
Joseph Kimmell, *Exec VP*
Mark Yost, *Exec VP*
Roger Scholten, *Senior VP*
EMP: 1238 **EST:** 1951
SALES (est): 1.4B **Publicly Held**
WEB: www.skylinehomes.com
SIC: 2452 3792 2451 Prefabricated buildings, wood; travel trailers & campers; mobile homes, except recreational

(G-17357)
SNAP JAWS MANUFACTURING INC
33215 Dequindre Rd (48083-4628)
PHONE.................................248 588-1099
John Fitzpatrick, *President*
EMP: 7 **EST:** 1988

▲ = Import ▼=Export
◆ =Import/Export

SQ FT: 5,000
SALES (est): 819.4K **Privately Held**
WEB: www.snapjaws.com
SIC: 3541 3545 Numerically controlled metal cutting machine tools; machine tool attachments & accessories

(G-17358)
SOCK HOP LLC
371 Scottsdale Dr (48084-1743)
PHONE..................................248 689-2683
Marie Carozza, *Principal*
EMP: 5 EST: 2014
SALES (est): 73.4K **Privately Held**
WEB: www.sockhopcosmetics.com
SIC: 2252 Socks

(G-17359)
SOLIDBODY TECHNOLOGY COMPANY
Also Called: Commando Lock Company
395 Elmwood Dr (48083-2754)
PHONE..................................248 709-7901
Patrick Smith, *President*
EMP: 4 EST: 2013
SALES (est): 240K **Privately Held**
WEB: www.commandolock.com
SIC: 3429 Padlocks

(G-17360)
SOLIDTHINKING INC
1820 E Big Beaver Rd (48083-2031)
PHONE..................................248 526-1920
Robert Little, *President*
Jim T Hassberger, *Vice Pres*
David Roccaforte, *Engineer*
Noreen Gilbertsen, *Manager*
EMP: 1 EST: 2008
SALES (est): 5.4MM
SALES (corp-wide): 469.9MM **Publicly Held**
WEB: www.altair.com
SIC: 7372 Prepackaged software
PA: Altair Engineering Inc.
   1820 E Big Beaver Rd
   Troy MI 48083
   248 614-2400

(G-17361)
SOMANETICS
1653 E Maple Rd (48083-4208)
PHONE..................................248 689-3050
EMP: 12
SALES (est): 1.2MM **Privately Held**
SIC: 3841 Mfg Surgical/Medical Instruments

(G-17362)
SOMERSET COLLECTION LTD PARTNR
2801 W Big Beaver Rd (48084-3243)
PHONE..................................248 827-4600
Kyle Czuprenski, *Officer*
Bill Julius, *Asst Director*
EMP: 10 EST: 2014
SALES (est): 3MM **Privately Held**
WEB: www.thesomersetcollection.com
SIC: 2844 Toilet preparations

(G-17363)
SORT-TEK INSPTN SYSTEMS INC
1784 Larchwood Dr (48083-2223)
PHONE..................................248 273-5200
Patricia Richards, *President*
Patrick Richards, *Vice Pres*
EMP: 9 EST: 1999
SALES (est): 1.3MM **Privately Held**
WEB: www.sort-tek.com
SIC: 3714 Motor vehicle parts & accessories

(G-17364)
SOURCEHUB LLC
1875 Stephenson Hwy (48083-2150)
PHONE..................................800 246-1844
William Nick, *President*
Robert Long, *Vice Pres*
▲ EMP: 2 EST: 2007
SQ FT: 23,475
SALES (est): 2.9MM **Privately Held**
WEB: www.sourcehub.com
SIC: 5085 3423 Industrial supplies; hand & edge tools

(G-17365)
SOUTH HILL SAND AND GRAVEL (PA)
5877 Livernois Rd Ste 103 (48098-3100)
PHONE..................................248 828-1726
Joel Garrett, *President*
EMP: 1 EST: 1992
SQ FT: 2,000
SALES (est): 2.5MM **Privately Held**
SIC: 1442 Gravel mining

(G-17366)
SOUTHSTERN MICH ACCSORY CTR 2
1755 Maplelawn Dr (48084-4612)
PHONE..................................248 519-9848
Crieg Tannehill, *Sales Mgr*
Gordon Cepnick, *Regl Sales Mgr*
Danielle Cline, *Sales Staff*
John Schock, *Director*
David Butler,
EMP: 35 EST: 2003
SALES (est): 2.7MM **Privately Held**
SIC: 3714 Motor vehicle parts & accessories

(G-17367)
SPIRE INTEGRATED SYSTEMS INC
2786 Industrial Row Dr (48084-7016)
PHONE..................................248 544-0072
Navot Shoresh, *President*
Nicole Bonsall, *Manager*
Mike Waligorski, *Director*
Stuart Hannon, *Assistant*
EMP: 22 EST: 2001
SALES (est): 4.6MM **Privately Held**
WEB: www.spireintegrated.com
SIC: 5999 5719 7372 Audio-visual equipment & supplies; lighting fixtures; prepackaged software

(G-17368)
SRG GLOBAL LLC (DH)
800 Stephenson Hwy (48083-1120)
PHONE..................................248 509-1100
Thomas Pastore, *President*
Kevin Baird, *President*
Rick Cummings, *Vice Pres*
David Dunford, *Vice Pres*
Jose Ivorra, *Vice Pres*
EMP: 706 EST: 1932
SALES (est): 953.5MM
SALES (corp-wide): 36.9B **Privately Held**
WEB: www.srgglobal.com
SIC: 2396 Automotive & apparel trimmings
HQ: Guardian Industries, Llc
   2300 Harmon Rd
   Auburn Hills MI 48326
   248 340-1800

(G-17369)
SRG GLOBAL COATINGS LLC (DH)
Also Called: Srg Global Coatings, Inc.
800 Stephenson Hwy (48083-1120)
PHONE..................................248 509-1100
Dave Prater, *CEO*
Kenny Abernathy, *Engineer*
Michele McBride, *Supervisor*
Michele Drew, *Analyst*
◆ EMP: 230 EST: 1946
SQ FT: 25,000
SALES (est): 546.1MM
SALES (corp-wide): 36.9B **Privately Held**
WEB: www.srgglobal.com
SIC: 3089 3494 2522 3826 Blow molded finished plastic products; injection molded finished plastic products; thermoformed finished plastic products; valves & pipe fittings; office furniture, except wood; analytical instruments; instruments to measure electricity
HQ: Guardian Industries, Llc
   2300 Harmon Rd
   Auburn Hills MI 48326
   248 340-1800

(G-17370)
STAPELS MANUFACTURING LLC
Also Called: Wes Stabeck Industries
2612 Elliott Dr (48083-4633)
PHONE..................................248 577-5570
Mark Stapels,
Nicholas Stapels,
EMP: 14 EST: 2001
SQ FT: 15,000
SALES (est): 2.5MM **Privately Held**
WEB: www.stapelsmfg.com
SIC: 3599 Machine shop, jobbing & repair

(G-17371)
STARLIGHT TECHNOLOGIES INC
2055 Applewood Dr (48085-7032)
PHONE..................................248 250-9607
Andrew Tong, *President*
EMP: 6 EST: 1996
SALES (est): 467.7K **Privately Held**
WEB: www.starlight5.com
SIC: 3694 Harness wiring sets, internal combustion engines

(G-17372)
STEGMAN TOOL CO INC
1985 Ring Dr (48083-4229)
PHONE..................................248 588-4634
Robert J Begeny, *President*
Mazak Nexus, *Prgrmr*
Victoria Begeny, *Shareholder*
EMP: 25 EST: 1957
SQ FT: 20,000
SALES (est): 4.4MM **Privately Held**
WEB: www.stegmantool.com
SIC: 3369 8711 Castings, except die-castings, precision; sanitary engineers

(G-17373)
STEVES MACHINE SHOP LLC
2119 Garry Dr (48083-2359)
PHONE..................................248 563-1662
Steven Haskell, *Principal*
EMP: 5 EST: 2017
SALES (est): 85.4K **Privately Held**
SIC: 3599 Machine shop, jobbing & repair

(G-17374)
STORM SEAL CO INC
1687 Hillman Dr (48083-6902)
PHONE..................................248 689-1900
Edward A Barrington, *President*
Mark Barrington, *President*
EMP: 6 EST: 1954
SALES (est): 960.1K **Privately Held**
SIC: 3442 5211 Storm doors or windows, metal; lumber & other building materials

(G-17375)
STYLE CRAFT PROTOTYPE INC
1820 Brinston Dr (48083-2215)
PHONE..................................248 619-9048
Michael Muszynski, *President*
Eric Huntley, *Vice Pres*
Reinhart Egbert, *Treasurer*
EMP: 16 EST: 1981
SALES (est): 1.5MM **Privately Held**
WEB: www.stylecraft1.com
SIC: 3469 Stamping metal for the trade

(G-17376)
SUNERA TECHNOLOGIES INC (PA)
Also Called: Suneratech
631 E Big Beaver Rd # 105 (48084-1420)
PHONE..................................248 434-0808
Ravi Reddy, *CEO*
Harish Aramadaka, *Partner*
Sudheer Mareddi, *Managing Dir*
Srikanth Pakala, *Chairman*
Anil Thalakera, *COO*
EMP: 1388 EST: 2004
SQ FT: 2,500
SALES (est): 77.7MM **Privately Held**
WEB: www.suneratech.com
SIC: 7379 7372 Computer related consulting services; application computer software

(G-17377)
SUNGWOO HITECH CO LTD
3221 W Big Beavr Rd # 30 (48084-2803)
PHONE..................................248 561-0604
Mun Yong Lee, *President*
Hyejung Yun, *Corp Secy*
Jin Seok Park, *Mng Member*
EMP: 6 EST: 2016
SALES (est): 570.5K **Privately Held**
WEB: www.swhitechco.en.ec21.com
SIC: 3465 Body parts, automobile: stamped metal

(G-17378)
SUNNINGDALE TECH INC (DH)
100 W Big Beaver Rd (48084-5206)
PHONE..................................248 526-0517
Vincent Raja, *President*
Chan Tung Sing, *Principal*
EMP: 8 EST: 2016
SALES (est): 12.7MM **Privately Held**
WEB: www.sdaletech.com
SIC: 3089 Injection molding of plastics

(G-17379)
SUNRISE FIBERGLASS LLC
1732 Crooks Rd (48084-5501)
PHONE..................................651 462-5313
Bernard H Coyle, *CEO*
Ray Pixley, *President*
EMP: 55 EST: 1968
SALES (est): 1.4MM
SALES (corp-wide): 20.7MM **Privately Held**
WEB: www.sunrisefiberglass.com
SIC: 2221 Fiberglass fabrics
PA: North Central Equity Llc
   6210 Bury Dr
   Eden Prairie MN 55346
   612 465-0260

(G-17380)
SUPERIOR MANUFACTURING CORP (PA)
Also Called: ABC Industrial Supply
431 Stephenson Hwy (48083-1130)
PHONE..................................313 935-1550
Aaron Chernow, *President*
David Chernow, *Vice Pres*
EMP: 8 EST: 1993
SALES (est): 3.4MM **Privately Held**
WEB: www.ordersuperior.com
SIC: 2842 Degreasing solvent

(G-17381)
SURFACE ACTIVATION TECH LLC
Also Called: Sat Plating
1837 Thunderbird (48084-5402)
PHONE..................................248 273-0037
John Wallace, *President*
Will Wallace, *General Mgr*
Brad Radke, *Engineer*
Anastasia Plonkey, *Admin Mgr*
EMP: 4 EST: 2006
SALES (est): 1.4MM **Privately Held**
WEB: www.satplating.com
SIC: 2899 3471 Plating compounds; electroplating & plating

(G-17382)
SYSTEMS DUPLICATING CO INC
358 Robbins Dr (48083-4558)
PHONE..................................248 585-7590
Charles A De Vito Sr, *President*
Bernice De Vito, *Corp Secy*
Bernice Devito, *Vice Pres*
EMP: 10 EST: 1979
SQ FT: 5,000
SALES (est): 788.8K **Privately Held**
WEB: www.sdci.net
SIC: 2752 Commercial printing, offset

(G-17383)
T M SHEA PRODUCTS INC
1950 Austin Dr (48083-2205)
PHONE..................................800 992-5233
Thomas M Shea, *President*
Monica Spaulding, *Vice Pres*
Crystal Burns, *Opers Staff*
EMP: 10 EST: 1983
SQ FT: 14,800
SALES (est): 2MM **Privately Held**
WEB: www.tmshea.com
SIC: 2542 3993 Fixtures, store: except wood; signs & advertising specialties

(G-17384)
TARRS TREE SERVICE INC
2009 Milverton Dr (48083-2535)
PHONE..................................248 528-3313
Linda Tarr, *President*
Gary Tarr, *Vice Pres*
EMP: 32 EST: 1978
SALES (est): 1MM **Privately Held**
SIC: 2411 Logging

Troy - Oakland County (G-17385)   GEOGRAPHIC SECTION

(G-17385)
TATA AUTOCOMP SYSTEMS LIMITED
Also Called: Mechanical Engineer
200 E Big Beaver Rd # 145 (48083-1208)
PHONE.................................248 680-4608
EMP: 7 Privately Held
WEB: www.tataautocomp.com
SIC: 3714 Motor vehicle parts & accessories
PA: Tata Autocomp Systems Limited
  Taco House, Plot No- 20/B
  Pune MH 41100

(G-17386)
TEBIS AMERICA INC
400 E Big Beaver Rd # 300 (48083-1260)
PHONE.................................248 524-0430
John Kowalczyk, *President*
Gerardo Mueller, *Vice Pres*
Julie Crowe, *CFO*
Matt O'donnell, *Accounts Mgr*
Brittny Duquesnel, *Marketing Staff*
EMP: 23 EST: 1995
SALES (est): 5.5MM
SALES (corp-wide): 55.4MM Privately Held
WEB: www.tebisusa.com
SIC: 7372 Prepackaged software
PA: Tebis Technische Informationssysteme Ag
  Einsteinstr. 39
  Planegg BY 82152
  898 180-30

(G-17387)
TEDSON INDUSTRIES INC
1408 Allen Dr (48083-4013)
PHONE.................................248 588-9230
Steven Marek, *President*
Dennis Breslin, *Project Mgr*
Elyse Marek, *Admin Sec*
EMP: 13 EST: 1985
SQ FT: 20,000
SALES (est): 1.9MM Privately Held
WEB: www.tedsonindustries.com
SIC: 3543 Industrial patterns

(G-17388)
TENNANT & ASSOCIATES INC
1700 Stutz Dr Ste 61 (48084-4502)
PHONE.................................248 643-6140
Mary Tennant, *President*
Terrence J Tennant, *Treasurer*
Mark Reyers, *Accounts Mgr*
EMP: 5 EST: 1972
SQ FT: 4,200
SALES (est): 446.8K Privately Held
WEB: www.michigandesign.com
SIC: 2396 5131 Furniture trimmings, fabric; piece goods & notions

(G-17389)
TESLA INC
Also Called: Tesla Motors
2850 W Big Beaver Rd (48084-3205)
PHONE.................................248 205-3206
Pavel Dutov, *Engineer*
EMP: 7
SALES (corp-wide): 31.5B Publicly Held
WEB: www.tesla.com
SIC: 3711 Motor vehicles & car bodies
PA: Tesla, Inc.
  3500 Deer Creek Rd
  Palo Alto CA 94304
  650 681-5000

(G-17390)
THYSSENKRUPP BILSTEIN AMER INC
3155 W Big Beavr Rd # 26 (48084-3002)
PHONE.................................248 530-2900
Axel Boehne, *Branch Mgr*
EMP: 5007
SALES (corp-wide): 34B Privately Held
WEB: www.bilstein.com
SIC: 3714 5013 Shock absorbers, motor vehicle; springs, shock absorbers & struts
HQ: Thyssenkrupp Bilstein Of America, Inc.
  8685 Bilstein Blvd
  Hamilton OH 45015
  513 881-7600

(G-17391)
TI GROUP AUTO SYSTEMS LLC
Also Called: Fuel Systems
100 W Big Beaver Rd (48084-5206)
PHONE.................................248 494-5000
EMP: 7
SALES (corp-wide): 3.3B Privately Held
WEB: www.tifluidsystems.com
SIC: 3714 Fuel pumps, motor vehicle
HQ: Ti Group Automotive Systems, Llc
  2020 Taylor Rd
  Auburn Hills MI 48326
  248 296-8000

(G-17392)
TIMOTHY J TADE INC (PA)
Also Called: Tade Publishing Group
4798 Butler Dr (48085-3525)
P.O. Box 4803 (48099-4803)
PHONE.................................248 552-8583
Thomas James Lynch, *President*
Susan Marie Lynch, *Treasurer*
EMP: 6 EST: 1985
SQ FT: 1,450
SALES (est): 483K Privately Held
SIC: 2721 2741 4813 Trade journals: publishing only, not printed on site; miscellaneous publishing;

(G-17393)
TKS INDUSTRIAL COMPANY (HQ)
901 Tower Dr Ste 300 (48098-2817)
PHONE.................................248 786-5000
Bob Booth, *Exec VP*
Mark Sweeney, *VP Mfg*
James Asam, *Project Mgr*
Jason Sisler, *Project Mgr*
Sergio Ogura, *Engineer*
▲ EMP: 40 EST: 1981
SQ FT: 6,000
SALES: 129.3MM Privately Held
WEB: www.tksindustrial.com
SIC: 1721 3559 Interior commercial painting contractor; metal finishing equipment for plating, etc.

(G-17394)
TMT INVESTMENT COMPANY
900 Rochester Rd (48083-6009)
PHONE.................................248 616-8880
David F Galli, *President*
William S Hubar, *Admin Sec*
EMP: 28 EST: 1976
SALES (est): 4.6MM Privately Held
SIC: 3451 Screw machine products

(G-17395)
TORAY RESIN COMPANY
2800 Livernois Rd D115 (48083-1215)
PHONE.................................248 269-8800
Fred Hourigan, *Electrical Engi*
Mark Barton, *Manager*
Dan Marsicek, *Manager*
Sandy McColley, *Executive*
EMP: 4 Privately Held
SIC: 2821 Plastics materials & resins
HQ: Toray Resin Company
  821 W Mausoleum Rd
  Shelbyville IN 46176

(G-17396)
TOTAL FLOW PRODUCTS INC
1197 Rochester Rd Ste N (48083-6031)
PHONE.................................248 588-4490
Stephen Sanchez, *President*
EMP: 5 EST: 1978
SQ FT: 3,000
SALES (est): 629.6K Privately Held
WEB: www.totalflowproducts.com
SIC: 3714 Motor vehicle parts & accessories

(G-17397)
TOYODA GOSEI NORTH AMER CORP (HQ)
1400 Stephenson Hwy (48083-1189)
PHONE.................................248 280-2100
Hiromi Ikehata, *President*
Todd Braund, *General Mgr*
Gustavo Castillo, *General Mgr*
Pierre Lessard, *General Mgr*
John Baylis, *Vice Pres*
◆ EMP: 216 EST: 1991
SQ FT: 36,000
SALES (est): 1.2B Privately Held
WEB: www.toyodagosei.com
SIC: 3069 3089 Weather strip, sponge rubber; automotive parts, plastic

(G-17398)
TREXEL INC
101 W Big Beaver Rd (48084-5253)
PHONE.................................248 687-1353
William Person, *Principal*
Brian Bechard, *Info Tech Dir*
EMP: 10 EST: 2006
SALES (est): 255K Privately Held
WEB: www.trexel.com
SIC: 3465 Body parts, automobile: stamped metal

(G-17399)
TRIPLE INC
2321 John R Rd (48083-2567)
PHONE.................................248 817-5151
Ed Dominic, *Manager*
EMP: 5 EST: 2018
SALES (est): 193.5K Privately Held
WEB: www.tripleinc.com
SIC: 3812 Search & navigation equipment

(G-17400)
TROY METAL FABRICATING LLC
2341 Alger Dr (48083-2052)
PHONE.................................248 506-6142
Doris Pedersen, *Principal*
EMP: 7 EST: 2008
SALES (est): 119.1K Privately Held
SIC: 3499 Fabricated metal products

(G-17401)
TROY PUZZLES LLC
1339 Barton Way Dr (48098-2034)
PHONE.................................248 828-3153
EMP: 4 EST: 2015
SALES (est): 69.5K Privately Held
SIC: 3944 Puzzles

(G-17402)
TRUCK TRAILER TRANSIT INC
1400 Rochester Rd (48083-6014)
PHONE.................................313 516-7151
Ralph David Lawrence, *President*
◆ EMP: 18 EST: 1982
SQ FT: 40,000
SALES (est): 1MM Privately Held
SIC: 3714 Motor vehicle brake systems & parts

(G-17403)
TRUE FABRICATIONS & MACHINE
1731 Thorncroft Dr (48084-4613)
PHONE.................................248 288-0140
Steve Stelkic, *President*
Neil Stelkic, *Vice Pres*
EMP: 10 EST: 1980
SQ FT: 14,000 Privately Held
WEB: www.truefab.com
SIC: 3443 3541 Fabricated plate work (boiler shop); numerically controlled metal cutting machine tools

(G-17404)
TRUING SYSTEMS INC
1060 Chicago Rd (48083-4298)
PHONE.................................248 588-9060
Ronald Stempin, *President*
David Stempin, *Vice Pres*
EMP: 24 EST: 1978
SQ FT: 3,000
SALES (est): 1.3MM Privately Held
WEB: www.truingsystems.com
SIC: 3545 Diamond dressing & wheel crushing attachments

(G-17405)
TRUTRON CORPORATION
274 Executive Dr (48083-4530)
PHONE.................................248 583-9166
Lisa J Kingsley, *President*
▼ EMP: 35 EST: 1967
SQ FT: 14,029
SALES (est): 3.8MM Privately Held
WEB: www.trutron.com
SIC: 3544 Special dies & tools

(G-17406)
TUOCAI AMERICA LLC
5700 Crooks Rd Ste 222 (48098-2809)
PHONE.................................248 346-5910
Frank Yang,
EMP: 8 EST: 2018
SALES (est): 460.6K Privately Held
WEB: www.tuocaiamerica.com
SIC: 2899 Metal treating compounds

(G-17407)
TUWAY AMERICAN GROUP INC
Also Called: Tu Way
3155 W Big Beavr Rd # 104 (48084-3006)
PHONE.................................248 205-9999
Gertrude Koester, *CEO*
Douglas Koester, *President*
John Feeny, *General Mgr*
▲ EMP: 147 EST: 1947
SQ FT: 1,000
SALES (est): 17MM Privately Held
WEB: www.tuwaymops.com
SIC: 2392 Mops, floor & dust

(G-17408)
TYDE GROUP WORLDWIDE LLC
5700 Crooks Rd Ste 207 (48098-2809)
PHONE.................................248 879-7656
Steven Dow, *Principal*
EMP: 2088 EST: 2007
SALES (est): 177.5MM
SALES (corp-wide): 3.4B Privately Held
WEB: www.suncappart.com
SIC: 3592 Carburetors
PA: Sun Capital Partners, Inc.
  5200 Town Center Cir # 600
  Boca Raton FL 33486
  561 962-3400

(G-17409)
TYGRUS LLC
1134 E Big Beaver Rd (48083-1934)
PHONE.................................248 218-0347
Janine Runey, *Comptroller*
Lawrence Carlson, *CTO*
Daniel Jenuwine, *Exec Dir*
Andrew Yaksic, *Officer*
EMP: 5 EST: 2012
SQ FT: 500
SALES (est): 1.1MM Privately Held
WEB: www.tygrus.com
SIC: 2869 Industrial organic chemicals

(G-17410)
UFI FILTERS USA INC
50 W Big Beavr Rd Ste 440 (48084-5290)
PHONE.................................248 376-0441
EMP: 4
SALES (corp-wide): 507.8K Privately Held
SIC: 3714 Mfg Motor Vehicle Parts/Accessories
HQ: Ufi Filters Usa, Inc.
  110 Firestone Pt
  Duluth GA 48084

(G-17411)
UFI FILTERS USA INC
50 W Big Beavr Rd Ste 440 (48084-5290)
PHONE.................................248 376-0441
Richard Hubbell, *President*
Chelsey Cowley, *COO*
Juan Delgado, *Sales Mgr*
Matt Tenbusch, *Sales Staff*
Richard Belf, *Manager*
▲ EMP: 12 EST: 2001
SQ FT: 2,600
SALES (est): 10MM
SALES (corp-wide): 406.8K Privately Held
WEB: www.ufihyd.com
SIC: 3714 Filters: oil, fuel & air, motor vehicle
HQ: Ufi Filters Spa
  Via Europa 26
  Porto Mantovano MN 46047
  045 633-9911

(G-17412)
UNITED GLOBAL SOURCING INC (PA)
Also Called: Ugs
675 E Big Beaver Rd # 211 (48083-1428)
PHONE.................................248 952-5700
Kenneth Eisenbraun, *Ch of Bd*
Kevin De Hart, *President*

Roger Gregory, *Vice Pres*
Pam S Payne, *Vice Pres*
Pam Payne, *Vice Pres*
▲ **EMP:** 18 **EST:** 1981
SALES (est): 5.1MM **Privately Held**
WEB: www.unitedgs.com
SIC: 3334 2491 Primary aluminum; flooring, treated wood block

(G-17413)
UNITED SYSTEMS
Also Called: Western Press
525 Elmwood Dr (48083-2755)
P.O. Box 353, Clawson (48017-0353)
PHONE 248 583-9670
David A Thomas, *Owner*
David Thomas, *Principal*
EMP: 8 **EST:** 1971
SQ FT: 4,600
SALES (est): 2MM **Privately Held**
SIC: 1799 3599 Welding on site; custom machinery

(G-17414)
UNIVERSAL TOOL INC
552 Robbins Dr (48083-4514)
PHONE 248 733-9800
William Nordness, *President*
Todd Ballard, *Vice Pres*
▼ **EMP:** 7 **EST:** 1988
SALES (est): 796.8K **Privately Held**
WEB: www.universaltoolinc.net
SIC: 3545 Machine tool accessories

(G-17415)
US FARATHANE HOLDINGS CORP
Also Called: Chemcast
750 W Maple Rd (48084-5315)
PHONE 586 978-2800
Preston Miller, *General Mgr*
Steve Souders, *General Mgr*
Greg Schaff, *Principal*
Rodney Turton, *Vice Pres*
Quentin Cole, *Plant Mgr*
EMP: 5
SALES (corp-wide): 549.4MM **Privately Held**
WEB: www.usfarathane.com
SIC: 3089 Injection molding of plastics
PA: U.S. Farathane Holdings Corp.
2700 High Meadow Cir
Auburn Hills MI 48326
248 754-7000

(G-17416)
USA CARBIDE
1395 Wheaton Dr Ste 500 (48083-1926)
PHONE 248 817-5137
Ralph D Schiller III, *Administration*
EMP: 5 **EST:** 2013
SALES (est): 158.9K **Privately Held**
SIC: 2819 Carbides

(G-17417)
USA TODAY ADVERTISING
2800 Livernois Rd Ste 630 (48083-1231)
PHONE 248 680-6530
Marcia Bollard, *Principal*
EMP: 5 **EST:** 2007
SALES (est): 79K **Privately Held**
SIC: 2711 Newspapers, publishing & printing

(G-17418)
UTICA BODY & ASSEMBLY INC (HQ)
5750 New King Dr Ste 200 (48098-2611)
PHONE 586 726-4330
Thomas J Carter, *President*
Stefan Wanczyk, *Vice Pres*
EMP: 20 **EST:** 1992
SQ FT: 62,640
SALES (est): 30.8MM
SALES (corp-wide): 305MM **Privately Held**
WEB: www.uticaenterprises.com
SIC: 3549 8711 3541 Assembly machines, including robotic; designing: ship, boat, machine & product; machine tools, metal cutting type
PA: Utica Enterprises, Inc.
5750 New King Dr Ste 200
Troy MI 48098
586 726-4300

(G-17419)
UTICA ENTERPRISES INC (PA)
Also Called: Utica Laeser Systems
5750 New King Dr Ste 200 (48098-2611)
PHONE 586 726-4300
Thomas J Carter, *Ch of Bd*
Stefan Wanczyk, *President*
Dennis Lucas, *Vice Pres*
Rob Stojkovski, *Project Mgr*
Phil Tuszynski, *Mfg Staff*
▲ **EMP:** 200 **EST:** 1977
SQ FT: 160,000
SALES (est): 305MM **Privately Held**
WEB: www.uticaenterprises.com
SIC: 3548 3549 3545 3541 Welding apparatus; assembly machines, including robotic; broaches (machine tool accessories); machine tools, metal cutting type; broaching machines; special dies & tools; designing: ship, boat, machine & product

(G-17420)
UTICA INTERNATIONAL INC (HQ)
5750 New King Dr Ste 200 (48098-2611)
PHONE 586 726-4330
Thomas J Carter, *Ch of Bd*
Stefan Wanczyk, *President*
EMP: 200 **EST:** 1977
SALES (est): 155.3MM
SALES (corp-wide): 305MM **Privately Held**
WEB: www.uticaenterprises.com
SIC: 3549 3548 3544 Assembly machines, including robotic; electric welding equipment; special dies, tools, jigs & fixtures
PA: Utica Enterprises, Inc.
5750 New King Dr Ste 200
Troy MI 48098
586 726-4300

(G-17421)
UTICA PRODUCTS INC
5750 New King Dr Ste 200 (48098-2611)
PHONE 586 726-4300
Thomas Carter, *President*
Lawrence Stover, *General Mgr*
Stefan Wanczyk, *Treasurer*
EMP: 2 **EST:** 1986
SQ FT: 62,640
SALES (est): 1.6MM
SALES (corp-wide): 305MM **Privately Held**
WEB: www.uticaenterprises.com
SIC: 3549 Assembly machines, including robotic
PA: Utica Enterprises, Inc.
5750 New King Dr Ste 200
Troy MI 48098
586 726-4300

(G-17422)
V E S T INC
3250 W Big Beaver Rd # 440 (48084-2902)
PHONE 248 649-9550
Shruti Raina, *President*
EMP: 7 **EST:** 1997
SALES (est): 1MM **Privately Held**
WEB: www.vestusa.com
SIC: 7372 Prepackaged software

(G-17423)
V S AMERICA INC
1000 John R Rd Ste 111 (48083-4317)
PHONE 248 585-6715
Oliver Diehm, *President*
Elizabeth Roberson, *Office Mgr*
▲ **EMP:** 2 **EST:** 1979
SQ FT: 1,000
SALES (est): 9.4MM
SALES (corp-wide): 32.6MM **Privately Held**
WEB: www.vs-america.com
SIC: 7692 Welding repair
PA: Vs Guss Ag
Parallelstr. 17
Solingen NW 42719
212 384-0

(G-17424)
VAL MANUFACTURING CO LLC
4112 Marywood Dr (48085-3659)
PHONE 248 765-8694
Valerian Dubei, *Principal*
EMP: 4 **EST:** 2015
SALES (est): 93.8K **Privately Held**
SIC: 3999 Manufacturing industries

(G-17425)
VALEO INC
Also Called: Valeo Interior Controls
150 Stephenson Hwy (48083-1116)
PHONE 248 619-8300
▲ **EMP:** 5000 **EST:** 2014
SALES (est): 168.9MM
SALES (corp-wide): 177.9K **Privately Held**
SIC: 3714 Motor vehicle parts & accessories; radiators & radiator shells & cores, motor vehicle; clutches, motor vehicle; transmissions, motor vehicle
HQ: Valeo International Holding B.V.
Heibloemweg 1
Helmond
492 580-800

(G-17426)
VALEO FRICTION MATERIALS INC (DH)
Also Called: Valeo Wiper Systems
150 Stephenson Hwy (48083-1116)
PHONE 248 619-8300
Lionel Brenac, *President*
Geoffrey Bouquot, *Vice Pres*
Luc Charlemagne, *Treasurer*
▲ **EMP:** 4 **EST:** 1979
SQ FT: 40,000
SALES (est): 48.4MM
SALES (corp-wide): 177.9K **Privately Held**
SIC: 3714 Clutches, motor vehicle

(G-17427)
VALEO KAPEC NORTH AMERICA INC
150 Stephenson Hwy (48083-1116)
PHONE 248 619-8710
Jacques Aschenbroich, *Ch of Bd*
Satish Nadella, *Engineer*
Goran Stojanovski, *Engineer*
Ronald Wegener, *Senior Engr*
Cathy Kempenaar, *Accounts Mgr*
EMP: 27 **EST:** 2017
SALES (est): 3.3MM
SALES (corp-wide): 177.9K **Privately Held**
WEB: www.valeo.com
SIC: 3566 Torque converters, except automotive
PA: Valeo
43 Rue Bayen
Paris
140 687-476

(G-17428)
VALEO NORTH AMERICA INC
Also Called: Valeo Service Center
150 Stephenson Hwy (48083-1116)
PHONE 248 619-8300
James Schwyn, *General Mgr*
Tangi French, *General Mgr*
Curt Estes, *Vice Pres*
Dennis Linson, *Project Mgr*
Elwyn Davies, *Mfg Staff*
EMP: 200
SALES (corp-wide): 177.9K **Privately Held**
SIC: 3625 7336 8731 Switches, electric power; art design services; commercial physical research
HQ: Valeo North America, Inc.
150 Stephenson Hwy
Troy MI 48083

(G-17429)
VALEO NORTH AMERICA INC (HQ)
Also Called: Valeo Wiper Systems
150 Stephenson Hwy (48083-1116)
PHONE 248 619-8300
Francoise Colpron, *President*
Brian Sirbak, *Production*
Loic Brault, *Purchasing*
Scott Adaska, *Engineer*
Kenneth Cronk, *Engineer*
◆ **EMP:** 74 **EST:** 1993
SQ FT: 437,000
SALES (est): 1.1B
SALES (corp-wide): 177.9K **Privately Held**
WEB: www.valeo.com
SIC: 3714 Motor vehicle electrical equipment
PA: Valeo
43 Rue Bayen
Paris
140 687-476

(G-17430)
VALEO RADAR SYSTEMS INC (HQ)
150 Stephenson Hwy (48083-1116)
PHONE 248 619-8300
James Schwyn, *President*
Nicolas Retailleau, *CFO*
Manuel Sanchez-Gijon, *Director*
EMP: 10 **EST:** 2002
SALES (est): 43.9MM
SALES (corp-wide): 177.9K **Privately Held**
WEB: www.valeo.com
SIC: 5731 3714 Radio, television & electronic stores; motor vehicle electrical equipment
PA: Valeo
43 Rue Bayen
Paris
140 687-476

(G-17431)
VALEO SWITCHES & DETE (DH)
150 Stephenson Hwy (48083-1116)
PHONE 248 619-8300
James Schwyn, *President*
▲ **EMP:** 42 **EST:** 2001
SALES (est): 415.7MM
SALES (corp-wide): 177.9K **Privately Held**
SIC: 3714 Motor vehicle parts & accessories

(G-17432)
VAST PRODUCTION SERVICES INC
307 Robbins Dr (48083-4561)
PHONE 248 838-9680
Fred Norvell, *President*
David Swaim, *Technical Staff*
EMP: 58 **EST:** 1996
SALES (est): 18.1MM **Privately Held**
WEB: www.vastsolutions.com
SIC: 8711 3999 3679 Engineering services; barber & beauty shop equipment; electronic circuits

(G-17433)
VDL STEELWELD USA LLC
1095 Crooks Rd Ste 300 (48084-7132)
PHONE 248 781-8141
Utkarsh Kopargaonkar, *Engineer*
EMP: 25 **EST:** 2016
SALES (est): 408.1K **Privately Held**
WEB: www.vdlsteelweld.com
SIC: 3569 8711 8744 Robots, assembly line: industrial & commercial; mechanical engineering; base maintenance (providing personnel on continuing basis)

(G-17434)
VEHMA INTERNATIONAL AMER INC
Also Called: Cosma Engineering
1807 E Maple Rd (48083-4212)
PHONE 248 631-1100
EMP: 131
SALES (corp-wide): 32.6B **Privately Held**
SIC: 3714 Motor vehicle parts & accessories
HQ: Vehma International Of America, Inc.
750 Tower Dr 4000
Troy MI 48098

(G-17435)
VEHMA INTERNATIONAL AMER INC
1230 Chicago Rd (48083-4230)
PHONE 248 585-4800
Simon Bennett, *Manager*
EMP: 75

Troy - Oakland County (G-17436) — GEOGRAPHIC SECTION

SALES (corp-wide): 32.6B **Privately Held**
SIC: 8711 3714 Designing; ship, boat, machine & product; motor vehicle parts & accessories
HQ: Vehma International Of America, Inc.
750 Tower Dr 4000
Troy MI 48098

(G-17436)
VEHMA INTERNATIONAL AMER INC (DH)
Also Called: Cosma Engineering
750 Tower Dr 4000 (48098-2863)
PHONE 248 631-2800
Philip Bell, *President*
Swamy Kotagiri, *Exec VP*
Scott Turner, *Exec VP*
Arthur L Lee, *Vice Pres*
Gerd Brusius, *Vice Pres*
◆ **EMP:** 100 **EST:** 1987
SQ FT: 115,000
SALES (est): 96.1MM
SALES (corp-wide): 32.6B **Privately Held**
SIC: 3714 Motor vehicle parts & accessories
HQ: Cosma International Of America, Inc.
750 Tower Dr
Troy MI 48098
248 631-1100

(G-17437)
VELCRO USA INC
Velcro Automotives Division
1210 Souter Dr (48083-6020)
PHONE 248 583-6060
Fax: 248 585-7861
EMP: 7 **Privately Held**
SIC: 3713 Sales Office
HQ: Velcro Usa Inc.
95 Sundial Ave
Manchester NH 03103
603 669-4880

(G-17438)
VERSATUBE CORPORATION
4755 Rochester Rd Ste 200 (48085-4963)
PHONE 248 524-0299
Eugene Goodman, *President*
Sandra Goodman, *Admin Sec*
▲ **EMP:** 12 **EST:** 1959
SQ FT: 180,000
SALES (est): 1.8MM **Privately Held**
WEB: www.versatubecorp.com
SIC: 3465 3469 3599 Moldings or trim, automobile: stamped metal; metal stampings; tubing, flexible metallic

(G-17439)
VERTICALSCOPE USA INC
3290 W Big Beavr Rd # 500 (48084-2917)
PHONE 248 220-1451
Neil Rosenzweig, *Principal*
EMP: 9 **EST:** 2019
SALES (est): 190.1K **Privately Held**
WEB: www.verticalscope.com
SIC: 2741 Miscellaneous publishing

(G-17440)
VIBRATION CONTROLS TECH LLC
2075 W Big Beaver Rd # 500 (48084-3407)
PHONE 248 822-8010
Joseph B Anderson,
EMP: 5 **EST:** 2000
SALES (est): 400K **Privately Held**
SIC: 3822 Damper operators: pneumatic, thermostatic, electric

(G-17441)
VIRTUAL ADVANTAGE LLC
3290 W Big Beavr Rd # 310 (48084-2910)
PHONE 877 772-6886
Nick Daniels, *Managing Dir*
Ryan Robison,
EMP: 5 **EST:** 2009 **Privately Held**
WEB: www.scoutcms.com
SIC: 7372 Prepackaged software

(G-17442)
VIRTUAL TECHNOLOGY INC
1345 Wheaton Dr (48083-1994)
PHONE 248 528-6565
Michael Dolik, *General Mgr*
Mike Hockney, *Marketing Staff*
EMP: 18 **EST:** 1983
SQ FT: 20,000
SALES (est): 1.7MM **Privately Held**
WEB: www.virtualtechnology.com
SIC: 3572 5045 Computer storage devices; computer peripheral equipment

(G-17443)
VU ACQUISITIONS LLC (PA)
Also Called: Vu Manufacturing
2151 Livernois Rd 200a (48083-1641)
PHONE 248 269-0517
Elisha Cunningham,
Joseph Burkhart,
◆ **EMP:** 189 **EST:** 2009
SQ FT: 2,000
SALES (est): 13.3MM **Privately Held**
WEB: www.vumfg.com
SIC: 2396 Automotive & apparel trimmings

(G-17444)
WAGNER CASTINGS COMPANY
5445 Corporate Dr Ste 200 (48098-2683)
PHONE 248 952-2500
EMP: 10 **EST:** 2008
SALES (est): 234.7K **Privately Held**
SIC: 3714 Motor vehicle parts & accessories

(G-17445)
WATERLOO GROUP INC
2865 Waterloo Dr (48084-2682)
PHONE 248 840-6447
Ronald Garbinski, *President*
EMP: 2 **EST:** 1995
SALES (est): 1.1MM **Privately Held**
WEB: www.waterloogroup.com
SIC: 2731 8742 8999 Books: publishing only; marketing consulting services; writing for publication

(G-17446)
WCSCARTS LLC (PA)
Also Called: World Class Shopping Carts
900 Wilshire Dr Ste 202 (48084-1600)
P.O. Box 3355, Rocklin CA (95677-8468)
PHONE 248 901-0965
Ross Vincent, *Mng Member*
▲ **EMP:** 56 **EST:** 2013
SALES (est): 10MM **Privately Held**
WEB: www.wcsarts.com
SIC: 3496 Grocery carts, made from purchased wire

(G-17447)
WESTERN INTERNATIONAL INC
Also Called: Western Global
1707 Northwood Dr (48084-5524)
PHONE 866 814-2470
Daryl Neilson, *General Mgr*
James Truan, *General Mgr*
Michael Truan, *Business Mgr*
Barry Truan, *Vice Pres*
Greg Cornell, *Opers Staff*
▲ **EMP:** 36 **EST:** 2007
SQ FT: 26,000
SALES (est): 5.7MM **Privately Held**
WEB: www.western-global.com
SIC: 3443 5084 4225 5051 Fuel tanks (oil, gas, etc.); metal plate; industrial machinery & equipment; general warehousing & storage; metals service centers & offices

(G-17448)
WEYV INC
1820 E Big Beaver Rd (48083-2031)
PHONE 248 614-2400
Srinivasa Palepu, *Controller*
EMP: 10 **EST:** 2017
SALES (est): 2.2MM
SALES (corp-wide): 469.9MM **Publicly Held**
WEB: www.altair.com
SIC: 2741
PA: Altair Engineering Inc.
1820 E Big Beaver Rd
Troy MI 48083
248 614-2400

(G-17449)
WITZENMANN USA LLC (HQ)
1201 Stephenson Hwy (48083-1105)
PHONE 248 588-6033
Keith Shivnen, *Managing Dir*
◆ **EMP:** 403 **EST:** 2000
SQ FT: 60,000
SALES (est): 72.5MM
SALES (corp-wide): 712.3MM **Privately Held**
WEB: www.witzenmann-usa.com
SIC: 3449 Miscellaneous metalwork
PA: Witzenmann Gmbh
Ostliche Karl-Friedrich-Str. 134
Pforzheim BW 75175
723 158-10

(G-17450)
WOLVERINE CARBIDE & TOOL INC
684 Robbins Dr (48083-4563)
PHONE 248 247-3888
Derek J Stevens, *President*
Randall Grunewald, *General Mgr*
Thomas Dharte, *Vice Pres*
Gregory J Stevens, *Vice Pres*
James Nelson, *Project Mgr*
EMP: 35 **EST:** 1994
SQ FT: 19,400
SALES (est): 3.8MM **Privately Held**
WEB: www.wolverinecarbide.com
SIC: 3544 Special dies & tools

(G-17451)
WOODBRIDGE HOLDINGS INC (HQ)
1515 Equity Dr Ste 100 (48084-7129)
PHONE 248 288-0100
Hugh W Sloan Jr, *President*
Taleen Nigosian, *Business Mgr*
Scott Snyder, *Business Mgr*
Frank Youvon, *Business Mgr*
Robert Magee, *Exec VP*
▲ **EMP:** 6 **EST:** 1984
SQ FT: 20,000
SALES (est): 606.3MM
SALES (corp-wide): 157.8MM **Privately Held**
WEB: www.woodbridgegroup.com
SIC: 2531 3086 Seats, automobile; plastics foam products
PA: Woodbridge Foam Corporation
4240 Sherwoodtowne Blvd Suite 300
Mississauga ON L4Z 2
905 896-3626

(G-17452)
WOODBRIDGE SALES & ENGRG INC (DH)
1515 Equity Dr (48084-7129)
PHONE 248 288-0100
Bob Magee, *President*
Tom Potochney, *VP Opers*
Richard Jocsak, *Treasurer*
EMP: 120 **EST:** 1988
SALES (est): 48.3MM
SALES (corp-wide): 157.8MM **Privately Held**
WEB: www.woodbridgegroup.com
SIC: 5162 5013 2821 Plastics products; automotive supplies & parts; plastics materials & resins
HQ: Woodbridge Holdings Inc.
1515 Equity Dr Ste 100
Troy MI 48084
248 288-0100

(G-17453)
WORLD CLASS STEEL & PROC INC
2673 American Dr (48083-4619)
PHONE 586 585-1734
Jay Tlumak, *President*
EMP: 4 **EST:** 2002
SALES (est): 641.9K **Privately Held**
WEB: www.wcspinc.com
SIC: 3999 5051 Advertising curtains; steel

(G-17454)
WRIGHT COMMUNICATIONS INC
1229 Chicago Rd (48083-4231)
P.O. Box 71276, Madison Heights (48071-0276)
PHONE 248 585-3838
Kevin Wright, *President*
Bill Wright, *Treasurer*
EMP: 10 **EST:** 1983
SQ FT: 2,500
SALES (est): 594.8K **Privately Held**
WEB: www.wrightdigital.net
SIC: 5045 2721 Printers, computer; periodicals

(G-17455)
X-BAR AUTOMATION INC
961 Elmsford Dr (48083-2803)
PHONE 248 616-9890
Michael O'Hagan, *President*
Daniel Selonke, *Corp Secy*
Thomas McQuarter, *Vice Pres*
Dave Jerore, *Production*
EMP: 25 **EST:** 1990
SQ FT: 12,500
SALES (est): 4.5MM **Privately Held**
WEB: www.xbarauto.com
SIC: 3613 Control panels, electric

(G-17456)
YAPP USA AUTO SYSTEMS INC
800 Kirts Blvd (48084-4878)
PHONE 248 817-5653
Greg Brown, *Branch Mgr*
Kris Barton, *Program Mgr*
Shuye Pan, *Program Mgr*
EMP: 171 **Privately Held**
WEB: www.yappusa.com
SIC: 3089 6399 Automotive parts, plastic; warranty insurance, automobile
HQ: Yapp Usa Automotive Systems, Inc.
300 Abc Blvd
Gallatin TN 37066

(G-17457)
YAREMA DIE & ENGINEERING CO (PA)
300 Minnesota Dr (48083-4610)
PHONE 248 585-2830
Lester Fisher, *President*
George W Lukowski, *Chairman*
James Yarema, *Vice Chairman*
Kevin Bachert, *Manager*
Keith Noble, *Manager*
EMP: 116 **EST:** 1960
SQ FT: 43,272
SALES (est): 20.5MM **Privately Held**
WEB: www.yarema.com
SIC: 3544 3465 Die sets for metal stamping (presses); moldings or trim, automobile: stamped metal

(G-17458)
YTI OFFICE EXPRESS LLC
1280 E Big Beaver Rd A (48083-1946)
PHONE 866 996-8952
Devin Durrell, *General Mgr*
Michael Carr,
EMP: 5 **EST:** 2005
SQ FT: 12,000
SALES (est): 631K **Privately Held**
SIC: 5712 5112 2752 Office furniture; stationery & office supplies; commercial printing, offset

(G-17459)
ZHONGLI NORTH AMERICA INC
1511 E 14 Mile Rd (48083-4621)
PHONE 248 733-9300
Yaunpeng Dai, *President*
Anthony Valitutti, *Engineer*
Jason Thomas, *CFO*
Yacong Dai, *Treasurer*
Randy Aron, *Sales Staff*
▲ **EMP:** 94 **EST:** 2009
SALES (est): 8.2MM
SALES (corp-wide): 880.7K **Privately Held**
SIC: 3714 Motor vehicle engines & parts
PA: Shanghai Zhongli Investment Development Co., Ltd.
Rm.250, No.375, Pingshun Rd.
Shanghai 20043

(G-17460)
ZIEBART INTERNATIONAL CORP (PA)
1290 E Maple Rd (48083-2817)
PHONE 248 588-4100
Thomas E Wolfe, *President*
Daniel C Baker, *Exec VP*
Zachary Mattiacio, *Senior VP*
Michael W Riley, *Senior VP*
Thomas A Wolfe, *Senior VP*
▼ **EMP:** 44 **EST:** 1961
SQ FT: 35,000

GEOGRAPHIC SECTION

SALES (est): 23.8MM **Privately Held**
WEB: www.ziebart.com
SIC: **7549** 6794 5013 2842 Lubrication service, automotive; franchises, selling or licensing; automotive supplies; specialty cleaning, polishes & sanitation goods; adhesives & sealants; paints & allied products

(G-17461)
ZKW LIGHTING SYSTEMS USA INC
100 W Big Beavr Rd # 300 (48084-5283)
PHONE.....................................248 509-7300
Stefan Hauptmann, *Manager*
Lindsay Seigel, *Manager*
EMP: 19 EST: 2014
SALES (est): 4.2MM **Privately Held**
WEB: www.zkw-group.com
SIC: **3647** Automotive lighting fixtures
HQ: Zkw Lichtsysteme Gmbh
 Scheibbser StraBe 17
 Wieselburg An Der Erlauf 3250
 741 650-50

Turner
Arenac County

(G-17462)
BAY CITY CRANE INC
3951 Allen Rd (48765-9502)
PHONE.....................................989 867-4292
Brian Tressler, *CEO*
Gary Tressler, *Corp Secy*
EMP: 4 EST: 1993
SQ FT: 7,800
SALES (est): 390.7K **Privately Held**
WEB: www.bay-journal.com
SIC: **3599** Machine shop, jobbing & repair

(G-17463)
G & S LOGGING LLC
2215 Edmonds Rd (48765-9723)
PHONE.....................................989 876-6596
EMP: 5 EST: 2016
SALES (est): 115.4K **Privately Held**
SIC: **2411** Logging

(G-17464)
LIME GYPSUM PRODUCTS
3425 Britt Rd (48765-9524)
PHONE.....................................989 867-4611
Kathy Gibson, *Manager*
EMP: 4 EST: 2020
SALES (est): 105.2K **Privately Held**
SIC: **3275** Gypsum products

Tustin
Osceola County

(G-17465)
BELCHERS MAPLE SYRUP LLC
Also Called: Belchers' Maple Syrup
11671 22 Mile Rd (49688-8750)
PHONE.....................................231 942-1399
Lisa Ruppert, *Manager*
James Belcher, *Webmaster*
Jim Belcher,
EMP: 4 EST: 2018
SQ FT: 7,000
SALES (est): 385K **Privately Held**
WEB: www.belchersmaplesyrup.com
SIC: **2099** Food preparations

(G-17466)
NELSONS SAW MILL INC
8482 N Raymond Rd (49688-9603)
PHONE.....................................231 829-5220
Steve Nelson, *President*
Michael Nelson, *Vice Pres*
Robert Nelson, *Treasurer*
EMP: 5 EST: 1979
SALES (est): 395.8K **Privately Held**
SIC: **2421** Resawing lumber into smaller dimensions

Twin Lake
Muskegon County

(G-17467)
FISHALL LURES
5850 Holton Duck Lake Rd (49457-9717)
PHONE.....................................231 821-9020
Michael King, *Principal*
EMP: 4 EST: 2010
SALES (est): 168.7K **Privately Held**
WEB: www.bncustom.com
SIC: **3949** Lures, fishing: artificial

(G-17468)
GREAT LAKES LOG & FIREWD CO
11405 Russell Rd (49457-9469)
PHONE.....................................231 206-4073
Dennis Blankenship, *President*
Sharon Blankenship, *Vice Pres*
EMP: 4 EST: 2010 **Privately Held**
WEB: www.greatlakesloggingandfirewood.com
SIC: **2411** 5099 5734 Logging camps & contractors; firewood; word processing equipment & supplies

(G-17469)
KENNETH A GOULD
2790 W Raymond Rd (49457)
PHONE.....................................231 828-4705
Kenneth Gould, *Principal*
EMP: 7 EST: 2009
SALES (est): 182.6K **Privately Held**
SIC: **2411** Logging camps & contractors

(G-17470)
MAPLE ISLAND LOG HOMES INC (PA)
2387 Bayne Rd (49457-9736)
P.O. Box 223, Fremont (49412-0223)
PHONE.....................................231 821-2151
David Tuxbury, *President*
Richard Tuxbury, *Vice Pres*
Robert Tuxbury, *Treasurer*
Georgia Tuxbury, *Admin Sec*
EMP: 55 EST: 1977
SQ FT: 1,120
SALES (est): 5.8MM **Privately Held**
WEB: www.mapleisland.com
SIC: **1521** 2452 New construction, single-family houses; prefabricated wood buildings

(G-17471)
ORANGE OCTOBER PUBLISHING CO
2719 Duff Rd (49457-9002)
PHONE.....................................231 828-1039
Frank Warrick, *Principal*
EMP: 5 EST: 2008
SALES (est): 61.1K **Privately Held**
SIC: **2741** Miscellaneous publishing

(G-17472)
S&M LOGGING LLC
6141 16th St (49457-9709)
PHONE.....................................231 821-0588
Mark Sundberg, *Principal*
EMP: 4 EST: 2006
SALES (est): 84.3K **Privately Held**
SIC: **2411** Logging

(G-17473)
SUNSHINE MEADERY LLC
50 W Englewood Ave Ste B (49457-9536)
PHONE.....................................231 215-7956
Jacob Lemoine, *Principal*
EMP: 4 EST: 2014
SALES (est): 86.8K **Privately Held**
WEB: www.sunshinemead.com
SIC: **2084** Wines

(G-17474)
TEE PAL LLC
7099 Oakshore Dr (49457-8515)
PHONE.....................................231 563-3770
Brian J Botbyl, *Administration*
EMP: 4 EST: 2015
SALES (est): 62.6K **Privately Held**
WEB: www.teepalllc.com
SIC: **3949** Sporting & athletic goods

Ubly
Huron County

(G-17475)
BAD AXE METAL & IRON ART
7125 Frieburger Rd (48475-8727)
PHONE.....................................989 658-8324
Kennedy Brian Thomas, *Owner*
EMP: 5 EST: 2017
SALES (est): 84.5K **Privately Held**
WEB: www.badaxeiron.com
SIC: **3446** Architectural metalwork

(G-17476)
GEMINI PLASTICS INC
4385 Garfield St (48475-9553)
PHONE.....................................989 658-8557
John Moll, *President*
Lindsay Fry, *Plant Mgr*
EMP: 250 EST: 1977
SALES (est): 64.5MM **Privately Held**
WEB: www.geminigroup.net
SIC: **3086** 6531 Plastics foam products; real estate agents & managers
PA: Gemini Group, Inc.
 175 Thompson Rd Ste A
 Bad Axe MI 48413

(G-17477)
GEMINI PLASTICS DE MEXICO INC
4385 Garfield St (48475-9553)
PHONE.....................................989 658-8557
David Hyzer, *Principal*
EMP: 1 EST: 2010
SALES (est): 3.2MM **Privately Held**
WEB: www.geminigroup.net
SIC: **3089** Injection molding of plastics
PA: Gemini Group, Inc.
 175 Thompson Rd Ste A
 Bad Axe MI 48413

(G-17478)
MAURER MEAT PROCESSORS INC
4075 Purdy Rd (48475-9744)
PHONE.....................................989 658-8185
Jim Maurer, *President*
EMP: 15 EST: 1965
SQ FT: 7,500
SALES (est): 695.6K **Privately Held**
WEB: www.maurermeat.com
SIC: **2011** Meat packing plants

(G-17479)
PEPRO ENTERPRISES INC
Also Called: Valley Enterprises
2147 Leppek Rd (48475-9790)
PHONE.....................................989 658-3200
EMP: 96 **Privately Held**
SIC: **3089** Mfg Plastic Products
HQ: Pepro Enterprises, Inc.
 2147 Leppek Rd
 Ubly MI 48475
 989 658-3200

(G-17480)
PEPRO ENTERPRISES INC (HQ)
Also Called: Gemini Plastics
4385 Garfield St (48475-9553)
PHONE.....................................989 658-3200
Lyn Drake, *President*
Michelle Gunderman, *Safety Mgr*
Doug Edwards, *Sales Staff*
Rick Spurlock, *Sales Staff*
Brenda Hoffman, *Admin Asst*
▲ EMP: 180 EST: 1977
SQ FT: 100,000
SALES (est): 100.9MM **Privately Held**
WEB: www.geminigroup.net
SIC: **3089** Injection molding of plastics

(G-17481)
QUALITY WOOD PRODUCTS INC
3399 Bay Cy Frestville Rd (48475)
PHONE.....................................989 658-2160
Rick Vogel, *President*
EMP: 10 EST: 1990
SALES (est): 750K **Privately Held**
WEB: www.qualitywoodproductsonline.com
SIC: **2431** Millwork

(G-17482)
REGENCY PLASTICS - UBLY INC (HQ)
4147 N Ubly Rd (48475-9578)
PHONE.....................................989 658-8504
William Roberts, *President*
Frank Peplinski, *Corp Secy*
EMP: 100 EST: 1988
SQ FT: 42,000
SALES (est): 125.3MM **Privately Held**
WEB: www.geminigroup.net
SIC: **3089** 3714 Blow molded finished plastic products; motor vehicle parts & accessories

(G-17483)
TRU FLO CARBIDE INC
3999 N Ubly Rd (48475-9764)
P.O. Box 276 (48475-0276)
PHONE.....................................989 658-8515
Brian Gunn, *President*
EMP: 11 EST: 1983
SQ FT: 15,000
SALES (est): 593K **Privately Held**
SIC: **3544** 3545 3444 Special dies & tools; machine tool accessories; sheet metalwork

(G-17484)
VALLEY ENTERPRISES UBLY INC
Ubly Logistics Center
4175 N Ubly Rd (48475-9578)
PHONE.....................................989 269-6272
Lynette G Drake, *President*
EMP: 11 **Privately Held**
WEB: www.geminigroup.net
SIC: **2431** Interior & ornamental woodwork & trim
HQ: Valley Enterprises Ubly Inc.
 2147 Leppek Rd
 Ubly MI 48475

(G-17485)
VALLEY ENTERPRISES UBLY INC (HQ)
2147 Leppek Rd (48475-9790)
PHONE.....................................989 658-3200
Lynette Drake, *President*
Shari Quinn, *Exec VP*
Jeffrey Rochefort, *Vice Pres*
Dave Chumbler, *Opers Mgr*
Dawn Hurlburt, *Treasurer*
▲ EMP: 114 EST: 1996
SQ FT: 80,000
SALES (est): 31.4MM **Privately Held**
WEB: www.geminigroup.net
SIC: **3089** Injection molding of plastics

Union
Cass County

(G-17486)
ADMAT MANUFACTURING INC
16744 Us Highway 12 (49130-9224)
PHONE.....................................269 641-7453
Donald K Miller, *President*
Rosemary Miller, *Corp Secy*
Jeffrita L Colglazier, *Vice Pres*
EMP: 17 EST: 1961
SQ FT: 15,700
SALES (est): 1.1MM **Privately Held**
SIC: **3429** 3469 Manufactured hardware (general); stamping metal for the trade

(G-17487)
GARYS CUSTOM MEATS
Also Called: Gary's Custom Meat Processing
16237 Mason St (49130-9606)
P.O. Box 456 (49130-0456)
PHONE.....................................269 641-5683
Gary Lorenz, *Owner*
Jode Lorenz, *Corp Secy*
EMP: 4 EST: 1993
SQ FT: 2,800
SALES (est): 258.9K **Privately Held**
WEB: www.meatprocessingmichiana.com
SIC: **2011** Meat packing plants

Union - Cass County (G-17488)

(G-17488)
HARMAN LUMBER & SUPPLY INC
Also Called: Harman Builders
15479 Us Highway 12 Ste 7 (49130-9742)
PHONE..........................269 641-5424
William M Harman, *President*
Delores Harman, *Admin Sec*
EMP: 5 **EST:** 1950
SQ FT: 10,000
SALES (est): 355.5K **Privately Held**
SIC: 2452 1521 Log cabins, prefabricated, wood; new construction, single-family houses

(G-17489)
HIBSHMAN SCREW MCH PDTS INC
69351 Union Rd S (49130-9760)
P.O. Box 138 (49130-0138)
PHONE..........................269 641-7525
William M Hibshman, *President*
Gary A Vanderbeek, *Vice Pres*
▲ **EMP:** 50 **EST:** 1967
SQ FT: 27,000
SALES (est): 8.6MM **Privately Held**
WEB: www.hibshman.co
SIC: 3451 3469 Screw machine products; metal stampings

Union City
Branch County

(G-17490)
ARCOSA SHORING PRODUCTS INC (HQ)
8530 M 60 (49094-9345)
PHONE..........................517 741-4300
Ken Groenewold, *President*
▲ **EMP:** 100 **EST:** 2012
SALES: 25MM
SALES (corp-wide): 1.9B **Publicly Held**
WEB: www.gme-shields.com
SIC: 3731 3743 3531 Barges, building & repairing; freight cars & equipment; concrete plants
PA: Arcosa, Inc.
500 N Akard St Ste 400
Dallas TX 75201
972 942-6500

(G-17491)
COUNTRYSIDE QUALITY MEATS LLC
1184 Adolph Rd (49094-9757)
PHONE..........................517 741-4275
Pat Albright, *Mng Member*
Colleen Albright,
Brian Sexton,
Sandra Sexton,
EMP: 14 **EST:** 2003
SALES (est): 980.3K **Privately Held**
WEB: www.countrysidequalitymeats.com
SIC: 2011 Meat packing plants

(G-17492)
ENER-TEC INC
306 Railroad St (49094-1216)
P.O. Box 85 (49094-0085)
PHONE..........................517 741-5015
Larry Shroyer, *President*
Susan Shroyer, *Admin Sec*
EMP: 11 **EST:** 1977
SQ FT: 1,500
SALES (est): 319K **Privately Held**
WEB: www.ener-tec.com
SIC: 3589 Water treatment equipment, industrial; sewage & water treatment equipment

(G-17493)
GLOVE COATERS INCORPORATED
8380 M 60 (49094-9634)
P.O. Box 5 (49094-0005)
PHONE..........................517 741-8402
Gene Tassie, *President*
▲ **EMP:** 16 **EST:** 1961
SQ FT: 6,000
SALES (est): 1.7MM **Privately Held**
SIC: 3089 Casting of plastic

(G-17494)
GRISWOLD TOOL AND DIE INC
204 Railroad St (49094-1215)
PHONE..........................517 741-7433
James Griswold, *President*
EMP: 5 **EST:** 1995
SALES (est): 79K **Privately Held**
WEB: www.gtd-inc.com
SIC: 3544 Special dies & tools

(G-17495)
MARK EATON SALES AND MFG
8480 M 60 (49094-9338)
PHONE..........................517 741-5000
EMP: 5 **EST:** 2014
SALES (est): 65.4K **Privately Held**
SIC: 3999 Manufacturing industries

(G-17496)
MILLWORKS ENGINEERING INC
Also Called: Craft Room
584 W Girard Rd (49094-9797)
PHONE..........................517 741-5511
Vern Coffman, *Ch of Bd*
Marvin Herman, *Vice Pres*
Leon Edwards, *VP Sales*
◆ **EMP:** 10 **EST:** 1988
SQ FT: 15,000
SALES (est): 1.2MM **Privately Held**
WEB: www.millworkengineering.com
SIC: 2499 Picture frame molding, finished

(G-17497)
TEAM SPORTS COVERS LLC
123 Ellen St (49094-1023)
P.O. Box 191 (49094-0191)
PHONE..........................269 207-0241
EMP: 4 **EST:** 2016
SALES (est): 53.1K **Privately Held**
WEB: www.teamsportscovers.com
SIC: 3949 Sporting & athletic goods

(G-17498)
TRINITY INDUSTRIES INC
Also Called: GME
594 M 60 (49094-8740)
P.O. Box 98 (49094-0098)
PHONE..........................517 741-4300
Joe Zylman, *Manager*
EMP: 60
SALES (corp-wide): 2B **Publicly Held**
WEB: www.trin.net
SIC: 3599 Machine shop, jobbing & repair
PA: Trinity Industries, Inc.
14221 Dallas Pkwy # 1100
Dallas TX 75254
214 631-4420

Union Pier
Berrien County

(G-17499)
COLLINS CAVIAR COMPANY
9595 Union Pier Rd (49129-9411)
PHONE..........................269 469-4576
Rachel Collins, *Principal*
EMP: 7 **EST:** 2013
SALES (est): 130.4K **Privately Held**
WEB: www.collinscaviar.com
SIC: 2092 Fresh or frozen packaged fish

(G-17500)
JOYCE MIMS
9691 Community Hall Rd (49129-9427)
PHONE..........................616 469-5016
Joyce Mims, *COO*
EMP: 4 **EST:** 2017
SALES (est): 81.3K **Privately Held**
WEB: www.mediationprofessionals.wordpress.com
SIC: 3599 Industrial machinery

Utica
Macomb County

(G-17501)
21ST CENTURY GRAPHIC TECH LLC
8344 Hall Rd Ste 210 (48317-5554)
PHONE..........................586 463-9599
Arthur Zysk,
Ron Bracali,
Steve Buckler,
EMP: 5 **EST:** 1997
SQ FT: 1,200
SALES (est): 536.8K **Privately Held**
WEB: www.21cgt.com
SIC: 7372 7371 Prepackaged software; custom computer programming services

(G-17502)
HL MANUFACTURING INC
45399 Utica Park Blvd (48315-5903)
PHONE..........................586 731-2800
Perry Gibbs, *President*
EMP: 18 **EST:** 1977
SQ FT: 7,000
SALES (est): 789K **Privately Held**
WEB: www.hlmfg.com
SIC: 3911 3961 Jewelry, precious metal; costume jewelry

(G-17503)
J D RUSSELL COMPANY
44865 Utica Rd (48317-5474)
P.O. Box 183471, Shelby Township (48318-3471)
PHONE..........................586 254-8500
Dan Caffey, *General Mgr*
Pam Ruser, *Technology*
EMP: 43
SALES (corp-wide): 32.6MM **Privately Held**
WEB: www.jdrussellco.com
SIC: 3494 3446 Expansion joints pipe; architectural metalwork
PA: The J D Russell Company
4075 N Highway Dr
Tucson AZ 85705
520 742-6194

(G-17504)
MNP CORPORATION (PA)
Also Called: STEEL AND WIRE
44225 Utica Rd (48317-5464)
P.O. Box 189002 (48318-9002)
PHONE..........................586 254-1320
Terri Chapman, *CEO*
Thomas Klein, *President*
Sean Murphy, *Partner*
Rick Vella, *General Mgr*
George Fordham, *Principal*
▲ **EMP:** 600 **EST:** 1970
SQ FT: 500,000
SALES: 171.5MM **Privately Held**
WEB: www.mnp.com
SIC: 3452 5051 5072 3714 Bolts, metal; screws, metal; washers, metal; steel; wire; bolts; screws; washers (hardware); miscellaneous fasteners; motor vehicle parts & accessories

Van Buren Twp
Wayne County

(G-17505)
5W LLC
847 Sumpter Rd (48111-4905)
PHONE..........................313 505-3106
Corey Wilcox, *CEO*
EMP: 10 **EST:** 2019
SALES (est): 570K **Privately Held**
SIC: 5961 2721 Toys & games (including dolls & models), mail order; magazines: publishing & printing

(G-17506)
A & B HOME ESSENTIALS LLC
8808 Ironwood Dr (48111-7420)
PHONE..........................734 334-3041
Dwayna Allen,
EMP: 5 **EST:** 2020
SALES (est): 139.9K **Privately Held**
SIC: 2099 Food preparations

(G-17507)
AEL/SPAN LLC (PA)
41775 Ecorse Rd Ste 100 (48111-5165)
PHONE..........................734 957-1600
John Henderson, *President*
Albert B Louis, *Business Mgr*
Courtland Colding, *Vice Pres*
Kelly Asmussen, *Opers Staff*
Beth Lissner, *Controller*
▲ **EMP:** 40 **EST:** 2007
SQ FT: 185,000
SALES (est): 97.1MM **Privately Held**
WEB: www.aelspan.com
SIC: 4225 3625 General warehousing & storage; switches, electronic applications

(G-17508)
AMERICAN LITHO INC
8455 Haggerty Rd (48111-1607)
PHONE..........................734 394-1400
EMP: 4 **EST:** 2018
SALES (est): 70.8K **Privately Held**
SIC: 2752 Commercial printing, lithographic

(G-17509)
ANTHONY CASTELLANI
Also Called: Tsnap Services
7025 Fay Dr (48111-5316)
PHONE..........................248 579-3406
Anthony Castellani, *Principal*
EMP: 6 **EST:** 2011
SALES (est): 90.7K **Privately Held**
SIC: 3541 Machine tools, metal cutting type

(G-17510)
BAYLOFF STMPED PDTS DTROIT INC (PA)
5910 Belleville Rd (48111-1120)
PHONE..........................734 397-9116
Richard Bayer, *President*
Bob Richards, *General Mgr*
Trent Vondrasek, *General Mgr*
Chris Bayer, *Vice Pres*
Christopher Bayer, *Vice Pres*
▲ **EMP:** 98 **EST:** 1948
SALES (est): 25.2MM **Privately Held**
WEB: www.bayloff.com
SIC: 3469 Stamping metal for the trade

(G-17511)
BELL INDUCTION HEATING INC
41241 Edison Lake Rd (48111-2803)
P.O. Box 112, Belleville (48112-0112)
PHONE..........................734 697-0133
John P Dolski, *President*
John Dolski Jr, *Vice Pres*
Alta Dolski, *Treasurer*
EMP: 6 **EST:** 1978
SQ FT: 5,000
SALES (est): 608.8K **Privately Held**
SIC: 3398 Brazing (hardening) of metal

(G-17512)
BELLEVILLE LOUNGE LLC
Also Called: Belleville Hookah Lounge
9612 Belleville Rd (48111-1365)
PHONE..........................734 270-4977
Moe Chami, *Principal*
EMP: 5 **EST:** 2019
SALES (est): 133.1K **Privately Held**
SIC: 2253 Lounge, bed & leisurewear

(G-17513)
BOZZ LASHEZ LLC
9790 Andover Dr (48111-4368)
PHONE..........................734 799-7020
Dionna Townsend,
EMP: 4 **EST:** 2020
SALES (est): 39.6K **Privately Held**
SIC: 3999 Eyelashes, artificial

(G-17514)
CARSTILL WAGON PUB/TOASTY TOES
750 W Huron River Dr # 2 (48111-3321)
PHONE..........................734 325-7542
Marian Caldwell, *Principal*
EMP: 4 **EST:** 2016
SALES (est): 37.5K **Privately Held**
SIC: 2741 Miscellaneous publishing

(G-17515)
CARTER CREATIONS
847 Sumpter Rd (48111-4905)
PHONE..........................800 710-8055
Herman Carter, *Administration*
EMP: 4 **EST:** 2019
SALES (est): 173.4K **Privately Held**
SIC: 2759 Screen printing

GEOGRAPHIC SECTION
Van Buren Twp - Wayne County (G-17542)

(G-17516)
CASCADE EQUIPMENT COMPANY
43412 N Interstate 94 Ser (48111-2468)
P.O. Box 587, Belleville (48112-0587)
PHONE..................................734 697-7870
Timo Ruuskanen, *President*
EMP: 4 **EST:** 1982
SQ FT: 6,000
SALES (est): 800K **Privately Held**
WEB: www.cascadeequipment.net
SIC: 3589 7699 Car washing machinery; aircraft & heavy equipment repair services

(G-17517)
CENTURY FUEL PRODUCTS
51225 Martz Rd (48111-2565)
PHONE..................................734 728-0300
▲ **EMP:** 8 **EST:** 2012
SALES (est): 5.5MM **Privately Held**
WEB: www.centuryfuelproducts.com
SIC: 2869 Fuels

(G-17518)
CENTURY QUAL PRODUCTS
51225 Martz Rd (48111-2565)
PHONE..................................734 728-0300
EMP: 7 **EST:** 2017
SALES (est): 134.4K **Privately Held**
WEB: www.centuryfuelproducts.com
SIC: 3714 Motor vehicle parts & accessories

(G-17519)
CONSTELLIUM AUTOMOTIVE USA LLC (DH)
6331 Schooner St (48111-5366)
PHONE..................................734 879-9700
Pierre Vareille, *CEO*
Jeremy Leach, *President*
Nicolas Brun, *Vice Pres*
Ryan Jurkovic, *Vice Pres*
Jason Ellerson, *Project Mgr*
EMP: 137 **EST:** 2009
SALES (est): 99.9MM
SALES (corp-wide): 551.2K **Privately Held**
WEB: www.constellium.com
SIC: 3334 3341 Primary aluminum; aluminum smelting & refining (secondary)
HQ: Constellium Singen Gmbh
   Alusingenplatz 1
   Singen (Hohentwiel) BW 78224
   773 180-0

(G-17520)
CONTRACT WELDING AND FABG INC
385 Sumpter Rd (48111-2932)
P.O. Box 68, Belleville (48112-0068)
PHONE..................................734 699-5561
Harry Tinsley, *President*
Toni Golden, *Principal*
Thomas Tinsley, *Vice Pres*
EMP: 30 **EST:** 1980
SQ FT: 16,000
SALES (est): 7.1MM **Privately Held**
WEB: www.contractwelding.com
SIC: 3443 7692 3532 3531 Bins, prefabricated metal plate; welding repair; mining machinery; construction machinery; metal stampings; metal cans

(G-17521)
COUNTERPOINT BY HLF
44001 Van Born Rd (48111-1149)
PHONE..................................734 699-7100
Bob Bechthel, *Owner*
Charles Hood, *Owner*
EMP: 5 **EST:** 1972
SALES (est): 281.1K **Privately Held**
SIC: 2521 2531 2522 2426 Wood office furniture; public building & related furniture; office furniture, except wood; hardwood dimension & flooring mills

(G-17522)
D L R MANUFACTURING INC
44205 Yost Rd (48111-1125)
PHONE..................................734 394-0690
Dennis Hennells, *President*
EMP: 6 **EST:** 1996
SQ FT: 3,200
SALES (est): 599.6K **Privately Held**
WEB: www.dlrmanufacturing.com
SIC: 3599 Machine shop, jobbing & repair

(G-17523)
DENSO INTERNATIONAL AMER INC
Denso Manufacturing TN
8652 Haggerty Rd Ste 220 (48111-1848)
PHONE..................................248 359-4177
Glenn Puro, *Senior Mgr*
Aaron Walker, *Technician*
EMP: 5 **Privately Held**
WEB: www.denso.com
SIC: 3625 3694 Starter, electric motor; alternators, automotive
HQ: Denso International America, Inc.
   24777 Denso Dr
   Southfield MI 48033
   248 350-7500

(G-17524)
DIE SERVICES INTERNATIONAL LLC
45000 Van Born Rd (48111-1152)
PHONE..................................734 699-3400
Steven Rowe, *Exec VP*
Roy Perkins, *Safety Mgr*
Lester Grove, *Purch Mgr*
Gayle Ringrose, *Manager*
Daniel Solea, *Manager*
▲ **EMP:** 65 **EST:** 2010
SALES (est): 9.5MM **Privately Held**
WEB: www.dieservicesinternational.com
SIC: 3545 Machine tool accessories

(G-17525)
DIE-NAMIC INC
7565 Haggerty Rd (48111-1601)
PHONE..................................734 710-3200
Robert J Bologna, *President*
Jeff Carmack, *Vice Pres*
Chris Hayes, *Controller*
Candy Cook, *Bookkeeper*
EMP: 115 **EST:** 1978
SQ FT: 87,050
SALES (est): 15.4MM **Privately Held**
WEB: www.die-namic.com
SIC: 3544 Special dies & tools

(G-17526)
GENERAL MOTORS LLC
50000 Ecorse Rd (48111-1112)
PHONE..................................734 481-3555
Thomas Taylor, *Branch Mgr*
EMP: 7
SQ FT: 1,000,000 **Publicly Held**
WEB: www.gm.com
SIC: 3714 7538 Motor vehicle parts & accessories; general automotive repair shops
HQ: General Motors Llc
   300 Renaissance Ctr L1
   Detroit MI 48243

(G-17527)
GENTLE MACHINE TOOL & DIE
13600 Martinsville Rd (48111-2890)
PHONE..................................734 699-2013
Aaron R Gentle, *President*
William Majnaric, *Corp Secy*
EMP: 6 **EST:** 1940
SQ FT: 12,000
SALES (est): 634.3K **Privately Held**
SIC: 3599 Machine shop, jobbing & repair

(G-17528)
H L F FURNITURE INCORPORATED
44001 Van Born Rd (48111-1149)
PHONE..................................734 697-3000
Robert B Bechtel, *President*
Harold Becker Jr, *Exec VP*
Charles Hood Jr, *Treasurer*
EMP: 50 **EST:** 1972
SQ FT: 63,000
SALES (est): 9.7MM **Privately Held**
WEB: www.hlffurniture.com
SIC: 2521 5712 2541 2511 Wood office filing cabinets & bookcases; wood office desks & tables; furniture stores; wood partitions & fixtures; wood household furniture

(G-17529)
HONEY TREE
9624 Belleville Rd (48111-1365)
PHONE..................................734 697-1000
Al George, *Manager*
EMP: 6 **EST:** 2008
SALES (est): 235.9K **Privately Held**
WEB: www.honeytreegrille.com
SIC: 2099 Food preparations

(G-17530)
INDUSTRIAL COMPUTER & CONTROLS
43774 Bemis Rd (48111-8765)
PHONE..................................734 697-4152
Louis G Kovach II, *President*
EMP: 10 **EST:** 1991
SQ FT: 3,500
SALES (est): 790.5K **Privately Held**
SIC: 3625 3621 Relays & industrial controls; motors & generators

(G-17531)
JOHNSON CONTROLS INC
41873 Ecorse Rd (48111-5227)
PHONE..................................313 842-3479
Denise Stinson, *Branch Mgr*
EMP: 4 **Publicly Held**
WEB: www.johnsoncontrols.com
SIC: 3585 Refrigeration & heating equipment
HQ: Johnson Controls, Inc.
   5757 N Green Bay Ave
   Glendale WI 53209
   800 382-2804

(G-17532)
KAGE GROUP LLC
Also Called: Esgar Products
13835 Basswood Cir (48111-2018)
PHONE..................................734 604-5052
Kudakwashe Garaba,
EMP: 6 **EST:** 2006
SALES (est): 294.7K **Privately Held**
SIC: 2819 8748 Sodium compounds or salts, inorg., ex. refined sod. chloride; business consulting

(G-17533)
KERNS WOOD WORKS LLC
49946 W Huron River Dr (48111-2576)
PHONE..................................734 368-1951
Matthew Kerns, *Principal*
EMP: 4 **EST:** 2017
SALES (est): 60.5K **Privately Held**
SIC: 2431 Millwork

(G-17534)
KREBS TOOL INC
611 Savage Rd (48111-2954)
P.O. Box 398, Belleville (48112-0398)
PHONE..................................734 697-8611
Allan D Krebs, *President*
Jeff Krebs, *Vice Pres*
EMP: 5 **EST:** 1986
SQ FT: 6,000
SALES (est): 450.4K **Privately Held**
SIC: 3545 Cutting tools for machine tools

(G-17535)
L & W INC
Also Called: L&W Engineering Co Plant 1
6771 Haggerty Rd (48111-5271)
PHONE..................................734 397-8085
Kevin Pires, *Manager*
EMP: 7
SALES (corp-wide): 3.1B **Privately Held**
WEB: www.autokiniton.com
SIC: 3465 3469 3441 Automotive stampings; metal stampings; fabricated structural metal
HQ: L & W, Inc.
   17757 Woodland Dr
   New Boston MI 48164
   734 397-6300

(G-17536)
L & W INC
Also Called: L & W Engineering Co Plant 2
6201 Haggerty Rd (48111-1137)
PHONE..................................734 397-2212
Al Henry, *Branch Mgr*
EMP: 7

SALES (corp-wide): 3.1B **Privately Held**
WEB: www.autokiniton.com
SIC: 3465 3443 Automotive stampings; bins, prefabricated metal plate
HQ: L & W, Inc.
   17757 Woodland Dr
   New Boston MI 48164
   734 397-6300

(G-17537)
L & W MEXICO LLC (DH)
6301 Haggerty Rd (48111)
PHONE..................................734 397-6300
Scott Jones, *President*
EMP: 100 **EST:** 2007
SALES (est): 10MM
SALES (corp-wide): 3.1B **Privately Held**
WEB: www.autokiniton.com
SIC: 3465 Automotive stampings
HQ: L & W, Inc.
   17757 Woodland Dr
   New Boston MI 48164
   734 397-6300

(G-17538)
MAYSER USA INC
6200 Schooner St (48111-5312)
PHONE..................................734 858-1290
William Fournier, *CEO*
Carl Robertson, *COO*
Julius Rummel, *CFO*
Scott Behr, *Sales Engr*
Clay Mitchem, *Manager*
EMP: 85 **EST:** 2008
SALES (est): 8MM **Privately Held**
WEB: www.mayser.us
SIC: 3714 5013 Motor vehicle parts & accessories; motor vehicle supplies & new parts

(G-17539)
MICHIGAN PAVING AND MTLS CO
1785 Rawsonville Rd (48111-1242)
PHONE..................................734 485-1717
Alan Sandell, *Branch Mgr*
EMP: 20
SALES (corp-wide): 27.5B **Privately Held**
WEB: www.michiganpaving.com
SIC: 2951 1611 Asphalt paving mixtures & blocks; highway & street construction
HQ: Michigan Paving And Materials Company
   2575 S Haggerty Rd # 100
   Canton MI 48188
   734 397-2050

(G-17540)
MIRRAGE LTD
8300 Belleville Rd (48111-1380)
P.O. Box 607, Belleville (48112-0607)
PHONE..................................734 697-6447
Mr Raymond Price, *President*
Linda Price, *Admin Sec*
EMP: 9 **EST:** 1979
SALES (est): 370.8K **Privately Held**
WEB: www.vacuum-metallizer.com
SIC: 3479 Coating of metals & formed products

(G-17541)
MJS PUBLISHING GROUP
41500 Bellridge Blvd (48111-1524)
PHONE..................................734 391-7370
Tokay Stanley, *Principal*
EMP: 4 **EST:** 2016
SALES (est): 37.5K **Privately Held**
SIC: 2741 Miscellaneous publishing

(G-17542)
MOUNTAIN MACHINE LLC
7850 Rawsonville Rd (48111-2344)
PHONE..................................734 480-2200
Michael Palmer, *Vice Pres*
Edward Larsen, *Supervisor*
Brian Napier, *Asst Director*
Stephen Ortner,
EMP: 17 **EST:** 1992
SALES (est): 2.6MM **Privately Held**
WEB: www.mountainmachine.net
SIC: 3559 3451 3599 Automotive related machinery; screw machine products; machine & other job shop work; machine shop, jobbing & repair; custom machinery

Van Buren Twp - Wayne County (G-17543)

GEOGRAPHIC SECTION

(G-17543)
NEAPCO DRIVELINES LLC
Belleville Plant
6735 Haggerty Rd (48111-5271)
PHONE..................................734 447-1316
Scott Kalkofen, *Branch Mgr*
EMP: 400 **Privately Held**
WEB: www.neapco.com
SIC: 3714 Transmission housings or parts, motor vehicle
HQ: Neapco Drivelines, Llc
6735 Haggerty Rd
Van Buren Twp MI 48111

(G-17544)
NEAPCO DRIVELINES LLC (DH)
6735 Haggerty Rd (48111-5271)
PHONE..................................734 447-1300
Kenneth Hopkins, *CEO*
Robert Hawkey, *President*
J Robert Mangini, *COO*
Alia Comai, *Vice Pres*
Tim Goode, *Vice Pres*
▲ **EMP:** 105 **EST:** 2007
SALES (est): 97.6MM **Privately Held**
WEB: www.neapco.com
SIC: 3714 Transmission housings or parts, motor vehicle

(G-17545)
PACIFIC OIL RESOURCES INC
44141 Yost Rd (48111-1153)
PHONE..................................734 397-1120
James K Dowling Jr, *President*
Tim Dowling, *Officer*
EMP: 8
SALES (est): 411.1K **Privately Held**
WEB: www.justbloomsbyjen.com
SIC: 2911 5172 Oils, fuel; fuel oil

(G-17546)
PAICH RAILWORKS INC
41275 Van Born Rd (48111-1147)
PHONE..................................734 397-2424
Mike Paich, *President*
Michael B Paich, *Vice Pres*
EMP: 6 **EST:** 1987
SQ FT: 5,000
SALES (est): 836.8K **Privately Held**
SIC: 3312 Rails, steel or iron

(G-17547)
PISTON AUTOMOTIVE LLC
8500 Haggerty Rd (48111-1821)
PHONE..................................313 541-8789
Robert Ajersch, *General Mgr*
EMP: 70
SALES (corp-wide): 2.3B **Privately Held**
WEB: www.pistongroup.com
SIC: 3714 Motor vehicle parts & accessories
HQ: Piston Automotive, L.L.C.
12723 Telegraph Rd Ste 1
Redford MI 48239
313 541-8674

(G-17548)
PLANT DF
41133 Van Born Rd Ste 205 (48111-1199)
PHONE..................................734 397-0397
▲ **EMP:** 25 **EST:** 2008
SALES (est): 1.4MM **Privately Held**
SIC: 2273 Mfg Carpets/Rugs

(G-17549)
R E B TOOL INC
Also Called: REB Tool Company
5910 Belleville Rd (48111-1120)
PHONE..................................734 397-9116
Richard Bayer, *President*
▲ **EMP:** 52 **EST:** 1978
SALES (est): 484.7K **Privately Held**
WEB: www.bayloff.com
SIC: 3544 Special dies & tools; jigs & fixtures

(G-17550)
REAL INK PUBLISHING LLC
48450 Denton Rd Apt 103 (48111-1975)
PHONE..................................313 766-1344
Jerome Williams, *CEO*
EMP: 4 **EST:** 2014
SALES (est): 284.7K **Privately Held**
SIC: 2731 2711 Textbooks: publishing only, not printed on site; newspapers, publishing & printing

(G-17551)
REPUBLIC DIE & TOOL CO
45000 Van Born Rd (48111-1152)
P.O. Box 339, Belleville (48112-0339)
PHONE..................................734 699-3400
John C Lasko, *President*
Charles B Zimmerman, *Admin Sec*
EMP: 37 **EST:** 1947
SQ FT: 250,000
SALES (est): 373.2K **Privately Held**
WEB: www.dieservicesinternational.com
SIC: 3469 Stamping metal for the trade

(G-17552)
SHAW INDUSTRIES DETROIT RDC
41133 Van Born Rd Ste 205 (48111-1199)
PHONE..................................800 469-9516
Chad Filek, *Opers Staff*
EMP: 5 **EST:** 2016
SALES (est): 52.4K **Privately Held**
SIC: 3999 Manufacturing industries

(G-17553)
SMW MFG INC (HQ)
8707 Samuel Barton Dr (48111-1600)
PHONE..................................517 596-3300
Robert Dunford, *President*
Doug Lance, *Plant Mgr*
Mike Kavanaugh, *Materials Mgr*
Bobbie Dunford, *Mfg Staff*
Lou Hampton, *Production*
EMP: 58 **EST:** 2004
SALES (est): 53MM
SALES (corp-wide): 2.4B **Privately Held**
WEB: www.smw-mfg.com
SIC: 3599 Machine shop, jobbing & repair
PA: Amsted Industries Incorporated
180 N Stetson Ave # 1800
Chicago IL 60601
312 645-1700

(G-17554)
SPAN AMERICA DETROIT INC
41775 Ecorse Rd Ste 100 (48111-5165)
PHONE..................................734 957-1600
Birindra Singh Jind, *President*
◆ **EMP:** 11 **EST:** 2003
SQ FT: 100,000
SALES (est): 239.9K **Privately Held**
SIC: 4226 3465 Special warehousing & storage; automotive stampings

(G-17555)
STATEWIDE BORING AND MCH INC
6401 Haggerty Rd (48111-5116)
PHONE..................................734 397-5950
Michael William Thomas, *President*
EMP: 30 **EST:** 1989
SQ FT: 34,100
SALES (est): 3.2MM **Privately Held**
WEB: www.idealfab.com
SIC: 3599 Machine shop, jobbing & repair

(G-17556)
TAYLOR SCREW PRODUCTS COMPANY
16894 Haggerty Rd (48111-6008)
P.O. Box 549, Belleville (48112-0549)
PHONE..................................734 697-8018
Kathleen Kondzer, *President*
Kim Kondzer, *Vice Pres*
EMP: 7 **EST:** 1974
SQ FT: 6,000
SALES (est): 2MM **Privately Held**
WEB: www.taylorscrewproducts.com
SIC: 3451 Screw machine products

(G-17557)
THE ENVELOPE PRINTERY INC (PA)
8979 Samuel Barton Dr (48111-1600)
PHONE..................................734 398-7700
David Hamilton, *President*
Ken Hamilton, *Vice Pres*
John Marks, *Plant Engr*
EMP: 74 **EST:** 1985
SQ FT: 73,258
SALES (est): 14.6MM **Privately Held**
WEB: www.envelopeprintery.com
SIC: 2677 2759 2791 2752 Envelopes; envelopes: printing; typesetting; commercial printing, lithographic

(G-17558)
VISTEON CORPORATION (PA)
1 Village Center Dr (48111-5711)
PHONE..................................734 627-7384
Francis M Scricco, *Ch of Bd*
Sachin S Lawande, *President*
Matthew M Cole, *Senior VP*
Jochen Ladwig, *Senior VP*
Joao Paulo Ribeiro, *Senior VP*
EMP: 8672 **EST:** 2000
SALES (est): 2.5B **Publicly Held**
WEB: www.visteon.com
SIC: 3714 Motor vehicle engines & parts

(G-17559)
VISTEON ELECTRONICS CORP
1 Village Center Dr (48111-5711)
PHONE..................................800 847-8366
Timothy D Leuliette, *CEO*
EMP: 61 **EST:** 2007
SALES (est): 6.4MM
SALES (corp-wide): 2.5B **Publicly Held**
WEB: www.visteon.com
SIC: 3714 Motor vehicle parts & accessories
PA: Visteon Corporation
1 Village Center Dr
Van Buren Twp MI 48111
734 627-7384

(G-17560)
VISTEON GLOBAL ELECTRONICS INC (HQ)
1 Village Center Dr (48111-5711)
PHONE..................................800 847-8366
Martin T Thall, *President*
Robert R Krakowiak, *Treasurer*
Jennifer Pretzel, *Treasurer*
Heidi A Sepanik, *Admin Sec*
Peter M Ziparo, *Admin Sec*
EMP: 4 **EST:** 2014
SALES (est): 25.8MM
SALES (corp-wide): 2.5B **Publicly Held**
WEB: www.visteon.com
SIC: 3714 Motor vehicle parts & accessories
PA: Visteon Corporation
1 Village Center Dr
Van Buren Twp MI 48111
734 627-7384

(G-17561)
VISTEON INTL HOLDINGS INC (HQ)
Also Called: Visteon International Business
1 Village Center Dr (48111-5711)
PHONE..................................734 710-2000
Brian P Casey, *Treasurer*
EMP: 1175 **EST:** 1999
SALES (est): 11MM
SALES (corp-wide): 2.5B **Publicly Held**
WEB: www.visteon.com
SIC: 3711 Motor vehicles & car bodies
PA: Visteon Corporation
1 Village Center Dr
Van Buren Twp MI 48111
734 627-7384

(G-17562)
VISTEON SYSTEMS LLC (HQ)
1 Village Center Dr (48111-5711)
PHONE..................................800 847-8366
Sachin Lawande, *Mng Member*
EMP: 201 **EST:** 1998
SALES (est): 128.8MM
SALES (corp-wide): 2.5B **Publicly Held**
WEB: www.visteon.com
SIC: 3714 Motor vehicle engines & parts
PA: Visteon Corporation
1 Village Center Dr
Van Buren Twp MI 48111
734 627-7384

(G-17563)
VSP LOGIS INC
41873 Ecorse Rd Ste 200 (48111-5226)
PHONE..................................734 957-9880
EMP: 8
SALES (corp-wide): 160.4K **Privately Held**
SIC: 3714 Motor vehicle parts & accessories
PA: Vsp Logis, Inc.
815 3rd Ave
West Point GA

(G-17564)
WINTER
13928 Kahla Dr (48111-1033)
PHONE..................................734 699-6825
Jennifer Winter, *Principal*
EMP: 5 **EST:** 2010
SALES (est): 129.5K **Privately Held**
SIC: 3273 Ready-mixed concrete

Vandalia
Cass County

(G-17565)
CONNELLS RESTORATION & SEALAN
16011 Hoffman St (49095-9530)
PHONE..................................269 370-0805
Robert Connell, *Administration*
EMP: 5 **EST:** 2017
SALES (est): 409.8K **Privately Held**
SIC: 2891 Sealants

(G-17566)
J AND L CUSTOM SERVICES
66252 Rainbow Rd (49095-9739)
PHONE..................................269 641-7800
Jeremy Gross, *Administration*
EMP: 6 **EST:** 2014
SALES (est): 232.8K **Privately Held**
SIC: 3499 0191 Fabricated metal products; general farms, primarily crop

(G-17567)
LA EAST INC
Also Called: Middlebury Trailers
62702 Woodland Dr (49095-9745)
PHONE..................................269 476-7170
James Bergan, *President*
Georgia Vangilder, *Corp Secy*
EMP: 12 **EST:** 2004
SALES (est): 318.7K **Privately Held**
SIC: 3731 Cargo vessels, building & repairing

Vanderbilt
Otsego County

(G-17568)
BUNKER & SONS SAWMILL LLC
119 Alexander Rd (49795-9707)
PHONE..................................989 983-2715
Jim Bunker, *Mng Member*
Cathy Bunker,
Daniel Bunker,
EMP: 7 **EST:** 1961
SALES (est): 440.2K **Privately Held**
SIC: 2448 Pallets, wood

(G-17569)
DIRECTV DISH DOCTOR
11803 Dunham Rd (49795-9714)
PHONE..................................989 983-3214
Kelly Woodbury, *Principal*
EMP: 6 **EST:** 2010
SALES (est): 135.4K **Privately Held**
WEB: www.thedishdoctor.net
SIC: 3663 Space satellite communications equipment

(G-17570)
ELL TRON MANUFACTURING CO (PA)
11893 Old 27 Hwy N (49795-9713)
P.O. Box 416 (49795-0416)
PHONE..................................989 983-3181
Kay Anderson, *President*
Louis Holm, *Principal*
Craig Vantielen, *Vice Pres*
Lisa Holm, *Treasurer*
▲ **EMP:** 32 **EST:** 1972
SQ FT: 4,625
SALES (est): 2.9MM **Privately Held**
WEB: www.elltron.com
SIC: 3089 Injection molding of plastics

(G-17571)
JAMES R GOFF LOGGING
11328 Huffman Lake Rd (49795-9503)
P.O. Box 123 (49795-0123)
PHONE..................................231 420-3455
James R Goff, *Principal*

▲ = Import ▼ =Export
◆ =Import/Export

EMP: 6 **EST:** 2010
SALES (est): 106.4K **Privately Held**
SIC: 2411 Logging

(G-17572)
MAYVILLE ENGINEERING CO INC
1444 Alexander Rd (49795-9709)
PHONE.................989 748-6031
EMP: 84
SQ FT: 50,000
SALES (corp-wide): 357.6MM **Publicly Held**
WEB: www.mecinc.com
SIC: 3498 Tube fabricating (contract bending & shaping)
PA: Mayville Engineering Co Inc
  715 South St
  Mayville WI 53050
  920 387-4500

(G-17573)
MAYVILLE ENGINEERING CO INC
8276 Yuill Rd (49795-9528)
P.O. Box 426 (49795-0426)
PHONE.................989 983-3911
Greg Rippey, *Branch Mgr*
EMP: 84
SALES (corp-wide): 357.6MM **Publicly Held**
WEB: www.mecinc.com
SIC: 3498 Tube fabricating (contract bending & shaping)
PA: Mayville Engineering Co Inc
  715 South St
  Mayville WI 53050
  920 387-4500

(G-17574)
MEC
8276 Mill St (49795-9701)
P.O. Box 426 (49795-0426)
PHONE.................989 983-3911
Greg Rippley, *Principal*
EMP: 15 **EST:** 2017
SALES (est): 3MM **Privately Held**
WEB: www.mecinc.com
SIC: 3469 Stamping metal for the trade

(G-17575)
QUIGLEY CO
8276 Mill St (49795-9701)
PHONE.................989 983-3911
Carol Quigley, *Owner*
EMP: 6 **EST:** 2002
SALES (est): 89.8K **Privately Held**
SIC: 3714 Motor vehicle engines & parts

Vassar
Tuscola County

(G-17576)
ADVANCE VEHICLE ASSEMBLY INC
555 E Huron Ave (48768-1831)
PHONE.................989 823-3800
Asaf Cohen, *Principal*
EMP: 10 **EST:** 2015
SQ FT: 50,000
SALES (est): 654.6K **Privately Held**
WEB: www.civilianhumvee.com
SIC: 3711 Truck & tractor truck assembly

(G-17577)
ASTECH INC
5512 Scotch Rd (48768-9235)
PHONE.................989 823-7211
Alan Bukach, *President*
Rick Wark, *Shareholder*
EMP: 49 **EST:** 1987
SQ FT: 40,000
SALES (est): 9.5MM **Privately Held**
WEB: www.astechcast.com
SIC: 3624 3325 3369 3341 Carbon & graphite products; steel foundries; nonferrous foundries; secondary nonferrous metals

(G-17578)
C AND M CONSTRUCTION
5463 Van Wagnen Rd (48768-9738)
PHONE.................989 213-1955
Carrie Fisher, *Principal*
EMP: 5 **EST:** 2017
SALES (est): 63.6K **Privately Held**
SIC: 2431 Millwork

(G-17579)
LARSEN GRAPHICS INC
1065 E Huron Ave (48768-1816)
P.O. Box 1641 (48768-0641)
PHONE.................989 823-3000
Harold Larsen, *President*
Rita Whalen, *Accounting Mgr*
EMP: 21 **EST:** 1992
SQ FT: 17,000
SALES (est): 1.5MM **Privately Held**
WEB: www.larsengraphics.com
SIC: 2759 2752 2791 2396 Screen printing; commercial printing, lithographic; typesetting; automotive & apparel trimmings

(G-17580)
LOUIS J WICKINGS
4740 Waltan Rd (48768-8904)
PHONE.................989 823-8765
Louis Wickings, *Principal*
EMP: 4 **EST:** 2010
SALES (est): 201.9K **Privately Held**
SIC: 2241 Wicking

(G-17581)
SIMERSON INC
6088 Caro Rd (48768-9758)
PHONE.................989 233-1420
Matt Simerson, *President*
Matthew Simerson, *Principal*
EMP: 9 **EST:** 2005
SALES (est): 487.1K **Privately Held**
WEB: www.simersonsales.com
SIC: 3949 Bowling alleys & accessories

(G-17582)
STAR INK AND THREAD
221 N Water St (48768-1752)
PHONE.................989 823-3660
Shawn York, *Principal*
EMP: 5 **EST:** 2013
SALES (est): 124.1K **Privately Held**
SIC: 2759 Screen printing

(G-17583)
TUSCOLA COUNTY ADVERTISER INC
Also Called: Cass River Trader East
5881 Frankenmuth Rd (48768-9401)
PHONE.................989 823-8651
EMP: 12
SALES (corp-wide): 9.4MM **Privately Held**
WEB: www.tuscolatoday.com
SIC: 2741 7313 Miscellaneous publishing; newspaper advertising representative
PA: Tuscola County Advertiser, Inc.
  344 N State St
  Caro MI 48723
  989 673-3181

(G-17584)
US ENGINE PRODUCTION MI INC
555 E Huron Ave (48768-1831)
PHONE.................989 823-3800
Asaf Cohen, *Principal*
EMP: 5 **EST:** 2013
SALES (est): 460.2K **Privately Held**
WEB: www.usepinc.com
SIC: 3714 Motor vehicle parts & accessories

(G-17585)
WATERMAN TOOL & MACHINE CORP
1032 E Huron Ave (48768-1818)
P.O. Box 1674 (48768-0674)
PHONE.................989 823-8181
Francis Longuski, *President*
Elaine Zink, *Office Mgr*
EMP: 11 **EST:** 1972
SQ FT: 7,290
SALES (est): 1MM **Privately Held**
WEB: www.watermantoolandmachine.com
SIC: 3544 Special dies & tools

(G-17586)
WEBER STEEL INC
Also Called: Weber Steel & Body
3000 Bradford Rd (48768-9467)
PHONE.................989 868-4162
James Scherzer, *President*
Albert Scherzer, *Vice Pres*
EMP: 10
SQ FT: 25,000
SALES (est): 1.4MM **Privately Held**
SIC: 3599 5251 Machine shop, jobbing & repair; hardware

Vermontville
Eaton County

(G-17587)
DAD AND SONS FARMING LLC
790 S Shaytown Rd (49096-9529)
PHONE.................517 719-2048
Bryant Griffin, *Administration*
EMP: 6 **EST:** 2013
SALES (est): 339.5K **Privately Held**
SIC: 3523 Farm machinery & equipment

(G-17588)
HAIGHS MAPLE SYRUP & SUPS LLC
11756 Scipio Hwy (49096-9433)
PHONE.................517 202-6975
Larry Haigh, *Branch Mgr*
EMP: 4
SALES (corp-wide): 295.8K **Privately Held**
WEB: www.haighsmaplesyrup.com
SIC: 2099 Maple syrup
PA: Haighs Maple Syrup And Supplies Llc
  6903 S Lacey Lake Rd
  Bellevue MI 49021
  269 763-2210

(G-17589)
J&N CUSTOM WOODWORKING
2396 N Pease Rd (49096-9502)
PHONE.................517 726-0290
James Chupp, *Owner*
EMP: 5 **EST:** 2013
SALES (est): 205.2K **Privately Held**
SIC: 2431 1799 Millwork; kitchen cabinet installation

(G-17590)
MERITT TOOL & DIE
2354 N Pease Rd (49096-9502)
PHONE.................517 726-1452
Eugene Miller, *Owner*
EMP: 6 **EST:** 1989
SQ FT: 1,500
SALES (est): 2MM **Privately Held**
WEB: www.merittmanufacturing.com
SIC: 3599 Machine shop, jobbing & repair

(G-17591)
PRECISION TOOL INC
519 Allegan Rd (49096-9700)
P.O. Box 189 (49096-0189)
PHONE.................517 726-1060
James Noe, *President*
Benjamin Pierce, *Vice Pres*
John Johnson, *Technical Staff*
EMP: 20 **EST:** 1999 **Privately Held**
WEB: www.precision-tool-inc.com
SIC: 3599 Machine shop, jobbing & repair

(G-17592)
TIMBERVIEW WOODWORKING
6201 Brick Hwy (49096-9736)
PHONE.................517 726-0321
Eli Miller, *Principal*
EMP: 5 **EST:** 2019
SALES (est): 54.1K **Privately Held**
SIC: 2431 Millwork

Vestaburg
Montcalm County

(G-17593)
ADVANCED FARM EQUIPMENT LLC
5773 N Crystal Rd (48891-9706)
PHONE.................989 268-5711
Greg Merrihew,
EMP: 16 **EST:** 2004
SQ FT: 2,500
SALES (est): 2.4MM **Privately Held**
WEB: www.lenco-harvesters.com
SIC: 3523 Farm machinery & equipment

(G-17594)
M-A METALS INC
7470 N Crystal Rd (48891-8754)
P.O. Box 216 (48891-0216)
PHONE.................989 268-5080
Fax: 989 268-5080
EMP: 7
SQ FT: 7,300
SALES (est): 410K **Privately Held**
SIC: 3599 Mfg Industrial Machinery

(G-17595)
ROSE ACRES PALLETS LLC
4769 N Bollinger Rd (48891-9732)
PHONE.................989 268-3074
Allen Beachy, *Principal*
EMP: 6 **EST:** 2008
SALES (est): 93.7K **Privately Held**
SIC: 2448 Pallets, wood

(G-17596)
ROSE ACRES TALLETS
9932 E Kendaville Rd (48891-9738)
PHONE.................989 268-3074
Melvin River, *Office Mgr*
EMP: 5 **EST:** 2008
SALES (est): 86.9K **Privately Held**
SIC: 2448 Pallets, wood

Vicksburg
Kalamazoo County

(G-17597)
4 FLUTES MACHINING LLC
14024 S 36th St (49097-9542)
PHONE.................269 330-1313
EMP: 6 **EST:** 2015
SALES (est): 516K **Privately Held**
WEB: www.4flutesmachining.com
SIC: 3599 Crankshafts & camshafts, machining

(G-17598)
A & O MOLD AND ENG INC
301 N 4th St (49097-1045)
PHONE.................269 649-0600
Douglas Northup, *President*
Doug Northup, *President*
Dave Ellison, *Vice Pres*
Steve Harden, *Vice Pres*
Tom Rice, *Vice Pres*
▲ **EMP:** 45 **EST:** 1987
SQ FT: 15,000
SALES (est): 8.1MM **Privately Held**
WEB: www.aomold.com
SIC: 3544 Industrial molds

(G-17599)
BEACON TOOL INC
111 N Leja Dr (49097-1192)
PHONE.................269 649-3558
William A Gettig, *President*
Loene Gettig, *Treasurer*
Dale Schuring, *Admin Sec*
EMP: 13 **EST:** 1978
SALES (est): 861.1K **Privately Held**
WEB: www.springmillsmfg.com
SIC: 3544 Forms (molds), for foundry & plastics working machinery

(G-17600)
BRIDGE ORGANICS COMPANY
311 W Washington St (49097-1200)
PHONE.................269 649-4200
Edward J Hessler, *President*
Max Bruer, *Vice Pres*
Harold Karnes, *Vice Pres*
Verlan Van Rheenen, *Vice Pres*
David Buss, *Treasurer*
◆ **EMP:** 30 **EST:** 1997
SQ FT: 9,400
SALES (est): 4.3MM **Privately Held**
WEB: www.bridgeorganics.com
SIC: 2899 Chemical preparations

Vicksburg - Kalamazoo County (G-17601)

(G-17601)
CAL MANUFACTURING COMPANY INC
5500 E V Ave (49097-8315)
P.O. Box 180 (49097-0180)
PHONE..................269 649-2942
Barbara Morren, *CEO*
EMP: 6 **EST:** 1957
SQ FT: 15,500
SALES (est): 813.5K **Privately Held**
WEB: www.calmfginc.com
SIC: 7692 Welding repair

(G-17602)
CENTRAL ELEVATOR CO INC (PA)
18 Baur Ln (49097-8782)
PHONE..................269 329-0705
Suzanne M Schulz, *President*
Bertha Lindsley, *Vice Pres*
EMP: 11 **EST:** 1982
SQ FT: 5,000
SALES (est): 526.6K **Privately Held**
WEB: www.centralelevator.us
SIC: 7699 3534 Elevators: inspection, service & repair; elevators & equipment

(G-17603)
EIMO TECHNOLOGIES INC (DH)
Also Called: Eimo Americas
14320 Portage Rd (49097-7716)
P.O. Box 156 (49097-0156)
PHONE..................269 649-0545
Gary Hallam, *President*
Michael Nuyen, *Mfg Spvr*
Robert Hagle, *Engineer*
Jerry Pardeik, *Engineer*
Stephen Castronovo, *Senior Engr*
▲ **EMP:** 20 **EST:** 2003
SQ FT: 60,000
SALES (est): 20.5MM **Privately Held**
WEB: www.eimotech.com
SIC: 3089 3544 Injection molded finished plastic products; industrial molds
HQ: Nissha Usa, Inc.
1051 Perimeter Dr Ste 600
Schaumburg IL 60173
847 413-2665

(G-17604)
GREAT LAKES CHEMICAL SERV
125 N Leja Dr (49097-1192)
PHONE..................269 353-1841
EMP: 4 **EST:** 2020
SALES (est): 81.8K **Privately Held**
SIC: 2869 Industrial organic chemicals

(G-17605)
IMERYS PERLITE USA INC
Also Called: Harborlite
1950 E W Ave (49097-9777)
P.O. Box 100 (49097-0100)
PHONE..................269 649-1352
William G Blunt, *President*
Mark Miller, *Manager*
EMP: 10
SQ FT: 7,000
SALES (corp-wide): 3.2MM **Privately Held**
SIC: 2819 Industrial inorganic chemicals
HQ: Imerys Perlite Usa, Inc.
1732 N 1st St Ste 450
San Jose CA 95112

(G-17606)
KEN GORSLINE WELDING (PA)
2210 E Vw Ave (49097-7735)
PHONE..................269 649-0650
Ken Gorsline, *Owner*
EMP: 4 **EST:** 1989
SQ FT: 6,000
SALES (est): 150K **Privately Held**
SIC: 3441 Fabricated structural metal

(G-17607)
KEPCO INC
Also Called: Kalamazoo Electropolishing Co
145 N Leja Dr (49097-1192)
PHONE..................269 649-5800
Bill Hochstetler, *President*
Paula Hochstetler, *Vice Pres*
Nick Sertic, *Sales Mgr*
EMP: 18 **EST:** 1983
SQ FT: 20,000
SALES (est): 2.2MM **Privately Held**
WEB: www.kepcoinc.com
SIC: 3471 Finishing, metals or formed products

(G-17608)
MINIATURE CUSTOM MFG LLC
170 N Leja Dr (49097-1192)
PHONE..................269 998-1277
Steve Shoemaker, *Owner*
Tammy Waldron, *Purchasing*
▲ **EMP:** 22 **EST:** 2011
SALES (est): 11.7MM **Privately Held**
WEB: www.miniaturecustommfg.com
SIC: 3089 Injection molding of plastics

(G-17609)
NASH PRODUCTS INC
5750 E S Ave (49097-8479)
PHONE..................269 323-2980
Robert Kirsten, *President*
Richard Keith, *Treasurer*
EMP: 4
SQ FT: 5,000
SALES (est): 300K **Privately Held**
WEB: www.nashproducts.com
SIC: 3496 4225 4731 Miscellaneous fabricated wire products; traps, animal & fish; general warehousing & storage; freight transportation arrangement

(G-17610)
PRINTER INK WAREHOUSECOM LLC
Also Called: Ink-Refills-Ink.com
109 E Prairie St (49097-1256)
PHONE..................269 649-5492
Joe Briggs,
Fred M Medich,
▲ **EMP:** 9 **EST:** 2004
SQ FT: 5,500
SALES (est): 746.2K **Privately Held**
WEB: www.printerinkwarehouse.com
SIC: 2752 Commercial printing, lithographic

(G-17611)
RONNINGEN RESEARCH AND DEV CO
Also Called: Emergent Technologies Co
6700 E Yz Ave (49097-8374)
P.O. Box 70 (49097-0070)
PHONE..................269 649-0520
Darrel Myers, *CEO*
EMP: 175 **EST:** 1983
SQ FT: 50,000
SALES (est): 17.2MM **Privately Held**
WEB: www.ronningenresearch.com
SIC: 3544 8711 3089 Industrial molds; designing: ship, boat, machine & product; injection molded finished plastic products

(G-17612)
SCHMIDT GRINDING
202 E Raymond St (49097-1458)
PHONE..................269 649-4604
Jeff Schmidt, *Owner*
EMP: 4 **EST:** 2001
SALES (est): 347.4K **Privately Held**
SIC: 3479 Coating of metals & formed products

(G-17613)
STEWART SUTHERLAND INC
5411 E V Ave (49097-8387)
P.O. Box 162 (49097-0162)
PHONE..................269 649-0530
John C Stewart, *President*
William Moran, *Vice Pres*
Patricia Stewart, *Vice Pres*
Loretta Johnson, *Purch Agent*
Phil Bartholomew, *Engineer*
▲ **EMP:** 145 **EST:** 1958
SQ FT: 90,000
SALES (est): 22.2MM **Privately Held**
WEB: www.ssbags.com
SIC: 2671 2674 2672 Waxed paper: made from purchased material; paper bags: made from purchased materials; coated & laminated paper

(G-17614)
SUMMIT POLYMERS INC
115 S Leja Dr (49097-1193)
PHONE..................269 649-4900
Amy Clary, *Purchasing*
Cale Munson, *Purchasing*
Keith Bulifant, *QC Mgr*
Tracy Sibley, *Human Resources*
Jeff Mohney, *Manager*
EMP: 5
SALES (corp-wide): 590MM **Privately Held**
WEB: www.summitpolymers.com
SIC: 3089 Injection molding of plastics
PA: Summit Polymers, Inc.
6715 S Sprinkle Rd
Portage MI 49002
269 324-9330

(G-17615)
TWOSIXNINE STUDIOS
12140 Highview Shrs (49097-8351)
PHONE..................269 365-6719
Austin Estes, *Principal*
EMP: 5
SALES (est): 60.9K **Privately Held**
SIC: 7372 Application computer software

Vulcan
Dickinson County

(G-17616)
UNITED ABRASIVE INC (PA)
19100 Industrial Dr (49892-8825)
P.O. Box 98 (49892-0098)
PHONE..................906 563-9249
William R Paupore Jr, *Ch of Bd*
William R Paupore III, *President*
EMP: 11 **EST:** 1960
SQ FT: 35,000
SALES (est): 1MM **Privately Held**
WEB: www.unitedabrasive.com
SIC: 3291 5085 3829 2819 Abrasive products; industrial supplies; measuring & controlling devices; industrial inorganic chemicals

(G-17617)
VULCAN WOOD PRODUCTS INC
N1549 Sturgeon Mill Rd (49892-8679)
P.O. Box 125, Norway (49870-0125)
PHONE..................906 563-8995
Jeff Goudreau, *President*
Bob Kordus, *Vice Pres*
EMP: 12 **EST:** 2002
SALES (est): 561.8K **Privately Held**
WEB: www.vulcanwoodproducts.net
SIC: 2411 Fuel wood harvesting

Wakefield
Gogebic County

(G-17618)
COPPERWOOD RESOURCES INC
310 E Us Highway 2 (49968-1000)
PHONE..................906 229-3115
Denis Miville-Deschenes, *President*
Timothy Lynott, *Manager*
EMP: 12 **EST:** 2008
SALES (est): 711.8K **Privately Held**
SIC: 1021 Copper ore mining & preparation

(G-17619)
D & D DRIERS TIMBER PRODUCT
115 E Old Us 2 (49968-9217)
PHONE..................906 224-7251
Mike Drier, *President*
EMP: 5 **EST:** 2001
SALES (est): 362.3K **Privately Held**
SIC: 3469 Machine parts, stamped or pressed metal

(G-17620)
EXTREME TOOL AND ENGRG INC (PA)
999 Production Dr (49968-9210)
PHONE..................906 229-9100
Mike Zacharias, *President*
Trevor Meinke, *General Mgr*
Anthony Stella, *Prdtn Mgr*
Mike Haupert, *Production*
Chuck Hampston, *Project Engr*
▲ **EMP:** 76 **EST:** 1998
SQ FT: 30,000
SALES (est): 15.3MM **Privately Held**
WEB: www.extremetool.com
SIC: 3544 Industrial molds

(G-17621)
EXTREME TOOL AND ENGRG INC
703 Chippawa Dr (49968-9222)
PHONE..................906 229-9100
Mike Zacharias, *Branch Mgr*
EMP: 4
SALES (corp-wide): 15.3MM **Privately Held**
WEB: www.extremetool.com
SIC: 3089 Injection molding of plastics
PA: Extreme Tool And Engineering, Inc.
999 Production Dr
Wakefield MI 49968
906 229-9100

(G-17622)
GA DALBECK LOGGING LLC
205 N County Road 519 (49968-9580)
PHONE..................906 364-3300
George A Dalbeck, *Mng Member*
EMP: 12 **EST:** 2010
SALES (est): 0 **Privately Held**
SIC: 2411 Logging camps & contractors

(G-17623)
MILJEVICH CORPORATION
511 Putnam St (49968-1021)
PHONE..................906 224-2651
Kathleen Miljevich, *President*
Michael Miljevich, *Vice Pres*
Loralee Radowski, *Treasurer*
EMP: 9 **EST:** 1950
SALES (est): 508K **Privately Held**
SIC: 2411 Logging camps & contractors

(G-17624)
MLC OF WAKEFIELD INC
893 Cemetery Rd (49968-9443)
PHONE..................906 224-1120
Brian Miljevich, *President*
EMP: 16 **EST:** 1984
SQ FT: 4,000
SALES (est): 823.3K **Privately Held**
SIC: 2421 Sawmills & planing mills, general

(G-17625)
RANDALLS BAKERY
Also Called: Roger Randall Bakery
505 Sunday Lake St (49968-1339)
PHONE..................906 224-5401
Roger B Randall, *Owner*
Anamarie Randall, *Owner*
EMP: 9 **EST:** 1943
SQ FT: 1,250
SALES (est): 312K **Privately Held**
WEB: www.randallbakery.com
SIC: 5461 2051 Bakeries; bread, cake & related products

Wales
St. Clair County

(G-17626)
CUSTOM VINYL PRINTS
9001 Smiths Creek Rd (48027-3611)
PHONE..................810 841-4301
EMP: 4 **EST:** 2013
SALES (est): 146.8K **Privately Held**
SIC: 2752 Commercial printing, lithographic

(G-17627)
DLH ROLLFORM LLC
8990 Marquette Rd (48027-3710)
PHONE..................586 231-0507
Ken Hesse, *Owner*
Rick Humby, *Owner*
EMP: 4 **EST:** 2011
SALES (est): 437.6K **Privately Held**
WEB: www.dlhrollform.com
SIC: 3449 Custom roll formed products

GEOGRAPHIC SECTION

(G-17628)
GOODELLS EQUESTRIAN CENTER
8820 Sparling Rd (48027-1906)
PHONE..................586 615-8535
Charlotte Godfrey, *Executive Asst*
EMP: 4 **EST:** 2004
SALES (est): 107.7K **Privately Held**
SIC: 3111 Equestrian leather products

(G-17629)
INNOVATIVE MFG TECHNOLOGI
10086 Smiths Creek Rd (48027-3410)
PHONE..................810 941-4675
Robert A Hayes, *Administration*
EMP: 4 **EST:** 2018
SALES (est): 113.9K **Privately Held**
SIC: 3999 Manufacturing industries

(G-17630)
SIMPSON INDUSTRIAL SVCS LLC
9020 Green Rd (48027-2401)
P.O. Box 12, Goodells (48027-0012)
PHONE..................810 392-2717
Susan Dungan, *Mng Member*
EMP: 6 **EST:** 2004
SQ FT: 5,000
SALES (est): 782.4K **Privately Held**
SIC: 3531 3536 Cranes; hoists, cranes & monorails

Walker
Kent County

(G-17631)
ALTUS INDUSTRIES INC
3731 Northridge Dr Nw # 1 (49544-9140)
PHONE..................616 233-9530
Craig Vanderheide, *President*
Diane Schmitt, *General Mgr*
Eric Kahkonen, *Vice Pres*
Jeff Mirbaha, *Buyer*
Joe Hillebrand, *Accounts Mgr*
▲ **EMP:** 28 **EST:** 2001
SQ FT: 7,500
SALES (est): 5.5MM **Privately Held**
WEB: www.altus-inc.com
SIC: 3841 Surgical & medical instruments

(G-17632)
CHALLENGE MANUFACTURING
3079 3 Mile Rd Nw (49534-1323)
PHONE..................616 735-6500
EMP: 12 **EST:** 2019
SALES (est): 193.5K **Privately Held**
WEB: www.challenge-mfg.com
SIC: 3465 Automotive stampings

(G-17633)
CHALLENGE MFG COMPANY
3200 Fruit Ridge Ave Nw (49544-9707)
PHONE..................616 735-6530
Douglas Bradley, *Branch Mgr*
EMP: 10
SALES (corp-wide): 781.8MM **Privately Held**
WEB: www.challenge-mfg.com
SIC: 3465 Automotive stampings
PA: Challenge Mfg. Company, Llc
3200 Fruit Ridge Ave Nw
Walker MI 49544
616 735-6500

(G-17634)
CHALLENGE MFG COMPANY LLC
2969 3 Mile Rd Nw (49534-1321)
P.O. Box 141637, Grand Rapids (49514-1637)
PHONE..................616 735-6500
Doug Bradley, *Vice Pres*
EMP: 196
SALES (corp-wide): 781.8MM **Privately Held**
WEB: www.challenge-mfg.com
SIC: 3465 Body parts, automobile: stamped metal
PA: Challenge Mfg. Company, Llc
3200 Fruit Ridge Ave Nw
Walker MI 49544
616 735-6500

(G-17635)
CHALLENGE MFG COMPANY LLC (PA)
3200 Fruit Ridge Ave Nw (49544-9707)
PHONE..................616 735-6500
Bruce Vor Broker, *President*
Douglas N Bradley, *Vice Pres*
Douglas Bradley, *Vice Pres*
Boyd Vor Broker, *Vice Pres*
Keith O'brien, *Vice Pres*
▲ **EMP:** 500
SQ FT: 251,000
SALES (est): 781.8MM **Privately Held**
WEB: www.challenge-mfg.com
SIC: 3465 Automotive stampings

(G-17636)
DESIGN MANUFACTURING LLC
1700 Northridge Dr Nw (49544-9130)
PHONE..................616 647-2229
Brad Graham, *Mng Member*
Brian Cole, *Mng Member*
Bob Graham, *Mng Member*
Colleen Farrell, *Graphic Designe*
EMP: 20 **EST:** 2002
SALES (est): 3.6MM **Privately Held**
WEB: www.designmfg.com
SIC: 3089 Injection molding of plastics

(G-17637)
DIE TECH SERVICES INC
2457 Waldorf Ct Nw (49544-1472)
PHONE..................616 363-6604
Kelly C Darby, *President*
Casey Darby, *President*
Ron Bourque, *Vice Pres*
Kelly Darby, *Vice Pres*
Carey Gordon, *Human Res Mgr*
EMP: 48 **EST:** 2002
SQ FT: 27,000
SALES (est): 5.5MM **Privately Held**
WEB: www.dietechservices.com
SIC: 7361 3544 Labor contractors (employment agency); special dies, tools, jigs & fixtures; welding positioners (jigs)

(G-17638)
EMC EDUCATIONAL SERVICES LLC
1953 Kinney Ave Nw (49534-2115)
PHONE..................616 460-3345
Bogdan Adamczyk, *Principal*
EMP: 4 **EST:** 2016
SALES (est): 69.4K **Privately Held**
SIC: 3572 Computer storage devices

(G-17639)
FLEXIBLE STEEL LACING COMPANY
Also Called: Flexco
1854 Northbridge Dr Nw (49544)
PHONE..................616 459-3196
Gordon Meineke, *Principal*
Donald Twiss, *Project Mgr*
Doug Saunders, *Opers Mgr*
Joe Marchigiani, *Mfg Mgr*
Ken Rozhon, *Mfg Mgr*
EMP: 100
SALES (corp-wide): 106.6MM **Privately Held**
WEB: www.flexco.com
SIC: 3429 Metal fasteners
PA: Flexible Steel Lacing Company Inc
2525 Wisconsin Ave
Downers Grove IL 60515
800 323-3444

(G-17640)
HAVILAND CONTOURED PLASTICS
2168 Avastar Pkwy Nw (49544-1928)
PHONE..................616 361-6691
E Bernard Haviland, *President*
▲ **EMP:** 7 **EST:** 2010
SALES (est): 146.6K **Privately Held**
SIC: 3052 Plastic hose

(G-17641)
HERALD PUBLISHING COMPANY LLC (HQ)
Also Called: Advance Central Services Mich
3102 Walker Ridge Dr Nw (49544-9125)
PHONE..................616 222-5400
Michael Ply, *Vice Pres*
Craig Brown, *Sales Staff*
Kristofer Bego, *Manager*
Erin Sparks, *Manager*
Scott Beal, *Exec Dir*
EMP: 110 **EST:** 2007
SALES (est): 25.5MM
SALES (corp-wide): 2.8B **Privately Held**
WEB: www.advance.com
SIC: 2711 Newspapers, publishing & printing
PA: Advance Publications, Inc.
1 World Trade Ctr Fl 43
New York NY 10007
718 981-1234

(G-17642)
KENTWOOD PACKAGING CORPORATION
2102 Avastar Pkwy Nw (49544-1928)
PHONE..................616 698-9000
Thomas A Boluyt, *President*
Leonard R Vining, *Principal*
Jack Skoog, *Vice Pres*
Sharon Mesker, *Accountant*
Joe Wood, *Sales Mgr*
▲ **EMP:** 60 **EST:** 1977
SQ FT: 70,000
SALES (est): 18.5MM **Privately Held**
WEB: www.gokpc.com
SIC: 2653 3496 2821 2631 Boxes, corrugated: made from purchased materials; miscellaneous fabricated wire products; plastics materials & resins; paperboard mills

(G-17643)
KRUPP INDUSTRIES LLC (PA)
Also Called: Universal Spiral Air
2735 West River Dr Nw (49544-2013)
PHONE..................616 475-5905
Daniel Szleser, *Manager*
David C Krupp,
EMP: 87 **EST:** 2002
SQ FT: 18,000
SALES (est): 17.1MM **Privately Held**
WEB: www.usaduct.com
SIC: 3444 Ducts, sheet metal

(G-17644)
NBHX TRIM USA CORPORATION
3056 Wlker Ridge Ct Ste D (49544)
PHONE..................616 785-9400
Tim Theisen, *Engineer*
Tim Isley, *Branch Mgr*
Scott Miller, *Program Mgr*
Wayne Baatz, *Manager*
Dalynn Flinn, *Manager*
EMP: 16
SALES (corp-wide): 2.5B **Privately Held**
WEB: www.nbhx-trim.com
SIC: 3714 Motor vehicle parts & accessories
HQ: Nbhx Trim Usa Corporation
1020 7 Mile Rd Nw
Comstock Park MI 49321

(G-17645)
OLIVER PACKAGING AND EQP CO
3236 Wilson Dr Nw (49534-7505)
PHONE..................616 356-2950
Jerry Bennish, *President*
Matt Meyer, *Vice Pres*
Vance Matz, *Engineer*
Jennifer King, *Human Res Dir*
Aiemee Hendricks, *Accounts Mgr*
▲ **EMP:** 61 **EST:** 2010
SALES (est): 18.9MM
SALES (corp-wide): 1.8B **Privately Held**
WEB: www.oliverquality.com
SIC: 2675 3556 2672 Die-cut paper & board; bakery machinery; adhesive papers, labels or tapes: from purchased material
HQ: Oliver Healthcare Packaging Company
445 6th St Nw
Grand Rapids MI 49504
616 456-7711

(G-17646)
PIPP MBL STOR SYSTEMS HLDG COR
2966 Wilson Dr Nw (49534-7592)
PHONE..................616 735-9100
Craig J Umans, *President*
Erik E Maurer, *Chairman*
Tom French, *Opers Mgr*
Allen Jarboe, *CFO*
Keith Tolger, *CFO*
EMP: 150 **EST:** 2005
SALES (est): 5.8MM **Privately Held**
SIC: 5719 2542 Closet organizers & shelving units; fixtures: display, office or store: except wood

(G-17647)
PLASAN CARBON COMPOSITES INC (DH)
3195 Wilson Dr Nw (49534-7565)
PHONE..................616 965-9450
James Staargaard, *President*
Tricia Ong, *Business Mgr*
John Erhardt, *Mfg Staff*
Candace Bosch, *Production*
Melanie Kramer, *Buyer*
◆ **EMP:** 100 **EST:** 2006
SQ FT: 49,000
SALES (est): 49.6MM
SALES (corp-wide): 788.8K **Privately Held**
WEB: www.plasancarbon.com
SIC: 3714 Motor vehicle parts & accessories
HQ: Plasan Sasa Ltd.
Kibbutz
Sasa 13870
468 090-00

(G-17648)
PLASAN NORTH AMERICA INC
3195 Wilson Dr Nw (49534-7565)
P.O. Box 169, Bennington VT (05201-0169)
PHONE..................616 559-0032
John Cavedo Jr, *President*
Dalton Blackwell, *COO*
Christine Foley, *Engineer*
David Peterson, *Engineer*
Brett Maki, *VP Bus Dvlpt*
◆ **EMP:** 20 **EST:** 2009
SALES (est): 9.3MM **Privately Held**
WEB: www.plasan-na.com
SIC: 3795 Specialized tank components, military
PA: Plasan Us, Inc.
3195 Wilson Dr Nw
Walker MI 49534

(G-17649)
PLASAN US INC (PA)
3195 Wilson Dr Nw (49534-7565)
PHONE..................616 559-0032
Adrienne Stevens, *President*
Azriel Biberstain, *CFO*
Mary Beth Bennett, *Controller*
Molly Barnett, *Director*
EMP: 6 **EST:** 2011
SALES (est): 10.8MM **Privately Held**
WEB: www.plasan-na.com
SIC: 2655 8711 Cans, composite: foil-fiber & other: from purchased fiber; engineering services

(G-17650)
PREFERRED FLOORING MI LLC
2853 3 Mile Rd Nw Ste B (49534-1300)
PHONE..................616 279-2162
Daniel Gonzalez, *Mng Member*
Jose Gonzalez, *Mng Member*
EMP: 15 **EST:** 2010
SQ FT: 1,600
SALES (est): 381.3K **Privately Held**
WEB: www.preferredflooringmi.com
SIC: 5713 1752 2273 3069 Floor covering stores; resilient floor laying; floor coverings, textile fiber; flooring, rubber: tile or sheet; flooring contractor

(G-17651)
QUALITY EDGE INC (DH)
Also Called: Qe
2712 Walkent Dr Nw (49544-1439)
PHONE..................616 735-3833
Craig Rasmussen, *President*
Scott Rasmussen, *President*
Alex Wesseldyke, *Production*
Matthew Mercier, *Engineer*
Mark Bredeweg, *Design Engr*
◆ **EMP:** 72 **EST:** 2006
SQ FT: 180,000

Walker - Kent County (G-17652)

SALES (est): 30.3MM **Privately Held**
WEB: www.qualityedge.com
SIC: 3442 Metal doors, sash & trim
HQ: Marubeni-Itochu Steel America Inc.
150 E 42nd St Fl 7
New York NY 10017
212 660-6000

(G-17652)
QUIKRETE COMPANIES LLC
Also Called: Quikrete
20 N Park St Nw (49544-6906)
P.O. Box 89, Comstock Park (49321-0089)
PHONE 616 784-5790
Jeremy Burt, *Site Mgr*
Noel Nixon, *Branch Mgr*
Brenton Wallis, *Manager*
EMP: 5 **Privately Held**
WEB: www.quikrete.com
SIC: 3272 Dry mixture concrete
HQ: The Quikrete Companies Llc
5 Concourse Pkwy Ste 1900
Atlanta GA 30328
404 634-9100

(G-17653)
TECH GROUP GRAND RAPIDS INC
Also Called: West Pharmaceutical
3116 N Wilson Ct Nw (49534-7566)
PHONE 616 490-2197
Eric M Green, *President*
George L Miller, *Senior VP*
Daniel Malone, *Vice Pres*
Mike Treadaway, *Vice Pres*
Brian Meines, *Engineer*
EMP: 325 **EST:** 1984
SALES (est): 61.1MM
SALES (corp-wide): 2.1B **Publicly Held**
WEB: www.westpharma.com
SIC: 3089 Injection molding of plastics
PA: West Pharmaceutical Services, Inc.
530 Herman O West Dr
Exton PA 19341
610 594-2900

(G-17654)
TESA TAPE INC
2945 Walkent Ct Nw (49544-1481)
PHONE 616 785-6970
Bobbi Shoemaker, *Production*
Brian Walker, *Sales Staff*
Tom Dupont, *Branch Mgr*
Scott Smalley, *Technician*
EMP: 9
SALES (corp-wide): 12B **Privately Held**
WEB: www.tesa.com
SIC: 2672 3842 3644 2671 Tape, pressure sensitive: made from purchased materials; surgical appliances & supplies; noncurrent-carrying wiring services; packaging paper & plastics film, coated & laminated
HQ: Tesa Tape, Inc.
5825 Garnegie Blvd
Charlotte NC 28209

(G-17655)
TUBELITE INC (HQ)
3056 Walker Ridge Dr Nw (49544-9133)
PHONE 800 866-2227
Steve Green, *President*
W Robert Keyes, *Chairman*
Glen Barfknecht, *Vice Pres*
Tim Salach, *Vice Pres*
Dean Seger, *Vice Pres*
EMP: 127 **EST:** 1993
SQ FT: 250,000
SALES (est): 36.3MM
SALES (corp-wide): 1.2B **Publicly Held**
WEB: www.tubeliteinc.com
SIC: 3449 3442 3444 3354 Miscellaneous metalwork; window & door frames; sheet metalwork; aluminum extruded products
PA: Apogee Enterprises, Inc.
4400 W 78th St Ste 520
Minneapolis MN 55435
952 835-1874

(G-17656)
VISTA MANUFACTURING INC
Also Called: Facements
3110 Wilson Dr Nw (49534-7564)
PHONE 616 719-5520
Rick Nykamp, *President*
Ric Nykamp, *President*
Paul Knapp, *Vice Pres*
Dave Steil, *Vice Pres*
EMP: 50 **EST:** 2003
SALES (est): 10.1MM **Privately Held**
WEB: www.vistamfg-inc.com
SIC: 2542 Office & store showcases & display fixtures

(G-17657)
WEST MICHIGAN GAGE INC
4055 Rmmbrnce Rd Nw Ste 1 (49534)
PHONE 616 735-0585
Mike Zajac, *Owner*
Al Smith, *Principal*
EMP: 14 **EST:** 1999
SALES (est): 2.3MM **Privately Held**
WEB: www.wmgage.com
SIC: 2599 3714 3545 Factory furniture & fixtures; motor vehicle parts & accessories; machine tool accessories

Walkerville
Oceana County

(G-17658)
ARBRE FARMS CORPORATION
6362 N 192nd Ave (49459-8601)
PHONE 231 873-3337
C O Johnson, *President*
Jean Hovey, *Controller*
Andy Akins, *Manager*
Vince Miskosky, *Manager*
Alexander Marks, *Director*
▼ **EMP:** 300 **EST:** 2009
SALES (est): 28.4MM **Privately Held**
WEB: www.oregonpotato.com
SIC: 2099 0191 Food preparations; general farms, primarily crop

Wallace
Menominee County

(G-17659)
ADVANCED BLNDING SOLUTIONS LLC
W5649 County Road 342 (49893-9375)
P.O. Box 37 (49893-0037)
PHONE 920 664-1469
Keith Hanson, *Project Engr*
Paul Carter, *Regl Sales Mgr*
Nick Rhode, *Administration*
EMP: 29 **EST:** 2015
SALES (est): 4.2MM **Privately Held**
WEB: www.adv-blend.com
SIC: 3089 Plastic processing

(G-17660)
KOPACH FILTERS LLC
N3840 R 2 Ln (49893-9642)
PHONE 906 863-8611
James R Parrett, *Principal*
EMP: 8 **EST:** 2011
SALES (est): 669.4K **Privately Held**
WEB: www.kopachfilter.com
SIC: 3498 Piping systems for pulp paper & chemical industries

(G-17661)
PAL-TEC INC
14 Ln W5886 (49893)
PHONE 906 788-4229
Larry Palzewic, *President*
Barbara Palzewic, *Corp Secy*
EMP: 6
SALES (est): 250K **Privately Held**
SIC: 3325 Steel foundries

Walled Lake
Oakland County

(G-17662)
AERO INC
1010 W West Maple Rd (48390-2935)
PHONE 248 669-4085
Francis R Geisler III, *President*
Matt Koontz, *Sales Staff*
Steve Koontz, *Manager*
EMP: 18 **EST:** 1993
SQ FT: 21,000
SALES (est): 3.8MM **Privately Held**
WEB: www.aeroincmfg.com
SIC: 3441 Fabricated structural metal

(G-17663)
AMERICAN PLASTIC TOYS INC (PA)
799 Ladd Rd (48390-3025)
PHONE 248 624-4881
David B Littleton, *Ch of Bd*
John W Gessert, *President*
Jim Grau, *Treasurer*
Ruth W Littleton, *Admin Sec*
◆ **EMP:** 175 **EST:** 1962
SQ FT: 284,000
SALES (est): 44.6MM **Privately Held**
WEB: www.americanplastictoys.com
SIC: 3944 Craft & hobby kits & sets; automobiles & trucks, toy; dollhouses & furniture; doll carriages & carts

(G-17664)
BASIC RUBBER AND PLASTICS CO (PA)
8700 Boulder Ct (48390-4104)
PHONE 248 360-7400
David C Smith, *President*
Thomas P Smith, *Vice Pres*
Randy Klann, *Mfg Staff*
Mike Clemons, *Engineer*
Geraldine A Smith, *Treasurer*
EMP: 31 **EST:** 1972
SQ FT: 35,000
SALES (est): 5.1MM **Privately Held**
WEB: www.basicrubber.com
SIC: 3053 3069 3083 3061 Gaskets, all materials; sponge rubber & sponge rubber products; laminated plastics plate & sheet; mechanical rubber goods

(G-17665)
C F LONG & SONS INC
1555 E West Maple Rd (48390-3770)
P.O. Box 837 (48390-0837)
PHONE 248 624-1562
Craig Long, *President*
Ronald C Long, *Corp Secy*
John D Long, *Vice Pres*
EMP: 28 **EST:** 1950
SQ FT: 3,000
SALES (est): 2.4MM **Privately Held**
WEB: www.cflongandsons.com
SIC: 3273 5032 Ready-mixed concrete; concrete & cinder block

(G-17666)
DEDOES INDUSTRIES LLC (PA)
1060 W West Maple Rd (48390-2935)
PHONE 248 624-7710
David Pratt, *Manager*
EMP: 233 **EST:** 2017
SALES (est): 2.5MM **Privately Held**
WEB: www.dedoes.com
SIC: 3531 Construction machinery

(G-17667)
EAGLE GRAPHIC AND DESIGN INC
317 N Pontiac Trl (48390-3438)
PHONE 248 668-0344
Robert Williams, *President*
EMP: 4 **EST:** 2016
SALES (est): 69.8K **Privately Held**
WEB: www.eaglegraphics.com
SIC: 3993 Signs & advertising specialties

(G-17668)
ERIN INDUSTRIES INC (PA)
902 N Pontiac Trl (48390-3234)
PHONE 248 669-2050
Steve A Atwell, *President*
Steven A Atwell, *President*
Bruce A Robertson, *Vice Pres*
Mary E Bradburn, *Treasurer*
EMP: 22 **EST:** 1975
SQ FT: 20,000
SALES (est): 5.2MM **Privately Held**
WEB: www.erinindustries.com
SIC: 3498 5013 Tube fabricating (contract bending & shaping); automotive supplies & parts

(G-17669)
GREAT LAKES POWDER COATING LLC
1020 Decker Rd (48390-3218)
PHONE 248 522-6222
Dewain Diacono, *Mng Member*
EMP: 16 **EST:** 2009
SQ FT: 55,000
SALES (est): 1.9MM **Privately Held**
WEB: www.greatlakespowdercoating.com
SIC: 3479 3444 Coating of metals & formed products; sheet metalwork

(G-17670)
HUSKY ENVELOPE PRODUCTS INC (PA)
1225 E West Maple Rd (48390-3764)
P.O. Box 868 (48390-0868)
PHONE 248 624-7070
William Reske, *President*
Robert Muehl, *Vice Pres*
Brian Tabaczka, *CFO*
Brian S Tabaczka, *Treasurer*
Adam Muehl, *Sales Dir*
EMP: 90
SQ FT: 50,000
SALES (est): 21.2MM **Privately Held**
WEB: www.huskyenvelope.com
SIC: 2677 2759 Envelopes; commercial printing

(G-17671)
LAWSON MANUFACTURING INC
920 Ladd Rd (48390-3028)
PHONE 248 624-1818
Lillian Lawson, *President*
Edward Lawson, *Vice Pres*
EMP: 8 **EST:** 1968
SQ FT: 4,300
SALES (est): 231.9K **Privately Held**
SIC: 3599 Machine shop, jobbing & repair

(G-17672)
MEGA PRINTING INC
1600 W West Maple Rd D (48390-1915)
PHONE 248 624-6065
Mark Grimm, *President*
Ed Grimm, *Vice Pres*
EMP: 4
SQ FT: 1,800
SALES (est): 200K **Privately Held**
WEB: www.mega-printing.com
SIC: 2752 7334 Commercial printing, offset; photocopying & duplicating services

(G-17673)
PRO ADS AMERICA
19106 Alexa Dr (48390-5836)
PHONE 586 219-6040
Nabeel Shareer, *Administration*
EMP: 5 **EST:** 2015
SALES (est): 89.6K **Privately Held**
SIC: 2752 Commercial printing, lithographic

(G-17674)
RICHARDSON ACQSTIONS GROUP INC
Also Called: V-Line Precision Products
961 Decker Rd (48390-3217)
PHONE 248 624-2272
Mason Richardson, *President*
Thomas Leblanc, *General Mgr*
Robin Carano, *Plant Mgr*
Helen Ransom, *Finance Mgr*
Sean Zimmer, *Sales Executive*
EMP: 25 **EST:** 2015
SALES (est): 3.9MM **Privately Held**
WEB: www.vlineprecision.com
SIC: 3541 Drilling & boring machines

(G-17675)
SHAIS LDSCPG SNOW PLOWING LLC
995 N Pontiac Trl (48390-7055)
PHONE 248 234-3663
Shai Grossman, *Principal*
EMP: 5 **EST:** 2016
SALES (est): 69.9K **Privately Held**
SIC: 0782 3991 4959 Lawn & garden services; street sweeping brooms, hand or machine; snowplowing

GEOGRAPHIC SECTION

Warren - Macomb County (G-17703)

(G-17676)
TZAMCO INC (PA)
1060 W West Maple Rd (48390-2935)
PHONE..................248 624-7710
Nancy Amberger, *CEO*
Dave Pratt, *President*
Jason Strasser, *Engineer*
Paul Johnson, *Manager*
◆ **EMP:** 49 **EST:** 1941
SQ FT: 100,000
SALES (est): 6.7MM Privately Held
SIC: 3559 Paint making machinery

Warren
Macomb County

(G-17677)
313 INDUSTRIES INC
32518 Dequindre Rd (48092-1061)
PHONE..................313 338-9700
Rita Fields, *CEO*
EMP: 17 **EST:** 2018
SALES (est): 3.1MM Privately Held
WEB: www.313industriesinc.com
SIC: 3559 3812 Automotive related machinery; defense systems & equipment; acceleration indicators & systems components, aerospace

(G-17678)
A & B TUBE BENDERS INC (PA)
13465 E 9 Mile Rd (48089-2697)
PHONE..................586 773-0440
Joseph REA, *President*
Mary REA, *Vice Pres*
Salvatore REA, *Vice Pres*
Agnes REA, *Treasurer*
Nadalie REA, *Admin Sec*
EMP: 10 **EST:** 1960
SQ FT: 37,850
SALES (est): 1.7MM Privately Held
WEB: www.abtubebenders.com
SIC: 3429 3498 3732 3317 Marine hardware; tube fabricating (contract bending & shaping); boat building & repairing; steel pipe & tubes

(G-17679)
A & B TUBE BENDERS INC
23133 Schoenherr Rd (48089-4262)
PHONE..................586 773-0440
Diane Ashmore, *Branch Mgr*
EMP: 5
SALES (corp-wide): 1.7MM Privately Held
WEB: www.abtubebenders.com
SIC: 3498 Fabricated pipe & fittings
PA: A & B Tube Benders, Inc.
13465 E 9 Mile Rd
Warren MI 48089
586 773-0440

(G-17680)
A & M DISTRIBUTORS
31239 Mound Rd (48092-4736)
PHONE..................586 755-9045
David Agno, *Principal*
EMP: 4 **EST:** 1997
SALES (est): 354.2K Privately Held
SIC: 2951 Asphalt paving mixtures & blocks

(G-17681)
A C SUPPLY CO INC
21831 Schoenherr Rd (48089-2857)
PHONE..................586 776-2222
Thomas Devoogd, *President*
EMP: 11 **EST:** 1982
SALES (est): 87.2K Privately Held
SIC: 3589 Service industry machinery

(G-17682)
A G SIMPSON (USA) INC
Also Called: AGS Automotive Systems
24358 Groesbeck Hwy (48089-4718)
PHONE..................586 825-9000
EMP: 9
SALES (corp-wide): 365.5MM Privately Held
SIC: 3465 Body parts, automobile: stamped metal
HQ: A. G. Simpson (Usa), Inc.
6640 Sterling Dr S
Sterling Heights MI 48312

(G-17683)
A S I INSTRUMENTS INC
12900 E 10 Mile Rd (48089-2045)
PHONE..................586 756-1222
Chris Chiodo, *President*
David Chiodo, *Opers Staff*
EMP: 6 **EST:** 1981
SQ FT: 6,700
SALES (est): 1.3MM Privately Held
WEB: www.asi-instruments.com
SIC: 3829 Measuring & controlling devices

(G-17684)
AAA WATERJET AND MACHINING INC
23720 Hoover Rd (48089-1944)
PHONE..................586 759-3736
Cynthia Barna, *President*
EMP: 4 **EST:** 2008 Privately Held
SIC: 3499 Fabricated metal products

(G-17685)
AATANKS LLC
25110 Thomas Dr (48091-1336)
PHONE..................586 427-7700
Jeffery Martin, *Principal*
Samuel Miller, *Vice Pres*
Ralph Berg, *Treasurer*
EMP: 5 **EST:** 2000
SALES (est): 1MM Privately Held
WEB: www.aatanks.com
SIC: 3443 Tanks, standard or custom fabricated: metal plate

(G-17686)
ABC BORING CO INC
30600 Ryan Rd (48092-4953)
PHONE..................586 751-2580
Dave Duhaime, *President*
EMP: 40 **EST:** 1963
SQ FT: 25,000
SALES (est): 4.1MM Privately Held
WEB: www.abcboring.com
SIC: 3541 Boring mills

(G-17687)
ABC MACHINING & FABRICATING
6737 E 8 Mile Rd (48091-2989)
PHONE..................586 758-0680
Robert Kay, *President*
EMP: 10 **EST:** 1962
SQ FT: 11,000
SALES (est): 245.3K Privately Held
WEB: www.absmurraysprockets.com
SIC: 3599 Machine shop, jobbing & repair

(G-17688)
ACHS METAL PRODUCTS INC
22238 Schoenherr Rd (48089-5400)
PHONE..................586 772-2734
Richard Achs, *President*
Barbara Achs, *Vice Pres*
John Achs, *Vice Pres*
Michael Achs, *Vice Pres*
Patrick Achs, *Vice Pres*
EMP: 5 **EST:** 1967
SALES (est): 501.1K Privately Held
WEB: www.achsmetal.com
SIC: 7692 Welding repair

(G-17689)
ACME CASTING ENTERPRISES INC
2565 John B Ave (48091-4244)
PHONE..................586 755-0300
Jon Dooge, *President*
Eric Kriebel, *Vice Pres*
Kim Kriebel, *Admin Sec*
EMP: 4 **EST:** 1954
SQ FT: 12,250
SALES (est): 2MM Privately Held
WEB: www.acmecasting.net
SIC: 5051 3543 Castings, rough: iron or steel; foundry patternmaking

(G-17690)
ACME HOLDING COMPANY
Also Called: Acme Abrasive Co.
24200 Marmon Ave (48089-3808)
PHONE..................586 759-3332
Robert Beebe, *President*
EMP: 24 **EST:** 2003

SALES (est): 4.6MM Privately Held
WEB: www.acmeabrasive.com
SIC: 3291 Pumice & pumicite abrasive

(G-17691)
ADEMCO INC
Also Called: ADI Global Distribution
24749 Forterra Dr (48089-4376)
PHONE..................586 759-1455
Greg Carter, *Principal*
Roger Black, *Branch Mgr*
EMP: 6
SALES (corp-wide): 5B Publicly Held
SIC: 5063 3669 3822 Electrical apparatus & equipment; emergency alarms; auto controls regulating residntl & coml environmt & applncs
HQ: Ademco Inc.
1985 Douglas Dr N
Golden Valley MN 55422
800 468-1502

(G-17692)
ADIENT
Also Called: Johnson Controls
7500 Tank Ave (48092-2707)
PHONE..................586 753-3072
Todd Emmons, *Engineer*
EMP: 7 Privately Held
WEB: www.adient.com
SIC: 3714 Motor vehicle parts & accessories
HQ: Adient Global Holdings Ltd
3rd Floor 37 Esplanade
Jersey

(G-17693)
ADVANCED RUBBER & PLASTIC (PA)
3035 Otis Ave (48091-2325)
PHONE..................586 754-7398
Frank D Aquino, *President*
Karin Barachkov, *Corp Secy*
EMP: 2 **EST:** 1988
SALES (est): 1MM Privately Held
WEB: www.advancedrandp.com
SIC: 3069 3089 5085 Molded rubber products; injection molding of plastics; rubber goods, mechanical

(G-17694)
AIR SUPPLY INC
Also Called: A S I
21300 Groesbeck Hwy (48089-4920)
PHONE..................586 773-6600
Ronald Dicicco, *President*
Dean Huber, *Corp Secy*
EMP: 6 **EST:** 1993
SQ FT: 18,000
SALES (est): 827.6K Privately Held
WEB: www.airsupplymi.com
SIC: 3842 Respirators

(G-17695)
AJAX METAL PROCESSING INC
22105 Hoover Rd (48089-2566)
PHONE..................586 497-7000
Robert Holland, *Plant Mgr*
EMP: 189
SQ FT: 20,000
SALES (corp-wide): 21.8MM Privately Held
WEB: www.ajaxmetal.com
SIC: 3398 Annealing of metal
PA: Ajax Metal Processing, Inc.
4651 Bellevue St
Detroit MI 48207
313 267-2100

(G-17696)
AJAX TRAILERS INC (PA)
2089 E 10 Mile Rd (48091-1306)
PHONE..................586 757-7676
Michael G Paulina, *President*
Justin McMaster, *Sales Staff*
EMP: 14 **EST:** 1941
SQ FT: 16,800
SALES (est): 1.3MM Privately Held
WEB: www.ajaxtrailers.com
SIC: 3715 7539 5599 3792 Truck trailers; trailer repair; utility trailers; travel trailers & campers

(G-17697)
ALL PACKAGING SOLUTIONS INC
Also Called: Allpacks
20750 Hoover Rd (48089-3101)
PHONE..................248 880-1548
Robert Morales, *President*
Greg Morris, *Sales Staff*
EMP: 7 **EST:** 2016
SALES (est): 2.5MM Privately Held
WEB: www.allpacks.com
SIC: 2653 Boxes, corrugated: made from purchased materials

(G-17698)
ALTERNATIVE COMPONENTS LLC (PA)
24055 Mound Rd (48091-2039)
PHONE..................586 755-9177
Adam Clifton, *President*
Michelle Swallow, *Business Mgr*
Ty Oberlin, *Engineer*
Scott Warn, *Engineer*
Francis Steele, *Office Mgr*
EMP: 49 **EST:** 1995
SQ FT: 26,000
SALES (est): 8.6MM Privately Held
WEB: www.alternativecomponents.com
SIC: 3498 Coils, pipe: fabricated from purchased pipe

(G-17699)
ALUDYNE INC
24155 Wahl St (48089-2057)
PHONE..................248 506-1692
EMP: 1364
SALES (corp-wide): 1.5B Privately Held
WEB: www.aludyne.com
SIC: 3363 Aluminum die-castings
HQ: Aludyne, Inc.
300 Galleria Ofcntr # 501
Southfield MI 48034
248 728-8700

(G-17700)
AMERICAN AXLE & MFG INC
Also Called: AAM Metal Forming
30500 Ryan Rd (48092-1902)
PHONE..................586 573-4840
EMP: 7
SALES (corp-wide): 4.7B Publicly Held
WEB: www.aam.com
SIC: 3714 Motor vehicle engines & parts
HQ: American Axle & Manufacturing, Inc.
1 Dauch Dr
Detroit MI 48211

(G-17701)
AMERICAN BLOWER SUPPLY INC
Also Called: American Fan & Blower
14219 E 10 Mile Rd (48089-2162)
PHONE..................586 771-7337
Randall Morrow, *President*
▲ **EMP:** 30 **EST:** 1970
SALES (est): 6.4MM Privately Held
SIC: 5085 3444 Industrial supplies; sheet metalwork

(G-17702)
AMERICAN GRAPHITE CORPORATION
21756 Dequindre Rd (48091-2102)
PHONE..................586 757-3540
Kenneth R Smith, *President*
EMP: 6 **EST:** 1980
SQ FT: 5,000
SALES (est): 800K Privately Held
WEB: www.americangraphite.com
SIC: 3624 Carbon & graphite products

(G-17703)
AMERICAN METAL PROCESSING CO
22720 Nagel St (48089-3725)
PHONE..................586 757-7144
Gerald Pinkos, *President*
Ryan Currier, *Prdtn Mgr*
Dennis Pinkos, *Admin Sec*
▲ **EMP:** 33 **EST:** 1945
SQ FT: 30,000
SALES (est): 4.8MM Privately Held
WEB: www.amphт.com
SIC: 3398 Metal heat treating

Warren - Macomb County (G-17704)   GEOGRAPHIC SECTION

(G-17704)
AMERY TAPE & LABEL CO INC
4145 E 10 Mile Rd (48091-1508)
P.O. Box 1914 (48090-1914)
PHONE.................................586 759-3230
EMP: 8
SQ FT: 7,000
SALES (est): 390K **Privately Held**
SIC: 2759 Commercial Printing

(G-17705)
ANDROID INDUSTRIES-STERLING (HQ)
Also Called: Ai Warren
27767 George Merrelli Dr (48092-2792)
PHONE.................................586 486-5616
Darrel Reece, *Principal*
EMP: 19 **EST:** 2005
SALES (est): 12.8MM
SALES (corp-wide): 474.4MM **Privately Held**
WEB: www.android-ind.com
SIC: 3711 Motor vehicles & car bodies
PA: Android Industries, L.L.C.
2155 Executive Hills Dr
Auburn Hills MI 48326
248 454-0500

(G-17706)
ANGELOS CRUSHED CONCRETE INC (PA)
26300 Sherwood Ave (48091-4168)
PHONE.................................586 756-1070
Angelo Iafrate Jr, *President*
Dominic Iafrate, *Vice Pres*
EMP: 3 **EST:** 1970
SQ FT: 25,000
SALES (est): 1.2MM **Privately Held**
SIC: 2951 3273 5032 Asphalt & asphaltic paving mixtures (not from refineries); ready-mixed concrete; concrete mixtures

(G-17707)
ANTICIPATED PLASTICS INC
24392 Gibson Dr (48089-4310)
PHONE.................................586 427-9450
Glenn Pesti, *President*
Brian Pesti, *Plant Mgr*
EMP: 10 **EST:** 2006
SQ FT: 8,000
SALES (est): 1.3MM **Privately Held**
WEB: www.anticipatedplastics.us
SIC: 3089 Injection molding of plastics

(G-17708)
APEX BROACHING SYSTEMS INC
22862 Hoover Rd (48089-2568)
PHONE.................................586 758-2626
Leonard Bantleon Jr, *President*
Lisa Thomas, *Corp Secy*
Phil House, *Opers Mgr*
James See, *Opers Mgr*
EMP: 12 **EST:** 1990
SQ FT: 10,000
SALES (est): 2.1MM **Privately Held**
WEB: www.apbsi.com
SIC: 3541 3545 Broaching machines; machine tool accessories

(G-17709)
APPLIED VISUAL CONCEPTS LLC
Also Called: Ceiling Scenes
24680 Mound Rd (48091-2036)
PHONE.................................866 440-6888
Mark Jenzen,
▼ **EMP:** 6 **EST:** 2001
SALES (est): 100K **Privately Held**
WEB: www.ceilingscenes.com
SIC: 2759 Commercial printing

(G-17710)
ARCH MED SLTONS LEHIGH VLY LLC (HQ) ◆
25040 Easy St (48089-4100)
PHONE.................................603 760-1554
Elizabeth Rothwell, *President*
EMP: 100 **EST:** 2021
SALES (est): 22.2MM
SALES (corp-wide): 25.1MM **Privately Held**
WEB: www.archglobalprecision.com
SIC: 3841 Surgical & medical instruments

PA: Arch Medical Solutions Corp.
25040 Easy St
Warren MI 48089
603 760-1554

(G-17711)
ARCH MEDICAL SOLUTIONS CORP (PA)
25040 Easy St (48089-4100)
PHONE.................................603 760-1554
Paul Barck, *President*
EMP: 6 **EST:** 2019
SALES (est): 25.1MM **Privately Held**
WEB: www.archglobalprecision.com
SIC: 3841 Surgical & medical instruments

(G-17712)
ARM TOOLING SYSTEMS INC
2453 John B Ave (48091-4242)
PHONE.................................586 759-5677
Martin Merrell, *President*
Roger A Murrell, *Vice Pres*
Ronald E Murrell, *Vice Pres*
EMP: 18 **EST:** 1985
SQ FT: 3,000
SALES (est): 3.4MM **Privately Held**
WEB: www.armtoolingsystems.com
SIC: 5084 5251 3545 Machine tools & metalworking machinery; tools; measuring tools & machines, machinists' metalworking type

(G-17713)
ARTED CHROME PLATING
24657 Mound Rd (48091-2043)
PHONE.................................586 758-0050
EMP: 5
SALES (est): 504.7K **Privately Held**
SIC: 3471 Plating/Polishing Service

(G-17714)
ARTISAN BREAD CO LLC
Also Called: Bosco's Pizza Co.
25000 Guenther (48091-1375)
PHONE.................................586 756-0100
Donnie Smith, *President*
Donnie King, *President*
Wes Morris, *President*
Dennis Letherby, *CFO*
EMP: 38 **EST:** 2000
SALES (est): 4.1MM
SALES (corp-wide): 47B **Publicly Held**
WEB: www.tysonfoods.com
SIC: 2099 2052 Pizza, refrigerated: except frozen; pretzels
PA: Tyson Foods, Inc.
2200 W Don Tyson Pkwy
Springdale AR 72762
479 290-4000

(G-17715)
ARTJAY INDUSTRIES INCORPORATED
14200 E 10 Mile Rd (48089-2163)
PHONE.................................810 773-6450
Gerald W Imlay Jr, *President*
Gilles Teste, *Vice Pres*
Larry E Hughes, *Opers Mgr*
Gordon Raezler, *Controller*
Brian Susko, *Asst Controller*
EMP: 100
SQ FT: 6,000
SALES (est): 19MM **Privately Held**
SIC: 3089 Injection molding of plastics

(G-17716)
AS PROPERTY MANAGEMENT INC
Also Called: Admiral Box Company
25133 Thomas Dr (48091-1397)
PHONE.................................586 427-8000
Steven J Stanton, *President*
Annette Stanton, *Admin Sec*
EMP: 10 **EST:** 2000
SQ FT: 20,000
SALES (est): 1.9MM **Privately Held**
WEB: www.admiralboxco.com
SIC: 2449 Rectangular boxes & crates, wood

(G-17717)
ASC CUSTOM WOODWORKING LLC
31224 Gardendale Dr (48088-7355)
PHONE.................................586 855-8817

Adam Cuffar, *Principal*
EMP: 5 **EST:** 2016
SALES (est): 70.9K **Privately Held**
SIC: 2431 Millwork

(G-17718)
ASE INDUSTRIES INC
Also Called: Automation Service Equipment
23850 Pinewood St (48091-4763)
PHONE.................................586 754-7480
Carl Lepera, *President*
Robert Curtis, *Vice Pres*
Don Trewhella, *Technology*
EMP: 55 **EST:** 1988
SQ FT: 45,000
SALES (est): 6.9MM **Privately Held**
WEB: www.aseind.com
SIC: 3599 3535 1796 7699 Custom machinery; conveyors & conveying equipment; machinery installation; industrial machinery & equipment repair

(G-17719)
ASPRA WORLD INC
25160 Easy St (48089-4129)
PHONE.................................248 872-7030
Shalu Sinha,
Sameer Sinha,
▲ **EMP:** 100 **EST:** 2005
SQ FT: 8,300
SALES (est): 8.7MM **Privately Held**
WEB: www.aspraworld.com
SIC: 3714 Motor vehicle parts & accessories

(G-17720)
ASSI FUEL INC
8309 E 8 Mile Rd (48089-2955)
PHONE.................................586 759-4759
Samir Assi, *Principal*
EMP: 8 **EST:** 2013
SALES (est): 1.3MM **Privately Held**
SIC: 2869 Fuels

(G-17721)
B & B MOLD & ENGINEERING INC
25185 Easy St (48089-4132)
PHONE.................................586 773-6664
Gerald Kuhl, *President*
EMP: 5 **EST:** 1975
SQ FT: 7,500
SALES (est): 325K **Privately Held**
SIC: 3544 Special dies & tools; industrial molds

(G-17722)
B & L PLATING CO INC
21353 Edom Ave (48089-4953)
PHONE.................................586 778-9300
Eugene O Pirrami, *President*
Grace M Pirrami, *Admin Sec*
EMP: 6 **EST:** 1970
SQ FT: 5,000
SALES (est): 495.4K **Privately Held**
WEB: www.blplating.com
SIC: 3471 Plating of metals or formed products

(G-17723)
B & N PLASTICS INC
8100 E 9 Mile Rd (48089-2362)
PHONE.................................586 758-0030
EMP: 7
SQ FT: 8,400
SALES: 390K **Privately Held**
SIC: 3089 Mfg Plastic Products

(G-17724)
B-J INDUSTRIES INC
14440 Barber Ave (48088-4833)
PHONE.................................586 778-7200
Brian Drzewiecki, *President*
James Drzewiecki, *Treasurer*
Ann D Drzewiecki, *Admin Sec*
EMP: 5 **EST:** 1966
SQ FT: 5,000
SALES (est): 499.4K **Privately Held**
WEB: www.b-jindustries.com
SIC: 3599 Machine shop, jobbing & repair

(G-17725)
BAE INDUSTRIES INC (HQ)
26020 Sherwood Ave (48091-1252)
PHONE.................................586 754-3000
Jesse Lopez, *President*

Dutch Jones, *Exec VP*
Stephen Bruck, *Vice Pres*
Mark Doetsch, *Vice Pres*
Sam Bowers, *Buyer*
▲ **EMP:** 189 **EST:** 1970
SQ FT: 90,000
SALES (est): 47.5MM **Privately Held**
WEB: www.baeind.com
SIC: 3465 3469 Body parts, automobile: stamped metal; metal stampings

(G-17726)
BANNER BROACH INC
12978 E 10 Mile Rd (48089-2045)
PHONE.................................586 493-9219
Harold Porter, *President*
Ross Porter, *Vice Pres*
Amy Jeric, *Office Mgr*
EMP: 8 **EST:** 1992
SALES (est): 1MM **Privately Held**
WEB: www.bannerbroach.com
SIC: 3545 Cutting tools for machine tools

(G-17727)
BAR PROCESSING CORPORATION
22534 Groesbeck Hwy (48089-2680)
PHONE.................................734 782-4454
Fritz Michalk, *General Mgr*
Aeiph King, *Manager*
EMP: 13
SALES (corp-wide): 39.9MM **Privately Held**
WEB: www.barprocessingcorp.com
SIC: 3471 3444 3316 3312 Finishing, metals or formed products; polishing, metals or formed products; sheet metalwork; cold finishing of steel shapes; blast furnaces & steel mills
HQ: Bar Processing Corporation
26601 W Huron River Dr
Flat Rock MI 48134
734 782-4454

(G-17728)
BAUER PRECISION TOOL CO
Also Called: East Side Gear
8670 E 9 Mile Rd (48089-2453)
PHONE.................................586 758-7370
Anton Bauer, *President*
Melba Bauer, *Treasurer*
Jim Bauer, *Manager*
EMP: 5 **EST:** 1975
SQ FT: 4,000
SALES (est): 411.5K **Privately Held**
SIC: 3544 Special dies & tools

(G-17729)
BEHCO INC
23751 Amber Ave (48089-6000)
PHONE.................................586 755-0200
Stephen J Ellis, *President*
Mike Folster, *General Mgr*
Amanda Sprinkle, *Sales Staff*
Chris Cameron, *Manager*
Ron Clark, *Manager*
EMP: 19 **EST:** 1961
SALES (est): 7.4MM **Privately Held**
WEB: www.behco.com
SIC: 5084 3593 Hydraulic systems equipment & supplies; pneumatic tools & equipment; fluid power cylinders, hydraulic or pneumatic

(G-17730)
BELLE ISLE AWNING CO INC
13701 E 9 Mile Rd (48089-2766)
PHONE.................................586 294-6050
William J Belluomo, *President*
Gail Wilk, *Sales Staff*
EMP: 20 **EST:** 1930
SQ FT: 14,000
SALES (est): 1.2MM **Privately Held**
WEB: www.belleisleawning.com
SIC: 5999 2394 Canvas products; awnings; canvas & related products

(G-17731)
BERKLEY PHARMACY LLC
28577 Schoenherr Rd (48088-4330)
PHONE.................................586 573-8300
Munice Patel, *Owner*
Selma Dahalic, *Mktg Dir*
Chirag Modi, *Manager*
EMP: 13 **EST:** 2009

GEOGRAPHIC SECTION

Warren - Macomb County (G-17756)

SALES (est): 1.8MM **Privately Held**
WEB: www.berkleypharmacy.com
SIC: **2064** 2834 Cough drops, except pharmaceutical preparations; pharmaceutical preparations

(G-17732)
BEST BLOCK COMPANY (PA)
Also Called: Best Alloys
22001 Groesbeck Hwy (48089-4228)
PHONE..................................586 772-7000
Robert Pachota, *President*
David Pachota, *Vice Pres*
Michael Pachota, *Treasurer*
EMP: 40 EST: 1945
SQ FT: 60,000
SALES (est): 18.7MM **Privately Held**
WEB: www.bestblock.net
SIC: **5211** 3271 3272 0782 Concrete & cinder block; blocks, concrete or cinder: standard; concrete products; lawn & garden services

(G-17733)
BEST GRANITE AND MARBLE INC
11080 E 9 Mile Rd (48089-2455)
PHONE..................................313 247-3909
Elis Komnenovic, *Principal*
EMP: 8 EST: 2004
SALES (est): 1MM **Privately Held**
SIC: **1411** Granite, dimension-quarrying

(G-17734)
BEST INDUSTRIAL GROUP INC
7256 Murthum Ave (48092-1251)
PHONE..................................586 826-8800
John Edgell Sr, *President*
John Edgell II, *Vice Pres*
Dorothy Korgol, *Vice Pres*
Anita Edgell, *Treasurer*
EMP: 14 EST: 1986
SQ FT: 8,000
SALES (est): 6.5MM **Privately Held**
WEB: www.bestindustrialgroup.com
SIC: **5084** 1796 3535 Conveyor systems; machinery installation; conveyors & conveying equipment

(G-17735)
BI-RITE OFFICE PRODUCTS INC
Also Called: Copy Copy Center
3681 E 12 Mile Rd (48092-4184)
PHONE..................................586 751-1410
Brian Malinowski, *President*
David Malinowski, *President*
EMP: 4 EST: 1978
SQ FT: 1,650
SALES (est): 541.4K **Privately Held**
WEB: www.copycopycenter.com
SIC: **2752** Commercial printing, offset; menus, lithographed

(G-17736)
BILAR TOOL & DIE
24700 Mound Rd (48091-5332)
PHONE..................................248 740-3400
EMP: 4 EST: 2018
SALES (est): 88.9K **Privately Held**
SIC: **3544** Special dies & tools

(G-17737)
BILCO TOOL CORPORATION
30076 Dequindre Rd (48092-1899)
PHONE..................................586 574-9300
Gerald Ivey, *President*
Raymond Ivey, *Vice Pres*
EMP: 9 EST: 1970
SQ FT: 9,500
SALES (est): 934.3K **Privately Held**
WEB: www.bilcotool.com
SIC: **3544** 3545 Jigs & fixtures; gauges (machine tool accessories)

(G-17738)
BIOSAN LABORATORIES INC
1950 Tobsal Ct (48091-1351)
PHONE..................................586 755-8970
Leonard A Rossmoore, *President*
EMP: 15 EST: 1973
SQ FT: 10,000 **Privately Held**
WEB: www.biosan.com
SIC: **8731** 2835 3829 2836 Biological research; microbiology & virology diagnostic products; measuring & controlling devices; biological products, except diagnostic

(G-17739)
BOSCH AUTO SVC SOLUTIONS INC (HQ)
28635 Mound Rd (48092-5509)
PHONE..................................586 574-2332
Laura Manou, *Project Mgr*
Roy Rajeev, *Purch Dir*
Amber Fedyszyn, *Engineer*
Kevin Respondek, *Engineer*
Vickie Gamble, *Auditor*
▲ EMP: 89 EST: 2011
SALES (est): 101.2MM
SALES (corp-wide): 297.8MM **Privately Held**
WEB: www.otctools.com
SIC: **7549** 3714 Inspection & diagnostic service, automotive; motor vehicle parts & accessories
PA: R O B E R T B O S C H S T I F T U N G Gesellschaft Mit Beschrankter Haftung
Heidehofstr. 31
Stuttgart BW 70184
711 460-840

(G-17740)
BOSCH AUTO SVC SOLUTIONS INC
5775 Enterprise Ct (48092-3463)
PHONE..................................586 574-1820
Bob Wiegand, *Principal*
Denise Palazzolo, *Program Mgr*
Nathaniel Caudill, *Associate*
EMP: 64
SALES (corp-wide): 297.8MM **Privately Held**
WEB: www.otctools.com
SIC: **3443** Cooling towers, metal plate
HQ: Bosch Automotive Service Solutions Inc.
28635 Mound Rd
Warren MI 48092
586 574-2332

(G-17741)
BRAUER CLAMPS USA
25269 Mound Rd (48091-3857)
PHONE..................................586 427-5304
Mark Matzka, *President*
▲ EMP: 12 EST: 2004
SALES (est): 318.4K **Privately Held**
SIC: **3429** Manufactured hardware (general)

(G-17742)
BREAK-A-BEAM
25257 Mound Rd (48091-3857)
PHONE..................................586 758-7790
Tom Matzka, *CEO*
Mark Matzka, *President*
EMP: 5 EST: 1981
SALES (est): 173.7K **Privately Held**
WEB: www.new.break-a-beam.com
SIC: **5085** 3643 Bearings; current-carrying wiring devices

(G-17743)
BRIDGEWATER INTERIORS LLC
7500 Tank Ave (48092-2707)
PHONE..................................586 753-3072
Alison Sanders, *Manager*
George Gribbin, *Technology*
EMP: 600 **Privately Held**
WEB: www.bridgewater-interiors.com
SIC: **2531** Seats, automobile
HQ: Bridgewater Interiors, L.L.C.
4617 W Fort St
Detroit MI 48209
313 842-3300

(G-17744)
C & G NEWS INC
Also Called: Shelby Utica News, The
13650 E 11 Mile Rd (48089-1422)
PHONE..................................586 498-8000
Gil Demers, *President*
Jen Sakey, *COO*
Greg Demers, *Vice Pres*
Laura Gayan, *Accounts Exec*
Maria Kruse, *Accounts Exec*
EMP: 36 EST: 2001
SALES (est): 1.3MM **Privately Held**
WEB: www.candgnews.com
SIC: **2711** Commercial printing & newspaper publishing combined; newspapers: publishing only, not printed on site

(G-17745)
C & G PUBLISHING INC
Also Called: Advertiser, The
13650 E 11 Mile Rd (48089-1422)
PHONE..................................586 498-8000
Gregory A Demers, *President*
Charlotte Demers, *Principal*
Gilbert Demers, *Principal*
Michelle Moran, *Editor*
Nick Mordowanec, *Editor*
EMP: 67 EST: 1977
SQ FT: 10,000
SALES (est): 9.5MM **Privately Held**
WEB: www.candgnews.com
SIC: **2711** Newspapers, publishing & printing

(G-17746)
C E C CONTROLS COMPANY INC (HQ)
14555 Barber Ave (48088-6002)
PHONE..................................586 779-0222
Robert Scheper, *President*
Bob Scheper, *Vice Pres*
Dave Smith, *Vice Pres*
Chris Street, *Project Mgr*
Matthew Wezensky, *Buyer*
◆ EMP: 94 EST: 1966
SQ FT: 40,000
SALES (est): 42.5MM
SALES (corp-wide): 7.5B **Privately Held**
WEB: www.ceccontrols.com
SIC: **3823** Industrial instrmnts msrmnt display/control process variable
PA: John Wood Group Plc
15 Justice Mill Lane
Aberdeen AB11
122 485-1000

(G-17747)
C R B CRANE & SERVICE CO (PA)
3751 E 10 Mile Rd (48091-3722)
PHONE..................................586 757-1222
Craig R Benedict, *President*
Patricia Benedict, *Vice Pres*
EMP: 6 EST: 1983
SQ FT: 12,000
SALES (est): 548.6K **Privately Held**
WEB: www.crbcrane.com
SIC: **3536** 5084 7699 Cranes, overhead traveling; cranes, industrial; industrial equipment services

(G-17748)
CADILLAC PLATING CORPORATION
23849 Groesbeck Hwy (48089-6004)
PHONE..................................586 771-9191
Nick Salvati, *President*
Mahmood Ahmed, *Vice Pres*
John Kitchen, *Vice Pres*
EMP: 80 EST: 1957
SQ FT: 80,000
SALES (est): 6.8MM **Privately Held**
WEB: www.cadillacplating.com
SIC: **3471** Electroplating of metals or formed products

(G-17749)
CAEA AUTO ELCTRNIC SYSTEMS USA (DH)
30500 Van Dyke Ave Ste 20 (48093-2195)
PHONE..................................586 649-9036
Yi Zhu, *President*
Lei Liu, *General Mgr*
EMP: 18 EST: 2018
SALES (est): 1MM **Privately Held**
SIC: **3714** Motor vehicle parts & accessories

(G-17750)
CB FABRICATING & SERVICE
25215 Hoover Rd (48089-1101)
PHONE..................................586 758-4980
Chester Bulak, *Principal*
EMP: 13 EST: 2002
SALES (est): 90K **Privately Held**
WEB: www.cbfabricating.com
SIC: **3545** Machine tool accessories

(G-17751)
CERATIZIT USA INC
11355 Stephens Rd (48091-1802)
PHONE..................................586 759-2280
Tim Tisler, *President*
Chris Schulte, *Natl Sales Mgr*
Nathan Paxton, *Sales Staff*
Beckius Dawn, *Analyst*
▲ EMP: 200 EST: 1972
SQ FT: 75,000
SALES (est): 46.7MM
SALES (corp-wide): 6.5MM **Privately Held**
WEB: www.ceratizit.com
SIC: **3545** 2819 Cutting tools for machine tools; industrial inorganic chemicals
PA: Ceratizit S.A.
Route De Holzem 101
Mamer 8232
312 085-1

(G-17752)
CG LIQUIDATION INCORPORATED (HQ)
2111 Walter P Reuther Dr (48091-6108)
PHONE..................................586 575-9800
William P Baer, *CEO*
Frank Knoth, *President*
Ken Stallons, *President*
Jerry Makedonski, *Facilities Mgr*
Chris Wypych, *QC Mgr*
▲ EMP: 25 EST: 1965
SQ FT: 14,000
SALES (est): 56.2MM
SALES (corp-wide): 15.1B **Publicly Held**
WEB: www.ppg.com
SIC: **3479** 3471 Painting of metal products; plating & polishing
PA: Ppg Industries, Inc.
1 Ppg Pl
Pittsburgh PA 15272
412 434-3131

(G-17753)
CHASSIX BLACKSTONE OPERAT
23300 Blackstone Ave (48089-4206)
PHONE..................................586 782-7311
EMP: 5 EST: 2017
SALES (est): 139.4K **Privately Held**
WEB: www.aludyne.com
SIC: **3714** Motor vehicle parts & accessories

(G-17754)
CHEMICO SYSTEMS INC
6250 Chicago Rd (48092-2042)
PHONE..................................586 986-2343
Kurt Sladick, *Branch Mgr*
EMP: 4 **Privately Held**
WEB: www.thechemicogroup.com
SIC: **2819** Chemicals, high purity: refined from technical grade
PA: Chemico Systems, Inc.
25200 Telg Rd Ste 120
Southfield MI 48034

(G-17755)
CHROME CRAFT CORPORATION
5663 E 9 Mile Rd (48091-2562)
PHONE..................................313 868-2444
EMP: 120
SQ FT: 60,000
SALES (est): 12.6MM **Privately Held**
SIC: **3471** Plating/Polishing Service

(G-17756)
CLASSIC CAR PORT & CANOPIES
11800 E 9 Mile Rd (48089-2588)
PHONE..................................586 759-5490
Russ Dibartoloneo, *President*
Lisa Redd, *Administration*
EMP: 12 EST: 1989
SALES (est): 252.9K **Privately Held**
WEB: www.classiccarports.com
SIC: **3448** Prefabricated metal buildings

Warren - Macomb County (G-17757)

(G-17757)
CLASSIC WELDING INC
21500 Ryan Rd (48091-4669)
PHONE..................................586 758-2400
John Stoianov, *President*
Agnita Stoianov, *Vice Pres*
EMP: 10 EST: 1982
SQ FT: 3,000
SALES (est): 500K Privately Held
WEB: www.classicwelding.com
SIC: 7692 Automotive welding

(G-17758)
COLD HEADING CO (HQ)
21777 Hoover Rd (48089-2544)
PHONE..................................586 497-7000
Derek J Stevens, *Ch of Bd*
James R Joliet, *President*
William Buban, *Vice Pres*
Thomas Dharte, *Vice Pres*
Drayke Dondero, *Vice Pres*
◆ EMP: 74 EST: 1912
SQ FT: 602,000
SALES (est): 70.4MM Privately Held
WEB: www.coldheading.com
SIC: 3452 8711 Bolts, metal; engineering services
PA: Beachlawn Inc.
    21777 Hoover Rd
    Warren MI 48089
    586 497-7000

(G-17759)
COLD HEADING CO
22155 Hoover Rd (48089-2566)
PHONE..................................586 497-7016
Jim Yacks, *Plant Mgr*
EMP: 35
SALES (corp-wide): 70.4MM Privately Held
WEB: www.coldheading.com
SIC: 3452 3316 Bolts, metal; cold finishing of steel shapes
HQ: The Cold Heading Co
    21777 Hoover Rd
    Warren MI 48089
    586 497-7000

(G-17760)
COLLEGE PARK INDUSTRIES INC
27955 College Park Dr (48088-4877)
P.O. Box 1227 (48090-1227)
PHONE..................................586 294-7950
Charlie Lehman, *Production*
Jacob Drews, *Engineer*
Ryan Wahl, *Senior Engr*
Kim Taylor, *Credit Mgr*
Robin Surhigh, *Accountant*
EMP: 45 EST: 1988
SQ FT: 7,500
SALES (est): 13.2MM
SALES (corp-wide): 612.8MM Privately Held
WEB: www.college-park.com
SIC: 3842 Limbs, artificial
PA: Ossur Hf.
    Grjothalsi 5
    Reykjavik
    425 340-0

(G-17761)
COMMERCIAL TRCK TRANSF SIGNS
4133 E 10 Mile Rd (48091-1508)
PHONE..................................586 754-7100
Debra Cunningham, *President*
Sharon Salcpa, *Admin Sec*
EMP: 4 EST: 1957
SQ FT: 4,500
SALES (est): 311.8K Privately Held
WEB: www.commercialtrucksigns.com
SIC: 2752 Decals, lithographed

(G-17762)
COMPANY PRODUCTS INC
11800 Commerce St (48089-3878)
PHONE..................................586 757-6160
Karl Strang, *President*
David B Mills, *Treasurer*
EMP: 8 EST: 1945
SQ FT: 7,000
SALES (est): 913.7K Privately Held
WEB: www.companyproductsinc.com
SIC: 3639 3544 Sewing machines & attachments, domestic; special dies, tools, jigs & fixtures

(G-17763)
CONQUEST MANUFACTURING LLC
28408 Lorna Ave (48092-3937)
PHONE..................................586 576-7600
Gary McClain, *Plant Mgr*
Tim McCarthy, *Mfg Staff*
James D Miller, *Mng Member*
James Miller,
▲ EMP: 55 EST: 1998
SQ FT: 100,000
SALES (est): 13.3MM Privately Held
WEB: www.conquest-firespray.com
SIC: 3443 3444 5039 Ducting, metal plate; sheet metalwork; air ducts, sheet metal

(G-17764)
COOK INDUSTRIES INC
23515 Pinewood St (48091-3121)
PHONE..................................586 754-4070
Carlos Cook, *President*
EMP: 9 EST: 1989
SQ FT: 11,000
SALES (est): 648.6K Privately Held
SIC: 3599 Machine shop, jobbing & repair

(G-17765)
COUNTRYSIDE FOODS LLC (HQ)
Also Called: I & K Distributors
26661 Bunert Rd (48089-3650)
PHONE..................................586 447-3500
Robert Fishbein, *President*
Raymond Feldmeier, *Vice Pres*
Jeff Racheter, *Vice Pres*
Carl Warschausky, *CFO*
John Barry, *Treasurer*
EMP: 350 EST: 1993
SQ FT: 60,000
SALES (est): 119.4MM
SALES (corp-wide): 371.5MM Privately Held
WEB: www.liparifoods.com
SIC: 5141 2099 Groceries, general line; salads, fresh or refrigerated; pizza, refrigerated: except frozen; noodles, uncooked: packaged with other ingredients
PA: Lipari Foods Operating Company Llc
    26661 Bunert Rd
    Warren MI 48089
    586 447-3500

(G-17766)
CRYSTAL MACHINE & TOOL INC
21986 Schmeman Ave (48089-3281)
P.O. Box 480520, New Haven (48048-0520)
PHONE..................................586 552-1503
Harry Gann Jr, *President*
Ellen Hatcher, *Vice Pres*
EMP: 8 EST: 1994
SQ FT: 13,000
SALES (est): 806.5K Privately Held
SIC: 3444 Downspouts, sheet metal

(G-17767)
CUSTOM FAB INC
24440 Gibson Dr (48089-4311)
PHONE..................................586 755-7260
Michael Nixon, *Vice Pres*
Bonnie Beaumont, *Regl Sales Mgr*
Gregory E Simmons,
EMP: 6 EST: 1999
SQ FT: 8,500
SALES (est): 828.9K Privately Held
WEB: www.customfabmi.com
SIC: 1761 3444 Sheet metalwork; sheet metalwork

(G-17768)
CUSTOM TRENDS PRINTING LLC
8475 Farnum Ave (48093-4966)
PHONE..................................586 563-3946
Robert L Butler,
EMP: 4 EST: 2019
SALES (est): 104K Privately Held
SIC: 2395 Embroidery & art needlework

(G-17769)
CUSTOM WOODWORK & RMDLG LLC
23579 Lauren Ave (48089-2249)
PHONE..................................586 778-9224
Trudy Miesel, *Principal*
EMP: 5 EST: 2014
SALES (est): 70.4K Privately Held
SIC: 2431 Millwork

(G-17770)
D & W MANAGEMENT COMPANY INC
Also Called: All Type Truck and Trlr Repr
23660 Sherwood Ave (48091-5365)
PHONE..................................586 758-2284
Lynn Christel, *President*
Roger J Christel, *Admin Sec*
EMP: 10 EST: 1992
SQ FT: 50,000
SALES (est): 715.9K Privately Held
SIC: 7538 7539 3792 3713 General truck repair; trailer repair; automotive springs, rebuilding & repair; brake repair, automotive; travel trailers & campers; truck & bus bodies

(G-17771)
D K ENTERPRISES INC
Also Called: A & S Silver Brazing Co
21942 Dequindre Rd (48091-2107)
PHONE..................................586 756-7350
Dan Kalich, *President*
EMP: 4 EST: 1962
SQ FT: 3,000
SALES (est): 356.6K Privately Held
SIC: 7692 3567 Brazing; induction heating equipment

(G-17772)
D W HINES MANUFACTURING CORP
21887 Schoenherr Rd (48089-2856)
PHONE..................................586 775-1200
Donald W Hines, *President*
William Hines, *Vice Pres*
Joan M Hines, *Admin Sec*
EMP: 4 EST: 1951
SQ FT: 7,000
SALES (est): 364.2K Privately Held
SIC: 3541 Machine tools, metal cutting type

(G-17773)
D&D PLANNING DESIGN MLLWK LLC
8646 E 9 Mile Rd (48089-2453)
PHONE..................................586 754-6500
Douglas B Friedel Jr, *Mng Member*
EMP: 15 EST: 2006
SQ FT: 10,000
SALES (est): 2.1MM Privately Held
WEB: www.boothsandbars.com
SIC: 2431 Millwork

(G-17774)
DANA LIMITED
28201 Van Dyke Ave (48093-2713)
PHONE..................................586 467-1600
Rich Letnianchyn, *Engineer*
Holly Phillips, *Asst Controller*
EMP: 7 Publicly Held
WEB: www.dana.com
SIC: 3714 Motor vehicle parts & accessories
HQ: Dana Limited
    3939 Technology Dr
    Maumee OH 43537

(G-17775)
DART MACHINERY LTD
2097 Bart Ave (48091-3206)
PHONE..................................248 362-1188
Richard A Maskin, *President*
Gary St Denis, *Principal*
Dave Scillion, *Purch Mgr*
Jason Hahn, *Supervisor*
James Brewer, *Art Dir*
▲ EMP: 85 EST: 1982
SALES (est): 15MM Privately Held
WEB: www.dartheads.com
SIC: 3599 Machine shop, jobbing & repair

(G-17776)
DETROIT METAL ELEMENTS LLC
23334 Schoenherr Rd (48091-4261)
PHONE..................................313 300-9057
EMP: 5 EST: 2016
SALES (est): 90.8K Privately Held
WEB: www.detroitmetalelements.com
SIC: 3312 Structural shapes & pilings, steel

(G-17777)
DIAMOND BROACH COMPANY
3560 E 10 Mile Rd (48091-1392)
PHONE..................................586 757-5131
Ronald Fauquier, *President*
Patricia Fauquier, *Vice Pres*
EMP: 6
SQ FT: 3,000
SALES (est): 648.3K Privately Held
WEB: www.diamondbroach.com
SIC: 3545 Broaches (machine tool accessories)

(G-17778)
DIAMOND SIGN
7067 Continental Ave (48091-2608)
PHONE..................................586 519-4296
William Topping, *Principal*
EMP: 4 EST: 2018
SALES (est): 46K Privately Held
SIC: 3993 Signs & advertising specialties

(G-17779)
DIGIGRAPHX CO
24722 Forterra Dr (48089-4375)
PHONE..................................586 755-1130
Anthony Michael Tocco, *Owner*
Angela M Tocco, *Principal*
EMP: 5 EST: 1999
SALES (est): 436K Privately Held
WEB: www.digigraphx.net
SIC: 2395 Embroidery products, except schiffli machine

(G-17780)
DIVISION 6 FBRCTION INSTLLTION
Also Called: Division Six
27450 Gloede Dr (48088-6036)
PHONE..................................586 200-3030
Michael Short, *Mng Member*
Cindy Zieglowski, *Administration*
Dave Kurtz,
EMP: 18
SQ FT: 30,000
SALES (est): 1.1MM Privately Held
WEB: www.division6mfg.com
SIC: 1751 2431 3999 Cabinet & finish carpentry; planing mill, millwork; atomizers, toiletry

(G-17781)
DOUGH & SPICE INC
2150 E 10 Mile Rd (48091-1381)
PHONE..................................586 756-6100
Steve Antoon, *President*
EMP: 5 EST: 1999
SQ FT: 500 Privately Held
SIC: 2099 Food preparations

(G-17782)
DOUGH MASTERS
23412 Dequindre Rd (48091-1822)
PHONE..................................248 585-0600
George Kakouros, *Principal*
EMP: 17 EST: 2009
SALES (est): 1.1MM Privately Held
SIC: 2051 Bakery: wholesale or wholesale/retail combined

(G-17783)
DPR MANUFACTURING & SVCS INC
23675 Mound Rd (48091-5315)
PHONE..................................586 757-1421
Westliegh De Guvera, *President*
Emmett De Guvera, *Vice Pres*
EMP: 20 EST: 2005
SQ FT: 20,000
SALES (est): 2.6MM Privately Held
WEB: www.dprmfg.com
SIC: 3441 Fabricated structural metal

▲ = Import ▼= Export
◆ = Import/Export

GEOGRAPHIC SECTION

(G-17784)
DUNNE-RITE PERFORMANCE INC
26063 Newport Ave (48089-1326)
PHONE.................................616 828-0908
Jeffrey H Dunne, *President*
EMP: 10 **EST:** 2008
SALES (est): 629.5K **Privately Held**
WEB: www.dunne-rite.com
SIC: 3465 Body parts, automobile: stamped metal

(G-17785)
DURAMET CORPORATION
11350 Stephens Rd (48089-1833)
PHONE.................................586 759-2280
EMP: 4 **EST:** 2019
SALES (est): 120.5K **Privately Held**
WEB: www.durametcorp.com
SIC: 2819 Industrial inorganic chemicals

(G-17786)
DURAMIC ABRASIVE PRODUCTS INC
24135 Gibson Dr (48089-2068)
PHONE.................................586 755-7220
William Steele, *President*
John Kennedy, *Vice Pres*
Paul Westerfield, *Plant Mgr*
◆ **EMP:** 31 **EST:** 1960
SQ FT: 26,000
SALES (est): 1.1MM **Privately Held**
WEB: www.duramic.com
SIC: 3291 Wheels, abrasive

(G-17787)
DWM HOLDINGS INC
23171 Groesbeck Hwy (48089-4249)
PHONE.................................586 541-0013
Ryan Macvoy, *President*
Kelly Guffey, *Risk Mgmt Dir*
EMP: 95 **EST:** 2016
SALES (est): 28MM **Privately Held**
WEB: www.dwmholdings.com
SIC: 3317 Seamless pipes & tubes

(G-17788)
E & E CUSTOM PRODUCTS LLC
7200 Miller Dr (48092-4727)
PHONE.................................586 978-3377
Matthew Hirzel,
EMP: 12 **EST:** 2018
SALES (est): 771.9K **Privately Held**
SIC: 3545 Tools & accessories for machine tools

(G-17789)
E & E SPECIAL PRODUCTS LLC
7200 Miller Dr (48092-4727)
P.O. Box 808 (48090-0808)
PHONE.................................586 978-3377
Steve Hirzel, *General Mgr*
Patrick Miloser, *Vice Pres*
Wendy Kelly, *Controller*
Jeannett Kiel, *Accounting Mgr*
Brad Beels, *Sales Staff*
EMP: 19 **EST:** 2009
SALES (est): 4.3MM **Privately Held**
WEB: www.eesp.co
SIC: 3545 5084 Machine tool attachments & accessories; machine tools & accessories

(G-17790)
E R TOOL COMPANY INC
3720 E 10 Mile Rd Ste A (48091-6019)
PHONE.................................586 757-1159
Edward Ruth, *President*
EMP: 7 **EST:** 1994
SQ FT: 3,800
SALES (est): 501.5K **Privately Held**
SIC: 3599 Machine shop, jobbing & repair

(G-17791)
EASTERN MICHIGAN INDUSTRIES
23850 Ryan Rd (48091-1931)
PHONE.................................586 757-4140
Derrick Kemppainen, *President*
EMP: 41 **EST:** 2000
SALES (est): 7.7MM **Privately Held**
WEB: www.emifab.com
SIC: 3441 Fabricated structural metal

(G-17792)
EDE CO
26969 Ryan Rd (48091-4077)
PHONE.................................586 756-7555
David E Turowski, *President*
Edward R Turowski, *Vice Pres*
EMP: 5 **EST:** 1985
SQ FT: 20,000
SALES (est): 486.4K **Privately Held**
SIC: 3444 Pipe, sheet metal

(G-17793)
ELECTRA CABLE & COMMUNICATION
24846 Forterra Dr (48089-4367)
PHONE.................................586 754-3479
Mark Machowicz, *Owner*
EMP: 4 **Privately Held**
WEB: www.ecci-1.com
SIC: 3694 Automotive electrical equipment
PA: Electra Cable & Communication Inc
    24844 Marine Ave
    Eastpointe MI 48021

(G-17794)
ENGRAVE A REMEMBRANCE INC
28555 Flanders Ave (48088-4315)
PHONE.................................586 772-7480
Anthony J Russo, *President*
EMP: 5 **EST:** 1983
SALES (est): 150K **Privately Held**
WEB: www.engrave-a-remembrance.com
SIC: 3231 Cut & engraved glassware: made from purchased glass

(G-17795)
EQUIVALENT BASE CO
Also Called: Prompt Pattern
4175 E 10 Mile Rd (48091-1508)
PHONE.................................586 759-2030
Michael Healy, *President*
Erik Koseck, *Plant Mgr*
Mike Healy, *CFO*
EMP: 25 **EST:** 1994
SALES (est): 3.8MM **Privately Held**
WEB: www.equivalentbase.com
SIC: 3599 Machine shop, jobbing & repair

(G-17796)
ETCS INC
21275 Mullin Ave (48089-3086)
PHONE.................................586 268-4870
Ravi Kapur, *President*
Ron Stephens, *Vice Pres*
Ro Kapur, *Marketing Mgr*
Priya Kapur, *Program Mgr*
▲ **EMP:** 17 **EST:** 2003
SALES (est): 2.2MM **Privately Held**
WEB: www.etcsinc.com
SIC: 3545 8711 3679 7361 Tools & accessories for machine tools; engineering services; recording & playback apparatus, including phonograph; placement agencies

(G-17797)
EVEREST ENERGY FUND L L C
30078 Schoenherr Rd # 150 (48088-3179)
PHONE.................................586 445-2300
Rai Bhargava,
Vincent J Brennan,
EMP: 8 **EST:** 2001
SQ FT: 6,000
SALES (est): 1MM **Privately Held**
WEB: www.everestenergy.com
SIC: 1321 3569 Natural gasoline production; filters & strainers, pipeline

(G-17798)
EVERFRESH BEVERAGES INC
6600 E 9 Mile Rd (48091-2673)
PHONE.................................586 755-9500
Nick A Caporella, *Ch of Bd*
Joseph G Caporella, *President*
EMP: 60 **EST:** 1996
SALES (est): 11.9MM
SALES (corp-wide): 1B **Publicly Held**
WEB: www.everfreshjuice.com
SIC: 2033 2086 Fruit juices: packaged in cans, jars, etc.; fruit juices: concentrated, hot pack; fruit drinks (less than 100% juice): packaged in cans, etc.; water, pasteurized: packaged in cans, bottles, etc.

HQ: Newbevco, Inc.
    8100 Sw 10th St
    Plantation FL 33324

(G-17799)
EXCELLENT DESIGNS SWIMWEAR
5751 E 13 Mile Rd (48092-1504)
PHONE.................................586 977-9140
Patricia Karalla, *President*
EMP: 5 **EST:** 1985
SQ FT: 6,000
SALES (est): 239.1K **Privately Held**
WEB: www.customswimwear.com
SIC: 2339 2389 5699 Bathing suits: women's, misses' & juniors'; theatrical costumes; costumes, masquerade or theatrical; bathing suits

(G-17800)
EXPRESS COAT CORPORATION
27350 Gloede Dr (48088-4870)
PHONE.................................586 773-2682
Lawrence H Werner, *President*
Lawrence E Werner Jr, *Chairman*
EMP: 27 **EST:** 1967
SQ FT: 15,700
SALES (est): 591.5K **Privately Held**
WEB: www.expresscoat.com
SIC: 3479 Coating of metals & formed products

(G-17801)
F J LUCIDO & ASSOCIATES (PA)
Also Called: Lucido, F J & Associates
29400 Van Dyke Ave (48093-2320)
PHONE.................................586 574-3577
Frank J Lucido Jr, *President*
Bonnie Lucido, *Vice Pres*
EMP: 50 **EST:** 1974
SALES (est): 13.4MM **Privately Held**
WEB: www.michiganstaffing.com
SIC: 5013 7361 3544 Automotive supplies & parts; employment agencies; special dies, tools, jigs & fixtures

(G-17802)
FCA US LLC
Warren Truck Assembly Plant
21500 Mound Rd (48091-4840)
PHONE.................................586 497-2500
Robert Bowers, *Manager*
EMP: 7
SALES (corp-wide): 102.5B **Privately Held**
WEB: www.chrysler.com
SIC: 3714 Motor vehicle parts & accessories
HQ: Fca Us Llc
    1000 Chrysler Dr
    Auburn Hills MI 48326

(G-17803)
FCA US LLC
Also Called: ITM
6565 E 8 Mile Rd (48091-2949)
PHONE.................................248 576-5741
Mukul Kumar, *Manager*
EMP: 7
SALES (corp-wide): 102.5B **Privately Held**
WEB: www.chrysler.com
SIC: 3711 Motor vehicles & car bodies
HQ: Fca Us Llc
    1000 Chrysler Dr
    Auburn Hills MI 48326

(G-17804)
FEDERAL INDUSTRIAL SVCS INC (PA)
11223 E 8 Mile Rd (48089-3070)
PHONE.................................586 427-6383
Steve Hadwin, *President*
EMP: 9 **EST:** 1973
SQ FT: 4,000
SALES (est): 1MM **Privately Held**
WEB: www.fismi.com
SIC: 3398 Shot peening (treating steel to reduce fatigue)

(G-17805)
FERGUSON ENTERPRISES LLC
24425 Schoenherr Rd (48089-4773)
PHONE.................................586 459-4491
EMP: 5

SALES (corp-wide): 21.8B **Privately Held**
WEB: www.ferguson.com
SIC: 5074 3432 Plumbing fittings & supplies; plumbing fixture fittings & trim
HQ: Ferguson Enterprises, Llc
    12500 Jefferson Ave
    Newport News VA 23602
    757 874-7795

(G-17806)
FINI FINISH METAL FINISHING
24657 Mound Rd (48091-2043)
PHONE.................................586 758-0050
Ronald Borawski, *President*
EMP: 12 **EST:** 1991
SALES (est): 1.1MM **Privately Held**
WEB: www.finifinish.com
SIC: 3471 Electroplating of metals or formed products

(G-17807)
FLEET FUEL COMPANY LLC
12225 Stephens Rd (48089-2010)
PHONE.................................586 939-7000
Jude Beres, *CEO*
EMP: 2 **EST:** 1997
SALES (est): 1.4MM **Privately Held**
SIC: 2869 Fuels

(G-17808)
FLEX SLOTTER INC
3462 E 10 Mile Rd (48091-1309)
PHONE.................................586 756-6444
Steven T Perlik, *President*
Christopher Perlik, *Treasurer*
EMP: 6 **EST:** 1968
SQ FT: 2,800
SALES (est): 400K **Privately Held**
WEB: www.flex-slotter-inc.business.site
SIC: 3599 Machine shop, jobbing & repair

(G-17809)
FLEX-N-GATE LLC
Also Called: Ventra Plastics
5663 E 9 Mile Rd (48091-2562)
PHONE.................................586 759-8900
Kevin Hamilton, *Principal*
Karen Robertson, *Purchasing*
Paul Geiger, *Engineer*
Gerald Gromacki, *Engineer*
David Welacky, *Engineer*
▲ **EMP:** 150 **EST:** 1956
SALES (est): 62.2MM
SALES (corp-wide): 1.5B **Privately Held**
WEB: www.flex-n-gate.com
SIC: 3714 Motor vehicle parts & accessories
PA: Flex-N-Gate Llc
    1306 E University Ave
    Urbana IL 61802
    217 384-6600

(G-17810)
FLEX-N-GATE CORPORATION
Also Called: Flex-N-Gate Forming Tech
26269 Groesbeck Hwy (48089-4150)
PHONE.................................586 773-0800
Shahid Khan, *CEO*
David Decaussin, *Maint Spvr*
Gary Odell, *Purch Mgr*
Gerry Gialanella, *Buyer*
Michael Bertelsen, *Purchasing*
EMP: 7
SALES (corp-wide): 1.5B **Privately Held**
WEB: www.flex-n-gate.com
SIC: 3714 Motor vehicle parts & accessories
PA: Flex-N-Gate Llc
    1306 E University Ave
    Urbana IL 61802
    217 384-6600

(G-17811)
FLEX-N-GATE KNSHAN HLDINGS LLC (HQ)
5663 E 9 Mile Rd (48091-2562)
PHONE.................................586 759-8900
EMP: 65 **EST:** 2020
SALES (est): 48.4MM
SALES (corp-wide): 1.5B **Privately Held**
WEB: www.flex-n-gate.com
SIC: 3714 Motor vehicle parts & accessories

Warren - Macomb County (G-17812) — GEOGRAPHIC SECTION

PA: Flex-N-Gate Llc
1306 E University Ave
Urbana IL 61802
217 384-6600

(G-17812)
FLEX-N-GATE MICHIGAN LLC
Also Called: Veltri Tooling Company
5663 E 9 Mile Rd (48091-2562)
PHONE 586 759-8900
Dave Papak, *President*
Andy Scheele, *General Mgr*
Brad Annis, *Business Mgr*
Scott Quartier, *Vice Pres*
Keith Nail, *Maint Spvr*
▲ **EMP:** 74 **EST:** 2000
SALES (est): 35.5MM
SALES (corp-wide): 1.5B **Privately Held**
WEB: www.flex-n-gate.com
SIC: 3714 Bumpers & bumperettes, motor vehicle
PA: Flex-N-Gate Llc
1306 E University Ave
Urbana IL 61802
217 384-6600

(G-17813)
FLEX-N-GATE STAMPING LLC (HQ)
5663 E 9 Mile Rd (48091-2562)
PHONE 586 759-8900
Shahid Khan,
Rubina Ali,
▲ **EMP:** 45 **EST:** 2000
SALES (est): 20.8MM
SALES (corp-wide): 1.5B **Privately Held**
WEB: www.flex-n-gate.com
SIC: 3444 3496 Sheet metalwork; miscellaneous fabricated wire products
PA: Flex-N-Gate Llc
1306 E University Ave
Urbana IL 61802
217 384-6600

(G-17814)
FLORKEYS CONVEYOR SERVICE
21810 Schemean Ave (48089-3280)
PHONE 810 772-1930
Frank F Hoffmann, *President*
Arnold R Hoffmann, *Vice Pres*
▼ **EMP:** 26
SQ FT: 11,000
SALES (est): 2.5MM **Privately Held**
SIC: 3535 Conveyors & conveying equipment

(G-17815)
FORDSELL MACHINE PRODUCTS CO
30400 Ryan Rd (48092-1997)
PHONE 586 751-4700
David H Redfield, *President*
Barry Marshall, *Vice Pres*
Jean Hicks, *Treasurer*
EMP: 43
SQ FT: 20,000
SALES (est): 8.4MM **Privately Held**
WEB: www.fordsell.com
SIC: 3451 Screw machine products

(G-17816)
FORMSPRAG LLC
Also Called: Marland Clutch
23601 Hoover Rd (48089-3994)
PHONE 586 758-5000
Carl Christenson, *CEO*
Tina Kostrubiec, *Production*
▲ **EMP:** 105 **EST:** 2004
SQ FT: 79,000
SALES (est): 27.3MM
SALES (corp-wide): 1.7B **Publicly Held**
WEB: www.formsprag.com
SIC: 3568 Clutches, except vehicular
PA: Altra Industrial Motion Corp.
300 Granite St Ste 201
Braintree MA 02184
781 917-0600

(G-17817)
FORST-USA INCORPORATED
23640 Hoover Rd (48089-1944)
PHONE 586 759-9380
▲ **EMP:** 4
SALES (est): 450K **Privately Held**
SIC: 3541 Mfg Machine Tools-Cutting

(G-17818)
FRANK TERLECKI COMPANY INC
Also Called: Creative Store Fixtures
4129 Kendall Rd (48091-1900)
PHONE 586 759-5770
Frank Terlecki, *President*
EMP: 10 **EST:** 1980
SQ FT: 9,000
SALES (est): 905.1K **Privately Held**
SIC: 2599 Factory furniture & fixtures

(G-17819)
FUTURAMIC TOOL & ENGRG CO (PA)
24680 Gibson D (48089)
PHONE 586 758-2200
Mark Jurcak, *President*
John Couch, *Vice Pres*
Chris Schanta, *Plant Mgr*
Scott Adams, *QC Mgr*
Mike Scott, *Controller*
EMP: 108 **EST:** 1955
SQ FT: 120,000
SALES (est): 33.2MM **Privately Held**
WEB: www.futuramic.com
SIC: 3544 Jigs & fixtures

(G-17820)
FUTURE MILL INC
25450 Ryan Rd (48091-1326)
PHONE 586 754-8088
Stephen Fitzpatrick, *President*
Lynda Fitzpatrick, *Vice Pres*
EMP: 7 **EST:** 1979
SQ FT: 12,000
SALES (est): 791.5K **Privately Held**
WEB: www.futuremill.com
SIC: 3599 Chemical milling job shop

(G-17821)
G & G STEEL FABRICATING CO
31154 Dequindre Rd (48092-3722)
PHONE 586 979-4112
Olimpio Giacomantonio, *President*
EMP: 5 **EST:** 1981
SQ FT: 8,000
SALES (est): 804.2K **Privately Held**
WEB: www.ggsteel.com
SIC: 3312 1791 Structural shapes & pilings, steel; structural steel erection

(G-17822)
GAGE EAGLE SPLINE INC
2357 E 9 Mile Rd (48091-2162)
PHONE 586 776-7240
Vincent V Spica III, *President*
EMP: 51 **EST:** 1960
SQ FT: 2,800
SALES (est): 365.6K
SALES (corp-wide): 4.6MM **Privately Held**
WEB: www.invospline.com
SIC: 3545 3829 3544 3462 Gauges (machine tool accessories); measuring & controlling devices; special dies, tools, jigs & fixtures; iron & steel forgings
PA: Invo Spline Inc
2357 E 9 Mile Rd
Warren MI 48091
586 757-8840

(G-17823)
GCH TOOL GROUP INC
13265 E 8 Mile Rd (48089-3275)
PHONE 586 777-6250
Daniel Geddes, *President*
Jim Housel, *COO*
Jeff Carter, *Vice Pres*
Joe Giacalone, *Vice Pres*
Alan Lee, *Vice Pres*
▲ **EMP:** 40 **EST:** 1998
SQ FT: 25,000
SALES (est): 6.4MM **Privately Held**
WEB: www.gchtoolgroup.openfos.com
SIC: 3544 Special dies & tools

(G-17824)
GENERAL MOTORS COMPANY
7015 Edward Cole Blvd (48093-1809)
PHONE 586 218-9240
Jim Robeson, *Branch Mgr*
James Galonski, *Manager*
Cristina Learman, *Manager*
EMP: 300 **Publicly Held**
WEB: www.gm.com
SIC: 5511 3714 7371 Automobiles, new & used; motor vehicle parts & accessories; custom computer programming services
PA: General Motors Company
300 Renaissance Ctr L1
Detroit MI 48243

(G-17825)
GENERAL MOTORS LLC
28720 Lorna Ave (48092-3930)
PHONE 586 441-8483
Jeffrey Bordner, *Manager*
Christopher Thompson, *Manager*
EMP: 20 **Publicly Held**
WEB: www.gm.com
SIC: 3711 Motor vehicles & car bodies
HQ: General Motors Llc
300 Renaissance Ctr L1
Detroit MI 48243

(G-17826)
GENERAL STRUCTURES INC
23171 Groesbeck Hwy (48089-4249)
PHONE 586 774-6105
Douglas W Macvoy, *President*
Cathy Lee, *Partner*
Mary Szydzik, *Partner*
Gerald Fossett, *QC Mgr*
Tripti Sharma, *Engineer*
EMP: 19 **EST:** 1986
SALES (est): 1MM
SALES (corp-wide): 9.8MM **Privately Held**
WEB: www.generalstructuresinc.com
SIC: 3648 3354 3317 3355 Lighting equipment; aluminum extruded products; steel pipe & tubes; aluminum rolling & drawing
PA: United Lighting Standards, Inc.
23171 Groesbeck Hwy
Warren MI 48089
586 774-5650

(G-17827)
GENEX WINDOW INC
23110 Sherwood Ave (48091-2025)
PHONE 586 754-2917
Geno Hodzic, *President*
EMP: 4 **EST:** 1997
SQ FT: 5,000
SALES (est): 1.1MM **Privately Held**
WEB: www.genexwindows.com
SIC: 3089 5211 Windows, plastic; door & window products

(G-17828)
GENTRY SERVICES OF ALABAMA
31943 Red Run Dr (48093-1143)
PHONE 248 321-6368
James Gentry, *CEO*
EMP: 5
SALES (est): 349.2K **Privately Held**
SIC: 7372 Application computer software; business oriented computer software

(G-17829)
GENTZ INDUSTRY
14132 E 10 Mile Rd (48089-2153)
PHONE 586 772-2501
Ray Holm, *President*
EMP: 8 **EST:** 2007
SALES (est): 180.5K **Privately Held**
WEB: www.gentz.net
SIC: 3812 Aircraft/aerospace flight instruments & guidance systems

(G-17830)
GLOBAL COMPONENTS LLC
4175 E 10 Mile Rd (48091-1508)
PHONE 586 755-9134
Patrick Healy, *President*
Michael Healy Jr, *Co-President*
EMP: 9 **EST:** 2007
SALES (est): 318.2K **Privately Held**
WEB: www.globalcomponents.co
SIC: 3541 Machine tools, metal cutting type

(G-17831)
GLS INDUSTRIES LLC (PA)
Also Called: Global Logistics Services
7111 E 11 Mile Rd (48092-2709)
PHONE 586 255-9221
EMP: 46 **EST:** 2016
SALES (est): 2.4MM **Privately Held**
SIC: 3089 Fittings for pipe, plastic

(G-17832)
GLS INDUSTRIES LLC
8333 E 11 Mile Rd (48093-2875)
PHONE 586 255-9221
EMP: 20
SALES (corp-wide): 2.4MM **Privately Held**
SIC: 3089 Fittings for pipe, plastic
PA: Gls Industries Llc
7111 E 11 Mile Rd
Warren MI 48092
586 255-9221

(G-17833)
GNU SOFTWARE DEVELOPMENT INC
14156 E 11 Mile Rd (48089-1468)
PHONE 586 778-9182
EMP: 8
SALES (est): 620K **Privately Held**
SIC: 7372 Prepackaged Software Services

(G-17834)
GOLLNICK TOOL CO
24300 Marmon Ave (48089-3874)
PHONE 586 755-0100
Arden Gollnick, *Owner*
Kevin Bohannon, *Manager*
EMP: 5 **EST:** 1954
SQ FT: 7,000 **Privately Held**
WEB: www.gollnicktool.ambz.com
SIC: 3544 Special dies & tools

(G-17835)
GRANDADS SWEET TEA LLC
26532 Joe Dr (48091-3954)
PHONE 313 320-4446
Ricky McQueen, *Mng Member*
Mark Baldwin,
Darrell Goolsby,
Charles Richardson,
EMP: 4 **EST:** 2008 **Privately Held**
SIC: 2086 Tea, iced: packaged in cans, bottles, etc.

(G-17836)
GREAT LAKES TIRE LLC
12225 Stephens Rd (48089-2010)
PHONE 586 939-7000
Hal Briand, *President*
EMP: 19 **EST:** 2010
SQ FT: 120,000
SALES (est): 2.4MM
SALES (corp-wide): 1.1B **Privately Held**
WEB: www.centraltransportint.com
SIC: 3011 Retreading materials, tire
PA: Centra Inc.
12225 Stephens Rd
Warren MI 48089
586 939-7000

(G-17837)
GREAT LAKES TOOL LLC
24027 Ryan Rd (48091-1644)
PHONE 586 759-5253
Stanley Sznitka, *Mng Member*
EMP: 10 **EST:** 2008
SQ FT: 8,000
SALES (est): 900K **Privately Held**
SIC: 3599 Machine shop, jobbing & repair

(G-17838)
GREENDALE SCREW PDTS CO INC
11500 Hupp Ave (48089-3720)
PHONE 586 759-8100
Bernard J Damman, *President*
John Taylor, *Engineer*
Angelia Moore, *Office Mgr*
EMP: 40 **EST:** 1945
SQ FT: 20,000
SALES (est): 3.6MM **Privately Held**
WEB: www.greendalescrewproducts.com
SIC: 3451 Screw machine products

GEOGRAPHIC SECTION

Warren - Macomb County (G-17867)

(G-17839)
GREENFIELD CABINETRY INC
23811 Ryan Rd (48091-1932)
PHONE..................................586 759-3300
Joseph Salet, *President*
Audrey Salet, *Admin Sec*
▲ EMP: 17 EST: 1975
SQ FT: 10,000
SALES (est): 1.3MM **Privately Held**
WEB: www.cabinetselect.com
SIC: 2522 2541 2542 5031 Cabinets, office: except wood; table or counter tops, plastic laminated; partitions & fixtures, except wood; kitchen cabinets

(G-17840)
GRINDERS CLEARINGHOUSE INC (PA)
Also Called: Gch Machinery Division
13301 E 8 Mile Rd (48089-3218)
PHONE..................................586 771-1500
Dennis P Nicholas, *CEO*
Dennis Nicholas, *President*
Jason Wilzek, *Opers Staff*
Tony Bologna, *Engineer*
Dan Hutchinson, *CFO*
▼ EMP: 30 EST: 1966
SALES (est): 5.5MM **Privately Held**
WEB: www.grindersclearinghouse.com
SIC: 3599 Machine shop, jobbing & repair

(G-17841)
GRINDING PRODUCTS COMPANY INC
11084 E 9 Mile Rd (48089-2493)
PHONE..................................586 757-2118
Clyde Olivero, *President*
Clifford Olivero, *Vice Pres*
EMP: 20 EST: 1950
SQ FT: 11,500
SALES (est): 1MM **Privately Held**
WEB: www.grindingproducts.net
SIC: 3599 Machine shop, jobbing & repair

(G-17842)
GROSSE TOOL AND MACHINE CO
23080 Groesbeck Hwy (48089-2690)
PHONE..................................586 773-6770
Douglas Mack, *President*
Walter Grosse, *Vice Pres*
Mathias Kirsch, *Treasurer*
Kristi Barnett, *Cust Mgr*
Kurt Mack, *Admin Sec*
EMP: 30 EST: 1965
SQ FT: 15,000
SALES (est): 2.4MM **Privately Held**
WEB: www.grossetool.com
SIC: 3369 3544 Castings, except die-castings, precision; special dies, tools, jigs & fixtures

(G-17843)
GUELPH TOOL SALES INC
24150 Gibson Dr (48089-4308)
PHONE..................................586 755-3333
Robert Ireland, *President*
Jesse Lieb, *Manager*
EMP: 500 EST: 1990
SALES (est): 37MM
SALES (corp-wide): 218.9MM **Privately Held**
WEB: www.guelphmanufacturing.com
SIC: 3465 8744 Body parts, automobile: stamped metal; facilities support services
PA: Guelph Manufacturing Group Inc
    39 Royal Rd
    Guelph ON N1H 1
    519 822-5401

(G-17844)
GYB LLC
31065 Ryan Rd (48092-1332)
PHONE..................................586 218-3222
Raymond Ouillette Jr, *Mng Member*
EMP: 10 EST: 2015
SALES (est): 508.7K **Privately Held**
SIC: 3645 Motor vehicle lighting equipment

(G-17845)
H & G TOOL COMPANY
30700 Ryan Rd (48092-1995)
PHONE..................................586 573-7040
Donald Hunt, *President*
EMP: 11 EST: 1961
SQ FT: 8,000
SALES (est): 370.7K **Privately Held**
SIC: 3545 3541 Tools & accessories for machine tools; machine tools, metal cutting type

(G-17846)
H & L TOOL & ENGINEERING INC
23701 Blackstone Ave (48089-4217)
PHONE..................................586 755-2806
Bill Lapierre, *President*
Tom Bhavsar, *Accountant*
Bill La Pierre, *Manager*
EMP: 6 EST: 1993
SQ FT: 2,500
SALES (est): 770.7K **Privately Held**
WEB: www.hltool.com
SIC: 3599 Machine shop, jobbing & repair

(G-17847)
HANWHA AZDEL INC
2200 Centerwood Dr (48091-5867)
PHONE..................................810 629-2496
Kim Forgette, *Accounts Mgr*
Erich Vorenkamp, *Branch Mgr*
Dave Meriwether, *Manager*
Chris Wesley, *Manager*
EMP: 5 **Privately Held**
WEB: www.azdel.com
SIC: 3083 3089 Thermoplastic laminates: rods, tubes, plates & sheet; spouting, plastic & glass fiber reinforced
HQ: Hanwha Azdel, Inc.
    2000 Enterprise Dr
    Forest VA 24551
    434 385-6524

(G-17848)
HAPPY CANDY
2325 John B Ave (48091-4240)
PHONE..................................248 629-9819
EMP: 5 EST: 2015
SALES (est): 1.3MM **Privately Held**
SIC: 5145 2064 Confectionery; candy & other confectionery products

(G-17849)
HARPER MACHINE TOOL INC
21410 Ryan Rd (48091-4667)
PHONE..................................586 756-0140
John Crawford, *President*
Carol Crawford, *Vice Pres*
EMP: 5 EST: 1976
SQ FT: 2,300
SALES (est): 412.6K **Privately Held**
SIC: 3544 Special dies & tools

(G-17850)
HB STUBBS COMPANY LLC
27027 Mound Rd (48092-2699)
P.O. Box 910, Birmingham (48012-0910)
PHONE..................................586 574-9700
Jeff Laverty, *Administration*
EMP: 19 EST: 2015
SALES (est): 1.5MM **Privately Held**
WEB: www.hbstubbs.com
SIC: 3993 Signs & advertising specialties

(G-17851)
HEMCO MACHINE CO INC
6785 Chicago Rd (48092-1659)
PHONE..................................586 264-8911
Ralph W Ascroft, *President*
Sandy Ascroft, *Treasurer*
EMP: 5 EST: 1985
SQ FT: 20,000
SALES (est): 750K **Privately Held**
WEB: www.hemcomachine.com
SIC: 3714 5531 Motor vehicle engines & parts; automotive & home supply stores

(G-17852)
HENKEL US OPERATIONS CORP
23343 Sherwood Ave (48091-2097)
PHONE..................................586 759-5555
Joe Dunn, *Business Mgr*
Linda Chase, *Vice Pres*
Juliane Hefel, *Vice Pres*
Corey Peck, *Project Mgr*
Doug Sanders, *Prdtn Mgr*
EMP: 125
SQ FT: 19,000
SALES (corp-wide): 22.7B **Privately Held**
WEB: www.henkel.com
SIC: 2819 2899 Industrial inorganic chemicals; chemical preparations
HQ: Henkel Us Operations Corporation
    1 Henkel Way
    Rocky Hill CT 06067
    860 571-5100

(G-17853)
HI-TECH COATINGS INC (PA)
24600 Industrial Hwy (48089-4346)
PHONE..................................586 759-3559
Kenneth Pape, *Ch of Bd*
Fred Pape, *President*
EMP: 50 EST: 1995
SQ FT: 44,000
SALES (est): 6.6MM **Privately Held**
WEB: www.pioneermetal.com
SIC: 3479 Coating of metals & formed products

(G-17854)
HIPPIWIC CANDLES
21090 Elroy Ave (48089-5109)
PHONE..................................586 488-8931
Jessica Walsh, *Principal*
EMP: 4 EST: 2016
SALES (est): 46.8K **Privately Held**
SIC: 3999 Candles

(G-17855)
HOTFAB LLC
13118 E 9 Mile Rd (48089-2618)
PHONE..................................586 489-7989
EMP: 4 EST: 2013
SALES (est): 48.7K **Privately Held**
SIC: 7692 Welding repair

(G-17856)
HYDRO ABRASIVE PRODUCTS LLC
21750 Schoenherr Rd (48089-2837)
PHONE..................................313 456-9410
EMP: 6 EST: 2019
SALES (est): 432K **Privately Held**
WEB: www.hydroabrasiveproducts.com
SIC: 3291 Abrasive products

(G-17857)
HYDRO-LOGIC INC
24832 Romano St (48091-3379)
PHONE..................................586 757-7477
Ronald Reed, *President*
Paul Mazetti, *Vice Pres*
EMP: 35 EST: 1980
SQ FT: 9,500
SALES (est): 7.7MM **Privately Held**
SIC: 3625 3613 Relays & industrial controls; switchgear & switchboard apparatus

(G-17858)
HYDRONIC COMPONENTS INC
Also Called: Hci
7243 Miller Dr Ste 200 (48092-4746)
PHONE..................................586 268-1640
Joseph Martin, *Ch of Bd*
Michael Puysse, *Manager*
Mark Waligora, *Manager*
◆ EMP: 10 EST: 1994
SALES (est): 1.6MM **Privately Held**
WEB: www.hciterminator.com
SIC: 3491 Industrial valves

(G-17859)
INALFA ROOF SYSTEMS INC
12500 E 9 Mile Rd (48089-2634)
PHONE..................................586 758-6620
Larry Wojciechowski, *Branch Mgr*
Russell Anglebrandt, *Director*
EMP: 7 **Privately Held**
WEB: www.inalfa.com
SIC: 3714 Motor vehicle parts & accessories
HQ: Inalfa Roof Systems, Inc.
    1370 Pacific Dr
    Auburn Hills MI 48326
    248 371-3060

(G-17860)
INALFA/SSI ROOF SYSTEMS LLC
12500 E 9 Mile Rd (48089-2634)
PHONE..................................586 758-6620
Les Morrell, *Mng Member*

▲ EMP: 91 EST: 1997
SALES (est): 10.1MM **Privately Held**
WEB: www.inalfa.com
SIC: 3465 3544 3469 Automotive stampings; special dies, tools, jigs & fixtures; metal stampings
HQ: Inalfa Roof Systems, Inc.
    1370 Pacific Dr
    Auburn Hills MI 48326
    248 371-3060

(G-17861)
INDEPENDENT DIE ASSOCIATION
Also Called: I.D.A.
14689 E 11 Mile Rd (48088-4887)
PHONE..................................586 773-9000
Greg Smith, *President*
Francis M Smith, *President*
EMP: 6 EST: 1974
SQ FT: 3,000
SALES (est): 621.5K **Privately Held**
SIC: 3544 Special dies & tools

(G-17862)
INDUCTION PROCESSING INC
24872 Gibson Dr (48089-4315)
PHONE..................................586 756-5101
Albert Schult, *President*
Katherine Schult, *Vice Pres*
EMP: 14 EST: 1994
SQ FT: 7,200
SALES (est): 510.7K **Privately Held**
SIC: 3398 Metal heat treating

(G-17863)
INDUCTION SERVICES INC
24800 Mound Rd (48091-5334)
PHONE..................................586 754-1640
David De Arment, *President*
Mike Oberg, *General Mgr*
Mike Miles, *QC Mgr*
Eric Lorentzen, *Sales Staff*
Kevin Geisler,
EMP: 40 EST: 1956
SQ FT: 33,000
SALES (est): 9.2MM **Privately Held**
WEB: www.inductionservicesinc.com
SIC: 3398 Metal burning

(G-17864)
INDUSTRIAL CONVERTING INC
21650 Hoover Rd (48089-3158)
PHONE..................................586 757-8820
Kenneth Bugno, *President*
Tom Polsuk, *Vice Pres*
EMP: 25 EST: 1983
SQ FT: 2,500
SALES (est): 549.7K **Privately Held**
WEB: www.industrialconvertinginc.com
SIC: 3544 3053 Dies & die holders for metal cutting, forming, die casting; dies, steel rule; gaskets, packing & sealing devices

(G-17865)
INNOVATE INDUSTRIES INC
5600 Enterprise Ct (48092-3474)
PHONE..................................586 558-8990
Norb Spinski, *CEO*
EMP: 4 EST: 1965
SQ FT: 8,000
SALES (est): 521.4K **Privately Held**
WEB: www.innovative-industries-inc.com
SIC: 3444 3448 Sheet metalwork; panels for prefabricated metal buildings

(G-17866)
INNOVATIVE THERMAL SYSTEMS LLC
21400 Hoover Rd (48089-3162)
PHONE..................................586 920-2900
EMP: 4 EST: 2014
SALES (est): 114.1K **Privately Held**
WEB: www.innovativethermalsystems.com
SIC: 3999 8711 Barber & beauty shop equipment; engineering services

(G-17867)
INTEGRATED INTERIORS INC
21221 Hoover Rd (48089-3164)
PHONE..................................586 756-4840
Lawrence Barnes, *President*
Bob Barnes, *Vice Pres*
Stephanie Morrison, *CFO*

Warren - Macomb County (G-17868) — GEOGRAPHIC SECTION

Laurie Gottman, *Office Mgr*
Dave Pendley,
EMP: 17 **EST:** 1988
SQ FT: 18,000
SALES (est): 4.2MM **Privately Held**
WEB: www.integratedinteriors.com
SIC: 3296 Acoustical board & tile, mineral wool

(G-17868)
INTER CITY NEON INC
23920 Amber Ave (48089-4203)
P.O. Box 3762, Center Line (48015-0762)
PHONE 586 754-6020
Walter Schafer, *President*
Joyce Schafer, *Corp Secy*
EMP: 8 **EST:** 1948
SQ FT: 6,400
SALES (est): 961.2K **Privately Held**
WEB: www.intercityneon.com
SIC: 3993 Neon signs

(G-17869)
INVECAST CORPORATION
25737 Sherwood Ave (48091-4159)
PHONE 586 755-4050
Gregory P Kurze, *President*
Judy Riley, *Office Mgr*
EMP: 25 **EST:** 1992
SQ FT: 16,000
SALES (est): 3.8MM **Privately Held**
WEB: www.invecast.com
SIC: 3324 3369 3325 Commercial investment castings, ferrous; nonferrous foundries; steel foundries

(G-17870)
INVO SPLINE INC (PA)
2357 E 9 Mile Rd (48091-2162)
PHONE 586 757-8840
Vincent Spica III, *President*
Terry Spear, *Accountant*
Brenda Smith, *Administration*
EMP: 30 **EST:** 1947
SQ FT: 20,000
SALES (est): 4.6MM **Privately Held**
WEB: www.invospline.com
SIC: 3545 3599 3829 3566 Gauges (machine tool accessories); machine shop, jobbing & repair; measuring & controlling devices; speed changers, drives & gears; special dies, tools, jigs & fixtures; iron & steel forgings

(G-17871)
IRON CAPITAL OF AMERICA CO
21550 Groesbeck Hwy (48089-3133)
PHONE 586 771-5840
Jerry Noto Jr, *President*
Bud Baxters, *General Mgr*
EMP: 5 **EST:** 1985
SQ FT: 6,000
SALES (est): 908.5K **Privately Held**
WEB: www.ironcapital.net
SIC: 3446 Architectural metalwork

(G-17872)
IROQUOIS ASSEMBLY SYSTEMS INC
23220 Pinewood St (48091-4753)
PHONE 586 771-5734
Reinhard Eschbach, *President*
Ramon Santos, *Opers Staff*
EMP: 10 **EST:** 2009
SALES (est): 2.2MM **Privately Held**
SIC: 3559 Automotive related machinery

(G-17873)
IROQUOIS INDUSTRIES INC (PA)
25101 Groesbeck Hwy (48089-1425)
PHONE 586 771-5734
Reinhard Eschbach, *President*
Al Godin, *General Mgr*
Kurt Lang, *Business Mgr*
Mark Thompson, *Exec VP*
Jim Carleton, *Vice Pres*
◆ **EMP:** 85
SALES (est): 54.4MM **Privately Held**
WEB: www.iroquoisind.com
SIC: 3469 Stamping metal for the trade

(G-17874)
IROQUOIS INDUSTRIES INC
23750 Regency Park Dr (48089-2649)
PHONE 586 353-1410
Ryan Hart-Bachbrook, *President*
EMP: 23
SALES (corp-wide): 54.4MM **Privately Held**
WEB: www.iroquoisind.com
SIC: 3469 Stamping metal for the trade
PA: Iroquois Industries, Inc.
25101 Groesbeck Hwy
Warren MI 48089
586 771-5734

(G-17875)
J & L MFG CO (PA)
23334 Schoenherr Rd (48089-2672)
PHONE 586 445-9530
John L Metzger Sr, *President*
Lance L Metzger, *Vice Pres*
Lance Metzger, *Vice Pres*
Kelly Harris, *Buyer*
Betty Lynn Wills, *Controller*
EMP: 20 **EST:** 1961
SQ FT: 7,000
SALES (est): 2.9MM **Privately Held**
WEB: www.jnlmfg.com
SIC: 3444 3469 3465 Sheet metalwork; metal stampings; automotive stampings

(G-17876)
J AND N FABRICATIONS INC
30130 Ryan Rd (48092-3337)
PHONE 586 751-6350
Nick Kuzatko Sr, *President*
Nick Kuzatko Jr, *Vice Pres*
Carol Kuzatko, *Admin Sec*
EMP: 6 **EST:** 1972
SQ FT: 13,000
SALES (est): 777K **Privately Held**
SIC: 3444 Sheet metal specialties, not stamped

(G-17877)
J C MANUFACTURING COMPANY
23900 Ryan Rd (48091-4556)
PHONE 586 757-2713
Dan Crawford, *President*
Ann Crawford, *Admin Sec*
EMP: 4 **EST:** 1946
SQ FT: 7,040
SALES (est): 366.3K **Privately Held**
WEB: www.jcmanufacturinginc.com
SIC: 3544 3599 3541 Special dies & tools; electrical discharge machining (EDM); die sinking machines

(G-17878)
J L SCHROTH CO
24074 Gibson Dr (48089-2001)
PHONE 586 759-4240
Richrad Davidson, *President*
Robert A Connelly, *Vice Pres*
EMP: 4 **EST:** 1968
SALES (est): 508.8K
SALES (corp-wide): 11.6MM **Privately Held**
SIC: 3053 Gaskets, packing & sealing devices
PA: Schroth Enterprises Inc
95 Tonnacour Pl
Grosse Pointe Farms MI 48236
586 759-4240

(G-17879)
J M L CONTRACTING & SALES INC
5649 E 8 Mile Rd (48091-2844)
PHONE 586 756-4133
Jay M Lifshay, *President*
EMP: 10 **EST:** 1988
SALES (est): 1.1MM **Privately Held**
WEB: www.jmlsheetmetal.com
SIC: 1761 3444 3353 3351 Sheet metalwork; sheet metalwork; aluminum sheet, plate & foil; copper rolling & drawing

(G-17880)
J M MOLD TECHNOLOGIES INC
25185 Easy St (48089-4132)
PHONE 586 773-6664
Marion Danak, *President*
Johnny Bossio, *Vice Pres*
EMP: 12 **EST:** 2005
SQ FT: 7,200
SALES (est): 1.5MM **Privately Held**
WEB: www.jmmold.com
SIC: 3089 Injection molding of plastics

(G-17881)
J&J FREON REMOVAL
32344 Newcastle Dr (48093-1257)
PHONE 586 264-6379
EMP: 4
SALES (est): 368.4K **Privately Held**
SIC: 2869 Mfg Industrial Organic Chemicals

(G-17882)
JAIMES CUPCAKE HAVEN
26142 Fairfield Ave (48089-4520)
PHONE 586 596-6809
Jamie Keller, *Principal*
EMP: 4
SALES (est): 233.2K **Privately Held**
SIC: 2051 Bread, cake & related products

(G-17883)
JAX SERVICES LLC
25343 Masch Ave (48091-5025)
PHONE 586 703-3212
Austin Fletcher, *CEO*
EMP: 5
SALES (est): 238.3K **Privately Held**
SIC: 3569 8721 7291 8711 Robots, assembly line: industrial & commercial; billing & bookkeeping service; tax return preparation services; consulting engineer

(G-17884)
JDL ENTERPRISES INC
7200 Miller Dr (48092-4727)
PHONE 586 977-8863
John Dominka, *President*
Sue Krajenke, *Manager*
EMP: 13 **EST:** 1987
SALES (est): 1MM **Privately Held**
WEB: www.jdlent.com
SIC: 3491 3541 3823 3494 Industrial valves; machine tools, metal cutting type; industrial instrmnts msrmnt display/control process variable; valves & pipe fittings

(G-17885)
JHS GRINDING LLC
24700 Mound Rd (48091-5332)
PHONE 586 427-6006
Rudy Lipski, *Mng Member*
Coutnie Heikkinen,
Jody Sparks,
EMP: 29 **EST:** 2002
SQ FT: 25,000
SALES (est): 658.6K **Privately Held**
WEB: www.jhsgrinding.com
SIC: 3599 Machine shop, jobbing & repair

(G-17886)
JLM MANUFACTURING
14299 Frazho Rd (48089-1476)
P.O. Box 658 (48090-0658)
PHONE 586 447-3500
EMP: 1 **EST:** 2011
SALES (est): 9.8MM
SALES (corp-wide): 371.5MM **Privately Held**
WEB: www.zoppitty.com
SIC: 2064 Breakfast bars
PA: Lipari Foods Operating Company Llc
26661 Bunert Rd
Warren MI 48089
586 447-3500

(G-17887)
JMS PRINTING SVC LLC
Also Called: International Minute Press
14147 Edison Dr (48088-3755)
PHONE 734 414-6203
Tim Higgins, *President*
EMP: 8 **EST:** 1998
SALES (est): 822.2K **Privately Held**
SIC: 2752 Commercial printing, offset

(G-17888)
JOHN SAMS TOOL CO
14478 E 9 Mile Rd (48089-2756)
PHONE 586 776-3560
John Samohin, *President*
Denetrios Samoin, *Vice Pres*
Alexander Samohin, *Shareholder*
EMP: 5 **EST:** 1969
SQ FT: 4,000 **Privately Held**
WEB: www.johnsamstoolco.com
SIC: 3599 Machine shop, jobbing & repair

(G-17889)
JORDAN TOOL CORPORATION
Also Called: Victoria Tool & Machine Div
11801 Commerce St (48089-3937)
PHONE 586 755-6700
Donna Pilarski, *President*
Dave Pilarski, *General Mgr*
Jimmy Pilarski, *Vice Pres*
Tami Roberts, *Office Mgr*
Dave Gerada, *Manager*
EMP: 33 **EST:** 1950
SQ FT: 22,500
SALES (est): 2.3MM **Privately Held**
WEB: www.jordantool.com
SIC: 3544 7389 Special dies & tools; grinding, precision: commercial or industrial

(G-17890)
KAREN SPRANGER
7520 Hudson Ave (48091-3015)
PHONE 719 359-4047
Karen Spranger, *Principal*
EMP: 5 **EST:** 2018
SALES (est): 128.6K **Privately Held**
SIC: 2711 Newspapers, publishing & printing

(G-17891)
KC JONES BRAZING INC
2845 E 10 Mile Rd (48091-1359)
PHONE 586 755-4900
Rick Stewart, *President*
EMP: 6 **EST:** 2006
SQ FT: 2,500
SALES (est): 616.6K **Privately Held**
WEB: www.kcjplating.com
SIC: 7692 Brazing

(G-17892)
KC JONES PLATING CO (PA)
2845 E 10 Mile Rd (48091-1359)
PHONE 586 755-4900
Robert H Burger, *CEO*
Lenard Berman, *Admin Sec*
◆ **EMP:** 25 **EST:** 1957
SQ FT: 36,000
SALES (est): 15.3MM **Privately Held**
WEB: www.kcjplating.com
SIC: 3471 3479 Electroplating of metals or formed products; coating of metals & formed products

(G-17893)
KEO CUTTERS INC
25040 Easy St (48089-4100)
PHONE 586 771-2050
Eli Crotzer, *President*
Michelle Connolly, *Vice Pres*
Pat Mulcahy, *Vice Pres*
Jeff Lederer, *Controller*
EMP: 50 **EST:** 1941
SQ FT: 45,000
SALES (est): 7.5MM
SALES (corp-wide): 98.6MM **Privately Held**
WEB: www.archcuttingtools.com
SIC: 3545 Machine tool accessories
PA: Scp Agp Llc
2600 S Telg Rd Ste 180
Bloomfield Hills MI 48302

(G-17894)
KERR INDUSTRIES OF MICHIGAN
24649 Mound Rd (48091-2043)
PHONE 586 578-9383
EMP: 6 **EST:** 2018
SALES (est): 149.7K **Privately Held**
SIC: 3999 Manufacturing industries

(G-17895)
KNIT AND CROCHET 4 CHARITY
32545 Greenbriar Ave (48092-3144)
PHONE 248 224-4965
Scott Glazer, *Principal*
EMP: 4 **EST:** 2016
SALES (est): 67.2K **Privately Held**
SIC: 2399 Hand woven & crocheted products

(G-17896)
KRAFT-WRAP INC
21650 Hoover Rd (48089-3158)
PHONE 586 755-2050

▲ = Import ▼ = Export
◆ = Import/Export

Kenneth Bugno, *President*
Patricia Bugno, *Treasurer*
Margaret Bugno, *Admin Sec*
EMP: 24 **EST:** 1975
SQ FT: 14,000
SALES (est): 1.5MM **Privately Held**
WEB: www.kraftwrap.com
SIC: 2653 3081 2655 Boxes, corrugated: made from purchased materials; unsupported plastics film & sheet; fiber cans, drums & similar products

(G-17897)
KRINGER INDUSTRIAL CORPORATION
24435 Forterra Dr (48089-4379)
PHONE.................519 818-3509
EMP: 10
SALES: 100K **Privately Held**
SIC: 3086 7389 Mfg Plastic Foam Products

(G-17898)
KUHNHENN BREWING CO LLC (PA)
Also Called: Brewing World
5951 Chicago Rd (48092-1606)
PHONE.................586 979-8361
Eric Kuhnhenn, *President*
▲ **EMP:** 15 **EST:** 1998
SQ FT: 3,150
SALES (est): 2.7MM **Privately Held**
WEB: www.brewingworld.com
SIC: 2082 Brewers' grain

(G-17899)
L & M MACHINING & MFG INC
14200 E 10 Mile Rd (48089-2163)
PHONE.................586 498-7110
Jan Linthorst, *President*
Lawrence Morath, *Principal*
Gene Zyjewski, *Mfg Staff*
Thomas Taylor, *Engineer*
Clinton Westover, *Engineer*
EMP: 5 **EST:** 1999
SALES (est): 694.7K **Privately Held**
WEB: www.landmmachine.com
SIC: 3599 Machine shop, jobbing & repair

(G-17900)
L D S SHEET METAL INC
21831 Schoenherr Rd (48089-2857)
PHONE.................313 892-2624
Kirk Lambert, *President*
Matt Lambert, *Vice Pres*
EMP: 5 **EST:** 1979
SQ FT: 6,000
SALES (est): 931.7K **Privately Held**
WEB: www.ldssheetmetal.com
SIC: 3444 Metal ventilating equipment; guard rails, highway; sheet metal

(G-17901)
LAY MANUFACTURING INC
31614 Iroquois Dr (48088-7011)
PHONE.................313 369-1627
Paul Lay, *President*
EMP: 7 **EST:** 1984
SQ FT: 44,000
SALES (est): 686.3K **Privately Held**
SIC: 3452 Nuts, metal; bolts, metal

(G-17902)
LEEWARD TOOL INC
23781 Blackstone Ave (48089-4217)
PHONE.................586 754-7200
Fax: 586 756-2434
EMP: 5
SALES (est): 526.5K **Privately Held**
SIC: 3544 Mfg Dies/Tools/Jigs/Fixtures

(G-17903)
LEONARD MACHINE TOOL SYSTEMS
22800 Hoover Rd (48089-2568)
PHONE.................586 757-8040
Leonard Bantleon, *President*
Leonard Bantle, *President*
Lisa Thomas, *Treasurer*
Rhonda Martinez, *VP Finance*
David Hunter, *Manager*
EMP: 21 **EST:** 1951
SQ FT: 26,000
SALES (est): 3.9MM **Privately Held**
WEB: www.lmtsi.com
SIC: 3549 3544 Metalworking machinery; special dies, tools, jigs & fixtures

(G-17904)
LG ENERGY SOLUTION MICH INC
12850 E 9 Mile Rd (48089-2664)
PHONE.................616 494-7100
EMP: 179 **Privately Held**
SIC: 3694 Battery charging generators, automobile & aircraft
HQ: Lg Energy Solution Michigan, Inc.
1 Lg Way
Holland MI 49423

(G-17905)
LOGAN TOOL AND ENGINEERING
23919 Blackstone Ave (48089-4200)
PHONE.................586 755-3555
John R Ugo, *President*
EMP: 7 **EST:** 1979
SQ FT: 4,000
SALES (est): 493K **Privately Held**
SIC: 3599 Machine shop, jobbing & repair

(G-17906)
LOGISTICS ON THE GO INC
142 N Lafayette Blvd (48091-2206)
PHONE.................248 750-6654
Darryl Taylor, *President*
EMP: 6 **EST:** 2020
SALES (est): 600K **Privately Held**
SIC: 3537 Truck trailers, used in plants, docks, terminals, etc.

(G-17907)
LORNA ICR LLC
Also Called: I C R
28601 Lorna Ave (48092-3931)
PHONE.................586 582-1500
Allison Kirby, *Managing Dir*
Andrew Johnson, *Financial Analy*
Colette Schneider, *Manager*
Tim Douglas, *Technician*
Chris Stein, *Technician*
EMP: 18 **EST:** 2005
SALES (est): 3MM **Privately Held**
WEB: www.icrservices.com
SIC: 7694 7699 8742 Motor repair services; cash register repair; automation & robotics consultant

(G-17908)
LUMERICA CORPORATION
21400 Hoover Rd (48089-3162)
PHONE.................248 543-8085
Justin Palm, *President*
▼ **EMP:** 10 **EST:** 2012
SQ FT: 15,000
SALES (est): 1MM **Privately Held**
WEB: www.lumerica.com
SIC: 3648 Lighting equipment

(G-17909)
LUXURY BATH SYSTEMS
31239 Mound Rd (48092-4736)
PHONE.................586 264-2561
EMP: 4 **EST:** 2019
SALES (est): 73.4K **Privately Held**
WEB: www.luxurybath.com
SIC: 3432 Plumbing fixture fittings & trim

(G-17910)
LYONS TOOL & ENGINEERING INC
13720 E 9 Mile Rd (48089-2767)
PHONE.................586 200-3003
Mary A Lyons, *President*
Steven J Botwin, *Vice Pres*
William J Lyons, *Vice Pres*
Nancy Skerchock, *Treasurer*
Nancy M Skerchock, *Admin Sec*
EMP: 20 **EST:** 1960
SQ FT: 10,000
SALES (est): 2.4MM **Privately Held**
WEB: www.lyonstoolandengineering.com
SIC: 3544 3545 3462 Special dies & tools; machine tool accessories; iron & steel forgings

(G-17911)
LYTE POLES INCORPORATED
24874 Groesbeck Hwy (48089-4726)
PHONE.................586 771-4610
Ryan Macvoy, *President*
Richard Duff, *QC Mgr*
Justin Snowden, *Engineer*
Jeff Aliotta, *Finance*
Jessica Schultz, *Sr Project Mgr*
EMP: 90 **EST:** 1989
SALES (est): 5.5MM **Privately Held**
WEB: www.lytepoles.com
SIC: 3646 Commercial indusl & institutional electric lighting fixtures

(G-17912)
MACOMB TUBE FABRICATING CO
13403 E 9 Mile Rd (48089-2658)
PHONE.................586 445-6770
Walter Magreta, *General Mgr*
EMP: 26 **EST:** 1982
SQ FT: 12,000
SALES (est): 1.1MM **Privately Held**
WEB: www.macombtube.com
SIC: 3498 Tube fabricating (contract bending & shaping)

(G-17913)
MADISON ELECTRIC COMPANY (PA)
Also Called: Madison Electronics
31855 Van Dyke Ave (48093-1047)
PHONE.................586 825-0200
Brett Schneider, *President*
Scott Leemaster, *Vice Pres*
Phil Snider, *Vice Pres*
Richard Sonenklar, *Vice Pres*
Jon Waitz, *Vice Pres*
EMP: 63 **EST:** 1914
SQ FT: 93,000
SALES (est): 91.4MM **Privately Held**
WEB: www.madisonelectric.com
SIC: 5063 3679 Electrical construction materials; harness assemblies for electronic use: wire or cable

(G-17914)
MAGNA MODULAR SYSTEMS LLC
Also Called: Magna Exteriors & Interiors
14253 Frazho Rd (48089-1476)
PHONE.................586 279-2000
Keith McMahon, *General Mgr*
EMP: 225
SALES (corp-wide): 32.6B **Privately Held**
WEB: www.magna.com
SIC: 3714 Motor vehicle body components & frame
HQ: Magna Modular Systems Llc
1800 Nathan Dr
Toledo OH 43611

(G-17915)
MARISA MANUFACTURING INC
26020 Sherwood Ave (48091-1252)
PHONE.................586 754-3000
Roger Clark, *Director*
EMP: 7 **EST:** 2013
SALES (est): 250K **Privately Held**
WEB: www.marisamfg.com
SIC: 3399 Spikes, nonferrous metal or wire

(G-17916)
MARIX SPECIALTY WELDING CO
3822 Kiefer Ave (48091-3765)
PHONE.................586 754-9685
Henry R Di Laura, *President*
David Jackf, *Supervisor*
EMP: 37 **EST:** 1971
SQ FT: 12,000
SALES (est): 7.9MM **Privately Held**
SIC: 3443 Metal parts

(G-17917)
MARTINREA HOT STAMPINGS INC
14401 Frazho Rd (48089-1512)
PHONE.................859 509-3031
EMP: 50
SALES (corp-wide): 2.8B **Privately Held**
SIC: 3465 Mfg Automotive Stampings

HQ: Martinrea Hot Stampings, Inc.
19200 Glendale St
Detroit MI 48223
313 272-8400

(G-17918)
MARYSVILLE HYDROCARBONS LLC
30078 Schoenherr Rd # 150 (48088-3179)
PHONE.................586 445-2300
Rai Bhergava, *Branch Mgr*
EMP: 5 **Publicly Held**
SIC: 2911 Petroleum refining
HQ: Marysville Hydrocarbons Llc
2510 Busha Hwy
Marysville MI 48040

(G-17919)
MAYCO INTERNATIONAL LLC
27027 Mound Rd (48092-2699)
P.O. Box 180149, Utica (48318-0149)
PHONE.................586 803-6000
Nicholas Demiro, *Manager*
EMP: 125 **Privately Held**
WEB: www.maycointernational.com
SIC: 3089 Injection molding of plastics
PA: Mayco International Llc
42400 Merrill Rd
Sterling Heights MI 48314

(G-17920)
MB AEROSPACE WARREN LLC
Also Called: Gentz Aero
25250 Easy St (48089-4130)
PHONE.................586 772-2500
John Birch, *General Mgr*
Enrique Hernandez, *General Mgr*
Doug Loudon, *Managing Dir*
Bill Evans II, *Senior VP*
John Kozma, *Vice Pres*
EMP: 210 **EST:** 2006
SQ FT: 132,000
SALES (est): 37.8MM
SALES (corp-wide): 55.5MM **Privately Held**
WEB: www.mbaerospace.com
SIC: 3769 3443 3444 3724 Guided missile & space vehicle parts & auxiliary equipment; fabricated plate work (boiler shop); sheet metalwork; aircraft engines & engine parts; metal heat treating
HQ: Mb Aerospace Us Holdings, Inc.
25250 Easy St
Warren MI 48089
586 772-2500

(G-17921)
MCCORMICK & COMPANY INC
28650 Dequindre Rd (48092-2467)
PHONE.................586 558-8424
Khanitha Sookanit, *Branch Mgr*
EMP: 7
SALES (corp-wide): 5.6B **Publicly Held**
WEB: www.mccormick.com
SIC: 2099 Spices, including grinding; seasonings: dry mixes; gravy mixes, dry; sauces: dry mixes
PA: Mccormick & Company Incorporated
24 Schilling Rd Ste 1
Hunt Valley MD 21031
410 771-7301

(G-17922)
MCKEON PRODUCTS INC (PA)
Also Called: Mack's Ear Plugs
25460 Guenther (48091-6801)
PHONE.................586 427-7560
Devin Benner, *CEO*
Pete Benner, *Sales Staff*
Emily Hilsabeck, *Sales Staff*
Dominic Rosiek, *Manager*
David Adinarayan, *Information Mgr*
▲ **EMP:** 49 **EST:** 1962
SQ FT: 21,000
SALES (est): 6.9MM **Privately Held**
WEB: www.macksearplugs.com
SIC: 3842 3949 3851 Ear plugs; sporting & athletic goods; ophthalmic goods

(G-17923)
MELODY DIGIGLIO
Also Called: McBf
8088 E 9 Mile Rd (48089-2320)
PHONE.................586 754-4405
Melody Digiglio, *Owner*
Frank Digiglio, *Principal*

Warren - Macomb County (G-17924) — GEOGRAPHIC SECTION

EMP: 7 **EST:** 1985
SQ FT: 15,000
SALES (est): 1.8MM Privately Held
SIC: 5023 2591 1799 Window furnishings; drapery hardware & blinds & shades; window treatment installation

(G-17924)
METAL MART USA INC
31164 Dequindre Rd (48092-3722)
PHONE.................................586 977-5820
Bruno Tome, *CEO*
John Vandermark, *CEO*
EMP: 6 **EST:** 1997
SQ FT: 10,000
SALES (est): 1.7MM Privately Held
WEB: www.metalmartusa.com
SIC: 5051 3441 Steel; fabricated structural metal

(G-17925)
METALLURGICAL PROCESSING LLC
Also Called: Metallurgical Processing Co.
23075 Warner Ave (48091-1919)
PHONE.................................586 758-3100
Jeff Pyne, *President*
James L Schroth, *President*
Kevin Brown, *Vice Pres*
Robert A Connelly, *Vice Pres*
Robert Connelly, *Vice Pres*
EMP: 1 **EST:** 1954
SQ FT: 30,000
SALES (est): 9.9MM
SALES (corp-wide): 11.6MM Privately Held
WEB: www.metallurgicalprocessing.com
SIC: 3398 Metal heat treating
PA: Schroth Enterprises Inc
    95 Tonnacour Pl
    Grosse Pointe Farms MI 48236
    586 759-4240

(G-17926)
METRO BROACH INC
2160 E 9 Mile Rd (48091-2145)
PHONE.................................586 758-2340
Clyde Hishok, *CEO*
Josephine Hishok, *President*
Karen Houde, *Office Mgr*
EMP: 10 **EST:** 1980
SQ FT: 14,000
SALES (est): 750K Privately Held
WEB: www.metrobroach.com
SIC: 3599 Machine shop, jobbing & repair

(G-17927)
MI SOY CANDLE COMPANY LLC
27550 Liberty Dr (48092-2866)
PHONE.................................586 350-7654
Kristina Sparks, *Principal*
EMP: 4 **EST:** 2017
SALES (est): 81K Privately Held
SIC: 3999 Candles

(G-17928)
MICA TEC INC
Also Called: Jon F Canty
21325 Hoover Rd (48089-3156)
PHONE.................................586 758-4404
Jon F Canty, *President*
EMP: 6 **EST:** 1950
SQ FT: 11,900
SALES (est): 784.2K Privately Held
WEB: www.micatec.net
SIC: 2434 Wood kitchen cabinets

(G-17929)
MICHIGAN METAL FABRICATORS
24575 Hoover Rd (48089-1930)
PHONE.................................586 754-0421
John Sweet, *President*
Kenneth Sweet, *Corp Secy*
Richard Sweet, *Vice Pres*
EMP: 8 **EST:** 1949
SQ FT: 9,000
SALES (est): 648.4K Privately Held
SIC: 3443 3444 Weldments; sheet metal-work

(G-17930)
MICHIGAN SLOTTING COMPANY INC
22214 Schoenherr Rd (48089-5458)
PHONE.................................586 772-1270
Fax: 586 772-6013
EMP: 4
SQ FT: 3,200
SALES (est): 280K Privately Held
SIC: 3599 Mfg Industrial Machinery

(G-17931)
MIDWEST BRAKE BOND CO
Also Called: Sommer Co.
26255 Groesbeck Hwy (48089-1587)
PHONE.................................586 775-3000
James L Taylor Jr, *President*
Joan Coyle, *Vice Pres*
Joyce Johnston, *Treasurer*
Sue Vansteel, *Accounting Mgr*
Kurt Liebold, *Sales Staff*
EMP: 27 **EST:** 1939
SALES (est): 4.3MM Privately Held
WEB: www.midwestbrake.com
SIC: 3714 Motor vehicle brake systems & parts; transmission housings or parts, motor vehicle

(G-17932)
MITSUBISHI CHEMICAL AMER INC
Also Called: McPp-Detroit
24060 Hoover Rd (48089-1942)
PHONE.................................586 755-1660
Ryan Gainey, *Plant Supt*
Keith Thomas, *Plant Mgr*
Steve Cummings, *Manager*
EMP: 127 Privately Held
WEB:
    www.mitsubishichemicalholdings.com
SIC: 2821 2822 Plastics materials & resins; synthetic rubber
HQ: Mitsubishi Chemical America, Inc.
    9115 Hrris Crners Pkwy St
    Charlotte NC 28269
    980 580-2839

(G-17933)
MMI ENGINEERED SOLUTIONS INC
12700 Stephens Rd (48089-4334)
PHONE.................................734 429-5130
Paul Larson, *CFO*
EMP: 50 Privately Held
WEB: www.mmi-es.com
SIC: 3089 8711 Injection molding of plastics; engineering services
HQ: Mmi Engineered Solutions, Inc.
    1715 Woodland Dr
    Saline MI 48176
    734 429-4664

(G-17934)
MOBILITY HOWELL PRODUCTS
11374 Common Rd (48093-2549)
PHONE.................................586 558-8308
Jerry Howell, *President*
EMP: 5 **EST:** 2000
SALES (est): 39.6K Privately Held
WEB: www.howellmobility.com
SIC: 3999 Manufacturing industries

(G-17935)
MOTION SYSTEMS INCORPORATED
21335 Schoenherr Rd (48089-3332)
PHONE.................................586 774-5666
William Ericson, *President*
◆ **EMP:** 15 **EST:** 1978
SQ FT: 10,000
SALES (est): 2.4MM Privately Held
WEB: www.motionsystems.us
SIC: 3429 3462 Pulleys metal; gears, forged steel

(G-17936)
MOTOR CITY NATURALS LLC
24201 Hoover Rd (48089-1973)
PHONE.................................313 329-4071
Maddy Frechette,
Nick Parker,
EMP: 7 **EST:** 2015
SQ FT: 7,800 Privately Held
WEB: www.motorcitynaturals.com

SIC: 2834 Vitamin, nutrient & hematinic preparations for human use

(G-17937)
MOTOR CITY RACKS INC
24445 Forterra Dr (48089-4379)
PHONE.................................519 776-9153
John Friesen, *President*
Abe Friesen, *Vice Pres*
Tony Van Noggeren, *Controller*
Matt Gleason, *Sales Staff*
Kevin Gross, *Program Mgr*
EMP: 40 **EST:** 2011
SQ FT: 1,200
SALES: 5MM
SALES (corp-wide): 24.6MM Privately Held
WEB: www.essexweldsolutions.com
SIC: 3496 Miscellaneous fabricated wire products
PA: Essex Weld Solutions Ltd
    340 Allen Ave
    Essex ON N8M 3
    519 776-9153

(G-17938)
MURRAY EQUIPMENT COMPANY INC (PA)
6737 E 8 Mile Rd (48091-2905)
PHONE.................................313 869-4444
Robert W Murray, *President*
James J Murray Jr, *Chairman*
Joseph Fillippi, *Admin Sec*
EMP: 15 **EST:** 1946
SQ FT: 11,000
SALES (est): 2MM Privately Held
SIC: 3568 3625 Power transmission equipment; relays & industrial controls

(G-17939)
N-P GRINDING INC
3700 E 10 Mile Rd (48091-3721)
PHONE.................................586 756-6262
Mark Hampton, *President*
EMP: 4 **EST:** 1967
SQ FT: 6,000
SALES (est): 444.7K Privately Held
SIC: 3599 Machine shop, jobbing & repair

(G-17940)
NAAMS LLC
25141 Easy St (48089-4132)
PHONE.................................586 285-5684
John Djurasaj, *Mng Member*
EMP: 8 **EST:** 2014
SALES (est): 444K Privately Held
WEB: www.naams.net
SIC: 3549 Metalworking machinery

(G-17941)
NATIONAL MANUFACTURING INC
25426 Ryan Rd (48091-1326)
PHONE.................................586 755-8983
Nelida Mari, *President*
EMP: 5 **EST:** 2014
SALES (est): 410.1K Privately Held
WEB: www.alltempairhvac.com
SIC: 3111 Industrial leather products; accessory products, leather

(G-17942)
NITRO-VAC HEAT TREAT INC
23080 Dequindre Rd (48091-1898)
PHONE.................................586 754-4350
Felix Stomber, *President*
Phyllis La Prairie, *Vice Pres*
William F Stomber, *Vice Pres*
Coleen Stomber, *Office Mgr*
Cheryl Trombley, *Admin Sec*
EMP: 13 **EST:** 1966
SQ FT: 5,400
SALES (est): 1.9MM Privately Held
WEB: www.nitrovac.com
SIC: 3398 Brazing (hardening) of metal

(G-17943)
NOLANS TOP TIN INC
8428 Republic Ave (48089-1716)
PHONE.................................586 899-3421
Nolan Brown, *Principal*
EMP: 4 **EST:** 2008
SALES (est): 116.1K Privately Held
SIC: 3356 Tin

(G-17944)
NOR-COTE INC
11425 Timken Ave (48089-3863)
PHONE.................................586 756-1200
Stanley C Grouse, *President*
Barbara A Grouse, *Corp Secy*
Christopher Grouse, *Vice Pres*
EMP: 33 **EST:** 1954
SQ FT: 43,000
SALES (est): 2.5MM Privately Held
WEB: www.nor-coteinc.com
SIC: 3471 5051 3398 Plating & polishing; metals service centers & offices; annealing of metal

(G-17945)
NORBROOK PLATING INC
11400 E 9 Mile Rd (48089-2583)
PHONE.................................586 755-4110
F Preston Kemp, *President*
Ken Otto, *Corp Secy*
Kathleen Kemp, *Vice Pres*
Abigai Vangheluwe, *Sales Staff*
EMP: 27 **EST:** 1953
SQ FT: 30,000
SALES (est): 3.3MM Privately Held
WEB: www.norbrookplating.com
SIC: 3471 Plating of metals or formed products; buffing for the trade; polishing, metals or formed products

(G-17946)
NORTH AMERICAN ASPHALT
11720 Susan Ave (48093-8338)
PHONE.................................586 754-0014
Daniel Bergen, *Principal*
EMP: 6 **EST:** 2005
SALES (est): 82.6K Privately Held
SIC: 2951 Asphalt paving mixtures & blocks

(G-17947)
NORTH AMERICAN GRAPHICS INC
24487 Gibson Dr (48089-2030)
PHONE.................................586 486-1110
John Mertz, *President*
EMP: 13 **EST:** 1970
SQ FT: 10,000
SALES (est): 1.4MM Privately Held
WEB: www.northamericangraphics.com
SIC: 2791 2796 2752 Typesetting; platemaking services; commercial printing, lithographic

(G-17948)
NOVUS CORPORATION
Also Called: Archangel's Jewelry
3077 Chard Ave (48092-3526)
PHONE.................................248 545-8600
Steven Arcangeli, *President*
EMP: 10 **EST:** 1979
SALES (est): 512.5K Privately Held
WEB: www.novuscorp.org
SIC: 3911 5944 5932 7631 Jewelry, precious metal; jewelry, precious stones & precious metals; pawnshop; jewelry repair services

(G-17949)
OAKLEY INDS SUB ASSMBLY DIV IN
25295 Guenther Ste 200 (48091-6020)
PHONE.................................586 754-5555
Matthew Sortor, *Plant Mgr*
John Jackson, *QC Mgr*
Doanald Amthor, *Branch Mgr*
EMP: 7
SALES (corp-wide): 89MM Privately Held
WEB: www.oakleysubassembly.com
SIC: 3714 3559 Motor vehicle wheels & parts; rubber working machinery, including tires
PA: Oakley Industries Sub Assembly Division, Inc.
    4333 Matthew
    Flint MI 48507
    810 720-4444

(G-17950)
OAKLEY INDS SUB ASSMBLY DIV IN
25295 Guenther Rear Rear (48091-6022)
PHONE.................................586 754-5555

Donald Amthor, *Manager*
EMP: 7
SALES (corp-wide): 89MM **Privately Held**
WEB: www.oakleysubassembly.com
SIC: 3714 Motor vehicle wheels & parts
PA: Oakley Industries Sub Assembly Division, Inc.
4333 Matthew
Flint MI 48507
810 720-4444

(G-17951)
OSHKOSH DEFENSE LLC
27600 Donald Ct (48092-5908)
PHONE 586 576-8301
Adam Hiltunen, *Engineer*
EMP: 28
SALES (corp-wide): 7.7B **Publicly Held**
WEB: www.oshkoshdefense.com
SIC: 3531 3715 3711 Mixers, concrete; truck trailers; military motor vehicle assembly
HQ: Oshkosh Defense, Llc
2307 Oregon St
Oshkosh WI 54902
920 235-9150

(G-17952)
PAINT WORK INCORPORATED
2088 Riggs Ave (48091-3771)
PHONE 586 759-6640
Elisabeth Weldhaddow, *President*
Mark Shamblin, *Vice Pres*
EMP: 10 **EST:** 1968
SQ FT: 8,000 **Privately Held**
SIC: 3479 Painting of metal products; coating of metals & formed products

(G-17953)
PALADINO PUBLICATIONS
24454 Curie St (48091-4428)
PHONE 586 759-2795
Lawrence Paladino, *Owner*
EMP: 4 **EST:** 2017
SALES (est): 69.5K **Privately Held**
SIC: 2741 Miscellaneous publishing

(G-17954)
PARTON & PREBLE INC
23507 Groesbeck Hwy (48089-2694)
PHONE 586 773-6000
Orville S Parton, *President*
Bruce Parton, *Vice Pres*
Shirley Parton, *Treasurer*
Louise Wilson, *Admin Sec*
EMP: 30 **EST:** 1959
SQ FT: 50,000
SALES (est): 4.5MM **Privately Held**
WEB: www.partonprebleinc.com
SIC: 3312 3444 3443 3441 Plate, steel; sheet metalwork; fabricated plate work (boiler shop); fabricated structural metal

(G-17955)
PARTS FINISHING GROUP INC
Also Called: Automted Dbrring A-1 Prts Wshg
13251 Stephens Rd (48089-4377)
PHONE 586 755-4053
Kenneth Pape, *CEO*
Sandra Pape, *President*
Fred Pape, *Vice Pres*
EMP: 65 **EST:** 1988
SQ FT: 50,000
SALES (est): 6MM
SALES (corp-wide): 27.3MM **Privately Held**
WEB: www.pioneermetal.com
SIC: 3599 Machine & other job shop work; machine shop, jobbing & repair
PA: Pfg Enterprises, Inc.
50271 E Rssell Smith Blvd
Chesterfield MI 48051
586 755-1053

(G-17956)
PASLIN COMPANY
23655 Hoover Rd (48089-1986)
PHONE 586 755-1693
Danny Pasque, *Owner*
David Taylor, *Exec VP*
Chris Ballach, *Project Mgr*
Jim Duval, *Project Mgr*
James Joo, *Project Mgr*
EMP: 202 **Privately Held**
WEB: www.paslin.com
SIC: 3545 Machine tool accessories
HQ: The Paslin Company
25303 Ryan Rd
Warren MI 48091
586 758-0200

(G-17957)
PASLIN COMPANY (HQ)
25303 Ryan Rd (48091-3778)
PHONE 586 758-0200
Kirk Goins, *CEO*
Ronald Pasque, *Vice Pres*
Mike Woodruff, *Buyer*
Jim Conover, *Engineer*
Therese Polk, *Corp Comm Staff*
▲ **EMP:** 175 **EST:** 1937
SQ FT: 700,000
SALES (est): 143.7MM **Privately Held**
WEB: www.paslin.com
SIC: 3548 3544 3545 Electric welding equipment; jigs & fixtures; machine tool accessories

(G-17958)
PASLIN COMPANY
Also Called: Paslin Controls Group
3400 E 10 Mile Rd (48091-3787)
PHONE 586 755-3606
Terry McKay, *Purch Mgr*
Luis Gutierrez, *Engineer*
Rufus Madison, *Engineer*
Tim Dory, *Manager*
EMP: 162 **Privately Held**
WEB: www.paslin.com
SIC: 7389 3548 Design services; welding apparatus
HQ: The Paslin Company
25303 Ryan Rd
Warren MI 48091
586 758-0200

(G-17959)
PATIO LAND MFG INC
Also Called: Russ Parke Awnings
8407 E 9 Mile Rd (48089-2460)
PHONE 586 758-5660
Russell K Parke, *President*
Joann Parke, *Vice Pres*
EMP: 7 **EST:** 1957
SQ FT: 3,000
SALES (est): 593.5K **Privately Held**
WEB: www.patiolandmanufacturing.com
SIC: 3444 5999 Awnings, sheet metal; awnings

(G-17960)
PESTI MANUFACTURING COMPANY
25211 Mound Rd (48091-3857)
PHONE 586 920-2731
EMP: 8 **EST:** 2019
SALES (est): 457.5K **Privately Held**
WEB: www.pestimfg.com
SIC: 3999 Manufacturing industries

(G-17961)
PET PATROL OF MACOMB-OAKLAND
25155 Rosenbusch Blvd (48089-1571)
PHONE 586 675-2451
Erica Smith, *Principal*
EMP: 5 **EST:** 2012
SALES (est): 118.5K **Privately Held**
SIC: 2711 Newspapers, publishing & printing

(G-17962)
PGM PRODUCTS INC
21034 Ryan Rd (48091-2740)
PHONE 586 757-4400
Ramo A Salerno Sr, *President*
Denise Marschner, *Admin Sec*
EMP: 10 **EST:** 1991
SALES (est): 715.3K **Privately Held**
SIC: 3452 7699 Bolts, nuts, rivets & washers; industrial machinery & equipment repair

(G-17963)
PIERCETEK INC
13201 Stephens Rd (48089-4378)
PHONE 586 757-0379
EMP: 9 **EST:** 2006
SALES (est): 12.7K **Privately Held**
SIC: 3452 Bolts, nuts, rivets & washers

(G-17964)
PIONEER METAL FINISHING LLC
13251 Stephens Rd (48089-4377)
PHONE 877 721-1100
Scott Kettler, *President*
EMP: 65
SALES (corp-wide): 93MM **Privately Held**
WEB: www.pioneermetal.com
SIC: 3599 Machine & other job shop work; machine shop, jobbing & repair
PA: Pioneer Metal Finishing, Llc
480 Pilgrim Way Ste 1400
Green Bay WI 54304
877 721-1100

(G-17965)
PIONEER METAL FINISHING LLC
13251 Stephens Rd (48089-4377)
PHONE 877 721-1100
▲ **EMP:** 6
SALES (est): 233.8K **Privately Held**
SIC: 3471 Plating/Polishing Service

(G-17966)
PIONEER PLASTICS INC (PA)
Also Called: Pioneer Molding
2295 Bart Ave (48091-3207)
PHONE 586 262-0159
Rajeev Gandhi, *President*
Vinita Gandhi, *Owner*
EMP: 29 **EST:** 2002
SQ FT: 40,000 **Privately Held**
WEB: www.pioneermolding.com
SIC: 3089 Automotive parts, plastic; injection molding of plastics

(G-17967)
PLATING PRODUCTS CONSULTA
27318 Dover Ave (48088-4778)
PHONE 586 755-7210
Laurie Pollett, *Principal*
EMP: 5 **EST:** 2003
SALES (est): 15.7K **Privately Held**
SIC: 3471 Plating of metals or formed products

(G-17968)
PLATING TECHNOLOGIES
21225 Mullin Ave (48089-3086)
PHONE 586 756-1825
William Coffie, *Principal*
William C Coffie, *Purch Mgr*
EMP: 7 **EST:** 2016
SALES (est): 84.6K **Privately Held**
SIC: 3471 Electroplating of metals or formed products

(G-17969)
POLYTEC FOHA INC (HQ)
7020 Murthum Ave (48092-3831)
PHONE 586 978-9386
Howard Lipman, *President*
Sieglinde Kaiser, *Vice Pres*
Steffen Richter, *Human Res Dir*
▲ **EMP:** 19 **EST:** 1989
SQ FT: 70,000
SALES (est): 10.8MM
SALES (corp-wide): 617.3MM **Privately Held**
WEB: www.polytec-group.com
SIC: 5013 3429 3089 Automotive supplies & parts; furniture builders' & other household hardware; plastic containers, except foam
PA: Polytec Holding Ag
Polytec-Str. 1
HOrsching 4063
722 170-10

(G-17970)
PPG INDUSTRIES INC
Also Called: PPG 5628
13344 E 11 Mile Rd (48091-1367)
PHONE 586 755-2011
Jason Macauley, *Branch Mgr*
EMP: 4
SALES (corp-wide): 15.1B **Publicly Held**
WEB: www.ppg.com
SIC: 2851 Paints & allied products
PA: Ppg Industries, Inc.
1 Ppg Pl
Pittsburgh PA 15272
412 434-3131

(G-17971)
PPI LLC (PA)
Also Called: Ppi Aerospace
23514 Groesbeck Hwy (48089-4246)
PHONE 586 772-7736
Paul Clark, *President*
Sheila McLain, *Purchasing*
Scott Thams, *Director*
Layne Joss, *Technician*
EMP: 29 **EST:** 2003
SQ FT: 80,000
SALES (est): 5MM **Privately Held**
WEB: www.ppiaerospace.com
SIC: 3471 Electroplating of metals or formed products

(G-17972)
PRECISION MOLD MACHINING SVCS
13143 E 9 Mile Rd (48089-2620)
PHONE 586 774-2330
David Loehr, *President*
▲ **EMP:** 20 **EST:** 1984
SQ FT: 16,500
SALES (est): 3.5MM **Privately Held**
WEB: www.precisionmold.com
SIC: 3089 Injection molding of plastics

(G-17973)
PRECISION PACKING CORPORATION
2145 Centerwood Dr (48091-5866)
PHONE 586 756-8700
Anthony Pappas, *President*
John Whitefoot, *Vice Pres*
Michael Pappas, *Treasurer*
Terry Daubenmeyer, *Admin Sec*
EMP: 30 **EST:** 1984
SQ FT: 12,600
SALES (est): 2.4MM **Privately Held**
WEB: www.precpack.com
SIC: 2891 3492 3053 Sealants; fluid power valves & hose fittings; gaskets, packing & sealing devices

(G-17974)
PREMIER MALT PRODUCTS INC
25760 Groesbeck Hwy # 103 (48089-1589)
P.O. Box 898, Saddle Brook NJ (07663-0898)
PHONE 586 443-3355
M Stuart Andreas, *President*
▼ **EMP:** 28 **EST:** 1933
SQ FT: 1,440
SALES (est): 930.2K **Privately Held**
WEB: www.premiermalt.com
SIC: 2082 5149 Malt syrups; malt extract; sugar, honey, molasses & syrups

(G-17975)
PRESTIGE ENGRG RSRCES TECH INC
26155 Groesbeck Hwy (48089-4149)
PHONE 586 777-1820
William Fritts, *Branch Mgr*
Perry Russo, *Executive*
▲ **EMP:** 13
SALES (corp-wide): 8MM **Privately Held**
WEB: www.prestige-grp.com
SIC: 3714 Motor vehicle parts & accessories
PA: Prestige Engineering Resources & Technologies Inc.
24700 Capital Blvd
Clinton Township MI 48036
586 868-4000

(G-17976)
PRESTIGE STAMPING LLC
23513 Groesbeck Hwy (48089-6001)
PHONE 586 773-2700
Christopher Rink, *CEO*
Jeff Rink, *Sales Mgr*
Jeffrey Rink, *Sales Staff*
Barb Wisniewski, *Sales Staff*
Alison Elmes, *Manager*
EMP: 120 **EST:** 1967
SQ FT: 105,000

Warren - Macomb County (G-17977) GEOGRAPHIC SECTION

SALES (est): 22.9MM
SALES (corp-wide): 116.4MM **Privately Held**
WEB: www.prestigestamping.com
SIC: 3452 3465 Washers, metal; automotive stampings
PA: Auxo Investment Partners, Llc
146 Monroe Center St Nw # 1125
Grand Rapids MI 49503
616 200-4454

(G-17977)
PROCESS SYSTEMS INC (HQ)
23633 Pinewood St (48091-4760)
P.O. Box 344 (48090-0344)
PHONE.....................586 757-5711
Thomas Ruthman, *President*
Dan Torongo, *Manager*
◆ EMP: 43 EST: 2007
SALES (est): 9.2MM
SALES (corp-wide): 29.7MM **Privately Held**
WEB: www.psi4pumps.com
SIC: 2448 3561 3564 5084 Wood pallets & skids; industrial pumps & parts; blowers & fans; pumps & pumping equipment; pumps & pumping equipment repair; fabricated plate work (boiler shop)
PA: Ruthman Pump And Engineering, Inc
7236 Tylers Corner Dr
West Chester OH 45069
513 559-1901

(G-17978)
PROGRESSIVE METAL MFG CO (PA)
Also Called: Pmmco
3100 E 10 Mile Rd (48091-3713)
PHONE.....................248 546-2827
Nathan Hendrix, *President*
Eric Borman, *Principal*
Julie Borman, *Chairman*
Bernie Fornwald, *Purch Agent*
Lewis Buko, *Engineer*
EMP: 25 EST: 1962
SQ FT: 55,000
SALES (est): 33.5MM **Privately Held**
WEB: www.pmmco.com
SIC: 3537 Trucks, tractors, loaders, carriers & similar equipment

(G-17979)
PROMPT PATTERN INC
4175 E 10 Mile Rd (48091-1508)
PHONE.....................586 759-2030
Michael J Healy, *President*
EMP: 16 EST: 1961
SALES (est): 554.2K **Privately Held**
SIC: 3543 3369 3366 3365 Industrial patterns; nonferrous foundries; copper foundries; aluminum foundries; malleable iron foundries

(G-17980)
PROMPT PLASTICS
5524 E 10 Mile Rd (48091-3899)
PHONE.....................586 307-8525
Greg Keoenig, *Owner*
EMP: 7 EST: 2004
SALES (est): 161.1K **Privately Held**
SIC: 3089 Plastics products

(G-17981)
PROPER AROSPC & MACHINING LLC
13870 E 11 Mile Rd (48089-1471)
PHONE.....................586 779-8787
Mark A Rusch,
EMP: 6 EST: 2009
SALES (est): 597.6K **Privately Held**
WEB: www.propergroupintl.com
SIC: 3499 Fabricated metal products

(G-17982)
PROPER GROUP INTERNATIONAL INC
Also Called: Proper Polymers
14575 E 11 Mile Rd (48088-4861)
PHONE.....................586 552-5267
EMP: 175 **Privately Held**
WEB: www.propergroupintl.com
SIC: 3089 Vulcanized fiber plates, sheets, rods or tubes
PA: Proper Group International, Llc
13870 E 11 Mile Rd
Warren MI 48089

(G-17983)
PROPER GROUP INTERNATIONAL LLC (PA)
Also Called: Proper Tooling
13870 E 11 Mile Rd (48089-1471)
PHONE.....................586 779-8787
Geoff O'Brien, *CEO*
Raymond Scott, *Plant Mgr*
Ronald Truett, *Facilities Mgr*
Tarin Gibson, *Purchasing*
Tara Sides, *Purchasing*
▲ EMP: 6 EST: 1971
SALES (est): 106.6MM **Privately Held**
WEB: www.propergroupintl.com
SIC: 3089 Automotive parts, plastic

(G-17984)
PROPER POLYMERS - WARREN LLC (PA)
Also Called: PME - Croswell
13870 E 11 Mile Rd (48089-1471)
PHONE.....................586 552-5267
Michael J Brody, *Mng Member*
EMP: 1 EST: 2007
SALES (est): 3.1MM **Privately Held**
WEB: www.propergroupintl.com
SIC: 3089 Injection molding of plastics

(G-17985)
PROPER POLYMERS-TENNESSEE INC
Also Called: Proper Polymers Pulaski
13870 E 11 Mile Rd (48089-1471)
PHONE.....................586 779-8787
Mark Rusch, *CFO*
EMP: 1 EST: 2013
SALES (est): 1.1MM **Privately Held**
WEB: www.propergroupintl.com
SIC: 3089 3544 Molding primary plastic; special dies, tools, jigs & fixtures

(G-17986)
PROPER POLYMERS-PULASKI LLC
13870 E 11 Mile Rd (48089-1471)
PHONE.....................931 371-3147
EMP: 184
SALES (corp-wide): 14.1MM **Privately Held**
WEB: www.propergroupintl.com
SIC: 3089 Injection molding of plastics
PA: Proper Polymers-Pulaski, Llc
102 Magneti Marelli Dr
Pulaski TN 38478
931 371-3147

(G-17987)
PUNCHCRAFT MCHNING TOOLING LLC
Also Called: Warren Mfg Facility
30500 Ryan Rd (48092-1902)
PHONE.....................586 573-4840
Doug Grimm, *Mng Member*
▲ EMP: 1 EST: 1971
SQ FT: 25,000
SALES (est): 9.6MM
SALES (corp-wide): 4.7B **Publicly Held**
WEB: www.aam.com
SIC: 5084 3544 Machine tools & accessories; special dies & tools
HQ: Metaldyne Powertrain Components, Inc.
1 Dauch Dr
Detroit MI 48211
313 758-2000

(G-17988)
QUALITY CRAFT FABRICATORS LLC
24631 Gibson Dr (48089-4321)
PHONE.....................586 353-2104
Mark Fecteau,
EMP: 8
SALES (est): 160K **Privately Held**
SIC: 3444 Sheet metalwork

(G-17989)
QUANTUM DIGITAL VENTURES LLC
24680 Mound Rd (48091-2036)
PHONE.....................248 292-5686
Nicole Walsh, *Marketing Staff*
Dirk Grizzle,
Jaime Merrywether,
Lee Skandalaris,
EMP: 20 EST: 2006
SQ FT: 15,000
SALES (est): 1.5MM **Privately Held**
WEB: www.qdvllc.com
SIC: 2752 Promotional printing, lithographic

(G-17990)
R & M MACHINE INC
23895 Regency Park Dr (48089-2677)
PHONE.....................586 754-8447
Randy Tunison, *President*
Steve Tunison, *General Mgr*
EMP: 27 EST: 1986
SQ FT: 14,000
SALES (est): 2.5MM **Privately Held**
WEB: www.randm-machine.com
SIC: 3544 Special dies & tools

(G-17991)
R+R MFG/ENG INC
21448 Mullin Ave (48089-3083)
PHONE.....................586 758-4420
Joseph Duguay, *President*
EMP: 5 EST: 1974
SQ FT: 8,000
SALES (est): 469.2K **Privately Held**
SIC: 3599 Machine shop, jobbing & repair

(G-17992)
RADAR MEXICAN INVESTMENTS LLC
27101 Groesbeck Hwy (48089-4162)
PHONE.....................586 779-0300
David Zmyslowski, *President*
Mark Zmyslowski, *Vice Pres*
EMP: 34 EST: 2009
SQ FT: 75,000
SALES (est): 2.5MM
SALES (corp-wide): 1.6B **Privately Held**
WEB: www.shiloh.com
SIC: 3465 3469 Automotive stampings; metal stampings
HQ: Shiloh Industries, Inc.
880 Steel Dr
Valley City OH 44280

(G-17993)
RADAR TOOL & MANUFACTURING CO
22800 Hoover Rd (48089-2568)
PHONE.....................586 759-2800
Fred Deckert, *President*
Mark Deckert, *Vice Pres*
Paul Deckert, *Treasurer*
Karen Robinson, *Admin Sec*
EMP: 8 EST: 1945
SALES (est): 370K **Privately Held**
SIC: 3544 Special dies & tools

(G-17994)
REHMANN INDUSTRIES INC
23051 Roseberry Ave (48089-2214)
PHONE.....................810 748-7793
Robert Rehmann, *President*
▲ EMP: 10 EST: 1968
SQ FT: 9,600
SALES (est): 1.5MM **Privately Held**
WEB: www.rehmannind.com
SIC: 3599 Machine shop, jobbing & repair

(G-17995)
REIF CARBIDE TOOL CO INC
11055 E 9 Mile Rd (48089-2454)
P.O. Box 862 (48090-0862)
PHONE.....................586 754-1890
Fred John Reif, *President*
James Dennis, *Exec VP*
Vincent F Locicero, *Admin Sec*
EMP: 28 EST: 1946
SQ FT: 10,000
SALES (est): 1.7MM **Privately Held**
WEB: www.reifcarbidetool.com
SIC: 3545 5084 Cutting tools for machine tools; tools & accessories for machine tools; industrial machinery & equipment

(G-17996)
RENS LLC
Also Called: Maxi-Grip
24871 Gibson Dr (48089-4323)
PHONE.....................586 756-6777
Nathan Brower, *Owner*
Sagar Sheth, *Owner*
Nathan Bowers, *Principal*
EMP: 14 EST: 1976
SQ FT: 11,000
SALES (est): 1.6MM **Privately Held**
WEB: www.maxigrip.com
SIC: 3544 Jigs & fixtures

(G-17997)
RIZK NATIONAL INDUSTRIES INC
24422 Ryan Rd (48091-1654)
PHONE.....................586 757-4700
George Rizk, *President*
EMP: 14 EST: 1963
SQ FT: 30,000
SALES (est): 1.1MM **Privately Held**
WEB: www.usabatterychargers.com
SIC: 3612 3694 Autotransformers, electric (power transformers); battery charging generators, automobile & aircraft

(G-17998)
ROYAL FLEX-N-GATE OAK LLC
5663 E 9 Mile Rd (48091-2562)
PHONE.....................248 549-3800
Malcolm Koresh, *Controller*
Kevin Hamilton, *Mng Member*
Timothy Graham,
James Zsebok,
▲ EMP: 350 EST: 2004
SQ FT: 250,000
SALES (est): 86.2MM
SALES (corp-wide): 1.5B **Privately Held**
WEB: www.flex-n-gate.com
SIC: 3469 3465 Metal stampings; body parts, automobile: stamped metal
PA: Flex-N-Gate Llc
1306 E University Ave
Urbana IL 61802
217 384-6600

(G-17999)
ROYCE CORPORATION
23042 Sherwood Ave (48091-2024)
PHONE.....................586 758-1500
Glen B Brown, *President*
EMP: 5 EST: 1968
SQ FT: 8,000
SALES (est): 719.6K **Privately Held**
WEB: www.roycecorporation.com
SIC: 3714 Motor vehicle parts & accessories

(G-18000)
RTO AUTO REPAIR SERVICE
28837 Bunert Rd (48088-3885)
PHONE.....................586 779-9450
Roz Oskui, *Principal*
EMP: 5 EST: 2009
SALES (est): 37.4K **Privately Held**
SIC: 7694 7549 5531 Armature rewinding shops; lubrication service, automotive; automobile & truck equipment & parts

(G-18001)
SALERNO TOOL WORKS INC
21034 Ryan Rd (48091-2740)
PHONE.....................586 755-5000
Ramo A Salerno Sr, *President*
Ramo A Salerno Jr, *Vice Pres*
Rhonda Salerno, *Admin Sec*
EMP: 8 EST: 1964
SQ FT: 7,000
SALES (est): 558.9K **Privately Held**
WEB: www.salernotoolworks.amlnk.com
SIC: 3545 Precision tools, machinists'

(G-18002)
SAS GLOBAL CORPORATION (PA)
21601 Mullin Ave (48089-3008)
PHONE.....................248 414-4470
Robert Wark, *President*
Samuel Avetisyan, *Principal*
Tim Foley, *Vice Pres*
Brian Henkel, *Vice Pres*
Phil Lizak, *Plant Mgr*
▲ EMP: 110

▲ = Import ▼ = Export
◆ = Import/Export

GEOGRAPHIC SECTION

SQ FT: 185,000
SALES (est): 44.4MM **Privately Held**
WEB: www.sasglobalcorp.com
SIC: 3441 3479 5051 Fabricated structural metal; coating of metals & formed products; metals service centers & offices; steel

(G-18003)
SAS GLOBAL CORPORATION
Also Called: Sure Alloy Steel
21601 Mullin Ave (48089-3008)
PHONE 248 414-4470
Brian Henkel, *Vice Pres*
Chuck Stage, *Purchasing*
EMP: 51
SALES (corp-wide): 44.4MM **Privately Held**
WEB: www.sasglobalcorp.com
SIC: 5051 3548 3441 Steel; welding & cutting apparatus & accessories; fabricated structural metal
PA: Sas Global Corporation
 21601 Mullin Ave
 Warren MI 48089
 248 414-4470

(G-18004)
SAWING LOGZ LLC
28634 Milton Ave (48092-2368)
PHONE 586 883-5649
Jeff Shelby, *President*
EMP: 9 **EST:** 2003
SALES (est): 468.4K **Privately Held**
SIC: 2421 Sawmills & planing mills, general

(G-18005)
SCHWARTZ INDUSTRIES INC
6909 E 11 Mile Rd (48092-2799)
PHONE 586 759-1777
Keith Pratt, *Ch of Bd*
John Channing, *General Mgr*
Deborah Krause, *Controller*
EMP: 35 **EST:** 1963
SQ FT: 19,000
SALES (est): 4.3MM
SALES (corp-wide): 7.3MM **Privately Held**
WEB: www.sharedvision.net
SIC: 3599 Machine shop, jobbing & repair
PA: Shared Vision, L.L.C.
 6909 E 11 Mile Rd
 Warren MI 48092
 586 759-1777

(G-18006)
SCHWARTZ MACHINE CO
4441 E 8 Mile Rd (48091-2798)
PHONE 586 756-2300
Robert C Schwartz, *Ch of Bd*
Cheryl Zeglin, *President*
Kenneth Sabo, *President*
Eleanor Kidwell, *Principal*
Doug Rose, *Principal*
EMP: 35 **EST:** 1951
SQ FT: 36,000
SALES (est): 7.8MM **Privately Held**
WEB: www.schwartzmachine.com
SIC: 3599 Machine shop, jobbing & repair

(G-18007)
SD OIL ENTERPRISES INC
28851 Hoover Rd (48093-4102)
PHONE 248 688-1419
Vikas Tandan, *Principal*
EMP: 7 **EST:** 2016
SALES (est): 791.6K **Privately Held**
SIC: 1311 Crude petroleum & natural gas

(G-18008)
SELECT DISTRIBUTORS LLC
2324 Morrissey Ave (48091-3271)
PHONE 586 510-4647
EMP: 11
SQ FT: 1,600
SALES (est): 907.2K **Privately Held**
SIC: 2086 3999 5074 Mfg Soft Drinks Mfg Misc Products Whol Plumbing Equip/Supp

(G-18009)
SELECT GRAPHICS CORPORATION
24024 Gibson Dr (48089-2001)
PHONE 586 755-7700
Jeff Angelosante, *President*
EMP: 15 **EST:** 1996
SQ FT: 12,500
SALES (est): 1.3MM **Privately Held**
WEB: www.select-graphics.com
SIC: 2752 Commercial printing, lithographic

(G-18010)
SHARED VISION LLC (PA)
6909 E 11 Mile Rd (48092-3907)
PHONE 586 759-1777
Steve Elwell, *General Mgr*
John Braine, *CFO*
Michelle Tannu, *Director*
Keith Pratt,
EMP: 19 **EST:** 2001
SQ FT: 25,000
SALES (est): 7.3MM **Privately Held**
WEB: www.sharedvision.net
SIC: 3599 Machine shop, jobbing & repair

(G-18011)
SHEILA J EATON PHD PC
12200 E 13 Mile Rd Ste 11 (48093-3093)
PHONE 586 215-1035
Sheila Eaton, *Principal*
EMP: 5 **EST:** 2016
SALES (est): 90.9K **Privately Held**
SIC: 3625 Motor controls & accessories

(G-18012)
SHEPTIME MUSIC
27035 Lorraine Ave (48093-4443)
PHONE 586 806-9058
Sean Shepard, *Owner*
EMP: 5 **EST:** 2012
SALES (est): 76.6K **Privately Held**
SIC: 2731 7389 Book music: publishing & printing;

(G-18013)
SIGN STUDIO INC
11450 Stephens Rd (48089-3861)
PHONE 214 526-6940
Lyester Billhymer, *Manager*
EMP: 4 **EST:** 2018
SALES (est): 103.7K **Privately Held**
SIC: 3993 Signs & advertising specialties

(G-18014)
SKYBLADE FAN COMPANY
24501 Hoover Rd (48089-1930)
PHONE 586 806-5107
EMP: 11 **EST:** 2012
SALES (est): 609.4K **Privately Held**
WEB: www.skybladefans.com
SIC: 3564 Blowing fans: industrial or commercial; air cleaning systems; exhaust fans: industrial or commercial

(G-18015)
SMO INTERNATIONAL INC
Also Called: Bigdaddybeauty.com
31745 Mound St (48092-1611)
PHONE 248 275-1091
Dennis Smolinski, *President*
▲ **EMP:** 16 **EST:** 2007
SALES (est): 571.6K **Privately Held**
WEB: www.infinityhair.com
SIC: 2844 5122 Toilet preparations; drugs & drug proprietaries

(G-18016)
SMS TECHNICAL SERVICES
12880 E 9 Mile Rd (48089-2664)
PHONE 586 445-0330
Doug Dunworth, *Administration*
EMP: 10 **EST:** 2015
SALES (est): 2.3MM **Privately Held**
SIC: 3569 General industrial machinery

(G-18017)
SONUS ENGINEERED SOLUTIONS LLC
23031 Sherwood Ave (48091-2044)
PHONE 586 427-3838
Tim Droege, *CEO*
Edin Jakupovic, *Mfg Staff*
Richard Krause, *Mfg Staff*
Rachael Carmichael, *Buyer*
Rachael Jablonski, *Buyer*
◆ **EMP:** 120
SQ FT: 120,000
SALES (est): 23.4MM **Privately Held**
WEB: www.sonus-es.com
SIC: 3089 Plastic containers, except foam

(G-18018)
SPECILTY VHCL ACQUISITION CORP
Also Called: ASC
6115 E 13 Mile Rd (48092-2050)
PHONE 586 446-4701
Joe Bione, *CEO*
Heinz Prechter, *Principal*
Marcus Shelley, *Controller*
▲ **EMP:** 94 **EST:** 2007
SQ FT: 38,000
SALES (est): 19.6MM
SALES (corp-wide): 79.1MM **Privately Held**
WEB: www.hpcap.com
SIC: 8748 2394 Systems analysis or design; convertible tops, canvas or boat: from purchased materials
PA: Hancock Park Associates Ii, L.P.
 10350 Santa Monica Blvd # 295
 Los Angeles CA 90025
 310 228-6900

(G-18019)
SPENCE INDUSTRIES INC
23888 Dequindre Rd (48091-1823)
PHONE 586 758-3800
Charles Dillon, *President*
EMP: 4 **EST:** 1958
SQ FT: 2,500
SALES (est): 350.5K **Privately Held**
WEB: www.jo-plug.com
SIC: 3545 Gauges (machine tool accessories)

(G-18020)
SPINA ELECTRIC COMPANY
26801 Groesbeck Hwy (48089-1583)
PHONE 586 771-8080
John Spina, *President*
Paul Spina, *President*
Albert Spina, *Chairman*
Timothy Spina, *Vice Pres*
Rick Gudenau, *Sales Mgr*
EMP: 35 **EST:** 1948
SQ FT: 29,000
SALES (est): 14.9MM **Privately Held**
WEB: www.spinaelectric.com
SIC: 5063 7694 7629 Motors, electric; electric motor repair; electrical repair shops

(G-18021)
SPINA WIND LLC
26801 Groesbeck Hwy (48089-4160)
PHONE 586 771-8080
John Spina,
Timothy Spina,
EMP: 9 **EST:** 2011 **Privately Held**
SIC: 3621 Windmills, electric generating

(G-18022)
SPM INDUSTRIES INC
2455 E 10 Mile Rd (48091-3704)
PHONE 586 758-1100
Frank C Bellisario, *President*
Ronald A Di Mambro, *Vice Pres*
EMP: 25 **EST:** 1972
SQ FT: 20,000
SALES (est): 3MM **Privately Held**
WEB: www.spmind.com
SIC: 3599 Machine shop, jobbing & repair

(G-18023)
SPRINGER PUBLISHING CO INC (PA)
Also Called: New Center News
31201 Chicago Rd S A101 (48093-5500)
P.O. Box 1046, New Baltimore (48047-8046)
PHONE 586 939-6800
William L Springer IL, *President*
Mary Gatsch, *Publisher*
Azarya Feig, *Opers Staff*
Lisa Torretta, *Opers Staff*
Shaun Duffy, *Sales Staff*
EMP: 18 **EST:** 1933
SQ FT: 2,400
SALES (est): 1.6MM **Privately Held**
WEB: www.springerpublishing.com
SIC: 2711 Newspapers, publishing & printing

(G-18024)
SRG GLOBAL AUTOMOTIVE LLC (DH)
Also Called: Guardian Automotive Trim
23751 Amber Ave (48089-6000)
PHONE 586 757-7800
Daniel J Davis, *CEO*
Kevin Myers, *Senior VP*
Joseph Abbruzzi, *Vice Pres*
Chuck Wilson, *Vice Pres*
David Serpa, *Plant Mgr*
▲ **EMP:** 70 **EST:** 1949
SQ FT: 25,000
SALES (est): 352.8MM
SALES (corp-wide): 36.9B **Privately Held**
WEB: www.guardian.com
SIC: 3089 3465 Extruded finished plastic products; molding primary plastic; moldings or trim, automobile: stamped metal

(G-18025)
ST CLAIR STEEL CORPORATION
Also Called: Steal Leading and Drum Company
27720 College Park Dr (48088-4882)
PHONE 586 758-4356
Thomas Taylor, *President*
EMP: 4 **EST:** 1998
SALES (est): 451.3K **Privately Held**
SIC: 3312 Hot-rolled iron & steel products

(G-18026)
STANDARD PRINTING OF WARREN
13647 E 10 Mile Rd (48089-4799)
PHONE 586 771-3770
William Ventimiglia Jr, *President*
EMP: 5
SQ FT: 6,100
SALES (est): 328.8K **Privately Held**
WEB: www.standardprintingmi.com
SIC: 2752 2759 Commercial printing, offset; letterpress printing

(G-18027)
STANHOPE TOOL INC
Also Called: J E Wood Comp
2357 E 9 Mile Rd (48091-2162)
PHONE 248 585-5711
Brian Fish, *President*
James Dayf, *Vice Pres*
EMP: 32 **EST:** 1962
SALES (est): 1MM **Privately Held**
WEB: www.stanhopetool.com
SIC: 3545 3541 3599 3544 Gauges (machine tool accessories); precision measuring tools; machine tools, metal cutting type; machine & other job shop work; special dies, tools, jigs & fixtures

(G-18028)
STATE BUILDING PRODUCT INC
21751 Schmeman Ave (48089-3219)
PHONE 586 772-8878
Andrew Stark, *CEO*
Troy Frank, *President*
Peter Stark, *President*
Eric Griswold, *CFO*
Jodi Kurzyniec, *Controller*
EMP: 45 **EST:** 1999
SQ FT: 144,500
SALES (est): 8.5MM **Privately Held**
WEB: www.statebp.com
SIC: 3444 Studs & joists, sheet metal

(G-18029)
STEEL MILL COMPONENTS INC
22522 Hoover Rd (48089-2575)
PHONE 586 920-2595
Robert Appleyard, *Manager*
EMP: 16 **Privately Held**
WEB: www.steelmillcomponents.com
SIC: 3312 Blast furnaces & steel mills
PA: Steel Mill Components, Inc.
 17000 Ecorse Rd
 Allen Park MI 48101

(G-18030)
SUNDANCE BEVERAGES INC
Also Called: Sundance Beverage Company
6600 E 9 Mile Rd (48091-2673)
PHONE 586 755-9470
Nick A Caporella, *Ch of Bd*
Eric Hellman, *Plant Mgr*
David Paul, *QC Mgr*

Warren - Macomb County (G-18031) GEOGRAPHIC SECTION

EMP: 69 **EST:** 2005
SALES (est): 12.3MM
SALES (corp-wide): 1B Publicly Held
WEB: www.everfreshjuice.com
SIC: 2086 Fruit drinks (less than 100% juice); packaged in cans, etc.
PA: National Beverage Corp.
8100 Sw 10th St Ste 4000
Plantation FL 33324
954 581-0922

(G-18031)
SUPER STEEL TREATING INC
6227 Rinke Ave (48091-2070)
PHONE 586 755-9140
Terence D Farrar, *President*
Jim Farrar, *General Mgr*
Don Huldin, *Principal*
Sue Nash, *COO*
Charles H Farrar, *Vice Pres*
▲ **EMP:** 65 **EST:** 1967
SQ FT: 300,000
SALES (est): 10.2MM Privately Held
WEB: www.supersteeltreating.com
SIC: 3398 Annealing of metal

(G-18032)
T M WOOD PRODUCTS MFG INC
24301 Hoover Rd (48089-1971)
PHONE 586 427-2364
Antonio Mattarelli, *Principal*
EMP: 16 **EST:** 1991
SALES (est): 1MM Privately Held
WEB: www.tmwood.com
SIC: 2431 Millwork

(G-18033)
T SHIRT GUY
31368 Beechwood Dr (48088-2080)
PHONE 586 944-5900
Vince Williams, *Principal*
EMP: 4 **EST:** 2008
SALES (est): 70.3K Privately Held
SIC: 2759 Screen printing

(G-18034)
TADEY FRANK R RADIAN TOOL CO
23823 Blackstone Ave (48089-4218)
PHONE 586 754-7422
Kris Tadey, *CEO*
Ann Tadey, *Corp Secy*
EMP: 4 **EST:** 1973
SQ FT: 3,200
SALES (est): 448.9K Privately Held
SIC: 3544 Special dies, tools, jigs & fixtures

(G-18035)
TAMBRA INVESTMENTS INC
Also Called: Real Time Diagnostics
23247 Pinewood St (48091-4754)
PHONE 866 662-7897
Michael D Evans, *CEO*
Brent Devooght, *CFO*
Beth Thibault, *Comp Spec*
Nicole Simpson, *Director*
EMP: 3 **EST:** 2009
SALES (est): 1.2MM Privately Held
WEB: www.rtdlabs.com
SIC: 3841 Surgical instruments & apparatus

(G-18036)
TANK TRUCK SERVICE & SALES INC (PA)
25150 Dequindre Rd (48091-1384)
PHONE 586 757-6500
James H Lawler, *President*
David M Lawler, *Vice Pres*
Karen Lawler, *Treasurer*
Jeff Quagliani, *Sales Staff*
John Marsack, *Manager*
EMP: 32 **EST:** 1978
SQ FT: 18,000
SALES (est): 8.9MM Privately Held
WEB: www.tanktruckservice.com
SIC: 3541 3795 Machine tool replacement & repair parts, metal cutting types; tanks & tank components

(G-18037)
TECHNICAL ROTARY SERVICES INC
14020 Hovey Ave (48089-1457)
PHONE 586 772-6755
Craig Barker, *President*
EMP: 7 **EST:** 1984
SQ FT: 6,000
SALES (est): 1MM Privately Held
WEB: www.precisionrotarytables.com
SIC: 3545 Rotary tables

(G-18038)
TESLA MACHINE & TOOL LTD
5415 E 8 Mile Rd (48091-2842)
PHONE 586 441-2402
Nikola Glusac, *President*
EMP: 7 **EST:** 2010
SALES (est): 69.1K Privately Held
SIC: 3599 Machine & other job shop work

(G-18039)
TICKET AVENGERS INC
28599 Wauketa Ave (48092-2531)
PHONE 248 635-3279
Deangelo Smith, *Principal*
EMP: 5 **EST:** 2020
SALES (est): 117.2K Privately Held
SIC: 7372 Application computer software

(G-18040)
TONY S DIE MACHINE COMPANY
24358 Groesbeck Hwy (48089-4718)
PHONE 586 773-7379
Douglas Wolfbauer, *Partner*
Doug Wolfbauer, *Partner*
Robert Wolfbauer, *Partner*
Dave Kohler, *Plant Mgr*
EMP: 11 **EST:** 1969
SQ FT: 44,000
SALES (est): 160.9K Privately Held
SIC: 3544 Industrial molds; jigs & fixtures

(G-18041)
TOTAL GRINDING SOLUTIONS LLC
13265 E 8 Mile Rd (48089-3275)
PHONE 586 541-5300
Chanley Chambers, *Sales Staff*
Dan Geddes, *Manager*
EMP: 17 **EST:** 2015
SALES (est): 696.3K Privately Held
WEB: www.totalgrindingsolutions.com
SIC: 3999 Custom pulverizing & grinding of plastic materials

(G-18042)
TRI COUNTY PRECISION GRINDING
Also Called: Tri-County Precision Grinding
21960 Schmeman Ave (48089-3281)
PHONE 586 776-6600
Lee Roy Hall, *President*
Ellen L Hall, *Corp Secy*
EMP: 21 **EST:** 1973
SQ FT: 17,300
SALES (est): 1.3MM Privately Held
WEB: www.tricountygrinding.com
SIC: 3599 Machine shop, jobbing & repair

(G-18043)
TRIG TOOL INC
26657 Haverhill Dr (48091-1119)
PHONE 248 543-2550
Andrey Duzyt, *President*
Andrey Duzyj, *Corp Secy*
EMP: 6 **EST:** 1995
SALES (est): 476K Privately Held
WEB: www.1000-oaks.com
SIC: 3599 Machine shop, jobbing & repair

(G-18044)
TRUEMNER ENTERPRISES INC
25418 Ryan Rd (48091-1326)
PHONE 586 756-6470
Dale Truemner, *President*
Mary Truemner, *Vice Pres*
EMP: 7 **EST:** 1900
SQ FT: 5,000 Privately Held
SIC: 3566 Gears, power transmission, except automotive; reduction gears & gear units for turbines, except automotive

(G-18045)
TSS INC
Also Called: TSS
21000 Hoover Rd (48089-3153)
PHONE 586 427-0070
Ismael Mosa Sasha, *President*
Mike Mustedanagic, *Mfg Staff*
Bobby Jones, *Sales Staff*
Ryan Caldwell, *Graphic Designe*
▲ **EMP:** 20 **EST:** 1990
SQ FT: 2,400
SALES (est): 10.4MM Privately Held
WEB: www.tsscws.com
SIC: 3993 Signs, not made in custom sign painting shops; electric signs

(G-18046)
TUBE-CO INC
23094 Schoenherr Rd (48089-2668)
PHONE 586 775-0244
Melissa Shevela, *President*
EMP: 7 **EST:** 1962
SQ FT: 15,000
SALES (est): 1.1MM Privately Held
WEB: www.tubecoinc.com
SIC: 3498 Tube fabricating (contract bending & shaping)

(G-18047)
UNITED LIGHTING STANDARDS INC (PA)
23171 Groesbeck Hwy (48089-6002)
PHONE 586 774-5650
Cathy Lee, *Partner*
Ben Tassin, *Partner*
Andrew Wojcik, *Partner*
Bob Wesch, *COO*
Cheryl Kowalski, *Technical Staff*
EMP: 65 **EST:** 1971
SQ FT: 57,500
SALES (est): 9.8MM Privately Held
WEB: www.unitedlightingstandards.com
SIC: 3446 Architectural metalwork

(G-18048)
US BORING INC
24895 Mound Rd Ste D (48091-5398)
PHONE 586 756-7511
EMP: 4
SQ FT: 5,000
SALES (est): 370K Privately Held
SIC: 3544 Mfg Dies/Tools/Jigs/Fixtures

(G-18049)
US METALS LLC
11675 E 8 Mile Rd (48089-3147)
PHONE 586 915-2885
Louie Kristovski, *Owner*
Destin Clark, *Owner*
EMP: 11 **EST:** 2012
SALES (est): 264.4K Privately Held
SIC: 3549 3559 Coil winding machines for springs; metal finishing equipment for plating, etc.

(G-18050)
VAC-MET INC
7236 Murthum Ave (48092-1296)
PHONE 586 264-8100
Robert F Gunow Jr, *President*
EMP: 20 **EST:** 1981
SQ FT: 14,000
SALES (est): 4.6MM Privately Held
WEB: www.vac-met.com
SIC: 3398 Brazing (hardening) of metal

(G-18051)
VARIETY FOODS INC (PA)
7001 Chicago Rd (48092-1615)
PHONE 586 268-4900
James Champane Jr, *CEO*
Dean Champane, *President*
Chris Champane, *Vice Pres*
George Champane, *Treasurer*
EMP: 61 **EST:** 1928
SQ FT: 55,000
SALES (est): 4.4MM Privately Held
WEB: www.varietyfoodsinc.com
SIC: 2068 2099 2096 Salted & roasted nuts & seeds; food preparations; potato chips & other potato-based snacks

(G-18052)
VEET AXELSON LIBERTY INDUSTRY
14322 E 9 Mile Rd (48089-5032)
PHONE 586 776-3000
Robert Veet, *Owner*
EMP: 10 **EST:** 1925
SALES (est): 621.2K Privately Held
SIC: 3599 Machine shop, jobbing & repair

(G-18053)
VEET INDUSTRIES INC
Also Called: Axelson-Veet-Liberty Inds
14322 E 9 Mile Rd (48089-5032)
PHONE 586 776-3000
Robert C Veit, *President*
EMP: 10 **EST:** 1921
SQ FT: 240,000
SALES (est): 694.8K Privately Held
SIC: 3714 3549 3728 Motor vehicle parts & accessories; metalworking machinery; aircraft parts & equipment

(G-18054)
VENTRA GREENWICH HOLDINGS CORP
Also Called: Ventra Greenwich Tooling Co
5663 E 9 Mile Rd (48091-2562)
PHONE 586 759-8900
Tom Orr, *Director*
EMP: 49 **EST:** 2009
SALES (est): 5.4MM Privately Held
SIC: 3541 Machine tools, metal cutting type

(G-18055)
VERTICAL TECHNOLOGIES LLC
12901 Stephens Rd (48089-4333)
PHONE 586 619-0141
Tim McShane, *Sales Mgr*
Brian Burns,
EMP: 26 **EST:** 2001
SQ FT: 48,000
SALES (est): 2.5MM Privately Held
WEB: www.verticaltechnologies.org
SIC: 3544 Special dies & tools

(G-18056)
VIROTECH BIOMATERIALS INC
8260 Dartmouth Dr (48093-2815)
PHONE 313 421-1648
WEI Song, *President*
EMP: 5 **EST:** 2014
SALES (est): 184.5K Privately Held
SIC: 3841 7389 Medical instruments & equipment, blood & bone work; business services

(G-18057)
WARLOCK LURES
4444 Reader Dr (48092-1751)
PHONE 586 977-1606
Dennis Osborn, *Principal*
EMP: 4 **EST:** 2016
SALES (est): 51.7K Privately Held
SIC: 3949 Sporting & athletic goods

(G-18058)
WARREN ABRASIVES INC
25800 Groesbeck Hwy (48089-4143)
P.O. Box 530, Roseville (48066-0530)
PHONE 586 772-0002
EMP: 14
SQ FT: 12,000
SALES: 840K Privately Held
SIC: 3291 Manufacturor Of Abrasive Grinding Wheels

(G-18059)
WARREN INDUSTRIAL WELDING CO (PA)
24275 Hoover Rd (48089-1973)
PHONE 586 756-0230
Gregory Lee, *President*
Lester Hall, *Assistant VP*
EMP: 16 **EST:** 1965
SQ FT: 10,000
SALES (est): 1.4MM Privately Held
WEB: www.warrenindustrialwelding.com
SIC: 7692 Welding repair

GEOGRAPHIC SECTION
Washington - Macomb County (G-18087)

(G-18060)
WARREN MANUFACTURING LLC
Also Called: Warren Mfg Acquisition
28201 Van Dyke Ave (48093-2713)
PHONE...................................586 467-1600
Jeff Cwiek, *Purch Dir*
Jeffery Zarling, *Supervisor*
Brian A Simon,
EMP: 1 **EST:** 2017
SQ FT: 630,000
SALES (est): 2.2MM **Publicly Held**
WEB: www.dana.com
SIC: 3356 3462 3714 Nonferrous rolling & drawing; iron & steel forgings; differentials & parts, motor vehicle
PA: Dana Incorporated
3939 Technology Dr
Maumee OH 43537

(G-18061)
WARREN SCREW PRODUCTS INC
13201 Stephens Rd (48089-4378)
PHONE...................................586 757-1280
Chris Kaspari, *CEO*
Carl Kaspari III, *President*
Steven G Kaspari, *Vice Pres*
Sue Ann Wessel, *Controller*
EMP: 110 **EST:** 1957
SQ FT: 140,000
SALES (est): 19.4MM **Privately Held**
WEB: www.warrenscrew.com
SIC: 3451 3714 Screw machine products; motor vehicle parts & accessories

(G-18062)
WARREN STEEL CO
21601 Hoover Rd Ste Ams (48089-3157)
P.O. Box 183552, Utica (48318-3552)
PHONE...................................586 756-6600
Jerry Serediuk, *President*
EMP: 8 **EST:** 2003
SQ FT: 40,000
SALES (est): 574.8K **Privately Held**
SIC: 3316 7694 Strip steel, flat bright, cold-rolled: purchased hot-rolled; coil winding service

(G-18063)
WARRIOR SPORTS INC (DH)
Also Called: Brine
32125 Hollingsworth Ave (48092-3804)
PHONE...................................800 968-7845
David K Morrow, *President*
Kevin Klucka, *Senior Buyer*
John Vader, *Buyer*
Twain Glaser, *Engineer*
Fredrick Sohm, *CFO*
▲ **EMP:** 198 **EST:** 1992
SQ FT: 120,000
SALES (est): 63.6MM
SALES (corp-wide): 1B **Privately Held**
WEB: www.warrior.com
SIC: 3949 3149 Hockey equipment & supplies, general; athletic shoes, except rubber or plastic
HQ: New Balance Athletics, Inc.
100 Guest St Fl 5
Boston MA 02135
617 783-4000

(G-18064)
WELDALOY PRODUCTS COMPANY
24011 Hoover Rd (48089-1931)
PHONE...................................586 758-5550
Jim Smietana, *CEO*
Katelynne McDougall, *General Mgr*
Richard E Warren, *Chairman*
Ramachandra Canumalla, *Vice Pres*
Kurt Ruppenthal, *Vice Pres*
▲ **EMP:** 58 **EST:** 1946
SQ FT: 33,000
SALES (est): 16.8MM **Privately Held**
WEB: www.weldaloy.com
SIC: 3449 3463 Miscellaneous metalwork; nonferrous forgings

(G-18065)
WELDMET INDUSTRIES INC
21799 Schmeman Ave (48089-3219)
PHONE...................................586 773-0533
Andrew Stark, *President*
EMP: 5 **EST:** 1993
SQ FT: 9,000
SALES (est): 434.5K **Privately Held**
SIC: 3544 Special dies & tools

(G-18066)
WELFORM ELECTRODES INC
2147 Kenney Ave (48091-1379)
PHONE...................................586 755-1184
Charles S Beach, *President*
John Pippin, *General Mgr*
C Edward Slade, *Vice Pres*
Blaise Flack, *CFO*
EMP: 20 **EST:** 1970
SQ FT: 12,700
SALES (est): 3.1MM **Privately Held**
WEB: www.welform.com
SIC: 3699 3823 3548 Electrical welding equipment; industrial instrmnts msrmnt display/control process variable; welding apparatus

(G-18067)
WICO METAL PRODUCTS COMPANY (PA)
23500 Sherwood Ave (48091-5363)
PHONE...................................586 755-9600
Richard A Brodie, *President*
Mike Bennett, *Exec VP*
Suzette Katopodes, *Vice Pres*
Elmer Kretsch, *Vice Pres*
Mike Piatt, *Vice Pres*
▲ **EMP:** 137 **EST:** 1964
SQ FT: 100,000
SALES (est): 43.3MM **Privately Held**
WEB: www.wicometal.com
SIC: 3465 3469 3452 3429 Automotive stampings; metal stampings; bolts, nuts, rivets & washers; manufactured hardware (general)

(G-18068)
WITHERS CORPORATION
23801 Mound Rd (48091-5319)
PHONE...................................586 758-2750
Kathleen M Withers, *President*
Mike Withers, *Vice Pres*
Brian Withers, *Treasurer*
EMP: 22 **EST:** 1973
SQ FT: 22,000
SALES (est): 1.6MM **Privately Held**
SIC: 3544 Special dies & tools

(G-18069)
WOCHEN-POST
Also Called: German/American Newspaper Age
12200 E 13 Mile Rd Ste 14 (48093-3093)
PHONE...................................248 641-9944
Knuth Beth, *Owner*
EMP: 4 **EST:** 1854
SALES (est): 81.9K **Privately Held**
WEB: www.wochenpostusa.com
SIC: 2711 Newspapers, publishing & printing

(G-18070)
WOLVERINE CARBIDE AND TOO
21777 Hoover Rd (48089-2544)
PHONE...................................586 497-7000
EMP: 9 **EST:** 2017
SALES (est): 697.2K **Privately Held**
WEB: www.wolverinecarbide.com
SIC: 2819 Carbides

(G-18071)
WOLVERINE DIE CAST LTD PRTNR O
30418 Saint Onge Cir (48088-3325)
PHONE...................................586 757-1900
Michael Karadimas, *Partner*
◆ **EMP:** 40 **EST:** 1960
SALES (est): 16.5MM **Privately Held**
WEB: www.wolverinediecast.com
SIC: 3364 3365 3363 Zinc & zinc-base alloy die-castings; aluminum foundries; aluminum die-castings

(G-18072)
WORKBLADES INC
21535 Groesbeck Hwy (48089-4921)
PHONE...................................586 778-0060
Edward P Bard, *President*
Edward P Bard Jr, *Vice Pres*
EMP: 22 **EST:** 1984
SQ FT: 21,000
SALES (est): 2.8MM **Privately Held**
WEB: www.workbladesinc.com
SIC: 3545 3425 Cutting tools for machine tools; saw blades & handsaws

(G-18073)
WRIGHT & FILIPPIS LLC
13384 E 11 Mile Rd (48089-1367)
PHONE...................................586 756-4020
Les Van Kuren, *Manager*
EMP: 19
SALES (corp-wide): 77.5MM **Privately Held**
WEB: www.firsttoserve.com
SIC: 3842 5999 7352 Surgical appliances & supplies; convalescent equipment & supplies; medical equipment rental
PA: Wright & Filippis, Llc
2845 Crooks Rd
Rochester Hills MI 48309
248 829-8292

(G-18074)
XC LLC
24060 Hoover Rd (48089-1942)
PHONE...................................586 755-1660
Chain S Sandhu,
EMP: 19 **EST:** 1994
SQ FT: 110,000
SALES (est): 1MM **Privately Held**
SIC: 2821 Molding compounds, plastics

(G-18075)
XMCO INC
5501 Entp Ct Ste 400 (48092)
PHONE...................................586 558-8510
Linda Czajka, *President*
Ann Lee, *Publisher*
Billy Gragg, *General Mgr*
Neva Carter, *Editor*
Thomas Panamaroff, *Chairman*
EMP: 58
SALES: 11.1MM
SALES (corp-wide): 323.8MM **Privately Held**
WEB: www.xmcoinc.com
SIC: 2731 Book publishing
HQ: Koniag Government Services, Llc
3800 Centerpoint Dr # 502
Anchorage AK 99503
907 561-2668

(G-18076)
XPLOR OUTSIDE BOX LLC
31487 Pinto Dr (48093-7624)
PHONE...................................248 961-0536
Del C Schroeder,
EMP: 10 **EST:** 2014
SALES (est): 345.9K **Privately Held**
WEB: www.xplor.org
SIC: 3999 Manufacturing industries

(G-18077)
XTREME SIGNS INC
27209 Van Dyke Ave (48093-2845)
PHONE...................................586 486-5068
EMP: 6 **EST:** 2016
SALES (est): 112.5K **Privately Held**
WEB: www.xtremesignsdesign.com
SIC: 3993 Signs & advertising specialties

Washington
Macomb County

(G-18078)
ARTFUL SCRAPBOOKING & RUBBER
7220 Smale St (48094-2750)
PHONE...................................586 651-1577
Pam Planitz, *Owner*
EMP: 5 **EST:** 2005
SALES (est): 183.7K **Privately Held**
SIC: 2782 Scrapbooks

(G-18079)
DEMMAK INDUSTRIES LLC
Also Called: Iridium Manufacturing
12475 31 Mile Rd Ste B (48095-1483)
PHONE...................................586 884-6441
Walter Demock, *Mng Member*
EMP: 12 **EST:** 2002
SALES (est): 1.3MM **Privately Held**
SIC: 3599 Machine shop, jobbing & repair

(G-18080)
GREEN AGE PRODUCTS & SVCS LLC
Also Called: Green Age Organics
64155 Van Dyke Rd Ste 238 (48095-2580)
PHONE...................................586 207-5724
Harold W Parslow Jr,
EMP: 10 **EST:** 2007
SQ FT: 12,500
SALES (est): 909.6K **Privately Held**
WEB: www.greenageproducts.com
SIC: 5084 3599 Industrial machinery & equipment; custom machinery

(G-18081)
INNOVATIVE MOLD INC
Also Called: I M I
12500 31 Mile Rd (48095-1466)
PHONE...................................586 752-2996
George Kasper, *President*
Dave Kasper, *Vice Pres*
Robert Auger, *Opers Mgr*
Jason Owens, *Manager*
Quinn Sova, *Manager*
EMP: 22
SQ FT: 9,500
SALES (est): 3.9MM **Privately Held**
WEB: www.innovativemoldinc.com
SIC: 3544 Special dies & tools; industrial molds

(G-18082)
INSTALLERS GLASS BLOCK
6177 Trailside Dr (48094-3845)
PHONE...................................586 463-1214
Joe Winokur, *Owner*
EMP: 4 **EST:** 2011
SALES (est): 43.7K **Privately Held**
WEB: www.gbi-glassblock.net
SIC: 3229 Pressed & blown glass

(G-18083)
LONGSHOT GOLF INC
60750 Stonecrest Dr (48094-1498)
PHONE...................................586 764-9847
James Krause, *Owner*
EMP: 4 **EST:** 1988
SALES (est): 51.7K **Privately Held**
WEB: www.longshotgolf.com
SIC: 3949 Sporting & athletic goods

(G-18084)
LOW COST SURCING SOLUTIONS LLC
Also Called: Lcss Worldwide
57253 Willow Way Ct (48094-4220)
P.O. Box 80672, Rochester (48308-0672)
PHONE...................................248 535-7721
Douglas Stahl, *Mng Member*
▲ **EMP:** 4 **EST:** 2009
SQ FT: 15,000
SALES (est): 259K **Privately Held**
SIC: 3469 3199 Metal stampings; harness or harness parts

(G-18085)
MARCEAU ENTERPRISES INC
Also Called: Puroclean Restoration Services
11517 Laurel Woods Dr (48094-3764)
PHONE...................................586 697-8100
EMP: 9 **EST:** 2009
SALES (est): 131.9K **Privately Held**
SIC: 7342 2273 Disinfecting services; carpets & rugs

(G-18086)
NORCROSS VISCOSITY CONTROLS
12427 31 Mile Rd (48095-1419)
PHONE...................................586 336-0700
Andrew Norcross, *Engineer*
EMP: 5 **EST:** 2016
SALES (est): 86.5K **Privately Held**
WEB: www.viscosity.com
SIC: 3823 Industrial instrmnts msrmnt display/control process variable

(G-18087)
STOP & GO TRANSPORTATION LLC
13425 Amberglen Dr (48094-3152)
PHONE...................................313 346-7114
EMP: 5 **EST:** 2014
SALES (est): 103.3K **Privately Held**
SIC: 2911 Petroleum refining

Washington - Macomb County (G-18088)

(G-18088)
T & C TOOL & SALES INC
60950 Van Dyke Rd (48094-3902)
PHONE.................................586 677-8390
Thomas Beard, *President*
EMP: 10 EST: 1986
SQ FT: 6,000
SALES (est): 1MM **Privately Held**
WEB: www.tc-tool.net
SIC: 3544 Special dies & tools; jigs & fixtures

(G-18089)
THM PUBLISHING DETROIT LLC
6303 26 Mile Rd (48094-3825)
PHONE.................................586 232-3037
Kathryn Andros, *President*
EMP: 4 EST: 2017
SALES (est): 44.7K **Privately Held**
SIC: 2741 Miscellaneous publishing

(G-18090)
VERTICAL WRKS BLINDS & DRAPERY
57597 Suffield Dr (48094-3558)
PHONE.................................586 992-2600
EMP: 7 EST: 2018
SALES (est): 57.3K **Privately Held**
WEB: www.verticalvics.com
SIC: 2591 Blinds vertical

(G-18091)
WG SWEIS INVESTMENTS LLC
Also Called: Cold Stone Creamery
57155 Covington Dr (48094-3160)
PHONE.................................313 477-8433
Gassab Sweis,
William Sweis,
EMP: 10 EST: 2004
SQ FT: 1,300
SALES (est): 201.8K **Privately Held**
WEB: www.coldstonecreamery.com
SIC: 2024 Ice cream & frozen desserts

(G-18092)
ZF ACTIVE SAFETY & ELEC US LLC
4585 26 Mile Rd (48094-2600)
PHONE.................................586 232-7200
EMP: 36
SALES (corp-wide): 216.2K **Privately Held**
WEB: www.zf.com
SIC: 3679 3469 3089 Electronic switches; metal stampings; plastic processing
HQ: Zf Active Safety & Electronics Us Llc
12001 Tech Center Dr
Livonia MI 48150
734 855-2600

(G-18093)
ZF ACTIVE SAFETY & ELEC US LLC
Also Called: North American Oss Operations
4505 26 Mile Rd (48094-2600)
PHONE.................................586 232-7200
Annmarie McMillan, *Engrg Mgr*
Ronald Lambert, *Engineer*
Thomas Ruhlman, *Design Engr*
Elizabeth Landry, *Human Res Mgr*
Dennis Boir, *Branch Mgr*
EMP: 36
SALES (corp-wide): 216.2K **Privately Held**
WEB: www.zf.com
SIC: 3679 3469 3089 Electronic switches; metal stampings; plastic processing
HQ: Zf Active Safety & Electronics Us Llc
12001 Tech Center Dr
Livonia MI 48150
734 855-2600

(G-18094)
ZF PASSIVE SAFETY US INC
4505 26 Mile Rd (48094-2600)
PHONE.................................586 232-7200
EMP: 7
SALES (corp-wide): 216.2K **Privately Held**
SIC: 3714 Motor vehicle parts & accessories
HQ: Zf Passive Safety Us Inc.
12001 Tech Center Dr
Livonia MI 48150
734 855-2600

(G-18095)
ZF PASSIVE SFETY SYSTEMS US IN
4505 26 Mile Rd (48094-2600)
PHONE.................................586 781-5511
Julieta Santacruz, *Manager*
EMP: 7
SALES (corp-wide): 216.2K **Privately Held**
WEB: www.zf.com
SIC: 3714 Motor vehicle parts & accessories
HQ: Zf Passive Safety Systems Us Inc.
12001 Tech Center Dr
Livonia MI 48150

Washington Township
Macomb County

(G-18096)
SOLE INDUSTRIES LLC
5253 Suncreek Ct (48094-4229)
PHONE.................................586 322-5492
James Wisniewski, *Principal*
EMP: 4 EST: 2017
SALES (est): 87.7K **Privately Held**
SIC: 3999 Manufacturing industries

(G-18097)
YAKEL ENTERPRISES LLC
Also Called: Favi Entertainment
8679 26 Mile Rd Ste 305 (48094-2967)
PHONE.................................586 943-5885
Jeff Yakel, *COO*
Jeremy Yakel, *Mng Member*
Karen Yakel, *Manager*
Leah Welch, *Assistant*
▲ EMP: 7 EST: 2007
SQ FT: 5,000
SALES (est): 1MM **Privately Held**
WEB: www.favientertainment.com
SIC: 3577 Computer peripheral equipment

Waterford
Oakland County

(G-18098)
AMERICAN STRONG
155 Lochaven Rd (48327-3865)
PHONE.................................248 978-6483
Gwen Hunt, *Principal*
EMP: 4 EST: 2019
SALES (est): 76.6K **Privately Held**
WEB: www.americanstrong.com
SIC: 7692 Welding repair

(G-18099)
AMK ENTERPRISE LLC
3575 Pontiac Lake Rd (48328-2341)
PHONE.................................248 977-3039
EMP: 4 EST: 2019
SALES (est): 108.5K **Privately Held**
SIC: 2399 Fabricated textile products

(G-18100)
ANNES CANVAS
1081 Airport Rd (48327-1805)
PHONE.................................248 623-3443
Patrick Kelley, *Principal*
EMP: 6 EST: 2010
SALES (est): 97.7K **Privately Held**
SIC: 2394 Canvas & related products

(G-18101)
ARCHITECTURAL PLANNERS INC
Also Called: API Plan Design Build
5101 Williams Lake Rd (48329-3555)
PHONE.................................248 674-1340
Keith Lutz, *President*
William Moustakeas, *Principal*
Alan Hall, *Vice Pres*
Alisha Robinson, *CFO*
Boyd Robinson, *Manager*
EMP: 29 EST: 2012
SQ FT: 2,500
SALES (est): 6.4MM **Privately Held**
WEB: www.api-mi.com
SIC: 1542 2431 8712 Commercial & office building, new construction; shopping center construction; restaurant construction; religious building construction; millwork; architectural services

(G-18102)
ARTBOX DESIGN INC
Also Called: Art Box Design
5085 Williams Lake Rd Si (48329-3571)
PHONE.................................248 461-2555
Veronica Peters, *President*
EMP: 5 EST: 1992
SQ FT: 2,400
SALES (est): 439.4K **Privately Held**
WEB: www.inkpressions.com
SIC: 2759 Screen printing

(G-18103)
BABY PALLET
1367 Forest Bay Dr (48328-4293)
PHONE.................................248 210-3851
Emilie Roper, *Principal*
EMP: 4 EST: 2014
SALES (est): 107.3K **Privately Held**
WEB: www.thebabypallet.com
SIC: 2448 Pallets, wood & wood with metal

(G-18104)
BLUE FIRE MANUFACTURING LLC
5405 Perry Dr (48329-3462)
PHONE.................................248 714-7166
Timothy Harris, *Mng Member*
EMP: 20 EST: 2013
SALES (est): 2.5MM **Privately Held**
WEB: www.bluefirellc.com
SIC: 3089 3469 3321 Automotive parts, plastic; metal stampings; gray iron castings

(G-18105)
BROADSWORD SOLUTIONS CORP
3795 Dorothy Ln (48329-1110)
PHONE.................................248 341-3367
Jeffrey Dalton, *President*
Jill Mannaioni, *Partner*
Amy Wilson, *Marketing Staff*
Jacob Dalton, *Manager*
Michelle Rauch, *Sr Consultant*
EMP: 12 EST: 2004
SALES (est): 452.2K **Privately Held**
WEB: www.broadswordsolutions.com
SIC: 7372 Business oriented computer software

(G-18106)
BROADTEQ INCORPORATED
5119 Highland Rd Ste 386 (48327-1915)
PHONE.................................248 794-9323
Jeff Vancamp, *President*
EMP: 5 EST: 2012
SALES (est): 156.3K **Privately Held**
WEB: www.broadteq.com
SIC: 3823 Industrial instrmnts msrmnt display/control process variable

(G-18107)
C T & T INC
Also Called: Waterfall Jewelers
5619 Dixie Hwy (48329-1619)
PHONE.................................248 623-9422
Thomas F Brown Jr, *President*
Christine Strong, *Treasurer*
Deanna Meyers, *Sales Staff*
Chris Strong, *Webmaster*
John Strong, *Shareholder*
EMP: 23 EST: 1979
SALES (est): 3.3MM **Privately Held**
WEB: www.waterfalljewelers.com
SIC: 5944 7631 3911 Jewelry, precious stones & precious metals; watches; diamond setter; jewelry repair services; jewelry, precious metal

(G-18108)
CARLTON SGNATURE PUB RELATIONS
553 Pingree Ct (48327-3076)
PHONE.................................248 387-9849
EMP: 4 EST: 2017
SALES (est): 70.6K **Privately Held**
SIC: 2741 Miscellaneous publishing

(G-18109)
CBARK MANUFACTURING INC
4812 Lore Dr (48329-1641)
PHONE.................................810 922-3092
Cory Barkiewicz, *Principal*
EMP: 4 EST: 2016
SALES (est): 54.6K **Privately Held**
SIC: 3999 Manufacturing industries

(G-18110)
CONNOLLY
5805 Pontiac Lake Rd (48327-2118)
PHONE.................................248 683-7985
D Connolly, *Principal*
EMP: 6 EST: 2005
SALES (est): 83.5K **Privately Held**
SIC: 3699 Electrical equipment & supplies

(G-18111)
CUSTOM FIREPLACE DOORS INC
3809 Lakewood Dr (48329-3952)
PHONE.................................248 673-3121
Stuart R Taylor, *President*
Bruce M Taylor, *Treasurer*
EMP: 10 EST: 1977
SQ FT: 6,000
SALES (est): 647K **Privately Held**
SIC: 3429 Fireplace equipment, hardware: andirons, grates, screens

(G-18112)
CYGNET FINANCIAL PLANNING INC
Also Called: Cygnet Financial Freedom House
4139 W Walton Blvd Ste D (48329-4187)
P.O. Box 301000 (48330-1000)
PHONE.................................248 673-2900
Ted Lakkides, *President*
Brian Lakkides, *Vice Pres*
EMP: 9 EST: 1983
SALES (est): 665K **Privately Held**
SIC: 8742 7372 Financial consultant; application computer software

(G-18113)
D & D PRODUCTION INC
2500 Williams Dr (48328-1868)
PHONE.................................248 334-2112
Scott Kather, *President*
Kraig Kather, *Vice Pres*
EMP: 10 EST: 1972
SQ FT: 5,000
SALES (est): 963.6K **Privately Held**
WEB: www.ddproductioninc.com
SIC: 3546 3541 Saws, portable & handheld: power driven; machine tools, metal cutting type

(G-18114)
DALTON INDUSTRIES LLC
2800 Alliance Ste B (48328-1800)
PHONE.................................248 673-0755
Terry Eichbrecht, *General Mgr*
Thomas Tolliver, *Vice Pres*
David Gray, *CFO*
Steve Tolliver, *Mktg Dir*
Thomas Fairbrother, *Software Dev*
▲ EMP: 50 EST: 1999
SQ FT: 80,000
SALES (est): 13.7MM **Privately Held**
WEB: www.daltonind.com
SIC: 3547 3599 Rolling mill machinery; machine shop, jobbing & repair

(G-18115)
DIVERSIFIED DAVITCO LLC
2569 Dixie Hwy (48328-1705)
PHONE.................................248 681-9197
EMP: 12
SALES (est): 1.9MM **Privately Held**
SIC: 2842 5087 Mfg Polish/Sanitation Goods Whol Service Establishment Equipment

(G-18116)
DONALD E ROGERS ASSOCIATES
Also Called: D E Rogers & Assoc.
2627 Williams Dr (48328-1872)
PHONE.................................248 673-9878

GEOGRAPHIC SECTION

Waterford - Oakland County (G-18145)

Donald Kather, *President*
EMP: 6 **EST:** 1964
SQ FT: 3,000
SALES (est): 604.2K **Privately Held**
WEB: www.rogersratchetwrenches.com
SIC: 3541 Machine tool replacement & repair parts, metal cutting types

(G-18117)
DOUGLAS WATER CONDITIONING (PA)
7234 Cooley Lake Rd (48327-4188)
PHONE 248 363-8383
Douglas R Lanni, *President*
Jerry Tiefenback, *Vice Pres*
Stephen Wolfe, *Vice Pres*
Deb Perczak, *Bookkeeper*
Eric Smith, *Sales Staff*
EMP: 15 **EST:** 1974
SALES (est): 3.4MM **Privately Held**
WEB: www.douglaswater.com
SIC: 3589 5999 7389 5084 Water treatment equipment, industrial; water purification equipment; water softener service; industrial machinery & equipment

(G-18118)
DOVETAILS INC
5600 Williams Lake Rd B (48329-3283)
PHONE 248 674-8777
Kevin Evanson, *Owner*
Ralph Rexroat, *Treasurer*
Denice Evanson, *Admin Sec*
EMP: 8 **EST:** 1992
SQ FT: 6,500
SALES (est): 258.6K **Privately Held**
SIC: 2431 Millwork

(G-18119)
DOWNEYS POTATO CHIPS-WATERFORD
Also Called: Downey's & Design
4709 Highland Rd (48328-1136)
PHONE 248 673-3636
Rosemary Hogarth, *President*
Richard Downey, *President*
Donald Hogarth, *Corp Secy*
Rebecca Hogarth, *Vice Pres*
Elizabeth Wieland, *Vice Pres*
EMP: 5 **EST:** 1984
SALES (est): 553.9K **Privately Held**
WEB: www.downeyspotatochips.com
SIC: 2096 5499 2099 Potato chips & other potato-based snacks; gourmet food stores; food preparations

(G-18120)
DRAYTON IRON & METAL INC (PA)
5229 Williams Lake Rd (48329-3557)
PHONE 248 673-1269
Lloyd L Spurgeon, *President*
Eddie E Spurgeon, *Vice Pres*
Tom Spurgeon, *Treasurer*
EMP: 13 **EST:** 1975
SALES (est): 2.7MM **Privately Held**
SIC: 5093 3273 Ferrous metal scrap & waste; ready-mixed concrete

(G-18121)
EAGLE GRAPHICS AND DESIGN
2040 Airport Rd (48327-1204)
PHONE 248 618-0000
Arthur T Lucero, *President*
Arthur Lucero, *President*
Edward Lucero, *Vice Pres*
Aaron Lucero, *Treasurer*
Patricia Lucero, *Admin Sec*
EMP: 5 **EST:** 1994
SQ FT: 3,500 **Privately Held**
WEB: www.eaglegraphics.com
SIC: 3993 Signs, not made in custom sign painting shops

(G-18122)
EARTHWORM CSTNGS UNLIMITED LLC
1179 Sylvertis Dr (48328-2042)
PHONE 248 882-3329
Dean Weston, *CEO*
Beverly Beaudoin, *Mng Member*
Ruth Beaudoin, *Mng Member*
Jared Weston, *Mng Member*
EMP: 13 **EST:** 2013
SQ FT: 10,000
SALES (est): 1.3MM **Privately Held**
WEB: www.earthwormcastingsunlimited.com
SIC: 2873 Fertilizers: natural (organic), except compost

(G-18123)
FORSTERS AND SONS OIL CHANGE
4773 Dixie Hwy (48329-3523)
P.O. Box 300815, Drayton Plains (48330-0815)
PHONE 248 618-6860
Matt Perry, *President*
EMP: 12 **EST:** 1982
SQ FT: 2,000
SALES (est): 1.1MM **Privately Held**
SIC: 1389 Oil field services

(G-18124)
FREE STATE BORING INC
5425 Perry Dr Ste 105 (48329-4826)
PHONE 248 821-8860
EMP: 6 **EST:** 2013
SALES (est): 343.2K **Privately Held**
WEB: www.freestateboring.com
SIC: 3599 Machine shop, jobbing & repair

(G-18125)
GRAPHICS DEPOT INC
7625 Highland Rd (48327-1408)
PHONE 248 383-5055
Joji Ahmed, *Principal*
EMP: 4 **EST:** 2007
SALES (est): 89K **Privately Held**
WEB: www.graphicsdepot.us
SIC: 3993 5099 5699 5949 Signs & advertising specialties; signs, except electric; miscellaneous apparel & accessories; sewing, needlework & piece goods

(G-18126)
GREYSTONE MEDICAL LLC
7433 Pine Creek Trl Ste B (48327-4521)
PHONE 248 955-3069
Kwamina Beecham, *Mng Member*
EMP: 4 **EST:** 2017
SALES (est): 218.5K **Privately Held**
WEB: www.greystoneclinic.com
SIC: 3841 Surgical & medical instruments

(G-18127)
HEAT TREATING SVCS CORP AMER
Also Called: Heating Treating Services
2501 Williams Dr (48328-1869)
PHONE 248 253-9560
Troy Hynes, *Plant Mgr*
Kenneth Rogghe, *Engineer*
Bob Burton, *Controller*
John Lund, *VP Sales*
Jeffrey Hynes, *Marketing Staff*
EMP: 6
SALES (corp-wide): 26MM **Privately Held**
WEB: www.htsmi.com
SIC: 3398 Metal heat treating
PA: Heat Treating Services Corporation Of America
217 Central Ave
Pontiac MI 48341
248 858-2230

(G-18128)
IDEAL MILLWORK ENTERPRISES LLC
5724 Williams Lake Rd A (48329-3286)
PHONE 248 461-6460
Gregory Schwartz,
EMP: 15 **EST:** 2016
SALES (est): 516.4K **Privately Held**
SIC: 2431 Millwork

(G-18129)
INFRA CORPORATION
5454 Dixie Hwy (48329-1615)
P.O. Box 300997 (48330-0997)
PHONE 248 623-0400
Bryan A McGraw, *President*
Cindy McGraw, *CFO*
EMP: 10 **EST:** 1938
SQ FT: 12,000 **Privately Held**
WEB: www.infracorp.wordpress.com

SIC: 3541 3569 3613 3914 Drilling machine tools (metal cutting); assembly machines, non-metalworking; control panels, electric; stainless steel ware

(G-18130)
JEWEL ALBRIGHT COHEN PUBG LLC
4885 Oak Hill Dr (48329-1748)
PHONE 248 672-8889
Jean Norman, *Principal*
EMP: 4 **EST:** 2017
SALES (est): 67.8K **Privately Held**
SIC: 2741 Miscellaneous publishing

(G-18131)
KEVIN LARKIN INC
Also Called: Lake Superior Soap Co
2611 Woodbourne Dr (48329-2479)
PHONE 248 736-8203
Kevin F Larkin, *President*
EMP: 4 **EST:** 2001
SALES (est): 77K **Privately Held**
WEB: www.lakesuperiorsoapcompany.com
SIC: 3999 Hair & hair-based products

(G-18132)
L E Q INC
Also Called: Architrave Woodworking
5600 Williams Lake Rd B (48329-3283)
PHONE 248 257-5466
Marilyn Nehring, *Principal*
EMP: 12 **EST:** 2015
SALES (est): 744K **Privately Held**
SIC: 2431 Millwork

(G-18133)
LANDMESSER TOOLS COMPANY INC
960 S Cass Lake Rd (48328-4121)
PHONE 248 682-4689
Lawrence E Landmesser, *President*
▼ **EMP:** 8 **EST:** 1970
SALES (est): 901.5K **Privately Held**
WEB: www.landmessertools.com
SIC: 3423 Hand & edge tools

(G-18134)
LINE-X OF WATERFORD
6650 Highland Rd Ste 101 (48327-1661)
PHONE 248 270-8848
EMP: 4 **EST:** 2019
SALES (est): 263.2K **Privately Held**
WEB: www.truckaccessorieswaterfordtownship.com
SIC: 2821 Plastics materials & resins

(G-18135)
LSM SYSTEMS ENGINEERING INC
4670 Hatchery Rd (48329-3633)
PHONE 248 674-4967
Gail Lowe, *Vice Pres*
Kathy Paulson, *Consultant*
Steve Lowe, *Administration*
EMP: 21 **EST:** 1990
SQ FT: 36,000
SALES (est): 5.3MM **Privately Held**
WEB: www.lsmeng.com
SIC: 3714 Motor vehicle parts & accessories

(G-18136)
MICHIGAN INTERLOCK LLC
2911 Pontiac Lake Rd A (48328-2681)
PHONE 248 481-9743
Michele Compton,
EMP: 5 **EST:** 2008
SALES (est): 941.1K **Privately Held**
WEB: www.miinterlock.com
SIC: 3694 Engine electrical equipment

(G-18137)
MIDLAND SILICON COMPANY LLC
3840 Island Park Dr (48329-1906)
PHONE 248 674-3736
James May, *CEO*
Virago Capital,
EMP: 15 **EST:** 2003
SALES (est): 903.6K **Privately Held**
WEB: www.mscsilicon.com
SIC: 3479 Coating of metals with silicon

(G-18138)
MIDWEST QUALITY BEDDING INC
Also Called: Mattress Mart
1384 Glenview Dr (48327-2978)
PHONE 614 504-5971
John Fogt, *Vice Pres*
EMP: 6 **EST:** 2011
SALES (est): 78K **Privately Held**
SIC: 2515 Mattresses & bedsprings

(G-18139)
NEOTECH INDUSTRIES INC
1034 Meadowcrest Dr (48327-2936)
PHONE 248 681-6667
EMP: 4 **EST:** 2011
SALES (est): 53.5K **Privately Held**
SIC: 3999 Manufacturing industries

(G-18140)
NETCON ENTERPRISES INC
5085 Williams Lake Rd A (48329-3573)
PHONE 248 673-7855
Gary L Leonard, *President*
Stacy Behrens, *General Mgr*
Terrence P Mirabito, *Vice Pres*
Terry Mirabito, *VP Sales*
EMP: 25 **EST:** 1985
SQ FT: 10,000
SALES (est): 1MM **Privately Held**
WEB: www.netconenterprises.com
SIC: 3679 Harness assemblies for electronic use: wire or cable

(G-18141)
NICOLE LENNOX LMT
3093 Sashabaw Rd Ste A (48329-4089)
PHONE 248 509-4433
Nicole Lennox Lmt, *Principal*
EMP: 5 **EST:** 2019
SALES (est): 111.8K **Privately Held**
WEB: www.hellobabybirth.com
SIC: 3585 Refrigeration & heating equipment

(G-18142)
OAKLAND MACHINE COMPANY
4865 Highland Rd Ste G (48328-1171)
PHONE 248 674-2201
William H Weber, *President*
Peggy Madsen, *Office Mgr*
EMP: 10 **EST:** 1969
SQ FT: 10,000
SALES (est): 919.9K **Privately Held**
WEB: www.oaklandmachine.com
SIC: 3599 Machine shop, jobbing & repair

(G-18143)
OMTRON INC
2560 Silverside Rd (48328-1760)
PHONE 248 673-3896
Kenneth Richardson, *President*
EMP: 5 **EST:** 1982
SQ FT: 2,200
SALES (est): 486.1K **Privately Held**
WEB: www.omtroninc.com
SIC: 3679 Electronic circuits

(G-18144)
OPENINGS INC
Also Called: Total Door An Openings
6145 Delfield Dr (48329-1388)
PHONE 248 623-6899
Leon Yulkowski, *Partner*
Susan Roldan, *Purch Mgr*
▲ **EMP:** 50 **EST:** 1974
SQ FT: 200,000
SALES (est): 9.3MM **Privately Held**
WEB: www.totaldoor.com
SIC: 3442 Metal doors

(G-18145)
ORRI CORP
5385 Perry Dr (48329-3460)
PHONE 248 618-1104
Lori Doa, *President*
Les Mikula, *General Mgr*
Angelo Doa, *Vice Pres*
▲ **EMP:** 16 **EST:** 2001
SALES (est): 1.7MM **Privately Held**
WEB: www.orricorp.com
SIC: 3496 3552 Cable, uninsulated wire: made from purchased wire; heddles for loom harnesses, wire

Waterford - Oakland County (G-18146)

(G-18146)
PAPER PETAL PRESS
6847 Saline Dr (48329-1256)
PHONE....................248 935-5193
Annessa Campian, *Principal*
EMP: 5 **EST:** 2019
SALES (est): 37.5K **Privately Held**
SIC: 2741 Miscellaneous publishing

(G-18147)
PARAGON READY MIX INC
4389 Lessing (48329-1425)
PHONE....................248 623-0100
Mandy Neihsl, *Vice Pres*
Steve Simpson, *Branch Mgr*
EMP: 8
SALES (corp-wide): 4.6MM **Privately Held**
WEB: www.paragonreadymix.com
SIC: 3273 Ready-mixed concrete
PA: Paragon Ready Mix Inc
48000 Hixson Ave
Shelby Township MI 48317
586 731-8000

(G-18148)
PAUL HORN AND ASSOCIATES
2525 Sylvan Shores Dr (48328-3934)
PHONE....................248 682-8490
EMP: 3
SALES: 1MM **Privately Held**
SIC: 3564 5075 Mfg Air Blowoff & Antistatic Equip & Whol Air Blowoff & Antistatic Equip

(G-18149)
PENCIL PUSHERS LLC
2570 Maplecrest Dr (48329-3149)
PHONE....................248 252-7839
Aubrey Oslund, *Principal*
EMP: 4 **EST:** 2018
SALES (est): 73.9K **Privately Held**
SIC: 3545 Pushers

(G-18150)
PENN AUTOMOTIVE INC (DH)
Also Called: Profile Steel and Wire
5331 Dixie Hwy (48329-1612)
P.O. Box 380643, Clinton Township
(48038-0069)
PHONE....................248 599-3700
Jeff Lewis, *Vice Pres*
Cathy Tinnley, *Accountant*
Judy McLauckin, *Bookkeeper*
Eric Wolk, *Manager*
Elliott Israel, *Admin Sec*
▲ **EMP:** 9 **EST:** 2004
SALES (est): 49.1MM **Privately Held**
WEB: www.pemnet.com
SIC: 3965 5085 3429 Fasteners; fasteners & fastening equipment; metal fasteners
HQ: Penn Engineering & Manufacturing Corp.
5190 Old Easton Rd
Danboro PA 18916
215 766-8853

(G-18151)
PENN ENGINEERING & MFG CORP
5331 Dixie Hwy (48329-1612)
PHONE....................313 299-8500
Mark Petty, *President*
Dale Boka, *Business Mgr*
EMP: 280 **Privately Held**
WEB: www.pemnet.com
SIC: 3965 5085 3429 Fasteners; fasteners & fastening equipment; metal fasteners
HQ: Penn Engineering & Manufacturing Corp.
5190 Old Easton Rd
Danboro PA 18916
215 766-8853

(G-18152)
PENN ENGINEERING & MFG CORP
5331 Dixie Hwy (48329-1612)
PHONE....................586 731-3560
Mike Mosher, *General Mgr*
EMP: 5 **Privately Held**
WEB: www.pemnet.com
SIC: 3429 Manufactured hardware (general)
HQ: Penn Engineering & Manufacturing Corp.
5190 Old Easton Rd
Danboro PA 18916
215 766-8853

(G-18153)
PERPETUAL MEASUREMENT INC
3185 Seebaldt Ave (48329-4152)
PHONE....................248 343-2952
Todd A Wyatt, *President*
EMP: 4 **EST:** 1999
SALES (est): 600K **Privately Held**
SIC: 3823 Industrial process measurement equipment

(G-18154)
PLASTICS IN PAINT
7251 Ida Ter (48329-2833)
PHONE....................248 520-7177
Patrick Pawloske, *Principal*
EMP: 5 **EST:** 2012
SALES (est): 178.1K **Privately Held**
SIC: 2752 Commercial printing, lithographic

(G-18155)
POWER WHEELS PRO
4895 Highland Rd Ste D (48329-1173)
PHONE....................248 686-2035
▲ **EMP:** 6 **EST:** 2010
SALES (est): 170.3K **Privately Held**
WEB: www.powerwheelspro.com
SIC: 3312 Wheels, locomotive & car: iron & steel

(G-18156)
PPG INDUSTRIES INC
Also Called: PPG 5629
497 Elizabeth Lake Rd (48328-3302)
PHONE....................248 683-8052
Joe Brunet, *Branch Mgr*
EMP: 4
SALES (corp-wide): 15.1B **Publicly Held**
WEB: www.ppg.com
SIC: 2851 Paints & allied products
PA: Ppg Industries, Inc.
1 Ppg Pl
Pittsburgh PA 15272
412 434-3131

(G-18157)
PRINTED MEMORIES
730 Globe Rd (48328-2130)
PHONE....................248 388-7788
Karen Walker, *Principal*
EMP: 5 **EST:** 2008
SALES (est): 68.4K **Privately Held**
SIC: 2752 Commercial printing, lithographic

(G-18158)
PRIVATE LIFE CORP
4353 S Meadow Dr (48329-4641)
PHONE....................248 922-9800
Dave Gromow, *Principal*
EMP: 4 **EST:** 2016
SALES (est): 55.8K **Privately Held**
SIC: 2741 Miscellaneous publishing

(G-18159)
PROFIL SYSTEM INC
5331 Dixie Hwy (48329-1612)
PHONE....................248 536-2130
Mark Wenzel, *Finance Dir*
EMP: 15 **EST:** 2009
SALES (est): 535.1K **Privately Held**
WEB: www.profil-global.com
SIC: 3429 Manufactured hardware (general)

(G-18160)
QQUEST CORPORATION
5119 Highland Rd Ste 397 (48327-1915)
PHONE....................313 441-0022
EMP: 5 **EST:** 2019
SALES (est): 233.9K **Privately Held**
WEB: www.qquest.com
SIC: 7372 Prepackaged software

(G-18161)
RIVAL SHOP
3526 Sashabaw Rd Ste B (48329-2682)
PHONE....................248 461-6281
Dmitry Petrov, *Administration*
EMP: 4 **EST:** 2017
SALES (est): 129.3K **Privately Held**
WEB: www.therivalshop.com
SIC: 2759 Screen printing

(G-18162)
SAFETY TECHNOLOGY INTL INC (PA)
Also Called: Safety Technology Intl
2306 Airport Rd (48327-1209)
PHONE....................248 673-9898
Margie Gobler, *President*
John F Taylor, *Vice Pres*
Robert Petrach, *Mfg Mgr*
Renee Diedrick, *Buyer*
Vincent Jones, *Buyer*
◆ **EMP:** 29 **EST:** 1980
SQ FT: 20,000
SALES (est): 9.8MM **Privately Held**
WEB: www.safetytechnologyinternational.com
SIC: 3669 Burglar alarm apparatus, electric

(G-18163)
SAFETY TECHNOLOGY INTL INC
Also Called: S T I
3777 Airport Rd (48329-1355)
PHONE....................248 673-9898
Margie Gobler, *President*
EMP: 6
SALES (corp-wide): 9.8MM **Privately Held**
WEB: www.safetytechnologyinternational.com
SIC: 3669 Burglar alarm apparatus, electric
PA: Safety Technology International, Inc.
2306 Airport Rd
Waterford MI 48327
248 673-9898

(G-18164)
SILENT CALL CORPORATION
Also Called: Silent Call Communications
5095 Williams Lake Rd (48329-3553)
PHONE....................248 673-7353
George J Elwell, *President*
Suzie Wright, *Vice Pres*
Cindy Larocque, *Prdtn Mgr*
Alfred Wright, *Engineer*
Silent Call, *Corp Comm Staff*
▲ **EMP:** 11 **EST:** 1986
SQ FT: 4,000
SALES (est): 1.9MM **Privately Held**
WEB: www.silentcall.com
SIC: 5999 3699 Audio-visual equipment & supplies; accelerating waveguide structures

(G-18165)
SLADES PRINTING COMPANY INC
2697 Costa Mesa Rd (48329-2432)
PHONE....................248 334-6257
Richard L Slade, *President*
EMP: 8 **EST:** 1956
SALES (est): 250K **Privately Held**
SIC: 2752 Commercial printing, offset

(G-18166)
STEVE TONKOVICH
3109 Lansdowne Rd (48329-2991)
PHONE....................810 348-4046
Steve Tonkovich II, *Principal*
EMP: 5 **EST:** 2016
SALES (est): 171.5K **Privately Held**
SIC: 3462 Iron & steel forgings

(G-18167)
SUNBURST SHUTTERS
5499 Perry Dr Ste M (48329-4827)
PHONE....................248 674-4600
Steve Hill, *Manager*
Stephen Hill, *Manager*
EMP: 6 **EST:** 2009
SALES (est): 458.8K **Privately Held**
WEB: www.sunburstshuttersdetroit.com
SIC: 5211 5023 2591 Door & window products; venetian blinds; window blinds

(G-18168)
SUPREME TOOL & MACHINE INC
Also Called: Stm Powersports
5409 Perry Dr (48329-3462)
PHONE....................248 673-8408
Mark E Beyer, *President*
Dawn M Beyer, *Vice Pres*
EMP: 10 **EST:** 1991
SQ FT: 4,000
SALES (est): 1.9MM **Privately Held**
SIC: 3544 3599 Special dies & tools; machine shop, jobbing & repair

(G-18169)
T F BOYER INDUSTRIES INC
5489 Perry Dr Ste C (48329-4832)
PHONE....................248 674-8420
Thomas F Boyer, *President*
EMP: 6 **EST:** 1977
SQ FT: 5,500
SALES (est): 510K **Privately Held**
WEB: www.tfboyer.com
SIC: 2521 Bookcases, office: wood

(G-18170)
TENNECO INC
7151 Astro Dr N (48327-1066)
PHONE....................248 886-0900
Karl Kazmirski, *Chief Engr*
Fred Baumgartner, *Engineer*
Tim Rolling, *Finance Dir*
William Hovest, *Manager*
Sharon Rangel, *Manager*
EMP: 7
SALES (corp-wide): 15.3B **Publicly Held**
WEB: www.tenneco.com
SIC: 3714 Motor vehicle parts & accessories
PA: Tenneco Inc.
500 N Field Dr
Lake Forest IL 60045
847 482-5000

(G-18171)
TOTAL DOOR II INC
6145 Delfield Dr (48329-1388)
PHONE....................866 781-2069
Patricia Yulkowski, *President*
Jeanne Kitchen, *COO*
Brian Butler, *Manager*
EMP: 50 **EST:** 2009
SALES (est): 5.5MM **Privately Held**
WEB: www.totaldoor.com
SIC: 3442 Metal doors

(G-18172)
VAN HORN BROS INC (PA)
Also Called: Van Horn Concrete
3700 Airport Rd (48329-1303)
PHONE....................248 623-4830
Richard B Clark, *Ch of Bd*
Gale Wigner, *Vice Pres*
Kenneth Clark, *Treasurer*
EMP: 30 **EST:** 1959
SQ FT: 2,000
SALES (est): 6.2MM **Privately Held**
WEB: www.vanhornconcrete.com
SIC: 3273 Ready-mixed concrete

(G-18173)
VAN HORN BROS INC
Also Called: Van Horn Concrete
3770 Airport Rd (48329-1303)
PHONE....................248 623-6000
Richard B Clark, *President*
Gale Wigner, *Vice Pres*
Ken Clark, *Treasurer*
EMP: 25 **EST:** 1959
SALES (est): 5.6MM
SALES (corp-wide): 6.2MM **Privately Held**
WEB: www.vanhornconcrete.com
SIC: 3273 Ready-mixed concrete
PA: Van Horn Bros., Inc.
3700 Airport Rd
Waterford MI 48329
248 623-4830

(G-18174)
VHB-123 CORPORATION
3770 Airport Rd (48329-1303)
PHONE....................248 623-4830
Kenneth Clark, *Manager*
EMP: 4 **EST:** 1950

SALES (est): 398.4K **Privately Held**
SIC: 3273 Ready-mixed concrete

(G-18175)
WHITESELL FRMED COMPONENTS INC
Fabristeel Taylor
5331 Dixie Hwy (48329-1612)
PHONE...................................313 299-1178
EMP: 75
SALES (corp-wide): 50MM **Privately Held**
SIC: 3452 3544 Mfg Bolts/Screws/Rivets Mfg Dies/Tools/Jigs/Fixtures
PA: Whitesell Formed Components, Inc.
5331 Dixie Hwy
Waterford MI 48329
313 299-8500

(G-18176)
WOLVERINE WATER WORKS INC
Also Called: Wolverine Waterworks
2469 Airport Rd (48327-1213)
PHONE...................................248 673-4310
Ron Gobler, *President*
Juli Philips, *Manager*
EMP: 4 EST: 1974
SALES (est): 338.1K **Privately Held**
WEB: www.wolverinewater.com
SIC: 3569 3594 Assembly machines, non-metalworking; fluid power pumps & motors

(G-18177)
ZIMBELL HOUSE PUBLISHING LLC
1093 Irwin Dr (48327-2020)
P.O. Box 1172, Union Lake (48387-1172)
PHONE...................................248 909-0143
Kelli Hunter, *Editor*
Paul Reeves, *Editor*
Evelyn M Zimmer, *Mng Member*
EMP: 5 EST: 2014
SALES (est): 93.5K **Privately Held**
WEB: www.zimbellhousepublishing.com
SIC: 2741 Miscellaneous publishing

Watersmeet
Gogebic County

(G-18178)
RUBBER ROPE PRODUCTS COMPANY
25760 Old Hwy 2e 2 E (49969)
PHONE...................................906 358-4143
Sharon J Rehling, *President*
Fay Diethert, *President*
C William Rehling, *Admin Sec*
EMP: 9 EST: 1973
SALES (est): 564.2K **Privately Held**
SIC: 3732 Non-motorized boat, building & repairing

Watervliet
Berrien County

(G-18179)
CUSTOM BUILT BRUSH COMPANY
7390 Dan Smith Rd (49098-9740)
PHONE...................................269 463-3171
G Jack Clark, *President*
Carol Lenz, *Admin Sec*
EMP: 10
SQ FT: 26,000
SALES (est): 1.2MM **Privately Held**
WEB: www.custombuiltbrush.com
SIC: 3991 Brushes, household or industrial

(G-18180)
DRAPERY WORKROOM
5864 N County Line Rd (49098-9798)
PHONE...................................269 463-5633
Eileen Kolosowsky, *Owner*
James Kolosowsky Jr, *Manager*
EMP: 5 EST: 1992
SQ FT: 1,500

SALES (est): 248.3K **Privately Held**
WEB: www.williamcaligari.com
SIC: 2211 Draperies & drapery fabrics, cotton

(G-18181)
JARVIS CONCRETE PRODUCTS INC
7584 Red Arrow Hwy (49098-8552)
P.O. Box 658 (49098-0658)
PHONE...................................269 463-3000
Eugene Jarvis, *President*
James Jarvis, *President*
EMP: 4 EST: 1967
SQ FT: 6,000
SALES (est): 250K **Privately Held**
WEB: www.jarvisconcreteproducts.net
SIC: 3272 Burial vaults, concrete or precast terrazzo; steps, prefabricated concrete

(G-18182)
LANE AUTOMOTIVE INC
Also Called: Motor State Distributing
8300 Lane Dr (49098-9583)
PHONE...................................269 463-4113
George Lane, *President*
Bryan Postelli, *President*
Doug Lane, *Vice Pres*
John Motycka, *Vice Pres*
Joe Stewart, *Vice Pres*
▲ EMP: 200 EST: 1965
SQ FT: 80,000
SALES (est): 55.7MM **Privately Held**
WEB: www.laneautomotive.com
SIC: 5013 5531 3714 Automotive supplies & parts; speed shops, including race car supplies; air brakes, motor vehicle

(G-18183)
TECHNICAL MACHINING WELDING
3008 N County Line Rd (49098-9550)
PHONE...................................269 463-3738
Thomas Carter, *President*
EMP: 8 EST: 2000
SALES (est): 253.1K **Privately Held**
SIC: 3599 1799 Machine shop, jobbing & repair; welding on site

(G-18184)
TRI CITY RECORD LLC
138 N Main St (49098-9787)
P.O. Box 7, Vandalia (49095-0007)
PHONE...................................269 463-6397
Karl Bayer, *Mng Member*
Anne Bayer,
EMP: 4 EST: 1891
SALES (est): 293.1K **Privately Held**
WEB: www.tricityrecord.com
SIC: 2711 Job printing & newspaper publishing combined; newspapers, publishing & printing

Watton
Baraga County

(G-18185)
SANTTI BROTHERS INC
26339 Ford Rd (49970-9016)
PHONE...................................906 355-2347
Donald Santti, *President*
EMP: 5 EST: 1999
SALES (est): 496K **Privately Held**
SIC: 2411 Logging camps & contractors

Wayland
Allegan County

(G-18186)
4 ONE 2 DISTILLERY
152 S Main St (49348-1209)
PHONE...................................269 205-3223
Nissa Smith, *Principal*
EMP: 5 EST: 2020
SALES (est): 237.7K **Privately Held**
SIC: 2085 Distilled & blended liquors

(G-18187)
ADVANTAGE HOUSING INC
3555 12th St (49348-9133)
PHONE...................................269 792-6291
Jiten Shah, *CEO*
Mike Mead, *President*
EMP: 8 EST: 1973
SQ FT: 3,040
SALES (est): 12MM **Privately Held**
WEB: www.advantagehousing.com
SIC: 5271 2451 Mobile homes; mobile homes

(G-18188)
AZTEC PRODUCING CO INC
3312 12th St (49348-9545)
PHONE...................................269 792-0505
Marcelino Candia, *Bd of Directors*
EMP: 6 EST: 2010
SALES (est): 1MM **Privately Held**
SIC: 1311 Crude petroleum production

(G-18189)
BAY VALLEY FOODS LLC
652 W Elm St (49348-1088)
PHONE...................................269 792-2277
Doug Shafer, *Engineer*
Dave Carter, *Manager*
EMP: 20
SALES (corp-wide): 4.3B **Publicly Held**
WEB: www.bayvalleyfoods.com
SIC: 2023 2043 2026 Cream substitutes; dietary supplements, dairy & non-dairy based; cereal breakfast foods; fluid milk
HQ: Bay Valley Foods, Llc
3200 Riverside Dr Ste A
Green Bay WI 54301
800 526-4700

(G-18190)
BEST MFG TOOLING SOLUTIONS LTD
1158 Morren Ct (49348-8944)
PHONE...................................616 877-0504
Brian Schaidt, *President*
EMP: 5 EST: 2016
SALES (est): 1MM **Privately Held**
WEB: www.best-mts.com
SIC: 3559 Automotive related machinery

(G-18191)
BLAIN MACHINING INC
1115 142nd Ave Ste 1 (49348-8966)
PHONE...................................616 877-0426
Kevin Blain, *President*
EMP: 7 EST: 1988
SQ FT: 5,000
SALES (est): 997.1K **Privately Held**
SIC: 3599 Machine shop, jobbing & repair

(G-18192)
BUCK-SPICA EQUIPMENT LTD
Also Called: Bakery Equipment/Design
631 W Cherry St (49348-1012)
PHONE...................................269 792-2251
Gerald Rose, *President*
Dan Rose, *Vice Pres*
Jon Rose, *Vice Pres*
EMP: 10 EST: 1987
SQ FT: 15,000
SALES (est): 1.8MM **Privately Held**
WEB: www.discountbakeryequip.com
SIC: 2499 Bakers' equipment, wood

(G-18193)
CONSUMERS CONCRETE CORPORATION
3316 12th St (49348-9545)
PHONE...................................269 792-9009
Tom Thomas, *Branch Mgr*
EMP: 4
SALES (corp-wide): 42.6MM **Privately Held**
WEB: www.consumerscrete.com
SIC: 3273 Ready-mixed concrete
PA: Consumers Concrete Corporation
3506 Lovers Ln
Kalamazoo MI 49001
269 342-0136

(G-18194)
DIGITRACE MACHINE WORKS LTD
Also Called: Digitrace Limited
1158 Morren Ct (49348-8944)
PHONE...................................616 877-4818
Lawrance Schaidt, *President*
Tom Woodward, *General Mgr*
Brian Schaidt, *Vice Pres*
Phil Hilaski, *Purchasing*
Scott Vanderhoning, *Accounts Exec*
EMP: 32 EST: 1996
SQ FT: 20,000
SALES (est): 5MM **Privately Held**
WEB: www.digitraceltd.com
SIC: 3599 Machine shop, jobbing & repair

(G-18195)
ECLIPSE TOOL & DIE INC
4713 Circuit Ct Ste A (49348-8992)
PHONE...................................616 877-3717
Calvin De Good, *President*
Paul Bogardus III, *Vice Pres*
Mark Stoutjesdyk, *Vice Pres*
Brian Merdzinski, *Plant Mgr*
Scott Degoed, *Purchasing*
EMP: 50 EST: 1997
SQ FT: 52,900
SALES (est): 8.1MM **Privately Held**
WEB: www.eclipsetd.com
SIC: 3544 Special dies & tools

(G-18196)
INTRIC GROUTING SOLUTIONS LLC
1159 Electric Ave (49348-8986)
PHONE...................................855 801-7453
Alexander Runkowski, *President*
Wendy Hoving, *Manager*
EMP: 15 EST: 2017
SALES (est): 1.4MM **Privately Held**
SIC: 3531 Concrete grouting equipment

(G-18197)
JAYDA GALE DISTILLING INC
152 S Main St (49348-1209)
PHONE...................................269 397-1132
EMP: 6 EST: 2017
SALES (est): 364.6K **Privately Held**
SIC: 2085 Distilled & blended liquors

(G-18198)
MAYVILLE ENGINEERING CO INC
4714 Circuit Ct (49348-8908)
PHONE...................................616 877-2073
Missy Moederzoon, *Principal*
EMP: 84
SALES (corp-wide): 357.6MM **Publicly Held**
WEB: www.mecinc.com
SIC: 3498 Tube fabricating (contract bending & shaping)
PA: Mayville Engineering Co Inc
715 South St
Mayville WI 53050
920 387-4500

(G-18199)
MOBILE PALLET SERVICE INC (PA)
858 S Main St (49348-1323)
PHONE...................................269 792-4200
Michael Kamps, *President*
Steve Kamps, *Vice Pres*
Nathan Kamps, *Treasurer*
EMP: 47 EST: 1987
SQ FT: 37,000
SALES (est): 6.9MM **Privately Held**
WEB: www.mobilepalletservice.com
SIC: 7699 5031 2448 Pallet repair; pallets, wood; wood pallets & skids

(G-18200)
NATIONAL PILING PRODUCTS INC
1159 Electric Ave Ste B (49348-8987)
PHONE...................................855 801-7453
Ben Vanderweide, *President*
Scott Tebben, *Vice Pres*
▲ EMP: 15 EST: 2011

Wayland - Allegan County (G-18201)

SALES (est): 1.1MM **Privately Held**
WEB: www.nppius.com
SIC: 3532 Drills & drilling equipment, mining (except oil & gas)

(G-18201)
PRECISION MICRO MILL
210 Commerce St (49348-1235)
PHONE.................................269 290-3603
EMP: 5 **EST:** 2012
SALES (est): 187.1K **Privately Held**
SIC: 3599 Machine shop, jobbing & repair

(G-18202)
RECCO PRODUCTS INC
702 S Main St (49348-1319)
P.O. Box 443 (49348-0443)
PHONE.................................269 792-2243
Brandon Cooper, *CEO*
Brian Cooper, *Vice Pres*
Jesse Schenkoske, *Design Engr*
Laura Cooper, *CFO*
EMP: 36 **EST:** 1967
SALES (est): 8.3MM **Privately Held**
WEB: www.reccofilters.com
SIC: 3569 Filters, general line: industrial; filters

(G-18203)
RHINO SEED & LANDSCAPE SUP LLC (PA)
1093 129th Ave (49348-9542)
PHONE.................................800 482-3130
Scott Hilbert,
▲ **EMP:** 10 **EST:** 1998
SALES (est): 8.9MM **Privately Held**
WEB: www.rhinoseed.com
SIC: 2499 5191 Mulch, wood & bark; seeds: field, garden & flower

(G-18204)
ROCKWELL AUTOMATION INC
1121 133rd Ave (49348-9535)
PHONE.................................269 792-9137
Thomas Adamczak, *Accounts Mgr*
Steven Stpierre, *Accounts Mgr*
Bruce Merrill, *Branch Mgr*
Carl Rossi, *Manager*
EMP: 5 **Publicly Held**
WEB: www.rockwellautomation.com
SIC: 3625 Relays & industrial controls
PA: Rockwell Automation, Inc.
1201 S 2nd St
Milwaukee WI 53204

(G-18205)
SAWMILL ESTATES
Also Called: Kmg Prestige
1185 Eagle Dr (49348-1714)
PHONE.................................269 792-7500
Jennifer Troud, *Principal*
EMP: 9 **EST:** 2008
SALES (est): 587.8K **Privately Held**
SIC: 2421 Sawmills & planing mills, general

(G-18206)
SEBRIGHT PRODUCTS INC
Also Called: Bright Technologies
2631 12th St (49348)
PHONE.................................269 792-6229
Dave Kaminski, *Business Mgr*
Renee Wilson, *Human Res Mgr*
Gary Brinkman, *Sales Staff*
Adisa Bajric, *Mktg Dir*
Mark Schwartz, *Branch Mgr*
EMP: 55
SALES (corp-wide): 16.1MM **Privately Held**
WEB: www.sebrightproducts.com
SIC: 3589 Sewage & water treatment equipment
PA: Sebright Products, Inc.
127 N Water St
Hopkins MI 49328
269 793-7183

(G-18207)
SERVO INNOVATIONS LLC
2560 Patterson Ave (49348-9458)
PHONE.................................269 792-9279
Troy Diller, *Owner*
EMP: 8 **EST:** 2005
SQ FT: 864
SALES (est): 2.8MM **Privately Held**
WEB: www.servoinnovations.com
SIC: 3825 Standards & calibrating equipment, laboratory

(G-18208)
STAMPEDE DIE CORP
Also Called: Stampede Die & Engineering
1142 Electric Ave (49348-8901)
PHONE.................................616 877-0100
Lee Vandyk, *President*
Adam Swann, *Vice Pres*
EMP: 75 **EST:** 2006
SQ FT: 40,000
SALES (est): 19.2MM **Privately Held**
WEB: www.stampededie.com
SIC: 3544 Special dies & tools

(G-18209)
WEST MICHIGAN FORKLIFT INC
4155 12th St (49348-9589)
PHONE.................................616 262-4949
EMP: 7 **EST:** 2016
SALES (est): 1.2MM **Privately Held**
WEB: www.westmichiganforklift.com
SIC: 3537 Forklift trucks

(G-18210)
WOODWORKING CONNECTION INC
3763 N Spur Ct (49348-8995)
PHONE.................................616 389-5481
Douglas Deater, *Principal*
EMP: 6 **EST:** 2019
SALES (est): 219.8K **Privately Held**
SIC: 2431 Millwork

Wayne
Wayne County

(G-18211)
AKA SPORTS
34932 W Michigan Ave (48184-1766)
PHONE.................................734 260-1023
Jeff Auer, *Owner*
EMP: 5 **EST:** 2001
SALES (est): 94.4K **Privately Held**
WEB: www.akasportsinc.com
SIC: 2759 Screen printing

(G-18212)
ALLIED TUBE & CONDUIT CORP
4205 Elizabeth St (48184-2162)
PHONE.................................734 721-4040
Chucks Neahls, *Manager*
EMP: 5
SQ FT: 300,000 **Publicly Held**
WEB: www.alliedeg.us
SIC: 3644 Noncurrent-carrying wiring services
HQ: Allied Tube & Conduit Corporation
16100 Lathrop Ave
Harvey IL 60426
708 339-1610

(G-18213)
AMERICAN JETWAY CORPORATION
34136 Myrtle St (48184-1729)
PHONE.................................734 721-5930
Gordon Jones, *President*
Charles Quint, *President*
Jan Germann, *COO*
Janice Germann, *COO*
Bill Dick, *Vice Pres*
◆ **EMP:** 78 **EST:** 1963
SQ FT: 36,000
SALES (est): 23MM **Privately Held**
WEB: www.americanjetwaycorp.com
SIC: 2842 2899 Specialty cleaning preparations; fuel tank or engine cleaning chemicals

(G-18214)
AXCHEM INC
38070 Van Born Rd (48184-1577)
PHONE.................................734 641-9842
Donald Kay, *Manager*
EMP: 9 **EST:** 2010
SALES (est): 248.7K **Privately Held**
WEB: www.axchemgroup.com
SIC: 2819 Industrial inorganic chemicals

(G-18215)
BACKDRAFT BREWING COMPANY
Also Called: Fire Acadamy
35122 W Michigan Ave (48184-1614)
PHONE.................................734 722-7639
Michael Reddy, *Partner*
George Riley, *Partner*
EMP: 10 **EST:** 1997
SQ FT: 8,000
SALES (est): 185.3K **Privately Held**
SIC: 2082 5812 5813 Beer (alcoholic beverage); eating places; drinking places

(G-18216)
BE A BOSS NOT A BOSSY BIH LLC ✪
35700 E Michigan Ave # 505 (48184-1648)
PHONE.................................734 833-8106
Latoya Miller, *CEO*
EMP: 5 **EST:** 2021
SALES (est): 15K **Privately Held**
SIC: 3999 5999 Manufacturing industries; miscellaneous retail stores

(G-18217)
BLAST OF THE PAST CORP
34860 Stellwagen St (48184-2354)
PHONE.................................734 772-4394
Robert Vincent, *Principal*
EMP: 4 **EST:** 2015
SALES (est): 68.2K **Privately Held**
SIC: 7692 Welding repair

(G-18218)
COMPLEX STEEL & WIRE CORP
36254 Annapolis St (48184-2094)
P.O. Box 446 (48184-0446)
PHONE.................................734 326-1600
Vincent Fedell, *President*
▼ **EMP:** 15 **EST:** 1966
SQ FT: 45,000
SALES (est): 1.5MM **Privately Held**
WEB: www.complexsteel.com
SIC: 3441 Fabricated structural metal

(G-18219)
CUL-MAC INDUSTRIES INC
Also Called: Tech Group
3720 Venoy Rd (48184-1837)
PHONE.................................734 728-9700
William Mc Laughlin, *President*
Scott Crighton, *Vice Pres*
Jon McGuire, *Sales Staff*
Dean Tabin, *Sales Staff*
EMP: 50
SQ FT: 120,000
SALES (est): 19.8MM **Privately Held**
WEB: www.cul-mac.com
SIC: 2841 2842 Soap: granulated, liquid, cake, flaked or chip; disinfectants, household or industrial plant

(G-18220)
FRENCHYS SKIRTING INC
34111 Michigan Ave (48184-1738)
PHONE.................................734 721-3013
Eddy Fournier, *President*
Daniel Fournier, *Vice Pres*
Serge Fournier, *Treasurer*
Lina Fournier, *Admin Sec*
EMP: 4 **EST:** 1972
SQ FT: 6,000
SALES (est): 813.7K **Privately Held**
WEB: www.frenchys-skirting.com
SIC: 3444 1799 Sheet metalwork; building site preparation

(G-18221)
GENERAL ELECTRIC COMPANY
38303 Michigan Ave (48184-1042)
PHONE.................................734 728-1472
Chad Russell, *Manager*
Lisa Wolski, *Government*
EMP: 5
SALES (corp-wide): 79.6B **Publicly Held**
WEB: www.ge.com
SIC: 4911 3699 Electric services; electrical equipment & supplies
PA: General Electric Company
5 Necco St
Boston MA 02210
617 443-3000

(G-18222)
GENERAL ELECTRIC COMPANY
1 Village Center Dr (48184)
PHONE.................................734 727-4619
Rob Hafer, *Project Mgr*
Dara Perry, *Project Mgr*
Antonio Valentini, *Project Mgr*
Sanjay Das, *Technical Mgr*
Nicole Calvert, *Manager*
EMP: 6
SALES (corp-wide): 79.6B **Publicly Held**
WEB: www.ge.com
SIC: 3724 Aircraft engines & engine parts
PA: General Electric Company
5 Necco St
Boston MA 02210
617 443-3000

(G-18223)
HELIUM STUDIO
3127 S Wayne Rd (48184-1220)
PHONE.................................734 725-3811
EMP: 6 **EST:** 2015
SALES (est): 169.4K **Privately Held**
SIC: 2813 Helium

(G-18224)
IMPERIAL PRESS INC
36024 W Michigan Ave (48184-1671)
PHONE.................................734 728-5430
Charles Rushlow, *President*
EMP: 5 **EST:** 1986
SQ FT: 1,650
SALES (est): 602K **Privately Held**
WEB: www.imperialpress.net
SIC: 2752 Commercial printing, offset

(G-18225)
INNOVATIVE LEATHER TECH LLC
36255 Michigan Ave (48184-1652)
PHONE.................................734 953-1100
James Conley, *Principal*
Michael Ferrantino,
EMP: 9 **EST:** 1999
SQ FT: 17,000
SALES (est): 200.6K **Privately Held**
SIC: 2843 Leather finishing agents

(G-18226)
KOENIG FUEL & SUPPLY CO
5501 Cogswell Rd (48184-1504)
P.O. Box 6349, Plymouth (48170-0353)
PHONE.................................313 368-1870
Dave Folkerson, *Principal*
EMP: 6 **EST:** 2005
SALES (est): 150.3K **Privately Held**
SIC: 3273 5983 Ready-mixed concrete; fuel oil dealers

(G-18227)
KWIK-SITE CORPORATION
5555 Treadwell St (48184-1599)
PHONE.................................734 326-1500
Irving N Rubin, *President*
Ivan Jimenez, *Corp Secy*
EMP: 10 **EST:** 1969
SQ FT: 10,000
SALES (est): 1.1MM **Privately Held**
SIC: 3827 Lens mounts; gun sights, optical

(G-18228)
L A S LEASING INC
36253 Michigan Ave (48184-1652)
PHONE.................................734 727-5148
Lisa Russo, *President*
EMP: 34 **EST:** 1994
SQ FT: 15,000
SALES (est): 1.4MM **Privately Held**
SIC: 3537 Industrial trucks & tractors

(G-18229)
LENAWEE INDUSTRIAL PNT SUP INC (PA)
Also Called: Stage 5 Coatings
5645 Cogswell Rd (48184-1544)
PHONE.................................734 729-8080
Kevin Stricker, *President*
Robert Wipe, *Principal*
EMP: 5 **EST:** 2003
SQ FT: 20,000
SALES (est): 1.5MM **Privately Held**
WEB: www.lenaweepaint.com
SIC: 2851 Paints & allied products

▲ = Import ▼ = Export
◆ = Import/Export

GEOGRAPHIC SECTION

(G-18230)
LOTTERY INFO
8432 Hannan Rd (48184-1558)
P.O. Box 87361, Canton (48187-0361)
PHONE..................734 326-0097
Warren Haley, *Owner*
EMP: 8 **EST:** 1981
SALES (est): 392.3K **Privately Held**
WEB: www.lotteryinfoinc.com
SIC: 2732 Pamphlets: printing & binding, not published on site

(G-18231)
MORKIN AND SOWARDS INC
38058 Van Born Rd (48184-1577)
PHONE..................734 729-4242
James Sowards, *President*
EMP: 29 **EST:** 1968
SQ FT: 22,000
SALES (est): 2.9MM **Privately Held**
SIC: 3441 Fabricated structural metal

(G-18232)
POWER PROPERTY SOLUTIONS LLC
34516 John St (48184-2326)
PHONE..................734 306-0299
Lamar Davis, *CEO*
EMP: 8 **EST:** 2020
SALES (est): 136.3K **Privately Held**
SIC: 0781 6531 6519 7299 Landscape services; real estate agent, residential; real estate leasing & rentals; real property lessors; home improvement & renovation contractor agency; removal services, bush & tree; removers & cleaners

(G-18233)
POWERSTROKE PRINTING
3019 S Wayne Rd (48184-1218)
PHONE..................734 740-7616
Brenna Wade, *Principal*
EMP: 5 **EST:** 2019
SALES (est): 136.9K **Privately Held**
WEB: www.powerstrokeprinting.com
SIC: 2752 Commercial printing, offset

(G-18234)
REALM
34950 Van Born Rd (48184-2731)
PHONE..................313 706-4401
Larry Sheffield, *President*
EMP: 4 **EST:** 2000
SALES (est): 303.9K **Privately Held**
SIC: 5084 3699 Robots, industrial; teaching machines & aids, electronic

(G-18235)
RINGMASTERS MFG LLC
36502 Van Born Rd (48184-1510)
PHONE..................734 729-6110
Carol Marshall, *Human Res Mgr*
Robert Krysiak,
Sharon Haverstock,
Michael Klingenberg,
EMP: 42 **EST:** 1996
SALES (est): 7.5MM **Privately Held**
WEB: www.ringmastersmfg.com
SIC: 3462 Iron & steel forgings

(G-18236)
STAMPING PLANT
37500 Van Born Rd (48184-1553)
PHONE..................734 467-0008
John Teresko, *Director*
EMP: 5 **EST:** 2018
SALES (est): 141.4K **Privately Held**
SIC: 3711 Motor vehicles & car bodies

(G-18237)
STAMPING SUPPORT GROUP
4935 Hannan Rd (48184-1568)
PHONE..................734 727-0605
EMP: 10 **EST:** 2019
SALES (est): 1.2MM **Privately Held**
WEB: www.stampingsupportgroup.com
SIC: 3599 Machine shop, jobbing & repair

(G-18238)
TOLEDO PRESS INDUSTRIES INC
4935 Hannan Rd (48184-1568)
PHONE..................734 727-0605
EMP: 8 **EST:** 2016

SALES (est): 367.7K **Privately Held**
WEB: www.toledopress.com
SIC: 2741 Miscellaneous publishing

(G-18239)
TORTILLAS TITA LLC
3763 Commerce Ct (48184-2803)
PHONE..................734 756-7646
Martha Jaramillo, *Mng Member*
EMP: 5 **EST:** 2010
SALES (est): 325K **Privately Held**
WEB: www.tortillastita.com
SIC: 2099 2096 Tortillas, fresh or refrigerated; tortilla chips

(G-18240)
UNISTRUT INTERNATIONAL CORP
Also Called: Unistrut Diversified Products
4205 Elizabeth St (48184-2091)
PHONE..................734 721-4040
J Piwok, *Plant Mgr*
EMP: 250 **Publicly Held**
WEB: www.unistrut.us
SIC: 3441 Fabricated structural metal
HQ: Unistrut International Corporation
2171 W Executive Dr # 100
Addison IL 60101
800 882-5543

Webberville
Ingham County

(G-18241)
APPLEGATE INSUL SYSTEMS INC (PA)
1000 Highview Dr (48892-9007)
PHONE..................517 521-3545
Aaron Applegate, *CEO*
Terry Applegate, *President*
Randy Beckett, *General Mgr*
Bob Thorp, *General Mgr*
Kelly Abell, *Plant Mgr*
▼ **EMP:** 25
SQ FT: 30,000
SALES (est): 19.1MM **Privately Held**
WEB: www.applegateinsulation.com
SIC: 2499 2493 2823 2421 Mulch or sawdust products, wood; insulation & roofing material, reconstituted wood; cellulosic manmade fibers; sawmills & planing mills, general; recycling, waste materials

(G-18242)
BEAVERS WELDING & FABRACATING
400 W Grand River Rd (48892-9325)
PHONE..................517 375-0443
Chris Beavers, *Principal*
EMP: 5 **EST:** 2017
SALES (est): 28.1K **Privately Held**
SIC: 7692 Welding repair

(G-18243)
CAR-MIN-VU FARM
2965 E Howell Rd (48892-9215)
PHONE..................517 749-9112
Carl Minnis, *Partner*
EMP: 5 **EST:** 1996
SALES (est): 762.6K **Privately Held**
SIC: 2241 Narrow fabric mills

(G-18244)
CONTROLS FOR INDUSTRIES INC
5279 Royce Rd (48892-9760)
PHONE..................517 468-3385
David M Jackson, *President*
Dan Jackson, *Vice Pres*
Thomas Jackson, *Vice Pres*
EMP: 7 **EST:** 1982
SALES (est): 300K **Privately Held**
SIC: 3625 Relays & industrial controls

(G-18245)
FORMRITE INC
2060 Elm Rd (48892-8206)
P.O. Box 12 (48892-0012)
PHONE..................517 521-1373
Joseph Bonadeo, *President*
EMP: 8 **EST:** 2011

SALES (est): 124.7K **Privately Held**
WEB: www.formriteinc.com
SIC: 3443 Chutes, metal plate

(G-18246)
MS PLASTIC WELDERS LLC
1101 Highview Dr (48892-9290)
P.O. Box 769 (48892-0769)
PHONE..................517 223-1059
Volker Amann, *President*
Peter Wall, *COO*
Andreas Kriegler, *Vice Pres*
Mark Pucel, *Vice Pres*
Jessica Malloy, *Project Mgr*
▲ **EMP:** 26 **EST:** 2007
SQ FT: 32,000
SALES (est): 13.4MM
SALES (corp-wide): 194MM **Privately Held**
WEB: www.ms-ultrasonic.com
SIC: 3699 Welding machines & equipment, ultrasonic
PA: Ms Industrie Ag
Briennerstr. 7
Munchen BY 80333
892 050-0900

(G-18247)
SA AUTOMOTIVE LTD (PA)
1307 Highview Dr (48892-9300)
PHONE..................517 521-4205
Andrea Savonuzzi, *Mng Member*
David Dare, *Manager*
Trent Holman, *Manager*
Paul Crawford,
Shahriar Hedayat,
◆ **EMP:** 120
SQ FT: 63,000
SALES (est): 49.5MM **Privately Held**
WEB: www.saautomotive.com
SIC: 3089 Automotive parts, plastic

(G-18248)
SAKAIYA COMPANY AMERICA LTD
901 Highview Dr (48892-9270)
PHONE..................517 521-5633
Akira Sakaitani, *President*
Toshi Kazuma, *General Mgr*
Rob Cox, *Prdtn Mgr*
Heather Walser, *Purch Mgr*
Heather Kline, *QC Mgr*
▲ **EMP:** 30 **EST:** 1961
SQ FT: 29,000
SALES (est): 6MM **Privately Held**
WEB: www.sakaiyameiban.co.jp
SIC: 3465 Moldings or trim, automobile: stamped metal

Weidman
Isabella County

(G-18249)
AGGIE WELDING
4518 W Vernon Rd (48893-9728)
PHONE..................989 824-1316
Jeffery Pierson, *Principal*
EMP: 4 **EST:** 2019
SALES (est): 68.3K **Privately Held**
SIC: 7692 Welding repair

(G-18250)
CONCENTRIC MFG SVCS LLC
6755 W Shore Dr (48893-8779)
PHONE..................989 506-8636
Matthew Lyon, *Principal*
EMP: 4 **EST:** 2014
SALES (est): 42.8K **Privately Held**
SIC: 3999 Manufacturing industries

(G-18251)
DYNAMIC MANUFACTURING LLC
5059 W Weidman Rd (48893-9718)
P.O. Box 39 (48893-0039)
PHONE..................989 644-8109
Fax: 989 644-6697
▼ **EMP:** 20 **EST:** 2010
SQ FT: 12,000
SALES (est): 2.4MM **Privately Held**
SIC: 3524 Mfg Lawn/Garden Equipment

(G-18252)
HARDCRETE INC
3610 N Rolland Rd (48893-9241)
PHONE..................989 644-5543
Ed Oneil, *Owner*
EMP: 6 **EST:** 2000
SALES (est): 430.2K **Privately Held**
WEB: www.hardcreteinc.com
SIC: 3273 Ready-mixed concrete

(G-18253)
INTERNATIONAL ASSN LIONS CLUBS
1100 El Camino Grande (48893-9671)
PHONE..................989 644-6562
Bernard Baldwin, *Executive*
EMP: 4 **EST:** 2013
SALES (est): 61.2K **Privately Held**
WEB: www.lionsclubs.org
SIC: 2741 Miscellaneous publishing

(G-18254)
LOR MANUFACTURING CO INC
7131 W Drew Rd (48893-9634)
PHONE..................989 644-2581
Lawrence O Rescoe, *President*
David Price, *Engineer*
Fred Bland, *Electrical Engi*
Jayson Galla, *Marketing Mgr*
Blake Sisco, *Technology*
EMP: 8 **EST:** 1991
SALES (est): 1.2MM **Privately Held**
WEB: www.lormnfg.com
SIC: 3625 3663 3593 Electric controls & control accessories, industrial; radio & TV communications equipment; fluid power cylinders & actuators

(G-18255)
MAEDER BROS INC
Also Called: Maeder Bros Saw Mill
5016 W Weidman Rd (48893-9718)
PHONE..................989 644-2235
Richard Maeder, *President*
Gerald Maeder, *Shareholder*
Jane Atkinson, *Admin Sec*
EMP: 20 **EST:** 1948
SALES (est): 2.8MM **Privately Held**
WEB: www.maederwoodpellets.com
SIC: 2421 5211 Lumber: rough, sawed or planed; millwork & lumber

(G-18256)
MAEDER BROS QLTY WD PLLETS INC
5180 W Weidman Rd (48893-9718)
PHONE..................989 644-3500
Richard Maeder, *President*
Gerald Maeder, *Shareholder*
Jane Atkinson, *Admin Sec*
EMP: 13 **EST:** 2006
SALES (est): 1.2MM **Privately Held**
WEB: www.maederwoodpellets.com
SIC: 2421 Sawmills & planing mills, general

(G-18257)
MID MCHIGAN INDUS COATINGS LLC
5059 W Weidman Rd (48893-9718)
PHONE..................989 441-1277
EMP: 4 **EST:** 2016
SALES (est): 80.2K **Privately Held**
WEB: www.midmichcoatings.com
SIC: 3479 Metal coating & allied service

Wellston
Manistee County

(G-18258)
NORMAN TOWNSHIP
Also Called: Norman Township Fire Dept
17201 6th St (49689-9347)
P.O. Box 143 (49689-0143)
PHONE..................231 848-4495
Brook Schaffer, *Manager*
EMP: 19 **Privately Held**
WEB: www.normantownship.org
SIC: 3569 Firefighting apparatus & related equipment

Wellston - Manistee County (G-18259)

PA: Norman Township
1738 Maple St
Wellston MI 49689
231 848-4138

(G-18259)
PINE CREEK LOG HOME
14746 Pine Lake Rd (49689-9501)
PHONE.....................231 848-4436
Larry Meyer, *Principal*
EMP: 4 EST: 2008
SALES (est): 157.4K **Privately Held**
SIC: 2452 Log cabins, prefabricated, wood

(G-18260)
SELECT CUT LOGGING LLC
20962 Hoxeyville Rd (49689-9764)
PHONE.....................231 690-6085
Erick Earl, *President*
Wendy Earl, *President*
EMP: 4 EST: 2010
SALES (est): 241K **Privately Held**
SIC: 2411 Logging

West Bloomfield
Oakland County

(G-18261)
ADVANCE PET SOLUTIONS LLC
5720 Pt Of The Woods Dr (48324-2155)
PHONE.....................248 334-6150
EMP: 4 EST: 2016
SALES (est): 43.4K **Privately Held**
WEB: www.advancepetproduct.com
SIC: 3999 Manufacturing industries

(G-18262)
ALLEGRA NETWORK LLC
7015 Cooley Lake Rd (48324-3902)
PHONE.....................248 360-1290
Tim Venus, *President*
Karen Venus, *President*
Bill Medlen, *Principal*
Jim Miller, *Prdtn Mgr*
EMP: 12 EST: 2000
SALES (est): 1.1MM **Privately Held**
WEB: www.allegramarketingprint.com
SIC: 2752 Commercial printing, offset

(G-18263)
APPLIED COMPUTER TECHNOLOGIES
4301 Orchard Lake Rd # 160 (48323-1604)
PHONE.....................248 388-0211
EMP: 10
SALES (est): 760K **Privately Held**
SIC: 7372 Automotive Industry Consultant

(G-18264)
BJB ENTERPRISES
3915 Lone Pine Rd Apt 100 (48323-2941)
PHONE.....................248 737-0760
Brenda Branoff, *Principal*
Terry McGinnis, *Technical Staff*
John Pyle, *Technical Staff*
EMP: 7 EST: 2007
SALES (est): 185.1K **Privately Held**
WEB: www.bjbenterprises.com
SIC: 2821 Plastics materials & resins

(G-18265)
BLACK SKI WEEKEND LLC
7650 Cooley Lk Rd Ste 955 (48324)
PHONE.....................313 879-7150
Shed Amin, *Mng Member*
EMP: 2 EST: 2006
SALES (est): 1MM **Privately Held**
WEB: www.blackskiweekend.com
SIC: 4724 7372 Travel agencies; application computer software

(G-18266)
BLUE LAGOON
3217 Shadydale Ct (48323-1847)
PHONE.....................248 515-1363
Melanee Radner, *Principal*
EMP: 4 EST: 2010
SALES (est): 144.9K **Privately Held**
WEB: www.bluelagoonbc.com
SIC: 2389 Apparel & accessories

(G-18267)
BMS ENTERPRISE LLC
6334 Timberwood S (48322-2007)
PHONE.....................281 516-9100
EMP: 4 EST: 2018
SALES (est): 354.7K **Privately Held**
SIC: 2879 Agricultural chemicals

(G-18268)
BRAPOS LLC
4271 Stoddard Rd (48323-3259)
PHONE.....................248 677-6700
Igor Braginsky, *Principal*
EMP: 5 EST: 2016
SALES (est): 70.2K **Privately Held**
WEB: www.eastonfranklinbooks.com
SIC: 2741 Miscellaneous publishing

(G-18269)
BROWN HOUSE PUBLISHING
2263 Timberridge Dr (48324-1473)
PHONE.....................248 470-4690
Timothy Brown, *Principal*
EMP: 4 EST: 2018
SALES (est): 67K **Privately Held**
SIC: 2741 Miscellaneous publishing

(G-18270)
CENTER CUPCAKES
6271 Bromley Ct (48322-3242)
PHONE.....................248 302-6503
EMP: 4
SALES (est): 320.9K **Privately Held**
SIC: 3331 Primary Copper Producer

(G-18271)
CHRONOTECH SWISS LLC
5367 Hauser Way (48323-2422)
PHONE.....................818 415-5039
EMP: 6 EST: 2018
SALES (est): 117.1K **Privately Held**
WEB: www.chronotechswiss.com
SIC: 3599 Machine shop, jobbing & repair

(G-18272)
CRAZY RED HEAD PUBLISHING
3900 Walnut Lake Rd (48323-2769)
PHONE.....................248 862-6096
Jeanette Copeland, *Principal*
EMP: 5 EST: 2015
SALES (est): 95K **Privately Held**
SIC: 2741 Miscellaneous publishing

(G-18273)
CREATIVE EMBOSSING
6730 E Dartmoor Rd (48322-4327)
PHONE.....................248 851-1302
Kathleen Sleder, *Principal*
EMP: 4 EST: 2010
SALES (est): 76.5K **Privately Held**
SIC: 2759 Embossing on paper

(G-18274)
CROWN STEEL RAIL CO (PA)
6347 Northfield Rd (48322-2435)
P.O. Box 2703, Birmingham (48012-2703)
PHONE.....................248 593-7100
Roger S Trunsky, *President*
Leonard H Trunsky, *Corp Secy*
Barbara Trunsky, *Vice Pres*
▲ EMP: 7 EST: 1980
SALES (est): 3.6MM **Privately Held**
WEB: www.crownrail.com
SIC: 5088 3312 Railroad equipment & supplies; railroad crossings, steel or iron

(G-18275)
CVK PUBLISHING INC
Also Called: Cvk Ink
6689 Orchard Lake Rd # 324 (48322-3404)
PHONE.....................248 877-6384
David M Freund, *Principal*
Vicky Freund, *Principal*
EMP: 8 EST: 1995
SALES (est): 52.1K **Privately Held**
WEB: www.houseinprovence.net
SIC: 2741 Miscellaneous publishing

(G-18276)
D J ROTUNDA ASSOCIATES INC
2634 Peterboro Ct (48323-3121)
PHONE.....................586 772-3350
Donald D Rotunda, *President*
EMP: 5 EST: 1971
SQ FT: 5,300
SALES (est): 364K **Privately Held**
WEB: www.djrotunda.com
SIC: 2752 2759 Commercial printing, offset; advertising literature: printing

(G-18277)
DAISY CHAIN ONLINE
4999 Crabapple Ct (48324-1291)
PHONE.....................330 259-6457
Nayeem Mahmud, *Owner*
EMP: 5 EST: 2015
SALES (est): 146.2K **Privately Held**
SIC: 3499 5099 5947 5699 Novelties & giftware, including trophies; antiques, souvenirs & novelties; gifts & novelties; T-shirts, custom printed

(G-18278)
DANDY DELIGHTS
2460 Lakena Rd (48324-4770)
PHONE.....................248 496-8523
Jeffery Dandy, *Principal*
EMP: 4 EST: 2010
SALES (est): 61.8K **Privately Held**
SIC: 3999 Framed artwork

(G-18279)
DETROIT AUTO SPECIALTIES INC
6960 Orchard Lake Rd # 301 (48322-4515)
PHONE.....................248 496-3856
Gary F Wyner, *President*
▲ EMP: 4 EST: 1977
SQ FT: 1,100
SALES (est): 415.2K **Privately Held**
SIC: 3429 Animal traps, iron or steel; motor vehicle hardware

(G-18280)
DIGITAL XPRESS
5262 Potomac Run E (48322-2132)
PHONE.....................248 325-9061
Eric Tuttleman, *Owner*
EMP: 4 EST: 2009
SALES (est): 61.4K **Privately Held**
SIC: 2752 Commercial printing, lithographic

(G-18281)
EMBROIDER IT LLC
6785 Candlewood Trl (48322-3921)
PHONE.....................248 538-9965
Heather Sherman, *Principal*
EMP: 5 EST: 2010
SALES (est): 46.6K **Privately Held**
SIC: 2395 Embroidery & art needlework

(G-18282)
ENERGY EFFICIENT LTG LLC EEL
3297 Wdview Lk Rd Ste 200 (48323)
PHONE.....................586 214-5557
Derryl Reed,
EMP: 4 EST: 2012
SALES (est): 167.7K **Privately Held**
WEB: www.eel-gogreen.com
SIC: 1731 3641 Electronic controls installation; lighting contractor; general electrical contractor; electric lamps; lamps, fluorescent, electric

(G-18283)
GENESIS SAND AND GRAVEL INC
6689 Orchard Lake Rd # 219 (48322-3404)
PHONE.....................313 587-8530
Jason Coleman, *Principal*
EMP: 4 EST: 2009
SALES (est): 146.5K **Privately Held**
SIC: 1442 Construction sand & gravel

(G-18284)
GENIX LLC
3151 Walnut Lake Rd (48323-3446)
PHONE.....................248 761-3030
EMP: 108
SALES (corp-wide): 6.7MM **Privately Held**
SIC: 3559 Ammunition & explosives, loading machinery
PA: Genix, Llc
43665 Utica Rd
Sterling Heights MI 48314
248 419-0231

(G-18285)
GRAND OCCASIONS
6904 Covington Ct (48322-2962)
PHONE.....................248 622-7144
Stephanie Langwell, *Principal*
EMP: 5 EST: 2009
SALES (est): 69.4K **Privately Held**
WEB: www.yourgrandoccasion.com
SIC: 2754 Stationery & invitation printing, gravure

(G-18286)
GUYS YOU ARE REAL HEROES PUBG
5047 Shenandoah Ct (48323-2344)
PHONE.....................248 682-2537
Meagan Burbidge, *Principal*
EMP: 4 EST: 2008
SALES (est): 74K **Privately Held**
SIC: 2741 Miscellaneous publishing

(G-18287)
HARVEY S FREEMAN
Also Called: Independent Engineering Co
4159 Ladysmith St (48323-3108)
PHONE.....................248 852-2222
Harvey S Freeman, *Owner*
EMP: 5 EST: 1949
SALES (est): 291.8K **Privately Held**
SIC: 3569 3714 3563 3549 Assembly machines, non-metalworking; motor vehicle parts & accessories; air & gas compressors; metalworking machinery; industrial trucks & tractors; conveyors & conveying equipment

(G-18288)
HENRY BATH LLC
6725 Daly Rd Unit 250662 (48325-3228)
PHONE.....................410 633-7055
Sean Ginnane, *General Mgr*
Paul Fok, *General Mgr*
Yong Shen, *General Mgr*
Michael Eanes, *Opers Spvr*
Zachary Spencer, *Manager*
EMP: 3 EST: 2002
SALES (est): 1.2MM **Privately Held**
WEB: www.henrybath.com
SIC: 3431 Bathroom fixtures, including sinks
HQ: Henry Bath & Son Limited
12 Princes Parade Princes Dock
Liverpool
151 224-1800

(G-18289)
HYDRO GIANT 4 INC
7480 Haggerty Rd (48322-1067)
PHONE.....................248 661-0034
EMP: 12
SALES (est): 123.2K
SALES (corp-wide): 3.4MM **Privately Held**
SIC: 0782 3524 Lawn And Garden Services
PA: Hg Management, Inc.
21651 W 8 Mile Rd
Detroit MI 48219
313 693-4916

(G-18290)
IGAN MICH PUBLISHING LLC
7025 Dandison Blvd (48324-2828)
PHONE.....................248 877-4649
Udo Neumann, *Principal*
EMP: 6 EST: 2015
SALES (est): 150.9K **Privately Held**
SIC: 2711 Newspapers, publishing & printing

(G-18291)
INDRATECH LLC
2482 Wickfield Rd (48323-3269)
PHONE.....................502 381-5798
EMP: 7
SALES (corp-wide): 11.5MM **Privately Held**
WEB: www.indratech.com
SIC: 2515 Mattresses & foundations
PA: Indratech Llc
1212 E Maple Rd
Troy MI 48083
248 377-1877

GEOGRAPHIC SECTION

West Branch - Ogemaw County (G-18324)

(G-18292)
JA SPORTSWEAR & PRINTING LLC
4382 Foxpointe Dr (48323-2622)
PHONE.....................248 706-1213
Gerard Ashe, *Administration*
EMP: 4 **EST:** 2019
SALES (est): 92.3K **Privately Held**
SIC: 2752 Commercial printing, lithographic

(G-18293)
JANICE MORSE INC
Also Called: Designs Unlimited
3160 Haggerty Rd Ste N (48323-2002)
PHONE.....................248 624-7300
Janice Morse, *President*
Kevin Grahl, *Manager*
EMP: 23 **EST:** 1986
SALES (est): 1.1MM **Privately Held**
SIC: 3083 2511 2434 Plastic finished products, laminated; wood household furniture; vanities, bathroom: wood

(G-18294)
LSPEDIA LLC
6230 Orchard Lake Rd # 280 (48322-2323)
PHONE.....................248 320-1909
Michael Ventura, *Vice Pres*
Kevin Burcroff, *Project Mgr*
Sean Mustonen, *Engineer*
Riya Cao, *Mng Member*
EMP: 8 **EST:** 2013
SALES (est): 904.8K **Privately Held**
WEB: www.lspedia.com
SIC: 7372 7371 Prepackaged software; application computer software; computer software development & applications

(G-18295)
MARINE PROPULSION LLC
6897 Chimney Hill Dr # 207 (48322-3463)
PHONE.....................248 396-2353
Allan Kaplan, *President*
EMP: 6 **EST:** 2016
SALES (est): 353.6K **Privately Held**
SIC: 5551 3531 Marine supplies & equipment; marine related equipment

(G-18296)
MARO PRECISION TOOL COMPANY
Also Called: Triple R Precision Boring Co
5041 Pheasant Cv (48323-2082)
PHONE.....................734 261-3100
Laurence S Rothenberg, *President*
Sol Rothenberg, *Vice Pres*
Alan Rothenberg, *Treasurer*
EMP: 11 **EST:** 1956
SQ FT: 11,000
SALES (est): 535.8K **Privately Held**
SIC: 3545 Precision tools, machinists'

(G-18297)
METRO REBAR INC
4275 Middlebelt Rd (48323-3220)
PHONE.....................248 851-5894
Kenneth W Dudzinski, *President*
EMP: 6 **EST:** 1991
SQ FT: 10,000
SALES (est): 492.9K **Privately Held**
SIC: 3449 Bars, concrete reinforcing: fabricated steel

(G-18298)
MH INDUSTRIES LTD
Also Called: Detroit Washer & Specials
6960 Orchard Lake Rd # 301 (48322-4515)
PHONE.....................734 261-7560
Gary Wyner, *President*
Mike Eastman, *Manager*
EMP: 35 **EST:** 2002
SALES (est): 5MM **Privately Held**
WEB: www.mhind.com
SIC: 3411 3465 Metal cans; automotive stampings

(G-18299)
MICRO LOGIC
4710 Rolling Ridge Rd (48323-3342)
PHONE.....................248 432-7209
Sheldon Wolberg, *Administration*
EMP: 4 **EST:** 2016
SALES (est): 357.7K **Privately Held**
WEB: www.micro-logic-inc.com
SIC: 3672 Printed circuit boards

(G-18300)
MY PERMIT PAL INC
5030 Meadowbrook Dr (48322-1570)
PHONE.....................248 432-2699
Franci Silver, *President*
Carolann Goode, *Senior VP*
Robert Goode, *Shareholder*
Larry Silver, *Shareholder*
EMP: 4 **EST:** 2005
SALES (est): 234.5K **Privately Held**
SIC: 3264 Magnets, permanent: ceramic or ferrite

(G-18301)
NAKED FUEL JUICE BAR
6718 Orchard Lake Rd (48322-3491)
PHONE.....................248 325-9735
EMP: 7 **EST:** 2015
SALES (est): 289.5K **Privately Held**
WEB: www.nakedfueljuice.com
SIC: 2869 Fuels

(G-18302)
NATIONAL CREDIT CORPORATION (PA)
7091 Orchard Lake Rd # 300 (48322-3654)
PHONE.....................734 459-8100
Fax: 248 855-6246
EMP: 10 **EST:** 1962
SALES (est): 20.4MM **Privately Held**
SIC: 6153 6512 3949 6111 S-Term Bus Credit Instn Nonresdentl Bldg Operatr Mfg Sport/Athletic Goods Federal Credit Agency

(G-18303)
PAPER PRESS
7335 Woodlore Dr (48323-1391)
PHONE.....................248 438-6238
Franci Hirsch, *Principal*
EMP: 6 **EST:** 2015
SALES (est): 102.3K **Privately Held**
WEB: www.thepaperpress.net
SIC: 2741 Miscellaneous publishing

(G-18304)
PETZPAWS LLC
4448 Rolling Pine Dr (48323-1443)
PHONE.....................313 414-9894
Brian Aho, *Mng Member*
Sultan Aho, *Webmaster*
Claire Aho,
EMP: 4 **EST:** 2011
SALES (est): 116.7K **Privately Held**
WEB: www.petzpaws.com
SIC: 3999 Pet supplies

(G-18305)
PHILLIPS-MEDISIZE LLC
Also Called: Detroit Sales Office
5706 Stonington Ct (48322-1432)
PHONE.....................248 592-2144
Caesar Weston, *Branch Mgr*
EMP: 10
SALES (corp-wide): 36.9B **Privately Held**
SIC: 3089 Injection molded finished plastic products
HQ: Phillips-Medisize Corporation
1201 Hanley Rd
Hudson WI 54016
715 386-4320

(G-18306)
PRINT JULEP
5345 Sunnycrest Dr (48323-3860)
PHONE.....................614 937-5114
Katie Parker, *Principal*
EMP: 4 **EST:** 2019
SALES (est): 70.6K **Privately Held**
SIC: 2752 Commercial printing, lithographic

(G-18307)
PURE GREEN PHARMACEUTICALS INC
4761 Tara Ct (48323-3646)
PHONE.....................248 515-0097
Stephen Goldner, *CEO*
EMP: 12 **EST:** 2019
SALES (est): 500K **Privately Held**
SIC: 2834 Pharmaceutical preparations

(G-18308)
PURESCRIPTION GRADE LLC
5364 W Doherty Dr (48323-2708)
PHONE.....................313 410-5686
Jessica Kado,
EMP: 6 **EST:** 2017
SALES (est): 39.6K **Privately Held**
SIC: 3999 Manufacturing industries

(G-18309)
RAZE IT PRINTING INC
1784 Heron View Ct (48323-3997)
PHONE.....................248 366-8691
Barbara Schmitz, *Principal*
EMP: 6 **EST:** 2005
SALES (est): 170.7K **Privately Held**
SIC: 2752 Commercial printing, offset

(G-18310)
ROHR WOODWORKING
2813 Bay Dr (48324-2031)
PHONE.....................248 363-9743
Steve Rohr, *Owner*
EMP: 4 **EST:** 2011
SALES (est): 170.1K **Privately Held**
WEB: www.rohrwoodworking.com
SIC: 2431 Millwork

(G-18311)
SANFORD CUSTOMS LLC
7355 Heather Heath (48322-3646)
PHONE.....................586 722-7274
Jason Sanford, *Administration*
EMP: 4 **EST:** 2016
SALES (est): 105.1K **Privately Held**
WEB: www.sanfordcustoms.com
SIC: 2434 Wood kitchen cabinets

(G-18312)
SHERWOOD STUDIOS INC (PA)
Also Called: Sherwood Furniture
6644 Orchard Lake Rd (48322-3402)
PHONE.....................248 855-1600
Mark Morganroth, *President*
◆ **EMP:** 30 **EST:** 1944
SQ FT: 23,000
SALES (est): 2.7MM **Privately Held**
WEB: www.sherwoodstudiosinc.com
SIC: 2512 7389 Upholstered household furniture; interior design services

(G-18313)
SHUTTERBOOTH
2441 Burleigh St (48324-3623)
PHONE.....................586 747-4110
EMP: 4 **EST:** 2018
SALES (est): 126.3K **Privately Held**
WEB: www.shutterbooth.com
SIC: 3442 Shutters, door or window: metal

(G-18314)
SNAVELY GORDON A ATTY RESERV
3240 Pine Lake Rd (48324-1951)
PHONE.....................248 760-0617
Keith Meriedeth, *Owner*
EMP: 4 **EST:** 2015
SALES (est): 101.7K **Privately Held**
SIC: 3812 Search & navigation equipment

(G-18315)
SOCKS DIRECT USA LLC
5400 Crispin Way Rd (48323-3402)
PHONE.....................248 535-7590
Alina Jafri, *Principal*
EMP: 4 **EST:** 2017
SALES (est): 73K **Privately Held**
SIC: 2252 Socks

(G-18316)
STARTECH-SOLUTIONS LLC
6689 Orchard Lake Rd # 267 (48322-3404)
PHONE.....................248 419-0650
Joseph Williams, *Mng Member*
Joyce Williams, *Director*
Kevin Williams,
EMP: 5 **EST:** 2010
SALES (est): 438.9K **Privately Held**
WEB: www.startechsolutions.net
SIC: 7373 1731 5099 7629 Computer integrated systems design; voice, data & video wiring contractor; video & audio equipment; telecommunication equipment repair (except telephones); radio receiver networks; telephone/video communications

(G-18317)
TANDIS LLC
6357 Branford Dr (48322-1098)
PHONE.....................248 345-3448
Igor Dykhno, *President*
EMP: 4 **EST:** 2015
SALES (est): 213K **Privately Held**
SIC: 3699 Electron beam metal cutting, forming or welding machines

(G-18318)
TRU COLOR PRINTING
5538 Abington (48322-4013)
PHONE.....................248 737-2041
Stanley Weinberger, *Owner*
EMP: 4 **EST:** 2015
SALES (est): 94.1K **Privately Held**
SIC: 2752 Commercial printing, offset

(G-18319)
TRU-FIT INTERNATIONAL INC
Also Called: Raydiance
5799 W Maple Rd Ste 167 (48322-4458)
PHONE.....................248 855-8845
Lisa Lano, *President*
EMP: 4 **EST:** 1985
SALES (est): 378.6K **Privately Held**
WEB: www.raydianceforwomen.com
SIC: 3999 Wigs, including doll wigs, toupees or wiglets

(G-18320)
TWIST
6331 Haggerty Rd (48322-5031)
PHONE.....................248 859-2169
Scott Simonovic, *Principal*
EMP: 7 **EST:** 2012
SALES (est): 99.8K **Privately Held**
SIC: 2026 Yogurt

(G-18321)
UNIQUE REPRODUCTIONS INC
5470 Carol Run S (48322-2110)
PHONE.....................248 788-2887
EMP: 4
SALES (est): 315.2K **Privately Held**
SIC: 2759 Commercial Printing

(G-18322)
VERISHOW
5640 W Maple Rd Ste 101 (48322-3717)
PHONE.....................212 913-0600
EMP: 9 **EST:** 2017
SALES (est): 99.8K **Privately Held**
WEB: www.verishow.com
SIC: 7372 Prepackaged software

(G-18323)
WE HAUL CARZ LLC
6247 Eastbrooke (48322-1046)
PHONE.....................248 933-2246
Ashley Walker, *Mng Member*
Tamara Walker,
EMP: 4 **EST:** 2020
SALES (est): 100K **Privately Held**
SIC: 3537 Trucks, tractors, loaders, carriers & similar equipment

West Branch
Ogemaw County

(G-18324)
AMERICAN THERMOFORMING MCH LLC (PA)
2525 Griffin Rd (48661-9296)
PHONE.....................989 345-0935
Danny Blasch, *Mng Member*
EMP: 23 **EST:** 2005
SALES (est): 968K **Privately Held**
WEB: www.americanthermoformingmachinery.com
SIC: 3599 Machine shop, jobbing & repair

West Branch – Ogemaw County

(G-18325)
ASSOCIATE MFG INC
3977 S M 30 (48661-9106)
PHONE..................................989 345-0025
Jeff Dunlap, *President*
Jeff A Dunlap, *Manager*
EMP: 4 **EST:** 2004
SALES (est): 402.4K **Privately Held**
WEB: www.associateandcastings.com
SIC: 3543 Industrial patterns

(G-18326)
BRANCH WEST CONCRETE PRODUCTS
3350 Rau Rd (48661-8723)
P.O. Box 336 (48661-0336)
PHONE..................................989 345-0794
Alan Gildner, *President*
Doris Gildner, *Corp Secy*
Rodger Gildner, *Vice Pres*
EMP: 10 **EST:** 1938
SQ FT: 3,500
SALES (est): 991.3K **Privately Held**
WEB: www.finishedconcrete.com
SIC: 3271 3273 1442 Blocks, concrete or cinder: standard; ready-mixed concrete; gravel mining

(G-18327)
BUNTING SAND & GRAVEL PRODUCTS
3247 Cook Rd (48661-9318)
P.O. Box 217 (48661-0217)
PHONE..................................989 345-2373
Robert A Resteiner, *President*
EMP: 48 **EST:** 1971
SQ FT: 800
SALES (est): 10.8MM **Privately Held**
WEB: www.buntingsandandgravel.com
SIC: 1442 Construction sand mining

(G-18328)
GREAT LAKES MOBILE WELDING
276 E Finerty Rd (48661-9795)
PHONE..................................406 890-5757
Craig Trout, *Principal*
EMP: 4 **EST:** 2017
SALES (est): 48.6K **Privately Held**
WEB: www.greatlakesweldingandfab.com
SIC: 7692 Welding repair

(G-18329)
JMC CUSTOM CABINETRY
960 W Houghton Ave (48661-1234)
PHONE..................................989 345-0475
EMP: 5 **EST:** 2013
SALES (est): 181.6K **Privately Held**
SIC: 2434 Wood kitchen cabinets

(G-18330)
LAY PRECISION MACHINE INC
620 Parkway Dr (48661-9201)
PHONE..................................989 726-5022
Kyle Hawley, *President*
Melinda Hawley, *Vice Pres*
EMP: 9 **EST:** 2017
SALES (est): 967.3K **Privately Held**
WEB: www.layprecision.com
SIC: 3724 Aircraft engines & engine parts

(G-18331)
MJ-HICK INC
2367 S M 76 (48661-9380)
PHONE..................................989 345-7610
Mark Hickey, *President*
EMP: 8 **EST:** 1995
SQ FT: 1,500
SALES (est): 990K **Privately Held**
WEB: www.balsm.com
SIC: 6531 7692 Real estate managers; welding repair

(G-18332)
NORTHERN MICHIGAN LOG HOMES
Also Called: Northern Log Homes
1968 Lost Lake Trl (48661-9448)
PHONE..................................989 345-7463
Larry Miles, *President*
Cheryl Miles, *Admin Sec*
EMP: 4 **EST:** 1983
SALES (est): 382.1K **Privately Held**
WEB: www.northernmichiganlogcabin.com
SIC: 2452 Log cabins, prefabricated, wood

(G-18333)
OGEMAW COUNTY HERALD INC (PA)
Also Called: Northland Ad-Liner
215 W Houghton Ave (48661-1219)
P.O. Box 247 (48661-0247)
PHONE..................................989 345-0044
Robert E Perlberg, *President*
Ed Perlberg, *Admin Sec*
EMP: 23 **EST:** 1974
SALES (est): 2.4MM **Privately Held**
WEB: www.ogemawherald.com
SIC: 2711 2791 2789 2759 Newspapers: publishing only, not printed on site; typesetting; bookbinding & related work; commercial printing; commercial printing, lithographic

(G-18334)
PAR EXCELLENCE PUBLICATION
2548 Caribou Trl (48661-8025)
PHONE..................................989 345-8305
Joe Peterson, *Principal*
EMP: 5 **EST:** 2008
SALES (est): 91.9K **Privately Held**
SIC: 2741 Miscellaneous publishing

(G-18335)
PBG MICHIGAN LLC
610 Parkway Dr (48661-9201)
PHONE..................................989 345-2595
EMP: 4 **EST:** 2012
SALES (est): 70.2K **Privately Held**
SIC: 2086 Bottled & canned soft drinks

(G-18336)
PEPSI-COLA METRO BTLG CO INC
610 Parkway Dr (48661-9205)
PHONE..................................989 345-2595
Brian Secorski, *Manager*
EMP: 6
SALES (corp-wide): 70.3B **Publicly Held**
WEB: www.pepsico.com
SIC: 2086 Carbonated soft drinks, bottled & canned
HQ: Pepsi-Cola Metropolitan Bottling Company, Inc.
1111 Westchester Ave
White Plains NY 10604
914 767-6000

(G-18337)
PVH CORP
Also Called: Van Heusen
2990 Cook Rd Ste 104 (48661-9389)
PHONE..................................989 345-7939
EMP: 4
SALES (corp-wide): 8.2B **Publicly Held**
SIC: 2321 Mfg Men's/Boy's Furnishings
PA: Pvh Corp.
200 Madison Ave Bsmt 1
New York NY 10016
212 381-3500

(G-18338)
ROSE TOOL & DIE INC
640 S Valley St (48661-9292)
P.O. Box 218 (48661-0218)
PHONE..................................989 343-1015
Les Fetters, *President*
Patti Fetters, *Admin Sec*
EMP: 28 **EST:** 1993
SQ FT: 11,000
SALES (est): 2.6MM **Privately Held**
SIC: 3545 Machine tool accessories

(G-18339)
SANDVIK INC
510 Griffin Rd (48661-9251)
PHONE..................................989 345-6138
John Suhadolnik, *Prdtn Mgr*
EMP: 8 **EST:** 2018
SALES (est): 891.7K **Privately Held**
WEB: www.home.sandvik
SIC: 3341 Secondary nonferrous metals

(G-18340)
SAPPINGTON CRUDE OIL INC
123 N 6th St (48661-1263)
P.O. Box 279 (48661-0279)
PHONE..................................989 345-1052
Walter Sappington, *President*
Dianne M Sappington, *Corp Secy*
EMP: 8 **EST:** 1975
SQ FT: 2,400
SALES (est): 1.6MM **Privately Held**
WEB: www.sappingtonresidential.com
SIC: 1311 1389 Crude petroleum production; natural gas production; servicing oil & gas wells

(G-18341)
SAWYER LOGGING LLC
4523 S M 76 (48661-9323)
P.O. Box 623 (48661-0623)
PHONE..................................989 942-6324
EMP: 4 **EST:** 2019
SALES (est): 166.8K **Privately Held**
SIC: 2411 Logging

(G-18342)
SUNRISE PRINT CMMNICATIONS INC
118 W Houghton Ave (48661-1276)
P.O. Box 806 (48661-0806)
PHONE..................................989 345-4475
Chris Dack, *Principal*
EMP: 6 **EST:** 2004
SALES (est): 211.6K **Privately Held**
WEB: www.sunriseprint.com
SIC: 2752 Commercial printing, offset

(G-18343)
THUNDER BAY PRESS MICHIGAN LLC
4503 S M 76 (48661-9323)
PHONE..................................989 701-2430
William Joseph Penrose, *Principal*
EMP: 7 **EST:** 2016
SALES (est): 253K **Privately Held**
SIC: 2741 Miscellaneous publishing

(G-18344)
TR TIMBER CO
502 E State Rd (48661-9762)
PHONE..................................989 345-5350
Tony Rosebrugh, *President*
Todd Rosebrugh, *Vice Pres*
Rebeka Rosebrugh, *Treasurer*
Tamara Grezeszak, *Admin Sec*
Amanda Podojak, *Admin Sec*
EMP: 17 **EST:** 1974
SQ FT: 4,000
SALES (est): 3.3MM **Privately Held**
SIC: 2411 Logging

(G-18345)
VANTAGE POINT MFG INC
614 Parkway Dr (48661-9201)
P.O. Box 859 (48661-0859)
PHONE..................................989 343-1070
Mike Harris, *President*
EMP: 10 **EST:** 2013
SALES (est): 283.4K **Privately Held**
WEB: www.vantagepointmanufacturing.com
SIC: 3999 Manufacturing industries

(G-18346)
WEST BRANCH WOOD TREATING INC
3800 S M 30 (48661-9170)
PHONE..................................989 343-0066
Eugene Zapczynski, *Principal*
EMP: 9 **EST:** 2013
SALES (est): 590.5K **Privately Held**
SIC: 2491 Wood preserving

West Olive – Ottawa County

(G-18347)
BBC COMMUNICATIONS INC
6463 Lakeshore Dr (49460-9743)
PHONE..................................616 399-0432
Marilyn Benson, *President*
EMP: 4 **EST:** 1990
SALES (est): 157.4K **Privately Held**
SIC: 3651 Household audio & video equipment

(G-18348)
BUNDEZE LLC
9717 Cottontail St (49460-8507)
PHONE..................................248 343-9179
Aaron Schradin,
Todd Ireland,
EMP: 4 **EST:** 2013
SALES (est): 162K **Privately Held**
WEB: www.bundeze.com
SIC: 2298 Slings, rope

(G-18349)
LAKE EFFECT EMBROIDERY LLC
9896 Basswood Dr (49460-8842)
PHONE..................................616 502-7844
Joan Crawford, *Principal*
EMP: 5 **EST:** 2018
SALES (est): 42.4K **Privately Held**
WEB: www.lakeeffectemb.espwebsite.com
SIC: 2395 Embroidery & art needlework

(G-18350)
PINNACLE MOLD & MACHINE INC
9900 Lake Michigan Dr (49460-9645)
PHONE..................................616 892-9018
Don Morren, *President*
EMP: 4 **EST:** 1995
SQ FT: 5,000
SALES (est): 410.8K **Privately Held**
WEB: www.pinnaclemoldandmachine.com
SIC: 3544 Dies, plastics forming

Westland – Wayne County

(G-18351)
ACME CARBIDE DIE INC (PA)
6202 E Executive Dr (48185-5694)
PHONE..................................734 722-2303
Allen Schmitt, *President*
Sharon K Schmitt, *Corp Secy*
EMP: 20 **EST:** 1960
SQ FT: 12,200
SALES (est): 2MM **Privately Held**
WEB: www.acmecarbidedie.com
SIC: 3544 3545 3444 Die sets for metal stamping (presses); machine tool accessories; sheet metalwork

(G-18352)
ALTO MANUFACTURING INC
38338 Abruzzi Dr (48185-3282)
PHONE..................................734 641-8800
Rudolph Ureste, *President*
Paul Ureste, *Vice Pres*
John Kraly, *Admin Sec*
EMP: 24 **EST:** 1948
SQ FT: 10,000
SALES (est): 1MM **Privately Held**
WEB: www.altomfg.com
SIC: 3541 Machine tool replacement & repair parts, metal cutting types

(G-18353)
AMERICAN GEAR & ENGRG CO INC
38200 Abruzzi Dr (48185-3280)
PHONE..................................734 595-6400
Jeffrey L Emerson, *President*
Gerry Kmet, *Plant Mgr*
Jake Teahan, *Engineer*
Julie Leon, *Manager*
EMP: 40 **EST:** 1985
SQ FT: 28,500
SALES (est): 6MM **Privately Held**
WEB: www.americangear.net
SIC: 3566 3545 3541 Gears, power transmission, except automotive; machine tool accessories; cutting tools for machine tools; machine tool replacement & repair parts, metal cutting types

(G-18354)
APOLLO BROACH INC
39001 Webb Ct (48185-7606)
PHONE..................................734 467-5750
Kenneth Ahlgren Jr, *President*
Cheri Ahlgren, *Corp Secy*
John Knecht Jr, *Vice Pres*
EMP: 9 **EST:** 1985
SQ FT: 10,500
SALES (est): 868.5K **Privately Held**
WEB: www.apollobroach.com
SIC: 3545 Broaches (machine tool accessories)

GEOGRAPHIC SECTION

Westland - Wayne County (G-18383)

(G-18355)
ARTCRAFT PATTERN WORKS INC
6430 Commerce Dr (48185-5677)
PHONE.................................734 729-0022
Blair Mc Kendrick, *President*
Maria Mc Kendrick, *Corp Secy*
EMP: 15 **EST:** 1946
SQ FT: 8,000
SALES (est): 1.7MM **Privately Held**
WEB: www.artcraftgages.com
SIC: 3545 8711 8742 Gauges (machine tool accessories); designing: ship, boat, machine & product; quality assurance consultant

(G-18356)
ATM INTERNATIONAL SERVICES LLC
8351 N Wayne Rd (48185-1351)
PHONE.................................734 524-9771
Fouad Dabaja,
EMP: 20 **EST:** 2001
SALES (est): 866.7K **Privately Held**
WEB: www.atminternationalservices.com
SIC: 3578 Automatic teller machines (ATM)

(G-18357)
AUSTIN DISTRIBUTORS LLC
29126 Currier Ave Ste 4a (48186-5605)
PHONE.................................248 665-2077
Sheare Austin,
EMP: 5 **EST:** 2020
SALES (est): 100K **Privately Held**
SIC: 3612 Distribution transformers, electric

(G-18358)
AYOTTE CSTM MSCAL ENGRVNGS LLC
36688 Rolf St (48186-4071)
PHONE.................................734 595-1901
Benjamin Ayotte,
EMP: 5 **EST:** 2010
SALES (est): 252.6K **Privately Held**
WEB: www.ayottemusic.com
SIC: 2741 Music book & sheet music publishing; music books: publishing & printing; music books: publishing only, not printed on site; music, sheet: publishing & printing

(G-18359)
B C I COLLET INC
6125 E Executive Dr (48185-1932)
P.O. Box 85718 (48185-0718)
PHONE.................................734 326-1222
Richard T Baruk, *President*
David Baruk, *Vice Pres*
EMP: 18 **EST:** 1941
SQ FT: 11,000
SALES (est): 557.2K **Privately Held**
WEB: www.bcicollet.com
SIC: 3545 Collets (machine tool accessories); pushers; tools & accessories for machine tools

(G-18360)
BATH BOMBS BY LORI
2538 Muirfield Dr (48186-5491)
PHONE.................................734 890-3832
Lori Hinch, *Principal*
EMP: 4 **EST:** 2016
SALES (est): 76.1K **Privately Held**
SIC: 2844 Bath salts

(G-18361)
COOLER KING LLC
35500 Central City Pkwy (48185-6746)
PHONE.................................248 789-3699
EMP: 9 **EST:** 2018
SALES (est): 1.3MM **Privately Held**
WEB: www.thecoolerking.net
SIC: 3585 Refrigeration equipment, complete

(G-18362)
CROSS TECHNOLOGIES GROUP INC
Also Called: Cross Chemical Company
1210 Manufacturers Dr (48186-4064)
PHONE.................................734 895-8084
Mark Brown, *President*
Dennis Kendall Sr, *Vice Pres*
Robert Dyla, *Treasurer*
Julie Tomanica, *Marketing Staff*
▲ **EMP:** 15 **EST:** 1959
SQ FT: 25,000
SALES (est): 4.1MM **Privately Held**
WEB: www.crosstechgrp.com
SIC: 2899 Metal treating compounds

(G-18363)
DETROIT CSTM TRCK TRAILOR LLC
Also Called: Food Truck Shop, The
33234 Beechwood St (48185-2827)
PHONE.................................734 925-2233
Karl Boston, *Mng Member*
EMP: 4 **EST:** 2016
SALES (est): 259.8K **Privately Held**
SIC: 3715 Truck trailers

(G-18364)
DISCOUNT JEWELRY CENTER INC
8339 N Wayne Rd (48185-1351)
PHONE.................................734 266-8200
Jay Benjamin, *President*
Brad Smith, *Vice Pres*
EMP: 5 **EST:** 1987
SQ FT: 1,000
SALES (est): 700K **Privately Held**
WEB: www.discountjewelrycenter.com
SIC: 5944 3911 7631 Jewelry, precious stones & precious metals; jewelry, precious metal; jewelry repair services

(G-18365)
DNR INC (PA)
38475 Webb Dr (48185-1975)
PHONE.................................734 722-4000
Dale V Roberts, *President*
Guy Roberts, *Vice Pres*
EMP: 18 **EST:** 1988
SQ FT: 10,200 **Privately Held**
WEB: www.dnrpartscleaning.com
SIC: 3471 Tumbling (cleaning & polishing) of machine parts

(G-18366)
DOUBLE H MFG INC
6171 Commerce Dr (48185-7629)
PHONE.................................734 729-3450
Frank J Hradil, *President*
Michael Houghton, *General Mgr*
Olive Crysler, *Vice Pres*
EMP: 21 **EST:** 1982
SQ FT: 20,000
SALES (est): 2.1MM **Privately Held**
WEB: www.doublehmfg.com
SIC: 3519 Engines, diesel & semi-diesel or dual-fuel

(G-18367)
EMBROIDERY SHOPPE LLC
39017 Cherry Hill Rd (48186-3250)
PHONE.................................734 595-7612
Eva Johnson, *Manager*
Jean Napolitano,
EMP: 7 **EST:** 1993
SQ FT: 2,800 **Privately Held**
WEB: www.theembroideryshoppe.com
SIC: 5699 2395 Uniforms; embroidery & art needlework

(G-18368)
ENRINITY SUPPLEMENTS INC
6480 Commerce Dr (48185-5677)
PHONE.................................734 322-4966
Udayan Chokshi, *President*
Parimal Bhatt, *Shareholder*
EMP: 8 **EST:** 2011
SQ FT: 10,000
SALES (est): 500K **Privately Held**
WEB: www.enrinity.com
SIC: 2023 Dietary supplements, dairy & non-dairy based

(G-18369)
ERNEST INDUSTRIES ACQUISITION, (PA)
Also Called: Ernest Industries Company
39133 Webb Dr (48185-1986)
PHONE.................................734 595-9500
EMP: 20 **EST:** 1967
SALES (est): 5.5MM **Privately Held**
SIC: 3469 3315 3317 3824 Metal stampings; welded steel wire fabric; welded pipe & tubes; mechanical & electromechanical counters & devices

(G-18370)
FLEETWOOD TOOL & GAGE INC
39050 Webb Ct (48185-7606)
PHONE.................................734 326-6737
Jurgen Schnepel, *CEO*
David Schnepel, *President*
David Jones, *QC Mgr*
Josee Schultz, *Office Mgr*
EMP: 15 **EST:** 1987
SQ FT: 10,000
SALES (est): 2.4MM **Privately Held**
WEB: www.fleetwoodtool.com
SIC: 3599 Machine shop, jobbing & repair

(G-18371)
FLODRAULIC GROUP INCORPORATED
Also Called: Rhm Fluid Power
375 Manufacturers Dr (48186-4038)
PHONE.................................734 326-5400
Mark Jackson, *General Mgr*
Matthew Verona, *General Mgr*
Paul Brown, *Project Mgr*
EMP: 4
SALES (corp-wide): 85.8MM **Privately Held**
WEB: www.flodraulic.com
SIC: 5084 3569 Hydraulic systems equipment & supplies; compressors, except air conditioning; filter elements, fluid, hydraulic line; jacks, hydraulic
PA: Flodraulic Group Incorporated
   3539 N 700 W
   Greenfield IN 46140
   317 890-3700

(G-18372)
G & L TOOL INC
Also Called: G & L Tool & Die
5874 E Executive Dr (48185-9115)
PHONE.................................734 728-1990
David Jackson, *President*
James Hill, *Vice Pres*
EMP: 17 **EST:** 1984
SQ FT: 6,950
SALES (est): 2MM **Privately Held**
SIC: 3544 Special dies & tools

(G-18373)
G&J PRODUCTS & SERVICES
8219 Roselawn St (48185-1613)
PHONE.................................734 522-2984
John Mendler, *Owner*
EMP: 6 **EST:** 1995
SALES (est): 406.7K **Privately Held**
SIC: 2511 Camp furniture: wood

(G-18374)
GENERATION TOOL INC
307 Manufacturers Dr (48186-4038)
PHONE.................................734 641-6937
Michael E Rotter, *President*
EMP: 6 **EST:** 1995
SQ FT: 10,000
SALES (est): 669K **Privately Held**
SIC: 3559 3544 Automotive related machinery; jigs & fixtures

(G-18375)
GRANOLA PROJECT LLC
38233 Hyman St (48186-3834)
PHONE.................................919 219-7158
Jesse Osoria, *Principal*
EMP: 4 **EST:** 2018
SALES (est): 45.2K **Privately Held**
SIC: 2043 Granola & muesli, except bars & clusters

(G-18376)
GREAT AMERICAN BASE COMPANY
5697 E Executive Dr (48185-1932)
PHONE.................................734 722-7700
William Knoll, *President*
▲ **EMP:** 20 **EST:** 2000
SQ FT: 20,000
SALES (est): 2MM **Privately Held**
WEB: www.gearchitecturalproducts.com
SIC: 2541 Cabinets, lockers & shelving

(G-18377)
GRINDING SPECIALISTS INC
38310 Abruzzi Dr (48185-3282)
PHONE.................................734 729-1775
Dennis Johnson, *President*
Cindy Johnson, *Vice Pres*
Jennifer Johnson, *Consultant*
EMP: 30 **EST:** 1987
SQ FT: 12,000
SALES (est): 2.6MM **Privately Held**
WEB: www.gsi1.com
SIC: 3599 3317 Grinding castings for the trade; welded pipe & tubes

(G-18378)
GT TECHNOLOGIES INC (HQ)
Also Called: Defiance Group, The
5859 E Executive Dr (48185-1932)
PHONE.................................734 467-8371
Paul Schwarzbaum, *President*
Dan Brinker, *Vice Pres*
Daniel Brinker, *Vice Pres*
John Brune, *Vice Pres*
Jim Porcaro, *Vice Pres*
◆ **EMP:** 40 **EST:** 1985
SALES (est): 283.2MM **Privately Held**
WEB: www.gttechnologies.com
SIC: 8711 3714 3545 3089 Designing: ship, boat, machine & product; motor vehicle engines & parts; machine tool attachments & accessories; injection molded finished plastic products

(G-18379)
H & A PHARMACY II   LLC
2379 S Venoy Rd (48185-4662)
PHONE.................................313 995-4552
Hassan Saaad, *Mng Member*
EMP: 5 **EST:** 2014
SALES (est): 147.7K **Privately Held**
SIC: 2834 Tablets, pharmaceutical

(G-18380)
HELIUM HOME BASE LLC
2600 Nichols Ct (48186-9376)
PHONE.................................734 895-3608
David Jenkins, *Principal*
EMP: 4 **EST:** 2015
SALES (est): 88.9K **Privately Held**
SIC: 2813 Helium

(G-18381)
HIGH-STAR CORPORATION
Also Called: Engineering and Mfg Svcs
6171 Commerce Dr (48185-5683)
PHONE.................................734 743-1503
Son Do, *CEO*
◆ **EMP:** 5 **EST:** 2002
SQ FT: 6,000
SALES (est): 734.4K **Privately Held**
WEB: www.high-star.us
SIC: 3541 3469 8711 Lathes, metal cutting & polishing; numerically controlled metal cutting machine tools; metal stampings; designing: ship, boat, machine & product

(G-18382)
HILL SCREW MACHINE PRODUCTS
8463 Hugh St (48185-1840)
PHONE.................................734 427-8237
William F Hill, *President*
John Fowler, *Vice Pres*
EMP: 8 **EST:** 1945
SQ FT: 12,000
SALES (est): 798.7K **Privately Held**
WEB: www.hrscrew.com
SIC: 3599 Machine shop, jobbing & repair

(G-18383)
HOLLYWOOD DRY CLEANERS
5999 N Wayne Rd (48185-7123)
PHONE.................................734 922-2630
Helwe Mahmoud, *Principal*
EMP: 4 **EST:** 2016
SALES (est): 72.1K **Privately Held**
SIC: 2499 Wood products

Westland - Wayne County (G-18384)

(G-18384)
HOME CHEF LTD
Also Called: Glocatch
39005 Webb Dr (48185-1979)
PHONE.................................734 468-2544
Jeffrey Vicars, *President*
EMP: 6 **EST:** 2013
SQ FT: 500
SALES (est): 55K **Privately Held**
SIC: 5064 3949 Appliance parts, household; fishing tackle, general

(G-18385)
IMPECCABLE MACHINING INC
1021 Manufacturers Dr (48186-4036)
PHONE.................................734 844-3855
Jerome Harvey, *Owner*
EMP: 6 **EST:** 2018
SALES (est): 323.3K **Privately Held**
SIC: 3599 Industrial machinery

(G-18386)
INTRA CORPORATION (PA)
885 Manufacturers Dr (48186-4036)
PHONE.................................734 326-7030
John Battista Sr, *CEO*
John Battista Jr, *President*
Eric Headrick, *Plant Mgr*
Clifford Norris, *Plant Mgr*
John Pfeiffer, *Purch Agent*
▲ **EMP:** 100 **EST:** 1976
SQ FT: 55,000
SALES (est): 24.1MM **Privately Held**
WEB: www.intra-corp.net
SIC: 3544 Special dies & tools

(G-18387)
JADE SCIENTIFIC INC (PA)
39103 Warren Rd (48185-1928)
PHONE.................................734 207-3775
Jheri Len Smolin, *President*
Michael Smolin, *President*
Charles Holleran, *Owner*
Les Freitag, *CFO*
Angela Belcher, *Sales Staff*
EMP: 10 **EST:** 1995
SQ FT: 9,500
SALES (est): 10.2MM **Privately Held**
WEB: www.jadesci.com
SIC: 5049 5169 3821 2869 Analytical instruments; laboratory equipment, except medical or dental; scientific instruments; chemicals & allied products; laboratory equipment: fume hoods, distillation racks, etc.; worktables, laboratory; laboratory chemicals, organic; industrial inorganic chemicals; microscopes, electron & proton

(G-18388)
JEDTCO CORP
5899 E Executive Dr (48185-5696)
PHONE.................................734 326-3010
Nancy Siwik, *President*
Michael Siwik, *Corp Secy*
S Ann Elliott, *Vice Pres*
EMP: 23 **EST:** 1971
SALES (est): 1.1MM **Privately Held**
WEB: www.jedtco.com
SIC: 3069 Custom compounding of rubber materials

(G-18389)
JET INDUSTRIES INC
38379 Abruzzi Dr (48185-3283)
PHONE.................................734 641-0900
Debra Kansier, *President*
Maureen Trainor, *Senior VP*
Daniel Trainor, *Vice Pres*
▲ **EMP:** 25 **EST:** 1969
SQ FT: 7,500
SALES (est): 1.5MM **Privately Held**
SIC: 3714 3494 Exhaust systems & parts, motor vehicle; mufflers (exhaust), motor vehicle; valves & pipe fittings

(G-18390)
KAH
Also Called: Universal Laundry Machinery
38700 Webb Dr (48185-1978)
PHONE.................................734 727-0478
Mark Hubbard, *President*
Ted Jaeckel, *Controller*
▲ **EMP:** 3 **EST:** 1997

SALES (est): 1.1MM **Privately Held**
WEB: www.univlaundry.net
SIC: 3582 Commercial laundry equipment

(G-18391)
KAP BUILDING SERVICES INC
6220 Commerce Dr (48185-9120)
PHONE.................................888 622-0527
Khalil Hakkani, *CEO*
EMP: 8 **EST:** 2019
SALES (est): 288.6K **Privately Held**
WEB: www.kapbuilding.com
SIC: 1389 Construction, repair & dismantling services

(G-18392)
LINK TOOL & MFG CO LLC
Also Called: Linktool Group
39115 Warren Rd (48185-1928)
PHONE.................................734 710-0010
Mark Petty, *President*
EMP: 80 **EST:** 1994
SQ FT: 28,000
SALES (est): 5.7MM **Privately Held**
WEB: www.linktoolgroup.com
SIC: 3544 Extrusion dies
HQ: Penn Engineering & Manufacturing Corp.
5190 Old Easton Rd
Danboro PA 18916
215 766-8853

(G-18393)
MASTER COAT LLC
6120 Commerce Dr (48185-9119)
PHONE.................................734 405-2340
Leonard Stephenson,
EMP: 9 **EST:** 2004
SQ FT: 33,000
SALES (est): 1MM **Privately Held**
WEB: www.mastercoatwestland.com
SIC: 3479 Coating of metals & formed products

(G-18394)
MAXPOW INTERNATIONAL LLC
37570 Avondale St (48186-3828)
PHONE.................................734 578-5369
Martin Mitkovski,
EMP: 4
SALES (est): 100K **Privately Held**
SIC: 2051 Bakery: wholesale or wholesale/retail combined

(G-18395)
METRO CAST CORPORATION
6170 Commerce Dr (48185-9119)
PHONE.................................734 728-0210
Constantin Bodea, *President*
Ramon Escobar, *Officer*
EMP: 6 **EST:** 1976
SQ FT: 14,000
SALES (est): 1MM **Privately Held**
WEB: www.metrocastcorp.com
SIC: 3272 Concrete products

(G-18396)
MIKES CABINET SHOP INC
Also Called: MCS Custom Design
37100 Enterprise Dr (48186-4028)
PHONE.................................734 722-1800
Mikhail Chalhoub, *Branch Mgr*
EMP: 6 **Privately Held**
WEB: www.choosemcs.com
SIC: 2434 Wood kitchen cabinets
PA: Mike's Cabinet Shop, Inc.
27031 W 7 Mile Rd
Redford MI
313 533-5800

(G-18397)
MODERNO INDUSTRIAL LLC
Also Called: Magnum Manufacturing
39140 Webb Dr (48185-7628)
PHONE.................................734 727-0560
David Lagrow,
EMP: 11 **EST:** 2009
SALES (est): 1.2MM **Privately Held**
WEB: www.magnum-mfg.com
SIC: 3599 Machine shop, jobbing & repair

(G-18398)
MONARCH PRINT AND MAIL LLC
1461 Selma St (48186-4024)
PHONE.................................734 620-8378

Scott Wolkhamer, *Principal*
EMP: 4 **EST:** 2015
SALES (est): 98.8K **Privately Held**
SIC: 2752 Commercial printing, offset

(G-18399)
NATIONAL BLOCK COMPANY
Also Called: National Ready-Mix
39000 Ford Rd (48185-1998)
PHONE.................................734 721-4050
Marty Eisenstein, *President*
James Gendron, *Vice Pres*
Amy Hollinshead, *Human Resources*
EMP: 25 **EST:** 1946
SQ FT: 4,800
SALES (est): 4.7MM **Privately Held**
WEB: www.nationalblock.com
SIC: 3273 3271 5211 3272 Ready-mixed concrete; blocks, concrete or cinder: standard; cement; masonry materials & supplies; concrete products

(G-18400)
NEW GENESIS ENTERPRISE INC
37774 Willow Ln Apt S2 (48185-3326)
PHONE.................................313 220-0365
David Lyles, *CEO*
EMP: 4 **EST:** 2015
SALES (est): 34.4K **Privately Held**
SIC: 7929 2741 Entertainment service; miscellaneous publishing

(G-18401)
NORTHFIELD MANUFACTURING INC
38549 Webb Dr (48185-1983)
PHONE.................................734 729-2890
Dennis Tynan, *CEO*
Dave Sylvester, *COO*
Christopher Tynan, *Vice Pres*
EMP: 45 **EST:** 1975
SQ FT: 30,000
SALES (est): 7.2MM **Privately Held**
WEB: www.northfieldfoundry.com
SIC: 3366 Copper foundries

(G-18402)
NYX LLC
Nyx Cherryhill Division
1000 Manufacturers Dr (48186-4064)
PHONE.................................734 467-7200
Dennis Dunlop, *Manager*
EMP: 63
SALES (corp-wide): 556.1MM **Privately Held**
WEB: www.nyxinc.com
SIC: 3089 Injection molding of plastics
PA: Nyx, Llc
36111 Schoolcraft Rd
Livonia MI 48150
734 462-2385

(G-18403)
PARKER ENGINEERING AMER CO LTD
38147 Abruzzi Dr (48185-3279)
PHONE.................................734 326-7630
John M Cole, *President*
EMP: 13 **EST:** 2018
SALES (est): 1.5MM **Privately Held**
WEB: www.parker-eng.us
SIC: 3563 Robots for industrial spraying, painting, etc.

(G-18404)
PENGUIN JUICE CO (PA)
39002 Webb Ct (48185-7606)
PHONE.................................734 467-6991
Jack D Pauley, *President*
Victoria Kohlstrand, *Corp Secy*
Linda Pauley, *Vice Pres*
Donald Kohlstrand, *Purch Agent*
▲ **EMP:** 15 **EST:** 1991
SQ FT: 11,150
SALES (est): 2.5MM **Privately Held**
WEB: www.penguinjuice.com
SIC: 2087 5149 Beverage bases, concentrates, syrups, powders & mixes; fruit juices: concentrated for fountain use; syrups, drink; extracts, flavoring; beverage concentrates

(G-18405)
PITTSBURGH GLASS WORKS LLC
1515 S Newburgh Rd Unit B (48186-4077)
PHONE.................................734 727-5001
Carolyn Rowland, *Opers Mgr*
Horacio Trujillo, *Marketing Mgr*
Luis Corona, *Branch Mgr*
Doug Harts, *CTO*
EMP: 50 **Privately Held**
WEB: www.vitro.com
SIC: 3211 5013 Flat glass; automobile glass
HQ: Pittsburgh Glass Works, Llc
323 N Shore Dr Ste 600
Pittsburgh PA 15212

(G-18406)
PLASTIPAK PACKAGING INC
1351 N Hix Rd (48185-3258)
PHONE.................................734 326-6184
William C Young, *President*
Catherine Brodehl, *Human Res Dir*
Laith Abduljabbar, *IT/INT Sup*
EMP: 5
SALES (corp-wide): 2.9B **Privately Held**
WEB: www.plastipak.com
SIC: 3089 3085 Pallets, plastic; plastics bottles
HQ: Plastipak Packaging, Inc.
41605 Ann Arbor Rd E
Plymouth MI 48170
734 455-3600

(G-18407)
PLYMOUTH BRAZING INC
6140 N Hix Rd (48185-1962)
PHONE.................................734 453-6274
Dallas Gibson, *President*
Jason Tell, *Vice Pres*
Diane Gibson, *Office Mgr*
Diana Gibson, *Manager*
Rob McComb, *Manager*
EMP: 65 **EST:** 2000
SQ FT: 32,000
SALES (est): 9.8MM **Privately Held**
WEB: www.plymouthbrazing.net
SIC: 3599 Machine shop, jobbing & repair

(G-18408)
PROMAX ENGINEERING LLC
6035 E Executive Dr (48185-1932)
PHONE.................................734 979-0888
John Zheng, *General Mgr*
Angelina Lai, *Marketing Staff*
Jun Zheng,
▲ **EMP:** 110 **EST:** 2003
SALES (est): 10.6MM **Privately Held**
WEB: www.promaxeng.com
SIC: 2531 Seats, automobile

(G-18409)
PROVIDENCE WORLDWIDE LLC
39005 Webb Dr (48185-1979)
PHONE.................................313 586-4144
Jeff Bucher,
EMP: 13 **EST:** 2007
SQ FT: 33,000
SALES (est): 3.2MM **Privately Held**
WEB: www.providenceworldwide.com
SIC: 3444 Metal housings, enclosures, casings & other containers

(G-18410)
PUNKTUAL PRINTING INC
8045 N Middlebelt Rd (48185-1809)
PHONE.................................734 664-8045
Sean Cullen, *Principal*
EMP: 5 **EST:** 2018
SALES (est): 107.9K **Privately Held**
SIC: 2752 Commercial printing, lithographic

(G-18411)
R & A TOOL & ENGINEERING CO
39127 Ford Rd (48185-1985)
PHONE.................................734 981-2000
Richard L Raymond, *President*
Gregory J Raymond, *Vice Pres*
Robert P Raymond, *Vice Pres*
Ron Raymond, *Vice Pres*
▲ **EMP:** 32 **EST:** 1945
SQ FT: 26,000

GEOGRAPHIC SECTION

White Cloud - Newaygo County (G-18439)

SALES (est): 3.4MM Privately Held
WEB: www.randatool.com
SIC: 3545 3544 Tools & accessories for machine tools; dies & die holders for metal cutting, forming, die casting

(G-18412)
RAMZAK WOODWORKING
37109 Gilchrist St (48186-9363)
PHONE 734 595-8155
Robert Schultz, *Principal*
EMP: 4 EST: 2014
SALES (est): 54.1K Privately Held
SIC: 2431 Millwork

(G-18413)
RED SPOT WESTLAND INC
550 Edwin St (48186-3801)
PHONE 734 729-1913
Charles D Storms, *President*
Madelyn Kraemer, *Admin Sec*
Robert Zamensky, *Maintence Staff*
▲ EMP: 106 EST: 1986
SQ FT: 85,000
SALES (est): 10.4MM Privately Held
WEB: www.redspot.com
SIC: 2851 Paints & paint additives; lacquers, varnishes, enamels & other coatings
HQ: Red Spot Paint & Varnish Co Inc
1107 E Louisiana St
Evansville IN 47711
812 428-9100

(G-18414)
RELIANCE METAL PRODUCTS INC
38289 Abruzzi Dr (48185-3281)
PHONE 734 641-3334
Thomas P Malysz, *President*
▲ EMP: 7 EST: 2000 Privately Held
SIC: 3469 Machine parts, stamped or pressed metal

(G-18415)
RELIANCE RUBBER INDUSTRIES INC
38230 N Executive Dr (48185-1972)
PHONE 734 641-4100
Gordhan Akbari, *President*
EMP: 9 EST: 1990
SQ FT: 11,000
SALES (est): 997K Privately Held
WEB: www.reliancerubberindustries.com
SIC: 3061 Mechanical rubber goods

(G-18416)
ROBMAR PRECISION MFG INC
38189 Abruzzi Dr (48185-3279)
PHONE 734 326-2664
Greg S Doss, *President*
Robert King, *Exec VP*
EMP: 41 EST: 1981
SQ FT: 12,000
SALES (est): 1.7MM Privately Held
WEB: www.robmar.com
SIC: 3599 Machine shop, jobbing & repair

(G-18417)
SCRIBLICAL VIBEZ PUBLISHING
6800 Central City Pkwy (48185-9135)
PHONE 313 544-3042
Kai Mann, *Principal*
EMP: 4 EST: 2016
SALES (est): 64.3K Privately Held
WEB: www.scriblicalvibez.com
SIC: 2741 Miscellaneous publishing

(G-18418)
SPECTRUM METAL PRODUCTS INC
38289 Abruzzi Dr (48185-3281)
PHONE 734 595-7600
Paul Massimilla, *President*
Dolores Massimilla, *Vice Pres*
EMP: 7 EST: 1988
SQ FT: 6,800
SALES (est): 700K Privately Held
SIC: 3444 Sheet metalwork

(G-18419)
SUNDAI IMPORTS INC
Also Called: Mz. Tilly Sunday ACC Bra Plug
36500 Ford Rd Ste 241 (48185-3769)
PHONE 877 517-7788
Latria Harrison, *Principal*
EMP: 5 EST: 2014
SALES (est): 250K Privately Held
SIC: 2339 Women's & misses' accessories

(G-18420)
TECRA SYSTEMS INC (PA)
6005 E Executive Dr (48185-1932)
PHONE 248 888-1116
Giridhar Gondi, *President*
Rod Lowe, *Minister*
SAI Parvataneni, *Vice Pres*
Ravi Musunuru, *Technical Mgr*
Giri Vinnakota, *Programmer Anys*
EMP: 18 EST: 1998
SQ FT: 2,500
SALES (est): 4MM Privately Held
WEB: www.tecra.com
SIC: 7372 7379 7371 Prepackaged software; data processing consultant; computer software development

(G-18421)
THERMAL ONE INC (PA)
Also Called: Special Div
39026 Webb Ct (48185-7606)
PHONE 734 721-8500
Ted Gaderick, *CEO*
Robert Gaderick, *Vice Pres*
EMP: 15 EST: 1960
SALES (est): 3MM Privately Held
WEB: www.thermal-one.com
SIC: 3398 Metal heat treating

(G-18422)
TOP NOTCH COOKIES & CAKES INC
1849 Knolson St (48185-3256)
PHONE 734 467-9550
Theresa Wheelock, *President*
Greg Wheelock, *Vice Pres*
EMP: 8 EST: 1983
SALES (est): 500K Privately Held
WEB: www.topnotchcookiescakes.com
SIC: 2052 2051 5461 Cookies; cakes, bakery: except frozen; bread, all types (white, wheat, rye, etc): fresh or frozen; bakeries

(G-18423)
TRI-STAR TOOL & MACHINE CO
613 Manufacturers Dr (48186-4036)
PHONE 734 729-5700
Kenneth Pelland, *President*
Winifred Pelland, *Corp Secy*
EMP: 10 EST: 1973
SQ FT: 13,600
SALES (est): 780.4K Privately Held
SIC: 3599 3544 Machine shop, jobbing & repair; jigs & fixtures

(G-18424)
TRU LINE CO
35562 Dove Trl (48185-9101)
PHONE 313 215-1935
Joseph Walker, *Principal*
EMP: 15 EST: 2015
SALES (est): 111.3K Privately Held
WEB: www.trulinecorp.com
SIC: 3599 Industrial machinery

(G-18425)
TRU-BORE MACHINE TOOL CO INC
6262 E Executive Dr (48185-1940)
PHONE 734 729-9590
Jon Horgas, *President*
EMP: 8 EST: 1986
SQ FT: 4,000
SALES (est): 638.1K Privately Held
SIC: 3599 Machine shop, jobbing & repair

(G-18426)
US FARATHANE HOLDINGS CORP
39200 Ford Rd (48185-9131)
PHONE 586 978-2800
Mike Sermo, *Principal*
David Mize, *Purchasing*
Steven Berger, *QC Mgr*
Ken Eklund, *Engineer*
Brian Young, *Engineer*
EMP: 5
SALES (corp-wide): 549.4MM Privately Held
WEB: www.usfarathane.com
SIC: 3089 Injection molding of plastics
PA: U.S. Farathane Holdings Corp.
2700 High Meadow Cir
Auburn Hills MI 48326
248 754-7000

(G-18427)
VITANORTH USA LLC
38309 Abruzzi Dr (48185-3283)
PHONE 734 595-4000
Rajendra Subudhi, *Principal*
Hitha Daida, *Principal*
EMP: 7 EST: 2015
SALES (est): 1MM Privately Held
WEB: www.vitanorthusa.com
SIC: 2834 Druggists' preparations (pharmaceuticals)

(G-18428)
VVP AUTO GLASS INC
1515 S Newburgh Rd (48186-4077)
PHONE 734 727-5001
Luis Corona, *Administration*
EMP: 41 EST: 1995
SALES (est): 2.9MM Privately Held
WEB: www.vitro.com
SIC: 3231 5013 Doors, glass: made from purchased glass; automobile glass
PA: Vitro, S.A.B. De C.V.
Av. Ricardo Margain Zozaya No. 400
San Pedro Garza Garcia N.L. 64410

(G-18429)
WARFIELD ELECTRIC COMPANY INC
5920 N Hix Rd (48185-7674)
PHONE 734 722-4044
Ed Hazelrigg, *Manager*
EMP: 5
SALES (corp-wide): 6MM Privately Held
WEB: www.warfieldelectric.com
SIC: 7694 Rewinding stators; rebuilding motors, except automotive; coil winding service
PA: Warfield Electric Company, Inc.
175 Industry Ave
Frankfort IL 60423
815 469-4094

(G-18430)
WEBB PARTNERS INC
39140 Webb Dr (48185-7628)
PHONE 734 727-0560
David Lagrow, *President*
Cynthia Lagrow, *CFO*
EMP: 25 EST: 1978
SQ FT: 230,000
SALES (est): 2.3MM Privately Held
SIC: 3599 Machine shop, jobbing & repair

(G-18431)
WEST SIDE FLAMEHARDENING INC
38200 N Executive Dr (48185-1972)
PHONE 734 729-1665
Michael Seror, *President*
EMP: 16 EST: 1978
SQ FT: 10,500
SALES (est): 2.2MM Privately Held
WEB: www.westsideflame.com
SIC: 3398 Brazing (hardening) of metal

(G-18432)
WESTMOUNTAIN SOFTWARE
36702 Cherry Oak Dr (48186-3449)
PHONE 734 776-3966
John McLeod, *Principal*
EMP: 5 EST: 2011
SALES (est): 85.5K Privately Held
SIC: 7372 Prepackaged software

Weston
Lenawee County

(G-18433)
SILBOND CORPORATION
9901 Sand Creek Hwy (49289)
PHONE 517 436-3171
Larry Brown, *COO*
John Gruber, *CFO*
◆ EMP: 50 EST: 1994
SALES (est): 14.4MM Privately Held
WEB: www.dynasylan.com
SIC: 2819 Industrial inorganic chemicals

Westphalia
Clinton County

(G-18434)
GROSS MACHINE SHOP
319 E Main St (48894-5113)
P.O. Box 65 (48894-0065)
PHONE 989 587-4021
Gerard A Gross, *Partner*
Gerard Gross, *Partner*
Michael Gross, *Partner*
EMP: 4 EST: 1937
SALES (est): 499.9K Privately Held
SIC: 3599 Machine shop, jobbing & repair

Wetmore
Alger County

(G-18435)
MODERN WOODSMITH LLC
E9998 State Highway M28 (49895-9567)
PHONE 906 387-5577
Joni Flynn, *Info Tech Mgr*
Timothy Flynn,
EMP: 5 EST: 2002
SALES (est): 615K Privately Held
SIC: 5031 2431 Kitchen cabinets; millwork

Wheeler
Gratiot County

(G-18436)
PATCH WORKS FARMS INC
Also Called: Double B'S Steel and Mfg
9710 E Monroe Rd (48662-9772)
PHONE 989 430-3610
Greg Baxter, *General Mgr*
William Butcher, *Principal*
Chuck Baxter, *Manager*
EMP: 4 EST: 2016
SALES (est): 338.8K Privately Held
WEB: www.doublebsteel.com
SIC: 3599 3291 Custom machinery; abrasive metal & steel products

---

White Cloud
Newaygo County

(G-18437)
ACAT GLOBAL LLC
66 N North St (49349-8832)
PHONE 231 437-5000
Joe Moch, *Branch Mgr*
EMP: 10
SALES (corp-wide): 2.3MM Privately Held
WEB: www.acatglobal.com
SIC: 3621 Rotary converters (electrical equipment)
PA: Acat Global, Llc
5339 M 66 N
Charlevoix MI 49720
231 330-2553

(G-18438)
ARROW DIE & MOLD REPAIR
8527 E Wilderness Trl (49349-9127)
PHONE 231 689-1829
Roger Mollema, *Owner*
EMP: 4 EST: 1985
SQ FT: 6,000
SALES (est): 296.5K Privately Held
SIC: 3544 Special dies & tools

(G-18439)
BP LUBRICANTS USA INC
201 N Webster St (49349-9678)
PHONE 231 689-0002
John Vollmar, *Business Mgr*
Christina Warren, *Buyer*
Scott Johnson, *Engineer*
Pam Myers, *Human Res Mgr*

White Cloud - Newaygo County (G-18440)

GEOGRAPHIC SECTION

Marcela Jaramillo, *Sales Mgr*
EMP: 47
SALES (corp-wide): 180.3B **Privately Held**
WEB: www.bp.com
SIC: 5171 2992 Petroleum bulk stations & terminals; lubricating oils & greases
HQ: Bp Lubricants Usa Inc.
1500 Valley Rd
Wayne NJ 07470
973 633-2200

(G-18440)
COUNTRY CANDLES
2832 S Laurel Dr (49349-9393)
PHONE..................................231.327-2730
Joshua Houle, *Principal*
EMP: 4 **EST:** 2018
SALES (est): 70.6K **Privately Held**
SIC: 3999 Candles

(G-18441)
GREAT LAKES ALLIED LLC
87 N Benson St (49349-9485)
PHONE..................................231 924-5794
Chris Drake, *Manager*
Gary Anderson,
Pam Anderson,
◆ **EMP:** 8 **EST:** 2001
SQ FT: 10,000
SALES (est): 1.4MM **Privately Held**
WEB: www.greatlakesallied.com
SIC: 5084 3559 5999 5941 Materials handling machinery; ; cleaning equipment & supplies; golf goods & equipment; truck equipment & parts

(G-18442)
HARBISONWALKER INTL INC
1301 E 8th St (49349-9746)
PHONE..................................231 689-6641
Carol Jackson, *CEO*
Mary Eichelberger, *Sales Executive*
Crawford Murton, *Marketing Staff*
Garret Childs, *Manager*
Alicia LI, *Manager*
EMP: 4
SALES (corp-wide): 542.2MM **Privately Held**
WEB: www.thinkhwi.com
SIC: 3255 3297 Clay refractories; nonclay refractories
HQ: Harbisonwalker International, Inc.
1305 Cherrington Pkwy # 1
Moon Township PA 15108

(G-18443)
HERITAGE FORESTRY LLC
3729 N Evergreen Dr (49349-9414)
PHONE..................................231 689-5721
James Ryan Coon, *Principal*
EMP: 4 **EST:** 2004
SALES (est): 229.1K **Privately Held**
SIC: 2411 Logging camps & contractors

(G-18444)
HI-TECH FASTENERS LLC
1341 E Pine Hill Ave (49349-9152)
PHONE..................................231 689-6000
Cory Newman,
EMP: 17
SALES (est): 574.9K **Privately Held**
SIC: 3965 Fasteners

(G-18445)
LUBECON SYSTEMS INC
Also Called: Lubetronics
201 N Webster St (49349-9678)
PHONE..................................231 689-0002
Lyle G Myers, *President*
Helen Myers, *Admin Sec*
EMP: 1 **EST:** 1977
SQ FT: 8,000
SALES (est): 15.8MM
SALES (corp-wide): 180.3B **Privately Held**
WEB: www.castrol.com
SIC: 5084 5172 2992 Industrial machinery & equipment; lubricating oils & greases; lubricating oils & greases
HQ: Castrol Industrial North America Inc.
150 W Warrenville Rd
Naperville IL 60563

(G-18446)
M 37 CONCRETE PRODUCTS INC
Also Called: Elmer's
1231 E 16th St M (49349-9748)
PHONE..................................231 689-1785
Mark C Holbrook, *Manager*
EMP: 9
SALES (corp-wide): 5.7MM **Privately Held**
SIC: 5032 5211 3273 3272 Concrete & cinder building products; concrete building products; lumber & other building materials; concrete & cinder block; ready-mixed concrete; concrete products
PA: M 37 Concrete Products Inc
767 E Sherman Blvd
Muskegon MI 49444
231 733-8247

(G-18447)
WHITE CLOUD MFG CO
19 N Charles St (49349-8769)
PHONE..................................231 689-6087
Jack Benedict, *President*
Fred K Benedict, *Vice Pres*
EMP: 7 **EST:** 1964
SQ FT: 12,000
SALES (est): 447.5K **Privately Held**
WEB: www.cityofwhitecloud.org
SIC: 3366 Bronze foundry

White Lake
Oakland County

(G-18448)
A&W WELDING
228 Abbey Blvd (48383-2881)
PHONE..................................248 949-4344
Scott Willman, *Principal*
EMP: 4 **EST:** 2016
SALES (est): 72.2K **Privately Held**
WEB: www.awwelding.net
SIC: 7692 Welding repair

(G-18449)
AMICUS SOFTWARE
11231 Sugden Lake Rd (48386-3661)
PHONE..................................313 417-9550
Ted Williford, *Owner*
Janie Williford, *Co-Owner*
Brad Affolder, *Marketing Staff*
EMP: 7 **EST:** 1973
SQ FT: 500
SALES (est): 500K **Privately Held**
WEB: www.amicussoftware.com
SIC: 7371 7372 Computer software development; prepackaged software

(G-18450)
ASHLEY GARCIA
9105 Huron Bluffs Dr (48386-4613)
PHONE..................................248 396-8138
Ashley Garcia, *Principal*
EMP: 4 **EST:** 2016
SALES (est): 206.2K **Privately Held**
SIC: 3441 Fabricated structural metal

(G-18451)
BIRD LOFTS & STUFF WOODWORKING
9211 Blondell Ave (48386-4211)
PHONE..................................248 882-1242
Patricia A Lidster, *Owner*
EMP: 5 **EST:** 2017
SALES (est): 93.8K **Privately Held**
SIC: 2431 Millwork

(G-18452)
CATHERINE PAWLOWSKI
301 Hurondale Dr (48386-2532)
PHONE..................................248 698-3614
Catherine Pawlowski, *Administration*
EMP: 5 **EST:** 2016
SALES (est): 62.9K **Privately Held**
SIC: 2711 Newspapers

(G-18453)
COLLAGECOM LLC
1471 Lynwood Ln (48383-3056)
P.O. Box 1684, Brighton (48116-5484)
PHONE..................................248 971-0538
Kevin Borders,
Joe Golden,
EMP: 7 **EST:** 2008
SALES (est): 748.7K **Privately Held**
SIC: 7372 Application computer software

(G-18454)
DAVISON-RITE PRODUCTS CO
2736 Havenwood Dr (48383-3917)
PHONE..................................734 513-0505
Arthur G Krol, *President*
Allen Brumbelow, *Purch Mgr*
EMP: 22 **EST:** 1947
SALES (est): 792.5K **Privately Held**
WEB: www.davison-rite.com
SIC: 3451 3545 3541 Screw machine products; machine tool accessories; machine tools, metal cutting type

(G-18455)
GATHERING PLACE OF WHITE LAKE
825 Oxbow Lake Rd (48386-3843)
PHONE..................................248 379-9582
Margaret White, *Principal*
EMP: 5 **EST:** 2010
SALES (est): 127.3K **Privately Held**
SIC: 2782 Scrapbooks

(G-18456)
GENERL-LCTRICAL-MECHANICAL INC
Also Called: G-E-M
10415 Highland Rd (48386-1810)
PHONE..................................248 698-1110
Vernon G Hooper, *President*
Louis Hooper, *Vice Pres*
Robin Hooper, *Admin Sec*
EMP: 8 **EST:** 1958
SQ FT: 14,800
SALES (est): 1.4MM **Privately Held**
WEB: www.g-e-m-inc.com
SIC: 3613 3599 Control panels, electric; machine shop, jobbing & repair

(G-18457)
GLOBAL WARMING SALSA
6900 Telluride Dr (48383-2397)
PHONE..................................248 882-3266
Daniel J Houston, *Owner*
EMP: 4 **EST:** 2013
SALES (est): 60.4K **Privately Held**
SIC: 2099 Dips, except cheese & sour cream based

(G-18458)
GOOD DO UP SKATEBOARDS
440 Rosario Ln (48386-4406)
PHONE..................................248 301-5188
Brandon Ash, *Principal*
EMP: 4 **EST:** 2018
SALES (est): 47K **Privately Held**
SIC: 3949 Skateboards

(G-18459)
KO INDUSTRIES
748 Rachelle St (48386-2959)
PHONE..................................248 882-6888
Kevin Oconnor, *Principal*
EMP: 13 **EST:** 2007
SALES (est): 86.7K **Privately Held**
WEB: www.koindustries.biz
SIC: 3599 Machine shop, jobbing & repair

(G-18460)
LL BECKER PUBLICATIONS
11375 Brigham Ln (48386-3638)
PHONE..................................248 366-9037
Laura Becker, *Principal*
EMP: 5 **EST:** 2008
SALES (est): 132.3K **Privately Held**
SIC: 2741 Miscellaneous publishing

(G-18461)
MACK INDUSTRIES MICHIGAN INC
8265 White Lake Rd (48386-1157)
PHONE..................................248 620-7400
Howard J Mack, *President*
Richard W Mack, *Vice Pres*
EMP: 30 **EST:** 1993
SALES (est): 4.6MM **Privately Held**
WEB: www.mackconcrete.com
SIC: 3272 Concrete products, precast

(G-18462)
NEW ALEXANDRIA PRESS
2870 Eric Dr (48383-3240)
PHONE..................................248 529-3108
Jeffrey Caminsky, *Principal*
Jeff Caminsky, *Author*
EMP: 5 **EST:** 2016
SALES (est): 40.4K **Privately Held**
SIC: 2741 Miscellaneous publishing

(G-18463)
PREACHER INDUSTRIES
5387 Touraine Dr (48383-2689)
PHONE..................................248 881-6590
Kenneth Fouty II, *CEO*
EMP: 4 **EST:** 2017
SALES (est): 51.3K **Privately Held**
SIC: 3999 Manufacturing industries

(G-18464)
SLIP DEFENSE INC
10279 Lakeside Dr (48386-2241)
PHONE..................................248 366-4423
Brian Greenstein, *Principal*
EMP: 5 **EST:** 2016
SALES (est): 155K **Privately Held**
SIC: 3812 Defense systems & equipment

(G-18465)
SOLID EPOXY COATINGS LLC
2975 Ford Rd (48383-3135)
PHONE..................................248 785-7313
Anthony Steckle, *Principal*
EMP: 4 **EST:** 2017
SALES (est): 80.7K **Privately Held**
SIC: 2851 Epoxy coatings

(G-18466)
SOLTIS PLASTICS CORP
10479 Highland Rd (48386-1810)
PHONE..................................248 698-1440
Joseph A Soltis, *President*
Gregory Soltis, *Vice Pres*
EMP: 6 **EST:** 1957
SQ FT: 8,000 **Privately Held**
WEB: www.soltisplastics.com
SIC: 3089 Injection molding of plastics

(G-18467)
STITCH INVENTIONS
8953 Haymarket St (48386-3394)
PHONE..................................248 698-7773
Lisa Mohr, *Principal*
EMP: 4 **EST:** 2018
SALES (est): 65.3K **Privately Held**
WEB: www.stitchinventions.com
SIC: 2395 Embroidery & art needlework

(G-18468)
TAGS R US LLC
920 Lake Jason Dr (48386-3832)
PHONE..................................248 880-4062
Sheelagh Tuza,
EMP: 5 **EST:** 2017
SALES (est): 39.6K **Privately Held**
WEB: www.tagsrus.us
SIC: 3999 Manufacturing industries

(G-18469)
TIME FOR BLINDS INC
9633 Highland Rd (48386-2315)
PHONE..................................248 363-9174
Mark F Sause, *President*
EMP: 6 **EST:** 1990
SQ FT: 5,000
SALES (est): 723.7K **Privately Held**
WEB: www.timeforblinds.com
SIC: 2591 5719 Blinds vertical; mini blinds; window furnishings; vertical blinds; window shades

(G-18470)
UNLIMITED MARINE INC
7775 Highland Rd (48383-2947)
PHONE..................................248 249-0222
Douglas M Henn, *President*
EMP: 7 **EST:** 2010
SALES (est): 521.9K **Privately Held**
SIC: 3732 4959 4226 Boat building & repairing; snowplowing; special warehousing & storage

(G-18471)
WHAT A STITCH
10164 Elizabeth Lake Rd (48386-2734)
PHONE.....................................248 698-1104
Karen Pipkin, *Owner*
EMP: 5 **EST:** 2015
SALES (est): 63.5K **Privately Held**
SIC: 2395 Embroidery & art needlework

White Pigeon
St. Joseph County

(G-18472)
BANKS HARDWOODS INC (PA)
Also Called: Banks Hardwoods Florida
69937 M 103 (49099-9449)
PHONE.....................................269 483-2323
Spencer Lutz, *President*
Stephen G Banks, *President*
Greg Ritchie, *Exec VP*
Brian Farrier, *Plant Mgr*
James F Clarke, *CFO*
◆ **EMP:** 100 **EST:** 1979
SQ FT: 2,500
SALES (est): 24.1MM **Privately Held**
WEB: www.bankshardwoods.com
SIC: 2421 5031 2426 Kiln drying of lumber; lumber: rough, dressed & finished; hardwood dimension & flooring mills

(G-18473)
CARGO KING MANUFACTURING INC
600 S Miller Rd (49099-8423)
PHONE.....................................269 483-9900
Robert L Dodson, *President*
Robert Dodson, *President*
Vickie Dodson, *Corp Secy*
EMP: 30 **EST:** 2004
SQ FT: 46,000
SALES (est): 2.6MM **Privately Held**
SIC: 3715 Demountable cargo containers

(G-18474)
DARKHORSE CARGO INC
500 S Miller Rd (49099-8436)
PHONE.....................................269 464-2620
EMP: 12 **EST:** 2019
SALES (est): 1.4MM **Privately Held**
WEB: www.darkhorsecargoinc.com
SIC: 3715 Truck trailers

(G-18475)
DECKORATORS INC
Also Called: Ucp
68956 Us Highway 131 (49099-8156)
PHONE.....................................616 365-4201
Larry Beck, *Purch Agent*
Ryan Hossman, *Manager*
EMP: 65
SALES (corp-wide): 5.1B **Publicly Held**
SIC: 3089 Fences, gates & accessories: plastic
HQ: Deckorators, Inc.
   1801 E Lessard St
   Prairie Du Chien WI 53821

(G-18476)
ELKHART PLASTICS LLC
Also Called: Elkhart Plastics - 08
605 Sol Morris Ave (49099-9501)
PHONE.....................................269 464-4107
EMP: 35
SALES (corp-wide): 510.3MM **Publicly Held**
WEB: www.epi-roto.com
SIC: 3089 Plastic containers, except foam
HQ: Elkhart Plastics Llc
   3300 N Kenmore St
   South Bend IN 46628
   574 232-8066

(G-18477)
FIBER BY-PRODUCTS CORP (PA)
70721 Us Highway 131 (49099-9473)
PHONE.....................................269 483-0066
Chad Schrock, *President*
Matt Myers, *Maintence Staff*
EMP: 19 **EST:** 2006
SALES (est): 5.3MM **Privately Held**
WEB: www.fiberby-products.com
SIC: 2421 Sawmills & planing mills, general

(G-18478)
GRAY BROS STAMPING & MCH INC
424 W Chicago Rd (49099-9111)
P.O. Box 338 (49099-0338)
PHONE.....................................269 483-7615
James Reilly, *President*
Dean Rentfrow, *General Mgr*
Donald C Grant, *Vice Pres*
Adele Gray, *Vice Pres*
James Gray, *Vice Pres*
EMP: 46 **EST:** 1948
SQ FT: 51,000
SALES (est): 2.6MM **Privately Held**
SIC: 3469 3498 3544 Stamping metal for the trade; tube fabricating (contract bending & shaping); special dies & tools

(G-18479)
GRAY BROTHERS MFG INC
424 W Chicago Rd (49099-9111)
P.O. Box 338 (49099-0338)
PHONE.....................................269 483-7615
James Gray, *President*
James Riley, *Corp Secy*
Phyllis Gray, *Vice Pres*
James Reilly, *Finance*
EMP: 12 **EST:** 1987
SALES (est): 521.5K **Privately Held**
SIC: 3498 3469 3444 3441 Fabricated pipe & fittings; metal stampings; sheet metalwork; fabricated structural metal

(G-18480)
HAGEN CEMENT PRODUCTS INC
17149 Us Highway 12 (49099-9779)
P.O. Box 606 (49099-0606)
PHONE.....................................269 483-9641
Sidney Hagen, *President*
Scott Hagen, *Vice Pres*
Terry Hagen, *Treasurer*
Jean Hagen, *Admin Sec*
EMP: 9 **EST:** 1945
SQ FT: 7,000
SALES (est): 800.6K **Privately Held**
WEB: www.theblockplant.com
SIC: 3271 5032 Blocks, concrete or cinder: standard; brick, stone & related material; brick, except refractory; sand, construction; gravel

(G-18481)
LAKELAND PAPER CORPORATION (PA)
68345 Edgewater Beach Rd (49099-8762)
PHONE.....................................269 651-5474
Graydon C Fox, *Ch of Bd*
Charlie Schmidt, *President*
Marvin A Weingard, *Corp Secy*
EMP: 50 **EST:** 1972
SQ FT: 200,000
SALES (est): 5.6MM **Privately Held**
WEB: www.lakelandpaper.com
SIC: 2631 Paperboard mills

(G-18482)
MAINE ORNAMENTAL LLC
Also Called: Deckorators
68956 Us Highway 131 (49099-8156)
PHONE.....................................800 556-8449
John Teller,
▲ **EMP:** 19 **EST:** 1989
SALES (est): 5.5MM
SALES (corp-wide): 5.1B **Publicly Held**
WEB: www.ufpi.com
SIC: 2499 5031 3496 Fencing, wood; lumber: rough, dressed & finished; miscellaneous fabricated wire products
HQ: Deckorators, Inc.
   1801 E Lessard St
   Prairie Du Chien WI 53821

(G-18483)
MENTOR ENTERPRISES INC
70431 M 103 (49099-9448)
PHONE.....................................269 483-7675
Mike Mentor, *Principal*
EMP: 7 **EST:** 2016
SALES (est): 286.7K **Privately Held**
SIC: 3543 Industrial patterns

(G-18484)
MORRIS EXCAVATING INC
69067 S Kalamazoo St (49099-9414)
P.O. Box 308 (49099-0308)
PHONE.....................................269 483-7773
John Morris, *President*
EMP: 10 **EST:** 1969
SQ FT: 28,000
SALES (est): 1MM **Privately Held**
WEB: www.whitepigeonexcavation.com
SIC: 1794 1611 1623 1442 Excavation work; concrete construction: roads, highways, sidewalks, etc.; underground utilities contractor; gravel mining

(G-18485)
PREMIER PALLET INC
11097 Us Highway 12 (49099-9176)
P.O. Box 383 (49099-0383)
PHONE.....................................269 483-8000
Joshua Royce, *Principal*
EMP: 13 **EST:** 2007
SALES (est): 513.5K **Privately Held**
WEB: www.premierpallet.net
SIC: 2448 Pallets, wood

(G-18486)
WARREN MANUFACTURING
68635 Suszek Rd (49099-9029)
PHONE.....................................269 483-0603
Ken Warren, *President*
Barbara Warren, *Vice Pres*
George Lasseigne, *Technology*
EMP: 8 **EST:** 1999 **Privately Held**
WEB: www.warrenmfg.com
SIC: 3599 5084 Machine shop, jobbing & repair; industrial machinery & equipment

White Pine
Ontonagon County

(G-18487)
PM POWER GROUP INC
29639 Willow Rd (49971-5001)
P.O. Box 695 (49971-0695)
PHONE.....................................906 885-7100
Brant Zettl, *President*
Zachary Halkola, *COO*
Suzanne Davey, *Officer*
EMP: 7 **EST:** 2017
SALES (est): 565.6K **Privately Held**
WEB: www.pmpowergroup.com
SIC: 8742 1731 3331 Administrative services consultant; general electrical contractor; primary copper

Whitehall
Muskegon County

(G-18488)
ACUTEX INC
Also Called: Acutex Division
2001 Peach St (49461-1844)
PHONE.....................................231 894-3200
Ron Overway, *President*
Chad Whitton, *Principal*
Thomas Buckingham, *Vice Pres*
Tom Buckingham, *Vice Pres*
Richard Smith, *Vice Pres*
EMP: 230 **Privately Held**
WEB: www.hilite.com
SIC: 3492 3594 3593 Fluid power valves & hose fittings; fluid power pumps & motors; fluid power cylinders & actuators
HQ: Hilite International, Inc.
   1671 S Broadway St
   Carrollton TX 75006
   972 242-2116

(G-18489)
ACUTEX INC
Also Called: Hilite International
2001 Peach St (49461-1844)
PHONE.....................................231 894-3200
Tom Buckingham, *President*
EMP: 1000 **EST:** 1999
SALES (est): 53.3MM **Privately Held**
SIC: 3714 Motor vehicle parts & accessories

(G-18490)
ALCOA HOWMET
1 Misco Dr (49461-1755)
PHONE.....................................231 894-5686
Michael A Pepper, *President*
Dirk Bauer, *Vice Pres*
Jack Bodner, *Vice Pres*
Marissa Earnest, *Vice Pres*
Boyd Mueller, *Vice Pres*
EMP: 12 **EST:** 2012
SALES (est): 501.5K **Privately Held**
SIC: 3353 Aluminum sheet, plate & foil

(G-18491)
ARCONIC
1600 Warner St (49461-1828)
PHONE.....................................231 894-7802
David Johnston, *Vice Pres*
Eric Rasmussen, *Vice Pres*
David Strate, *Engineer*
Adam Sylvester, *Engineer*
Mark Vrablec, *Ch Credit Ofcr*
EMP: 14 **EST:** 2018
SALES (est): 2.5MM **Privately Held**
WEB: www.arconic.com
SIC: 2834 Pharmaceutical preparations

(G-18492)
CONRAD MACHINE COMPANY
1525 Warner St (49461-1826)
PHONE.....................................231 893-7455
Earl Conrad, *Ch of Bd*
Thomas Conrad, *President*
Doug Conrad, *Vice Pres*
▲ **EMP:** 10 **EST:** 1947
SQ FT: 6,800 **Privately Held**
WEB: www.conradmachine.com
SIC: 3599 Machine shop, jobbing & repair

(G-18493)
CONSUMERS CONCRETE CORPORATION
2259 Holton Whitehall Rd (49461-9115)
PHONE.....................................231 894-2705
Mike Woodward, *Manager*
EMP: 12
SALES (corp-wide): 42.6MM **Privately Held**
WEB: www.consumersconcrete.com
SIC: 3273 Ready-mixed concrete
PA: Consumers Concrete Corporation
   3506 Lovers Ln
   Kalamazoo MI 49001
   269 342-0136

(G-18494)
D & D RETAINING WALLS INC
1481 Crystal Lake Rd (49461-9554)
PHONE.....................................260 341-8496
W David Macdonald, *President*
EMP: 5 **EST:** 2020
SALES (est): 159.6K **Privately Held**
SIC: 3999 Manufacturing industries

(G-18495)
ERDMAN MACHINE CO
8529 Silver Creek Rd (49461-9125)
PHONE.....................................231 894-1010
Scott Erdman, *President*
Ken Lahey, *Vice Pres*
Nancy Erdman, *Production*
Kevin Jacobs, *QC Mgr*
EMP: 35 **EST:** 1995
SQ FT: 20,000
SALES (est): 4.2MM **Privately Held**
WEB: www.erdmanmachine.com
SIC: 3545 Machine tool accessories

(G-18496)
FORM ALL TOOL COMPANY
803 S Mears Ave (49461-1521)
P.O. Box 413 (49461-0413)
PHONE.....................................231 894-6303
Thomas J Peterson, *President*
Cynthia Lombard, *Corp Secy*
EMP: 19 **EST:** 1968
SQ FT: 4,185
SALES (est): 997.3K **Privately Held**
WEB: www.formalltool.com
SIC: 3451 Screw machine products

Whitehall - Muskegon County (G-18497)

(G-18497)
FRETTY MEDIA LLC
Also Called: Barrels of Yum
201 W Obell St (49461-1742)
PHONE.................................231 894-8055
Liz Downey, *Marketing Staff*
Peter Fretty, *Mng Member*
Zackery Fretty, *Mng Member*
EMP: 5 **EST:** 2013
SALES (est): 408K **Privately Held**
SIC: 2064 Candy & other confectionery products

(G-18498)
HOWMET AEROSPACE INC
3850 White Lake Dr (49461-9345)
PHONE.................................231 981-3002
Weston Persons, *Marketing Staff*
William Zahrt, *Marketing Staff*
EMP: 7
SALES (corp-wide): 5.2B **Publicly Held**
WEB: www.howmet.com
SIC: 3334 Primary aluminum
PA: Howmet Aerospace Inc.
    201 Isabella St Ste 200
    Pittsburgh PA 15212
    412 553-1950

(G-18499)
HOWMET AEROSPACE INC
1500 Warner St (49461-1895)
PHONE.................................231 894-7290
Boyd Mueller, *Manager*
EMP: 170
SALES (corp-wide): 5.2B **Publicly Held**
WEB: www.howmet.com
SIC: 3324 Commercial investment castings, ferrous
PA: Howmet Aerospace Inc.
    201 Isabella St Ste 200
    Pittsburgh PA 15212
    412 553-1950

(G-18500)
HOWMET AEROSPACE INC
1 Misco Dr (49461-1799)
PHONE.................................231 894-5686
Leon Brown, *Production*
Thomas Marble, *QC Mgr*
Jerry Blackmer, *Research*
Bill Dewitt, *Engineer*
Randall Diehm, *Engineer*
EMP: 7
SALES (corp-wide): 5.2B **Publicly Held**
WEB: www.howmet.com
SIC: 3334 3353 1099 Primary aluminum; aluminum sheet & strip; coils, sheet aluminum; plates, aluminum; foil, aluminum; bauxite mining
PA: Howmet Aerospace Inc.
    201 Isabella St Ste 200
    Pittsburgh PA 15212
    412 553-1950

(G-18501)
HOWMET CORPORATION (DH)
Also Called: Alcoa Power & Propulsion
1 Misco Dr (49461-1799)
PHONE.................................231 894-5686
David L Squier, *President*
Marklin Lasker, *Senior VP*
James R Stanley, *Senior VP*
Roland A Paul, *Vice Pres*
B Dennis Albrechtsen, *VP Mfg*
◆ **EMP:** 30 **EST:** 1975
SQ FT: 10,000
SALES (est): 1.8B
SALES (corp-wide): 5.2B **Publicly Held**
WEB: www.theplayhouseatwhitelake.org
SIC: 3324 3542 5051 3479 Commercial investment castings, ferrous; machine tools, metal forming type; ferroalloys; ingots; coating of metals & formed products
HQ: Howmet Holdings Corporation
    1 Misco Dr
    Whitehall MI 49461
    231 894-5686

(G-18502)
HOWMET CORPORATION
Alcoa Howmet Ti-Ingot
555 Benston Rd (49461-1899)
PHONE.................................231 894-7183
Allen Zwierzchowski, *President*
Don Larsen, *Manager*
EMP: 126

SALES (corp-wide): 5.2B **Publicly Held**
WEB: www.theplayhouseatwhitelake.org
SIC: 3324 Commercial investment castings, ferrous
HQ: Howmet Corporation
    1 Misco Dr
    Whitehall MI 49461
    231 894-5686

(G-18503)
HOWMET CORPORATION
Alcoa Howmet, Ti-Cast
1600 Warner St (49461-1897)
PHONE.................................231 981-3269
Brian Plummer, *Engineer*
Trezelle Jenkins, *Manager*
EMP: 220
SALES (corp-wide): 5.2B **Publicly Held**
WEB: www.theplayhouseatwhitelake.org
SIC: 3324 Commercial investment castings, ferrous
HQ: Howmet Corporation
    1 Misco Dr
    Whitehall MI 49461
    231 894-5686

(G-18504)
HOWMET CORPORATION
Also Called: Alcoa Howmet, Thermatech
555 Benston Rd (49461-1899)
PHONE.................................231 894-5686
Laura Carpenter, *Manager*
EMP: 126
SALES (corp-wide): 5.2B **Publicly Held**
WEB: www.theplayhouseatwhitelake.org
SIC: 3353 Aluminum sheet, plate & foil
HQ: Howmet Corporation
    1 Misco Dr
    Whitehall MI 49461
    231 894-5686

(G-18505)
HOWMET CORPORATION
Also Called: Alcoa Hwmet Whthall Cast Oprto
1 Misco Dr (49461-1799)
PHONE.................................231 894-5686
Nicholas Stibitz, *Engineer*
Dan Grozskiewicz, *Manager*
EMP: 126
SALES (corp-wide): 5.2B **Publicly Held**
WEB: www.theplayhouseatwhitelake.org
SIC: 3353 Aluminum sheet, plate & foil
HQ: Howmet Corporation
    1 Misco Dr
    Whitehall MI 49461
    231 894-5686

(G-18506)
HOWMET HOLDINGS CORPORATION (HQ)
1 Misco Dr (49461-1799)
PHONE.................................231 894-5686
Mario Longhi, *CEO*
Raymond B Mitchell, *President*
James R Stanley, *Vice Pres*
▲ **EMP:** 1 **EST:** 1970
SALES (est): 1.8B
SALES (corp-wide): 5.2B **Publicly Held**
WEB: www.arconic.com
SIC: 3324 3542 5051 3479 Commercial investment castings, ferrous; machine tools, metal forming type; ferroalloys; ingots; coating of metals & formed products
PA: Howmet Aerospace Inc.
    201 Isabella St Ste 200
    Pittsburgh PA 15212
    412 553-1950

(G-18507)
LOOKING AFT PUBLICATIONS
409 Mill Pond Rd (49461-9603)
PHONE.................................231 759-8581
Daniel Yakes, *Principal*
EMP: 5 **EST:** 2016
SALES (est): 45.7K **Privately Held**
SIC: 2741 Miscellaneous publishing

(G-18508)
MAS INC
2100 Cogswell Dr (49461-1852)
PHONE.................................231 894-0409
EMP: 18 **EST:** 2014
SALES (est): 1.8MM **Privately Held**
SIC: 3728 Aircraft parts & equipment

(G-18509)
SIDEKICK DEVICE
7426 Wiczer Dr (49461-9263)
PHONE.................................231 894-6905
Jim Bundt, *Principal*
EMP: 4 **EST:** 2010
SALES (est): 176K **Privately Held**
WEB: www.sidekickdevice.com
SIC: 3824 Mechanical & electromechanical counters & devices

(G-18510)
TROPHY CENTER WEST MICHIGAN
8060 Whitehall Rd (49461-9496)
PHONE.................................231 893-1686
Pamela Semelbauer, *Owner*
EMP: 6 **EST:** 1990
SQ FT: 50,000
SALES (est): 370.9K **Privately Held**
WEB: www.trophycenterllc.com
SIC: 2261 2395 5999 7389 Screen printing of cotton broadwoven fabrics; embroidery & art needlework; trophies & plaques; engraving service; sporting goods & bicycle shops

(G-18511)
VIKING TOOL & ENGINEERING INC
2780 Colby Rd (49461-9254)
P.O. Box 278 (49461-0278)
PHONE.................................231 893-0031
Richard Seaver, *President*
Jeff Cussimanio, *Vice Pres*
Fred Danz, *Program Mgr*
Tom Burrous, *Manager*
◆ **EMP:** 30 **EST:** 1964
SQ FT: 24,000
SALES (est): 3.7MM **Privately Held**
WEB: www.vikingtooleng.com
SIC: 3544 Special dies & tools

(G-18512)
WHITE LAKE BEACON INC
432 E Spring St (49461-1153)
P.O. Box 340, Ludington (49431-0340)
PHONE.................................231 894-5356
Richard Lound, *President*
Greg Means, *Publisher*
Jared Leatzow, *Chief*
Dan Heller, *Sales Staff*
Katy Teitgen, *Internal Med*
EMP: 6 **EST:** 1983
SALES (est): 314.5K **Privately Held**
WEB: www.shorelinemedia.net
SIC: 2711 Newspapers, publishing & printing

(G-18513)
WHITE LAKE EXCAVATING INC
2571 Holton Whitehall Rd (49461-9169)
PHONE.................................231 894-6918
Tom Waruszewski, *President*
EMP: 20 **EST:** 1978
SQ FT: 6,280
SALES (est): 2.4MM **Privately Held**
WEB: www.whitelakeexcavating.com
SIC: 3531 5032 3272 1794 Asphalt plant, including gravel-mix type; gravel; concrete products; cast stone, concrete; excavation work; gravel or dirt road construction; surfacing & paving; paving stones; sand & gravel

(G-18514)
WHITEHALL PRODUCTS LLC
1625 Warner St (49461-1827)
PHONE.................................231 894-2688
Tim Swainston, *Purch Agent*
Roger Buter, *CFO*
Nicholas Hesse, *Natl Sales Mgr*
Brenda Bean, *Sales Staff*
Carolyn Dykman, *Marketing Staff*
▲ **EMP:** 75 **EST:** 1941
SQ FT: 110,000
SALES (est): 17.1MM **Privately Held**
WEB: www.whitehallproducts.com
SIC: 3599 3993 3365 3524 Weather vanes; signs & advertising specialties; aluminum foundries; lawn & garden equipment

Whitmore Lake
Washtenaw County

(G-18515)
A E C INC
Also Called: Littlite
10087 Industrial Dr (48189-9180)
P.O. Box 218, Hamburg (48139-0218)
PHONE.................................810 231-9546
James H Fackert, *President*
Rhonda Fackert, *Corp Secy*
Julie Sanders, *Marketing Mgr*
Jim Fackert, *Marketing Staff*
Donn Deniston, *Products*
▲ **EMP:** 55 **EST:** 1971
SQ FT: 21,500
SALES (est): 8.6MM **Privately Held**
WEB: www.caeinc.com
SIC: 3645 3648 3643 3625 Residential lighting fixtures; stage lighting equipment; current-carrying wiring devices; relays & industrial controls

(G-18516)
A&E MACHINE & FABRICATION INC
7540 Wheeler Rd (48189-9696)
PHONE.................................740 820-4701
Adam Mdoll, *Branch Mgr*
EMP: 4 **Privately Held**
SIC: 3599 Machine shop, jobbing & repair
PA: A & E Machine And Fabrication Inc
    384 State Route 335
    Beaver OH 45613

(G-18517)
AERO AUTO STUD SPECIALISTS INC
10769 Plaza Dr (48189-9737)
P.O. Box 140, New Hudson (48165-0330)
PHONE.................................248 437-2171
David L Stanton Jr, *President*
Michael J Stanton, *Vice Pres*
Gerry Gow, *Plant Mgr*
Liane Heinz, *Director*
EMP: 20 **EST:** 1960
SQ FT: 20,000
SALES (est): 2.5MM **Privately Held**
WEB: www.aeroandautostud.com
SIC: 3452 Rivets, metal; bolts, metal

(G-18518)
AL DENTE INC
9815 Main St (48189-9438)
PHONE.................................734 449-8522
Monique Deschaine, *President*
Nanette Carson, *General Mgr*
Dennis Deschaine, *Vice Pres*
EMP: 31 **EST:** 1981
SQ FT: 6,000
SALES (est): 3.5MM **Privately Held**
WEB: www.aldentepasta.com
SIC: 2099 Pasta, uncooked: packaged with other ingredients

(G-18519)
AMERICAN MODELS
11770 Green Oak Indus Dr (48189-9064)
PHONE.................................248 437-6800
Ronald Bashista, *Owner*
▲ **EMP:** 5 **EST:** 1987
SALES (est): 281.4K **Privately Held**
WEB: www.americanmodels.com
SIC: 3944 5945 Trains & equipment, toy: electric & mechanical; hobby, toy & game shops

(G-18520)
BALANCE TECHNOLOGY INC (PA)
Also Called: Bti Precision Measurement Tstg
7035 Jomar Dr (48189)
PHONE.................................734 769-2100
Thomas P Plunkett, *President*
Marco Iacono, *Accounts Mgr*
Carlos Zaragoza, *Technology*
Gary Grim, *Analyst*
▲ **EMP:** 100 **EST:** 1968
SQ FT: 53,000

▲ = Import ▼ = Export
◆ = Import/Export

SALES (est): 30.2MM Privately Held
WEB: www.balancetechnology.com
SIC: 3829 3825 3823 3821 Testing equipment: abrasion, shearing strength, etc.; vibration meters, analyzers & calibrators; instruments to measure electricity; industrial instrmnts msrmnt display/control process variable; laboratory apparatus & furniture; hand & edge tools

(G-18521)
BISNETT INSURANCE
7035 Jo Mar Dr (48189-8241)
PHONE.....................734 214-2676
Brian Plunkett, *Opers Staff*
Chad Hennemann, *Engineer*
Ryan Steele, *Engineer*
Mike Vizzini, *Engineer*
Ryan Borchert, *Software Engr*
EMP: 6 EST: 2017
SALES (est): 146.1K Privately Held
SIC: 3829 Measuring & controlling devices

(G-18522)
BLANK SLATE CREAMERY LLC
4090 Lori Lynn Ln (48189-9018)
PHONE.....................734 218-3242
Janice Sigler, *Principal*
EMP: 11 EST: 2013
SALES (est): 782.7K Privately Held
WEB: www.blankslatecreamery.com
SIC: 2021 Creamery butter

(G-18523)
BOOSTBUTTON LLC
9340 Wildwood Lake Dr (48189-9429)
PHONE.....................734 223-0813
EMP: 4 EST: 2010
SALES (est): 143.9K Privately Held
WEB: www.boostbutton.com
SIC: 3714 Motor vehicle parts & accessories

(G-18524)
BTI MEASUREMENT TSTG SVCS LLC (PA)
7035 Jomar Dr (48189)
PHONE.....................734 769-2100
David Benci, *Design Engr*
Tom Askew, *Marketing Staff*
Mike Takacs, *Program Mgr*
Stephen Simon, *Manager*
Thomas P Plunkett,
EMP: 6 EST: 2015
SALES (est): 1.1MM Privately Held
WEB: www.balancetechnology.com
SIC: 3829 Testing equipment: abrasion, shearing strength, etc.

(G-18525)
C R STITCHING
7870 Kearney Rd (48189-9572)
PHONE.....................734 449-2633
Cindi Moll, *Principal*
EMP: 4 EST: 2017
SALES (est): 72.9K Privately Held
SIC: 2395 Embroidery & art needlework

(G-18526)
CARPE CANDLE
11633 N Shore Dr (48189-9125)
PHONE.....................734 837-3053
Rachael Paul, *Principal*
EMP: 4 EST: 2019
SALES (est): 39.6K Privately Held
WEB: www.carpecandle.com
SIC: 3999 Candles

(G-18527)
CONCEPT ALLOYS INC
11234 Lemen Rd (48189-8115)
PHONE.....................734 449-9680
Robert Biermann, *President*
Tim Peters, *Principal*
▲ EMP: 6 EST: 2002
SALES (est): 1.5MM Privately Held
WEB: www.conceptalloys.com
SIC: 3356 Nonferrous rolling & drawing

(G-18528)
CONTROLLED MAGNETICS INC
10766 Plaza Dr (48189-9737)
PHONE.....................734 449-7225
Michael J Jagiela, *President*
Steven T Krause, *Admin Sec*
EMP: 10 EST: 1988

SQ FT: 5,000
SALES (est): 1.6MM Privately Held
WEB: www.controlledmagnetics.com
SIC: 3612 Autotransformers, electric (power transformers)

(G-18529)
COPY CONNECTION LLC
6500 Nollar Rd (48189-9252)
PHONE.....................734 425-3150
Bob Cowie, *Owner*
EMP: 4 EST: 2015
SALES (est): 68.7K Privately Held
WEB: www.copyconnectionllc.com
SIC: 2752 Commercial printing, lithographic

(G-18530)
DISTILLERY 9 LLC
8040 Apple Creek Ct (48189-9039)
PHONE.....................517 990-2929
Nicole Barczak, *Principal*
EMP: 5 EST: 2016
SALES (est): 103K Privately Held
WEB: www.distillery9.com
SIC: 2085 Distilled & blended liquors

(G-18531)
EJW CONTRACT INC
7930 Forest Creek Ct (48189-9142)
PHONE.....................616 293-5181
Erin Wallis, *President*
Steven Gottbreht, *Treasurer*
EMP: 2 EST: 2004
SALES (est): 3MM Privately Held
SIC: 2511 Wood household furniture

(G-18532)
ENERGY DESIGN SVC SYSTEMS LLC
7050 Jo Mar Dr (48189-8241)
PHONE.....................810 227-3377
David Ely, *CEO*
Kyle Leighton, *Sales Staff*
Simon Ren, *Director*
Laurie Anderson, *Executive Asst*
EMP: 75 EST: 2007
SALES (est): 9.6MM Privately Held
WEB: www.edssenergy.com
SIC: 3646 3648 8711 5063 Commercial indusl & institutional electric lighting fixtures; lighting equipment; engineering services; electrical apparatus & equipment

(G-18533)
ENGINEERED PRFMCE MTLS CO LLC
Also Called: EPM
11228 Lemen Rd Ste A (48189-9194)
PHONE.....................734 904-4023
Phil Young,
EMP: 4 EST: 2005
SALES (est): 323.6K Privately Held
WEB: www.epm-us.com
SIC: 3357 Nonferrous wiredrawing & insulating

(G-18534)
EXTREME MACHINE INC
10125 Industrial Dr (48189-9706)
PHONE.....................810 231-0521
Michael Barackman, *President*
EMP: 5 Privately Held
WEB: www.extrememachineinc.com
SIC: 3599 Machine shop, jobbing & repair
PA: Extreme Machine, Inc.
    10034 Industrial Dr
    Whitmore Lake MI 48189

(G-18535)
EXTREME MACHINE INC
10068 Industrial Dr (48189-9180)
PHONE.....................810 231-0521
Michael Barackman, *President*
EMP: 5
SQ FT: 31,000 Privately Held
WEB: www.extrememachineinc.com
SIC: 3599 3519 3714 Machine shop, jobbing & repair; parts & accessories, internal combustion engines; transmission housings or parts, motor vehicle
PA: Extreme Machine, Inc.
    10034 Industrial Dr
    Whitmore Lake MI 48189

(G-18536)
EXTREME MACHINE INC (PA)
10034 Industrial Dr (48189-9180)
PHONE.....................810 231-0521
Michael Barackman, *President*
Kim Barackman, *Vice Pres*
Lester Vincent, *Vice Pres*
Dennis Courter, *Plant Mgr*
Larry Pashnick, *Sales Staff*
EMP: 54 EST: 1992
SQ FT: 31,000
SALES (est): 10MM Privately Held
WEB: www.extrememachineinc.com
SIC: 3599 3519 8711 3714 Machine shop, jobbing & repair; internal combustion engines; engineering services; transmissions, motor vehicle

(G-18537)
GARY L MELCHI INC
11275 Merrill Rd (48189-9754)
P.O. Box 1331, Ann Arbor (48106-1331)
PHONE.....................810 231-0262
Gary L Melchi, *Principal*
EMP: 4 EST: 2009
SALES (est): 84.2K Privately Held
WEB: www.garylmelchi.com
SIC: 3643 Lightning arrestors & coils

(G-18538)
HIGH EFFCNCY PWR SOLUTIONS INC
11060 Hi Tech Dr (48189-9133)
PHONE.....................800 833-7094
Henry Grell Jr, *President*
Dean K Brown, *President*
Robert Rose, *Principal*
Teresa Smalley, *Director*
EMP: 9 EST: 2009
SALES (est): 1.5MM Privately Held
WEB: www.higheff.com
SIC: 3679 Electronic loads & power supplies

(G-18539)
M-36 COFFEE ROASTERS LLC
10815 Plaza Dr (48189-9737)
PHONE.....................734 449-8910
Kenneth Pargulski,
EMP: 4 EST: 2020
SALES (est): 425K Privately Held
WEB: www.m36coffeeroasters.com
SIC: 2095 Coffee roasting (except by wholesale grocers)

(G-18540)
MCMANUS SOFTWARE DEVELOPMENT
5171 Lisch Dr (48189-9774)
PHONE.....................810 231-6589
William McManus, *Principal*
EMP: 4 EST: 2014
SALES (est): 77.5K Privately Held
SIC: 7372 Prepackaged software

(G-18541)
MICHIGAN CNC TOOL INC
Also Called: Machine Shop
11710 Green Oak Indus Dr (48189-9064)
P.O. Box 626, Lakeland (48143-0626)
PHONE.....................734 449-9590
John Dziuban, *CEO*
EMP: 15 EST: 2005
SQ FT: 11,500
SALES (est): 2.3MM Privately Held
WEB: www.micnctool.com
SIC: 3599 Machine shop, jobbing & repair

(G-18542)
PACIFIC INDUSTRIES INC
11768 Freedom Dr (48189-9176)
PHONE.....................810 360-9141
Ken Ritchie, *Principal*
EMP: 5 EST: 2010
SALES (est): 108.8K Privately Held
WEB: www.pacificindustries.com
SIC: 3999 Manufacturing industries

(G-18543)
POP DADDY POPCORN LLC
11234 Lemen Industrial Dr C (48189-8149)
PHONE.....................734 550-9900
Mark Sarafa, *Mng Member*
EMP: 15 EST: 2013
SQ FT: 9,100

SALES (est): 4.4MM Privately Held
WEB: www.popdaddypopcorn.com
SIC: 5145 5461 5441 2064 Popcorn & supplies; pretzels; popcorn, including caramel corn; breakfast bars

(G-18544)
PRECISE POWER SYSTEMS LLC
10520 Plaza Dr (48189-9156)
PHONE.....................734 550-9505
Frank Taube, *Mng Member*
EMP: 8 EST: 2017
SALES (est): 592.9K Privately Held
WEB: www.precisepowersystems.com
SIC: 3625 Marine & navy auxiliary controls

(G-18545)
RHE-TECH LLC
1550 E N Territorial Rd (48189-9481)
PHONE.....................734 769-3558
EMP: 5
SALES (corp-wide): 1.5B Privately Held
WEB: www.hexpol.com
SIC: 3087 Custom compound purchased resins
HQ: Rhe-Tech, Llc
    1500 E N Territorial Rd
    Whitmore Lake MI 48189
    734 769-0585

(G-18546)
STELLAR MATERIALS INTL LLC
777 Eight Mile Rd (48189-9190)
PHONE.....................561 504-3924
David Mintz, *President*
EMP: 45
SQ FT: 82,000
SALES (est): 22MM Privately Held
WEB: www.thermbond.com
SIC: 3297 Cement refractories

(G-18547)
THERMBOND REFRACTORY SOLUTIONS
777 Eight Mile Rd (48189-9190)
PHONE.....................561 330-9300
EMP: 6 EST: 2019
SALES (est): 204.3K Privately Held
WEB: www.thermbond.com
SIC: 3297 Nonclay refractories

(G-18548)
TOTAL VINYL PRODUCTS INC
10750 Hi Tech Dr Ste B (48189-8138)
PHONE.....................734 485-7280
Bill Kindness, *CEO*
Robert Wiehagen, *Vice Pres*
EMP: 10 EST: 1976
SALES (est): 2.9MM Privately Held
WEB: www.totalvinyl.com
SIC: 3081 Vinyl film & sheet

(G-18549)
TUBE WRIGHT INC
10781 Plaza Dr (48189-9737)
PHONE.....................734 449-9129
Barney Raysor, *Principal*
EMP: 5 EST: 2016
SALES (est): 113.7K Privately Held
SIC: 3498 Tube fabricating (contract bending & shaping)

Whittemore
Iosco County

(G-18550)
LANGES BEEF & BULL INC
6750 Plant Rd (48770-9211)
PHONE.....................989 756-2941
Craig Lange, *President*
Carl A Lange Jr, *Principal*
Sandra Lange, *Admin Sec*
EMP: 9 EST: 1998
SALES (est): 165.4K Privately Held
SIC: 2011 Beef products from beef slaughtered on site

Williamsburg
Grand Traverse County

(G-18551)
ATWATER FOODS LLC
10106 Hgwy 31 Us (49690)
PHONE..................................231 264-5598
Randy Atwater,
EMP: 5 **EST:** 2006
SALES (est): 103.4K **Privately Held**
SIC: 2033 Canned fruits & specialties

(G-18552)
CHERRY BLOSSOM
8365 Park Rd (49690-9590)
PHONE..................................231 342-3635
Chris Hubbell, *Owner*
EMP: 7 **EST:** 2010
SALES (est): 217.9K **Privately Held**
SIC: 2099 Food preparations

(G-18553)
DOUBLE CHECK TOOLS SERVICE
6937 M 72 E (49690-9446)
PHONE..................................231 947-1632
Jim Munn, *Manager*
EMP: 7 **EST:** 1994
SALES (est): 294.1K **Privately Held**
SIC: 1389 Oil field services

(G-18554)
GRACE METAL PRODS INC
6322 Yuba Rd (49690-9525)
PHONE..................................231 264-8133
Dan Morrison, *President*
EMP: 4 **EST:** 1941
SALES (est): 188.2K **Privately Held**
WEB: www.graceusatools.com
SIC: 3423 Hand & edge tools

(G-18555)
GREAT LAKES TRIM INC
6183 S Railway Cmn (49690-8545)
PHONE..................................231 267-3000
Michael McNulty, *President*
Alan Agemy, *Controller*
EMP: 100 **EST:** 2002
SQ FT: 20,000
SALES (est): 16.4MM **Privately Held**
WEB: www.greatlakestrim.com
SIC: 3465 3429 3442 Moldings or trim, automobile; stamped metal; manufactured hardware (general); metal doors, sash & trim

(G-18556)
GRIT MANUFACTURING LLC
7646 Skegemog Point Rd (49690-8700)
PHONE..................................517 285-5277
Jon Dreher, *Principal*
EMP: 4 **EST:** 2018
SALES (est): 66.1K **Privately Held**
SIC: 3999 Manufacturing industries

(G-18557)
KDK DOWNHOLE TOOLING LLC
6671 M 72 E (49690-9360)
PHONE..................................231 590-3137
Kenneth Flannery, *Principal*
EMP: 7 **EST:** 2014
SALES (est): 767.2K **Privately Held**
SIC: 1389 Construction, repair & dismantling services

(G-18558)
MIKES STEAMER SERVICE INC
11825 Russell Ridge Rd (49690-9810)
PHONE..................................231 258-8500
Michael Beehler, *President*
EMP: 17 **EST:** 1977
SALES (est): 5.3MM **Privately Held**
WEB: www.mikessteamer.com
SIC: 1389 Oil field services

(G-18559)
NORTHERN MICH WDDING OFFCIANTS
4617 Bartlett Rd (49690-9325)
PHONE..................................231 938-1683
Crystal Yarlott, *Principal*
EMP: 4 **EST:** 2012
SALES (est): 179.8K **Privately Held**
WEB: www.northern-michiganweddingofficiants.com
SIC: 2435 Hardwood veneer & plywood

(G-18560)
NORTHERN MICHIGAN SAWMILL
4593 Hampshire Dr (49690-9633)
PHONE..................................231 409-1314
Vincenzo Festa, *Principal*
EMP: 4 **EST:** 2015
SALES (est): 79K **Privately Held**
SIC: 2421 Sawmills & planing mills, general

(G-18561)
NOWAK CABINETS INC
11744 S Us Highway 31 (49690-9449)
PHONE..................................231 264-8603
Joseph Nowak, *Owner*
Tracey Nowak, *Software Dev*
EMP: 8 **EST:** 2007
SALES (est): 475.4K **Privately Held**
WEB: www.nowakcabinets.com
SIC: 2434 Wood kitchen cabinets

(G-18562)
PHOENIX OPERATING COMPANY INC
4480b Mount Hope Rd (49690-9209)
PHONE..................................231 929-7171
Jeffrey Critchfield, *President*
EMP: 8 **EST:** 1990
SALES (est): 617K **Privately Held**
SIC: 1389 Oil field services; gas field services

(G-18563)
SAINT-GOBAIN PRFMCE PLAS CORP
Also Called: Twin Bay Medical
11590 S Us Highway 31 (49690-9434)
PHONE..................................231 264-0101
Albert Werth, *Branch Mgr*
EMP: 4
SALES (corp-wide): 2.1B **Privately Held**
WEB: www.plastics.saint-gobain.com
SIC: 2821 Plastics materials & resins
HQ: Saint-Gobain Performance Plastics Corporation
31500 Solon Rd
Solon OH 44139
440 836-6900

(G-18564)
SHORELINE FRUIT LLC (PA)
10106 Us Highway 31 N (49690-9521)
P.O. Box 987, Traverse City (49685-0987)
PHONE..................................231 941-4336
Duncan Morrison, *Plant Mgr*
Bryan Travis, *Transportation*
Justin Schumacher, *QC Mgr*
Mandi Twining, *Engineer*
Anne Moeller, *Controller*
◆ **EMP:** 178 **EST:** 2007
SALES (est): 33.6MM **Privately Held**
WEB: www.shorelinefruit.com
SIC: 2034 Fruits, dried or dehydrated, except freeze-dried

(G-18565)
THOMAS A DESPRES INC
Also Called: Cold Saw Precision
4229 Williamston Ct (49690-8627)
PHONE..................................313 633-9648
Thomas A Despres, *President*
Dolores Despres, *Corp Secy*
EMP: 17 **EST:** 1967
SQ FT: 27,000
SALES (est): 303.8K **Privately Held**
SIC: 3599 Machine shop, jobbing & repair

(G-18566)
TOP OF LINE CRANE SERVICE LLC
6925 M 72 E (49690-9446)
P.O. Box 101 (49690-0101)
PHONE..................................231 267-5326
Carl Baker, *Mng Member*
EMP: 7 **EST:** 2002
SALES (est): 562.5K **Privately Held**
WEB: www.topofthelinecrane.com
SIC: 3531 Cranes

(G-18567)
WOODHAVEN LOG AND LUMBER
3504 Kirkland Ct (49690-9388)
PHONE..................................231 938-2200
Randy Rhoads, *Manager*
EMP: 5 **EST:** 2017
SALES (est): 114K **Privately Held**
WEB: www.woodhavenlog.com
SIC: 2421 Sawmills & planing mills, general

Williamston
Ingham County

(G-18568)
BECK MOBILE CONCRETE LLC
2303 E Grand River Rd (48895-9158)
P.O. Box 354 (48895-0354)
PHONE..................................517 655-4996
Kevin Beck,
EMP: 4 **EST:** 1997
SALES (est): 308.6K **Privately Held**
SIC: 3273 3272 Ready-mixed concrete; concrete products, precast

(G-18569)
BEKUM AMERICA CORPORATION
1140 W Grand River Ave (48895-1394)
P.O. Box 567 (48895-0567)
PHONE..................................517 655-4331
Martin Stark, *Ch of Bd*
Gottfried Mehnert, *Ch of Bd*
Steven D London, *Exec VP*
Chad Hendges, *Production*
Charles Downer, *Buyer*
▲ **EMP:** 102 **EST:** 1979
SQ FT: 120,000
SALES (est): 26.6MM
SALES (corp-wide): 27.7MM **Privately Held**
WEB: www.bekumamerica.com
SIC: 3559 3544 Plastics working machinery; special dies, tools, jigs & fixtures
PA: Bekum - Maschinenfabriken
Gesellschaft Mit Beschrankter Haftung
Kitzingstr. 15-19
Berlin BE 12277
307 490-0

(G-18570)
CARDINAL FABRICATING INC
3394 Corwin Rd (48895-9711)
P.O. Box 69 (48895-0069)
PHONE..................................517 655-2155
Michael G Kavanagh, *President*
Stephen Zynda, *Principal*
Brad Tostevin, *Vice Pres*
EMP: 20
SQ FT: 13,000
SALES (est): 3.3MM **Privately Held**
WEB: www.cardfab.com
SIC: 3441 Fabricated structural metal

(G-18571)
ELAREE FABRICATION&WELDING
4531 Meridian Rd (48895-9417)
PHONE..................................517 505-5998
James C Potter, *Principal*
EMP: 4 **EST:** 2014
SALES (est): 39.1K **Privately Held**
SIC: 7692 Welding repair

(G-18572)
GEOTECH ENVIRONMENTAL EQP INC
1099 W Grnd Riv 6 (48895)
PHONE..................................517 655-5616
David Bean, *Manager*
EMP: 7
SALES (corp-wide): 18.3MM **Privately Held**
WEB: www.geotechenv.com
SIC: 3823 Water quality monitoring & control systems
PA: Geotech Environmental Equipment, Inc.
2650 E 40th Ave
Denver CO 80205
303 320-4764

(G-18573)
HUTSON INC
Also Called: D&G Equipment
2 Industrial Park Dr (48895-1600)
PHONE..................................517 655-4606
EMP: 124 **Privately Held**
WEB: www.hutsoninc.com
SIC: 5999 5261 7629 3648 Farm equipment & supplies; lawn & garden supplies; electrical repair shops; outdoor lighting equipment; construction & mining machinery
PA: Hutson, Inc.
306 Andrus Dr
Murray KY 42071

(G-18574)
JAMES AVE CATERING
1311 James Ave (48895-9702)
PHONE..................................517 655-4532
Colleen Gilmore, *Principal*
EMP: 4 **EST:** 2010
SALES (est): 210.1K **Privately Held**
WEB: www.jamesavecatering.com
SIC: 2051 Cakes, bakery: except frozen

(G-18575)
JBJ PRODUCTS AND MACHINERY
1432 E Grand River Rd (48895-9336)
PHONE..................................517 655-4734
John Palazzolo, *President*
James Palazzolo, *Vice Pres*
Robert Palazzolo, *Treasurer*
EMP: 5 **EST:** 1993 **Privately Held**
WEB: www.jbjpam.com
SIC: 3599 Machine shop, jobbing & repair

(G-18576)
M C MOLDS INC
125 Industrial Park Dr (48895-1656)
PHONE..................................517 655-5481
Robert J Palazzolo, *President*
William Russell, *Corp Secy*
Edward Fitzgerald, *Supervisor*
EMP: 39 **EST:** 1984
SQ FT: 12,000
SALES (est): 6.4MM **Privately Held**
WEB: www.mcmolds.com
SIC: 3089 3544 3542 Blow molded finished plastic products; special dies, tools, jigs & fixtures; machine tools, metal forming type

(G-18577)
MACHINE CONTROL TECHNOLOGY
4033 Vanneter Rd (48895-9172)
PHONE..................................517 655-3506
Jay Merkle, *Principal*
EMP: 5 **EST:** 1992
SQ FT: 10,000
SALES (est): 283.5K **Privately Held**
SIC: 7373 3541 7699 5084 Systems integration services; grinding machines, metalworking; industrial machinery & equipment repair; machine tools & accessories

(G-18578)
MODERN METAL PROCESSING CORP
3448 Corwin Rd (48895-9711)
P.O. Box 22 (48895-0022)
PHONE..................................517 655-4402
Chester Wesolek, *President*
Carolyn Wesolek, *Corp Secy*
Edward Wesolek, *Vice Pres*
Chris Piper, *Prdtn Mgr*
Sue Woodward, *Purchasing*
EMP: 5 **EST:** 1977
SQ FT: 15,000
SALES (est): 1MM **Privately Held**
WEB: www.modernmetalprocessing.com
SIC: 3398 Brazing (hardening) of metal

(G-18579)
PERFORMANCE PRINT AND MKTG
Also Called: Proforma
1907 Burkley Rd (48895-9755)
PHONE..................................517 896-9682
Timm Wiseley, *Accounts Exec*
EMP: 6 **EST:** 2011

GEOGRAPHIC SECTION

Wixom - Oakland County (G-18603)

SALES (est): 198.4K **Privately Held**
WEB: www.proforma.com
SIC: 2752 Commercial printing, lithographic

(G-18580)
R N FINK MANUFACTURING CO
1530 Noble Rd (48895-9354)
P.O. Box 245 (48895-0245)
PHONE.....................517 655-4351
Raymond N Fink, *Ch of Bd*
Eric Fink, *President*
Judy Jones, *Purch Mgr*
Dan Feldpausch, *Finance Mgr*
Vance Boyd, *Sales Mgr*
▼ EMP: 23 EST: 1960
SQ FT: 47,489
SALES (est): 2.6MM **Privately Held**
WEB: www.rnfink.com
SIC: 3085 Plastics bottles

(G-18581)
ROYAL STONE LLC
3014 Dietz Rd (48895-9214)
PHONE.....................248 343-6232
Jamey Palazeti, *General Mgr*
Randy Beverage, *Vice Pres*
Greg Hitchcock, *Vice Pres*
Chad Dunckel, *Plant Supt*
Mike Funk, *Treasurer*
EMP: 25 EST: 2000
SALES (est): 3.1MM **Privately Held**
WEB: www.royalstoneinc.com
SIC: 3272 3281 Cast stone, concrete; concrete products, precast; cut stone & stone products

(G-18582)
SEELEY INC
Also Called: Midway Rotary Die Solutions
811 Progress Ct (48895-1658)
PHONE.....................517 655-5631
Richard B Seeley, *President*
Betsy Seeley, *Vice Pres*
Elizabeth L Seeley, *Vice Pres*
Mike Graham, *Controller*
Joseph Lumsden, *Accounts Mgr*
EMP: 30 EST: 1974
SQ FT: 100,000
SALES (est): 5.5MM **Privately Held**
WEB: www.midwayrotary.com
SIC: 2754 Rotary photogravure printing

(G-18583)
SPECTRUM MAP PUBLISHING INC
795 Progress Ct (48895-1661)
PHONE.....................517 655-5641
EMP: 5 EST: 2016
SALES (est): 162.2K **Privately Held**
SIC: 5112 2741 Carbon paper; posters: publishing only, not printed on site

(G-18584)
UPPERHAND TACK CO LLC
2950 Burkley Rd (48895-9764)
PHONE.....................906 424-0401
Tyler Cappaert, *Mng Member*
EMP: 6 EST: 2020
SALES (est): 40.9K **Privately Held**
SIC: 2399 Horse & pet accessories, textile

(G-18585)
WILLIAMSTON PRODUCTS INC (PA)
Also Called: Wpi
845 Progress Ct (48895-1658)
PHONE.....................517 655-2131
Frank Remesch, *President*
Nigam Tripathi, *Principal*
Aashir Patel, *COO*
Ron Phillips, *Vice Pres*
Mike Metzger, *Plant Mgr*
◆ EMP: 65 EST: 2007
SQ FT: 36,000
SALES (est): 90MM **Privately Held**
WEB: www.wpius.com
SIC: 3089 Automotive parts, plastic

(G-18586)
WILLIAMSTON PRODUCTS INC
1560 Noble Rd (48895-9354)
PHONE.....................517 655-2273
Frank J Remesch, *Branch Mgr*
EMP: 5 **Privately Held**
WEB: www.wpius.com

SIC: 3089 Automotive parts, plastic
PA: Williamston Products, Inc.
845 Progress Ct
Williamston MI 48895

Willis
Washtenaw County

(G-18587)
QUANTUM WHATEVER LLC
9250 Macey Rd (48191-9765)
PHONE.....................734 546-4353
Brian C Moorhead, *Administration*
EMP: 5 EST: 2014
SALES (est): 75.4K **Privately Held**
SIC: 3572 Computer storage devices

(G-18588)
UNITED MILL & CABINET COMPANY
8842 Bunton Rd (48191-9619)
P.O. Box 339 (48191-0339)
PHONE.....................734 482-1981
Dennis Ruppert, *CEO*
Mark Boatwright, *President*
Marjorie Boatwright, *Chairman*
EMP: 10 EST: 1956
SQ FT: 19,900
SALES (est): 893.8K **Privately Held**
WEB: www.unitedmill.com
SIC: 2431 5211 Millwork; lumber & other building materials

Winn
Isabella County

(G-18589)
BOXER EQUIPMENT/MORBARK INC
8507 S Winn Rd (48896)
P.O. Box 1000 (48896-1000)
PHONE.....................989 866-2381
Jim Shoemaker Jr, *President*
Brian Macdonald, *Regional Mgr*
Gary Bardos, *Vice Pres*
Larry C Burkholder, *Vice Pres*
John Foote, *Vice Pres*
EMP: 3 EST: 1989
SALES (est): 6.3MM
SALES (corp-wide): 1.1B **Publicly Held**
WEB: www.morbark.com
SIC: 3599 3553 3549 3523 Machine shop, jobbing & repair; woodworking machinery; metalworking machinery; farm machinery & equipment
HQ: Morbark, Llc
8507 S Winn Rd
Winn MI 48896
989 866-2381

(G-18590)
MORBARK LLC (HQ)
8507 S Winn Rd (48896)
P.O. Box 1000 (48896-1000)
PHONE.....................989 866-2381
Dan Ruskin, *CEO*
John Foote, *Vice Pres*
Debbie Lehmann, *Vice Pres*
Miland Robinson, *Vice Pres*
David Schaufele, *Purchasing*
◆ EMP: 413 EST: 1965
SQ FT: 1,500,000
SALES (est): 146.8MM
SALES (corp-wide): 1.1B **Publicly Held**
WEB: www.morbark.com
SIC: 3599 3553 3549 3523 Machine shop, jobbing & repair; woodworking machinery; metalworking machinery; farm machinery & equipment
PA: Alamo Group Inc.
1627 E Walnut St
Seguin TX 78155
830 379-1480

Wixom
Oakland County

(G-18591)
3CON CORPORATION
47295 Cartier Dr (48393-2874)
PHONE.....................248 859-5440
Hannes Auer, *CEO*
Raymond Costello, *President*
Roman Pumpernick, *COO*
◆ EMP: 25 EST: 2014
SQ FT: 32,000
SALES (est): 3.5MM
SALES (corp-wide): 70.8MM **Privately Held**
WEB: www.3con.com
SIC: 3694 Automotive electrical equipment; motor generator sets, automotive
PA: 3con Anlagenbau Gmbh
Kleinfeld 16
Ebbs 6341
537 342-1110

(G-18592)
3M TECHNICAL CERAMICS INC
Also Called: Vehicle Armor Systems
50370 Dennis Ct (48393-2025)
PHONE.....................248 960-9339
Michael Kurilla, *Branch Mgr*
EMP: 11
SALES (corp-wide): 32.1B **Publicly Held**
WEB: www.ceradyne.com
SIC: 3299 3264 Ceramic fiber; porcelain electrical supplies
HQ: 3m Technical Ceramics, Inc.
1922 Barranca Pkwy
Irvine CA 92606
949 862-9600

(G-18593)
ABC MERCHANDISE
28900 Wall St (48393-3520)
PHONE.....................248 348-1560
Linda Iagee, *Owner*
▲ EMP: 4 EST: 1993
SALES (est): 156.5K **Privately Held**
SIC: 2399 Pet collars, leashes, etc.: non-leather

(G-18594)
ACROMAG INCORPORATED (PA)
30765 S Wixom Rd (48393-2417)
P.O. Box 437 (48393-0379)
PHONE.....................248 624-1541
John G Venious, *Ch of Bd*
Marc Brown, *Vice Pres*
Reg Crawford, *Purch Agent*
James Bowles, *Design Engr*
Kurt Lipsky, *Treasurer*
EMP: 57 EST: 1957
SQ FT: 33,480
SALES (est): 12.5MM **Privately Held**
WEB: www.acromag.com
SIC: 3823 3829 3672 3625 Industrial process control instruments; measuring & controlling devices; printed circuit boards; relays & industrial controls; computer peripheral equipment

(G-18595)
ADEMCO INC
Also Called: ADI Global Distribution
47247 Cartier Dr (48393-2874)
PHONE.....................248 926-5510
Mike Sampson, *Manager*
EMP: 5
SALES (corp-wide): 5B **Publicly Held**
SIC: 5063 3669 3822 Electrical apparatus & equipment; emergency alarms; auto controls regulating residntl & coml environmt & applncs
HQ: Ademco Inc.
1985 Douglas Dr N
Golden Valley MN 55422
800 468-1502

(G-18596)
ADEPT PLASTIC FINISHING INC
30540 Beck Rd (48393-2882)
PHONE.....................248 863-5930
David J Connell, *President*
Shane Gibson, *Principal*
EMP: 6 EST: 2019

SALES (est): 864.7K **Privately Held**
SIC: 3089 Injection molding of plastics

(G-18597)
ADEPT PLASTIC FINISHING INC
48668 Alpha Dr (48393-3445)
PHONE.....................248 374-5870
Bob Bretz, *President*
Carl Jacobson, *Corp Secy*
EMP: 1 EST: 2019
SALES (est): 7.2MM
SALES (corp-wide): 318MM **Privately Held**
SIC: 3089 Injection molding of plastics
PA: Tribar Technologies, Inc.
48668 Alpha Dr
Wixom MI 48393
248 516-1600

(G-18598)
AFC-HOLCROFT LLC (HQ)
Also Called: Pacific Industrial Furnace Div
49630 Pontiac Trl (48393-2009)
PHONE.....................248 624-8191
William Disler, *President*
Michael Hull, *CFO*
◆ EMP: 98 EST: 1962
SQ FT: 63,000
SALES (est): 17.5MM
SALES (corp-wide): 23.6MM **Privately Held**
WEB: www.afc-holcroft.com
SIC: 3567 Industrial furnaces & ovens
PA: Atmosphere Group Inc.
49630 Pontiac Trl
Wixom MI 48393
248 624-8191

(G-18599)
AG PRECISION GAGE INC
28317 Beck Rd Ste E6 (48393-4729)
PHONE.....................248 374-0063
John Baldwin, *President*
Joe Schmidt, *Exec VP*
EMP: 4 EST: 2004
SALES (est): 600K **Privately Held**
SIC: 3674 Strain gages, solid state

(G-18600)
AIC ACQUISITION COMPANY LLC
Also Called: Aic Eqpment Cntrls Plst-Co Eqp
51100 Grand River Ave (48393-3327)
PHONE.....................810 227-5510
Douglas Hugo, *President*
EMP: 35 EST: 2019
SALES: 4.6MM **Privately Held**
SIC: 3999 3545 Manufacturing industries; precision tools, machinists'

(G-18601)
AICHELIN HEAT TREATMENT SYST
49630 Pontiac Trl (48393-2009)
PHONE.....................734 459-9850
Udo Prenner, *President*
▲ EMP: 7 EST: 1989
SALES (est): 2.8MM
SALES (corp-wide): 544.5MM **Privately Held**
WEB: www.aichelin.com
SIC: 3567 Electrical furnaces, ovens & heating devices, exc. induction
HQ: Aichelin Holding Gmbh
Fabrikgasse 3
MOdling 2340
223 623-6460

(G-18602)
AIRMAN INC
46968 Liberty Dr (48393-3693)
PHONE.....................248 926-1409
Angelo Fratarcangeli, *Executive*
EMP: 6 EST: 2018
SALES (est): 60K **Privately Held**
SIC: 3531 Construction machinery

(G-18603)
AKTV8 LLC
50660 Century Ct (48393-2066)
PHONE.....................517 775-1270
Paul White, *VP Opers*
Gary M Meyers,
EMP: 7 EST: 2014

Wixom - Oakland County (G-18604)

SALES (est): 1.4MM **Privately Held**
WEB: www.aktv8.com
SIC: 3679 3694 Electronic switches; automotive electrical equipment

(G-18604)
ALLFI ROBOTICS INC
Also Called: Robotic System Integration
48829 West Rd (48393-3556)
P.O. Box 255, Walled Lake (48390-0255)
PHONE..................................586 248-1198
Samuel Song, *President*
◆ EMP: 3 EST: 2016
SQ FT: 6,000
SALES (est): 2MM **Privately Held**
WEB: www.allfirobotics.com
SIC: 3569 3541 Robots, assembly line: industrial & commercial; cutoff machines (metalworking machinery); drilling machine tools (metal cutting)

(G-18605)
ALLIGATOR NORTH AMERICA INC
50164 Pontiac Trl Unit 1 (48393-2079)
PHONE..................................248 914-0597
Josef Seidl, *Director*
EMP: 6 EST: 2013
SALES (est): 184.1K **Privately Held**
SIC: 3592 Valves

(G-18606)
ALTAIR SYSTEMS INC
30553 S Wixom Rd Ste 400 (48393-4420)
PHONE..................................248 668-0116
EMP: 15
SQ FT: 15,000
SALES: 780K **Privately Held**
SIC: 3625 3823 Mfg Relays/Industrial Controls Mfg Process Control Instruments

(G-18607)
AMERICAN AGGREGATES MICH INC (HQ)
Also Called: Natural Aggregate
51445 W 12 Mile Rd (48393-3100)
P.O. Box H, New Hudson (48165-0337)
PHONE..................................248 348-8511
Edward C Levy Jr, *President*
EMP: 100 EST: 1966
SALES (est): 9.7MM
SALES (corp-wide): 521.9MM **Privately Held**
WEB: www.edwclevy.com
SIC: 1442 Sand mining
PA: Edw. C. Levy Co.
9300 Dix
Dearborn MI 48120
313 429-2200

(G-18608)
APOLLO IDEMITSU CORPORATION
48325 Alpha Dr Ste 200 (48393-3451)
PHONE..................................248 675-4345
EMP: 7 **Privately Held**
WEB: www.idemitsuapollo.com
SIC: 2992 Lubricating oils & greases
HQ: Apollo Idemitsu Corporation
1831 16th St
Sacramento CA 95811
916 443-0890

(G-18609)
ATMOSPHERE GROUP INC (PA)
49630 Pontiac Trl (48393-2009)
PHONE..................................248 624-8191
William M Keough, *Ch of Bd*
Gary G Dawson, *CFO*
Mark R Lezotte, *Admin Sec*
EMP: 4 EST: 1977
SQ FT: 40,000
SALES (est): 23.6MM **Privately Held**
WEB: www.afc-holcroft.com
SIC: 3567 3398 Industrial furnaces & ovens; metal heat treating

(G-18610)
ATMOSPHERE HEAT TREATING INC
30760 Century Dr (48393-2063)
PHONE..................................248 960-4700
William Keough, *Ch of Bd*
James Haase, *President*
Wallace James, *Vice Pres*
Gary Dauson, *CFO*
EMP: 36 EST: 1997
SQ FT: 41,000
SALES (est): 4.1MM **Privately Held**
WEB: www.atmosphereheattreat.com
SIC: 3398 Metal heat treating

(G-18611)
ATS ASSEMBLY AND TEST INC (HQ)
1 Ats Dr (48393-2446)
PHONE..................................937 222-3030
David McAusland, *Ch of Bd*
John Donaldson, *Safety Mgr*
Michael Gondhi, *Cust Mgr*
▲ EMP: 189 EST: 1994
SQ FT: 140,000
SALES (est): 14.6MM
SALES (corp-wide): 1B **Privately Held**
WEB: www.atsautomation.com
SIC: 3599 Machine shop, jobbing & repair
PA: Ats Automation Tooling Systems Inc
730 Fountain St N Suite 2b
Cambridge ON N3H 4
519 653-6500

(G-18612)
ATS ASSEMBLY AND TEST INC
Advanced Assembly Automation
1 Ats Dr (48393-2446)
PHONE..................................937 222-3030
Bill Budde, *Director*
EMP: 10
SALES (corp-wide): 1B **Privately Held**
WEB: www.atsautomation.com
SIC: 3569 3825 Assembly machines, non-metalworking; instruments to measure electricity
HQ: Ats Assembly And Test, Inc.
1 Ats Dr
Wixom MI 48393
937 222-3030

(G-18613)
ATS ATMTION GLOBL SVCS USA INC
1 Ats Dr (48393-2446)
PHONE..................................734 522-1900
Steve Gedeon, *Mfg Staff*
Joann Middlestead, *Buyer*
Craig Anderson, *Treasurer*
Bill Bailey, *Manager*
EMP: 32 EST: 2010
SALES (est): 2MM
SALES (corp-wide): 1B **Privately Held**
WEB: www.atsautomation.com
SIC: 3823 Industrial instrmnts msrmnt display/control process variable
PA: Ats Automation Tooling Systems Inc
730 Fountain St N Suite 2b
Cambridge ON N3H 4
519 653-6500

(G-18614)
AUSTEMPER INC (HQ)
30760 Century Dr (48393-2063)
PHONE..................................586 293-4554
Lee C Price, *President*
Gary Dawson, *CFO*
EMP: 18 EST: 1984
SQ FT: 30,000
SALES (est): 6.1MM
SALES (corp-wide): 23.6MM **Privately Held**
WEB: www.austemperinc.com
SIC: 3398 Metal heat treating
PA: Atmosphere Group Inc.
49630 Pontiac Trl
Wixom MI 48393
248 624-8191

(G-18615)
AUSWELLA LLC
Also Called: Auswella Plush
3458 Castlewood Ct (48393-1749)
PHONE..................................248 630-5965
Jacqueline Sultana, *Mng Member*
Anthony Sciberras,
EMP: 4
SALES (est): 139.8K **Privately Held**
SIC: 3942 Dolls & stuffed toys

(G-18616)
AXSYS INC
29627 West Tech Dr (48393-3561)
PHONE..................................248 926-8810
Steven Braykovich, *President*
Roy Howard, *Vice Pres*
Bob Delisle, *Engineer*
George Lineman, *Engineer*
Eric Wennerstrom, *Engineer*
EMP: 24 EST: 1994
SQ FT: 8,000
SALES (est): 7MM **Privately Held**
WEB: www.axsysinc.com
SIC: 5045 3843 7373 Computer software; dental equipment; furnaces, laboratory, dental; computer-aided design (CAD) systems service

(G-18617)
B C MANUFACTURING INC
29431 Lorie Ln (48393-3686)
PHONE..................................248 344-0101
Louis Conrad, *President*
EMP: 10 EST: 1988
SALES (est): 826K **Privately Held**
SIC: 3544 Special dies & tools

(G-18618)
BAD AXE PRINTS
1012 Yorick Path (48393-4523)
PHONE..................................248 207-6999
Matthew Green, *Principal*
EMP: 4 EST: 2019
SALES (est): 83.9K **Privately Held**
WEB: www.badaxeprints.com
SIC: 2752 Commercial printing, lithographic

(G-18619)
BELASH INC
Also Called: Simplicabinets
2111 N Wixom Rd (48393-4249)
PHONE..................................248 379-4444
Kawkab Matti, *Principal*
EMP: 5 EST: 2018
SALES (est): 2.1MM **Privately Held**
SIC: 2434 Wood kitchen cabinets

(G-18620)
BENNY GAGE INC
Also Called: Zero Gage Division
4875 Product Dr Ste A (48393-2050)
PHONE..................................734 455-3080
Benny Dorenzo Jr, *President*
John Vogel, *Admin Sec*
EMP: 33 EST: 1929
SALES (est): 2.2MM **Privately Held**
WEB: www.zerogage.com
SIC: 3545 5084 3823 Gauges (machine tool accessories); industrial machinery & equipment; industrial instrmnts msrmnt display/control process variable

(G-18621)
BLADE INDUSTRIAL PRODUCTS INC
29289 Lorie Ln (48393-3682)
PHONE..................................248 773-7400
Joseph Smotherman, *President*
Joseph Mancos, *Vice Pres*
EMP: 7 EST: 1999
SALES (est): 730.7K **Privately Held**
WEB: www.bladeindustrial.com
SIC: 3069 3089 2499 3053 Rubber hardware; injection molded finished plastic products; cork & cork products; gaskets, packing & sealing devices

(G-18622)
BLADES ENTERPRISES LLC
47570 Avante Dr (48393-3617)
PHONE..................................734 449-4479
Bill Berry, *Business Mgr*
William Berry, *Business Mgr*
Edward Blades, *Mng Member*
Daniel Blades,
EMP: 10 EST: 2008
SALES (est): 1.5MM **Privately Held**
WEB: www.bladestool.com
SIC: 3312 Tool & die steel & alloys

(G-18623)
BLINDS AND DESIGNS INC
29988 Anthony Dr (48393-3609)
PHONE..................................770 971-5524
Neil S Lullove, *President*
Arlene Lullove, *Vice Pres*
EMP: 12 EST: 1977
SQ FT: 31,000
SALES (est): 221.4K **Privately Held**
WEB: www.blindsanddesignsltd.com
SIC: 2591 Window blinds; micro blinds; mini blinds

(G-18624)
BLUEWATER TECH GROUP INC (HQ)
Also Called: Bluewater Visual Services
30303 Beck Rd (48393-2840)
PHONE..................................248 356-4399
John Tracy, *CEO*
Suzanne Schoeneberger, *President*
Tobi Tungl, *President*
Robert Bolzman, *Business Mgr*
Jim Crowley, *Vice Pres*
EMP: 182 EST: 1985
SQ FT: 58,000
SALES (est): 77.2MM
SALES (corp-wide): 78.5MM **Privately Held**
WEB: www.bluewatertech.com
SIC: 3651 5064 7622 7359 Household audio & video equipment; electrical entertainment equipment; video repair; audio-visual equipment & supply rental
PA: M10 Group Holding Company
24050 Northwestern Hwy
Southfield MI 48075
248 356-4399

(G-18625)
BORAL BUILDING PRODUCTS INC (DH)
Also Called: Tapco Group, The
29797 Beck Rd (48393-2834)
P.O. Box 930316 (48393-0316)
PHONE..................................800 521-8486
Brian Below, *President*
Lynn Turner, *Treasurer*
Oren Post, *Director*
Mike Mildenhall, *Admin Sec*
EMP: 117 EST: 1999
SQ FT: 50,000
SALES (est): 124.7MM **Privately Held**
WEB: www.boralbuildingproducts.com
SIC: 8711 3542 3089 3531 Building construction consultant; sheet metalworking machines; shutters, plastic; construction machinery; sheet metalwork; hand & edge tools

(G-18626)
BROWN JIG GRINDING CO
Also Called: Bjg
28005 Oakland Oaks Ct (48393-3342)
PHONE..................................248 349-7744
Michael Brown, *President*
EMP: 12 EST: 1966
SQ FT: 12,000
SALES (est): 2MM **Privately Held**
WEB: www.brownjig.com
SIC: 3599 Machine shop, jobbing & repair

(G-18627)
BRUNT ASSOCIATES INC
47689 Avante Dr (48393-3697)
PHONE..................................248 960-8295
Denis P Brunt, *President*
Brian J Brunt, *Vice Pres*
Steve Fromm, *Manager*
EMP: 21 EST: 1984
SQ FT: 30,000
SALES (est): 2.5MM **Privately Held**
WEB: www.bruntassociates.com
SIC: 2431 1751 Millwork; carpentry work

(G-18628)
BUTTER COBBLER & THINGS LLC
714 Natures Cove Ct (48393-4578)
PHONE..................................810 391-8432
Gilbert Ruhumbika, *CEO*
EMP: 6 EST: 2017
SALES (est): 64K **Privately Held**
WEB: www.buttercobbler.ecwid.com
SIC: 2051 Bakery, for home service delivery

(G-18629)
C E C CONTROLS COMPANY INC
50208 Pontiac Trl (48393-2023)
PHONE..................................248 926-5701
Darren Pendley, *Branch Mgr*

GEOGRAPHIC SECTION
Wixom - Oakland County (G-18656)

Christopher Byrne, *Manager*
EMP: 7
SALES (corp-wide): 7.5B **Privately Held**
WEB: www.cec-controls.com
SIC: 3823 Industrial instrmnts msrmnt display/control process variable
HQ: C E C Controls Company, Inc.
  14555 Barber Ave
  Warren MI 48088
  586 779-0222

(G-18630)
CENTRAL CONVEYOR COMPANY LLC (DH)
52800 Pontiac Trl (48393-1928)
PHONE 248 446-0118
James Puscas, *CEO*
Jeremy Payne, *Division Mgr*
Jeff Debrabander, *Vice Pres*
Don Huffman, *Opers Staff*
Brian Castle, *Mfg Staff*
▲ **EMP:** 70 **EST:** 1993
SQ FT: 85,000
SALES: 180.1MM **Privately Held**
WEB: www.centralconveyor.com
SIC: 3535 Conveyors & conveying equipment
HQ: U.S. Tsubaki Holdings, Inc.
  301 E Marquardt Dr
  Wheeling IL 60090
  847 459-9500

(G-18631)
CHAIN INDUSTRIES INC (PA)
51035 Grand River Ave (48393-3329)
PHONE 248 348-7722
James M Chain, *President*
Timothy Doherty, *Vice Pres*
Russell Holman, *Vice Pres*
▲ **EMP:** 25 **EST:** 1982
SQ FT: 33,000
SALES (est): 25.8MM **Privately Held**
WEB: www.chainindustries.com
SIC: 3324 6798 Steel investment foundries; real estate investment trusts

(G-18632)
CHAMPION SCREW MCH ENGRG INC (PA)
30419 Beck Rd (48393-2841)
PHONE 248 624-4545
Katharine L Coffman, *President*
Susan Gorniak, *Vice Pres*
Kevin Coffman, *Treasurer*
Rhonda Long, *Finance Mgr*
Jim Merritt, *Sales Mgr*
EMP: 15 **EST:** 1945
SQ FT: 23,000
SALES (est): 5.3MM **Privately Held**
WEB: www.championscrew.com
SIC: 5084 3541 Machine tools & accessories; industrial machine parts; screw machines, automatic

(G-18633)
CHASE NEDROW MANUFACTURING INC
150 Landrow Dr (48393-2057)
P.O. Box 930313 (48393-0313)
PHONE 248 669-9886
James A Chase, *President*
Brian Nedrow, *Vice Pres*
Patrick Triest, *Marketing Staff*
EMP: 33 **EST:** 1992
SQ FT: 20,000
SALES (est): 2.9MM **Privately Held**
WEB: www.chasenedrow.com
SIC: 3297 Cement refractories

(G-18634)
CLIO MASSENA LLC
28214 Beck Rd (48393-3623)
P.O. Box 46129, Mount Clemens (48046-6129)
PHONE 248 477-5148
Vernon Guillermo,
▲ **EMP:** 30 **EST:** 2006
SQ FT: 10,000
SALES (est): 9.2MM **Privately Held**
SIC: 5015 3714 Motor vehicle parts, used; motor vehicle parts & accessories

(G-18635)
COMPLETE CUTTING TL & MFG INC
47577 Avante Dr (48393-3618)
PHONE 248 662-9811
Wendell Branton, *President*
Denise Branton, *Corp Secy*
EMP: 4 **EST:** 1994
SQ FT: 2,000
SALES (est): 368.1K **Privately Held**
WEB: www.completecuttingtools.com
SIC: 3545 Cutting tools for machine tools

(G-18636)
COUNTER REACTION LLC
46915 Liberty Dr (48393-3602)
PHONE 248 624-7900
Craig Fry, *Mng Member*
Ed Bear,
Jim Grover,
Mike Harris,
▲ **EMP:** 7 **EST:** 2013
SALES (est): 3.2MM **Privately Held**
WEB: www.counterreaction.net
SIC: 3821 Laboratory furniture

(G-18637)
COVENANT CPITL INVESTMENTS INC
Also Called: CCI Companies
49175 West Rd (48393-3552)
PHONE 248 477-4230
David Setsuda, *President*
EMP: 10 **EST:** 2001
SALES (est): 1.7MM **Privately Held**
WEB: www.cci-companies.com
SIC: 3469 8741 5085 Machine parts, stamped or pressed metal; management services; industrial supplies

(G-18638)
CP ACQUISITION LLC
Also Called: Classic Precision, LLC
28016 Oakland Oaks Ct (48393-3341)
PHONE 248 349-8811
Bill Maki, *Plant Mgr*
Lawrence J Waligorski, *Engr R&D*
Richard Przywara, *Sales & Mktg St*
Jo Ann Przywara, *Finance Other*
EMP: 20 **EST:** 1984
SQ FT: 12,000
SALES (est): 2.4MM **Privately Held**
WEB: www.classicprecision.net
SIC: 3599 Machine shop, jobbing & repair

(G-18639)
CPM SERVICES GROUP INC
47924 West Rd (48393-3669)
P.O. Box 301, Walled Lake (48390-0301)
PHONE 248 624-5100
Kevin Wadsworth, *President*
EMP: 4 **EST:** 2001
SQ FT: 5,300
SALES (est): 600K **Privately Held**
SIC: 7331 2752 Mailing service; commercial printing, offset

(G-18640)
CRACKER PUBLISHING LLC
28339 Beck Rd Ste F6 (48393-4753)
PHONE 248 429-9098
Robert J Poulos, *Principal*
EMP: 6 **EST:** 2013
SALES (est): 154.9K **Privately Held**
SIC: 2741 Miscellaneous publishing

(G-18641)
CREATIVE MACHINE COMPANY
50140 Pontiac Trl (48393-2019)
PHONE 248 669-4230
Gordon K Boring, *President*
EMP: 20 **EST:** 1980
SALES (est): 4.9MM **Privately Held**
WEB: www.creativemachinecompany.com
SIC: 3599 Custom machinery; machine shop, jobbing & repair

(G-18642)
CUSTOM ELECTRIC MFG LLC
48941 West Rd (48393-3555)
PHONE 248 305-7700
Bob Edwards, *President*
Vic Lafata, *General Mgr*
Jim Strauss, *Project Engr*
Bob Fouquette, *Manager*

EMP: 20 **EST:** 2018
SALES (est): 2.6MM
SALES (corp-wide): 9.9B **Privately Held**
WEB: www.custom-electric.com
SIC: 3567 Heating units & devices, industrial: electric
HQ: Kanthal Ab
  Sorkvarnsvagen 3
  Hallstahammar 734 4
  220 210-00

(G-18643)
DART CONTAINER MICHIGAN LLC
46918 Liberty Dr (48393-3600)
PHONE 248 669-3767
Jessica Spinner, *Accounts Mgr*
Andrew Farrar, *Analyst*
EMP: 2628 **Privately Held**
WEB: www.dartcontainer.com
SIC: 3086 Plastics foam products
HQ: Dart Container Of Michigan Llc
  500 Hogsback Rd
  Mason MI 48854
  800 248-5960

(G-18644)
DATALYZER INTERNATIONAL INC
29445 Beck Rd Ste A207 (48393-2879)
PHONE 248 960-3535
Robert Flores, *Engineer*
EMP: 7 **EST:** 2019
SALES (est): 37.5K **Privately Held**
WEB: www.datalyzer.com
SIC: 2741 Miscellaneous publishing

(G-18645)
DISCRAFT INC
51000 Grand River Ave (48393-3326)
PHONE 248 624-2250
James F Kenner, *President*
Mike Wagner, *General Mgr*
Pad Timmons, *Managing Dir*
Gail E Mc Coll, *Corp Secy*
Michelle Walsh, *Accounts Mgr*
▲ **EMP:** 25 **EST:** 1987
SALES (est): 4.6MM **Privately Held**
WEB: www.discraft.com
SIC: 3949 Sporting & athletic goods

(G-18646)
DISTINCTIVE APPLIANCES DISTRG
51155 Grand River Ave (48393-3330)
PHONE 248 380-2007
Michel Benoit, *President*
Nadia Amiel, *Vice Pres*
Mike Kanack, *Technical Mgr*
Suzanne Pataro, *Regl Sales Mgr*
Jason Manning, *Sales Staff*
▲ **EMP:** 10 **EST:** 2007
SQ FT: 30,740
SALES (est): 3.6MM
SALES (corp-wide): 900K **Privately Held**
WEB: www.distinctiveappliances.net
SIC: 3634 Housewares, excluding cooking appliances & utensils
HQ: Distinctive Appliances Inc
  2025 Rue Cunard
  Montreal QC H7S 2
  450 687-6311

(G-18647)
DOT SIGN
31158 Woodland St (48393-2690)
PHONE 248 760-8236
Henry Joshua, *Principal*
EMP: 4 **EST:** 2009
SALES (est): 56K **Privately Held**
WEB: www.dot-sign.com
SIC: 3993 Signs & advertising specialties

(G-18648)
DS SALES INC
Also Called: Premier International
46903 West Rd (48393-3654)
P.O. Box 88, Fenton (48430-0088)
PHONE 248 960-6411
David S Strach, *President*
Jason Linton, *Vice Pres*
Erica Crabb, *Controller*
Paul Moran, *Sales Mgr*
Gerrit Mortensen, *Accounts Mgr*
EMP: 38 **EST:** 2005

SQ FT: 15,000
SALES (est): 4.7MM **Privately Held**
WEB: www.premierdiecut.com
SIC: 3069 Foam rubber

(G-18649)
DYSON SERVICE CENTER
50160 Pontiac Trl Unit 1 (48393-2078)
PHONE 248 960-0052
EMP: 5 **EST:** 2018
SALES (est): 128.7K **Privately Held**
WEB: www.dyson.com
SIC: 3635 Household vacuum cleaners

(G-18650)
EAGLE INDUSTRIES INC
51135 Century Ct (48393-2077)
PHONE 248 624-4266
Peter Woolcox, *Branch Mgr*
EMP: 20 **Privately Held**
WEB: www.eagleindinc.com
SIC: 3089 Injection molding of plastics
PA: Eagle Industries, Inc.
  30926 Century Dr
  Wixom MI 48393

(G-18651)
EAGLE INDUSTRIES INC (PA)
30926 Century Dr (48393-2064)
PHONE 248 624-4266
John R Bull Jr, *President*
Keith Byer, *Maint Spvr*
Stuart Vukas, *Project Engr*
Linda Craig, *Sales Staff*
▲ **EMP:** 45 **EST:** 1992
SQ FT: 42,000
SALES: 34.4MM **Privately Held**
WEB: www.eagleindinc.com
SIC: 3089 Injection molding of plastics

(G-18652)
ECLIPSE PRINT SERVICES
46980 Liberty Dr (48393-3601)
PHONE 517 304-2151
EMP: 5 **EST:** 2011
SALES (est): 117.4K **Privately Held**
SIC: 2752 Commercial printing, lithographic

(G-18653)
ELECTROJET INC
50164 Pontiac Trl Unit 5 (48393-2079)
PHONE 734 272-4709
Kyle Schwulst, *CEO*
▲ **EMP:** 6 **EST:** 2003
SALES (est): 926.8K **Privately Held**
WEB: www.electrojet.org
SIC: 3625 Control equipment, electric

(G-18654)
ELK SOFTWARE LLC
28345 Beck Rd Ste 103 (48393-4733)
PHONE 800 658-3420
Yvonne Arnold, *Agent*
Timothy Damschroder, *Administration*
EMP: 14 **EST:** 2009
SALES (est): 488.3K **Privately Held**
SIC: 7372 Prepackaged software

(G-18655)
ELOPAK INC
46962 Liberty Dr (48393-3693)
PHONE 248 486-4600
Robert B Gillis, *President*
Nils Erik Aaby, *Vice Pres*
Gunnar Engen, *Vice Pres*
Thomas Marchioni, *Treasurer*
◆ **EMP:** 1 **EST:** 1987
SQ FT: 175,000
SALES (est): 11.5MM
SALES (corp-wide): 718MM **Privately Held**
WEB: www.elopak.com
SIC: 3565 Carton packing machines
HQ: Elopak-Americas, Inc.
  46962 Liberty Dr
  Wixom MI 48393

(G-18656)
ENA NORTH AMERICA CORPORATION
51150 Century Ct (48393-2077)
PHONE 248 926-0011
Cheol SOO Shin, *Ch of Bd*
Hobum Shin, *Vice Pres*
▲ **EMP:** 27 **EST:** 2005

Wixom - Oakland County (G-18657) GEOGRAPHIC SECTION

SQ FT: 32,000
SALES (est): 2.5MM Privately Held
WEB: www.ena.co.kr
SIC: 5013 3052 Automotive supplies & parts; rubber & plastics hose & beltings
PA: Ena Industryco., Ltd.
71 Gongdan 1-Ro, Jillyang-Eup
Gyeongsan 38459

(G-18657)
ENGAI
27056 Pinewood Dr Apt 203 (48393-3294)
PHONE.................................313 605-8220
EMP: 4 EST: 2018
SALES (est): 127.8K Privately Held
SIC: 2741 Miscellaneous publishing

(G-18658)
ESOC INC
Also Called: Environmental Safe Oil Change
48553 West Rd (48393-3537)
PHONE.................................248 624-7992
Ram Bedi, *President*
Michele Collins, *Business Mgr*
EMP: 10 EST: 1995
SALES (est): 1.3MM Privately Held
WEB: www.esocinc.com
SIC: 3559 5084 Automotive maintenance equipment; industrial machinery & equipment

(G-18659)
EXATEC LLC
31220 Oak Creek Dr (48393-2432)
PHONE.................................248 926-4200
Mr Ciemens Kaiser, *CEO*
Dominic McMahon, *General Mgr*
▲ EMP: 40 EST: 1998
SQ FT: 100,000
SALES (est): 8.4MM Privately Held
WEB: www.exatec.de
SIC: 3231 Windshields, glass: made from purchased glass

(G-18660)
EXCEL REAL ESTATE HOLDINGS LLC
28011 Grand Oaks Ct (48393-3340)
PHONE.................................919 250-1973
EMP: 7 EST: 2014
SALES (est): 74.9K Privately Held
WEB: www.excelrealtyholdings.com
SIC: 3089 Plastics products

(G-18661)
FIREBOLT GROUP INC (PA)
Also Called: Firebolt Igniting Brand Prfmce
28059 Center Oaks Ct (48393-3347)
PHONE.................................248 624-8880
Philip Ochtman, *CEO*
Brian Sciackitano, *COO*
Paul Norton, *Vice Pres*
Alex Topsfield, *Project Mgr*
Tony Lobaito, *Opers Staff*
▲ EMP: 9 EST: 2003
SQ FT: 4,800
SALES (est): 5.9MM Privately Held
WEB: www.firebolt-group.com
SIC: 3993 Signs & advertising specialties

(G-18662)
FLAGG DISTRIBUTION LLC
48155 West Rd Ste 6 (48393-4740)
PHONE.................................248 926-0510
Warren A Flagg Jr,
EMP: 5 EST: 2012
SALES (est): 212.7K Privately Held
SIC: 2434 Wood kitchen cabinets

(G-18663)
FLUID AUTOMATION INC
49175 West Rd (48393-3552)
P.O. Box 930302 (48393-0302)
PHONE.................................248 669-3717
EMP: 6 EST: 2019
SALES (est): 376.6K Privately Held
SIC: 3561 Pumps & pumping equipment

(G-18664)
FORTIS SLTIONS GROUP CENTL LLC (PA)
Also Called: A & M Label
28505 Automation Blvd (48393-3154)
PHONE.................................248 437-5200
James Listerman, *Ch of Bd*
Pauline Listerman, *President*
John O Wynne Jr, *Principal*
Pat Watson, *Director*
William Smith, *Officer*
EMP: 67 EST: 1971
SQ FT: 30,000
SALES (est): 8.8MM Privately Held
WEB: www.fortissolutionsgroup.com
SIC: 2759 2796 Flexographic printing; platemaking services

(G-18665)
FORTUNE TOOL & MACHINE INC
29650 Beck Rd (48393-2822)
PHONE.................................248 669-9119
Donna Dancik, *President*
Michael Dancik, *Vice Pres*
EMP: 14 EST: 1989
SQ FT: 8,000
SALES (est): 830.6K Privately Held
WEB: www.fortune-tool-and-machine.net
SIC: 7699 3544 3541 Industrial machinery & equipment repair; special dies, tools, jigs & fixtures; machine tools, metal cutting type

(G-18666)
FRIMO INC (DH)
50685 Century Ct (48393-2066)
PHONE.................................248 668-3160
Jeff Daily, *President*
Brent Gawne, *Business Mgr*
Trish Kirkman, *Controller*
Ralf Peters, *Sales Staff*
Jos Debruijn, *Manager*
▲ EMP: 199 EST: 1990
SQ FT: 25,000
SALES (est): 50.4MM
SALES (corp-wide): 167.1K Privately Held
WEB: www.frimo.com
SIC: 3544 Special dies & tools
HQ: Frimo Group Gmbh
Hansaring 1
Lotte NW 49504
540 488-60

(G-18667)
GENERAL MILL SUPPLY COMPANY
50690 General Mill Dr (48393-2085)
PHONE.................................248 668-0800
Stuart Rotenberg, *President*
Bob Rotenberg, *Treasurer*
Robert Rotenberg, *Treasurer*
Joshua Rotenberg, *Accounts Exec*
Gen Mill, *Manager*
EMP: 35 EST: 1970
SQ FT: 65,000
SALES (est): 12.8MM Privately Held
WEB: www.genmill.com
SIC: 5093 2611 Metal scrap & waste materials; pulp mills

(G-18668)
GENERAL TAPE LABEL LIQUIDATING
Also Called: A & M Label
28505 Automation Blvd (48393-3154)
PHONE.................................248 437-5200
James Listerman, *Ch of Bd*
Pauline Listerman, *President*
Pat Watson, *President*
EMP: 17 EST: 1949
SQ FT: 22,000
SALES (est): 1.7MM
SALES (corp-wide): 8.8MM Privately Held
WEB: www.fortissolutionsgroup.com
SIC: 5085 2759 5169 2671 Adhesives, tape & plasters; labels & seals: printing, chemicals & allied products; packaging paper & plastics film, coated & laminated
PA: Fortis Solutions Group Central Llc
28505 Automation Blvd
Wixom MI 48393
248 437-5200

(G-18669)
GREAT LAKES RUBBER CO
30573 Anderson Ct (48393-2817)
P.O. Box 930199 (48393-0199)
PHONE.................................248 624-5710
Don Demallie, *President*
Tom Leonardo, *General Mgr*
Grant Deedee, *Vice Pres*
Martha C Welch, *Vice Pres*
David Stachlewitz, *Engineer*
EMP: 37 EST: 1979
SQ FT: 21,000
SALES (est): 10.5MM
SALES (corp-wide): 157.8MM Privately Held
WEB: www.macvalves.com
SIC: 3069 Molded rubber products
PA: Mac Valves, Inc.
30569 Beck Rd
Wixom MI 48393
248 624-7700

(G-18670)
GREATECH INTEGRATION USA INC
47119 Cartier Ct (48393-2872)
PHONE.................................734 673-5985
Phillip Brooks, *Exec Dir*
EMP: 7 EST: 2020
SALES (est): 338.6K Privately Held
SIC: 3569 Assembly machines, non-metalworking

(G-18671)
GREEN INDUSTRIES INC
48145 West Rd (48393-3674)
PHONE.................................248 446-8900
David W Green, *President*
EMP: 15 EST: 1976
SALES (est): 846.8K Privately Held
WEB: www.greenindinc.com
SIC: 3451 Screw machine products

(G-18672)
GRESHAM DRIVING AIDS INC (PA)
30800 S Wixom Rd (48393-2418)
P.O. Box 930334 (48393-0334)
PHONE.................................248 624-1533
William J Dillon, *President*
Joyce Martell, *Cust Mgr*
Alan Anderson, *Manager*
Rich Campbell, *Manager*
Ohrt Dave, *Manager*
EMP: 18 EST: 1958
SQ FT: 7,000
SALES (est): 2.9MM Privately Held
WEB: www.greshamdrivingaids.com
SIC: 3842 Technical aids for the handicapped

(G-18673)
HALLMARK TOOL AND GAGE CO INC
51200 Pontiac Trl (48393-2043)
PHONE.................................248 669-4010
George H Richards, *President*
Scott A Richards, *Vice Pres*
Scott Richards, *Vice Pres*
EMP: 37 EST: 1982
SQ FT: 22,353
SALES: 6.4MM Privately Held
WEB: www.hallmarktool.com
SIC: 3544 3599 Special dies & tools; jigs & fixtures; machine shop, jobbing & repair

(G-18674)
HAMATON INC
47815 West Rd Ste D-109 (48393-4741)
PHONE.................................248 308-3856
Josh Lopez, *Sales Staff*
EMP: 10 EST: 2016
SALES (est): 1.9MM Privately Held
WEB: www.hamaton-tpms.com
SIC: 3714 Motor vehicle parts & accessories

(G-18675)
HANK THORN CO
Also Called: Van F Belknap Company
29164 Wall St (48393-3524)
PHONE.................................248 348-7800
Mayford W Thorn, *President*
Julie Acosta, *Corp Secy*
Enrique Acosta, *Vice Pres*
Vicki Thorn, *Controller*
Glenda Reaves,
EMP: 18 EST: 1938
SQ FT: 12,000
SALES (est): 5MM Privately Held
WEB: www.belknaptools.com
SIC: 5072 3546 3545 3423 Hand tools; power handtools; power-driven handtools; machine tool accessories; hand & edge tools

(G-18676)
HARMON SIGN INC (PA)
Also Called: Planet Neon
28054 Center Oaks Ct A (48393-3363)
PHONE.................................248 348-8150
Jeffrey Kasper, *President*
Daniel C Kasper, *Vice Pres*
Scott Brady, *Sales Staff*
EMP: 5 EST: 1983
SQ FT: 7,500
SALES (est): 1.6MM Privately Held
SIC: 3993 3599 Neon signs; custom machinery

(G-18677)
HAWK TOOL AND MACHINE INC
29183 Lorie Ln (48393-3680)
P.O. Box 930351 (48393-0351)
PHONE.................................248 349-0121
George L Hawkins, *President*
EMP: 18 EST: 1979
SALES (est): 2.1MM Privately Held
WEB: www.hawktool.com
SIC: 3599 Machine shop, jobbing & repair

(G-18678)
HOSCO INC (PA)
28026 Oakland Oaks Ct (48393-3341)
PHONE.................................248 912-1750
Jan Pitzer, *Vice Pres*
Debbie Bennett, *Office Mgr*
EMP: 11 EST: 1995
SALES (est): 9.2MM Privately Held
WEB: www.carlisleft.com
SIC: 3599 3498 3451 Flexible metal hose, tubing & bellows; pipe fittings, fabricated from purchased pipe; pipe sections fabricated from purchased pipe; screw machine products

(G-18679)
HOSCO FITTINGS LLC
28026 Oakland Oaks Ct (48393-3341)
PHONE.................................248 912-1750
Gary Newbold, *Business Mgr*
Tom Murray, *Mng Member*
Mike Vincent, *Supervisor*
EMP: 24 EST: 2010
SQ FT: 22,000 Privately Held
WEB: www.carlisleft.com
SIC: 3492 Fluid power valves & hose fittings

(G-18680)
HUGO BENZING LLC
29233 Haas Rd (48393-3024)
PHONE.................................248 264-6478
Reimund Hofstetter, *Mng Member*
▲ EMP: 35 EST: 2014
SALES (est): 5.4MM
SALES (corp-wide): 127.5MM Privately Held
WEB: www.hugobenzing.de
SIC: 3613 Switchgear & switchboard apparatus
PA: Hugo Benzing Gmbh & Co. Kg
Daimlerstr. 49-53
Korntal-Munchingen BW 70825
711 800-060

(G-18681)
HURON TOOL & GAGE CO INC
28005 Oakland Oaks Ct (48393-3342)
PHONE.................................313 381-1900
EMP: 5
SQ FT: 5,000
SALES: 300K Privately Held
SIC: 3544 3545 Mfg Metalworking Dies & Tools

(G-18682)
HURON VLLEYS HRSE BLNKET HDQTR
28525 Beck Rd Unit 102 (48393-4742)
PHONE.................................248 859-2398
Bread Kraust, *Principal*
EMP: 4 EST: 2013
SALES (est): 197.2K Privately Held
SIC: 2399 Horse blankets

GEOGRAPHIC SECTION

Wixom - Oakland County (G-18709)

(G-18683)
HUSSMANN CORPORATION
46974 Liberty Dr (48393-3601)
PHONE..................................248 668-0790
Ray Lima, *Manager*
EMP: 4 **Privately Held**
WEB: www.hussmann.com
SIC: 3585 Refrigeration & heating equipment
HQ: Hussmann Corporation
  12999 St Charles Rock Rd
  Bridgeton MO 63044
  314 291-2000

(G-18684)
INDEPENDENT MFG SOLUTIONS CORP
46918 Liberty Dr (48393-3600)
PHONE..................................248 960-3550
EMP: 23 **EST:** 2005
SQ FT: 13,500
SALES: 20MM **Privately Held**
SIC: 3561 3562 3569 3621 Mfg Pumps/Pumping Equip Mfg Ball/Roller Bearings Mfg General Indstl Mach Mfg Motors/Generators Elementary/Secondary Sch

(G-18685)
INNOVATION TECH LLC
Also Called: Robot Systems and Engineering
29020 S Wixom Rd (48393-3466)
PHONE..................................248 797-2686
Jan Nielsson, *Mng Member*
EMP: 10 **EST:** 2010
SALES (est): 544.5K **Privately Held**
WEB: www.innovationtechllc.com
SIC: 8742 8711 3563 3549 Automation & robotics consultant; electrical or electronic engineering; robots for industrial spraying, painting, etc.; assembly machines, including robotic; robots, industrial

(G-18686)
INNOVTIVE SRGCAL SOLUTIONS LLC
Also Called: Sentio
50461 Pontiac Trl (48393-2028)
P.O. Box 701846, Plymouth (48170-0971)
PHONE..................................248 595-0420
Christopher Wybo, *President*
EMP: 12 **EST:** 2007
SALES (est): 5.6MM
SALES (corp-wide): 82.5B **Publicly Held**
SIC: 3841 Surgical & medical instruments
HQ: Depuy Synthes Products, Inc.
  325 Paramount Dr
  Raynham MA 02767
  508 880-8100

(G-18687)
INTEGRITY BEVERAGE INC
28004 Center Oaks Ct # 206 (48393-3360)
PHONE..................................248 348-1010
Dan Abrams, *President*
Tim Sunder, *CFO*
Sunder Tim, *Technology*
EMP: 30 **EST:** 2004
SQ FT: 20,000
SALES (est): 3.3MM **Privately Held**
WEB: www.integritybev.com
SIC: 2033 Fruit juices: concentrated, hot pack

(G-18688)
J&B PHARMACY SERVICES INC
50496 Pontiac Trl Ste 15 (48393-2088)
PHONE..................................888 611-2941
Mary Shaya, *President*
EMP: 5 **EST:** 2020
SALES (est): 250.3K **Privately Held**
SIC: 2834 Druggists' preparations (pharmaceuticals)

(G-18689)
JCU INTERNATIONAL INC
51004 Century Ct (48393-2087)
PHONE..................................248 313-6630
Keiji Ozawa, *CEO*
EMP: 5 **EST:** 2015
SALES (est): 449.4K **Privately Held**
WEB: www.jcu-intl.com
SIC: 3559 Chemical machinery & equipment

(G-18690)
JTEKT TOYODA AMERICAS CORP
51300 Pontiac Trl (48393-2045)
PHONE..................................847 506-2415
Graham Roeder, *Manager*
Michele Richardson, *Executive*
EMP: 28 **Privately Held**
WEB: www.toyoda.com
SIC: 3541 Machine tools, metal cutting type
HQ: Jtekt Toyoda Americas Corporation
  316 W University Dr
  Arlington Heights IL 60004
  847 253-0340

(G-18691)
KENNEDY INDUSTRIES INC
Also Called: K.I.S.M.
4925 Holtz Dr (48393-2094)
P.O. Box 930079 (48393-0079)
PHONE..................................248 684-1200
Jeffrey Nachtweih, *President*
Nick Heintz, *Business Mgr*
Shirley Schmitz, *Corp Secy*
Marcus Hemeyer, *Vice Pres*
Christine Huepenbecker, *Project Mgr*
EMP: 70 **EST:** 1959
SQ FT: 19,600
SALES (est): 18.3MM
SALES (corp-wide): 36.2MM **Privately Held**
WEB: www.kennedyind.com
SIC: 7699 5085 3594 Pumps & pumping equipment repair; industrial machinery & equipment repair; valves & fittings; valves, pistons & fittings; fluid power pumps
PA: Vessco, Inc.
  8217 Upland Cir
  Chanhassen MN 55317
  952 941-2678

(G-18692)
KIEKERT USA INC
50695 Varsity Ct (48393-2067)
PHONE..................................248 960-4100
Mike Hietbrink, *Branch Mgr*
EMP: 75 **Privately Held**
WEB: www.kiekert.com
SIC: 3714 Motor vehicle parts & accessories
HQ: Kiekert Usa, Inc.
  46941 Liberty Dr
  Wixom MI 48393

(G-18693)
KIEKERT USA INC (DH)
Also Called: Keykert
46941 Liberty Dr (48393-3603)
PHONE..................................248 960-4100
Guido Hanel, *CEO*
Matthias Berg, *Exec VP*
Guglielmo Guastella, *Exec VP*
Andrea Kusemann, *Exec VP*
Jrgen Peulen, *Exec VP*
▲ **EMP:** 119 **EST:** 1987
SQ FT: 40,000
SALES (est): 53.5MM **Privately Held**
WEB: www.kiekert.com
SIC: 3714 Motor vehicle body components & frame
HQ: Kiekert Ag
  Hoseler Platz 2
  Heiligenhaus NW 42579
  205 615-0

(G-18694)
KORD INDUSTRIAL INC
47845 Anna Ct (48393-3688)
PHONE..................................248 374-8900
Edward J Bowler, *President*
Kathy Mercier, *Sales Staff*
EMP: 8 **EST:** 1970
SQ FT: 10,800
SALES (est): 2.5MM **Privately Held**
WEB: www.kordindustrial.com
SIC: 5084 3492 Hydraulic systems equipment & supplies; hose & tube fittings & assemblies, hydraulic/pneumatic

(G-18695)
LANCER TOOL CO
29289 Lorie Ln (48393-3682)
PHONE..................................248 380-8830
EMP: 12 **EST:** 1969
SQ FT: 8,500
SALES (est): 1.8MM **Privately Held**
SIC: 3545 Mfg Precision Machine Tools

(G-18696)
LEE STEVENS MACHINERY INC
49650 Martin Dr (48393-2400)
PHONE..................................248 926-8400
Randy Stevens, *President*
EMP: 6 **EST:** 2020
SALES (est): 301.3K **Privately Held**
WEB: www.stevensmachinery.com
SIC: 3541 Machine tools, metal cutting type

(G-18697)
LESCO DESIGN & MFG CO INC
28243 Beck Rd Ste B1 (48393-4722)
PHONE..................................248 596-9301
Lance Kaufman, *President*
Tom Violante, *Project Mgr*
Phillip Bollinger, *Sr Project Mgr*
Jennifer Hignite, *Manager*
EMP: 411
SALES (corp-wide): 93.4MM **Privately Held**
WEB: www.lescodesign.com
SIC: 3496 Conveyor belts
PA: Lesco Design & Manufacturing Company, Inc.
  1120 Fort Pickens Rd
  La Grange KY 40031
  502 222-7101

(G-18698)
LIGHTGUIDE INC ✪
48443 Alpha Dr (48393-3462)
PHONE..................................248 374-8000
Paul Ryznar, *CEO*
EMP: 6 **EST:** 2021
SALES (est): 87.2K **Privately Held**
SIC: 3711 Automobile assembly, including specialty automobiles

(G-18699)
LIMBRIGHT CONSULTING INC
Also Called: Plasti-Co Equipment Co
51100 Grand River Ave (48393-3327)
PHONE..................................810 227-5510
Robert W Limbright, *President*
Carol Limbright, *Corp Secy*
Wayne Limbright, *Vice Pres*
Mike Ervin, *Sales Mgr*
Abby Collett, *Sales Staff*
▲ **EMP:** 26 **EST:** 1974
SALES (est): 7.5MM **Privately Held**
WEB: www.aic-plastico.com
SIC: 7699 5084 3559 3452 Professional instrument repair services; controlling instruments & accessories; plastics working machinery; bolts, nuts, rivets & washers

(G-18700)
LMP WORLDWIDE INC
51135 Pontiac Trl (48393-2042)
PHONE..................................248 669-6103
Mark Arthurs, *President*
EMP: 5 **EST:** 2020
SALES (est): 96.8K **Privately Held**
WEB: www.seiauto.com
SIC: 2392 Household furnishings

(G-18701)
LYON SAND & GRAVEL CO
Also Called: Div Edw C Levy Co
51455 W 12 Mile Rd (48393-3100)
PHONE..................................248 348-8511
Mike Taylor, *Manager*
EMP: 14
SQ FT: 8,510
SALES (corp-wide): 10MM **Privately Held**
SIC: 1442 Gravel mining
PA: Lyon Sand & Gravel Co
  9300 Dix
  Dearborn MI 48120
  313 843-7200

(G-18702)
LYONS TOOL AND MFG CORP
47840 Anna Ct (48393-3687)
PHONE..................................248 344-9644
Michael J Murray, *President*
EMP: 29 **EST:** 1951
SQ FT: 12,000
SALES (est): 1.6MM **Privately Held**
SIC: 3599 Machine shop, jobbing & repair

(G-18703)
M C CARBIDE TOOL CO
28565 Automation Blvd (48393-3154)
PHONE..................................248 486-9590
Mark Boksha, *President*
Myron Boksha, *Vice Pres*
Jerry Brandemihl, *Vice Pres*
EMP: 23 **EST:** 1970
SQ FT: 23,000
SALES (est): 2.4MM **Privately Held**
WEB: www.mccarbidetool.com
SIC: 3545 3568 3541 Cutting tools for machine tools; power transmission equipment; machine tools, metal cutting type

(G-18704)
MAC VALVE ASIA INC (HQ)
30569 Beck Rd (48393-2842)
PHONE..................................248 624-7700
Robert Neff, *President*
EMP: 67 **EST:** 1984
SALES (est): 569.4K
SALES (corp-wide): 157.8MM **Privately Held**
WEB: www.macvalves.com
SIC: 3492 3494 3491 Control valves, fluid power; hydraulic & pneumatic; valves & pipe fittings; industrial valves
PA: Mac Valves, Inc.
  30569 Beck Rd
  Wixom MI 48393
  248 624-7700

(G-18705)
MAC VALVES INC (PA)
Also Called: M A C
30569 Beck Rd (48393-2842)
P.O. Box 111 (48393-0679)
PHONE..................................248 624-7700
Robert H Neff, *President*
Douglas Mc Cuiston, *Vice Pres*
Matthew Neff, *Vice Pres*
John Haar, *Plant Mgr*
Ed Bradley, *Mfg Staff*
◆ **EMP:** 740
SQ FT: 108,000
SALES (est): 157.8MM **Privately Held**
WEB: www.macvalves.com
SIC: 3492 3494 3491 Control valves, fluid power; hydraulic & pneumatic; valves & pipe fittings; industrial valves

(G-18706)
MASTER JIG GRINDING & GAGE CO
28005 Oakland Oaks Ct (48393-3342)
PHONE..................................248 380-8515
Lyle F Vidergar, *President*
EMP: 5 **EST:** 1962
SALES (est): 594K **Privately Held**
WEB: www.masterjig.net
SIC: 3545 3544 Gauges (machine tool accessories); jigs: inspection, gauging & checking

(G-18707)
MATRIX CONTROLS GROUP INC
28287 Beck Rd Ste D16 (48393-4706)
PHONE..................................248 380-7600
Ronald Larson, *Owner*
EMP: 4 **EST:** 2018
SALES (est): 163.9K **Privately Held**
WEB: www.matrixcontrols.com
SIC: 3822 Auto controls regulating residntl & coml environmt & applncs

(G-18708)
MAXXAR
28033 Center Oaks Ct (48393-3344)
PHONE..................................248 675-1040
EMP: 6 **EST:** 2019
SALES (est): 144.3K **Privately Held**
WEB: www.maxxar.com
SIC: 3661 Telephone & telegraph apparatus

(G-18709)
METHODS MACHINE TOOLS INC
50531 Varsity Ct (48393-2081)
PHONE..................................248 624-8601
Kevin Davidson, *Opers Mgr*
Lisa Kiser, *Purch Agent*

Lisa Kaiser, *CFO*
Michael Coughlin, *Accounts Mgr*
Kevin Fite, *Accounts Mgr*
EMP: 20
SALES (corp-wide): 93.9MM **Privately Held**
WEB: www.methodsmachine.com
SIC: 3541 Machine tools, metal cutting type
PA: Methods Machine Tools, Inc.
65 Union Ave
Sudbury MA 01776
978 443-5388

(G-18710)
MIDWEST SALES ASSOCIATES INC
Also Called: Michael Schafer and Associates
29445 Beck Rd Ste A103 (48393-2880)
PHONE..................248 348-9600
Michael Schafer, *President*
John Chappelle, *Sales Staff*
EMP: 5 **EST:** 1990
SALES (est): 728.1K **Privately Held**
WEB: www.midwestsales.com
SIC: 3678 3699 Electronic connectors; electrical equipment & supplies

(G-18711)
MINTH GROUP US HOLDING INC (HQ)
51331 Pontiac Trl (48393-2046)
PHONE..................248 848-8530
Patricia Ncube, *President*
Brandon Colvin, *Maint Spvr*
Megan Braun, *Accounts Mgr*
Thomas McKahan, *Program Mgr*
Christen Powers, *Director*
EMP: 50 **EST:** 2017
SALES (est): 37MM **Privately Held**
SIC: 8711 3465 Engineering services; automotive stampings

(G-18712)
MINTH NORTH AMERICA INC
Also Called: Pti International
51331 Pontiac Trl (48393-2046)
PHONE..................248 259-7468
Howard Boyer, *CEO*
Art Delusky, *General Mgr*
Alan Liang, *Opers Mgr*
Mark Fore, *QC Mgr*
Douglas Vargo, *Project Engr*
EMP: 95 **EST:** 2007
SQ FT: 15,000
SALES (est): 17MM **Privately Held**
SIC: 8711 3465 Consulting engineer; body parts, automobile: stamped metal
HQ: Minth Group Us Holding Inc
51331 Pontiac Trl
Wixom MI 48393
248 848-8530

(G-18713)
MODERN MILLWORK INC
29020 S Wixom Rd Ste 100 (48393-3467)
P.O. Box 930347 (48393-0347)
PHONE..................248 347-4777
Jeffery K Weinger, *President*
Sandy Stcharles, *Office Mgr*
EMP: 10 **EST:** 1979
SQ FT: 14,000
SALES (est): 1.5MM **Privately Held**
WEB: www.modernmillworkinc.com
SIC: 2431 Millwork

(G-18714)
MOLLEWOOD EXPORT INC
Also Called: Pak-Rite Michigan
46921 Enterprise Ct (48393-4728)
PHONE..................248 624-1885
Scott De Henau, *President*
EMP: 23 **EST:** 1987
SQ FT: 25,000
SALES (est): 5.9MM **Privately Held**
SIC: 4783 2441 2449 3089 Packing goods for shipping; nailed wood boxes & shook; rectangular boxes & crates, wood; shipping cases & drums, wood; wirebound & plywood; prefabricated plastic buildings

(G-18715)
MOTOR CITY WASH WORKS INC
48285 Frank St (48393-4712)
PHONE..................248 313-0272
Lionel G Belanger, *President*
Bob Wentworth, *VP Engrg*
Mark Vivyan, *Engineer*
Christian Vandam, *Regl Sales Mgr*
Eric Davis, *Sales Staff*
▲ **EMP:** 45 **EST:** 2003
SALES (est): 9.1MM **Privately Held**
WEB: www.motorcitywashworks.com
SIC: 3589 Car washing machinery

(G-18716)
NATIONAL INTGRATED SYSTEMS INC
29241 Beck Rd (48393-3679)
PHONE..................734 927-3030
Jay Park, *President*
Russell Gregg, *Accounts Mgr*
Scott Testerman, *Accounts Mgr*
▲ **EMP:** 12 **EST:** 2003
SALES (est): 3.4MM **Privately Held**
WEB: www.nisusa.com
SIC: 2542 Racks, merchandise display or storage: except wood

(G-18717)
NAVTECH LLC
47906 West Rd (48393-3669)
PHONE..................248 427-1080
EMP: 8
SQ FT: 5,000
SALES (est): 590K **Privately Held**
SIC: 2821 Mfg Plastic Materials/Resins

(G-18718)
NEDROW REFRACTORIES CO
150 Landrow Dr (48393-2057)
P.O. Box 930313 (48393-0313)
PHONE..................248 669-2500
James A Chase, *President*
Barbara A Nedrow Sitzler, *Vice Pres*
David Carmon, *Mfg Spvr*
Brian T Nedrow, *Treasurer*
Brad Nedrow, *Accounts Mgr*
EMP: 71 **EST:** 1976
SQ FT: 8,000
SALES (est): 6.2MM **Privately Held**
WEB: www.chasenedrow.com
SIC: 7699 3297 Industrial machinery & equipment repair; nonclay refractories

(G-18719)
NEWTECH 3 INC
28373 Beck Rd Ste H7 (48393-4735)
P.O. Box 441123, Detroit (48244-1123)
PHONE..................248 912-0807
Jack Long, *President*
Gail Gyenese, *Sales Staff*
EMP: 25
SALES (est): 35.8K **Privately Held**
WEB: www.newtech3.com
SIC: 3714 Automotive wiring harness sets

(G-18720)
NGK SPARK PLUG MFG USA INC (DH)
Also Called: NGK Spark Plugs USA
46929 Magellan (48393-3699)
PHONE..................248 926-6900
Goro Ogawa, *CEO*
Kenta Hachiya, *President*
Shin Odo, *President*
Mark Boyle, *General Mgr*
Todd Cullums, *General Mgr*
▲ **EMP:** 150
SQ FT: 18,000
SALES (est): 126.9MM **Privately Held**
WEB: www.ngksparkplugs.com
SIC: 3643 3264 Current-carrying wiring devices; porcelain parts for electrical devices, molded

(G-18721)
NORDSON CORPORATION
28775 Beck Rd (48393-3637)
PHONE..................734 459-7600
Travis Dobson, *Sales Staff*
EMP: 60
SALES (corp-wide): 2.1B **Publicly Held**
WEB: www.nordson.com
SIC: 3823 3586 3563 3531 Industrial flow & liquid measuring instruments; measuring & dispensing pumps; air & gas compressors; construction machinery; valves & pipe fittings; industrial valves
PA: Nordson Corporation
28601 Clemens Rd
Westlake OH 44145
440 892-1580

(G-18722)
NORTHERN MICH AGGREGATES LLC
Also Called: Ledgestone
51445 W12 Mile Rd (48393)
P.O. Box 678, Alpena (49707-0678)
PHONE..................989 354-3502
S Evan Weiner, *President*
Edward C Levy Jr, *Chairman*
Robert P Scholz, *CFO*
EMP: 10 **EST:** 1987
SALES (est): 1.8MM
SALES (corp-wide): 521.9MM **Privately Held**
WEB: www.edwclevy.com
SIC: 1411 Limestone, dimension-quarrying
HQ: Levy Indiana Slag Co.
9300 Dix
Dearborn MI 48120

(G-18723)
NORTHERN PROCESSES & SALES LLC
49700 Martin Dr (48393-2402)
PHONE..................248 669-3918
Rex Shefferly, *Engineer*
Richard Shefferly, *Mng Member*
EMP: 8 **EST:** 2004
SALES (est): 1MM **Privately Held**
WEB: www.npsmi.com
SIC: 5085 3569 Industrial supplies; assembly machines, non-metalworking

(G-18724)
O & S TOOL AND MACHINE INC
50400 Dennis Ct Unit B (48393-2048)
PHONE..................248 926-8045
Ray Orlando, *President*
Joanne Orlando, *Corp Secy*
Terri Orlando,
EMP: 9 **EST:** 1993
SQ FT: 3,200
SALES (est): 1.1MM **Privately Held**
WEB: www.ostool.net
SIC: 3599 Machine shop, jobbing & repair

(G-18725)
OAKS CONCRETE PRODUCTS INC
51744 Pontiac Trl (48393-1906)
PHONE..................248 684-5004
Lanzy Fuchs, *Marketing Staff*
▲ **EMP:** 19 **EST:** 2002
SALES (est): 6.7MM
SALES (corp-wide): 114.4MM **Privately Held**
WEB: www.bramptonbrick.com
SIC: 3272 Concrete products
PA: Brampton Brick Limited
225 Wanless Dr
Brampton ON L7A 1
905 840-1010

(G-18726)
OPS SOLUTIONS LLC (PA)
48443 Alpha Dr Ste 175 (48393-3464)
PHONE..................248 374-8000
Paul Ryznar, *CEO*
Chris Bala, *Exec VP*
William Coe, *Vice Pres*
John Morelli, *Vice Pres*
Brad Foley, *Engineer*
◆ **EMP:** 27 **EST:** 2005
SQ FT: 10,000
SALES (est): 6.8MM **Privately Held**
WEB: www.lightguidesys.com
SIC: 7372 Application computer software

(G-18727)
OSHINO LAMPS AMERICA LTD
47550 Avante Dr (48393-3617)
PHONE..................262 226-8620
Greg Winchell, *Managing Dir*
EMP: 4 **EST:** 2012
SALES (est): 618.5K **Privately Held**
WEB: www.oshinolamps.com
SIC: 5088 5013 7363 3641 Aircraft equipment & supplies; automotive supplies & parts; pilot service, aviation; electric lamps

(G-18728)
PARAGON MODEL AND TOOL INC
Also Called: Paragon Tool
46934 Magellan (48393-3699)
PHONE..................248 960-1223
S Lee Brithinee, *President*
EMP: 7 **EST:** 1994
SALES (est): 855K **Privately Held**
SIC: 3599 Machine shop, jobbing & repair

(G-18729)
PEAK EDM INC
28221 Beck Rd Ste A2 (48393-4701)
PHONE..................248 380-0871
Robert Palmer, *President*
Laura Palmer, *Controller*
EMP: 8 **EST:** 1995
SQ FT: 3,100
SALES (est): 1.3MM **Privately Held**
WEB: www.peakedm.com
SIC: 5084 3699 Machine tools & accessories; electrical equipment & supplies

(G-18730)
PLASAN CARBON COMPOSITES INC
47000 Liberty Dr (48393-3696)
PHONE..................616 965-9450
Jason Krapohl, *Project Engr*
Heidi Hayes, *Human Resources*
EMP: 60 **EST:** 2006
SALES (est): 271.7K **Privately Held**
WEB: www.plasancarbon.com
SIC: 3714 Motor vehicle parts & accessories

(G-18731)
POWER CLEANING SYSTEMS INC
28294 Beck Rd (48393-3623)
PHONE..................248 347-7727
Richard H Mc Carthy, *President*
Pamela Mc Carthy, *Vice Pres*
EMP: 5 **EST:** 1990
SALES (est): 900K **Privately Held**
WEB: www.powercleaningsystems.com
SIC: 5087 3699 Janitors' supplies; cleaning equipment, ultrasonic, except medical & dental

(G-18732)
PRECISE TOOL & CUTTER INC
51143 Pontiac Trl (48393-2042)
PHONE..................248 684-8480
Nash Sinishtaj, *President*
EMP: 5 **EST:** 2000
SQ FT: 2,000
SALES (est): 487.4K **Privately Held**
WEB: www.ptcgrinding.com
SIC: 3599 Machine shop, jobbing & repair

(G-18733)
PRECISION KARTING TECH LLC
28718 Wall St (48393-3516)
PHONE..................248 924-3272
EMP: 5 **EST:** 2016
SALES (est): 163.9K **Privately Held**
WEB: www.pktaxles.com
SIC: 3714 Motor vehicle parts & accessories

(G-18734)
PREMIER PRINTIN
28389 Beck Rd (48393-4732)
PHONE..................248 924-3213
EMP: 6 **EST:** 2019
SALES (est): 519.9K **Privately Held**
WEB: www.premierprintingmi.com
SIC: 2752 Commercial printing, lithographic

(G-18735)
PRO-MOTION TECH GROUP LLC
29755 Beck Rd (48393-2834)
PHONE..................248 668-3100

GEOGRAPHIC SECTION

Wixom - Oakland County (G-18762)

Lynn Matson, *CEO*
Michael Kowalczyk, *President*
Bill Fons, *Exec VP*
Jackie French, *Opers Staff*
Mark Pavlish, *Opers Staff*
▲ **EMP:** 60 **EST:** 2003
SQ FT: 65,000
SALES: 21.1MM **Privately Held**
WEB: www.promotion.tech
SIC: 5063 3993 5999 Wire & cable; signs & advertising specialties; audio-visual equipment & supplies

(G-18736)
PUREM NOVI INC
30220 Oak Creek Dr (48393-2430)
PHONE.................248 632-2731
Martin Peters, *CFO*
EMP: 117
SALES (corp-wide): 5.4B **Privately Held**
SIC: 3714 Exhaust systems & parts, motor vehicle
HQ: Purem Novi Inc.
29101 Haggerty Rd
Novi MI 48377
248 994-7010

(G-18737)
PURITAN AUTOMATION LLC
Also Called: Ventech
28389 Beck Rd Ste J2 (48393-4732)
PHONE.................248 668-1114
Jeremy Sanger, *CEO*
Jeff Diederich, *Business Mgr*
EMP: 15 **EST:** 2000
SQ FT: 15,000
SALES (est): 2MM **Privately Held**
WEB: www.puritanautomation.com
SIC: 3545 3569 Precision tools, machinists'; assembly machines, non-metalworking

(G-18738)
QUALITY ENGINEERING COMPANY
30194 S Wixom Rd (48393-3440)
PHONE.................248 351-9000
Abraham Varkovitzky, *President*
Bill Iordanou, *Vice Pres*
Lou Iordanou, *Vice Pres*
▲ **EMP:** 15 **EST:** 1981
SQ FT: 43,700
SALES: 8.3MM **Privately Held**
WEB: www.qen.com
SIC: 8711 3714 8742 8744 Consulting engineer; motor vehicle parts & accessories; productivity improvement consultant; facilities support services

(G-18739)
RED LASER INC
51200 Pontiac Trl 3b (48393-2043)
PHONE.................517 540-1300
Teresa Deacon, *President*
EMP: 12
SALES (est): 2MM **Privately Held**
WEB: www.redlasercutting.com
SIC: 3441 Fabricated structural metal

(G-18740)
RESA POWER LLC
50613 Varsity Ct (48393-2067)
PHONE.................763 784-4040
EMP: 8
SALES (corp-wide): 134.5MM **Privately Held**
WEB: www.resapower.com
SIC: 3699 Electrical equipment & supplies
PA: Resa Power, Llc
8300 Cypress Pkwy Ste 225
Houston TX 77070
832 900-8340

(G-18741)
REYNOLDA MFG SOLUTIONS INC
30419 Beck Rd (48393-2841)
PHONE.................336 699-4204
EMP: 9 **EST:** 2019
SALES (est): 43.6K **Privately Held**
WEB: www.reynolda.com
SIC: 3599 Machine shop, jobbing & repair

(G-18742)
RGM NEW VENTURES INC (PA)
Also Called: Barracuda Mfg
48230 West Rd (48393-3675)
P.O. Box 930439 (48393-0439)
PHONE.................248 624-5050
Bob Muse, *President*
Martin Agrest, *Vice Pres*
Herb Kindt, *Opers Staff*
▲ **EMP:** 60 **EST:** 1964
SQ FT: 42,000
SALES (est): 8MM **Privately Held**
WEB: www.glassandmetalcraft.com
SIC: 3229 2511 3231 Pressed & blown glass; wood household furniture; mirrored glass

(G-18743)
RICO TECHNOLOGIES
50250 Dennis Ct (48393-2024)
PHONE.................248 896-0110
Ricardo Joaquin, *Owner*
EMP: 4 **EST:** 2007
SALES (est): 49.9K **Privately Held**
SIC: 7692 Welding repair

(G-18744)
ROCKWELL MEDICAL INC (PA)
30142 S Wixom Rd (48393-3440)
PHONE.................248 960-9009
John P McLaughlin, *Ch of Bd*
Russell H Ellison, *President*
Paul E McGarry, *Vice Pres*
Russell Skibsted, *CFO*
Marc Hoffman, *Chief Mktg Ofcr*
EMP: 234 **EST:** 1995
SQ FT: 17,500
SALES (est): 62.2MM **Publicly Held**
WEB: www.rockwellmed.com
SIC: 2834 Pharmaceutical preparations

(G-18745)
S & M MACHINING COMPANY
47590 Avante Dr (48393-3617)
PHONE.................248 348-0310
Scott W McFarland, *Owner*
EMP: 7 **EST:** 2010
SQ FT: 3,500
SALES (est): 850.8K **Privately Held**
SIC: 3599 Amusement park equipment

(G-18746)
S F R PRECISION TURNING INC
29431 Lorie Ln (48393-3686)
PHONE.................517 709-3367
Harvey Wright, *President*
Kevin Jurus, *Vice Pres*
Allen Dase, *Treasurer*
EMP: 5 **EST:** 1952
SALES (est): 459.7K **Privately Held**
SIC: 3312 3544 Tubes, steel & iron; special dies, tools, jigs & fixtures

(G-18747)
S MAIN COMPANY LLC
Also Called: The South Main Company
50489 Pontiac Trl (48393-2028)
P.O. Box 3464, Farmington (48333-3464)
PHONE.................248 960-1540
Edmund J Swain,
Peter Bracco,
Mark Mosher,
EMP: 24 **EST:** 1997
SQ FT: 10,000
SALES (est): 2.5MM **Privately Held**
WEB: www.southmain.net
SIC: 3613 Panel & distribution boards & other related apparatus

(G-18748)
SCODELLER CONSTRUCTION INC
51722 Grand River Ave (48393-2303)
PHONE.................248 374-1102
Peter D Scodeller, *President*
EMP: 95 **EST:** 1985
SQ FT: 4,000
SALES (est): 8.9MM **Privately Held**
WEB: www.scodellerconstruction.com
SIC: 2891 1771 Sealing compounds for pipe threads or joints; concrete repair

(G-18749)
SEBRO PLASTICS INC (DH)
29200 Wall St (48393-3526)
PHONE.................248 348-4121
Rodger D Fuller, *President*
Joseph Bolton, *Vice Pres*
Harold G Cummings, *Treasurer*
Julie C Albrecht, *Director*
R Howard Coker, *Director*
▲ **EMP:** 50 **EST:** 1969
SQ FT: 18,500
SALES (est): 7.3MM
SALES (corp-wide): 5.2B **Publicly Held**
SIC: 3089 Injection molding of plastics
HQ: Sonoco-Crellin International, Inc.
87 Center St
Chatham NY 12037
518 392-2000

(G-18750)
SEKISUI PLASTICS US A INC
28345 Beck Rd Ste 406 (48393-4745)
PHONE.................248 308-3000
Tom Missentzis, *Director*
EMP: 10 **Privately Held**
WEB: www.sekisuiplastics.com
SIC: 3086 5199 Packaging & shipping materials, foamed plastic; packaging materials
PA: Sekisui Plastics U.S. A., Inc.
110 Clifton Way Dr
Mount Pleasant TN 38474

(G-18751)
SEMICNDCTOR HYBRID ASSMBLY INC
Also Called: S H A
49113 Wixom Tech Dr (48393-3559)
P.O. Box 930835 (48393-0835)
PHONE.................248 668-9050
Yassin Burgol, *President*
Hisham Burgol, *Vice Pres*
EMP: 10 **EST:** 1989
SQ FT: 5,500
SALES (est): 2.5MM **Privately Held**
WEB: www.shainc.net
SIC: 3672 Printed circuit boards

(G-18752)
SIMPLY CABINETS
29200 Lyon Oaks Dr (48393-2340)
PHONE.................810 923-8792
Nicholas Vanderhovel, *Principal*
EMP: 5 **EST:** 2017
SALES (est): 129.6K **Privately Held**
SIC: 2434 Wood kitchen cabinets

(G-18753)
SLM SOLUTIONS NA INC
48561 Alpha Dr Ste 300 (48393-3458)
PHONE.................248 243-5400
Andreas Frahm, *President*
Jill K Christner, *President*
Mark Hoefing, *Exec VP*
Steve West, *Vice Pres*
Mark Bashor, *Engineer*
EMP: 24 **EST:** 2013
SALES (est): 4.7MM **Privately Held**
WEB: www.slm-solutions.com
SIC: 3699 Laser welding, drilling & cutting equipment

(G-18754)
SPARTAN PRCISION MACHINING INC
Also Called: Spartan PMI
29431 Lorie Ln (48393-3686)
PHONE.................248 344-0101
Mike Benoit, *President*
Tina Barone, *Finance*
EMP: 25 **EST:** 2018
SALES (est): 1.9MM **Privately Held**
WEB: www.spartanpmi.com
SIC: 3599 Machine shop, jobbing & repair

(G-18755)
SPURT INDUSTRIES
2041 Charms Rd (48393-1127)
P.O. Box 930818 (48393-0818)
PHONE.................248 956-7643
Tom Turner, *General Mgr*
EMP: 5 **EST:** 2016
SALES (est): 164.8K **Privately Held**
WEB: www.spurtindustries.com
SIC: 3999 Manufacturing industries

(G-18756)
SQUIRES INDUSTRIES INC
Also Called: Petronis Industries
29181 Beck Rd (48393-3642)
PHONE.................248 449-6092
Edwin L Squires Jr, *President*
EMP: 20 **EST:** 1970
SQ FT: 8,000
SALES (est): 568.9K **Privately Held**
WEB: www.petronisind.com
SIC: 3599 Machine shop, jobbing & repair

(G-18757)
STATIC CONTROLS CORP
30460 S Wixom Rd (48393-2410)
PHONE.................248 926-4400
Robert Gassman, *President*
William Yonish, *Owner*
Judith Yonish, *Admin Sec*
▲ **EMP:** 22 **EST:** 1968
SQ FT: 26,500
SALES (est): 4.3MM **Privately Held**
WEB: www.scccontrols.com
SIC: 3625 5999 5065 Industrial controls: push button, selector switches, pilot; electronic parts & equipment; electronic parts

(G-18758)
STERLING EDGE INC
50230 Dennis Ct (48393-2024)
PHONE.................248 438-6034
Albert L Robitaille, *President*
David Brochu, *Vice Pres*
Chris Sellers, *Vice Pres*
EMP: 6 **EST:** 1997
SQ FT: 3,000
SALES (est): 539.5K **Privately Held**
WEB: www.sterlingedge.net
SIC: 3599 Machine shop, jobbing & repair

(G-18759)
STT USA INC
47815 West Rd Ste D-101 (48393-4741)
PHONE.................248 522-9655
Calvin Hashisaka, *President*
Takafumi Sugasawa, *Vice Pres*
Shigetaka Mori, *Director*
Hirohisa Takata, *Director*
EMP: 5 **EST:** 2010
SQ FT: 2,400
SALES (est): 1.3MM **Privately Held**
WEB: www.stt-inc.co.jp
SIC: 2992 Lubricating oils & greases
PA: Stt Inc.
2-6-1, Tatenodai
Hadano KNG 257-0

(G-18760)
SUMMIT CUTTING TOOL AND MFG IN
2069 Devonshire Dr (48393-4412)
PHONE.................248 624-3949
Jennifer Dreyer, *Principal*
EMP: 5 **EST:** 2014
SALES (est): 153.7K **Privately Held**
SIC: 3999 Manufacturing industries

(G-18761)
SUNSET SPORTSWEAR INC
676 Shady Maple Dr (48393-4308)
PHONE.................248 437-7611
Jeffrey C Wixom, *President*
EMP: 10 **EST:** 1979
SALES (est): 574.3K **Privately Held**
WEB: www.sunsetsportswear.com
SIC: 2396 Screen printing on fabric articles

(G-18762)
SUPERABRASIVES INC
28047 Grand Oaks Ct (48393-3340)
PHONE.................248 348-7670
Charles Halprin, *President*
Jerry Maxwell, *Engineer*
Linda Halrin, *CFO*
Michael J Sidley, *Treasurer*
Melvin Keck, *Business Dir*
▲ **EMP:** 30 **EST:** 1978
SQ FT: 25,000
SALES (est): 5MM **Privately Held**
WEB: www.superabrasives.com
SIC: 3541 3291 Grinding machines, metalworking; abrasive products

Wixom - Oakland County (G-18763) — **GEOGRAPHIC SECTION**

(G-18763)
SURE CONVEYORS INC
48155 West Rd Ste 6 (48393-4740)
PHONE..................248 926-2100
Ray Blanchet, *Vice Pres*
EMP: 14 **EST:** 2015
SALES (est): 2.6MM **Privately Held**
WEB: www.sureconveyors.com
SIC: 3535 Conveyors & conveying equipment

(G-18764)
SURE FLOW PRODUCTS LLC
28265 Beck Rd Ste C11 (48393-4724)
PHONE..................248 380-3569
Marty Petrill, *Executive*
Martin Petrill,
Lori Petrill,
EMP: 5 **EST:** 2001 **Privately Held**
WEB: www.flowmetersource.com
SIC: 3823 Industrial instrmnts msrmnt display/control process variable

(G-18765)
TACTICAL SIMPLICITY LLC
Also Called: Detroit Bullet Works
2817 Beck Rd Ste E-16 (48393)
PHONE..................248 410-4523
Christopher Jones,
EMP: 9 **EST:** 2012
SALES (est): 611.1K **Privately Held**
SIC: 3482 Small arms ammunition

(G-18766)
TAPCO HOLDINGS INC (DH)
Also Called: Mid America Building Pdts Div
29797 Beck Rd (48393-2834)
PHONE..................248 668-6400
Allen Gurney, *Vice Pres*
Jack Wallace III, *Vice Pres*
Matt Greenberg, *Purchasing*
Barb Rakowski, *Sales Staff*
EMP: 117
SQ FT: 50,000
SALES (est): 18.5MM **Privately Held**
WEB: www.boralbuildingproducts.com
SIC: 3542 3089 3531 3444 Sheet metalworking machines; shutters, plastic; construction machinery; sheet metalwork; hand & edge tools; millwork

(G-18767)
TAYLOR TURNING INC
29632 West Tech Dr (48393-3561)
PHONE..................248 960-7920
Russell J Taylor, *President*
EMP: 25 **EST:** 1984
SQ FT: 11,500
SALES (est): 2.4MM **Privately Held**
WEB: www.taylorturning.ambz.com
SIC: 3544 3545 Special dies & tools; machine tool accessories

(G-18768)
TECART INDUSTRIES INC
28059 Center Oaks Ct (48393-3347)
PHONE..................248 624-8880
Kimberly Perrigan, *CEO*
H Halstead Scudder, *President*
▲ **EMP:** 18 **EST:** 1989
SQ FT: 34,000
SALES (est): 3MM **Privately Held**
WEB: www.tecartinc.com
SIC: 3993 Electric signs

(G-18769)
TECHNIQUE GOLF LLC
Also Called: Superstroke Golf
29706 West Tech Dr (48393-3562)
PHONE..................586 758-7807
Dean Dingman, *Mng Member*
Darin Dingman,
Frank Vega,
▲ **EMP:** 4 **EST:** 1998
SQ FT: 4,500
SALES (est): 415.8K **Privately Held**
WEB: www.superstrokeusa.com
SIC: 3949 Sporting & athletic goods

(G-18770)
TEPSO GEN-X PLASTICS LLC
28525 Beck Rd Unit 111 (48393-4742)
PHONE..................248 869-2130
Pere Vazquez, *Vice Pres*
Carles Marti, *CFO*
Troy Isaacson, *Mng Member*
EMP: 8 **EST:** 2006
SALES (est): 5MM
SALES (corp-wide): 549.4MM **Privately Held**
WEB: www.usfarathane.com
SIC: 3089 Automotive parts, plastic
HQ: U.S. Farathane, S.A. De C.V.
Carretera A Huinala Km 1.5
Apodaca N.L. 66634

(G-18771)
TESTEK LLC
28320 Lakeview Dr (48393-3157)
PHONE..................248 573-4980
Harish Patel, *CEO*
Mona Patel, *President*
Jamie Whisner, *Vice Pres*
Tony Joseph, *Project Mgr*
Jeff Starr, *Mfg Staff*
◆ **EMP:** 90 **EST:** 1969
SQ FT: 120,000
SALES (est): 25.7MM **Privately Held**
WEB: www.testek.com
SIC: 3829 3699 8711 Physical property testing equipment; electrical equipment & supplies; engineering services

(G-18772)
THAI PARADIZE LLC
47516 Pontiac Trl (48393-2541)
PHONE..................248 331-7355
EMP: 4 **EST:** 2014
SALES (est): 58.8K **Privately Held**
SIC: 2395 Embroidery & art needlework

(G-18773)
TOMCO FABRICATING & ENGRG INC
50853 Century Ct (48393-2066)
PHONE..................248 669-2900
Donald Henry, *President*
Joan Henry, *Treasurer*
EMP: 10 **EST:** 1979
SQ FT: 7,800
SALES (est): 2MM **Privately Held**
WEB: www.tomcofab.com
SIC: 3599 Machine shop, jobbing & repair

(G-18774)
TOSHIBA AMERICA ELECTRONIC
48679 Alpha Dr Ste 120 (48393-3455)
PHONE..................248 347-2608
Mark Downing, *Branch Mgr*
EMP: 126 **Privately Held**
SIC: 3674 Semiconductors & related devices
HQ: Toshiba America Electronic Components Inc
5231 California Ave
Irvine CA 92617

(G-18775)
TRAFFIC SFETY CTRL SYSTEMS INC
Also Called: Traffic & Safety
48584 Downing St (48393-3501)
PHONE..................248 348-0570
Keith E Hay, *President*
Deborah Cantlon, *Exec VP*
Anthony Jaworowski, *Electrical Engi*
Lisa Vendittelli, *Controller*
Jason Wiitala, *Sales Staff*
EMP: 25 **EST:** 1974
SQ FT: 9,000
SALES (est): 10MM **Privately Held**
WEB: www.trafficandsafety.com
SIC: 5065 3559 1799 7382 Security control equipment & systems; parking facility equipment & supplies; parking facility equipment installation; security systems services

(G-18776)
TRAILER TECH HOLDINGS LLC
Also Called: Kentucky Trailer Technologies
48282 Frank St (48393-4711)
PHONE..................248 960-9700
Gary A Smith, *President*
Kenneth McAfee, *Partner*
Larry Roy, *Exec VP*
Bob Bachman, *Vice Pres*
Greg Larkin, *Vice Pres*
◆ **EMP:** 50 **EST:** 2002
SQ FT: 35,000
SALES (est): 13.2MM
SALES (corp-wide): 8.9B **Publicly Held**
WEB: www.kytrailer.com
SIC: 3715 Semitrailers for truck tractors
HQ: R. C. Tway Company
7201 Logistics Dr
Louisville KY 40258
502 637-2551

(G-18777)
TRIBAR MANUFACTURING LLC
30517 Anderson Ct (48393-2817)
P.O. Box 930359 (48393-0359)
PHONE..................248 669-0077
Dave Connell, *Manager*
EMP: 40
SALES (corp-wide): 318MM **Privately Held**
WEB: www.tribar.com
SIC: 3089 2789 2759 Coloring & finishing of plastic products; bookbinding & related work; commercial printing
HQ: Tribar Manufacturing, L.L.C.
2211 Grand Commerce Dr
Howell MI 48855

(G-18778)
TRIBAR MANUFACTURING LLC
Also Called: Adept Plastic Finishing
29883 Beck Rd (48393-2835)
PHONE..................248 374-5870
EMP: 336
SALES (corp-wide): 318MM **Privately Held**
WEB: www.tribar.com
SIC: 3089 Coloring & finishing of plastic products
HQ: Tribar Manufacturing, L.L.C.
2211 Grand Commerce Dr
Howell MI 48855

(G-18779)
TRIBAR TECHNOLOGIES INC (PA)
48668 Alpha Dr (48393-3445)
PHONE..................248 516-1600
Jordan Collins, *Finance*
John Dragonov, *Manager*
Mike Fallow, *Manager*
EMP: 350 **EST:** 2018
SALES (est): 318MM **Privately Held**
SIC: 3089 Automotive parts, plastic

(G-18780)
TRIJICON INC (PA)
49385 Shafer Ct (48393-2869)
P.O. Box 930059 (48393-0059)
PHONE..................248 960-7700
Stephen Bindon, *President*
John Rupp, *President*
Charles L Motley, *Vice Pres*
Jeannie Stone, *Vice Pres*
Greg Alaska, *Opers Mgr*
EMP: 182 **EST:** 1971
SQ FT: 42,000
SALES (est): 69.7MM **Privately Held**
WEB: www.trijicon.com
SIC: 3827 Gun sights, optical; telescopic sights

(G-18781)
ULB LLC
Also Called: Universal Load Banks
28200 Lakeview Dr (48393-3157)
PHONE..................734 233-0961
Yash Patel, *VP Opers*
Shilpa Patel, *Administration*
EMP: 30 **EST:** 2016
SALES (est): 2.9MM **Privately Held**
WEB: www.universalloadbanks.com
SIC: 5084 1731 3629 Industrial machinery & equipment; electric power systems contractors; electrical industrial apparatus

(G-18782)
USA SWITCH INC (PA)
49030 Pontiac Trl Ste 100 (48393-2586)
PHONE..................248 960-8500
Thomas P Petrillo, *President*
▲ **EMP:** 13 **EST:** 1992
SQ FT: 20,000
SALES (est): 1MM **Privately Held**
SIC: 3694 Engine electrical equipment

(G-18783)
V & V INDUSTRIES INC
Also Called: 2v Industries
48553 West Rd (48393-3537)
PHONE..................248 624-7943
Ram Bedi, *President*
Uma Bedi, *Chairman*
Vijay Bedi, *COO*
Vivek Bedi, *CFO*
Wendy Hayse, *Cust Mgr*
EMP: 15 **EST:** 1968
SQ FT: 27,800
SALES (est): 3.5MM **Privately Held**
WEB: www.2vindustries.com
SIC: 2899 8999 Metal treating compounds; chemical consultant

(G-18784)
VALLEY MANUFACTURING
28525 Beck Rd Unit 108 (48393-4742)
PHONE..................248 767-5078
EMP: 4 **EST:** 2008
SALES (est): 56.7K **Privately Held**
SIC: 3999 Manufacturing industries

(G-18785)
VELESCO PHRM SVCS INC
28036 Oakland Oaks Ct (48393-3348)
PHONE..................734 545-0696
Dave Barnes, *Branch Mgr*
EMP: 7
SALES (corp-wide): 64.8MM **Privately Held**
WEB: www.velescopharma.com
SIC: 3559 2834 Pharmaceutical machinery; druggists' preparations (pharmaceuticals)
HQ: Velesco Pharmaceutical Services, Inc.
46701 Commerce Center Dr
Plymouth MI 48170

(G-18786)
VENTURA AEROSPACE LLC
51170 Grand River Ave A (48393-3361)
PHONE..................734 357-0114
Mark Snow, *Vice Pres*
Troy Ingram, *Design Engr*
Jack Akey, *Sales Staff*
Brad Blanchard, *Manager*
EMP: 45 **EST:** 2003
SALES (est): 10.9MM **Privately Held**
WEB: www.venturaaerospace.net
SIC: 3494 3433 3728 3492 Valves & pipe fittings; heating equipment, except electric; aircraft assemblies, subassemblies & parts; valves, hydraulic, aircraft

(G-18787)
VENTURE GRAFIX LLC
47757 West Rd Ste C-105 (48393-4739)
PHONE..................248 449-1330
Michael J Cortis,
EMP: 7 **EST:** 2007
SQ FT: 5,000
SALES (est): 922.4K **Privately Held**
WEB: www.venturegrafix.com
SIC: 7319 3993 Display advertising service; electric signs

(G-18788)
VEXA GROUP LLC
52500 Grand River Ave (48393-2318)
PHONE..................734 330-8858
Andrew Meloeny, *Principal*
Harold Cunningham, *Principal*
Steffin Bader, *Business Dir*
EMP: 7 **EST:** 2016
SALES (est): 806.9K **Privately Held**
WEB: www.vexagroup.net
SIC: 3825 Network analyzers

(G-18789)
WAGON AUTOMOTIVE INC
28025 Oakland Oaks Ct (48393-3342)
PHONE..................248 262-2020
Ben Orler, *General Mgr*
▲ **EMP:** 132 **EST:** 1999
SQ FT: 78,000
SALES (est): 2.6MM
SALES (corp-wide): 171.4MM **Privately Held**
WEB: www.wagon-usa.com
SIC: 3441 Fabricated structural metal

PA: Modineer Co. Llc
2190 Industrial Dr
Niles MI 49120
269 683-2550

(G-18790)
WEST SIDE MFG FABRICATION INC
28776 Wall St (48393-3516)
PHONE................................248 380-6640
Glenn D Viazanko, *President*
EMP: 24 **EST:** 1989
SQ FT: 12,000
SALES (est): 1.6MM **Privately Held**
WEB: www.westsidemanufacturing.net
SIC: 3444 7692 Sheet metalwork; welding repair

(G-18791)
WETZEL TOOL & ENGINEERING INC
46952 Liberty Dr (48393-3693)
PHONE................................248 960-0430
Wieland H Wetzel, *President*
Frank Myers, *Foreman/Supr*
Hanna Wetzel, *Purchasing*
Hannelore C Wetzel, *Office Mgr*
EMP: 21 **EST:** 1973
SQ FT: 10,000
SALES (est): 3.8MM **Privately Held**
WEB: www.wetzeltool.net
SIC: 3544 Special dies & tools

(G-18792)
WILSONART LLC
50768 Varsity Ct (48393-2072)
PHONE................................248 960-3388
Mike Locke, *Branch Mgr*
EMP: 4
SALES (corp-wide): 1.6B **Privately Held**
WEB: www.wilsonart.com
SIC: 2821 Plastics materials & resins
HQ: Wilsonart Llc
2501 Wilsonart Dr
Temple TX 76504
254 207-7000

(G-18793)
YOUNGTRONICS LLC
49197 Wixom Tech Dr Ste A (48393-3572)
PHONE................................248 896-5790
Rupesh Srivastava, *CEO*
Kumar Arbind, *General Mgr*
Pratibha Srivastava, *Purchasing*
Nick Horlock, *Manager*
EMP: 10 **EST:** 2005
SALES (est): 2MM **Privately Held**
WEB: www.youngtronicsindia.com
SIC: 3569 Assembly machines, non-metalworking

(G-18794)
ZEISS INT
29295 Lyon Oaks Dr (48393-2340)
PHONE................................734 895-6004
EMP: 6 **EST:** 2017
SALES (est): 160.5K **Privately Held**
WEB: www.zeiss.com
SIC: 3827 Optical instruments & lenses

Wolverine
Cheboygan County

(G-18795)
JAROCHE BROTHERS INC
Also Called: M & J Forest Products
4250 Secord Rd (49799-9718)
PHONE................................231 525-8100
EMP: 10
SALES (est): 1.3MM **Privately Held**
SIC: 2421 2426 Sawmill/Planing Mill Hardwood Dimension/Floor Mill

Wolverine Lake
Oakland County

(G-18796)
CASTANO PLASTICS INC
2337 Solano Dr (48390-2460)
PHONE................................248 624-3724
Blanca Castano, *President*

John Castano, *Admin Sec*
EMP: 7 **EST:** 1987
SQ FT: 29,800
SALES (est): 600K **Privately Held**
SIC: 3089 Injection molding of plastics

(G-18797)
SERNIUK SOFTWARE
818 Wolverine Dr (48390-2377)
PHONE................................248 668-3826
Mike Serniuk, *Principal*
EMP: 4 **EST:** 2010
SALES (est): 135.4K **Privately Held**
SIC: 7372 Prepackaged software

Woodhaven
Wayne County

(G-18798)
CIRCLE S PRODUCTS INC (PA)
16415 Carter Rd (48183-2254)
PHONE................................734 675-2960
John Scharboneau, *President*
Carolyn Scharboneau, *Treasurer*
▼ **EMP:** 5 **EST:** 1998
SALES (est): 545.2K **Privately Held**
WEB: www.dryflo.com
SIC: 3441 7389 Fabricated structural metal;

(G-18799)
DIEZ GROUP LLC (PA)
Also Called: Integrated Terminals
25325 Hall Rd (48183-5101)
PHONE................................734 675-1700
April Diez, *CEO*
Gerald Diez Jr, *President*
Michael Roualet, *Vice Pres*
Lori Fricano, *VP Finance*
EMP: 59
SQ FT: 250,000
SALES (est): 15MM **Privately Held**
WEB: www.thediezgroup.com
SIC: 3316 3353 5051 Cold finishing of steel shapes; aluminum sheet, plate & foil; metals service centers & offices

(G-18800)
EWC WOODHAVEN INC
26747 Kirkway Cir (48183-1971)
PHONE................................734 552-3731
Mary Karp, *Principal*
EMP: 5 **EST:** 2016
SALES (est): 93.5K **Privately Held**
SIC: 2499 Wood products

(G-18801)
PARKER MACHINE & ENGINEERING
25028 Research Way (48183-5107)
PHONE................................734 692-4600
Robert W Parker, *President*
EMP: 4 **EST:** 1974
SQ FT: 5,000
SALES (est): 300K **Privately Held**
SIC: 3599 Machine shop, jobbing & repair

(G-18802)
PIPPA CUSTOM DESIGN PRINTING
22025 King Rd (48183-1026)
PHONE................................734 552-1598
Nancy L Weil, *Principal*
EMP: 6 **EST:** 2010
SALES (est): 120.6K **Privately Held**
SIC: 2752 Commercial printing, lithographic

(G-18803)
RUSNAK TOOL & MFG LLC
22452 Devonshire St (48183-1460)
PHONE................................734 362-8656
Richard T Rusnak, *Principal*
EMP: 4 **EST:** 2018
SALES (est): 39.6K **Privately Held**
SIC: 3999 Manufacturing industries

(G-18804)
YAMATO INTERNATIONAL CORP
22036 Commerce Dr (48183-5105)
PHONE................................734 675-6055
Yutaka Hasegawa, *President*
Minal Patel, *Purchasing*

Mikio Sato, *Treasurer*
▲ **EMP:** 32 **EST:** 1986
SQ FT: 14,000
SALES (est): 7.6MM **Privately Held**
WEB: www.yamatousa.com
SIC: 2672 Tape, pressure sensitive: made from purchased materials
PA: Yamato Co., Ltd.
9-10, Nihombashiodemmacho
Chuo-Ku TKY 103-0

Wyandotte
Wayne County

(G-18805)
ABBOTT LABORATORIES
1609 Biddle Ave Lot 4 (48192-3729)
PHONE................................734 324-6666
Tom Soblesky, *Manager*
EMP: 4
SALES (corp-wide): 34.6B **Publicly Held**
WEB: www.abbott.com
SIC: 2834 Druggists' preparations (pharmaceuticals)
PA: Abbott Laboratories
100 Abbott Park Rd
Abbott Park IL 60064
224 667-6100

(G-18806)
ABBVIE INC
1609 Biddle Ave (48192-3729)
PHONE................................734 324-6650
Miles D White, *Ch of Bd*
Martin McMillan, *QC Mgr*
Kierstyn Hibner, *Research*
Krista Miller, *Sales Staff*
EMP: 4
SALES (corp-wide): 45.8B **Publicly Held**
WEB: www.abbvie.com
SIC: 2834 Druggists' preparations (pharmaceuticals)
PA: Abbvie Inc.
1 N Waukegan Rd
North Chicago IL 60064
847 932-7900

(G-18807)
ARROW MOTOR & PUMP INC
629 Cent St (48192)
PHONE................................734 285-7860
Nancy Prohaska, *President*
Don Fischer, *Sales Staff*
Harry Geister, *Sales Staff*
Bob Wilson, *Sales Staff*
EMP: 30 **EST:** 1988
SQ FT: 11,500
SALES (est): 5.5MM **Privately Held**
WEB: www.arrowmotor.net
SIC: 7694 5063 7699 5084 Electric motor repair; motors, electric; pumps & pumping equipment repair; pumps & pumping equipment

(G-18808)
BASF CORPORATION
40 James Desana Dr (48192-4691)
PHONE................................734 324-6963
EMP: 4
SALES (corp-wide): 69.9B **Privately Held**
WEB: www.basf.com
SIC: 2869 Industrial organic chemicals
HQ: Basf Corporation
100 Park Ave
Florham Park NJ 07932
859 577-5797

(G-18809)
BASF CORPORATION
BASF Cellasto
1609 Biddle Ave (48192-3729)
PHONE................................734 324-6000
Oleksandra Korotchuk, *Business Mgr*
Sergio Franyutti, *Vice Pres*
Terri Willman, *Production*
Erin Wagner, *Buyer*
Michael Krupa, *Technical Mgr*
EMP: 200
SALES (corp-wide): 69.9B **Privately Held**
WEB: www.basf.com
SIC: 2869 2843 Industrial organic chemicals; surface active agents

HQ: Basf Corporation
100 Park Ave
Florham Park NJ 07932
859 577-5797

(G-18810)
BASF CORPORATION
1609 Biddle Ave (48192-3729)
PHONE................................734 324-6100
James Taft, *Business Mgr*
Greg Pflum, *Branch Mgr*
Bobby Daugherty, *Manager*
EMP: 4
SALES (corp-wide): 69.9B **Privately Held**
WEB: www.basf.com
SIC: 2869 Industrial organic chemicals
HQ: Basf Corporation
100 Park Ave
Florham Park NJ 07932
859 577-5797

(G-18811)
BASF CORPORATION
800 Central St (48192-7319)
PHONE................................734 759-2011
EMP: 101
SALES (corp-wide): 69.9B **Privately Held**
SIC: 2869 Industrial organic chemicals
HQ: Basf Corporation
100 Park Ave
Florham Park NJ 07932
859 577-5797

(G-18812)
BENCHMARK INC
4660 13th St (48192-7007)
P.O. Box 36068, Grosse Pointe (48236-0068)
PHONE................................734 285-0900
Richard F Cook, *President*
Paul Cook, *Vice Pres*
Laura Martin, *Manager*
EMP: 7 **EST:** 1956
SQ FT: 16,000 **Privately Held**
WEB: www.benchmark-inc.com
SIC: 2842 Specialty cleaning, polishes & sanitation goods

(G-18813)
CADON PLATING & COATINGS LLC
3715 11th St (48192-6496)
PHONE................................734 282-8100
Craig L Stormer,
Allen Ensign,
Tom Klein,
Gerald Lorenz,
William Sheets,
EMP: 80 **EST:** 1963
SQ FT: 85,000
SALES (est): 9.6MM **Privately Held**
WEB: www.cadonplating.com
SIC: 3471 Electroplating of metals or formed products

(G-18814)
CAP COLLET & TOOL CO INC
4082 6th St (48192-7104)
PHONE................................734 283-4040
Jerry Potter, *President*
John D Potter Jr, *President*
EMP: 11 **EST:** 1964
SQ FT: 32,000
SALES (est): 750K **Privately Held**
SIC: 3545 3451 Chucks: drill, lathe or magnetic (machine tool accessories); screw machine products

(G-18815)
CONCEPP TECHNOLOGIES
1609 Biddle Ave (48192-3729)
PHONE................................734 324-6750
EMP: 4
SALES (corp-wide): 9.8MM **Privately Held**
WEB: www.concepptechnologies.com
SIC: 2821 Polypropylene resins
PA: Concepp Technologies Incorporated
454 Rue Edouard
Granby QC J2G 3
450 378-9093

Wyandotte - Wayne County (G-18816) — GEOGRAPHIC SECTION

(G-18816)
DETROIT TUBULAR RIVET INC (PA)
1213 Grove St (48192-7045)
P.O. Box 279 (48192-0279)
PHONE..................................734 282-7979
Gerald Keast, *President*
Gary Sadonis, *Vice Pres*
EMP: 35 EST: 1954
SQ FT: 55,000
SALES (est): 3.1MM **Privately Held**
SIC: 3452 Rivets, metal

(G-18817)
ECORSE MCHY SLS & RBLDRS INC
Also Called: Ecorse Precision Products
4621 13th St (48192-7006)
PHONE..................................313 383-2100
Ivan Doverspike, *President*
Craig Neal, *Director*
EMP: 25 EST: 1963
SQ FT: 25,000
SALES (est): 4.4MM **Privately Held**
WEB: www.ecorse.com
SIC: 3491 8711 3541 Automatic regulating & control valves; engineering services; machine tools, metal cutting type

(G-18818)
ELECTRO OPTICS MFG INC
4459 13th St (48192-7004)
PHONE..................................734 283-3000
Kathryn Chambers, *CEO*
Russell Chambers, *President*
EMP: 10
SQ FT: 20,000 **Privately Held**
WEB: www.electroopticsmfg.com
SIC: 3469 Stamping metal for the trade

(G-18819)
EMPIRE TOOL CO
4261 13th St (48192-7002)
PHONE..................................734 283-8600
Butch Tittle, *Manager*
EMP: 7 EST: 2014
SALES (est): 126K **Privately Held**
SIC: 3599 Machine shop, jobbing & repair

(G-18820)
GEE & MISSLER INC
744 Vinewood St (48192-5007)
PHONE..................................734 284-1224
Elmer M Gee, *President*
EMP: 20 EST: 1945
SQ FT: 7,500
SALES (est): 2.7MM **Privately Held**
WEB: www.geeandmissler.com
SIC: 1711 3444 Mechanical contractor; sheet metalwork

(G-18821)
HESS PRINTING
201 Elm St Apt A (48192-5962)
PHONE..................................734 285-4377
Rachel Hess, *Principal*
EMP: 4 EST: 2006
SALES (est): 244.4K **Privately Held**
SIC: 2752 Commercial printing, offset

(G-18822)
HPS FABRICATIONS INC
4410 13th St (48192-7005)
PHONE..................................734 282-2285
Robert Lang, *CEO*
Gerald Page, *President*
Mitch Saari, *Purch Mgr*
EMP: 15 EST: 1994
SQ FT: 12,000
SALES (est): 2.9MM **Privately Held**
WEB: www.hpsfab.com
SIC: 3441 Fabricated structural metal

(G-18823)
II ENTERPRISES INC
555 Grove St (48192-6837)
P.O. Box 526 (48192-0526)
PHONE..................................734 285-6030
William Iverson, *President*
Jeffery Scott, *General Mgr*
Anthony Sawicki, *COO*
Thomas Iverson, *Vice Pres*
Bill Roy, *Opers Mgr*
▲ EMP: 10 EST: 2008
SALES (est): 2MM **Privately Held**
WEB: www.iienterprises.com
SIC: 3559 4225 Glass making machinery: blowing, molding, forming, etc.; general warehousing

(G-18824)
JCI JONES CHEMICALS INC
18000 Payne Ave (48192)
P.O. Box 2208, Riverview (48193-1208)
PHONE..................................734 283-0677
Lisa Gavilanez, *Office Mgr*
Norma Hudson, *Office Mgr*
Janet Smith, *Office Mgr*
D W Skidmore, *Branch Mgr*
Teresa Smith, *Manager*
EMP: 18
SALES (corp-wide): 196.9MM **Privately Held**
WEB: www.jcichem.com
SIC: 2812 5169 2819 Alkalies & chlorine; industrial chemicals; industrial inorganic chemicals
PA: Jci Jones Chemicals, Inc.
  1765 Ringling Blvd # 200
  Sarasota FL 34236
  941 330-1537

(G-18825)
JEANIES LLC
918 Oak St (48192-4904)
PHONE..................................313 412-8760
Richard Manigault, *Principal*
EMP: 5 EST: 2018
SALES (est): 182K **Privately Held**
SIC: 3651 Household audio & video equipment

(G-18826)
JEFFREY SCHEIBER
285 Biddle Ave (48192-2514)
PHONE..................................248 207-7036
EMP: 5 EST: 2018
SALES (est): 162.3K **Privately Held**
SIC: 2741 Miscellaneous publishing

(G-18827)
KULICK ENTERPRISES INC
4082 Biddle Ave (48192-7116)
PHONE..................................734 283-6999
Robert Kulick, *President*
EMP: 4 EST: 1999
SALES (est): 489.3K **Privately Held**
SIC: 3444 Sheet metal specialties, not stamped

(G-18828)
LAKE SHORE SERVICES INC
4354 Biddle Ave (48192-7304)
PHONE..................................734 285-7007
Robert Lemay, *President*
Jennifer McConnell, *Business Mgr*
EMP: 13 EST: 1985
SQ FT: 10,000
SALES (est): 1MM **Privately Held**
WEB: www.lakeshoreservicesinc.com
SIC: 7692 3441 Welding repair; fabricated structural metal

(G-18829)
LINDE GAS & EQUIPMENT INC
Also Called: Praxair
2025 Eureka Rd (48192-6001)
PHONE..................................734 282-3830
EMP: 4 **Privately Held**
WEB: www.lindeus.com
SIC: 5084 5999 2813 Welding machinery & equipment; welding supplies; carbon dioxide
HQ: Linde Gas & Equipment Inc.
  10 Riverview Dr
  Danbury CT 06810
  203 837-2000

(G-18830)
MADDEN ENTERPRISES INC
Also Called: American Speedy Printing
3557 Fort St (48192-6315)
PHONE..................................734 284-5330
Janell Madden, *President*
EMP: 5 EST: 1977
SALES (est): 507.1K **Privately Held**
WEB: www.americanspeedy.com
SIC: 2752 Commercial printing, offset

(G-18831)
MANRAY PRESS LLC
1788 Oak St (48192-5424)
PHONE..................................734 558-0580
Ray Ackley, *Mng Member*
EMP: 4 EST: 2020
SALES (est): 119.1K **Privately Held**
SIC: 2741 Miscellaneous publishing

(G-18832)
MECHANICAL SHEET METAL CO
723 Walnut St (48192-4338)
PHONE..................................734 284-1006
David Karl, *President*
Daniel Karl, *Treasurer*
EMP: 10 EST: 1952
SQ FT: 4,000
SALES (est): 1.7MM **Privately Held**
SIC: 3444 Sheet metalwork

(G-18833)
MERCURY MANUFACTURING COMPANY
Also Called: Apg - Spclty Vlve McHined Pdts
1212 Grove St (48192-7099)
PHONE..................................734 285-5150
Janice Wiegand, *President*
Alan Piurkowski, *Plant Mgr*
Lorenzo Tuff, *Buyer*
▲ EMP: 68
SQ FT: 53,000
SALES (est): 16.9MM **Privately Held**
WEB: www.mercurymfg.com
SIC: 3451 3491 Screw machine products; pressure valves & regulators, industrial
PA: Alpha Precision Group, Llc
  95 Mason Run Rd
  Ridgway PA 15857
  814 773-3191

(G-18834)
MR LUBE INC
6915 Airport Hwy (48192)
PHONE..................................313 615-6161
Mohamed Hameed, *Principal*
EMP: 4 EST: 2011
SALES (est): 283.7K **Privately Held**
SIC: 2992 Lubricating oils

(G-18835)
ORION BUS ACCNTING SLTIONS LLC
1611 Ford Ave (48192-2303)
PHONE..................................248 893-1060
Jeffrey Smith, *Partner*
Jim Steele, *Sales Staff*
Jeff Smith, *Mng Member*
EMP: 4 EST: 2002
SALES (est): 400K **Privately Held**
WEB: www.orionbas.com
SIC: 8721 7372 Accounting services, except auditing; business oriented computer software

(G-18836)
RAPP & SON INC (PA)
3767 11th St (48192-6431)
PHONE..................................734 283-1000
Roy W Rapp Jr, *President*
Roy W Rapp III, *Vice Pres*
Nora Teagan, *Controller*
Cheryl L Rapp, *Admin Sec*
EMP: 60 EST: 1939
SALES (est): 36.6MM **Privately Held**
SIC: 3724 3812 3769 3678 Engine mount parts, aircraft; search & navigation equipment; guided missile & space vehicle parts & auxiliary equipment; electronic connectors; motor vehicle parts & accessories

(G-18837)
S S GRAPHICS INC
Also Called: Signoutfitters.com
4176 6th St (48192-7106)
PHONE..................................734 246-4420
Russ Kissel, *President*
Russ Kissle, *President*
Scott Smiddy, *Vice Pres*
Rhonda Kilian, *Cust Mgr*
EMP: 9 EST: 2001
SQ FT: 7,500 **Privately Held**
WEB: www.signoutfitters.com
SIC: 3993 Signs, not made in custom sign painting shops

(G-18838)
SCAPEGOAT PRESS INC
1112 Mollno St (48192-4113)
PHONE..................................586 439-8381
Stephanie Manard, *Administration*
EMP: 4 EST: 2019
SALES (est): 68K **Privately Held**
SIC: 2741 Miscellaneous publishing

(G-18839)
SIMPLY CUSTOM
1732 Eureka Rd (48192-6002)
PHONE..................................734 558-4051
Noel Wegher, *Owner*
EMP: 4 EST: 2007
SALES (est): 219.7K **Privately Held**
SIC: 3479 Coating of metals & formed products

(G-18840)
STEWART PRINTING COMPANY INC
2715 Fort St (48192-4820)
PHONE..................................734 283-8440
Louis George, *President*
Cindy Scott, *Manager*
EMP: 8 EST: 1950
SQ FT: 2,000
SALES (est): 638.5K **Privately Held**
WEB: www.printingservicesdownriver.com
SIC: 2752 Commercial printing, offset

(G-18841)
STROHS
3162 Biddle Ave (48192-5916)
PHONE..................................734 285-5480
Julie Volante, *Owner*
EMP: 7 EST: 2011
SALES (est): 174.1K **Privately Held**
SIC: 2024 Ice cream, bulk

(G-18842)
TRI-TECH ENGINEERING INC
3663 11th St (48192-6406)
PHONE..................................734 283-3700
George Balint, *President*
David Isham, *Corp Secy*
Mark Fielhauer, *Purch Mgr*
EMP: 28 EST: 1950
SQ FT: 13,000
SALES (est): 4.5MM **Privately Held**
WEB: www.tri-techeng.com
SIC: 3593 7699 Fluid power cylinders, hydraulic or pneumatic; hydraulic equipment repair

(G-18843)
WAYNE COUNTY LABORATORY
797 Central St (48192-7307)
PHONE..................................734 285-5215
Walter Syrkowski, *Director*
EMP: 6 EST: 1938
SALES (est): 818.3K **Privately Held**
WEB: www.waynecounty.com
SIC: 3589 Sewage & water treatment equipment

(G-18844)
WELZIN HEALTH SERVICES LLC
3218 20th St (48192-5431)
PHONE..................................313 953-8768
Tiffani Welzin, *CEO*
EMP: 5 EST: 2019
SALES (est): 500K **Privately Held**
SIC: 8099 7381 2899 Health & allied services; blood related health services; health screening service; fingerprint service;

(G-18845)
WYANDOTTE COLLET AND TOOL INC
4070 5th St (48192-7102)
PHONE..................................734 283-8055
Victor Forsman, *President*
Phillip A Robinson III, *Vice Pres*
EMP: 17 EST: 1970
SQ FT: 6,000
SALES (est): 409.3K **Privately Held**
SIC: 3545 3599 Collets (machine tool accessories); pushers; sockets (machine tool accessories); machine shop, jobbing & repair

GEOGRAPHIC SECTION

Wyoming — Kent County (G-18874)

Wyoming
Kent County

(G-18846)
2K TOOL LLC
3025 Madison Ave Se (49548-1209)
PHONE.................................616 452-4927
Heidi Smith, *President*
Amanda Smith, *Opers Staff*
Kevin Smith,
EMP: 8
SQ FT: 8,500
SALES (est): 1.4MM **Privately Held**
WEB: www.2ktool.com
SIC: 3544 Special dies & tools

(G-18847)
4D INDUSTRIES INC
Also Called: Line-X of Grand Rapids
2290 28th St Sw Ste B (49519-2305)
PHONE.................................310 710-3955
Jason Dykstra, *Principal*
EMP: 7 **EST:** 2017
SALES (est): 313.9K **Privately Held**
WEB: www.linexgr.com
SIC: 3999 Manufacturing industries

(G-18848)
ADVANCED SHEET METAL
2630 Prairie St Sw (49519-2461)
PHONE.................................616 301-3828
EMP: 7 **EST:** 2014
SALES (est): 1.2MM **Privately Held**
WEB: www.advancedsheetmetal.us
SIC: 3444 Sheet metalwork

(G-18849)
AEC SYSTEMS USA INC
2663 44th St Sw (49519-4189)
P.O. Box 10, Grandville (49468-0010)
PHONE.................................616 257-9502
Darrel Wilcox, *CEO*
Ryan Westphal, *Manager*
EMP: 11 **EST:** 2007
SALES (est): 532.8K **Privately Held**
WEB: www.aecsystemsusa.com
SIC: 3582 Commercial laundry equipment

(G-18850)
AFP CONSULTING
2759 Golfbury Dr Sw (49519-4755)
PHONE.................................616 534-9858
Deb Hekman, *Manager*
EMP: 5 **EST:** 1952
SALES (est): 62.3K **Privately Held**
SIC: 2099 Food preparations

(G-18851)
ALL-TECH INC (PA)
Also Called: All-Tech Engineering
1030 58th St Sw (49509-9365)
PHONE.................................616 406-0681
Bruce Bunker, *President*
Ron Goldwater, *Project Engr*
Hunter Engels, *Design Engr*
Danielle Kondrat, *Accounting Mgr*
Denice Bunker, *Persnl Dir*
EMP: 45 **EST:** 1989
SQ FT: 32,000
SALES (est): 8.9MM **Privately Held**
WEB: www.alltech-eng.com
SIC: 3599 Machine shop, jobbing & repair

(G-18852)
BIHL+WIEDEMANN INC
5570 Wilson Ave Sw Ste E (49418-8867)
PHONE.................................616 345-0680
Ron Dibling, *President*
EMP: 1 **EST:** 2015
SALES (est): 1.5MM
SALES (corp-wide): 49.1MM **Privately Held**
WEB: www.bihl-wiedemann.de
SIC: 3823 Computer interface equipment for industrial process control
PA: Bihl + Wiedemann Gmbh
   FloBworthstr. 41
   Mannheim BW 68199
   621 339-960

(G-18853)
BNW WEST SIDE SCRNPRINTING LLC
2219 Holliday Dr Sw (49549-4238)
PHONE.................................616 717-1082
Annette Whitt, *Principal*
EMP: 5 **EST:** 2010
SALES (est): 151.5K **Privately Held**
SIC: 2752 Commercial printing, lithographic

(G-18854)
BOSS ELECTRO STATIC INC
3974 Linden Ave Se (49548-3432)
PHONE.................................616 575-0577
Kathi S Lynch, *President*
Michael Lynch, *Vice Pres*
▲ **EMP:** 28 **EST:** 2001
SQ FT: 30,000
SALES (est): 2.2MM **Privately Held**
SIC: 3479 1721 Etching & engraving; painting & paper hanging

(G-18855)
BUSTER MATHIS FOUNDATION
Also Called: Soul of The City Classics Socc
4409 Carol Ave Sw (49519-4519)
PHONE.................................616 843-4433
Buster Mathis, *President*
Joe Gonnella, *Principal*
Robert Woonacott, *Principal*
EMP: 4 **EST:** 2010
SALES (est): 128.9K **Privately Held**
WEB: www.bustermathisfoundation.org
SIC: 8331 3542 3545 1522 Job training & vocational rehabilitation services; robots for metal forming: pressing, extruding, etc.; measuring tools & machines, machinists' metalworking type; residential construction; sports promotion

(G-18856)
CHAMBERS INDUSTRIAL TECH INC
2220 Byron Center Ave Sw (49519-1652)
PHONE.................................616 249-8190
Anna Chambers, *President*
Dick Chambers, *Vice Pres*
Richard Chambers, *Vice Pres*
Nate V Kamp, *Manager*
▲ **EMP:** 8 **EST:** 2008
SALES (est): 1.2MM **Privately Held**
WEB: www.chamberstech.net
SIC: 3089 Injection molding of plastics

(G-18857)
CHEAP RECENTLY ACQUIRED PDTS
2405 Porter St Sw (49519-2182)
PHONE.................................616 272-4212
Jordan Green, *Principal*
EMP: 8 **EST:** 2015
SALES (est): 903.9K **Privately Held**
WEB: www.crapstores.com
SIC: 3639 Major kitchen appliances, except refrigerators & stoves

(G-18858)
CONSUMERS CONCRETE CORP
1505 Burlingame Ave Sw (49509-1001)
PHONE.................................616 243-3651
Tom Thomas, *President*
Steve Thomas, *Vice Pres*
Bruce Stanley, *CFO*
Daniel Kalee, *Director*
Mike Kline, *Products*
EMP: 166 **EST:** 1945
SQ FT: 12,000
SALES (est): 1.7MM
SALES (corp-wide): 42.6MM **Privately Held**
WEB: www.consumersconcrete.com
SIC: 3271 3272 Blocks, concrete or cinder: standard; concrete products
PA: Consumers Concrete Corporation
   3506 Lovers Ln
   Kalamazoo MI 49001
   269 342-0136

(G-18859)
CONTROL DEKK LLC
4035 Oak Valley Ct Sw (49519-3775)
PHONE.................................616 828-4862
Len Logsdon, *Mng Member*
Jared Dekker,
Jordan Dekker,
EMP: 4 **EST:** 2015
SALES (est): 7K **Privately Held**
WEB: www.controldekk.com
SIC: 3448 Greenhouses: prefabricated metal

(G-18860)
CONTROL SOLUTIONS INC
5805 Weller Ct Sw Ste A (49509-9602)
PHONE.................................616 247-9422
Ryan E Kauffman, *President*
Michael D Heavner, *Vice Pres*
Liz Pearson, *CFO*
Reed Kauffman, *Director*
EMP: 75 **EST:** 2008
SQ FT: 3,600
SALES (est): 8.1MM **Privately Held**
WEB: www.controlyourbuilding.com
SIC: 3822 Temperature controls, automatic

(G-18861)
COUNTRY CHOICE INC
2511 Ancient Dr Sw (49519-4564)
PHONE.................................616 241-6043
EMP: 5 **EST:** 2010
SALES (est): 108.4K **Privately Held**
SIC: 3421 Table & food cutlery, including butchers'

(G-18862)
CREATIVE MACHINING INC
2620 Remico St Sw (49519-2408)
PHONE.................................616 772-2328
James A Schutte, *President*
Dawn Schutte, *Vice Pres*
Rick Iacovoni, *Sales Staff*
Chris Mouw, *Program Mgr*
Jason Metzger, *Manager*
EMP: 2 **EST:** 1988
SALES (est): 1.3MM **Privately Held**
WEB: www.creativemachininginc.com
SIC: 3599 Machine shop, jobbing & repair

(G-18863)
DAKODA LOVE MANUFACTURING
1701 Clyde Park Ave Sw # 3 (49509-1500)
PHONE.................................616 840-0804
EMP: 5 **EST:** 2019
SALES (est): 226K **Privately Held**
WEB: www.dakodalove.com
SIC: 3999 Manufacturing industries

(G-18864)
DANKA
4489 Byron Center Ave Sw B (49519-4804)
PHONE.................................616 249-8199
Bill Kramer, *Manager*
EMP: 4 **EST:** 2010
SALES (est): 120.1K **Privately Held**
SIC: 3579 Office machines

(G-18865)
DAVIS DENTAL LABORATORY
5830 Crossroads Cmmrce (49519-9572)
PHONE.................................616 261-9191
Bob Ditta, *President*
Kim Jones, *Vice Pres*
EMP: 5 **EST:** 1923
SALES (est): 482.5K **Privately Held**
SIC: 8072 3842 Crown & bridge production; surgical appliances & supplies

(G-18866)
DETAIL TECHNOLOGIES LLC
5900 Crssrds Cmmrce Pkwy (49519)
PHONE.................................616 261-1313
Christopher Ostosh, *CEO*
Josh Schwab, *Vice Pres*
Josh Bylsma, *Engineer*
Tom Corcoran, *Manager*
Shawn Sytsma, *Manager*
EMP: 48 **EST:** 1994
SQ FT: 20,000
SALES (est): 10MM **Privately Held**
WEB: www.detailtechnologies.com
SIC: 3599 Electrical discharge machining (EDM)

(G-18867)
DIE-MATIC TOOL AND DIE INC
4309 Aldrich Ave Sw (49509-4031)
PHONE.................................616 531-0060
Chad Folkema, *President*
Bob Berthiaume, *Opers Mgr*
Rose David, *Mfg Staff*
Steve Sund, *Manager*
EMP: 21 **EST:** 2015
SQ FT: 47,500
SALES (est): 3.4MM **Privately Held**
WEB: www.diematic.net
SIC: 3469 Stamping metal for the trade

(G-18868)
DIE-MATIC USA LLC
4309 Aldrich Ave Sw (49509-4031)
PHONE.................................616 531-0060
Chad Folkema, *President*
Julie Sjaarda, *Office Mgr*
Robert Berthiaume, *Manager*
EMP: 35 **EST:** 1972
SALES (est): 2.9MM **Privately Held**
WEB: www.diematic.net
SIC: 3544 Special dies & tools

(G-18869)
DISCOUNT RESTAURANT & SUPPLY
2035 28th St Sw (49519-2515)
PHONE.................................574 370-9574
Daniel Palomelo, *Manager*
EMP: 4 **EST:** 2016
SALES (est): 80K **Privately Held**
SIC: 2599 Furniture & fixtures

(G-18870)
EJ USA INC
5075 Clyde Park Ave Sw (49509-5119)
PHONE.................................616 538-2040
Mike Warmouth, *Manager*
EMP: 7 **Privately Held**
WEB: www.eastjordancity.org
SIC: 3321 Manhole covers, metal
HQ: Ej Usa, Inc.
   301 Spring St
   East Jordan MI 49727
   800 874-4100

(G-18871)
EL INFORMADOR LLC
2000 28th St Sw Ste 4 (49519-2609)
P.O. Box 9625 (49509-0625)
PHONE.................................616 272-1092
Alma Molina, *Mng Member*
EMP: 6 **EST:** 2010
SALES (est): 269.1K **Privately Held**
WEB: www.elinformadorusa.com
SIC: 2711 7371 Newspapers, publishing & printing; computer software development & applications

(G-18872)
FHC HOLDING COMPANY (PA)
Also Called: F H C
2509 29th St Sw (49519-2468)
P.O. Box 9100, Grand Rapids (49509-0100)
PHONE.................................616 538-3231
Robert W Holt Jr, *CEO*
Thomas R Butterworth, *President*
Robert Holt, *Project Mgr*
Larry Lind, *Project Mgr*
Thomas Butterworth, *Consultant*
EMP: 4 **EST:** 1981
SQ FT: 18,000
SALES (est): 16MM **Privately Held**
WEB: www.franklinholwerda.com
SIC: 1711 3498 3444 Warm air heating & air conditioning contractor; fabricated pipe & fittings; sheet metalwork

(G-18873)
FISK PRECISION TECH LLC
3403 Lousma Dr Se (49548-2265)
PHONE.................................616 514-1415
Amy Steketee, *Principal*
EMP: 5 **EST:** 2011
SALES (est): 269.7K **Privately Held**
SIC: 3545 Precision measuring tools

(G-18874)
GIPSON FABRICATIONS
2151 Chicago Dr Sw (49519-1214)
PHONE.................................616 245-7331
Joe Weber, *General Mgr*
John Gipson, *Principal*
EMP: 8 **EST:** 2010
SALES (est): 709K **Privately Held**
WEB: www.gipsonfabrication.com
SIC: 3842 Welders' hoods

Wyoming - Kent County (G-18875)

(G-18875)
GOLDEN EAGLE PALLETS LLC
1701 Clyde Park Ave Sw # 8 (49509-1500)
PHONE..................................616 233-0970
Manuel Juarez, *Principal*
EMP: 15 **EST:** 2010
SALES (est): 2.9MM **Privately Held**
WEB: www.goldeneaglepallets.com
SIC: 2448 Pallets, wood; pallets, wood & wood with metal

(G-18876)
GRAND RAPIDS GRAPHIX
3853 Llewellyn Ct Sw (49519-3128)
PHONE..................................616 359-2383
Adam Lamos, *Partner*
Joseph Brunet, *Partner*
EMP: 4 **EST:** 2009
SALES (est): 154.9K **Privately Held**
WEB: www.grandrapidsgraphix.com
SIC: 2759 7389 Screen printing;

(G-18877)
GREEN INK WORKS
3637 Clyde Park Ave Sw # 2 (49509-4095)
PHONE..................................616 254-7350
EMP: 4 **EST:** 2013
SALES (est): 158.1K **Privately Held**
SIC: 2752 Commercial printing, lithographic

(G-18878)
GRT AVIONICS INC
3133 Madison Ave Se Ste B (49548-1277)
PHONE..................................616 245-7700
Greg Toman, *President*
Jonathan Francois, *Opers Staff*
EMP: 8 **EST:** 2004
SALES (est): 393K **Privately Held**
WEB: www.grtavionics.com
SIC: 3699 Electrical equipment & supplies

(G-18879)
HAGER WOOD PRESERVING LLC
1211 Judd Ave Sw (49509-1018)
P.O. Box 9371 (49509-0371)
PHONE..................................616 248-0905
Brian Hager,
EMP: 7 **EST:** 2009
SALES (est): 927.6K **Privately Held**
WEB: www.hagerwood.com
SIC: 2491 Wood preserving

(G-18880)
HALDEX BRAKE PRODUCTS CORP
5801 Weller Ct Sw Ste D (49509-9601)
PHONE..................................616 827-9641
EMP: 116
SALES (corp-wide): 534.6MM **Privately Held**
SIC: 3714 Mfg Motor Vehicle Parts/Accessories
HQ: Haldex Brake Products Corporation
10930 N Pomona Ave
Kansas City MO 64153
816 891-2470

(G-18881)
HASKELL OFFICE
3770 Hagen Dr Se (49548-2343)
PHONE..................................616 988-0880
Alan Robins, *Owner*
EMP: 6 **EST:** 2010
SALES (est): 950K **Privately Held**
WEB: www.haskelloffice.com
SIC: 2522 Office furniture, except wood

(G-18882)
HEYS FABRICATION AND MCH CO
3059 Hillcroft Ave Sw (49548-1034)
PHONE..................................616 247-0065
Rick Heys, *CEO*
EMP: 17 **EST:** 2005
SALES (est): 659.6K **Privately Held**
WEB: www.heysfab.com
SIC: 3441 Fabricated structural metal

(G-18883)
HIGH RIZE CANDLES
136 41st St Sw (49548-3138)
PHONE..................................616 818-9527
Michelle Flora, *Principal*
EMP: 4 **EST:** 2017
SALES (est): 39.6K **Privately Held**
SIC: 3999 Candles

(G-18884)
HIGHLIGHT INDUSTRIES INC
2694 Prairie St Sw (49519-2461)
PHONE..................................616 531-2464
Kurt Riemenschneider, *President*
Jim Krawczyk, *General Mgr*
Alan Martens, *Vice Pres*
Karen Riemenschneider, *Vice Pres*
Linda Wiersma, *Purch Mgr*
▲ **EMP:** 69 **EST:** 1981
SQ FT: 57,000
SALES (est): 20.4MM **Privately Held**
WEB: www.highlightindustries.com
SIC: 3565 Wrapping machines

(G-18885)
HME INC
Also Called: Hme Ahrens-Fox
1950 Byron Center Ave Sw (49519-1223)
PHONE..................................616 534-1463
Jim Monterusso, *CEO*
Rex Troost, *Principal*
Ken Lenz, *Vice Pres*
Rod McNeil, *Vice Pres*
EMP: 120 **EST:** 1913
SQ FT: 140,000
SALES (est): 32.5MM
SALES (corp-wide): 49.1MM **Privately Held**
WEB: www.firetrucks.com
SIC: 3713 3546 3537 3536 Truck & bus bodies; power-driven handtools; industrial trucks & tractors; hoists, cranes & monorails; motor vehicles & car bodies
PA: Valley Truck Parts, Inc.
1900 Chicago Dr Sw
Grand Rapids MI 49519
616 241-5431

(G-18886)
JASPER WELLER LLC
Also Called: Weller Truck Parts
5960 Burlingame Ave Sw (49509-9398)
PHONE..................................616 249-8596
Chris Jolie, *Branch Mgr*
EMP: 44
SALES (corp-wide): 791.6MM **Privately Held**
WEB: www.wellertruck.com
SIC: 3713 Truck bodies & parts
HQ: Jasper Weller, Llc
1500 Gezon Pkwy Sw
Wyoming MI 49509

(G-18887)
JASPER WELLER LLC (HQ)
Also Called: Weller Truck Parts
1500 Gezon Pkwy Sw (49509-9585)
PHONE..................................616 724-2000
Terry Stranz, *President*
Stephen Donahue, *Regional Mgr*
Bill Lewis, *Regional Mgr*
Amy Hurley, *Business Mgr*
Paul Weller, *COO*
▲ **EMP:** 200 **EST:** 2010
SALES (est): 268.4MM
SALES (corp-wide): 791.6MM **Privately Held**
WEB: www.wellertruck.com
SIC: 3713 3714 Truck bodies & parts; transmissions, motor vehicle
PA: Jasper Engine Exchange, Inc.
815 Wernsing Rd
Jasper IN 47546
812 482-1041

(G-18888)
KALAMAZOO PACKG SYSTEMS LLC
900 47th St Sw Ste J (49509-5142)
P.O. Box 88141, Grand Rapids (49518-0141)
PHONE..................................616 534-2600
Richard Wietczak, *President*
Teresa McClure, *Director*
EMP: 10 **EST:** 1980
SALES (est): 1MM **Privately Held**
WEB: www.kalpack.com
SIC: 3565 5084 Packing & wrapping machinery; industrial machinery & equipment

(G-18889)
KELLOGG COMPANY
3300 Rger B Chffee Mem Dr (49548-2324)
PHONE..................................269 961-6693
EMP: 4
SALES (corp-wide): 13.7B **Publicly Held**
WEB: www.kelloggcompany.com
SIC: 2041 Flour & other grain mill products
PA: Kellogg Company
1 Kellogg Sq
Battle Creek MI 49017
269 961-2000

(G-18890)
LEWIS WELDING INC
274 Mart St Sw (49548-1000)
PHONE..................................616 452-9226
Lyman Lewis, *President*
EMP: 20 **EST:** 1997
SQ FT: 5,200
SALES (est): 2.6MM **Privately Held**
WEB: www.lewisweldinginc.com
SIC: 7692 Welding repair

(G-18891)
LIGHT METALS CORPORATION
Also Called: LMC
2740 Prairie St Sw (49519-6098)
PHONE..................................616 538-3030
George T Boylan, *President*
Jeff Boylan, *Vice Pres*
Linus Schwartz, *Foreman/Supr*
David Moore, *Production*
Brandon Grantham, *Engineer*
▼ **EMP:** 270 **EST:** 1944
SQ FT: 170,000
SALES (est): 28.5MM **Privately Held**
WEB: www.light-metals.com
SIC: 3354 3444 Aluminum extruded products; sheet metalwork

(G-18892)
LOWING PRODUCTS LLC
1500 Whiting St Sw (49509-1056)
PHONE..................................616 530-7440
David Lowing,
Adam Boeskool,
Matthew Lowing,
Stephen Paulsen,
EMP: 4 **EST:** 2017
SQ FT: 18,000
SALES (est): 296.3K **Privately Held**
WEB: www.lowinglight.com
SIC: 3599 Tubing, flexible metallic

(G-18893)
METAL COMPONENTS INC
2000 Chicago Dr Sw (49519-1213)
PHONE..................................616 389-2400
EMP: 6 **EST:** 2011
SALES (est): 170.6K **Privately Held**
SIC: 3499 Fabricated metal products

(G-18894)
MICHIGAN TRKEY PRDCERS COOP IN
2140 Chicago Dr Sw (49519-1215)
PHONE..................................616 245-2221
Don Rae, *Regional Mgr*
Rob Rotterdam, *Regional Mgr*
Don Delordo, *Vice Pres*
Maria Santoyo, *QC Mgr*
Diane Ketchum, *Sales Mgr*
EMP: 63
SALES (corp-wide): 81.5MM **Privately Held**
WEB: www.miturkey.com
SIC: 2015 Turkey processing & slaughtering
PA: Michigan Turkey Producers Cooperative, Inc.
1100 Hall St Sw
Grand Rapids MI 49503
616 245-2221

(G-18895)
MITTEN SPRAY FOAM INSUL LLC
4010 Milan Ave Sw (49509-4410)
PHONE..................................616 250-8355
Gerrit Sonke,
EMP: 6 **EST:** 2017

SALES (est): 77.4K **Privately Held**
WEB: www.michigansprayfoamllc.com
SIC: 3086 Insulation or cushioning material, foamed plastic

(G-18896)
NATIONAL PRINTING SERVICES
5360 Pine Slope Dr Sw (49519-9641)
PHONE..................................616 813-0758
Dave Lange, *VP Sls/Mktg*
Ken Filary, *Sales Staff*
EMP: 4 **EST:** 2014
SALES (est): 178.1K **Privately Held**
WEB: www.nationalprintingservices.com
SIC: 2752 Commercial printing, offset

(G-18897)
NU-TRAN LLC
2947 Buchanan Ave Sw (49548-1043)
PHONE..................................616 350-9575
Chanh Nguyen, *Owner*
EMP: 8 **EST:** 2014
SALES (est): 745.7K **Privately Held**
WEB: www.nutranmfg.com
SIC: 2421 2511 2541 Building & structural materials, wood; wood household furniture; table or counter tops, plastic laminated

(G-18898)
P D P LLC
Also Called: Peninsula Prestress Company
2675 Chicago Dr Sw (49519-1677)
PHONE..................................616 437-9618
Fernando Roldan, *Plant Mgr*
Paul A Marsh, *Mng Member*
David Marsh, *Mng Member*
EMP: 23 **EST:** 2012
SALES (est): 13.5MM **Privately Held**
SIC: 3273 Ready-mixed concrete

(G-18899)
PINNACLE TOOL INCORPORATED
1150 Gezon Pkwy Sw (49509-9582)
PHONE..................................616 257-2700
Tim Hitson, *President*
Dick Gerke, *Vice Pres*
Brian Rieth, *Engineer*
Jamie Vanbeek, *Project Engr*
John Botner, *Sales Staff*
▲ **EMP:** 37
SQ FT: 41,000
SALES (est): 7.9MM **Privately Held**
WEB: www.pinntool.com
SIC: 3469 Machine parts, stamped or pressed metal

(G-18900)
PLEXICASE INC
2431 Clyde Park Ave Sw (49509-1935)
PHONE..................................616 246-6400
Steven Ries, *President*
Robert R Ries, *President*
Paul Geelhoed, *Treasurer*
EMP: 5 **EST:** 1990
SALES (est): 834.4K **Privately Held**
WEB: www.plexicase.com
SIC: 3089 Thermoformed finished plastic products

(G-18901)
PRECISION AUTOMOTIVE MCH SP
2320 Chicago Dr Sw (49519-1219)
PHONE..................................616 534-6946
Arnie Snyder, *Mng Member*
EMP: 5
SALES (est): 155.8K **Privately Held**
SIC: 3599 Machine shop, jobbing & repair

(G-18902)
RAM-PAK INDUSTRIES LLC
2629 Prairie St Sw Ste E (49519-2611)
PHONE..................................616 334-1443
Eric Schuyler,
EMP: 10 **EST:** 2020
SALES (est): 662.7K **Privately Held**
WEB: www.rampakindustries.com
SIC: 3399 Metal fasteners

(G-18903)
REFLECTIVE ART INC
2662 Prairie St Sw (49519-2461)
PHONE..................................616 452-0712

▲ = Import ▼ = Export
◆ = Import/Export

Thomas Hoover, *President*
Cindy Rousell, *Accountant*
◆ **EMP:** 21 **EST:** 1984
SALES (est): 1.4MM **Privately Held**
WEB: www.reflectiveartinc.com
SIC: 2741 Miscellaneous publishing

(G-18904)
RIETH-RILEY CNSTR CO INC
2100 Chicago Dr Sw (49519-1215)
P.O. Box 278, Ada (49301-0278)
PHONE 616 248-0920
Chad Loney, *Branch Mgr*
EMP: 14
SALES (corp-wide): 174.4MM **Privately Held**
WEB: www.rieth-riley.com
SIC: 1611 2951 Surfacing & paving; asphalt paving mixtures & blocks
PA: Rieth-Riley Construction Co., Inc.
3626 Elkhart Rd
Goshen IN 46526
574 875-5183

(G-18905)
RIVERSIDE CNC LLC
3331 Lousma Dr Se (49548-2251)
PHONE 616 246-6000
Bryan Roodvoets, *Principal*
EMP: 15 **EST:** 2013
SALES (est): 259.5K **Privately Held**
WEB: www.riversidecnc.com
SIC: 3541 3674 Milling machines; vertical turning & boring machines (metalworking); strain gages, solid state

(G-18906)
ROSE EMBROIDERY LLC
1118 Burton St Sw (49509-5509)
PHONE 616 245-9191
Noreen Rose,
EMP: 4 **EST:** 2008
SALES (est): 157K **Privately Held**
WEB: www.rosesembroidery.net
SIC: 2395 Embroidery products, except schiffli machine

(G-18907)
SPRINGER MACHINE
4785 Stafford Ave Sw (49548-4231)
PHONE 616 531-9816
Randy Wiebanga, *Principal*
EMP: 7 **EST:** 2007
SALES (est): 194.9K **Privately Held**
WEB: www.springermach.com
SIC: 3599 Machine shop, jobbing & repair

(G-18908)
STOPPA SIGNS & ENGRAVING LLC
3540 Raven Ave Sw (49509-3430)
PHONE 616 532-0230
Niel Stoppa, *Principal*
EMP: 4 **EST:** 2015
SALES (est): 169.9K **Privately Held**
SIC: 2759 Commercial printing

(G-18909)
SUCCESS BY DESIGN INC
3741 Linden Ave Se (49548-3474)
PHONE 800 327-0057
Steve Landheer, *President*
Matt Landheer, *Chief Mktg Ofcr*
Bill Rutherford, *Mktg Dir*
Amy Cole, *Graphic Designe*
EMP: 14 **EST:** 1984
SQ FT: 21,000
SALES (est): 2.5MM **Privately Held**
WEB: www.successbydesign.com
SIC: 2732 Book printing

(G-18910)
SWEETWATER BREW LLC
1760 44th St Sw (49519-6441)
PHONE 616 805-5077
EMP: 4 **EST:** 2016
SALES (est): 83K **Privately Held**
SIC: 2082 Malt beverages

(G-18911)
TORQSTORM SUPERCHARGERS
2909 Buchanan Ave Sw (49548-1027)
PHONE 616 706-5580
EMP: 4 **EST:** 2019

SALES (est): 102.8K **Privately Held**
WEB: www.torqstorm.com
SIC: 3714 Motor vehicle parts & accessories

(G-18912)
TOUCHSTONE SYSTEMS & SVCS INC
1817 Porter St Sw (49519-1765)
PHONE 616 532-0060
Jayma Kamerling, *President*
EMP: 8 **EST:** 1993
SQ FT: 6,500
SALES (est): 550.2K **Privately Held**
WEB: www.touchstone-testing.com
SIC: 8748 3679 3676 Testing services; electronic circuits; electronic loads & power supplies; electronic crystals; electronic switches; electronic resistors

(G-18913)
TRANE INC
5805 Weller Ct Sw Ste C (49509-9602)
PHONE 616 222-3750
Mark Switzer, *Branch Mgr*
EMP: 4 **Privately Held**
WEB: www.trane.com
SIC: 3585 Refrigeration & heating equipment
HQ: Trane Inc.
1 Centennial Ave Ste 101
Piscataway NJ 08854
732 652-7100

(G-18914)
TRIANGLE WINDOW FASHIONS INC
2625 Buchanan Ave Sw A (49548-1056)
PHONE 616 538-9676
Carol Limber, *President*
Mark Weih, *Vice Pres*
Jennifer Barnes, *Sales Staff*
Savanna Weih, *Manager*
EMP: 20 **EST:** 1969
SQ FT: 7,200
SALES (est): 3.4MM **Privately Held**
WEB: www.trianglewindowfashions.com
SIC: 2391 2591 5023 Draperies, plastic & textile: from purchased materials; blinds vertical; window shades; window furnishings

(G-18915)
ULTRA-TECH PRINTING CO
5851 Crossrds Cmmrce Pkwy (49519)
PHONE 616 249-0500
Thomas Gunn, *President*
Justin Noordeloos, *General Mgr*
Charles Piette, *VP Opers*
EMP: 16 **EST:** 1994
SQ FT: 25,000
SALES (est): 2.4MM **Privately Held**
WEB: www.utprinting.com
SIC: 2752 2759 Commercial printing, offset; commercial printing

(G-18916)
UNDERCAR PRODUCTS GROUP INC
4247 Eastern Ave Se (49508-3400)
PHONE 616 719-4571
Mike Schmidt, *President*
James Augustine, *Treasurer*
▲ **EMP:** 450 **EST:** 1992
SQ FT: 440,000
SALES (est): 91.2MM **Publicly Held**
WEB: www.abctechnologies.com
SIC: 3089 Injection molding of plastics
HQ: Abc Group Holdings Inc.
24133 Northwestern Hwy
Southfield MI 48075
248 352-3706

(G-18917)
VIKING SPAS INC
Also Called: Destiny River
2725 Prairie St Sw (49519-2458)
PHONE 616 248-7800
Tom Veneklase, *President*
Paul Kantor, *Exec VP*
John Gallagher, *Vice Pres*
Cary Glonek, *Vice Pres*
Matt Losey, *Purchasing*
▼ **EMP:** 12 **EST:** 1998
SQ FT: 30,000

SALES (est): 2.6MM **Privately Held**
WEB: www.vikingspas.com
SIC: 3999 Hot tubs

(G-18918)
VINYL SPECTRUM
4727 Clyde Park Ave Sw # 6 (49509-5162)
PHONE 616 591-3410
EMP: 10 **EST:** 2016
SALES (est): 242.2K **Privately Held**
WEB: www.thevinylspectrum.com
SIC: 2759 Commercial printing

Yale
St. Clair County

(G-18919)
MARGATE INDUSTRIES INC
129 N Main St (48097-2840)
PHONE 810 387-4300
William H Hopton, *President*
David A Widlak, *Vice Pres*
EMP: 4 **EST:** 1984
SQ FT: 70,000
SALES (est): 361.7K **Privately Held**
SIC: 3471 Finishing, metals or formed products

(G-18920)
TARTAN INDUSTRIES INC
2 1st St (48097-2800)
PHONE 810 387-4255
Dennis Hughes, *President*
Tim Hughes, *Manager*
EMP: 8 **EST:** 1993
SALES (est): 550K **Privately Held**
WEB: www.tartanindustries.com
SIC: 3441 3544 Fabricated structural metal; special dies, tools, jigs & fixtures

(G-18921)
YALE EXPOSITOR
21 S Main St (48097-3317)
P.O. Box 158 (48097-0158)
PHONE 810 387-2300
Arthur Brown, *Owner*
Bonnie Brown, *Co-Owner*
EMP: 5 **EST:** 1874
SQ FT: 1,320
SALES (est): 256.6K **Privately Held**
WEB: www.yalechamber.com
SIC: 2711 2752 Newspapers, publishing & printing; commercial printing, lithographic

Ypsilanti
Washtenaw County

(G-18922)
A NATURALLY EMPOWERED LF ANEL
6276 Aspen Way (48197-1038)
PHONE 734 572-8857
Dante Watson, *Principal*
EMP: 5 **EST:** 2013
SALES (est): 105.4K **Privately Held**
WEB: www.anelproducts.com
SIC: 2844 Toilet preparations

(G-18923)
ADVANCING BUS SOLUTIONS LLC
Also Called: Iron Pot Soups
235 Spencer Ln Ste B (48198-4247)
PHONE 734 905-7455
Kijuana Butler, *Mng Member*
EMP: 5 **EST:** 2019
SALES (est): 62.3K **Privately Held**
SIC: 2032 Soups & broths: canned, jarred, etc.

(G-18924)
AMERICAN BROACH & MACHINE CO
Also Called: American Gear Tools
575 S Mansfield St (48197-5157)
PHONE 734 961-0300
Xingyuan Long, *Ch of Bd*
Mike Castro, *President*
Mike Casto, *President*
Feng Mao, *Principal*
Sha Tian, *Principal*

◆ **EMP:** 46 **EST:** 1919
SQ FT: 75,000
SALES (est): 10.2MM **Privately Held**
WEB: www.americanbroach.com
SIC: 3541 3545 Broaching machines; tools & accessories for machine tools

(G-18925)
AUNT MILLIES BAKERIES INC (HQ)
5331 W Michigan Ave (48197-4900)
PHONE 734 528-1475
Tom Miskowski, *Manager*
EMP: 27 **EST:** 1985
SALES (est): 5.9MM
SALES (corp-wide): 457.7MM **Privately Held**
WEB: www.auntmillies.com
SIC: 2051 4225 4215 Bread, all types (white, wheat, rye, etc): fresh or frozen; general warehousing & storage; courier services, except by air
PA: Perfection Bakeries, Inc.
350 Pearl St
Fort Wayne IN 46802
260 424-8245

(G-18926)
BOSAL INDUSTRIES-GEORGIA INC
Bosal United States Ypsilanti
1476 Seaver Way Bldg C (48197-8300)
PHONE 734 547-7038
Bruce Wagar, *Opers Mgr*
EMP: 13
SALES (corp-wide): 514.6MM **Privately Held**
SIC: 3714 Exhaust systems & parts, motor vehicle
HQ: Bosal Industries-Georgia, Inc.
1476 Seaver Way Bldg A
Ypsilanti MI 48197

(G-18927)
BOSAL INDUSTRIES-GEORGIA INC
Bosal International North Amer
1476 Seaver Way Bldg B (48197-8300)
P.O. Box 230, Lavonia GA (30553-0230)
PHONE 734 547-7023
Phillip Koehler, *Controller*
Buddy Monroe, *Supervisor*
Dawn Brogdon, *Technology*
Todd Payne, *Director*
EMP: 50
SALES (corp-wide): 514.6MM **Privately Held**
SIC: 3714 Exhaust systems & parts, motor vehicle
HQ: Bosal Industries-Georgia, Inc.
1476 Seaver Way Bldg A
Ypsilanti MI 48197

(G-18928)
BOSAL INDUSTRIES-GEORGIA INC (HQ)
Also Called: Bosal International North Amer
1476 Seaver Way Bldg A (48197-8300)
PHONE 734 547-7022
Rene De Wit, *President*
Steve Steeden, *President*
Philip De Bruyn, *Regional Mgr*
Steve Molnar, *Purchasing*
Chris Masters, *Engineer*
◆ **EMP:** 50 **EST:** 1994
SQ FT: 100,000
SALES (est): 22MM
SALES (corp-wide): 514.6MM **Privately Held**
WEB: www.bosal.com
SIC: 3714 Exhaust systems & parts, motor vehicle
PA: Bosal Nederland B.V.
Kamerlingh Onnesweg 5
Vianen Ut 4131
347 362-911

(G-18929)
BREASCO LLC
3840 Carpenter Rd (48197-9635)
PHONE 734 961-9020
Carol Worthing, *Partner*
Carole Worthing,
EMP: 6 **EST:** 1997

Ypsilanti - Washtenaw County (G-18930) GEOGRAPHIC SECTION

SALES (est): 495.2K **Privately Held**
WEB: www.breasco.com
SIC: 3315 Steel wire & related products

(G-18930)
BURRELL TRI-COUNTY VAULTS INC
1106 E Michigan Ave (48198-5881)
P.O. Box 981112 (48198-1112)
PHONE.................................734 483-2024
Douglas Stark, *President*
Leonard Stark, *Admin Sec*
EMP: 15 EST: 1982
SQ FT: 13,000
SALES (est): 674.6K **Privately Held**
SIC: 3272 5087 5211 Burial vaults, concrete or precast terrazzo; caskets; concrete & cinder block

(G-18931)
CAFLOR INDUSTRIES LLC
2375 Parkwood (48198-7830)
PHONE.................................734 604-1168
Cesar A Flores, *Mng Member*
EMP: 9 EST: 2002
SQ FT: 10,000 **Privately Held**
WEB: www.caflor.net
SIC: 3999 Atomizers, toiletry

(G-18932)
CANTON EMBROIDERY LLC
3901 Bestech Rd Ste 800 (48197-9815)
PHONE.................................734 216-3374
EMP: 5 EST: 2016
SALES (est): 113.6K **Privately Held**
WEB: www.mswprint.com
SIC: 2752 Commercial printing, offset

(G-18933)
COOPER ROLLAND
5546 Grayfield Cir (48197-8434)
PHONE.................................734 482-8705
Rolland Cooper, *Administration*
EMP: 6 EST: 2018
SALES (est): 73.4K **Privately Held**
SIC: 3469 Metal stampings

(G-18934)
CORNER BREWERY LLC
720 Norris St (48198-2825)
PHONE.................................734 480-2739
Renee Greff, *President*
Kari Whitman, *Manager*
EMP: 22 EST: 2006
SALES (est): 3.2MM **Privately Held**
WEB: www.arborbrewing.com
SIC: 2082 5812 Beer (alcoholic beverage); American restaurant; restaurant, family: independent

(G-18935)
CROWN INDUSTRIAL SERVICES INC (PA)
Also Called: Crown Tumbling
2480 Airport Dr (48198-8038)
P.O. Box 970197 (48198-0026)
PHONE.................................734 483-7270
Kimberly Bullock, *President*
Jeffery Bullock, *Corp Secy*
Mark Beck, *Vice Pres*
Aaron Engel, *QC Mgr*
Jeffery Bullock, *Treasurer*
EMP: 66 EST: 1994
SQ FT: 150,000
SALES (est): 10.4MM **Privately Held**
WEB: www.crownindservices.com
SIC: 3471 Tumbling (cleaning & polishing) of machine parts

(G-18936)
CROWN INDUSTRIAL SERVICES INC
924 Minion St (48198-5811)
PHONE.................................734 483-7270
EMP: 7
SALES (corp-wide): 10.4MM **Privately Held**
WEB: www.crownindservices.com
SIC: 3471 Tumbling (cleaning & polishing) of machine parts
PA: Crown Industrial Services Inc
2480 Airport Dr
Ypsilanti MI 48198
734 483-7270

(G-18937)
CTMF INC
924 Minion St (48198-5811)
P.O. Box 970197 (48197-0026)
PHONE.................................734 482-3086
Jeffery Bullock, *President*
Kimberly Bullock, *Corp Secy*
EMP: 10 EST: 2004
SALES (est): 469.2K **Privately Held**
SIC: 3559 Metal finishing equipment for plating, etc.

(G-18938)
CURRY FRESH INC
2874 Washtenaw Rd (48197-1507)
PHONE.................................734 262-0560
Priya Dass, *Exec Dir*
Mamta Tiwari,
EMP: 4 EST: 2020
SQ FT: 4,000
SALES (est): 179K **Privately Held**
WEB: www.disruptiveeating.com
SIC: 2099 Sauces: gravy, dressing & dip mixes

(G-18939)
DIGITALLY ASSURED
1320 Warner St (48197-4658)
PHONE.................................734 730-8800
Brian Aeschliman, *Owner*
EMP: 5 EST: 2010
SALES (est): 181.8K **Privately Held**
SIC: 2759 Laser printing

(G-18940)
DOAN CONSTRUCTION CO (PA)
Also Called: Doan Companies
3670 Carpenter Rd (48197-9614)
PHONE.................................734 971-4678
Dennis Doan, *CEO*
Matt Doan, *President*
Jim McInnis, *General Mgr*
Kevin Hoatlin, *CFO*
Laurie Russell, *Administration*
EMP: 19 EST: 1970
SQ FT: 3,000
SALES (est): 24.8MM **Privately Held**
WEB: www.doancompanies.com
SIC: 8741 3273 Construction management; ready-mixed concrete

(G-18941)
ELECTRONICS FOR IMAGING INC
1260 James L Hart Pkwy (48197-7194)
PHONE.................................734 641-3062
Brad Scott, *Branch Mgr*
EMP: 5
SALES (corp-wide): 1B **Privately Held**
WEB: www.efi.com
SIC: 3577 Printers & plotters
HQ: Electronics For Imaging, Inc.
6453 Kaiser Dr
Fremont CA 94555

(G-18942)
EMBRACE PREMIUM VODKA LLC
515 Ferris St (48197-5303)
PHONE.................................616 617-5602
Carlos Robinson, *President*
EMP: 1
SALES (est): 20MM **Privately Held**
SIC: 2085 7389 Vodka (alcoholic beverage);

(G-18943)
ENGINEERED PLASTIC PRODUCTS (PA)
Also Called: Engineered Plastic Pdts Mfg
699 James L Hart Pkwy (48197-9791)
PHONE.................................734 439-0310
Gerald D Edwards, *CEO*
Norman Falk, *QC Dir*
Leroy Williams, *Controller*
Theresa Dubay, *Human Resources*
Michelle Jones, *IT/INT Sup*
EMP: 150 EST: 1987
SQ FT: 85,000
SALES (est): 15.6MM **Privately Held**
WEB: www.eppmfg.com
SIC: 3089 Injection molded finished plastic products

(G-18944)
ENSURE TECHNOLOGIES INC
135 S Prospect St Ste 100 (48198-7914)
PHONE.................................734 547-1600
John Dunlop, *President*
Mary Shindell, *Partner*
Barton Neulieb, *Technical Staff*
▲ EMP: 19 EST: 1997
SQ FT: 5,200
SALES (est): 1.1MM **Privately Held**
WEB: www.ensuretech.com
SIC: 3577 7382 Computer peripheral equipment; security systems services

(G-18945)
FINISHING SERVICES INC
877 Ann St (48197-2474)
PHONE.................................734 484-1700
Mitchell Marsh, *President*
James Nelson, *Corp Secy*
Matthew T Marsh, *Vice Pres*
▲ EMP: 73 EST: 1975
SQ FT: 23,000
SALES (est): 2.4MM
SALES (corp-wide): 11.7MM **Privately Held**
WEB: www.finishingservices.com
SIC: 3471 3479 Electroplating of metals or formed products; coating of metals & formed products
PA: Marsh Plating Corporation
103 N Grove St
Ypsilanti MI 48198
734 483-5767

(G-18946)
FOCUS CLEANING LLC
609 Calder Ave (48198-8031)
PHONE.................................734 883-9560
Vernard Pattersonvernard,
EMP: 4 EST: 2019
SALES (est): 175.1K **Privately Held**
SIC: 3589 Commercial cleaning equipment

(G-18947)
FORD MOTOR COMPANY
10300 Textile Rd (48197-9200)
PHONE.................................734 484-8626
Mark Willis, *Manager*
William Treharne, *Supervisor*
EMP: 2000
SALES (corp-wide): 127.1B **Publicly Held**
WEB: www.ford.com
SIC: 5511 3694 3677 3625 Automobiles, new & used; engine electrical equipment; electronic coils, transformers & other inductors; relays & industrial controls; motors & generators; pumps & pumping equipment
PA: Ford Motor Company
1 American Rd
Dearborn MI 48126
313 322-3000

(G-18948)
FRIENDS OF LIZ BRATER
8205 Starling Ct (48197-6009)
PHONE.................................734 547-1953
Bob June, *Principal*
EMP: 4 EST: 2016
SALES (est): 76.3K **Privately Held**
WEB: www.brater2002.com
SIC: 3677 Electronic coils, transformers & other inductors

(G-18949)
GEAR GEAR INC
129 Bell St (48197-5519)
PHONE.................................517 861-7757
EMP: 6 EST: 2018
SALES (est): 225.3K **Privately Held**
WEB: www.geargearinc.com
SIC: 3566 Speed changers, drives & gears

(G-18950)
GENERAL DYNMICS MSSION SYSTEMS
1200 Joe Hall Dr (48197-7523)
P.O. Box B (48197)
PHONE.................................734 480-5000
Karen Melancon, *President*
Christopher Marzilli, *President*
Sean Murphy, *Engineer*
Bill Wolters, *Manager*
Ben Van Tuyl, *Director*
EMP: 5
SALES (corp-wide): 37.9B **Publicly Held**
WEB: www.gdmissionsystems.com
SIC: 3571 8731 Electronic computers; commercial physical research
HQ: General Dynamics Mission Systems, Inc.
12450 Fair Lakes Cir
Fairfax VA 22033
877 449-0600

(G-18951)
GENERAL DYNMICS MSSION SYSTEMS
Also Called: General Dynmics Advnced Info S
1200 Joe Hall Dr (48197-7523)
PHONE.................................734 480-5000
Ben Tuyl, *Director*
Barbara Butchko, *Admin Asst*
EMP: 5
SALES (corp-wide): 37.9B **Publicly Held**
WEB: www.gdmissionsystems.com
SIC: 3571 8731 Electronic computers; commercial physical research
HQ: General Dynamics Mission Systems, Inc.
12450 Fair Lakes Cir
Fairfax VA 22033
877 449-0600

(G-18952)
HURON ADVERTISING COMPANY INC
Also Called: Huron Sign Co
663 S Mansfield St (48197-5156)
P.O. Box 980423 (48198-0423)
PHONE.................................734 483-2000
William J Short III, *President*
Barbara Hagadorn, *Treasurer*
Tom Short, *Supervisor*
Scott Wilkie, *Art Dir*
Kevin Short, *Executive*
EMP: 21 EST: 1966
SQ FT: 24,000
SALES (est): 2.6MM **Privately Held**
WEB: www.johnsonsign.com
SIC: 1799 3993 Sign installation & maintenance; electric signs

(G-18953)
IHA VSCLAR ENDVSCLAR SPCALISTS
5325 Elliott Dr Ste 104 (48197-8633)
PHONE.................................734 712-8150
Mark Lepage MD, *CEO*
EMP: 8 EST: 2014
SALES (est): 386.8K **Privately Held**
SIC: 3845 8011 Endoscopic equipment, electromedical; cardiologist & cardio-vascular specialist

(G-18954)
IMAGILLATION INC
Also Called: Hikking Production Embroidery
133 W Michigan Ave Ste 2 (48197-5550)
PHONE.................................734 481-0140
David W Heikkinen, *President*
Linda Hikking, *Corp Secy*
EMP: 4 EST: 2001
SALES (est): 286.7K **Privately Held**
WEB: www.menofcone.com
SIC: 3999 Music boxes

(G-18955)
INDUS TECHNOLOGIES INC
1922 Savannah Ln (48198-3676)
PHONE.................................630 915-8034
Arhum Arshad, *CEO*
EMP: 10 EST: 2020
SALES (est): 357.7K **Privately Held**
SIC: 2499 Food handling & processing products, wood

(G-18956)
INNOVATIVE DRONE SERVICES LLC
875 S Grove St (48198-6372)
PHONE.................................313 333-6956
EMP: 4 EST: 2016
SALES (est): 84.5K **Privately Held**
SIC: 3728 Aircraft parts & equipment

Ypsilanti - Washtenaw County (G-18986)

(G-18957)
INTEGRATED SENSING SYSTEMS INC (PA)
Also Called: Issys
391 Airport Industrial Dr (48198-7812)
PHONE.................................734 547-9896
Nader Najafi, *President*
Sonbol Massoud-Ansari, *Vice Pres*
Tim Hubbard, *Opers Staff*
Tina Bey, *Sales Mgr*
Jay Patel, *Director*
EMP: 29 **EST:** 1995
SQ FT: 16,000
SALES (est): 4.9MM **Privately Held**
WEB: www.mems-iss.com
SIC: 3829 Measuring & controlling devices

(G-18958)
INTERCLEAN EQUIPMENT LLC (PA)
709 James L Hart Pkwy (48197-9791)
PHONE.................................734 961-3300
Dan Bickersteth, *CEO*
Greg Harvey, *Vice Pres*
Scott Hessling, *Purch Mgr*
Troy Adams, *Controller*
Les Gale, *Sales Staff*
◆ **EMP:** 34 **EST:** 1984
SQ FT: 20,000
SALES (est): 10MM **Privately Held**
WEB: www.interclean.com
SIC: 3589 7542 Car washing machinery; truck wash

(G-18959)
JOPLINS SALSA
1565 Harvest Ln (48198-3316)
PHONE.................................419 787-8195
Sedric Joplin, *Principal*
EMP: 4 **EST:** 2015
SALES (est): 73.8K **Privately Held**
SIC: 2099 Dips, except cheese & sour cream based

(G-18960)
K AND S 39 CORPORATION
8933 Ringneck Dr (48197-1059)
PHONE.................................734 883-3868
EMP: 4 **EST:** 2019
SALES (est): 129.2K **Privately Held**
SIC: 3732 Boat building & repairing

(G-18961)
LADDER CAROLINA COMPANY INC
12 E Forest Ave (48198-2803)
P.O. Box 981307 (48198-1307)
PHONE.................................734 482-5946
Robert F Nissly, *President*
David Nissly, *Treasurer*
EMP: 16 **EST:** 1953
SQ FT: 75,000
SALES (est): 324.9K **Privately Held**
SIC: 2499 Ladders, wood

(G-18962)
LE FORGES PIPE & FAB INC
64 Wiard Rd (48198-4233)
PHONE.................................734 482-2100
Eric Le Forge, *President*
EMP: 4 **EST:** 1962
SQ FT: 8,000
SALES (est): 262.2K **Privately Held**
WEB: www.leforgepipe.com
SIC: 7692 Welding repair

(G-18963)
LIQUIDGOLDCONCEPT INC
3858 Bestech Rd Ste C (48197-3294)
PHONE.................................734 926-9197
Anna Sadovnikova, *CEO*
Jeffrey Plott, *CTO*
EMP: 6 **EST:** 2014
SALES (est): 503.5K **Privately Held**
WEB: www.liquidgoldconcept.com
SIC: 8099 5047 3999 Childbirth preparation clinic; medical equipment & supplies; education aids, devices & supplies

(G-18964)
MAGNUM FABRICATING
1754 E Michigan Ave (48198-6008)
PHONE.................................734 484-5800
EMP: 4
SALES (est): 325.7K **Privately Held**
WEB: www.magnumfabricating.com
SIC: 3499 3441 Fabricated metal products; fabricated structural metal

(G-18965)
MARSH PLATING CORPORATION (PA)
103 N Grove St (48198-2906)
PHONE.................................734 483-5767
David Marsh, *Principal*
David Willox, *Vice Pres*
Vikas Joshi, *Research*
Sue Henderson, *Controller*
Jeff Ramsey, *Technical Staff*
▲ **EMP:** 80 **EST:** 1959
SQ FT: 80,000
SALES (est): 11.7MM **Privately Held**
WEB: www.marshplating.com
SIC: 3471 3511 3441 Electroplating of metals or formed products; hydraulic turbine generator set units, complete; fabricated structural metal

(G-18966)
MASTER MIX COMPANY
Also Called: Mastermix
612 S Mansfield St (48198-5167)
PHONE.................................734 487-7870
Frederick McCants, *President*
EMP: 7 **EST:** 1990
SALES (est): 289.9K **Privately Held**
WEB: www.mastermixco.com
SIC: 3479 2891 Coating, rust preventive; adhesives

(G-18967)
MICHIGAN LADDER COMPANY LLC
12 E Forest Ave (48198-2803)
P.O. Box 981307 (48198-1307)
PHONE.................................734 482-5946
▲ **EMP:** 15
SQ FT: 75,000
SALES (est): 2.6MM **Privately Held**
WEB: www.michiganladder.com
SIC: 2499 5082 Wood Products, Nec, Nsk

(G-18968)
MISHIGAMA BREWING COMPANY
124 Pearl St (48197-2663)
PHONE.................................734 547-5840
William Anhut, *Principal*
EMP: 6 **EST:** 2015
SALES (est): 174K **Privately Held**
WEB: www.ypsialehouse.com
SIC: 5921 2082 Beer (packaged); malt beverages

(G-18969)
MSW PRINT AND IMAGING
3901 Bestech Rd (48197-9815)
PHONE.................................734 544-1626
Scott Katke, *Owner*
EMP: 11 **EST:** 2009
SALES (est): 970.3K **Privately Held**
WEB: www.mswprint.com
SIC: 2752 Commercial printing, offset

(G-18970)
PIERIAN PRESS INC
3196 Maple Dr (48197-3788)
PHONE.................................734 434-4074
Carroll Edward Wall, *President*
Edward Prezbiemda, *Vice Pres*
EMP: 4 **EST:** 1968
SQ FT: 8,000
SALES (est): 273K **Privately Held**
WEB: www.pierianpress.com
SIC: 2731 2741 2721 Books: publishing only; miscellaneous publishing; periodicals

(G-18971)
PRINTING PLUS INC
Also Called: Q P S Printing
989 James L Hart Pkwy (48197-9791)
PHONE.................................734 482-1680
Kim Craddick, *President*
EMP: 5 **EST:** 1985
SQ FT: 1,500
SALES (est): 441.5K **Privately Held**
WEB: www.printingplusus.com
SIC: 2752 2789 Commercial printing, offset; bookbinding & related work

(G-18972)
QC AMERICAN LLC
575 S Mansfield St (48197-5157)
PHONE.................................734 961-0300
Fran Mao, *Managing Dir*
Aaron Huyan, *Engineer*
Selene Zhong, *CFO*
▲ **EMP:** 4 **EST:** 2007
SALES (corp-wide): 622.1MM **Privately Held**
WEB: www.qcamerican.com
SIC: 3545 Cutting tools for machine tools
PA: Qinchuan Machine Tool & Tool Group Share Co.,Ltd.
No.22, Jiangtan Road, Weibin District
Baoji 72100
917 367-0665

(G-18973)
QUANTUM COMPLIANCE SYSTEMS
2111 Golfside Rd Ste B (48197-1146)
PHONE.................................734 930-0009
Patricia L Brooks, *President*
EMP: 13 **EST:** 1986
SQ FT: 12,000
SALES (est): 364.1K **Privately Held**
WEB: www.usequantum.com
SIC: 7371 7372 Computer software development; prepackaged software

(G-18974)
RISE BEYOND LLC
7825 Newbury Dr (48197-3195)
PHONE.................................734 203-0644
Kevin B Thomas,
EMP: 4 **EST:** 2017
SALES (est): 39.6K **Privately Held**
WEB: www.risebeyond.org
SIC: 3999 Manufacturing industries

(G-18975)
ROWERDINK INC
252 Airport Industrial Dr (48198-6061)
PHONE.................................734 487-1911
EMP: 9
SALES (corp-wide): 28.4MM **Privately Held**
WEB: www.rowerdink.com
SIC: 5013 5063 3691 Automotive supplies & parts; circuit breakers; storage batteries
PA: Rowerdink, Inc.
211 Fuller Ave Ne
Grand Rapids MI 49503
616 459-3274

(G-18976)
SENSATNAL SMLLS FROM MESHA LLC ✪
570 Kansas Ave (48198-6131)
PHONE.................................734 905-1058
Tamesha Smith,
EMP: 6 **EST:** 2021
SALES (est): 40K **Privately Held**
SIC: 3999 Candles

(G-18977)
SENSITILE SYSTEMS LLC
1735 Holmes Rd (48197-4155)
PHONE.................................313 872-6314
Vanika Lath, *CFO*
Abhinand Lath, *Mng Member*
◆ **EMP:** 30 **EST:** 2004
SQ FT: 36,000
SALES (est): 5.2MM **Privately Held**
WEB: www.sensitile.com
SIC: 2421 Building & structural materials, wood

(G-18978)
STANDARD PRINTING
120 E Cross St (48198-2878)
PHONE.................................734 483-0339
John Harrington,
EMP: 6 **EST:** 1946
SQ FT: 2,000
SALES (est): 801.5K **Privately Held**
WEB: www.ypsistandard.com
SIC: 2752 2759 Commercial printing, offset; letterpress printing

(G-18979)
STARWOOD HOMES
1998 White Oak Ln (48198-9549)
PHONE.................................734 340-2326
Linda Damitz, *Manager*
EMP: 6 **EST:** 2018
SALES (est): 110.1K **Privately Held**
WEB: www.suncommunities.com
SIC: 2452 Prefabricated wood buildings

(G-18980)
SUPERIOR TEXT LLC
151 Airport Industrial Dr (48198-7811)
PHONE.................................866 482-8762
Robert Voorheis, *Purchasing*
Joseph Lewandowski, *Controller*
Luke Oskvarek, *Accountant*
Mike Bartholomay, *Sales Mgr*
Diane Goldsmith, *Sales Mgr*
EMP: 15 **EST:** 2005
SALES (est): 6.8MM **Privately Held**
WEB: www.superiortext.com
SIC: 5192 2732 Books; textbooks: printing & binding, not publishing

(G-18981)
TRITON GLOBAL SOURCES INC
3914 Bestech Rd Ste C (48197-2262)
P.O. Box 130603, Ann Arbor (48113-0603)
PHONE.................................734 668-7107
Eric He, *Vice Pres*
Wen Huang, *CFO*
▲ **EMP:** 4 **EST:** 2000
SALES (est): 452.6K **Privately Held**
WEB: www.tritonsources.com
SIC: 3363 3369 3321 3324 Aluminum die-castings; zinc & zinc-base alloy castings, except die-castings; ductile iron castings; commercial investment castings, ferrous; marine hardware; stampings, metal

(G-18982)
TROY SYNCHRO SHARKETTES
1328 Rue Willette Blvd (48198-7554)
PHONE.................................734 395-8899
Alice Seipelt, *Principal*
EMP: 5 **EST:** 2016
SALES (est): 88.3K **Privately Held**
WEB: www.troysynchrosharkettes.com
SIC: 3621 Synchros

(G-18983)
VG KIDS
815 W Michigan Ave (48197-5201)
PHONE.................................734 480-0667
EMP: 6 **EST:** 2019
SALES (est): 112.7K **Privately Held**
WEB: www.vgkids.com
SIC: 2759 Screen printing

(G-18984)
VGKIDS INC
884 Railroad St Ste C (48197-3503)
PHONE.................................734 485-5128
James Marks, *Owner*
Aaron Bobzien, *Manager*
EMP: 16 **EST:** 1998
SQ FT: 6,000
SALES (est): 1MM **Privately Held**
WEB: www.vgkids.com
SIC: 2759 Screen printing

(G-18985)
VIEW PUBLICATION CO
5892 New Meadow Dr (48197-7175)
P.O. Box 87423, Canton (48187-0423)
PHONE.................................734 461-1579
EMP: 4 **EST:** 2006
SALES (est): 84.5K **Privately Held**
SIC: 2741 Miscellaneous publishing

(G-18986)
X-RAY AND SPECIALTY INSTRS INC
Also Called: Xsi
1980 E Michigan Ave (48198-6010)
PHONE.................................734 485-6300
Daniel Gorzen, *President*
Lisa Teets, *Vice Pres*
EMP: 4 **EST:** 1992
SQ FT: 2,500 **Privately Held**
WEB: www.web.archive.org
SIC: 3826 Analytical instruments

Ypsilanti - Washtenaw County (G-18987) GEOGRAPHIC SECTION

(G-18987)
YPSINEWSCOM
118 S Washington St (48197-5427)
PHONE.................................734 487-8109
EMP: 8 EST: 2017
SALES (est): 101.8K Privately Held
SIC: 2711 Newspapers, publishing & printing

Zeeland
Ottawa County

(G-18988)
ACTIVE TOOLING LLC
6017 Chicago Dr (49464-9515)
PHONE.................................616 875-8111
Tim Van Dam, *Vice Pres*
Gary Lubbers, *Mng Member*
EMP: 10 EST: 2011
SALES (est): 1.5MM Privately Held
WEB: www.activetooling.com
SIC: 3545 Tool holders

(G-18989)
AJ PALLETS
9471 Henry Ct (49464-8944)
PHONE.................................616 875-8900
Jasmin Ademovic, *Principal*
EMP: 13 EST: 2018
SALES (est): 1.6MM Privately Held
SIC: 2448 Pallets, wood

(G-18990)
ALLIED ENGINEERING INC
3424 88th Ave Ste 6 (49464-8534)
PHONE.................................616 748-7990
Michael Johnson, *President*
Kurt Vugteveen, *Vice Pres*
EMP: 4 EST: 2000
SQ FT: 2,400
SALES (est): 600K Privately Held
WEB: www.aei-alliedeng.com
SIC: 3465 Automotive stampings

(G-18991)
ALLROUT INC
3382 Production Ct (49464-8528)
PHONE.................................616 748-7696
Jeff Robinson, *President*
Mike Viletstre, *Vice Pres*
EMP: 6 EST: 2003
SALES (est): 900K Privately Held
WEB: www.allrout.com
SIC: 3823 Computer interface equipment for industrial process control

(G-18992)
ARTEX LABEL & GRAPHICS INC
740 Case Karsten Dr (49464-9693)
P.O. Box 331 (49464-0331)
PHONE.................................616 748-9655
Terry Gruppen, *President*
Kim Williams, *Purch Agent*
Bob Schippers, *Human Res Mgr*
Jan Wiersma, *Accounts Exec*
Brandi Bredeway, *Sales Staff*
EMP: 30 EST: 1999
SQ FT: 22,000
SALES (est): 6.6MM Privately Held
WEB: www.artexlabel.com
SIC: 2759 Labels & seals: printing

(G-18993)
ARTISAN MEDICAL DISPLAYS LLC
Also Called: Medical ACC & Reseach Co
3340 84th Ave (49464-9757)
PHONE.................................616 748-8950
Kris Wickens, *Business Mgr*
Jordan Vander Kolk, *Mng Member*
▼ EMP: 35 EST: 1988
SALES (est): 3.4MM Privately Held
WEB: www.artisanmedicaldisplays.com
SIC: 3841 Surgical & medical instruments

(G-18994)
ASTRO WOOD STAKE INC
6017 Chicago Dr (49464-9515)
PHONE.................................616 875-8118
Gary Lubbers, *President*
Troy Karsemeyer, *Marketing Staff*
Carol Karsemeyer, *Manager*
EMP: 8 EST: 1986

SQ FT: 30,000
SALES (est): 1.1MM Privately Held
WEB: www.astrowoodstake.com
SIC: 2499 Surveyors' stakes, wood

(G-18995)
BAUMANN TOOL & DIE
232 E Roosevelt Ave (49464-1240)
PHONE.................................616 772-6768
David Baumann, *Partner*
Lester Baumann, *Partner*
Ron Laduke, *Plant Mgr*
Chad Levalley, *Plant Mgr*
Dan Tidball, *Program Mgr*
EMP: 6 EST: 1980
SQ FT: 13,500
SALES (est): 800.3K Privately Held
WEB: www.baumanntd.com
SIC: 3544 Special dies & tools

(G-18996)
BENNETT WOOD SPECIALTIES INC
Also Called: Carlton, Robert Hanger Company
109 N Carlton St (49464-1303)
P.O. Box 279 (49464-0279)
PHONE.................................616 772-6683
Joe Bennett, *President*
Norraine Bennett, *Admin Sec*
▲ EMP: 16 EST: 1906
SQ FT: 25,000
SALES (est): 506.9K Privately Held
WEB: www.robertcarltonhangers.com
SIC: 2441 2541 Cases, wood; wood partitions & fixtures

(G-18997)
BERRY GLOBAL INC
200 N Franklin St (49464-1075)
PHONE.................................616 772-4635
Steve McDonough, *President*
EMP: 5 Publicly Held
WEB: www.berryplastics.com
SIC: 3081 3089 Plastic film & sheet; bottle caps, molded plastic
HQ: Berry Global, Inc.
101 Oakley St
Evansville IN 47710

(G-18998)
BESSER COMPANY USA
Also Called: Besser Lithibar
201 W Washington Ave # 202 (49464-1085)
P.O. Box 2008, Holland (49422-2008)
PHONE.................................616 399-5215
Kevin Curtis, *President*
Kevin Krentz, *Engineer*
Larry Dutkiewicz, *Controller*
Sandra V Munster, *Office Mgr*
▲ EMP: 67 EST: 1929
SQ FT: 93,000
SALES (est): 12.2MM
SALES (corp-wide): 213.4MM Privately Held
WEB: www.besser.com
SIC: 3536 3537 Hoists; industrial trucks & tractors; pallet loaders & unloaders; palletizers & depalletizers
PA: Besser Company
801 Johnson St
Alpena MI 49707
989 354-4111

(G-18999)
BIOTEC INCORPORATED
652 E Main Ave (49464-1399)
PHONE.................................616 772-2733
Harold Tai, *CEO*
Charles De Pree, *President*
EMP: 60 EST: 1969
SQ FT: 20,000
SALES (est): 9.1MM Privately Held
SIC: 3843 2434 Cabinets, dental; dental tools; wood kitchen cabinets

(G-19000)
BLACK RIVER PALLET COMPANY
410 E Roosevelt Ave (49464-1342)
PHONE.................................616 772-6211
Larry Slagh, *President*
Bryan Slagh, *Vice Pres*
EMP: 21 EST: 1962
SQ FT: 16,000

SALES (est): 1.2MM Privately Held
WEB: www.blackriverpallet.com
SIC: 2448 2449 Pallets, wood; wood containers

(G-19001)
BLACK SWAMP PERCUSSION LLC
11114 James St (49464-9125)
PHONE.................................800 557-0988
Tim Church, *Vice Pres*
Jamel Taylor, *Vice Pres*
Kristi Warren, *Bookkeeper*
Kristina Warren, *Bookkeeper*
Nathan Coles, *Manager*
▲ EMP: 8 EST: 1994
SQ FT: 9,000
SALES (est): 775.6K Privately Held
WEB: www.blackswamp.com
SIC: 3931 5736 Guitars & parts, electric & nonelectric; musical instrument stores

(G-19002)
BREMER AUTHENTIC INGREDIENTS
420 100th Ave (49464-2061)
PHONE.................................616 772-9100
Dan Nagelkerke, *General Mgr*
Joan Broersma, *Bookkeeper*
Tim Richards, *Sales Executive*
EMP: 22 EST: 2015
SALES (est): 2.5MM Privately Held
WEB: www.bremeringredients.com
SIC: 2499 Bakers' equipment, wood

(G-19003)
CENTENNIAL COATINGS LLC
371 N Centennial St (49464-1311)
PHONE.................................616 748-9410
Brenda Diekema, *Mng Member*
Paul McVane,
EMP: 50 EST: 2003
SALES (est): 5.9MM Privately Held
WEB: www.centennialcoatings.com
SIC: 3479 Coating of metals & formed products

(G-19004)
CHARTER HOUSE HOLDINGS LLC
200 N Franklin St Ste B (49464-1075)
PHONE.................................616 399-6000
George Kinsella, *Production*
Chris Arens, *Manager*
Stephanie Huddleston, *Manager*
Bill Smit, *Manager*
Charles Reid,
◆ EMP: 186
SQ FT: 72,000
SALES (est): 33.7MM Privately Held
WEB: www.gotochi.com
SIC: 3999 Advertising display products

(G-19005)
CONCEPT TOOL & DIE INC
9371 Henry Ct (49464-9216)
PHONE.................................616 875-4600
Michael Cooper, *President*
Daniel Cooper, *Vice Pres*
EMP: 4 EST: 1988
SQ FT: 1,000
SALES (est): 340K Privately Held
SIC: 3544 Dies & die holders for metal cutting, forming, die casting

(G-19006)
CONTOUR TOOL & ENGINEERING INC
2425 104th Ave (49464-6800)
PHONE.................................616 772-6360
Timothy Rietsma, *President*
Mike Rietsma, *Vice Pres*
EMP: 8 EST: 2000
SQ FT: 12,000
SALES (est): 724.6K Privately Held
SIC: 3544 Special dies & tools

(G-19007)
CORLETT-TURNER CO
2500 104th Ave (49464-9824)
PHONE.................................616 772-9082
Jesse Massengill, *President*
Jessie Massengill, *Vice Pres*
Harry Armstrong, *Treasurer*
Carolyn Palmer, *Info Tech Mgr*

Roger Klynstra, *Admin Sec*
EMP: 90 EST: 1943
SQ FT: 58,000
SALES (est): 9.6MM Privately Held
WEB: www.garichards.com
SIC: 3451 Screw machine products

(G-19008)
CREATIVE PRINTING SOLUTIONS
201 W Washington Ave # 66 (49464-1085)
PHONE.................................616 931-1040
Lori Lynn Hibma, *Administration*
EMP: 4 EST: 2011
SALES (est): 189.7K Privately Held
SIC: 2752 Commercial printing, lithographic

(G-19009)
CROSSBROOK LLC
3255 Production Ct Unit B (49464-8581)
PHONE.................................616 772-5921
Ned Laughlin,
EMP: 9 EST: 2011
SALES (est): 381.4K Privately Held
SIC: 2099 5411 Salads, fresh or refrigerated; grocery stores

(G-19010)
CULTURED LOVE LLC
2752 Meadow Dr (49464-9025)
PHONE.................................703 362-5991
Jodie Krumpe, *Administration*
EMP: 8 EST: 2014
SALES (est): 251.8K Privately Held
WEB: www.shop.culturedlove.com
SIC: 2035 Sauerkraut, bulk

(G-19011)
CUSTOM ARCHITECTURAL PRODUCTS
430 100th Ave (49464-2061)
PHONE.................................616 748-1905
Dave Quist, *Manager*
EMP: 6 Privately Held
WEB: www.allwheelsrecovery.com
SIC: 3441 Fabricated structural metal
PA: Custom Architectural Products Inc
4155 Yorkshire Ct
Hudsonville MI 49426

(G-19012)
CUSTOM TOOLING SYSTEMS INC
3331 80th Ave (49464-9583)
PHONE.................................616 748-9880
John Bouwkamp, *President*
Sean Devoe, *Engineer*
Todd Kane, *Treasurer*
Kevin Bouwkamp, *Manager*
EMP: 60 EST: 1990
SQ FT: 50,000
SALES (est): 6.6MM Privately Held
WEB: www.ctooling.com
SIC: 3544 Special dies & tools

(G-19013)
D & D TOOL INC
218 E Harrison Ave (49464-1207)
PHONE.................................616 772-2416
Paul Dannenberg, *President*
Jill Dannenberg, *Vice Pres*
EMP: 6 EST: 1984
SQ FT: 3,750
SALES (est): 838.2K Privately Held
WEB: www.ddtoolinc.com
SIC: 3599 Machine shop, jobbing & repair

(G-19014)
DAVON MANUFACTURING
3625 80th Ave (49464-9565)
PHONE.................................616 745-8453
EMP: 5 EST: 2019
SALES (est): 336.4K Privately Held
WEB: www.davonmfg.com
SIC: 3999 Manufacturing industries

(G-19015)
DISTINCTIVE MFG GROUP LLC
Also Called: Distinctive Machining
759 Construction Ct Ste 2 (49464-8755)
PHONE.................................616 953-8999
Ray Blackburn, *Partner*
EMP: 14 EST: 2012

GEOGRAPHIC SECTION

Zeeland - Ottawa County (G-19041)

SALES (est): 1.9MM **Privately Held**
WEB: www.distinctivemfg.co
SIC: 3569 Liquid automation machinery & equipment

(G-19016)
DUN-RITE MACHINE CO
4526 Adams St (49464-9318)
PHONE..............................616 688-5266
Mike Zuverink, *Owner*
▲ EMP: 8 EST: 1984
SALES (est): 579.9K **Privately Held**
WEB: www.dunritemachine.net
SIC: 3599 Machine shop, jobbing & repair

(G-19017)
EAGLE DESIGN & TECHNOLOGY INC
55 E Roosevelt Ave (49464-1235)
PHONE..............................616 748-1022
Bruce Okkema, *President*
Mike Horan, *Sales Engr*
Mary Okkema, *Consultant*
Rick Huizenga, *Shareholder*
EMP: 29 EST: 1994
SQ FT: 22,000
SALES (est): 5.9MM **Privately Held**
WEB: www.dianeolsenstudio.com
SIC: 2821 Plastics materials & resins

(G-19018)
ENVIRNMNTAL PLLET SLUTIONS INC
9500 Henry Ct Ste 350 (49464-8945)
PHONE..............................616 283-1784
EMP: 18 EST: 2007
SALES (est): 2.1MM **Privately Held**
WEB: www.envpallets.com
SIC: 2448 Pallets, wood

(G-19019)
EXTOL INC (PA)
Also Called: Affinity Solutions
651 Case Karsten Dr (49464-8729)
PHONE..............................616 741-0231
Randy Antaya, *CEO*
Ross Van Klompenberg, *President*
Andrew Van Klompenberg, *Vice Pres*
Don Wire, *Project Mgr*
Andrew Roderick, *Engineer*
◆ EMP: 89 EST: 1985
SQ FT: 53,000
SALES (est): 22.9MM **Privately Held**
WEB: www.extolinc.com
SIC: 3559 Automotive related machinery

(G-19020)
F2 INDUSTRIES LLC
11129 Autumn Dr (49464-9100)
P.O. Box 192 (49464-0192)
PHONE..............................616 610-0894
Andrew Ong, *Principal*
EMP: 8 EST: 2016
SALES (est): 317.3K **Privately Held**
WEB: www.f2ind.com
SIC: 3599 Industrial machinery

(G-19021)
FILLER SPECIALTIES INC
440 100th Ave (49464-2061)
PHONE..............................616 772-9235
Norman Slagh, *President*
Barbara Slagh, *Vice Pres*
Vern Slagh, *Vice Pres*
John Raak, *Manager*
◆ EMP: 20 EST: 1973
SQ FT: 9,000
SALES (est): 4.6MM **Privately Held**
WEB: www.filler-specialties.com
SIC: 3565 Bottling machinery: filling, capping, labeling

(G-19022)
FORGE INDUSTRIES LC
4191 88th Ave (49464-9713)
PHONE..............................616 402-7887
Daly Adam, *Administration*
EMP: 5 EST: 2008
SALES (est): 126K **Privately Held**
SIC: 3999 Manufacturing industries

(G-19023)
GALLANT INC
600 E Riley St (49464-9699)
PHONE..............................616 772-1880
Jerry Wolf, *President*
Susan Duncan, *General Mgr*
Jerry M Wolf, *Vice Pres*
Randy Wolf, *Vice Pres*
Sean Roush, *Engineer*
▲ EMP: 17 EST: 1997
SQ FT: 40,000
SALES (est): 2.3MM **Privately Held**
SIC: 3296 Acoustical board & tile, mineral wool

(G-19024)
GENTEX CORPORATION (PA)
600 N Centennial St (49464-1374)
PHONE..............................616 772-1800
Steve Downing, *President*
Scott Ryan, *Vice Pres*
John Arnold, *VP Opers*
Rocco Baldasare, *Mfg Staff*
Josh Hodgkinson, *Mfg Staff*
EMP: 250 EST: 1974
SALES (est): 1.6B **Publicly Held**
WEB: www.gentex.com
SIC: 3231 3714 3669 Mirrors, truck & automobile: made from purchased glass; motor vehicle parts & accessories; smoke detectors

(G-19025)
GENTEX CORPORATION
9001 Riley St (49464-9717)
PHONE..............................616 772-1800
Kevin Nash, *Vice Pres*
EMP: 5
SALES (corp-wide): 1.6B **Publicly Held**
WEB: www.gentex.com
SIC: 3231 Mirrors, truck & automobile: made from purchased glass
PA: Gentex Corporation
  600 N Centennial St
  Zeeland MI 49464
  616 772-1800

(G-19026)
GENTEX CORPORATION
58 E Riley St (49464-9610)
PHONE..............................616 772-1800
Paul Flynn, *Vice Pres*
Sue Franz, *Vice Pres*
Bryce Bodtke, *Production*
Nathan Reeder, *Production*
Dan Suman, *Branch Mgr*
EMP: 5
SALES (corp-wide): 1.6B **Publicly Held**
WEB: www.gentex.com
SIC: 3231 3669 Mirrors, truck & automobile: made from purchased glass; smoke detectors
PA: Gentex Corporation
  600 N Centennial St
  Zeeland MI 49464
  616 772-1800

(G-19027)
GENTEX CORPORATION
675 N State St (49464-1232)
PHONE..............................616 772-1800
Joe Matthews, *Vice Pres*
Steve McDaniels, *Project Mgr*
Jessica Eskridge, *Production*
Steven Essenburgh, *Production*
Justin Franchville, *Production*
EMP: 5
SALES (corp-wide): 1.6B **Publicly Held**
WEB: www.gentex.com
SIC: 3231 Mirrors, truck & automobile: made from purchased glass
PA: Gentex Corporation
  600 N Centennial St
  Zeeland MI 49464
  616 772-1800

(G-19028)
GENTEX CORPORATION
10985 Chicago Dr (49464-8101)
PHONE..............................616 392-7195
Keifer Sestric, *Vice Pres*
Dave Christian, *QC Dir*
EMP: 6
SALES (corp-wide): 1.6B **Publicly Held**
WEB: www.gentex.com
SIC: 3669 1731 Fire alarm apparatus, electric; fire detection systems, electric; smoke detectors; fire detection & burglar alarm systems specialization
PA: Gentex Corporation
  600 N Centennial St
  Zeeland MI 49464
  616 772-1800

(G-19029)
GENTEX CORPORATION
310 E Riley St (49464-9789)
PHONE..............................616 772-1800
Rosalie McCormick, *Manager*
EMP: 5
SALES (corp-wide): 1.6B **Publicly Held**
WEB: www.gentex.com
SIC: 3231 Mirrors, truck & automobile: made from purchased glass
PA: Gentex Corporation
  600 N Centennial St
  Zeeland MI 49464
  616 772-1800

(G-19030)
GIBRALTAR INC
421 N Centennial St (49464-1371)
PHONE..............................616 748-4857
Paul Koning, *CEO*
◆ EMP: 38
SQ FT: 70,000
SALES (est): 8.2MM **Privately Held**
WEB: www.gibraltarinc.com
SIC: 3499 Furniture parts, metal

(G-19031)
GRAND RAPIDS CUSTOM TOOLING
232 E Roosevelt Ave (49464-1240)
PHONE..............................616 836-0274
EMP: 6 EST: 2017
SALES (est): 165.7K **Privately Held**
WEB: www.grcustomtooling.com
SIC: 3599 Machine shop, jobbing & repair

(G-19032)
GRAPHIX GURUS
550 W Main Ave (49464-1545)
PHONE..............................616 217-6470
Adam Thompson, *Principal*
EMP: 4 EST: 2015
SALES (est): 287.7K **Privately Held**
WEB: www.graphixgurus.com
SIC: 3993 Signs & advertising specialties

(G-19033)
HARP COLUMN LLC
304 E Central Ave (49464-1706)
P.O. Box 441 (49464-0441)
PHONE..............................215 564-3232
Stephanie Gustafson, *Editor*
Kimberly Rowe,
Alison Reese,
EMP: 7 EST: 2015
SALES (est): 330K **Privately Held**
WEB: www.harpcolumn.com
SIC: 2721 Magazines: publishing only, not printed on site

(G-19034)
HEKMAN FURNITURE COMPANY (HQ)
Also Called: Woodmark Originals
860 E Main Ave (49464-1365)
PHONE..............................616 748-2660
Jack Miller, *CEO*
Dan Masters, *President*
Alan Forist, *CFO*
Andrew Christmann, *Marketing Mgr*
Ann Stephanie Pabon, *Manager*
▲ EMP: 20 EST: 1922
SQ FT: 200,000
SALES (est): 154K
SALES (corp-wide): 855.6K **Privately Held**
WEB: www.hekman.com
SIC: 2511 Wood household furniture
PA: Howard Miller Company
  860 E Main Ave
  Zeeland MI 49464
  616 772-9131

(G-19035)
HIGGINS MARINE METALS LLC
8717 Riley St (49464-9585)
PHONE..............................616 990-2732
EMP: 5 EST: 2019
SALES (est): 262K **Privately Held**
WEB: www.higginsmarinemetals.com
SIC: 3441 Fabricated structural metal

(G-19036)
HIGHPOINT FINSHG SOLUTIONS INC
541 E Roosevelt Ave (49464-1378)
PHONE..............................616 772-4425
James Davis, *President*
EMP: 70 EST: 2010
SQ FT: 4,000 **Privately Held**
WEB: www.highpointfinishingsolutions.com
SIC: 3471 Electroplating of metals or formed products

(G-19037)
HIL-MAN AUTOMATION LLC
260 E Roosevelt Ave (49464-1261)
PHONE..............................616 741-9099
Rick Mannes, *President*
Seth Hembree, *Opers Mgr*
Julie Blakely, *Office Mgr*
EMP: 13 EST: 2003
SALES (est): 2.5MM **Privately Held**
WEB: www.hil-manautomation.com
SIC: 3451 Screw machine products

(G-19038)
HILLSHIRE BRANDS COMPANY
Bil Mar Foods
8300 96th Ave (49464-9177)
PHONE..............................616 875-8131
Ross Myers, *Plant Mgr*
Timothy Forton, *Prdtn Mgr*
Andy Brewer, *Production*
Gary Dewitt, *Branch Mgr*
Jessica Brown, *Director*
EMP: 7
SALES (corp-wide): 47B **Publicly Held**
WEB: www.tysonfoods.com
SIC: 2013 2099 2015 Sausages & other prepared meats; food preparations; poultry slaughtering & processing
HQ: The Hillshire Brands Company
  400 S Jefferson St Ste 1n
  Chicago IL 60607
  312 614-6000

(G-19039)
HOLLAND LITHO SERVICE INC
Also Called: Holland Litho Printing Service
10972 Chicago Dr (49464-8100)
PHONE..............................616 392-4644
Jerry Baarman, *President*
Brian Baarman, *Exec VP*
Rick Baarman, *Vice Pres*
Tamas Baarman, *Vice Pres*
Tiffany Senabandith, *HR Admin*
EMP: 100
SQ FT: 40,000
SALES (est): 20.6MM **Privately Held**
WEB: www.hollandlitho.com
SIC: 2752 Commercial printing, offset

(G-19040)
HOWARD MILLER COMPANY (PA)
860 E Main Ave (49464-1365)
PHONE..............................616 772-9131
Philip Miller, *Ch of Bd*
Howard C Miller, *President*
Dennis Palasek, *Vice Pres*
Paul Van Noord, *Mfg Staff*
Steve Richel, *Engineer*
◆ EMP: 300 EST: 1946
SQ FT: 50,000
SALES (est): 855.6K **Privately Held**
WEB: www.howardmiller.com
SIC: 3873 3829 3823 Clocks, except timeclocks; measuring & controlling devices; industrial instrmnts msrmnt display/control process variable

(G-19041)
HUIZENGA & SONS INC
Also Called: Huizenga Redi-Mix
10075 Gordon St (49464-1491)
PHONE..............................616 772-6241
Phil Huizenga, *President*
EMP: 22 EST: 1926
SQ FT: 16,320
SALES (est): 1.8MM **Privately Held**
WEB: www.huizengaandsons.com
SIC: 3273 Ready-mixed concrete

Zeeland - Ottawa County (G-19042) GEOGRAPHIC SECTION

(G-19042)
HUIZENGA GRAVEL COMPANY INC (PA)
10075 Gordon St (49464-1491)
PHONE..................616 772-6241
Phil Huizenga, *President*
Bruce Huizenga, *Vice Pres*
▲ **EMP:** 15 **EST:** 1926
SQ FT: 15,000
SALES (est): 4.5MM **Privately Held**
SIC: 1442 Construction sand & gravel

(G-19043)
IFR INC
Also Called: Holland Awning Co.
10875 Chicago Dr (49464-8126)
PHONE..................616 772-2052
Steven Schaftenaar, *CEO*
Doug Buma, *President*
Scott Smith, *Vice Pres*
Todd Stockdale, *Vice Pres*
Jason Locke, *Project Engr*
▲ **EMP:** 250
SQ FT: 162,000
SALES (est): 26.2MM **Privately Held**
WEB: www.ifrinc.com
SIC: 2394 Tents: made from purchased materials
PA: Integrated Fabric Resource De Mexico, S. De R.L. De C.V.
Av. Rio Mississippi No. 672 Mod. 1
Irapuato GTO. 36810

(G-19044)
ILLINOIS TOOL WORKS INC
ITW Drawform
500 N Fairview Rd (49464-9419)
PHONE..................616 772-1910
John Bisset, *Division Mgr*
Ben V Sloten, *Purch Mgr*
Tom Crum, *Engineer*
Brandon Dykstra, *Engineer*
Brian Lackey, *Engineer*
EMP: 280
SALES (corp-wide): 12.5B **Publicly Held**
WEB: www.itw.com
SIC: 3469 Stamping metal for the trade
PA: Illinois Tool Works Inc.
155 Harlem Ave
Glenview IL 60025
847 724-7500

(G-19045)
INDUSTRIAL WOODWORKING CORP
9380 Pentatech Dr (49464-9090)
P.O. Box 286 (49464-0286)
PHONE..................616 741-9663
Bradford Davis, *President*
Greg Raczok, *Vice Pres*
Steve Huizinga, *Purch Mgr*
Dave Stumpfig, *Lab Dir*
▼ **EMP:** 44 **EST:** 1995
SQ FT: 22,000
SALES (est): 6.4MM **Privately Held**
WEB: www.industrialwoodworking.com
SIC: 2511 5047 Wood household furniture; hospital equipment & furniture

(G-19046)
INFORMATION STN SPECIALISTS
Also Called: ISS
3368 88th Ave (49464-9674)
P.O. Box 51 (49464-0051)
PHONE..................616 772-2300
William W Baker, *President*
Tom Coviak, *Project Mgr*
Frank Dopkiss, *Sales Staff*
Linda Folland, *Marketing Mgr*
John Cotten, *Manager*
EMP: 10 **EST:** 1980
SQ FT: 2,400
SALES (est): 2MM **Privately Held**
WEB: www.theradiosource.com
SIC: 3663 Radio & TV communications equipment

(G-19047)
INNOTEC CORP (PA)
Also Called: Innotec Automation
441 E Roosevelt Ave (49464-1278)
PHONE..................616 772-5959
Michael Lanser, *President*
Nicholas Devries, *Corp Secy*
Vince Boraas, *Engineer*
Luke Bredeweg, *Engineer*
Jason Cook, *Engineer*
▲ **EMP:** 87 **EST:** 1992
SQ FT: 12,000
SALES (est): 28.1MM **Privately Held**
WEB: www.innotecgroup.com
SIC: 3469 3679 Metal stampings; electronic circuits

(G-19048)
INTEGRITY MUNICIPAL SERVICE
500 E Washington Ave (49464-1385)
PHONE..................858 218-3750
Sandra Valero, *Principal*
EMP: 11 **EST:** 2015
SALES (est): 278.7K **Privately Held**
WEB: www.integritymunicipalsystems.com
SIC: 3589 Water treatment equipment, industrial

(G-19049)
JSK SPECIALTIES
11007 Chicago Dr Ste 34 (49464-9186)
PHONE..................616 218-2416
EMP: 7 **EST:** 2016
SALES (est): 368.2K **Privately Held**
WEB: www.jskspecialties.com
SIC: 3599 Machine shop, jobbing & repair

(G-19050)
LAKESHORE VISION & ROBOTICS
11007 Chicago Dr (49464-9186)
PHONE..................616 394-9201
Gregory Thomas Caskey, *Administration*
EMP: 6 **EST:** 2018
SALES (est): 180.3K **Privately Held**
SIC: 3599 Machine shop, jobbing & repair

(G-19051)
MEAD JOHNSON & COMPANY LLC
725 E Main Ave (49464-1368)
PHONE..................616 748-7100
Marcus Jordan, *Engineer*
Adam Vogt, *Engineer*
Mike Sanger, *Manager*
Jeremy Manning, *Manager*
Sean Miller, *Manager*
EMP: 7
SALES (corp-wide): 18.6B **Privately Held**
WEB: www.meadjohnson.com
SIC: 2099 Food preparations
HQ: Mead Johnson & Company, Llc
2400 W Lloyd Expy
Evansville IN 47712
812 429-5000

(G-19052)
MICHIGAN TURKEY PRODUCERS
9983 Polk St (49464-9778)
PHONE..................616 875-1838
Daniel Lennon, *Branch Mgr*
EMP: 63
SALES (corp-wide): 81.5MM **Privately Held**
WEB: www.miturkey.com
SIC: 2015 Turkey processing & slaughtering
PA: Michigan Turkey Producers Cooperative, Inc.
1100 Hall St Sw
Grand Rapids MI 49503
616 245-2211

(G-19053)
MICHIGAN WOOD FIBERS LLC
9426 Henry Ct (49464-8944)
PHONE..................616 875-2241
Charles Weaver, *President*
Nathan Weaver, *General Mgr*
Tim Guikema, *Sales Executive*
EMP: 9 **EST:** 1995
SQ FT: 40,000
SALES (est): 2.5MM **Privately Held**
WEB: www.michiganwoodfibers.com
SIC: 2499 5083 Mulch, wood & bark; landscaping equipment

(G-19054)
MIDWAY MACHINE TECH INC
555 N State St (49464-1230)
PHONE..................616 772-0808
Jerry Geertman, *President*
Terry Geertman, *Exec VP*
Jack Timmer, *Project Engr*
Tammy Theodore, *Info Tech Mgr*
EMP: 25 **EST:** 1988
SQ FT: 19,000
SALES (est): 5.1MM **Privately Held**
WEB: www.midwaymachine.com
SIC: 3599 Machine shop, jobbing & repair

(G-19055)
MILCARE INC (HQ)
855 E Main Ave (49464-1366)
PHONE..................616 654-8000
David Reid, *President*
EMP: 350 **EST:** 1985
SQ FT: 63,400
SALES (est): 54.9MM
SALES (corp-wide): 2.4B **Publicly Held**
WEB: www.hermanmiller.com
SIC: 2531 Public building & related furniture
PA: Millerknoll, Inc.
855 E Main Ave
Zeeland MI 49464
616 654-3000

(G-19056)
MILLERKNOLL INC (PA)
855 E Main Ave (49464-1366)
P.O. Box 302 (49464-0302)
PHONE..................616 654-3000
Michael A Volkema, *Ch of Bd*
Andrea R Owen, *President*
Jeremy Hocking, *President*
John Michael, *President*
Debbie Propst, *President*
◆ **EMP:** 2145 **EST:** 1905
SQ FT: 771,000
SALES: 2.4B **Publicly Held**
WEB: www.hermanmiller.com
SIC: 2521 2522 2541 2542 Wood office furniture; office furniture, except wood; wood partitions & fixtures; partitions & fixtures, except wood; public building & related furniture

(G-19057)
MOODY BIBLE INST OF CHICAGO
Also Called: Wgnb
3764 84th Ave (49464-9706)
P.O. Box 40 (49464-0040)
PHONE..................616 772-7300
Jack Haveman, *Branch Mgr*
EMP: 4
SALES (corp-wide): 109MM **Privately Held**
WEB: www.moody.edu
SIC: 3663 Radio & TV communications equipment
PA: The Moody Bible Institute Of Chicago
820 N La Salle Dr
Chicago IL 60610
312 329-4000

(G-19058)
NACS USA INC (DH)
Also Called: Novo Building Products
8181 Logistics Dr (49464-9378)
PHONE..................800 253-9000
George Judd, *CEO*
Jeffrey Broene, *Vice Pres*
Libby Dickinson, *Manager*
Mike Muir, *Manager*
Rhonda Rodriguez, *Manager*
EMP: 1 **EST:** 2003
SALES (est): 409.3MM
SALES (corp-wide): 805MM **Privately Held**
SIC: 2431 Millwork
HQ: Bw Empire Holdings, Llc
1 Liberty Plz Fl 52
New York NY 10006
864 675-9800

(G-19059)
NEPHEW FABRICATION INC
10752 Polk St (49464-9779)
PHONE..................616 875-2121
Mike Nephew, *President*
Adel Nephew, *Vice Pres*
EMP: 4 **EST:** 1991
SQ FT: 1,200
SALES (est): 434.5K **Privately Held**
SIC: 3599 1799 Machine & other job shop work; welding on site

(G-19060)
NEPTUNE COATING SERVICES
10996 Campanel Dr (49464-9117)
PHONE..................616 403-9034
EMP: 4 **EST:** 2017
SALES (est): 69.9K **Privately Held**
WEB: www.neptunecoatingservices.com
SIC: 3479 Metal coating & allied service

(G-19061)
NOVO DISTRIBUTION LLC (DH)
Also Called: Empire Moulding and Milwork
8181 Logistics Dr (49464-9378)
P.O. Box 17 (49464-0017)
PHONE..................616 772-7272
George Judd, *CEO*
Jonathan Solursh, *President*
Doug Sawyer, *Division Mgr*
Robin Sobota, *General Mgr*
Jeremy Johnson, *Area Mgr*
◆ **EMP:** 408 **EST:** 1993
SQ FT: 220,000
SALES (est): 349.8MM
SALES (corp-wide): 950.6MM **Privately Held**
WEB: www.empireco.com
SIC: 5031 2431 Lumber: rough, dressed & finished; millwork; molding, all materials; staircases, stairs & railings
HQ: Novo Building Products Holdings, Llc
8181 Logistics Dr
Zeeland MI 49464
616 772-7272

(G-19062)
ODL INCORPORATED (PA)
Also Called: O D L
215 E Roosevelt Ave (49464-1239)
PHONE..................616 772-9111
Jeffrey Mulder, *CEO*
Dave Killoran, *Ch of Bd*
Scot Harder, *Vice Pres*
Jim Oren, *Vice Pres*
Townes Parsley, *Vice Pres*
▲ **EMP:** 301
SQ FT: 14,000
SALES (est): 154.7MM **Privately Held**
WEB: www.odl.com
SIC: 2431 Doors & door parts & trim, wood

(G-19063)
ODL INCORPORATED
100 Mulder Rd (49464-8001)
PHONE..................616 772-9111
Jim Allardyce, *Senior Engr*
Gave Kiallol, *Branch Mgr*
EMP: 5
SALES (corp-wide): 154.7MM **Privately Held**
WEB: www.odl.com
SIC: 2431 Millwork
PA: Odl, Incorporated
215 E Roosevelt Ave
Zeeland MI 49464
616 772-9111

(G-19064)
ODOR GONE INC
2849 Air Park Dr (49464-9412)
PHONE..................888 636-7292
Kathy Pittsley, *President*
Mark Pittsley, *Vice Pres*
EMP: 10 **EST:** 1996
SALES (est): 569.9K **Privately Held**
WEB: www.ultraodorsgone.com
SIC: 2842 5169 Sanitation preparations, disinfectants & deodorants; aromatic chemicals

(G-19065)
ORNAMENTAL MOULDINGS LLC
8181 Logistics Dr (49464-9378)
P.O. Box 17 (49464-0017)
PHONE..................616 748-0188
Eric Harrison, *Opers Mgr*
EMP: 17
SALES (corp-wide): 805MM **Privately Held**
WEB: www.ornamental.com
SIC: 2431 Millwork

GEOGRAPHIC SECTION
Zeeland - Ottawa County (G-19093)

HQ: Ornamental Mouldings, Llc
3804 Comanche Rd
Archdale NC 27263

(G-19066)
OTTAWA COUNTY WINDOW CLG LLC
520 Gordon St Ste 2 (49464-2002)
PHONE.................................248 878-5377
EMP: 6 EST: 2019
SALES (est): 465.3K Privately Held
WEB: www.mainewindowcleaning.com
SIC: 2842 Window cleaning preparations

(G-19067)
P L OPTIMA INC
2734 84th Ave (49464-9594)
PHONE.................................616 828-8377
Kyrt Holstete, President
EMP: 7 EST: 2018
SALES (est): 188.4K Privately Held
SIC: 3599 Machine shop, jobbing & repair

(G-19068)
PI OPTIMA INC
Also Called: Industrial Machining Services
2734 84th Ave (49464-9594)
PHONE.................................616 772-2138
Nelson Zeerip, President
Julie Geerlings, Admin Asst
EMP: 21 EST: 1985
SQ FT: 7,500
SALES (est): 981.8K Privately Held
SIC: 3599 Machine shop, jobbing & repair

(G-19069)
PI OPTIMA MANUFACTURING LLC
2734 84th Ave (49464-9594)
PHONE.................................616 931-9750
Jason Beecham,
Julie Geerlings, Admin Asst
Kyle Snyder,
EMP: 10 EST: 2015
SALES (est): 819.3K Privately Held
WEB: www.pioptima.com
SIC: 3599 Machine shop, jobbing & repair

(G-19070)
PLASCORE INC
581 E Roosevelt Ave (49464-1379)
PHONE.................................616 772-1220
Ed Gasper, Controller
Fritz Huebner, Branch Mgr
EMP: 44
SALES (corp-wide): 72.4MM Privately Held
WEB: www.plascore.com
SIC: 3354 Aluminum extruded products
PA: Plascore, Inc.
615 N Fairview Rd
Zeeland MI 49464
616 772-1220

(G-19071)
PLASCORE INC
500a E Roosevelt Ave (49464-1344)
PHONE.................................616 772-1220
Dave Vander Ploeg, Principal
Joseph Forrest, Mfg Spvr
Jason Anderson, Production
Todd Dykman, Production
Steve Hessel, Production
EMP: 31
SALES (corp-wide): 72.4MM Privately Held
WEB: www.plascore.com
SIC: 3086 3083 Plastics foam products; laminated plastics plate & sheet
PA: Plascore, Inc.
615 N Fairview Rd
Zeeland MI 49464
616 772-1220

(G-19072)
PRIMERA PLASTICS INC (PA)
Also Called: Primera Pathways
3424 Production Ct (49464-8546)
PHONE.................................616 748-6248
Noel Cuellar, President
Brittany Gamelin, Production
James Belinski, Engineer
Nick Rose, Engineer
Steve Berkenpas, CFO
EMP: 79 EST: 1994
SQ FT: 60,000
SALES (est): 15.5MM Privately Held
WEB: www.primera-inc.com
SIC: 3089 Injection molding of plastics

(G-19073)
PRO-CAM SERVICES LLC
323 E Roosevelt Ave (49464-1339)
PHONE.................................616 748-4200
Eric Johnson, Opers Mgr
Kyle Hammond, Sales Staff
Thomas E Bassett II, Mng Member
Malinda Bassett,
EMP: 24 EST: 1995
SALES (est): 700K Privately Held
WEB: www.procamservices.com
SIC: 3599 Machine shop, jobbing & repair

(G-19074)
PROGRESSIVE PANEL SYSTEMS INC
8095 Riley St (49464-8517)
PHONE.................................616 748-1384
Stanley Sluiter, President
Steve Sluiter, Corp Secy
Gail Carney, Vice Pres
Scott Sluiter, Vice Pres
Ken Harmsen, Plant Mgr
EMP: 25 EST: 1990
SQ FT: 22,500
SALES (est): 3.8MM Privately Held
WEB: www.progressivesystem.com
SIC: 3448 8711 Trusses & framing: prefabricated metal; acoustical engineering

(G-19075)
PROTO-TEC INC
260 N Church St (49464-1244)
PHONE.................................616 772-9511
Kalvin Vanden Bosch, President
EMP: 10 EST: 1988
SQ FT: 8,600
SALES (est): 1.4MM Privately Held
WEB: www.proto-tec.com
SIC: 3089 3544 Injection molded finished plastic products; special dies, tools, jigs & fixtures

(G-19076)
R-BO CO INC
150 W Washington Ave (49464-1102)
PHONE.................................616 748-9733
Larry Rigterink, President
▲ EMP: 13 EST: 1989
SQ FT: 32,000
SALES (est): 1MM Privately Held
SIC: 3469 3646 3645 3441 Metal stampings; commercial indusl & institutional electric lighting fixtures; residential lighting fixtures; fabricated structural metal; wood household furniture

(G-19077)
ROWLAND MOLD & MACHINE INC
9395 Henry Ct (49464-9216)
PHONE.................................616 875-5400
Tim Rowland, President
EMP: 8 EST: 1998
SQ FT: 48,000
SALES (est): 1MM Privately Held
WEB: www.rowlandplastics.com
SIC: 3544 Special dies & tools

(G-19078)
ROWLAND PLASTICS LLC
9395 Henry Ct (49464-9216)
PHONE.................................616 875-5400
Kris Gaynor, Opers Mgr
Timothy Rowland,
EMP: 14 EST: 2017
SALES (est): 637.5K Privately Held
WEB: www.rowlandplastics.com
SIC: 3089 Injection molding of plastics

(G-19079)
SPOT ON MACHINE SHOP
2119 W Maple Ct (49464-9377)
PHONE.................................616 283-9830
EMP: 4 EST: 2019
SALES (est): 102.4K Privately Held
SIC: 3599 Machine shop, jobbing & repair

(G-19080)
SPURT INDUSTRIES LLC
Also Called: CST
5204 Adams St (49464-9005)
P.O. Box 930818, Wixom (48393-0818)
PHONE.................................616 688-5575
Tom Turner, General Mgr
EMP: 6 EST: 1992
SQ FT: 1,200
SALES (est): 988.8K Privately Held
WEB: www.spurtindustries.com
SIC: 2875 Compost

(G-19081)
STAINLESS CONCEPTS LLC
221 E Washington Ave # 4 (49464-1223)
PHONE.................................616 427-6682
Derrick Boetsma,
EMP: 6 EST: 2017
SALES (est): 211K Privately Held
SIC: 3999 Manufacturing industries

(G-19082)
STONE PLASTICS AND MFG INC
8245 Riley St Ste 100 (49464-8568)
PHONE.................................616 748-9740
Mark J Mason, President
Michael Kibben, Mfg Staff
Tim Vanderkooi, Buyer
Jim Weinmann, Engineer
Drew Coppess, Human Res Mgr
▲ EMP: 120 EST: 1999
SQ FT: 136
SALES (est): 40.8MM Privately Held
WEB: www.stoneplasticsmfg.com
SIC: 5162 3089 Plastics products; injection molding of plastics

(G-19083)
SYMBIOTE INC
300 N Centennial St (49464-1312)
PHONE.................................616 772-1790
Travis Randolph, President
Sandra Randolph, Vice Pres
John Lomonaco, Engineer
Heather Boeve, Project Engr
Steve Smith, Natl Sales Mgr
▲ EMP: 47 EST: 1982
SALES (est): 10.8MM Privately Held
WEB: www.symbiote.com
SIC: 3535 3821 2599 3446 Conveyors & conveying equipment; laboratory apparatus & furniture; factory furniture & fixtures; architectural metalwork

(G-19084)
TRUE DIE INC
2425 104th Ave (49464-6800)
PHONE.................................616 772-6360
Brian Brown, Principal
Mitchell Stahl, Technical Staff
EMP: 1 EST: 2015
SALES (est): 1.3MM Privately Held
WEB: www.truedie.com
SIC: 3499 Machine bases, metal

(G-19085)
TYSON FOODS /HR
8300 96th Ave (49464-9177)
PHONE.................................616 875-2311
Denise Brown, Principal
EMP: 12 EST: 2016
SALES (est): 3.5MM Privately Held
SIC: 2015 Poultry slaughtering & processing

(G-19086)
VAN ENK WOODCRAFTERS LLC
500 E Washington Ave # 50 (49464-1385)
P.O. Box 79 (49464-0079)
PHONE.................................616 931-0090
Ben Van Enk, Mng Member
David Van Enk, Mng Member
EMP: 12 EST: 2003
SQ FT: 21,000
SALES (est): 503.9K Privately Held
WEB: www.vanenkwoodcrafters.com
SIC: 2431 Millwork

(G-19087)
VENTURA MANUFACTURING INC
551 Case Karsten Dr (49464-1301)
PHONE.................................616 772-7405
Tim Sigelko, Principal
Lisa Goetsch, Engineer
EMP: 8
SALES (corp-wide): 55.2MM Privately Held
WEB: www.venturamfg.com
SIC: 3315 Steel wire & related products
PA: Ventura Manufacturing, Inc.
471 E Roosevelt Ave # 100
Zeeland MI 49464
616 772-7405

(G-19088)
VENTURA MANUFACTURING INC (PA)
471 E Roosevelt Ave # 100 (49464-1257)
PHONE.................................616 772-7405
France Allen, President
Michael Allen, Vice Pres
Kris Dibble, Mfg Staff
Joshua Driscoll, Mfg Staff
Terry Gort, Mfg Staff
◆ EMP: 159 EST: 1997
SQ FT: 95,000
SALES (est): 55.2MM Privately Held
WEB: www.venturamfg.com
SIC: 3315 2522 3714 Steel wire & related products; office furniture, except wood; motor vehicle electrical equipment

(G-19089)
VERTELLUS HLTH SPCLTY PDTS LLC
Also Called: Vertellus Specialty Materials
215 N Centennial St (49464-1309)
PHONE.................................616 772-2193
◆ EMP: 6
SALES (est): 610K Privately Held
SIC: 2899 Mfg Chemical Preparations

(G-19090)
VERTELLUS LLC
Also Called: Vertellus Zeeland
215 N Centennial St (49464-1309)
PHONE.................................616 772-2193
Liz Rich, Human Res Dir
Tod Hammond, Manager
EMP: 150
SALES (corp-wide): 587.7MM Privately Held
WEB: www.vertellus.com
SIC: 2869 Industrial organic chemicals
HQ: Vertellus Llc
201 N Illinois St # 1800
Indianapolis IN 46204
317 247-8141

(G-19091)
VORTEC
201 W Washington Ave # 110 (49464-1086)
PHONE.................................616 292-2401
Matthew D Potts, Administration
EMP: 8 EST: 2007
SALES (est): 2.8MM Privately Held
WEB: www.vortectooling.com
SIC: 3544 Special dies & tools

(G-19092)
WOODWARD FST INC
700 N Centennial St (49464-1369)
PHONE.................................616 772-9171
Thomas A Gendron, Ch of Bd
James R Rulseh, President
John D Cohn, Senior VP
Halil Kinaci, Purch Dir
Greg Phillips, Engineer
EMP: 230 EST: 1986
SALES (est): 52MM
SALES (corp-wide): 2.5B Publicly Held
WEB: www.woodward.com
SIC: 3724 Aircraft engines & engine parts
PA: Woodward, Inc.
1081 Woodward Way
Fort Collins CO 80524
970 482-5811

(G-19093)
WOODWAYS INC
665 Construction Ct (49464-8946)
P.O. Box 337, Grandville (49468-0337)
PHONE.................................616 956-3070
Timothy Waterway, President
EMP: 8 EST: 1991

Zeeland - Ottawa County (G-19094)

SALES (est): 321.4K **Privately Held**
WEB: www.woodwayscustom.com
SIC: **2434** 2511 2521 2517 Wood kitchen cabinets; wood household furniture; wood office furniture; wood television & radio cabinets; cabinet & finish carpentry

(G-19094)
ZCS INTERCONNECT LLC
138 W Washington Ave (49464-1120)
P.O. Box 222 (49464-0222)
PHONE.................................616 399-8614
Douglas Lincicum,
EMP: 5 **EST:** 2013
SALES (est): 748.1K **Privately Held**
WEB: www.zcsinterconnect.com
SIC: **3531** 5999 Subgraders (construction equipment); batteries, non-automotive

(G-19095)
ZEELAND BIO-BASED PRODUCTS LLC
2525 84th Ave (49464-9501)
P.O. Box 290 (49464-0290)
PHONE.................................616 748-1831
Robert D Meeuwsen,
EMP: 9
SALES (est): 950K **Privately Held**
SIC: **2075** Soybean oil mills

(G-19096)
ZEELAND FARM SERVICES INC (PA)
Also Called: Zeeland Freight Services
2525 84th Ave (49464-9501)
P.O. Box 290 (49464-0290)
PHONE.................................616 772-9042
Cliff Meeuwsen, *President*
Arlen Meeuwsen, *Vice Pres*
Eric Musen, *Vice Pres*
Eric Meeuwsen, *Plant Mgr*
Kurt Meeuwsen, *Opers Mgr*
◆ **EMP:** 130 **EST:** 1950
SQ FT: 40,000
SALES (est): 137.5MM **Privately Held**
WEB: www.zfsinc.com
SIC: **2075** 5153 4212 Soybean oil mills; grains; dump truck haulage; steel hauling, local

(G-19097)
ZEELAND FARM SOYA LLC
2525 84th Ave (49464-9501)
PHONE.................................616 772-9042
Brian Terborg, *Mng Member*
EMP: 13 **EST:** 1995
SALES (est): 208.5K **Privately Held**
WEB: www.zfsinc.com
SIC: **2075** Soybean oil mills

(G-19098)
ZEELAND PRINT SHOP CO
145 E Main Ave (49464-1735)
PHONE.................................616 772-6636
Brian Van Hoven, *President*
EMP: 6 **EST:** 1932
SQ FT: 2,400
SALES (est): 958K **Privately Held**
WEB: www.zeelandprint.com
SIC: **2752** Commercial printing, offset

(G-19099)
ZEELAND RECORD CO
16 S Elm St (49464-1751)
PHONE.................................616 772-2131
Paul Van Koevering, *President*
Kraig Van Koevering, *Corp Secy*
Kurt Van Koevering, *Vice Pres*
EMP: 6 **EST:** 1893
SQ FT: 12,000
SALES (est): 810K **Privately Held**
WEB: www.zrgraphics.com
SIC: **2759** Commercial printing

(G-19100)
ZFS CRESTON LLC
2525 84th Ave (49464-9501)
PHONE.................................616 748-1825
EMP: 17 **EST:** 2018
SALES (est): 2.6MM **Privately Held**
WEB: www.zfsinc.com
SIC: **2075** Soybean oil mills

(G-19101)
ZFS ITHACA LLC (PA)
2525 84th Ave (49464-9501)
PHONE.................................616 772-9042
Robert Garland, *Project Mgr*
Brian Terborg, *Mng Member*
Scott Duncan, *Manager*
Kirby Kerschner, *Manager*
EMP: 49 **EST:** 2014
SALES (est): 8.5MM **Privately Held**
WEB: www.zfsinc.com
SIC: **2075** Soybean oil mills

SIC INDEX

Standard Industrial Classification Alphabetical Index

SIC NO   PRODUCT

A

3291 Abrasive Prdts
2891 Adhesives & Sealants
3563 Air & Gas Compressors
3585 Air Conditioning & Heating Eqpt
3721 Aircraft
3724 Aircraft Engines & Engine Parts
3728 Aircraft Parts & Eqpt, NEC
2812 Alkalies & Chlorine
3363 Aluminum Die Castings
3354 Aluminum Extruded Prdts
3365 Aluminum Foundries
3355 Aluminum Rolling & Drawing, NEC
3353 Aluminum Sheet, Plate & Foil
3483 Ammunition, Large
3826 Analytical Instruments
2077 Animal, Marine Fats & Oils
2389 Apparel & Accessories, NEC
3446 Architectural & Ornamental Metal Work
7694 Armature Rewinding Shops
3292 Asbestos products
2952 Asphalt Felts & Coatings
3822 Automatic Temperature Controls
3581 Automatic Vending Machines
3465 Automotive Stampings
2396 Automotive Trimmings, Apparel Findings, Related Prdts

B

2673 Bags: Plastics, Laminated & Coated
2674 Bags: Uncoated Paper & Multiwall
3562 Ball & Roller Bearings
2836 Biological Prdts, Exc Diagnostic Substances
1221 Bituminous Coal & Lignite: Surface Mining
2782 Blankbooks & Looseleaf Binders
3312 Blast Furnaces, Coke Ovens, Steel & Rolling Mills
3564 Blowers & Fans
3732 Boat Building & Repairing
3452 Bolts, Nuts, Screws, Rivets & Washers
2732 Book Printing, Not Publishing
2789 Bookbinding
2731 Books: Publishing & Printing
3131 Boot & Shoe Cut Stock & Findings
2342 Brassieres, Girdles & Garments
2051 Bread, Bakery Prdts Exc Cookies & Crackers
3251 Brick & Structural Clay Tile
3991 Brooms & Brushes
3995 Burial Caskets
2021 Butter

C

3578 Calculating & Accounting Eqpt
2064 Candy & Confectionery Prdts
2033 Canned Fruits, Vegetables & Preserves
2032 Canned Specialties
2394 Canvas Prdts
3624 Carbon & Graphite Prdts
3955 Carbon Paper & Inked Ribbons
3592 Carburetors, Pistons, Rings & Valves
2273 Carpets & Rugs
2823 Cellulosic Man-Made Fibers
3241 Cement, Hydraulic
3253 Ceramic Tile
2043 Cereal Breakfast Foods
2022 Cheese
2899 Chemical Preparations, NEC
2067 Chewing Gum
2361 Children's & Infants' Dresses & Blouses
3261 China Plumbing Fixtures & Fittings
2066 Chocolate & Cocoa Prdts
2111 Cigarettes
3255 Clay Refractories
1241 Coal Mining Svcs
3479 Coating & Engraving, NEC
2095 Coffee
3316 Cold Rolled Steel Sheet, Strip & Bars
3582 Commercial Laundry, Dry Clean & Pressing Mchs
2759 Commercial Printing
2754 Commercial Printing: Gravure
2752 Commercial Printing: Lithographic
3646 Commercial, Indl & Institutional Lighting Fixtures
3669 Communications Eqpt, NEC
3577 Computer Peripheral Eqpt, NEC
3572 Computer Storage Devices

SIC NO   PRODUCT

3575 Computer Terminals
3271 Concrete Block & Brick
3272 Concrete Prdts
3531 Construction Machinery & Eqpt
1442 Construction Sand & Gravel
2679 Converted Paper Prdts, NEC
3535 Conveyors & Eqpt
2052 Cookies & Crackers
3366 Copper Foundries
1021 Copper Ores
2298 Cordage & Twine
2653 Corrugated & Solid Fiber Boxes
3961 Costume Jewelry & Novelties
2261 Cotton Fabric Finishers
2211 Cotton, Woven Fabric
3466 Crowns & Closures
1311 Crude Petroleum & Natural Gas
1423 Crushed & Broken Granite
1422 Crushed & Broken Limestone
1429 Crushed & Broken Stone, NEC
3643 Current-Carrying Wiring Devices
2391 Curtains & Draperies
3087 Custom Compounding Of Purchased Plastic Resins
3281 Cut Stone Prdts
3421 Cutlery
2865 Cyclic-Crudes, Intermediates, Dyes & Org Pigments

D

3843 Dental Eqpt & Splys
2835 Diagnostic Substances
2675 Die-Cut Paper & Board
3544 Dies, Tools, Jigs, Fixtures & Indl Molds
1411 Dimension Stone
2047 Dog & Cat Food
3942 Dolls & Stuffed Toys
2591 Drapery Hardware, Window Blinds & Shades
2381 Dress & Work Gloves
2034 Dried Fruits, Vegetables & Soup
1381 Drilling Oil & Gas Wells

E

3634 Electric Household Appliances
3641 Electric Lamps
3694 Electrical Eqpt For Internal Combustion Engines
3629 Electrical Indl Apparatus, NEC
3699 Electrical Machinery, Eqpt & Splys, NEC
3845 Electromedical & Electrotherapeutic Apparatus
3313 Electrometallurgical Prdts
3677 Electronic Coils & Transformers
3679 Electronic Components, NEC
3571 Electronic Computers
3678 Electronic Connectors
3676 Electronic Resistors
3471 Electroplating, Plating, Polishing, Anodizing & Coloring
3534 Elevators & Moving Stairways
3431 Enameled Iron & Metal Sanitary Ware
2677 Envelopes
2892 Explosives

F

2241 Fabric Mills, Cotton, Wool, Silk & Man-Made
3499 Fabricated Metal Prdts, NEC
3498 Fabricated Pipe & Pipe Fittings
3443 Fabricated Plate Work
3069 Fabricated Rubber Prdts, NEC
3441 Fabricated Structural Steel
2399 Fabricated Textile Prdts, NEC
2295 Fabrics Coated Not Rubberized
2297 Fabrics, Nonwoven
3523 Farm Machinery & Eqpt
3965 Fasteners, Buttons, Needles & Pins
2875 Fertilizers, Mixing Only
2655 Fiber Cans, Tubes & Drums
2091 Fish & Seafoods, Canned & Cured
2092 Fish & Seafoods, Fresh & Frozen
3211 Flat Glass
2087 Flavoring Extracts & Syrups
2045 Flour, Blended & Prepared
2041 Flour, Grain Milling
3824 Fluid Meters & Counters
3593 Fluid Power Cylinders & Actuators
3594 Fluid Power Pumps & Motors
3492 Fluid Power Valves & Hose Fittings
2657 Folding Paperboard Boxes

SIC NO   PRODUCT

3556 Food Prdts Machinery
2099 Food Preparations, NEC
3149 Footwear, NEC
2053 Frozen Bakery Prdts
2037 Frozen Fruits, Juices & Vegetables
2038 Frozen Specialties
2371 Fur Goods
2599 Furniture & Fixtures, NEC

G

3944 Games, Toys & Children's Vehicles
3524 Garden, Lawn Tractors & Eqpt
3053 Gaskets, Packing & Sealing Devices
2369 Girls' & Infants' Outerwear, NEC
3221 Glass Containers
3231 Glass Prdts Made Of Purchased Glass
1041 Gold Ores
3321 Gray Iron Foundries
2771 Greeting Card Publishing
3769 Guided Missile/Space Vehicle Parts & Eqpt, NEC
3764 Guided Missile/Space Vehicle Propulsion Units & parts
3761 Guided Missiles & Space Vehicles
2861 Gum & Wood Chemicals
3275 Gypsum Prdts

H

3423 Hand & Edge Tools
3425 Hand Saws & Saw Blades
3171 Handbags & Purses
3429 Hardware, NEC
2426 Hardwood Dimension & Flooring Mills
2435 Hardwood Veneer & Plywood
2353 Hats, Caps & Millinery
3433 Heating Eqpt
3536 Hoists, Cranes & Monorails
2252 Hosiery, Except Women's
2392 House furnishings: Textile
3142 House Slippers
3639 Household Appliances, NEC
3651 Household Audio & Video Eqpt
3631 Household Cooking Eqpt
2519 Household Furniture, NEC
3633 Household Laundry Eqpt
3632 Household Refrigerators & Freezers
3635 Household Vacuum Cleaners

I

2097 Ice
2024 Ice Cream
2819 Indl Inorganic Chemicals, NEC
3823 Indl Instruments For Meas, Display & Control
3569 Indl Machinery & Eqpt, NEC
3567 Indl Process Furnaces & Ovens
3537 Indl Trucks, Tractors, Trailers & Stackers
2813 Industrial Gases
2869 Industrial Organic Chemicals, NEC
3543 Industrial Patterns
1446 Industrial Sand
3491 Industrial Valves
2816 Inorganic Pigments
3825 Instrs For Measuring & Testing Electricity
3519 Internal Combustion Engines, NEC
3462 Iron & Steel Forgings
1011 Iron Ores

J

3915 Jewelers Findings & Lapidary Work
3911 Jewelry: Precious Metal

K

2253 Knit Outerwear Mills
2259 Knitting Mills, NEC

L

3821 Laboratory Apparatus & Furniture
2258 Lace & Warp Knit Fabric Mills
1031 Lead & Zinc Ores
3952 Lead Pencils, Crayons & Artist's Mtrls
2386 Leather & Sheep Lined Clothing
3151 Leather Gloves & Mittens
3199 Leather Goods, NEC
3111 Leather Tanning & Finishing
3648 Lighting Eqpt, NEC
3996 Linoleum & Hard Surface Floor Coverings, NEC
2085 Liquors, Distilled, Rectified & Blended

SIC INDEX

SIC NO	PRODUCT
2411	Logging
2992	Lubricating Oils & Greases
3161	Luggage

M

SIC NO	PRODUCT
2098	Macaroni, Spaghetti & Noodles
3545	Machine Tool Access
3541	Machine Tools: Cutting
3542	Machine Tools: Forming
3599	Machinery & Eqpt, Indl & Commercial, NEC
3322	Malleable Iron Foundries
2083	Malt
2082	Malt Beverages
2761	Manifold Business Forms
3999	Manufacturing Industries, NEC
3953	Marking Devices
2515	Mattresses & Bedsprings
3829	Measuring & Controlling Devices, NEC
3586	Measuring & Dispensing Pumps
2011	Meat Packing Plants
3568	Mechanical Power Transmission Eqpt, NEC
2833	Medicinal Chemicals & Botanical Prdts
2329	Men's & Boys' Clothing, NEC
2323	Men's & Boys' Neckwear
2325	Men's & Boys' Separate Trousers & Casual Slacks
2321	Men's & Boys' Shirts
2311	Men's & Boys' Suits, Coats & Overcoats
2322	Men's & Boys' Underwear & Nightwear
2326	Men's & Boys' Work Clothing
3143	Men's Footwear, Exc Athletic
3412	Metal Barrels, Drums, Kegs & Pails
3411	Metal Cans
3442	Metal Doors, Sash, Frames, Molding & Trim
3497	Metal Foil & Leaf
3398	Metal Heat Treating
2514	Metal Household Furniture
1081	Metal Mining Svcs
1099	Metal Ores, NEC
3469	Metal Stampings, NEC
3549	Metalworking Machinery, NEC
2026	Milk
2023	Milk, Condensed & Evaporated
2431	Millwork
3296	Mineral Wool
3295	Minerals & Earths: Ground Or Treated
3532	Mining Machinery & Eqpt
3496	Misc Fabricated Wire Prdts
2741	Misc Publishing
3449	Misc Structural Metal Work
1499	Miscellaneous Nonmetallic Mining
2451	Mobile Homes
3061	Molded, Extruded & Lathe-Cut Rubber Mechanical Goods
3716	Motor Homes
3714	Motor Vehicle Parts & Access
3711	Motor Vehicles & Car Bodies
3751	Motorcycles, Bicycles & Parts
3621	Motors & Generators
3931	Musical Instruments

N

SIC NO	PRODUCT
1321	Natural Gas Liquids
2711	Newspapers: Publishing & Printing
2873	Nitrogenous Fertilizers
3297	Nonclay Refractories
3644	Noncurrent-Carrying Wiring Devices
3364	Nonferrous Die Castings, Exc Aluminum
3463	Nonferrous Forgings
3369	Nonferrous Foundries: Castings, NEC
3357	Nonferrous Wire Drawing
3299	Nonmetallic Mineral Prdts, NEC
1481	Nonmetallic Minerals Svcs, Except Fuels

O

SIC NO	PRODUCT
2522	Office Furniture, Except Wood
3579	Office Machines, NEC
1382	Oil & Gas Field Exploration Svcs
1389	Oil & Gas Field Svcs, NEC
3533	Oil Field Machinery & Eqpt
3851	Ophthalmic Goods
3827	Optical Instruments
3489	Ordnance & Access, NEC
3842	Orthopedic, Prosthetic & Surgical Appliances/Splys

P

SIC NO	PRODUCT
3565	Packaging Machinery
2851	Paints, Varnishes, Lacquers, Enamels
2671	Paper Coating & Laminating for Packaging
2672	Paper Coating & Laminating, Exc for Packaging
3554	Paper Inds Machinery
2621	Paper Mills
2631	Paperboard Mills
2542	Partitions & Fixtures, Except Wood
2951	Paving Mixtures & Blocks
3951	Pens & Mechanical Pencils
2844	Perfumes, Cosmetics & Toilet Preparations
2721	Periodicals: Publishing & Printing
3172	Personal Leather Goods
2879	Pesticides & Agricultural Chemicals, NEC
2911	Petroleum Refining
2834	Pharmaceuticals
3652	Phonograph Records & Magnetic Tape
2874	Phosphatic Fertilizers
3861	Photographic Eqpt & Splys
2035	Pickled Fruits, Vegetables, Sauces & Dressings
3085	Plastic Bottles
3086	Plastic Foam Prdts
3083	Plastic Laminated Plate & Sheet
3084	Plastic Pipe
3088	Plastic Plumbing Fixtures
3089	Plastic Prdts
3082	Plastic Unsupported Profile Shapes
3081	Plastic Unsupported Sheet & Film
2821	Plastics, Mtrls & Nonvulcanizable Elastomers
2796	Platemaking & Related Svcs
2395	Pleating & Stitching For The Trade
3432	Plumbing Fixture Fittings & Trim, Brass
3264	Porcelain Electrical Splys
1474	Potash, Soda & Borate Minerals
2096	Potato Chips & Similar Prdts
3269	Pottery Prdts, NEC
2015	Poultry Slaughtering, Dressing & Processing
3546	Power Hand Tools
3612	Power, Distribution & Specialty Transformers
3448	Prefabricated Metal Buildings & Cmpnts
2452	Prefabricated Wood Buildings & Cmpnts
7372	Prepackaged Software
2048	Prepared Feeds For Animals & Fowls
3229	Pressed & Blown Glassware, NEC
3692	Primary Batteries: Dry & Wet
3399	Primary Metal Prdts, NEC
3339	Primary Nonferrous Metals, NEC
3334	Primary Production Of Aluminum
3331	Primary Smelting & Refining Of Copper
3672	Printed Circuit Boards
2893	Printing Ink
3555	Printing Trades Machinery & Eqpt
2999	Products Of Petroleum & Coal, NEC
2531	Public Building & Related Furniture
2611	Pulp Mills
3561	Pumps & Pumping Eqpt

R

SIC NO	PRODUCT
3663	Radio & T V Communications, Systs & Eqpt, Broadcast/Studio
3671	Radio & T V Receiving Electron Tubes
3743	Railroad Eqpt
3273	Ready-Mixed Concrete
2493	Reconstituted Wood Prdts
3695	Recording Media
3625	Relays & Indl Controls
3645	Residential Lighting Fixtures
3547	Rolling Mill Machinery & Eqpt
3351	Rolling, Drawing & Extruding Of Copper
3356	Rolling, Drawing-Extruding Of Nonferrous Metals
3021	Rubber & Plastic Footwear
3052	Rubber & Plastic Hose & Belting

S

SIC NO	PRODUCT
2068	Salted & Roasted Nuts & Seeds
2656	Sanitary Food Containers
2676	Sanitary Paper Prdts
2013	Sausages & Meat Prdts
2421	Saw & Planing Mills
3596	Scales & Balances, Exc Laboratory
2397	Schiffli Machine Embroideries
3451	Screw Machine Prdts
3812	Search, Detection, Navigation & Guidance Systs & Instrs
3341	Secondary Smelting & Refining Of Nonferrous Metals
3674	Semiconductors
3589	Service Ind Machines, NEC
2652	Set-Up Paperboard Boxes
3444	Sheet Metal Work
3731	Shipbuilding & Repairing
2079	Shortening, Oils & Margarine
3993	Signs & Advertising Displays
2262	Silk & Man-Made Fabric Finishers
2221	Silk & Man-Made Fiber
1044	Silver Ores
3914	Silverware, Plated & Stainless Steel Ware
3484	Small Arms
3482	Small Arms Ammunition
2841	Soap & Detergents
2086	Soft Drinks
2436	Softwood Veneer & Plywood
2075	Soybean Oil Mills
2842	Spec Cleaning, Polishing & Sanitation Preparations
3559	Special Ind Machinery, NEC
2429	Special Prdt Sawmills, NEC
3566	Speed Changers, Drives & Gears
3949	Sporting & Athletic Goods, NEC
2678	Stationery Prdts
3511	Steam, Gas & Hydraulic Turbines & Engines
3325	Steel Foundries, NEC
3324	Steel Investment Foundries
3317	Steel Pipe & Tubes
3493	Steel Springs, Except Wire
3315	Steel Wire Drawing & Nails & Spikes
3691	Storage Batteries
3259	Structural Clay Prdts, NEC
2439	Structural Wood Members, NEC
2063	Sugar, Beet
2061	Sugar, Cane
2062	Sugar, Cane Refining
2843	Surface Active & Finishing Agents, Sulfonated Oils
3841	Surgical & Medical Instrs & Apparatus
3613	Switchgear & Switchboard Apparatus
2824	Synthetic Organic Fibers, Exc Cellulosic
2822	Synthetic Rubber (Vulcanizable Elastomers)

T

SIC NO	PRODUCT
3795	Tanks & Tank Components
3661	Telephone & Telegraph Apparatus
2393	Textile Bags
2299	Textile Goods, NEC
3552	Textile Machinery
2284	Thread Mills
2296	Tire Cord & Fabric
3011	Tires & Inner Tubes
2141	Tobacco Stemming & Redrying
2131	Tobacco, Chewing & Snuff
3799	Transportation Eqpt, NEC
3792	Travel Trailers & Campers
3713	Truck & Bus Bodies
3715	Truck Trailers
2791	Typesetting

V

SIC NO	PRODUCT
3494	Valves & Pipe Fittings, NEC
2076	Vegetable Oil Mills
3647	Vehicular Lighting Eqpt

W

SIC NO	PRODUCT
3873	Watch & Clock Devices & Parts
2385	Waterproof Outerwear
3548	Welding Apparatus
7692	Welding Repair
2046	Wet Corn Milling
2084	Wine & Brandy
3495	Wire Springs
2331	Women's & Misses' Blouses
2335	Women's & Misses' Dresses
2339	Women's & Misses' Outerwear, NEC
3144	Women's Footwear, Exc Athletic
2341	Women's, Misses' & Children's Underwear & Nightwear
2441	Wood Boxes
2449	Wood Containers, NEC
2511	Wood Household Furniture
2512	Wood Household Furniture, Upholstered
2434	Wood Kitchen Cabinets
2521	Wood Office Furniture
2448	Wood Pallets & Skids
2499	Wood Prdts, NEC
2491	Wood Preserving
2517	Wood T V, Radio, Phono & Sewing Cabinets
2541	Wood, Office & Store Fixtures
3553	Woodworking Machinery
2231	Wool, Woven Fabric

X

SIC NO	PRODUCT
3844	X-ray Apparatus & Tubes

Y

SIC NO	PRODUCT
2281	Yarn Spinning Mills
2282	Yarn Texturizing, Throwing, Twisting & Winding Mills

SIC INDEX

Standard Industrial Classification Numerical Index

SIC NO	PRODUCT

10 metal mining
1011 Iron Ores
1021 Copper Ores
1031 Lead & Zinc Ores
1041 Gold Ores
1044 Silver Ores
1081 Metal Mining Svcs
1099 Metal Ores, NEC

12 coal mining
1221 Bituminous Coal & Lignite: Surface Mining
1241 Coal Mining Svcs

13 oil and gas extraction
1311 Crude Petroleum & Natural Gas
1321 Natural Gas Liquids
1381 Drilling Oil & Gas Wells
1382 Oil & Gas Field Exploration Svcs
1389 Oil & Gas Field Svcs, NEC

14 mining and quarrying of nonmetallic minerals, except fuels
1411 Dimension Stone
1422 Crushed & Broken Limestone
1423 Crushed & Broken Granite
1429 Crushed & Broken Stone, NEC
1442 Construction Sand & Gravel
1446 Industrial Sand
1474 Potash, Soda & Borate Minerals
1481 Nonmetallic Minerals, Except Fuels
1499 Miscellaneous Nonmetallic Mining

20 food and kindred products
2011 Meat Packing Plants
2013 Sausages & Meat Prdts
2015 Poultry Slaughtering, Dressing & Processing
2021 Butter
2022 Cheese
2023 Milk, Condensed & Evaporated
2024 Ice Cream
2026 Milk
2032 Canned Specialties
2033 Canned Fruits, Vegetables & Preserves
2034 Dried Fruits, Vegetables & Soup
2035 Pickled Fruits, Vegetables, Sauces & Dressings
2037 Frozen Fruits, Juices & Vegetables
2038 Frozen Specialties
2041 Flour, Grain Milling
2043 Cereal Breakfast Foods
2045 Flour, Blended & Prepared
2046 Wet Corn Milling
2047 Dog & Cat Food
2048 Prepared Feeds For Animals & Fowls
2051 Bread, Bakery Prdts Exc Cookies & Crackers
2052 Cookies & Crackers
2053 Frozen Bakery Prdts
2061 Sugar, Cane
2062 Sugar, Cane Refining
2063 Sugar, Beet
2064 Candy & Confectionery Prdts
2066 Chocolate & Cocoa Prdts
2067 Chewing Gum
2068 Salted & Roasted Nuts & Seeds
2075 Soybean Oil Mills
2076 Vegetable Oil Mills
2077 Animal, Marine Fats & Oils
2079 Shortening, Oils & Margarine
2082 Malt Beverages
2083 Malt
2084 Wine & Brandy
2085 Liquors, Distilled, Rectified & Blended
2086 Soft Drinks
2087 Flavoring Extracts & Syrups
2091 Fish & Seafoods, Canned & Cured
2092 Fish & Seafoods, Fresh & Frozen
2095 Coffee
2096 Potato Chips & Similar Prdts
2097 Ice
2098 Macaroni, Spaghetti & Noodles
2099 Food Preparations, NEC

21 tobacco products
2111 Cigarettes
2131 Tobacco, Chewing & Snuff
2141 Tobacco Stemming & Redrying

22 textile mill products
2211 Cotton, Woven Fabric
2221 Silk & Man-Made Fiber
2231 Wool, Woven Fabric
2241 Fabric Mills, Cotton, Wool, Silk & Man-Made
2252 Hosiery, Except Women's
2253 Knit Outerwear Mills
2258 Lace & Warp Knit Fabric Mills
2259 Knitting Mills, NEC
2261 Cotton Fabric Finishers
2262 Silk & Man-Made Fabric Finishers
2273 Carpets & Rugs
2281 Yarn Spinning Mills
2282 Yarn Texturizing, Throwing, Twisting & Winding Mills
2284 Thread Mills
2295 Fabrics Coated Not Rubberized
2296 Tire Cord & Fabric
2297 Fabrics, Nonwoven
2298 Cordage & Twine
2299 Textile Goods, NEC

23 apparel and other finished products made from fabrics and similar material
2311 Men's & Boys' Suits, Coats & Overcoats
2321 Men's & Boys' Shirts
2322 Men's & Boys' Underwear & Nightwear
2323 Men's & Boys' Neckwear
2325 Men's & Boys' Separate Trousers & Casual Slacks
2326 Men's & Boys' Work Clothing
2329 Men's & Boys' Clothing, NEC
2331 Women's & Misses' Blouses
2335 Women's & Misses' Dresses
2339 Women's & Misses' Outerwear, NEC
2341 Women's, Misses' & Children's Underwear & Nightwear
2342 Brassieres, Girdles & Garments
2353 Hats, Caps & Millinery
2361 Children's & Infants' Dresses & Blouses
2369 Girls' & Infants' Outerwear, NEC
2371 Fur Goods
2381 Dress & Work Gloves
2385 Waterproof Outerwear
2386 Leather & Sheep Lined Clothing
2389 Apparel & Accessories, NEC
2391 Curtains & Draperies
2392 House furnishings: Textile
2393 Textile Bags
2394 Canvas Prdts
2395 Pleating & Stitching For The Trade
2396 Automotive Trimmings, Apparel Findings, Related Prdts
2397 Schiffli Machine Embroideries
2399 Fabricated Textile Prdts, NEC

24 lumber and wood products, except furniture
2411 Logging
2421 Saw & Planing Mills
2426 Hardwood Dimension & Flooring Mills
2429 Special Prdt Sawmills, NEC
2431 Millwork
2434 Wood Kitchen Cabinets
2435 Hardwood Veneer & Plywood
2436 Softwood Veneer & Plywood
2439 Structural Wood Members, NEC
2441 Wood Boxes
2448 Wood Pallets & Skids
2449 Wood Containers, NEC
2451 Mobile Homes
2452 Prefabricated Wood Buildings & Cmpnts
2491 Wood Preserving
2493 Reconstituted Wood Prdts
2499 Wood Prdts, NEC

25 furniture and fixtures
2511 Wood Household Furniture
2512 Wood Household Furniture, Upholstered
2514 Metal Household Furniture
2515 Mattresses & Bedsprings
2517 Wood T V, Radio, Phono & Sewing Cabinets
2519 Household Furniture, NEC
2521 Wood Office Furniture
2522 Office Furniture, Except Wood
2531 Public Building & Related Furniture
2541 Wood, Office & Store Fixtures
2542 Partitions & Fixtures, Except Wood
2591 Drapery Hardware, Window Blinds & Shades
2599 Furniture & Fixtures, NEC

26 paper and allied products
2611 Pulp Mills
2621 Paper Mills
2631 Paperboard Mills
2652 Set-Up Paperboard Boxes
2653 Corrugated & Solid Fiber Boxes
2655 Fiber Cans, Tubes & Drums
2656 Sanitary Food Containers
2657 Folding Paperboard Boxes
2671 Paper Coating & Laminating for Packaging
2672 Paper Coating & Laminating, Exc for Packaging
2673 Bags: Plastics, Laminated & Coated
2674 Bags: Uncoated Paper & Multiwall
2675 Die-Cut Paper & Board
2676 Sanitary Paper Prdts
2677 Envelopes
2678 Stationery Prdts
2679 Converted Paper Prdts, NEC

27 printing, publishing, and allied industries
2711 Newspapers: Publishing & Printing
2721 Periodicals: Publishing & Printing
2731 Books: Publishing & Printing
2732 Book Printing, Not Publishing
2741 Misc Publishing
2752 Commercial Printing: Lithographic
2754 Commercial Printing: Gravure
2759 Commercial Printing
2761 Manifold Business Forms
2771 Greeting Card Publishing
2782 Blankbooks & Looseleaf Binders
2789 Bookbinding
2791 Typesetting
2796 Platemaking & Related Svcs

28 chemicals and allied products
2812 Alkalies & Chlorine
2813 Industrial Gases
2816 Inorganic Pigments
2819 Indl Inorganic Chemicals, NEC
2821 Plastics, Mtrls & Nonvulcanizable Elastomers
2822 Synthetic Rubber (Vulcanizable Elastomers)
2823 Cellulosic Man-Made Fibers
2824 Synthetic Organic Fibers, Exc Cellulosic
2833 Medicinal Chemicals & Botanical Prdts
2834 Pharmaceuticals
2835 Diagnostic Substances
2836 Biological Prdts, Exc Diagnostic Substances
2841 Soap & Detergents
2842 Spec Cleaning, Polishing & Sanitation Preparations
2843 Surface Active & Finishing Agents, Sulfonated Oils
2844 Perfumes, Cosmetics & Toilet Preparations
2851 Paints, Varnishes, Lacquers, Enamels
2861 Gum & Wood Chemicals
2865 Cyclic-Crudes, Intermediates, Dyes & Org Pigments
2869 Industrial Organic Chemicals, NEC
2873 Nitrogenous Fertilizers
2874 Phosphatic Fertilizers
2875 Fertilizers, Mixing Only
2879 Pesticides & Agricultural Chemicals, NEC
2891 Adhesives & Sealants
2892 Explosives
2893 Printing Ink
2899 Chemical Preparations, NEC

29 petroleum refining and related industries
2911 Petroleum Refining
2951 Paving Mixtures & Blocks
2952 Asphalt Felts & Coatings
2992 Lubricating Oils & Greases
2999 Products Of Petroleum & Coal, NEC

30 rubber and miscellaneous plastics products
3011 Tires & Inner Tubes
3021 Rubber & Plastic Footwear
3052 Rubber & Plastic Hose & Belting
3053 Gaskets, Packing & Sealing Devices
3061 Molded, Extruded & Lathe-Cut Rubber Mechanical

SIC INDEX

SIC NO	PRODUCT
	Goods
3069	Fabricated Rubber Prdts, NEC
3081	Plastic Unsupported Sheet & Film
3082	Plastic Unsupported Profile Shapes
3083	Plastic Laminated Plate & Sheet
3084	Plastic Pipe
3085	Plastic Bottles
3086	Plastic Foam Prdts
3087	Custom Compounding Of Purchased Plastic Resins
3088	Plastic Plumbing Fixtures
3089	Plastic Prdts

31 leather and leather products

SIC NO	PRODUCT
3111	Leather Tanning & Finishing
3131	Boot & Shoe Cut Stock & Findings
3142	House Slippers
3143	Men's Footwear, Exc Athletic
3144	Women's Footwear, Exc Athletic
3149	Footwear, NEC
3151	Leather Gloves & Mittens
3161	Luggage
3171	Handbags & Purses
3172	Personal Leather Goods
3199	Leather Goods, NEC

32 stone, clay, glass, and concrete products

SIC NO	PRODUCT
3211	Flat Glass
3221	Glass Containers
3229	Pressed & Blown Glassware, NEC
3231	Glass Prdts Made Of Purchased Glass
3241	Cement, Hydraulic
3251	Brick & Structural Clay Tile
3253	Ceramic Tile
3255	Clay Refractories
3259	Structural Clay Prdts, NEC
3261	China Plumbing Fixtures & Fittings
3264	Porcelain Electrical Splys
3269	Pottery Prdts, NEC
3271	Concrete Block & Brick
3272	Concrete Prdts
3273	Ready-Mixed Concrete
3275	Gypsum Prdts
3281	Cut Stone Prdts
3291	Abrasive Prdts
3292	Asbestos products
3295	Minerals & Earths: Ground Or Treated
3296	Mineral Wool
3297	Nonclay Refractories
3299	Nonmetallic Mineral Prdts, NEC

33 primary metal industries

SIC NO	PRODUCT
3312	Blast Furnaces, Coke Ovens, Steel & Rolling Mills
3313	Electrometallurgical Prdts
3315	Steel Wire Drawing & Nails & Spikes
3316	Cold Rolled Steel Sheet, Strip & Bars
3317	Steel Pipe & Tubes
3321	Gray Iron Foundries
3322	Malleable Iron Foundries
3324	Steel Investment Foundries
3325	Steel Foundries, NEC
3331	Primary Smelting & Refining Of Copper
3334	Primary Production Of Aluminum
3339	Primary Nonferrous Metals, NEC
3341	Secondary Smelting & Refining Of Nonferrous Metals
3351	Rolling, Drawing & Extruding Of Copper
3353	Aluminum Sheet, Plate & Foil
3354	Aluminum Extruded Prdts
3355	Aluminum Rolling & Drawing, NEC
3356	Rolling, Drawing-Extruding Of Nonferrous Metals
3357	Nonferrous Wire Drawing
3363	Aluminum Die Castings
3364	Nonferrous Die Castings, Exc Aluminum
3365	Aluminum Foundries
3366	Copper Foundries
3369	Nonferrous Foundries: Castings, NEC
3398	Metal Heat Treating
3399	Primary Metal Prdts, NEC

34 fabricated metal products, except machinery and transportation equipment

SIC NO	PRODUCT
3411	Metal Cans
3412	Metal Barrels, Drums, Kegs & Pails
3421	Cutlery
3423	Hand & Edge Tools
3425	Hand Saws & Saw Blades
3429	Hardware, NEC
3431	Enameled Iron & Metal Sanitary Ware
3432	Plumbing Fixture Fittings & Trim, Brass
3433	Heating Eqpt
3441	Fabricated Structural Steel
3442	Metal Doors, Sash, Frames, Molding & Trim
3443	Fabricated Plate Work
3444	Sheet Metal Work
3446	Architectural & Ornamental Metal Work
3448	Prefabricated Metal Buildings & Cmpnts
3449	Misc Structural Metal Work
3451	Screw Machine Prdts
3452	Bolts, Nuts, Screws, Rivets & Washers
3462	Iron & Steel Forgings
3463	Nonferrous Forgings
3465	Automotive Stampings
3466	Crowns & Closures
3469	Metal Stampings, NEC
3471	Electroplating, Plating, Polishing, Anodizing & Coloring
3479	Coating & Engraving, NEC
3482	Small Arms Ammunition
3483	Ammunition, Large
3484	Small Arms
3489	Ordnance & Access, NEC
3491	Industrial Valves
3492	Fluid Power Valves & Hose Fittings
3493	Steel Springs, Except Wire
3494	Valves & Pipe Fittings, NEC
3495	Wire Springs
3496	Misc Fabricated Wire Prdts
3497	Metal Foil & Leaf
3498	Fabricated Pipe & Pipe Fittings
3499	Fabricated Metal Prdts, NEC

35 industrial and commercial machinery and computer equipment

SIC NO	PRODUCT
3511	Steam, Gas & Hydraulic Turbines & Engines
3519	Internal Combustion Engines, NEC
3523	Farm Machinery & Eqpt
3524	Garden, Lawn Tractors & Eqpt
3531	Construction Machinery & Eqpt
3532	Mining Machinery & Eqpt
3533	Oil Field Machinery & Eqpt
3534	Elevators & Moving Stairways
3535	Conveyors & Eqpt
3536	Hoists, Cranes & Monorails
3537	Indl Trucks, Tractors, Trailers & Stackers
3541	Machine Tools: Cutting
3542	Machine Tools: Forming
3543	Industrial Patterns
3544	Dies, Tools, Jigs, Fixtures & Indl Molds
3545	Machine Tool Access
3546	Power Hand Tools
3547	Rolling Mill Machinery & Eqpt
3548	Welding Apparatus
3549	Metalworking Machinery, NEC
3552	Textile Machinery
3553	Woodworking Machinery
3554	Paper Inds Machinery
3555	Printing Trades Machinery & Eqpt
3556	Food Prdts Machinery
3559	Special Ind Machinery, NEC
3561	Pumps & Pumping Eqpt
3562	Ball & Roller Bearings
3563	Air & Gas Compressors
3564	Blowers & Fans
3565	Packaging Machinery
3566	Speed Changers, Drives & Gears
3567	Indl Process Furnaces & Ovens
3568	Mechanical Power Transmission Eqpt, NEC
3569	Indl Machinery & Eqpt, NEC
3571	Electronic Computers
3572	Computer Storage Devices
3575	Computer Terminals
3577	Computer Peripheral Eqpt, NEC
3578	Calculating & Accounting Eqpt
3579	Office Machines, NEC
3581	Automatic Vending Machines
3582	Commercial Laundry, Dry Clean & Pressing Mchs
3585	Air Conditioning & Heating Eqpt
3586	Measuring & Dispensing Pumps
3589	Service Ind Machines, NEC
3592	Carburetors, Pistons, Rings & Valves
3593	Fluid Power Cylinders & Actuators
3594	Fluid Power Pumps & Motors
3596	Scales & Balances, Exc Laboratory
3599	Machinery & Eqpt, Indl & Commercial, NEC

36 electronic and other electrical equipment and components, except computer

SIC NO	PRODUCT
3612	Power, Distribution & Specialty Transformers
3613	Switchgear & Switchboard Apparatus
3621	Motors & Generators
3624	Carbon & Graphite Prdts
3625	Relays & Indl Controls
3629	Electrical Indl Apparatus, NEC
3631	Household Cooking Eqpt
3632	Household Refrigerators & Freezers
3633	Household Laundry Eqpt
3634	Electric Household Appliances
3635	Household Vacuum Cleaners
3639	Household Appliances, NEC
3641	Electric Lamps
3643	Current-Carrying Wiring Devices
3644	Noncurrent-Carrying Wiring Devices
3645	Residential Lighting Fixtures
3646	Commercial, Indl & Institutional Lighting Fixtures
3647	Vehicular Lighting Eqpt
3648	Lighting Eqpt, NEC
3651	Household Audio & Video Eqpt
3652	Phonograph Records & Magnetic Tape
3661	Telephone & Telegraph Apparatus
3663	Radio & T V Communications, Systs & Eqpt, Broadcast/Studio
3669	Communications Eqpt, NEC
3671	Radio & T V Receiving Electron Tubes
3672	Printed Circuit Boards
3674	Semiconductors
3676	Electronic Resistors
3677	Electronic Coils & Transformers
3678	Electronic Connectors
3679	Electronic Components, NEC
3691	Storage Batteries
3692	Primary Batteries: Dry & Wet
3694	Electrical Eqpt For Internal Combustion Engines
3695	Recording Media
3699	Electrical Machinery, Eqpt & Splys, NEC

37 transportation equipment

SIC NO	PRODUCT
3711	Motor Vehicles & Car Bodies
3713	Truck & Bus Bodies
3714	Motor Vehicle Parts & Access
3715	Truck Trailers
3716	Motor Homes
3721	Aircraft
3724	Aircraft Engines & Engine Parts
3728	Aircraft Parts & Eqpt, NEC
3731	Shipbuilding & Repairing
3732	Boat Building & Repairing
3743	Railroad Eqpt
3751	Motorcycles, Bicycles & Parts
3761	Guided Missiles & Space Vehicles
3764	Guided Missile/Space Vehicle Propulsion Units & parts
3769	Guided Missile/Space Vehicle Parts & Eqpt, NEC
3792	Travel Trailers & Campers
3795	Tanks & Tank Components
3799	Transportation Eqpt, NEC

38 measuring, analyzing and controlling instruments; photographic, medical an

SIC NO	PRODUCT
3812	Search, Detection, Navigation & Guidance Systs & Instrs
3821	Laboratory Apparatus & Furniture
3822	Automatic Temperature Controls
3823	Indl Instruments For Meas, Display & Control
3824	Fluid Meters & Counters
3825	Instrs For Measuring & Testing Electricity
3826	Analytical Instruments
3827	Optical Instruments
3829	Measuring & Controlling Devices, NEC
3841	Surgical & Medical Instrs & Apparatus
3842	Orthopedic, Prosthetic & Surgical Appliances/Splys
3843	Dental Eqpt & Splys
3844	X-ray Apparatus & Tubes
3845	Electromedical & Electrotherapeutic Apparatus
3851	Ophthalmic Goods
3861	Photographic Eqpt & Splys
3873	Watch & Clock Devices & Parts

39 miscellaneous manufacturing industries

SIC NO	PRODUCT
3911	Jewelry: Precious Metal
3914	Silverware, Plated & Stainless Steel Ware
3915	Jewelers Findings & Lapidary Work
3931	Musical Instruments
3942	Dolls & Stuffed Toys
3944	Games, Toys & Children's Vehicles
3949	Sporting & Athletic Goods, NEC
3951	Pens & Mechanical Pencils
3952	Lead Pencils, Crayons & Artist's Mtrls
3953	Marking Devices
3955	Carbon Paper & Inked Ribbons
3961	Costume Jewelry & Novelties
3965	Fasteners, Buttons, Needles & Pins
3991	Brooms & Brushes
3993	Signs & Advertising Displays
3995	Burial Caskets

SIC INDEX

SIC NO	PRODUCT
3996	Linoleum & Hard Surface Floor Coverings, NEC
3999	Manufacturing Industries, NEC

73 business services

7372	Prepackaged Software

76 miscellaneous repair services

7692	Welding Repair
7694	Armature Rewinding Shops

SIC SECTION

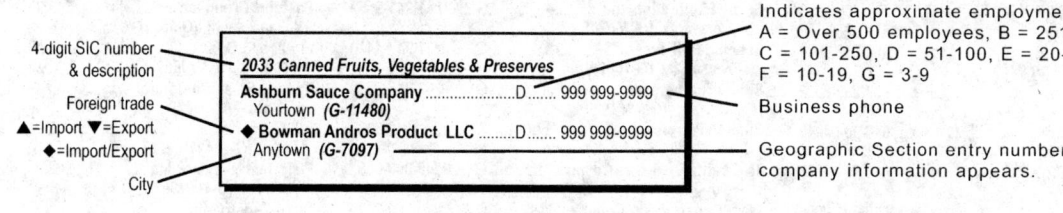

- 4-digit SIC number & description
- Foreign trade ▲=Import ▼=Export ◆=Import/Export
- City

2033 Canned Fruits, Vegetables & Preserves
Ashburn Sauce Company ....D...... 999 999-9999
  Yourtown (G-11480)
◆ Bowman Andros Product LLC ....D...... 999 999-9999
  Anytown (G-7097)

- Indicates approximate employment figure
  A = Over 500 employees, B = 251-500
  C = 101-250, D = 51-100, E = 20-50
  F = 10-19, G = 3-9
- Business phone
- Geographic Section entry number where full company information appears.

See footnotes for symbols and codes identification.

- The SIC codes in this section are from the latest Standard Industrial Classification manual published by the U.S. Government's Office of Management and Budget. For more information regarding SICs, see the Explanatory Notes.
- Companies may be listed under multiple classifications.

10 METAL MINING

1011 Iron Ores
Cleveland-Cliffs Inc.................A...... 906 475-3547
  Ishpeming (G-8775)
Constine Inc.................E...... 989 723-6043
  Owosso (G-12827)
Empire Iron Mining Partnership....A...... 906 475-3600
  Palmer (G-12930)
Tilden Mining Company LC............A...... 906 475-3400
  Ishpeming (G-8783)

1021 Copper Ores
Copperwood Resources Inc..........F...... 906 229-3115
  Wakefield (G-17618)
Eagle Mine LLC..........B...... 906 339-7000
  Champion (G-2704)
◆ Trelleborg Corporation..........G...... 269 639-9891
  South Haven (G-15419)

1031 Lead & Zinc Ores
National Zinc Processors Inc..........F...... 269 926-1161
  Benton Harbor (G-1577)
◆ Trelleborg Corporation..........G...... 269 639-9891
  South Haven (G-15419)

1041 Gold Ores
Sulugu Corporation USA Inc..........D...... 478 714-0325
  Grand Rapids (G-7232)
◆ Trelleborg Corporation..........G...... 269 639-9891
  South Haven (G-15419)

1044 Silver Ores
Aghog Inc..........G...... 313 277-2037
  Livonia (G-10105)
◆ Trelleborg Corporation..........G...... 269 639-9891
  South Haven (G-15419)

1081 Metal Mining Svcs
Angels of Detroit LLC..........G...... 248 796-1079
  Redford (G-13714)
Blade Excavating Inc..........G...... 810 287-6457
  Flint (G-5656)
Meridian Lightweight Tech Inc..........E...... 248 663-8100
  Plymouth (G-13241)
Minerals Processing Corp..........G...... 906 352-4024
  Menominee (G-11252)
URS Energy & Construction Inc..........C...... 989 642-4190
  Hemlock (G-7857)

1099 Metal Ores, NEC
Howmet Aerospace Inc..........G...... 231 894-5686
  Whitehall (G-18500)

12 COAL MINING

1221 Bituminous Coal & Lignite: Surface Mining
◆ Lotus International Company..........A...... 734 245-0140
  Canton (G-2486)
Silver Slate LLC..........F...... 248 486-3989
  Milford (G-11488)

1241 Coal Mining Svcs
Peak Manufacturing Inc..........E...... 517 769-6900
  Pleasant Lake (G-13104)

13 OIL AND GAS EXTRACTION

1311 Crude Petroleum & Natural Gas
A1 Utility Contractor Inc..........D...... 989 324-8581
  Evart (G-5118)
Aztec Producing Co Inc..........G...... 269 792-0505
  Wayland (G-18188)
Bailer and De Shaw..........G...... 989 684-3610
  Kawkawlin (G-9414)
Blarney Castle Inc..........G...... 231 864-3111
  Bear Lake (G-1416)
Breitburn Operating LP..........G...... 989 348-8459
  Grayling (G-7457)
Christian Oil Company..........F...... 269 673-2218
  Allegan (G-151)
Cima Energy LP..........G...... 231 941-0633
  Traverse City (G-16652)
Columbus Oil & Gas LLC..........G...... 810 385-9140
  Burtchville (G-2218)
Dart Energy Corporation..........F...... 231 885-1665
  Mesick (G-11271)
Dcp Midstream LLC..........G...... 936 615-5189
  Marysville (G-11086)
▼ DTE Energy Company..........E...... 313 235-4000
  Detroit (G-4193)
DTE Energy Trust II..........G...... 313 235-8822
  Detroit (G-4194)
DTE Energy Ventures Inc..........G...... 313 235-8000
  Detroit (G-4195)
E Smart Fuels America Inc..........G...... 248 687-8003
  Detroit (G-4198)
Energy Acquisition..........G...... 616 350-9129
  Grandville (G-7373)
Goodale Enterprises LLC..........G...... 616 453-7690
  Grand Rapids (G-6750)
Jordan Exploration Co LLC..........E...... 231 935-4220
  Traverse City (G-16731)
Kelly Oil & Gas Inc..........G...... 231 929-0591
  Traverse City (G-16732)
Landman..........G...... 231 946-4678
  Traverse City (G-16738)
Lease Management Inc..........G...... 989 773-5948
  Mount Pleasant (G-11707)
Mack Oil Corporation..........G...... 231 590-5903
  Traverse City (G-16751)
Michigan Reef Development..........G...... 989 288-2172
  Durand (G-4842)
Miller Exploration Company..........F...... 231 941-0004
  Traverse City (G-16758)
Muskegon Development Company..........E...... 989 772-4900
  Mount Pleasant (G-11724)
Oil City Venture Inc..........G...... 989 832-8071
  Midland (G-11399)
Omimex Energy Inc..........G...... 231 845-7358
  Ludington (G-10549)
Omimex Energy Inc..........G...... 517 628-2820
  Mason (G-11148)
Option Energy LLC..........G...... 269 329-4317
  Traverse City (G-16784)
Petroleum Resources Inc..........G...... 586 752-7856
  Romeo (G-14232)
Refinery Corporation America..........G...... 877 881-0336
  Harper Woods (G-7671)
Route 66 Pennzoil..........G...... 313 382-8888
  Taylor (G-16468)
Sappington Crude Oil Inc..........G...... 989 345-1052
  West Branch (G-18340)
SD Oil Enterprises Inc..........G...... 248 688-1419
  Warren (G-18007)
Somoco Inc..........G...... 231 946-0200
  Traverse City (G-16837)
Southwestern Mich Dust Ctrl..........E...... 269 521-7638
  Bloomingdale (G-1879)
Speedway LLC..........F...... 231 775-8101
  Cadillac (G-2355)
Summit-Reed City Inc..........E...... 989 433-5716
  Rosebush (G-14367)
TEs Filer Cy Stn Ltd Partnr..........G...... 231 723-6573
  Filer City (G-5611)
Trendwell Energy Corporation..........F...... 616 866-5024
  Rockford (G-14191)
Tronox Incorporated..........G...... 231 328-4986
  Merritt (G-11268)
Ward Lake Drilling Inc..........E...... 989 732-8499
  Gaylord (G-6166)
West Bay Exploration Company..........F...... 231 946-3529
  Traverse City (G-16877)
William R Hall Kimberly..........G...... 989 426-4605
  Gladwin (G-6208)

1321 Natural Gas Liquids
Altagas Marketing (us) Inc..........E...... 810 887-4105
  Port Huron (G-13435)
Altagas Power Holdings US Inc..........D...... 810 887-4105
  Port Huron (G-13436)
Everest Energy Fund L L C..........G...... 586 445-2300
  Warren (G-17797)
Tronox Incorporated..........G...... 231 328-4986
  Merritt (G-11268)
▲ Westport Fuel Systems US Inc..........D...... 734 233-6850
  Plymouth (G-13338)

1381 Drilling Oil & Gas Wells
5 Star Drctional Drlg Svcs Ind..........G...... 231 263-2050
  Kingsley (G-9520)
Advanced Energy Services LLC..........D...... 231 369-2602
  South Boardman (G-15395)
Alexander Directional Boring..........G...... 989 362-9506
  East Tawas (G-4916)
Alpha Directional Boring..........G...... 586 405-0171
  Davisburg (G-3756)
Comet Energy Services LLC..........G...... 231 933-3600
  Traverse City (G-16657)
Diamondbck-Directional Drlg LLC..........F...... 231 943-3000
  Traverse City (G-16668)
Edgemarc Energy Holdings LLC..........E...... 724 749-8466
  Birmingham (G-1726)
Eis Inc..........G...... 734 266-6500
  Livonia (G-10192)
Finn Directional Inc..........G...... 231 944-0923
  Roscommon (G-14349)
Fortis Energy Services Inc..........D...... 248 283-7100
  Troy (G-17119)
GTM Steamer Service Inc..........G...... 989 732-7678
  Gaylord (G-6132)
Industrial Control Systems LLC..........G...... 269 689-3241
  Sturgis (G-16294)
Key Energy Services Inc..........G...... 231 258-9637
  Kalkaska (G-9393)
Michiwest Energy Inc..........G...... 989 772-2107
  Mount Pleasant (G-11713)
Middleton Well Drilling..........G...... 989 465-1078
  Coleman (G-3469)
Navigator Wireline Service Inc..........F...... 989 275-9112
  Roscommon (G-14352)
Phoenix Technology Svcs USA..........F...... 231 995-0100
  Traverse City (G-16790)
Rafalski CPA..........G...... 248 689-1685
  Troy (G-17328)

13 OIL AND GAS EXTRACTION

▲ S and P Drctnal Boring Svc LLC .... G 989 832-7716
  Midland *(G-11412)*
Sedco Directional Drilling .... G 231 258-5318
  Kalkaska *(G-9403)*
Srw Inc .... F 989 732-8884
  Traverse City *(G-16840)*
Srw Inc .... F 989 269-8528
  Bad Axe *(G-1111)*
Stovall Well Drilling Co .... G 616 364-4144
  Grand Rapids *(G-7228)*
Thompson Well Drilling .... G 616 754-5032
  Gowen *(G-6230)*
Tip Top Drilling LLC .... G 616 291-8006
  Sparta *(G-15787)*
Walters Plumbing Company .... F 269 962-6253
  Battle Creek *(G-1310)*
Ward Lake Drilling Inc .... E 989 732-8499
  Gaylord *(G-6166)*

1382 Oil & Gas Field Exploration Svcs

American Wireline Services Inc .... G 231 218-6849
  Traverse City *(G-16601)*
Apollo Exploration Dev Inc .... G 989 773-2854
  Mount Pleasant *(G-11680)*
Arbor Operating LLC .... G 231 941-2237
  Traverse City *(G-16602)*
Baker Hghes Olfld Oprtions LLC .... G 989 773-7992
  Mount Pleasant *(G-11685)*
Baygeo Inc .... E 231 941-7660
  Traverse City *(G-16617)*
Bobcat Oil & Gas Inc .... G 989 426-4375
  Gladwin *(G-6190)*
Capital Assets Resources LLC .... G 248 252-7854
  Southfield *(G-15516)*
▼ CMS Enterprises Company .... C 517 788-0550
  Jackson *(G-8845)*
Core Energy LLC .... G 231 946-2419
  Traverse City *(G-16661)*
Dart Energy Corporation .... F 231 885-1665
  Mesick *(G-11271)*
Dcr Services & Cnstr Inc .... F 313 297-6544
  Detroit *(G-4123)*
Don Yohe Enterprises Inc .... F 586 784-5556
  Armada *(G-733)*
DTE Gas & Oil Company .... F 231 995-4000
  Traverse City *(G-16672)*
Dynamic Development Inc .... G 231 723-8318
  Manistee *(G-10897)*
Eagle Exploration Inc .... G 231 252-4624
  Grawn *(G-7450)*
Emerson Geophysical LLC .... E 231 943-1400
  Traverse City *(G-16677)*
Energy Acquisition Corp .... F 517 339-0249
  Holt *(G-8310)*
Energy Exploration .... G 248 579-6531
  Novi *(G-12413)*
Express Care of South Lyon .... G 248 437-6919
  South Lyon *(G-15436)*
Horizontal Lift Technologies .... G 231 421-9696
  Traverse City *(G-16715)*
Howard Energy Co Inc .... E 231 995-7850
  Traverse City *(G-16716)*
HRF Exploration & Prod LLC .... E 989 732-6950
  Gaylord *(G-6134)*
John T Stoliker Enterprises .... G 586 727-1402
  Columbus *(G-3499)*
Lgc Global Energy Fm Llc .... G 313 989-4141
  Detroit *(G-4396)*
Linn Energy .... F 989 786-7592
  Lewiston *(G-10024)*
Loneys Welding & Excvtg Inc .... G 231 328-4408
  Merritt *(G-11267)*
Maness Petroleum Corp .... G 989 773-5475
  Mount Pleasant *(G-11709)*
Martec Land Services Inc .... F 231 929-3971
  Traverse City *(G-16754)*
Maverick Exploration Prod Inc .... G 231 929-3923
  Traverse City *(G-16755)*
Meridian Energy Corporation .... E 517 339-8444
  Haslett *(G-7775)*
Miller Energy Inc .... F 269 352-5960
  Kalamazoo *(G-9272)*
Miracle Petroleum LLC .... G 231 946-8090
  Traverse City *(G-16760)*
OIL Energy Corp .... F 231 933-3600
  Traverse City *(G-16777)*
Peninslar Oil Gas Cmpny-Mchgan .... G 616 676-2090
  Grand Rapids *(G-7075)*
Pinnacle Energy LLC .... G 248 623-6091
  Clarkston *(G-3056)*

Ranch Production LLC .... F 231 869-2050
  Pentwater *(G-12973)*
Savoy Exploration Inc .... G 231 941-9552
  Traverse City *(G-16824)*
Schmude Oil Inc .... G 231 947-4410
  Traverse City *(G-16826)*
Sturak Brothers Inc .... G 269 345-2929
  Kalamazoo *(G-9344)*
Summit Petroleum Company LLC ..... F 231 942-8134
  Traverse City *(G-16845)*
Tri County Oil & Gas Co Inc .... G 248 390-0682
  Shelby Township *(G-15356)*
Wara Construction Company LLC ..... D 248 299-2410
  Rochester Hills *(G-14141)*
Ward-Williston Company .... D 248 594-6622
  Bloomfield *(G-1786)*
West Bay Geophysical Inc .... G 231 946-3529
  Traverse City *(G-16878)*
Western Land Services Inc .... D 231 843-8878
  Ludington *(G-10557)*
Wolverine Gas and Oil Corp .... E 616 458-1150
  Grand Rapids *(G-7346)*

1389 Oil & Gas Field Svcs, NEC

1st Choice Trckg & Rentl Inc .... G 231 258-0417
  Kalkaska *(G-9381)*
5 By 5 LLC .... F 855 369-6757
  Traverse City *(G-16594)*
917 Chittock Street LLC .... F 866 945-0269
  Lansing *(G-9798)*
Acme Septic Tank Co .... F 989 684-3852
  Kawkawlin *(G-9413)*
All About Bus Cnstr Aabc LLC .... G 248 229-3031
  Redford *(G-13712)*
Ally Servicing LLC .... A 248 948-7702
  Detroit *(G-4003)*
Altered Stone Realty Co LLC .... F 313 800-0362
  Detroit *(G-4005)*
Aspn Wood Construction LLC .... F 810 246-8044
  Royal Oak *(G-14514)*
B & H Cementing Services Inc .... G 989 773-5975
  Mount Pleasant *(G-11682)*
B & H Tractor & Truck Inc .... G 989 773-5975
  Mount Pleasant *(G-11683)*
Bach Services & Mfg Co LLC .... F 231 263-2777
  Kingsley *(G-9521)*
Baker Hghes Olfld Oprtions LLC .... G 989 772-1600
  Mount Pleasant *(G-11684)*
Baker Hghes Olfld Oprtions LLC .... G 989 773-7992
  Mount Pleasant *(G-11685)*
Baker Hghes Olfld Oprtions LLC .... G 231 342-9408
  Traverse City *(G-16611)*
Baker Hughes Holdings LLC .... G 989 506-2167
  Mount Pleasant *(G-11686)*
Baker Hughes Holdings LLC .... G 989 732-2082
  Gaylord *(G-6119)*
Bdr Inc .... G 989 732-1608
  Johannesburg *(G-9080)*
Beckman Production Svcs Inc .... C 231 258-9524
  Kalkaska *(G-9384)*
Bruno Wojcik .... G 989 785-5555
  Atlanta *(G-744)*
Burkholder Excavating Inc .... G 269 426-4227
  Sawyer *(G-15107)*
Cbbn Restoration LLc .... G 231 220-9892
  Traverse City *(G-16640)*
Central Michigan Tank Rental .... G 989 681-5963
  Saint Louis *(G-14989)*
Cheboygan Cnty Hbtat For Hmnit ..... G 231 597-4663
  Cheboygan *(G-2783)*
Coil Drilling Technologies Inc .... G 989 773-6504
  Mount Pleasant *(G-11693)*
Columbus Oil & Gas LLC .... G 810 385-9140
  Burtchville *(G-2218)*
Counts Investment Group LLC .... F 313 613-6866
  Detroit *(G-4105)*
Cross Country Oilfld Svcs Inc .... G 337 366-3840
  Metamora *(G-11278)*
D D Quality Servicing .... G 517 709-3705
  Holt *(G-8306)*
Dama Tool & Gauge Company .... E 616 842-9631
  Norton Shores *(G-12287)*
Deperez Contracting LLC .... G 947 224-1999
  Detroit *(G-4132)*
Diversified Prof Rlty Svcs .... G 313 215-1840
  Hazel Park *(G-7824)*
Double Check Tools Service .... G 231 947-1632
  Williamsburg *(G-18553)*
▼ DTE Energy Resources Inc .... D 734 302-4800
  Ann Arbor *(G-459)*

Dynamic Exploration Inc .... G 231 723-7879
  Manistee *(G-10898)*
Eastport Group Inc .... F 989 732-0030
  Johannesburg *(G-9081)*
El Paso LLC .... G 231 587-0704
  Mancelona *(G-10869)*
Exodus Pressure Control .... G 231 258-8001
  Kalkaska *(G-9387)*
F & M Gas .... G 313 292-2519
  Taylor *(G-16415)*
Field Tech Services Inc .... G 989 786-7046
  Lewiston *(G-10019)*
Fiore Construction .... G 517 404-0000
  Howell *(G-8454)*
Fisher McCall Oil Gas .... G 616 318-9155
  Grosse Pointe Farms *(G-7535)*
Forsters and Sons Oil Change .... F 248 618-6860
  Waterford *(G-18123)*
FTC LLC .... F 313 622-1583
  Novi *(G-12420)*
Gas Recovery Systems LLC .... E 248 305-7774
  Northville *(G-12222)*
Gjm Property LLC .... F 248 592-7323
  Boon *(G-1881)*
Go Frac LLC .... G 817 731-0301
  Detroit *(G-4268)*
Grace Contracting Services LLC ...... G 906 630-4680
  Mc Millan *(G-11188)*
Great Lakes Compression Inc .... E 989 786-3788
  Lewiston *(G-10020)*
Great Lakes Wellhead Inc .... G 231 943-9100
  Grawn *(G-7451)*
Greenlight Home Inspection Svc ...... G 313 885-5616
  Saint Clair Shores *(G-14863)*
GTM Steamer Service Inc .... F 989 732-7678
  Gaylord *(G-6132)*
Harmonie International LLC .... F 248 737-9933
  Farmington Hills *(G-5258)*
Hassan Sons Spcial HM Svcs LLC ... G 313 558-1031
  Inkster *(G-8665)*
Integrity Sltons Feld Svcs Inc .... E 517 481-4724
  Alma *(G-242)*
Jet Subsurface Rod Pumps Corp ..... F 989 732-7513
  Gaylord *(G-6136)*
Jn Newman Construction LLC .... G 269 968-1290
  Springfield *(G-15870)*
JO Well Service and Tstg Inc .... G 989 772-4221
  Mount Pleasant *(G-11705)*
Jones Ray Well Servicing Inc .... F 989 832-8071
  Midland *(G-11379)*
Jrj Energy Services LLC .... F 231 823-2171
  Stanwood *(G-15904)*
◆ Kadant Johnson LLC .... C 269 278-1715
  Three Rivers *(G-16577)*
Kap Building Services Inc .... G 888 622-0527
  Westland *(G-18391)*
Kdk Downhole Tooling LLC .... G 231 590-3137
  Williamsburg *(G-18557)*
Kingston Prperty Advisers Corp .... G 248 825-9657
  Redford *(G-13741)*
Lapeer Fuel Ventures Inc .... G 810 664-8770
  Lapeer *(G-9938)*
Layline Oil and Gas LLC .... F 231 743-2452
  Marion *(G-10972)*
Lease Management Inc .... G 989 773-5948
  Mount Pleasant *(G-11707)*
Lgc Global Inc .... E 313 989-4141
  Detroit *(G-4395)*
Loshaw Bros Inc .... G 989 732-7263
  Gaylord *(G-6143)*
Maximum Oilfield Service Inc .... E 989 731-0099
  Elmira *(G-5039)*
McConnell & Scully Inc .... G 517 568-4104
  Homer *(G-8353)*
McNaughton-Mckay Electric Co .... B 248 399-7500
  Madison Heights *(G-10779)*
Melix Services Inc .... G 248 387-9303
  Hamtramck *(G-7612)*
Michigan Wireline Service .... E 989 772-5075
  Mount Pleasant *(G-11712)*
Mid State Oil Tools Inc .... F 989 773-4114
  Mount Pleasant *(G-11714)*
Mikes Steamer Service Inc .... F 231 258-8500
  Williamsburg *(G-18558)*
Miller Investment Company LLC ...... F 231 933-3233
  Traverse City *(G-16759)*
Mr Everything LLC .... G 248 301-2580
  Redford *(G-13748)*
N G S G I Natural Gas Ser .... F 989 786-3788
  Lewiston *(G-10025)*

SIC SECTION 14 MINING AND QUARRYING OF NONMETALLIC MINERALS, EXCEPT FUELS

Natural Gas Cmprssion Systems ....E 231 941-0107
  Traverse City (G-16767)
Navigator Wireline Service Inc ....F....... 989 275-9112
  Roscommon (G-14352)
Northern A 1 Services Inc ....D....... 231 258-9961
  Kalkaska (G-9399)
Northern Tank LLC ....E....... 989 386-2389
  Clare (G-2992)
Northern Tank Truck Service ....G....... 989 732-7531
  Gaylord (G-6151)
Nse Property Group LLC ....G....... 313 605-1646
  Detroit (G-4493)
Oil Exchange 6 Inc ....G....... 734 641-4310
  Inkster (G-8669)
Oncourse Inc ....F....... 231 946-1259
  Traverse City (G-16782)
Pelhams Construction LLC ....G....... 517 549-8276
  Jonesville (G-9098)
Peninslar Oil Gas Cmpny-Mchgan ....G....... 616 676-2090
  Grand Rapids (G-7075)
Phoenix Operating Company Inc ....G....... 231 929-7171
  Williamsburg (G-18562)
Pioneer Oil Tools Inc ....G....... 989 644-6999
  Mount Pleasant (G-11732)
PRC Commercial Services LLC ....G....... 313 445-1760
  Dearborn (G-3884)
Premier Casing Crews Inc ....G....... 989 775-7436
  Mount Pleasant (G-11734)
Rcs Services Company LLC ....G....... 989 732-7999
  Johannesburg (G-9082)
Red Carpet Capital Inc ....G....... 248 952-8583
  Orchard Lake (G-12719)
Riverside Energy Michigan LLC ....G....... 231 995-4000
  Traverse City (G-16821)
Road To Freedom ....F....... 810 775-0992
  Brighton (G-2066)
Rock Industries Inc ....E....... 248 338-2800
  Bloomfield Hills (G-1858)
Rowsey Construction & Dev LLC ....G....... 313 675-2464
  Detroit (G-4572)
Sadie Oil LLC ....G....... 517 675-1325
  Perry (G-12980)
Saginaw Valley Inst Mtls Inc ....G....... 989 496-2307
  Midland (G-11413)
Sappington Crude Oil Inc ....G....... 989 345-1052
  West Branch (G-18340)
Schunk Oil Field Service Inc ....G....... 517 676-8900
  Mason (G-11152)
Seal Right Services Inc ....G....... 231 357-5595
  Buckley (G-2208)
Soli-Bond Inc ....G....... 989 684-9611
  Bay City (G-1404)
SOS Well Services LLC ....D....... 586 580-2576
  Shelby Township (G-15339)
Srw Inc ....F....... 989 732-8884
  Traverse City (G-16840)
Srw Inc ....F....... 989 269-8528
  Bad Axe (G-1111)
Steiner Associates ....G....... 734 422-5188
  Livonia (G-10421)
Stovall Well Drilling Co ....G....... 616 364-4144
  Grand Rapids (G-7228)
Superior Inspection Svc ....G....... 231 258-9400
  Kalkaska (G-9405)
Superior Mar & Envmtl Svcs LLC ....G....... 906 253-9448
  Sault Sainte Marie (G-15101)
Team Services LLC ....E....... 231 258-9130
  Kalkaska (G-9406)
Team Spooling Services LLC ....G....... 231 258-9130
  Kalkaska (G-9407)
Technical Enterprises LLC ....G....... 313 333-1438
  Detroit (G-4629)
Technical Environmental Svcs ....E....... 810 229-6323
  Brighton (G-2075)
Top Shelf Painter Inc ....F....... 586 465-0867
  Fraser (G-6004)
Trend Services Company ....G....... 231 258-9951
  Kalkaska (G-9409)
Ttadevelopment LLC ....G....... 626 399-4225
  Detroit (G-4648)
Union Oil Co ....G....... 989 348-8459
  Grayling (G-7470)
Verbio North America Corp ....E....... 866 306-4471
  Livonia (G-10459)
Veterans Utility Services LLC ....D....... 888 878-4191
  Lansing (G-9901)
Wara Construction Company LLC ....D....... 248 299-2410
  Rochester Hills (G-14141)
Wellmaster Consulting Inc ....F....... 231 893-9266
  Rothbury (G-14499)

Wentzel Energy Partners LLC ....G....... 817 713-3283
  Madison Heights (G-10861)
Woder Construction Inc ....F....... 989 731-6371
  Gaylord (G-6167)
Zellars Group LLC ....G....... 313 828-2309
  Detroit (G-4702)

14 MINING AND QUARRYING OF NONMETALLIC MINERALS, EXCEPT FUELS

1411 Dimension Stone

Best Granite and Marble Inc ....G....... 313 247-3909
  Warren (G-17733)
Doug Wirt Enterprises Inc ....G....... 989 684-5777
  Bay City (G-1347)
▲ Levy Indiana Slag Co ....D....... 313 843-7200
  Dearborn (G-3862)
Manigg Enterprises Inc ....F....... 989 356-4986
  Alpena (G-301)
▲ Michigan Tile and Marble Co ....E....... 313 931-1700
  Detroit (G-4453)
Northern Mich Aggregates LLC ....F....... 989 354-3502
  Wixom (G-18722)
O-N Minerals Michigan Company ....C....... 989 734-2131
  Rogers City (G-14215)
Take Us-4-Granite Inc ....F....... 586 803-1305
  Shelby Township (G-15349)
TNT Marble and Stone Inc ....G....... 248 887-8237
  Hartland (G-7772)

1422 Crushed & Broken Limestone

Aggregate and Developing LLC ....G....... 269 217-5492
  Allegan (G-144)
Carmeuse Lime Inc ....C....... 906 484-2201
  Cedarville (G-2668)
Carmeuse Lime Inc ....C....... 313 849-9268
  River Rouge (G-13853)
Dufferin Aggregates ....G....... 734 529-2411
  Dundee (G-4814)
Eggers Excavating LLC ....F....... 989 695-5205
  Freeland (G-6022)
F G Cheney Limestone Co ....G....... 269 763-9541
  Bellevue (G-1498)
Falcon Trucking Company ....E....... 989 656-2831
  Bay Port (G-1414)
Flint Lime Industries Inc ....G....... 313 843-6050
  Detroit (G-4238)
▲ Genesee Cut Stone & Marble Co .....E....... 810 743-1800
  Grand Blanc (G-6242)
Grand Rapids Gravel Company ....F....... 616 538-9000
  Grand Rapids (G-6759)
O N Minerals ....G....... 906 484-2201
  Cedarville (G-2671)
O-N Minerals Michigan Company ....C....... 906 484-2201
  Cedarville (G-2672)
O-N Minerals Michigan Company ....C....... 989 734-2131
  Rogers City (G-14214)
O-N Minerals Michigan Company ....C....... 906 484-2201
  Cedarville (G-2673)
O-N Minerals Michigan Company ....C....... 989 734-2131
  Rogers City (G-14215)
R E Glancy Inc ....G....... 989 362-0997
  Tawas City (G-16367)
Stoneco Inc ....G....... 734 587-7125
  Maybee (G-11172)
Trout Enterprises LLC ....G....... 810 309-4289
  Flint (G-5784)
Waanders Concrete Co ....F....... 269 673-6352
  Allegan (G-184)

1423 Crushed & Broken Granite

▲ Genesee Cut Stone & Marble Co .....E....... 810 743-1800
  Grand Blanc (G-6242)
Graniteonecom Inc ....G....... 616 452-8372
  Grand Rapids (G-6780)

1429 Crushed & Broken Stone, NEC

American Aggregate Inc ....G....... 269 683-6160
  Niles (G-12110)
Sandys Contracting ....G....... 810 629-2259
  Fenton (G-5502)

1442 Construction Sand & Gravel

1johnson Erling ....G....... 231 625-2247
  Cheboygan (G-2779)

A & E Agg Inc ....E....... 248 547-4711
  Berkley (G-1617)
A Lindberg & Sons Inc ....E....... 906 485-5705
  Ishpeming (G-8774)
Afgco Sand & Gravel Co Inc ....G....... 810 798-3293
  Almont (G-255)
Albrecht Sand & Gravel Co ....G....... 810 672-9272
  Snover (G-15390)
Alpena Aggregate Inc ....E....... 989 595-2511
  Alpena (G-275)
American Aggregate Inc ....G....... 269 683-6160
  Niles (G-12110)
American Aggregates Mich Inc ....D....... 248 348-8511
  Wixom (G-18607)
Bailey Sand & Gravel Co ....F....... 517 750-4889
  Jackson (G-8820)
Barber Creek Sand & Gravel ....E....... 616 675-7619
  Kent City (G-9427)
Bdk Group Northern Mich Inc ....F....... 574 875-5183
  Charlevoix (G-2711)
Bear Creek Sand & Gravel LLC ....G....... 989 681-3641
  Saint Louis (G-14987)
Bechtel Sand & Gravel ....G....... 810 346-2041
  Brown City (G-2135)
Bently Sand & Gravel ....G....... 810 629-6172
  Fenton (G-5458)
Bouchey and Sons Inc ....G....... 989 588-4118
  Farwell (G-5421)
Branch West Concrete Products ....F....... 989 345-0794
  West Branch (G-18326)
Briggs Contracting ....G....... 989 687-7331
  Sanford (G-15072)
Bunting Sand & Gravel Products ....E....... 989 345-2373
  West Branch (G-18327)
Cardinal Economic Sand Finance ....G....... 734 926-6989
  Ann Arbor (G-414)
Carr Brothers and Sons Inc ....E....... 517 629-3549
  Albion (G-119)
Carr Brothers and Sons Inc ....F....... 517 531-3358
  Albion (G-120)
Cheboygan Cement Products Inc ....E....... 231 627-5631
  Cheboygan (G-2782)
Chippewa Stone & Gravel Inc ....G....... 231 867-5757
  Rodney (G-14206)
Cliffs Sand & Gravel Inc ....G....... 989 422-3463
  Houghton Lake (G-8396)
Crandell Bros Trucking Co ....G....... 517 543-2930
  Charlotte (G-2747)
Downriver Crushed Concrete ....G....... 734 283-1833
  Taylor (G-16405)
Dugrees Sand and Gravel ....G....... 906 295-1569
  Hermansville (G-7861)
Elmers Crane and Dozer Inc ....C....... 231 943-3443
  Traverse City (G-16676)
Falcon Trucking Company ....G....... 313 843-7200
  Dearborn (G-3839)
Falcon Trucking Company ....E....... 989 656-2831
  Bay Port (G-1414)
Falcon Trucking Company ....E....... 248 634-9471
  Davisburg (G-3768)
Familygradegravel Yahoocom ....G....... 517 202-4121
  Mason (G-11132)
Finch Sand & Gravel LLC ....G....... 734 439-1044
  Milan (G-11435)
Fritz Enterprises ....E....... 734 283-7272
  Trenton (G-16888)
Fuoss Gravel Company ....F....... 989 725-2084
  Owosso (G-12834)
Fyke Washed Sand Gravel ....G....... 248 547-4714
  Berkley (G-1626)
Gale Briggs Inc ....G....... 517 543-1320
  Charlotte (G-2758)
Genesis Sand and Gravel Inc ....G....... 313 587-8530
  West Bloomfield (G-18283)
Genoak Materials Inc ....C....... 248 634-8276
  Holly (G-8273)
Grand Rapids Gravel Company ....E....... 616 538-9000
  Belmont (G-1507)
Grand Rapids Gravel Company ....F....... 616 538-9000
  Grand Rapids (G-6759)
Halliday Sand & Gravel Inc ....E....... 989 422-3463
  Houghton Lake (G-8397)
Heritage Resources Inc ....G....... 616 554-9888
  Caledonia (G-2379)
High Grade Materials Company ....E....... 616 754-5545
  Greenville (G-7492)
Hubscher & Son Inc ....G....... 989 773-5369
  Mount Pleasant (G-11702)
Hubscher & Son Inc ....G....... 989 875-2151
  Sumner (G-16332)

14 MINING AND QUARRYING OF NONMETALLIC MINERALS, EXCEPT FUELS

Huizenga Gravel Company Inc .... F 616 772-6241
  Zeeland (G-19042)
J T Express Ltd .... G 810 724-6471
  Brown City (G-2138)
Jack Millikin Inc .... G 989 348-8411
  Grayling (G-7464)
John R Sand & Gravel Co Inc .... G 810 678-3715
  Metamora (G-11282)
Kasson Sand & Gravel Co Inc .... F 231 228-5455
  Maple City (G-10942)
Ken Measel Supply Inc .... G 810 798-3293
  Almont (G-263)
Kurtz Gravel Company Inc .... E 810 787-6543
  Farmington Hills (G-5286)
Lafarge North America Inc .... G 231 726-3291
  Muskegon (G-11855)
Lafarge North America Inc .... G 703 480-3600
  Dundee (G-4827)
Lakeside Aggregate LLC .... D 616 837-5858
  Nunica (G-12583)
Levy Environmental Services Co .... E 313 429-2272
  Dearborn (G-3861)
Lyon Sand & Gravel Co .... G 313 843-7200
  Dearborn (G-3864)
Lyon Sand & Gravel Co .... F 248 348-8511
  Wixom (G-18701)
M-52 Sand & Gravel LLC .... G 734 453-3695
  Plymouth (G-13230)
M-57 Aggregate Company .... G 810 639-7516
  Montrose (G-11605)
Marsack Sand & Gravel Inc .... G 586 293-4414
  Roseville (G-14435)
Mbcd Inc .... E 517 484-4426
  Lansing (G-9867)
Michiana Aggregate Inc .... G 269 695-7669
  Niles (G-12144)
Michigan Aggr Sand/Gravel Haul .... F 231 258-8237
  Kalkaska (G-9397)
Michigan Aggregates Corp .... F 517 688-4414
  Jerome (G-9079)
Miller Sand & Gravel Company .... G 269 672-5601
  Hopkins (G-8367)
Mineral Visions Inc .... G 800 255-7263
  Bridgman (G-1932)
Modern Industries Inc .... E 810 767-3330
  Flint (G-5735)
Morris Excavating Inc .... F 269 483-7773
  White Pigeon (G-18484)
Mottes Materials Inc .... G 906 265-9955
  Iron River (G-8749)
Natural Aggregates Corporation .... F 248 685-1502
  Milford (G-11476)
Newark Gravel Company .... F 810 796-3072
  Dryden (G-4807)
Next-Level Sandbag LLC .... G 231 350-6738
  East Jordan (G-4877)
Nivers Sand Gravel .... G 231 743-6126
  Marion (G-10975)
Nugent Sand Company Inc .... G 231 755-1686
  Norton Shores (G-12322)
Parker Excvtg Grav & Recycle .... F 616 784-1681
  Comstock Park (G-3633)
Peters Sand and Gravel Inc .... G 906 595-7223
  Naubinway (G-11961)
R H Huhtala Aggregates Inc .... G 906 524-7758
  Lanse (G-9668)
Round Lake Sand & Gravel Inc .... G 517 467-4458
  Addison (G-44)
Ruby Sand & Gravel .... G 810 364-6100
  Clyde (G-3416)
Ruppe Manufacturing Company .... E 906 932-3540
  Ironwood (G-8771)
◆ Saginaw Rock Products Co .... F 989 754-6589
  Saginaw (G-14751)
Sandman Inc .... G 248 652-3432
  Troy (G-17343)
▲ Searles Construction Inc .... E 989 224-3297
  Saint Johns (G-14915)
Shimp Sand & Gravel LLC .... F 517 369-1632
  Bronson (G-2120)
South Flint Gravel Inc .... G 810 232-8911
  Holly (G-8295)
South Hill Sand and Gravel .... G 248 828-1726
  Troy (G-17365)
South Hill Sand and Gravel .... G 248 685-7020
  Milford (G-11490)
Southwest Gravel Inc .... G 269 673-4665
  Allegan (G-182)
Srm Concrete LLC .... D 231 839-4319
  Lake City (G-9555)

Stansley Mineral Resources Inc .... G 517 456-6310
  Clinton (G-3142)
Summers Road Gravel & Dev LLC .... G 810 798-8533
  Almont (G-268)
Technisand Inc .... G 269 465-5833
  Benton Harbor (G-1592)
Tip Top Gravel Co Inc .... G 616 897-8342
  Ada (G-37)
Top OMichigan Reclaimers Inc .... G 989 705-7983
  Gaylord (G-6164)
Tri County Sand and Stone Inc .... G 231 331-6549
  Alden (G-136)
Tri-City Aggregates Inc .... E 248 634-8276
  Holly (G-8298)
Trillacorpe/Bk LLC .... G 248 433-0585
  Bingham Farms (G-1705)
Trojan Sand and Gravel LLC .... G 517 712-5086
  Springport (G-15884)
Trp Enterprises Inc .... G 810 329-4027
  East China (G-4859)
Truth Sand Contemplations .... G 269 342-0369
  Portage (G-13627)
Van Sloten Enterprises Inc .... F 906 635-5151
  Sault Sainte Marie (G-15102)
Waanders Concrete Co .... F 269 673-6352
  Allegan (G-184)
Weber Sand and Gravel Inc .... F 248 373-0900
  Lake Orion (G-9637)

1446 Industrial Sand

Atlantic Precision Pdts Inc .... F 586 532-9420
  Shelby Township (G-15174)
Carrollton Paving Co .... F 989 752-7139
  Saginaw (G-14623)
Covia Solutions Inc .... G 800 255-7263
  Benton Harbor (G-1543)
Eggers Excavating LLC .... F 989 695-5205
  Freeland (G-6022)
Sand Products Corporation .... G 906 292-5432
  Moran (G-11610)
Sargent Sand Co .... G 989 792-8734
  Midland (G-11414)

1474 Potash, Soda & Borate Minerals

Mosiac Potash Hersey LLC .... G 231 832-3755
  Hersey (G-7868)

1481 Nonmetallic Minerals Svcs, Except Fuels

Aquila Resources Inc .... G 906 352-4024
  Menominee (G-11227)
Bourque H James & Assoc Inc .... G 906 635-9191
  Brimley (G-2101)
Detroit Salt Company LC .... E 313 554-0456
  Detroit (G-4164)

1499 Miscellaneous Nonmetallic Mining

Bay-Houston Towing Company .... F 810 648-2210
  Sandusky (G-15056)
Discovery Gold Corp .... G 269 429-7002
  Stevensville (G-16247)
Eggers Excavating LLC .... F 989 695-5205
  Freeland (G-6022)
J M Longyear Heirs Inc .... G 906 228-7960
  Marquette (G-11023)
Markham Peat Corp .... F 800 851-7230
  Lakeview (G-9643)
Michigan Gypsum Co .... F 989 792-8734
  Midland (G-11389)
Mmgg Inc .... G 989 324-7319
  Freeland (G-6026)
Ms International Holdings LLC .... G 443 210-1446
  Sterling Heights (G-16105)

20 FOOD AND KINDRED PRODUCTS

2011 Meat Packing Plants

A & R Packing Co Inc .... E 734 422-2060
  Livonia (G-10092)
Bellinger Packing .... E 989 838-2274
  Ashley (G-741)
Bernthal Packing Inc .... F 989 652-2648
  Frankenmuth (G-5859)
Berry Sns-Rbbeh Islmic Slghtrh .... G 313 259-6925
  Detroit (G-4051)
Bert Hazekamp & Son Inc .... C 231 773-8302
  Muskegon (G-11778)

Berthiaume Slaughter House .... G 989 879-4921
  Pinconning (G-13059)
Boars Head Provisions Co Inc .... C 941 955-0994
  Holland (G-7978)
Bob Evans Farms Inc .... A 517 437-3349
  Hillsdale (G-7926)
Boyers Meat Processing Inc .... G 734 495-1342
  Canton (G-2443)
Cargill Incorporated .... F 608 868-5150
  Owosso (G-12825)
Carol Packing House .... G 989 673-2688
  Caro (G-2566)
Clemens Welcome Center .... G 517 278-2500
  Coldwater (G-3426)
Cole Carter Inc .... G 269 626-8891
  Scotts (G-15131)
Cornbelt Beef Corporation .... G 313 237-0087
  Oak Park (G-12598)
Countryside Quality Meats LLC .... F 517 741-4275
  Union City (G-17491)
Erlas Inc .... D 989 872-2191
  Cass City (G-2614)
Gainors Meat Packing Inc .... G 989 269-8161
  Bad Axe (G-1101)
Garys Custom Meats .... G 269 641-5683
  Union (G-17487)
Gibbies Deer Processing .... G 231 924-6042
  Fremont (G-6044)
Hormel Foods Corporation .... G 616 454-0418
  Grand Rapids (G-6820)
Jbs Packerland Inc .... F 269 685-6886
  Plainwell (G-13078)
Jbs Plainwell Inc .... C 269 685-6886
  Plainwell (G-13079)
Kent Quality Foods Inc .... C 616 459-4595
  Hudsonville (G-8589)
Langes Beef & Bull Inc .... G 989 756-2941
  Whittemore (G-18550)
Lloyd Johnson Livestock Inc .... F 906 786-4878
  Escanaba (G-5081)
Makkedah Mt Proc & Bulk Fd Str .... G 231 873-2113
  Hart (G-7757)
Maurer Meat Processors Inc .... F 989 658-8185
  Ubly (G-17478)
Michigan Brand Inc .... G 989 395-4345
  Frankenmuth (G-5870)
Michigan Veal Inc .... E 616 669-6688
  Hudsonville (G-8596)
Mikes Meat Processing .... G 269 468-6173
  Coloma (G-3480)
Nagel Meat Processing .... G 517 568-5035
  Homer (G-8355)
Northern Processing .... G 989 734-9007
  Rogers City (G-14213)
Northwest Market .... G 517 787-5005
  Jackson (G-8977)
Papa Joes Grmet Mkt Hnry Ford .... F 248 609-5670
  Detroit (G-4504)
Pinkney Hill Meat Co .... G 616 897-4921
  Saranac (G-15080)
Pleasant Valley Packing LLC .... D 517 278-2500
  Coldwater (G-3446)
Pooles Meat Processing .... G 989 846-6348
  Standish (G-15894)
Prime Cuts of Jackson LLC .... E 517 768-8090
  Jackson (G-8991)
Rays Game .... G 810 346-2628
  Brown City (G-2141)
Ricks Meat Processing LLC .... G 517 628-2263
  Eaton Rapids (G-4971)
Rogers Beef Farms .... G 906 632-1584
  Sault Sainte Marie (G-15098)
Safari Meats Llc .... G 313 539-3367
  Oak Park (G-12644)
Smith & Sons Meat Proc Inc .... G 989 772-6048
  Mount Pleasant (G-11738)
Smith - Sons ME .... G 989 772-6048
  Mount Pleasant (G-11739)
Smith Meat Packing Inc .... E 810 985-5900
  Port Huron (G-13528)
Spillson Ltd .... G 734 384-0284
  Monroe (G-11575)
Standard Provision LLC .... G 989 354-4975
  Alpena (G-319)
Tyson Foods Inc .... G 231 922-3214
  Traverse City (G-16870)
Tyson Foods Inc .... G 231 929-2456
  Traverse City (G-16871)
Tyson Fresh Meats Inc .... G 248 213-1000
  Southfield (G-15729)

SIC SECTION
20 FOOD AND KINDRED PRODUCTS20 FOOD AND KINDRED PRODUCTS

Vin-Lee-Ron Meat Packing LLC ....F 574 353-1386
Cassopolis *(G-2635)*

◆ **Wolverine Packing Co** ....D 313 259-7500
Detroit *(G-4688)*

2013 Sausages & Meat Prdts

A & R Packing Co Inc ....E 734 422-2060
Livonia *(G-10092)*

Bernthal Packing Inc ....F 989 652-2648
Frankenmuth *(G-5859)*

Bert Hazekamp & Son Inc ....C 231 773-8302
Muskegon *(G-11778)*

Big O Smokehouse Inc ....E 616 891-5555
Caledonia *(G-2368)*

Boars Head Provisions Co Inc ....C 941 955-0994
Holland *(G-7978)*

Cattlemans Meat Company ....B 734 287-8260
Taylor *(G-16391)*

Darling Ingredients Inc ....G 269 751-0560
Hamilton *(G-7597)*

Deerings Jerky Co LLC ....G 231 590-5687
Interlochen *(G-8682)*

Dina Mia Kitchens Inc ....E 906 265-9082
Iron River *(G-8740)*

Erlas Inc ....D 989 872-2191
Cass City *(G-2614)*

Freds Jerky Products ....G 517 202-1908
Charlotte *(G-2756)*

Great Fresh Foods Co LLC ....E 734 904-0731
Taylor *(G-16422)*

Hillshire Brands Company ....G 616 875-8131
Zeeland *(G-19038)*

Hillshire Brands Company ....G 231 947-2100
Traverse City *(G-16711)*

Jerky Stock LLc ....G 616 481-2329
Grand Rapids *(G-6869)*

Kent Quality Foods Inc ....C 616 459-4595
Hudsonville *(G-8589)*

Kerns Sausages Inc ....F 989 652-2684
Frankenmuth *(G-5867)*

Koegel Meats Inc ....C 810 238-3685
Flint *(G-5722)*

Kowalski Companies Inc ....C 313 873-8200
Detroit *(G-4366)*

Krzysiak Family Restaurant ....D 989 894-5531
Bay City *(G-1372)*

Louies Meats Inc ....E 231 946-4811
Traverse City *(G-16748)*

Macomb Smoked Meats LLC ....D 313 842-2375
Dearborn *(G-3867)*

Mello Meats Inc ....F 800 852-5019
Auburn Hills *(G-972)*

Pioneer Meats LLC ....F 248 862-1988
Birmingham *(G-1744)*

Pleasant Valley Packing LLC ....D 517 278-2500
Coldwater *(G-3446)*

Quincy Street Inc ....C 616 399-3330
Holland *(G-8174)*

Smigelski Properties LLC ....G 989 255-6252
Alpena *(G-317)*

T Wigley Inc ....F 313 831-6881
Detroit *(G-4624)*

Vandco Incorporated ....E 906 482-1550
Hancock *(G-7623)*

Viaus Super Market ....G 906 786-1950
Escanaba *(G-5106)*

2015 Poultry Slaughtering, Dressing & Processing

Cargill Incorporated ....F 608 868-5150
Owosso *(G-12825)*

Cargill Americas Inc ....D 810 989-7689
New Haven *(G-12029)*

Farmers Egg Cooperative ....G 517 649-8957
Charlotte *(G-2754)*

Hillshire Brands Company ....G 616 875-8131
Zeeland *(G-19038)*

Michigan Trkey Prdcers Coop In ....B 616 245-2221
Grand Rapids *(G-6994)*

Michigan Trkey Prdcers Coop In ....D 616 245-2221
Wyoming *(G-18894)*

Michigan Turkey Producers ....D 616 875-1838
Zeeland *(G-19052)*

Michigan Turkey Producers LLC ....F 616 243-4186
Grand Rapids *(G-6995)*

Tyson Foods /Hr ....F 616 875-2311
Zeeland *(G-19085)*

◆ **Zoet Poultry** ....E 269 751-2776
Holland *(G-8259)*

2021 Butter

Blank Slate Creamery LLC ....F 734 218-3242
Whitmore Lake *(G-18522)*

Brinks Family Creamery LLC ....G 231 826-0099
Mc Bain *(G-11179)*

Browndog Creamery LLC ....F 248 361-3759
Northville *(G-12199)*

Greenville Ventr Partners LLC ....E 616 303-2400
Greenville *(G-7490)*

Inverness Dairy Inc ....E 231 627-4655
Cheboygan *(G-2787)*

Michigan Milk Producers Assn ....D 269 435-2835
Constantine *(G-3671)*

Michigan Milk Producers Assn ....E 248 474-6672
Novi *(G-12481)*

Michigan Milk Producers Assn ....D 989 834-2221
Ovid *(G-12815)*

Moo-Ville Inc ....F 517 852-9003
Nashville *(G-11958)*

2022 Cheese

Agropur Inc ....E 616 538-3822
Grand Rapids *(G-6439)*

Cheese Lady LLC ....G 231 728-3000
Muskegon *(G-11792)*

Country Home Creations Inc ....E 810 244-7348
Flint *(G-5674)*

Greenville Ventr Partners LLC ....E 616 303-2400
Greenville *(G-7490)*

Kraft Outdoor Svc ....G 517 404-8023
Fowlerville *(G-5848)*

Krafts & Thingz ....G 810 689-2457
Chesterfield *(G-2904)*

Kross Kraft LLC ....G 616 399-9167
Holland *(G-8116)*

Leprino Foods Company ....B 989 967-3635
Remus *(G-13815)*

Leprino Foods Company ....B 616 895-5800
Allendale *(G-223)*

Liberty Dairy Company ....C 800 632-5552
Evart *(G-5125)*

Litehouse Inc ....C 616 897-5911
Lowell *(G-10509)*

Michigan Chese Prtein Pdts LLC ....G 517 403-5247
Tipton *(G-16591)*

Michigan Farm Cheese Dairy ....G 231 462-3301
Fountain *(G-5827)*

MWC (michigan) LLC ....G 575 791-9559
Saint Johns *(G-14910)*

Natural Way Cheese ....G 989 935-9380
Clare *(G-2988)*

OH So Cheesy LLC ....G 616 835-1249
Grand Rapids *(G-7055)*

Schreiber Foods Inc ....E 616 538-3822
Grand Rapids *(G-7184)*

White Lotus Farms Inc ....G 734 904-1379
Ann Arbor *(G-716)*

Williams Cheese Co ....E 989 697-4492
Linwood *(G-10075)*

Windshadow Farm & Dairy LLC ....G 269 599-0467
Bangor *(G-1132)*

2023 Milk, Condensed & Evaporated

Bay Valley Foods LLC ....E 269 792-2277
Wayland *(G-18189)*

Castle Remedies Inc ....F 734 973-8990
Ann Arbor *(G-415)*

Cherryflex Inc ....G 888 947-4047
Traverse City *(G-16651)*

▲ **Continental Dar Facilities LLC** ....D 616 837-7641
Coopersville *(G-3682)*

Dairy Farmers America Inc ....D 517 265-5045
Adrian *(G-58)*

Enrinity Supplements Inc ....G 734 322-4966
Westland *(G-18368)*

Gerber Products Company ....E 231 928-2076
Fremont *(G-6042)*

Gerber Products Company ....E 231 928-2000
Fremont *(G-6043)*

Green Room Michigan LLC ....F 248 289-3288
Farmington Hills *(G-5255)*

Greenville Ventr Partners LLC ....E 616 303-2400
Greenville *(G-7490)*

Jaaz Management LLC ....G 248 957-9197
Novi *(G-12447)*

Kerry Inc ....E 616 871-9940
Detroit *(G-4358)*

Michigan Herbal Remedies LLC ....G 616 818-0823
Jenison *(G-9062)*

Michigan Milk Producers Assn ....E 248 474-6672
Novi *(G-12481)*

Michigan Milk Producers Assn ....D 989 834-2221
Ovid *(G-12815)*

Michigan Milk Producers Assn ....D 269 435-2835
Constantine *(G-3671)*

Nestle Usa Inc ....C 231 928-2000
Fremont *(G-6048)*

Nestle Usa Inc ....C 989 755-7940
Saginaw *(G-14709)*

Verndale Products Inc ....E 313 834-4190
Detroit *(G-4666)*

2024 Ice Cream

Aj Hometown LLC ....G 313 415-0843
Eastpointe *(G-4927)*

Alinosi French Ice Cream Co ....G 313 527-3195
Detroit *(G-3997)*

Berkley Frosty Freeze Inc ....G 248 336-2634
Berkley *(G-1622)*

Blossom Berry ....G 517 775-6978
Novi *(G-12374)*

Cold Stone Creamery ....F 313 886-4020
Grosse Pointe Park *(G-7550)*

Custard Corner Inc ....G 734 771-4396
Grosse Ile *(G-7517)*

D Sharp Masonry ....G 313 292-2375
Taylor *(G-16399)*

Deans Ice Cream Inc ....F 269 685-6641
Plainwell *(G-13075)*

Frosty Cove ....G 231 343-6643
Muskegon *(G-11822)*

Froyo Pinckney LLC ....G 248 310-4465
Pinckney *(G-13048)*

Gnass Masonry LLC ....G 616 530-3214
Byron Center *(G-2273)*

Guernsey Dairy Stores Inc ....C 248 349-1466
Northville *(G-12227)*

Hattiegirl Ice Cream Foods LLC ....G 877 444-3738
Detroit *(G-4296)*

▼ **House of Flavors Inc** ....C 231 845-7369
Ludington *(G-10540)*

Independent Dairy Inc ....E 734 241-6016
Monroe *(G-11550)*

Iorio Gelato Kentwood LLC ....F 517 927-9928
Grand Rapids *(G-6853)*

Loven Spoonful ....G 517 522-3953
Grass Lake *(G-7440)*

May Venture Inc ....G 248 481-3890
Lake Orion *(G-9618)*

Moo-Ville Inc ....F 517 852-9003
Nashville *(G-11958)*

Moomers Homemade Ice Cream LLC ....F 231 941-4122
Traverse City *(G-16763)*

PGI of Saugatuck Inc ....E 800 443-5286
Fennville *(G-5441)*

Plainwell Ice Cream Co ....F 269 685-8586
Plainwell *(G-13088)*

Pump House ....G 616 647-5481
Grand Rapids *(G-7125)*

Quality Dairy Company ....E 517 367-2400
Lansing *(G-9887)*

Rays Ice Cream Co Inc ....F 248 549-5256
Royal Oak *(G-14573)*

Sherman Dairy Products Co Inc ....E 269 637-8251
Holland *(G-8190)*

Strohs ....G 734 285-5480
Wyandotte *(G-18841)*

Stuarts of Novi ....F 248 615-2955
Novi *(G-12547)*

Sugar Kissed Cupcakes LLC ....G 231 421-9156
Traverse City *(G-16844)*

Sweet Tmpttons Ice Cream Prlor ....G 616 842-8108
Grand Haven *(G-6369)*

Swirlberry ....G 734 779-0830
Livonia *(G-10426)*

That French Place ....F 231 437-6037
Charlevoix *(G-2736)*

WG Sweis Investments LLC ....F 313 477-8433
Washington *(G-18091)*

Whats Scoop ....G 616 662-6423
Hudsonville *(G-8618)*

2026 Milk

Bay Valley Foods LLC ....E 269 792-2277
Wayland *(G-18189)*

Bloomberry ....G 586 212-9510
East China *(G-4856)*

◆ **C F Burger Creamery Co** ....D 313 584-4040
Detroit *(G-4084)*

SIC

Employee Codes: A=Over 500 employees, B=251-500
C=101-250, D=51-100, E=20-50, F=10-19, G=3-9
2022 Harris Michigan
Industrial Directory
729

20 FOOD AND KINDRED PRODUCTS

Calder Bros Dairy Inc .... E 313 381-8858
  Lincoln Park *(G-10044)*
Chocolate Vault Llc .... G 517 688-3388
  Horton *(G-8372)*
Country Dairy Inc .... D 231 861-4636
  New ERA *(G-12027)*
Country Fresh LLC .... B 734 261-7980
  Romulus *(G-14264)*
Cream Cup Dairy .... G 231 889-4158
  Kaleva *(G-9377)*
Dairy Farmers America Inc .... D 517 265-5045
  Adrian *(G-58)*
Fruit Fro Yo .... G 517 580-3967
  Okemos *(G-12668)*
General Mills Inc .... E 231 832-3285
  Reed City *(G-13790)*
Greenville Ventr Partners LLC ... E 616 303-2400
  Greenville *(G-7490)*
Instantwhip Detroit Inc .... G 734 379-9474
  Rockwood *(G-14200)*
Inverness Dairy Inc .... E 231 627-4655
  Cheboygan *(G-2787)*
Langs Inc .... G 248 634-6048
  Holly *(G-8280)*
Liberty Dairy Company .... C 800 632-5552
  Evart *(G-5125)*
Melody Farms LLC .... F 734 261-7980
  Livonia *(G-10310)*
Michigan Milk Producers Assn .. D 989 834-2221
  Ovid *(G-12815)*
Michigan Milk Producers Assn .. D 269 435-2835
  Constantine *(G-3671)*
Michigan Milk Producers Assn .. D 248 474-6672
  Novi *(G-12481)*
Quality Dairy Company .... E 517 367-2400
  Lansing *(G-9887)*
Rocky Mtn Choclat Fctry Inc ...... D 810 606-8550
  Grand Blanc *(G-6261)*
Sugar Berry .... G 517 321-0177
  Lansing *(G-9792)*
Sweet Earth .... G 248 850-8031
  Royal Oak *(G-14583)*
Twist .... G 248 859-2169
  West Bloomfield *(G-18320)*
Yogurtown Inc .... F 313 908-9376
  Dearborn *(G-3917)*
Yoplait USA .... F 231 832-3285
  Reed City *(G-13804)*

2032 Canned Specialties

Advancing Bus Solutions LLC .... G 734 905-7455
  Ypsilanti *(G-18923)*
American Spoon Foods Inc .... E 231 347-9030
  Petoskey *(G-12988)*
◆ Amway International Inc .... E 616 787-1000
  Ada *(G-8)*
Emesa Foods Company .... G 248 982-3908
  Farmington Hills *(G-5230)*
Global Restaurant Group Inc ..... G 313 271-2777
  Dearborn *(G-3847)*
Kraft Heinz Foods Company ...... G 616 396-6557
  Holland *(G-8115)*
National Coney Island Chili Co .. F 313 365-5611
  Roseville *(G-14451)*
Onion Crock of Michigan Inc ..... G 616 458-2922
  Grand Rapids *(G-7060)*
Randall Foods Inc .... F 517 767-3247
  Tekonsha *(G-16524)*

2033 Canned Fruits, Vegetables & Preserves

Almar Orchards LLC .... F 810 659-6568
  Flushing *(G-5801)*
American Spoon Foods Inc .... E 231 347-9030
  Petoskey *(G-12988)*
Atwater Foods LLC .... G 231 264-5598
  Williamsburg *(G-18551)*
Birds Eye Foods Inc .... D 269 561-8211
  Fennville *(G-5434)*
Blakes Orchard Inc .... G 586 784-5343
  Armada *(G-732)*
Brownwood Acres Foods Inc ..... F 231 599-3101
  Eastport *(G-4949)*
◆ Burnette Foods Inc .... D 231 264-8116
  Elk Rapids *(G-5022)*
Burnette Foods Inc .... C 269 621-3181
  Hartford *(G-7762)*
Burnette Foods Inc .... G 231 536-2284
  East Jordan *(G-4860)*
Burnette Foods Inc .... C 231 861-2151
  New ERA *(G-12026)*

Campbell Soup Company .... G 313 295-6884
  Taylor *(G-16390)*
Campbell Soup Company .... G 248 336-8486
  Ferndale *(G-5532)*
◆ Cherry Central Cooperative Inc .. E 231 946-1860
  Traverse City *(G-16648)*
Cherry Central Cooperative Inc .. E 231 861-2141
  Shelby *(G-15149)*
◆ Cherry Growers Inc .... C 231 276-9241
  Birmingham *(G-1720)*
Cherry Growers Inc .... G 231 947-2502
  Traverse City *(G-16650)*
Cherry Hut Products LLC .... G 231 882-4431
  Benzonia *(G-1613)*
Cherry Republic Inc .... G 231 334-3150
  Glen Arbor *(G-6209)*
Coca-Cola Refreshments USA Inc ...... G 616 913-0400
  Grand Rapids *(G-6578)*
Country Mill Farms LLC .... G 517 543-1019
  Charlotte *(G-2745)*
Everfresh Beverages Inc .... G 586 755-9500
  Warren *(G-17798)*
Fairview Farms .... G 269 449-0500
  Berrien Springs *(G-1640)*
Food For Thought Inc .... E 231 326-5444
  Traverse City *(G-16684)*
◆ Gray & Company .... C 231 873-5628
  Hart *(G-7753)*
▼ Great Lakes Packing Co .... E 231 264-5561
  Kewadin *(G-9487)*
Hirzel Canning Company .... G 419 360-3220
  Troy *(G-17144)*
Hopeful Harvest Foods Inc .... G 248 967-1500
  Oak Park *(G-12617)*
◆ Indian Summer Cooperative Inc .. C 231 845-6248
  Ludington *(G-10541)*
Integrity Beverage Inc .... E 248 348-1010
  Wixom *(G-18687)*
J House LLC .... G 313 220-4449
  Grosse Pointe Farms *(G-7536)*
Knouse Foods Cooperative Inc ..... C 269 657-5524
  Paw Paw *(G-12950)*
Kraft Heinz Foods Company ...... G 616 396-6557
  Holland *(G-8115)*
Lakewood Organics LLC .... E 231 861-6333
  Shelby *(G-15156)*
M Forche Farms Inc .... G 517 447-3488
  Blissfield *(G-1768)*
Materne North America Corp .... E 231 346-6600
  Grawn *(G-7452)*
▼ McClures Pickles LLC .... E 248 837-9323
  Detroit *(G-4422)*
Mitten Fruit Company LLC .... G 269 585-8541
  Kalamazoo *(G-9273)*
Mizkan America Inc .... D 616 794-0226
  Belding *(G-1457)*
Mpc Company Inc .... G 269 927-3371
  Benton Harbor *(G-1576)*
Northville Cider Mill Inc .... F 248 349-3181
  Northville *(G-12245)*
▲ Oceana Foods Inc .... C 231 861-2141
  Shelby *(G-15157)*
◆ Old Orchard Brands LLC .... D 616 887-1745
  Sparta *(G-15774)*
◆ Packers Canning Co Inc .... D 269 624-4681
  Lawton *(G-9989)*
Panther James LLC .... F 248 850-7522
  Berkley *(G-1634)*
Pantless Jams LLC .... G 419 283-8470
  Temperance *(G-16544)*
◆ Peterson Farms Inc .... B 231 861-6333
  Shelby *(G-15159)*
Randall Foods Inc .... F 517 767-3247
  Tekonsha *(G-16524)*
Rice Juice Company Inc .... G 906 774-1733
  Iron Mountain *(G-8730)*
Society of Saint John Inc .... G 906 289-4484
  Eagle Harbor *(G-4853)*
St Julian Wine Company Inc ..... E 269 657-5568
  Paw Paw *(G-12957)*
Thomas Cooper .... G 231 599-2251
  Ellsworth *(G-5037)*
Twin City Foods Inc .... G 616 374-4002
  Lake Odessa *(G-9579)*
Uncle Johns Cider Mill Inc .... E 989 224-3686
  Saint Johns *(G-14919)*
Wasem Fruit Farm .... G 734 482-2342
  Milan *(G-11451)*
Welch Foods Inc A Cooperative ..... D 269 624-4141
  Lawton *(G-9990)*

2034 Dried Fruits, Vegetables & Soup

American Spoon Foods Inc .... E 231 347-9030
  Petoskey *(G-12988)*
Angel Kisses Inc .... G 248 219-8577
  Ferndale *(G-5526)*
Apple Quest Inc .... E 616 299-4834
  Conklin *(G-3659)*
Cherry Central Cooperative Inc .. E 231 861-2141
  Shelby *(G-15149)*
◆ Graceland Fruit Inc .... C 231 352-7181
  Frankfort *(G-5877)*
J Rettenmaier USA LP .... G 269 323-1588
  Portage *(G-13569)*
◆ Shoreline Fruit LLC .... C 231 941-4336
  Williamsburg *(G-18564)*
▼ Smeltzer Companies Inc .... C 231 882-4421
  Frankfort *(G-5881)*

2035 Pickled Fruits, Vegetables, Sauces & Dressings

American Spoon Foods Inc .... E 231 347-9030
  Petoskey *(G-12988)*
Bessinger Pickle Co Inc .... G 989 876-8008
  Au Gres *(G-756)*
Brede Inc .... G 313 273-1079
  Bloomfield Hills *(G-1806)*
Cultured Love LLC .... G 703 362-5991
  Zeeland *(G-19010)*
Custom Foods Inc .... F 989 249-8061
  Saginaw *(G-14634)*
DForte Inc .... F 269 657-6996
  Paw Paw *(G-12946)*
Dimitri Mansour .... G 248 684-4545
  Milford *(G-11462)*
Dina Mia Kitchens Inc .... E 906 265-9082
  Iron River *(G-8740)*
Flamm Pickle and Packaging Co .. F 269 461-6916
  Eau Claire *(G-4977)*
Garden Fresh Gourmet LLC .... D 866 725-7239
  Ferndale *(G-5558)*
◆ Gielow Pickles Inc .... C 810 359-7680
  Lexington *(G-10028)*
◆ Great Lakes Food Center LLC .... G 248 397-8166
  Madison Heights *(G-10734)*
Harrison Packing Co Inc .... F 269 381-3837
  Kalamazoo *(G-9209)*
◆ Hausbeck Pickle Company .... D 989 754-4721
  Saginaw *(G-14661)*
Hopeful Harvest Foods Inc .... G 248 967-1500
  Oak Park *(G-12617)*
◆ Indian Summer Cooperative Inc .. C 231 845-6248
  Ludington *(G-10541)*
Jabars Complements LLC .... G 810 966-8371
  Port Huron *(G-13489)*
Knouse Foods Cooperative Inc .. C 269 657-5524
  Paw Paw *(G-12950)*
Litehouse Inc .... C 616 897-5911
  Lowell *(G-10509)*
McClures Pickles LLC .... G 248 837-9323
  Royal Oak *(G-14562)*
▲ Mr Chips Inc .... G 989 879-3555
  Pinconning *(G-13063)*
Pickled Door LLC .... G 616 916-6836
  Caledonia *(G-2392)*
Swanson Grading & Brining Inc .. F 231 853-2289
  Ravenna *(G-13695)*
Swanson Pickle Co Inc .... E 231 853-2289
  Ravenna *(G-13696)*
Tall Pauls Pickles LLC .... G 734 476-2424
  Ann Arbor *(G-671)*

2037 Frozen Fruits, Juices & Vegetables

All American Whse & Cold Stor ..... F 313 865-3870
  Detroit *(G-3998)*
◆ Cherry Growers Inc .... C 231 276-9241
  Birmingham *(G-1720)*
Cherry Growers Inc .... G 231 947-2502
  Traverse City *(G-16650)*
Coloma Frozen Foods Inc .... D 269 849-0500
  Coloma *(G-3475)*
Dole Packaged Foods LLC .... B 269 423-6375
  Decatur *(G-3947)*
Farber Concessions Inc .... E 313 387-1600
  Redford *(G-13733)*
◆ Graceland Fruit Inc .... C 231 352-7181
  Frankfort *(G-5877)*
Hart Freeze Pack LlC .... F 231 873-2175
  Hart *(G-7754)*

Jar-ME LLC ... G ... 313 319-7765
Detroit *(G-4334)*

▲ **Juvenex Inc** ... F ... 248 436-2866
Southfield *(G-15615)*

MI Frozen Food LLC ... G ... 231 357-4334
Manistee *(G-10909)*

◆ **Old Orchard Brands LLC** ... D ... 616 887-1745
Sparta *(G-15774)*

◆ **Peterson Farms Inc** ... B ... 231 861-6333
Shelby *(G-15159)*

Sill Farms & Market Inc ... E ... 269 674-3755
Lawrence *(G-9985)*

▼ **Smeltzer Companies Inc** ... C ... 231 882-4421
Frankfort *(G-5881)*

Smoothies ... G ... 231 498-2374
Kewadin *(G-9489)*

Standale Smoothie LLC ... G ... 810 691-9625
Fenton *(G-5504)*

Super Fluids LLC ... G ... 313 409-6522
Detroit *(G-4615)*

Svf Bloomingdale Inc ... F ... 269 521-3026
Bloomingdale *(G-1880)*

Twin City Foods Inc ... D ... 616 374-4002
Lake Odessa *(G-9579)*

Welch Foods Inc A Cooperative ... D ... 269 624-4141
Lawton *(G-9990)*

2038 Frozen Specialties

Achatzs Hand Made Pie Co ... E ... 586 749-2882
Chesterfield *(G-2834)*

Beagios Franchises Inc ... G ... 989 635-7173
Marlette *(G-10979)*

Campbell Soup Company ... G ... 313 295-6884
Taylor *(G-16390)*

Campbell Soup Company ... G ... 248 336-8486
Ferndale *(G-5532)*

Cole King Foods ... G ... 313 872-0220
Detroit *(G-4097)*

Coles Quality Foods Inc ... D ... 231 722-1651
Muskegon *(G-11793)*

DForte Inc ... F ... 269 657-6996
Paw Paw *(G-12946)*

Dina Mia Kitchens Inc ... E ... 906 265-9082
Iron River *(G-8740)*

Farber Concessions Inc ... E ... 313 387-1600
Redford *(G-13733)*

Frandale Sub Shop ... F ... 616 446-6311
Allendale *(G-218)*

◆ **Kellogg Company** ... A ... 269 961-2000
Battle Creek *(G-1255)*

Kring Pizza Inc ... G ... 586 792-0049
Harrison Township *(G-7704)*

Linda Mia Inc ... G ... 906 265-9082
Iron River *(G-8747)*

McDonalds ... F ... 248 851-7310
Oxford *(G-12900)*

▲ **Mid America Commodities LLC** ... G ... 810 936-0108
Linden *(G-10068)*

▲ **Pasty Oven Inc** ... G ... 906 774-2328
Quinnesec *(G-13676)*

▲ **Pierino Frozen Foods Inc** ... E ... 313 928-0950
Lincoln Park *(G-10053)*

Pietrzyk Foods LLC ... G ... 313 614-9393
Detroit *(G-4523)*

Pinnacle Foods Group LLC ... B ... 810 724-6144
Imlay City *(G-8643)*

Rays Ice Cream Co Inc ... F ... 248 549-5256
Royal Oak *(G-14573)*

◆ **Request Foods Inc** ... B ... 616 786-0900
Holland *(G-8180)*

▲ **Turris Italian Foods Inc** ... D ... 586 773-6010
Roseville *(G-14488)*

Twin City Foods Inc ... D ... 616 374-4002
Lake Odessa *(G-9579)*

2041 Flour, Grain Milling

▲ **Advanced Food Technologies Inc** ... D ... 616 574-4144
Grand Rapids *(G-6434)*

Archer-Daniels-Midland Company ... G ... 269 968-2900
Battle Creek *(G-1185)*

Archer-Daniels-Midland Company ... G ... 517 627-4017
Grand Ledge *(G-6385)*

Archer-Daniels-Midland Company ... G ... 517 647-4155
Portland *(G-13637)*

Cake Flour ... G ... 231 571-3054
Norton Shores *(G-12283)*

Chelsea Milling Company ... B ... 734 475-1361
Chelsea *(G-2806)*

Citizens LLC ... G ... 517 541-1449
Charlotte *(G-2743)*

Dorothy Dawson Food Products ... E ... 517 788-9830
Jackson *(G-8870)*

Freeport Milling ... G ... 616 765-8421
Freeport *(G-6033)*

General Mills Inc ... E ... 231 832-3285
Reed City *(G-13790)*

General Mills Inc ... F ... 269 337-0288
Kalamazoo *(G-9194)*

▲ **Ittner Bean & Grain Inc** ... F ... 989 662-4461
Auburn *(G-766)*

◆ **Kellogg Company** ... A ... 269 961-2000
Battle Creek *(G-1255)*

Kellogg Company ... G ... 269 961-6693
Wyoming *(G-18889)*

Kelloggs Corporation ... C ... 616 219-6100
Grand Rapids *(G-6882)*

◆ **King Milling Company** ... D ... 616 897-9264
Lowell *(G-10508)*

Knappen Milling Company ... E ... 269 731-4141
Augusta *(G-1092)*

Mennel Milling Co of Mich Inc ... E ... 269 782-5175
Dowagiac *(G-4788)*

◆ **Purity Foods Inc** ... E ... 517 448-7440
Hudson *(G-8560)*

Right Brain Brewery ... G ... 231 922-9662
Traverse City *(G-16820)*

▼ **Star of West Milling Company** ... D ... 989 652-9971
Frankenmuth *(G-5873)*

2043 Cereal Breakfast Foods

Austin Quality Sales Company ... E ... 269 961-2000
Battle Creek *(G-1187)*

Bay Valley Foods LLC ... E ... 269 792-2277
Wayland *(G-18189)*

Daddy DZ Granola Co ... G ... 616 374-0229
Lake Odessa *(G-9574)*

General Mills Inc ... G ... 763 764-7600
Kalamazoo *(G-9193)*

Granola Project Llc ... G ... 919 219-7158
Westland *(G-18375)*

◆ **K-Two Inc** ... D ... 269 961-2000
Battle Creek *(G-1249)*

Kellogg (thailand) Limited ... E ... 269 969-8937
Battle Creek *(G-1251)*

Kellogg Asia Marketing Inc ... G ... 269 961-2000
Battle Creek *(G-1252)*

Kellogg Chile Inc ... D ... 269 961-2000
Battle Creek *(G-1253)*

Kellogg Company ... B ... 269 961-2000
Battle Creek *(G-1254)*

Kellogg Company ... G ... 810 653-5625
Davison *(G-3788)*

Kellogg Company ... G ... 269 961-9387
Mulliken *(G-11749)*

Kellogg Company ... G ... 269 964-8525
Battle Creek *(G-1256)*

Kellogg Company ... G ... 269 969-8107
Battle Creek *(G-1257)*

Kellogg Company ... E ... 616 247-4841
Grand Rapids *(G-6881)*

Kellogg Company ... G ... 269 961-6693
Battle Creek *(G-1259)*

Kellogg Company ... G ... 269 961-2000
Battle Creek *(G-1258)*

◆ **Kellogg Company** ... A ... 269 961-2000
Battle Creek *(G-1255)*

▼ **Kellogg USA Inc** ... C ... 269 961-2000
Battle Creek *(G-1261)*

Kellogg USA Inc ... A ... 269 961-2000
Battle Creek *(G-1262)*

Post Foods LLC ... B ... 269 966-1000
Battle Creek *(G-1281)*

▲ **Roskam Baking Company** ... C ... 616 574-5757
Grand Rapids *(G-7166)*

Rothbury Farms Inc ... E ... 616 574-5757
Grand Rapids *(G-7171)*

Snackwerks of Michigan LLC ... E ... 269 719-8282
Battle Creek *(G-1296)*

2045 Flour, Blended & Prepared

▲ **Advanced Food Technologies Inc** ... D ... 616 574-4144
Grand Rapids *(G-6434)*

Bektrom Foods Inc ... G ... 734 241-3796
Monroe *(G-11531)*

Big Dipper Dough Co Inc ... G ... 231 883-6035
Traverse City *(G-16620)*

Dawn Food Products Inc ... G ... 517 789-4400
Jackson *(G-8862)*

Dawn Food Products Inc ... G ... 800 654-4843
Grand Rapids *(G-6634)*

◆ **Dawn Food Products Inc** ... C ... 517 789-4400
Jackson *(G-8863)*

◆ **Dawn Foods Inc** ... C ... 517 789-4400
Jackson *(G-8864)*

Dawn Foods International Corp ... C ... 517 789-4400
Jackson *(G-8865)*

▲ **Dominos Pizza LLC** ... C ... 734 930-3030
Ann Arbor *(G-456)*

Dorothy Dawson Food Products ... E ... 517 788-9830
Jackson *(G-8870)*

Ezbake Technologies LLC ... G ... 817 430-1621
Fenton *(G-5474)*

Fry Krisp Food Products Inc ... F ... 517 784-8531
Jackson *(G-8887)*

MA MA La Rosa Foods Inc ... E ... 734 946-7878
Taylor *(G-16437)*

Pizza Crust Company Inc ... F ... 517 482-3368
Lansing *(G-9730)*

2046 Wet Corn Milling

Cargill Incorporated ... F ... 608 868-5150
Owosso *(G-12825)*

Darwin Sneller ... G ... 989 977-3718
Sebewaing *(G-15139)*

Jamie Byrnes ... G ... 248 872-2513
Commerce Township *(G-3547)*

Prime Land Farm ... G ... 989 550-6120
Harbor Beach *(G-7635)*

Schuette Farms ... G ... 989 550-0563
Elkton *(G-5032)*

2047 Dog & Cat Food

Archer-Daniels-Midland Company ... G ... 517 647-4155
Portland *(G-13637)*

Blendco LLC ... F ... 269 350-2914
Kalamazoo *(G-9138)*

Free Rnge Ntrals Dog Trats Inc ... G ... 586 737-0797
Sterling Heights *(G-16022)*

▲ **Happy Howies Inc** ... F ... 313 537-7200
Detroit *(G-4294)*

Nestle Purina Petcare Company ... E ... 888 202-4554
Troy *(G-17274)*

▲ **Prestige Pet Products Inc** ... G ... 248 615-1526
Southfield *(G-15680)*

Pro Pet L L C ... G ... 248 930-2880
Ferndale *(G-5582)*

Videka LLC ... F ... 269 353-5536
Kalamazoo *(G-9362)*

Wysong Medical Corporation ... F ... 989 631-0009
Midland *(G-11424)*

2048 Prepared Feeds For Animals & Fowls

▲ **Active Feed Company** ... D ... 989 453-2472
Pigeon *(G-13034)*

Armada Grain Co ... E ... 586 784-5911
Armada *(G-729)*

Bake N Cakes LP ... G ... 517 337-2253
Lansing *(G-9811)*

Belle Feeds ... G ... 269 628-1231
Paw Paw *(G-12942)*

Cargill Incorporated ... F ... 608 868-5150
Owosso *(G-12825)*

Chippewa Farm Supply LLC ... G ... 989 471-5523
Spruce *(G-15885)*

Corunna Mills Feed LLC ... G ... 989 743-3110
Corunna *(G-3707)*

Custom Blend Feeds Inc ... G ... 810 798-3265
Bruce Twp *(G-2165)*

Darling Ingredients Inc ... C ... 517 279-9731
Coldwater *(G-3431)*

Darling Ingredients Inc ... G ... 269 751-0560
Hamilton *(G-7597)*

Darwin Sneller ... G ... 989 977-3718
Sebewaing *(G-15139)*

Elite Dog and Pet Supply LLC ... F ... 947 900-1101
Southfield *(G-15553)*

Equus Magnificus ... G ... 651 407-0023
Harbor Springs *(G-7646)*

Fishes & Loaves Food Pantry ... G ... 517 759-4421
Adrian *(G-66)*

Harveys Commodities LLC ... F ... 616 920-1805
Carson City *(G-2593)*

Hatfield Enterprises ... G ... 616 677-5215
Marne *(G-10993)*

▲ **Heath Manufacturing Company** ... E ... 616 997-8181
Coopersville *(G-3688)*

Holmquist Feed Mill ... G ... 906 446-3325
Trenary *(G-16885)*

Jk Outdoors LLC ... G ... 906 863-2932
Menominee *(G-11240)*

20 FOOD AND KINDRED PRODUCTS

John A Van Den Bosch Co ....E 616 848-2000
  Holland (G-8101)
Kemin Industries Inc ....F 248 869-3080
  Plymouth (G-13211)
Kilobar Compacting Mich LLC ....G 989 460-1981
  Bay City (G-1371)
Mar-Vo Mineral Company Inc ....E 517 523-2669
  Hillsdale (G-7940)
Markham Peat Corp ....F 800 851-7230
  Lakeview (G-9643)
Meal and More Incorporated ....E 517 625-3186
  Morrice (G-11625)
Mid McHgan Feed Ingrdients LLC ......G 989 236-5014
  Middleton (G-11299)
Midwest Marketing Inc ....G 989 793-9393
  Saginaw (G-14700)
N F P Inc ....G 989 631-0009
  Midland (G-11397)
Pet Treats Plus ....F 313 533-1701
  Redford (G-13755)
Prime Land Farm ....G 989 550-6120
  Harbor Beach (G-7635)
Purina Mills LLC ....E 517 322-0200
  Lansing (G-9786)
Quality Liquid Feeds Inc ....G 616 784-2930
  Comstock Park (G-3640)
Reconserve of Michigan Inc ....G 269 965-0427
  Battle Creek (G-1287)
Wysong Medical Corporation ....F 989 631-0009
  Midland (G-11424)

2051 Bread, Bakery Prdts Exc Cookies & Crackers

A & D Distribution Inc ....F 248 378-1418
  Troy (G-16899)
Achatzs Hand Made Pie Co ....E 586 749-2882
  Chesterfield (G-2834)
All Around Beauty Shop LLC ....G 313 704-2494
  Garden City (G-6091)
Almar Orchards LLC ....F 810 659-6568
  Flushing (G-5801)
Amys Baking Company ....G 313 530-9694
  Bloomfield Hills (G-1797)
Annas Kitchen LLC ....G 248 499-4774
  Detroit (G-4022)
Apple Valley Natural Foods ....C 269 471-3234
  Berrien Springs (G-1637)
Aunt Millies Bakeries ....G 989 356-6688
  Alpena (G-280)
Aunt Millies Bakeries Inc ....E 734 528-1475
  Ypsilanti (G-18925)
Avalon Intl New Ctr LLC ....E 313 308-0150
  Detroit (G-4033)
Bake Station Bakeries Mich Inc ....F 248 352-9000
  Southfield (G-15501)
Bakewell Company ....G 269 459-8030
  Portage (G-13545)
Baking Company LLC ....E 616 241-2583
  Grand Rapids (G-6493)
Bay Bread Co ....G 231 922-8022
  Traverse City (G-16614)
Beirut Bakery Inc ....F 313 533-4422
  Redford (G-13718)
Big Boy Restaurants Intl LLC ....D 586 263-6220
  Clinton Township (G-3184)
Bread of Life Bakery & Cafe ....F 906 663-4005
  Bessemer (G-1647)
Brothers Baking Company ....E 269 663-8591
  Edwardsburg (G-5001)
Butter Cobbler & Things LLC ....G 810 391-8432
  Wixom (G-18628)
Cake Connection Tc LLC ....G 231 943-3531
  Traverse City (G-16637)
Campbell Soup Company ....G 313 295-6884
  Taylor (G-16390)
Campbell Soup Company ....G 248 336-8486
  Ferndale (G-5532)
Carlson Enterprises Inc ....G 248 656-1442
  Rochester Hills (G-13972)
Cesere Enterprises Inc ....E 989 799-3350
  Saginaw (G-14626)
Chewys Gourmet Kitchen LLC ....F 313 757-2595
  Detroit (G-4092)
Coles Quality Foods Inc ....F 231 722-1651
  Grand Rapids (G-6582)
Coles Quality Foods Inc ....D 231 722-1651
  Muskegon (G-11793)
Country Mill Farms LLC ....G 517 543-1019
  Charlotte (G-2745)

Creme Curls Bakery Inc ....C 616 669-6230
  Hudsonville (G-8575)
Crew Family Rest & Bky LLC ....G 269 337-9800
  Kalamazoo (G-9158)
Cupcakes and Kisses ....G 248 382-5314
  Holly (G-8264)
Darwin Sneller ....G 989 977-3718
  Sebewaing (G-15139)
Divine Dessert ....G 313 278-3322
  Dearborn Heights (G-3924)
Doll Face Chef LLC ....G 248 495-8280
  Bloomfield Hills (G-1815)
Dorothy Dawson Food Products ....E 517 788-9830
  Jackson (G-8870)
Dough Masters ....F 248 585-0600
  Warren (G-17782)
Dunkin Donuts & Baskin-Robbins .....F 989 835-8412
  Midland (G-11357)
Emesa Foods Company ....G 248 982-3908
  Farmington Hills (G-5230)
Emesa Foods Company LLC ....G 248 982-3908
  Taylor (G-16413)
For The Love of Cupcakes ....G 906 399-3004
  Bark River (G-1154)
G M Paris Bakery Inc ....G 734 425-2060
  Livonia (G-10217)
Great Harvest Bread Co ....F 586 566-9500
  Shelby Township (G-15231)
Great Lakes Pot Pies LLC ....G 248 266-1160
  Bloomfield Hills (G-1824)
Hand 2 Hand Whl & Dist LLC ....G 313 574-2861
  Detroit (G-4293)
Haulin Oats Inc ....G 248 225-1672
  Roseville (G-14420)
Home Bakery ....G 248 651-4830
  Rochester (G-13904)
Hostess Cake ITT Contntl Bkg ....G 231 775-4629
  Cadillac (G-2335)
Italian BTR Bread Sticks Bky ....G 313 893-4945
  Detroit (G-4327)
Jaimes Cupcake Haven ....G 586 596-6809
  Warren (G-17882)
James Ave Catering ....G 517 655-4532
  Williamston (G-18574)
Jorgensens Inc ....E 989 831-8338
  Greenville (G-7494)
Josefs French Pastry Shop Co ....G 313 881-5710
  Grosse Pointe Woods (G-7568)
Jt Bakers ....G 989 424-5102
  Clare (G-2983)
Julian Brothers Inc ....F 248 588-0280
  Clawson (G-3100)
Kays Glrous Bked Gds Dist LLC ....G 248 830-1717
  Pontiac (G-13391)
◆ Keebler Company ....B 269 961-2000
  Battle Creek (G-1250)
◆ Kellogg Company ....A 269 961-2000
  Battle Creek (G-1255)
Kind Crumbs LLC ....G 616 881-6388
  Grand Rapids (G-6895)
Klaus Nixdorf ....G 269 429-3259
  Stevensville (G-16256)
Knickerbocker Baking Inc ....D 248 541-2110
  Madison Heights (G-10763)
La Azteca Foods LLC ....G 313 413-2014
  Ecorse (G-4983)
Lg Essentials LLC ....G 313 312-3813
  Detroit (G-4394)
Looney Baker of Livonia Inc ....F 734 425-8569
  Livonia (G-10292)
Mackenzies Bakery ....E 269 343-8440
  Kalamazoo (G-9263)
Magic Treatz LLC ....G 248 989-9956
  Oak Park (G-12624)
Marias Italian Bakery Inc ....F 734 981-1200
  Canton (G-2488)
Marie Minnie Bakers Inc ....C 734 522-1100
  Livonia (G-10300)
Maxpow International LLC ....G 734 578-5369
  Westland (G-18394)
Metropolitan Baking Company ....D 313 875-7246
  Detroit (G-4439)
Michigan State University ....G 517 353-9310
  East Lansing (G-4906)
Milano Bakery Inc ....E 313 833-3500
  Detroit (G-4457)
More Signature Cakes LLC ....G 248 266-0504
  Troy (G-17265)
National Bakery ....G 313 891-7803
  Detroit (G-4475)

New Martha Washington Bakery ......G 313 872-1988
  Detroit (G-4483)
New Yasmeen Detroit Inc ....F 313 582-6035
  Dearborn (G-3876)
New York Bagel Baking Co ....F 248 548-2580
  Ferndale (G-5572)
Old Mission Multigrain LLC ....G 231 366-4121
  Traverse City (G-16781)
Paladin Baking Company LLC ....F 248 601-1542
  Rochester (G-13919)
Palm Sweets LLC ....G 586 554-7979
  Sterling Heights (G-16123)
Paramount Baking Company ....F 313 690-4844
  Roseville (G-14459)
Prime Land Farm ....G 989 550-6120
  Harbor Beach (G-7635)
Rainbow Pizza Inc ....G 734 246-4250
  Taylor (G-16465)
Raleigh & Ron Corporation ....D 248 280-2820
  Royal Oak (G-14571)
Randalls Bakery ....G 906 224-5401
  Wakefield (G-17625)
Ripe Harvest Foods LLC ....F 630 863-2440
  Hillman (G-7916)
▲ Roskam Baking Company ....C 616 574-5757
  Grand Rapids (G-7166)
Roskam Baking Company ....B 616 419-1863
  Kentwood (G-9478)
Roskam Baking Company ....B 616 574-5757
  Grand Rapids (G-7167)
Roskam Baking Company ....B 616 574-5757
  Grand Rapids (G-7168)
Roskam Baking Company ....B 616 554-9160
  Grand Rapids (G-7169)
Roskam Baking Company ....B 616 574-5757
  Grand Rapids (G-7170)
Rothbury Farms Inc ....G 616 574-5757
  Grand Rapids (G-7171)
▲ Russos Bakery Inc ....G 586 791-7320
  Clinton Township (G-3346)
▲ Savory Foods Inc ....D 616 241-2583
  Grand Rapids (G-7181)
Schnitzelstein Baking Co ....G 616 988-2316
  Grand Rapids (G-7183)
Schuette Farms ....G 989 550-0563
  Elkton (G-5032)
Shakes and Cakes LLC ....G 313 707-0923
  Highland Park (G-7909)
▲ Shatila Food Products Inc ....E 313 934-1520
  Dearborn (G-3896)
Simply Divine Baking LLC ....G 313 903-2881
  Southfield (G-15704)
Simply Zara S Treats LLC ....F 313 327-5002
  Detroit (G-4595)
Skinny Petes LLc ....G 906 369-1431
  Lake Linden (G-9570)
Sophias Bakery Inc ....F 313 582-6992
  Detroit (G-4599)
Spatz Bakery Inc ....F 989 755-5551
  Saginaw (G-14760)
Stone Circle Bakehouse LLC ....E 517 881-0603
  Holt (G-8334)
Stone House Bread LLC ....E 231 933-8864
  Traverse City (G-16841)
Stone House Bread Inc ....E 231 933-8864
  Traverse City (G-16842)
Supreme Baking Company ....G 313 894-0222
  Detroit (G-4618)
Sweet & Sweeter Inc ....G 586 977-9338
  Sterling Heights (G-16198)
Sweet Mellisas Cupcakes ....G 616 889-3998
  Lowell (G-10519)
Sweet Sugas Inc ....G 313 444-8570
  Clinton Township (G-3368)
Sweetest Taboo LLC ....G 313 575-4642
  Detroit (G-4620)
Sweetheart Bakery Inc ....E 313 839-6330
  Detroit (G-4621)
Sweetheart Bakery of Michigan ....F 586 795-1660
  Harper Woods (G-7673)
Sweetwaters Donut Mill ....G 269 979-1944
  Battle Creek (G-1303)
Telo ....G 810 845-8051
  Fenton (G-5507)
Top Notch Cookies & Cakes Inc ....G 734 467-9550
  Westland (G-18422)
Traverse City Pie Company LLC ......F 231 929-7437
  Traverse City (G-16864)
Uncle Johns Cider Mill Inc ....E 989 224-3686
  Saint Johns (G-14919)

Vargas & Sons .... F ...... 989 754-4636 Saginaw (G-14789)	◆ Dawn Foods Inc .... C ...... 517 789-4400 Jackson (G-8864)	Mr Peel Inc .... G ...... 734 266-2022 Livonia (G-10326)
W Bay Cupcakes .... G ...... 231 632-2010 Traverse City (G-16876)	Julian Brothers Inc .... F ...... 248 588-0280 Clawson (G-3100)	Northwest Confections Mich LLC ..... E ...... 971 666-8282 Lapeer (G-9950)
Walmart Inc .... F ...... 517 541-1481 Charlotte (G-2774)	Ludwicks Frozen Donuts Inc .... F ...... 616 453-6880 Grand Rapids (G-6951)	Optisource LLC .... G ...... 616 554-9048 Comstock Park (G-3631)
Way Bakery .... C ...... 517 787-6720 Jackson (G-9033)	Marie Minnie Bakers Inc .... C ...... 734 522-1100 Livonia (G-10300)	Opus Products LLC .... G ...... 586 202-1870 Oakland Twp (G-12653)
▼ West Thomas Partners LLC .... E ...... 616 430-7585 Grand Rapids (G-7336)	Pepperidge Farm Incorporated ..... G ...... 734 953-6729 Livonia (G-10362)	Original Murdicks Fudge Co .... G ...... 906 847-3530 Mackinac Island (G-10567)
White Lotus Farms Inc .... G ...... 734 904-1379 Ann Arbor (G-716)	▲ Savory Foods Inc .... D ...... 616 241-2583 Grand Rapids (G-7181)	Pop Daddy Popcorn LLC .... F ...... 734 550-9900 Whitmore Lake (G-18543)
Wow Factor Tables and Events .... G ...... 248 550-5922 Howell (G-8543)	Sweet Creations .... G ...... 989 327-1157 Saginaw (G-14770)	Popped Kernel .... G ...... 586 295-4977 Shelby Township (G-15306)
Yell Sweets LLC .... G ...... 586 799-4560 Shelby Township (G-15372)	**2061 Sugar, Cane**	Ranis Granola .... G ...... 734 223-2995 Ann Arbor (G-631)
Zingermans Bakehouse Inc .... D ...... 734 761-2095 Ann Arbor (G-725)	Michigan Sugar Company .... 989 883-3200 Sebewaing (G-15141)	Renas Fudge Shops Inc .... F ...... 586 293-0600 Fraser (G-5987)
2052 Cookies & Crackers	Michigan Sugar Company .... 989 673-2223 Caro (G-2575)	Rochester Fudge Company LLC .... G ...... 248 402-3444 Rochester Hills (G-14101)
Actt Management LLC .... E ...... 616 803-8734 Grand Rapids (G-6425)	**2062 Sugar, Cane Refining**	Rocky Mtn Choclat Fctry Inc .... D ...... 810 606-8550 Grand Blanc (G-6261)
Among Friends LLC .... F ...... 734 997-9720 Ann Arbor (G-365)	Farber Concessions Inc .... E ...... 313 387-1600 Redford (G-13733)	▲ Sanders Candy LLC .... D ...... 800 651-7263 Clinton Township (G-3349)
Artisan Bread Co LLC .... E ...... 586 756-0100 Warren (G-17714)	Michigan Sugar Company .... C ...... 989 673-3126 Caro (G-2574)	Simply Suzanne LLC .... G ...... 917 364-4549 Detroit (G-4594)
Bear Naked Inc .... F ...... 203 662-1136 Battle Creek (G-1193)	**2063 Sugar, Beet**	Spagnuolo George & Sons .... G ...... 810 229-4424 Brighton (G-2073)
Campbell Soup Company .... G ...... 313 295-6884 Taylor (G-16390)	Darwin Sneller .... 989 977-3718 Sebewaing (G-15139)	Sugar Free Specialties LLC .... F ...... 616 734-6999 Comstock Park (G-3646)
Campbell Soup Company .... G ...... 248 336-8486 Ferndale (G-5532)	Michigan Sugar Company .... C ...... 989 673-3126 Caro (G-2574)	Sugar Sugar Cotton Candy Co ...... G ...... 248 847-0070 Burton (G-2247)
Cherry Cone LLC .... G ...... 231 944-1036 Traverse City (G-16649)	Michigan Sugar Company .... C ...... 989 686-0161 Bay City (G-1378)	Truans Candies Inc .... F ...... 313 281-0185 Plymouth (G-13326)
Cherry Republic Inc .... D ...... 231 334-3150 Glen Arbor (G-6209)	Michigan Sugar Company .... C ...... 989 883-3200 Sebewaing (G-15141)	W2 Inc .... G ...... 517 764-3141 Jackson (G-9032)
Chewys Gourmet Kitchen LLC ...... F ...... 313 757-2595 Detroit (G-4092)	Michigan Sugar Company .... 810 679-2241 Croswell (G-3733)	**2066 Chocolate & Cocoa Prdts**
Dick and Jane Baking Co LLC .... G ...... 248 519-2418 Troy (G-17060)	▲ Michigan Sugar Company .... D ...... 989 686-0161 Bay City (G-1379)	Alinosi French Ice Cream Co .... G ...... 313 527-3195 Detroit (G-3997)
DVine Cookies .... E ...... 248 417-7850 Bloomfield Hills (G-1817)	Michigan Sugar Company .... C ...... 989 673-2223 Caro (G-2575)	Crow and Moss LLC .... G ...... 231 838-9875 Petoskey (G-12995)
Frito-Lay North America Inc .... G ...... 989 754-0435 Saginaw (G-14647)	Schuette Farms .... 989 550-0563 Elkton (G-5032)	▲ Gayles Chocolates Limited .... E ...... 248 398-0001 Royal Oak (G-14539)
Karemor Inc .... G ...... 517 323-3042 Lansing (G-9770)	**2064 Candy & Confectionery Prdts**	Kemnitz Fine Candies .... 734 453-0480 Plymouth (G-13213)
◆ Keebler Company .... B ...... 269 961-2000 Battle Creek (G-1250)	American Gourmet Snacks LLC .... G ...... 989 892-4856 Essexville (G-5108)	Kilwins Qulty Confections Inc .... C ...... 231 347-3800 Petoskey (G-13001)
Keebler Company .... C ...... 231 445-0335 Cheboygan (G-2790)	Berkley Pharmacy LLC .... F ...... 586 573-8300 Warren (G-17731)	Marshalls Trail Inc .... F ...... 231 436-5082 Mackinaw City (G-10568)
◆ Kellogg Company .... A ...... 269 961-2000 Battle Creek (G-1255)	BS Bars .... G ...... 734 358-3832 Ann Arbor (G-407)	Original Murdicks Fudge Co .... G ...... 906 847-3530 Mackinac Island (G-10567)
Kellogg North America Company ... C ...... 269 961-2000 Battle Creek (G-1260)	Chocolate Vault Llc .... 517 688-3388 Horton (G-8372)	Renas Fudge Shops Inc .... F ...... 586 293-0600 Fraser (G-5987)
Kmj Global Inc .... G ...... 240 594-5050 Birmingham (G-1732)	Detroit Fd Entrprnrship Acdemy .... F ...... 248 894-8941 Detroit (G-4147)	Rocky Mtn Choclat Fctry Inc .... D ...... 810 606-8550 Grand Blanc (G-6261)
Krumb Snatcher Cookie Co LLC ... G ...... 313 408-6802 Battle Creek (G-1266)	Detroit Fudge Company Inc .... G ...... 734 369-8573 Ann Arbor (G-449)	Rocky Mtn Choclat Fctry Inc .... G ...... 989 624-4784 Birch Run (G-1714)
Krumbsnatcher Enterprises LLC ... F ...... 313 408-6802 Detroit (G-4368)	Doug Murdicks Fudge Inc .... G ...... 231 938-2330 Traverse City (G-16670)	▲ Sanders Candy LLC .... D ...... 800 651-7263 Clinton Township (G-3349)
◆ Lotte USA Incorporated .... F ...... 269 963-6664 Battle Creek (G-1269)	Elsa Enterprises Inc. .... G ...... 248 816-1454 Troy (G-17085)	Sugar Free Specialties LLC .... F ...... 616 734-6999 Comstock Park (G-3646)
Ludwicks Frozen Donuts Inc .... F ...... 616 453-6880 Grand Rapids (G-6951)	Emesa Foods Company LLC .... G ...... 248 982-3908 Taylor (G-16413)	Verse Chocolate LLC .... G ...... 816 325-0208 Holland (G-8238)
Marias Italian Bakery Inc .... F ...... 734 981-1200 Canton (G-2488)	Fretty Media LLC .... G ...... 231 894-8055 Whitehall (G-18497)	**2067 Chewing Gum**
Nautical Knots .... G ...... 231 206-0400 Grand Haven (G-6339)	▲ Gayles Chocolates Limited .... E ...... 248 398-0001 Royal Oak (G-14539)	◆ Lotte USA Incorporated .... F ...... 269 963-6664 Battle Creek (G-1269)
Otb Enterprises LLC .... G ...... 248 266-5568 Troy (G-17293)	Gerbers Home Made Sweets .... G ...... 231 348-3743 Charlevoix (G-2715)	**2068 Salted & Roasted Nuts & Seeds**
Pepperidge Farm Incorporated ..... G ...... 734 953-6729 Livonia (G-10362)	Happy Candy .... G ...... 248 629-9819 Warren (G-17848)	All Natural Bites LLC .... F ...... 248 470-6252 Lathrup Village (G-9974)
▲ Savory Foods Inc .... D ...... 616 241-2583 Grand Rapids (G-7181)	Jlm Manufacturing .... G ...... 586 447-3500 Warren (G-17886)	Kar Nut Products Company LLC ... C ...... 248 588-1903 Madison Heights (G-10758)
▲ Shatila Food Products Inc .... E ...... 313 934-1520 Dearborn (G-3896)	Junkless Foods Inc .... F ...... 616 560-7895 Portage (G-13570)	Knpc Holdco LLC .... G ...... 248 588-1903 Madison Heights (G-10764)
Stone House Bread Inc .... E ...... 231 933-8864 Traverse City (G-16842)	Kernel Bennys .... 989 928-3950 Frankenmuth (G-5866)	◆ Koeze Company .... E ...... 616 724-2601 Grand Rapids (G-6902)
Supreme Baking Company .... G ...... 313 894-0222 Detroit (G-4618)	Klopp Group LLC .... 877 256-4528 Saginaw (G-14679)	Nutco Inc .... E ...... 800 872-4006 Detroit (G-4494)
Sweetie Pie Pantry .... F ...... 517 669-9300 Dewitt (G-4716)	Liquid Otc LLC .... 248 214-7771 Commerce Township (G-3551)	St Laurent Brothers Inc .... E ...... 989 893-7522 Bay City (G-1405)
Syd Enterprises .... 517 719-2740 Howell (G-8524)	◆ Lotte USA Incorporated .... F ...... 269 963-6664 Battle Creek (G-1269)	Variety Foods Inc .... D ...... 586 268-4900 Warren (G-18051)
Top Notch Cookies & Cakes Inc .... G ...... 734 467-9550 Westland (G-18422)	Marshalls Trail Inc .... F ...... 231 436-5082 Mackinaw City (G-10568)	**2075 Soybean Oil Mills**
2053 Frozen Bakery Prdts	Morley Brands LLC .... E ...... 586 468-4300 Clinton Township (G-3304)	Cargill Incorporated .... F ...... 608 868-5150 Owosso (G-12825)
Bakers Rhapsody .... G ...... 269 767-1368 Dowagiac (G-4777)		

Employee Codes: A=Over 500 employees, B=251-500
C=101-250, D=51-100, E=20-50, F=10-19, G=3-9

2022 Harris Michigan
Industrial Directory

20 FOOD AND KINDRED PRODUCTS20 FOOD AND KINDRED PRODUCTS SIC SECTION

Nubreed Nutrition Inc ....F 734 272-7395
Troy *(G-17283)*
Zeeland Bio-Based Products LLC ....G 616 748-1831
Zeeland *(G-19095)*
◆ **Zeeland Farm Services Inc** ....C 616 772-9042
Zeeland *(G-19096)*
Zeeland Farm Soya LLC ....F 616 772-9042
Zeeland *(G-19097)*
Zfs Creston LLC ....F 616 748-1825
Zeeland *(G-19100)*
Zfs Ithaca LLC ....E 616 772-9042
Zeeland *(G-19101)*

2076 Vegetable Oil Mills

Darling Ingredients Inc ....G 269 751-0560
Hamilton *(G-7597)*
Go Beyond Healthy LLC ....G 407 255-0314
Grand Rapids *(G-6746)*

2077 Animal, Marine Fats & Oils

Asao LLC ....F 734 522-6333
Livonia *(G-10125)*
Darling Ingredients Inc ....F 989 752-4340
Carrollton *(G-2588)*
Darling Ingredients Inc ....C 517 279-9731
Coldwater *(G-3431)*
Darling Ingredients Inc ....G 269 751-0560
Hamilton *(G-7597)*
Evergreen Grease Service Inc ....G 517 264-9913
Adrian *(G-65)*
Kellys Recycling Service Inc ....G 313 389-7870
Detroit *(G-4357)*
Michigan Protein Inc ....F 877 869-0630
Cedar Springs *(G-2657)*
Northern Lkes Safood Meats LLC ....E 313 368-4234
Detroit *(G-4489)*

2079 Shortening, Oils & Margarine

Asao LLC ....F 734 522-6333
Livonia *(G-10125)*
Cozart Producers ....G 810 736-1046
Flint *(G-5675)*
Michigan Biodiesel LLC ....G 269 427-0804
Kalamazoo *(G-9269)*
Old World Olive Press ....G 734 667-2755
Plymouth *(G-13255)*
Priorat Importers Corporation ....G 248 217-4608
Royal Oak *(G-14570)*
Stamatopolos & Sons ....G 734 369-2995
Ann Arbor *(G-664)*

2082 Malt Beverages

127 Brewing ....G 517 258-1346
Jackson *(G-8797)*
▲ **Abaco Partners LLC** ....C 616 532-1700
Kentwood *(G-9441)*
Acoustic Tap Room ....G 231 714-5028
Traverse City *(G-16596)*
American Brewers Inc ....F 616 318-9230
Kalamazoo *(G-9113)*
Apple Blossom Winery LLC ....G 269 668-3724
Kalamazoo *(G-9114)*
Atwater In Park ....G 313 344-5104
Grosse Pointe Park *(G-7548)*
Backdraft Brewing Company ....F 734 722-7639
Wayne *(G-18215)*
Barkshanty Hops LLC ....G 810 300-8049
Grosse Pointe Park *(G-7549)*
Beards Brewery LLC ....E 231 753-2221
Petoskey *(G-12991)*
Bells Brewery Inc ....F 906 233-5002
Escanaba *(G-5060)*
Bells Brewery Inc ....G 269 382-1402
Kalamazoo *(G-9134)*
Black Bottom Brewing Co Inc ....G 313 205-5493
Detroit *(G-4057)*
Blackrocks Brewery LLC ....G 906 273-1333
Marquette *(G-11008)*
Blackrocks Brewery LLC ....G 906 360-6674
Marquette *(G-11009)*
Brew Detroit LLC ....F 313 974-7366
Detroit *(G-4069)*
Century Lanes Inc ....D 616 392-7086
Holland *(G-7992)*
Clarkston Courts LLC ....C 248 383-8444
Clarkston *(G-3025)*
Corner Brewery LLC ....E 734 480-2739
Ypsilanti *(G-18934)*
Detroit Cycle Pub LLC ....G 231 286-5257
Macomb *(G-10587)*
Detroit Rvrtown Brwing Cmpay L ....C 313 877-9205
Detroit *(G-4163)*
Dg Brewing Company LLC ....G 616 427-3242
Ada *(G-16)*
Draught Horse Group LLC ....G 231 631-5218
New Hudson *(G-12051)*
Eastside Spot Inc ....G 906 226-9431
Marquette *(G-11016)*
Elk Brewing ....G 616 214-8172
Comstock Park *(G-3606)*
Fabiano Bros Dev - Wscnsin LLC ....F 989 509-0200
Bay City *(G-1356)*
Frankenmuth Brewery LLC ....E 989 262-8300
Frankenmuth *(G-5861)*
Ghost Island Brewery ....G 219 242-4800
New Buffalo *(G-12024)*
Gilligan Steele Tastings LLC ....G 269 808-3455
Kalamazoo *(G-9196)*
Global Draught Service ....G 810 844-6888
Pinckney *(G-13049)*
Gpbc Inc ....F 734 741-7325
Ann Arbor *(G-503)*
Gravel Capital Brewing LLC ....F 248 895-8399
Oxford *(G-12885)*
Im A Beer Hound ....G 517 331-0528
Lansing *(G-9767)*
James Joy LLC ....G 989 317-6629
Farwell *(G-5424)*
Knickerbocker ....G 616 345-5642
Grand Rapids *(G-6901)*
Kraftbrau Brewery Inc ....G 269 384-0288
Kalamazoo *(G-9256)*
▲ **Kuhnhenn Brewing Co LLC** ....F 586 979-8361
Warren *(G-17898)*
Kuhnhenn Brewing Co LLC ....G 586 231-0249
Clinton Township *(G-3274)*
Loggers Brewing Co ....G 989 401-3085
Saginaw *(G-14684)*
Lucky Girl Brwing - Cross Rads ....G 630 723-4285
Paw Paw *(G-12951)*
M4 CIC LLC ....G 734 436-8507
Ann Arbor *(G-559)*
Marquette Distillery ....G 906 869-4933
Marquette *(G-11033)*
Midland Brewing Co LLC ....G 989 259-7210
Midland *(G-11391)*
Mishigama Brewing Company ....G 734 547-5840
Ypsilanti *(G-18968)*
▲ **Mor-Dall Enterprises Inc** ....G 269 558-4915
Marshall *(G-11071)*
Mountain Town Stn Brew Pub LLC ....D 989 775-2337
Mount Pleasant *(G-11719)*
Mug Shots Burgers and Brews ....G 616 895-2337
Allendale *(G-227)*
New Holland Brewery ....F 616 202-7200
Grand Rapids *(G-7042)*
▲ **New Holland Brewing Co LLC** ....C 616 355-2941
Holland *(G-8154)*
North Pier Brewing Company LLC ....G 312 545-0446
Saint Joseph *(G-14952)*
Northern Oak Brewery Inc ....F 248 634-7515
Holly *(G-8285)*
Null Taphouse ....G 734 792-9124
Dexter *(G-4747)*
One Beer At A Time LLC ....E 616 719-1604
Grand Rapids *(G-7059)*
Oracle Brewing Company LLC ....F 989 401-7446
Breckenridge *(G-1913)*
Ore Dock Brewing Company LLC ....F 906 228-8888
Marquette *(G-11039)*
Paddle Hard Distributing LLC ....G 513 309-1192
Grayling *(G-7468)*
Plow Point Brewing Co ....G 734 562-9102
Chelsea *(G-2823)*
Pollard Brewing ....G 734 207-3886
Canton *(G-2510)*
▼ **Premier Malt Products Inc** ....E 586 443-3355
Warren *(G-17974)*
Rare Bird Holdings LLC ....G 616 335-9463
Holland *(G-8176)*
S B C Holdings Inc ....F 313 446-2000
Detroit *(G-4574)*
Salt Brewing Company LLC ....E 517 446-0375
Lansing *(G-9890)*
Saugatuck Brewing Company Inc ....E 269 857-7222
Douglas *(G-4774)*
Schelde Enterprises Inc ....G 231 941-7325
Traverse City *(G-16825)*
Speciation Artisan Ales LLC ....G 616 279-3929
Grand Rapids *(G-7215)*
Stony Lake Corporation ....G 734 944-9426
Saline *(G-15041)*
Stroh Companies Inc ....G 313 446-2000
Detroit *(G-4612)*
Sweetwater Brew LLC ....G 616 805-5077
Wyoming *(G-18910)*
Thorn Apple Brewing Company ....G 616 288-6907
Grand Rapids *(G-7261)*

2083 Malt

Apple Blossom Winery LLC ....G 269 668-3724
Kalamazoo *(G-9114)*
Brydges Group LLC ....G 734 649-6635
Battle Creek *(G-1200)*

2084 Wine & Brandy

12 Corners Vineyards ....G 269 926-7597
Benton Harbor *(G-1524)*
▲ **45 North Vineyard & Winery** ....F 231 271-1188
Lake Leelanau *(G-9557)*
American Brewers Inc ....F 616 318-9230
Kalamazoo *(G-9113)*
American Vintners LLC ....F 248 310-0575
Rochester *(G-13891)*
▲ **Andretta & Associates Inc** ....F 586 557-6226
Macomb *(G-10577)*
Aurora Cellars 2015 LLC ....F 231 994-3188
Lake Leelanau *(G-9558)*
B Nektar LLC ....F 313 744-6323
Ferndale *(G-5530)*
Big Lttle Wines Traverse Cy MI ....G 231 714-4854
Suttons Bay *(G-16338)*
Black Barn Vinyrd & Winery LLC ....G 517 569-2164
Rives Junction *(G-13885)*
Black Owl Distillery LLC ....G 616 901-9003
Grand Rapids *(G-6514)*
▲ **Black Star Farms LLC** ....F 231 271-4970
Suttons Bay *(G-16339)*
Blue Collar Winery LLC ....G 419 344-4715
Dundee *(G-4810)*
Bowers Harbor Vinyrd & Winery ....G 231 223-7615
Traverse City *(G-16626)*
Brys Winery Lc ....G 231 223-8446
Traverse City *(G-16631)*
Burrone Family Vineyards ....G 989 379-3786
Lachine *(G-9531)*
Caprice Brands LLC ....G 989 745-1286
Livonia *(G-10144)*
Cellar 849 Winery ....G 734 254-0275
Plymouth *(G-13143)*
Chateau Aronautique Winery LLC ....G 517 569-2132
Jackson *(G-8840)*
Chateau Grand Travers Ltd ....G 231 223-7355
Traverse City *(G-16646)*
▲ **Chateau Operations Ltd** ....E 231 223-4110
Traverse City *(G-16647)*
▲ **CHI Co/Tabor Hill Winery** ....D 269 422-1161
Buchanan *(G-2192)*
Circus Procession LLC ....G 616 834-8048
Holland *(G-7997)*
Cody Kresta Vineyard & Winery ....G 269 668-3800
Mattawan *(G-11164)*
Contessa Wine Cellars ....G 269 468-5534
Coloma *(G-3476)*
Continent Wines Inc ....G 248 467-7383
Clarkston *(G-3029)*
Crystal Vista Vineyard LLC ....G 231 269-4165
Thompsonville *(G-16553)*
Dablon Vineyards LLC ....F 269 422-2846
Baroda *(G-1159)*
Detroit Original Winery ....G 248 924-2920
Northville *(G-12213)*
Divino Intl Wine & Spirit LLC ....G 586 770-9409
Lake Orion *(G-9603)*
Dunn Beverage Intl LLC ....G 269 420-1547
Battle Creek *(G-1222)*
Evergreen Winery LLC ....G 989 392-2044
Bay City *(G-1353)*
Fenn Valley Vineyards Inc ....F 269 561-2396
Fennville *(G-5435)*
Fieldstone Hard Cider ....G 248 923-1742
Rochester *(G-13901)*
Flying Otter Winery LLC ....G 517 424-7107
Adrian *(G-68)*
Fontaine Chateau ....G 231 256-0000
Lake Leelanau *(G-9560)*
◆ **French Road Cellars LLC** ....G 231 256-0680
Lake Leelanau *(G-9561)*

SIC SECTION 20 FOOD AND KINDRED PRODUCTS20 FOOD AND KINDRED PRODUCTS

French Valley Vineyard L L C.....G..... 231 228-2616
Cedar *(G-2639)*
Glenn Vineyards LLC.....G..... 269 330-2350
Fennville *(G-5436)*
Good Harbor Vineyards Winery.....G..... 231 632-0703
Lake Leelanau *(G-9562)*
Good Neighbor Organic.....G..... 231 386-5636
Northport *(G-12187)*
▲ Great Lakes Wine & Spirits LLC.....C..... 313 278-5400
Highland Park *(G-7908)*
Harbor Sprng Vnyrds Winery LLC.....G..... 231 242-4062
Harbor Springs *(G-7647)*
Hearth & Vine.....G..... 231 944-1297
Suttons Bay *(G-16341)*
Heavenly Vineyards LLC.....G..... 616 710-2751
Cedar Springs *(G-2653)*
Hello Vino.....G..... 231 350-7138
Bellaire *(G-1475)*
Home Winery Supply LLC.....G..... 734 529-3296
Dundee *(G-4825)*
Howells Mainstreet Winery.....G..... 517 545-9463
Howell *(G-8466)*
J & Z Distribution Co LLC.....G..... 925 828-6260
Riverview *(G-13876)*
JB Whiskey Creek.....G..... 269 965-4052
Springfield *(G-15869)*
Lake Michigan Vintners LLC.....G..... 269 326-7195
Baroda *(G-1163)*
Lawton Ridge Winery LLC.....G..... 269 372-9463
Kalamazoo *(G-9259)*
Lazy Ballerina Winery LLC.....F..... 269 363-6218
Saint Joseph *(G-14945)*
Lazy Ballerina Winery LLC.....F..... 269 759-8486
Bridgman *(G-1931)*
▲ Leelanau Wine Cellars Ltd.....F..... 231 386-5201
Northport *(G-12189)*
Left Foot Charley.....G..... 231 995-0500
Traverse City *(G-16744)*
Leighs Garden Winery Inc.....G..... 906 553-7799
Escanaba *(G-5080)*
Lemon Creek Fruit Farm.....F..... 269 471-1321
Berrien Springs *(G-1642)*
Lemon Creek Winery Ltd.....E..... 269 471-1321
Berrien Springs *(G-1643)*
Little Man Winery.....G..... 269 637-2229
South Haven *(G-15408)*
Lost Cellars Inc.....G..... 734 626-0969
Boyne City *(G-1895)*
Mari Villa Vineyards.....F..... 231 935-4513
Traverse City *(G-16753)*
Mario Anthony Tabone.....G..... 734 667-2946
Plymouth *(G-13234)*
Michigan Wine Trail.....G..... 231 944-5220
Traverse City *(G-16756)*
Modern Craft Winery LLC.....G..... 989 876-4948
Au Gres *(G-760)*
Moraine Vineyards LLC.....G..... 269 422-1309
Baroda *(G-1166)*
Nate Ronald.....G..... 269 424-3777
Dowagiac *(G-4792)*
Nathaniel Rose Wine.....G..... 989 302-3297
Traverse City *(G-16766)*
▲ Nicholass Black River Vineyar.....G..... 231 625-9060
Cheboygan *(G-2793)*
Nomad Cidery LLC.....G..... 231 313-8627
Traverse City *(G-16769)*
Northville Cider Mill Inc.....F..... 248 349-3181
Northville *(G-12245)*
Northville Winery.....G..... 248 320-6507
Northville *(G-12248)*
▲ OKeefe Centre Ltd.....G..... 231 223-7355
Traverse City *(G-16779)*
Old Woodward Cellar.....G..... 248 792-5452
Birmingham *(G-1741)*
Owl Wineries.....G..... 586 229-7217
Roseville *(G-14457)*
Peninsula Cellars.....F..... 231 223-4050
Traverse City *(G-16787)*
Pentamere Winery.....F..... 517 423-9000
Tecumseh *(G-16511)*
Perrone Vineyards.....G..... 231 330-1493
Levering *(G-10016)*
Petoskey Frms Vnyrd Winery LLC.....G..... 231 290-9463
Petoskey *(G-13014)*
Provemont Hill Vineyard.....G..... 231 256-8839
Lake Leelanau *(G-9565)*
R C M S Inc.....G..... 269 422-1617
Baroda *(G-1169)*
Saint Julian Winery.....G..... 248 951-2113
Troy *(G-17341)*
Sandhill Crane Vineyards LLC.....G..... 517 764-0679
Jackson *(G-9006)*
Schramms Mead.....G..... 248 439-5000
Ferndale *(G-5584)*
▲ Shady Lane Orchards Inc.....F..... 231 935-1620
Suttons Bay *(G-16342)*
Signal 7 Wines LLC.....F..... 616 581-8900
Ann Arbor *(G-653)*
Spare Key Winery LLC.....G..... 231 250-7442
Charlevoix *(G-2733)*
Speciation Artisan Ales LLC.....G..... 616 279-3929
Grand Rapids *(G-7215)*
St Ambrose Cellars.....G..... 231 383-4262
Beulah *(G-1659)*
St Julian Wine Company Inc.....G..... 734 529-3700
Dundee *(G-4836)*
St Julian Wine Company Inc.....E..... 269 657-5568
Paw Paw *(G-12957)*
St Julian Wine Company Inc.....G..... 989 652-3281
Frankenmuth *(G-5872)*
St Julian Winery.....G..... 616 263-9087
Rockford *(G-14190)*
Stoney Acres Winery.....G..... 989 356-1041
Alpena *(G-323)*
Stoney Ridge Vineyards LLC.....G..... 616 540-4318
Kent City *(G-9437)*
Sunshine Meadery LLC.....G..... 231 215-7956
Twin Lake *(G-17473)*
Suttons Bay Ciders.....G..... 734 646-3196
Suttons Bay *(G-16343)*
T/D Village Winery LLC.....G..... 586 752-5510
Romeo *(G-14236)*
Tabone Vineyards LLC.....G..... 734 354-7271
Traverse City *(G-16850)*
Tandem Ciders Inc.....G..... 231 271-0050
Suttons Bay *(G-16344)*
Teeq Spirits Inc.....G..... 866 877-1840
Canton *(G-2532)*
Tempo Vino Winery Kalamazoo.....G..... 269 342-9463
Kalamazoo *(G-9353)*
Terrace Hill Vineyards.....G..... 269 428-2168
Saint Joseph *(G-14965)*
Three Fires Wine.....G..... 231 620-9463
Suttons Bay *(G-16345)*
Thunder Bay Winery.....G..... 989 358-9463
Alpena *(G-326)*
To Willow Harbor Vineyard.....G..... 269 369-3900
Three Oaks *(G-16560)*
Uva Mare Inc.....G..... 858 848-4440
Shelby Township *(G-15362)*
Vander Mill LLC.....D..... 616 259-8828
Grand Rapids *(G-7307)*
Veritas Vineyard LLC.....E..... 517 962-2427
Jackson *(G-9030)*
Vine-N-Berry Wines.....G..... 989 551-1616
Bad Axe *(G-1117)*
Vineyard 2121 LLC.....F..... 269 429-0555
Benton Harbor *(G-1599)*
Vineyard On Plainfield.....G..... 616 570-0659
Grand Rapids *(G-7318)*
Vineyard Ventures LLC.....G..... 517 420-4771
Lansing *(G-9902)*
Vintners Cellar Winery of Kal.....G..... 269 342-9463
Kalamazoo *(G-9363)*
Virgils Vineyard LLC.....G..... 248 719-2808
Farmington Hills *(G-5411)*
Virtue Cider.....F..... 269 455-0526
Fennville *(G-5444)*
Waloon Lake Winery.....G..... 231 622-8645
Petoskey *(G-13026)*
Weathervane Vinyards Inc.....G..... 231 228-4800
Cedar *(G-2640)*
White Pine Winery.....G..... 269 281-0098
Saint Joseph *(G-14979)*
Willow Vineyards Inc.....G..... 231 271-4810
Suttons Bay *(G-16347)*
Winery At Young Farms LLC.....F..... 989 506-5142
Mecosta *(G-11194)*
Yooper Winery LLC.....G..... 906 361-0318
Menominee *(G-11262)*

2085 Liquors, Distilled, Rectified & Blended

4 Detroiters Liquor LLC.....G..... 248 756-3678
Farmington Hills *(G-5156)*
4 One 2 Distillery.....G..... 269 205-3223
Wayland *(G-18186)*
Artesian Distillers.....G..... 616 252-1700
Grand Rapids *(G-6472)*
Bier Barrel Distillery LLC.....G..... 616 633-8601
Comstock Park *(G-3591)*
Bier Distillery Company.....G..... 616 633-8601
Rockford *(G-14157)*
Brown Forman.....G..... 248 464-2011
Clawson *(G-3089)*
Copper Kettle Distilling Co.....G..... 989 366-4412
Prudenville *(G-13657)*
Coppercraft Distillery LLC.....E..... 616 796-8274
Holland *(G-8005)*
Detroit City Distillery LLC.....F..... 313 338-3760
Detroit *(G-4141)*
Distilled Kalamazoo LLC.....G..... 269 993-2859
Kalamazoo *(G-9170)*
Distillery 9 LLC.....G..... 517 990-2929
Whitmore Lake *(G-18530)*
Embrace Premium Vodka LLC.....G..... 616 617-5602
Ypsilanti *(G-18942)*
Grand Traverse Dist Tasting Rm.....G..... 269 254-8113
Kalamazoo *(G-9199)*
Gray Skies Distillery.....F..... 616 437-1119
Grand Rapids *(G-6785)*
Great Legs Wnery Brwry Dist LL.....G..... 616 298-7600
Holland *(G-8060)*
Green Door Distilling Co LLC.....F..... 269 207-2298
Kalamazoo *(G-9203)*
High Five Spirits LLC.....G..... 248 217-6057
Bingham Farms *(G-1699)*
Jayda Gale Distilling Inc.....G..... 269 397-1132
Wayland *(G-18197)*
Journeyman Distillery LLC.....G..... 269 820-2050
Three Oaks *(G-16557)*
Kalamazoo Stillhouse.....G..... 269 352-0250
Kalamazoo *(G-9249)*
Legacy Distillers Inc.....F..... 231 933-0631
Traverse City *(G-16745)*
Les Cheneaux Distillers Inc.....E..... 906 748-0505
Cedarville *(G-2670)*
▲ Liquid Manufacturing LLC.....E..... 810 220-2802
Ann Arbor *(G-550)*
Long Road Distillers LLC.....F..... 616 356-1770
Grand Rapids *(G-6948)*
Mammoth Distilling LLC.....G..... 773 841-4242
Central Lake *(G-2695)*
Michigrain Distillery.....G..... 517 580-8624
Lansing *(G-9871)*
▲ RGI Brands LLC.....F..... 312 253-7400
Bloomfield Hills *(G-1856)*
Tcwc LLC.....E..... 231 922-8292
Traverse City *(G-16852)*
Temperance Distilling Company.....F..... 734 847-5262
Temperance *(G-16550)*
▲ Two James Spirits LLC.....G..... 313 964-4800
Detroit *(G-4650)*
Valentine Distilling.....G..... 248 629-9951
Ferndale *(G-5595)*
Valentine Distilling Co.....G..... 646 286-2690
Ferndale *(G-5596)*

2086 Soft Drinks

Absopure Water Company LLC.....B..... 734 459-8000
Plymouth *(G-13111)*
American Bottling Company.....F..... 810 564-1432
Mount Morris *(G-11667)*
American Bottling Company.....F..... 616 396-1281
Holland *(G-7962)*
American Bottling Company.....F..... 616 392-2124
Holland *(G-7963)*
American Bottling Company.....E..... 989 731-5392
Gaylord *(G-6118)*
American Bottling Company.....F..... 231 775-7393
Cadillac *(G-2312)*
American Bottling Company.....F..... 517 622-8605
Grand Ledge *(G-6384)*
Arbor Springs Water Company.....E..... 734 668-8270
Ann Arbor *(G-376)*
Binks Coca-Cola Bottling Co.....E..... 906 786-4144
Escanaba *(G-5063)*
Binks Coca-Cola Bottling Co.....F..... 906 774-3202
Iron Mountain *(G-8718)*
Bottling Group Inc.....G..... 517 545-2624
Howell *(G-8432)*
Coca-Cola Bottling Co.....F..... 313 868-2167
Highland Park *(G-7902)*
Coca-Cola Company.....G..... 269 657-3171
Paw Paw *(G-12943)*
Coca-Cola Refreshments USA Inc.....G..... 616 913-0400
Grand Rapids *(G-6578)*
Coca-Cola Refreshments USA Inc.....G..... 231 947-4150
Traverse City *(G-16655)*
Coca-Cola Refreshments USA Inc.....G..... 616 458-4536
Grand Rapids *(G-6579)*

S I C

Employee Codes: A=Over 500 employees, B=251-500
C=101-250, D=51-100, E=20-50, F=10-19, G=3-9
2022 Harris Michigan
Industrial Directory
735

20 FOOD AND KINDRED PRODUCTS20 FOOD AND KINDRED PRODUCTS SIC SECTION

Coca-Cola Refreshments USA Inc ....G....... 269 657-8538
Paw Paw *(G-12944)*

Coca-Cola Refreshments USA Inc ....G....... 313 897-5000
Farmington Hills *(G-5204)*

Coke Bottle ....G....... 810 424-3352
Flint *(G-5668)*

Crystal Falls Springs Inc ....G....... 906 875-3191
Crystal Falls *(G-3741)*

Detroit Bubble Tea Company ....G....... 248 239-1131
Ferndale *(G-5542)*

Dr Pepper Snapple Group ....F....... 616 393-5800
Holland *(G-8016)*

Ellis Infinity LLC ....G....... 313 570-0840
Detroit *(G-4203)*

Everfresh Beverages Inc ....D....... 586 755-9500
Warren *(G-17798)*

Faygo Beverages Inc ....B....... 313 925-1600
Detroit *(G-4227)*

Florida Coca-Cola Bottling Co ....B....... 906 495-2261
Kincheloe *(G-9503)*

Global Restaurant Group Inc ....G....... 313 271-2777
Dearborn *(G-3847)*

Grandads Sweet Tea LLC ....G....... 313 320-4446
Warren *(G-17835)*

Great Lakes Coca-Cola Dist LLC ....F....... 989 895-8537
Bay City *(G-1363)*

Great Lakes Coca-Cola Dist LLC ....F....... 906 475-7003
Negaunee *(G-11966)*

Great Lakes Coca-Cola Dist LLC ....F....... 517 322-2349
Lansing *(G-9762)*

Great Lakes Coca-Cola Dist LLC ....F....... 734 397-2700
Belleville *(G-1485)*

Hancock Bottling Co Inc ....E....... 906 482-3701
Hancock *(G-7618)*

Hill Brothers ....G....... 616 784-2767
Grand Rapids *(G-6816)*

Jbt Bottling LLC ....G....... 269 377-4905
Kalamazoo *(G-9230)*

Jumpin Johnnys Inc ....G....... 989 832-0160
Midland *(G-11380)*

Keurig Dr Pepper Inc ....G....... 231 775-7393
Cadillac *(G-2339)*

Keurig Dr Pepper Inc ....G....... 313 937-3500
Detroit *(G-4359)*

▲ Liquid Manufacturing LLC ....E....... 810 220-2802
Ann Arbor *(G-550)*

▲ Michigan Btlg & Cstm Pack Co ....D....... 313 846-1717
Detroit *(G-4446)*

Minute Maid Co ....G....... 269 657-3171
Paw Paw *(G-12953)*

Newberry Bottling Co Inc ....G....... 906 293-5189
Newberry *(G-12095)*

Northville Cider Mill Inc ....F....... 248 349-3181
Northville *(G-12245)*

Pbg Michigan LLC ....G....... 989 345-2595
West Branch *(G-18335)*

Pepsi ....G....... 231 627-2290
Cheboygan *(G-2795)*

Pepsi Beverages Co ....G....... 989 754-0435
Saginaw *(G-14726)*

Pepsi Bottling Group ....F....... 810 966-8060
Kimball *(G-9497)*

Pepsi Bottling Group ....F....... 517 546-2777
Howell *(G-8493)*

Pepsi Co Wixom ....F....... 248 305-3500
Milan *(G-11448)*

Pepsi Cola Botling Co Houghton ....F....... 906 482-0161
Houghton *(G-8389)*

Pepsi-Cola Metro Btlg Co Inc ....G....... 517 321-0231
Lansing *(G-9726)*

Pepsi-Cola Metro Btlg Co Inc ....G....... 248 335-3528
Pontiac *(G-13406)*

Pepsi-Cola Metro Btlg Co Inc ....G....... 989 345-2595
West Branch *(G-18336)*

Pepsi-Cola Metro Btlg Co Inc ....G....... 231 946-0452
Traverse City *(G-16788)*

Pepsi-Cola Metro Btlg Co Inc ....G....... 989 755-1020
Saginaw *(G-14727)*

Pepsi-Cola Metro Btlg Co Inc ....G....... 517 546-2777
Howell *(G-8494)*

Pepsi-Cola Metro Btlg Co Inc ....G....... 269 226-6400
Kalamazoo *(G-9291)*

Pepsi-Cola Metro Btlg Co Inc ....G....... 810 232-3925
Flint *(G-5744)*

Pepsi-Cola Metro Btlg Co Inc ....G....... 616 285-8200
Grand Rapids *(G-7077)*

Pepsi-Cola Metro Btlg Co Inc ....G....... 989 772-3158
Mount Pleasant *(G-11730)*

Pepsi-Cola Metro Btlg Co Inc ....G....... 517 279-8436
Coldwater *(G-3445)*

Pepsi-Cola Metro Btlg Co Inc ....G....... 313 832-0910
Detroit *(G-4516)*

Pepsi-Cola Metro Btlg Co Inc ....G....... 231 798-1274
Norton Shores *(G-12325)*

Pepsi-Cola Metro Btlg Co Inc ....G....... 810 987-2181
Kimball *(G-9498)*

Pepsi-New Bern-Howell-151 ....F....... 517 546-7542
Howell *(G-8495)*

Pepsico Inc ....F....... 734 374-9841
Southgate *(G-15755)*

Pepsico Inc ....G....... 586 276-4102
Sterling Heights *(G-16124)*

Pond Biologics LLC ....F....... 800 527-9420
Shelby Township *(G-15305)*

Refreshment Product Svcs Inc ....G....... 906 475-7003
Negaunee *(G-11972)*

S B C Holdings Inc ....F....... 313 446-2000
Detroit *(G-4574)*

Select Distributors LLC ....F....... 586 510-4647
Warren *(G-18008)*

Simplify Inventions LLC ....D....... 248 960-1700
Farmington Hills *(G-5382)*

South Range Bottling Works Inc ....G....... 906 370-2295
South Range *(G-15462)*

St Julian Wine Company Inc ....G....... 989 652-3281
Frankenmuth *(G-5872)*

Stroh Companies Inc ....G....... 313 446-2000
Detroit *(G-4612)*

Sundance Beverages Inc ....D....... 586 755-9470
Warren *(G-18030)*

◆ Viva Beverages LLC ....G....... 248 746-7044
Southfield *(G-15739)*

Wasem Fruit Farm ....G....... 734 482-2342
Milan *(G-11451)*

2087 Flavoring Extracts & Syrups

▲ Coffee Beanery Ltd ....E....... 810 733-1020
Flushing *(G-5805)*

Contract Flavors Inc ....F....... 616 454-5950
Grand Rapids *(G-6598)*

Farber Concessions Inc ....E....... 313 387-1600
Redford *(G-13733)*

Flavorsum LLC ....E....... 800 525-2431
Kalamazoo *(G-9188)*

▼ Glcc Co ....E....... 269 657-3167
Paw Paw *(G-12948)*

Great Lakes Coca-Cola Dist LLC ....F....... 517 322-2349
Lansing *(G-9762)*

Gsb & Associates Inc ....G....... 770 424-1886
Kalamazoo *(G-9206)*

Jogue Inc ....G....... 248 349-1501
Northville *(G-12233)*

◆ Jogue Inc ....E....... 734 207-0100
Plymouth *(G-13203)*

Jogue Inc ....G....... 313 921-4802
Detroit *(G-4339)*

◆ John L Hinkle Holding Co Inc ....E....... 269 344-3640
Kalamazoo *(G-9233)*

◆ Kalsec Inc ....G....... 269 349-9711
Kalamazoo *(G-9250)*

Leonard Fountain Spc Inc ....D....... 313 891-4141
Detroit *(G-4390)*

Leroy Worden ....G....... 231 325-3837
Beulah *(G-1655)*

▼ Lorann Oils Inc ....F....... 517 882-0215
Lansing *(G-9865)*

Moore Ingredients Ltd ....G....... 513 881-7144
Kalamazoo *(G-9275)*

National Product Co ....F....... 269 344-3640
Kalamazoo *(G-9280)*

Northville Laboratories Inc ....F....... 248 349-1500
Northville *(G-12246)*

▲ Penguin Juice Co ....F....... 734 467-6991
Westland *(G-18404)*

Pure Herbs Ltd ....F....... 586 446-8200
Sterling Heights *(G-16139)*

Refreshment Product Svcs Inc ....G....... 906 475-7003
Negaunee *(G-11972)*

Sensient Flavors LLC ....E....... 989 479-3211
Harbor Beach *(G-7636)*

Sensient Technologies Corp ....G....... 989 479-3211
Harbor Beach *(G-7637)*

Sunopta Ingredients Inc ....E....... 502 587-7999
Schoolcraft *(G-15129)*

Tcwc LLC ....E....... 231 922-8292
Traverse City *(G-16852)*

Wild Flavors Inc ....E....... 269 216-2603
Kalamazoo *(G-9370)*

2091 Fish & Seafoods, Canned & Cured

Big O Smokehouse Inc ....E....... 616 891-5555
Caledonia *(G-2368)*

Gustafson Smoked Fish ....G....... 906 292-5424
Moran *(G-11609)*

▼ Ruleau Brothers Inc ....E....... 906 753-4767
Stephenson *(G-15911)*

Sea Fare Foods Inc ....F....... 313 568-0223
Detroit *(G-4586)*

2092 Fish & Seafoods, Fresh & Frozen

Collins Caviar Company ....G....... 269 469-4576
Union Pier *(G-17499)*

▼ Ruleau Brothers Inc ....E....... 906 753-4767
Stephenson *(G-15911)*

Sea Fare Foods Inc ....F....... 313 568-0223
Detroit *(G-4586)*

2095 Coffee

Ad Astra Roasters LLC ....G....... 517 914-2487
Hillsdale *(G-7922)*

Becharas Bros Coffee Co ....E....... 313 869-4700
Detroit *(G-4047)*

▲ Coffee Beanery Ltd ....E....... 810 733-1020
Flushing *(G-5805)*

Cozy Cup Coffee Company Llc ....G....... 989 984-7619
Oscoda *(G-12755)*

Fireside Coffee Company Inc ....F....... 810 635-9196
Swartz Creek *(G-16353)*

Good Sense Coffee LLC ....E....... 810 355-2349
Brighton *(G-2003)*

Hermans Boy ....G....... 616 866-2900
Rockford *(G-14169)*

Infusco Coffee Roasters LLC ....G....... 269 213-5282
Sawyer *(G-15109)*

Inter State Foods Inc ....F....... 517 372-5500
Lansing *(G-9706)*

◆ Koeze Company ....E....... 616 724-2601
Grand Rapids *(G-6902)*

M-36 Coffee Roasters LLC ....G....... 734 449-8910
Whitmore Lake *(G-18539)*

Prospectors LLC ....G....... 616 634-8260
Grand Rapids *(G-7122)*

Rowster Coffee Inc ....E....... 616 780-7777
Grand Rapids *(G-7172)*

Shift Roasting Company LLC ....G....... 734 915-3666
Saline *(G-15040)*

Stickmann Baeckerei ....G....... 269 205-2444
Middleville *(G-11314)*

Treat of Day LLC ....G....... 616 706-1717
Grand Rapids *(G-7271)*

Two Cups Coffee Co LLC ....F....... 616 953-0534
Holland *(G-8232)*

2096 Potato Chips & Similar Prdts

Better Made Snack Foods Inc ....C....... 313 925-4774
Detroit *(G-4054)*

Cambridge Sharpe Inc ....F....... 248 613-5562
South Lyon *(G-15429)*

Campbell Soup Company ....G....... 313 295-6884
Taylor *(G-16390)*

Campbell Soup Company ....G....... 248 336-8486
Ferndale *(G-5532)*

▲ Cheeze Kurls LLC ....D....... 616 784-6095
Grand Rapids *(G-6567)*

Detroit Frends Potato Chip LLC ....G....... 313 924-0085
Detroit *(G-4149)*

Doc Popcorn ....G....... 734 250-8133
Taylor *(G-16402)*

Downeys Potato Chips-Waterford ....G....... 248 673-3636
Waterford *(G-18119)*

▼ Grandpapas Inc ....E....... 313 891-6830
Detroit *(G-4274)*

Gvb Group-La Fiesta LLC ....F....... 231 843-7600
Montague *(G-11597)*

Hacienda Mexican Foods LLC ....D....... 313 895-8823
Detroit *(G-4289)*

Hippies Chippies Inc ....G....... 616 259-2133
Grand Rapids *(G-6818)*

Manos Authentic LLC ....G....... 800 242-2796
Clinton Township *(G-3293)*

▲ Mexamerica Foods LLC ....F....... 814 781-1447
Grand Rapids *(G-6984)*

Tortillas Tita LLC ....G....... 734 756-7646
Wayne *(G-18239)*

◆ Uncle Rays LLC ....C....... 313 834-0800
Detroit *(G-4652)*

Variety Foods Inc ....D....... 586 268-4900
Warren *(G-18051)*

SIC SECTION

20 FOOD AND KINDRED PRODUCTS

We Pop Corn LLC	F	313 387-1600
Redford (G-13786)		
Whm Investments Inc	G	269 432-3251
Colon (G-3492)		

2097 Ice

Arctic Glacier Grayling Inc	F	810 987-7100
Port Huron (G-13440)		
▲ Arctic Glacier Inc	E	734 485-0430
Port Huron (G-13441)		
Arctic Glacier Newburgh Inc	F	845 561-0549
Port Huron (G-13442)		
Arctic Glacier Texas Inc	G	517 999-3500
Lansing (G-9806)		
Arctic Glacier USA Inc	F	215 283-0326
Port Huron (G-13443)		
Arctic Glacier USA Inc	E	204 772-2473
Port Huron (G-13444)		
Arctic Glacier USA Inc	E	204 772-2473
Port Huron (G-13445)		
Arctic Glacier USA Inc	E	204 772-2473
Port Huron (G-13446)		
Arctic Glacier USA Inc	E	204 772-2473
Port Huron (G-13447)		
Arctic Glacier USA Inc	E	204 772-2473
Port Huron (G-13448)		
Arctic Glacier USA Inc	E	204 772-2473
Port Huron (G-13449)		
Arctic Glacier USA Inc	E	204 772-2473
Port Huron (G-13450)		
Arctic Glacier USA Inc	E	204 772-2473
Port Huron (G-13451)		
Arctic Glacier USA Inc	E	204 772-2473
Port Huron (G-13452)		
Arctic Glacier USA Inc	E	204 772-2473
Port Huron (G-13453)		
Cosner Ice Company Inc	B	812 279-8930
Port Huron (G-13466)		
Daneks Goodtime Ice Co Inc	E	989 725-5920
Owosso (G-12830)		
Gold Coast Ice Makers LLC	G	231 845-2745
Ludington (G-10537)		
▲ Hanson Cold Storage LLC	F	269 982-1390
Saint Joseph (G-14933)		
Home City Ice Company	E	734 955-9094
Romulus (G-14283)		
Knowlton Enterprises Inc	D	810 987-7100
Port Huron (G-13495)		
Lansing Ice and Fuel Company	F	517 372-3850
Lansing (G-9710)		
Michigan Pure Ice Co LLC	G	231 420-9896
Indian River (G-8655)		
Northern Pure Ice Co L L C	F	989 344-2088
Port Huron (G-13510)		
U S Ice Corp	E	313 862-3344
Detroit (G-4651)		

2098 Macaroni, Spaghetti & Noodles

Asian Noodle LLC	G	989 316-2380
Grand Rapids (G-6476)		
Dina Mia Kitchens Inc	E	906 265-9082
Iron River (G-8740)		
Greenfield Noodle Specialty Co	F	313 873-2212
Detroit (G-4281)		
International Noodle Co Inc	G	248 583-2479
Madison Heights (G-10747)		
Krzysiak Family Restaurant	D	989 894-5531
Bay City (G-1372)		
Northside Noodle Company	G	906 779-2181
Iron Mountain (G-8728)		
▲ Pierino Frozen Foods Inc	E	313 928-0950
Lincoln Park (G-10053)		
Tomukun Noodle Bar	G	734 995-8668
Ann Arbor (G-695)		
▲ Turris Italian Foods Inc	D	586 773-6010
Roseville (G-14488)		

2099 Food Preparations, NEC

18th Street Deli Inc	G	313 921-7710
Hamtramck (G-7610)		
A & B Home Essentials LLC	G	734 334-3041
Van Buren Twp (G-17506)		
Ace Vending Service Inc	F	616 243-7983
Grand Rapids (G-6422)		
AFP Consulting	G	616 534-9858
Wyoming (G-18850)		
Al Dente Inc	E	734 449-8522
Whitmore Lake (G-18518)		
Albies Food Products LLC	F	989 732-2800
Gaylord (G-6117)		
American Classics Corp	G	231 843-0523
Ludington (G-10525)		
▲ American Soy Products Inc	D	734 429-2310
Saline (G-15001)		
Among Friends LLC	F	734 997-9720
Ann Arbor (G-365)		
◆ Amway International Inc	E	616 787-1000
Ada (G-8)		
▼ Arbre Farms Corporation	B	231 873-3337
Walkerville (G-17658)		
Artisan Bread Co LLC	E	586 756-0100
Warren (G-17714)		
Aseltine Cider Company Inc	G	616 784-7676
Comstock Park (G-3588)		
Asmus Seasoning Inc	F	586 939-4505
Sterling Heights (G-15934)		
B & B Pretzels Inc	F	248 358-1655
Southfield (G-15500)		
Battels Sugar Bush	G	989 872-4794
Cass City (G-2611)		
Belchers Maple Syrup LLC	G	231 942-1399
Tustin (G-17465)		
Better Made Snack Foods Inc	C	313 925-4774
Detroit (G-4054)		
Big Boy Restaurants Intl LLC	F	586 759-6000
Southfield (G-15507)		
Blakes Orchard Inc	G	586 784-5343
Armada (G-732)		
Bliss & Vinegar LLC	G	616 970-0732
Grand Rapids (G-6515)		
Bovvy Mkt LLC	G	313 706-7922
Detroit (G-4065)		
Bowtie Catering LLC	G	313 989-3952
Eastpointe (G-4928)		
Brewts LLC	G	616 291-1117
Byron Center (G-2262)		
Brians Foods LLC	G	248 739-5280
Southfield (G-15511)		
Buddies Foods LLC	E	586 776-4036
Fraser (G-5907)		
Burnette Foods Inc	F	231 223-4282
Traverse City (G-16633)		
Butterball Farms Inc	C	616 243-0105
Grand Rapids (G-6541)		
Canadian Harvest LP	G	952 835-6429
Schoolcraft (G-15113)		
Champion Foods LLC	B	734 753-3663
New Boston (G-12006)		
Charidimos Inc	G	248 827-7733
Southfield (G-15519)		
Cheesecake and Ecetera LLC	G	734 335-8757
Livonia (G-10156)		
▲ Cheeze Kurls LLC	D	616 784-6095
Grand Rapids (G-6567)		
Cherry Blossom	G	231 342-3635
Williamsburg (G-18552)		
▲ Coffee Beanery Ltd	E	810 733-1020
Flushing (G-5805)		
Conagra Brands Inc	G	810 724-2715
Imlay City (G-8629)		
Conagra Brands Inc	G	402 240-8210
Quincy (G-13665)		
Conagra Brands Inc	E	616 392-2359
Holland (G-8003)		
Country Home Creations Inc	E	810 244-7348
Flint (G-5674)		
Countryside Foods LLC	B	586 447-3500
Warren (G-17765)		
Crossbrook LLC	G	616 772-5921
Zeeland (G-19009)		
Curry Fresh Inc	G	734 262-0560
Ypsilanti (G-18938)		
Custom Foods Inc	F	989 249-8061
Saginaw (G-14634)		
Daniel Olson	G	269 816-1838
Jones (G-9083)		
Danjos Foods Inc	G	517 543-2260
Charlotte (G-2749)		
Detroit Peanuts LLC	G	313 826-4327
Detroit (G-4158)		
Dexter Cider Mill Inc	G	734 475-6419
Chelsea (G-2809)		
DForte Inc	F	269 657-6996
Paw Paw (G-12946)		
Diehl Inc	G	517 265-5045
Adrian (G-62)		
Do & Co Detroit Inc	D	424 288-9025
Detroit (G-4184)		
Dorothy Dawson Food Products	E	517 788-9830
Jackson (G-8870)		
Dough & Spice Inc	G	586 756-6100
Warren (G-17781)		
Downeys Potato Chips-Waterford	G	248 673-3636
Waterford (G-18119)		
◆ Eden Foods Inc	D	517 456-7424
Clinton (G-3137)		
Eden Foods Inc	E	313 921-2053
Detroit (G-4201)		
El-Milagro of Michigan Inc	G	616 452-6625
Grand Rapids (G-6667)		
Frandale Sub Shop	F	616 446-6311
Allendale (G-218)		
Fudge and Frosting	G	517 763-2040
Lansing (G-9839)		
▲ Giovannis Apptzing Fd Pdts Inc	F	773 960-1945
Richmond (G-13838)		
Global Warming Salsa	G	248 882-3266
White Lake (G-18457)		
Good Life Naturals LLC	G	616 207-9230
Alto (G-333)		
Grand Rapids Salsa	G	616 780-1801
Grand Rapids (G-6769)		
▲ Great Lkes Fstida Holdings Inc	F	616 241-0400
Grand Rapids (G-6789)		
Green Dreamzz LLC	G	313 377-2926
Detroit (G-4279)		
Haighs Maple Syrup & Sups LLC	G	517 202-6975
Vermontville (G-17588)		
Hashems of Dearborn Heights	F	313 278-2000
Dearborn Heights (G-3928)		
Herman Hillbillies Farm LLC	G	906 201-0760
Lanse (G-9661)		
Highland Hills Maple Syrup LLC	G	231 920-1589
Mc Bain (G-11180)		
Hill Brothers	G	616 784-2767
Grand Rapids (G-6816)		
Hillshire Brands Company	G	616 875-8131
Zeeland (G-19038)		
Home Style Foods Inc	F	313 874-3250
Detroit (G-4303)		
Honey Tree	G	734 697-1000
Van Buren Twp (G-17529)		
Indian Summer Cooperative Inc	C	231 873-7504
Hart (G-7755)		
Intl Giuseppes Oils & Vinegars	G	586 698-2754
Sterling Hts (G-16236)		
J B Dough Co	G	269 944-4160
Benton Harbor (G-1558)		
Jarmans Pure Maple Syrup LLC	G	231 818-5315
Cheboygan (G-2789)		
Jaspers Sugar Bush LLC	G	906 639-2588
Carney (G-2563)		
Jiffy Mix	G	734 475-1361
Chelsea (G-2817)		
Jogue Inc	G	248 349-1501
Northville (G-12233)		
◆ Jogue Inc	E	734 207-0100
Plymouth (G-13203)		
Joplins Salsa	G	419 787-8195
Ypsilanti (G-18959)		
◆ Kalamazoo Holdings Inc	G	269 349-9711
Kalamazoo (G-9240)		
◆ Kalsec Inc	G	269 349-9711
Kalamazoo (G-9250)		
Kasza Sugar Bush	G	231 742-1930
Shelby (G-15152)		
Kerry Foods	F	616 871-9940
Grand Rapids (G-6893)		
Knouse Foods Cooperative Inc	C	269 657-5524
Paw Paw (G-12950)		
Kraft Heinz Foods Company	G	616 447-0481
Grand Rapids (G-6904)		
Kraft Heinz Foods Company	G	616 396-6557
Holland (G-8115)		
Kring Pizza Inc	G	586 792-0049
Harrison Township (G-7704)		
L & J Enterprises Inc	G	586 995-4153
Metamora (G-11283)		
L & J Products K Huntington	G	810 919-3550
Brighton (G-2015)		
L & P LLC	G	231 733-1415
Muskegon (G-11854)		
La Jalisciense Inc	F	313 237-0008
Farmington Hills (G-5288)		
Lafrontera Tortillas Inc	G	734 231-1701
Rockwood (G-14201)		
Las Brazas Tortillas	G	616 886-0737
Holland (G-8124)		
Lesley Elizabeth Inc	G	810 667-0706
Lapeer (G-9940)		

Employee Codes: A=Over 500 employees, B=251-500
C=101-250, D=51-100, E=20-50, F=10-19, G=3-9

20 FOOD AND KINDRED PRODUCTS20 FOOD AND KINDRED PRODUCTS SIC SECTION

▲ **Lesley Elizabeth Inc**..........G....... 810 667-0706
Lapeer *(G-9941)*
Levi Ohman Micah..........F....... 612 251-1293
Marquette *(G-11030)*
Litehouse Inc..........C....... 616 897-5911
Lowell *(G-10509)*
Ludhaven Sugarvush..........G....... 906 647-2400
Barbeau *(G-1152)*
Marfood USA..........G....... 313 292-4100
Taylor *(G-16438)*
Marshalls Trail Inc..........F....... 231 436-5082
Mackinaw City *(G-10568)*
▼ **McClures Pickles LLC**..........E....... 248 837-9323
Detroit *(G-4422)*
McCormick & Company Inc..........G....... 586 558-8424
Warren *(G-17921)*
Mead Johnson & Company LLC..........G....... 616 748-7100
Zeeland *(G-19051)*
▲ **Mexamerica Foods LLC**..........F....... 814 781-1447
Grand Rapids *(G-6984)*
Mexican Food Specialties Inc..........G....... 734 779-2370
Southfield *(G-15656)*
Michaelenes Inc..........G....... 248 625-0156
Clarkston *(G-3050)*
Michigan Celery Promotion Coop..........F....... 616 669-1250
Hudsonville *(G-8595)*
Michigan Dessert Corporation..........E....... 248 544-4574
Oak Park *(G-12628)*
Michigan Soy Products Company..........G....... 248 544-7742
Royal Oak *(G-14563)*
Mizkan America Inc..........D....... 616 794-0226
Belding *(G-1457)*
Mizkan America Inc..........D....... 616 794-3670
Belding *(G-1458)*
N F P Inc..........G....... 989 631-0009
Midland *(G-11397)*
▲ **Natural American Foods LLC**..........E....... 517 467-2065
Onsted *(G-12707)*
New Harper Seasoning Inc..........G....... 734 767-6290
Detroit *(G-4482)*
New Moon Noodle Incorporated..........F....... 269 962-8820
Battle Creek *(G-1278)*
Nuts & Coffee Gallery..........G....... 313 581-3212
Dearborn *(G-3878)*
On Base Food Group LLC..........G....... 248 672-7659
Birmingham *(G-1742)*
Onion Crock of Michigan Inc..........G....... 616 458-2922
Grand Rapids *(G-7060)*
Parshallville Cider Mill..........G....... 810 629-9079
Fenton *(G-5494)*
Parsons Centennial Farm LLC..........G....... 231 547-2038
Charlevoix *(G-2727)*
Pepperidge Farm Incorporated..........G....... 734 953-6729
Livonia *(G-10362)*
▲ **Pierino Frozen Foods Inc**..........E....... 313 928-0950
Lincoln Park *(G-10053)*
Poppin Top Hat LLC..........G....... 313 427-0400
Detroit *(G-4530)*
Porters Orchards Farm Market..........G....... 810 636-7156
Goodrich *(G-6226)*
Postma Brothers Maple Syrup..........G....... 906 478-3051
Rudyard *(G-14594)*
Priorat Importers Corporation..........G....... 248 217-4608
Royal Oak *(G-14570)*
◆ **Questor Partners Fund II LP**..........G....... 248 593-1930
Birmingham *(G-1745)*
Radical Plants LLC..........G....... 586 243-8128
Saint Clair Shores *(G-14880)*
Rays Ice Cream Co Inc..........F....... 248 549-5256
Royal Oak *(G-14573)*
Rays Pure Mple Syrup Pdts LLC..........G....... 269 601-7694
Fulton *(G-6072)*
Red Headed Honey LLC..........G....... 707 616-4278
Camden *(G-2424)*
Ridge Cider..........G....... 231 674-2040
Grant *(G-7432)*
Riveridge Cider Co LLC..........G....... 616 887-6873
Sparta *(G-15777)*
Rmg Family Sugar Bush Inc..........G....... 906 478-3038
Rudyard *(G-14595)*
Rmg Maple Products Inc..........G....... 906 478-3038
Rudyard *(G-14596)*
Russo Bros Inc..........F....... 906 485-5250
Ishpeming *(G-8781)*
Safie Specialty Foods Co Inc..........E....... 586 598-8282
Chesterfield *(G-2945)*
Salad Specialist LLC..........G....... 734 325-4032
Canton *(G-2520)*
▲ **Savory Foods Inc**..........D....... 616 241-2583
Grand Rapids *(G-7181)*
Sensient Flavors LLC..........E....... 989 479-3211
Harbor Beach *(G-7636)*
Sensient Technologies Corp..........G....... 989 479-3211
Harbor Beach *(G-7637)*
Shady Nook Farms..........G....... 989 236-7240
Middleton *(G-11300)*
Six Lugs LLC..........F....... 231 275-0600
Interlochen *(G-8685)*
Sleeping Bear Apiaries Ltd..........F....... 231 882-4456
Beulah *(G-1657)*
Spartan Central Kitchen..........G....... 616 878-8940
Grand Rapids *(G-7209)*
Ssa Consumer Brands Inc..........F....... 734 430-0565
Ann Arbor *(G-663)*
St Laurent Brothers Inc..........E....... 989 893-7522
Bay City *(G-1405)*
Stephen Haas..........G....... 906 475-4826
Negaunee *(G-11975)*
Steves Backroom LLC..........F....... 313 527-7240
Dearborn *(G-3901)*
Subway Restaurant..........G....... 248 625-5739
Clarkston *(G-3070)*
Sunopta Ingredients Inc..........E....... 502 587-7999
Schoolcraft *(G-15129)*
Tortillas Tita LLC..........G....... 734 756-7646
Wayne *(G-18239)*
Tree Line Maple Syrup..........G....... 616 889-6016
Grand Rapids *(G-7273)*
Twin City Foods Inc..........D....... 616 374-4002
Lake Odessa *(G-9579)*
Twinlab Holdings Inc..........G....... 800 645-5626
Grand Rapids *(G-7284)*
Uncle Johns Cider Mill Inc..........E....... 989 224-3686
Saint Johns *(G-14919)*
Union Commissary LLC..........F....... 248 795-2483
Clarkston *(G-3075)*
Unique Food Management Inc..........E....... 248 738-9393
Pontiac *(G-13421)*
Variety Foods Inc..........D....... 586 268-4900
Warren *(G-18051)*
Villanuevo Soledad..........G....... 989 770-4309
Burt *(G-2216)*
West Brothers LLC..........G....... 734 457-0083
Monroe *(G-11591)*
Wysong Medical Corporation..........F....... 989 631-0009
Midland *(G-11424)*
Yates Cider Mill Inc..........G....... 248 651-8300
Rochester Hills *(G-14149)*

21 TOBACCO PRODUCTS

2111 Cigarettes

Cheeba Hut Smoke Shop LLC..........G....... 586 213-5156
Chesterfield *(G-2858)*
Cloud 9 Pipe Tobacco Inc..........F....... 313 522-1957
Sterling Heights *(G-15962)*
Unique Hooka and Tobacco..........G....... 586 883-7674
Sterling Heights *(G-16215)*

2131 Tobacco, Chewing & Snuff

Akston Hughes Intl LLC..........F....... 989 448-2322
Gaylord *(G-6116)*
Qfc..........E....... 248 786-0272
Troy *(G-17322)*
Smoke-Free Kids Inc..........G....... 989 772-4063
Mount Pleasant *(G-11740)*

2141 Tobacco Stemming & Redrying

Veteran Liquids LLC..........G....... 586 698-2100
Rochester Hills *(G-14140)*

22 TEXTILE MILL PRODUCTS

2211 Cotton, Woven Fabric

24 Canvas..........G....... 517 902-5870
Manitou Beach *(G-10925)*
3 Ten Denim Ko LLc..........G....... 248 556-1725
Ferndale *(G-5517)*
▲ **Ace-Tex Enterprises Inc**..........E....... 313 834-4000
Detroit *(G-3982)*
American Soft Trim Inc..........G....... 989 681-0037
Saint Louis *(G-14984)*
Bahwse/Bahwse Brand LLC..........G....... 313 704-7376
Detroit *(G-4042)*
Bearcub Outfitters LLC..........F....... 231 439-9500
Petoskey *(G-12990)*
Better Built Gates Canvas LLC..........G....... 616 818-9103
Cedar Springs *(G-2642)*
BLAack&co LLC..........E....... 313 971-1857
Southfield *(G-15509)*
Blanck Canvas Photography LLC..........G....... 248 342-4935
Clarkston *(G-3019)*
Border Line Rich Apparel LLC..........G....... 866 959-3003
Clinton Township *(G-3187)*
Border Line Rich Clothing LLC..........G....... 586 267-5251
Clinton Township *(G-3188)*
Canvas Innovations LLC..........G....... 616 393-4400
Holland *(G-7990)*
Canvas Townhomes Allendale..........G....... 616 499-2680
Allendale *(G-216)*
Carry-All Products Inc..........G....... 616 399-8080
Holland *(G-7991)*
Cut Once LLC..........G....... 616 245-3136
Grand Rapids *(G-6624)*
D&E Incorporated..........G....... 313 673-3284
Southfield *(G-15535)*
Denim & Roses Childrens CL LLC..........G....... 313 363-0387
Detroit *(G-4130)*
Denim City LLC..........G....... 313 270-2942
Detroit *(G-4131)*
Detroit Denim Company LLC..........G....... 313 626-9216
Highland Park *(G-7904)*
Detroit Denim LLC..........G....... 313 351-1040
Detroit *(G-4143)*
Detroit Sewn Inc..........E....... 248 722-8407
Pontiac *(G-13360)*
Drapery Workroom..........G....... 269 463-5633
Watervliet *(G-18180)*
Elite Canvas LLC..........G....... 231 343-7649
Fruitport *(G-6062)*
◆ **Floracraft Corporation**..........C....... 231 845-5127
Ludington *(G-10536)*
G T Jerseys LLC..........F....... 248 588-3231
Troy *(G-17124)*
Gogettaz Clothing Company LLC..........D....... 630 800-3279
Southfield *(G-15578)*
Grand Strategy LLC..........G....... 269 637-8330
South Haven *(G-15407)*
Great Lkes Tex Restoration LLC..........G....... 989 448-8600
Gaylord *(G-6131)*
Guilford Performance Textiles..........F....... 910 794-5810
Southfield *(G-15588)*
Huxl Denim..........G....... 248 595-8480
Southfield *(G-15595)*
Inovation Services LLC..........F....... 586 932-7653
Detroit *(G-4321)*
J David Inc..........G....... 888 274-0669
Troy *(G-17177)*
JIT..........G....... 248 799-9210
Southfield *(G-15613)*
Joan Arnoudse..........G....... 616 364-9075
Grand Rapids *(G-6871)*
Legacy Canvas & Upholstery LLC..........G....... 231 578-9972
Muskegon *(G-11859)*
Lusciously Silked LLC..........G....... 313 878-7058
Detroit *(G-4411)*
M M Custom Canvas Shrink..........G....... 734 658-0497
Dearborn *(G-3866)*
Mansa Denim Company..........G....... 313 384-3929
Detroit *(G-4419)*
Michael E Nipke LLC..........G....... 616 350-0200
Grand Rapids *(G-6985)*
▲ **Nanosystems Inc**..........F....... 734 274-0020
Ann Arbor *(G-589)*
Northern Canvas & Upholstery..........G....... 989 735-2150
Glennie *(G-6215)*
Northwest Canvas..........G....... 231 676-1757
Charlevoix *(G-2723)*
Paper Chase American Dream LLC..........G....... 248 819-0939
Detroit *(G-4505)*
Rooms of Grand Rapids LLC..........G....... 616 260-1452
Spring Lake *(G-15847)*
Rose Denim..........G....... 517 694-3020
Holt *(G-8327)*
Simco Automotive Trim..........D....... 800 372-3172
Macomb *(G-10635)*
Street Denim & Co..........G....... 313 837-1200
Detroit *(G-4611)*
T and RC Anvas Awning LLC..........G....... 810 230-1740
Flint *(G-5775)*
Truly Tees & Co LLc..........G....... 313 266-1819
Detroit *(G-4647)*
Window Designs Inc..........F....... 616 396-5295
Holland *(G-8250)*
Wine and Canvas of Ann Arbor..........G....... 734 277-9253
Canton *(G-2542)*
Wine ND Canvas Grand Rapids..........G....... 616 970-1082
Grand Rapids *(G-7341)*

Wnc of Grand Rapids 2 LLC ....G....... 269 986-5066
Grand Rapids *(G-7343)*

2221 Silk & Man-Made Fiber

Advanced Composite Tech Inc ....G....... 248 709-9097
Rochester *(G-13889)*
Airhug LLC ....G....... 734 262-0431
Canton *(G-2432)*
C & J Fabrication Inc ....G....... 586 791-6269
Clinton Township *(G-3192)*
Glassline Incorporated ....F....... 734 453-2728
Plymouth *(G-13176)*
▲ J America Licensed Pdts Inc ....G....... 517 655-8800
Fowlerville *(G-5844)*
JAC Custom Pouches Inc ....E....... 269 782-3190
Dowagiac *(G-4784)*
▲ John Johnson Company ....D....... 313 496-0600
Romulus *(G-14291)*
Loonar Stn Two The 2 or 2nd ....G....... 419 720-1222
Temperance *(G-16537)*
Nickels Boat Works Inc ....F....... 810 767-4050
Flint *(G-5738)*
P I W Corporation ....G....... 989 448-2501
Gaylord *(G-6152)*
Performance Sailing Inc ....G....... 586 790-7500
Clinton Township *(G-3318)*
Satin Petals LLC ....G....... 248 905-3866
Southfield *(G-15694)*
SRS Fiberglass Products LLC ....D....... 231 747-6839
Muskegon *(G-11925)*
Sunrise Fiberglass LLC ....D....... 651 462-5313
Troy *(G-17379)*
Takata Americas ....A....... 336 547-1600
Auburn Hills *(G-1044)*
Three Sheep LLC ....F....... 616 215-1848
Grand Rapids *(G-7262)*
West Michigan Canvas Company ....G....... 616 355-7855
Holland *(G-8245)*
Window Designs Inc ....F....... 616 396-5295
Holland *(G-8250)*

2231 Wool, Woven Fabric

Lake Effect Alpacas ....G....... 616 836-7906
Holland *(G-8120)*
Loneys Alpaca Junction ....G....... 231 229-4530
Lake City *(G-9549)*
Majestic Sonrise Alpacas ....G....... 616 848-7414
Holland *(G-8138)*
Stonehedge Farm ....G....... 231 536-2779
East Jordan *(G-4881)*
West Michigan Alpacas ....G....... 616 990-0556
Holland *(G-8244)*
Whitefeather Creek Alpacas ....G....... 517 368-5493
Montgomery *(G-11604)*

2241 Fabric Mills, Cotton, Wool, Silk & Man-Made

▲ B Erickson Manufacturing Ltd ....F....... 810 765-1144
Marine City *(G-10955)*
Car-Min-Vu Farm ....G....... 517 749-9112
Webberville *(G-18243)*
Chambers Enterprises II LLC ....F....... 810 688-3750
North Branch *(G-12177)*
Fresh Heir LLC ....G....... 313 312-4492
Farmington *(G-5138)*
Louis J Wickings ....G....... 989 823-8765
Vassar *(G-17580)*
Rhino Products Inc ....G....... 269 674-8309
Lawrence *(G-9984)*
Superior Spindle Services LLC ....F....... 734 946-4646
Taylor *(G-16482)*
Tapex American Corporation ....F....... 810 987-4722
Port Huron *(G-13531)*

2252 Hosiery, Except Women's

Al Beck ....G....... 906 249-1645
Marquette *(G-11003)*
Argyle Socks LLC ....G....... 269 615-0097
Kalamazoo *(G-9120)*
Bold Endeavors LLC ....G....... 616 389-3902
Grand Rapids *(G-6520)*
Detroit Sock & Stocking Co LLC ....G....... 313 409-8735
Grosse Pointe Park *(G-7552)*
P&K Socks LLC ....G....... 586 295-5427
Grosse Pointe Farms *(G-7539)*
Rudys Sock Drive ....G....... 313 409-1778
Taylor *(G-16469)*
Skechers USA Inc ....F....... 989 624-9336
Birch Run *(G-1715)*

Sock Hop LLC ....G....... 248 689-2683
Troy *(G-17358)*
Socks & Associates Development ....G....... 231 421-5150
Traverse City *(G-16836)*
Socks Direct USA LLC ....G....... 248 535-7590
West Bloomfield *(G-18315)*
Socks Kick LLC ....G....... 231 222-2402
East Jordan *(G-4880)*
▲ Soyad Brothers Textile Corp ....E....... 586 755-5700
Fraser *(G-5994)*
Turbosocks Performance ....G....... 586 864-3252
Shelby Township *(G-15358)*
Warmerscom ....G....... 800 518-0938
Byron Center *(G-2302)*

2253 Knit Outerwear Mills

◆ Ajaxx Design Inc ....G....... 206 522-4545
Grosse Pointe Park *(G-7543)*
Belleville Lounge LLC ....G....... 734 270-4977
Van Buren Twp *(G-17512)*
Bustedtees LLC ....G....... 989 448-3179
Gaylord *(G-6121)*
Fuzzybutz ....G....... 269 983-9663
Saint Joseph *(G-14931)*
Noir Sportswear Corp ....F....... 248 607-3615
Oak Park *(G-12634)*
Spalding ....G....... 734 414-1567
Canton *(G-2525)*
Wickedglow Industries Inc ....G....... 586 776-4132
Mount Clemens *(G-11663)*

2258 Lace & Warp Knit Fabric Mills

J David Inc ....G....... 888 274-0669
Troy *(G-17177)*

2259 Knitting Mills, NEC

▲ Star Textile Inc ....E....... 888 527-5700
Madison Heights *(G-10836)*

2261 Cotton Fabric Finishers

Adco Specialties Inc ....G....... 616 452-6882
Grand Rapids *(G-6430)*
Advanced Printwear Inc ....G....... 248 585-4412
Madison Heights *(G-10662)*
Advertising Accents Inc ....G....... 313 937-3890
Redford *(G-13711)*
Allgraphics Corp ....G....... 248 994-7373
Farmington Hills *(G-5167)*
Baumans Running Center Inc ....G....... 810 238-5981
Flint *(G-5652)*
Charlevoix Screen Masters Inc ....G....... 231 547-5111
Charlevoix *(G-2713)*
Great Put On Inc ....G....... 810 733-8021
Flint *(G-5709)*
Hilton Screeners Inc ....G....... 810 653-0711
Davison *(G-3787)*
Inkpressions LLC ....E....... 248 461-2555
Commerce Township *(G-3543)*
Janet Kelly ....F....... 231 775-2313
Cadillac *(G-2338)*
Meridian Screen Prtg & Design ....G....... 517 351-2525
Okemos *(G-12674)*
Perrin Screen Printing Inc ....F....... 616 785-9900
Comstock Park *(G-3635)*
Pro Shop The/P S Graphics ....G....... 517 448-8490
Hudson *(G-8559)*
Prong Horn ....G....... 616 456-1903
Grand Rapids *(G-7120)*
Sign of The Loon Gifts Inc ....G....... 231 436-5155
Mackinaw City *(G-10569)*
Slick Shirts Screen Printing ....F....... 517 371-3600
Lansing *(G-9895)*
Trophy Center West Michigan ....G....... 231 893-1686
Whitehall *(G-18510)*

2262 Silk & Man-Made Fabric Finishers

Armada Printwear Inc ....G....... 586 784-5553
Armada *(G-730)*
◆ Stahls Inc ....E....... 800 478-2457
Saint Clair Shores *(G-14887)*

2273 Carpets & Rugs

Ability Weavers LLC ....G....... 616 929-0211
Lowell *(G-10493)*
Apparelmaster-Muskegon Inc ....E....... 231 728-5406
Muskegon *(G-11772)*
Classic Boat Decks LLC ....G....... 586 465-3606
Harrison Township *(G-7693)*

▼ Custom Marine Carpet ....G....... 269 684-1922
Niles *(G-12122)*
Great Lakes Right of Way LLC ....G....... 616 263-9898
Cedar Springs *(G-2652)*
▲ HP Pelzer Auto Systems Inc ....E....... 248 280-1010
Troy *(G-17155)*
▲ HR Technologies Inc ....G....... 248 284-1170
Madison Heights *(G-10743)*
Isingularis Inc ....G....... 248 347-0742
Novi *(G-12442)*
James E Sullivan & Associates ....G....... 616 453-0345
Grand Rapids *(G-6860)*
Marceau Enterprises Inc ....G....... 586 697-8100
Washington *(G-18085)*
Michigan -Bsed Frdman Dscndnts ....G....... 810 820-3017
Flint *(G-5731)*
▲ N A Visscher-Caravelle Inc ....G....... 248 851-9800
Bloomfield Hills *(G-1842)*
▲ Plant Df ....E....... 734 397-0397
Van Buren Twp *(G-17548)*
Preferred Flooring MI LLC ....F....... 616 279-2162
Walker *(G-17650)*
Pwv Studios Ltd ....G....... 616 361-5659
Grand Rapids *(G-7126)*
▲ Scott Group Custom Carpets LLC ....C....... 616 954-3200
Grand Rapids *(G-7187)*
Seelye Group Ltd ....G....... 517 267-2001
Lansing *(G-9894)*
Shelter Carpet Specialties ....G....... 616 475-4944
Grand Rapids *(G-7192)*
Treves N Kotobukiya Amer Inc ....F....... 248 513-4255
Novi *(G-12558)*
Usmats Inc ....G....... 810 765-4545
Marine City *(G-10968)*
W A Thomas Company ....G....... 734 955-6500
Taylor *(G-16487)*
Willie N Eicher ....G....... 269 432-3707
Colon *(G-3493)*

2281 Yarn Spinning Mills

True Teknit Inc ....F....... 616 656-5111
Grand Rapids *(G-7278)*
▲ Woolly & Co LLC ....G....... 248 480-4354
Birmingham *(G-1757)*

2282 Yarn Texturizing, Throwing, Twisting & Winding Mills

Janesville LLC ....G....... 269 964-5400
Battle Creek *(G-1244)*

2284 Thread Mills

American & Efird LLC ....G....... 248 399-1166
Berkley *(G-1619)*
Notions Marketing Intl Corp ....B....... 616 243-8424
Grand Rapids *(G-7050)*
RPC Company ....F....... 989 752-3618
Saginaw *(G-14741)*

2295 Fabrics Coated Not Rubberized

APS Machine LLC ....F....... 906 212-5600
Escanaba *(G-5058)*
Bentzer Enterprises ....G....... 269 663-2289
Edwardsburg *(G-4999)*
▼ Duro-Last Inc ....B....... 800 248-0280
Saginaw *(G-14641)*
Duro-Last Inc ....E....... 800 248-0280
Saginaw *(G-14642)*
Elden Industries Corp ....F....... 734 946-6900
Taylor *(G-16412)*
Haartz Corporation ....G....... 248 646-8200
Bloomfield Hills *(G-1825)*
Hig Recovery Fund Inc ....G....... 269 435-8414
Constantine *(G-3668)*
Maher Group LLC ....G....... 616 863-6046
Rockford *(G-14176)*
Mp-Tec Inc ....F....... 734 367-1284
Livonia *(G-10325)*
Pioneer Plastics Inc ....F....... 586 262-0159
Sterling Heights *(G-16128)*
Plastatech Engineering Ltd ....D....... 989 754-6500
Saginaw *(G-14729)*
Shawmut Inc ....G....... 810 987-2222
Port Huron *(G-13526)*
Tpi Industries LLC ....D....... 810 987-2222
Port Huron *(G-13535)*
Tri-City Vinyl Inc ....G....... 989 401-7992
Saginaw *(G-14779)*
Witchcraft Tape Products Inc ....D....... 269 468-3399
Coloma *(G-3485)*

2296 Tire Cord & Fabric

Ferro Fab LLC .... F 586 791-3561
  Clinton Township *(G-3237)*
Flatrock Tire .... G 734 783-0100
  Flat Rock *(G-5619)*
Takata Americas .... A 336 547-1600
  Auburn Hills *(G-1044)*
Ton-Tex Corporation .... F 616 957-3200
  Greenville *(G-7508)*

2297 Fabrics, Nonwoven

Nanotex LLC .... G 248 855-6000
  Bloomfield Hills *(G-1843)*

2298 Cordage & Twine

▲ American Twisting Company .... E 269 637-8581
  South Haven *(G-15398)*
Bundeze LLC .... G 248 343-9179
  West Olive *(G-18348)*
Cascade Paper Converters LLC .... F 616 974-9165
  Grand Rapids *(G-6555)*
▲ Great Lakes Cordage Inc .... F 616 842-4455
  Spring Lake *(G-15819)*
Hestia Inc .... G 616 296-0533
  Norton Shores *(G-12297)*
▲ Mason Tackle Company .... E 810 631-4571
  Otisville *(G-12783)*
Nelson Rapids Co Inc .... G 616 691-8041
  Belding *(G-1460)*
Networks Enterprises Inc .... G 248 446-8590
  New Hudson *(G-12063)*
Quickmitt Inc .... G 517 849-2141
  Jonesville *(G-9099)*

2299 Textile Goods, NEC

Acoufelt LLC .... G 800 966-8557
  Clawson *(G-3083)*
Airlite Synthetics Mfg Inc .... F 248 335-8131
  Pontiac *(G-13345)*
Chaotic Cotton Company LLC .... G 810 624-6153
  Linden *(G-10060)*
Clamp Industries Incorporated .... G 248 335-8131
  Pontiac *(G-13353)*
Golden Fashion .... G 616 288-9465
  Grand Rapids *(G-6747)*
Guilford of Maine Marketing Co .... D 616 554-2250
  Grand Rapids *(G-6794)*
Homestead Elements LLC .... G 248 560-7122
  Saginaw *(G-14668)*
J David Inc .... G 888 274-0669
  Troy *(G-17177)*
L & R Limited LLC .... G 910 308-7278
  Auburn Hills *(G-955)*
Nanotex LLC .... G 248 855-6000
  Bloomfield Hills *(G-1843)*
Six Collection LLC .... G 313 516-9999
  Harper Woods *(G-7672)*
Zeilinger Wool Co LLC .... E 989 652-2920
  Frankenmuth *(G-5874)*

23 APPAREL AND OTHER FINISHED PRODUCTS MADE FROM FABRICS AND SIMILAR MATERIAL

2311 Men's & Boys' Suits, Coats & Overcoats

Allie Brothers Inc .... F 248 477-4434
  Livonia *(G-10109)*
Baryames Tux Shop Inc .... G 517 349-6555
  Okemos *(G-12659)*
Labeled Lucky Brand Inc .... G 517 962-1729
  Romulus *(G-14297)*
Peckham Vocational Inds Inc .... A 517 316-4000
  Lansing *(G-9724)*
Peckham Vocational Inds Inc .... D 517 316-4478
  Lansing *(G-9725)*
Priority One Emergency Inc .... G 734 398-5900
  Canton *(G-2512)*
Zink .... G 586 781-5314
  Shelby Township *(G-15373)*

2321 Men's & Boys' Shirts

Pvh Corp .... G 989 345-7939
  West Branch *(G-18337)*
Pvh Corp .... G 989 624-5651
  Birch Run *(G-1713)*
Zemis 5 LLC .... G 317 946-7015
  Detroit *(G-4703)*

2322 Men's & Boys' Underwear & Nightwear

Harrys Meme LLC .... G 248 977-0168
  Novi *(G-12429)*

2323 Men's & Boys' Neckwear

Get Customized .... G 586 909-3881
  Rochester Hills *(G-14025)*

2325 Men's & Boys' Separate Trousers & Casual Slacks

◆ Carhartt Inc .... B 313 271-8460
  Dearborn *(G-3818)*
Guess Inc .... G 517 546-2933
  Howell *(G-8457)*

2326 Men's & Boys' Work Clothing

Acme Mills Company .... E 517 437-8940
  Hillsdale *(G-7919)*
Apex Apparel LLC .... F 248 915-1073
  Detroit *(G-4023)*
◆ Carhartt Inc .... B 313 271-8460
  Dearborn *(G-3818)*
Carhartt Inc .... G 517 282-4193
  Dewitt *(G-4709)*
Genstone LLC .... G 517 902-4730
  Adrian *(G-70)*
Just Right Duplications LLC .... F 313 655-3555
  Oak Park *(G-12619)*
Repairers of The Brach Mskegon ..... F 231 375-0990
  Muskegon *(G-11908)*
Scrubs Myway LLC .... G 616 201-8366
  Grand Haven *(G-6357)*
Traverse Bay Manufacturing Inc ...... D 231 264-8111
  Elk Rapids *(G-5029)*
Wealth Club Nation LLC .... G 323 695-1636
  Royal Oak *(G-14591)*

2329 Men's & Boys' Clothing, NEC

Avidasports LLC .... F 313 447-5670
  Harper Woods *(G-7662)*
◆ Carhartt Inc .... B 313 271-8460
  Dearborn *(G-3818)*
▲ Cliff Keen Wrestling Pdts Inc .... E 734 975-8800
  Ann Arbor *(G-428)*
Custom Giant LLC .... G 313 799-2085
  Southfield *(G-15534)*
Daulinas LLC .... G 313 258-0958
  Detroit *(G-4122)*
Fisll Media LLC .... G 646 492-8533
  Troy *(G-17111)*
Graphic Gear Inc .... G 734 283-3864
  Lincoln Park *(G-10048)*
Harvard Clothing Company .... F 517 542-2986
  Litchfield *(G-10078)*
Hemp Global Products Inc .... G 616 617-6476
  Holland *(G-8069)*
Kinder Company Inc .... G 810 240-3065
  Mount Morris *(G-11673)*
Little Legends Creations LLC .... G 313 828-7292
  Eastpointe *(G-4940)*
Puck Hogs Pro Shop Inc .... G 419 540-1388
  Grosse Pointe Woods *(G-7574)*
Sams Suit Fctry & Alteration .... G 248 424-8666
  Southfield *(G-15693)*
Thomas Porchea Collection LLC ..... G 313 693-6308
  Detroit *(G-4631)*
Traverse Bay Manufacturing Inc ...... D 231 264-8111
  Elk Rapids *(G-5029)*
Trims Unlimited LLC .... E 810 724-3500
  Almont *(G-269)*
Van Boven Incorporated .... G 734 665-7228
  Ann Arbor *(G-708)*

2331 Women's & Misses' Blouses

Law Offices Towana Tate PC .... G 248 560-7250
  Farmington Hills *(G-5290)*
Peckham Vocational Inds Inc .... A 517 316-4000
  Lansing *(G-9724)*
Peckham Vocational Inds Inc .... D 517 316-4478
  Lansing *(G-9725)*

2335 Women's & Misses' Dresses

Ashley Rose .... G 616 634-4919
  Rockford *(G-14155)*
Demmem Enterprises LLC .... F 810 564-9500
  Clio *(G-3396)*
Detroit Sewn Inc .... E 248 722-8407
  Pontiac *(G-13360)*

My Dream Dress Brdal Salon LLC ... G 248 327-6049
  Southfield *(G-15663)*
Recollections Co .... F 989 734-0566
  Hawks *(G-7816)*
Xtra-Ordinary-You LLC .... G 313 285-4472
  Ecorse *(G-4989)*

2339 Women's & Misses' Outerwear, NEC

Bedrock Manufacturing Co LLC ...... E 972 422-4372
  Detroit *(G-4048)*
Brintley Enterprises .... G 248 991-4086
  Detroit *(G-4074)*
▲ Cliff Keen Wrestling Pdts Inc .... E 734 975-8800
  Ann Arbor *(G-428)*
Cute N Classy Collection LLC .... G 313 279-8217
  Detroit *(G-4114)*
Diamond Boutique .... G 313 451-4217
  Dearborn *(G-3828)*
Excellent Designs Swimwear .... G 586 977-9140
  Warren *(G-17799)*
Fisll Media LLC .... G 646 492-8533
  Troy *(G-17111)*
Graphic Gear Inc .... G 734 283-3864
  Lincoln Park *(G-10048)*
Guess Inc .... G 517 546-2933
  Howell *(G-8457)*
Harvard Clothing Company .... F 517 542-2986
  Litchfield *(G-10078)*
Hemp Global Products Inc .... G 616 617-6476
  Holland *(G-8069)*
Keetz Kloset Kollection LLC .... G 313 878-1032
  Detroit *(G-4356)*
Lululemon USA Inc .... F 586 690-6001
  Clinton Township *(G-3281)*
Noir Sportswear Corp .... F 248 607-3615
  Oak Park *(G-12634)*
Pure Luxe LLC .... G 248 987-8734
  Farmington Hills *(G-5357)*
Pvh Corp .... E 989 624-5575
  Birch Run *(G-1712)*
Reed Sportswear Mfg Co .... G 313 963-7980
  Detroit *(G-4561)*
St John .... G 313 576-8212
  Detroit *(G-4603)*
Sundai Imports Inc .... G 877 517-7788
  Westland *(G-18419)*
Tall City LLC .... G 248 854-0713
  Auburn Hills *(G-1045)*
Traverse Bay Manufacturing Inc ...... D 231 264-8111
  Elk Rapids *(G-5029)*
Yore Creations LLC .... G 313 463-8652
  Detroit *(G-4698)*

2341 Women's, Misses' & Children's Underwear & Nightwear

▲ Minor Creations Incorporated ...... E 517 347-2900
  Okemos *(G-12676)*

2342 Brassieres, Girdles & Garments

Busted Bra Shop LLC .... G 313 288-0449
  Detroit *(G-4078)*
Shefit Operating Company LLC .... G 616 209-7003
  Hudsonville *(G-8611)*
Xrs Holdings Inc .... F 616 209-7003
  Hudsonville *(G-8619)*

2353 Hats, Caps & Millinery

B Pretty Hats LLC .... G 616 726-0002
  Hudsonville *(G-8568)*
Bahama Souvenirs Inc .... G 269 964-8275
  Battle Creek *(G-1189)*
Derby Hats By Rachelle .... G 248 489-0971
  Farmington Hills *(G-5212)*
J and W Dolphin LLC .... G 267 686-3713
  Marquette *(G-11022)*

2361 Children's & Infants' Dresses & Blouses

Justice .... G 517 780-4035
  Jackson *(G-8926)*
Justice .... G 616 531-4534
  Grandville *(G-7394)*
Renes Inc .... G 810 294-5008
  Croswell *(G-3735)*

2369 Girls' & Infants' Outerwear, NEC

Carters Inc .... G 616 647-9452
  Grand Rapids *(G-6549)*

SIC SECTION 23 APPAREL AND OTHER FINISHED PRODUCTS MADE FROM FABRICS AND SIMILAR MATERIAL

Just Girls LLC .... G 248 952-1967
  Troy *(G-17190)*
Renes Inc .... G 810 294-5008
  Croswell *(G-3735)*
Shefit Operating Company LLC .... G 616 209-7003
  Hudsonville *(G-8611)*

2371 Fur Goods

Inn Settle & Suites .... G 214 606-3531
  Marquette *(G-11021)*
Wolvering Fur .... G 313 961-0620
  Detroit *(G-4689)*

2381 Dress & Work Gloves

Kaul Glove and Mfg Co .... E 313 894-9494
  Detroit *(G-4353)*

2385 Waterproof Outerwear

Geckobrands LLC .... G 561 704-8400
  Grandville *(G-7378)*

2386 Leather & Sheep Lined Clothing

▲ Lee-Cobb Company .... G 269 553-0873
  Kalamazoo *(G-9260)*
▲ Reed Sportswear Mfg Co .... E 313 963-7980
  Detroit *(G-4560)*

2389 Apparel & Accessories, NEC

Bedrock Manufacturing Co LLC .... E 972 422-4372
  Detroit *(G-4048)*
Bioflex Inc .... G 734 327-2946
  Ann Arbor *(G-401)*
Blue Lagoon .... G 248 515-1363
  West Bloomfield *(G-18266)*
Bond Manufacturing LLC .... G 313 671-0799
  Detroit *(G-4062)*
Brandon Bernard Collection LLC .... G 888 611-7011
  Detroit *(G-4068)*
Curb Apparel LLC .... G 248 548-2324
  Huntington Woods *(G-8621)*
Detroit Denim LLC .... G 313 351-1040
  Detroit *(G-4143)*
Excellent Designs Swimwear .... G 586 977-9140
  Warren *(G-17799)*
Foxys Leotards .... G 616 949-1847
  Grand Rapids *(G-6718)*
▲ Gags and Games Inc .... E 734 591-1717
  Livonia *(G-10218)*
GLS Enterprises Inc .... G 616 243-2574
  Comstock Park *(G-3608)*
Impressions Promotional Group .... G 313 299-3140
  Taylor *(G-16427)*
Industrial Sew Innvtion Ctr Is .... G 313 870-1898
  Detroit *(G-4316)*
Just Right Duplications LLC .... G 313 655-3555
  Oak Park *(G-12619)*
Kalamazoo Regalia Inc .... F 269 344-4299
  Kalamazoo *(G-9247)*
Lewmar Custom Designs Inc .... G 586 677-5135
  Shelby Township *(G-15262)*
▲ Logofit LLC .... E 810 715-1980
  Flint *(G-5727)*
Michael Kors .... G 616 730-7071
  Byron Center *(G-2284)*
Mopega LLC .... G 231 631-2580
  Traverse City *(G-16764)*
Power Capes .... G 313 454-1492
  Livonia *(G-10368)*
▲ Retro-A-Go-go LLC .... G 734 476-0300
  Howell *(G-8507)*
Spiffys Slay Station LLC .... G 313 401-8906
  Detroit *(G-4601)*
▲ Superfly Manufacturing Co .... F 313 454-1492
  Farmington *(G-5152)*
Trims Unlimited LLC .... E 810 724-3500
  Almont *(G-269)*

2391 Curtains & Draperies

Barons Inc .... E 517 484-1366
  Lansing *(G-9813)*
Benton Harbor Awning & Tent .... E 800 272-2187
  Benton Harbor *(G-1535)*
Cardinal Custom Designs Inc .... G 586 296-2060
  Fraser *(G-5911)*
Designer Window Fashions .... G 734 421-1600
  Northville *(G-12212)*
Detroit Custom Services Inc .... E 586 465-3631
  Mount Clemens *(G-11636)*

Lorne Hanley .... G 248 547-9865
  Huntington Woods *(G-8622)*
Parkway Drapery & Uphl Co Inc .... G 734 779-1300
  Livonia *(G-10360)*
▲ Signature Designs Inc .... G 248 426-9735
  Farmington Hills *(G-5378)*
Triangle Window Fashions Inc .... E 616 538-9676
  Wyoming *(G-18914)*

2392 House furnishings: Textile

▲ Anchor Wiping Cloth Inc .... D 313 892-4000
  Detroit *(G-4019)*
▲ Arden Companies LLC .... E 248 415-8500
  Bingham Farms *(G-1691)*
Cellulose Mtl Solutions LLC .... G 616 669-2990
  Jenison *(G-9049)*
Colcha Linens Inc .... F 313 355-8300
  Plymouth *(G-13148)*
◆ Down Inc .... G 616 241-3922
  Grand Rapids *(G-6658)*
▲ Gamco Inc .... F 269 683-4280
  Niles *(G-12132)*
Grabber Inc .... G 616 940-1914
  Byron Center *(G-2274)*
Intramode LLC .... G 313 964-6990
  Detroit *(G-4324)*
▲ Jacquart Fabric Products Inc .... C 906 932-1339
  Ironwood *(G-8765)*
K and J Absorbent Products LLC .... G 517 486-3110
  Blissfield *(G-1766)*
▲ Krams Enterprises Inc .... A 248 415-8500
  Bingham Farms *(G-1702)*
Lmp Worldwide Inc .... G 248 669-6103
  Wixom *(G-18700)*
Preferred Products Inc .... F 248 255-0200
  Commerce Township *(G-3565)*
Spec International Inc .... D 616 248-9116
  Grand Rapids *(G-7210)*
▲ Star Textile Inc .... E 888 527-5700
  Madison Heights *(G-10836)*
▲ Tuway American Group Inc .... C 248 205-9999
  Troy *(G-17407)*

2393 Textile Bags

Acme Mills Company .... E 517 437-8940
  Hillsdale *(G-7919)*
Birlon Group LLC .... G 313 551-5341
  Inkster *(G-8659)*
Foreward Logistics LLC .... G 877 488-9724
  Oak Park *(G-12612)*
Industrial Bag & Spc Inc .... F 248 559-5550
  Southfield *(G-15603)*
JAC Custom Pouches Inc .... E 269 782-3190
  Dowagiac *(G-4784)*
Lake State Cleaning Inc .... G 314 961-7939
  Oxford *(G-12895)*
Total Packaging Solutions LLC .... F 248 519-2376
  Detroit *(G-4639)*

2394 Canvas Prdts

Ace Canvas & Tent Co .... F 313 842-3011
  Troy *(G-16903)*
Acme Mills Company .... E 517 437-8940
  Hillsdale *(G-7919)*
Advanced Inc .... G 231 938-2233
  Acme *(G-2)*
▲ American Roll Shutter Awng Co ...... G 734 422-7110
  Livonia *(G-10116)*
Annes Canvas .... G 248 623-3443
  Waterford *(G-18100)*
Armstrong Display Concepts Inc .... F 231 652-1675
  Newaygo *(G-12077)*
Belle Isle Awning Co Inc .... G 586 294-6050
  Warren *(G-17730)*
Benton Harbor Awning & Tent .... E 800 272-2187
  Benton Harbor *(G-1535)*
Bestop Inc .... F 586 268-0602
  Sterling Heights *(G-15945)*
▲ Boat Guard Inc .... G 989 424-1490
  Gladwin *(G-6189)*
Canvas Shoppe Inc .... G 810 733-1841
  Flint *(G-5662)*
Case-Free Inc .... G 616 245-3136
  Grand Rapids *(G-6558)*
▲ Detroit Tarpaulin Repr Sp Inc .... E 734 955-8200
  Romulus *(G-14267)*
Dial Tent & Awning Co .... G 989 793-0741
  Saginaw *(G-14639)*
Dockside Canvas Co Inc .... F 586 463-1231
  Harrison Township *(G-7696)*

Facet Business Communications .... F 248 912-0800
  Novi *(G-12415)*
Feb Inc .... F 231 759-0911
  Muskegon *(G-11816)*
Grand Traverse Canvas Works .... F 231 947-3140
  Traverse City *(G-16697)*
Holiday Distributing Co .... E 517 782-7146
  Jackson *(G-8904)*
▲ Ifr Inc .... C 616 772-2052
  Zeeland *(G-19043)*
Industrial Bag & Spc Inc .... F 248 559-5550
  Southfield *(G-15603)*
◆ Industrial Fabric Products Inc .... F 269 932-4440
  Saint Joseph *(G-14937)*
JAC Custom Pouches Inc .... E 269 782-3190
  Dowagiac *(G-4784)*
Jackson Canvas Company .... E 517 768-8459
  Jackson *(G-8913)*
▲ Jacquart Fabric Products Inc .... C 906 932-1339
  Ironwood *(G-8765)*
Lakeside Canvas & Upholstery .... G 231 755-2514
  Muskegon *(G-11857)*
Larrys Tarpaulin Shop LLC .... G 313 563-2292
  Inkster *(G-8668)*
▲ Magna Car Top Systems Amer Inc ... C 248 836-4500
  Rochester Hills *(G-14057)*
Millers Custom Boat Top Inc .... G 586 468-5533
  Harrison Township *(G-7710)*
Muskegon Awning & Mfg Co .... E 231 759-0911
  Muskegon *(G-11879)*
National Case Corporation .... G 586 726-1710
  Sterling Heights *(G-16112)*
North Sails Group LLC .... G 586 776-1330
  Saint Clair Shores *(G-14874)*
Odin International Inc .... G 262 569-7171
  Curtis *(G-3751)*
Paddle King Inc .... F 989 235-6776
  Carson City *(G-2594)*
Peerless Canvas Products Inc .... G 269 429-0600
  Saint Joseph *(G-14954)*
Performance Sailing Inc .... G 586 790-7500
  Clinton Township *(G-3318)*
Quality Awning Shops Inc .... G 517 882-2491
  Lansing *(G-9885)*
Quick Draw Tarpaulin Systems .... F 313 561-0554
  Inkster *(G-8674)*
▲ Quick Draw Tarpaulin Systems .... F 313 945-0766
  Dearborn *(G-3889)*
R L Canvas .... G 989 837-6352
  Midland *(G-11407)*
Royal Oak & Birmingham Tent .... F 248 542-5552
  Royal Oak *(G-14578)*
Shelby Auto Trim Inc .... E 586 939-9090
  Sterling Heights *(G-16175)*
▲ Specilty Vhcl Acquisition Corp .... D 586 446-4701
  Warren *(G-18018)*
▲ TD Industrial Coverings Inc .... D 586 731-2080
  Sterling Heights *(G-16202)*
Textile Fabrication & Dist Inc .... G 586 566-9100
  Mount Clemens *(G-11660)*
Traverse Bay Canvas Inc .... G 231 347-3001
  Harbor Springs *(G-7659)*
Tumacs Corporation .... G 517 816-8141
  Lansing *(G-9794)*
US Tarp Inc .... D 269 639-3010
  South Haven *(G-15420)*

2395 Pleating & Stitching For The Trade

A & Js Embroidery .... G 734 417-3694
  Milan *(G-11429)*
Adlib Grafix & Apparel .... G 269 964-2810
  Battle Creek *(G-1178)*
Advanced Printwear Inc .... G 248 585-4412
  Madison Heights *(G-10662)*
Aisin Holdings America Inc .... G 734 453-5551
  Northville *(G-12195)*
Alfie Embroidery Inc .... F 231 935-1488
  Traverse City *(G-16599)*
Alis Custom Embroidery .... G 586 744-9442
  Sterling Heights *(G-15927)*
Angel Embroidery .... G 517 515-4836
  Eaton Rapids *(G-4951)*
AP Impressions Inc .... G 734 464-8009
  Livonia *(G-10121)*
▲ Apparel Sales Inc .... G 616 842-5650
  Jenison *(G-9045)*
Authority Customwear Ltd .... E 248 588-8075
  Madison Heights *(G-10676)*
Bag Stitchery .... G 231 276-3163
  Traverse City *(G-16610)*

Employee Codes: A=Over 500 employees, B=251-500, C=101-250, D=51-100, E=20-50, F=10-19, G=3-9

23 APPAREL AND OTHER FINISHED PRODUCTS MADE FROM FABRICS AND SIMILAR MATERIAL23 APPAREL AND OTHER FINISHED PROD-

Bay Supply & Marketing Inc.......G....... 231 943-3249
Traverse City ***(G-16616)***

Bd Classic Sewing.......G....... 231 825-2628
Mc Bain ***(G-11176)***

Beck & Boys Custom Apparel.......G....... 734 458-4015
Livonia ***(G-10134)***

Bella Bleu Embroidery LLC.......G....... 810 797-2286
Metamora ***(G-11277)***

Bewitching Stitchng Embroidery.......G....... 810 289-3978
China ***(G-2969)***

Broadway Embroidery.......G....... 248 838-8074
Lake Orion ***(G-9590)***

C R Stitching.......G....... 734 449-2633
Whitmore Lake ***(G-18525)***

C R Stitching.......G....... 313 538-1660
Redford ***(G-13722)***

Carom L Embroidery.......G....... 231 690-0571
Ludington ***(G-10530)***

CC Embroidery Vinyl Designs.......G....... 517 996-6030
Dansville ***(G-3755)***

Charlevoix Screen Masters Inc.......G....... 231 547-5111
Charlevoix ***(G-2713)***

Classic Images Embroidery.......G....... 616 844-1702
Grand Haven ***(G-6286)***

Classic Stitch.......G....... 586 737-7767
Sterling Heights ***(G-15960)***

Classy Threadz.......G....... 989 479-9595
Harbor Beach ***(G-7629)***

Court-Side Inc.......G....... 269 948-2811
Hastings ***(G-7785)***

Creative Loop.......G....... 231 629-8228
Paris ***(G-12932)***

Creative Stitching.......G....... 248 210-9584
Howell ***(G-8443)***

Custom Embroidery Plus LLC.......G....... 989 227-9432
Saint Johns ***(G-14899)***

Custom Trends Printing LLc.......G....... 586 563-3946
Warren ***(G-17768)***

D & M Silkscreening.......G....... 517 694-4199
Holt ***(G-8305)***

Delta Sports Service & EMB.......G....... 517 482-6565
Lansing ***(G-9686)***

Digigraphx Co.......G....... 586 755-1130
Warren ***(G-17779)***

Dun Mor Embroidery & Designs.......F....... 248 577-1155
Troy ***(G-17071)***

E Q R 2 Inc.......G....... 586 731-3383
Sterling Heights ***(G-15995)***

Earthbound Inc.......G....... 616 774-0096
Grand Rapids ***(G-6662)***

Embroider It LLC.......G....... 248 538-9965
West Bloomfield ***(G-18281)***

Embroidery & Much More LLC.......F....... 586 771-3832
Saint Clair Shores ***(G-14857)***

Embroidery House Inc.......G....... 616 669-6400
Jenison ***(G-9054)***

Embroidery Hutch.......G....... 810 459-8728
Grand Blanc ***(G-6241)***

Embroidery Shoppe LLC.......G....... 734 595-7612
Westland ***(G-18367)***

Embroidery Wearhouse.......G....... 906 228-5818
Marquette ***(G-11017)***

Embroidme Grand Rapids.......G....... 616 974-1033
Grand Rapids ***(G-6675)***

Ensign Emblem Ltd.......D....... 231 946-7703
Traverse City ***(G-16678)***

Fido & Stitch.......G....... 616 288-7992
Grand Rapids ***(G-6705)***

Fully Promoted.......G....... 616 285-8009
Grand Rapids ***(G-6727)***

Gramma N Stitches.......G....... 810 664-8606
Lapeer ***(G-9932)***

Grand Rapids Embroidery.......G....... 616 451-2827
Grand Rapids ***(G-6757)***

Grasel Graphics Inc.......G....... 989 652-5151
Frankenmuth ***(G-5865)***

Gratefulthreadembroider.......G....... 231 855-1340
Pentwater ***(G-12972)***

Great Lakes Custom Embroidery.......G....... 734 844-7347
Canton ***(G-2467)***

Hoyt & Company LLC.......G....... 810 624-4445
Clio ***(G-3401)***

I D Pro Embroidery LLC.......G....... 734 847-6650
Temperance ***(G-16535)***

Ideal Wholesale Inc.......G....... 989 873-5850
Prescott ***(G-13651)***

Impact Label Corporation.......D....... 269 381-4280
Galesburg ***(G-6079)***

Imprint House LLC.......G....... 810 985-8203
Port Huron ***(G-13487)***

Initial Attraction.......G....... 269 341-4444
Kalamazoo ***(G-9223)***

Inkpressions LLC.......E....... 248 461-2555
Commerce Township ***(G-3543)***

▲ J2 Licensing Inc.......G....... 586 307-3400
Troy ***(G-17180)***

Janet Kelly.......F....... 231 775-2313
Cadillac ***(G-2338)***

Jean Smith Designs.......G....... 616 942-9212
Grand Rapids ***(G-6866)***

Jene Holly Designs Inc.......G....... 586 954-0255
Harrison Township ***(G-7703)***

JJ Jinkleheimer & Co Inc.......F....... 517 546-4345
Howell ***(G-8468)***

Just Wear It.......G....... 734 458-4015
Livonia ***(G-10263)***

K&S Custom Embroidery LLC.......G....... 734 709-2689
Canton ***(G-2483)***

Lake Effect Embroidery LLC.......G....... 616 502-7844
West Olive ***(G-18349)***

Lansing Athletics.......G....... 517 327-8828
Lansing ***(G-9772)***

Laughing Needles EMB LLC.......G....... 231 720-5789
Holton ***(G-8340)***

Lazer Graphics.......F....... 269 926-1066
Benton Harbor ***(G-1565)***

Liberty Embroidery.......G....... 269 419-0327
Battle Creek ***(G-1268)***

Logospot.......G....... 616 785-7170
Belmont ***(G-1512)***

Mach II Enterprises Inc.......G....... 248 347-8822
Northville ***(G-12238)***

Markit Products.......G....... 616 458-7881
Grand Rapids ***(G-6960)***

Meridian Screen Prtg & Design.......G....... 517 351-2525
Okemos ***(G-12674)***

Michigan Graphic Arts.......G....... 517 278-4120
Coldwater ***(G-3444)***

Midwest Custom Embroidery Co.......G....... 269 381-7660
Kalamazoo ***(G-9271)***

Mom & ME Embroidery.......G....... 231 590-0256
Bear Lake ***(G-1419)***

Monogram Etc.......G....... 989 743-5999
Corunna ***(G-3712)***

Monogram Goods Naples LLC.......G....... 231 526-7700
Harbor Springs ***(G-7652)***

Monogram Lady.......G....... 313 649-2160
Grosse Pointe Woods ***(G-7572)***

Monograms & More Inc.......E....... 313 299-3140
Taylor ***(G-16449)***

Nobby Inc.......F....... 810 984-3300
Fort Gratiot ***(G-5822)***

Northville Stitching Post.......G....... 248 347-7622
Northville ***(G-12247)***

One Stop Embroidery.......G....... 248 799-8662
Southfield ***(G-15669)***

Perfect Stitch Inc.......G....... 407 797-5527
Clio ***(G-3409)***

▲ Perrin Souvenir Distrs Inc.......B....... 616 785-9700
Comstock Park ***(G-3636)***

Personal Graphics.......G....... 231 347-6347
Petoskey ***(G-13013)***

Precision Embroidery.......G....... 248 684-1359
Milford ***(G-11481)***

Rose Embroidery LLC.......G....... 616 245-9191
Wyoming ***(G-18906)***

▲ Royal Stewart Enterprises.......G....... 734 224-7994
Temperance ***(G-16548)***

Saginaw Knitting Mills Inc.......F....... 989 695-2481
Freeland ***(G-6029)***

Sew Saintly.......G....... 586 773-8480
Saint Clair ***(G-14843)***

Sewphisticated Stitching.......G....... 269 428-4402
Saint Joseph ***(G-14960)***

Silk Screenstuff.......G....... 517 543-7716
Charlotte ***(G-2770)***

Slick Shirts Screen Printing.......F....... 517 371-3600
Lansing ***(G-9895)***

Special T Custom Products.......G....... 810 654-9602
Davison ***(G-3797)***

Spirit of Livingston Inc.......G....... 517 545-8831
Howell ***(G-8522)***

Sporting Image Inc.......F....... 269 657-5646
Paw Paw ***(G-12956)***

Sports Junction.......G....... 989 791-5900
Saginaw ***(G-14765)***

Sports Stop.......G....... 517 676-2199
Mason ***(G-11158)***

Sportswear Specialties Inc.......G....... 734 416-9941
Canton ***(G-2526)***

◆ Stahls Inc.......E....... 800 478-2457
Saint Clair Shores ***(G-14887)***

Stephanies Unlimited Creat LLC.......G....... 616 379-5392
Jenison ***(G-9072)***

Stitch Alley Customs.......G....... 616 377-7082
Holland ***(G-8203)***

Stitch Inventions.......G....... 248 698-7773
White Lake ***(G-18467)***

Stitch Kustoms.......G....... 248 622-4563
Pontiac ***(G-13418)***

Stitch N Lyds Embroidery.......G....... 231 675-1916
Charlevoix ***(G-2735)***

Stitches and Steel.......G....... 248 330-6302
Harrison ***(G-7682)***

Student Book Store Inc.......G....... 517 351-6768
East Lansing ***(G-4910)***

Superior Stitch.......G....... 734 347-1956
Petersburg ***(G-12986)***

T - Shirt Printing Plus Inc.......E....... 269 383-3666
Kalamazoo ***(G-9351)***

Thai Paradize LLC.......G....... 248 331-7355
Wixom ***(G-18772)***

Thread West - Michigan.......G....... 231 755-5229
Norton Shores ***(G-12339)***

Threads By Bb.......G....... 989 401-7525
Saginaw ***(G-14775)***

Threads Invisable.......G....... 248 516-5051
Farmington Hills ***(G-5400)***

Top Shelf Embroidery LLC.......G....... 231 932-0688
Traverse City ***(G-16862)***

Top Shells Embroidery LLC.......G....... 231 932-0688
Traverse City ***(G-16863)***

TP Logos LLC.......G....... 810 956-9484
Marysville ***(G-11110)***

Trophy Center West Michigan.......G....... 231 893-1686
Whitehall ***(G-18510)***

Twin City Engraving Company.......G....... 269 983-0601
Saint Joseph ***(G-14968)***

Ultra Stitch Embroidery.......F....... 586 498-5600
Madison Heights ***(G-10849)***

Vision Quest Embroidery LLC.......G....... 517 375-1518
Howell ***(G-8539)***

Watson Embroidery.......G....... 313 459-5070
Detroit ***(G-4675)***

What A Stitch.......G....... 248 698-1104
White Lake ***(G-18471)***

2396 Automotive Trimmings, Apparel Findings, Related Prdts

A Game Apparel.......G....... 810 564-2600
Mount Morris ***(G-11665)***

Advance Graphic Systems Inc.......E....... 248 656-8000
Rochester Hills ***(G-13943)***

Advanced Composite Tech Inc.......G....... 248 709-9097
Rochester ***(G-13889)***

▲ AGM Automotive LLC.......D....... 248 776-0600
Farmington Hills ***(G-5162)***

All For Love Prints LLC.......G....... 313 207-1547
Detroit ***(G-4000)***

American Silk Screen & EMB.......F....... 248 474-1000
Farmington Hills ***(G-5169)***

▲ American Twisting Company.......E....... 269 637-8581
South Haven ***(G-15398)***

AP Impressions Inc.......G....... 734 464-8009
Livonia ***(G-10121)***

Applause Inc.......G....... 517 485-9880
Holt ***(G-8303)***

Applied Graphics & Fabricating.......F....... 989 662-3334
Auburn ***(G-764)***

Ascott Corporation.......G....... 734 663-2023
Ann Arbor ***(G-381)***

Athletic Uniform Lettering.......G....... 313 533-9071
Redford ***(G-13717)***

Authority Customwear Ltd.......E....... 248 588-8075
Madison Heights ***(G-10676)***

▲ Automotive Trim Technologies.......E....... 734 947-0344
Taylor ***(G-16382)***

Bay Supply & Marketing Inc.......G....... 231 943-3249
Traverse City ***(G-16616)***

Bivins Graphics.......G....... 616 453-2211
Grand Rapids ***(G-6512)***

Blts Wearable Art Inc.......G....... 517 669-9659
Dewitt ***(G-4706)***

Britten Inc.......C....... 231 941-8200
Traverse City ***(G-16627)***

◆ Britten Banners LLC.......C....... 231 941-8200
Traverse City ***(G-16628)***

C & C Enterprises Inc.......G....... 989 772-5095
Mount Pleasant ***(G-11689)***

▲ Cadillac Prsentation Solutions ....E 248 288-9777
  Troy (G-16994)
▲ Canadian Amrcn Rstoration Sups ....E 248 853-8900
  Rochester Hills (G-13970)
Cedar Springs Sales LLC ....G 616 696-2111
  Cedar Springs (G-2645)
Chromatic Graphics Inc ....G 616 393-0034
  Holland (G-7996)
▲ Cni Enterprises Inc ....G 248 581-0200
  Madison Heights (G-10691)
▲ Cni-Owosso LLC ....G 248 586-3300
  Madison Heights (G-10692)
Crawford Associates Inc ....G 248 549-9494
  Royal Oak (G-14527)
Custom Ptint Ink LLC ....G 586 799-2465
  Eastpointe (G-4935)
▲ Detroit Name Plate Etching Inc ....E 248 543-5200
  Ferndale (G-5547)
Donbar LLC ....F 313 784-3519
  Inkster (G-8662)
Doorstep Printing LLC ....G 248 470-9567
  Detroit (G-4186)
E Q R 2 Inc ....G 586 731-3383
  Sterling Heights (G-15995)
E&S Sales LLC ....G 586 212-6018
  Sterling Heights (G-15996)
▲ Eissmann Auto Port Huron LLC ....C 810 216-6300
  Port Huron (G-13474)
Eissmann Auto Port Huron LLC .....E 248 829-4990
  Rochester Hills (G-14002)
Emaculate Enterprises LLC ....G 313 805-0654
  Detroit (G-4205)
Embroidery House Inc ....G 616 669-6400
  Jenison (G-9054)
Ethnic Artwork Inc ....F 586 726-1400
  Sterling Heights (G-16006)
Exclusive Imagery Inc ....G 248 436-2999
  Royal Oak (G-14536)
Federal Heath Sign Company LLC ...E 248 656-8000
  Rochester Hills (G-14010)
Fibre Converters Inc ....E 269 279-1700
  Constantine (G-3666)
Field Crafts Inc ....F 231 325-1122
  Honor (G-8359)
Flaunt It Sportswear ....G 616 696-9084
  Cedar Springs (G-2651)
Flint Group Pckg Inks N Amer C ...C 734 781-4600
  Livonia (G-10209)
Flint Group Pckg Inks N Amer H ...G 734 781-4600
  Livonia (G-10210)
▲ Futuris Automotive (ca) LLC ....B 510 771-2300
  Plymouth (G-13172)
▲ Futuris Automotive (us) Inc ....E 248 439-7800
  Oak Park (G-12614)
Futuris Global Holdings LLC ....G 248 439-7800
  Oak Park (G-12615)
Hayes-Albion Corporation ....F 517 629-2141
  Jackson (G-8900)
Hexon Corporation ....E 248 585-7585
  Farmington Hills (G-5259)
Image Projections Inc ....F 810 629-0700
  Fenton (G-5486)
Imprint House LLC ....G 810 985-8203
  Port Huron (G-13487)
Innovative Material Handling ....G 586 291-3694
  Detroit (G-4320)
Interntnal Auto Cmpnnts Group ...G 810 987-8500
  Port Huron (G-13488)
Irvin Acquisition LLC ....B 248 451-4100
  Pontiac (G-13382)
▲ Irvin Automotive Products LLC ....C 248 451-4100
  Pontiac (G-13383)
▲ J2 Licensing Inc ....G 586 307-3400
  Troy (G-17180)
Jam Enterprises ....G 313 417-9200
  Detroit (G-4332)
▲ Janet and Company Inc ....G 248 887-2050
  Highland (G-7893)
Janet Kelly ....F 231 775-2313
  Cadillac (G-2338)
Jbl Enterprises ....G 616 530-8647
  Grand Rapids (G-6863)
Jean Smith Designs ....G 616 942-9212
  Grand Rapids (G-6866)
JS Original Silkscreens LLC ....G 586 779-5456
  Eastpointe (G-4938)
Just Right Duplications LLC ....F 313 655-3555
  Oak Park (G-12619)
Kalamazoo Regalia Inc ....F 269 344-4299
  Kalamazoo (G-9247)

▲ Kay Screen Printing Inc ....B 248 377-4999
  Lake Orion (G-9611)
Lacks Exterior Systems LLC ....E 616 949-6570
  Grand Rapids (G-6914)
Lacks Industries Inc ....C 616 698-9852
  Grand Rapids (G-6918)
Larsen Graphics Inc ....E 989 823-3000
  Vassar (G-17579)
Lazer Graphics ....F 269 926-1066
  Benton Harbor (G-1565)
Lear Corporation ....E 248 447-1500
  Mason (G-11141)
◆ Lear Corporation ....B 248 447-1500
  Southfield (G-15628)
◆ Logofit LLC ....G 810 715-1980
  Flint (G-5727)
Loyalty 1977 Ink ....G 313 759-1006
  Detroit (G-4409)
◆ Marketing Displays Inc ....C 248 553-1900
  Farmington Hills (G-5310)
◆ Mayfair Golf Accessories ....G 989 732-8400
  Gaylord (G-6147)
Michael Anderson ....G 231 652-5717
  Newaygo (G-12088)
Mid-Michigan Industries Inc ....D 989 773-6918
  Mount Pleasant (G-11715)
Mid-Michigan Industries Inc ....E 989 386-7707
  Clare (G-2986)
◆ Mollertech LLC ....D 586 615-9154
  Macomb (G-10619)
Morgan Sofa Co ....G 347 262-5995
  Detroit (G-4465)
Mvp Sports Store ....G 517 764-5165
  Jackson (G-8973)
▲ Nalcor LLC ....D 248 541-1140
  Ferndale (G-5570)
Neighborhood Artisans Inc ....G 313 865-5373
  Detroit (G-4479)
Nobby Inc ....F 810 984-3300
  Fort Gratiot (G-5822)
Pangea Made Inc ....A 248 436-2300
  Rochester Hills (G-14078)
Peckham Vocational Inds Inc ....A 517 316-4000
  Lansing (G-9724)
Peckham Vocational Inds Inc ....E 517 316-4478
  Lansing (G-9725)
Perrin Screen Printing Inc ....F 616 785-9900
  Comstock Park (G-3635)
▲ Perrin Souvenir Distrs Inc ....B 616 785-9700
  Comstock Park (G-3636)
Plasti-Fab Inc ....F 248 543-1415
  Ferndale (G-5579)
Qmi Group Inc ....E 248 589-0505
  Madison Heights (G-10814)
R H & Company Inc ....F 269 345-7814
  Kalamazoo (G-9313)
▲ Real Green Systems Inc ....D 888 345-2154
  Commerce Township (G-3570)
▲ Rj Corp ....G 616 396-0552
  Holland (G-8181)
Rsls Corp ....G 248 726-0675
  Shelby Township (G-15319)
Rtlf-Hope LLC ....G 313 538-1700
  Detroit (G-4573)
Saginaw Knitting Mills Inc ....F 989 695-2481
  Freeland (G-6029)
Shirt Works ....G 989 448-8889
  Gaylord (G-6159)
◆ Sigma International Inc ....F 248 230-9681
  Livonia (G-10408)
Sign Screen Inc ....G 810 239-1100
  Flint (G-5762)
Silk Screenstuff ....G 517 543-7716
  Charlotte (G-2770)
Sporting Image Inc ....F 269 657-5646
  Paw Paw (G-12956)
Sports Stop ....G 517 676-2199
  Mason (G-11158)
Srg Global Inc ....G 586 757-7800
  Taylor (G-16479)
Srg Global LLC ....A 248 509-1100
  Troy (G-17368)
▲ Strattec Power Access LLC ....E 248 649-9742
  Auburn Hills (G-1039)
Sunset Sportswear Inc ....F 248 437-7611
  Wixom (G-18761)
T - Shirt Printing Plus Inc ....E 269 383-3666
  Kalamazoo (G-9351)
Takata Americas ....A 336 547-1600
  Auburn Hills (G-1044)

Tempro Industries Inc ....E 734 451-5900
  Plymouth (G-13312)
Tennant & Associates Inc ....G 248 643-6140
  Troy (G-17388)
Tesca Usa Inc ....E 586 991-0744
  Rochester Hills (G-14124)
Timbertech Inc ....F 231 348-2750
  Harbor Springs (G-7658)
Trims Unlimited LLC ....E 810 724-3500
  Almont (G-269)
Twin City Engraving Company .....G 269 983-0601
  Saint Joseph (G-14968)
Ultimate Graphic and Sign LLC ...G 989 865-5200
  Saint Charles (G-14812)
Vomela Specialty Company ....G 269 927-6500
  Benton Harbor (G-1600)
◆ Vu Acquisitions LLC ....C 248 269-0517
  Troy (G-17443)
Wec Group LLC ....E 248 260-4252
  Rochester Hills (G-14146)
▲ Yanfeng USA Auto Trim Systems ...E 586 354-2101
  Harrison Township (G-7736)

2397 Schiffli Machine Embroideries

Chromatic Graphics Inc ....G 616 393-0034
  Holland (G-7996)
Circles Way To Go Around Inc ....F 313 384-1193
  Clinton Township (G-3202)
Ideal Wholesale Inc ....G 989 873-5850
  Prescott (G-13651)
Ultimate Graphic and Sign LLC ...G 989 865-5200
  Saint Charles (G-14812)

2399 Fabricated Textile Prdts, NEC

▲ ABC Merchandise ....E 248 348-1560
  Wixom (G-18593)
▲ AGM Automotive LLC ....D 248 776-0600
  Farmington Hills (G-5162)
American Flag & Banner Company ...G 248 288-3010
  Clawson (G-3085)
Amk Enterprise LLC ....G 248 977-3039
  Waterford (G-18099)
Amk Enterprise LLC ....G 248 564-2549
  Auburn Hills (G-783)
▲ Bannergalaxycom LLC ....F 231 941-8200
  Traverse City (G-16612)
Bay Supply & Marketing Inc ....G 231 943-3249
  Traverse City (G-16616)
Belt-Tech USA Inc ....C 450 372-5826
  Grand Rapids (G-6498)
Britten Inc ....C 231 941-8200
  Traverse City (G-16627)
◆ Britten Banners LLC ....C 231 941-8200
  Traverse City (G-16628)
Brollytime Inc ....F 312 854-7606
  Royal Oak (G-14521)
Commonwealth Sewing Company ...G 313 319-2417
  Detroit (G-4098)
Consort Corporation ....E 269 388-4532
  Kalamazoo (G-9151)
▲ Dag Ltd LLC ....F 586 276-9310
  Sterling Heights (G-15979)
▲ Ed Cumings Inc ....E 810 736-0130
  Flint (G-5693)
Engineering Reproduction Inc .....G 313 366-3390
  Detroit (G-4209)
Faurecia North America Inc ....F 248 288-1000
  Auburn Hills (G-890)
Get In Game Marketing LLC ....G 231 846-1976
  Traverse City (G-16694)
Hogge Crochet ....G 313 808-1302
  Royal Oak (G-14548)
Huron Vlleys Hrse Blnket Hdqtr ...G 248 859-2398
  Wixom (G-18682)
Jack Ripper & Associates Inc .....G 734 453-7333
  Plymouth (G-13200)
Just Adorable Crocheting ....G 586 746-7137
  Clinton Township (G-3266)
▲ Key Safety Systems Inc ....C 248 373-8040
  Auburn Hills (G-951)
Key Safety Systems Inc ....F 586 726-3905
  Auburn Hills (G-952)
◆ Key Sfety Rstraint Systems Inc ...A 586 726-3800
  Auburn Hills (G-953)
Knit and Crochet 4 Charity ....G 248 224-4965
  Warren (G-17895)
Lamacs Inc ....G 248 643-9210
  Troy (G-17204)
◆ McCarthy Group Incorporated ....F 616 977-2900
  Grand Rapids (G-6970)

23 APPAREL AND OTHER FINISHED PRODUCTS MADE FROM FABRICS AND SIMILAR MATERIAL

Michigan Industrial Trim Inc .... F 734 947-0344
   Taylor *(G-16445)*

Midori Auto Leather N Amer Inc .... G 248 305-6437
   Novi *(G-12483)*

Olympus Group .... G 616 965-2671
   Kentwood *(G-9468)*

Outerwears Inc .... E 269 679-3301
   Schoolcraft *(G-15126)*

Powder It Inc .... G 586 949-0395
   Chesterfield *(G-2927)*

Priority One Emergency Inc .... G 734 398-5900
   Canton *(G-2512)*

Rampant Media LLC .... G 231 218-0401
   Traverse City *(G-16815)*

Ruff Love Pet LLC .... G 734 351-6289
   Maybee *(G-11171)*

Sage Automotive Interiors Inc .... G 248 355-9055
   Southfield *(G-15692)*

Silk Reflections .... G 313 292-1150
   Taylor *(G-16473)*

Spartan Flag Company Inc .... F 231 386-5150
   Northport *(G-12192)*

Spartan Village LLC .... G 661 724-6438
   Standish *(G-15896)*

◆ Stahls Inc .... E 800 478-2457
   Saint Clair Shores *(G-14887)*

Stitched Now .... G 586 460-6175
   Detroit *(G-4610)*

Takata Americas .... A 336 547-1600
   Auburn Hills *(G-1044)*

Teamtech Motorsports Safety .... G 989 792-4880
   Saginaw *(G-14773)*

Technotrim Inc .... A 734 254-5000
   Plymouth *(G-13311)*

Telescopic Seating Systems LLC .... G 616 566-9232
   Holland *(G-8214)*

Thorpe Printing Services Inc .... G 810 364-6222
   Marysville *(G-11107)*

Tk Holdings Inc .... A 517 545-9535
   Howell *(G-8534)*

Tk Mexico Inc .... C 248 373-8040
   Auburn Hills *(G-1059)*

Triple A Crochet LLC .... G 248 534-0818
   Clarkston *(G-3072)*

Upperhand Tack Co LLC .... G 906 424-0401
   Williamston *(G-18584)*

▲ Verduyn Tarps Detroit Inc .... G 313 270-4890
   Detroit *(G-4665)*

24 LUMBER AND WOOD PRODUCTS, EXCEPT FURNITURE

2411 Logging

4 Generation Logging Inc .... G 989 350-0337
   Curran *(G-3749)*

Abcor Partners LLC .... E 616 994-9577
   Holland *(G-7953)*

Aj Logging .... G 989 725-9610
   Henderson *(G-7859)*

Alexa Forest Products .... G 906 265-2347
   Iron River *(G-8739)*

Allen Whitehouse .... G 231 824-3000
   Manton *(G-10929)*

Antilla Logging Inc .... G 906 376-2374
   Republic *(G-13819)*

▼ Atwood Forest Products Inc .... E 616 696-0081
   Cedar Springs *(G-2641)*

B and C Logging .... G 906 753-2425
   Stephenson *(G-15906)*

B&T Logging .... G 810 417-6167
   Marlette *(G-10977)*

Beacom Enterprises Inc .... G 906 647-3831
   Pickford *(G-13030)*

Bear Creek Logging .... G 269 317-7475
   Ceresco *(G-2702)*

Bellmore Logging .... G 906 498-2528
   Hermansville *(G-7860)*

Bennett Sawmill .... G 231 734-5733
   Evart *(G-5121)*

Bills Logging Inc .... G 989 546-7164
   Comins *(G-3503)*

Bob Jutila Logging .... G 906 296-0753
   Lake Linden *(G-9567)*

Bosanic Lwrnce Sons Tmber Pdts .... G 906 341-5609
   Manistique *(G-10917)*

Bourdo Logging .... G 269 623-4981
   Delton *(G-3962)*

Brent Bastian Logging LLC .... G 906 482-6378
   Hancock *(G-7616)*

▲ Bruning Forest Products .... G 989 733-2880
   Onaway *(G-12697)*

Bryan K Sergent .... G 231 670-2106
   Stanwood *(G-15903)*

Bugay Logging .... G 906 428-2125
   Gladstone *(G-6176)*

C D C Logging .... G 906 524-6369
   Lanse *(G-9656)*

Cain Brothers Logging Inc .... G 906 345-9252
   Negaunee *(G-11964)*

Casselman Logging .... G 231 885-1040
   Mesick *(G-11270)*

Cg Logging .... G 906 322-1018
   Brimley *(G-2102)*

Chris Muma Forest Products .... E 989 426-5916
   Gladwin *(G-6193)*

Crawford Forest Products .... F 989 742-3855
   Hillman *(G-7912)*

D&L Logging .... G 231 709-5477
   Kingsley *(G-9522)*

Dale Routley Logging .... G 231 861-2596
   Hart *(G-7750)*

Dales LLC .... G 734 444-4620
   Lapeer *(G-9927)*

Danny K Bundy .... G 231 590-6924
   Manton *(G-10931)*

Darrell A Curtice .... G 231 745-9890
   Bitely *(G-1758)*

David Gauss Logging .... G 517 851-8102
   Stockbridge *(G-16273)*

David Jenks .... G 810 793-7340
   North Branch *(G-12178)*

David Newman Logging .... G 906 201-1125
   Baraga *(G-1137)*

Dawzye Excavation Inc .... G 906 786-5276
   Gladstone *(G-6179)*

Dehaan Forest Products Inc .... F 906 883-3417
   Mass City *(G-11161)*

Dillon Forest Products Inc .... G 906 869-4671
   Republic *(G-13820)*

DJL Logging Inc .... G 231 590-2012
   Manton *(G-10933)*

Donald LII Sons Logging .... G 231 420-3800
   Pellston *(G-12967)*

Doug Anderson Logging .... G 906 337-3707
   Calumet *(G-2409)*

Doyle Forest Products Inc .... G 231 832-5586
   Paris *(G-12933)*

Duane F Proehl Inc .... G 906 474-6630
   Rapid River *(G-13684)*

Duberville Logging .... G 906 586-6267
   Curtis *(G-3750)*

E H Tulgestka & Sons Inc .... F 989 734-2129
   Rogers City *(G-14209)*

Earl St John Forest Products .... F 906 497-5667
   Spalding *(G-15759)*

East Branch Forest Products .... G 906 852-3315
   Kenton *(G-9439)*

Ej Timber Producers Inc .... F 231 544-9866
   East Jordan *(G-4869)*

Elenz Inc .... G 989 732-7233
   Gaylord *(G-6127)*

Erickson Logging Inc .... G 906 481-4021
   Chassell *(G-2777)*

Eup Wood Shavings Inc .... F 586 943-7199
   Kincheloe *(G-9502)*

Fahl Forest Products Inc .... F 231 587-5388
   Mancelona *(G-10870)*

Forest Blake Products Inc .... G 231 879-3913
   Fife Lake *(G-5606)*

From Log Up LLC .... G 989 728-0611
   Hale *(G-7589)*

G & D Wood Products Inc .... G 517 254-4463
   Camden *(G-2422)*

G & S Logging LLC .... G 989 876-6596
   Turner *(G-17463)*

GA Dalbeck Logging LLC .... F 906 364-3300
   Wakefield *(G-17622)*

Gary Nankervis Logging .... G 906 524-7735
   Lanse *(G-9660)*

Giguere Logging Inc .... G 906 786-3975
   Escanaba *(G-5073)*

Great Lakes Log & Firewd Co .... G 231 206-4073
   Twin Lake *(G-17468)*

Heidtman Logging Inc .... G 906 249-3914
   Marquette *(G-11020)*

Heritage Forestry LLC .... G 231 689-5721
   White Cloud *(G-18443)*

Hincka Logging LLC .... G 989 766-8893
   Posen *(G-13643)*

Holli Forest Products .... F 906 486-9352
   Ishpeming *(G-8777)*

Hydrolake Inc .... G 231 825-2233
   Mc Bain *(G-11182)*

Iron Eagle Logging .... G 269 945-9617
   Hastings *(G-7799)*

J Carey Logging Inc .... F 906 542-3420
   Channing *(G-2706)*

Jacobson Logging Inc .... F 906 246-3497
   Felch *(G-5431)*

Jaimes Trusses and Wall Panels .... G 734 462-6100
   Livonia *(G-10257)*

James L Miller .... G 989 539-5540
   Harrison *(G-7679)*

James Pollard Logging .... G 906 884-6744
   Ontonagon *(G-12709)*

James R Goff Logging .... G 231 420-3455
   Vanderbilt *(G-17571)*

James Spicer Inc .... G 906 265-2385
   Iron River *(G-8743)*

Jason Breneman & Son Logging .... G 269 432-1378
   Mendon *(G-11217)*

Jason Laponsie .... G 906 440-3567
   Brimley *(G-2104)*

Jason Lutke .... E 231 824-6655
   Manton *(G-10934)*

Jeffery Lucas .... G 231 797-5152
   Luther *(G-10563)*

Jerome Miller Lumber Co .... G 231 745-3694
   Baldwin *(G-1123)*

Jesse James Logging .... G 906 395-6819
   Lanse *(G-9662)*

Jim Detweiler .... G 269 467-7728
   Sturgis *(G-16295)*

JM Longyear LLC .... G 906 228-7960
   Marquette *(G-11026)*

Jns Sawmill .... G 989 352-5430
   Coral *(G-3699)*

Joe Bosanic Forest Products .... G 906 341-2037
   Manistique *(G-10919)*

John Fuller Logging .... G 517 304-3298
   Fowlerville *(G-5847)*

John Vuk & Son Inc .... G 906 524-6074
   Lanse *(G-9663)*

Joseph Lakosky Logging .... G 906 573-2783
   Manistique *(G-10920)*

Jungnitsch Bros Logging .... G 989 233-8091
   Saint Charles *(G-14803)*

K & M Industrial LLC .... G 906 420-8770
   Gladstone *(G-6182)*

Kanerva Forest Products Inc .... G 906 356-6061
   Rock *(G-14150)*

Karttunen Logging .... G 906 884-4312
   Ontonagon *(G-12712)*

Keith Falan .... G 231 834-7358
   Grant *(G-7429)*

Kells Sawmill Inc .... G 906 753-2778
   Stephenson *(G-15908)*

Kenneth A Gould .... G 231 828-4705
   Twin Lake *(G-17469)*

Kk Logging .... G 906 524-6047
   Lanse *(G-9665)*

Kostamo Logging .... G 906 353-6171
   Pelkie *(G-12964)*

Laws & Ponies Logging Show .... G 269 838-3942
   Delton *(G-3964)*

Lawsons Logging .... G 517 567-0025
   Camden *(G-2423)*

Leep Logging Inc .... G 517 852-1540
   Nashville *(G-11956)*

Leonard J Hill Logging Co .... F 906 337-3435
   Calumet *(G-2411)*

Lindsay Nettell Inc .... G 906 482-3549
   Atlantic Mine *(G-750)*

Logging-In Com Inc .... G 248 466-0708
   Farmington Hills *(G-5294)*

Logging-Incom LLC .... F 248 662-7864
   Farmington Hills *(G-5295)*

Low Impact Logging Inc .... G 906 250-5117
   Iron River *(G-8748)*

Lucas Logging .... G 906 246-3629
   Bark River *(G-1155)*

Lumberjack Logging LLC .... G 616 799-4657
   Pierson *(G-13033)*

Manigg Enterprises Inc .... F 989 356-4986
   Alpena *(G-301)*

Mark A Nelson .... G 989 305-5769
   Lupton *(G-10562)*

Martens Logging .... G 616 675-5473
   Casnovia *(G-2607)*

Marvin Nelson Forest Products ....F .... 906 384-6700 Cornell *(G-3701)*

McNamara & Mcnamara ....F .... 906 293-5281 Newberry *(G-12093)*

Mid Michigan Logging ....F .... 231 229-4501 Lake City *(G-9551)*

Midnight Logging LLC ....G .... 202 521-1484 Howard City *(G-8412)*

Mike Hughes ....G .... 269 377-3578 Nashville *(G-11957)*

Miljevich Corporation ....G .... 906 224-2651 Wakefield *(G-17623)*

Minerick Logging Inc ....F .... 906 542-3583 Sagola *(G-14798)*

Moeke Foresty ....G .... 231 631-9600 Boyne City *(G-1898)*

Motto Cedar Products Inc ....G .... 906 753-4892 Daggett *(G-3753)*

Ndsay Nettell Logging ....G .... 906 482-3549 Atlantic Mine *(G-751)*

Nears Logging ....G .... 989 390-4951 Roscommon *(G-14353)*

Neumeier Logging Inc ....G .... 906 786-5242 Escanaba *(G-5086)*

Nickels Logging ....G .... 906 563-5880 Norway *(G-12354)*

Noble Forestry Inc ....G .... 989 866-6495 Blanchard *(G-1759)*

P G K Enterprises LLC ....G .... 248 535-4411 Southfield *(G-15671)*

Patrick Newland Logging Ltd ....G .... 906 524-2255 Lanse *(G-9667)*

Peacocks Eco Log & Sawmill LLC ....G .... 231 250-3462 Morley *(G-11621)*

Phelps Services ....G .... 231 942-8044 Lake City *(G-9553)*

Piwarski Brothers Logging Inc ....G .... 906 265-2914 Iron River *(G-8752)*

Plum Creek Timber Company Inc ....G .... 715 453-7952 Escanaba *(G-5090)*

Pomeroy Forest Products Inc ....G .... 906 474-6780 Rapid River *(G-13685)*

Precision Forestry ....F .... 989 619-1016 Onaway *(G-12702)*

Proctor Logging Inc ....G .... 231 775-3820 Cadillac *(G-2349)*

R&H Logging Inc ....G .... 906 241-7248 Cornell *(G-3702)*

Rapid River Rustic Inc ....E .... 906 474-6404 Rapid River *(G-13686)*

Richard Teachworht ....G .... 231 527-8227 Morley *(G-11622)*

Robert Craig Logging LLC ....G .... 906 287-0906 Newberry *(G-12101)*

Robert Crawford & Son Logging ....G .... 989 379-2712 Lachine *(G-9534)*

Robert Gentz Forest Pdts Inc ....F .... 231 398-9194 Manistee *(G-10912)*

Rodney E Harter ....G .... 231 796-6734 Big Rapids *(G-1686)*

Roger Bazuin & Sons Inc ....E .... 231 825-2889 Mc Bain *(G-11187)*

Rosenthal Logging ....G .... 231 348-8168 Petoskey *(G-13021)*

Rothig Forest Products Inc ....F .... 231 266-8292 Irons *(G-8757)*

Roxbury Creek LLC ....G .... 989 731-2062 Gaylord *(G-6156)*

S & M Logging LLC ....G .... 231 830-7317 Muskegon *(G-11912)*

S & S Forest Products ....G .... 906 892-8268 Munising *(G-11754)*

S&M Logging LLC ....G .... 231 821-0588 Twin Lake *(G-17472)*

Saninocencio Logging ....G .... 269 945-3567 Hastings *(G-7809)*

Santti Brothers Inc ....G .... 906 355-2347 Watton *(G-18185)*

Sawyer Logging LLC ....G .... 989 942-6324 West Branch *(G-18341)*

Schultz Logging ....G .... 906 863-5719 Menominee *(G-11259)*

Scott Johnson Forest Pdts Co ....G .... 906 482-3978 Houghton *(G-8391)*

Select Cut Logging LLC ....G .... 231 690-6085 Wellston *(G-18260)*

Shamco Inc ....G .... 906 265-5065 Iron River *(G-8753)*

Shamco Lumber Inc ....G .... 906 265-5065 Iron River *(G-8754)*

Shamion Brothers ....F .... 906 265-5065 Iron River *(G-8755)*

Shawn Muma ....G .... 989 426-9505 Gladwin *(G-6205)*

Shawn Muma Logging ....G .... 989 426-6852 Gladwin *(G-6206)*

Sheski Logging ....G .... 906 786-1886 Escanaba *(G-5098)*

Smith Logging LLC ....G .... 616 558-0729 Hopkins *(G-8371)*

Speedy Blaze Inc ....G .... 989 340-2028 Alpena *(G-318)*

Spencer Farms and Timber LLC ....G .... 810 459-4487 Ada *(G-35)*

Steigers Timber Operations ....G .... 906 667-0266 Bessemer *(G-1650)*

Stephen Rex Fetterley Jr ....G .... 269 215-2035 Delton *(G-3967)*

Steven Crandell ....G .... 231 582-7445 Charlevoix *(G-2734)*

Styx & Twigs LLC ....G .... 231 245-6083 Howard City *(G-8419)*

Sv Logging LLC ....G .... 715 360-0035 Iron River *(G-8756)*

Tarrs Tree Service Inc ....E .... 248 528-3313 Troy *(G-17384)*

Timberline Logging Inc ....E .... 989 731-2794 Gaylord *(G-6163)*

Tom Clisch Logging Inc ....G .... 906 338-2900 Pelkie *(G-12965)*

Total Chips Company Inc ....F .... 989 866-2610 Shepherd *(G-15379)*

TR Timber Co ....F .... 989 345-5350 West Branch *(G-18344)*

Turpeinen Bros Inc ....G .... 906 338-2870 Pelkie *(G-12966)*

Tuscola Logging ....G .... 517 231-2905 Grand Rapids *(G-7282)*

Tuttle Forest Products ....G .... 906 283-3871 Gulliver *(G-7578)*

Usher Logging LLC ....G .... 906 238-4261 Arnold *(G-740)*

Usher Logging LLC ....G .... 906 238-4261 Cornell *(G-3703)*

Usimaki Logging Inc ....G .... 920 869-4183 Baraga *(G-1149)*

Utility Supply and Cnstr Co ....G .... 231 832-2297 Reed City *(G-13802)*

Van Duinen Forest Products ....F .... 231 328-4507 Lake City *(G-9556)*

Vulcan Wood Products Inc ....F .... 906 563-8995 Vulcan *(G-17617)*

Wade Logging ....G .... 231 463-0363 Fife Lake *(G-5609)*

Weyerhaeuser Company ....G .... 906 524-2040 Lanse *(G-9669)*

Whittaker Timber Corporation ....G .... 989 872-3065 Cass City *(G-2624)*

Woods 2 G Logging LLC ....G .... 248 469-7416 Howell *(G-8542)*

Yates Forest Products Inc ....G .... 989 739-8412 Oscoda *(G-12774)*

Younggren Farm & Forest Inc ....G .... 906 355-2272 Covington *(G-3727)*

Younggren Timber Company ....G .... 906 355-2272 Covington *(G-3728)*

Zellar Forest Products ....G .... 906 586-9817 Germfask *(G-6169)*

2421 Saw & Planing Mills

/// 702 Cedar River Lbr Inc ....E .... 906 497-5365 Powers *(G-13648)*

A J D Forest Pdts Ltd Partnr ....D .... 989 348-5412 Grayling *(G-7454)*

All-Wood Inc ....G .... 906 353-6642 Baraga *(G-1133)*

American Classic Homes Inc ....G .... 616 594-5900 Holland *(G-7964)*

▼ Applegate Insul Systems Inc ....E .... 517 521-3545 Webberville *(G-18241)*

▼ Atwood Forest Products Inc ....E .... 616 696-0081 Cedar Springs *(G-2641)*

◆ Banks Hardwoods Inc ....D .... 269 483-2323 White Pigeon *(G-18472)*

Barnes Wood Works ....G .... 269 599-3479 Portage *(G-13546)*

Bennett Sawmill ....G .... 231 734-5733 Evart *(G-5121)*

Besse Forest Products Inc ....F .... 906 353-7193 Baraga *(G-1135)*

Biewer Forest Management LLC ....G .... 231 825-2855 Mc Bain *(G-11177)*

Biewer Sawmill Winona Inc ....C .... 810 329-4789 Saint Clair *(G-14815)*

Biewer Sawmill-Lake City LLC ....F .... 231 839-7646 Lake City *(G-9544)*

Blough Hardwoods Inc ....G .... 616 693-2174 Clarksville *(G-3078)*

Burt Moeke & Son Hardwoods ....E .... 231 587-5388 Mancelona *(G-10868)*

Buskirk Lumber Company ....E .... 616 765-5103 Freeport *(G-6032)*

Caledonia Cmnty Sawmill LLC ....G .... 616 891-8561 Alto *(G-330)*

Casselman Logging ....G .... 231 885-1040 Mesick *(G-11270)*

Collins Brothers Sawmill Inc ....F .... 906 524-5511 Lanse *(G-9658)*

Country Side Sawmill ....G .... 989 352-7198 Lakeview *(G-9640)*

Crawford Forest Products ....F .... 989 742-3855 Hillman *(G-7912)*

Creekside Lumber ....G .... 231 924-1934 Newaygo *(G-12079)*

Cruse Hardwood Lumber Inc ....G .... 517 688-4891 Birmingham *(G-1723)*

Cyrus Forest Products ....G .... 269 751-6535 Allegan *(G-152)*

Daniel D Slater ....G .... 989 833-7135 Riverdale *(G-13863)*

▲ Decatur Wood Products Inc ....E .... 269 657-6041 Decatur *(G-3946)*

Decorative Panels Intl Inc ....E .... 989 354-2121 Alpena *(G-290)*

▼ Devereaux Saw Mill Inc ....D .... 989 593-2552 Pewamo *(G-13027)*

Diversified Pdts & Svcs LLC ....G .... 616 836-6600 Holland *(G-8014)*

Don Sawmill Inc ....G .... 989 733-2780 Onaway *(G-12698)*

Dowd Brothers Forestry ....G .... 989 345-7459 Alger *(G-137)*

Dyers Sawmill Inc ....E .... 231 768-4438 Leroy *(G-10006)*

E H Tulgestka & Sons Inc ....F .... 989 734-2129 Rogers City *(G-14209)*

E U P Woods Shavings ....G .... 906 495-1141 Kincheloe *(G-9501)*

Elenz Inc ....F .... 989 732-7233 Gaylord *(G-6128)*

Elenz Inc ....G .... 989 732-7233 Gaylord *(G-6127)*

Eovations LLC ....F .... 616 361-7136 Grand Rapids *(G-6682)*

Fairview Sawmill Inc ....G .... 989 848-5238 Fairview *(G-5130)*

Fiber By-Products Corp ....F .... 269 483-0066 White Pigeon *(G-18477)*

Forest Blake Products Inc ....G .... 231 879-3913 Fife Lake *(G-5606)*

Forest Corullo Products Corp ....E .... 906 667-0275 Bessemer *(G-1649)*

Forest Elders Products Inc ....E .... 616 866-9317 Rockford *(G-14168)*

◆ Forestry Management Svcs Inc ....C .... 517 456-7431 Clinton *(G-3138)*

◆ Forte Industries Mill Inc ....E .... 906 753-6256 Stephenson *(G-15907)*

Gilchrist Premium Lumber Pdts ....F .... 989 826-8300 Mio *(G-11507)*

Grand Traverse Assembly Inc ....E .... 231 588-2406 Ellsworth *(G-5036)*

Great Northern Lumber Mich LLC ....G .... 989 736-6192 Lincoln *(G-10034)*

Green Gables Saw Mill ....G .... 989 386-7846 Clare *(G-2980)*

Gyms Sawmill ....G .... 989 826-8299 Mio *(G-11508)*

Hmi Hardwoods LLC ....D .... 517 456-7431 Clinton *(G-3141)*

Hochstetler Sawmill ....G .... 269 467-7018 Centreville *(G-2697)*

Housler Sawmill Inc ....F .... 231 824-6353 Mesick *(G-11272)*

Ida D Byler ....G .... 810 672-9355 Cass City *(G-2615)*

Integrity Forest Products LLC ....G .... 513 871-8988 Kenton *(G-9440)*

J and K Lumber Inc ....G .... 906 265-9130 Iron River *(G-8742)*

SIC

24 LUMBER AND WOOD PRODUCTS, EXCEPT FURNITURE24 LUMBER AND WOOD PRODUCTS, EXCEPT FURNITURE SIC SECTION

Jaroche Brothers Inc ....F 231 525-8100
Wolverine *(G-18795)*
Jerome Miller Lumber Co ....G 231 745-3694
Baldwin *(G-1122)*
Jerome Miller Lumber Co ....G 231 745-3694
Baldwin *(G-1123)*
John A Biewer Lumber Company ....E 231 839-7646
Lake City *(G-9547)*
John A Biewer Lumber Company ....E 231 825-2855
Mc Bain *(G-11183)*
Kappen Saw Mill ....G 989 872-4410
Cass City *(G-2616)*
Kells Sawmill Inc ....G 906 753-2778
Stephenson *(G-15908)*
Louisiana-Pacific Corporation ....G 906 293-3265
Newberry *(G-12092)*
Lumber Jack Hardwoods Inc ....F 906 863-7090
Menominee *(G-11243)*
Maeder Bros Inc ....E 989 644-2235
Weidman *(G-18255)*
Maeder Bros Qlty WD Pllets Inc ....F 989 644-3500
Weidman *(G-18256)*
Maple Ridge Hardwoods Inc ....E 989 873-5305
Sterling *(G-15913)*
Maples Sawmill Inc ....E 906 484-3926
Hessel *(G-7874)*
Master Woodworks ....G 269 240-3262
Saint Joseph *(G-14949)*
Matthews Mill Inc ....F 989 257-3271
South Branch *(G-15396)*
Mc Guire Mill & Lumber ....G 989 735-3851
Glennie *(G-6214)*
Meeders Lumber Co ....G 231 587-8611
Mancelona *(G-10875)*
Met Inc ....G 231 845-1737
Ludington *(G-10545)*
Michigan Lumber & Wood Fiber I ....E 989 848-2100
Comins *(G-3504)*
Michigan Sawmill Sales LLC ....G 810 625-3848
Linden *(G-10067)*
Michigan Timber Sawmill LLC ....F 989 266-2417
Hillman *(G-7914)*
Midwest Timber Inc ....E 269 663-5315
Edwardsburg *(G-5011)*
Mlc of Wakefield Inc ....F 906 224-1120
Wakefield *(G-17624)*
Nelsons Saw Mill Inc ....G 231 829-5220
Tustin *(G-17466)*
Nettleton Wood Products Inc ....G 906 297-5791
De Tour Village *(G-3802)*
▲ North American Forest Products ....C 269 663-8500
Edwardsburg *(G-5013)*
North American Forest Products ....G 269 663-8500
Edwardsburg *(G-5014)*
Northern Hardwoods Oper Co LLC ....D 860 632-3505
South Range *(G-15461)*
Northern Industrial Wood Inc ....E 989 736-6192
Lincoln *(G-10038)*
Northern Mich Hardwoods Inc ....F 231 347-4575
Petoskey *(G-13008)*
Northern Michigan Sawmill ....G 231 409-1314
Williamsburg *(G-18560)*
Northern Products of Wisconsin ....G 715 589-4417
Iron Mountain *(G-8727)*
Northwest Hardwoods Inc ....G 989 786-6100
Lewiston *(G-10026)*
Northwood Lumber ....G 989 826-1751
Mio *(G-11513)*
Nu-Tran LLC ....G 616 350-9575
Wyoming *(G-18897)*
Oceana Forest Products Inc ....G 231 861-6115
Shelby *(G-15158)*
Old Sawmill Woodworking Co ....G 248 366-6245
Commerce Township *(G-3559)*
Ottawa Forest Products Inc ....E 906 932-9701
Ironwood *(G-8769)*
Paris North Hardwood Lumber ....F 231 584-2500
Elmira *(G-5040)*
Pine Tech Inc ....E 989 426-0006
Plymouth *(G-13264)*
Pollums Natural Resources ....G 810 245-7268
Lapeer *(G-9955)*
Post Hardwoods Inc ....E 269 751-2221
Hamilton *(G-7604)*
◆ Precision Hrdwood Rsources Inc ....F 734 475-0144
Chelsea *(G-2824)*
Prells Saw Mill Inc ....E 989 734-2939
Hawks *(G-7815)*
Pure Products International In ....G 989 471-1104
Ossineke *(G-12779)*
Quigley Lumber Inc ....G 989 257-5116
South Branch *(G-15397)*
R & N Lumber ....G 989 848-5553
Mio *(G-11515)*
Rapid River Rustic Inc ....E 906 474-6404
Rapid River *(G-13686)*
Richter Sawmill ....G 231 829-3071
Leroy *(G-10011)*
Ridgewood Stoves LLC ....G 989 488-3397
Hersey *(G-7869)*
Riverbend Timber Framing Inc ....E 517 486-3629
Blissfield *(G-1776)*
Robert E Nelson & Son ....G 810 664-6091
Lapeer *(G-9959)*
Sabertooth Enterprises LLC ....F 989 539-9842
Harrison *(G-7681)*
Sagola Hardwoods Inc ....D 906 542-7200
Sagola *(G-14799)*
Sawing Logz LLC ....G 586 883-5649
Warren *(G-18004)*
Sawmill Estates ....G 269 792-7500
Wayland *(G-18205)*
Schleben Forest Products Inc ....G 989 734-2858
Rogers City *(G-14218)*
◆ Sensitile Systems LLC ....E 313 872-6314
Ypsilanti *(G-18977)*
Speedy Blaze Inc ....G 989 340-2028
Alpena *(G-318)*
St Charles Hardwood Michigan ....F 989 865-9299
Saint Charles *(G-14809)*
Terry Heiden ....G 906 753-6248
Stephenson *(G-15912)*
Thorn Creek Lumber LLC ....G 231 832-1600
Reed City *(G-13800)*
Timber Products Co Ltd Partnr ....C 906 452-6221
Munising *(G-11755)*
Total Chips Company Inc ....F 989 866-2610
Shepherd *(G-15379)*
Ufp Atlantic LLC ....G 616 364-6161
Grand Rapids *(G-7286)*
◆ Ufp Eastern Division Inc ....B 616 364-6161
Grand Rapids *(G-7287)*
Ufp Grand Rapids LLC ....F 616 464-1650
Grand Rapids *(G-7288)*
▼ Ufp Industries Inc ....C 616 364-6161
Grand Rapids *(G-7289)*
Ufp Southwest LLC ....G 616 364-6161
Grand Rapids *(G-7293)*
Ufp West Central LLC ....D 616 364-6161
Grand Rapids *(G-7295)*
Vickeryville Lumber Co LLC ....G 989 261-3100
Sheridan *(G-15385)*
Weber Bros Sawmill Inc ....E 989 644-2206
Mount Pleasant *(G-11746)*
West Michigan Sawmill ....G 616 693-0044
Clarksville *(G-3082)*
Weyerhaeuser Company ....G 989 348-2881
Grayling *(G-7471)*
Wheelers Wolf Lake Sawmill ....G 231 745-7078
Baldwin *(G-1125)*
Whitens Kiln & Lumber Inc ....F 906 498-2116
Hermansville *(G-7865)*
William S Wixtrom ....G 906 376-8247
Republic *(G-13821)*
Williams Milling & Moulding In ....G 906 474-9222
Rapid River *(G-13687)*
Willsie Lumber Company ....F 989 695-5094
Freeland *(G-6031)*
Woodhaven Log and Lumber ....G 231 938-2200
Williamsburg *(G-18567)*
Yard & Home LLC ....F 844 927-3466
Grand Rapids *(G-7354)*
Zulski Lumber Inc ....G 231 539-8909
Pellston *(G-12969)*

2426 Hardwood Dimension & Flooring Mills

▼ Atwood Forest Products Inc ....E 616 696-0081
Cedar Springs *(G-2641)*
B & B Heartwoods Inc ....G 734 332-9525
Ann Arbor *(G-394)*
◆ Banks Hardwoods Inc ....D 269 483-2323
White Pigeon *(G-18472)*
Besse Forest Products Inc ....F 906 353-7193
Baraga *(G-1135)*
Burt Moeke & Son Hardwoods ....E 231 587-5388
Mancelona *(G-10868)*
Component Solutions LLC ....E 906 863-2682
Menominee *(G-11230)*
Connor Sports Flooring LLC ....F 906 822-7311
Amasa *(G-338)*
Counterpoint By Hlf ....G 734 699-7100
Van Buren Twp *(G-17521)*
Craftwood Industries Inc ....E 616 796-1209
Holland *(G-8006)*
Demeester Wood Products Inc ....F 616 677-5995
Coopersville *(G-3685)*
▼ Devereaux Saw Mill Inc ....D 989 593-2552
Pewamo *(G-13027)*
Doltek Enterprises Inc ....E 616 837-7828
Nunica *(G-12579)*
Dyers Sawmill Inc ....E 231 768-4438
Leroy *(G-10006)*
Erickson Lumber & True Value ....G 906 524-6295
Lanse *(G-9659)*
Forest Elders Products Inc ....E 616 866-9317
Rockford *(G-14168)*
◆ Forestry Management Svcs Inc ....C 517 456-7431
Clinton *(G-3138)*
◆ Forte Industries Mill Inc ....E 906 753-6256
Stephenson *(G-15907)*
Ganas LLC ....F 313 646-9966
Detroit *(G-4250)*
◆ Genesis Seating Inc ....D 616 954-1040
Grand Rapids *(G-6739)*
Grand Rapids Carvers Inc ....E 616 538-0022
Grand Rapids *(G-6754)*
H & R Wood Specialties Inc ....E 269 628-2181
Gobles *(G-6217)*
Hunt & Noyer LLC ....G 517 914-6259
Berkley *(G-1627)*
IKEA Chip LLC ....G 877 218-9931
Troy *(G-17160)*
Jaroche Brothers Inc ....F 231 525-8100
Wolverine *(G-18795)*
Jarvis Saw Mill Inc ....G 231 861-2078
Shelby *(G-15150)*
John A Biewer Lumber Company ....E 231 825-2855
Mc Bain *(G-11183)*
▲ Kentwood Manufacturing Co ....E 616 698-6370
Byron Center *(G-2279)*
Lumber Jack Hardwoods Inc ....F 906 863-7090
Menominee *(G-11243)*
Maple Ridge Hardwoods Inc ....E 989 873-5305
Sterling *(G-15913)*
Matelski Lumber Company ....E 231 549-2780
Boyne Falls *(G-1909)*
Meeders Dim & Lbr Pdts Co ....G 231 587-8611
Mancelona *(G-10874)*
▲ Menomnee Rver Lbr Dmnsions LLC ....G 906 863-2682
Menominee *(G-11250)*
Metter Flooring LLC ....G 517 914-2004
Rives Junction *(G-13887)*
Motto Cedar Products Inc ....G 906 753-4892
Daggett *(G-3753)*
Nettleton Wood Products Inc ....G 906 297-5791
De Tour Village *(G-3802)*
North American Forest Products ....G 269 663-8500
Edwardsburg *(G-5014)*
Northern Hardwoods ....G 906 487-6400
Newberry *(G-12099)*
Northern Mich Hardwoods Inc ....F 231 347-4575
Petoskey *(G-13008)*
Omara Sprung Floors Inc ....G 810 743-8281
Burton *(G-2242)*
Ottawa Forest Products Inc ....E 906 932-9701
Ironwood *(G-8769)*
Paris North Hardwood Lumber ....F 231 584-2500
Elmira *(G-5040)*
PAW Enterprises LLC ....F 269 329-1865
Kalamazoo *(G-9290)*
Pine Tech Inc ....E 989 426-0006
Plymouth *(G-13264)*
Quigley Lumber Inc ....G 989 257-5116
South Branch *(G-15397)*
▲ Rare Earth Hardwoods Inc ....F 231 946-0043
Traverse City *(G-16817)*
▲ Richwood Industries Inc ....E 616 243-2700
Grand Rapids *(G-7154)*
Robbins Inc ....G 513 619-5936
Negaunee *(G-11973)*
Rt Baldwin Enterprises Inc ....G 616 669-1626
Hudsonville *(G-8610)*
Schafer Hardwood Flooring Co ....E 989 732-8800
Tecumseh *(G-16515)*
Solaire Medical Storage LLC ....D 888 435-2256
Marne *(G-10999)*
Timber Pdts Mich Ltd Partnr ....G 906 779-2000
Iron Mountain *(G-8736)*
Ufp Lansing LLC ....G 517 325-5572
Grand Rapids *(G-7291)*

SIC SECTION — 24 LUMBER AND WOOD PRODUCTS, EXCEPT FURNITURE

Vocational Strategies Inc .... F 906 482-6142
　Calumet *(G-2415)*
Weber Bros Sawmill Inc .... E 989 644-2206
　Mount Pleasant *(G-11746)*
Whitens Kiln & Lumber Inc .... F 906 498-2116
　Hermansville *(G-7865)*
William S Wixtrom .... G 906 376-8247
　Republic *(G-13821)*
Yooper WD Wrks Restoration LLC ..... G 906 203-0056
　Sault Sainte Marie *(G-15105)*
Zemis 5 LLC .... G 317 946-7015
　Detroit *(G-4703)*

2429 Special Prdt Sawmills, NEC

Biewer Sawmill Inc .... E 231 825-2855
　Mc Bain *(G-11178)*
Holmquist Feed Mill .... G 906 446-3325
　Trenary *(G-16885)*

2431 Millwork

2 Sg Wookworks LLC .... G 586 884-7090
　Clinton Township *(G-3143)*
Acadian Woodworking LLC .... G 989 356-0229
　Alpena *(G-273)*
Action Outdoor Services LLC .... G 719 596-5341
　Ann Arbor *(G-348)*
▲ Air Conditioning Products Co .... E 734 326-0050
　Romulus *(G-14247)*
Allen and Sons Woodworking .... G 313 492-1382
　Linden *(G-10059)*
American Bldrs Contrs Sup Inc .... G 906 226-9665
　Marquette *(G-11004)*
American Wood Moldings LLC .... G 586 726-9050
　Shelby Township *(G-15169)*
Andersen Corporation .... G 734 237-1052
　Livonia *(G-10119)*
Andoor Craftmaster .... G 989 672-2020
　Caro *(G-2565)*
Architectural Door & Mllwk Inc .... E 248 442-9222
　New Hudson *(G-12043)*
Architectural Planners Inc .... E 248 674-1340
　Waterford *(G-18101)*
Architectural Products Inc .... G 248 585-8272
　Royal Oak *(G-14511)*
Architectural Trim & Wdwrk LLC .... G 586 321-1860
　Shelby Township *(G-15171)*
Arctel Corp .... F 616 241-6001
　Grand Rapids *(G-6468)*
Area Exteriors .... G 248 544-0706
　Leonard *(G-10001)*
Ark Woodworks LLC .... G 269 364-1397
　Kalamazoo *(G-9121)*
Armstrong Millworks Inc .... G 248 887-1037
　Highland *(G-7881)*
ASC Custom Woodworking LLC .... G 586 855-8817
　Warren *(G-17717)*
Aspen Door Supply LLC .... G 248 291-5303
　Troy *(G-16959)*
Audia Woodworking & Fine Furn .... F 586 296-6330
　Clinton Township *(G-3174)*
Autumn Ridge Woodworks .... G 517 420-8185
　Mason *(G-11117)*
B & W Woodwork Inc .... G 616 772-4577
　Holland *(G-7969)*
Barlow Custom Woodworking .... G 810 220-0648
　Brighton *(G-1949)*
Bay Wood Homes Inc .... F 989 245-4156
　Fenton *(G-5456)*
Bc Woodworks .... G 989 820-7680
　Oscoda *(G-12754)*
Beaver Stair Company .... G 248 628-0441
　Oxford *(G-12879)*
Beechcraft Products Inc .... E 989 288-2606
　Durand *(G-4840)*
Birch Point Woodworks .... G 906 322-8761
　Brimley *(G-2100)*
Bird Lofts & Stuff Woodworking ...... G 248 882-1242
　White Lake *(G-18451)*
Birds-Eye Creations Inc .... G 906 337-5095
　Mohawk *(G-11517)*
Boattown Woodshop .... G 586 703-0538
　Mount Clemens *(G-11631)*
Brambles Boodwork LLC .... G 616 446-9118
　Ada *(G-13)*
Britten Woodworks Inc .... F 231 275-5457
　Traverse City *(G-16630)*
Brunt Associates Inc .... E 248 960-8295
　Wixom *(G-18627)*
C & A Wood Products Inc .... F 313 365-8400
　Detroit *(G-4083)*

C & K Hardwoods LLC .... G 269 231-0048
　Three Oaks *(G-16554)*
C & S Millwork Inc .... F 586 465-6470
　Clinton Township *(G-3193)*
C and M Construction .... G 989 213-1955
　Vassar *(G-17578)*
Canusa Inc .... G 906 446-3327
　Gwinn *(G-7583)*
Carlee Woodworking .... G 734 660-0491
　Pinckney *(G-13044)*
Carpenters Friend Woodworking ...... G 231 218-2736
　Interlochen *(G-8680)*
Carson Wood Specialties Inc .... G 269 465-6091
　Stevensville *(G-16242)*
Cedar Log Lbr Millersburg Inc .... G 989 733-2676
　Millersburg *(G-11497)*
Cedar Ridge Custom Wdwkg LLC .... G 248 425-0185
　Oxford *(G-12881)*
Charles A Specialties LLC .... G 231 946-3389
　Traverse City *(G-16645)*
▼ Chippewa Development Inc .... F 269 685-2646
　Plainwell *(G-13071)*
Crossroads Industries Inc .... E 989 732-1233
　Gaylord *(G-6124)*
Ctc Fabricators LLC .... G 586 242-8809
　Clay *(G-3118)*
Custom Craftsmen Woodworking .... G 616 638-4768
　Spring Lake *(G-15810)*
Custom Woodwork & Rmdlg LLC .... G 586 778-9224
　Warren *(G-17769)*
D & D Building Inc .... F 616 248-7908
　Grand Rapids *(G-6626)*
D&D Planning Design Mllwk LLC ..... F 586 754-6500
　Warren *(G-17773)*
Dads Panels Inc .... G 810 245-1871
　Lapeer *(G-9926)*
Dagenham Millworks LLC .... G 616 698-8883
　Grand Rapids *(G-6630)*
Daniel D Slater .... G 989 833-7135
　Riverdale *(G-13863)*
Dean Richard Woodworking .... G 586 764-6586
　Sylvan Lake *(G-16360)*
▲ Decatur Wood Products Inc .... E 269 657-6041
　Decatur *(G-3946)*
Division 6 Fbrction Instlltion .... F 586 200-3030
　Warren *(G-17780)*
Doltek Enterprises Inc .... E 616 837-7828
　Nunica *(G-12579)*
Donato Woodworks .... G 586 899-7430
　Center Line *(G-2681)*
Double Otis Inc .... E 616 878-3998
　Grand Rapids *(G-6656)*
Dovetails Inc .... G 248 674-8777
　Waterford *(G-18118)*
Downriver Creative Woodworking ... G 313 274-4090
　Allen Park *(G-193)*
E Leet Woodworking .... G 269 664-5203
　Plainwell *(G-13076)*
▲ E-Zee Set Wood Products Inc .... G 248 398-0090
　Oak Park *(G-12608)*
Elan Designs Inc .... G 248 682-3000
　Pontiac *(G-13365)*
Elegant Wood Craftsmanship .... G 231 742-0706
　Hart *(G-7751)*
Elegant Woodworking .... G 248 363-3804
　Commerce Township *(G-3526)*
Elenbaas Hardwood Incorporated ... G 269 343-7791
　Kalamazoo *(G-9176)*
Eliason Corporation .... E 269 621-2100
　Hartford *(G-7763)*
Elite Woodworking LLC .... E 586 204-5882
　Saint Clair Shores *(G-14856)*
Emery Design & Woodwork LLC ..... G 734 709-1687
　South Lyon *(G-15434)*
End Grain Woodwork .... G 248 420-3228
　Livonia *(G-10197)*
Eric Henry Woodworks .... G 248 613-5696
　Clarkston *(G-3033)*
▲ Euclid Industries Inc .... C 989 686-8920
　Bay City *(G-1352)*
Family Tradition Wdwkg Plans ...... G 989 871-6688
　Millington *(G-11500)*
Farmhouse Woodworking LLC .... G 269 350-0582
　Baroda *(G-1161)*
▼ Fiber-Char Corporation .... E 989 356-5501
　Alpena *(G-294)*
Five Lakes Manufacturing Inc .... F 586 463-4123
　Clinton Township *(G-3239)*
Foggy Mountain Woodworks .... G 231 675-1757
　Boyne Falls *(G-1907)*

Forsyth Millwork and Farms .... G 810 266-4000
　Byron *(G-2253)*
Freelands Country Upolstery .... G 269 330-2416
　Delton *(G-3963)*
Fwi Inc .... E 231 798-8324
　Norton Shores *(G-12294)*
G F Inc .... G 231 946-5330
　Traverse City *(G-16691)*
G P Woodworking L L C .... G 313 600-9414
　Brighton *(G-1995)*
◆ G-M Wood Products Inc .... D 231 652-2201
　Newaygo *(G-12081)*
General Hardwood Company .... F 313 365-7733
　Detroit *(G-4253)*
George Washburn .... G 269 694-2930
　Otsego *(G-12786)*
GI Millworks Inc .... F 734 451-1100
　Plymouth *(G-13175)*
Goodrich Brothers Inc .... G 989 224-4944
　Saint Johns *(G-14900)*
Goodrich Brothers Inc .... E 989 593-2104
　Pewamo *(G-13028)*
Goodwill Inds Nthrn Mich Inc ..... G 231 779-1311
　Cadillac *(G-2332)*
Goodwill Inds Nthrn Mich Inc ..... G 231 779-1361
　Cadillac *(G-2333)*
Goodwill Inds Nthrn Mich Inc ..... G 231 922-4890
　Traverse City *(G-16696)*
Gordon Woodwork LLC .... G 734 612-3586
　Belleville *(G-1484)*
Grabill Windows & Doors LLC .... E 810 798-2817
　Almont *(G-261)*
Grand Rapids Carvers Inc .... G 616 538-0022
　Grand Rapids *(G-6754)*
Grand Rapids Wood Works .... G 616 690-2889
　Grandville *(G-7380)*
Grand Rapids Woodworking ..... G 616 780-7137
　Grand Rapids *(G-6773)*
Grand Rapids Woodworking LLC .. G 616 301-8719
　Grand Rapids *(G-6774)*
Grand Valley Wood Products Inc .. E 616 475-5890
　Grand Rapids *(G-6779)*
Gravelle Woods .... G 616 617-7712
　Ada *(G-20)*
▼ Great Lake Woods Inc .... C 616 399-3300
　Holland *(G-8057)*
Great Lakes Stair & Case Co .. G 269 465-3777
　Bridgman *(G-1928)*
Great Lakes Wood Products ... G 906 228-3737
　Negaunee *(G-11967)*
Great Lakes Woodworking LLC .. E 248 550-1991
　Orion *(G-12732)*
Great North Woodworks .... G 231 622-6200
　Petoskey *(G-12998)*
Greggs Wood Duck Boxes ...... G 989 770-5204
　Burt *(G-2215)*
Guzman Woodworks .... G 313 436-1912
　Detroit *(G-4287)*
H & R Wood Specialties Inc ... E 269 628-2181
　Gobles *(G-6217)*
Hall Wood Creations .... G 248 645-0983
　Beverly Hills *(G-1664)*
Hambones Wood Works .... G 313 304-5590
　Newport *(G-12102)*
Harris Obrien Woodworks .... G 616 292-2613
　Caledonia *(G-2377)*
Hazeltree Woodworking .... G 517 320-2954
　Marshall *(G-11060)*
▼ Heartland Mills LLC .... F 888 829-5909
　Boyne Falls *(G-1908)*
Heritage Wdwrks Grnd Rpids LLC .. G 616 780-9499
　Grand Rapids *(G-6812)*
Heritage Woodworking .... G 734 753-3368
　New Boston *(G-12009)*
Hickmans Woodworking LLC .. G 616 678-4180
　Kent City *(G-9433)*
Holland Panel Products Inc .. E 616 392-1826
　Holland *(G-8081)*
Hollow Hill Woodworks .... G 906 493-6913
　Drummond Island *(G-4801)*
Homeworks .... G 810 533-2030
　Saint Clair Shores *(G-14865)*
Honey Creek Woodworks .... G 616 706-2539
　Ada *(G-22)*
Hornshaw Wood Works LLC .. G 616 566-0720
　Holland *(G-8088)*
Hunt & Noyer LLC .... G 517 914-6259
　Berkley *(G-1627)*
Iannuzzi Millwork Inc .... E 586 285-1000
　Fraser *(G-5941)*

Employee Codes: A=Over 500 employees, B=251-500
C=101-250, D=51-100, E=20-50, F=10-19, G=3-9

Ideal Millwork Enterprises LLC.............F 248 461-6460
Waterford *(G-18128)*
▲ Idp Inc ....E 248 352-0044
Southfield *(G-15601)*
Industrial Assemblies Inc.......................E 231 865-6500
Fruitport *(G-6063)*
Innovative Woodworking ....G....... 269 926-9663
Benton Harbor *(G-1557)*
Innovative Woodworking ....G....... 616 638-1139
Muskegon *(G-11840)*
Innovtive Dsplay Solutions LLC...........F 616 896-6080
Hudsonville *(G-8586)*
J J Wohlferts Custom Furniture...........F 989 593-3283
Fowler *(G-5829)*
J&N Custom Woodworking....................G....... 517 726-0290
Vermontville *(G-17589)*
Jackieswoodworks..................................G....... 616 914-2961
Norton Shores *(G-12304)*
James Gordon Marsh ....G....... 517 372-8685
Lansing *(G-9856)*
Jeld-Wen Inc...C....... 616 554-3551
Caledonia *(G-2385)*
Jeld-Wen Inc...D....... 616 531-5440
Grand Rapids *(G-6868)*
Jlm Whlsale S/Verett Dukes Inc............F 800 522-2940
Oxford *(G-12891)*
Joe Beam Woodworking ....G....... 269 873-0160
Stevensville *(G-16254)*
Justinscstmgatesandwoodworking......G....... 906 748-1999
Mason *(G-11140)*
Kent Door & Specialty Inc.....................E 616 534-9691
Grand Rapids *(G-6888)*
Kerns Wood Works LLC.........................G....... 734 368-1951
Van Buren Twp *(G-17533)*
Klise Manufacturing Company ....E 616 459-4283
Grand Rapids *(G-6899)*
Kpl Custom Woodworking LLC.............G....... 313 530-5507
Livonia *(G-10267)*
Kropp Woodworking Inc ....F 586 463-2300
Mount Clemens *(G-11646)*
Kropp Woodworking Inc ....G....... 586 997-3000
Sterling Heights *(G-16064)*
Krumrie Saw Mill Services.....................G....... 269 838-9060
Galien *(G-6089)*
L & M Woodworking LLC ....G....... 404 391-3868
Oxford *(G-12894)*
L E Q Inc ....F 248 257-5466
Waterford *(G-18132)*
Lamay Woodworking...............................G....... 734 421-6032
Livonia *(G-10274)*
Lapeer Plating & Plastics Inc................C....... 810 667-4240
Lapeer *(G-9939)*
Lavern Beechy ....G....... 269 651-5095
Sturgis *(G-16300)*
Leelanau Woodworking..........................G....... 231 946-4437
Traverse City *(G-16743)*
Legendary Millwork Inc ....G....... 248 588-5663
Troy *(G-17207)*
Lemica Corporation................................E 313 839-2150
Detroit *(G-4388)*
Lifetime Company...................................G....... 248 862-2578
Bloomfield Hills *(G-1830)*
Live Edge Detroit ....G....... 248 909-2259
Troy *(G-17213)*
Livingston Stairway................................G....... 517 546-7132
Howell *(G-8473)*
Loduca Woodworks LLC........................G....... 734 626-2525
Clinton Township *(G-3280)*
Louisiana-Pacific Corporation..............G....... 906 293-3265
Newberry *(G-12092)*
Lsd Investments Inc ....G....... 248 333-9085
Bloomfield Hills *(G-1832)*
Macb Woodworking LLC........................G....... 734 645-8990
Ann Arbor *(G-560)*
Macomb Stairs Inc ....F 586 226-2800
Shelby Township *(G-15267)*
Magiglide Inc ....F 906 822-7321
Crystal Falls *(G-3743)*
Manufacturing Dynamics Co ....G....... 248 670-0264
Madison Heights *(G-10774)*
Maple Leaf Woodworking.......................G....... 616 262-9754
Orleans *(G-12740)*
Marquis Wood Works ....G....... 810 488-9406
Burtchville *(G-2222)*
Masonite International Corp ....F....... 517 545-5811
Howell *(G-8476)*
Masters Millwork LLC............................F....... 248 987-4511
Madison Heights *(G-10777)*
Maw Ventures Inc...................................E 231 798-8324
Norton Shores *(G-12309)*

MB Woodworks and Co..........................G....... 231 452-6321
Newaygo *(G-12087)*
McCoy Craftsman LLC ....F 616 634-7455
Grand Rapids *(G-6972)*
Mendota Mantels LLC.............................G....... 651 271-7544
Ironwood *(G-8767)*
Metrie Inc..E 313 299-1860
Taylor *(G-16443)*
Michigan Woodwork..............................G....... 517 204-4394
Mason *(G-11145)*
▲ Milliken Millwork Inc..........................B 586 264-0950
Sterling Heights *(G-16101)*
MJB Stairs LLC ....G....... 586 822-9559
Shelby Township *(G-15278)*
Mjbcustomwoodworking.........................G....... 989 695-2737
Freeland *(G-6025)*
▲ Mlc Window Co Inc.............................E 586 731-3500
Shelby Township *(G-15279)*
Mod Interiors Inc.....................................E 586 725-8227
Ira *(G-8702)*
Modern Millwork Inc ....F 248 347-4777
Wixom *(G-18713)*
Modern Woodsmith LLC.........................G....... 906 387-5577
Wetmore *(G-18435)*
Monarch Millwork Inc ....G....... 989 348-8292
Grayling *(G-7467)*
Nacs USA Inc..G....... 800 253-9000
Zeeland *(G-19058)*
North American Forest Products ....G....... 269 663-8500
Edwardsburg *(G-5014)*
▲ North Amrcn Mlding Lqdtion LLC ....E 269 663-5300
Edwardsburg *(G-5015)*
Northern Blind Co....................................G....... 616 299-9399
Sparta *(G-15773)*
Northern Mich Hardwoods Inc...............F 231 347-4575
Petoskey *(G-13008)*
Northern Millwork Co.............................F 313 365-7733
Detroit *(G-4490)*
Northern Outdoor Woodworks LLC ......G....... 231 275-1181
Lake Ann *(G-9543)*
Northern Staircase Co Inc......................F 248 836-0652
Pontiac *(G-13402)*
◆ Novo Distribution LLC ....B 616 772-7272
Zeeland *(G-19061)*
Oak North Manufacturing Inc.................E 906 475-7992
Negaunee *(G-11971)*
▲ Odl Incorporated.................................B....... 616 772-9111
Zeeland *(G-19062)*
Odl Incorporated......................................G 616 772-9111
Zeeland *(G-19063)*
On The Level Woodworking....................G....... 269 429-4570
Stevensville *(G-16262)*
Ornamental Mouldings LLC...................F 616 748-0188
Zeeland *(G-19065)*
Owens Building Co Inc...........................E 989 835-1293
Midland *(G-11401)*
Oxford Woodworks..................................G....... 248 736-3090
Traverse City *(G-16785)*
Pacific Door & Trim.................................G...., 619 887-1786
Harper Woods *(G-7669)*
Parkway Drapery & Uphl Co Inc ....G....... 734 779-1300
Livonia *(G-10360)*
Pete Pullum Company Inc.......................G....... 313 837-9440
Detroit *(G-4521)*
Phil Elenbaas Millwork Inc....................G....... 231 526-8399
Harbor Springs *(G-7655)*
Phil Elenbaas Millwork Inc....................E 616 791-1616
Grand Rapids *(G-7085)*
Pine Tech Inc...E 989 426-0006
Plymouth *(G-13264)*
Poor Boy Woodworks Inc ....F 989 799-9440
Saginaw *(G-14730)*
Prime Wood Products Inc ....G....... 616 399-4700
Holland *(G-8170)*
Quality Craft Woodworking....................G....... 248 343-6358
Milford *(G-11483)*
Quality Wood Products Inc.....................F 989 658-2160
Ubly *(G-17481)*
R & K Woodworking ....G....... 734 741-3664
Howell *(G-8503)*
R Chamberlin Woodworking...................G....... 269 377-7232
Kalamazoo *(G-9312)*
R J Woodworking Inc ....E 231 766-2511
Muskegon *(G-11904)*
Ramzak Woodworking..............................G....... 734 595-8155
Westland *(G-18412)*
Redbird WD Pdts Bldwin Twnship ....G....... 989 362-7670
East Tawas *(G-4922)*
Rekmakker Millwork Inc ....G....... 616 546-3680
Holland *(G-8178)*

Resurgo LLC ....G....... 313 559-2325
Detroit *(G-4570)*
Rfc Woodworks..G....... 810 357-9072
Kalamazoo *(G-9315)*
Richmond Millwork Inc...........................F 586 727-6747
Ira *(G-8710)*
Rohr Woodworking...................................G....... 248 363-9743
West Bloomfield *(G-18310)*
Rosati Specialties LLC.............................G....... 586 783-3866
Clinton Township *(G-3341)*
Royal Enterprises......................................G....... 269 429-5878
Saint Joseph *(G-14959)*
Saurs Custom Woodworking...................G....... 906 288-3202
Toivola *(G-16592)*
Sawdust and Lace.....................................G....... 517 331-4535
Lansing *(G-9735)*
Sawmill Bill Lumber Inc..........................G....... 231 275-3000
Interlochen *(G-8684)*
Schrams Custom Woodworking..............G....... 989 335-0847
Lincoln *(G-10040)*
Scotco Woodworking ....G....... 586 749-9805
Ray *(G-13703)*
Scott Philip Custom Wdwkg LLC ....G....... 616 723-9074
Belmont *(G-1516)*
Select Millwork..G....... 269 685-2646
Plainwell *(G-13095)*
Serenity Woodworking LLC....................G....... 734 812-5429
South Lyon *(G-15456)*
SGS Wood Works LLC ....G....... 239 564-8449
Saline *(G-15038)*
Shayn Allen Marquetry............................G....... 586 991-0445
Shelby Township *(G-15329)*
Simply Woodworking LLC ....G....... 586 405-1080
Grosse Pointe Park *(G-7559)*
Sindelar Fine Woodworking Co..............G....... 269 663-8841
Edwardsburg *(G-5016)*
Snd Manufacturing LLC ....G....... 313 996-5088
Dearborn *(G-3898)*
Specialty Hardwood Moldings................F 734 847-3997
Temperance *(G-16549)*
Sprik Custom Woodworks LLC ....G....... 616 826-0858
Grand Haven *(G-6365)*
Ss Custom Market.....................................G....... 269 816-1311
Three Rivers *(G-16585)*
Stair Specialist Inc...................................G....... 269 420-0486
Battle Creek *(G-1299)*
Standale Lumber and Supply Co............D....... 616 530-8200
Grandville *(G-7419)*
Sterling Millwork Inc................................D....... 248 427-1400
Farmington Hills *(G-5389)*
Strongs Woodworking..............................G....... 989 350-9113
Boyne Falls *(G-1910)*
T & K Woodworks ....G....... 734 868-0028
La Salle *(G-9530)*
T M Wood Products Mfg Inc....................F 586 427-2364
Warren *(G-18032)*
▼ Tafcor Inc...F 269 471-2351
Berrien Springs *(G-1646)*
Tapco Holdings Inc...................................C....... 248 668-6400
Wixom *(G-18766)*
Thomas and Milliken Mllwk Inc..............F 231 386-7236
Northport *(G-12193)*
Thomas Cheal ....G....... 906 288-3487
Toivola *(G-16593)*
Thompson Custom Woodworking ....G....... 616 446-1058
Grand Rapids *(G-7260)*
Three Roses Woodwork ....G....... 248 763-1837
Romeo *(G-14237)*
Timber Coast Woodworks........................G....... 231 287-3042
Spring Lake *(G-15857)*
Timberstone Cstm Woodworks LLC.......G....... 810 227-6404
Brighton *(G-2082)*
Timberview Woodworking ....G....... 517 726-0321
Vermontville *(G-17592)*
Tiq Woodworking LLC...............................G....... 616 206-9369
Clarksville *(G-3080)*
Trend Millwork LLC..................................E 313 383-6300
Lincoln Park *(G-10057)*
Troy Millwork Inc......................................G....... 248 852-8383
Rochester Hills *(G-14133)*
Turner Custom Woodworking..................G....... 810 324-6254
Kenockee *(G-9424)*
Uncle Rons Woodworking ....G....... 248 585-7837
Madison Heights *(G-10851)*
United Mill & Cabinet Company..............F 734 482-1981
Willis *(G-18588)*
Valley Enterprises Ubly Inc.....................F 989 269-6272
Ubly *(G-17484)*
Van Beeks Custom Wood Products......F 616 583-9002
Byron Center *(G-2298)*

SIC SECTION 24 LUMBER AND WOOD PRODUCTS, EXCEPT FURNITURE24 LUMBER AND WOOD PRODUCTS, EXCEPT FURNITURE

Van Enk Woodcrafters LLC ....F 616 931-0090
Zeeland *(G-19086)*
Venture Woodworks ....G....... 616 262-1930
Grand Rapids *(G-7311)*
Virtuoso Custom Creations LLC ....G....... 313 332-1299
Detroit *(G-4668)*
Walton Woodworking ....G....... 248 730-2017
Southfield *(G-15742)*
Wayne-Craft Inc ....F 734 421-8800
Livonia *(G-10468)*
Weatherproof Inc ....E 517 764-1330
Jackson *(G-9034)*
Webber Woodworks LLC ....G....... 517 896-8636
Bath *(G-1174)*
Webers Woodwork LLC ....G....... 989 798-7210
Millington *(G-11504)*
Weyerhaeuser Company ....G....... 906 524-2040
Lanse *(G-9669)*
Wheatons Woodworking LLC ....G....... 616 288-8159
Cedar Springs *(G-2667)*
White Dove Woodworks ....G....... 734 717-6042
Manchester *(G-10892)*
Wholesalemillworkcom ....G....... 616 241-6011
Grand Rapids *(G-7338)*
William S Wixtrom ....G....... 906 376-8247
Republic *(G-13821)*
Winterset Woodworks LLC ....G....... 248 207-8795
Roseville *(G-14494)*
Wismer Wood Works ....G....... 616 262-9444
Lake Odessa *(G-9580)*
Wisner Woodworking ....G....... 231 924-5711
Newaygo *(G-12091)*
▲ **Wood Smiths Inc** ....F 269 372-6432
Kalamazoo *(G-9373)*
Woodcrafters ....G....... 517 741-7423
Sherwood *(G-15387)*
Woodcreek Customs ....G....... 248 761-5652
Bloomfield Hills *(G-1875)*
Woodland Pixie ....G....... 503 330-8033
Bessemer *(G-1651)*
Woodworking Connection Inc ....G....... 616 389-5481
Wayland *(G-18210)*
Woodworks & Design Company ....G....... 517 482-6665
Lansing *(G-9905)*
Wrights Woodworks ....G....... 989 295-7456
Saginaw *(G-14796)*

2434 Wood Kitchen Cabinets

A K Services Inc ....G....... 313 972-1010
Detroit *(G-3972)*
▼ **Albers Cabinet Company** ....G....... 586 727-9090
Lenox *(G-9997)*
Antells Custom Cabinetry ....G....... 616 318-8637
Grand Rapids *(G-6460)*
Autumn Designs LLC ....G....... 269 455-0490
South Haven *(G-15400)*
Avon Cabinets Atkins ....G....... 248 237-1103
Rochester Hills *(G-13959)*
Beaver Creek Cabinets LLC ....G....... 231 821-2861
Holton *(G-8337)*
Behrens Custom Cabinetry LLC ....G....... 269 720-4950
Paw Paw *(G-12941)*
Belash Inc ....G....... 248 379-4444
Wixom *(G-18619)*
Berrien Custom Cabinet Inc ....G....... 269 473-3404
Berrien Springs *(G-1638)*
Better-Bilt Cabinet Co ....G....... 586 469-0080
Mount Clemens *(G-11630)*
Biotec Incorporated ....D....... 616 772-2133
Zeeland *(G-18999)*
Blue Water Cabinetry AMP ....G....... 231 246-2293
Muskegon *(G-11779)*
Bradley Allen Interiors Inc ....G....... 989 689-6770
Rhodes *(G-13822)*
Cabinet Finishers ....G....... 248 635-7584
Farmington Hills *(G-5193)*
Cabinet Headquarters LLC ....G....... 231 286-3207
Norton Shores *(G-12282)*
Cabinet Install Shop ....G....... 586 946-0500
Chesterfield *(G-2856)*
Cabinet One Inc ....G....... 248 625-9440
Clarkston *(G-3022)*
Cabinets By H & K Inc ....G....... 313 903-8500
Inkster *(G-8660)*
Cabinets By Robert Inc ....F 231 947-3261
Traverse City *(G-16636)*
Cabinets Cuntertops Direct LLC ....G....... 616 238-6608
Jenison *(G-9048)*
Cabinets Express ....G....... 810 494-0511
Brighton *(G-1959)*

◆ **Cabinetworks Group Mich LLC** ....B 734 205-4600
Ann Arbor *(G-413)*
Carson Wood Specialties Inc ....G....... 269 465-6091
Stevensville *(G-16242)*
Case Systems Inc ....C....... 989 496-9510
Midland *(G-11327)*
Cg Cabinet Wholesale ....G....... 269 459-6833
Portage *(G-13552)*
Cg Cabinets Wholesale ....G....... 248 583-9666
Madison Heights *(G-10686)*
Charlotte Cabinets Inc ....G....... 517 543-1522
Charlotte *(G-2742)*
Classic Cabinets Interiors LLC ....G....... 517 423-2600
Tecumseh *(G-16491)*
Coast To Coast Cabinets LLC ....G....... 517 719-0118
Okemos *(G-12661)*
Cobblestone Cabinets ....G....... 248 398-3700
Berkley *(G-1624)*
Cole Wagner Cabinetry ....G....... 248 642-5330
Birmingham *(G-1721)*
Cole Wagner Cabinetry ....F 248 852-2406
Rochester Hills *(G-13976)*
Country Custom Cabinets ....G....... 937 354-2163
Lawrence *(G-9981)*
▲ **Crystal Lk Aprtmnts Fmly Ltd P** ....E 586 731-3500
Shelby Township *(G-15199)*
Custom Cabinets & More ....G....... 517 285-7286
Charlotte *(G-2748)*
Custom Cabinets & More LLC ....G....... 734 231-9086
Brownstown *(G-2145)*
Custom Line Cabinets ....G....... 810 459-0414
Commerce Township *(G-3520)*
D & M Cabinet Shop Inc ....G....... 989 479-9271
Ruth *(G-14597)*
Daniel Snderson Cstm Cabinetry ....G....... 231 421-5743
Traverse City *(G-16667)*
David Hirn Cabinets and Contg ....G....... 906 428-1935
Gladstone *(G-6178)*
Dejon Cabinetry Inc ....G....... 586 468-8611
Clinton Township *(G-3218)*
Designtech Custom Interiors ....G....... 989 695-6306
Freeland *(G-6020)*
Dexter Cabinet Works Inc ....G....... 734 426-5035
Dexter *(G-4735)*
Dibbleville Woodwork Co ....G....... 810 750-1139
Fenton *(G-5470)*
Display Cses By Grndpas Cbnets ....G....... 586 506-2222
Macomb *(G-10588)*
Donald K Stappert ....G....... 734 459-0004
Plymouth *(G-13161)*
Dream Custom Cabinets ....G....... 586 718-4812
Fraser *(G-5920)*
Elan Designs Inc ....G....... 248 682-3000
Pontiac *(G-13365)*
Esmies Cabinet ....G....... 269 921-1578
Stevensville *(G-16249)*
Euro-Craft Interiors Inc ....F 586 254-9130
Sterling Heights *(G-16007)*
▲ **European Cabinet Mfg Co** ....E 586 445-8909
Roseville *(G-14406)*
Fallen Oaks Cabinet Shop Inc ....G....... 586 463-4454
Troy *(G-17106)*
Farmington Cabinet Company ....F 248 476-2666
Livonia *(G-10205)*
Flagg Distribution LLC ....G....... 248 926-0510
Wixom *(G-18662)*
Fort Grtiot Cbnets Counter LLC ....G....... 810 364-1924
Port Huron *(G-13478)*
Fwi Inc ....E 231 798-8324
Norton Shores *(G-12294)*
G & G Wood & Supply Inc ....E 586 293-0450
Roseville *(G-14408)*
Gast Cabinet Co ....G....... 269 422-1587
Baroda *(G-1162)*
George Washburn ....G....... 269 694-2930
Otsego *(G-12786)*
Great Lakes Fine Cabinetry ....G....... 906 493-5780
Sault Sainte Marie *(G-15091)*
Greenia Custom Woodworking Inc ....E 989 868-9790
Reese *(G-13806)*
Greenville Cabinet Distri ....G....... 616 225-2424
Greenville *(G-7487)*
Gsa Direct Supply LLC ....G....... 313 739-6375
Detroit *(G-4285)*
Handorn Inc ....E 616 241-6181
Grand Rapids *(G-6801)*
Harbor Kitchen & Bath LLC ....G....... 231 624-8060
Traverse City *(G-16710)*
Hidden Lake Cabinet Trim ....G....... 586 246-9119
Clarkston *(G-3039)*

I S Two ....G....... 616 396-5634
Holland *(G-8091)*
Instyle Cabinets LLC ....G....... 248 589-0300
Royal Oak *(G-14550)*
Interior Spc of Holland ....F 616 396-5634
Holland *(G-8096)*
J B Cutting Inc ....G....... 586 468-4765
Mount Clemens *(G-11644)*
Janice Morse Inc ....E 248 624-7300
West Bloomfield *(G-18293)*
Jmc Custom Cabinetry ....G....... 989 345-0475
West Branch *(G-18329)*
Kaliniak Design LLC ....G....... 616 675-3850
Kent City *(G-9434)*
Kraft Maid Cabinetry ....G....... 734 205-4600
Ann Arbor *(G-543)*
Kurtis Mfg & Distrg Corp ....E 734 522-7600
Livonia *(G-10270)*
Lafata Cabinet Shop ....D....... 586 247-6536
Shelby Township *(G-15255)*
Lakeshore Marble Company Inc ....F 269 429-8241
Stevensville *(G-16257)*
Lakeside Cstm Cbinets Bldg LLC ....G....... 269 718-7960
Sturgis *(G-16299)*
Lakeview Cabinetry ....G....... 810 650-1420
Port Hope *(G-13429)*
Lesso Kitchen and Bath ....G....... 517 662-3230
Adrian *(G-79)*
Lifestyle Kitchen Studio ....G....... 616 454-2563
Grand Rapids *(G-6942)*
Lindas Woodcrafts & Cabinets ....G....... 989 734-2903
Rogers City *(G-14212)*
Ljs Kitchens & Interiors Ltd ....G....... 989 773-2132
Mount Pleasant *(G-11708)*
Lloyds Cabinet Shop Inc ....F 989 879-3015
Pinconning *(G-13061)*
M & K Cabinets LLC ....G....... 313 744-2755
Dearborn Heights *(G-3931)*
M and G Laminated Products ....G....... 517 784-4974
Jackson *(G-8938)*
Marbelite Corp ....E 248 348-1900
Novi *(G-12470)*
Masco Cabinetry LLC ....C....... 517 263-0771
Adrian *(G-82)*
◆ **Masco Corporation** ....A....... 313 274-7400
Livonia *(G-10302)*
Masco Services Inc ....E 313 274-7400
Livonia *(G-10303)*
Merillat Industries LLC ....F 517 263-0269
Adrian *(G-83)*
▲ **Merillat LP** ....C....... 517 263-0771
Adrian *(G-84)*
Mica TEC Inc ....G....... 586 758-4404
Warren *(G-17928)*
Mid Michigan Wood Specialites ....F 989 855-3667
Lyons *(G-10564)*
Mikes Cabinet Shop Inc ....G....... 734 722-1800
Westland *(G-18396)*
Millennium Cabinetry ....F 248 477-4420
Farmington Hills *(G-5321)*
Millennm-The Inside Sltion Inc ....F 248 645-9005
Farmington Hills *(G-5323)*
Millwork Design Group LLC ....G....... 248 472-2178
Milford *(G-11473)*
Miltons Cabinet Shop Inc ....G....... 269 473-2743
Berrien Springs *(G-1645)*
Mj Cabinet Designs ....G....... 734 354-9633
Plymouth *(G-13245)*
New Line Inc ....G....... 586 228-4820
Shelby Township *(G-15289)*
Newcraft Cabinetry ....G....... 269 220-5440
Kalamazoo *(G-9281)*
North State Sales ....G....... 989 681-2806
Saint Louis *(G-14994)*
Nowak Cabinets Inc ....G....... 231 264-8603
Williamsburg *(G-18561)*
Oak North Manufacturing Inc ....E 906 475-7992
Negaunee *(G-11971)*
OBrien Harris Woodworks LLc ....E 616 248-0779
Grand Rapids *(G-7054)*
Options ....G....... 248 855-6151
Franklin *(G-5884)*
Owens Building Co Inc ....E 989 835-1293
Midland *(G-11401)*
Pazzel Inc ....G....... 616 291-0257
Grand Rapids *(G-7074)*
Perry Creek Woodworking Inc ....G....... 989 848-2125
Mio *(G-11514)*
Perspectives Custom Cabinetry ....E 248 288-4100
Troy *(G-17298)*

SIC

Employee Codes: A=Over 500 employees, B=251-500
C=101-250, D=51-100, E=20-50, F=10-19, G=3-9
2022 Harris Michigan
Industrial Directory
749

24 LUMBER AND WOOD PRODUCTS, EXCEPT FURNITURE

Company		Phone
Pinnacle Cabinet Company Inc	E	989 772-3866
Mount Pleasant (G-11731)		
Pioneer Cabinetry Inc	D	810 658-2075
Davison (G-3793)		
Premier Kitchen Cabinetry Inc	G	248 375-0124
Rochester Hills (G-14090)		
Prime Wood Products Inc	G	616 399-4700
Holland (G-8170)		
Putnam Cabinetry	G	248 442-0118
Farmington Hills (G-5358)		
RC Cabinetry	G	734 513-2677
Livonia (G-10383)		
Rich-Wall Custom Cabine	G	734 237-4934
Livonia (G-10387)		
Rohloff Builders Inc	G	989 868-3191
Reese (G-13808)		
Rose Corporation	E	734 426-0005
Dexter (G-4753)		
Ross Cabinets II Inc	F	586 752-7750
Shelby Township (G-15317)		
Rowe Custom Cabinetry	G	517 526-1413
Portland (G-13641)		
Royal Cabinets	G	313 541-1190
Redford (G-13767)		
Sanford Customs LLC	G	586 722-7274
West Bloomfield (G-18311)		
Sawdust Bin Inc	F	906 932-5518
Ironwood (G-8772)		
Shayn Allen Marquetry	G	586 991-0445
Shelby Township (G-15329)		
Silver Creek Cabinets	G	989 387-0858
Gladwin (G-6207)		
Simply Cabinets	G	810 923-8792
Wixom (G-18752)		
Stanisci Design and Mfg Inc	G	248 572-6880
Oxford (G-12920)		
Straight Line Design	G	616 296-0920
Spring Lake (G-15853)		
Surface Expressions LLC	G	231 843-8282
Ludington (G-10552)		
Symphony Cabinetry LLC	G	231 421-5421
Traverse City (G-16847)		
Tims Cabinet Inc	G	989 846-9831
Pinconning (G-13065)		
Tims Custom Cabinets LLC	G	248 912-4154
Commerce Township (G-3578)		
Top Fabricators	G	313 563-7126
Taylor (G-16485)		
USA Custom Cabinet Inc	G	313 945-9796
Dearborn (G-3907)		
Van Daeles Inc	G	734 587-7165
Monroe (G-11588)		
Venetian Cabinets	G	586 580-3288
Shelby Township (G-15365)		
Village Cabinet Shoppe Inc	G	586 264-6464
Sterling Heights (G-16223)		
Visionary Cabinetry and Design	G	248 850-7178
Clawson (G-3111)		
W S Townsend Company	G	517 393-7300
Lansing (G-9903)		
W S Townsend Company	C	269 781-5131
Marshall (G-11078)		
Welker Cabinetry & Millwork	F	248 477-6600
Livonia (G-10471)		
West Michigan Cabinet Supply	F	616 896-6990
Hudsonville (G-8617)		
Woodways Inc	G	616 956-3070
Zeeland (G-19093)		
Woodways Industries LLC	E	616 956-3070
Grand Rapids (G-7350)		
World Wide Cabinets Inc	F	248 683-2680
Sylvan Lake (G-16363)		
Young Cabinetry Inc	G	734 316-2896
Saline (G-15047)		

2435 Hardwood Veneer & Plywood

Company		Phone
August Lilia Family Memorl Fund	G	906 228-6088
Marquette (G-11006)		
Bay Wood Homes Inc	F	989 245-4156
Fenton (G-5456)		
◆ Coldwater Veneer Inc	C	517 278-5676
Coldwater (G-3427)		
▲ Decatur Wood Products Inc	E	269 657-6041
Decatur (G-3946)		
Dyers Sawmill Inc	E	231 768-4438
Leroy (G-10006)		
Forest Corullo Products Corp	E	906 667-0275
Bessemer (G-1649)		
◆ Forte Industries Mill Inc	E	906 753-6256
Stephenson (G-15907)		
J A S Veneer & Lumber Inc	E	906 635-0710
Sault Sainte Marie (G-15092)		
Louisiana-Pacific Corporation	G	906 293-3265
Newberry (G-12092)		
▲ Manthei Inc	C	231 347-4672
Petoskey (G-13004)		
Midwest Panel Systems Inc	F	517 486-4844
Blissfield (G-1770)		
Northern Mich Endocrine Pllc	G	989 281-1125
Roscommon (G-14355)		
Northern Mich Hardwoods Inc	F	231 347-4575
Petoskey (G-13008)		
Northern Mich Mmrals Monuments	G	231 290-2333
Cheboygan (G-2794)		
Northern Mich Supportive Hsing	G	231 929-1309
Traverse City (G-16772)		
Northern Mich Wdding Offciants	G	231 938-1683
Williamsburg (G-18559)		
▲ Northern Michigan Veneers Inc	G	906 428-1082
Gladstone (G-6184)		
Ply-Forms Incorporated	E	989 686-5681
Bay City (G-1387)		
Precision Framing Systems Inc	E	704 588-6680
Taylor (G-16458)		
▼ Programmed Products Corp	D	248 348-7755
Novi (G-12517)		
Quincy Woodwrights LLC	G	808 397-0818
Houghton (G-8390)		
◆ Richelieu America Ltd	E	586 264-1240
Sterling Heights (G-16151)		
Rosati Specialties LLC	G	586 783-3866
Clinton Township (G-3341)		
Timber Pdts Mich Ltd Partnr	G	906 779-2000
Iron Mountain (G-8736)		
Timber Products Co Ltd Partnr	G	906 452-6221
Munising (G-11755)		
Ufp Sauk Rapids LLC	E	320 259-5190
Grand Rapids (G-7292)		

2436 Softwood Veneer & Plywood

Company		Phone
Forest Corullo Products Corp	E	906 667-0275
Bessemer (G-1649)		
◆ Forte Industries Mill Inc	E	906 753-6256
Stephenson (G-15907)		
Louisiana-Pacific Corporation	G	906 293-3265
Newberry (G-12092)		
Ply-Forms Incorporated	E	989 686-5681
Bay City (G-1387)		

2439 Structural Wood Members, NEC

Company		Phone
Allwood Building Components	D	586 727-2731
Richmond (G-13832)		
Bay Wood Homes Inc	F	989 245-4156
Fenton (G-5456)		
Bear Truss - US Lbm LLC	F	989 681-5774
Saint Louis (G-14988)		
Better-Bilt Cabinet Co	G	586 469-0080
Mount Clemens (G-11630)		
Calderwood WD Pdts & Svcs LLC	G	906 852-3232
Trout Creek (G-16897)		
Century Truss	G	248 486-4000
Livonia (G-10153)		
Custom Components Truss Co	E	810 744-0771
Burton (G-2234)		
G & G Wood & Supply Inc	E	586 293-0450
Roseville (G-14408)		
Heart Truss & Engineering Corp	C	517 372-0850
Lansing (G-9703)		
Joseph Miller	G	231 821-2430
Holton (G-8339)		
Ken Luneack Construction Inc	C	989 681-5774
Saint Louis (G-14992)		
Laketon Truss Inc	G	231 798-3467
Norton Shores (G-12308)		
Letherer Truss Inc	D	989 386-4999
Clare (G-2985)		
▲ Lumber & Truss Inc	F	810 664-7290
Lapeer (G-9945)		
Maple Valley Truss Co	F	989 389-4267
Prudenville (G-13658)		
Marshall Bldg Components Corp	E	269 781-4236
Marshall (G-11064)		
Maverick Building Systems LLC	F	248 366-9410
Commerce Township (G-3555)		
Midwest Panel Systems Inc	F	517 486-4844
Blissfield (G-1770)		
North American Forest Products	G	269 663-8500
Edwardsburg (G-5014)		
Precision Framing Systems Inc	E	704 588-6680
Taylor (G-16458)		
Rapid River Rustic Inc	E	906 474-6404
Rapid River (G-13686)		
Riverbend Timber Framing Inc	E	517 486-3629
Blissfield (G-1776)		
Truss Development	G	248 624-8100
Bloomfield Hills (G-1870)		
Truss Technologies Inc	E	231 788-6330
Muskegon (G-11939)		
Trussway	F	713 691-6900
Jenison (G-9074)		
Wendricks Truss Inc	E	906 635-8822
Sault Sainte Marie (G-15104)		
Wendricks Truss Inc	E	906 498-7709
Hermansville (G-7864)		
Wood Tech Inc	G	616 455-0800
Byron Center (G-2303)		

2441 Wood Boxes

Company		Phone
Anbren Inc	G	269 944-5066
Benton Harbor (G-1529)		
Auto Pallets-Boxes Inc	F	248 559-7744
Lathrup Village (G-9975)		
▲ Bennett Wood Specialties Inc	F	616 772-6683
Zeeland (G-18996)		
C & K Box Company Inc	F	517 784-1779
Jackson (G-8830)		
Complete Packaging Inc	D	734 241-2794
Monroe (G-11534)		
Crossroads Industries Inc	G	989 732-1233
Gaylord (G-6124)		
Demeester Wood Products Inc	F	616 677-5995
Coopersville (G-3685)		
Diversified Pdts & Svcs LLC	G	616 836-6600
Holland (G-8014)		
◆ Export Corporation	C	810 227-6153
Brighton (G-1987)		
Garcia Company	G	248 459-0952
Holly (G-8270)		
▼ Michigan Box Company	D	313 873-9500
Detroit (G-4444)		
Mollewood Export Inc	E	248 624-1885
Wixom (G-18714)		
National Case Corporation	G	586 726-1710
Sterling Heights (G-16112)		
▲ Packaging Specialties Inc	E	586 473-6703
Romulus (G-14315)		
Scotts Enterprises Inc	F	989 275-5011
Roscommon (G-14356)		
Shields Classic Toys	G	888 806-2632
Saline (G-15039)		
Vaive Wood Products Co	E	586 949-4900
Macomb (G-10648)		

2448 Wood Pallets & Skids

Company		Phone
AAR Manufacturing Inc	E	231 779-8800
Cadillac (G-2306)		
Acme Pallet Inc	E	616 738-6452
Holland (G-7956)		
Action Pallets Inc	G	248 557-9017
Lathrup Village (G-9973)		
Aj Pallets	F	616 875-8900
Zeeland (G-18989)		
Akers Wood Products Inc	G	269 962-3802
Battle Creek (G-1182)		
All American Container Corp	F	586 949-0000
Macomb (G-10573)		
All Size Pallets	E	810 721-1999
Imlay City (G-8626)		
American Pallet Company LLC	G	231 834-5056
Grant (G-7426)		
Anayas Pallets & Transport Inc	F	313 843-6570
Detroit (G-4018)		
Anbren Inc	G	269 944-5066
Benton Harbor (G-1529)		
Artists Pallet	G	248 889-2440
Highland (G-7882)		
Auto Pallets-Boxes Inc	F	248 559-7744
Lathrup Village (G-9975)		
Auto Pallets-Boxes Inc	G	734 782-1110
Flat Rock (G-5614)		
Baby Pallet	G	248 210-3851
Waterford (G-18103)		
Black River Pallet Company	E	616 772-6211
Zeeland (G-19000)		
Breiten Box & Packaging Co Inc	G	586 469-0800
Harrison Township (G-7690)		
Brindley Lumber & Pallet Co	G	989 345-3497
Lupton (G-10561)		
Bunker & Sons Sawmill LLC	G	989 983-2715
Vanderbilt (G-17568)		

SIC SECTION 24 LUMBER AND WOOD PRODUCTS, EXCEPT FURNITURE24 LUMBER AND WOOD PRODUCTS, EXCEPT FURNITURE

Burnrite Pellet Corporation....G.... 989 429-1067
Clare *(G-2974)*
C & J Pallets Inc....G.... 517 263-7415
Adrian *(G-55)*
C & K Box Company Inc....F.... 517 784-1779
Jackson *(G-8830)*
C&D Pallets Inc....G.... 517 285-5228
Eagle *(G-4851)*
Cannonsburg Wood Products Inc....E.... 616 866-4459
Rockford *(G-14162)*
Caveman Pallets LLC....G.... 616 675-7270
Conklin *(G-3660)*
Complete Packaging Inc....D.... 734 241-2794
Monroe *(G-11534)*
County Line Pallet....G.... 231 834-8416
Kent City *(G-9430)*
Curtis Country Connection LLC....F.... 517 368-5542
Camden *(G-2420)*
D T Fowler Mfg Co Inc....G.... 810 245-9336
Lapeer *(G-9925)*
▲ Delta Containers Inc....C.... 810 742-2730
Bay City *(G-1342)*
▲ Delta Packaging International....G.... 517 321-6548
Lansing *(G-9685)*
Demeester Wood Products Inc....F.... 616 677-5995
Coopersville *(G-3685)*
Discount Pallets....G.... 616 453-5455
Grand Rapids *(G-6650)*
Diversified Pdts & Svcs LLC....G.... 616 836-6600
Holland *(G-8014)*
DRYE Custom Pallets Inc....E.... 313 381-2681
Melvindale *(G-11199)*
Envirnmntal Pllet Slutions Inc....F.... 616 283-1784
Zeeland *(G-19018)*
Fair & Square Pallet & Lbr Co....G.... 989 727-3949
Hubbard Lake *(G-8546)*
Four Way Pallet Service....G.... 734 782-5914
Flat Rock *(G-5621)*
G & D Wood Products Inc....G.... 517 254-4463
Camden *(G-2422)*
Golden Eagle Pallets LLC....F.... 616 233-0970
Wyoming *(G-18875)*
Gonzalez Jr Pallets LLC....G.... 616 885-0201
Grand Rapids *(G-6748)*
Gonzalez Universal Pallets LLC....G.... 616 243-5524
Grand Rapids *(G-6749)*
Grand Industries Inc....E.... 616 846-7120
Grand Haven *(G-6307)*
Great Lakes Pallet Inc....G.... 989 883-9220
Sebewaing *(G-15140)*
Great Northern Lumber Mich LLC....G.... 989 736-6192
Lincoln *(G-10034)*
H & M Pallet LLC....F.... 231 821-8800
Holton *(G-8338)*
Hills Crate Mill Inc....G.... 616 761-3555
Belding *(G-1451)*
Hillsdale Pallet LLC....F.... 517 254-4777
Hillsdale *(G-7937)*
Holland Pallet Repair Inc....E.... 616 875-8642
Holland *(G-8080)*
Hugo Brothers Pallet Mfg....G.... 989 684-5564
Kawkawlin *(G-9417)*
I Pallet LLC....G.... 586 625-2238
Sterling Heights *(G-16045)*
Industrial Packaging Corp....F.... 248 677-0084
Berkley *(G-1628)*
J & G Pallets Inc....G.... 313 921-0222
Detroit *(G-4331)*
Jarvis Saw Mill Inc....G.... 231 861-2078
Shelby *(G-15150)*
Jerrys Pallets....G.... 734 242-1577
Monroe *(G-11552)*
Just Cover It Up....G.... 734 247-4729
Romulus *(G-14293)*
Kamps Inc....E.... 313 381-2681
Detroit *(G-4349)*
Kamps Inc....D.... 616 453-9676
Grand Rapids *(G-6878)*
Kamps Inc....E.... 517 645-2800
Potterville *(G-13646)*
Kamps Inc....E.... 734 281-3300
Taylor *(G-16433)*
Kamps Inc....E.... 269 683-6372
Niles *(G-12140)*
Kamps Inc....E.... 269 342-8113
Kalamazoo *(G-9251)*
▲ Karjo Trucking Inc....F.... 248 597-3700
Troy *(G-17192)*
Kerry J McNeely....G.... 734 776-1928
Livonia *(G-10265)*
Krauter Forest Products LLC....F.... 815 317-6561
Reed City *(G-13794)*
L & M Hardwood & Skids LLC....G.... 734 281-3043
Southgate *(G-15752)*
Lakeland Pallets Inc....E.... 616 949-9515
Grand Rapids *(G-6924)*
Las Tortugas Pallet Co....G.... 313 283-3279
Lincoln Park *(G-10051)*
Less Pay Pallets Inc....G.... 586 649-3800
Harrison Township *(G-7706)*
Lightning Technologies Inc....E.... 248 572-6700
Oxford *(G-12896)*
Lock and Load Corp....G.... 800 975-9658
Marion *(G-10973)*
Luberda Wood Products Inc....G.... 989 876-4334
Omer *(G-12696)*
Maple Valley Pallet Co....F.... 231 228-6641
Maple City *(G-10944)*
Marion Pallet....G.... 231 743-6124
Marion *(G-10974)*
Matelski Lumber Company....E.... 231 549-2780
Boyne Falls *(G-1909)*
Matthews Mill Inc....F.... 989 257-3271
South Branch *(G-15396)*
Metzger Sawmill....G.... 269 963-3022
Battle Creek *(G-1273)*
Michael Chris Storms....G.... 231 263-7516
Kingsley *(G-9525)*
Michigan Pallet Inc....F.... 989 865-9915
Saint Charles *(G-14805)*
Mid West Pallet....G.... 810 919-3072
Burton *(G-2240)*
Midwest Heat Treat Inc....E.... 616 395-9763
Holland *(G-8148)*
Mobile Pallet Service Inc....E.... 269 792-4200
Wayland *(G-18199)*
Nelson Company....G.... 517 788-6117
Jackson *(G-8976)*
Northern Pallet....G.... 989 386-7556
Clare *(G-2991)*
Ottawa Forest Products Inc....E.... 906 932-9701
Ironwood *(G-8769)*
Paliot Solutions LLC....G.... 616 648-5939
Plymouth *(G-13260)*
Pallet Man....G.... 269 274-8825
Springfield *(G-15873)*
Pallet Pros LLC....G.... 586 864-3353
Center Line *(G-2684)*
Patchwood Products Inc....G.... 989 742-2605
Hillman *(G-7915)*
Patchwood Products Inc....F.... 989 742-2605
Lachine *(G-9533)*
Pink Pallet LLC....G.... 586 873-2982
Grand Blanc *(G-6256)*
Prairie Wood Products Inc....F.... 269 659-1163
Sturgis *(G-16319)*
Precision Pallet LLC....G.... 252 943-5193
Charlevoix *(G-2729)*
Premier Pallet Inc....F.... 269 483-8000
White Pigeon *(G-18485)*
◆ Process Systems Inc....E.... 586 757-5711
Warren *(G-17977)*
Quality Pallet Inc....G.... 231 788-5161
Muskegon *(G-11901)*
Quality Pallets LLC....F.... 231 825-8361
Mc Bain *(G-11186)*
R Andrews Pallet Co Inc....F.... 616 677-3270
Marne *(G-10998)*
Rochester Pallet....G.... 248 266-1094
Rochester Hills *(G-14102)*
Rose Acres Pallets LLC....G.... 989 268-3074
Vestaburg *(G-17595)*
Rose Acres Tallets....G.... 989 268-3074
Vestaburg *(G-17596)*
Ross Pallet Co....G.... 810 966-4945
Port Huron *(G-13524)*
Royal Pallets Inc....E.... 616 261-2884
Grandville *(G-7415)*
Scotts Enterprises Inc....F.... 989 275-5011
Roscommon *(G-14356)*
Sfi Acquisition Inc....E.... 248 471-1500
Farmington Hills *(G-5377)*
Spartan Pallet LLC....G.... 586 291-8898
Clinton Township *(G-3361)*
Stoutenburg Inc....E.... 810 648-4400
Sandusky *(G-15068)*
Tamsco Inc....E.... 586 415-1500
Clinton Township *(G-3372)*
Tk Enterprises Inc....F.... 989 865-9915
Saint Charles *(G-14810)*
Tommy Joe Reed....G.... 989 291-5768
Sheridan *(G-15384)*
Union Pallet & Cont Co Inc....E.... 517 279-4888
Coldwater *(G-3459)*
Vaive Wood Products Co....E.... 586 949-4900
Macomb *(G-10648)*
Vocational Strategies Inc....F.... 906 482-6142
Calumet *(G-2415)*
WB Pallets Inc....E.... 616 669-3000
Hudsonville *(G-8615)*
White Pallet Chair....G.... 989 424-8771
Clare *(G-3001)*
World of Pallets and Trucking....G.... 313 899-2000
Detroit *(G-4691)*

2449 Wood Containers, NEC

AAR Manufacturing Inc....E.... 231 779-8800
Cadillac *(G-2306)*
▲ Action Wood Technologies Inc....E.... 586 468-2300
Clinton Township *(G-3155)*
AS Property Management Inc....F.... 586 427-8000
Warren *(G-17716)*
Black River Pallet Company....E.... 616 772-6211
Zeeland *(G-19000)*
C & K Box Company Inc....F.... 517 784-1779
Jackson *(G-8830)*
Classic Container Corporation....C.... 734 853-3000
Livonia *(G-10159)*
Croze Nest Cooperage LLC....G.... 616 805-9132
Grand Rapids *(G-6615)*
▲ Delta Packaging International....G.... 517 321-6548
Lansing *(G-9685)*
Demeester Wood Products Inc....F.... 616 677-5995
Coopersville *(G-3685)*
Diversified Pdts & Svcs LLC....G.... 616 836-6600
Holland *(G-8014)*
G & D Wood Products Inc....G.... 517 254-4463
Camden *(G-2422)*
Kamps Inc....E.... 517 645-2800
Potterville *(G-13646)*
Luberda Wood Products Inc....G.... 989 876-4334
Omer *(G-12696)*
Millers Woodworking....G.... 989 386-8110
Clare *(G-2987)*
Mollewood Export Inc....E.... 248 624-1885
Wixom *(G-18714)*
Monte Package Company LLC....E.... 269 849-1722
Riverside *(G-13864)*
Northern Packaging Mi Inc....F.... 734 692-4700
Grosse Ile *(G-7524)*
Scotts Enterprises Inc....F.... 989 275-5011
Roscommon *(G-14356)*
Tk Enterprises Inc....F.... 989 865-9915
Saint Charles *(G-14810)*
Union Pallet & Cont Co Inc....E.... 517 279-4888
Coldwater *(G-3459)*

2451 Mobile Homes

Advantage Housing Inc....G.... 269 792-6291
Wayland *(G-18187)*
CCI Arnheim Inc....G.... 906 353-6330
Baraga *(G-1136)*
Cedar Mobile Home Service Inc....G.... 616 696-1580
Cedar Springs *(G-2643)*
Champion Home Builders Inc....D.... 248 614-8200
Troy *(G-17007)*
Dream Clean Trucking Service....G.... 313 285-4029
New Boston *(G-12008)*
Flex Building Systems LLC....G.... 586 803-6000
Sterling Heights *(G-16017)*
Hometown America LLC....G.... 810 686-7020
Mount Morris *(G-11672)*
Larkhite Development System....G.... 616 457-6722
Jenison *(G-9060)*
Montrose Trailers Inc....G.... 810 639-7431
Montrose *(G-11607)*
Skyline Champion Corporation....A.... 248 614-8211
Troy *(G-17356)*
Sun Communities Inc....A.... 248 208-2500
Southfield *(G-15711)*
Woodland Park & Sales....G.... 810 229-2397
Brighton *(G-2098)*

2452 Prefabricated Wood Buildings & Cmp-nts

/// 702 Cedar River Lbr Inc....E.... 906 497-5365
Powers *(G-13648)*
4d Building Inc....F.... 248 799-7384
Milford *(G-11452)*

S I C

Employee Codes: A=Over 500 employees, B=251-500
C=101-250, D=51-100, E=20-50, F=10-19, G=3-9

2022 Harris Michigan
Industrial Directory

751

24 LUMBER AND WOOD PRODUCTS, EXCEPT FURNITURE

Ahs LLC .... G 888 355-3050
 Holland (G-7959)
▲ Backyard Products LLC .... G 734 242-6900
 Monroe (G-11526)
Bay Wood Homes Inc .... F 989 245-4156
 Fenton (G-5456)
Beaver Log Homes Inc .... F 231 258-5020
 Kalkaska (G-9383)
Classic Log Homes Incorporated .... F 989 821-6118
 Higgins Lake (G-7876)
Dickinson Homes Inc .... E 906 774-5800
 Kingsford (G-9508)
E B I Inc .... G 810 227-8180
 Brighton (G-1980)
G B Wolfgram and Sons Inc .... F 231 238-4638
 Indian River (G-8652)
Harman Lumber & Supply Inc .... G 269 641-5424
 Union (G-17488)
Higgins Lake Family Campground ...... G 989 821-6891
 Clinton Township (G-3253)
Home Inspection Protection .... G 906 370-6704
 Hancock (G-7619)
Hunt Hoppough Custom Crafted .... G 616 794-3455
 Belding (G-1452)
Koskis Log Homes Inc .... G 906 884-4937
 Ontonagon (G-12713)
Little Buildings Inc .... G 586 752-7100
 Romeo (G-14228)
Log Home Specialty .... G 231 943-9410
 Traverse City (G-16747)
Maple Island Log Homes Inc .... D 231 821-2151
 Twin Lake (G-17470)
Marshalls Crossing .... G 810 639-4740
 Montrose (G-11606)
Masons Lumber & Hardware Inc .... G 989 685-3999
 Rose City (G-14365)
Michigan Dutch Barns Inc .... F 616 693-2754
 Lake Odessa (G-9578)
Midwest Panel Systems Inc .... F 517 486-4844
 Blissfield (G-1770)
North Arrow Log Homes Inc .... G 906 484-5524
 Pickford (G-13031)
Northern Michigan Log Homes .... G 989 345-7463
 West Branch (G-18332)
Pageant Homes Inc .... G 517 694-0431
 Holt (G-8324)
Pine Creek Log Home .... G 231 848-4436
 Wellston (G-18259)
Pioneer Pole Buildings N Inc .... F 989 386-2570
 Clare (G-2994)
Premier Panel Company .... F 734 427-1700
 Livonia (G-10374)
Ritz-Craft Corp PA Inc .... C 517 849-7425
 Jonesville (G-9100)
Riverbend Timber Framing Inc .... F 517 486-3629
 Blissfield (G-1776)
Skyline Champion Corporation .... A 248 614-8211
 Troy (G-17356)
Source Capital Backyard LLC .... F 734 242-6900
 Monroe (G-11573)
Starwood Homes .... G 734 340-2326
 Ypsilanti (G-18979)
T & M Homes .... G 989 239-4699
 Saginaw (G-14772)
U P North Structures .... G 989 654-2350
 Sterling (G-15914)
Woodtech Builders Inc .... F 906 932-8055
 Ironwood (G-8773)

2491 Wood Preserving

/// 702 Cedar River Lbr Inc .... E 906 497-5365
 Powers (G-13648)
▲ 2nd Chance Wood Company .... G 989 472-4488
 Durand (G-4838)
Biewer of Lansing LLC .... E 810 326-3930
 Saint Clair (G-14814)
Biewer Sawmill Inc .... E 231 825-2855
 Mc Bain (G-11178)
▲ Charter Inds Extrusions LLC .... G 616 245-3388
 Kentwood (G-9448)
Hager Wood Preserving LLC .... G 616 248-0905
 Wyoming (G-18879)
Hoover Treated Wood Pdts Inc .... F 313 365-4200
 Detroit (G-4305)
Hydrolake Inc .... G 231 825-2233
 Mc Bain (G-11182)
JKL Hardwoods Inc .... F 906 265-9130
 Iron River (G-8744)
John A Biewer Co of Illinois .... C 810 326-3930
 Saint Clair (G-14833)

▲ John A Biewer Lumber Company .... E 810 329-4789
 Saint Clair (G-14834)
John A Biewer Lumber Company .... E 231 825-2855
 Mc Bain (G-11183)
Paris North Hardwood Lumber .... E 231 584-2500
 Elmira (G-5040)
Riverbend Woodworing .... G 231 869-4965
 Pentwater (G-12974)
Straits Corporation .... F 989 684-5088
 Tawas City (G-16368)
Straits Operations Company .... F 989 684-5088
 Tawas City (G-16369)
Straits Service Corporation .... G 989 684-5088
 Tawas City (G-16370)
Straits Wood Treating Inc .... G 989 684-5088
 Tawas City (G-16371)
Ufp Lansing LLC .... G 517 322-0025
 Lansing (G-9795)
▲ United Global Sourcing Inc .... F 248 952-5700
 Troy (G-17412)
Utility Supply and Cnstr Co .... G 231 832-2297
 Reed City (G-13802)
West Branch Wood Treating Inc .... G 989 343-0066
 West Branch (G-18346)
Yooper WD Wrks Restoration LLC ..... G 906 203-0056
 Sault Sainte Marie (G-15105)

2493 Reconstituted Wood Prdts

Abcor Industries LLC .... F 616 994-9577
 Holland (G-7952)
Alpena Biorefinery .... F 989 340-1190
 Alpena (G-276)
▼ Applegate Insul Systems Inc .... E 517 521-3545
 Webberville (G-18241)
Arauco North America Inc .... C 800 261-4896
 Grayling (G-7456)
Bourne Industries Inc .... E 989 743-3461
 Corunna (G-3705)
Brookfield Inc .... G 616 997-9663
 Coopersville (G-3681)
Central Wood and Strapping .... G 231 743-2800
 Marion (G-10971)
Dorel Home Furnishings Inc .... C 269 782-8661
 Dowagiac (G-4781)
Fultz Manufacturing Inc .... G 231 947-5801
 Traverse City (G-16690)
Hammond Publishing Company .... F 810 686-8879
 Mount Morris (G-11671)
Louisiana-Pacific Corporation .... G 906 293-3265
 Newberry (G-12092)
Norbord Panels USA Inc .... A 248 608-0387
 Rochester (G-13913)
Northeastern Products Corp .... E 906 265-6241
 Caspian (G-2608)
▲ Nu-Wool Co Inc .... D 800 748-0128
 Jenison (G-9065)
Ox Engineered Products LLC .... F 248 289-9950
 Northville (G-12250)
Ox Engineered Products LLC .... D 269 435-2425
 Constantine (G-3673)
Weyerhaeuser Company .... F 989 348-2881
 Grayling (G-7471)

2499 Wood Prdts, NEC

1732 Brentwood LLC .... G 248 457-9695
 Troy (G-16898)
Aisin Holdings America Inc .... G 734 453-5551
 Northville (G-12195)
◆ Anthony and Company .... F 906 786-7573
 Escanaba (G-5057)
Apple Fence Co .... F 231 276-9888
 Grawn (G-7449)
▼ Applegate Insul Systems Inc .... E 517 521-3545
 Webberville (G-18241)
Art of Custom Framing Inc .... G 248 435-3726
 Troy (G-16953)
Astro Wood Stake Inc .... G 616 875-8118
 Zeeland (G-18994)
Ausable Woodworking Co Inc .... E 989 348-7086
 Frederic (G-6014)
Bainbridge Manufacturing Inc .... G 616 447-7631
 Grand Rapids (G-6491)
Bally Block Co .... G 231 347-4170
 Petoskey (G-12989)
Beaver Creek Wood Products LLC ..... G 920 680-9663
 Menominee (G-11228)
Blade Industrial Products Inc .... G 248 773-7400
 Wixom (G-18621)
Bremer Authentic Ingredients .... E 616 772-9100
 Zeeland (G-19002)

Buck-Spica Equipment Ltd .... F 269 792-2251
 Wayland (G-18192)
Burlwoodbox .... G 734 662-7274
 Ann Arbor (G-410)
Cabin-N-Woods LLC .... G 248 828-4138
 Troy (G-16991)
◆ Cards of Wood Inc .... G 616 887-8680
 Belmont (G-1504)
Cherry Creek Post LLC .... G 231 734-2466
 Evart (G-5122)
Chivis Sportsman Cases .... G 231 834-1162
 Grant (G-7428)
CHR W LLC .... F 989 755-4000
 Saginaw (G-14628)
Clarey Custom Frmng & Art LLC .... G 989 415-4152
 Bay City (G-1339)
Clawson Custom Woodwork LLC ...... G 248 515-5336
 Clawson (G-3090)
Connexion Inc .... G 248 453-5177
 Pontiac (G-13355)
Contractors Fence Service .... E 313 592-1300
 Detroit (G-4102)
Custom Door Parts .... F 616 949-5000
 Byron Center (G-2265)
Derby Fabg Solutions LLC .... D 616 866-1650
 Rockford (G-14164)
Dko Intl .... F 248 926-9115
 Commerce Township (G-3523)
Doltek Enterprises Inc .... G 616 837-7828
 Nunica (G-12579)
Don Machalk Sons Fencing Corp .... E 906 753-4002
 Ingalls (G-8657)
Dynamic Wood Solutions .... G 616 935-7727
 Spring Lake (G-15811)
Easy Dock Corp .... G 231 750-5052
 Muskegon (G-11808)
Enviro Industries Inc .... G 906 492-3402
 Paradise (G-12931)
Ewc Woodhaven Inc .... G 734 552-3731
 Woodhaven (G-18800)
▲ Faulkner Fabricators Inc .... F 269 473-3073
 Berrien Springs (G-1641)
Genstone LLC .... G 517 902-4730
 Adrian (G-70)
▲ Heath Manufacturing Company ...... E 616 997-8181
 Coopersville (G-3688)
Holland Bowl Mill .... F 616 396-6513
 Holland (G-8075)
Hollywood Dry Cleaners .... G 734 922-2630
 Westland (G-18383)
Holy Art Framing .... G 248 634-8190
 Holly (G-8276)
Home Style Co .... G 989 871-3654
 Millington (G-11501)
Hydrolake Inc .... G 231 825-2233
 Reed City (G-13791)
Hydrolake Inc .... G 231 825-2233
 Mc Bain (G-11181)
Indus Technologies Inc .... F 630 915-8034
 Ypsilanti (G-18955)
Innovtive Dsplay Solutions LLC .... F 616 896-6080
 Hudsonville (G-8586)
Ironwood Consulting LLC .... G 616 916-9111
 Rockford (G-14171)
Jonathan Showalter .... G 269 496-7001
 Mendon (G-11218)
Joy of Moldings LLC .... G 248 543-9754
 Berkley (G-1629)
Kamps Inc .... E 313 381-2681
 Detroit (G-4349)
Kamps Inc .... D 616 453-9676
 Grand Rapids (G-6878)
Kells Sawmill Inc .... G 906 753-2778
 Stephenson (G-15908)
Klein Bros Fence & Stakes LLC .... G 248 684-6919
 Milford (G-11468)
Koetje Wood Products Inc .... G 616 393-9191
 Holland (G-8114)
Ladder Carolina Company Inc .... F 734 482-5946
 Ypsilanti (G-18961)
Larson-Juhl US LLC .... G 734 416-3302
 Plymouth (G-13217)
Lyle Jamieson Wood Turning .... G 231 947-2348
 Traverse City (G-16749)
▲ Maine Ornamental LLC .... F 800 556-8449
 White Pigeon (G-18482)
Mark Beem .... G 231 510-8122
 Lake City (G-9550)
Martin Products Company Inc .... G 269 651-1725
 Sturgis (G-16304)

Mbwwproducts Inc F 616 464-1650
Grand Rapids *(G-6969)*
▲ Michigan Ladder Company LLC F 734 482-5946
Ypsilanti *(G-18967)*
Michigan Wood Fibers Llc G 616 875-2241
Zeeland *(G-19053)*
Michigan Wood Fuels LLC F 616 355-4955
Holland *(G-8147)*
◆ Millworks Engineering Inc F 517 741-5511
Union City *(G-17496)*
Mitten Made Woodcrafts LLC G 616 430-2762
Grand Rapids *(G-7013)*
Nevill Supply Incorporated G 989 386-4522
Clare *(G-2989)*
Newberry Wood Enterprises Inc G 906 293-3131
Newberry *(G-12098)*
▲ Nu-Wool Co Inc D 800 748-0128
Jenison *(G-9065)*
Oakwood Sports Inc G 517 321-6852
Lansing *(G-9782)*
◆ Oakwood Veneer Company F 248 720-0288
Troy *(G-17285)*
Paddle King Inc F 989 235-6776
Carson City *(G-2594)*
▲ Paddlesports Warehouse Inc G 231 757-9051
Scottville *(G-15136)*
Paddletek LLC F 269 340-5967
Niles *(G-12156)*
Panel Processing New Jersey G 856 317-1998
Alpena *(G-308)*
Randy & Sandy Davis G 248 887-7124
Highland *(G-7899)*
Rapid River Rustic Inc E 906 474-6404
Rapid River *(G-13686)*
▲ Rhino Seed & Landscape Sup LLC F 800 482-3130
Wayland *(G-18203)*
▲ Richwood Industries Inc E 616 243-2700
Grand Rapids *(G-7154)*
Russell Farms Inc G 269 349-6120
Kalamazoo *(G-9322)*
S Wood Enterprises LLC G 989 673-8150
Caro *(G-2580)*
▲ Sheffler Manufacturing LLC F 248 409-0966
Clarkston *(G-3064)*
▲ Silver Street Incorporated E 231 861-2194
Shelby *(G-15160)*
Smith Manufacturing Co Inc F 269 925-8155
Benton Harbor *(G-1586)*
Sparkling Woodsby LLC G 313 724-0455
Dearborn *(G-3900)*
T J Northwoods Services LLC G 906 250-3509
Ishpeming *(G-8782)*
Thompson Art Glass Inc G 810 225-8766
Brighton *(G-2081)*
Timeless Picture Framing G 231 233-2221
Fountain *(G-5828)*
Toms World of Wood G 517 264-2836
Adrian *(G-99)*
Tree Tech G 248 543-2166
Royal Oak *(G-14585)*
Ufp Lansing LLC G 517 322-0025
Lansing *(G-9795)*
▲ Veldheer Tulip Garden Inc E 616 399-1900
Holland *(G-8235)*
Wellwood Solutions LLC G 734 368-0368
Saline *(G-15044)*
Williams Management Group LLC G 248 506-7967
Detroit *(G-4684)*
Wood Contracting LLC G 989 479-6037
Harbor Beach *(G-7638)*
Wood Plus Cloth G 231 421-8710
Traverse City *(G-16881)*
Wood Shop Inc G 231 582-9835
Boyne City *(G-1906)*
Wood Wonders G 313 461-2369
Belleville *(G-1496)*
Woodrum Services LLC G 616 827-1197
Kentwood *(G-9483)*

25 FURNITURE AND FIXTURES

2511 Wood Household Furniture

A K Services Inc G 313 972-1010
Detroit *(G-3972)*
A Lasting Impression Inc G 616 847-2380
Spring Lake *(G-15800)*
Alo LLC G 313 318-9029
Detroit *(G-4004)*
Anderson Manufacturing Co Inc F 906 863-8223
Menominee *(G-11226)*
Audia Woodworking & Fine Furn F 586 296-6330
Clinton Township *(G-3174)*
▲ Backyard Play Systems LLC G 734 242-6900
Monroe *(G-11525)*
▲ Backyard Products LLC G 734 242-6900
Monroe *(G-11526)*
Backyard Services LLC G 734 242-6900
Monroe *(G-11527)*
Best Self Storage G 810 227-7050
Brighton *(G-1951)*
Center of World Woodshop Inc G 269 469-5687
Three Oaks *(G-16555)*
Charles Phipps and Sons Ltd F 810 359-7141
Lexington *(G-10027)*
Charlotte Cabinets Inc G 517 543-1522
Charlotte *(G-2742)*
Compass Interiors LLC F 231 348-5353
Petoskey *(G-12994)*
Context Furniture L L C G 248 200-0724
Ferndale *(G-5535)*
Contract Furn Solutions Inc E 734 941-2750
Brownstown *(G-2144)*
Craftwood Industries Inc E 616 796-1209
Holland *(G-8006)*
Custom Interiors of Toledo G 419 865-3090
Ottawa Lake *(G-12805)*
Deweys Lumberville Inc G 313 885-0960
Grosse Pointe *(G-7530)*
Dorel Home Furnishings Inc C 269 782-8661
Dowagiac *(G-4781)*
Ejw Contract Inc G 616 293-5181
Whitmore Lake *(G-18531)*
▲ European Cabinet Mfg Co E 586 445-8909
Roseville *(G-14406)*
Fwi Inc E 231 798-8324
Norton Shores *(G-12294)*
G&J Products & Services G 734 522-2984
Westland *(G-18373)*
◆ Genesis Seating Inc D 616 954-1040
Grand Rapids *(G-6739)*
Grand Rapids Carvers Inc E 616 538-0022
Grand Rapids *(G-6754)*
▲ Grand Rapids Chair Company C 616 774-0561
Byron Center *(G-2275)*
Great Lakes Wood Products G 906 228-3737
Negaunee *(G-11967)*
H L F Furniture Incorporated E 734 697-3000
Van Buren Twp *(G-17528)*
Hearthwoods Ltd Inc G 269 469-5551
Lakeside *(G-9639)*
▲ Hekman Furniture Company E 616 748-2660
Zeeland *(G-19034)*
▼ Industrial Woodworking Corp E 616 741-9663
Zeeland *(G-19045)*
◆ Jack-Post Corporation E 269 695-7000
Buchanan *(G-2197)*
Janice Morse Inc E 248 624-7300
West Bloomfield *(G-18293)*
Kaliniak Design LLC G 616 675-3850
Kent City *(G-9434)*
▲ Kent Upholstery Inc G 248 332-7260
Pontiac *(G-13392)*
▲ Kentwood Manufacturing Co E 616 698-6370
Byron Center *(G-2279)*
▲ Kindel Furniture Company LLC C 616 243-3676
Grand Rapids *(G-6896)*
▲ La-Z-Boy Casegoods Inc E 734 242-1444
Monroe *(G-11555)*
◆ La-Z-Boy Incorporated A 734 242-1444
Monroe *(G-11557)*
▼ Lakeland Mills Inc E 989 427-5133
Edmore *(G-4993)*
Lapointe Cedar Products Inc G 906 753-4072
Ingalls *(G-8658)*
M C M Fixture Company Inc F 248 547-9280
Hazel Park *(G-7830)*
Meeders Dim & Lbr Pdts Co G 231 587-8611
Mancelona *(G-10874)*
▲ Merdel Game Manufacturing Co G 231 845-1263
Ludington *(G-10544)*
◆ Mien Company Inc F 616 818-1970
Grand Rapids *(G-7008)*
Millennm-The Inside Sltion Inc F 248 645-9005
Farmington Hills *(G-5323)*
Nicholas E Kappel G 810 404-9486
Sandusky *(G-15064)*
Nu-Tran LLC G 616 350-9575
Wyoming *(G-18897)*
◆ Nuvar Inc E 616 394-5779
Holland *(G-8157)*
Perspectives Custom Cabinetry E 248 288-4100
Troy *(G-17298)*
Picwood USA LLC G 844 802-1599
Kalamazoo *(G-9295)*
Prime Wood Products Inc G 616 399-4700
Holland *(G-8170)*
▲ R-Bo Co Inc F 616 748-9733
Zeeland *(G-19076)*
▲ Rgm New Ventures Inc D 248 624-5050
Wixom *(G-18742)*
Rooms of Grand Rapids LLC G 616 260-1452
Spring Lake *(G-15847)*
Sawdust Bin Inc F 906 932-5518
Ironwood *(G-8772)*
Serendipity Woods G 269 217-8197
Kalamazoo *(G-9331)*
Shelfgenie Southeastern Mich G 248 805-1834
Rochester *(G-13929)*
Shields Classic Toys G 888 806-2632
Saline *(G-15039)*
Shop Makarios LLC F 800 479-0032
Byron Center *(G-2295)*
Source Capital Backyard LLC F 734 242-6900
Monroe *(G-11573)*
▲ Stow Company C 616 399-3311
Holland *(G-8205)*
▲ Van Zee Acquisitions Inc F 616 855-7000
Grand Rapids *(G-7305)*
White Pine Furniture LLC G 269 366-4469
Kalamazoo *(G-9368)*
Woodard—Cm LLC C 989 725-4265
Owosso *(G-12869)*
Woodcraft Customs LLC G 248 987-4473
Farmington Hills *(G-5415)*
Woodcrafters G 517 741-7423
Sherwood *(G-15387)*
▲ Woodland Creek Furniture Inc E 231 258-2146
Kalkaska *(G-9412)*
Woodways Inc G 616 956-3070
Zeeland *(G-19093)*
Woodways Industries LLC E 616 956-3070
Grand Rapids *(G-7350)*

2512 Wood Household Furniture, Upholstered

Debbink and Sons Inc G 231 845-6421
Ludington *(G-10533)*
Eid Real Estates LLC G 717 471-5996
Rochester Hills *(G-14001)*
Homespun Furniture Inc F 734 284-6277
Riverview *(G-13874)*
▲ Kent Upholstery Inc G 248 332-7260
Pontiac *(G-13392)*
La-Z-Boy Global Limited G 734 241-2438
Monroe *(G-11556)*
◆ La-Z-Boy Incorporated A 734 242-1444
Monroe *(G-11557)*
◆ Lzb Manufacturing Inc G 734 242-1444
Monroe *(G-11559)*
◆ Sherwood Studios Inc E 248 855-1600
West Bloomfield *(G-18312)*

2514 Metal Household Furniture

Crazy Metals LLC G 810 730-9489
Grand Blanc *(G-6239)*
CTS Welding G 269 521-4481
Bloomingdale *(G-1876)*
◆ Flanders Industries Inc C 906 863-4491
Menominee *(G-11238)*
◆ Jack-Post Corporation E 269 695-7000
Buchanan *(G-2197)*
M C M Fixture Company Inc F 248 547-9280
Hazel Park *(G-7830)*
Martin and Hattie Rasche Inc D 616 245-1223
Grand Rapids *(G-6962)*
▼ MTS Burgess LLC D 734 847-2937
Temperance *(G-16542)*
Premium Machine & Tool Inc F 989 855-3326
Lyons *(G-10565)*
Rivmax Manufacturing Inc F 517 784-2556
Jackson *(G-8996)*
Spec International Inc F 616 248-3022
Grand Rapids *(G-7211)*

2515 Mattresses & Bedsprings

Artisans Cstm Mmory Mattresses F 989 793-3208
Saginaw *(G-14605)*
Capitol Bedding Co Inc F 615 370-7000
Lansing *(G-9677)*

Employee Codes: A=Over 500 employees, B=251-500
C=101-250, D=51-100, E=20-50, F=10-19, G=3-9

25 FURNITURE AND FIXTURES25 FURNITURE AND FIXTURES SIC SECTION

Clare Bedding Mfg Co ....E.... 906 789-9902
Escanaba *(G-5065)*
▲ **Comfort Mattress Co** ....D.... 586 293-4000
Roseville *(G-14387)*
Helping Hearts Helping Hands ....G.... 248 980-5090
Constantine *(G-3667)*
Indratech LLC ....G.... 502 381-5798
West Bloomfield *(G-18291)*
Indratech LLC ....E.... 248 377-1877
Troy *(G-17165)*
Jonathan Stevens Mattress Co ....G.... 616 243-4342
Grand Rapids *(G-6873)*
Leggett & Platt Incorporated ....G.... 417 358-8131
Detroit *(G-4387)*
Leggett Platt Components Inc ....D.... 616 784-7000
Sparta *(G-15771)*
Marrs Discount Furniture ....G.... 989 720-5436
Owosso *(G-12840)*
Mattress Wholesale ....G.... 248 968-2200
Oak Park *(G-12626)*
Midwest Quality Bedding Inc ....G.... 614 504-5971
Waterford *(G-18138)*
◆ **Recticel Foam Corporation** ....G.... 248 241-9100
Clarkston *(G-3059)*
Richards Quality Bedding Co ....E.... 616 363-0070
Grand Rapids *(G-7153)*

2517 Wood T V, Radio, Phono & Sewing Cabinets

▲ **European Cabinet Mfg Co** ....E.... 586 445-8909
Roseville *(G-14406)*
George Washburn ....G.... 269 694-2930
Otsego *(G-12786)*
Millennm-The Inside Sltion Inc ....F.... 248 645-9005
Farmington Hills *(G-5323)*
Pazzel Inc ....G.... 616 291-0257
Grand Rapids *(G-7074)*
Ross Cabinets II Inc ....F.... 586 752-7750
Shelby Township *(G-15317)*
Sterling Millwork Inc ....D.... 248 427-1400
Farmington Hills *(G-5389)*
Woodways Inc ....G.... 616 956-3070
Zeeland *(G-19093)*

2519 Household Furniture, NEC

Allstate HM Leisure Strlng Hts ....G.... 734 838-6500
Sterling Heights *(G-15928)*
D & R Fabrication Inc ....D.... 616 794-1130
Belding *(G-1444)*
◆ **Flanders Industries Inc** ....C.... 906 863-4491
Menominee *(G-11238)*
▲ **Innovative Pdts Unlimited Inc** ....E.... 269 684-5050
Niles *(G-12138)*
New Line Inc ....G.... 586 228-4820
Shelby Township *(G-15289)*
Nickels Boat Works Inc ....F.... 810 767-4050
Flint *(G-5738)*
Vita Talalay ....G.... 425 214-4732
Grandville *(G-7423)*

2521 Wood Office Furniture

Behrens Custom Cabinetry LLC ....G.... 269 720-4950
Paw Paw *(G-12941)*
Bold Companies Inc ....D.... 231 773-8026
Muskegon *(G-11782)*
Bourne Industries Inc ....E.... 989 743-3461
Corunna *(G-3705)*
Case Systems Inc ....C.... 989 496-9510
Midland *(G-11327)*
Cornerstone Furniture Inc ....G.... 269 795-3379
Hastings *(G-7784)*
Counterpoint By Hlf ....G.... 734 699-7100
Van Buren Twp *(G-17521)*
Craftwood Industries Inc ....E.... 616 796-1209
Holland *(G-8006)*
Custom Components Corporation ....F.... 616 523-1111
Ionia *(G-8688)*
Custom Crafters ....G.... 269 763-9180
Bellevue *(G-1497)*
Cygnus Inc ....E.... 231 347-5404
Petoskey *(G-12996)*
D & M Cabinet Shop Inc ....G.... 989 479-9271
Ruth *(G-14597)*
Debbink and Sons Inc ....G.... 231 845-6421
Ludington *(G-10533)*
Dynamic Wood Products Inc ....G.... 616 897-8114
Saranac *(G-15077)*
Farnell Contracting Inc ....F.... 810 714-3421
Linden *(G-10061)*
Fwi Inc ....E.... 231 798-8324
Norton Shores *(G-12294)*
◆ **Genesis Seating Inc** ....D.... 616 954-1040
Grand Rapids *(G-6739)*
Grand Rapids Carvers Inc ....E.... 616 538-0022
Grand Rapids *(G-6754)*
Grand Valley Wood Products Inc ....E.... 616 475-5890
Grand Rapids *(G-6779)*
Great Lakes Woodworking Co Inc ....E.... 313 892-8500
Detroit *(G-4277)*
H L F Furniture Incorporated ....E.... 734 697-3000
Van Buren Twp *(G-17528)*
◆ **Haworth Inc** ....A.... 616 393-3000
Holland *(G-8067)*
Haworth Hong Kong LLC ....G.... 616 393-3484
Gladstone *(G-6181)*
◆ **Haworth International Ltd** ....A.... 616 393-3000
Holland *(G-8068)*
Holland Stitchcraft Inc ....F.... 616 399-3868
Holland *(G-8085)*
Howe US Inc ....D.... 616 419-2226
Grand Rapids *(G-6821)*
▼ **Interior Concepts Corporation** ....E.... 616 842-5550
Spring Lake *(G-15827)*
Jsj Corporation ....C.... 616 847-7000
Spring Lake *(G-15828)*
◆ **Jsj Furniture Corporation** ....B.... 616 847-6534
Grand Haven *(G-6326)*
Konwinski Kabnets Inc ....G.... 989 773-2906
Mount Pleasant *(G-11706)*
◆ **Michigan Tube Swgers Fbrctors** ....B.... 734 847-3875
Temperance *(G-16541)*
◆ **Millerknoll Inc** ....A.... 616 654-3000
Zeeland *(G-19056)*
Millerknoll Inc ....G.... 616 949-3660
Grand Rapids *(G-7012)*
Mooreco Inc ....E.... 616 451-7800
Grand Rapids *(G-7028)*
▼ **Nucraft Furniture Company** ....C.... 616 784-6016
Comstock Park *(G-3630)*
Paladin Ind Inc ....E.... 616 698-7495
Grand Rapids *(G-7068)*
Pazzel Inc ....G.... 616 291-0257
Grand Rapids *(G-7074)*
Primeway Inc ....F.... 248 583-6922
Royal Oak *(G-14569)*
▲ **R T London Company** ....D.... 616 364-4800
Grand Rapids *(G-7135)*
Rose Corporation ....E.... 734 426-0005
Dexter *(G-4753)*
S & J Inc ....G.... 248 299-0822
Rochester Hills *(G-14104)*
▲ **S F Gilmore Inc** ....C.... 616 475-5100
Grand Rapids *(G-7175)*
▲ **Silver Street Incorporated** ....E.... 231 861-2194
Shelby *(G-15160)*
◆ **Steelcase Inc** ....A.... 616 247-2710
Grand Rapids *(G-7224)*
T F Boyer Industries Inc ....G.... 248 674-8420
Waterford *(G-18169)*
Tims Cabinet Inc ....G.... 989 846-9831
Pinconning *(G-13065)*
Tranquil Systems Intl LLC ....F.... 800 631-0212
Clare *(G-3000)*
◆ **Trendway Corporation** ....B.... 616 399-3900
Holland *(G-8226)*
West Mich Off Interiors Inc ....G.... 269 344-0768
Kalamazoo *(G-9367)*
West Shore Services Inc ....E.... 616 895-4347
Allendale *(G-229)*
Woodard—Cm LLC ....C.... 989 725-4265
Owosso *(G-12869)*
Woodways Inc ....G.... 616 956-3070
Zeeland *(G-19093)*

2522 Office Furniture, Except Wood

▲ **Agritek Industries Inc** ....D.... 616 786-9200
Holland *(G-7958)*
◆ **American Seating Company** ....B.... 616 732-6561
Grand Rapids *(G-6454)*
American Seating Company ....F.... 616 732-6600
Grand Rapids *(G-6455)*
Amneon Acquisitions LLC ....F.... 616 895-6640
Holland *(G-7965)*
Anso Products ....G.... 248 357-2300
Southfield *(G-15489)*
▲ **Autoexec Inc** ....G.... 616 971-0080
Grand Rapids *(G-6484)*
▲ **Avantis Inc** ....G.... 616 285-8000
Grand Rapids *(G-6486)*
▼ **Bostontec Inc** ....G.... 989 496-9510
Midland *(G-11324)*
Cerny Industries LLC ....E.... 231 929-2140
Traverse City *(G-16643)*
▲ **Contract Source & Assembly Inc** ....F.... 616 897-2186
Grand Rapids *(G-6599)*
Counterpoint By Hlf ....G.... 734 699-7100
Van Buren Twp *(G-17521)*
Craftwood Industries Inc ....E.... 616 796-1209
Holland *(G-8006)*
Custom Components Corporation ....F.... 616 523-1111
Ionia *(G-8688)*
▲ **Electra-Tec Inc** ....G.... 269 694-6652
Otsego *(G-12785)*
▲ **Greenfield Cabinetry Inc** ....F.... 586 759-3300
Warren *(G-17839)*
Haskell Office ....G.... 616 988-0880
Wyoming *(G-18881)*
◆ **Haworth Inc** ....A.... 616 393-3000
Holland *(G-8067)*
Haworth Hong Kong LLC ....G.... 616 393-3484
Gladstone *(G-6181)*
◆ **Haworth International Ltd** ....A.... 616 393-3000
Holland *(G-8068)*
Integrated Metal Tech Inc ....C.... 616 844-3032
Spring Lake *(G-15825)*
▼ **Interior Concepts Corporation** ....E.... 616 842-5550
Spring Lake *(G-15827)*
Jem Computers Inc ....F.... 586 783-3400
Clinton Township *(G-3264)*
◆ **Jsj Corporation** ....E.... 616 842-6350
Grand Haven *(G-6324)*
Kessebohmer Ergonomie Amer Inc ....G.... 616 202-1239
Grand Rapids *(G-6894)*
▲ **Metal Arc Inc** ....E.... 231 865-3111
Muskegon *(G-11868)*
▲ **Metal Components LLC** ....D.... 616 252-1900
Grand Rapids *(G-6978)*
◆ **Millerknoll Inc** ....A.... 616 654-3000
Zeeland *(G-19056)*
◆ **Mobile Office Vehicle Inc** ....G.... 616 971-0080
Grand Rapids *(G-7016)*
Mooreco Inc ....E.... 616 451-7800
Grand Rapids *(G-7028)*
Office Design & Furn LLC ....G.... 734 217-2717
Jackson *(G-8979)*
Office Station Enterprises Inc ....F.... 616 633-3339
Grandville *(G-7406)*
Premium Machine & Tool Inc ....F.... 989 855-3326
Lyons *(G-10565)*
◆ **Srg Global Coatings LLC** ....C.... 248 509-1100
Troy *(G-17369)*
◆ **Steelcase Inc** ....A.... 616 247-2710
Grand Rapids *(G-7224)*
Systems Design & Installation ....G.... 269 543-4204
Fennville *(G-5442)*
Total Innovative Mfg LLC ....F.... 616 399-9903
Holland *(G-8222)*
◆ **Trendway Corporation** ....B.... 616 399-3900
Holland *(G-8226)*
Trendway Svcs Organization LLC ....G.... 616 994-5327
Holland *(G-8227)*
Tvb Inc ....G.... 616 456-9629
Grand Rapids *(G-7283)*
◆ **Ventura Manufacturing Inc** ....C.... 616 772-7405
Zeeland *(G-19088)*
West Mich Off Interiors Inc ....G.... 269 344-0768
Kalamazoo *(G-9367)*

2531 Public Building & Related Furniture

Adient Inc ....A.... 734 254-5000
Plymouth *(G-13114)*
Alr Products Inc ....F.... 517 649-2243
Mulliken *(G-11748)*
American Athletic ....F.... 231 798-7300
Muskegon *(G-11768)*
American Metal Fab Inc ....D.... 269 279-5108
Three Rivers *(G-16563)*
◆ **American Seating Company** ....B.... 616 732-6561
Grand Rapids *(G-6454)*
Baker Road Upholstery Inc ....G.... 616 794-3027
Belding *(G-1436)*
Bourne Industries Inc ....E.... 989 743-3461
Corunna *(G-3705)*
Bracy & Associates Ltd ....G.... 616 298-8120
Holland *(G-7980)*
Bridgewater Interiors LLC ....A.... 586 753-3072
Warren *(G-17743)*
▲ **Bridgewater Interiors LLC** ....C.... 313 842-3300
Detroit *(G-4070)*

▲ Brill Company Inc ....E 231 843-2430
Ludington (G-10528)
Carson Wood Specialties Inc........G....... 269 465-6091
Stevensville (G-16242)
Counterpoint By Hlf........G....... 734 699-7100
Van Buren Twp (G-17521)
Craftwood Industries Inc........E 616 796-1209
Holland (G-8006)
Everest Expedition LLC........D....... 616 392-1848
Holland (G-8032)
Faurecia Auto Seating LLC........B 248 563-9241
Highland Park (G-7905)
Faurecia Auto Seating LLC........C 248 563-9241
Highland Park (G-7906)
▲ Fisher & Company Incorporated .....B 586 746-2000
Saint Clair Shores (G-14858)
Flint Stool & Chair Co Inc........G....... 810 235-7001
Flint (G-5702)
Four Lkes Spcial Asssment Dst ....G....... 989 941-3005
Midland (G-11365)
Furniture Partners LLC........G....... 616 355-3051
Holland (G-8044)
Grand Rapids Carvers Inc........E 616 538-0022
Grand Rapids (G-6754)
Greene Manufacturing Inc........E 734 428-8304
Chelsea (G-2813)
▲ Hoover Universal Inc ....E 734 454-0994
Plymouth (G-13190)
▲ Integrated Mfg & Assembly LLC.......B 734 530-5600
Detroit (G-4322)
◆ Interkal LLC........C....... 269 349-1521
Kalamazoo (G-9224)
◆ Irwin Seating Holding Company ....B 616 574-7400
Grand Rapids (G-6854)
▼ ITW Dahti Seating ....E 616 866-1323
Rockford (G-14172)
Joes Tables LLC........G....... 989 846-4970
Standish (G-15889)
Johnson Controls Inc........G....... 734 254-5000
Plymouth (G-13204)
Kawkawlin Manufacturing Co........G....... 989 684-5470
Midland (G-11381)
Kingdom Building Merchandise........G....... 313 334-3866
Detroit (G-4363)
▲ Knoedler Manufacturers Inc ....F 269 969-7722
Battle Creek (G-1264)
◆ Kotocorp (usa) Inc........G....... 269 349-1521
Kalamazoo (G-9255)
▲ Lanzen Incorporated........E 586 771-7070
Bruce Twp (G-2174)
Lear Corporation........B 248 447-1563
Detroit (G-4384)
Lear Corporation........G....... 248 447-1500
Mason (G-11141)
◆ Lear Corporation ....B 248 447-1500
Southfield (G-15628)
Lear European Operations Corp ....G....... 248 447-1500
Southfield (G-15629)
Midwest Seating Solutions Inc ....F 616 222-0636
Grand Rapids (G-7007)
Milcare Inc ....B 616 654-8000
Zeeland (G-19055)
◆ Millerknoll Inc ....A 616 654-3000
Zeeland (G-19056)
Milsco LLC........E 517 787-3650
Jackson (G-8965)
Multiform Studios LLC ....G....... 248 437-5964
South Lyon (G-15447)
▲ Promax Engineering LLC ....C 734 979-0888
Westland (G-18408)
▲ R T London Company........D....... 616 364-4800
Grand Rapids (G-7135)
Raven Acquisition LLC........B 734 254-5000
Holly (G-8291)
◆ Recaro Automotive North Amer........D 586 210-2600
Clinton Township (G-3331)
Recaro North America Inc........B 734 254-4704
Clinton Township (G-3332)
Recycletech Products Inc ....F 517 649-2243
Mulliken (G-11750)
Stadium Bleachers LLC........G....... 810 245-6258
Lapeer (G-9962)
Subassembly Plus Inc........E 616 395-2075
Holland (G-8207)
▲ Tachi-S Engineering USA Inc........D 248 478-5050
Farmington Hills (G-5397)
Telescopic Seating Systems LLC........F 855 713-0118
Grand Haven (G-6370)
TMC Furniture Inc ....G....... 734 622-0080
Ann Arbor (G-694)
TMC Furniture Inc ....G....... 734 622-0080
Kentwood (G-9482)
▲ Toyo Seat USA Corporation ....C 810 724-0300
Imlay City (G-8648)
Woodard—Cm LLC ....C 989 725-4265
Owosso (G-12869)
▲ Woodbridge Holdings Inc........G....... 248 288-0100
Troy (G-17451)
Worden Group LLC........D....... 616 392-1848
Holland (G-8252)
Yanfeng US Automotive ....G....... 616 394-1523
Holland (G-8257)

2541 Wood, Office & Store Fixtures

A Lasting Impression Inc ....G....... 616 847-2380
Spring Lake (G-15800)
AME For Auto Dealers Inc........G....... 248 720-0245
Auburn Hills (G-780)
Ameristeel Inc ....E 586 585-5250
Fraser (G-5894)
Bay Wood Homes Inc ....F 989 245-4156
Fenton (G-5456)
Behrens Custom Cabinetry LLC........G....... 269 720-4950
Paw Paw (G-12941)
▲ Bennett Wood Specialties Inc........F 616 772-6683
Zeeland (G-18996)
Bourne Industries Inc ....E 989 743-3461
Corunna (G-3705)
Carpenters Cabinets........G....... 989 777-1070
Saginaw (G-14621)
Competitive Edge Wood Spc Inc........D....... 616 842-1063
Muskegon (G-11794)
Custom Components Corporation ....F 616 523-1111
Ionia (G-8688)
Custom Crafters........G....... 269 763-9180
Bellevue (G-1497)
Dads Panels Inc ....G....... 810 245-1871
Lapeer (G-9926)
Dallas Design Inc ....G....... 810 238-4546
Flint (G-5682)
▲ Design Fabrications Inc ....D....... 248 597-0988
Madison Heights (G-10705)
▲ European Cabinet Mfg Co........E 586 445-8909
Roseville (G-14406)
Ferrante Manufacturing Co ....E 313 571-1111
Detroit (G-4231)
Fwi Inc........E 231 798-8324
Norton Shores (G-12294)
G & G Wood & Supply Inc ....E 586 293-0450
Roseville (G-14408)
G & W Display Fixtures Inc ....E 517 369-7110
Bronson (G-2112)
Gast Cabinet Co........G....... 269 422-1587
Baroda (G-1162)
Grand Valley Wood Products Inc ....E 616 475-5890
Grand Rapids (G-6779)
▲ Great American Base Company ....E 734 722-7700
Westland (G-18376)
▲ Greenfield Cabinetry Inc ....F 586 759-3300
Warren (G-17839)
H & R Wood Specialties Inc ....E 269 628-2181
Gobles (G-6217)
H L F Furniture Incorporated ....E 734 697-3000
Van Buren Twp (G-17528)
◆ Harbor Industries Inc ....D....... 616 842-5330
Grand Haven (G-6312)
Harbor Industries Inc........D....... 616 842-5330
Charlevoix (G-2718)
Harbor Industries Inc........D....... 616 842-5330
Grand Haven (G-6313)
Harbor Industries Inc........D....... 231 547-3280
Charlevoix (G-2717)
▼ Hilco Fixture Finders LLC ....E 616 453-1300
Grand Rapids (G-6815)
Holsinger Manufacturing Corp ....E 989 684-3101
Kawkawlin (G-9416)
Hudsonville Products LLC........G....... 616 836-1904
Grand Rapids (G-6824)
J & J Laminate Connection Inc........G....... 810 227-1824
Brighton (G-2014)
◆ Knape & Vogt Manufacturing Co........A 616 459-3311
Grand Rapids (G-6900)
Korcast Products Incorporated........G....... 248 740-2340
Troy (G-17196)
Korcast Products Incorporated........G....... 248 740-2340
Troy (G-17197)
Kreations Inc ....F 313 255-1230
Detroit (G-4367)
KS Liquidating LLC........G....... 248 577-8220
Madison Heights (G-10765)
Kurtis Mfg & Distrg Corp........E 734 522-7600
Livonia (G-10270)
Lafata Cabinet Shop ....D....... 586 247-6536
Shelby Township (G-15255)
M and G Laminated Products ....G....... 517 784-4974
Jackson (G-8938)
Maw Ventures Inc........E 231 798-8324
Norton Shores (G-12309)
Mica Crafters Inc........F 517 548-2924
Howell (G-8479)
Michigan Maple Block Company........D....... 231 347-4170
Petoskey (G-13006)
Millennm-The Inside Sltion Inc ....F 248 645-9005
Farmington Hills (G-5323)
◆ Millerknoll Inc ....A 616 654-3000
Zeeland (G-19056)
▲ Modular Systems Inc ....G....... 231 865-3167
Fruitport (G-6067)
National Millwork Inc ....E 248 307-1299
Madison Heights (G-10788)
Nieboers Pit Stop........G....... 616 997-2026
Coopersville (G-3694)
Nu-Tran LLC ....G....... 616 350-9575
Wyoming (G-18897)
Owens Building Co Inc........E 989 835-1293
Midland (G-11401)
Pageant Homes Inc........G....... 517 694-0431
Holt (G-8324)
Panel Processing Oregon Inc ....D....... 989 356-9007
Alpena (G-309)
Panel Processing Texas Inc........E 903 586-2423
Alpena (G-310)
Paxton Products Inc ....E 517 627-3688
Lansing (G-9783)
PCI Industries Inc........D....... 248 542-2570
Oak Park (G-12637)
▲ PDC ....F 269 651-9975
Sturgis (G-16317)
Pohls Custom Counter Tops........G....... 989 593-2174
Fowler (G-5831)
▼ Programmed Products Corp........D....... 248 348-7755
Novi (G-12517)
Reis Custom Cabinets........G....... 586 791-4925
Reese (G-13807)
Ross Cabinets II Inc........F 586 752-7750
Shelby Township (G-15317)
Royal Cabinet Inc........F 517 787-2940
Jackson (G-8999)
Sterling Millwork Inc........D....... 248 427-1400
Farmington Hills (G-5389)
Unislat LLC........G....... 616 844-4211
Grand Haven (G-6374)
Van Zee Corporation........E 616 245-9000
Grand Rapids (G-7306)
Village Cabinet Shoppe Inc........G....... 586 264-6464
Sterling Heights (G-16223)
W S Townsend Company ....C 269 781-5131
Marshall (G-11078)
Zuckero & Sons Inc ....E 586 772-3377
Roseville (G-14497)

2542 Partitions & Fixtures, Except Wood

Allen Pattern of Michigan........F 269 963-4131
Battle Creek (G-1184)
Arbor Gage & Tooling Inc........E 616 454-8266
Grand Rapids (G-6466)
Arlington Display Inds Inc........G....... 313 837-1212
Detroit (G-4027)
Associated Rack Corporation........G....... 616 554-6004
Grand Rapids (G-6477)
Basc Manufacturing Inc ....G....... 248 360-2272
Commerce Township (G-3514)
◆ Borroughs LLC ....D....... 269 342-0161
Kalamazoo (G-9139)
Casper Corporation ....E 248 442-9000
Farmington Hills (G-5200)
CF Plastic Fabricating Inc........G....... 586 954-1296
Harrison Township (G-7692)
Construction Retail Svcs Inc ....G....... 586 469-2289
Clinton Township (G-3210)
▲ Creative Solutions Group Inc ....D....... 248 288-9700
Clawson (G-3092)
Creative Solutions Group Inc ....G....... 734 425-2257
Redford (G-13727)
Dads Panels Inc........G....... 810 245-1871
Lapeer (G-9926)
Dee-Blast Corporation........F 269 428-2400
Stevensville (G-16246)
F F Industries ....G....... 313 291-7600
Taylor (G-16416)

S I C

Employee Codes: A=Over 500 employees, B=251-500
C=101-250, D=51-100, E=20-50, F=10-19, G=3-9
2022 Harris Michigan
Industrial Directory
755

25 FURNITURE AND FIXTURES

Company		Phone
Ferrante Manufacturing Co	E	313 571-1111
Detroit (G-4231)		
Fixture Max Inc	G	517 376-6421
Howell (G-8455)		
Fmmb LLC	E	313 372-7420
Detroit (G-4239)		
G & W Display Fixtures Inc	E	517 369-7110
Bronson (G-2112)		
◆ Glastender Inc	B	989 752-4275
Saginaw (G-14652)		
Grand Valley Wood Products Inc	E	616 475-5890
Grand Rapids (G-6779)		
▲ Greenfield Cabinetry Inc	F	586 759-3300
Warren (G-17839)		
H G Geiger Manufacturing Co	E	517 369-7357
Bronson (G-2114)		
Harbor Industries Inc	D	231 547-3280
Charlevoix (G-2717)		
▲ Hss Industries Inc	E	231 946-6101
Traverse City (G-16717)		
Impert Industries Inc	G	269 694-2727
Otsego (G-12788)		
J H P Inc	G	248 588-0110
Madison Heights (G-10750)		
▼ JMJ Inc	F	269 948-2828
Hastings (G-7801)		
◆ Knape & Vogt Manufacturing Co	A	616 459-3311
Grand Rapids (G-6900)		
▲ L & S Products LLC	G	517 238-4645
Coldwater (G-3442)		
Loudon Steel Inc	E	989 871-9353
Millington (G-11502)		
▲ Mega Wall Inc	F	616 647-4190
Comstock Park (G-3624)		
Michalski Enterprises Inc	E	517 703-0777
Lansing (G-9716)		
◆ Millerknoll Inc	A	616 654-3000
Zeeland (G-19056)		
National Case Corporation	G	586 726-1710
Sterling Heights (G-16112)		
▲ National Intgrated Systems Inc	F	734 927-3030
Wixom (G-18716)		
Phoenix Fixtures LLC (az)	G	616 847-0895
Spring Lake (G-15842)		
Pinnacle Cabinet Company Inc	E	989 772-3866
Mount Pleasant (G-11731)		
Pipp MBL Stor Systems Hldg Cor	C	616 735-9100
Walker (G-17646)		
▼ Royal Design & Manufacturing	D	248 588-0110
Madison Heights (G-10821)		
SC Custom Display Inc	G	616 940-0563
Kentwood (G-9479)		
Sfi Acquisition Inc	E	248 471-1500
Farmington Hills (G-5377)		
▲ Shaw & Slavsky Inc	E	313 834-3990
Detroit (G-4589)		
Shaw & Slavsky Inc	F	313 834-3990
Detroit (G-4590)		
Shield Material Handling Inc	D	248 418-0986
Auburn Hills (G-1032)		
Signature Wall Solutions Inc	F	616 366-4242
Midland (G-11417)		
◆ Structural Concepts Corp	A	231 798-8888
Norton Shores (G-12335)		
Structural Plastics Inc	E	810 953-9400
Holly (G-8296)		
T M Shea Products Inc	F	800 992-5233
Troy (G-17383)		
Tarpon Industries Inc	E	810 364-7421
Marysville (G-11105)		
Top Shop Inc	G	517 323-9085
Lansing (G-9744)		
Vista Manufacturing Inc	E	616 719-5520
Walker (G-17656)		

2591 Drapery Hardware, Window Blinds & Shades

Company		Phone
A ME Vertical Incorporated	G	248 720-0245
Troy (G-16900)		
Advantage Blnds Shds Shtters L	F	248 399-2154
Royal Oak (G-14504)		
All About Interiors	G	616 452-8998
Grand Rapids (G-6444)		
Blind Bull LLC	G	616 516-4881
Allendale (G-215)		
Blind Spot and More LLC	G	616 828-6495
Byron Center (G-2260)		
Blinds and Designs Inc	F	770 971-5524
Wixom (G-18623)		
Custom Verticals Unlimited	G	734 522-1615
Oak Park (G-12603)		
Dave Brand	G	269 651-4693
Sturgis (G-16287)		
Detroit Custom Services Inc	E	586 465-3631
Mount Clemens (G-11636)		
Elsie Inc	G	734 421-8844
Livonia (G-10196)		
Expressive Window Fashions	G	269 663-8833
Edwardsburg (G-5006)		
Kyler Industries Inc	G	616 392-1042
Holland (G-8117)		
Lorne Hanley	G	248 547-9865
Huntington Woods (G-8622)		
McDonald Wholesale Distributor	G	313 273-2870
Detroit (G-4423)		
Melody Digiglio	G	586 754-4405
Warren (G-17923)		
Mid-Michigan Blinds	G	810 225-8488
Brighton (G-2034)		
MSC Blinds & Shades Inc	G	269 489-5188
Bronson (G-2119)		
Muskegon Awning & Mfg Co	E	231 759-0911
Muskegon (G-11879)		
Parkway Drapery & Uphl Co Inc	G	734 779-1300
Livonia (G-10360)		
PCI Industries Inc	D	248 542-2570
Oak Park (G-12637)		
Protein Cheesecake Company	G	248 495-3258
Rochester (G-13923)		
Royal Crest Inc	G	248 399-2476
Oak Park (G-12642)		
Sheer Madness Drap & Blinds	G	248 379-2145
Macomb (G-10634)		
▲ Signature Designs Inc	G	248 426-9735
Farmington Hills (G-5378)		
▲ Sophias Textiles & Furn Inc	G	586 759-6231
Center Line (G-2687)		
Sunburst Shutters	G	248 674-4600
Waterford (G-18167)		
Time For Blinds Inc	G	248 363-9174
White Lake (G-18469)		
Triangle Window Fashions Inc	G	616 538-9676
Wyoming (G-18914)		
Vertical Detroit	G	313 732-9463
Detroit (G-4667)		
Vertical Wrks Blinds & Drapery	G	586 992-2600
Washington (G-18090)		

2599 Furniture & Fixtures, NEC

Company		Phone
At Home	G	313 769-4200
Dearborn (G-3811)		
B & W Woodwork Inc	G	616 772-4577
Holland (G-7969)		
Bakes & Kropp Ltd	F	888 206-0015
Mount Clemens (G-11629)		
Banta Furniture Company	F	616 575-8180
Grand Rapids (G-6494)		
Benchwork Inc	G	586 464-6699
Clinton Township (G-3182)		
▲ Billco Acquisition LLC	E	616 928-0637
Holland (G-7976)		
Boars Belly	G	231 722-2627
Muskegon (G-11781)		
▲ Brill Company Inc	G	231 843-2430
Ludington (G-10528)		
Consort Corporation	G	269 388-4532
Kalamazoo (G-9151)		
CTS Welding	G	269 521-4481
Bloomingdale (G-1876)		
Custom Components Corporation	F	616 523-1111
Ionia (G-8688)		
Discount Restaurant & Supply	G	574 370-9574
Wyoming (G-18869)		
Firehouse Woodworks LLC	G	616 285-2300
Grand Rapids (G-6707)		
Frank Terlecki Company Inc	F	586 759-5770
Warren (G-17818)		
H E Lyons Inc	F	517 467-2232
Adrian (G-72)		
Harborfront Interiors Inc	G	231 777-3838
Muskegon (G-11835)		
◆ Holland Bar Stool Company	F	616 399-5530
Holland (G-8074)		
Holland Stitchcraft Inc	F	616 399-3868
Holland (G-8085)		
Holsinger Manufacturing Corp	F	989 684-3101
Kawkawlin (G-9416)		
▲ Innovative Pdts Unlimited Inc	E	269 684-5050
Niles (G-12138)		
Jays Famous Fd Hotdogs & More	G	313 648-7225
Detroit (G-4336)		
Karps Kitchens & Baths Inc	G	989 732-7676
Gaylord (G-6137)		
Kci Prentis Building	F	313 578-4400
Detroit (G-4355)		
La Rosa Refrigeration & Eqp Co	G	313 368-6620
Detroit (G-4371)		
M and G Laminated Products	G	517 784-4974
Jackson (G-8938)		
Mr ES Eatery LLC	G	313 502-9256
Sterling Heights (G-16104)		
Newkirk and Associates Inc	G	616 863-9899
Rockford (G-14181)		
Orangebox Us Inc	G	616 988-8624
Grand Rapids (G-7062)		
Paladin Ind Inc	G	616 698-7495
Grand Rapids (G-7068)		
Perfect Dish LLC	G	734 272-9871
Taylor (G-16456)		
Pinnacle Cabinet Company Inc	E	989 772-3866
Mount Pleasant (G-11731)		
Robbie DS LLC	G	989 992-0153
Saginaw (G-14738)		
Schmaltz Hsptlity Westland LLC	G	734 728-6170
Bloomfield Hills (G-1861)		
Shop Makarios LLC	F	800 479-0032
Byron Center (G-2295)		
Sista Roles Cuisine LLC	G	313 588-1142
Detroit (G-4596)		
Stryker Far East Inc	A	269 385-2600
Portage (G-13618)		
Superior Fixture & Tooling LLC	G	616 828-1566
Grand Rapids (G-7237)		
▲ Symbiote Inc	G	616 772-1790
Zeeland (G-19083)		
West Michigan Gage Inc	F	616 735-0585
Walker (G-17657)		
Wm Kloeffler Industries Inc	G	810 765-4068
Marine City (G-10969)		
Woodard—Cm LLC	C	989 725-4265
Owosso (G-12869)		
Wright Time Foods LLc	G	810 835-9219
Flint (G-5797)		

26 PAPER AND ALLIED PRODUCTS

2611 Pulp Mills

Company		Phone
Anchor Recycling Inc	G	810 984-5545
Port Huron (G-13439)		
Bpv LLC	E	616 281-4502
Byron Center (G-2261)		
Fibrek Inc	C	906 864-9125
Menominee (G-11235)		
◆ Fibrek Recycling US Inc	D	906 863-8137
Menominee (G-11236)		
Fibrek US Inc	F	906 864-9125
Menominee (G-11237)		
Forest Blake Products Inc	G	231 879-3913
Fife Lake (G-5606)		
Forest Corullo Products Corp	E	906 667-0275
Bessemer (G-1649)		
Friedland Industries Inc	F	517 482-3000
Lansing (G-9701)		
General Mill Supply Company	E	248 668-0800
Wixom (G-18667)		
Gfl Envronmental Real Property	E	888 877-4996
Southfield (G-15575)		
Great Lakes Paper Stock Corp	D	586 779-1310
Roseville (G-14416)		
Infinity Recycling LLC	F	248 939-2563
Clinton Township (G-3258)		
Midland Cmpnding Cnsulting Inc	G	989 495-9367
Midland (G-11392)		
Mshiikenh Rnwble Resources LLC	G	231 818-9353
Cheboygan (G-2792)		
Recycling Concepts W Mich Inc	D	616 942-8888
Grand Rapids (G-7146)		
Recycling Rizzo Services LLC	G	248 541-4020
Royal Oak (G-14574)		
Southast Berrien Cnty Landfill	E	269 695-2500
Niles (G-12168)		
Star Paper Converters	G	313 254-9833
Ecorse (G-4986)		
United For Srvval St Jsphs Rcy	G	269 983-3820
Saint Joseph (G-14969)		
Upcycle Polymers LLC	G	248 446-8750
Howell (G-8537)		
V & M Corporation	E	248 591-6580
Royal Oak (G-14588)		

SIC SECTION

26 PAPER AND ALLIED PRODUCTS 26 PAPER AND ALLIED PRODUCTS

Verso Paper Holding LLC ....F 906 779-3200
  Quinnesec *(G-13678)*

2621 Paper Mills

▲ Ace-Tex Enterprises Inc ....E 313 834-4000
  Detroit *(G-3982)*
▲ American Twisting Company ....E 269 637-8581
  South Haven *(G-15398)*
Anchor Bay Manufacturing Corp ....F 586 949-1195
  Chesterfield *(G-2840)*
Anchor Bay Manufacturing Corp ....C 586 949-4040
  Chesterfield *(G-2841)*
Cadillac Products Inc ....F 989 766-2294
  Rogers City *(G-14208)*
Cascades Enviropac HPM LLC ....D 616 243-4870
  Grand Rapids *(G-6557)*
Domtar Industries LLC ....D 810 982-0191
  Port Huron *(G-13469)*
Dunn Paper Holdings Inc ....G 810 984-5521
  Port Huron *(G-13472)*
E B Eddy Paper Inc ....B 810 982-0191
  Port Huron *(G-13473)*
Eagle Ridge Paper Ltd ....F 248 376-9503
  Romulus *(G-14269)*
Esv Precision LLC ....G 810 441-0953
  Imlay City *(G-8631)*
◆ French Paper Company ....D 269 683-1100
  Niles *(G-12131)*
Gold Bond Building Pdts LLC ....E 989 756-2741
  National City *(G-11959)*
Great Lakes Tissue Company ....D 231 627-0200
  Cheboygan *(G-2785)*
▲ Handy Wacks Corporation ....G 616 887-8268
  Sparta *(G-15766)*
International Paper Company ....G 269 273-8461
  Three Rivers *(G-16576)*
Kimberly-Clark Corporation ....G 586 949-1649
  Macomb *(G-10609)*
Kimberly-Clark Corporation ....G 810 985-1830
  Port Huron *(G-13494)*
Kolossos Printing Inc ....G 734 741-1600
  Ann Arbor *(G-541)*
Meca Systeme USA ....G 616 294-1439
  Holland *(G-8141)*
▼ Menominee Acquisition Corp ....C 906 863-5595
  Menominee *(G-11246)*
Mextor Disposable LLC ....G 313 921-6860
  Detroit *(G-4441)*
Neenah Paper Inc ....B 906 387-2700
  Munising *(G-11752)*
North Coast Paper & Packg LLC ....G 586 648-7600
  New Baltimore *(G-11990)*
Northstar Sourcing LLC ....G 313 782-4749
  Troy *(G-17281)*
Otsego Paper Inc ....D 269 692-6141
  Otsego *(G-12793)*
Package Design & Mfg Inc ....E 248 486-4390
  Brighton *(G-2046)*
▼ Portage Paper Co Inc ....C 616 345-7131
  Kalamazoo *(G-9298)*
Pure Pulp Products Inc ....A 269 385-5050
  Kalamazoo *(G-9309)*
Recycled Paperboard Pdts Corp ....G 313 579-6608
  Detroit *(G-4558)*
Resolute FP US Inc ....G 877 547-2737
  Menominee *(G-11258)*
Rizzo Packaging Inc ....E 269 685-5808
  Plainwell *(G-13093)*
▼ Sanitor Mfg Co ....F 269 327-3001
  Portage *(G-13605)*
Star Paper Converters Inc ....F 313 963-5200
  Detroit *(G-4606)*
◆ Thetford Corporation ....C 734 769-6000
  Ann Arbor *(G-688)*
Vandelay Services LLC ....G 810 279-8550
  Howell *(G-8538)*
Verso Corporation ....A 906 786-1660
  Escanaba *(G-5105)*
Verso Paper Holding LLC ....F 906 779-3200
  Quinnesec *(G-13678)*
Verso Quinnesec LLC ....G 877 447-2737
  Quinnesec *(G-13679)*
Verso Quinnesec Rep LLC ....F 906 779-3200
  Quinnesec *(G-13680)*
Vision Solutions Inc ....G 810 695-9569
  Grand Blanc *(G-6267)*

2631 Paperboard Mills

Aactus Inc ....G 734 425-1212
  Livonia *(G-10096)*

Aldez North America ....F 586 530-5314
  Clinton Township *(G-3161)*
Anchor Bay Packaging Corp ....G 586 949-1500
  Chesterfield *(G-2843)*
Campbell Industrial Force LLC ....G 989 427-0011
  Edmore *(G-4990)*
Cardboard Prophets ....G 517 512-1267
  Eaton Rapids *(G-4957)*
Cardboard Robot Visuals LLC ....G 231 577-8710
  Buckley *(G-2206)*
Cascade Paper Converters LLC ....F 616 974-9165
  Grand Rapids *(G-6555)*
Classic Container Corporation ....C 734 853-3000
  Livonia *(G-10159)*
Coveris ....C 269 964-1130
  Battle Creek *(G-1212)*
Display Pack Disc Vdh Inc ....G 616 451-3061
  Cedar Springs *(G-2650)*
Everything Edbl Trats For Stne ....G 313 725-0118
  Detroit *(G-4220)*
Fibre Converters Inc ....E 269 279-1700
  Constantine *(G-3666)*
Handy Wacks Corporation ....G 616 887-8268
  Sparta *(G-15767)*
Highland Supply Inc ....G 248 714-8355
  Highland *(G-7892)*
Hydrolake Inc ....G 231 825-2233
  Mc Bain *(G-11182)*
▲ IBC North America Inc ....F 248 625-8700
  Clarkston *(G-3042)*
▲ Kentwood Packaging Corporation ...D 616 698-9000
  Walker *(G-17642)*
Lakeland Paper Corporation ....E 269 651-5474
  White Pigeon *(G-18481)*
Lotis Technologies Inc ....G 248 340-6065
  Orion *(G-12733)*
Lydall Performance Mtls US Inc ....G 248 596-2800
  Northville *(G-12236)*
M & J Entp Grnd Rapids LLC ....F 616 485-9775
  Comstock Park *(G-3620)*
M-Industries LLC ....E 616 682-4642
  Ada *(G-28)*
MRC Industries Inc ....E 269 343-0747
  Kalamazoo *(G-9278)*
Ox Paperboard Michigan LLC ....D 800 345-8881
  Constantine *(G-3674)*
▲ Packaging Specialties Inc ....E 586 473-6703
  Romulus *(G-14315)*
Rizzo Packaging Inc ....E 269 685-5808
  Plainwell *(G-13093)*
Sonoco Products Company ....G 586 978-0808
  Sterling Heights *(G-16182)*
Sonoco Products Company ....G 269 408-0182
  Saint Joseph *(G-14961)*
South Park Sales & Mfg Inc ....G 313 381-7579
  Dearborn *(G-3899)*
Trim Pac Inc ....G 269 279-9498
  Three Rivers *(G-16589)*
Utility Supply and Cnstr Co ....G 231 832-2297
  Reed City *(G-13802)*

2652 Set-Up Paperboard Boxes

Chelsea Milling Company ....F 269 781-2823
  Marshall *(G-11055)*
▼ Michigan Box Company ....D 313 873-9500
  Detroit *(G-4444)*
▲ Packaging Specialties Inc ....E 586 473-6703
  Romulus *(G-14315)*

2653 Corrugated & Solid Fiber Boxes

Aaa1 Box Division Container ....G 269 983-1563
  Saint Joseph *(G-14921)*
Action Packaging LLC ....E 616 871-5200
  Caledonia *(G-2366)*
▲ Advance Packaging Acquisition ......D 616 949-6610
  Grand Rapids *(G-6432)*
Advance Packaging Corporation ....C 616 949-6610
  Grand Rapids *(G-6433)*
Aero Box Company ....G 586 415-0000
  Roseville *(G-14370)*
Aldez North America ....F 586 530-5314
  Clinton Township *(G-3161)*
All Packaging Solutions Inc ....G 248 880-1548
  Warren *(G-17697)*
Alma Container Corporation ....E 989 463-2106
  Alma *(G-235)*
▲ Anchor Bay Packaging Corp ....E 586 949-4040
  Chesterfield *(G-2842)*
Anchor Bay Packaging Corp ....G 586 949-1500
  Chesterfield *(G-2843)*

Armstrong Display Concepts Inc ....F 231 652-1675
  Newaygo *(G-12077)*
▲ Arvco Container Corporation ....E 269 381-0900
  Kalamazoo *(G-9123)*
Arvco Container Corporation ....E 269 381-0900
  Kalamazoo *(G-9124)*
Arvco Container Corporation ....E 269 381-0900
  Kalamazoo *(G-9125)*
Arvco Container Corporation ....E 269 381-0900
  Kalamazoo *(G-9126)*
Arvco Container Corporation ....E 231 876-0935
  Cadillac *(G-2313)*
▲ Bay Corrugated Container Inc ....C 734 243-5400
  Monroe *(G-11530)*
◆ Bradford Company ....C 616 399-3000
  Holland *(G-7981)*
Bramco Containers Inc ....G 906 428-2855
  Gladstone *(G-6174)*
▼ Brickers Box Board Inc ....G 734 981-0828
  Canton *(G-2444)*
C/W South Inc ....E 810 767-2806
  Burton *(G-2230)*
Caraustar Cstm Packg Group Inc ....D 616 247-0330
  Grand Rapids *(G-6547)*
Classic Container Corporation ....C 734 853-3000
  Livonia *(G-10159)*
Coastal Container Corporation ....D 616 355-9800
  Holland *(G-7999)*
Compak Inc ....G 989 288-3199
  Burton *(G-2233)*
Complete Packaging Inc ....D 734 241-2794
  Monroe *(G-11534)*
Corr Pack In ....G 248 348-4188
  Northville *(G-12210)*
Corrugated Pratt ....E 734 853-3030
  Livonia *(G-10167)*
D T Fowler Mfg Co Inc ....G 810 245-9336
  Lapeer *(G-9925)*
▲ Delta Containers Inc ....C 810 742-2730
  Bay City *(G-1342)*
Dewitt Packaging Corporation ....E 616 698-0210
  Grand Rapids *(G-6644)*
Eco Paper ....G 248 652-3601
  Rochester Hills *(G-13999)*
Flint Boxmakers Inc ....G 810 743-0400
  Burton *(G-2235)*
Gdc Worldwide ....G 248 348-4189
  Northville *(G-12223)*
Genesee Group Inc ....E 810 235-6120
  Flint *(G-5707)*
Georgia-Pacific LLC ....G 734 439-2441
  Milan *(G-11436)*
Georgia-Pacific LLC ....G 989 725-5191
  Owosso *(G-12835)*
Grand Traverse Reels Inc ....C 231 946-1057
  Traverse City *(G-16700)*
Great Lakes-Triad Plastic ....D 616 241-6441
  Grand Rapids *(G-6788)*
Green Bay Packaging Inc ....C 269 552-1000
  Kalamazoo *(G-9202)*
Industrial Packaging Corp ....F 248 677-0084
  Berkley *(G-1628)*
Inter-Pack Corporation ....E 734 242-7755
  Monroe *(G-11551)*
Jet Box Co Inc ....F 248 362-1260
  Troy *(G-17185)*
Jetco Packaging Solutions LLC ....F 616 588-2492
  Grand Rapids *(G-6870)*
▲ Kentwood Packaging Corporation ...D 616 698-9000
  Walker *(G-17642)*
Kraft-Wrap Inc ....E 586 755-2050
  Warren *(G-17896)*
▲ Lepages 2000 Inc ....G 416 357-0041
  Melvindale *(G-11203)*
Loope Enterprises Inc ....G 269 639-1567
  South Haven *(G-15409)*
McC Kalamazoo Inc ....E 269 381-2706
  Kalamazoo *(G-9267)*
Michcor Container Inc ....G 616 452-7089
  Grand Rapids *(G-6986)*
Michiana Corrugated Pdts Co ....E 269 651-5225
  Sturgis *(G-16306)*
▼ Michigan Box Company ....D 313 873-9500
  Detroit *(G-4444)*
▲ Michigan Packaging Company ....D 517 676-8700
  Mason *(G-11144)*
Monte Package Company LLC ....E 269 849-1722
  Riverside *(G-13864)*
MRC Industries Inc ....E 269 343-0747
  Kalamazoo *(G-9278)*

Employee Codes: A=Over 500 employees, B=251-500
C=101-250, D=51-100, E=20-50, F=10-19, G=3-9

Msr-Pallets & Packaging LLC ....G 810 360-0425
Brighton *(G-2036)*
National Packaging Corporation ....F 248 652-3600
Rochester Hills *(G-14068)*
Opus Packaging - Kalamazoo LLC ....G 800 643-6721
Kalamazoo *(G-9283)*
Opus Packaging Group Inc ....D 616 871-5200
Caledonia *(G-2391)*
Packaging Corporation America ....G 616 530-5700
Grandville *(G-7407)*
Packaging Corporation America ....D 734 453-6262
Plymouth *(G-13259)*
Packaging Corporation America ....G 734 266-1877
Livonia *(G-10358)*
Packaging Corporation America ....G 269 567-7340
Kalamazoo *(G-9284)*
Packaging Corporation America ....B 231 723-1442
Filer City *(G-5610)*
Packaging Corporation America ....G 989 427-2130
Edmore *(G-4994)*
Packaging Corporation America ....G 989 427-5129
Edmore *(G-4995)*
▲ **Packaging Specialties Inc** ....E 586 473-6703
Romulus *(G-14315)*
Patriot Solutions LLC ....G 616 240-8164
Grand Rapids *(G-7072)*
Pratt Industries Inc ....G 616 452-2111
Grand Rapids *(G-7096)*
Pratt Industries Inc ....G 734 853-3000
Livonia *(G-10373)*
Preferred Packg Solutions Inc ....G 734 844-9092
Taylor *(G-16459)*
Premier Corrugated Inc ....C 517 629-5700
Albion *(G-130)*
Roberts Movable Walls Inc ....G 269 626-0227
Scotts *(G-15133)*
Royal Container Inc ....E 248 967-0910
Oak Park *(G-12641)*
Russell R Peters Co LLC ....G 989 732-0660
Gaylord *(G-6157)*
S & C Industries Inc ....E 269 381-6022
Kalamazoo *(G-9326)*
Scotts Enterprises Inc ....F 989 275-5011
Roscommon *(G-14356)*
Shipping Container Corporation ....E 313 937-2411
Redford *(G-13771)*
Shoreline Container LLC ....C 616 399-2088
Holland *(G-8191)*
South Haven Packaging Inc ....C 269 639-1567
South Haven *(G-15414)*
▲ **St Clair Packaging Inc** ....E 810 364-4230
Marysville *(G-11104)*
Tecumseh Packg Solutions Inc ....E 517 423-2126
Tecumseh *(G-16518)*
Understated Corrugated LLC ....G 248 880-5767
Northville *(G-12268)*
Universal Container Corp ....E 248 543-2788
Ferndale *(G-5594)*
US Gbc Wm ....G 616 691-1340
Greenville *(G-7509)*
▲ **Webcor Packaging Corporation** ....G 810 767-2806
Burton *(G-2251)*
Westrock Rkt LLC ....G 269 963-5511
Battle Creek *(G-1311)*
World Corrugated Container Inc ....F 517 629-9400
Albion *(G-135)*
Wrkco Inc ....E 269 964-7181
Battle Creek *(G-1312)*
Wrkco Inc ....E 734 453-6700
Plymouth *(G-13339)*
Zoomer Display LLC ....G 616 734-0300
Grand Rapids *(G-7359)*

2655 Fiber Cans, Tubes & Drums

Action Packaging LLC ....E 616 871-5200
Caledonia *(G-2366)*
Cascade Paper Converters LLC ....F 616 974-9165
Grand Rapids *(G-6555)*
E & M Cores Inc ....G 989 386-9223
Clare *(G-2978)*
Eteron Inc ....E 248 478-2900
Farmington Hills *(G-5236)*
Goodpack ....G 248 458-0041
Troy *(G-17131)*
Greif Inc ....G 586 415-0000
Roseville *(G-14417)*
Kraft-Wrap Inc ....E 586 755-2050
Warren *(G-17896)*
▲ **Mauser** ....E 248 795-2330
Clarkston *(G-3048)*
▲ **Nagel Paper Inc** ....E 810 644-7043
Swartz Creek *(G-16357)*
Plasan Us Inc ....G 616 559-0032
Walker *(G-17649)*
Quanta Containers LLC ....G 734 282-3044
Taylor *(G-16464)*
Rokan Corp ....G 810 735-9170
Linden *(G-10070)*
Russell R Peters Co LLC ....G 989 732-0660
Gaylord *(G-6157)*
Technova Corporation ....G 517 485-1402
Okemos *(G-12690)*
Xpress Packaging Solutions LLC ....G 231 629-0463
Shelby Township *(G-15371)*

2656 Sanitary Food Containers

Acumedia Manufacturers Inc ....E 517 372-9200
Lansing *(G-9799)*
▲ **AJM Packaging Corporation** ....D 248 901-0040
Bloomfield Hills *(G-1794)*
AJM Packaging Corporation ....D 313 842-7530
Detroit *(G-3993)*
◆ **Dart Container Michigan LLC** ....A 800 248-5960
Mason *(G-11128)*
Dart Container Michigan LLC ....A 888 327-8001
Lansing *(G-9828)*
Dart Container Michigan LLC ....A 517 694-9455
Holt *(G-8309)*
Hot Rods Bbq Services ....G 989 375-2191
Elkton *(G-5031)*
Huhtamaki Inc ....D 989 633-8900
Coleman *(G-3467)*
◆ **Letica Corporation** ....C 248 652-0557
Rochester Hills *(G-14053)*
Moving & Shipping Solutions ....G 231 824-4190
Manton *(G-10938)*
▼ **Scic LLC** ....D 800 248-5960
Mason *(G-11153)*
◆ **SF Holdings Group Inc** ....D 800 248-5960
Mason *(G-11154)*
▲ **Solo Cup Company LLC** ....C 800 248-5960
Mason *(G-11155)*
◆ **Solo Cup Operating Corporation** ....D 800 248-5960
Mason *(G-11156)*

2657 Folding Paperboard Boxes

Caraustar Cstm Packg Group Inc ....D 616 247-0330
Grand Rapids *(G-6547)*
Complete Packaging Inc ....D 734 241-2794
Monroe *(G-11534)*
Graphic Packaging Intl LLC ....D 269 651-2365
Sturgis *(G-16289)*
Graphic Packaging Intl LLC ....G 269 343-6104
Kalamazoo *(G-9200)*
Michigan Carton Paper Boy ....G 269 963-4004
Battle Creek *(G-1274)*
▲ **Packaging Specialties Inc** ....E 586 473-6703
Romulus *(G-14315)*
Rapid-Packaging Corporation ....E 616 949-0950
Grand Rapids *(G-7141)*
Steketee-Van Huis Inc ....B 616 392-2326
Holland *(G-8202)*
Wrkco Inc ....E 269 964-7181
Battle Creek *(G-1312)*
Wynalda International LLC ....F 616 866-1561
Belmont *(G-1522)*
◆ **Wynalda Litho Inc** ....C 616 866-1561
Belmont *(G-1523)*

2671 Paper Coating & Laminating for Packaging

Advance Engineering Company ....E 989 435-3641
Beaverton *(G-1423)*
Allsales Enterprises Inc ....F 616 437-0639
Grand Rapids *(G-6451)*
Alpha Data Business Forms Inc ....G 248 540-5930
Birmingham *(G-1718)*
American Label & Tag Inc ....E 734 454-7600
Canton *(G-2433)*
Anchor Bay Packaging Corp ....G 586 949-1500
Chesterfield *(G-2843)*
Andex Industries Inc ....E 906 786-7588
Escanaba *(G-5056)*
Argent Tape & Label Inc ....G 734 582-9956
Plymouth *(G-13125)*
Cadillac Products Packaging Co ....C 248 879-5000
Troy *(G-16993)*
CAM Packaging LLC ....F 989 426-1200
Gladwin *(G-6191)*
Cello-Foil Products Inc ....C 229 435-4777
Battle Creek *(G-1206)*
Classic Container Corporation ....C 734 853-3000
Livonia *(G-10159)*
Creative Foam Corporation ....G 810 714-0140
Fenton *(G-5468)*
Cummins Label Company ....E 269 345-3386
Kalamazoo *(G-9159)*
▲ **Delta Containers Inc** ....C 810 742-2730
Bay City *(G-1342)*
Dunn Paper Inc ....G 810 984-5521
Menominee *(G-11232)*
◆ **Dunn Paper Inc** ....F 810 984-5521
Port Huron *(G-13470)*
Dunn Paper - Wiggins LLC ....G 810 984-5521
Port Huron *(G-13471)*
Fibre Converters Inc ....E 269 279-1700
Constantine *(G-3666)*
▲ **Filcon Inc** ....F 989 386-2986
Clare *(G-2979)*
General Tape Label Liquidating ....F 248 437-5200
Wixom *(G-18668)*
Harbor Packaging ....G 616 494-9913
Holland *(G-8066)*
◆ **Holo-Source Corporation** ....G 734 427-1530
Livonia *(G-10242)*
Impact Label Corporation ....D 269 381-4280
Galesburg *(G-6079)*
International Master Pdts Corp ....C 231 894-5651
Montague *(G-11598)*
J W Manchester Company Inc ....G 810 632-5409
Hartland *(G-7771)*
Jetco Packaging Solutions LLC ....F 616 588-2492
Grand Rapids *(G-6870)*
Lotus Technologies LLC ....F 313 550-1889
Detroit *(G-4406)*
Macarthur Corp ....E 810 606-1777
Grand Blanc *(G-6252)*
◆ **MPS Lansing Inc** ....A 517 323-9000
Lansing *(G-9719)*
▲ **Noble Films Corporation** ....G 616 977-3770
Ada *(G-31)*
▲ **Nyx LLC** ....C 734 462-2385
Livonia *(G-10343)*
Nyx LLC ....D 734 261-7535
Livonia *(G-10347)*
Opus Packaging Group Inc ....D 616 871-5200
Caledonia *(G-2391)*
▲ **Packaging Specialties Inc** ....E 586 473-6703
Romulus *(G-14315)*
Profile Industrial Packg Corp ....C 616 245-7260
Grand Rapids *(G-7116)*
Quality Transparent Bag Inc ....F 989 893-3561
Bay City *(G-1391)*
Shawmut LLC ....G 810 987-2222
Port Huron *(G-13526)*
Shoreline Container LLC ....C 616 399-2088
Holland *(G-8191)*
Siliconature Corporation ....E 312 987-1848
Caledonia *(G-2400)*
Smart USA Inc ....G 248 214-1022
Ann Arbor *(G-656)*
Stamp-Rite Incorporated ....E 517 487-5071
Lansing *(G-9741)*
▲ **Stewart Sutherland Inc** ....C 269 649-0530
Vicksburg *(G-17613)*
Svrc Industries Inc ....C 989 723-8205
Owosso *(G-12860)*
Tesa Tape Inc ....G 616 785-6970
Walker *(G-17654)*
Tesa Tape Inc ....G 616 887-3107
Sparta *(G-15786)*
Timbertech Inc ....F 231 348-2750
Harbor Springs *(G-7658)*
Tryco Inc ....F 734 953-6800
Farmington Hills *(G-5406)*
◆ **Ufp Technologies Inc** ....D 616 949-8100
Grand Rapids *(G-7294)*
Unique Fabricating Inc ....A 248 853-2333
Auburn Hills *(G-1068)*
▲ **Unique Fabricating Na Inc** ....B 248 853-2333
Auburn Hills *(G-1069)*
▲ **Venchurs Inc** ....C 517 263-8937
Adrian *(G-100)*
Verso Paper Holding LLC ....F 906 779-3200
Quinnesec *(G-13678)*
Zajac Industries Inc ....E 586 489-6746
Clinton Township *(G-3392)*

2672 Paper Coating & Laminating, Exc for Packaging

Alpha Data Business Forms Inc .... G 248 540-5930
  Birmingham *(G-1718)*
American Label & Tag Inc .... E 734 454-7600
  Canton *(G-2433)*
Argent Tape & Label Inc .... G 734 582-9956
  Plymouth *(G-13125)*
▲ Celia Corporation .... G 616 887-7387
  Sparta *(G-15763)*
Cummins Label Company .... E 269 345-3386
  Kalamazoo *(G-9159)*
Cytec Industries Inc .... G 269 349-6677
  Kalamazoo *(G-9161)*
Dunn Paper Inc .... G 810 984-5521
  Menominee *(G-11232)*
◆ Dunn Paper Inc .... F 810 984-5521
  Port Huron *(G-13470)*
Dunn Paper Holdings Inc .... G 810 984-5521
  Port Huron *(G-13472)*
▲ Elliott Tape Inc .... E 248 475-2000
  Auburn Hills *(G-878)*
Grand Haven Gasket Company .... G 616 842-7682
  Grand Haven *(G-6303)*
Impact Label Corporation .... D 269 381-4280
  Galesburg *(G-6079)*
Independent Die Cutting Inc .... F 616 452-3197
  Grand Rapids *(G-6842)*
Kent Manufacturing Company .... D 616 454-9495
  Grand Rapids *(G-6889)*
▲ Laminin Medical Products Inc ...... G 616 871-3390
  Grand Rapids *(G-6926)*
Lawson Printers Inc .... G 269 965-0525
  Battle Creek *(G-1267)*
▲ Lepages 2000 Inc .... G 416 357-0041
  Melvindale *(G-11203)*
Litsenberger Print Shop .... G 906 482-3903
  Houghton *(G-8386)*
◆ Lowry Holding Company Inc .... C 810 229-7200
  Brighton *(G-2023)*
Macarthur Corp .... E 810 606-1777
  Grand Blanc *(G-6252)*
Macarthur Corp .... G 810 744-1380
  Flint *(G-5729)*
McCray Press .... F 989 792-8681
  Saginaw *(G-14689)*
Mead Westvaco Paper Div .... G 906 233-2362
  Escanaba *(G-5082)*
Michigan Shippers Supply Inc .... F 616 935-6680
  Spring Lake *(G-15835)*
▲ Oliver Packaging and Eqp Co ...... D 616 356-2950
  Walker *(G-17645)*
Plasti-Fab Inc .... E 248 543-1415
  Ferndale *(G-5579)*
Qrp Inc .... G 989 496-2955
  Midland *(G-11405)*
Shawmut LLC .... G 810 987-2222
  Port Huron *(G-13526)*
▲ Stewart Sutherland Inc .... C 269 649-0530
  Vicksburg *(G-17613)*
Technology MGT & Budgt Dept .... E 517 322-1897
  Lansing *(G-9899)*
Tesa Plant Sparta LLC .... G 616 887-1757
  Sparta *(G-15785)*
Tesa Tape Inc .... F 616 785-6970
  Walker *(G-17654)*
Tesa Tape Inc .... G 616 887-3107
  Sparta *(G-15786)*
◆ Trimas Corporation .... B 248 631-5450
  Bloomfield Hills *(G-1869)*
Witchcraft Tape Products Inc .... D 269 468-3399
  Coloma *(G-3485)*
▲ Yamato International Corp .... E 734 675-6055
  Woodhaven *(G-18804)*

2673 Bags: Plastics, Laminated & Coated

A-Pac Manufacturing Company .... E 616 791-7222
  Grand Rapids *(G-6412)*
Bioplstic Plymers Cmpsites LLC ...... G 517 349-2970
  Okemos *(G-12660)*
Cadillac Products Inc .... E 586 774-1700
  Roseville *(G-14382)*
▲ Cadillac Products Inc .... B 248 813-8200
  Troy *(G-16992)*
Cadillac Products Inc .... F 989 766-2294
  Rogers City *(G-14208)*
Coveris .... C 269 964-1130
  Battle Creek *(G-1212)*
D&Js Plastics LLC .... F 616 745-5798
  Hudsonville *(G-8578)*

▲ Idea Mia LLC .... G 248 891-8939
  Lathrup Village *(G-9976)*
Lbv Sales LLC .... G 616 874-9390
  Belmont *(G-1510)*
Opus Packaging Group Inc .... D 616 871-5200
  Caledonia *(G-2391)*
▲ Plasport Inc .... E 231 935-1580
  Traverse City *(G-16798)*
Quality Transparent Bag Inc .... F 989 893-3561
  Bay City *(G-1391)*
Superior Polyolefin Films Inc .... G 248 334-8074
  Bloomfield Hills *(G-1863)*

2674 Bags: Uncoated Paper & Multiwall

Acme Mills Company .... E 517 437-8940
  Hillsdale *(G-7919)*
AJM Packaging Corporation .... D 313 291-6500
  Taylor *(G-16375)*
▲ AJM Packaging Corporation .... D 248 901-0040
  Bloomfield Hills *(G-1794)*
AJM Packaging Corporation .... G 313 842-7530
  Detroit *(G-3993)*
Concorde Inc .... F 248 391-8177
  Auburn Hills *(G-846)*
Lisa Bain .... G 313 389-9661
  Allen Park *(G-198)*
McKenna Enterprises Inc .... G 248 375-3388
  Rochester Hills *(G-14061)*
◆ Pak-Rite Industries Inc .... D 313 388-6400
  Ecorse *(G-4984)*
▲ Stewart Sutherland Inc .... C 269 649-0530
  Vicksburg *(G-17613)*

2675 Die-Cut Paper & Board

▲ Accu-Shape Die Cutting Inc .... E 810 230-2445
  Flint *(G-5634)*
▲ Bradford Company .... C 616 399-3000
  Holland *(G-7981)*
▲ Cadillac Prsentation Solutions ..... E 248 288-9777
  Troy *(G-16994)*
Classic Container Corporation .... C 734 853-3000
  Livonia *(G-10159)*
▲ Delta Containers Inc .... C 810 742-2730
  Bay City *(G-1342)*
Design Converting Inc .... F 616 942-7780
  Grand Rapids *(G-6642)*
Diecutting Service Inc .... F 734 426-0290
  Dexter *(G-4740)*
Edgewater Apartments .... G 517 663-8123
  Eaton Rapids *(G-4962)*
Graphic Specialties Inc .... E 616 247-0060
  Grand Rapids *(G-6783)*
Hamblin Company .... E 517 423-7491
  Bloomfield Hills *(G-1826)*
Hexon Corporation .... E 248 585-7585
  Farmington Hills *(G-5259)*
Industrial Imprntng & Die Ctng .... G 586 778-9470
  Eastpointe *(G-4937)*
▲ Jacobsen Industries Inc .... D 734 591-6111
  Livonia *(G-10255)*
Lefty Love LLC .... G 248 795-3858
  Detroit *(G-4385)*
Macarthur Corp .... E 810 606-1777
  Grand Blanc *(G-6252)*
Michigan Paper Die Inc .... E 313 873-0404
  Detroit *(G-4451)*
▲ Oliver Packaging and Eqp Co ...... D 616 356-2950
  Walker *(G-17645)*
Rizzo Packaging Inc .... E 269 685-5808
  Plainwell *(G-13093)*
Russell R Peters Co LLC .... G 989 732-0660
  Gaylord *(G-6157)*
Trim Pac Inc .... G 269 279-9498
  Three Rivers *(G-16589)*

2676 Sanitary Paper Prdts

AJM Packaging Corporation .... D 313 842-7530
  Detroit *(G-3993)*
Chambers Ottawa Inc .... G 231 238-2122
  Cheboygan *(G-2781)*
Happy Bums .... G 616 987-3159
  Lowell *(G-10502)*
Kimberly-Clark Corporation .... C 586 949-1649
  Macomb *(G-10609)*
Kimberly-Clark Corporation .... G 810 985-1830
  Port Huron *(G-13494)*

2677 Envelopes

Husky Envelope Products Inc .... D 248 624-7070
  Walled Lake *(G-17670)*
Michigan Envelope Inc .... G 616 554-3404
  Grand Rapids *(G-6988)*
The Envelope Printery Inc .... D 734 398-7700
  Van Buren Twp *(G-17557)*

2678 Stationery Prdts

Barcroft Technology LLC .... G 313 378-0133
  Southfield *(G-15502)*
Edward and Cole Inc .... G 734 996-9074
  Ann Arbor *(G-467)*
Presscraft Papers Inc .... F 231 882-5505
  Benzonia *(G-1616)*
Scientific Notebook Company .... F 269 429-8285
  Stevensville *(G-16264)*
Williams Parts & Supply Co .... F 906 337-3813
  Calumet *(G-2418)*

2679 Converted Paper Prdts, NEC

AJM Packaging Corporation .... D 313 291-6500
  Taylor *(G-16375)*
B & B Entps Prtg Cnvrting Inc .... G 313 891-9840
  Detroit *(G-4037)*
Everest Manufacturing Inc .... F 313 401-2608
  Farmington Hills *(G-5238)*
Fibers of Kalamazoo Inc .... E 269 344-3122
  Kalamazoo *(G-9186)*
▲ Fineeye Color Solutions Inc .... G 616 988-6119
  Muskegon *(G-11817)*
Macarthur Corp .... E 810 606-1777
  Grand Blanc *(G-6252)*
Manchester Industries Inc VA .... E 269 496-2715
  Mendon *(G-11219)*
Marshall Floral Products .... G 517 787-7620
  Jackson *(G-8945)*
Middleton Printing Inc .... G 616 247-8742
  Grand Rapids *(G-7004)*
Progressive Paper Corp .... G 269 279-6320
  Three Rivers *(G-16582)*
◆ Shepherd Speciality Papers Inc ... G 269 629-8001
  Richland *(G-13829)*
▼ Sks Industries Inc .... F 517 546-1117
  Howell *(G-8518)*
Str Company .... G 517 206-6058
  Grass Lake *(G-7446)*
Trim Pac Inc .... G 269 279-9498
  Three Rivers *(G-16589)*
Tru Blu Industries LLC .... G 269 684-4989
  Niles *(G-12172)*
Venture Label Inc .... G 313 928-2545
  Detroit *(G-4664)*
W H Green & Associates .... G 616 682-5202
  Grand Rapids *(G-7322)*
Walters Seed Co LLC .... F 616 355-7333
  Holland *(G-8241)*

27 PRINTING, PUBLISHING, AND ALLIED INDUSTRIES

2711 Newspapers: Publishing & Printing

201 E Exchange .... G 989 725-6397
  Owosso *(G-12818)*
21st Century Newspapers Inc .... C 586 469-4510
  Sterling Heights *(G-15915)*
21st Century Newspapers Inc .... F 810 664-0811
  Lapeer *(G-9910)*
21st Century Newspapers Inc .... F 586 469-4510
  Pontiac *(G-13343)*
A B Rusgo Inc .... G 586 296-7714
  Fraser *(G-5886)*
ABC Printing Corporation Inc .... G 248 887-0010
  Highland *(G-7879)*
Action Ad Newspapers Inc .... G 734 740-6966
  Belleville *(G-1478)*
Adrian Team LLC .... F 517 264-6148
  Adrian *(G-51)*
Advance BCI Inc .... D 616 669-1366
  Grand Rapids *(G-6431)*
Alcona County Review .... G 989 724-6384
  Harrisville *(G-7740)*
Allegan Vocal Studio .... G 719 209-8957
  Allegan *(G-147)*
Angler Strategies LLC .... G 248 439-1420
  Royal Oak *(G-14508)*
Ann Arbor Chronicle .... G 734 645-2633
  Ann Arbor *(G-367)*

27 PRINTING, PUBLISHING, AND ALLIED INDUSTRIES

Company	Code	Phone
Ann Arbor Journal	G	734 429-7380
Saline (G-15002)		
Ann Arbor Observer Company	E	734 769-3175
Ann Arbor (G-368)		
Ann Arbor Offset	G	734 926-4500
Ann Arbor (G-369)		
Anteebo Publishers Inc	E	313 882-6900
Grosse Pointe Park (G-7546)		
Antrim Review	G	231 533-5651
Bellaire (G-1470)		
Arab American News Inc	G	313 582-4888
Dearborn (G-3809)		
Argus Press Company	E	989 725-5136
Owosso (G-12824)		
Beacon Billboards LLC	G	734 421-7512
Livonia (G-10132)		
Beaumont Enterprise	G	989 269-6464
Bad Axe (G-1098)		
Belleville Area Independent	G	734 699-9020
Belleville (G-1480)		
Benson Distribution Inc	G	269 344-5529
Kalamazoo (G-9135)		
Blue Shamrock Publishing Inc	G	269 687-7097
Niles (G-12114)		
Board For Student Publications	D	734 418-4115
Ann Arbor (G-402)		
Booth Newspaper	G	517 487-8888
Lansing (G-9814)		
Boyne City Gazette	G	231 582-2799
Boyne City (G-1884)		
Budget Europe Travel Service	G	734 668-0529
Ann Arbor (G-408)		
Bulletin Moon	G	734 453-9985
Plymouth (G-13140)		
Bulletin of Concerned Asi	G	231 228-7116
Cedar (G-2636)		
Business News	G	231 929-7919
Traverse City (G-16634)		
Buyers Guide	G	616 897-9261
Lowell (G-10497)		
C & G News Inc	E	586 498-8000
Warren (G-17744)		
C & G Publishing Inc	D	586 498-8000
Warren (G-17745)		
Calcomco Inc	G	313 885-9228
Kalamazoo (G-9143)		
Calhoun Communications Inc	E	517 629-0041
Albion (G-118)		
Campub Inc	F	517 368-0365
Camden (G-2419)		
Cass City Chronicle Inc	G	989 872-2010
Cass City (G-2612)		
Catherine Pawlowski	G	248 698-3614
White Lake (G-18452)		
Cedar Springs Post Inc	G	616 696-3655
Cedar Springs (G-2644)		
Chicago Tribune Company LLC	G	734 464-6500
Livonia (G-10157)		
Choice Publications Inc	G	989 732-8160
Gaylord (G-6122)		
Chris Faulknor	G	231 645-1970
Boyne City (G-1886)		
City of Greenville	E	616 754-0100
Greenville (G-7478)		
Clare County Cleaver Inc	G	989 539-7496
Harrison (G-7675)		
Clare County Review	G	989 386-4414
Clare (G-2975)		
Cmu	F	989 774-7143
Mount Pleasant (G-11692)		
Community Shoppers Guide Inc	G	269 694-9431
Otsego (G-12784)		
Conine Publishing Inc	E	231 723-3592
Manistee (G-10896)		
Coopersville Observer Inc	G	616 997-5049
Coopersville (G-3684)		
County Journal Inc	F	517 543-1099
Charlotte (G-2746)		
County of St Clair	F	810 982-4111
Port Huron (G-13467)		
Crain Communications Inc	B	313 446-6000
Detroit (G-4106)		
Crawford County Avalanche	G	989 348-6811
Grayling (G-7458)		
Daily Bill	G	989 631-2068
Midland (G-11332)		
Daily Contracts LLC	G	734 676-0903
Grosse Ile (G-7518)		
Daily De-Lish	G	616 450-9562
Ada (G-15)		
Daily Gardener LLC	G	734 754-6527
Ann Arbor (G-442)		
Daily Oakland Press	B	248 332-8181
Bloomfield Hills (G-1811)		
Daily Oakland Press	B	248 332-8181
Pontiac (G-13357)		
Daily Recycling of Michigan	G	734 654-9800
Carleton (G-2550)		
Daily Reporter	E	517 278-2318
Coldwater (G-3430)		
Daughtry Nwspapers Investments	G	269 683-2100
Niles (G-12123)		
Deadline Detroit	G	248 219-5985
Detroit (G-4125)		
Deadline Detroit	G	586 863-8397
Detroit (G-4126)		
Deadline Detroit	G	202 309-5555
Detroit (G-4127)		
Detroit Free Press Inc	B	313 222-2300
Detroit (G-4148)		
Detroit Jewish News Ltd Partnr	D	248 354-6060
Farmington Hills (G-5213)		
▲ Detroit Legal News Company	D	313 961-6000
Detroit (G-4150)		
Detroit Legal News Pubg LLC	E	248 577-6100
Troy (G-17057)		
Detroit Legal News Pubg LLC	F	734 477-0201
Ann Arbor (G-450)		
Detroit News Inc	B	313 222-6400
Detroit (G-4153)		
Detroit News Inc	B	313 222-6400
Sterling Heights (G-15983)		
Detroit News Inc	B	313 222-6400
Detroit (G-4154)		
Detroit Newspaper Partnr LP	G	989 752-3023
Saginaw (G-14638)		
Detroit Newspaper Partnr LP	A	586 826-7187
Sterling Heights (G-15984)		
Detroit Newspaper Partnr LP	A	313 222-2300
Detroit (G-4155)		
Detroit Newspaper Partnr LP	A	313 222-6400
Detroit (G-4156)		
El Informador LLC	G	616 272-1092
Wyoming (G-18871)		
El Vocero Hispano Inc	F	616 246-6023
Grand Rapids (G-6666)		
Eldon Publishing LLC	G	810 648-5282
Sandusky (G-15058)		
Evening News	G	734 242-1100
Monroe (G-11539)		
Express Publications Inc	F	231 947-8787
Traverse City (G-16679)		
Fedex Office & Print Svcs Inc	G	248 651-2679
Rochester (G-13900)		
Forum and Link Inc	G	313 945-5465
Dearborn (G-3845)		
Four Seasons Publishing Inc	G	906 341-5200
Manistique (G-10918)		
Fowlerville News & Views	G	517 223-8760
Fowlerville (G-5841)		
Frankenmuth News LLC	G	989 652-3246
Frankenmuth (G-5863)		
Frushour Publishers	G	248 701-2548
Clarkston (G-3035)		
Gannett Stllite Info Ntwrk Inc	G	734 229-1150
Detroit (G-4251)		
Gatehouse Media LLC	E	517 265-5111
Adrian (G-69)		
Gatehouse Media LLC	G	269 651-5407
Sturgis (G-16288)		
Gazelle Publishing	G	734 529-2688
Dundee (G-4821)		
Gazette Newspapers Inc	G	248 524-4868
Troy (G-17128)		
Gemini Corporation	E	616 459-4545
Grand Rapids (G-6737)		
General Media LLC	E	586 541-0075
Saint Clair Shores (G-14862)		
Genesee County Herald Inc	F	810 686-3840
Clio (G-3399)		
Gladwin County Newspapers LLC	G	989 426-9411
Gladwin (G-6196)		
GLS Diocesan Reports	G	989 793-7661
Saginaw (G-14653)		
Grand Haven Publishing Corp	G	616 842-6400
Grand Haven (G-6305)		
Grand Rapids Legal News	G	616 454-9293
Grand Rapids (G-6761)		
Grand Rapids Press Inc	E	616 459-1400
Grand Rapids (G-6767)		
Grand Rapids Times Inc	F	616 245-8737
Grand Rapids (G-6772)		
Graph-ADS Printing Inc	D	989 779-6000
Mount Pleasant (G-11700)		
Graphics Hse Spt Prmotions Inc	E	231 739-4004
Muskegon (G-11828)		
Great American Publishing Co	E	616 887-9008
Sparta (G-15765)		
Great Atlantic News LLC	C	517 784-7163
Jackson (G-8893)		
Great Lakes Post LLC	G	248 941-1349
Milford (G-11465)		
Grosse Pointe News	G	734 674-0131
Canton (G-2468)		
Hamp	G	989 366-5341
Houghton Lake (G-8398)		
Hamtramck Review Inc	G	313 874-2100
Detroit (G-4292)		
Harbor Beach Times	G	989 479-3605
Harbor Beach (G-7631)		
Harold K Schultz	G	517 279-9764
Coldwater (G-3438)		
Herald Newspapers Company Inc	G	269 345-3511
Kalamazoo (G-9213)		
Herald Newspapers Company Inc	G	231 722-3161
Muskegon (G-11836)		
Herald Newspapers Company Inc	G	616 222-5400
Grand Rapids (G-6810)		
Herald Newspapers Company Inc	G	734 926-4510
Ann Arbor (G-513)		
Herald Newspapers Company Inc	G	989 752-7171
Flint (G-5713)		
Herald Newspapers Company Inc	G	810 766-6100
Flint (G-5714)		
Herald Newspapers Company Inc	G	517 787-2300
Jackson (G-8902)		
Herald Newspapers Company Inc	G	734 834-6376
Grand Rapids (G-6811)		
Herald Newspapers Company Inc	G	989 895-8551
Flint (G-5715)		
Herald Newspapers Company Inc	D	269 388-8501
Kalamazoo (G-9214)		
Herald Publishing Company	E	517 423-2174
Tecumseh (G-16504)		
Herald Publishing Company LLC	E	734 623-2500
Ann Arbor (G-514)		
Herald Publishing Company LLC	C	616 222-5400
Walker (G-17641)		
Heritage Newspapers	F	586 783-0300
Pontiac (G-13379)		
Homer Index	E	517 568-4646
Homer (G-8352)		
Hometown Publishing Inc	G	989 834-2264
Ovid (G-12814)		
Houghton Cmnty Brdcstg Corp	G	906 482-7700
Houghton (G-8383)		
Houghton Lake Resorter Inc	F	989 366-5341
Houghton Lake (G-8400)		
Hudson Post Gazette	G	517 448-2611
Hudson (G-8552)		
Huron Publishing Company Inc	D	989 269-6461
Bad Axe (G-1107)		
Hydraulic Press Service	G	586 859-7099
Shelby Township (G-15237)		
Igan Mich Publishing LLC	G	248 877-4649
West Bloomfield (G-18290)		
Increase Enterprises LLC	G	616 550-8553
Grand Rapids (G-6840)		
▲ Independent Newspapers Inc	C	586 469-4510
Mount Clemens (G-11642)		
Indepndnt Advsor Nwsppr Group	F	989 723-1118
Owosso (G-12838)		
Indiana Newspapers LLC	D	248 680-9905
Troy (G-17164)		
Infoguys Inc	G	517 482-2125
Lansing (G-9854)		
Iosco News Press Publishing Co	G	989 739-2054
Oscoda (G-12762)		
Iosco News Press Publishing Co	G	989 362-3456
East Tawas (G-4917)		
Island Sun Times Inc	E	810 230-1735
Flint (G-5717)		
Italian Tribune	F	586 783-3260
Shelby Township (G-15240)		
J R C Inc	F	810 648-4000
Sandusky (G-15061)		
J-Ad Graphics Inc	D	800 870-7085
Hastings (G-7800)		
J-Ad Graphics Inc	F	269 965-3955
Battle Creek (G-1243)		

SIC SECTION 27 PRINTING, PUBLISHING, AND ALLIED INDUSTRIES27 PRINTING, PUBLISHING, AND ALLIED INDUSTRIES

J-Ad Graphics Inc....G....269 945-9554
Marshall *(G-11062)*

Jams Media LLC....F....810 664-0811
Lapeer *(G-9935)*

Joseph D Eckenswiller....G....586 784-8542
Riley *(G-13851)*

Jss - Macomb LLC....F....586 709-6305
Shelby Township *(G-15247)*

Kaechele Publications Inc....F....269 673-5534
Allegan *(G-162)*

Karen Spranger....G....719 359-4047
Warren *(G-17890)*

Kids World News Too....G....517 202-1808
Alma *(G-244)*

L D J Inc....F....906 524-6194
Lanse *(G-9666)*

Lansing Eastside Gateway....G....517 894-6125
Lansing *(G-9858)*

Lansing Labor News Inc....G....517 484-7408
East Lansing *(G-4899)*

Latino Press Inc....G....313 361-3000
Detroit *(G-4378)*

Leader Publications LLC....D....269 683-2100
Niles *(G-12141)*

Leelanau Enterprise Inc....E....231 256-9827
Lake Leelanau *(G-9563)*

Livonia Observer....G....734 525-4657
Livonia *(G-10288)*

Local Media Group Inc....D....313 885-2612
Detroit *(G-4403)*

Ludington Daily News Inc....E....231 845-5181
Ludington *(G-10543)*

Macdonald Publications Inc....F....989 875-4151
Ithaca *(G-8793)*

Macomb 4x4 LLC....G....586 744-0335
Chesterfield *(G-2907)*

Macomb County Cougars....G....586 231-5543
Clinton Township *(G-3287)*

Macomb North Clinton Advisor....G....586 731-1000
Shelby Township *(G-15266)*

Maquet Monthly....G....906 226-6500
Marquette *(G-11032)*

Menominee Cnty Jurnl Print Sp....F....906 753-2296
Stephenson *(G-15909)*

Michigan Chronicle Pubg Co....E....313 963-5522
Detroit *(G-4447)*

Michigan Front Page LLC....G....313 963-5522
Detroit *(G-4450)*

Michigan Maps Inc....G....231 264-6800
Elk Rapids *(G-5027)*

Michigan Metro Times Inc....C....313 961-4060
Ferndale *(G-5568)*

Michigan Peaceworks....F....734 262-4283
Ann Arbor *(G-572)*

Michigan Peaceworks....G....734 232-3079
Ann Arbor *(G-573)*

Michigan Peaceworks....G....734 764-1717
Ann Arbor *(G-574)*

Michigan Snowmobiler Inc....G....231 536-2371
East Jordan *(G-4876)*

Midland Publishing Company....C....989 835-7171
Midland *(G-11394)*

Milliman Communications Inc....G....517 327-8407
Lansing *(G-9778)*

Mining Jrnl Bsness Offc-Dtrial....E....906 228-2500
Marquette *(G-11036)*

Mlive Com....G....517 768-4984
Jackson *(G-8966)*

Mlive Media Group....G....212 286-2860
Ann Arbor *(G-580)*

Mlivecom....G....231 725-6343
Muskegon *(G-11875)*

Monroe Atellos 19....G....734 682-3467
Monroe *(G-11561)*

Monroe Evening News....F....734 242-1100
Monroe *(G-11563)*

Monroe Publishing Company....D....734 242-1100
Monroe *(G-11565)*

Monroe Success Vlc....G....734 682-3720
Monroe *(G-11566)*

Montmorency Press Inc....G....989 785-4214
Atlanta *(G-746)*

Moormann Printing Inc....G....269 423-2411
Decatur *(G-3950)*

Morning Star....G....989 755-2660
Saginaw *(G-14704)*

Morning Star Publishing Co....F....989 463-6071
Alma *(G-248)*

Morning Star Publishing Co....C....989 779-6000
Alma *(G-249)*

Morning Star Publishing Co....G....989 779-6000
Alma *(G-250)*

Morning Star Publishing Co....E....989 732-5125
Pontiac *(G-13399)*

Mt Pleasant Buyers Guide....G....989 779-6000
Mount Pleasant *(G-11720)*

Ndex....F....248 432-9000
Farmington Hills *(G-5332)*

Neumann Enterprises Inc....G....906 293-8122
Newberry *(G-12094)*

New Monitor....G....248 439-1863
Hazel Park *(G-7836)*

Newark Morning Ledger Co....D....517 487-8888
Lansing *(G-9875)*

Newberry News Inc....G....906 293-8401
Newberry *(G-12096)*

News One Inc....E....231 798-4669
Norton Shores *(G-12316)*

North Country Sun Inc....G....906 932-3530
Ironwood *(G-8768)*

Northern Michigan Review Inc....E....231 547-6558
Gaylord *(G-6150)*

Northern Michigan Review Inc....G....231 547-6558
Petoskey *(G-13009)*

Northland Publishers Inc....F....906 265-9927
Iron River *(G-8751)*

Npi Wireless....E....231 922-9273
Traverse City *(G-16776)*

Oakland Sail Inc....F....248 370-4268
Rochester *(G-13915)*

Oceanas Herald-Journal Inc....F....231 873-5602
Hart *(G-7759)*

Ogden Newspapers Inc....G....906 497-5652
Powers *(G-13649)*

Ogden Newspapers Virginia LLC....F....906 228-8920
Marquette *(G-11038)*

Ogemaw County Herald Inc....E....989 345-0044
West Branch *(G-18333)*

Old Mission Gazette....G....231 590-4715
Traverse City *(G-16780)*

Onesian Enterprises Inc....F....313 382-5875
Allen Park *(G-201)*

Ontonagon Herald Co Inc....G....906 884-2826
Ontonagon *(G-12714)*

Page One Inc....E....810 724-0254
Imlay City *(G-8642)*

Paxton Media Group LLC....D....269 429-2400
Saint Joseph *(G-14953)*

Pepperlee Paper Company....G....313 949-5917
Rochester Hills *(G-14081)*

Pet Patrol of Macomb-Oakland....G....586 675-2451
Warren *(G-17961)*

Peterson Publishing Inc....G....906 387-3282
Marquette *(G-11040)*

Pgi Holdings Inc....G....231 937-4740
Big Rapids *(G-1684)*

Pgi Holdings Inc....E....231 796-4831
Big Rapids *(G-1683)*

Plymouth-Canton Cmnty Crier....E....734 453-6900
Plymouth *(G-13268)*

Pontiac Properties LLC....G....248 639-4360
Pontiac *(G-13409)*

Porcupine Press Inc....G....906 439-5111
Chatham *(G-2778)*

Prescott Inc....G....517 515-0007
Lansing *(G-9785)*

Presque Isle Newspapers Inc....F....989 734-2105
Rogers City *(G-14217)*

Psa Courier C....G....810 234-8770
Flint *(G-5750)*

Punkin Dsign Seds Orgnlity LLC....G....313 347-8488
Detroit *(G-4542)*

Qp Acquisition 2 Inc....A....248 594-7432
Southfield *(G-15685)*

Real Ink Publishing LLC....G....313 766-1344
Van Buren Twp *(G-17550)*

Real Times Media LLC....G....313 963-8100
Detroit *(G-4556)*

Relationship Examiner....G....256 653-7374
Niles *(G-12162)*

Reminder Shopping Guide Inc....G....269 427-7474
Bangor *(G-1131)*

Reporter Papers Inc....G....734 429-5428
Saline *(G-15036)*

River Raisin Publications....G....517 486-2400
Blissfield *(G-1775)*

Rockman & Sons Publishing LLC....F....810 750-6011
Fenton *(G-5499)*

Rockman Communications Inc....E....810 433-6800
Fenton *(G-5500)*

Royal Lux Magazine....G....248 602-6565
Southfield *(G-15690)*

Sault Tribe News....F....906 632-6398
Sault Sainte Marie *(G-15099)*

Schepeler Corporation....E....517 592-6811
Brooklyn *(G-2132)*

Sciaccess Publishers....G....616 676-7012
Grand Rapids *(G-7186)*

Sherman Publications Inc....E....248 628-4801
Oxford *(G-12916)*

Sherman Publications Inc....G....248 627-4332
Ortonville *(G-12752)*

Shiawassee County 9/12 Comm....G....989 288-5049
Durand *(G-4847)*

Shoppers Fair Inc....E....231 627-7144
Cheboygan *(G-2799)*

Silent Observer....F....269 966-3550
Battle Creek *(G-1295)*

South Haven Tribune....G....269 637-1104
South Haven *(G-15415)*

Spin Lo Angler....G....231 882-6450
Beulah *(G-1658)*

Springer Publishing Co Inc....F....586 939-6800
Warren *(G-18023)*

St Ignace News....F....906 643-9150
Saint Ignace *(G-14895)*

Stafford Media Inc....E....616 754-9301
Greenville *(G-7505)*

State News Inc....D....517 295-1680
East Lansing *(G-4909)*

Sun Daily....G....248 842-2925
Orchard Lake *(G-12721)*

Super Woman Productions Pubg L....G....313 491-6819
Detroit *(G-4616)*

Textiss USA....G....310 909-6062
Three Rivers *(G-16587)*

The Sun....G....800 878-6397
Jackson *(G-9020)*

Three Rivers Commercial News....E....269 279-7488
Three Rivers *(G-16588)*

Thumbprint News....G....810 794-2300
Clay *(G-3127)*

Times and Titles....G....616 828-5640
Ada *(G-36)*

Times Herald Company....D....810 985-7171
Port Huron *(G-13532)*

Times Indicator Publications....G....231 924-4400
Fremont *(G-6056)*

Traverse Cy Record- Eagle Inc....G....231 946-2000
Traverse City *(G-16866)*

Treasure Enterprise LLC....F....810 233-7128
Flint *(G-5783)*

Tri City Record LLC....G....269 463-6397
Watervliet *(G-18184)*

Tuscola County Advertiser Inc....E....989 673-3181
Caro *(G-2583)*

Univesity Michigan-Dearborn....F....313 593-5428
Dearborn *(G-3906)*

Up Catholic Newspaper....G....906 226-8821
Marquette *(G-11046)*

Urban Aging L3c....G....313 204-5140
Detroit *(G-4654)*

USA Today Advertising....G....248 680-6530
Troy *(G-17417)*

Vegetable Growers News....G....616 887-9008
Sparta *(G-15788)*

View Newspaper....G....734 697-8255
Belleville *(G-1494)*

Vineyard Press Inc....F....269 657-5080
Paw Paw *(G-12959)*

Vintage Views Press....G....616 475-7662
Grand Rapids *(G-7319)*

Voice Communications Corp....E....586 716-8100
Sterling Heights *(G-16226)*

W Vbh....G....269 927-1527
Benton Harbor *(G-1601)*

Wall Street Journal Gate A 20....G....734 941-4139
Detroit *(G-4674)*

Washtenaw Voice....G....734 677-5405
Ann Arbor *(G-715)*

West Michigan Medical....G....269 673-2141
Allegan *(G-185)*

White Lake Beacon Inc....G....231 894-5356
Whitehall *(G-18512)*

Wings of Sturgis LLC....G....269 689-9326
Sturgis *(G-16330)*

Wochen-Post....G....248 641-9944
Warren *(G-18069)*

Yale Expositor....G....810 387-2300
Yale *(G-18921)*

SIC

Employee Codes: A=Over 500 employees, B=251-500
C=101-250, D=51-100, E=20-50, F=10-19, G=3-9

2022 Harris Michigan
Industrial Directory

761

27 PRINTING, PUBLISHING, AND ALLIED INDUSTRIES27 PRINTING, PUBLISHING, AND ALLIED INDUSTRIES SIC SECTION

Your Custom Image G 989 621-2250
Mount Pleasant *(G-11747)*

Your Hometown Shopper LLC F 586 412-8500
Bruce Twp *(G-2187)*

Ypsinewscom G 734 487-8109
Ypsilanti *(G-18987)*

Z & A News G 231 747-6232
Muskegon *(G-11952)*

2721 Periodicals: Publishing & Printing

5w LLC F 313 505-3106
Van Buren Twp *(G-17505)*

A & F Enterprises Inc F 248 714-6529
Milford *(G-11453)*

Advisor Inc G 906 341-2424
Manistique *(G-10916)*

African Amercn Parent Pubg Inc G 313 312-1611
Detroit *(G-3989)*

Agenda 2020 Inc F 616 581-6271
Grand Rapids *(G-6438)*

All Dealer Inventory LLC F 231 342-9823
Lake Ann *(G-9541)*

All Kids Cnsdred Pubg Group In E 248 398-3400
Ferndale *(G-5521)*

All Seasons Agency Inc G 586 752-6381
Bruce Twp *(G-2162)*

Ambassador Magazine G 313 965-6789
Detroit *(G-4008)*

American Public Works Assn G 816 472-6100
Springfield *(G-15859)*

Ann Arbor Observer Company E 734 769-3175
Ann Arbor *(G-368)*

Auto Connection G 586 752-6371
Bruce Twp *(G-2164)*

Blac Inc G 313 690-3372
Detroit *(G-4056)*

BNP Media Inc C 248 362-3700
Troy *(G-16978)*

Bob Allison Enterprises G 248 540-8467
Bloomfield Hills *(G-1804)*

Bowman Enterprises Inc G 269 720-1946
Portage *(G-13548)*

Business Direct Review G 269 373-7100
Kalamazoo *(G-9142)*

Business News Publishing F 248 362-3700
Troy *(G-16988)*

Caribbean Adventure LLC F 269 441-5675
Battle Creek *(G-1205)*

Castine Communications Inc G 248 477-1600
Farmington *(G-5134)*

Chaldean News LLC G 248 996-8360
Bingham Farms *(G-1693)*

Community Publishing & Mktg G 866 822-0101
Taylor *(G-16396)*

Consider Magazine G 734 769-0500
Ann Arbor *(G-435)*

Crain Communications Inc B 313 446-6000
Detroit *(G-4106)*

Cs Vendetta Pub LLC G 616 422-7555
Grand Rapids *(G-6616)*

Cte Publishing LLC G 313 338-4335
Detroit *(G-4111)*

Dbusiness F 313 929-0090
Troy *(G-17049)*

Dental Consultants Inc F 734 663-6777
Ann Arbor *(G-447)*

Denton Bobeldyk G 616 669-2076
Jenison *(G-9051)*

▲ Detroit Legal News Company D 313 961-6000
Detroit *(G-4150)*

Detroit Savings LLC G 313 971-5696
Detroit *(G-4165)*

Diocese of Lansing G 517 484-4449
Lansing *(G-9831)*

Double Gun Journal G 231 536-7439
East Jordan *(G-4862)*

Dynamic Color Publications G 248 553-3115
Farmington Hills *(G-5220)*

Elsie Publishing Institute F 517 371-5257
Lansing *(G-9835)*

▲ Faith Alive Christn Resources E 800 333-8300
Grand Rapids *(G-6698)*

Faith Publishing Service E 517 853-7600
Lansing *(G-9697)*

Farago & Associates LLC F 248 546-7070
Farmington Hills *(G-5240)*

Foreword Magazine Inc F 231 933-3699
Traverse City *(G-16685)*

G L Nelson Inc G 630 682-5958
Indian River *(G-8653)*

Gemini Corporation E 616 459-4545
Grand Rapids *(G-6737)*

Gongwer News Service Inc G 517 482-3500
Lansing *(G-9843)*

Graphics Hse Spt Prmotions Inc E 231 739-4004
Muskegon *(G-11828)*

Greater Lansing Bus Monthly G 517 203-0123
Lansing *(G-9844)*

Harp Column LLC G 215 564-3232
Zeeland *(G-19033)*

Hour Media LLC E 248 691-1800
Troy *(G-17152)*

Hour Media Group LLC G 248 691-1800
Troy *(G-17153)*

Infoguys Inc G 517 482-2125
Lansing *(G-9854)*

Informa Business Media Inc E 248 357-0800
Southfield *(G-15605)*

International Smart Tan Netwrk E 517 841-4920
Jackson *(G-8910)*

Jordan Barnett G 734 243-9565
Monroe *(G-11553)*

K and A Publishing Co LLC G 734 743-1541
Detroit *(G-4346)*

Kissman Consulting LLC G 517 256-1077
Okemos *(G-12672)*

Land & Homes Inc G 616 534-5792
Grand Rapids *(G-6927)*

Lansing Nwsppers In Edcatn Inc G 517 377-1000
Lansing *(G-9862)*

Lightworks Magazine Inc G 248 626-8026
Bloomfield *(G-1783)*

Living Word International Inc E 989 832-7547
Midland *(G-11384)*

Magazines In Motion Inc G 248 310-7647
Farmington Hills *(G-5299)*

Michigan Oil and Gas Assn G 517 487-0480
Lansing *(G-9870)*

Nationwide Network Inc G 989 793-0123
Saginaw *(G-14708)*

Opensystems Publishing LLC F 586 415-6500
Saint Clair Shores *(G-14876)*

Pathway Publishing Corporation F 269 521-3025
Bloomingdale *(G-1878)*

Pierian Press Inc G 734 434-4074
Ypsilanti *(G-18970)*

Planning & Zoning Center Inc G 517 886-0555
Lansing *(G-9731)*

Prakken Publications Inc F 734 975-2800
Ann Arbor *(G-618)*

Pressure Releases Corporation F 616 531-8116
Grand Rapids *(G-7103)*

Pride Source Corporation F 734 293-7200
Farmington Hills *(G-5352)*

Prism Publications Inc E 231 941-8174
Traverse City *(G-16802)*

Publishing Xpress G 248 582-1834
Madison Heights *(G-10811)*

R J Michaels Inc E 517 783-2637
Jackson *(G-8993)*

Renaissance Media LLC F 248 354-6060
Farmington Hills *(G-5367)*

Revue Holding Company G 616 608-6170
Grand Rapids *(G-7151)*

Rider Report Magazine G 248 854-8460
Auburn Hills *(G-1019)*

Rockman & Sons Publishing LLC F 810 750-6011
Fenton *(G-5499)*

Roe LLC G 231 755-5043
Muskegon *(G-11909)*

Saddle Up Magazine G 810 714-9000
Fenton *(G-5501)*

Shoreline Creations Ltd E 616 393-2077
Holland *(G-8192)*

Slaughterhouse Collective LLC G 248 259-5257
Ferndale *(G-5585)*

SPD America LLC G 734 709-7624
Pinckney *(G-13056)*

Stoney Creek Collection Inc F 616 363-4858
Grand Rapids *(G-7227)*

Tabs Floor Covering LLC G 616 846-1684
Nunica *(G-12587)*

Timothy J Tade Inc G 248 552-8583
Troy *(G-17392)*

Toastmasters International G 810 385-5477
Burtchville *(G-2223)*

Toastmasters International G 517 651-6507
Laingsburg *(G-9538)*

Towing & Equipment Magazine G 248 601-1385
Rochester Hills *(G-14130)*

Ukc Liquidating Inc G 269 343-9020
Portage *(G-13628)*

Unique U Magazine LLC G 586 696-1839
Madison Heights *(G-10852)*

Upston Associates Inc G 269 349-2782
Battle Creek *(G-1308)*

Vanguard Publications Inc G 517 336-1600
Okemos *(G-12692)*

Varsity Monthly Thumb G 810 404-5297
Caro *(G-2585)*

Verdoni Productions Inc G 989 790-0845
Saginaw *(G-14790)*

Vicrodesigns Global LLC G 616 307-3701
Grand Rapids *(G-7316)*

▲ Village Shop Inc E 231 946-3712
Traverse City *(G-16875)*

W W Thayne Advertising Cons F 269 979-1411
Battle Creek *(G-1309)*

West Michigan Printing Inc G 616 676-2190
Ada *(G-41)*

Wright Communications Inc F 248 585-3838
Troy *(G-17454)*

Your Home Town USA Inc G 517 529-9421
Clarklake *(G-3010)*

2731 Books: Publishing & Printing

▲ A B Publishing Inc G 989 875-4985
Ithaca *(G-8784)*

American Soc AG Blgcal Engners E 269 429-0300
Saint Joseph *(G-14922)*

◆ Baker Book House Company C 616 676-9185
Ada *(G-10)*

Banggameus G 734 904-1916
Ann Arbor *(G-395)*

Blackgirlperception LLC G 313 398-4275
Detroit *(G-4058)*

Boskage Commerce Publications G 269 673-7242
Portage *(G-13547)*

Caligirlbooks LLC G 415 361-1533
Macomb *(G-10582)*

Central Michigan University G 989 774-3216
Mount Pleasant *(G-11691)*

Chaosium Inc G 734 972-9551
Ann Arbor *(G-421)*

Childrens Bible Hour Inc F 616 647-4500
Grand Rapids *(G-6568)*

Christian Schools Intl E 616 957-1070
Grandville *(G-7369)*

Complete Services LLC F 248 470-8247
Livonia *(G-10161)*

Conant Gardeners G 313 863-2624
Detroit *(G-4101)*

Concord Editorial & Design LLC G 616 868-0148
Alto *(G-331)*

Cooper Publishing Group LLC G 231 933-9958
Traverse City *(G-16659)*

Creative Characters Inc G 231 544-6084
Central Lake *(G-2692)*

Dac Inc G 313 388-4342
Detroit *(G-4119)*

Dalton Armond Publishers Inc G 517 351-8520
Okemos *(G-12662)*

Developmental Services Inc G 313 653-1185
Detroit *(G-4173)*

Diocese of Lansing G 517 484-4449
Lansing *(G-9831)*

Duscha Management LLC F 352 247-2113
Luna Pier *(G-10560)*

E D C O Publishing Inc G 248 690-9184
Clarkston *(G-3031)*

Elmont District Library G 810 798-3100
Almont *(G-259)*

Entertainment Publications Inc D 248 404-1000
Troy *(G-17093)*

Evia Learning Inc G 616 393-8803
Holland *(G-8033)*

▲ Faith Alive Christn Resources E 800 333-8300
Grand Rapids *(G-6698)*

Foreword Magazine Inc F 231 933-3699
Traverse City *(G-16685)*

Harper Arrington Pubg LLC G 313 282-6751
Detroit *(G-4295)*

Harvest Time Partners Inc G 269 254-8999
Portage *(G-13564)*

Hayden - McNeil LLC E 734 455-7900
Plymouth *(G-13185)*

HSP Epi Acquisition LLC C 248 404-1520
Troy *(G-17156)*

Hummus & Co G 313 769-5557
Allen Park *(G-196)*

SIC SECTION
27 PRINTING, PUBLISHING, AND ALLIED INDUSTRIES

In-Depth Editions LLC .... G 616 566-6009
  Holland *(G-8095)*
Iris Design & Print Inc .... G 313 277-0505
  Dearborn *(G-3855)*
▲ Jenkins Group Inc .... G 231 933-4954
  Traverse City *(G-16728)*
◆ Kregel Inc .... E 616 531-7707
  Grandville *(G-7396)*
Literati LLC .... F 909 921-5242
  Ann Arbor *(G-551)*
Living Word International Inc .... E 989 832-7547
  Midland *(G-11384)*
Maria Dismondy Inc .... G 248 302-1800
  Novi *(G-12471)*
McGraw Hill Co .... G 616 802-3000
  Grand Rapids *(G-6973)*
Meghan March LLC .... G 231 740-8114
  Muskegon *(G-11865)*
Mehring Books Inc .... G 248 967-2924
  Oak Park *(G-12627)*
Mendenhall Associates Inc .... G 734 741-4710
  Ann Arbor *(G-569)*
▲ Michigan State Univ Press .... E 517 355-9543
  East Lansing *(G-4905)*
Mott Media LLC .... G 810 714-4280
  Fenton *(G-5492)*
◆ MPS Lansing Inc .... A 517 323-9000
  Lansing *(G-9719)*
Next Level Media Inc .... G 248 762-7043
  Southfield *(G-15666)*
Pagekicker Corporation .... G 734 646-6277
  Ann Arbor *(G-605)*
Pierian Press Inc .... G 734 434-4074
  Ypsilanti *(G-18970)*
Pink Diamond LLC .... G 586 298-7863
  Harrison Township *(G-7715)*
Prakken Publications Inc .... F 734 975-2800
  Ann Arbor *(G-618)*
Publishing Xpress .... G 248 582-1834
  Madison Heights *(G-10811)*
Quirkroberts Publishing Ltd .... G 248 879-2598
  Troy *(G-17326)*
▲ Rbc Ministries .... B 616 942-6770
  Grand Rapids *(G-7142)*
Real Ink Publishing LLC .... G 313 766-1344
  Van Buren Twp *(G-17550)*
▲ Remnant Publications Inc .... E 517 279-1304
  Coldwater *(G-3450)*
▲ Robbie Dean Press LLC .... G 734 973-9511
  Ann Arbor *(G-642)*
Rockman & Sons Publishing LLC ... F 810 750-6011
  Fenton *(G-5499)*
Roger D Rapoport .... G 231 755-6665
  Muskegon *(G-11910)*
Sheptime Music .... G 586 806-9058
  Warren *(G-18012)*
Short Books Inc .... G 231 796-2167
  Grand Rapids *(G-7194)*
Sprouting Sunflowers LLC .... G 248 982-2406
  Lathrup Village *(G-9977)*
Stoney Creek Collection Inc .... F 616 363-4858
  Grand Rapids *(G-7227)*
Team Breadwinner LLC .... G 313 460-0152
  Detroit *(G-4627)*
▲ Thunder Bay Press Inc .... E 517 694-3205
  Holt *(G-8335)*
Tri-C Publications Inc .... G 616 581-7967
  Grand Rapids *(G-7275)*
Truth & Tidings .... G 517 782-9798
  Jackson *(G-9027)*
Waterloo Group Inc .... G 248 840-6447
  Troy *(G-17445)*
▲ William B Eerdmans Pubg Co .... E 616 459-4591
  Grand Rapids *(G-7340)*
XMCO Inc .... D 586 558-8510
  Warren *(G-18075)*
Zonya Health International .... G 517 467-6995
  Onsted *(G-12708)*

2732 Book Printing, Not Publishing

Best Binding LLC .... G 734 459-7785
  Plymouth *(G-13136)*
Creative Graphics Inc .... G 517 784-0391
  Jackson *(G-8857)*
Cushing-Malloy Inc .... E 734 663-8554
  Ann Arbor *(G-440)*
Epi Printers Inc .... D 734 261-9400
  Livonia *(G-10198)*
Great Lakes Photo Inc .... G 586 784-5446
  Richmond *(G-13839)*

▼ Imperial Clinical RES Svcs Inc .... C 616 784-0100
  Grand Rapids *(G-6836)*
▲ Jenkins Group Inc .... G 231 933-4954
  Traverse City *(G-16728)*
Lottery Info .... G 734 326-0097
  Wayne *(G-18230)*
▼ McNaughton & Gunn Inc .... C 734 429-5411
  Saline *(G-15025)*
Mel Printing Co Inc .... E 313 928-5440
  Taylor *(G-16440)*
Practical Paper Inc .... F 616 887-1723
  Cedar Springs *(G-2658)*
R W Patterson Printing Co .... D 269 925-2177
  Benton Harbor *(G-1579)*
Rogers Printing Inc .... G 231 853-2244
  Ravenna *(G-13694)*
Sande-Wells Company .... G 248 276-9313
  Rochester Hills *(G-14106)*
Sheridan Pubg Grnd Rapids Inc ... D 616 957-5100
  Grand Rapids *(G-7193)*
SPD America LLC .... G 734 709-7624
  Pinckney *(G-13056)*
Success By Design Inc .... F 800 327-0057
  Wyoming *(G-18909)*
Superior Text LLC .... G 866 482-8762
  Ypsilanti *(G-18980)*
▲ Tweddle Group Inc .... C 586 307-3700
  Clinton Township *(G-3380)*
▲ William B Eerdmans Pubg Co .... E 616 459-4591
  Grand Rapids *(G-7340)*

2741 Misc Publishing

2 Donkeys Publishing .... G 616 554-3958
  Caledonia *(G-2365)*
▲ 4-Health Inc .... G 989 686-3377
  Bay City *(G-1313)*
Aaron Jagt .... G 517 304-4844
  Howell *(G-8425)*
ABC Printing Corporation Inc ...... G 248 887-0010
  Highland *(G-7879)*
Acra Training Center .... G 269 326-7088
  Baroda *(G-1158)*
Adams Street Publishing .... G 734 668-4044
  Ann Arbor *(G-350)*
Adtek Graphics Inc .... F 517 663-2460
  Eaton Rapids *(G-4950)*
Advance BCI Inc .... D 616 669-1366
  Grand Rapids *(G-6431)*
Advertiser Publishing Co Inc .... G 616 642-9411
  Saranac *(G-15076)*
Agri Blowers Express .... G 616 662-9999
  Jenison *(G-9043)*
All Kids Considered Pubg Group ... G 248 398-3400
  Ferndale *(G-5522)*
Alpha Omega Publishing .... G 517 879-1286
  Jackson *(G-8812)*
American Mathematical Society ... F 734 996-5250
  Ann Arbor *(G-364)*
Animo Games LLC .... G 586 201-9699
  Rochester Hills *(G-13948)*
Ariana Press Inc .... G 313 885-7581
  Grosse Pointe Farms *(G-7534)*
Ascribe .... G 616 726-2490
  Grand Rapids *(G-6475)*
Authors Coalition America LLC ... G 231 869-2011
  Pentwater *(G-12970)*
Avabella Press .... G 734 662-0048
  Ann Arbor *(G-386)*
Avanti Press Inc .... E 800 228-2684
  Detroit *(G-4034)*
Avery Color Studios Inc .... G 906 346-3908
  Gwinn *(G-7582)*
Aye Money Promotions Pubg LLC ... G 313 808-8173
  Detroit *(G-4036)*
Ayotte Cstm Mscal Engrvngs LLC ... G 734 595-1901
  Westland *(G-18358)*
B & D Publishing LLC .... G 586 651-3623
  Richmond *(G-13833)*
Ball Hard Music Group LLC .... G 833 246-4552
  Monroe *(G-11528)*
Bethany House Publishers .... G 616 676-9185
  Ada *(G-11)*
Big Maple Press .... G 231 313-4059
  Traverse City *(G-16621)*
Blackberry Publications .... G 313 627-1520
  Ecorse *(G-4980)*
Boch Publishing LLC .... G 734 718-2973
  Canton *(G-2441)*
Boone Express .... G 248 583-7080
  Ortonville *(G-12743)*

Bramin Enterprises .... G 313 960-1528
  Detroit *(G-4067)*
Brapos LLC .... G 248 677-6700
  West Bloomfield *(G-18268)*
Breakaway Media Marketing LLC ... G 734 787-3382
  Belleville *(G-1482)*
Broadside Press .... G 313 736-5338
  Detroit *(G-4075)*
Brother Mike Pubg & Mus Co LLC ... G 313 506-8866
  Bloomfield Hills *(G-1807)*
Brown House Publishing .... G 248 470-4690
  West Bloomfield *(G-18269)*
Buyers Guide .... G 616 897-9261
  Lowell *(G-10497)*
Buyers Guide .... G 231 722-3784
  Muskegon *(G-11787)*
C and N Press WD Enhncents LLC ... G 810 712-7771
  Berkley *(G-1623)*
Cabell Publishing LLC .... G 906 361-6828
  Marquette *(G-11011)*
CAM Publishing Inc .... G 248 848-3148
  Farmington Hills *(G-5194)*
Campbell and Co Publishing LLC ... G 810 320-0224
  Fort Gratiot *(G-5820)*
Campub Inc .... F 517 368-0365
  Camden *(G-2419)*
Candlelite Publishing LLC .... G 248 841-8925
  Rochester Hills *(G-13971)*
Capacity House Publishing .... G 586 209-3924
  Eastpointe *(G-4930)*
Carlton Sgnature Pub Relations ... G 248 387-9849
  Waterford *(G-18108)*
Carolyns Publication .... G 810 787-4114
  Flint *(G-5663)*
Carriage Town Press .... G 810 410-5113
  Flint *(G-5664)*
Carstill Wagon Pub/Toasty Toes ... G 734 325-7542
  Van Buren Twp *(G-17514)*
Cbm LLC .... G 800 487-2323
  Ann Arbor *(G-418)*
Chatman Walker Publishing LLC ... G 586 604-7534
  Clinton Township *(G-3197)*
City Press Inc .... G 800 867-2626
  Ortonville *(G-12744)*
Claire Aldin Publications .... G 313 702-4028
  Southfield *(G-15524)*
Cloud White Publishing .... G 248 684-6460
  Milford *(G-11459)*
Cobblestone Press .... G 989 832-0166
  Midland *(G-11330)*
Color Detroit Publishing LLC ...... G 313 974-9000
  Rochester Hills *(G-13977)*
Command Publishing LLC .... G 734 776-2692
  Canton *(G-2451)*
Common Earth Press LLC .... G 313 407-2919
  Huntington Woods *(G-8620)*
Complete Services LLC .... F 248 470-8247
  Livonia *(G-10161)*
Concordant Publishing Concern ... G 810 798-3563
  Almont *(G-257)*
Conine Publishing Inc .... E 231 723-3592
  Manistee *(G-10896)*
Conteur Publishing LLC .... G 248 602-9749
  Sterling Heights *(G-15968)*
Contribute A Verse Publishing .... G 616 447-2271
  Grand Rapids *(G-6601)*
Conway Publications .... G 517 424-1614
  Tecumseh *(G-16494)*
Corey .... G 313 565-8501
  Dearborn *(G-3822)*
Cornell Publications LLC .... G 810 225-3075
  Brighton *(G-1587)*
Country Register of Mich Inc ...... G 989 793-4211
  Saginaw *(G-14632)*
Cracker Publishing LLC .... G 248 429-9098
  Wixom *(G-18640)*
Crain Family Bible .... G 734 673-8620
  Pinckney *(G-13045)*
Crazy Red Head Publishing .... G 248 862-6096
  West Bloomfield *(G-18272)*
Creative Visions Publishing Co ... G 248 545-3528
  Oak Park *(G-12599)*
Crushing Hearts and Black .... G 224 234-9677
  Novi *(G-12386)*
Cs Express Inc .... G 248 425-1726
  Rochester Hills *(G-13987)*
Cs X Press Inc .... G 586 864-3360
  Sterling Heights *(G-15975)*
Cubbie Publications .... G 248 852-5297
  Rochester Hills *(G-13988)*

Employee Codes: A=Over 500 employees, B=251-500
C=101-250, D=51-100, E=20-50, F=10-19, G=3-9

27 PRINTING, PUBLISHING, AND ALLIED INDUSTRIES27 PRINTING, PUBLISHING, AND ALLIED INDUSTRIES SIC SECTION

Cvk Publishing Inc......G...... 248 877-6384
West Bloomfield *(G-18275)*
D L W Publishing Co......G...... 313 593-4554
Detroit *(G-4118)*
D2 Ink Inc......G...... 248 590-7076
Farmington Hills *(G-5209)*
Daily News......G...... 616 754-9301
Greenville *(G-7481)*
Dark Star Publishing......G...... 810 858-1135
Richmond *(G-13835)*
Datalyzer International Inc......G...... 248 960-3535
Wixom *(G-18644)*
Datamartz LLC......G...... 248 202-1559
Ann Arbor *(G-444)*
Deep Wood Press......G...... 231 587-0506
Bellaire *(G-1474)*
Denny Davis......G...... 989 785-3433
Atlanta *(G-745)*
Deslatae......G...... 313 820-4321
Detroit *(G-4133)*
Different Music Group Ent LLC......G...... 313 980-6159
Clinton Township *(G-3224)*
Diggypod Inc......G...... 734 429-3307
Tecumseh *(G-16496)*
Digiscroll Press......G...... 214 846-1826
Belmont *(G-1505)*
Digital Success Network......E...... 517 244-0771
Mason *(G-11130)*
Dillion Renee Entities......G...... 989 443-0654
Lansing *(G-9830)*
Diocesan Publications......E...... 616 878-5200
Byron Center *(G-2267)*
Diocese of Lansing......G...... 517 484-4449
Lansing *(G-9831)*
Direct Aim Media LLC......E...... 800 817-7101
Grand Rapids *(G-6649)*
▲ Discovery House Publishers......D...... 616 942-9218
Grand Rapids *(G-6651)*
Discovery Map......G...... 231 421-1466
Traverse City *(G-16669)*
Diva Publications......G...... 517 887-8271
Lansing *(G-9832)*
Dln Publications LLC......G...... 248 410-7337
Novi *(G-12402)*
Drake Publishing......G...... 269 963-4810
Battle Creek *(G-1221)*
Dream Catchers Publishing LLC......G...... 313 575-3933
Detroit *(G-4191)*
Dreambuilder Publications......G...... 989 465-1583
Coleman *(G-3463)*
Drummond Press Inc......G...... 248 834-7007
Lake Orion *(G-9604)*
Dust & Ashes Publications......G...... 231 722-6657
Byron Center *(G-2268)*
E D C O Publishing Inc......G...... 248 690-9184
Clarkston *(G-3031)*
E-Snap Publications LLC......G...... 708 740-0910
Ferndale *(G-5550)*
Edwards Publications In......G...... 864 882-3272
Caro *(G-2570)*
Eiklae Products......G...... 734 671-0752
Grosse Ile *(G-7521)*
▲ Elm International Inc......G...... 517 332-4900
Okemos *(G-12665)*
Encore Music Publishers......G...... 231 432-8322
Maple City *(G-10941)*
Encore Publications......G...... 269 488-3143
Kalamazoo *(G-9179)*
Engai......G...... 313 605-8220
Wixom *(G-18657)*
Ensign Publishing House......G...... 734 369-3983
Ann Arbor *(G-475)*
Ethnicemedia LLC......G...... 248 762-8904
Troy *(G-17097)*
Exie Smith Publications LLC......G...... 248 360-2917
Commerce Township *(G-3527)*
Express Expediting......G...... 313 347-9975
Harper Woods *(G-7666)*
Eyry of Eagle Publish......G...... 734 623-0337
Ann Arbor *(G-483)*
EZ Vent LLC......G...... 616 874-2787
Rockford *(G-14167)*
Fl Publishing......G...... 248 282-9905
Bloomfield Hills *(G-1821)*
First Wilson Inc......G...... 586 935-2687
Shelby Township *(G-15226)*
Fishkorn Publishing LLC......G...... 734 624-2211
Novi *(G-12416)*
Five Count Publishing LLC......G...... 616 308-6148
Gowen *(G-6229)*

Flashes Publishers Inc......E...... 269 673-2141
Holland *(G-8035)*
Flipsnack LLC......E...... 650 741-1328
Troy *(G-17115)*
Forerunner Press LLC......G...... 248 677-3272
Royal Oak *(G-14537)*
Forever Young Publishers......G...... 574 276-1805
Niles *(G-12130)*
Foreword Magazine Inc......G...... 231 933-3699
Traverse City *(G-16686)*
Foreword Reviews......G...... 231 933-5397
Traverse City *(G-16687)*
Forsons Inc......G...... 517 787-4562
Jackson *(G-8885)*
Foundations Press Inc......G...... 517 625-3052
Perry *(G-12977)*
Four Seasons Mobile Press......G...... 616 902-6233
Ionia *(G-8689)*
Fourth Seacoast Publishing Co......G...... 586 779-5570
Saint Clair Shores *(G-14861)*
French Press Knits LLC......G...... 810 623-0650
Fenton *(G-5480)*
Fresh Start Cmnty Initiative......G...... 941 225-9693
Detroit *(G-4246)*
Frontlines Publishing......E...... 616 887-6256
Grand Rapids *(G-6720)*
Fusion Design Group Ltd......G...... 269 469-8226
New Buffalo *(G-12023)*
G L Nelson Inc......G...... 630 682-5958
Indian River *(G-8653)*
Gaty......G...... 313 381-2853
Allen Park *(G-195)*
Gaus......G...... 517 764-6178
Jackson *(G-8889)*
Gemini Corporation......E...... 616 459-4545
Grand Rapids *(G-6737)*
George Moses Co......G...... 810 227-1575
Brighton *(G-2000)*
Ginger Tree Press......G...... 269 779-5780
Kalamazoo *(G-9197)*
Giving Press......G...... 702 302-2039
Spring Lake *(G-15817)*
Gossamer Press LLC......G...... 616 363-4608
Grand Rapids *(G-6751)*
Gpi-X LLC......G...... 616 453-4170
Grand Rapids *(G-6752)*
Grand Valley State University......G...... 847 744-0508
Allendale *(G-219)*
Graphics Hse Spt Prmotions Inc......E...... 231 739-4004
Muskegon *(G-11828)*
Grapho LLC......G...... 734 223-2144
Ann Arbor *(G-505)*
Great Lakes Publishing Inc......G...... 517 647-4444
Portland *(G-13638)*
Great Lakes Spt Publications......G...... 734 507-0241
Ann Arbor *(G-507)*
Great Northern Publishing Inc......D...... 810 648-4000
Sandusky *(G-15059)*
Gregg Publishing Co......G...... 906 789-1139
Escanaba *(G-5074)*
Grey Wolfe Publishing LLC......G...... 248 914-4027
Bingham Farms *(G-1698)*
Guest Publications LLC......G...... 231 651-9281
Traverse City *(G-16707)*
Guys You Are Real Heroes Pubg......G...... 248 682-2537
West Bloomfield *(G-18286)*
Hammond Publishing Company......G...... 810 686-8879
Mount Morris *(G-11671)*
Hang On Express......G...... 231 271-0202
Suttons Bay *(G-16340)*
Harpercollins Christn Pubg Inc......F...... 616 698-3230
Grand Rapids *(G-6804)*
Hatchback Publishing......G...... 810 394-8612
Genesee *(G-6168)*
Hawkshadow Publishing Company......G...... 586 979-5046
Sterling Heights *(G-16035)*
Health Enhancement Systems Inc......G...... 989 839-0852
Midland *(G-11372)*
▲ Helm Incorporated......D...... 734 468-3700
Plymouth *(G-13186)*
Herald Bi-County Inc......G...... 517 448-2201
Hudson *(G-8550)*
Hermiz Publishing In......G...... 586 212-4490
Sterling Heights *(G-16039)*
Hi-Lites Graphic Inc......E...... 231 924-0630
Fremont *(G-6045)*
Hmg Agency......F...... 989 443-3819
Saginaw *(G-14666)*
House of Hero LLC......G...... 248 260-8300
Bloomfield Hills *(G-1829)*

Human Synergistics Inc......E...... 734 459-1030
Plymouth *(G-13193)*
Ideation Inc......E...... 734 761-4360
Ann Arbor *(G-522)*
If and or But Publishing......G...... 269 274-6102
Battle Creek *(G-1239)*
Ifca International Inc......G...... 616 531-1840
Grandville *(G-7391)*
In Know Inc......G...... 734 827-9711
Ann Arbor *(G-526)*
Inside English......G...... 586 801-4351
Fraser *(G-5943)*
International Assn Lions Clubs......G...... 989 644-6562
Weidman *(G-18253)*
Internet Publishing Inc......G...... 248 438-8192
Novi *(G-12439)*
Intheknow313 LLC......G...... 248 445-1953
Lincoln Park *(G-10050)*
J B Express LLC......G...... 313 903-4601
Dearborn Heights *(G-3929)*
J-Ad Graphics Inc......D...... 800 870-7085
Hastings *(G-7800)*
J-Ad Graphics Inc......F...... 269 965-3955
Battle Creek *(G-1243)*
J-Ad Graphics Inc......G...... 269 945-9554
Marshall *(G-11062)*
Jeffrey Scheiber......G...... 248 207-7036
Wyandotte *(G-18826)*
Jewel Albright Cohen Pubg LLC......G...... 248 672-8889
Waterford *(G-18130)*
Jga Press/Jackson Gates Assoc......G...... 313 957-0200
Detroit *(G-4337)*
Jn Press......G...... 517 708-0300
Lansing *(G-9708)*
Johnson Multimedia Group LLC......G...... 989 753-1151
Bay City *(G-1369)*
Jones Music Co......G...... 313 521-6471
Detroit *(G-4342)*
Joseph Scott Falbe......G...... 269 282-1597
Battle Creek *(G-1247)*
Just Press Play......G...... 248 470-7797
Livonia *(G-10262)*
Kitchen Joy......G...... 616 682-7327
Grand Rapids *(G-6898)*
Kvga Publishing......G...... 517 545-0841
Howell *(G-8471)*
Lady Lazarus LLC......G...... 810 441-9115
Ferndale *(G-5564)*
Lake House Publishing LLC......G...... 231 377-2017
Bellaire *(G-1477)*
Lakeshore Publishing......G...... 616 846-0620
Spring Lake *(G-15829)*
Lakeview Publishing Company......G...... 586 443-5913
Saint Clair Shores *(G-14867)*
Lca International Publishing......G...... 313 908-4583
Dearborn *(G-3860)*
Leader Publications LLC......D...... 269 683-2100
Niles *(G-12141)*
Leann Kelley Enterprises LLC......G...... 505 270-5687
Hamilton *(G-7601)*
Leather Lore......G...... 269 548-7160
Coopersville *(G-3690)*
Lebutt Publishing LLC......G...... 248 756-1613
Commerce Township *(G-3550)*
Lehman Publishingcom......G...... 810 395-4535
Allenton *(G-230)*
Little Bird Press LLC......G...... 616 676-9052
Ada *(G-26)*
Little Blue Book Inc......F...... 313 469-0052
Grosse Pointe Woods *(G-7570)*
Little Spoke Big Wheel Pubg......G...... 313 779-9327
Southfield *(G-15637)*
Live Track Productions Inc......G...... 313 704-2224
Detroit *(G-4402)*
LL Becker Publications......G...... 248 366-9037
White Lake *(G-18460)*
Llomen Inc......G...... 269 345-3555
Portage *(G-13579)*
Local Logic Media......G...... 517 914-2486
Spring Arbor *(G-15794)*
Looking Aft Publications......G...... 231 759-8581
Whitehall *(G-18507)*
Lou Jack City Publishing LLC......G...... 404 863-7124
Detroit *(G-4407)*
Love Publicity......G...... 313 288-8342
Detroit *(G-4408)*
Lsjd Publications LLC......G...... 843 576-9040
Sault Sainte Marie *(G-15094)*
Lucky Press LLC......G...... 614 309-0048
Harbor Springs *(G-7650)*

27 PRINTING, PUBLISHING, AND ALLIED INDUSTRIES

Ludington Daily News Inc ... E ... 231 845-5181
Ludington *(G-10543)*

Luke Legacy Publications LLC ... G ... 313 363-5949
Plymouth *(G-13229)*

Macdonald Publications Inc ... F ... 989 875-4151
Ithaca *(G-8793)*

Manistee News Advocate ... F ... 231 723-3592
Manistee *(G-10905)*

Manray Press LLC ... G ... 734 558-0580
Wyandotte *(G-18831)*

Masters Publishing ... G ... 586 323-2723
Sterling Heights *(G-16086)*

McMackon Mktg ADM Pubg Svcs LL ... G ... 734 878-3198
Pinckney *(G-13051)*

Medwin Publishers LLC ... G ... 248 247-6042
Troy *(G-17244)*

Meech Road Ltd ... G ... 734 255-9119
Mason *(G-11143)*

Metra Inc ... G ... 248 543-3500
Hazel Park *(G-7831)*

Metro Graphic Arts Inc ... F ... 616 245-2271
Grand Rapids *(G-6982)*

Mh Publishing LLC ... G ... 313 881-3724
Grosse Pointe Farms *(G-7537)*

MI Classical Press ... G ... 734 747-6337
Ann Arbor *(G-571)*

Michigan Acdemy Fmly Physcians ... G ... 517 347-0098
Okemos *(G-12675)*

Michigan Legal Publishing Ltd ... F ... 877 525-1990
Grandville *(G-7400)*

Michiganensian ... G ... 734 418-4115
Ann Arbor *(G-576)*

Mission Point Press ... G ... 231 421-9513
Traverse City *(G-16761)*

Mjs Publishing Group ... G ... 734 391-7370
Van Buren Twp *(G-17541)*

Morning Star ... G ... 989 755-2660
Saginaw *(G-14704)*

Morning Star Publishing Co ... F ... 989 463-6071
Alma *(G-248)*

Morning Star Publishing Co ... G ... 989 779-6000
Alma *(G-250)*

Mpress Desighns LLC ... G ... 313 627-9727
Eastpointe *(G-4941)*

Music ... G ... 313 854-3606
Detroit *(G-4472)*

Musicalia Press ... G ... 734 433-1289
Chelsea *(G-2821)*

N2 Publications ... G ... 517 488-2607
Mason *(G-11146)*

Native Detroiter Pubg Inc ... G ... 313 822-1958
Detroit *(G-4477)*

Nb Media Solutions LLC ... G ... 616 724-7175
Grand Rapids *(G-7037)*

New Alexandria Press ... G ... 248 529-3108
White Lake *(G-18462)*

New Classics Press LLC ... G ... 616 975-9070
Grand Rapids *(G-7041)*

New Genesis Enterprise Inc ... G ... 313 220-0365
Westland *(G-18400)*

Next In Line Publishing LLc ... G ... 248 954-1280
Livonia *(G-10335)*

Ninja Pants Press LLC ... G ... 248 669-6577
Commerce Township *(G-3557)*

Nord Publications Inc ... G ... 734 455-5271
Canton *(G-2501)*

Northern Michigan Publishing ... G ... 231 946-7878
Traverse City *(G-16774)*

Novel Publicity LLC ... G ... 248 563-6637
Brighton *(G-2043)*

Npi Wireless ... E ... 231 922-9273
Traverse City *(G-16776)*

Oak Leaf Publishing Inc ... G ... 248 547-7103
Oak Park *(G-12635)*

Oceanas Herald-Journal Inc ... F ... 231 873-5602
Hart *(G-7759)*

One Tree Research Group LLC ... G ... 616 466-4880
Ada *(G-32)*

Online Publications Inc ... G ... 248 879-2133
Troy *(G-17289)*

Orange October Publishing Co ... G ... 231 828-1039
Twin Lake *(G-17471)*

Paine Press LLC ... G ... 231 645-1970
Boyne City *(G-1900)*

Paladino Publications ... G ... 586 759-2795
Warren *(G-17953)*

Panda King Express ... G ... 616 796-3286
Holland *(G-8159)*

Panther Publishing ... G ... 586 202-9814
Grand Blanc *(G-6255)*

Paper Petal Press ... G ... 248 935-5193
Waterford *(G-18146)*

Paper Press ... G ... 248 438-6238
West Bloomfield *(G-18303)*

Par Excellence Publication ... G ... 989 345-8305
West Branch *(G-18334)*

Parish Publications ... G ... 248 613-2384
Bloomfield Hills *(G-1847)*

▲ **Parker & Associates** ... G ... 269 694-6709
Otsego *(G-12794)*

Partridge Pointe Press LLC ... G ... 248 321-0475
Belmont *(G-1515)*

Pat Ro Publishing ... G ... 248 553-4935
Farmington Hills *(G-5343)*

Personal Power Press Inc ... G ... 989 239-8628
Bay City *(G-1386)*

Peter Dehaan Publishing Inc ... G ... 616 284-1305
Hudsonville *(G-8600)*

Pgi Holdings Inc ... G ... 231 937-4740
Big Rapids *(G-1684)*

Phalanx Press ... G ... 517 213-9393
Charlotte *(G-2764)*

Pick Energy Savings LLC ... G ... 248 343-8354
Highland *(G-7898)*

Pierian Press Inc ... G ... 734 434-4074
Ypsilanti *(G-18970)*

Pigeon River Publishing LLC ... G ... 616 528-4027
Haslett *(G-7776)*

Pinstripe Publishing LLC ... G ... 734 276-0554
Ann Arbor *(G-611)*

Poppyseed Press LLC ... G ... 616 450-8521
Grand Rapids *(G-7093)*

Prankster Press LLC ... G ... 616 550-3099
Detroit *(G-4531)*

Presque Isle Newspapers Inc ... F ... 989 734-2105
Rogers City *(G-14217)*

Press On Juice ... G ... 231 409-9971
Traverse City *(G-16800)*

Press Play ... G ... 231 753-2841
Traverse City *(G-16801)*

Press Play LLC ... G ... 248 802-3837
Auburn Hills *(G-1004)*

Private Life Corp ... G ... 248 922-9800
Waterford *(G-18158)*

Proquest Outdoor Solutions Inc ... E ... 734 761-4700
Ann Arbor *(G-626)*

Prs & PIP Ftrs L 506 ... G ... 906 789-9784
Escanaba *(G-5092)*

Prs Judd ... G ... 734 470-6162
Saline *(G-15033)*

Publishing Systems Inc ... G ... 248 852-0185
Rochester Hills *(G-14092)*

Quality Guest Publishing Inc ... F ... 616 894-1111
Cedar Springs *(G-2660)*

R & R Harwood Inc ... G ... 616 669-6400
Jenison *(G-9069)*

R S C Productions ... G ... 586 532-9200
Shelby Township *(G-15313)*

Rainbow Hollow Press ... G ... 231 825-2962
Rodney *(G-14207)*

Raychris ... G ... 734 404-5485
Plymouth *(G-13276)*

Red Falcon Press ... G ... 248 439-0432
Royal Oak *(G-14575)*

◆ **Reflective Art Inc** ... E ... 616 452-0712
Wyoming *(G-18903)*

Reg Publishers LLC ... G ... 616 889-4232
Hopkins *(G-8368)*

Reveal Publishing LLC ... G ... 248 798-3440
Bloomfield Hills *(G-1855)*

Review Directories Inc ... F ... 231 347-8606
Petoskey *(G-13020)*

Rhys World Publishing LLC ... G ... 248 974-7408
Northville *(G-12254)*

Ridge Pointe Publishing LLC ... G ... 586 948-4660
Macomb *(G-10632)*

Roaring River Press ... G ... 248 342-2281
New Haven *(G-12036)*

Robbins Publishing Group Inc ... G ... 734 260-3258
Lake Angelus *(G-9539)*

Roe Publishing Department ... G ... 517 522-3598
Jackson *(G-8997)*

Rosemary Felice ... G ... 517 861-7434
Howell *(G-8511)*

Royal Publishing ... G ... 810 768-3057
Flint *(G-5758)*

Rrr Training & Publishing ... G ... 906 396-9546
Iron Mountain *(G-8731)*

S G Publications Inc ... F ... 517 676-5100
Mason *(G-11151)*

S Hasan Publishing LLC ... G ... 734 858-8800
Inkster *(G-8675)*

Salesman Inc ... G ... 517 592-5886
Brooklyn *(G-2131)*

Salesman Inc ... G ... 517 783-4080
Jackson *(G-9005)*

Samhita Press ... G ... 248 747-7792
Sterling Heights *(G-16162)*

Sanders Information Publishing ... G ... 248 669-0991
Novi *(G-12531)*

Sandkey Publishing LLC ... G ... 248 475-3662
Rochester Hills *(G-14107)*

Scapegoat Press Inc ... G ... 586 439-8381
Wyandotte *(G-18838)*

Scriblical Vibez Publishing ... G ... 313 544-3042
Westland *(G-18417)*

Shamrock Publications ... G ... 269 459-1099
Portage *(G-13606)*

Shamrock Publishing ... G ... 313 881-1721
Grosse Pointe Woods *(G-7575)*

Sharedbook Inc ... E ... 734 302-6500
Ann Arbor *(G-650)*

Shepherd Jnes Pblcations Press ... G ... 313 221-3000
Southfield *(G-15698)*

Shoreline Creations Ltd ... E ... 616 393-2077
Holland *(G-8192)*

Source Point Press ... G ... 269 501-3690
Midland *(G-11419)*

Spectrum Map Publishing Inc ... G ... 517 655-5641
Williamston *(G-18583)*

Spes Publishing Co LLC ... G ... 734 741-1241
Ann Arbor *(G-661)*

Spirit Publishing LLC ... G ... 231 399-1538
Traverse City *(G-16838)*

Spitting Image Pblications LLC ... G ... 989 498-9459
Saginaw *(G-14764)*

Spoonful Press ... G ... 313 862-6579
Detroit *(G-4602)*

Spunky Duck Press ... G ... 269 365-7285
Plainwell *(G-13096)*

Stafford Media Inc ... E ... 616 754-9301
Greenville *(G-7505)*

Standard Register ... G ... 616 987-3128
Lowell *(G-10517)*

Star Buyers Guide ... G ... 989 366-8341
Houghton Lake *(G-8405)*

Star Design Metro Detroit LLC ... E ... 734 740-0189
Livonia *(G-10419)*

Subterranean Press ... G ... 810 232-1489
Flint *(G-5772)*

Summit Training Source Inc ... E ... 800 842-0466
Grand Rapids *(G-7233)*

Sunset Coast Publishing LLC ... G ... 574 440-3228
Edwardsburg *(G-5018)*

Svk Media and Publishing LLC ... G ... 616 379-4001
Hudsonville *(G-8613)*

Synod of Great Lakes ... E ... 616 698-7071
Grand Rapids *(G-7243)*

Taletyano Press ... G ... 517 381-1960
Okemos *(G-12688)*

Tapoos LLC ... G ... 619 319-4872
Taylor *(G-16483)*

Technical Illustration Corp ... F ... 313 982-9660
Canton *(G-2530)*

Think Club Publication ... G ... 248 651-3106
Rochester *(G-13933)*

Think Social Media ... G ... 810 360-0170
Brighton *(G-2080)*

Thm Publishing Detroit LLC ... G ... 586 232-3037
Washington *(G-18089)*

Thumb Blanket ... G ... 989 269-9918
Bad Axe *(G-1113)*

Thunder Bay Press Michigan LLC ... G ... 989 701-2430
West Branch *(G-18343)*

Time Traveling DJS ... G ... 517 402-0976
Eaton Rapids *(G-4973)*

Timothy J Tade Inc ... G ... 248 552-8583
Troy *(G-17392)*

Toledo Press Industries Inc ... G ... 734 727-0605
Wayne *(G-18238)*

Total Local Acquisitions LLC ... G ... 517 663-2405
Eaton Rapids *(G-4974)*

Triple S Publications LLC ... G ... 231 775-6113
Cadillac *(G-2362)*

Triumph Publishing House Inc ... G ... 248 423-1765
Southfield *(G-15727)*

Tuscola County Advertiser Inc ... F ... 989 823-8651
Vassar *(G-17583)*

Tuscola County Advertiser Inc ... E ... 989 673-3181
Caro *(G-2583)*

SIC

Employee Codes: A=Over 500 employees, B=251-500
C=101-250, D=51-100, E=20-50, F=10-19, G=3-9

2022 Harris Michigan
Industrial Directory

765

▲ Tweddle Group Inc ....C 586 307-3700
Clinton Township *(G-3380)*
Unique Connection Pubg Co ....G 248 304-0030
Southfield *(G-15731)*
◆ Upper Michigan Newspapers LLC ....G 989 732-5125
Gaylord *(G-6165)*
Upper Pnnsula Pbls Athors Assn ....G 906 226-1543
Marquette *(G-11048)*
US Suburban Press ....G 616 662-6420
Hudsonville *(G-8614)*
Valley Publishing ....G 989 671-1200
Grand Rapids *(G-7302)*
Van Buren Publishing LLC ....G 734 740-8668
Belleville *(G-1492)*
Vanguard Publications Inc ....G 517 336-1600
Okemos *(G-12692)*
Verdoni Productions Inc ....G 989 790-0845
Saginaw *(G-14790)*
Verticalscope USA Inc ....G 248 220-1451
Troy *(G-17439)*
View Publication Co ....G 734 461-1579
Ypsilanti *(G-18985)*
Village Press Inc ....G 231 946-3712
Traverse City *(G-16874)*
Vimax Publishing ....G 248 563-2367
Bloomfield Hills *(G-1873)*
Vineyard Press Inc ....F 269 657-5080
Paw Paw *(G-12959)*
Vivid Publishing ....G 614 282-6479
Monroe *(G-11589)*
Wade Printing & Publishing LLC ....G 616 894-6350
Lowell *(G-10521)*
Wallace Publishing LLC ....E 248 416-7259
Hazel Park *(G-7848)*
Walsworth Publishing Co Inc ....E 269 428-2054
Saint Joseph *(G-14973)*
Wardlaw Press LLC ....G 313 806-4603
Grosse Pointe Farms *(G-7542)*
Watersong Publications ....G 248 592-0109
Farmington Hills *(G-5412)*
Waub Ajijaak Press ....G 248 802-8630
Manistee *(G-10915)*
Wave Music and Publishing ....G 313 290-2193
Detroit *(G-4676)*
Wendy Williamson ....G 321 345-8297
Saint Joseph *(G-14975)*
West Mich Cmnty Help Netwrk ....F 231 727-5007
Muskegon *(G-11942)*
Weyv Inc ....F 248 614-2400
Troy *(G-17448)*
Whos Who Publishing Co LLC ....G 614 481-7300
Detroit *(G-4683)*
Wicwas Press ....G 269 344-8027
Kalamazoo *(G-9369)*
Winding Road Publishing Inc ....G 248 545-8360
Ferndale *(G-5598)*
Winning Publications ....G 269 342-8547
Kalamazoo *(G-9371)*
Writers Bible LLc ....G 734 286-7793
Romulus *(G-14341)*
Yeungs Lotus Express ....G 248 380-3820
Novi *(G-12573)*
Your Personal Memoir LLC ....G 248 629-0697
Pleasant Ridge *(G-13107)*
Zimbell House Publishing LLC ....G 248 909-0143
Waterford *(G-18177)*
◆ Zondervan Corporation LLC ....B 616 698-6900
Grand Rapids *(G-7358)*
Zoomer Display LLC ....G 616 734-0300
Grand Rapids *(G-7359)*

2752 Commercial Printing: Lithographic

20/20 Printing ....G 616 635-9690
Grand Rapids *(G-6403)*
3d Printed Parts ....G 616 516-3074
Grand Rapids *(G-6404)*
A B C Printing Inc ....G 248 887-0010
Highland *(G-7877)*
A Koppel Color Image Company ....G 616 534-3600
Grandville *(G-7360)*
Aalpha Tinadawn Inc ....G 517 351-1200
East Lansing *(G-4884)*
ABC Printing Corporation Inc ....G 248 887-0010
Highland *(G-7879)*
Acadia Group LLC ....E 734 944-1404
Saline *(G-14997)*
Accelerated Press Inc ....G 248 524-1850
Troy *(G-16902)*
Action Printech Inc ....F 734 207-6000
Plymouth *(G-13112)*
Adair Printing Company ....E 734 426-2822
Dexter *(G-4721)*
Adams Design & Print LLC ....G 269 612-8613
New Buffalo *(G-12022)*
ADM Graphics & Print Prod LLC ....G 586 598-1821
Chesterfield *(G-2835)*
Admore Inc ....C 586 949-8200
Macomb *(G-10571)*
Advance BCI Inc ....D 616 669-1366
Grand Rapids *(G-6431)*
Advance Graphic Systems Inc ....E 248 656-8000
Rochester Hills *(G-13943)*
Advance Print & Graphics Inc ....E 734 663-6816
Ann Arbor *(G-354)*
Advanced Eco Print ....G 231 292-1688
Fountain *(G-5826)*
Advanced Systems & Forms ....G 734 422-7180
Livonia *(G-10102)*
Afb Corporate Operations LLC ....E 248 669-1188
Plymouth *(G-13120)*
Affordable Prints ....G 231 679-2606
Evart *(G-5119)*
Afj Woodhaven LLC ....G 248 593-6200
Bloomfield Hills *(G-1793)*
Aladdin Printing ....G 248 360-2842
Commerce Township *(G-3507)*
All In Printing ....G 567 219-3660
New Boston *(G-11999)*
Allbrite Printing & Lettershop ....G 734 516-2623
New Boston *(G-12000)*
Allegra Marketing Print Mail ....G 586 335-2596
Grosse Pointe Park *(G-7544)*
Allegra Marketing Print Mail ....G 248 602-0545
Troy *(G-16926)*
Allegra Marketing Print Mail ....G 313 382-8033
Allen Park *(G-188)*
Allegra Marketing Print Mail ....G 517 879-2444
Jackson *(G-8809)*
Allegra Marketing Print Mail ....G 313 429-0916
Allen Park *(G-189)*
Allegra Marketing Print Mail ....G 269 213-8840
Battle Creek *(G-1183)*
Allegra Network LLC ....F 248 360-1290
West Bloomfield *(G-18262)*
Allegra Print & Imaging ....G 248 354-1313
Southfield *(G-15475)*
Allegra Print and Imaging ....G 616 784-6699
Grand Rapids *(G-6447)*
Allegra Print Imaging ....G 616 446-6269
Allendale *(G-212)*
Allegra-Marketing Design Print ....G 313 561-8000
Dearborn Heights *(G-3919)*
Allesk Enterprises Inc ....G 231 941-5770
Traverse City *(G-16600)*
Alliance Franchise Brands LLC ....F 248 596-8600
Plymouth *(G-13122)*
Alliance Prints LLC ....G 313 484-0700
Detroit *(G-4002)*
Allied Mailing and Prtg Inc ....E 810 750-8291
Fenton *(G-5448)*
Allied Printing Co Inc ....E 248 541-0551
Ferndale *(G-5523)*
Allied Printing Co Inc ....E 248 514-7394
Ferndale *(G-5524)*
Allprints Plus LLC ....G 248 906-2977
Madison Heights *(G-10665)*
Alpha Data Business Forms Inc ....G 248 540-5930
Birmingham *(G-1718)*
American Graphics Inc ....G 586 774-8880
Saint Clair Shores *(G-14848)*
American Ink USA Prntg & Grphc ....G 586 790-2555
Clinton Township *(G-3165)*
American Litho Inc ....G 734 394-1400
Van Buren Twp *(G-17508)*
American Printing Services Inc ....G 248 568-5543
Troy *(G-16934)*
American Speedy Printing Ctrs ....G 989 723-5196
Owosso *(G-12823)*
American Speedy Printing Ctrs ....G 313 928-5820
Taylor *(G-16376)*
Americas Finest Prtg Graphics ....G 586 296-1312
Fraser *(G-5893)*
Amped Electric LLC ....G 419 436-1818
Grand Blanc *(G-6232)*
▲ Anchor Printing Company ....E 248 335-7440
Novi *(G-12362)*
Andex Industries Inc ....E 906 786-7588
Escanaba *(G-5056)*
AP Impressions Inc ....G 734 464-8009
Livonia *(G-10121)*
Apb Inc ....G 248 528-2990
Troy *(G-16939)*
Apms Incorporated ....G 248 268-1477
Madison Heights *(G-10670)*
Aquaprintingcom ....G 269 779-2734
Kalamazoo *(G-9116)*
Arbor Press LLC ....D 248 549-0150
Royal Oak *(G-14510)*
Argus Press Company ....E 989 725-5136
Owosso *(G-12824)*
Artcraft Printing Corporation ....G 734 455-8893
Plymouth *(G-13126)*
Artech Printing Inc ....G 248 545-0088
Madison Heights *(G-10673)*
Artigy Printing ....G 269 373-6591
Kalamazoo *(G-9122)*
Artistic Flair EMB & Prtg ....G 810 487-9074
Flushing *(G-5802)*
Artistic Printing Inc ....G 248 356-1004
Southfield *(G-15491)*
ASAP Printing Inc ....F 517 882-3500
Lansing *(G-9807)*
ASAP Printing Inc ....G 517 882-3500
Okemos *(G-12657)*
Associated Print & Graphics ....G 734 676-8896
Grosse Ile *(G-7516)*
Associated Print Marketing ....G 248 268-2726
Madison Heights *(G-10674)*
August Communications Inc ....G 313 561-8000
Dearborn Heights *(G-3921)*
Automotive Media LLC ....C 248 537-8500
Troy *(G-16966)*
▲ Avanzado LLC ....E 248 615-0538
Farmington Hills *(G-5178)*
Avery Color Studios Inc ....G 906 346-3908
Gwinn *(G-7582)*
B & M Imaging Inc ....G 269 968-2403
Battle Creek *(G-1188)*
B-Quick Instant Printing ....G 616 243-6562
Grand Rapids *(G-6490)*
Bad Axe Prints ....G 248 207-6999
Wixom *(G-18618)*
▲ Batson Printing Inc ....D 269 926-6011
Benton Harbor *(G-1532)*
Battle Creek Flyers LLC ....G 269 579-2914
Battle Creek *(G-1192)*
BCT Internet LLC ....G 810 771-9117
Grand Blanc *(G-6235)*
Bearded Vinyl LLC ....G 989 786-9994
Lewiston *(G-10018)*
Behrmann Printing Company Inc ....F 248 799-7771
Southfield *(G-15505)*
Benzie Printing ....G 231 714-7565
Interlochen *(G-8679)*
Berci Printing Services Inc ....G 248 350-0206
Southfield *(G-15506)*
Bi-Rite Office Products Inc ....G 586 751-1410
Warren *(G-17735)*
Bizcard Xpress ....G 248 288-4800
Rochester *(G-13893)*
Blue Print Studio ....G 616 283-2893
Holland *(G-7977)*
Blue Water Printing Co Inc ....G 810 664-0643
Lapeer *(G-9914)*
Bnw West Side Scrnprinting LLC ....G 616 717-1082
Wyoming *(G-18853)*
Bowman Printing Inc ....G 810 982-8202
Port Huron *(G-13462)*
Bradford Printing Inc ....G 517 887-0044
Lansing *(G-9815)*
Bradley Jacob Printing LLC ....G 248 953-9010
Lake Orion *(G-9589)*
Brd Printing Inc ....E 517 372-0268
Lansing *(G-9816)*
Breck Graphics Incorporated ....E 616 248-4110
Grand Rapids *(G-6523)*
Bretts Printing Service ....G 517 482-2256
Lansing *(G-9818)*
Bronco Printing Company ....G 248 544-1120
Hazel Park *(G-7821)*
Brophy Engraving Co Inc ....E 313 871-2333
Detroit *(G-4076)*
Bruce Inc ....G 517 371-5205
Lansing *(G-9819)*
Business Cards Plus Inc ....F 269 327-7727
Portage *(G-13551)*
Business Design Solutions Inc ....G 248 672-8007
Southfield *(G-15514)*
Business Press Inc ....G 248 652-8855
Rochester *(G-13895)*

Bwjs Printing LLC G 248 678-3610
Detroit *(G-4081)*

C H M Graphics & Litho Inc G 586 777-4550
Saint Clair Shores *(G-14851)*

C J Graphics Inc G 906 774-8636
Kingsford *(G-9506)*

C L Mailing Printing G 248 471-3330
Farmington Hills *(G-5191)*

C S L Inc G 248 549-4434
Royal Oak *(G-14522)*

C W Enterprises Inc G 810 385-9100
Fort Gratiot *(G-5819)*

C&P Hoover LLC G 248 887-2400
Highland *(G-7886)*

Cadillac Printing Company F 231 775-2488
Cadillac *(G-2323)*

Cambridge Financial Services G 248 840-6650
Troy *(G-16995)*

Cameron S Roat G 810 620-7628
Burton *(G-2231)*

Canton Embroidery LLC G 734 216-3374
Ypsilanti *(G-18932)*

Capital City Blue Print Inc G 517 482-5431
Lansing *(G-9676)*

Capital Imaging Inc F 517 482-2292
Lansing *(G-9822)*

Carbonless 365 G 810 969-4014
Lapeer *(G-9921)*

Carmens Screen Printing & EMB G 248 535-4161
Lake Orion *(G-9593)*

Carrigan Graphics Inc G 734 455-6550
Canton *(G-2445)*

Cascade Prtg & Graphics Inc G 616 222-2937
Grand Rapids *(G-6556)*

Celani Printing Co G 810 395-1609
Capac *(G-2546)*

Cheap Fast Prints LLC G 517 490-0864
Lansing *(G-9824)*

Child Evngelism Fellowship Inc E 269 461-6953
Berrien Center *(G-1635)*

Christman Screenprint Inc E 800 962-9330
Springfield *(G-15863)*

Clare Print & Pulp G 989 386-3497
Clare *(G-2976)*

Clemco Printing Inc G 989 269-8364
Bad Axe *(G-1099)*

Color Connection G 248 351-0920
Southfield *(G-15527)*

Color Express Printing Inc G 734 213-4980
Ann Arbor *(G-433)*

▲ Color House Graphics Inc E 616 241-1916
Grand Rapids *(G-6583)*

Color Source Graphics Inc G 248 458-2040
Troy *(G-17018)*

Colorhub LLC F 616 333-4411
Grand Rapids *(G-6584)*

Colortech Graphics Inc D 586 779-7800
Roseville *(G-14386)*

Columbus Printing Inc G 614 534-0266
Grand Rapids *(G-6585)*

Commercial Graphics Company G 517 278-2159
Coldwater *(G-3429)*

Commercial Graphics Inc G 586 726-8150
Sterling Heights *(G-15965)*

Commercial Trck Transf Signs G 586 754-7100
Warren *(G-17761)*

Complete HM Advg Mdia Prmtnal G 586 254-9555
Shelby Township *(G-15192)*

Compton Press Industries LLC G 248 473-8210
Farmington Hills *(G-5207)*

Conventional Graphics Inc G 231 943-4301
Interlochen *(G-8681)*

Copilot Printing G 248 797-0150
Berkley *(G-1625)*

Copy Central Inc G 231 941-2298
Traverse City *(G-16660)*

Copy Connection LLC G 734 425-3150
Whitmore Lake *(G-18529)*

Copyrite Printing Inc G 586 774-0006
Roseville *(G-14390)*

Copytwo Inc E 734 665-9200
Ann Arbor *(G-437)*

Corporate Electronic Sty Inc D 248 583-7070
Troy *(G-17030)*

CPM Services Group Inc G 248 624-5100
Wixom *(G-18639)*

Craft Press Printing Inc G 269 683-9694
Niles *(G-12121)*

Creative Characters Inc G 231 544-6084
Central Lake *(G-2692)*

Creative Eyeball Agency G 517 398-8008
Quincy *(G-13667)*

Creative Image & Printing LLC G 586 222-4288
Sterling Heights *(G-15974)*

Creative Print Crew LLC G 248 629-9404
Troy *(G-17033)*

Creative Printing & Graphics G 810 235-8815
Flint *(G-5677)*

Creative Printing Solutions G 616 931-1040
Zeeland *(G-19008)*

Curtis Printing Inc G 810 230-6711
Flint *(G-5679)*

Cushing-Malloy Inc E 734 663-8554
Ann Arbor *(G-440)*

Custom Printers Inc D 616 454-9224
Grand Rapids *(G-6623)*

Custom Printing G 248 509-7134
Troy *(G-17039)*

Custom Printing of Michigan F 248 585-9222
Troy *(G-17040)*

Custom Service Printers Inc F 231 726-3297
Muskegon *(G-11797)*

Custom Vinyl Prints G 810 841-4301
Wales *(G-17626)*

D & D Printing Co E 616 454-7710
Grand Rapids *(G-6628)*

D and WP Rints LLC G 313 646-6571
Detroit *(G-4117)*

D J Rotunda Associates Inc G 586 772-3350
West Bloomfield *(G-18276)*

D2 Print Inc G 248 229-7633
Madison Heights *(G-10703)*

Daily Oakland Press B 248 332-8181
Bloomfield Hills *(G-1811)*

Daily Reporter E 517 278-2318
Coldwater *(G-3430)*

Daniel Ward G 810 965-6535
Mount Morris *(G-11670)*

▼ Data Reproductions Corporation D 248 371-3700
Auburn Hills *(G-859)*

Daves Printing G 989 355-1204
Saginaw *(G-14636)*

De Vru Printing Co G 616 452-5451
Grand Rapids *(G-6636)*

Dearborn Lithograph Inc E 734 464-4242
Livonia *(G-10176)*

Dearborn Offset Printing Inc G 313 561-1173
Dearborn *(G-3824)*

Dekoff & Sons Inc G 269 344-5816
Kalamazoo *(G-9165)*

Derk Pieter Co Inc G 616 554-7777
Grand Rapids *(G-6641)*

Designotype Printers Inc G 906 482-2424
Laurium *(G-9979)*

Detroit Business Centercom Inc G 313 255-4300
Detroit *(G-4138)*

Detroit CLB Prtg Hse Craftsmen G 734 953-9729
Livonia *(G-10182)*

Detroit Litho Inc G 313 993-6186
Detroit *(G-4151)*

Detroit News Inc G 313 222-6400
Sterling Heights *(G-15983)*

Detroit Newspaper Partnr LP A 586 826-7187
Sterling Heights *(G-15984)*

Detroit Printed Products G 586 226-3860
Clinton Township *(G-3220)*

Dexter Print & Stitch G 734 580-2181
Dexter *(G-4738)*

DGa Printing Inc G 586 979-2244
Troy *(G-17058)*

Digimax Business Corporation G 313 255-4300
Detroit *(G-4176)*

Digital Imaging Group Inc D 269 686-8744
Allegan *(G-155)*

Digital Print Specialties G 248 545-5888
Detroit *(G-4177)*

Digital Printing & Graphics G 586 566-9499
Shelby Township *(G-15206)*

Digital Printing Solutions LLC G 586 566-4910
Shelby Township *(G-15207)*

Digital Xpress G 248 325-9061
West Bloomfield *(G-18280)*

Dobb Printing Inc E 231 722-1060
Muskegon *(G-11799)*

Donalyn Enterprises Inc F 517 546-9798
Howell *(G-8447)*

Doorstep Printing LLC G 248 470-9567
Detroit *(G-4186)*

DPrinter Inc G 517 423-6554
Tecumseh *(G-16499)*

Dtm Inc G 734 944-1109
Saline *(G-15013)*

Dynamic Print & Imaging G 586 738-4367
Sterling Heights *(G-15994)*

E & R Bindery Service Inc G 734 464-7954
Livonia *(G-10188)*

E & S Graphics Inc G 989 875-2828
Ithaca *(G-8790)*

Earle Press Inc E 231 773-2111
Muskegon *(G-11805)*

Eclipse Print Services G 517 304-2151
Wixom *(G-18652)*

Econo Print Inc G 734 878-5806
Pinckney *(G-13047)*

Edgemen Screen Printing G 586 465-6820
Clinton Township *(G-3229)*

▲ Egt Printing Solutions LLC C 248 583-2500
Madison Heights *(G-10718)*

Elston Enterprises Inc F 313 561-8000
Dearborn Heights *(G-3926)*

Embroidery House Inc G 616 669-6400
Jenison *(G-9054)*

Empire Printing G 248 547-9223
Farmington Hills *(G-5232)*

Eon Project G 313 717-5976
Detroit *(G-4213)*

◆ Epi Printers Inc E 800 562-9733
Battle Creek *(G-1224)*

Epi Printers Inc D 269 968-2221
Battle Creek *(G-1225)*

Epi Printers Inc D 269 968-2221
Battle Creek *(G-1226)*

Epi Printers Inc D 734 261-9400
Livonia *(G-10198)*

Epi Printers Inc D 269 964-6744
Battle Creek *(G-1228)*

Epi Printers Inc D 269 964-4600
Battle Creek *(G-1227)*

Excel Graphics G 248 442-9390
Livonia *(G-10200)*

Exclusive Imagery Inc G 248 436-2999
Royal Oak *(G-14536)*

Express Press Inc G 269 684-2080
Niles *(G-12128)*

Eze Prints A Div Allied G 616 281-2406
Grand Rapids *(G-6697)*

F P Horak Company C 989 892-6505
Bay City *(G-1355)*

Fabulous Printing Inc G 734 422-5555
Livonia *(G-10203)*

Fairfax Prints Ltd G 517 321-5590
Lansing *(G-9696)*

Falcon Printing Inc E 616 676-3737
Ada *(G-17)*

Federal Heath Sign Company LLC E 248 656-8000
Rochester Hills *(G-14010)*

Flashes Publishers Inc E 269 673-2141
Holland *(G-8035)*

Floodwell Print Studio G 231 943-2930
Traverse City *(G-16683)*

Fluir Creative LLC G 734 494-0308
Livonia *(G-10213)*

Foremost Graphics LLC D 616 453-4747
Grand Rapids *(G-6715)*

Forerunner 3d Printing G 231 722-1144
Coopersville *(G-3687)*

Forsons Inc G 517 787-4562
Jackson *(G-8885)*

Forward Inking Design & Print G 231 714-8646
Traverse City *(G-16689)*

Franklin Press Inc F 616 538-5320
Grand Rapids *(G-6719)*

Fresh Baked Prints G 888 327-4137
Oak Park *(G-12613)*

From Photos To Canvas Prints G 248 760-4694
Rochester Hills *(G-14016)*

Frye Printing Company Inc F 517 456-4124
Clinton *(G-3139)*

Fudge Business Forms Inc G 248 299-3666
Rochester Hills *(G-14017)*

Fuller Printing G 989 304-0230
Stanton *(G-15901)*

Future Reproductions Inc F 248 350-2060
Southfield *(G-15571)*

G G & D Inc G 248 623-1212
Clarkston *(G-3037)*

Gage Company G 269 965-4279
Springfield *(G-15865)*

Garants Office Sups & Prtg Inc G 989 356-3930
Alpena *(G-296)*

S I C

Employee Codes: A=Over 500 employees, B=251-500
C=101-250, D=51-100, E=20-50, F=10-19, G=3-9

2022 Harris Michigan
Industrial Directory

767

Gary Cork Incorporated.......G....... 231 946-1061
Traverse City *(G-16692)*

Generation Press Inc.......G....... 616 392-4405
Holland *(G-8048)*

Genesee County Herald Inc.......F....... 810 686-3840
Clio *(G-3399)*

Genesis Service Associates LLC.......G....... 734 994-3900
Dexter *(G-4742)*

Global Digital Printing.......G....... 734 244-5010
Monroe *(G-11544)*

Globe Printing & Specialties.......F....... 906 485-1033
Ishpeming *(G-8776)*

Goetz Craft Printers Inc.......F....... 734 973-7604
Brooklyn *(G-2125)*

Gombar Corp.......G....... 989 793-9427
Saginaw *(G-14655)*

Good God Printing.......G....... 313 694-2985
Detroit *(G-4270)*

Grahams Printing Company Inc.......G....... 313 925-1188
Detroit *(G-4272)*

Grand Apps LLC.......G....... 517 927-5140
Grand Ledge *(G-6391)*

Grand Blanc Printing Inc.......E....... 810 694-1155
Grand Blanc *(G-6245)*

Grand Haven Publishing Corp.......G....... 616 842-6400
Grand Haven *(G-6305)*

Grand Rapids Letter Service.......G....... 616 459-4711
Grand Rapids *(G-6762)*

Grand Traverse Continuous Inc.......E....... 231 941-5400
Traverse City *(G-16698)*

▼ Grandville Printing Co.......C....... 616 534-8647
Grandville *(G-7382)*

Graphic Enterprises Inc.......D....... 248 616-4900
Madison Heights *(G-10732)*

Graphic Impressions Inc.......G....... 616 455-0303
Grand Rapids *(G-6782)*

Graphics & Printing Co Inc.......G....... 269 381-1482
Kalamazoo *(G-9201)*

Graphics 3 Inc.......E....... 517 278-2159
Coldwater *(G-3435)*

Graphics East Inc.......E....... 586 598-1500
Roseville *(G-14415)*

Graphics House Publishing.......E....... 231 739-4004
Muskegon *(G-11827)*

Graphics Unlimited Inc.......G....... 231 773-2696
Norton Shores *(G-12295)*

Great Lakes Graphics Inc.......G....... 517 783-5500
Jackson *(G-8894)*

Great Lakes Prtg Solutions Inc.......E....... 231 799-6000
Norton Shores *(G-12296)*

Green Ink Works.......G....... 616 254-7350
Wyoming *(G-18877)*

Greenmans Speedy Printing.......G....... 248 478-2600
Farmington Hills *(G-5256)*

Greko Print & Imaging Inc.......F....... 734 453-0341
Plymouth *(G-13180)*

Grigg Graphic Services Inc.......E....... 248 356-5005
Southfield *(G-15585)*

H & J Printing.......G....... 734 344-9447
Rockwood *(G-14199)*

H E L P Printers Inc.......G....... 734 847-0554
Temperance *(G-16533)*

Hamblin Company.......E....... 517 423-7491
Bloomfield Hills *(G-1826)*

Hanon Printing Company.......G....... 248 541-9099
Pleasant Ridge *(G-13105)*

Harold K Schultz.......G....... 517 279-9764
Coldwater *(G-3438)*

Hatteras Inc.......E....... 734 525-5500
Plymouth *(G-13183)*

Hawk Design Inc.......G....... 989 781-1152
Saginaw *(G-14662)*

Herald Bi-County Inc.......G....... 517 448-2201
Hudson *(G-8550)*

Herald Publishing Company.......E....... 517 423-2174
Tecumseh *(G-16504)*

Hess Printing.......G....... 734 285-4377
Wyandotte *(G-18821)*

Hi-Lites Graphic Inc.......E....... 231 924-0630
Fremont *(G-6045)*

Hodges & Irvine Inc.......F....... 810 329-4787
Saint Clair *(G-14831)*

Holland Litho Service Inc.......D....... 616 392-4644
Zeeland *(G-19039)*

Holland Printing Center Inc.......F....... 616 786-3101
Holland *(G-8083)*

Homestead Graphics Design Inc.......G....... 906 353-6741
Baraga *(G-1140)*

Hooper Printing LLC.......G....... 616 897-6719
Lowell *(G-10504)*

Horn Corporation.......F....... 248 583-7789
Troy *(G-17151)*

Hot Prints Inc.......G....... 989 627-6463
Saint Johns *(G-14901)*

Houghton Lake Resorter Inc.......F....... 989 366-5341
Houghton Lake *(G-8400)*

Huron Publishing Company Inc.......D....... 989 269-6461
Bad Axe *(G-1107)*

Ideal Printing.......G....... 616 453-5556
Grand Rapids *(G-6830)*

Ideal Printing Company.......E....... 616 454-9224
Grand Rapids *(G-6831)*

Image Factory Inc.......G....... 989 732-2712
Gaylord *(G-6135)*

Image Printing Inc.......G....... 248 585-4080
Royal Oak *(G-14549)*

Images 2 Print.......G....... 616 383-1121
Sparta *(G-15769)*

Images2printcom.......G....... 616 821-7143
Comstock Park *(G-3611)*

Imperial Press Inc.......G....... 734 728-5430
Wayne *(G-18224)*

Index Prints.......G....... 248 327-6621
Southfield *(G-15602)*

Industrial Imprntng & Die Ctng.......G....... 586 778-9470
Eastpointe *(G-4937)*

Inkwell Screen Printing.......G....... 586 292-4050
Rochester *(G-13907)*

Innovative Apparel Printing.......G....... 989 395-1204
Saginaw *(G-14671)*

Instant Car Credit Inc.......G....... 231 922-8180
Traverse City *(G-16722)*

Instant Framer.......G....... 231 947-8908
Traverse City *(G-16723)*

International Master Pdts Corp.......C....... 231 894-5651
Montague *(G-11598)*

Interntnal Mnute Press Clawson.......G....... 248 629-4220
Clawson *(G-3099)*

Iris Design & Print Inc.......G....... 313 277-0505
Dearborn *(G-3855)*

Irwin Enterprises Inc.......E....... 810 732-0770
Flint *(G-5716)*

J R C Inc.......F....... 810 648-4000
Sandusky *(G-15061)*

J&J Custom Print Services.......G....... 616 581-0545
Commerce Township *(G-3546)*

J-Ad Graphics Inc.......D....... 800 870-7085
Hastings *(G-7800)*

J-Ad Graphics Inc.......F....... 269 965-3955
Battle Creek *(G-1243)*

Ja Sportswear & Printing LLC.......G....... 248 706-1213
West Bloomfield *(G-18292)*

Jack Batdorss.......E....... 231 796-4831
Big Rapids *(G-1678)*

Jackpine Press Incorporated.......F....... 231 723-8344
Manistee *(G-10903)*

Janet Kelly.......F....... 231 775-2313
Cadillac *(G-2338)*

Janutol Printing Co Inc.......G....... 313 526-6196
Detroit *(G-4333)*

Jeffrey S Zimmer.......G....... 810 385-0726
Burtchville *(G-2221)*

Jerrys Quality Quick Print.......G....... 248 354-1313
Southfield *(G-15612)*

Jet Speed Printing Company.......G....... 989 224-6475
Saint Johns *(G-14903)*

Jiffy Print.......G....... 269 692-3128
Otsego *(G-12789)*

Jlc Print and Ship Inc.......G....... 517 544-0404
Jackson *(G-8921)*

Jlr Printing Inc.......G....... 734 728-0250
Romulus *(G-14290)*

JMS Printing Svc LLC.......G....... 734 414-6203
Warren *(G-17887)*

Job Shop Ink Inc.......G....... 517 372-3900
Lansing *(G-9768)*

Johnson-Clark Printers Inc.......F....... 231 947-6898
Traverse City *(G-16730)*

Johnston Printing & Offset.......G....... 906 786-1493
Escanaba *(G-5079)*

Jomark Inc.......E....... 248 478-2600
Farmington Hills *(G-5275)*

Journal Disposition Corp.......D....... 269 428-2054
Saint Joseph *(G-14938)*

Js Printing.......G....... 734 266-3350
Livonia *(G-10261)*

Just Right Duplications LLC.......F....... 313 655-3555
Oak Park *(G-12619)*

K & S Printing Centers Inc.......G....... 734 482-1680
Ann Arbor *(G-536)*

Kalamazoo Prtg & Promotions.......G....... 269 818-1122
Kalamazoo *(G-9246)*

Kaufman Enterprises Inc.......G....... 269 324-0040
Portage *(G-13573)*

▲ Kay Screen Printing Inc.......B....... 248 377-4999
Lake Orion *(G-9611)*

Kendall & Company Inc.......G....... 810 733-7330
Flint *(G-5721)*

Kent Communications Inc.......D....... 616 957-2120
Grand Rapids *(G-6886)*

Kimprint Inc.......E....... 734 459-2960
Plymouth *(G-13215)*

Kings Time Printing Press LLC.......G....... 734 426-8169
Ann Arbor *(G-539)*

Kleins 3d Prtg Solutions LLC.......G....... 586 212-9763
Fraser *(G-5951)*

Kmak Inc.......G....... 517 784-8800
Jackson *(G-8929)*

Knapp Printing Services Inc.......G....... 616 754-9159
Greenville *(G-7497)*

Kolossos Printing Inc.......F....... 734 994-5400
Ann Arbor *(G-540)*

Ktd Print.......G....... 248 670-4200
Royal Oak *(G-14554)*

▲ Ktr Printing Inc.......F....... 989 386-9740
Clare *(G-2984)*

Kwikie Inc.......G....... 231 946-9942
Traverse City *(G-16735)*

L D J Inc.......F....... 906 524-6194
Lanse *(G-9666)*

L&L Printing Inc.......G....... 586 263-0060
Clinton Township *(G-3278)*

Lake Michigan Mailers Inc.......D....... 269 383-9333
Kalamazoo *(G-9257)*

Lake Superior Press Inc.......F....... 906 228-7450
Marquette *(G-11027)*

Lakeside Custom Printing LLC.......G....... 517 936-5904
Jerome *(G-9078)*

Lamour Printing Co.......G....... 734 241-6006
Monroe *(G-11558)*

Larsen Graphics Inc.......E....... 989 823-3000
Vassar *(G-17579)*

Laser Printer Technologies Inc.......G....... 231 941-5273
Traverse City *(G-16739)*

Lawson Printers Inc.......E....... 269 965-0525
Battle Creek *(G-1267)*

Leader Printing and Design Inc.......F....... 313 565-0061
Dearborn Heights *(G-3930)*

Leader Publications LLC.......D....... 269 683-2100
Niles *(G-12141)*

Lee Printing Company.......F....... 586 463-1564
Clinton Township *(G-3279)*

Leelanau Prints.......G....... 231 386-7616
Northport *(G-12188)*

Lesnau Printing Company.......E....... 586 795-9200
Sterling Heights *(G-16071)*

Lighthouse Direct Buy LLC.......G....... 313 340-1850
Detroit *(G-4398)*

Lighting Printing.......G....... 989 792-2793
Birch Run *(G-1709)*

Lightning Litho Inc.......F....... 517 394-2995
Lansing *(G-9864)*

Limelite Printing LLC.......G....... 313 839-7321
Detroit *(G-4400)*

Lindy Press Inc.......G....... 231 937-6169
Howard City *(G-8411)*

Litho Photo Enterprises LLC.......G....... 313 717-6615
Taylor *(G-16436)*

Litho Printers Inc.......F....... 269 651-7309
Sturgis *(G-16302)*

Litho Printing Service Inc.......G....... 586 772-6067
Eastpointe *(G-4939)*

Litho-Graphics Printing Pdts.......G....... 586 775-1670
Roseville *(G-14433)*

Litsenberger Print Shop.......G....... 906 482-3903
Houghton *(G-8386)*

Lloyd Waters & Associates.......G....... 734 525-2777
Livonia *(G-10291)*

Logan Brothers Printing Inc.......G....... 517 485-3771
Dewitt *(G-4711)*

Logospot.......G....... 616 785-7170
Belmont *(G-1512)*

Lopez Reproductions Inc.......G....... 313 386-4526
Detroit *(G-4404)*

Lynn Shaler Fine Prints LLC.......G....... 248 644-5148
Bloomfield Hills *(G-1834)*

M & R Printing Inc.......G....... 248 543-8080
Redford *(G-13743)*

M Beshara Inc.......G....... 248 542-9220
Oak Park *(G-12623)*

27 PRINTING, PUBLISHING, AND ALLIED INDUSTRIES

M Print G 248 550-4405 — Livonia *(G-10296)*
M Print Dance Company G 616 575-9969 — Kentwood *(G-9464)*
Macdonald Publications Inc F 989 875-4151 — Ithaca *(G-8793)*
Macomb Business Forms Inc F 586 790-8500 — Clinton Township *(G-3286)*
Macomb Printing Inc E 586 463-2301 — Clinton Township *(G-3288)*
Madain Postal Services LLC G 586 323-3573 — Sterling Heights *(G-16080)*
Madden Enterprises Inc G 734 284-5330 — Wyandotte *(G-18830)*
Maleports Sault Prtg Co Inc E 906 632-3369 — Sault Sainte Marie *(G-15095)*
Maple Press LLC E 248 733-9669 — Madison Heights *(G-10775)*
Marketing VI Group Inc G 989 793-3933 — Saginaw *(G-14686)*
Maslin Corporation G 586 777-7500 — Harper Woods *(G-7667)*
MBA Printing Inc G 616 243-1600 — Comstock Park *(G-3623)*
McKay Press Inc C 989 631-2360 — Midland *(G-11387)*
Mega Printing Inc G 248 624-6065 — Walled Lake *(G-17672)*
Megee Printing Inc F 269 344-3226 — Kalamazoo *(G-9268)*
Mel Printing Co Inc E 313 928-5440 — Taylor *(G-16440)*
Menominee Cnty Jurnl Print Sp F 906 753-2296 — Stephenson *(G-15909)*
Merritt Press Inc F 517 394-0118 — Lansing *(G-9868)*
Messenger Printing & Copy Svc G 616 669-5620 — Hudsonville *(G-8593)*
Messenger Printing Service Inc F 313 381-0300 — Taylor *(G-16441)*
◆ **Metro Printing Service Inc** G 248 545-4444 — Troy *(G-17253)*
Metro Prints Inc F 586 979-9690 — Sterling Heights *(G-16093)*
Metropolitan Indus Lithography G 269 323-9333 — Portage *(G-13585)*
Mettes Printery Inc G 734 261-6262 — Livonia *(G-10314)*
Michigan State Medical Society E 517 337-1351 — East Lansing *(G-4904)*
Michigan Wholesale Prtg Inc G 248 350-8230 — Farmington Hills *(G-5319)*
Micrgraphics Printing Inc F 231 739-6575 — Norton Shores *(G-12311)*
Microforms Inc E 586 939-7900 — Beverly Hills *(G-1667)*
Mid-Michigan Screen Printing G 989 624-9827 — Birch Run *(G-1711)*
Mid-State Printing Inc F 989 875-4163 — Ithaca *(G-8794)*
Midland Publishing Company C 989 835-7171 — Midland *(G-11394)*
Millbrook Press Works G 517 323-2111 — Lansing *(G-9777)*
Miss Print Rocks G 517 639-8785 — Quincy *(G-13672)*
▲ **Mitchell Graphics Inc** E 231 347-4635 — Petoskey *(G-13007)*
Mj Creative Printing LLC G 248 891-1117 — Livonia *(G-10319)*
Mj Print & Imaging G 734 216-6273 — Grass Lake *(G-7441)*
MKP Enterprises Inc G 248 809-2525 — Southfield *(G-15660)*
Model Printing Service Inc F 989 356-0834 — Alpena *(G-304)*
Monarch Print and Mail LLC G 734 620-8378 — Westland *(G-18398)*
Moonlight Graphics Inc G 616 243-3166 — Grand Rapids *(G-7027)*
Moormann Printing Inc G 269 423-2411 — Decatur *(G-3950)*
MPS/Ih LLC E 517 323-9001 — Lansing *(G-9720)*
Msw Print and Imaging F 734 544-1626 — Ypsilanti *(G-18969)*
Muhleck Enterprises Inc E 517 333-0713 — Okemos *(G-12679)*
Munro Printing G 586 773-9579 — Eastpointe *(G-4942)*
My Little Prints G 248 613-8439 — Franklin *(G-5883)*
My Print Works MI G 269 344-3226 — Kalamazoo *(G-9279)*
Nafa Printing LLC G 734 338-2103 — Livonia *(G-10329)*
Naked Shirt Custom Prtg LLC G 269 625-7235 — Burr Oak *(G-2213)*
National Printing Services G 616 813-0758 — Wyoming *(G-18896)*
National Wholesale Prtg Corp G 734 416-8400 — Plymouth *(G-13252)*
Neetz Printing Inc G 989 684-4620 — Bay City *(G-1382)*
Neptix G 248 520-6181 — Birmingham *(G-1739)*
Newberry News Inc G 906 293-8401 — Newberry *(G-12096)*
Niereschers Print G 248 736-4501 — Oxford *(G-12905)*
Nikkis Printing & More LLC G 313 532-0281 — Detroit *(G-4485)*
Nje Enterprises LLC G 313 963-3600 — Detroit *(G-4486)*
North American Color Inc E 269 323-0552 — Portage *(G-13588)*
North American Graphics Inc F 586 486-1110 — Warren *(G-17947)*
Northamerican Reproduction G 734 421-6800 — Livonia *(G-10336)*
Npi Wireless E 231 922-9273 — Traverse City *(G-16776)*
Ntvb Media Inc E 248 583-4190 — Troy *(G-17282)*
Office Connection Inc E 248 871-2003 — Farmington Hills *(G-5339)*
Office Express Inc E 248 307-1850 — Troy *(G-17288)*
Ogemaw County Herald Inc E 989 345-0044 — West Branch *(G-18333)*
On The Side Sign Dsign Grphics G 810 266-7446 — Byron *(G-2255)*
P J Printing G 269 673-3372 — Allegan *(G-172)*
Page Litho Inc F 313 885-8555 — Grosse Pointe *(G-7532)*
Painless Printing G 517 812-6852 — Jackson *(G-8982)*
Pak Mail Center of America G 248 543-3097 — Ferndale *(G-5575)*
Palmer Envelope Co F 269 965-1336 — Battle Creek *(G-1280)*
Paper and Print Usa LLC G 616 940-8311 — Grand Rapids *(G-7069)*
Parallax Printing LLC G 248 397-5156 — Ferndale *(G-5576)*
Pariseaus Printing Inc G 810 653-8420 — Davison *(G-3792)*
Parkside Speedy Print Inc G 810 985-8484 — Port Huron *(G-13516)*
Paul C Doerr G 734 242-2058 — Monroe *(G-11568)*
Paw Print Creations LLC G 810 577-0410 — Mount Morris *(G-11676)*
Paw Print Gardens G 616 791-4758 — Grand Rapids *(G-7073)*
PDQ Ink Inc E 810 229-2989 — Brighton *(G-2048)*
Peg-Master Business Forms Inc G 586 566-8694 — Shelby Township *(G-15298)*
Performance Print and Mktg G 517 896-9682 — Williamston *(G-18579)*
Perrigo Printing Inc G 616 454-6761 — Grand Rapids *(G-7082)*
Personal Graphics G 231 347-6347 — Petoskey *(G-13013)*
Pgi Holdings Inc E 231 796-4831 — Big Rapids *(G-1683)*
Phase III Graphics Inc G 616 949-9290 — Grand Rapids *(G-7084)*
Phiber Printing LLC G 248 471-9435 — Livonia *(G-10364)*
Phoenix Press Incorporated E 248 435-8040 — Troy *(G-17300)*
Photo Offset Inc G 906 786-5800 — Escanaba *(G-5089)*
Pickle Print & Marketing LLC G 231 668-4148 — Traverse City *(G-16792)*
Pioneer Press Printing G 231 864-2404 — Bear Lake *(G-1421)*
Piping Plover Prints G 231 929-0261 — Traverse City *(G-16793)*
Pippa Custom Design Printing G 734 552-1598 — Woodhaven *(G-18802)*
Pixel Rush Printing G 248 231-4642 — South Lyon *(G-15455)*
Plastics In Paint G 248 520-7177 — Waterford *(G-18154)*
▲ **Pleasant Graphics Inc** F 989 773-7777 — Mount Pleasant *(G-11733)*
Pointe Printing Inc G 313 821-0030 — Grosse Pointe Park *(G-7558)*
Popcorn Press Inc F 248 588-4444 — Madison Heights *(G-10805)*
Postal Savings Direct Mktg F 810 238-8866 — Flint *(G-5745)*
Powerstroke Printing G 734 740-7616 — Wayne *(G-18233)*
Precision Print Label G 248 853-9007 — Rochester Hills *(G-14089)*
Preferred Printing Inc F 269 782-5488 — Dowagiac *(G-4793)*
Premier Printin G 248 924-3213 — Wixom *(G-18734)*
Presscraft Papers Inc F 231 882-5505 — Benzonia *(G-1616)*
Prestige Printing Inc G 616 532-5133 — Grand Rapids *(G-7104)*
Pride Printing Inc G 906 228-8182 — Marquette *(G-11042)*
Prins Bethesda LLC G 269 903-2237 — Portage *(G-13595)*
Print 4 U Promotional Prtg LLC G 313 575-1080 — Redford *(G-13759)*
Print All G 586 430-4383 — Richmond *(G-13844)*
Print and Save Now G 989 352-8171 — Edmore *(G-4996)*
Print Haus G 616 786-4030 — Holland *(G-8171)*
Print House Inc F 248 473-1414 — Farmington Hills *(G-5353)*
Print Julep G 614 937-5114 — West Bloomfield *(G-18306)*
Print Masters Inc F 248 548-7100 — Madison Heights *(G-10810)*
Print Metro Inc G 616 887-1723 — Sparta *(G-15775)*
Print n go G 989 362-6041 — East Tawas *(G-4921)*
Print Plus Inc G 586 888-8000 — Saint Clair Shores *(G-14878)*
Print Rapids LLC G 616 202-6508 — Hudsonville *(G-8601)*
Print Room G 231 489-8181 — Petoskey *(G-13017)*
Print Shop G 313 499-8444 — Harper Woods *(G-7670)*
Print Shop G 231 347-2000 — Petoskey *(G-13018)*
Print Xpress G 313 886-6850 — Grosse Pointe Woods *(G-7573)*
Print Zone G 313 278-0800 — Dearborn *(G-3886)*
▲ **Print-Tech Inc** E 734 996-2345 — Ann Arbor *(G-624)*
Printcomm Inc D 810 239-5763 — Flint *(G-5749)*
Printed Impressions Inc G 248 473-5333 — Farmington Hills *(G-5354)*
Printed Memories G 248 388-7788 — Waterford *(G-18157)*
▲ **Printer Ink Warehousecom LLC** G 269 649-5492 — Vicksburg *(G-17610)*
Printery Inc E 616 396-4655 — Holland *(G-8172)*
Printex Printing & Graphics G 269 629-0122 — Richland *(G-13827)*
Printing Buying Service G 586 907-2011 — Saint Clair Shores *(G-14879)*
▲ **Printing By Marc** G 248 355-0848 — Southfield *(G-15682)*
Printing Centre Inc F 517 694-2400 — Holt *(G-8326)*
Printing Industries of Mich G 248 946-5895 — Novi *(G-12516)*
Printing King G 517 367-7066 — Lansing *(G-9884)*
Printing Plus Inc G 734 482-1680 — Ypsilanti *(G-18971)*

SIC

Employee Codes: A=Over 500 employees, B=251-500
C=101-250, D=51-100, E=20-50, F=10-19, G=3-9
2022 Harris Michigan Industrial Directory
769

27 PRINTING, PUBLISHING, AND ALLIED INDUSTRIES

Company	Location	Code	Phone
Printing Productions Ink	Grand Rapids (G-7109)	G	616 871-9292
Printing Services	Portage (G-13596)	G	269 321-9826
Printing Services Inc	Saline (G-15032)	F	734 944-1404
Printing Systems Inc	Taylor (G-16461)	G	734 946-5111
Printing Xpress AMP Promo	Troy (G-17315)	G	586 915-9043
▲ Printlink Shrt Run Bus Frms In	Battle Creek (G-1283)	F	269 965-1336
Printmill Inc	Kalamazoo (G-9308)	G	269 382-0428
Prism Printing	Macomb (G-10629)	G	586 786-1250
Pro ADS America	Walled Lake (G-17673)	G	586 219-6040
Procolrcopy A Div Prclor Group	Rochester Hills (G-14091)	G	248 458-2040
Proforma Pltnum Prtg Prmotions	Clawson (G-3104)	G	248 341-3814
Progress Printers Inc	Traverse City (G-16805)	G	231 947-5311
▼ Progressive Prtg & Graphics	Battle Creek (G-1284)	G	269 965-8909
Pronto Printing	Macomb (G-10630)	G	586 215-9670
Prontoprinting LLC	Detroit (G-4538)	G	313 622-7565
Provisions Print LLC	Auburn Hills (G-1007)	G	248 214-1766
Pummill Print Services Lc	Comstock Park (G-3639)	G	616 785-7960
Punktual Printing Inc	Westland (G-18410)	G	734 664-8045
Qg LLC	Midland (G-11404)	D	989 496-3333
Qrp Inc	Midland (G-11405)	G	989 496-2955
Qrp Inc	Midland (G-11406)	E	989 496-2955
Quad/Graphics Inc	Troy (G-17324)	G	248 637-9950
Quality Press	Clawson (G-3106)	G	248 541-0753
Quality Printing & Graphics	Grand Rapids (G-7130)	G	616 949-3400
Quantum Digital Ventures LLC	Warren (G-17989)	E	248 292-5686
Quantum Graphics Inc	Shelby Township (G-15312)	E	586 566-5656
Quick Printing Company Inc	Grand Rapids (G-7131)	G	616 241-0506
Quickprint of Adrian Inc	Adrian (G-90)	F	517 263-2290
Quirky 3d Printing	Corunna (G-3716)	G	810 247-6732
R & L Color Graphics Inc	Detroit (G-4549)	G	313 345-3838
R & R Harwood Inc	Jenison (G-9069)	G	616 669-6400
R JS Printing Inc	Kalamazoo (G-9314)	G	773 936-7825
R N E Business Enterprises	Detroit (G-4551)	G	313 963-3600
R W Patterson Printing Co	Benton Harbor (G-1579)	D	269 925-2177
Raenell Press LLC	Grand Rapids (G-7137)	G	616 534-8890
Rapid Graphics Inc	Benton Harbor (G-1580)	G	269 925-7087
Rar Group Inc	Redford (G-13761)	G	248 353-2266
Ray Printing Company Inc	Jackson (G-8994)	F	517 787-4130
Raze It Printing Inc	West Bloomfield (G-18309)	G	248 366-8691
Raze-It Printing	Hazel Park (G-7839)	G	248 543-3813
Real Estate One Inc	Commerce Township (G-3569)	G	248 851-2600
Reimold Printing Corporation	Saginaw (G-14736)	G	989 799-0784
Renegade Cstm Screen Prtg LLC	Lincoln Park (G-10055)	G	313 475-8489
Renegade Screen Printing	Clawson (G-3108)	G	248 632-0207
Richard Larabee	Southfield (G-15689)	G	248 827-7755
Richards Printing	Escanaba (G-5095)	G	906 786-3540
Rider Type & Design	Midland (G-11408)	G	989 839-0015
Riegle Press Inc	Davison (G-3795)	E	810 653-9631
Rite Way Printing	Romulus (G-14325)	G	734 721-2746
River Run Press Inc	Kalamazoo (G-9320)	E	269 349-7603
Riverside Prtg of Grnd Rapids	Grand Rapids (G-7160)	G	616 458-8011
Rocket Copy Print Ship Inc	Royal Oak (G-14577)	G	248 336-3636
Rogers Printing Inc	Ravenna (G-13694)	C	231 853-2244
Romeo Printing Company Inc	Romeo (G-14234)	G	586 752-9003
Rtr Alpha Inc	Auburn Hills (G-1023)	F	248 377-4060
Rumler Brothers Inc	Hillsdale (G-7947)	G	517 437-2990
Rusas Printing Co Inc	Redford (G-13769)	G	313 952-2977
Rush Print and Pack	Midland (G-11410)	G	989 835-5161
S & N Graphic Solutions LLC	Canton (G-2519)	G	734 495-3314
Safran Printing Company Inc	Beverly Hills (G-1668)	C	586 939-7600
Sales Mfg	Flint (G-5759)	G	810 597-7707
Save On Printing	Sterling Heights (G-16165)	G	586 202-4469
▲ SBR Printing USA Inc	Port Huron (G-13525)	F	810 388-9441
Schepeler Corporation	Brooklyn (G-2132)	E	517 592-6811
Seifert City-Wide Printing Co	Farmington (G-5148)	G	248 477-9525
Select Graphics Corporation	Warren (G-18009)	F	586 755-7700
Shawnieboy Enterprises Inc	Grand Rapids (G-7191)	F	616 871-9292
Shayleslie Corporation	Holt (G-8332)	G	517 694-4115
◆ Sheridan Books Inc	Chelsea (G-2826)	B	734 475-9145
Skip Printing and Dup Co	Roseville (G-14477)	G	586 779-2640
Slades Printing Company Inc	Waterford (G-18165)	G	248 334-6257
Smm Printing Inc	Bay City (G-1402)	G	989 893-8788
Sourceone Imaging LLC	Grand Rapids (G-7204)	G	616 452-2001
Spartan Graphics Inc	Sparta (G-15780)	D	616 887-1073
▲ Spartan Printing Inc	Lansing (G-9738)	E	517 372-6910
Specialty Business Forms Inc	Kalamazoo (G-9340)	G	269 345-0828
Specifications Service Company	Bloomfield (G-1785)	G	248 353-0244
Spectrum Printers Inc	Tecumseh (G-16517)	E	517 423-5735
Spinnaker Forms Systems Corp	Grand Rapids (G-7219)	G	616 956-7677
Splash of Vinyl	Grandville (G-7418)	G	616 723-0311
Sports Ink Screen Prtg EMB LLC	Manistee (G-10913)	G	231 723-5696
Stafford Media Inc	Greenville (G-7505)	E	616 754-9301
Stamp-Rite Incorporated	Lansing (G-9741)	E	517 487-5071
Standard Printing	Ypsilanti (G-18978)	G	734 483-0339
Standard Printing of Warren	Warren (G-18026)	G	586 771-3770
Steketee-Van Huis Inc	Holland (G-8202)	B	616 392-2326
Stewart Printing Company Inc	Wyandotte (G-18840)	G	734 283-8440
Straits Area Printing Corp	Cheboygan (G-2800)	G	231 627-5647
▲ Stylecraft Printing Co	Canton (G-2528)	D	734 455-5500
Sunrise Print Cmmnications Inc	West Branch (G-18342)	G	989 345-4475
Superior Imaging Services Inc	Kalamazoo (G-9348)	G	269 382-0428
Superior Typesetting Service	Kalamazoo (G-9349)	G	269 382-0428
Swift Printing Co	Grand Rapids (G-7241)	F	616 459-4263
Systems Duplicating Co Inc	Troy (G-17382)	F	248 585-7590
T J K Inc	Sterling Heights (G-16199)	G	586 731-9639
T-Print USA	Hamilton (G-7607)	G	269 751-4603
Technology MGT & Budgt Dept	Lansing (G-9899)	G	517 322-1897
Temperance Printing	Lambertville (G-9654)		419 290-6846
Terry Butler Prints LLC	Ann Arbor (G-682)	G	734 255-8592
TGI Direct Inc	Ann Arbor (G-685)	G	810 239-5553
The Envelope Printery Inc	Van Buren Twp (G-17557)	D	734 398-7700
◆ Thomson-Shore Inc	Dexter (G-4758)	C	734 426-3939
Thorpe Printing Services Inc	Marysville (G-11107)	G	810 364-6222
Thought Prvoking Tees Prtg LLC	Detroit (G-4632)	G	313 673-6632
Tigner Printing Inc	Coleman (G-3473)	G	989 465-6916
Timbertech Inc	Harbor Springs (G-7658)	F	231 348-2750
Times Herald Company	Port Huron (G-13532)	D	810 985-7171
Top Notch Printing LLC	Hazel Park (G-7844)	G	248 268-3257
Total Business Systems Inc	Madison Heights (G-10845)	F	248 307-1076
Tourist Printing	Muskegon (G-11935)	G	231 733-5687
Transfigure Print Co	Grand Rapids (G-7270)	G	810 404-4569
Traverse Cy Record- Eagle Inc	Traverse City (G-16866)	G	231 946-2000
Tri Vector Printing	Livonia (G-10443)	G	734 748-7006
Triangle Printing Inc	Roseville (G-14486)	G	586 293-7530
Tru Color Printing	West Bloomfield (G-18318)	G	248 737-2041
Tsunami Inc	Saginaw (G-14780)	G	989 497-5200
Turner Business Forms Inc	Saginaw (G-14782)	E	989 752-5540
Tuteur Inc	Saint Joseph (G-14966)	G	269 983-1246
▲ Tweddle Group Inc	Clinton Township (G-3380)	C	586 307-3700
Tweddle Litho Inc	Sterling Heights (G-16213)	G	586 795-0515
Ultra-Tech Printing Co	Wyoming (G-18915)	F	616 249-0500
Unique-Intasco Usa Inc	Auburn Hills (G-1071)	G	810 982-3360
Universal Print	Bay City (G-1409)	G	989 525-5055
Universal Printing Company Inc	Bay City (G-1410)	E	989 671-9409
US Printers	Daggett (G-3754)	G	906 639-3100
Valassis International Inc	Livonia (G-10457)	B	734 591-3000
Verns Threedprinting	Burton (G-2250)	G	810 564-5184
Village Printing & Supply Inc	Lapeer (G-9966)	G	810 664-2270
▲ Village Shop Inc	Traverse City (G-16875)	E	231 946-3712
Vistaprint	Detroit (G-4670)	G	260 615-0027
Voila Print Inc	Livonia (G-10461)	G	866 942-1677
Vtec Graphics Inc	Livonia (G-10463)	G	734 953-9729
W B Mason Co Inc	Taylor (G-16488)	E	734 947-6370
▲ Walker Printery Inc	Oak Park (G-12650)	F	248 548-5100
Washington Street Printers LLC	Monroe (G-11590)	G	734 240-5541

SIC SECTION 27 PRINTING, PUBLISHING, AND ALLIED INDUSTRIES27 PRINTING, PUBLISHING, AND ALLIED INDUSTRIES

Web Litho Inc ....G.... 586 803-9000
Rochester Hills *(G-14142)*
Web Printing & Mktg Concepts ....G.... 269 983-4646
Saint Joseph *(G-14974)*
Wedo Custom Screen Printing ....G.... 616 965-7332
Grand Rapids *(G-7328)*
Weighman Enterprises Inc ....G.... 989 755-2116
Saginaw *(G-14792)*
West Colony Graphic Inc ....G.... 269 375-6625
Kalamazoo *(G-9366)*
West Michigan Printing Inc ....G.... 616 676-2190
Ada *(G-41)*
West Michigan Tag & Label Inc ....E.... 616 235-0120
Grand Rapids *(G-7335)*
Whipple Printing Inc ....G.... 313 382-8033
Allen Park *(G-210)*
Wide Eyed 3d Printing ....G.... 517 376-6612
Howell *(G-8541)*
William C Fox Enterprises Inc ....F.... 231 775-2732
Cadillac *(G-2364)*
Willoughby Press ....G.... 989 723-3360
Owosso *(G-12868)*
Wines Printing Co ....G.... 586 924-6229
Sterling Heights *(G-16231)*
Wolverine Printing Company LLC ....E.... 616 451-2075
Grand Rapids *(G-7347)*
Word Baron Inc ....F.... 248 471-4080
Ann Arbor *(G-717)*
Workman Printing Inc ....G.... 231 744-5500
Muskegon *(G-11951)*
Worten Copy Center Inc ....G.... 231 845-7030
Ludington *(G-10558)*
Write Idea ....G.... 313 967-5881
Detroit *(G-4693)*
Wynalda International LLC ....F.... 616 866-1561
Belmont *(G-1522)*
◆ **Wynalda Litho Inc** ....C.... 616 866-1561
Belmont *(G-1523)*
X-Treme Printing Inc ....G.... 810 232-3232
Flint *(G-5798)*
Yale Expositor ....G.... 810 387-2300
Yale *(G-18921)*
Yti Office Express LLC ....G.... 866 996-8952
Troy *(G-17458)*
Zak Brothers Printing LLC ....G.... 313 831-3216
Detroit *(G-4700)*
Zeeland Print Shop Co ....G.... 616 772-6636
Zeeland *(G-19098)*

2754 Commercial Printing: Gravure

Advantage Label and Packg Inc ....E.... 616 656-1900
Grand Rapids *(G-6435)*
Aip Group Inc ....G.... 248 828-4400
Troy *(G-16911)*
Capital Imaging Inc ....F.... 517 482-2292
Lansing *(G-9822)*
▼ **Eagile Incorporated** ....F.... 616 243-1200
Grand Rapids *(G-6660)*
▲ **Exone Americas LLC** ....G.... 248 740-1580
Troy *(G-17102)*
Grand Occasions ....G.... 248 622-7144
West Bloomfield *(G-18285)*
High Impact Solutions Inc ....G.... 248 473-9804
Farmington Hills *(G-5260)*
Hodges & Irvine Inc ....F.... 810 329-4787
Saint Clair *(G-14831)*
Ivy Snow LLC ....G.... 248 842-1242
Detroit *(G-4330)*
Just Write Invites LLC ....G.... 248 797-7844
Farmington Hills *(G-5278)*
Occasions ....F.... 517 694-6437
Holt *(G-8320)*
Rainbow Wrap ....F.... 586 949-3976
Chesterfield *(G-2937)*
Safran Printing Company Inc ....C.... 586 939-7600
Beverly Hills *(G-1668)*
Seeley Inc ....E.... 517 655-5631
Williamston *(G-18582)*
Taylor Communications Inc ....F.... 248 304-4800
Southfield *(G-15717)*
◆ **Tentcraft LLC** ....D.... 800 950-4553
Traverse City *(G-16854)*

2759 Commercial Printing

4 Seasons Gym LLC ....G.... 989 681-8175
Saint Louis *(G-14983)*
A B C Printing Inc ....G.... 248 887-0010
Highland *(G-7877)*
A-1 Screenprinting LLC ....D.... 734 665-2692
Ann Arbor *(G-342)*
ABC Printing Corporation Inc ....G.... 248 887-0010
Highland *(G-7879)*
Adair Printing Company ....E.... 734 426-2822
Dexter *(G-4721)*
Adlib Grafix & Apparel ....G.... 269 964-2810
Battle Creek *(G-1178)*
Adrians Screen Print ....G.... 734 994-1367
Holland *(G-7957)*
ADS Plus Printing LLC ....G.... 810 659-7190
Flushing *(G-5800)*
Advance Graphic Systems Inc ....E.... 248 656-8000
Rochester Hills *(G-13943)*
▼ **Advanced Tex Screen Printing** ....E.... 989 643-7288
Bay City *(G-1318)*
Advantage Label and Packg Inc ....E.... 616 656-1900
Grand Rapids *(G-6435)*
Afb Corporate Operations LLC ....E.... 248 669-1188
Plymouth *(G-13120)*
Aka Sports ....G.... 734 260-1023
Wayne *(G-18211)*
Al Corp ....F.... 734 475-7357
Chelsea *(G-2804)*
All Access Name Tags ....G.... 866 955-8247
Troy *(G-16923)*
Allesk Enterprises Inc ....G.... 231 941-5770
Traverse City *(G-16600)*
Alley T & Gifts ....G.... 989 875-4793
Carson City *(G-2591)*
Allgraphics Corp ....G.... 248 994-7373
Farmington Hills *(G-5167)*
Alpha Data Business Forms Inc ....G.... 248 540-5930
Birmingham *(G-1718)*
American Reprographics Co LLC ....G.... 248 299-8900
Clawson *(G-3086)*
American Thermographers ....F.... 248 398-3810
Madison Heights *(G-10668)*
Americas Finest Prtg Graphics ....G.... 586 296-1312
Fraser *(G-5893)*
Amery Tape & Label Co Inc ....G.... 586 759-3230
Warren *(G-17704)*
▲ **Anchor Printing Company** ....E.... 248 335-7440
Novi *(G-12362)*
Ancor Information MGT LLC ....D.... 248 740-8866
Troy *(G-16936)*
AP Impressions Inc ....G.... 734 464-8009
Livonia *(G-10121)*
Apb Inc ....G.... 248 528-2990
Troy *(G-16939)*
▲ **Apparel Sales Inc** ....G.... 616 842-5650
Jenison *(G-9045)*
Applied Graphics & Fabricating ....F.... 989 662-3334
Auburn *(G-764)*
▼ **Applied Visual Concepts LLC** ....G.... 866 440-6888
Warren *(G-17709)*
Ar-Tee Enterprises LLC ....G.... 989 433-5546
Rosebush *(G-14366)*
Ar2 Engineering LLC ....E.... 248 735-9999
Novi *(G-12364)*
▼ **ARC Print Solutions LLC** ....F.... 248 917-7052
Beverly Hills *(G-1661)*
Argent Tape & Label Inc ....F.... 248 588-4600
Livonia *(G-10124)*
Art Craft Display Inc ....D.... 517 485-2221
Lansing *(G-9756)*
Artbox Design Inc ....G.... 248 461-2555
Waterford *(G-18102)*
Artex Label & Graphics Inc ....E.... 616 748-9655
Zeeland *(G-18992)*
Artistic Printing Inc ....G.... 248 356-1004
Southfield *(G-15491)*
Autumn Endeavors LLC ....G.... 906 296-0601
Lake Linden *(G-9566)*
Azoth LLC ....F.... 734 669-3797
Ann Arbor *(G-392)*
B F S Printing and Promot ....G.... 248 685-2456
Milford *(G-11454)*
Beamer Laser Marking ....D.... 810 471-3044
Flushing *(G-5803)*
Behrmann Printing Company Inc ....F.... 248 799-7771
Southfield *(G-15505)*
Berci Printing Services Inc ....G.... 248 350-0206
Southfield *(G-15506)*
Beyond Embroidery ....G.... 616 726-7000
Grand Rapids *(G-6505)*
Bible Doctrines To Live By Inc ....G.... 616 453-0493
Comstock Park *(G-3590)*
Big D LLC ....G.... 248 787-2724
Redford *(G-13720)*
Big Rapids Printing ....G.... 231 796-8588
Grand Rapids *(G-6508)*
Bivins Graphics ....G.... 616 453-2211
Grand Rapids *(G-6512)*
Black Label Customs LLC ....G.... 231 924-8044
Grant *(G-7427)*
Blts Wearable Art Inc ....G.... 517 669-9659
Dewitt *(G-4706)*
Blue Water Printing Co Inc ....G.... 810 664-0643
Lapeer *(G-9914)*
Brightformat Inc ....E.... 616 247-1161
Grand Rapids *(G-6524)*
Bronco Printing Company ....G.... 248 544-1120
Hazel Park *(G-7821)*
Brooklyn Special Tees ....G.... 623 521-3230
Brooklyn *(G-2123)*
Brophy Engraving Co Inc ....E.... 313 871-2333
Detroit *(G-4076)*
Busy Bees EMB & Gifts LLC ....G.... 989 261-7446
Sheridan *(G-15381)*
C2 Imaging LLC ....C.... 248 743-2903
Troy *(G-16990)*
▲ **Cadillac Prsentation Solutions** ....E.... 248 288-9777
Troy *(G-16994)*
Carter Creations ....G.... 800 710-8055
Van Buren Twp *(G-17515)*
Carters Imagewear & Awards ....G.... 231 881-9324
Petoskey *(G-12992)*
Cartidge World ....G.... 810 229-5599
Brighton *(G-1962)*
Cedar Springs Sales LLC ....G.... 616 696-2111
Cedar Springs *(G-2645)*
Celebrations ....G.... 906 482-4946
Hancock *(G-7617)*
▲ **Celia Corporation** ....G.... 616 887-7387
Sparta *(G-15763)*
Cerva Screen Printing ....G.... 616 272-2635
Grand Rapids *(G-6561)*
Champion Screen Printers ....G.... 616 881-0760
Byron Center *(G-2263)*
Chosen Tees LLC ....G.... 313 766-4550
Redford *(G-13723)*
Christian Unity Press Inc ....G.... 810 732-1831
Flint *(G-5667)*
Clemco Printing Inc ....G.... 989 269-8364
Bad Axe *(G-1099)*
Cobrex Ltd ....G.... 734 429-9758
Saline *(G-15008)*
Columbia Marking Tools Inc ....E.... 586 949-8400
Chesterfield *(G-2860)*
Commercial Blueprint Inc ....E.... 517 372-8360
Lansing *(G-9825)*
Community Mntal Hlth Auth Clnt ....F.... 517 323-9558
Lansing *(G-9682)*
Complete Source Inc ....G.... 616 285-9110
Grand Rapids *(G-6587)*
Consoldted Dcment Slutions LLC ....F.... 586 293-8100
Fraser *(G-5914)*
Corporate Electronic Sty Inc ....D.... 248 583-7070
Troy *(G-17030)*
Coventry Creations Inc ....F.... 248 545-8360
Ferndale *(G-5537)*
Creation Highway ....G.... 307 220-7309
Milan *(G-11434)*
Creative Embossing ....G.... 248 851-1302
West Bloomfield *(G-18273)*
Creativitees Studio ....G.... 586 565-2213
Shelby Township *(G-15198)*
Cujographyx LLC ....G.... 248 318-6407
Redford *(G-13728)*
Cummins Label Company ....E.... 269 345-3386
Kalamazoo *(G-9159)*
Custom Printers Inc ....D.... 616 454-9224
Grand Rapids *(G-6623)*
Custom Threads and Sports LLC ....G.... 248 391-0088
Lake Orion *(G-9599)*
D & M Silkscreening ....G.... 517 694-4199
Holt *(G-8305)*
D J Rotunda Associates Inc ....G.... 586 772-3350
West Bloomfield *(G-18276)*
D4 Apparel LLC ....G.... 586 207-1841
Ray *(G-13698)*
Danmark Graphics LLC ....G.... 616 675-7499
Casnovia *(G-2606)*
Darson Corporation ....F.... 313 875-7781
Ferndale *(G-5538)*
Data Mail Services Inc ....E.... 248 588-2415
Madison Heights *(G-10704)*
De Vru Printing Co ....G.... 616 452-5451
Grand Rapids *(G-6636)*
Dekoff & Sons Inc ....G.... 269 344-5816
Kalamazoo *(G-9165)*

S I C

Employee Codes: A=Over 500 employees, B=251-500
C=101-250, D=51-100, E=20-50, F=10-19, G=3-9
2022 Harris Michigan
Industrial Directory
771

27 PRINTING, PUBLISHING, AND ALLIED INDUSTRIES

Delta Sports Service & EMB .... G 517 482-6565
  Lansing (G-9686)
Dennco LLC .... G 866 977-4467
  Sault Sainte Marie (G-15089)
Designshirtscom Inc .... G 734 414-7604
  Plymouth (G-13155)
Detroit Impression Company Inc .... G 313 921-9077
  Grosse Pointe Park (G-7551)
DI Tee Pee LLC .... G 906 493-6929
  Drummond Island (G-4800)
Digital Imaging Group Inc .... D 269 686-8744
  Allegan (G-155)
Digitally Assured .... G 734 730-8800
  Ypsilanti (G-18939)
Display Pack Inc .... C 616 451-3061
  Cedar Springs (G-2649)
Dobb Printing Inc .... E 231 722-1060
  Muskegon (G-11799)
Domart LLC .... G 616 285-9177
  Grand Rapids (G-6653)
Dome Production LLC .... G 517 787-9178
  Jackson (G-8869)
Domer Industries LLC .... F 269 226-4000
  Kalamazoo (G-9173)
Drink Branders LLC .... F 231 668-4121
  Traverse City (G-16671)
Dyemurex Inc .... G 586 447-2509
  Roseville (G-14403)
E & S Graphics Inc .... G 989 875-2828
  Ithaca (G-8790)
Eagle Grafix .... G 989 624-4638
  Birch Run (G-1706)
Earle Press Inc .... E 231 773-2111
  Muskegon (G-11805)
Earthbound Inc .... G 616 774-0096
  Grand Rapids (G-6662)
Eclipse Print Emporium Inc .... G 248 477-8337
  Livonia (G-10190)
Ecoprint Services LLC .... G 616 254-8019
  Grand Rapids (G-6664)
Edens Political .... G 313 277-0700
  Dearborn (G-3834)
EDM Inc .... G 586 933-3187
  Troy (G-17077)
Edwards Sign & Screen Printing .... G 989 725-2988
  Owosso (G-12832)
Elite Bus Svcs Exec Stffing In .... G 734 956-4550
  Bloomfield Hills (G-1818)
Emerald Graphics Inc .... G 616 871-3020
  Grand Rapids (G-6676)
Endless Engravings .... G 517 962-4293
  Jackson (G-8880)
Epi Printers Inc .... D 734 261-9400
  Livonia (G-10198)
Essential Screen Printing LLC .... G 313 300-6411
  Detroit (G-4215)
Express Sportswear Inc .... E 989 773-7515
  Mount Pleasant (G-11697)
Extreme Screen Prints .... G 616 889-8305
  Grand Rapids (G-6694)
Extreme Screenprints .... G 616 889-8305
  Grandville (G-7375)
F & A Enterprises of Michigan .... G 906 228-3222
  Marquette (G-11018)
F P Horak Company .... C 989 892-6505
  Bay City (G-1355)
Fabricated Customs .... G 517 488-7273
  Okemos (G-12667)
Faro Screen Process Inc .... F 734 207-8400
  Canton (G-2461)
Federal Heath Sign Company LLC .... E 248 656-8000
  Rochester Hills (G-14010)
Field Crafts Inc .... F 231 325-1122
  Honor (G-8359)
Figment Screen Printing .... G 269 858-9998
  Three Rivers (G-16573)
Flamingo Label Co .... F 586 469-9587
  Clinton Township (G-3240)
Flavored Group LLC .... G 517 775-4371
  Lansing (G-9760)
Flowing Well Publications .... G 231 622-8630
  Petoskey (G-12997)
Focus Marketing .... E 616 355-4362
  Holland (G-8037)
Foltz Screen Printing .... G 989 772-3947
  Mount Pleasant (G-11699)
Fonts About Inc .... G 248 767-7504
  Northville (G-12219)
Foresight Group Inc .... E 517 485-5700
  Lansing (G-9699)

Fortis Sltions Group Centl LLC .... D 248 437-5200
  Wixom (G-18664)
Frye Printing Company Inc .... F 517 456-4124
  Clinton (G-3139)
FSI Label Company .... F 586 776-4110
  Holland (G-8043)
Fug Inc .... G 269 781-8036
  Marshall (G-11058)
Futuristic Artwear Inc .... F 248 680-0200
  Rochester Hills (G-14018)
General Tape Label Liquidating .... F 248 437-5200
  Wixom (G-18668)
Genesee County Herald Inc .... F 810 686-3840
  Clio (G-3399)
Genesis Graphics Inc .... G 906 786-4913
  Escanaba (G-5072)
Gifts Engraved Inc .... G 248 321-8900
  Royal Oak (G-14540)
Globe Printing & Specialties .... F 906 485-1033
  Ishpeming (G-8776)
Grafaktri Inc .... G 734 665-0717
  Ann Arbor (G-504)
Grand Apps LLC .... G 517 927-5140
  Grand Ledge (G-6391)
Grand Blanc Printing Inc .... G 810 694-1155
  Grand Blanc (G-6245)
Grand Rapids Graphix .... G 616 359-2383
  Wyoming (G-18876)
Grand Rapids Graphix LLC .... G 616 359-2383
  Grand Rapids (G-6758)
Grand Rapids Graphix LLC .... G 616 359-2383
  Caledonia (G-2376)
Grand Rapids Label Company .... D 616 459-8134
  Grand Rapids (G-6760)
Grand Rapids Letter Service .... G 616 459-4711
  Grand Rapids (G-6762)
Grand Traverse Continuous Inc .... E 231 941-5400
  Traverse City (G-16698)
Graphic Enterprises Inc .... D 248 616-4900
  Madison Heights (G-10732)
Graphic Impressions Inc .... G 616 455-0303
  Grand Rapids (G-6782)
Graphic Specialties Inc .... G 616 247-0060
  Grand Rapids (G-6783)
Graphicolor Systems Inc .... G 248 347-0271
  Livonia (G-10229)
Graphics Embossed Images Inc .... G 616 791-0404
  Grand Rapids (G-6784)
Graphix 2 Go Inc .... G 269 969-7321
  Battle Creek (G-1235)
Grasel Graphics Inc .... G 989 652-5151
  Frankenmuth (G-5865)
Graveldinger Graphix .... G 248 535-8074
  Ortonville (G-12747)
Great Lakes Label LLC .... E 616 647-9880
  Comstock Park (G-3610)
Great Put On Inc .... G 810 771-4174
  Grand Blanc (G-6246)
Greystone Imaging LLC .... G 616 742-3810
  Grand Rapids (G-6790)
Group 7500 Inc .... F 313 875-9026
  Detroit (G-4284)
Group Infotech Inc .... E 517 336-7110
  Lansing (G-9848)
H E L P Printers Inc .... G 734 847-0554
  Temperance (G-16533)
Hamblin Company .... E 517 423-7491
  Bloomfield Hills (G-1826)
Handy Bindery Co Inc .... E 586 469-2240
  Clinton Township (G-3251)
Hankerds Sportswear Basic TS .... G 989 725-2979
  Owosso (G-12836)
Harbinger Laser .... G 269 445-1499
  Cassopolis (G-2629)
Help-U-Sell RE Big Rapids .... F 231 796-3966
  Big Rapids (G-1677)
Herald Newspapers Company Inc .... G 989 895-8551
  Flint (G-5715)
High Winds Graphix .... G 313 363-3434
  Grosse Pointe Park (G-7556)
Hilton Screeners Inc .... G 810 653-0711
  Davison (G-3787)
Hodges & Irvine Inc .... F 810 329-4787
  Saint Clair (G-14831)
Holland Screen Print Inc .... G 616 396-7630
  Holland (G-8084)
Homestead Graphics Design Inc .... G 906 353-6741
  Baraga (G-1140)
Honeybees Custom Tees .... G 248 421-0817
  Milford (G-11466)

Houghton Lake Resorter Inc .... F 989 366-5341
  Houghton Lake (G-8400)
Hoyt & Company LLC .... G 810 624-4445
  Clio (G-3401)
Husky Envelope Products Inc .... D 248 624-7070
  Walled Lake (G-17670)
I D Merch .... G 734 237-4111
  Garden City (G-6096)
I-94 Enterprises .... G 269 945-3185
  Hastings (G-7798)
IAC Creative LLC .... E 248 455-7000
  Southfield (G-15597)
Image Projections Inc .... F 810 629-0700
  Fenton (G-5486)
▲ Imagemaster LLC .... E 734 821-2500
  Ann Arbor (G-523)
Impact Label Corporation .... D 269 381-4280
  Galesburg (G-6079)
▼ Imperial Clinical RES Svcs Inc .... C 616 784-0100
  Grand Rapids (G-6836)
Impression Center Co .... E 248 989-8080
  Troy (G-17162)
Impressions Custom Graphics .... E 989 429-0079
  Harrison (G-7678)
Imprint House LLC .... G 810 985-8203
  Port Huron (G-13487)
Industrial Imprntng & Die Ctng .... E 586 778-9470
  Eastpointe (G-4937)
Industrial Mtal Idntfction Inc .... G 616 847-0060
  Spring Lake (G-15824)
Ink Chemistry Screen Printing .... G 810 429-9095
  Holly (G-8278)
Ink Frenzy .... E 734 562-2621
  Chelsea (G-2815)
Inkorporate .... G 734 261-4657
  Garden City (G-6097)
Inkpressions .... G 248 956-7974
  Commerce Township (G-3542)
Integrity Marketing Products .... E 734 522-5050
  Garden City (G-6099)
International Master Pdts Corp .... C 231 894-5651
  Montague (G-11598)
Invest Positive LLC .... G 313 205-9815
  Southfield (G-15607)
Invitations By Design .... G 269 342-8551
  Kalamazoo (G-9226)
Irwin Enterprises Inc .... E 810 732-0770
  Flint (G-5716)
IXL Graphics .... G 313 350-2800
  Taylor (G-16429)
J B M Technology .... G 269 344-5716
  Kalamazoo (G-9227)
J-Ad Graphics Inc .... D 800 870-7085
  Hastings (G-7800)
▲ J2 Licensing Inc .... G 586 307-3400
  Troy (G-17180)
Jack Batdorss .... F 231 723-3592
  Manistee (G-10902)
JD Group Inc .... F 248 735-9999
  Novi (G-12448)
Jentees Custom Screen Prtg LLC .... F 231 929-3610
  Traverse City (G-16729)
Job Shop Ink Inc .... G 517 372-3900
  Lansing (G-9768)
Johnson-Clark Printers Inc .... F 231 947-6898
  Traverse City (G-16730)
Jomar Inc .... E 269 925-2222
  Benton Harbor (G-1560)
Jomark Inc .... E 248 478-2600
  Farmington Hills (G-5275)
Just Wing It Inc .... G 248 549-9338
  Madison Heights (G-10756)
K G S Screen Process Inc .... G 313 794-2777
  Detroit (G-4347)
Kalamazoo Sportswear Inc .... E 269 344-4242
  Kalamazoo (G-9248)
Kenewell Group .... G 810 714-4290
  Fenton (G-5487)
Kennedy Acquisition Inc .... G 616 871-3020
  Grand Rapids (G-6884)
Kent County .... F 616 632-7580
  Grand Rapids (G-6887)
Kingdom Geekdom LLC .... G 517 610-5016
  Hillsdale (G-7939)
Kpmf Usa Inc .... F 248 377-4999
  Lake Orion (G-9612)
Label Tech Inc .... F 586 247-6444
  Shelby Township (G-15254)
Labor Education and Res Prj .... G 313 842-6262
  Detroit (G-4373)

▲ **Lamon Group Inc** F 616 710-3169
Byron Center *(G-2280)*
Lamour Printing Co G 734 241-6006
Monroe *(G-11558)*
Lansing Athletics G 517 327-8828
Lansing *(G-9772)*
Larsen Graphics Inc E 989 823-3000
Vassar *(G-17579)*
Lasertec Inc E 586 274-4500
Madison Heights *(G-10769)*
Lawson Printers Inc E 269 965-0525
Battle Creek *(G-1267)*
Legacy Design Studio LLC G 248 710-3219
Rochester Hills *(G-14052)*
Lesnau Printing Company E 586 795-9200
Sterling Heights *(G-16071)*
Let Love Rule G 734 749-7435
Rockwood *(G-14202)*
Litho-Graphics Printing Pdts G 586 775-1670
Roseville *(G-14433)*
Lithotech G 269 471-6027
Berrien Springs *(G-1644)*
Livonia Trophy & Screen Prtg G 734 464-9191
Livonia *(G-10289)*
Logos and Letters G 248 795-2093
Clarkston *(G-3045)*
Lowery Corporation C 616 554-5200
Grand Rapids *(G-6949)*
Lyons Graphics and Tees G 586 770-9630
New Haven *(G-12034)*
M & J Graphics Enterprises Inc F 734 542-8800
Livonia *(G-10294)*
Macarthur Corp E 810 606-1777
Grand Blanc *(G-6252)*
Macomb Residential Opprtnts G 586 231-0363
Clinton Township *(G-3289)*
Make It Mine Dsign EMB Screen G 989 448-8678
Gaylord *(G-6144)*
Malachi Printing LLC G 517 395-4813
Edwardsburg *(G-5008)*
Maleports Sault Prtg Co Inc E 906 632-3369
Sault Sainte Marie *(G-15095)*
Marking Machine Co F 517 767-4155
Tekonsha *(G-16523)*
Marquee Engraving Inc G 810 686-7550
Clio *(G-3404)*
Materialise Usa LLC D 734 259-6445
Plymouth *(G-13236)*
Mayfair Accessories Inc G 989 732-8400
Gaylord *(G-6146)*
Mega Screen Corp G 517 849-7057
Jonesville *(G-9094)*
Memories Xpress G 248 582-1836
Madison Heights *(G-10780)*
Meta4mat LLC G 616 214-7418
Comstock Park *(G-3625)*
Meteor Web Marketing Inc F 734 822-4999
Ann Arbor *(G-570)*
Metro Detroit Screen Prtg LLC G 586 337-5167
Shelby Township *(G-15276)*
Metroastyling G 586 991-6854
Sterling Heights *(G-16094)*
Mettek LLC G 616 895-2033
Allendale *(G-225)*
Michael Anderson G 231 652-5717
Newaygo *(G-12088)*
Michael Niederpruem G 231 935-0241
Kalkaska *(G-9396)*
Michigan Screen Printing G 810 687-5550
Clio *(G-3406)*
Micrgraphics Printing Inc F 231 739-6575
Norton Shores *(G-12311)*
Microforms Inc E 586 939-7900
Beverly Hills *(G-1667)*
Mid-State Printing Inc F 989 875-4163
Ithaca *(G-8794)*
Middleton Printing Inc G 616 247-8742
Grand Rapids *(G-7004)*
Midwest Graphics & Awards Inc G 734 424-3700
Dexter *(G-4746)*
Monograms & More Inc E 313 299-3140
Taylor *(G-16449)*
Monroe Publishing Company D 734 242-1100
Monroe *(G-11565)*
Monroe Sp Inc G 517 374-6544
Lansing *(G-9779)*
Moormann Printing Inc G 269 423-2411
Decatur *(G-3950)*
MPS Holdco Inc B 517 886-2526
Lansing *(G-9717)*
MPS Hrl LLC G 800 748-0517
Lansing *(G-9718)*
◆ **MPS Lansing Inc** A 517 323-9000
Lansing *(G-9719)*
Mr Cs Custom Tees G 989 965-2222
Clarksville *(G-3079)*
Multi Packg Solutions Intl Ltd A 517 323-9000
Lansing *(G-9721)*
▲ **Mylockercom LLC** B 877 898-3366
Detroit *(G-4473)*
▲ **Nalcor LLC** D 248 541-1140
Ferndale *(G-5570)*
New World Etching N Amer Ve G 586 296-8082
Fraser *(G-5968)*
Ninja Tees N More G 248 541-2547
Hazel Park *(G-7837)*
Nje Enterprises LLC G 313 963-3600
Detroit *(G-4486)*
North Country Publishing Corp G 231 526-2191
Harbor Springs *(G-7653)*
Northern Label Inc G 231 854-6301
Hesperia *(G-7871)*
Nu-Tech North Inc G 231 347-1992
Petoskey *(G-13010)*
Oc Tees G 248 858-9191
Pontiac *(G-13405)*
Ogemaw County Herald Inc E 989 345-0044
West Branch *(G-18333)*
P D Q Press Inc G 586 725-1888
Ira *(G-8706)*
Pds Plastics Inc F 616 896-1109
Dorr *(G-4769)*
Peg-Master Business Forms Inc G 586 566-8694
Shelby Township *(G-15298)*
▲ **Perrin Souvenir Distrs Inc** B 616 785-9700
Comstock Park *(G-3636)*
Personal Graphics G 231 347-6347
Petoskey *(G-13013)*
Pioneer Press Printing G 231 864-2404
Bear Lake *(G-1421)*
Plexus Cards G 231 652-5355
Newaygo *(G-12089)*
Pointe Printing Inc G 313 821-0030
Grosse Pointe Park *(G-7558)*
Precision Dial Co G 269 375-5601
Kalamazoo *(G-9302)*
Precision Label Inc G 616 534-9935
Grandville *(G-7412)*
Presscraft Papers Inc F 231 882-5505
Benzonia *(G-1616)*
Primo Crafts G 248 373-3229
Pontiac *(G-13411)*
Print Shop 4u LLC G 810 721-7500
Imlay City *(G-8644)*
Printcomm Inc D 810 239-5763
Flint *(G-5749)*
Printery Inc E 616 396-4655
Holland *(G-8172)*
Printing Consolidation Co LLC E 616 233-3161
Grand Rapids *(G-7108)*
▲ **Printwell Acquisition Co Inc** D 734 941-6300
Taylor *(G-16462)*
Printxpress Inc G 313 846-1644
Dearborn *(G-3887)*
Pro Gear Printing LLC G 734 386-1105
Canton *(G-2514)*
Pro Shop The/P S Graphics G 517 448-8490
Hudson *(G-8559)*
Progress Custom Screen Prtg G 248 982-4247
Ferndale *(G-5583)*
Progressive Graphics G 269 945-9249
Hastings *(G-7806)*
Prop Art Studio Inc G 313 824-2200
Detroit *(G-4539)*
Publishing Xpress G 248 582-1834
Madison Heights *(G-10811)*
Qrp Inc E 989 496-2955
Midland *(G-11406)*
R & R Harwood Inc G 616 669-6400
Jenison *(G-9069)*
R R Donnelley & Sons Company G 248 583-2500
Madison Heights *(G-10816)*
Raenell Press LLC G 616 534-8890
Grand Rapids *(G-7137)*
Rainbow Tape & Label Inc F 734 941-6090
Romulus *(G-14324)*
Ray Printing Company Inc F 517 787-4130
Jackson *(G-8994)*
Rbd Creative G 313 259-5507
Plymouth *(G-13278)*
Reborn Wear G 313 680-6806
Rockwood *(G-14204)*
Religious Communications LLC G 313 822-3361
Detroit *(G-4563)*
Riegle Press Inc E 810 653-9631
Davison *(G-3795)*
Rival Shop G 248 461-6281
Waterford *(G-18161)*
River Run Press Inc E 269 349-7603
Kalamazoo *(G-9320)*
Riverhill Publications & Prtg F 586 468-6011
Ira *(G-8711)*
Rodzina Industries Inc G 810 235-2341
Flint *(G-5755)*
Rogers Printing Inc C 231 853-2244
Ravenna *(G-13694)*
Romeo Printing Company Inc G 586 752-9003
Romeo *(G-14234)*
▲ **Royal Stewart Enterprises** G 734 224-7994
Temperance *(G-16548)*
RPC Company F 989 752-3618
Saginaw *(G-14741)*
RR Donnelley G 248 588-2941
Madison Heights *(G-10822)*
Safran Printing Company Inc C 586 939-7600
Beverly Hills *(G-1668)*
Sage Direct Inc F 616 940-8311
Grand Rapids *(G-7178)*
Sandlot Sports G 989 391-9684
Bay City *(G-1397)*
Sandlot Sports F 989 835-9696
Saginaw *(G-14752)*
Save On Everything LLC D 248 362-9119
Troy *(G-17345)*
Sboy LLC G 313 350-0496
Detroit *(G-4583)*
Screen Graphics Co Inc G 231 238-4499
Indian River *(G-8656)*
Screen Ideas Inc G 616 458-5119
Grand Rapids *(G-7188)*
Screen Print Department E 616 235-2200
Grand Rapids *(G-7189)*
Serviscreen Inc D 616 669-1640
Jenison *(G-9071)*
Shirt Razor LLC G 810 623-7116
Brighton *(G-2070)*
Shirt Traveler G 800 403-4117
Swartz Creek *(G-16358)*
Sign Screen Inc G 810 239-1100
Flint *(G-5762)*
Signal-Return Inc G 313 567-8970
Detroit *(G-4593)*
Signs365com LLC G 800 265-8830
Shelby Township *(G-15333)*
Silk Screenstuff G 517 543-7716
Charlotte *(G-2770)*
Sisters In Inc G 269 857-4085
Saugatuck *(G-15085)*
Slick Shirts Screen Printing F 517 371-3600
Lansing *(G-9895)*
SM & AM Enterprise Inc G 906 786-0373
Escanaba *(G-5100)*
Solutionsnowbiz G 269 321-5062
Portage *(G-13609)*
Source One Digital LLC E 231 759-3160
Norton Shores *(G-12334)*
Source One Dist Svcs Inc F 248 399-5060
Madison Heights *(G-10831)*
Spartan Graphics Inc D 616 887-1073
Sparta *(G-15780)*
Sports Junction G 989 791-5900
Saginaw *(G-14765)*
Stamp-Rite Incorporated E 517 487-5071
Lansing *(G-9741)*
Standard Printing G 734 483-0339
Ypsilanti *(G-18978)*
Standard Printing of Warren G 586 771-3770
Warren *(G-18026)*
Star Ink and Thread G 989 823-3660
Vassar *(G-17582)*
Star Line Commercial Printing G 810 733-1152
Flushing *(G-5813)*
Step Into Success Inc G 734 426-1075
Pinckney *(G-13057)*
Stepscreen Printing G 734 770-5009
Monroe *(G-11577)*
Stoppa Signs & Engraving LLC G 616 532-0230
Wyoming *(G-18908)*
Strait Astrid G 269 672-4110
Shelbyville *(G-15374)*

S I C

Employee Codes: A=Over 500 employees, B=251-500
C=101-250, D=51-100, E=20-50, F=10-19, G=3-9

2022 Harris Michigan
Industrial Directory

773

Straits Area Printing Corp ... G ... 231 627-5647 — Cheboygan *(G-2800)*
Stylerite Label Corporation ... E ... 248 853-7977 — Rochester Hills *(G-14120)*
Sublime Prints ... G ... 231 335-7799 — Hesperia *(G-7872)*
Sweet N Sporty Tees ... G ... 313 693-9793 — Detroit *(G-4619)*
Swift Printing Co ... F ... 616 459-4263 — Grand Rapids *(G-7241)*
T J K Inc ... G ... 586 731-9639 — Sterling Heights *(G-16199)*
T Shirt Guy ... G ... 586 944-5900 — Warren *(G-18033)*
T Shirt Shop ... G ... 810 285-8857 — Flint *(G-5776)*
Tallon Printing ... G ... 517 721-1307 — Okemos *(G-12689)*
Tc Office Express ... G ... 231 929-3549 — Traverse City *(G-16851)*
Tectonics Industries LLC ... E ... 248 597-1600 — Auburn Hills *(G-1046)*
Tee ... G ... 810 231-2764 — Brighton *(G-2076)*
Tee - The Extra Effort LLC ... G ... 734 891-4789 — Royal Oak *(G-14584)*
Tee Quilters ... G ... 248 336-9779 — Ferndale *(G-5588)*
Teesnitch Screen Printing ... G ... 734 667-1636 — Canton *(G-2533)*
▲ TGI Direct Inc ... E ... 810 239-5553 — Flint *(G-5778)*
TGI Direct Inc ... G ... 810 239-5553 — Ann Arbor *(G-685)*
The Envelope Printery Inc ... D ... 734 398-7700 — Van Buren Twp *(G-17557)*
Thorpe Printing Services Inc ... G ... 810 364-6222 — Marysville *(G-11107)*
Timbertech Inc ... F ... 231 348-2750 — Harbor Springs *(G-7658)*
Total Lee Sports Inc ... G ... 989 772-6121 — Mount Pleasant *(G-11745)*
Touched By Cupids ... G ... 313 704-6334 — Detroit *(G-4640)*
TP Logos LLC ... G ... 810 956-9484 — Marysville *(G-11110)*
Travel Information Services ... F ... 989 275-8042 — Roscommon *(G-14357)*
Tribar Manufacturing LLC ... E ... 248 669-0077 — Wixom *(G-18777)*
Trikala Inc ... G ... 517 646-8188 — Dimondale *(G-4765)*
Triple Creek Shirts and More ... G ... 269 273-5154 — Constantine *(G-3676)*
Triton 3d LLC ... G ... 616 405-8662 — Grand Rapids *(G-7277)*
Troy Haygood ... G ... 313 478-3308 — Ferndale *(G-5589)*
Turner Business Forms Inc ... E ... 989 752-5540 — Saginaw *(G-14782)*
Tuscola County Advertiser Inc ... B ... 517 673-3181 — Caro *(G-2584)*
Tvdn Group LLC ... G ... 248 255-6402 — Bloomfield Hills *(G-1871)*
▲ Tweddle Group Inc ... C ... 586 307-3700 — Clinton Township *(G-3380)*
Ultimate Graphic and Sign LLC ... G ... 989 865-5200 — Saint Charles *(G-14812)*
Ultra-Tech Printing Co ... F ... 616 249-0500 — Wyoming *(G-18915)*
Underground Shirts ... G ... 734 274-5494 — Ann Arbor *(G-705)*
Unique Embroidery ... G ... 517 321-8647 — Lansing *(G-9746)*
Unique Reproductions Inc ... G ... 248 788-2887 — West Bloomfield *(G-18321)*
Valassis International Inc ... B ... 734 591-3000 — Livonia *(G-10457)*
Van Kehrberg Vern ... G ... 810 364-1066 — Marysville *(G-11111)*
▲ Vector Distribution LLC ... G ... 616 361-2021 — Grand Rapids *(G-7308)*
Verso Services Inc ... G ... 734 368-0989 — Ann Arbor *(G-710)*
Vg Kids ... G ... 734 480-0667 — Ypsilanti *(G-18983)*
Vgkids Inc ... F ... 734 485-5128 — Ypsilanti *(G-18984)*
Village Printing & Supply Inc ... G ... 810 664-2270 — Lapeer *(G-9966)*
Villagebees ... G ... 810 217-2962 — Lapeer *(G-9967)*
Vinyl Spectrum ... F ... 616 591-3410 — Wyoming *(G-18918)*
Weighman Enterprises Inc ... G ... 989 755-2116 — Saginaw *(G-14792)*
Wesman Designs ... G ... 616 669-3290 — Hudsonville *(G-8616)*
Whipple Printing Inc ... G ... 313 382-8033 — Allen Park *(G-210)*
Whitlam Group Inc ... C ... 586 757-5100 — Center Line *(G-2689)*
Whitlock Distribution Svcs LLC ... F ... 248 548-1040 — Madison Heights *(G-10863)*
Yooper Shirts Mqt ... G ... 906 273-1837 — Marquette *(G-11051)*
Your Home Town USA Inc ... G ... 517 529-9421 — Clarklake *(G-3010)*
Zak Brothers Printing LLC ... G ... 313 831-3216 — Detroit *(G-4700)*
Zakoors ... G ... 313 831-6969 — Detroit *(G-4701)*
Zeeland Record Co ... G ... 616 772-2131 — Zeeland *(G-19099)*
Zodiac Enterprises LLC ... G ... 810 640-7146 — Mount Morris *(G-11677)*

2761 Manifold Business Forms

Alpha Data Business Forms Inc ... G ... 248 540-5930 — Birmingham *(G-1718)*
Business Press Inc ... G ... 248 652-8855 — Rochester *(G-13895)*
Earle Press Inc ... E ... 231 773-2111 — Muskegon *(G-11805)*
F P Horak Company ... C ... 989 892-6505 — Bay City *(G-1355)*
Forms Trac Enterprises Inc ... G ... 248 524-0006 — Sterling Heights *(G-16019)*
Frye Printing Company Inc ... F ... 517 456-4124 — Clinton *(G-3139)*
Grand Traverse Continuous Inc ... E ... 231 941-5400 — Traverse City *(G-16698)*
▼ Imperial Clinical RES Svcs Inc ... C ... 616 784-0100 — Grand Rapids *(G-6836)*
Micrgraphics Printing Inc ... F ... 231 739-6575 — Norton Shores *(G-12311)*
Microforms Inc ... E ... 586 939-7900 — Beverly Hills *(G-1667)*
◆ MPS Lansing Inc ... A ... 517 323-9000 — Lansing *(G-9719)*
Peg-Master Business Forms Inc ... G ... 586 566-8694 — Shelby Township *(G-15298)*
Riegle Press Inc ... E ... 810 653-9631 — Davison *(G-3795)*
Rotary Multiforms Inc ... G ... 586 558-7960 — Madison Heights *(G-10819)*
Spinnaker Corp ... G ... 616 956-7677 — Grand Rapids *(G-7218)*
Timbertech Inc ... F ... 231 348-2750 — Harbor Springs *(G-7658)*
Total Business Systems Inc ... F ... 248 307-1076 — Madison Heights *(G-10845)*
Ultra Forms Plus Inc ... F ... 269 337-6000 — Kalamazoo *(G-9360)*
Whitlock Business Systems Inc ... E ... 248 548-1040 — Madison Heights *(G-10862)*

2771 Greeting Card Publishing

Avanti Press Inc ... E ... 800 228-2684 — Detroit *(G-4034)*
Avanti Press Inc ... E ... 313 961-0022 — Taylor *(G-16383)*
Cards4heroescom LLC ... G ... 877 640-8206 — Hartland *(G-7767)*
◆ Design Design Inc ... C ... 866 935-2648 — Grand Rapids *(G-6643)*
Mr Sogs Creatures ... G ... 901 413-0291 — Farmington Hills *(G-5328)*
Notes From Man Cave LLC ... G ... 586 604-1997 — Detroit *(G-4492)*
Reyers Company Inc ... F ... 616 414-5530 — Spring Lake *(G-15846)*

2782 Blankbooks & Looseleaf Binders

Artful Scrapbooking & Rubber ... G ... 586 651-1577 — Washington *(G-18078)*
▲ Cadillac Prsentation Solutions ... E ... 248 288-9777 — Troy *(G-16994)*
Cookie Music Ent LLC ... G ... 209 851-6633 — Detroit *(G-4103)*
Gathering Place of White Lake ... G ... 248 379-9582 — White Lake *(G-18455)*
Hexon Corporation ... E ... 248 585-7585 — Farmington Hills *(G-5259)*
Janelle Peterson ... G ... 616 447-9070 — Grand Rapids *(G-6861)*
Memories Manor ... G ... 810 329-2800 — Saint Clair *(G-14836)*
Microforms Inc ... E ... 586 939-7900 — Beverly Hills *(G-1667)*
Scrapaloo ... G ... 269 623-7310 — Delton *(G-3966)*
Scrappy Chic ... G ... 248 426-9020 — Livonia *(G-10402)*
Superior Receipt Book Co Inc ... F ... 269 467-8265 — Centreville *(G-2698)*
Top Quality Cleaning LLC ... F ... 810 493-4211 — Flint *(G-5779)*

2789 Bookbinding

A Koppel Color Image Company ... G ... 616 534-3600 — Grandville *(G-7360)*
Afb Corporate Operations LLC ... E ... 248 669-1188 — Plymouth *(G-13120)*
Aladdin Printing ... G ... 248 360-2842 — Commerce Township *(G-3507)*
American Label & Tag Inc ... E ... 734 454-7600 — Canton *(G-2433)*
Americas Finest Prtg Graphics ... G ... 586 296-1312 — Fraser *(G-5893)*
Apb Inc ... G ... 248 528-2990 — Troy *(G-16939)*
ASAP Printing Inc ... G ... 517 882-3500 — Okemos *(G-12657)*
Bessenberg Bindery Corporation ... G ... 734 996-9696 — Ann Arbor *(G-400)*
Brd Printing Inc ... E ... 517 372-0268 — Lansing *(G-9816)*
Breck Graphics Incorporated ... E ... 616 248-4110 — Grand Rapids *(G-6523)*
Bronco Printing Company ... G ... 248 544-1120 — Hazel Park *(G-7821)*
Bruce Inc ... G ... 517 371-5205 — Lansing *(G-9819)*
Business Press Inc ... G ... 248 652-8855 — Rochester *(G-13895)*
Color Connection ... G ... 248 351-0920 — Southfield *(G-15527)*
Copy Central Inc ... G ... 231 941-2298 — Traverse City *(G-16660)*
Cushing-Malloy Inc ... E ... 734 663-8554 — Ann Arbor *(G-440)*
Custom Printers Inc ... D ... 616 454-9224 — Grand Rapids *(G-6623)*
De Vru Printing Co ... G ... 616 452-5451 — Grand Rapids *(G-6636)*
Derk Pieter Co Inc ... G ... 616 554-7777 — Grand Rapids *(G-6641)*
Dobb Printing Inc ... E ... 231 722-1060 — Muskegon *(G-11799)*
DPrinter Inc ... G ... 517 423-6554 — Tecumseh *(G-16499)*
Earle Press Inc ... E ... 231 773-2111 — Muskegon *(G-11805)*
Econo Print Inc ... G ... 734 878-5806 — Pinckney *(G-13047)*
F P Horak Company ... C ... 989 892-6505 — Bay City *(G-1355)*
Fedex Office & Print Svcs Inc ... F ... 734 761-4539 — Ann Arbor *(G-487)*
Fedex Office & Print Svcs Inc ... G ... 517 332-5855 — East Lansing *(G-4892)*
Foremost Graphics LLC ... D ... 616 453-4747 — Grand Rapids *(G-6715)*
Forsons Inc ... G ... 517 787-4562 — Jackson *(G-8885)*
Frye Printing Company Inc ... F ... 517 456-4124 — Clinton *(G-3139)*
Future Reproductions Inc ... F ... 248 350-2060 — Southfield *(G-15571)*
Gatherall Bindery Inc ... G ... 248 669-6850 — Roseville *(G-14410)*
Gatherall Bindery Inc ... G ... 248 669-6850 — Roseville *(G-14411)*
Gombar Corp ... G ... 989 793-9427 — Saginaw *(G-14655)*
Grand Blanc Printing Inc ... E ... 810 694-1155 — Grand Blanc *(G-6245)*
Graphic Impressions Inc ... G ... 616 455-0303 — Grand Rapids *(G-6782)*

Graphic Specialties Inc ....E 616 247-0060
Grand Rapids *(G-6783)*
Great Lakes Bindery Inc ....F 616 245-5264
Grand Rapids *(G-6786)*
Hamblin Company ....E 517 423-7491
Bloomfield Hills *(G-1826)*
Handy Bindery Co Inc ....E 586 469-2240
Clinton Township *(G-3251)*
Hatteras Inc ....E 734 525-5500
Plymouth *(G-13183)*
Hi-Lites Graphic Inc ....E 231 924-0630
Fremont *(G-6045)*
Hoag & Sons Book Bindery Inc ....F 517 857-2033
Eaton Rapids *(G-4965)*
Hodges & Irvine Inc ....F 810 329-4787
Saint Clair *(G-14831)*
J-Ad Graphics Inc ....F 269 965-3955
Battle Creek *(G-1243)*
J-Ad Graphics Inc ....D 800 870-7085
Hastings *(G-7800)*
▼ John H Dekker & Sons Inc ....D 616 257-4120
Grand Rapids *(G-6872)*
Kent Communications Inc ....D 616 957-2120
Grand Rapids *(G-6886)*
Litsenberger Print Shop ....G 906 482-3903
Houghton *(G-8386)*
Logan Brothers Printing Inc ....G 517 485-3771
Dewitt *(G-4711)*
Macomb Printing Inc ....E 586 463-2301
Clinton Township *(G-3288)*
Maleports Sault Prtg Co Inc ....E 906 632-3369
Sault Sainte Marie *(G-15095)*
▼ McNaughton & Gunn Inc ....C 734 429-5411
Saline *(G-15025)*
Mel Printing Co Inc ....E 313 928-5440
Taylor *(G-16440)*
Metropolitan Indus Lithography ....G 269 323-9333
Portage *(G-13585)*
Micrgraphics Printing Inc ....F 231 739-6575
Norton Shores *(G-12311)*
Mid-State Printing Inc ....F 989 875-4163
Ithaca *(G-8794)*
▲ Mitchell Graphics Inc ....E 231 347-4635
Petoskey *(G-13007)*
Ogemaw County Herald Inc ....E 989 345-0044
West Branch *(G-18333)*
▲ Owosso Graphic Arts Inc ....E 989 725-7112
Owosso *(G-12849)*
Page Litho Inc ....F 313 885-8555
Grosse Pointe *(G-7532)*
Parkside Speedy Print Inc ....G 810 985-8484
Port Huron *(G-13516)*
Paul C Doerr ....G 734 242-2058
Monroe *(G-11568)*
Phase III Graphics Inc ....G 616 949-9290
Grand Rapids *(G-7084)*
▲ Print-Tech Inc ....E 734 996-2345
Ann Arbor *(G-624)*
Printcomm Inc ....D 810 239-5763
Flint *(G-5749)*
Printery Inc ....E 616 396-4655
Holland *(G-8172)*
Printing Plus Inc ....G 734 482-1680
Ypsilanti *(G-18971)*
▲ Printwell Acquisition Co Inc ....D 734 941-6300
Taylor *(G-16462)*
Qrp Inc ....E 989 496-2955
Midland *(G-11406)*
Qrp Inc ....G 989 496-2955
Midland *(G-11405)*
R & R Harwood Inc ....G 616 669-6400
Jenison *(G-9069)*
R W Patterson Printing Co ....D 269 925-2177
Benton Harbor *(G-1579)*
Reyers Company Inc ....F 616 414-5530
Spring Lake *(G-15846)*
Riegle Press Inc ....E 810 653-9631
Davison *(G-3795)*
River Run Press Inc ....E 269 349-7603
Kalamazoo *(G-9320)*
Skyapple LLC ....E 248 588-5990
Madison Heights *(G-10830)*
Spartan Graphics Inc ....D 616 887-1073
Sparta *(G-15780)*
▲ Spartan Printing Inc ....E 517 372-6910
Lansing *(G-9738)*
Spectrum Printers Inc ....E 517 423-5735
Tecumseh *(G-16517)*
T J K Inc ....G 586 731-9639
Sterling Heights *(G-16199)*

Technology MGT & Budgt Dept ....G 517 322-1897
Lansing *(G-9899)*
Thorpe Printing Services Inc ....G 810 364-6222
Marysville *(G-11107)*
Tribar Manufacturing LLC ....E 248 669-0077
Wixom *(G-18777)*
Turner Business Forms Inc ....E 989 752-5540
Saginaw *(G-14782)*
▲ Village Shop Inc ....E 231 946-3712
Traverse City *(G-16875)*
Wolverine Printing Company LLC ....E 616 451-2075
Grand Rapids *(G-7347)*

2791 Typesetting

A Koppel Color Image Company ....G 616 534-3600
Grandville *(G-7360)*
AAA Language Services ....F 248 239-1138
Bloomfield *(G-1780)*
Adgravers Inc ....F 313 259-3780
Detroit *(G-3986)*
Advance Graphic Systems Inc ....E 248 656-8000
Rochester Hills *(G-13943)*
Al Corp ....F 734 475-7357
Chelsea *(G-2804)*
Aladdin Printing ....G 248 360-2842
Commerce Township *(G-3507)*
American Reprographics Co LLC ....G 248 299-8900
Clawson *(G-3086)*
Americas Finest Prtg Graphics ....G 586 296-1312
Fraser *(G-5893)*
Anteebo Publishers Inc ....E 313 882-6900
Grosse Pointe Park *(G-7546)*
AP Impressions Inc ....G 734 464-8009
Livonia *(G-10121)*
Apb Inc ....G 248 528-2990
Troy *(G-16939)*
Argus Press Company ....E 989 725-5136
Owosso *(G-12824)*
ASAP Printing Inc ....G 517 882-3500
Okemos *(G-12657)*
Beljan Ltd Inc ....F 734 426-3503
Dexter *(G-4726)*
Bookcomp Inc ....F 616 774-9700
Belmont *(G-1503)*
Breck Graphics Incorporated ....E 616 248-4110
Grand Rapids *(G-6523)*
Bronco Printing Company ....G 248 544-1120
Hazel Park *(G-7821)*
Brophy Engraving Co Inc ....E 313 871-2333
Detroit *(G-4076)*
Bruce Inc ....G 517 371-5205
Lansing *(G-9819)*
Business Press Inc ....G 248 652-8855
Rochester *(G-13895)*
Color Connection ....G 248 351-0920
Southfield *(G-15527)*
Copy Central Inc ....G 231 941-2298
Traverse City *(G-16660)*
Corporate Electronic Sty Inc ....D 248 583-7070
Troy *(G-17030)*
Daily Oakland Press ....B 248 332-8181
Bloomfield Hills *(G-1811)*
De Vru Printing Co ....G 616 452-5451
Grand Rapids *(G-6636)*
Dekoff & Sons Inc ....G 269 344-5816
Kalamazoo *(G-9165)*
Delmas Typesetting ....G 734 662-8899
Ann Arbor *(G-446)*
Derk Pieter Co Inc ....G 616 554-7777
Grand Rapids *(G-6641)*
Detroit Legal News Pubg LLC ....E 248 577-6100
Troy *(G-17057)*
Different By Design Inc ....G 248 588-4840
Farmington Hills *(G-5217)*
DPrinter Inc ....G 517 423-6554
Tecumseh *(G-16499)*
Earle Press Inc ....E 231 773-2111
Muskegon *(G-11805)*
Econo Print Inc ....G 734 878-5806
Pinckney *(G-13047)*
F P Horak Company ....C 989 892-6505
Bay City *(G-1355)*
Federal Heath Sign Company LLC ....E 248 656-8000
Rochester Hills *(G-14010)*
Fedex Office & Print Svcs Inc ....F 734 761-4539
Ann Arbor *(G-487)*
Fedex Office & Print Svcs Inc ....G 517 332-5855
East Lansing *(G-4892)*
Foremost Graphics LLC ....D 616 453-4747
Grand Rapids *(G-6715)*

Forsons Inc ....G 517 787-4562
Jackson *(G-8885)*
Future Reproductions Inc ....F 248 350-2060
Southfield *(G-15571)*
Gazette Newspapers Inc ....G 248 524-4868
Troy *(G-17128)*
Genesee County Herald Inc ....F 810 686-3840
Clio *(G-3399)*
Gombar Corp ....G 989 793-9427
Saginaw *(G-14655)*
Grand Blanc Printing Inc ....E 810 694-1155
Grand Blanc *(G-6245)*
Graphics Unlimited Inc ....G 231 773-2696
Norton Shores *(G-12295)*
Hatteras Inc ....E 734 525-5500
Plymouth *(G-13183)*
Hi-Lites Graphic Inc ....E 231 924-0630
Fremont *(G-6045)*
Infotel ....G 313 879-0820
Detroit *(G-4317)*
J-Ad Graphics Inc ....D 800 870-7085
Hastings *(G-7800)*
Jomark Inc ....E 248 478-2600
Farmington Hills *(G-5275)*
Jtc Inc ....G 517 784-0576
Jackson *(G-8925)*
Kalamazoo Photo Comp Svcs ....G 269 345-3706
Kalamazoo *(G-9245)*
Larsen Graphics Inc ....E 989 823-3000
Vassar *(G-17579)*
Lasertec Inc ....E 586 274-4500
Madison Heights *(G-10769)*
Litsenberger Print Shop ....G 906 482-3903
Houghton *(G-8386)*
Macomb Printing Inc ....E 586 463-2301
Clinton Township *(G-3288)*
Marketing VI Group Inc ....G 989 793-3933
Saginaw *(G-14686)*
Metropolitan Indus Lithography ....G 269 323-9333
Portage *(G-13585)*
Micrgraphics Printing Inc ....F 231 739-6575
Norton Shores *(G-12311)*
Microforms Inc ....E 586 939-7900
Beverly Hills *(G-1667)*
Mid-State Printing Inc ....F 989 875-4163
Ithaca *(G-8794)*
▲ Mitchell Graphics Inc ....E 231 347-4635
Petoskey *(G-13007)*
Moormann Printing Inc ....G 269 423-2411
Decatur *(G-3950)*
North American Graphics Inc ....F 586 486-1110
Warren *(G-17947)*
Ogemaw County Herald Inc ....E 989 345-0044
West Branch *(G-18333)*
P D Q Press Inc ....G 586 725-1888
Ira *(G-8706)*
Parkside Speedy Print Inc ....G 810 985-8484
Port Huron *(G-13516)*
Paul C Doerr ....G 734 242-2058
Monroe *(G-11568)*
Peg-Master Business Forms Inc ....G 586 566-8694
Shelby Township *(G-15298)*
Phase III Graphics Inc ....G 616 949-9290
Grand Rapids *(G-7084)*
Poly Tech Industries Inc ....G 248 589-9950
Madison Heights *(G-10804)*
Print Masters Inc ....F 248 548-7100
Madison Heights *(G-10810)*
▲ Print-Tech Inc ....E 734 996-2345
Ann Arbor *(G-624)*
Printcomm Inc ....D 810 239-5763
Flint *(G-5749)*
Printery Inc ....E 616 396-4655
Holland *(G-8172)*
Printing Centre Inc ....F 517 694-2400
Holt *(G-8326)*
▼ Progressive Prtg & Graphics ....G 269 965-8909
Battle Creek *(G-1284)*
Qrp Inc ....E 989 496-2955
Midland *(G-11406)*
Qrp Inc ....G 989 496-2955
Midland *(G-11405)*
Quick Printing Company Inc ....G 616 241-0506
Grand Rapids *(G-7131)*
Richard Larabee ....G 248 827-7755
Southfield *(G-15689)*
Rider Type & Design ....G 989 839-0015
Midland *(G-11408)*
River Run Press Inc ....E 269 349-7603
Kalamazoo *(G-9320)*

S I C

Safran Printing Company Inc .... C 586 939-7600
  Beverly Hills *(G-1668)*
Skip Printing and Dup Co .... G 586 779-2640
  Roseville *(G-14477)*
▲ Spartan Printing Inc .... E 517 372-6910
  Lansing *(G-9738)*
Spectrum Printers Inc 517 423-5735
  Tecumseh *(G-16517)*
Stafford Media Inc .... E 616 754-9301
  Greenville *(G-7505)*
Stafford Media Inc .... D 616 754-1178
  Greenville *(G-7506)*
T J K Inc .... G 586 731-9639
  Sterling Heights *(G-16199)*
Technology MGT & Budgt Dept ..... G 517 322-1897
  Lansing *(G-9899)*
TGI Direct Inc .... G 810 239-5553
  Ann Arbor *(G-685)*
The Envelope Printery Inc .... D 734 398-7700
  Van Buren Twp *(G-17557)*
Thorpe Printing Services Inc .... G 810 364-6222
  Marysville *(G-11107)*
Times Herald Company .... E 810 985-7171
  Port Huron *(G-13532)*
Turner Business Forms Inc .... G 989 752-5540
  Saginaw *(G-14782)*
▲ Tweddle Group Inc .... C 586 307-3700
  Clinton Township *(G-3380)*
▲ Village Shop Inc .... E 231 946-3712
  Traverse City *(G-16875)*
Whiteside Consulting Group LLC ... G 313 288-6598
  Detroit *(G-4681)*
Wolverine Printing Company LLC .. E 616 451-2075
  Grand Rapids *(G-7347)*
Worten Copy Center Inc .... G 231 845-7030
  Ludington *(G-10558)*

2796 Platemaking & Related Svcs

A D Johnson Engraving Co Inc ..... F 269 385-0044
  Kalamazoo *(G-9106)*
A-1 Engraving & Signs Inc .... G 810 231-2227
  Brighton *(G-1935)*
Adgravers Inc .... F 313 259-3780
  Detroit *(G-3986)*
AI Corp .... F 734 475-7357
  Chelsea *(G-2804)*
Alpha 21 LLC .... G 248 352-7330
  Southfield *(G-15476)*
Behrmann Printing Company Inc ... F 248 799-7771
  Southfield *(G-15505)*
Breck Graphics Incorporated .... E 616 248-4110
  Grand Rapids *(G-6523)*
Britten Inc .... C 231 941-8200
  Traverse City *(G-16627)*
◆ Britten Banners LLC .... C 231 941-8200
  Traverse City *(G-16628)*
Brophy Engraving Co Inc .... E 313 871-2333
  Detroit *(G-4076)*
Dearborn Lithograph Inc .... E 734 464-4242
  Livonia *(G-10176)*
Diamond Graphics Inc .... G 269 345-1164
  Kalamazoo *(G-9167)*
F & A Enterprises of Michigan ...... G 906 228-3222
  Marquette *(G-11018)*
Fortis Sltions Group Centl LLC ..... D 248 437-5200
  Wixom *(G-18664)*
Fusion Flexo LLC .... G 269 685-5827
  Richland *(G-13825)*
Fusion Flexo LLC .... G 269 685-5827
  Plainwell *(G-13077)*
Graphic Enterprises Inc .... D 248 616-4900
  Madison Heights *(G-10732)*
Graphic Specialties Inc .... E 616 247-0060
  Grand Rapids *(G-6783)*
Group Infotech Inc .... E 517 336-7110
  Lansing *(G-9848)*
Hamblin Company .... E 517 423-7491
  Bloomfield Hills *(G-1826)*
Industrial Imprntng & Die Ctng ...... G 586 778-9470
  Eastpointe *(G-4937)*
Kalamazoo Photo Comp Svcs ...... G 269 345-3706
  Kalamazoo *(G-9245)*
Mark Maker Company Inc .... E 616 538-6980
  Grand Rapids *(G-6959)*
Marketing VI Group Inc .... G 989 793-3933
  Saginaw *(G-14686)*
Mel Printing Co Inc .... E 313 928-5440
  Taylor *(G-16440)*
Microforms Inc .... E 586 939-7900
  Beverly Hills *(G-1667)*

North American Color Inc .... E 269 323-0552
  Portage *(G-13588)*
North American Graphics Inc .... F 586 486-1110
  Warren *(G-17947)*
▲ Owosso Graphic Arts Inc .... E 989 725-7112
  Owosso *(G-12849)*
Panoplate Lithographics Inc .... G 269 343-4644
  Kalamazoo *(G-9285)*
Qrp Inc .... G 989 496-2955
  Midland *(G-11405)*
Rob Enterprises Inc .... G 269 685-5827
  Plainwell *(G-13094)*
Safran Printing Company Inc .... C 586 939-7600
  Beverly Hills *(G-1668)*
Schawk Inc .... C 269 381-3820
  Kalamazoo *(G-9329)*
Sgk LLC .... G 269 381-3820
  Battle Creek *(G-1292)*
Spartan Graphics Inc .... D 616 887-1073
  Sparta *(G-15780)*
Stamp-Rite Incorporated .... E 517 487-5071
  Lansing *(G-9741)*
Standex International Corp .... E 586 296-5500
  Fraser *(G-6000)*
Trico Incorporated .... G 517 764-1780
  Jackson *(G-9023)*
Twin City Engraving Company ..... G 269 983-0601
  Saint Joseph *(G-14968)*
Weighman Enterprises Inc .... G 989 755-2116
  Saginaw *(G-14792)*

28 CHEMICALS AND ALLIED PRODUCTS

2812 Alkalies & Chlorine

◆ Dow Chemical Company .... A 989 636-1000
  Midland *(G-11341)*
Dow Chemical Company .... D 989 636-5409
  Midland *(G-11352)*
Jci Jones Chemicals Inc .... F 734 283-0677
  Wyandotte *(G-18824)*
▲ Kassouni Manufacturing Inc .... G 616 794-0989
  Belding *(G-1455)*
Pittsburgh Glass Works LLC .... C 248 371-1700
  Rochester Hills *(G-14084)*
PPG Industries Inc .... F 248 641-2000
  Troy *(G-17309)*

2813 Industrial Gases

Airserve LLC .... G 586 427-5349
  Center Line *(G-2677)*
Canton Renewables LLC .... G 248 380-3920
  Novi *(G-12379)*
Fremont Community Digester LLC F 248 735-6684
  Novi *(G-12418)*
Great Lakes Neon .... E 517 582-7451
  Grand Ledge *(G-6392)*
Greenville Trck Wldg Sups LLC ... F 616 754-6120
  Greenville *(G-7489)*
Helium Home Base LLC .... F 734 895-3608
  Westland *(G-18380)*
Helium Studio .... G 734 725-3811
  Wayne *(G-18223)*
Linde Gas & Equipment Inc .... G 630 857-6460
  Southfield *(G-15636)*
Linde Gas & Equipment Inc .... G 734 282-3830
  Wyandotte *(G-18829)*
Linde Inc .... E 269 317-7225
  Hudsonville *(G-8590)*
Matheson .... G 586 498-8315
  Roseville *(G-14437)*
Neon Roehler Services LLC .... G 248 895-8705
  Lake Orion *(G-9621)*
South Park Welding Sups LLC .... F 810 364-6521
  Marysville *(G-11103)*
Summit Industrial Services LLC ... E 248 762-0982
  Auburn Hills *(G-1041)*

2816 Inorganic Pigments

Alloying Surfaces Inc .... G 248 524-9200
  Troy *(G-16927)*
Boston Bioscience Inc .... G 617 515-5336
  Royal Oak *(G-14520)*
Douglas Corp .... E 517 767-4112
  Tekonsha *(G-16522)*
▲ Ebonex Corporation .... E 313 388-0063
  Melvindale *(G-11200)*
Oerlikon Metco (us) Inc .... E 248 288-0027
  Troy *(G-17287)*

Sun Chemical Corporation .... C 231 788-2371
  Muskegon *(G-11927)*
Titanium Industries .... G 734 335-2808
  Plymouth *(G-13315)*

2819 Indl Inorganic Chemicals, NEC

Access Technologies LLC .... G 574 286-1255
  Niles *(G-12109)*
Algoma Products Inc .... F 616 285-6440
  Grand Rapids *(G-6443)*
Antonios Leather Experts .... G 734 762-5000
  Livonia *(G-10120)*
Arkema Inc .... G 616 243-4578
  Grand Rapids *(G-6470)*
Assay Designs Inc .... G 734 214-0923
  Ann Arbor *(G-383)*
Axchem Inc .... G 734 641-9842
  Wayne *(G-18214)*
Blue Cube Holding LLC .... C 989 636-1000
  Midland *(G-11323)*
Boropharm Inc .... G 248 348-5776
  Novi *(G-12375)*
Cal-Chlor Corp .... D 231 843-1147
  Ludington *(G-10529)*
Caravan Technologies Inc .... F 313 632-8545
  Detroit *(G-4088)*
Carbide Savers .... G 248 388-1572
  Plymouth *(G-13141)*
▲ Ceratizit Usa Inc .... C 586 759-2280
  Warren *(G-17751)*
Chemico Systems Inc .... G 586 986-2343
  Warren *(G-17754)*
Chemico Systems Inc .... E 248 723-3263
  Southfield *(G-15521)*
Chemtrade Chemicals US LLC ... G 313 842-5222
  Detroit *(G-4091)*
▲ Cht USA Inc .... E 269 445-0847
  Cassopolis *(G-2626)*
Cole King LLC .... G 248 276-1278
  Orion *(G-12725)*
Continental Carbide Ltd Inc .... E 586 463-9577
  Clinton Township *(G-3211)*
Cytec Industries Inc .... G 269 349-6677
  Kalamazoo *(G-9161)*
Diazem Corp .... G 989 832-3612
  Midland *(G-11339)*
Drw Systems Carbide LLC .... G 810 392-3526
  Riley *(G-13849)*
Durametal Corporation .... G 586 759-2280
  Warren *(G-17785)*
El 903 Element LLC .... E 517 655-3492
  East Lansing *(G-4891)*
Element 22 Coml Group LLC ...... G 269 910-6739
  Kalamazoo *(G-9175)*
Element 80 Engraving LLC .... E 616 318-7407
  Grand Rapids *(G-6670)*
Element Facility Services .... G 734 895-8716
  Romulus *(G-14270)*
Element Services LLC .... G 517 672-1005
  Howell *(G-8452)*
Empirical Bioscience Inc .... G 877 479-9949
  Grand Rapids *(G-6677)*
Genomic Diagnostics Na Inc .... G 734 730-8399
  Ann Arbor *(G-499)*
Great Lakes Chemical Services .. E 269 372-6886
  Portage *(G-13562)*
Henkel US Operations Corp .... C 586 759-5555
  Warren *(G-17852)*
Henkel US Operations Corp .... B 248 588-1082
  Madison Heights *(G-10739)*
High-Po-Chlor Inc .... G 734 942-1500
  Ann Arbor *(G-515)*
I C S Corporation America Inc .... F 616 554-9300
  Grand Rapids *(G-6827)*
▲ Icmp Inc .... E 269 445-0847
  Cassopolis *(G-2630)*
Imerys Perlite Usa Inc .... F 269 649-1352
  Vicksburg *(G-17605)*
Inpore Technologies Inc .... G 517 481-2270
  East Lansing *(G-4897)*
Jade Scientific Inc .... F 734 207-3775
  Westland *(G-18387)*
Jci Jones Chemicals Inc .... F 734 283-0677
  Wyandotte *(G-18824)*
Kage Group LLC .... G 734 604-5052
  Van Buren Twp *(G-17532)*
Lily Products Michigan Inc .... G 616 245-9193
  Grand Rapids *(G-6944)*
Liquid Dustlayer Inc .... G 231 723-3750
  Manistee *(G-10904)*

McGean-Rohco Inc ....E.... 216 441-4900
Livonia *(G-10306)*
Metrex Research LLC ....D.... 734 947-6700
Romulus *(G-14303)*
Nanocerox Inc ....G.... 734 741-9522
Ann Arbor *(G-588)*
Nelsonite Chemical Pdts Inc ....G.... 616 456-7098
Grand Rapids *(G-7038)*
Nugentec Oilfield Chem LLC ....G.... 517 518-2712
Howell *(G-8486)*
Oerlikon Metco (us) Inc ....E.... 248 288-0027
Troy *(G-17287)*
Oils and Elements LLC ....G.... 989 450-4081
Bay City *(G-1385)*
▲ **Pacific Industrial Dev Corp** ....D.... 734 930-9292
Ann Arbor *(G-604)*
◆ **Pressure Vessel Service Inc** ....E.... 313 921-1200
Detroit *(G-4533)*
R L Schmitt Company Inc ....E.... 734 525-9310
Livonia *(G-10382)*
Rap Products Inc ....G.... 989 893-5583
Bay City *(G-1394)*
Sbz Corporation ....G.... 248 649-1166
Troy *(G-17346)*
Sean Michael Brines ....G.... 517 404-5481
Fowlerville *(G-5856)*
Shipston Group US Inc ....E.... 248 372-9018
Southfield *(G-15702)*
◆ **Silbond Corporation** ....E.... 517 436-3171
Weston *(G-18433)*
Solutia Inc ....G.... 734 676-4400
Trenton *(G-16892)*
Sterling Diagnostics Inc ....F.... 586 979-2141
Sterling Heights *(G-16192)*
Sumitomo Electric Carbide Inc ....F.... 734 451-0200
Novi *(G-12549)*
◆ **Transtar Autobody Tech LLC** ....C.... 810 220-3000
Brighton *(G-2084)*
United Abrasive Inc ....F.... 906 563-9249
Vulcan *(G-17616)*
USA Carbide ....G.... 248 817-5137
Troy *(G-17416)*
W R Grace & Co-Conn ....C.... 410 531-4000
South Haven *(G-15424)*
Weiser Metal Products Inc ....G.... 989 736-6055
Harrisville *(G-7746)*
Wilkinson Chemical Corporation ....F.... 989 843-6163
Mayville *(G-11174)*
Wilkinson Corporation ....G.... 989 843-6163
Mayville *(G-11175)*
Wolverine Carbide and Too ....G.... 586 497-7000
Warren *(G-18070)*
▼ **Xg Sciences Inc** ....G.... 517 703-1110
Lansing *(G-9908)*
▲ **Zhuzhou Cmntd Crbid Wrks USA** ....G.... 734 302-0125
Ann Arbor *(G-723)*

2821 Plastics, Mtrls & Nonvulcanizable Elastomers

Aci/Wipag Recycling LLC ....F.... 810 767-4424
Flint *(G-5638)*
Acp Technologies LLC ....G.... 586 322-3511
Saint Clair Shores *(G-14846)*
Advanced Elastomers Corp ....G.... 734 458-4194
Livonia *(G-10101)*
Advanced Polymers Composites ....G.... 248 766-1507
Clarkston *(G-3014)*
Allnex USA Inc ....D.... 269 385-1205
Kalamazoo *(G-9109)*
▲ **Alumilite Corporation** ....F.... 269 488-4000
Galesburg *(G-6073)*
American Compounding Spc LLC ....D.... 810 227-3500
Brighton *(G-1944)*
Amplas Compounding LLC ....F.... 586 795-2555
Sterling Heights *(G-15931)*
◆ **Anderson Development Company** ....C.... 517 263-2121
Adrian *(G-53)*
APS Compounding LLC ....F.... 734 710-6702
Romulus *(G-14251)*
◆ **Arbor Plastic Technologies LLC** ....F.... 734 678-5765
Bloomfield Hills *(G-1799)*
▼ **Argonics Inc** ....D.... 906 226-9747
Gwinn *(G-7580)*
▲ **Arvron Inc** ....E.... 616 530-1888
Grand Rapids *(G-6474)*
◆ **Asahi Kasei Plas N Amer Inc** ....C.... 517 223-2000
Fowlerville *(G-5833)*
▲ **Asahi Kasei Plastics Amer Inc** ....D.... 517 223-2000
Fowlerville *(G-5834)*

Bakelite N Sumitomo Amer Inc ....G.... 248 313-7000
Novi *(G-12373)*
BASF Corporation ....G.... 734 591-5560
Livonia *(G-10131)*
Bjb Enterprises ....G.... 248 737-0760
West Bloomfield *(G-18264)*
Byk USA Inc ....D.... 203 265-2086
Rochester Hills *(G-13969)*
C & D Enterprises Inc ....E.... 248 373-0011
Burton *(G-2229)*
▲ **Camryn Industries LLC** ....C.... 248 663-5850
Southfield *(G-15515)*
Cartex Corporation ....D.... 734 857-5961
Romulus *(G-14260)*
Cass Polymers ....E.... 517 543-7510
Charlotte *(G-2739)*
Celanese Americas LLC ....G.... 248 377-2700
Auburn Hills *(G-841)*
Chase Plastic Services Inc ....G.... 616 246-7190
Grand Rapids *(G-6566)*
▲ **Chase Plastic Services Inc** ....E.... 248 620-2120
Clarkston *(G-3023)*
Chelsea-Megan Holding Inc ....F.... 248 307-9160
Troy *(G-17009)*
CMC Plastyk LLC ....G.... 989 588-4468
Farwell *(G-5422)*
Concepp Technologies ....G.... 734 324-6750
Wyandotte *(G-18815)*
Coplas Inc ....G.... 586 739-8940
Sterling Heights *(G-15972)*
Covestro LLC ....B.... 248 475-7700
Auburn Hills *(G-851)*
Csn Manufacturing Inc ....E.... 616 364-0027
Grand Rapids *(G-6617)*
Cytec Industries Inc ....G.... 269 349-6677
Kalamazoo *(G-9161)*
▲ **D T M 1 Inc** ....E.... 248 889-9210
Highland *(G-7890)*
◆ **Dart Container Corp Kentucky** ....F.... 517 676-3800
Mason *(G-11124)*
Ddp Spclty Elctrnic Mtls US In ....D.... 989 708-6737
Midland *(G-11334)*
Ddp Spclty Elctrnic Mtls US LL ....D.... 989 636-9953
Midland *(G-11335)*
▲ **Delta Polymers Co** ....E.... 586 795-2900
Sterling Heights *(G-15980)*
Destiny Plastics Incorporated ....F.... 810 622-0018
Deckerville *(G-3953)*
Dn Plastics Corporation ....F.... 616 942-6060
Grand Rapids *(G-6652)*
◆ **Dow Chemical Company** ....A.... 989 636-1000
Midland *(G-11341)*
Dow Chemical Company ....G.... 231 845-4285
Ludington *(G-10534)*
Dow Chemical Company ....D.... 989 636-1000
Midland *(G-11342)*
Dow Chemical Company ....D.... 810 966-9816
Clyde *(G-3412)*
Dow Chemical Company ....G.... 989 636-1000
Midland *(G-11344)*
Dow Chemical Company ....G.... 989 636-1000
Midland *(G-11345)*
Dow Chemical Company ....D.... 989 636-5430
Midland *(G-11346)*
Dow Chemical Company ....G.... 989 636-1000
Midland *(G-11347)*
Dow Chemical Company ....C.... 989 832-1000
Midland *(G-11348)*
Dow Chemical Company ....G.... 989 636-0540
Midland *(G-11349)*
Dow Chemical Company ....D.... 989 636-5409
Midland *(G-11352)*
Dow Inc ....A.... 989 636-1000
Midland *(G-11354)*
Dow International Holdings Co ....G.... 989 636-1000
Midland *(G-11355)*
◆ **Dow Silicones Corporation** ....A.... 989 496-4000
Auburn *(G-765)*
DSM Engineering Plastics Inc ....G.... 608 477-0157
Troy *(G-17070)*
◆ **Durez Corporation** ....C.... 248 313-7000
Novi *(G-12406)*
E I Du Pont De Nemours & Co ....G.... 302 999-6566
Auburn Hills *(G-872)*
Eagle Design & Technology Inc ....E.... 616 748-1022
Zeeland *(G-19017)*
Envisiontec US LLC ....D.... 313 436-4300
Dearborn *(G-3837)*
Eovations LLC ....G.... 989 671-1460
Freeland *(G-6023)*

Florida Production Engrg Inc ....F.... 248 588-4870
Troy *(G-17116)*
FM Research Management LLC ....G.... 906 360-5833
Trenary *(G-16884)*
▲ **Foampartner Americas Inc** ....G.... 248 243-3100
Rochester Hills *(G-14012)*
◆ **Freudenberg N Amer Ltd Partnr** ....G.... 734 354-5505
Plymouth *(G-13169)*
◆ **Freudenberg-Nok General Partnr** ....C.... 734 451-0020
Plymouth *(G-13170)*
Freudenberg-Nok General Partnr ....G.... 734 451-0020
Plymouth *(G-13171)*
General Plymers Thrmplstic Mtl ....G.... 800 920-8033
Rochester Hills *(G-14023)*
Geomembrane Research ....F.... 231 943-2266
Traverse City *(G-16693)*
Georgia-Pacific LLC ....G.... 989 348-7275
Grayling *(G-7461)*
Grand Traverse Tool Inc ....G.... 231 929-4743
Traverse City *(G-16702)*
Harbor Green Solutions LLC ....G.... 269 352-0265
Benton Harbor *(G-1553)*
Heritage Mfg Inc ....G.... 586 949-7446
Chesterfield *(G-2890)*
Huntsman Advnced Mtls Amrcas L ....D.... 517 351-5900
East Lansing *(G-4896)*
Huntsman Corporation ....G.... 248 322-8682
Auburn Hills *(G-929)*
Huntsman-Cooper LLC ....E.... 248 322-7300
Auburn Hills *(G-930)*
Indelco Plastics Corporation ....G.... 616 452-7077
Grand Rapids *(G-6841)*
◆ **Innovative Polymers Inc** ....F.... 989 224-9500
Saint Johns *(G-14902)*
Interfibe Corporation ....F.... 269 327-6141
Schoolcraft *(G-15118)*
▲ **JB Products Inc** ....G.... 248 549-1900
Troy *(G-17183)*
Jsp International LLC ....G.... 517 748-5200
Jackson *(G-8924)*
Kayler Mold & Engineering Inc ....G.... 586 739-0699
Sterling Heights *(G-16062)*
▲ **Kentwood Packaging Corporation** ....D.... 616 698-9000
Walker *(G-17642)*
L Lewallen Co Inc ....F.... 586 792-9930
Clinton Township *(G-3276)*
Lakeshore Marble Company Inc ....F.... 269 429-8241
Stevensville *(G-16257)*
Lej Investments LLC ....F.... 616 452-3707
Grandville *(G-7398)*
Line-X of Livonia ....G.... 734 237-3115
Livonia *(G-10280)*
Line-X of Waterford ....G.... 248 270-8848
Waterford *(G-18134)*
Mac Material Acquisition Co ....G.... 248 685-8393
Highland *(G-7895)*
▲ **Materials Group LLC** ....F.... 616 863-6046
Rockford *(G-14178)*
McKechnie Vhcl Cmpnnts USA Inc ....B.... 218 894-1218
Roseville *(G-14438)*
Michigan Polymer Reclaim Inc ....F.... 989 227-0497
Saint Johns *(G-14909)*
Midwest Resin Inc ....G.... 586 803-3417
Roseville *(G-14444)*
Mitsubishi Chemical Amer Inc ....C.... 586 755-1660
Warren *(G-17932)*
Nano Materials & Processes Inc ....G.... 248 529-3873
Milford *(G-11475)*
Navtech LLC ....G.... 248 427-1080
Wixom *(G-18717)*
New Boston Rtm Inc ....E.... 734 753-9956
New Boston *(G-12015)*
Oscoda Plastics Inc ....G.... 989 739-6900
Saginaw *(G-14723)*
Oscoda Plastics Inc ....E.... 989 739-6900
Oscoda *(G-12767)*
Pacific Epoxy Polymers Inc ....G.... 616 949-1634
Grand Rapids *(G-7066)*
Package Design & Mfg Inc ....E.... 248 486-4390
Brighton *(G-2046)*
◆ **Palmer Distributors Inc** ....D.... 586 772-4225
Fraser *(G-5973)*
▲ **Pier One Polymers Incorporated** ....F.... 810 326-1456
Saint Clair *(G-14839)*
Pittsburgh Glass Works LLC ....C.... 248 371-1700
Rochester Hills *(G-14084)*
Pivot Materials LLC ....G.... 248 982-7970
Okemos *(G-12681)*
▲ **Plascon Inc** ....E.... 231 935-1580
Traverse City *(G-16796)*

S I C

Employee Codes: A=Over 500 employees, B=251-500
C=101-250, D=51-100, E=20-50, F=10-19, G=3-9

2022 Harris Michigan
Industrial Directory

777

Plascon Films Inc ... E ... 231 935-1580
Traverse City *(G-16797)*
▲ Plasteel Corporation ... E ... 313 562-5400
Inkster *(G-8670)*
Plastic Service Centers Inc ... F ... 586 307-3900
Clinton Township *(G-3320)*
Plasticos Inc ... G ... 586 493-1908
Clinton Township *(G-3321)*
▲ Plastics Plus Inc ... E ... 800 975-8694
Auburn Hills *(G-999)*
Plastics Recycling Tech Inc ... G ... 248 486-1449
Howell *(G-8496)*
PPG Industries Inc ... F ... 248 641-2000
Troy *(G-17309)*
Premier Plastic Resins Inc ... G ... 248 766-7578
Lake Orion *(G-9627)*
▲ Pro Polymers Inc ... G ... 734 222-8820
Stockbridge *(G-16277)*
Profile Industrial Packg Corp ... C ... 616 245-7260
Grand Rapids *(G-7116)*
Quality Dairy Company ... G ... 517 319-4302
Lansing *(G-9886)*
▲ Quantum Composites Inc ... F ... 989 922-3863
Bay City *(G-1392)*
Ravago Americas ... G ... 810 225-0029
Brighton *(G-2061)*
Ravago Americas LLC ... E ... 517 548-4140
Fowlerville *(G-5853)*
Recycled Polymetric Materials ... G ... 313 957-6373
Detroit *(G-4559)*
Reklein Plastics Incorporated ... G ... 586 739-8850
Sterling Heights *(G-16145)*
Resin Services Inc ... F ... 586 254-6770
Sterling Heights *(G-16147)*
Resins Unlimited LLC ... G ... 586 725-6873
Chesterfield *(G-2938)*
Revstone Industries LLC ... G ... 248 351-1000
Troy *(G-17331)*
Revstone Industries LLC ... G ... 248 351-8800
Southfield *(G-15688)*
Rhe-Tech LLC ... G ... 517 223-4874
Fowlerville *(G-5855)*
Rohm Haas Dnmark Invstmnts LLC ... F ... 989 636-1463
Midland *(G-11409)*
▲ Rosler Metal Finishing USA LLC ... E ... 269 441-3000
Battle Creek *(G-1290)*
Rubber & Plastics Co ... F ... 248 370-0700
Auburn Hills *(G-1024)*
S A Trinseo ... G ... 989 636-5409
Midland *(G-11411)*
Saint-Gobain Prfmce Plas Corp ... G ... 989 435-9533
Beaverton *(G-1430)*
Saint-Gobain Prfmce Plas Corp ... G ... 231 264-0101
Williamsburg *(G-18563)*
Saint-Gobain Prfmce Plas Corp ... G ... 586 884-9237
Shelby Township *(G-15321)*
Sekisui America Corporation ... G ... 517 279-7587
Coldwater *(G-3453)*
Sekisui Kydex LLC ... D ... 616 394-3810
Holland *(G-8188)*
▲ Sekisui Voltek LLC ... C ... 800 225-0668
Coldwater *(G-3454)*
◆ Sigma International Inc ... F ... 248 230-9681
Livonia *(G-10408)*
▲ Sika Auto Eaton Rapids Inc ... F ... 248 588-2270
Madison Heights *(G-10828)*
Solutia Inc ... G ... 734 676-4400
Trenton *(G-16892)*
Springfield Industries LLC ... F ... 248 601-1445
Imlay City *(G-8646)*
Stonecrafters Inc ... F ... 517 529-4990
Clarklake *(G-3009)*
Styrolution ... G ... 248 320-7230
Farmington Hills *(G-5391)*
▲ Sulfo-Technologies LLC ... G ... 248 307-9150
Madison Heights *(G-10838)*
▲ Sumika Polymers North Amer LLC ... E ... 248 284-4797
Farmington Hills *(G-5392)*
Ticona Polymers Inc ... E ... 248 377-6868
Auburn Hills *(G-1058)*
Topas Advanced Polymes Inc ... G ... 859 746-6447
Farmington Hills *(G-5403)*
Toray Resin Company ... G ... 248 269-8800
Troy *(G-17395)*
Trinseo LLC ... G ... 248 340-0109
Auburn Hills *(G-1065)*
◆ Ufp Technologies Inc ... D ... 616 949-8100
Grand Rapids *(G-7294)*
United Resin Inc ... E ... 800 521-4757
Royal Oak *(G-14587)*
▲ Vi-Chem Corp ... C ... 616 247-8501
Grand Rapids *(G-7314)*
Vibracoustic North America LP ... G ... 248 410-5066
Farmington Hills *(G-5410)*
◆ Vibracoustic North America LP ... E ... 269 637-2116
South Haven *(G-15421)*
Washington Penn Plastic Co Inc ... G ... 248 276-2275
Auburn Hills *(G-1087)*
Weatherproof Inc ... E ... 517 764-1330
Jackson *(G-9034)*
Wilsonart LLC ... G ... 248 960-3388
Wixom *(G-18792)*
▲ Wmc LLC ... E ... 616 560-4142
Greenville *(G-7510)*
Woodbridge Sales & Engrg Inc ... C ... 248 288-0100
Troy *(G-17452)*
Xc LLC ... F ... 586 755-1660
Warren *(G-18074)*
Xg Sciences Inc ... E ... 517 316-2038
Lansing *(G-9907)*
▲ Zander Colloids Lc ... G ... 810 714-1623
Fenton *(G-5514)*

2822 Synthetic Rubber (Vulcanizable Elastomers)

A-Line Products Corporation ... F ... 313 571-8300
Detroit *(G-3975)*
Aptargroup Inc ... G ... 989 631-8030
Midland *(G-11322)*
▲ Argonics Inc ... F ... 303 664-9467
Gwinn *(G-7581)*
Armada Rubber Manufacturing Co ... D ... 586 784-9135
Armada *(G-731)*
▲ Cht USA Inc ... E ... 269 445-0847
Cassopolis *(G-2626)*
Covestro LLC ... B ... 248 475-7700
Auburn Hills *(G-851)*
Dawson Manufacturing Company ... C ... 269 925-0100
Benton Harbor *(G-1545)*
Dendritech Inc ... G ... 989 496-1152
Midland *(G-11337)*
Dow Corning Corporation ... F ... 989 839-2808
Midland *(G-11353)*
▲ Flexfab Horizons Intl Inc ... E ... 269 945-4700
Hastings *(G-7791)*
▲ Flexfab LLC ... G ... 800 331-0003
Hastings *(G-7792)*
Grm Corporation ... E ... 989 453-2322
Pigeon *(G-13037)*
Mitsubishi Chemical Amer Inc ... C ... 586 755-1660
Warren *(G-17932)*
◆ Mykin Inc ... F ... 248 667-8030
South Lyon *(G-15448)*
Saint-Gobain Prfmce Plas Corp ... G ... 989 435-9533
Beaverton *(G-1431)*

2823 Cellulosic Man-Made Fibers

▼ Applegate Insul Systems Inc ... E ... 517 521-3545
Webberville *(G-18241)*
◆ J Rettenmaier USA LP ... C ... 269 679-2340
Schoolcraft *(G-15120)*
Kraig Biocraft Labs Inc ... G ... 734 619-8066
Ann Arbor *(G-544)*

2824 Synthetic Organic Fibers, Exc Cellulosic

ABC Nails LLC ... G ... 616 776-6000
Grand Rapids *(G-6416)*
Cytec Industries Inc ... G ... 269 349-6677
Kalamazoo *(G-9161)*
Dal-Tile Corporation ... F ... 248 471-7150
Farmington Hills *(G-5210)*
Protein Procurement Svcs Inc ... G ... 248 738-7970
Bloomfield Hills *(G-1853)*
Solutia Inc ... G ... 734 676-4400
Trenton *(G-16892)*

2833 Medicinal Chemicals & Botanical Prdts

Aapharmasyn LLC ... F ... 734 213-2123
Ann Arbor *(G-344)*
▲ Access Business Group LLC ... A ... 616 787-6000
Ada *(G-3)*
Alticor Global Holdings Inc ... F ... 616 787-1000
Ada *(G-5)*
◆ Alticor Inc ... A ... 616 787-1000
Ada *(G-6)*
Aureogen Inc ... G ... 269 353-3805
Kalamazoo *(G-9127)*
Bmu International LLC ... G ... 248 342-4032
Clarkston *(G-3020)*
C3 Industries Inc ... G ... 248 255-1283
Ann Arbor *(G-412)*
Cbd With B Wellness Ltd Lblty ... G ... 248 595-3583
Harper Woods *(G-7665)*
Degrasyn Biosciences LLC ... G ... 713 582-3395
Ann Arbor *(G-445)*
Heals & Herbs LLC ... G ... 888 604-1474
Southfield *(G-15591)*
Hearing Health Science Inc ... G ... 734 476-9490
Ann Arbor *(G-511)*
Kinder Products Unlimited LLC ... G ... 586 557-3453
Sterling Heights *(G-16063)*
Metabolic Solutions Dev Co LLC ... E ... 269 343-6732
Grand Rapids *(G-6977)*
Pharmacia & Upjohn Company LLC ... D ... 908 901-8000
Kalamazoo *(G-9294)*
Saja Natural Herbs ... G ... 313 769-6411
Dearborn *(G-3892)*
Savage Seamoss LLC ... G ... 313 288-6899
Detroit *(G-4580)*
Solohill Engineering Inc ... E ... 734 973-2956
Ann Arbor *(G-660)*
Visionary Vitamin Co ... G ... 734 788-5934
Melvindale *(G-11211)*
Viva Zen Sales LLC ... G ... 248 481-3605
Auburn Hills *(G-1081)*

2834 Pharmaceuticals

▲ Abaco Partners LLC ... C ... 616 532-1700
Kentwood *(G-9441)*
Abbott Laboratories ... B ... 269 651-0600
Sturgis *(G-16279)*
Abbott Laboratories ... G ... 734 324-6666
Wyandotte *(G-18805)*
Abbvie Inc ... G ... 734 324-6650
Wyandotte *(G-18806)*
Affiliated Troy Dermatologist ... F ... 248 267-5020
Troy *(G-16910)*
Akorn Inc ... E ... 800 579-8327
Ann Arbor *(G-359)*
Alphacore Pharma LLC ... G ... 734 330-0265
Ann Arbor *(G-361)*
Arconic ... F ... 231 894-7802
Whitehall *(G-18491)*
Aspire Pharmacy ... G ... 989 773-7849
Mount Pleasant *(G-11681)*
Astellas Pharma Us Inc ... G ... 616 698-8825
Grand Rapids *(G-6478)*
Atterocor Inc ... G ... 734 845-9300
Ann Arbor *(G-385)*
Avomeen LLC ... D ... 734 222-1090
Ann Arbor *(G-390)*
Axalta ... G ... 248 379-6913
Lake Orion *(G-9586)*
Barclay Pharmacy ... G ... 248 852-4600
Rochester Hills *(G-13961)*
Berkley Pharmacy LLC ... F ... 586 573-8300
Warren *(G-17731)*
Biolyte Laboratories LLC ... F ... 616 350-9055
Grand Rapids *(G-6509)*
Biopolymer Innovations LLC ... G ... 517 432-3044
East Lansing *(G-4887)*
Bristol-Myers Squibb Company ... G ... 248 528-2476
Troy *(G-16986)*
◆ Bryllan LLC ... G ... 248 442-7620
Brighton *(G-1954)*
▲ Caraco Pharma Inc ... G ... 313 871-8400
Detroit *(G-4087)*
Cayman Chemical Company Inc ... D ... 734 971-3335
Ann Arbor *(G-417)*
Central Admxture Phrm Svcs Inc ... G ... 734 953-6760
Livonia *(G-10151)*
◆ Charles Bowman & Company ... F ... 616 786-4000
Holland *(G-7994)*
Corium Inc ... E ... 616 656-4563
Grand Rapids *(G-6605)*
Corium Inc ... C ... 650 298-8255
Grand Rapids *(G-6606)*
Diplomat Spclty Phrm Flint LLC ... B ... 810 768-9000
Flint *(G-5688)*
Dow Chemical Company ... C ... 989 636-4406
Midland *(G-11343)*
Drip Therapi LLC ... G ... 586 488-1256
Shelby Township *(G-15210)*
▲ DSC Laboratories Inc ... E ... 800 492-5988
Muskegon *(G-11801)*
DSM Engineering Materials Inc ... G ... 616 667-2643
Jenison *(G-9053)*

SIC SECTION 28 CHEMICALS AND ALLIED PRODUCTS28 CHEMICALS AND ALLIED PRODUCTS

▲ **Elba Inc** ... E ... 248 288-6098
Troy *(G-17081)*
Emergent Biodef Oper Lnsng LLC ... B ... 517 327-1500
Lansing *(G-9690)*
Emergent Biosolutions Inc ... G ... 517 327-1500
Lansing *(G-9691)*
Esperion Therapeutics Inc ... D ... 734 887-3903
Ann Arbor *(G-479)*
▲ **Ferndale Laboratories Inc** ... C ... 248 548-0900
Ferndale *(G-5553)*
Ferndale Pharma Group Inc ... B ... 248 548-0900
Ferndale *(G-5554)*
Fremont Generate Digester LLC ... G ... 231 924-9401
Fremont *(G-6041)*
Genentech Inc ... C ... 650 225-1000
Lake Orion *(G-9606)*
Glaxosmithkline LLC ... G ... 989 450-9859
Frankenmuth *(G-5864)*
Glaxosmithkline LLC ... G ... 989 928-6535
Oxford *(G-12884)*
Glaxosmithkline LLC ... G ... 989 280-1225
Midland *(G-11369)*
Glaxosmithkline LLC ... G ... 248 561-3022
Bloomfield Hills *(G-1822)*
Grand River Aseptic Mfg Inc ... C ... 616 678-2400
Grand Rapids *(G-6776)*
Grass Lake Community Pharmacy ... G ... 517 522-4100
Grass Lake *(G-7438)*
Greenmark Biomedical Inc ... G ... 517 336-4665
Lansing *(G-9847)*
H & A Pharmacy II LLC ... G ... 313 995-4552
Westland *(G-18379)*
Harper Dermatology PC ... G ... 586 776-7546
Grosse Pointe Shores *(G-7562)*
▲ **Hello Life Inc** ... E ... 616 808-3290
Grand Rapids *(G-6809)*
Hibiskus Biopharma Inc ... G ... 616 234-2841
Kalamazoo *(G-9217)*
High Frequency Healing Co LLC ... G ... 313 938-9711
Detroit *(G-4301)*
Housey Phrm RES Labs LLC ... G ... 248 663-7000
Southfield *(G-15593)*
Innovative Pharmaceuticals LLC ... F ... 248 789-0999
Brighton *(G-2013)*
Inscribd LLC ... G ... 231 445-9104
Cheboygan *(G-2786)*
Integrated Sensing Systems ... G ... 734 604-4301
Ann Arbor *(G-530)*
Interntnal Hrvest Ventures LLC ... G ... 248 387-9944
Livonia *(G-10250)*
Ionxhealth Inc ... E ... 616 808-3290
Grand Rapids *(G-6852)*
J&B Pharmacy Services Inc ... G ... 888 611-2941
Wixom *(G-18688)*
Jade Pharmaceuticals Entp LLC ... G ... 248 716-8333
Livonia *(G-10256)*
▲ **Kassouni Manufacturing Inc** ... E ... 616 794-0989
Belding *(G-1455)*
Kure Products Distribution Inc ... G ... 248 330-3933
Farmington Hills *(G-5285)*
◆ **L Perrigo Company** ... A ... 269 673-8451
Allegan *(G-164)*
L Perrigo Company ... G ... 269 673-7962
Allegan *(G-165)*
L Perrigo Company ... G ... 616 738-0150
Holland *(G-8119)*
L Perrigo Company ... G ... 269 673-7962
Allegan *(G-166)*
L Perrigo Company ... G ... 269 673-1608
Allegan *(G-167)*
L Perrigo Company ... G ... 248 687-1036
Troy *(G-17201)*
LLC Ash Stevens ... D ... 734 282-3370
Riverview *(G-13879)*
Lxr Biotech LLC ... E ... 248 860-4246
Rochester Hills *(G-14055)*
Lxr Biotech LLC ... E ... 248 860-4246
Auburn Hills *(G-961)*
M Beard Solutions LLC ... G ... 734 441-0660
Dearborn *(G-3865)*
McKesson Corporation ... G ... 734 953-2523
Livonia *(G-10308)*
MD Hiller Corp ... G ... 877 751-9010
Dearborn *(G-3869)*
Meridianrx LLC ... D ... 855 323-4580
Detroit *(G-4429)*
Millendo Transactionsub Inc ... G ... 734 845-9300
Ann Arbor *(G-578)*
Mills Phrm & Apothecary LLC ... G ... 248 633-2872
Birmingham *(G-1737)*
Motor City Naturals LLC ... G ... 313 329-4071
Warren *(G-17936)*
N F P Inc ... G ... 989 631-0009
Midland *(G-11397)*
Natural Therapeutics LLC ... G ... 734 604-7313
Ann Arbor *(G-591)*
Nopras Technologies Inc ... G ... 248 486-6684
South Lyon *(G-15451)*
Norman A Lewis ... G ... 248 219-5736
Farmington Hills *(G-5334)*
Ocuphire Pharma Inc ... G ... 248 681-9815
Farmington Hills *(G-5338)*
Painexx Corporation ... G ... 313 863-1200
Detroit *(G-4503)*
Pancheck LLC ... F ... 989 288-6886
Durand *(G-4844)*
Par Sterile Products LLC ... B ... 248 651-9081
Rochester *(G-13920)*
Parkedale Pharmaceuticals Inc ... D ... 248 650-6400
Rochester *(G-13921)*
PBM Nutritionals LLC ... E ... 269 673-8451
Allegan *(G-173)*
Pcs Pharmaceuticals LLC ... G ... 248 289-7054
Bloomfield Hills *(G-1848)*
Penrose Therapeutix LLC ... G ... 847 370-0303
Plymouth *(G-13262)*
Perrigo China Bus Trustee LLC ... E ... 269 673-8451
Allegan *(G-174)*
Perrigo Company ... G ... 269 686-1973
Allegan *(G-175)*
◆ **Perrigo Company** ... A ... 269 673-8451
Allegan *(G-176)*
Perrigo Company ... G ... 616 396-0941
Holland *(G-8163)*
Perrigo Company ... G ... 269 686-1782
Holland *(G-8164)*
Perrigo Company ... F ... 269 673-7962
Allegan *(G-177)*
Perrigo New York Inc ... F ... 269 673-8451
Allegan *(G-178)*
Pfizer Inc ... G ... 248 867-9067
Clarkston *(G-3055)*
Pfizer Inc ... G ... 734 679-7368
Grosse Ile *(G-7525)*
Pfizer Inc ... G ... 734 671-9315
Trenton *(G-16890)*
Pfizer Inc ... G ... 269 833-5143
Kalamazoo *(G-9292)*
Pfizer Inc ... C ... 269 833-2358
Kalamazoo *(G-9293)*
Pharmacia & Upjohn Company LLC ... D ... 908 901-8000
Kalamazoo *(G-9294)*
Phenomics Health Inc ... E ... 410 336-2404
Ann Arbor *(G-609)*
Physicians Compounding Phrm ... G ... 248 758-9100
Bloomfield Hills *(G-1852)*
Plasma Biolife Services L P ... G ... 616 667-0264
Grandville *(G-7409)*
PMI Branded Pharmaceuticals ... F ... 269 673-8451
Allegan *(G-179)*
Port Huron Medical Assoc ... G ... 810 982-0100
Fort Gratiot *(G-5823)*
Pure Green Pharmaceuticals Inc ... F ... 248 515-0097
West Bloomfield *(G-18307)*
Qsv Pharma LLC ... G ... 269 324-2358
Portage *(G-13597)*
Quality Care Products LLC ... F ... 734 847-3847
Temperance *(G-16546)*
Renucell ... G ... 888 400-6032
Grand Haven *(G-6353)*
Rockwell Medical Inc ... C ... 248 960-9009
Wixom *(G-18744)*
▲ **Safe N Simple LLC** ... F ... 248 875-0840
Clarkston *(G-3062)*
Sepracor Inc ... G ... 508 481-6700
Northville *(G-12259)*
Soleo Health Inc ... F ... 248 513-8687
Novi *(G-12539)*
Stroyko Construction Group Inc ... G ... 281 240-3332
Orchard Lake *(G-12720)*
Sun Pharmaceutical Inds Inc ... F ... 248 346-7302
Farmington Hills *(G-5393)*
Supplement Group Inc ... F ... 248 588-2055
Madison Heights *(G-10840)*
Tabletting Inc ... G ... 616 957-0281
Grand Rapids *(G-7246)*
Team Pharma ... G ... 269 344-8326
Kalamazoo *(G-9352)*
Tetra Corporation ... E ... 401 529-1630
Eaton Rapids *(G-4972)*
▲ **Total Life Changes LLC** ... B ... 810 471-3812
Ira *(G-8716)*
Tower Laboratories Ltd ... G ... 860 767-2127
Norton Shores *(G-12341)*
Tower Laboratories Ltd ... E ... 231 893-1472
Montague *(G-11602)*
◆ **Uckele Health and Nutrition** ... C ... 800 248-0330
Blissfield *(G-1779)*
Urban Specialty Apparel Inc ... F ... 248 395-9500
Southfield *(G-15734)*
USA Health LLC ... G ... 248 846-0575
Dearborn *(G-3908)*
Vectech Pharmaceutical Cons ... F ... 248 478-5820
Brighton *(G-2092)*
Velesco Phrm Svcs Inc ... G ... 734 545-0696
Wixom *(G-18785)*
Velesco Phrm Svcs Inc ... G ... 734 274-9877
Plymouth *(G-13330)*
Vitanorth USA LLC ... G ... 734 595-4000
Westland *(G-18427)*
Vortech Pharmaceutical Ltd ... F ... 313 584-4088
Dearborn *(G-3912)*
Wandas Barium Cookie LLC ... G ... 906 281-1788
Calumet *(G-2416)*
▲ **Welchdry Inc** ... E ... 616 399-2711
Holland *(G-8243)*
Zoetis LLC ... G ... 888 963-8471
Kalamazoo *(G-9375)*
Zomedica Pharmaceuticals Inc ... E ... 734 369-2555
Ann Arbor *(G-726)*

2835 Diagnostic Substances

Applied Genomics ... G ... 313 458-7318
Grosse Pointe Park *(G-7547)*
Biosan Laboratories Inc ... F ... 586 755-8970
Warren *(G-17738)*
Cooper Genomics ... G ... 313 579-9650
Plymouth *(G-13150)*
Great Lakes Diagnostics Inc ... G ... 248 307-9494
Troy *(G-17133)*
Greenmark Biomedical Inc ... G ... 517 336-4665
Lansing *(G-9847)*
Life Otreach Ctr Houghton Cnty ... G ... 906 482-8681
Hancock *(G-7621)*
Microx Labs Inc ... G ... 248 318-3548
Bloomfield Hills *(G-1838)*
Nanorete Inc ... G ... 517 336-4680
Lansing *(G-9873)*
Nanosynthons LLC ... G ... 989 317-3737
Mount Pleasant *(G-11726)*
Neogen Corporation ... G ... 800 327-5487
Saint Joseph *(G-14951)*
▲ **Neogen Corporation** ... A ... 517 372-9200
Lansing *(G-9874)*
Ortho-Clinical Diagnostics Inc ... G ... 248 797-8087
Troy *(G-17292)*
Ovascience Inc ... G ... 617 351-2590
Ann Arbor *(G-603)*
Petnet Solutions Inc ... G ... 865 218-2000
Royal Oak *(G-14567)*
Plasma Biolife Services L P ... G ... 616 667-0264
Grandville *(G-7409)*
Retrosense Therapeutics LLC ... G ... 734 369-9333
Ann Arbor *(G-639)*
▲ **Sigma Diagnostics Inc** ... G ... 734 744-4846
Livonia *(G-10407)*
Swift Biosciences Inc ... G ... 734 330-2568
Ann Arbor *(G-669)*
Versant Med Physics Rdtion SFE ... E ... 888 316-3644
Kalamazoo *(G-9361)*

2836 Biological Prdts, Exc Diagnostic Substances

87 Grams LLC ... F ... 248 558-0424
Redford *(G-13708)*
A Taste of Leone LLC ... G ... 616 238-8881
Grand Rapids *(G-6411)*
Arbor Assays Inc ... F ... 734 677-1774
Ann Arbor *(G-373)*
Axonia Medical Inc ... G ... 269 615-6632
Kalamazoo *(G-9128)*
Biosan Laboratories Inc ... F ... 586 755-8970
Warren *(G-17738)*
Bruce Kane Enterprises LLC ... G ... 410 727-0637
Farmington Hills *(G-5187)*
Corium Inc ... C ... 650 298-8255
Grand Rapids *(G-6606)*
Deru Extracts LLC ... G ... 734 497-2963
Carleton *(G-2551)*

SIC

28 CHEMICALS AND ALLIED PRODUCTS

Emergent Biodef Oper Lnsng LLC ....B 517 327-1500
 Lansing *(G-9690)*
Extract ....G 269 362-4879
 Rockford *(G-14166)*
Immuno Concepts NA Ltd ....E 734 464-0701
 Livonia *(G-10246)*
◆ Koppert Biological Systems Inc ....E 734 641-3763
 Howell *(G-8470)*
Loud N Clear Extracts LLC ....G 312 320-4970
 Galien *(G-6090)*
Michigan For Vaccine Choice ....G 586 294-3074
 Saint Clair Shores *(G-14871)*
▲ Neogen Corporation ....A 517 372-9200
 Lansing *(G-9874)*
Novavax Inc ....G 248 656-5336
 Rochester *(G-13914)*
Oxford Biomedical Research Inc ....G 248 852-8815
 Metamora *(G-11284)*
S and N Products Inc ....G 810 542-9635
 Lake Orion *(G-9629)*
Vivica Miller LLC ....G 313 434-3280
 Detroit *(G-4673)*

2841 Soap & Detergents

Amway International Dev Inc ....A 616 787-6000
 Ada *(G-7)*
Caravan Technologies Inc ....F 313 632-8545
 Detroit *(G-4088)*
Chem Station ....F 517 371-8068
 Lansing *(G-9681)*
Continntal Bldg Svcs of Cncnna ....F 313 336-8543
 Grosse Pointe Woods *(G-7566)*
Cul-Mac Industries Inc ....E 734 728-9700
 Wayne *(G-18219)*
Diversified Chemical Tech Inc ....C 313 867-5444
 Detroit *(G-4180)*
▲ DSC Laboratories Inc ....E 800 492-5988
 Muskegon *(G-11801)*
Ecolab Inc ....G 248 697-0202
 Novi *(G-12410)*
Gage Global Services Inc ....D 248 541-3824
 Ferndale *(G-5556)*
Great Lakes Bath & Body Inc ....G 231 421-9160
 Traverse City *(G-16703)*
Huron Soap Candle Company ....G 810 989-5952
 Port Huron *(G-13486)*
Hydro-Chem Systems Inc ....E 616 531-6420
 Caledonia *(G-2383)*
Ipax Atlantic LLC ....G 313 933-4211
 Detroit *(G-4325)*
K C M Inc ....F 616 245-8599
 Grand Rapids *(G-6875)*
L I S Manufacturing Inc ....F 734 525-3070
 Livonia *(G-10272)*
Marjeannes Creations ....G 810 798-7278
 Almont *(G-264)*
Mom of Shire Apothecary LLC ....G 734 751-9443
 Garden City *(G-6104)*
Moon River Soap Co LLC ....G 248 930-9467
 Rochester *(G-13912)*
National Soap Company Inc ....G 248 545-8180
 Royal Oak *(G-14565)*
Nature Patch Soaps ....G 734 847-3759
 Temperance *(G-16543)*
Oil Chem Inc ....E 810 235-3040
 Flint *(G-5742)*
Rhema Products Inc ....G 313 561-6800
 Dearborn Heights *(G-3938)*
Richard D Matzke ....G 517 320-0964
 Hillsdale *(G-7945)*
Sanitation Strategies LLC ....F 517 268-3303
 Holt *(G-8328)*
Selestial Soap LLC ....E 231 944-1978
 Traverse City *(G-16828)*
South / Win LLC ....G 734 525-9000
 Livonia *(G-10414)*
▲ Stone Soap Company Inc ....E 248 706-1000
 Sylvan Lake *(G-16362)*
Take Care Natural Products ....G 989 280-3947
 Cass City *(G-2621)*
Vaughan Industries Inc ....F 313 935-2040
 Detroit *(G-4663)*

2842 Spec Cleaning, Polishing & Sanitation Preparations

2020 Mobile Detailing LLC ....G 313 953-6363
 Detroit *(G-3969)*
Able Solutions LLC ....G 810 216-6106
 Port Huron *(G-13430)*

▲ Access Business Group LLC ....A 616 787-6000
 Ada *(G-3)*
Affordable Pool and Spa Inc ....F 810 422-5058
 Burton *(G-2225)*
▲ American Jetway Corporation ....F 734 721-5930
 Wayne *(G-18213)*
▲ Anchor Wiping Cloth Inc ....D 313 892-4000
 Detroit *(G-4019)*
Arrow Chemical Products Inc ....E 313 237-0277
 Detroit *(G-4028)*
Benchmark Inc ....G 734 285-0900
 Wyandotte *(G-18812)*
▼ Bio Kleen Products Inc ....F 269 567-9400
 Kalamazoo *(G-9136)*
Biosolutions LLC ....F 616 846-1210
 Grand Haven *(G-6280)*
Bissell Better Life LLC ....G 800 237-7691
 Grand Rapids *(G-6510)*
Burge Incorporated ....G 616 791-2214
 Grand Rapids *(G-6533)*
Cal Chemical Manufacturing Co ....G 586 778-7006
 Saint Clair Shores *(G-14853)*
Caravan Technologies Inc ....F 313 632-8545
 Detroit *(G-4088)*
Chemetall US Inc ....G 517 787-4846
 Jackson *(G-8841)*
Chemloc Inc ....F 989 465-6541
 Coleman *(G-3462)*
◆ Chrysan Industries Inc ....E 734 451-5411
 Plymouth *(G-13146)*
Cleaning Solutions Inc ....G 616 243-0555
 Grand Rapids *(G-6572)*
Coastal Concierge ....G 269 639-1515
 South Haven *(G-15402)*
▲ Colonial Chemical Corp ....E 517 789-8161
 Jackson *(G-8848)*
◆ Coxen Enterprises Inc ....D 248 486-3800
 Brighton *(G-1971)*
Cul-Mac Industries Inc ....E 734 728-9700
 Wayne *(G-18219)*
Diversified Chemical Tech Inc ....C 313 867-5444
 Detroit *(G-4180)*
Diversified Davitco LLC ....F 248 681-9197
 Waterford *(G-18115)*
▲ DSC Laboratories Inc ....E 800 492-5988
 Muskegon *(G-11801)*
Enviro-Brite Solutions LLC ....E 989 387-2758
 Oscoda *(G-12758)*
Formax Manufacturing Corp ....E 616 456-5458
 Grand Rapids *(G-6716)*
Full Upholstery LLC ....F 248 760-3985
 Pontiac *(G-13373)*
Global Wholesale & Marketing ....G 248 910-8302
 Sterling Heights *(G-16030)*
Grav Co LLC ....G 269 651-5467
 Sturgis *(G-16290)*
H & J Mfg Consulting Svcs Corp ....G 734 941-8314
 Romulus *(G-14282)*
Healthcure LLC ....G 313 743-2331
 Detroit *(G-4297)*
▲ Henkel Surface Technologies ....G 248 307-0240
 Madison Heights *(G-10738)*
High-Po-Chlor Inc ....G 734 942-1500
 Ann Arbor *(G-515)*
Hydro-Chem Systems Inc ....E 616 531-6420
 Caledonia *(G-2383)*
Hygiene of Sweden USA LLC ....G 248 760-3241
 Sylvan Lake *(G-16361)*
Innovative Fluids LLC ....F 734 241-5699
 Milan *(G-11438)*
Ipax Atlantic LLC ....G 313 933-4211
 Detroit *(G-4325)*
▼ Ipax Cleanogel Inc ....G 313 933-4211
 Detroit *(G-4326)*
Joy Carpet Cleaning LLC ....G 734 656-8827
 Inkster *(G-8667)*
▲ Kath Khemicals LLC ....F 586 275-2646
 Sterling Heights *(G-16061)*
Katrina Love-Jones LLC ....G 248 779-6017
 Detroit *(G-4352)*
Kmi Cleaning Solutions Inc ....F 269 964-2557
 Battle Creek *(G-1263)*
Labtech Corporation ....F 313 862-1737
 Detroit *(G-4374)*
Lee Cleaners Inc ....G 517 351-5655
 East Lansing *(G-4900)*
Liedel Power Cleaning ....F 734 848-2827
 Erie *(G-5049)*
McGean-Rohco Inc ....E 216 441-4900
 Livonia *(G-10306)*

Mdla Inc ....F 248 643-0807
 Troy *(G-17242)*
Metals Preservation Group LLC ....F 586 944-2720
 Saint Clair Shores *(G-14870)*
Michigan Chimneys ....F 810 640-7961
 Clio *(G-3405)*
Nano Magic Holdings Inc ....G 844 273-6462
 Madison Heights *(G-10787)*
Native Green LLC ....F 248 365-4200
 Orion *(G-12736)*
Oden Sanitation LLC ....G 248 513-5763
 Roseville *(G-14456)*
Odor Gone Inc ....F 888 636-7292
 Zeeland *(G-19064)*
Ottawa County Window Clg LLC ....G 248 878-5377
 Zeeland *(G-19066)*
Peerless Quality Products ....F 313 933-7525
 Detroit *(G-4514)*
▲ Premiere Packaging Inc ....D 810 239-7650
 Flint *(G-5748)*
▼ Punati Chemical Corp ....D 248 276-0101
 Auburn Hills *(G-1008)*
Quaker Houghton Pa Inc ....E 248 265-7745
 Troy *(G-17325)*
Rhino Linings of Grand Rapids ....G 616 361-9786
 Grand Rapids *(G-7152)*
Rooto Corporation ....F 517 546-8330
 Howell *(G-8510)*
S C Johnson & Son Inc ....G 248 822-2174
 Troy *(G-17339)*
S C Johnson & Son Inc ....G 989 667-0211
 Bay City *(G-1396)*
Sabo Creative ....G 616 842-7226
 Spring Lake *(G-15848)*
Saniones LLC ....G 833 726-4111
 Auburn Hills *(G-1027)*
SC Johnson & Son ....G 989 667-0235
 Bay City *(G-1398)*
Spartans Finishing LLC ....G 517 528-5510
 Haslett *(G-7779)*
Superior Manufacturing Corp ....G 313 935-1550
 Troy *(G-17380)*
◆ Tennant Commercial ....D 616 994-4000
 Holland *(G-8215)*
◆ Thetford Corporation ....C 734 769-6000
 Ann Arbor *(G-688)*
◆ Transtar Autobody Tech LLC ....C 810 220-3000
 Brighton *(G-2084)*
Vira Clean LLC ....G 313 455-1020
 Canton *(G-2538)*
Wilbur Products Inc ....G 231 755-3805
 Muskegon *(G-11948)*
▼ Ziebart International Corp ....E 248 588-4100
 Troy *(G-17460)*

2843 Surface Active & Finishing Agents, Sulfonated Oils

BASF Corporation ....C 734 324-6000
 Wyandotte *(G-18809)*
Innovative Leather Tech LLC ....G 734 953-1100
 Wayne *(G-18225)*
Ipax Atlantic LLC ....G 313 933-4211
 Detroit *(G-4325)*
◆ McCarthy Group Incorporated ....F 616 977-2900
 Grand Rapids *(G-6970)*
▲ Metalworking Lubricants Co ....D 248 332-3500
 Pontiac *(G-13397)*
Quaker Houghton Pa Inc ....E 248 265-7745
 Troy *(G-17325)*
Tsw Technologies LLC ....G 248 773-5026
 Novi *(G-12559)*

2844 Perfumes, Cosmetics & Toilet Preparations

A Naturally Empowered Lf Anel ....G 734 572-8857
 Ypsilanti *(G-18922)*
▲ Abaco Partners LLC ....C 616 532-1700
 Kentwood *(G-9441)*
Akilahs Beauty Salon LLC ....G 602 607-8503
 Grand Rapids *(G-6441)*
Amour Your Body LLC ....G 586 846-3100
 Clinton Township *(G-3168)*
Amway International Dev Inc ....A 616 787-6000
 Ada *(G-7)*
Aroma Taba ....G 313 782-4076
 Hamtramck *(G-7611)*
Art of Shaving - Fl LLC ....G 248 649-5872
 Troy *(G-16954)*

Avissa Skin+body ....G....... 734 316-5556
Ann Arbor *(G-389)*
Babybops Melanin Collection ....F....... 313 770-4997
Detroit *(G-4041)*
Bath Bombs By Lori ....G....... 734 890-3832
Westland *(G-18360)*
Beard Balm LLC ....G....... 313 451-3653
Detroit *(G-4045)*
Bella Skyy Llc ....G....... 313 623-9296
Harper Woods *(G-7663)*
Bio Source Naturals LLC ....G....... 877 577-8223
New Boston *(G-12002)*
Body Exotics ....F....... 231 753-8590
Traverse City *(G-16623)*
Brighter Smile By Tierra LLC ....G....... 248 278-3117
Detroit *(G-4072)*
Brun Laboratories Inc ....G....... 616 456-1114
Grand Rapids *(G-6527)*
Buttered Body Essentials LLC ....G....... 313 687-3847
Detroit *(G-4080)*
Can You Handlebar LLC ....F....... 248 821-2171
Mount Clemens *(G-11632)*
Canyouhandlebar LLC ....G....... 313 354-5851
Royal Oak *(G-14524)*
Colors & Effects USA LLC ....D....... 973 245-6000
Southfield *(G-15528)*
Conquest Scents ....F....... 810 653-2759
Davison *(G-3778)*
Damionisha 823 Cosmetics LLC ....G....... 586 557-9893
Detroit *(G-4120)*
David Lee Naturals ....G....... 248 328-1131
Holly *(G-8266)*
Detroit Fine Products LLC ....G....... 877 294-5826
Ferndale *(G-5546)*
Diop Collection LLC ....G....... 313 522-6029
Detroit *(G-4178)*
Dollars From Scents ....G....... 847 650-0317
New ERA *(G-12028)*
Entrepreneur Solutions LLC ....G....... 248 660-2858
Clinton Township *(G-3232)*
Eve Salonspa ....G....... 269 327-4811
Portage *(G-13559)*
Fragrance Outlet Inc ....G....... 517 552-9545
Howell *(G-8456)*
Fresh Heir LLC ....G....... 313 312-4492
Farmington *(G-5138)*
Full of Scents ....G....... 734 972-6542
Northville *(G-12220)*
Function Inc ....C....... 570 317-0737
Caledonia *(G-2373)*
Garden of Edyn ....G....... 517 410-9931
Holt *(G-8313)*
◆ Homedics Usa LLC ....C....... 248 863-3000
Commerce Township *(G-3539)*
Honeyworks LLC ....G....... 313 575-0871
Detroit *(G-4304)*
Inscribd LLC ....G....... 231 445-9104
Cheboygan *(G-2786)*
Jogue Inc ....G....... 248 349-1501
Northville *(G-12233)*
◆ Jogue Inc ....E....... 734 207-0100
Plymouth *(G-13203)*
Jogue Inc ....G....... 313 921-4802
Detroit *(G-4339)*
Judah Scents ....G....... 810 219-9956
Flint *(G-5719)*
Kae Organics LLC ....G....... 248 832-0403
Detroit *(G-4348)*
Katarina Naturals ....G....... 517 333-6880
East Lansing *(G-4898)*
Kd Essentials LLC ....G....... 248 632-7180
Oak Park *(G-12620)*
Le Host LLC ....G....... 248 546-4247
Ferndale *(G-5565)*
Lipstick Jodi LLC ....G....... 616 430-5389
Cedar Springs *(G-2655)*
Lush ....G....... 586 228-1594
Clinton Township *(G-3282)*
Marc Molina ....G....... 810 701-3587
Davison *(G-3790)*
Merchandising Productions ....D....... 616 676-6000
Ada *(G-29)*
Microcide Inc ....G....... 248 526-9663
Troy *(G-17258)*
Mid-West Behavioral Associates ....G....... 517 267-5502
Lansing *(G-9776)*
Mineral Cosmetics Inc ....G....... 248 542-7733
Southfield *(G-15659)*
Mizjayzbraidz LLC ....G....... 313 799-7756
Detroit *(G-4460)*
◆ Murrays Worldwide Inc ....F....... 248 691-9156
Oak Park *(G-12629)*
Nail Time ....G....... 313 837-3871
Detroit *(G-4474)*
Oxford Brands LLC ....G....... 248 408-4020
Oxford *(G-12906)*
Ravenwood ....G....... 231 421-5682
Traverse City *(G-16818)*
Rejoice International Corp ....G....... 855 345-5575
Northville *(G-12253)*
Rose Nail ....G....... 313 271-8804
Allen Park *(G-204)*
S C Johnson & Son Inc ....G....... 248 822-2174
Troy *(G-17339)*
Scentmatchers LLC ....G....... 231 878-9918
Gaylord *(G-6158)*
Senica LLC ....G....... 248 426-2200
Southfield *(G-15697)*
Sensual Scents ....G....... 586 306-4233
Sterling Heights *(G-16169)*
Sephora Inside Jcpenney ....G....... 810 385-9800
Fort Gratiot *(G-5824)*
Sephora Inside Jcpenney ....G....... 517 323-4000
Lansing *(G-9790)*
▲ Smo International Inc ....F....... 248 275-1091
Warren *(G-18015)*
Somerset Collection Ltd Partnr ....F....... 248 827-4600
Troy *(G-17362)*
Square M LLC ....F....... 720 988-5836
Sterling Heights *(G-16185)*
Stinkn Pretty LLC ....G....... 517 694-8659
Holt *(G-8333)*
▲ Stone Soap Company Inc ....E....... 248 706-1000
Sylvan Lake *(G-16362)*
Sweed Dreams LLC ....G....... 313 704-6694
Livonia *(G-10425)*
Uber Hair and Nails Llc ....G....... 248 268-3227
Ferndale *(G-5592)*
Viladon Corporation ....G....... 248 548-0043
Oak Park *(G-12649)*
◆ Wellington Fragrance ....G....... 734 261-5531
Livonia *(G-10472)*
Whimsical Fusions LLC ....G....... 248 956-0952
Detroit *(G-4680)*

2851 Paints, Varnishes, Lacquers, Enamels

A-Line Products Corporation ....F....... 313 571-8300
Detroit *(G-3975)*
Akzo Nobel Coatings Inc ....E....... 248 451-6231
Pontiac *(G-13346)*
Akzo Nobel Coatings Inc ....E....... 248 637-0400
Troy *(G-16914)*
Akzo Nobel Coatings Inc ....E....... 248 451-6231
Troy *(G-16915)*
Akzo Nobel Coatings Inc ....G....... 248 528-0715
Troy *(G-16916)*
Akzo Nobel Coatings Inc ....E....... 248 637-0400
Pontiac *(G-13347)*
Allied Photochemical Inc ....F....... 810 364-6910
Macomb *(G-10575)*
Alloying Surfaces Inc ....G....... 248 524-9200
Troy *(G-16927)*
Axalta Coating Systems LLC ....G....... 586 846-4160
Clinton Township *(G-3178)*
Axson Tech Us Inc ....E....... 517 663-8191
Eaton Rapids *(G-4953)*
BASF Corporation ....G....... 269 668-3371
Mattawan *(G-11162)*
Benchmark Coating Systems LLC ....G....... 517 782-4061
Ann Arbor *(G-399)*
Carboline Company ....G....... 734 525-2824
Livonia *(G-10145)*
Cass Polymers ....E....... 517 543-7510
Charlotte *(G-2739)*
Chemetall US Inc ....G....... 517 787-4846
Jackson *(G-8841)*
Coat It Inc of Detroit ....G....... 313 869-8500
Detroit *(G-4096)*
▼ Coatings By Pcd Inc ....G....... 616 952-0032
Kent City *(G-9429)*
▲ Conway-Cleveland Corp ....G....... 616 458-0056
Grand Rapids *(G-6604)*
Creative Surfaces Inc ....F....... 586 226-2950
Clinton Township *(G-3213)*
Dhake Industries Inc ....E....... 734 420-0101
Plymouth *(G-13156)*
Douglas Corp ....E....... 517 767-4112
Tekonsha *(G-16522)*
▲ Eftec North America LLC ....D....... 248 585-2200
Taylor *(G-16410)*
◆ General Chemical Corporation ....G....... 248 587-5600
Brighton *(G-1998)*
Gougeon Holding Co ....G....... 989 684-7286
Bay City *(G-1361)*
▼ Great Lake Woods Inc ....C....... 616 399-3300
Holland *(G-8057)*
Great Lakes Epoxy Coatings LLC ....G....... 810 820-7073
Burton *(G-2236)*
Greenglow Products LLC ....G....... 248 827-1451
Southfield *(G-15584)*
▼ Helen Inc ....F....... 616 698-8102
Caledonia *(G-2378)*
Hygratek LLC ....G....... 847 962-6180
Ann Arbor *(G-520)*
Innovative Engineering Mich ....G....... 517 977-0460
Lansing *(G-9705)*
◆ Innovative Polymers Inc ....F....... 989 224-9500
Saint Johns *(G-14902)*
Innovative Solutions Tech Inc ....G....... 734 335-6665
Canton *(G-2477)*
Instacoat Premium Product ....G....... 877 552-6724
Oscoda *(G-12760)*
◆ Instacoat Premium Products LLC ....G....... 586 770-1773
Oscoda *(G-12761)*
Jbr Junk Removal LLC ....G....... 248 818-3471
Sterling Heights *(G-16055)*
Kelley Laboratories Inc ....F....... 231 861-6257
Shelby *(G-15153)*
Lakeshore Paints & Coating ....G....... 616 831-6990
Grand Rapids *(G-6925)*
Lancast Urethane Inc ....G....... 517 485-6070
Commerce Township *(G-3549)*
Lenawee Industrial Pnt Sup Inc ....G....... 734 729-8080
Wayne *(G-18229)*
▼ Lymtal International Inc ....E....... 248 373-8100
Orion *(G-12734)*
▲ Magni-Industries Inc ....E....... 313 843-7855
Detroit *(G-4416)*
Malach Group Plutonium Paint ....G....... 248 827-4844
Southfield *(G-15641)*
Marshall Ryerson Co ....F....... 616 299-1751
Grand Rapids *(G-6961)*
◆ Materials Processing Inc ....D....... 734 282-1888
Riverview *(G-13880)*
Michigan Coating Products Inc ....G....... 616 456-8800
Grand Rapids *(G-6987)*
Michigan Industrial Finishes ....F....... 248 553-7014
Farmington Hills *(G-5318)*
MPS Trading Group LLC ....E....... 313 841-7588
Farmington Hills *(G-5327)*
▼ Ncoc Inc ....E....... 248 548-5950
Oak Park *(G-12632)*
Ncp Coatings Inc ....D....... 269 683-3377
Niles *(G-12152)*
Nelson Paint Co of Mich Inc ....G....... 906 774-5566
Kingsford *(G-9514)*
Nelson Paint Company Ala Inc ....G....... 906 774-5566
Kingsford *(G-9515)*
Nelson Paint Company Mich Inc ....G....... 906 774-5566
Iron Mountain *(G-8726)*
New Layer Customs LLC ....G....... 313 358-3629
Troy *(G-17275)*
Nippon Paint Auto Americas Inc ....G....... 248 365-1100
Troy *(G-17278)*
▼ Northern Coatings & Chem Co ....E....... 906 863-2641
Menominee *(G-11254)*
Northwest Paint Pros ....G....... 231 944-3446
Traverse City *(G-16775)*
Ot Dynamics LLC ....F....... 734 984-7022
Flat Rock *(G-5624)*
Pacific Epoxy Polymers Inc ....G....... 616 949-1634
Grand Rapids *(G-7066)*
▲ Palmer Paint Products Inc ....D....... 248 588-4500
Troy *(G-17295)*
▲ Peter-Lacke Usa LLC ....G....... 248 588-9400
Troy *(G-17299)*
Pittsburgh Glass Works LLC ....C....... 248 371-1700
Rochester Hills *(G-14084)*
▲ Polymer Inc ....D....... 248 353-3035
Southfield *(G-15677)*
Port City Paints Mfg Inc ....G....... 231 726-5911
Muskegon *(G-11895)*
▲ Portland Plastics Co ....F....... 517 647-4115
Portland *(G-13640)*
Power Property Solutions LLC ....G....... 734 306-0299
Wayne *(G-18232)*
PPG Industrial Coatings ....G....... 616 844-4391
Grand Haven *(G-6345)*
PPG Industries Inc ....G....... 248 640-4174
Macomb *(G-10626)*

SIC

Employee Codes: A=Over 500 employees, B=251-500
C=101-250, D=51-100, E=20-50, F=10-19, G=3-9
2022 Harris Michigan
Industrial Directory
781

PPG Industries Inc.....G.......833 279-7021
Norton Shores *(G-12351)*

PPG Industries Inc.....G.......810 767-8030
Flint *(G-5746)*

PPG Industries Inc.....E.......616 846-4400
Grand Haven *(G-6346)*

PPG Industries Inc.....G.......248 625-7282
Clarkston *(G-3058)*

PPG Industries Inc.....G.......517 784-6138
Jackson *(G-8989)*

PPG Industries Inc.....G.......248 478-1300
Novi *(G-12510)*

PPG Industries Inc.....G.......586 566-3789
Shelby Township *(G-15307)*

PPG Industries Inc.....G.......248 357-4817
Southfield *(G-15678)*

PPG Industries Inc.....G.......734 287-2110
Southfield *(G-15679)*

PPG Industries Inc.....G.......586 755-2011
Warren *(G-17970)*

PPG Industries Inc.....G.......248 683-8052
Waterford *(G-18156)*

PPG Industries Inc.....F.......248 641-2000
Troy *(G-17309)*

Pro Coatings Inc.....E.......616 887-8808
Sparta *(G-15776)*

Quantum Chemical LLC.....G.......734 429-0033
Livonia *(G-10379)*

Rap Products Inc.....G.......989 893-5583
Bay City *(G-1394)*

▲ Red Spot Westland Inc.....C.......734 729-1913
Westland *(G-18413)*

Repcolite Paints Inc.....D.......616 396-5213
Holland *(G-8179)*

Richter Precision Inc.....E.......586 465-0500
Fraser *(G-5989)*

Riverside Spline & Gear Inc.....E.......810 765-8302
Marine City *(G-10965)*

◆ Rolled Alloys Inc.....D.......734 847-0561
Temperance *(G-16547)*

Rollie Williams Paint Spot.....G.......269 321-3174
Portage *(G-13600)*

▼ S P Kish Industries Inc.....E.......517 543-2650
Charlotte *(G-2766)*

Shadvin Industries LLC.....G.......509 263-7128
Bay City *(G-1400)*

▲ Simiron Inc.....E.......248 585-7500
Rochester Hills *(G-14112)*

Single Source Inc.....G.......765 825-4111
Flat Rock *(G-5630)*

Solid Epoxy Coatings LLC.....G.......248 785-7313
White Lake *(G-18465)*

▼ Specialty Coatings Inc.....G.......586 294-8343
Fraser *(G-5997)*

Statistical Processed Products.....F.......586 792-6900
Clinton Township *(G-3363)*

Supreme Media Blasting and Pow.....G.......586 792-7705
Clinton Township *(G-3366)*

Titan Sales International LLC.....G.......313 469-7105
Detroit *(G-4634)*

Top Quality Cleaning LLC.....F.......810 493-4211
Flint *(G-5779)*

Tru Custom Blends Inc.....F.......810 407-6207
Flint *(G-5785)*

United Paint and Chemical Corp.....D.......248 353-3035
Southfield *(G-15732)*

Wall Pro Painting.....G.......248 632-8525
Royal Oak *(G-14590)*

West System Inc.....D.......989 684-7286
Bay City *(G-1411)*

Wiesen Edm Inc.....E.......616 208-0000
Belding *(G-1466)*

▲ Z Technologies Corporation.....E.......313 937-0710
Redford *(G-13787)*

▼ Ziebart International Corp.....E.......248 588-4100
Troy *(G-17460)*

2861 Gum & Wood Chemicals

▲ Conway-Cleveland Corp.....G.......616 458-0056
Grand Rapids *(G-6604)*

Country Schoolhouse Kingsford.....G.......906 828-1971
Kingsford *(G-9507)*

2865 Cyclic-Crudes, Intermediates, Dyes & Org Pigments

▲ Chromatech Inc.....F.......734 451-1230
Canton *(G-2449)*

Diversfied Chem Tchnlgies Oprt.....G.......313 867-5444
Detroit *(G-4179)*

◆ Durez Corporation.....C.......248 313-7000
Novi *(G-12406)*

Esco Co Ltd Partnership.....F.......231 726-3106
Muskegon *(G-11813)*

▲ Esco Company LLC.....D.......231 726-3106
Grand Rapids *(G-6684)*

Flint CPS Inks North Amer LLC.....C.......734 781-4600
Livonia *(G-10208)*

◆ Flint Group US LLC.....B.......734 781-4600
Livonia *(G-10211)*

International Isocyanate Inst.....G.......989 878-0336
Midland *(G-11376)*

Mis Associates Inc.....G.......844 225-8156
Pontiac *(G-13398)*

Sun Chemical Corporation.....C.......231 788-2371
Muskegon *(G-11927)*

2869 Industrial Organic Chemicals, NEC

Aapharmasyn LLC.....F.......734 213-2123
Ann Arbor *(G-344)*

Adrian Lva Biofuel LLC.....G.......517 920-4863
Adrian *(G-48)*

▲ Advanced Urethanes Inc.....G.......313 273-5705
Detroit *(G-3988)*

Ahlusion LLC.....G.......888 277-0001
Swartz Creek *(G-16348)*

Akzo Nobel Coatings Inc.....E.......248 451-6231
Pontiac *(G-13346)*

Albasara Fuel LLC.....G.......313 443-6581
Dearborn *(G-3806)*

Amcol International Corp.....G.......517 629-6808
Albion *(G-116)*

▼ Amerchol Corporation.....G.......989 636-2441
Midland *(G-11320)*

▲ American Chemical Tech Inc.....E.......866 945-1041
Howell *(G-8428)*

American Farm Products Inc.....F.......734 484-4180
Saline *(G-15000)*

Ana Fuel Inc.....G.......810 422-5659
Ann Arbor *(G-366)*

Assi Fuel Inc.....G.......586 759-4759
Warren *(G-17720)*

Avient Colorants USA LLC.....C.......517 629-9101
Albion *(G-117)*

BASF.....F.......231 719-3019
Muskegon *(G-11774)*

BASF Corporation.....G.......734 324-6963
Wyandotte *(G-18808)*

BASF Corporation.....C.......734 324-6000
Wyandotte *(G-18809)*

BASF Corporation.....G.......734 324-6100
Wyandotte *(G-18810)*

BASF Corporation.....C.......734 759-2011
Wyandotte *(G-18811)*

BASF Corporation.....G.......734 591-5560
Livonia *(G-10131)*

BASF Corporation.....C.......248 827-4670
Southfield *(G-15503)*

Beebe Fuel Systems Inc.....G.......248 437-3322
South Lyon *(G-15427)*

Berry & Associates Inc.....F.......734 426-3787
Dexter *(G-4727)*

BKM Fuels LLC.....G.......269 342-9576
Kalamazoo *(G-9137)*

Boropharm Inc.....E.......517 455-7847
Ann Arbor *(G-403)*

BP Gas/ JB Fuel.....G.......517 531-3400
Parma *(G-12936)*

Burhani Labs Inc.....G.......313 212-3842
Detroit *(G-4077)*

Camerons of Jackson LLC.....G.......517 531-3400
Parma *(G-12937)*

Caravan Technologies Inc.....F.......313 632-8545
Detroit *(G-4088)*

Carbon Green Bioenergy LLC.....E.......616 374-4000
Lake Odessa *(G-9573)*

▲ Century Fuel Products.....G.......734 728-0300
Van Buren Twp *(G-17517)*

◆ Chem-Trend Limited Partnership.....C.......517 546-4520
Howell *(G-8438)*

Chouteau Fuels Company LLC.....G.......734 302-4800
Ann Arbor *(G-424)*

CJ Chemicals LLC.....F.......888 274-1044
Howell *(G-8440)*

Cjg LLC.....F.......734 793-1400
Livonia *(G-10158)*

Cldd LLC.....G.......517 748-9326
Jackson *(G-8844)*

Colors & Effects USA LLC.....E.......248 304-5753
Southfield *(G-15529)*

D M J Corp.....G.......810 239-9071
Flint *(G-5681)*

Ddp Spclty Elctrnic Mtls US LL.....D.......517 439-4440
Hillsdale *(G-7932)*

Dow Chemical Company.....G.......989 695-2584
Freeland *(G-6021)*

Dow Chemical Company.....E.......989 638-6441
Midland *(G-11350)*

Dow Chemical Company.....G.......925 432-5000
Midland *(G-11351)*

Dow Corning Corporation.....F.......989 839-2808
Midland *(G-11353)*

Dow Silicones Corporation.....C.......800 248-2481
Hemlock *(G-7852)*

Dow Silicones Corporation.....G.......989 895-3397
Bay City *(G-1348)*

◆ Dow Silicones Corporation.....A.......989 496-4000
Auburn *(G-765)*

Draths Corporation.....F.......517 349-0668
Howell *(G-8450)*

Dynamic Staffing Solutions.....G.......616 399-5220
Holland *(G-8019)*

Ecovia Renewables Inc.....G.......248 953-0594
Ann Arbor *(G-466)*

Eq Resource Recovery Inc.....G.......734 727-5500
Romulus *(G-14272)*

Ether LLC.....G.......248 795-8830
Ortonville *(G-12746)*

▼ Ex Soli LLC.....G.......800 525-2431
Kalamazoo *(G-9182)*

EZ Fuel Inc.....G.......810 744-4452
Flint *(G-5699)*

Fit Fuel By Kt LLC.....G.......517 643-8827
East Lansing *(G-4893)*

Fk Fuel Inc.....G.......313 383-6005
Lincoln Park *(G-10047)*

Flat Iron LLC.....F.......248 268-1668
Roseville *(G-14407)*

Fleet Fuel Company LLC.....G.......586 939-7000
Warren *(G-17807)*

Freal Fuel Inc.....G.......248 790-7202
Chesterfield *(G-2886)*

Frontier Rnwable Resources LLC.....G.......906 228-7960
Marquette *(G-11019)*

Fuel Tobacco Stop.....G.......810 487-2040
Flushing *(G-5809)*

Gage Corporation.....F.......248 541-3824
Ferndale *(G-5555)*

Gage Products Company.....G.......248 541-3824
Ferndale *(G-5557)*

Gb Dynamics Inc.....G.......313 400-3570
Port Huron *(G-13479)*

Georgia-Pacific LLC.....G.......989 348-7275
Grayling *(G-7461)*

Great Lakes Chemical Serv.....G.......269 353-1841
Vicksburg *(G-17604)*

Green Fuels Llc.....G.......734 735-6802
Carleton *(G-2554)*

Grm Corporation.....E.......989 453-2322
Pigeon *(G-13037)*

Hampshire Chemical Corp.....E.......989 636-1000
Midland *(G-11370)*

Henkel US Operations Corp.....B.......248 588-1082
Madison Heights *(G-10739)*

Hercules LLC.....G.......269 388-8676
Kalamazoo *(G-9215)*

Horiba Instruments Inc.....D.......866 540-2715
Canton *(G-2471)*

Ibidltd-Blue Green Energy.....E.......909 547-5160
Dearborn *(G-3852)*

Il Adrian LLC W2fuel.....G.......517 920-4863
Adrian *(G-73)*

Inkster Fuel & Food Inc.....G.......313 565-8230
Inkster *(G-8666)*

J&J Freon Removal.....G.......586 264-6379
Warren *(G-17881)*

Jade Scientific Inc.....F.......734 207-3775
Westland *(G-18387)*

K&S Fuel Ventures.....G.......248 360-0055
Commerce Township *(G-3548)*

Kelley Laboratories Inc.....F.......231 861-6257
Shelby *(G-15153)*

▲ Kemai (usa) Chemical Co Ltd.....G.......248 924-2225
Northville *(G-12234)*

Kentwood Fuel Inc.....G.......616 455-2387
Kentwood *(G-9459)*

Kern Auto Sales and Svc LLC.....F.......734 475-2722
Chelsea *(G-2818)*

Lab Link Testing LLC.....G.......419 283-6387
Madison Heights *(G-10766)*

SIC SECTION 28 CHEMICALS AND ALLIED PRODUCTS

Lansing Fuel Ventures Inc .... G 517 371-1198
  Lansing *(G-9860)*
Lillian Fuel Inc .... G 734 439-8505
  Milan *(G-11442)*
Lin Adam Fuel Inc .... G 313 733-6631
  Detroit *(G-4401)*
M and A Fuels .... G 313 397-7141
  Detroit *(G-4413)*
Medtest Holdings Inc .... D 866 540-2715
  Canton *(G-2492)*
Metal Mates Inc .... G 248 646-9831
  Beverly Hills *(G-1666)*
▲ Metalworking Lubricants Co .... D 248 332-3500
  Pontiac *(G-13397)*
Michigan Fuels .... G 313 886-7110
  Grosse Pointe Woods *(G-7571)*
Microcide Inc .... G 248 526-9663
  Troy *(G-17258)*
Monroe Fuel Company LLC .... G 734 302-4824
  Ann Arbor *(G-582)*
Naked Fuel Juice Bar .... G 248 325-9735
  West Bloomfield *(G-18301)*
Nation Wide Fuel Inc .... G 734 721-7110
  Dearborn *(G-3875)*
National Fuels Inc .... G 734 895-7836
  Canton *(G-2499)*
New Port Fuel Stop .... G 734 586-1401
  Newport *(G-12105)*
▼ Northern Coatings & Chem Co ...... E 906 863-2641
  Menominee *(G-11254)*
Paw Paw Fuel Stop .... G 269 657-7357
  Paw Paw *(G-12955)*
Performance Fuels Systems Inc .... G 248 202-1789
  Troy *(G-17297)*
Pira Testing LLC .... F 517 574-4297
  Lansing *(G-9784)*
Poet Biorefining - Caro LLC .... E 989 672-1222
  Caro *(G-2577)*
Quaker Houghton Pa Inc .... G 248 641-3231
  Livonia *(G-10376)*
Quaker Houghton Pa Inc .... E 248 265-7745
  Troy *(G-17325)*
Rap Products Inc .... G 989 893-5583
  Bay City *(G-1394)*
Reed Fuel LLC .... G 574 520-3101
  Niles *(G-12161)*
S & A Fuel LLC .... G 313 945-6555
  Dearborn *(G-3891)*
Seven Mile and Grnd River Fuel .... G 313 535-3000
  Hamtramck *(G-7613)*
Suite Spa Manufacturing LLC .... G 616 560-2713
  Caledonia *(G-2403)*
Superior Fuels LLC .... G 586 738-6851
  Dearborn *(G-3902)*
Sy Fuel Inc .... G 313 531-5894
  Redford *(G-13776)*
Taiz Fuel Inc .... G 313 485-2972
  Dearborn Heights *(G-3941)*
Temperance Fuel Stop Inc .... G 734 206-2676
  Grosse Pointe Woods *(G-7577)*
Thumb Bioenergy LLC .... F 810 404-2466
  Sandusky *(G-15069)*
Tpa Inc .... G 248 302-9131
  Detroit *(G-4641)*
Tygrus LLC .... G 248 218-0347
  Troy *(G-17409)*
Vertellus LLC .... C 616 772-2193
  Zeeland *(G-19090)*
Vision Fuels LLC .... G 586 997-3286
  Shelby Township *(G-15366)*
◆ Wacker Chemical Corporation ...... A 517 264-8500
  Adrian *(G-103)*
Wacker Chemical Corporation .... G 734 882-4055
  Ann Arbor *(G-712)*
Wamu Fuel LLC .... G 313 386-8700
  Livonia *(G-10465)*
Warren City Fuel .... G 586 759-4759
  Dearborn *(G-3914)*
Wild Flavors Inc .... E 269 216-2603
  Kalamazoo *(G-9370)*
Zunairah Fuels Inc .... G 647 405-1606
  Clinton Township *(G-3393)*

2873 Nitrogenous Fertilizers

◆ Advanced McRonutrient Pdts Inc ... E 989 752-2138
  Reese *(G-13805)*
Agrigenetics Inc .... D 317 337-3000
  Midland *(G-11318)*
Earthworm Cstngs Unlimited LLC ..... F 248 882-3329
  Waterford *(G-18122)*

Gantec Inc .... G 989 631-9300
  Midland *(G-11367)*
Hummus Goodness LLC .... G 248 229-9606
  Birmingham *(G-1731)*
Hyponex Corporation .... C 810 724-2875
  Imlay City *(G-8635)*
Scotts Company LLC .... G 586 254-6849
  Sterling Heights *(G-16167)*

2874 Phosphatic Fertilizers

Andersons Inc .... G 989 642-5291
  Hemlock *(G-7849)*
Cog Marketers Ltd .... F 989 224-4117
  Saint Johns *(G-14897)*
F C Simpson Lime Co .... G 810 367-3510
  Kimball *(G-9492)*

2875 Fertilizers, Mixing Only

Bay-Houston Towing Company .... F 810 648-2210
  Sandusky *(G-15056)*
Cog Marketers Ltd .... F 434 455-3209
  Ashley *(G-742)*
Cog Marketers Ltd .... F 989 224-4117
  Saint Johns *(G-14898)*
Great Lakes Nursery Soils Inc .... F 231 788-2770
  Muskegon *(G-11831)*
▲ Hydrodynamics International .... G 517 887-2007
  Lansing *(G-9853)*
Hyponex Corporation .... C 810 724-2875
  Imlay City *(G-8635)*
Markham Peat Corp .... G 800 851-7230
  Lakeview *(G-9643)*
Michigan Grower Products Inc .... F 269 665-7071
  Galesburg *(G-6080)*
Morgan Composting Inc .... G 231 734-2451
  Sears *(G-15137)*
Morgan Composting Inc .... E 231 734-2790
  Sears *(G-15138)*
Natures Best Top Soil Compost .... G 810 657-9528
  Carsonville *(G-2596)*
Nutrien AG Solutions Inc .... G 989 842-1185
  Breckenridge *(G-1912)*
Spurt Industries LLC .... G 616 688-5575
  Zeeland *(G-19080)*
Sun Gro Horticulture Dist Inc .... G 517 639-3115
  Quincy *(G-13675)*
Taylor Hills Compost Facility .... G 734 991-3902
  Taylor *(G-16484)*
Trp Enterprises Inc .... G 810 329-4027
  East China *(G-4859)*

2879 Pesticides & Agricultural Chemicals, NEC

Avian Enterprises LLC .... E 888 366-0709
  Sylvan Lake *(G-16359)*
Bayer Crop Science .... G 517 676-3586
  Mason *(G-11118)*
Bayer Cropscience LP .... F 231 744-4711
  Muskegon *(G-11776)*
Biobest USA Inc .... G 734 626-5693
  Romulus *(G-14258)*
Bms Enterprise LLC .... G 281 516-9100
  West Bloomfield *(G-18267)*
Centen AG LLC .... B 989 636-1000
  Midland *(G-11328)*
Corteva Agriscience LLC .... G 989 479-3245
  Harbor Beach *(G-7630)*
Dow Agrosciences LLC .... E 989 636-4400
  Midland *(G-11340)*
Dow Chemical Company .... C 989 636-4406
  Midland *(G-11343)*
Dow Chemical Company .... G 989 636-0540
  Midland *(G-11349)*
◆ Dow Chemical Company .... A 989 636-1000
  Midland *(G-11341)*
Dow Chemical Company .... D 989 636-5409
  Midland *(G-11352)*
Dupont .... E 651 767-2527
  Midland *(G-11358)*
Dupont Office and Self St .... G 206 471-3700
  Kewadin *(G-9486)*
Emerald Bioagriculture Corp .... G 517 882-7370
  Okemos *(G-12666)*
Gantec Inc .... G 989 631-9300
  Midland *(G-11367)*
Hpi Products Inc .... G 248 773-7460
  Northville *(G-12229)*
Monsanto Company .... G 269 483-1300
  Constantine *(G-3672)*

Rohm and Monsanto PLC .... G 313 886-1966
  Saint Clair Shores *(G-14882)*

2891 Adhesives & Sealants

A & B Display Systems Inc .... F 989 893-6642
  Bay City *(G-1314)*
Action Fabricators Inc .... C 616 957-2032
  Grand Rapids *(G-6423)*
Adco Products LLC .... C 517 841-7238
  Michigan Center *(G-11290)*
▲ Adhesive Systems Inc .... E 313 865-4448
  Detroit *(G-3987)*
Alco Products LLC .... C 313 823-7500
  Detroit *(G-3996)*
American Sealants Inc .... G 313 534-2500
  Detroit *(G-4014)*
Applied Molecules LLC .... G 810 355-1475
  Dexter *(G-4724)*
◆ Argent International Inc .... C 734 582-9800
  Plymouth *(G-13124)*
▲ Bars Products Inc .... E 248 634-8278
  Holly *(G-8262)*
Bear Cub Holdings Inc .... G 231 242-1152
  Harbor Springs *(G-7641)*
Bostik Inc .... G 269 781-8246
  Marshall *(G-11054)*
Cass Polymers .... E 517 543-7510
  Charlotte *(G-2739)*
Chem Link Inc .... D 269 679-4440
  Schoolcraft *(G-15114)*
Concrete Manufacturing Inc .... G 586 777-3320
  Roseville *(G-14388)*
▲ Conley Composites LLC .... E 918 299-5051
  Grand Rapids *(G-6594)*
Connells Restoration & Sealan .... G 269 370-0805
  Vandalia *(G-17565)*
Covalent Medical Inc .... G 734 604-0688
  Ann Arbor *(G-438)*
Daring Company .... G 248 340-0741
  Orion *(G-12728)*
Denarco Inc .... G 269 435-8404
  Constantine *(G-3664)*
Dico Manufacturing LLC .... G 586 731-3008
  Chesterfield *(G-2871)*
Diversified Chemical Tech Inc .... C 313 867-5444
  Detroit *(G-4180)*
▲ Diversitak Inc .... E 313 869-8500
  Detroit *(G-4181)*
Dow Chemical Company .... G 517 439-4400
  Hillsdale *(G-7933)*
▲ Eftec North America LLC .... D 248 585-2200
  Taylor *(G-16410)*
▲ Eternabond Inc .... G 847 540-0600
  Michigan Center *(G-11292)*
Henniges Auto Holdings Inc .... B 248 340-4100
  Auburn Hills *(G-924)*
◆ Henniges Auto Sling Systems N ... C 248 340-4100
  Auburn Hills *(G-925)*
Highland Industrial Inc .... G 989 391-9992
  Bay City *(G-1365)*
Huntler Industries Inc .... F 586 566-7684
  Shelby Township *(G-15236)*
▼ Huron Industries Inc .... G 810 984-4213
  Port Huron *(G-13485)*
Kent Manufacturing Company .... C 616 454-9495
  Grand Rapids *(G-6889)*
▲ Kiilunen Mfg Group Inc .... G 906 337-2433
  Calumet *(G-2410)*
Kleiberit Adhesives USA Inc .... C 248 709-9308
  Royal Oak *(G-14553)*
L & L Products Inc .... B 586 752-6681
  Bruce Twp *(G-2172)*
Lenderink Inc .... F 616 887-8257
  Belmont *(G-1511)*
Leonards Newcorp Inc .... F 313 366-9300
  Detroit *(G-4391)*
Lj/Hah Holdings Corporation .... C 248 340-4100
  Auburn Hills *(G-958)*
▼ Lymtal International Inc .... E 248 373-8100
  Orion *(G-12734)*
Master Mix Company .... G 734 487-7870
  Ypsilanti *(G-18966)*
◆ Materials Processing Inc .... D 734 282-1888
  Riverview *(G-13880)*
Millennium Adhesive Products .... G 800 248-4010
  Michigan Center *(G-11294)*
▼ Ncoc Inc .... E 248 548-5950
  Oak Park *(G-12632)*
▲ ND Industries Inc .... C 248 288-0000
  Clawson *(G-3101)*

Nyatex Chemical Company F 517 546-4046
Howell *(G-8487)*

▲ Parson Adhesives Inc G 248 299-5585
Rochester Hills *(G-14079)*

▲ Portland Plastics Co F 517 647-4115
Portland *(G-13640)*

Precision Packing Corporation E 586 756-8700
Warren *(G-17973)*

Precision Sealant G 616 667-9447
Jenison *(G-9066)*

Pro Sealants G 616 318-6067
Grand Rapids *(G-7110)*

Scodeller Construction Inc D 248 374-1102
Wixom *(G-18748)*

Seal Support Systems Inc E 918 258-6484
Romeo *(G-14235)*

Sealex Inc G 231 348-5020
Harbor Springs *(G-7656)*

Sika Corporation D 248 577-0020
Madison Heights *(G-10829)*

Specilty Adhesives Coating Inc G 269 345-3801
Kalamazoo *(G-9341)*

◆ Stahls Inc E 800 478-2457
Saint Clair Shores *(G-14887)*

Sugru Inc E 877 990-9888
Livonia *(G-10423)*

◆ Transtar Autobody Tech LLC C 810 220-3000
Brighton *(G-2084)*

◆ Trenton Corporation E 734 424-3600
Ann Arbor *(G-697)*

◆ Wall Colmonoy Corporation E 248 585-6400
Madison Heights *(G-10860)*

West System Inc D 989 684-7286
Bay City *(G-1411)*

Western Adhesive Inc F 616 874-5869
Rockford *(G-14193)*

Wilbur Products Inc F 231 755-3805
Muskegon *(G-11948)*

Xileh Holding Inc G 248 340-4100
Auburn Hills *(G-1090)*

▲ Z Technologies Corporation E 313 937-0710
Redford *(G-13787)*

▼ Ziebart International Corp E 248 588-4100
Troy *(G-17460)*

2892 Explosives

Austin Powder Company F 989 595-2400
Presque Isle *(G-13653)*

Pepin-Ireco Inc G 906 486-4473
Ishpeming *(G-8780)*

2893 Printing Ink

America Ink and Technology G 269 345-4657
Portage *(G-13543)*

▲ Celia Corporation G 616 887-7387
Sparta *(G-15763)*

D & D Business Machines Inc G 616 364-8446
Grand Rapids *(G-6627)*

Flint CPS Inks North Amer LLC C 734 781-4600
Livonia *(G-10208)*

◆ Flint Group US LLC B 734 781-4600
Livonia *(G-10211)*

Flint Ink Receivables Corp G 734 781-4600
Livonia *(G-10212)*

▲ Grand Rapids Printing Ink Co G 616 241-5681
Grand Rapids *(G-6768)*

▲ Great Lakes Toll Services G 616 847-1868
Spring Lake *(G-15820)*

Intra Business LLC G 269 262-0863
Niles *(G-12139)*

Jbr Associates G 586 693-5666
Sterling Heights *(G-16054)*

Pittsburgh Glass Works LLC C 248 371-1700
Rochester Hills *(G-14084)*

Pressburg LLC G 269 873-0775
Kalamazoo *(G-9307)*

▲ Sun Chemical Corporation F 513 681-5950
Muskegon *(G-11926)*

Wikoff Color Corporation E 616 245-3930
Grand Rapids *(G-7339)*

2899 Chemical Preparations, NEC

A-Line Products Corporation F 313 571-8300
Detroit *(G-3975)*

Aapharmasyn LLC F 734 213-2123
Ann Arbor *(G-344)*

Afton Chemical Corporation G 248 350-0640
Southfield *(G-15471)*

Ambers Essentials G 313 282-4615
Southfield *(G-15484)*

◆ American Jetway Corporation D 734 721-5930
Wayne *(G-18213)*

▲ Antimicrobial Specialist Assoc F 989 662-0377
Auburn *(G-763)*

Atotech Usa LLC F 586 939-3040
Sterling Heights *(G-15936)*

◆ Aurora Spclty Chemistries Corp E 517 372-9121
Lansing *(G-9810)*

▲ Bars Products Inc E 248 634-8278
Holly *(G-8262)*

BASF Corporation G 269 668-3371
Mattawan *(G-11162)*

BASF Corporation G 734 591-5560
Livonia *(G-10131)*

Bay City Fireworks Festival G 989 892-2264
Bay City *(G-1328)*

Beebe Fuel Systems G 734 261-3500
Livonia *(G-10135)*

Bio Source Naturals LLC G 877 577-8223
New Boston *(G-12002)*

◆ Bohning Company Ltd E 231 229-4247
Lake City *(G-9545)*

◆ Bridge Organics Company E 269 649-4200
Vicksburg *(G-17600)*

Brighton Laboratories Inc F 810 225-9520
Brighton *(G-1953)*

BV Technology LLC G 616 558-1746
Alto *(G-329)*

Caravan Technologies Inc F 313 632-8545
Detroit *(G-4088)*

Carco Inc E 313 925-1053
Detroit *(G-4089)*

Cargill Incorporated B 810 329-2736
Saint Clair *(G-14816)*

▲ Cau Acquisition Company LLC D 989 875-8133
Ithaca *(G-8787)*

Cayman Chemical Company Inc D 734 971-3335
Ann Arbor *(G-417)*

Cerco Inc E 734 362-8664
Brownstown Twp *(G-2153)*

Chames LLC G 616 363-0000
Grand Rapids *(G-6564)*

◆ Chem-Trend Holding Inc G 517 545-7980
Howell *(G-8437)*

◆ Chem-Trend Limited Partnership C 517 546-4520
Howell *(G-8438)*

Chem-Trend Limited Partnership G 517 546-4520
Howell *(G-8439)*

Chemetall US Inc G 517 787-4846
Jackson *(G-8841)*

Cleaning Solutions Inc G 616 243-0555
Grand Rapids *(G-6572)*

Clearwater Treatment Systems G 517 688-9316
Clarklake *(G-3004)*

CRC Industries Inc E 313 883-6977
Detroit *(G-4107)*

▲ Cross Technologies Group Inc F 734 895-8084
Westland *(G-18362)*

▲ Cummings-Moore Graphite Co E 313 841-1615
Detroit *(G-4112)*

Cytec Industries Inc G 269 349-6677
Kalamazoo *(G-9161)*

Dell Marking Systems G 248 481-2119
Pontiac *(G-13359)*

◆ Dell Marking Systems Inc G 248 547-7750
Rochester Hills *(G-13994)*

Diversified Chemical Tech Inc C 313 867-5444
Detroit *(G-4180)*

▲ Doerken Corporation G 517 522-4600
Grass Lake *(G-7437)*

Dow Chemical Company G 517 439-4400
Hillsdale *(G-7933)*

Dsw Holdings Inc E 313 567-4500
Detroit *(G-4192)*

▲ Duall Division G 989 725-8184
Lennon *(G-9993)*

Eastern Oil Company E 248 333-1333
Pontiac *(G-13364)*

▲ Eftec North America LLC D 248 585-2200
Taylor *(G-16410)*

Emco Chemical Inc F 313 894-7650
Detroit *(G-4207)*

Enerco Corporation F 517 627-1669
Grand Ledge *(G-6390)*

Engraved Memories G 586 703-7983
Shelby Township *(G-15221)*

Ernie Romanco G 517 531-3686
Albion *(G-125)*

Freiborne Industries Inc E 248 333-2490
Pontiac *(G-13371)*

◆ General Chemical Corporation G 248 587-5600
Brighton *(G-1998)*

◆ Ginsan Liquidating Company LLC D 616 791-8100
Grand Rapids *(G-6744)*

Great Lakes Treatment Corp G 517 566-8008
Sunfield *(G-16335)*

H M Products Inc G 313 875-5148
Detroit *(G-4288)*

H-O-H Water Technology Inc E 248 669-6667
Commerce Township *(G-3534)*

Haas Group International LLC G 810 236-0032
Flint *(G-5712)*

Haltermann Carless Us Inc E 248 422-6548
Troy *(G-17136)*

Henkel US Operations Corp B 248 588-1082
Madison Heights *(G-10739)*

Henkel US Operations Corp C 586 759-5555
Warren *(G-17852)*

Hercules LLC G 269 388-8676
Kalamazoo *(G-9215)*

Hill Machine Works LLC F 586 238-2897
Fraser *(G-5937)*

Hydro Chem Laboratories Inc G 248 348-1737
Commerce Township *(G-3541)*

Jones Chemical Inc G 734 283-0677
Riverview *(G-13878)*

▼ Kolene Corporation D 313 273-9220
Detroit *(G-4365)*

Lenderink Inc F 616 887-8257
Belmont *(G-1511)*

Lubrizol Corporation G 989 496-3780
Midland *(G-11385)*

▼ Lymtal International Inc E 248 373-8100
Orion *(G-12734)*

Macdermid Incorporated G 248 399-3553
Ferndale *(G-5566)*

Macdermid Incorporated G 248 437-8161
New Hudson *(G-12060)*

Mackenzie Company G 231 335-1997
Detroit *(G-4414)*

▲ Magni Group Inc F 248 647-4500
Birmingham *(G-1735)*

Marshall Ryerson Co F 616 299-1751
Grand Rapids *(G-6961)*

McGean-Rohco Inc E 216 441-4900
Livonia *(G-10306)*

Midland Cmpnding Cnsulting Inc G 989 495-9367
Midland *(G-11392)*

Morning Star Land Company LLC F 734 459-8022
Canton *(G-2498)*

Morton Salt Inc G 231 398-0758
Manistee *(G-10910)*

Natural Hlth Essntial Oils LLC G 906 495-5404
Kinross *(G-9527)*

▼ Ncoc Inc E 248 548-5950
Oak Park *(G-12632)*

Nelsonite Chemical Pdts Inc G 616 456-7098
Grand Rapids *(G-7038)*

▼ Northern Coatings & Chem Co E 906 863-2641
Menominee *(G-11254)*

Npworld Co G 586 826-9702
Sterling Heights *(G-16119)*

NV Labs Inc D 248 358-9022
Southfield *(G-15668)*

Patriot Pyrotechnics G 989 831-7788
Sheridan *(G-15382)*

Patty Raymond G 517 256-6673
Eagle *(G-4852)*

Pfb Manufacturing LLC G 517 486-4844
Blissfield *(G-1773)*

◆ Photo Systems Inc E 734 424-9625
Dexter *(G-4749)*

▲ Plating Systems and Tech Inc G 517 783-4776
Jackson *(G-8988)*

◆ Pressure Vessel Service Inc E 313 921-1200
Detroit *(G-4533)*

Quaker Houghton Pa Inc E 248 265-7745
Troy *(G-17325)*

Questron Packaging LLC G 313 657-1630
Detroit *(G-4547)*

Ralrube Inc G 734 429-0033
Saline *(G-15035)*

Rbm Chemical Company LLC G 248 766-1974
Rochester *(G-13924)*

Recycling Fluid Technologies F 269 788-0488
Battle Creek *(G-1288)*

◆ Rolled Alloys Inc D 734 847-0561
Temperance *(G-16547)*

Rooto Corporation F 517 546-8330
Howell *(G-8510)*

29 PETROLEUM REFINING AND RELATED INDUSTRIES

▼ Rustop Technologies LLC .... G 517 223-5098
  Howell *(G-8512)*
Selkey Fabricators LLC .... F 906 353-7104
  Baraga *(G-1148)*
Shay Water Co Inc .... E 989 755-3221
  Saginaw *(G-14755)*
Sika Corporation .... D 248 577-0020
  Madison Heights *(G-10829)*
▼ Sks Industries Inc .... F 517 546-1117
  Howell *(G-8518)*
Smith Wa Inc .... G 313 883-6977
  Detroit *(G-4598)*
Solar Flare Bar .... G 269 830-0499
  Battle Creek *(G-1297)*
▲ St Evans Inc .... G 269 663-6100
  Edwardsburg *(G-5017)*
Stony Creek Essential Oils .... G 989 227-5500
  Saint Johns *(G-14917)*
Suez Water Indiana LLC .... E 734 379-3855
  Rockwood *(G-14205)*
Surface Activation Tech LLC .... G 248 273-0037
  Troy *(G-17381)*
Svn Inc .... F 734 707-7131
  Saline *(G-15042)*
Teachout and Associates Inc .... G 269 729-4440
  Athens *(G-743)*
Technichem .... G 810 744-3770
  Flint *(G-5777)*
◆ Thetford Corporation .... C 734 769-6000
  Ann Arbor *(G-688)*
◆ Toda America Incorporated .... G 269 962-0353
  Battle Creek *(G-1305)*
Topduck Products LLC .... F 517 322-3202
  Saint Johns *(G-14918)*
▲ Trace Zero Inc .... F 248 289-1277
  Auburn Hills *(G-1062)*
◆ Transtar Autobody Tech LLC .... C 810 220-3000
  Brighton *(G-2084)*
Tuocai America LLC .... G 248 346-5910
  Troy *(G-17406)*
V & V Industries Inc .... F 248 624-7943
  Wixom *(G-18783)*
Valuable Services LLC .... G 512 667-7490
  Brighton *(G-2091)*
Varn International Inc .... F 734 781-4600
  Livonia *(G-10458)*
◆ Vertellus Hlth Spclty Pdts LLC ...... G 616 772-2193
  Zeeland *(G-19089)*
Wabco Group International Inc .... G 248 260-9025
  Auburn Hills *(G-1085)*
▲ Wacker Biochem Corporation .... C 517 264-8500
  Adrian *(G-102)*
Welzin Health Services LLC .... G 313 953-8768
  Wyandotte *(G-18844)*
Wilbur Products Inc .... F 231 755-3805
  Muskegon *(G-11948)*
Xaerus Performance Fluids LLC ..... C 989 631-7871
  Midland *(G-11425)*

29 PETROLEUM REFINING AND RELATED INDUSTRIES

2911 Petroleum Refining

Admiral .... G 989 684-8314
  Bay City *(G-1317)*
Admiral .... G 989 835-9160
  Midland *(G-11317)*
Americanlubricationcom .... G 586 219-9119
  Macomb *(G-10576)*
Amrican Petro Inc .... G 313 520-8404
  Detroit *(G-4017)*
Avflight Corporation .... G 734 663-6466
  Ann Arbor *(G-388)*
Bertoldi Oil Service Inc .... G 906 774-1707
  Iron Mountain *(G-8717)*
Buckeye Terminals LLC .... G 616 842-2450
  Ferrysburg *(G-5601)*
◆ Bva Inc .... E 248 348-4920
  New Hudson *(G-12044)*
Cfb Michigan Inc .... G 269 663-8855
  Edwardsburg *(G-5002)*
Corrigan Enterprises Inc .... E 810 229-6323
  Brighton *(G-1969)*
Ees Coke Battery LLC .... G 313 235-4000
  Ann Arbor *(G-468)*
▲ Fortech Products Inc .... E 248 446-9500
  Brighton *(G-1992)*
Hitachi America Ltd .... G 248 477-5400
  Farmington Hills *(G-5261)*

▼ Huron Industries Inc .... G 810 984-4213
  Port Huron *(G-13485)*
Jet Fuel .... G 231 767-9566
  Muskegon *(G-11845)*
Kerosene Fragrances .... G 810 292-5772
  Port Huron *(G-13493)*
Marysville Hydrocarbons LLC .... G 586 445-2300
  Warren *(G-17918)*
Marysville Hydrocarbons LLC .... E 586 445-2300
  Marysville *(G-11090)*
Matrix Construction Pdts LLC .... G 720 961-5454
  Marquette *(G-11035)*
Merritt Energy .... G 231 723-6587
  Manistee *(G-10908)*
▲ Michigan Paving and Mtls Co .... E 734 397-2050
  Canton *(G-2496)*
Miller Exploration Company .... F 231 941-0004
  Traverse City *(G-16758)*
Motor City Quick Lube One Inc .... G 734 367-6457
  Livonia *(G-10323)*
Mpc .... G 313 297-6386
  Detroit *(G-4468)*
Nano Materials & Processes Inc ..... G 248 529-3873
  Milford *(G-11475)*
Pacific Oil Resources Inc .... G 734 397-1120
  Van Buren Twp *(G-17545)*
Stop & Go Transportation LLC .... G 313 346-7114
  Washington *(G-18087)*
W2fuel LLC .... E 517 920-4868
  Adrian *(G-101)*

2951 Paving Mixtures & Blocks

A & M Distributors .... G 586 755-9045
  Warren *(G-17680)*
A Plus Asphalt LLC .... E 888 754-1125
  Bloomfield Hills *(G-1788)*
Ajax Materials Corporation .... G 248 244-3300
  Troy *(G-16912)*
Ajax Paving Industries Inc .... C 248 244-3300
  Troy *(G-16913)*
Alco Products LLC .... E 313 823-7500
  Detroit *(G-3996)*
Allied Asp Sealcoat & Repr LLC ...... G 810 797-6080
  Flint *(G-5643)*
Angelos Crushed Concrete Inc .... G 586 756-1070
  Warren *(G-17706)*
Asphalt Services .... G 313 971-5005
  Clarkston *(G-3018)*
Barrett Paving Materials Inc .... E 734 941-0200
  Romulus *(G-14255)*
Bdk Group Northern Mich Inc .... F 574 875-5183
  Charlevoix *(G-2711)*
Carlo John Inc .... E 586 254-3800
  Shelby Township *(G-15181)*
Celia Deboer .... G 269 279-9102
  Three Rivers *(G-16569)*
Central Asphalt Inc .... F 989 772-0720
  Mount Pleasant *(G-11690)*
Colorado Pavers & Walls Inc .... E 517 881-1704
  Flint *(G-5669)*
D O W Asphalt Paving LLC .... G 810 743-2633
  Swartz Creek *(G-16352)*
Dans Concrete LLC .... G 517 242-0754
  Grand Ledge *(G-6388)*
Delta Paving Inc .... F 810 232-0220
  Flint *(G-5685)*
Edw C Levy Co .... G 248 634-0879
  Davisburg *(G-3765)*
▲ Edw C Levy Co .... B 313 429-2200
  Dearborn *(G-3835)*
Edw C Levy Co .... G 248 349-8600
  Novi *(G-12411)*
Edw C Levy Co .... G 313 843-7200
  Detroit *(G-4202)*
Elmers Crane and Dozer Inc .... C 231 943-3443
  Traverse City *(G-16676)*
Eric Rogers LLC .... G 517 543-7126
  Charlotte *(G-2752)*
Fendt Builders Supply Inc .... E 248 474-3211
  Farmington Hills *(G-5242)*
Gem Asset Acquisition LLC .... G 248 338-0335
  Auburn Hills *(G-906)*
Hd Selcating Pav Solutions LLC ..... G 248 241-6526
  Clarkston *(G-3038)*
Hess Asphalt Pav Sand Cnstr Co ... E 810 984-4466
  Clyde *(G-3413)*
Hhj Holdings Limited .... F 248 652-9716
  Troy *(G-17143)*
J L Milling Inc .... F 269 679-5769
  Schoolcraft *(G-15119)*

Lafarge North America Inc .... G 231-726-3291
  Muskegon *(G-11855)*
Lafarge North America Inc .... G 703 480-3600
  Dundee *(G-4827)*
Laser Mfg Inc .... G 313 292-2299
  Plymouth *(G-13218)*
Lite Load Services LLC .... F 269 751-6037
  Hamilton *(G-7603)*
Mdc Contracting LLC .... G 231 547-6595
  Charlevoix *(G-2720)*
Michigan Paving and Mtls Co .... E 734 485-1717
  Van Buren Twp *(G-17539)*
Michigan Paving and Mtls Co .... F 989 463-1323
  Alma *(G-247)*
Michigan Paving and Mtls Co .... E 517 787-4200
  Jackson *(G-8956)*
Nagle Paving Company .... F 248 553-0600
  Novi *(G-12486)*
Nagle Paving Company .... C 734 591-1484
  Livonia *(G-10330)*
North American Asphalt .... G 586 754-0014
  Warren *(G-17946)*
Payne & Dolan Inc .... E 989 731-0700
  Gaylord *(G-6153)*
Peake Asphalt Inc .... F 586 254-4567
  Shelby Township *(G-15297)*
Pyramid Paving and Contg Co .... D 989 895-5861
  Bay City *(G-1390)*
Rieth-Riley Cnstr Co Inc .... F 231 263-2100
  Grawn *(G-7453)*
Rieth-Riley Cnstr Co Inc .... F 616 248-0920
  Wyoming *(G-18904)*
Rite Way Asphalt Inc .... G 586 264-1020
  Sterling Heights *(G-16154)*
RWS & Associates LLC .... E 517 278-3134
  Coldwater *(G-3451)*
▲ Saginaw Asphalt Paving Co .... D 989 755-8147
  Carrollton *(G-2590)*
Sealmaster/Michigan .... G 313 779-8415
  Plymouth *(G-13295)*
Shooks Asphalt Paving Co Inc .... E 989 236-7740
  Perrinton *(G-12976)*
Surface Coatings Co .... G 248 977-9478
  Metamora *(G-11288)*
Tri-City Aggregates Inc .... E 248 634-8276
  Holly *(G-8298)*
Woodland Paving Co .... E 616 784-5220
  Comstock Park *(G-3652)*

2952 Asphalt Felts & Coatings

Alco Products LLC .... E 313 823-7500
  Detroit *(G-3996)*
Ameripave .... G 843 509-5502
  Romulus *(G-14248)*
Arnt Asphalt Sealing Inc .... D 269 927-1532
  Benton Harbor *(G-1530)*
Curbco Inc .... D 810 232-2121
  Flint *(G-5678)*
▲ De Witt Products Co .... E 313 554-0575
  Detroit *(G-4124)*
Detroit Cornice & Slate Co Inc .... E 248 398-7690
  Ferndale *(G-5544)*
Green Link Inc .... F 269 216-9229
  Kalamazoo *(G-9204)*
Liveroof LLC .... E 616 842-1392
  Nunica *(G-12584)*
Marshall Ryerson Co .... F 616 299-1751
  Grand Rapids *(G-6961)*
McElroy Metal Mill Inc .... D 269 781-8313
  Marshall *(G-11069)*
Michigan Paving and Mtls Co .... E 517 787-4200
  Jackson *(G-8956)*
Michigan Steel and Trim Inc .... G 517 647-4555
  Portland *(G-13639)*
Oak Way Manufacturing Inc .... F 248 335-9476
  Pontiac *(G-13404)*
Over Top Steel Coating LLC .... G 616 647-9140
  Comstock Park *(G-3632)*
Pine River Inc .... F 231 758-3400
  Charlevoix *(G-2728)*
Randys Seal Coat .... G 231 342-8031
  Traverse City *(G-16816)*
Ravenna Sealcoating Inc .... G 231 766-0571
  Muskegon *(G-11905)*
Reurink Roof Maint & Coating .... G 269 795-2337
  Middleville *(G-11312)*
SM Andia Sealcoating LLC .... G 586 997-1750
  Shelby Township *(G-15334)*
UP Seal-Coating .... G 906 283-3433
  Gulliver *(G-7579)*

Employee Codes: A=Over 500 employees, B=251-500
C=101-250, D=51-100, E=20-50, F=10-19, G=3-9

29 PETROLEUM REFINING AND RELATED INDUSTRIES

2992 Lubricating Oils & Greases

A K Oil LLC DBA Speedy Oil and ....G...... 616 233-9505
  Grand Rapids (G-6410)
Agscap Inc..G...... 231 733-2101
  Muskegon (G-11766)
◆ Amcol Corporation ....E...... 248 414-5700
  Hazel Park (G-7819)
Apollo Idemitsu Corporation ....G...... 248 675-4345
  Wixom (G-18608)
Argent Limited ....G...... 734 427-5533
  Livonia (G-10123)
Bostik Inc ....G...... 269 781-8246
  Marshall (G-11054)
BP Lubricants USA Inc ....G...... 231 689-0002
  White Cloud (G-18439)
▼ Cadillac Oil Company ....E...... 313 365-6200
  Detroit (G-4085)
Chemtool Incorporated ....G...... 734 439-7010
  Milan (G-11432)
◆ Chrysan Industries Inc ....E...... 734 451-5411
  Plymouth (G-13146)
◆ Condat Corporation ....E...... 734 944-4994
  Saline (G-15009)
◆ Coxen Enterprises Inc ....D...... 248 486-3800
  Brighton (G-1971)
▲ Cummings-Moore Graphite Co ....E...... 313 841-1615
  Detroit (G-4112)
Diversified Chemical Tech Inc ....C...... 313 867-5444
  Detroit (G-4180)
Eastern Oil Company ....E...... 248 333-1333
  Pontiac (G-13364)
Edrich Products Inc ....F...... 586 296-3350
  Fraser (G-5922)
Excelda Mfg Holdg LLC ....F...... 517 223-8000
  Fowlerville (G-5838)
▲ Fortech Products Inc ....E...... 248 446-9500
  Brighton (G-1992)
Fuel Source LLC ....G...... 313 506-0448
  Grosse Ile (G-7522)
H and M Lube DBA Jlube ....G...... 231 929-1197
  Traverse City (G-16708)
▼ Huron Industries Inc ....G...... 810 984-4213
  Port Huron (G-13485)
Idemitsu Lubricants Amer Corp ....E...... 248 355-0666
  Southfield (G-15600)
▲ Lub-Tech Inc ....G...... 616 299-3540
  Grand Rapids (G-6950)
Lube-Tech Inc ....G...... 269 329-1269
  Portage (G-13580)
Lubecon Systems Inc ....G...... 231 689-0002
  White Cloud (G-18445)
MB Fluid Services LLC ....F...... 616 392-7036
  Holland (G-8140)
▲ Metalworking Lubricants Co ....D...... 248 332-3500
  Pontiac (G-13397)
Mr Lube Inc ....G...... 313 615-6161
  Wyandotte (G-18834)
Oil Chem Inc ....E...... 810 235-3040
  Flint (G-5742)
▲ Permawick Company Inc ....G...... 248 433-3500
  Birmingham (G-1743)
Persons Inc ....G...... 989 734-3835
  Rogers City (G-14216)
Quaker Houghton Pa Inc ....G...... 313 273-7374
  Detroit (G-4545)
Quaker Houghton Pa Inc ....E...... 248 265-7745
  Troy (G-17325)
Quality Lube Express Inc ....G...... 586 421-0600
  Chesterfield (G-2935)
Rap Products Inc ....G...... 989 893-5583
  Bay City (G-1394)
Shell Lubricants ....G...... 313 354-1187
  River Rouge (G-13860)
Stt Usa Inc ....G...... 248 522-9655
  Wixom (G-18759)
TMC Group Inc ....G...... 248 819-6063
  Pleasant Ridge (G-13106)
Vaughan Industries Inc ....F...... 313 935-2040
  Detroit (G-4663)
Warner Oil Company ....G...... 517 278-5844
  Coldwater (G-3461)
Wilbur Products Inc ....F...... 231 755-3805
  Muskegon (G-11948)

2999 Products Of Petroleum & Coal, NEC

B and R Oil Company Inc ....G...... 313 292-5500
  Taylor (G-16385)

30 RUBBER AND MISCELLANEOUS PLASTICS PRODUCTS

3011 Tires & Inner Tubes

Anh Enterprises LLC ....F...... 313 887-0800
  Taylor (G-16379)
▲ Avon Machining LLC ....D...... 586 884-2200
  Shelby Township (G-15175)
Avon Machining Holdings Inc ....C...... 586 884-2200
  Shelby Township (G-15176)
BF Franchising ....G...... 313 565-2713
  Dearborn (G-3814)
Goodyear Tire & Rubber Company ....G...... 248 336-0153
  Royal Oak (G-14541)
Great Lakes Tire LLC ....F...... 586 939-7000
  Warren (G-17836)
◆ Hutchinson Corporation ....G...... 616 459-4541
  Grand Rapids (G-6825)
Jam Tire Inc ....F...... 586 772-2900
  Clinton Township (G-3263)
Omni United (usa) Inc ....G...... 855 906-6646
  Charlevoix (G-2725)
Plastic Omnium Inc ....G...... 248 458-0772
  Troy (G-17304)
Polytek Michigan Inc ....G...... 734 782-0378
  Flat Rock (G-5625)
Tire Wholesalers Company ....D...... 269 349-9401
  Kalamazoo (G-9357)

3021 Rubber & Plastic Footwear

Atlantic Precision Pdts Inc ....F...... 586 532-9420
  Shelby Township (G-15174)
Fernand Corporation ....G...... 231 882-9622
  Kalamazoo (G-9185)
Musical Sneakers Incorporated ....F...... 888 410-7050
  Grandville (G-7405)
Nike Inc ....G...... 616 583-0754
  Byron Center (G-2289)
Original Footwear Company ....B...... 231 796-5828
  Big Rapids (G-1681)
▲ Wolverine Procurement Inc ....F...... 616 866-5500
  Rockford (G-14195)

3052 Rubber & Plastic Hose & Belting

Akwel Cadillac Usa Inc ....G...... 248 848-9599
  Farmington Hills (G-5166)
▲ Anand Nvh North America Inc ....C...... 810 724-2400
  Imlay City (G-8627)
Andronaco Inc ....G...... 616 554-4600
  Kentwood (G-9442)
Atcoflex Inc ....F...... 616 842-4661
  Grand Haven (G-6277)
Dayco Products LLC ....G...... 248 404-6506
  Troy (G-17047)
Dayco Products LLC ....G...... 248 404-6537
  Roseville (G-14393)
Eaton Aeroquip LLC ....B...... 949 452-9575
  Jackson (G-8873)
▲ Ena North America Corporation ....E...... 248 926-0011
  Wixom (G-18656)
Flexfab LLC ....E...... 269 945-3523
  Grand Rapids (G-6711)
▲ Flexfab Horizons Intl Inc ....E...... 269 945-4700
  Hastings (G-7791)
▲ Flexfab LLC ....G...... 800 331-0003
  Hastings (G-7792)
Gates Corporation ....G...... 248 260-2300
  Rochester Hills (G-14020)
Grenell Manufacturing LLC ....G...... 616 304-1593
  Lakeview (G-9641)
H P P ....G...... 248 307-4263
  Madison Heights (G-10737)
▲ Haviland Contoured Plastics ....G...... 616 361-6691
  Walker (G-17640)
◆ Kadant Johnson LLC ....C...... 269 278-1715
  Three Rivers (G-16577)
Lauren Zinn ....G...... 734 996-3524
  Ann Arbor (G-549)
◆ Mol Belting Systems Inc ....D...... 616 453-2484
  Grand Rapids (G-7020)
▲ Piranha Hose Products Inc ....E...... 231 779-4390
  Cadillac (G-2348)
◆ Pureflex Inc ....C...... 616 554-1100
  Kentwood (G-9473)
▲ Sejasmi Industries Inc ....G...... 586 725-5300
  Ira (G-8713)
Snook Inc ....F...... 231 799-3333
  Norton Shores (G-12332)

▲ Sparks Belting Company Inc ....D...... 616 949-2750
  Grand Rapids (G-7207)
Stephen A James ....G...... 269 641-5879
  Cassopolis (G-2634)
Thunder Technologies LLC ....F...... 248 844-4875
  Rochester Hills (G-14126)
▼ TI Fluid Systems LLC ....A...... 248 494-5000
  Auburn Hills (G-1054)
◆ TI Group Auto Systems LLC ....B...... 248 296-8000
  Auburn Hills (G-1055)
Ton-Tex Corporation ....F...... 616 957-3200
  Greenville (G-7508)

3053 Gaskets, Packing & Sealing Devices

Action Fabricators Inc ....C...... 616 957-2032
  Grand Rapids (G-6423)
Aircraft Precision Pdts Inc ....D...... 989 875-4186
  Ithaca (G-8785)
Armada Rubber Manufacturing Co ....D...... 586 784-9135
  Armada (G-731)
Basic Rubber and Plastics Co ....E...... 248 360-7400
  Walled Lake (G-17664)
Blade Industrial Products Inc ....G...... 248 773-7400
  Wixom (G-18621)
C W Marsh Company ....E...... 231 722-3781
  Muskegon (G-11788)
Champion Gasket & Rubber Inc ....E...... 248 624-6140
  Commerce Township (G-3518)
Copeland-Gibson Products Corp ....E...... 248 740-4400
  Troy (G-17028)
Cpj Company Inc ....E...... 616 784-6355
  Comstock Park (G-3598)
Creative Foam Corporation ....G...... 810 714-0140
  Fenton (G-5468)
▲ Creative Foam Corporation ....C...... 810 629-4149
  Fenton (G-5467)
Crk Ltd ....G...... 586 779-5240
  Eastpointe (G-4933)
Derby Fabg Solutions LLC ....D...... 616 866-1650
  Rockford (G-14164)
DMS Mnufacturing Solutions Inc ....G...... 517 423-6691
  Tecumseh (G-16498)
▲ Federal-Mogul Piston Rings Inc ....F...... 248 354-7700
  Southfield (G-15564)
Federl-Mgul Dutch Holdings Inc ....D...... 248 354-7700
  Southfield (G-15569)
▲ Flexfab Horizons Intl Inc ....E...... 269 945-4700
  Hastings (G-7791)
Flowserve US Inc ....C...... 269 381-2650
  Kalamazoo (G-9189)
FM International LLC ....G...... 248 354-7700
  Southfield (G-15570)
◆ Freudenberg N Amer Ltd Partnr ....G...... 734 354-5505
  Plymouth (G-13169)
◆ Freudenberg-Nok General Partnr ....C...... 734 451-0020
  Plymouth (G-13170)
Green Polymeric Materials Inc ....E...... 313 933-7390
  Detroit (G-4280)
Grm Corporation ....G...... 989 453-2322
  Pigeon (G-13038)
◆ Henniges Auto Sling Systems N ....C...... 248 340-4100
  Auburn Hills (G-925)
▲ Henniges Automotive N Amer Inc ....C...... 248 340-4100
  Auburn Hills (G-926)
Industrial Converting Inc ....E...... 586 757-8820
  Warren (G-17864)
J L Schroth Co ....G...... 586 759-4240
  Warren (G-17878)
▲ Jacobsen Industries Inc ....D...... 734 591-6111
  Livonia (G-10255)
John Crane Inc ....F...... 989 496-9292
  Midland (G-11378)
◆ Kaydon Corporation ....B...... 734 747-7025
  Ann Arbor (G-538)
Kent Manufacturing Company ....D...... 616 454-9495
  Grand Rapids (G-6889)
Ksb Dubric Inc ....E...... 616 784-6355
  Comstock Park (G-3618)
◆ L & L Products Inc ....B...... 586 336-1600
  Bruce Twp (G-2171)
L & L Products Inc ....B...... 586 752-6681
  Bruce Twp (G-2172)
L & L Products Inc ....E...... 586 336-1600
  Bruce Twp (G-2173)
Lamons ....G...... 989 488-4580
  Midland (G-11383)
Lydall Sealing Solutions Inc ....E...... 248 596-2800
  Northville (G-12237)
M-Seal Products Co LLC ....G...... 313 884-6147
  Grosse Pointe Shores (G-7563)

30 RUBBER AND MISCELLANEOUS PLASTICS PRODUCTS

Macarthur Corp ....E 810 606-1777
Grand Blanc *(G-6252)*

Manufacturing Hero ....G 269 271-0031
Portage *(G-13583)*

◆ **Marshall Excelsior Co** ....E 269 789-6700
Marshall *(G-11065)*

◆ **Martin Fluid Power Company** ....F 248 585-8170
Madison Heights *(G-10776)*

Memtech Inc ....F 734 455-8550
Plymouth *(G-13240)*

Michael-Stephens Company ....G 248 583-7767
Troy *(G-17256)*

Midwest Fbrglas Fbricators Inc ....F 810 765-7445
Marine City *(G-10963)*

Milfab Systems LLC ....F 248 391-8100
Lake Orion *(G-9619)*

N-K Sealing Technologies LLC ....G 616 248-3200
Grand Rapids *(G-7035)*

Nci Mfg Inc ....F 248 380-4151
Livonia *(G-10334)*

Oliver Healthcare Packaging Co ....C 616 456-7711
Grand Rapids *(G-7057)*

Package Design & Mfg Inc ....E 248 486-4390
Brighton *(G-2046)*

Parker-Hannifin Corporation ....G 330 253-5239
Otsego *(G-12797)*

Pipeline Packaging ....G 248 743-0248
Troy *(G-17302)*

Precision Packing Corporation ....E 586 756-8700
Warren *(G-17973)*

R & J Manufacturing Company ....F 248 669-2460
Commerce Township *(G-3568)*

R H M Rubber & Manufacturing ....G 248 624-8277
Novi *(G-12522)*

Rhino Strapping Products Inc ....F 734 442-4040
Taylor *(G-16467)*

Rodzina Industries Inc ....G 810 235-2341
Flint *(G-5755)*

▲ **Roger Zatkoff Company** ....E 248 478-2400
Farmington Hills *(G-5372)*

Snyder Plastics Inc ....E 989 684-8355
Bay City *(G-1403)*

Speyside Real Estate LLC ....F 248 354-7700
Southfield *(G-15707)*

Spray Booth Products Inc ....E 313 766-4400
Redford *(G-13773)*

▲ **Tts Oldco LLC** ....E 810 655-3900
Fenton *(G-5511)*

▲ **U S Graphite Inc** ....E 989 755-0441
Saginaw *(G-14783)*

Uniflex Inc ....G 248 486-6000
Brighton *(G-2088)*

Unique Fabricating Inc ....A 248 853-2333
Auburn Hills *(G-1068)*

▲ **Unique Fabricating Na Inc** ....B 248 853-2333
Auburn Hills *(G-1069)*

Unique Fabricating Na Inc ....G 517 524-9010
Concord *(G-3656)*

Unique Fabricating Na Inc ....G 248 853-2333
Rochester Hills *(G-14136)*

Upper Peninsula Rubber Co Inc ....G 906 786-0460
Escanaba *(G-5104)*

◆ **Vibracoustic North America LP** ....E 269 637-2116
South Haven *(G-15421)*

▲ **Yates Industries Inc** ....D 586 778-7680
Saint Clair Shores *(G-14892)*

Zephyros Inc ....G 586 336-1600
Bruce Twp *(G-2188)*

3061 Molded, Extruded & Lathe-Cut Rubber Mechanical Goods

Advanced Manufacturing LLC ....G 231 826-3859
Falmouth *(G-5131)*

▲ **Akwel Cadillac Usa Inc** ....B 231 775-6571
Cadillac *(G-2309)*

Akwel Cadillac Usa Inc ....F 248 476-8072
Novi *(G-12361)*

Akwel Mexico Usa Inc ....E 231 775-6571
Cadillac *(G-2310)*

▲ **Akwel Usa Inc** ....F 231 775-6571
Cadillac *(G-2311)*

▲ **Anand Nvh North America Inc** ....C 810 724-2400
Imlay City *(G-8627)*

Armada Rubber Manufacturing Co ....D 586 784-9135
Armada *(G-731)*

Basic Rubber and Plastics Co ....E 248 360-7400
Walled Lake *(G-17664)*

Black River Manufacturing Inc ....E 810 982-9812
Port Huron *(G-13459)*

BRC Rubber & Plastics Inc ....G 248 745-9200
Auburn Hills *(G-833)*

▲ **Cooper-Stndard Indus Spclty Gr** ....D 248 596-5900
Northville *(G-12209)*

▲ **Creative Foam Corporation** ....C 810 629-4149
Fenton *(G-5467)*

Dawson Manufacturing Company ....C 269 925-0100
Benton Harbor *(G-1545)*

Die Stampco Inc ....F 989 893-7790
Bay City *(G-1344)*

▲ **Fluid Hutchinson Management** ....D 248 679-1327
Auburn Hills *(G-903)*

Four Star Rubber Inc ....G 810 632-3335
Commerce Township *(G-3532)*

◆ **Freudenberg N Amer Ltd Partnr** ....G 734 354-5505
Plymouth *(G-13169)*

◆ **Freudenberg-Nok General Partnr** ....C 734 451-0020
Plymouth *(G-13170)*

▲ **HP Pelzer Auto Systems Inc** ....E 248 280-1010
Troy *(G-17155)*

▲ **Hutchnson Antvbrtion Systems I** ....B 616 459-4541
Grand Rapids *(G-6826)*

Hutchnson Antvbrtion Systems I ....C 231 775-9737
Cadillac *(G-2336)*

▲ **Pullman Company** ....F 734 243-8000
Monroe *(G-11571)*

R & J Manufacturing Company ....F 248 669-2460
Commerce Township *(G-3568)*

R H M Rubber & Manufacturing ....G 248 624-8277
Novi *(G-12522)*

Reliance Rubber Industries Inc ....G 734 641-4100
Westland *(G-18415)*

Rosta USA Corp ....F 269 841-5448
Benton Harbor *(G-1581)*

Uchiyama Mktg & Dev Amer LLC ....F 248 859-3986
Novi *(G-12562)*

Uniflex Inc ....G 248 486-6000
Brighton *(G-2088)*

◆ **Vibracoustic North America LP** ....E 269 637-2116
South Haven *(G-15421)*

Vibracoustic Usa Inc ....G 734 254-9140
Northville *(G-12269)*

▲ **Vibracoustic Usa Inc** ....C 269 637-2116
South Haven *(G-15422)*

Vibracoustic Usa Inc ....B 810 648-2100
Sandusky *(G-15070)*

Vibracoustic Usa Inc ....G 810 648-2100
Sandusky *(G-15071)*

3069 Fabricated Rubber Prdts, NEC

Advanced Rubber & Plastic ....G 586 754-7398
Warren *(G-17693)*

Advanced Rubber Tech Inc ....F 231 775-3112
Cadillac *(G-2308)*

Aerofab Company Inc ....F 248 542-0051
Ferndale *(G-5519)*

▲ **Airboss Flexible Products Co** ....C 248 852-5500
Auburn Hills *(G-776)*

Americo Corporation ....G 313 565-6550
Dearborn *(G-3807)*

▲ **Anand Nvh North America Inc** ....C 810 724-2400
Imlay City *(G-8627)*

▼ **Apex Marine Inc** ....D 989 681-4300
Saint Louis *(G-14986)*

Aptargroup Inc ....G 989 631-8030
Midland *(G-11322)*

Armada Rubber Manufacturing Co ....D 586 784-9135
Armada *(G-731)*

Basic Rubber and Plastics Co ....E 248 360-7400
Walled Lake *(G-17664)*

Blade Industrial Products Inc ....G 248 773-7400
Wixom *(G-18621)*

◆ **Bushings Inc** ....F 248 650-0603
Rochester Hills *(G-13968)*

Cartex Corporation ....G 610 759-1650
Troy *(G-17005)*

▲ **Changan US RES & Dev Ctr Inc** ....G 734 259-6440
Plymouth *(G-13145)*

Cooper-Stndard Indus Spclty Gr ....F 330 339-3373
Northville *(G-12208)*

▲ **Cooper-Stndard Indus Spclty Gr** ....D 248 596-5900
Northville *(G-12209)*

▲ **Creative Foam Corporation** ....C 810 629-4149
Fenton *(G-5467)*

◆ **Dawson Manufacturing Company** ....C 269 925-0100
Benton Harbor *(G-1544)*

◆ **Day International Inc** ....E 734 781-4600
Livonia *(G-10174)*

Derby Fabg Solutions LLC ....D 616 866-1650
Rockford *(G-14164)*

Ds Sales Inc ....E 248 960-6411
Wixom *(G-18648)*

Dti Molded Products Inc ....F 248 647-0400
Bingham Farms *(G-1695)*

▲ **Ehc Inc** ....G 313 259-2266
Troy *(G-17079)*

▲ **Evans Industries Inc** ....G 313 259-2266
Troy *(G-17100)*

Exotic Rubber & Plastics Corp ....D 248 477-2122
New Hudson *(G-12053)*

First Class Tire Shredders Inc ....F 810 639-4466
Clio *(G-3398)*

▲ **Gaco Sourcing LLC** ....G 248 633-2656
Birmingham *(G-1728)*

▲ **Go Cat Feather Toys** ....G 517 543-7519
Charlotte *(G-2759)*

Great Lake Foam Technologies ....F 517 563-8030
Hanover *(G-7624)*

Great Lakes Rubber Co ....E 248 624-5710
Wixom *(G-18669)*

Green Polymeric Materials Inc ....E 313 933-7390
Detroit *(G-4280)*

H A King Co Inc ....G 248 280-0006
Royal Oak *(G-14542)*

Henniges Auto Holdings Inc ....B 248 340-4100
Auburn Hills *(G-924)*

HI-Tech Flexible Products Inc ....E 517 783-5911
Jackson *(G-8903)*

Hold-It Inc ....G 810 984-4213
Port Huron *(G-13482)*

◆ **Hutchinson Corporation** ....G 616 459-4541
Grand Rapids *(G-6825)*

Hutchinson Seal Corporation ....E 248 375-4190
Auburn Hills *(G-931)*

▲ **Hutchinson Sealing Systems Inc** ....D 248 375-3720
Auburn Hills *(G-932)*

▲ **Hutchnson Antvbrtion Systems I** ....B 616 459-4541
Grand Rapids *(G-6826)*

Hutchnson Antvbrtion Systems I ....C 231 775-9737
Cadillac *(G-2336)*

Inoac Interior Systems LLC ....F 248 488-7610
Farmington Hills *(G-5270)*

Interdyne Inc ....F 517 849-2281
Jonesville *(G-9089)*

Jedtco Corp ....E 734 326-3010
Westland *(G-18388)*

Jfp Acquisition LLC ....E 517 787-8877
Jackson *(G-8920)*

Kent Manufacturing Company ....D 616 454-9495
Grand Rapids *(G-6889)*

Korens ....G 248 817-5188
Rochester Hills *(G-14046)*

◆ **Luebke & Vogt Corporation** ....G 248 449-3232
Novi *(G-12466)*

Massee Products Ltd ....G 269 684-8255
Niles *(G-12142)*

MCS Consultants Inc ....G 810 229-4222
Brighton *(G-2029)*

Meccom Industrial Products Co ....F 586 463-2828
Clinton Township *(G-3297)*

Michigan Roller Inc ....G 269 651-2304
Sturgis *(G-16307)*

Midwest Rubber Company ....C 810 376-2085
Deckerville *(G-3955)*

Milsco LLC ....E 517 787-3650
Jackson *(G-8965)*

Missaukee Molded Rubber Inc ....F 231 839-5309
Lake City *(G-9552)*

◆ **Mykin Inc** ....F 248 667-8030
South Lyon *(G-15448)*

Northern Michigan Leather ....G 231 675-4712
Charlevoix *(G-2722)*

Northern Tire Inc ....F 906 486-4463
Ishpeming *(G-8779)*

Peck Engineering Inc ....E 313 534-2950
Redford *(G-13753)*

Pegasus Tool LLC ....G 313 255-5900
Detroit *(G-4515)*

Plasticore Inc ....F 877 573-3090
Detroit *(G-4528)*

PRA Company ....D 989 846-1029
Standish *(G-15895)*

Preferred Flooring MI LLC ....F 616 279-2162
Walker *(G-17650)*

R H M Rubber & Manufacturing ....G 248 624-8277
Novi *(G-12522)*

R5 Construction Inc ....F 855 480-7663
Middleville *(G-11311)*

Rehau Incorporated ....G 269 651-7845
Sturgis *(G-16321)*

S I C

Employee Codes: A=Over 500 employees, B=251-500
C=101-250, D=51-100, E=20-50, F=10-19, G=3-9

2022 Harris Michigan
Industrial Directory

787

30 RUBBER AND MISCELLANEOUS PLASTICS PRODUCTS

Republic Roller Corporation .... E 269 273-9591
  Three Rivers *(G-16583)*
Rex M Tubbs .... G 734 459-3180
  Plymouth *(G-13281)*
Rubber Enterprises Inc .... G 810 724-9200
  Imlay City *(G-8645)*
Rubber Tucker LLC .... G 586 216-7071
  Clinton Township *(G-3345)*
Schroth Enterprises Inc .... F 586 759-4240
  Grosse Pointe Farms *(G-7540)*
Simolex Rubber Corporation .... F 734 453-4500
  Plymouth *(G-13299)*
▲ Specialty Pdts & Polymers Inc .... E 269 684-5931
  Niles *(G-12170)*
Thunder Technologies LLC .... F 248 844-4875
  Rochester Hills *(G-14126)*
Tillerman Jfp LLC .... G 616 443-8346
  Middleville *(G-11315)*
Tissue Seal LLC .... F 734 213-5530
  Ann Arbor *(G-692)*
◆ Toyoda Gosei North Amer Corp ..... C 248 280-2100
  Troy *(G-17397)*
◆ Trico Products Corporation .... C 248 371-1700
  Rochester Hills *(G-14132)*
Uniflex Inc .... F 248 486-6000
  Brighton *(G-2088)*
▲ Vte Inc .... E 231 539-8000
  Pellston *(G-12968)*
WI Molding of Michigan LLC .... D 269 327-3075
  Portage *(G-13633)*
▲ Zhongding Saling Parts USA Inc .... G 734 241-8870
  Plymouth *(G-13342)*

3081 Plastic Unsupported Sheet & Film

A-Pac Manufacturing Company .... E 616 791-7222
  Grand Rapids *(G-6412)*
Berry Global Inc .... G 616 772-4635
  Zeeland *(G-18997)*
Berry Global Inc .... G 269 435-2425
  Constantine *(G-3663)*
▲ Cadillac Products Inc .... B 248 813-8200
  Troy *(G-16992)*
Cadillac Products Inc .... E 586 774-1700
  Roseville *(G-14382)*
Cadillac Products Inc .... F 989 766-2294
  Rogers City *(G-14208)*
Cadillac Products Packaging Co .... C 248 879-5000
  Troy *(G-16993)*
Dow Chemical Company .... C 989 636-4406
  Midland *(G-11343)*
◆ Dow Chemical Company .... A 989 636-1000
  Midland *(G-11341)*
Dow Chemical Company .... G 989 636-1000
  Midland *(G-11345)*
Dow Chemical Company .... G 989 636-0540
  Midland *(G-11349)*
Dow Chemical Company .... D 989 636-5409
  Midland *(G-11352)*
Dow Inc .... A 989 636-1000
  Midland *(G-11354)*
▲ Durakon Industries Inc .... G 608 742-5301
  Lapeer *(G-9928)*
▲ Encore Commercial Products Inc .. F 248 354-4090
  Farmington Hills *(G-5233)*
▲ Filcon Inc .... F 989 386-2986
  Clare *(G-2979)*
Jsp International LLC .... G 248 397-3200
  Madison Heights *(G-10755)*
Jsp International LLC .... G 724 477-5100
  Detroit *(G-4343)*
Kraft-Wrap Inc .... E 586 755-2050
  Warren *(G-17896)*
◆ Link Tech Inc .... G 269 427-8297
  Bangor *(G-1129)*
Lotus Technologies LLC .... F 313 550-1889
  Detroit *(G-4406)*
▲ Mpf Acquisitions Inc .... E 269 672-5511
  Martin *(G-11080)*
Petoskey Plastics Inc .... D 231 347-2602
  Petoskey *(G-13016)*
Quality Transparent Bag Inc .... F 989 893-3561
  Bay City *(G-1391)*
Spire Michigan Acquisition LLC .... G 616 458-4924
  Grand Rapids *(G-7220)*
◆ Thyssenkrupp Materials NA Inc .... E 248 233-5600
  Southfield *(G-15722)*
Total Vinyl Products Inc .... F 734 485-7280
  Whitmore Lake *(G-18548)*
Zenith Global LLC .... G 517 546-7402
  Howell *(G-8544)*

3082 Plastic Unsupported Profile Shapes

Alloy Exchange Inc .... F 616 863-0640
  Rockford *(G-14154)*
Dlhbowles Inc .... F 248 569-0652
  Southfield *(G-15541)*
Gazelle Prototype LLC .... G 616 844-1820
  Spring Lake *(G-15816)*
▲ Idemitsu Chemicals USA Corp ...... G 248 355-0666
  Southfield *(G-15599)*
Plastic Plaque Inc .... F 810 982-9591
  Port Huron *(G-13518)*
Porex Technologies Corp .... E 989 865-8200
  Saint Charles *(G-14807)*
Spiratex Company .... D 734 289-4800
  Monroe *(G-11576)*
◆ Tg Fluid Systems USA Corp .... B 810 220-6161
  Brighton *(G-2078)*
◆ Trico Products Corporation .... C 248 371-1700
  Rochester Hills *(G-14132)*

3083 Plastic Laminated Plate & Sheet

Advanced Drainage Systems Inc .... G 989 723-5208
  Owosso *(G-12819)*
Bangor Plastics Inc .... E 269 427-7971
  Bangor *(G-1128)*
Basic Rubber and Plastics Co .... E 248 360-7400
  Walled Lake *(G-17664)*
▼ Duo-Gard Industries Inc .... D 734 207-9700
  Canton *(G-2456)*
H & R Wood Specialties Inc .... E 269 628-2181
  Gobles *(G-6217)*
Hanwha Azdel Inc .... G 810 629-2496
  Warren *(G-17847)*
J Kaltz & Co .... G 616 942-6070
  Grand Rapids *(G-6856)*
Janice Morse Inc .... E 248 624-7300
  West Bloomfield *(G-18293)*
Kent Manufacturing Company .... D 616 454-9495
  Grand Rapids *(G-6889)*
Key Plastics LLC .... F 248 449-6100
  Plymouth *(G-13214)*
Lwhs Ltd .... D 616 452-5300
  Grand Rapids *(G-6954)*
Max3 LLC .... E 269 925-2044
  Benton Harbor *(G-1570)*
McKechnie Vhcl Cmpnnts USA Inc ... B 218 894-1218
  Roseville *(G-14438)*
Paramount Solutions Inc .... G 586 914-0708
  Ray *(G-13702)*
Paul Murphy Plastics Co .... E 586 774-4880
  Roseville *(G-14460)*
Plascore Inc .... G 616 772-1220
  Zeeland *(G-19071)*
Polyply Composites LLC .... E 616 842-6330
  Grand Haven *(G-6344)*
Rehau Incorporated .... G 269 651-7845
  Sturgis *(G-16321)*
Shawmut LLC .... G 810 987-2222
  Port Huron *(G-13526)*
Spiratex Company .... D 734 289-4800
  Monroe *(G-11576)*
Summit Polymers Inc .... B 269 323-1301
  Portage *(G-13624)*
Summit Polymers Inc .... G 269 651-1643
  Sturgis *(G-16326)*
◆ Total Plastics Resources LLC .... D 269 344-0009
  Kalamazoo *(G-9358)*
Tuscarora Inc -Vs .... G 989 729-2780
  Owosso *(G-12864)*
▼ Vidon Plastics Inc .... D 810 667-0634
  Lapeer *(G-9965)*

3084 Plastic Pipe

Advanced Drainage Systems Inc .... G 989 761-7610
  Clifford *(G-3130)*
Advanced Drainage Systems Inc .... G 989 723-5208
  Owosso *(G-12819)*
Cff Inc .... G 517 242-6903
  Battle Creek *(G-1208)*
▲ Conley Composites LLC .... G 918 299-5051
  Grand Rapids *(G-6594)*
Creek Plastics LLC .... F 517 423-1003
  Adrian *(G-57)*
▲ Ethylene LLC .... E 616 554-3464
  Kentwood *(G-9451)*
▼ Vidon Plastics Inc .... D 810 667-0634
  Lapeer *(G-9965)*

3085 Plastic Bottles

▲ Inoac Usa Inc .... E 248 619-7031
  Troy *(G-17169)*
Novares US LLC .... G 616 554-3555
  Grand Rapids *(G-7051)*
Plastipak Packaging Inc .... G 734 326-6184
  Westland *(G-18406)*
▲ Plastipak Packaging Inc .... F 734 467-7519
  Romulus *(G-14320)*
▼ R N Fink Manufacturing Co .... E 517 655-4351
  Williamston *(G-18580)*

3086 Plastic Foam Prdts

Action Fabricators Inc .... C 616 957-2032
  Grand Rapids *(G-6423)*
Advance Engineering Company .... E 989 435-3641
  Beaverton *(G-1423)*
Aldez North America .... F 586 530-5314
  Clinton Township *(G-3161)*
◆ Armaly Sponge Company .... E 248 669-2100
  Commerce Township *(G-3512)*
▲ Aspen Technologies Inc .... D 248 446-1485
  Brighton *(G-1947)*
Bespro Pattern Inc .... E 586 268-6970
  Madison Heights *(G-10681)*
Bremen Corp .... F 574 546-4238
  Fenton *(G-5460)*
Briggs Industries Inc .... E 586 749-5191
  Chesterfield *(G-2852)*
◆ Brooklyn Products Intl .... E 517 592-2185
  Brooklyn *(G-2122)*
Cantrick Kip Co .... G 248 644-7622
  Birmingham *(G-1719)*
▲ Carcoustics Usa Inc .... D 517 548-6700
  Howell *(G-8435)*
Classic Container Corporation .... C 734 853-3000
  Livonia *(G-10159)*
Creative Foam Cmpsite Systems ...... G 810 629-4149
  Flint *(G-5676)*
Creative Foam Corporation .... G 269 782-3483
  Dowagiac *(G-4779)*
▲ Creative Foam Corporation .... C 810 629-4149
  Fenton *(G-5467)*
Creative Foam Corporation .... G 810 714-0140
  Fenton *(G-5468)*
Dart Container Corp California .... D 517 244-6408
  Mason *(G-11121)*
Dart Container Corp Florida .... G 800 248-5960
  Mason *(G-11122)*
◆ Dart Container Corp Georgia .... B 517 676-3800
  Mason *(G-11123)*
◆ Dart Container Corp Kentucky ...... F 517 676-3800
  Mason *(G-11124)*
◆ Dart Container Corporation .... A 517 676-3800
  Mason *(G-11126)*
Dart Container Michigan LLC .... A 248 669-3767
  Wixom *(G-18643)*
Dart Container Michigan LLC .... A 517 244-6249
  Mason *(G-11127)*
Dart Container Michigan LLC .... A 888 327-8001
  Lansing *(G-9828)*
Dart Container Michigan LLC .... A 517 694-9455
  Holt *(G-8309)*
Dart Container Michigan LLC .... A 517 676-3803
  Mason *(G-11129)*
◆ Dart Container Michigan LLC .... A 800 248-5960
  Mason *(G-11128)*
Derby Fabg Solutions LLC .... D 616 866-1650
  Rockford *(G-14164)*
Dow Chemical Company .... C 989 636-4406
  Midland *(G-11343)*
◆ Dow Chemical Company .... A 989 636-1000
  Midland *(G-11341)*
Dow Chemical Company .... G 989 636-0540
  Midland *(G-11349)*
Dow Chemical Company .... D 989 636-5409
  Midland *(G-11352)*
Dow Inc .... A 989 636-1000
  Midland *(G-11354)*
Envirolite LLC .... D 888 222-2191
  Coldwater *(G-3432)*
▲ Envirolite LLC .... F 248 792-3184
  Troy *(G-17094)*
Everest Manufacturing Inc .... F 313 401-2608
  Farmington Hills *(G-5238)*
◆ Floracraft Corporation .... C 231 845-5127
  Ludington *(G-10536)*
◆ Foam Factory Incorporated .... E 586 739-7449
  Macomb *(G-10596)*

Fomcore LLC .... D 231 366-4791
  Muskegon *(G-11819)*
Fxi Novi .... G 248 994-0630
  Novi *(G-12421)*
▲ G & T Industries Inc .... D 616 452-8611
  Byron Center *(G-2271)*
Gemini Plastics Inc .... C 989 658-8557
  Ubly *(G-17476)*
Grand Haven Gasket Company ...... E 616 842-7682
  Grand Haven *(G-6303)*
Green Polymeric Materials Inc .... E 313 933-7390
  Detroit *(G-4280)*
▲ Harbor Foam Inc .... G 616 855-8150
  Grandville *(G-7386)*
High Tech Insulators Inc .... F 734 525-9030
  Livonia *(G-10239)*
Huntington Foam LLC .... C 661 225-9951
  Greenville *(G-7493)*
Integrity Spray Foam LLC .... G 231 631-6084
  Traverse City *(G-16724)*
Inter-Pack Corporation .... F 734 242-7755
  Monroe *(G-11551)*
Janesville LLC .... D 248 948-1811
  Southfield *(G-15611)*
◆ Jsj Corporation .... E 616 842-6350
  Grand Haven *(G-6324)*
Kent Manufacturing Company .... D 616 454-9495
  Grand Rapids *(G-6889)*
Kringer Industrial Corporation .... F 519 818-3509
  Warren *(G-17897)*
◆ Leon Interiors Inc .... B 616 422-7557
  Holland *(G-8125)*
Light Metal Forming Corp .... F 248 851-3984
  Bloomfield Hills *(G-1831)*
▲ Michigan Foam Products Inc ..... F 616 452-9611
  Grand Rapids *(G-6989)*
Mitten Spray Foam Insul LLC .... G 616 250-8355
  Wyoming *(G-18895)*
N Pack Ship Center .... G 906 863-4095
  Menominee *(G-11253)*
▲ Nanosystems Inc .... F 734 274-0020
  Ann Arbor *(G-589)*
Nu-Pak Solutions Inc .... F 231 755-1662
  Norton Shores *(G-12321)*
Package Design & Mfg Inc .... E 248 486-4390
  Brighton *(G-2046)*
Packaging Engineering LLC .... G 248 437-9444
  Brighton *(G-2047)*
Pedmic Converting Inc .... F 810 679-9600
  Croswell *(G-3734)*
Plascore Inc .... E 616 772-1220
  Zeeland *(G-19071)*
▲ Plasteel Corporation .... E 313 562-5400
  Inkster *(G-8670)*
Pratt Classic Container Inc .... E 734 525-0410
  Livonia *(G-10372)*
Reklein Plastics Incorporated .... G 586 739-8850
  Sterling Heights *(G-16145)*
Revstone Industries LLC .... G 248 351-1000
  Troy *(G-17331)*
▲ Rogers Foam Automotive Corp .. E 810 820-6323
  Flint *(G-5756)*
Russell R Peters Co LLC .... G 989 732-0660
  Gaylord *(G-6157)*
Schmitz Foam Products LLC .... E 517 781-6615
  Coldwater *(G-3452)*
Sekisui America Corporation .... G 517 279-7587
  Coldwater *(G-3453)*
Sekisui Plastics US A Inc .... F 248 308-3000
  Wixom *(G-18750)*
Sekisui Voltek LLC .... C 517 279-7587
  Coldwater *(G-3455)*
▲ Simco Automotive Trim Inc .... E 616 608-9818
  Grand Rapids *(G-7199)*
Sonoco Prtective Solutions Inc .... G 989 723-3720
  Owosso *(G-12857)*
Southwestern Foam Tech Inc .... G 616 726-1677
  Grand Rapids *(G-7205)*
▲ Special Projects Engineering ..... G 517 676-8525
  Mason *(G-11157)*
Surrey USA LLC .... G 800 248-5960
  Mason *(G-11159)*
Sweetheart Corp .... G 847 405-2100
  Mason *(G-11160)*
Transpak Inc .... E 586 264-2064
  Sterling Heights *(G-16209)*
◆ Ufp Technologies Inc .... D 616 949-8100
  Grand Rapids *(G-7294)*
Unique Fabricating Inc .... A 248 853-2333
  Auburn Hills *(G-1068)*

▲ Unique Fabricating Na Inc .... B 248 853-2333
  Auburn Hills *(G-1069)*
Unique Fabricating Na Inc .... G 248 853-2333
  Rochester Hills *(G-14136)*
Unique Molded Foam Tech Inc ...... F 517 524-9010
  Concord *(G-3657)*
Unique-Chardan Inc .... D 419 636-6900
  Auburn Hills *(G-1070)*
▲ Woodbridge Holdings Inc .... G 248 288-0100
  Troy *(G-17451)*

3087 Custom Compounding Of Purchased Plastic Resins

Aci Plastics Inc .... E 810 767-3800
  Flint *(G-5636)*
▲ Aci Plastics Inc .... E 810 767-3800
  Flint *(G-5637)*
▲ Alumilite Corporation .... F 269 488-4000
  Galesburg *(G-6073)*
Amplas Compounding LLC .... E 586 795-2555
  Sterling Heights *(G-15931)*
▲ Azon Usa Inc .... F 269 385-5942
  Kalamazoo *(G-9129)*
Azon Usa Inc .... G 269 385-5942
  Kalamazoo *(G-9130)*
Cass Polymers .... E 517 543-7510
  Charlotte *(G-2739)*
Clean Tech Inc .... G 734 529-2475
  Dundee *(G-4812)*
▲ Clean Tech Inc .... E 734 455-3600
  Plymouth *(G-13147)*
Clean Tech Inc .... E 734 529-2475
  Dundee *(G-4811)*
▲ Eco Bio Plastics Midland Inc .... F 989 496-1934
  Midland *(G-11360)*
Georgia-Pacific LLC .... G 989 348-7275
  Grayling *(G-7461)*
Material Difference Tech LLC .... F 888 818-1283
  Macomb *(G-10614)*
Nano Materials & Processes Inc ... G 248 529-3873
  Milford *(G-11475)*
▲ Portland Plastics Co .... F 517 647-4115
  Portland *(G-13640)*
Rhe-Tech LLC .... G 517 223-4874
  Fowlerville *(G-5855)*
Rhe-Tech LLC .... G 734 769-3558
  Whitmore Lake *(G-18545)*
Ssb Holdings Inc .... E 586 755-1660
  Rochester Hills *(G-14117)*

3088 Plastic Plumbing Fixtures

Aquatic Co .... C 269 279-7461
  Three Rivers *(G-16564)*
◆ Conway Products Corporation .. E 616 698-2601
  Grand Rapids *(G-6603)*
Duo-Form Acquisition Corp .... C 269 663-8525
  Edwardsburg *(G-5005)*
Lakeshore Marble Company Inc ... F 269 429-8241
  Stevensville *(G-16257)*
▼ Lyons Industries Inc .... C 269 782-3404
  Dowagiac *(G-4787)*
◆ Masco Corporation .... A 313 274-7400
  Livonia *(G-10302)*
Masco Corporation of Indiana .... G 810 664-8501
  Lapeer *(G-9947)*
▼ Nordic Products Inc .... C 616 940-4036
  Grand Rapids *(G-7046)*
R A Townsend Company .... F 989 498-7000
  Saginaw *(G-14734)*
Rick Owen & Jason Vogel Partnr .. G 734 417-3401
  Dexter *(G-4752)*
Warm Rain Corporation .... D 906 482-3750
  Calumet *(G-2417)*
Zimmer Marble Co Inc .... F 517 787-1500
  Jackson *(G-9041)*

3089 Plastic Prdts

▲ 21st Century Plastics Corp .... D 517 645-2695
  Potterville *(G-13645)*
2255srv LLC .... F 616 678-4900
  Kent City *(G-9425)*
3d Polymers Inc .... F 248 588-5562
  Orchard Lake *(G-12715)*
A & D Plastics Inc .... E 734 455-2255
  Plymouth *(G-13108)*
A M R Inc .... G 810 329-9049
  East China *(G-4854)*
A S Plus Industries Inc .... G 586 741-0400
  Clinton Township *(G-3148)*

Aak Fabrication & Plastics Inc .... G 734 525-1391
  Southfield *(G-15468)*
◆ ABC Group Holdings Inc .... G 248 352-3706
  Southfield *(G-15470)*
ABC Packaging Eqp & Mtls Inc ..... F 616 784-2330
  Comstock Park *(G-3584)*
Able Solutions LLC .... G 810 216-6106
  Port Huron *(G-13430)*
Accurate Injection Molds Inc .... E 586 954-2553
  Clinton Township *(G-3152)*
▲ Acm Plastic Products Inc .... D 269 651-7888
  Sturgis *(G-16280)*
Acrylic Specialties .... G 248 588-4390
  Madison Heights *(G-10658)*
Active Plastics Inc .... F 616 813-5109
  Caledonia *(G-2367)*
▲ Adac Door Components Inc ..... B 616 957-0311
  Grand Rapids *(G-6427)*
▲ Adac Plastics Inc .... E 616 957-0311
  Grand Rapids *(G-6428)*
Adac Plastics Inc .... E 231 777-2645
  Muskegon *(G-11762)*
Adac Plastics Inc .... F 616 957-0311
  Grand Rapids *(G-6429)*
Adac Plastics Inc .... F 616 957-0520
  Muskegon *(G-11763)*
Adac Plastics Inc .... E 616 957-0311
  Muskegon *(G-11764)*
▲ Adduxi .... E 248 564-2000
  Rochester Hills *(G-13942)*
Adept Plastic Finishing Inc .... G 248 863-5930
  Wixom *(G-18596)*
Adept Plastic Finishing Inc .... G 248 374-5870
  Wixom *(G-18597)*
Advance Engineering Company .... E 989 435-3641
  Beaverton *(G-1423)*
▲ Advanced Auto Trends Inc .... E 248 628-6111
  Oxford *(G-12871)*
Advanced Auto Trends Inc .... E 810 672-9203
  Snover *(G-15389)*
Advanced Auto Trends Inc .... E 248 628-4850
  Oxford *(G-12872)*
Advanced BInding Solutions LLC .. E 920 664-1469
  Wallace *(G-17659)*
Advanced Composite Tech Inc ..... G 248 709-9097
  Rochester *(G-13889)*
Advanced Fibermolding Inc .... E 231 768-5177
  Leroy *(G-10004)*
Advanced Rubber & Plastic .... G 586 754-7398
  Warren *(G-17693)*
▲ Advanced Special Tools Inc ..... C 269 962-9697
  Battle Creek *(G-1179)*
Aees Power Systems Ltd Partnr ... G 269 668-4429
  Farmington Hills *(G-5160)*
▲ Affinity Custom Molding Inc ..... E 269 496-8423
  Mendon *(G-11215)*
Agape Plastics Inc .... C 616 735-4091
  Grand Rapids *(G-6437)*
Aim Plastics Inc .... E 586 954-2553
  Clinton Township *(G-3159)*
AIN Plastics .... F 248 356-4000
  Southfield *(G-15472)*
Airpark Plastics LLC .... F 989 846-1029
  Standish *(G-15886)*
Aktis Engrg Solutions Inc .... G 313 450-2420
  Southfield *(G-15474)*
Akwel Cadillac Usa Inc .... G 248 848-9599
  Farmington Hills *(G-5166)*
▲ Akwel Cadillac Usa Inc .... B 231 775-6571
  Cadillac *(G-2309)*
Akwel Cadillac Usa Inc .... F 248 476-8072
  Novi *(G-12361)*
▲ Akwel Usa Inc .... F 231 775-6571
  Cadillac *(G-2311)*
Albar Industries Inc .... B 810 667-0150
  Lapeer *(G-9911)*
Alco Plastics Inc .... D 586 752-4527
  Romeo *(G-14219)*
Alp Lghting Cmpnnts Charlevoix .. F 231 547-6584
  Charlevoix *(G-2708)*
Alp Lighting Ceiling Pdts Inc .... G 231 547-6584
  Charlevoix *(G-2709)*
Alternative Systems Inc .... F 269 384-2008
  Kalamazoo *(G-9111)*
▲ Alumilite Corporation .... F 269 488-4000
  Galesburg *(G-6073)*
Aluminum Textures Inc .... E 616 538-3144
  Grandville *(G-7364)*
◆ Amcor Rigid Packaging Usa LLC .. D 734 428-9741
  Manchester *(G-10880)*

Employee Codes: A=Over 500 employees, B=251-500
C=101-250, D=51-100, E=20-50, F=10-19, G=3-9

30 RUBBER AND MISCELLANEOUS PLASTICS PRODUCTS

Company	Code	Phone
▲ Ameri-Kart(mi) Corp — Cassopolis (G-2625)	C	269 641-5811
American Standard Windows — Farmington Hills (G-5170)	F	734 788-2261
Americo Corporation — Dearborn (G-3807)	G	313 565-6550
AMP Innovative Tech LLC — Harrison Township (G-7686)	E	586 465-2700
Amplas Compounding LLC — Sterling Heights (G-15931)	F	586 795-2555
Ann Arbor Plastics Inc — Saline (G-15003)	G	734 944-0800
Antara Systems LLC — Allendale (G-214)	D	616 895-7766
Anticipated Plastics Inc — Warren (G-17707)	F	586 427-9450
Antolin St Clair LLC — China (G-2968)	C	810 329-1045
ARC Group Worldwide Inc — Hudson (G-8547)	G	517 448-8954
◆ Armaly Sponge Company — Commerce Township (G-3512)	E	248 669-2100
Armoured Rsstnce McHanisms Inc — Fowlerville (G-5832)	F	517 223-7618
Artjay Industries Incorporated — Warren (G-17715)	D	810 773-6450
Astar Inc — Niles (G-12111)	E	574 234-2137
Atlantic Precision Pdts Inc — Shelby Township (G-15173)	G	586 532-9420
Atlantic Precision Pdts Inc — Shelby Township (G-15174)	F	586 532-9420
Atra Plastics Inc — Plymouth (G-13128)	F	734 237-3393
Automotive Manufacturing — Sunfield (G-16333)	G	517 566-8174
Automotive Plastics Recycling — Flint (G-5648)	F	810 767-3800
Avon Plastic Products Inc — Rochester Hills (G-13960)	E	248 852-1000
B & H Plastic Co Inc — Richmond (G-13834)	F	586 727-7100
B & N Plastics Inc — Warren (G-17723)	G	586 758-0030
B C & A Co — Saline (G-15005)	E	734 429-3129
Bangor Plastics Inc — Bangor (G-1128)	E	269 427-7971
Batts Group Ltd — Grand Rapids (G-6496)	G	616 956-3053
Bdgn Corporation — Hudsonville (G-8570)	C	616 669-9040
Beechcraft Products Inc — Durand (G-4840)	E	989 288-2606
▲ Belmont Engineered Plas LLC — Belmont (G-1501)	D	616 785-6279
Belmont Plastics Solutions LLC — Belmont (G-1502)	F	616 340-3147
Bentzer Incorporated — Edwardsburg (G-5000)	F	269 663-3649
Bermar Associates Inc — Troy (G-16975)	F	248 589-2460
Berry Global Inc — Constantine (G-3663)	G	269 435-2425
Berry Global Inc — Zeeland (G-18997)	G	616 772-4635
Best Impressions Inc — Fraser (G-5904)	G	313 839-9000
◆ Blackmore Co Inc — Belleville (G-1481)	D	734 483-8661
Blade Industrial Products Inc — Wixom (G-18621)	G	248 773-7400
Bloem LLC — Hudsonville (G-8571)	E	616 622-6344
Blue Fire Manufacturing LLC — Waterford (G-18104)	E	248 714-7166
▲ Blue Thumb Distributing Inc — Saginaw (G-14617)	E	989 921-3474
Bomaur Quality Plastics Inc — Fenton (G-5459)	F	810 629-9701
Boral Building Products Inc — Wixom (G-18625)	C	800 521-8486
Bradys Fence Company Inc — South Rockwood (G-15463)	G	313 492-8804
Bridgville Plastics Inc — Stevensville (G-16241)	F	269 465-6516
▼ Butler Plastics Company — Marine City (G-10956)	F	810 765-8811
C E B Tooling Inc — Burr Oak (G-2211)	G	269 489-2251
C-Plastics Inc — Nunica (G-12577)	E	616 837-7396
▲ Cadillac Engineered Plas Inc — Cadillac (G-2321)	F	231 775-2900
Cadillac Products Inc — Rogers City (G-14208)	F	989 766-2294
▲ Cadillac Products Inc — Troy (G-16992)	B	248 813-8200
Camcar Plastics Inc — Muskegon (G-11789)	F	231 726-5000
Capsonic Automotive Inc — Auburn Hills (G-839)	E	248 754-1100
Carcostics Tech Ctr N Amer Inc — Howell (G-8434)	G	248 251-1737
▲ Cascade Engineering Inc — Grand Rapids (G-6552)	A	616 975-4800
Cascade Engineering Inc — Grand Rapids (G-6553)	G	616 975-4767
Case-Free Inc — Grand Rapids (G-6558)	G	616 245-3136
Castano Plastics Inc — Wolverine Lake (G-18796)	C	248 624-3724
Castino Corporation — Romulus (G-14261)	E	734 941-7200
Cel Plastics Inc — Muskegon (G-11790)	F	231 777-3941
Century Plastics LLC — Macomb (G-10584)	F	586 697-5752
▲ Century Plastics LLC — Shelby Township (G-15184)	C	586 566-3900
Certainteed LLC — Jackson (G-8837)	G	517 787-8898
Cg Plastics Inc — Comstock Park (G-3594)	F	616 785-1900
Chadko LLC — Grand Haven (G-6284)	F	616 402-9207
▲ Chambers Industrial Tech Inc — Wyoming (G-18856)	F	616 249-8190
Champion Plastics Inc — Auburn Hills (G-842)	E	248 373-8995
CIE Automotive Usa Inc — Shelby Township (G-15187)	D	734 793-5320
CK Technologies — Hudsonville (G-8574)	F	616 836-6384
◆ Clarion Technologies Inc — Holland (G-7998)	F	616 698-7277
Clarion Technologies Inc — Greenville (G-7479)	F	616 754-1199
▲ Classic Die Inc — Grand Rapids (G-6570)	F	616 454-3760
Clearform — Caledonia (G-2372)	F	616 656-5359
Cme Plastics — Tecumseh (G-16492)	F	517 456-7722
Cni Plastics LLC — Charlotte (G-2744)	F	517 541-4960
◆ Colonial Engineering Inc — Portage (G-13553)	F	269 323-2495
▲ Colonial Manufacturing LLC — Benton Harbor (G-1540)	G	269 926-1000
Colonial Plastics Incorporated — Shelby Township (G-15191)	F	586 469-4944
Composite Techniques Inc — Grand Rapids (G-6589)	F	616 878-9795
Concord Industrial Corporation — Bloomfield Hills (G-1810)	G	248 646-9225
▲ Conley Composites LLC — Grand Rapids (G-6594)	F	918 299-5051
◆ Continental Plastics Co — Shelby Township (G-15195)	A	586 294-4600
Contour Engineering Inc — Shepherd (G-15376)	F	989 828-6526
▲ Craig Assembly Inc — Saint Clair (G-14821)	C	810 326-1374
Creative Foam Corporation — Fenton (G-5468)	G	810 714-0140
▲ Creative Foam Corporation — Fenton (G-5467)	C	810 629-4149
Creative Form Corp — Fenton (G-5467)	G	810 714-5860
Creative Repair Solutions LLC — Macomb (G-10586)	F	586 615-1517
Creative Techniques Inc — Orion (G-12727)	F	248 373-3050
Crescent Machining Inc — Oak Park (G-12601)	G	248 541-7010
◆ Cs Manufacturing Inc — Cedar Springs (G-2647)	F	616 696-2772
CSP Holding Corp — Auburn Hills (G-853)	D	248 237-7800
CSP Holding Corp — Auburn Hills (G-854)	G	248 724-4410
Cup Acquisition LLC — Grand Rapids (G-6619)	C	616 735-4410
Cusolar Industries Inc — Chesterfield (G-2863)	E	586 949-3880
D & W Awning and Window Co — Davison (G-3779)	E	810 742-0340
D B International LLC — Holland (G-8011)	E	616 796-0679
▲ D Find Corporation — Troy (G-17043)	E	248 641-2858
▲ D T M 1 Inc — Highland (G-7890)	E	248 889-9210
D&Js Plastics LLC — Hudsonville (G-8578)	E	616 745-5798
D&W Fine Pack LLC — Gladwin (G-6194)	D	866 296-2020
Dag Technology Inc — Grand Blanc (G-6240)	E	586 276-9310
▲ Daiek Products Inc — Troy (G-17044)	F	248 816-1360
Dana Incorporated — Novi (G-12392)	F	734 629-1200
▲ Dare Products Inc — Springfield (G-15864)	E	269 965-2307
Dart Container Corporation — Lansing (G-9684)	G	517 327-0613
Dart Container Corporation — Mason (G-11125)	G	517 676-3800
Datacover Inc — Pontiac (G-13358)	G	844 875-4076
Datacover Inc — Lake Orion (G-9601)	F	248 391-2163
Davalor Mold Company LLC — Chesterfield (G-2868)	C	586 598-0100
◆ Decade Products LLC — Grand Rapids (G-6637)	F	616 975-4965
Deckorators Inc — White Pigeon (G-18475)	D	616 365-4201
◆ Delfingen Us Inc — Rochester Hills (G-13991)	E	716 215-0300
Delfingen Us-Central Amer Inc — Rochester Hills (G-13992)	E	248 230-3500
◆ Delfingen Us-Holding Inc — Rochester Hills (G-13993)	E	248 230-3500
Deluxe Frame Company Inc — Auburn Hills (G-862)	E	248 373-8811
Denali Incorporated — Hartland (G-7768)	G	517 574-0047
Dendritic Nanotechnologies Inc — Midland (G-11338)	G	989 774-3096
Denso Manufacturing NC Inc — Battle Creek (G-1217)	A	269 441-2040
Derby Fabg Solutions LLC — Rockford (G-14164)	D	616 866-1650
Design Manufacturing LLC — Walker (G-17636)	E	616 647-2229
Die Stampco Inc — Bay City (G-1344)	F	989 893-7790
Display Pack Inc — Cedar Springs (G-2649)	C	616 451-3061
Diversified Engrg & Plas LLC — Jackson (G-8868)	D	517 789-8118
Djw Enterprises Inc — Crystal Falls (G-3742)	G	414 791-6192
DI Engineering & Tech Inc — Rochester Hills (G-13996)	G	248 852-6900
Dlhbowles Inc — Southfield (G-15541)	F	248 569-0652
Do-All Plastic Inc — Detroit (G-4185)	G	313 824-6565
◆ Do-It Corporation — South Haven (G-15404)	D	269 637-1121
Dr Schneider Auto Systems Inc — Brighton (G-1978)	G	270 858-5400
Dse Industries LLC — Macomb (G-10589)	G	313 530-6668
▲ Dunnage Engineering Inc — Brighton (G-1979)	E	810 229-9501
▼ Duo-Gard Industries Inc — Canton (G-2456)	D	734 207-9700
Dupearl Technology LLC — Bloomfield Hills (G-1816)	G	248 390-9609
▼ E & D Engineering Systems LLC — Gladwin (G-6195)	G	989 246-0770
▲ E-T-M Enterprises I Inc — Grand Ledge (G-6389)	C	517 627-8461
▲ Eagle Fasteners Inc — Troy (G-17076)	F	248 577-1441

SIC SECTION — 30 RUBBER AND MISCELLANEOUS PLASTICS PRODUCTS

Company	Code	Phone
Eagle Industries Inc — Wixom (G-18650)	E	248 624-4266
▲ Eagle Industries Inc — Wixom (G-18651)	E	248 624-4266
Eagle Manufacturing Corp — Shelby Township (G-15218)	F	586 323-0303
Eakas Corp — Novi (G-12408)	G	815 488-1879
▲ Eaton Inoac Company — Southfield (G-15549)	E	248 226-6200
Echo Engrg & Prod Sups Inc — Monroe (G-11538)	D	734 241-9622
Eckert Mfg Co — Fowlerville (G-5837)	G	517 521-4905
Eco - Composites LLC — Holland (G-8022)	G	616 395-8902
Edston Plastics Company — Brighton (G-1983)	G	734 941-3750
▲ Ehc Inc — Troy (G-17079)	G	313 259-2266
▲ Eimo Technologies Inc — Vicksburg (G-17603)	E	269 649-0545
◆ Eliason Corporation — Portage (G-13557)	D	269 327-7003
Elite Plastic Products Inc — Shelby Township (G-15220)	E	586 247-5800
Elkhart Plastics LLC — White Pigeon (G-18476)	G	269 464-4107
▲ Ell Tron Manufacturing Co — Vanderbilt (G-17570)	E	989 983-3181
Elmet North America Inc — Lansing (G-9834)	G	517 664-9011
Emabond Solutions LLC — Auburn Hills (G-879)	F	248 481-8048
Engineered Plastic Products — Ypsilanti (G-18943)	C	734 439-0310
Engineered Polymer Products — Eau Claire (G-4976)	E	269 461-6955
Enginred Plstic Components Inc — Saint Clair (G-14826)	G	810 326-1650
Enginred Plstic Components Inc — Troy (G-17092)	G	248 825-4508
Enginred Plstic Components Inc — Saint Clair (G-14827)	G	810 326-1650
Enginred Plstic Components Inc — Romeo (G-14225)	B	586 336-9500
Enginred Plstic Components Inc — Saint Clair (G-14828)	G	810 326-3010
Engtechnik Inc — Canton (G-2459)	G	734 667-4237
Enkon LLC — Manchester (G-10883)	E	937 890-5678
Enovapremier LLC — Charlotte (G-2751)	G	517 541-3200
Enterprise Plastics LLC — Shelby Township (G-15222)	G	586 665-1030
Epc-Columbia Inc — Saint Clair (G-14829)	D	810 326-1650
▲ Erwin Quarder Inc — Grand Rapids (G-6683)	D	616 575-1600
Ess Tec Inc — Holland (G-8031)	D	616 394-0230
▲ Ethylene LLC — Kentwood (G-9451)	E	616 554-3464
▼ Etx Holdings Inc — Alma (G-241)	F	989 463-1151
▲ Evans Industries Inc — Troy (G-17100)	E	313 259-2266
Excel Real Estate Holdings LLC — Wixom (G-18660)	F	919 250-1973
Exo-S US LLC — Troy (G-17101)	G	248 614-9707
Exo-S US LLC — Coldwater (G-3433)	C	517 278-8567
Exotic Rubber & Plastics Corp — New Hudson (G-12053)	D	248 477-2122
Extreme Tool and Engrg Inc — Wakefield (G-17621)	G	906 229-9100
Extrusions Division Inc — Grand Rapids (G-6796)	G	616 247-3611
Fabri-Kal Corporation — Kalamazoo (G-9183)	F	269 385-5050
Faith Plastics LLC — Marcellus (G-10948)	E	269 646-2294
Ferro Industries Inc — Harrison Township (G-7699)	G	586 792-6001
Fiberglass Technology Inds Inc — Cadillac (G-2329)	F	740 335-9400
▲ Fido Enterprises Inc — Clinton Township (G-3238)	G	586 790-8200
▲ Filcon Inc — Clare (G-2979)	F	989 386-2986
◆ Fischer America Inc — Auburn Hills (G-899)	C	248 276-1940
Fitness Finders Inc — Jackson (G-8884)	F	517 750-1500
◆ Five Peaks Technology LLC — Muskegon (G-11818)	F	231 830-8099
Flex-N-Gate Detroit LLC — Detroit (G-4236)	B	586 759-8092
Flex-N-Gate Shelby LLC — Shelby Township (G-15227)	C	586 251-2300
Flight Mold & Engineering Inc — Saint Clair (G-14830)	E	810 329-2900
◆ Formed Solutions Inc — Holland (G-8039)	F	616 395-5455
Forming Technologies LLC — Muskegon (G-11820)	D	231 777-7030
Gem Plastics Inc — Grand Rapids (G-6736)	G	616 538-5966
Gemini Group Inc — Bad Axe (G-1102)	F	989 269-6272
Gemini Group ME & T — Bad Axe (G-1103)	G	989 553-5685
Gemini Group Services Inc — Bad Axe (G-1104)	F	248 435-7271
Gemini Plastics De Mexico Inc — Ubly (G-17477)	G	989 658-8557
Genex Window Inc — Warren (G-17827)	E	586 754-2917
▼ Genova-Minnesota Inc — Davison (G-3784)	D	810 744-4500
Ghsp Inc — Hart (G-7752)	G	231 873-3300
Gilsbach Fabricating LLC — Gibraltar (G-6170)	G	734 379-9169
▲ Global Automotive Products Inc — Romulus (G-14278)	F	734 589-6179
Global Enterprise Limited — Chesterfield (G-2888)	G	586 948-4100
Global Mfg & Assembly Corp — Jackson (G-8892)	E	517 789-8116
Global Supply Integrator LLC — Davisburg (G-3770)	G	586 484-0734
▲ Global Technology Ventures Inc — Farmington Hills (G-5252)	E	248 324-3707
Glov Enterprises LLC — Tecumseh (G-16502)	G	517 423-9700
▲ Glove Coaters Incorporated — Union City (G-17493)	F	517 741-8402
GLS Industries LLC — Warren (G-17831)	G	586 255-9221
GLS Industries LLC — Warren (G-17832)	E	586 255-9221
▲ GMI Composites Inc — Muskegon (G-11825)	D	231 755-1611
Golden Pointe Inc — Detroit (G-4269)	G	313 581-8284
Grace Production Services LLC — Chesterfield (G-2889)	G	810 643-8070
Grand Haven Custom Molding LLC — Grand Haven (G-6302)	D	616 935-3160
Green Plastics LLC — Holland (G-8061)	F	616 295-2718
Greg Linska Sales Inc — Troy (G-17134)	F	248 765-6354
Grimm Industries LLC — New Baltimore (G-11981)	G	810 335-3188
Grm Corporation — Pigeon (G-13037)	F	989 453-2322
▲ Grw Technologies Inc — Grand Rapids (G-6792)	C	616 575-8119
Gt Plastics & Equipment LLC — Kent City (G-9432)	F	616 678-7445
Gt Plastics Incorporated — Oscoda (G-12759)	E	989 739-7803
◆ Gt Technologies Inc — Westland (G-18378)	F	734 467-8371
Gwinnett Plastics Inc — Grand Rapids (G-6796)	G	765 215-6593
▲ Handley Industries Inc — Jackson (G-8898)	F	517 787-8821
Hanwha Azdel Inc — Warren (G-17847)	G	810 629-2496
Harbor Green Solutions LLC — Benton Harbor (G-1553)	F	269 352-0265
▲ Harbor Isle Plastics LLC — Stevensville (G-16253)	F	269 465-6004
▲ Harman Corporation — Rochester (G-13903)	E	248 651-4477
Hi-Craft Engineering Inc — Fraser (G-5936)	D	586 293-0551
Hicks Plastics Company Inc — Macomb (G-10602)	D	586 786-5640
Hilco Industrial Plastics LLC — Caledonia (G-2381)	G	616 554-8833
Hilco Industrial Plastics LLC — Caledonia (G-2382)	E	616 554-8833
▲ HMS Mfg Co — Troy (G-17145)	D	248 689-3232
HMS Mfg Co — Bloomfield Hills (G-1828)	E	248 740-7040
▼ Hold It Products Corporation — Commerce Township (G-3538)	G	248 624-1195
▲ Holland Plastics Corporation — Grand Haven (G-6318)	E	616 844-2505
Homestead Products Inc — Coleman (G-3464)	F	989 465-6182
Hpi — Coleman (G-3466)	F	989 465-6141
Hubble Enterprises Inc — Ada (G-23)	G	616 676-4485
Huhtamaki Inc — Coleman (G-3467)	D	989 633-8900
Humphrey Companies LLC — Grandville (G-7389)	C	616 530-1717
I-Drink Products Inc — Ann Arbor (G-521)	G	734 531-6324
IAC Mexico Holdings Inc — Southfield (G-15598)	A	248 455-7000
IAC Plymouth LLC — Plymouth (G-13195)	E	734 207-7000
Iceberg Enterprises LLC — Sturgis (G-16293)	G	269 651-9488
Icon Industries Inc — Grand Rapids (G-6829)	G	616 241-1877
▼ Ideal Shield LLC — Detroit (G-4311)	E	866 825-8659
▲ Iig-Dss Technologies LLC — Ira (G-8699)	F	586 725-5300
Illinois Tool Works Inc — Oxford (G-12888)	D	248 969-4248
Illinois Tool Works Inc — Troy (G-17161)	G	248 589-2500
Imlay City Molded Pdts Corp — Imlay City (G-8637)	E	810 721-9100
◆ Ims/Chinatool Jv LLC — Livonia (G-10247)	F	734 466-5151
Industries Unlimited Inc — Chesterfield (G-2893)	F	586 949-4300
Inflatable Marine Products Inc — Howard City (G-8410)	G	616 723-8140
Innovative Engineering Mich — Lansing (G-9705)	G	517 977-0460
Innovative Packg Solutions LLC — Holt (G-8315)	G	517 213-3169
Inoac Interior Systems LLC — Farmington Hills (G-5270)	F	248 488-7610
Installations Inc — Redford (G-13740)	F	313 532-9000
▲ Instaset Plastics Company LLC — Anchorville (G-339)	C	586 725-0229
Integra Mold Inc — Portage (G-13568)	G	269 327-4337
Interntnal Auto Cmpnnts Group — Plymouth (G-13198)	G	734 456-2800
Interntnal Auto Cmpnnts Group — Sterling Heights (G-16051)	G	586 795-7800
Inteva Products LLC — Adrian (G-74)	B	517 266-8030
Intrepid Plastics Mfg Inc — Lakeview (G-9642)	G	616 901-5718
▲ Ironwood Plastics Inc — Ironwood (G-8764)	C	906 932-5025
J M Mold Technologies Inc — Warren (G-17880)	F	586 773-6664
◆ Jac Holding Corporation — Pontiac (G-13384)	G	248 874-1800
Jac Products Inc — Saline (G-15022)	G	734 944-8844
Jac Products Inc — Pontiac (G-13385)	D	248 874-1800
Jcim Mexico Holdings LLC — Plymouth (G-13201)	F	734 254-3100
Jelaga Inc — Adrian (G-77)	G	517 263-5190
Jer-Den Plastics Inc — Saint Louis (G-14991)	F	989 681-4303
Jgr Plastics LLC — Port Huron (G-13490)	E	810 990-1957

Employee Codes: A=Over 500 employees, B=251-500, C=101-250, D=51-100, E=20-50, F=10-19, G=3-9

2022 Harris Michigan Industrial Directory

30 RUBBER AND MISCELLANEOUS PLASTICS PRODUCTS30 RUBBER AND MISCELLANEOUS PLASTICS PRODUCTS SIC SECTION

▲ **Jimdi Receivables Inc** E 616 895-7766 Allendale *(G-221)*

JK Machining Inc F 269 344-0870 Kalamazoo *(G-9232)*

Jma Tool Company Inc F 586 270-6706 New Haven *(G-12033)*

▲ **John Allen Enterprises** G 734 426-2507 Ann Arbor *(G-535)*

Johnson Walker & Assoc LLC G 810 688-1600 North Branch *(G-12179)*

Jolicor Manufacturing Services E 586 323-5090 Shelby Township *(G-15246)*

Jsj Corporation G 231 873-3300 Hart *(G-7756)*

◆ **Jsj Corporation** E 616 842-6350 Grand Haven *(G-6324)*

Jvis - Usa LLC F 586 884-5700 Shelby Township *(G-15248)*

▲ **Jvis International LLC** C 586 739-9542 Shelby Township *(G-15249)*

Jvis Manufacturing LLC C 586 405-1950 Clinton Township *(G-3268)*

▲ **Kam Plastics Corp** D 616 355-5900 Holland *(G-8107)*

Kamex Molded Products LLC C 616 355-5900 Holland *(G-8108)*

Kautex Inc B 313 633-2254 Detroit *(G-4354)*

Kautex Inc A 248 616-0327 Madison Heights *(G-10760)*

Keltrol Enterprises Inc G 734 697-3011 Belleville *(G-1487)*

Kent City Plastics LLC F 616 678-4900 Kent City *(G-9435)*

Kinne Plastics Inc G 989 435-4373 Beaverton *(G-1427)*

Klann G 313 565-4135 Dearborn *(G-3858)*

Km and I G 248 792-2782 Troy *(G-17195)*

Kruger Plastic Products LLC C 269 545-3311 Galien *(G-6088)*

▲ **Kunststoff Tchnik Schrer Trier** E 734 944-5080 Troy *(G-17200)*

Kurt Dubowski G 231 796-0055 Big Rapids *(G-1680)*

Kyrie Enterprises LLC F 248 549-8690 Royal Oak *(G-14555)*

Lacks Enterprises Inc D 616 949-6570 Grand Rapids *(G-6908)*

▲ **Lacks Exterior Systems LLC** A 616 949-6570 Grand Rapids *(G-6909)*

Lacks Exterior Systems LLC E 616 949-6570 Grand Rapids *(G-6910)*

Lacks Exterior Systems LLC E 248 351-0555 Novi *(G-12462)*

Lacks Exterior Systems LLC E 616 949-6570 Grand Rapids *(G-6911)*

Lacks Exterior Systems LLC E 616 554-7805 Kentwood *(G-9461)*

Lacks Exterior Systems LLC C 616 949-6570 Grand Rapids *(G-6912)*

Lacks Exterior Systems LLC C 616 949-6570 Grand Rapids *(G-6913)*

Lacks Industries Inc C 616 698-6890 Grand Rapids *(G-6915)*

Lacks Industries Inc C 616 698-3600 Grand Rapids *(G-6916)*

Lacks Industries Inc C 616 554-7135 Kentwood *(G-9463)*

Lacks Industries Inc C 616 698-6854 Grand Rapids *(G-6917)*

Lacks Industries Inc C 616 554-7134 Grand Rapids *(G-6919)*

Lacks Industries Inc C 616 698-2776 Grand Rapids *(G-6920)*

Lacks Industries Inc C 616 656-2910 Grand Rapids *(G-6921)*

Lacks Wheel Trim Systems LLC F 248 351-0555 Novi *(G-12463)*

Lacks Wheel Trim Systems LLC E 616 949-6570 Grand Rapids *(G-6922)*

Lapeer Plating & Plastics Inc C 810 667-4240 Lapeer *(G-9939)*

Latin American Industries LLC G 616 301-1878 Grand Rapids *(G-6932)*

▼ **Lawrence Plastics LLC** D 248 475-0186 Clarkston *(G-3044)*

▼ **LDB Plastics Inc** G 586 566-9698 Shelby Township *(G-15259)*

LDM Technologies Inc A 248 858-2800 Auburn Hills *(G-956)*

◆ **Lear Operations Corporation** G 248 447-1500 Southfield *(G-15632)*

Leeann Plastics Inc F 269 489-5035 Burr Oak *(G-2212)*

◆ **Leon Interiors Inc** B 616 422-7557 Holland *(G-8125)*

◆ **Letica Corporation** C 248 652-0557 Rochester Hills *(G-14053)*

Lexamar Corporation B 231 582-3163 Boyne City *(G-1894)*

Liberty Plastics Inc G 616 994-7033 Holland *(G-8128)*

Lincoln Industries G 989 736-6421 Lincoln *(G-10036)*

Linear Mold & Engineering LLC F 734 422-6060 Livonia *(G-10283)*

Lites Alternative Inc F 989 685-3476 Rose City *(G-14364)*

Loose Plastics Inc C 989 246-1880 Gladwin *(G-6200)*

Luckmarr Plastics Inc D 586 978-8498 Sterling Heights *(G-16077)*

M & E Plastics LLC F 989 875-4191 Ithaca *(G-8792)*

M C Molds Inc E 517 655-5481 Williamston *(G-18576)*

M-R Products Inc G 231 378-2251 Copemish *(G-3698)*

Macauto Usa Inc E 248 556-5256 Troy *(G-17218)*

Machine Star LLC G 616 245-6400 Grand Rapids *(G-6955)*

Machine Tool & Gear Inc B 989 761-7521 Clifford *(G-3132)*

Machine Tool & Gear Inc D 989 743-3936 Corunna *(G-3711)*

Majestic Formed Plastics G 269 663-2870 Edwardsburg *(G-5007)*

Mann + Hummel Usa Inc E 248 857-8501 Kalamazoo *(G-9265)*

◆ **Mann + Hummel Usa Inc** F 269 329-3900 Portage *(G-13582)*

Mantissa Industries Inc G 517 694-2260 Holt *(G-8317)*

Manufacturers Services Inds G 906 493-6685 Drummond Island *(G-4802)*

Maple Valley Plastics LLC E 810 346-3040 Brown City *(G-2140)*

▲ **Marcon Technologies LLC** G 269 279-1701 Constantine *(G-3669)*

Marjo Plastics Company Inc G 734 455-4130 Plymouth *(G-13235)*

▲ **Mark Schwager Inc** F 248 275-1978 Shelby Township *(G-15269)*

Markdom of America Inc G 716 681-8306 Eaton Rapids *(G-4966)*

Martinrea Industries Inc E 231 832-5504 Reed City *(G-13795)*

▲ **Martinrea Industries Inc** E 734 428-2400 Manchester *(G-10886)*

▲ **Mason Tackle Company** E 810 631-4571 Otisville *(G-12783)*

Mathson Group Inc G 248 821-5478 Troy *(G-17241)*

▲ **Matrix Manufacturing Inc** G 616 532-6000 Grand Rapids *(G-6966)*

May-Day Window Manufacturing G 989 348-2809 Grayling *(G-7465)*

Maya Plastics Inc E 586 997-6000 Shelby Township *(G-15271)*

Mayco International LLC C 586 803-6000 Clinton Township *(G-3296)*

Mayco International LLC E 586 803-6000 Auburn Hills *(G-971)*

Mayco International LLC C 586 803-6000 Warren *(G-17919)*

▲ **Mayco International LLC** A 586 803-6000 Sterling Heights *(G-16087)*

▲ **Mayfair Plastics Inc** D 989 732-2441 Gaylord *(G-6148)*

Mc Pherson Plastics Inc D 269 694-9487 Otsego *(G-12790)*

McCray Press F 989 792-8681 Saginaw *(G-14689)*

McG Plastics Inc E 989 667-4349 Bay City *(G-1373)*

McKechnie Vhcl Cmpnnts USA Inc B 218 894-1218 Roseville *(G-14438)*

McKechnie Vhcl Cmpnnts USA Inc F 586 491-2600 Roseville *(G-14439)*

▲ **Medbio LLC** D 616 245-0214 Grand Rapids *(G-6975)*

Mega Screen Corp G 517 849-7057 Jonesville *(G-9094)*

Meyers Boat Company Inc E 517 265-9821 Adrian *(G-85)*

◆ **MGR Molds Inc** F 586 254-6020 Sterling Heights *(G-16096)*

Michiana Rtational Molding LLC F 574 849-7077 Constantine *(G-3670)*

Michigan Church Supply Co Inc F 810 686-8877 Mount Morris *(G-11674)*

▲ **Midwest Plastic Engineering** D 269 651-5223 Sturgis *(G-16309)*

Mig Molding LLC G 810 660-8435 Almont *(G-266)*

▲ **Miniature Custom Mfg LLC** E 269 998-1277 Vicksburg *(G-17608)*

Mmi Companies LLC E 248 528-1680 Troy *(G-17263)*

▲ **Mmi Engineered Solutions Inc** D 734 429-4664 Saline *(G-15028)*

Mmi Engineered Solutions Inc E 734 429-5130 Warren *(G-17933)*

Modern Builders Supply Inc G 517 787-3633 Jackson *(G-8968)*

▲ **Modern Plastics Technology LLC** D 810 966-3376 Port Huron *(G-13503)*

Mohr Engineering Inc E 810 227-4598 Brighton *(G-2035)*

▲ **Mold Masters Co** C 810 245-4100 Lapeer *(G-9948)*

Mold-Rite LLC G 586 296-3970 Fraser *(G-5965)*

▲ **Molded Materials** F 734 927-1989 Plymouth *(G-13247)*

Molded Plastic Industries Inc E 517 694-7434 Holt *(G-8318)*

Molded Plastics & Tooling F 517 268-0849 Holt *(G-8319)*

Moldex3d Northern America Inc F 248 946-4570 Farmington Hills *(G-5326)*

Molding Concepts Inc E 586 264-6990 Sterling Heights *(G-16103)*

▲ **Molding Solutions Inc** E 616 847-6822 Grand Haven *(G-6337)*

▲ **Moller Group North America Inc** D 586 532-0860 Shelby Township *(G-15284)*

Mollewood Export Inc E 248 624-1885 Wixom *(G-18714)*

Monroe LLC B 616 942-9820 Grand Rapids *(G-7025)*

Monroe Inc G 616 284-3358 Grand Rapids *(G-7026)*

Montaplast North America Inc E 248 353-5553 Auburn Hills *(G-973)*

Moon Roof Corporation America E 586 772-8730 Roseville *(G-14446)*

Moon Roof Corporation America E 586 552-1901 Roseville *(G-14447)*

Morren Mold & Machine Inc G 616 892-7474 Allendale *(G-226)*

Mp6 LLC G 231 409-7530 Traverse City *(G-16765)*

Mpi Plastics G 201 502-1534 Macomb *(G-10620)*

◆ **MPS Lansing Inc** A 517 323-9000 Lansing *(G-9719)*

▲ **Msinc** F 248 275-1978 Shelby Township *(G-15286)*

Mubea Inc G 248 393-9600 Auburn Hills *(G-976)*

Mueller Industries Inc G 248 446-3720 Brighton *(G-2037)*

Multi-Form Plastics Inc F 586 786-4229 Macomb *(G-10621)*

Multiform Plastics Inc F 586 726-2688 Sterling Heights *(G-16109)*

Munimula Inc F 517 605-5343 Quincy *(G-13673)*

▲ **N A Actuaplast Inc** F 734 744-4010 Livonia *(G-10328)*

▲ **N-K Manufacturing Tech LLC** E 616 248-3200 Grand Rapids *(G-7034)*

Narburgh & Tidd LLC G 734 281-1959 Riverview *(G-13881)*

National Case Corporation G 586 726-1710 Sterling Heights *(G-16112)*

30 RUBBER AND MISCELLANEOUS PLASTICS PRODUCTS

National Plastek Inc ....E.... 616 698-9559
Caledonia *(G-2390)*
New Gldc LLC ....D.... 231 726-4002
Muskegon *(G-11885)*
New Product Development LLC ....G.... 616 399-6253
Holland *(G-8155)*
Noack Ventures LLC ....G.... 248 583-0311
Troy *(G-17280)*
Noble Polymers LLC ....F.... 616 975-4800
Grand Rapids *(G-7045)*
North American Assembly LLC ....E.... 248 335-6702
Auburn Hills *(G-985)*
North American Mold LLC ....E.... 248 335-6702
Auburn Hills *(G-986)*
Northern Logistics LLC ....E.... 989 386-2389
Clare *(G-2990)*
Northern Mold ....G.... 231 629-1342
Howard City *(G-8414)*
Northern Plastics Inc ....E.... 586 979-7737
Sterling Heights *(G-16118)*
Nova Industries Inc ....E.... 586 294-9182
Fraser *(G-5970)*
Novares Corporation US Inc ....C.... 248 449-6100
Livonia *(G-10338)*
Novares US Eng Components Inc ....G.... 248 799-8949
Southfield *(G-15667)*
▲ **Novares US LLC** ....D.... 248 449-6100
Livonia *(G-10339)*
Novares US LLC ....G.... 517 546-1900
Howell *(G-8485)*
Novares US LLC ....G.... 616 554-3555
Grand Rapids *(G-7051)*
▲ **Nyloncraft of Michigan LLC** ....B.... 517 849-9911
Jonesville *(G-9097)*
▲ **Nyx LLC** ....C.... 734 462-2385
Livonia *(G-10343)*
Nyx LLC ....D.... 734 467-7200
Westland *(G-18402)*
Nyx LLC ....D.... 734 421-3850
Livonia *(G-10345)*
Nyx LLC ....D.... 734 261-7535
Livonia *(G-10347)*
Oakley Industries Inc ....E.... 586 791-3194
Clinton Township *(G-3310)*
▲ **Oakwood Energy Management Inc** ..F.... 734 947-7700
Taylor *(G-16453)*
▲ **Oakwood Metal Fabricating Co** ....E.... 313 561-7740
Dearborn *(G-3879)*
Omega Plastic Inc ....E.... 816 246-3115
Clinton Township *(G-3313)*
Omega Plastics Inc ....D.... 586 954-2100
Clinton Township *(G-3314)*
One Plus Boats Inc ....G.... 586 493-9900
Harrison Township *(G-7714)*
Orbis Corporation ....G.... 248 616-3232
Troy *(G-17291)*
Osco Inc ....E.... 248 852-7310
Rochester Hills *(G-14077)*
Oscoda Plastics Inc ....E.... 989 739-6900
Oscoda *(G-12767)*
Oth Consultants Inc ....C.... 586 598-0100
Chesterfield *(G-2920)*
Otr Performance Inc ....G.... 586 799-4375
Macomb *(G-10624)*
Overhead Door Company Alpena ....G.... 989 354-8316
Alpena *(G-307)*
P & K Technologies Inc ....G.... 586 336-9545
Romeo *(G-14231)*
Pace Industries LLC ....G.... 231 777-3941
Muskegon *(G-11890)*
◆ **Palmer Distributors Inc** ....D.... 586 772-4225
Fraser *(G-5973)*
Parousia Plastics Inc ....G.... 989 832-4054
Midland *(G-11402)*
Patton Tool and Die Inc ....F.... 810 359-5336
Lexington *(G-10031)*
Paul Murphy Plastics Co ....E.... 586 774-4880
Roseville *(G-14460)*
PDM Industries Inc ....E.... 231 943-9601
Traverse City *(G-16786)*
Pds Plastics Inc ....F.... 616 896-1109
Dorr *(G-4769)*
Pearce Plastics LLC ....F.... 231 519-5994
Fremont *(G-6053)*
Pegasus Tool LLC ....G.... 313 255-5900
Detroit *(G-4515)*
▲ **Penguin LLC** ....C.... 269 651-9488
Sturgis *(G-16318)*
Peninsula Plastics Company Inc ....D.... 248 852-3731
Auburn Hills *(G-995)*

Pepro Enterprises Inc ....D.... 989 658-3200
Ubly *(G-17479)*
▲ **Pepro Enterprises Inc** ....C.... 989 658-3200
Ubly *(G-17480)*
Pepro Enterprises Inc ....G.... 248 435-7271
Clawson *(G-3103)*
▲ **Performance Systematix LLC** ....E.... 616 949-9090
Grand Rapids *(G-7080)*
Petersen Products Inc ....E.... 248 446-0500
Brighton *(G-2051)*
◆ **Petoskey Plastics Inc** ....E.... 231 347-2602
Petoskey *(G-13015)*
Phillips-Medisize LLC ....F.... 248 592-2144
West Bloomfield *(G-18305)*
Pierburg Pump Tech US LLC ....D.... 864 688-1322
Auburn Hills *(G-996)*
Pinconning Metals Inc ....G.... 989 879-3144
Pinconning *(G-13064)*
Pioneer Automotive Inc ....F.... 586 758-7730
Sterling Heights *(G-16127)*
▲ **Pioneer Molded Products Inc** ....E.... 616 977-4172
Grand Rapids *(G-7087)*
Pioneer Plastics Inc ....E.... 586 262-0159
Warren *(G-17966)*
▲ **Plast-O-Foam LLC** ....D.... 586 307-3790
Clinton Township *(G-3319)*
Plastechs of Michigan LLC ....E.... 734 429-3129
Saline *(G-15031)*
Plasti-Fab Inc ....E.... 248 543-1415
Ferndale *(G-5579)*
Plastic Dress-Up Service Inc ....F.... 586 727-7878
Port Huron *(G-13517)*
▲ **Plastic Mold Technology Inc** ....D.... 616 698-9810
Kentwood *(G-9469)*
Plastic Mold Technology Inc ....G.... 616 698-9810
Grand Rapids *(G-7089)*
Plastic Molding Development ....G.... 586 739-4500
Sterling Heights *(G-16129)*
Plastic Omnium Auto Inrgy USA ....C.... 517 265-1100
Adrian *(G-88)*
Plastic Plate LLC ....E.... 616 455-5288
Grand Rapids *(G-7091)*
Plastic Solutions LLC ....G.... 231 824-7350
Traverse City *(G-16799)*
◆ **Plastic Trends Inc** ....D.... 586 232-4167
Shelby Township *(G-15303)*
▲ **Plastic Trim Inc** ....F.... 937 429-1100
Tawas City *(G-16365)*
Plastic Trim International Inc ....E.... 989 362-4419
Tawas City *(G-16366)*
Plastic Trim International Inc ....C.... 989 362-4419
East Tawas *(G-4920)*
Plastico Industries Inc ....F.... 616 304-6289
Carson City *(G-2595)*
▲ **Plasticrafts Inc** ....G.... 313 532-1900
Redford *(G-13757)*
Plastics By Design Inc ....G.... 269 646-3388
Marcellus *(G-10950)*
Plastipak Holdings Inc ....A.... 209 681-9919
Canton *(G-2508)*
◆ **Plastipak Holdings Inc** ....F.... 734 455-3600
Plymouth *(G-13266)*
Plastipak Packaging Inc ....G.... 734 326-6184
Westland *(G-18406)*
▲ **Plastomer Corporation** ....C.... 734 464-0700
Livonia *(G-10366)*
Plexicase Inc ....G.... 616 246-6400
Wyoming *(G-18900)*
▲ **Pliant Plastics Corp** ....D.... 616 844-0300
Spring Lake *(G-15843)*
Pliant Plastics Corp ....F.... 616 844-3215
Spring Lake *(G-15844)*
Pmd Automotive LLC ....G.... 248 732-7554
Pontiac *(G-13407)*
◆ **Poly Flex Products Inc** ....E.... 734 458-4194
Farmington Hills *(G-5349)*
Polymer Process Dev LLC ....D.... 586 464-6400
Shelby Township *(G-15304)*
Polymer Products Group Inc ....G.... 989 723-9510
Owosso *(G-12851)*
▲ **Polymerica Limited Company** ....E.... 248 542-2000
Huntington Woods *(G-8623)*
Polyply Composites LLC ....E.... 616 842-6330
Grand Haven *(G-6344)*
▲ **Polytec Foha Inc** ....F.... 586 978-9386
Warren *(G-17969)*
Poncraft Door Co Inc ....F.... 248 373-6060
Auburn Hills *(G-1000)*
PR Solo Cup Inc ....G.... 517 244-2837
Mason *(G-11150)*

PRA Company ....D.... 989 846-1029
Standish *(G-15895)*
Precision Industries Inc ....F.... 810 239-5816
Flint *(G-5747)*
Precision Masters Inc ....E.... 248 648-8071
Auburn Hills *(G-1003)*
▲ **Precision Mold Machining Svcs** ....E.... 586 774-2330
Warren *(G-17972)*
▲ **Precision Polymer Mfg Inc** ....E.... 269 344-2044
Kalamazoo *(G-9305)*
Precision Tool & Mold LLC ....F.... 906 932-3440
Ironwood *(G-8770)*
Preferred Plastics Inc ....D.... 269 685-5873
Plainwell *(G-13091)*
Primera Plastics Inc ....D.... 616 748-6248
Zeeland *(G-19072)*
Prism Plastics Inc ....F.... 810 292-6300
Chesterfield *(G-2928)*
Prism Plastics Inc ....E.... 810 292-6300
Shelby Township *(G-15308)*
▲ **Pro Slot Ltd** ....G.... 616 897-6000
Hartford *(G-7766)*
Profile Mfg Inc ....E.... 586 598-0007
Chesterfield *(G-2931)*
Prompt Plastics ....G.... 586 307-8525
Warren *(G-17980)*
Proper Group International Inc ....C.... 586 552-5267
Warren *(G-17982)*
▲ **Proper Group International LLC** ....G.... 586 779-8787
Warren *(G-17983)*
Proper Polymers - Warren LLC ....G.... 586 552-5267
Warren *(G-17984)*
Proper Polymers- Tennessee Inc ....G.... 586 779-8787
Warren *(G-17985)*
Proper Polymers-Pulaski LLC ....C.... 931 371-3147
Warren *(G-17986)*
Proto Crafts Inc ....E.... 810 376-3665
Deckerville *(G-3956)*
▲ **Proto Shapes Inc** ....F.... 517 278-3947
Coldwater *(G-3447)*
Proto-TEC Inc ....F.... 616 772-9511
Zeeland *(G-19075)*
Protojet LLC ....F.... 810 956-8000
Fraser *(G-5981)*
▲ **Pti Engineered Plastics Inc** ....B.... 586 263-5100
Macomb *(G-10631)*
▼ **Purforms Inc** ....E.... 616 897-3000
Lowell *(G-10514)*
Qcq Design & Fab Inc ....G.... 810 735-4033
Linden *(G-10069)*
Qfd Recycling ....E.... 810 733-2335
Flint *(G-5751)*
Quality Assured Plastics Inc ....E.... 269 674-3888
Lawrence *(G-9983)*
▲ **R B L Plastics Incorporated** ....E.... 313 873-8800
Detroit *(G-4550)*
◆ **R C Plastics Inc** ....F.... 517 523-2112
Osseo *(G-12776)*
R L Adams Plastics Inc ....D.... 616 261-4400
Grand Rapids *(G-7134)*
Rak-O-Nizer LLC ....G.... 810 444-9807
Marysville *(G-11098)*
Ray Scott Industries Inc ....G.... 248 535-2528
Port Huron *(G-13522)*
▲ **Rbl Products Inc** ....F.... 313 873-8806
Detroit *(G-4555)*
▲ **Reed City Group LLC** ....D.... 231 832-7500
Reed City *(G-13797)*
Reeves Plastics LLC ....E.... 616 997-0777
Coopersville *(G-3696)*
Regal Finishing Co Inc ....E.... 269 849-2963
Coloma *(G-3482)*
Regency Plastics - Ubly Inc ....D.... 989 658-8504
Ubly *(G-17482)*
Reklein Plastics Incorporated ....G.... 586 739-8850
Sterling Heights *(G-16145)*
Reliable Reasonable Tl Svc LLC ....F.... 586 630-6016
Clinton Township *(G-3335)*
Retro Enterprises Inc ....G.... 269 435-8583
Constantine *(G-3675)*
◆ **Reutter LLC** ....G.... 248 466-0652
Ann Arbor *(G-640)*
Revere Plastics Systems LLC ....C.... 586 415-4823
Fraser *(G-5988)*
▲ **Revere Plastics Systems LLC** ....B.... 833 300-4043
Novi *(G-12525)*
Riverside Plastic Co ....F.... 231 937-7333
Howard City *(G-8417)*
▲ **Rkaa Business LLC** ....E.... 231 734-5517
Evart *(G-5127)*

SIC

Employee Codes: A=Over 500 employees, B=251-500
C=101-250, D=51-100, E=20-50, F=10-19, G=3-9

2022 Harris Michigan
Industrial Directory

793

30 RUBBER AND MISCELLANEOUS PLASTICS PRODUCTS30 RUBBER AND MISCELLANEOUS PLASTICS PRODUCTS SIC SECTION

▼ **Robinson Industries Inc** ... C ... 989 465-6111
Coleman *(G-3472)*
Robmar Plastics Inc ... G ... 989 386-9600
Clare *(G-2995)*
Rockford Molding & Trim ... G ... 616 874-8997
Rockford *(G-14189)*
Rocktech Systems LLC ... E ... 586 330-9031
Chesterfield *(G-2940)*
▲ **Romeo-Rim Inc** ... C ... 586 336-5800
Bruce Twp *(G-2179)*
Ronningen Research and Dev Co ... C ... 269 649-0520
Vicksburg *(G-17611)*
Roto-Plastics Corporation ... D ... 517 263-8981
Adrian *(G-92)*
Rowland Plastics LLC ... F ... 616 875-5400
Zeeland *(G-19078)*
Royal Plastics LLC ... E ... 616 669-3393
Hudsonville *(G-8604)*
Royal Technologies Corporation ... D ... 616 669-3393
Hudsonville *(G-8605)*
Royal Technologies Corporation ... B ... 616 667-4102
Hudsonville *(G-8606)*
◆ **Royal Technologies Corporation** ... D ... 616 669-3393
Hudsonville *(G-8607)*
Royal Technologies Corporation ... B ... 616 667-4102
Hudsonville *(G-8608)*
Royal Technologies Corporation ... B ... 616 669-3393
Hudsonville *(G-8609)*
RPS Tool and Engineering Inc ... E ... 586 298-6590
Roseville *(G-14474)*
◆ **SA Automotive Ltd** ... C ... 517 521-4205
Webberville *(G-18247)*
Sac Plastics Inc ... G ... 616 846-0820
Spring Lake *(G-15849)*
▲ **Saginaw Bay Plastics Inc** ... D ... 989 686-7860
Kawkawlin *(G-9418)*
Saint-Gobain Prfmce Plas Corp ... G ... 989 435-9533
Beaverton *(G-1431)*
▲ **SCC Plastics Inc** ... E ... 231 759-8820
Norton Shores *(G-12329)*
Schrier Plastics Corp ... E ... 616 669-7174
Jenison *(G-9070)*
◆ **Schwintek Inc** ... G ... 269 445-9999
Cassopolis *(G-2633)*
▼ **Scic LLC** ... D ... 800 248-5960
Mason *(G-11153)*
Seagate Plastics Company ... G ... 517 547-8123
Addison *(G-45)*
▲ **Sebro Plastics Inc** ... E ... 248 348-4121
Wixom *(G-18749)*
Sequoia Molding ... G ... 586 463-4400
Grosse Pointe *(G-7533)*
◆ **Shape Corp** ... B ... 616 846-8700
Grand Haven *(G-6361)*
Sheffler Mfg Intl Lgistics LLC ... E ... 248 409-0960
Clarkston *(G-3065)*
Shinwon USA Inc ... E ... 734 469-2550
Livonia *(G-10405)*
Shoreline Mold & Engrg LLC ... G ... 269 926-2223
Benton Harbor *(G-1584)*
Sierra Plastics Inc ... G ... 989 269-6272
Bad Axe *(G-1110)*
▲ **Silikids Inc** ... G ... 866 789-7454
Traverse City *(G-16833)*
▲ **Sohner Plastics LLC** ... F ... 734 222-4847
Dexter *(G-4756)*
▲ **Solo Cup Company LLC** ... C ... 800 248-5960
Mason *(G-11155)*
◆ **Solo Cup Operating Corporation** ... D ... 800 248-5960
Mason *(G-11156)*
Soltis Plastics Corp ... G ... 248 698-1440
White Lake *(G-18466)*
◆ **Sonus Engineered Solutions LLC** ... C ... 586 427-3838
Warren *(G-18017)*
Soroc Products Inc ... E ... 810 743-2660
Burton *(G-2246)*
Special Mold Engineering Inc ... E ... 248 652-6600
Rochester Hills *(G-14116)*
Special-Lite Inc ... C ... 800 821-6531
Decatur *(G-3951)*
Specialty Manufacturing Inc ... E ... 989 790-9011
Saginaw *(G-14763)*
▼ **Speed Cinch Inc** ... G ... 269 646-2016
Marcellus *(G-10952)*
Spencer Plastics Inc ... E ... 231 942-7100
Cadillac *(G-2356)*
SPI Blow Molding LLC ... E ... 269 849-3200
Coloma *(G-3483)*
SPI LLC ... E ... 586 566-5870
Shelby Township *(G-15341)*

Spiratex Company ... D ... 734 289-4800
Monroe *(G-11576)*
Spirit Industries Inc ... G ... 517 371-7840
Lansing *(G-9740)*
Sr Injection Molding Inc ... G ... 586 260-2360
Harrison Township *(G-7726)*
▲ **Srg Global Automotive LLC** ... D ... 586 757-7800
Warren *(G-18024)*
◆ **Srg Global Coatings LLC** ... C ... 248 509-1100
Troy *(G-17369)*
Ssb Holdings Inc ... E ... 586 755-1660
Rochester Hills *(G-14117)*
Standard Plaque Incorporated ... F ... 313 383-7233
Melvindale *(G-11210)*
Statistical Processed Products ... F ... 586 792-6900
Clinton Township *(G-3363)*
Stellar Plastics Fabg LLC ... G ... 313 527-7337
Detroit *(G-4609)*
▲ **Stone Plastics and Mfg Inc** ... C ... 616 748-9740
Zeeland *(G-19082)*
Sturgis Molded Products Co ... C ... 269 651-9381
Sturgis *(G-16324)*
Styroloution ... G ... 734 676-3616
Trenton *(G-16894)*
Su-Dan Plastics Inc ... C ... 248 651-6035
Rochester *(G-13932)*
Su-Dan Plastics Inc ... F ... 248 651-6035
Rochester Hills *(G-14121)*
Sumitomo Chemical America Inc ... G ... 248 284-4797
Novi *(G-12548)*
▲ **Summit Plastic Molding Inc** ... E ... 586 262-4500
Shelby Township *(G-15344)*
▲ **Summit Plastic Molding II Inc** ... G ... 586 262-4500
Shelby Township *(G-15345)*
▲ **Summit Polymers Inc** ... C ... 269 324-9330
Portage *(G-13622)*
Summit Polymers Inc ... G ... 269 324-9320
Portage *(G-13623)*
Summit Polymers Inc ... B ... 269 324-9330
Kalamazoo *(G-9345)*
Summit Polymers Inc ... B ... 269 323-1301
Portage *(G-13624)*
Summit Polymers Inc ... B ... 269 651-1643
Sturgis *(G-16326)*
Summit Polymers Inc ... G ... 269 649-4900
Vicksburg *(G-17614)*
Sunningdale Tech Inc ... G ... 248 526-0517
Troy *(G-17378)*
Supreme Industries LLC ... G ... 586 725-2500
Ira *(G-8715)*
Sur-Form LLC ... E ... 586 221-1950
Chesterfield *(G-2951)*
Svrc Industries Inc ... E ... 989 280-3038
Saginaw *(G-14768)*
▲ **Systex Products Corporation** ... C ... 269 964-8800
Battle Creek *(G-1304)*
Szymanowski Electric LLC ... G ... 612 928-8370
Plainwell *(G-13097)*
T & K Industries Inc ... G ... 586 212-9100
Clinton Township *(G-3371)*
Talco Industries ... G ... 989 269-6260
Bad Axe *(G-1112)*
Tapco Holdings Inc ... C ... 248 668-6400
Wixom *(G-18766)*
TAW Plastics LLC ... G ... 616 302-0954
Greenville *(G-7507)*
Tech Group Grand Rapids Inc ... B ... 616 490-2197
Walker *(G-17653)*
Technimold Inc ... F ... 906 284-1921
Caspian *(G-2609)*
Techniplas LLC ... B ... 517 849-9911
Jonesville *(G-9103)*
▲ **Tecla Company Inc** ... E ... 248 624-8200
Commerce Township *(G-3576)*
▲ **Tecnoma LLC** ... F ... 248 354-8888
Southfield *(G-15718)*
▲ **Teijin Advan Compo Ameri Inc** ... G ... 248 365-6600
Auburn Hills *(G-1047)*
▲ **Teijin Auto Tech Mnchester LLC** ... D ... 734 428-8301
Manchester *(G-10890)*
Teijin Auto Tech NA Hldngs Cor ... C ... 248 237-7800
Auburn Hills *(G-1048)*
▲ **Teijin Automotive Tech Inc** ... C ... 248 237-7800
Auburn Hills *(G-1049)*
Ten X Plastics LLC ... G ... 616 813-3037
Grand Rapids *(G-7252)*
Tepso Gen-X Plastics LLC ... G ... 248 869-2130
Wixom *(G-18770)*
Tesca Usa Inc ... E ... 586 991-0744
Rochester Hills *(G-14124)*

◆ **Tg Fluid Systems USA Corp** ... B ... 810 220-6161
Brighton *(G-2078)*
▲ **Th Plastics Inc** ... C ... 269 496-8495
Mendon *(G-11222)*
Th Plastics Inc ... D ... 269 496-8495
Mendon *(G-11223)*
Thermo Flex LLC ... G ... 734 458-4194
Farmington Hills *(G-5398)*
Thermoforms Inc ... F ... 616 974-0055
Kentwood *(G-9481)*
◆ **Thetford Corporation** ... C ... 734 769-6000
Ann Arbor *(G-688)*
Thomson Plastics Inc ... E ... 517 545-5026
Howell *(G-8531)*
▲ **Three 60 Roto LLC** ... F ... 517 545-3600
Howell *(G-8532)*
Thumb Plastics Inc ... B ... 989 269-9791
Bad Axe *(G-1114)*
Thunder Bay Pattern Works Inc ... F ... 586 783-1126
Clinton Township *(G-3376)*
TI Group Auto Systems LLC ... G ... 810 364-3277
Marysville *(G-11108)*
◆ **Tk Mold & Engineering Inc** ... E ... 586 752-5840
Romeo *(G-14238)*
Tnj Manufacturing LLC ... E ... 586 251-1900
Shelby Township *(G-15353)*
Tomas Plastics Inc ... G ... 734 455-4706
Canton *(G-2535)*
Tomas Plastics Inc ... G ... 734 455-4706
Plymouth *(G-13318)*
Tooling Cncepts Design Not Inc ... F ... 810 444-9807
Port Huron *(G-13533)*
Total Molding Solutions Inc ... E ... 517 424-5900
Tecumseh *(G-16519)*
Total Plastics Resources LLC ... F ... 248 299-9500
Rochester Hills *(G-14129)*
▼ **Tower Tag & Label LLC** ... F ... 269 927-1065
Benton Harbor *(G-1593)*
◆ **Toyoda Gosei North Amer Corp** ... C ... 248 280-2100
Troy *(G-17397)*
Trans Industries Plastics LLC ... E ... 248 310-0008
Rochester *(G-13934)*
Transnav Holdings Inc ... C ... 586 716-5600
New Baltimore *(G-11996)*
▲ **Transnav Technologies Inc** ... C ... 888 249-9955
New Baltimore *(G-11997)*
Trellborg Sling Sltions US Inc ... G ... 269 639-4217
Benton Harbor *(G-1594)*
Trellborg Sling Sltions US Inc ... G ... 734 354-1250
Northville *(G-12266)*
Trellborg Sling Sltions US Inc ... G ... 810 655-3900
Fenton *(G-5509)*
Trestle Plastic Services LLC ... G ... 616 262-5484
Hamilton *(G-7608)*
Tri-Star Molding Inc ... E ... 269 646-0062
Marcellus *(G-10953)*
▲ **Tri-Way Manufacturing Inc** ... E ... 586 776-0700
Roseville *(G-14485)*
Tribar Manufacturing LLC ... E ... 248 669-0077
Wixom *(G-18777)*
Tribar Manufacturing LLC ... B ... 248 374-5870
Wixom *(G-18778)*
Tribar Manufacturing LLC ... B ... 248 516-1600
Howell *(G-8536)*
Tribar Technologies Inc ... B ... 248 516-1600
Wixom *(G-18779)*
Triple C Geothermal Inc ... G ... 517 282-7249
Muskegon *(G-11938)*
Truck Acquisition Inc ... G ... 877 875-4376
Ann Arbor *(G-699)*
Two Mitts Inc ... G ... 800 888-5054
Kalamazoo *(G-9359)*
U S Farathane Port Huron LLC ... F ... 248 754-7000
Auburn Hills *(G-1067)*
▲ **Undercar Products Group Inc** ... B ... 616 719-4571
Wyoming *(G-18916)*
Uniflex Inc ... G ... 248 486-6000
Brighton *(G-2088)*
Uniloy Inc ... D ... 514 424-8900
Tecumseh *(G-16520)*
Unique-Chardan Inc ... D ... 419 636-6900
Auburn Hills *(G-1070)*
▲ **Universal Products Inc** ... E ... 231 937-5555
Rockford *(G-14192)*
University Plastics Inc ... G ... 734 668-8773
Ann Arbor *(G-706)*
Urgent Plastic Services Inc ... G ... 248 852-8999
Rochester Hills *(G-14138)*
US Farathane LLC ... C ... 248 754-7000
Auburn Hills *(G-1072)*

US Farathane Holdings Corp .... G 586 726-1200
  Sterling Heights *(G-16218)*
◆ US Farathane Holdings Corp .... B 248 754-7000
  Auburn Hills *(G-1073)*
US Farathane Holdings Corp .... G 586 978-2800
  Troy *(G-17415)*
US Farathane Holdings Corp .... G 248 754-7000
  Port Huron *(G-13536)*
US Farathane Holdings Corp .... G 248 754-7000
  Shelby Township *(G-15360)*
US Farathane Holdings Corp .... G 248 754-7000
  Lake Orion *(G-9636)*
US Farathane Holdings Corp .... C 780 246-1034
  Auburn Hills *(G-1074)*
US Farathane Holdings Corp .... G 586 978-2800
  Westland *(G-18426)*
US Farathane Holdings Corp .... G 586 685-4000
  Sterling Heights *(G-16220)*
US Farathane Holdings Corp .... G 586 726-1200
  Shelby Township *(G-15361)*
US Farathane Holdings Corp .... G 248 754-7000
  Orion *(G-12739)*
US Mold LLC .... G 586 719-7239
  Hazel Park *(G-7846)*
USA Summit Plas Silao 1 LLC .... C 269 324-9330
  Portage *(G-13630)*
USF Westland LLC .... F 248 754-7000
  Auburn Hills *(G-1076)*
Vacuum Orna Metal Company Inc .... E 734 941-9100
  Romulus *(G-14336)*
▲ Valley Enterprises Ubly Inc .... C 989 658-3200
  Ubly *(G-17485)*
Valtec LLC .... C 810 724-5048
  Imlay City *(G-8649)*
Vaupell Molding & Tooling Inc .... F 269 435-8414
  Constantine *(G-3677)*
▲ Ventra Evart LLC .... G 231 734-9000
  Evart *(G-5128)*
▲ Ventra Ionia Main LLC .... A 616 597-3220
  Ionia *(G-8693)*
▼ Vidon Plastics Inc .... D 810 667-0634
  Lapeer *(G-9965)*
▲ Vintech Industries Inc .... C 810 724-7400
  Imlay City *(G-8650)*
Vinyl Tech Window Systems Inc .... E 248 634-8900
  Holly *(G-8300)*
▲ Vitec LLC .... B 313 633-2254
  Detroit *(G-4671)*
Vivatar Inc .... E 616 928-0750
  Holland *(G-8239)*
▲ W T Beresford Co .... F 248 350-2900
  Southfield *(G-15741)*
▲ Weather King Windows Doors Inc .... D 313 933-1234
  Farmington *(G-5154)*
Weather King Windows Doors Inc .... E 248 478-7788
  Farmington *(G-5155)*
Weather Pane Inc .... G 810 798-8695
  Almont *(G-272)*
Weathergard Window Company Inc .... D 248 967-8822
  Oak Park *(G-12651)*
▲ West Michigan Molding Inc .... C 616 846-4950
  Grand Haven *(G-6382)*
Western Diversified Plas LLC .... G 269 668-3393
  Mattawan *(G-11169)*
▲ Western Michigan Plastics .... F 616 394-9269
  Holland *(G-8247)*
◆ Williamston Products Inc .... D 517 655-2131
  Williamston *(G-18585)*
Williamston Products Inc .... G 517 655-2273
  Williamston *(G-18586)*
Williamston Products Inc .... D 989 723-0149
  Owosso *(G-12867)*
Windsor Mold Inc .... G 734 944-5080
  Saline *(G-15045)*
Windsor Mold USA Inc .... E 734 944-5080
  Saline *(G-15046)*
WI Molding of Michigan LLC .... D 269 327-3075
  Portage *(G-13633)*
Woco Tech Usa Inc .... F 248 385-2854
  Novi *(G-12569)*
World Class Prototypes Inc .... F 616 355-0200
  Holland *(G-8253)*
Worswick Mold & Tool Inc .... F 810 765-1700
  Marine City *(G-10970)*
Wow Products USA .... G 989 672-1300
  Caro *(G-2586)*
Wright Plastic Products Co LLC .... G 586 336-3000
  Saint Clair *(G-14845)*
▲ Wright Plastic Products Co LLC .... D 989 291-3211
  Sheridan *(G-15386)*

Xcentric Mold & Engrg LLC .... D 586 598-4636
  Clinton Township *(G-3390)*
Xxtar Associates LLC .... G 888 946-6066
  Detroit *(G-4695)*
Yanfeng US Auto Intr Systems I .... G 313 259-3226
  Detroit *(G-4697)*
Yanfeng US Auto Intr Systems I .... G 734 946-0600
  Romulus *(G-14342)*
Yanfeng US Automotive .... F 517 721-0179
  Novi *(G-12572)*
Yapp USA Auto Systems Inc .... G 248 817-5653
  Troy *(G-17456)*
Yapp USA Auto Systems Inc .... G 248 404-8696
  Romulus *(G-14343)*
Zayna LLC .... G 616 452-4522
  Grand Rapids *(G-7356)*
ZF Active Safety & Elec US LLC .... E 586 232-7200
  Washington *(G-18092)*
◆ ZF Active Safety & Elec US LLC .... C 734 855-2600
  Livonia *(G-10481)*
ZF Active Safety & Elec US LLC .... E 586 232-7200
  Washington *(G-18093)*

31 LEATHER AND LEATHER PRODUCTS

3111 Leather Tanning & Finishing

▲ Afx Industries LLC .... G 810 966-4650
  Port Huron *(G-13431)*
Afx Industries LLC .... G 810 966-4650
  Port Huron *(G-13432)*
Afx Industries LLC .... G 517 768-8993
  Jackson *(G-8805)*
Beau Satchelle LLC .... G 313 374-8462
  Ann Arbor *(G-398)*
Goodells Equestrian Center .... G 586 615-8535
  Wales *(G-17628)*
Horn Corp .... G 248 358-8883
  Brighton *(G-2009)*
K & K Tannery LLC .... G 517 849-9720
  Jonesville *(G-9091)*
Larrys Taxidermy Inc .... G 517 769-6104
  Pleasant Lake *(G-13103)*
Lear Corporation .... G 248 853-3122
  Rochester Hills *(G-14051)*
Mexico Express .... F 313 843-6717
  Detroit *(G-4440)*
Michigan Diversfd Holdings Inc .... F 248 280-0450
  Madison Heights *(G-10782)*
Modern Fur Dressing LLC .... G 517 589-5575
  Leslie *(G-10015)*
National Manufacturing Inc .... G 586 755-8983
  Warren *(G-17941)*
Russell Farms Inc .... G 269 349-6120
  Kalamazoo *(G-9322)*
Transnav Holdings Inc .... C 586 716-5600
  New Baltimore *(G-11996)*
◆ Wolverine World Wide Inc .... A 616 866-5500
  Rockford *(G-14197)*

3131 Boot & Shoe Cut Stock & Findings

Bean Counter Inc .... G 906 523-5027
  Calumet *(G-2408)*
Bond Manufacturing LLC .... G 313 671-0799
  Detroit *(G-4062)*
Canusa LLC .... F 906 259-0800
  Sault Sainte Marie *(G-15088)*
▲ David Epstein Inc .... F 248 542-0802
  Ferndale *(G-5539)*
Living Quarters .... G 616 874-6160
  Coral *(G-3700)*
Midwest Cabinet Counters .... G 248 586-4260
  Madison Heights *(G-10783)*
Paul Murphy Plastics Co .... E 586 774-4880
  Roseville *(G-14460)*
Quarters Vending LLC .... G 313 510-5555
  Commerce Township *(G-3567)*
Rand L Industries Inc .... G 989 657-5175
  Alpena *(G-315)*
Rand Worldwide Subsidiary Inc .... G 616 261-8183
  Grandville *(G-7413)*
S A S .... G 586 725-6381
  Chesterfield *(G-2943)*
Security Countermeasures Tech .... G 248 237-6263
  Livonia *(G-10403)*
Stoney Creek Tmber Qrter Hrses .... G 517 677-9661
  Reading *(G-13706)*
Wolverine Procurement Inc .... C 616 866-9521
  Rockford *(G-14194)*

3142 House Slippers

Wolverine Slipper Group Inc .... B 616 866-5500
  Rockford *(G-14196)*

3143 Men's Footwear, Exc Athletic

Hush Puppies Retail LLC .... E 231 937-1004
  Howard City *(G-8409)*
Hy-Test Inc .... G 616 866-5500
  Rockford *(G-14170)*
Kalamazoo Orthotics & Dbtc .... F 269 349-2247
  Kalamazoo *(G-9244)*
Millers Shoe Parlor Inc .... G 517 783-1258
  Jackson *(G-8964)*
Original Footwear Company .... B 231 796-5828
  Big Rapids *(G-1681)*
Original Footwear Mfg BR Inc .... F 231 796-5828
  Big Rapids *(G-1682)*
Orthotool LLC .... G 734 455-8103
  Plymouth *(G-13258)*
Shoe Shop .... G 231 739-2174
  Muskegon *(G-11918)*
▲ Veldheer Tulip Garden Inc .... E 616 399-1900
  Holland *(G-8235)*
Wolverine Procurement Inc .... C 616 866-9521
  Rockford *(G-14194)*
▲ Wolverine Procurement Inc .... F 616 866-5500
  Rockford *(G-14195)*
◆ Wolverine World Wide Inc .... A 616 866-5500
  Rockford *(G-14197)*

3144 Women's Footwear, Exc Athletic

Millers Shoe Parlor Inc .... G 517 783-1258
  Jackson *(G-8964)*
Original Footwear Mfg BR Inc .... F 231 796-5828
  Big Rapids *(G-1682)*
Orthotool LLC .... G 734 455-8103
  Plymouth *(G-13258)*
Wolverine Procurement Inc .... C 616 866-9521
  Rockford *(G-14194)*
◆ Wolverine World Wide Inc .... A 616 866-5500
  Rockford *(G-14197)*

3149 Footwear, NEC

Orthotool LLC .... G 734 455-8103
  Plymouth *(G-13258)*
▲ Warrior Sports Inc .... C 800 968-7845
  Warren *(G-18063)*
◆ Wolverine World Wide Inc .... A 616 866-5500
  Rockford *(G-14197)*

3151 Leather Gloves & Mittens

Kaul Glove and Mfg Co .... E 313 894-9494
  Detroit *(G-4353)*

3161 Luggage

Activerse LLC .... G 313 463-9344
  Detroit *(G-3985)*
Birlon Group LLC .... G 313 551-5341
  Inkster *(G-8659)*
Detroit Couture .... G 734 237-6826
  Southfield *(G-15539)*
Gionl LLC .... G 313 957-9247
  Detroit *(G-4263)*
Golden Satchel LLC .... G 248 636-0550
  River Rouge *(G-13855)*
Invest Buy Own LLC .... G 248 467-2048
  Commerce Township *(G-3544)*
Kash St James LLC .... G 248 571-1160
  Detroit *(G-4351)*
Motor City Designs LLC .... G 313 686-1025
  Dearborn *(G-3874)*
Restricted Area LLC .... G 419 975-8109
  Detroit *(G-4569)*
Rhino Products Inc .... G 269 674-8309
  Lawrence *(G-9984)*
Sound Productions Entrmt .... F 989 386-2221
  Clare *(G-2998)*
Stoned Like Willy LLC .... G 833 378-6633
  Southfield *(G-15710)*
Tallulahs Satchels .... G 231 775-4082
  Cadillac *(G-2360)*
Travis Fulmore LLC .... F 810 701-6981
  Flint *(G-5782)*
Viva Salon Nouvelle LLC .... F 947 800-9115
  Detroit *(G-4672)*

31 LEATHER AND LEATHER PRODUCTS

3171 Handbags & Purses

Fisll Media LLC .... G 646 492-8533
  Troy *(G-17111)*
Military Apparel Co .... G 810 637-1542
  Port Huron *(G-13502)*
Rose Laila 989 598-0950
  Saginaw *(G-14740)*
Sandusky Concrete & Supply .... G 810 648-2627
  Sandusky *(G-15066)*
Tapestry Inc .... G 631 724-8066
  Sterling Heights *(G-16200)*

3172 Personal Leather Goods

Bianco Inc .... G 313 682-2612
  Livonia *(G-10137)*
Birlon Group LLC .... G 313 551-5341
  Inkster *(G-8659)*
C W Marsh Company .... E 231 722-3781
  Muskegon *(G-11788)*
Original Footwear Company .... B 231 796-5828
  Big Rapids *(G-1681)*
Shields Classic Toys .... G 888 806-2632
  Saline *(G-15039)*

3199 Leather Goods, NEC

Adams Holsters .... G 906 662-4212
  Channing *(G-2705)*
Birlon Group LLC .... G 313 551-5341
  Inkster *(G-8659)*
C W Marsh Company .... E 231 722-3781
  Muskegon *(G-11788)*
Custom Built Holsters LLC .... G 517 825-9856
  Jonesville *(G-9086)*
Erich Jaeger USA Inc .... G 734 404-5940
  Livonia *(G-10199)*
Gst Autoleather Holdco Corp .... F 248 436-2300
  Rochester Hills *(G-14028)*
Leathercrafts By Bear .... G 616 453-8308
  Grand Rapids *(G-6933)*
Lebalab Inc .... G 519 542-4236
  Kimball *(G-9494)*
▲ Low Cost Surcing Solutions LLC ... G 248 535-7721
  Washington *(G-18084)*
Lyon Hide Leather Goods LLC .... G 517 997-6067
  Charlotte *(G-2761)*
Paragon Leather Inc USA .... G 269 323-9483
  Portage *(G-13590)*
Perras Holster Sales LLC .... G 248 467-4254
  South Lyon *(G-15452)*
▲ Shinola/Detroit LLC .... C 888 304-2534
  Detroit *(G-4591)*
Tapestry Inc .... G 616 538-5802
  Grandville *(G-7420)*
Topsydekennel LLC .... G 313 655-5804
  Detroit *(G-4638)*

32 STONE, CLAY, GLASS, AND CONCRETE PRODUCTS

3211 Flat Glass

Antique Botl & GL Collectr LLC ...... G 248 486-0530
  New Hudson *(G-12042)*
Beechcraft Products Inc .... E 989 288-2606
  Durand *(G-4840)*
Ford Motor Company .... A 313 446-5945
  Detroit *(G-4240)*
Furniture City Glass Corp .... F 616 784-5500
  Grand Rapids *(G-6728)*
Golich Glass .... G 248 667-9084
  Brighton *(G-2002)*
Guardian Fabrication LLC .... D 248 340-1800
  Auburn Hills *(G-919)*
Guardian Fabrication Inc .... C 248 340-1800
  Auburn Hills *(G-920)*
Guardian Glass LLC .... D 248 340-1800
  Auburn Hills *(G-921)*
Guardian Industries LLC .... F 517 629-9464
  Albion *(G-127)*
Guardian Industries LLC .... B 734 654-4285
  Carleton *(G-2555)*
◆ Guardian Industries LLC .... B 248 340-1800
  Auburn Hills *(G-922)*
Guardian Industries LLC .... D 734 654-1111
  Carleton *(G-2556)*
I2 International Dev LLC .... G 616 534-8100
  Grandville *(G-7390)*
Pilkington North America Inc .... G 989 754-2956
  Saginaw *(G-14728)*
Pilkington North America Inc .... F 248 542-8300
  Royal Oak *(G-14568)*
Pilkington North America Inc .... G 269 687-2100
  Niles *(G-12159)*
Pittsburgh Glass Works LLC .... C 248 371-1700
  Rochester Hills *(G-14084)*
Pittsburgh Glass Works LLC .... E 734 727-5001
  Westland *(G-18405)*
PPG Industries Inc .... F 248 641-2000
  Troy *(G-17309)*
Single Vision Solution Inc .... F 586 464-1522
  Mount Clemens *(G-11657)*
Superior Auto Glass of Mich .... G 989 366-9691
  Houghton Lake *(G-8406)*
Valley Glass Co Inc .... G 989 790-9342
  Saginaw *(G-14786)*
Weatherproof Inc 517 764-1330
  Jackson *(G-9034)*

3221 Glass Containers

Amcor Phrm Packg USA LLC .... C 734 428-9741
  Ann Arbor *(G-363)*
Iron Heart Canning Company LLC .. F 231 675-1839
  Kewadin *(G-9488)*

3229 Pressed & Blown Glassware, NEC

Bare Bulb Companies LLC .... G 616 644-8251
  Grand Rapids *(G-6495)*
Brand Logoed Barware .... G 517 763-1044
  East Lansing *(G-4888)*
▲ City Auto Glass Co .... G 616 842-3235
  Grand Haven *(G-6285)*
Corning Incorporated .... G 248 680-4701
  Troy *(G-17029)*
▲ Dare Products Inc .... E 269 965-2307
  Springfield *(G-15864)*
▲ General Scientific Corporation .... E 734 996-9200
  Ann Arbor *(G-498)*
Glassicart Decorative Glwr .... G 231 739-5956
  Muskegon *(G-11824)*
Great Lakes Aero Products .... F 810 235-1402
  Flint *(G-5708)*
Guardian Industries LLC .... B 734 654-4285
  Carleton *(G-2555)*
Hudson Industries Inc .... G 313 777-5622
  Sterling Heights *(G-16044)*
Installers Glass Block .... G 586 463-1214
  Washington *(G-18082)*
Jordan Valley Glassworks .... G 231 536-0539
  East Jordan *(G-4874)*
Keweenaw Bay Indian Community .. F 906 524-5757
  Baraga *(G-1141)*
Laidco Sales Inc .... G 231 832-1327
  Hersey *(G-7867)*
Light Speed Usa LLC .... A 616 308-0054
  Grand Rapids *(G-6943)*
Linden Art Glass .... G 734 459-5060
  Plymouth *(G-13221)*
Living On Etch .... G 810 229-7955
  Brighton *(G-2021)*
▲ Lumecon LLC .... G 248 505-1090
  Farmington Hills *(G-5296)*
Optrand Inc .... E 734 451-3480
  Plymouth *(G-13257)*
PPG Industries Inc .... F 248 641-2000
  Troy *(G-17309)*
▲ Precision Polymer Mfg Inc .... E 269 344-2044
  Kalamazoo *(G-9305)*
▲ Rgm New Ventures Inc .... D 248 624-5050
  Wixom *(G-18742)*
Robroy Enclosures Inc .... C 616 794-0700
  Belding *(G-1462)*
Thompson John .... G 810 225-8780
  Howell *(G-8530)*
Tig Entity LLC .... E 810 629-9558
  Fenton *(G-5508)*
Twins Studio .... G 248 676-8157
  Milford *(G-11495)*

3231 Glass Prdts Made Of Purchased Glass

A & B Display Systems Inc .... F 989 893-6642
  Bay City *(G-1314)*
A K Services Inc .... G 313 972-1010
  Detroit *(G-3972)*
Beans Best LLC .... G 734 707-7378
  Ann Arbor *(G-397)*
Boyer Glassworks Inc .... G 231 526-6359
  Harbor Springs *(G-7642)*
Burco Inc .... E 616 453-7771
  Grand Rapids *(G-6532)*

SIC SECTION

Carlex Glass America LLC .... A 248 824-8800
  Troy *(G-17000)*
Case Island Glass LLC .... G 810 252-1704
  Flint *(G-5665)*
▲ City Auto Glass Co .... G 616 842-3235
  Grand Haven *(G-6285)*
Classic Glass Battle Creek Inc .... F 269 968-2791
  Battle Creek *(G-1209)*
▼ Duo-Gard Industries Inc .... D 734 207-9700
  Canton *(G-2456)*
Elegant Glassworks 734 845-1901
  Saline *(G-15015)*
Engrave A Remembrance Inc .... G 586 772-7480
  Warren *(G-17794)*
▲ Exatec LLC .... E 248 926-4200
  Wixom *(G-18659)*
Fox Fire Glass LLC .... G 248 332-2442
  Fenton *(G-5479)*
Full Spectrum Stained GL Inc .... G 269 432-2610
  Colon *(G-3487)*
Furniture City Glass Corp .... F 616 784-5500
  Grand Rapids *(G-6728)*
Gentex Corporation .... C 616 772-1800
  Zeeland *(G-19024)*
Gentex Corporation 616 772-1800
  Zeeland *(G-19025)*
Gentex Corporation 616 772-1800
  Zeeland *(G-19026)*
Gentex Corporation 616 772-1800
  Zeeland *(G-19027)*
Gentex Corporation 616 772-1800
  Zeeland *(G-19029)*
Glass Recyclers Ltd .... E 313 584-3434
  Dearborn *(G-3846)*
Grand River Interiors Inc .... E 616 454-2800
  Grand Rapids *(G-6777)*
Guardian Fabrication LLC .... D 248 340-1800
  Auburn Hills *(G-919)*
Guardian Industries LLC .... B 734 654-4285
  Carleton *(G-2555)*
▲ Hensley Mfg Inc .... F 810 653-3226
  Davison *(G-3786)*
▲ Inalfa Holding Inc .... F 248 371-3060
  Auburn Hills *(G-934)*
Jordan Valley Glassworks .... G 231 536-0539
  East Jordan *(G-4874)*
Keeler-Glasgow Company Inc .... F 269 621-2415
  Hartford *(G-7764)*
▲ Kentwood Manufacturing Co .... E 616 698-6370
  Byron Center *(G-2279)*
Knight Tonya .... G 313 255-3434
  Southfield *(G-15618)*
Lippert Components Mfg Inc .... D 989 845-3061
  Chesaning *(G-2829)*
Luxottica of America Inc .... G 989 624-8958
  Birch Run *(G-1710)*
M2 Scientifics LLC .... F 616 379-9080
  Allendale *(G-224)*
Magna .... F 616 786-7403
  Holland *(G-8133)*
◆ Magna Mirrors America Inc .... E 616 786-7000
  Grand Rapids *(G-6956)*
Magna Mirrors America Inc .... G 616 786-7300
  Holland *(G-8134)*
Magna Mirrors America Inc .... G 616 942-0163
  Newaygo *(G-12085)*
Magna Mirrors America Inc .... G 616 738-0115
  Holland *(G-8135)*
Magna Mirrors America Inc .... G 616 786-7000
  Grand Haven *(G-6333)*
Magna Mirrors America Inc .... A 616 786-7772
  Holland *(G-8137)*
Magna Mirrors America Inc .... B 231 652-4450
  Newaygo *(G-12086)*
Magna Mirrors America Inc .... G 616 786-7000
  Holland *(G-8136)*
◆ Magna Mirrors North Amer LLC .. A 616 868-6122
  Alto *(G-336)*
Oldcastle Buildingenvelope Inc ...... F 734 947-9670
  Taylor *(G-16455)*
Oldcastle Buildingenvelope Inc ...... G 616 896-8341
  Burnips *(G-2210)*
On The Side Sign Dsign Grphics ... G 810 266-7446
  Byron *(G-2255)*
Paragon Tempered Glass LLC .... G 269 684-5060
  Niles *(G-12157)*
Penstone Inc .... E 734 379-3160
  Rockwood *(G-14203)*
Polymer Process Dev LLC .... D 586 464-6400
  Shelby Township *(G-15304)*

PPG Industries Inc................F....... 248 641-2000
Troy *(G-17309)*
▲ **Rgm New Ventures Inc**..................D....... 248 624-5050
Wixom *(G-18742)*
Sciencekitwarhousecom..................G....... 800 992-8338
Commerce Township *(G-3572)*
Se-Kure Domes & Mirrors Inc..............F....... 269 651-9351
Sturgis *(G-16322)*
▲ **SMR Atmtive Mrror Intl USA Inc**........B....... 810 364-4141
Marysville *(G-11100)*
▲ **SMR Atmtive Tech Hldngs USA PR**..D....... 810 364-4141
Marysville *(G-11101)*
SMR Automotive Systems USA Inc.......F....... 810 937-2456
Port Huron *(G-13529)*
▲ **SMR Automotive Systems USA Inc**..A....... 810 364-4141
Marysville *(G-11102)*
Solutia Inc..................G....... 734 676-4400
Trenton *(G-16892)*
Stained Glass and Gifts..................G....... 810 736-6766
Flint *(G-5768)*
Thermaglas Corporation..................D....... 517 754-7461
Saginaw *(G-14774)*
Thompson Art Glass Inc..................G....... 810 225-8766
Brighton *(G-2081)*
Valley Glass Co Inc..................G....... 989 790-9342
Saginaw *(G-14786)*
Vvp Auto Glass Inc..................E....... 734 727-5001
Westland *(G-18428)*

3241 Cement, Hydraulic

Blue Circle Cement..................G....... 313 842-4600
Detroit *(G-4059)*
Holcim (us) Inc..................D....... 734 529-2411
Dundee *(G-4823)*
Holcim (us) Inc..................G....... 734 529-4600
Dundee *(G-4824)*
Holcim (us) Inc..................G....... 989 755-7515
Saginaw *(G-14667)*
Joe Davis Crushing Inc..................G....... 586 757-3612
Sterling Heights *(G-16056)*
Knust Masonry..................G....... 231 322-2587
Rapid City *(G-13681)*
Lafarge North America Inc..................G....... 989 399-1005
Saginaw *(G-14682)*
Lafarge North America Inc..................G....... 989 894-0157
Essexville *(G-5116)*
Lafarge North America Inc..................G....... 989 595-3820
Presque Isle *(G-13654)*
Lafarge North America Inc..................G....... 269 983-6333
Saint Joseph *(G-14944)*
Lafarge North America Inc..................G....... 989 354-4171
Alpena *(G-299)*
Lafarge North America Inc..................G....... 231 726-3291
Muskegon *(G-11855)*
Lafarge North America Inc..................G....... 703 480-3600
Dundee *(G-4827)*
Nb Cement Co..................G....... 313 278-8299
Dearborn Heights *(G-3935)*

3251 Brick & Structural Clay Tile

Heb Development LLC..................E....... 616 363-3825
Grand Rapids *(G-6807)*

3253 Ceramic Tile

Earthwerks LLC..................G....... 800 275-7943
Grand Haven *(G-6294)*
Haarala Ceramic Tile & Marble..........G....... 734 422-1168
Livonia *(G-10232)*
Mannino Tile & Marble Inc..................G....... 586 978-3390
Sterling Heights *(G-16084)*
Motawi Tileworks Inc..................E....... 734 213-0017
Ann Arbor *(G-584)*
Yoxheimer Tile Co..................F....... 517 788-7542
Jackson *(G-9040)*

3255 Clay Refractories

Alco Products LLC..................E....... 313 823-7500
Detroit *(G-3996)*
◆ **Alpha Resources LLC**..................E....... 269 465-5559
Stevensville *(G-16239)*
Harbisonwalker Intl Inc..................G....... 231 689-6641
White Cloud *(G-18442)*
◆ **Marshall-Gruber Company LLC**.......F....... 248 353-4100
Southfield *(G-15647)*
▲ **Mono Ceramics Inc**..................E....... 269 925-0212
Benton Harbor *(G-1575)*
Pewabic Society Inc..................E....... 313 626-2000
Detroit *(G-4522)*

Schad Boiler Setting Company..........D....... 313 273-2235
Detroit *(G-4584)*

3259 Structural Clay Prdts, NEC

St Onge Masonry LLC..................G....... 248 709-8161
Auburn Hills *(G-1036)*

3261 China Plumbing Fixtures & Fittings

Americast LLC..................G....... 989 681-4800
Saint Louis *(G-14985)*
Cucina Moda - Birmingham LLC..........F....... 248 792-2285
Troy *(G-17037)*
National Composites LLC..................E....... 989 723-8997
Owosso *(G-12846)*
York Electric Inc..................G....... 517 487-6400
Lansing *(G-9909)*

3264 Porcelain Electrical Splys

3M Technical Ceramics Inc..................F....... 248 960-9339
Wixom *(G-18592)*
◆ **Leco Corporation**..................B....... 269 983-5531
Saint Joseph *(G-14946)*
Livonia Magnetics Co Inc..................E....... 734 397-8844
Farmington Hills *(G-5293)*
My Permit Pal Inc..................G....... 248 432-2699
West Bloomfield *(G-18300)*
▲ **NGK Spark Plug Mfg USA Inc**..........C....... 248 926-6900
Wixom *(G-18720)*
▲ **Tengam Engineering Inc**..................E....... 269 694-9466
Otsego *(G-12800)*

3269 Pottery Prdts, NEC

Make It Yours..................G....... 517 990-6799
Jackson *(G-8943)*
New Pioneer Ceramics LLC..................G....... 248 200-9893
Auburn Hills *(G-981)*
Paint Your Masterpiece..................G....... 231 622-8824
Petoskey *(G-13011)*
Penzo America Inc..................G....... 248 723-0802
Bloomfield Hills *(G-1850)*
Reilchz Inc..................G....... 231 421-9600
Traverse City *(G-16819)*
Terra Green Ceramics Inc..................G....... 810 742-4611
Burton *(G-2248)*
▲ **Veldheer Tulip Garden Inc**..................E....... 616 399-1900
Holland *(G-8235)*

3271 Concrete Block & Brick

Bark River Concrete Pdts Co..................G....... 906 466-9940
Bark River *(G-1153)*
Best Block Company..................E....... 586 772-7000
Warren *(G-17732)*
Branch West Concrete Products..........F....... 989 345-0794
West Branch *(G-18326)*
Carlesimo Products Inc..................E....... 248 474-0415
Farmington Hills *(G-5198)*
Cheboygan Cement Products Inc..........E....... 231 627-5631
Cheboygan *(G-2782)*
Cherry Oak Landscaping LLC..................F....... 517 339-2881
East Lansing *(G-4890)*
Clay & Graham Inc..................G....... 989 354-5292
Alpena *(G-287)*
Consumers Concrete Corp..................C....... 616 243-3651
Wyoming *(G-18858)*
Consumers Concrete Corp..................E....... 269 384-0977
Kalamazoo *(G-9152)*
Consumers Concrete Corporation........E....... 269 342-0136
Kalamazoo *(G-9153)*
Consumers Concrete Corporation........F....... 231 777-3981
Muskegon *(G-11795)*
Declarks Landscaping Inc..................E....... 586 752-7200
Bruce Twp *(G-2166)*
Fendt Builders Supply Inc..................F....... 734 663-4277
Ann Arbor *(G-488)*
Fendt Builders Supply Inc..................E....... 248 474-3211
Farmington Hills *(G-5242)*
Ferguson Block Co Inc..................E....... 810 653-2812
Davison *(G-3781)*
Grand Blanc Cement Pdts Inc..................E....... 810 694-7500
Grand Blanc *(G-6244)*
Hagen Cement Products Inc..................G....... 269 483-9641
White Pigeon *(G-18480)*
Hampton Block Co..................G....... 248 628-1333
Oxford *(G-12886)*
Hobe Inc..................G....... 231 845-5196
Ludington *(G-10539)*
Interlock Design..................F....... 616 784-5901
Comstock Park *(G-3612)*

K-Tel Corporation..................F....... 517 543-6174
Charlotte *(G-2760)*
Kurtz Gravel Company Inc..................E....... 810 787-6543
Farmington Hills *(G-5286)*
Lafarge North America Inc..................G....... 231 726-3291
Muskegon *(G-11855)*
Lafarge North America Inc..................G....... 703 480-3600
Dundee *(G-4827)*
Livingston County Concrete Inc..........E....... 810 632-3030
Brighton *(G-2022)*
Ludvanwall Inc..................E....... 616 842-4500
Spring Lake *(G-15830)*
Mbcd Inc..................E....... 517 484-4426
Lansing *(G-9867)*
Miller Products & Supply Co..................F....... 906 774-1243
Iron Mountain *(G-8725)*
National Block Company..................E....... 734 721-4050
Westland *(G-18399)*
Port Huron Building Supply Co..........F....... 810 987-2666
Port Huron *(G-13519)*
Ruppe Manufacturing Company..........E....... 906 932-3540
Ironwood *(G-8771)*
Simply Green Outdoor Svcs LLC..........G....... 734 385-6190
Dexter *(G-4755)*
St Marys Cement Inc (us)..................G....... 269 679-5253
Schoolcraft *(G-15128)*
Superior Block Company Inc..................E....... 906 482-2731
Houghton *(G-8392)*
Swartzmiller Lumber Company..........G....... 989 845-6625
Chesaning *(G-2830)*
Theut Concrete Products Inc..................F....... 810 679-3376
Croswell *(G-3737)*
Waanders Concrete Co..................F....... 269 673-6352
Allegan *(G-184)*
Zaremba & Co Inc..................G....... 248 922-3300
Davisburg *(G-3773)*

3272 Concrete Prdts

Acme Septic Tank Co..................F....... 989 684-3852
Kawkawlin *(G-9413)*
Advance Concrete Products Co..........E....... 248 887-4173
Highland *(G-7880)*
Ajax Paving Industries Inc..................C....... 248 244-3300
Troy *(G-16913)*
All About Drainage LLC..................G....... 248 921-0766
Commerce Township *(G-3508)*
▲ **Arnets Inc**..................F....... 734 665-3650
Ann Arbor *(G-379)*
Asphalt Paving Inc..................E....... 231 733-1409
Muskegon *(G-11773)*
Atlas Cut Stone Inc..................G....... 248 545-5100
Oak Park *(G-12592)*
Beck Mobile Concrete LLC..................G....... 517 655-4996
Williamston *(G-18568)*
Becker & Scrivens Con Pdts Inc..........E....... 517 437-4250
Hillsdale *(G-7924)*
Best Block Company..................E....... 586 772-7000
Warren *(G-17732)*
Bonsal American Inc..................F....... 248 338-0335
Auburn Hills *(G-813)*
Bonsal American Inc..................G....... 734 753-4413
New Boston *(G-12003)*
Bostwick Enterprises Inc..................G....... 231 946-8613
Traverse City *(G-16624)*
Brutsche Concrete Products Co..........F....... 269 963-1554
Battle Creek *(G-1199)*
Burrell Tri-County Vaults Inc..................F....... 734 483-2024
Ypsilanti *(G-18930)*
Bush Concrete Products Inc..................F....... 231 733-1904
Norton Shores *(G-12281)*
Busscher Septic Tank Service..........G....... 616 392-9653
Holland *(G-7988)*
Carlesimo Products Inc..................E....... 248 474-0415
Farmington Hills *(G-5198)*
Central Michigan Crematory..................F....... 269 963-1554
Battle Creek *(G-1207)*
Cheboygan Cement Products Inc..........G....... 989 742-4107
Hillman *(G-7911)*
Cheboygan Cement Products Inc..........E....... 231 627-5631
Cheboygan *(G-2782)*
Christy Vault Company Inc..................G....... 415 994-1378
Grand Rapids *(G-6569)*
Clancy Excavating Co..................G....... 586 294-2900
Roseville *(G-14384)*
Co-Pipe Products Inc..................E....... 734 287-1000
Taylor *(G-16393)*
Concrete Manufacturing Inc..................G....... 586 777-3320
Roseville *(G-14388)*
Concrete Step Co..................G....... 810 789-3061
Flint *(G-5671)*

S I C

32 STONE, CLAY, GLASS, AND CONCRETE PRODUCTS

Consumers Concrete Corp ....C 616 243-3651
Wyoming *(G-18858)*
Consumers Concrete Corporation ....F 517 784-9108
Jackson *(G-8852)*
Cosella Dorken Products Inc ....G 888 433-5824
Rochester *(G-13896)*
Darby Ready Mix Concrete Co ....E 517 547-7004
Addison *(G-43)*
Daves Concrete Products Inc ....F 269 624-4100
Lawton *(G-9988)*
Decorative Concrete By John ....G 616 862-7152
Grand Rapids *(G-6639)*
Deforest & Bloom Septic Tanks ....G 231 544-3599
Central Lake *(G-2693)*
Detroit Wilbert Vault Corp ....E 313 862-1616
Detroit *(G-4170)*
Detroit Wlbert Crmtion Svcs LL ....G 248 853-0559
Auburn Hills *(G-863)*
Dlh World LLC ....G 313 915-0274
Detroit *(G-4182)*
Dm Vault Forms ....G 989 275-4797
Roscommon *(G-14348)*
E & M Cores Inc ....G 989 386-9223
Clare *(G-2978)*
Ej Ardmore Inc ....F 231 536-2261
East Jordan *(G-4864)*
Espinoza Bros ....G 313 468-7775
Detroit *(G-4214)*
Fendt Builders Supply Inc ....E 248 474-3211
Farmington Hills *(G-5242)*
Fenton Corporation ....G 810 629-2858
Fenton *(G-5476)*
Fenton Memorials & Vaults Inc ....G 810 629-2858
Fenton *(G-5477)*
Flambeau Inc ....G 248 364-3357
Auburn Hills *(G-901)*
Fogelsonger Vault Co Inc ....G 989 684-0262
Bay City *(G-1358)*
Forbes Sanitation & Excavation ....F 231 723-2311
Manistee *(G-10900)*
Fraco Products Ltd ....G 248 667-9260
Troy *(G-17122)*
Franke Salisbury Virginia ....G 231 775-7014
Cadillac *(G-2330)*
Gambles Redi-Mix Inc ....E 989 539-6460
Harrison *(G-7677)*
Genesee Valley Vault Inc ....G 810 629-3909
Holly *(G-8272)*
Gibraltar National Corporation ....E 248 634-8257
Holly *(G-8274)*
Gnap LLC ....G 616 583-5000
Byron Center *(G-2272)*
Grand Rpids Wilbert Burial Vlt ....E 616 453-9429
Grand Rapids *(G-6778)*
High Grade Materials Company ....E 616 754-5545
Greenville *(G-7492)*
Holcim (us) Inc ....G 734 529-4600
Dundee *(G-4824)*
Imlay City Concrete Inc ....F 810 724-3905
Imlay City *(G-8636)*
Interntnal Prcast Slutions LLC ....D 313 843-0073
River Rouge *(G-13856)*
Jarvis Concrete Products Inc ....G 269 463-3000
Watervliet *(G-18181)*
Jordan Valley Concrete Service ....F 231 536-7701
East Jordan *(G-4873)*
K-Mar Structures LLC ....F 231 924-3895
Fremont *(G-6046)*
Kelder LLC ....F 231 757-3000
Scottville *(G-15135)*
◆ **Kerkstra Precast LLC** ....C 616 457-4920
Grandville *(G-7395)*
Kurtz Gravel Company Inc ....E 810 787-6543
Farmington Hills *(G-5286)*
Lafarge North America Inc ....G 703 480-3600
Dundee *(G-4827)*
Lake Orion Concrete Orna Pdts ....G 248 693-8683
Lake Orion *(G-9614)*
Lakeshore Cement Products ....G 989 739-9341
Oscoda *(G-12763)*
Leelanau Redi-Mix Inc ....E 231 228-5005
Maple City *(G-10943)*
Lenox Inc ....G 586 727-1488
Lenox *(G-9999)*
Liberty Transit Mix LLC ....F 586 254-2212
Shelby Township *(G-15263)*
M 37 Concrete Products Inc ....G 231 689-1785
White Cloud *(G-18446)*
Mack Industries Michigan Inc ....E 248 620-7400
White Lake *(G-18461)*
Marquette Castings LLC ....G 248 798-8035
Royal Oak *(G-14560)*
Maxs Concrete Inc ....G 231 972-7558
Mecosta *(G-11193)*
Mbcd Inc ....E 517 484-4426
Lansing *(G-9867)*
MEGA Precast Inc ....F 586 477-5959
Shelby Township *(G-15272)*
Metro Cast Corporation ....G 734 728-0210
Westland *(G-18395)*
Milan Burial Vault Inc ....E 734 439-1538
Milan *(G-11444)*
National Block Company ....E 734 721-4050
Westland *(G-18399)*
▲ **National Precast Strl Inc** ....F 586 294-6430
Shelby Township *(G-15288)*
Newberry Redi-Mix Inc ....G 906 293-5178
Newberry *(G-12097)*
Northern Concrete Pipe Inc ....G 517 645-2777
Charlotte *(G-2763)*
Northern Concrete Pipe Inc ....E 989 892-3545
Bay City *(G-1383)*
Nucast LLC ....G 313 532-4610
Redford *(G-13750)*
▲ **Oaks Concrete Products Inc** ....F 248 684-5004
Wixom *(G-18725)*
Paschal Burial Vault Svc LLC ....G 517 448-8868
Hudson *(G-8558)*
Paul Murphy Plastics Co ....E 586 774-4880
Roseville *(G-14460)*
Pearson Precast Concrete Pdts ....G 517 486-4060
Blissfield *(G-1772)*
Peninsula Products Inc ....G 906 296-9801
Lake Linden *(G-9569)*
Perfected Grave Vault Co ....G 616 243-3375
Grand Rapids *(G-7078)*
Polycem LLC ....E 231 799-1040
Norton Shores *(G-12350)*
Port Huron Building Supply Co ....F 810 987-2666
Port Huron *(G-13519)*
Prestressed Group ....G 313 962-9189
River Rouge *(G-13859)*
Quality Precast Inc ....E 269 342-0539
Kalamazoo *(G-9310)*
Quality Precast Con Pdts LLC ....G 269 342-0539
Kalamazoo *(G-9311)*
Quality Way Products LLC ....F 248 634-2401
Holly *(G-8287)*
Quikrete Companies LLC ....G 616 784-5790
Walker *(G-17652)*
▲ **Quikrete Detroit** ....F 313 491-3500
Detroit *(G-4548)*
Redi-Rock International LLC ....F 866 222-8400
Petoskey *(G-13019)*
Royal Stone LLC ....E 248 343-6232
Williamston *(G-18581)*
Rudy Goupille & Sons Inc ....G 906 475-9816
Negaunee *(G-11974)*
Ruth Drain Tile Inc ....G 989 864-3406
Ruth *(G-14598)*
Sandusky Concrete & Supply ....G 810 648-2627
Sandusky *(G-15066)*
Sanilac Drain and Tile Co ....G 810 648-4100
Sandusky *(G-15067)*
Shores Cremation & Burial ....G 616 395-3630
Holland *(G-8195)*
Smith Concrete Products ....G 989 875-4687
North Star *(G-12185)*
Superior Monuments Co ....G 231 728-2211
Muskegon *(G-11928)*
Superior Vault Co ....G 989 643-4200
Merrill *(G-11265)*
Surface Mausoleum Company Inc ....G 989 864-3460
Minden City *(G-11506)*
Ufp International LLC ....F 770 472-3050
Grand Rapids *(G-7290)*
Unit Step Company Inc ....G 989 684-9361
Bay City *(G-1408)*
Upper Peninsula Con Pipe Co ....F 906 786-0934
Escanaba *(G-5103)*
Van Sloten Enterprises Inc ....F 906 635-5151
Sault Sainte Marie *(G-15102)*
White Lake Excavating Inc ....E 231 894-6918
Whitehall *(G-18513)*
Wilbert Burial Vault Company ....G 231 773-6631
Muskegon *(G-11946)*
Wilbert Burial Vault Company ....G 231 773-6631
Muskegon *(G-11947)*
Wilbert Burial Vault Works ....G 906 786-0261
Kingsford *(G-9519)*
Wilbert Saginaw Vault Corp ....G 989 753-3065
Saginaw *(G-14794)*
Willbee Concrete Products Co ....F 517 782-8246
Jackson *(G-9035)*
Wolverine Concrete Products ....G 313 931-7189
Detroit *(G-4687)*

3273 Ready-Mixed Concrete

Aggregate Industries - Mwr Inc ....G 734 475-2531
Grass Lake *(G-7434)*
Ajax Paving Industries Inc ....C 248 244-3300
Troy *(G-16913)*
Alma Concrete Products Company ....G 989 463-5476
Alma *(G-234)*
Angelos Crushed Concrete Inc ....G 586 756-1070
Warren *(G-17706)*
Are You Ready ....G 616 935-1133
Fruitport *(G-6058)*
Arquette Concrete & Supply ....G 989 846-4131
Standish *(G-15887)*
Associated Constructors LLC ....D 906 226-6505
Negaunee *(G-11963)*
Baraga County Concrete Company ....G 906 353-6595
Baraga *(G-1134)*
Beck Mobile Concrete LLC ....G 517 655-4996
Williamston *(G-18568)*
Becker & Scrivens Con Pdts Inc ....E 517 437-4250
Hillsdale *(G-7924)*
Beckman Brothers Inc ....E 231 861-2031
Shelby *(G-15148)*
Beechbed Mix ....G 616 263-7422
Holland *(G-7972)*
Best Concrete & Supply Inc ....G 734 283-7055
Brownstown *(G-2143)*
Best-Block Co ....G 313 933-8676
Detroit *(G-4053)*
Bichler Gravel & Concrete Co ....F 906 786-0343
Escanaba *(G-5062)*
Bigos Precast ....G 517 223-5000
Fowlerville *(G-5835)*
Bogen Concrete Inc ....G 269 651-6751
Sturgis *(G-16281)*
Bonsal American Inc ....G 734 753-4413
New Boston *(G-12003)*
Bozzer Brothers Inc ....G 989 732-9684
Gaylord *(G-6120)*
Branch West Concrete Products ....F 989 345-0794
West Branch *(G-18326)*
Brewers City Dock Inc ....E 616 396-6563
Holland *(G-7983)*
Bwb LLC ....F 231 439-9200
Farmington Hills *(G-5189)*
C F Long & Sons Inc ....E 248 624-1562
Walled Lake *(G-17665)*
Callahan Supply LLC ....G 231 878-9023
Cadillac *(G-2325)*
Carrollton Concrete Mix Inc ....G 989 753-7737
Saginaw *(G-14622)*
Carrollton Paving Co ....F 989 752-7139
Saginaw *(G-14623)*
Cemex Cement Inc ....C 231 547-9971
Charlevoix *(G-2712)*
Central Concrete Products Inc ....E 810 659-7488
Flushing *(G-5804)*
Cheboygan Cement Products Inc ....E 231 627-5631
Cheboygan *(G-2782)*
Cheboygan Cement Products Inc ....G 989 356-5156
Alpena *(G-286)*
Cheboygan Cement Products Inc ....G 989 742-4107
Hillman *(G-7911)*
Coit Avenue Gravel Co Inc ....E 616 363-7777
Grand Rapids *(G-6581)*
Concrete Store ....G 231 577-3433
Cadillac *(G-2326)*
Consumers Concrete Corp ....E 269 384-0977
Kalamazoo *(G-9152)*
Consumers Concrete Corporation ....E 269 342-0136
Kalamazoo *(G-9153)*
Consumers Concrete Corporation ....G 800 643-4235
Plainwell *(G-13072)*
Consumers Concrete Corporation ....F 231 777-3981
Muskegon *(G-11795)*
Consumers Concrete Corporation ....G 269 792-9009
Wayland *(G-18193)*
Consumers Concrete Corporation ....F 231 924-6131
Fremont *(G-6037)*
Consumers Concrete Corporation ....F 269 925-3109
Benton Harbor *(G-1542)*
Consumers Concrete Corporation ....F 517 267-8428
Lansing *(G-9826)*

32 STONE, CLAY, GLASS, AND CONCRETE PRODUCTS

Consumers Concrete Corporation ....G 616 827-0063
Byron Center *(G-2264)*
Consumers Concrete Corporation ....F 269 342-5983
Kalamazoo *(G-9154)*
Consumers Concrete Corporation ....G 269 965-2321
Battle Creek *(G-1211)*
Consumers Concrete Corporation ....G 616 392-6190
Holland *(G-8004)*
Consumers Concrete Corporation ....G 269 684-8760
Niles *(G-12120)*
Consumers Concrete Corporation ....F 231 894-2705
Whitehall *(G-18493)*
Consumers Concrete Corporation ....F 517 784-9108
Jackson *(G-8852)*
Cornillie Concrete ....G 231 439-9200
Harbor Springs *(G-7645)*
Crete Dry-Mix & Supply Co ....F 616 784-5790
Comstock Park *(G-3599)*
Darby Ready Mix Concrete Co ....E 517 547-7004
Addison *(G-43)*
Darby Ready Mix-Dundee LLC ....F 734 529-7100
Dundee *(G-4813)*
Daves Concrete Products Inc ....F 269 624-4100
Lawton *(G-9988)*
Dekes Concrete Inc ....F 810 686-5570
Clarkston *(G-3030)*
Detroit Ready Mix Concrete ....F 313 931-7043
Detroit *(G-4160)*
Detroit Recycled Concrete Co ....G 248 553-0600
Novi *(G-12395)*
Detroit Recycled Concrete Co ....G 313 934-7677
Detroit *(G-4161)*
Dewent Redi-Mix LLC ....G 616 457-2100
Jenison *(G-9052)*
Doan Construction Co ....F 734 971-4678
Ypsilanti *(G-18940)*
Downriver Crushed Concrete ....G 734 283-1833
Taylor *(G-16405)*
Drayton Iron & Metal Inc ....F 248 673-1269
Waterford *(G-18120)*
E A Wood Inc ....F 989 739-9118
Oscoda *(G-12757)*
Edw C Levy Co ....F 248 334-4302
Auburn Hills *(G-875)*
Edw C Levy Co ....G 313 843-7200
Detroit *(G-4202)*
Edward E Yates ....G 517 467-4961
Onsted *(G-12705)*
Elmers Crane and Dozer Inc ....F 231 943-3443
Mount Pleasant *(G-11696)*
Elmers Crane and Dozer Inc ....C 231 943-3443
Traverse City *(G-16676)*
Fenton Concrete Inc ....G 810 629-0783
Fenton *(G-5475)*
Ferguson Block Co Inc ....E 810 653-2812
Davison *(G-3781)*
Fisher Cnstr Aggregates Inc ....F 989 539-6431
Mount Pleasant *(G-11698)*
Fisher Redi Mix Concrete ....G 989 723-1622
Owosso *(G-12833)*
Fisher Sand and Gravel Company ....E 989 835-7187
Midland *(G-11363)*
Gale Briggs Inc ....G 517 543-1320
Charlotte *(G-2758)*
Gambles Redi-Mix Inc ....E 989 539-6460
Harrison *(G-7677)*
Gene Brow & Sons Inc ....F 906 635-0859
Sault Sainte Marie *(G-15090)*
Gotts Transit Mix Inc ....F 734 439-1528
Milan *(G-11437)*
Grand Rapids Gravel Company ....F 616 538-9000
Grand Rapids *(G-6759)*
Grand Rapids Gravel Company ....E 616 538-9000
Belmont *(G-1507)*
Grand Rapids Gravel Company ....E 616 538-9000
Holland *(G-8055)*
Grand Rapids Gravel Company ....E 231 777-2777
Muskegon *(G-11826)*
Great Lakes Aggregates LLC ....C 734 379-0311
South Rockwood *(G-15464)*
Great Lakes Sand & Gravel LLC ....G 616 374-3169
Lake Odessa *(G-9576)*
Guidobono Concrete Inc ....F 810 229-2666
Brighton *(G-2006)*
Hamilton Block & Ready Mix Co ....E 269 751-5129
Hamilton *(G-7598)*
Hanson Lehigh Inc ....F 989 233-5343
Corunna *(G-3708)*
Hardcrete Inc ....G 989 644-5543
Weidman *(G-18252)*
Hart Concrete LLC ....G 231 873-2183
Spring Lake *(G-15821)*
High Grade Concrete Pdts Co ....F 616 842-8630
Spring Lake *(G-15822)*
High Grade Materials Company ....G 616 554-8828
Caledonia *(G-2380)*
High Grade Materials Company ....E 616 754-5545
Greenville *(G-7492)*
High Grade Materials Company ....G 269 926-6900
Benton Harbor *(G-1555)*
High Grade Materials Company ....G 269 349-8222
Kalamazoo *(G-9218)*
High Grade Materials Company ....F 616 677-1271
Grand Rapids *(G-6814)*
High Grade Materials Company ....G 517 374-1029
Lansing *(G-9704)*
High Grade Materials Company ....G 989 365-3010
Six Lakes *(G-15388)*
High Grade Materials Company ....G 616 696-9540
Sand Lake *(G-15048)*
Huizenga & Sons Inc ....E 616 772-6241
Zeeland *(G-19041)*
Imlay City Concrete Inc ....F 810 724-3905
Imlay City *(G-8636)*
Jordan Valley Concrete Service ....F 231 536-7701
East Jordan *(G-4873)*
Kens Redi Mix Inc ....F 810 687-6000
Clio *(G-3402)*
Kens Redi Mix Inc ....G 810 636-2630
Goodrich *(G-6224)*
Koenig Fuel & Supply Co ....G 313 368-1870
Wayne *(G-18226)*
Kuhlman Corporation ....G 734 241-8692
Monroe *(G-11554)*
Kurtz Gravel Company Inc ....E 810 787-6543
Farmington Hills *(G-5286)*
▲ L & S Transit Mix Concrete Co ....E 989 354-5363
Alpena *(G-298)*
Lafarge North America Inc ....G 216 566-0545
Essexville *(G-5117)*
Lafarge North America Inc ....G 703 480-3600
Dundee *(G-4827)*
Lafarge North America Inc ....G 231 726-3291
Muskegon *(G-11855)*
Lafarge North America Inc ....G 313 842-9258
Detroit *(G-4375)*
Lafarghlcim Acm Nwco Tx-La LLC ....G 972 837-2462
Dundee *(G-4828)*
Lakeside Building Products ....G 248 349-3500
Detroit *(G-4376)*
Land Star Inc ....G 313 834-2366
Detroit *(G-4377)*
Lattimore Material ....E 972 837-2462
Dundee *(G-4829)*
Lc Materials LLC ....G 231 946-5600
Cadillac *(G-2342)*
Lc Materials LLC ....C 817 835-4100
Harbor Springs *(G-7649)*
Lc Materials LLC ....C 231 946-5600
Bear Lake *(G-1418)*
Leelanau Redi-Mix Inc ....E 231 228-5005
Maple City *(G-10943)*
Lees Ready Mix Inc ....G 989 734-7666
Rogers City *(G-14211)*
Little Bay Concrete Products ....G 906 428-9859
Gladstone *(G-6183)*
Livingston County Concrete Inc ....E 810 632-3030
Brighton *(G-2022)*
M 37 Concrete Products Inc ....E 231 733-8247
Muskegon *(G-11863)*
M 37 Concrete Products Inc ....G 231 689-1785
White Cloud *(G-18446)*
Manistique Rentals Inc ....G 906 341-6955
Manistique *(G-10921)*
Manthei Development Corp ....G 231 347-6282
Petoskey *(G-13005)*
Massive Mineral Mix LLC ....G 517 857-4544
Springport *(G-15883)*
Maxs Concrete Inc ....G 231 972-7558
Mecosta *(G-11193)*
McCoig Materials LLC ....E 734 414-6179
Plymouth *(G-13238)*
Meredith Lea Sand Gravel ....G 517 930-3662
Charlotte *(G-2762)*
Messina Concrete Inc ....E 734 783-1020
Flat Rock *(G-5623)*
Michigan Crushed Concrete Inc ....G 313 534-1500
Detroit *(G-4448)*
Midway Group LLC ....F 586 264-5380
Sterling Heights *(G-16099)*
Milford Redi-Mix Company ....E 248 684-1465
Milford *(G-11472)*
Miller Sand & Gravel Company ....G 269 672-5601
Hopkins *(G-8367)*
Millers Redi-Mix Inc ....E 989 587-6511
Fowler *(G-5830)*
Mini-Mix Inc ....E 586 792-2260
Clinton Township *(G-3302)*
Mirkwood Properties Inc ....G 586 727-3363
Richmond *(G-13842)*
Mix Masters Inc ....G 616 490-8520
Byron Center *(G-2287)*
Modern Industries Inc ....E 810 767-3330
Flint *(G-5735)*
Morse Concrete & Excavating ....F 989 826-3975
Mio *(G-11512)*
Mottes Materials Inc ....G 906 265-9955
Iron River *(G-8749)*
Mt Pleasant Centl Con Pdts Co ....G 989 772-3695
Mount Pleasant *(G-11721)*
National Block Company ....E 734 721-4050
Westland *(G-18399)*
Newberry Redi-Mix Inc ....G 906 293-5178
Newberry *(G-12097)*
Northfork Readi Mix Inc ....G 906 341-3445
Manistique *(G-10922)*
Novi Crushed Concrete LLC ....G 248 305-6020
Novi *(G-12493)*
Osborne Concrete Co ....G 734 941-3008
Romulus *(G-14314)*
Osborne Materials Company ....E 906 493-5211
Drummond Island *(G-4803)*
Owosso Ready Mix Co ....G 989 723-1295
Owosso *(G-12850)*
Ozinga Bros Inc ....E 269 469-2515
New Buffalo *(G-12025)*
P D P LLC ....E 616 437-9618
Wyoming *(G-18898)*
Paragon Ready Mix Inc ....E 586 731-8000
Shelby Township *(G-15295)*
Paragon Ready Mix Inc ....G 248 623-0100
Waterford *(G-18147)*
Peterman Mobile Concrete Inc ....E 269 324-1211
Portage *(G-13592)*
Piedmont Concrete Inc ....E 248 474-7740
Farmington Hills *(G-5347)*
Port Huron Building Supply Co ....F 810 987-2666
Port Huron *(G-13519)*
Quarrystone Inc ....E 906 786-0343
Escanaba *(G-5093)*
R & C Redi-Mix Inc ....G 616 636-5650
Sand Lake *(G-15051)*
R & R Ready-Mix Inc ....F 989 753-3862
Saginaw *(G-14732)*
R & R Ready-Mix Inc ....G 989 892-9313
Bay City *(G-1393)*
Rock Redi Mix LLC ....G 989 754-5861
Saginaw *(G-14739)*
Rock Redi Mix Inc ....G 989 752-0795
Carrollton *(G-2589)*
Roger Mix Storage ....G 231 352-9762
Frankfort *(G-5880)*
Rudy Goupille & Sons Inc ....G 906 475-9816
Negaunee *(G-11974)*
Ruppe Manufacturing Company ....E 906 932-3540
Ironwood *(G-8771)*
Ruth Drain Tile Inc ....G 989 864-3406
Ruth *(G-14598)*
◆ Saginaw Rock Products Co ....F 989 754-6589
Saginaw *(G-14751)*
Scheels Concrete Inc ....G 734 782-1464
Livonia *(G-10401)*
Sebewaing Concrete Pdts Inc ....E 989 883-3860
Sebewaing *(G-15143)*
Shafer Bros Inc ....F 517 629-4800
Albion *(G-131)*
Shafer Redi-Mix Inc ....F 517 629-4800
Albion *(G-132)*
Shafer Redi-Mix Inc ....D 517 764-0517
Jackson *(G-9009)*
Srm Concrete LLC ....G 231 796-8685
Big Rapids *(G-1688)*
Srm Concrete LLC ....G 989 422-4202
Houghton Lake *(G-8404)*
Srm Concrete LLC ....D 231 943-4818
Traverse City *(G-16839)*
Srm Concrete LLC ....G 231 775-9301
Cadillac *(G-2357)*
Srm Concrete LLC ....F 231 258-8633
Kalkaska *(G-9404)*

Employee Codes: A=Over 500 employees, B=251-500
C=101-250, D=51-100, E=20-50, F=10-19, G=3-9

Srm Concrete LLC G 231 832-5460
Reed City *(G-13799)*
Srm Concrete LLC G 989 344-0235
Grayling *(G-7469)*
Stevenson Building and Sup Co G 734 856-3931
Lambertville *(G-9653)*
Superior Materials LLC D 248 788-8000
Farmington Hills *(G-5394)*
Superior Materials LLC E 734 941-2479
Romulus *(G-14332)*
Superior Materials Holdings G 586 468-3544
Mount Clemens *(G-11658)*
Superior Materials Inc G 248 788-8000
Farmington Hills *(G-5395)*
Superior Mtls Holdings LLC E 248 788-8000
Farmington Hills *(G-5396)*
Swansons Excavating Inc G 989 873-4419
Prescott *(G-13652)*
Swartzmiller Lumber Company G 989 845-6625
Chesaning *(G-2830)*
The Mix G 269 382-1300
Kalamazoo *(G-9354)*
Theut Concrete Products Inc F 810 679-3376
Croswell *(G-3737)*
Theut Products Inc G 810 364-7132
Marysville *(G-11106)*
Theut Products Inc G 810 765-9321
Marine City *(G-10967)*
Theut Products Inc G 586 949-1300
Chesterfield *(G-2955)*
Van Horn Bros Inc E 248 623-4830
Waterford *(G-18172)*
Van Horn Bros Inc E 248 623-6000
Waterford *(G-18173)*
Van Sloten Enterprises Inc F 906 635-5151
Sault Sainte Marie *(G-15102)*
Vhb-123 Corporation G 248 623-4830
Waterford *(G-18174)*
Vollmer Ready-Mix Inc G 989 453-2262
Pigeon *(G-13042)*
Voorheis Hausbeck Excavating E 989 752-9666
Reese *(G-13810)*
Waanders Concrete Co F 269 673-6352
Allegan *(G-184)*
Westendorff Transit Mix G 989 593-2488
Pewamo *(G-13029)*
Whats Your Mix Menchies LLC G 248 840-1668
Shelby Township *(G-15368)*
Willbee Transit-Mix Co Inc E 517 782-9493
Jackson *(G-9036)*
Williams Reddi Mix Inc G 906 875-6952
Crystal Falls *(G-3747)*
Williams Redi Mix G 906 875-6839
Crystal Falls *(G-3748)*
Winter G 734 699-6825
Van Buren Twp *(G-17564)*

3275 Gypsum Prdts

Certainteed Gypsum Inc A 906 524-6101
Lanse *(G-9657)*
Lime Gypsum Products G 989 867-4611
Turner *(G-17464)*
Ng Operations LLC G 989 756-2741
National City *(G-11960)*
United States Gypsum Company D 269 384-6335
Otsego *(G-12801)*
United States Gypsum Company D 313 624-4232
River Rouge *(G-13861)*
United States Gypsum Company D 313 842-4455
Detroit *(G-4653)*
US Gypsum Co G 313 842-5800
River Rouge *(G-13862)*

3281 Cut Stone Prdts

A E G M Inc G 313 304-5279
Dearborn *(G-3804)*
▲ **Booms Stone Company** D 313 531-3000
Redford *(G-13721)*
▲ **Botsg Inc** D 231 929-2121
Traverse City *(G-16625)*
Cig Jan Products Ltd E 616 698-9070
Caledonia *(G-2371)*
Classic Stone MBL & Gran Inc F 248 588-1599
Troy *(G-17014)*
Dura Sill Corporation G 248 348-2490
Novi *(G-12405)*
▲ **Genesee Cut Stone & Marble Co** E 810 743-1800
Grand Blanc *(G-6242)*
▲ **Gmr Stone Products LLC** F 586 739-2700
Sterling Heights *(G-16032)*
Granite City Inc F 248 478-0033
Livonia *(G-10228)*
K2 Stoneworks LLC F 989 790-3250
Saginaw *(G-14675)*
Korcast Products Incorporated G 248 740-2340
Troy *(G-17197)*
Lakeshore Marble Company Inc F 269 429-8241
Stevensville *(G-16257)*
Landscape Stone Supply Inc G 616 953-2028
Holland *(G-8123)*
Lewiston Sand & Gravel Inc G 989 786-2742
Lewiston *(G-10023)*
Marbelite Corp E 248 348-1900
Novi *(G-12470)*
Marblecast of Michigan Inc F 248 398-0600
Oak Park *(G-12625)*
Mellemas Cut Stone G 616 984-2493
Sand Lake *(G-15049)*
▲ **Michigan Tile and Marble Co** E 313 931-1700
Detroit *(G-4453)*
Mis Controls Inc E 586 339-3900
Rochester Hills *(G-14064)*
Moderne Slate Inc G 231 584-3499
Mancelona *(G-10877)*
Muskegon Monument & Stone Co G 231 722-2730
Muskegon *(G-11882)*
Parker Property Dev Inc F 616 842-6118
Grand Haven *(G-6343)*
Patten Monument Company D 616 785-4141
Comstock Park *(G-3634)*
Pearson Precast Concrete Pdts G 517 486-4060
Blissfield *(G-1772)*
Quarry Ridge Stone Inc F 616 827-8244
Byron Center *(G-2294)*
Rockwood Quarry LLC C 734 783-7415
South Rockwood *(G-15465)*
Rockwood Quarry LLC G 734 783-7400
Newport *(G-12106)*
Royal Stone LLC E 248 343-6232
Williamston *(G-18581)*
Solutions In Stone Inc G 734 453-4444
Plymouth *(G-13301)*
Steinbrecher Stone Corp G 906 563-5852
Norway *(G-12357)*
Stone Shop Inc F 248 852-4700
Port Huron *(G-13530)*
Stonecrafters Inc F 517 529-4990
Clarklake *(G-3009)*
Superior Monuments Co G 231 728-2211
Muskegon *(G-11928)*
▲ **Tile Craft Inc** F 231 929-7207
Traverse City *(G-16860)*
TNT Marble and Stone Inc G 248 887-8237
Hartland *(G-7772)*
▲ **Unilock Michigan Inc** E 248 437-7037
Brighton *(G-2089)*
Yellowstone Products Inc G 616 299-7855
Comstock Park *(G-3653)*
Zimmer Marble Co Inc F 517 787-1500
Jackson *(G-9041)*

3291 Abrasive Prdts

3M Company E 313 372-4200
Detroit *(G-3970)*
Abrasive Diamond Tool Company E 248 588-4800
Madison Heights *(G-10657)*
◆ **Abrasive Finishing Inc** G 734 433-9236
Chelsea *(G-2801)*
▲ **Abrasive Materials LLC** G 517 437-4796
Battle Creek *(G-1176)*
Acme Holding Company E 586 759-3332
Warren *(G-17690)*
◆ **Afi Enterprises Inc** E 734 475-9111
Chelsea *(G-2803)*
Auto Quip Inc F 810 364-3366
Kimball *(G-9491)*
Beans Best LLC G 734 707-7378
Ann Arbor *(G-397)*
Belanger Inc D 248 349-7010
Northville *(G-12197)*
▲ **Botsg Inc** D 231 929-2121
Traverse City *(G-16625)*
▼ **Calumet Abrasives Co Inc** E 219 844-2695
Grand Rapids *(G-6545)*
Cdp Diamond Products Inc E 734 591-1041
Livonia *(G-10149)*
▲ **Cincinnati Tyrolit Inc** C 513 458-8121
Shelby Township *(G-15188)*
▼ **Crippen Manufacturing Company** E 989 681-4323
Saint Louis *(G-14990)*
D R W Systems G 989 874-4663
Filion *(G-5612)*
Detroit Abrasives Company G 989 725-2405
Owosso *(G-12831)*
▲ **Detroit Abrasives Company** G 734 475-1651
Chelsea *(G-2808)*
Di-Coat Corporation E 248 349-1211
Novi *(G-12399)*
Diamond Tool Manufacturing Inc E 734 416-1900
Plymouth *(G-13157)*
Diamondback Corp F 248 960-8260
Commerce Township *(G-3522)*
Dianamic Abrasive Products F 248 280-1185
Troy *(G-17059)*
Dryden Steel LLC G 586 777-7600
Dryden *(G-4805)*
◆ **Duramic Abrasive Products Inc** E 586 755-7220
Warren *(G-17786)*
▲ **E C Moore Company** E 313 581-7878
Dearborn *(G-3832)*
E S I Industries G 231 256-9345
Lake Leelanau *(G-9559)*
Enkon LLC E 937 890-5678
Manchester *(G-10883)*
Ervin Industries Inc D 517 265-6118
Adrian *(G-64)*
◆ **Ervin Industries Inc** E 734 769-4600
Ann Arbor *(G-478)*
Ervin Industries Inc E 517 423-5477
Tecumseh *(G-16500)*
▲ **Even-Cut Abrasive Company** D 216 881-9595
Grand Rapids *(G-6689)*
Ferro Industries Inc E 586 792-6001
Harrison Township *(G-7699)*
▲ **Finishing Technologies Inc** F 616 794-4001
Belding *(G-1449)*
Formax Manufacturing Corp E 616 456-5458
Grand Rapids *(G-6716)*
▲ **GMA Industries Inc** E 734 595-7300
Romulus *(G-14280)*
Hammond Machinery Inc D 269 345-7151
Kalamazoo *(G-9207)*
Howell Tool Service Inc F 517 548-1114
Howell *(G-8465)*
Hydro Abrasive Products LLC G 313 456-9410
Warren *(G-17856)*
Hydro-Abrasive Products LLC G 734 459-1544
Plymouth *(G-13194)*
▼ **IGA Abrasives LLC** E 616 243-5566
Grand Rapids *(G-6832)*
▲ **Inland Diamond Products Co** E 248 585-1762
Madison Heights *(G-10746)*
Internal Grinding Abrasives E 616 243-5566
Grand Rapids *(G-6849)*
◆ **International Abrasives Inc** G 586 778-8490
Roseville *(G-14424)*
Kalamazoo Company E 269 345-7151
Kalamazoo *(G-9237)*
▲ **Krmc LLC** G 734 955-9311
Romulus *(G-14296)*
▲ **L R Oliver and Company Inc** E 810 765-1000
Cottrellville *(G-3724)*
◆ **Metaltec Steel Abrasive Co** E 734 459-7900
Canton *(G-2495)*
Michigan Carbide Company Inc F 586 264-8780
Troy *(G-17257)*
▼ **Mid-West Waltham Abrasives Co** E 517 725-7161
Owosso *(G-12843)*
Nakagawa Special Stl Amer Inc E 248 449-6050
Novi *(G-12487)*
Nutek Industries LLC F 800 637-9194
Novi *(G-12495)*
Patch Works Farms Inc G 989 430-3610
Wheeler *(G-18436)*
Peerless Mtal Pwders Abrsive L G 313 841-5400
Detroit *(G-4513)*
▲ **Roll It Up Inc** E 248 735-8900
Northville *(G-12255)*
▲ **Sam Brown Sales LLC** E 248 358-2626
Farmington *(G-5147)*
▲ **Sandbox Solutions Inc** C 248 349-7010
Northville *(G-12257)*
Schwab Industries Inc E 586 566-8090
Shelby Township *(G-15326)*
▲ **Sidley Diamond Tool Company** E 734 261-7970
Garden City *(G-6109)*
South Bay Supply LLC G 313 882-8090
Saint Clair Shores *(G-14885)*
Stan Sax Corp F 248 683-9199
Detroit *(G-4604)*

▲ **Superabrasives Inc** ....E 248 348-7670
Wixom *(G-18762)*
Superior Abrasive Products ....F 248 969-4090
Oxford *(G-12921)*
▼ **Trinity Tool Co** ....E 586 296-5900
Fraser *(G-6006)*
United Abrasive Inc ....F 906 563-9249
Vulcan *(G-17616)*
▲ **Vachon Industries Inc** ....F 517 278-2354
Coldwater *(G-3460)*
Van Industries Inc ....F 248 398-6990
Ferndale *(G-5597)*
Warren Abrasives Inc ....F 586 772-0002
Warren *(G-18058)*

3292 Asbestos products

Cobalt Friction Technologies ....F 734 274-3030
Ann Arbor *(G-430)*
K-Value Insulation LLC ....G 248 688-5816
Troy *(G-17191)*

3295 Minerals & Earths: Ground Or Treated

D J McQuestion & Sons Inc ....F 231 768-4403
Leroy *(G-10005)*
Edw C Levy Co ....G 313 843-7200
Detroit *(G-4202)*
▲ **Edw C Levy Co** ....B 313 429-2200
Dearborn *(G-3835)*
Fritz Enterprises ....E 734 283-7272
Trenton *(G-16888)*
Graphite Machining Inc ....F 810 678-2227
Metamora *(G-11279)*
Michigan Metals and Mfg Inc ....G 248 910-7674
Southfield *(G-15657)*
Montcalm Aggregates Inc ....G 989 772-7038
Mount Pleasant *(G-11717)*
Mw Minerals ....G 517 294-6709
Milford *(G-11474)*
Novaceuticals LLC ....G 248 309-3402
Auburn Hills *(G-988)*
▲ **R J Marshall Company** ....F 248 353-4100
Southfield *(G-15687)*
R5 Construxtion Inc ....F 855 480-7663
Middleville *(G-11311)*
Sgl Technic LLC ....G 248 540-9508
Shelby Township *(G-15328)*
Techni Sand Inc ....G 269 465-5833
Benton Harbor *(G-1590)*
Tms International LLC ....F 734 241-3007
Monroe *(G-11584)*

3296 Mineral Wool

Autoneum North America Inc ....G 248 848-0100
Farmington Hills *(G-5176)*
Dgp Inc ....E 989 635-7531
Marlette *(G-10980)*
▲ **Eftec North America LLC** ....D 248 585-2200
Taylor *(G-16410)*
▲ **Gallant Inc** ....F 616 772-1880
Zeeland *(G-19023)*
HP Pelzer Auto Systems Inc ....B 810 987-4444
Port Huron *(G-13483)*
Integrated Interiors Inc ....F 586 756-4840
Warren *(G-17867)*
Knauf Insulation Inc ....C 517 630-2000
Albion *(G-128)*
Manta Group LLC ....F 248 325-8264
Pontiac *(G-13395)*
Mbcd Inc ....E 517 484-4426
Lansing *(G-9867)*
Midwest Fbrglas Fbricators Inc ....F 810 765-7445
Marine City *(G-10963)*
◆ **Ufp Technologies Inc** ....D 616 949-8100
Grand Rapids *(G-7294)*
Unique Fabricating Inc ....A 248 853-2333
Auburn Hills *(G-1068)*
▲ **Unique Fabricating Na Inc** ....B 248 853-2333
Auburn Hills *(G-1069)*

3297 Nonclay Refractories

▲ **Ajf Inc** ....E 734 753-4410
New Boston *(G-11998)*
Cerco Inc ....E 734 362-8664
Brownstown Twp *(G-2153)*
Chase Nedrow Manufacturing Inc ....E 248 669-9886
Wixom *(G-18633)*
Harbisonwalker Intl Inc ....G 231 689-6641
White Cloud *(G-18442)*
Martin Mretta Magnesia Spc LLC ....E 231 723-2577
Manistee *(G-10907)*
▲ **Midwest Product Spc Inc** ....G 231 767-9942
Muskegon *(G-11874)*
Nedrow Refractories Co ....D 248 669-2500
Wixom *(G-18718)*
Rex Materials Inc ....E 517 223-3787
Howell *(G-8509)*
Stellar Materials Intl LLC ....E 561 504-3924
Whitmore Lake *(G-18546)*
Taylor Controls Inc ....F 269 637-8521
South Haven *(G-15418)*
Thermbond Refractory Solutions ....G 561 330-9300
Whitmore Lake *(G-18547)*

3299 Nonmetallic Mineral Prdts, NEC

3M Technical Ceramics Inc ....F 248 960-9339
Wixom *(G-18592)*
Darren McCaffery Stucco ....G 321 303-0988
Manton *(G-10932)*
Delicate Creations Inc ....G 313 406-6268
Dearborn Heights *(G-3923)*
Huron Glass Block ....G 586 598-6900
Macomb *(G-10603)*
Maker Works ....G 734 222-4911
Ann Arbor *(G-565)*
Nano Innovations LLC ....G 906 231-2101
Houghton *(G-8387)*
Neuvokas Corporation ....G 906 934-2661
Ahmeek *(G-109)*
▲ **Vico Company** ....G 734 453-3777
Plymouth *(G-13332)*
Wonderland Graphics Inc ....G 616 452-0712
Grand Rapids *(G-7349)*

33 PRIMARY METAL INDUSTRIES

3312 Blast Furnaces, Coke Ovens, Steel & Rolling Mills

ABC Coating Company Inc ....F 616 245-4626
Grand Rapids *(G-6415)*
Accutek Mold & Engineering ....E 586 978-1335
Sterling Heights *(G-15922)*
Acme Tool & Die Co ....G 231 938-1260
Acme *(G-1)*
Alan Bruce Enterprises ....G 616 262-4609
Byron Center *(G-2257)*
America Wireless ....G 810 820-3273
Flint *(G-5644)*
Ann Arbor Stainless ....G 734 741-9499
Ann Arbor *(G-370)*
Apex Tooling Solutions LLC ....G 616 283-7439
Jenison *(G-9044)*
Araymond Mfg Ctr N Amer Inc ....G 248 537-3147
Rochester Hills *(G-13950)*
ARC Mit ....G 248 399-4800
Ferndale *(G-5527)*
Arcanum Steel Technologies Inc ....E 630 715-4899
Grand Rapids *(G-6467)*
Arlington Metals Corporation ....E 269 426-3371
Sawyer *(G-15106)*
ATI Marketing ....G 231 590-9600
Traverse City *(G-16605)*
Atlantis Tech Corp ....G 989 356-6954
Alpena *(G-279)*
▲ **Autocam-Pax Inc** ....C 269 782-5186
Dowagiac *(G-4776)*
Avatar Inc ....G 586 846-3195
Clinton Township *(G-3177)*
▲ **Aweba Tool & Die Corp** ....F 478 296-2002
Hastings *(G-7781)*
▲ **Axle of Dearborn Inc** ....C 248 543-5995
Ferndale *(G-5529)*
Bar Processing Corporation ....F 734 782-4454
Warren *(G-17727)*
Bazzi Tire & Wheels ....G 313 846-8888
Detroit *(G-4043)*
Bbg North America Ltd Partnr ....F 248 572-6550
Oxford *(G-12878)*
Benteler Automotive Corp ....B 616 247-3936
Auburn Hills *(G-810)*
Blades Enterprises LLC ....F 734 449-4479
Wixom *(G-18622)*
Bnb Welding & Fabrication Inc ....G 810 820-1508
Burton *(G-2227)*
Borneman & Peterson Inc ....F 810 744-1890
Flint *(G-5659)*
Brake Roller Co Inc ....F 269 965-2371
Battle Creek *(G-1197)*
Broaching Industries Inc ....E 586 949-3775
Chesterfield *(G-2853)*
Burnham & Northern Inc ....G 517 279-7501
Coldwater *(G-3422)*
C & M Manufacturing Corp Inc ....E 586 749-3455
Chesterfield *(G-2854)*
C P I Inc ....G 810 664-8686
Lapeer *(G-9919)*
▲ **Cannon-Muskegon Corporation** ....C 231 755-1681
Norton Shores *(G-12284)*
Carry Manufacturing Inc ....G 989 672-2779
Caro *(G-2567)*
◆ **Central Lake Armor Express Inc** ....C 231 544-6090
Central Lake *(G-2691)*
Champlain Specialty Metals Inc ....E 269 926-7241
Benton Harbor *(G-1539)*
Cleveland-Cliffs Steel Corp ....B 313 317-8900
Dearborn *(G-3820)*
Cleveland-Cliffs Steel Corp ....A 800 532-8857
Dearborn *(G-3821)*
Coach House Iron Inc ....G 616 785-8967
Sparta *(G-15764)*
Creform Corporation ....E 248 926-2555
Novi *(G-12385)*
▲ **Crown Steel Rail Co** ....G 248 593-7100
West Bloomfield *(G-18274)*
De Luxe Die Set Inc ....G 810 227-2556
Brighton *(G-1974)*
Delaco Steel Corporation ....C 313 491-1200
Dearborn *(G-3826)*
Delaware Dynamics Michigan LLC ....F 586 997-1717
Shelby Township *(G-15203)*
Detroit Metal Elements LLC ....G 313 300-9057
Warren *(G-17776)*
Detroit Steel Group Inc ....G 248 298-2900
Royal Oak *(G-14530)*
Die Cast Press Mfg Co Inc ....E 269 657-6060
Paw Paw *(G-12947)*
Domestic Forge & Forming Inc ....G 586 749-9559
New Haven *(G-12031)*
Doylen Albring Jr ....G 989 427-2919
Edmore *(G-4991)*
Dundee Products Company ....E 734 529-2441
Dundee *(G-4817)*
◆ **Eaton Steel Corporation** ....D 248 398-3434
Oak Park *(G-12609)*
Eaton Steel Corporation ....D 248 398-3434
Livonia *(G-10189)*
Euridium Solutions LLC ....G 248 535-7005
Troy *(G-17098)*
F and R Associates ....G 734 316-7763
Saline *(G-15016)*
Fab Concepts ....G 586 466-6411
Chesterfield *(G-2879)*
Fabtronic Inc ....E 586 786-6114
Macomb *(G-10594)*
◆ **First Place Manufacturing LLC** ....G 231 798-1694
Norton Shores *(G-12293)*
Fritz Enterprises ....E 734 283-7272
Trenton *(G-16888)*
G & G Steel Fabricating Co ....G 586 979-4112
Warren *(G-17821)*
General Motors LLC ....G 810 236-1970
Flint *(G-5706)*
Gerdau Macsteel Inc ....B 517 764-0311
Jackson *(G-8890)*
Gerdau Macsteel Inc ....A 734 243-2446
Monroe *(G-11542)*
Gerdau Macsteel Inc ....B 734 243-2446
Monroe *(G-11543)*
◆ **Gerdau Macsteel Inc** ....E 517 782-0415
Jackson *(G-8891)*
▲ **Gill Corporation** ....B 616 453-4491
Grand Rapids *(G-6740)*
Gladiator Quality Sorting LLC ....G 734 578-1950
Canton *(G-2465)*
Grant Industries Incorporated ....E 586 293-9200
Fraser *(G-5931)*
Greenbrook Tms Neurohealth Ctr ....G 855 940-4867
Lansing *(G-9846)*
Harrison Steel LLC ....G 586 247-1230
Shelby Township *(G-15232)*
▲ **Hayes Lmmerz Intrntnl-Grgia LL** ....D 734 737-5000
Novi *(G-12431)*
Industrial Engineering Service ....F 616 794-1330
Belding *(G-1453)*
Industrial Marking Products ....G 517 699-2160
Holt *(G-8314)*
Ivan Doverspike ....F 313 579-3000
Detroit *(G-4328)*

Employee Codes: A=Over 500 employees, B=251-500
C=101-250, D=51-100, E=20-50, F=10-19, G=3-9
2022 Harris Michigan
Industrial Directory
801

JIT Steel Corp F 313 491-3212
Dearborn *(G-3856)*

▲ King Steel Corporation E 800 638-2530
Grand Blanc *(G-6250)*

Lake Michigan Wire LLC F 616 786-9200
Holland *(G-8121)*

▲ Major Industries Ltd F 810 985-9372
Port Huron *(G-13499)*

Manistee Wldg & Piping Svc Inc G 231 723-2551
Manistee *(G-10906)*

Mean Erectors Inc F 989 737-3285
Saginaw *(G-14690)*

Metal Dynamics Detroit G 313 841-1800
Detroit *(G-4431)*

▲ Michigan Rod Products Inc D 517 552-9812
Howell *(G-8481)*

Michigan Wheel Corp G 616 647-1078
Grand Rapids *(G-6996)*

Mill Steel Co D 616 949-6700
Grand Rapids *(G-7010)*

Mueller Industrial Realty Co G 810 987-7770
Port Huron *(G-13507)*

National Galvanizing LP A 734 243-1882
Monroe *(G-11567)*

Nelson Manufacturing Inc G 810 648-0065
Sandusky *(G-15063)*

Nobilis Pipe Company F 248 470-5692
Novi *(G-12490)*

Oakland Welding Industries E 586 949-4090
Chesterfield *(G-2916)*

OEM Wheels G 248 556-9993
Harper Woods *(G-7668)*

Paich Railworks Inc G 734 397-2424
Van Buren Twp *(G-17546)*

Parton & Preble Inc E 586 773-6000
Warren *(G-17954)*

Patterson Precision Mfg Inc E 231 733-1913
Norton Shores *(G-12324)*

Pdf Mfg Inc G 517 522-8431
Grass Lake *(G-7443)*

Peerless Steel Company E 616 530-6695
Grandville *(G-7408)*

▲ Power Wheels Pro G 248 686-2035
Waterford *(G-18155)*

Premium Air Systems Inc E 248 680-8800
Troy *(G-17312)*

Prime Wheel Corporation G 248 207-4739
Canton *(G-2511)*

Proservice Machine Ltd F 734 317-7266
Erie *(G-5054)*

Quality Cavity Inc F 248 344-9995
Canton *(G-2516)*

Ram Die Corp F 616 647-2855
Grand Rapids *(G-7138)*

Repair Industries Michigan Inc C 313 365-5300
Detroit *(G-4568)*

Resetar Equipment Inc G 313 291-0500
Dearborn Heights *(G-3937)*

River Valley Machine Inc F 269 673-8070
Allegan *(G-181)*

▼ Rod Chomper Inc F 616 392-9677
Holland *(G-8182)*

Rucci Forged Wheels Inc G 248 577-3500
Sterling Heights *(G-16161)*

S F R Precision Turning Inc G 517 709-3367
Wixom *(G-18746)*

Sabre Manufacturing G 269 945-4120
Hastings *(G-7808)*

Sandvik Inc D 269 926-7241
Benton Harbor *(G-1582)*

Service Iron Works Inc E 248 446-9750
South Lyon *(G-15457)*

Set Enterprises Inc E 586 573-3600
Royal Oak *(G-14580)*

Shoreline Recycling & Supply E 231 722-6081
Muskegon *(G-11920)*

▲ SL Wheels Inc G 734 744-8500
Livonia *(G-10411)*

St Clair Steel Corporation G 586 758-4356
Warren *(G-18025)*

St Johns Computer Machining G 989 224-7664
Saint Johns *(G-14916)*

Stage Stop G 989 838-4039
Ithaca *(G-8795)*

Steel 21 LLC E 616 884-2121
Cedar Springs *(G-2662)*

◆ Steel Industries Inc C 313 535-8505
Redford *(G-13774)*

Steel Mill Components Inc F 586 920-2595
Warren *(G-18029)*

Strong Steel Products LLC F 313 267-3300
Detroit *(G-4613)*

Superalloy North America LLC G 810 252-1552
Bingham Farms *(G-1704)*

The Pom Group Inc E 248 409-7900
Auburn Hills *(G-1051)*

▼ TI Fluid Systems LLC A 248 494-5000
Auburn Hills *(G-1054)*

◆ TI Group Auto Systems LLC B 248 296-8000
Auburn Hills *(G-1055)*

Tms International LLC G 734 241-3007
Monroe *(G-11583)*

Tms International LLC G 517 764-5123
Jackson *(G-9021)*

Tms International LLC G 313 378-6502
Ecorse *(G-4987)*

TNT Pipe and Tube LLC E 419 466-1144
Erie *(G-5055)*

▲ Twb Company LLC C 734 289-6400
Monroe *(G-11586)*

Universal Hdlg Eqp Owosso LLC E 989 720-1650
Owosso *(G-12865)*

Versa Handling Co G 313 491-0500
Sterling Heights *(G-16222)*

W A Thomas Company G 734 955-6500
Taylor *(G-16487)*

Welk-Ko Fabricators Inc G 248 486-2598
New Hudson *(G-12074)*

Westwood Lands Inc F 906 475-9544
Marquette *(G-11050)*

Wiesen EDM Inc E 616 794-9870
Belding *(G-1467)*

Wire Nets G 248 669-5312
Commerce Township *(G-3581)*

WM Tube & Wire Forming Inc F 231 830-9393
Muskegon *(G-11950)*

▲ Worthington Steel of Michigan C 734 374-3260
Taylor *(G-16490)*

3313 Electrometallurgical Prdts

Alloying Surfaces Inc G 248 524-9200
Troy *(G-16927)*

◆ Alpha Resources LLC E 269 465-5559
Stevensville *(G-16239)*

▲ Cannon-Muskegon Corporation C 231 755-1681
Norton Shores *(G-12284)*

▲ H C Starck Inc G 517 279-9511
Coldwater *(G-3437)*

▲ Miccus Inc F 616 604-4449
Howell *(G-8480)*

3315 Steel Wire Drawing & Nails & Spikes

▲ AG Manufacturing Inc E 989 479-9590
Harbor Beach *(G-7628)*

Autonertia Inc F 810 882-1002
Fenton *(G-5453)*

Barrette Outdoor Living Inc G 810 235-0400
Flint *(G-5650)*

Breasco LLC G 734 961-9020
Ypsilanti *(G-18929)*

▲ Dw-National Standard-Niles LLC C 269 683-8100
Niles *(G-12127)*

▲ Elco Enterprises Inc E 517 782-8040
Jackson *(G-8878)*

Ernest Industries Acquisition, E 734 595-9500
Westland *(G-18369)*

Flexpost Inc G 616 928-0829
Holland *(G-8036)*

Jems of Litchfield Inc F 517 542-5367
Litchfield *(G-10081)*

Kyungshin Cable Intl Corp F 248 679-7578
Livonia *(G-10271)*

Lee Spring Company LLC F 586 296-9850
Fraser *(G-5957)*

Marathon Weld Group LLC F 517 782-8040
Jackson *(G-8944)*

▲ McClure Metals Group Inc G 616 957-5955
Grand Rapids *(G-6971)*

Metter Flooring LLC G 517 914-2004
Rives Junction *(G-13887)*

Morstar Inc F 248 605-3291
Livonia *(G-10322)*

◆ National Nail Corp C 616 538-8000
Grand Rapids *(G-7036)*

▲ National-Standard LLC C 269 683-9902
Niles *(G-12151)*

Philips Machining Company F 616 997-7777
Coopersville *(G-3695)*

Pro-Soil Site Services Inc F 517 267-8767
Lansing *(G-9733)*

Stephens Pipe & Steel LLC E 616 248-3433
Grand Rapids *(G-7226)*

◆ Straits Steel and Wire Company D 231 843-3416
Ludington *(G-10551)*

Transportation Tech Group Inc F 810 233-0440
Flint *(G-5781)*

Van Ron Steel Services LLC F 616 813-6907
Marne *(G-11001)*

Vandelay Services LLC G 810 279-8550
Howell *(G-8538)*

Ventura Manufacturing Inc G 616 772-7405
Zeeland *(G-19087)*

◆ Ventura Manufacturing Inc C 616 772-7405
Zeeland *(G-19088)*

Wapc Holdings Inc F 586 939-0770
Sterling Heights *(G-16228)*

▲ West Michigan Wire Co D 231 845-1281
Ludington *(G-10556)*

WM Tube & Wire Forming Inc F 231 830-9393
Muskegon *(G-11950)*

3316 Cold Rolled Steel Sheet, Strip & Bars

Alro Steel Corporation G 517 371-9600
Lansing *(G-9803)*

Bar Processing Corporation F 734 782-4454
Warren *(G-17727)*

BR Safety Products Inc G 734 582-4499
Plymouth *(G-13137)*

Cold Heading Co E 586 497-7016
Warren *(G-17759)*

Diez Group LLC D 734 675-1700
Woodhaven *(G-18799)*

Eikos Holdings Inc E 248 280-0300
Troy *(G-17080)*

Fabtec Enterprises Inc F 616 878-9288
Byron Center *(G-2269)*

Flat Rock Metal Inc C 734 782-4454
Flat Rock *(G-5618)*

◆ Gerdau Macsteel Inc E 517 782-0415
Jackson *(G-8891)*

Gerdau Macsteel Inc B 517 764-0311
Jackson *(G-8890)*

Gerdau Macsteel Inc B 734 243-2446
Monroe *(G-11543)*

Grant Industries Incorporated E 586 293-9200
Fraser *(G-5931)*

H & L Tool Company Inc E 248 585-7474
Madison Heights *(G-10736)*

Kamax Inc C 810 272-2090
Lapeer *(G-9936)*

National Galvanizing LP A 734 243-1882
Monroe *(G-11567)*

◆ Nss Technologies Inc E 734 459-9500
Canton *(G-2502)*

Peerless Steel Company E 616 530-6695
Grandville *(G-7408)*

Sandvik Inc D 269 926-7241
Benton Harbor *(G-1582)*

Van Emon Bruce G 269 467-7803
Centreville *(G-2699)*

Warren Steel Co G 586 756-6600
Warren *(G-18062)*

Worthington Industries Inc G 734 397-6187
Canton *(G-2543)*

Worthington Industries Inc G 734 289-5416
Monroe *(G-11592)*

▲ Worthington Steel of Michigan C 734 374-3260
Taylor *(G-16490)*

3317 Steel Pipe & Tubes

A & B Tube Benders Inc F 586 773-0440
Warren *(G-17678)*

▲ Ace Consulting & MGT Inc E 989 821-7040
Roscommon *(G-14346)*

Advanced Drainage Systems Inc G 989 723-5208
Owosso *(G-12819)*

All Bending & Tubular Pdts LLC F 616 333-2364
Grand Rapids *(G-6446)*

◆ Angstrom USA LLC E 313 295-0100
Southfield *(G-15488)*

◆ Atlas Tube (plymouth) Inc D 734 738-5600
Plymouth *(G-13127)*

Austin Tube Products Inc F 231 745-2741
Baldwin *(G-1121)*

Benteler Automotive Corp B 616 245-4607
Grand Rapids *(G-6501)*

Benteler Automotive Corp B 616 247-3936
Auburn Hills *(G-810)*

Berkley Industries Inc E 989 656-2171
Bay Port *(G-1413)*

SIC SECTION
33 PRIMARY METAL INDUSTRIES33 PRIMARY METAL INDUSTRIES

▼ **Burgaflex North America Inc** ... F ... 810 584-7296
Grand Blanc *(G-6237)*

◆ **Burr Oak Tool Inc** ... B ... 269 651-9393
Sturgis *(G-16282)*

Delta Tube & Fabricating Corp ... E ... 248 634-8267
Holly *(G-8267)*

Detroit Tubing Mill Inc ... E ... 313 491-8823
Detroit *(G-4169)*

Diversified Tube LLC ... F ... 313 790-7348
Southfield *(G-15540)*

Dwm Holdings Inc ... D ... 586 541-0013
Warren *(G-17787)*

▼ **Energy Steel & Supply Co** ... D ... 810 538-4990
Rochester Hills *(G-14004)*

Ernest Industries Acquisition, ... E ... 734 595-9500
Westland *(G-18369)*

Exceptional Product Sales LLC ... F ... 586 286-3240
Sterling Heights *(G-16008)*

Forged Tubular Products Inc ... F ... 313 843-6720
Detroit *(G-4242)*

Formfab LLC ... E ... 248 844-3676
Rochester Hills *(G-14013)*

General Structures Inc ... F ... 586 774-6105
Warren *(G-17826)*

Grinding Specialists Inc ... E ... 734 729-1775
Westland *(G-18377)*

James Steel & Tube Company ... F ... 248 547-4200
Madison Heights *(G-10752)*

M & W Manufacturing Co LLC ... F ... 586 741-8897
Chesterfield *(G-2906)*

Martinrea Industries Inc ... E ... 231 832-5504
Reed City *(G-13795)*

▲ **Martinrea Industries Inc** ... E ... 734 428-2400
Manchester *(G-10886)*

Midway Strl Pipe & Sup Inc ... G ... 517 787-1350
Jackson *(G-8961)*

New 11 Inc ... E ... 616 494-9370
Holland *(G-8153)*

◆ **New Hudson Corporation** ... E ... 248 437-3970
New Hudson *(G-12064)*

Parma Tube Corp ... E ... 269 651-2351
Sturgis *(G-16316)*

Perforated Tubes Inc ... E ... 616 942-4550
Ada *(G-33)*

RB Christian Ironworks LLC ... G ... 269 963-2222
Battle Creek *(G-1286)*

Rbc Enterprises Inc ... E ... 313 491-3350
Detroit *(G-4554)*

Rock River Fabrications Inc ... E ... 616 281-5769
Grand Rapids *(G-7162)*

◆ **Rolled Alloys Inc** ... D ... 734 847-0561
Temperance *(G-16547)*

Roman Engineering ... E ... 231 238-7644
Afton *(G-107)*

S & S Tube Inc ... E ... 989 656-7211
Bay Port *(G-1415)*

Specialty Tube Solutions ... G ... 989 848-0880
Mio *(G-11516)*

Tarpon Industries Inc ... E ... 810 364-7421
Marysville *(G-11105)*

▼ **TI Fluid Systems LLC** ... A ... 248 494-5000
Auburn Hills *(G-1054)*

◆ **TI Group Auto Systems LLC** ... B ... 248 296-8000
Auburn Hills *(G-1055)*

TI Group Auto Systems LLC ... G ... 859 235-5420
Auburn Hills *(G-1056)*

TI Group Auto Systems LLC ... G ... 248 475-4663
Auburn Hills *(G-1057)*

Trans Tube Inc ... F ... 248 334-5720
Pontiac *(G-13420)*

Transportation Tech Group Inc ... F ... 810 233-0440
Flint *(G-5781)*

◆ **Usui International Corporation** ... E ... 734 354-3626
Plymouth *(G-13328)*

Van Pelt Corporation ... F ... 313 365-6500
Detroit *(G-4662)*

3321 Gray Iron Foundries

Awcco USA Incorporated ... G ... 586 336-9135
Romeo *(G-14220)*

Berne Enterprises Inc ... F ... 989 453-3235
Pigeon *(G-13036)*

Bernier Cast Metals Inc ... G ... 989 754-7571
Saginaw *(G-14615)*

▲ **Betz Industries Inc** ... D ... 616 453-4429
Grand Rapids *(G-6504)*

Blue Fire Manufacturing LLC ... E ... 248 714-7166
Waterford *(G-18104)*

Cadillac Casting Inc ... B ... 231 779-9600
Cadillac *(G-2319)*

Calhoun Foundry Company Inc ... D ... 517 568-4415
Homer *(G-8349)*

Casting Industries Inc ... F ... 586 776-5700
Saint Clair *(G-14817)*

City of East Jordan ... G ... 231 536-2561
East Jordan *(G-4861)*

Dock Foundry Company ... G ... 269 278-1765
Three Rivers *(G-16571)*

E & M Cores Inc ... G ... 989 386-9223
Clare *(G-2978)*

◆ **Eagle Quest International Ltd** ... F ... 616 850-2630
Spring Lake *(G-15812)*

East Jordan Ironworks Inc ... G ... 517 566-7211
Sunfield *(G-16334)*

Ej Americas LLC ... G ... 231 536-2261
East Jordan *(G-4863)*

Ej Asia-Pacific Inc ... B ... 231 536-2261
East Jordan *(G-4865)*

Ej Co ... F ... 231 536-4527
East Jordan *(G-4866)*

Ej Europe LLC ... C ... 231 536-2261
East Jordan *(G-4867)*

Ej Group Inc ... E ... 231 536-2261
East Jordan *(G-4868)*

◆ **Ej Usa Inc** ... B ... 800 874-4100
East Jordan *(G-4870)*

Ej Usa Inc ... G ... 248 546-2004
Oak Park *(G-12610)*

Ej Usa Inc ... G ... 616 538-2040
Wyoming *(G-18870)*

Ej Usa Inc ... G ... 231 536-2261
East Jordan *(G-4871)*

Eqi Ltd ... G ... 616 850-2630
Norton Shores *(G-12292)*

▲ **Federal Group Usa Inc** ... F ... 248 545-5000
Southfield *(G-15559)*

General Motors LLC ... G ... 989 757-0528
Saginaw *(G-14651)*

▲ **Global Technology Ventures Inc** ... G ... 248 324-3707
Farmington Hills *(G-5252)*

Great Lakes Castings LLC ... C ... 231 843-2501
Ludington *(G-10538)*

Great Lakes Castings LLC ... E ... 616 399-9710
Holland *(G-8058)*

Grede Holdings LLC ... E ... 248 440-9500
Southfield *(G-15579)*

▲ **Grede II LLC** ... E ... 248 440-9500
Southfield *(G-15580)*

Grede LLC ... B ... 906 774-7250
Kingsford *(G-9509)*

▲ **Grede LLC** ... B ... 248 440-9500
Southfield *(G-15581)*

▼ **Grede Wscnsin Subsidiaries LLC** ... C ... 248 727-1800
Southfield *(G-15583)*

GSC Riii - Grede LLC ... G ... 248 440-9500
Southfield *(G-15586)*

Holland Alloys Inc ... E ... 616 396-6444
Holland *(G-8073)*

JP Castings Inc ... E ... 517 857-3660
Springport *(G-15882)*

Kent Foundry Company ... E ... 616 754-1100
Greenville *(G-7496)*

Michigan Poly Pipe Inc ... G ... 517 709-8100
Grand Ledge *(G-6396)*

Midland Iron Works Inc ... F ... 989 832-3041
Midland *(G-11393)*

Northland Castings Corporation ... E ... 231 873-4974
Hart *(G-7758)*

▲ **Paragon Metals LLC** ... G ... 517 639-4629
Hillsdale *(G-7941)*

Pioneer Foundry Company Inc ... F ... 517 782-9469
Jackson *(G-8986)*

Ravenna Casting Center Inc ... G ... 231 853-0300
Ravenna *(G-13692)*

Robert Bosch LLC ... G ... 269 429-3221
Saint Joseph *(G-14957)*

Shop IV Sbsuid Inv Grede LLC ... G ... 248 440-9515
Southfield *(G-15703)*

Smith Castings Inc ... F ... 906 774-4956
Iron Mountain *(G-8733)*

Smith Castings Incorporated ... F ... 906 774-4956
Kingsford *(G-9517)*

▲ **Steeltech Ltd** ... D ... 616 243-7920
Grand Rapids *(G-7225)*

Steeltech Ltd ... G ... 616 696-1130
Cedar Springs *(G-2663)*

Threaded Products Co ... E ... 586 727-3435
Richmond *(G-13846)*

▲ **Triton Global Sources Inc** ... G ... 734 668-7107
Ypsilanti *(G-18981)*

◆ **Triumph Gear Systems - McOmb I** ... C ... 586 781-2800
Macomb *(G-10644)*

Vx-LLC ... F ... 734 854-8700
Lambertville *(G-9655)*

3322 Malleable Iron Foundries

CB Marcellus Metalcasters Inc ... F ... 269 646-0202
Marcellus *(G-10946)*

Grede LLC ... B ... 906 774-7250
Kingsford *(G-9509)*

Holland Alloys Inc ... E ... 616 396-6444
Holland *(G-8073)*

International Casting Corp ... G ... 586 293-8220
Roseville *(G-14425)*

Kramer International Inc ... F ... 586 726-4300
Troy *(G-17199)*

▲ **Paragon Metals LLC** ... G ... 517 639-4629
Hillsdale *(G-7941)*

Peerless Steel Company ... E ... 616 530-6695
Grandville *(G-7408)*

Prompt Pattern Inc ... F ... 586 759-2030
Warren *(G-17979)*

Robert Bosch LLC ... G ... 269 429-3221
Saint Joseph *(G-14957)*

Smith Castings Inc ... F ... 906 774-4956
Iron Mountain *(G-8733)*

◆ **Teksid Inc** ... E ... 734 846-5492
Farmington *(G-5153)*

Tooling Technology LLC ... D ... 937 381-9211
Macomb *(G-10643)*

Wolverine Bronze Company ... D ... 586 776-8180
Roseville *(G-14495)*

3324 Steel Investment Foundries

▼ **Acra Cast Inc** ... E ... 989 893-3961
Bay City *(G-1316)*

Barron Group Inc ... D ... 248 628-4300
Oxford *(G-12875)*

Barron Industries Inc ... F ... 248 628-4300
Oxford *(G-12877)*

◆ **Barron Industries Inc** ... D ... 248 628-4300
Oxford *(G-12876)*

▲ **Chain Industries Inc** ... E ... 248 348-7722
Wixom *(G-18631)*

Douglas King Industries Inc ... G ... 989 642-2865
Hemlock *(G-7851)*

Eagle Precision Cast Parts Inc ... E ... 231 788-3318
Muskegon *(G-11803)*

Eps Industries Inc ... E ... 616 844-9220
Ferrysburg *(G-5602)*

Eutectic Engineering Co Inc ... E ... 313 892-2248
Bloomfield Hills *(G-1820)*

▲ **Federal Group Usa Inc** ... F ... 248 545-5000
Southfield *(G-15559)*

Howmet Aerospace Inc ... C ... 231 894-7290
Whitehall *(G-18499)*

◆ **Howmet Corporation** ... E ... 231 894-5686
Whitehall *(G-18501)*

Howmet Corporation ... C ... 231 894-7183
Whitehall *(G-18502)*

Howmet Corporation ... C ... 231 981-3269
Whitehall *(G-18503)*

▲ **Howmet Holdings Corporation** ... G ... 231 894-5686
Whitehall *(G-18506)*

Invecast Corporation ... E ... 586 755-4050
Warren *(G-17869)*

▲ **Onodi Tool & Engineering Co** ... E ... 313 386-6682
Melvindale *(G-11208)*

▲ **Paragon Metals LLC** ... G ... 517 639-4629
Hillsdale *(G-7941)*

Precision Castparts Corp ... G ... 586 690-8659
Macomb *(G-10628)*

▲ **R L M Industries Inc** ... D ... 248 628-5103
Oxford *(G-12910)*

Robe Aerospace ... G ... 231 933-9355
Traverse City *(G-16823)*

▲ **Triton Global Sources Inc** ... G ... 734 668-7107
Ypsilanti *(G-18981)*

3325 Steel Foundries, NEC

◆ **Allied Metals Corp** ... E ... 248 680-2400
Auburn Hills *(G-778)*

Alloying Surfaces Inc ... G ... 248 524-9200
Troy *(G-16927)*

Ancast Inc ... E ... 269 927-1985
Sodus *(G-15392)*

Arcanum Alloys Inc ... G ... 312 810-4479
Kentwood *(G-9443)*

Astech Inc ... E ... 989 823-7211
Vassar *(G-17577)*

S
I
C

33 PRIMARY METAL INDUSTRIES

Company	Code	Phone
Axly Production Machining Inc	G	989 269-2444
Bad Axe (G-1096)		
Berne Enterprises Inc	F	989 453-3235
Pigeon (G-13036)		
▲ Bico Michigan Inc	E	616 453-2400
Grand Rapids (G-6506)		
Detroit Materials Inc	G	248 924-5436
Farmington (G-5136)		
Federal Screw Works	G	231 922-9500
Traverse City (G-16681)		
GAL Gage Co	F	269 465-5750
Bridgman (G-1926)		
General Motors Company	G	989 757-1576
Saginaw (G-14650)		
General Motors LLC	G	989 757-0528
Saginaw (G-14651)		
Hackett Brass Foundry Co	G	313 331-6005
Detroit (G-4291)		
Holland Alloys Inc	E	616 396-6444
Holland (G-8073)		
◆ Huron Casting Inc	B	989 453-3933
Pigeon (G-13039)		
▲ International Casting Corp	F	586 293-8220
New Baltimore (G-11984)		
International Casting Corp	G	586 293-8220
Roseville (G-14425)		
Invecast Corporation	E	586 755-4050
Warren (G-17869)		
▲ J & M Machine Products Inc	D	231 755-1622
Norton Shores (G-12302)		
Mannix RE Holdings LLC	G	231 972-0088
Mecosta (G-11192)		
Pal-TEC Inc	G	906 788-4229
Wallace (G-17661)		
▲ Paragon Metals LLC	F	517 639-4629
Hillsdale (G-7941)		
Pennisular Packaging LLC	G	313 304-4724
Plymouth (G-13261)		
▼ Saarsteel Incorporated	G	248 608-0849
Rochester Hills (G-14105)		
Smith Castings Inc	F	906 774-4956
Iron Mountain (G-8733)		
▲ Steeltech Ltd	D	616 243-7920
Grand Rapids (G-7225)		
Steeltech Ltd	G	616 696-1130
Cedar Springs (G-2663)		
◆ Temperform LLC	E	248 349-5230
Novi (G-12554)		
Temperform Corp	F	248 851-9611
Bloomfield Hills (G-1864)		

3331 Primary Smelting & Refining Of Copper

Company	Code	Phone
Center Cupcakes	G	248 302-6503
West Bloomfield (G-18270)		
PM Power Group Inc	G	906 885-7100
White Pine (G-18487)		
Specialty Steel Treating Inc	E	586 293-5355
Fraser (G-5998)		

3334 Primary Production Of Aluminum

Company	Code	Phone
Aleris International Inc	F	517 279-9596
Coldwater (G-3418)		
Constellium Automotive USA LLC	C	734 879-9700
Van Buren Twp (G-17519)		
Fritz Enterprises	G	313 841-9460
Detroit (G-4247)		
General Motors LLC	G	989 757-0528
Saginaw (G-14651)		
Howmet Aerospace Inc	G	231 981-3002
Whitehall (G-18498)		
Howmet Aerospace Inc	G	231 894-5686
Whitehall (G-18500)		
Kaiser Aluminum Fab Pdts LLC	G	269 250-8400
Kalamazoo (G-9235)		
Nemak International Inc	E	248 350-3999
Southfield (G-15664)		
Shipston Group US Inc	G	248 372-9018
Southfield (G-15702)		
▲ United Global Sourcing Inc	F	248 952-5700
Troy (G-17412)		
Viking Industries Inc	F	734 421-5416
Garden City (G-6115)		
Wayne-Craft Inc	F	734 421-8800
Livonia (G-10468)		

3339 Primary Nonferrous Metals, NEC

Company	Code	Phone
Airtec Corporation	E	313 892-7800
Detroit (G-3991)		
Arco Alloys Corp	E	313 871-2680
Detroit (G-4026)		
▲ Cannon-Muskegon Corporation	C	231 755-1681
Norton Shores (G-12284)		
Carrington Precious Metals LLC	G	517 323-9154
Lansing (G-9678)		
◆ Comau LLC	B	248 353-8888
Southfield (G-15530)		
Eclectic Metal Arts LLC	G	248 251-5924
Detroit (G-4200)		
◆ Expan Inc	E	586 725-0405
New Baltimore (G-11980)		
▲ H C Starck Inc	G	517 279-9511
Coldwater (G-3437)		
Mayer Alloys Corporation	G	248 399-2233
Ferndale (G-5567)		
Metropolitan Alloys Corp	E	313 366-4443
Detroit (G-4438)		
Resource Rcovery Solutions Inc	G	248 454-3442
Pontiac (G-13413)		
Snyder Plastics Inc	E	989 684-8355
Bay City (G-1403)		
Specialty Steel Treating Inc	E	586 293-5355
Fraser (G-5998)		
Usmfg Inc	E	262 993-9197
East Lansing (G-4914)		

3341 Secondary Smelting & Refining Of Nonferrous Metals

Company	Code	Phone
All Care Team Inc	G	313 533-7057
Detroit (G-3999)		
◆ Allied Metals Corp	E	248 680-2400
Auburn Hills (G-778)		
Alloying Surfaces Inc	G	248 524-9200
Troy (G-16927)		
▲ Aluminum Blanking Co Inc	D	248 338-4422
Pontiac (G-13349)		
Arco Alloys Corp	E	313 871-2680
Detroit (G-4026)		
Astech Inc	E	989 823-7211
Vassar (G-17577)		
◆ Benteler Auto Holland Inc	C	616 396-6591
Holland (G-7974)		
▲ Cannon-Muskegon Corporation	C	231 755-1681
Norton Shores (G-12284)		
Colfran Industrial Sales Inc	G	734 595-8920
Romulus (G-14262)		
Constellium Automotive USA LLC	C	734 879-9700
Van Buren Twp (G-17519)		
Eutectic Engineering Co Inc	E	313 892-2248
Bloomfield Hills (G-1820)		
▲ Fpt Schlafer	E	313 925-8200
Detroit (G-4245)		
Franklin Iron & Metal Co Inc	F	269 968-6111
Battle Creek (G-1233)		
Franklin Metal Trading Corp	E	616 374-7171
Lake Odessa (G-9575)		
Friedland Industries Inc	G	517 482-3000
Lansing (G-9701)		
Great Lakes Paper Stock Corp	D	586 779-1310
Roseville (G-14416)		
◆ Huron Valley Steel Corporation	C	734 479-3500
Trenton (G-16889)		
Intern Metals and Energy	G	248 765-7747
Jackson (G-8909)		
Johnson Matthey North Amer Inc	G	734 946-9856
Taylor (G-16432)		
▼ Lorbec Metals - Usa Ltd	E	810 736-0961
Flint (G-5728)		
Louis Padnos Iron and Metal Co	G	517 372-6600
Lansing (G-9773)		
Martin Bros Mill Fndry Sup Co	G	269 927-1355
Benton Harbor (G-1567)		
Metropolitan Alloys Corp	E	313 366-4443
Detroit (G-4438)		
Milfab Systems LLC	F	248 391-8100
Lake Orion (G-9619)		
National Galvanizing LP	A	734 243-1882
Monroe (G-11567)		
National Zinc Processors Inc	E	269 926-1161
Benton Harbor (G-1577)		
Oerlikon Metco (us) Inc	E	248 288-0027
Troy (G-17287)		
Revstone Industries LLC	E	248 351-1000
Troy (G-17331)		
◆ Rolled Alloys Inc	D	734 847-0561
Temperance (G-16547)		
Sandvik Inc	E	989 345-6138
West Branch (G-18339)		
Schneider Iron & Metal Inc	G	906 774-0644
Iron Mountain (G-8732)		
Shoreline Recycling & Supply	E	231 722-6081
Muskegon (G-11920)		
Strong Steel Products LLC	F	313 267-3300
Detroit (G-4613)		
◆ Trelleborg Corporation	G	269 639-9891
South Haven (G-15419)		
V & M Corporation	E	248 591-6580
Royal Oak (G-14588)		
Wls Processing LLC	G	313 378-5743
Detroit (G-4686)		

3351 Rolling, Drawing & Extruding Of Copper

Company	Code	Phone
▲ Aluminum Blanking Co Inc	D	248 338-4422
Pontiac (G-13349)		
Anchor Lamina America Inc	C	231 533-8646
Bellaire (G-1468)		
Bradhart Products Inc	E	248 437-3746
Brighton (G-1952)		
J M L Contracting & Sales Inc	F	586 756-4133
Warren (G-17879)		
Midbrook LLC	G	800 966-9274
Jackson (G-8960)		
Mueller Brass Co	D	810 987-7770
Port Huron (G-13505)		
◆ Mueller Brass Co		810 987-7770
Port Huron (G-13504)		
Mueller Industries Inc	E	248 446-3720
Brighton (G-2037)		
Vx-LLC	F	734 854-8700
Lambertville (G-9655)		

3353 Aluminum Sheet, Plate & Foil

Company	Code	Phone
Alcoa Howmet	F	231 894-5686
Whitehall (G-18490)		
▲ Aluminum Blanking Co Inc	D	248 338-4422
Pontiac (G-13349)		
▲ Arconic Automotive Castings	C	248 489-4900
Farmington Hills (G-5171)		
◆ Brazeway LLC	D	517 265-2121
Adrian (G-54)		
Diez Group LLC	D	734 675-1700
Woodhaven (G-18799)		
▲ Erbsloeh Alum Solutions Inc	B	269 323-2565
Portage (G-13558)		
Howmet Aerospace Inc	G	231 894-5686
Whitehall (G-18500)		
Howmet Corporation	C	231 894-5686
Whitehall (G-18504)		
Howmet Corporation	G	231 894-5686
Whitehall (G-18505)		
J M L Contracting & Sales Inc	F	586 756-4133
Warren (G-17879)		
Kaiser Aluminum Fab Pdts LLC	G	269 250-8400
Kalamazoo (G-9235)		
Novelis Corporation	E	248 668-5111
Novi (G-12492)		
On The Side Sign Dsign Grphics	G	810 266-7446
Byron (G-2255)		
▼ Permaloc Corporation	F	616 399-9600
Holland (G-8162)		
Richmond Steel Inc	E	586 948-4700
Chesterfield (G-2939)		
Shipston Group US Inc	G	248 372-9018
Southfield (G-15702)		
▲ Tech Forms Metal Ltd	E	616 956-0430
Grand Rapids (G-7250)		
▲ Twb Company LLC	C	734 289-6400
Monroe (G-11586)		

3354 Aluminum Extruded Prdts

Company	Code	Phone
▲ Air Conditioning Products Co	E	734 326-0050
Romulus (G-14247)		
Aluminum Textures Inc	E	616 538-3144
Grandville (G-7364)		
Arconic Corporation	G	248 489-4900
Farmington Hills (G-5172)		
Austin Tube Products Inc	F	231 745-2741
Baldwin (G-1121)		
Belding McHy & Eqp Lsg Corp	C	616 794-0300
Belding (G-1439)		
◆ Benteler Auto Holland Inc	C	616 396-6591
Holland (G-7974)		
Bonnell Aluminum (niles) LLC	C	269 697-6063
Niles (G-12115)		
◆ Brazeway LLC	D	517 265-2121
Adrian (G-54)		
Christianson Industries Inc	E	269 663-8502
Edwardsburg (G-5003)		
D & W Awning and Window Co	E	810 742-0340
Davison (G-3779)		

SIC SECTION

33 PRIMARY METAL INDUSTRIES

▲ Erbsloeh Alum Solutions Inc ....B 269 323-2565
  Portage (G-13558)
Extruded Aluminum Corporation ....C 616 794-0300
  Belding (G-1448)
Flotronics Automation Inc ....E 248 625-8890
  Auburn Hills (G-902)
General Structures Inc ....F 586 774-6105
  Warren (G-17826)
▲ Hancock Enterprises Inc ....D 734 287-8840
  Taylor (G-16424)
Heatsinkusa LLC ....G 800 901-2395
  Greenville (G-7491)
Hydro Extrusion North Amer LLC ....B 269 349-6626
  Kalamazoo (G-9220)
International Extrusion ....G 734 427-1934
  Garden City (G-6100)
International Extrusions ....F 734 956-6841
  Garden City (G-6101)
International Extrusions Inc ....C 734 427-8700
  Garden City (G-6102)
Kaiser Aluminum Corporation ....G 269 488-0957
  Kalamazoo (G-9234)
Kaiser Aluminum Fab Pdts LLC ....G 269 250-8400
  Kalamazoo (G-9235)
▼ Light Metals Corporation ....B 616 538-3030
  Wyoming (G-18891)
Lippert Components Mfg Inc ....D 989 845-3061
  Chesaning (G-2829)
Loftis Alumi-TEC Inc ....G 616 846-1990
  Grand Haven (G-6330)
◆ Lorin Industries Inc ....D 231 722-1631
  Muskegon (G-11861)
◆ Marketing Displays Inc ....C 248 553-1900
  Farmington Hills (G-5310)
◆ Mueller Brass Co ....C 810 987-7770
  Port Huron (G-13504)
▼ Mueller Impacts Company Inc ....C 810 364-3700
  Marysville (G-11093)
Petschke Manufacturing Company .....F 586 463-0841
  Mount Clemens (G-11652)
Plascore Inc ....C 616 772-1220
  Zeeland (G-19070)
Quality Alum Acquisition LLC ....F 734 783-0990
  Flat Rock (G-5626)
Quality Alum Acquisition LLC ....D 800 550-1667
  Hastings (G-7807)
Quality Model & Pattern Co ....E 616 791-1456
  Grand Rapids (G-7129)
Sign Cabinets Inc ....G 231 725-7187
  Muskegon (G-11922)
Special-Lite Inc ....C 800 821-6531
  Decatur (G-3951)
◆ Superior Extrusion Inc ....C 906 346-7308
  Gwinn (G-7587)
Tubelite Inc ....C 800 866-2227
  Walker (G-17655)
Uacj Auto Whitehall Inds Inc ....D 231 845-5101
  Ludington (G-10554)
◆ Ube Machinery Inc ....D 734 741-7000
  Ann Arbor (G-702)

3355 Aluminum Rolling & Drawing, NEC

AAR Manufacturing Inc ....E 231 779-8800
  Cadillac (G-2306)
▲ Alcotec Wire Corporation ....D 800 228-0750
  Traverse City (G-16598)
▲ Brooks & Perkins Inc ....D 231 775-2229
  Cadillac (G-2318)
CPM Acquisition Corp ....G 231 947-6400
  Traverse City (G-16663)
▲ Extrunet America Inc ....G 517 301-4504
  Tecumseh (G-16501)
General Structures Inc ....F 586 774-6105
  Warren (G-17826)
Madison Electric Company ....E 586 294-8300
  Fraser (G-5960)
Turn Key Harness & Wire LLC ....E 248 236-9915
  Oxford (G-12927)

3356 Rolling, Drawing-Extruding Of Nonferrous Metals

Anchor Lamina America Inc ....C 231 533-8646
  Bellaire (G-1468)
▲ Anchor Lamina America Inc ....E 248 489-9122
  Bellaire (G-1469)
▲ Autocam-Pax Inc ....G 269 782-5186
  Dowagiac (G-4776)
Carbide Technologies Inc ....E 586 296-5200
  Fraser (G-5910)

▲ Concept Alloys Inc ....G 734 449-9680
  Whitmore Lake (G-18527)
▲ Dirksen Screw Products Co ....E 586 247-5400
  Shelby Township (G-15208)
Dodge West Joe Nickel ....G 810 691-2133
  Clio (G-3397)
◆ Eureka Welding Alloys Inc ....E 248 588-0001
  Madison Heights (G-10724)
Fine Arts ....G 269 695-6263
  Buchanan (G-2193)
▲ H C Starck Inc ....G 517 279-9511
  Coldwater (G-3437)
Jay Titanium Sports LLC ....G 616 502-5945
  Norton Shores (G-12349)
Moheco Products Company ....G 734 855-4194
  Livonia (G-10321)
Nanomag LLC ....G 734 261-2800
  Livonia (G-10331)
▼ Ncoc Inc ....E 248 548-5950
  Oak Park (G-12632)
Nolans Top Tin Inc ....G 586 899-3421
  Warren (G-17943)
Norton Equipment Corporation ....G 517 486-2113
  Blissfield (G-1771)
Oerlikon Metco (us) Inc ....E 248 288-0027
  Troy (G-17287)
Radiolgical Fabrication Design ....G 810 632-6000
  Howell (G-8506)
Red Tin Boat ....G 734 239-3796
  Ann Arbor (G-635)
Scitex LLC ....G 517 694-7449
  Holt (G-8329)
Scitex LLC ....G 517 694-7449
  Holt (G-8330)
Scitex Trick Titanium LLC ....G 517 349-3736
  Okemos (G-12685)
Tico Titanium Inc ....G 248 446-0400
  New Hudson (G-12073)
Titanium Building Co Inc ....G 586 634-8580
  Macomb (G-10642)
Titanium Elite MTS Global LLC ....G 616 262-5222
  Clarksville (G-3081)
Titanium Operations LLC ....G 616 717-0218
  Ada (G-38)
Titanium Sports LLC ....G 734 818-0904
  Dundee (G-4837)
Traverse City Products LLC ....D 231 946-4414
  Traverse City (G-16865)
Warren Manufacturing LLC ....G 586 467-1600
  Warren (G-18060)
Weldall Corporation ....G 989 375-2251
  Elkton (G-5034)

3357 Nonferrous Wire Drawing

Active Solutions Group Inc ....G 313 278-4522
  Dearborn (G-3805)
▲ AGM Automotive LLC ....D 248 776-0600
  Farmington Hills (G-5162)
◆ American Furukawa Inc ....E 734 446-2200
  Plymouth (G-13123)
Bulls-Eye Wire & Cable Inc ....G 810 245-8600
  Lapeer (G-9916)
Cardell Corporation ....E 248 371-9700
  Auburn Hills (G-840)
◆ Coppertec Inc ....E 313 278-0139
  Inkster (G-8661)
Ddp Spclty Elctrnc Mtls US 9 ....E 989 496-6000
  Midland (G-11333)
Engineered Prfmce Mtls Co LLC ....G 734 904-4023
  Whitmore Lake (G-18533)
◆ Ews Legacy LLC ....C 248 853-6363
  Rochester Hills (G-14006)
Federal Screw Works ....C 734 941-4211
  Romulus (G-14275)
Gemo Hopkins Usa Inc ....G 734 330-1271
  Auburn Hills (G-907)
▲ Glassmaster Controls Co Inc ....E 269 382-2010
  Kalamazoo (G-9198)
▲ Hi-Lex America Incorporated ....B 269 968-0781
  Battle Creek (G-1237)
▲ Kurabe America Corporation ....F 248 939-5803
  Farmington Hills (G-5284)
Lumen North America Inc ....F 248 289-6100
  Rochester Hills (G-14054)
Madison Electric Company ....E 586 294-8300
  Fraser (G-5960)
Matrix Engineering and Sls Inc. ....G 734 981-7321
  Canton (G-2491)
◆ Morrell Incorporated ....D 248 373-1600
  Auburn Hills (G-975)

▲ Quad Electronics Inc ....C 800 969-9220
  Troy (G-17323)
Reeling Systems LLC ....G 810 364-3900
  Saint Clair (G-14841)
Sanderson Insulation ....G 269 496-7660
  Mendon (G-11221)
▲ Sine Systems Corporation ....C 586 465-3131
  Clinton Township (G-3359)
T R S Fieldbus Systems Inc ....G 586 826-9696
  Birmingham (G-1751)
Tack Electronics Inc ....G 616 698-0960
  Grand Rapids (G-7247)
Temprel Inc ....E 231 582-6585
  Boyne City (G-1902)
Tsk of America Inc ....A 517 542-2955
  Litchfield (G-10086)
▼ Weather-Rite LLC ....E 612 338-1401
  Comstock Park (G-3651)

3363 Aluminum Die Castings

Aludyne Inc ....A 248 506-1692
  Warren (G-17699)
Aludyne North America LLC ....B 989 463-6166
  Alma (G-238)
Angstrom Aluminum Castings LLC ...E 616 309-1208
  Grand Rapids (G-6459)
▲ Cascade Die Casting Group Inc ......G 616 281-1774
  Grand Rapids (G-6550)
Cascade Die Casting Group Inc ....D 616 887-1771
  Sparta (G-15762)
Centracore De Mexico LLC ....E 586 776-5700
  Saint Clair (G-14819)
Charles Group Inc ....B 336 882-0186
  Grand Rapids (G-6565)
Connell Limited Partnership ....G 989 875-5135
  Ithaca (G-8789)
Cooper Foundry Inc ....E 269 343-2808
  Kalamazoo (G-9155)
Eagle Alum Prmnt Mold Cstngs I .....G 231 788-4884
  Muskegon (G-11802)
▲ Evans Industries Inc ....G 313 259-2266
  Troy (G-17100)
▲ Federal Group Usa Inc ....F 248 545-5000
  Southfield (G-15559)
Hackett Brass Foundry Co ....E 313 822-1214
  Detroit (G-4290)
Hanson International Inc ....C 269 429-5555
  Saint Joseph (G-14935)
Hoffmann Die Cast LLC ....C 269 983-1102
  Saint Joseph (G-14936)
Homestead Tool and Machine ....E 989 465-6182
  Coleman (G-3465)
Husite Engineering Co Inc ....F 248 588-0337
  Clinton Township (G-3255)
Key Casting Company Inc ....G 269 426-3800
  Sawyer (G-15110)
Lakeshore Die Cast Inc ....F 269 422-1523
  Baroda (G-1164)
M and A Castings Ltd ....F 517 879-2222
  Pinconning (G-13062)
▲ Mag-TEC Casting Corporation ....E 517 789-8505
  Jackson (G-8941)
Michigan Die Casting LLC ....D 269 471-7715
  Dowagiac (G-4789)
Montague Metal Products Inc ....E 231 893-0547
  Montague (G-11599)
Mv Metal Pdts & Solutions LLC ....D 269 462-4010
  Dowagiac (G-4791)
New Gldc LLC ....D 231 726-4002
  Muskegon (G-11885)
▲ North Shore Mfg Corp ....E 269 849-2551
  Coloma (G-3481)
Pace Industries LLC ....G 231 777-3941
  Muskegon (G-11888)
Pace Industries LLC ....G 231 773-4491
  Muskegon (G-11889)
Pace Industries LLC ....A 231 777-3941
  Norton Shores (G-12323)
Pace Industries LLC ....F 231 777-5615
  Muskegon (G-11891)
▲ Paragon Metals LLC ....G 517 639-4629
  Hillsdale (G-7941)
Precision Die Cast Inc ....G 586 463-1800
  Kimball (G-9499)
▲ Prototype Cast Mfg Inc ....G 586 739-0180
  Shelby Township (G-15311)
Prototype Cast Mfg Inc ....G 586 615-8524
  Sterling Heights (G-16137)
Soper Manufacturing Company ....F 269 429-5245
  Saint Joseph (G-14962)

33 PRIMARY METAL INDUSTRIES

SPX Corporation .... C 248 669-5100
  Commerce Township *(G-3574)*
Supreme Casting Inc .... D 269 465-5757
  Stevensville *(G-16267)*
T C H Industries Incorporated .... D 616 942-0505
  Grand Rapids *(G-7245)*
Tooling Technology LLC .... D 937 381-9211
  Macomb *(G-10643)*
▲ Triton Global Sources Inc .... G 734 668-7107
  Ypsilanti *(G-18981)*
▲ Tru Die Cast Corporation .... E 269 426-3361
  New Troy *(G-12075)*
◆ Ube Machinery Inc .... D 734 741-7000
  Ann Arbor *(G-702)*
◆ Wolverine Die Cast Ltd Prtnr O ..... E 586 757-1900
  Warren *(G-18071)*

3364 Nonferrous Die Castings, Exc Aluminum

▲ Cascade Die Casting Group Inc ... G 616 281-1774
  Grand Rapids *(G-6550)*
Cascade Die Casting Group Inc .... D 616 887-1771
  Sparta *(G-15762)*
Cascade Die Casting Group Inc .... G 616 455-4010
  Grand Rapids *(G-6551)*
Charles Group Inc .... B 336 882-0186
  Grand Rapids *(G-6565)*
Cobra Patterns & Models Inc .... E 248 588-2669
  Madison Heights *(G-10694)*
Cooper Foundry Inc .... E 269 343-2808
  Kalamazoo *(G-9155)*
▲ Evans Industries Inc .... G 313 259-2266
  Troy *(G-17100)*
▲ Flare Fittings Incorporated .... E 269 344-7600
  Kalamazoo *(G-9187)*
Hackett Brass Foundry Co .... E 313 822-1214
  Detroit *(G-4290)*
Hoffmann Die Cast LLC .... C 269 983-1102
  Saint Joseph *(G-14936)*
Key Casting Company Inc .... G 269 426-3800
  Sawyer *(G-15110)*
Lakeshore Die Cast Inc .... F 269 422-1523
  Baroda *(G-1164)*
Lubo Inc .... G 248 632-1185
  Madison Heights *(G-10771)*
▲ Lubo Usa Inc .... G 810 244-5826
  Madison Heights *(G-10772)*
M and A Castings Ltd .... F 517 879-2222
  Pinconning *(G-13062)*
▲ Mag-TEC Casting Corporation ..... E 517 789-8505
  Jackson *(G-8941)*
▲ Magnesium Products America Inc ..B 734 416-8600
  Plymouth *(G-13231)*
Mv Metal Pdts & Solutions LLC .... D 269 462-4010
  Dowagiac *(G-4791)*
Mv Metal Pdts & Solutions LLC .... G 269 471-7715
  Portage *(G-13586)*
▲ North Shore Mfg Corp .... E 269 849-2551
  Coloma *(G-3481)*
Proto-Cast Inc .... E 313 565-5400
  Inkster *(G-8672)*
T C H Industries Incorporated .... D 616 942-0505
  Grand Rapids *(G-7245)*
▲ Tru Die Cast Corporation .... E 269 426-3361
  New Troy *(G-12075)*
Wolverine Bronze Company .... D 586 776-8180
  Roseville *(G-14495)*
◆ Wolverine Die Cast Ltd Prtnr O ..... E 586 757-1900
  Warren *(G-18071)*

3365 Aluminum Foundries

A C Foundry Incorporated .... F 269 963-4131
  Battle Creek *(G-1175)*
▼ Acra Cast Inc .... E 989 893-3961
  Bay City *(G-1316)*
Algonac Marine Cast LLC .... E 810 794-9391
  Clay *(G-3114)*
Bernier Cast Metals Inc .... G 989 754-7571
  Saginaw *(G-14615)*
Birkhold Pattern Company Inc .... E 269 467-8705
  Centreville *(G-2696)*
Cascade Die Casting Group Inc .... D 616 887-1771
  Sparta *(G-15762)*
Casting Industries Inc .... F 586 776-5700
  Saint Clair *(G-14817)*
▲ Centracore LLC .... F 586 776-5700
  Saint Clair *(G-14818)*
Chassix Holdings Inc .... E 248 728-8700
  Southfield *(G-15520)*
Continental Aluminum LLC .... D 248 437-1001
  New Hudson *(G-12046)*
Cytec Industries Inc .... G 269 349-6677
  Kalamazoo *(G-9161)*
▲ Dundee Castings Company .... D 734 529-2455
  Dundee *(G-4815)*
▲ Ehc Inc .... E 313 259-2266
  Troy *(G-17079)*
Eps Industries Inc .... E 616 844-9220
  Ferrysburg *(G-5602)*
Gen3 Defense and Aerospace LLC ... F 616 345-8031
  Comstock Park *(G-3607)*
Hackett Brass Foundry Co .... E 313 331-6005
  Detroit *(G-4291)*
Hoffmann Die Cast LLC .... C 269 983-1102
  Saint Joseph *(G-14936)*
Holland Alloys Inc .... E 616 396-6444
  Holland *(G-8073)*
IBC Precision Inc .... D 248 373-8202
  Auburn Hills *(G-933)*
▲ J & M Machine Products Inc .... D 231 755-1622
  Norton Shores *(G-12302)*
Line Precision Inc .... E 248 474-5280
  Farmington Hills *(G-5291)*
Mall City Aluminum Inc .... G 269 349-5088
  Kalamazoo *(G-9264)*
Max Casting Company Inc .... F 269 925-8081
  Benton Harbor *(G-1568)*
Mpi Products LLC .... D 248 237-3007
  Rochester Hills *(G-14067)*
▼ Non-Ferrous Cast Alloys Inc .... D 231 799-0550
  Norton Shores *(G-12318)*
▲ Onodi Tool & Engineering Co ...... E 313 386-6682
  Melvindale *(G-11208)*
Patterson Precision Mfg Inc .... E 231 733-1913
  Norton Shores *(G-12324)*
Prompt Pattern Inc .... F 586 759-2030
  Warren *(G-17979)*
Shipston Alum Tech Intl Inc .... C 317 738-0282
  Southfield *(G-15699)*
Shipston Alum Tech Intl LLC .... C 317 738-0282
  Southfield *(G-15700)*
◆ Shipston Alum Tech Mich Inc .... E 616 842-3500
  Fruitport *(G-6070)*
Shipston Aluminum Tech Ind Inc ...... D 317 738-0282
  Southfield *(G-15701)*
Specialty Steel Treating Inc .... E 586 293-5355
  Fraser *(G-5998)*
Sterling Metal Works LLC .... G 586 977-9577
  Sterling Heights *(G-16193)*
Supreme Casting Inc .... D 269 465-5757
  Stevensville *(G-16267)*
Tooling & Equipment Intl Corp .... D 734 522-1422
  Livonia *(G-10433)*
Tooling Technology LLC .... D 937 381-9211
  Macomb *(G-10643)*
▲ Tower Defense & Aerospace LLC ... E 248 675-6000
  Livonia *(G-10439)*
Tri-State Aluminum LLC .... F 231 722-7825
  Muskegon *(G-11936)*
Tri-State Cast Technologies Co .... G 231 582-0452
  Boyne City *(G-1904)*
▲ Whitehall Products LLC .... E 231 894-2688
  Whitehall *(G-18514)*
Wolverine Bronze Company .... D 586 776-8180
  Roseville *(G-14495)*
◆ Wolverine Die Cast Ltd Prtnr O ..... E 586 757-1900
  Warren *(G-18071)*

3366 Copper Foundries

Anchor Lamina America Inc .... C 231 533-8646
  Bellaire *(G-1468)*
▲ Anchor Lamina America Inc .... E 248 489-9122
  Bellaire *(G-1469)*
Axly Production Machining Inc .... G 989 269-2444
  Bad Axe *(G-1096)*
Barron Group Inc .... D 248 628-4300
  Oxford *(G-12875)*
◆ Barron Industries Inc .... D 248 628-4300
  Oxford *(G-12876)*
Belwith Products LLC .... F 616 247-4000
  Grandville *(G-7367)*
Bernier Cast Metals Inc .... G 989 754-7571
  Saginaw *(G-14615)*
Bradhart Products Inc .... E 248 437-3746
  Brighton *(G-1952)*
Century Foundry Inc .... E 231 733-1572
  Muskegon *(G-11791)*
▲ Conway Detroit Corporation .... E 586 552-8413
  Roseville *(G-14389)*
Duplicast Corporation .... G 586 756-5900
  Sterling Heights *(G-15992)*
▲ Ehc Inc .... G 313 259-2266
  Troy *(G-17079)*
Enterprise Tool and Gear Inc .... F 989 269-9797
  Bad Axe *(G-1100)*
Eps Industries Inc .... E 616 844-9220
  Ferrysburg *(G-5602)*
▲ Federal-Mogul Powertrain LLC .... D 248 354-7700
  Southfield *(G-15565)*
◆ GKN Sinter Metals LLC .... D 248 883-4500
  Auburn Hills *(G-914)*
▲ Global CNC Industries Ltd .... E 734 464-1920
  Plymouth *(G-13177)*
Hackett Brass Foundry Co .... E 313 331-6005
  Detroit *(G-4291)*
Holland Alloys Inc .... E 616 396-6444
  Holland *(G-8073)*
▲ Huron Tool & Engineering Co ..... E 989 269-9927
  Bad Axe *(G-1108)*
◆ Jsj Corporation .... E 616 842-6350
  Grand Haven *(G-6324)*
L & L Pattern Inc .... G 231 733-2646
  Muskegon *(G-11853)*
Lewkowicz Corporation .... F 734 941-0411
  Romulus *(G-14298)*
Marcellus Metalcasters Inc .... F 269 646-0202
  Marcellus *(G-10949)*
◆ Michigan Wheel Operations LLC ... D 616 452-6941
  Grand Rapids *(G-6997)*
Milan Cast Metal Corporation .... E 734 439-0510
  Milan *(G-11445)*
Mssb LLC .... G 616 868-9730
  Alto *(G-337)*
Mueller Brass Co .... D 810 987-7770
  Port Huron *(G-13505)*
▼ Non-Ferrous Cast Alloys Inc .... D 231 799-0550
  Norton Shores *(G-12318)*
Northfield Manufacturing Inc .... F 734 729-2890
  Westland *(G-18401)*
Parker-Hannifin Corporation .... B 269 694-9411
  Otsego *(G-12795)*
Production Tube Company Inc .... G 313 259-3990
  Detroit *(G-4537)*
Prompt Pattern Inc .... F 586 759-2030
  Warren *(G-17979)*
Smith Castings Inc .... F 906 774-4956
  Iron Mountain *(G-8733)*
Sterling Metal Works LLC .... G 586 977-9577
  Sterling Heights *(G-16193)*
Threaded Products Co .... E 586 727-3435
  Richmond *(G-13846)*
White Cloud Mfg Co .... G 231 689-6087
  White Cloud *(G-18447)*

3369 Nonferrous Foundries: Castings, NEC

A C Foundry Incorporated .... F 269 963-4131
  Battle Creek *(G-1175)*
▼ Acra Cast Inc .... E 989 893-3961
  Bay City *(G-1316)*
Algonac Marine Cast LLC .... E 810 794-9391
  Clay *(G-3114)*
Alloy Machining LLC .... G 517 204-3306
  Lansing *(G-9753)*
Ancast Inc .... E 269 927-1985
  Sodus *(G-15392)*
Apollo Trick Titanium Inc .... E 517 694-7449
  Troy *(G-16940)*
Ascent Integrated Platforms .... F 586 726-0500
  Macomb *(G-10580)*
Astech Inc .... E 989 823-7211
  Vassar *(G-17577)*
Awcco USA Incorporated .... G 586 336-9135
  Romeo *(G-14220)*
◆ Barron Industries Inc .... D 248 628-4300
  Oxford *(G-12876)*
Berne Enterprises Inc .... F 989 453-3235
  Pigeon *(G-13036)*
Cascade Die Casting Group Inc .... G 616 455-4010
  Grand Rapids *(G-6551)*
Computer Operated Mfg .... E 989 686-1333
  Bay City *(G-1340)*
Douglas King Industries Inc .... G 989 642-2865
  Hemlock *(G-7851)*
▲ Dundee Castings Company .... D 734 529-2455
  Dundee *(G-4815)*
Elden Industries Corp .... E 734 946-6900
  Taylor *(G-16412)*
▲ Federal Group Usa Inc .... F 248 545-5000
  Southfield *(G-15559)*

▲ Federal-Mogul Piston Rings Inc .... F 248 354-7700
Southfield *(G-15564)*
◆ GKN Sinter Metals LLC .... G 248 883-4500
Auburn Hills *(G-914)*
Gokoh Coldwater Incorporated .... F 517 279-1080
Coldwater *(G-3434)*
Grosse Tool and Machine Co .... E 586 773-6770
Warren *(G-17842)*
Hackett Brass Foundry Co .... G 313 331-6005
Detroit *(G-4291)*
High-Tech Inds of Holland .... E 616 399-5430
Holland *(G-8072)*
Hoffmann Die Cast LLC .... C 269 983-1102
Saint Joseph *(G-14936)*
Holland Alloys Inc .... E 616 396-6444
Holland *(G-8073)*
Holland Pattern Co .... G 616 396-6348
Holland *(G-8082)*
◆ Huron Casting Inc .... B 989 453-3933
Pigeon *(G-13039)*
Husite Engineering Co Inc .... F 248 588-0337
Clinton Township *(G-3255)*
Inland Lakes Machine Inc .... E 231 775-6543
Cadillac *(G-2337)*
Invecast Corporation .... E 586 755-4050
Warren *(G-17869)*
Kuhlman Casting Co Inc .... F 248 853-2382
Detroit *(G-4369)*
Line Precision Inc .... E 248 474-5280
Farmington Hills *(G-5291)*
▲ Magnesium Products America Inc ... B 734 416-8600
Plymouth *(G-13231)*
▼ Non-Ferrous Cast Alloys Inc .... D 231 799-0550
Norton Shores *(G-12318)*
▲ Onodi Tool & Engineering Co .... E 313 386-6682
Melvindale *(G-11208)*
▲ Paragon Metals LLC .... G 517 639-4629
Hillsdale *(G-7941)*
Patterson Precision Mfg Inc .... E 231 733-1913
Norton Shores *(G-12324)*
Premiere Tool & Die Cast .... G 269 782-3030
Kalamazoo *(G-9306)*
Prompt Pattern Inc .... F 586 759-2030
Warren *(G-17979)*
Proto-Cast Inc .... E 313 565-5400
Inkster *(G-8672)*
◆ Rolled Alloys Inc .... D 734 847-0561
Temperance *(G-16547)*
Shellcast Inc .... E 231 893-8245
Montague *(G-11600)*
Smith Castings Inc .... F 906 774-4956
Iron Mountain *(G-8733)*
Soper Manufacturing Company .... F 269 429-5245
Saint Joseph *(G-14962)*
Stegman Tool Co Inc .... E 248 588-4634
Troy *(G-17372)*
Superior Brass & Alum Cast Co .... F 517 351-7534
East Lansing *(G-4911)*
Trin-Mac Company Inc .... G 586 774-1900
Saint Clair Shores *(G-14889)*
▲ Triton Global Sources Inc .... G 734 668-7107
Ypsilanti *(G-18981)*
White Cloud Manufacturing Co .... E 231 796-8603
Big Rapids *(G-1689)*

3398 Metal Heat Treating

Advanced Heat Treat Corp .... F 734 243-0063
Monroe *(G-11521)*
Ajax Metal Processing Inc .... C 586 497-7000
Warren *(G-17695)*
▲ Ajax Metal Processing Inc .... G 313 267-2100
Detroit *(G-3992)*
Al Fe Heat Treating-Ohio Inc .... F 260 747-9422
Lansing *(G-9800)*
Al-Fe Heat Treating LLC .... D 260 747-9422
Lansing *(G-9801)*
Al-Fe Heat Treating LLC .... E 989 752-2819
Saginaw *(G-14603)*
Al-Fe Heat Treating LLC .... E 888 747-2533
Lansing *(G-9802)*
▲ Ald Thermal Treatment Inc .... C 810 357-0693
Port Huron *(G-13434)*
Alloy Steel Treating Company .... E 269 628-2154
Gobles *(G-6216)*
Alpha Steel Treating Inc .... F 734 523-1035
Livonia *(G-10111)*
▲ American Metal Processing Co .... E 586 757-7144
Warren *(G-17703)*
American Metallurgical Svcs .... F 313 893-8328
Detroit *(G-4013)*
Apollo Heat Treating Proc LLC .... F 248 398-3434
Oak Park *(G-12591)*
▲ Applied Process Inc .... E 734 464-8000
Livonia *(G-10122)*
Atmosphere Annealing LLC .... D 517 485-5090
Lansing *(G-9808)*
Atmosphere Annealing LLC .... E 517 482-1374
Lansing *(G-9809)*
Atmosphere Group Inc .... G 248 624-8191
Wixom *(G-18609)*
Atmosphere Heat Treating Inc .... E 248 960-4700
Wixom *(G-18610)*
Austemper Inc .... F 586 293-4554
Wixom *(G-18614)*
Austemper Inc .... E 616 458-7061
Grand Rapids *(G-6479)*
Authority Flame Hrdning Strght .... E 586 598-5887
Chesterfield *(G-2848)*
▲ Autocam-Pax Inc .... C 269 782-5186
Dowagiac *(G-4776)*
Bell Induction Heating Inc .... G 734 697-0133
Van Buren Twp *(G-17511)*
Bellaire Log Homes Indus Hm .... G 231 533-6669
Bellaire *(G-1471)*
Bellevue Proc Met Prep Inc .... C 313 921-1931
Detroit *(G-4050)*
Benton Harbor LLC .... E 269 925-6581
Benton Harbor *(G-1536)*
Bluewater Thermal Solutions .... G 269 925-6581
Benton Harbor *(G-1537)*
Bluewater Thermal Solutions .... G 989 753-7770
Saginaw *(G-14618)*
Bodycote Thermal Proc Inc .... G 616 399-6880
Holland *(G-7979)*
Bodycote Thermal Proc Inc .... G 616 245-0465
Grand Rapids *(G-6519)*
Bodycote Thermal Proc Inc .... G 734 623-3436
Livonia *(G-10138)*
Bodycote Thermal Proc Inc .... G 734 451-0338
Canton *(G-2442)*
Bodycote Thermal Proc Inc .... F 734 427-6814
Livonia *(G-10139)*
Burkk Inc .... F 616 365-0354
Grand Rapids *(G-6536)*
◆ Century Inc .... C 231 947-6400
Traverse City *(G-16641)*
▲ Commercial Steel Treating Corp .... C 248 588-3300
Madison Heights *(G-10696)*
Curtis Metal Finishing Co .... F 248 588-3300
Madison Heights *(G-10701)*
Curtiss-Wright Surface Tech .... G 734 728-8600
Romulus *(G-14266)*
Cyprium Induction LLC .... G 586 884-4982
Sterling Heights *(G-15976)*
Darby Metal Treating Inc .... F 269 204-6504
Plainwell *(G-13073)*
Detroit Edge Tool Company .... G 586 776-3727
Roseville *(G-14397)*
Detroit Flame Hardening Co .... G 586 484-1726
Clinton Township *(G-3219)*
Detroit Steel Treating Company .... E 248 334-7436
Pontiac *(G-13361)*
▲ Dynamic Mtal Treating Intl Inc .... E 734 459-8022
Canton *(G-2457)*
East - Lind Heat Treat Inc .... E 248 585-1415
Madison Heights *(G-10715)*
◆ Engineered Heat Treat Inc .... E 248 588-5141
Madison Heights *(G-10723)*
Federal Industrial Services .... G 313 533-9888
Redford *(G-13734)*
Federal Industrial Svcs Inc .... G 586 427-6383
Warren *(G-17804)*
▲ Fire-Rite Inc .... E 313 273-3730
Detroit *(G-4234)*
▲ Gerdau McSteel Atmsphere Annli .... F 517 782-0415
Lansing *(G-9841)*
Gerdau McSteel Atmsphere Annli .... E 517 482-1374
Lansing *(G-9842)*
◆ Gestamp Mason LLC .... B 517 244-8800
Mason *(G-11135)*
▲ Grand Blanc Processing LLC .... D 810 694-6000
Holly *(G-8275)*
Grand Rapids Polsg & Buffing .... E 616 241-2233
Grand Rapids *(G-6766)*
Heat Treating Svcs Corp Amer .... E 248 858-2230
Pontiac *(G-13377)*
Heat Treating Svcs Corp Amer .... G 248 332-1510
Pontiac *(G-13378)*
Heat Treating Svcs Corp Amer .... G 248 253-9560
Waterford *(G-18127)*
Hi-Tech Steel Treating Inc .... D 800 835-8294
Saginaw *(G-14664)*
Houston Flame Hardening Co .... G 713 926-8017
Clinton Township *(G-3254)*
Hycal Corp .... F 216 671-6161
Gibraltar *(G-6171)*
Induction Engineering Inc .... F 586 716-4700
New Baltimore *(G-11982)*
Induction Processing Inc .... F 586 756-5101
Warren *(G-17862)*
Induction Services Inc .... E 586 754-1640
Warren *(G-17863)*
Industrial Steel Treating Co .... D 517 787-6312
Jackson *(G-8908)*
▲ Ionbond LLC .... D 248 398-9100
Madison Heights *(G-10748)*
J Hansen-Balk Stl Treating Co .... E 616 458-1414
Grand Rapids *(G-6855)*
Laydon Enterprises Inc .... E 906 774-4633
Iron Mountain *(G-8724)*
M P D Welding Inc .... D 248 340-0330
Orion *(G-12735)*
Magnum Induction Inc .... E 586 716-4700
New Baltimore *(G-11986)*
MB Aerospace Warren LLC .... C 586 772-2500
Warren *(G-17920)*
Metal Improvement Company LLC .... D 734 728-8600
Romulus *(G-14302)*
Metal Prep Technology Inc .... G 313 843-2890
Dearborn *(G-3870)*
Metallurgical Processing LLC .... G 586 758-3100
Warren *(G-17925)*
Metro Machine Works Inc .... D 734 941-4571
Romulus *(G-14304)*
Midwest Heat Treat Inc .... E 616 395-9763
Holland *(G-8148)*
Miller Tool Die Co .... G 734 738-1970
Plymouth *(G-13244)*
Mjc Industries Inc .... E 313 838-2800
Detroit *(G-4461)*
Modern Metal Processing Corp .... G 517 655-4402
Williamston *(G-18578)*
Mpd Welding - Grand Rapids Inc .... E 616 248-9353
Grand Rapids *(G-7031)*
▼ Ncoc Inc .... E 248 548-5950
Oak Park *(G-12632)*
◆ New Hudson Corporation .... E 248 437-3970
New Hudson *(G-12064)*
▲ Nitrex Inc .... E 517 676-6370
Mason *(G-11147)*
Nitro-Vac Heat Treat Inc .... F 586 754-4350
Warren *(G-17942)*
Nor-Cote Inc .... E 586 756-1200
Warren *(G-17944)*
Omc Archtrim .... G 517 482-9411
Lansing *(G-9877)*
Pioneer Metal Finishing LLC .... D 734 384-9000
Monroe *(G-11569)*
Precision Heat Treating Co .... F 269 382-4660
Kalamazoo *(G-9303)*
Production Tube Company Inc .... G 313 259-3990
Detroit *(G-4537)*
Richter Precision Inc .... E 586 465-0500
Fraser *(G-5989)*
Rmt Acquisition Company LLC .... G 248 353-4229
Plymouth *(G-13286)*
Savanna Inc .... E 734 254-0566
Plymouth *(G-13294)*
▲ Savanna Inc .... E 248 353-8180
Southfield *(G-15695)*
Schroth Enterprises Inc .... E 586 759-4240
Grosse Pointe Farms *(G-7540)*
Solution Steel Treating LLC .... F 586 247-9250
Shelby Township *(G-15338)*
South Haven Finishing Inc .... E 269 637-2047
South Haven *(G-15413)*
Specialty Steel Treating Inc .... D 586 293-5355
Farmington Hills *(G-5384)*
Specialty Steel Treating Inc .... E 586 293-5355
Fraser *(G-5998)*
State Heat Treating Company .... E 616 243-0178
Grand Rapids *(G-7222)*
◆ Steel Industries Inc .... C 313 535-8505
Redford *(G-13774)*
Steelworks Inc .... F 734 692-3020
Trenton *(G-16893)*
Stokes Steel Treating Company .... E 810 235-3573
Flint *(G-5771)*
Sun Steel Treating Inc .... D 877 471-0844
South Lyon *(G-15459)*

SIC

33 PRIMARY METAL INDUSTRIES

▲ Super Steel Treating Inc ....D 586 755-9140
  Warren (G-18031)
Superior Heat Treat LLC ....E 586 792-9500
  Clinton Township (G-3365)
Temp Rite Steel Treating Inc ....E 586 469-3071
  Harrison Township (G-7729)
Thermal One Inc ....F 734 721-8500
  Westland (G-18421)
Trojan Heat Treat Inc ....D 517 568-4403
  Homer (G-8358)
Universal Induction Inc ....G 269 925-9890
  Benton Harbor (G-1595)
Vac-Met Inc ....E 586 264-8100
  Warren (G-18050)
Walker Wire (ispat) Inc ....G 248 399-4800
  Sterling Heights (G-16227)
◆ Wall Co Incorporated ....E 248 585-6400
  Madison Heights (G-10859)
West Side Flamehardening Inc ....F 734 729-1665
  Westland (G-18431)
Western Engineered Products ....G 248 371-9259
  Lake Orion (G-9638)
Woodworth Inc ....E 810 820-6780
  Flint (G-5794)
Woodworth Inc ....E 248 481-2354
  Pontiac (G-13426)
Woodworth Rassini Holding LLC ....D 248 481-2354
  Pontiac (G-13427)
Wyatt Services Inc ....F 586 264-8000
  Sterling Heights (G-16233)
Zion Industries Inc ....F 517 622-3409
  Grand Ledge (G-6401)

3399 Primary Metal Prdts, NEC

▲ Advantage Sintered Metals Inc .....C 269 964-1212
  Battle Creek (G-1180)
Arch Cutting Tools LLC ....C 734 266-6900
  Bloomfield Hills (G-1800)
◆ Century Inc ....C 231 947-6400
  Traverse City (G-16641)
Cox Industries Inc ....E 586 749-6650
  Chesterfield (G-2862)
Custom Powder Coating LLC ....G 616 454-9730
  Grand Rapids (G-6622)
Hill Machine Works LLC ....F 586 238-2897
  Fraser (G-5937)
Hoeganaes Corporation ....D 248 435-6764
  Royal Oak (G-14547)
Lisi Automotive HI Vol Inc ....F 734 266-6958
  Livonia (G-10285)
Marisa Manufacturing Inc ....G 586 754-3000
  Warren (G-17915)
▲ Mueller Brass Co ....F 616 794-1200
  Belding (G-1459)
▲ Nitto Seiko Co Ltd ....G 248 588-0133
  Troy (G-17279)
Nylok LLC ....C 586 786-0100
  Macomb (G-10623)
Peerless Mtal Pwders Abrsive L ....E 313 841-5400
  Detroit (G-4512)
Qc Tech LLC ....D 248 597-3984
  Madison Heights (G-10813)
Ram-Pak Industries LLC ....F 616 334-1443
  Wyoming (G-18902)
Rayce Americas Inc ....E 248 537-3159
  Auburn Hills (G-1015)
Revwires LLC ....G 269 683-8100
  Niles (G-12163)
Tapex American Corporation ....F 810 987-4722
  Port Huron (G-13531)
Tpi Powder Metallurgy Inc ....E 989 865-9921
  Saint Charles (G-14811)
Traction Tech Holdings LLC ....E 313 923-0400
  Detroit (G-4642)
◆ Wall Co Incorporated ....E 248 585-6400
  Madison Heights (G-10859)
Wes Corp ....G 231 536-2500
  East Jordan (G-4882)

34 FABRICATED METAL PRODUCTS, EXCEPT MACHINERY AND TRANSPORTATION EQUIPMENT

3411 Metal Cans

AAR Manufacturing Inc ....E 231 779-8800
  Cadillac (G-2306)
Contract Welding and Fabg Inc ....E 734 699-5561
  Van Buren Twp (G-17520)
Delta Tube & Fabricating Corp ....C 248 634-8267
  Holly (G-8268)
Mh Industries Ltd ....E 734 261-7560
  West Bloomfield (G-18298)
▼ Oktober LLC ....G 231 750-1998
  Grand Rapids (G-7056)
▼ Royal Design & Manufacturing .....D 248 588-0110
  Madison Heights (G-10821)
Tin Can Dewitt ....G 517 624-2078
  Dewitt (G-4717)

3412 Metal Barrels, Drums, Kegs & Pails

Actron Steel Inc ....E 231 947-3981
  Traverse City (G-16597)
Advance Packaging Corporation ......C 616 949-6610
  Grand Rapids (G-6433)
Associated Metals Inc ....G 734 369-3851
  Ann Arbor (G-384)
Chemtool Incorporated ....G 734 439-7010
  Milan (G-11432)
Delta Tube & Fabricating Corp ....C 248 634-8267
  Holly (G-8268)
Fluid-Bag LLC ....F 513 310-9550
  Lansing (G-9698)
▲ Geerpres Inc ....E 231 773-3211
  Muskegon (G-11823)
Georgia-Pacific LLC ....F 734 439-2441
  Milan (G-11436)
Georgia-Pacific LLC ....G 989 725-5191
  Owosso (G-12835)
Green Bay Packaging Inc ....C 269 552-1000
  Kalamazoo (G-9202)
▲ Mauser ....E 248 795-2330
  Clarkston (G-3048)
Quiktap LLC ....G 855 784-5827
  Grand Rapids (G-7132)
Rap Products Inc ....G 989 893-5583
  Bay City (G-1394)
Repair Industries Michigan Inc ....C 313 365-5300
  Detroit (G-4568)
Royal ARC Welding Company ....E 734 789-9099
  Flat Rock (G-5628)
Shamrock Fabricating Inc ....F 810 744-0677
  Burton (G-2245)
Zayna LLC ....G 616 452-4522
  Grand Rapids (G-7356)

3421 Cutlery

Alamin Super Market LLC ....G 313 305-7281
  Detroit (G-3994)
Art of Shaving - FI LLC ....G 248 649-5872
  Troy (G-16954)
Country Choice Inc ....G 616 241-6043
  Wyoming (G-18861)
◆ Crl Inc ....E 906 428-3710
  Gladstone (G-6177)
Edgewell Personal Care Company ...G 866 462-8669
  Taylor (G-16409)
Los Cuarto Amigos ....G 989 984-0200
  East Tawas (G-4918)
Meijer Inc ....D 269 556-2400
  Stevensville (G-16260)
Midwest Tool and Cutlery Co ....F 231 258-2341
  Kalkaska (G-9398)
▼ Midwest Tool and Cutlery Co ......D 269 651-2476
  Sturgis (G-16310)
Stewart Knives LLC ....E 906 789-1801
  Escanaba (G-5101)
T S M Foods LLC ....G 313 262-6556
  Detroit (G-4623)
Yacks Dry Dock ....G 989 689-6749
  Hope (G-8365)

3423 Hand & Edge Tools

Allied Mask & Tooling ....G 419 470-2555
  Temperance (G-16527)
◆ Assembly Technologies Intl Inc ....F 248 280-2810
  Troy (G-16960)
Atlas Die LLC ....E 413 289-1276
  Rochester Hills (G-13953)
Atlas Die LLC ....F 770 981-6585
  Rochester Hills (G-13954)
Atlas Welding Accessories Inc ....D 248 588-4666
  Troy (G-16962)
▲ Aven Inc ....F 734 973-0099
  Ann Arbor (G-387)
▲ Balance Technology Inc ....D 734 769-2100
  Whitmore Lake (G-18520)
Bartlett Manufacturing Co LLC ....F 989 635-8900
  Marlette (G-10978)
Bay-Houston Towing Company ....F 810 648-2210
  Sandusky (G-15056)
Boral Building Products Inc ....C 800 521-8486
  Wixom (G-18625)
Cobra Maufacturing ....F 248 585-1606
  Troy (G-17017)
▲ Detroit Edge Tool Company ....D 313 366-4120
  Detroit (G-4146)
Detroit Steel Treating Company ......E 248 334-7436
  Pontiac (G-13361)
▼ E M I Construction Products ....F 616 392-7207
  Holland (G-8020)
Eagle Tool Group LLC ....F 586 997-0800
  Sterling Heights (G-16000)
Ferrees Tools Inc ....E 269 965-0511
  Battle Creek (G-1230)
Gill Industries Inc ....G 616 559-2700
  Grand Rapids (G-6743)
Grace Metal Prods Inc ....E 231 264-8133
  Williamsburg (G-18554)
Grace Metal Products Inc ....E 231 264-8133
  Elk Rapids (G-5025)
Growgeneration Michigan Corp ....G 248 473-0450
  Lansing (G-9849)
Hanchett Manufacturing Inc ....E 231 796-7678
  Big Rapids (G-1676)
Hank Thorn Co ....F 248 348-7800
  Wixom (G-18675)
◆ Hastings Fiber Glass Pdts Inc ......D 269 945-9541
  Hastings (G-7795)
Lach Diamond ....E 616 698-0101
  Grand Rapids (G-6907)
▼ Lakeland Mills Inc ....E 989 427-5133
  Edmore (G-4993)
▼ Landmesser Tools Company Inc ..G 248 682-4689
  Waterford (G-18133)
Megapro Marketing Usa Inc ....F 866 522-3652
  Niles (G-12143)
Mercedes-Benz Extra LLC ....E 205 747-8006
  Farmington Hills (G-5315)
Micro Engineering Inc ....G 616 534-9681
  Byron Center (G-2285)
MJB Stairs LLC ....E 586 822-9559
  Shelby Township (G-15278)
Muskegon Tools LLC ....G 231 788-4633
  Muskegon (G-11883)
Next Level Die Cutting LLC ....F 888 819-9959
  Jenison (G-9063)
▲ Ontario Die Company America ...D 810 987-5060
  Marysville (G-11095)
Patco Air Tool Inc ....D 248 648-8830
  Orion (G-12738)
Performnce Dcutting Finshg LLC ....F 616 245-3636
  Grand Rapids (G-7081)
◆ Persico Usa Inc ....D 248 299-5100
  Shelby Township (G-15300)
Port Austin Level & TI Mfg Co ....F 989 738-5291
  Port Austin (G-13428)
R J S Tool & Gage Co ....E 248 642-8620
  Birmingham (G-1746)
▲ Rock Tool & Machine Co Inc ....E 734 455-9840
  Plymouth (G-13289)
Roesch Maufacturing Co LLC ....G 517 424-6300
  Tecumseh (G-16514)
RTS Cutting Tools Inc ....E 586 954-1900
  Clinton Township (G-3344)
▲ Saginaw Products Corporation ...E 989 753-1411
  Saginaw (G-14748)
▲ Shaws Enterprises Inc ....E 810 664-2981
  Lapeer (G-9960)
Simonds International LLC ....G 231 527-2322
  Big Rapids (G-1687)
▲ Sourcehub LLC ....G 800 246-1844
  Troy (G-17364)
Specialty Steel Treating Inc ....E 586 293-5355
  Fraser (G-5998)
Steelcraft Tool Co Inc ....F 734 522-7130
  Livonia (G-10420)
Summit Tooling & Mfg Inc ....G 231 856-7037
  Morley (G-11623)
◆ Sure-Loc Aluminum Edging Inc ...E 616 392-3209
  Holland (G-8210)
Swarovski ....E 248 344-2922
  Novi (G-12552)
Tapco Holdings Inc ....C 248 668-6400
  Wixom (G-18766)
◆ Tekton Inc ....D 616 243-2443
  Grand Rapids (G-7251)
▲ Umix Dissoultion Corp ....F 586 446-9950
  Sterling Heights (G-16214)

Wranosky & Sons Inc ..... G 586 336-9761
Romeo (G-14240)

3425 Hand Saws & Saw Blades

▼ Edge Industries Inc ..... G 616 453-5458
Grand Rapids (G-6665)
Martin Saw & Tool Inc ..... G 906 863-6812
Menominee (G-11245)
▼ Menominee Saw and Supply Co ..... E 906 863-2609
Menominee (G-11248)
Saw Tubergen Service Inc ..... G 616 534-0701
Grand Rapids (G-7182)
Schott Saw Co ..... G 269 782-3203
Dowagiac (G-4795)
Workblades Inc ..... E 586 778-0060
Warren (G-18072)

3429 Hardware, NEC

A & B Tube Benders Inc ..... F 586 773-0440
Warren (G-17678)
◆ Aba of America Inc ..... F 815 332-5170
Auburn Hills (G-772)
Acme Mills Company ..... E 517 437-8940
Hillsdale (G-7919)
Adjustable Locking Tech LLC ..... G 248 443-9664
Bloomfield Hills (G-1792)
Admat Manufacturing Inc ..... F 269 641-7453
Union (G-17486)
▲ ADS Us Inc ..... D 989 871-4550
Millington (G-11498)
▲ Albion Industries LLC ..... C 800 835-8911
Albion (G-114)
Allegion S&S Holding Co Inc ..... G 734 680-7429
Plymouth (G-13121)
▲ Alpha Technology Corporation ..... E 517 546-9700
Howell (G-8426)
American Arrow Corp Inc ..... G 248 435-6115
Madison Heights (G-10666)
◆ Anchor Coupling Inc ..... C 906 863-2672
Menominee (G-11225)
Antolin Interiors Usa Inc ..... A 517 548-0052
Howell (G-8429)
Apex Spring & Stamping Corp ..... D 616 453-5463
Grand Rapids (G-6462)
Ardy Inc ..... G 231 845-7318
Ludington (G-10527)
◆ Attwood Corporation ..... C 616 897-2301
Lowell (G-10495)
▲ Bauer Products Inc ..... E 616 245-4540
Grand Rapids (G-6497)
▲ BDS Company Inc ..... F 517 279-2135
Coldwater (G-3421)
Belwith Products LLC ..... F 616 247-4000
Grandville (G-7367)
Berkley Screw Machine Pdts Inc ..... E 248 853-0044
Rochester Hills (G-13962)
Big Dog Marine LLC ..... G 248 705-2875
Highland (G-7884)
▲ Brauer Clamps USA ..... F 586 427-5304
Warren (G-17741)
C & S Security Inc ..... G 989 821-5759
Roscommon (G-14347)
Caillau Usa Inc ..... G 248 446-1900
Brighton (G-1960)
Caster Concepts Inc ..... G 517 629-2456
Albion (G-121)
Clamptech LLC ..... G 989 832-8027
Bay City (G-1338)
▲ Commando Lock Company LLC ..... F 248 709-7901
Troy (G-17020)
Consolidated Clips Clamps Inc ..... D 734 455-0880
Plymouth (G-13149)
Consort Corporation ..... E 269 388-4532
Kalamazoo (G-9151)
Cube Tracker LLC ..... G 269 436-1270
Decatur (G-3945)
Custom Fireplace Doors Inc ..... F 248 673-3121
Waterford (G-18111)
D A C Industries Inc ..... G 616 235-0140
Grand Rapids (G-6629)
David Kimberly Door Company ..... F 248 652-8833
Rochester (G-13898)
▲ Detmar Corporation ..... E 313 831-1155
Detroit (G-4134)
▲ Detroit Auto Specialties Inc ..... G 248 496-3856
West Bloomfield (G-18279)
Dgh Enterprises Inc ..... G 269 925-0657
Benton Harbor (G-1547)
Die Cast Press Mfg Co Inc ..... E 269 657-6060
Paw Paw (G-12947)
Dolphin Manufacturing Inc ..... E 734 946-6322
Taylor (G-16403)
Door SEC Solutions of Mich ..... F 616 301-1991
Grand Rapids (G-6655)
▲ Dover Energy Inc ..... C 248 836-6700
Auburn Hills (G-866)
▲ Dowding Industries Inc ..... E 517 663-5455
Eaton Rapids (G-4959)
Dundee Manufacturing Co Inc ..... E 734 529-2540
Dundee (G-4816)
◆ Dura Operating LLC ..... C 248 299-7500
Auburn Hills (G-868)
Eaton Aeroquip LLC ..... B 949 452-9575
Jackson (G-8873)
Elemental Artistry LLC ..... G 616 326-1758
Grand Rapids (G-6671)
▲ Engineered Products Company ..... E 810 767-2050
Flint (G-5696)
▲ Enterprise Hinge Inc ..... G 269 857-2111
Douglas (G-4773)
Ervins Group LLC ..... E 248 203-2000
Bloomfield Hills (G-1819)
Evans Industries Inc ..... G 313 272-8200
Detroit (G-4219)
Fathom Drones Inc ..... G 586 216-7047
Grand Rapids (G-6703)
Five Star Manufacturing Inc ..... F 815 723-2245
Auburn Hills (G-900)
Flambeau Inc ..... G 248 364-3357
Auburn Hills (G-901)
Flexible Steel Lacing Company ..... D 616 459-3196
Walker (G-17639)
Flue Sentinel LLC ..... G 586 739-4373
Shelby Township (G-15228)
▲ Fluid Hutchinson Management ..... D 248 679-1327
Auburn Hills (G-903)
▼ Franklin Fastener Company ..... E 313 537-8900
Redford (G-13735)
G T Gundrilling Inc ..... G 586 992-3301
Macomb (G-10598)
▲ G&G Industries Inc ..... E 586 726-6000
Shelby Township (G-15229)
GAL Gage Co ..... F 269 465-5750
Bridgman (G-1926)
Gates Corporation ..... G 248 260-2300
Rochester Hills (G-14020)
Grant Industries Incorporated ..... E 586 293-9200
Fraser (G-5931)
Great Lakes Trim Inc ..... D 231 267-3000
Williamsburg (G-18555)
▲ H & L Advantage Inc ..... E 616 532-1012
Grandville (G-7384)
Hearth-N-Home Inc ..... F 517 625-5586
Owosso (G-12837)
HI TEC Stainless Inc ..... E 269 543-4205
Fennville (G-5438)
Hydro-Craft Inc ..... G 248 652-8100
Rochester Hills (G-14037)
Incoe Corporation ..... C 248 616-0220
Auburn Hills (G-936)
▲ International Engrg & Mfg Inc ..... D 989 689-4911
Hope (G-8361)
Interntnal Auto Cmpnnts Group ..... G 810 987-8500
Port Huron (G-13488)
▼ Jay & Kay Manufacturing LLC ..... E 810 679-2333
Croswell (G-3730)
Jay & Kay Manufacturing LLC ..... G 810 679-3079
Croswell (G-3731)
▲ Jay Cee Sales & Rivet Inc ..... F 248 478-2150
Farmington (G-5140)
K & W Manufacturing Co Inc ..... E 517 369-9708
Bronson (G-2117)
Keglove LLC ..... G 616 610-7289
Holland (G-8110)
Keys N More ..... G 248 260-1967
Rochester Hills (G-14045)
Keys Plus In 15 Minute ..... G 248 581-0112
Madison Heights (G-10762)
◆ Knape & Vogt Manufacturing Co ..... A 616 459-3311
Grand Rapids (G-6900)
Kriewall Enterprises Inc ..... E 586 336-0600
Romeo (G-14227)
▲ L & W Inc ..... D 734 397-6300
New Boston (G-12012)
Lacks Industries Inc ..... C 616 698-6890
Grand Rapids (G-6915)
Magna Mirrors America Inc ..... B 231 652-4450
Newaygo (G-12086)
Marine Industries Inc ..... F 989 635-3644
Marlette (G-10985)
Masco Building Products Corp ..... G 313 274-7400
Livonia (G-10301)
◆ Masco Corporation ..... A 313 274-7400
Livonia (G-10302)
◆ Michigan Wheel Operations LLC ..... D 616 452-6941
Grand Rapids (G-6997)
Milan Screw Products Inc ..... F 734 439-2431
Milan (G-11447)
Miller Industrial Products Inc ..... E 517 783-2756
Jackson (G-8962)
Millerknoll Inc ..... G 616 453-5995
Grand Rapids (G-7011)
Milton Manufacturing Inc ..... E 313 366-2450
Detroit (G-4458)
Moheco Products Company ..... G 734 855-4194
Livonia (G-10321)
◆ Motion Systems Incorporated ..... F 586 774-5666
Warren (G-17935)
Mvc Holdings LLC ..... F 586 491-2600
Roseville (G-14450)
▲ Myrtle Industries Inc ..... F 517 784-8579
Jackson (G-8974)
Norma Michigan Inc ..... G 248 373-4300
Lake Orion (G-9622)
▲ Norma Michigan Inc ..... C 248 373-4300
Auburn Hills (G-984)
Northwest Metal Products Inc ..... F 616 453-0556
Grand Rapids (G-7049)
OBrien Engineered Products ..... F 517 447-3602
Deerfield (G-3959)
Options Cabinetry Inc ..... F 248 669-0000
Commerce Township (G-3561)
Orion Manufacturing Inc ..... F 616 527-5994
Ionia (G-8691)
Peninsular Inc ..... E 586 775-7211
Roseville (G-14461)
Penn Automotive Inc ..... C 734 595-3000
Romulus (G-14317)
▲ Penn Automotive Inc ..... G 248 599-3700
Waterford (G-18150)
Penn Engineering & Mfg Corp ..... G 586 731-3560
Waterford (G-18152)
Penn Engineering & Mfg Corp ..... B 313 299-8500
Waterford (G-18151)
Penstone Inc ..... E 734 379-3160
Rockwood (G-14203)
Peterson American Corporation ..... D 269 279-7421
Three Rivers (G-16580)
▲ Polytec Foha Inc ..... F 586 978-9386
Warren (G-17969)
▲ Precision Polymer Mfg Inc ..... E 269 344-2044
Kalamazoo (G-9305)
Probe-TEC ..... G 765 252-0257
Chesterfield (G-2930)
Profil System Inc ..... F 248 536-2130
Waterford (G-18159)
◆ R & D Enterprises Inc ..... E 248 349-7077
Plymouth (G-13274)
▲ R G Ray Corporation ..... D 248 373-4300
Auburn Hills (G-1011)
R M Wright Company Inc ..... E 248 476-9800
Farmington Hills (G-5363)
R T Gordon Inc ..... E 586 294-6100
Fraser (G-5985)
▲ R W Fernstrum & Company ..... E 906 863-5553
Menominee (G-11257)
▲ Refrigeration Sales Inc ..... G 517 784-8579
Jackson (G-8995)
Regency Construction Corp ..... E 586 741-8000
Clinton Township (G-3334)
River Valley Machine Inc ..... F 269 673-8070
Allegan (G-181)
▲ RSR Sales Inc ..... E 734 668-8166
Ann Arbor (G-645)
Scaff-All Inc ..... G 888 204-9990
Clay (G-3124)
Select Products Limited ..... E 269 323-4433
Kalamazoo (G-9330)
▲ Shane Group LLC ..... G 517 439-4316
Hillsdale (G-7949)
Shark Tool & Die Inc ..... G 586 749-7400
Columbus (G-3502)
▲ Shepherd Hardware Products Inc ..... D 269 756-3830
Three Oaks (G-16558)
Shurco LLC ..... F 616 366-2367
Caledonia (G-2398)
Shwayder Company ..... G 248 645-9511
Birmingham (G-1749)
Solidbody Technology Company ..... G 248 709-7901
Troy (G-17359)

S I C

34 FABRICATED METAL PRODUCTS, EXCEPT MACHINERY AND TRANSPORTATION EQUIPMENT

Company		Phone
Souris Enterprises Inc .... F	810 664-2964
Lapeer (G-9961)	
Spiral Industries Inc .... E	810 632-6300
Howell (G-8521)	
Srg Global Automotive LLC .... B	586 757-7800
Sterling Heights (G-16186)	
Startech-Solutions LLC .... G	248 419-0650
Southfield (G-15708)	
Sterling Die & Engineering Inc .... E	586 677-0707
Macomb (G-10637)	
Strattec Security Corporation .... G	248 649-9742
Auburn Hills (G-1040)	
▲ Stromberg-Carlson Products Inc .... F	231 947-8600
Traverse City (G-16843)	
T & L Products .... G	989 868-4428
Reese (G-13809)	
Teamtech Motorsports Safety .... G	989 792-4880
Saginaw (G-14773)	
TEC-3 Prototypes Inc .... E	810 678-8909
Metamora (G-11289)	
▲ Tecla Company Inc .... E	248 624-8200
Commerce Township (G-3576)	
TI Group Auto Systems LLC .... G	586 948-6006
Chesterfield (G-2956)	
Tops-In-Quality Inc .... G	810 364-7150
Marysville (G-11109)	
▲ Toyo Seat USA Corporation C	810 724-0300
Imlay City (G-8648)	
▲ Triton Global Sources Inc .... G	734 668-7107
Ypsilanti (G-18981)	
Twb of Indiana Inc .... G	734 289-6400
Monroe (G-11587)	
Unist Inc .... G	616 949-0853
Grand Rapids (G-7297)	
US RAC .... G	248 505-0413
Southfield (G-15735)	
Vacuum Orna Metal Company Inc ... E	734 941-9100
Romulus (G-14336)	
W-Lok Corporation .... G	616 355-4015
Holland (G-8240)	
▲ Wartian Lock Company .... G	586 777-2244
Saint Clair Shores (G-14891)	
Weber Security Group Inc .... G	586 582-0000
Mount Clemens (G-11662)	
▲ Wico Metal Products Company C	586 755-9600
Warren (G-18067)	
◆ Zsi-Foster Inc .... E	734 844-0055
Canton (G-2545)	

3431 Enameled Iron & Metal Sanitary Ware

▲ Aviv Global LLC .... G	248 737-5777
Farmington Hills (G-5179)	
Henry Bath LLC .... G	410 633-7055
West Bloomfield (G-18288)	
▲ Hotwater Works Inc .... G	517 364-8827
Lansing (G-9852)	
Lakeshore Marble Company Inc ...... F	269 429-8241
Stevensville (G-16257)	
Marbelite Corp .... E	248 348-1900
Novi (G-12470)	
▲ Pure Liberty Manufacturing LLC .... F	734 224-0333
Ottawa Lake (G-12811)	
Sloan Valve Company .... D	248 446-5300
New Hudson (G-12070)	
◆ Thetford Corporation C	734 769-6000
Ann Arbor (G-688)	
Zurn Industries LLC .... F	313 864-2800
Detroit (G-4704)	

3432 Plumbing Fixture Fittings & Trim, Brass

▲ American Beverage Equipment Co .. E	586 773-0094
Roseville (G-14373)	
Barbron Corporation .... E	586 716-3530
Kalkaska (G-9382)	
Beans Best LLC .... G	734 707-7378
Ann Arbor (G-397)	
▲ Brasscraft Manufacturing Co C	248 305-6000
Novi (G-12376)	
Builders Plbg Sup Traverse Cy .... G	800 466-5160
Traverse City (G-16632)	
▲ Decker Manufacturing Corp .... D	517 629-3955
Albion (G-124)	
Epic Fine Arts Company Inc .... G	313 274-7400
Taylor (G-16414)	
Etna Distributors LLC .... F	810 232-4760
Flint (G-5697)	
Ferguson Enterprises LLC .... G	616 803-7521
Kentwood (G-9452)	
Ferguson Enterprises LLC .... G	269 383-1200
Kalamazoo (G-9184)	
Ferguson Enterprises LLC .... G	586 459-4491
Warren (G-17805)	
◆ Fernco Inc C	810 503-9000
Davison (G-3782)	
Incoe Corporation C	248 616-0220
Auburn Hills (G-936)	
Joe S Handyman Service .... G	616 642-6038
Saranac (G-15079)	
◆ Kerkstra Precast LLC C	616 457-4920
Grandville (G-7395)	
Key Gas Components Inc .... E	269 673-2151
Allegan (G-163)	
Luxury Bath Systems .... G	586 264-2561
Warren (G-17909)	
Machine Guard & Cover Co .... E	616 392-8188
Holland (G-8131)	
▲ Marquis Industries Inc .... E	616 842-2810
Spring Lake (G-15832)	
◆ Masco Corporation .... A	313 274-7400
Livonia (G-10302)	
Masco De Puerto Rico Inc C	313 274-7400
Taylor (G-16439)	
Parker-Hannifin Corporation .... B	269 694-9411
Otsego (G-12795)	
S H Leggitt Company .... E	269 781-3901
Marshall (G-11073)	
Titan Sprinkler LLC .... G	517 540-1851
Howell (G-8533)	
Trane Technologies Company LLC .. E	248 398-6200
Madison Heights (G-10846)	
United Brass Manufacturers Inc ..... E	734 941-0700
Romulus (G-14334)	
United Brass Manufacturers Inc ..... E	734 942-9224
Romulus (G-14335)	
Village & Cntry Wtr Trtmnt Inc .... F	810 632-7880
Hartland (G-7773)	
Wittock Supply Company .... F	810 721-8000
Imlay City (G-8651)	

3433 Heating Eqpt

Alhern-Martin Indus Frnc Co .... E	248 689-6363
Troy (G-16922)	
▲ Armstrong Hot Water Inc .... E	269 278-1413
Three Rivers (G-16566)	
Banner Engineering & Sales Inc ..... F	989 755-0584
Saginaw (G-14609)	
▲ Burners Inc .... G	248 676-9141
Milford (G-11457)	
Commercial Works .... F	269 795-2060
Middleville (G-11304)	
Crown Heating Inc .... G	248 352-1688
Detroit (G-4109)	
D S C Services Inc .... G	734 241-9500
Monroe (G-11535)	
▲ Detroit Stoker Company C	734 241-9500
Monroe (G-11537)	
Great Lakes Electric LLC .... G	269 408-8276
Saint Joseph (G-14932)	
◆ Hamilton Engineering Inc .... G	734 419-0200
Livonia (G-10234)	
Log Jam Forest Products Inc .... G	616 677-2560
Marne (G-10995)	
◆ Marshall Excelsior Co .... E	269 789-6700
Marshall (G-11065)	
Messersmith Manufacturing Inc ...... G	906 466-9010
Bark River (G-1156)	
▲ Nu-Way Stove Inc .... G	989 733-8792
Onaway (G-12701)	
▲ Pyrinas LLC .... G	810 422-7535
Traverse City (G-16807)	
Refrigeration Research Inc .... D	810 227-1151
Brighton (G-2064)	
River Valley Machine Inc .... G	269 673-8070
Allegan (G-181)	
Rlh Industries Inc .... F	989 732-0493
Gaylord (G-6155)	
Solar Control Systems .... G	734 671-6899
Grosse Ile (G-7526)	
Solar EZ Inc .... F	989 773-3347
Mount Pleasant (G-11741)	
▲ Solaronics Inc .... E	248 651-5333
Auburn Hills (G-1035)	
U S Distributing Inc .... E	248 646-0550
Birmingham (G-1755)	
Ventura Aerospace LLC .... E	734 357-0114
Wixom (G-18786)	
Whittaker Orgname Assoc Inc .... G	616 786-2255
Holland (G-8249)	
Wood Burn LLC .... G	810 614-4204
Millington (G-11505)	

3441 Fabricated Structural Steel

A & S Industrial LLC .... G	906 482-8007
Hancock (G-7614)	
A-1 Roll Co .... F	586 783-6677
Mount Clemens (G-11626)	
Aarons Fabrictions-Tube Steel .... F	586 883-0652
Macomb (G-10570)	
AB Custom Fabricating LLC .... F	269 663-8100
Edwardsburg (G-4998)	
Ability Mfg & Engrg Co .... D	269 227-3292
Fennville (G-5433)	
Ace Welding & Machine Inc .... F	231 941-9664
Traverse City (G-16595)	
Actron Steel Inc .... E	231 947-3981
Traverse City (G-16597)	
Admin Industries LLC .... G	989 685-3438
Rose City (G-14358)	
Adrian Tool Corporation .... F	517 263-6530
Adrian (G-52)	
ADW Industries Inc .... E	989 466-4742
Alma (G-233)	
Aero Inc .... F	248 669-4085
Walled Lake (G-17662)	
Afco Manufacturing Corp .... F	248 634-4415
Holly (G-8260)	
Alco Products LLC .... F	313 823-7500
Detroit (G-3996)	
Allegan Metal Fabricators Inc .... G	269 751-7130
Hamilton (G-7595)	
Allen Partners LLC .... F	269 673-4010
Allegan (G-148)	
▲ Allor Manufacturing Inc .... D	248 486-4500
Brighton (G-1943)	
Alloy Construction Service Inc .... E	989 486-6960
Midland (G-11319)	
Alro Steel Corporation .... G	810 695-7300
Grand Blanc (G-6231)	
Alumabridge LLC .... F	855 373-7500
Ann Arbor (G-362)	
Ambassador Steel Corporation .... E	517 455-7216
Lansing (G-9804)	
American Steel Works Inc .... F	734 282-0300
Riverview (G-13869)	
Amerikam Inc .... D	616 243-5833
Grand Rapids (G-6457)	
Amhawk LLC .... F	269 468-4141
Coloma (G-3474)	
Amhawk LLC .... E	269 468-4177
Hartford (G-7761)	
◆ Amigo Mobility Intl Inc .... D	989 777-0910
Bridgeport (G-1914)	
ARC Archer LLC .... E	616 439-3014
Kent City (G-9426)	
Ashley Garcia .... G	248 396-8138
White Lake (G-18450)	
Assembly Source One Inc .... G	616 844-5250
Grand Haven (G-6276)	
Austin Tube Products Inc .... F	231 745-2741
Baldwin (G-1121)	
B & D Metal Fab .... G	616 255-1796
Morley (G-11619)	
B & G Custom Works Inc .... F	269 686-9420
Allegan (G-149)	
Baker Enterprises Inc .... E	989 354-2189
Alpena (G-281)	
Bauer Sheet Metal & Fabg Inc .... E	231 773-3244
Muskegon (G-11775)	
Bell Metals .... G	248 227-0407
Troy (G-16972)	
Bennett Steel LLC .... F	616 401-5271
Grand Rapids (G-6500)	
Berrien Metal Products Inc .... F	269 695-5000
Buchanan (G-2189)	
Black River Manufacturing Inc .... E	810 982-9812
Port Huron (G-13459)	
▲ Boomer Company .... E	313 832-5050
Detroit (G-4063)	
Boones Welding & Fabricating .... G	517 782-7461
Jackson (G-8825)	
Bridgeport Manufacturing Inc .... G	989 777-4314
Bridgeport (G-1915)	
Bristol Steel & Conveyor Corp .... G	810 658-9510
Davison (G-3775)	
Builders Iron Inc .... E	616 647-9288
Sparta (G-15761)	
Bulldog Innovative Mfg LLC .... E	517 223-2500
Fowlerville (G-5836)	
Burnham & Northern Inc .... G	517 279-7501
Coldwater (G-3422)	

Busch Industries Inc ..... G ..... 616 957-3737 Grand Rapids *(G-6539)*
C & C Manufacturing Inc ..... F ..... 586 268-3650 Sterling Heights *(G-15949)*
C & J Fabrication Inc ..... G ..... 586 791-6269 Clinton Township *(G-3192)*
C & M Manufacturing Inc ..... E ..... 517 279-0013 Coldwater *(G-3423)*
Cadillac Fabrication Inc ..... E ..... 231 775-7386 Cadillac *(G-2322)*
Campbell & Shaw Steel Inc ..... F ..... 810 364-5100 Marysville *(G-11083)*
Camryn Fabrication LLC ..... F ..... 586 949-0818 Chesterfield *(G-2857)*
Capital Steel & Builders Sup ..... E ..... 517 694-0451 Holt *(G-8304)*
Capital Welding Inc ..... E ..... 248 355-0410 Detroit *(G-4086)*
Cardinal Fabricating Inc ..... E ..... 517 655-2155 Williamston *(G-18570)*
Casadei Structural Steel Inc ..... E ..... 586 698-2898 Sterling Heights *(G-15953)*
Cbp Fabrication Inc ..... E ..... 313 653-4220 Detroit *(G-4090)*
Century Roll Inc ..... F ..... 810 743-5065 Burton *(G-2232)*
Cerco Inc ..... E ..... 734 362-8664 Brownstown Twp *(G-2153)*
Chicago Blow Pipe Company ..... F ..... 773 533-6100 Marquette *(G-11012)*
▼ Circle S Products Inc ..... G ..... 734 675-2960 Woodhaven *(G-18798)*
Clair Sawyer ..... G ..... 906 228-8242 Marquette *(G-11013)*
▼ Complex Steel & Wire Corp ..... F ..... 734 326-1600 Wayne *(G-18218)*
Concept Metal Machining LLC ..... E ..... 616 647-9200 Comstock Park *(G-3597)*
Concept Metal Products Inc ..... D ..... 231 799-3202 Spring Lake *(G-15808)*
Cooper & Cooper Sales Inc ..... G ..... 810 327-6247 Port Huron *(G-13465)*
Corban Industries Inc ..... E ..... 248 393-2720 Orion *(G-12726)*
Cornerstone Fabg & Cnstr Inc ..... E ..... 989 642-5241 Hemlock *(G-7850)*
Corsair Engineering Inc ..... C ..... 810 234-3664 Flint *(G-5673)*
Cox Brothers Machining Inc ..... E ..... 517 796-4662 Jackson *(G-8855)*
Custom Architectural Products ..... G ..... 616 748-1905 Zeeland *(G-19011)*
Custom Design & Manufacturing ..... F ..... 989 754-9962 Carrollton *(G-2587)*
Custom Metal Products Corp ..... G ..... 734 591-2500 Livonia *(G-10171)*
Custom Powder and Fabricators ..... F ..... 616 915-9995 Grand Rapids *(G-6621)*
D&M Metal Products Company ..... E ..... 616 784-0601 Comstock Park *(G-3600)*
Delta Steel Inc ..... G ..... 989 752-5129 Saginaw *(G-14637)*
Delta Tube & Fabricating Corp ..... C ..... 810 239-0154 Flint *(G-5686)*
Delta Tube & Fabrication ..... F ..... 810 233-0440 Flint *(G-5687)*
Demaria Building Company Inc ..... G ..... 248 486-2598 New Hudson *(G-12050)*
▲ Demmer Corporation ..... C ..... 517 321-3600 Lansing *(G-9687)*
▲ Digital Fabrication Inc ..... F ..... 616 794-2848 Belding *(G-1445)*
Diversified Fabricators Inc ..... F ..... 586 868-1000 Clinton Township *(G-3225)*
Diversiform LLC ..... G ..... 989 278-9605 Oscoda *(G-12756)*
Djd Mfg LLC ..... G ..... 586 359-2090 Roseville *(G-14400)*
▲ Dobson Industrial Inc ..... E ..... 800 298-6063 Bay City *(G-1346)*
Douglas King Industries Inc ..... G ..... 989 642-2865 Hemlock *(G-7851)*
Douglas Steel Fabricating Corp ..... D ..... 517 322-2050 Lansing *(G-9759)*
▲ Dowding Industries Inc ..... E ..... 517 663-5455 Eaton Rapids *(G-4959)*
Dowding Industries Inc ..... C ..... 517 663-5455 Eaton Rapids *(G-4960)*
Dpr Manufacturing & Svcs Inc ..... E ..... 586 757-1421 Warren *(G-17783)*
Drushal Fabricating LLC ..... G ..... 517 539-5921 Jackson *(G-8871)*
Dumas Concepts In Building Inc ..... F ..... 313 895-2555 Detroit *(G-4196)*
▲ Dunnage Engineering Inc ..... E ..... 810 229-9501 Brighton *(G-1979)*
Dunns Welding Inc ..... G ..... 248 356-3866 Southfield *(G-15543)*
Eab Fabrication Inc ..... E ..... 517 639-7080 Quincy *(G-13668)*
Eab Fabrication Inc ..... E ..... 517 639-7080 Quincy *(G-13669)*
Eagle Engineering & Supply Co ..... E ..... 989 356-4526 Alpena *(G-291)*
Eastern Michigan Industries ..... E ..... 586 757-4140 Warren *(G-17791)*
EMC Welding & Fabrication Inc ..... G ..... 231 788-4172 Muskegon *(G-11811)*
Empire Machine & Conveyors Inc ..... F ..... 989 541-2060 Durand *(G-4841)*
▲ Engineered Alum Fabricators Co ..... G ..... 248 582-3430 Ferndale *(G-5551)*
▲ Envirodyne Technologies Inc ..... E ..... 269 342-1918 Kalamazoo *(G-9181)*
▲ Ethylene LLC ..... E ..... 616 554-3464 Kentwood *(G-9451)*
Fab Masters Company Inc ..... D ..... 269 646-5315 Marcellus *(G-10947)*
Fab-Lite Inc ..... E ..... 231 398-8280 Manistee *(G-10899)*
Fabrication Plus ..... G ..... 231 730-9374 Montague *(G-11596)*
Fabricted Cmpnnts Assmblies In ..... F ..... 269 673-7100 Allegan *(G-157)*
Ferguson Steel Inc ..... F ..... 810 984-3918 Fort Gratiot *(G-5821)*
Ferro Fab LLC ..... F ..... 586 791-3561 Clinton Township *(G-3237)*
Flat-To-Form Metal Spc Inc ..... F ..... 231 924-1288 Fremont *(G-6040)*
Focal Point Metal Fab LLC ..... F ..... 616 844-7670 Spring Lake *(G-15814)*
Frankenmuth Industrial Svcs ..... E ..... 989 652-3322 Frankenmuth *(G-5862)*
▲ Genco Alliance LLC ..... G ..... 269 216-5500 Kalamazoo *(G-9192)*
General Motors LLC ..... F ..... 989 894-7210 Bay City *(G-1359)*
Gerref Industries Inc ..... E ..... 616 794-3110 Belding *(G-1450)*
◆ Global Strgc Sup Solutions LLC ..... D ..... 734 525-9100 Livonia *(G-10226)*
Gosen Tool & Machine Inc ..... F ..... 989 777-6493 Saginaw *(G-14656)*
Gray Brothers Mfg Inc ..... F ..... 269 483-7615 White Pigeon *(G-18479)*
Great Lakes Contracting Inc ..... E ..... 616 846-8888 Grand Haven *(G-6308)*
Great Lakes Custom Metalworks ..... G ..... 231 818-5888 Cheboygan *(G-2784)*
Great Lakes Metal Fabrication ..... G ..... 248 218-0540 Livonia *(G-10230)*
Great Lakes Metal Works ..... G ..... 269 789-2342 Marshall *(G-11059)*
Great Lakes Stainless Inc ..... E ..... 231 943-7648 Traverse City *(G-16705)*
▲ Great Lakes Towers LLC ..... C ..... 734 682-4000 Monroe *(G-11545)*
▲ Greene Metal Products Inc ..... E ..... 586 465-6800 Clinton Township *(G-3249)*
Griffen Fab Works LLC ..... G ..... 616 890-0621 Byron Center *(G-2276)*
▲ Griptrac Inc ..... F ..... 231 853-2284 Ravenna *(G-13689)*
H & M Welding and Fabricating ..... G ..... 517 764-3630 Jackson *(G-8897)*
Hamilton Steel Fabrications ..... G ..... 269 751-8757 Hamilton *(G-7600)*
Harrington Construction Co ..... G ..... 269 543-4251 Fennville *(G-5437)*
Hayden Neitzke LLC ..... G ..... 989 875-2440 Sumner *(G-16331)*
Heartland Steel Products LLC ..... E ..... 810 364-7421 Marysville *(G-11088)*
Heys Fabrication and Mch Co ..... F ..... 616 247-0065 Wyoming *(G-18882)*
Higgins Marine Metals LLC ..... G ..... 616 990-2732 Zeeland *(G-19035)*
▼ Highland Engineering Inc ..... E ..... 517 548-4372 Howell *(G-8460)*
Howard Structural Steel Inc ..... E ..... 989 752-3000 Saginaw *(G-14670)*
HPS Fabrications Inc ..... F ..... 734 282-2285 Wyandotte *(G-18822)*
Ideal Steel & Bldrs Sups LLC ..... E ..... 313 849-0000 Detroit *(G-4312)*
IEC Fabrication LLC ..... F ..... 810 623-1546 Fowlerville *(G-5842)*
Imm Inc ..... E ..... 989 344-7662 Grayling *(G-7463)*
Industrial Fabricating Inc ..... F ..... 734 676-2710 Brownstown Twp *(G-2155)*
Industrial Fabrication LLC ..... E ..... 269 465-5960 Bridgman *(G-1929)*
Innovative Iron Inc ..... G ..... 616 248-4250 Grand Rapids *(G-6846)*
Inter-Lakes Bases Inc ..... E ..... 586 294-8120 Fraser *(G-5944)*
International Extrusions Inc ..... C ..... 734 427-8700 Garden City *(G-6102)*
Iron Fetish Metalworks Inc ..... F ..... 586 776-8311 Roseville *(G-14426)*
J & J United Industries LLC ..... F ..... 734 443-3737 Livonia *(G-10252)*
▲ J & M Machine Products Inc ..... D ..... 231 755-1622 Norton Shores *(G-12302)*
J & S Livonia Inc ..... G ..... 734 793-9000 Livonia *(G-10253)*
Jack & Sons Welding & Fabg LLC ..... G ..... 248 302-6496 Lewiston *(G-10022)*
Jaimes Liquidation Inc ..... E ..... 248 356-8600 Southfield *(G-15610)*
Jay Industries Inc ..... G ..... 313 240-7535 Northville *(G-12232)*
JC Metal Fabricating Inc ..... F ..... 231 629-0425 Reed City *(G-13792)*
Jic Metalworks ..... G ..... 989 390-2077 Mio *(G-11509)*
JRC Fabricating Sales and Mfg ..... G ..... 734 459-6711 Canton *(G-2481)*
K & L Sheet Metal LLC ..... G ..... 269 965-0027 Battle Creek *(G-1248)*
K & M Industrial LLC ..... G ..... 906 420-8770 Gladstone *(G-6182)*
K-R Metal Engineers Corp ..... G ..... 989 892-1901 Bay City *(G-1370)*
Kalamazoo Metal Muncher Inc ..... G ..... 269 492-0268 Plainwell *(G-13080)*
Kehrig Steel Inc ..... G ..... 586 716-9700 Ira *(G-8700)*
Ken Gorsline Welding ..... G ..... 269 649-0650 Vicksburg *(G-17606)*
Kenowa Industries Inc ..... G ..... 517 322-0311 Lansing *(G-9771)*
Kirby Metal Corporation ..... E ..... 810 743-3360 Burton *(G-2237)*
▲ Kraftube Inc ..... C ..... 231 832-5562 Reed City *(G-13793)*
Kriewall Enterprises Inc ..... E ..... 586 336-0600 Romeo *(G-14227)*
L & W Inc ..... G ..... 734 397-8085 Van Buren Twp *(G-17535)*
▲ L & W Inc ..... D ..... 734 397-6300 New Boston *(G-12012)*
Laduke Corporation ..... E ..... 248 414-6600 Oak Park *(G-12622)*
Lake Shore Services Inc ..... F ..... 734 285-7007 Wyandotte *(G-18828)*
Laser Craft LLC ..... E ..... 248 340-8922 Lake Orion *(G-9615)*
Lasers Unlimited Inc ..... F ..... 616 977-2668 Grand Rapids *(G-6931)*
Legacy Metal Services Inc ..... G ..... 810 721-7775 Imlay City *(G-8639)*
Legendary Fabrication Wldg LLC ..... G ..... 989 872-9353 Cass City *(G-2617)*
Lewis Metals LLC ..... G ..... 231 468-3435 Cadillac *(G-2343)*
Liberty Fabricators Inc ..... F ..... 810 877-7117 Flint *(G-5724)*
Lincoln Welding Company ..... G ..... 313 292-2299 Stockbridge *(G-16276)*
▲ Lna Solutions Inc ..... F ..... 734 677-2305 Ann Arbor *(G-553)*
Loudon Steel Inc ..... E ..... 989 871-9353 Millington *(G-11502)*
Lyndon Fabricators Inc ..... G ..... 313 937-3640 Detroit *(G-4412)*
M & J Manufacturing Inc ..... G ..... 586 778-6322 Clinton Township *(G-3283)*

Employee Codes: A=Over 500 employees, B=251-500
C=101-250, D=51-100, E=20-50, F=10-19, G=3-9

2022 Harris Michigan
Industrial Directory

811

Madar Metal Fabricating LLC................F....... 517 267-9610
Lansing ***(G-9714)***
Magnum Fabricating..............................G....... 734 484-5800
Ypsilanti ***(G-18964)***
Manistee Wldg & Piping Svc Inc...........G....... 231 723-2551
Manistee ***(G-10906)***
▲ Marsh Plating Corporation................D....... 734 483-5767
Ypsilanti ***(G-18965)***
Maslo Fabrication LLC ....G....... 616 298-7700
Holland ***(G-8139)***
Matrix North Amercn Cnstr Inc..............D....... 734 847-4605
Temperance ***(G-16539)***
Mayo Welding & Fabricating Co............G....... 248 435-2730
Royal Oak ***(G-14561)***
Mbm Fabricators Co Inc........................C....... 734 941-0100
Romulus ***(G-14301)***
MCS Industries Inc.................................F....... 517 568-4161
Homer ***(G-8354)***
Meccom Corporation..............................G....... 313 895-4900
Detroit ***(G-4426)***
Mechanical Fabricators Inc...................E....... 810 765-8853
Marine City ***(G-10962)***
Men of Steel Inc......................................F....... 989 635-4866
Marlette ***(G-10986)***
Merrill Institute Inc................................G....... 989 462-0330
Alma ***(G-245)***
Metal Mart USA Inc ....G....... 586 977-5820
Warren ***(G-17924)***
Metalbuilt LLC..E....... 586 786-9106
Chesterfield ***(G-2911)***
Metaldyne Tblar Components LLC........D....... 248 727-1800
Southfield ***(G-15655)***
Metalfab Inc..G....... 313 381-7579
Dearborn ***(G-3871)***
Metalfab Manufacturing Inc ....E....... 989 826-2301
Mio ***(G-11510)***
Michigan Diversified Metals...................G....... 517 223-7730
Fowlerville ***(G-5851)***
Michigan Fab and Engrg LLC................G....... 248 297-5268
Detroit ***(G-4449)***
Michigan Indus Met Pdts Inc.................F....... 616 786-3922
Muskegon ***(G-11870)***
Michigan Steel Fabricators Inc.............E....... 810 785-1478
Flint ***(G-5732)***
Mid Michigan Pipe Inc............................G....... 989 772-5664
Grand Rapids ***(G-7003)***
Midco 2 Inc..G....... 517 467-2222
Onsted ***(G-12706)***
Midwest Fabricating Inc.........................G....... 734 921-3914
Taylor ***(G-16447)***
Midwest Steel Inc....................................E....... 313 873-2220
Detroit ***(G-4456)***
Milton Manufacturing Inc ....E....... 313 366-2450
Detroit ***(G-4458)***
Minuteman Metal Works Inc...................G....... 989 269-8342
Bad Axe ***(G-1109)***
Mkr Fabricating Inc................................F....... 989 753-8100
Saginaw ***(G-14703)***
Modern Engrg Solutions LLC ....G....... 616 835-2711
Grand Rapids ***(G-7018)***
Moore Flame Cutting Co ....F....... 586 978-1090
Bloomfield Hills ***(G-1840)***
Moran Iron Works Inc ....D....... 989 733-2011
Onaway ***(G-12700)***
Morkin and Sowards Inc.........................E....... 734 729-4242
Wayne ***(G-18231)***
Morrison Indust Ries North...................F....... 248 859-4864
Novi ***(G-12484)***
Mound Steel & Supply Inc......................F....... 248 852-6630
Troy ***(G-17266)***
Mtw Industries Inc..................................F....... 989 317-3301
Mount Pleasant ***(G-11722)***
Mtw Performance & Fab.........................G....... 989 317-3301
Mount Pleasant ***(G-11723)***
National Metal Sales Inc........................G....... 734 942-3000
Romulus ***(G-14308)***
National Ordanace Auto Mfg LLC..........G....... 248 853-8822
Auburn Hills ***(G-979)***
NBC Truck Equipment Inc.......................E....... 586 774-4900
Roseville ***(G-14452)***
Nelson Iron Works Inc............................G....... 313 925-5355
Detroit ***(G-4480)***
Newco Industries LLC...........................E....... 517 542-0105
Litchfield ***(G-10084)***
Niles Aluminum Products Inc ....E....... 269 683-1191
Niles ***(G-12153)***
Nisshinbo Automotive Mfg Inc ....E....... 586 997-1000
Sterling Heights ***(G-16117)***
Northern Chain Specialties....................F....... 231 889-3151
Kaleva ***(G-9380)***
Northern Concrete Pipe Inc ....E....... 989 892-3545
Bay City ***(G-1383)***
Northern Machining & Repr Inc.............E....... 906 786-0526
Escanaba ***(G-5088)***
Northwest Fabrication Inc.......................G....... 231 536-3229
East Jordan ***(G-4878)***
▲ Northwoods Manufacturing Inc.........D....... 906 779-2370
Kingsford ***(G-9516)***
Nova International LLC..........................E....... 269 381-6779
Portage ***(G-13589)***
Nt Fabricating Inc....................................F....... 586 566-7280
Shelby Township ***(G-15293)***
Oakland Welding Industries...................E....... 586 949-4090
Chesterfield ***(G-2916)***
▲ Oakwood Energy Management Inc ..F....... 734 947-7700
Taylor ***(G-16453)***
▲ Oakwood Metal Fabricating Co ....E....... 313 561-7740
Dearborn ***(G-3879)***
P I W Corporation....................................G....... 989 448-2501
Gaylord ***(G-6152)***
Parton & Preble Inc..................................E....... 586 773-6000
Warren ***(G-17954)***
Pioneer Machine and Tech Inc...............G....... 248 546-4451
Madison Heights ***(G-10800)***
Pk Fabricating Inc....................................F....... 248 398-4500
Ferndale ***(G-5578)***
Plutchak Fab..G....... 906 864-4650
Menominee ***(G-11256)***
Ponder Industrial Incorporated ....E....... 989 684-9841
Bay City ***(G-1389)***
▼ Powell Fabrication & Mfg LLC ....E....... 989 681-2158
Saint Louis ***(G-14996)***
Power Industries Corp............................G....... 586 783-3818
Harrison Township ***(G-7716)***
Precision Metals Plus Inc........................G....... 269 342-6330
Kalamazoo ***(G-9304)***
Precision Mtl Hdlg Eqp LLC....................D....... 313 789-8101
Inkster ***(G-8671)***
Precision Mtl Hdlg Eqp LLC....................D....... 734 351-7350
Romulus ***(G-14322)***
Premier Prototype Inc.............................E....... 586 323-6114
Sterling Heights ***(G-16132)***
▲ Production Fabricators Inc ....E....... 231 777-3822
Muskegon ***(G-11900)***
Professional Metal Works Inc ....E....... 517 351-7411
Haslett ***(G-7777)***
▼ PSI Marine Inc ....F....... 989 695-2646
Saginaw ***(G-14731)***
Quality Bending Threading Inc...............F....... 313 898-5100
Detroit ***(G-4546)***
Quality Finishing Systems.......................F....... 231 834-9131
Grant ***(G-7431)***
Quality Metal Fabricating ....G....... 616 901-5510
Grand Rapids ***(G-7128)***
R T C Enviro Fab Inc ....E....... 517 596-2987
Munith ***(G-11757)***
▲ R-Bo Co Inc ....F....... 616 748-9733
Zeeland ***(G-19076)***
Red Laser Inc ....F....... 517 540-1300
Wixom ***(G-18739)***
Refab Metal Fabrication LLC ....E....... 616 842-9705
Grand Haven ***(G-6352)***
REO Fab LLC..G....... 810 969-4667
Lapeer ***(G-9958)***
Richard Bennett & Associates................G....... 313 831-4262
Detroit ***(G-4571)***
Richmonds Steel Inc.................................F....... 989 453-7010
Pigeon ***(G-13040)***
Ridgefield Company LLC ....G....... 888 226-8665
Grand Rapids ***(G-7155)***
River City Metal Products Inc ....D....... 616 235-3746
Grand Rapids ***(G-7159)***
River City Steel Svc.................................G....... 616 301-7227
Grandville ***(G-7414)***
Rives Manufacturing Inc ....E....... 517 569-3380
Rives Junction ***(G-13888)***
▲ RKP Consulting Inc ....E....... 616 698-0300
Caledonia ***(G-2397)***
Rochester Welding Company Inc............E....... 248 628-0801
Oxford ***(G-12913)***
Rocksteady Manufacturing LLC ....F....... 586 778-5028
Roseville ***(G-14472)***
Rohmann Iron Works Inc ....E....... 810 233-5611
Flint ***(G-5757)***
Roth Fabricating Inc ....E....... 517 458-7541
Morenci ***(G-11615)***
Royal ARC Welding Company ....E....... 734 789-9099
Flat Rock ***(G-5628)***
RSI..G....... 586 566-7716
Shelby Township ***(G-15318)***
RSI Global Sourcing LLC ....G....... 734 604-2448
Novi ***(G-12529)***
Rt Manufacturing Inc ....F....... 906 233-9158
Escanaba ***(G-5097)***
Ruess Winchester Inc...............................F....... 989 725-5809
Owosso ***(G-12852)***
S & G Erection Company ....E....... 517 546-9240
Howell ***(G-8513)***
S & N Machine & Fabricating..................E....... 231 894-2658
Rothbury ***(G-14498)***
S & P Fabricating Inc...............................G....... 586 421-1950
Chesterfield ***(G-2942)***
S L H Metals Inc ....F....... 989 743-3467
Corunna ***(G-3717)***
S N D Steel Fabrication Inc ....F....... 586 997-1500
Shelby Township ***(G-15320)***
Sales & Engineering Inc............................E....... 734 525-9030
Livonia ***(G-10398)***
Sanilac Steel Inc.......................................F....... 989 635-2992
Marlette ***(G-10987)***
▲ Sas Global Corporation.........................C....... 248 414-4470
Warren ***(G-18002)***
Sas Global Corporation.............................D....... 248 414-4470
Warren ***(G-18003)***
Savs Welding Services Inc........................F....... 313 841-3430
Detroit ***(G-4582)***
Service Iron Works Inc ....E....... 248 446-9750
South Lyon ***(G-15457)***
Servotech Industries Inc ....G....... 734 697-5555
Taylor ***(G-16471)***
Sherwood Manufacturing Corp ....F....... 231 386-5132
Northport ***(G-12191)***
Shoreline Mtal Fabricators Inc.................E....... 231 722-4443
Muskegon ***(G-11919)***
Short Iron Fabrication ....G....... 231 375-8825
Muskegon ***(G-11921)***
Signa Group Inc ....B....... 231 845-5101
Ludington ***(G-10550)***
SL Holdings Inc...E....... 586 949-0912
Chesterfield ***(G-2948)***
Smede-Son Steel and Sup Co Inc ....D....... 313 937-8300
Redford ***(G-13772)***
SMI American Inc ....G....... 313 438-0096
Taylor ***(G-16474)***
Sol-I-Cor Industries....................................G....... 248 476-0670
Livonia ***(G-10413)***
South Park Sales & Mfg Inc ....G....... 313 381-7579
Dearborn ***(G-3899)***
Spartan Metal Fab LLC...............................G....... 517 322-9050
Lansing ***(G-9737)***
Special Fabricators Inc...............................G....... 248 588-6717
Madison Heights ***(G-10833)***
Special Projects Inc.....................................E....... 734 455-7130
Plymouth ***(G-13302)***
Steel Craft Inc..G....... 989 358-7196
Alpena ***(G-320)***
Steel Mill Components Inc ....G....... 313 386-0893
Allen Park ***(G-207)***
Steel Supply & Engineering Co ....E....... 616 452-3281
Grand Rapids ***(G-7223)***
Stevens Custom Fabrication ....G....... 989 340-1184
Alpena ***(G-321)***
Stevens Custom Fabrication ....G....... 989 340-1184
Alpena ***(G-322)***
Stone For You...G....... 248 651-9940
Rochester ***(G-13930)***
Structural Standards Inc ....E....... 616 813-1798
Sparta ***(G-15784)***
Superior Fabricating Inc...............................F....... 989 354-8877
Alpena ***(G-324)***
Superior Suppliers Network LLC..................F....... 906 284-1561
Crystal Falls ***(G-3746)***
Synergy Additive Mfg LLC ....G....... 248 719-2194
Clinton Township ***(G-3369)***
Tartan Industries Inc.....................................G....... 810 387-4255
Yale ***(G-18920)***
Tbl Fabrications Inc.......................................G....... 586 294-2087
Roseville ***(G-14483)***
Tfi Inc ....E....... 231 728-2310
Muskegon ***(G-11931)***
Tg Manufacturing LLC...................................G....... 616 935-7575
Byron Center ***(G-2296)***
◆ Thyssenkrupp Materials NA Inc................C....... 248 233-5600
Southfield ***(G-15722)***
Toolpak Solutions LLC ....G....... 586 646-5655
New Baltimore ***(G-11995)***
Tower International Inc..................................G....... 616 802-1600
Grand Rapids ***(G-7267)***
Trimet Industries Inc.....................................E....... 231 929-9100
Traverse City ***(G-16867)***

Tube Fab/Roman Engrg Co Inc ... C ... 231 238-9366
Afton *(G-108)*
U P Fabricating Co Inc ... F ... 906 475-4400
Negaunee *(G-11976)*
U S Fabrication & Design LLC ... F ... 248 919-2910
Livonia *(G-10452)*
Unistrut International Corp ... C ... 734 721-4040
Wayne *(G-18240)*
United Fabricating Company ... G ... 248 887-7289
Highland *(G-7901)*
Universal Induction Inc ... G ... 269 983-5543
Saint Joseph *(G-14970)*
▼ **Universal Manufacturing Co** ... E ... 586 463-2560
Clinton Township *(G-3383)*
Utica Steel Inc ... D ... 586 949-1900
Chesterfield *(G-2962)*
Valley Steel Company ... E ... 989 799-2600
Saginaw *(G-14788)*
Van Dam Iron Works LLC ... E ... 616 452-8627
Grand Rapids *(G-7304)*
Van Dellen Steel Inc ... E ... 616 698-9950
Caledonia *(G-2405)*
▲ **Van Pelt Corporation** ... G ... 313 365-3600
Sterling Heights *(G-16221)*
Van Pelt Corporation ... G ... 313 733-0073
Detroit *(G-4661)*
Van Pelt Corporation ... F ... 313 365-6500
Detroit *(G-4662)*
Vanco Steel Inc ... E ... 810 688-4333
North Branch *(G-12184)*
Varneys Fab & Weld LLC ... G ... 231 865-6856
Nunica *(G-12589)*
▲ **Vci Inc** ... D ... 269 659-3676
Sturgis *(G-16328)*
Versatile Fabrication Co Inc ... E ... 231 739-7115
Muskegon *(G-11941)*
Vertex Steel Inc ... E ... 248 684-4177
Milford *(G-11496)*
Very Best Steel LLC ... G ... 734 697-8609
Belleville *(G-1493)*
Vochaska Engineering ... G ... 269 637-5670
South Haven *(G-15423)*
▲ **Wagon Automotive Inc** ... C ... 248 262-2020
Wixom *(G-18789)*
Wahmhoff Farms LLC ... F ... 269 628-4308
Gobles *(G-6220)*
▲ **Webasto Roof Systems Inc** ... B ... 248 997-5100
Auburn Hills *(G-1088)*
Webasto Roof Systems Inc ... C ... 248 997-5100
Rochester Hills *(G-14145)*
Weir Fabrication LLC ... G ... 248 953-8363
Sterling Heights *(G-16230)*
Wenstrom Dsign Fabrication LLC ... G ... 269 760-2358
Brohman *(G-2109)*
West Michigan Fab Corp ... G ... 616 794-3750
Belding *(G-1465)*
West Michigan Fabrication ... G ... 269 637-2415
South Haven *(G-15425)*
West Michigan Metals LLC ... G ... 269 978-7021
Allegan *(G-186)*
Wm Kloeffler Industries Inc ... G ... 810 765-4068
Marine City *(G-10969)*
Wolverine Steel and Welding ... E ... 517 524-7300
Concord *(G-3658)*
Worldtek Industries LLC ... C ... 734 494-5204
Romulus *(G-14340)*
Wpw Inc ... F ... 810 785-1478
Flint *(G-5796)*

3442 Metal Doors, Sash, Frames, Molding & Trim

1-800-Hansons ... G ... 269 234-1670
Kalamazoo *(G-9105)*
Alliance Engnred Sltons NA Ltd ... C ... 586 291-3694
Detroit *(G-4001)*
Aluminum Textures Inc ... E ... 616 538-3144
Grandville *(G-7364)*
▲ **American Roll Shutter Awng Co** ... E ... 734 422-7110
Livonia *(G-10116)*
Andoor Craftmaster ... G ... 989 672-2020
Caro *(G-2565)*
Architectural Glass & Mtls Inc ... F ... 269 375-6165
Kalamazoo *(G-9118)*
Arnold & Sautter Co ... F ... 989 684-7557
Bay City *(G-1322)*
Astro Building Products Inc ... G ... 231 941-0324
Traverse City *(G-16604)*
Beechcraft Products Inc ... E ... 989 288-2606
Durand *(G-4840)*
Behind Shutter LLC ... G ... 248 467-7237
Grand Blanc *(G-6236)*
Caliber Metals Inc ... E ... 586 465-7650
New Baltimore *(G-11979)*
Curbs & Damper Products Inc ... F ... 586 776-7890
Roseville *(G-14392)*
▲ **Daiek Products Inc** ... F ... 248 816-1360
Troy *(G-17044)*
▼ **Duo-Gard Industries Inc** ... D ... 734 207-9700
Canton *(G-2456)*
▲ **E-Zee Set Wood Products Inc** ... G ... 248 398-0090
Oak Park *(G-12608)*
Elemental Artistry LLC ... G ... 616 326-1758
Grand Rapids *(G-6671)*
◆ **Eliason Corporation** ... D ... 269 327-7003
Portage *(G-13557)*
Eliason Corporation ... E ... 269 621-2100
Hartford *(G-7763)*
Forma-Kool Manufacturing Inc ... E ... 586 949-4813
Chesterfield *(G-2884)*
▲ **Fox Aluminum Products Inc** ... E ... 248 399-4288
Hazel Park *(G-7826)*
George W Trapp Co ... E ... 313 531-7180
Redford *(G-13737)*
Gissing North America LLC ... D ... 248 647-0400
Bingham Farms *(G-1697)*
Grabill Windows & Doors LLC ... E ... 810 798-2817
Almont *(G-261)*
Grand Valley Wood Products Inc ... E ... 616 475-5890
Grand Rapids *(G-6779)*
Great Lakes Trim Inc ... D ... 231 267-3000
Williamsburg *(G-18555)*
Hacks Key Shop Inc ... E ... 517 485-9488
Lansing *(G-9850)*
HS Inc ... G ... 248 373-4048
Rochester Hills *(G-14035)*
Integrity Door LLC ... G ... 616 896-8077
Dorr *(G-4768)*
International Door Inc ... E ... 248 547-7240
Canton *(G-2478)*
Ken Rodenhouse Door & Window ... F ... 616 784-3365
Comstock Park *(G-3614)*
Laforce LLC ... G ... 248 588-5601
Troy *(G-17203)*
◆ **Lean Factory America LLC** ... G ... 513 297-3086
Buchanan *(G-2199)*
Lippert Components Mfg Inc ... D ... 989 845-3061
Chesaning *(G-2829)*
▲ **Llink Technologies LLC** ... E ... 586 336-9370
Brown City *(G-2139)*
Lorenzo White ... G ... 313 943-3667
Detroit *(G-4405)*
Magna ... F ... 616 786-7403
Holland *(G-8133)*
◆ **Magna Mirrors North Amer LLC** ... A ... 616 868-6122
Alto *(G-336)*
Memtech Inc ... F ... 734 455-8550
Plymouth *(G-13240)*
Midynaco LLC ... G ... 989 550-8552
Kingston *(G-9526)*
Mt Clemens Glass & Mirror Co ... G ... 586 465-1733
Clinton Township *(G-3306)*
◆ **National Nail Corp** ... C ... 616 538-8000
Grand Rapids *(G-7036)*
Northern Mich Hardwoods Inc ... F ... 231 347-4575
Petoskey *(G-13008)*
▲ **Openings Inc** ... E ... 248 623-6899
Waterford *(G-18144)*
Panel Processing Oregon Inc ... D ... 989 356-9007
Alpena *(G-309)*
Paul Murphy Plastics Co ... E ... 586 774-4880
Roseville *(G-14460)*
Plymouth Garage LLC ... G ... 734 459-3667
Livonia *(G-10367)*
Pro-Line Doors LLC ... G ... 586 765-1657
Clinton Township *(G-3329)*
Proto-Form Engineering Inc ... F ... 586 727-9803
Columbus *(G-3501)*
PTL Engineering Inc ... F ... 810 664-2310
Lapeer *(G-9956)*
◆ **Quality Edge Inc** ... D ... 616 735-3833
Walker *(G-17651)*
Reliable Glass Company ... E ... 313 924-9750
Detroit *(G-4562)*
Replacement West Glass ... G ... 248 974-4635
Livonia *(G-10386)*
Rubbair LLC ... E ... 269 327-7003
Portage *(G-13602)*
Scott Iron Works Inc ... F ... 248 548-2822
Hazel Park *(G-7841)*
Shure Star LLC ... E ... 248 365-4382
Auburn Hills *(G-1033)*
Shutterbooth ... G ... 734 680-6067
Ann Arbor *(G-651)*
Shutterbooth ... G ... 586 747-4110
West Bloomfield *(G-18313)*
Special-Lite Inc ... C ... 800 821-6531
Decatur *(G-3951)*
Srg Global Automotive LLC ... B ... 586 757-7800
Sterling Heights *(G-16186)*
Storm Seal Co Inc ... G ... 248 689-1900
Troy *(G-17374)*
Total Door II Inc ... E ... 866 781-2069
Waterford *(G-18171)*
Tubelite Inc ... C ... 800 866-2227
Walker *(G-17655)*
Vinyl Sash of Flint Inc ... E ... 810 234-4831
Grand Blanc *(G-6266)*
Wallside Inc ... F ... 313 292-4400
Taylor *(G-16489)*
▲ **Weather King Windows Doors Inc** ... D ... 313 933-1234
Farmington *(G-5154)*
Weather King Windows Doors Inc ... E ... 248 478-7788
Farmington *(G-5155)*
Weatherproof Inc ... E ... 517 764-1330
Jackson *(G-9034)*

3443 Fabricated Plate Work

A & B Welding & Fabricating ... G ... 231 733-2661
Muskegon *(G-11759)*
Aatanks Llc ... G ... 586 427-7700
Warren *(G-17685)*
▲ **Acorn Stamping Inc** ... F ... 248 628-5216
Oxford *(G-12870)*
Actron Steel Inc ... E ... 231 947-3981
Traverse City *(G-16597)*
Admin Industries LLC ... F ... 989 685-3438
Rose City *(G-14358)*
Alro Riverside LLC ... G ... 517 782-8322
Jackson *(G-8813)*
Ambassador Steel Corporation ... E ... 517 455-7216
Lansing *(G-9804)*
American Dumpster Services LLC ... G ... 586 501-3600
Center Line *(G-2679)*
American Metal Fab Inc ... D ... 269 279-5108
Three Rivers *(G-16563)*
American Tank Fabrication LLC ... F ... 780 663-3552
Okemos *(G-12656)*
Amhawk LLC ... E ... 269 468-4177
Hartford *(G-7761)*
▲ **Anchor Lamina America Inc** ... E ... 248 489-9122
Bellaire *(G-1469)*
Anderson Welding & Mfg Inc ... F ... 906 523-4661
Houghton *(G-8380)*
Apex Rack and Coating Co ... E ... 616 530-6811
Grandville *(G-7365)*
Aqua Systems Inc ... G ... 810 346-2525
Brown City *(G-2133)*
Arctic Solutions Inc ... E ... 586 331-2600
Bruce Twp *(G-2163)*
Astro Dumpster Rental LLC ... G ... 313 444-7905
Royal Oak *(G-14515)*
B & G Products Inc ... F ... 616 698-9050
Grand Rapids *(G-6488)*
Baker Enterprises Inc ... E ... 989 354-2189
Alpena *(G-281)*
◆ **Besser Company** ... B ... 989 354-4111
Alpena *(G-284)*
Best Rate Dumpster Rental Inc ... G ... 248 391-5956
Ortonville *(G-12742)*
Bills Custom Fab Inc ... F ... 989 772-5817
Mount Pleasant *(G-11687)*
BMC Global LLC ... D ... 517 486-2121
Blissfield *(G-1762)*
Bosch Auto Svc Solutions Inc ... D ... 586 574-1820
Warren *(G-17740)*
Brian A Broomfield ... G ... 989 309-0709
Remus *(G-13814)*
Brockie Fabricating & Wldg LLC ... F ... 517 750-7500
Jackson *(G-8828)*
◆ **Burr Oak Tool Inc** ... B ... 269 651-9393
Sturgis *(G-16282)*
CA Picard Inc ... G ... 269 962-2231
Battle Creek *(G-1202)*
Chicago Blow Pipe Company ... F ... 773 533-6100
Marquette *(G-11012)*
Clawson Container Company ... E ... 248 625-8700
Clarkston *(G-3026)*
Clawson Tank Company ... E ... 248 625-8700
Clarkston *(G-3027)*

SIC

Cmi-Schneible Group C 810 354-0404
Fenton *(G-5465)*
Commercial Welding Company Inc G 269 782-5252
Dowagiac *(G-4778)*
Conner Steel Products F 248 852-5110
Rochester Hills *(G-13983)*
▲ **Conquest Manufacturing LLC** D 586 576-7600
Warren *(G-17763)*
Constructive Sheet Metal Inc E 616 245-5306
Allendale *(G-217)*
Contech Engnered Solutions LLC G 517 676-3000
Mason *(G-11120)*
Contract Welding and Fabg Inc E 734 699-5561
Van Buren Twp *(G-17520)*
◆ **D-M-E USA Inc** D 616 754-4601
Greenville *(G-7480)*
Davco Manufacturing LLC G 734 429-5665
Saline *(G-15011)*
Delta Iron Works Inc E 313 579-1445
Grosse Pointe *(G-7529)*
Detroit Boiler Company F 313 921-7060
Detroit *(G-4137)*
Detroit Dumpster Inc G 313 466-3174
Detroit *(G-4145)*
Detroit Plate Fabricators Inc G 313 921-7020
Detroit *(G-4159)*
Die-Mold-Automation Component G 313 581-6510
Dearborn *(G-3829)*
Dino S Dumpsters LLC G 989 225-5635
Bay City *(G-1345)*
Diversfied Prcurement Svcs LLC G 248 821-1147
Ferndale *(G-5548)*
Diversified Mech Svcs Inc F 616 785-2735
Comstock Park *(G-3602)*
Diversified Tooling Group Inc E 248 837-5828
Madison Heights *(G-10708)*
Dolphin Dumpsters LLC G 734 272-8981
Farmington Hills *(G-5219)*
E L Nickell Co F 269 435-2475
Constantine *(G-3665)*
Elden Cylinder Testing Inc G 734 946-6900
Taylor *(G-16411)*
Fab-Alloy Company G 517 787-4313
Jackson *(G-8883)*
Fabrications Unlimited Inc G 313 567-9616
Shelby Township *(G-15224)*
Fabrications Unlimited Inc G 313 567-9616
Detroit *(G-4224)*
Fabrilaser Mfg LLC E 269 789-9490
Marshall *(G-11057)*
Fischer Tanks LLC D 231 362-8265
Kaleva *(G-9378)*
▲ **Fluid Hutchinson Management** D 248 679-1327
Auburn Hills *(G-903)*
Formrite Inc G 517 521-1373
Webberville *(G-18245)*
Gladwin Tank Manufacturing Inc F 989 426-4768
Gladwin *(G-6199)*
Gld Holdings Inc E 616 877-4288
Moline *(G-11518)*
Glycon Corp E 517 423-8356
Tecumseh *(G-16503)*
Great Lakes Gauge Company E 989 652-6136
Bridgeport *(G-1916)*
Great Lakes Laser Dynamics Inc D 616 892-7070
Allendale *(G-220)*
▲ **Greene Metal Products Inc** E 586 465-6800
Clinton Township *(G-3249)*
Grossel Tool Co E 586 294-3660
Fraser *(G-5932)*
H & M Welding and Fabricating G 517 764-3630
Jackson *(G-8897)*
Hammars Contracting LLC E 810 367-3037
Kimball *(G-9493)*
▼ **Highland Engineering Inc** E 517 548-4372
Howell *(G-8460)*
◆ **Hines Corporation** F 231 799-6240
Norton Shores *(G-12348)*
Hydro-Craft Inc G 248 652-8100
Rochester Hills *(G-14037)*
Ideal Fabricators Inc E 734 422-5320
Livonia *(G-10245)*
Impert Industries Inc G 269 694-2727
Otsego *(G-12788)*
Industrial Container Inc F 313 923-8778
Detroit *(G-4314)*
Industrial Fabg Systems Inc E 248 685-7373
Milford *(G-11467)*
Jl Dumpsters LLC G 313 258-0767
Belleville *(G-1486)*
John Crowley Inc F 517 782-0491
Jackson *(G-8922)*
Johnston Boiler Company E 616 842-5050
Ferrysburg *(G-5603)*
K & W Manufacturing Co Inc E 517 369-9708
Bronson *(G-2117)*
K and W Landfill Inc D 906 883-3504
Ontonagon *(G-12711)*
Kerr Pump and Supply Inc E 248 543-3880
Oak Park *(G-12621)*
Krista Messer G 734 459-1952
Canton *(G-2484)*
Kurrent Welding Inc G 734 753-9197
New Boston *(G-12011)*
L & W Inc G 734 397-2212
Van Buren Twp *(G-17536)*
L & W Inc G 616 394-9665
Holland *(G-8118)*
L Barge & Associates Inc E 248 582-3430
Ferndale *(G-5563)*
Larsen Service Inc G 810 374-6132
Otisville *(G-12782)*
Laser North Inc G 906 353-6090
Baraga *(G-1144)*
▲ **Lasl Inc** E 586 331-2600
Bruce Twp *(G-2175)*
Liberty Steel Fabricating Inc E 269 556-9792
Saint Joseph *(G-14948)*
Lochinvar LLC E 734 454-4480
Plymouth *(G-13225)*
M&D Dumpsters LLC G 616 299-0234
Hudsonville *(G-8591)*
▲ **Magnetic Products Inc** D 248 887-5600
Highland *(G-7896)*
Mahle Eng Components USA Inc G 248 305-8200
Farmington Hills *(G-5302)*
Marix Specialty Welding Co E 586 754-9685
Warren *(G-17916)*
Marsh Industrial Services Inc F 231 258-4870
Kalkaska *(G-9395)*
Massie Mfg Inc E 906 353-6381
Baraga *(G-1145)*
Matrix North Amercn Cnstr Inc D 734 847-4605
Temperance *(G-16539)*
Mayo Welding & Fabricating Co G 248 435-2730
Royal Oak *(G-14561)*
MB Aerospace Warren LLC C 586 772-2500
Warren *(G-17920)*
McM Disposal LLC G 616 656-4049
Byron Center *(G-2283)*
▲ **Merrill Technologies Group Inc** D 989 791-6676
Saginaw *(G-14697)*
Merrill Technologies Group Inc C 989 462-0330
Alma *(G-246)*
Metal Quest Inc G 989 733-2011
Onaway *(G-12699)*
Metal Tech Products Inc E 313 533-5277
Detroit *(G-4432)*
Michigan Metal Fabricators G 586 754-0421
Warren *(G-17929)*
Moore Flame Cutting Co F 586 978-1090
Bloomfield Hills *(G-1840)*
Nelson Steel Products Inc D 616 396-1515
Holland *(G-8152)*
▲ **Nicholson Terminal & Dock Co** D 313 842-4300
River Rouge *(G-13858)*
North Central Welding Co E 989 275-8054
Roscommon *(G-14354)*
Northern Fab & Machine LLC F 906 863-8506
Menominee *(G-11255)*
Northern Machining & Repr Inc E 906 786-0526
Escanaba *(G-5088)*
Northwest Fabrication Inc G 231 536-3229
East Jordan *(G-4878)*
Oakland Welding Industries E 586 949-4090
Chesterfield *(G-2916)*
Old Xembedded LLC G 734 975-0577
Ann Arbor *(G-600)*
Parton & Preble Inc E 586 773-6000
Warren *(G-17954)*
Peninsular Inc E 586 775-7211
Roseville *(G-14461)*
Plesh Industries Inc E 716 873-4916
Brighton *(G-2052)*
Power Industries Corp G 586 783-3818
Harrison Township *(G-7716)*
Power Marine LLC G 586 344-1192
Harrison Township *(G-7717)*
Precise Finishing Systems Inc E 517 552-9200
Howell *(G-8499)*
Priority Waste LLC E 586 228-1200
Clinton Township *(G-3327)*
◆ **Process Systems Inc** E 586 757-5711
Warren *(G-17977)*
▲ **Production Fabricators Inc** E 231 777-3822
Muskegon *(G-11900)*
PSC Industrial Outsourcing LP E 313 824-5859
Detroit *(G-4540)*
Quigley Industries Inc E 248 426-8600
Farmington Hills *(G-5361)*
◆ **R & D Enterprises Inc** E 248 349-7077
Plymouth *(G-13274)*
R and J Dumpsters LLC G 248 863-8579
Howell *(G-8504)*
R T C Enviro Fab Inc E 517 596-2987
Munith *(G-11757)*
▲ **R W Fernstrum & Company** E 906 863-5553
Menominee *(G-11257)*
RC Metal Products Inc G 616 696-1694
Sand Lake *(G-15053)*
Refrigeration Research Inc D 810 227-1151
Brighton *(G-2064)*
Rendon & Sons Machining Inc F 269 628-2200
Gobles *(G-6219)*
Returnable Packaging Corp F 586 206-8050
Clinton Township *(G-3336)*
▼ **Riverside Tank & Mfg Corp** E 810 329-7143
Saint Clair *(G-14842)*
RK Wojan Inc E 231 347-1160
Charlevoix *(G-2730)*
Rlh Industries Inc F 989 732-0493
Gaylord *(G-6155)*
Rocksteady Manufacturing LLC F 586 778-5028
Roseville *(G-14472)*
Rss Baker LLC E 616 844-5429
Grand Haven *(G-6356)*
Saline Manufacturing Inc F 586 294-4701
Roseville *(G-14475)*
Saranac Tank Inc G 616 642-9481
Saranac *(G-15081)*
SBS Corp G 248 844-8200
Auburn Hills *(G-1029)*
Schad Boiler Setting Company D 313 273-2235
Detroit *(G-4584)*
Schrader Stoves of Michiana E 269 684-4494
Niles *(G-12166)*
Seal Support Systems Inc E 918 258-6484
Romeo *(G-14235)*
Sfi Acquisition Inc E 248 471-1500
Farmington Hills *(G-5377)*
Sloan Valve Company D 248 446-5300
New Hudson *(G-12070)*
Smith Dumpsters G 616 675-9399
Kent City *(G-9436)*
Special Mold Engineering Inc E 248 652-6600
Rochester Hills *(G-14116)*
SPX Corporation C 248 669-5100
Commerce Township *(G-3574)*
◆ **Steel Tank & Fabricating Co** D 248 625-8700
Clarkston *(G-3069)*
Steel Tank & Fabricating Co D 231 587-8412
Mancelona *(G-10879)*
Superior Steel Components Inc E 616 866-4759
Grand Rapids *(G-7238)*
Taylor Controls Inc F 269 637-8521
South Haven *(G-15418)*
▲ **Tower Defense & Aerospace LLC** E 248 675-6000
Livonia *(G-10439)*
◆ **Trimas Corporation** B 248 631-5450
Bloomfield Hills *(G-1869)*
True Fabrications & Machine F 248 288-0140
Troy *(G-17403)*
Unified Equipment Systems Inc G 586 307-3770
Clinton Township *(G-3382)*
Van Loon Industries Inc E 586 532-8530
Shelby Township *(G-15363)*
Vent-Rite Valve Corp E 269 925-8812
Benton Harbor *(G-1598)*
Vierson Boiler & Repair Co F 616 949-0500
Grand Rapids *(G-7317)*
Walbro LLC D 989 872-2131
Cass City *(G-2622)*
Waltz-Holst Blow Pipe Company E 616 676-8119
Ada *(G-40)*
Welding & Joining Tech LLC G 734 926-9353
Clarkston *(G-3076)*
▲ **Western International Inc** E 866 814-2470
Troy *(G-17447)*
▲ **Wolverine Metal Stamping Inc** D 269 429-6600
Saint Joseph *(G-14980)*

Yale Steel Inc … G … 810 387-2567
Brockway *(G-2108)*

Yello Dumpster … G … 616 915-0506
Grand Rapids *(G-7355)*

3444 Sheet Metal Work

A & B Welding & Fabricating … G … 231 733-2661
Muskegon *(G-11759)*

Access Heating & Cooling Inc … G … 734 464-0566
Livonia *(G-10098)*

Accuform Industries Inc … F … 616 363-3801
Grand Rapids *(G-6419)*

Accuform Industries Inc … G … 616 363-3801
Grand Rapids *(G-6420)*

Ace Welding & Machine Inc … F … 231 941-9664
Traverse City *(G-16595)*

Ackerman Brothers Inc … G … 989 892-4122
Bay City *(G-1315)*

Acme Carbide Die Inc … E … 734 722-2303
Westland *(G-18351)*

Acme Tool & Die Co … G … 231 938-1260
Acme *(G-1)*

Admin Industries LLC … F … 989 685-3438
Rose City *(G-14358)*

Advanced Sheet Metal … G … 616 301-3828
Wyoming *(G-18848)*

Advantage Laser Inc … G … 734 367-9936
Livonia *(G-10103)*

▲ Air Conditioning Products Co … E … 734 326-0050
Romulus *(G-14247)*

Alliance Sheet Metal Inc … F … 269 795-2954
Middleville *(G-11302)*

Allied Machine Inc … F … 231 834-0050
Grant *(G-7425)*

▲ Allor Manufacturing Inc … D … 248 486-4500
Brighton *(G-1943)*

▲ Aluminum Blanking Co Inc … D … 248 338-4422
Pontiac *(G-13349)*

▲ American Blower Supply Inc … E … 586 771-7337
Warren *(G-17701)*

American Fabricated Pdts Inc … E … 616 607-8785
Spring Lake *(G-15803)*

American Metal Fab Inc … D … 269 279-5108
Three Rivers *(G-16563)*

▲ American Roll Shutter Awng Co … E … 734 422-7110
Livonia *(G-10116)*

American Tchncal Fbrcators LLC … E … 989 269-6262
Bad Axe *(G-1095)*

Amhawk LLC … E … 269 468-4177
Hartford *(G-7761)*

Amjs Incorporated … G …
Lawton *(G-9987)*

Anderson Welding & Mfg Inc … F … 906 523-4661
Houghton *(G-8380)*

Arnold & Sautter Co … F … 989 684-7557
Bay City *(G-1322)*

Attentive Industries Inc … F … 810 233-7077
Flint *(G-5646)*

▲ Attentive Industries Inc … G … 810 233-7077
Flint *(G-5647)*

Austin Tube Products Inc … F … 231 745-2741
Baldwin *(G-1121)*

▲ B & D Thread Rolling Inc … D … 734 728-7070
Taylor *(G-16384)*

B & L Industries Inc … E … 810 987-9121
Port Huron *(G-13456)*

▲ Baldauf Enterprises Inc … D … 989 686-0350
Bay City *(G-1324)*

Bar Processing Corporation … F … 734 782-4454
Warren *(G-17727)*

Bauer Sheet Metal & Fabg Inc … E … 231 773-3244
Muskegon *(G-11775)*

Belco Industries Inc … E … 616 794-0410
Belding *(G-1437)*

▲ Belco Industries Inc … E … 616 794-0410
Belding *(G-1438)*

Benteler Automotive Corp … B … 616 247-3936
Auburn Hills *(G-810)*

▲ Beswick Corporation … F … 248 589-0562
Troy *(G-16976)*

▲ Bico Michigan Inc … E … 616 453-2400
Grand Rapids *(G-6506)*

Blue Water Fabricators Inc … G … 586 307-3550
Clinton Township *(G-3185)*

Bmc/Industrial Eductl Svcs Inc … E … 231 733-1206
Muskegon *(G-11780)*

Boral Building Products Inc … C … 800 521-8486
Wixom *(G-18625)*

Borchers Sheet Metal … G … 260 413-0632
Hudsonville *(G-8573)*

Bradhart Products Inc … E … 248 437-3746
Brighton *(G-1952)*

Bristol Steel & Conveyor Corp … E … 810 658-9510
Davison *(G-3775)*

Britten Inc … C … 231 941-8200
Traverse City *(G-16627)*

Burnham & Northern Inc … G … 517 279-7501
Coldwater *(G-3422)*

Buy Best Manufacturing LLC … F … 248 875-2491
Brighton *(G-1955)*

▲ C & T Fabrication LLC … G … 616 678-5133
Kent City *(G-9428)*

▲ C L Rieckhoff Company Inc … C … 734 946-8220
Taylor *(G-16388)*

Carlson … E … 248 824-7600
Troy *(G-17001)*

Carlson Metal Products Inc … E … 248 528-1931
Troy *(G-17002)*

Case-Free Inc … G … 616 245-3136
Grand Rapids *(G-6558)*

Cdp Environmental Inc … E … 586 776-7890
Roseville *(G-14383)*

Ceeflow Inc … G … 231 526-5579
Harbor Springs *(G-7643)*

Certainteed LLC … G … 517 787-8898
Jackson *(G-8837)*

Certainteed LLC … G … 517 787-1737
Jackson *(G-8838)*

Chicago Blow Pipe Company … F … 773 533-6100
Marquette *(G-11012)*

◆ Classic Gutter Systems LLC … F … 269 665-2700
Galesburg *(G-6074)*

Cmn Fabrication Inc … G … 586 294-1941
Roseville *(G-14385)*

CNC Products LLC … E … 269 684-5500
Niles *(G-12118)*

Commercial Fabricating & Engrg … F … 248 887-1595
Highland *(G-7887)*

Commercial Indus A Sltions LLC … G … 269 373-8797
Kalamazoo *(G-9147)*

▲ Commercial Mfg & Assembly Inc … E … 616 847-9980
Grand Haven *(G-6287)*

Conner Steel Products … F … 248 852-5110
Rochester Hills *(G-13983)*

▲ Conquest Manufacturing LLC … D … 586 576-7600
Warren *(G-17763)*

Consolidated Metal Pdts Inc … G … 616 538-1000
Grand Rapids *(G-6596)*

Constructive Sheet Metal Inc … E … 616 245-5306
Allendale *(G-217)*

Corlett-Turner Co … F … 616 772-9082
Grand Rapids *(G-6607)*

Coxline Inc … E … 269 345-1132
Kalamazoo *(G-9157)*

Crystal Machine & Tool Inc … G … 586 552-1503
Warren *(G-17766)*

Cse Morse Inc … D … 269 962-5548
Battle Creek *(G-1213)*

Curbs & Damper Products Inc … F … 586 776-7890
Roseville *(G-14392)*

Custom Archtctral Shtmtl Spcls … F … 313 571-2277
Detroit *(G-4113)*

Custom Design & Manufacturing … F … 989 754-9962
Carrollton *(G-2587)*

Custom Fab Inc … G … 586 755-7260
Warren *(G-17767)*

Custom Metal Works Inc … G … 810 420-0390
Marine City *(G-10957)*

Custom Products Inc … F … 269 983-9500
Saint Joseph *(G-14925)*

Customer Metal Fabrication Inc … E … 906 774-3216
Iron Mountain *(G-8721)*

D & W Awning and Window Co … E … 810 742-0340
Davison *(G-3779)*

Delta Iron Works Inc … E … 313 579-1445
Grosse Pointe *(G-7529)*

Delta Tube & Fabricating Corp … C … 248 634-8267
Holly *(G-8268)*

Denlin Industries Inc … G … 586 303-5209
Milford *(G-11461)*

Design Metal Inc … F … 248 547-4170
Oak Park *(G-12605)*

Designers Sheet Metal Inc … G … 269 429-4133
Saint Joseph *(G-14926)*

Detroit Blow Pipe & Shtmtl … G … 313 365-8970
Detroit *(G-4136)*

Detroit Cornice & Slate Co Inc … E … 248 398-7690
Ferndale *(G-5544)*

Detronic Industries Inc … D … 586 977-5660
Sterling Heights *(G-15985)*

▲ Dewys Manufacturing Inc … C … 616 677-5281
Marne *(G-10991)*

Diversified Fabricators Inc … F … 586 868-1000
Clinton Township *(G-3225)*

Diversified Metal Fabricators … E … 248 541-0500
Ferndale *(G-5549)*

DMC Service Group … G … 313 526-2431
Detroit *(G-4183)*

Dmi Sheet Metal LLC … G … 517 242-6005
Grand Haven *(G-6293)*

Dorris Company … F … 586 293-5260
Fraser *(G-5919)*

Douglas King Industries Inc … G … 989 642-2865
Hemlock *(G-7851)*

Douglas West Company Inc … G … 734 676-8882
Grosse Ile *(G-7520)*

▲ Dowding Industries Inc … E … 517 663-5455
Eaton Rapids *(G-4959)*

Dowding Tool Products LLC … F … 517 541-2795
Springport *(G-15880)*

Dri-Design Inc … E … 616 355-2970
Holland *(G-8017)*

Dts Enterprises Inc … E … 231 599-3123
Ellsworth *(G-5035)*

Dubois Production Services Inc … F … 616 785-0088
Comstock Park *(G-3604)*

▼ Duo-Gard Industries Inc … D … 734 207-9700
Canton *(G-2456)*

East Muskegon Roofg Shtmtl Co … D … 231 744-2461
Muskegon *(G-11806)*

Ecolo-Tech Inc … E … 248 541-1100
Madison Heights *(G-10716)*

Ede Co … G … 586 756-7555
Warren *(G-17792)*

Electrolabs Inc … F … 586 294-4150
Fraser *(G-5924)*

Elevated Technologies Inc … E … 616 288-9817
Grand Rapids *(G-6672)*

Eliason Corporation … E … 269 621-2100
Hartford *(G-7763)*

▲ Envision Engineering LLC … G … 616 897-0599
Lowell *(G-10500)*

▲ Erbsloeh Alum Solutions Inc … B … 269 323-2565
Portage *(G-13558)*

Experi-Metal Inc … C … 586 977-7800
Sterling Heights *(G-16009)*

Fab-Alloy Company … G … 517 787-4313
Jackson *(G-8883)*

Fabrication Specialties Inc … G … 313 891-7181
Davisburg *(G-3767)*

Fabrications Plus Inc … G … 269 749-3050
Olivet *(G-12693)*

Fabrilaser Mfg LLC … E … 269 789-9490
Marshall *(G-11057)*

▲ Federal Screw Works … F … 734 941-4211
Romulus *(G-14274)*

Fenixx Technologies LLC … G … 586 254-6000
Sterling Heights *(G-16012)*

Fhc Holding Company … G … 616 538-3231
Wyoming *(G-18872)*

▲ Flex-N-Gate Stamping LLC … E … 586 759-8900
Warren *(G-17813)*

Fortress Manufacturing Inc … F … 269 925-1336
Benton Harbor *(G-1549)*

Frankenmuth Welding & Fabg … G … 989 754-9457
Saginaw *(G-14646)*

Frenchys Skirting Inc … G … 734 721-3013
Wayne *(G-18220)*

▲ G A Richards Company … D … 616 243-2800
Grand Rapids *(G-6730)*

G A Richards Company … G … 616 850-8528
Spring Lake *(G-15815)*

◆ Gallagher-Kaiser Corporation … D … 313 368-3100
Troy *(G-17126)*

Gee & Missler Inc … E … 734 284-1224
Wyandotte *(G-18820)*

▲ Geerpres Inc … E … 231 773-3211
Muskegon *(G-11823)*

General Motors LLC … F … 810 234-2710
Flint *(G-5704)*

Gladwin Tank Manufacturing Inc … F … 989 426-4768
Gladwin *(G-6199)*

Gokoh Coldwater Incorporated … F … 517 279-1080
Coldwater *(G-3434)*

Gray Brothers Mfg Inc … F … 269 483-7615
White Pigeon *(G-18479)*

Great Lakes Mechanical Corp … C … 313 581-1400
Dearborn *(G-3849)*

Great Lakes Powder Coating LLC … F … 248 522-6222
Walled Lake *(G-17669)*

Employee Codes: A=Over 500 employees, B=251-500
C=101-250, D=51-100, E=20-50, F=10-19, G=3-9

2022 Harris Michigan
Industrial Directory

815

34 FABRICATED METAL PRODUCTS, EXCEPT MACHINERY AND TRANSPORTATION EQUIPMENT

Company	Location	Phone
Greene Manufacturing Inc	E	734 428-8304
Chelsea (G-2813)		
▲ Greene Metal Products Inc	E	586 465-6800
Clinton Township (G-3249)		
H & M Welding and Fabricating	G	517 764-3630
Jackson (G-8897)		
▲ Hancock Enterprises Inc	D	734 287-8840
Taylor (G-16424)		
Harris Sheet Metal Co	E	989 496-3080
Midland (G-11371)		
Hart Acquisition Company LLC	E	313 537-0490
Redford (G-13738)		
Hart Fabrication Inc	F	517 924-1109
Quincy (G-13670)		
Hdn F&A Inc	D	269 965-3268
Battle Creek (G-1236)		
Historic Denver Inc	G	989 354-2121
Alpena (G-297)		
Hmw Contracting LLC	C	313 531-8477
Detroit (G-4302)		
Hydro Extrusion North Amer LLC	B	269 349-6626
Kalamazoo (G-9220)		
Industrial Duct Systems Inc	E	586 498-3993
Roseville (G-14422)		
Industrial Mtal Fbricators LLC	E	810 765-8960
Cottrellville (G-3722)		
Innovate Industries Inc	G	586 558-8990
Warren (G-17865)		
Innovative Sheet Metals LLC	F	231 788-5751
Muskegon (G-11839)		
Integrated Industries Inc	F	586 790-1550
Clinton Township (G-3259)		
Integrated Metal Tech Inc	C	616 844-3032
Spring Lake (G-15825)		
J & J Metal Products Inc	G	586 792-2680
Clinton Township (G-3261)		
J & L Mfg Co	E	586 445-9530
Warren (G-17875)		
▲ J & M Machine Products Inc	D	231 755-1622
Norton Shores (G-12302)		
J and N Fabrications Inc	G	586 751-6350
Warren (G-17876)		
J M L Contracting & Sales Inc	F	586 756-4133
Warren (G-17879)		
Jackson Archtctral Met Fbrctor	G	517 782-8884
Jackson (G-8912)		
Jbs Sheet Metal Inc	G	231 777-2802
Muskegon (G-11844)		
Jensen Bridge & Supply Company	E	810 648-3000
Sandusky (G-15062)		
Jones Mfg & Sup Co Inc	E	616 877-4442
Moline (G-11519)		
K & W Manufacturing Co Inc	E	517 369-9708
Bronson (G-2117)		
K-R Metal Engineers Corp	E	989 892-1901
Bay City (G-1370)		
Kalamazoo Mechanical Inc	F	269 343-5351
Kalamazoo (G-9241)		
Kamax Inc	C	810 272-2090
Lapeer (G-9936)		
Kehrig Manufacturing Company	G	586 949-9610
Chesterfield (G-2900)		
Kimbow Inc	F	616 774-4680
Comstock Park (G-3616)		
▲ Kraftube Inc	C	231 832-5562
Reed City (G-13793)		
Kriewall Enterprises Inc	E	586 336-0600
Romeo (G-14227)		
Krupp Industries LLC	E	734 261-0410
Livonia (G-10268)		
Krupp Industries LLC	D	616 475-5905
Walker (G-17643)		
Kulick Enterprises Inc	G	734 283-6999
Wyandotte (G-18827)		
L D S Sheet Metal Inc	G	313 892-2624
Warren (G-17900)		
Lahti Fabrication Inc	E	989 343-0420
Alger (G-138)		
▲ Lanzen Incorporated	E	586 771-7070
Bruce Twp (G-2174)		
Lanzen-Petoskey LLC	E	231 881-9602
Petoskey (G-13002)		
Laser Fab Inc	G	586 415-8090
Fraser (G-5955)		
Laser North Inc	G	906 353-6090
Baraga (G-1144)		
Laser Specialists Inc	E	586 294-8830
Fraser (G-5956)		
Legacy Metal Fabricating LLC	E	616 258-8406
Grand Rapids (G-6936)		
Liberty Steel Fabricating Inc	E	269 556-9792
Saint Joseph (G-14948)		
▼ Light Metals Corporation	B	616 538-3030
Wyoming (G-18891)		
▲ Llink Technologies LLC	E	586 336-9370
Brown City (G-2139)		
Loftis Machine Company	E	616 846-1990
Grand Haven (G-6331)		
Longstreet Group LLC	F	517 278-4487
Coldwater (G-3443)		
Lv Metals Inc	G	734 654-8081
Carleton (G-2559)		
M C M Fixture Company Inc	F	248 547-9280
Hazel Park (G-7830)		
M J Mechanical Inc	E	989 865-9633
Saint Charles (G-14804)		
▲ Magnetic Products Inc	D	248 887-5600
Highland (G-7896)		
Manning Enterprises Inc	E	269 657-2346
Paw Paw (G-12952)		
Mardan Fabrication Inc	G	586 466-6401
Harrison Township (G-7708)		
Marsh Industrial Services Inc	G	231 258-4870
Kalkaska (G-9395)		
▲ Material Handling Tech Inc	E	586 725-5546
Ira (G-8701)		
Matrix Mtlcraft LLP A Ltd Prtn	E	586 469-9611
Macomb (G-10615)		
Mayo Welding & Fabricating Co	E	248 435-2730
Royal Oak (G-14561)		
MB Aerospace Warren LLC	C	586 772-2500
Warren (G-17920)		
McElroy Metal Mill Inc	D	269 781-8313
Marshall (G-11069)		
Mechanical Sheet Metal Co	F	734 284-1006
Wyandotte (G-18832)		
Metal Components LLC	D	616 252-1900
Grand Rapids (G-6979)		
▲ Metal Components LLC	D	616 252-1900
Grand Rapids (G-6979)		
Metal Design Manufacturing LLC	G	313 893-9810
Detroit (G-4430)		
Metal Merchants of Michigan	F	248 293-0621
Rochester Hills (G-14062)		
Metal Plus LLC	F	616 459-7587
Grand Rapids (G-6980)		
Metal Sales Manufacturing Corp	F	989 686-5879
Bay City (G-1376)		
▲ Metal Standard Corp	D	616 396-6356
Holland (G-8144)		
Metalworks Inc	C	231 845-5136
Ludington (G-10546)		
▲ Meter Devices Company Inc	D	330 455-0301
Farmington Hills (G-5317)		
Metro Duct Inc	F	517 783-2646
Jackson (G-8955)		
Metro-Fabricating LLC	D	989 667-8100
Bay City (G-1379)		
Michigan Metal Fabricators	G	586 754-0421
Warren (G-17929)		
Michigan Tooling Solutions LLC	G	616 681-2210
Sparta (G-15772)		
▲ Midbrook Inc	D	800 966-9274
Jackson (G-8959)		
Midwest Wall Company LLC	F	517 881-3701
Dewitt (G-4713)		
Mill Creek Fabrication LLC	G	616 419-4857
Comstock Park (G-3626)		
Milton Manufacturing Inc	F	313 366-2450
Detroit (G-4458)		
Mlp Mfg Inc	F	616 842-8767
Spring Lake (G-15837)		
Modern Metalcraft Inc	F	989 835-3716
Midland (G-11396)		
Modulated Metals Inc	F	586 749-8400
Chesterfield (G-2914)		
Monarch Metal Mfg Inc	F	616 247-0412
Grand Rapids (G-7023)		
Monarch Welding & Engrg Inc	E	231 733-7222
Muskegon (G-11876)		
MSE Fabrication LLC	F	586 991-6138
Sterling Heights (G-16107)		
Muskegon Awning & Mfg Co	E	231 759-0911
Muskegon (G-11879)		
National Ordnance Auto Mfg LLC	G	248 853-8822
Auburn Hills (G-980)		
National Roofg & Shtmtl Co Inc	D	989 964-0557
Saginaw (G-14707)		
Nelson Steel Products Inc	D	616 396-1515
Holland (G-8152)		
▲ Nicholson Terminal & Dock Co	D	313 842-4300
River Rouge (G-13858)		
North Woods Industrial	G	616 784-2840
Comstock Park (G-3629)		
Northern Machining & Repr Inc	G	906 786-0526
Escanaba (G-5088)		
Northland Corporation	E	616 754-5601
Greenville (G-7502)		
◆ Northland Corporation	C	616 754-5601
Greenville (G-7503)		
Northwest Fabrication Inc	G	231 536-3229
East Jordan (G-4878)		
▲ Northwoods Manufacturing Inc	D	906 779-2370
Kingsford (G-9516)		
Oakland Welding Industries	E	586 949-4090
Chesterfield (G-2916)		
Pardon Inc	E	906 428-3494
Gladstone (G-6185)		
Parton & Preble Inc	E	586 773-6000
Warren (G-17954)		
Patio Land Mfg Inc	G	586 758-5660
Warren (G-17959)		
Portage Wire Systems Inc	E	231 889-4215
Onekama (G-12703)		
Precision Prototype & Mfg Inc	F	517 663-4114
Eaton Rapids (G-4967)		
▲ Production Fabricators Inc	E	231 777-3822
Muskegon (G-11900)		
Production Tube Company Inc	C	313 259-3990
Detroit (G-4537)		
Professional Fabricating Inc	E	616 531-1240
Grand Rapids (G-7113)		
Progressive Manufacturing LLC	G	231 924-9975
Fremont (G-6055)		
Prototech Laser Inc	E	586 598-6900
Chesterfield (G-2934)		
Providence Worldwide LLC	F	313 586-4144
Westland (G-18409)		
Quality Alum Acquisition LLC	F	734 783-0990
Flat Rock (G-5626)		
Quality Alum Acquisition LLC	F	800 550-1667
Hastings (G-7807)		
Quality Craft Fabricators LLC	E	586 353-2104
Warren (G-17988)		
Quality Finishing Systems	F	231 834-9131
Grant (G-7431)		
▲ Quality Metalcraft Inc	E	734 261-6700
Livonia (G-10377)		
Quality Stainless Mfg Co	F	248 546-4141
Madison Heights (G-10815)		
R & DS Manufacturing LLC	G	586 716-9900
New Baltimore (G-11992)		
Rainbow Seamless Systems Inc	G	231 933-8888
Traverse City (G-16814)		
Rick Wykle LLC	G	734 839-6376
Trenton (G-16891)		
Robo-Fence LLC	E	586 232-3909
Clinton Township (G-3340)		
▲ Roura Acquisition Inc	F	586 790-6100
Clinton Township (G-3343)		
S & N Machine & Fabricating	E	231 894-2658
Rothbury (G-14498)		
▲ Saginaw Control & Engrg Inc	B	989 799-6871
Saginaw (G-14745)		
Salem/Savard Industries LLC	F	313 931-6880
Detroit (G-4579)		
Sandvik Inc	D	269 926-7241
Benton Harbor (G-1582)		
Schneider Iron & Metal Inc	G	906 774-0644
Iron Mountain (G-8732)		
Schneider Sheet Metal Sup Inc	G	517 694-7661
Lansing (G-9892)		
Schrader Stoves of Michiana	E	269 684-4494
Niles (G-12166)		
◆ Schuler Incorporated	D	734 207-7200
Canton (G-2522)		
Scotten Steel Processing Inc	F	313 897-8837
Detroit (G-4585)		
Security Steelcraft Corp	F	231 733-1101
Muskegon (G-11917)		
◆ Selkirk Corporation	E	616 656-8200
Grand Rapids (G-7190)		
Servotech Industries Inc	G	734 697-5555
Taylor (G-16471)		
Set Duct Manufacturing LLC	E	313 491-4380
Detroit (G-4588)		
Set Enterprises of Mi Inc	D	586 573-3600
Sterling Heights (G-16174)		
Sfi Acquisition Inc	E	248 471-1500
Farmington Hills (G-5377)		

SIC SECTION 34 FABRICATED METAL PRODUCTS, EXCEPT MACHINERY AND TRANSPORTATION EQUIPMENT 34 FABRICATED METAL PROD-

Sheet Metal Workers Local ....G 231 590-1112
 Traverse City (G-16830)
Sheren Plumbing & Heating Inc ....E 231 943-7916
 Traverse City (G-16831)
Shouldice Indus Mfrs Cntrs Inc ....D 269 962-5579
 Battle Creek (G-1293)
Sintel Inc ....E 616 842-6960
 Spring Lake (G-15852)
Sparta Sheet Metal Inc ....F 616 784-9035
 Grand Rapids (G-7208)
Spectrum Metal Products Inc ....G 734 595-7600
 Westland (G-18418)
Spinform Inc ....G 810 767-4660
 Flint (G-5766)
◆ Stageright Corporation ....C 989 386-7393
 Clare (G-2999)
State Building Product Inc ....E 586 772-8878
 Warren (G-18028)
Steinke-Fenton Fabricators ....F 517 782-8174
 Jackson (G-9013)
Stelmatic Industries Inc ....F 586 949-0160
 Chesterfield (G-2950)
Stewart Steel Specialties ....G 248 477-0680
 Farmington Hills (G-5390)
Stus Welding & Fabrication ....G 616 392-8459
 Holland (G-8206)
Sure-Weld & Plating Rack Co ....G 248 304-9430
 Southfield (G-15714)
Tapco Holdings Inc ....C 248 668-6400
 Wixom (G-18766)
Tara Industries Inc ....G 248 477-6520
 Livonia (G-10429)
Target Construction Inc ....F 616 866-7728
 Cedar Springs (G-2664)
TEC-3 Prototypes Inc ....E 810 678-8909
 Metamora (G-11289)
Tel-X Corporation ....F 734 425-2225
 Garden City (G-6112)
Ter Molen & Hart Inc ....G 616 458-4832
 Grand Rapids (G-7253)
Thermal Designs & Manufacturng ......F 586 773-5231
 Roseville (G-14484)
▼ Thierica Equipment Corporation ....E 616 453-6570
 Grand Rapids (G-7259)
Tigmaster Co ....E 800 824-4830
 Baroda (G-1171)
Tops-In-Quality Inc ....E 810 364-7150
 Marysville (G-11109)
Trade Specific Solutions LLC ....G 734 752-7124
 Southgate (G-15758)
Tri-Vision LLC ....F 313 526-6020
 Detroit (G-4644)
Trigon Metal Products Inc ....G 734 513-3488
 Livonia (G-10444)
◆ Triumph Gear Systems - McOmb I ...C 586 781-2800
 Macomb (G-10644)
Tru Flo Carbide Inc ....F 989 658-8515
 Ubly (G-17483)
Tubelite Inc ....C 800 866-2227
 Walker (G-17655)
Turnkey Fabrication LLC ....F 616 248-9116
 Grand Rapids (G-7281)
Unifab Corporation ....E 269 382-2803
 Portage (G-13629)
Universal Fabricators Inc ....F 248 399-7565
 Madison Heights (G-10853)
Universal Spiral Air Npp ....G 616 475-5905
 Grand Rapids (G-7299)
Van Loon Industries Inc ....E 586 532-8530
 Shelby Township (G-15363)
Vanmeer Corporation ....F 269 694-6090
 Otsego (G-12802)
Ventcon Inc ....C 313 336-4000
 Allen Park (G-209)
Ventilation + Plus Eqp Inc ....G 231 487-1156
 Harbor Springs (G-7661)
Versatile Fabrication Co Inc ....E 231 739-7115
 Muskegon (G-11941)
W Soule & Co ....D 269 324-7001
 Portage (G-13631)
Waltz-Holst Blow Pipe Company ....E 616 676-8119
 Ada (G-40)
Weather Tight ....G 989 817-2149
 Midland (G-11422)
Welk-Ko Fabricators Inc ....F 734 425-6840
 Livonia (G-10470)
Welk-Ko Fabricators Inc ....G 810 227-7500
 Brighton (G-2096)
Wendling Sheet Metal Inc ....E 989 753-5286
 Saginaw (G-14793)

West Side Mfg Fabrication Inc ....E 248 380-6640
 Wixom (G-18790)
Westco Metalcraft Inc ....F 734 425-0900
 Livonia (G-10474)
Wm Kloeffler Industries Inc ....G 810 765-4068
 Marine City (G-10969)
Worthington Armstrong Venture ....F 269 934-6200
 Benton Harbor (G-1611)
Zinger Sheet Metal Inc ....F 616 532-3121
 Grand Rapids (G-7357)

3446 Architectural & Ornamental Metal Work

A D Johnson Engraving Co Inc ....F 269 385-0044
 Kalamazoo (G-9106)
Adaptive Metal Works LLC ....G 419 386-9336
 Blissfield (G-1760)
▲ Alliance Interiors LLC ....C 517 322-0711
 Lansing (G-9752)
Alro Steel Corporation ....C 989 893-9553
 Bay City (G-1320)
Aluminum Architectural Met Co ....C 313 895-2555
 Detroit (G-4006)
▲ Aluminum Blanking Co Inc ....D 248 338-4422
 Pontiac (G-13349)
Aluminum Supply Company Inc ....E 313 491-5040
 Detroit (G-4007)
▲ Amanda Products LLC ....C 248 547-3870
 Ferndale (G-5525)
Aquarius Recreational Products ....G 586 469-4600
 Harrison Township (G-7687)
Arnold & Sautter Co ....C 989 684-7557
 Bay City (G-1322)
Bad Axe Metal & Iron Art ....G 989 658-8324
 Ubly (G-17475)
Blacksmith Shop LLC ....G 616 754-4719
 Greenville (G-7477)
Bradys Fence Company Inc ....G 313 492-8804
 South Rockwood (G-15463)
Britten Inc ....C 231 941-8200
 Traverse City (G-16627)
◆ Brown-Campbell Company ....F 586 884-2180
 Shelby Township (G-15179)
CEi Composite Materials LLC ....E 734 212-3006
 Manchester (G-10882)
Cr Forge LLC ....F 231 924-2033
 Fremont (G-6038)
Creative Composites Inc ....E 906 474-9941
 Rapid River (G-13683)
CTS Welding ....G 269 521-4481
 Bloomingdale (G-1876)
Davis Iron Works Inc ....E 248 624-5960
 Commerce Township (G-3521)
Elemental Artistry LLC ....G 616 326-1758
 Grand Rapids (G-6671)
Greenwell Machine Shop Inc ....G 231 347-3346
 Petoskey (G-12999)
Guile & Son Inc ....G 517 376-2116
 Byron (G-2254)
Hamiltons Custom Stairs ....G 810 686-5698
 Clio (G-3400)
Harlow Sheet Metal LLC ....G 734 996-1509
 Ann Arbor (G-509)
◆ Hart & Cooley LLC ....C 616 656-6200
 Grand Rapids (G-6805)
Iron Capital of America Co ....G 586 771-5840
 Warren (G-17871)
Iron Fetish Metalworks Inc ....F 586 776-8311
 Roseville (G-14426)
▲ ITT Motion Tech Amer LLC ....F 248 863-2161
 Novi (G-12444)
J D Russell Company ....E 586 254-8500
 Utica (G-17503)
◆ Jack-Post Corporation ....F 269 695-7000
 Buchanan (G-2197)
Kern-Liebers Pieron Inc ....D 248 427-1100
 Farmington Hills (G-5280)
Land Enterprises Inc ....E 248 398-7276
 Madison Heights (G-10768)
Marquette Fence Company Inc ....G 906 249-8000
 Marquette (G-11034)
Mayo Welding & Fabricating Co ....G 248 435-2730
 Royal Oak (G-14561)
Merrill Technologies Group Inc ....C 989 462-0330
 Alma (G-246)
Michigan Ornamental Ir & Fabg ....F 616 899-2441
 Conklin (G-3661)
◆ Mol Belting Systems Inc ....D 616 453-2484
 Grand Rapids (G-7020)
O I K Industries Inc ....E 269 382-1210
 Kalamazoo (G-9282)

Parker Fluid Syst Connectors ....G 989 352-7264
 Lakeview (G-9644)
▲ Phoenix Wire Cloth Inc ....E 248 585-6350
 Troy (G-17301)
R B Christian Inc ....G 269 963-9327
 Battle Creek (G-1285)
Rka Design Build ....G 269 362-5558
 Buchanan (G-2203)
Scott Iron Works Inc ....F 248 548-2822
 Hazel Park (G-7841)
Spartan Metal Fab LLC ....G 517 322-9050
 Lansing (G-9737)
St USA Holding Corp ....D 517 278-7144
 Coldwater (G-3456)
St USA Holding Corp ....C 800 637-3303
 Coldwater (G-3457)
Stus Welding & Fabrication ....G 616 392-8459
 Holland (G-8206)
Swing-Lo Suspended Scaffold Co ....F 269 764-8989
 Covert (G-3726)
▲ Symbiote Inc ....E 616 772-1790
 Zeeland (G-19083)
Under Stairs ....G 586 781-6202
 Macomb (G-10645)
United Lighting Standards Inc ....D 586 774-5650
 Warren (G-18047)
Valley City Sign Company ....E 616 784-5711
 Comstock Park (G-3649)
Versatile Stair System ....G 269 983-5437
 Saint Joseph (G-14972)
Won-Door Corp ....G 248 478-5757
 Farmington Hills (G-5414)
Worthington Armstrong Venture ....F 269 934-6200
 Benton Harbor (G-1611)

3448 Prefabricated Metal Buildings & Cmpnts

4ever Aluminum Products Inc ....F 517 368-0000
 Coldwater (G-3417)
All Season Enclosures ....G 248 650-8020
 Shelby Township (G-15168)
Alumiramp Inc ....F 517 639-8777
 Quincy (G-13661)
Berlin Holdings LLC ....G 517 523-2444
 Pittsford (G-13067)
Biologcal Mdiation Systems LLC ......F 970 221-5949
 Hillsdale (G-7925)
◆ Brasco International Inc ....D 313 393-0393
 Madison Heights (G-10684)
Bulmann Enterprises Inc ....E 231 549-5020
 Boyne City (G-1885)
Classic Car Port & Canopies ....F 586 759-5490
 Warren (G-17756)
Con-De Manufacturing Inc ....G 269 651-3756
 Sturgis (G-16285)
Control Dekk LLC ....G 616 828-4862
 Wyoming (G-18859)
▼ Duo-Gard Industries Inc ....D 734 207-9700
 Canton (G-2456)
Falk Production LLC ....G 616 540-1053
 Grand Rapids (G-6699)
G & C Carports ....G 616 678-4308
 Kent City (G-9431)
Gd Enterprises LLC ....G 248 207-1366
 Holly (G-8271)
Great Lakes Lift Inc ....G 989 673-2109
 Caro (G-2572)
I B P Inc ....F 248 588-4710
 Clarkston (G-3041)
Icon Shelters Inc ....E 616 396-0919
 Holland (G-8092)
Innovate Industries Inc ....G 586 558-8990
 Warren (G-17865)
Keeler-Glasgow Company Inc ....F 269 621-2415
 Hartford (G-7764)
Laser North Inc ....G 906 353-6090
 Baraga (G-1143)
Little Buildings Inc ....G 586 752-7100
 Romeo (G-14228)
Marine Automated Doc System ....F 989 539-9010
 Harrison (G-7680)
Mark Adler Homes ....G 586 850-0630
 Birmingham (G-1736)
Mast Mini Barns LLC ....G 231 924-3895
 Holton (G-8341)
McElroy Metal Mill Inc ....D 269 781-8313
 Marshall (G-11069)
Midwest Steel Carports Inc ....G 877 235-5210
 Grant (G-7430)

34 FABRICATED METAL PRODUCTS, EXCEPT MACHINERY AND TRANSPORTATION EQUIPMENT

Mini Storage of Manton ...... G 231 645-6727
  Manton *(G-10937)*
Morton Buildings Inc ...... G 616 696-4747
  Three Rivers *(G-16579)*
Mpi Products Holdings LLC ...... D 248 237-3007
  Rochester Hills *(G-14066)*
Nathan Shetler ...... F 269 521-4554
  Bloomingdale *(G-1877)*
Pioneer Pole Buildings N Inc ...... F 989 386-2570
  Clare *(G-2994)*
Porter Corp ...... D 616 399-1963
  Holland *(G-8167)*
Pro Tool & Die LLC ...... G 586 840-7040
  Chesterfield *(G-2929)*
Progressive Panel Systems Inc ...... E 616 748-1384
  Zeeland *(G-19074)*
RB Construction Company ...... E 586 264-9478
  Mount Clemens *(G-11655)*
Serenus Johnson Portables LLC ...... F 800 605-0693
  Midland *(G-11416)*
▼ Thoreson-Mc Cosh Inc ...... E 248 362-0960
  Lake Orion *(G-9634)*
Trigon Steel Components Inc ...... E 616 834-0506
  Holland *(G-8231)*
Twin Bay Dock and Products ...... G 231 943-8420
  Traverse City *(G-16869)*
Vets Access LLC ...... G 810 639-2222
  Flushing *(G-5815)*
Wheelock & Son Welding Shop ...... G 231 947-6557
  Traverse City *(G-16879)*
Wildcat Buildings Inc ...... F 231 824-6406
  Manton *(G-10939)*

3449 Misc Structural Metal Work

A & B Welding & Fabricating ...... G 231 733-2661
  Muskegon *(G-11759)*
Aarons Fabrication of Steel ...... G 586 883-0652
  Clinton Township *(G-3151)*
Ambassador Steel Corporation ...... E 517 455-7216
  Lansing *(G-9804)*
Aristo-Cote Inc ...... E 586 447-9049
  Harrison Township *(G-7688)*
Bowling Enterprises Inc ...... G 231 864-2653
  Kaleva *(G-9376)*
Bristol Steel & Conveyor Corp ...... E 810 658-9510
  Davison *(G-3775)*
Butler Mill Service Company ...... E 313 429-2486
  Detroit *(G-4079)*
Campbell & Shaw Steel Inc ...... F 810 364-5100
  Marysville *(G-11083)*
Challenge Mfg Company ...... G 616 735-6500
  Lansing *(G-9680)*
Corson Fabricating LLC ...... E 810 326-0532
  Saint Clair *(G-14820)*
Cotson Fabricating Inc ...... E 248 589-2758
  Sterling Heights *(G-15973)*
Creform Corporation ...... E 248 926-2555
  Novi *(G-12385)*
Ctc Fabricators LLC ...... G 586 242-8809
  Clay *(G-3118)*
D & D Fabrications Inc ...... G 810 798-2491
  Almont *(G-258)*
Daughtery Group Inc ...... E 313 452-7918
  Detroit *(G-4121)*
Depottey Acquisition Inc ...... F 616 846-4150
  Grand Haven *(G-6291)*
Die Stampco Inc ...... F 989 893-7790
  Bay City *(G-1344)*
Dlh Rollform LLC ...... G 586 231-0507
  Wales *(G-17627)*
▲ Dowding Industries Inc ...... E 517 663-5455
  Eaton Rapids *(G-4959)*
Econ-O-Line Abrasive Products ...... F 616 846-4150
  Grand Haven *(G-6295)*
F&B Technologies ...... F 734 856-2118
  Ottawa Lake *(G-12806)*
Frankenmuth Welding & Fabg ...... G 989 754-9457
  Saginaw *(G-14646)*
Global Lift Corp ...... F 989 269-5900
  Bad Axe *(G-1106)*
Howard Finishing LLC ...... E 248 588-9050
  Madison Heights *(G-10742)*
▼ Ideal Shield LLC ...... E 866 825-8659
  Detroit *(G-4311)*
Jcr Fabrication LLC ...... G 906 235-2683
  Ontonagon *(G-12710)*
Kenowa Industries Inc ...... E 616 392-7080
  Holland *(G-8111)*
Kenowa Industries Inc ...... G 517 322-0311
  Lansing *(G-9771)*

Kustom Creations Inc ...... G 586 997-4141
  Sterling Heights *(G-16068)*
▲ Llink Technologies LLC ...... E 586 336-9370
  Brown City *(G-2139)*
Lor Products Inc ...... G 989 382-9020
  Remus *(G-13816)*
M J Day Machine Tool Company ...... G 313 730-1200
  Allen Park *(G-199)*
Metro Rebar Inc ...... G 248 851-5894
  West Bloomfield *(G-18297)*
Mig Molding LLC ...... F 810 724-7400
  Imlay City *(G-8641)*
N & K Fulbright LLC ...... F 269 695-4580
  Niles *(G-12149)*
Netshape International LLC ...... D 616 846-8700
  Grand Haven *(G-6340)*
Northern Michigan Glass LLC ...... E 231 941-0050
  Traverse City *(G-16773)*
Porter Steel & Welding Company ...... G 231 733-4495
  Muskegon *(G-11897)*
R & S Propeller Inc ...... F 616 636-8202
  Sand Lake *(G-15052)*
Raq LLC ...... F 313 473-7271
  Pontiac *(G-13412)*
Robert Anderson ...... F 586 552-5648
  Saint Clair Shores *(G-14881)*
Rocksteady Manufacturing LLC ...... F 586 778-5028
  Roseville *(G-14472)*
S & N Machine & Fabricating ...... E 231 894-2658
  Rothbury *(G-14498)*
◆ Shape Corp ...... B 616 846-8700
  Grand Haven *(G-6361)*
Shape Corp ...... G 616 846-8700
  Spring Lake *(G-15851)*
Shape Corp ...... G 616 846-8700
  Grand Haven *(G-6362)*
Speedrack Products Group Ltd ...... C 517 639-8781
  Quincy *(G-13674)*
▼ Speedrack Products Group Ltd ...... E 616 887-0002
  Sparta *(G-15782)*
Standard Coating Inc ...... D 248 297-6650
  Madison Heights *(G-10835)*
Tennessee Fabricators LLC ...... G 615 793-4444
  Sterling Heights *(G-16203)*
Tubelite Inc ...... C 800 866-2227
  Walker *(G-17655)*
Tubelite Inc ...... D 800 866-2227
  Reed City *(G-13801)*
Vanermen Smith Products Inc ...... F 517 575-6618
  Lansing *(G-9748)*
◆ Walther Trowal LLC ...... F 616 455-8940
  Byron Center *(G-2301)*
▲ Weldaloy Products Company ...... D 586 758-5550
  Warren *(G-18064)*
Welk-Ko Fabricators Inc ...... G 248 486-2598
  New Hudson *(G-12074)*
◆ Witzenmann Usa LLC ...... B 248 588-6033
  Troy *(G-17449)*
Worthington Armstrong Venture ...... F 269 934-6200
  Benton Harbor *(G-1611)*

3451 Screw Machine Prdts

AAA Industries Inc ...... E 313 255-0420
  Redford *(G-13709)*
Accuspec Grinding Inc ...... E 269 556-1410
  Stevensville *(G-16238)*
Advance Turning and Mfg Inc ...... C 517 783-2713
  Jackson *(G-8802)*
Air-Matic Products Company Inc ...... E 248 356-4200
  Southfield *(G-15473)*
Alco Manufacturing Corp ...... E 734 426-3941
  Dexter *(G-4722)*
▲ Allan Tool & Machine Co Inc ...... D 248 585-2910
  Troy *(G-16925)*
American Screw Products Inc ...... G 248 543-0991
  Madison Heights *(G-10667)*
Amerikam Inc ...... D 616 243-5833
  Grand Rapids *(G-6457)*
Atf Inc ...... E 989 685-2468
  Rose City *(G-14362)*
Atg Precision Products LLC ...... E 586 247-5400
  Canton *(G-2437)*
▲ Autocam-Pax Inc ...... C 269 782-5186
  Dowagiac *(G-4776)*
B M Industries Inc ...... G 810 658-0052
  Lapeer *(G-9913)*
Berkley Screw Machine Pdts Inc ...... E 248 853-0044
  Rochester Hills *(G-13962)*
Black River Manufacturing Inc ...... E 810 982-9812
  Port Huron *(G-13459)*

BMC Bil-Mac Corporation ...... D 616 538-1930
  Grandville *(G-7368)*
Borneman & Peterson Inc ...... F 810 744-1890
  Flint *(G-5659)*
C S M Manufacturing Corp ...... D 248 471-0700
  Farmington Hills *(G-5192)*
▲ C Thorrez Industries Inc ...... F 517 750-3160
  Jackson *(G-8831)*
Cap Collet & Tool Co Inc ...... F 734 283-4040
  Wyandotte *(G-18814)*
Cardinal Group Industries Corp ...... F 517 437-6000
  Hillsdale *(G-7929)*
▲ Central Screw Products Company ...... F 313 893-9100
  Troy *(G-17006)*
Comtronics ...... G 517 750-3160
  Jackson *(G-8850)*
Core Electric Company Inc ...... F 313 382-7140
  Melvindale *(G-11198)*
Corlett-Turner Co ...... D 616 772-9082
  Zeeland *(G-19007)*
▲ CPM Acquisition Corp ...... D 231 947-6400
  Traverse City *(G-16664)*
Davison-Rite Products Co ...... E 734 513-0505
  White Lake *(G-18454)*
▼ Dawlen Corporation ...... E 517 787-2200
  Jackson *(G-8860)*
Dennison Automatics LLC ...... E 616 837-7063
  Nunica *(G-12578)*
Denny Grice Inc ...... E 269 279-6113
  Three Rivers *(G-16570)*
Dexter Automatic Products Co ...... C 734 426-8900
  Dexter *(G-4734)*
Dimension Machine Tech LLC ...... F 586 649-4747
  Bloomfield Hills *(G-1814)*
▲ Dirksen Screw Products Co ...... E 586 247-5400
  Shelby Township *(G-15208)*
Dynamic Corporation ...... F 616 399-2200
  Holland *(G-8018)*
E and P Form Tool Company Inc ...... F 734 261-3530
  Garden City *(G-6093)*
Eagle Creek Mfg & Sales ...... E 989 643-7521
  Saint Charles *(G-14802)*
ECM Specialties Inc ...... G 810 736-0299
  Flint *(G-5692)*
Edmore Tool & Grinding Inc ...... F 989 427-3790
  Edmore *(G-4992)*
Elkins Machine & Tool Co Inc ...... E 734 941-0266
  Romulus *(G-14271)*
Embers Ballscrew Repair ...... G 586 216-8444
  Detroit *(G-4206)*
Extreme Precision Screw Pdts ...... E 810 744-1980
  Flint *(G-5698)*
Federal Screw Works ...... D 734 941-4211
  Big Rapids *(G-1673)*
Federal Screw Works ...... D 810 227-7712
  Brighton *(G-1989)*
Fettes Manufacturing Co ...... E 586 939-8500
  Sterling Heights *(G-16013)*
Fordsell Machine Products Co ...... G 586 751-4700
  Warren *(G-17815)*
Form All Tool Company ...... G 231 894-6303
  Whitehall *(G-18496)*
Fox Mfg Co ...... E 586 468-1421
  Harrison Township *(G-7700)*
▲ Grace Engineering Corp ...... F 810 392-2181
  Memphis *(G-11213)*
Grand Haven Steel Products Inc ...... D 616 842-2740
  Grand Haven *(G-6306)*
Green Industries Inc ...... F 248 446-8900
  Wixom *(G-18671)*
Greendale Screw Pdts Co Inc ...... E 586 759-8100
  Warren *(G-17838)*
H & K Machine Company Inc ...... G 269 756-7339
  Three Oaks *(G-16556)*
H & L Tool Company Inc ...... E 248 585-7474
  Madison Heights *(G-10736)*
H G Geiger Manufacturing Co ...... E 517 369-7357
  Bronson *(G-2114)*
Harbor Screw Machine Products ...... G 269 925-5855
  Benton Harbor *(G-1554)*
Hemingway Screw Products Inc ...... E 313 383-7300
  Melvindale *(G-11201)*
▲ Hibshman Screw Mch Pdts Inc ...... E 269 641-7525
  Union *(G-17489)*
Hil-Man Automation LLC ...... F 616 741-9099
  Zeeland *(G-19037)*
Holt Products Company ...... E 517 927-4198
  Mason *(G-11138)*
Hosco Inc ...... F 248 912-1750
  Wixom *(G-18678)*

SIC SECTION34 FABRICATED METAL PRODUCTS, EXCEPT MACHINERY AND TRANSPORTATION EQUIPMENT34 FABRICATED METAL PROD-

▲ **Huron Inc** .... E 810 359-5344
Lexington *(G-10029)*
Inland Lakes Machine Inc .... E 231 775-6543
Cadillac *(G-2337)*
J & J Industries Inc .... G 517 784-3586
Jackson *(G-8911)*
J C Gibbons Mfg Inc .... E 734 266-5544
Livonia *(G-10254)*
Jamco Manufacturing Inc .... G 248 852-1988
Auburn Hills *(G-943)*
▲ **K & Y Manufacturing LLC** .... E 734 414-7000
Canton *(G-2482)*
Kalkaska Screw Products Inc .... E 231 258-2560
Kalkaska *(G-9392)*
Kerr Screw Products Co Inc .... G 248 589-2200
Madison Heights *(G-10761)*
L A Martin Company .... E 313 581-3444
Dearborn *(G-3859)*
Lakeshore Fittings Inc .... D 616 846-5090
Grand Haven *(G-6328)*
Lester Detterbeck Entps Ltd .... E 906 265-5121
Iron River *(G-8746)*
Liberty Research Co Inc .... G 734 508-6237
Milan *(G-11440)*
Liberty Turned Components LLC .... E 734 508-6237
Milan *(G-11441)*
Livonia Automatic Incorporated .... G 734 591-0321
Livonia *(G-10287)*
Lyon Manufacturing Inc .... E 734 359-3000
Canton *(G-2487)*
Malabar Manufacturing Inc .... F 517 448-2155
Hudson *(G-8555)*
◆ **Maynard L Maclean L C** .... D 586 949-0471
Chesterfield *(G-2908)*
McNees Manufacturing Inc .... E 616 675-7480
Bailey *(G-1120)*
Melling Do Brasil LLC .... F 517 787-8172
Jackson *(G-8948)*
◆ **Melling Tool Co** .... B 517 787-8172
Jackson *(G-8951)*
▲ **Merchants Automatic Pdts Inc** .... E 734 829-0020
Canton *(G-2493)*
▲ **Mercury Manufacturing Company** .... D 734 285-5150
Wyandotte *(G-18833)*
Michigan Prcsion Swiss Prts In .... E 810 329-2270
Saint Clair *(G-14837)*
Micromatic Screw Products Inc .... E 517 787-3666
Jackson *(G-8957)*
Mid-West Screw Products Co .... F 734 591-1800
Livonia *(G-10316)*
Milan Screw Products Inc .... F 734 439-2431
Milan *(G-11447)*
▲ **MK Chambers Company** .... E 810 688-3750
North Branch *(G-12181)*
Modern Tech Machining LLC .... G 810 531-7992
Marysville *(G-11092)*
Mohr Engineering Inc .... E 810 227-4598
Brighton *(G-2035)*
Mountain Machine LLC .... F 734 480-2200
Van Buren Twp *(G-17542)*
Nelms Technologies Inc .... E 734 955-6500
Romulus *(G-14309)*
North Shore Machine Works Inc .... E 616 842-8360
Spring Lake *(G-15840)*
▲ **Nuko Precision LLC** .... F 734 464-6856
Livonia *(G-10342)*
Petschke Manufacturing Company .... F 586 463-0841
Mount Clemens *(G-11652)*
Phillips Bros Screw Pdts Co .... G 517 882-0279
Lansing *(G-9880)*
Pinckney Automatic & Mfg .... G 734 878-3430
Pinckney *(G-13053)*
▲ **Pro Slot Ltd** .... G 616 897-6000
Hartford *(G-7766)*
R & D Screw Products Inc .... E 517 546-2380
Howell *(G-8502)*
R E Gallaher Corp .... G 586 725-3333
Ira *(G-8709)*
Rempco Acquisition Inc .... E 231 775-0108
Cadillac *(G-2351)*
Rima Manufacturing Company .... C 517 448-8921
Hudson *(G-8561)*
▲ **Riverside Screw Mch Pdts Inc** .... F 269 962-5449
Battle Creek *(G-1289)*
Ryan Polishing Corporation .... E 248 548-6832
Oak Park *(G-12643)*
S H Leggitt Company .... B 269 781-3901
Marshall *(G-11073)*
Sigma Machine Inc .... D 269 806-5679
Kalamazoo *(G-9333)*
Slater Tools Inc .... E 586 465-5000
Clinton Township *(G-3360)*
South Park Sales & Mfg Inc .... G 313 381-7579
Dearborn *(G-3899)*
Springdale Automatics Inc .... G 517 523-2424
Osseo *(G-12777)*
St Joe Tool Co .... E 269 426-4300
Bridgman *(G-1934)*
Stagg Machine Products Inc .... G 231 775-2355
Cadillac *(G-2359)*
Steadfast Engineered Pdts LLC .... F 616 846-4747
Grand Haven *(G-6368)*
Stockbridge Manufacturing Co .... G 517 851-7865
Stockbridge *(G-16278)*
▲ **Stonebridge Industries Inc** .... B 586 323-0348
Sterling Heights *(G-16195)*
Supreme Domestic Intl Sls Corp .... F 616 842-6550
Spring Lake *(G-15854)*
▲ **Supreme Machined Pdts Co Inc** .... C 616 842-6550
Spring Lake *(G-15855)*
Swiss American Screw Pdts Inc .... E 734 397-1600
Canton *(G-2529)*
Swiss Industries Inc .... G 517 437-3682
Hillsdale *(G-7950)*
Taylor Machine Products Inc .... F 734 287-3550
Plymouth *(G-13309)*
Taylor Screw Products Company .... G 734 697-8018
Van Buren Twp *(G-17556)*
Terry Tool & Die Co .... F 517 750-1771
Jackson *(G-9019)*
Tmt Investment Company .... E 248 616-8880
Troy *(G-17394)*
◆ **Tompkins Products Inc** .... D 313 894-2222
Detroit *(G-4637)*
Tri-Matic Screw Products Co .... E 517 548-6414
Howell *(G-8535)*
▲ **Tribal Manufacturing Inc** .... D 269 781-3901
Marshall *(G-11076)*
Trinity Holding Inc .... F 517 787-3100
Jackson *(G-9024)*
Tru-Line Screw Products Inc .... F 734 261-8780
Livonia *(G-10445)*
United Precision Pdts Co Inc .... E 313 292-0100
Dearborn Heights *(G-3943)*
Victor Screw Products Co .... G 269 489-2760
Burr Oak *(G-2214)*
Warren Screw Products Inc .... C 586 757-1280
Warren *(G-18061)*
Westgood Manufacturing Co .... F 586 771-3970
Roseville *(G-14493)*
Wolverine Machine Products Co .... E 248 634-9952
Holly *(G-8301)*
Yankee Scrw Products Company .... G 248 634-3011
Holly *(G-8302)*
Yarbrough Precision Screws LLC .... F 586 776-0752
Fraser *(G-6013)*
Zimmermann Engineering Co Inc .... G 248 358-0044
Southfield *(G-15746)*
Zygot Operations Limited .... E 810 736-2900
Flint *(G-5799)*

3452 Bolts, Nuts, Screws, Rivets & Washers

A A Anchor Bolt Inc .... F 248 349-6565
Northville *(G-12194)*
AAA Industries Inc .... E 313 255-0420
Redford *(G-13709)*
Aero Auto Stud Specialists Inc .... E 248 437-2171
Whitmore Lake *(G-18517)*
▲ **Ajax Spring and Mfg Co** .... E 248 588-5700
Madison Heights *(G-10664)*
Amanda Manufacturing LLC .... E 740 385-9380
Livonia *(G-10113)*
Anchor Lamina America Inc .... C 231 533-8646
Bellaire *(G-1468)*
Ankara Industries Incorporated .... E 586 749-1190
Chesterfield *(G-2845)*
Apex Spring & Stamping Corp .... D 616 453-5463
Grand Rapids *(G-6462)*
▲ **B & D Thread Rolling Inc** .... D 734 728-7070
Taylor *(G-16384)*
Basch Olovson Engineering Co .... G 231 865-2027
Fruitport *(G-6060)*
▲ **BDS Company Inc** .... F 517 279-2135
Coldwater *(G-3421)*
◆ **Beaver Aerospace & Defense Inc** .... C 734 853-5003
Livonia *(G-10133)*
Belwith Products LLC .... F 616 247-4000
Grandville *(G-7367)*
Bollhoff .... G 313 506-0150
Troy *(G-16979)*
Bollhoff Rivnut .... G 248 269-0475
Troy *(G-16980)*
Broaching Industries Inc .... E 586 949-3775
Chesterfield *(G-2853)*
Camcar LLC .... D 586 254-3900
Sterling Heights *(G-15950)*
◆ **Cold Heading Co** .... D 586 497-7000
Warren *(G-17758)*
Cold Heading Co .... E 586 497-7016
Warren *(G-17759)*
▲ **Connection Service Company** .... E 269 926-2658
Benton Harbor *(G-1541)*
Consolidated Metal Pdts Inc .... G 616 538-1000
Grand Rapids *(G-6596)*
▲ **Decker Manufacturing Corp** .... D 517 629-3955
Albion *(G-124)*
Detroit Tubular Rivet Inc .... E 734 282-7979
Wyandotte *(G-18816)*
▲ **Dexter Fastener Tech Inc** .... C 734 426-0311
Dexter *(G-4736)*
Dexter Fastener Tech Inc .... G 734 426-5200
Dexter *(G-4737)*
Dias Holding Inc .... F 313 928-1254
Allen Park *(G-192)*
Die Cast Press Mfg Co Inc .... E 269 657-6060
Paw Paw *(G-12947)*
▲ **Dirksen Screw Products Co** .... E 586 247-5400
Shelby Township *(G-15208)*
E & E Manufacturing Co Inc .... E 248 616-1300
Clawson *(G-3095)*
E J M Ball Screw LLC .... F 989 893-7674
Bay City *(G-1349)*
E M P Manufacturing Corp .... F 586 949-8277
Chesterfield *(G-2873)*
▲ **Ecoclean Inc** .... C 248 450-2000
Southfield *(G-15552)*
▲ **Fastco Industries Inc** .... C 616 453-5428
Grand Rapids *(G-6700)*
Fastco Industries Inc .... G 616 389-1390
Grand Rapids *(G-6701)*
Fastco Industries Inc .... G 616 453-5428
Grand Rapids *(G-6702)*
▲ **Fastener Advance PDT Co Ltd** .... F 734 428-8070
Manchester *(G-10884)*
Federal Screw Works .... D 231 796-7664
Big Rapids *(G-1674)*
Federal Screw Works .... G 231 922-9500
Traverse City *(G-16681)*
Federal Screw Works .... C 734 941-4211
Romulus *(G-14275)*
▲ **Federal Screw Works** .... F 734 941-4211
Romulus *(G-14274)*
Federal Screw Works .... D 734 941-4211
Big Rapids *(G-1673)*
▼ **Franklin Fastener Company** .... E 313 537-8900
Redford *(G-13735)*
Fred Oswalts Pins Unltd .... G 269 342-1387
Portage *(G-13561)*
Gage Bilt Inc .... E 586 226-1500
Clinton Township *(G-3247)*
General Motors LLC .... F 989 894-7210
Bay City *(G-1359)*
Glycon Corp .... E 517 423-8356
Tecumseh *(G-16503)*
Grant Industries Incorporated .... E 586 293-9200
Fraser *(G-5931)*
H & L Tool Company Inc .... E 248 585-7474
Madison Heights *(G-10736)*
Headqrter Strlng Hts Oprations .... G 765 654-0477
Sterling Heights *(G-16037)*
◆ **Henrob Corporation** .... D 248 493-3800
New Hudson *(G-12057)*
Henry Plambeck .... G 586 463-3410
Harrison Township *(G-7701)*
Hexagon Enterprises Inc .... F 248 583-0550
Troy *(G-17142)*
▲ **Huron Tool & Engineering Co** .... E 989 269-9927
Bad Axe *(G-1108)*
◆ **Kamax Inc** .... E 248 879-0200
Rochester Hills *(G-14044)*
Kamax Inc .... C 810 272-2090
Lapeer *(G-9936)*
Kamax Inc .... B 810 664-7741
Lapeer *(G-9937)*
Lay Manufacturing Inc .... G 313 369-1627
Warren *(G-17901)*
Leader Tool Company - HB Inc .... E 989 479-3281
Harbor Beach *(G-7634)*
▲ **Limbright Consulting Inc** .... E 810 227-5510
Wixom *(G-18699)*

SIC

Employee Codes: A=Over 500 employees, B=251-500
C=101-250, D=51-100, E=20-50, F=10-19, G=3-9

2022 Harris Michigan
Industrial Directory

819

34 FABRICATED METAL PRODUCTS, EXCEPT MACHINERY AND TRANSPORTATION EQUIPMENT34 FABRICATED METAL PRODUCTS, EXCEPT

Mac Lean-Fogg Company ... C ... 248 280-0880
Royal Oak *(G-14558)*

◆ Maynard L Maclean L C ... D ... 586 949-0471
Chesterfield *(G-2908)*

▲ Merchants Automatic Pdts Inc ... E ... 734 829-0020
Canton *(G-2493)*

▲ Michigan Rod Products Inc ... D ... 517 552-9812
Howell *(G-8481)*

Michigan Steel Finishing Co ... F ... 313 838-3925
Detroit *(G-4452)*

Mid-States Bolt & Screw Co ... F ... 989 732-3265
Gaylord *(G-6149)*

Midwest Acorn Nut Company ... E ... 800 422-6887
Troy *(G-17261)*

▲ MNP Corporation ... A ... 586 254-1320
Utica *(G-17504)*

▲ Modular Systems Inc ... G ... 231 865-3167
Fruitport *(G-6067)*

Mycdbdmk Services LLC ... G ... 586 994-7910
Sterling Heights *(G-16110)*

Northern Industrial Mfg Corp ... E ... 586 468-2790
Harrison Township *(G-7712)*

◆ Nss Technologies Inc ... E ... 734 459-9500
Canton *(G-2502)*

Oakland Bolt & Nut Co LLC ... G ... 313 659-1677
Detroit *(G-4495)*

Perigee Manufacturing Co Inc ... F ... 313 933-4420
Detroit *(G-4519)*

Pgm Products Inc ... F ... 586 757-4400
Warren *(G-17962)*

Phillips Service Inds Inc ... F ... 734 853-5000
Ann Arbor *(G-610)*

Piercetek Inc ... G ... 586 757-0379
Warren *(G-17963)*

Pinckney Automatic & Mfg ... G ... 734 878-3430
Pinckney *(G-13053)*

Pink Pin Lady LLC ... G ... 586 731-1532
Shelby Township *(G-15302)*

Prestige Stamping LLC ... C ... 586 773-2700
Warren *(G-17976)*

PSI Hydraulics ... E ... 734 261-4160
Plymouth *(G-13271)*

Ring Screw LLC ... D ... 810 695-0800
Holly *(G-8292)*

▲ Ring Screw LLC ... D ... 586 997-5600
Sterling Heights *(G-16152)*

Rippa Products Inc ... E ... 906 337-0010
Calumet *(G-2414)*

Roy A Hutchins Company ... G ... 248 437-3470
New Hudson *(G-12069)*

Rush Machining Inc ... E ... 248 583-0550
Troy *(G-17338)*

SA Industries 2 Inc ... F ... 248 391-5705
Jonesville *(G-9102)*

SA Industries 2 Inc ... D ... 248 693-9100
Lake Orion *(G-9630)*

◆ Saf-Holland Inc ... A ... 231 773-3271
Muskegon *(G-11913)*

▼ Securit Metal Products Co ... E ... 269 782-7076
Dowagiac *(G-4796)*

Shannon Precision Fastener LLC ... D ... 248 589-9670
Auburn Hills *(G-1031)*

▲ Shannon Precision Fastener LLC ... D ... 248 589-9670
Madison Heights *(G-10827)*

Shannon Precision Fastener LLC ... D ... 248 658-3015
Madison Heights *(G-10826)*

Smsg LLC ... G ... 517 787-9447
Jackson *(G-9011)*

Steel Master LLC ... E ... 810 771-4943
Grand Blanc *(G-6264)*

Taper-Line Inc ... G ... 586 775-5960
Clinton Township *(G-3373)*

Tip-Top Screw Mfg Inc ... E ... 989 739-5157
Oscoda *(G-12773)*

◆ Trimas Corporation ... B ... 248 631-5450
Bloomfield Hills *(G-1869)*

Under Pressure Pwr Washers LLC ... G ... 616 292-4289
Marne *(G-11000)*

United Precision Pdts Co Inc ... E ... 313 292-0100
Dearborn Heights *(G-3943)*

Utica Washers ... F ... 313 571-1568
Detroit *(G-4659)*

▲ Vamp Screw Products Company ... E ... 734 676-8020
Brownstown Twp *(G-2161)*

◆ Vico Products Co ... D ... 734 453-3777
Plymouth *(G-13334)*

W G Benjey Inc ... G ... 989 356-0027
Alpena *(G-328)*

Warren Screw Works Inc ... G ... 734 525-2920
Livonia *(G-10466)*

Washers Incorporated ... C ... 734 523-1000
Livonia *(G-10467)*

Wedin International Inc ... E ... 231 779-8650
Cadillac *(G-2363)*

Whitesell Frmed Components Inc ... D ... 313 299-1178
Waterford *(G-18175)*

▲ Wico Metal Products Company ... C ... 586 755-9600
Warren *(G-18067)*

◆ Williams Form Engineering Corp ... D ... 616 866-0815
Belmont *(G-1521)*

Wilson-Garner Company ... E ... 586 466-5880
Harrison Township *(G-7732)*

3462 Iron & Steel Forgings

▲ Allor Manufacturing Inc ... D ... 248 486-4500
Brighton *(G-1943)*

Amk Ironworks ... G ... 248 620-9027
Clarkston *(G-3016)*

▲ Avon Machining LLC ... D ... 586 884-2200
Shelby Township *(G-15175)*

Avon Machining Holdings Inc ... C ... 586 884-2200
Shelby Township *(G-15176)*

Boos Products Inc ... F ... 734 498-2207
Gregory *(G-7513)*

Borgwarner Powdered Metals Inc ... C ... 734 261-5322
Livonia *(G-10140)*

▲ Buchanan Metal Forming Inc ... E ... 269 695-3836
Buchanan *(G-2190)*

Cambric Corporation ... E ... 801 415-7300
Novi *(G-12378)*

Chardam Gear Company Inc ... C ... 586 795-8900
Sterling Heights *(G-15957)*

▼ Composite Forgings Ltd Partnr ... D ... 313 496-1226
Detroit *(G-4099)*

Computer Operated Mfg ... E ... 989 686-1333
Bay City *(G-1340)*

Decker Gear Inc ... F ... 810 388-1500
Saint Clair *(G-14825)*

Detail Precision Products Inc ... E ... 248 544-3390
Ferndale *(G-5540)*

Dias Holding Inc ... F ... 313 928-1254
Allen Park *(G-192)*

Dorris Company ... F ... 586 293-5260
Fraser *(G-5919)*

Enterprise Tool and Gear Inc ... F ... 989 269-9797
Bad Axe *(G-1100)*

Equitable Engineering Co Inc ... E ... 248 689-9700
Troy *(G-17096)*

Fairlane Gear Inc ... G ... 734 459-2440
Canton *(G-2460)*

Formax Precision Gear Inc ... F ... 586 323-9067
Sterling Heights *(G-16018)*

Gage Eagle Spline Inc ... D ... 586 776-7240
Warren *(G-17822)*

Global Engine Mfg Aliance LLC ... G ... 734 529-9888
Dundee *(G-4822)*

▲ Great Lakes Forge Inc ... G ... 231 947-4931
Traverse City *(G-16704)*

▲ Great Lakes Industry Inc ... E ... 517 784-3153
Jackson *(G-8895)*

Hephaestus Holdings LLC ... G ... 248 479-2700
Novi *(G-12432)*

Hhi Forging LLC ... E ... 248 284-2900
Royal Oak *(G-14544)*

▲ Hhi Formtech LLC ... B ... 248 597-3800
Royal Oak *(G-14545)*

Hhi Formtech LLC ... E ... 586 415-2000
Fraser *(G-5935)*

Hog Forging LLC ... G ... 248 765-7180
Birmingham *(G-1729)*

Invo Spline Inc ... E ... 586 757-8840
Warren *(G-17870)*

▲ Iwis Engine Systems LP ... G ... 248 247-3178
Troy *(G-17176)*

◆ Jervis B Webb Company ... B ... 248 553-1000
Novi *(G-12449)*

Kendor Steel Rule Die Inc ... F ... 586 293-7111
Fraser *(G-5950)*

Khearma Group LLC ... F ... 248 513-5763
Detroit *(G-4361)*

Lansing Forge Inc ... F ... 517 882-2056
Lansing *(G-9859)*

Lansing Holding Company Inc ... G ... 517 882-2056
Lansing *(G-9861)*

Lc Manufacturing LLC ... C ... 231 839-7102
Lake City *(G-9548)*

Lc Manufacturing LLC ... E ... 734 753-3990
New Boston *(G-12013)*

▲ Letts Industries Inc ... G ... 313 579-1100
Detroit *(G-4392)*

▼ Lincoln Park Die & Tool Co ... E ... 734 285-1680
Brownstown *(G-2149)*

Linear Mold & Engineering LLC ... E ... 734 744-4548
Livonia *(G-10281)*

▲ Linear Mold & Engineering LLC ... F ... 734 422-6060
Livonia *(G-10282)*

Lisi Automotive Hl Vol Inc ... C ... 734 266-6900
Livonia *(G-10286)*

Lucerne Forging Inc ... G ... 248 674-7210
Auburn Hills *(G-960)*

Lyons Tool & Engineering Inc ... E ... 586 200-3003
Warren *(G-17910)*

M P I International Inc ... B ... 608 764-5416
Rochester Hills *(G-14056)*

Mason Forge & Die Inc ... F ... 517 676-2992
Mason *(G-11142)*

Metal Forming & Coining Corp ... G ... 586 731-2003
Shelby Township *(G-15273)*

▲ Metal Forming Technology Inc ... F ... 586 949-4586
Chesterfield *(G-2910)*

Metalcraft Impression Die Co ... G ... 734 513-8058
Livonia *(G-10311)*

MFC Netform Inc ... F ... 586 731-2003
Shelby Township *(G-15277)*

Michigan Forge Company LLC ... E ... 815 758-6400
Lansing *(G-9869)*

Midwest Gear & Tool Inc ... E ... 586 779-1300
Roseville *(G-14442)*

◆ Motion Systems Incorporated ... F ... 586 774-5666
Warren *(G-17935)*

Plesh Industries Inc ... E ... 716 873-4916
Brighton *(G-2052)*

Power Industries Corp ... G ... 586 783-3818
Harrison Township *(G-7716)*

Quality Steel Products Inc ... E ... 248 684-0555
Milford *(G-11484)*

Rack & Pinion Inc ... G ... 517 563-8872
Horton *(G-8378)*

Ringmasters Mfg LLC ... E ... 734 729-6110
Wayne *(G-18235)*

Riverside Spline & Gear Inc ... E ... 810 765-8302
Marine City *(G-10965)*

Shadko Enterprises Inc ... G ... 248 816-1712
Troy *(G-17348)*

Steve Tonkovich ... G ... 810 348-4046
Waterford *(G-18166)*

▲ Stonebridge Industries Inc ... B ... 586 323-0348
Sterling Heights *(G-16195)*

Superalloy North America LLC ... G ... 810 252-1552
Bingham Farms *(G-1704)*

Tech Tool Company Inc ... G ... 313 836-4131
Detroit *(G-4628)*

Trenton Forging Company ... D ... 734 675-1620
Trenton *(G-16895)*

◆ Triumph Gear Systems - McOmb I ... C ... 586 781-2800
Macomb *(G-10644)*

Vectorall Manufacturing Inc ... E ... 248 486-4570
Brighton *(G-2093)*

Vico Louisville LLC ... E ... 502 245-1616
Plymouth *(G-13333)*

Warren Manufacturing LLC ... G ... 586 467-1600
Warren *(G-18060)*

▲ Wartian Lock Company ... G ... 586 777-2244
Saint Clair Shores *(G-14891)*

Webster Cold Forge Co ... F ... 313 554-4500
Northville *(G-12271)*

Wedin International Inc ... E ... 231 779-8650
Cadillac *(G-2363)*

▼ Wilkie Bros Conveyors Inc ... E ... 810 364-4820
Marysville *(G-11113)*

▲ Wkw Roof Rail Systems LLC ... G ... 205 338-4242
Portage *(G-13632)*

Wyman-Gordon Forgings Inc ... B ... 810 229-9550
Brighton *(G-2099)*

3463 Nonferrous Forgings

▲ AGC Grand Haven LLC ... G ... 616 842-1820
Grand Haven *(G-6271)*

▲ Alliance Automation LLC ... F ... 810 953-9539
Flint *(G-5642)*

Borgwarner Powdered Metals Inc ... C ... 734 261-5322
Livonia *(G-10140)*

D Mac Industries Inc ... F ... 734 536-7754
Livonia *(G-10173)*

Global Fmi LLC ... D ... 810 964-5555
Fenton *(G-5481)*

Greenseed LLC ... G ... 313 295-0100
Taylor *(G-16423)*

Hephaestus Holdings LLC ... G ... 248 479-2700
Novi *(G-12432)*

SIC SECTION34 FABRICATED METAL PRODUCTS, EXCEPT MACHINERY AND TRANSPORTATION EQUIPMENT34 FABRICATED METAL PROD-

Hhi Formtech LLC....E....586 415-2000
Fraser (G-5935)
▼ Lincoln Park Die & Tool Co....E....734 285-1680
Brownstown (G-2149)
◆ Mueller Brass Co....C....810 987-7770
Port Huron (G-13504)
Mueller Brass Forging Co Inc....D....810 987-7770
Port Huron (G-13506)
▼ Mueller Impacts Company Inc....C....810 364-3700
Marysville (G-11093)
Mueller Industries Inc....G....248 446-3720
Brighton (G-2037)
▲ Resistnce Wldg Mch Accssory LL....F....269 428-4770
Saint Joseph (G-14956)
United Brass Manufacturers Inc....F....734 942-9224
Romulus (G-14335)
United Brass Manufacturers Inc....E....734 941-0700
Romulus (G-14334)
▲ Weldaloy Products Company....D....586 758-5550
Warren (G-18064)
Wonder Makers Environmental....F....269 382-4154
Kalamazoo (G-9372)

3465 Automotive Stampings

3715-11th Street Corp....E....734 523-1000
Livonia (G-10089)
A G Simpson (usa) Inc....G....586 268-4817
Sterling Heights (G-15918)
A G Simpson (usa) Inc....F....586 268-4817
Sterling Heights (G-15919)
A G Simpson (usa) Inc....G....586 825-9000
Warren (G-17682)
A G Simpson (usa) Inc....E....586 268-5844
Sterling Heights (G-15920)
A-1 Stampings Inc....G....586 294-7790
Fraser (G-5887)
Aaron Incorporated....G....586 791-0320
Clinton Township (G-3150)
▲ Acemco Incorporated....C....231 799-8612
Norton Shores (G-12344)
Advance Engineering Company....D....313 537-3500
Canton (G-2429)
▲ Advanced Auto Trends Inc....E....248 628-6111
Oxford (G-12871)
Advanced Auto Trends Inc....E....248 628-4850
Oxford (G-12872)
▲ Ajax Spring and Mfg Co....E....248 588-5700
Madison Heights (G-10664)
Allied Engineering Inc....G....616 748-7990
Zeeland (G-18990)
Aludyne US LLC....D....810 987-1112
Port Huron (G-13438)
AMI Livonia LLC....D....734 428-3132
Livonia (G-10117)
Anderton Equity LLC....G....248 430-6650
Troy (G-16937)
Android Indstrs-Shreveport LLC....E....248 454-0500
Auburn Hills (G-785)
▲ Anjun America Inc....G....248 680-8825
Auburn Hills (G-787)
Ankara Industries Incorporated....E....586 749-1190
Chesterfield (G-2845)
Aphase II Inc....D....586 977-0790
Sterling Heights (G-15933)
ARC-Kecy LLC....D....517 448-8954
Hudson (G-8549)
Arcturian LLC....G....313 643-5326
Dearborn (G-3810)
Auto Metal Craft Inc....E....248 398-2240
Oak Park (G-12594)
Autokiniton US Holdings Inc....C....734 397-6300
New Boston (G-12001)
Automatic Spring Products Corp....C....616 842-2284
Grand Haven (G-6278)
Automobili Lamborghini Amer LLC....F....866 681-6276
Auburn Hills (G-806)
Autowares Inc....G....248 473-0928
Farmington Hills (G-5177)
▲ Avon Machining LLC....D....586 884-2200
Shelby Township (G-15175)
Avon Machining Holdings Inc....C....586 884-2200
Shelby Township (G-15176)
▲ Bae Industries Inc....C....586 754-3000
Warren (G-17725)
Bae Industries Inc....C....248 475-9600
Auburn Hills (G-809)
Benesh Corporation....F....734 244-4143
Monroe (G-11532)
Benteler Automotive Corp....B....616 247-3936
Auburn Hills (G-810)
◆ Benteler Automotive Corp....C....248 364-7190
Auburn Hills (G-811)
Bopp-Busch Manufacturing Co....E....989 876-7924
Au Gres (G-758)
Britten Metalworks LLC....G....231 421-1615
Traverse City (G-16629)
▲ Burkland Inc....C....810 636-2233
Goodrich (G-6222)
C & H Stamping Inc....E....517 750-3600
Jackson (G-8829)
C & M Manufacturing Corp Inc....E....586 749-3455
Chesterfield (G-2854)
Capco Automovite....G....248 616-8888
Troy (G-16997)
Capital Stamping & Machine Inc....G....248 471-0700
Farmington Hills (G-5197)
Challenge Manufacturing....F....616 735-6500
Walker (G-17632)
Challenge Mfg Company....F....616 735-6530
Walker (G-17633)
Challenge Mfg Company LLC....C....616 735-6500
Walker (G-17634)
▲ Challenge Mfg Company LLC....B....616 735-6500
Walker (G-17635)
Challenge Mfg Company LLC....C....616 735-6500
Grand Rapids (G-6562)
Challenge Mfg Company LLC....C....616 396-2079
Holland (G-7993)
▲ Concord Tool and Mfg Inc....C....586 465-6537
Mount Clemens (G-11634)
Cooper-Standard Automotive Inc....G....248 630-7262
Auburn Hills (G-850)
Crescive Die and Tool Inc....F....734 482-0303
Saline (G-15010)
▲ D & N Bending Corp....E....586 752-5511
Romeo (G-14223)
▲ D T M 1 Inc....E....248 889-9210
Highland (G-7890)
Dajaco Industries Inc....D....586 949-1590
Chesterfield (G-2866)
Dayco Incorporated....D....248 404-6500
Troy (G-17046)
Delaco Steel Corporation....C....313 491-1200
Dearborn (G-3826)
▲ Demmer Corporation....C....517 321-3600
Lansing (G-9687)
Design Metal Inc....F....248 547-4170
Oak Park (G-12605)
▼ Dgh Enterprises Inc....E....269 925-0657
Benton Harbor (G-1546)
Diversfied Prcurement Svcs LLC....G....248 821-1147
Ferndale (G-5548)
◆ Dongah America Inc....E....734 946-7940
Taylor (G-16404)
Douglas Stamping Company....F....248 542-3940
Madison Heights (G-10711)
Dowding Industries Inc....C....517 663-5455
Eaton Rapids (G-4960)
▲ Dst Industries Inc....C....734 941-0300
Romulus (G-14268)
Dti Molded Products Inc....F....248 647-0400
Bingham Farms (G-1695)
Dunne-Rite Performance Inc....F....616 828-0908
Warren (G-17784)
Dynamic Metals Group LLC....F....586 790-5615
Birmingham (G-1724)
Dynetics Inc....G....248 619-1681
Troy (G-17073)
E & E Manufacturing Co Inc....F....734 451-7600
Plymouth (G-13165)
E & E Manufacturing Co Inc....E....248 616-1300
Clawson (G-3095)
◆ Elringklinger North Amer Inc....D....734 738-1800
Plymouth (G-13166)
Emerging Advanced Products LLC....D....734 942-1060
Belleville (G-1483)
F & S Diversified Products Inc....F....248 409-0960
Auburn Hills (G-885)
Fab-All Manufacturing Inc....D....248 585-6700
Troy (G-17103)
FCA US LLC....A....248 512-2950
Auburn Hills (G-894)
Fisher & Company Incorporated....G....248 280-0808
Troy (G-17109)
Flex-N-Gate Troy LLC....E....586 759-8900
Troy (G-17114)
Ford Global Technologies LLC....A....313 312-3000
Bingham Farms (G-1696)
Forward Metal Craft Inc....F....616 459-6051
Grand Rapids (G-6717)
▼ Franklin Fastener Company....E....313 537-8900
Redford (G-13735)
Gedia Michigan LLC....E....248 392-9090
Orion (G-12730)
Gedia Michigan LLC....E....248 392-9090
Lake Orion (G-9605)
General Motors LLC....F....810 234-2710
Flint (G-5704)
General Motors LLC....F....810 234-2710
Flint (G-5705)
General Motors LLC....G....810 236-1970
Flint (G-5706)
◆ Gestamp Mason LLC....B....517 244-8800
Mason (G-11135)
Gestamp Washtenaw LLC....E....734 593-9036
Chelsea (G-2812)
Gfm LLC....E....586 859-4587
Roseville (G-14412)
▲ Gill Corporation....B....616 453-4491
Grand Rapids (G-6740)
Gill Holding Company Inc....D....616 559-2700
Grand Rapids (G-6741)
◆ Gill Industries Inc....C....616 559-2700
Grand Rapids (G-6742)
Global Fmi LLC....D....810 964-5555
Fenton (G-5481)
▲ Globe Tech LLC....E....734 656-2200
Plymouth (G-13178)
▲ Gns Canton LLC....C....734 927-9520
Canton (G-2466)
Gns North America Inc....G....616 796-0433
Holland (G-8054)
Grant Industries Incorporated....E....586 293-9200
Fraser (G-5931)
Great Lakes Trim Inc....D....231 267-3000
Williamsburg (G-18555)
Grouper Wild LLC....G....248 299-7500
Auburn Hills (G-917)
Guelph Tool Sales Inc....B....586 755-3333
Warren (G-17843)
▲ Guyoung Tech Usa Inc....D....248 746-4261
Southfield (G-15589)
Hamlin Tool & Machine Co Inc....E....248 651-6302
Rochester Hills (G-14029)
Hatch Stamping Co....G....734 475-6507
Spring Arbor (G-15792)
◆ Hatch Stamping Company LLC....C....734 475-8628
Chelsea (G-2814)
▼ Hawthorne Metal Products Co....B....248 549-1375
Royal Oak (G-14543)
Hbpo North America Inc....C....248 823-7076
Troy (G-17138)
Henze Stamping & Mfg Co....G....248 588-5620
Troy (G-17141)
Illinois Tool Works Inc....G....248 589-2500
Troy (G-17161)
▲ Inalfa/Ssi Roof Systems LLC....D....586 758-6620
Warren (G-17860)
Invention Evolution Comp LLC....E....517 219-0180
Fowlerville (G-5843)
Iroquois Industries Inc....E....586 465-1023
Cottrellville (G-3723)
J & J Spring Co Inc....F....586 566-7600
Shelby Township (G-15241)
J & L Mfg Co....E....586 445-9530
Warren (G-17875)
Jaytec LLC....F....734 713-4500
Milan (G-11439)
Jaytec LLC....F....734 397-6300
Chelsea (G-2816)
▲ Jaytec LLC....F....517 451-8272
New Boston (G-12010)
◆ Jsj Corporation....E....616 842-6350
Grand Haven (G-6324)
▲ K & K Mfg Inc....G....616 784-4286
Sparta (G-15770)
▲ K&K Stamping Company....E....586 443-7900
Saint Clair Shores (G-14866)
▲ Kecy Products Inc....E....517 448-8954
Hudson (G-8554)
▲ Kirchhoff Auto Tecumseh Inc....B....517 423-2400
Tecumseh (G-16506)
Kirchhoff Automotive USA Inc....F....248 247-3740
Troy (G-17194)
Kirmin Die & Tool Inc....E....734 722-9210
Romulus (G-14295)
L & W Inc....G....734 397-8085
Van Buren Twp (G-17535)
L & W Inc....G....517 486-6321
Blissfield (G-1767)

S I C

Employee Codes: A=Over 500 employees, B=251-500
C=101-250, D=51-100, E=20-50, F=10-19, G=3-9
2022 Harris Michigan
Industrial Directory
821

34 FABRICATED METAL PRODUCTS, EXCEPT MACHINERY AND TRANSPORTATION EQUIPMENT

L & W Inc ....F   734 529-7290
  Dundee (G-4826)
▲ L & W Inc ....D   734 397-6300
  New Boston (G-12012)
L & W Inc ....G   734 397-2212
  Van Buren Twp (G-17536)
L & W Inc ....G   616 394-9665
  Holland (G-8118)
L & W Mexico LLC ....D   734 397-6300
  Van Buren Twp (G-17537)
L Barge & Associates Inc ....E   248 582-3430
  Ferndale (G-5563)
Lacks Exterior Systems LLC ....F   616 554-7180
  Kentwood (G-9462)
Lacy Tool Company Inc ....G   248 476-5250
  Novi (G-12464)
Laser Cutting Co ....E   586 468-5300
  Harrison Township (G-7705)
Lgb USA Inc ....E   586 777-4542
  Roseville (G-14432)
▲ Llink Technologies LLC ....E   586 336-9370
  Brown City (G-2139)
Manufacturing Products & Svcs ....F   734 927-1964
  Plymouth (G-13233)
▲ Manufcturing Assembly Intl LLC ....F   248 549-4700
  Royal Oak (G-14559)
Martinrea Hot Stampings Inc ....E   859 509-3031
  Warren (G-17917)
▲ Martinrea Jonesville LLC ....A   517 849-2195
  Jonesville (G-9093)
Martinrea Jonesville LLC ....G   248 630-7730
  Auburn Hills (G-968)
Matcor Automotive Michigan Inc C   616 527-4050
  Ionia (G-8690)
Means Industries Inc ....G   989 754-3300
  Saginaw (G-14693)
◆ Means Industries Inc C   989 754-1433
  Saginaw (G-14691)
Means Industries Inc ....F   989 754-0312
  Saginaw (G-14692)
Melling Products North LLC ....D   989 588-6147
  Farwell (G-5426)
◆ Meritor Inc C   248 435-1000
  Troy (G-17246)
Mh Industries Ltd ....E   734 261-7560
  West Bloomfield (G-18298)
Michigan Vehicle Solutions LLC ....G   734 720-7649
  Southgate (G-15754)
Microgauge Machining Inc ....G   248 446-3720
  Brighton (G-2032)
Middleville Tool & Die Co Inc ....D   269 795-3646
  Middleville (G-11309)
Midstates Industrial Group Inc ....E   586 307-3414
  Clinton Township (G-3300)
Minth Group US Holding Inc ....E   248 848-8530
  Wixom (G-18711)
Minth North America Inc ....D   248 259-7468
  Wixom (G-18712)
▲ Motor City Stampings Inc ....B   586 949-8420
  Chesterfield (G-2915)
Motus Holdings LLC ....G   616 422-7557
  Holland (G-8149)
▲ Motus LLC C   616 422-7557
  Holland (G-8150)
Multimatic Michigan LLC ....E   517 962-7190
  Jackson (G-8971)
Mvc Holdings LLC ....F   586 491-2600
  Roseville (G-14450)
▲ N A Sodecia Inc ....B   586 879-8969
  Center Line (G-2683)
Northern Industrial Mfg Corp ....E   586 468-2790
  Harrison Township (G-7712)
Northern Metalcraft Inc ....F   586 997-3632
  Shelby Township (G-15292)
Oakley Industries Inc ....E   586 791-3194
  Clinton Township (G-3310)
Oakley Industries Inc C   586 792-1261
  Clinton Township (G-3311)
Oakwood Metal Fabricating Co ....E   734 947-7740
  Taylor (G-16454)
Oblut Limited ....F   810 241-4029
  Clarkston (G-3054)
Orion Manufacturing Inc ....F   616 527-5994
  Ionia (G-8691)
▲ P & C Group I Inc ....E   248 442-6800
  Farmington Hills (G-5341)
Pacific Engineering Corp ....G   248 359-7823
  Novi (G-12502)
Pinconning Metals Inc ....G   989 879-3144
  Pinconning (G-13064)

▲ Plastic Trim International Inc ....B   248 259-7468
  East Tawas (G-4919)
Precision Parts Holdings Inc ....A   248 853-9010
  Rochester Hills (G-14088)
Precision Stamping Co Inc ....E   517 546-5656
  Howell (G-8500)
Press-Way Inc ....E   586 790-3324
  Clinton Township (G-3325)
Prestige Advanced Inc ....F   586 868-4000
  Madison Heights (G-10807)
Prestige Stamping LLC C   586 773-2700
  Warren (G-17976)
▲ Pridgeon & Clay Inc ....A   616 241-5675
  Grand Rapids (G-7106)
Pt Tech Stamping Inc ....E   586 293-1810
  Fraser (G-5982)
Qp Acquisition 2 Inc ....A   248 594-7432
  Southfield (G-15685)
▲ Quality Metalcraft Inc C   734 261-6700
  Livonia (G-10377)
Quigley Industries Inc ....E   248 426-8600
  Farmington Hills (G-5361)
Quigley Manufacturing Inc ....E   248 426-8600
  Farmington Hills (G-5362)
R D M Enterprises Co Inc C   810 985-4721
  Port Huron (G-13520)
Radar Mexican Investments LLC ....E   586 779-0300
  Warren (G-17992)
Ralco Industries Inc ....A   248 853-3200
  Auburn Hills (G-1014)
Reko International Holdings ....E   519 737-6974
  Bloomfield Hills (G-1854)
Reliant Industries Inc C   586 275-0479
  Sterling Heights (G-16146)
▲ Royal Flex-N-Gate Oak LLC ....B   248 549-3800
  Warren (G-17998)
S & G Prototype Inc ....F   586 716-3600
  New Baltimore (G-11993)
▲ Sakaiya Company America Ltd ....E   517 521-5633
  Webberville (G-18248)
Sales & Engineering Inc ....E   734 525-9030
  Livonia (G-10398)
Schwab Industries Inc ....E   586 566-8090
  Shelby Township (G-15326)
Set Enterprises Inc ....E   586 573-3600
  Royal Oak (G-14580)
Sodecia Auto Detroit Corp ....B   586 759-2200
  Roseville (G-14478)
▲ Sodecia Auto Detroit Corp C   586 759-2200
  Center Line (G-2686)
◆ Span America Detroit Inc ....F   734 957-1600
  Van Buren Twp (G-17554)
Spoiler Wing King ....G   810 733-9464
  Flint (G-5767)
Srg Global Automotive LLC ....B   586 757-7800
  Sterling Heights (G-16186)
▲ Srg Global Automotive LLC ....D   586 757-7800
  Warren (G-18024)
◆ Stanco Metal Products Inc ....E   616 842-5000
  Grand Haven (G-6366)
Statistical Processed Products ....F   586 792-6900
  Clinton Township (G-3363)
Stemco Products Inc ....G   888 854-6474
  Millington (G-11503)
Sterling Die & Engineering Inc ....E   586 677-0707
  Macomb (G-10637)
▲ Su-Dan Company ....D   248 651-6035
  Lake Orion (G-9632)
Su-Dan Company ....E   248 754-1430
  Rochester (G-13931)
Sungwoo Hitech Co Ltd ....G   248 561-0604
  Troy (G-17377)
Superior Cam Inc ....D   248 588-1100
  Madison Heights (G-10839)
Superior Machining Inc ....F   248 446-9451
  New Hudson (G-12071)
Ta Delaware Inc ....E   248 675-6000
  Novi (G-12553)
▲ Tajco North America Inc ....G   248 418-7550
  Auburn Hills (G-1043)
TEC-3 Prototypes Inc ....B   810 678-8909
  Metamora (G-11289)
Technique Inc ....D   517 789-8988
  Jackson (G-9017)
Tel-X Corporation ....E   734 425-2225
  Garden City (G-6112)
Tesca Usa Inc ....E   586 991-0744
  Rochester Hills (G-14124)
Tower Acquisition Co II LLC ....E   248 675-6000
  Livonia (G-10434)

Tower Atmtive Oprtons USA I LL ....D   989 375-2201
  Elkton (G-5033)
▲ Tower Atmtive Oprtons USA I LL ....D   734 397-6300
  New Boston (G-12021)
Tower Atmtive Oprtons USA I LL 616 802-1600
  Grand Rapids (G-7266)
Tower Atmtive Oprtons USA I LL 586 465-5158
  Clinton Township (G-3379)
Tower Atmtive Oprtons USA I LL 734 414-3100
  Plymouth (G-13320)
▲ Tower Atmtive Oprtons USA II L 248 675-6000
  Livonia (G-10435)
Tower Atmtive Oprtons USA III ....D   248 675-6000
  Livonia (G-10436)
Tower Auto Holdings II A LLC 248 675-6000
  Livonia (G-10437)
▲ Tower Auto Holdings USA LLC C   248 675-6000
  Livonia (G-10438)
▲ Tower Defense & Aerospace LLC .....E   248 675-6000
  Livonia (G-10439)
▲ Tower International Inc ....B   248 675-6000
  Livonia (G-10440)
▲ Trans-Matic Mfg Co Inc 616 820-2500
  Holland (G-8225)
Traverse City Products LLC 231 946-4414
  Traverse City (G-16865)
Trexel Inc ....F   248 687-1353
  Troy (G-17398)
Trianon Industries Corporation ....E   586 759-2200
  Center Line (G-2688)
▲ Troy Design & Manufacturing Co C   734 738-2300
  Plymouth (G-13325)
▲ Tubular Metal Systems LLC C   989 879-2611
  Pinconning (G-13066)
Twb Company LLC 734 454-4000
  Canton (G-2536)
Unique Tool & Mfg Co Inc ....E   336 498-2614
  Temperance (G-16551)
Van-Rob Inc 517 657-2450
  Lansing (G-9747)
▲ Variety Die & Stamping Co ....D   734 426-4488
  Dexter (G-4761)
▲ Versatube Corporation ....F   248 524-0299
  Troy (G-17438)
Visor Frames LLC ....F   586 864-6058
  Sterling Heights (G-16225)
Washers Incorporated C   734 523-1000
  Livonia (G-10467)
Webster Cold Forge Co 313 554-4500
  Northville (G-12271)
Wellington-Almont LLC 734 942-1060
  Belleville (G-1495)
▲ Wico Metal Products Company C   586 755-9600
  Warren (G-18067)
Wirco Inc 586 267-1300
  Clinton Township (G-3388)
▼ Wirco Manufacturing LLC ....F   810 984-5576
  Port Huron (G-13538)
Wirco Products Inc 810 984-5576
  Port Huron (G-13539)
Yarema Die & Engineering Co C   248 585-2830
  Troy (G-17457)
Zeledyne Glass Corp ....G   615 350-7500
  Allen Park (G-211)

3466 Crowns & Closures

Adcaa LLC ....G   734 623-4236
  Ann Arbor (G-352)
▲ Roll Rite Corporation ....E   989 345-3434
  Gladwin (G-6202)

3469 Metal Stampings, NEC

A & A Manufacturing Co ....G   616 846-1730
  Spring Lake (G-15799)
A & R Specialty Services Corp ....E   313 933-8750
  Detroit (G-3971)
A & S Reel & Tackle Inc ....G   313 928-1667
  Ecorse (G-4979)
A Raymond Corp N Amer Inc ....E   248 853-2500
  Rochester Hills (G-13938)
A-1 Stampings Inc ....G   586 294-7790
  Fraser (G-5887)
▲ Acemco Incorporated C   231 799-8612
  Norton Shores (G-12344)
Acme Tool & Die Co 231 938-1260
  Acme (G-1)
▲ Acorn Stamping Inc ....E   248 628-5216
  Oxford (G-12870)
Actron Steel Inc ....E   231 947-3981
  Traverse City (G-16597)

Admat Manufacturing Inc .... F 269 641-7453
Union *(G-17486)*

▼ Adrian Steel Company .... B 517 265-6194
Adrian *(G-50)*

Advance Engineering Company .... D 313 537-3500
Canton *(G-2429)*

▲ Advanced Auto Trends Inc .... E 248 628-6111
Oxford *(G-12871)*

▲ Ajax Spring and Mfg Co .... E 248 588-5700
Madison Heights *(G-10664)*

Alternate Number Five Inc .... D 616 842-2581
Grand Haven *(G-6272)*

▲ Aluminum Blanking Co Inc .... D 248 338-4422
Pontiac *(G-13349)*

Aluminum Textures Inc .... E 616 538-3144
Grandville *(G-7364)*

▲ Amanda Products LLC .... E 248 547-3870
Ferndale *(G-5525)*

American Engnred Cmponents Inc .... C 734 428-8301
Manchester *(G-10881)*

American Fabricated Pdts Inc .... E 616 607-8785
Spring Lake *(G-15803)*

American Metal Fab Inc .... D 269 279-5108
Three Rivers *(G-16563)*

American Trim .... G 269 281-0651
Saint Joseph *(G-14923)*

▲ Anand Nvh North America Inc .... C 810 724-2400
Imlay City *(G-8627)*

Anrod Screen Cylinder Company .... E 989 872-2101
Cass City *(G-2610)*

Apex Spring & Stamping Corp .... D 616 453-5463
Grand Rapids *(G-6462)*

ARC Metal Stamping LLC .... D 517 448-8954
Hudson *(G-8548)*

Arnold Tool & Die Co .... E 586 598-0099
Chesterfield *(G-2846)*

Automatic Spring Products Corp .... C 616 842-2284
Grand Haven *(G-6278)*

Automotive Prototype Stamping .... G 586 445-6792
Clinton Township *(G-3176)*

▲ Bae Industries Inc .... C 586 754-3000
Warren *(G-17725)*

Bae Industries Inc .... C 248 475-9600
Auburn Hills *(G-809)*

Barnes Group Inc .... G 586 415-6677
Fraser *(G-5900)*

Bay Manufacturing Corporation .... F 989 358-7198
Alpena *(G-282)*

▲ Bayloff Stmped Pdts Dtroit Inc .... D 734 397-9116
Van Buren Twp *(G-17510)*

Belwith Products LLC .... F 616 247-4000
Grandville *(G-7367)*

Benteler Automotive Corp .... B 616 247-3936
Auburn Hills *(G-810)*

Big Rapids Products Inc .... D 231 796-3593
Big Rapids *(G-1669)*

Blue Fire Manufacturing LLC .... E 248 714-7166
Waterford *(G-18104)*

▲ Bopp-Busch Manufacturing Co .... E 989 876-7121
Au Gres *(G-757)*

Bopp-Busch Manufacturing Co .... E 989 876-7924
Au Gres *(G-758)*

Broaching Industries Inc .... E 586 949-3775
Chesterfield *(G-2853)*

◆ Brooks Utility Products Group .... D 248 477-0250
Novi *(G-12377)*

▲ Burkland Inc .... C 810 636-2233
Goodrich *(G-6222)*

Burnside Acquisition LLC .... G 616 243-2800
Grand Rapids *(G-6538)*

Burnside Acquisition LLC .... C 231 798-3394
Norton Shores *(G-12346)*

Burnside Industries LLC .... G 231 798-3394
Norton Shores *(G-12347)*

▲ CA Picard Surface Engrg Inc .... E 440 366-5400
Battle Creek *(G-1203)*

▲ Cameron Tool Corporation .... D 517 487-3671
Lansing *(G-9820)*

Challenge Mfg Company LLC .... C 616 396-2079
Holland *(G-7993)*

Clark Perforating Company Inc .... F 734 439-1170
Milan *(G-11433)*

Cleveland L&W Inc .... G 440 882-5195
New Boston *(G-12007)*

▲ Commercial Mfg & Assembly Inc .... E 616 847-9980
Grand Haven *(G-6287)*

Complete Metalcraft LLC .... G 248 952-8002
Highland *(G-7888)*

Conner Steel Products .... F 248 852-5110
Rochester Hills *(G-13983)*

Consolidated Clips Clamps Inc .... D 734 455-0880
Plymouth *(G-13149)*

Consolidated Metal Pdts Inc .... G 616 538-1000
Grand Rapids *(G-6596)*

Contour Engineering Inc .... F 989 828-6526
Shepherd *(G-15376)*

Contract Welding and Fabg Inc .... E 734 699-5561
Van Buren Twp *(G-17520)*

Cooper Rolland .... G 734 482-8705
Ypsilanti *(G-18933)*

Corban Industries Inc .... E 248 393-2720
Orion *(G-12726)*

Covenant Cpitl Investments Inc .... F 248 477-4230
Wixom *(G-18637)*

Craft Steel Products Inc .... G 616 935-7575
Spring Lake *(G-15809)*

D & D Driers Timber Product .... G 906 224-7251
Wakefield *(G-17619)*

Dajaco Ind Inc .... F 586 949-1590
Chesterfield *(G-2865)*

Dajaco Industries Inc .... D 586 949-1590
Chesterfield *(G-2866)*

Dee-Blast Corporation .... F 269 428-2400
Stevensville *(G-16246)*

Degele Manufacturing Inc .... E 586 949-3550
Chesterfield *(G-2869)*

Demmer Investments Inc .... G 517 321-3600
Lansing *(G-9688)*

▲ Dexter Stamping Company LLC .... D 517 750-3414
Jackson *(G-8866)*

▼ Dgh Enterprises Inc .... E 269 925-0657
Benton Harbor *(G-1546)*

Dgh Enterprises Inc .... G 269 925-0657
Benton Harbor *(G-1547)*

Diamond Press Solutions LLC .... G 269 945-1997
Hastings *(G-7789)*

Die-Matic Tool and Die Inc .... E 616 531-0060
Wyoming *(G-18867)*

Dietech Tool & Mfg Inc .... D 810 724-0505
Imlay City *(G-8630)*

Diversfied Prcurement Svcs LLC .... G 248 821-1147
Ferndale *(G-5548)*

Douglas Stamping Company .... F 248 542-3940
Madison Heights *(G-10711)*

Duggans Limited LLC .... E 586 254-7400
Shelby Township *(G-15213)*

Duquaine Incorporated .... G 906 228-7290
Marquette *(G-11015)*

Dynamic Corporation .... F 616 399-2200
Holland *(G-8018)*

▲ E & E Manufacturing Co Inc .... C 734 451-7600
Plymouth *(G-13164)*

E & E Manufacturing Co Inc .... E 248 616-1300
Clawson *(G-3095)*

Echo Quality Grinding Inc .... F 231 544-6637
Central Lake *(G-2694)*

▲ Edmar Manufacturing Inc .... D 616 392-7218
Holland *(G-8023)*

Electro Optics Mfg Inc .... F 734 283-3000
Wyandotte *(G-18818)*

Elkins Machine & Tool Co Inc .... E 734 941-0266
Romulus *(G-14271)*

Elmhirst Industries Inc .... E 586 731-8663
Sterling Heights *(G-16002)*

Ernest Inds Acquisition LLC .... G 734 459-8881
Plymouth *(G-13168)*

Ernest Industries Acquisition, ... E 734 595-9500
Westland *(G-18369)*

Euclid Manufacturing Co Inc .... E 734 397-6300
Detroit *(G-4216)*

▲ European Cabinet Mfg Co .... E 586 445-8909
Roseville *(G-14406)*

◆ Expan Inc .... E 586 725-0405
New Baltimore *(G-11980)*

Experi-Metal Inc .... C 586 977-7800
Sterling Heights *(G-16009)*

▼ Falcon Stamping Inc .... G 517 540-6197
Howell *(G-8453)*

Fast Tech Mfg Inc .... G 586 783-1741
Harrison Township *(G-7698)*

Fisher & Company Incorporated .... G 248 280-0808
Troy *(G-17109)*

Fortress Manufacturing Inc .... F 269 925-1336
Benton Harbor *(G-1549)*

Forward Metal Craft Inc .... F 616 459-6051
Grand Rapids *(G-6717)*

Four Star Tooling & Engrg Inc .... G 586 264-4090
Sterling Heights *(G-16020)*

Four Way Industries Inc .... F 248 588-5421
Clawson *(G-3097)*

Four-Slide Technology Inc .... F 586 755-7778
Fraser *(G-5929)*

▲ Frank Condon Inc .... E 517 849-2505
Hillsdale *(G-7935)*

▼ Franklin Fastener Company .... E 313 537-8900
Redford *(G-13735)*

Future Industries Inc .... E 616 844-0772
Grand Haven *(G-6299)*

Gar-V Manufacturing Inc .... G 269 279-5134
Three Rivers *(G-16574)*

Gestamp Alabama LLC .... D 810 245-3100
Lapeer *(G-9931)*

▲ Gill Corporation .... B 616 453-4491
Grand Rapids *(G-6740)*

▲ Global Advanced Products LLC .... D 586 749-6800
Chesterfield *(G-2887)*

▲ Globe Tech LLC .... E 734 656-2200
Plymouth *(G-13178)*

▲ Globe Technologies Corporation .... E 989 846-9591
Standish *(G-15888)*

▲ Gns Holland Inc .... G 616 796-0433
Holland *(G-8053)*

Gordon Metal Products Inc .... F 586 445-0960
Detroit *(G-4271)*

Grand Traverse Stamping Co .... E 231 929-4215
Traverse City *(G-16701)*

Grant Industries Incorporated .... E 586 293-9200
Fraser *(G-5931)*

Gray Bros Stamping & Mch Inc .... E 269 483-7615
White Pigeon *(G-18478)*

Gray Brothers Mfg Inc .... F 269 483-7615
White Pigeon *(G-18479)*

▲ Great Lakes Metal Stamping Inc .... E 269 465-4415
Bridgman *(G-1927)*

◆ Haerter Stamping LLC .... D 616 871-9400
Kentwood *(G-9457)*

Heinzmann D Tool & Die Inc .... F 248 363-5115
Commerce Township *(G-3535)*

Henze Stamping & Mfg Co .... G 248 588-5620
Troy *(G-17141)*

▲ Hibshman Screw Mch Pdts Inc .... E 269 641-7525
Union *(G-17489)*

◆ High-Star Corporation .... G 734 743-1503
Westland *(G-18381)*

▼ Highland Engineering Inc .... E 517 548-4372
Howell *(G-8460)*

Highwood Die & Engineering Inc .... E 248 338-1807
Pontiac *(G-13380)*

Hilite Industries Inc .... G 248 475-4580
Lake Orion *(G-9608)*

Hope Network West Michigan .... E 231 775-3425
Cadillac *(G-2334)*

Hope Network West Michigan .... E 231 796-4801
Paris *(G-12934)*

Hti Associates LLC .... E 616 399-5430
Holland *(G-8089)*

Illinois Tool Works Inc .... B 616 772-1910
Zeeland *(G-19044)*

Impeccable Machining Inc .... G 734 844-3855
Canton *(G-2473)*

▲ Inalfa/Ssi Roof Systems LLC .... D 586 758-6620
Warren *(G-17860)*

Independent Tool and Mfg Co .... E 269 521-4811
Allegan *(G-161)*

Industrial Engineering Service .... F 616 794-1330
Belding *(G-1453)*

Industrial Innovations Inc .... F 616 249-1525
Grandville *(G-7392)*

Industrial Machine Pdts Inc .... D 248 628-3621
Oxford *(G-12889)*

Industrial Stamping & Mfg Co .... E 586 772-8430
Roseville *(G-14423)*

▲ Innotec Corp .... D 616 772-5959
Zeeland *(G-19047)*

Innovation Fab Inc .... G 586 752-3092
Bruce Twp *(G-2168)*

◆ Innovative Tool and Design Inc .... E 248 542-1831
Oak Park *(G-12618)*

◆ Iroquois Industries Inc .... D 586 771-5734
Warren *(G-17873)*

Iroquois Industries Inc .... E 586 353-1410
Warren *(G-17874)*

J & L Mfg Co .... E 586 445-9530
Warren *(G-17875)*

Jackson Precision Inds Inc .... E 517 782-8103
Jackson *(G-8917)*

Jireh Metal Products Inc .... D 616 531-7581
Grandville *(G-7393)*

▼ JMS of Holland Inc .... D 616 796-2727
Holland *(G-8100)*

SIC

34 FABRICATED METAL PRODUCTS, EXCEPT MACHINERY AND TRANSPORTATION EQUIPMENT

John Lamantia Corporation .... G 269 428-8100
Stevensville *(G-16255)*
Jordan Manufacturing Company .... E 616 794-0900
Belding *(G-1454)*
◆ Jsj Corporation .... E 616 842-6350
Grand Haven *(G-6324)*
K & K Die Inc 586 268-8812
Sterling Heights *(G-16059)*
▲ K&K Stamping Company .... E 586 443-7900
Saint Clair Shores *(G-14866)*
KB Stamping Inc .... F 616 866-5917
Belmont *(G-1509)*
▲ Kecy Corporation .... G 517 448-8954
Hudson *(G-8553)*
▲ Kecy Products Inc 517 448-8954
Hudson *(G-8554)*
Kendor Steel Rule Die Inc .... F 586 293-7111
Fraser *(G-5950)*
Keyes-Davis Company .... E 269 962-7505
Springfield *(G-15871)*
Kinney Tool and Die Inc .... D 616 997-0901
Coopersville *(G-3689)*
Kriewall Enterprises Inc 586 336-0600
Romeo *(G-14227)*
L & W Inc 517 627-7333
Grand Ledge *(G-6394)*
L & W Inc .... G 734 397-8085
Van Buren Twp *(G-17535)*
L & W Inc .... G 517 486-6321
Blissfield *(G-1767)*
L & W Inc .... F 734 529-7290
Dundee *(G-4826)*
▲ L & W Inc .... D 734 397-6300
New Boston *(G-12012)*
L Barge & Associates Inc .... E 248 582-3430
Ferndale *(G-5563)*
▲ L T C Roll & Engineering Co 586 465-1023
Clinton Township *(G-3277)*
Lab Tool and Engineering Corp .... F 517 750-4131
Spring Arbor *(G-15793)*
Lacy Tool Company Inc .... G 248 476-5250
Novi *(G-12464)*
Lake Fabricators Inc .... E 269 651-1935
Sturgis *(G-16298)*
Laser Cutting Co .... E 586 468-5300
Harrison Township *(G-7705)*
Lecreuset .... G 248 209-7025
Auburn Hills *(G-957)*
▲ Llink Technologies LLC .... E 586 336-9370
Brown City *(G-2139)*
▲ Low Cost Surcing Solutions LLC .... G 248 535-7721
Washington *(G-18084)*
Luckmarr Plastics Inc .... D 586 978-8498
Sterling Heights *(G-16077)*
Lupaul Industries Inc .... F 517 783-3223
Saint Johns *(G-14904)*
▼ M D Hubbard Spring Co Inc .... E 248 628-2528
Oxford *(G-12898)*
M P I International Inc .... B 608 764-5416
Rochester Hills *(G-14056)*
Marshall Metal Products Inc .... G 269 781-3924
Marshall *(G-11067)*
Max2 LLC .... F 269 468-3452
Benton Harbor *(G-1569)*
Mayville Engineering Co Inc .... D 616 878-5235
Byron Center *(G-2281)*
Means Industries Inc .... G 989 754-3300
Saginaw *(G-14693)*
Mec .... F 989 983-3911
Vanderbilt *(G-17574)*
Mercury Metal Forming Tech LLC .... F 586 778-4444
Roseville *(G-14440)*
Mercury Products Corp .... F 586 749-6800
Chesterfield *(G-2909)*
▼ Metal Flow Corporation .... C 616 392-7976
Holland *(G-8143)*
Metal Spinning Specialists .... G 810 743-6797
Burton *(G-2239)*
Metro Stamping & Mfg Co .... E 313 538-6464
Redford *(G-13746)*
▲ Michigan Rod Products Inc .... D 517 552-9812
Howell *(G-8481)*
Michigan Scientific Corp .... D 231 547-5511
Charlevoix *(G-2721)*
Mico Industries Inc .... D 616 245-6426
Grand Rapids *(G-6999)*
Mico Industries Inc .... F 616 245-6426
Grand Rapids *(G-7000)*
Mico Industries Inc .... E 616 514-1143
Grand Rapids *(G-7001)*

Mid-Tech Inc .... G 734 426-4327
Ann Arbor *(G-577)*
Middleville Tool & Die Co Inc .... D 269 795-3646
Middleville *(G-11309)*
▲ Midway Products Group Inc .... C 734 241-7242
Monroe *(G-11560)*
◆ Modineer Co LLC .... E 269 683-2550
Niles *(G-12145)*
Modineer Co LLC .... E 269 683-2550
Niles *(G-12146)*
Modineer Co LLC .... E 269 684-3138
Niles *(G-12147)*
Modineer P-K Tool LLC .... E 269 683-2550
Niles *(G-12148)*
Mpi Engineered Tech LLC .... F 248 237-3007
Troy *(G-17267)*
▼ Mueller Impacts Company Inc .... C 810 364-3700
Marysville *(G-11093)*
Munn Manufacturing Company .... E 616 765-3067
Freeport *(G-6035)*
Nelson Manufacturing Inc .... G 810 648-0065
Sandusky *(G-15063)*
Nelson Steel Products Inc .... D 616 396-1515
Holland *(G-8152)*
New 11 Inc .... G 616 494-9370
Holland *(G-8153)*
New Center Stamping Inc .... C 313 872-3500
Detroit *(G-4481)*
New Line Inc .... G 586 228-4820
Shelby Township *(G-15289)*
Nidec Chs LLC .... F 586 777-7440
Romeo *(G-14230)*
Nor-Dic Tool Company Inc .... F 734 326-3610
Romulus *(G-14312)*
Northern Industrial Mfg Corp .... E 586 468-2790
Harrison Township *(G-7712)*
Northern Stampings Inc .... F 586 598-6969
Rochester Hills *(G-14072)*
Northwest Pattern Company .... G 248 477-7070
Farmington Hills *(G-5335)*
▲ Oakland Stamping LLC .... C 734 397-6300
Detroit *(G-4496)*
Oakland Stamping LLC .... E 248 340-2520
Lake Orion *(G-9623)*
Ort Tool & Die Corporation .... D 419 242-9553
Erie *(G-5052)*
Os Holdings LLc .... E 734 397-6300
New Boston *(G-12017)*
Ovidon Manufacturing LLC .... D 517 548-4005
Howell *(G-8489)*
Pac-Cnc Inc .... E 616 288-3389
Grand Rapids *(G-7065)*
Palmer Engineering Inc .... E 517 321-3600
Lansing *(G-9723)*
Paradigm Engineering Inc .... G 586 776-5910
Roseville *(G-14458)*
Patton Tool and Die Inc .... F 810 359-5336
Lexington *(G-10031)*
Paw Paw Everlast Label Company .... F 269 657-4921
Paw Paw *(G-12954)*
▲ PEC of America Corporation .... F 248 675-3130
Novi *(G-12504)*
Pentar Stamping Inc .... E 517 782-0700
Jackson *(G-8984)*
▼ Permaloc Corporation .... F 616 399-9600
Holland *(G-8162)*
Pinconning Metals Inc .... G 989 879-3144
Pinconning *(G-13064)*
▲ Pinnacle Tool Incorporated .... E 616 257-2700
Wyoming *(G-18899)*
Precision Parts Holdings Inc .... A 248 853-9010
Rochester Hills *(G-14088)*
Precision Prototype & Mfg Inc .... F 517 663-4114
Eaton Rapids *(G-4967)*
Precision Stamping Co Inc .... E 517 546-5656
Howell *(G-8500)*
Premier Prototype Inc .... E 586 323-6114
Sterling Heights *(G-16132)*
Press-Way Inc .... E 586 790-3324
Clinton Township *(G-3325)*
Pro Stamp Plus LLC .... G 616 447-2988
Grand Rapids *(G-7111)*
▲ Production Fabricators Inc .... E 231 777-3822
Muskegon *(G-11900)*
Production Spring LLC .... E 248 583-0036
Troy *(G-17318)*
Profile Inc .... E 517 224-8012
Potterville *(G-13647)*
Proos Manufacturing LLC .... C 616 454-5622
Grand Rapids *(G-7121)*

Punching Concepts Inc .... F 989 358-7070
Alpena *(G-313)*
▲ Quality Metalcraft Inc .... C 734 261-6700
Livonia *(G-10377)*
▲ Quality Tool & Stamping Co Inc .... C 231 733-2538
Muskegon *(G-11902)*
Quantum Custom Designs LLC .... E 989 293-7372
Fraser *(G-5984)*
Quigley Industries Inc .... E 248 426-8600
Farmington Hills *(G-5361)*
Quigley Manufacturing Inc .... G 248 426-8600
Farmington Hills *(G-5362)*
R E D Industries Inc .... F 248 542-2211
Hazel Park *(G-7838)*
▲ R-Bo Co Inc .... F 616 748-9733
Zeeland *(G-19076)*
Radar Mexican Investments LLC .... E 586 779-0300
Warren *(G-17992)*
Ranger Tool & Die Co .... E 989 754-1403
Saginaw *(G-14735)*
▲ Reliance Metal Products Inc .... G 734 641-3334
Westland *(G-18414)*
Reliant Industries Inc .... E 586 275-0479
Sterling Heights *(G-16146)*
Republic Die & Tool Co .... E 734 699-3400
Van Buren Twp *(G-17551)*
Rew Industries Inc .... E 586 803-1150
Shelby Township *(G-15316)*
Ridgeview Industries Inc .... B 616 453-8636
Grand Rapids *(G-7156)*
Ridgeview Industries Inc .... D 616 414-6500
Nunica *(G-12585)*
▲ Ridgeview Industries Inc .... C 616 453-8636
Grand Rapids *(G-7157)*
▲ Rj Acquisition Corp Rj USA .... E 586 268-2300
Sterling Heights *(G-16156)*
▲ Royal Flex-N-Gate Oak LLC .... B 248 549-3800
Warren *(G-17998)*
Schaller Corporation .... C 586 949-6000
Chesterfield *(G-2946)*
Schwab Industries Inc .... E 586 566-8090
Shelby Township *(G-15326)*
SDrol Metals Inc .... D 734 753-3410
New Boston *(G-12020)*
Selective Industries Inc .... D 810 765-4666
Marine City *(G-10966)*
Set Enterprises of Mi Inc .... D 586 573-3600
Sterling Heights *(G-16174)*
Silver Creek Manufacturing Inc .... F 231 798-3003
Norton Shores *(G-12330)*
Sinclair Designs & Engrg LLC .... E 877 517-0311
Albion *(G-133)*
Sintel Inc .... C 616 842-6960
Spring Lake *(G-15852)*
SOS Engineering Inc .... F 616 846-5767
Grand Haven *(G-6364)*
Specialty Tube LLC .... F 616 949-5990
Grand Rapids *(G-7214)*
Spinform Inc .... G 810 767-4660
Flint *(G-5766)*
Spirit Industries Inc .... G 517 371-7840
Lansing *(G-9740)*
◆ Stanco Metal Products Inc .... E 616 842-5000
Grand Haven *(G-6366)*
Standard Die International Inc .... E 800 838-5464
Livonia *(G-10417)*
Sterling Die & Engineering Inc .... E 586 677-0707
Macomb *(G-10637)*
Stus Welding & Fabrication .... G 616 392-8459
Holland *(G-8206)*
Style Craft Prototype Inc .... F 248 619-9048
Troy *(G-17375)*
Su-Dan Company .... C 248 754-1430
Rochester *(G-13931)*
▲ Su-Dan Company .... D 248 651-6035
Lake Orion *(G-9632)*
Synergy Prototype Stamping LLC .... E 586 961-6109
Clinton Township *(G-3370)*
Technical Stamping Inc .... G 586 948-3285
Chesterfield *(G-2954)*
Technique Inc .... D 517 789-8988
Jackson *(G-9017)*
Tenibac-Graphion Inc .... E 586 792-0150
Clinton Township *(G-3375)*
Tg Manufacturing LLC .... E 616 842-1503
Grand Rapids *(G-7255)*
Tg Manufacturing LLC .... F 616 935-7575
Byron Center *(G-2296)*
◆ Thai Summit America Corp .... D 517 548-4900
Howell *(G-8529)*

▲ Thomas Industrial Rolls Inc F 313 584-9696
Dearborn ***(G-3905)***

▲ Trans-Matic Mfg Co Inc C 616 820-2500
Holland ***(G-8225)***

Transfer Tool Systems LLC C 616 846-8510
Grand Haven ***(G-6372)***

TRW Automotive US LLC E 248 426-3901
Farmington Hills ***(G-5405)***

Uei Inc E 616 361-6093
Grand Rapids ***(G-7285)***

Ultraform Industries Inc D 586 752-4508
Bruce Twp ***(G-2185)***

Unique Tool & Mfg Co Inc E 336 498-2614
Temperance ***(G-16551)***

United Manufacturing Inc E 616 738-8888
Holland ***(G-8233)***

Universal Stamping Inc E 269 925-5300
Benton Harbor ***(G-1596)***

Usher Tool & Die Inc E 616 583-9160
Byron Center ***(G-2297)***

Van Loon Industries Inc E 586 532-8530
Shelby Township ***(G-15363)***

Van S Fabrications Inc G 810 679-2115
Croswell ***(G-3738)***

Van-Dies Engineering Inc E 586 293-1430
Fraser ***(G-6010)***

▲ Variety Die & Stamping Co D 734 426-4488
Dexter ***(G-4761)***

▲ Ventra Ionia Main LLC A 616 597-3220
Ionia ***(G-8693)***

▲ Versatube Corporation F 248 524-0299
Troy ***(G-17438)***

Vinewood Metalcraft Inc E 734 946-8733
Taylor ***(G-16486)***

Wallin Brothers Inc G 734 525-7750
Livonia ***(G-10464)***

Webasto Roof Systems Inc C 248 997-5100
Rochester Hills ***(G-14145)***

Weber Bros & White Metal Works G 269 751-5193
Hamilton ***(G-7609)***

Webster Cold Forge Co F 313 554-4500
Northville ***(G-12271)***

West Mich Auto Stl & Engrg Inc E 616 560-8198
Belding ***(G-1464)***

Western Engineered Products G 248 371-9259
Lake Orion ***(G-9638)***

▲ Wico Metal Products Company C 586 755-9600
Warren ***(G-18067)***

▲ Wolverine Metal Stamping Inc D 269 429-6600
Saint Joseph ***(G-14980)***

ZF Active Safety & Elec US LLC E 734 855-3631
Livonia ***(G-10480)***

ZF Active Safety & Elec US LLC E 586 232-7200
Washington ***(G-18092)***

◆ ZF Active Safety & Elec US LLC C 734 855-2600
Livonia ***(G-10481)***

ZF Active Safety & Elec US LLC E 586 232-7200
Washington ***(G-18093)***

Zygot Operations Limited E 810 736-2900
Flint ***(G-5799)***

3471 Electroplating, Plating, Polishing, Anodizing & Coloring

A-W Custom Chrome Inc G 586 775-2040
Eastpointe ***(G-4926)***

Able Welding Inc G 989 865-9611
Saint Charles ***(G-14800)***

Abrasive Services Incorporated G 734 941-2144
Romulus ***(G-14244)***

Abrasive Solutions LLC G 517 592-2668
Cement City ***(G-2675)***

Accurate Coating Inc G 616 452-0016
Grand Rapids ***(G-6421)***

Acme Plating Inc G 313 838-3870
Detroit ***(G-3983)***

Acorn Industries Inc E 734 261-2940
Livonia ***(G-10100)***

▲ Ajax Metal Processing Inc G 313 267-2100
Detroit ***(G-3992)***

▲ Allan Tool & Machine Co Inc D 248 585-2910
Troy ***(G-16925)***

Allied Finishing Inc C 616 698-7550
Grand Rapids ***(G-6450)***

Almond Products Inc D 616 844-1813
Spring Lake ***(G-15802)***

Alpha Metal Finishing Co F 734 426-2855
Dexter ***(G-4723)***

Aluminum Finishing Company G 269 382-4010
Kalamazoo ***(G-9112)***

◆ American Metal Restoration G 810 364-4820
Marysville ***(G-11081)***

Ano-Kal Company F 269 685-5743
Plainwell ***(G-13070)***

Apollo Plating Inc C 586 777-0070
Roseville ***(G-14374)***

ARC Services of Macomb Inc E 586 469-1600
Clinton Township ***(G-3173)***

Armorclad G 248 477-7785
Farmington Hills ***(G-5173)***

Arted Chrome Plating G 586 758-0050
Warren ***(G-17713)***

Arted Chrome Plating Inc F 313 871-3331
Detroit ***(G-4029)***

Asp Plating Company G 616 842-8080
Grand Haven ***(G-6273)***

Auto Anodics Inc E 810 984-5600
Port Huron ***(G-13455)***

Automotive Tumbling Co Inc G 313 925-7450
Detroit ***(G-4032)***

B & K Buffing Inc G 734 941-2144
Romulus ***(G-14254)***

B & L Plating Co Inc G 586 778-9300
Warren ***(G-17722)***

B and L Metal Finishing LLC G 269 767-2225
Allegan ***(G-150)***

Bar Processing Corporation F 734 243-8937
Monroe ***(G-11529)***

▲ Bar Processing Corporation C 734 782-4454
Flat Rock ***(G-5616)***

Bar Processing Corporation F 734 782-4454
Warren ***(G-17727)***

Beacon Park Finishing LLC F 248 318-4286
Roseville ***(G-14380)***

Beech & Rich Inc E 269 968-8012
Springfield ***(G-15861)***

Bellevue Proc Met Prep Inc C 313 921-1931
Detroit ***(G-4050)***

Blough Inc D 616 897-8407
Lowell ***(G-10496)***

Bopp-Busch Manufacturing Co E 989 876-7924
Au Gres ***(G-758)***

Bowers Aluminum G 269 251-8625
Springfield ***(G-15862)***

Bush Polishing Buffing LLC G 989 855-2248
Ionia ***(G-8687)***

Cadillac Plating Corporation D 586 771-9191
Warren ***(G-17748)***

Cadon Plating & Coatings LLC D 734 282-8100
Wyandotte ***(G-18813)***

Cal Grinding Inc E 906 786-8749
Escanaba ***(G-5064)***

Cds Specialty Coatings LLC G 313 300-8997
Ecorse ***(G-4981)***

▲ Cg Liquidation Incorporated E 586 575-9800
Warren ***(G-17752)***

Changeover Integration LLC F 231 845-5320
Ludington ***(G-10532)***

Charlotte Anodizing Pdts Inc D 517 543-1911
Charlotte ***(G-2741)***

Chemical Process Inds LLC F 248 547-5200
Madison Heights ***(G-10687)***

Chemical Processing Inc E 313 925-3400
Madison Heights ***(G-10688)***

Chor Industries Inc E 248 585-3323
Troy ***(G-17011)***

Chrome Craft Corporation C 313 868-2444
Warren ***(G-17755)***

Classic Metal Finishing Inc E 517 990-0011
Jackson ***(G-8842)***

Classic Plating Inc G 313 532-1440
Redford ***(G-13725)***

Color Coat Plating Company E 248 744-0445
Madison Heights ***(G-10695)***

Complete Automation CMF G 269 343-0500
Kalamazoo ***(G-9149)***

Complete Metal Finishing Inc F 269 343-0500
Kalamazoo ***(G-9150)***

Controlled Plating Tech Inc E 616 243-6622
Grand Rapids ***(G-6602)***

Crown Industrial Services Inc D 734 483-7270
Ypsilanti ***(G-18935)***

Crown Industrial Services Inc G 734 483-7270
Ypsilanti ***(G-18936)***

Crown Industrial Services Inc G 517 905-5300
Jackson ***(G-8858)***

Cyclone Manufacturing Inc G 269 782-9670
Dowagiac ***(G-4780)***

D & B Metal Finishing G 586 725-6056
Chesterfield ***(G-2864)***

DC Byers Co/Grand Rapids Inc F 616 538-7300
Grand Rapids ***(G-6635)***

Deburring Company E 734 542-9800
Livonia ***(G-10177)***

Detroit Chrome Inc E 313 341-9478
Detroit ***(G-4140)***

Detroit Steel Treating Company E 248 334-7436
Pontiac ***(G-13361)***

Di-Anodic Finishing Corp F 616 454-0470
Grand Rapids ***(G-6645)***

Diamond Chrome Plating Inc D 517 546-0150
Howell ***(G-8445)***

Diamond Tool Manufacturing Inc E 734 416-1900
Plymouth ***(G-13157)***

Dmi Automotive Inc F 517 548-1414
Howell ***(G-8446)***

Dn-Lawrence Industries Inc F 269 552-4999
Kalamazoo ***(G-9172)***

DNR Inc G 734 722-4000
Plymouth ***(G-13160)***

DNR Inc F 734 722-4000
Westland ***(G-18365)***

Downriver Deburring Inc G 313 388-2640
Taylor ***(G-16406)***

Dyna Plate Inc E 616 452-6763
Grand Rapids ***(G-6659)***

Eastern Oil Company E 248 333-1333
Pontiac ***(G-13364)***

ECJ Processing G 248 540-2336
Southfield ***(G-15550)***

Electro Chemical Finishing Co D 616 531-1250
Grand Rapids ***(G-6669)***

Electro Chemical Finishing Co F 616 531-0670
Grandville ***(G-7372)***

Electro-Plating Service Inc F 248 541-0035
Madison Heights ***(G-10719)***

Electroplating Industries Inc F 586 469-2390
Clinton Township ***(G-3230)***

Empire Hardchrome G 810 392-3122
Richmond ***(G-13837)***

▲ Erbsloeh Alum Solutions Inc B 269 323-2565
Portage ***(G-13558)***

Expert Coating Company Inc F 616 453-8261
Grand Rapids ***(G-6693)***

Fini Finish Metal Finishing F 586 758-0050
Warren ***(G-17806)***

▲ Finishing Services Inc D 734 484-1700
Ypsilanti ***(G-18945)***

Finishing Touch Inc E 517 542-5581
Litchfield ***(G-10077)***

▲ Fintex LLC E 734 946-3100
Romulus ***(G-14276)***

▲ Fire-Rite Inc E 313 273-3730
Detroit ***(G-4234)***

Fitzgerald Finishing LLC D 313 368-3630
Detroit ***(G-4235)***

Flat Rock Metal Inc C 734 782-4454
Flat Rock ***(G-5618)***

Flexible Controls Corporation E 313 368-3630
Detroit ***(G-4237)***

Garys Polishing G 810 621-4137
Lennon ***(G-9994)***

Gj Prey Coml & Indus Pntg Cov G 248 250-4792
Clawson ***(G-3098)***

Gladwin Metal Processing Inc G 989 426-9038
Gladwin ***(G-6198)***

Gokoh Coldwater Incorporated F 517 279-1080
Coldwater ***(G-3434)***

Grand Rapids Polsg & Buffing E 616 241-2233
Grand Rapids ***(G-6766)***

Grand Rapids Stripping Co G 616 361-0794
Grand Rapids ***(G-6770)***

Grand River Polishing Co Corp E 616 846-1420
Spring Lake ***(G-15818)***

Great Lakes Finishing Inc F 231 733-9566
Muskegon ***(G-11830)***

Great Lakes Metal Finshg LLC D 517 764-1335
Jackson ***(G-8896)***

Hayes-Albion Corporation F 517 629-2141
Jackson ***(G-8900)***

High Prfmce Met Finshg Inc F 269 327-8897
Portage ***(G-13565)***

Highpoint Finshg Solutions Inc D 616 772-4425
Zeeland ***(G-19036)***

Honhart Mid-Nite Black Co F 248 588-1515
Troy ***(G-17148)***

Hpc Holdings Inc E 248 634-9361
Holly ***(G-8277)***

Hpc Holdings Inc E 810 714-9213
Fenton ***(G-5485)***

S
I
C

Employee Codes: A=Over 500 employees, B=251-500
C=101-250, D=51-100, E=20-50, F=10-19, G=3-9

2022 Harris Michigan
Industrial Directory

825

34 FABRICATED METAL PRODUCTS, EXCEPT MACHINERY AND TRANSPORTATION EQUIPMENT

Ihc Inc..C 313 535-3210
  Detroit *(G-4313)*
Impact Operations LLC ....F 616 642-9570
  Saranac *(G-15078)*
International Paint Stripping ....F 734 942-0500
  Romulus *(G-14286)*
International Paint Stripping ....F 734 942-0500
  Romulus *(G-14287)*
Jackson Tumble Finish Corp ....E 517 787-0368
  Jackson *(G-8918)*
▲ JD Plating Company Inc ....E 248 547-5200
  Madison Heights *(G-10753)*
Jo-Mar Enterprises Inc ....G 313 365-9200
  Detroit *(G-4338)*
Kalamazoo Metal Finishers Inc ....F 269 382-1611
  Kalamazoo *(G-9242)*
Kalamazoo Stripping Derusting ....F 269 323-1340
  Portage *(G-13572)*
◆ KC Jones Plating Co ....E 586 755-4900
  Warren *(G-17892)*
KC Jones Plating Co ....E 248 399-8500
  Hazel Park *(G-7827)*
▲ Keen Point International Inc ....E 248 340-8732
  Auburn Hills *(G-950)*
Kenwal Pickling LLC ....E 313 739-1040
  Dearborn *(G-3857)*
Kepco Inc ....F 269 649-5800
  Vicksburg *(G-17607)*
Kriseler Welding Inc ....G 989 624-9266
  Birch Run *(G-1708)*
Lacks Industries Inc ....C 616 698-9852
  Grand Rapids *(G-6918)*
Lansing Plating Company ....G 517 485-6915
  Lansing *(G-9711)*
Lawrence Surface Tech Inc ....G 248 609-9001
  Troy *(G-17206)*
Liberty Burnishing Co ....G 313 366-7878
  Detroit *(G-4397)*
Mann Metal Finishing Inc ....D 269 621-6359
  Hartford *(G-7765)*
Margate Industries Inc ....G 810 387-4300
  Yale *(G-18919)*
▲ Marsh Plating Corporation ....D 734 483-5767
  Ypsilanti *(G-18965)*
Martin and Hattie Rasche Inc ....D 616 245-1223
  Grand Rapids *(G-6962)*
Master Finish Co 877 590-5819
  Grand Rapids *(G-6965)*
▲ Material Sciences Corporation ....F 734 207-4444
  Canton *(G-2490)*
Matthews Plating Inc ....E 517 784-3535
  Jackson *(G-8946)*
McGean-Rohco Inc ....E 216 441-4900
  Livonia *(G-10306)*
McNichols Polsg & Anodizing ....F 313 538-3470
  Redford *(G-13744)*
McNichols Polsg & Anodizing ....G 313 538-3470
  Redford *(G-13745)*
Metal Finishing Technology ....G 231 733-9736
  Muskegon *(G-11869)*
Metal Prep Technology Inc ....G 313 843-2890
  Dearborn *(G-3870)*
Michigan Plating LLC ....G 248 544-3500
  Hazel Park *(G-7832)*
▲ Micro Platers Sales Inc ....E 313 865-2293
  Detroit *(G-4454)*
Mid-Michigan Industries Inc ....D 989 773-6918
  Mount Pleasant *(G-11715)*
Mid-Michigan Industries Inc ....E 989 386-7707
  Clare *(G-2986)*
Mid-State Plating Co Inc ....E 810 767-1622
  Flint *(G-5733)*
Midwest II Inc ....C 734 856-5200
  Ottawa Lake *(G-12808)*
Midwest Plating Company Inc ....E 616 451-2007
  Grand Rapids *(G-7005)*
Modern Hard Chrome Service Co ....F 586 445-0330
  Grosse Pointe Farms *(G-7538)*
Muskegon Industrial Finishng ....G 231 733-7663
  Muskegon *(G-11881)*
Mvc Holdings LLC ....F 586 491-2600
  Roseville *(G-14450)*
National Galvanizing LP ....A 734 243-1882
  Monroe *(G-11567)*
National Zinc Processors Inc ....F 269 926-1161
  Benton Harbor *(G-1577)*
New Life Cop Brass Mint Free M ....G 586 725-3286
  Casco *(G-2601)*
▼ Non-Ferrous Cast Alloys Inc ....D 231 799-0550
  Norton Shores *(G-12318)*

Nor-Cote Inc ....E 586 756-1200
  Warren *(G-17944)*
Norbrook Plating Inc ....E 586 755-4110
  Warren *(G-17945)*
Norbrook Plating Inc ....G 313 369-9304
  Detroit *(G-4488)*
Northwest Fabrication Inc ....G 231 536-3229
  East Jordan *(G-4878)*
Oliver Industries Inc ....E 586 977-7750
  Sterling Heights *(G-16120)*
▲ Patmai Company Inc ....E 586 294-0370
  Fraser *(G-5975)*
Pearson Auto Service Inc ....G 313 538-6870
  Detroit *(G-4509)*
Perfection Industries Inc ....E 313 272-4040
  Detroit *(G-4518)*
Pfg Enterprises Inc ....E 586 755-1053
  Chesterfield *(G-2924)*
Pioneer Metal Finishing LLC ....D 734 384-9000
  Monroe *(G-11569)*
▲ Pioneer Metal Finishing LLC ....G 877 721-1100
  Warren *(G-17965)*
Plating Products Consulta ....E 586 755-7210
  Warren *(G-17967)*
Plating Specialties Inc ....F 248 547-8660
  Madison Heights *(G-10802)*
Plating Specialties Inc ....E 248 547-8660
  Madison Heights *(G-10803)*
Plating Technologies ....E 586 756-1825
  Warren *(G-17968)*
Plymouth Plating Works Inc ....F 734 453-1560
  Plymouth *(G-13267)*
Port City Industrial Finishing ....E 231 726-4288
  Muskegon *(G-11894)*
Ppi LLC ....E 586 772-7736
  Warren *(G-17971)*
Precision Finishing Co Inc ....F 616 245-2255
  Grand Rapids *(G-7099)*
Premier Finishing Inc ....E 616 785-3070
  Grand Rapids *(G-7102)*
Production Tube Company Inc ....G 313 259-3990
  Detroit *(G-4537)*
Professional Metal Finishers ....E 616 365-2620
  Grand Rapids *(G-7114)*
Prs Manufacturing Inc ....G 616 784-4409
  Grand Rapids *(G-7124)*
Qmi Group Inc ....F 248 589-0505
  Madison Heights *(G-10814)*
Quali Tone Corporation ....F 269 426-3664
  Sawyer *(G-15111)*
Richcoat LLC ....E 586 978-1311
  Sterling Heights *(G-16150)*
Robert & Son Black Ox Special ....E 586 778-7633
  Roseville *(G-14471)*
Ryan Polishing Corporation ....E 248 548-6832
  Oak Park *(G-12643)*
Sac Legacy Company LLC ....D 517 750-2903
  Chelsea *(G-2825)*
Schwartz Boiler Shop Inc ....E 231 627-2556
  Cheboygan *(G-2798)*
Seaver Industrial Finishing Co ....D 616 842-8560
  Grand Haven *(G-6359)*
Selfridge Plating Inc ....E 586 469-3141
  Harrison Township *(G-7724)*
Shields Acquisition Co Inc ....E 734 782-4454
  Flat Rock *(G-5629)*
◆ Sigma International Inc ....F 248 230-9681
  Livonia *(G-10408)*
Sodus Hard Chrome Inc ....E 269 925-2077
  Sodus *(G-15394)*
South Haven Finishing Inc ....E 269 637-2047
  South Haven *(G-15413)*
Spec Abrasives and Finishing ....F 231 722-1926
  Muskegon *(G-11924)*
▲ Spectrum Industries Inc ....D 616 451-0784
  Springfield *(G-7216)*
Spencer Zdanowitz Inc ....E 517 841-9380
  Jackson *(G-9012)*
Ss Stripping ....G 586 268-5799
  Sterling Heights *(G-16187)*
Superior Mtal Finshg Rustproof ....F 313 893-1050
  Detroit *(G-4617)*
Supreme Media Blasting and Pow ....G 586 792-7705
  Clinton Township *(G-3366)*
Surface Activation Tech LLC ....G 248 273-0037
  Troy *(G-17381)*
Tawas Plating Company ....E 989 362-2011
  Tawas City *(G-16372)*
Technickel Inc ....F 269 926-8505
  Benton Harbor *(G-1591)*

Togreencleancom ....G 269 428-4812
  Stevensville *(G-16268)*
Tri K Cylinder Service Inc ....G 269 965-3981
  Springfield *(G-15877)*
Troy Laboratories Inc ....F 248 652-6000
  Rochester *(G-13935)*
Tru-Coat Inc ....G 810 785-3331
  Montrose *(G-11608)*
Ultraseal America Inc ....G 734 222-9478
  Ann Arbor *(G-703)*
USA Quality Metal Finshg LLC ....G 269 427-9000
  Lawrence *(G-9986)*
V & V Inc ....E 616 842-8611
  Grand Haven *(G-6377)*
Vacuum Orna Metal Company Inc ....E 734 941-9100
  Romulus *(G-14336)*
W A Thomas Company ....G 734 955-6500
  Taylor *(G-16487)*
Western Engineered Products ....E 248 371-9259
  Lake Orion *(G-9638)*
Williams Diversified Inc ....E 734 421-6100
  Livonia *(G-10475)*
Williams Finishing Inc ....E 734 421-6100
  Livonia *(G-10476)*
▲ Wolverine Plating Corporation ....E 586 771-5000
  Roseville *(G-14496)*
WSi Industrial Services Inc ....E 734 942-9300
  Riverview *(G-13884)*
Zav-Tech Metal Finishing ....G 269 422-2559
  Stevensville *(G-16271)*

3479 Coating & Engraving, NEC

A & K Finishing Inc ....F 616 949-9100
  Grand Rapids *(G-6407)*
A1 Powder Coating ....G 616 238-0683
  Grand Rapids *(G-6413)*
A2z Coating ....G 616 805-3281
  Grand Rapids *(G-6414)*
Aactron Inc ....E 248 543-6740
  Madison Heights *(G-10655)*
AB Custom Fabricating LLC ....F 269 663-8100
  Edwardsburg *(G-4998)*
Able Machine Tooling ....G 586 783-7776
  Harrison Twp *(G-7737)*
▲ Act Test Panels LLC ....E 517 439-1485
  Hillsdale *(G-7921)*
Action Asphalt LLC ....F 734 449-8565
  Brighton *(G-1937)*
▲ Ajax Metal Processing Inc ....G 313 267-2100
  Detroit *(G-3992)*
All-Cote Coatings Company LLC ....G 586 427-0062
  Center Line *(G-2678)*
Almond Products Inc ....D 616 844-1813
  Spring Lake *(G-15802)*
Alpha Coatings Inc ....F 734 523-9000
  Livonia *(G-10110)*
American Porcelain Enamel Co ....F 231 744-3013
  Muskegon *(G-11770)*
Anchor Bay Powder Coat LLC ....F 586 725-3255
  New Baltimore *(G-11978)*
Apex Powder Coating LLC ....G 734 921-3177
  Taylor *(G-16381)*
Applied Coatings Solutions LLC ....G 269 341-9757
  Kalamazoo *(G-9115)*
Aristo-Cote Inc ....D 586 447-9049
  Shelby Township *(G-15172)*
Aristo-Cote Inc ....D 586 447-9049
  Fraser *(G-5896)*
Aristo-Cote Inc ....E 586 447-9049
  Harrison Township *(G-7688)*
B & J Enmeling Inc A Mich Corp ....F 313 365-6620
  Detroit *(G-4040)*
Baron Acquisition LLC ....E 248 585-0444
  Madison Heights *(G-10679)*
Beech & Rich Inc ....E 269 968-8012
  Springfield *(G-15861)*
Bio-Vac Inc ....E 248 350-2150
  Southfield *(G-15508)*
Bolyea Industries ....F 586 293-8600
  Fraser *(G-5906)*
▲ Boss Electro Static Inc ....E 616 575-0577
  Wyoming *(G-18854)*
▲ Burkard Industries Inc ....E 586 791-6520
  Clinton Township *(G-3191)*
C & M Coatings Inc ....F 616 842-1925
  Grand Haven *(G-6282)*
▼ Cadillac Oil Company ....E 313 365-6200
  Detroit *(G-4085)*
Carbide Surface Company ....G 586 465-6110
  Clinton Township *(G-3194)*

SIC SECTION34 FABRICATED METAL PRODUCTS, EXCEPT MACHINERY AND TRANSPORTATION EQUIPMENT34 FABRICATED METAL PROD-

Cast Coatings Inc.................E....... 269 545-8373
Galien *(G-6087)*
Centennial Coatings LLC.................E....... 616 748-9410
Zeeland *(G-19003)*
Cg Liquidation Incorporated.................D....... 586 803-1000
Shelby Township *(G-15185)*
▲ **Cg Liquidation Incorporated**.................E....... 586 575-9800
Warren *(G-17752)*
Changeover Integration LLC.................F....... 231 845-5320
Ludington *(G-10532)*
Chemical Processing Inc.................E....... 313 925-3400
Madison Heights *(G-10688)*
Chieftain Coating LLC.................E....... 586 791-1866
Clinton Township *(G-3198)*
Coatings Plus Inc.................E....... 616 451-2427
Grand Rapids *(G-6577)*
Coles Custom Con Coatings LLC.................G....... 231 651-0709
Beulah *(G-1653)*
Color Factory.................G....... 810 577-2974
Flushing *(G-5806)*
Commercial Coating Systems LLC.................G....... 616 490-6242
Cedar Springs *(G-2646)*
▲ **Commercial Steel Treating Corp**.................C....... 248 588-3300
Madison Heights *(G-10696)*
Conformance Coatings Prototype.................F....... 810 364-4333
Marysville *(G-11084)*
Corlin Company.................G....... 616 842-7093
Grand Haven *(G-6290)*
Cox Brothers Machining Inc.................E....... 517 796-4662
Jackson *(G-8855)*
Crm Inc.................D....... 231 947-0304
Traverse City *(G-16665)*
Crown Group Co.................D....... 313 922-8433
Eastpointe *(G-4934)*
Crown Group Co.................B....... 586 575-9800
Troy *(G-17035)*
Csquared Innovations Inc.................F....... 734 998-8330
Novi *(G-12388)*
Cushion Lrry Trphies Engrv LLC.................G....... 517 332-1667
Lansing *(G-9827)*
Custom Coating Tech Inc.................G....... 734 442-4074
Taylor *(G-16397)*
Custom Coating Technologies.................G....... 734 244-3610
Flat Rock *(G-5617)*
Custom Powder Coating LLC.................G....... 616 454-9730
Grand Rapids *(G-6622)*
▲ **Dag Ltd LLC**.................F....... 586 276-9310
Sterling Heights *(G-15979)*
▼ **Decc Company Inc**.................E....... 616 245-0431
Grand Rapids *(G-6638)*
Decorative Finishes Division.................G....... 616 450-4918
Grand Rapids *(G-6640)*
▲ **Depor Industries Inc**.................G....... 248 362-3900
Troy *(G-17056)*
Detroit Laser Co LLC.................G....... 313 338-9494
Farmington Hills *(G-5214)*
▲ **Detroit Name Plate Etching Inc**.................E....... 248 543-5200
Ferndale *(G-5547)*
Done Right Engraving Inc.................G....... 248 332-3133
Pontiac *(G-13362)*
Double Eagle Steel Coating Co.................C....... 313 203-9800
Dearborn *(G-3831)*
Douglas Corp.................E....... 517 767-4112
Tekonsha *(G-16522)*
▲ **Dunnage Engineering Inc**.................E....... 810 229-9501
Brighton *(G-1979)*
Duraflex Coatings LLC.................G....... 586 855-1087
Shelby Township *(G-15215)*
Eagle Powder Coating.................G....... 517 784-2556
Jackson *(G-8872)*
Eastside Coatings.................G....... 313 936-1000
Saint Clair Shores *(G-14855)*
Ecology Coatings.................G....... 248 370-9900
Auburn Hills *(G-874)*
Electro Chemical Finishing Co.................F....... 616 531-0670
Grandville *(G-7372)*
Engineered Prfmce Coatings Inc.................G....... 616 988-7927
Grand Rapids *(G-6680)*
Evans Coatings L L C.................G....... 248 583-9890
Troy *(G-17099)*
Exclusive Imagery Inc.................G....... 248 436-2999
Royal Oak *(G-14536)*
Expert Coating Company Inc.................F....... 616 453-8261
Grand Rapids *(G-6693)*
Express Coat Corporation.................E....... 586 773-2682
Warren *(G-17800)*
Fastener Coatings Inc.................F....... 269 279-5134
Three Rivers *(G-16572)*
Finishers Unlimited Monroe Inc.................E....... 734 243-3502
Monroe *(G-11540)*
▲ **Finishing Services Inc**.................D....... 734 484-1700
Ypsilanti *(G-18945)*
Flying Pig Coatings LLC.................G....... 616 947-1118
Grand Rapids *(G-6714)*
Fricia Enterprises Inc.................G....... 586 977-1900
Sterling Heights *(G-16023)*
Gannons General Contract.................G....... 734 429-5859
Saline *(G-15018)*
Gladwin Metal Processing Inc.................G....... 989 426-9038
Gladwin *(G-6198)*
Glw Finishing.................E....... 616 395-0112
Holland *(G-8052)*
Godfrey & Wing Inc.................G....... 330 562-1440
Saginaw *(G-14654)*
Grand Haven Powder Coating Inc.................E....... 616 850-8822
Grand Haven *(G-6304)*
Great Lakes Powder Coating LLC.................F....... 248 522-6222
Walled Lake *(G-17669)*
Gt Performance Coatings LLC.................F....... 248 627-5905
Ortonville *(G-12748)*
Gyro Powder Coating Inc.................F....... 616 846-2580
Grand Haven *(G-6311)*
H & H Powdercoating Inc.................F....... 810 750-1800
Fenton *(G-5483)*
H & J Mfg Consulting Svcs Corp.................G....... 734 941-8314
Romulus *(G-14282)*
HB Fuller Co.................G....... 248 585-2200
Taylor *(G-16425)*
Hi-Tech Coatings Inc.................E....... 586 759-3559
Warren *(G-17853)*
Hice and Summey Inc.................F....... 269 651-6217
Bronson *(G-2116)*
▲ **Hj Manufacturing Inc**.................F....... 906 233-1500
Escanaba *(G-5076)*
Hope Network West Michigan.................E....... 231 796-4801
Paris *(G-12934)*
◆ **Howmet Corporation**.................E....... 231 894-5686
Whitehall *(G-18501)*
▲ **Howmet Holdings Corporation**.................G....... 231 894-5686
Whitehall *(G-18506)*
I S P Coatings Corp.................F....... 586 752-5020
Romeo *(G-14226)*
Imagecraft.................G....... 517 750-0077
Jackson *(G-8907)*
Instacote Inc.................G....... 734 847-5260
Erie *(G-5048)*
Integricoat Inc.................E....... 616 935-7878
Spring Lake *(G-15826)*
▲ **Ionbond LLC**.................D....... 248 398-9100
Madison Heights *(G-10748)*
Jackson Industrial Coating Svc.................G....... 517 782-8169
Jackson *(G-8915)*
Jandron II.................G....... 906 225-9600
Marquette *(G-11024)*
Jbl Enterprises.................G....... 616 530-8647
Grand Rapids *(G-6863)*
Jbs Coating.................F....... 231 366-7159
Fruitport *(G-6064)*
▲ **JD Plating Company Inc**.................E....... 248 547-5200
Madison Heights *(G-10753)*
Joseph M Hoffman Inc.................F....... 586 774-8500
Roseville *(G-14428)*
Kalb & Associates Inc.................E....... 586 949-2735
Chesterfield *(G-2899)*
◆ **KC Jones Plating Co**.................E....... 586 755-4900
Warren *(G-17892)*
Kencoat Comp.................G....... 586 754-1400
Clinton Township *(G-3272)*
Kentwood Powder Coat Inc.................E....... 616 698-8181
Grand Rapids *(G-6891)*
◆ **Knape Industries Inc**.................E....... 616 866-1651
Rockford *(G-14174)*
Lakeshore Custom Powdr Coating.................G....... 616 296-9330
Grand Haven *(G-6327)*
Langley Powder Coating.................G....... 989 739-5203
Oscoda *(G-12764)*
Lasers Plus LLC.................G....... 734 926-1030
Holt *(G-8316)*
Liberty Bell Powdr Coating LLC.................G....... 586 557-6328
Highland *(G-7894)*
Lincoln Industries.................G....... 989 736-6421
Lincoln *(G-10036)*
Locpac Inc.................E....... 734 453-2300
Plymouth *(G-13226)*
▲ **Magni Group Inc**.................F....... 248 647-4500
Birmingham *(G-1735)*
Magnum Powder Coating Inc.................G....... 616 785-3155
Comstock Park *(G-3621)*
March Coatings Inc.................D....... 810 229-6464
Brighton *(G-2024)*
Martin Powder Coating.................G....... 517 625-4220
Perry *(G-12979)*
Martin Products Company Inc.................G....... 269 651-1721
Sturgis *(G-16304)*
Master Coat LLC.................G....... 734 405-2340
Westland *(G-18393)*
Master Mix Company.................G....... 734 487-7870
Ypsilanti *(G-18966)*
▲ **Material Sciences Corporation**.................F....... 734 207-4444
Canton *(G-2490)*
Matrix Mtlcraft LLP A Ltd Prtn.................G....... 248 724-1800
Auburn Hills *(G-970)*
Mdm Enterprises Inc.................F....... 616 452-1591
Grand Rapids *(G-6974)*
Metal Finishing Technology.................G....... 231 733-9736
Muskegon *(G-11869)*
Metro Powder Coating.................G....... 313 744-7134
Detroit *(G-4437)*
Michigan Machining Inc.................G....... 810 686-6655
Mount Morris *(G-11675)*
Michigan Metal Coatings Co.................D....... 810 966-9240
Port Huron *(G-13501)*
Mid McHigan Indus Coatings LLC.................G....... 989 441-1277
Weidman *(G-18257)*
Midland Silicon Company LLC.................F....... 248 674-3736
Waterford *(G-18137)*
Midwest Products Finshg Co Inc.................D....... 734 856-5200
Ottawa Lake *(G-12809)*
Mirrage Ltd.................G....... 734 697-6447
Van Buren Twp *(G-17540)*
Modineer Coatings Division.................F....... 269 925-0702
Benton Harbor *(G-1574)*
Monarch Powder Coating Inc.................G....... 231 798-1422
Norton Shores *(G-12312)*
▼ **Motor City Metal Fab Inc**.................E....... 734 345-1001
Taylor *(G-16450)*
Nano Materials & Processes Inc.................G....... 248 529-3873
Milford *(G-11475)*
National Indus Sp Coatings LLC.................F....... 989 894-8538
Sanford *(G-15074)*
▲ **ND Industries Inc**.................C....... 248 288-0000
Clawson *(G-3101)*
Neptune Coating Services.................G....... 616 403-9034
Zeeland *(G-19060)*
New Age Coatings.................G....... 248 217-1842
Pontiac *(G-13401)*
Nof Metal Coatings North Amer.................G....... 248 617-3033
New Hudson *(G-12065)*
Normic Industries Inc.................E....... 231 947-8860
Traverse City *(G-16771)*
▲ **Oakwood Energy Management Inc**.................F....... 734 947-7700
Taylor *(G-16453)*
Oerlikon Blzers Cating USA Inc.................E....... 248 409-5900
Lake Orion *(G-9625)*
Oerlikon Blzers Cating USA Inc.................G....... 989 463-6268
Alma *(G-251)*
Oerlikon Blzers Cating USA Inc.................E....... 586 465-0412
Harrison Township *(G-7713)*
On The Side Sign Dsign Grphics.................G....... 810 266-7446
Byron *(G-2255)*
P C S Companies Inc.................G....... 616 754-2229
Greenville *(G-7504)*
Paint Work Incorporated.................F....... 586 759-6640
Warren *(G-17952)*
PDM Industries Inc.................E....... 231 943-9601
Traverse City *(G-16786)*
Peninsula Powder Coating Inc.................E....... 906 353-7234
Baraga *(G-1146)*
Performcoat of Michigan LLC.................F....... 269 282-7030
Springfield *(G-15874)*
Permacoat Inc.................G....... 313 388-7798
Allen Park *(G-202)*
Plasma-Tec Inc.................E....... 616 455-2593
Holland *(G-8166)*
Plasti - Paint Inc.................E....... 989 285-2280
Saint Louis *(G-14995)*
Powco Inc.................F....... 269 646-5385
Marcellus *(G-10951)*
▲ **Powder Cote II Inc**.................C....... 586 463-7040
Mount Clemens *(G-11653)*
Powder Cote II Inc.................G....... 586 463-7040
Mount Clemens *(G-11654)*
Pre-Cut Patterns.................G....... 616 392-4415
Holland *(G-8168)*
Precision Coatings Inc.................D....... 248 363-8361
Commerce Township *(G-3564)*
Prestige Coating Solutions.................G....... 248 402-3732
Sterling Heights *(G-16133)*
Prestige Powder Coating.................G....... 616 401-0250
Caledonia *(G-2393)*

SIC

Employee Codes: A=Over 500 employees, B=251-500
C=101-250, D=51-100, E=20-50, F=10-19, G=3-9
2022 Harris Michigan
Industrial Directory
827

▲ Pro - Tech Graphics Ltd.................F........586 791-6363
    Clinton Township (G-3328)
Pro-Finish Powder Coating Inc............E........616 245-7550
    Grand Rapids (G-7112)
Progressive Cutter Grinding Co...........G........586 580-2367
    Shelby Township (G-15309)
Pti Qlity Cntnment Sltions LLC...........C........313 365-3999
    Detroit (G-4541)
Quali Tone Corporation.....................F........269 426-3664
    Sawyer (G-15111)
Quality Business Engraving................G........248 852-5123
    Rochester Hills (G-14094)
Quality Coatings...............................G........517 294-0394
    Fowlerville (G-5852)
Rapid Coating Solutions Llc...............G........586 255-7142
    Sterling Heights (G-16142)
Rcd Quality Coatings..........................G........313 575-8125
    Redford (G-13763)
Reliance Finishing Co.........................D........616 241-4436
    Grand Rapids (G-7148)
Reliance Plastisol Coating Co.............F........616 245-2297
    Grand Rapids (G-7149)
Richcoat LLC....................................F........586 978-1311
    Sterling Heights (G-16150)
Richter Precision Inc........................E........586 465-0500
    Fraser (G-5989)
Royal Oak Name Plate Company........G........586 774-8500
    Roseville (G-14473)
S&G Group LLC................................G........616 719-3124
    Grand Rapids (G-7177)
▲ Sas Global Corporation..................C........248 414-4470
    Warren (G-18002)
Schmidt Grinding..............................G........269 649-4604
    Vicksburg (G-17612)
Schroth Enterprises Inc......................E........586 759-4240
    Grosse Pointe Farms (G-7540)
Seaver Finishing Inc..........................E........616 844-8566
    Grand Haven (G-6358)
Seaver Industrial Finishing Co...........D........616 842-8560
    Grand Haven (G-6359)
Seaver-Smith Inc.............................E........616 842-8560
    Grand Haven (G-6360)
Serviscreen Inc................................D........616 669-1640
    Jenison (G-9071)
Simmons Crtrght Plstic Cntngs L........G........616 365-0045
    Grand Rapids (G-7200)
Simply Custom..................................G........734 558-4051
    Wyandotte (G-18839)
Skop Powder Coating........................G........231 881-9909
    Petoskey (G-13024)
Spartan Steel Coating LLC................D........734 289-5400
    Monroe (G-11574)
▲ Spectrum Industries Inc................D........616 451-0784
    Grand Rapids (G-7216)
▲ Spraytek Inc.................................F........248 546-3551
    Ferndale (G-5586)
◆ Star Cutter Co..............................E........248 474-8200
    Farmington Hills (G-5387)
Stechschulte/Wegerly AG LLC............D........586 739-0101
    Sterling Heights (G-16190)
Steplen Coatings LLC.......................G........810 653-6418
    Davison (G-3798)
◆ Straits Steel and Wire Company......D........231 843-3416
    Ludington (G-10551)
Sun Plastics Coating Company............F........734 453-0822
    Plymouth (G-13305)
Superior Collision Inc........................G........231 946-4983
    Traverse City (G-16846)
Superior Mtal Finshg Rustproof............F........313 893-1050
    Detroit (G-4617)
Sure-Weld & Plating Rack Co.............G........248 304-9430
    Southfield (G-15714)
Tawas Powder Coating Inc.................E........989 362-2011
    Tawas City (G-16373)
Techno-Coat Inc..............................C........616 396-6446
    Holland (G-8213)
▲ Thierica Inc.................................D........616 458-1538
    Grand Rapids (G-7257)
Three Oaks Engraving & Engrg............G........269 469-2124
    Three Oaks (G-16559)
Ti-Coating Inc................................E........586 726-1900
    Shelby Township (G-15351)
Tlr Coatings.....................................G........269 870-3083
    Scotts (G-15134)
Todd R Lrcque Pntg Wllcvring L.........G........989 252-9424
    Freeland (G-6030)
Toefco Engineering Inc......................E........269 683-0188
    Niles (G-12171)
Traction Tech Holdings LLC...............E........313 923-0400
    Detroit (G-4642)

Unicote Corporation..........................E........586 296-0700
    Fraser (G-6008)
Universal Coating Inc........................D........810 785-7555
    Flint (G-5788)
Universal Coating Technology.............G........616 847-6036
    Grand Haven (G-6375)
V & S Detroit Galvanizing LLC............E........313 535-2600
    Redford (G-13782)
Varners Pwr Coating & Sndblst..........G........517 448-3425
    Hudson (G-8563)
Vergason Technology Inc...................G........248 568-0120
    Rochester (G-13937)
Voigt Schwtzer Galvanizers Inc..........G........313 535-2600
    Redford (G-13784)
Volcor Finishing Inc..........................G........616 527-5555
    Ionia (G-8694)
Wealthy Street Corporation...............C........800 222-8116
    Belding (G-1463)
Wealthy Street Corporation...............E........616 451-0784
    Grand Rapids (G-7326)
West Michigan Coating LLC................E........616 647-9509
    Grand Rapids (G-7333)
West Michigan GL Coatings Inc..........G........616 970-4863
    Grand Rapids (G-7334)
Westside Powder Coat LLC................G........734 729-1667
    Romulus (G-14337)
Whites Industrial Service...................G........616 291-3706
    Lowell (G-10523)
▲ X-Cel Industries Inc......................C........248 226-6000
    Southfield (G-15744)
Yale Tool & Engraving Inc.................G........734 459-7171
    Plymouth (G-13340)
▲ Z Technologies Corporation...........E........313 937-0710
    Redford (G-13787)

3482 Small Arms Ammunition

Bold Ammo & Guns Inc....................G........616 826-0913
    Rockford (G-14158)
Boss Outdoors LLC..........................G........269 465-3631
    Bridgman (G-1922)
Brass Kings Inc..............................G........248 674-1860
    Manton (G-10930)
DLM Holding Group LLC....................G........269 465-3631
    Bridgman (G-1925)
Kenneth David Kent.........................G........906 475-7036
    Negaunee (G-11969)
Lairds Custom Cabinetry Inc..............G........810 494-5164
    Brighton (G-2020)
Oakland Tactical Supply LLC.............G........810 991-1436
    Howell (G-8488)
On The Mark Inc.............................G........989 317-8033
    Mount Pleasant (G-11729)
▲ Sage Control Ordnance Inc............E........989 739-2200
    Oscoda (G-12771)
Scorpion Reloads LLC.......................G........586 214-3843
    Fraser (G-5991)
Tactical Simplicity LLC......................G........248 410-4523
    Wixom (G-18765)

3483 Ammunition, Large

Bliss Munitions Equipment.................G........269 953-6655
    Hastings (G-7782)

3484 Small Arms

Aerospace America Inc......................E........989 684-2121
    Bay City (G-1319)
▲ Crl Inc..E........906 428-3710
    Gladstone (G-6177)
Kirtland Products LLC.......................F........231 582-7505
    Boyne City (G-1893)
Larson Tactical Arms........................G........906 204-8228
    Ishpeming (G-8778)
Manly Innovations LLC....................G........734 548-0200
    Chelsea (G-2820)
Oakland Tactical Supply LLC.............G........810 991-1436
    Howell (G-8488)
Pierce Engineers Inc........................G........517 321-5051
    Lansing (G-9727)
Rs Products LLC..............................G........801 722-9746
    Chesterfield (G-2941)
Sage International Limited................F........989 739-7000
    Oscoda (G-12772)
Timers Enterprises LLC.....................G........517 617-3092
    Reading (G-13707)

3489 Ordnance & Access, NEC

Autoneum North America Inc............G........248 848-0100
    Farmington Hills (G-5176)

Camdex Inc......................................G........248 528-2300
    Troy (G-16996)
▲ Lanzen Incorporated....................E........586 771-7070
    Bruce Twp (G-2174)
Plead Arms LLC...............................G........248 563-1822
    Troy (G-17307)
Walter Jerome Lelo..........................G........989 274-8895
    Bridgeport (G-1919)

3491 Industrial Valves

▲ Armstrong International Inc..........C........269 273-1415
    Three Rivers (G-16567)
Asco LP...C........810 648-9141
    Sandusky (G-15054)
Asco LP...C........248 596-3200
    Novi (G-12365)
▲ Automatic Valve Corp...................E........248 474-6761
    Novi (G-12370)
▲ Century Instrument Company........E........734 427-0340
    Livonia (G-10152)
Champion Charter Sls & Svc Inc........E........906 779-2300
    Iron Mountain (G-8719)
▲ Conley Composites LLC...............E........918 299-5051
    Grand Rapids (G-6594)
Dss Valve Products Inc....................E........269 340-7303
    Niles (G-12126)
Ecorse McHy Sls & Rbldrs Inc............E........313 383-2100
    Wyandotte (G-18817)
Fcx Performance Inc........................E........734 654-2201
    Carleton (G-2553)
Flaretite Inc....................................G........810 750-4140
    Brighton (G-1990)
Flowtek Inc.....................................F........231 734-3415
    Kalkaska (G-9388)
▲ Hills-Mccanna LLC.......................D........616 554-9308
    Kentwood (G-9458)
◆ Hydronic Components Inc............F........586 268-1640
    Warren (G-17858)
Instrument and Valve Services..........G........734 459-0375
    Plymouth (G-13197)
Jdl Enterprises Inc..........................F........586 977-8863
    Warren (G-17884)
Key Gas Components Inc...............E........269 673-2151
    Allegan (G-163)
Mac Valve Asia Inc..........................D........248 624-7700
    Wixom (G-18704)
◆ Mac Valves Inc...........................A........248 624-7700
    Wixom (G-18705)
Mac Valves Inc...............................G........734 529-5099
    Dundee (G-4830)
Marshall Gas Controls Inc.................G........269 781-3901
    Marshall (G-11066)
▲ Mercury Manufacturing Company..D........734 285-5150
    Wyandotte (G-18833)
Morgold Inc.....................................G........269 445-3844
    Cassopolis (G-2632)
Neptech Inc....................................E........810 225-2222
    Highland (G-7897)
▲ Nil-Cor LLC.................................C........616 554-3100
    Kentwood (G-9466)
Nordson Corporation........................D........734 459-8600
    Wixom (G-18721)
Novi Tool & Machine Company..........F........313 532-0900
    Redford (G-13749)
Primore Inc.....................................G........517 263-2220
    Adrian (G-89)
Rocon LLC.......................................G........248 542-9635
    Hazel Park (G-7840)
S H Leggitt Company........................B........269 781-3901
    Marshall (G-11073)
▼ Sedco Inc...................................E........517 263-2220
    Adrian (G-95)
▲ Sloan Transportation Pdts Inc.......E........616 395-5600
    Holland (G-8197)
▲ Triad Process Equipment Inc........G........248 685-9938
    Milford (G-11493)

3492 Fluid Power Valves & Hose Fittings

Acutex Inc......................................C........231 894-3200
    Whitehall (G-18488)
Aircraft Precision Pdts Inc.................D........989 875-4186
    Ithaca (G-8785)
Airman Inc......................................E........248 960-1354
    Brighton (G-1941)
▲ Airman Products LLC...................E........248 960-1354
    Brighton (G-1942)
Alco Manufacturing Corp..................G........734 426-3941
    Dexter (G-4722)
Austin Tube Products Inc..................F........231 745-2741
    Baldwin (G-1121)

▲ **Automatic Valve Corp** E 248 474-6761
Novi *(G-12370)*
▲ **Bucher Hydraulics Inc** C 616 458-1306
Grand Rapids *(G-6528)*
Bucher Hydraulics Inc G 231 652-2773
Newaygo *(G-12078)*
Buhler Technologies LLC E 248 652-1546
Rochester Hills *(G-13966)*
▲ **Burgaflex North America LLC** E 810 714-3285
Fenton *(G-5461)*
Central Industrial Corporation G 616 784-9612
Grand Rapids *(G-6560)*
▲ **Craig Assembly Inc** C 810 326-1374
Saint Clair *(G-14821)*
◆ **Dadco Inc** D 734 207-1100
Plymouth *(G-13151)*
Eaton Aeroquip LLC B 949 452-9575
Jackson *(G-8873)*
▲ **Fluid Hutchinson Management** D 248 679-1327
Auburn Hills *(G-903)*
Hlc Industries Inc D 810 477-9600
Farmington Hills *(G-5262)*
Hosco Fittings LLC E 248 912-1750
Wixom *(G-18679)*
Kord Industrial Inc G 248 374-8900
Wixom *(G-18694)*
Mac Valve Asia Inc D 248 624-7700
Wixom *(G-18704)*
◆ **Mac Valves Inc** A 248 624-7700
Wixom *(G-18705)*
McLaren Inc G 989 720-4328
Owosso *(G-12842)*
▲ **Nabtesco Motion Control Inc** F 248 553-3020
Farmington Hills *(G-5329)*
Novi Tool & Machine Company F 313 532-0900
Redford *(G-13749)*
▲ **Oilgear Company** D 231 929-1660
Traverse City *(G-16778)*
Parker-Hannifin Corporation G 330 253-5239
Otsego *(G-12797)*
Parker-Hannifin Corporation B 269 629-5000
Richland *(G-13826)*
Pinckney Automatic & Mfg G 734 878-3430
Pinckney *(G-13053)*
▲ **Piper Industries Inc** D 586 771-5100
Roseville *(G-14463)*
Precision Packing Corporation E 586 756-8700
Warren *(G-17973)*
▲ **Sames Kremlin Inc** C 734 979-0100
Plymouth *(G-13292)*
Scott Machine Inc E 517 787-6616
Jackson *(G-9008)*
Spiral Industries Inc E 810 632-6300
Howell *(G-8521)*
Stonebrdge Technical Entps Ltd F 810 750-0040
Fenton *(G-5505)*
Ventura Aerospace LLC E 734 357-0114
Wixom *(G-18786)*
Wmh Fluidpower Inc F 269 327-7011
Portage *(G-13634)*

3493 Steel Springs, Except Wire

A N L Spring Manufacturing G 313 837-0200
Detroit *(G-3973)*
▲ **Ajax Spring and Mfg Co** E 248 588-5700
Madison Heights *(G-10664)*
American MSC Inc F 248 589-7770
Troy *(G-16932)*
▲ **American MSC Inc** E 248 589-7770
Troy *(G-16933)*
American Ring Manufacturing E 734 402-0426
Livonia *(G-10115)*
Automatic Spring Products Corp C 616 842-2284
Grand Haven *(G-6278)*
Eaton Detroit Spring Svc Co F 313 963-3839
Detroit *(G-4199)*
▲ **Gill Corporation** B 616 453-4491
Grand Rapids *(G-6740)*
J & J Spring Co Inc F 586 566-7600
Shelby Township *(G-15241)*
Lee Spring Company LLC F 586 296-9850
Fraser *(G-5957)*
▲ **Llink Technologies LLC** E 586 336-9370
Brown City *(G-2139)*
▼ **M D Hubbard Spring Co Inc** E 248 628-2528
Oxford *(G-12898)*
◆ **Meritor Inc** C 248 435-1000
Troy *(G-17246)*
Mid-West Spring & Stamping Inc D 231 777-2707
Muskegon *(G-11872)*
Ms Chip Inc F 586 296-9850
Fraser *(G-5966)*
Muskegon Brake & Distrg Co LLC E 231 733-0874
Norton Shores *(G-12313)*
P J Wallbank Springs Inc D 810 987-2992
Port Huron *(G-13514)*
Qp Acquisition 2 Inc A 248 594-7432
Southfield *(G-15685)*
◆ **Quality Spring/Togo Inc** C 517 278-2391
Coldwater *(G-3449)*
Rhino Strapping Products Inc F 734 442-4040
Taylor *(G-16467)*
Weiser Metal Products Inc G 989 736-8151
Lincoln *(G-10041)*

3494 Valves & Pipe Fittings, NEC

2 Brothers Holdings LLC G 517 487-3900
Lansing *(G-9797)*
Anrod Screen Cylinder Company E 989 872-2101
Cass City *(G-2610)*
▲ **Autocam-Pax Inc** C 269 782-5186
Dowagiac *(G-4776)*
▲ **Automatic Valve Corp** E 248 474-6761
Novi *(G-12370)*
Barbron Corporation E 586 716-3530
Kalkaska *(G-9382)*
Beaden Screen Inc E 810 679-3119
Croswell *(G-3729)*
Bucher Hydraulics Inc G 231 652-2773
Newaygo *(G-12078)*
Cal Grinding Inc E 906 786-8749
Escanaba *(G-5064)*
◆ **Colonial Engineering Inc** F 269 323-2495
Portage *(G-13553)*
Computer Operated Mfg E 989 686-1333
Bay City *(G-1340)*
▲ **Conley Composites LLC** E 918 299-5051
Grand Rapids *(G-6594)*
Creform Corporation E 248 926-2555
Novi *(G-12385)*
▼ **Dcl Inc** C 231 547-5600
Charlevoix *(G-2714)*
▲ **Delta Machining Inc** D 269 683-7775
Niles *(G-12125)*
Dexter Automatic Products Co C 734 426-8900
Dexter *(G-4734)*
Dover Energy Inc C 248 836-6750
Auburn Hills *(G-865)*
Eaton Aeroquip LLC B 949 452-9575
Jackson *(G-8873)*
Eaton Corporation G 517 789-1148
Jackson *(G-8875)*
Extrusion Punch & Tool Company E 248 689-3300
Rochester Hills *(G-14007)*
Flow-Rite Controls Ltd E 616 583-1700
Byron Center *(G-2270)*
Great Lakes Hydra Corporation F 231 258-4338
Kalkaska *(G-9389)*
Hill Machinery Co D 616 940-2800
Grand Rapids *(G-6817)*
J D Russell Company E 586 254-8500
Utica *(G-17503)*
Jdl Enterprises Inc F 586 977-8863
Warren *(G-17884)*
▲ **Jet Industries Inc** E 734 641-0900
Westland *(G-18389)*
◆ **Kadant Johnson LLC** C 269 278-1715
Three Rivers *(G-16577)*
Key Gas Components Inc E 269 673-2151
Allegan *(G-163)*
Loftis Alumi-TEC Inc G 616 846-1990
Grand Haven *(G-6330)*
Mac Valve Asia Inc D 248 624-7700
Wixom *(G-18704)*
◆ **Mac Valves Inc** A 248 624-7700
Wixom *(G-18705)*
Mac Valves Inc G 734 529-5099
Dundee *(G-4830)*
◆ **Marshall Excelsior Co** E 269 789-6700
Marshall *(G-11065)*
▲ **Maxitrol Company** D 248 356-1400
Southfield *(G-15648)*
Maxitrol Company G 517 486-2820
Blissfield *(G-1769)*
◆ **Melling Tool Co** B 517 787-8172
Jackson *(G-8951)*
Metro Piping Inc F 313 872-4330
Detroit *(G-4436)*
◆ **Mueller Brass Co** C 810 987-7770
Port Huron *(G-13504)*
Mueller Industries Inc G 248 446-3720
Brighton *(G-2037)*
Nordson Corporation D 734 459-8600
Wixom *(G-18721)*
Novi Tool & Machine Company F 313 532-0900
Redford *(G-13749)*
Npi G 248 478-0010
Farmington Hills *(G-5336)*
O2/Specialty Mfg Holdings LLC G 248 554-4228
Bloomfield Hills *(G-1845)*
Parker-Hannifin Corporation B 269 629-5000
Richland *(G-13826)*
Parker-Hannifin Corporation B 269 694-9411
Otsego *(G-12795)*
Perfection Sprinkler Company G 734 761-5110
Ann Arbor *(G-607)*
▲ **Piper Industries Inc** D 586 771-5100
Roseville *(G-14463)*
▲ **Pittsfield Products Inc** E 734 665-3771
Ann Arbor *(G-612)*
Power Process Engrg Co Inc G 248 473-8450
Novi *(G-12508)*
Quality Filters Inc F 734 668-0211
Ann Arbor *(G-630)*
◆ **Quality Pipe Products Inc** E 734 606-5100
New Boston *(G-12019)*
R M Wright Company Inc E 248 476-9800
Farmington Hills *(G-5363)*
River Valley Machine Inc F 269 673-8070
Allegan *(G-181)*
◆ **Rosedale Products Inc** D 734 665-8201
Ann Arbor *(G-644)*
S H Leggitt Company B 269 781-3901
Marshall *(G-11073)*
Scott Machine Inc E 517 787-6616
Jackson *(G-9008)*
▲ **Set Liquidation Inc** D 517 694-2300
Holt *(G-8331)*
Sloan Valve Company D 248 446-5300
New Hudson *(G-12070)*
◆ **Srg Global Coatings LLC** C 248 509-1100
Troy *(G-17369)*
▲ **Tribal Manufacturing Inc** D 269 781-3901
Marshall *(G-11076)*
Unist Inc E 616 949-0853
Grand Rapids *(G-7297)*
Ventura Aerospace LLC E 734 357-0114
Wixom *(G-18786)*
▲ **W L Hamilton & Co** F 269 781-6941
Marshall *(G-11077)*
Wayne Wire Cloth Products Inc F 989 742-4591
Hillman *(G-7917)*

3495 Wire Springs

A N L Spring Manufacturing G 313 837-0200
Detroit *(G-3973)*
Apex Spring & Stamping Corp D 616 453-5463
Grand Rapids *(G-6462)*
Barnes Group Inc G 586 415-6677
Fraser *(G-5900)*
▲ **De-Sta-Co Cylinders Inc** B 248 836-6700
Auburn Hills *(G-860)*
Dover Energy Inc C 248 836-6750
Auburn Hills *(G-865)*
Dowsett Spring Company G 269 782-2138
Dowagiac *(G-4782)*
General Automatic Mch Pdts Co E 517 437-6000
Hillsdale *(G-7936)*
▲ **Gill Corporation** B 616 453-4491
Grand Rapids *(G-6740)*
Hilite Industries Inc G 248 475-4580
Lake Orion *(G-9608)*
Hyde Spring and Wire Company F 313 272-2201
Detroit *(G-4310)*
J & J Spring Co Inc F 586 566-7600
Shelby Township *(G-15241)*
J & J Spring Enterprises LLC G 586 566-7600
Shelby Township *(G-15242)*
Jade Mfg Inc G 734 942-1462
Romulus *(G-14289)*
Lee Spring Company LLC F 586 296-9850
Fraser *(G-5957)*
▼ **M D Hubbard Spring Co Inc** E 248 628-2528
Oxford *(G-12898)*
Magiera Holdings Inc E 269 685-1768
Plainwell *(G-13082)*
Mc Guire Spring Corporation G 517 546-7311
Brighton *(G-2028)*
▲ **Michigan Spring & Stamping LLC** C 231 755-1691
Muskegon *(G-11871)*

S I C

34 FABRICATED METAL PRODUCTS, EXCEPT MACHINERY AND TRANSPORTATION EQUIPMENT

Michigan Steel Finishing Co ....F 313 838-3925
Detroit (G-4452)
Mid-West Spring & Stamping Inc ....D 231 777-2707
Muskegon (G-11872)
Mid-West Spring Mfg Co ....F 231 777-2707
Muskegon (G-11873)
Motion Dynamics Corporation ....D 231 865-7400
Fruitport (G-6068)
Ms Chip Inc ....F 586 296-9850
Fraser (G-5966)
▲ Novi Spring Inc ....F 248 486-4220
Brighton (G-2045)
▲ Peterson American Corporation ....E 248 799-5400
Southfield (G-15673)
Peterson American Corporation ....G 248 799-5410
Commerce Township (G-3562)
Peterson American Corporation ....D 269 279-7421
Three Rivers (G-16580)
Peterson Spring ....G 248 799-5400
Madison Heights (G-10797)
◆ Quality Spring/Togo Inc ....C 517 278-2391
Coldwater (G-3449)
Rassini Chassis Systems LLC ....D 419 485-1524
Plymouth (G-13275)
▲ Scherdel Sales & Tech Inc ....C 231 777-7774
Muskegon (G-11916)
Serra Spring & Mfg LLC ....G 586 932-2202
Sterling Heights (G-16172)
Spring Design and Mfg Inc ....E 586 566-9741
Shelby Township (G-15342)
▲ Spring Dynamics Inc ....E 810 798-2622
Almont (G-267)
Spring Saginaw Company ....F 989 624-9333
Birch Run (G-1716)
▲ Stump Schlele Somappa Sprng ....E 616 361-2791
Grand Rapids (G-7230)
Stumpp Schuele Somappa USA Inc ......F 616 361-2791
Grand Rapids (G-7231)
TEC-3 Prototypes Inc ....E 810 678-8909
Metamora (G-11289)
Tokusen Hytech Inc ....C 269 685-1768
Plainwell (G-13099)
Tokusen Hytech Inc ....D 269 658-1768
Plainwell (G-13100)
Wolverine Coil Spring Company ....D 616 459-3504
Grand Rapids (G-7344)

3496 Misc Fabricated Wire Prdts

A A A Wire Rope & Splicing Inc ....F 734 283-1765
Riverview (G-13867)
Accra-Wire Controls Inc ....G 616 866-3434
Rockford (G-14152)
Acme Wire & Iron Works LLC ....F 313 923-7555
Detroit (G-3984)
▼ Adrian Steel Company ....B 517 265-6194
Adrian (G-50)
▲ Ajax Spring and Mfg Co ....E 248 588-5700
Madison Heights (G-10664)
Ambassador Steel Corporation ....E 517 455-7216
Lansing (G-9804)
American Industrial Training ....G 734 789-9099
Flat Rock (G-5613)
Anrod Screen Cylinder Company ....E 989 872-2101
Cass City (G-2610)
Apex Spring & Stamping Corp ....D 616 453-5463
Grand Rapids (G-6462)
Aspc International Inc ....G 616 842-7800
Grand Haven (G-6274)
Automatic Spring Products Corp ....C 616 842-2284
Grand Haven (G-6278)
Awcoa Inc ....G 313 892-4100
Detroit (G-4035)
Barbron Corporation ....E 586 716-3530
Kalkaska (G-9382)
Beaden Screen Inc ....E 810 679-3119
Croswell (G-3729)
▲ Benmill LLC ....E 616 243-7555
Grand Rapids (G-6499)
Big Foot Manufacturing Co ....E 231 775-5588
Cadillac (G-2315)
Bopp-Busch Manufacturing Co ....E 989 876-7924
Au Gres (G-758)
Burnside Industries LLC ....G 231 798-3394
Norton Shores (G-12347)
▼ Center Mass Inc ....G 734 207-8934
Canton (G-2447)
Clark Engineering Co ....E 989 723-7930
Owosso (G-12826)
▲ Clipper Belt Lacer Company ....D 616 459-3196
Grand Rapids (G-6574)

▼ Commercial Group Inc ....E 313 931-6100
Taylor (G-16395)
Consolidated Clips Clamps Inc ....D 734 455-0880
Plymouth (G-13149)
Constructive Sheet Metal Inc ....E 616 245-5306
Allendale (G-217)
◆ Cor-Met Inc ....E 810 227-0004
Brighton (G-1966)
Corners Limited ....G 269 353-8311
Kalamazoo (G-9156)
Corsair Engineering Inc ....C 810 234-3664
Flint (G-5673)
Corsair Engineering Inc ....F 810 233-0440
Flint (G-5672)
▲ Dare Products Inc ....E 269 965-2307
Springfield (G-15864)
Davon Manufacturing Company ....G 616 896-7888
Hudsonville (G-8579)
Delta Tube & Fabricating Corp ....E 248 634-8267
Holly (G-8267)
Deshler Group Inc ....C 734 525-9100
Livonia (G-10181)
Detroit Wire Rope Splcing Corp ....G 248 585-1063
Madison Heights (G-10706)
▼ E M I Construction Products ....F 616 392-7207
Holland (G-8020)
Fab-Jet Services LLC ....G 586 463-9622
Clinton Township (G-3234)
Fabric Patch Ltd ....F 906 932-5260
Ironwood (G-8762)
▲ Flex-N-Gate Stamping LLC ....E 586 759-8900
Warren (G-17813)
▼ Franklin Fastener Company ....E 313 537-8900
Redford (G-13735)
Fresh Water Buyer II LLC ....F 517 914-8284
Eaton Rapids (G-4963)
▲ Gill Corporation ....B 616 453-4491
Grand Rapids (G-6740)
▲ Glassmaster Controls Co Inc ....E 269 382-2010
Kalamazoo (G-9198)
Great Lakes Grilling Co ....F 616 791-8600
Grand Rapids (G-6787)
▲ Hi-Lex America Incorporated ....B 269 968-0781
Battle Creek (G-1237)
Hi-Lex America Incorporated ....C 517 542-2955
Litchfield (G-10079)
Hi-Lex America Incorporated ....B 248 844-0096
Rochester Hills (G-14030)
Hlc Industries Inc ....D 810 477-9600
Farmington Hills (G-5262)
Hohmann & Barnard Inc ....F 765 420-7940
East Lansing (G-4895)
Industries Unlimited Inc ....F 586 949-4300
Chesterfield (G-2893)
Jaslin Assembly Inc ....G 248 528-3024
Troy (G-17181)
Jon Bee Distribution LLC ....G 248 846-0491
Pontiac (G-13387)
▲ Kentwood Packaging Corporation ....D 616 698-9000
Walker (G-17642)
▲ King Steel Fasteners Inc ....E 810 721-0300
Oxford (G-12893)
Law Enforcement Supply Inc ....G 616 895-7875
Allendale (G-222)
Lesco Design & Mfg Co Inc ....B 248 596-9301
Wixom (G-18697)
Loudon Steel Inc ....E 989 871-9353
Millington (G-11502)
Lupaul Industries Inc ....F 517 783-3223
Saint Johns (G-14904)
▼ M D Hubbard Spring Co Inc ....E 248 628-2528
Oxford (G-12898)
Macomb Products LLC ....E 586 855-0223
Macomb (G-10610)
▲ Maine Ornamental LLC ....F 800 556-8449
White Pigeon (G-18482)
▲ Mason Tackle Company ....E 810 631-4571
Otisville (G-12783)
Mazzella Lifting Tech Inc ....F 734 953-7300
Livonia (G-10304)
Mazzella Lifting Tech Inc ....F 248 585-1063
Madison Heights (G-10778)
Memtech Inc ....F 734 455-8550
Plymouth (G-13240)
Merchants Metals LLC ....F 810 227-3036
Howell (G-8477)
▲ Michigan Rod Products Inc ....D 517 552-9812
Howell (G-8481)
Mid-West Spring & Stamping Inc ....D 231 777-2707
Muskegon (G-11872)

▼ Mid-West Wire Products Inc ....E 248 548-3200
Rochester Hills (G-14063)
Milton Manufacturing Inc ....F 313 366-2450
Detroit (G-4458)
Motor City Racks Inc ....E 519 776-9153
Warren (G-17937)
Nash Products Inc ....G 269 323-2980
Vicksburg (G-17609)
National Industrial Sup Co Inc ....F 248 588-1828
Troy (G-17273)
▲ National-Standard LLC ....C 269 683-9902
Niles (G-12151)
Northern Cable & Automtn LLC ....D 231 937-8000
Howard City (G-8413)
Omni Technical Services Inc ....F 989 227-8900
Saint Johns (G-14912)
▲ Orri Corp ....F 248 618-1104
Waterford (G-18145)
▲ PA Products Inc ....G 734 421-1060
Livonia (G-10357)
Petschke Manufacturing Company ......F 586 463-0841
Mount Clemens (G-11652)
▲ Phoenix Wire Cloth Inc ....E 248 585-6350
Troy (G-17301)
▲ Pittsfield Products Inc ....F 734 665-3771
Ann Arbor (G-612)
Plastgage Cstm Fabrication LLC ....G 517 817-0719
Jackson (G-8987)
◆ Polytorx LLC ....G 734 322-2114
Ann Arbor (G-614)
▲ Precision Wire Forms Inc ....E 269 279-0053
Three Rivers (G-16581)
▲ Production Fabricators Inc ....E 231 777-3822
Muskegon (G-11900)
Quality Filters Inc ....F 734 668-0211
Ann Arbor (G-630)
Rapid River Rustic Inc ....F 906 474-6404
Rapid River (G-13686)
Riverview Products Inc ....E 616 866-1305
Rockford (G-14187)
Rives Manufacturing Inc ....E 517 569-3380
Rives Junction (G-13888)
▼ Rod Chomper Inc ....F 616 392-9677
Holland (G-8182)
Salco Engineering and Mfg Inc ....F 517 789-9010
Jackson (G-9004)
Schroth Enterprises Inc ....E 586 939-0770
Sterling Heights (G-16166)
Schroth Enterprises Inc ....E 586 759-4240
Grosse Pointe Farms (G-7540)
Sterling Die & Engineering Inc ....E 586 677-0707
Macomb (G-10637)
▲ Stonebridge Industries Inc ....B 586 323-0348
Sterling Heights (G-16195)
◆ Straits Steel and Wire Company .....D 231 843-3416
Ludington (G-10551)
Strema Sales Corp ....E 248 645-0626
Bingham Farms (G-1703)
TEC-3 Prototypes Inc ....E 810 678-8909
Metamora (G-11289)
Tigmaster Co ....F 800 824-4830
Baroda (G-1171)
Ton-Tex Corporation ....F 616 957-3200
Greenville (G-7508)
Torque 2020 CMA Acqstion LLC D .....F 810 229-2534
Brighton (G-2083)
Ultraform Industries Inc ....D 586 752-4508
Bruce Twp (G-2185)
Unifab Corporation ....E 269 382-2803
Portage (G-13629)
Unified Scrning Crshing - MI L ....F 888 464-9473
Saint Johns (G-14920)
▲ US Wire Rope Supply Inc ....E 313 925-0444
Detroit (G-4655)
Vandelay Services LLC ....G 810 279-8550
Howell (G-8538)
▲ Wayne Wire A Bag Cmponents Inc ..B 231 258-9187
Kalkaska (G-9410)
Wayne Wire Cloth Products Inc ....D 231 258-9187
Kalkaska (G-9411)
Wayne Wire Cloth Products Inc ....F 989 742-4591
Hillman (G-7917)
▲ Wcscarts LLC ....D 248 901-0965
Troy (G-17446)
▲ West Michigan Wire Co ....D 231 845-1281
Ludington (G-10556)
Windy Lake LLC ....D 877 869-6911
Pentwater (G-12975)
Wire Fab Inc ....F 313 893-8816
Detroit (G-4685)

3497 Metal Foil & Leaf

Barbron Corporation ....E.... 586 716-3530
Kalkaska *(G-9382)*
Graphic Specialties Inc ....E.... 616 247-0060
Grand Rapids *(G-6783)*
Illinois Tool Works Inc ....D.... 231 258-5521
Kalkaska *(G-9390)*

3498 Fabricated Pipe & Pipe Fittings

A & B Tube Benders Inc ....G.... 586 773-0440
Warren *(G-17679)*
A & B Tube Benders Inc ....F.... 586 773-0440
Warren *(G-17678)*
◆ Acme Tube Bending Company ....G.... 248 545-8500
Berkley *(G-1618)*
Allegan Tubular Products Inc ....D.... 269 673-6636
Allegan *(G-146)*
Alro Steel Corporation ....G.... 989 893-9553
Bay City *(G-1320)*
Alternative Components LLC ....E.... 586 755-9177
Warren *(G-17698)*
Angstrom Automotive Group LLC ....E.... 248 627-2871
Ortonville *(G-12741)*
Austin Tube Products Inc ....F.... 231 745-2741
Baldwin *(G-1121)*
Avpi Limited ....G.... 616 842-1200
Spring Lake *(G-15804)*
B L Harroun and Son Inc ....E.... 269 345-8657
Kalamazoo *(G-9131)*
▲ Baldauf Enterprises Inc ....D.... 989 686-0350
Bay City *(G-1324)*
Berkley Industries Inc ....E.... 989 656-2171
Bay Port *(G-1413)*
Big Foot Manufacturing Co ....E.... 231 775-5588
Cadillac *(G-2315)*
▲ Blissfield Manufacturing Co ....C.... 517 486-2121
Blissfield *(G-1761)*
Bundy Corporation ....G.... 517 439-1132
Hillsdale *(G-7927)*
Burnham & Northern Inc ....G.... 517 279-7501
Coldwater *(G-3422)*
Cadillac Culvert Inc ....F.... 231 775-3761
Cadillac *(G-2320)*
Computer Operated Mfg ....E.... 989 686-1333
Bay City *(G-1340)*
▲ Denso Air Systems Michigan Inc ....B.... 269 962-9676
Battle Creek *(G-1215)*
Detroit Nipple Works Inc ....F.... 313 872-6370
Detroit *(G-4157)*
Detroit Tube Products LLC ....E.... 313 841-0300
Detroit *(G-4168)*
▲ Elringklinger Auto Mfg Inc ....E.... 248 727-6600
Southfield *(G-15554)*
Elringklinger Auto Mfg Inc ....E.... 248 727-6600
Southfield *(G-15555)*
Erin Industries Inc ....E.... 248 669-2050
Walled Lake *(G-17668)*
Ferguson Enterprises LLC ....G.... 989 790-2220
Saginaw *(G-14645)*
◆ Fernco Inc ....C.... 810 503-9000
Davison *(G-3782)*
Fhc Holding Company ....G.... 616 538-3231
Wyoming *(G-18872)*
Flexible Metal Inc ....D.... 810 231-1300
Hamburg *(G-7591)*
Formfab LLC ....E.... 248 844-3676
Rochester Hills *(G-14013)*
Future Industries Inc ....E.... 616 844-0772
Grand Haven *(G-6299)*
Gonzalez Group Jonesville LLC ....E.... 517 849-9908
Jonesville *(G-9088)*
Gray Bros Stamping & Mch Inc ....E.... 269 483-7615
White Pigeon *(G-18478)*
Gray Brothers Mfg Inc ....F.... 269 483-7615
White Pigeon *(G-18479)*
Hlc Industries Inc ....D.... 810 477-9600
Farmington Hills *(G-5262)*
Hosco Inc ....F.... 248 912-1750
Wixom *(G-18678)*
▲ Huron Inc ....E.... 810 359-5344
Lexington *(G-10029)*
▲ J & L Manufacturing Co Inc ....E.... 269 789-1507
Marshall *(G-11061)*
JCs Tool & Mfg Co Inc ....E.... 989 892-8975
Essexville *(G-5114)*
Jems of Litchfield Inc ....F.... 517 542-5367
Litchfield *(G-10081)*
Jep Industries LLC ....G.... 734 844-3506
Canton *(G-2480)*
Key Gas Components Inc ....E.... 269 673-2151
Allegan *(G-163)*
Kopach Filters LLC ....G.... 906 863-8611
Wallace *(G-17660)*
L A Burnhart Inc ....G.... 810 227-4567
Brighton *(G-2016)*
Lapine Metal Products Inc ....F.... 269 388-5900
Kalamazoo *(G-9258)*
Loftis Alumi-TEC Inc ....G.... 616 846-1990
Grand Haven *(G-6330)*
Macomb Tube Fabricating Co ....E.... 586 445-6770
Warren *(G-17912)*
Manistee Wldg & Piping Svc Inc ....G.... 231 723-2551
Manistee *(G-10906)*
◆ Marshall Excelsior Co ....E.... 269 789-6700
Marshall *(G-11065)*
Masterbilt Products Corp ....F.... 269 749-4841
Olivet *(G-12694)*
Mayville Engineering Co Inc ....D.... 989 748-6031
Vanderbilt *(G-17572)*
Mayville Engineering Co Inc ....D.... 616 877-2073
Wayland *(G-18198)*
Mayville Engineering Co Inc ....D.... 989 983-3911
Vanderbilt *(G-17573)*
Meccom Corporation ....G.... 313 895-4900
Detroit *(G-4426)*
Melling Products North LLC ....D.... 989 588-6147
Farwell *(G-5426)*
Metaldyne Tblar Components LLC ....D.... 248 727-1800
Southfield *(G-15655)*
▲ Midwest Tube Fabricators Inc ....E.... 586 264-9898
Sterling Heights *(G-16100)*
Motor City Bending & Rolling ....G.... 313 368-4400
Detroit *(G-4466)*
◆ Myco Enterprises Inc ....G.... 248 348-3806
Royal Oak *(G-14564)*
Nelson Hardware ....G.... 269 327-3583
Portage *(G-13587)*
▲ Norma Michigan Inc ....C.... 248 373-4300
Auburn Hills *(G-984)*
Novi Tool & Machine Company ....F.... 313 532-0900
Redford *(G-13749)*
Oilpatch Machine Tool Inc ....G.... 989 772-0637
Mount Pleasant *(G-11728)*
Parma Tube Corp ....E.... 269 651-2351
Sturgis *(G-16316)*
Patton Welding Inc ....F.... 231 258-9925
Kalkaska *(G-9401)*
Paumac Tubing LLC ....D.... 810 985-9400
Marysville *(G-11096)*
Picko Ferrum Fabricating LLC ....G.... 810 626-7086
Hamburg *(G-7593)*
Pipe Fabricators Inc ....G.... 269 345-8657
Kalamazoo *(G-9297)*
▲ Pontiac Coil Inc ....C.... 248 922-1100
Clarkston *(G-3057)*
Power Process Piping Inc ....E.... 734 451-0130
Plymouth *(G-13269)*
Production Tube Company Inc ....G.... 313 259-3990
Detroit *(G-4537)*
◆ Quality Pipe Products Inc ....E.... 734 606-5100
New Boston *(G-12019)*
Quigley Manufacturing Inc ....G.... 248 426-8600
Farmington Hills *(G-5362)*
Refrigeration Concepts Inc ....E.... 616 785-7335
Comstock Park *(G-3643)*
Ridgid Slotting LLC ....G.... 616 847-0332
Grand Haven *(G-6354)*
River Valley Machine Inc ....F.... 269 673-8070
Allegan *(G-181)*
Rock River Fabrications Inc ....E.... 616 281-5769
Grand Rapids *(G-7162)*
Roman Engineering ....E.... 231 238-7644
Afton *(G-107)*
Rss Baker LLC ....E.... 616 844-5429
Grand Haven *(G-6356)*
Ryson Tube Inc ....F.... 810 227-4567
Brighton *(G-2067)*
S & S Tube Inc ....E.... 989 656-7211
Bay Port *(G-1415)*
Sales & Engineering Inc ....E.... 734 525-9030
Livonia *(G-10398)*
South Park Sales & Mfg Inc ....G.... 313 381-7579
Dearborn *(G-3899)*
Spiral Industries Inc ....E.... 810 632-6300
Howell *(G-8521)*
St Regis Culvert Inc ....F.... 517 543-3430
Charlotte *(G-2773)*
Superior Fluid Systems ....F.... 734 246-4550
Taylor *(G-16481)*
Tempro Industries Inc ....E.... 734 451-5900
Plymouth *(G-13312)*
Tg Manufacturing LLC ....G.... 616 935-7575
Byron Center *(G-2296)*
TI Group Auto Systems LLC ....G.... 859 235-5420
Auburn Hills *(G-1056)*
Troy Tube & Manufacturing Co ....D.... 586 949-8700
Chesterfield *(G-2959)*
Tube Wright Inc ....E.... 810 227-4567
Brighton *(G-2085)*
Tube Wright Inc ....G.... 734 449-9129
Whitmore Lake *(G-18549)*
Tube-Co Inc ....G.... 586 775-0244
Warren *(G-18046)*
▲ Tubesource Manufacturing Inc ....E.... 248 543-4746
Ferndale *(G-5591)*
▲ Universal Tube Inc ....C.... 248 853-5100
Rochester Hills *(G-14137)*
Universal Warranty Corpor ....G.... 248 263-6900
Southfield *(G-15733)*
Van Pelt Industries LLC ....G.... 616 842-1200
Grand Haven *(G-6378)*
Volos Tube Form Inc ....E.... 586 416-3600
Macomb *(G-10650)*
Wooley Industries Inc ....G.... 810 341-8823
Flint *(G-5795)*

3499 Fabricated Metal Prdts, NEC

A & L Metal Products ....G.... 734 654-8990
Carleton *(G-2549)*
A&G Corporate Holdings LLC ....G.... 734 513-3488
Livonia *(G-10094)*
AAA Waterjet and Machining Inc ....G.... 586 759-3736
Warren *(G-17684)*
◆ Ace Controls Inc ....C.... 248 476-0213
Farmington Hills *(G-5158)*
▲ Advanced Magnet Source Corp ....G.... 734 398-7188
Canton *(G-2430)*
Advanced Metal Fabricators ....G.... 616 570-4847
Lowell *(G-10494)*
American Indus McHinery-Mc LLC ....G.... 810 420-0949
Marine City *(G-10954)*
Anchor Bay Fab ....G.... 586 231-0295
Chesterfield *(G-2839)*
Aquarius Recreational Products ....G.... 586 469-4600
Harrison Township *(G-7687)*
Arrowhead Industries Inc ....F.... 231 238-9366
Afton *(G-106)*
Atf Inc ....E.... 989 685-2468
Rose City *(G-14362)*
Avian Control Technologies LLC ....G.... 231 349-9050
Stanwood *(G-15902)*
Best Barricade Sysytem Inc ....G.... 989 778-1482
Bay City *(G-1332)*
Bulman Products Inc ....E.... 616 363-4416
Grand Rapids *(G-6531)*
▲ Camaco LLC ....E.... 248 442-6800
Farmington Hills *(G-5195)*
Campbell & Shaw Steel Inc ....F.... 810 364-5100
Marysville *(G-11083)*
Central Mich Met Fbrcation LLC ....G.... 989 875-9172
Ithaca *(G-8788)*
Challenger Manufacturing LLC ....F.... 248 930-9920
Farmington Hills *(G-5202)*
CNc Products Acquisition Inc ....F.... 269 684-5500
Niles *(G-12119)*
Colson Casters ....F.... 269 944-6063
Saint Joseph *(G-14924)*
Con-De Manufacturing Inc ....G.... 269 651-3756
Sturgis *(G-16285)*
Contemporary Industries Inc ....G.... 248 478-8850
Farmington Hills *(G-5208)*
Cruux LLC ....G.... 248 515-8411
Troy *(G-17036)*
Dag R&D ....G.... 248 444-0575
Milford *(G-11460)*
Daisy Chain Online ....G.... 330 259-6457
West Bloomfield *(G-18277)*
Down Home Inc ....G.... 517 545-5955
Howell *(G-8449)*
Dts Enterprises Inc ....E.... 231 599-3123
Ellsworth *(G-5035)*
Elemental Artistry LLC ....G.... 616 326-1758
Grand Rapids *(G-6671)*
Fab-Alloy Company ....G.... 517 787-4313
Jackson *(G-8883)*
Fluxtrol Inc ....G.... 248 393-2000
Auburn Hills *(G-904)*
Fournier Enterprises Inc ....G.... 586 323-9160
Mount Clemens *(G-11639)*

SIC

34 FABRICATED METAL PRODUCTS, EXCEPT MACHINERY AND TRANSPORTATION EQUIPMENT

Friendship Industries Inc .... E 586 323-0033
 Sterling Heights (G-16024)
◆ Gibraltar Inc .... E 616 748-4857
 Zeeland (G-19030)
Give-Em A Brake Safety LLC .... E 616 531-8705
 Grandville (G-7379)
Great Lakes Laser Dynamics Inc .... D 616 892-7070
 Allendale (G-220)
Greene Manufacturing Tech LLC .... C 810 982-9720
 Port Huron (G-13481)
▲ Heath Manufacturing Company .... E 616 997-8181
 Coopersville (G-3688)
Henshaw Inc .... D 586 752-0700
 Armada (G-736)
Hollingsworth Container LLC .... G 313 768-1400
 Dearborn (G-3850)
Incoe Corporation .... C 248 616-0220
 Auburn Hills (G-936)
▲ Industrial Magnetics Inc .... D 231 582-3100
 Boyne City (G-1890)
J and L Custom Services .... G 269 641-7800
 Vandalia (G-17566)
Jershon Inc .... G 231 861-2900
 Shelby (G-15151)
Johnson Systems Inc .... G 616 455-1900
 Caledonia (G-2386)
Lachman Enterprises Inc .... G 248 948-9944
 Southfield (G-15623)
Laddertech LLC .... F 248 437-7100
 Brighton (G-2019)
Lock and Load Corp .... G 800 975-9658
 Marion (G-10973)
Lsr Incorporated .... F 734 455-6530
 Plymouth (G-13228)
Lyncs Metal Fabrication .... G 616 813-2071
 Alto (G-335)
▲ Magnetic Systems Intl Inc .... E 231 582-9600
 Boyne City (G-1896)
Magnum Fabricating .... G 734 484-5800
 Ypsilanti (G-18964)
Management Training Inn .... G 734 439-1546
 Milan (G-11443)
Metal Components Inc .... G 616 389-2400
 Wyoming (G-18893)
Metalworks Inc .... C 231 845-5136
 Ludington (G-10546)
▲ Meter USA LLC .... F 810 388-9373
 Marysville (G-11091)
◆ Miba Hydramechanica Corp .... D 586 264-3094
 Sterling Heights (G-16097)
▲ Mpg Inc .... C 734 207-6200
 Plymouth (G-13249)
Multi Steel Services .... G 734 261-6201
 Livonia (G-10327)
My Metal Medium .... G 231 590-4051
 Mesick (G-11274)
National Innovation Center .... F 248 414-3913
 Oak Park (G-12630)
National Ordnance Auto Mfg LLC .... G 248 853-8822
 Auburn Hills (G-980)
Nortech LLC .... E 248 446-7575
 New Hudson (G-12066)
North East Fabrication Co Inc .... F 517 849-8090
 Jonesville (G-9095)
Northstar Metalcraft .... G 248 858-8484
 Pontiac (G-13403)
▲ Northwoods Manufacturing Inc .... D 906 779-2370
 Kingsford (G-9516)
▲ Omt Veyhl .... G 616 738-6688
 Holland (G-8158)
Oronoko Iron Works Inc .... G 269 326-7045
 Baroda (G-1167)
Ottawa Tool & Machine LLC .... G 616 677-1743
 Grand Rapids (G-7064)
▲ P & C Group I Inc .... E 248 442-6800
 Farmington Hills (G-5341)
Pak Mail Center of America .... G 248 543-3097
 Ferndale (G-5575)
Poco Inc .... E 313 220-6752
 Canton (G-2509)
Poetry Factory Ltd .... G 586 296-3125
 Fraser (G-5977)
Proper Arospc & Machining LLC .... G 586 779-8787
 Warren (G-17981)
Prototech Laser Inc .... E 586 598-6900
 Chesterfield (G-2934)
Prs Manufacturing Inc .... G 616 784-4409
 Grand Rapids (G-7124)
Rankam Metal Products .... G 586 799-4259
 Shelby Township (G-15314)

Scenario Systems Ltd .... G 586 532-1320
 Shelby Township (G-15324)
Signature Wall Solutions Inc .... F 616 366-4242
 Midland (G-11417)
Slik Metal Fabrication LLC .... G 586 344-5621
 Macomb (G-10636)
Spartan Barricading .... G 313 292-2488
 Romulus (G-14330)
Specialty Metal Fabricators .... G 616 698-9020
 Caledonia (G-2401)
Spraying Systems Co .... F 248 473-1331
 Farmington Hills (G-5385)
Steel Appeal .... G 231 326-6116
 Empire (G-5042)
▲ Synchronous Manufacturing Inc ...... F 517 764-6930
 Michigan Center (G-11296)
▲ Tengam Engineering Inc .... E 269 694-9466
 Otsego (G-12800)
Timberwolf Furnace Co .... G 231 924-6654
 Grant (G-7433)
Troy Metal Fabricating LLC .... G 248 506-6142
 Troy (G-17400)
True Die Inc .... G 616 772-6360
 Zeeland (G-19084)
▲ Unisorb Inc .... E 517 764-6060
 Michigan Center (G-11297)
Universal Magnetics Inc .... G 231 937-5555
 Howard City (G-8420)
Van Dyken Mechanical Inc .... G 616 224-7030
 Grandville (G-7422)
Vel-Kal Manufacturing Inc .... F 269 344-1204
 Galesburg (G-6086)
◆ Viking Corporation .... D 269 945-9501
 Hastings (G-7811)
▲ Viking Fabrication Svcs LLC .... B 269 945-9501
 Hastings (G-7812)
W International LLC .... D 248 577-0364
 Madison Heights (G-10858)
West Mich Auto Stl & Engrg Inc .... G 616 560-8198
 Belding (G-1464)
Zero Hour Parts .... F 734 997-0866
 Kentwood (G-9484)

35 INDUSTRIAL AND COMMERCIAL MACHINERY AND COMPUTER EQUIPMENT

3511 Steam, Gas & Hydraulic Turbines & Engines

3dfx Interactive Inc .... G 918 938-8967
 Saginaw (G-14599)
Ahd LLC .... G 586 922-6511
 Shelby Township (G-15167)
Alpena Antiq Trctr Stm Eng CL .... G 989 734-3859
 Hawks (G-7814)
Diamond Power Specialty Co .... G 734 429-8527
 Ann Arbor (G-452)
▲ Dowding Machining LLC .... F 517 663-5455
 Eaton Rapids (G-4961)
Dynamic Energy Tech LLC .... G 248 212-5904
 Oak Park (G-12607)
Elderberry Steam Engines .... G 989 245-0652
 Saginaw (G-14643)
Ener2 LLC .... G 248 842-2662
 Brighton (G-1984)
Horiba Instruments Inc .... D 734 213-6555
 Ann Arbor (G-518)
Kinetic Wave Power LLC .... G 989 839-9757
 Midland (G-11382)
Lutke Hydraulics .... G 231 824-9505
 Manton (G-10935)
▲ Marsh Plating Corporation .... D 734 483-5767
 Ypsilanti (G-18965)
Metro Machine Works Inc .... D 734 941-4571
 Romulus (G-14304)
Nu Con Corporation .... E 734 525-0770
 Livonia (G-10341)
Plasma-Tec Inc .... E 616 455-2593
 Holland (G-8166)
South Pointe Radiator .... G 734 941-1460
 Romulus (G-14329)
Steel Tool & Engineering Co .... D 734 692-8580
 Brownstown Twp (G-2157)
Wmh Fluidpower Inc .... F 269 327-7011
 Portage (G-13634)

3519 Internal Combustion Engines, NEC

Apex Competition Engines .... G 616 761-4010
 Fenwick (G-5516)
CF Components Inc .... G 248 670-2974
 Livonia (G-10154)
Chandas Engineering Inc .... F 313 582-8666
 Dearborn (G-3819)
Cobra Aero LLC .... G 517 437-9100
 Hillsdale (G-7930)
Creek Diesel Services Inc .... F 800 974-4600
 Grand Rapids (G-6611)
Cummins Bridgeway Grove Cy LLC .... C 614 604-6000
 New Hudson (G-12047)
Cummins Inc .... G 586 469-2010
 Clinton Township (G-3215)
Cummins Inc .... G 616 538-2250
 Grand Rapids (G-6618)
Cummins Inc .... G 313 843-6200
 Dearborn (G-3823)
Cummins Inc .... G 248 573-1900
 New Hudson (G-12048)
Cummins Inc .... G 989 752-5200
 Saginaw (G-14633)
Cummins Npower LLC .... E 906 475-8800
 Negaunee (G-11965)
D & S Engine Specialist Inc .... F 248 583-9240
 Clawson (G-3093)
◆ Detroit Diesel Corporation .... A 313 592-5000
 Detroit (G-4144)
Detroit Diesel Corporation .... F 313 592-8256
 Redford (G-13730)
Double H Mfg Inc .... E 734 729-3450
 Westland (G-18366)
▲ Ehc Inc .... G 313 259-2266
 Troy (G-17079)
▲ Emp Racing Inc .... G 906 786-8404
 Escanaba (G-5068)
◆ Engineered Machined Pdts Inc .... B 906 786-8404
 Escanaba (G-5069)
Extreme Machine Inc .... G 810 231-0521
 Whitmore Lake (G-18535)
Extreme Machine Inc .... D 810 231-0521
 Whitmore Lake (G-18536)
FCA US LLC .... G 313 957-7000
 Detroit (G-4229)
Fev Test Systems Inc .... G 248 373-6000
 Auburn Hills (G-897)
▲ Geislinger Corporation .... F 269 441-7000
 Battle Creek (G-1234)
Global Fmi LLC .... D 810 964-5555
 Fenton (G-5481)
GM Powertrain-Romulus Engine .... G 734 595-5203
 Romulus (G-14279)
Holbrook Racing Engines .... F 734 762-4315
 Livonia (G-10241)
K & S Property Inc .... D 248 573-1600
 New Hudson (G-12059)
Katech Inc .... E 586 791-4120
 Clinton Township (G-3270)
Logan Diesel Incorporated .... G 517 589-8811
 Leslie (G-10014)
Mtu America Inc .... G 248 560-8298
 Brownstown (G-2151)
Navarre Inc .... G 313 892-7300
 Detroit (G-4478)
Paice Technologies LLC .... G 248 376-1115
 Orchard Lake (G-12718)
▲ Peaker Services Inc .... D 248 437-4174
 Brighton (G-2049)
▲ Powertrain Integration LLC .... E 248 577-0010
 Madison Heights (G-10806)
▲ PSI Holding Company .... D 248 437-4174
 Brighton (G-2057)
◆ R & D Enterprises Inc .... E 248 349-7077
 Plymouth (G-13274)
Rolls-Royce Solutions Amer Inc .... G 734 261-0309
 Livonia (G-10390)
▲ Rolls-Royce Solutions Amer Inc ...... C 248 560-8000
 Novi (G-12528)
Shadowood Technology Inc .... G 810 358-2569
 Metamora (G-11286)
W W Williams Company LLC .... G 313 584-6150
 Dearborn (G-3913)

3523 Farm Machinery & Eqpt

▲ A & B Packing Equipment Inc .... C 269 539-4700
 Lawrence (G-9980)
A G Case LLC .... G 586 791-0125
 Clinton Township (G-3145)

SIC SECTION35 INDUSTRIAL AND COMMERCIAL MACHINERY AND COMPUTER EQUIPMENT35 INDUSTRIAL AND COMMERCIAL MACHINERY

Advanced Drainage Systems Inc .... G 989 723-5208
Owosso *(G-12819)*
Advanced Farm Equipment LLC .... F 989 268-5711
Vestaburg *(G-17593)*
AG Harvesters LLC .... G 989 876-7161
Au Gres *(G-754)*
▲ **Agritek Industries Inc** .... D 616 786-9200
Holland *(G-7958)*
Bader & Co .... F 810 648-2404
Sandusky *(G-15055)*
▼ **BEI International LLC** .... F 616 204-8274
Holland *(G-7973)*
Best Harvest .... G 888 947-6226
Bay City *(G-1333)*
◆ **Big Dutchman Inc** .... D 616 392-5981
Holland *(G-7975)*
Big Foot Manufacturing Co .... E 231 775-5588
Cadillac *(G-2315)*
Boxer Equipment/Morbark Inc .... G 989 866-2381
Winn *(G-18589)*
Brilar LLC .... D 248 547-6439
Oak Park *(G-12596)*
Burly Oak Builders Inc .... G 734 368-4912
Dexter *(G-4730)*
Case Quality Upkeep LLC .... G 231 233-8013
Pentwater *(G-12971)*
CPM Acquisition Corp .... G 231 947-6400
Traverse City *(G-16663)*
▼ **Crippen Manufacturing Company** .... E 989 681-4323
Saint Louis *(G-14990)*
Dad and Sons Farming LLC .... G 517 719-2048
Vermontville *(G-17587)*
◆ **Diamond Moba Americas Inc** .... C 248 476-7100
Farmington Hills *(G-5216)*
Eagle Group II Ltd .... E 616 754-7777
Greenville *(G-7483)*
Ebels Hardware Inc .... F 231 826-3334
Falmouth *(G-5133)*
Express Welding Inc .... G 906 786-8808
Escanaba *(G-5071)*
◆ **Gillisons Var Fabrication Inc** .... E 231 882-5921
Benzonia *(G-1614)*
Glenn Knochel .... G 989 684-7869
Kawkawlin *(G-9415)*
▲ **Griptrac Inc** .... F 231 853-2284
Ravenna *(G-13689)*
◆ **HD Hudson Manufacturing Co** .... D 800 977-8661
Lowell *(G-10503)*
▲ **Heath Manufacturing Company** .... E 616 997-8181
Coopersville *(G-3688)*
Holland Transplanter Co Inc .... F 616 392-3579
Holland *(G-8086)*
Howey Tree Baler Corporation .... G 231 328-4321
Merritt *(G-11266)*
Hy Capacity Inc .... G 616 558-5690
Brighton *(G-2012)*
Ikes Welding Shop and Mfg .... G 989 892-2783
Munger *(G-11751)*
Keays Family Truckin .... G 231 838-6430
Gaylord *(G-6139)*
Liver Transplant/Univ of Mich .... G 734 936-7670
Ann Arbor *(G-552)*
Local Bsket Case LLC - Rckford .... G 616 884-0749
Rockford *(G-14175)*
Logan Diesel Incorporated .... G 517 589-8811
Leslie *(G-10014)*
Mahindra Tractor Assembly Inc .... E 734 274-2239
Ann Arbor *(G-563)*
▲ **Mechanical Transplanter Co LLC** .... E 616 396-8738
Holland *(G-8142)*
Mensch Manufacturing LLC .... F 269 945-5300
Hastings *(G-7804)*
Mensch Mfg Mar Div Inc .... E 269 945-5300
Hastings *(G-7805)*
▲ **Michigan AG Services Inc** .... F 616 374-8803
Lake Odessa *(G-9577)*
◆ **Morbark LLC** .... B 989 866-2381
Winn *(G-18590)*
National Case Corp .... G 586 803-3245
Shelby Township *(G-15287)*
Nelson Farms .... G 989 560-1303
Elwell *(G-5041)*
Overstreet Property MGT Co .... G 269 281-3880
Benton Harbor *(G-1578)*
Packard Farms LLC .... E 989 386-3816
Clare *(G-2993)*
▲ **Phil Brown Welding Corporation** .... F 616 784-3046
Conklin *(G-3662)*
Prime Land Farm .... G 989 550-6120
Harbor Beach *(G-7635)*
Recon Technologies LLC .... G 616 241-1877
Grand Rapids *(G-7145)*
◆ **Root-Lowell Manufacturing Co** .... D 616 897-9211
Lowell *(G-10515)*
S & S Mowing Inc .... G 906 466-9009
Bark River *(G-1157)*
Schuette Farms .... G 989 550-0563
Elkton *(G-5032)*
Sprayerusa Inc .... G 800 253-4642
Lowell *(G-10516)*
▲ **Steiner Tractor Parts Inc** .... E 810 621-3000
Lennon *(G-9996)*
Stephens Pipe & Steel LLC .... E 616 248-3433
Grand Rapids *(G-7226)*
Stuff A Pal .... G 734 646-3775
Maybee *(G-11173)*
Superior Attachment Inc .... G 906 864-1708
Menominee *(G-11261)*
Tindall Packaging Inc .... G 269 649-1163
Portage *(G-13626)*
Triple K Farms Inc .... G 517 458-9741
Morenci *(G-11617)*
Ubly Bean Knife Mfg Inc .... G 231 723-3244
Manistee *(G-10914)*
Unist Inc .... E 616 949-0853
Grand Rapids *(G-7297)*

3524 Garden, Lawn Tractors & Eqpt

Ace Outdoor Services LLC .... E 810 820-8313
Flint *(G-5635)*
Big Green Tomato LLC .... G 269 282-1593
Battle Creek *(G-1194)*
Buyers Development Group LLC .... F 734 677-0009
Ann Arbor *(G-411)*
Coffman Electrical Eqp Co .... E 616 452-8708
Grand Rapids *(G-6580)*
◆ **Contech (us) Inc** .... F 616 459-4139
Grand Rapids *(G-6597)*
▼ **Dynamic Manufacturing LLC** .... E 989 644-8109
Weidman *(G-18251)*
Ebels Hardware Inc .... F 231 826-3334
Falmouth *(G-5133)*
Excellence Lawn Landscape .... G 810 623-9742
Brighton *(G-1985)*
Forest Grove Power Eqp LLC .... G 616 896-8344
Hudsonville *(G-8584)*
Grandville Tractor Svcs LLC .... F 616 530-2030
Grandville *(G-7383)*
Green Day Management LLC .... F 313 652-1390
Detroit *(G-4278)*
Harrells LLC .... G 248 446-8070
New Hudson *(G-12056)*
Hydro Giant 4 Inc .... F 248 661-0034
West Bloomfield *(G-18289)*
Lloyd Miller & Sons Inc .... G 517 223-3112
Corunna *(G-3710)*
Milsco LLC .... E 517 787-3650
Jackson *(G-8965)*
Randys Lawn Care Services LLC .... G 313 447-9536
Detroit *(G-4553)*
Reeds Equipment LLC .... G 517 567-4415
Pittsford *(G-13068)*
▼ **Root Spring Scraper Co** .... E 269 382-2025
Kalamazoo *(G-9321)*
Superior Cedar Products Inc .... E 906 639-2132
Carney *(G-2564)*
◆ **Sure-Loc Aluminum Edging Inc** .... G 616 392-3209
Holland *(G-8210)*
Surefit Parts LLC .... G 586 416-9150
Chesterfield *(G-2952)*
Wells Equipment Sales Inc .... F 517 542-2376
Litchfield *(G-10087)*
▲ **Whitehall Products LLC** .... D 231 894-2688
Whitehall *(G-18514)*

3531 Construction Machinery & Eqpt

ABI International .... F 248 583-7150
Madison Heights *(G-10656)*
Airman Inc .... G 248 926-1409
Wixom *(G-18602)*
Alta Construction Eqp LLC .... D 248 356-5200
New Hudson *(G-12041)*
AME For Auto Dealers Inc .... G 248 720-0245
Auburn Hills *(G-780)*
Arcosa Epi LLC .... E 517 676-8800
Mason *(G-11116)*
Arcosa Shoring Products Inc .... E 800 292-1225
Lansing *(G-9673)*
▲ **Arcosa Shoring Products Inc** .... D 517 741-4300
Union City *(G-17490)*
◆ **B&P Littleford LLC** .... E 989 757-1300
Saginaw *(G-14608)*
◆ **Bandit Industries Inc** .... B 989 561-2270
Remus *(G-13813)*
◆ **Besser Company** .... B 989 354-4111
Alpena *(G-284)*
Big Foot Manufacturing Co .... E 231 775-5588
Cadillac *(G-2315)*
Blackline Bear LLC .... G 616 291-1521
Norton Shores *(G-12279)*
Bme Inc .... G 810 937-2974
Port Huron *(G-13461)*
Bob-O-Link Associates LLC .... G 616 891-6939
Grand Rapids *(G-6518)*
Boral Building Products Inc .... C 800 521-8486
Wixom *(G-18625)*
Border City Tool and Mfg Co .... F 586 758-5574
Harper Woods *(G-7664)*
Brawn Mixer Inc .... E 616 399-5600
Holland *(G-7982)*
Capital Equipment Clare LLC .... F 517 669-5533
Dewitt *(G-4708)*
CB Industrial LLC .... F 248 264-9800
New Hudson *(G-12045)*
Contract Welding and Fabg Inc .... E 734 699-5561
Van Buren Twp *(G-17520)*
CPS LLC .... F 517 639-1464
Quincy *(G-13666)*
Creative Surfaces Inc .... F 586 226-2950
Clinton Township *(G-3213)*
Cutting Edge Poly .... G 269 953-2866
Hastings *(G-7787)*
D P Equipment Co .... F 517 368-5266
Camden *(G-2421)*
Dedoes Industries LLC .... C 248 624-7710
Walled Lake *(G-17666)*
Di-Coat Corporation .... E 248 349-1211
Novi *(G-12399)*
Douglas Dynamics LLC .... F 414 362-3890
Madison Heights *(G-10710)*
▲ **Drag Finishing Tech LLC** .... G 616 785-0400
Comstock Park *(G-3603)*
▼ **E M I Construction Products** .... F 616 392-7207
Holland *(G-8020)*
East Coast Finishers .... E 844 366-9966
Farmington Hills *(G-5222)*
Falcon Road Maint Eqp LLC .... F 989 495-9332
Midland *(G-11362)*
▲ **Fireboy-Xintex Inc** .... E 616 735-9380
Grand Rapids *(G-6706)*
Fw Shoring Company .... D 517 676-8800
Mason *(G-11133)*
Globe Industries Incorporated .... F 906 932-3540
Ironwood *(G-8763)*
Golde Auburn Hills LLC .... D 248 606-1912
Auburn Hills *(G-916)*
Great Lakes Exploration Inc .... G 906 352-4024
Menominee *(G-11239)*
Griff & Son Tree Service Inc .... G 989 735-5160
Glennie *(G-6212)*
◆ **Hines Corporation** .... F 231 799-6240
Norton Shores *(G-12348)*
Independent Machine Co Inc .... E 906 428-4524
Escanaba *(G-5077)*
Intric Grouting Solutions LLC .... F 855 801-7453
Wayland *(G-18196)*
Jackson Pandrol Inc .... E 231 843-3431
Ludington *(G-10542)*
JB Machinery LLC .... G 419 727-1772
Blissfield *(G-1765)*
JG Distributing Inc .... G 906 225-0882
Marquette *(G-11025)*
John Crowley Inc .... F 517 782-0491
Jackson *(G-8922)*
Jolman & Jolman Enterprises .... G 231 744-4500
Muskegon *(G-11848)*
JP Skidmore LLC .... G 906 424-4127
Menominee *(G-11241)*
K&H Supply of Lansing Inc .... E 517 482-7600
Lansing *(G-9769)*
Kaufman Cstm Shtmtl Fbrction L .... G 906 932-2130
Ironwood *(G-8766)*
Keizer-Morris Intl Inc .... E 810 688-1234
North Branch *(G-12180)*
▲ **Lang Tool Company** .... G 989 435-9864
Beaverton *(G-1428)*
Lawrence J Julio LLC .... G 906 483-4781
Houghton *(G-8384)*
Leadership Group LLC .... G 586 251-2090
Sterling Heights *(G-16069)*

SIC

Employee Codes: A=Over 500 employees, B=251-500
C=101-250, D=51-100, E=20-50, F=10-19, G=3-9

2022 Harris Michigan
Industrial Directory

833

▲ **Leedy Manufacturing Co LLC** ....D....... 616 245-0517
Grand Rapids ***(G-6934)***
Leica Geo Systems Gr LLC ....G....... 616 949-7430
Grand Rapids ***(G-6938)***
Lyonnais Inc ....G....... 616 868-6625
Lowell ***(G-10510)***
▲ **Magnum Toolscom LLC** ....F....... 734 595-4600
Romulus ***(G-14300)***
Marine Propulsion LLC ....G....... 248 396-2353
West Bloomfield ***(G-18295)***
Midwest Vibro Inc ....G....... 616 532-7670
Grandville ***(G-7401)***
Milan Metal Worx LLC ....G....... 734 369-7115
Petersburg ***(G-12984)***
Mull-It-Over Products LLC ....G....... 616 730-2162
Grandville ***(G-7403)***
New Wake Inc ....G....... 800 957-5606
Hudsonville ***(G-8599)***
Nordson Corporation ....D....... 734 459-8600
Wixom ***(G-18721)***
Oshkosh Defense LLC ....E....... 586 576-8301
Warren ***(G-17951)***
◆ **Paladin Brands Group Inc** ....F....... 319 378-3696
Dexter ***(G-4748)***
▲ **Petter Investments Inc** ....F....... 269 637-1997
South Haven ***(G-15411)***
Powerscreen of Michigan LLC ....G....... 586 690-7224
Clinton Township ***(G-3322)***
▼ **PSI Marine Inc** ....F....... 989 695-2646
Saginaw ***(G-14731)***
▼ **Root Spring Scraper Co** ....E....... 269 382-2025
Kalamazoo ***(G-9321)***
Rough Road Trucking LLC ....G....... 231 645-3355
Kalkaska ***(G-9402)***
◆ **Ryans Equipment Inc** ....E....... 989 427-2829
Edmore ***(G-4997)***
Shred-Pac Inc ....E....... 269 793-7978
Hopkins ***(G-8370)***
Simplicity Engineering Company ....G....... 989 288-3121
Durand ***(G-4848)***
Simpson Industrial Svcs LLC ....G....... 810 392-2717
Wales ***(G-17630)***
Spaulding Mfg Inc ....E....... 989 777-4550
Saginaw ***(G-14762)***
Stoneco of Michigan Inc ....G....... 734 236-6538
Newport ***(G-12107)***
Stoneco of Michigan Inc ....D....... 734 241-8966
Monroe ***(G-11578)***
▲ **Superior Fabrication Co LLC** ....D....... 906 495-5634
Kincheloe ***(G-9505)***
Syncon Inc ....E....... 313 914-4481
Livonia ***(G-10427)***
Tapco Holdings Inc ....C....... 248 668-6400
Wixom ***(G-18766)***
TCH Supply Inc ....G....... 517 545-4900
Howell ***(G-8526)***
Terex Corporation ....G....... 360 993-0515
Durand ***(G-4849)***
Thomas J Moyle Jr Incorporated ....F....... 906 482-3000
Houghton ***(G-8393)***
Timberland Forestry ....G....... 906 387-4350
Munising ***(G-11756)***
Top of Line Crane Service LLC ....G....... 231 267-5326
Williamsburg ***(G-18566)***
Trelan Manufacturing ....F....... 989 561-2280
Remus ***(G-13818)***
U P Fabricating Co Inc ....F....... 906 475-4400
Negaunee ***(G-11976)***
▼ **UNI-Vue Inc** ....E....... 248 564-3251
Ferndale ***(G-5593)***
W & S Development Inc ....F....... 989 724-5463
Greenbush ***(G-7473)***
Wacker Neuson Corporation ....F....... 231 799-4500
Norton Shores ***(G-12342)***
West Michigan Aerial LLc ....F....... 269 998-4455
Lawton ***(G-9991)***
White Knight Fluid Hdlg Inc ....G....... 435 783-6040
Hemlock ***(G-7858)***
White Lake Excavating Inc ....E....... 231 894-6918
Whitehall ***(G-18513)***
Wmc Sales LLC ....G....... 616 813-7237
Ada ***(G-42)***
Zcs Interconnect LLC ....G....... 616 399-8614
Zeeland ***(G-19094)***

3532 Mining Machinery & Eqpt

▼ **Classfcation Flotation Systems** ....G....... 810 714-5200
Fenton ***(G-5464)***
Contract Welding and Fabg Inc ....E....... 734 699-5561
Van Buren Twp ***(G-17520)***
▲ **General Machine Services** ....G....... 269 695-2244
Buchanan ***(G-2196)***
▲ **Lake Shore Systems Inc** ....D....... 906 774-1500
Kingsford ***(G-9512)***
Lake Shore Systems Inc ....E....... 906 265-5414
Iron River ***(G-8745)***
McLanahan Corporation ....G....... 517 614-2007
East Lansing ***(G-4902)***
Michigan Wood Pellet LLC ....F....... 989 348-4100
Grayling ***(G-7466)***
Mq Operating Company ....E....... 906 337-1515
Calumet ***(G-2412)***
▲ **National Piling Products Inc** ....F....... 855 801-7453
Wayland ***(G-18200)***
Oakland Welding Industries ....E....... 586 949-4090
Chesterfield ***(G-2916)***
▲ **Pillar Manufacturing Inc** ....F....... 269 628-5605
Gobles ***(G-6218)***
▲ **Ring Screw LLC** ....D....... 586 997-5600
Sterling Heights ***(G-16152)***
Thermo Vac Inc ....D....... 248 969-0300
Oxford ***(G-12923)***
U P Fabricating Co Inc ....F....... 906 475-4400
Negaunee ***(G-11976)***
Yerington Brothers Inc ....G....... 269 695-7669
Niles ***(G-12174)***

3533 Oil Field Machinery & Eqpt

▲ **General Machine Services** ....G....... 269 695-2244
Buchanan ***(G-2196)***
Merrill Technologies Group Inc ....C....... 989 462-0330
Alma ***(G-246)***
Millennium Planet LLC ....G....... 248 835-2331
Farmington Hills ***(G-5322)***
◆ **Murphys Water Well Bits** ....G....... 810 658-1554
Davison ***(G-3791)***
Titan Global Oil Services Inc ....F....... 248 594-5983
Birmingham ***(G-1753)***
United Metal Technology Inc ....E....... 517 787-7940
Jackson ***(G-9029)***

3534 Elevators & Moving Stairways

All Access Lift LLC ....G....... 616 250-1084
Hastings ***(G-7780)***
◆ **Automated Systems Inc** ....E....... 248 373-5600
Auburn Hills ***(G-804)***
Central Elevator Co Inc ....F....... 269 329-0705
Vicksburg ***(G-17602)***
▼ **Commercial Group Inc** ....E....... 313 931-6100
Taylor ***(G-16395)***
Detroit Elevator Company ....E....... 248 591-7484
Ferndale ***(G-5545)***
Elevated Technologies Inc ....E....... 616 288-9817
Grand Rapids ***(G-6672)***
Elevator Concepts Ltd ....G....... 734 246-4700
Riverview ***(G-13871)***
Lake Shore Systems Inc ....E....... 906 265-5414
Iron River ***(G-8745)***
Mc Nally Elevator Company ....F....... 269 381-1860
Kalamazoo ***(G-9266)***
Mitsubishi Electric Us Inc ....G....... 734 453-6200
Northville ***(G-12241)***
▲ **Nylube Products Company LLC** ....F....... 248 852-6500
Rochester Hills ***(G-14074)***
Schafers Elevator Co ....G....... 517 263-7202
Adrian ***(G-93)***
Schindler Elevator Corporation ....F....... 517 272-1234
Lansing ***(G-9891)***
Tk Elevator Corporation ....E....... 616 942-4710
Grand Rapids ***(G-7263)***

3535 Conveyors & Eqpt

ADW Industries Inc ....E....... 989 466-4742
Alma ***(G-233)***
Allied Indus Solutions LLC ....F....... 810 422-5093
Fenton ***(G-5447)***
▲ **Allor Manufacturing Inc** ....D....... 248 486-4500
Brighton ***(G-1943)***
Ally Equipment LLC ....G....... 810 422-5093
Fenton ***(G-5449)***
Alternative Engineering Inc ....E....... 616 785-7200
Belmont ***(G-1499)***
Altron Automation Inc ....D....... 616 669-7711
Hudsonville ***(G-8565)***
Altron Automation Group Inc ....C....... 616 669-7711
Hudsonville ***(G-8566)***
▲ **Anchor Conveyor Products Inc** ....G....... 313 582-5045
Dearborn ***(G-3808)***
Ase Industries Inc ....D....... 586 754-7480
Warren ***(G-17718)***
Auto/Con Services LLC ....G....... 586 791-7474
Fraser ***(G-5898)***
◆ **Automated Systems Inc** ....E....... 248 373-5600
Auburn Hills ***(G-804)***
▲ **Automatic Handling Intl Inc** ....D....... 734 847-0633
Erie ***(G-5044)***
Automation Contrls & Engrg LLC ....E....... 734 424-5500
Dexter ***(G-4725)***
▲ **Automtion Mdlar Components Inc** ....D....... 248 922-4740
Davisburg ***(G-3758)***
Bay Manufacturing Corporation ....F....... 989 358-7198
Alpena ***(G-282)***
Belco Industries Inc ....E....... 616 794-0410
Belding ***(G-1437)***
▲ **Belco Industries Inc** ....E....... 616 794-0410
Belding ***(G-1438)***
Benesh Corporation ....F....... 734 244-4143
Monroe ***(G-11532)***
Best Industrial Group Inc ....F....... 586 826-8800
Warren ***(G-17734)***
◆ **Blue Water Manufacturing Inc** ....E....... 810 364-6170
Marysville ***(G-11082)***
◆ **Bos Manufacturing LLC** ....F....... 231 398-3328
Manistee ***(G-10895)***
◆ **Bradford Company** ....C....... 616 399-3000
Holland ***(G-7981)***
Bristol Steel & Conveyor Corp ....E....... 810 658-9510
Davison ***(G-3775)***
Caliber Industries LLC ....F....... 586 774-6775
Romeo ***(G-14221)***
▲ **Central Conveyor Company LLC** ....D....... 248 446-0118
Wixom ***(G-18630)***
Change Parts Incorporated ....E....... 231 845-5107
Ludington ***(G-10531)***
▲ **Chip Systems International** ....F....... 269 626-8000
Scotts ***(G-15130)***
◆ **Cignys Inc** ....G....... 989 753-1411
Saginaw ***(G-14629)***
Clinton Machine Inc ....E....... 989 834-2235
Ovid ***(G-12813)***
Colombo Sales & Engrg Inc ....F....... 248 547-2820
Davisburg ***(G-3764)***
Colombo Sales and Engrg Inc ....F....... 248 547-2820
Oakley ***(G-12654)***
Constructive Sheet Metal Inc ....E....... 616 245-5306
Allendale ***(G-217)***
Continental Crane & Service ....E....... 586 294-7900
Fraser ***(G-5915)***
Conveyor Concepts Michigan LLC ....F....... 616 997-5200
Coopersville ***(G-3683)***
Cornerstone Fabg & Cnstr Inc ....E....... 989 642-5241
Hemlock ***(G-7850)***
▼ **Crippen Manufacturing Company** ....E....... 989 681-4323
Saint Louis ***(G-14990)***
Csi Service Parts Corp ....G....... 989 358-7199
Alpena ***(G-289)***
Daifuku North America Holdg Co ....C....... 248 553-1000
Novi ***(G-12391)***
▼ **Dcl Inc** ....C....... 231 547-5600
Charlevoix ***(G-2714)***
▲ **Dearborn Mid West Conveyor Co** ....G....... 313 273-2804
Detroit ***(G-4129)***
▲ **Dearborn Mid-West Company LLC** ....D....... 734 288-4400
Taylor ***(G-16400)***
◆ **Diamond Automation Ltd** ....G....... 734 838-7138
Livonia ***(G-10184)***
Dimension Machine Tech LLC ....F....... 586 649-4747
Bloomfield Hills ***(G-1814)***
Dumas Concepts In Building Inc ....F....... 313 895-2555
Detroit ***(G-4196)***
Dunkley International Inc ....C....... 269 343-5583
Kalamazoo ***(G-9174)***
Dynamic Conveyor Corporation ....E....... 231 798-0014
Norton Shores ***(G-12288)***
Eagle Engineering & Supply Co ....E....... 989 356-4526
Alpena ***(G-291)***
▼ **Edge Industries Inc** ....G....... 616 453-5458
Grand Rapids ***(G-6665)***
▲ **Egemin Automation Inc** ....C....... 616 393-0101
Holland ***(G-8025)***
Empire Machine & Conveyors Inc ....F....... 989 541-2060
Durand ***(G-4841)***
▼ **Endura-Veyor Inc** ....E....... 989 358-7060
Alpena ***(G-292)***
Ensign Equipment Inc ....G....... 616 738-9000
Holland ***(G-8028)***
Esys Automation LLC ....C....... 248 484-9927
Auburn Hills ***(G-881)***
Esys Automation LLC ....E....... 284 484-9724
Pontiac ***(G-13370)***

Esys Automation LLC E 248 484-9702
Sterling Heights *(G-16005)*
▲ Fata Automation Inc D 248 724-7660
Auburn Hills *(G-886)*
Fibro Laepple Technology Inc G 248 591-4494
Sterling Heights *(G-16014)*
▼ Florkeys Conveyor Service E 810 772-1930
Warren *(G-17814)*
Fraser Fab and Machine Inc E 248 852-9050
Rochester Hills *(G-14015)*
Frost Inc G 616 785-9030
Grand Rapids *(G-6721)*
◆ Frost Incorporated E 616 453-7781
Grand Rapids *(G-6722)*
Frost Incorporated G 616 785-9030
Grand Rapids *(G-6724)*
▲ Frost Links G 616 785-9030
Grand Rapids *(G-6725)*
GMI Packaging Co F 734 972-7389
Ann Arbor *(G-502)*
▲ Gudel Inc D 734 214-0000
Ann Arbor *(G-508)*
Hapman F 269 382-8257
Kalamazoo *(G-9208)*
Harvey S Freeman G 248 852-2222
West Bloomfield *(G-18287)*
Henshaw Inc D 586 752-0700
Armada *(G-736)*
▲ Herkules Equipment Corporation E 248 960-7100
Commerce Township *(G-3536)*
▼ Highland Engineering Inc E 517 548-4372
Howell *(G-8460)*
◆ Hines Corporation F 231 799-6240
Norton Shores *(G-12348)*
▲ HMS Products Co D 248 689-8120
Troy *(G-17146)*
Howard Structural Steel Inc E 989 752-3000
Saginaw *(G-14670)*
Industrial Kinetics Inc F 586 212-3894
New Baltimore *(G-11983)*
Integrated Conveyor Ltd G 231 747-6430
Muskegon *(G-11841)*
International Material Co F 616 355-2800
Holland *(G-8097)*
Intersrce Recovery Systems Inc E 269 375-5100
Kalamazoo *(G-9225)*
Jantec Incorporated E 231 941-4339
Traverse City *(G-16727)*
◆ Jervis B Webb Company B 248 553-1000
Novi *(G-12449)*
Kalamazoo Mfg Corp Globl C 269 382-8200
Kalamazoo *(G-9243)*
Livonia Magnetics Co Inc E 734 397-8844
Farmington Hills *(G-5293)*
Loudon Steel Inc E 989 871-9353
Millington *(G-11502)*
Magline Inc G 800 624-5463
Standish *(G-15891)*
▲ Magnetic Products Inc D 248 887-5600
Highland *(G-7896)*
Mark One Corporation D 989 732-2427
Gaylord *(G-6145)*
▼ Material Control Inc G 630 892-4274
Croswell *(G-3732)*
Material Hdlg Techniques Inc G 616 890-1475
Hopkins *(G-8366)*
Material Transfer and Stor Inc E 269 673-2125
Allegan *(G-170)*
McNichols Conveyor Company F 248 357-6077
Southfield *(G-15651)*
Metzgar Conveyor Co E 616 784-0930
Grand Rapids *(G-6983)*
MHS Conveyor Corp B 231 798-4547
Norton Shores *(G-12310)*
Milan Metal Worx LLC G 734 369-7115
Petersburg *(G-12984)*
◆ Mol Belting Systems Inc D 616 453-2484
Grand Rapids *(G-7020)*
Mondrella Process Systems LLC G 616 281-9836
Grand Rapids *(G-7024)*
◆ Motan Inc E 269 685-1050
Plainwell *(G-13083)*
Motion Industries Inc G 989 771-0200
Saginaw *(G-14705)*
Motion Machine Company F 810 664-9901
Lapeer *(G-9949)*
National Element Inc E 248 486-1810
Brighton *(G-2040)*
New Technologies Tool & Mfg F 810 694-5426
Grand Blanc *(G-6254)*
North Woods Industrial G 616 784-2840
Comstock Park *(G-3629)*
▲ Omni Metalcraft Corp E 989 354-4075
Alpena *(G-306)*
Overhead Conveyor Company E 248 547-3800
Ferndale *(G-5574)*
P & A Conveyor Sales Inc G 734 285-7970
Riverview *(G-13882)*
Paradigm Conveyor LLC F 616 667-4040
Marne *(G-10996)*
Paslin Company C 248 953-8419
Shelby Township *(G-15296)*
PCI Procal Inc F 989 358-7070
Alpena *(G-311)*
Peak Industries Co Inc E 313 846-8666
Dearborn *(G-3883)*
Powerscreen USA LLC G 989 288-3121
Durand *(G-4845)*
▲ Prab Inc C 269 382-8200
Kalamazoo *(G-9299)*
Prab Inc G 269 382-8200
Kalamazoo *(G-9300)*
Prab Inc G 269 343-1675
Kalamazoo *(G-9301)*
◆ Pressure Vessel Service Inc E 313 921-1200
Detroit *(G-4533)*
Production Accessories Co G 313 366-1500
Detroit *(G-4536)*
RK Wojan Inc E 231 347-1160
Charlevoix *(G-2730)*
▲ Roberts Sinto Corporation D 517 371-2460
Lansing *(G-9787)*
▲ Saginaw Products Corporation E 989 753-1411
Saginaw *(G-14748)*
Santanna Tool & Design LLC D 248 541-3500
Madison Heights *(G-10824)*
▲ Sinto America Inc E 517 371-2460
Lansing *(G-9791)*
Sparks Belting Company Inc G 800 451-4537
Grand Rapids *(G-7206)*
▲ Sparks Belting Company Inc D 616 949-2750
Grand Rapids *(G-7207)*
Spectrum Automation Company E 734 522-2160
Livonia *(G-10416)*
Steel Craft Inc G 989 358-7196
Alpena *(G-320)*
Steel Master LLC E 810 771-4943
Grand Blanc *(G-6264)*
◆ Storch Products Company Inc F 734 591-2200
Livonia *(G-10422)*
Structural Equipment Co F 248 547-3800
Ferndale *(G-5587)*
Sure Conveyors Inc F 248 926-2100
Wixom *(G-18763)*
▲ Symbiote Inc E 616 772-1790
Zeeland *(G-19083)*
Symorex Ltd F 734 971-6000
Ann Arbor *(G-670)*
◆ Tgw Systems Inc C 616 888-2595
Grand Rapids *(G-7256)*
▼ Thoreson-Mc Cosh Inc E 248 362-0960
Lake Orion *(G-9634)*
Ton-Tex Corporation F 616 957-3200
Greenville *(G-7508)*
▲ Triad Industrial Corp F 989 358-7191
Atlanta *(G-748)*
Ultimation Industries LLC E 586 771-1881
Roseville *(G-14489)*
▲ Uniband Usa LLC F 616 676-6011
Grand Rapids *(G-7296)*
Unified Scrning Crshing - MI L F 888 464-9473
Saint Johns *(G-14920)*
Versa Handling Co G 313 491-0500
Sterling Heights *(G-16222)*
Versa-Craft Inc G 586 465-5999
Clinton Township *(G-3385)*
Verstraete Conveyability Inc F 800 798-0410
Grand Rapids *(G-7313)*
Via-Tech Corp F 989 358-7028
Lachine *(G-9535)*
Wardcraft Industries LLC E 517 750-9100
Spring Arbor *(G-15798)*
Wedin International Inc E 231 779-8650
Cadillac *(G-2363)*
Whites Bridge Tooling Inc E 616 897-4151
Lowell *(G-10522)*
▼ Wilkie Bros Conveyors Inc E 810 364-4820
Marysville *(G-11113)*

3536 Hoists, Cranes & Monorails

Ats Assembly and Test Inc F 734 266-4713
Livonia *(G-10129)*
▲ Besser Company USA D 616 399-5215
Zeeland *(G-18998)*
Bulmann Enterprises Inc E 231 549-5020
Boyne City *(G-1885)*
C R B Crane & Service Co G 586 757-1222
Warren *(G-17747)*
Crane 1 Services Inc E 586 468-0909
Harrison Township *(G-7694)*
▲ Crane Technologies Group Inc E 248 652-8700
Rochester Hills *(G-13985)*
Crb Crane Services Inc E 517 552-5699
Howell *(G-8442)*
▲ Detroit Hoist & Crane Co L L C E 586 268-2600
Sterling Heights *(G-15982)*
F&B Technologies F 734 856-2118
Ottawa Lake *(G-12806)*
Frost Inc G 616 785-9030
Grand Rapids *(G-6721)*
Frost Incorporated G 616 453-7781
Grand Rapids *(G-6723)*
◆ Frost Incorporated E 616 453-7781
Grand Rapids *(G-6722)*
Great Lakes Lift Inc G 989 673-2109
Caro *(G-2572)*
Harbor Master Ltd F 616 669-3170
Hudsonville *(G-8585)*
Hme Inc C 616 534-1463
Wyoming *(G-18885)*
James W Liess Co Inc G 248 547-9160
Rochester Hills *(G-14042)*
Jered LLC G 906 776-1800
Iron Mountain *(G-8723)*
◆ Jervis B Webb Company B 248 553-1000
Novi *(G-12449)*
K&S Consultants LLC G 269 240-7767
Buchanan *(G-2198)*
Konecranes Inc E 248 380-2626
Novi *(G-12454)*
Konecranes Inc F 269 323-1222
Portage *(G-13574)*
L & C Enterprises Inc G 231 943-7787
Traverse City *(G-16736)*
L & M Mfg Inc G 989 689-4010
Hope *(G-8362)*
▲ Leedy Manufacturing Co LLC D 616 245-0517
Grand Rapids *(G-6934)*
North Central Welding Co E 989 275-8054
Roscommon *(G-14354)*
Odonnells Docks G 269 244-1446
Jones *(G-9084)*
Otsego Crane & Hoist LLC G 269 672-7222
Otsego *(G-12792)*
Royal ARC Welding Company E 734 789-9099
Flat Rock *(G-5628)*
Simpson Industrial Svcs LLC G 810 392-2717
Wales *(G-17630)*
Star Crane Hist Svc of Klmazoo G 269 321-8882
Portage *(G-13611)*
Symorex Ltd F 734 971-6000
Ann Arbor *(G-670)*
▲ Unified Industries Inc D 517 546-3220
Brighton *(G-2087)*
Versa Handling Co G 313 491-0500
Sterling Heights *(G-16222)*
▲ Wolverine Crane & Service Inc E 616 538-4870
Grand Rapids *(G-7345)*
Wolverine Crane & Service Inc F 734 467-9066
Romulus *(G-14339)*

3537 Indl Trucks, Tractors, Trailers & Stackers

AAR Manufacturing Inc E 231 779-8800
Cadillac *(G-2306)*
Aimrite LLC G 248 693-8925
Lake Orion *(G-9584)*
Air-Hydraulics Inc F 517 787-9444
Jackson *(G-8806)*
All Pointe Truck & Trailer Svc G 586 504-0364
New Baltimore *(G-11977)*
Alta Equipment Holdings Inc E 248 449-6700
Livonia *(G-10112)*
American Fabricated Pdts Inc E 616 607-8785
Spring Lake *(G-15803)*
Automated Machine Systems Inc E 616 662-1309
Jenison *(G-9046)*
Baker Enterprises Inc E 989 354-2189
Alpena *(G-281)*

S I C

Bay Wood Homes Inc F 989 245-4156 Fenton *(G-5456)*
Bell Fork Lift Inc F 313 841-1220 Detroit *(G-4049)*
Bell Forklifts G 586 469-7979 Clinton Township *(G-3181)*
▲ **Besser Company USA** D 616 399-5215 Zeeland *(G-18998)*
Bristol Manufacturing Inc E 810 658-9510 Davison *(G-3774)*
Brownlee Group LLC G 512 202-0568 Clinton Township *(G-3190)*
Bucher Hydraulics Inc G 231 652-2773 Newaygo *(G-12078)*
Budd Magnetic Products Inc G 248 353-2533 Southfield *(G-15512)*
C&C Forklift G 313 729-2850 Taylor *(G-16389)*
Charles Lange F 989 777-0110 Saginaw *(G-14627)*
Circle K Service Corporation E 989 496-0511 Midland *(G-11329)*
▼ **Commercial Group Inc** E 313 931-6100 Taylor *(G-16395)*
Crown Equipment Corporation G 616 530-3000 Traverse City *(G-16666)*
Crown Equipment Corporation E 616 530-3000 Grand Rapids *(G-6614)*
Delta Tube & Fabricating Corp C 248 634-8267 Holly *(G-8268)*
Dlr Logistics Inc G 248 499-2368 Ann Arbor *(G-453)*
Dr Forklift G 734 968-6576 Brighton *(G-1977)*
▲ **Egemin Automation Inc** C 616 393-0101 Holland *(G-8025)*
Forklift Parts Group G 248 792-7132 Troy *(G-17117)*
◆ **Frost Incorporated** E 616 453-7781 Grand Rapids *(G-6722)*
Gilmore Logistics LLC G 586 488-9895 Inkster *(G-8664)*
Great Lakes Dock & Door LLC E 313 368-6300 Detroit *(G-4276)*
Harlo Corporation D 616 538-0550 Grandville *(G-7387)*
▲ **Harlo Products Corporation** E 616 538-0550 Grandville *(G-7388)*
Hart Precision Products Inc E 313 537-0490 Redford *(G-13739)*
Harvey S Freeman G 248 852-2222 West Bloomfield *(G-18287)*
Hme Inc C 616 534-1463 Wyoming *(G-18885)*
Hobart Brothers LLC G 231 933-1234 Traverse City *(G-16712)*
Holland Transport Services LLC G 313 605-3103 New Haven *(G-12032)*
Humphrey Companies LLC C 616 530-1717 Grandville *(G-7389)*
Ihs Inc G 616 464-4224 Grand Rapids *(G-6833)*
Independent Machine Co Inc E 906 428-4524 Escanaba *(G-5077)*
Ipp Logistic LLC G 248 330-5379 Southfield *(G-15608)*
J & J Transport LLC G 231 582-6083 Boyne City *(G-1891)*
◆ **Jervis B Webb Company** B 248 553-1000 Novi *(G-12449)*
Keller Tool Ltd F 734 425-4500 Livonia *(G-10264)*
L A S Leasing Inc E 734 727-5148 Wayne *(G-18228)*
▲ **Lake Shore Systems Inc** D 906 774-1500 Kingsford *(G-9512)*
Lakewood Machine Products Co D 734 654-6677 Carleton *(G-2558)*
Lee Hamilton Gary Jr G 231 884-9600 Mc Bain *(G-11184)*
Lock and Load Corp G 800 975-9658 Marion *(G-10973)*
Logistics Insight Corp D 810 424-0511 Flint *(G-5726)*
Logistics On The Go Inc G 248 750-6654 Warren *(G-17906)*
Loudon Steel Inc E 989 871-9353 Millington *(G-11502)*
◆ **Magline Inc** C 800 624-5463 Standish *(G-15890)*
Magline Inc G 800 624-5463 Standish *(G-15891)*
Magline International LLC G 989 512-1000 Standish *(G-15892)*
Marsh Industrial Services Inc F 231 258-4870 Kalkaska *(G-9395)*
Metzgar Conveyor Co E 616 784-0930 Grand Rapids *(G-6983)*
Michiana Forklift G 269 663-2700 Edwardsburg *(G-5010)*
Midwest Forklift Parts LLC G 248 830-5982 Oxford *(G-12902)*
Midwest Tractor & Equipment Co F 231 269-4100 Buckley *(G-2207)*
Milsco LLC E 517 787-3650 Jackson *(G-8965)*
▲ **Mollers North America Inc** D 616 942-6504 Grand Rapids *(G-7022)*
Montrose Trailers Inc G 810 639-7431 Montrose *(G-11607)*
Nyx LLC D 734 464-0800 Livonia *(G-10346)*
O Keller Tool Engrg Co LLC D 734 425-4500 Livonia *(G-10349)*
One Source Trucking LLC G 855 999-7723 Detroit *(G-4499)*
PCI Procal Inc F 989 358-7070 Alpena *(G-311)*
Peninsular Inc E 586 775-7211 Roseville *(G-14461)*
◆ **Perfecto Industries Inc** E 989 732-2941 Gaylord *(G-6154)*
▲ **Pettibone/Traverse Lift LLC** E 906 353-4800 Baraga *(G-1147)*
Progressive Metal Mfg Co E 248 546-2827 Warren *(G-17978)*
Prophotonix Limited G 586 778-1100 Roseville *(G-14466)*
Ream Logistics Dlvry Svcs LLC G 877 246-7857 Belleville *(G-1490)*
Ross Joseph G 269 424-5448 Dowagiac *(G-4794)*
Sadia Enterprises Inc F 248 854-4666 Troy *(G-17340)*
◆ **Saf-Holland Inc** A 231 773-3271 Muskegon *(G-11913)*
Sfi Acquisition Inc E 248 471-1500 Farmington Hills *(G-5377)*
Skamp Industries Inc G 269 731-2666 Portage *(G-13608)*
Steelhead Industries LLC G 989 506-7416 Mount Pleasant *(G-11743)*
◆ **Sterling Truck and Wstn Star** E 313 592-4200 Redford *(G-13775)*
Superior Distribution Svcs LLC G 616 453-6358 Grand Rapids *(G-7236)*
Superior Equipment & Supply Co G 906 774-1789 Iron Mountain *(G-8734)*
T & L Transport Inc G 313 350-1535 Plymouth *(G-13308)*
▼ **Thoreson-Mc Cosh Inc** E 248 362-0960 Lake Orion *(G-9634)*
US Tarp Inc D 269 639-3010 South Haven *(G-15420)*
▲ **Vci Inc** D 269 659-3676 Sturgis *(G-16328)*
Versatile Fabrication Co Inc E 231 739-7115 Muskegon *(G-11941)*
We Haul Carz LLC G 248 933-2246 West Bloomfield *(G-18323)*
West Michigan Forklift Inc G 616 262-4949 Wayland *(G-18209)*
Windy Lake LLC D 877 869-6911 Pentwater *(G-12975)*

3541 Machine Tools: Cutting

A & D Run Off Inc G 231 759-0950 Muskegon *(G-11760)*
AAA Industries Inc E 313 255-0420 Redford *(G-13709)*
ABC Boring Co Inc E 586 751-2580 Warren *(G-17686)*
ABC Precision Machining Inc G 269 926-6322 Benton Harbor *(G-1525)*
Abrasive Services Incorporated G 734 941-2144 Romulus *(G-14244)*
Accra Tool Inc G 248 680-9936 Lake Orion *(G-9582)*
Accubilt Automated Systems LLC E 517 787-9353 Jackson *(G-8800)*
Accurate Machined Service Inc G 734 421-4660 Livonia *(G-10099)*
◆ **Acme Manufacturing Company** D 248 393-7300 Auburn Hills *(G-773)*
Acme Manufacturing Company F 248 393-7300 Lake Orion *(G-9583)*
Advanced Maintenance Tech G 810 820-2554 Flint *(G-5639)*
Advanced Stage Tooling LLC G 810 444-9807 East China *(G-4855)*
◆ **Allfi Robotics Inc** G 586 248-1198 Wixom *(G-18604)*
Alliance Tool G 586 465-3960 Harrison Township *(G-7685)*
Alto Manufacturing Inc E 734 641-8800 Westland *(G-18352)*
◆ **American Broach & Machine Co** E 734 961-0300 Ypsilanti *(G-18924)*
American Gator Tool Company G 231 347-3222 Harbor Springs *(G-7639)*
American Gear & Engrg Co Inc E 734 595-6400 Westland *(G-18353)*
American Lap Company G 231 526-7121 Harbor Springs *(G-7640)*
American Pride Machining Inc G 586 294-6404 Fraser *(G-5892)*
Americhip International Inc E 586 783-4598 Clinton Township *(G-3167)*
Amex Mfg & Distrg Co Inc G 734 439-8560 Milan *(G-11430)*
Antech Tool Inc F 734 207-3622 Canton *(G-2435)*
Anthony Castellani G 248 579-3406 Van Buren Twp *(G-17509)*
Apex Broaching Systems Inc F 586 758-2626 Warren *(G-17708)*
▲ **Atlas Technologies LLC** D 810 629-6663 Fenton *(G-5451)*
Aw Carbide Fabricators Inc E 586 294-1850 Sterling Heights *(G-15939)*
Axly Production Machining Inc G 989 269-2444 Bad Axe *(G-1096)*
B & O Saws Inc E 616 794-7297 Belding *(G-1435)*
B L Tool Products G 517 896-1624 Eaton Rapids *(G-4954)*
Barron LLC G 248 879-6203 Troy *(G-16968)*
Belco Industries Inc E 616 794-0410 Belding *(G-1437)*
▲ **Belco Industries Inc** E 616 794-0410 Belding *(G-1438)*
Berg Tool Inc F 586 646-7100 Chesterfield *(G-2850)*
▲ **Berger LLC** G 734 414-0402 Plymouth *(G-13135)*
Bielomatik USA Inc E 248 446-9910 Commerce Township *(G-3516)*
◆ **Bmt Aerospace Usa Inc** D 586 285-7700 Fraser *(G-5905)*
Bob G Machining LLC G 586 285-1400 Clinton Township *(G-3186)*
Broaching Industries Inc E 586 949-3775 Chesterfield *(G-2853)*
Car Pak G 248 280-1401 Troy *(G-16998)*
Carb-A-Tron Tool Co G 517 782-2249 Jackson *(G-8834)*
Casalbi Company Inc F 517 782-0345 Jackson *(G-8835)*
CB Industrial LLC F 248 264-9800 New Hudson *(G-12045)*
CBS Tool Inc F 586 566-5945 Shelby Township *(G-15182)*
▲ **Cellular Concepts Co Inc** G 313 371-4800 Rochester Hills *(G-13974)*
Champion Screw Mch Engrg Inc F 248 624-4545 Wixom *(G-18632)*
Changeover Integration LLC F 231 845-5320 Ludington *(G-10532)*
City Animation Co E 248 589-0600 Troy *(G-17012)*
City Animation Co F 989 743-3458 Corunna *(G-3706)*
Clausing Industrial Inc F 269 345-7155 Kalamazoo *(G-9144)*
▲ **Clausing Industrial Inc** D 269 345-7155 Kalamazoo *(G-9145)*
Clear Cut Water Jet Machining G 616 534-9119 Grand Rapids *(G-6573)*

SIC SECTION 35 INDUSTRIAL AND COMMERCIAL MACHINERY AND COMPUTER EQUIPMENT 35 INDUSTRIAL AND COMMERCIAL MACHINERY

▲ Cleary Developments Inc .... E 248 588-7011
  Madison Heights *(G-10689)*
Clm Vibetech Inc .... F 269 344-3878
  Kalamazoo *(G-9146)*
▲ Cold Forming Technology Inc .... F 586 254-4600
  Sterling Heights *(G-15963)*
Cole Carbide Industries Inc .... F 248 276-1278
  Lake Orion *(G-9595)*
Craft Industries Inc .... B 586 726-4300
  Shelby Township *(G-15197)*
Crankshaft Machine Company .... E 517 787-3791
  Jackson *(G-8856)*
Crow Forge .... G 269 948-5346
  Hastings *(G-7786)*
Crown Boring Industries LLC .... E 586 447-3900
  Roseville *(G-14391)*
Cutex Inc .... G 734 953-8908
  Livonia *(G-10172)*
D & D Production Inc .... F 248 334-2112
  Waterford *(G-18113)*
D W Hines Manufacturing Corp .... G 586 775-1200
  Warren *(G-17772)*
D W Machine Inc .... F 517 787-9929
  Jackson *(G-8859)*
Davison-Rite Products Co .... E 734 513-0505
  White Lake *(G-18454)*
Design Services Unlimited Inc .... G 586 463-3225
  Chesterfield *(G-2870)*
Detroit Boring & Mch Co LLC .... F 586 604-6506
  Sterling Heights *(G-15981)*
Detroit Edge Tool Company .... D 586 776-1598
  Roseville *(G-14398)*
Diamond Standard Mch Co LLC .... F 248 805-7144
  Oakland *(G-12652)*
Dikar Tool Company Inc .... E 248 348-0010
  Novi *(G-12400)*
Dimond Machinery Company Inc .... F 269 945-5908
  Hastings *(G-7790)*
Diversified Precision Pdts Inc .... E 517 750-2310
  Spring Arbor *(G-15790)*
Donald E Rogers Associates .... G 248 673-9878
  Waterford *(G-18116)*
Dons Quality Tools LLC .... G 248 701-5154
  Flint *(G-5689)*
DTe Hankin Inc .... G 734 279-1831
  Petersburg *(G-12983)*
Dvs Technology America Inc .... G 734 656-2080
  Plymouth *(G-13163)*
Dyna- Bignell Products LLC .... G 989 418-5050
  Clare *(G-2977)*
▲ Dynamic Robotic Solutions Inc .... G 248 829-2800
  Auburn Hills *(G-871)*
Ecorse McHy Sls & Rbldrs Inc .... E 313 383-2100
  Wyandotte *(G-18817)*
▼ Edge Industries Inc .... G 616 453-5458
  Grand Rapids *(G-6665)*
Eikos Holdings Inc .... E 248 280-0300
  Troy *(G-17080)*
Electro ARC Manufacturing Co .... F 734 483-4233
  Dexter *(G-4741)*
Elite Prcsion McHining Tooling .... G 269 383-9714
  Kalamazoo *(G-9177)*
Elk Rapids Engineering Inc .... F 231 264-5661
  Elk Rapids *(G-5024)*
◆ Emag LLC .... E 248 477-7440
  Farmington Hills *(G-5227)*
Emag USA Corporation .... C 248 477-7440
  Farmington Hills *(G-5228)*
Emcor Inc .... F 989 667-0652
  Bay City *(G-1350)*
Emhart Teknologies LLC .... F 586 949-0440
  Chesterfield *(G-2875)*
Emhart Teknologies LLC .... F 800 783-6427
  Chesterfield *(G-2876)*
Emhart Teknologies LLC .... G 800 783-6427
  Troy *(G-17088)*
Emhart Teknologies LLC .... G 800 783-6427
  Troy *(G-17089)*
Enagon LLC .... G 269 455-5110
  Saugatuck *(G-15083)*
Esco Group Inc .... F 616 453-5458
  Grand Rapids *(G-6685)*
Esr .... G 989 619-7160
  Harrisville *(G-7742)*
ExIterra Inc .... G 248 268-2336
  Hazel Park *(G-7825)*
Extrude Hone LLC .... F 616 647-9050
  Grand Rapids *(G-6695)*
Fair Industries LLC .... F 248 740-7841
  Troy *(G-17104)*

Falcon Motorsports Inc .... G 248 328-2222
  Holly *(G-8269)*
▲ Federal Broach & Mch Co LLC .... C 989 539-7420
  Harrison *(G-7676)*
Fitz-Rite Products Inc .... G 248 360-3730
  Commerce Township *(G-3529)*
Five Star Industries Inc .... E 586 786-0500
  Macomb *(G-10595)*
▲ Forst-Usa Incorporated .... G 586 759-9380
  Warren *(G-17817)*
Fortune Tool & Machine Inc .... F 248 669-9119
  Wixom *(G-18665)*
Fourway Machinery Sales Co .... F 517 782-9371
  Jackson *(G-8886)*
Framon Mfg Co Inc .... G 989 354-5623
  Alpena *(G-295)*
G & W Machine Co .... G 616 363-4435
  Grand Rapids *(G-6729)*
Gehring Corporation .... D 248 478-8060
  Farmington Hills *(G-5250)*
General Broach & Engrg Inc .... C 586 726-4300
  Troy *(G-17129)*
▲ General Broach Company .... F 517 458-7555
  Morenci *(G-11611)*
Gerald Harris .... G 985 774-0261
  Detroit *(G-4261)*
Global Components LLC .... G 586 755-9134
  Warren *(G-17830)*
▲ Globe Tech LLC .... E 734 656-2200
  Plymouth *(G-13178)*
Godin Tool Inc .... G 231 946-2210
  Traverse City *(G-16695)*
Govro-Nelson Co .... G 810 329-4727
  Commerce Township *(G-3533)*
Great Lakes Tech & Mfg LLC .... G 810 593-0257
  Fenton *(G-5482)*
Great Lakes Waterjet Laser LLC .... G 517 629-9900
  Albion *(G-126)*
Grindmaster Eqp & Mchs USA LLC .... G 517 455-3675
  Lansing *(G-9763)*
H & G Tool Company .... F 586 573-7040
  Warren *(G-17845)*
▲ Hal International Inc .... G 248 488-0440
  Livonia *(G-10233)*
Hammond Machinery Inc .... D 269 345-7151
  Kalamazoo *(G-9207)*
Heartland Machine & Engrg LLC .... G 616 437-1641
  Mason *(G-11137)*
▲ Hegenscheidt-Mfd Corporation .... E 586 274-4900
  Sterling Heights *(G-16038)*
Helical Lap & Manufacturing Co .... F 586 307-8322
  Mount Clemens *(G-11640)*
Heller Inc .... E 248 288-5000
  Troy *(G-17140)*
◆ High-Star Corporation .... G 734 743-1503
  Westland *(G-18381)*
Highland Machine Design Inc .... G 248 669-6150
  Commerce Township *(G-3537)*
Hill Machine Works LLC .... F 586 238-2897
  Fraser *(G-5937)*
Hot Tool Cutter Grinding Co .... G 586 790-4867
  Fraser *(G-5940)*
◆ Hougen Manufacturing Inc .... C 810 635-7111
  Swartz Creek *(G-16355)*
▲ Huron Tool & Engineering Co .... F 989 269-9927
  Bad Axe *(G-1108)*
Hydro-Craft Inc .... G 248 652-8100
  Rochester Hills *(G-14037)*
Ideal Tool Inc .... F 989 893-8336
  Bay City *(G-1366)*
Illinois Tool Works Inc .... G 248 589-2500
  Troy *(G-17161)*
Indexable Cutter Engineering .... E 586 598-1540
  Chesterfield *(G-2892)*
Infra Corporation .... F 248 623-0400
  Waterford *(G-18129)*
◆ Ingersoll CM Systems LLC .... D 989 495-5000
  Midland *(G-11373)*
Ingersoll Prod Systems LLC .... G 248 585-9130
  Troy *(G-17167)*
Inland Lakes Machine Inc .... E 231 775-6543
  Cadillac *(G-2337)*
Integrity Design & Mfg LLC .... G 248 628-6927
  Oxford *(G-12890)*
Internal Grinding Abrasives .... E 616 243-5566
  Grand Rapids *(G-6849)*
Iron River Mfg Co Inc .... G 906 265-5121
  Iron River *(G-8741)*
Ivan Doverspike .... F 313 579-3000
  Detroit *(G-4328)*

J & R Tool Inc .... G 989 662-0026
  Auburn *(G-767)*
J & W Machine Inc .... G 989 773-9951
  Mount Pleasant *(G-11704)*
J C Manufacturing Company .... E 586 757-2713
  Warren *(G-17877)*
J M Mold & Engineering .... E 586 783-3300
  Clinton Township *(G-3262)*
J W Holdings Inc .... E 616 530-9889
  Grand Rapids *(G-6858)*
J&M Group Industrial Svcs Inc .... G 248 957-0006
  Clay *(G-3121)*
Jag Enterprises Inc .... E 586 784-4231
  Chesterfield *(G-2898)*
Jdl Enterprises Inc .... E 586 977-8863
  Warren *(G-17884)*
JF Hubert Enterprises Inc .... F 586 293-8660
  Fraser *(G-5947)*
JPS Mfg Inc .... E 586 415-8702
  Fraser *(G-5948)*
Jtekt Toyoda Americas Corp .... E 847 506-2415
  Wixom *(G-18690)*
K&S Consultants LLC .... G 269 240-7767
  Buchanan *(G-2198)*
▲ K-Tool Corporation Michigan .... D 863 603-0777
  Plymouth *(G-13209)*
Kalamazoo Company .... E 269 345-7151
  Kalamazoo *(G-9237)*
▲ Kalamazoo Machine Tool Co Inc .... G 269 321-8860
  Portage *(G-13571)*
▲ Kasper Machine Co .... F 248 547-3150
  Madison Heights *(G-10759)*
Kbe Precision Products LLC .... G 586 725-4200
  New Baltimore *(G-11985)*
Koch Limited .... G 586 296-3103
  Fraser *(G-5952)*
▲ Krmc LLC .... G 734 955-9311
  Romulus *(G-14296)*
Laydon Enterprises Inc .... E 906 774-4633
  Iron Mountain *(G-8724)*
Leader Corporation .... E 586 566-7114
  Shelby Township *(G-15260)*
Lee Stevens Machinery Inc .... G 248 926-8400
  Wixom *(G-18696)*
Leitz Tooling Systems LP .... G 616 698-7010
  Grand Rapids *(G-6940)*
Leitz Tooling Systems LP .... G 616 698-7010
  Grand Rapids *(G-6941)*
Lester Detterbeck Entps Ltd .... E 906 265-5121
  Iron River *(G-8746)*
Liberty Steel Fabricating Inc .... E 269 556-9792
  Saint Joseph *(G-14948)*
Liberty Tool Inc .... E 586 726-2449
  Sterling Heights *(G-16073)*
Lincoln Precision Carbide Inc .... F 989 736-8113
  Lincoln *(G-10037)*
Liquid Drive Corporation .... E 248 634-5382
  Mount Clemens *(G-11647)*
Lloyd Tool & Mfg Corp .... F 810 694-3519
  Grand Blanc *(G-6251)*
Loc Performance Products Inc .... G 734 453-2300
  Sterling Heights *(G-16076)*
◆ Loc Performance Products LLC .... C 734 453-2300
  Plymouth *(G-13224)*
Loc Performance Products LLC .... E 734 453-2300
  Lansing *(G-9713)*
Loc Performance Products LLC .... E 734 453-2300
  Lapeer *(G-9944)*
Love Machinery Inc .... G 734 427-0824
  Livonia *(G-10293)*
M C Carbide Tool Co .... E 248 486-9590
  Wixom *(G-18703)*
M S Machining Systems Inc .... F 517 546-1170
  Howell *(G-8474)*
Machine Control Technology .... G 517 655-3506
  Williamston *(G-18577)*
Maes Tool & Die Co Inc .... F 517 750-3131
  Jackson *(G-8940)*
▲ Mag-Powertrain .... F 586 446-7000
  Sterling Heights *(G-16082)*
Manufacturing Associates Inc .... G 248 421-4943
  Livonia *(G-10299)*
Max2 LLC .... F 269 468-3452
  Benton Harbor *(G-1569)*
MB Liquidating Corporation .... D 810 638-5388
  Flushing *(G-5811)*
Mc Pherson Industrial Corp .... E 586 752-5555
  Romeo *(G-14229)*
▼ Menominee Saw and Supply Co .... E 906 863-2609
  Menominee *(G-11248)*

Employee Codes: A=Over 500 employees, B=251-500
C=101-250, D=51-100, E=20-50, F=10-19, G=3-9

2022 Harris Michigan Industrial Directory

837

35 INDUSTRIAL AND COMMERCIAL MACHINERY AND COMPUTER EQUIPMENT

Methods Machine Tools Inc ....E 248 624-8601
  Wixom (G-18709)
Mi-Tech Tooling Inc ....E 989 912-2440
  Cass City (G-2618)
Microform Tool Company Inc ....G 586 776-4840
  Saint Clair Shores (G-14872)
Microprecision Cleaning ....F 586 997-6960
  Sterling Heights (G-16098)
▼ Mid-West Waltham Abrasives Co ....E 517 725-7161
  Owosso (G-12843)
Migatron Precision Products ....F 989 739-1439
  Oscoda (G-12765)
Millennium Screw Machine Inc ....G 734 525-5235
  Livonia (G-10318)
Miller Broach Inc ....D 810 395-8810
  Capac (G-2547)
▼ Miller Tool & Die Co ....E 517 782-0347
  Jackson (G-8963)
Modern Machine Tool Co ....F 517 788-9120
  Jackson (G-8969)
Moore Production Tool Spc ....E 248 476-1200
  Farmington (G-5143)
◆ Nagel Precision Inc ....G 734 426-5650
  Ann Arbor (G-587)
Nagel Precision Inc ....G 248 380-4052
  Novi (G-12485)
New Dimension Laser Inc ....G 586 415-6041
  Roseville (G-14454)
▲ New Unison Corporation ....E 248 544-9500
  Ferndale (G-5571)
▼ Neway Manufacturing Inc ....G 989 743-3458
  Corunna (G-3714)
Niagara Cutter LLC ....G 248 528-5220
  Troy (G-17276)
Nidec Indl Automation USA ....G 203 735-6367
  Sterling Heights (G-16115)
Normac Incorporated ....F 248 349-2644
  Northville (G-12244)
Novi Tool & Machine Company ....F 313 532-0900
  Redford (G-13749)
Oliver of Adrian Inc ....G 517 263-2132
  Adrian (G-86)
Only Tool Co ....G 734 552-8875
  New Boston (G-12016)
◆ Ossineke Industries Inc ....F 989 471-2197
  Ossineke (G-12778)
Oster Manufacturing Company ....G 989 729-1160
  Owosso (G-12847)
P M R Industries Inc ....F 810 989-5020
  Port Huron (G-13515)
Palfam Industries Inc ....G 248 922-0590
  Ortonville (G-12750)
Paragon Tool Company ....G 734 326-1702
  Romulus (G-14316)
Pentech Industries Inc ....E 586 445-1070
  Roseville (G-14462)
Petty Machine & Tool Inc ....E 517 782-9355
  Jackson (G-8985)
Pinnacle Engineering Co Inc ....G 734 428-7039
  Manchester (G-10888)
Pioneer Broach Midwest Inc ....F 231 768-5800
  Leroy (G-10009)
Plason Scraping Co Inc ....G 248 588-7280
  Madison Heights (G-10801)
Posa-Cut Corporation ....E 248 474-5620
  Farmington Hills (G-5350)
Precision Guides LLC ....G 517 536-7234
  Michigan Center (G-11295)
Precision Honing ....G 586 757-0304
  Roseville (G-14464)
Precision Jig Grinding Inc ....G 989 865-7953
  Saint Charles (G-14808)
Prime Industries Inc ....E 734 946-8588
  Taylor (G-16460)
Pro Precision Inc ....G 586 247-6160
  Sterling Heights (G-16134)
Production Threaded Parts Co ....E 810 688-3186
  North Branch (G-12183)
Productivity Technologies ....G 810 714-0200
  Fenton (G-5496)
Promac North America Corp ....G 248 817-2346
  Troy (G-17319)
Punch Tech ....E 810 364-4811
  Marysville (G-11097)
◆ Quality Pipe Products Inc ....E 734 606-5100
  New Boston (G-12019)
R & R Broach Inc ....G 586 779-2227
  Clinton Township (G-3330)
R & T Tooling ....G 586 218-7644
  Roseville (G-14468)

▲ R F M Incorporated ....E 810 229-4567
  Brighton (G-2059)
▲ R P T Cincinnati Inc ....G 313 382-5880
  Lincoln Park (G-10054)
Ra Prcsion Grnding Mtlwrks Inc ....E 586 783-7776
  Harrison Township (G-7719)
▲ Rattunde Corporation ....F 616 940-3340
  Caledonia (G-2396)
▲ Raven Engineering Inc ....E 248 969-9450
  Oxford (G-12911)
Richardson Acqstions Group Inc ....E 248 624-2272
  Walled Lake (G-17674)
Riverside Cnc LLC ....F 616 246-6000
  Wyoming (G-18905)
Riverside Spline & Gear Inc ....E 810 765-8302
  Marine City (G-10965)
Rnd Engineering LLC ....G 734 328-8277
  Canton (G-2518)
◆ Robert Bosch LLC ....E 248 876-1000
  Farmington Hills (G-5371)
Robert Bosch LLC ....E 248 921-9054
  Novi (G-12527)
Robert Bosch LLC ....G 734 979-3000
  Plymouth (G-13287)
▲ Rock Tool & Machine Co Inc ....E 734 455-9840
  Plymouth (G-13289)
▼ Rod Chomper Inc ....F 616 392-9677
  Holland (G-8182)
Roussin M & Ubelhor R Inc ....E 586 783-6015
  Harrison Township (G-7723)
Roy A Hutchins Company ....G 248 437-3470
  New Hudson (G-12069)
RSI Global Sourcing LLC ....G 734 604-2448
  Novi (G-12529)
RTS Cutting Tools Inc ....E 586 954-1900
  Clinton Township (G-3344)
Rwc Inc ....D 989 684-4030
  Bay City (G-1395)
S & L Tool Inc ....G 734 464-4200
  Livonia (G-10397)
S & S Machine Tool Repair LLC ....G 616 877-4930
  Dorr (G-4770)
▲ Saginaw Machine Systems Inc .....E 989 753-8465
  Saginaw (G-14747)
Sauter North America Inc ....G 734 207-0900
  Auburn Hills (G-1028)
Schienke Products Inc ....G 586 752-5454
  Bruce Twp (G-2181)
◆ Schutte Corporation ....F 517 782-3600
  Jackson (G-9007)
Select Steel Fabricators Inc ....E 248 945-9582
  Southfield (G-15696)
SKF USA Inc ....E 810 231-2400
  Brighton (G-2072)
SMS Holding Co Inc ....C 989 753-8465
  Saginaw (G-14759)
Snap Jaws Manufacturing Inc ....G 248 588-1099
  Troy (G-17353)
Snyder Corporation ....C 586 726-4300
  Shelby Township (G-15337)
Soaring Concepts Aerospace LLC ....F 574 286-9670
  Hastings (G-7810)
Soils and Structures Inc ....D 800 933-3959
  Norton Shores (G-12333)
Solidica Inc ....F 734 222-4680
  Ann Arbor (G-659)
Stanhope Tool Inc ....E 248 585-5711
  Warren (G-18027)
◆ Star Cutter Co ....G 248 474-8200
  Farmington Hills (G-5387)
Star Cutter Company Inc ....E 248 474-8200
  East Tawas (G-4923)
Star Su Company LLC ....G 248 474-8200
  Farmington Hills (G-5388)
Steadfast Tool & Machine Inc ....G 989 856-8127
  Caseville (G-2605)
Stoney Crest Regrind Service ....F 989 777-7190
  Bridgeport (G-1918)
Sunrise Tool Products Inc ....F 989 724-6688
  Harrisville (G-7745)
▲ Superabrasives Inc ....E 248 348-7670
  Wixom (G-18762)
T E C Boring ....G 586 443-5437
  Roseville (G-14482)
Tank Truck Service & Sales Inc ....G 989 731-4887
  Gaylord (G-6162)
Tank Truck Service & Sales Inc ....E 586 757-6500
  Warren (G-18036)
▲ Tarus Products Inc ....D 586 977-1400
  Sterling Heights (G-16201)

Tawas Tool Co Inc ....D 989 362-0414
  East Tawas (G-4925)
Tech Tooling Specialties Inc ....E 517 782-8898
  Jackson (G-9016)
▲ Telsonic Ultrasonics Inc ....F 586 802-0033
  Shelby Township (G-15350)
▲ Thielenhaus Microfinish Corp ....E 248 349-9450
  Novi (G-12556)
◆ Thyssenkrupp System Engrg ....C 248 340-8000
  Auburn Hills (G-1052)
Transfer Tool Systems LLC ....C 616 846-8510
  Grand Haven (G-6372)
Triangle Broach Company ....E 313 838-2150
  Detroit (G-4645)
Troy Industries Inc ....E 586 739-7760
  Shelby Township (G-15357)
Tru Tech Systems LLC ....D 586 469-2700
  Mount Clemens (G-11661)
True Fabrications & Machine ....F 248 288-0140
  Troy (G-17403)
▲ U S Equipment Co ....E 313 526-8300
  Rochester Hills (G-14134)
Ultra-Dex USA LLC ....G 810 638-5388
  Flushing (G-5814)
United Mfg Netwrk Inc ....G 586 321-7887
  Chesterfield (G-2960)
Utica Body & Assembly Inc ....E 586 726-4330
  Troy (G-17418)
▲ Utica Enterprises Inc ....E 586 726-4300
  Troy (G-17419)
▼ Van-Mark Products Corporation ....E 248 478-1200
  Farmington Hills (G-5408)
Ventra Greenwich Holdings Corp .....E 586 759-8900
  Warren (G-18054)
Vertical Machining Services ....G 734 462-1800
  Livonia (G-10460)
Viper Tool Company LLC ....G 734 417-9974
  Ann Arbor (G-711)
Viscount Equipment Co Inc ....E 586 293-5900
  Hazel Park (G-7847)
W W J Form Tool Company Inc ....G 313 565-0015
  Inkster (G-8677)
Waber Tool & Engineering Co ....F 269 342-0765
  Kalamazoo (G-9365)
Warren Broach & Machine Corp ....F 586 254-7080
  Sterling Heights (G-16229)
Warren Industries Inc ....C 586 741-0420
  Clinton Township (G-3386)
Wave Tool LLC ....F 989 912-2116
  Cass City (G-2623)
Wolverine Machine Products Co ......E 248 634-9952
  Holly (G-8301)
Wright-K Technology Inc ....E 989 752-2588
  Saginaw (G-14795)

3542 Machine Tools: Forming

◆ A W B Industries Inc ....E 989 739-1447
  Oscoda (G-12753)
▲ Advance Products Corporation .....E 269 849-1000
  Benton Harbor (G-1527)
Advanced Feedlines LLC ....E 248 583-9400
  Troy (G-16908)
Air-Hydraulics Inc ....F 517 787-9444
  Jackson (G-8806)
Aladdin Machining Inc ....G 586 465-4280
  Clinton Township (G-3160)
American Brake and Clutch Inc ....F 586 948-3730
  Chesterfield (G-2838)
American Wldg & Press Repr Inc ....E 248 358-2050
  Southfield (G-15486)
▲ Anderson-Cook Inc ....D 586 954-0700
  Chesterfield (G-2844)
Anderson-Cook Inc ....G 586 293-0800
  Fraser (G-5895)
Arch Cutting Tools LLC ....C 734 266-6900
  Bloomfield Hills (G-1800)
▲ Atlas Technologies LLC ....D 810 629-6663
  Fenton (G-5451)
Automated Indus Motion Inc ....G 231 865-1800
  Fruitport (G-6059)
B & B Holdings Groesbeck LLC ......F 586 554-7600
  Sterling Heights (G-15940)
◆ B&P Littleford LLC ....E 989 757-1300
  Saginaw (G-14608)
Baldauf Enterprises Inc ....F 989 686-0350
  Bay City (G-1325)
▼ Birdsall Tool & Gage Co ....E 248 474-5150
  Farmington Hills (G-5181)
Birmingham Benders Co ....F 313 435-4200
  Clawson (G-3088)

Bmax USA LLC .... E 248 794-4176
Lake Orion *(G-9587)*
Boral Building Products Inc .... C 800 521-8486
Wixom *(G-18625)*
Brake Roller Co Inc .... F 269 965-2371
Battle Creek *(G-1197)*
▲ Buhlerprince Inc .... C 616 394-8248
Holland *(G-7986)*
Burton Press Co Inc .... G 248 853-0212
Rochester Hills *(G-13967)*
Buster Mathis Foundation .... G 616 843-4433
Wyoming *(G-18855)*
▲ Centerless Rebuilders Inc .... E 586 749-6529
New Haven *(G-12030)*
◆ Century Inc .... C 231 947-6400
Traverse City *(G-16641)*
Challenge Mfg Holdings LLC .... E 616 735-6500
Grand Rapids *(G-6563)*
▲ Clark Granco Inc .... D 616 794-2600
Belding *(G-1443)*
CNB International Inc .... D 269 948-3300
Hastings *(G-7783)*
Columbia Marking Tools Inc .... E 586 949-8400
Chesterfield *(G-2860)*
Contractors Steel Company .... E 616 531-4000
Grand Rapids *(G-6600)*
D M Tool & Fab Inc .... D 586 726-8390
Sterling Heights *(G-15978)*
Die Cast Press Mfg Co Inc .... E 269 657-6060
Paw Paw *(G-12947)*
Digital Die Solutions Inc .... F 734 542-2222
Livonia *(G-10185)*
Dimond Machinery Company Inc .... F 269 945-5908
Hastings *(G-7790)*
Diversified Metal Products Inc .... E 989 448-7120
Gaylord *(G-6126)*
Eagle Machine Tool Corporation .... G 231 798-8473
Norton Shores *(G-12289)*
Ems Parts Div .... G 517 319-5306
Lansing *(G-9692)*
Enprotech Industrial Tech LLC .... C 517 372-0950
Lansing *(G-9694)*
◆ Fanuc America Corporation .... B 248 377-7000
Rochester Hills *(G-14009)*
▲ Feed - Lease Corp .... E 248 377-0000
Auburn Hills *(G-896)*
Flagler Corporation .... E 586 749-6300
Chesterfield *(G-2882)*
▲ Fontijne Grotnes Inc .... E 269 262-4700
Niles *(G-12129)*
Gasbarre Products Inc .... G 734 425-5165
Livonia *(G-10220)*
◆ Global Strgc Sup Solutions LLC .... D 734 525-9100
Livonia *(G-10226)*
▲ Globe Tech LLC .... E 734 656-2200
Plymouth *(G-13178)*
Green Oak Tool and Svcs Inc .... F 586 531-2255
Brighton *(G-2005)*
Hamilton Industrial Products .... E 269 751-5153
Hamilton *(G-7599)*
▲ HMS Products Co .... D 248 689-8120
Troy *(G-17146)*
Howell Gear Company LLC .... D 517 273-5202
Howell *(G-8463)*
◆ Howmet Corporation .... E 231 894-5686
Whitehall *(G-18501)*
▲ Howmet Holdings Corporation .... G 231 894-5686
Whitehall *(G-18506)*
Hti Cybernetics .... G 586 826-8346
Sterling Heights *(G-16042)*
Hti Cybernetics Inc .... E 586 826-8346
Sterling Heights *(G-16043)*
Impel Industries Inc .... E 586 254-5800
Sterling Heights *(G-16046)*
Industrial Innovations Inc .... F 616 249-1525
Grandville *(G-7392)*
International Machinery .... G 248 619-9999
Troy *(G-17172)*
▲ Jier North America Inc .... F 734 404-6683
Plymouth *(G-13202)*
▼ Kasten Machinery Inc .... G 269 945-1999
Hastings *(G-7803)*
Lloyd Tool & Mfg Corp .... F 810 694-3519
Grand Blanc *(G-6251)*
M & M Turning Co .... E 586 791-7188
Clinton Township *(G-3284)*
M C Molds Inc .... E 517 655-5481
Williamston *(G-18576)*
▲ Magnetool Inc .... E 248 588-5400
Troy *(G-17228)*
Mak Press & Machinery Co .... G 734 266-3044
Farmington Hills *(G-5308)*
Martinrea Industries Inc .... E 231 832-5504
Reed City *(G-13795)*
Metal Mechanics Inc .... F 269 679-2525
Schoolcraft *(G-15124)*
Michigan Roll Form Inc .... E 248 669-3700
Commerce Township *(G-3556)*
Midwest Tool and Cutlery Co .... F 231 258-2341
Kalkaska *(G-9398)*
▼ Miller Tool & Die Co .... E 517 782-0347
Jackson *(G-8963)*
Monroe LLC .... B 616 942-9820
Grand Rapids *(G-7025)*
Moore Production Tool Spc .... F 248 476-1200
Farmington *(G-5143)*
Nn Inc .... E 616 698-0707
Kentwood *(G-9467)*
Nn Inc .... E 269 591-6951
Grand Rapids *(G-7044)*
◆ Oak Press Solutions Inc .... E 269 651-8513
Sturgis *(G-16314)*
Orbitform Group LLC .... D 800 957-4838
Jackson *(G-8980)*
P M R Industries Inc .... F 810 989-5020
Port Huron *(G-13515)*
Pace Industries LLC .... G 231 777-3941
Muskegon *(G-11890)*
Press Room Eqp Sls & Svc Co .... G 248 334-1880
Pontiac *(G-13410)*
Product and Tooling Tech Inc .... E 586 293-1810
Fraser *(G-5980)*
▲ Production Fabricators Inc .... E 231 777-3822
Muskegon *(G-11900)*
Productivity Technologies .... G 810 714-0200
Fenton *(G-5496)*
Prophotonix Limited .... G 586 778-1100
Roseville *(G-14466)*
Pt Tech Stamping Inc .... E 586 293-1810
Fraser *(G-5982)*
R and T West Michigan Inc .... E 616 698-9931
Caledonia *(G-2395)*
Reliable Sales Co .... G 248 969-0943
Oxford *(G-12912)*
Rempco Acquisition Inc .... E 231 775-0108
Cadillac *(G-2351)*
S & L Tool Inc .... G 734 464-4200
Livonia *(G-10397)*
Salvo Tool & Engineering Co .... F 810 346-2727
Brown City *(G-2142)*
Seg Automotive North Amer LLC .... E 248 465-2602
Novi *(G-12533)*
Selmuro Ltd .... E 810 603-2117
Grand Blanc *(G-6263)*
Sesco Inc .... D 313 843-7710
Detroit *(G-4587)*
Shannon Precision Fastener LLC .... D 248 658-3015
Madison Heights *(G-10826)*
Spline Specialist Inc .... G 586 731-4569
Sterling Heights *(G-16184)*
Stilson Products LLC .... F 586 778-1100
Roseville *(G-14481)*
Superior USA LLC .... G 586 786-4261
Macomb *(G-10638)*
Tapco Holdings Inc .... C 248 668-6400
Wixom *(G-18766)*
Tech Tooling Specialties Inc .... F 517 782-8898
Jackson *(G-9016)*
Triple Tool .... G 586 795-1785
Sterling Heights *(G-16211)*
U S Baird Corporation .... F 616 826-5013
Middleville *(G-11316)*
▲ United Sttes Sckt Screw Mfg C .... F 586 469-8811
Fraser *(G-6009)*
▼ Van-Mark Products Corporation .... E 248 478-1200
Farmington Hills *(G-5408)*
▲ West Michigan Spline Inc .... F 616 399-4078
Holland *(G-8246)*

3543 Industrial Patterns

Acme Casting Enterprises Inc .... G 586 755-0300
Warren *(G-17689)*
Advantage Industries Inc .... E 616 669-2400
Jenison *(G-9042)*
Al-Craft Design & Engrg Inc .... G 248 589-3827
Troy *(G-16918)*
Allen Pattern of Michigan .... F 269 963-4131
Battle Creek *(G-1184)*
▲ Anderson Global Inc .... C 231 733-2164
Muskegon *(G-11771)*
Arbor Gage & Tooling Inc .... E 616 454-8266
Grand Rapids *(G-6466)*
Associate Mfg Inc .... G 989 345-0025
West Branch *(G-18325)*
Aurora Cad CAM Inc .... F 810 678-2128
Metamora *(G-11276)*
Bespro Pattern Inc .... E 586 268-6970
Madison Heights *(G-10681)*
▲ Big Dome Holdings Inc .... D 616 735-6228
Grand Rapids *(G-6507)*
Briggs Industries Inc .... E 586 749-5191
Chesterfield *(G-2852)*
C & D Enterprises Inc .... E 248 373-0011
Burton *(G-2229)*
C & D Gage Inc .... G 517 548-7049
Howell *(G-8433)*
Champion Charter Sls & Svc Inc .... E 906 779-2300
Iron Mountain *(G-8719)*
Cobra Patterns & Models Inc .... E 248 588-2669
Madison Heights *(G-10694)*
Complete Prototype Svcs Inc .... C 586 690-8897
Clinton Township *(G-3207)*
Crescent Pattern Company .... E 248 541-1052
Oak Park *(G-12602)*
Decca Pattern Co Inc .... G 586 775-8450
Roseville *(G-14395)*
Dhs Inc .... G 313 724-6566
Detroit *(G-4174)*
Elmhirst Industries Inc .... E 586 731-8663
Sterling Heights *(G-16002)*
Gage Pattern & Model Inc .... D 248 361-6609
Madison Heights *(G-10729)*
GM Bassett Pattern Inc .... G 248 477-6454
Farmington Hills *(G-5253)*
Grand Rapids Carvers Inc .... E 616 538-0022
Grand Rapids *(G-6754)*
Harvey Pattern Works Inc .... F 906 774-4285
Kingsford *(G-9510)*
Holland Pattern Co .... G 616 396-6348
Holland *(G-8082)*
Homestead Tool and Machine .... E 989 465-6182
Coleman *(G-3465)*
Husite Engineering Co Inc .... F 248 588-0337
Clinton Township *(G-3255)*
Industrial Model Inc .... G 586 254-0450
Auburn Hills *(G-939)*
J J Pattern & Castings Inc .... G 248 543-7119
Madison Heights *(G-10751)*
Jay/Enn Corporation .... D 248 588-2393
Troy *(G-17182)*
L & L Pattern Inc .... G 231 733-2646
Muskegon *(G-11853)*
Majestic Pattern Company Inc .... G 313 892-5800
Detroit *(G-4417)*
Mantissa Industries Inc .... G 517 694-2260
Holt *(G-8317)*
Marten Models & Molds Inc .... F 586 293-2260
Fraser *(G-5962)*
Mentor Enterprises Inc .... G 269 483-7675
White Pigeon *(G-18483)*
Metro Technologies Ltd .... D 248 528-9240
Troy *(G-17254)*
Michalski Enterprises Inc .... E 517 703-0777
Lansing *(G-9716)*
Michigan Pattern Works Inc .... E 616 245-9259
Grand Rapids *(G-6993)*
▲ National Pattern Inc .... E 989 755-6274
Saginaw *(G-14706)*
Northern Sierra Corporation .... G 989 777-4784
Saginaw *(G-14722)*
Paragon Molds Corporation .... E 586 294-7630
Fraser *(G-5974)*
Parker Pattern Inc .... F 586 466-5900
Mount Clemens *(G-11651)*
Parker Tooling & Design Inc .... F 616 791-1080
Grand Rapids *(G-7071)*
Portenga Manufacturing Company .... G 616 846-2691
Ferrysburg *(G-5604)*
Prompt Pattern Inc .... F 586 759-2030
Warren *(G-17979)*
Proto-Cast Inc .... E 313 565-5400
Inkster *(G-8672)*
Quality Model & Pattern Co .... E 616 791-1156
Grand Rapids *(G-7129)*
Ravenna Pattern & Mfg .... E 231 853-2264
Ravenna *(G-13693)*
Rehau Incorporated .... G 269 651-7845
Sturgis *(G-16321)*
Sbti Company .... D 586 726-5756
Shelby Township *(G-15323)*

SIC

Employee Codes: A=Over 500 employees, B=251-500
C=101-250, D=51-100, E=20-50, F=10-19, G=3-9

2022 Harris Michigan
Industrial Directory

839

Company		Phone
Simpsons Enterprises Inc	F	269 279-7237
Three Rivers (G-16584)		
Tedson Industries Inc	F	248 588-9230
Troy (G-17387)		
Tri-Star Tooling LLC		586 978-0435
Sterling Heights (G-16210)		
U S Pattern Company Inc		586 727-2896
Richmond (G-13847)		
Vans Pattern Corp	F	616 364-9483
Marne (G-11002)		
Wing Pattern Inc	G	248 588-1121
Sterling Heights (G-16232)		
Wolverine Products Inc	F	586 792-3740
Clinton Township (G-3389)		

3544 Dies, Tools, Jigs, Fixtures & Indl Molds

Company		Phone
2k Tool LLC	G	616 452-4927
Wyoming (G-18846)		
3d Polymers Inc	F	248 588-5562
Orchard Lake (G-12715)		
A & A Manufacturing Co	G	616 846-1730
Spring Lake (G-15799)		
▲ A & O Mold and Eng Inc	E	269 649-0600
Vicksburg (G-17598)		
A B M Tool & Die Inc	G	734 432-6060
Livonia (G-10093)		
A C Steel Rule Dies Inc	G	248 588-5600
Madison Heights (G-10654)		
A D Johnson Engraving Co Inc	F	269 385-0044
Kalamazoo (G-9106)		
A J Tool Co	F	517 787-5755
Jackson (G-8798)		
A S A P Tool Inc	G	586 790-6550
Clinton Township (G-3147)		
Accu Die & Mold Inc	E	269 465-4020
Stevensville (G-16237)		
▲ Accu-Shape Die Cutting Inc	G	810 230-2445
Flint (G-5634)		
Accubilt Automated Systems LLC	E	517 787-9353
Jackson (G-8800)		
Acg Services Inc	G	586 232-4698
Shelby Township (G-15164)		
Acme Carbide Die Inc	E	734 722-2303
Westland (G-18351)		
Acme Tool & Die Co		231 938-1260
Acme (G-1)		
Action Die & Tool Inc	G	616 538-2326
Grandville (G-7362)		
▲ Action Mold & Machining Inc	E	616 452-1580
Grand Rapids (G-6424)		
Action Mold Removal	G	517 960-1928
Jackson (G-8801)		
Action Tool & Machine Inc	E	810 229-6300
Brighton (G-1938)		
Ada Gage Inc	G	616 676-3338
Ada (G-4)		
Adaptive Mfg Solutions LLC	G	810 743-1600
Burton (G-2224)		
Adrian Precision Machining LLC	F	517 263-4564
Adrian (G-49)		
Adrian Tool Corporation	E	517 263-6530
Adrian (G-52)		
Advance Tool Co	G	231 587-5286
Mancelona (G-10865)		
Advanced Auto Trends Inc	E	248 628-4850
Oxford (G-12872)		
▲ Advanced Integ Tooling Solns	C	586 749-5525
Chesterfield (G-2836)		
Advanced Mold Solutions	C	586 468-6883
Clinton Township (G-3157)		
▲ Advanced Special Tools Inc	C	269 962-9697
Battle Creek (G-1179)		
◆ Advanced Tooling Systems Inc	G	616 784-7513
Comstock Park (G-3586)		
Advantage Design & Tool Inc	G	586 463-2800
Clinton Township (G-3158)		
Advantage Design and Tool	G	586 801-7413
Richmond (G-13831)		
Advantage Industries Inc	E	616 669-2400
Jenison (G-9042)		
▼ Aero Foil International Inc	G	231 773-0200
Muskegon (G-11765)		
▲ Affinity Custom Molding Inc	E	269 496-8423
Mendon (G-11215)		
Aggressive Tool & Die Inc	E	616 837-1983
Coopersville (G-3679)		
Aggressive Tooling Inc	D	616 754-1404
Greenville (G-7475)		
Air-Hydraulics Inc	F	517 787-9444
Jackson (G-8806)		
Airmetal Corporation	F	517 784-6000
Jackson (G-8807)		
Al-Craft Design & Engrg Inc	G	248 589-3827
Troy (G-16918)		
Albion Machine and Tool LLC	F	517 629-8838
Albion (G-115)		
Alcona Tool & Machine Inc	G	989 736-8151
Harrisville (G-7741)		
Alcona Tool & Machine Inc	G	989 736-8151
Lincoln (G-10033)		
Allen Tool and Die LLC	G	734 224-7900
Temperance (G-16526)		
Alliance Industries Inc	E	248 656-3473
Macomb (G-10574)		
Alliance Tool and Machine Co	F	586 427-6411
Saint Clair Shores (G-14847)		
Allied Tool and Machine Co	E	989 755-5384
Saginaw (G-14604)		
Amber Manufacturing Inc	E	586 218-6080
Fraser (G-5890)		
American Assemblers Inc	E	248 334-9777
Pontiac (G-13350)		
American Die and Mold Inc	G	231 269-3788
Buckley (G-2204)		
American Die Corporation	E	810 794-4080
Clay (G-3115)		
American Tooling Center Inc	E	517 522-8411
Lansing (G-9672)		
American Tooling Center Inc	E	517 522-8411
Jackson (G-8815)		
▲ American Tooling Center Inc	D	517 522-8411
Grass Lake (G-7435)		
American Vault Service	G	989 366-8657
Prudenville (G-13655)		
Anchor Danly Inc	G	989 875-5400
Ithaca (G-8786)		
▲ Anchor Lamina America Inc	E	248 489-9122
Bellaire (G-1469)		
Anitom Automation LLC	G	517 278-6205
Coldwater (G-3419)		
Apex Spring & Stamping Corp	D	616 453-5463
Grand Rapids (G-6462)		
Applied Mechanics Corporation	G	616 677-1355
Grand Rapids (G-6464)		
Arbor Gage & Tooling Inc	G	616 454-8266
Grand Rapids (G-6466)		
Argus Corporation	E	313 937-2900
Redford (G-13716)		
Arnold Tool & Die Co	E	586 598-0099
Chesterfield (G-2846)		
Arrow Die & Mold Repair	G	231 689-1829
White Cloud (G-18438)		
Artiflex Manufacturing LLC	C	616 459-8285
Grand Rapids (G-6473)		
Assembly Concepts Inc	F	989 685-2603
Rose City (G-14361)		
Astar Inc	E	574 234-2137
Niles (G-12111)		
Athey Precision Inc	F	989 386-4523
Clare (G-2973)		
Atlas Die LLC	E	413 289-1276
Rochester Hills (G-13953)		
Atlas Die LLC	E	770 981-6585
Rochester Hills (G-13954)		
Atlas Die Inc	E	574 295-0050
Rochester Hills (G-13955)		
▲ Auto Craft Tool & Die Co	D	810 794-4929
Clay (G-3116)		
Auto Craft Tool & Die Co	E	810 794-4929
Clay (G-3117)		
Auto Metal Craft Inc	E	248 398-2240
Oak Park (G-12594)		
▲ Autodie LLC	C	616 454-9361
Grand Rapids (G-6483)		
Aw Carbide Fabricators Inc	E	586 294-1850
Sterling Heights (G-15939)		
Axis Machine & Tool Inc	G	616 738-2196
Holland (G-7968)		
Axis Mold Works Inc	F	616 866-2222
Rockford (G-14156)		
Axly Production Machining		989 269-9553
Bad Axe (G-1097)		
B & B Mold & Engineering Inc	G	586 773-6664
Warren (G-17721)		
B & M Machine & Tool Company		989 288-2934
Durand (G-4839)		
B C Manufacturing Inc	E	248 344-0101
Wixom (G-18617)		
Badger Tool LLC	G	586 246-1810
Sterling Heights (G-15941)		
Bauer Precision Tool Co	G	586 758-7370
Warren (G-17728)		
Baumann Tool & Die	G	616 772-6768
Zeeland (G-18995)		
Bawden Industries Inc	F	734 721-6414
Romulus (G-14256)		
Baxter Machine & Tool Co	E	517 782-2808
Jackson (G-8822)		
Bay Area Tool LLC	G	231 946-3500
Traverse City (G-16613)		
Bay Products Inc	E	586 296-7130
Fraser (G-5902)		
Beacon Tool Inc	F	269 649-3558
Vicksburg (G-17599)		
▲ Bekum America Corporation	C	517 655-4331
Williamston (G-18569)		
Bel-Kur Inc	E	734 847-0651
Temperance (G-16528)		
Benteler Automotive Corp	B	616 247-3936
Auburn Hills (G-810)		
Berg Tool Inc	F	586 646-7100
Chesterfield (G-2850)		
▲ Bernal LLC	D	248 299-3600
Rochester Hills (G-13964)		
Bessey Tool & Die Inc	F	616 887-8820
Sparta (G-15760)		
Best Tool & Engineering Co		586 792-4119
Clinton Township (G-3183)		
Betz Contracting Inc	G	269 746-3320
Climax (G-3134)		
Big 3 Precision Products Inc	F	313 846-6601
Dearborn (G-3815)		
Bilar Tool & Die	E	248 740-3400
Warren (G-17736)		
Bilco Tool Corporation	G	586 574-9300
Warren (G-17737)		
Birmingham Benders Co	E	313 435-4200
Clawson (G-3088)		
Blackledge Tool Inc	G	989 865-8393
Saint Charles (G-14801)		
Boda Corporation	G	906 353-7320
Chassell (G-2776)		
Bold Ammo & Guns Inc	G	616 826-0913
Rockford (G-14158)		
Bolman Die Services Inc	F	810 919-2262
Sterling Heights (G-15947)		
Bonal Technologies Inc	F	248 582-0900
Royal Oak (G-14519)		
Borgia Die & Engineering Inc	G	616 677-3595
Marne (G-10990)		
Borgman Tool & Engineering LLC	G	231 733-4133
Muskegon (G-11783)		
Boyers Tool and Die Inc	G	517 782-7869
Jackson (G-8826)		
Bradley-Thompson Tool Company	E	248 352-1466
Southfield (G-15510)		
Bridge Tool and Die LLC	G	231 269-3200
Buckley (G-2205)		
Briggs Industries Inc	E	586 749-5191
Chesterfield (G-2852)		
Briggs Mold & Die Inc	G	517 784-6908
Jackson (G-8827)		
Bry Mac Inc	G	231 799-2211
Norton Shores (G-12280)		
Btm National Holdings LLC	F	616 794-0100
Belding (G-1441)		
Btmc Holdings Inc		616 794-0100
Belding (G-1442)		
Buchanan Global Inc		269 635-5270
Niles (G-12116)		
Buckingham Tool Corp	E	734 591-2333
Livonia (G-10142)		
Buiter Tool & Die Inc	E	616 455-7410
Grand Rapids (G-6529)		
▲ Burkland Inc	C	810 636-2233
Goodrich (G-6222)		
Byrne Tool & Die Inc	E	616 866-4479
Rockford (G-14161)		
Byrnes Manufacturing Co LLC	G	810 664-3686
Lapeer (G-9917)		
Byrnes Tool Co Inc		810 664-3686
Lapeer (G-9918)		
C & D Tool & Die Company Inc	E	248 922-5937
Davisburg (G-3762)		
C & H Stamping Inc	E	517 750-3600
Jackson (G-8829)		
C & M Tool LLC		734 944-3355
Saline (G-15006)		
C & N Manufacturing Inc	E	586 293-9150
Fraser (G-5908)		

C & R Tool Die ... G ... 231 584-3588
Alba *(G-113)*

Cad CAM Services Inc ... F ... 616 554-5222
Grand Rapids *(G-6544)*

Cadillac Tool and Die Inc ... G ... 231 775-9007
Cadillac *(G-2324)*

Cambria Tool and Machine Inc ... F ... 517 437-3500
Hillsdale *(G-7928)*

Cambron Engineering Inc ... E ... 989 684-5890
Bay City *(G-1334)*

▲ **Cameron Tool Corporation** ... D ... 517 487-3671
Lansing *(G-9820)*

Cammand Machining LLC ... E ... 586 752-0366
Romeo *(G-14222)*

Carroll Tool and Die Co ... E ... 586 949-7670
Macomb *(G-10583)*

Cav Tool Company ... F ... 248 349-7860
Novi *(G-12381)*

CBS Tool Inc ... F ... 586 566-5945
Shelby Township *(G-15182)*

Centennial Technologies Inc ... E ... 989 752-6167
Saginaw *(G-14624)*

Center Line Gage Inc ... G ... 810 387-4300
Brockway *(G-2106)*

Centerline Engineering Inc ... D ... 616 735-2506
Comstock Park *(G-3592)*

Central Industrial Mfg Inc ... F ... 231 347-5920
Harbor Springs *(G-7644)*

◆ **Century Inc** ... C ... 231 947-6400
Traverse City *(G-16641)*

Century Inc ... G ... 231 946-7500
Traverse City *(G-16642)*

Century Tool & Gage LLC ... D ... 810 629-0784
Fenton *(G-5463)*

Certified Metal Products Inc ... F ... 586 598-1000
Clinton Township *(G-3196)*

Cfh Inc ... E ... 734 947-9574
Taylor *(G-16392)*

CG Automation & Fixture Inc ... E ... 616 785-5400
Comstock Park *(G-3593)*

Chalker Tool & Gauge Inc ... F ... 586 977-8660
Sterling Heights *(G-15956)*

Champion Die Incorporated ... E ... 616 784-2397
Comstock Park *(G-3595)*

Cherry Bend Tool & Die ... G ... 231 947-3046
Cedar *(G-2638)*

Christensen Fiberglass LLC ... E ... 616 738-1219
Holland *(G-7995)*

Circle C Mold & Plas Group Inc ... F ... 269 496-5515
Mendon *(G-11216)*

Circle Engineering Inc ... G ... 586 978-8120
Sterling Heights *(G-15959)*

▲ **Classic Die Inc** ... E ... 616 454-3760
Grand Rapids *(G-6570)*

Cleary Developments Inc ... F ... 248 588-6614
Madison Heights *(G-10690)*

Cole Tooling Systems Inc ... E ... 586 573-9450
Lake Orion *(G-9596)*

Coles Machine Service Inc ... E ... 810 658-5373
Davison *(G-3777)*

Colonial Mold Inc ... E ... 586 469-4944
Clinton Township *(G-3204)*

Columbia Marking Tools Inc ... E ... 586 949-8400
Chesterfield *(G-2860)*

▲ **Commercial Mfg & Assembly Inc** ... E ... 616 847-9980
Grand Haven *(G-6287)*

Company Products Inc ... G ... 586 757-6160
Warren *(G-17762)*

Complete Surface Technologies ... E ... 586 493-5800
Clinton Township *(G-3208)*

Concept Molds Inc ... F ... 269 679-2100
Schoolcraft *(G-15116)*

Concept Tool & Die Inc ... G ... 616 875-4600
Zeeland *(G-19005)*

Concept Tooling Systems Inc ... E ... 616 301-6906
Grand Rapids *(G-6591)*

▲ **Concord Tool and Mfg Inc** ... C ... 586 465-6537
Mount Clemens *(G-11634)*

Conley Manufacturing Inc ... G ... 586 262-4484
Shelby Township *(G-15193)*

Connell Limited Partnership ... G ... 989 875-5135
Ithaca *(G-8789)*

Contour Mold Corporation ... F ... 810 245-4070
Lapeer *(G-9922)*

Contour Tool & Engineering Inc ... G ... 616 772-6360
Zeeland *(G-19006)*

Convex Mold Inc ... G ... 586 978-0808
Sterling Heights *(G-15971)*

Corban Industries Inc ... E ... 248 393-2720
Orion *(G-12726)*

Craft Industries Inc ... B ... 586 726-4300
Shelby Township *(G-15197)*

Crash Tool Inc ... F ... 517 552-0250
Howell *(G-8441)*

Creative Steel Rule Dies Inc ... G ... 630 307-8880
Grand Rapids *(G-6610)*

Creative Techniques Inc ... D ... 248 373-3050
Orion *(G-12727)*

Cs Tool Engineering Inc ... E ... 616 696-0940
Cedar Springs *(G-2648)*

CTS Manufacturing Inc ... G ... 586 465-4594
Clinton Township *(G-3214)*

Custer Tool & Mfg LLC ... G ... 734 854-5943
Lambertville *(G-9651)*

Custom Design Inc ... E ... 269 323-8561
Portage *(G-13555)*

Custom Tool & Die Service Inc ... G ... 616 662-1068
Hudsonville *(G-8577)*

Custom Tool and Die Co ... E ... 269 465-9130
Stevensville *(G-16243)*

Custom Tooling Systems Inc ... D ... 616 748-9880
Zeeland *(G-19012)*

Cutting Edge Technologies Inc ... F ... 616 738-0800
Holland *(G-8009)*

D & F Corporation ... D ... 586 254-5300
Sterling Heights *(G-15977)*

D & F Mold LLC ... E ... 269 465-6633
Bridgman *(G-1923)*

D & L Tooling Inc ... G ... 517 369-5655
Bronson *(G-2110)*

D M Tool & Fab Inc ... D ... 586 726-8390
Sterling Heights *(G-15978)*

D W Machine Inc ... F ... 517 787-9929
Jackson *(G-8859)*

◆ **D-M-E USA Inc** ... D ... 616 754-4601
Greenville *(G-7480)*

Danly IEM ... G ... 800 243-2659
Grand Rapids *(G-6632)*

▲ **Datum Industries LLC** ... E ... 616 977-1995
Grand Rapids *(G-6633)*

Davis Steel Rule Die ... G ... 269 492-9908
Kalamazoo *(G-9164)*

Dayton Lamina Corp ... F ... 231 533-8646
Bellaire *(G-1473)*

DD Parker Enterprises Inc ... F ... 734 241-6898
Monroe *(G-11536)*

De Luxe Die Set Inc ... G ... 810 227-2556
Brighton *(G-1974)*

Dehring Mold E-D-M ... G ... 269 683-5970
Niles *(G-12124)*

Deland Manufacturing Inc ... E ... 586 323-2350
Shelby Township *(G-15202)*

Delta Precision Inc ... G ... 248 585-2344
Fraser *(G-5917)*

▲ **Demmer Corporation** ... C ... 517 321-3600
Lansing *(G-9687)*

Deppe Mold & Tooling Inc ... E ... 616 530-1331
Grandville *(G-7370)*

Detroit Steel Treating Company ... E ... 248 334-7436
Pontiac *(G-13361)*

Dexter Automatic Products Co ... C ... 734 426-8900
Dexter *(G-4734)*

Diamond Die and Mold Company ... F ... 586 791-0700
Clinton Township *(G-3221)*

Die Tech Services Inc ... E ... 616 363-6604
Walker *(G-17637)*

Die-Matic USA LLC ... E ... 616 531-0060
Wyoming *(G-18868)*

Die-Mold-Automation Component ... G ... 313 581-6510
Dearborn *(G-3829)*

Die-Namic Inc ... C ... 734 710-3200
Van Buren Twp *(G-17525)*

Die-Namic Tool & Design Llc ... F ... 517 787-4900
Jackson *(G-8867)*

Die-Namic Tool Corp ... G ... 616 954-7882
Grand Rapids *(G-6646)*

Die-Tech and Engineering Inc ... E ... 616 530-9030
Grand Rapids *(G-6647)*

Die-Verse Solutions LLC ... G ... 616 914-9427
Marne *(G-10992)*

Dies and Fixtures Mold Corp ... G ... 269 465-6633
Bridgman *(G-1924)*

Dietech North America LLC ... D ... 586 771-8580
Roseville *(G-14399)*

▲ **Digital Tool & Die Inc** ... E ... 616 532-8020
Grandville *(G-7371)*

Diversified Tool & Engineering ... F ... 734 692-1260
Grosse Ile *(G-7519)*

Dixon & Ryan Corporation ... F ... 248 549-4000
Royal Oak *(G-14531)*

▲ **Dme Company LLC** ... B ... 248 398-6000
Madison Heights *(G-10709)*

Do Rite Tool Inc ... G ... 734 522-7510
Brighton *(G-1976)*

Dolphin Manufacturing Inc ... E ... 734 946-6322
Taylor *(G-16403)*

Douglas King Industries Inc ... G ... 989 642-2865
Hemlock *(G-7851)*

Dr and Hl Mold and Mch Inc ... G ... 989 672-2192
Caro *(G-2569)*

Drive System Integration Inc ... G ... 248 568-7750
Beverly Hills *(G-1663)*

Dryden Mold Services Inc ... F ... 810 614-8621
Dryden *(G-4804)*

Ds Mold LLC ... E ... 616 794-1639
Belding *(G-1447)*

Du Val Industries LLC ... E ... 586 737-2710
Sterling Heights *(G-15991)*

Dubetsky K9 Academy LLC ... F ... 586 997-1717
Shelby Township *(G-15211)*

Dubois Production Services Inc ... F ... 616 785-0088
Comstock Park *(G-3604)*

▲ **Dura Mold Inc** ... D ... 269 465-3301
Stevensville *(G-16248)*

Dura Thread Gage Inc ... F ... 248 545-2890
Madison Heights *(G-10714)*

Dynamic Corporation ... F ... 616 399-2200
Holland *(G-8018)*

Dynamic Jig Grinding Corp ... E ... 248 589-3110
Troy *(G-17072)*

Dynamic Metals Group LLC ... F ... 586 790-5615
Birmingham *(G-1724)*

Dynamic Plastics Inc ... E ... 586 749-6100
Chesterfield *(G-2872)*

E & D Machine Company Inc ... E ... 248 473-0255
Farmington *(G-5137)*

E D M Specialties Inc ... G ... 248 344-4080
Novi *(G-12407)*

▲ **E-T-M Enterprises I Inc** ... C ... 517 627-8461
Grand Ledge *(G-6389)*

Eagle Indus Group Federal LLC ... G ... 616 863-8623
Grand Rapids *(G-6661)*

Eagle Masking Fabrication Inc ... G ... 586 992-3080
Sterling Heights *(G-15998)*

East River Machine & Tool Inc ... G ... 231 767-1701
Muskegon *(G-11807)*

Eclipse Tool & Die Inc ... E ... 616 877-3717
Wayland *(G-18195)*

▲ **Edmar Manufacturing Inc** ... D ... 616 392-7218
Holland *(G-8023)*

Edwards Machining Inc ... E ... 517 782-2568
Jackson *(G-8876)*

Eifel Mold & Engineering Inc ... E ... 586 296-9640
Fraser *(G-5923)*

Eikos Holdings Inc ... E ... 248 280-0300
Troy *(G-17080)*

▲ **Eimo Technologies Inc** ... E ... 269 649-0545
Vicksburg *(G-17603)*

▲ **Ekstrom Industries Inc** ... D ... 248 477-0040
Novi *(G-12412)*

Elite Mold & Engineering Inc ... E ... 586 314-4000
Shelby Township *(G-15219)*

Emcor Inc ... F ... 989 667-0652
Bay City *(G-1350)*

EMD Wire Tek ... G ... 810 235-5344
Flint *(G-5695)*

Emmie Die and Engineering Corp ... G ... 810 346-2914
Brown City *(G-2136)*

Empire Machine Company ... F ... 269 684-3713
Saint Joseph *(G-14929)*

▲ **Engineered Tooling Systems Inc** ... F ... 616 647-5063
Grand Rapids *(G-6681)*

Enkon LLC ... E ... 937 890-5678
Manchester *(G-10883)*

Enmark Tool Company ... E ... 586 293-2797
Fraser *(G-5925)*

Enterprise Tool & Die LLC ... D ... 616 538-0920
Grandville *(G-7374)*

Enterprise Tool and Gear Inc ... F ... 989 269-9797
Bad Axe *(G-1100)*

Envisiontec US LLC ... D ... 313 436-4300
Dearborn *(G-3837)*

Epic Machine Inc ... E ... 810 629-9400
Fenton *(G-5473)*

ERA Tool & Engineering Co ... F ... 734 464-7788
Farmington Hills *(G-5235)*

▲ **Erwin Quarder Inc** ... D ... 616 575-1600
Grand Rapids *(G-6683)*

Everson Tool & Machine Ltd ... F ... 906 932-3440
Ironwood *(G-8761)*

Employee Codes: A=Over 500 employees, B=251-500
C=101-250, D=51-100, E=20-50, F=10-19, G=3-9

2022 Harris Michigan
Industrial Directory

841

Evolution Tool Inc ....F.... 810 664-5500
Lapeer *(G-9930)*
Excell Machine & Tool Co LLC ....G.... 231 728-1210
Muskegon *(G-11814)*
▲ **Exco Extrusion Dies Inc** ....C.... 586 749-5400
Chesterfield *(G-2877)*
Exco USA ....F.... 586 749-5400
Chesterfield *(G-2878)*
Experi-Metal Inc ....C.... 586 977-7800
Sterling Heights *(G-16009)*
Experienced Concepts Inc ....F.... 586 752-4200
Armada *(G-735)*
Expert Machine & Tool Inc ....G.... 810 984-2323
Port Huron *(G-13477)*
▲ **Extreme Tool and Engrg Inc** ....D.... 906 229-9100
Wakefield *(G-17620)*
Extreme Wire EDM Service Inc ....G.... 616 249-3901
Grandville *(G-7376)*
Extrusion Punch & Tool Company ....E.... 248 689-3300
Rochester Hills *(G-14007)*
F & F Mold Inc ....G.... 517 287-5866
North Adams *(G-12176)*
F J Lucido & Associates ....E.... 586 574-3577
Warren *(G-17801)*
Fair Industries LLC ....F.... 248 740-7841
Troy *(G-17104)*
Fairlane Co ....E.... 586 294-6100
Fraser *(G-5926)*
Falcon Corporation ....D.... 616 842-7071
Spring Lake *(G-15813)*
Falcon Industry Inc ....F.... 586 468-7010
Clinton Township *(G-3235)*
Falcon Lakeside Mfg Inc ....E.... 269 429-6193
Stevensville *(G-16250)*
FCA US LLC ....G.... 313 369-7312
Detroit *(G-4228)*
Federal Screw Works ....D.... 810 227-7712
Brighton *(G-1989)*
Fega Tool & Gage Company ....F.... 586 469-4400
Clinton Township *(G-3236)*
Finazzo Tool & Die LLC ....G.... 586 598-5806
Chesterfield *(G-2880)*
◆ **Fischer Tool & Die Corp** ....E.... 734 847-4788
Temperance *(G-16530)*
◆ **Fisher Kellering Co** ....G.... 586 749-6616
Chesterfield *(G-2881)*
Fitz-Rite Products Inc ....E.... 248 528-8440
Troy *(G-17113)*
Five Star Industries Inc ....E.... 586 786-0500
Macomb *(G-10595)*
▲ **Fixtureworks LLC** ....G.... 586 294-6100
Fraser *(G-5928)*
Flagler Corporation ....E.... 586 749-6300
Chesterfield *(G-2882)*
Flannery Machine & Tool Inc ....E.... 231 587-5076
Mancelona *(G-10871)*
Florance Turning Company Inc ....G.... 248 347-0068
Northville *(G-12218)*
Forge Die & Tool Corp ....D.... 248 477-0020
Farmington Hills *(G-5245)*
Formfab LLC ....E.... 248 844-3676
Rochester Hills *(G-14013)*
Forrest Company ....G.... 269 384-6120
Kalamazoo *(G-9190)*
Fortune Tool & Machine Inc ....F.... 248 669-9119
Wixom *(G-18665)*
Four Star Tooling & Engrg Inc ....G.... 586 264-4090
Sterling Heights *(G-16020)*
Four-Way Tool and Die Inc ....E.... 248 585-8255
Troy *(G-17121)*
Foust Electro Mold Inc ....G.... 517 439-1062
Hillsdale *(G-7934)*
Fowlerville Machine Tool Inc ....G.... 517 223-8871
Fowlerville *(G-5840)*
Fra-Wod Company Inc ....G.... 586 254-4450
Sterling Heights *(G-16021)*
Franchino Mold & Engrg Co ....D.... 517 321-5609
Lansing *(G-9700)*
Frankfort Manufacturing Inc ....E.... 231 352-7551
Frankfort *(G-5876)*
Freedom Tool & Mfg Co ....G.... 231 788-2898
Muskegon *(G-11821)*
▲ **Freer Tool & Die Inc** ....E.... 586 463-3200
Clinton Township *(G-3243)*
Freer Tool & Die Inc ....G.... 586 741-5274
Clinton Township *(G-3244)*
▲ **Frimo Inc** ....C.... 248 668-3160
Wixom *(G-18666)*
Futuramic Tool & Engrg Co ....C.... 586 758-2200
Warren *(G-17819)*

Future Mold Corporation ....D.... 989 588-9948
Farwell *(G-5423)*
G & F Tool Products ....F.... 517 663-3646
Eaton Rapids *(G-4964)*
▲ **G & G Die and Engineering Inc** ....E.... 586 716-8099
Ira *(G-8697)*
G & L Tool Inc ....F.... 734 728-1990
Westland *(G-18372)*
G A Machine Company Inc ....G.... 313 836-5646
Detroit *(G-4249)*
Gage Eagle Spline Inc ....D.... 586 776-7240
Warren *(G-17822)*
Gage Pattern & Model Inc ....D.... 248 361-6609
Madison Heights *(G-10729)*
Garden City Products Inc ....E.... 269 684-6264
Niles *(G-12133)*
▲ **Gch Tool Group Inc** ....E.... 586 777-6250
Warren *(G-17823)*
Gemini Precision Machining Inc ....C.... 989 269-9702
Bad Axe *(G-1105)*
General Die & Engineering Inc ....D.... 616 698-6961
Grand Rapids *(G-6738)*
General Motors LLC ....G.... 810 236-1970
Flint *(G-5706)*
Generation Tool Inc ....G.... 734 641-6937
Westland *(G-18374)*
Gill Holding Company Inc ....D.... 616 559-2700
Grand Rapids *(G-6741)*
◆ **Gill Industries Inc** ....C.... 616 559-2700
Grand Rapids *(G-6742)*
Gladwin Machine Inc ....G.... 989 426-8753
Gladwin *(G-6197)*
Gleason Holbrook Mfg Co ....F.... 586 749-5519
Ray *(G-13699)*
Global Engineering Inc ....E.... 586 566-0423
Shelby Township *(G-15230)*
▲ **Globe Tech LLC** ....E.... 734 656-2200
Plymouth *(G-13178)*
Glycon Corp ....E.... 517 423-8356
Tecumseh *(G-16503)*
Gollnick Tool Co ....G.... 586 755-0100
Warren *(G-17834)*
Grace Engineering Corp ....E.... 810 392-2181
Riley *(G-13850)*
Grandville Industries Inc ....E.... 616 538-0920
Grandville *(G-7381)*
Granite Precision Tool Corp ....G.... 248 299-8317
Rochester Hills *(G-14027)*
Gray Bros Stamping & Mch Inc ....E.... 269 483-7615
White Pigeon *(G-18478)*
Great Lakes Jig & Fixture ....G.... 269 795-4349
Middleville *(G-11307)*
◆ **Greenville Tool & Die Co** ....C.... 616 754-5693
Greenville *(G-7488)*
Griffin Tool Inc ....E.... 269 429-4077
Stevensville *(G-16252)*
Griswold Tool and Die Inc ....G.... 517 741-7433
Union City *(G-17494)*
Grm Automation Inc ....F.... 616 559-2700
Grand Rapids *(G-6791)*
Grosse Tool and Machine Co ....E.... 586 773-6770
Warren *(G-17842)*
Group B Industries II Inc ....G.... 734 941-6640
Romulus *(G-14281)*
▲ **Grw Technologies Inc** ....C.... 616 575-8119
Grand Rapids *(G-6792)*
Guo Ji Tooling Systems LLC ....F.... 616 301-6906
Grand Rapids *(G-6795)*
H & M Machining Inc ....F.... 586 778-5028
Roseville *(G-14419)*
H & S Mold Inc ....F.... 989 732-3566
Gaylord *(G-6133)*
H B D M Inc ....F.... 269 273-1976
Three Rivers *(G-16575)*
H S Die & Engineering Inc ....G.... 616 453-5451
Grand Rapids *(G-6799)*
Hacker Machine Inc ....E.... 517 569-3348
Rives Junction *(G-13886)*
Hallmark Tool and Gage Co Inc ....E.... 248 669-4010
Wixom *(G-18673)*
Hanson Inc ....F.... 616 451-3061
Grand Rapids *(G-6802)*
Hanson International Inc ....G.... 269 429-5555
Saint Joseph *(G-14934)*
Hanson International Inc ....C.... 269 429-5555
Saint Joseph *(G-14935)*
Harbrook Tool Inc ....E.... 248 477-8040
Novi *(G-12427)*
Hard Milling Solutions Inc ....G.... 586 286-2300
Bruce Twp *(G-2167)*

Hardy-Reed Tool & Die Co Inc ....E.... 517 547-7107
Manitou Beach *(G-10927)*
Harper Machine Tool Inc ....G.... 586 756-0140
Warren *(G-17849)*
Havercroft Tool & Die Inc ....G.... 989 724-5913
Greenbush *(G-7472)*
HB Carbide Company ....D.... 989 786-4223
Lewiston *(G-10021)*
Heinzmann D Tool & Die Inc ....F.... 248 363-5115
Commerce Township *(G-3535)*
Henze Stamping & Mfg Co ....G.... 248 588-5620
Troy *(G-17141)*
Hercules Machine Tl & Die LLC ....G.... 586 778-4120
Fraser *(G-5934)*
Hhi Formtech LLC ....E.... 586 415-2000
Fraser *(G-5935)*
Hi-Craft Engineering Inc ....D.... 586 293-0551
Fraser *(G-5936)*
Hi-Tech Mold & Engineering Inc ....E.... 248 844-0722
Rochester Hills *(G-14031)*
▲ **Hi-Tech Mold & Engineering Inc** ....E.... 248 852-6600
Rochester Hills *(G-14032)*
▼ **Highland Engineering Inc** ....E.... 517 548-4372
Howell *(G-8460)*
Highwood Die & Engineering Inc ....E.... 248 338-1807
Pontiac *(G-13380)*
Hill Machinery Co ....D.... 616 940-2800
Grand Rapids *(G-6817)*
Hite Tool Co Inc ....G.... 734 422-1777
Garden City *(G-6095)*
Hogle Sales & Mfg LLC ....G.... 517 592-1980
Brooklyn *(G-2126)*
▲ **Holland Plastics Corporation** ....E.... 616 844-2505
Grand Haven *(G-6318)*
Homestead Tool and Machine ....E.... 989 465-6182
Coleman *(G-3465)*
Horizon Die Company ....G.... 248 590-2966
Bingham Farms *(G-1700)*
▼ **HS Inc** ....C.... 616 453-5451
Grand Rapids *(G-6823)*
Hti Cybernetics Inc ....E.... 586 826-8346
Sterling Heights *(G-16043)*
▲ **Huron Tool & Engineering Co** ....E.... 989 269-9927
Bad Axe *(G-1108)*
Huron Tool & Gage Co Inc ....G.... 313 381-1900
Wixom *(G-18681)*
I & G Tool Co Inc ....F.... 586 777-7690
Cottrellville *(G-3721)*
I E & E Industries Inc ....F.... 248 544-8181
Madison Heights *(G-10744)*
Idel LLC ....G.... 231 929-3195
Traverse City *(G-16718)*
Illinois Tool Works Inc ....G.... 248 589-2500
Troy *(G-17161)*
▲ **Inalfa/Ssi Roof Systems LLC** ....D.... 586 758-6620
Warren *(G-17860)*
Incoe Corporation ....C.... 248 616-0220
Auburn Hills *(G-936)*
Incoe International Inc ....B.... 248 616-0220
Auburn Hills *(G-937)*
Independent Die Association ....G.... 586 773-9000
Warren *(G-17861)*
Independent Tool and Mfg Co ....E.... 269 521-4811
Allegan *(G-161)*
Industrial Converting Inc ....E.... 586 757-8820
Warren *(G-17864)*
▲ **Inglass Usa Inc** ....E.... 616 228-6900
Byron Center *(G-2278)*
Innovative Mold Inc ....E.... 586 752-2996
Washington *(G-18081)*
Integrity Fab & Machine Inc ....F.... 989 481-3200
Breckenridge *(G-1911)*
International Mold ....G.... 586 727-7898
Columbus *(G-3498)*
▲ **International Mold Corporation** ....D.... 586 783-6890
Clinton Township *(G-3260)*
▲ **Intra Corporation** ....D.... 734 326-7030
Westland *(G-18386)*
Invo Spline Inc ....E.... 586 757-8840
Warren *(G-17870)*
Iq Manufacturing LLC ....G.... 586 634-7185
Auburn Hills *(G-940)*
ITT Gage Inc ....F.... 231 766-2155
Muskegon *(G-11842)*
J & K Spratt Enterprises Inc ....D.... 517 439-5010
Hillsdale *(G-7938)*
J C Manufacturing Company ....G.... 586 757-2713
Warren *(G-17877)*
J M Kusch Inc ....E.... 989 684-8820
Bay City *(G-1368)*

SIC SECTION35 INDUSTRIAL AND COMMERCIAL MACHINERY AND COMPUTER EQUIPMENT35 INDUSTRIAL AND COMMERCIAL MACHINERY

▲ **Jacobsen Industries Inc** ... D ... 734 591-6111
Livonia ***(G-10255)***
Jamesway Tool and Die Inc ... E ... 616 396-3731
Holland ***(G-8099)***
Jay/Enn Corporation ... D ... 248 588-2393
Troy ***(G-17182)***
Jbl Systems Inc ... G ... 586 802-6700
Shelby Township ***(G-15244)***
JCs Tool & Mfg Co Inc ... E ... 989 892-8975
Essexville ***(G-5114)***
JD Edwards MGT Group Inc ... G ... 586 727-4039
Casco ***(G-2599)***
▲ **Jemar Tool Inc** ... E ... 586 726-6960
Hudsonville ***(G-8588)***
Jems of Litchfield Inc ... F ... 517 542-5367
Litchfield ***(G-10081)***
Jet Gage & Tool Inc ... G ... 586 294-3770
Fraser ***(G-5946)***
▲ **Jimdi Receivables Inc** ... E ... 616 895-7766
Allendale ***(G-221)***
Jirgens Modern Tool Corp ... F ... 269 381-5588
Kalamazoo ***(G-9231)***
Jo-Ad Industries Inc ... E ... 248 588-4810
Madison Heights ***(G-10754)***
▼ **Jo-Mar Industries Inc** ... E ... 248 588-9625
Troy ***(G-17188)***
Joggle Tool & Die Co Inc ... G ... 586 792-7477
Clinton Township ***(G-3265)***
John Lamantia Corporation ... G ... 269 428-8100
Stevensville ***(G-16255)***
Johnson Precision Mold & Engrg ... G ... 269 651-2553
Sturgis ***(G-16296)***
Jolico/J-B Tool Inc ... E ... 586 739-5555
Shelby Township ***(G-15245)***
Jordan Manufacturing Company ... E ... 616 794-0900
Belding ***(G-1454)***
Jordan Tool Corporation ... E ... 586 755-6700
Warren ***(G-17889)***
K & T Tool and Die Inc ... F ... 616 884-5900
Rockford ***(G-14173)***
K and K Machine Tools Inc ... G ... 586 463-1177
Clinton Township ***(G-3269)***
▲ **K&K Stamping Company** ... E ... 586 443-7900
Saint Clair Shores ***(G-14866)***
K-B Tool Corporation ... G ... 586 795-9003
Sterling Heights ***(G-16060)***
▲ **K-Tool Corporation Michigan** ... D ... 863 603-0777
Plymouth ***(G-13209)***
Kapex Manufacturing LLC ... G ... 989 928-4993
Saginaw ***(G-14676)***
Karr Unlimited Inc ... G ... 231 652-9045
Newaygo ***(G-12083)***
Katai Machine Shop ... F ... 269 465-6051
Bridgman ***(G-1930)***
Keller Tool Ltd ... F ... 734 425-4500
Livonia ***(G-10264)***
Kendor Steel Rule Die Inc ... F ... 586 293-7111
Fraser ***(G-5950)***
Kent Tool and Die Inc ... E ... 586 949-6600
Chesterfield ***(G-2901)***
Kentwater Tool & Mfg Co ... G ... 616 784-7171
Comstock Park ***(G-3615)***
Kenyon Specialties Inc ... G ... 810 686-3190
Clio ***(G-3403)***
Kern Industries Inc ... E ... 248 349-4866
Novi ***(G-12451)***
Ketchum Machine Corporated ... F ... 616 765-5101
Freeport ***(G-6034)***
Key Casting Company Inc ... G ... 269 426-3800
Sawyer ***(G-15110)***
Kidder Machine Company ... G ... 231 775-9271
Cadillac ***(G-2340)***
Kimastle Corporation ... D ... 586 949-2355
Chesterfield ***(G-2902)***
Kinney Tool and Die Inc ... D ... 616 997-0901
Coopersville ***(G-3689)***
Kirmin Die & Tool Inc ... E ... 734 722-9210
Romulus ***(G-14295)***
Koch Limited ... G ... 586 296-3103
Fraser ***(G-5952)***
Komarnicki Tool & Die Company ... F ... 586 776-9300
Roseville ***(G-14431)***
▲ **Kraftube Inc** ... C ... 231 832-5562
Reed City ***(G-13793)***
Kremin Inc ... E ... 989 790-5147
Frankenmuth ***(G-5868)***
Krieger Craftsmen Inc ... E ... 616 735-9200
Grand Rapids ***(G-6905)***
Kriseler Welding Inc ... G ... 989 624-9266
Birch Run ***(G-1708)***
Krt Precision Tool & Mfg Co ... G ... 517 783-5715
Jackson ***(G-8930)***
▲ **Ktx America Inc** ... G ... 734 737-0100
Livonia ***(G-10269)***
Kurek Tool Inc ... F ... 989 777-5300
Saginaw ***(G-14681)***
Kwk Industries Inc ... G ... 269 423-6213
Decatur ***(G-3949)***
L S Machining Inc ... G ... 248 583-7277
Troy ***(G-17202)***
Lab Tool and Engineering Corp ... F ... 517 750-4131
Spring Arbor ***(G-15793)***
Labor Aiding Systems Corp ... E ... 517 768-7478
Jackson ***(G-8931)***
Laingsburg Screw Inc ... G ... 517 651-2757
Laingsburg ***(G-9536)***
Lake Design and Mfg Co ... G ... 616 794-0290
Belding ***(G-1456)***
Lakeshore Mold and Die LLC ... G ... 269 429-6764
Stevensville ***(G-16258)***
Lakeside Manufacturing Co ... E ... 269 429-6193
Stevensville ***(G-16259)***
Lakeview Quality Tool Inc ... G ... 989 732-6417
Gaylord ***(G-6141)***
Lambert Industries Inc ... F ... 734 668-6864
Ann Arbor ***(G-548)***
Lance Industries LLC ... G ... 248 549-1968
Madison Heights ***(G-10767)***
Lane Tool ... G ... 248 528-1606
Rochester Hills ***(G-14048)***
Lane Tool and Mfg Corp ... G ... 248 528-1606
Rochester Hills ***(G-14049)***
▲ **Lapeer Industries Inc** ... C ... 810 538-0589
Shelby Township ***(G-15257)***
Lasercutting Services Inc ... E ... 616 975-2000
Grand Rapids ***(G-6929)***
Latin American Industries LLC ... G ... 616 301-1878
Grand Rapids ***(G-6932)***
Lc Manufacturing LLC ... C ... 231 839-7102
Lake City ***(G-9548)***
Lca Mold & Engineering Inc ... G ... 269 651-1193
Sturgis ***(G-16301)***
Leader Tool Company - HB Inc ... E ... 989 479-3281
Harbor Beach ***(G-7634)***
Leeward Tool Inc ... G ... 586 754-7200
Warren ***(G-17902)***
Legacy Precision Molds Inc ... G ... 616 532-6536
Grandville ***(G-7397)***
Lenawee Tool & Automation Inc ... G ... 517 458-7222
Morenci ***(G-11614)***
Lenway Machine Company Inc ... G ... 269 751-5183
Hamilton ***(G-7602)***
Leonard Machine Tool Systems ... E ... 586 757-8040
Warren ***(G-17903)***
▲ **Leroy Tool & Die Inc** ... D ... 231 768-4336
Leroy ***(G-10007)***
Lester Detterbeck Entps Ltd ... E ... 906 265-5121
Iron River ***(G-8746)***
Levannes Inc ... E ... 269 327-4484
Portage ***(G-13575)***
▲ **Liberty Manufacturing Company** ... E ... 269 327-0997
Portage ***(G-13576)***
Liberty Tool Inc ... E ... 586 726-2449
Sterling Heights ***(G-16073)***
▼ **Lincoln Park Die & Tool Co** ... E ... 734 285-1680
Brownstown ***(G-2149)***
Lincoln Tool Co Inc ... G ... 989 736-8711
Harrisville ***(G-7743)***
Line Precision Inc ... E ... 248 474-5280
Farmington Hills ***(G-5291)***
Link Tool & Mfg Co LLC ... D ... 734 710-0010
Westland ***(G-18392)***
Linwood Tool Co Inc ... E ... 989 697-4403
Linwood ***(G-10074)***
Lloyd Tool & Mfg Corp ... F ... 810 694-3519
Grand Blanc ***(G-6251)***
Lomar Machine & Tool Co ... E ... 517 563-8136
Horton ***(G-8374)***
Lonero Engineering Co Inc ... E ... 248 689-9120
Troy ***(G-17215)***
Lotus Corporation ... G ... 616 494-0112
Holland ***(G-8130)***
▲ **Louca Mold Arspc Machining Inc** ... E ... 248 391-1616
Auburn Hills ***(G-959)***
LP Products ... G ... 989 465-0287
Coleman ***(G-3468)***
Lrs Inc ... G ... 734 416-5050
Plymouth ***(G-13227)***
Ls Precision Tool & Die Inc ... G ... 269 963-9910
Battle Creek ***(G-1270)***
Luckmarr Plastics Inc ... D ... 586 978-8498
Sterling Heights ***(G-16077)***
Lupaul Industries Inc ... F ... 517 783-3223
Saint Johns ***(G-14904)***
Lutco Inc ... G ... 231 972-5566
Mecosta ***(G-11191)***
Luttmann Precision Mold Inc ... E ... 269 651-1193
Sturgis ***(G-16303)***
Lyons Tool & Engineering Inc ... E ... 586 200-3003
Warren ***(G-17910)***
M & F Machine & Tool Inc ... E ... 734 847-0571
Erie ***(G-5050)***
M & M Services Inc ... G ... 248 619-9861
Troy ***(G-17216)***
M C Molds Inc ... E ... 517 655-5481
Williamston ***(G-18576)***
M C Ward Inc ... F ... 810 982-9720
Port Huron ***(G-13497)***
M Curry Corporation ... E ... 989 777-7950
Saginaw ***(G-14685)***
M P D Welding Inc ... D ... 248 340-0330
Orion ***(G-12735)***
M&M Polishing Inc ... F ... 269 468-4407
Coloma ***(G-3478)***
Mac-Mold Base Inc ... E ... 586 752-1956
Bruce Twp ***(G-2176)***
Maco Tool & Engineering Inc ... E ... 989 224-6723
Saint Johns ***(G-14905)***
Maddox Industries Inc ... E ... 517 369-8665
Bronson ***(G-2118)***
Maes Tool & Die Co Inc ... F ... 517 750-3131
Jackson ***(G-8940)***
◆ **Magna Exteriors America Inc** ... A ... 248 631-1100
Troy ***(G-17220)***
▲ **Majestic Industries Inc** ... D ... 586 786-9100
Macomb ***(G-10612)***
Malmac Tool and Fixture Inc ... G ... 517 448-8244
Hudson ***(G-8556)***
Manufax Inc ... G ... 231 929-3226
Traverse City ***(G-16752)***
Manufctring Solutions Tech LLC ... G ... 734 744-5050
Commerce Township ***(G-3552)***
Mark Carbide Co ... G ... 248 545-0606
Troy ***(G-17238)***
Mark Four CAM Inc ... G ... 586 204-5906
Saint Clair Shores ***(G-14869)***
Mark Maker Company Inc ... E ... 616 538-6980
Grand Rapids ***(G-6959)***
Mark Mold and Engineering ... F ... 989 687-9786
Sanford ***(G-15073)***
Mark Tool & Die Company Inc ... E ... 248 363-1567
Commerce Township ***(G-3554)***
Marked Tool Inc ... G ... 616 669-3201
Hudsonville ***(G-8592)***
Marten Models & Molds Inc ... F ... 586 293-2260
Fraser ***(G-5962)***
Martin Tool & Machine Inc ... G ... 586 775-1800
Roseville ***(G-14436)***
Martinrea Industries Inc ... E ... 231 832-5504
Reed City ***(G-13795)***
▲ **Martinrea Industries Inc** ... E ... 734 428-2400
Manchester ***(G-10886)***
Master Craft Extrusion Tls Inc ... F ... 231 386-5149
Northport ***(G-12190)***
Master Jig Grinding & Gage Co ... G ... 248 380-8515
Wixom ***(G-18706)***
Master Machine & Tool Co Inc ... G ... 586 469-4243
Clinton Township ***(G-3295)***
Master Model & Fixture Inc ... F ... 586 532-1153
Shelby Township ***(G-15270)***
◆ **Master Precision Products Inc** ... E ... 616 754-5483
Greenville ***(G-7499)***
Master Precision Tool Corp ... F ... 586 739-3240
Sterling Heights ***(G-16085)***
Masters Tool & Die Inc ... G ... 989 777-2450
Saginaw ***(G-14688)***
Matrix Engineering Inc ... G ... 810 231-0212
Brighton ***(G-2026)***
Mattson Tool & Die Corp ... G ... 616 447-9012
Grand Rapids ***(G-6967)***
Max3 LLC ... E ... 269 925-2044
Benton Harbor ***(G-1570)***
Maya Jig Grinding & Gage Co ... F ... 248 471-0820
Farmington Hills ***(G-5311)***
Mayco Tool ... G ... 616 785-7350
Comstock Park ***(G-3622)***
▲ **Mayer Tool & Engineering Inc** ... E ... 269 651-1428
Sturgis ***(G-16305)***
McKechnie Vhcl Cmpnnts USA Inc ... B ... 218 894-1218
Roseville ***(G-14438)***

S I C

Employee Codes: A=Over 500 employees, B=251-500
C=101-250, D=51-100, E=20-50, F=10-19, G=3-9
2022 Harris Michigan
Industrial Directory
843

35 INDUSTRIAL AND COMMERCIAL MACHINERY AND COMPUTER EQUIPMENT

Merriman Products Inc .... G 517 787-1825
Jackson *(G-8953)*
Mesick Mold Co .... E 231 885-1304
Mesick *(G-11273)*
Met-L-Tec LLC .... E 734 847-7004
Temperance *(G-16540)*
Meta Tool Technologies LLC .... F 616 295-2115
Spring Lake *(G-15834)*
Metal Punch Corporation .... F 231 775-8391
Cadillac *(G-2346)*
Metalfab Tool & Machine Inc .... G 989 826-6044
Mio *(G-11511)*
Metalform Industries LLC .... G 248 462-0056
Shelby Township *(G-15274)*
Metalform LLC .... G 517 569-3313
Jackson *(G-8954)*
Metalmite Corporation .... F 248 651-9415
Rochester *(G-13911)*
Metric Precision Tool LLC .... F 734 946-8114
Taylor *(G-16442)*
Metro Technologies Ltd .... D 248 528-9240
Troy *(G-17254)*
◆ MGR Molds Inc .... F 586 254-6020
Sterling Heights *(G-16096)*
Michalski Enterprises Inc .... E 517 703-0777
Lansing *(G-9716)*
Michigan Auto Bending Corp .... E 248 528-1150
Madison Heights *(G-10781)*
Michigan Metal Tech Inc .... E 586 598-7800
Chesterfield *(G-2913)*
Michigan Mold Inc .... E 269 468-4407
Coloma *(G-3479)*
Michigan Precision Tl & Engrg .... E 269 783-1300
Dowagiac *(G-4790)*
Michigan Tool & Gauge Inc .... E 517 548-4604
Howell *(G-8482)*
Micro Engineering Inc .... G 616 534-9681
Byron Center *(G-2285)*
Micro Precision Molds Inc .... E 269 344-2044
Kalamazoo *(G-9270)*
Mid Michigan Pipe Inc .... G 989 772-5664
Grand Rapids *(G-7003)*
Mid-Tech Inc .... G 734 426-4327
Ann Arbor *(G-577)*
Middleville Tool & Die Co Inc .... D 269 795-3646
Middleville *(G-11309)*
Midwest Die Corp .... E 269 422-2171
Baroda *(G-1165)*
Midwest Machining Inc .... E 616 837-0165
Coopersville *(G-3693)*
▲ Midwest Mold Services Inc .... E 586 888-8800
Roseville *(G-14443)*
▲ Midwest Plastic Engineering .... D 269 651-5223
Sturgis *(G-16309)*
Midwest Tool & Die Inc .... F 616 863-8187
Rockford *(G-14179)*
Millennium Mold & Tool Inc .... G 586 791-1711
Clinton Township *(G-3301)*
Miller Mold Co .... E 989 793-8881
Frankenmuth *(G-5871)*
▼ Miller Tool & Die Co .... E 517 782-0347
Jackson *(G-8963)*
Mistequay Group Ltd .... E 989 752-7700
Saginaw *(G-14701)*
▲ Mistequay Group Ltd .... E 989 752-7700
Saginaw *(G-14702)*
Model Pattern Company Inc .... E 616 878-9710
Byron Center *(G-2288)*
Model-Matic Inc .... F 248 528-1680
Troy *(G-17264)*
Models & Tools Inc .... C 586 580-6900
Shelby Township *(G-15281)*
Modified Technologies Inc .... D 586 725-0448
Ira *(G-8703)*
Modineer Co LLC .... E 269 683-2550
Niles *(G-12146)*
◆ Modineer Co LLC .... C 269 683-2550
Niles *(G-12145)*
Modineer Co LLC .... G 269 684-3138
Niles *(G-12147)*
Modineer P-K Tool LLC .... E 269 683-2550
Niles *(G-12148)*
Mol-Son Inc .... G 269 668-3377
Mattawan *(G-11165)*
Mold Matter .... G 231 933-6653
Traverse City *(G-16762)*
Mold Specialties Inc .... G 586 247-4660
Shelby Township *(G-15283)*
Mold Tooling Systems Inc .... F 616 735-6653
Grand Rapids *(G-7021)*

Momentum Industries Inc .... F 989 681-5735
Saint Louis *(G-14993)*
Monroe LLC .... B 616 942-9820
Grand Rapids *(G-7025)*
▲ Motor City Stampings Inc .... B 586 949-8420
Chesterfield *(G-2915)*
▲ Mpp Corp .... E 810 364-2939
Kimball *(G-9496)*
Msx International Inc .... C 248 585-6654
Madison Heights *(G-10786)*
Multi Precision Intl LLC .... E 248 373-3330
Auburn Hills *(G-977)*
Multi-Precision Detail Inc .... E 248 373-3330
Auburn Hills *(G-978)*
Nesco Tool & Fixture LLC .... E 517 618-7052
Howell *(G-8483)*
Next Tool LLC .... F 734 405-7079
Belleville *(G-1489)*
Northern Machine Tool Company .... E 231 755-1603
Norton Shores *(G-12319)*
Northern Precision Inc .... F 989 736-6322
Lincoln *(G-10039)*
Northland Tool & Die Inc .... E 616 866-4451
Rockford *(G-14182)*
Northwest Tool & Machine Inc .... E 517 750-1332
Jackson *(G-8978)*
▲ Novi Precision Products Inc .... E 810 227-1024
Brighton *(G-2044)*
O Keller Tool Engrg Co LLC .... D 734 425-4500
Livonia *(G-10349)*
▲ Oakwood Energy Management Inc .... F 734 947-7700
Taylor *(G-16453)*
Odyssey Tool LLC .... F 586 468-6696
Clinton Township *(G-3312)*
Olivet Machine Tool Engrg Co .... F 269 749-2671
Olivet *(G-12695)*
Olympian Tool LLC .... E 989 224-4817
Saint Johns *(G-14911)*
Omega Plastics Inc .... D 586 954-2100
Clinton Township *(G-3314)*
One-Way Tool & Die Inc .... G 248 477-2964
Livonia *(G-10353)*
▲ Ontario Die Company America .... D 810 987-5060
Marysville *(G-11095)*
Ort Tool & Die Corporation .... D 419 242-9553
Erie *(G-5052)*
Ovidon Manufacturing LLC .... D 517 548-4005
Howell *(G-8489)*
▲ Owosso Graphic Arts Inc .... E 989 725-7112
Owosso *(G-12849)*
Oxbow Machine Products Inc .... E 734 422-7730
Livonia *(G-10355)*
P X Tool Co .... G 248 585-9330
Madison Heights *(G-10794)*
Pacific Tool & Engineering Ltd .... G 586 737-2710
Sterling Heights *(G-16122)*
▲ Paragon Die & Engineering Co .... C 616 949-2220
Grand Rapids *(G-7070)*
Paragon Molds Corporation .... E 586 294-7630
Fraser *(G-5974)*
Paramount Tool and Die Inc .... F 616 677-0000
Marne *(G-10997)*
Paravis Industries Inc .... E 248 393-2300
Auburn Hills *(G-993)*
Park Street Machine Inc .... F 231 739-9165
Muskegon *(G-11893)*
Parker Tooling & Design Inc .... F 616 791-1080
Grand Rapids *(G-7071)*
Parry Precision Inc .... E 248 585-1234
Madison Heights *(G-10795)*
▲ Paslin Company .... C 586 758-0200
Warren *(G-17957)*
Paslin Company .... E 248 953-8419
Shelby Township *(G-15296)*
Paterek Mold & Engineering .... G 586 784-8030
Armada *(G-739)*
Patrick Carbide Die LLC .... E 517 546-5646
Howell *(G-8491)*
Patton Tool and Die Inc .... F 810 359-5336
Lexington *(G-10031)*
▲ PCS Company .... D 586 294-7780
Fraser *(G-5976)*
Pdf Mfg Inc .... E 517 522-8431
Grass Lake *(G-7443)*
Peak Industries Co Inc .... E 313 846-8666
Dearborn *(G-3883)*
Pedri Mold Inc .... G 586 598-0882
Chesterfield *(G-2923)*
Peerless Gage .... G 734 261-3000
Northville *(G-12251)*

Pegasus Industries Inc .... F 313 937-0770
Redford *(G-13754)*
Pegasus Mold & Die Inc .... G 517 423-2009
Tecumseh *(G-16510)*
Peloton Inc .... G 269 694-9702
Otsego *(G-12798)*
Penka Tool Corporation .... G 248 543-3940
Madison Heights *(G-10796)*
Pentagon Mold Co .... G 269 496-7072
Mendon *(G-11220)*
Pentel Tool & Die Inc .... E 734 782-9500
Romulus *(G-14319)*
Peterson Jig & Fixture Inc .... E 616 866-8296
Rockford *(G-14183)*
Philips Machining Company .... F 616 997-7777
Coopersville *(G-3695)*
Pinnacle Engineering Co Inc .... E 734 428-7039
Manchester *(G-10888)*
Pinnacle Mold & Machine Inc .... G 616 892-9018
West Olive *(G-18350)*
Pioneer Steel Corporation .... E 616 878-5800
Byron Center *(G-2291)*
Pioneer Steel Corporation .... E 313 933-9400
Detroit *(G-4525)*
Plas-TEC Inc .... G 248 853-7777
Rochester Hills *(G-14085)*
▲ Plas-Tech Mold and Design Inc .... G 269 225-1223
Plainwell *(G-13089)*
▲ Plastic Engrg Tchncal Svcs Inc .... E 248 373-0800
Auburn Hills *(G-998)*
Plastic Mold Technology Inc .... G 616 698-9810
Grand Rapids *(G-7089)*
Plastic-Plate Inc .... E 616 698-2030
Grand Rapids *(G-7092)*
▲ Pollington Machine Tool Inc .... E 231 743-2003
Marion *(G-10976)*
Poseidon Industries Inc .... E 586 949-3550
Chesterfield *(G-2926)*
Positive Tool & Engineering Co .... G 313 532-1674
Redford *(G-13758)*
Praet Tool & Engineering Inc .... E 586 677-3800
Macomb *(G-10627)*
▲ Pratt & Whitney Autoair Inc .... C 517 393-4040
Lansing *(G-9882)*
Pratt & Whitney Autoair Inc .... E 517 348-1416
Holt *(G-8325)*
Precise Machine & Tool Co .... G 517 787-7699
Jackson *(G-8990)*
Precision Die and Machine Co .... F 810 329-2861
Saint Clair *(G-14840)*
Precision Jig & Fixture Inc .... E 616 696-2595
Cedar Springs *(G-2659)*
Precision Masking Inc .... E 734 848-4200
Erie *(G-5053)*
▲ Precision Masters Inc .... E 248 853-0308
Rochester Hills *(G-14087)*
Precision Parts Holdings Inc .... A 248 853-9010
Rochester Hills *(G-14088)*
Precision Tool Company Inc .... E 231 733-0811
Muskegon *(G-11898)*
▲ Preferred Industries Inc .... E 810 364-4090
Kimball *(G-9500)*
▲ Preferred Tool & Die Co Inc .... E 616 784-6789
Comstock Park *(G-3638)*
Prima Technologies Inc .... F 586 759-0250
Center Line *(G-2685)*
Prime Industries Inc .... E 734 946-8588
Taylor *(G-16460)*
Prime Mold LLC .... F 586 221-2512
Clinton Township *(G-3326)*
Pro Tool LLC .... G 616 850-0556
Grand Haven *(G-6348)*
Pro-Tech Machine Inc .... E 810 743-1854
Burton *(G-2243)*
Product and Tooling Tech Inc .... E 586 293-1810
Fraser *(G-5980)*
Proficient Products Inc .... G 586 977-8630
Sterling Heights *(G-16135)*
Project Die and Mold Inc .... G 616 862-8689
Grand Rapids *(G-7119)*
Proper Polymers- Tennessee Inc .... G 586 779-8787
Warren *(G-17985)*
Prophotonix Limited .... F 586 778-1100
Roseville *(G-14466)*
Prosper-Tech Machine & Tl LLC .... F 586 727-8800
Richmond *(G-13845)*
Proto Gage Inc .... E 586 978-2783
Sterling Heights *(G-16136)*
Proto-TEC Inc .... F 616 772-9511
Zeeland *(G-19075)*

SIC SECTION35 INDUSTRIAL AND COMMERCIAL MACHINERY AND COMPUTER EQUIPMENT35 INDUSTRIAL AND COMMERCIAL MACHINERY

Proto-Tek Manufacturing Inc ....E 586 772-2663
Roseville *(G-14467)*
▲ **Pti Engineered Plastics Inc** ....B 586 263-5100
Macomb *(G-10631)*
Punch Tech ....E 810 364-4811
Marysville *(G-11097)*
▲ **Punchcraft McHning Tooling LLC** ....G 586 573-4840
Warren *(G-17987)*
▼ **Q M E Inc** ....E 269 422-2137
Baroda *(G-1168)*
Qc Tech LLC ....D 248 597-3984
Madison Heights *(G-10813)*
Quad Precision Tool Co Inc ....F 248 608-2400
Rochester Hills *(G-14093)*
▲ **Quality Metalcraft Inc** ....C 734 261-6700
Livonia *(G-10377)*
Quality Metalcraft Inc ....C 734 261-6700
Livonia *(G-10378)*
Quality Model & Pattern Co ....E 616 791-1156
Grand Rapids *(G-7129)*
Quality Steel Fabg & Erct ....G 989 672-2873
Caro *(G-2578)*
Quality Tool and Die LLC ....G 248 707-0060
Clawson *(G-3107)*
Quantum Mold & Engineering LLC ....F 586 276-0100
Sterling Heights *(G-16141)*
Quasar Industries Inc ....D 248 844-7190
Rochester Hills *(G-14096)*
Quasar Industries Inc ....E 248 852-0300
Rochester Hills *(G-14097)*
Qwik Tool & Mfg Inc ....G 231 739-8849
Muskegon *(G-11903)*
▲ **R & A Tool & Engineering Co** ....E 734 981-2000
Westland *(G-18411)*
▲ **R & B Plastics Machinery LLC** ....E 734 429-9421
Saline *(G-15034)*
R & D Machine and Tool Inc ....G 231 798-8500
Norton Shores *(G-12327)*
R & M Machine Inc ....E 586 754-8447
Warren *(G-17990)*
R & M Manufacturing Company ....E 269 683-9550
Niles *(G-12160)*
R & S Tool & Die Inc ....G 989 673-8511
Caro *(G-2579)*
R D M Enterprises Co Inc ....G 810 985-4721
Port Huron *(G-13520)*
▲ **R E B Tool Inc** ....D 734 397-9116
Van Buren Twp *(G-17549)*
R S L Tool LLC ....G 616 786-2880
Holland *(G-8175)*
R T Gordon Inc ....E 586 294-6100
Fraser *(G-5985)*
Radar Tool & Manufacturing Co ....G 586 759-2800
Warren *(G-17993)*
Ralco Industries Inc ....D 248 853-3200
Auburn Hills *(G-1012)*
Ralco Industries Inc ....E 248 853-3200
Auburn Hills *(G-1013)*
Ran-Mark Co ....F 231 873-5103
Hart *(G-7760)*
Ranger Tool & Die Co ....F 989 754-1403
Saginaw *(G-14735)*
Rapids Tool & Engineering ....G 517 663-8721
Eaton Rapids *(G-4970)*
Rare Tool Inc ....F 517 423-5000
Tecumseh *(G-16512)*
Ravenna Pattern & Mfg ....E 231 853-2264
Ravenna *(G-13693)*
Rdc Machine Inc ....G 810 695-5587
Grand Blanc *(G-6260)*
Ready Molds Inc ....F 248 474-4007
Farmington Hills *(G-5365)*
Reef Tool & Gage Co ....E 586 468-3000
Clinton Township *(G-3333)*
Reeves Plastics LLC ....E 616 997-0777
Coopersville *(G-3696)*
Reger Manufacturing Company ....G 586 293-5096
Fraser *(G-5986)*
Reliance Spray Mask Co Inc ....F 616 784-3664
Grand Rapids *(G-7150)*
Rens LLC ....F 586 756-6777
Warren *(G-17996)*
Republic Drill/Apt Corp ....C 248 689-5050
Troy *(G-17330)*
Research Tool Corporation ....E 989 834-2246
Ovid *(G-12816)*
▲ **Resistnce Wldg Mch Accssory LL** ....F 269 428-4770
Saint Joseph *(G-14956)*
▲ **Richard Tool & Die Corporation** ....D 248 486-0900
New Hudson *(G-12068)*
Rivercity Rollform Inc ....E 231 799-9550
Norton Shores *(G-12328)*
Rk Boring Inc ....G 734 542-7920
Livonia *(G-10388)*
▲ **Rkaa Business LLC** ....E 231 734-5517
Evart *(G-5127)*
Rm Machine & Mold ....G 734 721-8800
Romulus *(G-14326)*
Robb Machine Tool Co ....G 616 532-6642
Grand Rapids *(G-7161)*
Roll Tech Inc ....G 517 283-3811
Reading *(G-13704)*
Rolleigh Inc ....F 517 283-3811
Reading *(G-13705)*
Romeo Mold Technologies Inc ....F 586 336-1245
Bruce Twp *(G-2177)*
Romeo Technologies Inc ....D 586 336-5015
Bruce Twp *(G-2178)*
Ronald R Wellington ....F 586 488-3087
Bruce Twp *(G-2180)*
Ronningen Research and Dev Co ....C 269 649-0520
Vicksburg *(G-17611)*
Ross Design & Engineering Inc ....E 517 547-6033
Cement City *(G-2676)*
Roth-Williams Industries Inc ....E 586 792-0090
Clinton Township *(G-3342)*
Rowland Mold & Machine Inc ....G 616 875-5400
Zeeland *(G-19077)*
Royal ARC Inc ....G 586 758-0718
Madison Heights *(G-10820)*
S & K Tool & Die Company Inc ....E 269 345-2174
Portage *(G-13603)*
S & S Die Co ....E 517 272-1100
Lansing *(G-9889)*
S F R Precision Turning Inc ....G 517 709-3367
Wixom *(G-18746)*
Sampson Tool Incorporated ....G 248 651-3313
Rochester *(G-13927)*
Sbti Company ....D 586 726-5756
Shelby Township *(G-15323)*
Schaenzle Tool and Die Inc ....G 248 656-0596
Rochester Hills *(G-14109)*
Schaller Tool & Die Co ....E 586 949-5500
Chesterfield *(G-2947)*
Schmald Tool & Die Inc ....F 810 743-1600
Burton *(G-2244)*
Schrader Stoves of Michiana ....E 269 684-4494
Niles *(G-12166)*
Schwab Industries Inc ....E 586 566-8090
Shelby Township *(G-15326)*
Select Tool and Die Inc ....G 269 422-2812
Baroda *(G-1170)*
Sequoia Tool Inc ....D 586 463-4400
Clinton Township *(G-3351)*
Service Extrusion Die Co Inc ....G 616 784-6933
Comstock Park *(G-3644)*
Set Enterprises Inc ....E 586 573-3600
Royal Oak *(G-14580)*
Set Enterprises of Mi Inc ....D 586 573-3600
Sterling Heights *(G-16174)*
Sfi Acquisition Inc ....E 248 471-1500
Farmington Hills *(G-5377)*
Shark Tool & Die Inc ....G 586 749-7400
Columbus *(G-3502)*
Sharp Die & Mold Co ....F 586 293-8660
Fraser *(G-5993)*
Sharp Model Co ....D 586 752-3099
Bruce Twp *(G-2182)*
Shields Classic Toys ....G 888 806-2632
Saline *(G-15039)*
Shoreline Mold & Engrg LLC ....G 269 926-2223
Benton Harbor *(G-1584)*
Shores Engineering Co Inc ....E 586 792-2748
Clinton Township *(G-3353)*
Sigma Tool Mfg Inc ....G 586 792-3300
Clinton Township *(G-3354)*
Simpsons Enterprises Inc ....F 269 279-7237
Three Rivers *(G-16584)*
Sink Rite Die Company ....F 586 268-0000
Sterling Heights *(G-16178)*
Slater Tools Inc ....E 586 465-5000
Clinton Township *(G-3360)*
Smeko Inc ....E 586 254-5310
Sterling Heights *(G-16180)*
Smith Brothers Tool Company ....D 586 726-5756
Shelby Township *(G-15335)*
Soper Manufacturing Company ....F 269 429-5245
Saint Joseph *(G-14962)*
Spare Die Inc ....G 734 522-2508
Livonia *(G-10415)*
Special Mold Engineering Inc ....E 248 652-6600
Rochester Hills *(G-14116)*
Special Tool & Engineering Inc ....D 586 285-5900
Fraser *(G-5996)*
Specialty Tool & Mold Inc ....G 616 531-3870
Grand Rapids *(G-7212)*
Specialty Tooling Systems Inc ....E 616 784-2353
Grand Rapids *(G-7213)*
Spencer Tool ....F 248 628-3677
Oxford *(G-12919)*
Spray Metal Mold Technology ....G 269 781-7151
Marshall *(G-11074)*
Stampede Die Corp ....D 616 877-0100
Wayland *(G-18208)*
▼ **Standard Components LLC** ....E 586 323-9700
Sterling Heights *(G-16189)*
Standard Die International Inc ....E 800 838-5464
Livonia *(G-10417)*
▲ **Standard Tool & Die Inc** ....E 269 465-6004
Stevensville *(G-16266)*
Stanhope Tool Inc ....E 248 585-5711
Warren *(G-18027)*
Steenson Enterprises ....G 248 628-0036
Leonard *(G-10003)*
Steeplechase Tool & Die Inc ....E 989 352-5544
Lakeview *(G-9646)*
▲ **Stellar Forge Products Inc** ....F 313 535-7631
Bloomfield Hills *(G-1862)*
Sterling Die & Engineering Inc ....E 586 677-0707
Macomb *(G-10637)*
Stm Mfg Inc ....E 616 392-4656
Holland *(G-8204)*
Sturgis Molded Products Co ....C 269 651-9381
Sturgis *(G-16324)*
Sturgis Tool and Die Inc ....E 269 651-5435
Sturgis *(G-16325)*
Su-Dan Plastics Inc ....C 248 651-6035
Rochester *(G-13932)*
Su-Dan Plastics Inc ....F 248 651-6035
Rochester Hills *(G-14121)*
Suburban Industries Inc ....F 734 676-6141
Brownstown Twp *(G-2158)*
Summit Services Inc ....E 586 977-8300
Shelby Township *(G-15346)*
Superior Mold Services Inc ....F 586 264-9570
Sterling Heights *(G-16197)*
Superior Products Mfg Inc ....G 810 679-4479
Croswell *(G-3736)*
Supreme Tool & Machine Inc ....F 248 673-8408
Waterford *(G-18168)*
Sweeney Metalworking LLC ....F 989 401-6531
Saginaw *(G-14769)*
T & C Tool & Sales Inc ....F 586 677-8390
Washington *(G-18088)*
T & T Tools Inc ....F 800 521-6893
Holland *(G-8211)*
T & W Tool & Die Corporation ....E 248 548-5400
Oak Park *(G-12647)*
Tadey Frank R Radian Tool Co ....G 586 754-7422
Warren *(G-18034)*
Talent Industries Inc ....F 313 531-4700
Redford *(G-13777)*
Talon LLC ....F 313 392-1000
Detroit *(G-4625)*
Tamara Tool Inc ....F 269 273-1463
Three Rivers *(G-16586)*
Target Mold Corporation ....F 231 798-3535
Norton Shores *(G-12336)*
Tartan Industries Inc ....G 810 387-4255
Yale *(G-18920)*
Taylor Turning Inc ....E 248 960-7920
Wixom *(G-18767)*
Tech Tooling Specialties Inc ....F 517 782-8898
Jackson *(G-9016)*
▲ **Technical Manufacturers Inc** ....G 989 846-6885
Standish *(G-15897)*
▲ **Telco Tools** ....F 616 296-0253
Spring Lake *(G-15856)*
Terry Tool & Die Co ....F 517 750-1771
Jackson *(G-9019)*
▲ **Thumb Tool & Engineering Co** ....C 989 269-9731
Bad Axe *(G-1115)*
Tijer Inc ....G 586 741-0308
Clinton Township *(G-3377)*
Tiller Tool and Die Inc ....F 517 458-6602
Jonesville *(G-9104)*
Titan Tool & Die Inc ....G 231 799-8680
Norton Shores *(G-12340)*
Tnr Machine Inc ....E 269 623-2827
Dowling *(G-4799)*

SIC

Employee Codes: A=Over 500 employees, B=251-500
C=101-250, D=51-100, E=20-50, F=10-19, G=3-9

2022 Harris Michigan
Industrial Directory

845

35 INDUSTRIAL AND COMMERCIAL MACHINERY AND COMPUTER EQUIPMENT35 INDUSTRIAL AND COMMERCIAL MACHINERY AND COM-

TNT-Edm Inc E 734 459-1700
Plymouth *(G-13316)*

Tolerance Tool & Engineering E 313 592-4011
Detroit *(G-4635)*

Tony S Die Machine Company F 586 773-7379
Warren *(G-18040)*

Tool Company Inc G 586 598-1519
Chesterfield *(G-2957)*

Tool North Inc E 231 941-1150
Traverse City *(G-16861)*

Toolco Inc E 734 453-9911
Plymouth *(G-13319)*

▲ Tooling Systems Group Inc F 616 863-8623
Grand Rapids *(G-7265)*

Tooling Technology LLC D 937 381-9211
Macomb *(G-10643)*

Top Craft Tool Inc E 586 461-4600
Clinton Township *(G-3378)*

Trademark Die & Engineering E 616 863-6660
Belmont *(G-1520)*

Trainer Metal Forming Co Inc E 616 844-9982
Grand Haven *(G-6371)*

▲ Tranor Industries LLC F 313 733-4888
Detroit *(G-4643)*

Travis Creek Tooling G 269 685-2000
Plainwell *(G-13101)*

Tregets Tool & Engineering Co G 517 782-0044
Jackson *(G-9022)*

▲ Tri Tech Tooling Inc F 616 396-6000
Holland *(G-8228)*

Tri-M-Mold Inc E 269 465-3301
Stevensville *(G-16269)*

Tri-Mation Industries Inc E 269 668-4333
Mattawan *(G-11168)*

Tri-Star Tool & Machine Co F 734 729-5700
Westland *(G-18423)*

Tri-Star Tooling LLC E 586 978-0435
Sterling Heights *(G-16210)*

▲ Tri-Way Manufacturing Inc E 586 776-0700
Roseville *(G-14485)*

Triangle Broach Company E 313 838-2150
Detroit *(G-4645)*

Trianon Industries Corporation E 586 759-2200
Center Line *(G-2688)*

Tric Tool Ltd E 616 395-1530
Holland *(G-8230)*

Tru Flo Carbide Inc F 989 658-8515
Ubly *(G-17483)*

Tru Point Corporation G 313 897-9100
Detroit *(G-4646)*

▲ True Industrial Corporation D 586 771-3500
Roseville *(G-14487)*

▼ Trutron Corporation E 248 583-9166
Troy *(G-17405)*

Turbine Tool & Gage Inc E 734 427-2270
Livonia *(G-10451)*

Twin Mold and Engineering LLC E 586 532-8558
Shelby Township *(G-15359)*

Uei Inc E 616 361-6093
Grand Rapids *(G-7285)*

Ultra-Sonic Extrusion Dies Inc E 586 791-8550
Clinton Township *(G-3381)*

Unified Tool and Die Inc G 517 768-8070
Jackson *(G-9028)*

Unique Tool & Mfg Co Inc E 336 498-2614
Temperance *(G-16551)*

Unytrex Inc F 810 796-9074
Dryden *(G-4808)*

US Boring Inc G 586 756-7511
Warren *(G-18048)*

◆ USF Delta Tooling LLC C 248 391-6800
Auburn Hills *(G-1075)*

Usher Tool & Die Inc E 616 583-9160
Byron Center *(G-2297)*

▲ Utica Enterprises Inc C 586 726-4300
Troy *(G-17419)*

Utica International Inc C 586 726-4330
Troy *(G-17420)*

Van Emon Bruce G 269 467-7803
Centreville *(G-2699)*

Vanex Mold Inc G 616 662-4100
Jenison *(G-9076)*

Varco Precision Products Co G 313 538-4300
Redford *(G-13783)*

Veit Tool & Gage Inc E 810 658-4949
Davison *(G-3800)*

Venture Manufacturing Inc G 269 429-6337
Saint Joseph *(G-14971)*

Vertical Technologies LLC E 586 619-0141
Warren *(G-18055)*

◆ Viking Tool & Engineering Inc E 231 893-0031
Whitehall *(G-18511)*

Vision Global Industries D 248 390-5805
Macomb *(G-10649)*

▲ Visioneering Inc B 248 622-5600
Auburn Hills *(G-1079)*

Vortec G 616 292-2401
Zeeland *(G-19091)*

W & W Tool and Die Inc G 989 835-5522
Midland *(G-11421)*

Waber Tool & Engineering Co F 269 342-0765
Kalamazoo *(G-9365)*

◆ Walker Tool & Die Inc D 616 453-5471
Grand Rapids *(G-7323)*

Wallin Brothers Inc G 734 525-7750
Livonia *(G-10464)*

Wardcraft Industries LLC E 517 750-9100
Spring Arbor *(G-15798)*

Wartrom Machine Systems Inc E 586 469-1915
Clinton Township *(G-3387)*

Waterman Tool & Machine Corp F 989 823-8181
Vassar *(G-17585)*

Wayne Allen Lambert G 269 467-4624
Centreville *(G-2701)*

Wefa Cedar Inc F 616 696-0873
Cedar Springs *(G-2666)*

Weldmet Industries Inc G 586 773-0533
Warren *(G-18065)*

West Michigan Tool & Die Co E 269 925-0900
Benton Harbor *(G-1602)*

Westgood Manufacturing Co F 586 771-3970
Roseville *(G-14493)*

▲ Westool Corporation E 734 847-2520
Temperance *(G-16552)*

Wetzel Tool & Engineering Inc E 248 960-0430
Wixom *(G-18791)*

White Automation & Tool Co F 734 947-9822
Romulus *(G-14338)*

White Engineering Inc G 269 695-0825
Niles *(G-12173)*

White River Knife and Tool G 616 997-0026
Fremont *(G-6057)*

Whitesell Frmed Components Inc D 313 299-1178
Waterford *(G-18175)*

Wico Metal Products Company F 586 755-9600
Center Line *(G-2690)*

Widell Industries Inc E 989 742-4528
Hillman *(G-7918)*

Wieske Tool Inc G 989 288-2648
Durand *(G-4850)*

Williams Tooling & Mfg E 616 681-2093
Dorr *(G-4771)*

Wire Dynamics Inc G 586 879-0321
Fraser *(G-6012)*

Withers Corporation E 586 758-2750
Warren *(G-18068)*

Wolverine Carbide & Tool Inc E 248 247-3888
Troy *(G-17450)*

Wolverine Products Inc F 586 792-3740
Clinton Township *(G-3389)*

Wolverine Tool Co F 810 664-2964
Lapeer *(G-9968)*

Worswick Mold & Tool Inc F 810 765-1700
Marine City *(G-10970)*

Wright Plastic Products Co LLC G 810 326-3000
Saint Clair *(G-14845)*

Wyke Die & Engineering Inc G 616 871-1175
Grand Rapids *(G-7351)*

X L T Engineering Inc E 989 684-4344
Kawkawlin *(G-9420)*

Yarema Die & Engineering Co C 248 585-2830
Troy *(G-17457)*

Z Mold & Engineering Inc G 586 948-5000
Chesterfield *(G-2966)*

3545 Machine Tool Access

A & D Run Off Inc G 231 759-0950
Muskegon *(G-11760)*

A A Anchor Bolt Inc F 248 349-6565
Northville *(G-12194)*

Abrasive Diamond Tool Company E 248 588-4800
Madison Heights *(G-10657)*

Accell Technologies Inc G 248 360-3762
Commerce Township *(G-3505)*

▲ Accu Products International G 734 429-9571
Saline *(G-14998)*

Accurate Carbide Tool Co Inc E 989 755-0429
Saginaw *(G-14600)*

Ace Drill Corporation G 517 265-5184
Adrian *(G-47)*

Acg Services Inc G 586 232-4698
Shelby Township *(G-15164)*

Acme Carbide Die Inc E 734 722-2303
Westland *(G-18351)*

Acme Grooving Tool Co F 800 633-8828
Clarkston *(G-3011)*

Action Tool & Machine Inc E 810 229-6300
Brighton *(G-1938)*

Active Tooling LLC F 616 875-8111
Zeeland *(G-18988)*

Adaptable Tool Supply LLC F 248 439-0866
Clawson *(G-3084)*

▲ Admiral Broach Company Inc E 586 468-8411
Clinton Township *(G-3156)*

▲ Advance Products Corporation E 269 849-1000
Benton Harbor *(G-1527)*

Advanced Feedlines LLC E 248 583-9400
Troy *(G-16908)*

Advantage Design and Tool G 586 801-7413
Richmond *(G-13831)*

AG Davis Gage & Engrg Co E 586 977-9000
Sterling Heights *(G-15926)*

Aic Acquisition Company LLC E 810 227-5510
Wixom *(G-18600)*

◆ American Broach & Machine Co E 734 961-0300
Ypsilanti *(G-18924)*

American Gator Tool Company G 231 347-3222
Harbor Springs *(G-7639)*

American Gear & Engrg Co Inc E 734 595-6400
Westland *(G-18353)*

American Industrial Gauge Inc G 248 280-0048
Royal Oak *(G-14507)*

Anbo Tool & Manufacturing Inc G 586 465-7610
Clinton Township *(G-3171)*

Anchor Lamina America Inc C 231 533-8646
Bellaire *(G-1468)*

▲ Anderson-Cook Inc D 586 954-0700
Chesterfield *(G-2844)*

Anderson-Cook Inc G 586 293-0800
Fraser *(G-5895)*

Apex Broaching Systems Inc F 586 758-2626
Warren *(G-17708)*

Apollo Broach Inc G 734 467-5750
Westland *(G-18354)*

Apollo Tool & Engineering Inc F 616 735-4934
Grand Rapids *(G-6463)*

Arch Cutting Tools LLC C 734 266-6900
Bloomfield Hills *(G-1800)*

Arm Tooling Systems Inc F 586 759-5677
Warren *(G-17712)*

Art Laser Inc E 248 391-6600
Auburn Hills *(G-798)*

Artcraft Pattern Works Inc F 734 729-0022
Westland *(G-18355)*

Ashine Diamond Tools G 734 668-9067
Ann Arbor *(G-382)*

Associated Broach Corporation E 810 798-9112
Almont *(G-256)*

Atlas Thread Gage Inc G 248 477-3230
Farmington Hills *(G-5175)*

▲ Avon Broach & Prod Co LLC E 248 650-8080
Rochester Hills *(G-13958)*

Aw Carbide Fabricators Inc E 586 294-1850
Sterling Heights *(G-15939)*

Award Cutter Company Inc F 616 531-0430
Grand Rapids *(G-6487)*

B C I Collet Inc F 734 326-1222
Westland *(G-18359)*

Banner Broach Inc G 586 493-9219
Warren *(G-17726)*

Baxter Machine & Tool Co E 517 782-2808
Jackson *(G-8822)*

Benny Gage Inc E 734 455-3080
Wixom *(G-18620)*

Bilco Tool Corporation G 586 574-9300
Warren *(G-17737)*

Bob G Machining LLC G 586 285-1400
Clinton Township *(G-3186)*

Borite Manufacturing Corp G 248 588-7260
Madison Heights *(G-10683)*

Bower Tool & Manufacturing Inc G 734 522-0444
Livonia *(G-10141)*

Breckers ABC Tool Company Inc E 586 779-1122
Roseville *(G-14381)*

▼ Breesport Holdings Inc C 248 685-9500
Milford *(G-11456)*

Briggs Industries Inc E 586 749-5191
Chesterfield *(G-2852)*

Broaching Industries Inc E 586 949-3775
Chesterfield *(G-2853)*

SIC SECTION35 INDUSTRIAL AND COMMERCIAL MACHINERY AND COMPUTER EQUIPMENT35 INDUSTRIAL AND COMMERCIAL MACHINERY

Buster Mathis Foundation......G......616 843-4433
Wyoming **(G-18855)**

Cap Collet & Tool Co Inc......F......734 283-4040
Wyandotte **(G-18814)**

Carbide Form Master Inc......G......248 625-9373
Davisburg **(G-3763)**

Carbide Surface Company......G......586 465-6110
Clinton Township **(G-3194)**

Carbide Technologies Inc......E......586 296-5200
Fraser **(G-5910)**

Cardinal Machine Co......E......810 686-1190
Clio **(G-3394)**

Caro Carbide Corporation......F......248 588-4252
Troy **(G-17003)**

CB Fabricating & Service......F......586 758-4980
Warren **(G-17750)**

Cdp Diamond Products Inc......E......734 591-1041
Livonia **(G-10149)**

Center Line Gage Inc......G......810 387-4300
Brockway **(G-2106)**

Century Inc......G......231 946-7500
Traverse City **(G-16642)**

▲ Ceratizit Usa Inc......C......586 759-2280
Warren **(G-17751)**

Champagne Grinding & Mfg Co......E......734 459-1759
Canton **(G-2448)**

Clymer Manufacturing Company......G......248 853-5555
Rochester Hills **(G-13975)**

Cole Carbide Industries Inc......G......989 872-4348
Cass City **(G-2613)**

Coles Machine Service Inc......E......810 658-5373
Davison **(G-3777)**

Colonial Bushings Inc......E......586 954-3880
Clinton Township **(G-3203)**

▲ Colonial Tool Sales & Svc LLC......F......734 946-2733
Taylor **(G-16394)**

◆ Comau LLC......B......248 353-8888
Southfield **(G-15530)**

Complete Cutting Tl & Mfg Inc......G......248 662-9811
Wixom **(G-18635)**

Complex Tool & Machine Inc......G......248 625-0664
Clarkston **(G-3028)**

Conical Cutting Tools Inc......E......616 531-8500
Grand Rapids **(G-6593)**

Contour Tool and Machine Inc......G......517 787-6806
Jackson **(G-8853)**

▲ Control Gaging Inc......E......734 668-6750
Ann Arbor **(G-436)**

◆ Costello Machine LLC......E......586 749-0136
Chesterfield **(G-2861)**

Cougar Cutting Tools Inc......E......586 469-1310
Clinton Township **(G-3212)**

Cross Paths Corp......G......616 248-5371
Grand Rapids **(G-6613)**

Crystal Cut Tool Inc......G......734 946-0099
Romulus **(G-14265)**

▲ CWk International Corp......G......616 396-2063
Holland **(G-8010)**

Cz Industries Inc......G......248 475-4415
Auburn Hills **(G-856)**

D & F Corporation......D......586 254-5300
Sterling Heights **(G-15977)**

Davison-Rite Products Co......E......734 513-0505
White Lake **(G-18454)**

Dependable Gage & Tool Co......E......248 545-2100
Oak Park **(G-12604)**

Detail Precision Products Inc......E......248 544-3390
Ferndale **(G-5540)**

Detroit Edge Tool Company......D......586 776-1598
Roseville **(G-14398)**

▲ Detroit Edge Tool Company......D......313 366-4120
Detroit **(G-4146)**

Di-Coat Corporation......E......248 349-1211
Novi **(G-12399)**

Diamond Alternatives LLC......G......734 755-1505
Carleton **(G-2552)**

Diamond Broach Company......G......586 757-5131
Warren **(G-17777)**

Diamond Tool Manufacturing Inc......E......734 416-1900
Plymouth **(G-13157)**

▲ Die Services International LLC......D......734 699-3400
Van Buren Twp **(G-17524)**

▲ Dijet Incorporated......G......734 454-9100
Plymouth **(G-13158)**

Dixon & Ryan Corporation......F......248 549-4000
Royal Oak **(G-14531)**

▲ Dme Company LLC......B......248 398-6000
Madison Heights **(G-10709)**

Dobday Manufacturing Co Inc......F......586 254-6777
Sterling Heights **(G-15990)**

Douglas Gage Inc......F......586 727-2089
Richmond **(G-13836)**

▲ Dowding Machining LLC......F......517 663-5455
Eaton Rapids **(G-4961)**

Dumbarton Tool Inc......F......231 775-4342
Cadillac **(G-2328)**

Dura Thread Gage Inc......F......248 545-2890
Madison Heights **(G-10714)**

Dynamic Jig Grinding Corp......E......248 589-3110
Troy **(G-17072)**

E & E Custom Products LLC......F......586 978-3377
Warren **(G-17788)**

E & E Special Products LLC......F......586 978-3377
Warren **(G-17789)**

Ecco Tool Co Inc......G......248 349-0840
Novi **(G-12409)**

▼ Edge Industries Inc......G......616 453-5458
Grand Rapids **(G-6665)**

Elk Lake Tool Co......E......231 264-5616
Elk Rapids **(G-5023)**

Ellsworth Cutting Tools Ltd......F......586 598-6040
Chesterfield **(G-2874)**

Elmhirst Industries Inc......E......586 731-8663
Sterling Heights **(G-16002)**

Engineered Tools Corp......E......989 673-8733
Caro **(G-2571)**

Enmark Tool Company......E......586 293-2797
Fraser **(G-5925)**

Enterprise Tool and Gear Inc......F......989 269-9797
Bad Axe **(G-1100)**

Equitable Engineering Co Inc......E......248 689-9700
Troy **(G-17096)**

Erdman Machine Co......E......231 894-1010
Whitehall **(G-18495)**

Est Tools America Inc......F......810 824-3323
Ira **(G-8695)**

▲ Etcs Inc......F......586 268-4870
Warren **(G-17796)**

Evans Tool & Engineering Inc......F......616 791-6333
Grand Rapids **(G-6688)**

F & S Tool & Gauge Co Inc......G......517 787-2661
Jackson **(G-8882)**

Fab-Jet Services LLC......G......586 463-9622
Clinton Township **(G-3234)**

Falcon Motorsports Inc......G......248 328-2222
Holly **(G-8269)**

▲ Federal Broach & Mch Co LLC......C......989 539-7420
Harrison **(G-7676)**

▲ Feed - Lease Corp......E......248 377-0000
Auburn Hills **(G-896)**

Fega Tool & Gage Company......F......586 469-4400
Clinton Township **(G-3236)**

Fisk Precision Tech LLC......G......616 514-1415
Wyoming **(G-18873)**

Fitz-Rite Products Inc......E......248 528-8440
Troy **(G-17113)**

Five Star Industries Inc......E......586 786-0500
Macomb **(G-10595)**

FL Tool Holders LLC......E......734 591-0134
Livonia **(G-10207)**

▲ Fontijne Grotnes Inc......E......269 262-4700
Niles **(G-12129)**

Forkardt Inc......E......231 995-8300
Traverse City **(G-16688)**

Formula One Tool & Engineering......G......810 794-3617
Algonac **(G-142)**

▲ Fraser Tool & Gauge LLC......G......313 882-9192
Grosse Pointe Park **(G-7554)**

Fsp Inc......E......248 585-0760
Troy **(G-17123)**

Fullerton Tool Company Inc......C......989 799-4550
Saginaw **(G-14648)**

G A Machine Company Inc......G......313 836-5646
Detroit **(G-4249)**

▲ G&G Industries Inc......E......586 726-6000
Shelby Township **(G-15229)**

Gage Eagle Spline Inc......D......586 776-7240
Warren **(G-17822)**

Gage Numerical Inc......G......231 328-4426
Lake City **(G-9546)**

GAL Gage Co......F......269 465-5750
Bridgman **(G-1926)**

General Broach & Engrg Inc......C......586 726-4300
Troy **(G-17129)**

▲ General Broach Company......D......517 458-7555
Morenci **(G-11611)**

General Broach Company......G......517 458-7555
Morenci **(G-11612)**

▲ Global CNC Industries Ltd......E......734 464-1920
Plymouth **(G-13177)**

Global Engineering Inc......E......586 566-0423
Shelby Township **(G-15230)**

Global Retool Group Amer LLC......E......248 289-5820
Brighton **(G-2001)**

Global Thread Gage Inc......G......313 438-6789
Dearborn **(G-3848)**

▼ Global Tooling Systems LLC......B......586 726-0500
Macomb **(G-10599)**

Grand Rapids Metaltek Inc......E......616 791-2373
Grand Rapids **(G-6765)**

Green Manufacturing Inc......G......517 458-1500
Morenci **(G-11613)**

Green Oak Tool and Svcs Inc......F......586 531-2255
Brighton **(G-2005)**

Grind-All Precision Tool Co......F......586 954-3430
Clinton Township **(G-3250)**

Groholski Mfg Solutions LLC......E......517 278-9339
Coldwater **(G-3436)**

◆ Gt Technologies Inc......E......734 467-8371
Westland **(G-18378)**

Guardian Manufacturing Corp......E......734 591-1454
Livonia **(G-10231)**

Guhring Inc......E......262 784-6730
Novi **(G-12424)**

H & G Tool Company......F......586 573-7040
Warren **(G-17845)**

H E Morse Co......D......616 396-4604
Holland **(G-8065)**

Hanchett Manufacturing Inc......E......231 796-7678
Big Rapids **(G-1676)**

Hank Thorn Co......F......248 348-7800
Wixom **(G-18675)**

Hanlo Gauges & Engineering Co......G......734 422-4224
Livonia **(G-10235)**

Hardy-Reed Tool & Die Co Inc......E......517 547-7107
Manitou Beach **(G-10927)**

▲ Harroun Enterprises Inc......G......810 629-9885
Fenton **(G-5484)**

Hexagon Mfg Intelligence Inc......G......248 449-9400
Novi **(G-12434)**

▲ Hope Focus Companies Inc......E......313 494-5500
Detroit **(G-4308)**

◆ Hougen Manufacturing Inc......C......810 635-7111
Swartz Creek **(G-16355)**

Howell Tool Service Inc......F......517 548-1114
Howell **(G-8465)**

▲ Htc Sales Corporation......F......800 624-2027
Ira **(G-8698)**

Hti Cybernetics Inc......E......586 826-8346
Sterling Heights **(G-16043)**

▲ Huron Tool & Engineering Co......E......989 269-9927
Bad Axe **(G-1108)**

Huron Tool & Gage Co Inc......G......313 381-1900
Wixom **(G-18681)**

Hydra-Lock Corporation......E......586 783-5007
Mount Clemens **(G-11641)**

Hydro-Craft Inc......G......248 652-8100
Rochester Hills **(G-14037)**

I & G Tool Co Inc......F......586 777-7690
Cottrellville **(G-3721)**

Ideal Heated Knives Inc......G......248 437-1510
New Hudson **(G-12058)**

Illinois Tool Works Inc......G......231 947-5755
Traverse City **(G-16719)**

Illinois Tool Works Inc......G......231 947-5755
Traverse City **(G-16720)**

Image Machine & Tool Inc......G......586 466-3400
Fraser **(G-5942)**

Indepndnce Tling Solutions LLC......E......586 274-2300
Troy **(G-17163)**

Invo Spline Inc......E......586 757-8840
Warren **(G-17870)**

J & K Spratt Enterprises Inc......D......517 439-5010
Hillsdale **(G-7938)**

J & L Turning Inc......F......810 765-5755
East China **(G-4857)**

J E Wood Co......F......248 585-5711
Madison Heights **(G-10749)**

Jade Tool Inc......E......231 946-7710
Traverse City **(G-16726)**

Johan Van De Weerd Co Inc......G......517 542-3817
Litchfield **(G-10082)**

Joint Production Tech Inc......E......586 786-0080
Macomb **(G-10608)**

Jt Manufacturing Inc......E......517 849-2923
Jonesville **(G-9090)**

▲ K-Tool Corporation Michigan......D......863 603-0777
Plymouth **(G-13209)**

Kalamazoo Chuck Mfg Svc Ctr Co......F......269 679-2325
Schoolcraft **(G-15122)**

S I C

Employee Codes: A=Over 500 employees, B=251-500
C=101-250, D=51-100, E=20-50, F=10-19, G=3-9

2022 Harris Michigan
Industrial Directory

847

Kalamazoo Engrg & Mfg LLC .... G 269 569-5205
Kalamazoo (G-9239)
Karr Spring Company .... E 616 394-1277
Holland (G-8109)
▲ Kasper Machine Co .... F 248 547-3150
Madison Heights (G-10759)
Keller Tool Ltd .... F 734 425-4500
Livonia (G-10264)
Kennametal Inc .... G 231 946-2100
Traverse City (G-16733)
Kenrie Inc .... F 616 494-3200
Holland (G-8112)
Keo Cutters Inc .... E 586 771-2050
Warren (G-17893)
Khalsa Metal Products Inc .... G 616 791-4794
Kentwood (G-9460)
Kingsford Broach & Tool Inc .... E 906 774-4917
Kingsford (G-9511)
Knight Carbide Inc .... E 586 598-4888
Chesterfield (G-2903)
Kooiker Tool & Die Inc .... F 616 554-3630
Caledonia (G-2387)
Krebs Tool Inc .... G 734 697-8611
Van Buren Twp (G-17534)
▲ Krmc LLC .... G 734 955-9311
Romulus (G-14296)
Kurek Tool Inc .... F 989 777-5300
Saginaw (G-14681)
▲ Kyocera Unimerco Tooling Inc .... E 734 944-4433
Saline (G-15023)
▲ L E Jones Company .... B 906 863-1043
Menominee (G-11242)
Lab Tool and Engineering Corp .... F 517 750-4131
Spring Arbor (G-15793)
Lamina Inc .... D 248 489-9122
Farmington Hills (G-5289)
Lancer Tool Co .... F 248 380-8830
Wixom (G-18695)
Laydon Enterprises Inc .... E 906 774-4633
Iron Mountain (G-8724)
▼ Lead Screws International Inc .... D 262 786-1500
Traverse City (G-16740)
Leader Corporation .... E 586 566-7114
Shelby Township (G-15260)
Legacy Tool LLC .... G 231 335-8983
Newaygo (G-12084)
Lester Detterbeck Entps Ltd .... E 906 265-5121
Iron River (G-8746)
Lightning Machine Holland LLC .... F 616 786-9280
Holland (G-8129)
Linamar Holding Nevada Inc .... D 248 477-6240
Livonia (G-10278)
Lincoln Precision Carbide Inc .... E 989 736-8113
Lincoln (G-10037)
Line Precision Inc .... E 248 474-5280
Farmington Hills (G-5291)
Link Manufacturing Inc .... G 231 238-8741
Indian River (G-8654)
Lumco Manufacturing Company .... F 810 724-0582
Lum (G-10559)
Lyons Tool & Engineering Inc .... E 586 200-3003
Warren (G-17910)
M & M Thread & Assembly Inc .... G 248 583-9696
Sterling Heights (G-16079)
M C Carbide Tool Co .... E 248 486-9590
Wixom (G-18703)
M Curry Corporation .... E 989 777-7950
Saginaw (G-14685)
Mac-Tech Tooling Corporation .... G 248 743-1400
Troy (G-17217)
Machining & Fabricating Inc .... E 586 773-9288
Roseville (G-14434)
Machining Technologies LLC .... G 248 379-4201
Clarkston (G-3046)
Maes Tool & Die Co Inc .... F 517 750-3131
Jackson (G-8940)
Magnetic Chuck Services Co Inc .... G 586 822-9441
Casco (G-2600)
Majeske Machine Inc .... G 319 273-8905
Plymouth (G-13232)
Malmac Tool and Fixture Inc .... G 517 448-8244
Hudson (G-8556)
◆ Mapal Inc .... D 810 364-8020
Port Huron (G-13500)
Mark Tool & Die Company Inc .... E 248 363-1567
Commerce Township (G-3554)
Maro Precision Tool Company .... F 734 261-3100
West Bloomfield (G-18296)
◆ Marshall-Gruber Company LLC .... F 248 353-4100
Southfield (G-15647)

Martel Tool Corporation .... F 313 278-2420
Allen Park (G-200)
Master Jig Grinding & Gage Co .... G 248 380-8515
Wixom (G-18706)
Master Machine & Tool Co Inc .... G 586 469-4243
Clinton Township (G-3295)
MB Liquidating Corporation .... D 810 638-5388
Flushing (G-5811)
Mc Pherson Industrial Corp .... E 586 752-5555
Romeo (G-14229)
Merrifield McHy Solutions Inc .... E 248 494-7335
Sterling Heights (G-16091)
Metal Punch Corporation .... F 231 775-8391
Cadillac (G-2346)
Metro Machine Works Inc .... D 734 941-4571
Romulus (G-14304)
Michigan Spline Gage Co Inc .... F 248 544-7303
Hazel Park (G-7833)
Micro Form Inc .... G 517 750-3660
Spring Arbor (G-15796)
▼ Midwest Tool and Cutlery Co .... D 269 651-2476
Sturgis (G-16310)
Millennium Technology II Inc .... F 734 479-4440
Romulus (G-14306)
Miller Broach Inc .... D 810 395-8810
Capac (G-2547)
▼ Miller Tool & Die Co .... E 517 782-0347
Jackson (G-8963)
▲ Mistequay Group Ltd .... F 989 752-7700
Saginaw (G-14702)
Mjc Tool & Machine Co Inc .... G 586 790-4766
Clinton Township (G-3303)
Modern CAM and Tool Co .... G 734 946-9800
Taylor (G-16448)
Moehrle Inc .... F 734 761-2000
Ann Arbor (G-581)
Montague Tool and Mfg Co .... E 810 686-0000
Clio (G-3408)
Motor Tool Manufacturing Co .... G 734 425-3300
Livonia (G-10324)
Mp Tool & Engineering Company .... E 586 772-7730
Roseville (G-14448)
◆ Nagel Precision Inc .... C 734 426-5650
Ann Arbor (G-587)
Nexteer Automotive Corporation .... B 989 757-5000
Saginaw (G-14710)
North-East Gage Inc .... G 586 792-6790
Clinton Township (G-3309)
Northern Precision Inc .... F 989 736-6322
Lincoln (G-10039)
O Keller Tool Engrg Co LLC .... D 734 425-4500
Livonia (G-10349)
Olivet Machine Tool Engrg Co .... F 269 749-2671
Olivet (G-12695)
Olympian Tool LLC .... E 989 224-4817
Saint Johns (G-14911)
Omax Tool Products Inc .... F 517 768-0300
Ray (G-13701)
▲ Oneida Tool Corporation .... E 313 537-0770
Redford (G-13752)
P & P Manufacturing Co Inc .... E 810 667-2712
Lapeer (G-9952)
P L Schmitt Crbide Tooling LLC .... G 313 706-5756
Grass Lake (G-7442)
P T M Corporation .... G 586 725-2733
Ira (G-8708)
P T M Corporation .... D 586 725-2211
Ira (G-8707)
P&L Development & Mfg LLC .... D 989 739-5203
Oscoda (G-12768)
Paslin Company .... C 586 755-1693
Warren (G-17956)
▲ Paslin Company .... C 586 758-0200
Warren (G-17957)
Peak Industries Co Inc .... E 313 846-8666
Dearborn (G-3883)
Pencil Pushers LLC .... G 248 252-7839
Waterford (G-18149)
Perry Tool Company Inc .... G 734 283-7393
Riverview (G-13883)
Petal Pushers By Liz LLC .... G 616 481-9513
Comstock Park (G-3637)
Philips Machining Company .... F 616 997-7777
Coopersville (G-3695)
Pioneer Broach Midwest Inc .... F 231 768-5800
Leroy (G-10009)
Pioneer Michigan Broach Co .... F 231 768-5800
Leroy (G-10010)
PL Schmitt Crbide Toling LLC .... G 517 522-6891
Grass Lake (G-7444)

Posa-Cut Corporation .... E 248 474-5620
Farmington Hills (G-5350)
Precise Cnc Routing Inc .... E 616 538-8608
Grand Rapids (G-7097)
Precision Components .... F 248 588-5650
Troy (G-17310)
Precision Devices Inc .... E 734 439-2462
Milan (G-11449)
▲ Precision Threading Corp .... G 231 627-3133
Cheboygan (G-2796)
Precision Tool Company Inc .... E 231 733-0811
Muskegon (G-11898)
Primary Tool & Cutter Grinding .... E 248 588-1530
Madison Heights (G-10809)
Prime Industries Inc .... E 734 946-8588
Taylor (G-16460)
Productivity Technologies .... G 810 714-0200
Fenton (G-5496)
Puritan Automation LLC .... F 248 668-1114
Wixom (G-18737)
▲ Qc American LLC .... G 734 961-0300
Ypsilanti (G-18972)
▲ R & A Tool & Engineering Co .... E 734 981-2000
Westland (G-18411)
▼ R & B Industries Inc .... E 734 462-9478
Livonia (G-10380)
R & S Tool & Die Inc .... G 989 673-8511
Caro (G-2579)
R J S Tool & Gage Co .... E 248 642-8620
Birmingham (G-1746)
R L Schmitt Company Inc .... E 734 525-9310
Livonia (G-10382)
R T Gordon Inc .... E 586 294-6100
Fraser (G-5985)
Rayco Manufacturing Inc .... F 586 795-2884
Sterling Heights (G-16144)
Reef Tool & Gage Co .... E 586 468-3000
Clinton Township (G-3333)
Reif Carbide Tool Co Inc .... E 586 754-1890
Warren (G-17995)
Republic Drill/Apt Corp .... C 248 689-5050
Troy (G-17330)
◆ Reska Spline Gage Inc .... G 586 778-4000
Roseville (G-14470)
Rhinevault Olsen Machine & Tl .... G 989 753-4363
Saginaw (G-14737)
Riverside Spline & Gear Inc .... E 810 765-8302
Marine City (G-10965)
Riviera Industries Inc .... G 313 381-5500
Allen Park (G-203)
Rochester Machine Products .... G 586 466-6190
Harrison Township (G-7722)
Rodan Tool & Mold LLC .... G 248 926-9200
Commerce Township (G-3571)
Roesch Maufacturing Co LLC .... G 517 424-6300
Tecumseh (G-16514)
Rose Tool & Die Inc .... E 989 343-1015
West Branch (G-18338)
Roth-Williams Industries Inc .... E 586 792-0090
Clinton Township (G-3342)
▼ Royal Design & Manufacturing .... D 248 588-0110
Madison Heights (G-10821)
RTS Cutting Tools Inc .... E 586 954-1900
Clinton Township (G-3344)
S F S Carbide Tool .... G 989 777-3890
Saginaw (G-14742)
Salerno Tool Works Inc .... G 586 755-5000
Warren (G-18001)
SB Investments LLC .... E 734 462-9478
Livonia (G-10400)
Sbti Company .... D 586 726-5756
Shelby Township (G-15323)
SC Thread Cutting Tools Inc .... G 248 365-4044
Auburn Hills (G-1030)
Schaller Tool & Die Co .... E 586 949-5500
Chesterfield (G-2947)
▲ Seco Holding Co Inc .... D 248 528-5200
Troy (G-17347)
Select Steel Fabricators Inc .... E 248 945-9582
Southfield (G-15696)
Selector Spline Products Co .... F 586 254-4020
Sterling Heights (G-16168)
Selmuro Ltd .... E 810 603-2117
Grand Blanc (G-6263)
Service Diamond Tool Company .... G 248 669-3100
Novi (G-12535)
Sesco Products Group Inc .... F 586 979-4400
Sterling Heights (G-16173)
Severance Tool Industries Inc .... E 989 777-5500
Saginaw (G-14753)

Severance Tool Industries Inc ... G ... 989 777-5500
Saginaw *(G-14754)*
Shouse Tool Inc ... F ... 810 629-0391
Fenton *(G-5503)*
Shwayder Company ... G ... 248 645-9511
Birmingham *(G-1749)*
▲ **Sidley Diamond Tool Company** ... E ... 734 261-7970
Garden City *(G-6109)*
Skill-Craft Company Inc ... F ... 586 716-4300
Ira *(G-8714)*
Sme Holdings LLC ... E ... 586 254-5310
Sterling Heights *(G-16179)*
Smeko Inc ... E ... 586 254-5310
Sterling Heights *(G-16180)*
Snap Jaws Manufacturing Inc ... G ... 248 588-1099
Troy *(G-17357)*
Southwest Broach ... G ... 714 356-2967
Cadillac *(G-2354)*
Spartan Carbide Inc ... E ... 586 285-9786
Fraser *(G-5995)*
Spartan Tool Sales Inc ... G ... 586 268-1556
Sterling Heights *(G-16183)*
Spartans Finishing LLC ... G ... 517 528-5510
Haslett *(G-7779)*
Special Drill and Reamer Corp ... E ... 248 588-5333
Madison Heights *(G-10832)*
Spence Industries Inc ... G ... 586 758-3800
Warren *(G-18019)*
Stanhope Tool Inc ... E ... 248 585-5711
Warren *(G-18027)*
◆ **Star Cutter Co** ... E ... 248 474-8200
Farmington Hills *(G-5387)*
Star Ringmaster ... G ... 734 641-7147
Canton *(G-2527)*
Steel Craft Technologies Inc ... C ... 616 866-4400
Belmont *(G-1518)*
Steelcraft Tool Co Inc ... F ... 734 522-7130
Livonia *(G-10420)*
Stoney Crest Regrind Service ... F ... 989 777-7190
Bridgeport *(G-1918)*
Stratford-Cambridge Group Co ... G ... 734 404-6047
Plymouth *(G-13304)*
Superior Controls Inc ... C ... 734 454-0500
Plymouth *(G-13306)*
Superior Design & Mfg ... F ... 810 678-3950
Metamora *(G-11287)*
T M Smith Tool Intl Corp ... E ... 586 468-1465
Mount Clemens *(G-11659)*
Target Mold Corporation ... F ... 231 798-3535
Norton Shores *(G-12336)*
▲ **Tawas Tool Co Inc** ... D ... 989 362-6121
East Tawas *(G-4924)*
Tawas Tool Co Inc ... D ... 989 362-0414
East Tawas *(G-4925)*
Taylor Turning Inc ... E ... 248 960-7920
Wixom *(G-18767)*
Tazz Broach and Machine Inc ... G ... 586 296-7755
Harrison Township *(G-7728)*
TEC Industries Inc ... G ... 248 446-9560
New Hudson *(G-12072)*
Techni CAM and Manufacturing ... F ... 734 261-6477
Livonia *(G-10430)*
Technical Rotary Services Inc ... G ... 586 772-6755
Warren *(G-18037)*
Teknikut Corporation ... G ... 586 778-7150
Canton *(G-2534)*
▲ **Thielenhaus Microfinish Corp** ... E ... 248 349-9450
Novi *(G-12556)*
▲ **Thread-Craft Inc** ... D ... 586 323-1116
Sterling Heights *(G-16205)*
Three-Dimensional Services Inc ... C ... 248 852-1333
Rochester Hills *(G-14125)*
Tolerance Tool & Engineering ... E ... 313 592-4011
Detroit *(G-4635)*
Tool Service Company Inc ... G ... 586 296-2500
Fraser *(G-6003)*
Tool-Craft Industries Inc ... E ... 248 549-0077
Sterling Heights *(G-16206)*
Tooling Solutions Group LLC ... G ... 248 585-0222
Madison Heights *(G-10844)*
Tooltech Machinery Inc ... G ... 248 628-1813
Oxford *(G-12924)*
Total Tooling Concepts Inc ... G ... 616 785-8402
Comstock Park *(G-3648)*
Triangle Broach Company ... E ... 313 838-2150
Detroit *(G-4645)*
◆ **Trimas Corporation** ... B ... 248 631-5450
Bloomfield Hills *(G-1869)*
Tru Flo Carbide Inc ... F ... 989 658-8515
Ubly *(G-17483)*
Tru Point Corporation ... G ... 313 897-9100
Detroit *(G-4646)*
Trudex One Inc ... G ... 248 392-2036
Milford *(G-11494)*
Truing Systems Inc ... E ... 248 588-9060
Troy *(G-17404)*
Trusted Tool Mfg Inc ... G ... 810 750-6000
Fenton *(G-5510)*
TS Carbide Inc ... G ... 248 486-8330
Commerce Township *(G-3580)*
Turbine Tool & Gage Inc ... E ... 734 427-2270
Livonia *(G-10451)*
Universal / Devlieg Inc ... F ... 989 752-3077
Saginaw *(G-14784)*
▼ **Universal Tool Inc** ... G ... 248 733-9800
Troy *(G-17414)*
▲ **Universal/Devlieg LLC** ... F ... 989 752-7700
Saginaw *(G-14785)*
▲ **Utica Enterprises Inc** ... C ... 586 726-4300
Troy *(G-17419)*
Van Emon Bruce ... G ... 269 467-7803
Centreville *(G-2699)*
Vigel North America Inc ... G ... 734 947-9900
Madison Heights *(G-10855)*
Wachtel Tool & Broach Inc ... G ... 586 758-0110
Saint Clair *(G-14844)*
Warren Broach & Machine Corp ... F ... 586 254-7080
Sterling Heights *(G-16229)*
Weber Precision Grinding Inc ... G ... 616 842-1634
Spring Lake *(G-15858)*
Wedin International Inc ... E ... 231 779-8650
Cadillac *(G-2363)*
West Michigan Gage Inc ... F ... 616 735-0585
Walker *(G-17657)*
Westech Corp ... E ... 231 766-3914
Muskegon *(G-11943)*
Western Pegasus Inc ... G ... 616 393-9580
Holland *(G-8248)*
Widell Industries Inc ... E ... 989 742-4528
Hillman *(G-7918)*
Wire Fab Inc ... F ... 313 893-8816
Detroit *(G-4685)*
Wit-Son Carbide Tool Inc ... E ... 231 536-2247
East Jordan *(G-4883)*
Wit-Son Quality Tool & Mfg LLC ... G ... 989 335-4342
Harrisville *(G-7747)*
Wolverine Broach Co Inc ... E ... 586 468-4445
Harrison Township *(G-7733)*
Wolverine Production & Engrg ... E ... 586 468-2890
Harrison Township *(G-7734)*
Wolverine Special Tool Inc ... E ... 616 791-1027
Grand Rapids *(G-7348)*
Wolverine Tool Co ... F ... 810 664-2964
Lapeer *(G-9968)*
Wood-Cutters Tooling Inc ... G ... 616 257-7930
Grandville *(G-7424)*
Workblades Inc ... E ... 586 778-0060
Warren *(G-18072)*
Wyandotte Collet and Tool Inc ... F ... 734 283-8055
Wyandotte *(G-18845)*
Wyser Innovative Products LLC ... G ... 616 583-9225
Byron Center *(G-2304)*
X-Edge Products Inc ... G ... 866 591-9991
Grand Rapids *(G-7352)*
▲ **Yost Vises LLC** ... G ... 616 396-2063
Holland *(G-8258)*
▲ **Zcc USA Inc** ... F ... 734 997-3811
Ann Arbor *(G-721)*
Zimmermann Engineering Co Inc ... G ... 248 358-0044
Southfield *(G-15746)*

3546 Power Hand Tools

◆ **A W B Industries Inc** ... E ... 989 739-1447
Oscoda *(G-12753)*
Ace Drill Corporation ... G ... 517 265-5184
Adrian *(G-47)*
▲ **Anchor Lamina America Inc** ... E ... 248 489-9122
Bellaire *(G-1469)*
Anchor Lamina America Inc ... C ... 231 533-8646
Bellaire *(G-1468)*
Avalon Tools Inc ... G ... 248 269-0001
Troy *(G-16967)*
Black & Decker (us) Inc ... G ... 410 716-3900
Grand Rapids *(G-6513)*
Black & Decker Corporation ... F ... 248 597-5000
Madison Heights *(G-10682)*
Carbide Technologies Inc ... E ... 586 296-5200
Fraser *(G-5910)*
Clausing Industrial Inc ... F ... 269 345-7155
Kalamazoo *(G-9144)*
▲ **Clausing Industrial Inc** ... D ... 269 345-7155
Kalamazoo *(G-9145)*
▲ **Conway-Cleveland Corp** ... G ... 616 458-0056
Grand Rapids *(G-6604)*
Coxline Inc ... E ... 269 345-1132
Kalamazoo *(G-9157)*
D & D Production Inc ... F ... 248 334-2112
Waterford *(G-18113)*
Ebels Hardware Inc ... F ... 231 826-3334
Falmouth *(G-5133)*
Elmo Manufacturing Co Inc ... G ... 734 995-5966
Ann Arbor *(G-471)*
Falcon Global LLC ... F ... 734 302-3025
Ann Arbor *(G-486)*
Hank Thorn Co ... F ... 248 348-7800
Wixom *(G-18675)*
▲ **Heck Industries Incorporated** ... F ... 810 632-5400
Hartland *(G-7769)*
Hme Inc ... C ... 616 534-1463
Wyoming *(G-18885)*
◆ **Hougen Manufacturing Inc** ... C ... 810 635-7111
Swartz Creek *(G-16355)*
Jemms-Cascade Inc ... F ... 248 526-8100
Troy *(G-17184)*
Jones & Hollands Inc ... G ... 810 364-6400
Marysville *(G-11089)*
K M S Company ... G ... 616 994-7000
Holland *(G-8106)*
Lamina Inc ... D ... 248 489-9122
Farmington Hills *(G-5289)*
Lumberjack Shack Inc ... G ... 810 724-7230
Imlay City *(G-8640)*
Lutco Inc ... G ... 231 972-5566
Mecosta *(G-11191)*
▼ **Menominee Saw and Supply Co** ... E ... 906 863-2609
Menominee *(G-11248)*
Pitchford Bertie ... G ... 517 627-1151
Grand Ledge *(G-6397)*
Plum Brothers LLC ... G ... 734 947-8100
Romulus *(G-14321)*
Roesch Maufacturing Co LLC ... G ... 517 424-6300
Tecumseh *(G-16514)*
RTS Cutting Tools Inc ... E ... 586 954-1900
Clinton Township *(G-3344)*
◆ **Star Cutter Co** ... E ... 248 474-8200
Farmington Hills *(G-5387)*
Striker Tools LLC ... G ... 248 990-7767
Manitou Beach *(G-10928)*
▲ **Telco Tools** ... F ... 616 296-0253
Spring Lake *(G-15856)*
Waber Tool & Engineering Co ... F ... 269 342-0765
Kalamazoo *(G-9365)*

3547 Rolling Mill Machinery & Eqpt

Burger Iron Co ... G ... 330 794-1716
Grand Rapids *(G-6534)*
D-N-S Industries Inc ... E ... 586 465-2444
Clinton Township *(G-3216)*
▲ **Dalton Industries LLC** ... E ... 248 673-0755
Waterford *(G-18114)*
Delta Tube & Fabricating Corp ... C ... 248 634-8267
Holly *(G-8268)*
Enprotech Industrial Tech LLC ... E ... 216 883-3220
Lansing *(G-9695)*
▲ **Feed - Lease Corp** ... E ... 248 377-0000
Auburn Hills *(G-896)*
▲ **Fontijne Grotnes Inc** ... E ... 269 262-4700
Niles *(G-12129)*
Mill Assist Services Inc ... E ... 269 692-3211
Otsego *(G-12791)*
Novi Tool & Machine Company ... F ... 313 532-0900
Redford *(G-13749)*
◆ **Perfecto Industries Inc** ... E ... 989 732-2941
Gaylord *(G-6154)*
▼ **Rod Chomper Inc** ... F ... 616 392-9677
Holland *(G-8182)*
SMS Technical Service LLC ... F ... 313 322-4890
Dearborn *(G-3897)*

3548 Welding Apparatus

1271 Associates Inc ... D ... 586 948-4300
Chesterfield *(G-2832)*
Airgas Usa LLC ... G ... 248 545-9353
Ferndale *(G-5520)*
▲ **Alcotec Wire Corporation** ... D ... 800 228-0750
Traverse City *(G-16598)*
▲ **All-Fab Corporation** ... G ... 269 673-6572
Allegan *(G-145)*
Allied Indus Fabrication LLC ... E ... 810 422-5093
Fenton *(G-5446)*

S
I
C

Anroid Industries Inc ....D 248 732-0000
Auburn Hills *(G-788)*
▲ Aro Welding Technologies Inc ....D 586 949-9353
Chesterfield *(G-2847)*
Arplas USA LLC ....G 888 527-5553
Troy *(G-16952)*
◆ Assembly Technologies Intl Inc ....F 248 280-2810
Troy *(G-16960)*
Atlas Welding Accessories Inc ....D 248 588-4666
Troy *(G-16962)*
▲ Bielomatik Inc ....E 248 446-9910
Commerce Township *(G-3515)*
◆ Comau LLC ....B 248 353-8888
Southfield *(G-15530)*
◆ Cor-Met Inc ....E 810 227-0004
Brighton *(G-1966)*
Craft Industries Inc ....B 586 726-4300
Shelby Township *(G-15197)*
Delfab Inc ....E 906 428-9570
Gladstone *(G-6180)*
Dytron Corporation ....F 586 296-9600
Fraser *(G-5921)*
◆ Eureka Welding Alloys Inc ....E 248 588-0001
Madison Heights *(G-10724)*
Fair Industries LLC ....F 248 740-7841
Troy *(G-17104)*
◆ Fanuc America Corporation ....B 248 377-7000
Rochester Hills *(G-14009)*
GAL Gage Co ....F 269 465-5750
Bridgman *(G-1926)*
Great Lakes Laser Services ....G 248 584-1828
Madison Heights *(G-10735)*
Grossel Tool Co ....E 586 294-3660
Fraser *(G-5932)*
Hmr Fabrication Unlimited Inc ....F 586 569-4288
Fraser *(G-5938)*
Hobart Brothers LLC ....G 231 933-1234
Traverse City *(G-16712)*
Hti Cybernetics Inc ....E 586 826-8346
Sterling Heights *(G-16043)*
Huebner E W & Son Mfg Co Inc ....G 734 427-2600
Livonia *(G-10243)*
J W Holdings Inc ....E 616 530-9889
Grand Rapids *(G-6858)*
K&S Consultants LLC ....G 269 240-7767
Buchanan *(G-2198)*
Lakeland Elec Mtr Svcs Inc ....E 616 647-0331
Comstock Park *(G-3619)*
Lloyd Tool & Mfg Corp ....F 810 694-3519
Grand Blanc *(G-6251)*
Mc REA Corporation ....G 734 420-2116
Plymouth *(G-13237)*
Melttools LLC ....G 269 978-0968
Portage *(G-13584)*
Mid Michigan Repair Service ....G 989 835-6014
Midland *(G-11390)*
Miyachi Unitek Corp ....G 616 676-2634
Grand Rapids *(G-7015)*
▲ Nadex of America Corporation ....E 248 477-3900
Farmington Hills *(G-5330)*
▲ Northwoods Manufacturing Inc ....D 906 779-2370
Kingsford *(G-9516)*
▲ Nortronic Company ....G 313 893-3730
Detroit *(G-4491)*
▲ Paslin Company ....C 586 758-0200
Warren *(G-17957)*
Paslin Company ....C 248 953-8419
Shelby Township *(G-15296)*
Paslin Company ....C 586 755-3606
Warren *(G-17958)*
Peak Industries Co Inc ....E 313 846-8666
Dearborn *(G-3883)*
Purity Cylinder Gases Inc ....G 517 321-9555
Lansing *(G-9734)*
▲ Resistnce Wldg Mch Accssory LL ....F 269 428-4770
Saint Joseph *(G-14956)*
RSI Global Sourcing LLC ....G 734 604-2448
Novi *(G-12529)*
▲ Saginaw Machine Systems Inc ....E 989 753-8465
Saginaw *(G-14747)*
Santanna Tool & Design LLC ....D 248 541-3500
Madison Heights *(G-10824)*
▲ Sanyo Machine America Corp ....D 248 651-5911
Rochester Hills *(G-14108)*
Sas Global Corporation ....D 248 414-4470
Warren *(G-18003)*
Startec Training Institute ....F 313 808-7013
Detroit *(G-4608)*
Textile Fabrication & Dist Inc ....G 586 566-9100
Mount Clemens *(G-11660)*
◆ Thyssenkrupp System Engrg ....C 248 340-8000
Auburn Hills *(G-1052)*
▲ Tipaloy Inc ....F 313 875-5145
Detroit *(G-4633)*
Tupes of Saginaw Inc ....F 989 799-1550
Saginaw *(G-14781)*
▲ Utica Enterprises Inc ....C 586 726-4300
Troy *(G-17419)*
Utica International Inc ....C 586 726-4330
Troy *(G-17420)*
◆ Welding Technology Corp ....C 248 477-3900
Farmington Hills *(G-5413)*
Welform Electrodes Inc ....E 586 755-1184
Warren *(G-18066)*

3549 Metalworking Machinery, NEC

Accu-Rite Industries LLC ....E 586 247-0060
Shelby Township *(G-15161)*
Ace & 1 Logistics LLC ....G 601 335-3625
Shelby Township *(G-15163)*
Advanced Feedlines LLC ....E 248 583-9400
Troy *(G-16908)*
Allied Tool and Machine Co ....E 989 755-5384
Saginaw *(G-14604)*
Aludyne US LLC ....D 810 987-1112
Port Huron *(G-13438)*
▲ Anderson-Cook Inc ....D 586 954-0700
Chesterfield *(G-2844)*
Anderson-Cook Inc ....G 586 293-0800
Fraser *(G-5895)*
Apollo Seiko Ltd ....F 269 465-3400
Bridgman *(G-1920)*
▲ Atlas Technologies LLC ....D 810 629-6663
Fenton *(G-5451)*
Ats Assembly and Test Inc ....F 734 266-4713
Livonia *(G-10129)*
Auto/Con Corp ....D 586 791-7474
Fraser *(G-5897)*
Bay Plastics Machinery Co LLC ....E 989 671-9630
Bay City *(G-1330)*
Bel-Kur Inc ....E 734 847-0651
Temperance *(G-16528)*
Boxer Equipment/Morbark Inc ....G 989 866-2381
Winn *(G-18589)*
▲ Bulk AG Innovations LLC ....F 269 925-0900
Benton Harbor *(G-1538)*
◆ Burke E Porter Machinery Co ....C 616 234-1200
Grand Rapids *(G-6535)*
▲ Burton Industries Inc ....E 906 932-5970
Ironwood *(G-8758)*
Burton Press Co Inc ....G 248 853-0212
Rochester Hills *(G-13967)*
Cardinal Machine Co ....E 810 686-1190
Clio *(G-3394)*
▲ Carter Products Company Inc ....E 616 647-3380
Grand Rapids *(G-6548)*
▲ Coleman Machine Inc ....E 906 863-1113
Menominee *(G-11229)*
Columbia Marking Tools Inc ....E 586 949-8400
Chesterfield *(G-2860)*
▲ Dane Systems LLC ....D 269 465-3263
Stevensville *(G-16245)*
Das Group Inc ....F 248 670-2718
Royal Oak *(G-14529)*
▼ Dawlen Corporation ....E 517 787-2200
Jackson *(G-8860)*
Demmer Investments Inc ....G 517 321-3600
Lansing *(G-9688)*
◆ Diamond Automation Ltd ....G 734 838-7138
Livonia *(G-10184)*
Dnl Fabrication LLC ....E 586 872-2656
Roseville *(G-14401)*
◆ Dominion Tech Group Inc ....C 586 773-3303
Roseville *(G-14402)*
Duo Robotic Solutions Inc ....F 586 883-7559
Shelby Township *(G-15214)*
Esys Automation LLC ....C 248 484-9927
Auburn Hills *(G-881)*
Esys Automation LLC ....E 284 484-9724
Pontiac *(G-13370)*
Esys Automation LLC ....E 248 484-9702
Sterling Heights *(G-16005)*
Experienced Concepts Inc ....F 586 752-4200
Armada *(G-735)*
▲ Feed - Lease Corp ....E 248 377-0000
Auburn Hills *(G-896)*
Fives Cinetic Corp ....C 248 477-0800
Farmington Hills *(G-5244)*
Flagler Corporation ....E 586 749-6300
Chesterfield *(G-2882)*
▲ Fontijne Grotnes Inc ....E 269 262-4700
Niles *(G-12129)*
Friendship Industries Inc ....E 586 323-0033
Sterling Heights *(G-16024)*
Friendship Industries Inc ....F 586 997-1325
Sterling Heights *(G-16025)*
Gatco Incorporated ....F 734 453-2295
Plymouth *(G-13174)*
Hak Inc ....G 231 587-5322
Mancelona *(G-10872)*
Hanson International Inc ....C 269 429-5555
Saint Joseph *(G-14935)*
Harvey S Freeman ....G 248 852-2222
West Bloomfield *(G-18287)*
▲ HMS Products Co ....D 248 689-8120
Troy *(G-17146)*
Hti Cybernetics Inc ....E 586 826-8346
Sterling Heights *(G-16043)*
Ideal Tool Inc ....F 989 893-8336
Bay City *(G-1366)*
◆ Industrial Automation LLC ....D 248 598-5900
Rochester Hills *(G-14039)*
Innovation Tech LLC ....F 248 797-2686
Wixom *(G-18685)*
▲ J W Froehlich Inc ....G 586 580-0025
Sterling Heights *(G-16053)*
J W Holdings Inc ....E 616 530-9889
Grand Rapids *(G-6858)*
▲ JR Automation Tech LLC ....C 616 399-2168
Holland *(G-8104)*
Jr Technology Group LLC ....C 616 399-2168
Holland *(G-8105)*
▲ Jsj DC Holdings Inc ....D 616 842-7110
Grand Haven *(G-6325)*
Kapex Manufacturing LLC ....G 989 928-4993
Saginaw *(G-14676)*
▲ Kuka Assembly and Test Corp ....C 989 220-3088
Saginaw *(G-14680)*
Kuka Robotics Corporation ....E 586 795-2000
Shelby Township *(G-15250)*
Kuka Systems North America LLC ....F 586 795-2000
Sterling Heights *(G-16065)*
▲ Kuka Systems North America LLC ...B 586 795-2000
Sterling Heights *(G-16066)*
Kuka Systems North America LLC ....G 586 726-4300
Shelby Township *(G-15251)*
▲ Kuka US Holdings Company LLC ....D 586 795-2000
Sterling Heights *(G-16067)*
L & H Diversified Mfg USA LLC ....G 586 615-4873
Shelby Township *(G-15252)*
Lab Tool and Engineering Corp ....F 517 750-4131
Spring Arbor *(G-15793)*
Lampco Industries of MI Inc ....G 517 783-3414
Jackson *(G-8932)*
Leonard Machine Tool Systems ....E 586 757-8040
Warren *(G-17903)*
◆ Letnan Industries Inc ....E 586 726-1155
Sterling Heights *(G-16072)*
Linwood Tool Co Inc ....E 989 697-4403
Linwood *(G-10074)*
Lomar Machine & Tool Co ....E 517 563-8136
Horton *(G-8374)*
M & F Machine & Tool Inc ....E 734 847-0571
Erie *(G-5050)*
Manufacturers / Mch Bldrs Svcs ....G 734 748-3706
Livonia *(G-10298)*
Manufctring Solutions Tech LLC ....G 734 744-5050
Commerce Township *(G-3552)*
Mark One Corporation ....D 989 732-2427
Gaylord *(G-6145)*
Marking Machine Co ....F 517 767-4155
Tekonsha *(G-16523)*
Mega Screen Corp ....G 517 849-7057
Jonesville *(G-9094)*
Milacron LLC ....G 517 424-8981
Tecumseh *(G-16508)*
Modern Tool and Tapping Inc ....G 586 777-5144
Fraser *(G-5964)*
◆ Morbark LLC ....B 989 866-2381
Winn *(G-18590)*
Motion Machine Company ....F 810 664-9901
Lapeer *(G-9949)*
Naams LLC ....G 586 285-5684
Warren *(G-17940)*
National Advnced Mblity Cnsrti ....G 734 205-5920
Ann Arbor *(G-590)*
▲ New Unison Corporation ....E 248 544-9500
Ferndale *(G-5571)*
Nidec Chs LLC ....F 586 777-7440
Romeo *(G-14230)*

SIC SECTION 35 INDUSTRIAL AND COMMERCIAL MACHINERY AND COMPUTER EQUIPMENT 35 INDUSTRIAL AND COMMERCIAL MACHINERY

▲ Norgren Automtn Solutions LLC......C 734 429-4989
  Saline (G-15030)
Norgren Automtn Solutions LLC......F 586 463-3000
  Rochester Hills (G-14070)
Northwest Tool & Machine Inc......E 517 750-1332
  Jackson (G-8978)
▲ Novi Precision Products Inc......E 810 227-1024
  Brighton (G-2044)
On The Mark Inc......G 989 317-8033
  Mount Pleasant (G-11729)
◆ Perfecto Industries Inc......E 989 732-2941
  Gaylord (G-6154)
Precision Plus......G 906 553-7900
  Escanaba (G-5091)
Pro-Tech Machine Inc......E 810 743-1854
  Burton (G-2243)
Prosys Industries Inc......D 734 207-3710
  Canton (G-2515)
R & S Tool & Die Inc......G 989 673-8511
  Caro (G-2579)
Reger Manufacturing Company......G 586 293-5096
  Fraser (G-5986)
▲ Rock Tool & Machine Co Inc......E 734 455-9840
  Plymouth (G-13289)
▼ Rod Chomper Inc......E 616 392-9677
  Holland (G-8182)
Savard Corporation......F 313 931-6880
  Detroit (G-4581)
SB Investments LLC......E 734 462-9478
  Livonia (G-10400)
Sesco Inc......D 313 843-7710
  Detroit (G-4587)
Sharp Die & Mold Co......F 586 293-8660
  Fraser (G-5993)
SKW Automation Inc......G 517 563-8288
  Hanover (G-7626)
Smartcoast LLC......G 231 571-2020
  Grand Rapids (G-7202)
Spen-Tech Machine Engrg Corp......D 810 275-6800
  Flint (G-5765)
Standard Automation LLC......E 248 227-6964
  Rochester Hills (G-14118)
TA Systems Inc......D 248 656-5150
  Rochester Hills (G-14123)
◆ Tannewitz Inc......E 616 457-5999
  Jenison (G-9073)
▼ Tarpon Automation & Design Co......E 586 774-8020
  Clinton Township (G-3374)
▲ Thielenhaus Microfinish Corp......E 248 349-9450
  Novi (G-12556)
Toman Industries Inc......G 734 289-1393
  Monroe (G-11585)
Tri-Mation Industries Inc......E 269 668-4333
  Mattawan (G-11168)
▼ Trinity Tool Co......E 586 296-5900
  Fraser (G-6006)
US Metals LLC......F 586 915-2885
  Warren (G-18049)
Utica Body & Assembly Inc......E 586 726-4330
  Troy (G-17418)
▲ Utica Enterprises Inc......C 586 726-4300
  Troy (G-17419)
Utica International Inc......C 586 726-4330
  Troy (G-17420)
Utica Products Inc......G 586 726-4300
  Troy (G-17421)
▼ Van-Mark Products Corporation......E 248 478-1200
  Farmington Hills (G-5408)
Veet Industries Inc......F 586 776-3000
  Warren (G-18053)
▲ Weber Electric Mfg Co......E 586 323-9000
  Shelby Township (G-15367)
Wright-K Technology Inc......E 989 752-2588
  Saginaw (G-14795)

3552 Textile Machinery

All American Embroidery Inc......F 734 421-9292
  Livonia (G-10108)
B&P Littleford Day LLC......D 989 757-1300
  Saginaw (G-14607)
Becmar Corp......G 616 675-7479
  Bailey (G-1118)
Belding Bleacher Erectors Inc......G 616 794-3126
  Greenville (G-7476)
Bpg International Fin Co LLC......G 616 855-1480
  Ada (G-12)
Carry-All Products Inc......G 616 399-8080
  Holland (G-7991)
Craft Press Printing Inc......G 269 683-9694
  Niles (G-12121)

▲ Fabri-Tech Inc......E 616 662-0150
  Jenison (G-9055)
Groholski Mfg Solutions LLC......E 517 278-9339
  Coldwater (G-3436)
Howa USA Holdings Inc......E 248 715-4000
  Novi (G-12436)
Modern Monogram......G 248 792-6266
  Bloomfield Hills (G-1839)
Needles N Pins Inc......G 734 459-0625
  Plymouth (G-13253)
▲ Orri Corp......F 248 618-1104
  Waterford (G-18145)
Precision Spindle Service Co......F 248 544-0100
  Ferndale (G-5581)
Star Shade Cutter Co......F 269 983-2403
  Saint Joseph (G-14963)
Superior Threading Inc......F 989 729-1160
  Owosso (G-12859)
Tri-State Technical Services......G 517 563-8743
  Hanover (G-7627)

3553 Woodworking Machinery

▲ Alexander Dodds Company......G 616 784-6000
  Grand Rapids (G-6442)
Automated Precision Eqp LLC......E 517 481-2414
  Eaton Rapids (G-4952)
Bespro Pattern Inc......E 586 268-6970
  Madison Heights (G-10681)
Boxer Equipment/Morbark Inc......E 989 866-2381
  Winn (G-18589)
▲ Carter Products Company Inc......E 616 647-3380
  Grand Rapids (G-6548)
▲ Conway-Cleveland Corp......G 616 458-0056
  Grand Rapids (G-6604)
Coxline Inc......E 269 345-1132
  Kalamazoo (G-9157)
Crescent Casting Inc......F 248 541-1052
  Oak Park (G-12600)
Gudho USA Inc......G 616 682-7814
  Ada (G-21)
▲ Homag Machinery North Amer Inc......F 616 254-8181
  Grand Rapids (G-6819)
Moda Manufacturing LLC......F 586 204-5120
  Farmington Hills (G-5325)
▲ Morbark LLC......B 989 866-2381
  Winn (G-18590)
Northern Woodcrafters......G 989 348-2553
  Frederic (G-6016)
Northwest Pattern Company......G 248 477-7070
  Farmington Hills (G-5335)
R J Flood Professional Co......G 269 930-3608
  Stevensville (G-16263)
Saginaw Industries LLC......F 989 752-5514
  Saginaw (G-14746)
Straitoplane Inc......G 616 997-2211
  Coopersville (G-3697)
◆ Tannewitz Inc......E 616 457-5999
  Jenison (G-9073)
Wing Pattern Inc......G 248 588-1121
  Sterling Heights (G-16232)

3554 Paper Inds Machinery

A S R C Inc......G 517 545-7430
  Howell (G-8423)
▲ Accu-Shape Die Cutting Inc......E 810 230-2445
  Flint (G-5634)
B&P Littleford Day LLC......D 989 757-1300
  Saginaw (G-14607)
▲ Bernal LLC......D 248 299-3600
  Rochester Hills (G-13964)
▲ Challenge Machinery Company......E 231 799-8484
  Norton Shores (G-12285)
Euclid Coating Systems Inc......F 989 922-4789
  Bay City (G-1351)
Graphic Art Service & Supply......G 810 229-4700
  Brighton (G-2004)
▲ Graphic Arts Service & Sup Inc......F 616 698-9300
  Grand Rapids (G-6781)
Hycorr LLC......F 269 381-6349
  Kalamazoo (G-9219)
Paper Machine Service Inds......F 989 695-2646
  Saginaw (G-14724)
Pratt (bell Packaging) Inc......D 616 452-2111
  Grand Rapids (G-7095)
S & W Holdings Ltd......G 248 723-2870
  Birmingham (G-1748)

3555 Printing Trades Machinery & Eqpt

A C Steel Rule Dies Inc......G 248 588-5600
  Madison Heights (G-10654)

Alpine Sign and Prtg Sup Inc......F 517 487-1400
  Lansing (G-9754)
Benmar Communications LLC......F 313 593-0690
  Dearborn (G-3813)
◆ Brown Mch Group Intrmdate Hldn......C 989 435-7741
  Beaverton (G-1424)
▲ Douthitt Corporation......E 313 259-1565
  Detroit (G-4189)
Eagle Press Repairs & Ser......G 419 539-7206
  Adrian (G-63)
Elk Lake Tool Co......E 231 264-5616
  Elk Rapids (G-5023)
▲ F P Rosback Co......E 269 983-2582
  Saint Joseph (G-14930)
Haynie and Hess Realty Co LLC......F 586 296-2750
  Fraser (G-5933)
▲ Innovative Machines Inc......G 616 669-1649
  Jenison (G-9059)
Just Right Duplications LLC......F 313 655-3555
  Oak Park (G-12619)
Lavalier Corp......E 248 616-8880
  Troy (G-17205)
M & M Typewriter Service Inc......E 734 995-4033
  Ann Arbor (G-558)
Maple Leaf Press Inc......G 616 846-8844
  Grand Haven (G-6334)
Qmi Group Inc......E 248 589-0505
  Madison Heights (G-10814)
Sgk LLC......G 269 381-3820
  Battle Creek (G-1292)
▲ Sunraise Inc......F 810 359-7301
  Lexington (G-10032)
Thermoforming Tech Group LLC......E 989 435-7741
  Beaverton (G-1433)
Unique-Intasco Usa Inc......F 810 982-3360
  Auburn Hills (G-1071)
Varn International Inc......F 734 781-4600
  Livonia (G-10458)
▲ Voxeljet America Inc......E 734 709-8237
  Canton (G-2541)
Xyresic LLC......G 906 281-0021
  Jackson (G-9039)

3556 Food Prdts Machinery

Atwater Foods LLC......G 231 941-4336
  Traverse City (G-16607)
▼ Automated Process Equipment......E 616 374-1000
  Lake Odessa (G-9572)
B&P Littleford Day LLC......D 989 757-1300
  Saginaw (G-14607)
◆ Baker Perkins Inc......D 616 784-3111
  Grand Rapids (G-6492)
Banner Engineering & Sales Inc......F 989 755-0584
  Saginaw (G-14609)
Bermaxx LLC......E 248 299-3600
  Rochester Hills (G-13963)
Carb-A-Tron Tool Co......G 517 782-2249
  Jackson (G-8834)
Dawn Equipment Company Inc......C 517 789-4500
  Jackson (G-8861)
◆ Dawn Food Products Inc......C 517 789-4400
  Jackson (G-8863)
◆ Dawn Foods Inc......C 517 789-4400
  Jackson (G-8864)
◆ Duke De Jong LLC......G 734 403-1708
  Taylor (G-16407)
Dunkley International Inc......C 269 343-5583
  Kalamazoo (G-9174)
Foodtools Consolidated Inc......C 269 637-9969
  South Haven (G-15405)
▲ Frontier Technology Inc......F 269 673-9464
  Allegan (G-159)
Graf Acres LLC......G 517 851-8693
  Stockbridge (G-16275)
Indian Summer Cooperative Inc......C 231 873-7504
  Hart (G-7755)
Infusco Coffee Roasters LLC......G 269 213-5282
  Sawyer (G-15109)
▲ J J Steel Inc......E 269 964-0474
  Battle Creek (G-1242)
◆ Lematic Inc......D 517 787-3301
  Jackson (G-8934)
Lowry Joanellen......G 231 873-2323
  Hesperia (G-7870)
◆ Marshall Middleby Holding LLC......D 906 863-4401
  Menominee (G-11244)
Middleby Corporation......C 906 863-4401
  Menominee (G-11251)
Motembo Fine Foods LLC......G 800 692-4814
  Okemos (G-12678)

▲ **Oliver Packaging and Eqp Co**..........D....... 616 356-2950
Walker *(G-17645)*
Pappas Cutlery-Grinding Inc..........G....... 800 521-0888
Detroit *(G-4506)*
Peanut Shop Inc..........G....... 517 374-0008
Lansing *(G-9879)*
▲ **Pisces Fish Machinery Inc**..........E....... 906 789-1636
Gladstone *(G-6186)*
Precision Extraction Corp..........F....... 855 420-0020
Troy *(G-17311)*
Process Partners Inc..........G....... 616 875-2156
Hudsonville *(G-8602)*
◆ **Request Foods Inc**..........B....... 616 786-0900
Holland *(G-8180)*
Saa Tech Inc..........G....... 313 933-4960
Detroit *(G-4575)*
Spiral-Matic Inc..........G....... 248 486-5080
Brighton *(G-2074)*
Spotted Cow..........G....... 517 265-6188
Adrian *(G-97)*
Taylor Freezer Michigan Inc..........F....... 616 453-0531
Grand Rapids *(G-7249)*
Whirlpool Corporation..........G....... 800 541-6390
Benton Harbor *(G-1604)*

3559 Special Ind Machinery, NEC

313 Industries Inc..........F....... 313 338-9700
Warren *(G-17677)*
◆ **Ace Controls Inc**..........C....... 248 476-0213
Farmington Hills *(G-5158)*
▲ **AGC Grand Haven LLC**..........G....... 616 842-1820
Grand Haven *(G-6271)*
Air Tight Solutions LLC..........G....... 248 629-0461
Detroit *(G-3990)*
Air-Hydraulics Inc..........F....... 517 787-9444
Jackson *(G-8806)*
◆ **Aisin Technical Ctr Amer Inc**..........D....... 734 453-5551
Northville *(G-12196)*
▲ **Alliance Automation LLC**..........F....... 810 953-9539
Flint *(G-5642)*
AME For Auto Dealers Inc..........G....... 248 720-0245
Auburn Hills *(G-780)*
American Chem Solutions LLC..........E....... 231 655-5840
Muskegon *(G-11769)*
Amerivet Engineering LLC..........G....... 269 751-9092
Hamilton *(G-7596)*
▲ **AMI Industries Inc**..........D....... 989 786-3755
Lewiston *(G-10017)*
AMI Industries Inc..........G....... 989 786-3755
Sault Sainte Marie *(G-15086)*
Arcon Vernova Inc..........G....... 734 904-1895
Saline *(G-15004)*
Arctic Glacier Wisconsin Inc..........E....... 262 345-6999
Port Huron *(G-13454)*
Automotive Component Mfg..........G....... 705 549-7406
Sterling Heights *(G-15937)*
Automotive Technology LLC..........C....... 586 446-7000
Sterling Heights *(G-15938)*
Avancez LLC..........D....... 313 404-1962
Hazel Park *(G-7820)*
B & J Tool Services Inc..........F....... 810 629-8577
Fenton *(G-5455)*
B&P Littleford Day LLC..........D....... 989 757-1300
Saginaw *(G-14607)*
◆ **B&P Littleford LLC**..........E....... 989 757-1300
Saginaw *(G-14608)*
▲ **Bekum America Corporation**..........C....... 517 655-4331
Williamston *(G-18569)*
Berghof Group North Amer Inc..........F....... 313 720-6884
Troy *(G-16974)*
◆ **Besser Company**..........B....... 989 354-4111
Alpena *(G-284)*
Best Mfg Tooling Solutions Ltd..........G....... 616 877-0504
Wayland *(G-18190)*
Blockmatic Inc..........G....... 269 683-1655
Niles *(G-12113)*
▲ **Brothers Industrials Inc**..........G....... 248 794-5080
Farmington Hills *(G-5186)*
◆ **Brown Mch Group Intrmdate Hldn**....C....... 989 435-7741
Beaverton *(G-1424)*
Built Systems LLC..........F....... 616 834-5099
Holland *(G-7987)*
◆ **Burke E Porter Machinery Co**..........C....... 616 234-1200
Grand Rapids *(G-6535)*
▲ **Burton Industries Inc**..........E....... 906 932-5970
Ironwood *(G-8758)*
▲ **Busche Southfield Inc**..........C....... 248 357-5180
Southfield *(G-15513)*
CD Tool & Gage..........F....... 616 682-1111
Ada *(G-14)*
Centennial Technologies Inc..........E....... 989 752-6167
Saginaw *(G-14624)*
▲ **Centracore LLC**..........F....... 586 776-5700
Saint Clair *(G-14818)*
◆ **Century Inc**..........C....... 231 947-6400
Traverse City *(G-16641)*
Cfe Racing Products Inc..........G....... 586 773-6310
Eastpointe *(G-4931)*
Compac Specialties Inc..........F....... 616 786-9100
Holland *(G-8001)*
Considine Sales & Marketing..........G....... 248 889-7887
Highland *(G-7889)*
Corls Kiln..........G....... 989 673-4925
Caro *(G-2568)*
Corr-Fac Corporation..........G....... 989 358-7050
Alpena *(G-288)*
Corvac Composites LLC..........C....... 616 281-2430
Grand Rapids *(G-6608)*
◆ **Corvac Composites LLC**..........E....... 616 281-4028
Kentwood *(G-9449)*
Creative Performance Racg LLC..........G....... 248 250-6187
Troy *(G-17032)*
Ctmf Inc..........F....... 734 482-3086
Ypsilanti *(G-18937)*
D & F Corporation..........D....... 586 254-5300
Sterling Heights *(G-15977)*
Dayco Products LLC..........G....... 989 775-0689
Mount Pleasant *(G-11694)*
Dayco Products LLC..........G....... 517 439-0689
Hillsdale *(G-7931)*
Detroit Tech Innovation LLC..........G....... 734 259-4168
Redford *(G-13731)*
▲ **Dipsol of America Inc**..........E....... 734 367-0530
Livonia *(G-10186)*
▲ **Drew Technologies Inc**..........G....... 734 222-5228
Ann Arbor *(G-458)*
▲ **Durr Inc**..........G....... 734 459-6800
Southfield *(G-15544)*
◆ **Durr Systems Inc**..........B....... 248 450-2000
Southfield *(G-15545)*
Durr Systems Inc..........F....... 248 745-8500
Southfield *(G-15546)*
Eaton Aerospace LLC..........B....... 616 949-1090
Grand Rapids *(G-6663)*
Ebels Equipment LLC..........G....... 231 826-3334
Falmouth *(G-5132)*
▼ **Edge Industries Inc**..........G....... 616 453-5458
Grand Rapids *(G-6665)*
Energy Suppliers LLC..........F....... 269 342-9482
Kalamazoo *(G-9180)*
Environ Manufacturing Inc..........G....... 616 644-6846
Battle Creek *(G-1223)*
Epiphany Studios Ltd..........G....... 248 745-3786
Pontiac *(G-13367)*
Erae AMS USA Manufacturing LLC..........F....... 314 600-3434
Pontiac *(G-13369)*
Esoc Inc..........F....... 248 624-7992
Wixom *(G-18658)*
Ess Tec Inc..........D....... 616 394-0230
Holland *(G-8031)*
Euclid Coating Systems Inc..........F....... 989 922-4789
Bay City *(G-1351)*
◆ **Extol Inc**..........D....... 616 741-0231
Zeeland *(G-19019)*
◆ **Fanuc America Corporation**..........B....... 248 377-7000
Rochester Hills *(G-14009)*
▲ **Fata Aluminum LLC**..........E....... 248 802-9853
Orion *(G-12729)*
▲ **Firstronic LLC**..........B....... 616 456-9220
Grand Rapids *(G-6708)*
▲ **Frontier Technology Inc**..........F....... 269 673-9464
Allegan *(G-159)*
Gd Enterprises LLC..........G....... 248 486-9800
Brighton *(G-1997)*
Generation Tool Inc..........G....... 734 641-6937
Westland *(G-18374)*
Genix LLC..........C....... 248 761-3030
West Bloomfield *(G-18284)*
Genix LLC..........F....... 248 419-0231
Sterling Heights *(G-16029)*
George Koch Sons LLC..........E....... 248 237-1100
Rochester Hills *(G-14024)*
◆ **Global Strgc Sup Solutions LLC**..........D....... 734 525-9100
Livonia *(G-10226)*
Glycon Corp..........E....... 517 423-8356
Tecumseh *(G-16503)*
Gokoh Coldwater Incorporated..........F....... 517 279-1080
Coldwater *(G-3434)*
Graminex LLC..........G....... 989 797-5502
Saginaw *(G-14658)*
Grav Co LLC..........F....... 269 651-5467
Sturgis *(G-16290)*
Gravel Flow Inc..........G....... 269 651-5467
Sturgis *(G-16291)*
◆ **Great Lakes Allied LLC**..........G....... 231 924-5794
White Cloud *(G-18441)*
Greene Manufacturing Tech LLC..........C....... 810 982-9720
Port Huron *(G-13481)*
H A Eckhart & Associates Inc..........E....... 517 321-7700
Lansing *(G-9702)*
Hi-Tech/Fpa Inc..........G....... 616 942-0076
Grand Rapids *(G-6813)*
Higgins and Associates Inc..........F....... 989 772-8853
Mount Pleasant *(G-11701)*
HP Pelzer Auto Systems Inc..........B....... 810 987-4444
Port Huron *(G-13483)*
Hti Cybernetics Inc..........E....... 586 826-8346
Sterling Heights *(G-16043)*
◆ **Huron Valley Steel Corporation**..........C....... 734 479-3500
Trenton *(G-16889)*
Ied Inc..........G....... 231 728-9154
Muskegon *(G-11837)*
▲ **Il Enterprises Inc**..........F....... 734 285-6030
Wyandotte *(G-18823)*
◆ **Ims/Chinatool Jv LLC**..........F....... 734 466-5151
Livonia *(G-10247)*
◆ **Innovative Cleaning Eqp Inc**..........E....... 616 656-9225
Grand Rapids *(G-6845)*
Innovative Engineering Mich..........G....... 517 977-0460
Lansing *(G-9705)*
▼ **International Wheel & Tire Inc**..........E....... 248 298-0207
Farmington Hills *(G-5271)*
Iroquois Assembly Systems Inc..........F....... 586 771-5734
Warren *(G-17872)*
Itac Software Inc..........E....... 248 450-2446
Southfield *(G-15609)*
J H P Inc..........G....... 248 588-0110
Madison Heights *(G-10750)*
JB Autotech LLC..........E....... 734 838-3963
Livonia *(G-10258)*
Jcu International Inc..........G....... 248 313-6630
Wixom *(G-18689)*
Jvis - Usa LLC..........B....... 586 803-6056
Clinton Township *(G-3267)*
Kansmackers Manufacturing Co..........F....... 248 249-6666
Lansing *(G-9709)*
Kapex Manufacturing LLC..........G....... 989 928-4993
Saginaw *(G-14676)*
Kiln Kreations..........G....... 989 435-3296
Beaverton *(G-1426)*
Kimastle Corporation..........D....... 586 949-2355
Chesterfield *(G-2902)*
Knight Industries Inc..........G....... 248 377-4950
Auburn Hills *(G-954)*
Kolco Industries Inc..........G....... 248 486-1690
South Lyon *(G-15442)*
Kolene Corporation..........F....... 586 771-1200
Roseville *(G-14430)*
Koyo Corp..........G....... 269 962-9676
Battle Creek *(G-1265)*
Latitude Recycling Inc..........G....... 586 243-5153
Ray *(G-13700)*
Liberty Fabricators Inc..........F....... 810 877-7117
Flint *(G-5724)*
Libra Industries Inc Michigan..........G....... 517 787-5675
Jackson *(G-8935)*
▲ **Limbright Consulting Inc**..........E....... 810 227-5510
Wixom *(G-18699)*
◆ **Loadmaster Corporation**..........E....... 906 563-9226
Norway *(G-12353)*
Lumbee Custom Painting LLC..........G....... 586 296-5083
Fraser *(G-5958)*
Lumbertown Portable Sawmill..........G....... 231 206-4600
Muskegon *(G-11862)*
▲ **Lyle Industries**..........C....... 989 435-7717
Beaverton *(G-1429)*
Mag Automotive LLC..........C....... 586 446-7000
Sterling Heights *(G-16081)*
Mag Automotive LLC..........F....... 586 446-7000
Port Huron *(G-13498)*
▲ **Magnetic Products Inc**..........D....... 248 887-5600
Highland *(G-7896)*
▲ **Mann + Hummel Inc**..........G....... 269 329-3900
Portage *(G-13581)*
Met-L-Tec LLC..........E....... 734 847-7004
Temperance *(G-16540)*
Michigan Roll Form Inc..........E....... 248 669-3700
Commerce Township *(G-3556)*
▲ **Midbrook Inc**..........D....... 800 966-9274
Jackson *(G-8959)*

Miller Mold Co ... E ... 989 793-8881
Frankenmuth (G-5871)
Minland Machine Inc ... G ... 269 641-7998
Edwardsburg (G-5012)
Modern Builders ... G ... 989 773-1405
Mount Pleasant (G-11716)
◆ Morrell Incorporated ... D ... 248 373-1600
Auburn Hills (G-975)
Mountain Machine LLC ... F ... 734 480-2200
Van Buren Twp (G-17542)
Mp Tool & Engineering Company ... E ... 586 772-7730
Roseville (G-14448)
Nava Solar LLC ... F ... 734 707-8260
Mount Pleasant (G-11727)
New-Matic Industries Inc ... G ... 586 415-9801
Fraser (G-5969)
Northwods Prperty Holdings LLC ... G ... 231 334-3000
Glen Arbor (G-6211)
Nyx LLC ... D ... 734 464-0800
Livonia (G-10346)
Oakley Inds Sub Assmbly Div In ... G ... 586 754-5555
Warren (G-17949)
Omega Industries Michigan LLC ... G ... 616 460-0500
Grand Rapids (G-7058)
Oneiric Systems Inc ... G ... 248 554-3090
Madison Heights (G-10792)
Online Engineering Inc ... F ... 906 341-0090
Manistique (G-10923)
Ovshinsky Technologies LLC ... G ... 248 752-2344
Bloomfield Hills (G-1846)
Oxmaster Inc ... G ... 810 987-7600
Port Huron (G-13512)
Peloton Inc ... G ... 269 694-9702
Otsego (G-12798)
Perfected Grave Vault Co ... G ... 616 243-3375
Grand Rapids (G-7078)
▲ Pgp Corp ... D ... 313 291-7500
Taylor (G-16457)
Pine Needle People LLC ... G ... 517 242-4752
Lansing (G-9728)
▼ Powell Fabrication & Mfg LLC ... E ... 989 681-2158
Saint Louis (G-14996)
Pulverdryer Usa Inc ... G ... 269 552-5290
Galesburg (G-6082)
Purem Novi Inc ... C ... 810 225-4582
Brighton (G-2058)
Puritan Magnetics Inc ... F ... 248 628-3808
Oxford (G-12908)
Quantum Mold & Engineering LLC ... F ... 586 276-0100
Sterling Heights (G-16141)
▲ R & B Plastics Machinery LLC ... E ... 734 429-9421
Saline (G-15034)
R & S Tool & Die Inc ... G ... 989 673-8511
Caro (G-2579)
Race Ramps LLC ... F ... 866 464-2788
Escanaba (G-5094)
RB Oil Enterprises LLC ... G ... 734 354-0700
Plymouth (G-13277)
Reese Business Group LLC ... G ... 246 216-2605
Farmington Hills (G-5366)
Rnj Services Inc ... F ... 906 786-0585
Escanaba (G-5096)
▲ Roberts Sinto Corporation ... D ... 517 371-2460
Lansing (G-9787)
▲ Rosler Metal Finishing USA LLC ... E ... 269 441-3000
Battle Creek (G-1290)
▼ Royal Design & Manufacturing ... D ... 248 588-0110
Madison Heights (G-10821)
Safety-Kleen Systems Inc ... G ... 989 753-3261
Saginaw (G-14743)
Sarns Industries Inc ... E ... 586 463-5829
Harrison Twp (G-7739)
Schneider National Inc ... F ... 810 636-2220
Goodrich (G-6227)
Senstronic Inc ... F ... 586 466-4108
Clinton Township (G-3350)
SGC Industries Inc ... G ... 586 293-5260
Fraser (G-5992)
▲ Sinto America Inc ... E ... 517 371-2460
Lansing (G-9791)
Spirit Industries Inc ... G ... 517 371-7840
Lansing (G-9740)
Stec Usa Inc ... F ... 248 307-1440
Madison Heights (G-10837)
◆ Superior Automotive Eqp Inc ... G ... 231 829-9902
Leroy (G-10012)
▲ Sure Solutions Corporation ... G ... 248 674-7210
Auburn Hills (G-1042)
▲ Technology & Manufacturing Inc ... G ... 248 755-1444
Milford (G-11492)

Thermfrmer Parts Suppliers LLC ... G ... 989 435-3800
Beaverton (G-1432)
Thermoforming Tech Group LLC ... G ... 989 435-7741
Beaverton (G-1433)
Thomas-Ward Systems LLC ... G ... 734 929-0644
Ann Arbor (G-689)
▼ Thoreson-Mc Cosh Inc ... E ... 248 362-0960
Lake Orion (G-9634)
Ti-Coating Inc ... E ... 586 726-1900
Shelby Township (G-15351)
Titan Pharmaceutical McHy Inc ... G ... 248 220-7421
Shelby Township (G-15352)
▲ Tks Industrial Company ... E ... 248 786-5000
Troy (G-17393)
Toyota Industries Elctc Sys N ... G ... 248 489-7700
Novi (G-12557)
Traffic Sfety Ctrl Systems Inc ... E ... 248 348-0570
Wixom (G-18775)
◆ Tzamco Inc ... E ... 248 624-7710
Walled Lake (G-17676)
◆ Ube Machinery Inc ... D ... 734 741-7000
Ann Arbor (G-702)
Unified Equipment Systems Inc ... G ... 586 307-3770
Clinton Township (G-3382)
Universal Magnetics Inc ... G ... 231 937-5555
Howard City (G-8420)
Urgent Design and Mfg Inc ... F ... 810 245-1300
Lapeer (G-9964)
US Metals LLC ... F ... 586 915-2885
Warren (G-18049)
Usher Enterprises Inc ... E ... 313 834-7055
Detroit (G-4656)
Valley Gear and Machine Inc ... F ... 989 269-8177
Bad Axe (G-1116)
Van-Rob USA Holdings ... E ... 517 423-2400
Tecumseh (G-16521)
Velesco Phrm Svcs Inc ... G ... 734 545-0696
Wixom (G-18785)
Velesco Phrm Svcs Inc ... G ... 734 274-9877
Plymouth (G-13330)
W G Benjey Inc ... F ... 989 356-0016
Alpena (G-327)
Webasto Convertibles USA Inc ... E ... 734 582-5900
Rochester Hills (G-14143)
◆ Williams Form Engineering Corp ... D ... 616 866-0815
Belmont (G-1521)
◆ Wirtz Manufacturing Co Inc ... D ... 810 987-7600
Port Huron (G-13540)
◆ Wolverine Advanced Mtls LLC ... E ... 313 749-6100
Dearborn (G-3916)
Z-Brite Metal Finishing Inc ... F ... 269 422-2191
Stevensville (G-16270)

3561 Pumps & Pumping Eqpt

Advanced Pumps Intl LLC ... G ... 734 230-5013
Monroe (G-11522)
Automationsupply365 LLC ... G ... 248 912-7354
Auburn Hills (G-805)
▲ Becktold Enterprises Inc ... G ... 269 349-3656
Kalamazoo (G-9133)
▲ Benecor Inc ... F ... 248 437-4437
Fenton (G-5457)
Clyde Union (holdings) Inc ... B ... 269 966-4600
Battle Creek (G-1210)
Cpj Company Inc ... E ... 616 784-6355
Comstock Park (G-3598)
David Brown Union Pumps Co Pay ... G ... 269 966-4702
Battle Creek (G-1214)
Dover Pmps Prcess Sltons Sgmen ... B ... 616 241-1611
Grand Rapids (G-6657)
Emp Advanced Development LLC ... G ... 906 789-7497
Escanaba (G-5067)
◆ Engineered Machined Pdts Inc ... B ... 906 786-8404
Escanaba (G-5069)
Flowserve US Inc ... G ... 989 496-3897
Midland (G-11364)
Fluid Automation Inc ... G ... 248 669-3717
Wixom (G-18663)
Fluid Systems Engineering Inc ... E ... 586 790-8880
Clinton Township (G-3242)
Ford Motor Company ... A ... 734 484-8626
Ypsilanti (G-18947)
◆ Gast Manufacturing Inc ... B ... 269 926-6171
Benton Harbor (G-1551)
General Motors LLC ... F ... 989 894-7210
Bay City (G-1359)
◆ Global Pump Company LLC ... G ... 810 653-4828
Davison (G-3785)
H & R Industries Inc ... F ... 616 247-1165
Grand Rapids (G-6798)

Hydra-Tech Inc ... G ... 586 232-4479
Macomb (G-10604)
Independent Mfg Solutions Corp ... E ... 248 960-3550
Wixom (G-18684)
Jacksons Industrial Mfg ... F ... 616 531-1820
Grand Rapids (G-6859)
◆ Jetech Inc ... E ... 269 965-6311
Battle Creek (G-1246)
K & M Industrial LLC ... G ... 906 420-8770
Gladstone (G-6182)
K and K Machine Tools Inc ... G ... 586 463-1177
Clinton Township (G-3269)
Kerr Pump and Supply Inc ... E ... 248 543-3880
Oak Park (G-12621)
▲ Kristus Inc ... F ... 269 321-3330
Scotts (G-15132)
Ksb Dubric Inc ... E ... 616 784-6355
Comstock Park (G-3618)
▲ M P Pumps Inc ... D ... 586 293-8240
Fraser (G-5959)
◆ Melling Tool Co ... B ... 517 787-8172
Jackson (G-8951)
▲ Neptune Chemical Pump Company ... C ... 215 699-8700
Grand Rapids (G-7039)
Nortek Air Solutions LLC ... D ... 616 738-7148
Holland (G-8156)
Pinnacle Technology Group ... D ... 734 568-6600
Ottawa Lake (G-12810)
Plasma-Tec Inc ... E ... 616 455-2593
Holland (G-8166)
Preyde LLC ... G ... 517 333-1600
Lansing (G-9883)
◆ Process Systems Inc ... E ... 586 757-5711
Warren (G-17977)
▲ QEd Envmtl Systems Inc ... D ... 734 995-2547
Dexter (G-4751)
Ramparts LLC ... C ... 616 656-2250
Kentwood (G-9474)
◆ Sales Driven Ltd Liability Co ... E ... 269 254-8497
Kalamazoo (G-9327)
▲ Sales Driven Services LLC ... G ... 586 854-9494
Rochester (G-13926)
Sames Kremlin Inc ... G ... 734 979-0100
Plymouth (G-13293)
Shellback Manufacturing Co ... G ... 248 544-4600
Hazel Park (G-7842)
▲ Sloan Transportation Pdts Inc ... E ... 616 395-5600
Holland (G-8197)
SPX Flow Us LLC ... F ... 269 966-4782
Battle Creek (G-1298)
Standfast Industries Inc ... F ... 248 380-3223
Livonia (G-10418)
▲ Tramec Sloan LLC ... E ... 616 395-5600
Holland (G-8224)
Vent-Rite Valve Corp ... E ... 269 925-8812
Benton Harbor (G-1598)
Vogel Engineering Inc ... G ... 231 821-2125
Holton (G-8342)
Walbro LLC ... D ... 989 872-2131
Cass City (G-2622)
Water Department ... F ... 313 943-2307
Dearborn (G-3915)
Yoe Industries Inc ... G ... 586 791-7660
Clinton Township (G-3391)

3562 Ball & Roller Bearings

▲ ABC Acquisition Company LLC ... E ... 734 335-4083
Livonia (G-10097)
◆ Caster Concepts Inc ... E ... 888 781-1470
Albion (G-122)
Evans Industries Inc ... G ... 313 272-8200
Detroit (G-4219)
Ewellix USA LLC ... C ... 586 752-0060
Armada (G-734)
◆ Frost Incorporated ... E ... 616 453-7781
Grand Rapids (G-6722)
Independent Mfg Solutions Corp ... E ... 248 960-3550
Wixom (G-18684)
◆ Kaydon Corporation ... B ... 734 747-7025
Ann Arbor (G-538)
Kaydon Corporation ... C ... 231 755-3741
Norton Shores (G-12306)
Schaeffler Group USA Inc ... C ... 810 360-0294
Milford (G-11487)
▲ Sunhill America LLC ... E ... 616 249-3600
Grand Rapids (G-7234)
▲ USA Brngs Sup LLC DBA JSB Grea ... G ... 734 222-4177
Ann Arbor (G-707)

SIC

Employee Codes: A=Over 500 employees, B=251-500
C=101-250, D=51-100, E=20-50, F=10-19, G=3-9
2022 Harris Michigan
Industrial Directory
853

3563 Air & Gas Compressors

▲ Atlas Copco Ias LLC ....D 248 377-9722
Auburn Hills (G-799)
Autoliv Asp Inc ....C 248 475-9000
Auburn Hills (G-801)
Belco Industries Inc ....E 616 794-0410
Belding (G-1437)
▲ Blissfield Manufacturing Co ....C 517 486-2121
Blissfield (G-1761)
Correct Compression Inc ....G 231 864-2101
Bear Lake (G-1417)
◆ Gast Manufacturing Inc ....B 269 926-6171
Benton Harbor (G-1551)
Gast Manufacturing Inc ....D 269 926-6171
Benton Harbor (G-1552)
Harvey S Freeman ....G 248 852-2222
West Bloomfield (G-18287)
Innovation Tech LLC ....F 248 797-2686
Wixom (G-18685)
Metallurgical High Vacuum Corp ....F 269 543-4291
Fennville (G-5440)
◆ Michigan Auto Comprsr Inc ....A 517 796-3200
Parma (G-12938)
Millennium Planet LLC ....G 248 835-2331
Farmington Hills (G-5322)
Nordson Corporation ....D 734 459-8600
Wixom (G-18721)
▲ Okuno International Corp ....G 248 536-2727
Novi (G-12496)
Parker Engineering Amer Co Ltd ....F 734 326-7630
Westland (G-18403)
Pr39 Industries LLC ....G 248 481-8512
Auburn Hills (G-1001)
Precision Masking Inc ....E 734 848-4200
Erie (G-5053)
Primore Inc ....F 517 263-2220
Adrian (G-89)
Reeling Systems LLC ....G 810 364-3900
Saint Clair (G-14841)
Rochester Petroleum Inc ....G 507 533-9156
Birmingham (G-1747)
▲ Saylor-Beall Manufacturing Co ....B 989 224-2371
Saint Johns (G-14914)
Spray Foam Fabrication LLC ....G 517 745-7885
Parma (G-12939)
Stop & Go No 10 Inc ....G 734 281-7500
Southgate (G-15757)
▼ Thierica Equipment Corporation ....E 616 453-6570
Grand Rapids (G-7259)
Unist Inc ....E 616 949-0853
Grand Rapids (G-7297)

3564 Blowers & Fans

AC Covers Inc ....F 313 541-7770
Redford (G-13710)
▲ Advance Products Corporation ....E 269 849-1000
Benton Harbor (G-1527)
▲ Advanced Air Technologies Inc ....G 989 743-5544
Corunna (G-3704)
Aero Filter Inc ....E 248 837-4100
Madison Heights (G-10663)
Air Filter & Equipment Inc ....G 734 261-1860
Livonia (G-10106)
Air Solution Company ....F 800 819-2869
Farmington Hills (G-5164)
Airhug LLC ....G 734 262-0431
Canton (G-2432)
Anrod Screen Cylinder Company ....E 989 872-2101
Cass City (G-2610)
▲ Avl Test Systems Inc ....C 734 414-9600
Plymouth (G-13134)
Baker Enterprises Inc ....E 989 354-2189
Alpena (G-281)
Beckert & Hiester Inc ....G 989 793-2420
Saginaw (G-14612)
◆ Besser Company ....B 989 354-4111
Alpena (G-284)
Borgwarner Thermal Systems Inc ....G 231 779-7500
Cadillac (G-2317)
◆ Cdgjl Inc ....E 517 787-2100
Jackson (G-8836)
Chicago Blow Pipe Company ....F 773 533-6100
Marquette (G-11012)
Clarkson Controls & Eqp Co ....G 248 380-9915
Novi (G-12384)
Clean Air Technology Inc ....E 734 459-6320
Canton (G-2450)
Clean Rooms International Inc ....E 616 452-8700
Grand Rapids (G-6571)
◆ Combustion Research Corp ....E 248 852-3611
Rochester Hills (G-13979)
▲ Complete Filtration Inc ....F 248 693-0500
Lake Orion (G-9598)
Compressor Technologies Inc ....F 616 949-7000
Grand Rapids (G-6590)
Constructive Sheet Metal Inc ....E 616 245-5306
Allendale (G-217)
Custom Service & Design Inc ....F 248 340-9005
Auburn Hills (G-855)
D-Mark Inc ....E 586 949-3610
Mount Clemens (G-11635)
▼ Dcl Inc ....C 231 547-5600
Charlevoix (G-2714)
Depierre Industries Inc ....E 517 263-5781
Adrian (G-59)
Dexter Automatic Products Co ....C 734 426-8900
Dexter (G-4734)
Eagle Engineering & Supply Co ....E 989 356-4526
Alpena (G-291)
Ecoquest Intl Independent ....G 734 854-6080
Erie (G-5047)
Entrepreneurial Pursuits ....G 248 829-6903
Rochester Hills (G-14005)
Forma-Kool Manufacturing Inc ....E 586 949-4813
Chesterfield (G-2884)
Forrest Brothers Inc ....C 989 356-4011
Gaylord (G-6129)
◆ Gallagher-Kaiser Corporation ....D 313 368-3100
Troy (G-17126)
▲ Gelman Sciences Inc ....C 734 665-0651
Ann Arbor (G-496)
General Aire ....G 866 476-5101
Novi (G-12422)
◆ General Filters Inc ....E 248 476-5100
Novi (G-12423)
Hammond Machinery Inc ....D 269 345-7151
Kalamazoo (G-9207)
Key Gas Components Inc ....E 269 673-2151
Allegan (G-163)
Madison Street Holdings LLC ....E 517 252-2031
Adrian (G-81)
Manrisa ....G 248 364-4415
Auburn Hills (G-967)
Met-Pro Technologies LLC ....D 989 725-8184
Lennon (G-9995)
▼ Midwest Air Products Co Inc ....E 231 941-5865
Traverse City (G-16757)
Murtech Energy Services LLC ....G 810 653-5681
Port Huron (G-13508)
Nortek Air Solutions LLC ....D 616 738-7148
Holland (G-8156)
Parker-Hannifin Corporation ....B 269 629-5000
Richland (G-13826)
Paul Horn and Associates ....G 248 682-8490
Waterford (G-18148)
▲ Pittsfield Products Inc ....E 734 665-3771
Ann Arbor (G-612)
◆ Process Systems Inc ....E 586 757-5711
Warren (G-17977)
Quality Filters Inc ....F 734 668-0211
Ann Arbor (G-630)
◆ Robovent Products Group Inc ....E 586 698-1800
Sterling Heights (G-16157)
Ron Pair Enterprises Inc ....E 231 547-4000
Charlevoix (G-2731)
Ronal Industries Inc ....F 248 616-9691
Sterling Heights (G-16159)
◆ Rosedale Products Inc ....D 734 665-8201
Ann Arbor (G-644)
Salem/Savard Industries LLC ....F 313 931-6880
Detroit (G-4579)
▲ SER Inc ....E 586 725-0192
New Baltimore (G-11994)
Skyblade Fan Company ....F 586 806-5107
Warren (G-18014)
Tanis Technologies LLC ....G 616 796-2712
Holland (G-8212)
Technical Air Products LLC ....F 616 863-9115
Belmont (G-1519)
Therma-Tech Engineering Inc ....E 313 537-5330
Redford (G-13778)
Thermo Vac Inc ....D 248 969-0300
Oxford (G-12923)
◆ Viron International Corp ....D 254 773-9292
Owosso (G-12866)
Vision Air ....G 989 202-4100
Houghton Lake (G-8407)
Waltz-Holst Blow Pipe Company ....E 616 676-8119
Ada (G-40)
Wayne Wire Cloth Products Inc ....F 989 742-4591
Hillman (G-7917)
West Mich Auto Stl & Engrg Inc ....E 616 560-8198
Belding (G-1464)
Wh Filtration Inc ....G 248 633-4001
Detroit (G-4679)

3565 Packaging Machinery

A & B Packing Equipment Inc ....G 616 294-3539
Holland (G-7951)
A-OK Precision Prototype Inc ....G 586 758-3430
Ray (G-13697)
Ameri-Serv Group ....F 734 426-9700
Troy (G-16931)
▲ Anchor Bay Packaging Corp ....E 586 949-4040
Chesterfield (G-2842)
B & G Products Inc ....F 616 698-9050
Grand Rapids (G-6488)
BP Pack Inc ....G 612 594-0839
Bellaire (G-1472)
▲ British Cnvrtng Sltns Nrth AME ....E 281 764-6651
Kalamazoo (G-9141)
▲ Camaco LLC ....E 248 442-6800
Farmington Hills (G-5195)
Change Parts Incorporated ....E 231 845-5107
Ludington (G-10531)
Coleman Bowman & Associates ....G 248 642-8221
Bloomfield Hills (G-1809)
▲ D J S Systems Inc ....E 517 568-4444
Homer (G-8350)
▲ Dura-Pack Inc ....E 313 299-9600
Taylor (G-16408)
◆ Elopak Inc ....G 248 486-4600
Wixom (G-18655)
◆ Filler Specialties Inc ....E 616 772-9235
Zeeland (G-19021)
Gentile Packaging Machinery Co ....G 734 429-1177
Saline (G-15019)
▲ Highlight Industries Inc ....D 616 531-2464
Wyoming (G-18884)
▼ Hot Melt Technologies Inc ....E 248 853-2011
Rochester Hills (G-14034)
Industrial Model Inc ....G 586 254-0450
Auburn Hills (G-939)
Kalamazoo Packaging Systems ....G 616 534-2600
Grand Rapids (G-6877)
Kalamazoo Packg Systems LLC ....F 616 534-2600
Wyoming (G-18888)
◆ Korten Quality Inc ....D 586 752-6255
Bruce Twp (G-2170)
▲ Meca-Systeme Usa Inc ....G 616 843-5566
Grand Haven (G-6335)
▲ Nyx LLC ....C 734 462-2385
Livonia (G-10343)
Nyx LLC ....D 734 261-7535
Livonia (G-10347)
RED Stamp Inc ....E 616 878-7771
Grand Rapids (G-7147)
Robert Bosch LLC ....G 734 302-2000
Ann Arbor (G-643)
◆ Robert Bosch LLC ....G 248 876-1000
Farmington Hills (G-5371)
Robert Bosch LLC ....G 248 921-9054
Novi (G-12527)
Robert Bosch LLC ....G 734 979-3000
Plymouth (G-13287)
Rollstock Inc ....G 616 803-5370
Grand Rapids (G-7164)
Take-A-Label Inc ....F 616 837-9300
Nunica (G-12588)
Tekkra Systems Inc ....E 517 568-4121
Homer (G-8357)
Tindall Packaging Inc ....G 269 649-1163
Portage (G-13626)

3566 Speed Changers, Drives & Gears

Alma Products Company ....G 989 463-1151
Alma (G-236)
American Gear & Engrg Co Inc ....E 734 595-6400
Westland (G-18353)
Amk Automation Corp ....G 804 348-2125
Detroit (G-4016)
Arthur R Sommers ....G 586 469-1280
Harrison Township (G-7689)
▲ Atlas Gear Company ....F 248 583-2964
Madison Heights (G-10675)
Certified Reducer Rbldrs Inc ....F 248 585-0883
Sterling Heights (G-15955)
◆ Cone Drive Operations Inc ....C 231 946-8410
Traverse City (G-16658)

SIC SECTION35 INDUSTRIAL AND COMMERCIAL MACHINERY AND COMPUTER EQUIPMENT35 INDUSTRIAL AND COMMERCIAL MACHINERY

Custom Gears Inc ....G....... 616 243-2723
Grand Rapids *(G-6620)*
Dama Tool & Gauge Company ....E....... 616 842-9631
Norton Shores *(G-12287)*
Decker Gear Inc ....F....... 810 388-1500
Saint Clair *(G-14825)*
Dorris Company ....F....... 586 293-5260
Fraser *(G-5919)*
Eaton Corporation ....G....... 248 226-6347
Southfield *(G-15547)*
◆ **Gast Manufacturing Inc** ....B....... 269 926-6171
Benton Harbor *(G-1551)*
Gear Gear Inc ....G....... 517 861-7757
Ypsilanti *(G-18949)*
Geartec Inc ....E....... 810 987-4700
Port Huron *(G-13480)*
Good Parts ....G....... 248 656-7643
Rochester Hills *(G-14026)*
Great Lakes Hydra Corporation ....F....... 231 258-4338
Kalkaska *(G-9389)*
Invo Spline Inc ....E....... 586 757-8840
Warren *(G-17870)*
▲ **J G Kern Enterprises Inc** ....D....... 586 531-9472
Sterling Heights *(G-16052)*
▲ **Nabtesco Motion Control Inc** ....F....... 248 553-3020
Farmington Hills *(G-5329)*
Orlandi Gear Company Inc ....E....... 586 285-9900
Fraser *(G-5971)*
▲ **Porite USA Co Ltd** ....G....... 248 597-9988
Troy *(G-17308)*
Spindel Corp Specialized ....F....... 616 554-2200
Grand Rapids *(G-7217)*
Truemner Enterprises Inc ....G....... 586 756-6470
Warren *(G-18044)*
▲ **Tts Oldco LLC** ....E....... 810 655-3900
Fenton *(G-5511)*
Valeo Kapec North America Inc ....E....... 248 619-8710
Troy *(G-17427)*
Valley Gear and Machine Inc ....F....... 989 269-8177
Bad Axe *(G-1116)*
▼ **Wilkie Bros Conveyors Inc** ....E....... 810 364-4820
Marysville *(G-11113)*

3567 Indl Process Furnaces & Ovens

Able Htng Clng & Plmbng ....G....... 231 779-5430
Cadillac *(G-2307)*
◆ **Afc-Holcroft LLC** ....D....... 248 624-8191
Wixom *(G-18598)*
▲ **Aichelin Heat Treatment Syst** ....G....... 734 459-9850
Wixom *(G-18601)*
Alhern-Martin Indus Frnc Co ....E....... 248 689-6363
Troy *(G-16922)*
Allegan Tubular Products Inc ....D....... 269 673-6636
Allegan *(G-146)*
Atmosphere Group Inc ....G....... 248 624-8191
Wixom *(G-18609)*
Belco Industries Inc ....E....... 616 794-0410
Belding *(G-1437)*
▲ **Belco Industries Inc** ....E....... 616 794-0410
Belding *(G-1438)*
▼ **Capital Induction Inc** ....F....... 586 322-1444
Sterling Heights *(G-15951)*
▲ **Ce Il Holdings Inc** ....F....... 248 305-7700
Brighton *(G-1963)*
▲ **Clark Granco Inc** ....D....... 616 794-2600
Belding *(G-1443)*
▲ **Complete Filtration Inc** ....F....... 248 693-0500
Lake Orion *(G-9598)*
Custom Electric Mfg LLC ....E....... 248 305-7700
Wixom *(G-18642)*
Cyprium Induction LLC ....G....... 586 884-4982
Sterling Heights *(G-15976)*
D K Enterprises Inc ....G....... 586 756-7350
Warren *(G-17771)*
Davids Heating & Cooling Inc ....G....... 586 601-5108
Southfield *(G-15537)*
▲ **Ddr Heating Inc** ....E....... 269 673-2145
Allegan *(G-154)*
Detroit Steel Treating Company ....E....... 248 334-7436
Pontiac *(G-13361)*
Dfc Inc ....G....... 734 285-6749
Riverview *(G-13870)*
▲ **Durr Inc** ....G....... 734 459-6800
Southfield *(G-15544)*
◆ **Durr Systems Inc** ....B....... 248 450-2000
Southfield *(G-15545)*
▲ **E H Inc** ....F....... 269 673-6456
Allegan *(G-156)*
▲ **Efd Induction Inc** ....F....... 248 658-0700
Madison Heights *(G-10717)*
Eldec LLC ....F....... 248 364-4750
Auburn Hills *(G-876)*
Electroheat Technologies LLC ....E....... 810 798-2400
Auburn Hills *(G-877)*
Evenheat Kiln Inc ....E....... 989 856-2281
Caseville *(G-2604)*
Florheat Company ....G....... 517 272-4441
Lansing *(G-9836)*
▲ **Fluid Hutchinson Management** ....D....... 248 679-1327
Auburn Hills *(G-903)*
Fluidtherm Corp Michigan ....G....... 989 344-1500
Frederic *(G-6015)*
Fritz Enterprises ....G....... 313 841-9460
Detroit *(G-4247)*
Furnaces Ovens & Baths Inc ....G....... 248 625-7400
River Rouge *(G-13854)*
◆ **Gallagher-Kaiser Corporation** ....D....... 313 368-3100
Troy *(G-17126)*
Gerref Industries Inc ....E....... 616 794-3110
Belding *(G-1450)*
Great Lkes Indus Frnc Svcs Inc ....F....... 586 323-9200
Sterling Heights *(G-16033)*
Heating Induction Services Inc ....G....... 586 791-3160
Clinton Township *(G-3252)*
▲ **Hi-Tech Furnace Systems Inc** ....F....... 586 566-0600
Shelby Township *(G-15235)*
Hotset Corp ....G....... 269 964-0271
Battle Creek *(G-1238)*
Industrial Frnc Interiors Inc ....G....... 586 977-9600
Sterling Heights *(G-16048)*
Industrial Temperature Control ....G....... 734 451-8740
Canton *(G-2474)*
▲ **Inter-Power Corporation** ....E....... 810 798-9201
Almont *(G-262)*
Interpower Induction Svcs Inc ....F....... 586 296-7697
Fraser *(G-5945)*
J L Becker Acquisition LLC ....E....... 734 656-2000
Plymouth *(G-13199)*
Jackson Oven Supply Inc ....F....... 517 784-9660
Jackson *(G-8916)*
Kernel Burner ....G....... 989 792-2808
Saginaw *(G-14677)*
Kolene Corporation ....F....... 586 771-1200
Roseville *(G-14430)*
▼ **Kolene Corporation** ....D....... 313 273-9220
Detroit *(G-4365)*
▲ **National Appliance Parts Co** ....E....... 269 639-1469
South Haven *(G-15410)*
National Element Inc ....E....... 248 486-1810
Brighton *(G-2040)*
▲ **Nexthermal Corporation** ....D....... 269 964-0271
Battle Creek *(G-1279)*
Nortek Air Solutions LLC ....D....... 616 738-7148
Holland *(G-8156)*
North Woods Industrial ....G....... 616 784-2840
Comstock Park *(G-3629)*
Oakland Welding Industries ....E....... 586 949-4090
Chesterfield *(G-2916)*
Perceptive Industries Inc ....E....... 269 204-6768
Plainwell *(G-13086)*
Phoenix Induction Corporation ....F....... 248 486-7377
South Lyon *(G-15453)*
Pillar Induction ....F....... 586 254-8470
Madison Heights *(G-10799)*
R J Manufacturing Incorporated ....G....... 906 779-9151
Crystal Falls *(G-3745)*
▲ **Rapid Engineering LLC** ....D....... 616 784-0500
Comstock Park *(G-3642)*
Salem/Savard Industries LLC ....F....... 313 931-6880
Detroit *(G-4579)*
Sheler Corporation ....E....... 586 979-8560
Sterling Heights *(G-16176)*
SMS Elotherm North America LLC ....F....... 586 469-8324
Shelby Township *(G-15336)*
▲ **Solaronics Inc** ....E....... 248 651-5333
Auburn Hills *(G-1035)*
Specified A Sltons Hldings LLC ....D....... 616 784-0500
Comstock Park *(G-3645)*
Thermal Designs & Manufacturng ....F....... 586 773-5231
Roseville *(G-14484)*
Thermal Designs & Mfg ....E....... 248 476-2978
Novi *(G-12555)*
Thermalfab Products Inc ....F....... 517 486-2073
Blissfield *(G-1778)*
▼ **Thoreson-Mc Cosh Inc** ....E....... 248 362-0960
Lake Orion *(G-9634)*
Tps LLC ....D....... 269 849-2700
Riverside *(G-13866)*
Ultra-Temp Corporation ....G....... 810 794-4709
Clay *(G-3128)*
Vconverter Corporation ....C....... 248 388-0549
Novi *(G-12564)*

3568 Mechanical Power Transmission Eqpt, NEC

Accurate Gauge & Mfg Inc ....D....... 248 853-2400
Rochester Hills *(G-13940)*
▲ **Allor Manufacturing Inc** ....D....... 248 486-4500
Brighton *(G-1943)*
Arthur R Sommers ....G....... 586 469-1280
Harrison Township *(G-7689)*
Auburn Hills Manufacturing Inc ....C....... 313 758-2000
Auburn Hills *(G-800)*
B & H Machine Sales Inc ....E....... 313 843-6720
Detroit *(G-4039)*
Barnes Industries Inc ....E....... 248 541-2333
Madison Heights *(G-10678)*
▲ **BDS Company Inc** ....F....... 517 279-2135
Coldwater *(G-3421)*
Borgwarner Powdered Metals Inc ....C....... 734 261-5322
Livonia *(G-10140)*
Borgwarner Thermal Systems Inc ....G....... 231 779-7500
Cadillac *(G-2317)*
Bradhart Products Inc ....E....... 248 437-3746
Brighton *(G-1952)*
Bunting Bearings LLC ....E....... 269 345-8691
Portage *(G-13550)*
Colonial Bushings Inc ....E....... 586 954-3880
Clinton Township *(G-3203)*
Craft Steel Products Inc ....G....... 616 935-7575
Spring Lake *(G-15809)*
Dayco LLC ....E....... 248 404-6500
Troy *(G-17045)*
Dayco Products LLC ....D....... 248 404-6500
Troy *(G-17048)*
◆ **Engineered Machined Pdts Inc** ....B....... 906 786-8404
Escanaba *(G-5069)*
Equitable Engineering Co Inc ....E....... 248 689-9700
Troy *(G-17096)*
Evans Industries Inc ....G....... 313 272-8200
Detroit *(G-4219)*
Federal-Mogul Powertrain LLC ....B....... 616 754-5681
Greenville *(G-7485)*
▲ **Formsprag LLC** ....C....... 586 758-5000
Warren *(G-17816)*
Friction Control LLC ....G....... 586 741-8493
Clinton Township *(G-3246)*
Gates Corporation ....G....... 248 260-2300
Rochester Hills *(G-14020)*
Gateway Engineering Inc ....F....... 616 284-1425
Grand Rapids *(G-6732)*
▲ **Geislinger Corporation** ....F....... 269 441-7000
Battle Creek *(G-1234)*
◆ **GKN Sinter Metals LLC** ....G....... 248 883-4500
Auburn Hills *(G-914)*
▲ **Great Lakes Industry Inc** ....E....... 517 784-3153
Jackson *(G-8895)*
▲ **Hayes Manufacturing Inc** ....E....... 231 879-3372
Fife Lake *(G-5608)*
Hole Industries Incorporated ....G....... 517 548-4229
Howell *(G-8461)*
Idc Industries Inc ....E....... 586 427-4321
Clinton Township *(G-3257)*
Kaydon Corporation ....C....... 231 755-3741
Norton Shores *(G-12306)*
▲ **Leedy Manufacturing Co LLC** ....D....... 616 245-0517
Grand Rapids *(G-6934)*
Liquid Drive Corporation ....E....... 248 634-5382
Mount Clemens *(G-11647)*
M C Carbide Tool Co ....E....... 248 486-9590
Wixom *(G-18703)*
Masterline Design & Mfg ....E....... 586 463-5888
Harrison Township *(G-7709)*
◆ **Melling Tool Co** ....B....... 517 787-8172
Jackson *(G-8951)*
◆ **Michigan Auto Comprsr Inc** ....A....... 517 796-3200
Parma *(G-12938)*
Milan Screw Products Inc ....F....... 734 439-2431
Milan *(G-11447)*
Mq Operating Company ....E....... 906 337-1515
Calumet *(G-2412)*
Murray Equipment Company Inc ....F....... 313 869-4444
Warren *(G-17938)*
National Element Inc ....E....... 248 486-1810
Brighton *(G-2040)*
◆ **Neapco Holdings LLC** ....C....... 248 699-6500
Farmington Hills *(G-5333)*
PCI Procal Inc ....F....... 989 358-7070
Alpena *(G-311)*

S I C

Employee Codes: A=Over 500 employees, B=251-500
C=101-250, D=51-100, E=20-50, F=10-19, G=3-9

2022 Harris Michigan
Industrial Directory

855

▲ Powertrain Integration LLC .... E 248 577-0010
Madison Heights ***(G-10806)***

▲ Precision Torque Control Inc .... F 989 495-9330
Midland ***(G-11403)***

Production Industries II Inc .... G 231 352-7500
Traverse City ***(G-16804)***

Quality Steel Products Inc .... E 248 684-0555
Milford ***(G-11484)***

Riverside Spline & Gear Inc .... E 810 765-8302
Marine City ***(G-10965)***

S R P Inc .... F 517 784-3153
Jackson ***(G-9003)***

◆ Saf-Holland Inc .... A 231 773-3271
Muskegon ***(G-11913)***

Saginaw Bearing Company .... F 989 752-3169
Saginaw ***(G-14744)***

Supreme Gear Co .... E 586 775-6325
Fraser ***(G-6001)***

▲ System Components Inc .... E 269 637-2191
South Haven ***(G-15417)***

Ton-Tex Corporation .... F 616 957-3200
Greenville ***(G-7508)***

Ton-Tex Corporation .... E 616 957-3200
Grand Rapids ***(G-7264)***

Tractech Inc .... E 248 226-6800
Southfield ***(G-15725)***

▲ U S Graphite Inc .... E 989 755-0441
Saginaw ***(G-14783)***

▼ Wilkie Bros Conveyors Inc .... E 810 364-4820
Marysville ***(G-11113)***

Wolverine Machine Products Co .... E 248 634-9952
Holly ***(G-8301)***

3569 Indl Machinery & Eqpt, NEC

◆ +vantage Corporation .... E 734 432-5055
Livonia ***(G-10088)***

AA Anderson & Co Inc .... E 248 476-7782
Plymouth ***(G-13110)***

Acme Mills Company .... E 517 437-8940
Hillsdale ***(G-7920)***

Acme Mills Company .... G 800 521-8585
Bloomfield Hills ***(G-1791)***

Acumen Technologies Inc .... F 586 566-8600
Shelby Township ***(G-15165)***

▲ Advance Products Corporation .... E 269 849-1000
Benton Harbor ***(G-1527)***

Advanced Recovery Tech Corp .... G 231 788-2911
Nunica ***(G-12575)***

Airtificial Intelligent Robots .... G 989 799-6669
Saginaw ***(G-14602)***

◆ Allfi Robotics Inc .... G 586 248-1198
Wixom ***(G-18604)***

◆ Amcol Corporation .... E 248 414-5700
Hazel Park ***(G-7819)***

Applied & Integrated Mfg Inc .... G 248 370-8950
Auburn Hills ***(G-793)***

Arbor Fabricating LLC .... G 734 626-5864
Milan ***(G-11431)***

Arbor International Inc .... G 734 761-5200
Ann Arbor ***(G-374)***

Arrow Automation and Engrg Inc .... F 248 660-1520
Auburn Hills ***(G-797)***

Asw Amerca Inc .... G 248 957-9638
Farmington Hills ***(G-5174)***

Atlas Technologies Inc .... G 810 629-6663
Fenton ***(G-5452)***

Ats Assembly and Test Inc .... F 937 222-3030
Wixom ***(G-18612)***

Auto/Con Services LLC .... G 586 791-7474
Fraser ***(G-5898)***

Avl North Amer Corp Svcs Inc .... A 734 414-9600
Plymouth ***(G-13131)***

Baird Investments LLC .... G 586 665-0154
Sterling Heights ***(G-15943)***

Barbron Corporation .... E 586 716-3530
Kalkaska ***(G-9382)***

Bayshore Custom Assembly LLC .... G 616 396-5502
Holland ***(G-7971)***

Becker Robotic Equipment Corp .... G 470 249-7880
Orion ***(G-12724)***

▲ Beswick Corporation .... F 248 589-0562
Troy ***(G-16976)***

Bme Inc .... G 810 937-2974
Port Huron ***(G-13461)***

Bobier Tool Supply Inc .... E 810 732-4030
Flint ***(G-5658)***

Borneman & Peterson Inc .... F 810 744-1890
Flint ***(G-5659)***

Boulding Filtration Co LLC .... G 313 300-2388
Detroit ***(G-4064)***

Buhler Technologies LLC .... E 248 652-1546
Rochester Hills ***(G-13966)***

Bulldog Fabricating Corp .... G 734 761-3111
Ann Arbor ***(G-409)***

Centrum Force Fabrication LLC .... G 517 857-4774
Ann Arbor ***(G-420)***

Change Parts Incorporated .... E 231 845-5107
Ludington ***(G-10531)***

▲ Chip Systems International .... F 269 626-8000
Scotts ***(G-15130)***

Classic Systems LLC .... C 248 588-2738
Troy ***(G-17015)***

Comau LLC .... D 248 219-0756
Southfield ***(G-15531)***

Conair North America .... E 814 437-6861
Pinconning ***(G-13060)***

Craft Industries Inc .... B 586 726-4300
Shelby Township ***(G-15197)***

Dee-Blast Corporation .... F 269 428-2400
Stevensville ***(G-16246)***

Dispense Technologies LLC .... G 248 486-6244
Brighton ***(G-1975)***

Distinctive Mfg Group LLC .... F 616 953-8999
Zeeland ***(G-19015)***

▲ Duperon Corporation .... D 800 383-8479
Saginaw ***(G-14640)***

Edwards Machinery and Repa .... G 616 422-2584
Baroda ***(G-1160)***

Esirpal Inc .... G 586 337-7848
Macomb ***(G-10592)***

Everest Energy Fund L L C .... G 586 445-2300
Warren ***(G-17797)***

Fabrication Concepts LLC .... F 517 750-4742
Spring Arbor ***(G-15791)***

◆ Fanuc America Corporation .... B 248 377-7000
Rochester Hills ***(G-14009)***

▲ Fec Inc .... F 586 580-2622
Shelby Township ***(G-15225)***

Fergin & Associates Inc .... G 906 477-0040
Engadine ***(G-5043)***

Flodraulic Group Incorporated .... G 734 326-5400
Westland ***(G-18371)***

Flow Ezy Filters Inc .... F 734 665-8777
Ann Arbor ***(G-491)***

Front Line Services Inc .... F 989 695-6633
Freeland ***(G-6024)***

G P Reeves Inc .... E 616 399-8893
Holland ***(G-8045)***

Gallagher Fire Equipment Co .... E 248 477-1540
Livonia ***(G-10219)***

▲ Gelman Sciences Inc .... C 734 665-0651
Ann Arbor ***(G-496)***

General Electric Company .... F 616 676-0870
Ada ***(G-19)***

Geofabrica Inc .... F 810 728-2468
Auburn Hills ***(G-909)***

Global Electronics Limited .... F 248 353-0100
Bloomfield Hills ***(G-1823)***

▼ Global Tooling Systems LLC .... B 586 726-0500
Macomb ***(G-10599)***

Gr Tooling & Automation Inc .... F 616 299-1521
Comstock Park ***(G-3609)***

Greatech Integration USA Inc .... G 734 673-5985
Wixom ***(G-18670)***

Haosen Automation N Amer Inc .... G 248 556-6398
Auburn Hills ***(G-923)***

Harvey S Freeman .... G 248 852-2222
West Bloomfield ***(G-18287)***

▲ Haven Innovation Inc .... E 616 935-1040
Grand Haven ***(G-6315)***

◆ Hirotec America Inc .... B 248 836-5100
Auburn Hills ***(G-927)***

Hoff Engineering Co Inc .... G 248 969-8272
Oxford ***(G-12887)***

▲ Hoffmann Filter Corporation .... F 248 486-8430
Brighton ***(G-2008)***

▼ Hot Melt Technologies Inc .... E 248 853-2011
Rochester Hills ***(G-14034)***

Independent Mfg Solutions Corp .... E 248 960-3550
Wixom ***(G-18684)***

Industrial Atomated Design LLC .... F 810 648-9200
Sandusky ***(G-15060)***

Industrial Service Tech Inc .... F 616 247-1033
Grand Rapids ***(G-6843)***

Infra Corporation .... F 248 623-0400
Waterford ***(G-18129)***

Inovatech Automation Inc .... F 586 210-9010
Macomb ***(G-10606)***

Intellichem LLC .... F 810 765-4075
Marine City ***(G-10959)***

International Robot Support .... G 586 783-8000
Mount Clemens ***(G-11643)***

Intersrce Recovery Systems Inc .... E 269 375-5100
Kalamazoo ***(G-9225)***

Jack Weaver Corp .... G 517 263-6500
Adrian ***(G-76)***

Jax Services LLC .... G 586 703-3212
Warren ***(G-17883)***

Jomesa North America Inc .... F 248 457-0023
Troy ***(G-17189)***

K and J Absorbent Products LLC .... G 517 486-3110
Blissfield ***(G-1766)***

◆ Kaydon Corporation .... B 734 747-7025
Ann Arbor ***(G-538)***

Kdf Fluid Treatment Inc .... F 269 273-3300
Three Rivers ***(G-16578)***

Keane Saunders & Associates .... G 616 954-7088
Grand Rapids ***(G-6880)***

Krush Industries Inc .... G 248 238-2296
Taylor ***(G-16434)***

Lampco Industries of MI Inc .... G 517 783-3414
Jackson ***(G-8932)***

▲ Lube - Power Inc .... D 586 247-6500
Shelby Township ***(G-15264)***

M-B-M Manufacturing Inc .... G 231 924-9614
Fremont ***(G-6047)***

Mark One Corporation .... D 989 732-2427
Gaylord ***(G-6145)***

Metalform Industries LLC .... G 248 462-0056
Shelby Township ***(G-15274)***

Mhr Inc .... F 616 394-0191
Holland ***(G-8146)***

Microphoto Incorporated .... E 586 772-1999
Roseville ***(G-14441)***

Millennium Planet LLC .... G 248 835-2331
Farmington Hills ***(G-5322)***

Mosley .... G 734 654-2969
Carleton ***(G-2560)***

Muskegon Heights Water Filter .... G 231 780-3415
Norton Shores ***(G-12314)***

New 9 Inc .... E 616 459-8274
Grand Rapids ***(G-7040)***

Norman Township .... F 231 848-4495
Wellston ***(G-18258)***

Northern Processes & Sales LLC .... G 248 669-3918
Wixom ***(G-18723)***

Nu-ERA Holdings Inc .... E 810 794-4935
Clay ***(G-3123)***

Nu-Ice Age Inc .... F 517 990-0665
Clarklake ***(G-3006)***

Onyx Manufacturing Inc .... G 248 687-8611
Rochester Hills ***(G-14075)***

▼ Opco Lubrication Systems Inc .... G 231 924-6160
Fremont ***(G-6050)***

▲ Orsco Inc .... G 314 679-4200
Armada ***(G-738)***

P R Machining & Prototype Inc .... G 586 468-7146
Mount Clemens ***(G-11650)***

Parker-Hannifin Corporation .... G 330 253-5239
Otsego ***(G-12797)***

▲ Permawick Company Inc .... G 248 433-3500
Birmingham ***(G-1743)***

▲ Petter Investments Inc .... F 269 637-1997
South Haven ***(G-15411)***

▲ Pittsfield Products Inc .... E 734 665-3771
Ann Arbor ***(G-612)***

Plamondon Oil Co Inc .... G 231 256-9261
Lake Leelanau ***(G-9564)***

Polk Gas Producer LLC .... G 734 913-2970
Ann Arbor ***(G-613)***

Positech Inc .... G 616 949-4024
Grand Rapids ***(G-7094)***

Power Cleaning Systems Inc .... G 248 347-7727
Novi ***(G-12507)***

▼ Progressive Surface Inc .... D 616 957-0871
Grand Rapids ***(G-7117)***

Progressive Surface Inc .... F 616 957-0871
Grand Rapids ***(G-7118)***

Puritan Automation LLC .... F 248 668-1114
Wixom ***(G-18737)***

Quality Filters Inc .... F 734 668-0211
Ann Arbor ***(G-630)***

R Concepts Incorporated .... G 810 632-4857
Howell ***(G-8505)***

REB Research & Consulting Co .... G 248 545-0155
Oak Park ***(G-12639)***

Recco Products Inc .... E 269 792-2243
Wayland ***(G-18202)***

Reese Inspection Services LLC .... F 248 481-3598
Auburn Hills ***(G-1017)***

SIC SECTION 35 INDUSTRIAL AND COMMERCIAL MACHINERY AND COMPUTER EQUIPMENT 35 INDUSTRIAL AND COMMERCIAL MACHINERY

◆ **Rosedale Products Inc**......D...... 734 665-8201
Ann Arbor *(G-644)*
▲ **Sanyo Machine America Corp**......D...... 248 651-5911
Rochester Hills *(G-14108)*
Schap Specialty Machine Inc......F...... 616 846-6530
Spring Lake *(G-15850)*
▲ **Service Tectonics Inc**......E...... 517 263-0758
Adrian *(G-96)*
Sk Enterprises Inc......G...... 616 785-1070
Grand Rapids *(G-7201)*
Smart Diet Scale LLC......G...... 586 383-6734
Bruce Twp *(G-2183)*
SMS Group Inc......D...... 734 246-8230
Taylor *(G-16475)*
SMS Technical Services......F...... 586 445-0330
Warren *(G-18016)*
Smullen Fire App Sales & Svcs......G...... 517 546-8898
Howell *(G-8520)*
Stokes Automation......G...... 248 573-5277
Northville *(G-12264)*
Superior Design & Mfg......F...... 810 678-3950
Metamora *(G-11287)*
Terrell Manufacturing Svcs Inc......F...... 231 788-2000
Muskegon *(G-11930)*
◆ **Thyssenkrupp System Engrg**......C...... 248 340-8000
Auburn Hills *(G-1052)*
Tool North Inc......E...... 231 941-1150
Traverse City *(G-16861)*
▼ **Trinity Tool Co**......E...... 586 296-5900
Fraser *(G-6006)*
United Fbrcnts Strainrite Corp......E...... 800 487-3136
Pontiac *(G-13422)*
Universal Tl Eqp & Contrls Inc......D...... 586 268-4380
Sterling Heights *(G-16217)*
US Jack Company......G...... 269 925-7777
Benton Harbor *(G-1597)*
Vdl Steelweld Usa LLC......E...... 248 781-8141
Troy *(G-17433)*
Viking Group Inc......C...... 616 831-6448
Hastings *(G-7813)*
Viking Group Inc......G...... 616 432-6800
Caledonia *(G-2406)*
Volos Tube Form Inc......E...... 586 416-3600
Macomb *(G-10650)*
Wartrom Machine Systems Inc......E...... 586 469-1915
Clinton Township *(G-3387)*
Wayne Wire Cloth Products Inc......F...... 989 742-4591
Hillman *(G-7917)*
▲ **Weiss Technik North Amer Inc**......D...... 616 554-5020
Grand Rapids *(G-7329)*
West Mich Flcking Assembly LLC......E...... 269 639-1634
Grand Rapids *(G-7331)*
Whites Bridge Tooling Inc......E...... 616 897-4151
Lowell *(G-10522)*
William Shaw Inc......G...... 231 536-3569
Traverse City *(G-16880)*
Wolverine Water Works Inc......G...... 248 673-4310
Waterford *(G-18176)*
Yaskawa America Inc......G...... 248 668-8800
Rochester Hills *(G-14148)*
Youngtronics LLC......F...... 248 896-5790
Wixom *(G-18793)*

3571 Electronic Computers

3dfx Interactive Inc......G...... 918 938-8967
Saginaw *(G-14599)*
Advanced Integrated Mfg......G...... 586 439-0300
Fraser *(G-5888)*
Artemis Technologies Inc......E...... 517 336-9915
East Lansing *(G-4886)*
Bull Hn Info Systems Inc......G...... 616 942-7126
Grand Rapids *(G-6530)*
Compudyne Inc......F...... 906 360-9081
Marquette *(G-11014)*
▲ **Cypress Computer Systems Inc**......F...... 810 245-2300
Lapeer *(G-9924)*
Eaton Aerospace LLC......B...... 616 949-1090
Grand Rapids *(G-6663)*
Enovate It......F...... 248 721-8104
Ferndale *(G-5552)*
Entron Computer Systems Inc......G...... 248 349-8898
Northville *(G-12215)*
▲ **Ews Legacy LLC**......C...... 248 853-6363
Rochester Hills *(G-14006)*
Experimac Macomb......G...... 586 884-6292
Macomb *(G-10593)*
General Dynmics Mssion Systems......G...... 734 480-5000
Ypsilanti *(G-18950)*
General Dynmics Mssion Systems......G...... 734 480-5000
Ypsilanti *(G-18951)*
Hardware Exchange Inc......G...... 440 449-8006
Grand Rapids *(G-6803)*
Hp Inc......G...... 650 857-1501
Lansing *(G-9765)*
Hp Inc......G...... 248 614-6600
Troy *(G-17154)*
Indocomp Systems Inc......F...... 810 678-3990
Metamora *(G-11281)*
Innovation Unlimited LLC......G...... 574 635-1064
Bay City *(G-1367)*
▲ **Innovtive Design Solutions Inc**......C...... 248 583-1010
Sterling Heights *(G-16049)*
Intellibee Inc......E...... 313 586-4122
Detroit *(G-4323)*
International Bus Mchs Corp......E...... 989 832-6000
Midland *(G-11375)*
Jasons Apple Service & Sls LLC......G...... 586 530-4908
Macomb *(G-10607)*
Kismet Strategic Sourcing Part......G...... 269 932-4990
Saint Joseph *(G-14942)*
Lga Retail Inc......G...... 248 910-1918
South Lyon *(G-15443)*
Mesa Corporation......G...... 517 669-5656
Dewitt *(G-4712)*
Novastar Solutionscom LLC......D...... 734 453-8003
Livonia *(G-10340)*
Official Brand Limited......G...... 734 224-9942
Dearborn *(G-3880)*
Opto Solutions Inc......G...... 269 254-9716
Plainwell *(G-13084)*
PC Techs On Wheels......G...... 734 262-4424
Canton *(G-2505)*
PCI Procal Inc......F...... 989 358-7070
Alpena *(G-311)*
▲ **Pro-Face America LLC**......E...... 734 477-0600
Ann Arbor *(G-625)*
▼ **Protxs Inc**......C...... 989 255-3836
Jenison *(G-9068)*
Radio Advertising Bureau Inc......G...... 248 514-7048
Novi *(G-12523)*
Rave Computer Association Inc......E...... 586 939-8230
Sterling Heights *(G-16143)*
Reply Inc......C...... 248 686-2481
Auburn Hills *(G-1018)*
S T A Inc......E...... 248 328-5000
Holly *(G-8294)*
Secord Solutions LLC......G...... 734 363-8887
Ecorse *(G-4985)*
Stellar Computer Services LLC......G...... 989 732-7153
Gaylord *(G-6161)*
Tes America LLC......E...... 616 786-5353
Holland *(G-8217)*

3572 Computer Storage Devices

◆ **American Furukawa Inc**......E...... 734 446-2200
Plymouth *(G-13123)*
Aperion Information Tech Inc......F...... 248 969-9791
Oxford *(G-12874)*
▲ **Autocam Corporation**......B...... 616 698-0707
Kentwood *(G-9444)*
Cloudface LLC......G...... 248 756-1688
Northville *(G-12200)*
Digilink Technology Inc......F...... 517 381-8888
Okemos *(G-12664)*
Don Theyken......G...... 734 996-8359
Ann Arbor *(G-457)*
Donald Schilstra......G...... 616 534-1897
Grand Rapids *(G-6654)*
EMC Corporation......G...... 248 957-5800
Farmington Hills *(G-5229)*
EMC Educational Services LLC......G...... 616 460-3345
Walker *(G-17638)*
Laser Re-Nu LLC......G...... 248 630-1454
Pontiac *(G-13394)*
Magnetic Systems International......G...... 231 582-9600
Petoskey *(G-13003)*
Mass Mountain Technologies......G...... 855 722-7900
Grand Rapids *(G-6964)*
Piolax Corporation......D...... 734 668-6005
Plymouth *(G-13265)*
Quantam Solutions LLC......G...... 248 395-2200
Southfield *(G-15686)*
Quantum Data Analytics Inc......G...... 248 894-7442
Rochester Hills *(G-14095)*
Quantum Difference Corp......G...... 810 845-8765
Flint *(G-5753)*
Quantum Life LLC......G...... 248 634-2784
Holly *(G-8288)*
Quantum Manufacturing......G...... 248 690-9410
Auburn Hills *(G-1010)*
Quantum Ventures LLC......G...... 248 325-8380
Holly *(G-8289)*
Quantum Whatever LLC......G...... 734 546-4353
Willis *(G-18587)*
Rave Computer Association Inc......E...... 586 939-8230
Sterling Heights *(G-16143)*
Virtual Technology Inc......F...... 248 528-6565
Troy *(G-17442)*

3575 Computer Terminals

Dynics Inc......D...... 734 677-6100
Ann Arbor *(G-462)*
Freedom Technologies Corp......E...... 810 227-3737
Brighton *(G-1993)*
Geeks of Detroit LLC......G...... 734 576-2363
Detroit *(G-4252)*
Mmp Molded Magnesium Pdts LLC......G...... 517 789-8505
Jackson *(G-8967)*
Mobile Knowledge Group LLC......G...... 248 625-3327
Clarkston *(G-3052)*
▲ **Photodon LLC**......F...... 847 377-1185
Traverse City *(G-16791)*
▲ **Pro-Face America LLC**......E...... 734 477-0600
Ann Arbor *(G-625)*
Semisource Corporation......G...... 734 331-2104
Pinckney *(G-13055)*

3577 Computer Peripheral Eqpt, NEC

Acromag Incorporated......D...... 248 624-1541
Wixom *(G-18594)*
Advanced Integrated Mfg......G...... 586 439-0300
Fraser *(G-5888)*
Ampm Inc......E...... 989 837-8800
Midland *(G-11321)*
Appliction Spclist Kompany Inc......F...... 517 676-6633
Lansing *(G-9805)*
Artic Technologies Intl......G...... 248 689-9884
Troy *(G-16955)*
Bbcm Inc......G...... 248 410-2528
Bloomfield Hills *(G-1803)*
Bcc Distribution Inc......F...... 734 737-9300
Canton *(G-2439)*
Berkshire & Associates Inc......F...... 734 719-1822
Canton *(G-2440)*
Black Box Corporation......G...... 248 743-1320
Troy *(G-16977)*
Black Box Corporation......F...... 616 246-1320
Caledonia *(G-2369)*
Bull Hn Info Systems Inc......G...... 616 942-7126
Grand Rapids *(G-6530)*
Cisco Systems Inc......G...... 800 553-6387
Detroit *(G-4094)*
Comptek Inc......E...... 248 477-5215
Farmington Hills *(G-5206)*
Compunetics Systems Inc......G...... 248 531-0015
Rochester Hills *(G-13981)*
◆ **Daco Hand Controllers Inc**......F...... 248 982-3266
Novi *(G-12390)*
Electronics For Imaging Inc......G...... 734 641-3062
Ypsilanti *(G-18941)*
Elite Engineering Inc......E...... 517 304-3254
Rochester Hills *(G-14003)*
▲ **Ensure Technologies Inc**......F...... 734 547-1600
Ypsilanti *(G-18944)*
Envisiontec US LLC......D...... 313 436-4300
Dearborn *(G-3837)*
▲ **Graphic Resource Group Inc**......E...... 248 588-6100
Troy *(G-17132)*
Innovative Support Svcs Inc......F...... 248 585-3600
Troy *(G-17168)*
Jant Group LLC......G...... 616 863-6600
Belmont *(G-1508)*
Jem Computers Inc......F...... 586 783-3400
Clinton Township *(G-3264)*
▲ **Jo-Dan International Inc**......F...... 248 340-0300
Auburn Hills *(G-944)*
Kace Logistics LLC......E...... 734 946-8600
Carleton *(G-2557)*
Kingdom Cartridge Inc......G...... 734 564-1590
Plymouth *(G-13216)*
▲ **Law Enforcement Development Co**......E...... 734 656-4100
Plymouth *(G-13220)*
Lexmark International Inc......F...... 248 352-0616
Southfield *(G-15635)*
LMI Technologies Inc......F...... 248 298-2839
Royal Oak *(G-14557)*
Printek Inc......D...... 269 925-3200
Saint Joseph *(G-14955)*
▲ **Pro-Face America LLC**......E...... 734 477-0600
Ann Arbor *(G-625)*

SIC

Employee Codes: A=Over 500 employees, B=251-500
C=101-250, D=51-100, E=20-50, F=10-19, G=3-9

2022 Harris Michigan
Industrial Directory

857

Red Barn Maps ......G...... 906 346-2226
Gwinn *(G-7586)*
Sakor Technologies Inc ......F...... 989 720-2700
Owosso *(G-12855)*
▼ **Samsung Sdi America Inc** ......F...... 408 544-4470
Auburn Hills *(G-1025)*
Scs Embedded Tech LLC ......G...... 248 615-4441
Novi *(G-12532)*
Startech-Solutions LLC ......G...... 248 419-0650
Southfield *(G-15708)*
◆ **Triangle Product Distributors** ......E...... 970 609-9001
Holland *(G-8229)*
Visionit Supplies and Svcs Inc ......E...... 313 664-5650
Detroit *(G-4669)*
▲ **Yakel Enterprises LLC** ......G...... 586 943-5885
Washington Township *(G-18097)*

3578 Calculating & Accounting Eqpt

Atm International Services LLC ......E...... 734 524-9771
Westland *(G-18356)*
Baliko Pos Inc ......G...... 248 470-4652
Farmington Hills *(G-5180)*
Computer Decisions Intl Inc ......G...... 248 473-5900
Northville *(G-12202)*
Cornelius Systems Inc ......E...... 248 545-5558
Clawson *(G-3091)*
Daler Inc ......G...... 989 752-1582
Saginaw *(G-14635)*
PC Complete Inc ......G...... 248 545-4211
Ferndale *(G-5577)*
Robiccon Inc ......F...... 734 425-7080
Livonia *(G-10389)*
Wholesale Proc Systems LLC ......G...... 833 755-6696
Adrian *(G-104)*

3579 Office Machines, NEC

A A A Mailing & Packg Sups LLC ......G...... 616 481-9120
Grand Rapids *(G-6408)*
Central Michigan Engravers ......G...... 517 485-5865
Lansing *(G-9679)*
Danka ......G...... 616 249-8199
Wyoming *(G-18864)*
Debi Designs ......G...... 989 832-9598
Midland *(G-11336)*
Golden Apple ......G...... 231 477-5366
Manistee *(G-10901)*
Pitney Bowes Inc ......G...... 203 356-5000
South Lyon *(G-15454)*
Pitney Bowes Inc ......G...... 517 393-4101
Lansing *(G-9881)*
Pitney Bowes Inc ......D...... 616 285-9590
Grand Rapids *(G-7088)*

3581 Automatic Vending Machines

Kunzman & Associates West ......G...... 269 663-8978
Decatur *(G-3948)*
◆ **Maytag Corporation** ......C...... 269 923-5000
Benton Harbor *(G-1572)*
Quarters LLC ......G...... 313 510-5555
Plymouth *(G-13273)*

3582 Commercial Laundry, Dry Clean & Pressing Mchs

AEC Systems Usa Inc ......F...... 616 257-9502
Wyoming *(G-18849)*
▲ **Kah** ......G...... 734 727-0478
Westland *(G-18390)*

3585 Air Conditioning & Heating Eqpt

Acme Tool & Die Co ......G...... 231 938-1260
Acme *(G-1)*
▲ **Air International (us) Inc** ......D...... 248 391-7970
Auburn Hills *(G-775)*
Auction Masters ......G...... 586 576-7777
Oak Park *(G-12593)*
▲ **Blissfield Manufacturing Co** ......C...... 517 486-2121
Blissfield *(G-1761)*
◆ **Cdgjl Inc** ......E...... 517 787-2100
Jackson *(G-8836)*
▲ **Check Technology Solutions LLC** ......E...... 248 680-2323
Troy *(G-17008)*
Chrysler & Koppin Company ......F...... 313 491-7100
Grosse Pointe *(G-7527)*
◆ **Combustion Research Corp** ......E...... 248 852-3611
Rochester Hills *(G-13979)*
Compressor Industries LLC ......F...... 313 389-2800
Melvindale *(G-11197)*
Cooler King LLC ......G...... 248 789-3699
Westland *(G-18361)*
Crown Heating Inc ......G...... 248 352-1688
Detroit *(G-4109)*
Crystal Ice Resource LLC ......G...... 616 560-8102
Ravenna *(G-13688)*
D & B Heat Transfer Pdts Inc ......F...... 616 827-0028
Grand Rapids *(G-6625)*
▲ **Dimplex Thermal Solutions Inc** ......C...... 269 349-6800
Kalamazoo *(G-9169)*
Dynasty Mechanical Inc ......G...... 313 506-5504
Detroit *(G-4197)*
Enersave LLC ......F...... 616 785-1800
Grand Rapids *(G-6678)*
Espar Inc ......G...... 248 994-7010
Novi *(G-12414)*
▼ **Etx Holdings Inc** ......G...... 989 463-1151
Alma *(G-241)*
Evans Tempcon Delaware LLC ......G...... 616 361-2681
Grand Rapids *(G-6687)*
Exclusive Heating & Coolg Comp ......G...... 248 219-9528
Detroit *(G-4221)*
Fantastic Sams Hair Salon ......G...... 713 861-2500
Madison Heights *(G-10726)*
▼ **Fluid Chillers Inc** ......E...... 517 484-9190
Lansing *(G-9837)*
Forma-Kool Manufacturing Inc ......E...... 586 949-4813
Chesterfield *(G-2884)*
Forzza Corporation ......E...... 616 884-6121
Middleville *(G-11306)*
◆ **General Filters Inc** ......E...... 248 476-5100
Novi *(G-12423)*
◆ **Glastender Inc** ......B...... 989 752-4275
Saginaw *(G-14652)*
Hanon Systems Usa LLC ......B...... 248 907-8000
Novi *(G-12425)*
Heat Controller LLC ......F...... 517 787-2100
Jackson *(G-8901)*
Hussmann Corporation ......G...... 248 668-0790
Wixom *(G-18683)*
Johnson Controls Inc ......G...... 313 842-3479
Van Buren Twp *(G-17531)*
▲ **Kraftube Inc** ......C...... 231 832-5562
Reed City *(G-13793)*
La Rosa Refrigeration & Eqp Co ......E...... 313 368-6620
Detroit *(G-4371)*
Lenox Block Club Assn ......G...... 313 823-0941
Detroit *(G-4389)*
Lenox Pharmacy LLC ......G...... 313 971-5928
Lenox *(G-10000)*
▲ **Mahle Behr Industy America Lp** ......D...... 616 647-3490
Belmont *(G-1513)*
▲ **Mahle Behr USA Inc** ......C...... 248 743-3700
Troy *(G-17232)*
Manitwoc Fdsrvice Cmpanies LLC ......G...... 989 773-7981
Mount Pleasant *(G-11710)*
▲ **Mann + Hummel Inc** ......G...... 269 329-3900
Portage *(G-13581)*
◆ **Marelli North America Inc** ......A...... 931 684-4490
Southfield *(G-15644)*
Marelli North America Inc ......G...... 248 403-2033
Southfield *(G-15645)*
◆ **Michigan Auto Comprsr Inc** ......A...... 517 796-3200
Parma *(G-12938)*
Microtemp Fluid Systems LLC ......G...... 248 703-5056
Farmington Hills *(G-5320)*
Mjs Investing LLC ......E...... 734 455-6500
Plymouth *(G-13246)*
Murtech Energy Services LLC ......G...... 810 653-5681
Port Huron *(G-13508)*
National Aircraft Service Inc ......E...... 517 423-7589
Tecumseh *(G-16509)*
Nicole Lennox Lmt ......G...... 248 509-4433
Waterford *(G-18141)*
Nortek Inc ......G...... 616 719-5588
Grand Rapids *(G-7047)*
Nortek Air Solutions LLC ......D...... 616 738-7148
Holland *(G-8156)*
▲ **Northstar Wholesale** ......F...... 517 545-2379
Howell *(G-8484)*
Opti Temp Inc ......E...... 231 946-2931
Traverse City *(G-16783)*
Ostrander Company Inc ......G...... 248 646-6680
Madison Heights *(G-10793)*
Quality Draft Systems LLC ......G...... 616 259-9852
Grand Rapids *(G-7127)*
▲ **Rapid Engineering LLC** ......D...... 616 784-0500
Comstock Park *(G-3642)*
Refrigeration Research Inc ......G...... 989 773-7540
Mount Pleasant *(G-11736)*
Refrigeration Research Inc ......D...... 810 227-1151
Brighton *(G-2064)*
Remacon Compressors Inc ......G...... 313 842-8219
Detroit *(G-4564)*
Riedel USA Inc ......F...... 734 595-9820
Kalamazoo *(G-9317)*
▲ **Riedel USA Inc** ......G...... 734 595-9820
Kalamazoo *(G-9318)*
Rush Air Inc ......F...... 810 694-5763
Holly *(G-8293)*
Scientemp Corp ......E...... 517 263-6020
Adrian *(G-94)*
Service Control Inc ......E...... 248 478-1133
Howell *(G-8516)*
▲ **Snow Machines Incorporated** ......E...... 989 631-6091
Midland *(G-11418)*
Specified A Sltons Hldings LLC ......D...... 616 784-0500
Comstock Park *(G-3645)*
◆ **Stahls Inc** ......E...... 800 478-2457
Saint Clair Shores *(G-14887)*
Su-Tec Inc ......F...... 248 852-4711
Rochester Hills *(G-14122)*
Tecumseh Compressor Co LLC ......E...... 662 566-2231
Ann Arbor *(G-675)*
▲ **Tecumseh Compressor Company** ......D...... 734 585-9500
Ann Arbor *(G-676)*
◆ **Tecumseh Products Company LLC** ......A...... 734 585-9500
Ann Arbor *(G-677)*
Tecumseh Products Company LLC ......G...... 734 585-9500
Ann Arbor *(G-678)*
Tecumseh Products Company LLC ......G...... 734 585-9500
Ann Arbor *(G-679)*
Tecumseh Products Holdings LLC ......C...... 734 585-9500
Ann Arbor *(G-680)*
Terra Caloric LLC ......F...... 989 356-2113
Alpena *(G-325)*
Therma-Tech Engineering Inc ......E...... 313 537-5330
Redford *(G-13778)*
▼ **TI Fluid Systems LLC** ......A...... 248 494-5000
Auburn Hills *(G-1054)*
◆ **TI Group Auto Systems LLC** ......B...... 248 296-8000
Auburn Hills *(G-1055)*
TMI Climate Solutions Inc ......C...... 810 694-5763
Holly *(G-8297)*
Trane Inc ......G...... 616 222-3750
Wyoming *(G-18913)*
Trane US Inc ......E...... 800 245-3964
Flint *(G-5780)*
Trane US Inc ......G...... 734 367-0700
Livonia *(G-10441)*
Trane US Inc ......D...... 734 452-2000
Livonia *(G-10442)*
Trane US Inc ......G...... 616 971-1400
Grand Rapids *(G-7269)*
U S Distributing Inc ......E...... 248 646-0550
Birmingham *(G-1755)*
Way2go Tech LLC ......G...... 616 294-1301
Holland *(G-8242)*
▼ **Weather-Rite LLC** ......E...... 612 338-1401
Comstock Park *(G-3651)*
Whirlpool Corporation ......G...... 269 923-5000
Benton Harbor *(G-1609)*
▼ **Whirlpool Corporation** ......A...... 269 923-5000
Benton Harbor *(G-1603)*
Whirlpool Corporation ......G...... 269 923-5000
Benton Harbor *(G-1605)*
Whirlpool Corporation ......C...... 269 849-0907
Coloma *(G-3484)*
Whirlpool Corporation ......G...... 269 923-3009
Benton Harbor *(G-1610)*
▲ **Young Supply Company** ......E...... 313 875-3280
Detroit *(G-4699)*

3586 Measuring & Dispensing Pumps

Accurate Gauge & Mfg Inc ......D...... 248 853-2400
Rochester Hills *(G-13940)*
Automationsupply365 LLC ......G...... 248 912-7354
Auburn Hills *(G-805)*
▼ **Bpc Acquisition Company** ......C...... 231 798-1310
Norton Shores *(G-12345)*
Dispense Technologies LLC ......G...... 248 486-6244
Brighton *(G-1975)*
▼ **Edge Industries Inc** ......G...... 616 453-5458
Grand Rapids *(G-6665)*
▲ **Neptune Chemical Pump Company** ......C...... 215 699-8700
Grand Rapids *(G-7039)*
Nordson Corporation ......D...... 734 459-8600
Wixom *(G-18721)*

3589 Service Ind Machines, NEC

1st Rate Office Solutions LLC ......G...... 989 544-4009
Clare *(G-2971)*

A C Supply Co Inc ... F ... 586 776-2222
Warren *(G-17681)*

Admiral ... G ... 989 356-6419
Alpena *(G-274)*

Aerospace America Inc ... E ... 989 684-2121
Bay City *(G-1319)*

Amos Mfg Inc ... F ... 989 358-7187
Alpena *(G-278)*

Bauer Soft Water Co ... G ... 269 695-7900
Niles *(G-12112)*

Birks Works Environmental LLC ... G ... 313 891-1310
Detroit *(G-4055)*

Bissell Better Life LLC ... G ... 800 237-7691
Grand Rapids *(G-6510)*

Business Connect L3c ... G ... 833 229-6753
Grand Rapids *(G-6540)*

Cascade Equipment Company ... G ... 734 697-7870
Van Buren Twp *(G-17516)*

Caseville Village Government ... G ... 989 856-4407
Caseville *(G-2603)*

▲ Chip Systems International ... F ... 269 626-8000
Scotts *(G-15130)*

Clean Harbors Envmtl Svcs Inc ... F ... 231 258-8014
Kalkaska *(G-9385)*

▲ Creative Products Intl ... F ... 616 335-3333
Holland *(G-8007)*

Custom Service & Design Inc ... F ... 248 340-9005
Auburn Hills *(G-855)*

▲ D & L Water Control Inc ... E ... 734 455-6982
Canton *(G-2453)*

Dancorp Inc ... F ... 269 663-5566
Edwardsburg *(G-5004)*

▲ Delfield Company LLC ... A ... 989 773-7981
Mount Pleasant *(G-11695)*

Digested Organics LLC ... G ... 844 934-4378
Farmington Hills *(G-5218)*

Dihydro Services Inc ... E ... 586 978-0900
Sterling Heights *(G-15987)*

Douglas Water Conditioning ... F ... 248 363-8383
Waterford *(G-18117)*

Easy Scrub LLC ... G ... 586 565-1777
Roseville *(G-14404)*

Ener-TEC Inc ... F ... 517 741-5015
Union City *(G-17492)*

Evoqua Water Technologies LLC ... D ... 616 772-9011
Holland *(G-8034)*

Focus Cleaning LLC ... G ... 734 883-9560
Ypsilanti *(G-18946)*

Garbage Man LLC ... G ... 810 225-3001
Brighton *(G-1996)*

GCI Water Solutions LLC ... G ... 312 928-9992
Midland *(G-11368)*

▲ Geerpres Inc ... E ... 231 773-3211
Muskegon *(G-11823)*

◆ Ginsan Liquidating Company LLC ... D ... 616 791-8100
Grand Rapids *(G-6744)*

◆ Glastender Inc ... B ... 989 752-4275
Saginaw *(G-14652)*

Great Lakes Ncw LLC ... G ... 616 355-2626
Holland *(G-8059)*

H & R Electrical Contrs LLC ... E ... 517 669-2102
Dewitt *(G-4710)*

H-O-H Water Technology Inc ... E ... 248 669-6667
Commerce Township *(G-3534)*

◆ Hines Corporation ... F ... 231 799-6240
Norton Shores *(G-12348)*

Horizon Bros Painting Corp ... G ... 810 632-3362
Howell *(G-8462)*

Hot Logic LLC ... G ... 616 935-1040
Grand Haven *(G-6319)*

Hydrochem LLC ... F ... 313 841-5800
Monroe *(G-11549)*

Hygratek LLC ... G ... 847 962-6180
Ann Arbor *(G-520)*

Impressive Auto Care LLC ... F ... 734 306-4880
Romulus *(G-14285)*

▼ Inland Management Inc ... G ... 313 899-3014
Detroit *(G-4318)*

Integrity Municipal Service ... F ... 858 218-3750
Zeeland *(G-19048)*

◆ Interclean Equipment LLC ... E ... 734 961-3300
Ypsilanti *(G-18958)*

J Mark Systems Inc ... G ... 616 784-6005
Grand Rapids *(G-6857)*

Just-In Time Auto Dtailing LLC ... G ... 248 590-0085
Southfield *(G-15614)*

Lane Soft Water ... G ... 269 673-3272
Allegan *(G-169)*

Lions Pride Pressure Wshg LLC ... G ... 989 251-5577
Perry *(G-12978)*

Mar Cor Purification Inc ... E ... 248 373-7844
Lake Orion *(G-9616)*

McIntyres Soft Water Svc Ltd ... E ... 810 735-5778
Linden *(G-10065)*

Mdla Inc ... F ... 248 643-0807
Troy *(G-17242)*

Menominee City of Michigan ... G ... 906 863-3050
Menominee *(G-11247)*

Michigan Soft Water of Centr ... D ... 517 339-0722
East Lansing *(G-4903)*

Midwest Stainless Fabricating ... G ... 248 476-4502
Livonia *(G-10317)*

◆ Monroe Environmental Corp ... D ... 734 242-2420
Monroe *(G-11562)*

▲ Motor City Wash Works Inc ... E ... 248 313-0272
Wixom *(G-18715)*

MRM Ida Products Co Inc ... G ... 313 834-0200
Detroit *(G-4470)*

On Site Car Wash and Detail ... G ... 313 350-8357
Detroit *(G-4498)*

◆ Pacific Stamex Clg Systems Inc ... E ... 231 773-1330
Muskegon *(G-11892)*

▲ Plymouth Technology Inc ... F ... 248 537-0081
Rochester Hills *(G-14086)*

Power-Brite of Michigan Inc ... F ... 734 591-7911
Livonia *(G-10369)*

Priceless Dtils Auto Cncrge LL ... G ... 313 701-6851
Troy *(G-17314)*

Recovere LLC ... G ... 269 370-3165
Plainwell *(G-13092)*

▲ Reynolds Water Conditioning Co ... F ... 248 888-5000
Farmington Hills *(G-5368)*

Rich Mars Mobile Spa LLC ... G ... 734 210-2797
Redford *(G-13765)*

▲ Royal Accoutrements Inc ... G ... 517 347-7983
Okemos *(G-12683)*

Royce Rolls Ringer Company ... D ... 616 361-9266
Grand Rapids *(G-7173)*

▲ Sandbox Solutions Inc ... C ... 248 349-7010
Northville *(G-12257)*

Sebright Products Inc ... E ... 269 793-7183
Hopkins *(G-8369)*

Sebright Products Inc ... D ... 269 792-6229
Wayland *(G-18206)*

Servapure Company ... G ... 989 892-7745
Bay City *(G-1399)*

Shred-Pac Inc ... E ... 269 793-7978
Hopkins *(G-8370)*

Sludgehammer Group Ltd ... G ... 231 348-5866
Petoskey *(G-13025)*

▲ Solaronics Inc ... E ... 248 651-5333
Auburn Hills *(G-1035)*

Sparta Wash & Storage LLC ... G ... 616 887-1034
Sparta *(G-15779)*

▲ Spartan Tool LLC ... E ... 815 539-7411
Niles *(G-12169)*

Superior Washing and Pain ... G ... 616 293-5347
Lowell *(G-10518)*

Supply Pro ... G ... 810 239-8658
Flint *(G-5773)*

◆ Sweepster Attachments LLC ... A ... 734 996-9116
Dexter *(G-4757)*

Telespector Corporation ... E ... 248 373-5400
Auburn Hills *(G-1050)*

◆ Tennant Commercial ... D ... 616 994-4000
Holland *(G-8215)*

Tennant Company ... G ... 616 994-4000
Holland *(G-8216)*

Truly Free LLC ... E ... 231 252-4571
Traverse City *(G-16868)*

V & T Painting LLC ... G ... 248 497-1494
Farmington Hills *(G-5407)*

Vaclovers Inc ... F ... 616 246-1700
Grand Rapids *(G-7301)*

Vanaire Inc ... D ... 906 428-4656
Gladstone *(G-6187)*

Wayne County Laboratory ... G ... 734 285-5215
Wyandotte *(G-18843)*

Wesley Floor Care Company ... G ... 313 978-4539
Detroit *(G-4677)*

Wonder Makers Environmental ... F ... 269 382-4154
Kalamazoo *(G-9372)*

3592 Carburetors, Pistons, Rings & Valves

Aircraft Precision Pdts Inc ... D ... 989 875-4186
Ithaca *(G-8785)*

Alligator North America Inc ... G ... 248 914-0597
Wixom *(G-18605)*

Autocam Corp ... D ... 616 698-0707
Grand Rapids *(G-6481)*

▲ Autocam-Pax Inc ... C ... 269 782-5186
Dowagiac *(G-4776)*

British Carburetors LLC ... G ... 616 920-0203
Grand Rapids *(G-6526)*

Bucher Hydraulics Inc ... G ... 231 652-2773
Newaygo *(G-12078)*

Cal Grinding Inc ... E ... 906 786-8749
Escanaba *(G-5064)*

Ckd USA Corporation ... G ... 248 740-7004
Troy *(G-17013)*

Dexter Automatic Products Co ... C ... 734 426-8900
Dexter *(G-4734)*

▲ Federal Screw Works ... F ... 734 941-4211
Romulus *(G-14274)*

Federal Screw Works ... D ... 734 941-4211
Big Rapids *(G-1673)*

▲ Federal-Mogul Piston Rings Inc ... F ... 248 354-7700
Southfield *(G-15564)*

Federal-Mogul Valve Train Inte ... D ... 248 354-7700
Southfield *(G-15567)*

Flowcor LLC ... G ... 616 554-1100
Kentwood *(G-9454)*

General Motors LLC ... F ... 989 894-7210
Bay City *(G-1359)*

Geoffrey Manufacturing Inc ... G ... 734 479-4030
Brownstown Twp *(G-2154)*

▲ Hastings Manufacturing Company ... B ... 269 945-2491
Hastings *(G-7796)*

◆ Kaydon Corporation ... B ... 734 747-7025
Ann Arbor *(G-538)*

Kens Carburetor Service Inc ... G ... 517 627-1417
Grand Ledge *(G-6393)*

▲ L E Jones Company ... B ... 906 863-1043
Menominee *(G-11242)*

Mahle Eng Components USA Inc ... G ... 248 305-8200
Farmington Hills *(G-5302)*

Motor City Carburetor ... G ... 586 443-8048
Saint Clair Shores *(G-14873)*

Nelms Technologies Inc ... E ... 734 955-6500
Romulus *(G-14309)*

▲ Piston Modules LLC ... A ... 313 897-1540
Detroit *(G-4527)*

▲ Polyvalve LLC ... G ... 616 554-1100
Kentwood *(G-9472)*

Rotary Valve Systems LLC ... G ... 517 780-4002
Jackson *(G-8998)*

Tyde Group Worldwide LLC ... A ... 248 879-7656
Troy *(G-17408)*

Vortex Industries Inc ... F ... 855 867-8399
Plymouth *(G-13335)*

Walbro LLC ... D ... 989 872-2131
Cass City *(G-2622)*

3593 Fluid Power Cylinders & Actuators

◆ Ace Controls Inc ... C ... 248 476-0213
Farmington Hills *(G-5158)*

Acutex Inc ... C ... 231 894-3200
Whitehall *(G-18488)*

▲ Airman Products LLC ... E ... 248 960-1354
Brighton *(G-1942)*

◆ Beaver Aerospace & Defense Inc ... C ... 734 853-5003
Livonia *(G-10133)*

Behco Inc ... F ... 586 755-0200
Warren *(G-17729)*

▲ Best Metal Products Co Inc ... C ... 616 942-7141
Grand Rapids *(G-6502)*

Bucher Hydraulics Inc ... G ... 231 652-2773
Newaygo *(G-12078)*

Cpj Company Inc ... E ... 616 784-6355
Comstock Park *(G-3598)*

Crankshaft Machine Company ... E ... 517 787-3791
Jackson *(G-8856)*

◆ Dadco Inc ... D ... 734 207-1100
Plymouth *(G-13151)*

Dadco Inc ... G ... 616 785-2888
Comstock Park *(G-3601)*

▲ De-Sta-Co Cylinders Inc ... B ... 248 836-6700
Auburn Hills *(G-860)*

E J M Ball Screw LLC ... F ... 989 893-7674
Bay City *(G-1349)*

Eaton Corporation ... G ... 517 789-1148
Jackson *(G-8875)*

Ksb Dubric Inc ... E ... 616 784-6355
Comstock Park *(G-3618)*

Lor Manufacturing Co Inc ... G ... 989 644-2581
Weidman *(G-18254)*

▲ Nabtesco Motion Control Inc ... F ... 248 553-3020
Farmington Hills *(G-5329)*

Npi ... G ... 248 478-0010
Farmington Hills *(G-5336)*

Employee Codes: A=Over 500 employees, B=251-500
C=101-250, D=51-100, E=20-50, F=10-19, G=3-9

2022 Harris Michigan
Industrial Directory

859

Nu-ERA Holdings Inc........F....... 248 477-2288
Farmington Hills *(G-5337)*
Parker-Hannifin Corporation........G....... 330 253-5239
Otsego *(G-12797)*
Parker-Hannifin Corporation........B....... 269 629-5000
Richland *(G-13826)*
Parker-Hannifin Corporation........B....... 269 384-3459
Kalamazoo *(G-9288)*
Peninsular Inc........E....... 586 775-7211
Roseville *(G-14461)*
R M Wright Company Inc........E....... 248 476-9800
Farmington Hills *(G-5363)*
Superior Tool & Fabg LLC........G....... 906 353-7588
Keweenaw Bay *(G-9490)*
▲ Suspa Incorporated........C....... 616 241-4200
Grand Rapids *(G-7240)*
Tri-Tech Engineering Inc........E....... 734 283-3700
Wyandotte *(G-18842)*
▲ Yates Industries Inc........D....... 586 778-7680
Saint Clair Shores *(G-14892)*

3594 Fluid Power Pumps & Motors

◆ Ace Controls Inc........C....... 248 476-0213
Farmington Hills *(G-5158)*
Acutex Inc........C....... 231 894-3200
Whitehall *(G-18488)*
▲ Armstrong Fluid Handling Inc........D....... 269 279-3600
Three Rivers *(G-16565)*
▲ Bucher Hydraulics Inc........C....... 616 458-1306
Grand Rapids *(G-6528)*
Bucher Hydraulics Inc........G....... 231 652-2773
Newaygo *(G-12078)*
Dare Auto Inc........E....... 734 228-6243
Plymouth *(G-13152)*
▲ Ddks Industries LLC........G....... 586 323-5909
Shelby Township *(G-15201)*
Dover Pmps Prcess Sltons Sgmen........B....... 616 241-1611
Grand Rapids *(G-6657)*
Eaton Aeroquip LLC........B....... 949 452-9575
Jackson *(G-8873)*
Eaton Aerospace LLC........B....... 616 949-1090
Grand Rapids *(G-6663)*
Eaton Corporation........G....... 517 789-1148
Jackson *(G-8875)*
◆ Flint Hydrostatics Inc........F....... 901 794-2462
Chesterfield *(G-2883)*
Flow-Rite Controls Ltd........E....... 616 583-1700
Byron Center *(G-2270)*
◆ Gast Manufacturing Inc........B....... 269 926-6171
Benton Harbor *(G-1551)*
Great Lakes Hydra Corporation........F....... 231 258-4338
Kalkaska *(G-9389)*
Hydraulex Intl Holdings Inc........E....... 914 682-2700
Chesterfield *(G-2891)*
Hydro-Craft Inc........G....... 248 652-8100
Rochester Hills *(G-14037)*
▲ J H Bennett and Company Inc........E....... 248 596-5100
Novi *(G-12446)*
Jamco Manufacturing Inc........G....... 248 852-1988
Auburn Hills *(G-943)*
▲ Kawasaki Prcision McHy USA Inc........E....... 616 975-3100
Grand Rapids *(G-6879)*
Kennedy Industries Inc........D....... 248 684-1200
Wixom *(G-18691)*
Limo-Reid Inc........G....... 517 447-4164
Deerfield *(G-3957)*
Loftis Alumi-TEC Inc........G....... 616 846-1990
Grand Haven *(G-6330)*
▲ M P Pumps Inc........D....... 586 293-8240
Fraser *(G-5959)*
Matt and Dave LLC........F....... 734 439-1988
Dundee *(G-4831)*
Med-Kas Hydraulics Inc........F....... 248 585-3220
Troy *(G-17243)*
Metaris Hydraulics........G....... 586 949-4240
Chesterfield *(G-2912)*
Mfp Automation Engineering Inc........D....... 616 538-5700
Hudsonville *(G-8594)*
▲ Nabtesco Motion Control Inc........F....... 248 553-3020
Farmington Hills *(G-5329)*
Npi........G....... 248 478-0010
Farmington Hills *(G-5336)*
▲ Oilgear Company........D....... 231 929-1660
Traverse City *(G-16778)*
Parker HSD........F....... 269 384-3915
Kalamazoo *(G-9287)*
Parker-Hannifin Corporation........G....... 269 692-6254
Otsego *(G-12796)*
Parker-Hannifin Corporation........B....... 269 384-3459
Kalamazoo *(G-9288)*

▲ Piper Industries Inc........D....... 586 771-5100
Roseville *(G-14463)*
Prophotonix Limited........G....... 586 778-1100
Roseville *(G-14466)*
REO Hydraulic & Mfg Inc........F....... 313 891-2244
Detroit *(G-4566)*
Robert Bosch LLC........G....... 269 429-3221
Saint Joseph *(G-14957)*
Schrader Stoves of Michiana........E....... 269 684-4494
Niles *(G-12166)*
Truform Machine Inc........E....... 517 782-8523
Jackson *(G-9025)*
Usi Inc........F....... 248 583-9337
Madison Heights *(G-10854)*
Wmh Fluidpower Inc........F....... 269 327-7011
Portage *(G-13634)*
Wolverine Water Works Inc........G....... 248 673-4310
Waterford *(G-18176)*
▲ Yates Industries Inc........D....... 586 778-7680
Saint Clair Shores *(G-14892)*

3596 Scales & Balances, Exc Laboratory

Hanchett Manufacturing Inc........E....... 231 796-7678
Big Rapids *(G-1676)*
Heco Inc........E....... 269 381-7200
Kalamazoo *(G-9210)*
M2 Scientifics LLC........F....... 616 379-9080
Allendale *(G-224)*
Standard Scale & Supply Co........G....... 313 255-6700
Detroit *(G-4605)*
▼ Trucksforsalecom........G....... 989 883-3382
Sebewaing *(G-15145)*

3599 Machinery & Eqpt, Indl & Commercial, NEC

▲ 175 North Green Creek Inc........G....... 231 766-2155
Muskegon *(G-11758)*
2 E Fabricating........G....... 616 498-7036
Marne *(G-10988)*
4 Flutes Machining LLC........G....... 269 330-1313
Vicksburg *(G-17597)*
4-M Industries Incorporated........F....... 734 762-7200
Livonia *(G-10090)*
4-M Industries Incorporated........D....... 734 762-7200
Livonia *(G-10091)*
A & M Industries Inc........F....... 586 791-5610
Clinton Township *(G-3144)*
A C Machining LLC........G....... 616 455-3870
Grand Rapids *(G-6409)*
A S A P Machine Company........G....... 734 459-2447
Canton *(G-2426)*
A&E Machine & Fabrication Inc........G....... 740 820-4701
Whitmore Lake *(G-18516)*
AA EDM Corporation........F....... 734 253-2784
Dexter *(G-4719)*
ABC Grinding Inc........G....... 313 295-1060
Dearborn Heights *(G-3918)*
ABC Machining & Fabricating........F....... 586 758-0680
Warren *(G-17687)*
ABC-2100 Inc........E....... 616 647-9200
Comstock Park *(G-3585)*
Ability Mfg & Engrg Co........D....... 269 227-3292
Fennville *(G-5433)*
Able Manufacturing Inc........E....... 616 235-3322
Grand Rapids *(G-6417)*
Abrasive Diamond Tool Company........E....... 248 588-4800
Madison Heights *(G-10657)*
Absolute Machine LLC........G....... 517 745-5905
Jackson *(G-8799)*
Acal Universal Grinding Co........E....... 586 296-3900
Roseville *(G-14368)*
Accelerated Tooling LLC........F....... 616 293-9612
Grand Rapids *(G-6418)*
Accu Tech Michigan........G....... 616 953-0256
Holland *(G-7954)*
Accu-Tech Manufacturing Inc........E....... 586 532-4000
Shelby Township *(G-15162)*
Accurate Engineering & Mfg LLC........F....... 616 738-1261
Holland *(G-7955)*
Accurate Gauge & Mfg Inc........D....... 248 853-2400
Rochester Hills *(G-13940)*
Accurate Machine & Tl USA Ltd........G....... 269 205-2610
Middleville *(G-11301)*
Accurate Machining & Fabg Inc........G....... 989 426-5400
Gladwin *(G-6188)*
Accuworx LLC........E....... 734 847-6115
Temperance *(G-16525)*
Ace Tool & Engineering Inc........G....... 616 361-4800
Belding *(G-1434)*

Acme Gear Company Inc........E....... 586 465-7740
Clinton Township *(G-3154)*
Acro-Tech Manufacturing Inc........F....... 269 629-4300
Plainwell *(G-13069)*
Action Tool & Machine Inc........E....... 810 229-6300
Brighton *(G-1938)*
▲ Active Manufacturing Corp........E....... 616 842-0800
Spring Lake *(G-15801)*
Acubar Inc........G....... 269 927-3000
Benton Harbor *(G-1526)*
Acute Fixture & Tooling Inc........G....... 586 323-4132
Shelby Township *(G-15166)*
Adept Broaching Co........G....... 734 427-9221
Plymouth *(G-13113)*
Advance Cnc Machine Inc........G....... 269 751-7005
Hamilton *(G-7594)*
Advance Machine Corp........G....... 989 362-9192
Tawas City *(G-16364)*
Advance Precision Grinding Co........G....... 586 773-1330
Roseville *(G-14369)*
Advance Turning and Mfg Inc........D....... 517 750-3580
Jackson *(G-8803)*
Advance Turning and Mfg Inc........C....... 517 783-2713
Jackson *(G-8802)*
Advanced Automotive Group LLC........F....... 586 206-2478
Clay *(G-3113)*
Advanced Boring and Tool Co........D....... 586 598-9300
Troy *(G-16907)*
Advanced Cnc Machining LLC........G....... 616 226-6706
Grandville *(G-7363)*
Advanced Industries Inc........E....... 734 433-1800
Chelsea *(G-2802)*
▲ Ae Group LLC........C....... 734 942-0615
Romulus *(G-14246)*
Aero Grinding Inc........G....... 586 774-6450
Roseville *(G-14372)*
Aero Grinding Inc........D....... 586 774-6450
Roseville *(G-14371)*
Aertech Machining & Mfg Inc........E....... 517 782-4644
Jackson *(G-8804)*
Ai Machine Shop........G....... 615 855-1217
East Lansing *(G-4885)*
◆ Air Way Automation Inc........E....... 989 348-1802
Grayling *(G-7455)*
Airmetal Corporation........F....... 517 784-6000
Jackson *(G-8807)*
Alco Products........G....... 715 346-3174
Swartz Creek *(G-16349)*
Alcona Tool & Machine Inc........E....... 989 736-8151
Harrisville *(G-7741)*
All Metal Designs Inc........G....... 616 392-3696
Holland *(G-7960)*
All-Tech Inc........E....... 616 406-0681
Wyoming *(G-18851)*
Allen Pattern of Michigan........F....... 269 963-4131
Battle Creek *(G-1184)*
Alliance Cnc LLC........F....... 616 971-4700
Grand Rapids *(G-6448)*
Allied Chucker and Engrg Co........C....... 517 787-1370
Jackson *(G-8810)*
Allied Chucker and Engrg Co........D....... 517 787-1370
Jackson *(G-8811)*
Allied Machine & Tool Inc........F....... 269 623-7295
Delton *(G-3961)*
Allied Machine Inc........F....... 231 834-0050
Grant *(G-7425)*
Allmet Industries Inc........G....... 248 280-4600
Royal Oak *(G-14505)*
Alloy Industries Corporation........G....... 734 433-1112
Chelsea *(G-2805)*
Allynn Corp........G....... 269 383-1199
Kalamazoo *(G-9110)*
Alro Riverside LLC........G....... 517 782-8322
Jackson *(G-8813)*
American Grinding and Mac........F....... 517 467-5399
Onsted *(G-12704)*
American Grinding Machining Co........F....... 313 388-0440
Lincoln Park *(G-10043)*
American Mfg Innovators Inc........F....... 248 669-5990
Commerce Township *(G-3510)*
American Thermoforming Mch LLC........E....... 989 345-0935
West Branch *(G-18324)*
▲ Amphenol Borisch Tech Inc........C....... 616 554-9820
Grand Rapids *(G-6458)*
Amsco Champion LLC........G....... 734 728-8500
Romulus *(G-14249)*
Anderson Welding & Mfg Inc........F....... 906 523-4661
Houghton *(G-8380)*
▲ Anderson-Cook Inc........D....... 586 954-0700
Chesterfield *(G-2844)*

SIC SECTION35 INDUSTRIAL AND COMMERCIAL MACHINERY AND COMPUTER EQUIPMENT35 INDUSTRIAL AND COMMERCIAL MACHINERY

Anderson-Cook Inc G 586 293-0800
Fraser *(G-5895)*
Anderton Machining LLC G 517 905-5155
Jackson *(G-8816)*
Ansco Pattern & Machine Co G 248 625-1362
Clarkston *(G-3017)*
Antrim Machine Products Inc E 231 587-9114
Mancelona *(G-10866)*
Apollo Machining Inc G 248 961-3943
Auburn Hills *(G-792)*
Aqua Tool LLC F 248 307-1984
Madison Heights *(G-10671)*
Arch Precision Components D 866 935-5771
Bloomfield Hills *(G-1801)*
Arete Products & Mfg LLC G 269 383-0015
Kalamazoo *(G-9119)*
Arizona Tooling Inc G 810 533-8828
Columbus *(G-3496)*
ARL Service LLC G 248 625-6160
Davisburg *(G-3757)*
Arnold Tool & Die Co E 586 598-0099
Chesterfield *(G-2846)*
Art Laser Inc E 248 391-6600
Auburn Hills *(G-798)*
Ase Industries Inc D 586 754-7480
Warren *(G-17718)*
Ash Industries Inc E 269 672-9630
Martin *(G-11079)*
Assembly Concepts Inc F 989 685-2603
Rose City *(G-14361)*
Atd Engineering and Mch LLC E 989 876-7161
Au Gres *(G-755)*
▲ Ats Assembly and Test Inc C 937 222-3030
Wixom *(G-18611)*
Auto Builders Inc E 586 948-3780
Chesterfield *(G-2849)*
Autocam Corp D 616 698-0707
Grand Rapids *(G-6481)*
Autocam Corporation G 616 698-0707
Kentwood *(G-9445)*
Automate Industries Inc G 248 740-7022
Troy *(G-16965)*
Automated Indus Motion Inc G 231 865-1800
Fruitport *(G-6059)*
Automated Prod Assemblies E 586 293-3990
Fraser *(G-5899)*
Automated Techniques LLC G 810 346-4670
Brown City *(G-2134)*
Automation Specialists Inc F 616 738-8288
Holland *(G-7967)*
Autosport Development LLC G 734 675-1620
Trenton *(G-16886)*
Avid Industries Inc G 810 672-9100
Argyle *(G-728)*
▲ Avon Broach & Prod Co LLC E 248 650-8080
Rochester Hills *(G-13958)*
Awd Associates Inc F 248 922-9898
Davisburg *(G-3759)*
Axis Machining Inc E 989 453-3943
Pigeon *(G-13035)*
▲ Azon Usa Inc F 269 385-5942
Kalamazoo *(G-9129)*
Azon Usa Inc G 269 385-5942
Kalamazoo *(G-9130)*
◆ Aztec Manufacturing Corp C 734 942-7433
Romulus *(G-14253)*
B & B Custom and Prod Wldg F 517 524-7121
Spring Arbor *(G-15789)*
B & B Production LLC G 586 822-9960
Detroit *(G-4038)*
B & J Tool Co F 810 629-8577
Fenton *(G-5454)*
B & K Machine Products Inc F 269 637-3001
South Haven *(G-15401)*
B & M Machine & Tool Company G 989 288-2934
Durand *(G-4839)*
B & R Gear Company Inc F 517 787-8381
Jackson *(G-8819)*
B G Industries Inc F 313 292-5355
Taylor *(G-16386)*
B-J Industries Inc G 586 778-7200
Warren *(G-17724)*
Baade Fabricating & Engrg G 517 639-4536
Quincy *(G-13663)*
Back Machine Shop LLC G 269 963-7061
Springfield *(G-15860)*
Barron Group Inc D 248 628-4300
Oxford *(G-12875)*
Baxter Machine & Tool Co E 517 782-2808
Jackson *(G-8822)*

▼ Bay Cast Technologies Inc E 989 892-9500
Bay City *(G-1327)*
Bay City Crane Inc G 989 867-4292
Turner *(G-17462)*
Bay Design Inc E 586 296-7130
Fraser *(G-5901)*
Bay Machine Tool Co Inc F 989 894-2863
Essexville *(G-5111)*
Bay Machining and Sales Inc F 989 316-1801
Bay City *(G-1329)*
Bay Tool Inc G 989 894-2863
Essexville *(G-5112)*
BCT-2017 Inc E 231 832-3114
Reed City *(G-13789)*
Beck Industries Inc G 586 790-4060
Clinton Township *(G-3180)*
Beckan Industries Inc E 269 381-6984
Kalamazoo *(G-9132)*
Bedford Machinery Inc G 734 848-4980
Erie *(G-5045)*
Belding Tool Acquisition LLC F 586 816-4450
Belding *(G-1440)*
Bell Engineering Inc F 989 753-3127
Saginaw *(G-14613)*
Bell Engineering LLC G 989 753-3127
Saginaw *(G-14614)*
Bentley Mfg LLC G 810 621-3616
Lennon *(G-9992)*
Benton Chassix Harbor G 248 728-8700
Benton Harbor *(G-1534)*
Benzie Manufacturing LLC G 231 631-0498
Frankfort *(G-5875)*
▼ Bermont Gage & Automation Inc E 586 296-1103
Fraser *(G-5903)*
▲ Best Metal Products Co Inc C 616 942-7141
Grand Rapids *(G-6502)*
Bischoff Enterprises LLC G 734 856-8490
Ottawa Lake *(G-12804)*
Blackledge Tool Inc G 989 865-8393
Saint Charles *(G-14801)*
Blain Machining Inc G 616 877-0426
Wayland *(G-18191)*
Blevins Screw Products Inc E 810 744-1820
Flint *(G-5657)*
▲ Blissfield Manufacturing Co C 517 486-2121
Blissfield *(G-1761)*
Blue Water Boring LLC G 586 421-2100
Macomb *(G-10581)*
Bond Bailey and Smith Company G 313 496-0177
Detroit *(G-4061)*
Boomerang Amusements F 586 323-3327
Shelby Township *(G-15178)*
Boos Products Inc F 734 498-2207
Gregory *(G-7513)*
Borneman & Peterson Inc F 810 744-1890
Flint *(G-5659)*
BOS Field Machining Inc G 517 204-1688
Houghton Lake *(G-8394)*
Boxer Equipment/Morbark Inc G 989 866-2381
Winn *(G-18589)*
Boyne Machine Company Inc F 616 669-7178
Jenison *(G-9047)*
Bradhart Products Inc E 248 437-3746
Brighton *(G-1952)*
Break Mold LLC G 269 359-0822
Portage *(G-13549)*
Breco LLC F 517 317-2211
Quincy *(G-13664)*
▼ Breesport Holdings Inc C 248 685-9500
Milford *(G-11456)*
Brembo North America Inc G 517 568-3301
Homer *(G-8347)*
Brembo North America Homer Inc E 517 568-4398
Homer *(G-8348)*
Bridgeport Manufacturing Inc G 989 777-4314
Bridgeport *(G-1915)*
Bron Machine Inc F 616 392-5320
Holland *(G-7984)*
Brown Jig Grinding Co F 248 349-7744
Wixom *(G-18626)*
Buck-N-Ham Machines Inc G 231 587-5322
Mancelona *(G-10867)*
Buffoli North America Corp F 616 610-4362
Holland *(G-7985)*
▼ Burrow Industries Inc E 734 847-1842
Temperance *(G-16529)*
Byrne Tool & Die Inc E 616 866-4479
Rockford *(G-14161)*
C & C Machine Tool Inc G 248 693-3347
Lake Orion *(G-9592)*

C & N Manufacturing Inc E 586 293-9150
Fraser *(G-5908)*
C & S Automated Systems LLC G 586 265-1416
Fraser *(G-5909)*
C & S Machine Products Inc E 269 695-6859
Niles *(G-12117)*
C & S Machine Products Inc G 269 695-6859
Buchanan *(G-2191)*
C D Tool and Gage G 616 682-1111
Grand Rapids *(G-6542)*
C E S Industries Inc F 734 425-0522
Livonia *(G-10143)*
C L Design Inc G 248 474-4220
Farmington Hills *(G-5190)*
C S M Manufacturing Corp D 248 471-0700
Farmington Hills *(G-5192)*
C T Machining Inc G 586 772-0320
Saint Clair Shores *(G-14852)*
C W Industries G 586 465-4157
Chesterfield *(G-2855)*
Cambria Tool and Machine Inc F 517 437-3500
Hillsdale *(G-7928)*
Cannon Machine Inc G 616 363-4014
Grand Rapids *(G-6546)*
Car Quest Machine Shop G 989 686-3111
Bay City *(G-1335)*
Carbon Tool & Manufacturing E 734 422-0380
Livonia *(G-10146)*
Carmac Tool LLC G 586 649-7245
Clinton Township *(G-3195)*
▼ Casemer Tool & Machine Inc E 248 628-4807
Oxford *(G-12880)*
CDK Enterprises LLC E 586 296-9300
Fraser *(G-5912)*
CDM Machine Co G 313 538-9100
Southfield *(G-15518)*
Celano Precision Mfg Inc G 734 748-1744
Livonia *(G-10150)*
Centech Inc F 517 546-9185
Howell *(G-8436)*
Center Machine & Tool LLC G 517 748-2500
Michigan Center *(G-11291)*
Central Gear Inc E 800 589-1602
Madison Heights *(G-10685)*
Centurn Machine & Tool Inc G 231 947-4773
Cedar *(G-2637)*
Champion Fortune Corporation F 989 422-6130
Houghton Lake *(G-8395)*
Chelsea Grinding Company E 517 796-0343
Royal Oak *(G-14526)*
Chelsea Tool Inc G 734 475-9679
Chelsea *(G-2807)*
Chesterfield Engines Inc G 586 949-5777
Chesterfield *(G-2859)*
Choice Corporation E 586 783-5600
Clinton Township *(G-3199)*
▲ Choice Mold Components Inc E 586 783-5600
Clinton Township *(G-3200)*
Chronotech Swiss LLC G 818 415-5039
West Bloomfield *(G-18271)*
Clair Sawyer G 906 228-8242
Marquette *(G-11013)*
Clark Manufacturing Company D 231 946-5110
Traverse City *(G-16653)*
Clarklake Machine Incorporated E 517 529-9454
Clarklake *(G-3003)*
Clarkston Carbide Tool & Mch G 248 625-3182
Ortonville *(G-12745)*
Classic Metal Finishing Inc E 517 990-0011
Jackson *(G-8842)*
Classic Tool & Boring Inc G 586 795-8967
Sterling Heights *(G-15961)*
Classic Turning Inc D 517 764-1335
Jackson *(G-8843)*
Cleary Developments Inc F 248 588-6614
Madison Heights *(G-10690)*
▲ Cleary Developments Inc E 248 588-7011
Madison Heights *(G-10689)*
▲ Clipper Belt Lacer Company D 616 459-3196
Grand Rapids *(G-6574)*
Cnc Prototype of Michigan G 586 218-3291
Troy *(G-17016)*
Cnc Tooling Solutions LLC G 248 890-5625
Ferndale *(G-5534)*
Cobalt Friction Tech LLC G 734 930-6902
Ann Arbor *(G-429)*
Cobra Enterprises Inc F 248 588-2669
Madison Heights *(G-10693)*
Cochran Corporation E 517 857-2211
Springport *(G-15879)*

SIC

Employee Codes: A=Over 500 employees, B=251-500
C=101-250, D=51-100, E=20-50, F=10-19, G=3-9
2022 Harris Michigan
Industrial Directory
861

35 INDUSTRIAL AND COMMERCIAL MACHINERY AND COMPUTER EQUIPMENT

Codo Machine & Tool Inc ....G 517 789-5113
 Jackson (G-8846)
Cogsdill Tool Products Inc ....G 734 744-4500
 Livonia (G-10160)
Coldwater Sintered Met Pdts Inc ....E 517 278-8750
 Coldwater (G-3428)
Cole Tooling Systems Inc ....G 586 558-9450
 Sterling Heights (G-15964)
▲ Coleman Machine Inc ....E 906 863-1113
 Menominee (G-11229)
Coles Machine Service Inc ....E 810 658-5373
 Davison (G-3777)
Colt - 7 Corporation ....G 586 792-9050
 Clinton Township (G-3205)
▲ Commercial Tool & Die Inc ....C 616 785-8100
 Comstock Park (G-3596)
Competitive Edge Designs Inc ....G 616 257-0565
 Grand Rapids (G-6586)
Complex Tool & Machine Inc ....G 248 625-0664
 Clarkston (G-3028)
Component Engrg Solutions LLC .....E 616 514-1343
 Grand Rapids (G-6588)
Computer Operated Mfg ....E 989 686-1333
 Bay City (G-1340)
Concentric Industries Inc ....G 734 848-5133
 Erie (G-5046)
Conner Engineering LLC ....E 586 465-9590
 Clinton Township (G-3209)
▲ Conrad Machine Company ....F 231 893-7455
 Whitehall (G-18492)
Consolidated Metal Pdts Inc ....G 616 538-1000
 Grand Rapids (G-6596)
Continental Midland LLC ....G 734 367-7032
 Livonia (G-10162)
Contour Machining Inc ....F 734 525-4877
 Livonia (G-10163)
Contour Tool and Machine Inc ....G 517 787-6806
 Jackson (G-8853)
Controlled Turning Inc ....G 517 782-0517
 Jackson (G-8854)
Cook Industries Inc ....G 586 754-4070
 Warren (G-17764)
Cox Machine LLC ....F 269 953-5446
 Traverse City (G-16662)
CP Acquisition LLC ....E 248 349-8811
 Wixom (G-18638)
Craft Precision Inc ....E 269 679-5121
 Schoolcraft (G-15117)
Crandall Precision Inc ....G 231 775-7101
 Cadillac (G-2327)
Crankshaft Craftsman Inc ....G 313 366-0140
 Commerce Township (G-3519)
Creative Machine Company ....E 248 669-4230
 Wixom (G-18641)
Creative Machining Inc ....G 616 772-2328
 Wyoming (G-18862)
Cross Paths Corp ....G 616 248-5371
 Grand Rapids (G-6613)
Ctmi Group Inc ....E 248 542-1615
 Madison Heights (G-10700)
Custom Design Components Inc .....E 231 937-6166
 Howard City (G-8408)
Custom Machining By Farley ....G 616 896-8469
 Hudsonville (G-8576)
Custom Marine and Mch Servic ......G 989 732-5455
 Gaylord (G-6125)
Custom Molds ....F 574 326-7576
 Sturgis (G-16286)
Customer Metal Fabrication Inc ......E 906 774-3216
 Iron Mountain (G-8721)
Cut All Water Jet Cutting Inc ....G 734 946-7880
 Taylor (G-16398)
Cut-Rite EDM Services LLC ....F 586 566-0100
 Shelby Township (G-15200)
D & D Tool Inc ....G 616 772-2416
 Zeeland (G-19013)
D & J Mfg & Machining ....G 231 830-9522
 Muskegon (G-11798)
D & J Precision Machine Svcs ....G 269 673-4010
 Allegan (G-153)
D L R Manufacturing Inc ....G 734 394-0690
 Van Buren Twp (G-17522)
▲ D M C International Inc ....G 586 465-1112
 Harrison Township (G-7695)
D-N-S Industries Inc ....E 586 465-2444
 Clinton Township (G-3216)
▲ Dalton Industries LLC ....E 248 673-0755
 Waterford (G-18114)
Damar Machinery Co ....F 616 453-4655
 Grand Rapids (G-6631)

Damick Enterprises ....F 248 652-7500
 Rochester Hills (G-13989)
Daniel Pruitoff ....G 616 392-1371
 Holland (G-8013)
Darrell R Hanson ....G 810 364-7892
 Marysville (G-11085)
▲ Dart Machinery Ltd ....D 248 362-1188
 Warren (G-17775)
Das Group Inc ....F 248 670-2718
 Royal Oak (G-14529)
DAS Technologies Inc ....G 269 657-0541
 Paw Paw (G-12945)
Datum Precision Machine Inc ....G 586 790-1120
 Clinton Township (G-3217)
DD Parker Enterprises Inc ....G 734 241-6898
 Monroe (G-11536)
▲ Ddks Industries LLC ....G 586 323-5909
 Shelby Township (G-15201)
Decker Gear Inc ....G 810 388-1500
 Saint Clair (G-14825)
Deco Engineering Inc ....G 989 761-7521
 Clifford (G-3131)
Defense Component Detroit LLC ...E 248 393-2300
 Auburn Hills (G-861)
Defense Components America LLC ..G 248 789-1578
 Farmington Hills (G-5211)
Deford Engine ....G 989 872-3640
 Deford (G-3960)
Deland Manufacturing Inc ....E 586 323-2350
 Shelby Township (G-15202)
▲ Delta Machining Inc ....D 269 683-7775
 Niles (G-12125)
Demmak Industries LLC ....F 586 884-6441
 Washington (G-18079)
Deshler Group Inc ....C 734 525-9100
 Livonia (G-10181)
Desrochers Brothers Inc ....F 906 353-6346
 Baraga (G-1138)
Detail Technologies LLC ....E 616 261-1313
 Wyoming (G-18866)
Detroit Diameters Inc ....G 248 669-2330
 Novi (G-12394)
▲ Detroit Edge Tool Company ....D 313 366-4120
 Detroit (G-4146)
Detroit Edge Tool Company ....D 586 776-1598
 Roseville (G-14398)
Dexter Manufacturing Inc ....G 734 475-8046
 Chelsea (G-2810)
Diamond Racing Products ....F 586 792-6620
 Clinton Township (G-3222)
Diamond Racing Products Inc ....F 586 792-6620
 Clinton Township (G-3223)
Diamond Tool Manufacturing ....F 616 895-4007
 Hudsonville (G-8580)
Die Cad Group ....G 937 243-8327
 Byron Center (G-2266)
Digitrace Machine Works Ltd ....E 616 877-4818
 Wayland (G-18194)
Dimension Machine Tech LLC ....F 586 649-4747
 Bloomfield Hills (G-1814)
Distinctive Machine Corp ....G 616 433-4111
 Rockford (G-14165)
Diversified E D M Inc ....G 248 547-2320
 Madison Heights (G-10707)
Diversified Tool & Engineering ....F 734 692-1260
 Grosse Ile (G-7519)
Djc Products Inc ....G 586 992-1352
 Shelby Township (G-15209)
DMS Electric Apparatus Service ....G 269 349-7000
 Kalamazoo (G-9171)
Dobday Manufacturing Co Inc ....F 586 254-6777
 Sterling Heights (G-15990)
Double Eagle Defense LLC ....G 313 562-5550
 Dearborn (G-3830)
Douglas King Industries Inc ....G 989 642-2865
 Hemlock (G-7851)
▲ Dowding Industries Inc ....E 517 663-5455
 Eaton Rapids (G-4959)
▼ Draco Mfg Inc ....F 248 585-0320
 Troy (G-17068)
Driven Fabrication ....G 248 491-4940
 New Hudson (G-12052)
Dubois Production Services Inc .....F 616 785-0088
 Comstock Park (G-3604)
▼ Duggan Manufacturing LLC ....C 586 254-7400
 Shelby Township (G-15212)
▲ Dun-Rite Machine Co ....G 616 688-5266
 Zeeland (G-19016)
Dura Hog Inc ....G 586 825-0066
 Sterling Heights (G-15993)

Dusevoir Acquisitions LLC ....F 313 562-5550
 Howell (G-8451)
Dyna Sales & Service LLC ....G 231 734-4433
 Millington (G-11499)
Dynamic Jig Grinding Corp ....E 248 589-3110
 Troy (G-17072)
Dynamite Machining Inc ....F 586 247-8230
 Shelby Township (G-15216)
E & C Manufacturing LLC ....F 248 330-0400
 Troy (G-17075)
▼ E & D Engineering Systems LLC ..G 989 246-0770
 Gladwin (G-6195)
E D M Shuttle Inc ....G 586 468-9880
 Clinton Township (G-3227)
E R Tool Company Inc ....G 586 757-1159
 Warren (G-17790)
Eagle Machine Products Company .G 586 268-2460
 Sterling Heights (G-15997)
Eagle T M C Technologies ....F 231 766-3914
 Muskegon (G-11804)
Eca Enterprises LLC ....G 313 828-4098
 Inkster (G-8663)
Echo Quality Grinding Inc ....F 231 544-6637
 Central Lake (G-2694)
EDM Wire Tek ....G 810 235-5344
 Flint (G-5694)
Edmore Tool & Grinding Inc ....F 989 427-3790
 Edmore (G-4992)
Edstrom Prototype LLC ....G 616 566-4361
 Holland (G-8024)
Efesto LLC ....G 734 913-0428
 Superior Township (G-16336)
Eidemller Prcsion McHining Inc .....E 248 669-2660
 Milford (G-11463)
Eikos Holdings Inc ....E 248 280-0300
 Troy (G-17073)
Eiler Brothers Inc ....F 517 784-0970
 Jackson (G-8877)
Elite Machining LLC ....G 517 784-0986
 Jackson (G-8879)
Elkins Machine & Tool Co Inc ....E 734 941-0266
 Romulus (G-14271)
Elucidation Fabrication ....G 586 612-4601
 Port Huron (G-13475)
EMD Wire Tek ....G 810 235-5344
 Flint (G-5695)
Emerald Tool Inc ....G 231 799-9193
 Norton Shores (G-12291)
Emma Sogoian Inc ....E 248 549-8690
 Royal Oak (G-14533)
Empire Tool Co ....G 734 283-8600
 Wyandotte (G-18819)
Engineered Concepts Inc ....F 574 333-9110
 Cassopolis (G-2627)
◆ Engineered Machined Pdts Inc .....B 906 786-8404
 Escanaba (G-5069)
Engineered Resources Inc ....G 248 399-5500
 Oak Park (G-12611)
Enkon LLC ....E 937 890-5678
 Manchester (G-10883)
Enprotech Industrial Tech LLC ....E 216 883-3220
 Lansing (G-9695)
Envision Machine and Mfg LLC ......G 616 953-8580
 Holland (G-8029)
Epic Equipment & Engrg Inc ....D 586 314-0020
 Shelby Township (G-15223)
Epic Machine Inc ....E 810 629-9400
 Fenton (G-5473)
Epoch Robotics ....F 616 820-3369
 Holland (G-8030)
Eptech Inc ....G 586 254-2722
 Macomb (G-10591)
Equivalent Base Co ....E 586 759-2030
 Warren (G-17795)
Ervott Tool Co LLC ....G 616 842-3688
 Grand Haven (G-6298)
Esco Group Inc ....F 616 453-5458
 Grand Rapids (G-6685)
Esys Automation LLC ....C 248 484-9927
 Auburn Hills (G-881)
Esys Automation LLC ....E 284 484-9724
 Pontiac (G-13370)
Esys Automation LLC ....E 248 484-9702
 Sterling Heights (G-16005)
▲ Euclid Industries Inc ....C 989 686-8920
 Bay City (G-1352)
Euclid Machine & Mfg Co ....E 734 941-1080
 Romulus (G-14273)
Eversharp Tools Inc ....G 810 824-3323
 Ira (G-8696)

2022 Harris Michigan Industrial Directory

SIC SECTION35 INDUSTRIAL AND COMMERCIAL MACHINERY AND COMPUTER EQUIPMENT35 INDUSTRIAL AND COMMERCIAL MACHINERY

Excel Machinery Intl Corp G 810 348-9162
Davisburg ***(G-3766)***
Excell Manufacturing Inc G 989 496-0473
Bay City ***(G-1354)***
Experienced Concepts Inc F 586 752-4200
Armada ***(G-735)***
Expernced Prcsion McHining Inc G 989 635-2299
Marlette ***(G-10981)***
Express Cnc & Fabrication LLC G 517 937-8760
Jonesville ***(G-9087)***
Extreme Machine Inc G 810 231-0521
Whitmore Lake ***(G-18534)***
Extreme Machine Inc G 810 231-0521
Whitmore Lake ***(G-18535)***
Extreme Machine Inc D 810 231-0521
Whitmore Lake ***(G-18536)***
Extreme Precision Screw Pdts E 810 744-1980
Flint ***(G-5698)***
Extrusion Punch & Tool Company E 248 689-3300
Rochester Hills ***(G-14007)***
F & G Tool Company G 734 261-0022
Livonia ***(G-10202)***
F & H Manufacturing Co Inc E 517 783-2311
Jackson ***(G-8881)***
F J Manufacturing Co E 248 583-4777
Madison Heights ***(G-10725)***
F2 Industries LLC G 616 610-0894
Zeeland ***(G-19020)***
Fabx Industries Inc F 616 225-1724
Greenville ***(G-7484)***
Falcon Consulting Services LLC G 989 262-9325
Alpena ***(G-293)***
Family Machinists G 734 340-1848
Redford ***(G-13732)***
Far Associates Inc G 734 282-1881
Riverview ***(G-13872)***
Fega Tool & Gage Company F 586 469-4400
Clinton Township ***(G-3236)***
Fenton Radiator & Garage Inc G 810 629-0923
Fenton ***(G-5478)***
Ferris Wheel Innovation Center G 810 213-4720
Flint ***(G-5700)***
Fischell Machinery LLC G 517 445-2828
Clayton ***(G-3129)***
Fitz Manufacturing Inc F 248 589-1780
Troy ***(G-17112)***
Fjr Industrial Sales Inc F 616 427-3776
Kentwood ***(G-9453)***
Fleetwood Tool & Gage Inc F 734 326-6737
Westland ***(G-18370)***
Flex Manufacturing Inc F 586 469-1076
Clinton Township ***(G-3241)***
Flex Slotter Inc G 586 756-6444
Warren ***(G-17808)***
▲ **Flexfab Horizons Intl Inc** E 269 945-4700
Hastings ***(G-7791)***
Florida Machine & Casting Co G 561 655-3771
Boyne City ***(G-1888)***
Forge Precision Company E 248 477-0020
Farmington Hills ***(G-5246)***
▲ **Form G Tech Co** D 248 583-3610
Troy ***(G-17118)***
Franks Products G 269 350-7366
Cassopolis ***(G-2628)***
Fraser Fab and Machine Inc E 248 852-9050
Rochester Hills ***(G-14015)***
Fraser Grinding Co F 586 293-6060
Fraser ***(G-5930)***
Free State Boring Inc G 248 821-8860
Waterford ***(G-18124)***
Friction Coating Corporation E 586 731-0990
Clinton Township ***(G-3245)***
Frostys Ice Cream Machine Retn G 616 886-1418
Holland ***(G-8042)***
Fusion Mfg Solutions LLC F 734 224-7216
Temperance ***(G-16532)***
Future Mill Inc G 586 754-8088
Warren ***(G-17820)***
Future Tool and Machine Inc E 734 946-2100
Romulus ***(G-14277)***
G & G Metal Products Inc G 248 625-8099
Clarkston ***(G-3036)***
G & R Machine Tool Inc G 734 641-6560
Taylor ***(G-16420)***
G P Manufacturing Inc G 269 695-1202
Buchanan ***(G-2194)***
Gage Rite Products Inc F 248 588-7796
Troy ***(G-17125)***
Gaishin Manufacturing Inc E 269 934-9340
Benton Harbor ***(G-1550)***

Garden City Products Inc E 269 684-6264
Niles ***(G-12133)***
Gaylord Mch & Fabrication LLC F 989 732-0817
Gaylord ***(G-6130)***
Gc Boring Inc G 313 937-2320
Redford ***(G-13736)***
Gehring Honing Machs D 248 478-8061
Farmington Hills ***(G-5251)***
Geiger EDM Inc F 517 369-9752
Bronson ***(G-2113)***
▲ **Geisler Company** F 313 255-1450
Livonia ***(G-10221)***
Gem Industries Inc E 616 656-9779
Caledonia ***(G-2374)***
General Broach & Engrg Inc C 586 726-4300
Troy ***(G-17129)***
General Machine & Boring Inc G 810 220-1203
Brighton ***(G-1999)***
General Machine Service Inc E 989 752-5161
Saginaw ***(G-14649)***
▲ **General Machine Services** G 269 695-2244
Buchanan ***(G-2196)***
General Parts Inc G 989 686-3114
Bay City ***(G-1360)***
General Processing Systems Inc F 630 554-7804
Holland ***(G-8046)***
General Technology Inc F 269 751-7516
Holland ***(G-8047)***
Generl-Lctrical-Mechanical Inc G 248 698-1110
White Lake ***(G-18456)***
Genix LLC F 248 419-0231
Sterling Heights ***(G-16029)***
Gentle Machine Tool & Die G 734 699-2013
Van Buren Twp ***(G-17527)***
Geolean USA LLC F 313 859-9780
Livonia ***(G-10222)***
▲ **Gil-Mar Manufacturing Co** D 248 640-4303
Canton ***(G-2463)***
Gil-Mar Manufacturing Co G 734 422-1925
Livonia ***(G-10223)***
Gil-Mar Manufacturing Co G 734 459-4803
Canton ***(G-2464)***
◆ **Gillisons Var Fabrication Inc** E 231 882-5921
Benzonia ***(G-1614)***
Gladwin Machine Inc G 989 426-8753
Gladwin ***(G-6197)***
Gosen Tool & Machine Inc F 989 777-6493
Saginaw ***(G-14656)***
Grand Rapids Custom Tooling G 616 836-0274
Zeeland ***(G-19031)***
Grand Rapids Machine Repair G 616 248-4760
Grand Rapids ***(G-6763)***
Grand Rapids Metaltek Inc E 616 791-2373
Grand Rapids ***(G-6765)***
Grand Traverse Machine Co D 231 946-8006
Traverse City ***(G-16699)***
Graphite Electrodes Ltd E 989 893-3635
Bay City ***(G-1362)***
Graphite Engineering & Sls Co F 616 754-5671
Greenville ***(G-7486)***
Graphite Machining Inc F 810 678-2227
Metamora ***(G-11279)***
▲ **Graphite Products Corp** G 248 548-7800
Madison Heights ***(G-10733)***
Great Lakes Laser Services G 248 584-1828
Madison Heights ***(G-10735)***
Great Lakes Precision Machine E 269 695-4580
Niles ***(G-12134)***
Great Lakes Tool LLC F 586 759-5253
Warren ***(G-17837)***
Green Age Products & Svcs LLC F 586 207-5724
Washington ***(G-18080)***
Greenforces LLC G 906 231-7769
Houghton ***(G-8382)***
Greenwell Machine Shop Inc G 231 347-3346
Petoskey ***(G-12999)***
Greg Socha E 269 344-1204
Kalamazoo ***(G-9205)***
Gregory M Boese F 989 754-2990
Saginaw ***(G-14659)***
Grind-All Precision Tool Co F 586 954-3430
Clinton Township ***(G-3250)***
▼ **Grinders Clearinghouse Inc** E 586 771-1500
Warren ***(G-17840)***
Grinding Products Company Inc E 586 757-2118
Warren ***(G-17841)***
Grinding Specialists Inc E 734 729-1775
Westland ***(G-18377)***
Grippe Machining and Mfg Co E 586 778-3150
Roseville ***(G-14418)***

Gross Machine Shop G 989 587-4021
Westphalia ***(G-18434)***
Guerne Precision Machining G 231 834-7417
Bailey ***(G-1119)***
Gws Tool LLC G 616 971-4700
Grand Rapids ***(G-6797)***
H & L Tool & Engineering Inc G 586 755-2806
Warren ***(G-17846)***
H G Geiger Manufacturing Co E 517 369-7357
Bronson ***(G-2114)***
Hallmark Tool and Gage Co Inc E 248 669-4010
Wixom ***(G-18673)***
Hallstrom Company G 906 439-5439
Eben Junction ***(G-4978)***
Hamilton Industrial Products E 269 751-5153
Hamilton ***(G-7599)***
Hamtech Inc G 231 796-3917
Big Rapids ***(G-1675)***
Harbor Tool and Machine F 989 479-6708
Harbor Beach ***(G-7632)***
Hardy-Reed Tool & Die Co Inc E 517 547-7107
Manitou Beach ***(G-10927)***
Harloff Manufacturing Co LLC E 269 655-1097
Paw Paw ***(G-12949)***
Harmon Sign Inc G 248 348-8150
Wixom ***(G-18676)***
Harrington Construction Co G 269 543-4251
Fennville ***(G-5437)***
Hart Industries LLC F 313 588-1837
Sterling Heights ***(G-16034)***
Haven Manufacturing Company E 616 842-1260
Grand Haven ***(G-6316)***
Hawk Tool and Machine Inc F 248 349-0121
Wixom ***(G-18677)***
Hemingway Screw Products Inc G 313 383-7300
Melvindale ***(G-11201)***
Heritage Mfg Inc G 586 949-7446
Chesterfield ***(G-2890)***
HI Tech Mechanical Svcs LLC G 734 847-1831
Temperance ***(G-16534)***
▼ **Highland Engineering Inc** E 517 548-4372
Howell ***(G-8460)***
Highland Manufacturing Inc E 248 585-8040
Madison Heights ***(G-10740)***
Hill Machine Works LLC F 586 238-2897
Fraser ***(G-5937)***
Hill Screw Machine Products G 734 427-8237
Westland ***(G-18382)***
Holder Corporation G 517 484-5453
Lansing ***(G-9764)***
Holloway Equipment Co Inc G 810 748-9577
Harsens Island ***(G-7749)***
Hosco Inc F 248 912-1750
Wixom ***(G-18678)***
Hosford & Co Inc G 734 769-5660
Ann Arbor ***(G-519)***
Howell Machine Products Inc E 517 546-0580
Brighton ***(G-2010)***
Howell Penncraft Inc G 517 548-2250
Howell ***(G-8464)***
Hudson Industries Inc G 313 777-5622
Sterling Heights ***(G-16044)***
Huff Machine & Tool Co Inc F 231 734-3291
Evart ***(G-5123)***
Hurless Machine Shop Inc G 269 945-9362
Hastings ***(G-7797)***
Huron Quality Mfg Inc G 989 736-8121
Lincoln ***(G-10035)***
Hurricane Machine Inc G 313 383-8614
Lincoln Park ***(G-10049)***
Husky LLC F 586 774-6148
Roseville ***(G-14421)***
Hylite Tool & Machine Inc G 586 465-7878
Clinton Township ***(G-3256)***
IBC Precision Inc G 248 373-8202
Auburn Hills ***(G-933)***
Ideal Machine Tool Tech LLC G 248 320-4729
Troy ***(G-17158)***
Ideal Tool Inc F 989 893-8336
Bay City ***(G-1366)***
Illmatik Industries G 714 767-1296
Grand Rapids ***(G-6834)***
Impact Fab Inc F 616 399-9970
Holland ***(G-8093)***
Impeccable Machining Inc G 734 844-3855
Westland ***(G-18385)***
Imperial Metal Products Co E 616 452-1700
Grand Rapids ***(G-6838)***
Impres Engineering Svcs LLC F 616 796-8976
Holland ***(G-8094)***

SIC

Employee Codes: A=Over 500 employees, B=251-500
C=101-250, D=51-100, E=20-50, F=10-19, G=3-9
2022 Harris Michigan Industrial Directory
863

35 INDUSTRIAL AND COMMERCIAL MACHINERY AND COMPUTER EQUIPMENT35 INDUSTRIAL AND COMMERCIAL MACHINERY AND COM-

Inateg LLC ....G.... 734 276-3899
Livonia *(G-10248)*
Independent Machine Co Inc ....E.... 906 428-4524
Escanaba *(G-5077)*
Industrial Exprmental Tech LLC ....E.... 248 371-8000
Auburn Hills *(G-938)*
Industrial Exprmental Tech LLC ....E.... 248 948-1100
Southfield *(G-15604)*
Infinicoat LLC ....G.... 810 721-9631
Attica *(G-753)*
Ingham Tool LLC ....G.... 734 929-2390
Ann Arbor *(G-527)*
Inland Lakes Machine Inc ....E.... 231 775-6543
Cadillac *(G-2337)*
Innovation Machining Corp ....F.... 269 683-3343
Niles *(G-12137)*
Innovative Fab Inc ....G.... 269 782-9154
Dowagiac *(G-4783)*
Innovative Machine Technology ....E.... 248 348-1630
Northville *(G-12231)*
Innovative Tool Inc ....E.... 586 329-4922
Chesterfield *(G-2894)*
▼ **Innovative Works Inc** ....G.... 586 329-1557
Chesterfield *(G-2895)*
Integrity Machine Services ....G.... 989 386-0216
Clare *(G-2981)*
International Machine Too ....G.... 810 588-9591
Canton *(G-2479)*
International Machining Svc ....G.... 248 486-3600
South Lyon *(G-15440)*
International Mch Tl Svcs LLC ....G.... 734 667-2233
Hartland *(G-7770)*
Intricate Grinding Mch Spc Inc ....E.... 231 798-2154
Norton Shores *(G-12300)*
Invo Spline Inc ....E.... 586 757-8840
Warren *(G-17870)*
◆ **Ioperations Inc** ....F.... 616 607-9751
Norton Shores *(G-12301)*
Iq Manufacturing LLC ....G.... 586 634-7185
Auburn Hills *(G-940)*
Island Machine and Engrg LLC ....G.... 810 765-8228
Marine City *(G-10960)*
IXL Machine Shop Inc ....C.... 616 392-9803
Holland *(G-8098)*
J & B Precision Inc ....G.... 313 565-3431
Taylor *(G-16430)*
J & E Manufacturing Company ....G.... 586 777-5614
Roseville *(G-14427)*
J & J Engineering and Machine ....G.... 616 554-3302
Caledonia *(G-2384)*
J & J Machine Ltd ....F.... 231 773-4100
Muskegon *(G-11843)*
J & K Spratt Enterprises Inc ....D.... 517 439-5010
Hillsdale *(G-7938)*
J & L Turning Inc ....F.... 810 765-5755
East China *(G-4857)*
▲ **J & M Machine Products Inc** ....D.... 231 755-1622
Norton Shores *(G-12302)*
J & T Machining Inc ....G.... 616 897-6744
Lowell *(G-10507)*
J B Lunds & Sons Inc ....G.... 231 627-9070
Cheboygan *(G-2788)*
J C Manufacturing Company ....G.... 586 757-2713
Warren *(G-17877)*
J E Enterprises ....G.... 586 463-5129
Harrison Township *(G-7702)*
J I B Properties LLC ....G.... 313 382-3234
Melvindale *(G-11202)*
J N B Machinery LLC ....G.... 517 223-0725
Fowlerville *(G-5845)*
J&S Technologies Inc ....G.... 616 837-7080
Nunica *(G-12580)*
Jackson Grinding Co Inc ....F.... 517 782-8080
Jackson *(G-8914)*
Jamison Industries Inc ....E.... 734 946-3088
Taylor *(G-16431)*
Jansen Industries Inc ....E.... 517 788-6800
Jackson *(G-8919)*
Jbj Products and Machinery ....G.... 517 655-4734
Williamston *(G-18575)*
JD Machine ....F.... 906 233-7420
Escanaba *(G-5078)*
Je Machining LLC ....G.... 616 340-1786
Marne *(G-10994)*
Jefferson Iron Works Inc ....G.... 248 542-3554
Ferndale *(G-5561)*
Jems of Litchfield Inc ....F.... 517 542-5367
Litchfield *(G-10081)*
Jerz Machine Tool Corporation ....G.... 269 782-3535
Dowagiac *(G-4785)*
Jess Enterprises LLC ....G.... 517 546-5818
Howell *(G-8467)*
◆ **Jetech Inc** ....E.... 269 965-6311
Battle Creek *(G-1246)*
Jex Manufacturing Inc ....G.... 586 463-4274
Mount Clemens *(G-11645)*
Jhs Grinding LLC ....E.... 586 427-6006
Warren *(G-17885)*
▲ **JNB Machining Company Inc** ....E.... 517 223-0725
Fowlerville *(G-5846)*
▲ **Jobs Inc** ....G.... 810 714-0522
Allen Park *(G-197)*
John Sams Tool Co ....G.... 586 776-3560
Warren *(G-17888)*
Johns Small Engine and Outdoo ....G.... 517 523-1060
Osseo *(G-12775)*
Johnson & Berry Mfg Inc ....G.... 906 524-6433
Lanse *(G-9664)*
Johnson Precision Mold & Engrg ....G.... 269 651-2553
Sturgis *(G-16296)*
Jolico/J-B Tool Inc ....E.... 586 739-5555
Shelby Township *(G-15245)*
Jones Precision Jig Grinding ....G.... 248 549-4866
Royal Oak *(G-14552)*
Joyce Mims ....G.... 616 469-5016
Union Pier *(G-17500)*
Jsk Specialties ....G.... 616 218-2416
Zeeland *(G-19049)*
Jt Manufacturing Inc ....E.... 517 849-2923
Jonesville *(G-9090)*
JW Liess Machine Shop ....G.... 248 219-0444
Detroit *(G-4344)*
▲ **K & M Machine-Fabricating Inc** ....C.... 269 445-2495
Cassopolis *(G-2631)*
K & S Automation LLC ....G.... 248 861-2123
Oxford *(G-12892)*
K & W Manufacturing Co Inc ....E.... 517 369-9708
Bronson *(G-2117)*
K&A Machine and Tool Inc ....D.... 517 750-9244
Jackson *(G-8927)*
K&W Tool and Machine Inc ....F.... 616 754-7540
Greenville *(G-7495)*
Ka-Wood Gear & Machine Co ....E.... 248 585-8870
Madison Heights *(G-10757)*
Kasper Industries Inc ....E.... 989 705-1177
Gaylord *(G-6138)*
Kelley Machining Inc ....G.... 231 861-0951
Shelby *(G-15154)*
◆ **Kelm Acubar Lc** ....E.... 269 927-3000
Benton Harbor *(G-1561)*
Kelm Acubar Lc ....G.... 269 925-2007
Benton Harbor *(G-1562)*
Kentwater Tool & Mfg Co ....G.... 616 784-7171
Comstock Park *(G-3615)*
Ketchum Machine Corporated ....F.... 616 765-5101
Freeport *(G-6034)*
Keystone Manufacturing ....G.... 248 796-2546
River Rouge *(G-13857)*
▲ **King Tool & Die Inc** ....E.... 517 265-2741
Adrian *(G-78)*
Kiser Industrial Mfg Co ....F.... 269 934-9220
Benton Harbor *(G-1563)*
Kksp Precision Machining LLC ....E.... 810 329-4731
East China *(G-4858)*
Kmk Machining ....F.... 231 629-8068
Big Rapids *(G-1679)*
Knapp Manufacturing Inc ....E.... 517 279-9538
Coldwater *(G-3441)*
Ko Industries ....F.... 248 882-6888
White Lake *(G-18459)*
Kodiak Manufacturing Co Inc ....G.... 248 335-5552
Pontiac *(G-13393)*
Koehler Industries Inc ....G.... 269 934-9670
Benton Harbor *(G-1564)*
Kolenda Technologies LLC ....G.... 616 299-0126
Grand Rapids *(G-6903)*
Koppel Tool & Engineering LLC ....G.... 616 638-2611
Norton Shores *(G-12307)*
Koski Welding Inc ....G.... 906 353-7588
Baraga *(G-1142)*
Kotzian Tool Inc ....F.... 231 861-5377
Shelby *(G-15155)*
Kremin Inc ....E.... 989 790-5147
Frankenmuth *(G-5868)*
Kriewall Enterprises Inc ....E.... 586 336-0600
Romeo *(G-14227)*
Kriseler Welding Inc ....G.... 989 624-9266
Birch Run *(G-1708)*
Krontz General Machine & Tool ....G.... 269 651-5882
Sturgis *(G-16297)*
Krt Precision Tool & Mfg Co ....G.... 517 783-5715
Jackson *(G-8930)*
Kurt Machine Tool Co Inc ....F.... 586 296-5070
Fraser *(G-5953)*
Kuzimski Enterprises Inc ....G.... 989 422-5377
Houghton Lake *(G-8401)*
L & L Pattern Inc ....G.... 231 733-2646
Muskegon *(G-11853)*
L & M Machining & Mfg Inc ....G.... 586 498-7110
Warren *(G-17899)*
L & R Centerless Grinding ....G.... 734 397-3031
Canton *(G-2485)*
L A Burnhart Inc ....G.... 810 227-4567
Brighton *(G-2016)*
L F M Enterprises Inc ....E.... 586 792-7220
Clinton Township *(G-3275)*
L S Machining Inc ....G.... 248 583-7277
Troy *(G-17202)*
L T C Solutions Inc ....G.... 586 323-2071
Shelby Township *(G-15253)*
Lakeshore Fabrication LLC ....G.... 231 740-5861
Nunica *(G-12582)*
Lakeshore Vision & Robotics ....G.... 616 394-9201
Zeeland *(G-19050)*
Lakeside Manufacturing Co ....E.... 269 429-6193
Stevensville *(G-16259)*
Lakeside Spring LLC ....G.... 616 847-2706
Muskegon *(G-11858)*
Lakeview Quality Tool Inc ....G.... 989 732-6417
Gaylord *(G-6141)*
Lam Industries ....G.... 734 266-1404
Livonia *(G-10273)*
Lambert Industries Inc ....F.... 734 668-6864
Ann Arbor *(G-548)*
Langenberg Machine Pdts Inc ....G.... 517 485-9450
Lansing *(G-9857)*
Lanphear Tool Works Inc ....F.... 269 674-8877
Lawrence *(G-9982)*
Lanzen Incorporated ....E.... 231 587-8200
Mancelona *(G-10873)*
Laser Cutting Co ....E.... 586 468-5300
Harrison Township *(G-7705)*
Lawson Manufacturing Inc ....G.... 248 624-1818
Walled Lake *(G-17671)*
Laydon Enterprises Inc ....E.... 906 774-4633
Iron Mountain *(G-8724)*
LE Warren Inc ....E.... 517 784-8701
Jackson *(G-8933)*
Le-Q Fabricators Ltd ....G.... 906 246-3402
Felch *(G-5432)*
Leading Edge Engineering Inc ....F.... 586 786-0382
Shelby Township *(G-15261)*
Lee Manufacturing Inc ....F.... 231 865-3359
Fruitport *(G-6065)*
Leelanau Industries Inc ....E.... 231 947-0372
Traverse City *(G-16742)*
Lenway Machine Company Inc ....G.... 269 751-5183
Hamilton *(G-7602)*
Levy Machining LLC ....G.... 517 563-2013
Hanover *(G-7625)*
Lewkowicz Corporation ....F.... 734 941-0411
Romulus *(G-14298)*
Liberty Tool Inc ....E.... 586 726-2449
Sterling Heights *(G-16073)*
Libra Precision Machining Inc ....F.... 517 423-1365
Tecumseh *(G-16507)*
Lightning Machine Holland LLC ....F.... 616 786-9280
Holland *(G-8129)*
▲ **Lincoln Park Boring Co** ....E.... 734 946-8300
Romulus *(G-14299)*
Lindberg Hydraulic Systems ....F.... 517 787-3791
Jackson *(G-8936)*
Line Precision Inc ....E.... 248 474-5280
Farmington Hills *(G-5291)*
Linear Measurement Instrs Corp ....E.... 810 714-5811
Fenton *(G-5489)*
Link Mechanical Solutions LLC ....F.... 734 744-5616
Livonia *(G-10284)*
Livingston Machine Inc ....F.... 517 546-4253
Howell *(G-8472)*
Lmm Group Inc ....G.... 269 276-9909
Kalamazoo *(G-9261)*
Local Grind ....G.... 269 623-5777
Delton *(G-3965)*
Loftis Machine Company ....F.... 616 846-1990
Grand Haven *(G-6331)*
Logan Tool and Engineering ....G.... 586 755-3555
Warren *(G-17905)*
Lomar Machine & Tool Co ....E.... 517 563-8136
Horton *(G-8373)*

Lomar Machine & Tool Co E 517 750-4089
Spring Arbor ***(G-15795)***
Lomar Machine & Tool Co G 517 563-8136
Horton ***(G-8375)***
Lomar Machine & Tool Co E 517 563-8800
Horton ***(G-8376)***
Lowing Products LLC G 616 530-7440
Wyoming ***(G-18892)***
Ltek Industries Inc G 734 747-6105
Ann Arbor ***(G-556)***
Lyons Tool and Mfg Corp E 248 344-9644
Wixom ***(G-18702)***
M & A Machining Inc F 269 342-0026
Kalamazoo ***(G-9262)***
M & F Machine & Tool Inc E 734 847-0571
Erie ***(G-5050)***
M & M Automatic Products Inc F 517 782-0577
Jackson ***(G-8937)***
M & M Machining Inc G 586 997-9910
Sterling Heights ***(G-16078)***
M & M Services Inc G 248 619-9861
Troy ***(G-17216)***
M & R Machine Company G 313 277-1570
Dearborn Heights ***(G-3932)***
M&I Machine Inc F 269 849-3624
Coloma ***(G-3477)***
M-A Metals Inc G 989 268-5080
Vestaburg ***(G-17594)***
Machine Shop Beer Company LLC G 810 577-4202
Fenton ***(G-5490)***
Machine Shop Services LLC G 616 396-4898
Holland ***(G-8132)***
Machine Tool & Gear Inc C 989 723-5486
Owosso ***(G-12839)***
Machined Solutions G 517 759-4075
Adrian ***(G-80)***
Machining Speci G 248 589-4070
Madison Heights ***(G-10773)***
Machining Specialists Inc Mich G 517 881-2863
Flint ***(G-5730)***
Maclean Master LLC E 734 414-0500
Livonia ***(G-10297)***
Madison Machine Company G 517 265-8532
Alpena ***(G-300)***
Mag Machine Tool G 734 281-1700
Gibraltar ***(G-6172)***
Magiera Holdings Inc E 269 685-1768
Plainwell ***(G-13082)***
Magnum Tool Inc F 586 716-8075
New Baltimore ***(G-11987)***
Magnus Precision Tool LLC G 586 285-2500
Fraser ***(G-5961)***
Mahnke Machine Inc G 231 775-0581
Cadillac ***(G-2344)***
Main & Company E 517 789-7183
Jackson ***(G-8942)***
Man U TEC Inc G 586 262-4085
Sterling Heights ***(G-16083)***
Manor Industries Inc D 586 463-4604
Clinton Township ***(G-3292)***
Manufacturers Hardware Company F 313 892-6650
Detroit ***(G-4420)***
Manus Tool Inc E 989 724-7171
Harrisville ***(G-7744)***
Map To Elopak Precision G 417 467-7419
Commerce Township ***(G-3553)***
▼ **Marine Machining and Mfg** G 586 791-8800
Clinton Township ***(G-3294)***
◆ **Marshall Excelsior Co** E 269 789-6700
Marshall ***(G-11065)***
Marshall Tool Service Inc G 989 777-3137
Saginaw ***(G-14687)***
Martin Saw & Tool Inc G 906 863-6812
Menominee ***(G-11245)***
Master Machining Inc F 248 509-7185
Troy ***(G-17240)***
Master Mfg Inc E 248 628-9400
Oxford ***(G-12899)***
Mathew Parmelee G 248 894-5955
Rochester Hills ***(G-14059)***
Matteson Manufacturing Inc G 231 779-2898
Cadillac ***(G-2345)***
Maverick Machine Tool F 269 789-1617
Marshall ***(G-11068)***
▲ **Maximum Mold Inc** F 269 468-6291
Benton Harbor ***(G-1571)***
Maxum LLC G 248 726-7110
Rochester Hills ***(G-14060)***
MB Aerospace Holdings III Corp F 586 977-9200
Sterling Heights ***(G-16088)***
▲ **MB Aerospace Sterling Hts Inc** D 586 977-9200
Sterling Heights ***(G-16089)***
McDonald Acquisitions LLC E 616 878-7800
Byron Center ***(G-2282)***
McDonald Enterprises Inc F 734 464-4664
Livonia ***(G-10305)***
Meezherati Industries LLC G 734 931-0466
Detroit ***(G-4428)***
Meliss Company Inc F 248 398-1970
Clarkston ***(G-3049)***
Melling Industries Inc E 517 787-8172
Jackson ***(G-8949)***
Melling Manufacturing Inc D 517 750-3580
Jackson ***(G-8950)***
▲ **Merchants Automatic Pdts Inc** E 734 829-0020
Canton ***(G-2493)***
Merchants Industries Inc G 734 397-3031
Canton ***(G-2494)***
Meritt Tool & Die G 517 726-1452
Vermontville ***(G-17590)***
Merrill Technologies Group Inc C 989 643-7981
Merrill ***(G-11263)***
▲ **Merrill Technologies Group Inc** D 989 791-6676
Saginaw ***(G-14697)***
▲ **Metal Arc Inc** E 231 865-3111
Muskegon ***(G-11868)***
Metal Mechanics Inc F 269 679-2525
Schoolcraft ***(G-15124)***
Metalcraft Cutting Tools LLC G 586 243-5591
Clinton Township ***(G-3298)***
Metallurgical High Vacuum Corp F 269 543-4291
Fennville ***(G-5440)***
Metalmite Corporation F 248 651-9415
Rochester ***(G-13911)***
Metalution Tool Die F 616 355-9700
Holland ***(G-8145)***
Metric Manufacturing Co Inc C 616 897-5959
Lowell ***(G-10511)***
Metric Tool Company Inc F 313 369-9610
Detroit ***(G-4435)***
Metro Broach Inc F 586 758-2340
Warren ***(G-17926)***
Michigan Cnc Tool Inc F 734 449-9590
Whitmore Lake ***(G-18541)***
Michigan Custom Machines Inc E 248 347-7900
Novi ***(G-12480)***
Michigan General Grinding LLC G 616 454-5089
Grand Rapids ***(G-6990)***
▲ **Michigan Prod Machining Inc** B 586 228-9700
Macomb ***(G-10616)***
▼ **Michigan Rebuild & Automtn Inc** F 517 542-6000
Litchfield ***(G-10083)***
Michigan Slotting Company Inc G 586 772-1270
Warren ***(G-17930)***
Michigan Tool Works LLC E 269 651-5139
Sturgis ***(G-16308)***
◆ **Michigan Wheel Operations LLC** D 616 452-6941
Grand Rapids ***(G-6997)***
Michigan Wire EDM Services G 616 742-0940
Grand Rapids ***(G-6998)***
Micro EDM Co LLC G 989 872-4306
Cass City ***(G-2619)***
Micro Engineering Inc G 616 534-9681
Byron Center ***(G-2285)***
Micro Fixtures Inc G 313 382-9781
Taylor ***(G-16446)***
Micro Gauge Inc C 248 446-3720
Brighton ***(G-2031)***
Micro Grind Co Inc G 248 398-9770
Hazel Park ***(G-7834)***
Micro Manufacturing Inc E 616 554-9200
Caledonia ***(G-2389)***
Micron Mfg Company E 616 453-5486
Grand Rapids ***(G-7002)***
Micron Precision Machining Inc E 989 759-1030
Saginaw ***(G-14699)***
Microtech Machine Company G 517 750-4422
Jackson ***(G-8958)***
Mid-America Machining Inc D 517 592-4945
Brooklyn ***(G-2128)***
Mid-Tech Inc G 734 426-4327
Ann Arbor ***(G-577)***
Mid-West Innovators Inc E 989 358-7147
Alpena ***(G-303)***
Midway Machine Tech Inc E 616 772-0808
Zeeland ***(G-19054)***
Miedema Realty Inc G 616 538-4800
Grandville ***(G-7402)***
Mika Tool & Die Inc G 989 662-6979
Auburn ***(G-770)***
Milfab Systems LLC F 248 391-8100
Lake Orion ***(G-9619)***
Miller Machine Inc G 734 455-5333
Plymouth ***(G-13242)***
Miller Prod & Machining Inc F 810 395-8810
Capac ***(G-2548)***
Milo Boring & Machining Inc G 586 293-8611
Fraser ***(G-5963)***
Minland Machine Inc G 269 641-7998
Edwardsburg ***(G-5012)***
Mittler Supply G 616 451-3055
Grand Rapids ***(G-7014)***
Modern Machine Co E 989 895-8563
Bay City ***(G-1380)***
Modern Machining Inc G 269 964-4415
Battle Creek ***(G-1275)***
Modern Metalcraft Inc F 989 835-3716
Midland ***(G-11396)***
Moderno Industrial LLC F 734 727-0560
Westland ***(G-18397)***
Modified Gear and Spline Inc F 313 893-3511
Detroit ***(G-4463)***
◆ **Modineer Co LLC** C 269 683-2550
Niles ***(G-12145)***
Modineer Co LLC G 269 684-3138
Niles ***(G-12147)***
Modineer Co LLC E 269 683-2550
Niles ***(G-12146)***
Modineer P-K Tool LLC E 269 683-2550
Niles ***(G-12148)***
Moeller Mfg Company LLC G 616 285-5012
Grand Rapids ***(G-7019)***
Mogultech LLC G 734 944-5053
Saline ***(G-15029)***
Momentum Industries Inc F 989 681-5735
Saint Louis ***(G-14993)***
Monroe Machinining LLC G 734 457-2088
Monroe ***(G-11564)***
Monroe Sattler LLC E 586 725-1140
Ira ***(G-8704)***
Montague Tool and Mfg Co E 810 686-0000
Clio ***(G-3408)***
Montina Manufacturing Inc G 616 846-1080
Grand Haven ***(G-6338)***
◆ **Morbark LLC** B 989 866-2381
Winn ***(G-18590)***
Morgan Machining LLC F 248 293-3277
Auburn Hills ***(G-974)***
Morren Mold & Machine Inc G 616 892-7474
Allendale ***(G-226)***
Morrow Foundry G 231 582-0452
Boyne City ***(G-1899)***
Motion Machine Company F 810 664-9901
Lapeer ***(G-9949)***
Motor City Bending & Rolling G 313 368-4400
Detroit ***(G-4466)***
Mountain Machine LLC F 734 480-2200
Van Buren Twp ***(G-17542)***
Mr E Machine LLC G 810 407-0319
Au Gres ***(G-761)***
MSI Machine Tool Parts Inc F 248 589-0515
Madison Heights ***(G-10785)***
MTI Precision Machining Inc E 989 865-9880
Saint Charles ***(G-14806)***
Mtm Machine Inc G 586 443-5703
Sterling Heights ***(G-16108)***
Multi McHning Capabilities Inc G 734 955-5592
Romulus ***(G-14307)***
Multi Tech Precision Inc G 616 514-1415
Grand Rapids ***(G-7032)***
Munn Manufacturing Company E 616 765-3067
Freeport ***(G-6035)***
▲ **Murray Grinding Inc** E 313 295-6030
Dearborn Heights ***(G-3934)***
▲ **N C Brighton Machine Corp** C 810 227-6190
Brighton ***(G-2039)***
N-P Grinding Inc G 586 756-6262
Warren ***(G-17939)***
N/C Production & Grinding Inc G 586 731-2150
Sterling Heights ***(G-16111)***
◆ **National Bulk Equipment Inc** C 616 399-2220
Holland ***(G-8151)***
Nephew Fabrication Inc G 616 875-2121
Zeeland ***(G-19059)***
New Concept Products Inc G 269 679-5970
Schoolcraft ***(G-15125)***
New Gldc LLC F 989 879-4009
Muskegon ***(G-11884)***
New Technologies Tool & Mfg F 810 694-5426
Grand Blanc ***(G-6254)***

SIC

Employee Codes: A=Over 500 employees, B=251-500
C=101-250, D=51-100, E=20-50, F=10-19, G=3-9
2022 Harris Michigan
Industrial Directory
865

35 INDUSTRIAL AND COMMERCIAL MACHINERY AND COMPUTER EQUIPMENT

Next Level Manufacturing LLC .... G 616 965-1913
  Comstock Park (G-3628)
Nikolic Industries Inc .... E 586 254-4810
  Sterling Heights (G-16116)
Niles Machine & Tool Company .... G 269 684-2594
  Niles (G-12154)
Nims Precision Machining Inc .... G 248 446-1053
  South Lyon (G-15449)
Nitz Valve Hardware Inc .... F 989 883-9500
  Sebewaing (G-15142)
Nmp Inc .... E 231 798-8851
  Norton Shores (G-12317)
North American Mch & Engrg Co .... G 586 726-6700
  Shelby Township (G-15291)
North Branch Machining & Engrg .... G 989 795-2324
  Fostoria (G-5825)
North Kent Base LLC .... G 616 636-4300
  Sand Lake (G-15050)
North Shore Machine Works Inc .... G 616 842-8360
  Spring Lake (G-15840)
Northern Fab & Machine LLC .... F 906 863-8506
  Menominee (G-11255)
Northern Machining & Repr Inc .... E 906 786-0526
  Escanaba (G-5088)
Northern Precision Pdts Inc .... G 231 768-4435
  Leroy (G-10008)
Northwest Tool & Machine Inc .... E 517 750-1332
  Jackson (G-8978)
Norton Tool & Gage LLC .... G 231 750-9789
  Norton Shores (G-12320)
▲ Nu-Core Inc .... G 231 547-2600
  Charlevoix (G-2724)
Nuway Tool .... G 616 452-4366
  Grand Rapids (G-7053)
O & S Tool and Machine Inc .... G 248 926-8045
  Wixom (G-18724)
Oakland Automation LLC .... E 248 589-3350
  Livonia (G-10350)
Oakland Machine Company .... F 248 674-2201
  Waterford (G-18142)
▲ Oneida Tool Corporation .... E 313 537-0770
  Redford (G-13752)
Orion Machine Inc .... G 231 728-1229
  Muskegon (G-11887)
Oxid .... G 248 474-9817
  Farmington Hills (G-5340)
Oxid Corporation .... E 248 474-9817
  Novi (G-12501)
P & G Technologies Inc .... G 248 399-3135
  Sterling Heights (G-16121)
P & M Industries Inc .... F 517 223-1000
  Gregory (G-7515)
P D E Systems Inc .... F 586 725-3330
  Chesterfield (G-2921)
P L Optima Inc .... G 616 828-8377
  Zeeland (G-19067)
P M R Industries Inc .... F 810 989-5020
  Port Huron (G-13515)
P2r Metal Fabrication Inc .... F 586 606-5266
  Macomb (G-10625)
Padnos Leitelt Inc .... D 616 363-3817
  Grand Rapids (G-7067)
Panter Master Controls Inc .... F 810 687-5600
  Flint (G-5743)
Paragon Manufacturing Corp .... G 810 629-4100
  Fenton (G-5493)
Paragon Model and Tool Inc .... G 248 960-1223
  Wixom (G-18728)
Paragon Model Shop Inc .... G 616 693-3224
  Freeport (G-6036)
Paramont Machine Co LLC .... G 330 339-3489
  Kalamazoo (G-9286)
Paramount Industrial Machining .... E 248 543-2100
  Oak Park (G-12636)
Paravis Industries Inc .... E 248 393-2300
  Auburn Hills (G-993)
Park Street Machine Inc .... F 231 739-9165
  Muskegon (G-11893)
Parker Machine & Engineering .... G 734 692-4600
  Woodhaven (G-18801)
Parts Finishing Group Inc .... D 586 755-4053
  Warren (G-17955)
Patch Works Farms Inc .... G 989 430-3610
  Wheeler (G-18436)
Patriot Tool Inc .... G 313 299-1400
  Dearborn Heights (G-3936)
Patterson Precision Mfg Inc .... E 231 733-1913
  Norton Shores (G-12324)
Paul Jeffrey Kenny .... G 989 828-6109
  Shepherd (G-15378)

▲ Pavco MCR .... G 734 464-2220
  Livonia (G-10361)
Pdf Mfg Inc .... G 517 522-8431
  Grass Lake (G-7443)
Pentier Group Inc .... E 810 664-7997
  Lapeer (G-9954)
◆ Perfecto Industries Inc .... E 989 732-2941
  Gaylord (G-6154)
Performance Machinery LLC .... F 586 698-2508
  Sterling Heights (G-16125)
Performance Machining Inc .... G 269 683-4370
  Niles (G-12158)
Perman Industries LLC .... F 586 991-5600
  Shelby Township (G-15299)
Pezco Industries Inc .... G 248 589-1140
  Madison Heights (G-10798)
Photographic Support Inc .... G 586 264-9957
  Sterling Heights (G-16126)
PI Optima Inc .... G 616 772-2138
  Zeeland (G-19068)
PI Optima Manufacturing LLC .... F 616 931-9750
  Zeeland (G-19069)
Pioneer Machine and Tech Inc .... G 248 546-4451
  Madison Heights (G-10800)
Pioneer Metal Finishing LLC .... D 877 721-1100
  Warren (G-17964)
Pioneer Michigan Broach Co .... F 231 768-5800
  Leroy (G-10010)
Plascon .... G 231 421-3119
  Traverse City (G-16795)
Plasma-Tec Inc .... G 616 455-2593
  Holland (G-8166)
Platt Mounts - Usa Inc .... G 586 202-2920
  Lake Orion (G-9626)
Plesh Industries Inc .... G 716 873-4916
  Brighton (G-2052)
Plymouth Brazing Inc .... D 734 453-6274
  Westland (G-18407)
Polaris Engineering Inc .... F 586 296-1603
  Fraser (G-5978)
▲ Pollington Machine Tool Inc .... E 231 743-2003
  Marion (G-10976)
Post Production Solutions LLC .... F 734 428-7000
  Manchester (G-10889)
Power Precision Industries Inc .... G 586 997-0600
  Sterling Heights (G-16130)
Praet Tool & Engineering Inc .... E 586 677-3800
  Macomb (G-10627)
Precise Machining Inc .... G 231 937-7957
  Howard City (G-8415)
Precise McHining Unlimited LLC .... F 517 524-3104
  Concord (G-3654)
Precise Metal Components Inc .... E 734 769-0790
  Ann Arbor (G-8173)
Precise Tool & Cutter Inc .... E 248 684-8480
  Wixom (G-18732)
▲ Precision Advanced Machining .... D 586 463-3900
  Clinton Township (G-3323)
Precision Aerospace Corp .... E 616 243-8112
  Grand Rapids (G-7098)
Precision Automotive Mch Sp .... E 616 534-6946
  Wyoming (G-18901)
Precision Boring and Machine .... G 248 371-9140
  Auburn Hills (G-1002)
Precision Hone & Tool Inc .... F 313 493-9760
  Detroit (G-4532)
Precision Machining .... G 248 669-2660
  Milford (G-11482)
Precision Machining Company .... E 810 688-8674
  North Branch (G-12182)
Precision Manufacturing Svcs .... G 734 995-3505
  Ann Arbor (G-621)
Precision Micro Mill .... G 269 290-3603
  Wayland (G-18201)
Precision Tool Inc .... E 517 726-1060
  Vermontville (G-17591)
Precision Tool & Machine Inc .... F 989 291-3365
  Sheridan (G-15383)
Precision Wire EDM Service .... E 616 453-4360
  Grand Rapids (G-7100)
Precisioncraft Co .... F 586 954-9510
  Clinton Township (G-3324)
Preferred Machine LLC .... E 616 272-6334
  Jenison (G-9067)
Premach Engineering Ltd .... G 616 247-3750
  Grand Rapids (G-7101)
Prestige Engrg Rsrces Tech Inc .... G 586 573-3070
  Madison Heights (G-10808)
Prestige Machining .... G 248 879-1028
  Troy (G-17313)

Primo Tool & Manufacturing .... G 231 592-5262
  Big Rapids (G-1685)
Prk Holdings Inc .... E 231 728-1155
  Muskegon (G-11899)
Pro Source Manufacturing Inc .... G 616 607-2990
  Grand Haven (G-6347)
Pro-CAM Services LLC .... E 616 748-4200
  Zeeland (G-19073)
Production Dev Systems LLC .... F 810 648-2111
  Sandusky (G-15065)
▲ Production Machining of Alma .... E 989 463-1495
  Alma (G-253)
Production Saw & Machine Co .... D 517 529-4014
  Clarklake (G-3007)
Production Tooling Inc .... G 269 668-6789
  Mattawan (G-11166)
Proficient Machining Inc .... G 616 453-9496
  Grand Rapids (G-7115)
▲ Profile Gear Inc .... E 810 324-2731
  North Street (G-12186)
Progress Machine & Tool Inc .... E 231 798-3410
  Norton Shores (G-12352)
Progressive Finishing Inc .... E 586 949-6961
  Chesterfield (G-2932)
Prosper-Tech Machine & TI LLC .... F 586 727-8800
  Richmond (G-13845)
Proto-CAM Inc .... F 616 454-9810
  Grand Rapids (G-7123)
Proto-Tek Manufacturing Inc .... E 586 772-2663
  Roseville (G-14467)
Protomatic Inc .... E 734 426-3655
  Dexter (G-4750)
Prototech Laser Inc .... E 586 598-6900
  Chesterfield (G-2934)
▲ Prototype Cast Mfg Inc .... G 586 739-0180
  Shelby Township (G-15311)
Provision Cnc LLC .... G 616 309-4545
  Byron Center (G-2293)
PT&t Precise Machining LLC .... G 517 748-9325
  Jackson (G-8992)
Pushman Manufacturing Co Inc .... E 810 629-9688
  Fenton (G-5497)
Putnam Machine Products Inc .... E 517 278-2364
  Coldwater (G-3448)
▲ Pyxis Technologies LLC .... E 734 414-0261
  Plymouth (G-13272)
Quality Cavity Inc .... F 248 344-9995
  Canton (G-2516)
Quality Dial Inc .... G 231 947-1071
  Traverse City (G-16809)
Quality Grinding Inc .... E 586 293-3780
  Fraser (G-5983)
Quality Machine & Automation .... E 616 399-4415
  Holland (G-8173)
Quality Precision Inc .... G 313 254-9141
  Dearborn (G-3888)
Quality Tool & Gear Inc .... E 734 266-1500
  Redford (G-13760)
Quasar Industries Inc .... E 248 852-0300
  Rochester Hills (G-14097)
Quasar Industries Inc .... D 248 844-7190
  Rochester Hills (G-14096)
Quest Industries Inc .... E 810 245-4535
  Lapeer (G-9957)
Quest Precision LLC .... E 616 288-6101
  Rockford (G-14185)
R & B EDM Inc .... F 810 714-5050
  Fenton (G-5498)
▼ R & B Industries Inc .... E 734 462-9478
  Livonia (G-10380)
R & D Cnc Machining Inc .... F 269 751-4171
  Hamilton (G-7606)
R & D Machine and Tool Inc .... G 231 798-8500
  Norton Shores (G-12327)
R & L Machine Products Inc .... G 734 992-2574
  Romulus (G-14323)
R & M Machine Tool Inc .... E 989 695-6601
  Freeland (G-6027)
R & S Cutter Grind Inc .... E 989 791-3100
  Saginaw (G-14733)
R & S Tool & Die Inc .... G 989 673-8511
  Caro (G-2579)
R C Grinding and Tool Company .... E 586 949-4373
  Chesterfield (G-2936)
▲ R F M Incorporated .... E 810 229-4567
  Brighton (G-2059)
R K C Corporation .... G 231 627-9131
  Cheboygan (G-2797)
R N B Machine & Tool Inc .... G 616 784-6868
  Comstock Park (G-3641)

SIC SECTION 35 INDUSTRIAL AND COMMERCIAL MACHINERY AND COMPUTER EQUIPMENT 35 INDUSTRIAL AND COMMERCIAL MACHINERY

Company	Code	Phone
R+r Mfg/Eng Inc — Warren (G-17991)	G	586 758-4420
Rae Precision Products Inc — Port Huron (G-13521)	G	810 987-9170
Ramtec Corp — Romeo (G-14233)	F	586 752-9270
▲ Rassey Industries Inc — Shelby Township (G-15315)	E	586 803-9500
Ratio Machining Inc — Redford (G-13762)	G	313 531-5155
RB&w Detroit — Madison Heights (G-10817)	G	234 380-8544
Rdc Machine Inc — Grand Blanc (G-6260)	G	810 695-5587
Reau Manufacturing Co — Dundee (G-4833)	G	734 823-5603
Rebecca Eiben — Mount Clemens (G-11656)	G	586 231-0548
Reemco Incorporated — Livonia (G-10384)	G	734 522-8988
▲ Rehmann Industries Inc — Warren (G-17994)	F	810 748-7793
Rendon & Sons Machining Inc — Gobles (G-6219)	G	269 628-2200
▲ REO Hydro-Pierce Inc — Detroit (G-4567)	F	313 891-2244
Rep Innovations Inc — Livonia (G-10385)	F	734 744-6968
Resetar Equipment Inc — Dearborn Heights (G-3937)	G	313 291-0500
Revak Precision Grinding Inc — Taylor (G-16466)	G	313 388-2626
Rex Materials Inc — Howell (G-8509)	E	517 223-3787
Reynolda Mfg Solutions Inc — Wixom (G-18741)	G	336 699-4204
Richland Machine & Pump Co — Richland (G-13828)	G	269 629-4344
Ridgefield Company LLC — Grand Rapids (G-7155)	G	888 226-8665
Rima Manufacturing Company — Hudson (G-8561)	C	517 448-8921
Rise Machine Company Inc — Mount Pleasant (G-11737)	G	989 772-2151
Rite Machine Products Inc — Clinton Township (G-3338)	F	586 465-9393
Rite Hand Stamp Company — Auburn Hills (G-1021)	G	248 391-7600
Rite Tool Company Inc — Sterling Heights (G-16153)	G	586 264-1900
Ritsema Prcision Machining Inc — Kalamazoo (G-9319)	G	269 344-8882
Riverside Tool — Harrison Township (G-7721)	G	586 980-7630
Roberts Tool Company — Tecumseh (G-16513)	F	517 423-6691
Robmar Precision Mfg Inc — Westland (G-18416)	E	734 326-2664
Rocksteady Manufacturing LLC — Roseville (G-14472)	F	586 778-5028
Roma Tool Inc — Lake Orion (G-9628)	G	248 218-1889
Ronal Industries Inc — Sterling Heights (G-16159)	F	248 616-9691
Roush Industries Inc — Livonia (G-10394)	G	734 779-7000
Royal Oak Industries Inc — Oxford (G-12914)	D	248 628-2830
▲ Rsb Transmissions Na Inc — Homer (G-8356)	D	517 568-4171
RSI of West Michigan LLC — Muskegon (G-11911)	E	231 728-1155
RTD Manufacturing Inc — Jackson (G-9002)	E	517 783-1550
Ruelle Industries Inc — Clarkston (G-3061)	G	248 618-0333
Rvm Company of Toledo — Carleton (G-2562)	G	734 654-2201
S & C Tool & Manufacturing — Livonia (G-10396)	G	313 378-1003
S & L Machine Products Inc — Madison Heights (G-10823)	F	248 543-6633
S & M Machining Company — Wixom (G-18745)	G	248 348-0310
S & S Tool Inc — Grand Rapids (G-7174)	G	616 458-3219
S-3 Engineering Inc — Ann Arbor (G-646)	F	734 996-2303
Sabre-TEC Inc — Chesterfield (G-2944)	F	586 949-5386
Sage Tool & Engineering — Perry (G-12981)	G	517 625-7817
Saginaw Products Corporation — Saginaw (G-14749)	E	989 753-1411
Saginaw Products Corporation — Saginaw (G-14750)	E	989 753-1411
Salem Tool Company — Northville (G-12256)	G	248 349-2632
Sattler Inc — Ira (G-8712)	F	586 725-1140
Sb Tools LLC — Taylor (G-16470)	G	313 729-2759
▲ Schaefer Screw Products Co — Garden City (G-6108)	E	734 522-0020
Schaller Tool & Die Co — Chesterfield (G-2947)	F	586 949-5500
Schrader Stoves of Michiana — Niles (G-12166)	E	269 684-4494
◆ Schuler Incorporated — Canton (G-2522)	D	734 207-7200
Schwartz Industries Inc — Warren (G-18005)	E	586 759-1777
Schwartz Machine Co — Warren (G-18006)	F	586 756-2300
Scott & ITOH Machine Company — Madison Heights (G-10825)	E	248 585-5385
Scranton Machine Inc — Hillsdale (G-7948)	F	517 437-6000
◆ Sebewaing Tool and Engrg Co — Sebewaing (G-15144)	E	989 883-2000
Sebright Machining Inc — Holland (G-8187)	F	616 399-0445
Servotech Industries Inc — Taylor (G-16471)	G	734 697-5555
Sfs LLC — Taylor (G-16472)	G	734 947-4377
Shared Vision LLC — Warren (G-18010)	F	586 759-1777
Sharp Industries Incorporated — Brighton (G-2069)	G	810 229-6305
Sherwood Prototype Inc — Highland Park (G-7910)	F	313 883-3880
Shively Corp — Niles (G-12167)	F	269 683-9503
Siler Precision Machine Inc — Merrill (G-11264)	G	989 643-7793
◆ Skyway Precision Inc — Plymouth (G-13300)	C	734 454-3550
Slotting Ingram & Machine — Livonia (G-10412)	F	248 478-2430
Smith Metal LLC — Augusta (G-1093)	G	269 731-5211
Smith Metal Turning Inc — Augusta (G-1094)	G	269 731-5211
◆ Smiths Machine & Grinding Inc — Galesburg (G-6083)	E	269 665-4231
Smj Inc — Milford (G-11489)	G	248 343-6244
Smoracy LLC — Remus (G-13817)	G	989 561-2270
Smw Inc — Van Buren Twp (G-17553)	D	517 596-3300
Smw Mfg Inc — Taylor (G-16476)	E	517 596-3300
Smw Mfg Inc — Belleville (G-1491)	E	517 596-3300
SMW Tooling Inc — Holland (G-8198)	F	616 355-9822
Solid Manufacturing Inc — Grass Lake (G-7445)	E	517 522-5895
Sollman & Son Mold & Tool — Grand Junction (G-6383)	G	269 236-6700
SOO Welding Inc — Sault Sainte Marie (G-15100)	G	906 632-8241
Source 1 Cnc LLC — Ida (G-8624)	G	734 269-3381
South Shore Tool & Die Inc — Benton Harbor (G-1587)	E	269 925-9660
Spartan Grinding Inc — Roseville (G-14479)	G	586 774-1970
Spartan Prcision Machining Inc — Wixom (G-18754)	E	248 344-0101
Spaulding Machine Co Inc — Saginaw (G-14761)	G	989 777-0694
Spec Technologies Inc — Shelby Township (G-15340)	D	586 726-0000
Spec Tool Company — Sparta (G-15781)	D	888 887-1717
Specialty Engine Components — Romulus (G-14331)	F	734 955-6500
Spen-Tech Machine Engrg Corp — Flint (G-5765)	D	810 275-6800
Spindle Grinding Service Inc — Albion (G-134)	G	517 629-9334
Spirit Industries Inc — Lansing (G-9740)	G	517 371-7840
Spm Industries Inc — Warren (G-18022)	G	586 758-1100
Spot Design LLC — Ann Arbor (G-662)	E	734 997-0866
Spot On Machine Shop — Zeeland (G-19079)	G	616 283-9830
Springer Machine — Wyoming (G-18907)	G	616 531-9816
Springfield Machine and TI Inc — Springfield (G-15875)	G	269 968-8223
Squires Industries Inc — Wixom (G-18756)	F	248 449-6092
SRS Manufacturing Inc — Clinton Township (G-3362)	F	586 792-5693
St Johns Computer Machining — Saint Johns (G-14916)	G	989 224-7664
St Pierre Inc — Clarkston (G-3068)	G	248 620-2755
Stainless Fabg & Engrg Inc — Portage (G-13610)	G	269 329-6142
Stamping Support Group — Wayne (G-18237)	F	734 727-0605
Stanhope Tool Inc — Warren (G-18027)	E	248 585-5711
Stapels Manufacturing LLC — Troy (G-17370)	F	248 577-5570
Starbuck Machining Inc — Holland (G-8201)	E	616 399-9720
State Wide Grinding Co — Roseville (G-14480)	G	586 778-5700
Statewide Boring and Mch Inc — Van Buren Twp (G-17555)	E	734 397-5950
Steel Industries Inc — Northville (G-12263)	G	734 427-8550
Steel-Fab Wilson & Machine — Mount Pleasant (G-11742)	G	989 773-6046
Sterling Edge Inc — Wixom (G-18758)	E	248 438-6034
Sterling Prod Machining LLC — Harrison Township (G-7727)	G	586 493-0633
Stevens Custom Fabrication — Alpena (G-321)	G	989 340-1184
Steves Machine Shop LLC — Troy (G-17373)	G	248 563-1662
Stirnemann Tool & Mch Co Inc — Clawson (G-3110)	G	248 435-4040
Stoney Crest Regrind Service — Bridgeport (G-1918)	F	989 777-7190
Stork Industries Cbd LLC — Commerce Township (G-3575)	G	248 513-1778
Strauss Tool Inc — Corunna (G-3718)	G	989 743-4741
Sturdy Grinding Machining Inc — New Haven (G-12037)	F	586 463-8880
Stus Welding & Fabrication — Holland (G-8206)	G	616 392-8459
Sun Tool Company — Detroit (G-4614)	G	313 837-2442
Superb Machine Repair Inc — New Haven (G-12038)	F	586 749-8800
Superior Cutter Grinding Inc — Shelby Township (G-15347)	G	586 781-2365
Superior Cutting Service Inc — Holland (G-8209)	F	616 796-0114
Superior Design & Mfg — Metamora (G-11287)	F	810 678-3950
Superior Machine & Tool Inc — Lansing (G-9793)	F	800 822-9524
Superior Products Mfg Inc — Croswell (G-3736)	G	810 679-4479
Superior Roll LLC — Petersburg (G-12985)	F	734 279-1831
Supreme Tool & Machine Inc — Waterford (G-18168)	F	248 673-8408
Surface Induction Tech — Macomb (G-10639)	G	248 881-2481
Swiss Precision Machining Inc — Macomb (G-10640)	F	586 677-7558
Sws - Trimac Inc — Saginaw (G-14771)	E	989 791-4595
Symonds Machine Co Inc — Dowagiac (G-4798)	G	269 782-8051
Synchron Laser Service Inc — Plymouth (G-13307)	F	248 486-0402

Employee Codes: A=Over 500 employees, B=251-500 C=101-250, D=51-100, E=20-50, F=10-19, G=3-9

35 INDUSTRIAL AND COMMERCIAL MACHINERY AND COMPUTER EQUIPMENT

Systrand Prsta Eng Systems LLC ....F 734 479-8100
  Brownstown Twp (G-2160)
T & M Machining Inc ....G 586 294-5781
  Fraser (G-6002)
T Q Machining Inc ....E 231 726-5914
  Muskegon (G-11929)
T&K Machine ....G 989 836-0811
  Alger (G-139)
Tait Grinding Service Inc ....G 248 437-5100
  Howell (G-8525)
▲ Tec-Option Inc ....F 517 486-6055
  Blissfield (G-1777)
Tech Tooling Specialties Inc ....F 517 782-8898
  Jackson (G-9016)
Techni CAM and Manufacturing ....F 734 261-6477
  Livonia (G-10430)
Technical Machining Welding ....G 269 463-3738
  Watervliet (G-18183)
Ted Senk Tooling Inc ....F 989 725-6067
  Owosso (G-12861)
Tesla Machine & Tool Ltd ....G 586 441-2402
  Warren (G-18038)
Thermfrmer Parts Suppliers LLC ....E 989 435-3800
  Beaverton (G-1432)
Thermotron Industries Inc ....E 616 928-9044
  Holland (G-8218)
▼ Thierica Equipment Corporation ....E 616 453-6570
  Grand Rapids (G-7259)
Thomas A Despres Inc ....F 313 633-9648
  Williamsburg (G-18565)
▲ Thomas L Snarey & Assoc Inc ......F 734 241-8474
  Monroe (G-11582)
Thor Tool and Machine LLC ....G 248 628-3185
  Lakeville (G-9649)
Thread Grinding Service Inc ....G 248 474-5350
  Farmington Hills (G-5399)
▲ Thread-Craft Inc ....D 586 323-1116
  Sterling Heights (G-16205)
Three M Tool & Machine Inc ....E 248 363-0982
  Commerce Township (G-3577)
Thunder Technologies LLC ....F 248 844-4875
  Rochester Hills (G-14126)
▼ TI Fluid Systems LLC ....A 248 494-5000
  Auburn Hills (G-1054)
◆ TI Group Auto Systems LLC ....B 248 296-8000
  Auburn Hills (G-1055)
Tmd Machining Inc ....E 269 685-3091
  Plainwell (G-13098)
Tomco Fabricating & Engrg Inc ....F 248 669-2900
  Wixom (G-18773)
Tomkins Products Inc ....F 313 894-2222
  Detroit (G-4636)
Tommie Inc ....G 313 377-2931
  Redford (G-13779)
Tool House Inc ....G 248 481-7092
  Auburn Hills (G-1060)
Top Craft Tool Inc ....E 586 461-4600
  Clinton Township (G-3378)
Total Quality Machining Inc ....F 231 767-1825
  Muskegon (G-11934)
Tramm Tech Inc ....G 989 723-2944
  Owosso (G-12862)
Tree Cutting Stump Grinding ....G 231 856-9021
  Morley (G-11624)
Treib Inc ....F 989 752-4821
  Saginaw (G-14778)
Tri County Precision Grinding ....E 586 776-6600
  Warren (G-18042)
Tri Matics Mfg Inc ....G 586 469-3150
  Harrison Township (G-7730)
Tri-City Repair Company ....G 989 835-4784
  Hope (G-8364)
Tri-Master Inc ....G 248 541-1864
  Royal Oak (G-14586)
Tri-Power Manufacturing Inc ....G 734 414-8084
  Plymouth (G-13323)
Tri-Star Tool & Machine Co ....F 734 729-5700
  Westland (G-18423)
Tri-State Cast Technologies Co ....G 231 582-0452
  Boyne City (G-1904)
Tri-Tool Boring Machine Co ....F 586 598-0036
  Chesterfield (G-2958)
▲ Tri-Way Manufacturing Inc ....E 586 776-0700
  Roseville (G-14485)
Triad Manufacturing Co Inc ....G 248 583-9636
  Madison Heights (G-10847)
Triangle Grinding Company Inc ....E 586 749-6540
  New Haven (G-12040)
▲ Tribal Manufacturing Inc ....D 269 781-3901
  Marshall (G-11076)

Tric Tool Ltd ....E 616 395-1530
  Holland (G-8230)
Trig Tool Inc ....G 248 543-2550
  Warren (G-18043)
Trinity Industries Inc ....D 517 741-4300
  Union City (G-17498)
Triple E LLC ....E 517 531-4481
  Parma (G-12940)
Trison Tool and Machine Inc ....G 248 628-8770
  Oxford (G-12925)
◆ Triumph Gear Systems - McOmb I..E 586 781-2800
  Macomb (G-10644)
Tru Line Co ....F 313 215-1935
  Westland (G-18424)
Tru-Bore Machine Tool Co Inc ....G 734 729-9590
  Westland (G-18425)
Tru-Thread Co Inc ....G 248 399-0255
  Ferndale (G-5590)
True Tool Cnc Regrinding & Mfg ......E 616 677-1751
  Grand Rapids (G-7279)
Truform Machine Inc ....G 517 782-8523
  Jackson (G-9025)
Trusted Tool Mfg Grand Haven ....E 616 607-2023
  Grand Haven (G-6373)
Trusted Tool Mfg Inc ....G 810 750-6000
  Fenton (G-5510)
▲ Tsm Corporation ....D 248 276-4700
  Auburn Hills (G-1066)
▲ Tuff Automation Inc ....E 616 735-3939
  Grand Rapids (G-7280)
Turn Tech Inc ....E 586 415-8090
  Fraser (G-6007)
Tyrone Tool Company Inc ....G 810 742-4762
  Burton (G-2249)
U P Fabricating Co Inc ....G 906 341-2868
  Manistique (G-10924)
U P Machine & Engineering Co ....E 906 497-5278
  Powers (G-13650)
▼ U S Group Inc ....G 313 372-7900
  Rochester Hills (G-14135)
Ultimate Tube Bender Part ....G 810 599-7862
  Brighton (G-2086)
Ultra Fab & Machine Inc ....G 248 628-7065
  Oxford (G-12928)
Ultra Tool Grind Inc ....G 989 471-5169
  Ossineke (G-12780)
United Engineered Tooling ....E 231 947-3650
  Traverse City (G-16872)
United Systems ....G 248 583-9670
  Troy (G-17413)
Urgent Design and Mfg Inc ....E 810 245-1300
  Lapeer (G-9963)
Urgent Tool and Machine Inc ....E 616 288-5000
  Grand Rapids (G-7300)
Valade Precision Machining Inc ....G 586 771-7705
  Eastpointe (G-4947)
Van Machine Co ....G 269 729-9540
  East Leroy (G-4915)
Van S Fabrications Inc ....G 810 679-2115
  Croswell (G-3738)
Vectorall Manufacturing Inc ....E 248 486-4570
  Brighton (G-2093)
Veet Axelson Liberty Industry ....F 586 776-3000
  Warren (G-18052)
Veit Tool & Gage Inc ....G 810 658-4949
  Davison (G-3800)
Venture Tool & Metalizing ....G 989 883-9121
  Sebewaing (G-15146)
▲ Versatube Corporation ....F 248 524-0299
  Troy (G-17438)
Versi-Tech Incorporated ....F 586 944-2230
  Roseville (G-14490)
Vickers Engineering Inc ....F 269 756-9133
  Three Oaks (G-16561)
Vickers Engineering Inc ....C 269 426-8545
  New Troy (G-12076)
Viking Oil LLC ....G 989 366-4772
  Prudenville (G-13659)
Village Automatics Inc ....G 269 663-8521
  Edwardsburg (G-5020)
Vince Krstevski ....G 586 739-7600
  Sterling Heights (G-16224)
Vn Industries Inc ....G 616 540-2812
  Grand Rapids (G-7321)
W T & M Inc ....G 313 533-7888
  Redford (G-13785)
Waber Tool & Engineering Co ....F 269 342-0765
  Kalamazoo (G-9365)
Warren Manufacturing ....G 269 483-0603
  White Pigeon (G-18486)

We Are Urban Technology LLC ....F 313 779-4406
  Harper Woods (G-7674)
Webb Partners Inc ....E 734 727-0560
  Westland (G-18430)
Weber Steel Inc ....F 989 868-4162
  Vassar (G-17586)
Wedge Mill Tool Inc ....G 248 486-6400
  Brighton (G-2095)
Welz Tool Mch & Boring Co Inc ....E 734 425-3920
  Livonia (G-10473)
Werkema Machine Company Inc ......G 616 455-7650
  Grand Rapids (G-7330)
West Mich Prcsion McHining Inc ......F 616 791-1970
  Grand Rapids (G-7332)
West Michigan Grinding Svc Inc ......E 231 739-4245
  Norton Shores (G-12343)
Westech Corp ....E 231 766-3914
  Muskegon (G-11943)
▲ Whitehall Products LLC ....D 231 894-2688
  Whitehall (G-18514)
▲ Willenborg Associates Inc ....F 810 724-5678
  Bruce Twp (G-2186)
Willis Engine & Machining Svc ....E 616 842-4366
  Fruitport (G-6071)
Witco Inc ....F 810 387-4231
  Greenwood (G-7512)
Wmt Properties Inc ....F 248 486-6400
  Brighton (G-2097)
Wolverine Tool Co ....F 810 664-2964
  Lapeer (G-9968)
Woodie Manufacturing Inc ....E 517 782-7663
  Jackson (G-9038)
Woodville Heights Enterprises ....F 231 629-7750
  Big Rapids (G-1690)
World Class Equipment Company ....F 586 331-2121
  Shelby Township (G-15370)
Wyandotte Collet and Tool Inc ....F 734 283-8055
  Wyandotte (G-18845)
X L T Engineering Inc ....E 989 684-4344
  Kawkawlin (G-9420)
▲ X-L Machine Co Inc ....E 269 279-5128
  Three Rivers (G-16590)
Xl Engineering LLC ....G 616 656-0324
  Caledonia (G-2407)
Yale Tool & Engraving Inc ....F 734 459-7171
  Plymouth (G-13340)
Yen Group LLC ....F 810 201-6457
  Port Huron (G-13542)
Z & R Electric Service Inc ....E 906 774-0468
  Iron Mountain (G-8738)
Zalco Products LLC ....G 586 354-0227
  Macomb (G-10653)
Zellco Precision Inc ....G 269 684-1720
  Niles (G-12175)

36 ELECTRONIC AND OTHER ELECTRICAL EQUIPMENT AND COMPONENTS, EXCEPT COMPUTER

3612 Power, Distribution & Specialty Transformers

Actia Electronics Inc ....G 574 264-2373
  Romulus (G-14245)
▼ Aprotech Powertrain LLC ....E 248 649-9200
  Troy (G-16941)
Austin Distributors LLC ....G 248 665-2077
  Westland (G-18357)
Controlled Magnetics Inc ....F 734 449-7225
  Whitmore Lake (G-18528)
▼ Controlled Power Company ....C 248 528-3700
  Troy (G-17027)
D & W Square LLC ....G 313 493-4970
  Detroit (G-4116)
Detroit Renewable Energy LLC ....C 313 972-5700
  Detroit (G-4162)
Eastern Power and Lighting ....G 248 739-0908
  Dearborn Heights (G-3925)
▲ Ebw Electronics Inc ....B 616 786-0575
  Holland (G-8021)
Elite Industrial Mfg LLC ....F 616 377-7769
  Holland (G-8027)
Eugene ....E 313 217-9297
  Detroit (G-4217)
Gti Liquidating Inc ....D 616 842-5430
  Grand Haven (G-6309)
Gti Power Acquisition LLC ....C 616 842-5430
  Grand Haven (G-6310)

SIC SECTION36 ELECTRONIC AND OTHER ELECTRICAL EQUIPMENT AND COMPONENTS, EXCEPT COMPUTER36 ELECTRONIC AND OTHER

Heyboer Transformers Inc....E....616 842-5830 Grand Haven *(G-6317)*
▼ Houseart LLC....G....248 651-8124 Rochester *(G-13905)*
Lvc Technologies Inc....E....248 373-3778 Davison *(G-3789)*
Marcie Electric Inc....G....248 486-1200 Brighton *(G-2025)*
▲ Maxitrol Company....D....248 356-1400 Southfield *(G-15648)*
▲ Meiden America Inc....E....734 459-1781 Northville *(G-12239)*
▲ Nextek Power Systems Inc....G....313 887-1321 Detroit *(G-4484)*
Osborne Transformer Corp....F....586 218-6900 Fraser *(G-5972)*
Parker-Hannifin Corporation....B....269 629-5000 Richland *(G-13826)*
Power Control Systems Inc....G....517 339-1442 Okemos *(G-12682)*
Powertran Corporation....E....248 399-4300 Ferndale *(G-5580)*
Rizk National Industries Inc....F....586 757-4700 Warren *(G-17997)*
Rtg Products Inc....G....734 323-8916 Redford *(G-13768)*
S H Leggitt Company....B....269 781-3901 Marshall *(G-11073)*
Sgm Transformer LLC....G....734 922-2400 Ann Arbor *(G-649)*
Syndevco Inc....F....248 356-2839 Southfield *(G-15716)*
Tara Industries Inc....G....248 477-6520 Livonia *(G-10429)*
US Green Energy Solutions LLC....G....810 955-2992 Livonia *(G-10454)*

3613 Switchgear & Switchboard Apparatus

A & L Metal Products....G....734 654-8990 Carleton *(G-2549)*
Alpha Tran Engineering Co....E....616 837-7341 Nunica *(G-12576)*
Automation Enterprises Inc....G....586 774-0280 Roseville *(G-14377)*
Benesh Corporation....F....734 244-4143 Monroe *(G-11532)*
C L Design Inc....G....248 474-4220 Farmington Hills *(G-5190)*
Clarkston Control Products....G....248 394-1430 Clarkston *(G-3024)*
▲ Command Electronics Inc....E....269 679-4011 Schoolcraft *(G-15115)*
Control Technique Incorporated....D....586 997-3200 Sterling Heights *(G-15970)*
Danlyn Controls Inc....G....586 773-6797 Chesterfield *(G-2867)*
Eagle Engineering & Supply Co....E....989 356-4526 Alpena *(G-291)*
▲ Ews Legacy LLC....C....248 853-6363 Rochester Hills *(G-14006)*
Generl-Lctrical-Mechanical Inc....G....248 698-1110 White Lake *(G-18456)*
H H Barnum Co....G....248 486-5982 Brighton *(G-2007)*
Harlo Corporation....D....616 538-0550 Grandville *(G-7387)*
Hear Clear Inc....G....734 525-8467 Saline *(G-15020)*
Henshaw Inc....D....586 752-0700 Armada *(G-736)*
▲ Hugo Benzing LLC....E....248 264-6478 Wixom *(G-18680)*
Hydro-Logic Inc....E....586 757-7477 Warren *(G-17857)*
Indicon LLC....C....586 274-0505 Sterling Heights *(G-16047)*
Infra Corporation....F....248 623-0400 Waterford *(G-18129)*
Intec Automated Controls Inc....E....586 532-8881 Sterling Heights *(G-16050)*
International Door Inc....E....248 547-7240 Canton *(G-2478)*
Java Manufacturing Inc....G....616 784-3873 Comstock Park *(G-3613)*
◆ Jervis B Webb Company....B....248 553-1000 Novi *(G-12449)*
Kirk Enterprises Inc....G....248 357-5070 Southfield *(G-15617)*
M & N Controls Inc....E....734 850-2127 Temperance *(G-16538)*
▲ M P Jackson LLC....F....517 782-0391 Jackson *(G-8939)*
Memcon North America LLC....F....269 281-0478 Stevensville *(G-16261)*
Metro-Fabricating LLC....D....989 667-8100 Bay City *(G-1377)*
Motor City Electric Tech Inc....D....313 921-5300 Detroit *(G-4467)*
▲ Mp Hollywood LLC....F....517 782-0391 Jackson *(G-8970)*
Parker-Hannifin Corporation....B....269 629-5000 Richland *(G-13826)*
Patriot Sensors & Contrls Corp....F....810 378-5511 Peck *(G-12962)*
◆ Patriot Sensors & Contrls Corp....D....248 435-0700 Peck *(G-12963)*
▲ PEC of America Corporation....F....248 675-3130 Novi *(G-12504)*
Power Controllers LLC....G....248 888-9896 Farmington Hills *(G-5351)*
Quality Business Engraving....G....248 852-5123 Rochester Hills *(G-14094)*
S Main Company LLC....E....248 960-1540 Wixom *(G-18747)*
Schneider Electric Usa Inc....G....810 733-9400 Flint *(G-5760)*
Spec Corporation....G....517 529-4105 Clarklake *(G-3008)*
▲ Ssi Electronics Inc....E....616 866-8880 Belmont *(G-1517)*
Superior Controls Inc....C....734 454-0500 Plymouth *(G-13306)*
Systems Control Inc....A....906 774-0440 Iron Mountain *(G-8735)*
Tara Industries Inc....G....248 477-6520 Livonia *(G-10429)*
Thierica Controls Inc....G....616 956-5500 Grand Rapids *(G-7258)*
US Energia LLC....G....248 669-1462 Rochester *(G-13936)*
X-Bar Automation Inc....E....248 616-9890 Troy *(G-17455)*
▲ X-Rite Incorporated....C....616 803-2100 Grand Rapids *(G-7353)*

3621 Motors & Generators

3dfx Interactive Inc....G....918 938-8967 Saginaw *(G-14599)*
Acat Global LLC....F....231 437-5000 White Cloud *(G-18437)*
▲ Ainsworth Electric Inc....E....810 984-5768 Port Huron *(G-13433)*
Allied Motion Technologies Inc....G....989 725-5151 Owosso *(G-12822)*
American Mitsuba Corporation....C....989 773-0377 Mount Pleasant *(G-11678)*
Ametek Inc....G....248 435-7540 Peck *(G-12961)*
▲ Ballard Power Systems Corp....A....313 583-5980 Dearborn *(G-3812)*
Bay Motor Products Inc....E....231 941-0411 Traverse City *(G-16615)*
Celerity Systems N Amer Inc....G....248 994-7696 Novi *(G-12382)*
Continental Auto Systems Inc....G....248 267-9408 Troy *(G-17023)*
Denso Manufacturing NC Inc....A....269 441-2040 Battle Creek *(G-1217)*
▲ Detroit Coil Co....E....248 658-1543 Ferndale *(G-5543)*
Diamond Electric Mfg Corp....F....734 995-5525 Farmington Hills *(G-5215)*
DMS Electric Apparatus Service....E....269 349-7000 Kalamazoo *(G-9171)*
Edwards Industrial Sales Inc....G....517 887-6100 Lansing *(G-9833)*
▲ Ehc Inc....G....313 259-2266 Troy *(G-17079)*
Eltek Inc....G....616 363-6397 Belmont *(G-1506)*
Energy Products Inc....G....248 866-5622 Troy *(G-17090)*
▼ Etx Holdings Inc....G....989 463-1151 Alma *(G-241)*
Ev Anywhere LLC....G....313 653-9870 Detroit *(G-4218)*
▲ Feed - Lease Corp....E....248 377-0000 Auburn Hills *(G-896)*
◆ Flint Hydrostatics Inc....F....901 794-2462 Chesterfield *(G-2883)*
Ford Motor Company....A....734 484-8626 Ypsilanti *(G-18947)*
Fortis Energy Services Inc....D....248 283-7100 Troy *(G-17119)*
◆ Gast Manufacturing Inc....B....269 926-6171 Benton Harbor *(G-1551)*
▲ Genco Alliance LLC....G....269 216-5500 Kalamazoo *(G-9192)*
▼ Global Fleet Sales LLC....G....248 327-6483 Southfield *(G-15576)*
Great Lakes Pwr Generation LLC....G....231 492-3764 Elk Rapids *(G-5026)*
H W Jencks Incorporated....E....231 352-4422 Frankfort *(G-5878)*
Heco Inc....E....269 381-7200 Kalamazoo *(G-9210)*
Hydraulex Intl Holdings Inc....E....914 682-2700 Chesterfield *(G-2891)*
Ies-Synergy Inc....G....586 206-4410 Troy *(G-17159)*
Independent Mfg Solutions Corp....E....248 960-3550 Wixom *(G-18684)*
Induction Engineering Inc....F....586 716-4700 New Baltimore *(G-11982)*
Industrial Computer & Controls....F....734 697-4152 Van Buren Twp *(G-17530)*
Jlm Elec....G....989 486-3788 Midland *(G-11377)*
◆ Kaydon Corporation....B....734 747-7025 Ann Arbor *(G-538)*
Kraft Power Corporation....E....989 748-4040 Gaylord *(G-6140)*
Magna E-Car USA LLC....D....248 606-0600 Holly *(G-8281)*
Maxitrol Company....G....517 486-2820 Blissfield *(G-1769)*
Monarch Electric Service Co....G....313 388-7800 Melvindale *(G-11206)*
◆ Morrell Incorporated....D....248 373-1600 Auburn Hills *(G-975)*
▲ Motor Products Corporation....C....989 725-5151 Owosso *(G-12845)*
Nidec Motors & Actuators (usa)....G....248 340-9977 Auburn Hills *(G-983)*
North Country Power Generation....G....231 499-3951 Elk Rapids *(G-5028)*
◆ Patriot Sensors & Contrls Corp....D....248 435-0700 Peck *(G-12963)*
▲ Pontiac Coil Inc....C....248 922-1100 Clarkston *(G-3057)*
Power Controllers LLC....G....248 888-9896 Farmington Hills *(G-5351)*
Powerthru Inc....G....734 583-5004 Livonia *(G-10370)*
Powerthru Inc....F....734 853-5004 Livonia *(G-10371)*
▲ Prestolite Electric LLC....G....248 313-3807 Novi *(G-12512)*
Prestolite Electric Holding....A....248 313-3807 Novi *(G-12513)*
▲ Prestolite Electric Inc....F....866 463-7078 Novi *(G-12514)*
▲ Pro Slot Ltd....G....616 897-6000 Hartford *(G-7766)*
Reuland Electric Co....F....517 546-4400 Howell *(G-8508)*
Sfm LLC....G....248 719-0212 Northville *(G-12260)*
Smart Power Systems Inc....C....231 832-5525 Reed City *(G-13798)*
▲ Southern Auto Wholesalers Inc....F....248 335-5555 Pontiac *(G-13417)*
Spina Wind LLC....G....586 771-8080 Warren *(G-18021)*
Troy Synchro Sharkettes....G....734 395-8899 Ypsilanti *(G-18982)*
Twm Technology LLC....F....989 684-7050 Bay City *(G-1407)*
Vandervest Electric Mtr & Fabg....G....231 843-6196 Ludington *(G-10555)*
Vico Louisville LLC....E....502 245-1616 Plymouth *(G-13333)*
Z & R Electric Service Inc....E....906 774-0468 Iron Mountain *(G-8738)*

3624 Carbon & Graphite Prdts

Acp Technologies LLC....G....586 322-3511 Saint Clair Shores *(G-14846)*
American Graphite Corporation....G....586 757-3540 Warren *(G-17702)*

S I C

Employee Codes: A=Over 500 employees, B=251-500 C=101-250, D=51-100, E=20-50, F=10-19, G=3-9
2022 Harris Michigan Industrial Directory
869

36 ELECTRONIC AND OTHER ELECTRICAL EQUIPMENT AND COMPONENTS, EXCEPT COMPUTER

Company	Code	Phone
Astech Inc, Vassar (G-17577)	E	989 823-7211
Bay Carbon Inc, Bay City (G-1326)	E	989 686-8090
▲ Bay Composites Inc, Essexville (G-5110)	E	989 891-9159
Carbone of America, Bay City (G-1336)	F	989 894-2911
Composite Builders LLC, Holland (G-8002)	G	616 377-7767
▲ Cummings-Moore Graphite Co, Detroit (G-4112)	E	313 841-1615
Dowaksa Usa LLC, Midland (G-11356)	G	989 600-8610
Fortress Stblztion Systems LLC, Holland (G-8040)	G	616 355-1421
Graphite Electrodes Ltd, Bay City (G-1362)	E	989 893-3635
Graphite Machining Inc, Metamora (G-11279)	F	810 678-2227
Mersen, Bay City (G-1374)	E	989 894-2911
◆ Mersen USA Gs Corp, Greenville (G-7500)	D	616 754-5671
Mersen USA Gs Corp, Bay City (G-1375)	F	989 894-2911
Mersen USA Gs Corp, Greenville (G-7501)	C	616 754-5671
National Carbon Tech LLC, Gwinn (G-7585)	E	651 330-4063
Sankuer Composite Tech Inc, Sterling Heights (G-16163)	E	586 264-1880
▲ U S Graphite Inc, Saginaw (G-14783)	G	989 755-0441
Wahoo Composites LLC, Dexter (G-4762)	F	734 424-0966

3625 Relays & Indl Controls

Company	Code	Phone
▲ A E C Inc, Whitmore Lake (G-18515)	D	810 231-9546
A1 Noise Control, Bloomfield Hills (G-1789)	G	248 538-7585
Acculift Inc, Melvindale (G-11196)	G	313 382-5121
Acromag Incorporated, Wixom (G-18594)	D	248 624-1541
▲ Advanced Automation Group LLC, Madison Heights (G-10661)	G	248 299-8100
▲ AEL/Span LLC, Van Buren Twp (G-17507)	E	734 957-1600
AG Davis Gage & Engrg Co, Sterling Heights (G-15926)	E	586 977-9000
Altair Systems Inc, Wixom (G-18606)	F	248 668-0116
American Brake and Clutch Inc, Chesterfield (G-2838)	F	586 948-3730
Amtex Inc, Clinton Township (G-3170)	G	586 792-7888
Amx Corp, Sterling Heights (G-15932)	F	469 624-8000
▲ Apollo America Inc, Auburn Hills (G-791)	D	248 332-3900
Automated Control Systems Inc, Novi (G-12369)	G	248 476-9490
Bay Electronics Inc, Roseville (G-14376)	E	586 296-0900
Borgwarner Thermal Systems Inc, Cadillac (G-2317)	G	231 779-7500
▲ Burners Inc, Milford (G-11457)	G	248 676-9141
Burr Engineering & Dev Co, Battle Creek (G-1201)	G	269 966-3122
Carmel Township, Charlotte (G-2738)	G	888 805-6182
Complete Dsign Automtn Systems, Dexter (G-4732)	G	734 424-2789
Comptek Inc, Farmington Hills (G-5206)	E	248 477-5215
Concentric Labs Inc, Mason (G-11119)	G	517 969-3038
Control One Inc, Sterling Heights (G-15969)	G	586 979-6106
Controls For Industries Inc, Webberville (G-18244)	G	517 468-3385
▲ Ctc Acquisition Company LLC, Rockford (G-14163)	G	616 884-7100
Cusolar Industries Inc, Chesterfield (G-2863)	E	586 949-3880
Custom Engineering & Design, Troy (G-17038)	G	248 680-1435
Dare Auto Inc, Plymouth (G-13152)	E	734 228-6243
Data Acquisition Ctrl Systems, Brighton (G-1973)	F	248 437-6096
Denso International Amer Inc, Van Buren Twp (G-17523)	G	248 359-4177
▲ Detroit Coil Co, Ferndale (G-5543)	E	248 658-1543
Eagle Engineering & Supply Co, Alpena (G-291)	E	989 356-4526
Eaton Aerospace LLC, Grand Rapids (G-6663)	B	616 949-1090
Eaton Corporation, Clinton Township (G-3228)		586 228-2029
Edon Controls Inc, Troy (G-17078)	G	248 280-0420
Electrocraft Michigan Inc, Saline (G-15014)	E	603 516-1297
▲ Electrojet Inc, Wixom (G-18653)	E	734 272-4709
▲ Emergency Technology Inc, Hudsonville (G-8581)	D	616 896-7100
Energy Products Inc, Troy (G-17090)	G	248 866-5622
◆ Energy Products Inc, Madison Heights (G-10722)	G	248 545-7700
▲ Eto Magnetic Corp, Grand Rapids (G-6686)	C	616 957-2570
Fenton Systems Inc, Goodrich (G-6223)	G	810 636-6318
▲ Fidia Co, Rochester Hills (G-14011)	F	248 680-0700
Fitz-Rite Products Inc, Troy (G-17113)	E	248 528-8440
▲ Flextronics Automotive USA Inc, Coopersville (G-3686)	D	248 853-5724
Ford Motor Company, Ypsilanti (G-18947)	A	734 484-8626
Fortis Energy Services Inc, Troy (G-17119)	G	248 283-7100
Galco Industrial Elec Inc, Madison Heights (G-10730)	F	248 542-9090
Ghsp Inc, Grand Haven (G-6300)	G	248 588-5095
▲ Glassmaster Controls Co Inc, Kalamazoo (G-9198)	E	269 382-2010
Great Lakes Electric LLC, Saint Joseph (G-14932)	G	269 408-8276
Harold G Schaevitz Inds LLC, Bloomfield Hills (G-1827)	G	248 636-1515
Hi-Lex Controls Incorporated, Hudson (G-8551)	C	517 448-2752
Hydraulic Systems Technology, Rochester Hills (G-14036)	G	248 656-5810
Hydro-Logic Inc, Warren (G-17857)	E	586 757-7477
Incoe Corporation, Auburn Hills (G-936)	C	248 616-0220
Indicon LLC, Sterling Heights (G-16047)	C	586 274-0505
Industrial Computer & Controls, Van Buren Twp (G-17530)	F	734 697-4152
Industrial Temperature Control, Canton (G-2474)	G	734 451-8740
Infinity Controls & Engrg Inc, Lake Orion (G-9609)	G	248 397-8267
Innovative Support Svcs Inc, Troy (G-17168)	F	248 585-3600
ITT Industries Holdings Inc, Novi (G-12443)	F	248 863-2153
▲ ITT Motion Tech Amer LLC, Novi (G-12444)	F	248 863-2161
▲ ITT Motion Technologies LLC, Novi (G-12445)	F	248 863-2161
Jenda Controls Inc, Rochester (G-13910)	G	248 656-0090
Jered LLC, Iron Mountain (G-8723)	G	906 776-1800
▲ Johnson Electric N Amer Inc, Plymouth (G-13206)	D	734 392-5300
Linak US Inc, Grand Rapids (G-6945)	G	502 413-0387
Lor Manufacturing Co Inc, Weidman (G-18254)	G	989 644-2581
M K Eaton Services LLC, South Lyon (G-15444)	G	608 852-3118
▲ M P Jackson LLC, Jackson (G-8939)	F	517 782-0391
Mahle Powertrain LLC, Farmington Hills (G-5307)	D	248 305-8200
Manufacturing Ctrl Systems Inc, Rochester Hills (G-14058)	G	248 853-7400
▲ Maxitrol Company, Southfield (G-15648)	D	248 356-1400
Maxitrol Company, Colon (G-3488)	G	269 432-3291
Maxitrol Company, Blissfield (G-1769)		517 486-2820
◆ Melling Tool Co, Jackson (G-8951)	B	517 787-8172
▲ Mercury Displacement Inds Inc, Edwardsburg (G-5009)	D	269 663-8574
◆ Meritor Inc, Troy (G-17246)	C	248 435-1000
▲ Meter Devices Company Inc, Farmington Hills (G-5317)	D	330 455-0301
Motor Control Incorporated, Melvindale (G-11207)		313 389-4000
Murray Equipment Company Inc, Warren (G-17938)	F	313 869-4444
Nabco Inc, Reed City (G-13796)	E	231 832-2001
▲ Nadex of America Corporation, Farmington Hills (G-5330)	E	248 477-3900
National Control Systems Inc, Hamburg (G-7592)	G	810 231-2901
National Crane & Hoist Service, Leonard (G-10002)	G	248 789-4535
Noisemeters Inc, Berkley (G-1633)	G	248 840-6559
Parker-Hannifin Corporation, Kalamazoo (G-9288)	B	269 384-3459
Patriot Sensors & Contrls Corp, Peck (G-12962)	F	810 378-5511
◆ Patriot Sensors & Contrls Corp, Peck (G-12963)	D	248 435-0700
Peak Industries Co Inc, Dearborn (G-3883)	E	313 846-8666
▲ Peaker Services Inc, Brighton (G-2049)	E	248 437-4174
◆ Pilz Automtn Safety Ltd Partnr, Canton (G-2507)	E	734 354-0272
Precise Power Systems LLC, Whitmore Lake (G-18544)	G	734 550-9505
▲ Precision Controls Company, Ann Arbor (G-620)	F	734 663-3104
▲ Prestolite Electric LLC, Novi (G-12512)	G	248 313-3807
Radius LLC, Milford (G-11485)	G	248 685-0773
Rekey Luxury Homes LLC, Troy (G-17329)	G	586 747-0342
Rick Wykle LLC, Trenton (G-16891)	G	734 839-6376
Rjg Technologies Inc, Traverse City (G-16822)	D	231 947-3111
Rockwell Automation Inc, Troy (G-17335)	G	248 696-1200
Rockwell Automation Inc, Troy (G-17336)	E	248 435-2574
Rockwell Automation Inc, Wayland (G-18204)	G	269 792-9137
▲ Ross Decco Company, Troy (G-17337)	E	248 764-1845
▲ Safari Circuits Inc, Otsego (G-12799)	C	269 694-9471
▲ Serapid Inc, Sterling Heights (G-16171)	F	586 274-0774
Sheila J Eaton Phd PC, Warren (G-18011)	G	586 215-1035
Shelton Technology LLC, Troy (G-17349)	G	248 816-1585
▲ Sine Systems Corporation, Clinton Township (G-3359)	C	586 465-3131
Singh Automation LLC, Portage (G-13607)	G	269 267-6078
▲ Sloan Transportation Pdts Inc, Holland (G-8197)	E	616 395-5600
Solutions For Industry Inc, Hudson (G-8562)	G	517 448-8608
▲ Southern Auto Wholesalers Inc, Pontiac (G-13417)	F	248 335-5555
Ssi Technology Inc, Sterling Heights (G-16188)	D	248 582-0600
▲ Static Controls Corp, Wixom (G-18757)	E	248 926-4400
Stegner Controls LLC, Auburn Hills (G-1038)	E	248 904-0400
Stonebrdge Technical Entps Ltd, Fenton (G-5505)	F	810 750-0040

◆ Stoneridge Inc .... A 248 489-9300
  Novi *(G-12543)*
Stoneridge Control Devices Inc .... G 248 489-9300
  Novi *(G-12545)*
Superior Controls Inc .... C 734 454-0500
  Plymouth *(G-13306)*
Symorex Ltd .... F 734 971-6000
  Ann Arbor *(G-670)*
▲ Synchronous Manufacturing Inc ..... F 517 764-6930
  Michigan Center *(G-11296)*
▲ TAC Manufacturing Inc .... B 517 789-7000
  Jackson *(G-9014)*
Tachyon Corporation .... F 586 598-4320
  Chesterfield *(G-2953)*
Temcor Systems Inc .... G 810 229-0006
  Brighton *(G-2077)*
▲ Tramec Sloan LLC .... E 616 395-5600
  Holland *(G-8224)*
Valeo North America Inc .... C 248 619-8300
  Troy *(G-17428)*
Valley Group of Companies .... F 989 799-9669
  Saginaw *(G-14787)*
Valmec Inc .... G 810 629-8750
  Fenton *(G-5512)*
Versatile Systems LLC .... F 734 397-3957
  Canton *(G-2537)*
▲ Vibracoustic Usa Inc .... C 269 637-2116
  South Haven *(G-15422)*
▲ Von Weise LLC .... G 517 618-9763
  Eaton Rapids *(G-4975)*
Warner Instruments .... G 616 843-5342
  Grand Haven *(G-6379)*
◆ Welding Technology Corp .... C 248 477-3900
  Farmington Hills *(G-5413)*
Winford Engineering LLC .... G 989 671-9721
  Auburn *(G-771)*
Wired Technologies LLC .... G 313 800-1611
  Livonia *(G-10477)*

3629 Electrical Indl Apparatus, NEC

Actia Electronics Inc .... G 574 264-2373
  Romulus *(G-14245)*
Adam Electronics Incorporated .... E 248 583-2000
  Madison Heights *(G-10659)*
▲ Blissfield Manufacturing Co .... C 517 486-2121
  Blissfield *(G-1761)*
Comec USA .... G 810 299-3000
  Brighton *(G-1965)*
▼ Controlled Power Company .... C 248 528-3700
  Troy *(G-17027)*
Exide Technologies LLC .... G 248 853-5000
  Auburn Hills *(G-884)*
Inmatech Inc .... F 734 717-8247
  Ann Arbor *(G-528)*
Jem Computers Inc .... F 586 783-3400
  Clinton Township *(G-3264)*
Optimystic Enterprises Inc .... G 269 695-7741
  Buchanan *(G-2200)*
Questyme Usa Inc .... G 832 912-4994
  Farmington Hills *(G-5360)*
Redeem Power Services .... G 248 679-5277
  Novi *(G-12524)*
Rvi Management Inc .... G 580 531-5826
  Okemos *(G-12684)*
Sparta Outlets .... G 616 887-6010
  Sparta *(G-15778)*
Ssi Technology Inc .... D 248 582-0600
  Sterling Heights *(G-16188)*
Ulb LLC .... E 734 233-0961
  Wixom *(G-18781)*
Warner Power Conversion LLC .... E 603 456-3111
  Grand Haven *(G-6381)*
Winford Engineering LLC .... G 989 671-9721
  Auburn *(G-771)*
Xalt Energy LLC .... G 816 525-1153
  Midland *(G-11427)*

3631 Household Cooking Eqpt

American Household Inc .... G 601 296-5000
  Livonia *(G-10114)*
Delorean Associates Inc .... E 248 646-1930
  Bloomfield Hills *(G-1813)*
Lockett Enterprises LLC .... G 810 407-6644
  Flint *(G-5725)*
◆ Maytag Corporation .... C 269 923-5000
  Benton Harbor *(G-1572)*
Whirlpool Corporation .... G 269 923-5000
  Benton Harbor *(G-1609)*

3632 Household Refrigerators & Freezers

AGA Marvel .... G 616 754-5601
  Greenville *(G-7474)*
Flow Gas Misture Solutions Inc .... G 810 488-1492
  Marysville *(G-11087)*
Forma-Kool Manufacturing Inc .... E 586 949-4813
  Chesterfield *(G-2884)*
◆ Maytag Corporation .... C 269 923-5000
  Benton Harbor *(G-1572)*
◆ Northland Corporation .... C 616 754-5601
  Greenville *(G-7503)*
Scientemp Corp .... E 517 263-6020
  Adrian *(G-94)*
◆ Thetford Corporation .... C 734 769-6000
  Ann Arbor *(G-688)*
Whirlpool Corporation .... G 269 923-7400
  Benton Harbor *(G-1606)*
Whirlpool Corporation .... G 269 923-5000
  Benton Harbor *(G-1609)*
▼ Whirlpool Corporation .... A 269 923-5000
  Benton Harbor *(G-1603)*
Whirlpool Corporation .... G 269 923-5000
  Benton Harbor *(G-1605)*
Whirlpool Corporation .... G 269 849-0907
  Coloma *(G-3484)*
Whirlpool Corporation .... G 269 923-3009
  Benton Harbor *(G-1610)*

3633 Household Laundry Eqpt

◆ Maytag Corporation .... C 269 923-5000
  Benton Harbor *(G-1572)*
▼ Whirlpool Corporation .... A 269 923-5000
  Benton Harbor *(G-1603)*
Whirlpool Corporation .... G 269 923-7441
  Saint Joseph *(G-14976)*
Whirlpool Corporation .... G 404 547-3194
  Saint Joseph *(G-14977)*
Whirlpool Corporation .... G 269 923-5000
  Benton Harbor *(G-1605)*
Whirlpool Corporation .... G 269 923-7400
  Benton Harbor *(G-1606)*
Whirlpool Corporation .... G 269 849-0907
  Coloma *(G-3484)*
Whirlpool Corporation .... G 269 923-5000
  Benton Harbor *(G-1607)*
Whirlpool Corporation .... G 269 923-6057
  Saint Joseph *(G-14978)*
Whirlpool Corporation .... G 269 923-6486
  Benton Harbor *(G-1608)*
Whirlpool Corporation .... G 269 923-3009
  Benton Harbor *(G-1610)*
Whirlpool Corporation .... G 269 923-5000
  Benton Harbor *(G-1609)*

3634 Electric Household Appliances

▲ Advanced Blnding Solutions LLC .... F 906 914-4180
  Menominee *(G-11224)*
Aesthtic Affcts Stffing Agcy L .... G 734 436-1248
  Canton *(G-2431)*
◆ Cdgjl Inc .... E 517 787-2100
  Jackson *(G-8836)*
▲ Distinctive Appliances Distrg .... F 248 380-2007
  Wixom *(G-18646)*
▲ E H Inc .... F 269 673-6456
  Allegan *(G-156)*
◆ Fka Distributing Co LLC .... C 248 863-3000
  Commerce Township *(G-3530)*
Hands That Heal .... G 517 740-6930
  Jackson *(G-8899)*
Iscuplt LLC .... G 313 728-7982
  Taylor *(G-16428)*
National Element Inc .... C 248 486-1810
  Brighton *(G-2040)*
Neptech Inc .... E 810 225-2222
  Highland *(G-7897)*
Nippa Sauna Stoves LLC .... G 231 882-7707
  Beulah *(G-1656)*
Ogilvie Manufacturing Company ...... G 810 793-6598
  Lapeer *(G-9951)*
Sampling Bag Technologies LLC ...... G 734 525-8600
  Livonia *(G-10399)*
Sweed Dreams LLC .... G 313 704-6694
  Livonia *(G-10425)*
▲ Therm Technology Corp .... G 616 530-6540
  Grandville *(G-7421)*
▼ Thoreson-Mc Cosh Inc .... E 248 362-0960
  Lake Orion *(G-9634)*
▲ Weco International Inc .... F 810 686-7221
  Flushing *(G-5816)*

3635 Household Vacuum Cleaners

Bissell Better Life LLC .... G 800 237-7691
  Grand Rapids *(G-6510)*
◆ Bissell Homecare Inc .... A 800 237-7691
  Grand Rapids *(G-6511)*
Dyson Service Center .... G 248 808-6952
  Troy *(G-17074)*
Dyson Service Center .... G 248 960-0052
  Wixom *(G-18649)*
Electrolux Professional Inc .... G 248 338-4320
  Pontiac *(G-13366)*
◆ Maytag Corporation .... C 269 923-5000
  Benton Harbor *(G-1572)*
◆ Rexair Holdings Inc .... E 248 643-7222
  Troy *(G-17332)*
▼ Whirlpool Corporation .... A 269 923-5000
  Benton Harbor *(G-1603)*
Whirlpool Corporation .... G 269 923-5000
  Benton Harbor *(G-1605)*
Whirlpool Corporation .... G 269 923-5000
  Benton Harbor *(G-1609)*

3639 Household Appliances, NEC

Affordable Heat Llc .... G 517 673-0404
  Manitou Beach *(G-10926)*
Bradford-White Corporation .... A 269 795-3364
  Middleville *(G-11303)*
Cheap Recently Acquired Pdts .... G 616 272-4212
  Wyoming *(G-18857)*
Cleaning Up Detroit City LLC .... F 517 715-7010
  Detroit *(G-4095)*
Company Products Inc .... G 586 757-6160
  Warren *(G-17762)*
Complete Kitchen Design LLC .... G 586 790-2800
  Clinton Township *(G-3206)*
J & E Appliance Company Inc .... G 248 642-9191
  Beverly Hills *(G-1665)*
Masco Building Products Corp .... G 313 274-7400
  Livonia *(G-10301)*
◆ Maytag Corporation .... C 269 923-5000
  Benton Harbor *(G-1572)*
P and K Graphics Inc .... G 810 984-1575
  Port Huron *(G-13513)*
S A R Company LLC .... E 248 979-7590
  Novi *(G-12530)*
Whirlpool Corporation .... G 269 923-5000
  Benton Harbor *(G-1609)*
Whirlpool Corporation .... G 269 923-3009
  Benton Harbor *(G-1610)*

3641 Electric Lamps

▲ Chicl LLC .... A 859 294-5590
  Troy *(G-17010)*
Elumigen LLC .... G 855 912-0477
  Troy *(G-17086)*
Emitted Energy Inc .... F 855 752-3347
  Sterling Heights *(G-16004)*
Energy Efficient Ltg LLC Eel .... G 586 214-5557
  West Bloomfield *(G-18282)*
▲ Ews Legacy LLC .... C 248 853-6363
  Rochester Hills *(G-14006)*
G & L Powerup Inc .... G 586 200-2169
  Roseville *(G-14409)*
Global Connections & More LLC ...... G 248 990-2266
  Livonia *(G-10224)*
High Q Lighting Inc .... F 616 396-3591
  Holland *(G-8071)*
Illumination Machines LLC .... G 856 685-7403
  Rochester Hills *(G-14038)*
Inland Vapor of Michigan LLC .... G 734 738-6312
  Canton *(G-2475)*
Inland Vapor of Michigan LLC .... D 734 237-4389
  Garden City *(G-6098)*
Johnico LLC .... E 248 895-7820
  Detroit *(G-4340)*
Led Source Detroit .... G 586 983-9905
  Sterling Heights *(G-16070)*
Optic Edge Corporation .... G 231 547-6090
  Charlevoix *(G-2726)*
Oshino Lamps America Ltd .... G 262 226-8620
  Wixom *(G-18727)*
Philips North America LLC .... C 248 553-9080
  Farmington Hills *(G-5346)*
Rel Inc .... E 906 337-3018
  Calumet *(G-2413)*
▲ Trident Lighting LLC .... D 616 957-9500
  Grand Rapids *(G-7276)*
Wickedglow Industries Inc .... G 586 776-4132
  Mount Clemens *(G-11663)*

36 ELECTRONIC AND OTHER ELECTRICAL EQUIPMENT AND COMPONENTS, EXCEPT COMPUTER36 ELECTRONIC AND OTHER ELECTRICAL

3643 Current-Carrying Wiring Devices

▲ **A E C Inc** ....D.... 810 231-9546
Whitmore Lake *(G-18515)*
Aees Power Systems Ltd Partnr ....G.... 269 668-4429
Farmington Hills *(G-5160)*
▲ **American Pwr Cnnection Systems** ...F.... 989 686-6302
Bay City *(G-1321)*
Armada Rubber Manufacturing Co ....D.... 586 784-9135
Armada *(G-731)*
Astra Associates Inc ....E.... 586 254-6500
Sterling Heights *(G-15935)*
Break-A-Beam ....G.... 586 758-7790
Warren *(G-17742)*
◆ **Brooks Utility Products Group** ....D.... 248 477-0250
Novi *(G-12377)*
Cardell Corporation ....D.... 248 371-9700
Auburn Hills *(G-840)*
◆ **Coppertec Inc** ....E.... 313 278-0139
Inkster *(G-8661)*
Dollars Sense ....G.... 231 369-3610
Fife Lake *(G-5605)*
▲ **Ekstrom Industries Inc** ....D.... 248 477-0040
Novi *(G-12412)*
Electrical Product Sales Inc ....E.... 248 583-6100
Troy *(G-17084)*
Electrocom Midwest Sales Inc ....G.... 248 449-2643
Madison Heights *(G-10720)*
Emm Inc ....G.... 248 478-1182
Farmington Hills *(G-5231)*
Erich Jaeger USA Inc ....G.... 734 404-5940
Livonia *(G-10199)*
▲ **Ews Legacy LLC** ....C.... 248 853-6363
Rochester Hills *(G-14006)*
▲ **Flextronics Automotive USA Inc** ....D.... 248 853-5724
Coopersville *(G-3686)*
Four-Way Tool and Die Inc ....E.... 248 585-8255
Troy *(G-17121)*
Gary L Melchi Inc ....G.... 810 231-0262
Whitmore Lake *(G-18537)*
H W Jencks Incorporated ....E.... 231 352-4422
Frankfort *(G-5878)*
▲ **Harman Corporation** ....E.... 248 651-4477
Rochester *(G-13903)*
Hi-Lex America Incorporated ....B.... 248 844-0096
Rochester Hills *(G-14030)*
Hug-A-Plug Inc ....G.... 810 626-1224
Brighton *(G-2011)*
▲ **JST Sales America Inc** ....F.... 248 324-1957
Farmington Hills *(G-5276)*
◆ **Lear Corporation** ....B.... 248 447-1500
Southfield *(G-15628)*
▲ **Mercury Displacement Inds Inc** ....D.... 269 663-8574
Edwardsburg *(G-5009)*
▲ **Meter Devices Company Inc** ....D.... 330 455-0301
Farmington Hills *(G-5317)*
Metropolitan Alloys Corp ....E.... 313 366-4443
Detroit *(G-4438)*
◆ **Morrell Incorporated** ....D.... 248 373-1600
Auburn Hills *(G-975)*
National Zinc Processors Inc ....F.... 269 926-1161
Benton Harbor *(G-1577)*
▲ **NGK Spark Plug Mfg USA Inc** ....C.... 248 926-6900
Wixom *(G-18720)*
Nyx LLC ....D.... 734 464-0800
Livonia *(G-10346)*
▲ **Owosso Graphic Arts Inc** ....E.... 989 725-7112
Owosso *(G-12849)*
Panel Pro LLC ....G.... 734 427-1691
Livonia *(G-10359)*
Patriot Sensors & Contrls Corp ....F.... 810 378-5511
Peck *(G-12962)*
◆ **Patriot Sensors & Contrls Corp** ....D.... 248 435-0700
Peck *(G-12963)*
Plugs To Panels Electrical LLC ....G.... 248 318-5915
Howell *(G-8497)*
▲ **Prestolite Electric LLC** ....G.... 248 313-3807
Novi *(G-12512)*
Prime Assemblies Inc ....E.... 906 875-6420
Crystal Falls *(G-3744)*
Seeking ....G.... 586 489-2524
Macomb *(G-10633)*
▲ **Semtron Inc** ....F.... 810 732-9080
Flint *(G-5761)*
▲ **Sine Systems Corporation** ....C.... 586 465-3131
Clinton Township *(G-3359)*
▲ **Southern Auto Wholesalers Inc** ....F.... 248 335-5555
Pontiac *(G-13417)*
▲ **Ssi Electronics Inc** ....E.... 616 866-8880
Belmont *(G-1517)*
State Tool & Manufacturing Co ....D.... 269 927-3153
Benton Harbor *(G-1589)*
Syndevco Inc ....F.... 248 356-2839
Southfield *(G-15716)*
Teradyne Inc ....G.... 313 425-3900
Allen Park *(G-208)*
Testron Incorporated ....F.... 734 513-6820
Livonia *(G-10431)*
TI Group Auto Systems LLC ....G.... 586 948-6006
Chesterfield *(G-2956)*
▲ **Tram Inc** ....C.... 734 254-8500
Plymouth *(G-13322)*
Tram Inc ....G.... 269 966-0100
Battle Creek *(G-1306)*
▲ **Trmi Inc** ....A.... 269 966-0800
Battle Creek *(G-1307)*
◆ **Yazaki International Corp** ....G.... 734 983-1000
Canton *(G-2544)*

3644 Noncurrent-Carrying Wiring Devices

Adnic Products Co ....G.... 810 789-0321
Mount Morris *(G-11666)*
Allied Tube & Conduit Corp ....G.... 734 721-4040
Wayne *(G-18212)*
Austin Company ....F.... 269 329-1181
Portage *(G-13544)*
▲ **Dare Products Inc** ....E.... 269 965-2307
Springfield *(G-15864)*
▲ **Ews Legacy LLC** ....C.... 248 853-6363
Rochester Hills *(G-14006)*
Masco Building Products Corp ....G.... 313 274-7400
Livonia *(G-10301)*
Merritt Raceway LLC ....G.... 231 590-4431
Mancelona *(G-10876)*
▲ **Meter Devices Company Inc** ....D.... 330 455-0301
Farmington Hills *(G-5317)*
Tesa Tape Inc ....G.... 616 785-6970
Walker *(G-17654)*
Tesa Tape Inc ....G.... 616 887-3107
Sparta *(G-15786)*
Zygot Operations Limited ....E.... 810 736-2900
Flint *(G-5799)*

3645 Residential Lighting Fixtures

▲ **A E C Inc** ....D.... 810 231-9546
Whitmore Lake *(G-18515)*
Baylume Inc ....G.... 877 881-3641
Clawson *(G-3087)*
Casual Ptio Furn Rfnishing Inc ....G.... 586 254-1900
Canton *(G-2446)*
Douglas Milton Lamp Co ....G.... 888 738-3332
Battle Creek *(G-1220)*
▲ **Full Spectrum Solutions Inc** ....E.... 517 783-3800
Jackson *(G-8888)*
▲ **Lighting Enterprises Inc** ....G.... 313 693-9504
Detroit *(G-4399)*
Nitelights of SE Michigan ....G.... 248 684-4664
Milford *(G-11477)*
▲ **R-Bo Co Inc** ....F.... 616 748-9733
Zeeland *(G-19076)*

3646 Commercial, Indl & Institutional Lighting Fixtures

Alumalight LLC ....G.... 248 457-9302
Troy *(G-16929)*
Burst Led ....G.... 248 321-6262
Farmington Hills *(G-5188)*
Chandelier & More LLC ....E.... 248 214-1525
Jackson *(G-8839)*
▲ **Command Electronics Inc** ....E.... 269 679-4011
Schoolcraft *(G-15115)*
Douglas Milton Lamp Co ....G.... 888 738-3332
Battle Creek *(G-1220)*
E-Light LLC ....G.... 734 427-0600
Commerce Township *(G-3524)*
Earthtronics Inc ....F.... 231 332-1188
Norton Shores *(G-12290)*
▲ **El Sol Custom Lighting** ....F.... 269 281-0435
Saint Joseph *(G-14928)*
Elumigen LLC ....G.... 855 912-0477
Troy *(G-17086)*
Energy Design Svc Systems LLC ....D.... 810 227-3377
Whitmore Lake *(G-18532)*
Global Green Corporation ....F.... 734 560-1743
Ann Arbor *(G-501)*
GT Solutions LLC ....G.... 616 259-0700
Holland *(G-8062)*
High Q Lighting Inc ....F.... 616 396-3591
Holland *(G-8071)*
Illumination Machines LLC ....G.... 856 685-7403
Rochester Hills *(G-14038)*
▲ **Itc Incorporated** ....E.... 616 396-1355
Hudsonville *(G-8587)*
Johnico LLC ....E.... 248 895-7820
Detroit *(G-4340)*
▲ **Leif Distribution LLC** ....E.... 517 481-2122
Grand Rapids *(G-6939)*
▲ **Light Corp Inc** ....C.... 616 842-5100
Grand Haven *(G-6329)*
Lyte Poles Incorporated ....D.... 586 771-4610
Warren *(G-17911)*
▲ **Nylube Products Company LLC** ....F.... 248 852-6500
Rochester Hills *(G-14074)*
▼ **Pro Lighting Group Inc** ....G.... 810 229-5600
Brighton *(G-2054)*
▲ **R-Bo Co Inc** ....F.... 616 748-9733
Zeeland *(G-19076)*
Robogistics LLC ....F.... 409 234-1033
Adrian *(G-91)*
Skyworks LLC ....F.... 972 284-9093
Northville *(G-12261)*
Smart Vision Lights LLC ....D.... 231 722-1199
Norton Shores *(G-12331)*
Sound Productions Entrmt ....F.... 989 386-2221
Clare *(G-2998)*
Suntech Industrials LLC ....G.... 734 678-5922
Ann Arbor *(G-668)*
Woodward Energy Solutions LLC ....F.... 888 967-4533
Detroit *(G-4690)*

3647 Vehicular Lighting Eqpt

A S Auto Lights Inc ....G.... 734 941-1164
Romulus *(G-14242)*
Autosystems America Inc ....B.... 734 582-2300
Plymouth *(G-13129)*
Clarience Technologies LLC ....D.... 716 665-6214
Southfield *(G-15525)*
▲ **Emergency Technology Inc** ....D.... 616 896-7100
Hudsonville *(G-8581)*
Eoi Pioneer Inc ....G.... 626 823-5639
Dundee *(G-4818)*
▲ **Eto Magnetic Corp** ....C.... 616 957-2570
Grand Rapids *(G-6686)*
▲ **F M T Products Inc** ....G.... 517 568-3373
Homer *(G-8351)*
▲ **Fisher-Baker Corporation** ....G.... 810 765-3548
Marine City *(G-10958)*
Gyb LLC ....F.... 586 218-3222
Warren *(G-17844)*
HA Automotive Systems Inc ....F.... 248 781-0001
Troy *(G-17135)*
▲ **Il Stanley Co Inc** ....A.... 269 660-7777
Battle Creek *(G-1240)*
Illumination Machines LLC ....G.... 856 685-7403
Rochester Hills *(G-14038)*
Interntnal Auto Cmpnnts Group ....G.... 231 734-9000
Evart *(G-5124)*
Magna Mirrors America Inc ....G.... 616 786-7300
Holland *(G-8134)*
Magna Mirrors America Inc ....G.... 616 942-0163
Newaygo *(G-12085)*
Marelli Automotive Ltg LLC ....G.... 248 418-3000
Clarkston *(G-3047)*
◆ **Marelli Automotive Ltg LLC** ....E.... 248 418-3000
Southfield *(G-15642)*
Mid American AEL LLC ....G.... 810 229-5483
Brighton *(G-2033)*
MLS Automotive Incorporated ....F.... 844 453-3669
Farmington Hills *(G-5324)*
◆ **Penske Company LLC** ....G.... 248 648-2000
Bloomfield Hills *(G-1849)*
▲ **Progressive Dynamics Inc** ....D.... 269 781-4241
Marshall *(G-11072)*
Rebo Lighting & Elec LLC ....F.... 734 213-4159
Ann Arbor *(G-633)*
Shelton Technology LLC ....G.... 248 816-1585
Troy *(G-17349)*
▲ **Stanley Elc Holdg Amer Inc** ....D.... 269 660-7777
Battle Creek *(G-1300)*
▲ **Tecniq Inc** ....E.... 269 629-4440
Galesburg *(G-6085)*
▲ **Trident Lighting LLC** ....D.... 616 957-9500
Grand Rapids *(G-7276)*
Zkw Lighting Systems Usa Inc ....F.... 248 509-7300
Troy *(G-17461)*

3648 Lighting Eqpt, NEC

▲ **A E C Inc** ....D.... 810 231-9546
Whitmore Lake *(G-18515)*

A Lite In Nite ....G ... 231 275-5900
Lake Ann *(G-9540)*
Affordable OEM Autolighting ....G ... 989 400-6106
Stanton *(G-15898)*
Ci Lighting LLC ....G ... 248 997-4415
Auburn Hills *(G-843)*
Clearview Lighting LLC ....G ... 248 709-8707
Beverly Hills *(G-1662)*
Coreled Systems LLC ....G ... 734 516-2060
Livonia *(G-10166)*
Dakkota Lighting Tech LLC ....E ... 517 694-2823
Holt *(G-8308)*
Denali Lighting LLC ....G ... 586 731-0399
Shelby Township *(G-15204)*
▲ Emergency Technology Inc ....D ... 616 896-7100
Hudsonville *(G-8581)*
Energy Design Svc Systems LLC ....D ... 810 227-3377
Whitmore Lake *(G-18532)*
Firewater Lighting LLC ....G ... 616 570-0088
Alto *(G-332)*
Gadget Factory LLC ....G ... 517 449-1444
Lansing *(G-9840)*
General Structures Inc ....F ... 586 774-6105
Warren *(G-17826)*
Global Green Corporation ....F ... 734 560-1743
Ann Arbor *(G-501)*
GT Solutions LLC ....G ... 616 259-0700
Holland *(G-8062)*
High Q Lighting Inc ....F ... 616 396-3591
Holland *(G-8071)*
Hutson Inc ....C ... 517 655-4606
Williamston *(G-18573)*
▲ I Parth Inc ....G ... 248 548-9722
Ferndale *(G-5560)*
Illumination Machines LLC ....G ... 856 685-7403
Rochester Hills *(G-14038)*
Ilumigreen Corp ....G ... 616 318-3087
Norton Shores *(G-12299)*
Infection Prevention Tech LLC ....G ... 248 340-8800
Grand Blanc *(G-6248)*
Infusion Tanning Products LLC ....G ... 734 422-9826
Livonia *(G-10249)*
▼ J & B Products Ltd ....F ... 989 792-6119
Saginaw *(G-14672)*
J & M Products and Service LLC ....G ... 517 263-3082
Adrian *(G-75)*
Johnico LLC ....E ... 248 895-7820
Detroit *(G-4340)*
K and J Lighting ....G ... 586 625-2001
Roseville *(G-14429)*
▲ Leif Distribution LLC ....E ... 517 481-2122
Grand Rapids *(G-6939)*
▼ Lumerica Corporation ....F ... 248 543-8085
Warren *(G-17908)*
Michigan Lightning Protection ....G ... 866 712-4071
Grand Rapids *(G-6992)*
▼ Phoenix Imaging Inc ....F ... 248 476-4200
Livonia *(G-10365)*
▲ Qualite Inc ....E ... 517 439-4316
Hillsdale *(G-7943)*
Searchlight Safety LLC ....G ... 313 333-9200
Dundee *(G-4835)*
Solar Tonic LLC ....G ... 734 368-0215
Ann Arbor *(G-658)*
Sonrize LLC ....G ... 586 329-3225
Chesterfield *(G-2949)*
Sound Productions Entrmt ....F ... 989 386-2221
Clare *(G-2998)*
Spectrum Illumination Co Inc ....G ... 231 894-4590
Montague *(G-11601)*
Spotlight Couture LLC ....G ... 313 768-5305
Taylor *(G-16478)*
Spotlight Media LLC ....G ... 269 808-4473
Kalamazoo *(G-9343)*
◆ Steelcase Inc ....A ... 616 247-2710
Grand Rapids *(G-7224)*
Tls Productions Inc ....E ... 810 220-8577
Ann Arbor *(G-693)*
Total Source Led Inc ....G ... 313 575-8889
Dearborn Heights *(G-3942)*
▼ Universal Manufacturing Co ....E ... 586 463-2560
Clinton Township *(G-3383)*

3651 Household Audio & Video Eqpt

BBC Communications Inc ....G ... 616 399-0432
West Olive *(G-18347)*
Bluewater Tech Group Inc ....C ... 248 356-4399
Wixom *(G-18624)*
Bluewater Tech Group Inc ....G ... 231 885-2600
Mesick *(G-11269)*
Bluewater Tech Group Inc ....G ... 616 656-9380
Grand Rapids *(G-6517)*
Bluewater Tech Group Inc ....G ... 248 356-4399
Farmington Hills *(G-5182)*
Charter Communication ....G ... 989 634-1093
Bancroft *(G-1127)*
Charter Communication ....G ... 810 515-8418
Flint *(G-5666)*
Charter Communication ....G ... 810 360-2748
Brighton *(G-1964)*
Clarion Corporation America ....E ... 248 991-3100
Farmington Hills *(G-5203)*
▲ Cusack Music LLC ....E ... 616 546-8888
Holland *(G-8008)*
Donley Computer Services LLC ....G ... 231 750-1774
Muskegon *(G-11800)*
▲ Driven Designs Inc ....G ... 616 794-9977
Belding *(G-1446)*
Fast Cash ....G ... 269 966-0079
Battle Creek *(G-1229)*
Intaglio LLC ....E ... 616 243-3300
Grand Rapids *(G-6848)*
Intellitech Systems Inc ....G ... 586 219-3737
Troy *(G-17170)*
Jeanies LLC ....G ... 313 412-8760
Wyandotte *(G-18825)*
Lg Electronics USA Inc ....C ... 248 268-5100
Troy *(G-17209)*
Logical Digital Audio Video ....G ... 734 572-0022
Ann Arbor *(G-555)*
◆ Lotus International Company ....A ... 734 245-0140
Canton *(G-2486)*
M A S Information Age Tech ....G ... 248 352-0162
Southfield *(G-15638)*
M10 Group Holding Company ....G ... 248 356-4399
Southfield *(G-15639)*
Mark MSA ....G ... 586 716-5941
New Baltimore *(G-11988)*
Mitsubishi Elc Auto Amer Inc ....D ... 734 453-6200
Northville *(G-12240)*
Moss Audio Corporation ....D ... 616 451-9933
Grand Rapids *(G-7030)*
Osowet Collections Inc ....G ... 313 844-8171
Detroit *(G-4501)*
Premium Sund Slutions Amer LLC ....G ... 734 259-6142
Plymouth *(G-13270)*
▲ Pro-Vision Solutions LLC ....D ... 616 583-1520
Byron Center *(G-2292)*
Quantum Digital Group LLC ....G ... 888 408-3199
Auburn Hills *(G-1009)*
▲ Salk Communications Inc ....G ... 248 342-7109
Pontiac *(G-13415)*
▲ Sargam International Inc ....F ... 310 855-9694
Troy *(G-17344)*
▲ Shinola/Detroit LLC ....C ... 888 304-2534
Detroit *(G-4591)*
Startech-Solutions LLC ....G ... 248 419-0650
Southfield *(G-15708)*
Stedman Corp ....G ... 269 629-5930
Richland *(G-13830)*
Tf Entertainment LLC ....F ... 424 303-3407
Detroit *(G-4630)*

3652 Phonograph Records & Magnetic Tape

Amber Engine LLC ....F ... 313 373-4751
Detroit *(G-4009)*
Archer Record Pressing Co ....G ... 313 365-9545
Detroit *(G-4025)*
▲ Brilliance Publishing Inc ....C ... 616 846-5256
Grand Haven *(G-6281)*
Faulkner Tech Inc ....G ... 517 857-4241
Charlotte *(G-2755)*
Geeks and Gurus Inc ....G ... 313 549-2796
Farmington Hills *(G-5249)*
Logic Quantum LLC ....F ... 734 930-0009
Ann Arbor *(G-554)*
Megapixel Ideas LLC ....G ... 616 307-5220
Belmont *(G-1514)*
Passenger Inc ....G ... 323 556-5400
Howell *(G-8490)*
Summit Training Source Inc ....E ... 800 842-0466
Grand Rapids *(G-7233)*

3661 Telephone & Telegraph Apparatus

Balogh ....G ... 734 283-3972
Taylor *(G-16387)*
Central On Line Data Systems ....G ... 586 939-7000
Sterling Heights *(G-15954)*
Clarity Comm Advisors Inc ....E ... 248 327-4390
Southfield *(G-15526)*
▲ Code Blue Corporation ....E ... 616 392-8296
Holland *(G-8000)*
DB Communications Inc ....F ... 800 692-8200
Livonia *(G-10175)*
Maxxar ....G ... 248 675-1040
Wixom *(G-18708)*
Multiax International Inc ....G ... 616 534-4530
Grandville *(G-7404)*
Nuwave Technology Partners LLC ....F ... 616 942-7520
Grand Rapids *(G-7052)*
Omnilink Communications Corp ....E ... 517 336-1800
Lansing *(G-9878)*
▲ Rti Products LLC ....F ... 269 684-9960
Niles *(G-12164)*
▲ Safari Circuits Inc ....C ... 269 694-9471
Otsego *(G-12799)*
▲ Semtron Inc ....F ... 810 732-9080
Flint *(G-5761)*
Sigma Wireless LLC ....G ... 313 423-2629
Detroit *(G-4592)*
Spectra Link ....G ... 313 417-3723
Grosse Pointe Woods *(G-7576)*

3663 Radio & T V Communications, Systs & Eqpt, Broadcast/Studio

Amphenol T&M Antennas Inc ....G ... 847 478-5600
Brighton *(G-1946)*
Apem Solutions LLC ....G ... 616 848-5393
Grand Rapids *(G-6461)*
Asset Track Technologies LLC ....G ... 517 745-3879
Jackson *(G-8817)*
Balogh Inc ....G ... 810 360-0182
Brighton *(G-1948)*
Bob Allison Enterprises ....G ... 248 540-8467
Bloomfield Hills *(G-1804)*
C & A Wholesale Inc ....G ... 248 302-3555
Detroit *(G-4082)*
Cohda Wireless America LLC ....G ... 248 513-2105
Ann Arbor *(G-432)*
Community Access Center ....F ... 269 343-2211
Kalamazoo *(G-9148)*
Directv Dish Doctor ....G ... 989 983-3214
Vanderbilt *(G-17569)*
Emag Technologies Inc ....F ... 734 996-3624
Ann Arbor *(G-472)*
EMR Corp ....G ... 810 376-4710
Deckerville *(G-3954)*
▲ Harada Industry America Inc ....D ... 248 374-2587
Novi *(G-12426)*
Holland Vision Systems Inc ....E ... 616 494-9974
Holland *(G-8087)*
Hughes Network Systems LLC ....G ... 301 428-5500
Southfield *(G-15594)*
Information Stn Specialists ....F ... 616 772-2300
Zeeland *(G-19046)*
L3 Technologies Inc ....G ... 734 741-8868
Ann Arbor *(G-546)*
Livbig LLC ....G ... 888 519-8290
Portage *(G-13578)*
Livespace LLC ....F ... 616 929-0191
Grand Rapids *(G-6947)*
Lor Manufacturing Co Inc ....G ... 989 644-2581
Weidman *(G-18254)*
Michigan Satellite ....F ... 989 792-6666
Saginaw *(G-14698)*
Mobimogul Inc ....G ... 313 575-2795
Southfield *(G-15661)*
Moody Bible Inst of Chicago ....G ... 616 772-7300
Zeeland *(G-19057)*
Motorola Solutions Inc ....G ... 517 321-6655
Lansing *(G-9780)*
Parvox Technology ....G ... 231 924-4366
Fremont *(G-6051)*
Parvox Technology ....G ... 231 924-4366
Fremont *(G-6052)*
R A Miller Industries Inc ....C ... 888 845-9450
Grand Haven *(G-6349)*
Riprap ....G ... 734 945-0892
Durand *(G-4846)*
Rml Industries LLC ....G ... 616 935-3839
Grand Haven *(G-6355)*
Satellite Controls ....G ... 313 532-6848
Redford *(G-13770)*
Sinclair Designs & Engrg LLC ....E ... 877 517-0311
Albion *(G-133)*
Sound Productions Entrmt ....F ... 989 386-2221
Clare *(G-2998)*
South Lyon Bb Inc ....G ... 248 437-8000
South Lyon *(G-15458)*

S I C

36 ELECTRONIC AND OTHER ELECTRICAL EQUIPMENT AND COMPONENTS, EXCEPT COMPUTER36 ELECTRONIC AND OTHER ELECTRICAL

Spectrum Wireless (usa) Inc ...G... 586 693-7525
Saint Clair Shores *(G-14886)*

Startech-Solutions LLC ...G... 248 419-0650
West Bloomfield *(G-18316)*

Thalner Electronic Labs Inc ...E... 734 761-4506
Ann Arbor *(G-686)*

Washtenaw Communications Inc ...G... 734 662-7138
Ann Arbor *(G-714)*

3669 Communications Eqpt, NEC

Aaccess Entertainment ...G... 734 260-1002
Brighton *(G-1936)*

Ademco Inc ...G... 586 759-1455
Warren *(G-17691)*

Ademco Inc ...G... 248 926-5510
Wixom *(G-18595)*

Advanced-Cable LLC ...F... 586 491-3073
Troy *(G-16909)*

Aero Systems ...G... 253 269-3000
Livonia *(G-10104)*

▲ Apollo America Inc ...D... 248 332-3900
Auburn Hills *(G-791)*

Axis Tms Corp ...E... 248 509-2440
Clinton Township *(G-3179)*

Bluewater Tech Group Inc ...G... 248 356-4399
Farmington Hills *(G-5182)*

City of Saginaw ...G... 989 759-1670
Saginaw *(G-14630)*

▲ Code Blue Corporation ...E... 616 392-8296
Holland *(G-8000)*

Controller Systems Corporation ...E... 586 772-6100
Eastpointe *(G-4932)*

Curbell Plastics Inc ...G... 734 513-0531
Livonia *(G-10170)*

Em A Give Break Safety ...G... 231 263-6625
Kingsley *(G-9523)*

▲ Emergency Technology Inc ...D... 616 896-7100
Hudsonville *(G-8581)*

Gentex Corporation ...G... 616 392-7195
Zeeland *(G-19028)*

Gentex Corporation ...G... 616 772-1800
Zeeland *(G-19026)*

Gentex Corporation ...C... 616 772-1800
Zeeland *(G-19024)*

Give-Em A Brake Safety LLC ...E... 616 531-8705
Grandville *(G-7379)*

National Sign & Signal Co ...E... 269 963-2817
Battle Creek *(G-1277)*

National Time and Signal Corp ...E... 248 291-5867
Oak Park *(G-12631)*

Nationwide Communications LLC ...G... 517 990-1223
Jackson *(G-8975)*

Quality Metal Detectors ...G... 734 624-8462
Southgate *(G-15756)*

R A Miller Industries Inc ...C... 888 845-9450
Grand Haven *(G-6349)*

▲ R H K Technology Inc ...E... 248 577-5426
Troy *(G-17327)*

◆ Safety Technology Intl Inc ...E... 248 673-9898
Waterford *(G-18162)*

Safety Technology Intl Inc ...G... 248 673-9898
Waterford *(G-18163)*

Shield Material Handling Inc ...D... 248 418-0986
Auburn Hills *(G-1032)*

Techncal Audio Video Solutions ...G... 810 899-5546
Howell *(G-8527)*

▲ Tpk America LLC ...F... 616 786-5300
Holland *(G-8223)*

West Shore Services Inc ...E... 616 895-4347
Allendale *(G-229)*

3671 Radio & T V Receiving Electron Tubes

Puff Baby LLC ...G... 734 620-9991
Garden City *(G-6106)*

3672 Printed Circuit Boards

3dxtech LLC ...F... 616 717-3811
Grand Rapids *(G-6406)*

A and D Design Electronics ...G... 989 493-1884
Auburn *(G-762)*

Acromag Incorporated ...D... 248 624-1541
Wixom *(G-18594)*

▲ Adco Circuits Inc ...C... 248 853-6620
Rochester Hills *(G-13941)*

Aero Embedded Technologies Inc ...G... 586 251-2980
Sterling Heights *(G-15925)*

Ameritronix Inc ...G... 724 956-2356
Canton *(G-2434)*

Assem-Tech Inc ...E... 616 846-3410
Grand Haven *(G-6275)*

Assembltech Inc ...E... 734 769-2800
Ottawa Lake *(G-12803)*

Assembly Alternatives Inc ...G... 248 362-1616
Rochester Hills *(G-13952)*

Bralyn Inc ...G... 231 865-3186
Fruitport *(G-6061)*

Burton Industries Inc ...E... 906 932-5970
Ironwood *(G-8759)*

Ci Lighting LLC ...G... 248 997-4415
Auburn Hills *(G-843)*

Cusolar Industries Inc ...E... 586 949-3880
Chesterfield *(G-2863)*

Debron Industrial Elec LLC ...D... 248 588-7220
Troy *(G-17050)*

Dse Industries LLC ...G... 313 530-6668
Macomb *(G-10589)*

Dupearl Technology LLC ...G... 248 390-9609
Bloomfield Hills *(G-1816)*

Excel Circuits LLC ...F... 248 373-0700
Auburn Hills *(G-883)*

◆ Ghi Electronics LLC ...E... 248 397-8856
Madison Heights *(G-10731)*

▲ Glassmaster Controls Co Inc ...E... 269 382-2010
Kalamazoo *(G-9198)*

Hgc Westshore LLC ...D... 616 796-1218
Holland *(G-8070)*

Hughes Electronics Pdts Corp ...E... 734 427-8310
Livonia *(G-10244)*

▲ I Parth Inc ...G... 248 548-9722
Ferndale *(G-5560)*

Ips Assembly Corp ...F... 734 391-0080
Livonia *(G-10251)*

Jabil Circuit Michigan Inc ...C... 248 292-6000
Auburn Hills *(G-941)*

Jabil Inc ...A... 248 292-6000
Auburn Hills *(G-942)*

K & F Electronic Inc ...E... 586 294-8720
Fraser *(G-5949)*

Keska LLC ...G... 616 283-7056
Holland *(G-8113)*

M T S Chenault LLC ...G... 269 861-0053
Benton Harbor *(G-1566)*

▲ Magna Electronics Inc ...C... 248 729-2643
Auburn Hills *(G-962)*

Micro Logic ...G... 248 432-7209
West Bloomfield *(G-18299)*

▲ N S International Ltd ...C... 248 251-1600
Troy *(G-17272)*

Northville Circuits Inc ...G... 248 853-3232
Rochester Hills *(G-14073)*

Nu Tek Sales Parts Inc ...F... 616 258-0631
Muskegon *(G-11886)*

▲ Obertron Electronic Mfg Inc ...F... 734 428-0722
Manchester *(G-10887)*

▲ Odyssey Electronics Inc ...D... 734 421-8340
Livonia *(G-10352)*

P M Z Technology Inc ...G... 248 471-0447
Livonia *(G-10356)*

Petra Electronic Mfg Inc ...F... 616 877-1991
Holland *(G-8165)*

Pgf Technology Group Inc ...E... 248 852-2800
Rochester Hills *(G-14082)*

Posthaste Electronics LLC ...G... 616 794-9977
Belding *(G-1461)*

Protodesign Inc ...E... 586 739-4340
Shelby Township *(G-15310)*

Ram Electronics Inc ...F... 231 865-3186
Fruitport *(G-6069)*

Rockstar Digital Inc ...F... 888 808-5868
Sterling Heights *(G-16158)*

▲ Saline Lectronics Inc ...C... 734 944-2120
Saline *(G-15037)*

▲ Saturn Electronics Corp ...C... 734 941-8100
Romulus *(G-14327)*

Saturn Flex Systems Inc ...F... 734 532-4093
Romulus *(G-14328)*

Semicndctor Hybrid Assmbly Inc ...F... 248 668-9050
Wixom *(G-18751)*

3674 Semiconductors

ABB Enterprise Software Inc ...E... 313 863-1909
Detroit *(G-3979)*

Advanced Photonix Inc ...E... 734 864-5647
Ann Arbor *(G-355)*

AG Precision Gage Inc ...G... 248 374-0063
Wixom *(G-18599)*

Allegro Microsystems LLC ...G... 248 242-5044
Auburn Hills *(G-777)*

Alsentis LLC ...G... 616 395-8254
Holland *(G-7961)*

API / Inmet Inc ...C... 734 426-5553
Ann Arbor *(G-372)*

Bay Carbon Inc ...E... 989 686-8090
Bay City *(G-1326)*

▼ Birdsall Tool & Gage Co ...E... 248 474-5150
Farmington Hills *(G-5181)*

Compunetics Incorporated ...E... 248 524-6376
Troy *(G-17022)*

Convergent Solutions LLC ...G... 616 490-8747
Lowell *(G-10499)*

▲ Electro-Matic Ventures Inc ...C... 248 478-1182
Farmington Hills *(G-5225)*

Freescale Semiconductor Inc ...G... 248 324-3260
Novi *(G-12417)*

Fuel Cell System Mfg LLC ...G... 313 319-5571
Brownstown Township *(G-2152)*

Gan Systems Corp ...G... 248 609-7643
Ann Arbor *(G-494)*

Great Lakes Crystal Tech Inc ...G... 517 249-4395
East Lansing *(G-4894)*

Helian Technologies LLC ...G... 248 535-6545
Shelby Township *(G-15234)*

Helios Solar LLC ...G... 269 343-5581
Kalamazoo *(G-9212)*

Hemlock Semiconductor LLC ...G... 989 301-5000
Hemlock *(G-7853)*

▲ Hemlock Smcndctor Oprtions LLC ...B... 989 301-5000
Hemlock *(G-7854)*

Instrumented Sensor Tech Inc ...G... 517 349-8487
Okemos *(G-12670)*

J & K Spratt Enterprises Inc ...D... 517 439-5010
Hillsdale *(G-7938)*

▲ Johnson Electric N Amer Inc ...D... 734 392-5300
Plymouth *(G-13206)*

▲ Kimberly Lighting LLC ...E... 888 480-0070
Clarkston *(G-3043)*

Lexatronics LLC ...G... 734 878-6237
Pinckney *(G-13050)*

▲ Lumasmart Technology Intl Inc ...D... 586 232-4125
Shelby Township *(G-15265)*

Lumileds LLC ...E... 248 553-9080
Farmington Hills *(G-5297)*

Luna Optoeletronics ...G... 734 864-5611
Ann Arbor *(G-557)*

Macom Technology Solutions Inc ...G... 734 864-5664
Ann Arbor *(G-561)*

Maxim Integrated Products Inc ...G... 408 601-1000
Brighton *(G-2027)*

Moog Inc ...G... 734 738-5862
Plymouth *(G-13248)*

Nihil Ultra Corporation ...G... 413 723-3218
Troy *(G-17277)*

▲ Nuvosun Inc ...D... 408 514-6200
Midland *(G-11398)*

Optimems Technology Inc ...G... 248 660-0380
Novi *(G-12498)*

Ovshinsky Technologies LLC ...G... 248 752-2344
Bloomfield Hills *(G-1846)*

▲ Patriot Solar Group LLC ...E... 517 629-9292
Albion *(G-129)*

Powerlase Photonics Inc ...G... 248 305-2963
Novi *(G-12509)*

Promethient Inc ...G... 231 525-0500
Traverse City *(G-16806)*

Quantum Opus LLC ...G... 517 680-0011
Novi *(G-12521)*

Regener-Eyes LLC ...G... 248 207-4641
Ann Arbor *(G-636)*

Riverside Cnc LLC ...F... 616 246-6000
Wyoming *(G-18905)*

Siemens Industry Inc ...G... 248 307-3400
Troy *(G-17350)*

▲ Sigma Luminous LLC ...G... 866 755-3563
Saint Clair Shores *(G-14884)*

Sonima Corp ...F... 302 450-6452
Lake Orion *(G-9631)*

Star Board Multi Media Inc ...G... 616 296-0823
Grand Haven *(G-6367)*

◆ T E Technology Inc ...E... 231 929-3966
Traverse City *(G-16849)*

▲ Tellurex Corporation ...E... 231 947-0110
Traverse City *(G-16853)*

Teradyne Inc ...G... 313 425-3900
Allen Park *(G-208)*

Terametrix LLC ...C... 540 769-8430
Ann Arbor *(G-681)*

Teslir LLC ...G... 248 644-5500
Bloomfield Hills *(G-1865)*

Tetradyn Ltd ...G... 202 415-7295
Traverse City *(G-16855)*

SIC SECTION 36 ELECTRONIC AND OTHER ELECTRICAL EQUIPMENT AND COMPONENTS, EXCEPT COMPUTER 36 ELECTRONIC AND OTHER

Tinilite World Inc .... G 734 334-0839
  Ann Arbor *(G-691)*
Toshiba America Electronic .... C 248 347-2608
  Wixom *(G-18774)*
US Trade LLC .... G 800 676-0208
  Garden City *(G-6114)*
▲ Uusi LLC .... D 231 832-5513
  Reed City *(G-13803)*
Veoneer Us Inc .... B 248 223-8074
  Southfield *(G-15737)*
▼ Viking Technologies Inc .... G 586 914-0819
  Madison Heights *(G-10856)*
White River .... G 231 894-9216
  Montague *(G-11603)*
Ziel Optics Inc .... G 734 994-9803
  Ann Arbor *(G-724)*

3676 Electronic Resistors

Touchstone Systems & Svcs Inc .... G 616 532-0060
  Wyoming *(G-18912)*

3677 Electronic Coils & Transformers

Actia Electronics Inc .... G 574 264-2373
  Romulus *(G-14245)*
▼ Controlled Power Company .... C 248 528-3700
  Troy *(G-17027)*
Cusolar Industries Inc .... E 586 949-3880
  Chesterfield *(G-2863)*
▲ Ecoclean Inc .... C 248 450-2000
  Southfield *(G-15552)*
Ford Motor Company .... A 734 484-8626
  Ypsilanti *(G-18947)*
Friends of Liz Brater .... G 734 547-1953
  Ypsilanti *(G-18948)*
H W Jencks Incorporated .... E 231 352-4422
  Frankfort *(G-5878)*
Heco Inc .... E 269 381-7200
  Kalamazoo *(G-9210)*
Induction Engineering Inc .... F 586 716-4700
  New Baltimore *(G-11982)*
◆ La Solucion Corp .... G 313 893-9760
  Detroit *(G-4372)*
Ntf Manufacturing Usa LLC .... F 989 739-8560
  Oscoda *(G-12766)*
Osborne Transformer Corp .... F 586 218-6900
  Fraser *(G-5972)*
▲ Pontiac Coil Inc .... C 248 922-1100
  Clarkston *(G-3057)*
Prosys Industries Inc .... D 734 207-3710
  Canton *(G-2515)*
South Haven Coil Inc .... G 269 637-5201
  South Haven *(G-15412)*
Trucent Inc .... G 734 426-9015
  Dexter *(G-4759)*
Trucent Separation Tech LLC .... D 734 426-9015
  Dexter *(G-4760)*
V and F Transformer .... G 248 328-6288
  Holly *(G-8299)*

3678 Electronic Connectors

Aees Power Systems Ltd Partnr .... G 269 668-4429
  Farmington Hills *(G-5160)*
Amphenol Corporation .... B 586 465-3131
  Clinton Township *(G-3169)*
Cardell Corporation .... D 248 371-9700
  Auburn Hills *(G-840)*
Hirschmann Auto N Amer LLC .... G 248 495-2677
  Rochester Hills *(G-14033)*
▲ Iriso USA Inc .... E 248 324-9780
  Farmington Hills *(G-5273)*
▲ Kostal Kontakt Systeme Inc .... C 248 284-7600
  Rochester Hills *(G-14047)*
Mac Lean-Fogg Company .... C 248 280-0880
  Royal Oak *(G-14558)*
Maclean Royal Oak LLC .... G 248 840-0880
  Farmington Hills *(G-5298)*
Midwest Sales Associates Inc .... G 248 348-9600
  Wixom *(G-18710)*
Norma Group Craig Assembly .... G 810 326-1374
  Saint Clair *(G-14838)*
Nvent Thermal LLC .... E 248 273-3359
  Troy *(G-17284)*
Rapp & Son Inc .... D 734 283-1000
  Wyandotte *(G-18836)*
▲ Sine Systems Corporation .... C 586 465-3131
  Clinton Township *(G-3359)*
Teradyne Inc .... G 313 425-3900
  Allen Park *(G-208)*
Winford Engineering LLC .... G 989 671-9721
  Auburn *(G-771)*

3679 Electronic Components, NEC

Accessories Wholesale Inc .... F 248 755-7465
  Pontiac *(G-13344)*
Ace Electronics LLC Michigan .... G 443 327-6100
  Troy *(G-16904)*
Aees Inc .... A 248 489-4700
  Farmington Hills *(G-5159)*
Affinity Electronics Inc .... G 586 477-4920
  Fraser *(G-5889)*
Aktv8 LLC .... G 517 775-1270
  Wixom *(G-18603)*
▲ Amphenol Borisch Tech Inc .... G 616 554-9820
  Grand Rapids *(G-6458)*
▲ Amptech Inc .... G 231 464-5492
  Manistee *(G-10894)*
▲ Asimco International Inc .... G 248 213-5200
  Southfield *(G-15492)*
Assem-Tech Inc .... E 616 846-3410
  Grand Haven *(G-6275)*
Aztecnology LLC .... G 734 857-2045
  Southgate *(G-15748)*
Bay Electronics Inc .... E 586 296-0900
  Roseville *(G-14379)*
▲ Byrne Elec Specialists Inc .... G 616 866-3461
  Rockford *(G-14159)*
Byrne Elec Specialists Inc .... E 616 866-3461
  Rockford *(G-14160)*
Cardell Corporation .... D 248 371-9700
  Auburn Hills *(G-840)*
Chrouch Communications Inc .... G 231 972-0339
  Mecosta *(G-11190)*
Circuits of Sound .... G 313 886-5599
  Grosse Pointe Woods *(G-7565)*
Cobham McRIctrnic Slutions Inc .... G 734 426-1230
  Ann Arbor *(G-431)*
Code Systems Inc .... E 248 307-3884
  Auburn Hills *(G-845)*
Concept Circuits Corporation .... G 248 852-5200
  Rochester Hills *(G-13982)*
Connect With Us LLC .... G 586 262-4359
  Shelby Township *(G-15194)*
Contract People Corporation .... F 248 304-9900
  Southfield *(G-15532)*
Control Electronics .... G 734 941-5008
  Romulus *(G-14263)*
▲ Ctc Acquisition Company LLC .... C 616 884-7100
  Rockford *(G-14163)*
Debron Industrial Elec LLC .... D 248 588-7220
  Troy *(G-17050)*
Diversfied Tchncal Systems Inc .... E 248 513-6050
  Novi *(G-12401)*
Dupearl Technology LLC .... F 248 390-9609
  Bloomfield Hills *(G-1816)*
Dynamic Supply Solutions Inc .... G 248 987-2205
  Grosse Pointe Shores *(G-7561)*
▲ Ebw Electronics Inc .... B 616 786-0575
  Holland *(G-8021)*
▲ Electro-Matic Integrated Inc .... E 248 478-1182
  Farmington Hills *(G-5223)*
Enertech Corporation .... F 231 832-5587
  Hersey *(G-7866)*
▲ Etcs Inc .... F 586 268-4870
  Warren *(G-17796)*
▲ Eto Magnetic Corp .... C 616 957-2570
  Grand Rapids *(G-6686)*
Fema Corporation of Michigan .... C 269 323-1369
  Portage *(G-13560)*
Five-Way Switch Music .... G 269 425-2843
  Battle Creek *(G-1231)*
◆ Fka Distributing Co LLC .... C 248 863-3000
  Commerce Township *(G-3530)*
◆ Ghs Corporation .... E 269 968-3351
  Springfield *(G-15867)*
High Effcncy Pwr Solutions Inc .... G 800 833-7094
  Whitmore Lake *(G-18538)*
▲ Hirschmann Car Comm Inc .... F 248 373-7150
  Auburn Hills *(G-928)*
▲ House of Marley LLC .... C 248 863-3000
  Commerce Township *(G-3540)*
▲ Innotec Corp .... D 616 772-5959
  Zeeland *(G-19047)*
◆ Kaydon Corporation .... F 734 747-7025
  Ann Arbor *(G-538)*
Lappans of Gaylord Inc .... G 989 732-3274
  Gaylord *(G-6142)*
Lectronix Inc .... E 517 492-1900
  Lansing *(G-9863)*
Leoni Wiring Systems Inc .... F 586 782-4444
  Troy *(G-17208)*
Madison Electric Company .... D 586 825-0200
  Warren *(G-17913)*
Magna Electronics Inc .... E 810 606-8683
  Holly *(G-8282)*
Magna Electronics Inc .... E 248 606-0606
  Auburn Hills *(G-963)*
▲ Magna Electronics Inc .... C 248 729-2643
  Auburn Hills *(G-962)*
MAKS INCORPORATED .... E 248 733-9771
  Troy *(G-17235)*
Mark Griessel .... G 810 378-6060
  Melvin *(G-11195)*
▲ Memtron Technologies Co .... D 989 652-2656
  Frankenmuth *(G-5869)*
Mobile Knowledge Group LLC .... G 248 625-3327
  Clarkston *(G-3052)*
Movellus Circuits Inc .... G 877 321-7667
  Ann Arbor *(G-585)*
▲ Nass Corporation .... F 586 725-6610
  New Baltimore *(G-11989)*
Nelson Specialties Company .... F 269 983-1878
  Saint Joseph *(G-14950)*
Netcon Enterprises Inc .... E 248 673-7855
  Waterford *(G-18140)*
No Limit Wireless-Michigan Inc .... G 313 285-8402
  Detroit *(G-4487)*
Nova-Tron Controls Corp .... F 989 358-6126
  Alpena *(G-305)*
Omtron Inc .... E 248 673-3896
  Waterford *(G-18143)*
Parkway Elc Communications LLC .... D 616 392-2788
  Holland *(G-8160)*
Pcb Piezotronics Inc .... F 888 684-0014
  Novi *(G-12503)*
Photo-Tron Corp .... G 248 852-5200
  Rochester Hills *(G-14083)*
Pkc Group USA Inc .... A 248 489-4700
  Farmington Hills *(G-5348)*
Practical Power .... G 866 385-2961
  Rochester *(G-13922)*
Premier Passivation Services .... G 269 432-2244
  Colon *(G-3490)*
▲ Progressive Dynamics Inc .... D 269 781-4241
  Marshall *(G-11072)*
Quality Cable Assembly LLC .... F 248 236-9915
  Oxford *(G-12909)*
Rdi Switching Technologies .... G 951 699-8919
  Ann Arbor *(G-632)*
Renewable World Energies LLC .... G 906 828-0808
  Norway *(G-12356)*
Rockford Contract Mfg .... G 616 304-3837
  Rockford *(G-14188)*
▲ Safari Circuits Inc .... C 269 694-9471
  Otsego *(G-12799)*
Saldet Sales and Services Inc .... F 586 469-4312
  Clinton Township *(G-3348)*
Sensor Manufacturing Company .... F 248 474-7300
  Novi *(G-12534)*
▲ Ssi Electronics Inc .... E 616 866-8880
  Belmont *(G-1517)*
▲ Stanley Elc Holdg Amer Inc .... D 269 660-7777
  Battle Creek *(G-1300)*
◆ Stoneridge Inc .... A 248 489-9300
  Novi *(G-12543)*
◆ Tecumseh Products Company LLC .... A 734 585-9500
  Ann Arbor *(G-677)*
Tecumseh Products Holdings LLC .... C 734 585-9500
  Ann Arbor *(G-680)*
TMC Group Inc .... G 248 819-6063
  Pleasant Ridge *(G-13106)*
Touchstone Systems & Svcs Inc .... G 616 532-0060
  Wyoming *(G-18912)*
Turn Key Harness & Wire LLC .... E 248 236-9915
  Oxford *(G-12927)*
Vast Production Services Inc .... D 248 838-9680
  Troy *(G-17432)*
Venntis Technologies LLC .... F 616 395-8254
  Holland *(G-8236)*
Wh Manufacturing Inc .... E 616 534-7560
  Grand Rapids *(G-7337)*
▲ World Magnetics Company LLC .... E 231 946-3800
  Traverse City *(G-16882)*
Y Squared Inc .... G 248 435-0301
  Royal Oak *(G-14593)*
ZF Active Safety & Elec US LLC .... E 586 232-7200
  Washington *(G-18092)*
◆ ZF Active Safety & Elec US LLC .... C 734 855-2600
  Livonia *(G-10481)*
ZF Active Safety & Elec US LLC .... E 586 232-7200
  Washington *(G-18093)*

Employee Codes: A=Over 500 employees, B=251-500
C=101-250, D=51-100, E=20-50, F=10-19, G=3-9

36 ELECTRONIC AND OTHER ELECTRICAL EQUIPMENT AND COMPONENTS, EXCEPT COMPUTER36 ELECTRONIC AND OTHER ELECTRICAL

3691 Storage Batteries

A123 Systems LLC......G....... 734 466-6521
Livonia *(G-10095)*
A123 Systems LLC......G....... 734 772-0600
Romulus *(G-14243)*
▼ **A123 Systems LLC**......B....... 248 412-9249
Novi *(G-12359)*
Adana Voltaics LLC......G....... 734 622-0193
Ann Arbor *(G-351)*
▲ **Advanced Battery Concepts LLC**....E....... 989 424-6645
Clare *(G-2972)*
Akasol Inc......E....... 248 259-7843
Hazel Park *(G-7818)*
▼ **Alpine Power Systems Inc**......D....... 313 531-6600
Redford *(G-13713)*
American Battery Solutions Inc......C....... 248 462-6364
Lake Orion *(G-9585)*
Arotech Corporation......D....... 800 281-0356
Ann Arbor *(G-380)*
Batteries Plus......G....... 269 925-7367
Benton Harbor *(G-1533)*
Battery Center of America......G....... 248 399-5999
Ferndale *(G-5531)*
Clarios LLC......G....... 734 995-3016
Ann Arbor *(G-425)*
Contemporary Amperex Tech USA......G....... 248 289-6200
Rochester Hills *(G-13984)*
East Penn Manufacturing Co......G....... 586 979-5300
Sterling Heights *(G-16001)*
Ematrix Energy Systems Inc......F....... 248 797-2149
Southfield *(G-15556)*
Ematrix Energy Systems Inc......G....... 248 629-9111
Royal Oak *(G-14532)*
Exide Technologies LLC......G....... 248 853-5000
Auburn Hills *(G-884)*
G & L Powerup Inc......G....... 586 200-2169
Roseville *(G-14409)*
Global Battery Solutions LLC......E....... 800 456-4265
Holland *(G-8051)*
◆ **Harding Energy Inc**......E....... 231 798-7033
Grand Haven *(G-6314)*
Httm LLC......G....... 616 820-2500
Holland *(G-8090)*
Innovative Weld Solutions LLC......G....... 937 545-7695
Rochester *(G-13908)*
Lg Energy Solution Mich Inc......C....... 248 291-2385
Troy *(G-17211)*
Lg Energy Solution Mich Inc......C....... 248 307-1800
Troy *(G-17212)*
Lg Energy Solution Mich Inc......C....... 616 494-7153
Hazel Park *(G-7829)*
Lg Energy Solution Mich Inc......C....... 616 494-7100
Belleville *(G-1488)*
◆ **Lg Energy Solution Mich Inc**......C....... 616 494-7100
Holland *(G-8126)*
M & M Irish Enterprises Inc......G....... 248 644-0666
Birmingham *(G-1733)*
Navitas Advnced Sltons Group L......G....... 734 913-8176
Ann Arbor *(G-592)*
Our Next Energy Inc......E....... 408 623-1896
Novi *(G-12500)*
Redeem Power Services......G....... 248 679-5277
Novi *(G-12524)*
▲ **Robert Bosch Btry Systems LLC**......D....... 248 620-5700
Farmington Hills *(G-5370)*
Rowerdink Inc......G....... 734 487-1911
Ypsilanti *(G-18975)*
TMC Group Inc......G....... 248 819-6063
Pleasant Ridge *(G-13106)*
Wonch Battery Company......E....... 517 394-3600
Lansing *(G-9904)*
▲ **Xalt Energy LLC**......F....... 989 486-8501
Midland *(G-11426)*
◆ **Xalt Energy Mi LLC**......D....... 989 486-8501
Midland *(G-11428)*

3692 Primary Batteries: Dry & Wet

G & L Powerup Inc......G....... 586 200-2169
Roseville *(G-14409)*
▲ **Mophie LLC**......B....... 269 743-1340
Kalamazoo *(G-9276)*
▲ **Robert Bosch Btry Systems LLC**......D....... 248 620-5700
Farmington Hills *(G-5370)*

3694 Electrical Eqpt For Internal Combustion Engines

◆ **3con Corporation**......E....... 248 859-5440
Wixom *(G-18591)*
▲ **Aees Power Systems Ltd Partnr**......D....... 248 489-4900
Allen Park *(G-187)*
Aees Power Systems Ltd Partnr......G....... 269 668-4429
Farmington Hills *(G-5160)*
Aktv8 LLC......G....... 517 775-1270
Wixom *(G-18603)*
Arotech Corporation......D....... 800 281-0356
Ann Arbor *(G-380)*
▲ **Auto Electric International**......E....... 248 354-2082
Southfield *(G-15498)*
Autocam Corp......D....... 616 698-0707
Grand Rapids *(G-6481)*
Best Netwrk Design & Assoc LLC......E....... 313 680-2047
Detroit *(G-4052)*
▲ **Bontaz Centre Usa Inc**......F....... 248 588-8113
Troy *(G-16982)*
▲ **Brose New Boston Inc**......C....... 248 339-4021
New Boston *(G-12004)*
Case Tool Inc......G....... 734 261-2227
Livonia *(G-10148)*
Cignet LLC......E....... 586 307-3790
Clinton Township *(G-3201)*
Continental Auto Systems Inc......B....... 248 253-2969
Auburn Hills *(G-847)*
Continental Auto Systems Inc......G....... 248 874-2597
Auburn Hills *(G-848)*
◆ **Crosscon Industries LLC**......F....... 248 852-5888
Rochester Hills *(G-13986)*
Cusolar Industries Inc......E....... 586 949-3880
Chesterfield *(G-2863)*
Denso International Amer Inc......G....... 248 359-4177
Van Buren Twp *(G-17523)*
Diamond Electric Mfg Corp......F....... 734 995-5525
Farmington Hills *(G-5215)*
▲ **Don Duff Rebuilding**......G....... 734 522-7700
Livonia *(G-10187)*
Eldor Automotive N Amer Inc......E....... 248 878-9193
Troy *(G-17082)*
Electra Cable & Communication......G....... 586 754-3479
Warren *(G-17793)*
Electro-Matic Products Inc......G....... 248 478-1182
Farmington Hills *(G-5224)*
▲ **Electrodynamics Inc**......G....... 734 422-5420
Livonia *(G-10193)*
▲ **Emp Racing Inc**......G....... 906 786-8404
Escanaba *(G-5068)*
Ford Motor Company......A....... 734 484-8626
Ypsilanti *(G-18947)*
◆ **Fram Group Operations LLC**......G....... 800 890-2075
Rochester Hills *(G-14014)*
Freudnberg Btry Pwr Systems LL......E....... 989 698-3329
Midland *(G-11366)*
H & L Manufacturing Co......C....... 269 795-5000
Middleville *(G-11308)*
Jing-Jin Electric N Amer LLC......G....... 248 554-7247
Farmington Hills *(G-5274)*
Kathrein Automotive N Amer Inc......F....... 248 230-2951
Auburn Hills *(G-949)*
Keystone Cable Corporation......G....... 313 924-9720
Detroit *(G-4360)*
▲ **Kirks Automotive Incorporated**......E....... 313 933-7030
Detroit *(G-4364)*
Lg Elctrnics Vhcl Cmpnnts USA......C....... 248 268-5851
Hazel Park *(G-7828)*
Lg Electronics Vehicle Compone......C....... 248 268-5851
Troy *(G-17210)*
Lg Energy Solution Mich Inc......C....... 616 494-7100
Warren *(G-17904)*
Lumen North America Inc......F....... 248 289-6100
Rochester Hills *(G-14054)*
Magnecor Australia Limited......F....... 248 471-9505
Farmington Hills *(G-5300)*
Michigan Interlock LLC......G....... 248 481-9743
Waterford *(G-18136)*
Nabco Inc......E....... 231 832-2001
Reed City *(G-13796)*
Obdpros LLC......G....... 734 274-5315
Canton *(G-2503)*
Omron Automotive Electronics......E....... 248 893-0200
Novi *(G-12497)*
Overseas Auto Parts Inc......E....... 734 427-4840
Livonia *(G-10354)*
Portable Factory......F....... 586 883-6843
Saint Clair Shores *(G-14877)*
Portage Wire Systems Inc......E....... 231 889-4215
Onekama *(G-12703)*
Powermat Inc......E....... 616 259-4867
Grandville *(G-7410)*
▲ **Prestolite Electric LLC**......G....... 248 313-3807
Novi *(G-12512)*
Prestolite Electric Holding......A....... 248 313-3807
Novi *(G-12513)*
▲ **Prestolite Electric Inc**......F....... 866 463-7078
Novi *(G-12514)*
◆ **Prestolite Wire LLC**......E....... 248 355-4422
Southfield *(G-15681)*
Protean Electric Inc......D....... 248 504-4940
Auburn Hills *(G-1005)*
Protean Holdings Corp......G....... 248 504-4940
Auburn Hills *(G-1006)*
Rizk National Industries Inc......F....... 586 757-4700
Warren *(G-17997)*
◆ **Robert Bosch LLC**......G....... 248 876-1000
Farmington Hills *(G-5371)*
Robert Bosch LLC......G....... 248 921-9054
Novi *(G-12527)*
Robert Bosch LLC......G....... 734 979-3000
Plymouth *(G-13287)*
Seg Automotive North Amer LLC......E....... 248 465-2602
Novi *(G-12533)*
▲ **Southern Auto Wholesalers Inc**......F....... 248 335-5555
Pontiac *(G-13417)*
Starlight Technologies Inc......G....... 248 250-9607
Troy *(G-17371)*
▲ **USA Switch Inc**......F....... 248 960-8500
Wixom *(G-18782)*
Veoneer Inc......A....... 248 223-0600
Southfield *(G-15736)*
Veoneer Us Inc......B....... 248 223-8074
Southfield *(G-15737)*
Veoneer Us Inc......B....... 248 223-0600
Southfield *(G-15738)*
▲ **Vte Inc**......E....... 231 539-8000
Pellston *(G-12968)*
Walbro LLC......D....... 989 872-2131
Cass City *(G-2622)*
◆ **Walther Trowal LLC**......F....... 616 455-8940
Byron Center *(G-2301)*
◆ **Wiric Corporation**......E....... 248 598-5297
Rochester Hills *(G-14147)*
◆ **Wolverine Advanced Mtls LLC**......E....... 313 749-6100
Dearborn *(G-3916)*
Xytek Industries Inc......F....... 313 838-6961
Detroit *(G-4696)*

3695 Recording Media

Ade Inc......G....... 248 625-7200
Clarkston *(G-3012)*
▲ **Applied Automation Tech Inc**......E....... 248 656-4930
Rochester Hills *(G-13949)*
Livonia Magnetics Co Inc......E....... 734 397-8844
Farmington Hills *(G-5293)*
Rutherford & Associates Inc......E....... 616 392-5000
Holland *(G-8185)*
◆ **Storch Products Company Inc**......F....... 734 591-2200
Livonia *(G-10422)*

3699 Electrical Machinery, Eqpt & Splys, NEC

◆ **Ace Filtration Inc**......G....... 248 624-6300
Commerce Township *(G-3506)*
Advanced Avionics Inc......G....... 734 259-5300
Plymouth *(G-13119)*
Advanced Research Company......F....... 248 475-4770
Orion *(G-12723)*
Aerobee Electric Inc......F....... 248 549-2044
Ferndale *(G-5518)*
AMS Co Ltd......G....... 248 712-4435
Troy *(G-16935)*
Andex Laser Inc......G....... 734 947-9840
Taylor *(G-16378)*
Arch Cutting Tools LLC......C....... 734 266-6900
Bloomfield Hills *(G-1800)*
Arin Inc......F....... 586 779-3410
Roseville *(G-14375)*
Asco Power Technologies LP......G....... 248 957-9050
Troy *(G-16958)*
Azure Training Systems Jv LLC......G....... 734 761-5836
Ann Arbor *(G-393)*
Bailey Electrical Inc......G....... 906 478-8000
Hessel *(G-7873)*
Band-Ayd Systems Intl Inc......F....... 586 294-8851
Madison Heights *(G-10677)*
Branson Ultrasonics Corp......G....... 586 276-0150
Sterling Heights *(G-15948)*
◆ **Bronner Display Sign Advg Inc**......C....... 989 652-9931
Frankenmuth *(G-5860)*
BT Engineering LLC......G....... 734 417-2218
Spring Lake *(G-15807)*
Caniff Electric Supply......G....... 586 221-1663
Mount Clemens *(G-11633)*

Challenger Communications LLC ... F ... 517 680-0125 Albion *(G-123)*

Cheap Electric Contractors Co ... G ... 734 205-9591 Ann Arbor *(G-422)*

Cheap Electric Contractors Co ... G ... 734 452-1964 Livonia *(G-10155)*

Cheap Electric Contractors Co ... G ... 734 205-9596 Ann Arbor *(G-423)*

Cheap Electric Contractors Co ... G ... 734 286-9165 Southgate *(G-15749)*

Comptek Inc ... E ... 248 477-5215 Farmington Hills *(G-5206)*

▲ Computerized SEC Systems Inc ... C ... 248 837-3700 Madison Heights *(G-10697)*

Connolly ... G ... 248 683-7985 Waterford *(G-18110)*

Cortar Laser and Fab LLC ... G ... 248 446-1110 Brighton *(G-1970)*

Craft Electric ... G ... 517 529-7164 Clarklake *(G-3005)*

Csh Incorporated ... G ... 989 723-8985 Owosso *(G-12829)*

▲ Cypress Computer Systems Inc ... F ... 810 245-2300 Lapeer *(G-9924)*

▲ Dare Products Inc ... E ... 269 965-2307 Springfield *(G-15864)*

Dataspeed Inc ... E ... 248 243-8889 Rochester Hills *(G-13990)*

Diamond Electric ... G ... 734 995-5525 Ann Arbor *(G-451)*

Dice Corporation ... E ... 989 891-2800 Bay City *(G-1343)*

Dm3d Technology LLC ... F ... 248 409-7900 Auburn Hills *(G-864)*

Electric Beach Tanning Co ... G ... 313 423-6539 Grosse Pointe Park *(G-7553)*

Electric Contractors Company ... G ... 734 205-9594 Ann Arbor *(G-469)*

Electric Eye Cafe ... G ... 734 369-6904 Ann Arbor *(G-470)*

Electric Soul Tattoo and Fine ... G ... 616 930-3113 Grand Rapids *(G-6668)*

Electro-Matic Visual Inc ... F ... 248 478-1182 Farmington Hills *(G-5226)*

Electronic Design & Packg Co ... F ... 734 591-9176 Livonia *(G-10194)*

▲ Emergency Technology Inc ... D ... 616 896-7100 Hudsonville *(G-8581)*

Faac Incorporated ... G ... 734 761-5836 Ann Arbor *(G-484)*

Fabrilaser Mfg LLC ... E ... 269 789-9490 Marshall *(G-11057)*

Farr & Faron Associates Inc ... G ... 810 229-7730 Brighton *(G-1988)*

Fire Equipment Company ... E ... 313 891-3164 Detroit *(G-4233)*

G and R Laser Solutions Inc ... G ... 734 748-6603 Canton *(G-2462)*

▲ Gelman Sciences Inc ... C ... 734 665-0651 Ann Arbor *(G-496)*

General Electric Company ... G ... 734 728-1472 Wayne *(G-18221)*

Grt Avionics Inc ... G ... 616 245-7700 Wyoming *(G-18878)*

▲ Gvn Group Corp ... E ... 248 340-0342 Pontiac *(G-13376)*

H & R Industries Inc ... F ... 616 247-1165 Grand Rapids *(G-6798)*

Hanon Systems Usa LLC ... B ... 248 907-8000 Novi *(G-12425)*

Harold G Schaevitz Inds LLC ... G ... 248 636-1515 Bloomfield Hills *(G-1827)*

Heco Inc ... E ... 269 381-7200 Kalamazoo *(G-9210)*

Hirose Electric USA Inc ... G ... 734 542-9963 Livonia *(G-10240)*

Holland Vision Systems Inc ... E ... 616 494-9974 Holland *(G-8087)*

▼ Iaec Corporation ... G ... 586 354-5996 Armada *(G-737)*

Identify Inc ... E ... 313 802-2015 Madison Heights *(G-10745)*

Imperial Laser Inc ... G ... 616 735-9315 Grand Rapids *(G-6837)*

▲ Imra America Inc ... E ... 734 669-7377 Ann Arbor *(G-525)*

Innovative Groups Inc ... G ... 313 309-7064 Detroit *(G-4319)*

Insulation Wholesale Supply ... G ... 269 968-9746 Battle Creek *(G-1241)*

▼ Integrated Security Corp ... F ... 248 624-0700 Novi *(G-12438)*

Ipg Photonics Corporation ... G ... 248 863-5001 Novi *(G-12441)*

▲ Kore Inc ... E ... 616 785-5900 Comstock Park *(G-3617)*

Lakepoint Elec ... G ... 586 983-2510 Shelby Township *(G-15256)*

Laser Access Inc ... C ... 616 459-5496 Grand Rapids *(G-6928)*

Laser Fab Inc ... G ... 586 415-8090 Fraser *(G-5955)*

▲ Laser Marking Technologies LLC ... F ... 989 673-6690 Caro *(G-2573)*

Laser Mechanisms Inc ... D ... 248 474-9480 Novi *(G-12465)*

Laser Product Development LLC ... G ... 800 765-4424 Center Line *(G-2682)*

Lastek Industries LLC ... G ... 586 739-6666 Shelby Township *(G-15258)*

Lighthouse Elec Protection LLC ... G ... 586 932-2690 Sterling Heights *(G-16074)*

Macomb Sheet Metal Inc ... E ... 586 790-4600 Clinton Township *(G-3290)*

Magna Electronics Inc ... D ... 810 606-0444 Troy *(G-17219)*

Magna Mirrors America Inc ... B ... 231 652-4450 Newaygo *(G-12086)*

Metropoulos Amplification Inc ... G ... 810 614-3905 Holly *(G-8284)*

Midwest Sales Associates Inc ... G ... 248 348-9600 Wixom *(G-18710)*

Montronix Inc ... G ... 734 213-6500 Ann Arbor *(G-583)*

Morstar Inc ... F ... 248 605-3291 Livonia *(G-10322)*

▲ Ms Plastic Welders LLC ... E ... 517 223-1059 Webberville *(G-18246)*

Muskegon Charter Township Fire ... G ... 231 329-3068 Muskegon *(G-11880)*

New Electric ... F ... 586 580-2405 Sterling Heights *(G-16114)*

Niowave Inc ... G ... 517 999-3475 Lansing *(G-9722)*

Oleco Inc ... E ... 616 842-6790 Spring Lake *(G-15841)*

▲ Operator Specialty Company Inc ... D ... 616 675-5050 Grand Rapids *(G-7061)*

Passivebolt Inc ... F ... 734 972-0306 Ann Arbor *(G-606)*

Pct Security Inc ... G ... 888 567-3287 Clinton Township *(G-3317)*

Peak Edm Inc ... G ... 248 380-0871 Wixom *(G-18729)*

▼ Picpatch LLC ... G ... 248 670-2681 Milford *(G-11480)*

Power Cleaning Systems Inc ... G ... 248 347-7727 Wixom *(G-18731)*

Quad City Innovations LLC ... G ... 513 200-6980 Ann Arbor *(G-629)*

Quality Door & More Inc ... G ... 989 317-8314 Coleman *(G-3470)*

Ram Electronics Inc ... F ... 231 865-3186 Fruitport *(G-6069)*

Realm ... G ... 313 706-4401 Wayne *(G-18234)*

Reau Manufacturing Co ... G ... 734 823-5603 Dundee *(G-4833)*

Resa Power LLC ... G ... 763 784-4040 Wixom *(G-18740)*

Rofin-Sinar Technologies LLC ... G ... 734 416-0206 Plymouth *(G-13290)*

Rydin and Associates Inc ... F ... 586 783-9772 Clinton Township *(G-3347)*

▲ Saginaw Control & Engrg Inc ... B ... 989 799-6871 Saginaw *(G-14745)*

Secure Crossing RES & Dev Inc ... F ... 248 535-3800 Dearborn *(G-3894)*

Securecom Inc ... G ... 989 837-4005 Midland *(G-11415)*

Sensigma LLC ... G ... 734 998-8328 Ann Arbor *(G-648)*

Siemens Industry Software Inc ... G ... 734 953-2700 Livonia *(G-10406)*

▲ Silent Call Corporation ... F ... 248 673-7353 Waterford *(G-18164)*

SLM Solutions Na Inc ... E ... 248 243-5400 Wixom *(G-18753)*

Stanley Electric Sales America ... G ... 248 471-1300 Farmington Hills *(G-5386)*

Stoneridge Inc ... B ... 781 830-0340 Novi *(G-12544)*

Tandis LLC ... G ... 248 345-3448 West Bloomfield *(G-18317)*

Tech Electric Co LLC ... G ... 586 697-5095 Macomb *(G-10641)*

Tech-Source International Inc ... F ... 231 652-9100 Newaygo *(G-12090)*

▲ Telsonic Ultrasonics Inc ... F ... 586 802-0033 Shelby Township *(G-15350)*

Tenneco Automotive Oper Co Inc ... E ... 734 243-8000 Lansing *(G-9742)*

◆ Testek LLC ... D ... 248 573-4980 Wixom *(G-18771)*

Trumpf Inc ... E ... 734 354-9770 Plymouth *(G-13327)*

Twig Power LLC ... G ... 248 613-9652 Novi *(G-12561)*

Visotek Inc ... F ... 734 427-4800 Novi *(G-12568)*

Volkswagen Group America Inc ... F ... 248 754-5000 Auburn Hills *(G-1082)*

Walker Telecommunications ... G ... 989 274-7384 Saginaw *(G-14791)*

◆ Warner Power Acquisition LLC ... C ... 603 456-3111 Grand Haven *(G-6380)*

Weber Security Group Inc ... G ... 586 582-0000 Mount Clemens *(G-11662)*

Welform Electrodes Inc ... E ... 586 755-1184 Warren *(G-18066)*

Welk-Ko Fabricators Inc ... F ... 734 425-6840 Livonia *(G-10470)*

Yakkertech Limited ... G ... 734 568-6162 Ottawa Lake *(G-12812)*

37 TRANSPORTATION EQUIPMENT

3711 Motor Vehicles & Car Bodies

A & A Manufacturing Co ... G ... 616 846-1730 Spring Lake *(G-15799)*

AAM Mexico Holdings LLC ... D ... 313 758-2000 Detroit *(G-3977)*

AAM Travel Services LLC ... G ... 313 758-2000 Detroit *(G-3978)*

▲ Adac Door Components Inc ... B ... 616 957-0311 Grand Rapids *(G-6427)*

Advance Vehicle Assembly Inc ... F ... 989 823-3800 Vassar *(G-17576)*

Advanced Def Vhcl Systems Corp ... F ... 248 391-3200 Clarkston *(G-3013)*

Aftershock Motorsports ... G ... 586 273-1333 Casco *(G-2597)*

Ai-Genesee LLC ... F ... 810 720-4848 Flint *(G-5641)*

American Axle Mfg Holdings Inc ... A ... 313 758-2000 Detroit *(G-4012)*

American Fabricated Pdts Inc ... E ... 616 607-8785 Spring Lake *(G-15803)*

Android Industries-Sterling ... F ... 586 486-5616 Warren *(G-17705)*

Armartis Manufacturing Inc ... E ... 248 308-9622 Roseville *(G-14376)*

◆ Armored Group LLC ... E ... 602 840-2271 Dearborn Heights *(G-3920)*

Asp Grede Acquisitionco LLC ... E ... 248 440-9515 Southfield *(G-15493)*

Asp Hhi Acquisition Co Inc ... G ... 313 758-2000 Detroit *(G-4030)*

◆ Autoalliance Management Co ... D ... 734 782-7800 Flat Rock *(G-5615)*

Autoform Development Inc ... F ... 616 392-4909 Holland *(G-7966)*

▲ BDS Company Inc ... F ... 517 279-2135 Coldwater *(G-3421)*

Bearing Holdings LLC ... G ... 313 758-2000 Detroit *(G-4046)*

Bennett Funeral Coaches Inc ... G ... 616 538-8100 Byron Center *(G-2259)*

Bordrin Motor Corporation Inc ... F ... 877 507-3267 Oak Park *(G-12595)*

CATI Armor LLC ... G ... 269 788-4322 Charlotte *(G-2740)*

◆ Champion Bus Inc ... B ... 810 724-1753 Imlay City *(G-8628)*

Chassix Holdings Inc ... E ... 248 728-8700 Southfield *(G-15520)*

Chrysler Group LLC ... D ... 586 977-4900 Sterling Heights *(G-15958)*

▲ Comstar Automotive USA LLC ... F ... 517 266-2445 Tecumseh *(G-16493)*

Employee Codes: A=Over 500 employees, B=251-500 C=101-250, D=51-100, E=20-50, F=10-19, G=3-9

2022 Harris Michigan Industrial Directory

877

37 TRANSPORTATION EQUIPMENT

Company	Col	Phone
Creative Automation Solutions, Livonia (G-10168)	G	313 790-4848
CT Custom Collision LLC, Detroit (G-4110)	G	313 912-9776
▲ Dakkota Integrated Systems LLC, Brighton (G-1972)	B	517 694-6500
Dakkota Integrated Systems LLC, Lansing (G-9683)	G	517 321-3064
Dakkota Integrated Systems LLC, Hazel Park (G-7822)	G	517 694-6500
Dakkota Integrated Systems LLC, Holt (G-8307)	G	517 694-6500
▲ Detroit Chassis LLC, Detroit (G-4139)	G	313 571-2100
Detroit Custom Chassis LLC, Detroit (G-4142)	C	313 571-2100
Detroit Mfg Systems LLC, Detroit (G-4152)	D	313 243-0700
Dus Operating Inc, Auburn Hills (G-869)	B	248 299-7500
Dynamic Corporation, Auburn Hills (G-870)	E	248 338-1100
Electric Last Mile Inc, Troy (G-17083)	G	888 825-9111
FCA North America Holdings LLC, Auburn Hills (G-893)	A	248 512-2950
FCA US LLC, Mount Clemens (G-11638)	C	586 468-2891
FCA US LLC, Detroit (G-4230)	G	800 334-9200
FCA US LLC, Livonia (G-10206)	E	734 422-0557
FCA US LLC, Warren (G-17803)	G	248 576-5741
FCA US LLC, Sterling Heights (G-16011)	F	586 978-0067
◆ FCA US LLC, Auburn Hills (G-895)	A	248 576-5741
▲ Ficosa North America Corp, Madison Heights (G-10727)	E	248 307-2230
Finish Line Fabricating LLC, Allegan (G-158)	G	269 686-8400
Ford Investment Entps Corp, Dearborn (G-3841)	G	973 764-8783
Ford Motor Company, Dearborn (G-3842)	A	313 322-3000
Ford Motor Company, Dearborn (G-3844)	G	313 322-7715
Ford Motor Company, Flat Rock (G-5620)	G	734 782-7800
Ford Motor Company, Monroe (G-11541)	G	734 241-2498
Forging Holdings LLC, Detroit (G-4243)	G	313 758-2000
Frank Industries Inc, Brown City (G-2137)	E	810 346-3234
G Tech Sales LLC, Sterling Heights (G-16026)	G	586 803-9393
General Coach America Inc, Imlay City (G-8633)	D	810 724-6474
General Motors Company, Detroit (G-4255)	A	313 667-1500
General Motors LLC, Warren (G-17825)	E	586 441-8483
General Motors LLC, Auburn Hills (G-908)	G	313 408-3987
General Motors LLC, Detroit (G-4257)	A	313 972-6000
General Motors LLC, Pontiac (G-13374)	C	248 874-1737
General Motors LLC, Detroit (G-4259)	A	313 972-6000
General Motors LLC, Detroit (G-4260)	A	313 556-5000
General Motors LLC, Pontiac (G-13375)	A	248 857-3500
◆ Gestamp Mason LLC, Mason (G-11135)	B	517 244-8800
Gleason Race Cars, Benzonia (G-1615)	G	231 882-2336
Global Impact Group LLC, Grand Blanc (G-6243)	G	248 895-9900
GM Defense LLC, Detroit (G-4266)	C	313 462-8782
GM Defense LLC, Milford (G-11464)	E	586 359-8880
▲ GM Gdls Defense Group LLC, Sterling Heights (G-16031)	D	586 825-4000
GM Laam Holdings LLC, Detroit (G-4267)	D	313 556-5000
GM Orion Assembly, Lake Orion (G-9607)	E	248 377-5260
Grede Omaha LLC, Southfield (G-15582)	C	248 727-1800
Hayes-Albion Corporation, Jackson (G-8900)	F	517 629-2141
Hercules Electric Mobility Inc, Detroit (G-4298)	G	734 666-8078
Hhi Funding II LLC, Detroit (G-4299)	C	313 758-2000
Hhi Holdings LLC, Detroit (G-4300)	G	313 758-2000
Hme Inc, Wyoming (G-18885)	C	616 534-1463
Holbrook Racing Engines, Livonia (G-10241)	F	734 762-4315
Horizon Global Corporation, Plymouth (G-13192)	A	734 656-3000
Horstman Inc, Sterling Heights (G-16041)	E	586 737-2100
▲ HP Pelzer Automotive Systems, Port Huron (G-13484)	E	810 987-0725
Illinois Tool Works Inc, Troy (G-17161)	G	248 589-2500
Jasco International LLC, Detroit (G-4335)	G	313 841-5000
Jeff Schaller Transport Inc, Imlay City (G-8638)	G	810 724-7640
Junk Man LLC, Pontiac (G-13389)	G	248 459-7359
Jvis - Usa LLC, Shelby Township (G-15248)	F	586 884-5700
Kendrick Plastics Inc, Grand Rapids (G-6883)	B	616 975-4000
Kyklos Holdings Inc, Detroit (G-4370)	G	313 758-2000
Lemforder Corp, Northville (G-12235)	E	734 416-6200
Lightguide Inc, Wixom (G-18698)	G	248 374-8000
Lucasvarity Inc, Fowlerville (G-5849)	G	517 223-8330
M M R LLC, Livonia (G-10295)	G	734 502-5239
▲ Magna Steyr LLC, Troy (G-17227)	B	248 740-0214
Mahindra N Amercn Technical, Troy (G-17229)	G	248 268-6600
Mahindra N Amrcn Tchncal Ctr I, Auburn Hills (G-965)	C	248 268-6600
Manufacturing Products & Svcs, Plymouth (G-13233)	F	734 927-1964
▲ Marrel Corporation, Rockford (G-14177)	G	616 863-9155
Maven Drive LLC, Detroit (G-4421)	D	313 667-1541
May Mobility Inc, Ann Arbor (G-567)	F	312 869-2711
▲ Meritor Heavy Vhcl Systems LLC, Troy (G-17247)	A	248 435-1000
Meyers John, Middleton (G-11298)	G	989 236-5400
Mico Industries Inc, Grand Rapids (G-6999)	D	616 245-6426
Midstates Industrial Group Inc, Clinton Township (G-3300)	E	586 307-3414
Mobility Innovations LLC, Shelby Township (G-15280)	G	586 843-3816
Morris Associates Inc, Southfield (G-15662)	E	248 355-9055
Moser Racing Inc, Northville (G-12243)	F	248 348-6502
Nationwide Design Inc, Sterling Heights (G-16113)	F	586 254-5493
Nexteer Automotive Corporation, Saginaw (G-14710)	B	989 757-5000
Nyx LLC, Livonia (G-10348)	D	734 462-2385
Omaha Automation Inc, Detroit (G-4497)	G	313 557-3565
Omnico Agv LLC, Clinton Township (G-3315)	F	586 268-7700
▲ Onodi Tool & Engineering Co, Melvindale (G-11208)	E	313 386-6682
Onyx Manufacturing Inc, Rochester Hills (G-14075)	G	248 687-8611
Oshkosh Defense LLC, Warren (G-17951)	E	586 576-8301
P2r Metal Fabrication Inc, Macomb (G-10625)	F	586 606-5266
Pcm US Steering Holding LLC, Auburn Hills (G-994)	E	313 556-5000
Quality First Fire Alarm, Flint (G-5752)	G	810 736-4911
Quality Inspections Inc, Sterling Heights (G-16140)	G	586 323-6135
R V Wolverine, Gladwin (G-6201)	F	989 426-9241
Rattle Top Precision Assembly, Howard City (G-8416)	G	231 937-5333
Redline Fabrications, Clyde (G-3415)	G	810 984-5621
Rivian Automotive Inc, Plymouth (G-13283)	A	734 855-4350
Rivian Automotive Inc, Plymouth (G-13284)	A	408 483-1987
◆ Rivian Automotive LLC, Plymouth (G-13285)	D	734 855-4350
Robert Carmichael, Auburn Hills (G-1022)	G	248 576-5741
Rough Road Trucking LLC, Kalkaska (G-9402)	G	231 645-3355
Roush Enterprises Inc, Allen Park (G-205)	A	313 294-8200
Sakthi Auto Group USA Inc, Detroit (G-4576)	C	313 551-6001
Sakthi Auto Group USA Inc, Detroit (G-4577)	C	248 292-9328
◆ Sakthi Auto Group USA Inc, Detroit (G-4578)	C	313 652-5254
Saleen, Pontiac (G-13414)	G	248 499-5333
▲ Saleen Special Vehicles Inc, Troy (G-17342)	B	909 978-6700
▲ Sas Automotive Usa Inc, Sterling Heights (G-16164)	E	248 606-1152
Serena Hines, Benton Harbor (G-1583)	G	269 252-0895
SGC Industries Inc, Fraser (G-5992)	G	586 293-5260
◆ Shyft Group Inc, Novi (G-12536)	A	517 543-6400
Shyft Group Inc, Charlotte (G-2767)	G	517 543-6400
Shyft Group Inc, Charlotte (G-2768)	E	517 543-6400
◆ Shyft Group Usa Inc, Charlotte (G-2769)	D	517 543-6400
Skinny Kid Race Cars, Commerce Township (G-3573)	G	248 668-1040
▲ Smart Automation Systems Inc, Rochester Hills (G-14114)	G	248 651-5911
▼ Spartan Motors Chassis Inc, Charlotte (G-2772)	B	517 543-6400
Special Projects Inc, Plymouth (G-13302)	E	734 455-7130
Spectra Lmp LLC, Detroit (G-4600)	G	313 571-2100
Spencer Manufacturing Inc, South Haven (G-15416)	F	269 637-9459
Stamping Plant, Wayne (G-18236)	G	734 467-0008
Superalloy North America LLC, Bingham Farms (G-1704)	G	810 252-1552
Supreme Gear Co, Fraser (G-6001)	E	586 775-6325
Tesla Inc, Troy (G-17389)	G	248 205-3206
Think North America Inc, Dearborn (G-3904)	E	313 565-6781
Thomas Engineering, Clarkston (G-3071)	G	248 620-7916
Thor Industries Inc, Imlay City (G-8647)	G	810 724-6474
Trailer Tech Repair Inc, Plymouth (G-13321)	G	734 354-6680
Transglobal Design & Mfg LLC, Auburn Hills (G-1063)	D	734 525-2651
TRW Safety Systems Mexico LLC, Livonia (G-10450)	G	734 855-2600
▲ Trynex International LLC, Madison Heights (G-10848)	F	248 586-3500
▲ Tunkers Inc, Sterling Heights (G-16212)	E	734 744-5990
Turn Key Automotive LLC, Oxford (G-12926)	F	248 628-5556
UPF Inc, Flint (G-5789)	E	810 768-0001
Usm Holdings LLC, Detroit (G-4657)	F	313 758-2000

Usm Holdings LLC II.....................F.......313 758-2000 Detroit *(G-4658)*	Mobilitytrans LLC........................E.......734 262-3760 Livonia *(G-10320)*	Adient US LLC............................B.......734 254-5000 Plymouth *(G-13117)*
Valley Truck Parts Inc................D.......616 241-5431 Grand Rapids *(G-7303)*	Monroe Truck Equipment Inc....E.......810 238-4603 Flint *(G-5736)*	Adient US LLC............................G.......734 414-9215 Plymouth *(G-13118)*
Veigel North America LLC..........F.......586 843-3816 Shelby Township *(G-15364)*	◆ Morgan Olson LLC.....................A.......269 659-0200 Sturgis *(G-16311)*	Adient US LLC............................G.......510 771-2300 Madison Heights *(G-10660)*
Very Best Motors LLC.................G.......517 253-0707 Lansing *(G-9749)*	NBC Truck Equipment Inc.........E.......586 774-4900 Roseville *(G-14452)*	Adient US LLC............................B.......269 968-3000 Battle Creek *(G-1177)*
Visteon Intl Holdings Inc............A.......734 710-2000 Van Buren Twp *(G-17561)*	▲ Norma Michigan Inc..................C.......248 373-4300 Auburn Hills *(G-984)*	▲ ADS Us Inc................................D.......989 871-4550 Millington *(G-11498)*
▲ Visteon Systems LLC..................C.......313 755-9500 Dearborn *(G-3910)*	Norma Michigan Inc...................G.......248 373-4300 Lake Orion *(G-9622)*	▲ Advanced Assembly Products Inc...G.......248 543-2427 Hazel Park *(G-7817)*
▲ Wgs Global Services LC............B.......810 239-4947 Flint *(G-5792)*	Novi Manufacturing Co..............C.......248 476-4350 Novi *(G-12494)*	Advanced Auto Trends Inc........E.......248 628-4850 Oxford *(G-12872)*
Wgs Global Services LC.............D.......810 694-3843 Grand Blanc *(G-6268)*	◆ Off Site Mfg Tech Inc.................D.......586 598-3110 Chesterfield *(G-2917)*	▲ Advanced Auto Trends Inc........E.......248 628-6111 Oxford *(G-12871)*
▲ Workhorse Custom Chassis LLC...C.......248 588-5300 Madison Heights *(G-10864)*	Optimal Electric Vehicles LLC...E.......734 414-7933 Plymouth *(G-13256)*	Advanced Vhcl Assemblies LLC....A.......248 299-7500 Rochester Hills *(G-13944)*
◆ ZF TRW Auto Holdings Corp....A.......734 855-2600 Livonia *(G-10492)*	Perspective Enterprises Inc........G.......269 327-0869 Portage *(G-13591)*	▼ Advantage Truck ACC Inc........G.......800 773-3110 Ann Arbor *(G-356)*
3713 Truck & Bus Bodies	Precision Laser & Mfg LLC.........G.......519 733-8422 Sterling Heights *(G-16131)*	ADW Industries Inc....................E.......989 466-4742 Alma *(G-233)*
AM General LLC..........................B.......734 523-8098 Auburn Hills *(G-779)*	Roll Rite Group Holdings LLC....D.......989 345-3434 Gladwin *(G-6203)*	Aerospace America Inc..............E.......989 684-2121 Bay City *(G-1319)*
Armada Rubber Manufacturing Co.......D.......586 784-9135 Armada *(G-731)*	▲ Roll-Rite LLC..............................G.......989 345-3434 Gladwin *(G-6204)*	Affinia Group Inc.......................E.......734 827-5400 Ann Arbor *(G-357)*
Automotive Service Co................F.......517 784-6131 Jackson *(G-8818)*	▲ Tecnoma LLC.............................F.......248 354-8888 Southfield *(G-15718)*	Aftech Inc....................................G.......616 866-1650 Grand Rapids *(G-6436)*
▲ BDS Company Inc......................F.......517 279-2135 Coldwater *(G-3421)*	Tectum Holdings Inc..................D.......734 677-0444 Ann Arbor *(G-673)*	AGM Automotive Mexico LLC....C.......248 925-4152 Farmington Hills *(G-5163)*
Borgwarner Thermal Systems Inc...G.......231 779-7500 Cadillac *(G-2317)*	Tractech Inc................................E.......248 226-6800 Southfield *(G-15725)*	▲ Agritek Industries Inc...............D.......616 786-9200 Holland *(G-7958)*
Bucks Cement Inc.......................G.......810 233-4141 Burton *(G-2228)*	Transit Bus Rebuilders Inc.........F.......989 277-3645 Owosso *(G-12863)*	◆ Air Lift Company.......................E.......517 322-2144 Lansing *(G-9751)*
Cameron Kirk Forest Pdts Inc....G.......989 426-3439 Gladwin *(G-6192)*	Velcro USA Inc............................G.......248 583-6060 Troy *(G-17437)*	▲ Airboss Flexible Products Co...C.......248 852-5500 Auburn Hills *(G-776)*
Carter Industries Inc..................D.......510 324-6700 Adrian *(G-56)*	Weiderman Motorsports............G.......269 689-0264 Sturgis *(G-16329)*	◆ Akebono Brake Corporation....C.......248 489-7400 Farmington Hills *(G-5165)*
Central Mich Knwrth Lnsing LLC...G.......517 394-7000 Lansing *(G-9823)*	◆ Worldwide Marketing Svcs Inc...F.......269 556-2000 Saint Joseph *(G-14981)*	Albion Automotive Limited........G.......313 758-2000 Detroit *(G-3995)*
Central Mich Knwrth Sginaw LLC...G.......989 754-4500 Saginaw *(G-14625)*	**3714 Motor Vehicle Parts & Access**	Alfmeier Friedrichs & Rath LLC...G.......248 526-1650 Troy *(G-16921)*
Csi Emergency Apparatus LLC....F.......989 348-2877 Grayling *(G-7459)*	1st Quality LLC............................G.......313 908-4864 Dearborn *(G-3803)*	Allegan Tubular Products Inc....D.......269 673-6636 Allegan *(G-146)*
D & W Management Company Inc...F.......586 758-2284 Warren *(G-17770)*	3d Polymers Inc..........................F.......248 588-5562 Orchard Lake *(G-12715)*	Allison..G.......734 261-3735 Garden City *(G-6092)*
Dowding Industries Inc..............C.......517 663-5455 Eaton Rapids *(G-4960)*	751 Parts Company Inc.............F.......231 845-1221 Ludington *(G-10524)*	◆ Alma Products I LLC.................C.......989 463-1151 Alma *(G-237)*
▲ Durakon Industries Inc............G.......608 742-5301 Lapeer *(G-9928)*	A I Flint LLC................................A.......810 732-8760 Flint *(G-5633)*	▲ Alpha Technology Corporation...E.......517 546-9700 Howell *(G-8426)*
▲ E-T-M Enterprises I Inc............C.......517 627-8461 Grand Ledge *(G-6389)*	A&M Assembly and Machining LLC...E.......313 369-9475 Detroit *(G-3974)*	Alternative Fuel Tech LLC.........C.......313 417-9212 Grosse Pointe Park *(G-7545)*
Eleven Mile Trck Frame Axle In...E.......248 399-7536 Madison Heights *(G-10721)*	AA Gear LLC................................F.......517 552-3100 Howell *(G-8424)*	Aludyne Inc.................................C.......248 728-8700 Southfield *(G-15478)*
Ford Motor Company..................A.......313 322-3000 Dearborn *(G-3842)*	AAM Casting................................G.......313 758-5968 Southfield *(G-15469)*	▲ Aludyne East Michigan LLC.....D.......810 987-7633 Port Huron *(G-13437)*
Ford Motor Company..................G.......313 322-7715 Dearborn *(G-3844)*	AAM International Holdings Inc....A.......313 758-2000 Detroit *(G-3976)*	Aludyne International Inc.........G.......248 728-8642 Southfield *(G-15479)*
Ford Motor Company..................F.......910 381-7998 Taylor *(G-16419)*	AAM Mexico Holdings LLC.........D.......313 758-2000 Detroit *(G-3977)*	▲ Aludyne Mexico LLC.................C.......248 728-8642 Southfield *(G-15480)*
Ford Motor Company..................F.......734 523-3000 Livonia *(G-10215)*	AAM Pwder Metal Components Inc...G.......248 597-3800 Royal Oak *(G-14501)*	▲ Aludyne Montague LLC............A.......248 479-6455 Montague *(G-11594)*
Ford Motor Company..................F.......734 942-6248 Brownstown *(G-2146)*	AAM Travel Services LLC...........G.......313 758-2000 Detroit *(G-3978)*	▲ Aludyne North America Inc.....G.......248 728-8642 Southfield *(G-15481)*
▲ Gac..—.......269 639-3010 South Haven *(G-15406)*	ABC Precision Machining Inc....G.......269 926-6322 Benton Harbor *(G-1525)*	Aludyne North America Inc......C.......248 728-8642 Howell *(G-8427)*
Hme Inc.......................................C.......616 534-1463 Wyoming *(G-18885)*	Acat Global LLC..........................G.......231 330-2553 Charlevoix *(G-2707)*	Aludyne North America LLC.....D.......248 728-8700 Southfield *(G-15482)*
Hovertechnics LLC.....................G.......269 461-3934 Benton Harbor *(G-1556)*	Access Works Inc.......................G.......231 777-2537 Muskegon *(G-11761)*	Aludyne North America LLC.....B.......989 463-6166 Alma *(G-238)*
Hulet Body Co Inc......................F.......313 931-6000 Northville *(G-12230)*	▼ Accurate Automotive Engs Inc...E.......616 531-2050 Grandville *(G-7361)*	▲ Aludyne US LLC.........................D.......248 728-8700 Southfield *(G-15483)*
Jasper Weller LLC......................E.......616 249-8596 Wyoming *(G-18886)*	◆ Ace Controls Inc.........................C.......248 476-0213 Farmington Hills *(G-5158)*	Aludyne US LLC.........................D.......810 987-1112 Port Huron *(G-13438)*
▲ Jasper Weller LLC......................C.......616 724-2000 Wyoming *(G-18887)*	Acutex Inc....................................A.......231 894-3200 Whitehall *(G-18489)*	▲ Aludyne West Michigan LLC....E.......248 728-8642 Benton Harbor *(G-1528)*
Johnson Controls Inc.................B.......734 254-5000 Plymouth *(G-13204)*	▲ Adac Automotive Trim Inc.......C.......616 957-0311 Grand Rapids *(G-6426)*	▲ Aludyne West Michigan LLC....C.......248 728-8642 Stevensville *(G-16240)*
◆ Loadmaster Corporation...........E.......906 563-9226 Norway *(G-12353)*	Adac Plastics Inc........................D.......616 642-0109 Saranac *(G-15075)*	AM Specialties Inc......................F.......586 795-9000 Sterling Heights *(G-15929)*
◆ Lodal Inc.....................................D.......906 779-1700 Kingsford *(G-9513)*	Adac Plastics Inc........................E.......616 957-0520 Muskegon *(G-11763)*	Amalgamated Uaw......................G.......231 734-9286 Evart *(G-5120)*
Mahindra N Amrcn Tchncal Ctr I...C.......248 268-6600 Auburn Hills *(G-965)*	Adac Plastics Inc........................E.......616 957-0311 Muskegon *(G-11764)*	▲ Amanda Products LLC..............E.......248 547-3870 Ferndale *(G-5525)*
Marsh Industrial Services Inc....F.......231 258-4870 Kalkaska *(G-9395)*	Adient..G.......586 753-3072 Warren *(G-17692)*	American Axle & Mfg Inc..........G.......248 353-2155 Southfield *(G-15485)*
▲ Midwest Bus Corporation.........D.......989 723-5241 Owosso *(G-12844)*	Adient US Entps Ltd Partnr.......C.......734 254-5000 Plymouth *(G-13115)*	American Axle & Mfg Inc..........G.......248 475-3475 Auburn Hills *(G-781)*
Mobility Trnsp Svcs Inc..............E.......734 453-6452 Canton *(G-2497)*	◆ Adient US LLC............................A.......734 254-5000 Plymouth *(G-13116)*	American Axle & Mfg Inc..........G.......586 415-2000 Fraser *(G-5891)*

American Axle & Mfg Inc G 517 542-4241 Litchfield *(G-10076)*
American Axle & Mfg Inc G 586 573-4840 Warren *(G-17700)*
American Axle & Mfg Inc G 810 772-8778 Detroit *(G-4010)*
▲ **American Axle & Mfg Inc** B 313 758-3600 Detroit *(G-4011)*
American Axle & Mfg Inc A 269 278-0211 Three Rivers *(G-16562)*
American Axle & Mfg Inc G 248 299-2900 Rochester Hills *(G-13946)*
American Axle & Mfg Inc F 248 276-2328 Auburn Hills *(G-782)*
American Axle Mfg Holdings Inc A 313 758-2000 Detroit *(G-4012)*
American Axle Oxford G 248 361-6044 Oxford *(G-12873)*
▼ **American Cooling Systems LLC** E 616 954-0280 Grand Rapids *(G-6452)*
American Lear F 616 252-3643 Grand Rapids *(G-6453)*
◆ **American Mitsuba Corporation** B 989 779-4962 Mount Pleasant *(G-11679)*
American T-Mould LLC G 616 617-2422 Grand Rapids *(G-6456)*
American Undercar F 989 235-1427 Crystal *(G-3740)*
▲ **Anand Nvh North America Inc** C 810 724-2400 Imlay City *(G-8627)*
▲ **Anderson-Cook Inc** D 586 954-0700 Chesterfield *(G-2844)*
Anderson-Cook Inc G 586 293-0800 Fraser *(G-5895)*
▲ **Android Indstrs-Dlta Twnship L** D 517 322-0657 Lansing *(G-9755)*
Android Industries-Wixom LLC F 248 255-5434 Shelby Township *(G-15170)*
▲ **Android Industries-Wixom LLC** E 248 732-0000 Auburn Hills *(G-786)*
Angstrom Automotive Group LLC E 734 756-1164 Southfield *(G-15487)*
Angstrom Automotive Group LLC E 248 627-2871 Ortonville *(G-12741)*
▲ **Anjun America Inc** G 248 680-8825 Auburn Hills *(G-787)*
Anrod Screen Cylinder Company E 989 872-2101 Cass City *(G-2610)*
▲ **Antolin Interiors Usa Inc** B 248 373-1749 Auburn Hills *(G-789)*
Antolin Interiors Usa Inc A 517 548-0052 Howell *(G-8429)*
Antolin Interiors Usa Inc D 248 567-4000 Troy *(G-16938)*
Antolin Sprtnburg Assembly LLC E 248 373-1749 Auburn Hills *(G-790)*
Apply Prssure MBL Dtailing LLC G 248 794-7710 Redford *(G-13715)*
◆ **Aptiv Corporation** A 248 813-2000 Troy *(G-16942)*
Aptiv Corporation G 248 724-5900 Auburn Hills *(G-794)*
Aptiv Corporation A 248 813-3005 Troy *(G-16943)*
Aptiv Intl Svcs Co LLC G 248 813-2000 Troy *(G-16944)*
Aptiv Mexican Holdings US LLC C 248 813-2000 Troy *(G-16945)*
◆ **Aptiv Services 3 (us) LLC** G 248 813-2000 Troy *(G-16946)*
Aptiv Services 5 Us LLC G 248 813-2000 Troy *(G-16947)*
Aptiv Services Us LLC G 810 459-8809 Auburn Hills *(G-795)*
Aptiv Services Us LLC G 248 724-5900 Auburn Hills *(G-796)*
Aptiv Services Us LLC G 248 813-2000 Hudsonville *(G-8567)*
Aptiv Services Us LLC G 330 373-7666 Troy *(G-16948)*
Aptiv Services Us LLC G 248 813-2000 Troy *(G-16949)*
Aptiv Trade MGT Svcs US LLC E 248 813-2000 Troy *(G-16950)*
Aqueous Orbital Systems LLC G 269 501-7461 Kalamazoo *(G-9117)*
Arete Industries Inc F 231 582-4470 Boyne City *(G-1882)*
Argent Tape & Label Inc G 734 582-9956 Plymouth *(G-13125)*
Argo Ai LLC G 313 908-2447 Allen Park *(G-190)*
▲ **Argonics Inc** F 303 664-9467 Gwinn *(G-7581)*
Artisans Cstm Mmory Mattresses F 989 793-3208 Saginaw *(G-14605)*
▲ **Arvinmeritor Oe LLC** G 248 435-1000 Troy *(G-16957)*
▲ **Asama Coldwater Mfg Inc** B 517 279-1090 Coldwater *(G-3420)*
▲ **Asmo Detroit Inc** G 248 359-4440 Novi *(G-12366)*
Asp Grede Acquisitionco LLC E 248 440-9515 Southfield *(G-15493)*
Asp Hhi Acquisition Co Inc G 313 758-2000 Detroit *(G-4030)*
Asp Hhi Holdings Inc A 248 597-3800 Royal Oak *(G-14513)*
▲ **Aspra World Inc** D 248 872-7030 Warren *(G-17719)*
Atf Inc E 989 685-2468 Rose City *(G-14362)*
▲ **Atlas Gear Company** F 248 583-2964 Madison Heights *(G-10675)*
Auria Albemarle LLC D 248 728-8000 Southfield *(G-15495)*
Auria Solutions Intl Inc G 734 456-2800 Southfield *(G-15496)*
Auria Solutions USA Inc A 248 728-8000 Southfield *(G-15497)*
Auria St Clair LLC C 810 329-8400 Saint Clair *(G-14813)*
Auto-Tech Plastics Inc G 586 783-0103 Mount Clemens *(G-11628)*
Autocam Corp D 616 698-0707 Grand Rapids *(G-6481)*
Autocam Corporation G 269 789-4000 Marshall *(G-11052)*
Autocam Corporation G 269 782-5186 Dowagiac *(G-4775)*
Autocam Corporation C 616 698-0707 Kentwood *(G-9446)*
▲ **Autocam Corporation** B 616 698-0707 Kentwood *(G-9444)*
Autoform Development Inc F 616 392-4909 Holland *(G-7966)*
Autoliv Asp Inc C 248 761-0081 Pontiac *(G-13351)*
Autoliv Asp Inc C 248 475-9000 Auburn Hills *(G-801)*
Autoliv Asp Inc C 248 475-9000 Auburn Hills *(G-802)*
Autoliv Holding Inc B 248 475-9000 Auburn Hills *(G-803)*
◆ **Automotive LLC** C 248 712-1175 Southfield *(G-15499)*
Automotive Exteriors LLC G 248 458-0702 Auburn Hills *(G-807)*
Automotive International Svcs G 248 808-8112 Rochester Hills *(G-13957)*
▲ **Autoneum North America Inc** D 248 848-0100 Novi *(G-12372)*
Autotech Engrg R&D USA Inc G 248 743-3400 Auburn Hills *(G-808)*
Avl Powertrain Technologies G 734 414-9600 Plymouth *(G-13132)*
Avl Properties Inc E 734 414-9600 Plymouth *(G-13133)*
Avon Plastic Products Inc E 248 852-1000 Rochester Hills *(G-13960)*
Baldwin Precision Inc E 231 237-4515 Charlevoix *(G-2710)*
Bandit Utv Suspension G 586 419-9574 Columbus *(G-3497)*
Barker Manufacturing Co E 269 965-2371 Battle Creek *(G-1190)*
Barker Manufacturing Co F 269 965-2371 Battle Creek *(G-1191)*
▲ **Bartec USA LLC** E 586 685-1300 Sterling Heights *(G-15944)*
Bay Alphi Manufacturing Inc E 517 849-9945 Jonesville *(G-9085)*
Bdgn Corporation C 616 669-9040 Hudsonville *(G-8570)*
▲ **BDS Company Inc** F 517 279-2135 Coldwater *(G-3421)*
Bearing Holdings LLC G 313 758-2000 Detroit *(G-4046)*
Benteler Automotive Corp B 616 245-4607 Grand Rapids *(G-6501)*
◆ **Benteler Automotive Corp** C 248 364-7190 Auburn Hills *(G-811)*
Best Products Inc F 313 538-7414 Redford *(G-13719)*
Bestop Inc F 586 268-0602 Sterling Heights *(G-15945)*
Bgm Electronic Services LLC G 586 997-7090 Auburn Hills *(G-812)*
Black River Manufacturing Inc E 810 982-9812 Port Huron *(G-13459)*
Black River Manufacturing Inc D 810 982-9812 Port Huron *(G-13460)*
Bleistahl N Amer Ltd Partnr E 269 719-8585 Battle Creek *(G-1196)*
Boesch Built LLC G 248 318-2136 Highland *(G-7885)*
Boostbutton LLC G 734 223-0813 Whitmore Lake *(G-18523)*
Borgwarner Arden LLC E 248 754-9200 Auburn Hills *(G-814)*
Borgwarner Global Holding LLC A 248 754-9200 Auburn Hills *(G-815)*
Borgwarner Inc G 248 371-0040 Auburn Hills *(G-816)*
Borgwarner Inc G 231 779-7500 Cadillac *(G-2316)*
Borgwarner Inc A 248 754-9200 Auburn Hills *(G-817)*
Borgwarner Inc E 248 754-9600 Auburn Hills *(G-818)*
Borgwarner Inc G 248 754-9200 Auburn Hills *(G-819)*
Borgwarner Intl Svcs LLC F 248 813-2000 Auburn Hills *(G-820)*
Borgwarner Inv Holdg Inc E 248 754-9200 Auburn Hills *(G-821)*
Borgwarner Jersey Holdings LLC G 248 754-9200 Auburn Hills *(G-822)*
▲ **Borgwarner Pds (usa) Inc** B 248 754-9600 Auburn Hills *(G-823)*
Borgwarner Pds Anderson LLC G 248 641-3045 Troy *(G-16983)*
Borgwarner Powdered Metals Inc C 734 261-5322 Livonia *(G-10140)*
Borgwarner Tech Svcs LLC E 248 754-9200 Auburn Hills *(G-824)*
▲ **Borgwarner Thermal Systems Inc** C 269 781-1228 Marshall *(G-11053)*
Borgwarner Transm Pdts LLC D 248 754-9200 Auburn Hills *(G-825)*
▲ **Borgwarner Transm Systems LLC** B 248 754-9200 Auburn Hills *(G-826)*
Borgwarner US Holding LLC G 248 754-9200 Auburn Hills *(G-827)*
Borgwarner USA Corporation E 248 813-2000 Auburn Hills *(G-828)*
▲ **Borgwrner Emssions Systems LLC** C 248 754-9200 Auburn Hills *(G-829)*
▲ **Borgwrner Emssons Systems Mich** C 248 754-9600 Auburn Hills *(G-830)*
Borgwrner Prplsion Systems LLC G 248 707-5224 Auburn Hills *(G-831)*
Borgwrner Prplsion Systems LLC C 248 813-2000 Auburn Hills *(G-832)*
Borgwrner Prplsion Systems LLC C 248 813-2000 Troy *(G-16984)*
▲ **Bos Automotive Products Inc** E 248 289-6072 Rochester Hills *(G-13965)*
Bosal Industries-Georgia Inc F 734 547-7038 Ypsilanti *(G-18926)*
Bosal Industries-Georgia Inc E 734 547-7023 Ypsilanti *(G-18927)*
◆ **Bosal Industries-Georgia Inc** E 734 547-7022 Ypsilanti *(G-18928)*
▲ **Bosch Auto Svc Solutions Inc** D 586 574-2332 Warren *(G-17739)*
Bpi Holdings International Inc G 815 363-9000 Ann Arbor *(G-405)*
Brake Team G 313 914-6000 Saint Clair Shores *(G-14849)*
Brembo F 517 568-4398 Homer *(G-8345)*
Brembo North America Inc G 517 568-4398 Homer *(G-8346)*
◆ **Brembo North America Inc** D 734 416-1275 Plymouth *(G-13138)*
Brose Harmon Road F 248 339-4702 Auburn Hills *(G-834)*
Brose New Boston Inc G 248 340-1100 Auburn Hills *(G-835)*

SIC SECTION

37 TRANSPORTATION EQUIPMENT37 TRANSPORTATION EQUIPMENT

Brose New Boston Inc G 248 339-4000 Auburn Hills ***(G-836)***
▲ **Brose North America Inc** C 248 339-4000 Auburn Hills ***(G-837)***
▲ **Brose North America Inc** G 734 753-4902 New Boston ***(G-12005)***
▲ **Brugola Oeb Indstriale USA Inc** F 734 468-0009 Plymouth ***(G-13139)***
▲ **Bullseye Power** G 231 788-5209 Muskegon ***(G-11786)***
Burr Engineering & Dev Co G 269 966-3122 Battle Creek ***(G-1201)***
◆ **Bushings Inc** F 248 650-0603 Rochester Hills ***(G-13968)***
Bwa Receivables Corporation G 248 754-9200 Auburn Hills ***(G-838)***
Bwi Chassis Dynamics NA Inc G 937 455-5308 Brighton ***(G-1956)***
Bwi North America Inc F 810 494-4584 Brighton ***(G-1957)***
C W A Manufacturing Co Inc E 810 686-3030 Mount Morris ***(G-11669)***
▲ **Cadillac Products Inc** B 248 813-8200 Troy ***(G-16992)***
Cadillac Products Inc E 586 774-1700 Roseville ***(G-14382)***
Cadillac Products Inc F 989 766-2294 Rogers City ***(G-14208)***
Caea Auto Elctrnic Systems USA G 586 649-9036 Warren ***(G-17749)***
Cambria Tool and Machine Inc F 517 437-3500 Hillsdale ***(G-7928)***
Cambridge Sharpe Inc F 248 613-5562 South Lyon ***(G-15429)***
Cambro Products Inc F 586 468-8847 Harrison Township ***(G-7691)***
Camshaft Acquisition Inc F 517 787-2040 Jackson ***(G-8832)***
Camshaft Machine Company LLC E 517 787-2040 Jackson ***(G-8833)***
Carr Engineering G 248 447-4109 Southfield ***(G-15517)***
Carter Fuel Systems LLC E 248 371-8392 Rochester Hills ***(G-13973)***
Carter Industries Inc D 510 324-6700 Adrian ***(G-56)***
Cascade Engineering Inc G 616 975-4965 Grand Rapids ***(G-6554)***
Casco Products Corporation F 248 957-0400 Novi ***(G-12380)***
▲ **CC Industries LLC** D 269 426-3342 Sawyer ***(G-15108)***
Century Qual Products G 734 728-0300 Van Buren Twp ***(G-17518)***
Cequent Uk Ltd G 734 656-3000 Plymouth ***(G-13144)***
Cfe Racing Products Inc G 586 773-6310 Eastpointe ***(G-4931)***
Champion Laboratories Inc G 586 247-9044 Shelby Township ***(G-15186)***
Chassis Brakes Intl USA G 248 957-9997 Farmington ***(G-5135)***
Chassix Blackstone Operat G 586 782-7311 Warren ***(G-17753)***
▲ **Check Technology Solutions LLC** E 248 680-2323 Troy ***(G-17008)***
Chicago Blow Pipe Company F 773 533-6100 Marquette ***(G-11012)***
Cinnabar Engineering Inc F 810 648-2444 Sandusky ***(G-15057)***
◆ **Cipa Usa Inc** E 810 982-3555 Port Huron ***(G-13464)***
▲ **Circuit Controls Corporation** C 231 347-0760 Petoskey ***(G-12993)***
Citation Camden Cast Ctr LLC B 248 727-1800 Southfield ***(G-15523)***
▼ **Classic Design Concepts LLC** G 248 504-5202 Milford ***(G-11458)***
▲ **Clio Massena LLC** E 248 477-5148 Wixom ***(G-18634)***
Complete Prototype Svcs Inc C 586 690-8897 Clinton Township ***(G-3207)***
▲ **Concen Grinding Inc** G 517 787-8172 Jackson ***(G-8851)***
Concorde Inc F 248 391-8177 Auburn Hills ***(G-846)***
Conform Automotive LLC C 248 647-0400 Macomb ***(G-10585)***
Conform Automotive LLC F 248 647-0400 Grand Rapids ***(G-6592)***
Conform Automotive LLC D 517 322-0711 Lansing ***(G-9758)***
▲ **Conform Automotive LLC** F 248 647-0400 Bingham Farms ***(G-1694)***
Continental Auto Systems Inc G 906 248-6700 Brimley ***(G-2103)***
Continental Auto Systems Inc G 248 874-1801 Auburn Hills ***(G-849)***
Continental Auto Systems Inc G 248 267-9408 Troy ***(G-17023)***
Continntal Auto Systems US Inc D 248 764-6400 Troy ***(G-17024)***
Cooper-Standard Auto OH LLC G 248 596-5900 Northville ***(G-12203)***
▲ **Cooper-Standard Automotive Inc** B 248 596-5900 Northville ***(G-12204)***
Cooper-Standard Automotive Inc D 734 542-6300 Livonia ***(G-10164)***
Cooper-Standard Automotive Inc G 989 848-2272 Fairview ***(G-5129)***
▲ **Cooper-Standard Fhs LLC** C 248 596-5900 Northville ***(G-12205)***
Cooper-Standard Foundation Inc G 248 596-5900 Northville ***(G-12206)***
Cooper-Standard Holdings Inc G 248 596-5900 Northville ***(G-12207)***
▲ **Cosma International Amer Inc** B 248 631-1100 Troy ***(G-17031)***
▲ **Creative Controls Inc** E 248 577-9800 Madison Heights ***(G-10698)***
Creative Performance Racg LLC G 248 250-6187 Troy ***(G-17032)***
Crowne Group LLC G 734 855-4512 Livonia ***(G-10169)***
Cs Intermediate Holdco 1 LLC G 248 596-5900 Northville ***(G-12211)***
Csa Services Inc G 248 596-6184 Novi ***(G-12387)***
◆ **CTA Acoustics Inc** E 248 544-2580 Madison Heights ***(G-10699)***
▲ **CTC Distribution Inc** G 313 486-2225 Saint Clair Shores ***(G-14854)***
Cummins Inc G 906 774-2424 Iron Mountain ***(G-8720)***
Cummins Inc G 248 573-1600 New Hudson ***(G-12049)***
Cusolar Industries Inc E 586 949-3880 Chesterfield ***(G-2863)***
Custom Pro Products Inc G 734 558-2070 Rockwood ***(G-14198)***
Custom Wheel Solutions G 248 547-9587 Grosse Pointe ***(G-7528)***
D & M Truck Top Co Inc G 248 792-7972 Troy ***(G-17042)***
D M P E G 269 428-5070 Stevensville ***(G-16244)***
Daimay North America Auto Inc E 313 533-9680 Redford ***(G-13729)***
Dakkota Integrated Systems LLC G 517 694-6500 Holt ***(G-8307)***
Dana E 419 887-3000 Kalamazoo ***(G-9162)***
Dana Driveshaft Mfg LLC C 248 623-2185 Auburn Hills ***(G-857)***
Dana Incorporated C 269 567-1537 Kalamazoo ***(G-9163)***
Dana Limited G 586 467-1600 Warren ***(G-17774)***
Dana Limited G 810 329-2500 Saint Clair ***(G-14822)***
Dana Off-Hghway Components LLC E 586 467-1600 Flint ***(G-5683)***
Dana Thermal Products LLC E 810 329-2500 Saint Clair ***(G-14823)***
Dana Thermal Products LLC E 810 329-2500 Saint Clair ***(G-14824)***
Davco Manufacturing LLC G 734 429-5665 Saline ***(G-15011)***
◆ **Davco Technology LLC** D 734 429-5665 Saline ***(G-15012)***
Dawson Manufacturing Company C 269 925-0100 Benton Harbor ***(G-1545)***
Dayco Products LLC G 989 775-0689 Mount Pleasant ***(G-11694)***
Dayco Products LLC G 517 439-0689 Hillsdale ***(G-7931)***
Dcd Idid Enterprise LLC E 517 424-0577 Tecumseh ***(G-16495)***
Dearborn Total Auto Svc Ctr F 313 291-6300 Dearborn Heights ***(G-3922)***
Dearborne Cummins F 313 843-6200 Dearborn ***(G-3825)***
Debron Industrial Elec LLC D 248 588-7220 Troy ***(G-17050)***
Delco Elec Overseas Corp C 248 813-2000 Troy ***(G-17051)***
Delphi E 248 813-2000 Troy ***(G-17052)***
Delphi Automotive Systems D 248 813-2000 Troy ***(G-17053)***
Delphi Corp F 313 996-3429 Dearborn ***(G-3827)***
Delphi Pwrtrain Tech Gen Prtnr E 248 813-2000 Troy ***(G-17054)***
Delphi World Headquarters G 248 813-3045 Troy ***(G-17055)***
▲ **Delta Gear Inc** E 734 525-8000 Livonia ***(G-10179)***
▲ **Delta Research Corporation** E 734 261-6400 Livonia ***(G-10180)***
▲ **Denso Air Systems Michigan Inc** B 269 962-9676 Battle Creek ***(G-1215)***
◆ **Denso International Amer Inc** A 248 350-7500 Southfield ***(G-15538)***
◆ **Denso Manufacturing Mich Inc** A 269 965-3322 Battle Creek ***(G-1216)***
▼ **Denso Sales Michigan Inc** E 269 965-3322 Battle Creek ***(G-1218)***
Design Converting Inc F 616 942-7780 Grand Rapids ***(G-6642)***
Design Usa Inc G 734 233-8677 Plymouth ***(G-13154)***
Detail Production Company Inc F 248 544-3390 Ferndale ***(G-5541)***
◆ **Detroit Diesel Corporation** A 313 592-5000 Detroit ***(G-4144)***
Detroit Diesel Corporation F 313 592-8256 Redford ***(G-13730)***
Detroit Hitch Co F 248 379-0071 Clawson ***(G-3094)***
Detroit Radiator Corporation C 800 525-0011 Taylor ***(G-16401)***
Dewitts Radiator LLC F 517 548-0600 Howell ***(G-8444)***
▼ **Dgh Enterprises Inc** E 269 925-0657 Benton Harbor ***(G-1546)***
Dicastal North America Inc B 616 619-7500 Greenville ***(G-7482)***
Dieomatic Incorporated F 269 966-4900 Battle Creek ***(G-1219)***
Dieomatic Incorporated D 319 668-2031 Troy ***(G-17061)***
Diesel Performance Products G 586 726-7478 Shelby Township ***(G-15205)***
Diversified Machine Inc E 231 894-9562 Montague ***(G-11595)***
Diversified Mfg & Assembly LLC G 586 272-2431 Sterling Heights ***(G-15988)***
Dolphin Manufacturing Inc E 734 946-6322 Taylor ***(G-16403)***
▲ **Donnelly Corp** G 231 652-8425 Newaygo ***(G-12080)***
Dontech Solutions LLC F 248 789-3086 Howell ***(G-8448)***
◆ **Douglas Autotech Corporation** D 517 369-2315 Bronson ***(G-2111)***
Dowding Industries Inc C 517 663-5455 Eaton Rapids ***(G-4960)***
◆ **Dph LLC** A 248 813-2000 Troy ***(G-17065)***
▲ **Dph-Das Global (holdings) LLC** C 248 813-2000 Troy ***(G-17066)***
◆ **Dph-Das LLC** C 248 813-2000 Troy ***(G-17067)***
▲ **Drake Enterprises Inc** E 586 783-3009 Clinton Township ***(G-3226)***
Dreal Inc F 248 813-2000 Troy ***(G-17069)***
Dse Industries LLC G 313 530-6668 Macomb ***(G-10589)***
Dst Industries Inc F 734 941-0300 Clinton ***(G-3136)***
Dt Manufacturing One LLC D 248 889-9210 Highland ***(G-7891)***
Dura Global Technologies Inc E 248 299-7500 Rochester Hills ***(G-13997)***
◆ **Dura Operating LLC** C 248 299-7500 Auburn Hills ***(G-868)***
Dura Shifter LLC F 248 299-7500 Rochester Hills ***(G-13998)***

S I C

Employee Codes: A=Over 500 employees, B=251-500 C=101-250, D=51-100, E=20-50, F=10-19, G=3-9

2022 Harris Michigan Industrial Directory

881

37 TRANSPORTATION EQUIPMENT37 TRANSPORTATION EQUIPMENT SIC SECTION

▲ **Durakon Industries Inc** G 608 742-5301
Lapeer *(G-9928)*

Dus Operating Inc G 231 924-0930
Fremont *(G-6039)*

E & E Manufacturing Co Inc E 248 616-1300
Clawson *(G-3095)*

▲ **E-T-M Enterprises I Inc** C 517 627-8461
Grand Ledge *(G-6389)*

Eagle Thread Verifier LLC G 586 764-8218
Sterling Heights *(G-15999)*

Eaton Aerospace LLC B 616 949-1090
Grand Rapids *(G-6663)*

Eaton Corporation B 269 342-3000
Galesburg *(G-6076)*

Eaton Corporation G 269 342-3000
Galesburg *(G-6077)*

Eaton Corporation G 248 226-6200
Southfield *(G-15548)*

Eberspecher Contrls N Amer Inc E 248 994-7010
Brighton *(G-1981)*

◆ **Eklund Holdings Inc** C 231 777-2537
Muskegon *(G-11810)*

Elite Plastic Products Inc E 586 247-5800
Shelby Township *(G-15220)*

Elmwood Manufacturing Company G 313 571-1777
Detroit *(G-4204)*

Emergency Services LLC F 231 727-7400
Muskegon *(G-11812)*

Emma Sogoian Inc E 248 549-8690
Royal Oak *(G-14533)*

▲ **Emssons Faurecia Ctrl Systems** G 248 724-5100
Auburn Hills *(G-880)*

Enertrols Inc E 734 595-4500
Farmington Hills *(G-5234)*

◆ **Engine Power Components Inc** B 616 846-0110
Grand Haven *(G-6297)*

◆ **Engineered Machined Pdts Inc** B 906 786-8404
Escanaba *(G-5069)*

Engineering Service of America D 248 357-3800
Southfield *(G-15557)*

Enovapremier LLC G 517 541-3200
Charlotte *(G-2751)*

Environmental Catalysts LLC F 248 813-2000
Troy *(G-17095)*

Erae AMS America Corp F 419 386-8876
Pontiac *(G-13368)*

Ervins Group LLC E 248 203-2000
Bloomfield Hills *(G-1819)*

▲ **Erwin Quarder Inc** D 616 575-1600
Grand Rapids *(G-6683)*

▲ **Ese LLc** G 810 538-1000
Lapeer *(G-9929)*

Etx Inc A 989 463-1151
Alma *(G-240)*

▼ **Etx Holdings Inc** G 989 463-1151
Alma *(G-241)*

▲ **Euclid Industries Inc** C 989 686-8920
Bay City *(G-1352)*

Everblades Inc G 906 483-0174
Atlantic Mine *(G-749)*

Excellence Manufacturing Inc E 616 456-9928
Grand Rapids *(G-6691)*

Expernced Prcsion McHining Inc G 989 635-2299
Marlette *(G-10981)*

▲ **Extang Corporation** D 734 677-0444
Ann Arbor *(G-482)*

Extreme Machine Inc G 810 231-0521
Whitmore Lake *(G-18535)*

Extreme Machine Inc D 810 231-0521
Whitmore Lake *(G-18536)*

Fastime Racing Engines & Parts G 734 947-1600
Taylor *(G-16417)*

◆ **Faurecia Emssons Ctrl Tech USA** C 248 724-5100
Auburn Hills *(G-887)*

Faurecia Emssons Ctrl Tech USA B 734 947-1688
Taylor *(G-16418)*

Faurecia Exhaust Systems LLC E 248 409-3500
Auburn Hills *(G-888)*

▲ **Faurecia Intr Systems Sline LL** G 734 429-0030
Saline *(G-15017)*

▲ **Faurecia USA Holdings Inc** G 248 724-5100
Auburn Hills *(G-891)*

◆ **FCA Intrntional Operations LLC** E 800 334-9200
Auburn Hills *(G-892)*

FCA North America Holdings LLC A 248 512-2950
Auburn Hills *(G-893)*

FCA US LLC B 734 478-5658
Dundee *(G-4819)*

FCA US LLC G 586 497-2500
Warren *(G-17802)*

Fcaus Dundee Engine Plant A 734 529-9256
Dundee *(G-4820)*

Federal Screw Works D 231 796-7664
Big Rapids *(G-1674)*

Federal-Mogul Chassis LLC F 248 354-7700
Southfield *(G-15560)*

▲ **Federal-Mogul Corporation** E 248 354-7700
Southfield *(G-15561)*

▲ **Federal-Mogul Ignition LLC** D 248 354-7700
Southfield *(G-15562)*

Federal-Mogul Motorparts LLC D 248 354-7700
Southfield *(G-15563)*

Federal-Mogul Powertrain LLC B 616 754-5681
Greenville *(G-7485)*

▲ **Federal-Mogul Products US LLC** A 248 354-7700
Southfield *(G-15566)*

Federal-Mogul World Wide Inc D 248 354-7700
Southfield *(G-15568)*

◆ **Fiamm Technologies LLC** C 248 427-3200
Farmington Hills *(G-5243)*

Firefish Topco LLC D 248 299-7500
Auburn Hills *(G-898)*

Fisher & Company Incorporated G 248 280-0808
Troy *(G-17108)*

Fisher & Company Incorporated F 586 746-2280
Saint Clair Shores *(G-14859)*

Fisher & Company Incorporated F 586 746-2000
Sterling Heights *(G-16016)*

Fisher & Company Incorporated F 586 746-2101
Troy *(G-17110)*

Fisher Dynamics Corporation C 586 746-2000
Saint Clair Shores *(G-14860)*

▲ **Flex-N-Gate LLC** C 586 759-8900
Warren *(G-17809)*

▲ **Flex-N-Gate Battle Creek LLC** C 269 962-2982
Battle Creek *(G-1232)*

Flex-N-Gate Corporation G 586 773-0800
Warren *(G-17810)*

Flex-N-Gate Knshan Hldings LLC D 586 759-8900
Warren *(G-17811)*

Flex-N-Gate LLC G 616 222-3296
Grand Rapids *(G-6710)*

▲ **Flex-N-Gate Michigan LLC** D 586 759-8900
Warren *(G-17812)*

▲ **Flextronics Automotive USA Inc** D 248 853-5724
Coopersville *(G-3686)*

▲ **Fluid Hutchinson Management** D 248 679-1327
Auburn Hills *(G-903)*

▲ **Fontijne Grotnes Inc** E 269 262-4700
Niles *(G-12129)*

Ford Motor Company A 313 594-0050
Dearborn *(G-3843)*

Ford Motor Company F 734 523-3000
Livonia *(G-10214)*

Ford Motor Company F 313 594-4090
Allen Park *(G-194)*

Ford Motor Company A 313 322-3000
Dearborn *(G-3842)*

Ford Motor Company F 734 523-3000
Livonia *(G-10215)*

Ford Motor Company F 734 942-6248
Brownstown *(G-2146)*

Forged Tubular G 313 843-4870
Detroit *(G-4241)*

Forging Holdings LLC G 313 758-2000
Detroit *(G-4243)*

Formfab LLC E 248 844-3676
Rochester Hills *(G-14013)*

Formtech Inds Holdings LLC G 248 597-3800
Royal Oak *(G-14538)*

◆ **Fram Group Operations LLC** G 800 890-2075
Rochester Hills *(G-14014)*

Frank Industries Inc E 810 346-3234
Brown City *(G-2137)*

◆ **Freudenberg N Amer Ltd Partnr** G 734 354-5505
Plymouth *(G-13169)*

◆ **Freudenberg-Nok General Partnr** C 734 451-0020
Plymouth *(G-13170)*

◆ **Fte Automotive North Amer Inc** E 248 340-1262
Auburn Hills *(G-905)*

◆ **Fte Automotive USA Inc** C 248 209-8239
Highland Park *(G-7907)*

◆ **Fujikura Automotive Amer LLC** E 248 957-0130
Farmington Hills *(G-5247)*

G P Dura F 248 299-7500
Rochester Hills *(G-14019)*

Gabriel Ride Control LLC E 248 247-7600
Farmington Hills *(G-5248)*

Gage Pattern & Model Inc D 248 361-6609
Madison Heights *(G-10729)*

Garage Grus Fdrl-Mgul Mtrparts F 800 325-8886
Southfield *(G-15572)*

Garrett Motion Inc A 734 359-5901
Plymouth *(G-13173)*

Garrisons Hitch Center Inc G 810 239-5728
Flint *(G-5703)*

Gasket Holdings Inc G 248 354-7700
Southfield *(G-15573)*

Gates Corporation G 248 260-2300
Rochester Hills *(G-14020)*

General Motors China LLC G 313 556-5000
Detroit *(G-4254)*

General Motors Company F 248 249-6347
Brownstown *(G-2147)*

General Motors Company B 586 218-9240
Warren *(G-17824)*

General Motors Company A 313 667-1500
Detroit *(G-4255)*

▲ **General Motors Holdings LLC** C 313 667-1500
Detroit *(G-4256)*

General Motors LLC G 810 635-5281
Swartz Creek *(G-16354)*

General Motors LLC G 734 481-3555
Van Buren Twp *(G-17526)*

General Motors LLC F 989 894-7210
Bay City *(G-1359)*

General Motors LLC F 586 342-2728
Sterling Heights *(G-16027)*

General Motors LLC F 517 885-6669
Lansing *(G-9761)*

General Motors LLC G 313 408-3987
Auburn Hills *(G-908)*

General Motors LLC A 313 972-6000
Detroit *(G-4257)*

General Motors LLC C 248 874-1737
Pontiac *(G-13374)*

▼ **General Motors LLC** A 313 665-4919
Detroit *(G-4258)*

General Motors LLC A 313 556-5000
Detroit *(G-4260)*

Gentex Corporation C 616 772-1800
Zeeland *(G-19024)*

▲ **Gentherm Incorporated** A 248 504-0500
Northville *(G-12224)*

◆ **Gestamp Mason LLC** B 517 244-8800
Mason *(G-11135)*

▲ **Gestamp North America Inc** C 248 743-3400
Troy *(G-17130)*

▲ **Ghsp Inc** B 616 842-5500
Holland *(G-8050)*

Ghsp Inc G 248 588-5095
Grand Haven *(G-6300)*

Ghsp Inc G 248 581-0890
Grand Haven *(G-6301)*

Ghsp Inc G 231 873-3300
Hart *(G-7752)*

Gissing North America LLC D 248 647-0400
Bingham Farms *(G-1697)*

◆ **GKN Driveline North Amer Inc** B 248 296-7000
Auburn Hills *(G-911)*

GKN North America Inc C 248 296-7200
Auburn Hills *(G-912)*

GKN North America Services Inc G 248 377-1200
Auburn Hills *(G-913)*

◆ **GKN Sinter Metals LLC** G 248 883-4500
Auburn Hills *(G-914)*

▲ **Glassmaster Controls Co Inc** E 269 382-2010
Kalamazoo *(G-9198)*

Global Automotive Systems LLC E 248 299-7500
Auburn Hills *(G-915)*

Global Fmi LLC D 810 964-5555
Fenton *(G-5481)*

Global Rollforming Systems LLC G 586 218-5100
Roseville *(G-14413)*

▲ **GM Components Holdings LLC** C 870 594-0351
Detroit *(G-4265)*

GM Defense LLC C 313 462-8782
Detroit *(G-4266)*

GM Defense LLC E 586 359-8880
Milford *(G-11464)*

GM Laam Holdings LLC D 313 556-5000
Detroit *(G-4267)*

GMC (general Motors) G 517 265-4222
Adrian *(G-71)*

Grakon LLC G 734 462-1201
Livonia *(G-10227)*

Grede Omaha LLC C 248 727-1800
Southfield *(G-15582)*

Ground Effects LLC C 810 250-5560
Flint *(G-5710)*

Ground Effects LLC ....B 810 250-5560
Flint (G-5711)
Grouper Wild LLC ....G 269 665-4261
Galesburg (G-6078)
▲ Grupo Antolin Michigan Inc ....C 989 635-5055
Marlette (G-10982)
▲ Grupo Antolin North Amer Inc ....C 248 373-1749
Auburn Hills (G-918)
▲ Grupo Antolin Primera Auto Sys ....D 734 495-9180
Canton (G-2469)
◆ Gt Technologies Inc ....E 734 467-8371
Westland (G-18378)
H & L Manufacturing Co ....C 269 795-5000
Middleville (G-11308)
Hacker Machine Inc ....E 517 569-3348
Rives Junction (G-13886)
◆ Hadley Products Corporation ....C 616 530-1717
Grandville (G-7385)
Haldex Brake Products Corp ....C 616 827-9641
Wyoming (G-18880)
Hamaton Inc ....F 248 308-3856
Wixom (G-18674)
Hamlin Tool & Machine Co Inc ....E 248 651-6302
Rochester Hills (G-14029)
Hanho America Co Ltd ....G 248 422-6921
Troy (G-17137)
Hanon Systems Usa LLC ....B 248 907-8000
Novi (G-12425)
Hanwha Advanced Mtls Amer LLC ....F 810 629-2496
Monroe (G-11546)
Harrys Steering Gear Repair ....G 586 677-5580
Macomb (G-10601)
Harvey S Freeman ....G 248 852-2222
West Bloomfield (G-18287)
▲ Havis Inc ....F 734 414-0699
Plymouth (G-13184)
Hayes Lemmerz Intl Import LLC ....G 734 737-5000
Novi (G-12430)
▲ Hayes Lmmerz Intrntnl-Grgia LL ....D 734 737-5000
Novi (G-12431)
Hayes-Albion Corporation ....F 517 629-2141
Jackson (G-8900)
Hdt Automotive Solutions LLC ....G 810 359-5344
Livonia (G-10237)
Heavy Duty Radiator LLC ....E 800 525-0011
Taylor (G-16426)
Hemco Machine Co Inc ....G 586 264-8911
Warren (G-17851)
Henniges Auto Holdings Inc ....B 248 340-4100
Auburn Hills (G-924)
◆ Henniges Auto Sling Systems N ....C 248 340-4100
Auburn Hills (G-925)
Hhi Formtech LLC ....E 586 415-2000
Fraser (G-5935)
▼ Hhi Formtech Industries LLC ....D 248 597-3800
Royal Oak (G-14546)
Hhi Funding II LLC ....C 313 758-2000
Detroit (G-4299)
Hhi Holdings LLC ....G 313 758-2000
Detroit (G-4300)
Hi-Lex America Incorporated ....B 248 844-0096
Rochester Hills (G-14030)
HI-Lex Controls Incorporated ....C 517 448-2752
Hudson (G-8551)
▲ Hi-Lex Controls Incorporated ....F 517 542-2955
Litchfield (G-10080)
Highland Manufacturing Inc ....E 248 585-8040
Madison Heights (G-10740)
Hitachi America Ltd ....G 248 477-5400
Farmington Hills (G-5261)
Hoff Engineering Co Inc ....G 248 969-8272
Oxford (G-12887)
Hope Focus ....E 313 494-4500
Detroit (G-4306)
Hope Focus ....C 313 494-5500
Detroit (G-4307)
Hope Network West Michigan ....E 231 796-4801
Paris (G-12934)
◆ Horizon Global Americas Inc ....C 734 656-3000
Plymouth (G-13191)
Horizon Global Corporation ....A 734 656-3000
Plymouth (G-13192)
Horizon Intl Group LLC ....G 734 341-9336
Birmingham (G-1730)
Horstman Inc ....E 586 737-2100
Sterling Heights (G-16041)
Hot Rod Holdings Inc ....E 517 424-0577
Tecumseh (G-16505)
Howe Racing Enterprises Inc ....E 989 435-7080
Beaverton (G-1425)
Howell Engine Developments Inc ....F 810 765-5100
Cottrellville (G-3720)
HP Pelzer Auto Systems Inc ....B 810 987-4444
Port Huron (G-13483)
Hudson Industries Inc ....G 313 777-5622
Sterling Heights (G-16044)
Huf North America Automoti ....G 248 213-4605
Farmington Hills (G-5263)
Humphrey Companies LLC ....C 616 530-1717
Grandville (G-7389)
Hydraulic Tubes & Fittings LLC ....E 810 660-8088
Lapeer (G-9933)
Hydro-Craft Inc ....G 248 652-8100
Rochester Hills (G-14037)
Ihi Detroit Turbo Engrg Ctr ....G 947 777-4976
Novi (G-12437)
▲ Ilmor Engineering Inc ....D 734 456-3600
Plymouth (G-13196)
IMC Products Inc ....F 231 759-3430
Muskegon (G-11838)
▲ Inalfa Holding Inc ....F 248 371-3060
Auburn Hills (G-934)
◆ Inalfa Roof Systems Inc ....B 248 371-3060
Auburn Hills (G-935)
Inalfa Roof Systems Inc ....G 586 758-6620
Warren (G-17859)
▲ Inoac Usa Inc ....E 248 619-7031
Troy (G-17169)
International Auto Components ....F 248 755-3928
Troy (G-17171)
Interntnal Auto Cmpnnts Group ....C 989 620-7649
Alma (G-243)
◆ Interntnal Auto Cmpnnts Group ....A 248 455-7000
Southfield (G-15606)
Interntnal Auto Cmpnnts Group ....G 810 987-8500
Port Huron (G-13488)
▲ Intertec Systems LLC ....F 248 488-7610
Farmington Hills (G-5272)
Inteva Products LLC ....G 248 655-8886
Troy (G-17173)
◆ Inteva Products LLC ....B 248 655-8886
Troy (G-17174)
Inteva Products Usa LLC ....C 248 655-8886
Troy (G-17175)
▲ Inzi Controls Detroit LLC ....G 334 282-4237
Rochester Hills (G-14041)
Iochpe Holdings LLC ....D 734 737-5000
Novi (G-12440)
J & J Industries Inc ....G 517 784-3586
Jackson (G-8911)
J & K Spratt Enterprises Inc ....D 517 439-5010
Hillsdale (G-7938)
▲ J G Kern Enterprises Inc ....D 586 531-9472
Sterling Heights (G-16052)
J L International Inc ....C 734 941-0300
Romulus (G-14288)
Jac Products Inc ....G 586 254-1534
Shelby Township (G-15243)
Jac Products Inc ....D 248 874-1800
Pontiac (G-13385)
▲ Jasper Weller LLC ....C 616 724-2000
Wyoming (G-18887)
▼ Jay & Kay Manufacturing LLC ....E 810 679-2333
Croswell (G-3730)
Jay & Kay Manufacturing LLC ....G 810 679-3079
Croswell (G-3731)
▲ Jet Industries Inc ....E 734 641-0900
Westland (G-18389)
Johnson Controls Inc ....G 313 842-3300
Detroit (G-4341)
Johnson Controls Inc ....G 734 254-7200
Plymouth (G-13205)
Johnson Controls Inc ....G 616 394-6818
Holland (G-8102)
Johnson Controls Inc ....G 616 392-5151
Holland (G-8103)
Johnson Controls Inc ....G 586 826-8845
Sterling Heights (G-16057)
Joint Clutch & Gear Svc Inc ....E 734 641-7575
Romulus (G-14292)
Jomar Performance Products LLC ....G 248 322-3080
Pontiac (G-13386)
◆ Jost International Corp ....C 616 846-7700
Grand Haven (G-6322)
Joyson Sfety Systems Acqstion ....B 248 373-8040
Auburn Hills (G-946)
◆ Joyson Sfety Systems Acqstion ....A 248 373-8040
Auburn Hills (G-947)
Jsj Corporation ....G 616 842-5500
Grand Haven (G-6323)
Jtekt Automotive N Amer Inc ....A 734 454-1500
Plymouth (G-13208)
Kar-Bones Inc ....G 313 582-5551
Detroit (G-4350)
Katcon Global Usa Inc ....D 248 239-1362
Auburn Hills (G-948)
Kautex Inc ....B 231 739-2704
Muskegon (G-11850)
▲ Kautex Inc ....A 248 616-5100
Troy (G-17193)
Kay Manufacturing Company ....E 269 408-8344
Saint Joseph (G-14941)
Kearsley Lake Terrace LLC ....G 810 736-7000
Flint (G-5720)
Kellogg Crankshaft Co ....D 517 788-9200
Jackson (G-8928)
Kenona Industries LLC ....C 616 735-6228
Grand Rapids (G-6885)
Kerkstra Mechanical LLC ....G 616 532-6100
Grand Rapids (G-6892)
▲ Key Safety Systems Inc ....C 248 373-8040
Auburn Hills (G-951)
◆ Key Sfety Rstraint Systems Inc ....A 586 726-3800
Auburn Hills (G-953)
Kiekert Usa Inc ....D 248 960-4100
Wixom (G-18692)
▲ Kiekert Usa Inc ....C 248 960-4100
Wixom (G-18693)
▲ Knoedler Manufacturers Inc ....F 269 969-7722
Battle Creek (G-1264)
▲ Kongsberg Automotive Inc ....D 248 468-1300
Novi (G-12455)
Kongsberg Holding I Inc ....G 248 468-1300
Novi (G-12456)
Kongsberg Holding III Inc ....E 248 468-1300
Novi (G-12457)
▲ Kongsberg Intr Systems II LLC ....D 956 465-4541
Novi (G-12458)
▲ Kostal of America Inc ....C 248 284-6500
Troy (G-17198)
Ksr Industrial Corporation ....G 248 213-7208
Southfield (G-15621)
▲ Kurabe America Corporation ....F 248 939-5803
Farmington Hills (G-5284)
Kyklos Holdings Inc ....G 313 758-2000
Detroit (G-4370)
Kysor Industrial Corporation ....C 231 779-7500
Cadillac (G-2341)
L T C Roll & Engineering Co ....F 586 465-1023
Fraser (G-5954)
Lab Tool and Engineering Corp ....F 517 750-4131
Spring Arbor (G-15793)
Label Motorsports LLC ....G 616 288-7710
Ada (G-25)
Lacks Industries Inc ....C 616 698-6890
Grand Rapids (G-6915)
Lacks Industries Inc ....C 616 656-2910
Grand Rapids (G-6921)
Lakeland Finishing Corporation ....C 616 949-8001
Grand Rapids (G-6923)
▲ Lane Automotive Inc ....C 269 463-4113
Watervliet (G-18182)
Laserline Inc ....G 248 826-5041
Plymouth (G-13219)
LDM Technologies Inc ....A 248 858-2800
Auburn Hills (G-956)
Lear Automotive Mfg LLC ....F 248 447-1603
Detroit (G-4380)
Lear Automotive Mfg LLC ....F 248 447-1603
Detroit (G-4381)
▼ Lear Corp Eeds and Interiors ....G 248 447-1500
Southfield (G-15625)
Lear Corporation ....C 313 731-0840
Detroit (G-4382)
Lear Corporation ....G 313 852-7800
Southfield (G-15626)
Lear Corporation ....G 313 965-0507
Detroit (G-4383)
Lear Corporation ....B 989 588-6181
Farwell (G-5425)
Lear Corporation ....G 248 447-1500
Southfield (G-15627)
Lear Corporation ....G 248 299-7100
Rochester Hills (G-14050)
Lear Corporation ....C 989 275-5794
Roscommon (G-14351)
◆ Lear Corporation ....B 248 447-1500
Southfield (G-15628)
Lear Corporation ....G 231 947-0160
Traverse City (G-16741)

S I C

Employee Codes: A=Over 500 employees, B=251-500
C=101-250, D=51-100, E=20-50, F=10-19, G=3-9
2022 Harris Michigan
Industrial Directory
883

37 TRANSPORTATION EQUIPMENT

Company	Code	Phone
Lear Corporation Flint (G-5723)	A	313 731-0833
Lear European Operations Corp Southfield (G-15629)	G	248 447-1500
Lear Global Technology Corp Uk Southfield (G-15630)	F	248 447-1500
▲ Lear Mexican Seating Corp Southfield (G-15631)	G	248 447-1500
Lear Trim LP Southfield (G-15633)	C	248 447-1500
▲ Leedy Manufacturing Co LLC Grand Rapids (G-6934)	D	616 245-0517
◆ Leon Interiors Inc Holland (G-8125)	B	616 422-7557
▲ Letts Industries Inc Detroit (G-4392)	G	313 579-1100
Liberty Spring Lapeer Inc Lapeer (G-9942)	F	418 248-7781
▼ Libertys High Prfmce Pdts Inc Harrison Township (G-7707)	F	586 469-1140
Lippert Components Inc Sterling Heights (G-16075)	G	586 275-2107
Lippert Components Mfg Inc Chesaning (G-2829)	D	989 845-3061
Litebrake Tech LLC Houghton (G-8385)	G	906 523-2007
Lj/Hah Holdings Corporation Auburn Hills (G-958)	C	248 340-4100
▲ Longson International Corp Superior Township (G-16337)	G	734 657-8719
LSm Systems Engineering Inc Waterford (G-18135)	E	248 674-4967
M P I International Inc Rochester Hills (G-14056)	B	608 764-5416
M S Manufacturing Inc Clinton Township (G-3285)	F	586 463-2788
M-Tek Inc Novi (G-12467)	F	248 553-1581
Mac Lean-Fogg Company Royal Oak (G-14558)	C	248 280-0880
Machine Tool & Gear Inc Clifford (G-3132)	B	989 761-7521
Machine Tool & Gear Inc Corunna (G-3711)	D	989 743-3936
Machinery Prts Specialists LLC Auburn (G-769)	G	989 662-7810
Magna Donnelly Corp Grand Haven (G-6332)	G	616 844-8257
▲ Magna Electronics Tech Inc Holly (G-8283)	D	810 606-0145
◆ Magna Exteriors America Inc Troy (G-17220)	A	248 631-1100
Magna Extrors Intrors Amer Inc Troy (G-17221)	C	248 729-2400
Magna International Amer Inc Troy (G-17222)	B	248 729-2400
Magna Modular Systems LLC Warren (G-17914)	C	586 279-2000
Magna Powertrain America Inc Lansing (G-9866)	G	517 316-1013
▲ Magna Powertrain America Inc Troy (G-17223)	C	248 597-7811
▲ Magna Powertrain Usa Inc Troy (G-17224)	D	248 680-4900
Magna Powertrain Usa Inc Troy (G-17225)	E	248 524-1397
Magna Powertrain Usa Inc Troy (G-17226)	E	248 680-4900
Magna Seating America Inc Auburn Hills (G-964)	D	248 243-7158
▲ Magna Seating America Inc Novi (G-12469)	B	248 567-4000
Magna Seating America Inc Detroit (G-4415)	B	313 422-6000
Magna Seating America Inc Shelby Township (G-15268)	G	586 816-1400
Magna Services America Inc New Hudson (G-12061)	F	248 617-3200
Magna Services America Inc Saint Clair (G-14835)	D	816 602-5872
▲ Magnesium Products America Inc Plymouth (G-13231)	B	734 416-8600
Magneti Marelli Tennessee LLC Southfield (G-15640)	F	248 418-3000
Mahle Inc Farmington Hills (G-5301)	E	248 305-8200
Mahle Aftermarket Inc Saint Johns (G-14906)	G	717 840-0678
▲ Mahle Aftermarket Inc Farmington (G-5142)	D	248 347-9700
Mahle Behr Dayton LLc Troy (G-17230)	C	937 369-2900
Mahle Behr Mfg MGT Inc Troy (G-17231)	E	248 735-3623
Mahle Behr USA Inc Ann Arbor (G-564)	G	336 768-3429
Mahle Behr USA Inc Troy (G-17233)	D	248 735-3623
▲ Mahle Behr USA Inc Troy (G-17234)	B	248 743-3700
▲ Mahle Behr USA Inc Troy (G-17232)	C	248 743-3700
Mahle Eng Components USA Inc Saint Johns (G-14907)	D	989 224-2384
Mahle Industries Incorporated Farmington Hills (G-5303)	E	248 305-8200
▲ Mahle Industries Incorporated Farmington Hills (G-5304)	G	248 305-8200
Mahle Industries Incorporated Muskegon (G-11864)	G	248 305-8200
Mahle Industries Incorporated Farmington Hills (G-5305)	E	248 473-6511
▼ Mahle Manufacturing MGT Inc Farmington Hills (G-5306)	E	248 735-3623
Mall Tooling & Engineering Mount Clemens (G-11648)	G	586 463-6520
Mann + Hummel Usa Inc Kalamazoo (G-9265)	E	248 857-8501
◆ Mann + Hummel Usa Inc Portage (G-13582)	F	269 329-3900
Marcella Manifolds Milford (G-11469)	F	248 259-6696
Marelli Holding USA LLC Southfield (G-15643)	A	248 418-3000
◆ Marelli North America Inc Southfield (G-15644)	A	931 684-4490
Marelli Tennessee USA LLC Southfield (G-15646)	A	248 418-3000
Marelli Tennessee USA LLC Troy (G-17236)	A	248 680-8872
◆ Mariah Industries Inc Troy (G-17237)	E	248 237-0404
◆ Marimba Auto LLC Canton (G-2489)	G	734 398-9000
Mark Land Industries Inc Dearborn (G-3868)	E	313 615-0503
Marley Precision Inc Battle Creek (G-1272)	G	269 963-7374
▲ Martinrea Industries Inc Manchester (G-10886)	E	734 428-2400
Martinrea Metal Industries Inc Auburn Hills (G-969)	D	248 392-9700
Mason Forge & Die Inc Mason (G-11142)	F	517 676-2992
Master Mfg Inc Oxford (G-12899)	E	248 628-9400
▲ Maxable Inc Brooklyn (G-2127)	F	517 592-5638
Maxion Fumagalli Auto USA Novi (G-12473)	D	734 737-5000
◆ Maxion Import LLC Novi (G-12474)	F	734 737-5000
▲ Maxion Wheels Akron LLC Novi (G-12475)	C	330 794-2310
◆ Maxion Wheels LLC Novi (G-12476)	D	734 737-5000
Maxion Wheels USA LLC Novi (G-12477)	D	734 737-5000
Mayne McKenney Southfield (G-15649)	G	248 709-5250
Mayne-Mc Kenney Inc Bloomfield Hills (G-1835)	E	248 258-0300
Mayser Usa Inc Van Buren Twp (G-17538)	D	734 858-1290
MD Investors Corporation Detroit (G-4425)	C	734 207-6200
◆ Means Industries Inc Saginaw (G-14691)	E	989 754-1433
Means Industries Inc Saginaw (G-14692)	F	989 754-0312
Means Industries Inc Sterling Heights (G-16090)	F	586 826-8500
Means Industries Inc Southfield (G-15652)	F	989 754-1433
Med-Kas Hydraulics Inc Troy (G-17243)	E	248 585-3220
▲ Medallion Instrmnttion Systems Spring Lake (G-15833)	C	616 847-3700
Melling Do Brasil LLC Jackson (G-8948)	F	517 787-8172
Melling Products North LLC Farwell (G-5426)	D	989 588-6147
Melling Tool Co Jackson (G-8952)	G	517 787-8172
◆ Melling Tool Co Jackson (G-8951)	B	517 787-8172
◆ Meritor Inc Troy (G-17246)	C	248 435-1000
▲ Meritor Industrial Pdts LLC Troy (G-17248)	G	888 725-9355
Meritor Intl Holdings LLC Troy (G-17249)	C	248 435-1000
Meritor Specialty Products LLC Howell (G-8478)	D	517 545-5800
▲ Meritor Specialty Products LLC Troy (G-17250)	A	248 435-1000
Metaldyne LLC Detroit (G-4433)	C	734 207-6200
Metaldyne Prfmce Group Inc Southfield (G-15654)	A	248 727-1800
▲ Metaldyne Pwrtrain Cmpnnts Inc Detroit (G-4434)	C	313 758-2000
Metaldyne Tblar Components LLC Southfield (G-15655)	A	248 727-1800
Metalsa Structural Pdts Inc Sterling Heights (G-16092)	A	248 669-3704
▲ Metalsa Structural Pdts Inc Novi (G-12479)	D	248 669-3704
◆ Metavation LLC Troy (G-17251)	E	248 351-1000
◆ Michigan Auto Comprsr Inc Parma (G-12938)	A	517 796-3200
▲ Micro Rim Corporation Detroit (G-4455)	F	313 865-1090
Micron Holdings Inc Kentwood (G-9465)	A	616 698-0707
Midwest Brake Bond Co Warren (G-17931)	E	586 775-3000
▲ Milan Metal Systems LLC Milan (G-11446)	C	734 439-1546
▲ Millennium Steering LLC Cass City (G-2620)	D	989 872-8823
Miller Industrial Products Inc Jackson (G-8962)	E	517 783-2756
▲ Mint Steel Forge Inc Lake Orion (G-9620)	F	248 276-9000
▼ Misc Products Macomb (G-10617)	D	586 263-3300
▲ Mistequay Group Ltd Saginaw (G-14702)	F	989 752-7700
Mistequay Group Ltd Standish (G-15893)	E	989 846-1000
Mitsubishi Steel Mfg Co Ltd Troy (G-17262)	G	248 502-8000
Mj Mfg Co Burton (G-2241)	G	810 744-3840
▲ MNP Corporation Utica (G-17504)	A	586 254-1320
Model-Matic Inc Troy (G-17264)	F	248 528-1680
Moldex Crank Shaft Inc Redford (G-13747)	G	313 561-7676
Montaplast North America Inc Auburn Hills (G-973)	E	248 353-5553
Motor Parts Inc of Michigan Rochester Hills (G-14065)	E	248 852-1522
Mpg Holdco I Inc Plymouth (G-13250)	G	734 207-6200
Mpt Driveline Systems Troy (G-17268)	F	248 680-3786
◆ Mpt Lansing LLC Lansing (G-9872)	C	517 316-1013
Mr Axle Muskegon (G-11878)	G	231 788-4624
▲ MSP Industries Corporation Oxford (G-12904)	C	248 628-4150
▲ Mssc Inc Troy (G-17270)	C	248 502-8000
▲ Musashi Auto Parts Mich Inc Battle Creek (G-1276)	B	269 965-0057
Mvc Holdings LLC Roseville (G-14450)	F	586 491-2600
Nafta Benchmarking Center Pontiac (G-13400)	G	248 335-0366
▲ National Fleet Service LLC Detroit (G-4476)	E	313 923-1799
National Ordnance Auto Mfg LLC Auburn Hills (G-980)	G	248 853-8822
Nationwide Design Inc Sterling Heights (G-16113)	F	586 254-5493

Navarre Inc ....G....... 313 892-7300
Detroit *(G-4478)*

Nbhx Trim USA Corporation ....F....... 616 785-9400
Walker *(G-17644)*

▲ **Nbhx Trim USA Corporation** ....B....... 616 785-9400
Comstock Park *(G-3627)*

Neapco Drivelines LLC ....B....... 734 447-1316
Van Buren Twp *(G-17543)*

▲ **Neapco Drivelines LLC** ....C....... 734 447-1300
Van Buren Twp *(G-17544)*

◆ **Neapco Holdings LLC** ....C....... 248 699-6500
Farmington Hills *(G-5333)*

Newcor Inc ....C....... 248 537-0014
Corunna *(G-3715)*

Newtech 3 Inc ....E....... 248 912-0807
Wixom *(G-18719)*

Nexteer Automotive Corporation ....B....... 989 754-1920
Saginaw *(G-14711)*

Nexteer Automotive Corporation ....B....... 989 757-5000
Saginaw *(G-14712)*

Nexteer Automotive Corporation ....B....... 989 757-5000
Saginaw *(G-14713)*

Nexteer Automotive Corporation ....B....... 989 757-5000
Saginaw *(G-14714)*

Nexteer Automotive Corporation ....B....... 989 757-5000
Saginaw *(G-14715)*

Nexteer Automotive Corporation ....B....... 989 757-5000
Saginaw *(G-14716)*

Nexteer Automotive Corporation ....D....... 989 757-5000
Saginaw *(G-14717)*

Nexteer Automotive Corporation ....E....... 989 757-5000
Saginaw *(G-14718)*

Nexteer Automotive Corporation ....B....... 989 757-5000
Saginaw *(G-14719)*

Nexteer Automotive Corporation ....B....... 989 757-5000
Saginaw *(G-14720)*

◆ **Nexteer Automotive Corporation** ....A....... 248 340-8200
Auburn Hills *(G-982)*

Nexteer Automotive Corporation ....B....... 989 757-5000
Saginaw *(G-14710)*

Nexteer Automotive Group Ltd ....A....... 989 757-5000
Saginaw *(G-14721)*

Nisshinbo Automotive Mfg Inc ....E....... 586 997-1000
Sterling Heights *(G-16117)*

▲ **Nitrex Inc** ....E....... 517 676-6370
Mason *(G-11147)*

Nitto Inc ....D....... 732 276-1039
Romulus *(G-14310)*

Nitto Inc ....F....... 734 729-7800
Romulus *(G-14311)*

Nitto Inc ....D....... 248 449-2300
Novi *(G-12489)*

Nodel-Co ....F....... 248 543-1325
Ferndale *(G-5573)*

Norma Michigan Inc ....G....... 248 373-4300
Lake Orion *(G-9622)*

▲ **Norma Michigan Inc** ....C....... 248 373-4300
Auburn Hills *(G-984)*

Norplas Industries Inc ....D....... 517 999-1400
Lansing *(G-9781)*

North Amer Fuel Systems Rmnfct ....C....... 616 541-1100
Grand Rapids *(G-7048)*

Northrop Grmmn Spce & Mssn Sys ....A....... 734 266-2600
Livonia *(G-10337)*

Novares US LLC ....G....... 616 554-3555
Grand Rapids *(G-7051)*

Nr Racing LLC ....G....... 248 767-0421
Commerce Township *(G-3558)*

▲ **NSK Americas Inc** ....C....... 734 913-7500
Ann Arbor *(G-595)*

▲ **NSK Steering Systems Amer Inc** ....C....... 734 913-7500
Ann Arbor *(G-596)*

Nu Con Corporation ....E....... 734 525-0770
Livonia *(G-10341)*

Nyx LLC ....D....... 734 261-4324
Livonia *(G-10344)*

Nyx LLC ....D....... 734 261-7535
Livonia *(G-10347)*

▲ **Nyx LLC** ....C....... 734 462-2385
Livonia *(G-10343)*

O Flex Group Inc ....G....... 248 505-0322
Clarkston *(G-3053)*

Oakley Inds Sub Assmbly Div In ....G....... 586 754-5555
Warren *(G-17949)*

Oakley Inds Sub Assmbly Div In ....E....... 810 720-4444
Flint *(G-5739)*

Oakley Inds Sub Assmbly Div In ....G....... 586 754-5555
Warren *(G-17950)*

Oakley Sub Assembly Inc ....D....... 810 720-4444
Flint *(G-5740)*

Oakley Sub Assembly Intl Inc ....F....... 810 720-4444
Flint *(G-5741)*

▲ **Oakwood Metal Fabricating Co** ....E....... 313 561-7740
Dearborn *(G-3879)*

Obr Control Systems Inc ....G....... 248 672-3339
Livonia *(G-10351)*

Offsite Manufacturing Inc ....G....... 586 598-8850
Chesterfield *(G-2918)*

Ogura Corporation ....G....... 586 749-1900
Madison Heights *(G-10791)*

▲ **Ogura Corporation** ....C....... 586 749-1900
Chesterfield *(G-2919)*

Oiles America Corporation ....C....... 734 414-7400
Plymouth *(G-13254)*

▲ **Old Dura Inc** ....G....... 248 299-7500
Auburn Hills *(G-989)*

▲ **Orotex Corporation** ....C....... 248 773-8630
Novi *(G-12499)*

▼ **Owens Products Inc** ....E....... 269 651-2300
Sturgis *(G-16315)*

Oxford Forge Inc ....G....... 248 628-1303
Oxford *(G-12907)*

P G S Inc ....C....... 248 526-3800
Troy *(G-17294)*

P T M Corporation ....D....... 586 725-2211
Ira *(G-8707)*

P T M Corporation ....G....... 586 725-2733
Ira *(G-8708)*

Pardon Inc ....E....... 906 428-3494
Gladstone *(G-6185)*

Patent Lcnsing Clringhouse LLC ....F....... 248 299-7500
Rochester Hills *(G-14080)*

PCI Procal Inc ....F....... 989 358-7070
Alpena *(G-311)*

Pcm US Steering Holding LLC ....E....... 313 556-5000
Auburn Hills *(G-994)*

Peckham Vocational Inds Inc ....D....... 517 316-4478
Lansing *(G-9725)*

Pelzer ....G....... 248 250-6161
Troy *(G-17296)*

Performance Springs Inc ....F....... 248 486-3372
New Hudson *(G-12067)*

▲ **Performnce Assmbly Sltions LLC** ....E....... 734 466-6380
Livonia *(G-10363)*

Pgf Technology Group Inc ....E....... 248 852-2800
Rochester Hills *(G-14082)*

Pierburg Us LLC ....C....... 864 688-1322
Auburn Hills *(G-997)*

◆ **Piston Automotive LLC** ....B....... 313 541-8674
Redford *(G-13756)*

Piston Automotive LLC ....A....... 313 541-8789
Detroit *(G-4526)*

Piston Automotive LLC ....D....... 313 541-8789
Van Buren Twp *(G-17547)*

Piston Group LLC ....B....... 248 226-3976
Southfield *(G-15674)*

Plasan Carbon Composites Inc ....D....... 616 965-9450
Wixom *(G-18730)*

◆ **Plasan Carbon Composites Inc** ....D....... 616 965-9450
Walker *(G-17647)*

Plastic Omnium Auto Inrgy USA ....G....... 248 743-5700
Troy *(G-17305)*

Plastic Omnium Auto Inrgy USA ....B....... 734 753-1350
New Boston *(G-12018)*

▲ **Plastic Omnium Auto Inrgy USA** ....B....... 248 743-5700
Troy *(G-17306)*

Plastic Omnium Auto Inrgy USA ....C....... 517 265-1100
Adrian *(G-88)*

Plastic Plate LLC ....E....... 616 455-5240
Grand Rapids *(G-7090)*

Plastic Plate LLC ....D....... 616 698-3678
Kentwood *(G-9470)*

Plastic Plate LLC ....D....... 616 949-6570
Kentwood *(G-9471)*

▲ **Pontiac Coil Inc** ....C....... 248 922-1100
Clarkston *(G-3057)*

Power Cool Systems Inc ....G....... 317 852-4193
Brighton *(G-2053)*

Precision Karting Tech LLC ....G....... 248 924-3272
Wixom *(G-18733)*

Precision Race Services Inc ....G....... 248 634-4010
Davisburg *(G-3771)*

▲ **Precision Torque Control Inc** ....F....... 989 495-9330
Midland *(G-11403)*

▲ **Prestige Engrg Rsrces Tech Inc** ....F....... 586 777-1820
Warren *(G-17975)*

Prestige Engrg Rsrces Tech Inc ....G....... 586 573-3070
Madison Heights *(G-10808)*

▲ **Pridgeon & Clay Inc** ....A....... 616 241-5675
Grand Rapids *(G-7106)*

◆ **Pritech Corporation** ....G....... 248 488-9120
Canton *(G-2513)*

Product Assembly Group LLC ....G....... 586 549-8601
Troy *(G-17317)*

Propride Inc ....G....... 810 695-1127
Grand Blanc *(G-6258)*

Propride Inc ....G....... 810 962-0219
Grand Blanc *(G-6259)*

Prototech Laser Inc ....F....... 586 948-3032
Chesterfield *(G-2933)*

Prototypes Plus Inc ....G....... 269 751-7141
Hamilton *(G-7605)*

▲ **Pullman Company** ....F....... 734 243-8000
Monroe *(G-11571)*

Purem Novi Inc ....C....... 248 778-5231
Novi *(G-12518)*

▲ **Purem Novi Inc** ....E....... 248 994-7010
Novi *(G-12519)*

Purem Novi Inc ....C....... 248 632-2731
Wixom *(G-18736)*

Qp Acquisition 2 Inc ....A....... 248 594-7432
Southfield *(G-15685)*

Quality Clutches Inc ....G....... 734 782-0783
Flat Rock *(G-5627)*

Quality Customs Cons LLC ....F....... 313 564-9327
Inkster *(G-8673)*

▲ **Quality Engineering Company** ....F....... 248 351-9000
Wixom *(G-18738)*

◆ **Quality Spring/Togo Inc** ....C....... 517 278-2391
Coldwater *(G-3449)*

Quality Steel Products Inc ....E....... 248 684-0555
Milford *(G-11484)*

Quigley Co ....G....... 989 983-3911
Vanderbilt *(G-17575)*

▲ **R Cushman & Associates Inc** ....A....... 248 477-9900
Livonia *(G-10381)*

Rack & Pinion Inc ....G....... 517 563-8872
Horton *(G-8378)*

Ralco Industries Inc ....D....... 248 853-3200
Auburn Hills *(G-1012)*

Ralco Industries Inc ....E....... 248 853-3200
Auburn Hills *(G-1013)*

Rapp & Son Inc ....D....... 734 283-1000
Wyandotte *(G-18836)*

▲ **Rassey Industries Inc** ....E....... 586 803-9500
Shelby Township *(G-15315)*

▲ **Raval USA Inc** ....F....... 248 260-4050
Rochester Hills *(G-14099)*

Ravenna Casting Center Inc ....G....... 231 853-0300
Ravenna *(G-13692)*

Recardo North America Inc ....D....... 248 364-3818
Plymouth *(G-13280)*

Regency Plastics - Ubly Inc ....D....... 989 658-8504
Ubly *(G-17482)*

Remy International Inc ....G....... 765 778-6499
Rochester *(G-13925)*

Ricardo Defense Inc ....G....... 805 882-1884
Sterling Heights *(G-16149)*

◆ **Ride Control LLC** ....D....... 248 247-7600
Farmington Hills *(G-5369)*

Rieke-Arminak Corp ....E....... 248 631-5450
Bloomfield Hills *(G-1857)*

▲ **Rivas Inc** ....D....... 586 566-0326
Sterling Heights *(G-16155)*

▼ **Riverside Tank & Mfg Corp** ....E....... 810 329-7143
Saint Clair *(G-14842)*

◆ **Rivian Automotive LLC** ....D....... 734 855-4350
Plymouth *(G-13285)*

Robert Bosch Fuel Systems LLC ....E....... 616 554-6500
Kentwood *(G-9477)*

Robert Bosch LLC ....G....... 248 921-9054
Novi *(G-12527)*

Robert Bosch LLC ....G....... 734 979-3000
Plymouth *(G-13287)*

Robert Bosch LLC ....G....... 734 979-3412
Plymouth *(G-13288)*

Robert Bosch LLC ....G....... 269 429-3221
Saint Joseph *(G-14957)*

◆ **Robert Bosch LLC** ....G....... 248 876-1000
Farmington Hills *(G-5371)*

Rochester Gear Inc ....D....... 989 659-2899
Clifford *(G-3133)*

Roush Enterprises Inc ....A....... 734 779-7006
Livonia *(G-10391)*

Roush Enterprises Inc ....A....... 313 294-8200
Allen Park *(G-205)*

Roush Enterprises Inc ....C....... 734 805-4400
Farmington *(G-5145)*

Roush Industries Inc ....G....... 734 779-7016
Livonia *(G-10392)*

S
I
C

37 TRANSPORTATION EQUIPMENT

Roush Industries Inc .... G 734 779-7013
  Livonia (G-10393)
Roush Manufacturing Inc .... D 734 805-4400
  Farmington (G-5146)
▲ Roush Manufacturing Inc .... C 734 779-7006
  Livonia (G-10395)
Royce Corporation .... G 586 758-1500
  Warren (G-17999)
◆ Rugged Liner Inc .... E 989 725-8354
  Owosso (G-12853)
Ryder Integrated Logistics Inc ... F 517 492-4446
  Lansing (G-9789)
S & S Tube Inc .... E 989 656-7211
  Bay Port (G-1415)
S & W Holdings Ltd .... G 248 723-2870
  Birmingham (G-1748)
S H Leggitt Company .... B 269 781-3901
  Marshall (G-11073)
S K D L P .... G 517 849-2166
  Jonesville (G-9101)
SA Automotive Ltd LLC .... G 989 723-0425
  Owosso (G-12854)
Saf-Holland Inc .... G 616 396-6501
  Holland (G-8186)
◆ Saf-Holland Inc .... A 231 773-3271
  Muskegon (G-11913)
▲ Sam Brown Sales LLC .... E 248 358-2626
  Farmington (G-5147)
▲ Sanhua Automotive Usa Inc .. G 248 244-8870
  Auburn Hills (G-1026)
Sapa Transmission Inc .... F 954 608-0125
  Shelby Township (G-15322)
▲ Sas Automotive Usa Inc .... E 248 606-1152
  Sterling Heights (G-16164)
Schwab Industries Inc .... F 586 566-8090
  Shelby Township (G-15325)
Schwarzerobitec Inc .... G 616 278-3971
  Grand Rapids (G-7185)
Seg Automotive North Amer LLC ... E 248 465-2602
  Novi (G-12533)
Servotech Industries Inc .... G 734 697-5555
  Taylor (G-16471)
Shaftmasters .... G 313 383-6347
  Lincoln Park (G-10056)
Sharp Model Co .... D 586 752-3099
  Bruce Twp (G-2182)
Shelby Antolin Inc .... F 734 395-0328
  Shelby Township (G-15330)
◆ Shyft Group Inc .... A 517 543-6400
  Novi (G-12536)
Shyft Group Inc .... E 517 543-6400
  Charlotte (G-2767)
Signature Truck Systems LLC .. D 810 564-2294
  Clio (G-3411)
Sitronic North America Corp .... E 248 939-5910
  Southfield (G-15705)
Skg International Inc .... F 248 620-4139
  Clarkston (G-3067)
▲ Skilled Manufacturing Inc ..... C 231 941-0290
  Traverse City (G-16834)
Skokie Castings LLC .... D 248 727-1800
  Southfield (G-15706)
SL America Corporation .... D 586 731-8511
  Auburn Hills (G-1034)
Sliding Systems Inc .... F 517 339-1455
  Haslett (G-7778)
▲ Sloan Transportation Pdts Inc ... E 616 395-5600
  Holland (G-8197)
◆ Slw Automotive Inc .... D 248 464-6200
  Rochester Hills (G-14113)
Smartpat PLC .... G 248 854-2233
  Birmingham (G-1750)
Sort-Tek Insptn Systems Inc .... G 248 273-5200
  Troy (G-17363)
Southstern Mich Accsory Ctr 2 ... E 248 519-9848
  Troy (G-17366)
▲ Specialty Eng Components LLC ... E 734 955-6500
  Taylor (G-16477)
▲ Spectrum Cubic Inc .... D 616 451-0784
  Kentwood (G-9480)
▲ Spicer Heavy Axle & Brake Inc ... G 269 567-1000
  Kalamazoo (G-9242)
Sports Resorts International ..... E 989 725-8354
  Owosso (G-12858)
SRI Delaware Holdings LLC ..... G 248 489-9300
  Novi (G-12541)
Stackpole Pwrtrn Intl USA LLC ... G 248 481-4600
  Auburn Hills (G-1037)
Stant USA Corp .... C 765 827-8104
  Rochester Hills (G-14119)

Steering Solutions - Plant 3 ...... F 989 757-5000
  Saginaw (G-14767)
▲ Steinbauer Performance LLC ... G 704 587-0856
  Dowagiac (G-4797)
Stemco Products Inc .... G 888 854-6474
  Millington (G-11503)
▲ Sterling Performance Inc ...... E 248 685-7811
  Milford (G-11491)
Stewart Industries LLC .... D 269 660-9290
  Battle Creek (G-1301)
▲ Stoneridge Inc .... A 248 489-9300
  Novi (G-12543)
Stoneridge Inc .... B 781 830-0340
  Novi (G-12544)
Strattec Security Corporation ... G 248 649-9742
  Auburn Hills (G-1040)
▲ Stromberg-Carlson Products Inc ... F 231 947-8600
  Traverse City (G-16843)
Su-Dan Plastics Inc .... C 248 651-6035
  Lake Orion (G-9633)
▲ Superior Industries Intl Inc ... C 248 352-7300
  Southfield (G-15712)
▲ Superior Industries N Amer LLC ... D 248 352-7300
  Southfield (G-15713)
Supply Line International LLC .. E 248 242-7140
  Novi (G-12551)
Sweet Manufacturing Inc .... E 269 344-2086
  Kalamazoo (G-9350)
Swiss American Screw Pdts Inc ... E 734 397-1600
  Canton (G-2529)
▲ Swoboda Inc .... C 616 554-6161
  Grand Rapids (G-7242)
Sxs Gear .... G 810 265-7219
  Flint (G-5774)
▲ Synchronous Manufacturing Inc ... F 517 764-6930
  Michigan Center (G-11296)
◆ Systrand Manufacturing Corp ... C 734 479-8100
  Brownstown Twp (G-2159)
▲ TAC Manufacturing Inc .... B 517 789-7000
  Jackson (G-9014)
Takata Americas .... A 336 547-1600
  Auburn Hills (G-1044)
Tata Autocomp Systems Limited ... 248 680-4608
  Troy (G-17385)
Teamtech Motorsports Safety ... G 989 792-4880
  Saginaw (G-14773)
Technique Inc .... D 517 789-8988
  Jackson (G-9017)
Tectum Holdings Inc .... D 734 926-2362
  Ann Arbor (G-674)
Teksid Aluminum North Amer Inc ... E 248 304-4001
  Southfield (G-15719)
◆ Teksid Inc .... E 734 846-5492
  Farmington (G-5153)
Telmar Manufacturing Company ... 810 577-7050
  Fenton (G-5506)
Tenneco Automotive Oper Co ... B 248 849-1258
  Northville (G-12265)
Tenneco Automotive Oper Co Inc ... C 517 522-5520
  Grass Lake (G-7447)
Tenneco Automotive Oper Co Inc ... E 734 243-8000
  Lansing (G-9742)
Tenneco Automotive Oper Co Inc ... G 734 243-8039
  Monroe (G-11579)
Tenneco Automotive Oper Co Inc ... C 269 781-1350
  Marshall (G-11075)
Tenneco Automotive Oper Co Inc ... C 517 542-5511
  Litchfield (G-10085)
Tenneco Automotive Oper Co Inc ... G 517 522-5525
  Jackson (G-9018)
Tenneco Automotive Oper Co Inc ... F 734 243-4615
  Monroe (G-11580)
Tenneco Automotive Oper Co Inc ... G 734 243-8000
  Monroe (G-11581)
Tenneco Clean Air US Inc .... F 517 253-8902
  Lansing (G-9743)
Tenneco Inc .... G 734 254-1122
  Plymouth (G-13313)
Tenneco Inc .... G 248 354-7700
  Southfield (G-15720)
Tenneco Inc .... G 248 886-0900
  Waterford (G-18170)
Tesca Usa Inc .... E 586 991-0744
  Rochester Hills (G-14124)
Tg Fluid Systems USA Corporati ... G 248 486-8950
  Brighton (G-2079)
Th Plastics Inc .... D 269 496-8495
  Mendon (G-11223)
Therma-Tech Engineering Inc .. E 313 537-5330
  Redford (G-13778)

Thermal Solutions Mfg .... D 734 655-7145
  Livonia (G-10432)
Thk Rhythm Auto Mich Corp .... B 517 647-4121
  Portland (G-13642)
Thomas Engineering .... G 248 620-7916
  Clarkston (G-3071)
Thyssenkrupp Bilstein Amer Inc ... A 248 530-2900
  Troy (G-17390)
TI Fluid Systems .... D 586 948-6036
  New Haven (G-12039)
TI Fluid Systems .... G 248 393-4525
  Auburn Hills (G-1053)
▼ TI Fluid Systems LLC .... A 248 494-5000
  Auburn Hills (G-1054)
TI Group Auto Systems LLC .... G 989 672-1200
  Caro (G-2581)
TI Group Auto Systems LLC .... G 989 673-7727
  Caro (G-2582)
TI Group Auto Systems LLC .... G 248 494-5000
  Troy (G-17391)
TI Group Auto Systems LLC .... G 810 364-3277
  Marysville (G-11108)
TI Group Auto Systems LLC .... G 586 948-6006
  Chesterfield (G-2956)
TI Group Auto Systems LLC .... G 859 235-5420
  Auburn Hills (G-1056)
TI Group Auto Systems LLC .... G 248 475-4663
  Auburn Hills (G-1057)
◆ TI Group Auto Systems LLC .. B 248 296-8000
  Auburn Hills (G-1055)
◆ Tianhai Electric N Amer Inc .. D 248 987-2100
  Pontiac (G-13419)
Tomar Inc .... G 313 382-2293
  Ecorse (G-4988)
Torqstorm Superchargers .... G 616 706-5580
  Wyoming (G-18911)
Torsion Control Products Inc ... F 248 537-1900
  Rochester Hills (G-14128)
Total Flow Products Inc .... G 248 588-4490
  Troy (G-17396)
▲ Toyo Seat USA Corporation ... C 810 724-0300
  Imlay City (G-8648)
Tractech Inc .... E 248 226-6800
  Southfield (G-15725)
▲ Tram Inc .... C 734 254-8500
  Plymouth (G-13322)
Tram Inc .... G 269 966-0100
  Battle Creek (G-1306)
▲ Tramec Sloan LLC .... E 616 395-5600
  Holland (G-8224)
Trans Parts Plus Inc .... G 734 427-6844
  Garden City (G-6113)
Transform Automotive LLC ...... G 586 826-8500
  Shelby Township (G-15355)
Transform Automotive LLC ...... G 586 826-8500
  Sterling Heights (G-16207)
▲ Transform Automotive LLC ... C 586 826-8500
  Sterling Heights (G-16208)
Transpak Inc .... E 586 264-2064
  Sterling Heights (G-16209)
Trico Group Inc .... G 800 388-7426
  Rochester Hills (G-14131)
◆ Trico Products Corporation ... C 248 371-1700
  Rochester Hills (G-14132)
▲ Trident Lighting LLC .... D 616 957-9500
  Grand Rapids (G-7276)
◆ Trimas Corporation .... B 248 631-5450
  Bloomfield Hills (G-1869)
Trin Inc .... E 260 587-9282
  Plymouth (G-13324)
Tristone Flowtech USA Inc .... E 248 560-1724
  Southfield (G-15726)
▲ Trmi Inc .... A 269 966-0800
  Battle Creek (G-1307)
◆ Truck Trailer Transit Inc .... F 313 516-7151
  Troy (G-17402)
Truck Acquisition Inc .... G 877 875-4376
  Ann Arbor (G-699)
Truck Holdings Inc .... G 877 875-4376
  Ann Arbor (G-700)
TRW Atomotive Holdg Mexico LLC ... D 734 855-2600
  Livonia (G-10446)
TRW Automotive (Iv) Corp .... G 734 855-2600
  Livonia (G-10447)
TRW East Inc .... D 734 855-2600
  Livonia (G-10448)
TRW Occupant Safety Systems ... G 586 752-1409
  Bruce Twp (G-2184)
TRW Odyssey Mexico LLC .... D 734 855-2600
  Livonia (G-10449)

TRW Safety Systems Mexico LLC ....G.... 734 855-2600 — Livonia *(G-10450)*
Uc Holdings Inc ....D.... 248 728-8642 — Southfield *(G-15730)*
Ufi Filters Usa Inc ....G.... 248 376-0441 — Troy *(G-17410)*
▲ **Ufi Filters Usa Inc** ....F.... 248 376-0441 — Troy *(G-17411)*
◆ **Ufp Technologies Inc** ....D.... 616 949-8100 — Grand Rapids *(G-7294)*
Umlaut Product Solutions Inc ....F.... 248 703-7724 — Madison Heights *(G-10850)*
Unifilter Inc ....F.... 248 476-5100 — Novi *(G-12563)*
Unique Fabricating Inc ....A.... 248 853-2333 — Auburn Hills *(G-1068)*
Unique-Chardan Inc ....D.... 419 636-6900 — Auburn Hills *(G-1070)*
◆ **United Machining Inc** ....C.... 586 323-4300 — Sterling Heights *(G-16216)*
United Machining Inc ....G.... 586 323-4300 — Macomb *(G-10646)*
United Metal Technology Inc ....E.... 517 787-7940 — Jackson *(G-9029)*
United Systems Group LLC ....G.... 810 227-4567 — Brighton *(G-2090)*
US Engine Production MI Inc ....G.... 989 823-3800 — Vassar *(G-17584)*
US Farathane Holdings Corp ....E.... 586 991-6922 — Sterling Heights *(G-16219)*
Usm Holdings LLC ....F.... 313 758-2000 — Detroit *(G-4657)*
Usm Holdings LLC II ....F.... 313 758-2000 — Detroit *(G-4658)*
◆ **Usui International Corporation** ....E.... 734 354-3626 — Plymouth *(G-13328)*
▲ **Valeo Inc** ....A.... 248 619-8300 — Troy *(G-17425)*
▲ **Valeo Friction Materials Inc** ....G.... 248 619-8300 — Troy *(G-17426)*
Valeo North America Inc ....C.... 248 209-8253 — Auburn Hills *(G-1077)*
◆ **Valeo North America Inc** ....D.... 248 619-8300 — Troy *(G-17429)*
Valeo North America Inc ....C.... 313 883-8850 — Detroit *(G-4660)*
Valeo Radar Systems Inc ....F.... 248 619-8300 — Troy *(G-17430)*
▲ **Valeo Switches & Dete** ....E.... 248 619-8300 — Troy *(G-17431)*
Veet Industries Inc ....F.... 586 776-3000 — Warren *(G-18053)*
Vehicle Research and Dev ....G.... 586 504-1163 — Almont *(G-270)*
Vehma International Amer Inc ....C.... 248 631-1100 — Troy *(G-17434)*
◆ **Vehma International Amer Inc** ....D.... 248 631-2800 — Troy *(G-17436)*
Vehma International Amer Inc ....D.... 248 585-4800 — Troy *(G-17435)*
▲ **Ventra Fowlerville LLC** ....B.... 517 223-5900 — Fowlerville *(G-5857)*
Ventra Grand Rapids 5 LLC ....B.... 616 222-3296 — Grand Rapids *(G-7310)*
◆ **Ventura Manufacturing Inc** ....C.... 616 772-7405 — Zeeland *(G-19088)*
Veoneer Inc ....A.... 248 223-0600 — Southfield *(G-15736)*
Veritas USA Corporation ....E.... 248 374-5019 — Novi *(G-12567)*
◆ **Vibracoustic North America LP** ....E.... 269 637-2116 — South Haven *(G-15421)*
Vico Louisville LLC ....E.... 502 245-1616 — Plymouth *(G-13333)*
▲ **Victora Usa Inc** ....G.... 810 798-0253 — Almont *(G-271)*
Viking Laser LLC ....G.... 586 200-5369 — Roseville *(G-14491)*
Visiocorp Holding USA LLP ....G.... 810 388-2403 — Marysville *(G-11112)*
Visions Car & Truck Acc ....G.... 269 342-2962 — Kalamazoo *(G-9364)*
Visteon Corporation ....D.... 734 718-8927 — Canton *(G-2539)*
Visteon Corporation ....A.... 734 627-7384 — Van Buren Twp *(G-17558)*
Visteon Electronics Corp ....D.... 800 847-8366 — Van Buren Twp *(G-17559)*
Visteon Global Electronics Inc ....G.... 800 847-8366 — Van Buren Twp *(G-17560)*
Visteon Systems LLC ....C.... 800 847-8366 — Van Buren Twp *(G-17562)*
Vitesco Technologies Usa LLC ....C.... 313 583-5980 — Dearborn *(G-3911)*
Vitesco Technologies Usa LLC ....B.... 248 209-4000 — Auburn Hills *(G-1080)*
▲ **Von Weise LLC** ....G.... 517 618-9763 — Eaton Rapids *(G-4975)*
Vortek ....G.... 248 767-2992 — Pinckney *(G-13058)*
Vsp Logis Inc ....G.... 734 957-9880 — Van Buren Twp *(G-17563)*
Wabco Air Comprsr Holdings Inc ....F.... 248 260-9032 — Auburn Hills *(G-1083)*
Wabco Expats Inc ....E.... 248 260-9032 — Auburn Hills *(G-1084)*
▲ **Wabco Holdings Inc** ....A.... 248 260-9032 — Auburn Hills *(G-1086)*
Wagner Castings Company ....F.... 248 952-2500 — Troy *(G-17444)*
Walbro LLC ....D.... 989 872-2131 — Cass City *(G-2622)*
Waldrons Antique Exhaust ....G.... 269 467-7185 — Centreville *(G-2700)*
▲ **Walther Trowal GMBH & Co KG** ....F.... 616 871-0031 — Grand Rapids *(G-7324)*
Warren Chassix ....F.... 248 728-8700 — Southfield *(G-15743)*
Warren Manufacturing LLC ....G.... 586 467-1600 — Warren *(G-18060)*
Warren Screw Products Inc ....C.... 586 757-1280 — Warren *(G-18061)*
▲ **Webasto Convertibles USA Inc** ....C.... 734 582-5900 — Plymouth *(G-13336)*
▲ **Webasto Roof Systems Inc** ....B.... 248 997-5100 — Auburn Hills *(G-1088)*
Webasto Roof Systems Inc ....B.... 248 997-5100 — Plymouth *(G-13337)*
Webasto Roof Systems Inc ....B.... 248 299-2000 — Rochester Hills *(G-14144)*
Webasto Roof Systems Inc ....C.... 248 997-5100 — Rochester Hills *(G-14145)*
▲ **Weber Automotive Corporation** ....C.... 248 393-5520 — Auburn Hills *(G-1089)*
West Mich Auto Stl & Engrg Inc ....E.... 616 560-8198 — Belding *(G-1464)*
West Michigan Gage Inc ....F.... 616 735-0585 — Walker *(G-17657)*
◆ **Wiric Corporation** ....E.... 248 598-5297 — Rochester Hills *(G-14147)*
Xileh Holding Inc ....G.... 248 340-4100 — Auburn Hills *(G-1090)*
Yanfeng US Auto Intr Systems I ....G.... 616 394-1567 — Holland *(G-8254)*
Yanfeng US Auto Intr Systems I ....G.... 734 254-5000 — Plymouth *(G-13341)*
Yanfeng US Auto Intr Systems I ....C.... 248 319-7333 — Novi *(G-12570)*
Yanfeng US Auto Intr Systems I ....D.... 248 319-7333 — Novi *(G-12571)*
Yanfeng US Auto Intr Systems I ....G.... 616 283-1349 — Holland *(G-8255)*
Yanfeng US Auto Intr Systems I ....G.... 586 354-2101 — Harrison Township *(G-7735)*
Yanfeng US Auto Intr Systems I ....G.... 616 392-5151 — Holland *(G-8256)*
Yanfeng US Auto Intr Systems I ....G.... 734 289-4841 — Monroe *(G-11593)*
Yanfeng US Auto Intr Systems I ....G.... 810 987-2434 — Port Huron *(G-13541)*
Yapp USA Auto Systems Inc ....G.... 248 404-8696 — Romulus *(G-14343)*
Young Diversified Industries ....G.... 248 353-1867 — Southfield *(G-15745)*
ZF Active Safety & Elec US LLC ....D.... 586 843-2100 — Livonia *(G-10479)*
ZF Active Safety & Elec US LLC ....B.... 248 478-7210 — Farmington Hills *(G-5417)*
ZF Active Safety US Inc ....G.... 906 248-3882 — Brimley *(G-2105)*
ZF Active Safety US Inc ....G.... 248 478-7210 — Farmington Hills *(G-5418)*
ZF Active Safety US Inc ....G.... 956 491-9036 — Howell *(G-8545)*
ZF Active Safety US Inc ....G.... 517 223-8330 — Fowlerville *(G-5858)*
◆ **ZF Active Safety US Inc** ....F.... 734 812-6979 — Livonia *(G-10482)*
ZF Active Safety US Inc ....G.... 810 750-1036 — Fenton *(G-5515)*
ZF Active Safety US Inc ....G.... 586 899-2807 — Sterling Heights *(G-16234)*
ZF Active Safety US Inc ....G.... 734 855-2470 — Livonia *(G-10483)*
ZF Active Safety US Inc ....G.... 248 863-2412 — Saginaw *(G-14797)*
ZF Auto Holdings US Inc ....G.... 734 855-2600 — Livonia *(G-10484)*
ZF Automotive JV US LLC ....A.... 734 855-2787 — Livonia *(G-10485)*
▲ **ZF Automotive US Inc** ....B.... 734 855-2600 — Livonia *(G-10486)*
▲ **ZF Axle Drives Marysville LLC** ....B.... 810 989-8702 — Marysville *(G-11114)*
◆ **ZF Chassis Components LLC** ....C.... 810 245-2000 — Lapeer *(G-9969)*
ZF Chassis Components LLC ....E.... 810 245-2000 — Lapeer *(G-9970)*
ZF Chassis Components LLC ....E.... 810 245-2000 — Lapeer *(G-9971)*
ZF Friedrichshafen AG ....G.... 734 855-2600 — Livonia *(G-10487)*
ZF Lemforder Corp ....F.... 810 245-7136 — Lapeer *(G-9972)*
◆ **ZF North America Inc** ....B.... 734 416-6200 — Northville *(G-12272)*
ZF Passive Safety S Africa Inc ....E.... 734 855-2600 — Livonia *(G-10488)*
▲ **ZF Passive Safety US Inc** ....B.... 734 855-2600 — Livonia *(G-10489)*
ZF Passive Safety US Inc ....G.... 586 232-7200 — Washington *(G-18094)*
ZF Passive Sfety Systems US In ....G.... 586 752-1409 — Romeo *(G-14241)*
▲ **ZF Passive Sfety Systems US In** ....A.... 586 232-7200 — Livonia *(G-10490)*
ZF Passive Sfety Systems US In ....G.... 586 781-5511 — Washington *(G-18095)*
▲ **ZF String Active Safety US Inc** ....G.... 734 855-2600 — Livonia *(G-10491)*
◆ **ZF TRW Auto Holdings Corp** ....A.... 734 855-2600 — Livonia *(G-10492)*
▲ **Zhongli North America Inc** ....D.... 248 733-9300 — Troy *(G-17459)*
◆ **Zynp International Corp** ....E.... 734 947-1000 — Romulus *(G-14345)*

3715 Truck Trailers

Ajax Trailers Inc ....F.... 586 757-7676 — Warren *(G-17696)*
All-Star Equipment LLC ....F.... 855 273-8265 — Rockford *(G-14153)*
Anderson Welding & Mfg Inc ....F.... 906 523-4661 — Houghton *(G-8380)*
Arboc Ltd ....G.... 248 684-2895 — Commerce Township *(G-3511)*
Automotive Service Co ....F.... 517 784-6131 — Jackson *(G-8818)*
Benlee Inc ....E.... 586 791-1830 — Romulus *(G-14257)*
Bobbys Mobile Service LLC ....G.... 517 206-6026 — Jackson *(G-8824)*
Cargo King Manufacturing Inc ....E.... 269 483-9900 — White Pigeon *(G-18473)*
Clydes Frame & Wheel Service ....F.... 248 338-0323 — Pontiac *(G-13354)*
Complete Truck and Trailer ....G.... 989 732-9000 — Gaylord *(G-6123)*
Darkhorse Cargo Inc ....F.... 269 464-2620 — White Pigeon *(G-18474)*
Detroit Cstm Trck Trailor LLC ....G.... 734 925-2233 — Westland *(G-18363)*
Eddies Quick Stop Inc ....G.... 313 712-1818 — Dearborn *(G-3833)*
Executive Operations LLC ....E.... 313 312-0653 — Brighton *(G-1986)*
Express Welding Inc ....G.... 906 786-8808 — Escanaba *(G-5071)*
Hulet Body Co Inc ....F.... 313 931-6000 — Northville *(G-12230)*
Joes Trailer Manufacturing ....G.... 734 261-0050 — Livonia *(G-10260)*
Leonard & Randy Inc ....G.... 734 287-9500 — Taylor *(G-16435)*
Lupa R A and Sons Repair ....G.... 810 346-3579 — Marlette *(G-10983)*
Montrose Trailers Inc ....G.... 810 639-7431 — Montrose *(G-11607)*
Neo Manufacturing Inc ....F.... 269 503-7630 — Sturgis *(G-16313)*

Employee Codes: A=Over 500 employees, B=251-500
C=101-250, D=51-100, E=20-50, F=10-19, G=3-9
2022 Harris Michigan
Industrial Directory
887

Oshkosh Defense LLC E 586 576-8301
Warren *(G-17951)*

▲ **Pratt Industries Inc** D 269 465-7676
Bridgman *(G-1933)*

▲ **Pullman Company** F 734 243-8000
Monroe *(G-11571)*

◆ **Saf-Holland Inc** A 231 773-3271
Muskegon *(G-11913)*

Saf-Holland Inc G 616 396-6501
Holland *(G-8186)*

Technology Plus Trailers Inc F 734 928-0001
Canton *(G-2531)*

Thumb Truck and Trailer Co G 989 453-3133
Pigeon *(G-13041)*

Tow-Line Trailers G 989 752-0055
Saginaw *(G-14777)*

◆ **Trailer Tech Holdings LLC** E 248 960-9700
Wixom *(G-18776)*

Transport Trailers Co G 269 543-4405
Fennville *(G-5443)*

Trimas Company LLC D 248 631-5450
Bloomfield Hills *(G-1868)*

Wolverine Trailers Inc G 517 782-4950
Jackson *(G-9037)*

Woodland Industries G 989 686-6176
Kawkawlin *(G-9419)*

Xpo Cnw Inc C 734 757-1444
Ann Arbor *(G-720)*

3716 Motor Homes

Auto-Masters Inc F 616 455-4510
Grand Rapids *(G-6480)*

Frank Industries Inc E 810 346-3234
Brown City *(G-2137)*

Motor City Home Inc G 248 562-7296
Bloomfield Hills *(G-1841)*

Riverside Vans Inc F 269 432-3212
Colon *(G-3491)*

3721 Aircraft

▲ **Ascent Aerospace Holdings LLC** G 212 916-8142
Macomb *(G-10579)*

Boeing Company G 248 258-7191
Bloomfield Hills *(G-1805)*

C H Industries Inc F 586 997-1717
Shelby Township *(G-15180)*

Dakota Aerospace LLC G 787 403-3564
Pinckney *(G-13046)*

Delorean Aerospace LLC G 248 752-2380
Bloomfield Hills *(G-1812)*

Eaton Aerospace LLC C 517 787-8121
Jackson *(G-8874)*

G-Force Tooling LLC E 517 541-2747
Charlotte *(G-2757)*

Great Lakes Drone Company LLC G 317 430-5291
Stevensville *(G-16251)*

Midwest Build Center LLC G 989 672-1388
Caro *(G-2576)*

Mrd Aerospace G 586 468-1196
Harrison Township *(G-7711)*

Mustang Aeronautics Inc G 248 649-6818
Troy *(G-17271)*

P2r Metal Fabrication Inc F 586 606-5266
Macomb *(G-10625)*

Procore Drones LLC G 850 774-0604
Spring Lake *(G-15845)*

Sika Corporation D 248 577-0020
Madison Heights *(G-10829)*

Skywalker Drone Solutions LLC G 248 342-6747
Oxford *(G-12917)*

Soaring Concepts Aerospace LLC F 574 286-9670
Hastings *(G-7810)*

Temper Inc F 616 293-1349
Cedar Springs *(G-2665)*

Textron Inc G 248 545-2035
Madison Heights *(G-10841)*

3724 Aircraft Engines & Engine Parts

Advance Turning and Mfg Inc C 517 783-2713
Jackson *(G-8802)*

Aerovision Aircraft Svcs LLC E 231 799-9000
Norton Shores *(G-12274)*

Aerovision International LLC E 231 799-9000
Norton Shores *(G-12275)*

Aircraft Precision Pdts Inc D 989 875-4186
Ithaca *(G-8785)*

Approved Aircraft Accessories G 734 946-9000
Romulus *(G-14250)*

AVI Inventory Services LLC E 231 799-9000
Norton Shores *(G-12277)*

Barnes Group Inc A 517 393-5110
Lansing *(G-9812)*

Dorris Company F 586 293-5260
Fraser *(G-5919)*

◆ **Dry Coolers Inc** E 248 969-3400
Oxford *(G-12883)*

Eaton Corporation B 269 781-0200
Marshall *(G-11056)*

Expernced Prcsion McHining Inc G 989 635-2299
Marlette *(G-10981)*

Filtration Machine G 810 845-0536
Davison *(G-3783)*

General Electric Company G 734 727-4619
Wayne *(G-18222)*

Honeywell E 248 362-7154
Troy *(G-17147)*

Honeywell International Inc G 989 792-8707
Saginaw *(G-14669)*

Honeywell International Inc G 586 777-7870
Fraser *(G-5939)*

Honeywell International Inc G 734 392-5501
Plymouth *(G-13189)*

Johnson Technology Inc G 231 777-2685
Muskegon *(G-11846)*

Johnson Technology Inc B 231 777-2685
Norton Shores *(G-12305)*

▲ **Johnson Technology Inc** B 231 777-2685
Muskegon *(G-11847)*

LAY Precision Machine Inc G 989 726-5022
West Branch *(G-18330)*

Manufacturing & Indus Tech Inc E 248 522-6959
Farmington Hills *(G-5309)*

MB Aerospace Warren LLC C 586 772-2500
Warren *(G-17920)*

Merrill Technologies Group E 989 921-1490
Saginaw *(G-14696)*

▲ **Merrill Technologies Group Inc** D 989 791-6676
Saginaw *(G-14697)*

Metro Machine Works Inc D 734 941-4571
Romulus *(G-14304)*

Moeller Aerospace Tech Inc C 231 347-9575
Harbor Springs *(G-7651)*

Niles Precision Company C 269 683-0585
Niles *(G-12155)*

Nu Con Corporation E 734 525-0770
Livonia *(G-10341)*

▲ **Pratt & Whitney Autoair Inc** C 517 393-4040
Lansing *(G-9882)*

Pratt & Whitney Autoair Inc E 517 348-1416
Holt *(G-8325)*

Rapp & Son Inc D 734 283-1000
Wyandotte *(G-18836)*

SGC Industries Inc G 586 293-5260
Fraser *(G-5992)*

Steel Tool & Engineering Co D 734 692-8580
Brownstown Twp *(G-2157)*

Steven J Devlin G 734 439-1325
Milan *(G-11450)*

Stm Power Inc E 734 214-1448
Ann Arbor *(G-666)*

Supreme Gear Co E 586 775-6325
Fraser *(G-6001)*

Tidy Mro Enterprises LLC G 734 649-1122
Manchester *(G-10891)*

United Precision Pdts Co Inc E 313 292-0100
Dearborn Heights *(G-3943)*

▲ **Williams International Co LLC** A 248 624-5200
Pontiac *(G-13425)*

Woodward Fst Inc C 616 772-9171
Zeeland *(G-19092)*

3728 Aircraft Parts & Eqpt, NEC

AAR Corp F 231 779-4859
Cadillac *(G-2305)*

Advance Turning and Mfg Inc C 517 783-2713
Jackson *(G-8802)*

Advanced Integration Tech LP G 586 749-5525
Chesterfield *(G-2837)*

Aero Inspection & Tool LLC G 517 525-7373
Leslie *(G-10013)*

Aero Train Corp G 810 230-8096
Flint *(G-5640)*

Aerovision Aircraft Svcs LLC E 231 799-9000
Norton Shores *(G-12274)*

Aerovision International LLC E 231 799-9000
Norton Shores *(G-12275)*

Aircraft Precision Pdts Inc D 989 875-4186
Ithaca *(G-8785)*

Aj Aircraft G 734 244-4015
Monroe *(G-11523)*

American Aircraft Parts Mfg Co E 586 294-3300
Clinton Township *(G-3164)*

AVI Inventory Services LLC E 231 799-9000
Norton Shores *(G-12277)*

◆ **Beaver Aerospace & Defense Inc** C 734 853-5003
Livonia *(G-10133)*

◆ **Bmt Aerospace Usa Inc** D 586 285-7700
Fraser *(G-5905)*

Bradley-Thompson Tool Company E 248 352-1466
Southfield *(G-15510)*

Chardam Gear Company Inc C 586 795-8900
Sterling Heights *(G-15957)*

Detail Precision Products Inc E 248 544-3390
Ferndale *(G-5540)*

▲ **Detroit Coil Co** E 248 658-1543
Ferndale *(G-5543)*

Dhs/Cbp G 586 954-2214
Selfridge Angb *(G-15147)*

Dolphin Manufacturing Inc E 734 946-6322
Taylor *(G-16403)*

Dorris Company F 586 293-5260
Fraser *(G-5919)*

Eagle Industrial Group Inc E 616 647-9904
Comstock Park *(G-3605)*

Eaton Aeroquip LLC B 949 452-9575
Jackson *(G-8873)*

◆ **Enstrom Helicopter Corporation** C 906 863-1200
Menominee *(G-11233)*

Extreme Precision Screw Pdts E 810 744-1980
Flint *(G-5698)*

Fema Corporation of Michigan C 269 323-1369
Portage *(G-13560)*

Flow-Rite Controls Ltd E 616 583-1700
Byron Center *(G-2270)*

Gear Master Inc F 810 798-9254
Almont *(G-260)*

Grand Rapids Technologies Inc G 616 245-7700
Grand Rapids *(G-6771)*

Hart Precision Products Inc E 313 537-0490
Redford *(G-13739)*

Honeywell International Inc C 231 582-5686
Boyne City *(G-1889)*

Hytrol Manufacturing Inc E 734 261-8030
Jackson *(G-8906)*

Innovative Drone Services LLC G 313 333-6956
Ypsilanti *(G-18956)*

Intergrted Dspnse Slutions LLC F 586 554-7404
Shelby Township *(G-15239)*

Jedco Inc C 616 459-5161
Grand Rapids *(G-6867)*

▲ **Lapeer Industries Inc** C 810 538-0589
Shelby Township *(G-15257)*

Liberty Tool Inc E 586 726-2449
Sterling Heights *(G-16073)*

▲ **Liebherr Aerospace Saline Inc** C 734 429-7225
Saline *(G-15024)*

▲ **Linear Motion LLC** C 989 759-8300
Saginaw *(G-14683)*

Mas Inc F 231 894-0409
Whitehall *(G-18508)*

Masterbilt Products Corp F 269 749-4841
Olivet *(G-12694)*

Meggitt G 989 759-8327
Saginaw *(G-14694)*

Melling Manufacturing Inc D 517 750-3580
Jackson *(G-8950)*

Merrill Technologies Group E 989 921-1490
Saginaw *(G-14696)*

Military Vtrans Affirs Mich De C 231 775-7222
Cadillac *(G-2347)*

Moose Mfg & Machining LLC G 586 765-4686
Detroit *(G-4464)*

Motor City Aerospace G 616 916-5473
Rockford *(G-14180)*

National Aircraft Service Inc E 517 423-7589
Tecumseh *(G-16509)*

Niles Precision Company C 269 683-0585
Niles *(G-12155)*

◆ **Northern Wings Repair Inc** E 906 477-6176
Newberry *(G-12100)*

Nu Con Corporation E 734 525-0770
Livonia *(G-10341)*

Odyssey Industries LLC C 248 814-8800
Lake Orion *(G-9624)*

Parker-Hannifin Corporation B 269 384-3459
Kalamazoo *(G-9288)*

Parker-Hannifin Corporation G 269 384-3400
Kalamazoo *(G-9289)*

◆ **Phoenix Cmposite Solutions LLC** C 989 739-7108
Oscoda *(G-12770)*

Pifers Airmotive Inc ....G....... 248 674-0909
  Goodrich (G-6225)
Pontoon Rentals ....G....... 906 387-2685
  Munising (G-11753)
Prime Products Inc ....E....... 616 531-8970
  Grand Rapids (G-7107)
R & B Electronics Inc ....D....... 906 632-1542
  Sault Sainte Marie (G-15097)
Saf-Air Products Inc ....G....... 734 522-8360
  Garden City (G-6107)
Scott Machine Inc ....E....... 517 787-6616
  Jackson (G-9008)
SGC Industries Inc ....G....... 586 293-5260
  Fraser (G-5992)
Teamtech Motorsports Safety ....G....... 989 792-4880
  Saginaw (G-14773)
♦ Triumph Gear Systems - McOmb I ....C....... 586 781-2800
  Macomb (G-10644)
United Precision Pdts Co Inc ....G....... 313 292-0100
  Dearborn Heights (G-3943)
Veet Industries Inc ....F....... 586 776-3000
  Warren (G-18053)
Ventura Aerospace LLC ....E....... 734 357-0114
  Wixom (G-18786)
Ventura Industries Inc ....F....... 734 357-0114
  Plymouth (G-13331)
Visioneering Inc ....E....... 248 622-5600
  Fraser (G-6011)
Wmh Fluidpower Inc ....F....... 269 327-7011
  Portage (G-13634)

3731 Shipbuilding & Repairing

▲ Arcosa Shoring Products Inc ....D....... 517 741-4300
  Union City (G-17490)
Beardslee Investments Inc ....E....... 810 748-9951
  Harsens Island (G-7748)
Di Square America Inc ....F....... 248 374-5051
  Novi (G-12398)
▲ FD Lake Company ....F....... 616 241-5639
  Grand Rapids (G-6704)
Floatation Docking Inc ....E....... 906 484-3422
  Cedarville (G-2669)
K & N Transport LLC ....G....... 313 384-0037
  Detroit (G-4345)
LA East Inc ....F....... 269 476-7170
  Vandalia (G-17567)
Lake Shore Systems Inc ....E....... 906 265-5414
  Iron River (G-8745)
▲ Lake Shore Systems Inc ....D....... 906 774-1500
  Kingsford (G-9512)
Merchant Holdings Inc ....G....... 906 786-7120
  Escanaba (G-5085)
▲ Nicholson Terminal & Dock Co ....D....... 313 842-4300
  River Rouge (G-13858)
Nk Dockside Service & Repair ....G....... 906 420-0777
  Escanaba (G-5087)

3732 Boat Building & Repairing

A & B Tube Benders Inc ....F....... 586 773-0440
  Warren (G-17678)
American Pleasure Products Inc ....G....... 989 685-8484
  Rose City (G-14360)
♦ Ameriform Acquisition Co LLC ....B....... 231 733-2725
  Rochester Hills (G-13947)
Andersen Boat Works ....G....... 616 836-2502
  South Haven (G-15399)
Artisans Cstm Mmory Mattresses ....F....... 989 793-3208
  Saginaw (G-14605)
▼ Avalon & Tahoe Mfg Inc ....G....... 989 463-2112
  Alma (G-239)
Barton Boatworks ....G....... 616 240-5562
  Holland (G-7970)
Beardslee Investments Inc ....E....... 810 748-9951
  Harsens Island (G-7748)
Bingham Boat Works Ltd ....G....... 906 225-0050
  Marquette (G-11007)
C & C Sports Inc ....E....... 810 227-7068
  Brighton (G-1958)
Crest Marine LLC ....E....... 989 725-5188
  Owosso (G-12828)
▼ Douglas Marine Corporation ....E....... 269 857-1764
  Douglas (G-4772)
Downriver Boatworks Ltd ....G....... 313 335-4288
  Lincoln Park (G-10045)
Eldean Company ....E....... 616 335-5843
  Macatawa (G-10566)
Eldean Yacht Basin Ltd ....E....... 616 786-2205
  Holland (G-8026)
Finishing Touches By Odell ....G....... 231 947-3080
  Traverse City (G-16682)

Geelhoed Performance ....G....... 616 837-6666
  Grand Rapids (G-6735)
▼ Glastron LLC ....D....... 800 354-3141
  Cadillac (G-2331)
Gregs Dockside Marine Svc LLC ....G....... 810 874-8250
  Clay (G-3120)
Irish Boat Shop Inc ....E....... 231 547-9967
  Charlevoix (G-2719)
K and S 39 Corporation ....G....... 734 883-3868
  Ypsilanti (G-18960)
KI Companies Inc ....D....... 231 332-1700
  Muskegon (G-11851)
Macs Marina Motorsports ....F....... 248 486-8300
  South Lyon (G-15445)
Marsh Brothers Inc ....F....... 517 869-2653
  Quincy (G-13671)
▲ Maurell Products Inc ....E....... 989 725-5188
  Owosso (G-12841)
Max Manufacturing ....F....... 517 990-9180
  Jackson (G-8947)
Meyers Boat Company Inc ....E....... 517 265-9821
  Adrian (G-85)
Mid-Tech Inc ....G....... 734 426-4327
  Ann Arbor (G-577)
Midwest Aquatics Group Inc ....G....... 734 426-4155
  Pinckney (G-13052)
Morin Boats ....G....... 989 686-7353
  Bay City (G-1381)
Murleys Marine ....G....... 586 725-7446
  Ira (G-8705)
N D R Enterprises Inc ....G....... 269 857-4556
  Saugatuck (G-15084)
Nauticraft ....G....... 810 356-2942
  Columbiaville (G-3494)
Northern Michigan Prop Sp LLC ....G....... 231 275-7173
  Lake Ann (G-9542)
Northshore Pontoon ....G....... 517 547-9877
  Hudson (G-8557)
Paddle King Inc ....F....... 989 235-6776
  Carson City (G-2594)
Pender Boatworks LLC ....G....... 269 207-0627
  Hickory Corners (G-7875)
Pier Pressure Custom Boats ....G....... 231 723-0124
  Bear Lake (G-1420)
▼ Quantum Sails Design Group LLC ....E....... 231 941-1222
  Traverse City (G-16811)
▼ Rec Boat Holdings LLC ....B....... 231 779-2616
  Cadillac (G-2350)
Recon Fishing Systems Inc ....G....... 989 358-2923
  Alpena (G-316)
Reed Yacht Sales LLC ....G....... 419 304-4405
  La Salle (G-9529)
Reed Yacht Sales LLC ....G....... 616 842-8899
  Grand Haven (G-6351)
Rubber Rope Products Company ....G....... 906 358-4133
  Watersmeet (G-18178)
Spicers Boat Cy Hughton Lk Inc ....E....... 989 366-8384
  Houghton Lake (G-8403)
▲ Sterling Performance Inc ....E....... 248 685-7811
  Milford (G-11491)
Sunsation Products Inc ....F....... 810 794-4888
  Clay (G-3126)
▲ Swivl - Eze Marine ....E....... 616 897-9241
  Lowell (G-10520)
T D Vinette Company ....G....... 906 786-1884
  Escanaba (G-5102)
Tassier Boat Works Inc ....G....... 906 484-2573
  Cedarville (G-2674)
♦ Tiara Yachts Inc ....A....... 616 392-7163
  Holland (G-8220)
Tiara Yachts Inc ....C....... 616 335-3594
  Holland (G-8221)
Triton Industries Inc ....D....... 517 322-3822
  Lansing (G-9745)
Unlimited Marine Inc ....G....... 248 249-0222
  White Lake (G-18470)
▲ Van Dam Marine Co ....E....... 231 582-2323
  Boyne City (G-1905)
Wooden Runabout Co ....G....... 616 396-7248
  Holland (G-8251)

3743 Railroad Eqpt

Amsted Rail Company Inc ....C....... 517 568-4161
  Homer (G-8344)
▲ Arcosa Shoring Products Inc ....D....... 517 741-4300
  Union City (G-17490)
Delta Tube & Fabricating Corp ....E....... 248 634-8267
  Holly (G-8267)
Gorang Industries Inc ....G....... 248 651-9010
  Rochester (G-13902)

▲ Hj Manufacturing Inc ....F....... 906 233-1500
  Escanaba (G-5076)
McL Jasco Inc ....G....... 313 294-7414
  Detroit (G-4424)
▼ Mitchell Equipment Corporation ....E....... 734 529-3400
  Dundee (G-4832)
▲ Peaker Services Inc ....D....... 248 437-4174
  Brighton (G-2049)
Rescar Inc ....G....... 517 486-3130
  Blissfield (G-1774)
▲ Trinity Equipment Co ....G....... 231 719-1813
  Muskegon (G-11937)
Trinity Industries Inc ....G....... 586 285-1692
  Fraser (G-6005)
Union Tank Car Company ....G....... 989 615-3054
  Midland (G-11420)

3751 Motorcycles, Bicycles & Parts

Aerospoke Incorporated ....G....... 248 685-9009
  Brighton (G-1939)
Assenmacher Lightweight Cycles ....G....... 810 635-7844
  Swartz Creek (G-16350)
▲ Detroit Bikes LLC ....G....... 313 646-4109
  Detroit (G-4135)
♦ Discover Your Mobility Inc ....G....... 866 868-9694
  Hazel Park (G-7823)
Hamilton Harley-Davidson ....G....... 269 651-3424
  Sturgis (G-16292)
Icon Choppers ....G....... 616 292-0536
  Jenison (G-9056)
▲ ITT Motion Tech Amer LLC ....F....... 248 863-2161
  Novi (G-12444)
▲ Mahindra Tractor Assembly Inc ....E....... 650 779-5180
  Auburn Hills (G-966)
Mid Cost Grass Choppers ....G....... 985 445-7155
  Clarkston (G-3051)
♦ Pritech Corporation ....G....... 248 488-9120
  Canton (G-2513)
Ron Watkins ....G....... 517 439-5451
  Hillsdale (G-7946)
▲ Shinola/Detroit LLC ....C....... 888 304-2534
  Detroit (G-4591)
Technique Inc ....D....... 517 789-8988
  Jackson (G-9017)
Turtle Racing LLC ....G....... 517 918-3444
  Morenci (G-11618)
▲ Varroc Lighting Systems Inc ....D....... 734 446-4400
  Plymouth (G-13329)
▲ Velocity Worldwide Inc ....F....... 616 243-3400
  Grand Rapids (G-7309)
▲ Wiz Wheelz Inc ....E....... 616 455-5988
  Grand Rapids (G-7342)

3761 Guided Missiles & Space Vehicles

Morris Kall Incorporated ....G....... 815 528-8665
  Marquette (G-11037)

3764 Guided Missile/Space Vehicle Propulsion Units & parts

Hytrol Manufacturing Inc ....E....... 734 261-8030
  Jackson (G-8906)
Orbion Space Technology Inc ....E....... 906 362-2509
  Houghton (G-8388)
▲ Williams International Co LLC ....A....... 248 624-5200
  Pontiac (G-13425)

3769 Guided Missile/Space Vehicle Parts & Eqpt, NEC

Advance Turning and Mfg Inc ....C....... 517 783-2713
  Jackson (G-8802)
Dorris Company ....F....... 586 293-5260
  Fraser (G-5919)
MB Aerospace Warren LLC ....C....... 586 772-2500
  Warren (G-17920)
Mistequay Group Ltd ....E....... 989 846-1000
  Standish (G-15893)
Parker-Hannifin Corporation ....B....... 269 384-3459
  Kalamazoo (G-9288)
Rapp & Son Inc ....D....... 734 283-1000
  Wyandotte (G-18836)
RCO Aerospace Products LLC ....E....... 586 774-8400
  Roseville (G-14469)
SGC Industries Inc ....G....... 586 293-5260
  Fraser (G-5992)
Swiss American Screw Pdts Inc ....E....... 734 397-1600
  Canton (G-2529)
Truform Machine Inc ....E....... 517 782-8523
  Jackson (G-9025)

37 TRANSPORTATION EQUIPMENT

3792 Travel Trailers & Campers

Ajax Trailers Inc .... F 586 757-7676
  Warren (G-17696)
County of Muskegon .... E 231 744-3580
  Muskegon (G-11796)
D & W Management Company Inc ...... F 586 758-2284
  Warren (G-17770)
Frank Industries Inc .... E 810 346-3234
  Brown City (G-2137)
Gibbys Transport LLC .... G 269 838-2794
  Hastings (G-7793)
Kimble Auto and Rv LLC .... G 517 227-5089
  Coldwater (G-3440)
Michigan East Side Sales LLC .... G 989 354-6867
  Alpena (G-302)
Monroes Custom Campers Inc .... F 231 773-0005
  Muskegon (G-11877)
Montrose Trailers Inc .... G 810 639-7431
  Montrose (G-11607)
Mvm7 LLC .... E 989 317-3901
  Mount Pleasant (G-11725)
R V Wolverine .... F 989 426-9241
  Gladwin (G-6201)
Rough Road Trucking LLC .... G 231 645-3355
  Kalkaska (G-9402)
Skyline Champion Corporation .... A 248 614-8211
  Troy (G-17356)
Technology Plus Trailers Inc .... F 734 928-0001
  Canton (G-2531)
Van Kam Inc .... F 231 744-2658
  Muskegon (G-11940)

3795 Tanks & Tank Components

American Rhnmtall Vehicles LLC .... F 586 942-0139
  Sterling Heights (G-15930)
Burch Tank & Truck Inc .... G 989 495-0342
  Midland (G-11326)
Burch Tank & Truck Inc .... D 989 772-6266
  Mount Pleasant (G-11688)
▲ Demmer Corporation .... C 517 321-3600
  Lansing (G-9687)
Dynamic Metals Group LLC .... F 586 790-5615
  Birmingham (G-1724)
General Tactical Vehicles LLC .... G 586 825-7242
  Sterling Heights (G-16028)
Horstman Inc .... E 586 737-2100
  Sterling Heights (G-16041)
Interntnal Def Fabrication LLC .... G 810 643-1198
  Lapeer (G-9934)
Lipp America Tank Systems LLC ..... F 616 201-6761
  Grand Rapids (G-6946)
◆ Plasan North America Inc .... E 616 559-0032
  Walker (G-17648)
Renk America LLC .... D 231 724-2666
  Muskegon (G-11907)
◆ Reutter LLC .... G 248 466-0652
  Ann Arbor (G-640)
Ronal Industries Inc .... F 248 616-9691
  Sterling Heights (G-16159)
Supreme Gear Co .... E 586 775-6325
  Fraser (G-6001)
Tank Truck Service & Sales Inc .... E 586 757-6500
  Warren (G-18036)

3799 Transportation Eqpt, NEC

American Tool & Gage Inc .... G 313 587-7923
  Taylor (G-16377)
Annieraerv Co .... G 517 669-4103
  Dewitt (G-4705)
Bedford Machinery Inc .... G 734 848-4980
  Erie (G-5045)
Berg Marketing Group .... G 314 457-9400
  Troy (G-16973)
Bloodline Rich LLC .... G 734 719-1650
  Grosse Pointe Woods (G-7564)
Boat Customs Trailers LLC .... G 517 712-3512
  Caledonia (G-2370)
Chassis Shop Prfmce Pdts Inc .... G 231 873-3640
  Mears (G-11189)
Detroit Wrecker Sales Llc .... G 313 835-8700
  Detroit (G-4171)
Dexko Global Inc .... G 248 533-0029
  Novi (G-12397)
Dragon Acquisition Intermediat .... F 248 692-4367
  Novi (G-12403)
Dragon Acquisition Parent Inc .... F 248 692-4367
  Novi (G-12404)
Ds Automotion LLC .... G 248 370-8950
  Auburn Hills (G-867)

Erich Jaeger USA Inc .... G 734 404-5940
  Livonia (G-10199)
Expedite Freight LLC .... G 313 502-7572
  Detroit (G-4222)
George Brown Legacy Group .... G 313 770-9928
  Southfield (G-15574)
Great Lakes Lift Inc .... G 989 673-2109
  Caro (G-2572)
Guiding Our Destiny Ministry .... G 313 212-9063
  Detroit (G-4286)
H W Motor Homes Inc .... G 734 394-2000
  Canton (G-2470)
▲ Hensley Mfg Inc .... F 810 653-3226
  Davison (G-3786)
Holiday Rmbler Recrtl Vhcl CLB .... G 616 847-0582
  Spring Lake (G-15823)
Holz Enterprises Inc .... G 810 392-2840
  Richmond (G-13840)
◆ Horizon Global Americas Inc .... C 734 656-3000
  Plymouth (G-13191)
Hydro King Incorporated .... F 313 835-8700
  Southfield (G-15596)
JC and Associates .... G 616 401-5798
  Grand Rapids (G-6864)
Jrm Industries Inc .... G 616 837-9758
  Nunica (G-12581)
K & K Racing LLC .... F 906 322-1276
  Sault Sainte Marie (G-15093)
▲ Liberty Products Inc .... F 231 853-2323
  Ravenna (G-13691)
Michael John LLC .... G 734 560-9268
  Livonia (G-10315)
Midwest Direct Transport Inc .... F 616 698-8900
  Byron Center (G-2286)
Midwest Transportation Inc .... G 313 615-7282
  Dearborn Heights (G-3933)
Montrose Trailers Inc .... G 810 639-7431
  Montrose (G-11607)
Nash Car Trailer Corporation .... G 269 673-5776
  Allegan (G-171)
P2r Metal Fabrication Inc .... F 586 606-5266
  Macomb (G-10625)
Phoenix Trailer & Body Company ...... F 248 360-7184
  Commerce Township (G-3563)
Plt Express Transportation LLC .... G 248 809-3241
  Southfield (G-15676)
Power Sports Ann Arbor LLC .... G 734 585-3300
  Ann Arbor (G-617)
Premier Custom Trailers LLC .... F 877 327-0888
  Schoolcraft (G-15127)
Pro King Trucking Inc .... G 909 800-7885
  Detroit (G-4534)
Pro-Powersports .... G 734 457-0829
  Monroe (G-11570)
Pro-Tech Group LLC .... F 888 221-1505
  Southfield (G-15683)
▼ Rapidtek LLC .... G 616 662-0954
  Hudsonville (G-8603)
Rdz Racing Incorporated .... G 517 468-3254
  Fowlerville (G-5854)
Rieke-Arminak Corp .... E 248 631-5450
  Bloomfield Hills (G-1857)
▲ RSM & Associates Co .... E 517 750-9330
  Jackson (G-9001)
Sled Shed Enterprises LLC .... G 517 783-5136
  Jackson (G-9010)
Trimas Corporation .... G 248 631-5451
  Ann Arbor (G-698)
◆ Trimas Corporation .... B 248 631-5450
  Bloomfield Hills (G-1869)
Valley Ventures Mapping LLC .... G 989 879-5023
  Rhodes (G-13823)
▲ Viking Sales Inc .... F 810 227-2222
  Brighton (G-2094)
Z&G Auto Carriers LLC .... G 586 819-1809
  Romulus (G-14344)

38 MEASURING, ANALYZING AND CONTROLLING INSTRUMENTS; PHOTOGRAPHIC, MEDICAL AN

3812 Search, Detection, Navigation & Guidance Systs & Instrs

313 Industries Inc .... F 313 338-9700
  Warren (G-17677)
A2 Motus LLC .... G 734 780-7334
  Ann Arbor (G-343)

Adept Defense LLC .... G 231 758-2792
  Petoskey (G-12987)
Aertech Machining & Mfg Inc .... E 517 782-4644
  Jackson (G-8804)
Allied Defense .... G 810 252-9232
  Goodrich (G-6221)
Antrim Machine Products Inc .... E 231 587-9114
  Mancelona (G-10866)
Ascent Aerospace LLC .... A 586 726-0500
  Macomb (G-10578)
Bae Systems Land Armaments LP .... A 586 596-4123
  Sterling Heights (G-15942)
◆ Beaver Aerospace & Defense Inc ... C 734 853-5003
  Livonia (G-10133)
Brandons Defense .... G 517 669-5272
  Dewitt (G-4707)
Center For Qlty Trning Intl LL .... G 586 212-9524
  Shelby Township (G-15183)
Consoldted Rsource Imaging LLC ..... E 616 735-2080
  Grand Rapids (G-6595)
D&D Defense LLC .... C 248 255-8765
  Ceresco (G-2703)
▲ Demmer Corporation .... C 517 321-3600
  Lansing (G-9687)
Drs C3 & Aviation Company .... E 248 588-0365
  Madison Heights (G-10712)
Eaton Corporation .... G 517 787-8121
  Ann Arbor (G-463)
Electronic Design & Packg Co .... F 734 591-9176
  Livonia (G-10194)
Elite Prcsion McHining Tooling .... G 269 383-9714
  Kalamazoo (G-9177)
Eotech LLC .... C 248 971-4027
  Ann Arbor (G-477)
Equitable Engineering Co Inc .... E 248 689-9700
  Troy (G-17096)
G Defense Company B .... G 616 202-4500
  Grand Rapids (G-6731)
GE Aviation Systems LLC .... G 616 241-7000
  Grand Rapids (G-6733)
GE Aviation Systems LLC .... E 616 224-6480
  Grand Rapids (G-6734)
Gen3 Defense and Aerospace LLC ... F 616 345-8031
  Comstock Park (G-3607)
General Dynamics Corporation .... G 615 427-5768
  Taylor (G-16421)
Gentz Industry .... G 586 772-2501
  Warren (G-17829)
▲ Glassmaster Controls Co Inc .... E 269 382-2010
  Kalamazoo (G-9198)
Grand Rapids Machine Repr Inc .... E 616 245-9102
  Grand Rapids (G-6764)
Grupo Resilient Intl Inc .... G 810 410-8177
  Linden (G-10062)
◆ Harman Becker Auto Systems Inc .. B 248 785-2361
  Farmington Hills (G-5257)
Harman Becker Auto Systems Inc .... G 248 703-3010
  Novi (G-12428)
Hawtal Whiting .... G 248 262-2020
  Sterling Heights (G-16036)
Herrmann Aerospace .... G 810 695-1758
  Grand Blanc (G-6247)
Honeywell International Inc .... C 231 582-5686
  Boyne City (G-1889)
Hytrol Manufacturing Inc .... E 734 261-8030
  Jackson (G-8906)
Instrumented Sensor Tech Inc .... G 517 349-8487
  Okemos (G-12670)
Interactive Aerial Inc .... A 231 486-6007
  Traverse City (G-16725)
Kba Defense .... G 586 552-9268
  Lakeville (G-9648)
Kings Self Defense LLC .... G 910 890-4322
  Grand Rapids (G-6897)
Kva Engineering Inc .... G 616 745-7483
  Morley (G-11620)
L3 Aviation Products Inc .... B 616 949-6600
  Grand Rapids (G-6906)
Leviathan Defense Group .... G 419 575-7792
  Newport (G-12104)
Mercy Health Partners .... D 231 728-4032
  Muskegon (G-11866)
Micromet Corp .... G 231 885-1047
  Bloomfield Hills (G-1837)
▲ Mistequay Group Ltd .... F 989 752-7700
  Saginaw (G-14702)
▲ N S International Ltd .... C 248 251-1600
  Troy (G-17272)
Navistar Defense LLC .... G 248 680-7505
  Madison Heights (G-10789)

SIC SECTION38 MEASURING, ANALYZING AND CONTROLLING INSTRUMENTS; PHOTOGRAPHIC, MEDICAL AN38 MEASURING, ANALYZING

Niles Precision Company ....C 269 683-0585
Niles *(G-12155)*
Parker-Hannifin Corporation ....B 269 384-3459
Kalamazoo *(G-9288)*
Phg Aviation LLC ....G 231 526-7380
Harbor Springs *(G-7654)*
Pierce Personal Defense LLC ....G 269 664-6960
Plainwell *(G-13087)*
Preferred Avionics Instrs LLC ....E 800 521-5130
Howell *(G-8501)*
Project Echo LLC ....F 248 971-4027
Clawson *(G-3105)*
Quanenergy Systems Inc ....G 248 859-5587
Commerce Township *(G-3566)*
R A Miller Industries Inc ....C 888 845-9450
Grand Haven *(G-6349)*
Rapp & Son Inc ....D 734 283-1000
Wyandotte *(G-18836)*
Riverside Defense Training LLC ....G 231 825-2895
Lake City *(G-9554)*
Rocketplane Global Inc ....G 734 476-2888
Lansing *(G-9788)*
Sani Zeevi ....G 248 546-4489
Oak Park *(G-12646)*
Sextant Advisor Group Inc ....G 248 650-8280
Rochester *(G-13928)*
Slip Defense Inc ....G 248 366-4423
White Lake *(G-18464)*
Snavely Gordon A Atty Reserv ....G 248 760-0617
West Bloomfield *(G-18314)*
Sniffer Robotics LLC ....G 855 476-4333
Ann Arbor *(G-657)*
Split Second Defense LLC ....G 586 709-1385
Fraser *(G-5999)*
▲ Superior Fabrication Co LLC ....D 906 495-5634
Kincheloe *(G-9505)*
Swiss Precision Machining Inc ....F 586 677-7558
Macomb *(G-10640)*
Talkin Tackle LLC ....G 517 474-6241
Jackson *(G-9015)*
Teslir LLC ....G 248 644-5500
Bloomfield Hills *(G-1865)*
Tetradyn Ltd ....G 202 415-7295
Traverse City *(G-16855)*
▲ Thierica Inc ....D 616 458-1538
Grand Rapids *(G-7257)*
Triple Inc ....G 248 817-5151
Troy *(G-17399)*
Truform Machine Inc ....E 517 782-8523
Jackson *(G-9025)*
Universal Magnetics Inc ....G 231 937-5555
Howard City *(G-8420)*
Utica Aerospace Inc ....F 586 598-9300
Chesterfield *(G-2961)*
Valeo Radar Systems Inc ....E 248 340-3126
Auburn Hills *(G-1078)*

3821 Laboratory Apparatus & Furniture

Accuri Cytometers Inc ....E 734 994-8000
Ann Arbor *(G-346)*
AG Davis Gage & Engrg Co ....E 586 977-9000
Sterling Heights *(G-15926)*
Air Master Systems Corp ....E 231 798-1111
Norton Shores *(G-12276)*
◆ Alpha Resources LLC ....E 269 465-5559
Stevensville *(G-16239)*
▲ Balance Technology Inc ....D 734 769-2100
Whitmore Lake *(G-18520)*
Bmc/Industrial Eductl Svcs Inc ....E 231 733-1206
Muskegon *(G-11780)*
Case Systems Inc ....C 989 496-9510
Midland *(G-11327)*
▲ Cmg America Inc ....G 810 686-3064
Clio *(G-3395)*
Cmp Acquisitions LLC ....F 888 519-2286
Redford *(G-13726)*
▲ Counter Reaction LLC ....G 248 624-7900
Wixom *(G-18636)*
▼ Coy Laboratory Products Inc ....E 734 433-9296
Grass Lake *(G-7436)*
▲ Gelman Sciences Inc ....C 734 665-0651
Ann Arbor *(G-496)*
Gross Ventures Inc ....G 231 767-1301
Byron Center *(G-2277)*
Holland Community Hosp Aux Inc ....G 616 355-3926
Holland *(G-8076)*
ID Systems Inc ....F 231 799-8760
Norton Shores *(G-12298)*
Impert Industries Inc ....G 269 694-2727
Otsego *(G-12788)*
Jade Scientific Inc ....F 734 207-3775
Westland *(G-18387)*
◆ Leco Corporation ....B 269 983-5531
Saint Joseph *(G-14946)*
Leco Corporation ....G 269 985-5496
Saint Joseph *(G-14947)*
M2 Scientifics LLC ....F 616 379-9080
Allendale *(G-224)*
Marketlab Inc ....D 866 237-3722
Caledonia *(G-2388)*
▲ Metal Arc Inc ....E 231 865-3111
Muskegon *(G-11868)*
Multi-Lab LLC ....F 616 846-6990
Spring Lake *(G-15838)*
Peerless Waste Solutions LLC ....G 616 355-2800
Holland *(G-8161)*
▲ Plas-Labs Incorporated ....E 517 372-7178
Lansing *(G-9732)*
▲ QEd Envmtl Systems Inc ....D 734 995-2547
Dexter *(G-4751)*
▼ Rankin Biomedical Corporation ....F 248 625-4104
Holly *(G-8290)*
Security Steelcraft Corp ....F 231 733-1101
Muskegon *(G-11917)*
▲ Snow Machines Incorporated ....E 989 631-6091
Midland *(G-11418)*
Southwest Mich Innovation Ctr ....G 269 353-1823
Kalamazoo *(G-9339)*
▲ Symbiote Inc ....E 616 772-1790
Zeeland *(G-19083)*
Total Toxicology Labs LLC ....G 248 352-7171
Southfield *(G-15724)*
Xxtar Associates LLC ....G 888 946-6066
Detroit *(G-4695)*

3822 Automatic Temperature Controls

Actalent Services LLC ....E 248 712-2750
Troy *(G-16905)*
Ademco Inc ....G 586 759-1455
Warren *(G-17691)*
Ademco Inc ....G 248 926-5510
Wixom *(G-18595)*
American Controls Inc ....G 248 476-0663
Bloomfield Hills *(G-1796)*
Astra Associates Inc ....E 586 254-6500
Sterling Heights *(G-15935)*
▲ Century Instrument Company ....E 734 427-0340
Livonia *(G-10152)*
Commonwealth Associates Inc ....C 517 788-3000
Jackson *(G-8849)*
Control Solutions Inc ....D 616 247-9422
Wyoming *(G-18860)*
Core Energy and Automation LLC ....G 248 830-0476
Livonia *(G-10165)*
Crewbotiq LLC ....E 248 939-4229
Troy *(G-17034)*
Eaton Corporation ....G 248 226-6347
Southfield *(G-15547)*
Edmore Tool & Grinding Inc ....F 989 427-3790
Edmore *(G-4992)*
Energy Control Solutions Inc ....G 810 735-2800
Fenton *(G-5472)*
Energy Development Assoc LLC ....G 313 354-2644
Dearborn *(G-3836)*
Enertemp Inc ....E 616 243-2752
Grand Rapids *(G-6679)*
◆ Hart & Cooley LLC ....C 616 656-8200
Grand Rapids *(G-6805)*
Imeco Inc ....G 906 774-0202
Iron Mountain *(G-8722)*
Industrial Plant Svcs Nat LLC ....E 586 221-9017
Macomb *(G-10605)*
Industrial Temperature Control ....G 734 451-8740
Canton *(G-2474)*
Inland Vapor of Michigan LLC ....D 734 237-4389
Garden City *(G-6098)*
Integrated Building Solutions ....F 616 889-3070
Chesaning *(G-2828)*
Johnson Controls Inc ....D 248 276-6000
Auburn Hills *(G-945)*
Kva Inc ....F 269 982-2888
Saint Joseph *(G-14943)*
Matrix Controls Group Inc ....G 248 380-7600
Wixom *(G-18707)*
Maxitrol Company ....G 269 432-3291
Colon *(G-3488)*
▲ Maxitrol Company ....D 248 356-1400
Southfield *(G-15648)*
▲ Mercury Displacement Inds Inc ....D 269 663-8574
Edwardsburg *(G-5009)*
Peak Industries Co Inc ....E 313 846-8666
Dearborn *(G-3883)*
▲ Precision Speed Equipment Inc ....C 269 651-4303
Sturgis *(G-16320)*
▲ Pyro Service Company ....G 248 547-2552
Madison Heights *(G-10812)*
Rhombus Energy Solutions Inc ....G 313 406-3292
Dearborn *(G-3890)*
Softaire Diffusers Inc ....G 810 730-1668
Linden *(G-10071)*
Solidica Inc ....F 734 222-4680
Ann Arbor *(G-659)*
Sterling Security LLC ....E 248 809-9309
Southfield *(G-15709)*
Swat Environmental Inc ....E 517 322-2999
Lansing *(G-9898)*
System Controls Inc ....E 734 427-0440
Livonia *(G-10428)*
◆ T E Technology Inc ....E 231 929-3966
Traverse City *(G-16849)*
Taylor Controls Inc ....F 269 637-8521
South Haven *(G-15418)*
Therma-Tech Engineering Inc ....E 313 537-5330
Redford *(G-13778)*
Vibration Controls Tech LLC ....G 248 822-8010
Troy *(G-17440)*
Warner Instruments ....G 616 843-5342
Grand Haven *(G-6379)*

3823 Indl Instruments For Meas, Display & Control

▲ A&D Technology Inc ....D 734 973-1111
Ann Arbor *(G-341)*
ABB Inc ....D 248 471-0888
Farmington Hills *(G-5157)*
Accurate Home Insptn Svcs Inc ....G 303 530-9600
Harrison Township *(G-7684)*
Acromag Incorporated ....D 248 624-1541
Wixom *(G-18594)*
ADS LLC ....G 248 740-9593
Troy *(G-16906)*
Advance Engineering Company ....D 313 537-3500
Canton *(G-2429)*
Advanced Integrated Mfg ....G 586 439-0300
Fraser *(G-5888)*
AG Davis Gage & Engrg Co ....E 586 977-9000
Sterling Heights *(G-15926)*
Airflow Sciences Equipment LLC ....G 734 525-0300
Livonia *(G-10107)*
Allrout Inc ....G 616 748-7696
Zeeland *(G-18991)*
Altair Systems Inc ....F 248 668-0116
Wixom *(G-18606)*
Ametek Inc ....G 248 362-2777
Peck *(G-12960)*
Applied Synergistics Inc ....G 248 634-0151
Holly *(G-8261)*
Astra Associates Inc ....E 586 254-6500
Sterling Heights *(G-15935)*
Ateq Tpms Tools Lc ....F 734 838-3104
Livonia *(G-10127)*
Atmo-Seal Inc ....G 248 528-9640
Troy *(G-16963)*
Ats Atmtion Globl Svcs USA Inc ....E 734 522-1900
Wixom *(G-18613)*
Auric Enterprises Inc ....G 231 882-7251
Beulah *(G-1652)*
Avl Michigan Holding Corp ....D 734 414-9600
Plymouth *(G-13130)*
▲ Avl Test Systems Inc ....C 734 414-9600
Plymouth *(G-13134)*
▲ Balance Technology Inc ....D 734 769-2100
Whitmore Lake *(G-18520)*
Banner Engineering & Sales Inc ....F 989 755-0584
Saginaw *(G-14609)*
▼ Beet Inc ....F 248 432-0052
Troy *(G-16971)*
Benny Gage Inc ....E 734 455-3080
Wixom *(G-18620)*
Bihl+wiedemann Inc ....G 616 345-0680
Wyoming *(G-18852)*
Binsfeld Engineering Inc ....G 231 334-4383
Maple City *(G-10940)*
Bisbee Infrared Services Inc ....G 517 787-4620
Jackson *(G-8823)*
Broadteq Incorporated ....G 248 794-9323
Waterford *(G-18106)*
◆ Burke E Porter Machinery Co ....C 616 234-1200
Grand Rapids *(G-6535)*

SIC

Employee Codes: A=Over 500 employees, B=251-500
C=101-250, D=51-100, E=20-50, F=10-19, G=3-9

2022 Harris Michigan
Industrial Directory

891

38 MEASURING, ANALYZING AND CONTROLLING INSTRUMENTS; PHOTOGRAPHIC, MEDICAL AN38 MEASURING, ANALYZING AND CON-

◆ C E C Controls Company Inc .... D 586 779-0222
   Warren *(G-17746)*
C E C Controls Company Inc .... G 248 926-5701
   Wixom *(G-18629)*
Clarkson Controls & Eqp Co .... G 248 380-9915
   Novi *(G-12384)*
Complete Auto-Mation Inc .... D 248 693-0500
   Lake Orion *(G-9597)*
◆ Custom Valve Concepts Inc .... E 248 597-8999
   Madison Heights *(G-10702)*
D & C Investment Group Inc .... F 734 994-0591
   Ann Arbor *(G-441)*
Debron Industrial Elec LLC .... D 248 588-7220
   Troy *(G-17050)*
Dexter Research Center Inc .... D 734 426-3921
   Dexter *(G-4739)*
Digital Performance Tech .... F 877 983-4230
   Troy *(G-17062)*
Dura Thread Gage Inc .... F 248 545-2890
   Madison Heights *(G-10714)*
Emerson Electric Co .... G 616 846-3950
   Grand Haven *(G-6296)*
Emerson Electric Co .... G 586 268-3104
   Sterling Heights *(G-16003)*
Emerson Electric Co .... G 734 420-0832
   Plymouth *(G-13167)*
Emerson Prcess MGT Pwr Wtr Slt .... E 313 874-0860
   Detroit *(G-4208)*
Emitted Energy Inc .... F 855 752-3347
   Sterling Heights *(G-16004)*
Engineered Combustn Systems LLC .... G 248 549-1703
   Royal Oak *(G-14534)*
▲ Fannon Products LLC .... F 810 794-2000
   Algonac *(G-141)*
Flow-Rite Controls Ltd .... E 616 583-1700
   Byron Center *(G-2270)*
Forefront Control Systems LLC .... G 616 796-3495
   Holland *(G-8038)*
Forrest Brothers Inc .... C 989 356-4011
   Gaylord *(G-6129)*
George Instrument Company .... F 248 280-1111
   Orion *(G-12731)*
Geotech Environmental Eqp Inc .... G 517 655-5616
   Williamston *(G-18572)*
Gic LLC .... F 231 237-7000
   Charlevoix *(G-2716)*
Gordinier Electronics Corp .... G 586 778-0426
   Roseville *(G-14414)*
▲ H O Trerice Co Inc .... E 248 399-8000
   Oak Park *(G-12616)*
Harvest Energy Inc .... F 269 838-4595
   Grand Rapids *(G-6806)*
Henkel US Operations Corp .... B 248 588-1082
   Madison Heights *(G-10739)*
Henshaw Inc .... D 586 752-0700
   Armada *(G-736)*
Hexagon Mfg Intelligence Inc .... G 248 662-1740
   Novi *(G-12433)*
◆ Hines Corporation .... F 231 799-6240
   Norton Shores *(G-12348)*
◆ Hines Industries Inc .... E 734 769-2300
   Ann Arbor *(G-517)*
Hitec Sensor Developments Inc .... G 313 506-2460
   Plymouth *(G-13188)*
Honeywell International Inc .... F 231 582-5686
   Boyne City *(G-1889)*
Horiba Instruments Inc .... D 734 213-6555
   Ann Arbor *(G-518)*
Horiba Instruments Inc .... G 248 689-9000
   Troy *(G-17150)*
◆ Howard Miller Company .... B 616 772-9131
   Zeeland *(G-19040)*
IMC Dataworks LLC .... F 248 356-4311
   Ann Arbor *(G-524)*
Incoe Corporation .... C 248 616-0220
   Auburn Hills *(G-936)*
Industrial Temperature Control .... G 734 451-8740
   Canton *(G-2474)*
Infrared Telemetrics Inc .... F 906 482-0012
   Hancock *(G-7620)*
Innovative Support Svcs Inc .... F 248 585-3600
   Troy *(G-17168)*
Integrated Marketing Svcs LLC .... F 248 625-7444
   Pontiac *(G-13381)*
▼ Integrated Security Corp .... F 248 624-0700
   Novi *(G-12438)*
International Temperature Ctrl .... G 989 876-8075
   Au Gres *(G-759)*
Jay/Enn Corporation .... D 248 588-2393
   Troy *(G-17182)*

Jcp LLC .... E 989 754-7496
   Saginaw *(G-14673)*
Jdl Enterprises Inc .... F 586 977-8863
   Warren *(G-17884)*
K-Space Associates Inc .... E 734 426-7977
   Dexter *(G-4744)*
K-TEC Systems Inc .... G 248 414-4100
   Ferndale *(G-5562)*
▼ Kaltec Scientific Inc .... G 248 349-8100
   Novi *(G-12450)*
Kubica Corp .... F 248 344-7750
   Novi *(G-12459)*
Labortrio Elttrofisico USA Inc .... E 248 340-7040
   Lake Orion *(G-9613)*
Leader Corporation .... F 586 566-7114
   Shelby Township *(G-15260)*
◆ Leco Corporation .... B 269 983-5531
   Saint Joseph *(G-14946)*
Maes Tool & Die Co Inc .... F 517 750-3131
   Jackson *(G-8940)*
Mahle Powertrain LLC .... D 248 305-8200
   Farmington Hills *(G-5307)*
Martel Tool Corporation .... F 313 278-2420
   Allen Park *(G-200)*
Maxitrol Company .... G 517 486-2820
   Blissfield *(G-1769)*
▲ Maxitrol Company .... D 248 356-1400
   Southfield *(G-15648)*
Metric Hydrulic Components LLC .... F 586 786-6990
   Shelby Township *(G-15275)*
▲ Midwest Timer Service Inc .... D 269 849-2800
   Benton Harbor *(G-1573)*
▲ Montague Latch Company .... E 810 687-4242
   Clio *(G-3407)*
Mycrona Inc .... F 734 453-9348
   Plymouth *(G-13251)*
New Wake Inc .... F 800 957-5606
   Hudsonville *(G-8599)*
Norcross Viscosity Controls .... G 586 336-0700
   Washington *(G-18086)*
Nordson Corporation .... F 734 459-8600
   Wixom *(G-18721)*
Oflow-Rite Controls Ltd .... E 616 583-1700
   Byron Center *(G-2290)*
Online Engineering Inc .... F 906 341-0090
   Manistique *(G-10923)*
Parjana Distribution LLC .... F 313 915-5418
   Southfield *(G-15672)*
◆ Patriot Sensors & Contrls Corp .... E 248 435-0700
   Peck *(G-12963)*
Patriot Sensors & Contrls Corp .... E 810 378-5511
   Peck *(G-12962)*
▲ Peaker Services Inc .... D 248 437-4174
   Brighton *(G-2049)*
◆ Peaktronics Inc .... E 248 542-5640
   Clawson *(G-3102)*
Perceptive Controls Inc .... E 269 685-3040
   Plainwell *(G-13085)*
Perpetual Measurement Inc .... E 248 343-2952
   Waterford *(G-18153)*
Piping Components Inc .... G 313 382-6400
   Melvindale *(G-11209)*
Precise Finishing Systems Inc .... E 517 552-9200
   Howell *(G-8499)*
◆ Pyro Service Company .... G 248 547-2552
   Madison Heights *(G-10812)*
▲ QEd Envmtl Systems Inc .... D 734 995-2547
   Dexter *(G-4751)*
R Concepts Incorporated .... F 810 632-4857
   Howell *(G-8505)*
Rjg Technologies Inc .... D 231 947-3111
   Traverse City *(G-16822)*
▲ Sinto America Inc .... E 517 371-2460
   Lansing *(G-9791)*
Smarteye Corporation .... E 248 853-4495
   Rochester Hills *(G-14115)*
Ssi Technology Inc .... D 248 582-0600
   Sterling Heights *(G-16188)*
Superior Controls Inc .... C 734 454-0500
   Plymouth *(G-13306)*
Sure Flow Products LLC .... G 248 380-3569
   Wixom *(G-18764)*
Taylor Controls Inc .... F 269 637-8521
   South Haven *(G-15418)*
Tech Tool Supply LLC .... G 734 207-7700
   Plymouth *(G-13310)*
Temprel Inc .... E 231 582-6585
   Boyne City *(G-1902)*
Terametrix LLC .... C 540 769-8430
   Ann Arbor *(G-681)*

Testron Incorporated .... F 734 513-6820
   Livonia *(G-10431)*
Therm-O-Disc Incorporated .... A 231 799-4100
   Norton Shores *(G-12337)*
Therm-O-Disc Midwest Inc .... A 231 799-4100
   Norton Shores *(G-12338)*
Thermo Arl US Inc .... F 313 336-3901
   Dearborn *(G-3903)*
Toledo Molding & Die Inc .... G 734 233-6338
   Plymouth *(G-13317)*
Transology Associates .... F 517 694-8645
   East Lansing *(G-4913)*
Turbine Tool & Gage Inc .... E 734 427-2270
   Livonia *(G-10451)*
Universal Flow Monitors Inc .... E 248 542-9635
   Hazel Park *(G-7845)*
Warner Instruments .... G 616 843-5342
   Grand Haven *(G-6379)*
◆ Welding Technology Corp .... C 248 477-3900
   Farmington Hills *(G-5413)*
Welform Electrodes Inc .... E 586 755-1184
   Warren *(G-18066)*
▲ X-Rite Incorporated .... G 616 803-2100
   Grand Rapids *(G-7353)*

3824 Fluid Meters & Counters

Advance Tech Solutions LLC .... G 989 928-1806
   Saginaw *(G-14601)*
Advanced Integrated Mfg .... G 586 439-0300
   Fraser *(G-5888)*
▲ Carlon Meter Inc .... G 616 842-0420
   Grand Haven *(G-6283)*
▲ Clark Brothers Instrument Co .... F 586 781-7000
   Shelby Township *(G-15190)*
Ernest Industries Acquisition, ... E 734 595-9500
   Westland *(G-18369)*
▲ Medallion Instrmnttion Systems .... C 616 847-3700
   Spring Lake *(G-15833)*
Mitchs Slots .... G 586 739-5157
   Sterling Heights *(G-16102)*
Modular Data Systems Inc .... G 586 739-5870
   Shelby Township *(G-15282)*
▲ New Vintage Usa Inc .... F 248 259-4964
   Oak Park *(G-12633)*
Northville Circuits Inc .... G 248 853-3232
   Rochester Hills *(G-14073)*
▲ Prestolite Electric LLC .... G 248 313-3807
   Novi *(G-12512)*
Rap Electronics & Machines .... G 616 846-1437
   Grand Haven *(G-6350)*
Re-Sol LLC .... F 248 270-7777
   Auburn Hills *(G-1016)*
▼ Royal Design & Manufacturing .... D 248 588-0110
   Madison Heights *(G-10821)*
Sensus .... G 517 230-1529
   East Lansing *(G-4908)*
Sidekick Device .... G 231 894-6905
   Whitehall *(G-18509)*
Silversmith Inc .... E 989 732-8988
   Gaylord *(G-6160)*
SLC Meter LLC .... F 248 625-0667
   Pontiac *(G-13416)*
▲ Southern Auto Wholesalers Inc .... F 248 335-5555
   Pontiac *(G-13417)*
▲ U S Speedo Inc .... E 810 244-0909
   Flint *(G-5787)*

3825 Instrs For Measuring & Testing Electricity

▲ A&D Technology Inc .... D 734 973-1111
   Ann Arbor *(G-341)*
Abtech Installation & Svc Inc .... E 800 548-2381
   Southgate *(G-15747)*
Accurate Technologies Inc .... D 248 848-9200
   Novi *(G-12360)*
Advanced Systems & Contrls Inc .... E 586 992-9684
   Macomb *(G-10572)*
Aerospace America Inc .... E 989 684-2121
   Bay City *(G-1319)*
AG Davis Gage & Engrg Co .... E 586 977-9000
   Sterling Heights *(G-15926)*
Ats Assembly and Test Inc .... F 937 222-3030
   Wixom *(G-18612)*
Auric Enterprises Inc .... G 231 882-7251
   Beulah *(G-1652)*
▲ Balance Technology Inc .... D 734 769-2100
   Whitmore Lake *(G-18520)*
Benesh Corporation .... F 734 244-4143
   Monroe *(G-11532)*

Brothers Mead 3 LLC G 269 883-6241
Battle Creek *(G-1198)*
◆ **Burke E Porter Machinery Co** C 616 234-1200
Grand Rapids *(G-6535)*
▲ **Classic Instruments Inc** G 231 582-0461
Boyne City *(G-1887)*
Cobham McRlctrnic Slutions Inc G 734 426-1230
Ann Arbor *(G-431)*
Concept Technology Inc F 248 765-0100
Birmingham *(G-1722)*
CPR III Inc E 248 652-2900
Rochester *(G-13897)*
Creative Power Systems Inc F 313 961-2460
Detroit *(G-4108)*
CSM Products Inc F 248 836-4995
Auburn Hills *(G-852)*
Debron Industrial Elec LLC D 248 588-7220
Troy *(G-17050)*
Design & Test Technology Inc G 734 665-4111
Dexter *(G-4733)*
Design & Test Technology Inc G 734 665-4316
Ann Arbor *(G-448)*
Diagnostic Systems Assoc Inc F 269 544-9000
Kalamazoo *(G-9166)*
Dynamic Auto Test Engineering G 269 342-1334
Portage *(G-13556)*
▼ **Eagile Incorporated** F 616 243-1200
Grand Rapids *(G-6660)*
▲ **Electrodynamics Inc** G 734 422-5420
Livonia *(G-10193)*
Esirpal Inc G 586 337-7848
Macomb *(G-10592)*
Ezm LLC F 248 861-2602
Commerce Township *(G-3528)*
Frequency Finders LLC F 734 660-3357
Pontiac *(G-13372)*
Global Electronics Limited F 248 353-0100
Bloomfield Hills *(G-1823)*
▲ **Greening Associates Inc** E 313 366-7160
Detroit *(G-4283)*
Hale Manufacturing Inc G 231 529-6271
Alanson *(G-111)*
Higgins Corp G 269 365-7744
Roscommon *(G-14350)*
Hole Industries Incorporated G 517 548-4229
Howell *(G-8461)*
Honeywell International Inc C 231 582-5686
Boyne City *(G-1889)*
Horiba Instruments Inc D 734 213-6555
Ann Arbor *(G-518)*
Infrared Telemetrics Inc F 906 482-0012
Hancock *(G-7620)*
Instrumented Sensor Tech Inc G 517 349-8487
Okemos *(G-12670)*
Ix Innovations LLC G
Ann Arbor *(G-532)*
Jodon Engineering Assoc Inc F 734 761-4044
Ann Arbor *(G-534)*
Konrad Technologies Inc G 248 489-1200
Farmington Hills *(G-5283)*
◆ **Leco Corporation** B 269 983-5531
Saint Joseph *(G-14946)*
Lumileds LLC E 248 553-9080
Farmington Hills *(G-5297)*
Mahle Powertrain LLC D 248 305-8200
Farmington Hills *(G-5307)*
Medical Infrmtics Slutions LLC G 248 851-3124
Bloomfield Hills *(G-1836)*
▲ **Meiden America Inc** E 734 459-1781
Northville *(G-12239)*
Merc-O-Tronic Instruments Corp F 586 894-9529
Almont *(G-265)*
Michigan Scientific Corp D 231 547-5511
Charlevoix *(G-2721)*
My Electrician Grand Rapids G 616 208-4113
Grand Rapids *(G-7033)*
▲ **Nadex of America Corporation** E 248 477-3900
Farmington Hills *(G-5330)*
Nanorete Inc G 517 336-4680
Lansing *(G-9873)*
Netwave G 586 263-4469
Macomb *(G-10622)*
Opteos Inc G 734 929-3333
Ann Arbor *(G-601)*
▲ **Orion Test Systems Inc** D 248 373-9097
Auburn Hills *(G-990)*
▲ **Ptm-Electronics Inc** F 248 987-4446
Farmington Hills *(G-5356)*
Racelogic USA Corporation G 248 994-9050
Farmington Hills *(G-5364)*
Ram Meter Inc F 248 362-0990
Royal Oak *(G-14572)*
Sciemetric Inc F 248 509-2209
Rochester Hills *(G-14110)*
Seneca Enterprises LLC G 231 943-1171
Traverse City *(G-16829)*
Servo Innovations LLC G 269 792-9279
Wayland *(G-18207)*
Smart Label Solutions LLC G 800 996-7343
Howell *(G-8519)*
◆ **Srg Global Coatings LLC** C 248 509-1100
Troy *(G-17369)*
Standard Electric Company F 906 774-4455
Kingsford *(G-9518)*
Swain Company Inc G 989 773-3700
Farwell *(G-5429)*
Swain Meter Company G 989 773-3700
Farwell *(G-5430)*
Syscom Technologies Inc G 231 946-1411
Traverse City *(G-16848)*
▲ **Tengam Engineering Inc** E 269 694-9466
Otsego *(G-12800)*
Teradyne Inc G 313 425-3900
Allen Park *(G-208)*
Test Products Incorporated E 586 997-9600
Sterling Heights *(G-16204)*
Testron Incorporated F 734 513-6820
Livonia *(G-10431)*
Vexa Group LLC G 734 330-8858
Wixom *(G-18788)*
VSR Technologies Inc F 734 425-7172
Livonia *(G-10462)*

3826 Analytical Instruments

Alliance Hni LLC E 989 729-2804
Owosso *(G-12821)*
Auric Enterprises Inc G 231 882-7251
Beulah *(G-1652)*
Authentic 3d E 248 469-8809
Bingham Farms *(G-1692)*
Beckman Equipment G 231 420-4791
Cheboygan *(G-2780)*
Best Products Inc F 313 538-7414
Redford *(G-13719)*
◆ **Burke E Porter Machinery Co** C 616 234-1200
Grand Rapids *(G-6535)*
Celsee Inc D 866 748-1448
Ann Arbor *(G-419)*
Clark-Mxr Inc E 734 426-2803
Dexter *(G-4731)*
Cpr Inc G 734 459-7251
Canton *(G-2452)*
Espec Corp E 616 896-6100
Hudsonville *(G-8582)*
Essen Instruments Inc D 734 769-1600
Ann Arbor *(G-480)*
Fisher Scientific Intl LLC G 734 622-0413
Ann Arbor *(G-489)*
Full Spectrum Tech Inc G 810 225-4760
Brighton *(G-1994)*
Horiba Automotive Test Systems E 248 689-9000
Troy *(G-17149)*
Horiba Instruments Inc D 734 213-6555
Ann Arbor *(G-518)*
▲ **Hti Usa Inc** G 248 358-5533
Farmington *(G-5139)*
Jade Scientific Inc F 734 207-3775
Westland *(G-18387)*
Jodon Engineering Assoc Inc F 734 761-4044
Ann Arbor *(G-534)*
Kuka Assembly and Test Corp F 810 593-0350
Fenton *(G-5488)*
Lake Erie Med Surgical Sup Inc E 734 847-3847
Temperance *(G-16536)*
◆ **Leco Corporation** B 269 983-5531
Saint Joseph *(G-14946)*
Marshall Ryerson Co F 616 299-1751
Grand Rapids *(G-6961)*
▲ **Mectron Engineering Co Inc** E 734 944-8777
Saline *(G-15026)*
Neptech Inc E 810 225-2222
Highland *(G-7897)*
Opti 02 LLC G 517 381-9831
Okemos *(G-12680)*
▲ **Phadia US Inc** C 269 492-1940
Portage *(G-13593)*
Pioneer Technologies Corp G 702 806-3152
Fremont *(G-6054)*
Proto Manufacturing Inc E 734 946-0974
Taylor *(G-16463)*
◆ **Q-Photonics LLC** G 734 477-0133
Ann Arbor *(G-628)*
▲ **QEd Envmtl Systems Inc** D 734 995-2547
Dexter *(G-4751)*
▲ **R H K Technology Inc** E 248 577-5426
Troy *(G-17327)*
◆ **Richard-Allan Scientific Co** D 269 544-5600
Kalamazoo *(G-9316)*
Rigaku Innovative Tech Inc C 248 232-6400
Auburn Hills *(G-1020)*
◆ **Srg Global Coatings LLC** C 248 509-1100
Troy *(G-17369)*
Thermo Arl US Inc F 313 336-3901
Dearborn *(G-3903)*
Thermo Fisher Scientific Inc G 231 932-0242
Traverse City *(G-16856)*
Thermo Fisher Scientific Inc G 800 346-4364
Portage *(G-13625)*
Thermo Fisher Scientific Inc G 269 544-5600
Kalamazoo *(G-9356)*
Thermo Fisher Scientific Inc G 734 662-4117
Ann Arbor *(G-687)*
▲ **TS Enterprise Associates Inc** F 248 348-2963
Northville *(G-12267)*
Venturedyne Ltd G 616 392-6550
Holland *(G-8237)*
X-Ray and Specialty Instrs Inc G 734 485-6300
Ypsilanti *(G-18986)*
▲ **X-Rite Incorporated** C 616 803-2100
Grand Rapids *(G-7353)*

3827 Optical Instruments

Browe Inc G 248 877-3800
Clinton Township *(G-3189)*
Carl Zeiss Nts LLC E 248 486-7600
Brighton *(G-1961)*
Clark-Mxr Inc E 734 426-2803
Dexter *(G-4731)*
Contour Metrological & Mfg Inc G 248 273-1111
Troy *(G-17025)*
▲ **Crl Inc** E 906 428-3710
Gladstone *(G-6177)*
Diagnostic Instruments Inc E 586 731-6000
Sterling Heights *(G-15986)*
▲ **Electro-Optics Technology Inc** D 231 935-4044
Traverse City *(G-16675)*
Eotech Inc E 734 741-8868
Ann Arbor *(G-476)*
Eye 2 Eye Contact G 313 378-7883
Northville *(G-12216)*
Eyewear Detroit Company G 248 396-2214
Clarkston *(G-3034)*
First Optometry Lab G 248 546-1300
Madison Heights *(G-10728)*
General Dynamics Mission A 530 271-2500
Rochester Hills *(G-14021)*
▲ **General Dynmics Globl Imging T** A 248 293-2929
Rochester Hills *(G-14022)*
▲ **General Scientific Corporation** E 734 996-9200
Ann Arbor *(G-498)*
Genx Corporation G 269 341-4242
Kalamazoo *(G-9195)*
◆ **Jenoptik Automotive N Amer LLC** C 248 853-5888
Rochester Hills *(G-14043)*
▲ **Kaiser Optical Systems Inc** D 734 665-8083
Ann Arbor *(G-537)*
Kwik-Site Corporation F 734 326-1500
Wayne *(G-18227)*
▲ **Leapers Inc** D 734 542-1500
Livonia *(G-10275)*
Lumenflow Corp G 269 795-9007
Spring Lake *(G-15831)*
Magna Mirrors America Inc G 616 786-7300
Holland *(G-8134)*
Magna Mirrors America Inc G 616 942-0163
Newaygo *(G-12085)*
Meridian Mechatronics LLC G 517 447-4587
Deerfield *(G-3958)*
Optec Inc F 616 897-9351
Lowell *(G-10513)*
▲ **Perceptron Inc** B 734 414-6100
Plymouth *(G-13263)*
Perform3-D LLC G 734 604-4100
Ann Arbor *(G-608)*
Periscope Playschool G 989 875-4409
Alma *(G-252)*
▼ **Phoenix Imaging Inc** F 248 476-4200
Livonia *(G-10365)*
Planewave Instruments Inc D 310 639-1662
Adrian *(G-87)*

SIC

Employee Codes: A=Over 500 employees, B=251-500
C=101-250, D=51-100, E=20-50, F=10-19, G=3-9
2022 Harris Michigan
Industrial Directory
893

Rs Products LLC....G....801 722-9746
Chesterfield *(G-2941)*
Seneca Enterprises LLC....G....231 943-1171
Traverse City *(G-16829)*
Spencer Tool....G....877 956-6868
Oxford *(G-12918)*
Trijicon Inc....C....248 960-7700
Wixom *(G-18780)*
Visioncraft....G....586 949-6540
Chesterfield *(G-2964)*
Visotek Inc....F....734 427-4800
Novi *(G-12568)*
Visual Precision Inc....G....248 546-7984
Madison Heights *(G-10857)*
▼ **Williams Gun Sight Company**....D....800 530-9028
Davison *(G-3801)*
▲ **X-Rite Incorporated**....C....616 803-2100
Grand Rapids *(G-7353)*
Zeiss Int....G....734 895-6004
Wixom *(G-18794)*

3829 Measuring & Controlling Devices, NEC

2 Brothers Holdings LLC....G....517 487-3900
Lansing *(G-9797)*
A S I Instruments Inc....G....586 756-1222
Warren *(G-17683)*
▲ **A&D Technology Inc**....D....734 973-1111
Ann Arbor *(G-341)*
Abletech Industries LLC....G....734 677-2420
Dexter *(G-4720)*
Acromag Incorporated....D....248 624-1541
Wixom *(G-18594)*
Adcole Corporation....G....508 485-9100
Orion *(G-12722)*
Advanced Systems & Contrls Inc....E....586 992-9684
Macomb *(G-10572)*
Analytical Process Systems Inc....E....248 393-0700
Auburn Hills *(G-784)*
▲ **Apollo America Inc**....D....248 332-3900
Auburn Hills *(G-791)*
Assay Designs Inc....E....734 214-0923
Ann Arbor *(G-383)*
Astra Associates Inc....E....586 254-6500
Sterling Heights *(G-15935)*
▲ **Ateq Corporation**....G....734 838-3100
Livonia *(G-10126)*
Ats Assembly and Test Inc....F....734 266-4713
Livonia *(G-10129)*
Auric Enterprises Inc....G....231 882-7251
Beulah *(G-1652)*
Avidhrt Inc....G....517 214-9041
Okemos *(G-12658)*
▲ **Avl Test Systems Inc**....C....734 414-9600
Plymouth *(G-13134)*
B K Corporation....F....989 777-2111
Saginaw *(G-14606)*
▲ **Balance Technology Inc**....D....734 769-2100
Whitmore Lake *(G-18520)*
▼ **Beet Inc**....F....248 432-0052
Troy *(G-16971)*
Benesh Corporation....F....734 244-4143
Monroe *(G-11532)*
Biosan Laboratories Inc....F....586 755-8970
Warren *(G-17738)*
Bisnett Insurance....G....734 214-2676
Whitmore Lake *(G-18521)*
Bonal International Inc....F....248 582-0900
Royal Oak *(G-14518)*
Bonal Technologies Inc....F....248 582-0900
Royal Oak *(G-14519)*
Bti Measurement Tstg Svcs LLC....G....734 769-2100
Whitmore Lake *(G-18524)*
Bti Measurement Tstg Svcs LLC....G....734 769-2100
Dexter *(G-4729)*
Calhoun County Med Care Fcilty....E....269 962-5458
Battle Creek *(G-1204)*
Cammenga & Associates LLC....F....313 914-7160
Dearborn *(G-3817)*
Clark Instrument Inc....F....248 669-3100
Novi *(G-12383)*
◆ **Comau LLC**....B....248 353-8888
Southfield *(G-15530)*
Common Sensors LLC....G....248 722-8556
Farmington Hills *(G-5205)*
Control Power-Reliance LLC....G....248 583-1020
Troy *(G-17026)*
▲ **Conway-Cleveland Corp**....G....616 458-0056
Grand Rapids *(G-6604)*
Creative Engineering Inc....G....734 996-5900
Ann Arbor *(G-439)*
▼ **Crippen Manufacturing Company**....E....989 681-4323
Saint Louis *(G-14990)*
D & N Gage Inc....F....586 336-2110
Romeo *(G-14224)*
Demmer Investments Inc....G....517 321-3600
Lansing *(G-9688)*
Detroit Testing Machine Co....G....248 669-3100
Novi *(G-12396)*
Dietert Foundry Testing Eqp....G....313 491-4680
Detroit *(G-4175)*
Digitaleo Corporation....G....248 250-9205
Troy *(G-17063)*
Dimension Products Corporation....F....616 842-6050
Grand Haven *(G-6292)*
Electro ARC Manufacturing Co....E....734 483-4233
Dexter *(G-4741)*
Equitable Engineering Co Inc....E....248 689-9700
Troy *(G-17096)*
Exquise Inc....G....248 220-9048
Detroit *(G-4223)*
Ezm LLC....F....248 861-2602
Commerce Township *(G-3528)*
F I D Corporation....G....248 373-7005
Rochester Hills *(G-14008)*
Family Safety Products Inc....G....616 530-6540
Grandville *(G-7377)*
▲ **Froude Inc**....D....248 579-4295
Novi *(G-12419)*
Gage Eagle Spline Inc....D....586 776-7240
Warren *(G-17822)*
General Inspection LLC....F....248 625-0529
Davisburg *(G-3769)*
Gfg Instrumentation Inc....E....734 769-0573
Ann Arbor *(G-500)*
Gic LLC....F....231 237-7000
Charlevoix *(G-2716)*
Gravikor Inc....G....734 302-3200
Ann Arbor *(G-506)*
Great Lakes Gages LLC....G....810 797-8300
Metamora *(G-11280)*
▲ **Greening Incorporated**....G....313 366-7160
Detroit *(G-4282)*
▲ **Greening Associates Inc**....E....313 366-7160
Detroit *(G-4283)*
▲ **Hanse Environmental Inc**....G....269 673-8638
Allegan *(G-160)*
Hbm Inc....G....248 350-8300
Southfield *(G-15590)*
◆ **Hines Industries Inc**....E....734 769-2300
Ann Arbor *(G-517)*
Horiba Instruments Inc....D....734 213-6555
Ann Arbor *(G-518)*
◆ **Howard Miller Company**....B....616 772-9131
Zeeland *(G-19040)*
◆ **Humantics Innvtive Sltions Inc**....C....734 451-7878
Farmington Hills *(G-5264)*
Ifm Efector....G....800 441-8246
Farmington Hills *(G-5268)*
Infrared Telemetrics Inc....F....906 482-0012
Hancock *(G-7620)*
Innkeeper LLC....G....734 743-1707
Canton *(G-2476)*
Inora Technologies Inc....G....734 302-7488
Ann Arbor *(G-529)*
Instrumented Sensor Tech Inc....G....517 349-8487
Okemos *(G-12670)*
Integrated Sensing Systems Inc....E....734 547-9896
Ypsilanti *(G-18957)*
Intelligent Dynamics LLC....F....313 727-9920
Dearborn *(G-3854)*
▲ **International Met Systems Inc**....F....616 971-1005
Grand Rapids *(G-6850)*
Invertech Inc....G....734 944-4400
Saline *(G-15021)*
Invo Spline Inc....E....586 757-8840
Warren *(G-17870)*
J E Myles Inc....E....248 583-1020
Troy *(G-17178)*
Jgs Machining LLC....G....810 329-4210
Saint Clair *(G-14832)*
Jomat Industries Ltd....F....586 336-1801
Bruce Twp *(G-2169)*
K-Space Associates Inc....E....734 426-7977
Dexter *(G-4744)*
Kemkraft Engineering Inc....F....734 414-6500
Plymouth *(G-13212)*
▲ **Kistler Instrument Corporation**....D....248 668-6900
Novi *(G-12453)*
KLC Enterprises Inc....E....989 753-0496
Saginaw *(G-14678)*
▲ **Kuka Assembly and Test Corp**....C....989 220-3088
Saginaw *(G-14680)*
Labortrio Elttrofisico USA Inc....G....248 340-7040
Lake Orion *(G-9613)*
Lifesafer....G....888 294-7002
Marquette *(G-11031)*
▲ **Link Group Inc**....D....734 453-0800
Plymouth *(G-13222)*
▲ **Link Manufacturing Inc**....D....734 453-0800
Plymouth *(G-13223)*
Link Manufacturing Inc....G....734 387-1001
Ottawa Lake *(G-12807)*
M Antonik....G....248 236-0333
Oxford *(G-12897)*
Martel Tool Corporation....F....313 278-2420
Allen Park *(G-200)*
McCrea Controls Inc....G....248 544-1366
Berkley *(G-1630)*
Michael Engineering Ltd....E....989 772-4073
Mount Pleasant *(G-11711)*
◆ **Michigan Scientific Corp**....E....248 685-3939
Milford *(G-11470)*
Michigan Scientific Corp....D....231 547-5511
Charlevoix *(G-2721)*
Midwest Flex Systems Inc....F....810 424-0060
Flint *(G-5734)*
▲ **Miljoco Corp**....E....586 777-4280
Mount Clemens *(G-11649)*
Montronix Inc....G....734 213-6500
Ann Arbor *(G-583)*
Neptech Inc....E....810 225-2222
Highland *(G-7897)*
New Wake Inc....G....800 957-5606
Hudsonville *(G-8599)*
◆ **Nikon Metrology Inc**....E....810 220-4360
Brighton *(G-2041)*
Nikon Metrology Inc....G....810 220-4347
Brighton *(G-2042)*
▼ **North American Controls Inc**....E....586 532-7140
Shelby Township *(G-15290)*
◆ **Og Technologies Inc**....F....734 973-7500
Ann Arbor *(G-599)*
Parker-Hannifin Corporation....G....330 253-5239
Otsego *(G-12797)*
◆ **Patriot Sensors & Contrls Corp**....D....248 435-0700
Peck *(G-12963)*
Pcb Load & Torque Inc....E....248 471-0065
Farmington Hills *(G-5344)*
Pcb Piezotronics Inc....F....888 684-0014
Novi *(G-12503)*
Pcb Piezotronics Inc....G....716 684-0001
Farmington Hills *(G-5345)*
▲ **Perceptron Inc**....B....734 414-6100
Plymouth *(G-13263)*
▲ **Pharmaceutical Specialties LLC**....F....269 382-6402
Galesburg *(G-6081)*
Pinto Products Inc....G....269 383-0015
Kalamazoo *(G-9296)*
Port Austin Level & Tl Mfg Co....F....989 738-5291
Port Austin *(G-13428)*
Precision Devices Inc....E....734 439-2462
Milan *(G-11449)*
Precision Measurement Co....F....734 995-0041
Ann Arbor *(G-622)*
Promess Inc....D....810 229-9334
Brighton *(G-2055)*
Promess Incorporated....G....810 229-9334
Brighton *(G-2056)*
◆ **Quality First Systems Inc**....E....248 922-4780
Davisburg *(G-3772)*
Quigley Manufacturing Inc....G....248 426-8600
Farmington Hills *(G-5362)*
R & J Manufacturing Company....F....248 669-2460
Commerce Township *(G-3568)*
R M Young Company....E....231 946-3980
Traverse City *(G-16812)*
Ram Meter Inc....F....248 362-0990
Royal Oak *(G-14572)*
Ramer Products Inc....G....269 409-8583
Buchanan *(G-2201)*
Rayco Manufacturing Inc....F....586 795-2884
Sterling Heights *(G-16144)*
Rel Inc....E....906 337-3018
Calumet *(G-2413)*
Richmond Instrs & Systems Inc....F....586 954-3770
Clinton Township *(G-3337)*
Rs Technologies Ltd....F....248 888-8260
Farmington Hills *(G-5374)*
Russells Technical Pdts Inc....E....616 392-3161
Holland *(G-8184)*

SIC SECTION 38 MEASURING, ANALYZING AND CONTROLLING INSTRUMENTS; PHOTOGRAPHIC, MEDICAL AN38 MEASURING, ANALYZING

Company	Emp	Phone
Safety Technology Holdings Inc — Farmington Hills (G-5375)	F	415 983-2706
▲ Saginaw Machine Systems Inc — Saginaw (G-14747)	E	989 753-8465
Schap Specialty Machine Inc — Spring Lake (G-15850)	F	616 846-6530
Senscomp Inc — Livonia (G-10404)	G	734 953-4783
Sensordata Technologies Inc — Shelby Township (G-15327)	F	586 739-4254
Service Diamond Tool Company — Novi (G-12535)	G	248 669-3100
▲ Siko Products Inc — Dexter (G-4754)	G	734 426-3476
◆ Solar Street Lights Usa LLC — Holland (G-8199)	G	269 983-6361
Ssi Technology Inc — Sterling Heights (G-16188)	D	248 582-0600
Sterling Prmeasure Systems Inc — Sterling Heights (G-16194)	E	586 254-5310
▲ Storage Control Systems Inc — Sparta (G-15783)	E	616 887-7994
▲ Sun-Tec Corp — Novi (G-12550)	G	248 669-3100
Superior Controls Inc — Plymouth (G-13306)	C	734 454-0500
◆ T E Technology Inc — Traverse City (G-16849)	E	231 929-3966
Tecat Performance Systems LLC — Ann Arbor (G-672)	F	248 615-9862
Temprel Inc — Boyne City (G-1902)	E	231 582-6585
Teradyne Inc — Allen Park (G-208)	G	313 425-3900
Tessonics Corp — Birmingham (G-1752)	G	248 885-8335
◆ Testek LLC — Wixom (G-18771)	D	248 573-4980
Testron Incorporated — Livonia (G-10431)	G	734 513-6820
▼ Thermal Wave Imaging Inc — Madison Heights (G-10843)	F	248 414-3730
▼ Thermotron Industries Inc — Holland (G-8219)	B	616 392-1491
▲ Thielenhaus Microfinish Corp — Novi (G-12556)	F	248 349-9450
▲ Thierica Inc — Grand Rapids (G-7257)	G	616 458-1538
Trece Adhesive Division — Grand Rapids (G-7272)	G	918 785-3061
Triangle Broach Company — Detroit (G-4645)	E	313 838-2150
United Abrasive Inc — Vulcan (G-17616)	F	906 563-9249
United Testing Systems — Linden (G-10072)	G	989 494-3664
Verimation Technology Inc — Farmington Hills (G-5409)	E	248 471-0000
Versicor LLC — Royal Oak (G-14589)	F	734 306-9137
Vgage LLC — Oak Park (G-12648)	D	248 589-7455
Vibration Research Corporation — Jenison (G-9077)	E	616 669-3028
Waber Tool & Engineering Co — Kalamazoo (G-9365)	F	269 342-0765
▲ Wellsense USA Inc — Birmingham (G-1756)	G	888 335-0995
▲ World Magnetics Company LLC — Traverse City (G-16882)	E	231 946-3800

3841 Surgical & Medical Instrs & Apparatus

Company	Emp	Phone
Acousys Biodevices Inc — Ann Arbor (G-347)	G	573 823-3849
Aees Power Systems Ltd Partnr — Farmington Hills (G-5160)	G	269 668-4429
▲ Alliant Enterprises LLC — Grand Rapids (G-6449)	D	269 629-0300
▲ Altus Industries Inc — Walker (G-17631)	E	616 233-9530
American Laser Centers LLC — Farmington Hills (G-5168)	A	248 426-8250
Arch Med Sltons Lehigh Vly LLC — Warren (G-17710)	D	603 760-1554
Arch Medical Solutions Corp — Warren (G-17711)	G	603 760-1554
▼ Artisan Medical Displays LLC — Zeeland (G-18993)	E	616 748-8950
Autocam Corp — Grand Rapids (G-6481)	D	616 698-0707
▲ Autocam Corporation — Kentwood (G-9444)	B	616 698-0707
Autocam Med DVC Holdings LLC — Kentwood (G-9447)	G	616 541-8080
Autocam Medical Devices LLC — Grand Rapids (G-6482)	E	877 633-8080
Barron Precision Instruments — Grand Blanc (G-6234)	G	810 695-2080
Bd Diagnostic Systems — Detroit (G-4044)	G	313 442-8800
Bio-Vac Inc — Southfield (G-15508)	E	248 350-2150
Bonwrx Ltd — Lansing (G-9675)	G	517 481-2924
Bretton Square Industries — Lansing (G-9817)	G	517 346-9607
Brio Device LLC — Ann Arbor (G-406)	G	734 945-5728
C2dx Inc — Schoolcraft (G-15112)	F	269 409-0068
Capnesity Inc — Lapeer (G-9920)	G	317 401-6766
Cardiac Assist Holdings LLC — Plymouth (G-13142)	G	781 727-1391
Clear Image Devices LLC — Ann Arbor (G-427)	G	734 645-6459
Cnd Products LLC — Grand Rapids (G-6576)	G	616 361-1000
Complete Health System — Flint (G-5670)	G	810 720-3891
Concentric Medical Inc — Portage (G-13554)	E	269 385-2600
▼ Crippen Manufacturing Company — Saint Louis (G-14990)	E	989 681-4323
Darla Nagel — Flushing (G-5807)	G	810 624-9043
▲ David Epstein Inc — Ferndale (G-5539)	F	248 542-0802
Delphinus Medical Technologies — Novi (G-12393)	E	248 522-9600
Deuwave LLC — Northville (G-12214)	G	888 238-9283
DForte Inc — Paw Paw (G-12946)	F	269 657-6996
Di-Coat Corporation — Novi (G-12399)	E	248 349-1211
Domico Med-Device LLC — Fenton (G-5471)	D	810 750-5300
Drive Medical — Galesburg (G-6075)	G	404 349-0280
Evosys North America Corp — Auburn Hills (G-882)	F	248 973-1703
Femur Buyer Inc — Holt (G-8311)	E	517 694-2300
Ferndale Pharma Group Inc — Ferndale (G-5554)	B	248 548-0900
Filter Plus Inc — Chelsea (G-2811)	G	734 475-7403
Flexdex Inc — Brighton (G-1991)	F	810 522-9009
Fms Lansing LLC — Lansing (G-9838)	G	781 699-9000
Frontier Medical Devices Inc — Gwinn (G-7584)	F	906 232-1200
Functional Fluidics Inc — Detroit (G-4248)	G	410 493-8322
▲ Gelman Sciences Inc — Ann Arbor (G-496)	C	734 665-0651
Genesis Innovation Group LLC — Holland (G-8049)	E	616 294-1026
▲ Grace Engineering Corp — Memphis (G-11213)	D	810 392-2181
Graham Medical Tech LLC — Macomb (G-10600)	E	586 677-9600
Greystone Medical LLC — Waterford (G-18126)	G	248 955-3069
Hart Enterprises USA Inc — Sparta (G-15768)	D	616 887-0400
Healthcare Drble Med Eqpmnts L — Ann Arbor (G-510)	G	734 975-6668
Horiba Instruments Inc — Canton (G-2472)	E	734 487-8300
Innovtive Srgcal Solutions LLC — Wixom (G-18686)	G	248 595-0420
J Sterling Industries LLC — Kalamazoo (G-9228)	F	269 492-6922
J Sterling Industries Ltd — Kalamazoo (G-9229)	G	269 492-6920
Jodon Engineering Assoc Inc — Ann Arbor (G-534)	F	734 761-4044
▲ Keystone Manufacturing LLC — Kalamazoo (G-9254)	F	269 343-4108
Lake Erie Med Surgical Sup Inc — Temperance (G-16536)	E	734 847-3847
Link Technology Inc — Portage (G-13577)	F	269 324-8212
▲ Mar-Med Inc — Grand Rapids (G-6958)	E	616 454-3000
Marketlab Inc — Caledonia (G-2388)	D	866 237-3722
Med Michigan Holdings LLC — Plymouth (G-13239)	G	888 891-1200
Medical Engineering & Dev — Horton (G-8377)	G	517 563-2352
▲ Medical Laser Resources LLC — Oxford (G-12901)	G	248 628-8120
Medtronic Inc — Grand Rapids (G-6976)	G	616 643-5200
Medtronic Usa Inc — Novi (G-12478)	G	248 449-5027
Melling Manufacturing Inc — Jackson (G-8950)	D	517 750-3580
Michigan Instruments LLC — Grand Rapids (G-6991)	G	616 554-9696
Michigan Med Innovations LLC — Ada (G-30)	G	616 682-4848
Nel Group Inc — Ann Arbor (G-593)	G	734 730-9164
▲ Neogen Corporation — Lansing (G-9874)	A	517 372-9200
Orchid Macdee LLC — Chelsea (G-2822)	C	734 475-9165
Orchid MPS Holdings LLC — Holt (G-8321)	A	517 694-2300
Orchid Orthopedic Solutions — Mason (G-11149)	F	517 694-2300
Orchid Orthpd Sltons Organ Inc — Holt (G-8322)	C	203 877-3341
Orchid Orthpd Solutions LLC — Bridgeport (G-1917)	B	989 746-0780
Orchid Orthpd Solutions LLC — Holt (G-8323)	B	517 694-2300
▲ Oxus America Inc — Auburn Hills (G-991)	G	248 475-0925
Oxygenplus LLC — Clinton Township (G-3316)	G	586 221-9112
▲ Performance Systematix LLC — Grand Rapids (G-7080)	E	616 949-9090
Perspective Enterprises Inc — Portage (G-13591)	G	269 327-0869
Photonics Products Grou — Grand Rapids (G-7086)	F	616 301-7800
Pinnacle Technology Group — Ottawa Lake (G-12810)	D	734 568-6600
Pioneer Surgical Tech Inc — Marquette (G-11041)	C	906 226-9909
Plasma Biolife Services L P — Grandville (G-7409)	G	616 667-0264
Precision Edge Srgcal Pdts LLC — Boyne City (G-1901)	E	231 459-4304
Precision Edge Srgcal Pdts LLC — Sault Sainte Marie (G-15096)	C	906 632-5600
Professional Hearing Services — Hillsdale (G-7942)	G	517 439-1610
▲ Progressive Dynamics Inc — Marshall (G-11072)	D	269 781-4241
R H Cross Enterprises Inc — Portage (G-13598)	G	269 488-4009
RJL Sciences Inc — Clinton Township (G-3339)	F	800 528-4513
Rls Interventional Inc — Kentwood (G-9476)	F	616 301-7800
Rose Technologies Company — Grand Rapids (G-7165)	E	616 233-3000
◆ Salter Labs LLC — Grand Rapids (G-7179)		847 739-3224
Salter Medical Holdings Corp — Grand Rapids (G-7180)	D	800 421-0024
SGC Industries Inc — Fraser (G-5992)		586 293-5260
Shoulder Innovations Inc — Grand Rapids (G-7195)	F	616 294-1026
Slaughter Instrument Company — Stevensville (G-16265)	F	269 428-7471
Smith and Nephew — Grand Rapids (G-7203)	F	616 288-6153
Somanetics — Troy (G-17361)	F	248 689-3050
Steele Supply Co — Saint Joseph (G-14964)	G	269 983-0920

Employee Codes: A=Over 500 employees, B=251-500
C=101-250, D=51-100, E=20-50, F=10-19, G=3-9

38 MEASURING, ANALYZING AND CONTROLLING INSTRUMENTS; PHOTOGRAPHIC, MEDICAL AN38 MEASURING, ANALYZING AND CON-

Stryker Australia LLC ....C 269 385-2600
Portage *(G-13612)*
▲ **Stryker Communications Inc** ....C 972 410-7000
Portage *(G-13613)*
Stryker Corporation ....E 269 385-2600
Portage *(G-13615)*
Stryker Corporation ....G 248 374-6352
Novi *(G-12546)*
Stryker Corporation ....E 269 389-2300
Portage *(G-13616)*
Stryker Corporation ....E 269 389-3741
Portage *(G-13614)*
Stryker Far East Inc ....A 269 385-2600
Portage *(G-13618)*
Stryker Prfmce Solutions LLC ....F 269 385-2600
Portage *(G-13619)*
Stryker Sales LLC ....F 269 324-5346
Portage *(G-13620)*
Stryker Sales LLC ....E 269 323-1027
Portage *(G-13621)*
Sunmed Holdings LLC ....E 616 259-8400
Grand Rapids *(G-7235)*
Supreme Gear Co ....E 586 775-6325
Fraser *(G-6001)*
Surgitech Surgical Svcs Inc ....F 248 593-0797
Highland *(G-7900)*
Sybron Dental Specialti ....G 734 947-6927
Romulus *(G-14333)*
Tambra Investments Inc ....G 866 662-7897
Warren *(G-18035)*
Tecomet Inc ....B 517 882-4311
Lansing *(G-9900)*
▲ **Terumo Crdvscular Systems Corp** ....C 734 663-4145
Ann Arbor *(G-683)*
▲ **Terumo Heart Incorporated** ....E 734 663-4145
Ann Arbor *(G-684)*
Tesma Instruments LLC ....G 517 940-1362
Howell *(G-8528)*
Thompson Surgical Instrs Inc ....E 231 922-0177
Traverse City *(G-16857)*
Thompson Surgical Instrs Inc ....G 231 922-5169
Traverse City *(G-16858)*
Thompson Surgical Instrs Inc ....G 231 922-5169
Traverse City *(G-16859)*
Thoratec LLC ....C 734 827-7422
Ann Arbor *(G-690)*
Tiger Neuroscience LLC ....G 872 903-1904
Muskegon *(G-11932)*
Tilco Inc ....G 248 644-0901
Suttons Bay *(G-16346)*
TMJ Manufacturing LLC ....G 248 987-7857
Farmington Hills *(G-5402)*
Trelleborg Sealing Solutions ....D 231 264-0087
Elk Rapids *(G-5030)*
Truform Machine Inc ....E 517 782-8523
Jackson *(G-9025)*
TSC Group Inc ....G 269 544-9966
Springfield *(G-15878)*
Tulip US Holdings Inc ....E 517 694-2300
Holt *(G-8336)*
Versah LLC ....G 844 711-5585
Jackson *(G-9031)*
Viant Medical LLC ....E 616 643-5200
Grand Rapids *(G-7315)*
Virotech Biomaterials Inc ....G 313 421-1648
Warren *(G-18056)*
Vital Concepts Inc ....G 616 954-2890
Grand Rapids *(G-7320)*
Warmilu LLC ....G 855 927-6458
Ann Arbor *(G-713)*
Wright & Filippis LLC ....F 313 386-3330
Lincoln Park *(G-10058)*
Wright & Filippis LLC ....F 248 336-8460
Detroit *(G-3968)*
Wysong Medical Corporation ....F 989 631-0009
Midland *(G-11424)*

3842 Orthopedic, Prosthetic & Surgical Appliances/Splys

3dm Source Inc ....F 616 647-9513
Grand Rapids *(G-6405)*
Aactus Inc ....G 734 425-1212
Livonia *(G-10096)*
Able Entities LLC ....F 313 422-9555
Detroit *(G-3980)*
▲ **Abretec Group LLC** ....E 248 591-4000
Royal Oak *(G-14503)*
Accurate Safety Distrs Inc ....G 989 695-6446
Freeland *(G-6017)*
Agelessmage Fcial Asthtics LLC ....G 269 998-5547
Farmington Hills *(G-5161)*
Air Supply Inc ....G 586 773-6600
Warren *(G-17694)*
American Prosthetic Institute ....G 517 349-3130
Okemos *(G-12655)*
Americandiecast Releasants ....G 810 714-1964
Fenton *(G-5450)*
◆ **Amigo Mobility Intl Inc** ....D 989 777-0910
Bridgeport *(G-1914)*
Andersen Eye Prosthetics LLC ....G 989 249-1030
Detroit *(G-4020)*
Assistive Technology Mich Inc ....G 248 348-7161
Novi *(G-12367)*
Audionet America Inc ....F 586 944-0043
Clinton Township *(G-3175)*
Auric Enterprises Inc ....G 231 882-7251
Beulah *(G-1652)*
Autocam Med DVC Holdings LLC ....G 616 541-8080
Kentwood *(G-9447)*
Autocam Medical Devices LLC ....E 877 633-8080
Grand Rapids *(G-6482)*
Avasure Holdings Inc ....E 616 301-0129
Belmont *(G-1500)*
◆ **Avon Protection Systems Inc** ....C 231 779-6200
Cadillac *(G-2314)*
Axiobionics ....G 734 327-2946
Ann Arbor *(G-391)*
B B Wheelchair Services ....G 906 281-7202
Hancock *(G-7615)*
Becker Oregon Inc ....E 248 588-7480
Troy *(G-16969)*
▲ **Becker Orthopedic Appliance Co** ....D 248 588-7480
Troy *(G-16970)*
Beltone Skoric Hearng Aid Cntr ....G 906 379-0606
Sault Sainte Marie *(G-15087)*
Beltone Skoric Hearng Aid Cntr ....G 906 553-4660
Escanaba *(G-5061)*
Binson-Becker Inc ....F 888 246-7667
Center Line *(G-2680)*
Bio Cmmunication Solutions LLC ....G 616 502-0238
Spring Lake *(G-15805)*
Biocomsolutions LLC ....G 616 502-0238
Spring Lake *(G-15806)*
Biopro Inc ....E 810 982-7777
Port Huron *(G-13458)*
Bms Great Lakes LLC ....G 248 390-1598
Lake Orion *(G-9588)*
Bremer Prosthetic Design Inc ....G 810 733-3375
Flint *(G-5660)*
Bremer Prosthetics LLC ....G 989 249-9400
Saginaw *(G-14620)*
Bulletsafe Bulletproof Vests ....G 248 457-6877
Troy *(G-16987)*
Carlson Technology Inc ....G 248 476-0013
Livonia *(G-10147)*
◆ **Central Lake Armor Express Inc** ....C 231 544-6090
Central Lake *(G-2691)*
Clinton River Medical Pdts LLC ....G 248 289-1825
Auburn Hills *(G-844)*
College Park Industries Inc ....E 586 294-7950
Warren *(G-17760)*
Curbell Plastics Inc ....G 734 513-0531
Livonia *(G-10170)*
Danmar Products Inc ....E 734 761-1990
Ann Arbor *(G-443)*
▲ **David Epstein Inc** ....F 248 542-0802
Ferndale *(G-5539)*
Davis Dental Laboratory ....G 616 261-9191
Wyoming *(G-18865)*
Davismade Inc ....F 810 743-5262
Flint *(G-5684)*
Ever-Flex Inc ....E 313 389-2060
Lincoln Park *(G-10046)*
First Response Med Sups LLC ....F 313 731-2554
Dearborn *(G-3840)*
Gipson Fabrications ....G 616 245-7331
Wyoming *(G-18874)*
Greater Lansing Orthotic Clini ....G 517 337-0856
Lansing *(G-9845)*
Gresham Driving Aids Inc ....F 248 624-1533
Wixom *(G-18672)*
Hackley Health Ventures Inc ....G 231 728-5720
Muskegon *(G-11834)*
Hanger Prsthetcs & Ortho Inc ....F 517 394-5850
Lansing *(G-9851)*
Hear USA ....G 734 525-3900
Livonia *(G-10238)*
Hi-Tech Optical Inc ....E 989 799-9390
Saginaw *(G-14663)*
Hi-Trac Industries Inc ....G 810 625-7193
Linden *(G-10063)*
Hosmer ....G 248 541-9829
Madison Heights *(G-10741)*
Howmedica Osteonics Corp ....G 269 389-8959
Portage *(G-13566)*
J & K Spratt Enterprises Inc ....D 517 439-5010
Hillsdale *(G-7938)*
▲ **Jacquart Fabric Products Inc** ....C 906 932-1339
Ironwood *(G-8765)*
James Glove & Supply ....F 810 733-5780
Flint *(G-5718)*
Landra Prsthtics Orthotics Inc ....G 586 294-7188
Saint Clair Shores *(G-14868)*
Landra Prsthtics Orthotics Inc ....G 734 281-8144
Southgate *(G-15753)*
Luma Laser and Medi Spa ....G 248 817-5499
Bloomfield Hills *(G-1833)*
Mask Makers LLC ....G 313 790-1784
South Lyon *(G-15446)*
▲ **McKeon Products Inc** ....E 586 427-7560
Warren *(G-17922)*
Medtronic Inc ....G 616 643-5200
Grand Rapids *(G-6976)*
Mercy Health Partners ....E 231 672-4886
Muskegon *(G-11867)*
Metro Medical Eqp Mfg Inc ....E 734 522-8400
Livonia *(G-10313)*
Micro Engineering Inc ....G 616 534-9681
Byron Center *(G-2285)*
Mll Disposition Inc ....E 616 554-9696
Grand Rapids *(G-7009)*
▲ **Miller Technical Services Inc** ....F 734 207-3159
Plymouth *(G-13243)*
Mount Clemens Orthopedic Appls ....G 586 463-3600
Clinton Township *(G-3305)*
Noir Medical Technologies LLC ....F 248 486-3760
South Lyon *(G-15450)*
Northwest Orthotics-Prosthetic ....G 248 477-1443
Novi *(G-12491)*
O and P Sparton ....G 517 220-4960
East Lansing *(G-4907)*
Oakland Orthopedic Appls Inc ....F 989 893-7544
Bay City *(G-1384)*
Obsolete LLC ....G 616 843-0351
Lowell *(G-10512)*
Orthopaedic Associates Mich ....D 616 459-7101
Grand Rapids *(G-7063)*
Orthotic Shop Inc ....G 800 309-0412
Shelby Township *(G-15294)*
Out On A Limb Playhouses ....G 616 502-4251
Grand Haven *(G-6341)*
P & O Services Inc ....G 248 809-3072
Southfield *(G-15670)*
Paul W Reed DDS ....G 231 347-4145
Petoskey *(G-13012)*
▲ **Performance Fabrics Inc** ....C 616 459-4144
Grand Rapids *(G-7079)*
▲ **Pharmaceutical Specialties LLC** ....F 269 382-6402
Galesburg *(G-6081)*
Plasma Biolife Services L P ....G 616 667-0264
Grandville *(G-7409)*
Porex Technologies Corp ....E 989 865-8200
Saint Charles *(G-14807)*
Preferred Products Inc ....F 248 255-0200
Commerce Township *(G-3565)*
Prosthetic & Implant Dentistry ....G 248 254-3945
Farmington Hills *(G-5355)*
Prosthetic Center Inc ....G 517 372-7007
Dimondale *(G-4764)*
Radiolgical Fabrication Design ....G 810 632-6000
Howell *(G-8506)*
Regents of The University Mich ....E 734 973-2400
Ann Arbor *(G-638)*
S and L Associates ....G 616 608-6583
Grandville *(G-7416)*
▲ **Set Liquidation Inc** ....D 517 694-2300
Holt *(G-8331)*
Shock-Tek LLC ....G 313 886-0530
Saint Clair Shores *(G-14883)*
Signal Medical Corporation ....F 810 364-7070
Marysville *(G-11099)*
Sigvaris Inc ....E 616 741-4281
Holland *(G-8196)*
Skoric Hearing Aid Center LLC ....G 248 961-4329
Saginaw *(G-14758)*
Skyline Window Cleaning Inc ....E 616 895-4143
Allendale *(G-228)*
Springer Prsthtic Orthtic Svcs ....G 517 337-0300
Lansing *(G-9896)*

SIC SECTION38 MEASURING, ANALYZING AND CONTROLLING INSTRUMENTS; PHOTOGRAPHIC, MEDICAL AN38 MEASURING, ANALYZING

Standing Company .... F 989 746-9100
Saginaw *(G-14766)*
Steele Supply Co .... G 269 983-0920
Saint Joseph *(G-14964)*
Strive Orthtics Prsthetics LLC .... G 586 803-4325
Sterling Heights *(G-16196)*
Stryker Australia LLC .... C 269 385-2600
Portage *(G-13612)*
Stryker Corporation .... E 269 389-3741
Portage *(G-13614)*
Stryker Corporation .... E 269 385-2600
Portage *(G-13615)*
Stryker Customs Brokers LLC .... F 269 389-2300
Portage *(G-13617)*
Stryker Far East Inc .... A 269 385-2600
Portage *(G-13618)*
Stryker Sales LLC .... E 269 323-1027
Portage *(G-13621)*
Studio One Midwest Inc .... F 269 962-3475
Battle Creek *(G-1302)*
Tesa Tape Inc .... G 616 785-6970
Walker *(G-17654)*
Tesa Tape Inc .... G 616 887-3107
Sparta *(G-15786)*
▼ Thierica Equipment Corporation .... E 616 453-6570
Grand Rapids *(G-7259)*
Trackcore Inc .... F 616 632-2222
Grand Rapids *(G-7268)*
▲ Trulife Inc .... E 800 492-1088
Jackson *(G-9026)*
Twin Cities Orthotic & Prosthe .... G 269 428-2910
Saint Joseph *(G-14967)*
Ultralight Prosthetics Inc .... G 313 538-8500
Redford *(G-13781)*
Um Orthotics Pros Cntr .... G 734 764-3100
Ann Arbor *(G-704)*
Warwick Mas & Equipment Co .... G 810 966-3431
Port Huron *(G-13537)*
Wheelchair Barn .... G 231 730-1647
Muskegon *(G-11944)*
Wright & Filippis Inc .... G 313 832-5020
Detroit *(G-4692)*
Wright & Filippis LLC .... F 517 484-2624
Lansing *(G-9906)*
Wright & Filippis LLC .... F 586 756-4020
Warren *(G-18073)*
Wright & Filippis LLC .... F 313 386-3330
Lincoln Park *(G-10058)*
Wright & Filippis LLC .... F 248 336-8460
Detroit *(G-3968)*
XYZ McHine Tl Fabrications Inc .... G 517 482-3668
Lansing *(G-9796)*
Zimmer - Lieffring Inc .... F 734 953-1630
Novi *(G-12574)*

3843 Dental Eqpt & Splys

Akervall Technologies Inc .... F 800 444-0570
Saline *(G-14999)*
Aluwax Dental Products Co Inc .... G 616 895-4385
Allendale *(G-213)*
Andrew J Reisterer D D S Pllc .... G 231 845-8989
Ludington *(G-10526)*
Avo Dental Supplies LLC .... G 586 585-1210
Roseville *(G-14378)*
Axsys Inc .... E 248 926-8810
Wixom *(G-18616)*
Biotec Incorporated .... D 616 772-2133
Zeeland *(G-18999)*
David R Lacharite Lmsw .... G 517 347-0988
Okemos *(G-12663)*
Dental Art Laboratories Inc .... D 517 485-2200
Lansing *(G-9689)*
▲ E C Moore Company .... E 313 581-7878
Dearborn *(G-3832)*
End Product Results LLC .... F 586 585-1210
Roseville *(G-14405)*
Kerr Corporation .... B 734 946-7800
Romulus *(G-14294)*
Ktr Dental Lab & Pdts LLC .... F 248 224-9158
Southfield *(G-15622)*
Liquid Otc LLC .... G 248 214-7771
Commerce Township *(G-3551)*
Mary Palaszek Dr .... G 616 453-2255
Grand Rapids *(G-6963)*
Microdental Laboratories Inc .... G 877 711-8778
Troy *(G-17259)*
New Image Dental P C .... G 586 727-1100
Richmond *(G-13843)*
Pdl LLC .... G 810 844-3209
Howell *(G-8492)*
Phoenix Dental Inc .... G 810 750-2328
Fenton *(G-5495)*
Ranir LLC .... E 616 957-7790
Kentwood *(G-9475)*
▲ Ranir LLC .... B 616 698-8880
Grand Rapids *(G-7139)*
Ranir Global Holdings LLC .... A 616 698-8880
Grand Rapids *(G-7140)*
Select Dental Equipment LLC .... G 734 667-1194
Canton *(G-2523)*
Tokusen Hytech Inc .... C 269 685-1768
Plainwell *(G-13099)*
Visual Chimera .... F 586 585-1210
Eastpointe *(G-4948)*
Voco America Inc .... G 248 568-0964
Howell *(G-8540)*

3844 X-ray Apparatus & Tubes

I D Medical Systems Inc .... G 616 698-0535
Grand Rapids *(G-6828)*
Kgf Enterprise Inc .... G 586 430-4182
Columbus *(G-3500)*

3845 Electromedical & Electrotherapeutic Apparatus

American Lazer Centers .... G 248 798-6552
Clinton Township *(G-3166)*
Benesh Corporation .... F 734 244-4143
Monroe *(G-11532)*
Bieri Hearing Instruments Inc .... G 989 793-2701
Saginaw *(G-14616)*
Cerephex Corporation .... G 517 719-0414
Bancroft *(G-1126)*
Eaton Industries Inc .... G 734 428-0000
Ann Arbor *(G-464)*
Endoscopic Solutions .... F 248 625-4055
Clarkston *(G-3032)*
Endra Life Sciences Inc .... F 734 335-0468
Ann Arbor *(G-474)*
▲ Gelman Sciences Inc .... C 734 665-0651
Ann Arbor *(G-496)*
Gys Tech LLC .... F 269 385-2600
Portage *(G-13563)*
Healthcare Drble Med Eqpmnts L .... G 734 975-6668
Ann Arbor *(G-510)*
Heart Sync Inc .... F 734 213-5530
Ann Arbor *(G-512)*
Helping Hands Therapy .... G 313 492-6007
Southfield *(G-15592)*
Iha Vsclar Endvsclar Spcalists .... G 734 712-8150
Ypsilanti *(G-18953)*
Medtronic Inc .... G 616 643-5200
Grand Rapids *(G-6976)*
▲ Merlin Simulation Inc .... G 703 560-7203
Dexter *(G-4745)*
Metrex Research LLC .... D 734 947-6700
Romulus *(G-14303)*
Mll Disposition Inc .... E 616 554-9696
Grand Rapids *(G-7009)*
Omo Enterprises LLC .... G 248 392-6397
Redford *(G-13751)*
Oncofusion Therapeutics Inc .... F 248 361-3341
Northville *(G-12249)*
Rofin-Sinar Technologies LLC .... G 734 416-0206
Plymouth *(G-13290)*
Sobaks Pharmacy Inc .... F 989 725-2785
Owosso *(G-12856)*
▲ Terumo Crdvscular Systems Corp .... C 734 663-4145
Ann Arbor *(G-683)*
Thoratec LLC .... C 734 827-7422
Ann Arbor *(G-690)*
Uv Partners Inc .... G 888 277-2596
Grand Haven *(G-6376)*
Xoran Holdings LLC .... G 734 418-5108
Ann Arbor *(G-718)*
Xoran Technologies LLC .... D 734 663-7194
Ann Arbor *(G-719)*

3851 Ophthalmic Goods

Art Optical Contact Lens Inc .... C 616 453-1888
Grand Rapids *(G-6471)*
Council For Edctl Trvl US Amer .... E 949 940-1140
Grand Rapids *(G-6609)*
Delta Optical Supply Inc .... G 248 628-3977
Oxford *(G-12882)*
Diagnostic Instruments Inc .... E 586 731-6000
Sterling Heights *(G-15986)*
Fairway Optical Inc .... G 231 744-6168
Muskegon *(G-11815)*
Flint Optical Company Inc .... G 810 235-4607
Flint *(G-5701)*
▲ General Scientific Corporation .... E 734 996-9200
Ann Arbor *(G-498)*
Hi-Tech Optical Inc .... E 989 799-9390
Saginaw *(G-14663)*
▲ Inland Diamond Products Co .... E 248 585-1762
Madison Heights *(G-10746)*
Luxottica of America Inc .... G 517 349-0784
Okemos *(G-12673)*
Main Street Spectacles LLC .... G 231 429-7234
Mc Bain *(G-11185)*
▲ McKeon Products Inc .... E 586 427-7560
Warren *(G-17922)*
Noir Laser Company LLC .... E 800 521-9746
Milford *(G-11478)*
Noir Medical Technologies LLC .... F 734 769-5565
Milford *(G-11479)*
Noir Medical Technologies LLC .... F 248 486-3760
South Lyon *(G-15450)*
Perfect Eyes Optical .... G 248 275-7861
Detroit *(G-4517)*
▲ Performance Fabrics Inc .... C 616 459-4144
Grand Rapids *(G-7079)*
Rx Optical Laboratories Inc .... G 269 349-7627
Kalamazoo *(G-9325)*
Rx Optical Laboratories Inc .... G 269 965-5106
Battle Creek *(G-1291)*
Rx Optical Laboratories Inc .... D 269 342-5958
Kalamazoo *(G-9324)*
Rx-Rite Optical Co .... G 586 293-8888
Fraser *(G-5990)*
Tri State Optical Inc .... G 517 279-2701
Coldwater *(G-3458)*

3861 Photographic Eqpt & Splys

6df Research LLC .... G 906 281-1170
Houghton *(G-8379)*
Accuform Prtg & Graphics Inc .... F 313 271-5600
Detroit *(G-3981)*
American Information Services .... F 248 399-4848
Berkley *(G-1620)*
Arts Crafts Hardware .... F 586 231-5344
Mount Clemens *(G-11627)*
Cognisys Inc .... G 231 943-2425
Traverse City *(G-16656)*
Compatible Laser Products Inc .... F 810 629-0459
Fenton *(G-5466)*
DOT Bridge Inc .... G 248 921-7363
South Lyon *(G-15433)*
▲ Douthitt Corporation .... E 313 259-1565
Detroit *(G-4189)*
Douthitt Corporation .... F 313 259-1565
Detroit *(G-4190)*
Envirodrone Inc .... G 226 344-5614
Detroit *(G-4212)*
Essential Photo Gear .... G 502 244-2888
Rogers City *(G-14210)*
Former Company LLC .... G 248 202-0473
Detroit *(G-4244)*
General Dynamics Mission .... A 530 271-2500
Rochester Hills *(G-14021)*
▲ General Dynmics Globl Imging T .... A 248 293-2929
Rochester Hills *(G-14022)*
Just Rite Bracket .... G 248 477-0592
Farmington Hills *(G-5277)*
Kistler Instrument Corp .... G 248 489-1090
Farmington Hills *(G-5282)*
Laser Connection LLC .... E 989 662-4022
Auburn *(G-768)*
Lasers Resource Inc .... E 616 554-5555
Grand Rapids *(G-6930)*
Luxury Richland LLc .... F 269 222-7979
Grand Rapids *(G-6953)*
Macmichigan Inc .... G 248 613-6372
Novi *(G-12468)*
Nationwide Laser Technologies .... G 248 488-0155
Farmington Hills *(G-5331)*
Northern Mich Wldlife Art Fram .... F 989 340-1272
Lachine *(G-9532)*
▲ Orion Test Systems Inc .... D 248 373-9097
Auburn Hills *(G-990)*
Osowet Collections Inc .... G 313 844-8171
Detroit *(G-4501)*
Precision Printer Services Inc .... E 269 384-5725
Portage *(G-13594)*
Veronica K LLC .... G 248 251-5144
Clinton Township *(G-3384)*
▲ X-Rite Incorporated .... C 616 803-2100
Grand Rapids *(G-7353)*

SIC

Employee Codes: A=Over 500 employees, B=251-500
C=101-250, D=51-100, E=20-50, F=10-19, G=3-9
2022 Harris Michigan
Industrial Directory
897

3873 Watch & Clock Devices & Parts

Ausable Woodworking Co Inc ....E 989 348-7086
 Frederic (G-6014)
Eliason Corporation ....E 269 621-2100
 Hartford (G-7763)
▼ Ernst Benz Company LLC ....G 248 203-2323
 Birmingham (G-1727)
◆ Howard Miller Company ....B 616 772-9131
 Zeeland (G-19040)
◆ Lumichron Inc ....G 616 245-8888
 Grand Rapids (G-6952)
National Time and Signal Corp ....E 248 291-5867
 Oak Park (G-12631)
Quality Time Components ....F 231 947-1071
 Traverse City (G-16810)
▲ Shinola/Detroit LLC ....C 888 304-2534
 Detroit (G-4591)

39 MISCELLANEOUS MANUFACTURING INDUSTRIES

3911 Jewelry: Precious Metal

Abracadabra Jewelry ....G 734 994-4848
 Ann Arbor (G-345)
Alexander J Bongiorno Inc ....G 248 689-7766
 Troy (G-16920)
Amalgamations Ltd ....G 248 879-7345
 Troy (G-16930)
Au Enterprises Inc ....F 248 544-9700
 Berkley (G-1621)
Aurum Design Inc ....G 248 651-9040
 Rochester (G-13892)
Bauble Patch Inc ....G 616 785-1100
 Comstock Park (G-3589)
Bednarsh Mrris Jwly Design Mfg ....F 248 671-0087
 Bloomfield (G-1781)
Birmingham Jewelry Inc ....G 586 939-5100
 Sterling Heights (G-15946)
C I I Ltd ....G 248 585-9905
 Troy (G-16989)
C T & T Inc ....E 248 623-9422
 Waterford (G-18107)
◆ Combine International Inc ....C 248 585-9900
 Troy (G-17019)
Daves Diamond Inc ....G 248 693-2482
 Lake Orion (G-9602)
Discount Jewelry Center Inc ....G 734 266-8200
 Westland (G-18364)
HL Manufacturing Inc ....F 586 731-2800
 Utica (G-17502)
Hunters Jewelry Repair Ctr Inc ....G 313 892-7621
 Detroit (G-4309)
Joseph A Dimaggio ....G 313 881-5353
 Grosse Pointe Woods (G-7569)
Kayayan Hayk Jewelry Mfg Co ....E 248 626-3060
 Bloomfield (G-1782)
La Gold Mine Inc ....G 517 540-1050
 Brighton (G-2018)
LLC Stahl Cross ....G 810 688-2505
 Lapeer (G-9943)
▲ Michels Inc ....F 313 441-3620
 Dearborn (G-3872)
Milford Jewelers Inc ....G 248 676-0721
 Milford (G-11471)
Mount-N-Repair ....G 248 647-8670
 Birmingham (G-1738)
Newell Brands Inc ....F 734 284-2528
 Taylor (G-16452)
Novus Corporation ....F 248 545-8600
 Warren (G-17948)
Orin Jewelers Inc ....F 734 422-7030
 Garden City (G-6105)
▲ Pure & Simple Solutions LLC ....G 248 398-4600
 Troy (G-17320)
Rebel Nell L3c ....G 716 640-4267
 Detroit (G-4557)
Seoul International Inc ....G 586 275-2494
 Sterling Heights (G-16170)
Talisman ....G 616 458-1391
 Grand Rapids (G-7248)
▲ Terryberry Company LLC ....F 616 458-1391
 Grand Rapids (G-7254)
▲ Touchstone Distributing Inc ....G 517 669-8200
 Dewitt (G-4718)
Tva Kane Inc ....E 248 946-4670
 Novi (G-12560)
Wattsson & Wattsson Jewelers ....G 906 228-5775
 Marquette (G-11049)

3914 Silverware, Plated & Stainless Steel Ware

Carry Manufacturing Inc ....G 989 672-2779
 Caro (G-2567)
Collectors Zone ....G 517 788-8498
 Jackson (G-8847)
H M Products Inc ....G 313 875-5148
 Detroit (G-4288)
Infra Corporation ....F 248 623-0400
 Waterford (G-18129)
McCallum Fabricating LLC ....F 586 784-5555
 Allenton (G-231)
▲ Michigan Plaques & Awards Inc ....E 248 398-6400
 Berkley (G-1632)
Mp Acquisition LLC ....D 800 362-8491
 Madison Heights (G-10784)
▼ Quicktrophy LLC ....G 906 228-2604
 Marquette (G-11043)
Rivore Metals LLC ....G 800 248-1250
 Troy (G-17334)
Samco Industries LLC ....F 586 447-3900
 Roseville (G-14476)

3915 Jewelers Findings & Lapidary Work

Dtown Grillz LLC ....G 734 624-9657
 Oak Park (G-12606)
Grandkids Edcted Motivated Gem ....G 313 539-7330
 Detroit (G-4273)
Jostens Inc ....G 734 308-3879
 Ada (G-24)
Kevin Wheat & Assoc Ltd ....G 517 349-0101
 Okemos (G-12671)
L N T Inc ....G 248 347-6006
 Novi (G-12461)
Trenton Jewelers Ltd ....G 734 676-0188
 Trenton (G-16896)

3931 Musical Instruments

Alf Enterprises Inc ....G 734 665-2012
 Ann Arbor (G-360)
Awesome Musical Instrs LLC ....G 734 941-2927
 Romulus (G-14252)
▲ Black Swamp Percussion LLC ....G 800 557-0988
 Zeeland (G-19001)
Brian M Fowler Pipe Organs ....G 517 485-3748
 Eaton Rapids (G-4956)
Ferrees Tools Inc ....E 269 965-0511
 Battle Creek (G-1230)
Ghf Corp ....G 269 968-3351
 Springfield (G-15866)
◆ Ghs Corporation ....E 269 968-3351
 Springfield (G-15867)
GHS Corporation ....D 800 388-4447
 Springfield (G-15868)
Grip Studios ....G 248 757-0796
 Plymouth (G-13181)
◆ Harman Becker Auto Systems Inc ....B 248 785-2361
 Farmington Hills (G-5257)
Heritage Guitar Inc ....F 269 385-5721
 Kalamazoo (G-9216)
J Naylor LLC ....G 248 227-8250
 Troy (G-17179)
▲ Klingler Consulting & Mfg ....F 810 765-3700
 Marine City (G-10961)
Kyoei Electronics America Inc ....G 248 773-3690
 Novi (G-12460)
Lesson Rooms ....G 248 677-1341
 Royal Oak (G-14556)
Rebeats ....F 989 463-4757
 Alma (G-254)
Rt Swanson Inc ....G 517 627-4955
 Grand Ledge (G-6398)
School of Rock Canton ....G 734 845-7448
 Canton (G-2521)
Wlw Musical ....G 248 956-3060
 Commerce Township (G-3582)

3942 Dolls & Stuffed Toys

Auswella LLC ....G 248 630-5965
 Wixom (G-18615)
Marshal E Hyman and Associates ....G 248 643-0642
 Troy (G-17239)
Mr Sogs Creatures ....G 901 413-0291
 Farmington Hills (G-5328)

3944 Games, Toys & Children's Vehicles

Abbotts Magic Manufacturing Co ....G 269 432-3235
 Colon (G-3486)
▲ American Models ....G 248 437-6800
 Whitmore Lake (G-18519)
◆ American Plastic Toys Inc ....C 248 624-4881
 Walled Lake (G-17663)
American Plastic Toys Inc ....D 989 685-2455
 Rose City (G-14359)
Ann Williams Group LLC ....G 248 977-5831
 Bloomfield Hills (G-1798)
Designs By D LLC ....G 313 629-3617
 Highland Park (G-7903)
Dog Might LLC ....F 734 679-0646
 Ann Arbor (G-455)
Eca Educational Services Inc ....D 248 669-7170
 Commerce Township (G-3525)
Fourth Ave Birkenstock ....G 734 663-1644
 Ann Arbor (G-493)
Hampton Company Inc ....G 517 765-2222
 Burlington (G-2209)
Lejanae Designs LLC ....G 248 621-3677
 Southfield (G-15634)
▲ Mac Enterprises Inc ....F 313 846-4567
 Manchester (G-10885)
Melissa Fowler ....G 818 447-9903
 Fenton (G-5491)
▲ Merdel Game Manufacturing Co ....G 231 845-1263
 Ludington (G-10544)
Meteor Web Marketing Inc ....F 734 822-4999
 Ann Arbor (G-570)
National Ambucs Inc ....G 231 798-4244
 Norton Shores (G-12315)
Pauri Retail Store LLC ....F 415 980-1525
 Detroit (G-4508)
Promoquip Inc ....G 989 287-6211
 Lakeview (G-9645)
Puzzle Escape ....G 313 645-6405
 Detroit (G-4543)
▲ Shelti Inc ....F 989 893-1739
 Bay City (G-1401)
Shields Classic Toys ....G 888 806-2632
 Saline (G-15039)
Sly Fox Prints LLC ....G 616 900-9677
 Cedar Springs (G-2661)
Tdw Custom Apparel & More LLC ....G 248 934-0312
 Detroit (G-4626)
Troy Puzzles LLC ....G 248 828-3153
 Troy (G-17401)
Unique-Chardan Inc ....D 419 636-6900
 Auburn Hills (G-1070)

3949 Sporting & Athletic Goods, NEC

▲ 2-N-1 Grips Inc ....F 800 530-9878
 Chesterfield (G-2833)
305 N 3rd LLC ....G 517 404-1212
 Howell (G-8421)
Accessories & Specialties Inc ....G 989 235-3331
 Crystal (G-3739)
Aerospace America Inc ....E 989 684-2121
 Bay City (G-1319)
Assenmacher Lightweight Cycles ....G 810 232-2994
 Flint (G-5645)
Assra ....F 906 225-1828
 Marquette (G-11005)
B4 Sports Inc ....E 248 454-9700
 Bloomfield Hills (G-1802)
Bbp Investment Holdings LLC ....B 231 725-4966
 Muskegon (G-11777)
Bitzenburger Machine & Tool ....G 517 627-8433
 Grand Ledge (G-6386)
◆ Bohning Company Ltd ....E 231 229-4247
 Lake City (G-9545)
Boomerang Enterprises Inc ....G 269 547-9715
 Mattawan (G-11163)
Boomerang Exhibits ....G 315 525-6973
 Grand Rapids (G-6522)
Boomerang Retro & Relics ....G 906 362-7876
 Marquette (G-11010)
Boomerangs Gift Gallery ....G 248 228-0314
 Lapeer (G-9915)
◆ Brunswick Bowling Products LLC ....B 231 725-4966
 Muskegon (G-11784)
Brunswick Indoor Recreation ....E 231 725-4764
 Muskegon (G-11785)
Buck Stop Lure Company Inc ....G 989 762-5091
 Stanton (G-15899)
Bucks Sports Products Inc ....G 763 229-1331
 Gladstone (G-6175)
Canam Undrwtr Hockey Gear LLC ....G 906 399-7857
 Rapid River (G-13682)
Carbon Impact Inc ....G 231 929-8152
 Traverse City (G-16639)

Chiipss G 248 345-6112
Detroit *(G-4093)*

Container Specialties Inc E 989 728-4231
Hale *(G-7588)*

◆ **Conway Products Corporation** E 616 698-2601
Grand Rapids *(G-6603)*

▲ **Crl Inc** E 906 428-3710
Gladstone *(G-6177)*

Dave Lewishcky Fantsy Camp G 248 328-0891
Holly *(G-8265)*

Delta 6 LLC G 248 778-6414
Livonia *(G-10178)*

▲ **Discraft Inc** E 248 624-2250
Wixom *(G-18645)*

Double Six Sports Complex F 989 762-5342
Stanton *(G-15900)*

▲ **Dreamweaver Lure Company Inc** F 231 843-3652
Ludington *(G-10535)*

Dunhams Athleisure Corporation G 248 658-1382
Madison Heights *(G-10713)*

▲ **Ed Cumings Inc** E 810 736-0130
Flint *(G-5693)*

Elite Defense LLC F 734 424-9955
Clawson *(G-3096)*

Eppinger Mfg Co F 313 582-3205
Dearborn *(G-3838)*

Evolve Longboards USA LLC G 616 915-3876
Grand Rapids *(G-6690)*

Excalibur Crossbow Inc G 810 937-5864
Port Huron *(G-13476)*

Family Trdtons Tree Stands LLC G 517 543-3926
Charlotte *(G-2753)*

Fastball LLC G 810 955-8510
Davison *(G-3780)*

Fish On Sports Inc G 231 342-5231
Interlochen *(G-8683)*

Fishall Lures G 231 821-9020
Twin Lake *(G-17467)*

Forche Rd Welding G 517 920-3473
Blissfield *(G-1764)*

Forest View Lanes LLC E 734 847-4915
Temperance *(G-16531)*

▲ **G5 Outdoors LLC** G 866 456-8836
Memphis *(G-11212)*

Garneau Baits LLC G 616 676-0186
Ada *(G-18)*

Gb Sportz G 734 604-8919
Ann Arbor *(G-495)*

Golf Store G 517 347-8733
Okemos *(G-12669)*

Good Do Up Skateboards G 248 301-5188
White Lake *(G-18458)*

Grapentin Specialties Inc G 810 724-0636
Imlay City *(G-8634)*

Grayling Outdoor Products Inc F 989 348-2956
Grayling *(G-7462)*

Great Northern Quiver Co LLC G 269 838-5437
Nashville *(G-11954)*

Gw Fishing Lures Inc G 989 684-6431
Bay City *(G-1364)*

Hl Outdoors G 989 422-3264
Houghton Lake *(G-8399)*

Home Chef Ltd G 734 468-2544
Westland *(G-18384)*

▲ **Howies Hockey Incorporated** G 616 643-0594
Grand Rapids *(G-6822)*

In The Zone Sports Camps G 616 889-5571
Grand Rapids *(G-6839)*

▲ **Invis Inc** G 517 279-7585
Coldwater *(G-3439)*

Jon Morris G 269 967-2862
Marshall *(G-11063)*

K & E Tackle Inc F 269 945-4496
Hastings *(G-7802)*

Kaycee Lux LLC G 248 461-7117
Farmington Hills *(G-5279)*

Keller Sports-Optics G 248 894-0960
Farmington *(G-5141)*

Kennedy Game Calls LLC G 269 870-5001
Kalamazoo *(G-9253)*

Kennedy Sales Inc G 586 228-9390
Clinton Township *(G-3273)*

Killer Paint Ball G 248 491-0088
South Lyon *(G-15441)*

▲ **King Par LLC** D 810 732-2470
Flushing *(G-5810)*

Legends Game Call Co G 517 499-6962
Napoleon *(G-11953)*

Level 6 G 231 755-7000
Muskegon *(G-11860)*

Liebner Enterprises LLC G 231 331-3076
Cheboygan *(G-2791)*

Lone Wolf Custom Bows G 989 735-3358
Glennie *(G-6213)*

Longshot Golf Inc G 586 764-9847
Washington *(G-18083)*

M-22 Challenge G 231 392-2212
Traverse City *(G-16750)*

M-B-M Manufacturing Inc G 231 924-9614
Fremont *(G-6047)*

Malibu Skateboards LLC G 616 243-3154
Grand Rapids *(G-6957)*

Marhar Snowboards LLC G 616 432-3104
Fruitport *(G-6066)*

▲ **Mason Tackle Company** E 810 631-4571
Otisville *(G-12783)*

Maxair Trampoline G 616 929-0882
Grand Rapids *(G-6968)*

▲ **McClure Tables Inc** G 616 662-5974
Jenison *(G-9061)*

McKae Group LLC E 313 564-5100
Livonia *(G-10307)*

▲ **McKeon Products Inc** E 586 427-7560
Warren *(G-17922)*

Medalist G 269 789-4653
Marshall *(G-11070)*

▲ **Mike Vaughn Custom Sports Inc** E 248 969-8956
Oxford *(G-12903)*

Mitchell Coates D 231 582-5878
Boyne City *(G-1897)*

My Tec-Tronics LLC G 586 218-0118
Brighton *(G-2038)*

My-Can LLC G 989 288-7779
Durand *(G-4843)*

National Credit Corporation F 734 459-8100
West Bloomfield *(G-18302)*

Nipguards LLC G 734 544-4490
Ann Arbor *(G-594)*

Noir Sportswear Corp F 248 607-3615
Oak Park *(G-12634)*

North Coast Golf Company LLC G 810 547-4900
Port Huron *(G-13509)*

North Post Inc G 906 482-5210
Hancock *(G-7622)*

Northern Trading Group LLC G 248 885-8750
Birmingham *(G-1740)*

▲ **Nustep LLC** D 734 769-3939
Ann Arbor *(G-597)*

▲ **O2totes Llc** F 734 730-4472
Saint Clair Shores *(G-14875)*

Orion Hunting Products LLC G 906 563-1230
Norway *(G-12355)*

Outdoor Lines LLC G 616 844-7351
Grand Haven *(G-6342)*

Overkill Research & Dev Labs G 517 768-8155
Jackson *(G-8981)*

Owosso Country Club Pro Shop G 989 723-1470
Owosso *(G-12848)*

Pcs Outdoors G 989 569-3480
Oscoda *(G-12769)*

Penchura LLC F 810 229-6245
Brighton *(G-2050)*

Perfect Expressions G 248 640-1287
Bloomfield Hills *(G-1851)*

Plastisnow LLC G 414 397-1233
Plainwell *(G-13090)*

Play Wright LLC G 616 784-5437
Rockford *(G-14184)*

Pluskate Boarding Company G 248 426-0899
Farmington *(G-5144)*

Predator Products Company G 231 799-8300
Norton Shores *(G-12326)*

▲ **Pro Release Inc** G 810 512-4120
Marine City *(G-10964)*

Pro Shot Basketball Inc G 877 968-3865
Holly *(G-8286)*

Puck Hogs Pro Shop Inc G 419 540-1388
Grosse Pointe Woods *(G-7574)*

▲ **Pull-Buoy Inc** G 586 997-0900
Sterling Heights *(G-16138)*

Qsr Outdoor Products Inc G 989 354-0777
Alpena *(G-314)*

Quality Industries Inc E 517 439-1591
Hillsdale *(G-7944)*

R and T Sporting Clays Inc G 586 215-9861
Harrison Township *(G-7718)*

R W Summers Co G 231 946-7923
Traverse City *(G-16813)*

Ripper Ventures LLC G 248 808-2325
Plymouth *(G-13282)*

Riverfront Cycle Inc G 517 482-8585
Lansing *(G-9888)*

Rochester Sports LLC F 248 608-6000
Rochester Hills *(G-14103)*

Rogers Athletic G 989 386-7393
Clare *(G-2996)*

Rogers Athletic Company Inc E 800 457-5337
Farwell *(G-5427)*

Rolston Hockey Academy LLC G 248 450-5300
Oak Park *(G-12640)*

Royaltees Golf LLC G 517 783-5911
Jackson *(G-9000)*

Seal Bowling Balls LLC G 248 707-6482
Clarkston *(G-3063)*

See Our Designs G 866 431-0025
Royal Oak *(G-14579)*

▲ **Shane Group LLC** G 517 439-4316
Hillsdale *(G-7949)*

Simerson Inc G 989 233-1420
Vassar *(G-17581)*

Slayer Outdoor Products G 517 726-0221
Charlotte *(G-2771)*

Soupcan Inc F 269 381-2101
Galesburg *(G-6084)*

Spieth Anderson USA Lc F 817 536-3366
Lansing *(G-9739)*

Superior Hockey LLC F 906 225-9008
Marquette *(G-11045)*

Supertramp Cstm Trmpline LLC D G 616 634-2010
Grand Rapids *(G-7239)*

▲ **T L V Inc** F 989 773-4362
Mount Pleasant *(G-11744)*

Team Sports Covers LLC G 269 207-0241
Union City *(G-17497)*

▲ **Technique Golf LLC** G 586 758-7807
Wixom *(G-18769)*

Tee Pal LLC G 231 563-3770
Twin Lake *(G-17474)*

Thomson Plastics Inc E 517 545-5026
Howell *(G-8531)*

Thunderdome Media LLC G 800 978-0206
Plymouth *(G-13314)*

Total Tennis LLC G 248 594-1749
Bloomfield Hills *(G-1867)*

Trainingmask LLC F 888 407-7555
Cadillac *(G-2361)*

Two Tracks Bow Co G 989 834-0588
Ovid *(G-12817)*

Unique-Chardan Inc D 419 636-6900
Auburn Hills *(G-1070)*

▲ **United Shield Intl LLC** E 231 933-1179
Traverse City *(G-16873)*

UP Lure Company LLC G 906 249-3526
Marquette *(G-11047)*

Vanishing Point Lures G 260 316-7768
Bronson *(G-2121)*

Warlock Lures G 586 977-1606
Warren *(G-18057)*

▲ **Warrior Sports Inc** C 800 968-7845
Warren *(G-18063)*

Wilderness Treasures F 906 647-4002
Pickford *(G-13032)*

Witchcraft Tape Products Inc D 269 468-3399
Coloma *(G-3485)*

▲ **Xenith LLC** E 866 888-2322
Detroit *(G-4694)*

Y M C A Family Center G 269 428-9622
Saint Joseph *(G-14982)*

3951 Pens & Mechanical Pencils

Carco Inc E 313 925-1053
Detroit *(G-4089)*

Golden Apple G 231 477-5366
Manistee *(G-10901)*

3952 Lead Pencils, Crayons & Artist's Mtrls

E and K Arts and More G 855 285-0320
Pontiac *(G-13363)*

▲ **Mac Enterprises Inc** F 313 846-4567
Manchester *(G-10885)*

▲ **Markerboard People Inc** E 517 372-1666
Lansing *(G-9715)*

Panoplate Lithographics Inc G 269 343-4644
Kalamazoo *(G-9285)*

3953 Marking Devices

All American Embroidery Inc F 734 421-9292
Livonia *(G-10108)*

▲ **Argon Tool Inc** F 248 583-1605
Madison Heights *(G-10672)*

SIC

Borries Mkg Systems Partnr................G....... 734 761-9549
Ann Arbor *(G-404)*
Carco Inc................E....... 313 925-1053
Detroit *(G-4089)*
Collier Enterprise III................G....... 269 503-3402
Sturgis *(G-16284)*
Columbia Marking Tools Inc................E....... 586 949-8400
Chesterfield *(G-2860)*
Detroit Marking Products Corp................F....... 313 838-9760
Canton *(G-2454)*
Events To Envy................G....... 248 841-8400
Rochester *(G-13899)*
F & A Enterprises of Michigan................G....... 906 228-3222
Marquette *(G-11018)*
JL Geisler Sign Company................F....... 586 574-1800
Troy *(G-17187)*
Lakeside Property Services................G....... 863 455-9038
Holland *(G-8122)*
Mark Maker Company Inc................E....... 616 538-6980
Grand Rapids *(G-6959)*
Mark-Pack Inc................E....... 616 837-5400
Coopersville *(G-3691)*
Michigan Shippers Supply Inc................F....... 616 935-6680
Spring Lake *(G-15835)*
Mlh Services LLC................G....... 313 768-4403
Detroit *(G-4462)*
Nelson Paint Co of Mich Inc................G....... 906 774-5566
Kingsford *(G-9514)*
▼ **New Method Steel Stamps Inc**................G....... 586 293-0200
Fraser *(G-5967)*
Rite Mark Stamp Company................F....... 248 391-7600
Auburn Hills *(G-1021)*
Rodzina Industries Inc................G....... 810 235-2341
Flint *(G-5755)*
Rubber Stamps Unlimited Inc................F....... 734 451-7300
Plymouth *(G-13291)*
Stamp-Rite Incorporated................E....... 517 487-5071
Lansing *(G-9741)*
Volk Corporation................G....... 616 940-9900
Northville *(G-12270)*

3955 Carbon Paper & Inked Ribbons

▲ **Cau Acquisition Company LLC**................D....... 989 875-8133
Ithaca *(G-8787)*
Compatible Laser Products Inc................F....... 810 629-0459
Fenton *(G-5466)*
Lps-2 Inc................G....... 313 538-0181
Redford *(G-13742)*
Mikan Corporation................F....... 734 944-9447
Saline *(G-15027)*
Visionit Supplies and Svcs Inc................E....... 313 664-5650
Detroit *(G-4669)*

3961 Costume Jewelry & Novelties

Allymade................G....... 616 813-0591
Lake Odessa *(G-9571)*
Amalgamations Ltd................G....... 248 879-7345
Troy *(G-16930)*
Bead Gallery................F....... 734 663-6800
Ann Arbor *(G-396)*
Bracelet Shack................G....... 312 656-9191
Clarkston *(G-3021)*
Embracelets................G....... 616 719-3545
Grand Rapids *(G-6674)*
HL Manufacturing Inc................F....... 586 731-2800
Utica *(G-17502)*
Homes Bracelet................G....... 231 499-9402
Traverse City *(G-16713)*
Homes Bracelet LLC................G....... 231 463-9808
Traverse City *(G-16714)*
Preusser Jewelers................G....... 616 458-1425
Grand Rapids *(G-7105)*
Rosary Workshop................G....... 906 788-4846
Stephenson *(G-15910)*
Swarovski North America Ltd................G....... 586 226-4420
Clinton Township *(G-3367)*

3965 Fasteners, Buttons, Needles & Pins

A Raymond Tinnerman Mexico................G....... 248 537-3404
Rochester Hills *(G-13939)*
Aall American Fasteners................G....... 616 414-7688
Grand Haven *(G-6270)*
▲ **Acument Global Tech Inc**................E....... 586 254-3900
Sterling Heights *(G-15924)*
Axis Enterprises Inc................G....... 616 677-5281
Marne *(G-10989)*
▲ **Baker Fastening Systems Inc**................G....... 616 669-7400
Hudsonville *(G-8569)*
Decoties Inc................G....... 906 285-1286
Bessemer *(G-1648)*
▲ **Ebinger Manufacturing Company**................F....... 248 486-8880
Brighton *(G-1982)*
Elkay Industries Inc................F....... 269 381-4266
Kalamazoo *(G-9178)*
Fourslides Inc................F....... 313 564-5600
Chesterfield *(G-2885)*
Hi-Tech Fasteners LLC................F....... 231 689-6000
White Cloud *(G-18444)*
▲ **Michigan ATF Holdings LLC**................D....... 734 941-2220
Romulus *(G-14305)*
▲ **Penn Automotive Inc**................G....... 248 599-3700
Waterford *(G-18150)*
Penn Engineering & Mfg Corp................B....... 313 299-8500
Waterford *(G-18151)*
Punch Tech................E....... 810 364-4811
Marysville *(G-11097)*
Rhino Strapping Products Inc................F....... 734 442-4040
Taylor *(G-16467)*
Rodenhouse Inc................G....... 616 454-3100
Grand Rapids *(G-7163)*
Scs Fasteners LLC................G....... 586 563-0865
Eastpointe *(G-4944)*
Transfer Tool Systems LLC................C....... 616 846-8510
Grand Haven *(G-6372)*

3991 Brooms & Brushes

Brollytime Inc................F....... 312 854-7606
Royal Oak *(G-14521)*
Custom Built Brush Company................F....... 269 463-3171
Watervliet *(G-18179)*
▲ **Detroit Qulty Brush Mfg Co Inc**................D....... 734 525-5660
Livonia *(G-10183)*
Duff Brush LLC................G....... 906 863-3319
Menominee *(G-11231)*
Eco Brushes and Fibers................G....... 231 683-9202
Muskegon *(G-11809)*
Even Weight Brush LLC................G....... 906 863-3319
Menominee *(G-11234)*
▲ **Laco Inc**................E....... 231 929-3300
Traverse City *(G-16737)*
Mack Andrew & Son Brush Co................G....... 517 849-9272
Jonesville *(G-9092)*
Michigan Brush Mfg Co................E....... 313 834-1070
Detroit *(G-4445)*
R J Manufacturing Incorporated................G....... 906 779-9151
Crystal Falls *(G-3745)*
▲ **Ranir LLC**................B....... 616 698-8880
Grand Rapids *(G-7139)*
Rbt Mfg LLC................F....... 800 691-8204
Plymouth *(G-13279)*
Shais Ldscpg Snow Plowing LLC................G....... 248 234-3663
Walled Lake *(G-17675)*
Superior Equipment LLC................G....... 269 388-2871
Kalamazoo *(G-9347)*
◆ **Sweepster Attachments LLC**................A....... 734 996-9116
Dexter *(G-4757)*
▼ **Thierica Equipment Corporation**................E....... 616 453-6570
Grand Rapids *(G-7259)*

3993 Signs & Advertising Displays

5 Lakes Printing and Sign LLC................G....... 517 265-3202
Adrian *(G-46)*
5 Pyn Inc................G....... 906 228-2828
Negaunee *(G-11962)*
A D Johnson Engraving Co Inc................F....... 269 385-0044
Kalamazoo *(G-9106)*
A To Z Signs................G....... 248 887-7737
Highland *(G-7878)*
A-1 Engraving & Signs Inc................G....... 810 231-2227
Brighton *(G-1935)*
AC Design LLC................G....... 616 874-9007
Rockford *(G-14151)*
Accent Signs................G....... 860 693-6760
Canton *(G-2427)*
Acme Sign Co................G....... 248 930-9718
Sterling Heights *(G-15923)*
Adams Outdoor Advg Ltd Partnr................G....... 770 333-0399
Lansing *(G-9670)*
Adams Outdoor Advg Ltd Partnr................E....... 517 321-2121
Lansing *(G-9671)*
Add-Savvy Digital Signage................F....... 844 233-7288
Ann Arbor *(G-353)*
Advance Graphic Systems Inc................E....... 248 656-8000
Rochester Hills *(G-13943)*
Advanced Signs Incorporated................F....... 616 846-4667
Ferrysburg *(G-5600)*
▲ **Advantage Sign Supply Inc**................E....... 877 237-4464
Hudsonville *(G-8564)*
Advertsing Ntwrk Solutions Inc................G....... 248 475-7881
Rochester *(G-13890)*
Agnew Grphics Signs Promotions................G....... 989 723-4621
Owosso *(G-12820)*
Akzonobel Sign Finishes................G....... 770 317-6361
Troy *(G-16917)*
Al Bo Co................G....... 248 240-9155
Bloomfield Hills *(G-1795)*
Alex Delvecchio Entps Inc................F....... 248 619-9600
Troy *(G-16919)*
All American Embroidery Inc................F....... 734 421-9292
Livonia *(G-10108)*
All Signs LLC................G....... 231 755-5540
Muskegon *(G-11767)*
Allen Pattern of Michigan................F....... 269 963-4131
Battle Creek *(G-1184)*
Allied Screen & Grapics LLC................G....... 248 499-8204
Pontiac *(G-13348)*
Allied Signs Inc................F....... 586 791-7900
Clinton Township *(G-3162)*
Allstate Sign Company Inc................G....... 989 386-4045
Farwell *(G-5420)*
American Label & Tag Inc................E....... 734 454-7600
Canton *(G-2433)*
Amor Sign Studios Inc................E....... 231 723-8361
Manistee *(G-10893)*
Ar2 Engineering LLC................E....... 248 735-9999
Novi *(G-12364)*
Arlington Display Inds Inc................G....... 313 837-1212
Detroit *(G-4027)*
Armstrong Display Concepts Inc................F....... 231 652-1675
Newaygo *(G-12077)*
▲ **Arnets Inc**................F....... 734 665-3650
Ann Arbor *(G-379)*
Arrow Sign Co................F....... 586 939-9966
Sterling Hts *(G-16235)*
Arrow Signs................G....... 989 350-4357
Saint Ignace *(G-14894)*
Art & Image................G....... 800 566-4162
Benton Harbor *(G-1531)*
Art/Fx Sign Co................G....... 269 465-5706
Bridgman *(G-1921)*
Articulate Signs................G....... 248 577-1860
Troy *(G-16956)*
Attitude & Experience Inc................F....... 231 946-7446
Traverse City *(G-16606)*
Ausable Woodworking Co Inc................E....... 989 348-7086
Frederic *(G-6014)*
Auxier & Associates LLC................G....... 231 486-0641
Traverse City *(G-16608)*
Auxier & Associates LLC................G....... 231 933-7446
Traverse City *(G-16609)*
Banacom Instant Signs................G....... 810 230-0233
Flint *(G-5649)*
Barrett Signs................G....... 989 792-7446
Saginaw *(G-14611)*
Barrys Sign Company................G....... 810 234-9919
Flint *(G-5651)*
Bbj Graphics Inc................G....... 248 450-3149
Southfield *(G-15504)*
Bcs Creative LLC................G....... 248 917-1660
Davisburg *(G-3760)*
Beacon Sign Co................G....... 313 368-3410
Madison Heights *(G-10680)*
Bella Group LLC................G....... 586 789-7700
Harrison Twp *(G-7738)*
Berline Group Inc................E....... 248 203-0492
Royal Oak *(G-14516)*
Best Portable Sign................G....... 616 291-2911
Grand Rapids *(G-6503)*
Big Bore Signs LLC................G....... 313 701-5900
Dexter *(G-4728)*
Bigsignscom................F....... 800 790-7611
Grand Haven *(G-6279)*
Bill Carr Signs Inc................F....... 810 232-1569
Flint *(G-5655)*
Bill Daup Signs Inc................G....... 810 235-4080
Swartz Creek *(G-16351)*
Blue De-Signs LLC................G....... 248 808-2583
Royal Oak *(G-14517)*
Brews Brothers III Inc................G....... 228 255-5548
Dearborn *(G-3816)*
Bright Star Sign Inc................G....... 313 933-4460
Detroit *(G-4071)*
Brighter Sign Age................G....... 248 719-5389
Saint Clair Shores *(G-14850)*
Britten Inc................C....... 231 941-8200
Traverse City *(G-16627)*
◆ **Britten Banners LLC**................C....... 231 941-8200
Traverse City *(G-16628)*
Bronco Printing Company................G....... 248 544-1120
Hazel Park *(G-7821)*

39 MISCELLANEOUS MANUFACTURING INDUSTRIES

Brownie Signs LLC.....G..... 248 437-0800
South Lyon *(G-15428)*
Burkett Signs Corp.....F..... 269 746-4285
Climax *(G-3135)*
Business Signs of America.....G..... 810 814-3987
Fenton *(G-5462)*
C G Witvoet & Sons Company.....E..... 616 534-6677
Grand Rapids *(G-6543)*
C T L Enterprises Inc.....F..... 616 392-1159
Holland *(G-7989)*
Carrier & Gable Inc.....E..... 248 477-8700
Farmington Hills *(G-5199)*
Castleton Village Center Inc.....G..... 616 247-8100
Grand Rapids *(G-6559)*
Cg Detroit.....G..... 248 553-0202
Farmington Hills *(G-5201)*
Chad S Signs and Shirts.....G..... 248 821-3087
Davison *(G-3776)*
City Animation Co.....E..... 248 589-0600
Troy *(G-17012)*
City Animation Co.....F..... 989 743-3458
Corunna *(G-3706)*
Clips Coupons of Ann Arbo.....G..... 248 437-9294
South Lyon *(G-15431)*
Cobrex Ltd.....G..... 734 429-9758
Saline *(G-15008)*
Consort Corporation.....E..... 269 388-4532
Kalamazoo *(G-9151)*
Cook Sign Plus.....G..... 586 254-7000
Shelby Township *(G-15196)*
Copy Central Inc.....G..... 231 941-2298
Traverse City *(G-16660)*
Cornhole Stop LLC.....G..... 704 728-1550
Brighton *(G-1968)*
Cotton Concepts Printing LLC.....G..... 313 444-3857
Detroit *(G-4104)*
Craigs Signs.....G..... 810 667-7446
Lapeer *(G-9923)*
Creative Designs & Signs Inc.....G..... 248 334-5580
Pontiac *(G-13356)*
Crop Marks Printing.....G..... 616 356-5555
Grand Rapids *(G-6612)*
Custom Signs By Huntley.....G..... 810 399-8185
Flint *(G-5680)*
D Sign LLC.....G..... 616 392-3841
Holland *(G-8012)*
D T R Sign Co LLC.....G..... 616 889-8927
Hastings *(G-7788)*
Dagher Signs.....G..... 313 729-9555
Southfield *(G-15536)*
Dana & Sean Roberds.....G..... 989 382-7564
Barryton *(G-1172)*
Decor Group International Inc.....F..... 248 307-2430
Orchard Lake *(G-12716)*
▲ Design Fabrications Inc.....D..... 248 597-0988
Madison Heights *(G-10705)*
Designs N Signs LLC.....G..... 248 789-8797
Roseville *(G-14396)*
Detroit Marking Products Corp.....F..... 313 838-9760
Canton *(G-2454)*
▲ Detroit Name Plate Etching Inc.....E..... 248 543-5200
Ferndale *(G-5547)*
Detroit Sign Factory LLC.....G..... 313 782-4667
Detroit *(G-4166)*
Detroit Signs LLC.....G..... 313 345-5858
Detroit *(G-4167)*
Diamond Sign.....G..... 586 519-4296
Warren *(G-17778)*
Dicks Signs.....G..... 810 987-9002
Port Huron *(G-13468)*
Digital Impact Design Inc.....G..... 269 337-4200
Kalamazoo *(G-9168)*
Dimension Graphics Inc.....G..... 616 245-1447
Grand Rapids *(G-6648)*
Dj Customs LLC.....G..... 810 358-0236
Attica *(G-752)*
Dmp Sign Company.....G..... 248 996-9281
Southfield *(G-15542)*
Dornbos Sign Inc.....F..... 517 543-4000
Charlotte *(G-2750)*
DOT Sign.....G..... 248 760-8236
Wixom *(G-18647)*
Eagle Graphic and Design Inc.....G..... 248 668-0344
Walled Lake *(G-17667)*
Eagle Graphics and Design.....G..... 248 618-0000
Waterford *(G-18121)*
Earl Daup Signs.....F..... 810 767-2020
Flint *(G-5690)*
Eberhard and Father Signworks.....G..... 989 892-5566
Essexville *(G-5113)*
Eco Sign Solutions LLC.....G..... 734 276-8585
Ann Arbor *(G-465)*
Edston Plastics Company.....G..... 734 941-3750
Brighton *(G-1983)*
Eight Mile Signs.....G..... 248 762-3889
Livonia *(G-10191)*
Elder Creek Sign Design.....G..... 517 857-4252
Springport *(G-15881)*
Elite Sign Company.....G..... 906 481-7446
Big Rapids *(G-1672)*
Engineering Reproduction Inc.....G..... 313 366-3390
Detroit *(G-4209)*
Epi Printers Inc.....D..... 734 261-9400
Livonia *(G-10198)*
Epic Fine Arts Company Inc.....G..... 313 274-7400
Taylor *(G-16414)*
Erie Marking Inc.....F..... 989 754-8360
Saginaw *(G-14644)*
Euko Design-Signs Inc.....G..... 248 478-1330
Farmington Hills *(G-5237)*
Expressign Design.....G..... 734 747-7444
Ann Arbor *(G-481)*
Extreme Signs Inc.....G..... 586 846-3251
Clinton Township *(G-3233)*
▲ Fairfield Investment Co.....G..... 734 427-4141
Livonia *(G-10204)*
Fairmont Sign Company.....E..... 313 368-4000
Detroit *(G-4225)*
Fastsigns.....G..... 313 345-5858
Detroit *(G-4226)*
Fastsigns.....G..... 616 377-7491
Hudsonville *(G-8583)*
Fastsigns.....G..... 248 372-9554
Southfield *(G-15558)*
Fastsigns.....G..... 248 488-9010
Farmington Hills *(G-5241)*
Fastsigns International Inc.....G..... 231 941-0300
Traverse City *(G-16680)*
Federal Heath Sign Company LLC.....E..... 248 656-8000
Rochester Hills *(G-14010)*
Fire Fly.....G..... 586 601-8792
Sterling Heights *(G-16015)*
Fire Safety Displays Co.....G..... 313 274-7888
Dearborn Heights *(G-3927)*
▲ Firebolt Group Inc.....G..... 248 624-8880
Wixom *(G-18661)*
Flashpoint Sign LLC.....G..... 734 231-3361
Riverview *(G-13873)*
Flatlander Signs.....G..... 810 867-2207
Flushing *(G-5808)*
Folk Sign Studio LLC.....G..... 734 883-8259
Stockbridge *(G-16274)*
Fosters Ventures LLC.....F..... 248 519-7446
Troy *(G-17120)*
Freshwater Digital.....E..... 616 682-5470
Kentwood *(G-9455)*
Freshwter Dgtal Mdia Prtners L.....F..... 616 446-1771
Kentwood *(G-9456)*
Fug Inc.....G..... 269 781-8036
Marshall *(G-11058)*
Fwi Inc.....E..... 231 798-8324
Norton Shores *(G-12294)*
G & W Display Fixtures Inc.....E..... 517 369-7110
Bronson *(G-2112)*
Gardner Signs Inc.....F..... 248 689-9100
Troy *(G-17127)*
Gator Grafix & Signs.....G..... 269 362-2039
Buchanan *(G-2195)*
Genesee County Herald Inc.....F..... 810 686-3840
Clio *(G-3399)*
▲ George P Johnson Company.....D..... 248 475-2500
Auburn Hills *(G-910)*
Golden Pointe Inc.....G..... 313 581-8284
Detroit *(G-4269)*
Golden Sign Co.....G..... 313 580-4094
Ferndale *(G-5559)*
Grafaktri Inc.....G..... 734 665-0717
Ann Arbor *(G-504)*
Graph-X Signs.....G..... 734 420-0906
Plymouth *(G-13179)*
Graphic Visions Inc.....E..... 248 347-3355
Northville *(G-12225)*
Graphics Depot Inc.....G..... 248 383-5055
Waterford *(G-18125)*
Graphics Hse Spt Prmotions Inc.....G..... 231 733-1877
Muskegon *(G-11829)*
Graphicus Signs & Designs.....G..... 231 652-9160
Newaygo *(G-12082)*
Graphix Gurus.....G..... 616 217-6470
Zeeland *(G-19032)*
Graphix Signs & Embroidery.....G..... 616 396-0009
Holland *(G-8056)*
Graphx Shop.....G..... 248 678-5432
Keego Harbor *(G-9421)*
Grasshopper Signs Graphics LLC.....F..... 248 946-8475
Farmington Hills *(G-5254)*
Green Sign Man.....G..... 269 370-0554
Otsego *(G-12787)*
▼ Griffon Inc.....F..... 231 788-4630
Muskegon *(G-11833)*
H M Day Signs Inc.....G..... 231 946-7132
Traverse City *(G-16709)*
Handicap Sign Inc.....G..... 616 454-9416
Grand Rapids *(G-6800)*
Harbor Industries Inc.....D..... 231 547-3280
Charlevoix *(G-2717)*
◆ Harbor Industries Inc.....D..... 616 842-5330
Grand Haven *(G-6312)*
Hardy & Sons Sign Service Inc.....G..... 586 779-8018
Saint Clair Shores *(G-14864)*
Harmon Sign Inc.....G..... 248 348-8150
Wixom *(G-18676)*
Harvest Indus & Trade Co LLC.....G..... 636 675-6430
Northville *(G-12228)*
HB Stubbs Company LLC.....F..... 586 574-9700
Warren *(G-17850)*
Hexon Corporation.....E..... 248 585-7585
Farmington Hills *(G-5259)*
High End Signs Svc & Lighting.....G..... 248 596-9301
Sterling Heights *(G-16040)*
Higher Image Signs & Wraps LLC.....G..... 989 964-0443
Saginaw *(G-14665)*
Highlander Graphics LLC.....G..... 734 449-9733
Ann Arbor *(G-516)*
Holland Custom Signs.....G..... 616 566-4783
Holland *(G-8077)*
Hoppenjans Inc.....F..... 734 344-5304
Monroe *(G-11548)*
Huron Advertising Company Inc.....E..... 734 483-2000
Ypsilanti *(G-18952)*
Hy-Ko Products Company LLC.....E..... 330 467-7446
Portage *(G-13567)*
I Do Signs.....G..... 616 604-0431
Grand Haven *(G-6320)*
Icon Sign & Design Inc.....G..... 517 372-1104
Lansing *(G-9766)*
Icon Signs Inc.....G..... 906 401-0162
Negaunee *(G-11968)*
ID Enterprises.....G..... 248 442-4849
Farmington Hills *(G-5265)*
Idea MNP Com LLC.....G..... 269 459-8955
Kalamazoo *(G-9221)*
Idea Signs Visually.....G..... 269 779-9163
Kalamazoo *(G-9222)*
Identicom Sign Solutions LLC.....F..... 248 344-9590
Farmington Hills *(G-5267)*
Illusion Signs & Graphic Inc.....G..... 313 443-0567
Dearborn *(G-3853)*
Images Unlimited LLC.....G..... 248 608-8685
Rochester *(G-13906)*
Infonorm Inc.....G..... 248 276-9027
Lake Orion *(G-9610)*
Inter City Neon Inc.....G..... 586 754-6020
Warren *(G-17868)*
Its Yours.....G..... 517 676-7003
Mason *(G-11139)*
Janet Kelly.....F..... 231 775-2313
Cadillac *(G-2338)*
Japhil Inc.....G..... 616 455-0260
Grand Rapids *(G-6862)*
JD Group Inc.....F..... 248 735-9999
Novi *(G-12448)*
JD Hemp Inc.....G..... 248 549-0095
Royal Oak *(G-14551)*
Jetco Signs.....G..... 269 420-0202
Battle Creek *(G-1245)*
JL Geisler Sign Company.....F..... 586 574-1800
Troy *(G-17187)*
Johnson Sign Company Inc.....F..... 517 784-3720
Jackson *(G-8923)*
Johnson Sign Mint Cnslting LLC.....G..... 231 796-8880
Paris *(G-12935)*
Jordan Advertising Inc.....G..... 989 792-7446
Saginaw *(G-14674)*
Jra-Sign Supplies.....G..... 800 447-7365
Plymouth *(G-13207)*
Juanita L Signs.....G..... 269 429-7248
Saint Joseph *(G-14939)*
Just Signs Sometimes T-Shirts.....G..... 616 401-1215
Grand Rapids *(G-6874)*

SIC

Employee Codes: A=Over 500 employees, B=251-500
C=101-250, D=51-100, E=20-50, F=10-19, G=3-9

2022 Harris Michigan
Industrial Directory

901

Jvrf Unified Inc......G....... 248 973-2006
Sterling Heights *(G-16058)*
K-Bur Enterprises Inc......G....... 616 447-7446
Grand Rapids *(G-6876)*
Kore Group Inc......G....... 734 677-1500
Ann Arbor *(G-542)*
Lakeshore Graphics......G....... 810 359-2087
Lexington *(G-10030)*
Landers Drafting Inc......G....... 906 228-8690
Marquette *(G-11028)*
Laughabits LLC......G....... 248 990-3011
Detroit *(G-4379)*
Lavanway Sign Co Inc......G....... 248 356-1600
Southfield *(G-15624)*
Ledges Sign Company......G....... 517 925-1139
Grand Ledge *(G-6395)*
Legend Sign Company......G....... 616 447-7446
Grand Rapids *(G-6937)*
Lettering Inc......G....... 248 223-9700
Livonia *(G-10276)*
Lettering Inc of Michigan......F....... 248 223-9700
Livonia *(G-10277)*
Leutz Enterprise Inc......G....... 906 228-5887
Marquette *(G-11029)*
LLC Helton Brothers......G....... 517 927-6941
Livonia *(G-10290)*
Lobo Signs Inc......E....... 231 941-7739
Traverse City *(G-16746)*
Macomb Signs & Graphics......G....... 586 350-9789
Macomb *(G-10611)*
Majik Graphics Inc......G....... 586 792-8055
Clinton Township *(G-3291)*
Mamemarquees LLC......G....... 586 322-2215
Macomb *(G-10613)*
◆ **Marketing Displays Inc**......C....... 248 553-1900
Farmington Hills *(G-5310)*
Maw Ventures Inc......E....... 231 798-8324
Norton Shores *(G-12309)*
Maxxlite Led Signs......G....... 248 397-5769
Pontiac *(G-13396)*
▲ **Mayfair Golf Accessories**......G....... 989 732-8400
Gaylord *(G-6147)*
Mayrose Sign and Mktg Co LLC......G....... 616 837-1884
Coopersville *(G-3692)*
Media Solutions Inc......G....... 313 831-3152
Detroit *(G-4427)*
Meiers Signs Inc......G....... 906 786-3424
Escanaba *(G-5084)*
Metro Detroit Printing LLC......G....... 734 469-7174
Livonia *(G-10312)*
Metro Sign Fabricators Inc......G....... 586 493-0502
Clinton Township *(G-3299)*
MHR Investments Inc......F....... 989 832-5395
Midland *(G-11388)*
MI Custom Signs LLC......F....... 734 946-7446
Taylor *(G-16444)*
Michigan Graphic Arts......G....... 517 278-4120
Coldwater *(G-3444)*
Michigan Graphics & Signs......G....... 989 224-1936
Saint Johns *(G-14908)*
Michigan Highway Signs Inc......G....... 810 695-7529
Grand Blanc *(G-6253)*
▲ **Michigan Plaques & Awards Inc**......E....... 248 398-6400
Berkley *(G-1632)*
Michigan Signs Inc......G....... 734 662-1503
Ann Arbor *(G-575)*
Midwest Safety Products Inc......E....... 616 554-5155
Grand Rapids *(G-7006)*
Midwest Sign Install Inc......G....... 616 862-7568
Hudsonville *(G-8597)*
Miller Designworks LLC......G....... 313 562-4000
Dearborn *(G-3873)*
Miracle Sign......G....... 313 663-0145
Melvindale *(G-11205)*
Mitchart Inc......G....... 989 835-3964
Midland *(G-11395)*
MLS Signs Inc......F....... 586 948-0200
Macomb *(G-10618)*
Mod Signs Inc......F....... 616 455-0260
Grand Rapids *(G-7017)*
Modern Neon Sign Co Inc......F....... 269 349-8636
Kalamazoo *(G-9274)*
Moore Signs Investments Inc......F....... 586 783-9339
Shelby Township *(G-15285)*
Moreys Logo......G....... 989 772-4492
Mount Pleasant *(G-11718)*
Motor City Manufacturing Ltd......G....... 586 731-1086
Ferndale *(G-5569)*
Motor City Signs LLC......G....... 810 867-2207
Flushing *(G-5812)*
Motwon Sign Company LLC......G....... 313 580-4094
Hazel Park *(G-7835)*
Mrj Sign Company LLC......G....... 248 521-2431
Ortonville *(G-12749)*
▲ **Nalcor LLC**......D....... 248 541-1140
Ferndale *(G-5570)*
National Sign & Signal Co......E....... 269 963-2817
Battle Creek *(G-1277)*
Network Sign Company Inc......G....... 517 548-1232
Brooklyn *(G-2129)*
New Rules Marketing Inc......E....... 800 962-3119
Spring Lake *(G-15839)*
Nicolet Sign & Design......G....... 906 265-5220
Iron River *(G-8750)*
Normic Industries Inc......E....... 231 947-8860
Traverse City *(G-16771)*
Norris Graphics Inc......G....... 586 447-0646
Clinton Township *(G-3308)*
North Woods Sign Shop......G....... 231 843-3956
Ludington *(G-10547)*
Northern Laser Creations......G....... 517 581-7699
Jonesville *(G-9096)*
Northern Sign Co......G....... 248 333-7733
Auburn Hills *(G-987)*
Northwood Signs Inc......G....... 231 843-3956
Ludington *(G-10548)*
On The Side Sign Dsign Grphics......G....... 810 266-7446
Byron *(G-2255)*
One Stop Sign Services......G....... 810 358-1962
Marysville *(G-11094)*
Paramount Signs LLC......G....... 734 548-1721
Dearborn *(G-3882)*
Penn Sign......G....... 814 932-7181
Romulus *(G-14318)*
Perfect Signs......G....... 231 233-3721
Manistee *(G-10911)*
Phillips Enterprises Inc......E....... 586 615-6208
Shelby Township *(G-15301)*
▲ **Plasticrafts Inc**......G....... 313 532-1900
Redford *(G-13757)*
Poco Inc......E....... 313 220-6752
Canton *(G-2509)*
▲ **Port Cy Archtctral Signage LLC**......G....... 231 739-3463
Muskegon *(G-11896)*
Praise Sign Company......G....... 616 439-0315
Grandville *(G-7411)*
Premier Signs Plus Inc......G....... 248 633-5598
Novi *(G-12511)*
Princessa Designs Inc......G....... 616 285-6868
Ada *(G-34)*
Printastic LLC......F....... 248 761-5697
Novi *(G-12515)*
Pro Image Design......G....... 231 322-8052
Traverse City *(G-16803)*
Pro Linez of Ann Arbor......G....... 734 755-7309
Temperance *(G-16545)*
Pro Sign and Awning Inc......G....... 313 581-9333
Detroit *(G-4535)*
▲ **Pro-Motion Tech Group LLC**......D....... 248 668-3100
Wixom *(G-18735)*
▼ **Programmed Products Corp**......D....... 248 348-7755
Novi *(G-12517)*
Qmi Group Inc......E....... 248 589-0505
Madison Heights *(G-10814)*
Quality Business Engraving......G....... 248 852-5123
Rochester Hills *(G-14094)*
Quality Decals & Signs......G....... 517 441-1200
Eaton Rapids *(G-4969)*
▼ **Quicktrophy LLC**......F....... 906 228-2604
Marquette *(G-11043)*
R & R Harwood Inc......G....... 616 669-6400
Jenison *(G-9069)*
R Gari Sign and Display Inc......G....... 810 355-1245
Pinckney *(G-13054)*
R Gari Sign Studio Inc......G....... 810 355-1245
Brighton *(G-2060)*
R J Designers Inc......G....... 517 750-1990
Spring Arbor *(G-15797)*
Race Graphics Plus......G....... 989 465-9117
Coleman *(G-3471)*
Radiant Electric Sign Corp......G....... 313 835-1400
Detroit *(G-4552)*
Rathco Safety Supply Inc......E....... 269 323-0153
Portage *(G-13599)*
Reliable Sign Service Inc......G....... 586 465-6829
Harrison Township *(G-7720)*
Revolutions Signs Designs LLC......G....... 248 439-0727
Royal Oak *(G-14576)*
Rockstar Digital Inc......F....... 888 808-5868
Sterling Heights *(G-16158)*
Rodzina Industries Inc......G....... 810 235-2341
Flint *(G-5755)*
Rouhan Signs LLC......G....... 406 202-2369
Howard City *(G-8418)*
Royal Oak Name Plate Company......G....... 586 774-8500
Roseville *(G-14473)*
Rsls Corp......G....... 248 726-0675
Shelby Township *(G-15319)*
Rwl Sign Co LLC......G....... 269 372-3629
Kalamazoo *(G-9323)*
Ryan Daup......G....... 810 240-6016
Grand Blanc *(G-6262)*
S S Graphics Inc......G....... 734 246-4420
Wyandotte *(G-18837)*
Safari Signs......G....... 231 727-9200
Muskegon *(G-11914)*
Salient Sign Studio......G....... 248 532-0013
Oak Park *(G-12645)*
Scarlet Spartan Inc......F....... 810 224-5700
Brighton *(G-2068)*
Scotts Signs......G....... 616 532-2034
Grandville *(G-7417)*
Sgo Corporate Center LLC......F....... 248 596-8626
Plymouth *(G-13296)*
▲ **Shaw & Slavsky Inc**......E....... 313 834-3990
Detroit *(G-4589)*
Shelby Signarama Township......G....... 586 843-3702
Shelby Township *(G-15332)*
Shields & Shields Enterprises......G....... 269 345-7744
Kalamazoo *(G-9332)*
Shields Classic Toys......G....... 888 806-2632
Saline *(G-15039)*
Shop Makarios LLC......F....... 800 479-0032
Byron Center *(G-2295)*
Shorecrest Enterprises Inc......G....... 586 948-9226
Clinton Township *(G-3352)*
Sign & Graphics Operations LLC......E....... 248 596-8626
Plymouth *(G-13297)*
Sign & Vinyl Graphix Express......G....... 586 838-4741
Sterling Heights *(G-16177)*
Sign A Rama......G....... 517 489-4314
Okemos *(G-12686)*
Sign A Rama......G....... 517 489-4314
Lansing *(G-9736)*
Sign A Rama Inc......G....... 810 494-7446
Brighton *(G-2071)*
Sign and Banner World......G....... 248 957-1240
Farmington *(G-5149)*
Sign and Design......G....... 231 348-9256
Petoskey *(G-13023)*
Sign Art Inc......E....... 269 381-3012
Kalamazoo *(G-9334)*
Sign Center of Kalamazoo Inc......G....... 269 381-6869
Kalamazoo *(G-9335)*
Sign City Inc......G....... 269 375-1385
Kalamazoo *(G-9336)*
Sign Concepts Corporation......F....... 248 680-8970
Troy *(G-17351)*
Sign Division......G....... 269 548-8978
Benton Harbor *(G-1585)*
Sign Fabricators Inc......G....... 586 468-7360
Harrison Township *(G-7725)*
Sign Graphix......G....... 248 241-6531
Clarkston *(G-3066)*
Sign Image Inc......F....... 989 781-5229
Saginaw *(G-14756)*
Sign Impressions Inc......G....... 269 382-5152
Kalamazoo *(G-9337)*
Sign On Inc......G....... 269 381-6869
Kalamazoo *(G-9338)*
Sign Pal......G....... 989 755-7773
Saginaw *(G-14757)*
Sign Pros LLC......G....... 313 310-1010
Dearborn Heights *(G-3939)*
Sign Screen......G....... 231 942-2273
Cadillac *(G-2353)*
Sign Screen Inc......G....... 810 239-1100
Flint *(G-5762)*
Sign Studio Inc......G....... 214 526-6940
Warren *(G-18013)*
Sign Stuff Inc......G....... 734 458-1055
Livonia *(G-10409)*
Sign Up Inc......G....... 906 789-7446
Escanaba *(G-5099)*
Sign With Sally C LLC......G....... 586 612-5100
Algonac *(G-143)*
Sign Works Inc......G....... 517 546-3620
Howell *(G-8517)*
Sign-A-Rama......G....... 586 792-7446
Clinton Township *(G-3355)*

Sign-A-Rama Inc ....G 734 522-6661
Garden City *(G-6110)*
Sign-On Connect ....G 313 539-3246
Grosse Pointe Farms *(G-7541)*
Signarama Farmington ....G 248 957-1240
Farmington *(G-5150)*
◆ **Signcomp LLC** ....E 616 784-0405
Grand Rapids *(G-7196)*
Signcrafters Inc ....G 231 773-3343
Muskegon *(G-11923)*
Signing Savvy LLC ....G 517 455-7663
Okemos *(G-12687)*
Signmakers Ltd ....G 616 455-4220
Grand Rapids *(G-7197)*
Signplicity Sign Systems Inc ....G 231 943-3800
Traverse City *(G-16832)*
Signproco Inc ....F 248 585-6880
Troy *(G-17352)*
Signs & Designs Inc ....G 269 968-8909
Battle Creek *(G-1294)*
Signs & Laser Engraving ....G 248 577-6191
Troy *(G-17353)*
Signs & Wonders LLC ....G 618 694-4960
Dewitt *(G-4715)*
Signs and More ....G 810 820-9955
Flint *(G-5763)*
Signs By Crannie Inc ....E 810 487-0000
Flint *(G-5764)*
Signs By Rhonda LLC ....G 248 408-0552
Clinton Township *(G-3356)*
Signs By Tmrrow - Rchster Hlls ....G 248 299-9229
Rochester Hills *(G-14111)*
Signs By Tomorrow ....G 616 647-7446
Hudsonville *(G-8612)*
Signs By Tomorrow ....G 734 522-8440
Livonia *(G-10410)*
Signs By Tomorrow ....G 248 478-5600
Novi *(G-12537)*
Signs Direct LLC ....G 810 732-5067
Davison *(G-3796)*
Signs In LLC ....G 248 939-7446
Farmington Hills *(G-5379)*
Signs Letters & Graphics Inc ....G 231 536-7929
East Jordan *(G-4879)*
Signs of Love Inc ....G 586 413-1269
Clinton Township *(G-3357)*
Signs of Prosperity LLC ....G 248 488-9010
Farmington Hills *(G-5380)*
Signs Plus ....G 810 987-7446
Port Huron *(G-13527)*
Signs That Scream ....G 616 698-6284
Caledonia *(G-2399)*
Signs365com LLC ....G 800 265-8830
Shelby Township *(G-15333)*
Signtext Incorporated ....E 248 442-9080
Farmington Hills *(G-5381)*
Signworks of Michigan Inc ....G 616 954-2554
Grand Rapids *(G-7198)*
Simi Air ....G 517 401-0284
Morenci *(G-11616)*
Snap Display Frames ....G 616 846-7747
Grand Haven *(G-6363)*
Source One Digital LLC ....E 231 759-3160
Norton Shores *(G-12334)*
Spectrum Neon Company ....G 313 366-7333
Madison Heights *(G-10834)*
Sporting Image Inc ....F 269 657-5646
Paw Paw *(G-12956)*
Spry Sign & Graphics Co LLC ....G 517 524-7685
Concord *(G-3655)*
Stamp-Rite Incorporated ....E 517 487-5071
Lansing *(G-9741)*
Star Design Metro Detroit LLC ....E 734 740-0189
Livonia *(G-10419)*
Steel Skinz LLC ....G 517 545-9955
Howell *(G-8523)*
Sterling Creative Team Inc ....G 586 978-0100
Sterling Heights *(G-16191)*
Steves Custom Signs Inc ....F 734 662-5964
Ann Arbor *(G-665)*
Stickerchef LLC ....G 231 622-9900
Saint Ignace *(G-14896)*
Stimmel Construction LLC ....G 734 263-8949
Garden City *(G-6111)*
Stnj LLC ....F 810 230-6445
Flint *(G-5770)*
Sun Ray Sign Group Inc ....G 616 392-2824
Holland *(G-8208)*
Sunset Enterprises Inc ....F 269 373-6440
Kalamazoo *(G-9346)*
Supersine Company ....E 313 892-6200
Lathrup Village *(G-9978)*
▼ **System 2/90 Inc** ....D 616 656-4310
Grand Rapids *(G-7244)*
T M Shea Products Inc ....F 800 992-5233
Troy *(G-17383)*
▲ **Tecart Industries Inc** ....F 248 624-8880
Wixom *(G-18768)*
◆ **Tentcraft LLC** ....D 800 950-4553
Traverse City *(G-16854)*
The Sign Chap Inc ....G 248 585-6880
Madison Heights *(G-10842)*
Think Chromatic ....G 248 719-2058
Comstock Park *(G-3647)*
Tile By Bill & Sondra ....G 616 554-5413
Caledonia *(G-2404)*
Timothy Michael Goodwin ....G 586 322-3312
Memphis *(G-11214)*
Tischco Signs ....G 231 755-5529
Muskegon *(G-11933)*
Tj Pant LLC ....G 419 215-8434
Sturgis *(G-16327)*
Toms Sign Service ....G 248 852-3550
Rochester Hills *(G-14127)*
▲ **Top Deck Systems Inc** ....G 586 263-1550
Shelby Township *(G-15354)*
Traffic Signs Inc ....G 269 964-7511
Springfield *(G-15876)*
Transign LLC ....F 248 623-6400
Auburn Hills *(G-1064)*
▲ **TSS Inc** ....E 586 427-0070
Warren *(G-18045)*
Tyes Inc ....F 888 219-6301
Ludington *(G-10553)*
Ucb Advertising ....G 269 808-2411
Plainwell *(G-13102)*
Ultimate Graphic and Sign LLC ....G 989 865-5200
Saint Charles *(G-14812)*
United Sign Co ....G 616 642-0200
Saranac *(G-15082)*
Universal Sign Inc ....E 616 554-9999
Grand Rapids *(G-7298)*
Up North Sign LLC ....G 231 838-6328
Alanson *(G-112)*
USA Sign Frame & Stake Inc ....G 616 662-9100
Jenison *(G-9075)*
Valassis International Inc ....B 734 591-3000
Livonia *(G-10457)*
Valley City Sign Company ....E 616 784-5711
Comstock Park *(G-3649)*
Van Kehrberg Vern ....G 810 364-1066
Marysville *(G-11111)*
Venture Grafix LLC ....G 248 449-1330
Wixom *(G-18787)*
Versatility Inc ....G 616 957-5555
Grand Rapids *(G-7312)*
Vinyl Graphix Inc ....G 586 774-1188
Saint Clair Shores *(G-14890)*
Visual Productions Inc ....D 248 356-4399
Mesick *(G-11275)*
▲ **Visual Workplace Byron Ctr Inc** ....G 616 583-9400
Byron Center *(G-2299)*
▲ **Visual Workplace LLC** ....F 616 583-9400
Byron Center *(G-2300)*
Vital Signs Inc ....G 313 491-2010
Canton *(G-2540)*
Vocational Strategies Inc ....F 906 482-6142
Calumet *(G-2415)*
Wenz & Gibbens Enterprises ....G 248 333-7938
Pontiac *(G-13424)*
▲ **Westcott Displays Inc** ....E 313 872-1200
Detroit *(G-4678)*
Wheelhouse Graphix LLC ....F 800 732-0815
Bloomfield Hills *(G-1874)*
Whitcomb and Sons Sign Co Inc ....G 586 752-3576
Romeo *(G-14239)*
▲ **Whitehall Products LLC** ....D 231 894-2688
Whitehall *(G-18514)*
Wikid Vinyl ....G 313 585-7814
Shelby Township *(G-15369)*
Wilde Signs ....F 231 727-1200
Muskegon *(G-11949)*
Wildfire Signs & Graphics ....G 248 872-1998
Oxford *(G-12929)*
Wilfred Swartz & Swartz G ....G 989 652-6322
Reese *(G-13811)*
Windy Lake LLC ....D 877 869-6911
Pentwater *(G-12975)*
Wood Love Signs ....G 586 322-6400
Macomb *(G-10651)*
Wooden Moon Studio ....G 269 329-3229
Portage *(G-13635)*
Woods Graphics ....F 616 691-8025
Greenville *(G-7511)*
Wraps N Signs ....G 269 377-8488
Portage *(G-13636)*
X-Treme Graphics N Signs LLC ....G 989 277-7517
Perry *(G-12982)*
Xtreme Signs Inc ....G 586 486-5068
Warren *(G-18077)*
Your Big Sign ....G 248 881-9505
Hartland *(G-7774)*
Your Sign Lady LLC ....G 586 741-8585
Macomb *(G-10652)*
Zk Enterprises Inc ....G 989 728-4439
Alger *(G-140)*

3995 Burial Caskets

◆ **Genesis International LLC** ....E 317 777-6700
Mason *(G-11134)*

3996 Linoleum & Hard Surface Floor Coverings, NEC

Floorcovering Engineers LLC ....G 616 299-1007
Grand Rapids *(G-6712)*
Flor TEC Inc ....G 616 897-3122
Lowell *(G-10501)*
Innovative Surface Works ....F 734 261-3010
Farmington Hills *(G-5269)*
Pro Floor Service ....G 517 663-5012
Eaton Rapids *(G-4968)*

3999 Manufacturing Industries, NEC

2 Gen Manufacturing LLC ....G 616 443-7886
Grand Rapids *(G-6402)*
2stone Mfg LLC ....G 269 214-6560
Berrien Springs *(G-1636)*
313 Industries ....G 313 969-8570
Southfield *(G-15467)*
4 Wheels Industries ....G 989 323-2191
Chesaning *(G-2827)*
420 Group ....G 586 978-0420
Sterling Heights *(G-15916)*
4d Industries Inc ....G 310 710-3955
Wyoming *(G-18847)*
5 14 Candles ....G 231 944-9585
Interlochen *(G-8678)*
7 Seas Sourcing LLC ....G 734 357-8560
Novi *(G-12358)*
8th Candle LLC ....G 248 818-7625
Lake Orion *(G-9581)*
A & B Display Systems Inc ....F 989 893-6642
Bay City *(G-1314)*
A & R Tool & Mfg Co ....G 586 553-9623
Sterling Heights *(G-15917)*
A K Industries ....G 231 726-0134
Norton Shores *(G-12273)*
A&A Manufacturing ....G 800 473-1730
Coopersville *(G-3678)*
A&D Industries LLC ....G 586 291-6444
Clinton Township *(G-3149)*
A&S Industries ....G 269 903-1081
Kalamazoo *(G-9107)*
A2e Manufacturing ....G 734 622-9800
Plymouth *(G-13109)*
AAM Mtal Frming Troy Mfg Fclty ....G 248 362-8500
Troy *(G-16901)*
AAM Royal Oak Mfg ....G 248 597-3800
Royal Oak *(G-14502)*
Abbotts Magic Manufacturing Co ....G 269 432-3235
Colon *(G-3486)*
Abletech Industries LLC ....G 734 677-2420
Dexter *(G-4720)*
▲ **Access Manufacturing Techn** ....G 224 610-0171
Niles *(G-12108)*
Achieve Industries LLC ....G 586 493-9780
Clinton Township *(G-3153)*
Active Plastics Inc ....F 616 813-5109
Caledonia *(G-2367)*
Actuator Services LLC ....G 734 242-5456
Monroe *(G-11520)*
Adams Manufacturing ....G 313 383-7804
Lincoln Park *(G-10042)*
Admin Industries LLC ....F 989 685-3438
Rose City *(G-14358)*
Advance Pet Solutions LLC ....G 248 334-6150
West Bloomfield *(G-18261)*
Adventures Moni and Koko LLC ....G 269 589-2154
Battle Creek *(G-1181)*

S I C

Employee Codes: A=Over 500 employees, B=251-500
C=101-250, D=51-100, E=20-50, F=10-19, G=3-9
2022 Harris Michigan
Industrial Directory
903

Aerostar Manufacturing ....G.... 734 947-2558
Taylor *(G-16374)*
Aftermarket Industries LLC ....G.... 810 229-3200
Brighton *(G-1940)*
AG Industries ....F.... 248 564-2758
Rochester Hills *(G-13945)*
Aic Acquisition Company LLC ....E.... 810 227-5510
Wixom *(G-18600)*
Airman Inc ....E.... 248 960-1354
Brighton *(G-1941)*
Airplane Factory ....G.... 989 561-5381
Remus *(G-13812)*
Ajm Manufacturing Sales Inc ....G.... 269 447-2087
Kalamazoo *(G-9108)*
AJS Manufacturing LLC ....G.... 616 916-6521
Grand Rapids *(G-6440)*
AJW Industries Inc ....G.... 313 595-5554
Belleville *(G-1479)*
Aldez North America ....F.... 586 530-5314
Clinton Township *(G-3161)*
Aldridge Industries LLC ....G.... 248 379-5357
Beverly Hills *(G-1660)*
Allen Models of Michigan LLC ....G.... 989 284-8866
Freeland *(G-6018)*
Alta Distribution LLC ....F.... 313 363-1682
Southfield *(G-15477)*
◆ **Altus Brands LLC** ....F.... 231 421-3810
Grawn *(G-7448)*
Alynn Industries ....G.... 517 764-7783
Jackson *(G-8814)*
Ambrosia Inc ....G.... 734 529-7174
Dundee *(G-4809)*
AME International LLC ....E.... 586 532-8981
Clinton Township *(G-3163)*
American Laser Centers LLC ....A.... 248 426-8250
Farmington Hills *(G-5168)*
▲ **American MSC Inc** ....E.... 248 589-7770
Troy *(G-16933)*
Americana Manufacturing Co ....G.... 248 505-3277
Lapeer *(G-9912)*
Angel Affects Candles LLC ....G.... 313 288-6899
Detroit *(G-4021)*
Ann Barrette ....G.... 586 713-8145
Clinton Township *(G-3172)*
Annalux Candles LLC ....G.... 313 566-3289
Taylor *(G-16380)*
Arbor Kitchen LLC ....G.... 248 921-4602
Ann Arbor *(G-375)*
Arete Industries Inc ....G.... 248 352-7205
Southfield *(G-15490)*
Arrowhead Manufacturing ....G.... 248 688-8939
Royal Oak *(G-14512)*
ASC Industries Inc ....G.... 586 722-7871
Rochester Hills *(G-13951)*
Asher Brandon Industries ....G.... 231 313-3513
Traverse City *(G-16603)*
Aspidistra Naturals Inc ....G.... 269 317-0996
Battle Creek *(G-1186)*
Atlas Industries ....G.... 310 694-7457
Southfield *(G-15494)*
Atmore Industries Inc ....G.... 734 455-7655
Livonia *(G-10128)*
ATW Industries LLC ....G.... 616 318-6052
Byron Center *(G-2258)*
Aurora Preserved Flowers ....G.... 989 498-0290
Bay City *(G-1323)*
Automatic Valve Mfg Co In ....G.... 248 924-7671
Novi *(G-12371)*
Axline Advanced Industries ....G.... 231 679-7907
Reed City *(G-13788)*
B T I Industries ....F.... 586 532-8411
Shelby Township *(G-15177)*
B&B HAIr&co LLC ....G.... 616 600-4568
Grand Rapids *(G-6489)*
Bach Mobilities Inc ....G.... 906 789-9490
Escanaba *(G-5059)*
Bad Day Industries LLC ....G.... 844 213-6541
Clarksville *(G-3077)*
Bartz Mfg LLC ....G.... 517 281-2571
Eaton Rapids *(G-4955)*
Basan Cord Inc ....G.... 888 802-2726
Commerce Township *(G-3513)*
Bay Archery Sales Co ....G.... 989 894-5800
Essexville *(G-5109)*
Bay Home Medical and Rehab Inc ....F.... 231 933-1200
Grandville *(G-7366)*
Bayside Engineering and Mfg ....G.... 906 420-8770
Gladstone *(G-6173)*
Bayside Industries ....G.... 231 632-2222
Traverse City *(G-16618)*

Bbb Industries ....G.... 231 735-6060
Traverse City *(G-16619)*
Bcubed Manufacturing LLC ....G.... 989 356-2294
Alpena *(G-283)*
Be A Boss Not A Bossy Bih LLC ....G.... 734 833-8106
Wayne *(G-18216)*
Bee Dazzled Candle Works ....G.... 231 882-7765
Benzonia *(G-1612)*
Bellar Industries Inc ....G.... 810 227-1574
Brighton *(G-1950)*
Benchmark Manufacturing ....G.... 231 375-8172
Norton Shores *(G-12278)*
◆ **Benteler Automotive Corp** ....C.... 248 364-7190
Auburn Hills *(G-811)*
Bentley Industries ....G.... 810 625-0400
Flint *(G-5654)*
Berlin Holdings LLC ....G.... 517 523-2444
Pittsford *(G-13067)*
Best Buy Bones Inc ....G.... 810 631-6971
Mount Morris *(G-11668)*
Best Mfg Tooling Solutions ....G.... 616 877-5149
Dorr *(G-4767)*
Betko Manufacturing LLC ....G.... 734 854-1148
Lambertville *(G-9650)*
Bloom Industries LLC ....F.... 616 890-8029
Traverse City *(G-16622)*
Bloom Industries LLC ....G.... 616 453-2946
Grand Rapids *(G-6516)*
Bluefire Industries LLC ....G.... 269 235-9779
Augusta *(G-1091)*
Body Contour Ventures LLC ....E.... 248 579-6772
Farmington Hills *(G-5184)*
Body Language Scented Candles ....G.... 989 906-0354
Saginaw *(G-14619)*
Bohr Manufacturing LLC ....G.... 734 261-3010
Farmington Hills *(G-5185)*
Bolden Industries Inc ....F.... 248 387-9489
Detroit *(G-4060)*
Bomark Industries LLc ....G.... 248 879-9577
Troy *(G-16981)*
Boones Candle Co ....G.... 248 444-0621
Commerce Township *(G-3517)*
Bozz Lashez LLC ....G.... 734 799-7020
Van Buren Twp *(G-17513)*
Brady Worldwide Inc ....G.... 248 650-1952
Rochester *(G-13894)*
Brandt Manufacturing Inc ....G.... 517 851-7000
Stockbridge *(G-16272)*
Bridgewater Industries ....G.... 810 228-3963
Flint *(G-5661)*
Brightly Twisted ....G.... 313 303-1364
Detroit *(G-4073)*
Brilliant Industries LLC ....G.... 616 954-9209
Grand Rapids *(G-6525)*
Britt Manufacturing ....F.... 810 982-9720
Port Huron *(G-13463)*
Britt Mfg ....G.... 810 966-0223
Fort Gratiot *(G-5818)*
Brollytime Inc ....F.... 312 854-7606
Royal Oak *(G-14521)*
Brooks Manufacturing ....G.... 231 832-4961
Chase *(G-2775)*
Brothers In Arms Mfg LLC ....G.... 989 464-9615
Alpena *(G-285)*
Bucklin Township Candles LLC ....G.... 248 403-0600
River Rouge *(G-13852)*
Burlingame Industries Inc ....G.... 616 682-5691
Grand Rapids *(G-6537)*
◆ **Burr Oak Tool Inc** ....B.... 269 651-9393
Sturgis *(G-16282)*
Busch Machine Tool Supply LLC ....G.... 989 798-4794
Freeland *(G-6019)*
Caflor Industries LLC ....G.... 734 604-1168
Ypsilanti *(G-18931)*
Camoplast ....G.... 517 278-8567
Coldwater *(G-3424)*
Candle Factory Grand Traverse ....G.... 231 946-2280
Traverse City *(G-16638)*
Candle Knight Light ....G.... 248 291-5483
Oak Park *(G-12597)*
Candle Wick ....G.... 248 547-2987
Ferndale *(G-5533)*
Candles By Cottonwood ....G.... 734 344-2339
Monroe *(G-11533)*
Candles By Jugg ....G.... 313 732-1349
Eastpointe *(G-4929)*
Candles By Lori LLC ....G.... 734 474-6314
Saline *(G-15007)*
Capler Mfg ....G.... 586 264-7851
Sterling Heights *(G-15952)*

Car Pak Manufacturing Co ....G.... 480 625-3655
Troy *(G-16999)*
Carpathians Manufacturing ....G.... 248 291-6232
Troy *(G-17004)*
Carpe Candle ....G.... 734 837-3053
Whitmore Lake *(G-18526)*
Cbark Manufacturing Inc ....G.... 810 922-3092
Waterford *(G-18109)*
CBS Enterprises LLC ....G.... 248 335-6702
Pontiac *(G-13352)*
CF Manufacturing LLC ....G.... 231 409-9468
Traverse City *(G-16644)*
Changstar Industries LLC ....G.... 248 446-1811
South Lyon *(G-15430)*
Charboneau Inc ....G.... 989 293-1773
Bay City *(G-1337)*
◆ **Charter House Holdings LLC** ....C.... 616 399-6000
Zeeland *(G-19004)*
Chelsea Vlg Candles & Gifts ....G.... 734 385-6588
Brooklyn *(G-2124)*
Chris Brown Industries LLC ....G.... 734 323-5651
Southfield *(G-15522)*
Cirko LLC ....G.... 586 504-1313
Shelby Township *(G-15189)*
Ckc Industries Inc ....G.... 248 667-6286
Redford *(G-13724)*
Classic Mfg ....G.... 616 651-2921
Sturgis *(G-16283)*
Clossons Manufacturing LLC ....G.... 269 363-4261
Sodus *(G-15393)*
Clover Industries Inc ....G.... 231 929-1660
Traverse City *(G-16654)*
Coastline Manufacturing LLC ....G.... 231 798-1700
Norton Shores *(G-12286)*
Colwell Industries Inc ....G.... 248 841-1254
Rochester Hills *(G-13978)*
Compositech ....G.... 269 908-7846
Lowell *(G-10498)*
Concentric Mfg Svcs LLC ....G.... 989 506-8636
Weidman *(G-18250)*
◆ **Conway Products Corporation** ....E.... 616 698-2601
Grand Rapids *(G-6603)*
Core Lite Industries LLC ....G.... 616 481-3940
Jenison *(G-9050)*
Core-Lite Industries LLC ....G.... 616 843-5993
Grand Haven *(G-6288)*
Core-Lite Industries LLC ....G.... 616 822-7587
Grand Haven *(G-6289)*
Country Candles ....G.... 231 327-2730
White Cloud *(G-18440)*
Coventry Creations Inc ....E.... 248 547-2987
Ferndale *(G-5536)*
Coventry Industries LLC ....F.... 248 761-8462
Holly *(G-8263)*
Crescent Manufacturing Company ....G.... 517 486-2670
Blissfield *(G-1763)*
Crown Manufacturing LLC ....F.... 616 295-7018
Middleville *(G-11305)*
CSB Industries LLC ....G.... 231 651-9484
Beulah *(G-1654)*
Cultivation Station Inc ....G.... 313 383-1766
Allen Park *(G-191)*
Culver J Manufacturing Company ....G.... 248 541-0297
Royal Oak *(G-14528)*
Cunningham Industries LLC ....G.... 734 225-1044
Southgate *(G-15750)*
Cypress Industries Inc ....F.... 269 381-2160
Kalamazoo *(G-9160)*
D & D Retaining Walls Inc ....G.... 260 341-8496
Whitehall *(G-18494)*
D & F Corporation ....D.... 586 254-5300
Sterling Heights *(G-15977)*
D3w Industries Inc ....G.... 248 798-0703
Novi *(G-12389)*
Dakoda Love Manufacturing ....G.... 616 840-0804
Wyoming *(G-18863)*
Dandy Delights ....G.... 248 496-8523
West Bloomfield *(G-18278)*
Davon Manufacturing ....G.... 616 745-8453
Zeeland *(G-19014)*
▲ **Dawson Mfg Co Morganfield** ....F.... 269 639-4229
South Haven *(G-15403)*
Dayco Products LLC ....G.... 248 404-6500
Roseville *(G-14394)*
Dealer Aid Enterprises ....G.... 313 331-5800
Detroit *(G-4128)*
Deluxe Technologies LLC ....E.... 586 294-2340
Fraser *(G-5918)*
Denton Atd Inc ....E.... 734 451-7878
Plymouth *(G-13153)*

39 MISCELLANEOUS MANUFACTURING INDUSTRIES

Detroits Very Own CL Co LLC .... G 313 614-1033
  Detroit *(G-4172)*
Dewsbury Manufacturing Company ...... G 734 839-6376
  Trenton *(G-16887)*
▼ Dgh Enterprises Inc .... E 269 925-0657
  Benton Harbor *(G-1546)*
Diamond Tool Manufacturing .... F 616 895-4007
  Hudsonville *(G-8580)*
Dissrad Inc .... G 586 463-8722
  Mount Clemens *(G-11637)*
Diverse Manufacturing Soltion .... G 517 423-6691
  Tecumseh *(G-16497)*
Division 6 Fbrction Instlltion .... F 586 200-3030
  Warren *(G-17780)*
▲ Dorden & Company Inc .... G 313 834-7910
  Detroit *(G-4187)*
Dougco Industries LLC .... G 313 808-1689
  Detroit *(G-4188)*
Douglas Innovation LLC .... G 586 596-3641
  Troy *(G-17064)*
Dowding Industries .... F 319 294-9094
  Eaton Rapids *(G-4958)*
Dunlop Dreams Candles .... G 231 633-4064
  Traverse City *(G-16673)*
Duo Gard Industries Inc .... G 734 459-9166
  Plymouth *(G-13162)*
Dynatect Manufacturing In .... F 231 947-4124
  Traverse City *(G-16674)*
E M Smokers Inc .... G 586 207-1172
  Shelby Township *(G-15217)*
Eagleburgmann Industries LP .... G 989 486-1571
  Midland *(G-11359)*
▲ Ebinger Manufacturing Company .... F 248 486-8880
  Brighton *(G-1982)*
ECM Manufacturing Inc .... G 810 736-0299
  Flint *(G-5691)*
EDS Industries .... G 989 274-2551
  Rochester Hills *(G-14000)*
Eileen Smeltzer .... G 269 629-8056
  Richland *(G-13824)*
Elite Manufacturing Tech LLC .... F 586 846-2055
  Clinton Township *(G-3231)*
Elite Metal Manufacturing LLC .... G 734 718-0061
  Livonia *(G-10195)*
Emack Manufacturing .... G 616 241-3040
  Grand Rapids *(G-6673)*
◆ Emag LLC .... E 248 477-7440
  Farmington Hills *(G-5227)*
Emerald Growth Partners LLC .... F 248 756-0286
  Harrison Township *(G-7697)*
◆ Emhart Teknologies LLC .... D 248 677-9693
  Troy *(G-17087)*
▲ Endless Possibilities Inc .... G 248 262-7443
  Grayling *(G-7460)*
Engineering Graphics Inc .... G 517 485-5828
  Lansing *(G-9693)*
Enhanceher Collection LLC .... G 313 279-7308
  Detroit *(G-4210)*
Enuf Haircare and Lashes LLC .... G 586 354-1798
  Detroit *(G-4211)*
Esl Supplies LLC .... G 517 525-7877
  Mason *(G-11131)*
Esyntrk Industries LLC .... G 248 730-0640
  Orchard Lake *(G-12717)*
Exclusive Brands LLC .... F 734 210-0107
  Livonia *(G-10201)*
Exquise Inc .... G 248 220-9048
  Detroit *(G-4223)*
Faucher Industries .... G 248 515-4772
  Troy *(G-17107)*
Faucher Industries .... G 586 434-5115
  Sterling Heights *(G-16010)*
▲ Faurecia Interior Systems Inc .... B 248 724-5100
  Auburn Hills *(G-889)*
Feleo Mfg Strategies LLC .... F 517 795-1193
  Michigan Center *(G-11293)*
Fenixx Technologies LLC .... F 586 254-6000
  Fraser *(G-5927)*
Fifth Box Industries LLC .... G 734 323-6388
  Northville *(G-12217)*
◆ Flexi Display Marketing Inc .... G 800 875-1725
  Commerce Township *(G-3531)*
Fluresh LLC .... D 616 600-0420
  Grand Rapids *(G-6713)*
Fluresh LLC .... E 616 600-0420
  Adrian *(G-67)*
Forge Industries Lc .... G 616 402-7887
  Zeeland *(G-19022)*
Fowlerville Feed & Pet Sups .... G 517 223-9115
  Fowlerville *(G-5839)*

Fresh Coast Candles .... G 616 405-8518
  Holland *(G-8041)*
Friscos Mechanical & Fabg .... G 517 719-3933
  Holt *(G-8312)*
Fruit Haven Nursery Inc .... G 231 889-9973
  Kaleva *(G-9379)*
Fulcrum Industries Inc .... G 888 818-5121
  Grand Rapids *(G-6726)*
Fun Learning Company LLC .... G 269 362-0651
  Macomb *(G-10597)*
Fur Brained Ideas .... G 248 830-0764
  Grosse Pointe Woods *(G-7567)*
G & L Mfg Inc .... G 810 724-4101
  Imlay City *(G-8632)*
Gaishin Manufacturing .... G 269 459-6996
  Kalamazoo *(G-9191)*
Garbarino Industries LLC .... G 586 215-5479
  Clinton Township *(G-3248)*
Garden of Edyn .... G 517 410-9931
  Holt *(G-8313)*
Genstone LLC .... G 517 902-4730
  Adrian *(G-70)*
Glamour Girl Hair LLC .... F 313 204-4143
  Detroit *(G-4264)*
Global Industries Inc .... G 248 357-7211
  Southfield *(G-15577)*
Global Manufacturing Inds .... G 513 271-2180
  Hastings *(G-7794)*
Gmd Industries Inc .... G 616 245-1215
  Grand Rapids *(G-6745)*
Gopher Scope Manufacturing .... G 248 667-4025
  New Hudson *(G-12054)*
Gr Psp LLC .... G 616 785-1070
  Grand Rapids *(G-6753)*
Gr X Manufacturing .... F 616 541-7420
  Caledonia *(G-2375)*
Grand River Aseptic Mfg .... G 616 678-2400
  Grand Rapids *(G-6775)*
Great Lakes Cylinders LLC .... F 248 437-4141
  New Hudson *(G-12055)*
Greatlakespowertoolscom .... G 231 733-6200
  Muskegon *(G-11832)*
Green Peak Industries LLC .... G 517 408-0178
  Dimondale *(G-4763)*
Grit Manufacturing LLC .... G 517 285-5277
  Williamsburg *(G-18556)*
GRX Manufacturing .... F 616 570-0832
  Grand Rapids *(G-6793)*
Gvd Industries LLC .... G 616 836-4067
  Holland *(G-8063)*
Gvd Industries LLC .... G 616 298-7243
  Holland *(G-8064)*
H & B Machining LLC .... G 810 986-2423
  Howell *(G-8458)*
Hair Vault LLC .... G 586 649-8218
  Plymouth *(G-13182)*
Hammerhead Industries .... F 574 277-8911
  Niles *(G-12135)*
Hand Cast Covers .... G 810 225-7770
  Howell *(G-8459)*
Harrison Industries Inc .... G 231 881-4704
  Harbor Springs *(G-7648)*
Harry & Assoc LLC .... G 248 446-8820
  South Lyon *(G-15437)*
Harvest Oak Manufacturing .... G 517 781-4016
  Bronson *(G-2115)*
Harvey Industries LLC .... G 734 405-2430
  Livonia *(G-10236)*
Havers Heritage .... G 517 423-3455
  Clinton *(G-3140)*
HB Manufacturing LLC .... G 586 703-5269
  Shelby Township *(G-15233)*
Head Over Heels .... G 248 435-2954
  Troy *(G-17139)*
Heaven Scent Candle Co & Decor .... G 810 374-6279
  Otisville *(G-12781)*
Heed Industries .... G 906 233-7192
  Escanaba *(G-5075)*
Helion Industries LLC .... G 618 303-0214
  Kalamazoo *(G-9211)*
Heritage .... G 734 414-0343
  Plymouth *(G-13187)*
High Rize Candles .... G 616 818-9527
  Wyoming *(G-18883)*
Highland Tank & Mfg Co .... F 248 795-2000
  Clarkston *(G-3040)*
Hippiwic Candles .... G 586 488-8931
  Warren *(G-17854)*
Holland House Candles Inc .... G 800 238-8467
  Holland *(G-8079)*

Hoosier Tank and Manufacturing .... G 269 683-2550
  Niles *(G-12136)*
Horse Creek Candles LLC .... G 517 962-1476
  Jackson *(G-8905)*
Huys Industries .... G 734 895-3067
  Romulus *(G-14284)*
I & D Manufacturing LLC .... G 517 852-9215
  Nashville *(G-11955)*
Ict Industries .... G 586 727-2677
  Lenox *(G-9998)*
Ieq Industries .... G 616 902-1865
  Lowell *(G-10505)*
Imagillation Inc .... G 734 481-0140
  Ypsilanti *(G-18954)*
In The Stars Candles .... G 231 590-7407
  Traverse City *(G-16721)*
Income Waxcom .... G 616 457-4277
  Jenison *(G-9057)*
Industrial Mtal Idntfction Inc .... G 616 847-0060
  Spring Lake *(G-15824)*
Industrial Services Group .... F 269 945-5291
  Lowell *(G-10506)*
Industries Indy Bear .... F 248 446-1435
  South Lyon *(G-15438)*
Inflatable Industries .... G 517 505-0700
  Birch Run *(G-1707)*
Inhe Manufacturing LLC .... G 616 863-2222
  Jenison *(G-9058)*
Innovative Fabrication LLC .... E 734 789-9099
  Flat Rock *(G-5622)*
Innovative Mfg Technologi .... G 810 941-4675
  Wales *(G-17629)*
Innovative Thermal Systems LLC .... G 586 920-2900
  Warren *(G-17866)*
International Wood Inds Inc .... G 800 598-9663
  Grand Rapids *(G-6851)*
Intuitive Technology Inc .... G 602 249-5750
  Dexter *(G-4743)*
Irene Industries LLC .... G 757 696-3969
  Commerce Township *(G-3545)*
Ironmann Industries .... G 810 695-9177
  Holly *(G-8279)*
Ivory Industries Inc .... G 313 821-3291
  Detroit *(G-4329)*
J & K Industries LLC .... G 586 948-2747
  Chesterfield *(G-2897)*
▲ J F McCaughin Co .... E 231 759-7304
  Norton Shores *(G-12303)*
J&C Industries .... G 734 479-0069
  Riverview *(G-13877)*
J&D Industries LLC .... G 734 430-6582
  Newport *(G-12103)*
J&S Homemade Candles .... G 517 885-1983
  Lansing *(G-9855)*
Jac Mfg Inc .... G 269 679-3301
  Schoolcraft *(G-15121)*
Jamcat Candles LLC .... G 313 319-3125
  Grosse Pointe Park *(G-7557)*
Jandys Home .... G 616 446-7013
  Alto *(G-334)*
Jcr Industries Inc .... G 616 364-4856
  Grand Rapids *(G-6865)*
Jef-Scot Metal Industries .... F 231 582-0452
  Boyne City *(G-1892)*
Jetpack Industries LLC .... G 248 689-5083
  Troy *(G-17186)*
Jgs Manufacturing LLC .... G 248 376-1659
  Livonia *(G-10259)*
Jim Bennett .... G 517 323-9061
  Lansing *(G-9707)*
Jk Manufacturing Co .... F 231 258-2638
  Kalkaska *(G-9391)*
Jt General Industries LLC .... G 517 712-8481
  Howell *(G-8469)*
Jupiter Manufacturing .... G 989 551-0519
  Harbor Beach *(G-7633)*
Jus Kutz LLC .... G 248 882-5462
  Pontiac *(G-13390)*
Jwg Industries .... G 734 881-0312
  Garden City *(G-6103)*
K & L Manufacturing Ltd .... G 734 475-1009
  Grass Lake *(G-7439)*
Kalamazoo Candle Company .... F 269 532-9816
  Kalamazoo *(G-9236)*
Karmann Manufacturing LLC .... E 734 582-5900
  Plymouth *(G-13210)*
Katts Candles & More .... G 269 281-6805
  Saint Joseph *(G-14940)*
KB Property Holdings LLC .... E 269 344-0870
  Kalamazoo *(G-9252)*

Employee Codes: A=Over 500 employees, B=251-500
C=101-250, D=51-100, E=20-50, F=10-19, G=3-9

2022 Harris Michigan
Industrial Directory

Kelsheimer Industries LLC ....G.... 810 701-9455
Corunna (G-3709)
Ken Budowick Fabricating LLC ....G.... 586 263-1318
Clinton Township (G-3271)
Kenny G Mfg & Sls LLC ....G.... 313 218-6297
Brownstown (G-2148)
Kenyon Tj & Associates Inc ....G.... 231 544-1144
Bellaire (G-1476)
Kerr Industries of Michigan ....G.... 586 578-9383
Warren (G-17894)
Keviar Candles ....G.... 248 325-4087
Southfield (G-15616)
Kevin Larkin Inc ....G.... 248 736-8203
Waterford (G-18131)
Keyes-Davis Company ....E.... 269 962-7505
Springfield (G-15871)
Kharon Industries ....G.... 810 630-6355
Swartz Creek (G-16356)
Kidde Safety ....F.... 800 880-6788
Novi (G-12452)
Kims Mart Inc ....G.... 313 592-4929
Detroit (G-4362)
Kitty Condo LLC ....G.... 419 690-9063
Livonia (G-10266)
Kommar Industries ....G.... 231 334-3475
Glen Arbor (G-6210)
Kraus Fire Equipment Inc ....G.... 810 744-4780
Burton (G-2238)
Kriewall Enterprises Inc ....E.... 586 336-0600
Romeo (G-14227)
Krysak Industries LLC ....G.... 312 848-1952
Southfield (G-15620)
Ktc Industries LLC ....G.... 989 838-0388
Traverse City (G-16734)
Kymora Kandles LLC ....G.... 517 667-6067
Maple Rapids (G-10945)
L&W Products ....G.... 248 661-3889
Farmington Hills (G-5287)
L4 Manufacturing LLC ....G.... 810 217-3407
Brighton (G-2017)
Lake Michigan Candles LLC ....G.... 231 766-0412
Muskegon (G-11856)
Lawrence Industries Inc ....G.... 269 664-4614
Plainwell (G-13081)
Le Host LLC ....G.... 248 546-4247
Ferndale (G-5565)
Leanne Sowa ....G.... 616 225-8858
Cedar Springs (G-2654)
Legacy Barricades Inc ....G.... 616 656-9600
Grand Rapids (G-6935)
Legend Lllys Pet Grming Ret Sp ....G.... 734 346-6030
Detroit (G-4386)
Liberty Advisors Inc ....G.... 269 679-3281
Schoolcraft (G-15123)
Liberty Automotive Tech LLC ....G.... 269 487-8114
Holland (G-8127)
Limited Lblty Co Colormemink ....G.... 313 707-3366
Brownstown Twp (G-2156)
Lion Labs Ltd ....F.... 248 231-0753
Lansing (G-9712)
Liquidgoldconcept Inc ....G.... 734 926-9197
Ypsilanti (G-18963)
Lite N Go Inc ....G.... 248 414-7540
Dearborn (G-3863)
Loftis Manufacturing Inc ....G.... 855 564-8665
Chesterfield (G-2905)
Loonar Stn Two The 2 or 2nd ....G.... 419 720-1222
Temperance (G-16537)
LP Industries Ltd ....G.... 313 834-4847
Detroit (G-4410)
Lucky Bird Candle Co ....G.... 734 272-7338
Chelsea (G-2819)
Lummi Customs Lc ....G.... 702 713-8428
Linden (G-10064)
M Industries LLC ....G.... 616 745-4279
Ada (G-27)
M Three Manufacturing LLC ....G.... 810 824-4734
Kimball (G-9495)
Magnatron NC Pattern and Mfg ....G.... 810 522-7520
Howell (G-8475)
Mannetron ....F.... 269 962-3475
Battle Creek (G-1271)
Manufacturers Solutions LLC ....G.... 616 894-2964
Greenville (G-7498)
Manufacturing Options ....G.... 989 430-6770
Midland (G-11386)
Manufctring Partners Group LLC ....G.... 517 749-4050
Lapeer (G-9946)
Maple Ridge Companies Inc ....F.... 989 356-4807
Posen (G-13644)
Marada Industries ....G.... 586 264-4908
New Hudson (G-12062)
Mark Eaton Sales and Mfg ....G.... 517 741-5000
Union City (G-17495)
Marrone Michigan Manufactoring ....G.... 269 427-0300
Bangor (G-1130)
Matney Models ....G.... 734 848-8195
Erie (G-5051)
Maximum Manufacturing LLC ....G.... 810 272-0804
Lake Orion (G-9617)
Meridian Industries ....G.... 248 526-0444
Troy (G-17245)
Metalworking Industries of MI ....G.... 248 538-0680
Farmington Hills (G-5316)
Metro Engrg of Grnd Rapids ....F.... 616 458-2823
Grand Rapids (G-6981)
Mettle Craft Manufacturing LLC ....G.... 586 306-8962
Sterling Heights (G-16095)
Mfg United LLC ....G.... 313 928-1802
Melvindale (G-11204)
Mfr Enterprises Inc ....G.... 517 285-9555
Lansing (G-9775)
Mfr Enterprises LLC ....G.... 248 965-3220
Troy (G-17255)
MGM Industries Inc ....G.... 248 561-7558
Berkley (G-1631)
Mgs Horticultural USA Inc ....E.... 248 661-4378
Detroit (G-4442)
Mh Industries Ltd ....G.... 734 261-2600
Detroit (G-4443)
MI Soy Candle Company LLC ....G.... 586 350-7654
Warren (G-17927)
Michigan Laser Mfg LLC ....G.... 810 623-2783
Brighton (G-2030)
Midwest Grinding ....G.... 734 395-1033
Maybee (G-11170)
Mindchip Industries LLC ....G.... 313 355-2447
Brownstown (G-2150)
Mirus Industries Inc ....G.... 616 402-3256
Grand Haven (G-6336)
Mj Industries LLC ....G.... 586 200-3903
Roseville (G-14445)
Mlc Manufacturing ....E.... 616 846-6990
Spring Lake (G-15836)
Mobility Accessories LLC ....G.... 734 262-3760
Northville (G-12242)
Mobility Howell Products ....G.... 586 558-8308
Warren (G-17934)
Modern Fur Dressing LLC ....G.... 517 589-5575
Leslie (G-10015)
Monogram Market LLC ....G.... 517 455-9083
Dewitt (G-4714)
Morton Industries LLC ....F.... 616 453-7121
Grand Rapids (G-7029)
Mote Enterprises Inc ....G.... 248 613-3413
New Haven (G-12035)
Mount Mfg LLC ....G.... 231 487-2118
Negaunee (G-11970)
Mr McGooz Products Inc ....G.... 313 693-4003
Detroit (G-4469)
MRC Indsutries ....G.... 586 204-5241
Roseville (G-14449)
MRC Industries ....G.... 269 552-5586
Kalamazoo (G-9277)
Mse ....G.... 586 264-4120
Sterling Heights (G-16106)
Msmac Designs LLC ....G.... 313 521-6289
Detroit (G-4471)
Music Box ....G.... 517 539-5069
Jackson (G-8972)
My Secret Bundles LLC ....G.... 586 610-2804
Clinton Township (G-3307)
Neotech Industries Inc ....G.... 248 681-6667
Waterford (G-18139)
Neptune Candles LLC ....G.... 231 947-0554
Traverse City (G-16768)
New Boston Candle Company ....G.... 734 782-5809
New Boston (G-12014)
New Key Pet LLC ....G.... 734 716-5357
Canton (G-2500)
Next Chapter Mfg Corp ....G.... 616 773-1200
Grand Rapids (G-7043)
Next Level Manufacturing LLC ....E.... 269 397-1220
Jenison (G-9064)
Ngu Industries LLC ....G.... 313 283-9570
Lincoln Park (G-10052)
Noble Industries ....G.... 616 245-7400
Middleville (G-11310)
Nodel-Co ....F.... 248 543-1325
Ferndale (G-5573)
North Coast Studios Inc ....F.... 586 359-6630
Roseville (G-14455)
North Star Candle Company LLC ....G.... 248 430-4321
Dearborn (G-3877)
Northbound Industries LLC ....G.... 661 510-8537
Rochester Hills (G-14071)
▲ Northwoods Manufacturing Inc ....D.... 906 779-2370
Kingsford (G-9516)
Novelty House ....G.... 248 583-9900
Madison Heights (G-10790)
Nyman Industries LLC ....G.... 702 290-9433
Grosse Pointe (G-7531)
Oak Mountain Industries ....G.... 734 941-7000
Romulus (G-14313)
Octet Industries LLC ....G.... 225 302-0541
Ann Arbor (G-598)
Odin Defense Industries Inc ....G.... 248 434-5072
Troy (G-17286)
Pacific Industries Inc ....G.... 810 360-9141
Whitmore Lake (G-18542)
Packys Pet Supplies LLC ....G.... 989 422-5484
Houghton Lake (G-8402)
Palo Alto Manufacturing LLC ....G.... 248 266-3669
Auburn Hills (G-992)
Pandia Industries LLC ....G.... 269 386-2110
Colon (G-3489)
Panelcraft Inc ....G.... 734 646-2173
Canton (G-2504)
Paragon Molds Corporation ....E.... 586 294-7630
Fraser (G-5974)
Patriot Bars Mfg LLC ....G.... 248 342-3319
Chesterfield (G-2922)
Pearson Industries LLC ....G.... 740 584-9080
Detroit (G-4510)
Pegasus Industries ....F.... 810 356-5579
Lapeer (G-9953)
Personal Touch ....G.... 313 354-4255
Detroit (G-4520)
Pesti Manufacturing Company ....G.... 586 920-2731
Warren (G-17960)
Pet Supplies Plus ....G.... 616 554-3600
Grand Rapids (G-7083)
Petzpaws LLC ....G.... 313 414-9894
West Bloomfield (G-18304)
Pingree Mfg L3c ....G.... 313 444-8428
Detroit (G-4524)
Pinsmedalscoins LLC ....G.... 312 771-2973
Lansing (G-9729)
Plainview Industries LLC ....G.... 517 652-1466
Charlotte (G-2765)
Plush Products Mfg LLC ....G.... 586 871-8082
Clyde (G-3414)
Pmd Automotive LLC ....G.... 248 732-7554
Pontiac (G-13407)
Point A Organization ....G.... 313 971-4625
Detroit (G-4529)
Ponder Industrial ....G.... 989 391-4575
Bay City (G-1388)
Pr39 Industries LLC ....G.... 248 866-1445
Keego Harbor (G-9422)
Preacher Industries ....G.... 248 881-6590
White Lake (G-18463)
Prf Manufacturing USA Inc ....G.... 586 218-3055
Roseville (G-14465)
Price Industries LLC ....G.... 313 706-9862
Dearborn (G-3885)
Price Koch Industries ....G.... 616 871-0263
Caledonia (G-2394)
Pringles Manufacturing Company ....F.... 731 421-3148
Battle Creek (G-1282)
Pro-Built Mfg ....G.... 989 354-1321
Alpena (G-312)
Probus Technical Services Inc ....F.... 876 226-5692
Troy (G-17316)
Protojet LLC ....F.... 810 956-8000
Fraser (G-5981)
PSI Labs ....F.... 734 369-6273
Ann Arbor (G-627)
Purescription Grade LLC ....G.... 313 410-5686
West Bloomfield (G-18308)
Purus Candles ....G.... 586 876-7800
New Baltimore (G-11991)
Px2 Holdings LLC ....D.... 855 420-0020
Troy (G-17321)
Q Sage Inc ....F.... 989 775-2424
Mount Pleasant (G-11735)
Qsdg Manufacturing LLC ....F.... 231 941-1222
Traverse City (G-16808)
Qt Glamour Collection LLC ....G.... 248 605-5507
Detroit (G-4544)

Quality Stainless MGF G 248 866-6219
Metamora ***(G-11285)***
Quantum Custom Designs LLC G 989 293-7372
Fraser ***(G-5984)***
Quinco Tool G 313 353-1340
Oak Park ***(G-12638)***
R House Industries LLC F 616 890-7125
Grand Rapids ***(G-7133)***
R J Chemical Manufacturing LLC G 810 252-8425
Clio ***(G-3410)***
R J Manufacturing G 810 610-0205
Davison ***(G-3794)***
Race Fuel Candles LLC G 616 889-1674
Rockford ***(G-14186)***
Ravishing Wreaths G 248 613-6210
Brighton ***(G-2062)***
▲ Rayconnect Inc D 248 265-4000
Rochester Hills ***(G-14100)***
Real Steel Manufacturing LLC F 231 457-4673
Muskegon ***(G-11906)***
Recycledlps Com G 810 623-4498
Brighton ***(G-2063)***
Redbud Roots Lab I LLC F 312 656-3823
Buchanan ***(G-2202)***
Reemarkable Eyes LLC G 313 461-3006
Eastpointe ***(G-4943)***
Rel Inc E 906 337-3018
Calumet ***(G-2413)***
Remy Girls G 313 397-2870
Detroit ***(G-4565)***
Resourcemfg F 810 937-5058
Port Huron ***(G-13523)***
Reynolds Cntrless Grinding LLC G 313 418-5109
Redford ***(G-13764)***
Rfm Manufacturing G 810 522-6922
Brighton ***(G-2065)***
Rilas & Rogers LLC F 937 901-4228
Canton ***(G-2517)***
Rise Beyond LLC G 734 203-0644
Ypsilanti ***(G-18974)***
Rodzina Industries Inc G 810 235-2341
Flint ***(G-5755)***
Roi Rich Oles Industries LLC G 616 610-7050
Saint Joseph ***(G-14958)***
▲ Rol Usa Inc G 616 499-8484
Holland ***(G-8183)***
Roots Industries G 231 779-2865
Cadillac ***(G-2352)***
Roses Susies Feather G 989 689-6570
Hope ***(G-8363)***
Rottman Manufacturing Group G 586 693-5676
Sterling Heights ***(G-16160)***
Roush Industries Inc F 313 937-8603
Redford ***(G-13766)***
Rpd Manufacturing LLC G 248 760-4796
Milford ***(G-11486)***
Rta Industries LLC G 269 327-2916
Portage ***(G-13601)***
Ruf International Mfg Corp G 954 448-3454
Charlevoix ***(G-2732)***
Ruff Life LLC G 231 347-1214
Petoskey ***(G-13022)***
Rusnak Tool & Mfg LLC G 734 362-8656
Woodhaven ***(G-18803)***
S Sheree Collection LLC G 616 930-1416
Grand Rapids ***(G-7176)***
Saegertown Manufacturing Inc G 517 281-9789
Howell ***(G-8514)***
Saffe Furniture Corp G 231 329-1790
Muskegon ***(G-11915)***
Sashabaw Bead Co G 248 969-1353
Oxford ***(G-12915)***
Sawtelle Industries LLC G 248 645-1869
Bloomfield Hills ***(G-1860)***
Schlegel G 248 344-0997
Northville ***(G-12258)***
Schwartz Manufacturing G 517 552-3100
Howell ***(G-8515)***
Scw Industries LLC G 616 656-5959
Lansing ***(G-9893)***
SDS LLC G 231 492-5996
Traverse City ***(G-16827)***
Select Distributors LLC F 586 510-4647
Warren ***(G-18008)***
Sensatnal Smlls From Mesha LLC G 734 905-1058
Ypsilanti ***(G-18976)***
Services To Enhance Potential G 313 278-3040
Dearborn ***(G-3895)***
Shamrock Industries LLC F 616 566-6214
Holland ***(G-8189)***
Shaw Industries Detroit Rdc G 800 469-9516
Van Buren Twp ***(G-17552)***
Shelby Industries Inc G 586 884-4421
Shelby Township ***(G-15331)***
Sheri Boston G 248 627-9576
Ortonville ***(G-12751)***
Shoreline Manufacturing LLC G 616 834-1503
Holland ***(G-8193)***
Shoreline Manufacturing LLC G 616 834-1503
Holland ***(G-8194)***
▲ Sika Auto Eaton Rapids Inc F 248 588-2270
Madison Heights ***(G-10828)***
Sizmek Dsp Inc E 313 516-4482
Troy ***(G-17355)***
Sk Enterprises Inc G 616 785-1070
Grand Rapids ***(G-7201)***
Skin Bar VII LLC G 313 397-9919
Detroit ***(G-4597)***
Sky Industries G 810 614-6044
Columbiaville ***(G-3495)***
Slotbrokers LLC G 231 929-7568
Traverse City ***(G-16835)***
Smart Swatter LLC G 989 763-2626
Harbor Springs ***(G-7657)***
Sofia Rose Industries Inc G 810 278-4907
Clay ***(G-3125)***
Solarfall Industries LLC G 269 274-6108
Hemlock ***(G-7855)***
Sole Industries LLC G 586 322-5492
Washington Township ***(G-18096)***
Southwestern Industries Inc G 517 667-0466
Tecumseh ***(G-16516)***
Soy D-Lights & Scentsations G 989 728-5947
Hale ***(G-7590)***
Sparks Exhbits Envrnments Corp G 248 291-0007
Royal Oak ***(G-14582)***
Spec International Inc F 616 248-3022
Grand Rapids ***(G-7211)***
Special-Lite Inc - Benton G 269 423-7068
Benton Harbor ***(G-1588)***
Spring Air Co G 616 459-8234
Grand Rapids ***(G-7221)***
Spurt Industries G 248 956-7643
Wixom ***(G-18755)***
Sra Industries G 586 251-2000
Shelby Township ***(G-15343)***
◆ Stageright Corporation C 989 386-7393
Clare ***(G-2999)***
Stainless Concepts LLC G 616 427-6682
Zeeland ***(G-19081)***
Stansley Industries Inc G 810 515-1919
Flint ***(G-5769)***
Steadfast Lab G 248 242-2291
Hazel Park ***(G-7843)***
Stewart General Incorporated G 616 318-4971
Nunica ***(G-12586)***
▲ Stewart Manufacturing LLC D 906 498-7600
Hermansville ***(G-7862)***
Stoked & Bearded LLC G 248 513-2927
Clinton Township ***(G-3364)***
Stretchy Screens G 989 780-1624
Caledonia ***(G-2402)***
Stride Inc E 616 309-1600
Grand Rapids ***(G-7229)***
Studio One Midwest Inc F 269 962-3475
Battle Creek ***(G-1302)***
Studtmans Stuff G 269 673-3126
Allegan ***(G-183)***
Sues Scented Soy Candles G 989 642-3352
Hemlock ***(G-7856)***
Suiter Industries Inc G 989 277-1554
Lansing ***(G-9897)***
Summit Cutting Tool and Mfg In G 248 624-3949
Wixom ***(G-18760)***
Sun Coast Coverings LLC F 734 947-1230
Taylor ***(G-16480)***
T 4 Manufacturing G 616 952-0020
Kent City ***(G-9438)***
T K Industries Inc G 586 242-5969
Shelby Township ***(G-15348)***
Tags R Us LLC G 248 880-4062
White Lake ***(G-18468)***
Tech World LLC G 616 901-2611
Shelbyville ***(G-15375)***
▲ Tecla Company Inc E 248 624-8200
Commerce Township ***(G-3576)***
Telescopic Seating Systems LLC F 855 713-0118
Grand Haven ***(G-6370)***
Texwood Industries G 517 266-4739
Adrian ***(G-98)***
The Spott G 269 459-6462
Kalamazoo ***(G-9355)***
Therapeutic Health Choices LLC G 989 459-2020
Bay City ***(G-1406)***
Tide Rings LLC G 586 206-3142
Allenton ***(G-232)***
Tillman Manufacturing Com G 248 802-8430
Southfield ***(G-15723)***
Timberwolf Furnace Co G 231 924-6654
Grant ***(G-7433)***
Tip Top Screw Manufacturi G 989 739-5157
Saginaw ***(G-14776)***
To Z A Manufacturing G 734 782-3911
Flat Rock ***(G-5631)***
Toreson Industries Inc G 818 261-7249
Inkster ***(G-8676)***
Total Grinding Solutions LLC F 586 541-5300
Warren ***(G-18041)***
Total Repair Express MI LLC F 248 690-9410
Auburn Hills ***(G-1061)***
Tramar Industries G 313 387-3600
Redford ***(G-13780)***
Tremco Inc Sealex Mfg Pla G 231 348-5020
Harbor Springs ***(G-7660)***
Trident Mfg LLC F 989 875-5145
Ithaca ***(G-8796)***
Triunfar Industries Inc G 313 790-5592
South Lyon ***(G-15460)***
Triunfar Industries Inc I G 248 993-9302
Commerce Township ***(G-3579)***
Tru-Fit International Inc G 248 855-8845
West Bloomfield ***(G-18319)***
Truth Traxx LLC F 800 792-2239
Flint ***(G-5786)***
Twisted Scissor G 248 620-2626
Clarkston ***(G-3074)***
Uis Industries LLC G 734 443-3737
Livonia ***(G-10453)***
Unit City Wigs LLC G 313 264-8112
Eastpointe ***(G-4946)***
United Mfg Netwrk Inc G 586 321-7887
Chesterfield ***(G-2960)***
Universal Industries Inco G 248 259-2674
Macomb ***(G-10647)***
Universal Pultrusion G 269 423-7068
Decatur ***(G-3952)***
Unypos Manufacturing Inc G 810 701-8719
Grand Blanc ***(G-6265)***
▲ US Salon Supply LLC F 616 365-5790
Paw Paw ***(G-12958)***
◆ USF Delta Tooling LLC C 248 391-6800
Auburn Hills ***(G-1075)***
Uvsheltron Inc G 888 877-7946
Pontiac ***(G-13423)***
Val Manufacturing Co LLC G 248 765-8694
Troy ***(G-17424)***
Valley Manufacturing G 248 767-5078
Wixom ***(G-18784)***
Vantage Point Mfg Inc F 989 343-1070
West Branch ***(G-18345)***
Vast Production Services Inc D 248 838-9680
Troy ***(G-17432)***
Vb Chesaning LLC C 989 323-2333
Chesaning ***(G-2831)***
Venture Technology Groups Inc F 248 473-8450
Novi ***(G-12566)***
Vertex Industries Inc G 248 838-1827
Dearborn ***(G-3909)***
▼ Viking Spas Inc F 616 248-7800
Wyoming ***(G-18917)***
Viladon Corporation G 248 548-0043
Oak Park ***(G-12649)***
Vision Global Industries D 248 390-5805
Macomb ***(G-10649)***
Waters Industries LLC G 616 848-8050
Custer ***(G-3752)***
Wax Poetic G 616 272-4693
Grand Rapids ***(G-7325)***
Wende J Periard G 989 770-4542
Burt ***(G-2217)***
Weslope Industries Inc G 248 320-7007
Royal Oak ***(G-14592)***
West Mich Flcking Assembly LLC E 269 639-1634
Grand Rapids ***(G-7331)***
White Knight Industries G 269 823-4207
South Haven ***(G-15426)***
Wholesale Weave Inc F 800 762-2037
Detroit ***(G-4682)***
Wild Manufacturing G 586 719-2028
Harrison Township ***(G-7731)***

Employee Codes: A=Over 500 employees, B=251-500
C=101-250, D=51-100, E=20-50, F=10-19, G=3-9

2022 Harris Michigan
Industrial Directory
907

39 MISCELLANEOUS MANUFACTURING INDUSTRIES

Company	Code	Phone
Williams Diversified Inc	E	734 421-6100
Livonia (G-10475)		
Willies Wicks	G	810 730-4176
Flushing (G-5817)		
Willow Mfg Inc	G	231 275-1026
Interlochen (G-8686)		
Wings Mfg Inc	G	585 873-3105
Mount Clemens (G-11664)		
Winsol Electronics LLC	G	810 767-2987
Flint (G-5793)		
Wolfe Whistle	G	517 303-9197
Lansing (G-9750)		
Wood Haven Truss	G	231 821-0252
Holton (G-8343)		
Woody Hollow Candles	G	906 774-7839
Iron Mountain (G-8737)		
World Class Steel & Proc Inc	G	586 585-1734
Troy (G-17453)		
Wreathinkingbykathie LLC	G	248 432-7312
Farmington Hills (G-5416)		
Wright & Filippis LLC	F	517 484-2624
Lansing (G-9906)		
Xplor Outside Box LLC	F	248 961-0536
Warren (G-18076)		
Xtreme Mfg	G	906 353-8005
Baraga (G-1151)		
Y Not Candles	G	313 289-6299
Dearborn Heights (G-3944)		
Young Manufacturing Inc	G	906 483-3851
Dollar Bay (G-4766)		
Zerilli & Sesi LLC	G	586 741-8805
Chesterfield (G-2967)		
Zero Hour Production LLC	F	616 498-3545
Ann Arbor (G-722)		
Zoe Health	G	616 485-1909
Kentwood (G-9485)		
Zoyes East Inc	G	248 584-3300
Ferndale (G-5599)		

73 BUSINESS SERVICES

7372 Prepackaged Software

Company	Code	Phone
123go LLC	G	734 773-0049
Ann Arbor (G-340)		
21st Century Graphic Tech LLC	G	586 463-9599
Utica (G-17501)		
313 Certified LLC	G	248 915-8419
Bloomfield Hills (G-1787)		
360ofme Inc	G	844 360-6363
Royal Oak (G-14500)		
3dfx Interactive Inc	G	918 938-8967
Saginaw (G-14599)		
3r Info LLC	F	201 221-6133
Canton (G-2425)		
4d Systems LLC	E	800 380-9165
Flint (G-5632)		
Accessible Information LLC	G	248 338-4928
Bloomfield Hills (G-1790)		
Accord Software Solutions LLC	G	616 604-1699
Canton (G-2428)		
Adadapted Inc	F	313 744-3383
Ann Arbor (G-349)		
Advanced Tubular Tech Inc	G	248 674-2059
Clarkston (G-3015)		
AK Rewards LLC	G	734 272-7078
Ann Arbor (G-358)		
Akamai Technologies Inc	G	734 424-1142
Pinckney (G-13043)		
Alfa Financial Software Inc	D	855 680-7100
Birmingham (G-1717)		
Alta Vista Technology LLC	F	855 913-3228
Royal Oak (G-14506)		
Altair Engineering Inc	C	248 614-2400
Troy (G-16928)		
Amesite Inc	G	734 876-8141
Detroit (G-4015)		
Amicus Software	G	313 417-9550
White Lake (G-18449)		
Ansys Inc	G	248 613-2677
Ann Arbor (G-371)		
Apis North America LLC	G	800 470-8970
Royal Oak (G-14509)		
Appgraft LLC	G	734 546-8458
Canton (G-2436)		
Applied Computer Technologies	F	248 388-0211
West Bloomfield (G-18263)		
Appropos LLC	E	844 462-7776
Grand Rapids (G-6465)		
Aras Corp	F	248 385-5293
Troy (G-16951)		
Arbormetrix Inc	C	734 661-7944
Ann Arbor (G-377)		
Arbortext Inc	C	734 997-0200
Ann Arbor (G-378)		
Arctuition LLC	G	616 635-9959
Ada (G-9)		
Argus Technologies LLC	E	616 538-9895
Grand Rapids (G-6469)		
Artifcial Intllgnce Tech Sltn	E	877 787-6268
Ferndale (G-5528)		
Asset Health Inc	D	248 822-2870
Troy (G-16961)		
Atos Syntel Inc	A	248 619-2800
Troy (G-16964)		
Aurora Software	G	248 853-2358
Rochester Hills (G-13956)		
Autodesk Inc	G	248 347-9650
Novi (G-12368)		
Automated Bookkeeping Inc	G	866 617-3122
Detroit (G-4031)		
Automated Media Inc	D	313 937-5000
Canton (G-2438)		
Auvesy Inc	G	616 888-3770
Grand Rapids (G-6485)		
Auxant Software LLC	G	810 584-5947
Grand Blanc (G-6233)		
Azore Software LLC	E	734 525-0300
Livonia (G-10130)		
Bell and Howell LLC	G	734 421-1727
Livonia (G-10136)		
Betterlife	G	248 889-3245
Highland (G-7883)		
Biscayne and Associates Inc	G	248 304-0600
Milford (G-11455)		
Black Ski Weekend LLC	G	313 879-7150
West Bloomfield (G-18265)		
Blue Pony LLC	G	616 291-5554
Hudsonville (G-8572)		
BMC Software Inc	F	248 888-4600
Farmington Hills (G-5183)		
Boa Software LLC	G	517 540-0681
Howell (G-8430)		
Bokhara Pet Care Centers	G	231 264-6667
Elk Rapids (G-5021)		
Bond Street Software	G	616 847-8377
Grand Rapids (G-6521)		
Braiq Inc	G	858 729-4116
Detroit (G-4066)		
Brenton Consulting LLC	G	248 342-6590
Northville (G-12198)		
Brinston Acquisition LLC	D	248 269-1000
Troy (G-16985)		
Broadsword Solutions Corp	F	248 341-3367
Waterford (G-18105)		
C R T & Associates Inc	G	231 946-1680
Traverse City (G-16635)		
Capital Billing Systems Inc	G	248 478-7298
Farmington Hills (G-5196)		
Capital Software Inc Michigan	G	517 324-9100
East Lansing (G-4889)		
Catylist Inc	G	734 973-3185
Ann Arbor (G-416)		
Chain-Sys Corporation	G	517 627-1173
Lansing (G-9757)		
Change Dynamix Inc	G	248 671-6700
Royal Oak (G-14525)		
Circlebuilder Software LLC	G	248 770-3191
Franklin (G-5882)		
Clear Estimates Inc	F	734 368-9951
Ann Arbor (G-426)		
Click Care LLC	G	989 792-1544
Saginaw (G-14631)		
Cloud Apps Consulting LLC	G	616 528-0528
Grand Rapids (G-6575)		
Coeus LLC	G	248 564-1958
Bloomfield Hills (G-1808)		
Collagecom LLC	G	248 971-0538
White Lake (G-18453)		
Comet Information Systems LLC	G	248 686-2600
Grand Blanc (G-6238)		
Competitive Cmpt Info Tech Inc	F	732 829-9699
Northville (G-12201)		
Complete Data Products Inc	F	248 651-8602
Troy (G-17021)		
Computer Mail Services Inc	F	248 352-6700
Sterling Heights (G-15966)		
Computer Sciences Corp	G	734 761-8513
Ann Arbor (G-434)		
Computer Sciences Corporation	G	586 825-5043
Sterling Heights (G-15967)		
▲ Compuware Corporation	E	313 227-7300
Detroit (G-4100)		
Consistacom Inc	G	906 482-7653
Houghton (G-8381)		
Consolidated Computing Svcs	G	989 906-0467
Bay City (G-1341)		
Core Technology Corporation	F	517 627-1521
Grand Ledge (G-6387)		
Covisint Corporation	B	248 483-2000
Southfield (G-15533)		
Cq Simple LLC	G	989 492-7068
Midland (G-11331)		
Cyberlogic Technologies Inc	E	248 631-2200
Troy (G-17041)		
Cygnet Financial Planning Inc	G	248 673-2900
Waterford (G-18112)		
Cytk Corp	F	313 288-9360
South Lyon (G-15432)		
Dassault Systmes Americas Corp	C	248 267-9696
Auburn Hills (G-858)		
Data Pro Inc	G	269 685-9214
Plainwell (G-13074)		
Datamatic Processing Inc	E	517 882-4401
Lansing (G-9829)		
Diagknowstics Tutoring	G	877 382-1133
Canton (G-2455)		
Dna Software Inc	F	734 222-9080
Plymouth (G-13159)		
Docnetwork Inc	E	734 619-8300
Ann Arbor (G-454)		
Driven-4 LLC	G	269 281-7567
Saint Joseph (G-14927)		
Duo Security Inc	D	866 768-4247
Ann Arbor (G-460)		
Duo Security LLC	C	734 330-2673
Ann Arbor (G-461)		
E Z Logic Data Systems Inc	E	248 817-8800
Farmington Hills (G-5221)		
E-Con LLC	G	248 766-9000
Birmingham (G-1725)		
E-Procurement Services LLC	D	248 630-7200
Auburn Hills (G-873)		
Eca Educational Services Inc	D	248 669-7170
Commerce Township (G-3525)		
Eco Tax Group Inc	G	313 422-1300
Southfield (G-15551)		
Edge Fitnes Training Hdqtr LLC	G	989 486-9870
Midland (G-11361)		
Elk Software LLC	F	800 658-3420
Wixom (G-18654)		
EMC Corporation	G	248 957-5800
Farmington Hills (G-5229)		
Empatheticbot LLC	G	810 938-3168
Canton (G-2458)		
Empower Financials Inc	G	734 747-9393
Ann Arbor (G-473)		
Engineering Tech Assoc Inc	D	248 729-3010
Troy (G-17091)		
Epath Logic Inc	G	313 375-5375
Royal Oak (G-14535)		
Eview 360 LLC	E	248 306-5191
Farmington Hills (G-5239)		
Expectancy Learning LLC	G	866 829-9533
Grand Rapids (G-6692)		
Faac Incorporated	C	734 761-5836
Ann Arbor (G-485)		
Falcon Network Services Inc	G	248 726-0577
Troy (G-17105)		
Fbe Associates Inc	G	989 894-2785
Bay City (G-1357)		
Flashplays Live LLC	G	978 888-3935
Ann Arbor (G-490)		
Foresee Session Replay Inc	G	800 621-2850
Ann Arbor (G-492)		
Forty Eight Forty Solutions	F	713 332-6145
Livonia (G-10216)		
Fuzen Software Inc	G	248 504-6870
Northville (G-12221)		
Gene Codes Forensics Inc	G	734 769-7249
Ann Arbor (G-497)		
Gentry Services of Alabama	G	248 321-6368
Warren (G-17828)		
Genus Inc	G	810 580-9197
Grosse Pointe Park (G-7555)		
Ginkgotree Inc	G	734 707-7191
Detroit (G-4262)		
Global Information Systems Inc	C	248 223-9800
Livonia (G-10225)		
Gnu Software Development Inc	G	586 778-9182
Warren (G-17833)		

Gravity Software LLC ....G....... 844 464-7284
Detroit *(G-4275)*
Great Lakes Infotronics Inc ....E....... 248 476-2500
Northville *(G-12226)*
Great Lakes Technologies ....G....... 734 362-8217
Grosse Ile *(G-7523)*
Guardhat Inc ....G....... 248 281-6089
Southfield *(G-15587)*
Harbor Software Intl Inc ....G....... 231 347-8866
Petoskey *(G-13000)*
Harper Arrington Pubg LLC ....G....... 313 282-6751
Detroit *(G-4295)*
Herfert Software ....G....... 586 776-2880
Eastpointe *(G-4936)*
High Touch Healthcare LLC ....G....... 248 513-2425
Novi *(G-12435)*
Hilgraeve Inc ....G....... 734 243-0576
Monroe *(G-11547)*
Ht Computing Services ....G....... 313 563-0087
Dearborn *(G-3851)*
I-9 Advantage ....F....... 800 724-8546
Troy *(G-17157)*
Ideation International Inc ....F....... 248 737-8854
Farmington Hills *(G-5266)*
Imagesoft ....G....... 919 462-8505
Grand Rapids *(G-6835)*
Infor (us) LLC ....G....... 616 258-3311
Grand Rapids *(G-6844)*
Information Builders Inc ....G....... 248 641-8820
Troy *(G-17166)*
Innovative Programming Systems ....G....... 810 695-9332
Grand Blanc *(G-6249)*
Innovative Sftwr Solutions Ltd ....E....... 616 785-0745
Grand Rapids *(G-6847)*
Inora Technologies Inc ....G....... 734 302-7488
Ann Arbor *(G-529)*
Inovision Inc ....E....... 248 299-1915
Rochester Hills *(G-14040)*
Inovision Sftwr Solutions Inc ....G....... 586 598-8750
Chesterfield *(G-2896)*
Integrated Practice Service ....G....... 248 646-7009
South Lyon *(G-15439)*
Integrted Database Systems Inc ....F....... 989 546-4512
Mount Pleasant *(G-11703)*
Intellibee Inc ....E....... 313 586-4122
Detroit *(G-4323)*
Interact Websites Inc ....F....... 800 515-9672
Midland *(G-11374)*
Interplai Inc ....G....... 734 274-4628
Ann Arbor *(G-531)*
Interpro Technology Inc ....F....... 248 650-8695
Rochester *(G-13909)*
Intrinsic4d LLC ....G....... 248 469-8811
Bingham Farms *(G-1701)*
J H P Inc ....G....... 248 588-0110
Madison Heights *(G-10750)*
Jda Software Group Inc ....G....... 734 741-4205
Ann Arbor *(G-533)*
Kingston Educational Software ....G....... 248 895-4803
Farmington Hills *(G-5281)*
Kronos Inc ....G....... 248 357-5604
Southfield *(G-15619)*
Kumanu Inc ....E....... 734 822-6673
Ann Arbor *(G-545)*
Lakeside Software LLC ....G....... 248 686-1700
Ann Arbor *(G-547)*
Level Eleven LLC ....E....... 313 662-2000
Detroit *(G-4393)*
Linked Live Inc ....G....... 248 345-5993
Madison Heights *(G-10770)*
Lintech Global Inc ....D....... 248 553-8033
Farmington Hills *(G-5292)*
Livermore Software Tech LLC ....F....... 925 449-2500
Troy *(G-17214)*
Lspedia LLC ....G....... 248 320-1909
West Bloomfield *(G-18294)*
Luhu LLC ....G....... 320 469-3162
East Lansing *(G-4901)*
Mad Dog Software ....G....... 248 940-2963
Birmingham *(G-1734)*
Magnetic Michigan ....D....... 734 922-7068
Ann Arbor *(G-562)*
Magnus Software Inc ....G....... 517 294-0315
Fowlerville *(G-5850)*
Major One Electronics LLC ....G....... 313 652-3723
Detroit *(G-4418)*
Marc Schrreiber & Company LLC ....G....... 734 222-9930
Ann Arbor *(G-566)*
Marketplus Software Inc ....G....... 269 968-4240
Springfield *(G-15872)*

Mastery Technologies Inc ....F....... 248 888-8420
Novi *(G-12472)*
Mc Donald Computer Corporation ....E....... 248 350-9290
Southfield *(G-15650)*
McKesson Pharmacy Systems LLC ....A....... 800 521-1758
Livonia *(G-10309)*
McManus Software Development ....G....... 810 231-6589
Whitmore Lake *(G-18540)*
Medical Systems Resource Group ....G....... 248 476-5400
Farmington Hills *(G-5313)*
Medimage Inc ....G....... 734 665-5400
Ann Arbor *(G-568)*
Mejenta Systems Inc ....E....... 248 434-2583
Southfield *(G-15653)*
Melange Computer Services Inc ....F....... 517 321-8434
Lansing *(G-9774)*
Menu Pulse Inc ....G....... 989 708-1207
Saginaw *(G-14695)*
Methodica Technologies LLC ....E....... 312 622-7697
Troy *(G-17252)*
Micro Focus Software Inc ....G....... 248 353-8010
Southfield *(G-15658)*
Microsoft Corporation ....G....... 248 205-5990
Troy *(G-17260)*
Microworld Technologies Inc ....G....... 248 470-1119
Novi *(G-12482)*
Mighty Co ....E....... 616 822-1013
Hudsonville *(G-8598)*
Mintmesh Inc ....F....... 888 874-3644
Detroit *(G-4459)*
Mission Pathways LLC ....G....... 734 260-9411
Ann Arbor *(G-579)*
Mokasoft LLC ....G....... 517 703-0237
Okemos *(G-12677)*
Mscsoftware Corporation ....G....... 734 994-3800
Troy *(G-17269)*
Mscsoftware Corporation ....G....... 734 994-3800
Ann Arbor *(G-586)*
National Instruments Corp ....B....... 734 464-2310
Livonia *(G-10332)*
Nemo Capital Partners LLC ....D....... 855 944-2995
Southfield *(G-15665)*
New Concepts Software Inc ....G....... 586 776-2855
Roseville *(G-14453)*
Nexiq Technologies Inc ....F....... 248 293-8200
Rochester Hills *(G-14069)*
Nits Solutions Inc ....F....... 248 231-2267
Novi *(G-12488)*
Noora Health ....G....... 402 981-0421
Traverse City *(G-16770)*
Novation Analytics LLC ....G....... 313 910-3280
Bloomfield Hills *(G-1844)*
Nubill Corporation ....F....... 248 246-7640
Royal Oak *(G-14566)*
Oasys LLC ....G....... 414 529-3922
Lansing *(G-9876)*
Onestream Software Corp ....G....... 248 841-1356
Rochester *(G-13916)*
Onestream Software LLC ....G....... 248 342-1541
Rochester *(G-13917)*
Onstar LLC ....E....... 313 300-0106
Detroit *(G-4500)*
Openalpr Software Solutions L ....G....... 800 935-1699
Commerce Township *(G-3560)*
Opio LLc ....F....... 313 433-1098
Dearborn *(G-3881)*
◆ **Ops Solutions LLC** ....E....... 248 374-8000
Wixom *(G-18726)*
Optimizerx Corporation ....G....... 248 651-6568
Rochester *(G-13918)*
Optonomy Inc ....E....... 734 604-6472
Ann Arbor *(G-602)*
Oracle America Inc ....G....... 989 495-0465
Midland *(G-11400)*
Oracle Corporation ....G....... 248 393-2498
Orion *(G-12737)*
Oracle Systems Corporation ....G....... 248 614-5139
Rochester Hills *(G-14076)*
Oracle Systems Corporation ....G....... 248 816-8050
Troy *(G-17290)*
Orbit Technology Inc ....G....... 906 776-7248
Iron Mountain *(G-8729)*
Orion Bus Accnting Sltions LLC ....G....... 248 893-1060
Wyandotte *(G-18835)*
Owntheplay Inc ....G....... 248 514-0352
Detroit *(G-4502)*
Pace Software Systems Inc ....F....... 586 727-3189
Casco *(G-2602)*
Paragon Vciso Group LLC ....G....... 248 895-9866
Detroit *(G-4507)*

Parameter Driven Software Inc ....F....... 248 553-6410
Farmington Hills *(G-5342)*
Paramount Technologies Inc ....E....... 248 960-0909
Saginaw *(G-14725)*
PC Solutions ....E....... 517 787-9934
Jackson *(G-8983)*
Pearson Software Company ....G....... 313 878-2687
Detroit *(G-4511)*
Peninsular Technologies LLC ....E....... 616 676-9811
Grand Rapids *(G-7076)*
Perennial Software ....F....... 734 414-0760
Canton *(G-2506)*
Perfect Sync Inc ....G....... 231 947-9300
Traverse City *(G-16789)*
Perspective Software ....G....... 248 308-2418
Northville *(G-12252)*
Phoenix Intergration Inc ....G....... 586 484-8196
Novi *(G-12505)*
Pioneer Automotive Inc ....F....... 586 758-7730
Sterling Heights *(G-16127)*
Pitss America LLC ....E....... 248 740-0935
Troy *(G-17303)*
Platform Computing Inc ....G....... 248 359-7825
Southfield *(G-15675)*
Platformsh Inc ....D....... 734 707-9124
Brooklyn *(G-2130)*
Polyworks USA Training Center ....G....... 216 226-1617
Novi *(G-12506)*
Possibilities For Change LLC ....G....... 810 333-1347
Ann Arbor *(G-615)*
Power Rank Inc ....G....... 650 387-2336
Ann Arbor *(G-616)*
Practice Management Tech ....G....... 231 352-9844
Frankfort *(G-5879)*
Prehab Technologies LLC ....G....... 734 368-9983
Ann Arbor *(G-623)*
Prime Pdiatrics Adolescent PLC ....G....... 281 259-5785
Grand Blanc *(G-6257)*
Process Analytics Factory LLC ....G....... 929 350-4053
Southfield *(G-15684)*
Qad Inc ....G....... 248 324-9890
Farmington Hills *(G-5359)*
Qnx Software Systems ....G....... 248 513-3412
Novi *(G-12520)*
Qquest Corporation ....G....... 313 441-0022
Waterford *(G-18160)*
Quantum Compliance Systems ....F....... 734 930-0009
Ypsilanti *(G-18973)*
Quest - IV Incorporated ....F....... 734 847-5487
Lambertville *(G-9652)*
Quest Software LLC ....B....... 800 541-2593
Saint Johns *(G-14913)*
R E R Software Inc ....G....... 586 744-0881
Rochester Hills *(G-14098)*
Radley Corporation ....E....... 616 554-9060
Grand Rapids *(G-7136)*
Real View LLC ....F....... 616 524-5243
Grand Rapids *(G-7143)*
Rearden Development Corp ....G....... 616 464-4434
Grand Rapids *(G-7144)*
Recursive LLC ....G....... 904 449-2386
Holland *(G-8177)*
Red Hat Inc ....G....... 978 392-2459
Ann Arbor *(G-634)*
Redtail Software ....G....... 231 587-0720
Mancelona *(G-10878)*
Regents of The University Mich ....E....... 734 936-0435
Ann Arbor *(G-637)*
Reilly & Associates Inc ....E....... 248 605-9393
Clarkston *(G-3060)*
Rewardpal Inc ....G....... 800 377-6099
Novi *(G-12526)*
Rezoop LLC ....G....... 248 952-8070
Bloomfield *(G-1784)*
Ringmaster Software Corp ....F....... 802 383-1050
Troy *(G-17333)*
Ripple Science Corporation ....G....... 919 451-0241
Ann Arbor *(G-641)*
Rise Health LLC ....G....... 616 451-2775
Grand Rapids *(G-7158)*
Robal Tech LLC ....G....... 248 436-8105
Madison Heights *(G-10818)*
Rose Mobile Computer Repr LLC ....F....... 248 653-0865
Bloomfield Hills *(G-1859)*
Routeone Holdings LLC ....E....... 800 282-6308
Farmington Hills *(G-5373)*
Rutherford & Associates Inc ....E....... 616 392-5000
Holland *(G-8185)*
S2 Games LLC ....D....... 269 344-8020
Portage *(G-13604)*

Employee Codes: A=Over 500 employees, B=251-500
C=101-250, D=51-100, E=20-50, F=10-19, G=3-9
2022 Harris Michigan
Industrial Directory
909

Saagara LLC ... F ... 734 658-4693
Ann Arbor (G-647)
Saba Software Inc ... G ... 248 228-7300
Southfield (G-15691)
Salespage Technologies LLC ... E ... 269 567-7400
Kalamazoo (G-9328)
Sbsi Software Inc ... F ... 248 567-3044
Farmington Hills (G-5376)
Schindler Software LLC ... G ... 574 360-9045
Niles (G-12165)
Sensible Vision Inc ... G ... 734 478-1130
Covert (G-3725)
Serniuk Software ... G ... 248 668-3826
Wolverine Lake (G-18797)
Siemens Industry Software Inc ... G ... 313 317-6100
Allen Park (G-206)
Siemens Industry Software Inc ... G ... 734 994-7300
Ann Arbor (G-652)
Signalx Technologies LLC ... E ... 248 935-4237
Plymouth (G-13298)
Signmeupcom Inc ... G ... 312 343-1263
Monroe (G-11572)
Silkroute Global Inc ... E ... 248 854-3409
Troy (G-17354)
Simerics Inc ... G ... 248 513-3200
Novi (G-12538)
Sims Software II Inc ... G ... 586 491-0058
Clinton Township (G-3358)
Sirionlabs Inc ... G ... 313 300-0588
Grosse Pointe Park (G-7560)
Sizzl LLC ... F ... 201 454-1938
Ann Arbor (G-654)
Skysync Inc ... E ... 734 822-6858
Ann Arbor (G-655)
Sodius Corporation ... G ... 248 270-2950
Royal Oak (G-14581)
Software Advantage Consulting ... G ... 586 264-5632
Sterling Heights (G-16181)
Software Assoc Inc ... F ... 248 477-6112
Farmington (G-5151)
Software Bots Inc ... G ... 734 730-6526
Canton (G-2524)
Software Finesse LLC ... G ... 248 737-8990
Farmington Hills (G-5383)
Solid Logic LLC ... F ... 616 738-8922
Holland (G-8200)
Solidthinking Inc ... G ... 248 526-1920
Troy (G-17360)
Spiders Software Solutions LLC ... G ... 248 305-3225
Northville (G-12262)
Spire Integrated Systems Inc ... E ... 248 544-0072
Troy (G-17367)
SRP Software ... G ... 231 779-3602
Cadillac (G-2358)
Star Board Multi Media Inc ... G ... 616 296-0823
Grand Haven (G-6367)
Stardock Systems Inc ... E ... 734 927-0677
Plymouth (G-13303)
Startech Software Systems Inc ... G ... 248 344-2266
Novi (G-12542)
Strategic Computer Solutions ... G ... 248 888-0666
Ann Arbor (G-667)
Strider Software Inc ... G ... 906 863-7798
Menominee (G-11260)
Sunera Technologies Inc ... A ... 248 434-0808
Troy (G-17376)
Superior Information Tech LLC ... F ... 734 666-9963
Livonia (G-10424)
Supported Intelligence LLC ... G ... 517 908-4420
East Lansing (G-4912)
Suse LLC ... F ... 248 353-8010
Southfield (G-15715)
Sync Technologies Inc ... E ... 313 963-5353
Detroit (G-4622)
T4 Software ... G ... 313 610-3297
Dearborn Heights (G-3940)
Talbot & Associates Inc ... F ... 248 723-9700
Franklin (G-5885)
Tebis America Inc ... E ... 248 524-0430
Troy (G-17386)
Technology Network Svcs Inc ... F ... 586 294-7771
Saint Clair Shores (G-14888)
Tecra Systems Inc ... F ... 248 888-1116
Westland (G-18420)
Tequionbrookins LLC ... G ... 313 290-0303
Southfield (G-15721)
Ticket Avengers Inc ... G ... 248 635-3279
Warren (G-18039)
Torenzo Inc ... F ... 313 732-7874
Bloomfield Hills (G-1866)
Totle Inc ... G ... 248 645-1111
Birmingham (G-1754)
Touch World Inc ... E ... 248 539-3700
Farmington Hills (G-5404)
Tree House Software Inc ... G ... 503 208-6171
Ann Arbor (G-696)
Trend Software LLC ... G ... 616 452-8032
Grand Rapids (G-7274)
Tru-Syzygy Inc ... G ... 248 622-7211
Lake Orion (G-9635)
Truarx Inc ... F ... 248 538-7809
Southfield (G-15728)
True Anlytics Mfg Slutions LLC ... G ... 517 902-9700
Ida (G-8625)
TST Tooling Software Tech LLC ... F ... 248 922-9293
Clarkston (G-3073)
Tweddle Group Inc ... G ... 586 840-3275
Detroit (G-4649)
Twosixnine Studios ... G ... 269 365-6719
Vicksburg (G-17615)
Tyler Technologies Inc ... G ... 734 677-0550
Ann Arbor (G-701)
Ultimate Software Group Inc ... G ... 616 682-9639
Ada (G-39)
Umakanth Consultants Inc ... F ... 517 347-7500
Okemos (G-12691)
Uniprax LLC ... G ... 616 522-3158
Ionia (G-8692)
Universal Sftwr Solutions Inc ... E ... 810 653-5000
Davison (G-3799)
V E S T Inc ... G ... 248 649-9550
Troy (G-17422)
V2soft Inc ... D ... 248 904-1702
Bloomfield Hills (G-1872)
▲ Valassis Communications Inc ... A ... 734 591-3000
Livonia (G-10455)
Valassis Communications Inc ... G ... 734 432-8000
Livonia (G-10456)
Vanroth LLC ... F ... 734 929-5268
Ann Arbor (G-709)
Varatech Inc ... F ... 616 393-6408
Holland (G-8234)
Vector North America Inc ... D ... 248 449-9290
Novi (G-12565)
Ventuor LLC ... G ... 248 790-8700
Flint (G-5791)
Verishow ... G ... 212 913-0600
West Bloomfield (G-18322)
Vertigee Corporation ... G ... 313 999-1020
Saline (G-15043)
Vieth Consulting LLC ... F ... 517 622-3090
Grand Ledge (G-6400)
Virtual Advantage LLc ... G ... 877 772-6886
Troy (G-17441)
Vivian Enterprises LLC ... E ... 248 792-9925
Southfield (G-15740)
Warner Software Co LLC ... G ... 616 916-1182
Comstock Park (G-3650)
Weaver Instructional Systems ... G ... 616 942-2891
Grand Rapids (G-7327)
Westmountain Software ... G ... 734 776-3966
Westland (G-18432)
Wilson Technologies Inc ... G ... 248 655-0005
Clawson (G-3112)
Workforce Payhub Inc ... G ... 517 759-4026
Adrian (G-105)
Workforce Software LLC ... C ... 734 542-4100
Livonia (G-10478)
World of Cd-Rom ... F ... 269 382-3766
Kalamazoo (G-9374)
Xcell Software Inc ... G ... 248 760-3160
Commerce Township (G-3583)
Zume It Inc ... G ... 248 522-6868
Farmington Hills (G-5419)

76 MISCELLANEOUS REPAIR SERVICES

7692 Welding Repair

589 Fabrication LLC ... G ... 313 402-0586
Fenton (G-5445)
A & B Welding & Fabricating ... G ... 231 733-2661
Muskegon (G-11759)
A & M Mobile Welding & Fab LLC ... G ... 517 672-0289
Howell (G-8422)
A M T Welding Inc ... G ... 586 463-7030
Clinton Township (G-3146)
A R C Welding & Repair ... G ... 517 628-2475
Mason (G-11115)
A&W Welding ... G ... 248 949-4344
White Lake (G-18448)
Ability Mfg & Engrg Co ... D ... 269 227-3292
Fennville (G-5433)
Able Welding Inc ... G ... 989 865-9611
Saint Charles (G-14800)
Absolute Lser Wldg Sltions LLC ... G ... 586 932-2597
Sterling Heights (G-15921)
Ace Welding & Machine Inc ... F ... 231 941-9664
Traverse City (G-16595)
Achs Metal Products Inc ... G ... 586 772-2734
Warren (G-17688)
Ackerman Brothers Inc ... G ... 989 892-4122
Bay City (G-1315)
Advanced Metal Recyclers ... G ... 989 389-7708
Saint Helen (G-14893)
▲ Advanced Special Tools Inc ... C ... 269 962-9697
Battle Creek (G-1179)
Aegis Welding Supply ... G ... 248 475-9860
Auburn Hills (G-774)
Aggie Welding ... G ... 989 824-1316
Weidman (G-18249)
Aggressive Tooling Inc ... D ... 616 754-1404
Greenville (G-7475)
Airway Welding Inc ... F ... 517 789-6125
Jackson (G-8808)
All American Welding LLC ... G ... 517 294-2480
Byron (G-2252)
All Around Mobil Welding ... G ... 616 481-4267
Grand Rapids (G-6445)
All Phase Welding Service Inc ... G ... 616 235-6100
Comstock Park (G-3587)
All Welding and Fabg Co Inc ... F ... 248 689-0986
Troy (G-16924)
Allegan Metal Fabricators Inc ... G ... 269 751-7130
Hamilton (G-7595)
Allied Machine Inc ... F ... 231 834-0050
Grant (G-7425)
Allied Welding Incorporated ... G ... 248 360-1122
Commerce Township (G-3509)
Allynn Corp ... G ... 269 383-1199
Kalamazoo (G-9110)
American Strong ... G ... 248 978-6483
Waterford (G-18098)
American Wldg & Press Repr Inc ... F ... 248 358-2050
Southfield (G-15486)
Amerivet Services LLC ... G ... 810 299-3095
Brighton (G-1945)
◆ Amtrade Systems Inc ... G ... 734 522-9500
Livonia (G-10118)
Anderson Brazing Co Inc ... G ... 248 399-5155
Madison Heights (G-10669)
Andritz Metals USA Inc ... G ... 248 305-2969
Novi (G-12363)
Angstrom Automotive Group LLC ... E ... 734 756-1164
Southfield (G-15487)
Anywhere Welding ... G ... 906 250-7217
Trenary (G-16883)
ARC On Mobile Welding LLC ... G ... 734 344-7128
Monroe (G-11524)
ARC Rite Welding LLC ... G ... 989 545-8006
Linwood (G-10073)
Arcelrmttal Tlred Blnks Amrcas ... B ... 313 332-5300
Detroit (G-4024)
Arctech Precision Welding ... G ... 517 614-5722
Quincy (G-13662)
Autorack Technologies Inc ... F ... 517 437-4800
Hillsdale (G-7923)
B & G Custom Works Inc ... F ... 269 686-9420
Allegan (G-149)
B&M Welding Inc ... G ... 810 837-0742
Snover (G-15391)
Bakers Gas and Welding Sups ... G ... 517 539-5047
Jackson (G-8821)
Bakker Welding & Mechanics LLC ... G ... 616 828-8664
Coopersville (G-3680)
Bannasch Welding Inc ... F ... 517 482-2916
Lansing (G-9674)
Barnes Welding & Fab LLC ... G ... 989 287-0161
Sheridan (G-15380)
Barneys Welding and Fabg ... G ... 989 753-4892
Saginaw (G-14610)
Beattie Spring & Welding Svc ... G ... 810 239-9151
Flint (G-5653)
Beavers Welding & Fabracating ... G ... 517 375-0443
Webberville (G-18242)
Beishlag Welding LLC ... G ... 231 881-5023
Elmira (G-5038)
Bel-Kur Inc ... E ... 734 847-0651
Temperance (G-16528)

SIC SECTION 76 MISCELLANEOUS REPAIR SERVICES76 MISCELLANEOUS REPAIR SERVICES

Big Mikes Welding G 269 420-8017
Battle Creek *(G-1195)*

Bills Welding G 989 330-1014
Prudenville *(G-13656)*

Blast of The Past Corp G 734 772-4394
Wayne *(G-18217)*

Bnb Welding & Fabrication Inc G 810 820-1508
Burton *(G-2227)*

Bobs Welding & Fabricating F 810 324-2592
Kenockee *(G-9423)*

Bond Bailey and Smith Company G 313 496-0177
Detroit *(G-4061)*

Bopp-Busch Manufacturing Co E 989 876-7924
Au Gres *(G-758)*

Bowman Welding and Fabrication G 231 580-6438
Big Rapids *(G-1670)*

Boyne Area Wldg & Fabrication G 231 582-6078
Boyne City *(G-1883)*

Bradeen Specialties LLC G 269 349-0276
Kalamazoo *(G-9140)*

Brico Welding & Fab Inc E 586 948-8881
Chesterfield *(G-2851)*

Britten Metalworks LLC G 231 421-1615
Traverse City *(G-16629)*

Brockie Fabricating & Wldg LLC F 517 750-7500
Jackson *(G-8828)*

Bruce Weld Edwards LLC G 248 693-6222
Lake Orion *(G-9591)*

Buckeys Contracting & Service G 989 835-9512
Midland *(G-11325)*

Buiter Tool & Die Inc E 616 455-7410
Grand Rapids *(G-6529)*

Bulldog Welding G 248 342-1189
Davisburg *(G-3761)*

C & R Tool Die G 231 584-3588
Alba *(G-113)*

C S Mobile Welding LLC G 517 543-2339
Charlotte *(G-2737)*

C&E Welding G 248 990-3191
Royal Oak *(G-14523)*

Cal Manufacturing Company Inc G 269 649-2942
Vicksburg *(G-17601)*

Calm Welding G 417 358-8131
Three Rivers *(G-16568)*

▲ Campbell Inc Press Repair E 517 371-1034
Lansing *(G-9821)*

Case Welding & Fabrication Inc G 517 278-2729
Coldwater *(G-3425)*

Century Tool Welding Inc G 586 758-3330
Fraser *(G-5913)*

Clair Sawyer G 906 228-8242
Marquette *(G-11013)*

Classic Welding Inc F 586 758-2400
Warren *(G-17757)*

Cobra Torches Inc G 248 499-8122
Lake Orion *(G-9594)*

▲ Commercial Mfg & Assembly Inc E 616 847-9980
Grand Haven *(G-6287)*

Consolidated Metal Pdts Inc G 616 538-1000
Grand Rapids *(G-6596)*

Contract Welding and Fabg Inc E 734 699-5561
Van Buren Twp *(G-17520)*

Cooks Blacksmith Welding Inc G 231 796-6819
Big Rapids *(G-1671)*

◆ Coppertec Inc E 313 278-0139
Inkster *(G-8661)*

Corban Industries Inc E 248 393-2720
Orion *(G-12726)*

Cramblits Welding LLC G 906 932-3773
Ironwood *(G-8760)*

CTS Welding G 269 521-4481
Bloomingdale *(G-1876)*

Custom Design & Manufacturing F 989 754-9962
Carrollton *(G-2587)*

Custom Welding F 586 243-6298
Lake Orion *(G-9600)*

Customer Metal Fabrication Inc E 906 774-3216
Iron Mountain *(G-8721)*

Cw Champion Welding Alloys LLC G 906 296-9633
Lake Linden *(G-9568)*

Cw Creative Welding Inc G 586 294-1050
Fraser *(G-5916)*

D & A Welding & Fabg LLC G 313 220-2277
Detroit *(G-4115)*

D & J Precision Machine Svcs G 269 673-4010
Allegan *(G-153)*

D and D Welding G 810 824-3622
Burtchville *(G-2219)*

D J and G Enterprise Inc G 231 258-9925
Kalkaska *(G-9386)*

D K Enterprises Inc G 586 756-7350
Warren *(G-17771)*

Damonds Mobile Welding G 313 932-4135
Ecorse *(G-4982)*

Delta Welding Services G 906 786-4348
Escanaba *(G-5066)*

Denudts Portable Welding G 517 605-5154
Riga *(G-13848)*

Detroit Torch G 248 499-8122
Rochester Hills *(G-13995)*

DH Custom Fabrication G 517 264-8045
Adrian *(G-60)*

DH Custom Fabrication G 517 366-9067
Adrian *(G-61)*

Diversified Welding & Fabg G 616 738-0400
Holland *(G-8015)*

DK Concepts LLC G 586 222-5255
Sterling Heights *(G-15989)*

Dowding Industries Inc C 517 663-5455
Eaton Rapids *(G-4960)*

Dubois Production Services Inc F 616 785-0088
Comstock Park *(G-3604)*

Dunns Welding Inc G 248 356-3866
Southfield *(G-15543)*

Dutchmans Welding & Repair G 989 584-6861
Carson City *(G-2592)*

Dwayne Thomleys Redneck G 906 353-7376
Baraga *(G-1139)*

Dynasty Fab LLC F 586 623-0227
Macomb *(G-10590)*

Ebling & Son Inc G 616 532-8400
Kentwood *(G-9450)*

Edt Welding & Fabrication LLC G 978 257-4700
Gregory *(G-7514)*

Elaree FABrication&welding G 517 505-5998
Williamston *(G-18571)*

Elden Industries Corp F 734 946-6900
Taylor *(G-16412)*

▲ Erwin Quarder Inc D 616 575-1600
Grand Rapids *(G-6683)*

Escanaba and Lk Superior RR Co G 906 786-9399
Escanaba *(G-5070)*

Exact Fabrication G 248 240-4506
South Lyon *(G-15435)*

Express Welding Inc G 906 786-8808
Escanaba *(G-5071)*

Fab-N-Weld Sheetmetal G 269 471-7453
Berrien Springs *(G-1639)*

Forge Tech Inc G 989 685-3443
Rose City *(G-14363)*

Frankenmuth Industrial Svcs E 989 652-3322
Frankenmuth *(G-5862)*

Frankenmuth Welding & Fabg G 989 754-9457
Saginaw *(G-14646)*

Fraser Fab and Machine Inc E 248 852-9050
Rochester Hills *(G-14015)*

Garden City Products Inc E 269 684-6264
Niles *(G-12133)*

Grand Rapids Metaltek Inc E 616 791-2373
Grand Rapids *(G-6765)*

Great Lakes Mobile Welding G 406 890-5757
West Branch *(G-18328)*

Great Lakes Weld LLC G 231 943-4180
Traverse City *(G-16706)*

Great Lakes Welding Co G 810 689-8182
Burtchville *(G-2220)*

▲ Griptrac Inc F 231 853-2284
Ravenna *(G-13689)*

Gustos Quality Systems G 231 409-0219
Fife Lake *(G-5607)*

H & H Welding & Repair LLC D 517 676-1800
Mason *(G-11136)*

H & M Machining Inc F 586 778-5028
Roseville *(G-14419)*

H & M Welding and Fabricating G 517 764-3630
Jackson *(G-8897)*

◆ Hatch Stamping Company LLC C 734 475-8628
Chelsea *(G-2814)*

Hel Inc F 616 774-9032
Grand Rapids *(G-6808)*

High Point Group G 810 543-0448
Lakeville *(G-9647)*

Hotfab LLC G 586 489-7989
Warren *(G-17855)*

Huron High School F 734 782-2441
Riverview *(G-13875)*

Ianna Fab Inc G 586 739-2410
Shelby Township *(G-15238)*

Innovated Portable Weldin G 586 322-4442
Casco *(G-2598)*

Integrity Fab & Machine Inc F 989 481-3200
Breckenridge *(G-1911)*

Iron Clad Welding LLC G 810 304-1180
Brockway *(G-2107)*

Iron Fetish Metalworks Inc F 586 776-8311
Roseville *(G-14426)*

Ithaca Manufacturing Corp G 989 875-4949
Ithaca *(G-8791)*

J G Welding & Maintenance Inc G 586 758-0150
China *(G-2970)*

James L Barnett G 231 544-8118
East Jordan *(G-4872)*

JD Metalworks Inc D 989 386-3231
Clare *(G-2982)*

Jerrys Welding Inc G 231 853-6494
Ravenna *(G-13690)*

Jerz Machine Tool Corporation G 269 782-3535
Dowagiac *(G-4785)*

Johnnyamp Mobile Welding Svcs G 269 338-8013
Benton Harbor *(G-1559)*

Johnsons Fabrication and Wldg G 616 607-2202
Grand Haven *(G-6321)*

Joy Industries Inc F 248 334-4062
Pontiac *(G-13388)*

K Two Welding G 810 858-3072
Port Huron *(G-13491)*

K&G Welding LLC G 810 887-0560
Port Huron *(G-13492)*

K-C Welding Supply Inc F 989 893-6509
Essexville *(G-5115)*

Kbs Welding Service G 231 263-7164
Kingsley *(G-9524)*

KC Jones Brazing Inc G 586 755-4900
Warren *(G-17891)*

Kenkraft Industrial Weldi G 269 543-3153
Fennville *(G-5439)*

Kenowa Industries Inc E 616 392-7080
Holland *(G-8111)*

Kent Welding Inc G 616 363-4414
Grand Rapids *(G-6890)*

Kibby Welding LLC F 231 258-8838
Kalkaska *(G-9394)*

Kinross Fab & Machine Inc E 906 495-1900
Kincheloe *(G-9504)*

Kjm Specialty Welding LLC G 734 626-2442
Southgate *(G-15751)*

Koski Welding Inc G 906 353-7588
Baraga *(G-1142)*

Krause Welding Inc F 231 773-4443
Muskegon *(G-11852)*

Kriseler Welding Inc G 989 624-9266
Birch Run *(G-1708)*

Ktwo Welding G 810 216-6087
Port Huron *(G-13496)*

Kurrent Welding Inc G 734 753-9197
New Boston *(G-12011)*

Kustom Welding LLC G 231 823-2912
Stanwood *(G-15905)*

Lake Shore Services Inc F 734 285-7007
Wyandotte *(G-18828)*

Lakeside Mechanical Contrs E 616 786-0211
Allegan *(G-168)*

Lance Safford Welding LLC G 989 464-7841
Hillman *(G-7913)*

Laser Access Inc C 616 459-5496
Grand Rapids *(G-6928)*

Laylin Welding Inc G 269 782-2910
Dowagiac *(G-4786)*

Le Forges Pipe & Fab Inc G 734 482-2100
Ypsilanti *(G-18962)*

Lewis Welding Inc E 616 452-9226
Wyoming *(G-18890)*

Linwood Tool Co Inc E 989 697-4403
Linwood *(G-10074)*

Lite Bright Welding G 269 208-5698
Cedar Springs *(G-2656)*

Loneys Welding & Excvtg Inc G 231 328-4408
Merritt *(G-11267)*

Lutke Welding LLC G 231 590-6565
Manton *(G-10936)*

M & B Welding Inc G 989 635-8017
Marlette *(G-10984)*

M and L Fabrication LLC G 616 259-7754
Grandville *(G-7399)*

M P D Welding Inc D 248 340-0330
Orion *(G-12735)*

Manistee Wldg & Piping Svc Inc G 231 723-2551
Manistee *(G-10906)*

Manning Enterprises Inc E 269 657-2346
Paw Paw *(G-12952)*

SIC

Employee Codes: A=Over 500 employees, B=251-500
C=101-250, D=51-100, E=20-50, F=10-19, G=3-9

2022 Harris Michigan
Industrial Directory

911

Company	Location	Code	Phone
Marsh Industrial Services Inc	Kalkaska (G-9395)	F	231 258-4870
Martin Powder Coating	Perry (G-12979)	G	517 625-4220
▲ Material Handling Tech Inc	Ira (G-8701)	D	586 725-5546
Matteson Manufacturing Inc	Cadillac (G-2345)	G	231 779-2898
▲ Maxable Inc	Brooklyn (G-2127)	F	517 592-5638
Mayo Welding & Fabricating Co	Royal Oak (G-14561)	G	248 435-2730
McCullys Wldg Fabrication LLC	East Jordan (G-4875)	G	231 499-3842
Meccom Corporation	Detroit (G-4426)	G	313 895-4900
Mechancal Sup A Div Nthrn McHn	Escanaba (G-5083)	F	906 789-0355
Mechanic Evltion Crtfction For	Evart (G-5126)	G	231 734-3483
Menominee Saw and Supply Co	Menominee (G-11249)	G	906 863-8998
Metal Master Welding LLC	Dryden (G-4806)	G	810 706-0476
Metal Worxs Inc	Clay (G-3122)	G	586 484-9355
Methods Prtable Machining Wldg	Laingsburg (G-9537)	G	989 413-5022
Metro Machine Works Inc	Romulus (G-14304)	D	734 941-4571
Mg Welding Inc	Richmond (G-13841)	G	586 405-2909
Michigan Mobile Welding Co	Linden (G-10066)	G	810 569-0229
Mico Industries Inc	Grand Rapids (G-6999)	D	616 245-6426
Mid Michigan Repair Service	Midland (G-11390)	G	989 835-6014
Midwest Fabricating Inc	Taylor (G-16447)	G	734 921-3914
Mj-Hick Inc	West Branch (G-18331)	G	989 345-7610
Monarch Welding & Engrg Inc	Muskegon (G-11876)	E	231 733-7222
Moyer Wldg & Fabrication LLC	La Salle (G-9528)	G	734 243-1212
Mpd Welding - Grand Rapids Inc	Grand Rapids (G-7031)	E	616 248-9353
N & S Customs	Sturgis (G-16312)	G	269 651-8237
Nates Custom Welding	Niles (G-12150)	G	574 303-2254
National Tool & Die Welding	Livonia (G-10333)	F	734 522-0072
Nelson Steel Products Inc	Holland (G-8152)	D	616 396-1515
▲ Nicholson Terminal & Dock Co	River Rouge (G-13858)	D	313 842-4300
Northern Design Services Inc	Kalkaska (G-9400)	E	231 258-9900
Northern Machining & Repr Inc	Escanaba (G-5088)	E	906 786-0526
O E M Company Inc	Port Huron (G-13511)	F	810 985-9070
Oilpatch Machine Tool Inc	Mount Pleasant (G-11728)	G	989 772-0637
Olivet Machine Tool Engrg Co	Olivet (G-12695)	F	269 749-2671
Oreos Wldg & Fabrication LLC	Akron (G-110)	G	989 529-0815
Parker Tooling & Design Inc	Grand Rapids (G-7071)	F	616 791-1080
Parma Tube Corp	Sturgis (G-16316)	E	269 651-2351
Parsons Industrial Maintenance	Carleton (G-2561)	G	734 236-4163
Patrick D Duffy	Shepherd (G-15377)	G	989 828-5467
Peacock Industries Inc	Baldwin (G-1124)	E	231 745-4609
▲ Phil Brown Welding Corporation	Conklin (G-3662)	F	616 784-3046
Pin Point Welding Inc	Chesterfield (G-2925)	G	586 598-7382
Pinnacle Engineering Co Inc	Manchester (G-10888)	F	734 428-7039
Pipe Fabricators Inc	Kalamazoo (G-9297)	G	269 345-8657
Plamondons Welding/Fab LLC	Traverse City (G-16794)	G	231 632-0406
Porter Steel & Welding Company	Muskegon (G-11897)	F	231 733-4495
PR Plastic Welding Service	Howell (G-8498)	G	734 355-3341
▲ Precision Polymer Mfg Inc	Kalamazoo (G-9305)	E	269 344-2044
Precision Welding N Fab	Byron (G-2256)	G	810 931-6853
Precision Wldg & Mch Repr LLC	Barryton (G-1173)	G	989 309-0699
Preferred Welding LLC	Holland (G-8169)	G	616 294-1068
Prima Wldg & Experimental Inc	Fraser (G-5979)	G	586 415-8873
Pushard Welding LLC	Mattawan (G-11167)	G	269 760-9611
Pushman Manufacturing Co Inc	Fenton (G-5497)	G	810 629-9688
R E Cap Inc	Bear Lake (G-1422)	G	231 864-3959
Rak Welding	Honor (G-8360)	G	231 651-0732
Ranger Tool & Die Co	Saginaw (G-14735)	G	989 754-1403
Response Welding Inc	Sterling Heights (G-16148)	G	586 795-8090
Rhodes Welding Inc	Clawson (G-3109)	G	248 568-0857
Rico Technologies	Wixom (G-18743)	G	248 896-0110
Ridge Locomotive	Freeland (G-6028)	G	989 714-4671
▲ Ridgeview Industries Inc	Grand Rapids (G-7157)	C	616 453-8636
Rise Machine Company Inc	Mount Pleasant (G-11737)	G	989 772-2151
Rogue Welding Service LLC	Middleville (G-11313)	G	616 648-9723
Rss Baker LLC	Grand Haven (G-6356)	G	616 844-5429
Ryson Tube Inc	Brighton (G-2067)	F	810 227-4567
S and S Welding	Farwell (G-5428)	G	989 588-6916
Salenbien Welding Service Inc	Dundee (G-4834)	F	734 529-3280
Sams Welding Inc	Dearborn (G-3893)	G	313 350-5010
Savs Welding Services Inc	Detroit (G-4582)	F	313 841-3430
Schrader Stoves of Michiana	Niles (G-12166)	E	269 684-4494
Set Enterprises of Mi Inc	Sterling Heights (G-16174)	D	586 573-3600
Sharpco Wldg & Fabrication LLC	Clare (G-2997)	G	989 915-0556
Sherwood Manufacturing Corp	Northport (G-12191)	F	231 386-5132
Smith Welding	Atlanta (G-747)	G	989 306-0154
SOO Welding Inc	Sault Sainte Marie (G-15100)	G	906 632-8241
Soutec Div of Andritz Bricmont	Novi (G-12540)	E	248 305-2955
Spaulding Machine Co Inc	Saginaw (G-14761)	G	989 777-0694
Specialty Welding	Grand Ledge (G-6399)	G	517 627-5566
Starlite Tool & Die Welding	Detroit (G-4607)	G	313 533-3462
Stus Welding & Fabrication	Holland (G-8206)	G	616 392-8459
◆ Superior Welding & Mfg Inc	Hermansville (G-7863)	E	906 498-7616
Sws - Trimac Inc	Saginaw (G-14771)	E	989 791-4595
T and A Welding	Edwardsburg (G-5019)	G	269 228-1268
TEC Welding Sales Incorporated	Oxford (G-12922)	E	248 969-7490
▲ Tec-Option Inc	Blissfield (G-1777)	F	517 486-6055
Technique Inc	Jackson (G-9017)	D	517 789-8988
Thermal Designs & Manufacturng	Roseville (G-14484)	F	586 773-5231
Tigmaster Co	Baroda (G-1171)	E	800 824-4830
Tip of Mitt Welding LLC	Boyne City (G-1903)	G	231 582-2977
Titus Welding Company	Farmington Hills (G-5401)	F	248 476-9366
Todds Welding Service Inc	Kalkaska (G-9408)	G	231 587-9969
Tough Weld Fabrication	Port Huron (G-13534)	G	810 937-2038
Troy Tube & Manufacturing Co	Chesterfield (G-2959)	D	586 949-8700
Troys Welding Company	Applegate (G-727)	G	810 633-9388
True Welding LLC	Eastpointe (G-4945)	G	586 822-5398
Tupes of Saginaw Inc	Saginaw (G-14781)	F	989 799-1550
◆ UP Truck Center Inc	Quinnesec (G-13677)	E	906 774-0098
▲ V S America Inc	Troy (G-17423)	G	248 585-6715
Valiant Specialties Inc	Rochester Hills (G-14139)	E	248 656-1001
Van Straten Brothers Inc	Baraga (G-1150)	E	906 353-6490
Vehicle Cy Wldg Fbrication LLC	Flint (G-5790)	G	810 836-2385
Verstar Group Inc	Chesterfield (G-2963)	F	586 465-5033
Virtec Manufacturing LLC	Roseville (G-14492)	F	313 590-2367
Vochaska Engineering	South Haven (G-15423)	G	269 637-5670
Wallis Diesel Welding	Sault Sainte Marie (G-15103)	G	906 647-3245
Warren Industrial Welding Co	Warren (G-18059)	F	586 756-0230
Waynes Portable Welding Svc	South Rockwood (G-15466)	G	734 777-9888
Weldcraft Inc	Livonia (G-10469)	G	734 779-1303
Welders & Presses Inc	Chesterfield (G-2965)	F	586 948-4300
Welding & Joining Tech LLC	Clarkston (G-3076)	G	734 926-9353
Welding Wizard	Escanaba (G-5107)	G	906 786-4745
West Michigan Welding LLC	Nunica (G-12590)	G	231 578-3593
West Side Mfg Fabrication Inc	Wixom (G-18790)	E	248 380-6640
Whaley Welding and Mechine LLC	Fenton (G-5513)	G	810 835-5804
Wheelock & Son Welding Shop	Traverse City (G-16879)	G	231 947-6557
Whitaker Welding and Mech LLC	Muskegon (G-11945)	F	855 754-2548
Whites Bridge Tooling Inc	Lowell (G-10522)	E	616 897-4151
Wicked Wldg & Fabrication LLC	Grand Blanc (G-6269)	G	517 304-3709
William Barnes	Prudenville (G-13660)	G	989 424-1849
Williams Welding Custom Metal	Midland (G-11423)	G	989 941-2901
Wm Kloeffler Industries Inc	Marine City (G-10969)	F	810 765-4068
Wolverine Steel and Welding	Concord (G-3658)	E	517 524-7300
Wright Way Fabrication & Weldi	Gould City (G-6228)	G	602 703-1393
▲ Xcal Tools - Clare LLC	Clare (G-3002)	E	989 386-5376

7694 Armature Rewinding Shops

Company	Location	Code	Phone
A & C Electric Company	Harrison Township (G-7683)	E	586 773-2746
All City Electric Motor Repair	Riverview (G-13868)	G	734 284-2268
Alpena Electric Motor Service	Alpena (G-277)	G	989 354-8780
American Electric Motor Corp	Burton (G-2226)	F	810 743-6080
Arrow Motor & Pump Inc	Wyandotte (G-18807)	E	734 285-7860
Barry Electric-Rovill Co	Port Huron (G-13457)	D	810 985-8960
Bay United Motors Inc	Bay City (G-1331)	F	989 684-3972
Birclar Electric and Elec LLC	Romulus (G-14259)	F	734 941-7400
Bob Maxey Ford Howell Inc	Howell (G-8431)	G	517 545-5700

76 MISCELLANEOUS REPAIR SERVICES

Commonwealth Service Sls Corp..........G........ 313 581-8050
 Rochester Hills *(G-13980)*
Core Electric Company Inc ....F........ 313 382-7140
 Melvindale *(G-11198)*
DMS Electric Apparatus Service ....E........ 269 349-7000
 Kalamazoo *(G-9171)*
Electric Equipment Company ....G........ 269 925-3266
 Benton Harbor *(G-1548)*
Electric Motor & Contg Co ....F........ 313 871-3775
 Clay *(G-3119)*
Fife Pearce Electric Company ....F........ 313 369-2560
 Detroit *(G-4232)*
Fixall Electric Motor Service ....G........ 616 454-6863
 Grand Rapids *(G-6709)*
Franklin Electric Corporation ....F........ 248 442-8000
 Garden City *(G-6094)*
Gower Corporation ....G........ 989 249-5938
 Saginaw *(G-14657)*
Grand Rapids Elc Mtr Svc LLC ....G........ 616 243-8866
 Grand Rapids *(G-6755)*
Grand Rapids Elc Mtr Svcs LLC ....G........ 616 243-8866
 Grand Rapids *(G-6756)*
Gustos Quality Systems.........................G........ 231 409-0219
 Fife Lake *(G-5607)*
Hamilton Electric Co..............................F........ 989 799-6291
 Saginaw *(G-14660)*
Heco Inc ....E........ 269 381-7200
 Kalamazoo *(G-9210)*
Holland Electric Motor Co ....G........ 616 392-1115
 Holland *(G-8078)*
Industrial Elc Co Detroit Inc....................D........ 313 872-1133
 Detroit *(G-4315)*
Jones Electric Company ....E........ 231 726-5001
 Muskegon *(G-11849)*
Kalamazoo Electric Motor Inc.................G........ 269 345-7802
 Kalamazoo *(G-9238)*
Lincoln Service LLC ....G........ 734 793-0083
 Livonia *(G-10279)*
Lorna Icr LLC......................................F........ 586 582-1500
 Warren *(G-17907)*
Master Mfg Inc....................................E........ 248 628-9400
 Oxford *(G-12899)*
McElroys Automotive Svc LLC ....G........ 248 427-0501
 Farmington Hills *(G-5312)*
Medsker Electric Inc ....F........ 248 855-3383
 Farmington Hills *(G-5314)*
Monarch Electric Service Co ....G........ 313 388-7800
 Melvindale *(G-11206)*
Moore Brothers Electrical Co ....G........ 810 232-2148
 Flint *(G-5737)*
Motors Online LLC..............................F........ 989 723-8985
 Corunna *(G-3713)*
Motown Harley-Davidson Inc.................D........ 734 947-4647
 Taylor *(G-16451)*
Nieboer Inc ....F........ 231 924-0960
 Fremont *(G-6049)*
Phillips Service Inds Inc........................F........ 734 853-5000
 Ann Arbor *(G-610)*
Pontiac Electric Motor Works ....G........ 248 332-4622
 Pontiac *(G-13408)*
PSI Repair Services Inc........................C........ 734 853-5000
 Livonia *(G-10375)*
Rapa Electric Inc................................E........ 269 673-3157
 Allegan *(G-180)*
Reliance Electric Machine Co ....F........ 810 232-3355
 Flint *(G-5754)*
Riverside Electric Service Inc................G........ 269 849-1222
 Riverside *(G-13865)*
Rto Auto Repair Service.......................G........ 586 779-9450
 Warren *(G-18000)*
Spina Electric Company.......................E........ 586 771-8080
 Warren *(G-18020)*
Sturgis Electric Motor Service................G........ 269 651-2955
 Sturgis *(G-16323)*
Superior Elc Mtr Sls & Svc Inc...............G........ 906 226-9051
 Marquette *(G-11044)*
Valley Truck Parts Inc ....D........ 616 241-5431
 Grand Rapids *(G-7303)*
Warfield Electric Company Inc ....G........ 734 722-4044
 Westland *(G-18429)*
Warren Steel Co ....G........ 586 756-6600
 Warren *(G-18062)*
▼ Winans Inc ....G........ 810 744-1240
 Corunna *(G-3719)*
York Electric Inc................................D........ 989 684-7460
 Bay City *(G-1412)*
York Electric Inc................................G........ 517 487-6400
 Lansing *(G-9909)*
Z & R Electric Service Inc....................E........ 906 774-0468
 Iron Mountain *(G-8738)*

Employee Codes: A=Over 500 employees, B=251-500
C=101-250, D=51-100, E=20-50, F=10-19, G=3-9

ALPHABETIC SECTION

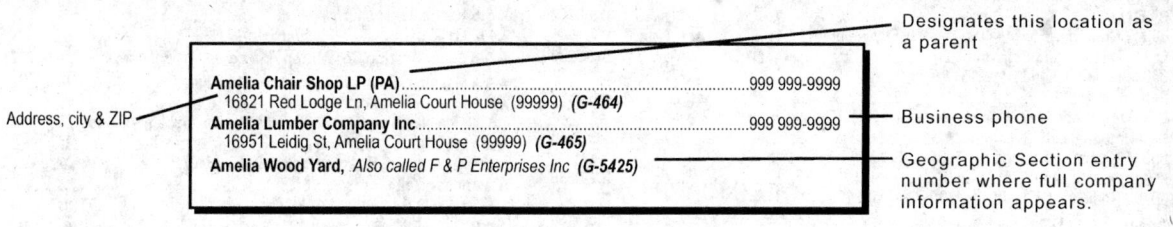

See footnotes for symbols and codes identification.
* Companies listed alphabetically.
* Complete physical or mailing address.

+vantage Corporation 734 432-5055
  12623 Newburgh Rd Livonia (48150) *(G-10088)*
/// 702 Cedar River Lbr Inc 906 497-5365
  W4249 Us Highway 2 Powers (49874) *(G-13648)*
1-800-Hansons 269 234-1670
  6475 Technology Ave Ste E Kalamazoo (49009) *(G-9105)*
12 Corners Vineyards (PA)...269 926-7597
  1201 N Benton Center Rd Benton Harbor (49022) *(G-1524)*
123go LLC 734 773-0049
  455 E Eisenhower Pkwy Ann Arbor (48108) *(G-340)*
127 Brewing 517 258-1346
  3090 Shirley Dr Jackson (49201) *(G-8797)*
1271 Associates Inc (PA)..586 948-4300
  27295 Luckino Dr Chesterfield (48047) *(G-2832)*
1732 Brentwood LLC..248 457-9695
  4909 Somerton Dr Troy (48085) *(G-16898)*
175 North Green Creek Inc 231 766-2155
  3253 Whitehall Rd Muskegon (49445) *(G-11758)*
18th Street Deli Inc 313 921-7710
  8800 Conant St Hamtramck (48211) *(G-7610)*
1johnson Erling..231 625-2247
  6564 N Black River Rd Cheboygan (49721) *(G-2779)*
1st Choice Trckg & Rentl Inc 231 258-0417
  1256 Thomas Rd Kalkaska (49646) *(G-9381)*
1st Quality LLC 313 908-4864
  6700 Wyoming St Ste A Dearborn (48126) *(G-3803)*
1st Rate Office Solutions LLC...989 544-4009
  1395 N Mcewan St Clare (48617) *(G-2971)*
2 Brothers Holdings LLC 517 487-3900
  1115 S Penn Ave Ste B Lansing (48912) *(G-9797)*
2 Donkeys Publishing 616 554-3958
  6550 Leisure Creek Dr Se Caledonia (49316) *(G-2365)*
2 E Fabricating 616 498-7036
  1202 Comstock St Marne (49435) *(G-10988)*
2 Gen Manufacturing LLC 616 443-7886
  3025 Madison Ave Se Grand Rapids (49548) *(G-6402)*
2 Sg Wookworks LLC 586 884-7090
  35360 Forton Ct Clinton Township (48035) *(G-3143)*
2-N-1 Grips Inc 800 530-9878
  46460 Continental Dr Chesterfield (48047) *(G-2833)*
2/90 Sign Systems, Grand Rapids *Also called System 2/90 Inc (G-7244)*
20/20 Printing 616 635-9690
  1702 Glenvale Ct Sw Grand Rapids (49519) *(G-6403)*
201 E Exchange 989 725-6397
  201 E Exchange St Owosso (48867) *(G-12818)*
2020 Mobile Detailing LLC 313 953-6363
  2493 S La Salle Gdns Detroit (48206) *(G-3969)*
21st Century Graphic Tech LLC 586 463-9599
  8344 Hall Rd Ste 210 Utica (48317) *(G-17501)*
21st Century Newspapers Inc (HQ) 586 469-4510
  6250 Metropolitan Pkwy Sterling Heights (48312) *(G-15915)*
21st Century Newspapers Inc 810 664-0811
  1521 Imlay City Rd Lapeer (48446) *(G-9910)*
21st Century Newspapers Inc 586 469-4510
  28 W Huron St Pontiac (48342) *(G-13343)*
21st Century Plastics Corp (PA)...517 645-2695
  300 Wright Pkwy Potterville (48876) *(G-13645)*
2255srv LLC 616 678-4900
  2825 17 Mile Rd Ste A Kent City (49330) *(G-9425)*
24 Canvas...517 902-5870
  4335 Geneva Hwy Manitou Beach (49253) *(G-10925)*
24 Hr Health, Dearborn *Also called USA Health LLC (G-3908)*
2k Tool LLC 616 452-4927
  3025 Madison Ave Se Wyoming (49548) *(G-18846)*
2nd Chance Wood Company 989 472-4488
  7505 E M 71 Ste B Durand (48429) *(G-4838)*
2stone Mfg LLC..269 214-6560
  109 N Main St Berrien Springs (49103) *(G-1636)*
2v Industries, Wixom *Also called V & V Industries Inc (G-18783)*

3 Dimensional Services, Lapeer *Also called Urgent Design and Mfg Inc (G-9963)*
3 Ten Denim Ko LLc..248 556-1725
  195 W 9 Mile Rd Ferndale (48220) *(G-5517)*
3-Dimensional Services, Rochester Hills *Also called Three-Dimensional Services Inc (G-14125)*
305 N 3rd LLC 517 404-1212
  140 Skyline Dr Howell (48843) *(G-8421)*
313 Certified LLC..248 915-8419
  6379 Muirfield Dr Bloomfield Hills (48301) *(G-1787)*
313 Industries 313 969-8570
  21686 Berg Rd Southfield (48033) *(G-15467)*
313 Industries Inc 313 338-9700
  32518 Dequindre Rd Warren (48092) *(G-17677)*
313certified, Bloomfield Hills *Also called 313 Certified LLC (G-1787)*
360ofme Inc 844 360-6363
  225 S Main St Ste 200 Royal Oak (48067) *(G-14500)*
3715-11th Street Corp...734 523-1000
  32711 Glendale St Livonia (48150) *(G-10089)*
3con Corporation 248 859-5440
  47295 Cartier Dr Wixom (48393) *(G-18591)*
3d Polymers Inc..248 588-5562
  4084 Commerce Rd Orchard Lake (48324) *(G-12715)*
3d Printed Parts 616 516-3074
  4355 Airwest Dr Se Grand Rapids (49512) *(G-6404)*
3dfx Interactive Inc..918 938-8967
  1813 Mackinaw St Saginaw (48602) *(G-14599)*
3dm Source Inc 616 647-9513
  555 Plymouth Ave Ne Grand Rapids (49505) *(G-6405)*
3dx Tech, Byron Center *Also called Lamon Group Inc (G-2280)*
3dxtech LLC..616 717-3811
  904 36th St Se Ste B Grand Rapids (49508) *(G-6406)*
3M Company 313 372-4200
  11900 E 8 Mile Rd Detroit (48205) *(G-3970)*
3M Technical Ceramics Inc...248 960-9339
  50370 Dennis Ct Wixom (48393) *(G-18592)*
3r Info LLC (PA)...201 221-6133
  5840 N Canton Center Rd # 2 Canton (48187) *(G-2425)*
4 Detroiters Liquor LLC 248 756-3678
  24125 Drake Rd Ste 102 Farmington Hills (48335) *(G-5156)*
4 Flutes Machining LLC..269 330-1313
  14024 S 36th St Vicksburg (49097) *(G-17597)*
4 Generation Logging Inc 989 350-0337
  2335 N Curran Rd Curran (48728) *(G-3749)*
4 One 2 Distillery 269 205-3223
  152 S Main St Wayland (49348) *(G-18186)*
4 Seasons Gym LLC..989 681-8175
  116 N Mill St Saint Louis (48880) *(G-14983)*
4 Wheels Industries 989 323-2191
  9980 Peet Rd Chesaning (48616) *(G-2827)*
4-Health Inc 989 686-3377
  701 5th St Bay City (48708) *(G-1313)*
4-M Industries Incorporated 734 762-7200
  33855 Capitol St Livonia (48150) *(G-10090)*
4-M Industries Incorporated (PA) 734 762-7200
  35300 Glendale St Livonia (48150) *(G-10091)*
420 Group 586 978-0420
  38300 Van Dyke Ave Sterling Heights (48312) *(G-15916)*
45 North Vineyard & Winery 231 271-1188
  8580 E Horn Rd Lake Leelanau (49653) *(G-9557)*
45th Parallel, Traverse City *Also called Bowers Harbor Vinyrd & Winery (G-16626)*
4d Building Inc..248 799-7384
  54500 Pontiac Trl Milford (48381) *(G-11452)*
4d Industries Inc 310 710-3955
  2290 28th St Sw Ste B Wyoming (49519) *(G-18847)*
4d Systems LLC 800 380-9165
  4130 Market Pl Flint (48507) *(G-5632)*
4ever Aluminum Products Inc..517 368-0000
  628 Pebblestone Dr Coldwater (49036) *(G-3417)*

(PA)=Parent Co (HQ)=Headquarters (DH)=Div Headquarters

5 14 Candles 231 944-9585
2801 Timber Ridge Rd Interlochen (49643) *(G-8678)*
5 By 5 LLC 855 369-6757
333 W Grandview Pkwy # 404 Traverse City (49684) *(G-16594)*
5 Lakes Printing and Sign LLC 517 265-3202
358 Mulzer Ave Adrian (49221) *(G-46)*
5 Pyn Inc 906 228-2828
363 Us Highway 41 E Ste 1 Negaunee (49866) *(G-11962)*
5 Star Drctional Drlg Svcs Ind 231 263-2050
8553 Blackman Rd Kingsley (49649) *(G-9520)*
589 Fabrication LLC 313 402-0586
10105 Gordon Rd Fenton (48430) *(G-5445)*
5w LLC 313 505-3106
847 Sumpter Rd Van Buren Twp (48111) *(G-17505)*
6df Research LLC 906 281-1170
101 W Lkshore Dr Ste 101g Houghton (49931) *(G-8379)*
7 Seas Sourcing LLC 734 357-8560
43000 W 9 Mile Rd Ste 308 Novi (48375) *(G-12358)*
7 Up Bottling Co, Cadillac *Also called American Bottling Company (G-2312)*
7 Up Holland, Holland *Also called American Bottling Company (G-7963)*
7 Up Lansing, Grand Ledge *Also called American Bottling Company (G-6384)*
7-Up Flint, Mount Morris *Also called American Bottling Company (G-11667)*
7-Up of Gaylord, Gaylord *Also called American Bottling Company (G-6118)*
751 Parts Company Inc 231 845-1221
3351 W Us Highway 10 Ludington (49431) *(G-10524)*
8 Mile Vodka, Farmington Hills *Also called 4 Detroiters Liquor LLC (G-5156)*
87 Grams LLC 248 558-0424
18226 Dalby Redford (48240) *(G-13708)*
8th Candle LLC 248 818-7625
2577 Huntington Dr Lake Orion (48360) *(G-9581)*
917 Chittock Street LLC 866 945-0269
114 Bank St Lansing (48910) *(G-9798)*
A & A Manufacturing Co 616 846-1730
19033 174th Ave Spring Lake (49456) *(G-15799)*
A & B Display Systems Inc 989 893-6642
1111 S Henry St Bay City (48706) *(G-1314)*
A & B Home Essentials LLC 734 334-3041
8808 Ironwood Dr Van Buren Twp (48111) *(G-17506)*
A & B Packing Equipment Inc (PA) 269 539-4700
732 W Saint Joseph St Lawrence (49064) *(G-9980)*
A & B Packing Equipment Inc 616 294-3539
414 E 40th St Holland (49423) *(G-7951)*
A & B Tube Benders Inc (PA) 586 773-0440
13465 E 9 Mile Rd Warren (48089) *(G-17678)*
A & B Tube Benders Inc 586 773-0440
23133 Schoenherr Rd Warren (48089) *(G-17679)*
A & B Welding & Fabricating 231 733-2661
2532 S Getty St Muskegon (49444) *(G-11759)*
A & C Electric Company 586 773-2746
41225 Irwin Dr Harrison Township (48045) *(G-7683)*
A & C Electric Motor Sls & Svc, Harrison Township *Also called A & C Electric Company (G-7683)*
A & D Distribution Inc 248 378-1418
2701 Troy Center Dr # 100 Troy (48084) *(G-16899)*
A & D Plastics Inc 734 455-2255
1255 S Mill St Plymouth (48170) *(G-13108)*
A & D Run Off Inc 231 759-0950
701 W Clay Ave Muskegon (49440) *(G-11760)*
A & E Agg Inc 248 547-4711
3500 11 Mile Rd Ste D Berkley (48072) *(G-1617)*
A & E Sign, Traverse City *Also called Attitude & Experience Inc (G-16606)*
A & F Enterprises Inc 248 714-6529
1203 N Milford Rd Milford (48381) *(G-11453)*
A & F Wood Products, Howell *Also called Masonite International Corp (G-8476)*
A & J Pallets, Sheridan *Also called Tommy Joe Reed (G-15384)*
A & Js Embroidery 734 417-3694
8666 Acorne Ave Milan (48160) *(G-11429)*
A & K Finishing Inc 616 949-9100
4175 Danvers Ct Se Grand Rapids (49512) *(G-6407)*
A & L Metal Products 734 654-8990
11984 Telegraph Rd Carleton (48117) *(G-2549)*
A & M Distributors 586 755-9045
31239 Mound Rd Warren (48092) *(G-17680)*
A & M Industries Inc 586 791-5610
35590 Groesbeck Hwy Clinton Township (48035) *(G-3144)*
A & M Label, Wixom *Also called General Tape Label Liquidating (G-18668)*
A & M Label, Wixom *Also called Fortis Sltions Group Centl LLC (G-18664)*
A & M Mobile Welding & Fab LLC 517 672-0289
159 Groveland Dr Howell (48843) *(G-8422)*
A & O Mold and Eng Inc 269 649-0600
301 N 4th St Vicksburg (49097) *(G-17598)*
A & R Packing Co Inc 734 422-2060
34165 Autry St Livonia (48150) *(G-10092)*
A & R Specialty Services Corp 313 933-8750
8101 Lyndon St Detroit (48238) *(G-3971)*
A & R Tool & Mfg Co 586 553-9623
36760 Metro Ct Sterling Heights (48312) *(G-15917)*

A & S Industrial LLC 906 482-8007
19273 Kiiskila Rd Hancock (49930) *(G-7614)*
A & S Reel & Tackle Inc 313 928-1667
4420 High St Ecorse (48229) *(G-4979)*
A & S Silver Brazing Co, Warren *Also called D K Enterprises Inc (G-17771)*
A A A Machine, Centreville *Also called Van Emon Bruce (G-2699)*
A A A Mailing & Packg Sups LLC 616 481-9120
3148 Plainfield Ave Ne # 258 Grand Rapids (49525) *(G-6408)*
A A A Wire Rope & Splicing Inc 734 283-1765
12650 Sibley Rd Riverview (48193) *(G-13867)*
A A Anchor Bolt Inc 248 349-6565
7390 Salem Rd Northville (48168) *(G-12194)*
A A P, Hazel Park *Also called Advanced Assembly Products Inc (G-7817)*
A and D Design Electronics 989 493-1884
301 W Midland Rd Auburn (48611) *(G-762)*
A B C Printing Inc 248 887-0010
2983 E Highland Rd Highland (48356) *(G-7877)*
A B M Tool & Die Inc 734 432-6060
38281 Schoolcraft Rd D Livonia (48150) *(G-10093)*
A B Publishing Inc 989 875-4985
3039 S Bagley Rd Ithaca (48847) *(G-8784)*
A B Rusgo Inc (PA) 586 296-7714
32064 Utica Rd Fraser (48026) *(G-5886)*
A C Foundry Incorporated 269 963-4131
202 Mcgrath Pl Battle Creek (49014) *(G-1175)*
A C I Plastics, Flint *Also called Aci Plastics Inc (G-5637)*
A C Machining LLC 616 455-3870
7490 Division Ave S Grand Rapids (49548) *(G-6409)*
A C Steel Rule Dies Inc 248 588-5600
324 E Mandoline Ave Madison Heights (48071) *(G-10654)*
A C Supply Co Inc 586 776-2222
21831 Schoenherr Rd Warren (48089) *(G-17681)*
A D Johnson Engraving Co Inc 269 385-0044
2129 Portage St Kalamazoo (49001) *(G-9106)*
A D S Environmental Srvs, Troy *Also called ADS LLC (G-16906)*
A Dependable Property MGT, Lansing *Also called 917 Chittock Street LLC (G-9798)*
A E C Inc 810 231-9546
10087 Industrial Dr Whitmore Lake (48189) *(G-18515)*
A E G M Inc 313 304-5279
335 S Telegraph Rd Dearborn (48124) *(G-3804)*
A F I, Plymouth *Also called American Furukawa Inc (G-13123)*
A G, Rochester Hills *Also called Accurate Gauge & Mfg Inc (G-13940)*
A G Case LLC 586 791-0125
36227 Eaton Dr Clinton Township (48035) *(G-3145)*
A G Simpson (usa) Inc 586 268-4817
6700 18 1/2 Mile Rd Sterling Heights (48314) *(G-15918)*
A G Simpson Inc 586 268-4817
6700 18 1/2 Sterling Heights (48314) *(G-15919)*
A G Simpson (usa) Inc 586 825-9000
24358 Groesbeck Hwy Warren (48089) *(G-17682)*
A G Simpson (usa) Inc (HQ) 586 268-5844
6640 Sterling Dr S Sterling Heights (48312) *(G-15920)*
A Game Apparel 810 564-2600
4330 W Mount Morris Rd # 1 Mount Morris (48458) *(G-11665)*
A H Webster, Saginaw *Also called RPC Company (G-14741)*
A I Flint LLC 810 732-8760
4444 W Maple Ave Flint (48507) *(G-5633)*
A I M I, Clinton Township *Also called Accurate Injection Molds Inc (G-3152)*
A J D Forest Pdts Ltd Partnr 989 348-5412
4440 W 4 Mile Rd Grayling (49738) *(G-7454)*
A J M, Bloomfield Hills *Also called AJM Packaging Corporation (G-1794)*
A J Tool Co 517 787-5755
3525 Scheele Dr Ste A Jackson (49202) *(G-8798)*
A K Industries 231 726-0134
1737 Ritter Dr Norton Shores (49441) *(G-12273)*
A K Oil LLC DBA Speedy Oil and 616 233-9505
925 Leonard St Nw Grand Rapids (49504) *(G-6410)*
A K Services Inc 313 972-1010
1604 Clay St Ste 137 Detroit (48211) *(G-3972)*
A Koppel Color Image Company 616 534-3600
4025 Chicago Dr Sw Grandville (49418) *(G-7360)*
A Lasting Impression Inc 616 847-2380
17796 North Shore Dr Spring Lake (49456) *(G-15800)*
A Lindberg & Sons Inc (PA) 906 485-5705
599 Washington St Ishpeming (49849) *(G-8774)*
A Lite In Nite 231 275-5900
15782 Hooker Rd Lake Ann (49650) *(G-9540)*
A M D, Holland *Also called All Metal Designs Inc (G-7960)*
A M F, Three Rivers *Also called American Metal Fab Inc (G-16563)*
A M I, Commerce Township *Also called American Mfg Innovators Inc (G-3510)*
A M P, Reese *Also called Advanced McRonutrient Pdts Inc (G-13805)*
A M R Inc 810 329-9049
671 Hathaway St East China (48054) *(G-4854)*
A M T Welding Inc 586 463-7030
21446 Carlo Dr Clinton Township (48038) *(G-3146)*
A ME Vertical Incorporated 248 720-0245
675 E Big Beaver Rd Troy (48083) *(G-16900)*

A N L Spring Manufacturing 313 837-0200
18307 Weaver St Detroit (48228) ***(G-3973)***
A Naturally Empowered Lf Anel 734 572-8857
6276 Aspen Way Ypsilanti (48197) ***(G-18922)***
A P Engineering, Holly *Also called Falcon Motorsports Inc* ***(G-8269)***
A P S, Auburn Hills *Also called Analytical Process Systems Inc* ***(G-784)***
A Plus Asphalt LLC 888 754-1125
41000 Woodward Ave Bloomfield Hills (48304) ***(G-1788)***
A R C Welding & Repair 517 628-2475
5261 Bunker Rd Mason (48854) ***(G-11115)***
A Raymond Corp N Amer Inc (HQ) 248 853-2500
2350 Austin Ave Ste 200 Rochester Hills (48309) ***(G-13938)***
A Raymond Tinnerman Mexico 248 537-3404
3091 Research Dr Rochester Hills (48309) ***(G-13939)***
A S A P Machine Company 734 459-2447
8575 Ronda Dr Canton (48187) ***(G-2426)***
A S A P Tool Inc 586 790-6550
35660 Groesbeck Hwy Clinton Township (48035) ***(G-3147)***
A S Auto Lights Inc 734 941-1164
15326 Oakwood Dr Romulus (48174) ***(G-14242)***
A S D, Freeland *Also called Accurate Safety Distrs Inc* ***(G-6017)***
A S I, Warren *Also called Air Supply Inc* ***(G-17694)***
A S I Instruments Inc 586 756-1222
12900 E 10 Mile Rd Warren (48089) ***(G-17683)***
A S P, Saline *Also called American Soy Products Inc* ***(G-15001)***
A S Plus Industries Inc 586 741-0400
34728 Centaur Dr Clinton Township (48035) ***(G-3148)***
A S R C Inc 517 545-7430
4285 Westhill Dr Howell (48843) ***(G-8423)***
A Taste of Leone LLC 616 238-8881
736 Cherry St Se Grand Rapids (49503) ***(G-6411)***
A To Z Signs 248 887-7737
2680 Morel Dr Highland (48356) ***(G-7878)***
A V L Instrumentation Test Sys, Plymouth *Also called Avl Powertrain Technologies* ***(G-13132)***
A W B Industries Inc 989 739-1447
1000 Ausable Rd Oscoda (48750) ***(G-12753)***
A W C, Rockford *Also called Accra-Wire Controls Inc* ***(G-14152)***
A&A Manufacturing 800 473-1730
18634 56th Ave Coopersville (49404) ***(G-3678)***
A&B Welding, Muskegon *Also called A & B Welding & Fabricating* ***(G-11759)***
A&D Industries LLC 586 291-6444
44645 Macomb Indus Dr Clinton Township (48036) ***(G-3149)***
A&D Technology Inc 734 973-1111
4622 Runway Blvd Ann Arbor (48108) ***(G-341)***
A&E Machine & Fabrication Inc 740 820-4701
7540 Wheeler Rd Whitmore Lake (48189) ***(G-18516)***
A&G Corporate Holdings LLC 734 513-3488
12725 Inkster Rd Livonia (48150) ***(G-10094)***
A&M Assembly and Machining LLC 313 369-9475
6400 E Hildale St Detroit (48234) ***(G-3974)***
A&S Industries 269 903-1081
5743 N 20th St Kalamazoo (49004) ***(G-9107)***
A&W Welding 248 949-4344
228 Abbey Blvd White Lake (48383) ***(G-18448)***
A-1 Engraving & Signs Inc 810 231-2227
397 Washington St Ste A Brighton (48116) ***(G-1935)***
A-1 Roll Co 586 783-6677
301 Church St Mount Clemens (48043) ***(G-11626)***
A-1 Screenprinting LLC (PA) 734 665-2692
260 Metty Dr Ste G Ann Arbor (48103) ***(G-342)***
A-1 Stampings Inc 586 294-7790
33381 Kelly Rd Fraser (48026) ***(G-5887)***
A-Day Badge Co, Detroit *Also called Dealer Aid Enterprises* ***(G-4128)***
A-Line Products Corporation 313 571-8300
2955 Bellevue St Detroit (48207) ***(G-3975)***
A-OK Precision Prototype Inc 586 758-3430
59539 Romeo Plank Rd Ray (48096) ***(G-13697)***
A-Pac Manufacturing Company 616 791-7222
2719 Courier Dr Nw Grand Rapids (49534) ***(G-6412)***
A-W Custom Chrome Inc 586 775-2040
17726 E 9 Mile Rd Eastpointe (48021) ***(G-4926)***
A. R. Lintern Division, Redford *Also called Therma-Tech Engineering Inc* ***(G-13778)***
A.M. Todd, Kalamazoo *Also called Wild Flavors Inc* ***(G-9370)***
A/C Covers, Redford *Also called AC Covers Inc* ***(G-13710)***
A1 Noise Control 248 538-7585
4578 Walden Dr Bloomfield Hills (48301) ***(G-1789)***
A1 Powder Coating 616 238-0683
3460 Fruit Ridge Ave Nw Grand Rapids (49544) ***(G-6413)***
A1 Utility Contractor Inc 989 324-8581
8399 Evergreen Rd Evart (49631) ***(G-5118)***
A123 Systems LLC (HQ) 248 412-9249
27101 Cabaret Dr Novi (48377) ***(G-12359)***
A123 Systems LLC 734 466-6521
28200 Plymouth Rd Livonia (48150) ***(G-10095)***
A123 Systems LLC 734 772-0600
38100 Ecorse Rd Romulus (48174) ***(G-14243)***
A123 Systems Rmulus Operations, Romulus *Also called A123 Systems LLC* ***(G-14243)***

A2 Motus LLC 734 780-7334
3575 Stanton Ct Ann Arbor (48105) ***(G-343)***
A2e Manufacturing 734 622-9800
45209 Helm St Plymouth (48170) ***(G-13109)***
A2z Coating 616 805-3281
200 Garden St Se Grand Rapids (49507) ***(G-6414)***
AA Anderson & Co Inc 248 476-7782
41304 Concept Dr Plymouth (48170) ***(G-13110)***
AA EDM Corporation 734 253-2784
7455 Newman Blvd Dexter (48130) ***(G-4719)***
AA Gear LLC 517 552-3100
1045 Durant Dr Howell (48843) ***(G-8424)***
Aa Gear & Manufacturing, Howell *Also called Meritor Specialty Products LLC* ***(G-8478)***
AAA Industries Inc 313 255-0420
24500 Capitol Redford (48239) ***(G-13709)***
AAA Language Services 248 239-1138
1573 S Telegraph Rd Bloomfield (48302) ***(G-1780)***
AAA Waterjet and Machining Inc 586 759-3736
23720 Hoover Rd Warren (48089) ***(G-17684)***
Aaa1 Box Division Container 269 983-1563
233 Hawthorne Ave Saint Joseph (49085) ***(G-14921)***
Aaccess Entertainment 734 260-1002
11552 Eagle Way Brighton (48114) ***(G-1936)***
Aactron Inc 248 543-6740
29306 Stephenson Hwy Madison Heights (48071) ***(G-10655)***
Aactus Inc 734 425-1212
12671 Richfield Ct Livonia (48150) ***(G-10096)***
Aak Fabrication & Plastics Inc 734 525-1391
26140 W 9 Mile Rd Southfield (48033) ***(G-15468)***
Aall American Fasteners 616 414-7688
1730 Airpark Dr Grand Haven (49417) ***(G-6270)***
Aalpha Tinadawn Inc 517 351-1200
974 Trwbrdge Rd Trwbrdge Trowbridge East Lansing (48823) ***(G-4884)***
AAM, Detroit *Also called American Axle Mfg Holdings Inc* ***(G-4012)***
AAM Casting 313 758-5968
26533 Evergreen Rd Ste 13 Southfield (48076) ***(G-15469)***
AAM Fraser Mfg Fcilty, Fraser *Also called American Axle & Mfg Inc* ***(G-5891)***
AAM International Holdings Inc (HQ) 313 758-2000
1 Dauch Dr Detroit (48211) ***(G-3976)***
AAM Metal Forming, Warren *Also called American Axle & Mfg Inc* ***(G-17700)***
AAM Mexico Holdings LLC (HQ) 313 758-2000
1 Dauch Dr Detroit (48211) ***(G-3977)***
AAM Mtal Frming Troy Mfg Fclty 248 362-8500
690 W Maple Rd Troy (48084) ***(G-16901)***
AAM Pwder Metal Components Inc 248 597-3800
2727 W 14 Mile Rd Royal Oak (48073) ***(G-14501)***
AAM Qality Engrg Technical Ctr, Auburn Hills *Also called American Axle & Mfg Inc* ***(G-781)***
AAM Royal Oak Mfg 248 597-3800
2727 W 14 Mile Rd Royal Oak (48073) ***(G-14502)***
AAM Technical Center, Rochester Hills *Also called American Axle & Mfg Inc* ***(G-13946)***
AAM Travel Services LLC 313 758-2000
1 Dauch Dr Detroit (48211) ***(G-3978)***
AAMCO Transmissions, Detroit *Also called American Axle & Mfg Inc* ***(G-4011)***
Aapharmasyn LLC 734 213-2123
3915 Res Pk Dr Ste A1 Ann Arbor (48108) ***(G-344)***
AAR Corp 231 779-4859
10732 Pine Shore Dr Cadillac (49601) ***(G-2305)***
AAR Manufacturing Inc 231 779-8800
201 Haynes St Cadillac (49601) ***(G-2306)***
AAR Mobility Systems, Cadillac *Also called AAR Manufacturing Inc* ***(G-2306)***
Aaron Incorporated 586 791-0320
33674 Kelly Rd Clinton Township (48035) ***(G-3150)***
Aaron Jagt 517 304-4844
3321 Sesame Dr Howell (48843) ***(G-8425)***
Aarons Fabrication of Steel 586 883-0652
21427 Carlo Dr Clinton Township (48038) ***(G-3151)***
Aarons Fabrictions-Tube Steel 586 883-0652
50220 Shenandoah Dr Macomb (48044) ***(G-10570)***
Aatanks Llc 586 427-7700
25110 Thomas Dr Warren (48091) ***(G-17685)***
Aati, Oxford *Also called Advanced Auto Trends Inc* ***(G-12872)***
AB Custom Fabricating LLC 269 663-8100
27531 May St Edwardsburg (49112) ***(G-4998)***
Aba of America Inc (HQ) 815 332-5170
2430 E Walton Blvd Auburn Hills (48326) ***(G-772)***
Abaco Partners LLC 616 532-1700
4560 Danvers Dr Se Kentwood (49512) ***(G-9441)***
ABB Enterprise Software Inc 313 863-1909
16503 Manor St Detroit (48221) ***(G-3979)***
ABB Inc 248 471-0888
23629 Industrial Park Dr Farmington Hills (48335) ***(G-5157)***
Abbott Laboratories 269 651-0600
901 N Centerville Rd Sturgis (49091) ***(G-16279)***
Abbott Laboratories 734 324-6666
1609 Biddle Ave Lot 4 Wyandotte (48192) ***(G-18805)***
Abbott Magic, Colon *Also called Abbotts Magic Manufacturing Co* ***(G-3486)***
Abbotts Magic Manufacturing Co 269 432-3235
124 S Saint Joseph St Colon (49040) ***(G-3486)***

Abbvie Inc 734 324-6650
  1609 Biddle Ave Wyandotte (48192) *(G-18806)*
Abby's Printing, Grand Rapids Also called Quality Printing & Graphics *(G-7130)*
ABC Acquisition Company LLC 734 335-4083
  31778 Enterprise Dr Livonia (48150) *(G-10097)*
ABC Boring Co Inc 586 751-2580
  30600 Ryan Rd Warren (48092) *(G-17686)*
ABC Coating Company Inc 616 245-4626
  1503 Burlingame Ave Sw Grand Rapids (49509) *(G-6415)*
ABC Coating Company Michigan, Grand Rapids Also called ABC Coating Company Inc *(G-6415)*
ABC Grinding Inc 313 295-1060
  26950 Van Born Rd Dearborn Heights (48125) *(G-3918)*
ABC Group Holdings Inc (HQ) 248 352-3706
  24133 Northwestern Hwy Southfield (48075) *(G-15470)*
ABC Group Sale & Marketing, Southfield Also called ABC Group Holdings Inc *(G-15470)*
ABC Industrial Supply, Troy Also called Superior Manufacturing Corp *(G-17380)*
ABC Machining & Fabricating 586 758-0680
  6737 E 8 Mile Rd Warren (48091) *(G-17687)*
ABC Merchandise 248 348-1560
  28900 Wall St Wixom (48393) *(G-18593)*
ABC Nails LLC 616 776-6000
  20 Monroe Center St Ne # 110 Grand Rapids (49503) *(G-6416)*
ABC Packaging Eqp & Mtls Inc 616 784-2330
  544 7 Mile Rd Nw Comstock Park (49321) *(G-3584)*
ABC Precision Machining Inc 269 926-6322
  2077 Yore Ave Benton Harbor (49022) *(G-1525)*
ABC Printing Corporation Inc 248 887-0010
  2983 E Highland Rd Highland (48356) *(G-7879)*
ABC Supply 693, Marquette Also called American Bldrs Contrs Sup Inc *(G-11004)*
ABC-2100 Inc 616 647-9200
  5320 6 Mile Ct Nw Comstock Park (49321) *(G-3585)*
Abco, Pontiac Also called Aluminum Blanking Co Inc *(G-13349)*
Abcor Industries LLC 616 994-9577
  4690 128th Ave Holland (49424) *(G-7952)*
Abcor Partners LLC 616 994-9577
  4690 128th Ave Holland (49424) *(G-7953)*
ABI International 248 583-7150
  32052 Edward Ave Madison Heights (48071) *(G-10656)*
Ability Mfg & Engrg Co 269 227-3292
  1585 68th St Fennville (49408) *(G-5433)*
Ability Weavers LLC 616 929-0211
  215 W Main St Lowell (49331) *(G-10493)*
Abl Enterprises, Grand Rapids Also called Jbl Enterprises *(G-6863)*
Able Entities LLC 313 422-9555
  3330 Stockton St Detroit (48234) *(G-3980)*
Able Htng Clng & Plmbng 231 779-5430
  9542 Peterson Dr Cadillac (49601) *(G-2307)*
Able Machine Tooling 586 783-7776
  40875 Irwin Dr Harrison Twp (48045) *(G-7737)*
Able Manufacturing Inc 616 235-3322
  601 Crosby St Nw Grand Rapids (49504) *(G-6417)*
Able Solutions LLC 810 216-6106
  2030 10th St Port Huron (48060) *(G-13430)*
Able Welding Inc 989 865-9611
  5265 S Graham Rd Saint Charles (48655) *(G-14800)*
Abletech Industries LLC 734 677-2420
  8383 Millview Ct Dexter (48130) *(G-4720)*
Abracadabra Jewelry 734 994-4848
  205 E Liberty St Ann Arbor (48104) *(G-345)*
Abrasive Diamond Tool Company 248 588-4800
  30231 Stephenson Hwy Madison Heights (48071) *(G-10657)*
Abrasive Finishing Inc 734 433-9236
  11770 Dexter Chelsea Rd Chelsea (48118) *(G-2801)*
Abrasive Materials LLC 517 437-4796
  7253 Tower Rd Battle Creek (49014) *(G-1176)*
Abrasive Services Incorporated 734 941-2144
  29040 Northline Rd Romulus (48174) *(G-14244)*
Abrasive Solutions LLC 517 592-2668
  12875 Mack Ave Cement City (49233) *(G-2675)*
Abretec Group LLC (PA) 248 591-4000
  2807 Samoset Rd Royal Oak (48073) *(G-14503)*
ABS, Menominee Also called Advanced Blnding Solutions LLC *(G-11224)*
Absolute Lser Wldg Sltions LLC 586 932-2597
  6545 19 Mile Rd Sterling Heights (48314) *(G-15921)*
Absolute Machine LLC 517 745-5905
  3233 Gregory Rd Jackson (49202) *(G-8799)*
Absopure Water Company LLC 734 459-8000
  8835 General Dr Plymouth (48170) *(G-13111)*
Abtech Installation & Svc Inc 800 548-2381
  11900 Reeck Rd Ste 100 Southgate (48195) *(G-15747)*
Abz Steel Systems, Clinton Township Also called Ferro Fab LLC *(G-3237)*
Abzac - US, Swartz Creek Also called Nagel Paper Inc *(G-16357)*
AC Covers Inc 313 541-7770
  25544 5 Mile Rd Redford (48239) *(G-13710)*
AC Design LLC 616 874-9007
  8550 Young Ave Ne Rockford (49341) *(G-14151)*
Academicpub Xanedu, Ann Arbor Also called Sharedbook Inc *(G-650)*

Acadia Group LLC 734 944-1404
  1283 Industrial Dr Saline (48176) *(G-14997)*
Acadian Woodworking LLC 989 356-0229
  4357 M 32 W Alpena (49707) *(G-273)*
Acal Precision Products, Roseville Also called Acal Universal Grinding Co *(G-14368)*
Acal Universal Grinding Co 586 296-3900
  20200 Cornillie Dr Roseville (48066) *(G-14368)*
Acat Global LLC (PA) 231 330-2553
  5339 M 66 N Charlevoix (49720) *(G-2707)*
Acat Global LLC 231 437-5000
  66 N North St White Cloud (49349) *(G-18437)*
Accelerated Press Inc 248 524-1850
  1337 Piedmont Dr Troy (48083) *(G-16902)*
Accelerated Tooling LLC 616 293-9612
  2909 Buchanan Ave Sw Grand Rapids (49548) *(G-6418)*
Accell Technologies Inc 248 360-3762
  4143 Pioneer Dr Commerce Township (48390) *(G-3505)*
Accent Signs 860 693-6760
  45721 Bryn Mawr Rd Canton (48187) *(G-2427)*
Accents Custom Printwear Plus, Lincoln Park Also called Graphic Gear Inc *(G-10048)*
Access Business Group LLC (HQ) 616 787-6000
  7575 Fulton St E Ada (49355) *(G-3)*
Access Heating & Cooling Inc 734 464-0566
  39001 Ann Arbor Trl Livonia (48150) *(G-10098)*
Access Manufacturing Techn 224 610-0171
  1530 W River Rd Niles (49120) *(G-12108)*
Access Technologies LLC (PA) 574 286-1255
  1530 W River Rd Niles (49120) *(G-12109)*
Access Works Inc 231 777-2537
  1800 E Keating Ave Muskegon (49442) *(G-11761)*
Accessible Information LLC 248 338-4928
  124 N Berkshire Rd Bloomfield Hills (48302) *(G-1790)*
Accessories & Specialties Inc 989 235-3331
  121 E Park St Crystal (48818) *(G-3739)*
Accessories R US, Pontiac Also called Accessories Wholesale Inc *(G-13344)*
Accessories Wholesale Inc 248 755-7465
  555 Friendly St Pontiac (48341) *(G-13344)*
Accord Paper and Packaging, Coopersville Also called Mark-Pack Inc *(G-3691)*
Accord Software Solutions LLC 616 604-1699
  42565 Laird Ln Canton (48187) *(G-2428)*
Accra Tool Inc 248 680-9936
  1218 Cottonwood St Lake Orion (48360) *(G-9582)*
Accra-Wire Controls Inc (PA) 616 866-3434
  10891 Northland Dr Ne A Rockford (49341) *(G-14152)*
Accu Die & Mold Inc 269 465-4020
  7473 Red Arrow Hwy Stevensville (49127) *(G-16237)*
Accu Products International 734 429-9571
  7836 Bethel Church Rd Saline (48176) *(G-14998)*
Accu Tech Michigan 616 953-0256
  9652 Black River Ct # 10 Holland (49424) *(G-7954)*
Accu-Form Metal Products, Grand Rapids Also called Accuform Industries Inc *(G-6420)*
Accu-Rite Industries LLC 586 247-0060
  51047 Oro Dr Shelby Township (48315) *(G-15161)*
Accu-Shape Die Cutting Inc 810 230-2445
  4050 Market Pl Flint (48507) *(G-5634)*
Accu-Tech Manufacturing Inc 586 532-4000
  51210 Oro Dr Shelby Township (48315) *(G-15162)*
Accubilt Automated Systems LLC 517 787-9353
  2365 Research Dr Jackson (49203) *(G-8800)*
Accuform Industries Inc (PA) 616 363-3801
  1701 Broadway Ave Nw Grand Rapids (49504) *(G-6419)*
Accuform Industries Inc 616 363-3801
  1701 Broadway Ave Nw Grand Rapids (49504) *(G-6420)*
Accuform Prtg & Graphics Inc 313 271-5600
  7231 Southfield Fwy Detroit (48228) *(G-3981)*
Acculift Inc 313 382-5121
  17516 Dix Rd Melvindale (48122) *(G-11196)*
Accurate Automotive Engs Inc 616 531-2050
  2840 Dormax St Sw Grandville (49418) *(G-7361)*
Accurate Carbide Tool Co Inc 989 755-0429
  5655 N Westervelt Rd Saginaw (48604) *(G-14600)*
Accurate Coating Inc 616 452-0016
  955 Godfrey Ave Sw Grand Rapids (49503) *(G-6421)*
Accurate Engineering & Mfg Inc 616 738-1261
  13569 New Holland St Holland (49424) *(G-7955)*
Accurate Engines, Grandville Also called Accurate Automotive Engs Inc *(G-7361)*
Accurate Gauge & Mfg Inc (PA) 248 853-2400
  2943 Technology Dr Rochester Hills (48309) *(G-13940)*
Accurate Home Insptn Svcs Inc 303 530-9600
  38457 Huron Pointe Dr Harrison Township (48045) *(G-7684)*
Accurate Injection Molds Inc 586 954-2553
  22264 Starks Dr Clinton Township (48036) *(G-3152)*
Accurate Machine & TI USA Ltd 269 205-2610
  987 Grand Rapids St Middleville (49333) *(G-11301)*
Accurate Machine Service, Livonia Also called Accurate Machined Service Inc *(G-10099)*
Accurate Machined Service Inc 734 421-4660
  30948 Industrial Rd Livonia (48150) *(G-10099)*
Accurate Machining & Fabg Inc 989 426-5400
  1650 S M 30 Gladwin (48624) *(G-6188)*

Accurate Safety Distrs Inc ... 989 695-6446
10320 Thor Dr Freeland (48623) *(G-6017)*
Accurate Technologies Inc (PA) ... 248 848-9200
26999 Meadowbrook Rd Novi (48377) *(G-12360)*
Accurate Tooling Solutions, Chesterfield *Also called Verstar Group Inc (G-2963)*
Accuri Cytometers Inc ... 734 994-8000
173 Parkland Plz Ann Arbor (48103) *(G-346)*
Accuspec Grinding Inc (PA) ... 269 556-1410
2660 Lawrence St Stevensville (49127) *(G-16238)*
Accutek Mold & Engineering ... 586 978-1335
35815 Stanley Dr Sterling Heights (48312) *(G-15922)*
Accuworx LLC (PA) ... 734 847-6115
7156 Sulier Dr Temperance (48182) *(G-16525)*
Ace, Dexter *Also called Automation Contrls & Engrg LLC (G-4725)*
Ace & 1 Logistics LLC ... 601 335-3625
2076 Jonathan Cir Shelby Township (48317) *(G-15163)*
Ace Canvas & Tent Co ... 313 842-3011
465 Stephenson Hwy Troy (48083) *(G-16903)*
Ace Consulting & MGT Inc ... 989 821-7040
10386 S Leline Rd Roscommon (48653) *(G-14346)*
Ace Controls Inc (HQ) ... 248 476-0213
23435 Industrial Park Dr Farmington Hills (48335) *(G-5158)*
Ace Drill Corporation ... 517 265-5184
2600 E Maumee St Adrian (49221) *(G-47)*
Ace Electronics LLC Michigan ... 443 327-6100
401 Minnesota Dr Troy (48083) *(G-16904)*
Ace Filtration Inc ... 248 624-6300
4123 Pioneer Dr Commerce Township (48390) *(G-3506)*
Ace Outdoor Services LLC ... 810 820-8313
5249 Miller Rd Flint (48507) *(G-5635)*
Ace Purification, Commerce Township *Also called Ace Filtration Inc (G-3506)*
Ace Tool & Engineering Inc ... 616 361-4800
500 Reed St Belding (48809) *(G-1434)*
ACE TOOLING, Norton Shores *Also called Patterson Precision Mfg Inc (G-12324)*
Ace Vending Service Inc ... 616 243-7983
3417 Rger B Chffee Mem Bl Grand Rapids (49548) *(G-6422)*
Ace Welding & Machine Inc ... 231 941-9664
1505 Premier St Traverse City (49686) *(G-16595)*
Ace Wiping Cloth, Detroit *Also called Ace-Tex Enterprises Inc (G-3982)*
Ace-Tex Enterprises Inc (PA) ... 313 834-4000
7601 Central St Detroit (48210) *(G-3982)*
Acecd, Jackson *Also called Allied Chucker and Engrg Co (G-8810)*
Acemco Automotive, Norton Shores *Also called Acemco Incorporated (G-12344)*
Acemco Incorporated ... 231 799-8612
7297 Enterprise Dr Norton Shores (49456) *(G-12344)*
Acg Services Inc ... 586 232-4698
51512 Schoenherr Rd Shelby Township (48315) *(G-15164)*
Achatzs Hand Made Pie Co (PA) ... 586 749-2882
30301 Commerce Blvd Chesterfield (48051) *(G-2834)*
Achieve Industries LLC ... 586 493-9780
44421 N Groesbeck Hwy Clinton Township (48036) *(G-3153)*
Achs Metal Products Inc ... 586 772-2734
22238 Schoenherr Rd Warren (48089) *(G-17688)*
Aci, Rose City *Also called Assembly Concepts Inc (G-14361)*
Aci Plastics Inc ... 810 767-3800
2945 Davison Rd Flint (48506) *(G-5636)*
Aci Plastics Inc (PA) ... 810 767-3800
2945 Davison Rd Flint (48506) *(G-5637)*
Aci/Wipag Recycling LLC ... 810 767-4424
2945 Davison Rd Flint (48506) *(G-5638)*
Ackerman Brothers Inc ... 989 892-4122
200 S Linn St Bay City (48706) *(G-1315)*
Acm, Coldwater *Also called Asama Coldwater Mfg Inc (G-3420)*
Acm, Sterling Heights *Also called Automotive Component Mfg (G-15937)*
Acm Plastic Products Inc ... 269 651-7888
507 Saint Joseph St Sturgis (49091) *(G-16280)*
Acme Abrasive Co., Warren *Also called Acme Holding Company (G-17690)*
Acme Bedding Company, Grand Rapids *Also called Jonathan Stevens Mattress Co (G-6873)*
Acme Carbide Die Inc (PA) ... 734 722-2303
6202 E Executive Dr Westland (48185) *(G-18351)*
Acme Casting Enterprises Inc ... 586 755-0300
2565 John B Ave Warren (48091) *(G-17689)*
Acme Gear Company Inc ... 586 465-7740
23402 Reynolds Ct Clinton Township (48036) *(G-3154)*
Acme Grooving Tool Co ... 800 633-8828
7409 S Village Dr Clarkston (48346) *(G-3011)*
Acme Holding Company ... 586 759-3332
24200 Marmon Ave Warren (48089) *(G-17690)*
Acme Manufacturing Company (PA) ... 248 393-7300
4240 N Atlantic Blvd Auburn Hills (48326) *(G-773)*
Acme Manufacturing Company ... 248 393-7300
101 Premier Dr Lake Orion (48359) *(G-9583)*
Acme Mills Company ... 517 437-8940
301 Arch Ave Hillsdale (49242) *(G-7919)*
Acme Mills Company ... 517 437-8940
301 Arch Ave Hillsdale (49242) *(G-7920)*
Acme Mills Company ... 800 521-8585
33 Bloomfield Hills Pkwy Bloomfield Hills (48304) *(G-1791)*
Acme Pallet Inc ... 616 738-6452
13450 New Holland St Holland (49424) *(G-7956)*
Acme Plating Inc ... 313 838-3870
18636 Fitzpatrick St Detroit (48228) *(G-3983)*
Acme Septic Tank Co ... 989 684-3852
2888 S Huron Rd Kawkawlin (48631) *(G-9413)*
Acme Sign Co ... 248 930-9718
42732 Merrill Rd Sterling Heights (48314) *(G-15923)*
Acme Small Log Sawmill, Holland *Also called Acme Pallet Inc (G-7956)*
Acme Tool & Die Co ... 231 938-1260
5181 S Lautner Rd Acme (49610) *(G-1)*
Acme Tube Bending Company ... 248 545-8500
3180 W 11 Mile Rd Berkley (48072) *(G-1618)*
Acme Wire & Iron Works LLC ... 313 923-7555
3527 E Canfield St Detroit (48207) *(G-3984)*
Acorn Industries Inc (PA) ... 734 261-2940
11844 Brookfield St Livonia (48150) *(G-10100)*
Acorn Stamping Inc ... 248 628-5216
600 S Glaspie St Oxford (48371) *(G-12870)*
Acoufelt LLC ... 800 966-8557
1238 Anderson Rd Fl 2 Clawson (48017) *(G-3083)*
Acoustic Tap Room ... 231 714-5028
119 N Maple St Traverse City (49684) *(G-16596)*
Acousys Biodevices Inc ... 573 823-3849
1777 Highland Dr Ste B Ann Arbor (48108) *(G-347)*
Acp Technologies LLC ... 586 322-3511
20527 Stephens St Saint Clair Shores (48080) *(G-14846)*
Acra Cast Inc ... 989 893-3961
1837 1st St Bay City (48708) *(G-1316)*
Acra Training Center ... 269 326-7088
9202 Cleveland Ave Baroda (49101) *(G-1158)*
Acro-Tech Manufacturing Inc ... 269 629-4300
12229 M 89 Plainwell (49080) *(G-13069)*
Acromag Incorporated (PA) ... 248 624-1541
30765 S Wixom Rd Wixom (48393) *(G-18594)*
Acrylic Specialties ... 248 588-4390
32336 Edward Ave Madison Heights (48071) *(G-10658)*
ACS, Fraser *Also called Auto/Con Services LLC (G-5898)*
ACS, Brighton *Also called American Compounding Spc LLC (G-1944)*
Act Test Panels LLC ... 517 439-1485
273 Industrial Dr Hillsdale (49242) *(G-7921)*
Actalent Services LLC ... 248 712-2750
340 E Big Beaver Rd Troy (48083) *(G-16905)*
Actia Electronics Inc ... 574 264-2373
15385 Pine Romulus (48174) *(G-14245)*
Action Ad Newspapers Inc ... 734 740-6966
45223 Wear Rd Belleville (48111) *(G-1478)*
Action Asphalt LLC ... 734 449-8565
12809 Silver Lake Rd Brighton (48116) *(G-1937)*
Action Die & Tool Inc ... 616 538-2326
4621 Spartan Indus Dr Sw Grandville (49418) *(G-7362)*
Action Fabricators Inc ... 616 957-2032
3760 East Paris Ave Se Grand Rapids (49512) *(G-6423)*
Action Mold & Machining Inc ... 616 452-1580
3120 Ken O Sha Ind Pk Ct Grand Rapids (49508) *(G-6424)*
Action Mold Removal ... 517 960-1928
129 Sagamore St Jackson (49203) *(G-8801)*
Action Outdoor Services LLC ... 719 596-5341
2543 Andrew Thomas Trl Ann Arbor (48103) *(G-348)*
Action Packaging LLC ... 616 871-5200
6995 Southbelt Dr Se Caledonia (49316) *(G-2366)*
Action Pallets Inc ... 248 557-9017
28000 Southfield Rd Fl 2 Lathrup Village (48076) *(G-9973)*
Action Printech Inc ... 734 207-6000
41079 Concept Dr Plymouth (48170) *(G-13112)*
Action Shopper, Marquette *Also called Ogden Newspapers Virginia LLC (G-11038)*
Action Tool & Machine Inc ... 810 229-6300
5976 Ford Ct Brighton (48116) *(G-1938)*
Action Wood 360, Clinton Township *Also called Action Wood Technologies Inc (G-3155)*
Action Wood Technologies Inc ... 586 468-2300
44500 Reynolds Dr Clinton Township (48036) *(G-3155)*
Active and Passive Safety, Livonia *Also called ZF Active Safety & Elec US LLC (G-10481)*
Active Feed Company (PA) ... 989 453-2472
7564 Pigeon Rd Pigeon (48755) *(G-13034)*
Active Manufacturing Corp ... 616 842-0800
17127 Hickory St Spring Lake (49456) *(G-15801)*
Active Plastics Inc ... 616 813-5109
125 Mill Ave Se Caledonia (49316) *(G-2367)*
Active Solutions Group Inc ... 313 278-4522
4 Parklane Blvd Ste 170 Dearborn (48126) *(G-3805)*
Active Tooling LLC ... 616 875-8111
6017 Chicago Dr Zeeland (49464) *(G-18988)*
Activerse LLC ... 313 463-9344
10577 Marne St Detroit (48224) *(G-3985)*
Actron Steel Inc ... 231 947-3981
2341 Molon Dr Traverse City (49684) *(G-16597)*
Actt Management LLC ... 616 803-8734
3577 28th St Se Ste G4 Grand Rapids (49512) *(G-6425)*
Actuator Services LLC ... 734 242-5456
1620 Rose St Monroe (48162) *(G-11520)*

ALPHABETIC

Actuator Specialties, Monroe *Also called Actuator Services LLC* ***(G-11520)***
Acubar Inc (PA)....269 927-3000
1055 N Shore Dr Benton Harbor (49022) ***(G-1526)***
Acumedia Manufacturers Inc....517 372-9200
620 Lesher Pl Lansing (48912) ***(G-9799)***
Acumen Technologies Inc....586 566-8600
51445 Celeste Shelby Township (48315) ***(G-15165)***
Acument Global Tech Inc (HQ)....586 254-3900
6125 18 Mile Rd Sterling Heights (48314) ***(G-15924)***
Acute Fixture & Tooling Inc....586 323-4132
13313 W Star Dr Shelby Township (48315) ***(G-15166)***
Acutex Inc....231 894-3200
2001 Peach St Whitehall (49461) ***(G-18488)***
Acutex Inc....231 894-3200
2001 Peach St Whitehall (49461) ***(G-18489)***
Acutex Division, Whitehall *Also called Acutex Inc* ***(G-18488)***
Acutus Gladwin Industries, Taylor *Also called SMS Group Inc* ***(G-16475)***
Ad Astra Roasters LLC....517 914-2487
106 N Broad St Hillsdale (49242) ***(G-7922)***
Ad-Tech Plastics Systems, Charlotte *Also called Cass Polymers* ***(G-2739)***
Ada Gage Inc....616 676-3338
9450 Grand River Dr Se Ada (49301) ***(G-4)***
Adac Automotive, Grand Rapids *Also called Adac Plastics Inc* ***(G-6428)***
Adac Automotive, Grand Rapids *Also called Adac Door Components Inc* ***(G-6427)***
Adac Automotive, Muskegon *Also called Adac Plastics Inc* ***(G-11762)***
Adac Automotive, Grand Rapids *Also called Adac Plastics Inc* ***(G-6429)***
Adac Automotive, Muskegon *Also called Adac Plastics Inc* ***(G-11764)***
Adac Automotive, Saranac *Also called Adac Plastics Inc* ***(G-15075)***
Adac Automotive Trim Inc (HQ)....616 957-0311
5690 Eagle Dr Se Grand Rapids (49512) ***(G-6426)***
Adac Door Components Inc....616 957-0311
5690 Eagle Dr Se Grand Rapids (49512) ***(G-6427)***
Adac Plastics Inc (PA)....616 957-0311
5690 Eagle Dr Se Grand Rapids (49512) ***(G-6428)***
Adac Plastics Inc....231 777-2645
2653 Olthoff St Muskegon (49444) ***(G-11762)***
Adac Plastics Inc....616 957-0311
2929 32nd St Se Grand Rapids (49512) ***(G-6429)***
Adac Plastics Inc....616 957-0520
2050 Port City Blvd Muskegon (49442) ***(G-11763)***
Adac Plastics Inc....616 957-0311
1801 E Keating Ave Muskegon (49442) ***(G-11764)***
Adac Plastics Inc....616 642-0109
6138 Riverside Dr Saranac (48881) ***(G-15075)***
Adadapted Inc....313 744-3383
330 E Liberty St Ann Arbor (48104) ***(G-349)***
Adair Printing Company (PA)....734 426-2822
7850 2nd St Dexter (48130) ***(G-4721)***
Adam, New Hudson *Also called Architectural Door & Mllwk Inc* ***(G-12043)***
Adam Electronics Incorporated....248 583-2000
32020 Edward Ave Madison Heights (48071) ***(G-10659)***
Adams Design & Print LLC....269 612-8613
18702 Oldfield Rd New Buffalo (49117) ***(G-12022)***
Adams Holsters....906 662-4212
W8941 Newberg Rd Channing (49815) ***(G-2705)***
Adams Manufacturing....313 383-7804
1586 Detroit Ave Lincoln Park (48146) ***(G-10042)***
Adams Outdoor Advg Ltd Partnr (PA)....770 333-0399
3801 Capitol City Blvd Lansing (48906) ***(G-9670)***
Adams Outdoor Advg Ltd Partnr....517 321-2121
3801 Capitol City Blvd Lansing (48906) ***(G-9671)***
Adams Street Publishing....734 668-4044
3003 Washtenaw Ave Ste 3 Ann Arbor (48104) ***(G-350)***
Adana Voltaics LLC....734 622-0193
5776 Cedar Ridge Dr Ann Arbor (48103) ***(G-351)***
Adaptable Tool Supply LLC....248 439-0866
309 N Chocolay Ave Clawson (48017) ***(G-3084)***
Adaptive Metal Works LLC....419 386-9336
8611 E Us Highway 223 Blissfield (49228) ***(G-1760)***
Adaptive Mfg Solutions LLC....810 743-1600
G4206 S Saginaw St Burton (48529) ***(G-2224)***
ADC, Adrian *Also called Anderson Development Company* ***(G-53)***
Adcaa LLC....734 623-4236
3110 W Liberty Rd Ste B Ann Arbor (48103) ***(G-352)***
Adco Circuits Inc (PA)....248 853-6620
2868 Bond St Rochester Hills (48309) ***(G-13941)***
Adco Products LLC....517 841-7238
4401 Page Ave Michigan Center (49254) ***(G-11290)***
Adco Products, Inc., Michigan Center *Also called Adco Products LLC* ***(G-11290)***
Adco Specialties Inc....616 452-6882
4331 E Beltline Ave Ne Grand Rapids (49525) ***(G-6430)***
Adcole Corporation....508 485-9100
40 Engelwood Dr Ste G Orion (48359) ***(G-12722)***
Adcr, Fenton *Also called Zander Colloids Lc* ***(G-5514)***
Add-Savvy Digital Signage....844 233-7288
2723 S State St Ann Arbor (48104) ***(G-353)***
Addison Awning Co, Jackson *Also called Holiday Distributing Co* ***(G-8904)***
Adduxi....248 564-2000
2791 Research Dr Rochester Hills (48309) ***(G-13942)***
Ade Inc....248 625-7200
8949 Dixie Hwy Clarkston (48348) ***(G-3012)***
Ademco Inc....586 759-1455
24749 Forterra Dr Warren (48089) ***(G-17691)***
Ademco Inc....248 926-5510
47247 Cartier Dr Wixom (48393) ***(G-18595)***
Adept Broaching Co....734 427-9221
6253 Barbara Ln Plymouth (48170) ***(G-13113)***
Adept Defense LLC....231 758-2792
1307 Howard St Petoskey (49770) ***(G-12987)***
Adept Plastic Finishing, Wixom *Also called Tribar Manufacturing LLC* ***(G-18778)***
Adept Plastic Finishing Inc....248 863-5930
30540 Beck Rd Wixom (48393) ***(G-18596)***
Adept Plastic Finishing Inc....248 374-5870
48668 Alpha Dr Wixom (48393) ***(G-18597)***
Adgravers Inc....313 259-3780
269 Walker St Detroit (48207) ***(G-3986)***
Adhesive Systems Inc....313 865-4448
15477 Woodrow Wilson St Detroit (48238) ***(G-3987)***
ADI Global Distribution, Warren *Also called Ademco Inc* ***(G-17691)***
ADI Global Distribution, Wixom *Also called Ademco Inc* ***(G-18595)***
Adient....586 753-3072
7500 Tank Ave Warren (48092) ***(G-17692)***
Adient Inc (HQ)....734 254-5000
49200 Halyard Dr Plymouth (48170) ***(G-13114)***
Adient Madison Heights, Madison Heights *Also called Adient US LLC* ***(G-10660)***
Adient US Entps Ltd Partnr....734 254-5000
49200 Halyard Dr Plymouth (48170) ***(G-13115)***
Adient US LLC (HQ)....734 254-5000
49200 Halyard Dr Plymouth (48170) ***(G-13116)***
Adient US LLC....734 254-5000
47700 Halyard Dr Plymouth (48170) ***(G-13117)***
Adient US LLC....734 414-9215
45000 Helm St Plymouth (48170) ***(G-13118)***
Adient US LLC....510 771-2300
1451 E Lincoln Ave Madison Heights (48071) ***(G-10660)***
Adient US LLC....269 968-3000
76 Armstrong Rd Battle Creek (49037) ***(G-1177)***
Adjustable Locking Tech LLC....248 443-9664
6632 Telegraph Rd Ste 298 Bloomfield Hills (48301) ***(G-1792)***
Adler Pelzer Group, Troy *Also called HP Pelzer Auto Systems Inc* ***(G-17155)***
Adler Pelzer Group, Port Huron *Also called HP Pelzer Auto Systems Inc* ***(G-13483)***
Adlib Grafix & Apparel....269 964-2810
10 Van Armon Ave Battle Creek (49017) ***(G-1178)***
ADM, Battle Creek *Also called Archer-Daniels-Midland Company* ***(G-1185)***
ADM, Grand Ledge *Also called Archer-Daniels-Midland Company* ***(G-6385)***
ADM, Portland *Also called Archer-Daniels-Midland Company* ***(G-13637)***
ADM Graphics & Print Prod LLC....586 598-1821
48505 Carmine Ct Chesterfield (48051) ***(G-2835)***
Admat Manufacturing Inc....269 641-7453
16744 Us Highway 12 Union (49130) ***(G-17486)***
Admin Industries LLC....989 685-3438
3049 Beechwood Rd Rose City (48654) ***(G-14358)***
Admiral....989 684-8314
212 S Euclid Ave Bay City (48706) ***(G-1317)***
Admiral....989 356-6419
2520 Us Highway 23 S Alpena (49707) ***(G-274)***
Admiral....989 835-9160
1801 S Saginaw Rd Midland (48640) ***(G-11317)***
Admiral Box Company, Warren *Also called AS Property Management Inc* ***(G-17716)***
Admiral Broach Company Inc....586 468-8411
21391 Carlo Dr Clinton Township (48038) ***(G-3156)***
Admore Inc....586 949-8200
24707 Wood Ct Macomb (48042) ***(G-10571)***
Adnic Products Co....810 789-0321
6261 N Saginaw St Mount Morris (48458) ***(G-11666)***
Adrian Lva Biofuel LLC....517 920-4863
1571 W Beecher Rd Adrian (49221) ***(G-48)***
Adrian Precision Machining LLC....517 263-4564
605 Industrial Dr Adrian (49221) ***(G-49)***
Adrian Sand & Stone, Clinton *Also called Stansley Mineral Resources Inc* ***(G-3142)***
Adrian Steel Company (PA)....517 265-6194
906 James St Adrian (49221) ***(G-50)***
Adrian Team LLC....517 264-6148
795 Richlyn Dr Adrian (49221) ***(G-51)***
Adrian Tool Corporation....517 263-6530
1441 Enterprise Ave Adrian (49221) ***(G-52)***
Adrian's T-Shirt Printery, Holland *Also called Adrians Screen Print* ***(G-7957)***
Adrians Screen Print....734 994-1367
3735 Hollywood Dr Holland (49424) ***(G-7957)***
ADS LLC....248 740-9593
1100 Owendale Dr Ste K Troy (48083) ***(G-16906)***
ADS Plus Printing LLC....810 659-7190
767 E Main St Flushing (48433) ***(G-5800)***
ADS Us Inc....989 871-4550
4705 Industrial Dr Millington (48746) ***(G-11498)***

ALPHABETIC SECTION
Advantage Design & Tool Inc

Adtco, Madison Heights *Also called Abrasive Diamond Tool Company* ***(G-10657)***

Adtek Graphics Inc ... 517 663-2460
228 1/2 S Main St Eaton Rapids (48827) ***(G-4950)***

Advance, Rogers City *Also called Presque Isle Newspapers Inc* ***(G-14217)***

Advance BCI Inc (PA) ... 616 669-1366
3102 Walker Ridge Dr Nw Grand Rapids (49544) ***(G-6431)***

Advance Central Services Mich, Walker *Also called Herald Publishing Company LLC* ***(G-17641)***

Advance Cnc Machine Inc ... 269 751-7005
3051 Lincoln Rd Hamilton (49419) ***(G-7594)***

Advance Concrete Products Co ... 248 887-4173
975 N Milford Rd Highland (48357) ***(G-7880)***

Advance Engineering Co Mich, Canton *Also called Advance Engineering Company* ***(G-2429)***

Advance Engineering Company (PA) ... 313 537-3500
7505 Baron Dr Canton (48187) ***(G-2429)***

Advance Engineering Company ... 989 435-3641
3982 Terry Dianne St Beaverton (48612) ***(G-1423)***

Advance Graphic Systems Inc ... 248 656-8000
1806 Rochester Indl Dr Rochester Hills (48309) ***(G-13943)***

Advance Machine Corp ... 989 362-9192
612 9th Ave Tawas City (48763) ***(G-16364)***

Advance Newspapers, Grand Rapids *Also called Advance BCI Inc* ***(G-6431)***

Advance Packaging Acquisition (HQ) ... 616 949-6610
4450 36th St Se Grand Rapids (49512) ***(G-6432)***

Advance Packaging Corporation (PA) ... 616 949-6610
4459 40th St Se Grand Rapids (49512) ***(G-6433)***

Advance Pet Solutions LLC ... 248 334-6150
5720 Pt Of The Woods Dr West Bloomfield (48324) ***(G-18261)***

Advance Precision Grinding Co ... 586 773-1330
29739 Groesbeck Hwy Roseville (48066) ***(G-14369)***

Advance Print & Graphics Inc ... 734 663-6816
4553 Concourse Dr Ann Arbor (48108) ***(G-354)***

Advance Products Corporation ... 269 849-1000
2527 N M 63 Benton Harbor (49022) ***(G-1527)***

Advance Publishing & Printing, Blissfield *Also called River Raisin Publications* ***(G-1775)***

Advance Specialties, Ann Arbor *Also called Advance Print & Graphics Inc* ***(G-354)***

Advance Tech Solutions LLC ... 989 928-1806
1348 Delta Dr Saginaw (48638) ***(G-14601)***

Advance Tool Co ... 231 587-5286
407 Rose St Mancelona (49659) ***(G-10865)***

Advance Turning and Mfg Inc (PA) ... 517 783-2713
4005 Morrill Rd Jackson (49201) ***(G-8802)***

Advance Turning and Mfg Inc ... 517 750-3580
4901 James Mcdevitt St Jackson (49201) ***(G-8803)***

Advance Vehicle Assembly Inc ... 989 823-3800
555 E Huron Ave Vassar (48768) ***(G-17576)***

Advanced Air Technologies Inc ... 989 743-5544
300 Sleeseman Dr Corunna (48817) ***(G-3704)***

Advanced Assembly Products Inc (PA) ... 248 543-2427
1300 E 9 Mile Rd Hazel Park (48030) ***(G-7817)***

Advanced Auto Trends Inc (PA) ... 248 628-6111
2230 Metamora Rd Oxford (48371) ***(G-12871)***

Advanced Auto Trends Inc ... 810 672-9203
3279 Washington St Snover (48472) ***(G-15389)***

Advanced Auto Trends Inc ... 248 628-4850
3485 Metamora Rd Oxford (48371) ***(G-12872)***

Advanced Automation Group LLC ... 248 299-8100
580 Ajax Dr Madison Heights (48071) ***(G-10661)***

Advanced Automotive Group LLC ... 586 206-2478
8784 Folkert Rd Clay (48001) ***(G-3113)***

Advanced Avionics Inc ... 734 259-5300
6118 Gotfredson Rd Plymouth (48170) ***(G-13119)***

Advanced Battery Concepts LLC ... 989 424-6645
8 Consumers Energy Pkwy Clare (48617) ***(G-2972)***

Advanced Blnding Solutions LLC ... 920 664-1469
W5649 County Road 342 Wallace (49893) ***(G-17659)***

Advanced Blnding Solutions LLC ... 906 914-4180
949 1st St Menominee (49858) ***(G-11224)***

Advanced Boring and Tool Co ... 586 598-9300
5750 New King Dr Ste 200 Troy (48098) ***(G-16907)***

Advanced Cnc Machining LLC ... 616 226-6706
3086 Dixie Ave Sw Ste E Grandville (49418) ***(G-7363)***

Advanced Composite Tech Inc ... 248 709-9097
417 E 2nd St Rochester (48307) ***(G-13889)***

Advanced Conveyor Systems, Allegan *Also called B & G Custom Works Inc* ***(G-149)***

Advanced Cutting Tool Systems, Taylor *Also called Colonial Tool Sales & Svc LLC* ***(G-16394)***

Advanced Decorative Systems, Millington *Also called ADS Us Inc* ***(G-11498)***

Advanced Def Vhcl Systems Corp ... 248 391-3200
6716 Ridgeview Dr Clarkston (48346) ***(G-3013)***

Advanced Drainage Systems Inc ... 989 761-7610
4800 Marlette Rd Clifford (48727) ***(G-3130)***

Advanced Drainage Systems Inc ... 989 723-5208
770 S Chestnut St Owosso (48867) ***(G-12819)***

Advanced Eco Print ... 231 292-1688
5884 E Ford Lake Dr Fountain (49410) ***(G-5826)***

Advanced Elastomers Corp ... 734 458-4194
34481 Industrial Rd Livonia (48150) ***(G-10101)***

Advanced Energy Services LLC ... 231 369-2602
5894 Puffer Rd Sw South Boardman (49680) ***(G-15395)***

Advanced Energy Svc, South Boardman *Also called Advanced Energy Services LLC* ***(G-15395)***

Advanced Farm Equipment LLC ... 989 268-5711
5773 N Crystal Rd Vestaburg (48891) ***(G-17593)***

Advanced Feedlines LLC ... 248 583-9400
103 Park Dr Troy (48083) ***(G-16908)***

Advanced Fibermolding Inc ... 231 768-5177
23095 14 Mile Rd Leroy (49655) ***(G-10004)***

Advanced Finishing Tech, Comstock Park *Also called Drag Finishing Tech LLC* ***(G-3603)***

Advanced Food Technologies Inc ... 616 574-4144
1140 Butterworth St Sw Grand Rapids (49504) ***(G-6434)***

Advanced Heat Treat Corp ... 734 243-0063
1625 Rose St Monroe (48162) ***(G-11521)***

Advanced Inc ... 231 938-2233
5474 Em 72 Acme (49610) ***(G-2)***

Advanced Industries Inc ... 734 433-1800
3955 S Fletcher Rd Chelsea (48118) ***(G-2802)***

Advanced Integ Tooling Solns ... 586 749-5525
29700 Commerce Blvd Chesterfield (48051) ***(G-2836)***

Advanced Integrated Mfg ... 586 439-0300
34673 Bennett Fraser (48026) ***(G-5888)***

Advanced Integration Tech LP ... 586 749-5525
29700 Commerce Blvd Chesterfield (48051) ***(G-2837)***

Advanced Integration Tech Mich, Chesterfield *Also called Advanced Integ Tooling Solns* ***(G-2836)***

Advanced Magnet Source Corp (PA) ... 734 398-7188
5033 Belleville Rd Canton (48188) ***(G-2430)***

Advanced Maintenance Tech ... 810 820-2554
3118 S Dye Rd Flint (48507) ***(G-5639)***

Advanced Manufacturing LLC ... 231 826-3859
311 E Prosper Rd Falmouth (49632) ***(G-5131)***

Advanced McRonutrient Pdts Inc ... 989 752-2138
2405 W Vassar Rd Reese (48757) ***(G-13805)***

Advanced Metal Fabricators ... 616 570-4847
12958 Christopher Dr Lowell (49331) ***(G-10494)***

Advanced Metal Recyclers ... 989 389-7708
2360 S Maple Valley Rd Saint Helen (48656) ***(G-14893)***

Advanced Mold Solutions ... 586 468-6883
43682 N Gratiot Ave Clinton Township (48036) ***(G-3157)***

Advanced Molding Solutions, Grand Haven *Also called Molding Solutions Inc* ***(G-6337)***

Advanced Photonix Inc (PA) ... 734 864-5647
2925 Boardwalk St Ann Arbor (48104) ***(G-355)***

Advanced Polymers Composites ... 248 766-1507
7111 Dixie Hwy 110 Clarkston (48346) ***(G-3014)***

Advanced Printing & Graphics, Muskegon *Also called Workman Printing Inc* ***(G-11951)***

Advanced Printwear Inc ... 248 585-4412
31171 Stephenson Hwy Madison Heights (48071) ***(G-10662)***

Advanced Pumps Intl LLC ... 734 230-5013
800 Ternes Dr Monroe (48162) ***(G-11522)***

Advanced Recovery Tech Corp ... 231 788-2911
16684 130th Ave Nunica (49448) ***(G-12575)***

Advanced Research Company ... 248 475-4770
4140 S Lapeer Rd Orion (48359) ***(G-12723)***

Advanced Rubber & Plastic (PA) ... 586 754-7398
3035 Otis Ave Warren (48091) ***(G-17693)***

Advanced Rubber Tech Inc ... 231 775-3112
10640 W Cadillac Rd Cadillac (49601) ***(G-2308)***

Advanced Sheet Metal ... 616 301-3828
2630 Prairie St Sw Wyoming (49519) ***(G-18848)***

Advanced Signs Incorporated ... 616 846-4667
401 2nd St Ferrysburg (49409) ***(G-5600)***

Advanced Special Tools Inc ... 269 962-9697
320 Clark Rd Battle Creek (49037) ***(G-1179)***

Advanced Stage Tooling LLC ... 810 444-9807
4317 River Rd East China (48054) ***(G-4855)***

Advanced Systems & Contrls Inc ... 586 992-9684
15773 Leone Dr Macomb (48042) ***(G-10572)***

Advanced Systems & Forms ... 734 422-7180
27690 Joy Rd Livonia (48150) ***(G-10102)***

Advanced Technologies Cons, Northville *Also called TS Enterprise Associates Inc* ***(G-12267)***

Advanced Tex Screen Printing ... 989 643-7288
4177 3 Mile Rd Bay City (48706) ***(G-1318)***

Advanced Tex Screenprinting, Bay City *Also called Advanced Tex Screen Printing* ***(G-1318)***

Advanced Tooling Systems Inc (HQ) ... 616 784-7513
1166 7 Mile Rd Nw Comstock Park (49321) ***(G-3586)***

Advanced Tubular Tech Inc ... 248 674-2059
1076 Blue Ridge Dr Clarkston (48348) ***(G-3015)***

Advanced Urethanes Inc ... 313 273-5705
12727 Westwood St Detroit (48223) ***(G-3988)***

Advanced Vhcl Assemblies LLC ... 248 299-7500
2917 Waterview Dr Rochester Hills (48309) ***(G-13944)***

Advanced-Cable LLC ... 586 491-3073
1179 Chicago Rd Troy (48083) ***(G-16909)***

Advancing Bus Solutions LLC ... 734 905-7455
235 Spencer Ln Ste B Ypsilanti (48198) ***(G-18923)***

Advantage Blnds Shds Shtters L ... 248 399-2154
815 Maplegrove Ave Royal Oak (48067) ***(G-14504)***

Advantage Design & Tool Inc ... 586 463-2800
44319 Macomb Indus Dr Clinton Township (48036) ***(G-3158)***

ALPHABETIC

Advantage Design and Tool 586 801-7413
35800 Big Hand Rd Richmond (48062) ***(G-13831)***
Advantage Housing Inc 269 792-6291
3555 12th St Wayland (49348) ***(G-18187)***
Advantage Industries Inc 616 669-2400
2196 Port Sheldon St Jenison (49428) ***(G-9042)***
Advantage Label & Packg Pdts, Grand Rapids *Also called Advantage Label and Packg Inc* ***(G-6435)***
Advantage Label and Packg Inc 616 656-1900
5575 Executive Pkwy Se Grand Rapids (49512) ***(G-6435)***
Advantage Laser Inc 734 367-9936
35684 Veronica St Livonia (48150) ***(G-10103)***
Advantage Millwork, Grand Rapids *Also called D & D Building Inc* ***(G-6626)***
Advantage Sign Grphic Slutions, Hudsonville *Also called Advantage Sign Supply Inc* ***(G-8564)***
Advantage Sign Supply Inc (PA) 877 237-4464
4182 Royal Ct Hudsonville (49426) ***(G-8564)***
Advantage Sintered Metals Inc 269 964-1212
5701 W Dickman Rd Ste A Battle Creek (49037) ***(G-1180)***
Advantage Truck ACC Inc 800 773-3110
5400 S State Rd Ann Arbor (48108) ***(G-356)***
Adventures Moni and Koko LLC 269 589-2154
188 Roosevelt Ave W Battle Creek (49037) ***(G-1181)***
Advertiser Publishing Co Inc 616 642-9411
13 N Bridge St Saranac (48881) ***(G-15076)***
Advertiser, The, Warren *Also called C & G Publishing Inc* ***(G-17745)***
Advertising Accents Inc 313 937-3890
18845 Denby Redford (48240) ***(G-13711)***
Advertsing Ntwrk Solutions Inc (PA) 248 475-7881
530 Pine St Ste F Rochester (48307) ***(G-13890)***
Advisor Inc 906 341-2424
311 Oak St Manistique (49854) ***(G-10916)***
Advisor The, Shelby Township *Also called Macomb North Clinton Advisor* ***(G-15266)***
Advs, Clarkston *Also called Advanced Def Vhcl Systems Corp* ***(G-3013)***
ADW Industries Inc 989 466-4742
130 Woodworth Ave Alma (48801) ***(G-233)***
Ae Group LLC 734 942-0615
28275 Northline Rd Romulus (48174) ***(G-14246)***
AEC Systems Usa Inc 616 257-9502
2663 44th St Sw Wyoming (49519) ***(G-18849)***
Aees Inc (HQ) 248 489-4700
36555 Corp Dr Ste 300 Farmington Hills (48331) ***(G-5159)***
Aees Power Systems Ltd Partnr 269 668-4429
36555 Corp Dr Ste 300 Farmington Hills (48331) ***(G-5160)***
Aees Power Systems Ltd Partnr (HQ) 248 489-4900
999 Republic Dr Allen Park (48101) ***(G-187)***
Aegis Welding Supply 248 475-9860
1080 Centre Rd Auburn Hills (48326) ***(G-774)***
AEL/Span LLC (PA) 734 957-1600
41775 Ecorse Rd Ste 100 Van Buren Twp (48111) ***(G-17507)***
Aero Inc 248 669-4085
1010 W West Maple Rd Walled Lake (48390) ***(G-17662)***
Aero Auto Stud Specialists Inc 248 437-2171
10769 Plaza Dr Whitmore Lake (48189) ***(G-18517)***
Aero Box Company 586 415-0000
20101 Cornillie Dr Roseville (48066) ***(G-14370)***
Aero Embedded Technologies Inc 586 251-2980
6580 Cotter Ave Sterling Heights (48314) ***(G-15925)***
Aero Filter Inc 248 837-4100
1604 E Avis Dr Madison Heights (48071) ***(G-10663)***
Aero Foil International Inc 231 773-0200
1920 Port City Blvd Muskegon (49442) ***(G-11765)***
Aero Grinding Inc (PA) 586 774-6450
28300 Groesbeck Hwy Roseville (48066) ***(G-14371)***
Aero Grinding Inc 586 774-6450
28240 Groesbeck Hwy Roseville (48066) ***(G-14372)***
Aero Inspection & Tool LLC 517 525-7373
856 Ewers Rd Leslie (49251) ***(G-10013)***
Aero Systems 253 269-3000
13475 Wayne Rd Livonia (48150) ***(G-10104)***
Aero Test, Romulus *Also called Approved Aircraft Accessories* ***(G-14250)***
Aero Train Corp 810 230-8096
5083 Miller Rd Flint (48507) ***(G-5640)***
Aerobee Electric Inc 248 549-2044
3030 Hilton Rd Ferndale (48220) ***(G-5518)***
Aerofab Company Inc 248 542-0051
2335 Goodrich St Ferndale (48220) ***(G-5519)***
Aerospace America Inc 989 684-2121
900 Harry S Truman Pkwy Bay City (48706) ***(G-1319)***
Aerospace Group, Jackson *Also called Eaton Aeroquip LLC* ***(G-8873)***
Aerospoke Incorporated 248 685-9009
5034 Walnut Hills Dr Brighton (48116) ***(G-1939)***
Aerostar Manufacturing, Romulus *Also called Ae Group LLC* ***(G-14246)***
Aerostar Manufacturing 734 947-2558
24340 Northline Rd Taylor (48180) ***(G-16374)***
Aerovision Aircraft Svcs LLC 231 799-9000
620 E Ellis Rd Norton Shores (49441) ***(G-12274)***
Aerovision International LLC 231 799-9000
620 E Ellis Rd Norton Shores (49441) ***(G-12275)***
Aertech Machining & Mfg Inc 517 782-4644
2020 Micor Dr Jackson (49203) ***(G-8804)***
Aerus Electrolux, Pontiac *Also called Electrolux Professional Inc* ***(G-13366)***
Aesthtic Affcts Stffing Agcy L 734 436-1248
50010 Cherry Hill Rd Canton (48187) ***(G-2431)***
Aetna Bearing Company, Livonia *Also called ABC Acquisition Company LLC* ***(G-10097)***
Aetna Engineering, Grand Rapids *Also called Fireboy-Xintex Inc* ***(G-6706)***
Afb Corporate Operations LLC 248 669-1188
47585 Galleon Dr Plymouth (48170) ***(G-13120)***
Afc-Holcroft LLC (HQ) 248 624-8191
49630 Pontiac Trl Wixom (48393) ***(G-18598)***
Afco Manufacturing Corp 248 634-4415
428 Cogshall St Holly (48442) ***(G-8260)***
Affiliated Troy Dermatologist 248 267-5020
4600 Investment Dr Troy (48098) ***(G-16910)***
Affinia Group Inc 734 827-5400
1101 Technology Dr Ann Arbor (48108) ***(G-357)***
Affinity Custom Molding Inc 269 496-8423
21198 M 60 Mendon (49072) ***(G-11215)***
Affinity Electronics Inc 586 477-4920
33710 Doreka Fraser (48026) ***(G-5889)***
Affinity Solutions, Zeeland *Also called Extol Inc* ***(G-19019)***
Affordable Heat Llc 517 673-0404
2068 Marsh Dr Manitou Beach (49253) ***(G-10926)***
Affordable OEM Autolighting 989 400-6106
3068 W Klees Rd Stanton (48888) ***(G-15898)***
Affordable Pool and Spa Inc 810 422-5058
3234 Associates Dr Burton (48529) ***(G-2225)***
Affordable Prints 231 679-2606
125 N Main St Evart (49631) ***(G-5119)***
Afgco Sand & Gravel Co Inc 810 798-3293
5171 Sandhill Rd Almont (48003) ***(G-255)***
Afi, Muskegon *Also called Aero Foil International Inc* ***(G-11765)***
Afi Enterprises Inc 734 475-9111
11770 Dexter Chelsea Rd Chelsea (48118) ***(G-2803)***
Afj Woodhaven LLC 248 593-6200
4036 Telegraph Rd Ste 201 Bloomfield Hills (48302) ***(G-1793)***
AFP Consulting 616 534-9858
2759 Golfbury Dr Sw Wyoming (49519) ***(G-18850)***
African Amercn Parent Pubg Inc 313 312-1611
6200 2nd Ave Detroit (48202) ***(G-3989)***
Aftech, Rockford *Also called Derby Fabg Solutions LLC* ***(G-14164)***
Aftech Inc 616 866-1650
3056 Walker Ridge Dr Nw A Grand Rapids (49544) ***(G-6436)***
Aftermarket Industries LLC 810 229-3200
315 E Main St Brighton (48116) ***(G-1940)***
Aftershock Motorsports 586 273-1333
5831 Church Rd Casco (48064) ***(G-2597)***
Afton Chemical Corporation 248 350-0640
2000 Town Ctr Ste 1160 Southfield (48075) ***(G-15471)***
Afx Industries LLC (HQ) 810 966-4650
1411 3rd St Ste G Port Huron (48060) ***(G-13431)***
Afx Industries LLC 810 966-4650
1411 3rd St Ste G Port Huron (48060) ***(G-13432)***
Afx Industries LLC 517 768-8993
4111 County Farm Rd Jackson (49201) ***(G-8805)***
Afx/Trim, Port Huron *Also called Afx Industries LLC* ***(G-13431)***
AG Davis, Sterling Heights *Also called AG Davis Gage & Engrg Co* ***(G-15926)***
AG Davis Gage & Engrg Co (PA) 586 977-9000
6533 Sims Dr Sterling Heights (48313) ***(G-15926)***
AG Harvesters LLC 989 876-7161
533 N Court St Au Gres (48703) ***(G-754)***
AG Industries 248 564-2758
1720 Star Batt Dr Rochester Hills (48309) ***(G-13945)***
AG Manufacturing Inc 989 479-9590
319 Industrial Dr Harbor Beach (48441) ***(G-7628)***
AG Precision Gage Inc 248 374-0063
28317 Beck Rd Ste E6 Wixom (48393) ***(G-18599)***
Ag-Pro, Grand Rapids *Also called Allsales Enterprises Inc* ***(G-6451)***
AGA Marvel 616 754-5601
1260 E Van Deinse St Greenville (48838) ***(G-7474)***
Agape Plastics Inc 616 735-4091
11474 1st Ave Nw Grand Rapids (49534) ***(G-6437)***
Agapy Publishing, Saint Joseph *Also called Wendy Williamson* ***(G-14975)***
AGC Grand Haven LLC 616 842-1820
16750 Comstock St Grand Haven (49417) ***(G-6271)***
Agelessmage Fcial Asthtics LLC 269 998-5547
28499 Orchard Lake Rd Farmington Hills (48334) ***(G-5161)***
Agenda 2020 Inc 616 581-6271
555 Cascade West Pkwy Se Grand Rapids (49546) ***(G-6438)***
Agent 18, Troy *Also called Sargam International Inc* ***(G-17344)***
Aget Manufacturing Company, Adrian *Also called Madison Street Holdings LLC* ***(G-81)***
Aget Manufacturing Company, Adrian *Also called Depierre Industries Inc* ***(G-59)***
Aggie Welding 989 824-1316
4518 W Vernon Rd Weidman (48893) ***(G-18249)***
Aggregate, Cedarville *Also called O-N Minerals Michigan Company* ***(G-2672)***
Aggregate and Developing LLC 269 217-5492
1108 Lincoln Rd Allegan (49010) ***(G-144)***

Aggregate Industries - Mwr Inc....734 475-2531
4950 Loveland Rd Grass Lake (49240) *(G-7434)*
Aggressive Mfg Innovations, Lewiston *Also called AMI Industries Inc (G-10017)*
Aggressive Tool & Die Inc....616 837-1983
728 Main St Coopersville (49404) *(G-3679)*
Aggressive Tooling Inc....616 754-1404
608 Industrial Park Dr Greenville (48838) *(G-7475)*
Aghog Inc....313 277-2037
30629 Puritan St Livonia (48154) *(G-10105)*
Agio Imaging, Kalamazoo *Also called Domer Industries LLC (G-9173)*
AGM Automotive LLC (HQ)....248 776-0600
27755 Stansbury Blvd # 300 Farmington Hills (48334) *(G-5162)*
AGM Automotive Mexico LLC (HQ)....248 925-4152
27755 Stansbury Blvd # 300 Farmington Hills (48334) *(G-5163)*
Agnew Grphics Signs Promotions....989 723-4621
1905 W M 21 A Owosso (48867) *(G-12820)*
Agri Blowers Express....616 662-9999
6665 Marcan Ave Ste 1 Jenison (49428) *(G-9043)*
Agribusiness, Grand Rapids *Also called Sulugu Corporation USA Inc (G-7232)*
Agriculture Liqiud Fertilizers, Saint Johns *Also called Cog Marketers Ltd (G-14897)*
Agrigenetics Inc....317 337-3000
2030 Dow Ctr Midland (48674) *(G-11318)*
Agritek Industries Inc....616 786-9200
4211 Hallacy Dr Holland (49424) *(G-7958)*
Agritemp, Livonia *Also called Hamilton Engineering Inc (G-10234)*
Agro-Clture Liquid Fertilizers, Ashley *Also called Cog Marketers Ltd (G-742)*
Agropur Inc....616 538-3822
5252 Clay Ave Sw Grand Rapids (49548) *(G-6439)*
AGS Automotive Systems, Warren *Also called A G Simpson (usa) Inc (G-17682)*
Agscap Inc....231 733-2101
2651 Hoyt St Muskegon (49444) *(G-11766)*
Ahd LLC....586 922-6511
50649 Central Indus Dr Shelby Township (48315) *(G-15167)*
Ahlusion LLC....888 277-0001
5118 Morrish Rd Swartz Creek (48473) *(G-16348)*
Ahs LLC (HQ)....888 355-3050
11261 James St Holland (49424) *(G-7959)*
Ai Machine Shop....615 855-1217
325 E Grand River Ave East Lansing (48823) *(G-4885)*
Ai Warren, Warren *Also called Android Industries-Sterling (G-17705)*
Ai-Delta Township, Lansing *Also called Android Indstrs-Dlta Twnship L (G-9755)*
Ai-Genesee LLC....810 720-4848
4400 Matthew Flint (48507) *(G-5641)*
Aic Acquisition Company LLC....810 227-5510
51100 Grand River Ave Wixom (48393) *(G-18600)*
Aic Eqpment Cntrls Plst-Co Eqp, Wixom *Also called Aic Acquisition Company LLC (G-18600)*
Aichelin Heat Treatment Syst....734 459-9850
49630 Pontiac Trl Wixom (48393) *(G-18601)*
Aim, Auburn Hills *Also called Applied & Integrated Mfg Inc (G-793)*
Aim Mail Centers, Fruitport *Also called Automated Indus Motion Inc (G-6059)*
Aim Plastics Inc....586 954-2553
22264 Starks Dr Clinton Township (48036) *(G-3159)*
Aim-Rite Hauling, Lake Orion *Also called Aimrite LLC (G-9584)*
Aimrite LLC....248 693-8925
941 Hinford Ave Lake Orion (48362) *(G-9584)*
AIN Plastics....248 356-4000
23235 Telegraph Rd Southfield (48033) *(G-15472)*
Ainsworth Electric Inc....810 984-5768
3200 Dove Rd Ste A Port Huron (48060) *(G-13433)*
Aip Aerospace, Macomb *Also called Ascent Integrated Platforms (G-10580)*
Aip Group Inc....248 828-4400
2041 E Square Lake Rd # 100 Troy (48085) *(G-16911)*
Air Conditioning Products Co (PA)....734 326-0050
30350 Ecorse Rd Romulus (48174) *(G-14247)*
Air Filter & Equipment Inc....734 261-1860
37007 Industrial Rd Livonia (48150) *(G-10106)*
Air Filter Sales & Service, Madison Heights *Also called Aero Filter Inc (G-10663)*
Air International (us) Inc (HQ)....248 391-7970
750 Standard Pkwy Auburn Hills (48326) *(G-775)*
Air Intrntonal Thermal Systems, Auburn Hills *Also called Air International (us) Inc (G-775)*
Air Lift Company (PA)....517 322-2144
2727 Snow Rd Lansing (48917) *(G-9751)*
Air Lift Performance, Lansing *Also called Air Lift Company (G-9751)*
Air Master Systems Corp....231 798-1111
6480 Norton Center Dr Norton Shores (49441) *(G-12276)*
Air Products and Controls, Auburn Hills *Also called Apollo America Inc (G-791)*
Air Solution Company....800 819-2869
23857 Industrial Park Dr Farmington Hills (48335) *(G-5164)*
Air Source, Stevensville *Also called Dee-Blast Corporation (G-16246)*
Air Supply Inc....586 773-6600
21300 Groesbeck Hwy Warren (48089) *(G-17694)*
Air Tight Solutions LLC....248 629-0461
18677 Robson St Detroit (48235) *(G-3990)*
Air Way Automation Inc....989 348-1802
2268 Industrial Dr Grayling (49738) *(G-7455)*
Air-Hydraulics Inc....517 787-9444
545 Hupp Ave Jackson (49203) *(G-8806)*
Air-Matic Products Company Inc (PA)....248 356-4200
22218 Telegraph Rd Southfield (48033) *(G-15473)*
Airboss Flexible Products Co....248 852-5500
2600 Auburn Ct Auburn Hills (48326) *(G-776)*
Aircraft Precision Pdts Inc....989 875-4186
185 Industrial Pkwy Ithaca (48847) *(G-8785)*
Aircraft Tool Supply, Oscoda *Also called A W B Industries Inc (G-12753)*
Airflow Sciences Equipment LLC....734 525-0300
12190 Hubbard St Livonia (48150) *(G-10107)*
Airgas Usa LLC....248 545-9353
1200 Farrow St Ferndale (48220) *(G-5520)*
Airhug LLC....734 262-0431
47960 Red Run Dr Canton (48187) *(G-2432)*
Airlite Synthetics Mfg Inc....248 335-8131
342 Irwin Ave Pontiac (48341) *(G-13345)*
Airman Inc....248 960-1354
6150 Whitmore Lake Rd Brighton (48116) *(G-1941)*
Airman Inc....248 926-1409
46968 Liberty Dr Wixom (48393) *(G-18602)*
Airman Products LLC....248 960-1354
6150 Whitmore Lake Rd Brighton (48116) *(G-1942)*
Airmetal Corporation....517 784-6000
1309 Bagley Ave Jackson (49203) *(G-8807)*
Airpark Plastics LLC....989 846-1029
1415 W Cedar St Standish (48658) *(G-15886)*
Airplane Factory....989 561-5381
6400 W Lake Shore Dr Remus (49340) *(G-13812)*
Airpower America, Scotts *Also called Kristus Inc (G-15132)*
Airserve LLC....586 427-5349
26770 Liberal Center Line (48015) *(G-2677)*
Airtec Corporation....313 892-7800
17565 Wlter P Chrysler Fw Detroit (48203) *(G-3991)*
Airtificial Intelligent Robots....989 799-6669
3175 Christy Way S Ste 5 Saginaw (48603) *(G-14602)*
Airway Welding Inc....517 789-6125
2415 E High St Jackson (49203) *(G-8808)*
Airwest Engineering, Grand Rapids *Also called Lacks Industries Inc (G-6920)*
Aisin Holdings America Inc....734 453-5551
15300 Centennial Dr Northville (48168) *(G-12195)*
Aisin Technical Ctr Amer Inc....734 453-5551
15300 Centennial Dr Northville (48168) *(G-12196)*
Ait Tooling, Chesterfield *Also called Advanced Integration Tech LP (G-2837)*
Aj Aircraft....734 244-4015
2410 N Monroe St Monroe (48162) *(G-11523)*
Aj Hometown LLC....313 415-0843
14700 E 9 Mile Rd Eastpointe (48021) *(G-4927)*
Aj Logging....989 725-9610
8203 N M 52 Henderson (48841) *(G-7859)*
Aj Pallets....616 875-8900
9471 Henry Ct Zeeland (49464) *(G-18989)*
Ajax Materials Corporation (HQ)....248 244-3300
1957 Crooks Rd A Troy (48084) *(G-16912)*
Ajax Metal Processing Inc (PA)....313 267-2100
4651 Bellevue St Detroit (48207) *(G-3992)*
Ajax Metal Processing Inc....586 497-7000
22105 Hoover Rd Warren (48089) *(G-17695)*
Ajax Paving Industries Inc (HQ)....248 244-3300
1957 Crooks Rd A Troy (48084) *(G-16913)*
Ajax Spring and Mfg Co....248 588-5700
700 Ajax Dr Madison Heights (48071) *(G-10664)*
Ajax Trailers Inc (PA)....586 757-7676
2089 E 10 Mile Rd Warren (48091) *(G-17696)*
Ajaxx 63, Grosse Pointe Park *Also called Ajaxx Design Inc (G-7543)*
Ajaxx Design Inc....206 522-4545
869 Whittier Rd Grosse Pointe Park (48230) *(G-7543)*
Ajf Inc....734 753-4410
37015 Pennsylvania Rd New Boston (48164) *(G-11998)*
Ajm Manufacturing Sales Inc....269 447-2087
8731 Mountain Pine Ln Kalamazoo (49009) *(G-9108)*
AJM Packaging Corporation (PA)....248 901-0040
E-4111 Andover Rd Bloomfield Hills (48302) *(G-1794)*
AJM Packaging Corporation....313 842-7530
6910 Dix St Detroit (48209) *(G-3993)*
AJM Packaging Corporation....313 291-6500
21130 Trolley Indus Dr Taylor (48180) *(G-16375)*
AJS Manufacturing LLC....616 916-6521
1940 Turner Ave Nw Ste D Grand Rapids (49504) *(G-6440)*
AJW Industries Inc....313 595-5554
43590 Harris Rd Belleville (48111) *(G-1479)*
AK Rewards LLC....734 272-7078
2723 S State St Ste 150 Ann Arbor (48104) *(G-358)*
Aka Sports....734 260-1023
34932 W Michigan Ave Wayne (48184) *(G-18211)*
Akamai Technologies Inc....734 424-1142
9394 Anne St Pinckney (48169) *(G-13043)*
Akasol Inc....248 259-7843
1400 E 10 Mile Rd Ste 150 Hazel Park (48030) *(G-7818)*
Akebono Brake Corporation (HQ)....248 489-7400
34385 W 12 Mile Rd Farmington Hills (48331) *(G-5165)*

Akers Wood Products Inc (PA)......269 962-3802
1124 River Rd W Battle Creek (49037) ***(G-1182)***
Akervall Technologies Inc......800 444-0570
1512 Woodland Dr Saline (48176) ***(G-14999)***
Akilahs Beauty Salon LLC......602 607-8503
509 Diamond Ave Se Grand Rapids (49506) ***(G-6441)***
Akki Products, Saline *Also called Mikan Corporation* ***(G-15027)***
Akorn Inc......800 579-8327
2929 Plymouth Rd Ann Arbor (48105) ***(G-359)***
Akorn Consumer Health, Ann Arbor *Also called Akorn Inc* ***(G-359)***
Akston Hughes Intl LLC......989 448-2322
1865 Orourke Blvd Ste A Gaylord (49735) ***(G-6116)***
Aktis Engrg Solutions Inc......313 450-2420
17340 W 12 Mile Rd Ste 20 Southfield (48076) ***(G-15474)***
Aktv8 LLC......517 775-1270
50660 Century Ct Wixom (48393) ***(G-18603)***
Akwel Cadillac Usa Inc (HQ)......231 775-6571
603 7th St Cadillac (49601) ***(G-2309)***
Akwel Cadillac Usa Inc......248 476-8072
39750 Grand River Ave Novi (48375) ***(G-12361)***
Akwel Cadillac Usa Inc......248 848-9599
39205 Country Club Dr C1 Farmington Hills (48331) ***(G-5166)***
Akwel Mexico Usa Inc......231 775-6571
603 7th St Cadillac (49601) ***(G-2310)***
Akwel Usa Inc (HQ)......231 775-6571
603 7th St Cadillac (49601) ***(G-2311)***
Akzo Nobel Coatings Inc......248 451-6231
120 Franklin Rd Pontiac (48341) ***(G-13346)***
Akzo Nobel Coatings Inc......248 637-0400
1845 Maxwell Dr Ste 100 Troy (48084) ***(G-16914)***
Akzo Nobel Coatings Inc......248 451-6231
27 Brush St Troy (48084) ***(G-16915)***
Akzo Nobel Coatings Inc......248 528-0715
2373 John R Rd Ste A Troy (48083) ***(G-16916)***
Akzo Nobel Coatings Inc......248 637-0400
117 Brush St Pontiac (48341) ***(G-13347)***
Akzonobel Sign Finishes......770 317-6361
1845 Maxwell Dr Troy (48084) ***(G-16917)***
Al Beck......906 249-1645
105 Poplar Trl Marquette (49855) ***(G-11003)***
Al Bo Co......248 240-9155
4115 Franklin Rd Bloomfield Hills (48302) ***(G-1795)***
Al Corp......734 475-7357
525 Glazier Rd Chelsea (48118) ***(G-2804)***
Al Dente Inc......734 449-8522
9815 Main St Whitmore Lake (48189) ***(G-18518)***
Al Fe Corporate Group, Lansing *Also called Al-Fe Heat Treating LLC* ***(G-9801)***
Al Fe Heat Treating-Ohio Inc (PA)......260 747-9422
209 W Mount Hope Ave # 1 Lansing (48910) ***(G-9800)***
Al's Cabinet Shop, Monroe *Also called Van Daeles Inc* ***(G-11588)***
Al-Craft Design & Engrg Inc (PA)......248 589-3827
710 Minnesota Dr Troy (48083) ***(G-16918)***
Al-Craft Industries, Troy *Also called Al-Craft Design & Engrg Inc* ***(G-16918)***
Al-Fe Heat Treating LLC (HQ)......260 747-9422
209 W Mount Hope Ave # 1 Lansing (48910) ***(G-9801)***
Al-Fe Heat Treating LLC......989 752-2819
1300 Leon Scott Ct Saginaw (48601) ***(G-14603)***
Al-Fe Heat Treating LLC......888 747-2533
209 W Mount Hope Ave # 1 Lansing (48910) ***(G-9802)***
Aladdin Machining Inc......586 465-4280
21240 Carlo Dr Clinton Township (48038) ***(G-3160)***
Aladdin Printing......248 360-2842
1546 Union Lake Rd Commerce Township (48382) ***(G-3507)***
Alamin Super Market LLC......313 305-7281
11920 Conant St Detroit (48212) ***(G-3994)***
Alan Bruce Enterprises......616 262-4609
4590 28th St Sw Byron Center (49315) ***(G-2257)***
Alba Plastics, Troy *Also called Noack Ventures LLC* ***(G-17280)***
Albar Industries Inc......810 667-0150
780 Whitney Dr Lapeer (48446) ***(G-9911)***
Albasara Fuel LLC......313 443-6581
10419 Ford Rd Dearborn (48126) ***(G-3806)***
Albers Cabinet Company......586 727-9090
65151 Gratiot Ave Lenox (48050) ***(G-9997)***
Albies Food Products LLC......989 732-2800
1534 Orourke Blvd Gaylord (49735) ***(G-6117)***
Albion Automotive Limited......313 758-2000
1 Dauch Dr Detroit (48211) ***(G-3995)***
Albion Industries LLC (PA)......800 835-8911
800 N Clark St Albion (49224) ***(G-114)***
Albion Machine and Tool LLC......517 629-8838
1001 Industrial Blvd Albion (49224) ***(G-115)***
Albion Recorder, Albion *Also called Calhoun Communications Inc* ***(G-118)***
Albrecht Sand & Gravel Co......810 672-9272
3790 W Sanilac Rd Snover (48472) ***(G-15390)***
Albring Auto Salvage, Edmore *Also called Doylen Albring Jr* ***(G-4991)***
Alco Manufacturing Corp......734 426-3941
8763 Dexter Chelsea Rd Dexter (48130) ***(G-4722)***
Alco Plastics Inc (PA)......586 752-4527
160 E Pond Dr Romeo (48065) ***(G-14219)***
Alco Products......715 346-3174
5217 Seymour Rd Swartz Creek (48473) ***(G-16349)***
Alco Products LLC......313 823-7500
580 Saint Jean St Detroit (48214) ***(G-3996)***
Alcoa Howmet......231 894-5686
1 Misco Dr Whitehall (49461) ***(G-18490)***
Alcoa Howmet, Thermatech, Whitehall *Also called Howmet Corporation* ***(G-18504)***
Alcoa Hwmet Whthall Cast Oprto, Whitehall *Also called Howmet Corporation* ***(G-18505)***
Alcoa Power & Propulsion, Whitehall *Also called Howmet Corporation* ***(G-18501)***
Alcona County Review......989 724-6384
111 N Lake St Harrisville (48740) ***(G-7740)***
Alcona Tool & Machine Inc (PA)......989 736-8151
3040 E Carbide Dr Harrisville (48740) ***(G-7741)***
Alcona Tool & Machine Inc......989 736-8151
325 N Lake St Lincoln (48742) ***(G-10033)***
Alcotec Wire Corporation (HQ)......800 228-0750
2750 Aero Park Dr Traverse City (49686) ***(G-16598)***
Ald Thermal Treatment Inc......810 357-0693
2656 24th St Port Huron (48060) ***(G-13434)***
Aldez North America......586 530-5314
42463 Garfield Rd Clinton Township (48038) ***(G-3161)***
Aldoa Company, Detroit *Also called Advanced Urethanes Inc* ***(G-3988)***
Aldridge Industries LLC......248 379-5357
18811 Riverside Dr Beverly Hills (48025) ***(G-1660)***
Aldridge Trucking, Holly *Also called South Flint Gravel Inc* ***(G-8295)***
Aleris International Inc......517 279-9596
368 W Garfield Ave Coldwater (49036) ***(G-3418)***
Alex Delvecchio Entps Inc......248 619-9600
1343 Piedmont Dr Troy (48083) ***(G-16919)***
Alexa Forest Products......906 265-2347
137 Dirkman Rd Iron River (49935) ***(G-8739)***
Alexander Directional Boring......989 362-9506
2395 Robinet Dr East Tawas (48730) ***(G-4916)***
Alexander Dodds Company......616 784-6000
3000 Walkent Dr Nw Grand Rapids (49544) ***(G-6442)***
Alexander J Bongiorno Inc......248 689-7766
101 W Big Beavr Rd # 135 Troy (48084) ***(G-16920)***
Alf Enterprises Inc......734 665-2012
1342 N Main St Ste 11a Ann Arbor (48104) ***(G-360)***
Alf Studios, Ann Arbor *Also called Alf Enterprises Inc* ***(G-360)***
Alfa Financial Software Inc......855 680-7100
350 N Old Woodward Ave Birmingham (48009) ***(G-1717)***
Alfie Embroidery Inc......231 935-1488
2425 Switch Dr Ste A Traverse City (49684) ***(G-16599)***
Alfmeier Friedrichs & Rath LLC......248 526-1650
340 E Big Beaver Rd # 135 Troy (48083) ***(G-16921)***
Algal Scientific, Plymouth *Also called Kemin Industries Inc* ***(G-13211)***
Algen County Shopper, Marquette *Also called Peterson Publishing Inc* ***(G-11040)***
Algoma Products Inc......616 285-6440
4201 Brockton Dr Se Grand Rapids (49512) ***(G-6443)***
Algonac Marine Cast LLC......810 794-9391
9300 Stone Rd Clay (48001) ***(G-3114)***
Alhern-Martin Indus Frnc Co......248 689-6363
2155 Austin Dr Troy (48083) ***(G-16922)***
Alien Resources, Lansing *Also called Pine Needle People LLC* ***(G-9728)***
Alinosi French Ice Cream Co......313 527-3195
12748 E Mcnichols Rd Detroit (48205) ***(G-3997)***
Alinosi Ice Cream Co., Detroit *Also called Alinosi French Ice Cream Co* ***(G-3997)***
Alis Custom Embroidery......586 744-9442
3031 Juanita Dr Sterling Heights (48310) ***(G-15927)***
All About Bus Cnstr Aabc LLC......248 229-3031
16935 Wakenden Redford (48240) ***(G-13712)***
All About Drainage LLC......248 921-0766
1940 Alton Cir Commerce Township (48390) ***(G-3508)***
All About Interiors......616 452-8998
974 Front Ave Nw Ste 1 Grand Rapids (49504) ***(G-6444)***
All Access Lift LLC......616 250-1084
407 Woods Edge Dr Hastings (49058) ***(G-7780)***
All Access Name Tags......866 955-8247
1435 Rochester Rd Troy (48083) ***(G-16923)***
All American Container Corp......586 949-0000
24600 Wood Ct Macomb (48042) ***(G-10573)***
All American Embroidery Inc......734 421-9292
31600 Plymouth Rd Livonia (48150) ***(G-10108)***
All American Essentials, Livonia *Also called All American Embroidery Inc* ***(G-10108)***
All American Welding LLC......517 294-2480
14392 Barnes Rd Byron (48418) ***(G-2252)***
All American Whse & Cold Stor......313 865-3870
14401 Dexter Ave Detroit (48238) ***(G-3998)***
All Around Beauty Shop LLC......313 704-2494
30106 Ford Rd Garden City (48135) ***(G-6091)***
All Around Mobil Welding......616 481-4267
3926 Edinboro St Nw Grand Rapids (49534) ***(G-6445)***
All Bending & Tubular Pdts LLC......616 333-2364
430 Cummings Ave Nw Ste G Grand Rapids (49534) ***(G-6446)***
All Care Team Inc......313 533-7057
22341 Karl St Detroit (48219) ***(G-3999)***

All City Electric Motor Repair....734 284-2268
18750 Fort St Apt 15 Riverview (48193) ***(G-13868)***
All Dealer Inventory LLC....231 342-9823
8148 Maple City Hwy Lake Ann (49650) ***(G-9541)***
All For Love Prints LLC....313 207-1547
1205 Harding St Detroit (48214) ***(G-4000)***
All In Printing....567 219-3660
24026 Waterview Dr New Boston (48164) ***(G-11999)***
All Kids Cnsdred Pubg Group In....248 398-3400
22041 Woodward Ave Ferndale (48220) ***(G-5521)***
All Kids Considered Pubg Group....248 398-3400
22041 Woodward Ave Ferndale (48220) ***(G-5522)***
All Metal Designs Inc....616 392-3696
13131 Reflections Dr Holland (49424) ***(G-7960)***
All Metal Finishing, Casco *Also called New Life Cop Brass Mint Free M* ***(G-2601)***
All Natural Bites LLC....248 470-6252
27400 Southfield Rd Lathrup Village (48076) ***(G-9974)***
All Overhead Door Operator Co, Detroit *Also called General Hardwood Company* ***(G-4253)***
All Packaging Solutions Inc....248 880-1548
20750 Hoover Rd Warren (48089) ***(G-17697)***
All Phase Welding Service Inc....616 235-6100
950 Vitality Dr Nw Ste G Comstock Park (49321) ***(G-3587)***
All Pointe Truck & Trailer Svc....586 504-0364
54137 Avondale Dr New Baltimore (48047) ***(G-11977)***
All Season Enclosures....248 650-8020
2760 Marissa Way Shelby Township (48316) ***(G-15168)***
All Seasons Agency Inc....586 752-6381
5455 34 Mile Rd Bruce Twp (48065) ***(G-2162)***
All Seasons Communications, Bruce Twp *Also called All Seasons Agency Inc* ***(G-2162)***
All Signs LLC....231 755-5540
1005 W Laketon Ave Muskegon (49441) ***(G-11767)***
All Size Pallets....810 721-1999
4005 N Van Dyke Rd Imlay City (48444) ***(G-8626)***
All Things Made In America, Ann Arbor *Also called Ideation Inc* ***(G-522)***
All Type Truck and Trlr Repr, Warren *Also called D & W Management Company Inc* ***(G-17770)***
All Welding and Fabg Co Inc....248 689-0986
1882 Woodslee Dr Troy (48083) ***(G-16924)***
All Wood Log Splitters, Petersburg *Also called Milan Metal Worx LLC* ***(G-12984)***
All-Cote Coatings Company LLC....586 427-0062
23896 Sherwood Center Line (48015) ***(G-2678)***
All-Fab Corporation....269 673-6572
1235 Lincoln Rd Unit 1235 # 1235 Allegan (49010) ***(G-145)***
All-Star Equipment LLC....855 273-8265
7205 10 Mile Rd Ne Rockford (49341) ***(G-14153)***
All-Tech Inc (PA)....616 406-0681
1030 58th St Sw Wyoming (49509) ***(G-18851)***
All-Tech Engineering, Wyoming *Also called All-Tech Inc* ***(G-18851)***
All-Wood Inc....906 353-6642
101 Us Highway 41 S Baraga (49908) ***(G-1133)***
Allan Tool & Machine Co Inc (PA)....248 585-2910
1822 E Maple Rd Troy (48083) ***(G-16925)***
Allbrite Printing & Lettershop....734 516-2623
28400 Van Horn Rd New Boston (48164) ***(G-12000)***
Allegan Flashes, Holland *Also called Flashes Publishers Inc* ***(G-8035)***
Allegan Metal Fabricators Inc....269 751-7130
3280 Lincoln Rd Hamilton (49419) ***(G-7595)***
Allegan News & Gazette, Allegan *Also called Kaechele Publications Inc* ***(G-162)***
Allegan Tubular Products Inc....269 673-6636
1276 Lincoln Rd Allegan (49010) ***(G-146)***
Allegan Vocal Studio....719 209-8957
1871 23rd St Allegan (49010) ***(G-147)***
Allegion S&S Holding Co Inc....734 680-7429
44704 Helm St Plymouth (48170) ***(G-13121)***
Allegra Alpena, Alpena *Also called Model Printing Service Inc* ***(G-304)***
Allegra Battle Creek, Battle Creek *Also called B & M Imaging Inc* ***(G-1188)***
Allegra Marketing Print Mail....586 335-2596
1201 Audubon Rd Grosse Pointe Park (48230) ***(G-7544)***
Allegra Marketing Print Mail....248 602-0545
1307 E Maple Rd Ste E Troy (48083) ***(G-16926)***
Allegra Marketing Print Mail....313 382-8033
17140 Ecorse Rd Allen Park (48101) ***(G-188)***
Allegra Marketing Print Mail....517 879-2444
1232 S West Ave Jackson (49203) ***(G-8809)***
Allegra Marketing Print Mail....313 429-0916
7307 Allen Rd Allen Park (48101) ***(G-189)***
Allegra Marketing Print Mail....269 213-8840
1514 Columbia Ave W Battle Creek (49015) ***(G-1183)***
Allegra Marketing Print Signs, Auburn Hills *Also called Rtr Alpha Inc* ***(G-1023)***
Allegra Network LLC....248 360-1290
7015 Cooley Lake Rd West Bloomfield (48324) ***(G-18262)***
Allegra Print & Imaging, Saline *Also called Acadia Group LLC* ***(G-14997)***
Allegra Print & Imaging, Grand Rapids *Also called Breck Graphics Incorporated* ***(G-6523)***
Allegra Print & Imaging, Troy *Also called Apb Inc* ***(G-16939)***
Allegra Print & Imaging, Holland *Also called Holland Printing Center Inc* ***(G-8083)***
Allegra Print & Imaging, Okemos *Also called Muhleck Enterprises Inc* ***(G-12679)***
Allegra Print & Imaging....248 354-1313
28810 Northwestern Hwy Southfield (48034) ***(G-15475)***
Allegra Print & Imaging No 38, Portage *Also called Kaufman Enterprises Inc* ***(G-13573)***
Allegra Print and Imaging....616 784-6699
929 Alpine Commerce Park Grand Rapids (49544) ***(G-6447)***
Allegra Print Imaging....616 446-6269
5985 Farmview Dr Allendale (49401) ***(G-212)***
Allegra Print Imaging Detroit, Detroit *Also called Nje Enterprises LLC* ***(G-4486)***
Allegra Print Imaging Highland, Highland *Also called C&P Hoover LLC* ***(G-7886)***
Allegra Print Imaging-Lansing, Lansing *Also called Lightning Litho Inc* ***(G-9864)***
Allegra Print Imging Port Hron, Fort Gratiot *Also called C W Enterprises Inc* ***(G-5819)***
Allegra Printing, Traverse City *Also called Allesk Enterprises Inc* ***(G-16600)***
Allegra Printing & Imaging, Saline *Also called Printing Services Inc* ***(G-15032)***
Allegra-Marketing Design Print....313 561-8000
22250 Ford Rd Dearborn Heights (48127) ***(G-3919)***
Allegra-Marketingdesign Print, Dearborn Heights *Also called August Communications Inc* ***(G-3921)***
Allegro Microsystems LLC....248 242-5044
691 N Squirrel Rd Ste 107 Auburn Hills (48326) ***(G-777)***
Allen and Sons Woodworking....313 492-1382
401 Tickner St Linden (48451) ***(G-10059)***
Allen Models of Michigan LLC....989 284-8866
9961 Buck Rd Freeland (48623) ***(G-6018)***
Allen Partners LLC....269 673-4010
611 N Eastern Ave Allegan (49010) ***(G-148)***
Allen Pattern of Michigan....269 963-4131
202 Mcgrath Pl Battle Creek (49014) ***(G-1184)***
Allen Tool and Die LLC....734 224-7900
7355 Sulier Dr Temperance (48182) ***(G-16526)***
Allen Whitehouse....231 824-3000
1270 E 16 1/2 Rd Manton (49663) ***(G-10929)***
Allesk Enterprises Inc (PA)....231 941-5770
1224 Centre St Traverse City (49686) ***(G-16600)***
Alley T & Gifts....989 875-4793
118 E Main St Carson City (48811) ***(G-2591)***
Allfi Robotics Inc....586 248-1198
48829 West Rd Wixom (48393) ***(G-18604)***
Allgraphics Corp....248 994-7373
28960 E King William Dr Farmington Hills (48331) ***(G-5167)***
Alliance Automation LLC....810 953-9539
4072 Market Pl Flint (48507) ***(G-5642)***
Alliance Broach and Tool, East China *Also called J & L Turning Inc* ***(G-4857)***
Alliance Cnc LLC....616 971-4700
3987 Brockton Dr Se Ste A Grand Rapids (49512) ***(G-6448)***
Alliance Cnc Ctter Grnding Svc, Grand Rapids *Also called Alliance Cnc LLC* ***(G-6448)***
Alliance Engnred Sltons NA Ltd....586 291-3694
18615 Sherwood St Detroit (48234) ***(G-4001)***
Alliance Franchise Brands LLC (PA)....248 596-8600
47585 Galleon Dr Plymouth (48170) ***(G-13122)***
Alliance Hni LLC....989 729-2804
525 S Gould St Owosso (48867) ***(G-12821)***
Alliance Industries Inc....248 656-3473
51820 Regency Center Dr Macomb (48042) ***(G-10574)***
Alliance Interiors LLC....517 322-0711
4521 W Mount Hope Hwy Lansing (48917) ***(G-9752)***
Alliance Prints LLC....313 484-0700
24502 W 7 Mile Rd Detroit (48219) ***(G-4002)***
Alliance Sheet Metal Inc....269 795-2954
6262 N Moe Rd Middleville (49333) ***(G-11302)***
Alliance Tool....586 465-3960
41239 Irwin Dr Harrison Township (48045) ***(G-7685)***
Alliance Tool and Machine Co....586 427-6411
21418 Timberidge St Saint Clair Shores (48082) ***(G-14847)***
Alliant Enterprises LLC....269 629-0300
2140 Oak Industrial Dr Ne Grand Rapids (49505) ***(G-6449)***
Alliant Healthcare Products, Grand Rapids *Also called Alliant Enterprises LLC* ***(G-6449)***
Allie Brothers Inc....248 477-4434
20295 Middlebelt Rd Livonia (48152) ***(G-10109)***
Allie Brothers Men's Wear, Livonia *Also called Allie Brothers Inc* ***(G-10109)***
Allied Asp Sealcoat & Repr LLC....810 797-6080
913 Markham St Flint (48507) ***(G-5643)***
Allied Bindery, Madison Heights *Also called Skyapple LLC* ***(G-10830)***
Allied Chucker and Engrg Co (PA)....517 787-1370
3529 Scheele Dr Jackson (49202) ***(G-8810)***
Allied Chucker and Engrg Co....517 787-1370
3525 Scheele Dr Jackson (49202) ***(G-8811)***
Allied Concrete Products, Midland *Also called Fisher Sand and Gravel Company* ***(G-11363)***
Allied Defense....810 252-9232
10420 Valley Creek Dr Goodrich (48438) ***(G-6221)***
Allied Distribution, Ferndale *Also called Allied Printing Co Inc* ***(G-5523)***
Allied Engineering Inc....616 748-7990
3424 88th Ave Ste 6 Zeeland (49464) ***(G-18990)***
Allied Finishing Inc....616 698-7550
4100 Broadmoor Ave Se Grand Rapids (49512) ***(G-6450)***
Allied Indus Fabrication LLC....810 422-5093
3061 W Thompson Rd Fenton (48430) ***(G-5446)***
Allied Indus Solutions LLC....810 422-5093
3061 W Thompson Rd Ste 1 Fenton (48430) ***(G-5447)***

Allied Kelite, New Hudson *Also called Macdermid Incorporated* ***(G-12060)***
Allied Machine & Tool Inc 269 623-7295
3590 Hope Industry Dr Delton (49046) ***(G-3961)***
Allied Machine Inc 231 834-0050
11171 Spruce Ave Grant (49327) ***(G-7425)***
Allied Mailing and Prtg Inc 810 750-8291
240 N Fenway Dr Fenton (48430) ***(G-5448)***
Allied Mask & Tooling 419 470-2555
7507 Willow Pointe Dr Temperance (48182) ***(G-16527)***
Allied Media.net, Fenton *Also called Allied Mailing and Prtg Inc* ***(G-5448)***
Allied Metals Corp (PA) 248 680-2400
2668 Lapeer Rd Auburn Hills (48326) ***(G-778)***
Allied Motion Technologies Inc 989 725-5151
201 S Delaney Rd Owosso (48867) ***(G-12822)***
Allied Photochemical Inc 810 364-6910
16024 Angelo Dr Macomb (48042) ***(G-10575)***
Allied Photopolymers, Macomb *Also called Allied Photochemical Inc* ***(G-10575)***
Allied Printing Co Inc (PA) 248 541-0551
2035 Hilton Rd Ferndale (48220) ***(G-5523)***
Allied Printing Co Inc 248 514-7394
965 Wanda St Ferndale (48220) ***(G-5524)***
Allied Screen & Graphics LLC 248 499-8204
73 W Walton Blvd Pontiac (48340) ***(G-13348)***
Allied Signs Inc 586 791-7900
33650 Giftos Dr Clinton Township (48035) ***(G-3162)***
Allied Tool and Machine Co 989 755-5384
3545 Janes Ave Saginaw (48601) ***(G-14604)***
Allied Tube & Conduit Corp 734 721-4040
4205 Elizabeth St Wayne (48184) ***(G-18212)***
Allied Welding Incorporated 248 360-1122
8240 Goldie St Commerce Township (48390) ***(G-3509)***
Alligator North America Inc 248 914-0597
50164 Pontiac Trl Unit 1 Wixom (48393) ***(G-18605)***
Allison 734 261-3735
1219 Farmington Rd Garden City (48135) ***(G-6092)***
Allmet Industries Inc 248 280-4600
5030 Leafdale Blvd Royal Oak (48073) ***(G-14505)***
Allnex USA Inc 269 385-1205
2715 Miller Rd Kalamazoo (49001) ***(G-9109)***
Allor Manufacturing Inc 248 486-4500
12534 Emerson Dr Brighton (48116) ***(G-1943)***
Alloy Construction Service Inc (PA) 989 486-6960
3500 Contractors Dr Midland (48642) ***(G-11319)***
Alloy Exchange Inc (PA) 616 863-0640
300 Rockford Park Dr Ne Rockford (49341) ***(G-14154)***
Alloy Industries Corporation 734 433-1112
13500 Luick Dr Chelsea (48118) ***(G-2805)***
Alloy Machining LLC 517 204-3306
437 N Rosemary St Lansing (48917) ***(G-9753)***
Alloy Steel Treating Company 269 628-2154
22138 M 40 Gobles (49055) ***(G-6216)***
Alloying Surfaces Inc 248 524-9200
1346 Wheaton Dr Troy (48083) ***(G-16927)***
Allpacks, Warren *Also called All Packaging Solutions Inc* ***(G-17697)***
Allprints Plus LLC 248 906-2977
27749 Dequindre Rd Madison Heights (48071) ***(G-10665)***
Allpro Vector Group, Northville *Also called Hpi Products Inc* ***(G-12229)***
Allrout Inc 616 748-7696
3382 Production Ct Zeeland (49464) ***(G-18991)***
Allsales Enterprises Inc 616 437-0639
1013 Country Gdns Nw Grand Rapids (49534) ***(G-6451)***
Allstate, Detroit *Also called Amrican Petro Inc* ***(G-4017)***
Allstate HM Leisure Strlng Hts 734 838-6500
44605 Schoenherr Rd Sterling Heights (48313) ***(G-15928)***
Allstate Sign Company Inc 989 386-4045
1291 E Surrey Rd Farwell (48622) ***(G-5420)***
Allwood Building Components 586 727-2731
35377 Division Rd Richmond (48062) ***(G-13832)***
Ally Equipment LLC 810 422-5093
3061 W Thompson Rd Ste 1 Fenton (48430) ***(G-5449)***
Ally Equipment Solutions, Fenton *Also called Allied Indus Solutions LLC* ***(G-5447)***
Ally Servicing LLC (HQ) 248 948-7702
500 Woodward Ave Fl 1 Detroit (48226) ***(G-4003)***
Allymade 616 813-0591
1037 4th Ave Lake Odessa (48849) ***(G-9571)***
Allynn Corp 269 383-1199
7868 Douglas Ave Kalamazoo (49009) ***(G-9110)***
Alma Concrete Products Company (PA) 989 463-5476
1277 Bridge Rd Alma (48801) ***(G-234)***
Alma Container Corporation 989 463-2106
1000 Charles Ave Alma (48801) ***(G-235)***
Alma Products Company, Alma *Also called Etx Inc* ***(G-240)***
Alma Products Company 989 463-1151
150 N Court Ave Alma (48801) ***(G-236)***
Alma Products I LLC (HQ) 989 463-1151
2000 Michigan Ave Alma (48801) ***(G-237)***
Alma Reminder, Alma *Also called Morning Star Publishing Co* ***(G-248)***
Almar Orchards LLC 810 659-6568
1431 Duffield Rd Flushing (48433) ***(G-5801)***
Almond Products Inc 616 844-1813
17150 148th Ave Spring Lake (49456) ***(G-15802)***
Almost Heaven Saunas, Holland *Also called Ahs LLC* ***(G-7959)***
Alnco, Constantine *Also called E L Nickell Co* ***(G-3665)***
Alo LLC 313 318-9029
3011 W Grand Blvd Ste 105 Detroit (48202) ***(G-4004)***
Alp Lghting Cmpnnts Charlevoix 231 547-6584
10163 Us Highway 31 N Charlevoix (49720) ***(G-2708)***
Alp Lighting Ceiling Pdts Inc 231 547-6584
10163 Us Highway 31 N Charlevoix (49720) ***(G-2709)***
Alpena Aggregate Inc 989 595-2511
7590 Weiss Rd Alpena (49707) ***(G-275)***
Alpena Antiq Trctr Stm Eng CL 989 734-3859
3219 Darga Hwy Hawks (49743) ***(G-7814)***
Alpena Biorefinery 989 340-1190
412 Ford Ave Alpena (49707) ***(G-276)***
Alpena Electric Motor Service 989 354-8780
1581 M 32 W Alpena (49707) ***(G-277)***
Alpha 21 LLC 248 352-7330
22400 Telegraph Rd Ste A Southfield (48033) ***(G-15476)***
Alpha Coatings Inc 734 523-9000
32711 Glendale St Livonia (48150) ***(G-10110)***
Alpha Data Business Forms Inc 248 540-5930
757 S Eton St Ste D Birmingham (48009) ***(G-1718)***
Alpha Directional Boring 586 405-0171
11910 Scott Rd Davisburg (48350) ***(G-3756)***
Alpha Engineered Refrigeration, Rochester Hills *Also called Su-Tec Inc* ***(G-14122)***
Alpha Group, Livonia *Also called Alpha Coatings Inc* ***(G-10110)***
Alpha Group of Companies, The, Livonia *Also called 3715-11th Street Corp* ***(G-10089)***
Alpha Metal Finishing Co 734 426-2855
8155 Huron St Dexter (48130) ***(G-4723)***
Alpha Omega Publishing 517 879-1286
322 Madison St Jackson (49202) ***(G-8812)***
Alpha Resources LLC 269 465-5559
3090 Johnson Rd Stevensville (49127) ***(G-16239)***
Alpha Steel Treating Inc 734 523-1035
32969 Glendale St Livonia (48150) ***(G-10111)***
Alpha Technology Corporation 517 546-9700
1450 Mcpherson Park Dr Howell (48843) ***(G-8426)***
Alpha Tran Engineering Co 616 837-7341
12575 Cleveland St Nunica (49448) ***(G-12576)***
Alphacore Pharma LLC 734 330-0265
2425 Meadowridge Ct Ann Arbor (48105) ***(G-361)***
AlphaGraphics 336, Canton *Also called Carrigan Graphics Inc* ***(G-2445)***
Alphausa, Livonia *Also called Washers Incorporated* ***(G-10467)***
Alpine Power Systems Inc (HQ) 313 531-6600
24355 Capitol Ste 1 Redford (48239) ***(G-13713)***
Alpine Sign and Prtg Sup Inc 517 487-1400
3105 Sanders Rd Lansing (48917) ***(G-9754)***
Alr Products Inc 517 649-2243
12 Charlotte St Mulliken (48861) ***(G-11748)***
Alro Riverside LLC 517 782-8322
829 Belden Rd Jackson (49203) ***(G-8813)***
Alro Steel Corporation 989 893-9553
3125 N Water St Bay City (48708) ***(G-1320)***
Alro Steel Corporation 810 695-7300
3000 Tri Park Dr Grand Blanc (48439) ***(G-6231)***
Alro Steel Corporation 517 371-9600
1800 W Willow St Lansing (48915) ***(G-9803)***
Alsentis LLC 616 395-8254
1261 S Waverly Rd Holland (49423) ***(G-7961)***
Alt, Bloomfield Hills *Also called Adjustable Locking Tech LLC* ***(G-1792)***
Alt House Malts, Battle Creek *Also called Brydges Group LLC* ***(G-1200)***
Alta Construction Eqp LLC 248 356-5200
56195 Pontiac Trl New Hudson (48165) ***(G-12041)***
Alta Distribution LLC 313 363-1682
21650 W 11 Mile Rd Southfield (48076) ***(G-15477)***
Alta Equipment Holdings Inc (HQ) 248 449-6700
13211 Merriman Rd Livonia (48150) ***(G-10112)***
Alta Vista Technology LLC 855 913-3228
26622 Woodward Ave # 105 Royal Oak (48067) ***(G-14506)***
Altagas Marketing (us) Inc 810 887-4105
1411 3rd St Ste A Port Huron (48060) ***(G-13435)***
Altagas Power Holdings US Inc (HQ) 810 887-4105
1411 3rd St Ste A Port Huron (48060) ***(G-13436)***
Altair Engineering Inc (PA) 248 614-2400
1820 E Big Beaver Rd Troy (48083) ***(G-16928)***
Altair Systems Inc 248 668-0116
30553 S Wixom Rd Ste 400 Wixom (48393) ***(G-18606)***
Altec, Howell *Also called Alpha Technology Corporation* ***(G-8426)***
Altered Stone Realty Co LLC 313 800-0362
16061 Fairmount Dr Detroit (48205) ***(G-4005)***
Alternate Number Five Inc (PA) 616 842-2581
11095 W Olive Rd Grand Haven (49417) ***(G-6272)***
Alternative Components LLC (PA) 586 755-9177
24055 Mound Rd Warren (48091) ***(G-17698)***
Alternative Engineering Inc 616 785-7200
5670 West River Dr Ne Belmont (49306) ***(G-1499)***

Alternative Fuel Tech LLC 313 417-9212
1350 Buckingham Rd Grosse Pointe Park (48230) *(G-7545)*
Alternative Systems Inc 269 384-2008
5519 E Cork St Ste A Kalamazoo (49048) *(G-9111)*
Alternatives In Advertising, Southfield *Also called MKP Enterprises Inc (G-15660)*
Alticor Global Holdings Inc (PA) 616 787-1000
7575 Fulton St E Ada (49301) *(G-5)*
Alticor Inc (HQ) 616 787-1000
7575 Fulton St E Ada (49355) *(G-6)*
Alto Manufacturing Inc 734 641-8800
38338 Abruzzi Dr Westland (48185) *(G-18352)*
Altron Automation Inc 616 669-7711
3523 Highland Dr Hudsonville (49426) *(G-8565)*
Altron Automation Group Inc 616 669-7711
3523 Highland Dr Hudsonville (49426) *(G-8566)*
Altus Brands LLC (PA) 231 421-3810
6893 Sullivan Rd Grawn (49637) *(G-7448)*
Altus Industries Inc 616 233-9530
3731 Northridge Dr Nw # 1 Walker (49544) *(G-17631)*
Aludyne Inc 248 506-1692
24155 Wahl St Warren (48089) *(G-17699)*
Aludyne Inc (HQ) 248 728-8700
300 Galleria Ofcntr # 501 Southfield (48034) *(G-15478)*
Aludyne East Michigan LLC 810 987-7633
2223 Dove St Port Huron (48060) *(G-13437)*
Aludyne International Inc (HQ) 248 728-8642
300 Galleria Ofcntr Ste 5 Southfield (48034) *(G-15479)*
Aludyne Mexico LLC (HQ) 248 728-8642
300 Gllria Ofc Ctr Ste 50 Southfield (48034) *(G-15480)*
Aludyne Montague LLC 248 479-6455
5353 Wilcox St Montague (49437) *(G-11594)*
Aludyne North America Inc (HQ) 248 728-8642
300 Galleria Ofcntr Ste 5 Southfield (48034) *(G-15481)*
Aludyne North America Inc 248 728-8642
2280 W Grand River Ave Howell (48843) *(G-8427)*
Aludyne North America LLC 989 463-6166
250 Adams St Alma (48801) *(G-238)*
Aludyne North America LLC (HQ) 248 728-8700
300 Galleria Ofcntr Ste 5 Southfield (48034) *(G-15482)*
Aludyne US LLC 810 987-1112
3150 Dove St Port Huron (48060) *(G-13438)*
Aludyne US LLC (HQ) 248 728-8700
300 Galleria Ofcntr Ste 5 Southfield (48034) *(G-15483)*
Aludyne West Michigan LLC 248 728-8642
1320 Paw Paw Ave Benton Harbor (49022) *(G-1528)*
Aludyne West Michigan LLC 248 728-8642
2800 Yasdick Dr Stevensville (49127) *(G-16240)*
Alumabridge LLC 855 373-7500
2723 S State St Ste 150 Ann Arbor (48104) *(G-362)*
Alumalight LLC 248 457-9302
1307 E Maple Rd Ste E Troy (48083) *(G-16929)*
Alumi Span, Pittsford *Also called Berlin Holdings LLC (G-13067)*
Alumilite Corporation 269 488-4000
1458 S 35th St Galesburg (49053) *(G-6073)*
Aluminum Architectural Met Co 313 895-2555
8711 Epworth St Detroit (48204) *(G-4006)*
Aluminum Blanking Co Inc 248 338-4422
360 W Sheffield Ave Pontiac (48340) *(G-13349)*
Aluminum Finishing Company 269 382-4010
615 W Ransom St Kalamazoo (49007) *(G-9112)*
Aluminum Supply Company Inc 313 491-5040
14359 Meyers Rd Detroit (48227) *(G-4007)*
Aluminum Textures Inc 616 538-3144
2925 Remico St Sw Ste A Grandville (49418) *(G-7364)*
Alumiramp Inc 517 639-8777
855 E Chicago Rd Quincy (49082) *(G-13661)*
Alure International, Bloomfield Hills *Also called Elite Bus Svcs Exec Stffing In (G-1818)*
Aluwax Dental Products Co Inc 616 895-4385
5260 Edgewater Dr Allendale (49401) *(G-213)*
Alynn Industries 517 764-7783
414 N Jackson St 97-11 Jackson (49201) *(G-8814)*
AM General LLC 734 523-8098
1399 Pacific Dr Auburn Hills (48326) *(G-779)*
AM Specialties Inc 586 795-9000
5985 Wall St Sterling Heights (48312) *(G-15929)*
AM Twist, South Haven *Also called American Twisting Company (G-15398)*
Amalgamated Uaw 231 734-9286
601 W 7th St Evart (49631) *(G-5120)*
Amalgamated Uaw Local 2270, Evart *Also called Amalgamated Uaw (G-5120)*
Amalgamations Ltd 248 879-7345
6181 Elmoor Dr Troy (48098) *(G-16930)*
Amanda Manufacturing LLC 740 385-9380
34450 Industrial Rd Livonia (48150) *(G-10113)*
Amanda Products LLC 248 547-3870
1350 Jarvis St Ferndale (48220) *(G-5525)*
Ambassador Magazine 313 965-6789
151 W Congress St 306 Detroit (48226) *(G-4008)*
Ambassador Steel Corporation 517 455-7216
1501 E Jolly Rd Lansing (48910) *(G-9804)*
Amber Engine LLC 313 373-4751
711 Griswold St Detroit (48226) *(G-4009)*
Amber Manufacturing Inc 586 218-6080
18320 Malyn Blvd Fraser (48026) *(G-5890)*
Ambers Essentials 313 282-4615
25504 Shiawassee Rd # 45 Southfield (48033) *(G-15484)*
Ambrosia Inc 734 529-7174
129 Riley St Dundee (48131) *(G-4809)*
Ambucs Muskegon Chapter, Norton Shores *Also called National Ambucs Inc (G-12315)*
AMC, Davisburg *Also called Automtion Mdlar Components Inc (G-3758)*
Amcol Corporation 248 414-5700
21435 Dequindre Rd Hazel Park (48030) *(G-7819)*
Amcol International Corp 517 629-6808
807 Austin Ave Albion (49224) *(G-116)*
Amcor, Grand Rapids *Also called Applied Mechanics Corporation (G-6464)*
Amcor Phrm Packg USA LLC 734 428-9741
935 Technology Dr Ste 100 Ann Arbor (48108) *(G-363)*
Amcor Rigid Packaging Usa LLC (HQ) 734 428-9741
10521 S M 52 Manchester (48158) *(G-10880)*
Amcor Rigid Plastics, Ann Arbor *Also called Amcor Phrm Packg USA LLC (G-363)*
AME For Auto Dealers Inc 248 720-0245
1000 N Opdyke Rd Ste J Auburn Hills (48326) *(G-780)*
AME International LLC 586 532-8981
21481 Carlo Dr Clinton Township (48038) *(G-3163)*
Ameco, Fennville *Also called Ability Mfg & Engrg Co (G-5433)*
Amerchol Corporation 989 636-2441
2030 Dow Ctr Midland (48674) *(G-11320)*
Ameri-Kart(mi) Corp 269 641-5811
19300 Grange St Cassopolis (49031) *(G-2625)*
Ameri-Serv Group 734 426-9700
2855 Coolidge Hwy Ste 112 Troy (48084) *(G-16931)*
America Ink and Technology 269 345-4657
8975 Shaver Rd Portage (49024) *(G-13543)*
America Wireless 810 820-3273
4205 Miller Rd Flint (48507) *(G-5644)*
America's Green Line, Detroit *Also called Johnico LLC (G-4340)*
American & Efird LLC 248 399-1166
1919 Coolidge Hwy Berkley (48072) *(G-1619)*
American Aggregate Inc 269 683-6160
2041 M 140 Niles (49120) *(G-12110)*
American Aggregates Mich Inc (HQ) 248 348-8511
51445 W 12 Mile Rd Wixom (48393) *(G-18607)*
American Aircraft Parts Mfg Co 586 294-3300
44801 Centre Ct E Clinton Township (48038) *(G-3164)*
American Arrow Corp Inc 248 435-6115
1609 Englewood Ave Madison Heights (48071) *(G-10666)*
American Assemblers Inc 248 334-9777
40 W Howard St Ste 222 Pontiac (48342) *(G-13350)*
American Athletic 231 798-7300
418 W Hackley Ave Muskegon (49444) *(G-11768)*
American Axle & Mfg Inc 248 353-2155
20750 Civic Center Dr Southfield (48076) *(G-15485)*
American Axle & Mfg Inc 248 475-3475
1987 Taylor Rd Auburn Hills (48326) *(G-781)*
American Axle & Mfg Inc 586 415-2000
18450 15 Mile Rd Fraser (48026) *(G-5891)*
American Axle & Mfg Inc 517 542-4241
917 Anderson Rd Litchfield (49252) *(G-10076)*
American Axle & Mfg Inc 586 573-4840
30500 Ryan Rd Warren (48092) *(G-17700)*
American Axle & Mfg Inc 810 772-8778
1840 Holbrook St Detroit (48212) *(G-4010)*
American Axle & Mfg Inc (HQ) 313 758-3600
1 Dauch Dr Detroit (48211) *(G-4011)*
American Axle & Mfg Inc 269 278-0211
1 Manufacturing Dr Three Rivers (49093) *(G-16562)*
American Axle & Mfg Inc 248 299-2900
2965 Technology Dr Rochester Hills (48309) *(G-13946)*
American Axle & Mfg Inc 248 276-2328
2007 Taylor Rd Auburn Hills (48326) *(G-782)*
American Axle Mfg Holdings Inc (PA) 313 758-2000
1 Dauch Dr Detroit (48211) *(G-4012)*
American Axle Oxford 248 361-6044
2300 Xcelsior Dr Ste 230 Oxford (48371) *(G-12873)*
American Battery Solutions Inc 248 462-6364
3768 S Lapeer Rd Lake Orion (48359) *(G-9585)*
American Beauty Tools, Troy *Also called Assembly Technologies Intl Inc (G-16960)*
American Beverage Equipment Co 586 773-0094
27560 Groesbeck Hwy Roseville (48066) *(G-14373)*
American Bldrs Contrs Sup Inc 906 226-9665
908 W Baraga Ave Marquette (49855) *(G-11004)*
American Blower Supply Inc 586 771-7337
14219 E 10 Mile Rd Warren (48089) *(G-17701)*
American Bottling Company 810 564-1432
7300 Enterprise Pkwy Mount Morris (48458) *(G-11667)*
American Bottling Company 616 396-1281
545 E 32nd St Holland (49423) *(G-7962)*
American Bottling Company 616 392-2124
900 Brooks Ave Ste 1 Holland (49423) *(G-7963)*

ALPHABETIC

American Bottling Company 989 731-5392
1923 Orourke Blvd Gaylord (49735) ***(G-6118)***
American Bottling Company 231 775-7393
1481 Potthoff St Cadillac (49601) ***(G-2312)***
American Bottling Company 517 622-8605
1145 Comet Ln Grand Ledge (48837) ***(G-6384)***
American Brake and Clutch Inc 586 948-3730
50631 E Russell Schmidt Chesterfield (48051) ***(G-2838)***
American Brewers Inc 616 318-9230
3408 Miller Rd Ste D Kalamazoo (49001) ***(G-9113)***
American Broach & Machine Co 734 961-0300
575 S Mansfield St Ypsilanti (48197) ***(G-18924)***
American Charcoal, Hazel Park *Also called Amcol Corporation* ***(G-7819)***
American Chem Solutions LLC 231 655-5840
2406 Roberts St Muskegon (49444) ***(G-11769)***
American Chemical Tech Inc (PA) 866 945-1041
1892 Hydralic Dr Howell (48855) ***(G-8428)***
American Classic Homes Inc 616 594-5900
13352 Van Buren St Holland (49424) ***(G-7964)***
American Classics Corp 231 843-0523
3750 W Hansen Rd Ludington (49431) ***(G-10525)***
American Cmmnities Media Group, Southfield *Also called Business Design Solutions Inc* ***(G-15514)***
American Commodities, Flint *Also called Automotive Plastics Recycling* ***(G-5648)***
American Compounding Spc LLC 810 227-3500
9984 Borderline Dr Brighton (48116) ***(G-1944)***
American Controls Inc 248 476-0663
3485 Bradway Blvd Bloomfield Hills (48301) ***(G-1796)***
American Cooling Systems LLC 616 954-0280
3099 Wilson Dr Nw Grand Rapids (49534) ***(G-6452)***
American Die and Mold Inc 231 269-3788
141 S Industrial Dr Buckley (49620) ***(G-2204)***
American Die Corporation 810 794-4080
6860 Holland Rd Clay (48001) ***(G-3115)***
American Dowel & Fastener, Harrison Township *Also called Henry Plambeck* ***(G-7701)***
American Dumpster Services LLC 586 501-3600
6490 E 10 Mile Rd Center Line (48015) ***(G-2679)***
American Eagle Systems, Commerce Township *Also called Michigan Roll Form Inc* ***(G-3556)***
American Electric Motor Corp (PA) 810 743-6080
4102 Davison Rd Burton (48509) ***(G-2226)***
American Engnred Cmponents Inc (PA) 734 428-8301
17951 W Austin Rd Manchester (48158) ***(G-10881)***
American Fabricated Pdts Inc 616 607-8785
16910 148th Ave Spring Lake (49456) ***(G-15803)***
American Fan & Blower, Warren *Also called American Blower Supply Inc* ***(G-17701)***
American Farm Products Inc 734 484-4180
1382 Industrial Dr Ste 4 Saline (48176) ***(G-15000)***
American Flag & Banner Company 248 288-3010
28 S Main St Clawson (48017) ***(G-3085)***
American Furukawa Inc (HQ) 734 446-2200
47677 Galleon Dr Plymouth (48170) ***(G-13123)***
American Gator Tool Company 231 347-3222
1225 W Conway Rd Unit C Harbor Springs (49740) ***(G-7639)***
American Gear & Engrg Co Inc 734 595-6400
38200 Abruzzi Dr Westland (48185) ***(G-18353)***
American Gear Tools, Ypsilanti *Also called American Broach & Machine Co* ***(G-18924)***
American Gourmet Snacks LLC 989 892-4856
1211 Woodside Ave Essexville (48732) ***(G-5108)***
American Graphics Inc 586 774-8880
27413 Harper Ave Saint Clair Shores (48081) ***(G-14848)***
American Graphics Printing, Clinton Township *Also called Macomb Business Forms Inc* ***(G-3286)***
American Graphite Corporation 586 757-3540
21756 Dequindre Rd Warren (48091) ***(G-17702)***
American Grinding and Mac 517 467-5399
9562 Sand Lake Hwy Onsted (49265) ***(G-12704)***
American Grinding Machining Co 313 388-0440
1415 Dix Hwy Lincoln Park (48146) ***(G-10043)***
American Grow Rack, Marne *Also called Dewys Manufacturing Inc* ***(G-10991)***
American Holoptics, Clawson *Also called Project Echo LLC* ***(G-3105)***
American Household Inc 601 296-5000
33067 Industrial Rd Livonia (48150) ***(G-10114)***
American Indus McHinery-Mc LLC 810 420-0949
2026 S Parker St Marine City (48039) ***(G-10954)***
American Industrial Door, Canton *Also called International Door Inc* ***(G-2478)***
American Industrial Gauge Inc 248 280-0048
4839 Leafdale Blvd Royal Oak (48073) ***(G-14507)***
American Industrial Partners, Macomb *Also called Ascent Aerospace Holdings LLC* ***(G-10579)***
American Industrial Training 734 789-9099
23851 Vreeland Rd Flat Rock (48134) ***(G-5613)***
American Information Services (HQ) 248 399-4848
3010 Coolidge Hwy Berkley (48072) ***(G-1620)***
American Ink USA Prntg & Grphc 586 790-2555
33812 Groesbeck Hwy Clinton Township (48035) ***(G-3165)***
American Jetway Corporation 734 721-5930
34136 Myrtle St Wayne (48184) ***(G-18213)***
American Label & Tag Inc 734 454-7600
41878 Koppernick Rd Canton (48187) ***(G-2433)***
American Lap Company 231 526-7121
220 Franklin Park Harbor Springs (49740) ***(G-7640)***
American Laser Centers LLC 248 426-8250
24555 Hallwood Ct Farmington Hills (48335) ***(G-5168)***
American Lazer Centers 248 798-6552
16010 19 Mile Rd Ste 100 Clinton Township (48038) ***(G-3166)***
American Lear 616 252-3643
2150 Alpine Ave Nw Grand Rapids (49544) ***(G-6453)***
American Litho Inc 734 394-1400
8455 Haggerty Rd Van Buren Twp (48111) ***(G-17508)***
American Made Tubcraft Plus, Baraga *Also called Keweenaw Bay Indian Community* ***(G-1141)***
American Mathematical Society 734 996-5250
416 4th St Ann Arbor (48103) ***(G-364)***
American Metal Fab Inc 269 279-5108
55515 Franklin Dr Three Rivers (49093) ***(G-16563)***
American Metal Processing Co 586 757-7144
22720 Nagel St Warren (48089) ***(G-17703)***
American Metal Restoration 810 364-4820
1765 Michigan Ave Ste 2 Marysville (48040) ***(G-11081)***
American Metallurgical Svcs 313 893-8328
2731 Jerome St Detroit (48212) ***(G-4013)***
American Mfg Innovators Inc 248 669-5990
1840 W West Maple Rd Commerce Township (48390) ***(G-3510)***
American Mitsuba Corporation 989 773-0377
2945 Three Leaves Dr Mount Pleasant (48858) ***(G-11678)***
American Mitsuba Corporation (HQ) 989 779-4962
2945 Three Leaves Dr Mount Pleasant (48858) ***(G-11679)***
American Models 248 437-6800
11770 Green Oak Indus Dr Whitmore Lake (48189) ***(G-18519)***
American MSC Inc 248 589-7770
2451 Elliott Dr Troy (48083) ***(G-16932)***
American MSC Inc (HQ) 248 589-7770
2401 Elliott Dr Troy (48083) ***(G-16933)***
American Mtsuba Corp Mich Plan, Mount Pleasant *Also called American Mitsuba Corporation* ***(G-11678)***
American Newspaper Solutions, Rochester *Also called Advertsing Ntwrk Solutions Inc* ***(G-13890)***
American Pallet Company LLC 231 834-5056
11421 S Peach Ave Grant (49327) ***(G-7426)***
American Panel, Norton Shores *Also called Hestia Inc* ***(G-12297)***
American Plastic Solutions, Saline *Also called Ann Arbor Plastics Inc* ***(G-15003)***
American Plastic Toys Inc (PA) 248 624-4881
799 Ladd Rd Walled Lake (48390) ***(G-17663)***
American Plastic Toys Inc 989 685-2455
3059 Beechwood Rd Rose City (48654) ***(G-14359)***
American Pleasure Products Inc 989 685-8484
2823 E Industrial Dr Rose City (48654) ***(G-14360)***
American Porcelain Enamel Co 231 744-3013
1709 Ruddiman Dr Muskegon (49445) ***(G-11770)***
American Pride Machining Inc 586 294-6404
34062 James J Pompo Dr Fraser (48026) ***(G-5892)***
American Printing Services Inc 248 568-5543
6931 Killarney Dr Troy (48098) ***(G-16934)***
American Prosthetic Institute 517 349-3130
2145 University Park Dr # 100 Okemos (48864) ***(G-12655)***
American Public Works Assn 816 472-6100
601 Avenue A Springfield (49037) ***(G-15859)***
American Pwr Cnnection Systems 989 686-6302
2460 Midland Rd Bay City (48706) ***(G-1321)***
American Reprographics Co LLC 248 299-8900
1009 W Maple Rd Clawson (48017) ***(G-3086)***
American Rhnmtall Vehicles LLC 586 942-0139
33844 Sterling Ponds Blvd Sterling Heights (48312) ***(G-15930)***
American Ring Manufacturing 734 402-0426
35955 Veronica St Livonia (48150) ***(G-10115)***
American Rod Consumers, Grand Blanc *Also called King Steel Corporation* ***(G-6250)***
American Roll Manufacturing, Clinton Township *Also called D-N-S Industries Inc* ***(G-3216)***
American Roll Shutter Awng Co 734 422-7110
12700 Merriman Rd Livonia (48150) ***(G-10116)***
American Screw Products Inc 248 543-0991
29866 John R Rd Madison Heights (48071) ***(G-10667)***
American Sealants Inc 313 534-2500
26112 W 7 Mile Rd Detroit (48240) ***(G-4014)***
American Seating Company (PA) 616 732-6561
801 Broadway Ave Nw # 200 Grand Rapids (49504) ***(G-6454)***
American Seating Company 616 732-6600
801 Broadway Ave Nw # 200 Grand Rapids (49504) ***(G-6455)***
American Shortening and Oil Co, Livonia *Also called Asao LLC* ***(G-10125)***
American Silk Screen & EMB 248 474-1000
24601 Hallwood Ct Farmington Hills (48335) ***(G-5169)***
American Soc AG Blgcal Engners 269 429-0300
2950 Niles Rd Saint Joseph (49085) ***(G-14922)***
American Soft Trim Inc 989 681-0037
300 Woodside Dr Saint Louis (48880) ***(G-14984)***
American Soy Products Inc 734 429-2310
1474 Woodland Dr Saline (48176) ***(G-15001)***

American Speedy Printing, Saint Clair Shores *Also called American Graphics Inc* ***(G-14848)***
American Speedy Printing, Rochester *Also called Business Press Inc* ***(G-13895)***
American Speedy Printing, Romulus *Also called Jlr Printing Inc* ***(G-14290)***
American Speedy Printing, Wyandotte *Also called Madden Enterprises Inc* ***(G-18830)***
American Speedy Printing, Plymouth *Also called Afb Corporate Operations LLC* ***(G-13120)***
American Speedy Printing, Detroit *Also called R N E Business Enterprises* ***(G-4551)***
American Speedy Printing, Southfield *Also called Jerrys Quality Quick Print* ***(G-15612)***
American Speedy Printing, Clinton Township *Also called L&L Printing Inc* ***(G-3278)***
American Speedy Printing, Jackson *Also called Kmak Inc* ***(G-8929)***
American Speedy Printing Ctrs....989 723-5196
111 S Washington St Owosso (48867) ***(G-12823)***
American Speedy Printing Ctrs....313 928-5820
20320 Ecorse Rd Taylor (48180) ***(G-16376)***
American Spoon Foods Inc (PA)....231 347-9030
1668 Clarion Ave Petoskey (49770) ***(G-12988)***
American Standard Windows....734 788-2261
30281 Pipers Ln Farmington Hills (48334) ***(G-5170)***
American Steel Works Inc....734 282-0300
12615 Nixon Ave Riverview (48193) ***(G-13869)***
American Strong....248 978-6483
155 Lochaven Rd Waterford (48327) ***(G-18098)***
American T-Mould LLC....616 617-2422
5090 Weeping Willow Dr Se Grand Rapids (49546) ***(G-6456)***
American Tank Fabrication LLC....780 663-3552
2222 W Grand Okemos (48864) ***(G-12656)***
American Tchncal Fbrcators LLC....989 269-6262
414 E Soper Rd Bad Axe (48413) ***(G-1095)***
American Thermoforming Mch LLC (PA)....989 345-0935
2525 Griffin Rd West Branch (48661) ***(G-18324)***
American Thermographers....248 398-3810
291 E 12 Mile Rd Madison Heights (48071) ***(G-10668)***
American Tool & Gage Inc....313 587-7923
26312 Susan St Taylor (48180) ***(G-16377)***
American Tooling Center Inc....517 522-8411
705 E Oakland Ave Lansing (48906) ***(G-9672)***
American Tooling Center Inc....517 522-8411
11505 Elm St Jackson (49202) ***(G-8815)***
American Tooling Center Inc (PA)....517 522-8411
4111 Mount Hope Rd Grass Lake (49240) ***(G-7435)***
American Trading International, Grand Rapids *Also called Sunhill America LLC* ***(G-7234)***
American Trim....269 281-0651
1010 Main St Saint Joseph (49085) ***(G-14923)***
American Twisting Company (PA)....269 637-8581
1675 Stieve Dr South Haven (49090) ***(G-15398)***
American Undercar....989 235-1427
10099 E Stanton Rd Crystal (48818) ***(G-3740)***
American Vault Service (PA)....989 366-8657
2063 Norway Ln Prudenville (48651) ***(G-13655)***
American Vintners LLC....248 310-0575
612 W University Dr # 200 Rochester (48307) ***(G-13891)***
American Wireline Services Inc....231 218-6849
820 Duell Rd Traverse City (49686) ***(G-16601)***
American Wldg & Press Repr Inc....248 358-2050
26500 W 8 Mile Rd Southfield (48033) ***(G-15486)***
American Wood Moldings LLC....586 726-9050
52976 Van Dyke Ave Shelby Township (48316) ***(G-15169)***
Americana Manufacturing Co....248 505-3277
1672 Morris Rd Lapeer (48446) ***(G-9912)***
Americandiecast Releasants....810 714-1964
2040 W Thompson Rd Fenton (48430) ***(G-5450)***
Americanlubricationcom....586 219-9119
45790 Meadows Cir W Macomb (48044) ***(G-10576)***
Americas Finest Prtg Graphics (PA)....586 296-1312
17060 Masonic Ste 101 Fraser (48026) ***(G-5893)***
Americast LLC....989 681-4800
107 Enterprize Dr Saint Louis (48880) ***(G-14985)***
Americhip International Inc....586 783-4598
24700 Capital Blvd Clinton Township (48036) ***(G-3167)***
Americo Corporation....313 565-6550
25120 Trowbridge St Dearborn (48124) ***(G-3807)***
Ameriform Acquisition Co LLC....231 733-2725
2619 Bond St Rochester Hills (48309) ***(G-13947)***
Amerikam Inc....616 243-5833
1337 Judd Ave Sw Grand Rapids (49509) ***(G-6457)***
Ameripave....843 509-5502
5931 Panam St Romulus (48174) ***(G-14248)***
Ameriplastic Imprinting Co, Flint *Also called Rodzina Industries Inc* ***(G-5755)***
Ameristeel Inc....586 585-5250
33900 Doreka Fraser (48026) ***(G-5894)***
Ameritronix Inc....724 956-2356
777 Kings Way Canton (48188) ***(G-2434)***
Amerivet Engineering LLC....269 751-9092
3146 53rd St Hamilton (49419) ***(G-7596)***
Amerivet Services LLC....810 299-3095
12795 Silver Lake Rd Brighton (48116) ***(G-1945)***
Amery Tape & Label Co Inc....586 759-3230
4145 E 10 Mile Rd Warren (48091) ***(G-17704)***
Amesite Inc (PA)....734 876-8141
607 Shelby St Ste 700 Detroit (48226) ***(G-4015)***
Ametek Inc....248 362-2777
6380 Brockway Rd Peck (48466) ***(G-12960)***
Ametek Inc....248 435-7540
6380 Brockway Rd Peck (48466) ***(G-12961)***
Ametek Automtn & Process Tech, Peck *Also called Ametek Inc* ***(G-12961)***
Ametek Patriot Sensors, Peck *Also called Patriot Sensors & Contrls Corp* ***(G-12962)***
Ametek-APT, Peck *Also called Patriot Sensors & Contrls Corp* ***(G-12963)***
Amex Mfg & Distrg Co Inc....734 439-8560
640 Ash St Milan (48160) ***(G-11430)***
Amhawk LLC....269 468-4141
236 N West St Coloma (49038) ***(G-3474)***
Amhawk LLC (PA)....269 468-4177
200 Dunbar St Hartford (49057) ***(G-7761)***
AMI Industries Inc (PA)....989 786-3755
5093 N Red Oak Rd Lewiston (49756) ***(G-10017)***
AMI Industries Inc....989 786-3755
1351 Industrial Park Dr Sault Sainte Marie (49783) ***(G-15086)***
AMI Livonia LLC....734 428-3132
36930 Industrial Rd Livonia (48150) ***(G-10117)***
Amicus Software....313 417-9550
11231 Sugden Lake Rd White Lake (48386) ***(G-18449)***
Amigo Mobility Intl Inc (PA)....989 777-0910
6693 Dixie Hwy Bridgeport (48722) ***(G-1914)***
Amish Country Cheese, Linwood *Also called Williams Cheese Co* ***(G-10075)***
Amjs Incorporated....
828 S Main St Lawton (49065) ***(G-9987)***
Amk Automation Corp....804 348-2125
500 Woodward Ave Ste 4000 Detroit (48226) ***(G-4016)***
Amk Enterprise LLC....248 977-3039
3575 Pontiac Lake Rd Waterford (48328) ***(G-18099)***
Amk Enterprise LLC....248 564-2549
201 N Squirrel Rd Auburn Hills (48326) ***(G-783)***
Amk Ironworks....248 620-9027
5543 Chickadee Ln Clarkston (48346) ***(G-3016)***
Ammex Plastics, Monroe *Also called Echo Engrg & Prod Sups Inc* ***(G-11538)***
Amneon Acquisitions LLC....616 895-6640
199 E 17th St Holland (49423) ***(G-7965)***
Among Friends LLC....734 997-9720
191 Orchard Hills Ct Ann Arbor (48104) ***(G-365)***
Among Friends Baking Mixes, Ann Arbor *Also called Among Friends LLC* ***(G-365)***
Amor Imagepro, Manistee *Also called Amor Sign Studios Inc* ***(G-10893)***
Amor Sign Studios Inc....231 723-8361
443 Water St Manistee (49660) ***(G-10893)***
Amos Mfg Inc....989 358-7187
3490 Us Highway 23 N Alpena (49707) ***(G-278)***
Amour Your Body LLC....586 846-3100
16518 Festian Dr Clinton Township (48035) ***(G-3168)***
AMP Innovative Tech LLC....586 465-2700
42050 Executive Dr Harrison Township (48045) ***(G-7686)***
Amped Electric LLC....419 436-1818
5384 Silverton Dr Grand Blanc (48439) ***(G-6232)***
Amphenol Borisch Tech Inc (HQ)....616 554-9820
4511 East Paris Ave Se Grand Rapids (49512) ***(G-6458)***
Amphenol Corporation....586 465-3131
44724 Morley Dr Clinton Township (48036) ***(G-3169)***
Amphenol Saa, Brighton *Also called Amphenol T&M Antennas Inc* ***(G-1946)***
Amphenol Sine Systems, Clinton Township *Also called Amphenol Corporation* ***(G-3169)***
Amphenol T&M Antennas Inc....847 478-5600
7117 Fieldcrest Dr Brighton (48116) ***(G-1946)***
Amplas Compounding LLC....586 795-2555
6675 Sterling Dr N Sterling Heights (48312) ***(G-15931)***
Ampm Inc....989 837-8800
7403 W Wackerly St Midland (48642) ***(G-11321)***
Amptech Inc (HQ)....231 464-5492
201 Glocheski Dr Manistee (49660) ***(G-10894)***
Amrican Petro Inc....313 520-8404
9210 Freeland St Detroit (48228) ***(G-4017)***
AMS America, Troy *Also called AMS Co Ltd* ***(G-16935)***
AMS Co Ltd....248 712-4435
3221 W Big Beaver Rd # 117 Troy (48084) ***(G-16935)***
Amsa, Auburn *Also called Antimicrobial Specialist Assoc* ***(G-763)***
Amsco Champion LLC....734 728-8500
6775 Brandt St Romulus (48174) ***(G-14249)***
Amsted Rail Company Inc....517 568-4161
124 W Platt St Homer (49245) ***(G-8344)***
Amtex Inc....586 792-7888
34680 Nova Dr Clinton Township (48035) ***(G-3170)***
Amtrade Systems Inc....734 522-9500
12885 Wayne Rd Livonia (48150) ***(G-10118)***
Amway, Ada *Also called Alticor Inc* ***(G-6)***
Amway International Dev Inc (HQ)....616 787-6000
7575 Fulton St E Ada (49301) ***(G-7)***
Amway International Inc (HQ)....616 787-1000
7575 Fulton St E Ada (49355) ***(G-8)***
Amx Corp....469 624-8000
38780 Hartwell Dr Sterling Heights (48312) ***(G-15932)***
Amys Baking Company....313 530-9694
6399 Muirfield Dr Bloomfield Hills (48301) ***(G-1797)***

ALPHABETIC

An Andronaco Industries Co, Grand Rapids   ALPHABETIC SECTION

An Andronaco Industries Co, Grand Rapids *Also called Conley Composites LLC* **(G-6594)**
An Andronaco Industries Co, Kentwood *Also called Polyvalve LLC* **(G-9472)**
Ana Fuel Inc 810 422-5659
   2759 Seminole Rd Ann Arbor (48108) **(G-366)**
Analytical Process Systems Inc 248 393-0700
   1771 Harmon Rd Ste 100 Auburn Hills (48326) **(G-784)**
Anand Nvh North America Inc 810 724-2400
   2083 Reek Rd Imlay City (48444) **(G-8627)**
Anantics, Livonia *Also called Superior Information Tech LLC* **(G-10424)**
Anayas Pallets & Transport Inc 313 843-6570
   163 Morrell St Detroit (48209) **(G-4018)**
Anbo Tool & Manufacturing Inc 586 465-7610
   22785 Macomb Indus Dr Clinton Township (48036) **(G-3171)**
Anbren Inc 269 944-5066
   1025 Point O Woods Dr Benton Harbor (49022) **(G-1529)**
Ancast Inc 269 927-1985
   3194 Townline Rd Sodus (49126) **(G-15392)**
Anchor Bay Fab 586 231-0295
   50545 Metzen Dr Chesterfield (48051) **(G-2839)**
Anchor Bay Manufacturing Corp 586 949-1195
   50900 E Russell Schmidt Chesterfield (48051) **(G-2840)**
Anchor Bay Manufacturing Corp (PA) 586 949-4040
   30905 23 Mile Rd Chesterfield (48047) **(G-2841)**
Anchor Bay Packaging Corp (PA) 586 949-4040
   30905 23 Mile Rd Chesterfield (48047) **(G-2842)**
Anchor Bay Packaging Corp 586 949-1500
   30871 23 Mile Rd Chesterfield (48047) **(G-2843)**
Anchor Bay Powder Coat LLC 586 725-3255
   51469 Birch St New Baltimore (48047) **(G-11978)**
Anchor Bay Tackle, Pickford *Also called Wilderness Treasures* **(G-13032)**
Anchor Conveyor Products Inc 313 582-5045
   6830 Kingsley St Dearborn (48126) **(G-3808)**
Anchor Coupling Inc (HQ) 906 863-2672
   5520 13th St Menominee (49858) **(G-11225)**
Anchor Danly, Farmington Hills *Also called Lamina Inc* **(G-5289)**
Anchor Danly Inc 989 875-5400
   255 Indtl Pkwy Ithaca (48847) **(G-8786)**
Anchor Die Supply, Bellaire *Also called Anchor Lamina America Inc* **(G-1469)**
Anchor Flexible Packg & Label, Novi *Also called Anchor Printing Company* **(G-12362)**
Anchor Lamina America Inc 231 533-8646
   3650 S Derenzy Rd Bellaire (49615) **(G-1468)**
Anchor Lamina America Inc (HQ) 248 489-9122
   3650 S Derenzy Rd Bellaire (49615) **(G-1469)**
Anchor Printing Company 248 335-7440
   22790 Heslip Dr Novi (48375) **(G-12362)**
Anchor Recycling Inc 810 984-5545
   2829 Goulden St Port Huron (48060) **(G-13439)**
Anchor Wiping Cloth Inc 313 892-4000
   3855 E Outer Dr Detroit (48234) **(G-4019)**
Ancor Information MGT LLC (PA) 248 740-8866
   1911 Woodslee Dr Troy (48083) **(G-16936)**
Anders University Lithotech, Berrien Springs *Also called Lithotech* **(G-1644)**
Andersen Boat Works 616 836-2502
   815 Wells St South Haven (49090) **(G-15399)**
Andersen Corporation 734 237-1052
   37720 Amrhein Rd Livonia (48150) **(G-10119)**
Andersen Eye Prosthetics LLC 989 249-1030
   4719 Saint Antoine St Detroit (48201) **(G-4020)**
Anderson Brazing Co Inc 248 399-5155
   1544 E 11 Mile Rd Madison Heights (48071) **(G-10669)**
Anderson Cook Machine Tool, Fraser *Also called Anderson-Cook Inc* **(G-5895)**
Anderson Development Company 517 263-2121
   1415 E Michigan St Adrian (49221) **(G-53)**
Anderson Global Inc 231 733-2164
   500 W Sherman Blvd Muskegon (49444) **(G-11771)**
Anderson Manufacturing Co Inc (PA) 906 863-8223
   5300 13th St Menominee (49858) **(G-11226)**
Anderson Process, Plymouth *Also called AA Anderson & Co Inc* **(G-13110)**
Anderson Screen Printing, Newaygo *Also called Michael Anderson* **(G-12088)**
Anderson Technologies, Grand Haven *Also called Holland Plastics Corporation* **(G-6318)**
Anderson Welding & Mfg Inc 906 523-4661
   301 W Edwards Ave Houghton (49931) **(G-8380)**
Anderson-Cook Inc (PA) 586 954-0700
   50550 E Rssell Schmidt Bl Chesterfield (48051) **(G-2844)**
Anderson-Cook Inc 586 293-0800
   17650 15 Mile Rd Fraser (48026) **(G-5895)**
Andersons Inc 989 642-5291
   485 S Hemlock Rd Hemlock (48626) **(G-7849)**
Anderton Equity LLC (PA) 248 430-6650
   3001 W Big Beaver Rd # 310 Troy (48084) **(G-16937)**
Anderton Machining LLC 517 905-5155
   2400 Enterprise St Ste 1 Jackson (49203) **(G-8816)**
Andex Industries Inc 906 786-7588
   2300 20th Ave N Escanaba (49829) **(G-5056)**
Andex Laser Inc 734 947-9840
   12222 Universal Dr Taylor (48180) **(G-16378)**
Andex Printing Division, Escanaba *Also called Andex Industries Inc* **(G-5056)**

Andoor Craftmaster 989 672-2020
   3521 Lobdell Rd Caro (48723) **(G-2565)**
Andretta & Associates Inc 586 557-6226
   48945 Austrian Pine Dr Macomb (48044) **(G-10577)**
Andrew J Reisterer D D S Pllc 231 845-8989
   902 E Ludington Ave Ludington (49431) **(G-10526)**
Andritz Metals USA Inc 248 305-2969
   26800 Meadowbrook Rd Novi (48377) **(G-12363)**
Android Indstrs-Dlta Twnship L 517 322-0657
   2051 S Canal Rd Lansing (48917) **(G-9755)**
Android Indstrs-Shreveport LLC 248 454-0500
   2155 Executive Hills Dr Auburn Hills (48326) **(G-785)**
Android Industries-Sterling (HQ) 586 486-5616
   27767 George Merrelli Dr Warren (48092) **(G-17705)**
Android Industries-Wixom LLC 248 255-5434
   50150 Ryan Rd Shelby Township (48317) **(G-15170)**
Android Industries-Wixom LLC (HQ) 248 732-0000
   4444 W Maple Dr Auburn Hills (48326) **(G-786)**
Andronaco Inc (PA) 616 554-4600
   4855 Broadmoor Ave Se Kentwood (49512) **(G-9442)**
Angel Affects Candles LLC 313 288-6899
   16250 Stansbury St Detroit (48235) **(G-4021)**
Angel Embroidery 517 515-4836
   9100 Deer Run Dr Eaton Rapids (48827) **(G-4951)**
Angel Kisses Inc 248 219-8577
   513 Allen St Ferndale (48220) **(G-5526)**
Angela's Book Shelf, Ithaca *Also called A B Publishing Inc* **(G-8784)**
Angelos Crushed Concrete Inc (PA) 586 756-1070
   26300 Sherwood Ave Warren (48091) **(G-17706)**
Angels of Detroit LLC 248 796-1079
   7741 Lamphere Redford (48239) **(G-13714)**
Angler Strategies LLC 248 439-1420
   2815 Benjamin Ave Royal Oak (48073) **(G-14508)**
Angstrom Aluminum Castings LLC 616 309-1208
   3559 Kraft Ave Se Grand Rapids (49512) **(G-6459)**
Angstrom Automotive Group LLC 248 627-2871
   85 Myron St Ortonville (48462) **(G-12741)**
Angstrom Automotive Group LLC (PA) 734 756-1164
   2000 Town Ctr Ste 100 Southfield (48075) **(G-15487)**
Angstrom USA LLC (HQ) 313 295-0100
   2000 Town Ctr Ste 1100 Southfield (48075) **(G-15488)**
Anh Enterprises LLC (PA) 313 887-0800
   21538 Goddard Rd Taylor (48180) **(G-16379)**
Animo Games LLC 586 201-9699
   864 Rambling Dr Rochester Hills (48307) **(G-13948)**
Anitom Automation LLC 517 278-6205
   349 S Clay St Coldwater (49036) **(G-3419)**
Anjun America Inc 248 680-8825
   2735 Paldan Dr Auburn Hills (48326) **(G-787)**
Ankara Industries Incorporated 586 749-1190
   56359 N Bay Dr Chesterfield (48051) **(G-2845)**
Ann Arbor Chronicle 734 645-2633
   330 Mulholland Ave Ann Arbor (48103) **(G-367)**
Ann Arbor Gear, Howell *Also called AA Gear LLC* **(G-8424)**
Ann Arbor Journal 734 429-7380
   106 W Michigan Ave Saline (48176) **(G-15002)**
Ann Arbor News, Grand Rapids *Also called Herald Newspapers Company Inc* **(G-6811)**
Ann Arbor News, The, Ann Arbor *Also called Herald Newspapers Company Inc* **(G-513)**
Ann Arbor Observer Company 734 769-3175
   2390 Winewood Ave Ann Arbor (48103) **(G-368)**
Ann Arbor Offset 734 926-4500
   5690 Hines Dr Ann Arbor (48108) **(G-369)**
Ann Arbor Plastics Inc 734 944-0800
   815 Woodland Dr Saline (48176) **(G-15003)**
Ann Arbor Stainless 734 741-9499
   1123 Pontiac Trl Ann Arbor (48105) **(G-370)**
Ann Barrette 586 713-8145
   44381 Manitou Dr Clinton Township (48038) **(G-3172)**
Ann Williams Group LLC 248 977-5831
   784 Industrial Ct Bloomfield Hills (48302) **(G-1798)**
Annalux Candles LLC 313 566-3289
   1546 Park Village Blvd Taylor (48180) **(G-16380)**
Annas Kitchen LLC 248 499-4774
   17910 Van Dyke St Detroit (48234) **(G-4022)**
Annes Canvas 248 623-3443
   1081 Airport Rd Waterford (48327) **(G-18100)**
Annieraerv Co 517 669-4103
   13200 S Us Highway 27 Dewitt (48820) **(G-4705)**
Ano-Kal Company 269 685-5743
   734 Jersey St Plainwell (49080) **(G-13070)**
Anrod Screen Cylinder Company 989 872-2101
   6160 Garfield Ave Cass City (48726) **(G-2610)**
Anroid Industries Inc 248 732-0000
   2155 Executive Hills Dr Auburn Hills (48326) **(G-788)**
Ansco Pattern & Machine Co 248 625-1362
   7945 Perry Lake Rd Clarkston (48348) **(G-3017)**
Anso Products 248 357-2300
   21380 Telegraph Rd Southfield (48033) **(G-15489)**
Ansys Inc 248 613-2677
   2805 S Industrial Hwy # 100 Ann Arbor (48104) **(G-371)**

ALPHABETIC SECTION

Antara Systems LLC 616 895-7766
   5375 Edgeway Dr Allendale (49401) *(G-214)*
Antech Tool Inc 734 207-3622
   7553 Baron Dr Canton (48187) *(G-2435)*
Anteebo Publishers Inc 313 882-6900
   16980 Kercheval Pl Grosse Pointe Park (48230) *(G-7546)*
Antells Custom Cabinetry 616 318-8637
   2581 Maguire Ave Ne Grand Rapids (49525) *(G-6460)*
Anterior Quest, Jenison *Also called Fabri-Tech Inc* *(G-9055)*
Anthony and Company 906 786-7573
   1503 N 23rd St Escanaba (49829) *(G-5057)*
Anthony Castellani 248 579-3406
   7025 Fay Dr Van Buren Twp (48111) *(G-17509)*
Anticipated Plastics Inc 586 427-9450
   24392 Gibson Dr Warren (48089) *(G-17707)*
Antilla Logging Inc 906 376-2374
   7794 State Highway M95 Republic (49879) *(G-13819)*
Antimicrobial Specialist Assoc 989 662-0377
   4714 Garfield Rd Auburn (48611) *(G-763)*
Antique Botl & GL Collectr LLC 248 486-0530
   28465 Coyote Ct New Hudson (48165) *(G-12042)*
Antolin Interiors Usa Inc (HQ) 248 373-1749
   1700 Atlantic Blvd Auburn Hills (48326) *(G-789)*
Antolin Interiors Usa Inc 517 548-0052
   3705 W Grand River Ave Howell (48855) *(G-8429)*
Antolin Interiors Usa Inc 248 567-4000
   600 Wilshire Dr Troy (48084) *(G-16938)*
Antolin Sprtnburg Assembly LLC (HQ) 248 373-1749
   1700 Atlantic Blvd Auburn Hills (48326) *(G-790)*
Antolin St Clair LLC 810 329-1045
   4662 Puttygut Rd China (48054) *(G-2968)*
Antonios Leather Experts 734 762-5000
   12409 Stark Rd Livonia (48150) *(G-10120)*
Antrim Machine Products Inc 231 587-9114
   9142 Johnson Rd Mancelona (49659) *(G-10866)*
Antrim Review 231 533-5651
   4470 S M 88 Hwy Bellaire (49615) *(G-1470)*
Anywhere Welding 906 250-7217
   N3550 Et Rd Trenary (49891) *(G-16883)*
AP Impressions Inc (PA) 734 464-8009
   17360 N Laurel Park Dr Livonia (48152) *(G-10121)*
AP Southridge, Livonia *Also called Applied Process Inc* *(G-10122)*
Apb Inc 248 528-2990
   3334 Rochester Rd Troy (48083) *(G-16939)*
Apec, Lake Odessa *Also called Automated Process Equipment* *(G-9572)*
Apem Solutions LLC 616 848-5393
   2508 Hufford Ave Nw Grand Rapids (49544) *(G-6461)*
Aperion Information Tech Inc (PA) 248 969-9791
   144 S Washington St Oxford (48371) *(G-12874)*
Apex Apparel LLC 248 915-1073
   22413 Lyndon St Detroit (48223) *(G-4023)*
Apex Broaching Systems Inc 586 758-2626
   22862 Hoover Rd Warren (48089) *(G-17708)*
Apex Competition Engines 616 761-4010
   119 E South Cnty Line Rd Fenwick (48834) *(G-5516)*
Apex Dental Milling, Ann Arbor *Also called Adcaa LLC* *(G-352)*
Apex Marine Inc 989 681-4300
   300 Woodside Dr Saint Louis (48880) *(G-14986)*
Apex Powder Coating LLC 734 921-3177
   27258 Wick Rd Taylor (48180) *(G-16381)*
Apex Rack and Coating Co 616 530-6811
   3434 Busch Dr Sw Grandville (49418) *(G-7365)*
Apex Spring & Stamping Corp 616 453-5463
   11420 1st Ave Nw Grand Rapids (49534) *(G-6462)*
Apex Tooling Solutions LLC 616 283-7439
   6854 Valley View Ave Jenison (49428) *(G-9044)*
Apg - Spclty Vlve McHined Pdts, Wyandotte *Also called Mercury Manufacturing Company* *(G-18833)*
Aphase II Inc (PA) 586 977-0790
   6120 Center Dr Sterling Heights (48312) *(G-15933)*
API / Inmet Inc 734 426-5553
   300 Dino Dr Ann Arbor (48103) *(G-372)*
API Plan Design Build, Waterford *Also called Architectural Planners Inc* *(G-18101)*
API Promotional Products, Armada *Also called Armada Printwear Inc* *(G-730)*
Apis North America LLC 800 470-8970
   938 N Washington Ave Royal Oak (48067) *(G-14509)*
Apms Incorporated 248 268-1477
   31211 Stvnson Hwy Ste 100 Madison Heights (48071) *(G-10670)*
Apollo America Inc 248 332-3900
   25 Corporate Dr Auburn Hills (48326) *(G-791)*
Apollo Broach Inc 734 467-5750
   39001 Webb Ct Westland (48185) *(G-18354)*
Apollo E.D.M. Company, Fraser *Also called CDK Enterprises LLC* *(G-5912)*
Apollo Exploration Dev Inc 989 773-2854
   1710 E Remus Rd Mount Pleasant (48858) *(G-11680)*
Apollo Heat Treating Proc LLC 248 398-3434
   10400 Capital St Oak Park (48237) *(G-12591)*
Apollo Idemitsu Corporation 248 675-4345
   48325 Alpha Dr Ste 200 Wixom (48393) *(G-18608)*

Apollo Machining Inc 248 961-3943
   70 S Squirrel Rd Ste W Auburn Hills (48326) *(G-792)*
Apollo Plating Inc 586 777-0070
   15765 Sturgeon St Roseville (48066) *(G-14374)*
Apollo Seiko Ltd 269 465-3400
   3969 Lemon Creek Rd Bridgman (49106) *(G-1920)*
Apollo Tool & Engineering Inc 616 735-4934
   3020 Wilson Dr Nw Grand Rapids (49534) *(G-6463)*
Apollo Trick Titanium Inc 517 694-7449
   321 Elmwood Dr Troy (48083) *(G-16940)*
Apparel Manufacturer, Detroit *Also called Detroit Denim LLC* *(G-4143)*
Apparel Sales Inc 616 842-5650
   2712 Edward St Ste A Jenison (49428) *(G-9045)*
Apparelmaster-Muskegon Inc 231 728-5406
   341 E Apple Ave Muskegon (49442) *(G-11772)*
Appgraft LLC 734 546-8458
   435 Innsbrook Dr Canton (48188) *(G-2436)*
Applause Inc 517 485-9880
   1655 Tuscany Ln Holt (48842) *(G-8303)*
Apple Blossom Winery LLC 269 668-3724
   6970 Texas Dr Kalamazoo (49009) *(G-9114)*
Apple Fence Co 231 276-9888
   1893 Pine Tree Grawn (49637) *(G-7449)*
Apple Quest Inc 616 299-4834
   1380 Coolidge St Conklin (49403) *(G-3659)*
Apple Valley Natural Foods (PA) 269 471-3234
   9067 Us Highway 31 Ofc A Berrien Springs (49103) *(G-1637)*
Applegate Insul Systems Inc (PA) 517 521-3545
   1000 Highview Dr Webberville (48892) *(G-18241)*
Application Specialists Co, Lansing *Also called Appliction Spclist Kompany Inc* *(G-9805)*
Appliction Spclist Kompany Inc 517 676-6633
   316 Moores River Dr Lansing (48910) *(G-9805)*
Applied & Integrated Mfg Inc 248 370-8950
   691 N Squirrel Rd 119 Auburn Hills (48326) *(G-793)*
Applied Automation Tech Inc 248 656-4930
   1688 Star Batt Dr Rochester Hills (48309) *(G-13949)*
Applied Coatings Solutions LLC 269 341-9757
   1830 Reed Ave Kalamazoo (49001) *(G-9115)*
Applied Computer Technologies 248 388-0211
   4301 Orchard Lake Rd # 160 West Bloomfield (48323) *(G-18263)*
Applied Electronics Group, Ann Arbor *Also called Tecumseh Products Company LLC* *(G-678)*
Applied Genomics 313 458-7318
   702 Middlesex Rd Grosse Pointe Park (48230) *(G-7547)*
Applied Graphics & Fabricating 989 662-3334
   1994 W Midland Rd Auburn (48611) *(G-764)*
Applied Imaging, Grand Rapids *Also called Lowery Corporation* *(G-6949)*
Applied Mechanics Corporation 616 677-1355
   14122 Ironwood Dr Nw Grand Rapids (49534) *(G-6464)*
Applied Molecules LLC 810 355-1475
   7275 Joy Rd Ste D Dexter (48130) *(G-4724)*
Applied Process Inc (HQ) 734 464-8000
   12202 Newburgh Rd Livonia (48150) *(G-10122)*
Applied Synergistics Inc 248 634-0151
   926 Running Brook Dr Holly (48442) *(G-8261)*
Applied Tech Industries, Chesterfield *Also called Kalb & Associates Inc* *(G-2899)*
Applied Visual Concepts LLC 866 440-6888
   24680 Mound Rd Warren (48091) *(G-17709)*
Apply Prssure MBL Dtailing LLC 248 794-7710
   11360 Garfield Redford (48239) *(G-13715)*
Appropos Digital, Grand Rapids *Also called Appropos LLC* *(G-6465)*
Appropos LLC 844 462-7776
   678 Front Ave Nw Ste 100 Grand Rapids (49504) *(G-6465)*
Approved Aircraft Accessories 734 946-9000
   29300 Goddard Rd Romulus (48174) *(G-14250)*
Aprotech Powertrain LLC (PA) 248 649-9200
   2150 Butterfield Dr Troy (48084) *(G-16941)*
APS Compounding LLC 734 710-6702
   30735 Cypress Rd Ste 400 Romulus (48174) *(G-14251)*
APS Machine LLC 906 212-5600
   2501 Danforth Rd Escanaba (49829) *(G-5058)*
APT Division, Southfield *Also called Durr Systems Inc* *(G-15546)*
Aptargroup Inc 989 631-8030
   2202 Ridgewood Dr Midland (48642) *(G-11322)*
Aptiv Corporation (HQ) 248 813-2000
   5725 Innovation Dr Troy (48098) *(G-16942)*
Aptiv Corporation 248 724-5900
   2611 Superior Ct Auburn Hills (48326) *(G-794)*
Aptiv Corporation (HQ) 248 813-3005
   5820 Innovation Dr Troy (48098) *(G-16943)*
Aptiv Intl Svcs Co LLC 248 813-2000
   5820 Innovation Dr Troy (48098) *(G-16944)*
Aptiv Mexican Holdings US LLC (HQ) 248 813-2000
   5820 Innovation Dr Troy (48098) *(G-16945)*
Aptiv Services 3 (us) LLC 248 813-2000
   5725 Innovation Dr Troy (48098) *(G-16946)*
Aptiv Services 5 Us LLC 248 813-2000
   5820 Innovation Dr Troy (48098) *(G-16947)*

(PA)=Parent Co (HQ)=Headquarters (DH)=Div Headquarters

Aptiv Services Us LLC 810 459-8809
3000 University Dr Auburn Hills (48326) ***(G-795)***
Aptiv Services Us LLC 248 724-5900
2611 Superior Ct Auburn Hills (48326) ***(G-796)***
Aptiv Services Us LLC 248 813-2000
4254 Oak Meadow Dr Hudsonville (49426) ***(G-8567)***
Aptiv Services Us LLC 330 373-7666
5820 Innovation Dr Troy (48098) ***(G-16948)***
Aptiv Services Us LLC 248 813-2000
5725 Innovation Dr Troy (48098) ***(G-16949)***
Aptiv Trade MGT Svcs US LLC 248 813-2000
5820 Innovation Dr Troy (48098) ***(G-16950)***
Aqua Systems Inc 810 346-2525
7070 Enterprise Dr Brown City (48416) ***(G-2133)***
Aqua Tool LLC 248 307-1984
32360 Edward Ave Ste 100 Madison Heights (48071) ***(G-10671)***
Aquaprintingcom 269 779-2734
410 The Dells Kalamazoo (49048) ***(G-9116)***
Aquarich Water Treatment Pdts, Fraser *Also called Edrich Products Inc* ***(G-5922)***
Aquarius Recreational Products 586 469-4600
41201 Production Dr Harrison Township (48045) ***(G-7687)***
Aquatic Co 269 279-7461
888 W Broadway St Three Rivers (49093) ***(G-16564)***
Aqueous Orbital Systems LLC 269 501-7461
301 N 26th St Kalamazoo (49048) ***(G-9117)***
Aquest Machining & Assembly, Greenville *Also called Fabx Industries Inc* ***(G-7484)***
Aquila Resources Inc (PA) 906 352-4024
414 10th Ave Ste 1 Menominee (49858) ***(G-11227)***
Ar-Tee Enterprises LLC 989 433-5546
4131 E Rosebush Rd Rosebush (48878) ***(G-14366)***
Ar2 Engineering LLC 248 735-9999
26600 Heyn Dr Novi (48374) ***(G-12364)***
Arab American News Inc 313 582-4888
5706 Chase Rd Dearborn (48126) ***(G-3809)***
Aras Corp 248 385-5293
3290 W Big Beaver Rd # 315 Troy (48084) ***(G-16951)***
Arauco North America Inc 800 261-4896
5851 Arauco Rd Grayling (49738) ***(G-7456)***
Araymond Mfg Ctr N Amer Inc 248 537-3147
2900 Technology Dr Rochester Hills (48309) ***(G-13950)***
Arboc Ltd (PA) 248 684-2895
3504 Car Dr Commerce Township (48382) ***(G-3511)***
Arbor Assays Inc 734 677-1774
1514 Eisenhower Pl Ann Arbor (48108) ***(G-373)***
Arbor Fabricating LLC 734 626-5864
14030 Tuttlehill Rd Milan (48160) ***(G-11431)***
Arbor Gage & Tooling Inc 616 454-8266
2031 Calvin Ave Se Grand Rapids (49507) ***(G-6466)***
Arbor International Inc 734 761-5200
143 Enterprise Dr Ann Arbor (48103) ***(G-374)***
Arbor Kitchen LLC 248 921-4602
124 W Summit St Ste B Ann Arbor (48103) ***(G-375)***
Arbor Operating LLC 231 941-2237
333 W Grandview Pkwy # 401 Traverse City (49684) ***(G-16602)***
Arbor Plastic Technologies LLC 734 678-5765
40900 Woodward Ave # 275 Bloomfield Hills (48304) ***(G-1799)***
Arbor Press LLC 248 549-0150
4303 Normandy Ct Royal Oak (48073) ***(G-14510)***
Arbor Springs Water Company (PA) 734 668-8270
1440 Plymouth Rd Ann Arbor (48105) ***(G-376)***
Arbormetrix Inc 734 661-7944
339 E Liberty St Ste 210 Ann Arbor (48104) ***(G-377)***
Arboroakland Group, Royal Oak *Also called Arbor Press LLC* ***(G-14510)***
Arbortext Inc (HQ) 734 997-0200
3767 Ranchero Dr Ste 100 Ann Arbor (48108) ***(G-378)***
Arbre Farms Corporation 231 873-3337
6362 N 192nd Ave Walkerville (49459) ***(G-17658)***
ARC Archer LLC 616 439-3014
380 W Muskegon St Kent City (49330) ***(G-9426)***
ARC Group Worldwide Inc 517 448-8954
4111 Munson Hwy Hudson (49247) ***(G-8547)***
ARC Metal Stamping LLC 517 448-8954
4111 Munson Hwy Hudson (49247) ***(G-8548)***
ARC Mit 248 399-4800
660 E 10 Mile Rd Ferndale (48220) ***(G-5527)***
ARC On Mobile Welding LLC 734 344-7128
7875 Forrestway Dr Monroe (48161) ***(G-11524)***
ARC Print Solutions LLC 248 917-7052
19625 Riverside Dr Beverly Hills (48025) ***(G-1661)***
ARC Rite Welding LLC 989 545-8006
606 N Elevator Rd Linwood (48634) ***(G-10073)***
ARC Services of Macomb Inc 586 469-1600
44050 N Gratiot Ave Clinton Township (48036) ***(G-3173)***
ARC-Kecy LLC 517 448-8954
4111 Munson Hwy Hudson (49247) ***(G-8549)***
Arcanum Alloys Inc 312 810-4479
4460 44th St Se Ste F Kentwood (49512) ***(G-9443)***
Arcanum Steel Technologies Inc 630 715-4899
265 Auburn Ave Se Grand Rapids (49506) ***(G-6467)***
Arcelrmttal Tlred Blnks Amrcas 313 332-5300
8650 Mount Elliott St Detroit (48211) ***(G-4024)***
Arch Cutting Tools LLC (PA) 734 266-6900
2600 S Telegraph Rd Bloomfield Hills (48302) ***(G-1800)***
Arch Med Sltons Lehigh Vly LLC (HQ) 603 760-1554
25040 Easy St Warren (48089) ***(G-17710)***
Arch Medical Solutions Corp (PA) 603 760-1554
25040 Easy St Warren (48089) ***(G-17711)***
Arch Precision Components (HQ) 866 935-5771
2600 S Telg Rd Ste 180 Bloomfield Hills (48302) ***(G-1801)***
Archangel's Jewelry, Warren *Also called Novus Corporation* ***(G-17948)***
Archer Record Pressing Co 313 365-9545
7401 E Davison St Detroit (48212) ***(G-4025)***
Archer-Daniels-Midland Company 269 968-2900
436 Porter St Unit F2 Battle Creek (49014) ***(G-1185)***
Archer-Daniels-Midland Company 517 627-4017
16994 Wright Rd Grand Ledge (48837) ***(G-6385)***
Archer-Daniels-Midland Company 517 647-4155
401 E Grand River Ave Portland (48875) ***(G-13637)***
Architectural Door & Mllwk Inc 248 442-9222
30150 S Hill Rd New Hudson (48165) ***(G-12043)***
Architectural Glass & Mtls Inc (PA) 269 375-6165
604 S 8th St Kalamazoo (49009) ***(G-9118)***
Architectural Model Studios, Ferndale *Also called Zoyes East Inc* ***(G-5599)***
Architectural Planners Inc 248 674-1340
5101 Williams Lake Rd Waterford (48329) ***(G-18101)***
Architectural Products Inc 248 585-8272
4850 Coolidge Hwy Unit B Royal Oak (48073) ***(G-14511)***
Architectural Trim & Wdwrk LLC 586 321-1860
15003 Totten Pl Shelby Township (48315) ***(G-15171)***
Architrave Woodworking, Waterford *Also called L E Q Inc* ***(G-18132)***
Arco Alloys Corp 313 871-2680
1891 Trombly St Detroit (48211) ***(G-4026)***
Arcon Vernova Inc 734 904-1895
271 Old Creek Dr Saline (48176) ***(G-15004)***
Arconic 231 894-7802
1600 Warner St Whitehall (49461) ***(G-18491)***
Arconic Automotive Castings 248 489-4900
37000 W 12 Mile Rd Ste 11 Farmington Hills (48331) ***(G-5171)***
Arconic Corporation 248 489-4900
37000 W 12 Mile Rd Ste 11 Farmington Hills (48331) ***(G-5172)***
Arcosa Epi LLC 517 676-8800
685 Hull Rd Mason (48854) ***(G-11116)***
Arcosa Shoring Products Inc (HQ) 517 741-4300
8530 M 60 Union City (49094) ***(G-17490)***
Arcosa Shoring Products Inc 800 292-1225
4837 W Grand River Ave Lansing (48906) ***(G-9673)***
Arctech Precision Welding 517 614-5722
929 E Chicago Rd Quincy (49082) ***(G-13662)***
Arctel Corp 616 241-6001
4707 40th St Se Grand Rapids (49512) ***(G-6468)***
Arctic Glacier Grayling Inc 810 987-7100
1755 Yeager St Port Huron (48060) ***(G-13440)***
Arctic Glacier Inc 734 485-0430
1755 Yeager St Port Huron (48060) ***(G-13441)***
Arctic Glacier Newburgh Inc (HQ) 845 561-0549
1755 Yeager St Port Huron (48060) ***(G-13442)***
Arctic Glacier Texas Inc 517 999-3500
5635 Commerce St Ste B Lansing (48911) ***(G-9806)***
Arctic Glacier USA Inc 215 283-0326
1755 Yeager St Port Huron (48060) ***(G-13443)***
Arctic Glacier USA Inc 204 772-2473
1755 Yeager St Port Huron (48060) ***(G-13444)***
Arctic Glacier USA Inc 204 772-2473
1755 Yeager St Port Huron (48060) ***(G-13445)***
Arctic Glacier USA Inc 204 772-2473
1755 Yeager St Port Huron (48060) ***(G-13446)***
Arctic Glacier USA Inc 204 772-2473
1755 Yeager St Port Huron (48060) ***(G-13447)***
Arctic Glacier USA Inc 204 772-2473
1755 Yeager St Port Huron (48060) ***(G-13448)***
Arctic Glacier USA Inc 204 772-2473
1755 Yeager St Port Huron (48060) ***(G-13449)***
Arctic Glacier USA Inc 204 772-2473
1755 Yeager St Port Huron (48060) ***(G-13450)***
Arctic Glacier USA Inc 204 772-2473
1755 Yeager St Port Huron (48060) ***(G-13451)***
Arctic Glacier USA Inc 204 772-2473
1755 Yeager St Port Huron (48060) ***(G-13452)***
Arctic Glacier USA Inc 204 772-2473
1755 Yeager St Port Huron (48060) ***(G-13453)***
Arctic Glacier Wisconsin Inc 262 345-6999
1755 Yeager St Port Huron (48060) ***(G-13454)***
Arctic Solutions Inc 586 331-2600
74100 Van Dyke Rd Bruce Twp (48065) ***(G-2163)***
Arctuition LLC 616 635-9959
8011 Thornapple Clb Dr Se Ada (49301) ***(G-9)***
Arcturian LLC 313 643-5326
3319 Greenfield Rd 423 Dearborn (48120) ***(G-3810)***

Arden Companies LLC (HQ) ... 248 415-8500
30400 Telg Rd Ste 200 Bingham Farms (48025) ***(G-1691)***

Arden-Benhar Mills, Bingham Farms *Also called Krams Enterprises Inc* ***(G-1702)***

Ardy Inc ... 231 845-7318
2999 S Palmer Blvd Ludington (49431) ***(G-10527)***

Are You Ready ... 616 935-1133
281 N 3rd Ave Fruitport (49415) ***(G-6058)***

Area Exteriors ... 248 544-0706
4075 Forest St Leonard (48367) ***(G-10001)***

Arete Industries Inc ... 231 582-4470
1 Altair Dr Boyne City (49712) ***(G-1882)***

Arete Industries Inc ... 248 352-7205
24001 Southfield Rd Southfield (48075) ***(G-15490)***

Arete Products & Mfg LLC ... 269 383-0015
2525 Miller Rd Kalamazoo (49001) ***(G-9119)***

Argent Automotive Systems, Plymouth *Also called Argent International Inc* ***(G-13124)***

Argent International Inc ... 734 582-9800
41016 Concept Dr Plymouth (48170) ***(G-13124)***

Argent Limited ... 734 427-5533
11966 Brookfield St Livonia (48150) ***(G-10123)***

Argent Tape & Label Inc (PA) ... 734 582-9956
41016 Concept Dr Ste A Plymouth (48170) ***(G-13125)***

Argent Tape & Label Inc ... 248 588-4600
37770 Amrhein Rd Livonia (48150) ***(G-10124)***

Argo Ai LLC ... 313 908-2447
17000 Federal Dr Allen Park (48101) ***(G-190)***

Argo Liquid, Saint Johns *Also called Cog Marketers Ltd* ***(G-14898)***

Argo Systems, Holland *Also called FSI Label Company* ***(G-8043)***

Argon & Tool Manufacturing Co, Madison Heights *Also called Argon Tool Inc* ***(G-10672)***

Argon Tool Inc ... 248 583-1605
32309 Milton Ave Madison Heights (48071) ***(G-10672)***

Argonics Inc (PA) ... 906 226-9747
520 9th St Gwinn (49841) ***(G-7580)***

Argonics Inc ... 303 664-9467
520 9th St Gwinn (49841) ***(G-7581)***

Argus Corporation (PA) ... 313 937-2900
12540 Beech Daly Rd Redford (48239) ***(G-13716)***

Argus Press Company ... 989 725-5136
201 E Exchange St Owosso (48867) ***(G-12824)***

Argus Technologies LLC ... 616 538-9895
560 5th St Nw Ste 100 Grand Rapids (49504) ***(G-6469)***

Argyle Socks LLC ... 269 615-0097
3800 Winding Way Kalamazoo (49004) ***(G-9120)***

Arhouzz, Kalkaska *Also called Woodland Creek Furniture Inc* ***(G-9412)***

Aria Furniture, Rochester Hills *Also called S & J Inc* ***(G-14104)***

Ariana Press Inc ... 313 885-7581
123 Cloverly Rd Grosse Pointe Farms (48236) ***(G-7534)***

Arin Inc ... 586 779-3410
29139 Calahan Rd Roseville (48066) ***(G-14375)***

Aristo Industries, Fraser *Also called Aristo-Cote Inc* ***(G-5896)***

Aristo Industries, Harrison Township *Also called Aristo-Cote Inc* ***(G-7688)***

Aristo-Cote Inc ... 586 447-9049
11655 Park Ct Shelby Township (48315) ***(G-15172)***

Aristo-Cote Inc ... 586 447-9049
32100 Groesbeck Hwy Fraser (48026) ***(G-5896)***

Aristo-Cote Inc (PA) ... 586 447-9049
24951 Henry B Joy Blvd Harrison Township (48045) ***(G-7688)***

Arizona Tooling Inc ... 810 533-8828
7964 Gratiot Ave Columbus (48063) ***(G-3496)***

Ark Industrial, Benton Harbor *Also called West Michigan Tool & Die Co* ***(G-1602)***

Ark Woodworks LLC ... 269 364-1397
2016 Lakeway Ave Kalamazoo (49001) ***(G-9121)***

Arkema Coating Resins, Grand Rapids *Also called Arkema Inc* ***(G-6470)***

Arkema Inc ... 616 243-4578
1415 Steele Ave Sw Grand Rapids (49507) ***(G-6470)***

ARL Service LLC ... 248 625-6160
10399 Enterprise Dr Davisburg (48350) ***(G-3757)***

Arlington Display Inds Inc ... 313 837-1212
19303 W Davison St Detroit (48223) ***(G-4027)***

Arlington Metals Corporation ... 269 426-3371
13100 Arlington Dr Sawyer (49125) ***(G-15106)***

Arm Fulfillment, Battle Creek *Also called Epi Printers Inc* ***(G-1227)***

Arm Tooling Systems Inc ... 586 759-5677
2453 John B Ave Warren (48091) ***(G-17712)***

Armada Grain Co (PA) ... 586 784-5911
73180 Fulton St Armada (48005) ***(G-729)***

Armada Printwear Inc ... 586 784-5553
74135 Church St Armada (48005) ***(G-730)***

Armada Rubber Manufacturing Co ... 586 784-9135
24586 Armada Ridge Rd Armada (48005) ***(G-731)***

Armaly Brands, Commerce Township *Also called Armaly Sponge Company* ***(G-3512)***

Armaly Sponge Company (PA) ... 248 669-2100
1900 Easy St Commerce Township (48390) ***(G-3512)***

Armartis Manufacturing Inc ... 248 308-9622
20815 Kraft Blvd Roseville (48066) ***(G-14376)***

Armi, Fowlerville *Also called Armoured Rsstnce McHanisms Inc* ***(G-5832)***

Armor Protective Packaging, Howell *Also called Sks Industries Inc* ***(G-8518)***

Armorclad ... 248 477-7785
24285 Indoplex Cir Farmington Hills (48335) ***(G-5173)***

Armored Group LLC ... 602 840-2271
2727 S Beech Daly St Dearborn Heights (48125) ***(G-3920)***

Armoured Rsstnce McHanisms Inc ... 517 223-7618
345 W Frank St Fowlerville (48836) ***(G-5832)***

Armstrong Display Concepts Inc ... 231 652-1675
480 S Industrial Dr Newaygo (49337) ***(G-12077)***

Armstrong Fluid Handling Inc ... 269 279-3600
221 Armstrong Blvd Three Rivers (49093) ***(G-16565)***

Armstrong Graphics, Milford *Also called A & F Enterprises Inc* ***(G-11453)***

Armstrong Hot Water Inc ... 269 278-1413
221 Armstrong Blvd Three Rivers (49093) ***(G-16566)***

Armstrong International Inc (PA) ... 269 273-1415
816 Maple St Three Rivers (49093) ***(G-16567)***

Armstrong Millworks Inc ... 248 887-1037
3039 W Highland Rd Highland (48357) ***(G-7881)***

Arnet's Memorials, Ann Arbor *Also called Arnets Inc* ***(G-379)***

Arnets Inc (PA) ... 734 665-3650
5060 Jackson Rd Ste H Ann Arbor (48103) ***(G-379)***

Arnold & Sautter Co (PA) ... 989 684-7557
408 N Euclid Ave Bay City (48706) ***(G-1322)***

Arnold Tool & Die Co (PA) ... 586 598-0099
48800 Structural Dr Chesterfield (48051) ***(G-2846)***

Arnt Asphalt Sealing Inc (PA) ... 269 927-1532
1240 S Crystal Ave Benton Harbor (49022) ***(G-1530)***

Aro Welding Technologies Inc ... 586 949-9353
48500 Structural Dr Chesterfield (48051) ***(G-2847)***

Aroma Taba ... 313 782-4076
10009 Joseph Campau St Hamtramck (48212) ***(G-7611)***

Arotech Corporation (PA) ... 800 281-0356
1229 Oak Valley Dr Ann Arbor (48108) ***(G-380)***

Arplas USA LLC ... 888 527-5553
1030 Chicago Rd Troy (48083) ***(G-16952)***

Arquette Concrete & Supply (PA) ... 989 846-4131
4374 Airpark Dr Standish (48658) ***(G-15887)***

Arrow Adtech Tool Co, Ray *Also called Omax Tool Products Inc* ***(G-13701)***

Arrow Automation and Engrg Inc ... 248 660-1520
4200 N Atlantic Blvd Auburn Hills (48326) ***(G-797)***

Arrow Chemical Products Inc ... 313 237-0277
2067 Sainte Anne St Detroit (48216) ***(G-4028)***

Arrow Die & Mold Repair ... 231 689-1829
8527 E Wilderness Trl White Cloud (49349) ***(G-18438)***

Arrow Motor & Pump Inc ... 734 285-7860
629 Cent St Wyandotte (48192) ***(G-18807)***

Arrow Sign Co ... 586 939-9966
13335 15 Mile Rd Sterling Hts (48312) ***(G-16235)***

Arrow Signs ... 989 350-4357
N975 Martin Lake Rd Saint Ignace (49781) ***(G-14894)***

Arrow Swift Printing, Hillsdale *Also called Rumler Brothers Inc* ***(G-7947)***

Arrow Swift Prtg & Copy Ctr, Greenville *Also called Knapp Printing Services Inc* ***(G-7497)***

Arrowhead Industries Inc ... 231 238-9366
1715 E M 68 Hwy Afton (49705) ***(G-106)***

Arrowhead Manufacturing ... 248 688-8939
1406 Woodsboro Dr Royal Oak (48067) ***(G-14512)***

Art & Image ... 800 566-4162
582 E Napier Ave Benton Harbor (49022) ***(G-1531)***

Art Box Design, Waterford *Also called Artbox Design Inc* ***(G-18102)***

Art Craft Display Inc (PA) ... 517 485-2221
500 Business Centre Dr Lansing (48917) ***(G-9756)***

Art Laser Inc ... 248 391-6600
4141 N Atlantic Blvd Auburn Hills (48326) ***(G-798)***

Art of Custom Framing Inc ... 248 435-3726
3863 Rochester Rd Troy (48083) ***(G-16953)***

Art of Shaving - Fl LLC ... 248 649-5872
2800 W Big Beavr Rd Fl 2 Troy (48084) ***(G-16954)***

Art Optical Contact Lens Inc ... 616 453-1888
3175 3 Mile Rd Nw Grand Rapids (49534) ***(G-6471)***

Art/Fx Sign Co ... 269 465-5706
9751 Red Arrow Hwy Bridgman (49106) ***(G-1921)***

Artbox Design Inc ... 248 461-2555
5085 Williams Lake Rd Si Waterford (48329) ***(G-18102)***

Artco Mfg, Livonia *Also called American Ring Manufacturing* ***(G-10115)***

Artcraft Pattern Works Inc ... 734 729-0022
6430 Commerce Dr Westland (48185) ***(G-18355)***

Artcraft Printing Corporation ... 734 455-8893
14919 Maplewood Ln Plymouth (48170) ***(G-13126)***

Artech Printing Inc ... 248 545-0088
26346 John R Rd Madison Heights (48071) ***(G-10673)***

Arted Chrome Plating ... 586 758-0050
24657 Mound Rd Warren (48091) ***(G-17713)***

Arted Chrome Plating Inc ... 313 871-3331
38 Piquette St Detroit (48202) ***(G-4029)***

Artemis Technologies Inc ... 517 336-9915
2501 Coolidge Rd Ste 503 East Lansing (48823) ***(G-4886)***

Artesian Distillers ... 616 252-1700
955 Ken O Sha Ind Park Grand Rapids (49508) ***(G-6472)***

Artex Label & Graphics Inc ... 616 748-9655
740 Case Karsten Dr Zeeland (49464) ***(G-18992)***

Artful Scrapbooking & Rubber 586 651-1577
7220 Smale St Washington (48094) *(G-18078)*

Arthur R Sommers 586 469-1280
41700 Conger Bay Dr Harrison Township (48045) *(G-7689)*

Artic Technologies Intl 248 689-9884
3456 Rochester Rd Troy (48083) *(G-16955)*

Articulate Signs 248 577-1860
1923 Ring Dr Troy (48083) *(G-16956)*

Artifcial Intllgnce Tech Slton 877 787-6268
10800 Galaxie Ave Ferndale (48220) *(G-5528)*

Artificial Sky, Northville Also called Skyworks LLC *(G-12261)*

Artiflex Manufacturing LLC 616 459-8285
731 Broadway Ave Nw Grand Rapids (49504) *(G-6473)*

Artigy Printing 269 373-6591
5285 E Fg Ave Kalamazoo (49004) *(G-9122)*

Artisan Bread Co LLC 586 756-0100
25000 Guenther Warren (48091) *(G-17714)*

Artisan Medical Displays LLC 616 748-8950
3340 84th Ave Zeeland (49464) *(G-18993)*

Artisans Cstm Mmory Mattresses 989 793-3208
2200 S Hamilton St Ste 3 Saginaw (48602) *(G-14605)*

Artisans Mattresses, Saginaw Also called Artisans Cstm Mmory Mattresses *(G-14605)*

Artistic, Troy Also called Combine International Inc *(G-17019)*

Artistic European Granich MBL, Dearborn Also called A E G M Inc *(G-3804)*

Artistic Flair EMB & Prtg 810 487-9074
11070 Potter Rd Flushing (48433) *(G-5802)*

Artistic Printing Inc 248 356-1004
26040 W 12 Mile Rd Southfield (48034) *(G-15491)*

Artists Pallet 248 889-2440
203 S Milford Rd Highland (48357) *(G-7882)*

Artjay Industries Incorporated 810 773-6450
14200 E 10 Mile Rd Warren (48089) *(G-17715)*

Arts Crafts Hardware 586 231-5344
169 Smith St Mount Clemens (48043) *(G-11627)*

Arvan Specialty Products, Kalamazoo Also called Arvco Container Corporation *(G-9124)*

Arvco Container Corporation (PA) 269 381-0900
845 Gibson St Kalamazoo (49001) *(G-9123)*

Arvco Container Corporation 269 381-0900
845 Gibson St Kalamazoo (49001) *(G-9124)*

Arvco Container Corporation 269 381-0900
351 Rochester Ave Kalamazoo (49007) *(G-9125)*

Arvco Container Corporation 269 381-0900
148 Parkway Dr Kalamazoo (49007) *(G-9126)*

Arvco Container Corporation 231 876-0935
1355 Marty Paul St Cadillac (49601) *(G-2313)*

Arvco Speciality Packaging, Kalamazoo Also called Arvco Container Corporation *(G-9123)*

Arvinmeritor Oe LLC (HQ) 248 435-1000
2135 W Maple Rd Troy (48084) *(G-16957)*

Arvron Inc 616 530-1888
4720 Clay Ave Sw Grand Rapids (49548) *(G-6474)*

As, Grand Rapids Also called Design Design Inc *(G-6643)*

AS Property Management Inc 586 427-8000
25133 Thomas Dr Warren (48091) *(G-17716)*

Asahi Kasei Plas N Amer Inc (HQ) 517 223-2000
1 Thermofil Way Fowlerville (48836) *(G-5833)*

Asahi Kasei Plastics Amer Inc 517 223-2000
1 Thermofil Way Fowlerville (48836) *(G-5834)*

Asama Coldwater Mfg Inc (HQ) 517 279-1090
180 Asama Pkwy Coldwater (49036) *(G-3420)*

Asao LLC 734 522-6333
34115 Industrial Rd Livonia (48150) *(G-10125)*

ASAP Printing Inc 517 882-3500
1110 Keystone Ave Lansing (48911) *(G-9807)*

ASAP Printing Inc (PA) 517 882-3500
2323 Jolly Rd Okemos (48864) *(G-12657)*

ASAP Source, Ann Arbor Also called Ltek Industries Inc *(G-556)*

ASC, Warren Also called Specilty Vhcl Acquisition Corp *(G-18018)*

ASC Custom Woodworking LLC 586 855-8817
31224 Gardendale Dr Warren (48088) *(G-17717)*

ASC Industries Inc 586 722-7871
3255 W Hamlin Rd Rochester Hills (48309) *(G-13951)*

Ascent Aerospace, Macomb Also called Global Tooling Systems LLC *(G-10599)*

Ascent Aerospace LLC 586 726-0500
16445 23 Mile Rd Macomb (48042) *(G-10578)*

Ascent Aerospace Holdings LLC (PA) 212 916-8142
16445 23 Mile Rd Macomb (48042) *(G-10579)*

Ascent Integrated Platforms 586 726-0500
16445 23 Mile Rd Macomb (48042) *(G-10580)*

Asco LP 810 648-9141
360 Thelma St Sandusky (48471) *(G-15054)*

Asco LP 248 596-3200
46280 Dylan Dr Ste 100 Novi (48377) *(G-12365)*

Asco Power Technologies LP 248 957-9050
1975 Technology Dr Ste B Troy (48083) *(G-16958)*

Ascott Corporation 734 663-2023
1202 N Main St Ann Arbor (48104) *(G-381)*

Ascribe 616 726-2490
100 Grandville Ave Sw Grand Rapids (49503) *(G-6475)*

Ase Industries Inc 586 754-7480
23850 Pinewood St Warren (48091) *(G-17718)*

Aseltine Cider Company Inc 616 784-7676
533 Lamoreaux Dr Nw Comstock Park (49321) *(G-3588)*

Ash Industries Inc 269 672-9630
362 116th Ave Martin (49070) *(G-11079)*

Asher Brandon Industries 231 313-3513
425 W Twelfth St Traverse City (49684) *(G-16603)*

Ashine Diamond Tools 734 668-9067
4872 S Ridgeside Cir Ann Arbor (48105) *(G-382)*

Ashland Slag Company, Dearborn Also called Levy Indiana Slag Co *(G-3862)*

Ashley Garcia 248 396-8138
9105 Huron Bluffs Dr White Lake (48386) *(G-18450)*

Ashley Rose 616 634-4919
11080 Angel Pond Dr Ne Rockford (49341) *(G-14155)*

Asi Signage Innovation, Troy Also called Sign Concepts Corporation *(G-17351)*

Asian Noodle LLC 989 316-2380
201 Fulton St W Apt 1415 Grand Rapids (49503) *(G-6476)*

Asimco International Inc (HQ) 248 213-5200
1000 Town Ctr Ste 1050 Southfield (48075) *(G-15492)*

Ask Your Neighbor, Bloomfield Hills Also called Bob Allison Enterprises *(G-1804)*

Asmo Detroit Inc 248 359-4440
39575 Lewis Dr Ste 800 Novi (48377) *(G-12366)*

Asmus Seasoning Inc 586 939-4505
36625 Metro Ct Ste A Sterling Heights (48312) *(G-15934)*

Asp Grede Acquisitionco LLC (PA) 248 440-9515
20750 Civic Center Dr # 100 Southfield (48076) *(G-15493)*

Asp Hhi Acquisition Co Inc (HQ) 313 758-2000
1 Dauch Dr Detroit (48211) *(G-4030)*

Asp Hhi Holdings Inc 248 597-3800
2727 W 14 Mile Rd Royal Oak (48073) *(G-14513)*

Asp Plating Company 616 842-8080
211 N Griffin St Grand Haven (49417) *(G-6273)*

Aspc International Inc 616 842-7800
803 Taylor Ave Grand Haven (49417) *(G-6274)*

Aspen Door Supply LLC 248 291-5303
1195 Rochester Rd Ste P Troy (48083) *(G-16959)*

Aspen Technologies Inc (PA) 248 446-1485
7963 Lochlin Dr Brighton (48116) *(G-1947)*

Asphalt Paving Inc 231 733-1409
1000 E Sherman Blvd Muskegon (49444) *(G-11773)*

Asphalt Services 313 971-5005
5052 Clntonville Pines Dr Clarkston (48346) *(G-3018)*

Aspidistra Naturals Inc 269 317-0996
191 N Eastway Dr Battle Creek (49015) *(G-1186)*

Aspire Pharmacy 989 773-7849
121 E Broadway St D Mount Pleasant (48858) *(G-11681)*

Aspn Wood Construction LLC 810 246-8044
418 N Main St Royal Oak (48067) *(G-14514)*

Aspra World Inc 248 872-7030
25160 Easy St Warren (48089) *(G-17719)*

Assay Designs Inc 734 214-0923
5777 Hines Dr Ann Arbor (48108) *(G-383)*

Assem-Tech Inc 616 846-3410
1600 Kooiman St Grand Haven (49417) *(G-6275)*

Assemacher's Cycling Center, Flint Also called Assenmacher Lightweight Cycles *(G-5645)*

Assembltech Inc 734 769-2800
7076 Schnipke Dr Ottawa Lake (49267) *(G-12803)*

Assembly Alternatives Inc 248 362-1616
501 Longford Dr Rochester Hills (48309) *(G-13952)*

Assembly Concepts Inc 989 685-2603
2651 S M 33 Rose City (48654) *(G-14361)*

Assembly Source One Inc 616 844-5250
17169 Hayes St Ste B Grand Haven (49417) *(G-6276)*

Assembly Technologies Intl Inc 248 280-2810
1937 Barrett Dr Troy (48084) *(G-16960)*

Assenmacher Lightweight Cycles (PA) 810 635-7844
8053 Miller Rd Swartz Creek (48473) *(G-16350)*

Assenmacher Lightweight Cycles 810 232-2994
1272 W Hill Rd Flint (48507) *(G-5645)*

Assenmachers Hill Road Cyclery, Swartz Creek Also called Assenmacher Lightweight Cycles *(G-16350)*

Asset Health Inc 248 822-2870
2250 Butterfield Dr # 100 Troy (48084) *(G-16961)*

Asset Track Gps Systems, Jackson Also called Asset Track Technologies LLC *(G-8817)*

Asset Track Technologies LLC 517 745-3879
510 W Michigan Ave Jackson (49201) *(G-8817)*

Assi Fuel Inc 586 759-4759
8309 E 8 Mile Rd Warren (48089) *(G-17720)*

Assistive Technology Cal, Novi Also called Assistive Technology Mich Inc *(G-12367)*

Assistive Technology Mich Inc 248 348-7161
43000 W 9 Mile Rd Ste 113 Novi (48375) *(G-12367)*

Associate Mfg Inc 989 345-0025
3977 S M 30 West Branch (48661) *(G-18325)*

Associated Broach Corporation 810 798-9112
7481 Research Dr Almont (48003) *(G-256)*

Associated Constructors LLC 906 226-6505
14 Industrial Park Dr Negaunee (49866) *(G-11963)*

Associated Metals Inc 734 369-3851
6235 Jackson Rd Ste B Ann Arbor (48103) ***(G-384)***
Associated Print & Graphics 734 676-8896
9617 Island Dr Grosse Ile (48138) ***(G-7516)***
Associated Print & Marketing, Madison Heights *Also called Apms Incorporated* ***(G-10670)***
Associated Print Marketing 248 268-2726
32350 Howard Ave Madison Heights (48071) ***(G-10674)***
Associated Rack Corporation 616 554-6004
4910 Kraft Ave Se Grand Rapids (49512) ***(G-6477)***
Associated Redi Mix and Block, Negaunee *Also called Associated Constructors LLC* ***(G-11963)***
Assra 906 225-1828
625 Pine St Marquette (49855) ***(G-11005)***
Astar Inc 574 234-2137
71135 Fir Rd Niles (49120) ***(G-12111)***
Astech Inc 989 823-7211
5512 Scotch Rd Vassar (48768) ***(G-17577)***
Astellas Pharma Us Inc 616 698-8825
5905 Kraft Ave Se Grand Rapids (49512) ***(G-6478)***
Astra Associates Inc 586 254-6500
6500 Dobry Dr Sterling Heights (48314) ***(G-15935)***
Astro Building Products Inc (HQ) 231 941-0324
221 W South Airport Rd Traverse City (49686) ***(G-16604)***
Astro Dumpster Rental LLC 313 444-7905
922 Forestdale Rd Royal Oak (48067) ***(G-14515)***
Astro Wood Stake Inc 616 875-8118
6017 Chicago Dr Zeeland (49464) ***(G-18994)***
Asw Amerca Inc 248 957-9638
24762 Crestview Ct Farmington Hills (48335) ***(G-5174)***
At Home 313 769-4200
5901 Mercury Dr Dearborn (48126) ***(G-3811)***
Atco Rubber Products, Grand Haven *Also called Atcoflex Inc* ***(G-6277)***
Atcoflex Inc 616 842-4661
14261 172nd Ave Grand Haven (49417) ***(G-6277)***
Atd Engineering and Mch LLC 989 876-7161
533 N Court St Au Gres (48703) ***(G-755)***
Ateq Corporation (HQ) 734 838-3100
35980 Industrial Rd Livonia (48150) ***(G-10126)***
Ateq Leak Detecting Service, Livonia *Also called Ateq Corporation* ***(G-10126)***
Ateq Tpms Tools Lc 734 838-3104
35990 Industrial Rd Livonia (48150) ***(G-10127)***
Atf Inc 989 685-2468
285 Casemaster Dr Rose City (48654) ***(G-14362)***
Atg Precision Products LLC 586 247-5400
7545 N Haggerty Rd Canton (48187) ***(G-2437)***
Athena Foods, Southfield *Also called Charidimos Inc* ***(G-15519)***
Athey Precision Inc 989 386-4523
2021 S Athey Ave Clare (48617) ***(G-2973)***
Athletic Uniform Lettering 313 533-9071
26114 W 6 Mile Rd Redford (48240) ***(G-13717)***
ATI, Novi *Also called Accurate Technologies Inc* ***(G-12360)***
ATI Marketing 231 590-9600
506 N Spruce St Traverse City (49684) ***(G-16605)***
Atlantic Precision Pdts Inc 586 532-9420
51745 Filomena Dr Shelby Township (48315) ***(G-15173)***
Atlantic Precision Pdts Inc 586 532-9420
51234 Filomena Dr Shelby Township (48315) ***(G-15174)***
Atlantis Tech Corp 989 356-6954
706 Island View Dr Alpena (49707) ***(G-279)***
Atlas Copco Ias LLC 248 377-9722
3301 Cross Creek Pkwy Auburn Hills (48326) ***(G-799)***
Atlas Cut Stone Inc 248 545-5100
12920 Northend Ave Oak Park (48237) ***(G-12592)***
Atlas Die LLC 413 289-1276
2960 Technology Dr Rochester Hills (48309) ***(G-13953)***
Atlas Die LLC 770 981-6585
2960 Technology Dr Rochester Hills (48309) ***(G-13954)***
Atlas Die Inc 574 295-0050
2960 Technology Dr Rochester Hills (48309) ***(G-13955)***
Atlas Gear Company 248 583-2964
32801 Edward Ave Madison Heights (48071) ***(G-10675)***
Atlas Industries 310 694-7457
26100 American Dr Ste 600 Southfield (48034) ***(G-15494)***
Atlas Technologies LLC 810 629-6663
14165 N Fenton Rd 102c Fenton (48430) ***(G-5451)***
Atlas Technologies Inc 810 629-6663
2100 Upper Ave Fenton (48430) ***(G-5452)***
Atlas Thread Gage Inc 248 477-3230
30990 W 8 Mile Rd Farmington Hills (48336) ***(G-5175)***
Atlas Tube (plymouth) Inc 734 738-5600
13101 Eckles Rd Plymouth (48170) ***(G-13127)***
Atlas Welding Accessories Inc 248 588-4666
501 Stephenson Hwy Troy (48083) ***(G-16962)***
Atm International Services LLC 734 524-9771
8351 N Wayne Rd Westland (48185) ***(G-18356)***
Atmo-Seal Enginering, Troy *Also called Atmo-Seal Inc* ***(G-16963)***
Atmo-Seal Inc 248 528-9640
1091 Wheaton Dr Troy (48083) ***(G-16963)***
Atmore Industries Inc 734 455-7655
12887 Fairlane St Livonia (48150) ***(G-10128)***
Atmosphere Annealing LLC (HQ) 517 485-5090
209 W Mount Hope Ave # 2 Lansing (48910) ***(G-9808)***
Atmosphere Annealing LLC 517 482-1374
1801 Bassett St Lansing (48915) ***(G-9809)***
Atmosphere Group Inc (PA) 248 624-8191
49630 Pontiac Trl Wixom (48393) ***(G-18609)***
Atmosphere Heat Treating Inc 248 960-4700
30760 Century Dr Wixom (48393) ***(G-18610)***
Atos Syntel Inc (HQ) 248 619-2800
525 E Big Beaver Rd # 300 Troy (48083) ***(G-16964)***
Atotech Usa LLC 586 939-3040
35840 Beattie Dr Sterling Heights (48312) ***(G-15936)***
Atra Plastics Inc 734 237-3393
43938 Plymouth Oaks Blvd Plymouth (48170) ***(G-13128)***
Atreum, Auburn Hills *Also called Antolin Interiors Usa Inc* ***(G-789)***
Ats Assembly and Test Inc 734 266-4713
12841 Stark Rd Livonia (48150) ***(G-10129)***
Ats Assembly and Test Inc (HQ) 937 222-3030
1 Ats Dr Wixom (48393) ***(G-18611)***
Ats Assembly and Test Inc 937 222-3030
1 Ats Dr Wixom (48393) ***(G-18612)***
Ats Atmtion Globl Svcs USA Inc 734 522-1900
1 Ats Dr Wixom (48393) ***(G-18613)***
Attentive Industries Inc 810 233-7077
1301 Alabama Ave Flint (48505) ***(G-5646)***
Attentive Industries Inc (PA) 810 233-7077
502 Kelso St Flint (48506) ***(G-5647)***
Atterocor Inc 734 845-9300
301 N Main St Ste 100 Ann Arbor (48104) ***(G-385)***
Attitude & Experience Inc 231 946-7446
1230 S M 37 Traverse City (49685) ***(G-16606)***
Attwood Corporation (HQ) 616 897-2301
1016 N Monroe St Lowell (49331) ***(G-10495)***
ATW Industries LLC 616 318-6052
525 100th St Sw Byron Center (49315) ***(G-2258)***
Atwater Brewery, Detroit *Also called Detroit Rvrtown Brwing Cmpay L* ***(G-4163)***
Atwater Foods LLC 231 941-4336
10850 E Traverse Hwy # 4001 Traverse City (49684) ***(G-16607)***
Atwater Foods LLC 231 264-5598
10106 Hgwy 31 Us Williamsburg (49690) ***(G-18551)***
Atwater In Park 313 344-5104
1175 Lakepointe St Grosse Pointe Park (48230) ***(G-7548)***
Atwood Forest Products Inc 616 696-0081
1177 17 Mile Rd Ne Cedar Springs (49319) ***(G-2641)***
Au Enterprises Inc 248 544-9700
3916 11 Mile Rd Berkley (48072) ***(G-1621)***
Auburn Hills Manufacturing Inc 313 758-2000
1987 Taylor Rd Auburn Hills (48326) ***(G-800)***
Auction Masters 586 576-7777
8700 Capital St Oak Park (48237) ***(G-12593)***
Audia Woodworking & Fine Furn 586 296-6330
16627 Millar Rd Clinton Township (48036) ***(G-3174)***
Audionet America Inc 586 944-0043
33900 Harper Ave Ste 101 Clinton Township (48035) ***(G-3175)***
Audiospace, Grand Rapids *Also called Livespace LLC* ***(G-6947)***
August Communications Inc 313 561-8000
22250 Ford Rd Dearborn Heights (48127) ***(G-3921)***
August Lilia Famly Memorl Fund 906 228-6088
1502 W Washington St Marquette (49855) ***(G-11006)***
Aunt Millies Bakeries 989 356-6688
3450 Us Highway 23 S Alpena (49707) ***(G-280)***
Aunt Millies Bakeries Inc (HQ) 734 528-1475
5331 W Michigan Ave Ypsilanti (48197) ***(G-18925)***
Auntie Anne's, Lansing *Also called Karemor Inc* ***(G-9770)***
Auntie Anne's, Southfield *Also called B & B Pretzels Inc* ***(G-15500)***
Aureogen Inc 269 353-3805
4717 Campus Dr Ste 2300 Kalamazoo (49008) ***(G-9127)***
Aureogen Biosciences, Kalamazoo *Also called Aureogen Inc* ***(G-9127)***
Auria Albemarle LLC (HQ) 248 728-8000
26999 Centrl Pk Blvd # 30 Southfield (48076) ***(G-15495)***
Auria Solutions Intl Inc 734 456-2800
26999 Centrl Pk Blvd # 30 Southfield (48076) ***(G-15496)***
Auria Solutions USA Inc (HQ) 248 728-8000
26999 Centrl Pk Blvd # 300 Southfield (48076) ***(G-15497)***
Auria St Clair LLC 810 329-8400
2001 Christian B Haas Dr Saint Clair (48079) ***(G-14813)***
Auric Enterprises Inc 231 882-7251
7755 Narrow Gauge Rd Beulah (49617) ***(G-1652)***
Aurora Cad CAM Inc 810 678-2128
1643 E Brocker Rd Metamora (48455) ***(G-11276)***
Aurora Cellars 2015 LLC 231 994-3188
7788 E Horn Rd Lake Leelanau (49653) ***(G-9558)***
Aurora Preserved Flowers 989 498-0290
7201 Westside Saginaw Rd # 5 Bay City (48706) ***(G-1323)***
Aurora Software 248 853-2358
3135 Primrose Dr Rochester Hills (48307) ***(G-13956)***
Aurora Spclty Chemistries Corp 517 372-9121
1520 Lake Lansing Rd Lansing (48912) ***(G-9810)***

ALPHABETIC

Aurum Design Inc 248 651-9040
　400 S Main St Rochester (48307) *(G-13892)*
Aurum Design Jewelry, Rochester Also called Aurum Design Inc *(G-13892)*
Ausable Woodworking Co Inc 989 348-7086
　6677 Frederic St Frederic (49733) *(G-6014)*
Austemper Inc (HQ) 586 293-4554
　30760 Century Dr Wixom (48393) *(G-18614)*
Austemper Inc 616 458-7061
　341 Grant St Sw Grand Rapids (49503) *(G-6479)*
Austin Company 269 329-1181
　9764 Portage Rd Portage (49002) *(G-13544)*
Austin Distributors LLC 248 665-2077
　29126 Currier Ave Ste 4a Westland (48186) *(G-18357)*
Austin Powder Company 989 595-2400
　11351 E Grand Lake Rd Presque Isle (49777) *(G-13653)*
Austin Quality Sales Company 269 961-2000
　1 Kellogg Sq Battle Creek (49017) *(G-1187)*
Austin Tube Products Inc 231 745-2741
　5629 S Forman Rd Baldwin (49304) *(G-1121)*
Auswella LLC 248 630-5965
　3458 Castlewood Ct Wixom (48393) *(G-18615)*
Auswella Plush, Wixom Also called Auswella LLC *(G-18615)*
Authentic 3d 248 469-8809
　30800 Telg Rd Ste 4775 Bingham Farms (48025) *(G-1692)*
Authority Customwear Ltd 248 588-8075
　32046 Edward Ave Madison Heights (48071) *(G-10676)*
Authority Flame Hrdning Strght 586 598-5887
　49803 Leona Dr Chesterfield (48051) *(G-2848)*
Authors Coalition America LLC 231 869-2011
　438 6th St Pentwater (49449) *(G-12970)*
Auto & Truck Components, Co., Port Huron Also called Cipa Usa Inc *(G-13464)*
Auto Anodics Inc 810 984-5600
　2407 16th St Port Huron (48060) *(G-13455)*
Auto Builders Inc 586 948-3780
　46571 Continental Dr Chesterfield (48047) *(G-2849)*
Auto Chem Craft, Oak Park Also called Auto Metal Craft Inc *(G-12594)*
Auto Connection 586 752-6371
　75903 Peters Dr Bruce Twp (48065) *(G-2164)*
Auto Craft Tool & Die Co 810 794-4929
　1800 Fruit St Clay (48001) *(G-3116)*
Auto Craft Tool & Die Co 810 794-4929
　1800 Fruit St Clay (48001) *(G-3117)*
Auto Electric International 248 354-2082
　22211 Telegraph Rd Southfield (48033) *(G-15498)*
Auto Metal Craft Inc 248 398-2240
　12741 Capital St Oak Park (48237) *(G-12594)*
Auto Pallets-Boxes Inc (PA) 248 559-7744
　28000 Southfield Rd Fl 2 Lathrup Village (48076) *(G-9975)*
Auto Pallets-Boxes Inc 734 782-1110
　27945 Cooke St Flat Rock (48134) *(G-5614)*
Auto Quip Inc 810 364-3366
　70 Airport Dr Kimball (48074) *(G-9491)*
Auto-Air Composites, Lansing Also called Pratt & Whitney Autoair Inc *(G-9882)*
Auto-Air Composites, Holt Also called Pratt & Whitney Autoair Inc *(G-8325)*
Auto-Masters Inc 616 455-4510
　6521 Division Ave S Grand Rapids (49548) *(G-6480)*
Auto-Tech Plastics Inc 586 783-0103
　164 Grand Ave Mount Clemens (48043) *(G-11628)*
Auto/Con Corp 586 791-7474
　33842 James J Pompo Dr Fraser (48026) *(G-5897)*
Auto/Con Services LLC 586 791-7474
　33661 James J Pompo Dr Fraser (48026) *(G-5898)*
Autoalliance Management Co 734 782-7800
　1 International Dr Flat Rock (48134) *(G-5615)*
Autocam Corp 616 698-0707
　4180 40th St Se Grand Rapids (49512) *(G-6481)*
Autocam Corporation 269 789-4000
　1511 George Brown Dr Marshall (49068) *(G-11052)*
Autocam Corporation 269 782-5186
　201 Percy St Dowagiac (49047) *(G-4775)*
Autocam Corporation (HQ) 616 698-0707
　4180 40th St Se Kentwood (49512) *(G-9444)*
Autocam Corporation 616 698-0707
　4060 East Paris Ave Se Kentwood (49512) *(G-9445)*
Autocam Corporation 616 698-0707
　4070 East Paris Ave Se Kentwood (49512) *(G-9446)*
Autocam Med DVC Holdings LLC (PA) 616 541-8080
　4152 East Paris Ave Se Kentwood (49512) *(G-9447)*
Autocam Medical Devices LLC (HQ) 877 633-8080
　4152 East Paris Ave Se Grand Rapids (49512) *(G-6482)*
Autocam Prcsion Cmpnents Group, Kentwood Also called Autocam Corporation *(G-9444)*
Autocam-Pax, Dowagiac Also called Autocam Corporation *(G-4775)*
Autocam-Pax Inc 269 782-5186
　201 Percy St Dowagiac (49047) *(G-4776)*
Autodesk Inc 248 347-9650
　26200 Town Center Dr # 300 Novi (48375) *(G-12368)*
Autodie LLC 616 454-9361
　44 Coldbrook St Nw Grand Rapids (49503) *(G-6483)*

Autoexec Inc 616 971-0080
　4477 East Paris Ave Se Grand Rapids (49512) *(G-6484)*
Autoform Development Inc 616 392-4909
　257 E 32nd St Ste 2 Holland (49423) *(G-7966)*
Autokiniton Global Group, New Boston Also called Autokiniton US Holdings Inc *(G-12001)*
Autokiniton US Holdings Inc (PA) 734 397-6300
　17757 Woodland Dr New Boston (48164) *(G-12001)*
Autoliv Americas, Auburn Hills Also called Autoliv Holding Inc *(G-803)*
Autoliv Asp Inc 248 761-0081
　856 Featherstone St Pontiac (48342) *(G-13351)*
Autoliv Asp Inc 248 475-9000
　2601 Cambridge Ct Auburn Hills (48326) *(G-801)*
Autoliv Asp Inc 248 475-9000
　1320 Pacific Dr Auburn Hills (48326) *(G-802)*
Autoliv Holding Inc (HQ) 248 475-9000
　1320 Pacific Dr Auburn Hills (48326) *(G-803)*
Autoliv N Amer Technical Cntr, Auburn Hills Also called Autoliv Asp Inc *(G-802)*
Autoliv Technical Center-W, Pontiac Also called Autoliv Asp Inc *(G-13351)*
Automate Industries Inc 248 740-7022
　1906 Brinston Dr Troy (48083) *(G-16965)*
Automated Bookkeeping Inc 866 617-3122
　1555 Broadway St Detroit (48226) *(G-4031)*
Automated Control Systems Inc 248 476-9490
　25168 Seeley Rd Novi (48375) *(G-12369)*
Automated Indus Motion Inc 231 865-1800
　5627 Airline Rd Fruitport (49415) *(G-6059)*
Automated Machine Systems Inc 616 662-1309
　6651 Pine Ridge Ct Sw Jenison (49428) *(G-9046)*
Automated Media Inc 313 937-5000
　5711 Research Dr Canton (48188) *(G-2438)*
Automated Precision Eqp LLC 517 481-2414
　770 Jackson St Ste A Eaton Rapids (48827) *(G-4952)*
Automated Process Equipment (PA) 616 374-1000
　1201 4th Ave Lake Odessa (48849) *(G-9572)*
Automated Prod Assemblies 586 293-3990
　33957 Doreka Fraser (48026) *(G-5899)*
Automated Systems Inc 248 373-5600
　2400 Commercial Dr Auburn Hills (48326) *(G-804)*
Automated Techniques LLC 810 346-4670
　7105 Enterprise Dr Brown City (48416) *(G-2134)*
Automatic Handling Intl Inc 734 847-0633
　360 La Voy Rd Erie (48133) *(G-5044)*
Automatic Spring Products Corp (PA) 616 842-2284
　803 Taylor Ave Grand Haven (49417) *(G-6278)*
Automatic Valve Corp 248 474-6761
　22550 Heslip Dr Novi (48375) *(G-12370)*
Automatic Valve Mfg Co In 248 924-7671
　22550 Heslip Dr Novi (48375) *(G-12371)*
Automatic Valve Nuclear, Novi Also called Automatic Valve Corp *(G-12370)*
Automation Contrls & Engrg LLC 734 424-5500
　2105 Bishop Cir W Dexter (48130) *(G-4725)*
Automation Enterprises Inc 586 774-0280
　29970 Parkway Roseville (48066) *(G-14377)*
Automation Service Equipment, Warren Also called Ase Industries Inc *(G-17718)*
Automation Specialists Inc 616 738-8288
　12555 Superior Ct Holland (49424) *(G-7967)*
Automationsupply365 LLC 248 912-7354
　1532 N Opdyke Rd Ste 800 Auburn Hills (48326) *(G-805)*
Automatrics, Grand Rapids Also called Thierica Controls Inc *(G-7258)*
Autombili Lamborghini Amer LLC 866 681-6276
　3800 Hamlin Rd Auburn Hills (48326) *(G-806)*
Automotive LLC 248 712-1175
　300 Galleria Office Ctr Southfield (48034) *(G-15499)*
Automotive Component Mfg (PA) 705 549-7406
　36155 Mound Rd Sterling Heights (48310) *(G-15937)*
Automotive Div, Auburn Hills Also called Washington Penn Plastic Co Inc *(G-1087)*
Automotive Exteriors LLC (HQ) 248 458-0702
　2800 High Meadow Cir Auburn Hills (48326) *(G-807)*
Automotive International Svcs 248 808-8112
　774 Snowmass Dr Rochester Hills (48309) *(G-13957)*
Automotive Lighting North Amer, Southfield Also called Marelli Automotive Ltg LLC *(G-15642)*
Automotive Manufacturing 517 566-8174
　101 Main St Sunfield (48890) *(G-16333)*
Automotive Media LLC 248 537-8500
　500 W Long Lake Rd Troy (48098) *(G-16966)*
Automotive Moulding, Sterling Heights Also called Srg Global Automotive LLC *(G-16186)*
Automotive Operations, Auburn Hills Also called Henniges Automotive N Amer Inc *(G-926)*
Automotive Plastics Recycling 810 767-3800
　2945 Davison Rd Flint (48506) *(G-5648)*
Automotive Prototype Stamping 586 445-6792
　17207 Millar Rd Clinton Township (48036) *(G-3176)*
Automotive Service Co 517 784-6131
　603 E Washington Ave Jackson (49203) *(G-8818)*
Automotive Technology LLC 586 446-7000
　6015 Center Dr Sterling Heights (48312) *(G-15938)*
Automotive Trim Technologies 734 947-0344
　12400 Universal Dr Taylor (48180) *(G-16382)*

Automotive Tumbling Co Inc....313 925-7450
3125 Meldrum St Detroit (48207) **(G-4032)**
Automted Dbrring A-1 Prts Wshg, Warren *Also called Parts Finishing Group Inc* **(G-17955)**
Automtion Mdlar Components Inc (PA)....248 922-4740
10301 Enterprise Dr Davisburg (48350) **(G-3758)**
Autonertia Inc....810 882-1002
6456 Hartland Rd Fenton (48430) **(G-5453)**
Autoneum North America Inc (HQ)....248 848-0100
29293 Haggerty Rd Novi (48377) **(G-12372)**
Autoneum North America Inc....248 848-0100
38555 Hills Tech Dr Farmington Hills (48331) **(G-5176)**
Autorack Technologies Inc....517 437-4800
20 Superior St Hillsdale (49242) **(G-7923)**
Autosport Development LLC....734 675-1620
2331 Toledo St Trenton (48183) **(G-16886)**
Autosystems America Inc....734 582-2300
46600 Port St Plymouth (48170) **(G-13129)**
Autotech Engrg R&D USA Inc....248 743-3400
1600 Harmon Rd Auburn Hills (48326) **(G-808)**
Autowares Inc....248 473-0928
23240 Industrial Park Dr Farmington Hills (48335) **(G-5177)**
Autumn Designs LLC....269 455-0490
225 Broadway St Ste 11 South Haven (49090) **(G-15400)**
Autumn Endeavors LLC....906 296-0601
51019 Paradise Ln Lake Linden (49945) **(G-9566)**
Autumn Ridge Woodworks....517 420-8185
2020 Kelly Rd Mason (48854) **(G-11117)**
Auvesy Inc....616 888-3770
146 Monroe Center St Nw # 1210 Grand Rapids (49503) **(G-6485)**
Auxant Software LLC....810 584-5947
8340 Loon Ln Grand Blanc (48439) **(G-6233)**
Auxier & Associates LLC....231 486-0641
1702 Barlow St Ste A Traverse City (49686) **(G-16608)**
Auxier & Associates LLC....231 933-7446
741 Woodmere Ave Traverse City (49686) **(G-16609)**
Avabella Press....734 662-0048
4299 Katie Jo Ct Ann Arbor (48103) **(G-386)**
Avalon & Tahoe Mfg Inc....989 463-2112
903 Michigan Ave Alma (48801) **(G-239)**
Avalon International Breads, Detroit *Also called Avalon Intl New Ctr LLC* **(G-4033)**
Avalon Intl New Ctr LLC....313 308-0150
4731 Bellevue St Detroit (48207) **(G-4033)**
Avalon Tools Inc....248 269-0001
1910 Barrett Dr Troy (48084) **(G-16967)**
Avancez LLC....313 404-1962
1430 E 10 Mile Rd Ste 30 Hazel Park (48030) **(G-7820)**
Avanti Greeting Cards, Detroit *Also called Avanti Press Inc* **(G-4034)**
Avanti Press Inc (PA)....800 228-2684
155 W Congress St Ste 200 Detroit (48226) **(G-4034)**
Avanti Press Inc....313 961-0022
22701 Trolley Industrial Taylor (48180) **(G-16383)**
Avantis Inc....616 285-8000
5441 36th St Se Grand Rapids (49512) **(G-6486)**
Avanzado LLC....248 615-0538
25330 Interchange Ct Farmington Hills (48335) **(G-5178)**
Avasure Holdings Inc (PA)....616 301-0129
5801 Safety Dr Ne Belmont (49306) **(G-1500)**
Avatar Inc....586 846-3195
44041 N Groesbeck Hwy Clinton Township (48036) **(G-3177)**
Aven Inc....734 973-0099
4330 Varsity Dr Ann Arbor (48108) **(G-387)**
Aven Tools, Ann Arbor *Also called Aven Inc* **(G-387)**
Avery Color Studios Inc....906 346-3908
511 Avenue D Gwinn (49841) **(G-7582)**
Avflight Corporation (HQ)....734 663-6466
47 W Ellsworth Rd Ann Arbor (48108) **(G-388)**
AVI Inventory Services LLC (PA)....231 799-9000
620 E Ellis Rd Norton Shores (49441) **(G-12277)**
Avian Control, Sylvan Lake *Also called Avian Enterprises LLC* **(G-16359)**
Avian Control Technologies LLC....231 349-9050
6800 Mayfair Dr Stanwood (49346) **(G-15902)**
Avian Enterprises LLC (PA)....888 366-0709
2000 Pontiac Dr Sylvan Lake (48320) **(G-16359)**
Avid Industries Inc....810 672-9100
4887 Ubly Rd Argyle (48410) **(G-728)**
Avidasports LLC....313 447-5670
20844 Harper Ave Ste 300 Harper Woods (48225) **(G-7662)**
Avidhrt Inc....517 214-9041
2721 Sophiea Pkwy Okemos (48864) **(G-12658)**
Avient Colorants USA LLC....517 629-9101
926 Elliott St Albion (49224) **(G-117)**
Avissa Skin+body....734 316-5556
1715 Plymouth Rd Ann Arbor (48105) **(G-389)**
Aviv Global LLC....248 737-5777
32430 Northwestern Hwy Farmington Hills (48334) **(G-5179)**
Avl Michigan Holding Corp (HQ)....734 414-9600
47519 Halyard Dr Plymouth (48170) **(G-13130)**
Avl North Amer Corp Svcs Inc....734 414-9600
47603 Halyard Dr Plymouth (48170) **(G-13131)**
Avl Powertrain Technologies (PA)....734 414-9600
47603 Halyard Dr Plymouth (48170) **(G-13132)**
Avl Properties Inc....734 414-9600
47603 Halyard Dr Plymouth (48170) **(G-13133)**
Avl Test Systems Inc....734 414-9600
47603 Halyard Dr Plymouth (48170) **(G-13134)**
Avo Dental Supplies LLC....586 585-1210
27251 Gratiot Ave Roseville (48066) **(G-14378)**
Avomeen LLC....734 222-1090
4840 Venture Dr Ann Arbor (48108) **(G-390)**
Avomeen Analytical Services, Ann Arbor *Also called Avomeen LLC* **(G-390)**
Avon Auotmotive, Novi *Also called Akwel Cadillac Usa Inc* **(G-12361)**
Avon Automotive, Cadillac *Also called Akwel Usa Inc* **(G-2311)**
Avon Automotive-Orizaba, Cadillac *Also called Akwel Cadillac Usa Inc* **(G-2309)**
Avon Broach & Prod Co LLC....248 650-8080
1089 John R Rd Rochester Hills (48307) **(G-13958)**
Avon Cabinets Atkins....248 237-1103
2596 Hessel Ave Rochester Hills (48307) **(G-13959)**
Avon Gear, Shelby Township *Also called Avon Machining LLC* **(G-15175)**
Avon Machining LLC....586 884-2200
11968 Investment Dr Shelby Township (48315) **(G-15175)**
Avon Machining Holdings Inc....586 884-2200
11968 Investment Dr Shelby Township (48315) **(G-15176)**
Avon Plastic Products Inc....248 852-1000
2890 Technology Dr Rochester Hills (48309) **(G-13960)**
Avon Protection Systems Inc (HQ)....231 779-6200
503 8th St Cadillac (49601) **(G-2314)**
Avpi Limited....616 842-1200
612 W Savidge St Spring Lake (49456) **(G-15804)**
Aw Carbide Fabricators Inc....586 294-1850
35434 Mound Rd Sterling Heights (48310) **(G-15939)**
Award Cutter Company Inc....616 531-0430
5577 Crippen Ave Sw Grand Rapids (49548) **(G-6487)**
Awarenessideas.com, Commerce Township *Also called Flexi Display Marketing Inc* **(G-3531)**
Awcco USA Incorporated....586 336-9135
171 Shafer Dr Romeo (48065) **(G-14220)**
Awcoa Inc....313 892-4100
17210 Gable St Detroit (48212) **(G-4035)**
Awd Associates Inc....248 922-9898
10560 Enterprise Dr Ste A Davisburg (48350) **(G-3759)**
Aweba Tool & Die Corp....478 296-2002
1004 E State St Hastings (49058) **(G-7781)**
Awesome Musical Instrs LLC....734 941-2927
16646 Mary Grace Ln Romulus (48174) **(G-14252)**
Awrey Bakeries, Livonia *Also called Marie Minnie Bakers Inc* **(G-10300)**
Axalta....248 379-6913
3136 Cedar Key Dr Lake Orion (48360) **(G-9586)**
Axalta Coating Systems LLC....586 846-4160
45000 River Ridge Dr # 200 Clinton Township (48038) **(G-3178)**
Axchem Inc....734 641-9842
38070 Van Born Rd Wayne (48184) **(G-18214)**
Axelson-Veet-Liberty Inds, Warren *Also called Veet Industries Inc* **(G-18053)**
Axiobionics....734 327-2946
6111 Jackson Rd Ste 200 Ann Arbor (48103) **(G-391)**
Axiom Business Book Awards, Traverse City *Also called Jenkins Group Inc* **(G-16728)**
Axis Engineering Div, Dundee *Also called L & W Inc* **(G-4826)**
Axis Enterprises Inc....616 677-5281
15300 8th Ave Marne (49435) **(G-10989)**
Axis Machine & Tool Inc....616 738-2196
7217 W Olive Rd Holland (49424) **(G-7968)**
Axis Machining Inc....989 453-3943
7061 Hartley St Pigeon (48755) **(G-13035)**
Axis Mold Works Inc....616 866-2222
8005 Childsdale Ave Ne Rockford (49341) **(G-14156)**
Axis Tms Corp....248 509-2440
36380 Garfield Rd Ste 2 Clinton Township (48035) **(G-3179)**
Axle of Dearborn Inc (PA)....248 543-5995
2000 W 8 Mile Rd Ferndale (48220) **(G-5529)**
Axline Advanced Industries....231 679-7907
229 W North Ave Reed City (49677) **(G-13788)**
Axly Production Machining, Bad Axe *Also called Gemini Precision Machining Inc* **(G-1105)**
Axly Production Machining Inc....989 269-2444
700 E Soper Rd Bad Axe (48413) **(G-1096)**
Axly Prodution Machining....989 269-9553
727 Skinner St Bad Axe (48413) **(G-1097)**
Axly-Briney Sales, Bad Axe *Also called Axly Production Machining Inc* **(G-1096)**
Axonia Medical Inc....269 615-6632
4321 Roxbury Ln Kalamazoo (49008) **(G-9128)**
Axson Tech Us Inc....517 663-8191
1611 Hults Dr Eaton Rapids (48827) **(G-4953)**
Axsys Inc....248 926-8810
29627 West Tech Dr Wixom (48393) **(G-18616)**
Ayb, Clinton Township *Also called Amour Your Body LLC* **(G-3168)**
Aye Money Promotions Pubg LLC....313 808-8173
20355 Plymouth Rd Detroit (48228) **(G-4036)**
Ayotte Cstm Mscal Engrvngs LLC....734 595-1901
36688 Rolf St Westland (48186) **(G-18358)**

ALPHABETIC

(PA)=Parent Co (HQ)=Headquarters (DH)=Div Headquarters

AZ Automotive, Roseville Also called Sodecia Auto Detroit Corp *(G-14478)*

Azon Elite Summaries, Southfield Also called Next Level Media Inc *(G-15666)*

Azon Usa Inc (PA) 269 385-5942
643 W Crosstown Pkwy Kalamazoo (49008) *(G-9129)*

Azon Usa Inc 269 385-5942
2204 Ravine Rd Kalamazoo (49004) *(G-9130)*

Azore Software LLC 734 525-0300
12190 Hubbard St Livonia (48150) *(G-10130)*

Azoth LLC 734 669-3797
1099 Highland Dr Ste F Ann Arbor (48108) *(G-392)*

Aztec Manufacturing Corp 734 942-7433
15378 Oakwood Dr Romulus (48174) *(G-14253)*

Aztec Producing Co Inc 269 792-0505
3312 12th St Wayland (49348) *(G-18188)*

Aztecnology LLC 734 857-2045
15677 Noecker Way Ste 100 Southgate (48195) *(G-15748)*

Azure Training Systems Jv LLC 734 761-5836
1229 Oak Valley Dr Ann Arbor (48108) *(G-393)*

B & B Custom and Prod Wldg 517 524-7121
10391 Spring Arbor Rd Spring Arbor (49283) *(G-15789)*

B & B Entps Prtg Cnvrtng Inc 313 891-9840
17800 Filer St Detroit (48212) *(G-4037)*

B & B Heartwoods Inc 734 332-9525
5444 Whitmore Lake Rd Ann Arbor (48105) *(G-394)*

B & B Holdings Groesbeck LLC 586 554-7600
42450 R Mancini Dr Sterling Heights (48314) *(G-15940)*

B & B Mold & Engineering Inc 586 773-6664
25185 Easy St Warren (48089) *(G-17721)*

B & B Pretzels Inc (PA) 248 358-1655
19155 Addison Dr Southfield (48075) *(G-15500)*

B & B Production LLC 586 822-9960
10103 Kercheval St Detroit (48214) *(G-4038)*

B & D Cold Heading, Taylor Also called B & D Thread Rolling Inc *(G-16384)*

B & D Metal Fab 616 255-1796
10717 Arbogast Rd Morley (49336) *(G-11619)*

B & D Publishing LLC 586 651-3623
35688 Diane Ln Richmond (48062) *(G-13833)*

B & D Sales and Service, Plymouth Also called Skyway Precision Inc *(G-13300)*

B & D Thread Rolling Inc 734 728-7070
25000 Brest Taylor (48180) *(G-16384)*

B & G Custom Works Inc 269 686-9420
2830 113th Ave Allegan (49010) *(G-149)*

B & G Products Inc 616 698-9050
3631 44th St Se Ste E Grand Rapids (49512) *(G-6488)*

B & H Cementing Services Inc 989 773-5975
5580 Venture Way Mount Pleasant (48858) *(G-11682)*

B & H Machine Sales, Detroit Also called Forged Tubular Products Inc *(G-4242)*

B & H Machine Sales Inc 313 843-6720
9339 W Fort St Detroit (48209) *(G-4039)*

B & H Plastic Co Inc 586 727-7100
66725 S Forest Ave Richmond (48062) *(G-13834)*

B & H Tractor & Truck Inc 989 773-5975
5580 Venture Way Mount Pleasant (48858) *(G-11683)*

B & J Enmeling Inc A Mich Corp 313 365-6620
6827 E Davison St Detroit (48212) *(G-4040)*

B & J Tool Co 810 629-8577
11289 Quality Dr Fenton (48430) *(G-5454)*

B & J Tool Services Inc 810 629-8577
11289 Quality Way Dr Fenton (48430) *(G-5455)*

B & K Buffing Inc 734 941-2144
29040 Northline Rd Romulus (48174) *(G-14254)*

B & K Machine Products Inc 269 637-3001
100 Aylworth Ave South Haven (49090) *(G-15401)*

B & L Industries Inc 810 987-9121
2121 16th St Port Huron (48060) *(G-13456)*

B & L Plating Co Inc 586 778-9300
21353 Edom Ave Warren (48089) *(G-17722)*

B & M Imaging Inc 269 968-2403
1514 Columbia Ave W Battle Creek (49015) *(G-1188)*

B & M Machine & Tool Company 989 288-2934
7665 E M 71 Durand (48429) *(G-4839)*

B & N Plastics Inc 586 758-0030
8100 E 9 Mile Rd Warren (48089) *(G-17723)*

B & O Saws Inc 616 794-7297
825 Reed St Belding (48809) *(G-1435)*

B & P Manufacturing, Cadillac Also called Brooks & Perkins Inc *(G-2318)*

B & R Gear Company Inc 517 787-8381
2102 River St Jackson (49202) *(G-8819)*

B & R Manufacturing Division, Grandville Also called Hadley Products Corporation *(G-7385)*

B & W Woodwork Inc 616 772-4577
11362 James St Holland (49424) *(G-7969)*

B and C Logging 906 753-2425
N8759 P 1 Rd Stephenson (49887) *(G-15906)*

B and L Metal Finishing LLC 269 767-2225
755 Airway Dr Allegan (49010) *(G-150)*

B and R Oil Company Inc 313 292-5500
24501 Ecorse Rd Taylor (48180) *(G-16385)*

B B Wheelchair Services 906 281-7202
1215 Jasberg St Hancock (49930) *(G-7615)*

B C & A Co 734 429-3129
1270 Barnes Ct Saline (48176) *(G-15005)*

B C I Collet Inc 734 326-1222
6125 E Executive Dr Westland (48185) *(G-18359)*

B C Manufacturing Inc 248 344-0101
29431 Lorie Ln Wixom (48393) *(G-18617)*

B Erickson Manufacturing Ltd 810 765-1144
6317 King Rd Marine City (48039) *(G-10955)*

B F S Printing and Promot 248 685-2456
786 Knolls Landing Dr Milford (48381) *(G-11454)*

B G Industries Inc 313 292-5355
6835 Monroe Blvd Taylor (48180) *(G-16386)*

B H Awning & Tent, Benton Harbor Also called Benton Harbor Awning & Tent *(G-1535)*

B K Corporation 989 777-2111
5675 Dixie Hwy Saginaw (48601) *(G-14606)*

B L Harroun and Son Inc (PA) 269 345-8657
1018 Staples Ave Kalamazoo (49007) *(G-9131)*

B L Tool Products 517 896-1624
6407 Ferris Rd Eaton Rapids (48827) *(G-4954)*

B M F, Buchanan Also called Buchanan Metal Forming Inc *(G-2190)*

B M Industries Inc 810 658-0052
130 Harsen Rd Lapeer (48446) *(G-9913)*

B Nektar LLC 313 744-6323
1511 Jarvis St Ferndale (48220) *(G-5530)*

B Nektar Meadery, Ferndale Also called B Nektar LLC *(G-5530)*

B Pretty Hats LLC 616 726-0002
4474 Equestrian Dr Hudsonville (49426) *(G-8568)*

B T I Industries 586 532-8411
49820 Oakland Dr Shelby Township (48315) *(G-15177)*

B W and F Excavating, Kenockee Also called Bobs Welding & Fabricating *(G-9423)*

B&B Dumpsters, Remus Also called Brian A Broomfield *(G-13814)*

B&B HAIr&co LLC 616 600-4568
625 Kenmoor Ave Se # 301 Grand Rapids (49546) *(G-6489)*

B&M Welding Inc 810 837-0742
2635 Wheeler Rd Snover (48472) *(G-15391)*

B&P Littleford Day LLC 989 757-1300
1000 Hess Ave Saginaw (48601) *(G-14607)*

B&P Littleford LLC (PA) 989 757-1300
1000 Hess Ave Saginaw (48601) *(G-14608)*

B&P Process Eqp & Systems, Saginaw Also called B&P Littleford LLC *(G-14608)*

B&T Logging 810 417-6167
4619 Frenchline Rd Marlette (48453) *(G-10977)*

B'Bites, Lathrup Village Also called All Natural Bites LLC *(G-9974)*

B-J Industries Inc 586 778-7200
14440 Barber Ave Warren (48088) *(G-17724)*

B-Quick Instant Printing 616 243-6562
3120 Division Ave S Grand Rapids (49548) *(G-6490)*

B.K. Vending, Saginaw Also called Klopp Group LLC *(G-14679)*

B4 Sports Inc 248 454-9700
2055 Franklin Rd Bloomfield Hills (48302) *(G-1802)*

Baade Fabricating & Engrg 517 639-4536
210 S Ray Quincy Rd Quincy (49082) *(G-13663)*

Baby Pallet 248 210-3851
1367 Forest Bay Dr Waterford (48328) *(G-18103)*

Babybops Melanin Collection 313 770-4997
607 Shelby St Detroit (48226) *(G-4041)*

Bach Mobilities Inc 906 789-9490
1617 N 28th St Escanaba (49829) *(G-5059)*

Bach Services & Mfg Co LLC 231 263-2777
2777 Lynx Ln Kingsley (49649) *(G-9521)*

Back Machine Shop LLC 269 963-7061
1300 W Dickman Rd Springfield (49037) *(G-15860)*

Backdraft Brewing Company 734 722-7639
35122 W Michigan Ave Wayne (48184) *(G-18215)*

Backyard Play Systems LLC 734 242-6900
1000 Ternes Dr Monroe (48162) *(G-11525)*

Backyard Products LLC (PA) 734 242-6900
1000 Ternes Dr Monroe (48162) *(G-11526)*

Backyard Services LLC 734 242-6900
1000 Ternes Dr Monroe (48162) *(G-11527)*

Bad Axe Metal & Iron Art 989 658-8324
7125 Frieburger Rd Ubly (48475) *(G-17475)*

Bad Axe Prints 248 207-6999
1012 Yorick Path Wixom (48393) *(G-18618)*

Bad Day Industries LLC 844 213-6541
9932 Bell Rd Clarksville (48815) *(G-3077)*

Bader & Co 810 648-2404
989 W Sanilac Rd Sandusky (48471) *(G-15055)*

Badger Tool LLC 586 246-1810
35425 Beattie Dr Sterling Heights (48312) *(G-15941)*

Bae Industries Inc (HQ) 586 754-3000
26020 Sherwood Ave Warren (48091) *(G-17725)*

Bae Industries Inc 248 475-9600
1426 Pacific Dr Auburn Hills (48326) *(G-809)*

Bae Systems Land Armaments LP 586 596-4123
34201 Van Dyke Ave Sterling Heights (48312) *(G-15942)*

Bag Stitchery 231 276-3163
536 Woodland Dr Traverse City (49686) *(G-16610)*

Bagel Brothers Cafe, Southfield Also called Vivian Enterprises LLC *(G-15740)*

ALPHABETIC SECTION
Barron Industries Inc

Bahama Souvenirs Inc (PA)....269 964-8275
20260 North Ave Battle Creek (49017) ***(G-1189)***
Bahwse/Bahwse Brand LLC....313 704-7376
2400 S Bassett St Detroit (48217) ***(G-4042)***
Bailer and De Shaw....989 684-3610
204 S Old Kawkawlin Rd Kawkawlin (48631) ***(G-9414)***
Bailey Electrical Inc....906 478-8000
4070 E Simmons Rd Hessel (49745) ***(G-7873)***
Bailey Sand & Gravel Co....517 750-4889
6505 W Michigan Ave Jackson (49201) ***(G-8820)***
Bainbridge Manufacturing Inc....616 447-7631
1931 Will Ave Nw Ste 1 Grand Rapids (49504) ***(G-6491)***
Baird Investments LLC (PA)....586 665-0154
43333 Westview Dr Sterling Heights (48313) ***(G-15943)***
Bake N Cakes LP....517 337-2253
3003 E Kalamazoo St Lansing (48912) ***(G-9811)***
Bake Station Bakeries Mich Inc....248 352-9000
26000 W 8 Mile Rd Southfield (48033) ***(G-15501)***
Bakelite N Sumitomo Amer Inc (HQ)....248 313-7000
46820 Magellan Dr Ste C Novi (48377) ***(G-12373)***
Baker Atlas, Mount Pleasant *Also called Baker Hghes Olfld Oprtions LLC* ***(G-11685)***
Baker Book House Company (PA)....616 676-9185
6030 Fulton St E Ada (49301) ***(G-10)***
Baker Enterprises Inc (HQ)....989 354-2189
801 Johnson St Alpena (49707) ***(G-281)***
Baker Fastening Systems Inc....616 669-7400
5030 40th Ave Hudsonville (49426) ***(G-8569)***
Baker Hghes Olfld Oprtions LLC....989 772-1600
1950 Commercial Dr Mount Pleasant (48858) ***(G-11684)***
Baker Hghes Olfld Oprtions LLC....989 773-7992
2222 Enterprise Dr Mount Pleasant (48858) ***(G-11685)***
Baker Hghes Olfld Oprtions LLC....231 342-9408
2397 Traversefield Dr Traverse City (49686) ***(G-16611)***
Baker Hughes Holdings LLC....989 506-2167
2222 Enterprise Dr Mount Pleasant (48858) ***(G-11686)***
Baker Hughes Holdings LLC....989 732-2082
526 Barnyard Gaylord (49735) ***(G-6119)***
Baker Hughes Incorporat..., Mount Pleasant *Also called Baker Hughes Holdings LLC* ***(G-11686)***
Baker Metal Products Corp., Grand Haven *Also called Rss Baker LLC* ***(G-6356)***
Baker Oil Tools, Mount Pleasant *Also called Baker Hghes Olfld Oprtions LLC* ***(G-11684)***
Baker Perkins Inc....616 784-3111
3223 Kraft Ave Se Grand Rapids (49512) ***(G-6492)***
Baker Publishing Group, Ada *Also called Baker Book House Company* ***(G-10)***
Baker Rd Seating & Restoration, Belding *Also called Baker Road Upholstery Inc* ***(G-1436)***
Baker Road Upholstery Inc....616 794-3027
1122 S Bridge St Belding (48809) ***(G-1436)***
Bakers Gas and Welding Sups....517 539-5047
3151 Cooper St Jackson (49201) ***(G-8821)***
Bakers Rhapsody....269 767-1368
144 S Front St Dowagiac (49047) ***(G-4777)***
Bakery Equipment/Design, Wayland *Also called Buck-Spica Equipment Ltd* ***(G-18192)***
Bakery Ingredient Mfg, Fenton *Also called Ezbake Technologies LLC* ***(G-5474)***
Bakes & Kropp Ltd....888 206-0015
154 S Rose St Mount Clemens (48043) ***(G-11629)***
Bakewell Company....269 459-8030
2725 E Milham Ave Portage (49002) ***(G-13545)***
Baking Company LLC....616 241-2583
1880 Turner Ave Nw Ste C Grand Rapids (49504) ***(G-6493)***
BAKKER METAL FABRICATION, Coopersville *Also called Bakker Welding & Mechanics LLC* ***(G-3680)***
Bakker Welding & Mechanics LLC (PA)....616 828-8664
15031 84th Ave Coopersville (49404) ***(G-3680)***
Balance Technology Inc (PA)....734 769-2100
7035 Jomar Dr Whitmore Lake (48189) ***(G-18520)***
Baldauf Enterprises Inc (PA)....989 686-0350
1321 S Valley Center Dr Bay City (48706) ***(G-1324)***
Baldauf Enterprises Inc....989 686-0350
910 Harry S Truman Pkwy Bay City (48706) ***(G-1325)***
Baldwin Precision Inc....231 237-4515
5339 M 66 N Charlevoix (49720) ***(G-2710)***
Baliko Pos Inc....248 470-4652
22338 Tredwell Ave Farmington Hills (48336) ***(G-5180)***
Ball Hard Music Group LLC (PA)....833 246-4552
330 E Elm Ave Monroe (48162) ***(G-11528)***
Ballard Power Systems Corp....313 583-5980
15001 N Commerce Dr Dearborn (48120) ***(G-3812)***
Bally Block Co....231 347-4170
1420 Standish Ave Petoskey (49770) ***(G-12989)***
Balogh....734 283-3972
14102 Jackson St Taylor (48180) ***(G-16387)***
Balogh Inc....810 360-0182
3637 S Old Us 23 Ste 100 Brighton (48114) ***(G-1948)***
Bam, Holland *Also called Century Lanes Inc* ***(G-7992)***
Banacom Instant Signs....810 230-0233
4463 Miller Rd Flint (48507) ***(G-5649)***
Band-Ayd Systems Intl Inc....586 294-8851
355 E Whitcomb Ave Madison Heights (48071) ***(G-10677)***

Bandit Industries Inc....989 561-2270
6750 W Millbrook Rd Remus (49340) ***(G-13813)***
Bandit Utv Suspension....586 419-9574
1631 Palms Rd Columbus (48063) ***(G-3497)***
Banggameus....734 904-1916
2590 Cook Creek Dr Ann Arbor (48103) ***(G-395)***
Bangor Plastics Inc....269 427-7971
809 Washington St Bangor (49013) ***(G-1128)***
Banks Hardwoods Inc (PA)....269 483-2323
69937 M 103 White Pigeon (49099) ***(G-18472)***
Banks Hardwoods Florida, White Pigeon *Also called Banks Hardwoods Inc* ***(G-18472)***
Bannasch Welding Inc....517 482-2916
807 Lake Lansing Rd Ste 1 Lansing (48906) ***(G-9674)***
Banner Broach Inc....586 493-9219
12978 E 10 Mile Rd Warren (48089) ***(G-17726)***
Banner Engineering & Sales Inc....989 755-0584
1840 N Michigan Ave Ste 1 Saginaw (48602) ***(G-14609)***
Banner Sign Specialties, Shelby Township *Also called Phillips Enterprises Inc* ***(G-15301)***
BANNER-DAY, Saginaw *Also called Banner Engineering & Sales Inc* ***(G-14609)***
Bannergalaxycom LLC....231 941-8200
2322 Cass Rd Traverse City (49684) ***(G-16612)***
Banta Furniture Company....616 575-8180
3390 Broadmoor Ave Se A Grand Rapids (49512) ***(G-6494)***
Banta Management Resources, Grand Rapids *Also called Banta Furniture Company* ***(G-6494)***
Bar Processing Corporation....734 243-8937
550 Ternes Dr Monroe (48162) ***(G-11529)***
Bar Processing Corporation (HQ)....734 782-4454
26601 W Huron River Dr Flat Rock (48134) ***(G-5616)***
Bar Processing Corporation....734 782-4454
22534 Groesbeck Hwy Warren (48089) ***(G-17727)***
Baraga County Concrete Company....906 353-6595
468 N Superior Ave Baraga (49908) ***(G-1134)***
Baraga Lumber Division, Baraga *Also called Besse Forest Products Inc* ***(G-1135)***
Barber Creek Sand & Gravel....616 675-7619
15666 Barber Creek Ave Kent City (49330) ***(G-9427)***
Barbron Corporation....586 716-3530
200 E Dresden St Kalkaska (49646) ***(G-9382)***
Barclay Pharmacy....248 852-4600
75 Barclay Cir Ste 114 Rochester Hills (48307) ***(G-13961)***
Barcroft Technology LLC....313 378-0133
29193 Nw Hwy St 715 Southfield (48034) ***(G-15502)***
Bare Bulb Companies LLC....616 644-8251
2090 Celebration Dr Ne # 204 Grand Rapids (49525) ***(G-6495)***
Bargain Hunter, Sandusky *Also called J R C Inc* ***(G-15061)***
Bark River Concrete Pdts Co (PA)....906 466-9940
1397 Us Highway 2 41 Bark River (49807) ***(G-1153)***
Barker Manufacturing Co (PA)....269 965-2371
1125 Watkins Rd Battle Creek (49015) ***(G-1190)***
Barker Manufacturing Co....269 965-2371
781 Watkins Rd Battle Creek (49015) ***(G-1191)***
Barkshanty Hops LLC....810 300-8049
1231 Bishop Rd Grosse Pointe Park (48230) ***(G-7549)***
Barlow Custom Woodworking....810 220-0648
1340 Baywood Cir Brighton (48116) ***(G-1949)***
Barnes Group Inc....517 393-5110
5300 Aurelius Rd Lansing (48911) ***(G-9812)***
Barnes Group Inc....586 415-6677
33280 Groesbeck Hwy Fraser (48026) ***(G-5900)***
Barnes Industries Inc....248 541-2333
1161 E 11 Mile Rd Madison Heights (48071) ***(G-10678)***
Barnes Welding & Fab LLC....989 287-0161
8200 S Holland Rd Sheridan (48884) ***(G-15380)***
Barnes Wood Works....269 599-3479
7531 Lake Wood Dr Portage (49002) ***(G-13546)***
Barneys Welding and Fabg....989 753-4892
965 Shattuck Rd Saginaw (48604) ***(G-14610)***
Baron Acquisition LLC (PA)....248 585-0444
999 E Mandoline Ave Madison Heights (48071) ***(G-10679)***
Baron Industries, Madison Heights *Also called Baron Acquisition LLC* ***(G-10679)***
Baron's Window Coverings, Lansing *Also called Barons Inc* ***(G-9813)***
Barons Inc....517 484-1366
325 S Washington Sq Lansing (48933) ***(G-9813)***
Barracuda Mfg, Wixom *Also called Rgm New Ventures Inc* ***(G-18742)***
Barrels of Yum, Whitehall *Also called Fretty Media LLC* ***(G-18497)***
Barrett Advertising, Saginaw *Also called Jordan Advertising Inc* ***(G-14674)***
Barrett Paving Materials Inc....734 941-0200
13501 S Huron River Dr Romulus (48174) ***(G-14255)***
Barrett Signs....989 792-7446
321 Lyon St Saginaw (48602) ***(G-14611)***
Barrette Outdoor Living Inc....810 235-0400
3200 Rbert T Longway Blvd Flint (48506) ***(G-5650)***
Barron Cast, Oxford *Also called Barron Industries Inc* ***(G-12876)***
Barron Group Inc....248 628-4300
215 Plexus Dr Oxford (48371) ***(G-12875)***
Barron Industries Inc (PA)....248 628-4300
215 Plexus Dr Oxford (48371) ***(G-12876)***

ALPHABETIC

(PA)=Parent Co (HQ)=Headquarters (DH)=Div Headquarters
2022 Harris Michigan Industrial Directory
939

Barron Industries Inc ALPHABETIC SECTION

Barron Industries Inc 248 628-4300
215 Plexus Dr Oxford (48371) *(G-12877)*
Barron LLC 248 879-6203
247 Minnesota Dr Troy (48083) *(G-16968)*
Barron Precision Instruments 810 695-2080
8170 Embury Rd Grand Blanc (48439) *(G-6234)*
Barry Electric-Rovill Co 810 985-8960
1431 White St Port Huron (48060) *(G-13457)*
Barrys Sign Company 810 234-9919
3501 Blackington Ave Flint (48503) *(G-5651)*
Bars Products Inc (PA) 248 634-8278
10386 N Holly Rd Holly (48442) *(G-8262)*
Bartec USA LLC 586 685-1300
44231 Phoenix Dr Sterling Heights (48314) *(G-15944)*
Bartlett Arborist Sup & Mfrs, Marlette *Also called Bartlett Manufacturing Co LLC (G-10978)*
Bartlett Manufacturing Co LLC 989 635-8900
7876 S Van Dyke Rd Ste 10 Marlette (48453) *(G-10978)*
Barton Boatworks 616 240-5562
4328 52nd St Holland (49423) *(G-7970)*
Bartz Mfg LLC 517 281-2571
1215 N Smith Rd Eaton Rapids (48827) *(G-4955)*
Baryames Tux Shop Inc 517 349-6555
2421 W Grand River Ave Okemos (48864) *(G-12659)*
Basan Cord Inc 888 802-2726
4170 Martin Rd Commerce Township (48390) *(G-3513)*
Basc Manufacturing Inc 248 360-2272
4325 Martin Rd Commerce Township (48390) *(G-3514)*
Basch Olovson Engineering Co 231 865-2027
3438 E Mount Garfield Rd Fruitport (49415) *(G-6060)*
BASF 231 719-3019
1740 Whitehall Rd Muskegon (49445) *(G-11774)*
BASF Corporation 734 324-6963
40 James Desana Dr Wyandotte (48192) *(G-18808)*
BASF Corporation 734 324-6000
1609 Biddle Ave Wyandotte (48192) *(G-18809)*
BASF Corporation 734 324-6100
1609 Biddle Ave Wyandotte (48192) *(G-18810)*
BASF Corporation 269 668-3371
23930 Concord Ave Mattawan (49071) *(G-11162)*
BASF Corporation 734 759-2011
800 Central St Wyandotte (48192) *(G-18811)*
BASF Corporation 734 591-5560
13000 Levan Rd Livonia (48150) *(G-10131)*
BASF Corporation 248 827-4670
26701 Telegraph Rd Southfield (48033) *(G-15503)*
Basic Rubber and Plastics Co (PA) 248 360-7400
8700 Boulder Ct Walled Lake (48390) *(G-17664)*
Basin Material Handling, Sturgis *Also called Vci Inc (G-16328)*
Bata Plastics, Grand Rapids *Also called Lwhs Ltd (G-6954)*
Bath Bombs By Lori 734 890-3832
2538 Muirfield Dr Westland (48186) *(G-18360)*
Batson Printing Inc 269 926-6011
195 Michigan St Benton Harbor (49022) *(G-1532)*
Battels Sugar Bush 989 872-4794
7964 Daus Rd Cass City (48726) *(G-2611)*
Batteries Plus, Birmingham *Also called M & M Irish Enterprises Inc (G-1733)*
Batteries Plus, Roseville *Also called G & L Powerup Inc (G-14409)*
Batteries Plus 269 925-7367
2061 M 139 Benton Harbor (49022) *(G-1533)*
Battery Center of America 248 399-5999
1805 E 9 Mile Rd Ferndale (48220) *(G-5531)*
Battle Creek Chamber Commerce, Battle Creek *Also called Silent Observer (G-1295)*
Battle Creek Flyers LLC 269 579-2914
36 Hiawatha Dr Battle Creek (49015) *(G-1192)*
Batts Group Ltd (PA) 616 956-3053
3855 Sparks Dr Se Ste 222 Grand Rapids (49546) *(G-6496)*
Bauble Patch Inc 616 785-1100
5228 Alpine Ave Nw Ste A Comstock Park (49321) *(G-3589)*
Bauer Precision Tool Co 586 758-7370
8670 E 9 Mile Rd Warren (48089) *(G-17728)*
Bauer Products Inc 616 245-4540
702 Evergreen St Se Grand Rapids (49507) *(G-6497)*
Bauer Sheet Metal & Fabg Inc (PA) 231 773-3244
1550 Evanston Ave Muskegon (49442) *(G-11775)*
Bauer Soft Water Co 269 695-7900
1760 Mayflower Rd Niles (49120) *(G-12112)*
Baumann Tool & Die 616 772-6768
232 E Roosevelt Ave Zeeland (49464) *(G-18995)*
Baumans Running & Walking Shop, Flint *Also called Baumans Running Center Inc (G-5652)*
Baumans Running Center Inc 810 238-5981
1473 W Hill Rd Flint (48507) *(G-5652)*
Bawden Industries Inc 734 721-6414
29909 Beverly Rd Romulus (48174) *(G-14256)*
Baxter Machine & Tool Co 517 782-2808
103 N Horton St Jackson (49202) *(G-8822)*
Bay Alphi Manufacturing Inc 517 849-9945
576 Beck St Jonesville (49250) *(G-9085)*
Bay Archery Sales Co 989 894-5800
2713 Center Ave Essexville (48732) *(G-5109)*
Bay Area Tool LLC 231 946-3500
466 Hughes Dr Traverse City (49696) *(G-16613)*
Bay Bread Co 231 922-8022
601 Randolph St Traverse City (49684) *(G-16614)*
Bay Carbon Inc 989 686-8090
800 Marquette St Ste 2 Bay City (48706) *(G-1326)*
Bay Cast Technologies Inc 989 892-9500
2611 Center Ave Bay City (48708) *(G-1327)*
Bay City Crane Inc 989 867-4292
3951 Allen Rd Turner (48765) *(G-17462)*
Bay City Division, Corunna *Also called Newcor Inc (G-3715)*
Bay City Fireworks Festival 989 892-2264
3296 E Fisher Rd Bay City (48706) *(G-1328)*
Bay City Times, Flint *Also called Herald Newspapers Company Inc (G-5715)*
Bay Composites Inc 989 891-9159
1801 Jarman Rd Essexville (48732) *(G-5110)*
Bay Corrugated Container Inc 734 243-5400
1655 W 7th St Monroe (48161) *(G-11530)*
Bay Design Inc 586 296-7130
17800 15 Mile Rd Fraser (48026) *(G-5901)*
Bay Electronics Inc 586 296-0900
20805 Kraft Blvd Roseville (48066) *(G-14379)*
Bay Geophysical, Traverse City *Also called Baygeo Inc (G-16617)*
Bay Home Medical and Rehab Inc (PA) 231 933-1200
5752 Stonebridge Dr Sw Grandville (49418) *(G-7366)*
Bay Machine Tool Co Inc 989 894-2863
110 Woodside Ave Essexville (48732) *(G-5111)*
Bay Machinery, Blissfield *Also called JB Machinery LLC (G-1765)*
Bay Machining and Sales Inc 989 316-1801
4421 Ace Commercial Ct Bay City (48706) *(G-1329)*
Bay Manufacturing Corporation 989 358-7198
3750 Us Highway 23 N Alpena (49707) *(G-282)*
Bay Motor Products Inc 231 941-0411
3100 Cass Rd Ste 1 Traverse City (49684) *(G-16615)*
Bay Plastics Machinery Co LLC 989 671-9630
3494 N Euclid Ave Bay City (48706) *(G-1330)*
Bay Products Inc 586 296-7130
17800 15 Mile Rd Fraser (48026) *(G-5902)*
Bay Supply & Marketing Inc 231 943-3249
520 Us Highway 31 S Traverse City (49685) *(G-16616)*
Bay Tool Inc 989 894-2863
110 Woodside Ave Essexville (48732) *(G-5112)*
Bay United Motors Inc 989 684-3972
4353 Wilder Rd Bay City (48706) *(G-1331)*
Bay Valley Foods LLC 269 792-2277
652 W Elm St Wayland (49348) *(G-18189)*
Bay Wood Homes Inc 989 245-4156
1393 Eden Gardens Dr Fenton (48430) *(G-5456)*
Bay-Houston Towing Company 810 648-2210
875 E Sanilac Rd Sandusky (48471) *(G-15056)*
Bayer Crop Science 517 676-3586
1440 Okemos Rd Mason (48854) *(G-11118)*
Bayer Cropscience LP 231 744-4711
1740 Whitehall Rd Muskegon (49445) *(G-11776)*
Baygeo Inc 231 941-7660
528 Hughes Dr Traverse City (49696) *(G-16617)*
Bayloff Stmped Pdts Dtroit Inc (PA) 734 397-9116
5910 Belleville Rd Van Buren Twp (48111) *(G-17510)*
Baylume Inc 877 881-3641
2832 High St Clawson (48017) *(G-3087)*
Bayshore Custom Assembly LLC 616 396-5502
13055 Riley St Ste 40 Holland (49424) *(G-7971)*
Bayside Engineering and Mfg 906 420-8770
80 Delta Ave Gladstone (49837) *(G-6173)*
Bayside Industries 231 632-2222
921 Mitchell St Traverse City (49686) *(G-16618)*
Bazzi Tire & Wheels 313 846-8888
8001 Schaefer Hwy Detroit (48228) *(G-4043)*
Bbb Industries 231 735-6060
10515 S Monaco Way Traverse City (49684) *(G-16619)*
BBC Communications Inc 616 399-0432
6463 Lakeshore Dr West Olive (49460) *(G-18347)*
Bbcm Inc 248 410-2528
1015 Golf Dr Bloomfield Hills (48302) *(G-1803)*
Bbg North America Ltd Partnr 248 572-6550
2371 Xcelsior Dr Oxford (48371) *(G-12878)*
Bbi Group, Lake Orion *Also called Complete Auto-Mation Inc (G-9597)*
Bbj Graphics Inc 248 450-3149
18940 W 8 Mile Rd Southfield (48075) *(G-15504)*
Bbp Investment Holdings LLC (PA) 231 725-4966
525 W Laketon Ave Muskegon (49441) *(G-11777)*
Bc Woodworks 989 820-7680
7015 Woodlea Rd W Oscoda (48750) *(G-12754)*
Bcc Distribution Inc 734 737-9300
7529 Baron Dr Canton (48187) *(G-2439)*
Bcs Creative LLC 248 917-1660
10012 Old Farm Trl Davisburg (48350) *(G-3760)*
BCT Internet LLC 810 771-9117
6076 Dort Hwy Grand Blanc (48439) *(G-6235)*

ALPHABETIC SECTION

BCT-2017 Inc (PA) 231 832-3114
  710 E Church Ave Reed City (49677) *(G-13789)*
Bcubed Manufacturing LLC 989 356-2294
  666 Mckinley Ave Alpena (49707) *(G-283)*
Bd Classic Sewing 231 825-2628
  1890 E Stoney Corners Rd Mc Bain (49657) *(G-11176)*
Bd Diagnostic Systems 313 442-8800
  920 Henry St Detroit (48201) *(G-4044)*
Bdgn Corporation 616 669-9040
  3565 Highland Dr Hudsonville (49426) *(G-8570)*
Bdk Group Northern Mich Inc 574 875-5183
  6795 Us Highway 31 N Charlevoix (49720) *(G-2711)*
Bdr Inc 989 732-1608
  9319 M 32 E Johannesburg (49751) *(G-9080)*
BDS Company Inc 517 279-2135
  491 W Garfield Ave Coldwater (49036) *(G-3421)*
Be A Boss Not A Bossy Bih LLC 734 833-8106
  35700 E Michigan Ave # 505 Wayne (48184) *(G-18216)*
Be At Ease Products, Clinton Township *Also called Entrepreneur Solutions LLC* *(G-3232)*
Beacom Enterprises Inc 906 647-3831
  6671 E Rockview Rd Pickford (49774) *(G-13030)*
Beacom's Chipping & Logging, Pickford *Also called Beacom Enterprises Inc* *(G-13030)*
Beacon Billboards LLC 734 421-7512
  11030 Brookfield St Livonia (48150) *(G-10132)*
Beacon Park Finishing LLC 248 318-4286
  15765 Sturgeon St Roseville (48066) *(G-14380)*
Beacon Sign Co (PA) 313 368-3410
  1280 Kempar Ave Madison Heights (48071) *(G-10680)*
Beacon Tool Inc 269 649-3558
  111 N Leja Dr Vicksburg (49097) *(G-17599)*
Bead Gallery 734 663-6800
  311 E Liberty St Ann Arbor (48104) *(G-396)*
Beaden Screen Inc 810 679-3119
  305 Melvin St Croswell (48422) *(G-3729)*
Beagio's 1, Marlette *Also called Beagios Franchises Inc* *(G-10979)*
Beagios Franchises Inc 989 635-7173
  3013 Main St Marlette (48453) *(G-10979)*
Beamer Laser Marking 810 471-3044
  7136 Sheridan Rd Flushing (48433) *(G-5803)*
Bean Counter Inc 906 523-5027
  25963 Cedar St Calumet (49913) *(G-2408)*
Beano's On Site Machining, Houghton Lake *Also called BOS Field Machining Inc* *(G-8394)*
Beans Best LLC 734 707-7378
  1240 Jewett St Ann Arbor (48104) *(G-397)*
Bear Creek Logging 269 317-7475
  123 Court St Ceresco (49033) *(G-2702)*
Bear Creek Sand & Gravel LLC 989 681-3641
  10907 Riverside Dr Saint Louis (48880) *(G-14987)*
Bear Cub Holdings Inc 231 242-1152
  8761 M 119 Harbor Springs (49740) *(G-7641)*
Bear Naked Inc 203 662-1136
  1 Kellogg Sq Battle Creek (49017) *(G-1193)*
Bear Truss & Components, Saint Louis *Also called Ken Luneack Construction Inc* *(G-14992)*
Bear Truss - US Lbm LLC 989 681-5774
  721 E Washington St Saint Louis (48880) *(G-14988)*
Bearcub Outfitters LLC 231 439-9500
  321 E Lake St Unit 1 Petoskey (49770) *(G-12990)*
Beard Balm LLC 313 451-3653
  1951 Temple St Detroit (48216) *(G-4045)*
Bearded Vinyl LLC 989 786-9994
  4085 Salling Ave Lewiston (49756) *(G-10018)*
Beards Brewery LLC 231 753-2221
  215 E Lake St Petoskey (49770) *(G-12991)*
Beardslee Investments Inc 810 748-9951
  2256 N Channel Dr Harsens Island (48028) *(G-7748)*
Bearing Holdings LLC (HQ) 313 758-2000
  1 Dauch Dr Detroit (48211) *(G-4046)*
Beattie Spring & Welding Svc 810 239-9151
  2840 Rbert T Longway Blvd Flint (48506) *(G-5653)*
Beau Satchelle LLC 313 374-8462
  4860 Washtenaw Ave Ste I Ann Arbor (48108) *(G-398)*
Beaumont Enterprise 989 269-6464
  211 N Heisterman St Bad Axe (48413) *(G-1098)*
Beauty Spot, Detroit *Also called Kims Mart Inc* *(G-4362)*
Beaver Aerospace & Defense Inc (HQ) 734 853-5003
  11850 Mayfield St Livonia (48150) *(G-10133)*
Beaver Creek Cabinets LLC 231 821-2861
  8636 Skeels Rd Holton (49425) *(G-8337)*
Beaver Creek Wood Products LLC 920 680-9663
  993 26th St Menominee (49858) *(G-11228)*
Beaver Log Homes Inc 231 258-5020
  850 S Cedar St Kalkaska (49646) *(G-9383)*
Beaver Stair Company 248 628-0441
  549 E Lakeville Rd Oxford (48371) *(G-12879)*
Beavers Welding & Fabracating 517 375-0443
  400 W Grand River Rd Webberville (48892) *(G-18242)*
Becharas Bros Coffee Co 313 869-4700
  14501 Hamilton Ave Detroit (48203) *(G-4047)*
Bechtel Sand & Gravel 810 346-2041
  5278 Churchill Rd Brown City (48416) *(G-2135)*

Beck & Boys Custom Apparel 734 458-4015
  33650 5 Mile Rd Livonia (48154) *(G-10134)*
Beck Industries Inc 586 790-4060
  24454 Sorrentino Ct Clinton Township (48035) *(G-3180)*
Beck Mobile Concrete LLC 517 655-4996
  2303 E Grand River Rd Williamston (48895) *(G-18568)*
Beckan Industries Inc 269 381-6984
  2700 N Pitcher St Kalamazoo (49004) *(G-9132)*
Becker & Scrivens Con Pdts Inc 517 437-4250
  3340 Beck Rd Hillsdale (49242) *(G-7924)*
Becker Oregon Inc 248 588-7480
  635 Executive Dr Troy (48083) *(G-16969)*
Becker Orthopedic Appliance Co (PA) 248 588-7480
  635 Executive Dr Troy (48083) *(G-16970)*
Becker Robotic Equipment Corp 470 249-7880
  260 Engelwood Dr Ste E Orion (48359) *(G-12724)*
Beckert & Hiester Inc 989 793-2420
  2025 Carman Dr Saginaw (48602) *(G-14612)*
Beckman Brothers Inc 231 861-2031
  3455 W Baker Rd Shelby (49455) *(G-15148)*
Beckman Equipment 231 420-4791
  12800 Airport Rd Cheboygan (49721) *(G-2780)*
Beckman Production Svcs Inc (HQ) 231 258-9524
  3786 Beebe Rd Kalkaska (49646) *(G-9384)*
Becktold Enterprises Inc 269 349-3656
  2101 Palmer Ave Kalamazoo (49001) *(G-9133)*
Becmar Corp 616 675-7479
  585 Canada Rd Bailey (49303) *(G-1118)*
Bedford Machinery Inc 734 848-4980
  9899 Telegraph Rd Erie (48133) *(G-5045)*
Bedford Press, Lambertville *Also called Temperance Printing* *(G-9654)*
Bednarsh Mrris Jwly Design Mfg 248 671-0087
  6600 Telegraph Rd Bloomfield (48301) *(G-1781)*
Bedrock Manufacturing Co LLC 972 422-4372
  485 W Milwaukee St Detroit (48202) *(G-4048)*
Bee Dazzled Candle Works 231 882-7765
  6289 River Rd Benzonia (49616) *(G-1612)*
Bee Line Apiaries & Woodenware, Mendon *Also called Jonathan Showalter* *(G-11218)*
Bee Queen Dairy & Ice Cream, Eastpointe *Also called Aj Hometown LLC* *(G-4927)*
Beebe Fuel Systems 734 261-3500
  13191 Wayne Rd Livonia (48150) *(G-10135)*
Beebe Fuel Systems Inc 248 437-3322
  6351 Wilderness Dr South Lyon (48178) *(G-15427)*
Beech & Rich Inc 269 968-8012
  525 20th St N Springfield (49037) *(G-15861)*
Beechbed Mix 616 263-7422
  120 James St Holland (49424) *(G-7972)*
Beechcraft Products Inc 989 288-2606
  1100 N Saginaw St Durand (48429) *(G-4840)*
Beechem Labs, Shelby *Also called Kelley Laboratories Inc* *(G-15153)*
Beem Fence, Lake City *Also called Mark Beem* *(G-9550)*
Beet Inc 248 432-0052
  1742 Crooks Rd Troy (48084) *(G-16971)*
Behavioral Health, Holland *Also called Holland Community Hosp Aux Inc* *(G-8076)*
Behco Inc 586 755-0200
  23751 Amber Ave Warren (48089) *(G-17729)*
Behind Shutter LLC 248 467-7237
  7070 Anna St Grand Blanc (48439) *(G-6236)*
Behr Climate Systems, Troy *Also called Mahle Behr USA Inc* *(G-17232)*
Behrens Custom Cabinetry LLC 269 720-4950
  200 S Gremps St Paw Paw (49079) *(G-12941)*
Behrmann Printing Company Inc 248 799-7771
  21063 Bridge St Southfield (48033) *(G-15505)*
BEI International LLC 616 204-8274
  10753 Macatawa St Holland (49424) *(G-7973)*
Beirut Bakery Inc 313 533-4422
  25706 Schoolcraft Redford (48239) *(G-13718)*
Beishlag Welding LLC 231 881-5023
  3935 Buell Rd Elmira (49730) *(G-5038)*
Bektrom Foods Inc 734 241-3796
  15610 S Telegraph Rd Monroe (48161) *(G-11531)*
Bekum America Corporation 517 655-4331
  1140 W Grand River Ave Williamston (48895) *(G-18569)*
Bel Lago, Cedar *Also called Weathervane Vinyards Inc* *(G-2640)*
Bel-Kur Inc 734 847-0651
  7297 Express Rd Temperance (48182) *(G-16528)*
Belanger Inc 248 349-7010
  1001 Doheny Dr Northville (48167) *(G-12197)*
Belanger Industrial Products, Northville *Also called Roll It Up Inc* *(G-12255)*
Belash Inc 248 379-4444
  2111 N Wixom Rd Wixom (48393) *(G-18619)*
Belchers Maple Syrup LLC 231 942-1399
  11671 22 Mile Rd Tustin (49688) *(G-17465)*
Belchers' Maple Syrup, Tustin *Also called Belchers Maple Syrup LLC* *(G-17465)*
Belco Industries Inc 616 794-0410
  9138 W Belding Rd Belding (48809) *(G-1437)*
Belco Industries Inc (PA) 616 794-0410
  9138 W Belding Rd Belding (48809) *(G-1438)*

Belding Bleacher Erectors Inc 616 794-3126
11467 Hart St Ne Greenville (48838) ***(G-7476)***
Belding McHy & Eqp Lsg Corp (HQ) 616 794-0300
7200 Industrial Dr Belding (48809) ***(G-1439)***
Belding Tank Technologies, Belding *Also called D & R Fabrication Inc* ***(G-1444)***
Belding Tool Acquisition LLC (PA) 586 816-4450
1114 S Bridge St Belding (48809) ***(G-1440)***
Belding Tool and Machine, Belding *Also called Belding Tool Acquisition LLC* ***(G-1440)***
Belding Tool and Machine, Belding *Also called Btm National Holdings LLC* ***(G-1441)***
Beljan Ltd Inc 734 426-3503
4635 Mcguiness Rd Dexter (48130) ***(G-4726)***
Bell and Howell LLC 734 421-1727
12794 Currie Ct Livonia (48150) ***(G-10136)***
Bell Engineering Inc 989 753-3127
735 S Outer Dr Saginaw (48601) ***(G-14613)***
Bell Engineering LLC 989 753-3127
735 S Outer Dr Saginaw (48601) ***(G-14614)***
Bell Fork Lift Inc 313 841-1220
13700 Mellon St Detroit (48217) ***(G-4049)***
Bell Forklifts 586 469-7979
4660 Centaur Ave Clinton Township (48035) ***(G-3181)***
Bell Induction Heating Inc 734 697-0133
41241 Edison Lake Rd Van Buren Twp (48111) ***(G-17511)***
Bell Metals 248 227-0407
1107 Wheaton Dr Troy (48083) ***(G-16972)***
Bella Bleu Embroidery LLC 810 797-2286
3423 Wynns Mill Rd Metamora (48455) ***(G-11277)***
Bella Group LLC 586 789-7700
24770 Trombley St Harrison Twp (48045) ***(G-7738)***
Bella Skyy Llc 313 623-9296
20441 Danbury Ln Harper Woods (48225) ***(G-7663)***
Bellaire Log Homes Indus Hm 231 533-6669
6633 Bellaire Hwy Bellaire (49615) ***(G-1471)***
Bellar Industries Inc 810 227-1574
3447 Charlotte Dr Brighton (48114) ***(G-1950)***
Belle Feeds 269 628-1231
34026 M 40 Paw Paw (49079) ***(G-12942)***
Belle Isle Awning Co Inc 586 294-6050
13701 E 9 Mile Rd Warren (48089) ***(G-17730)***
Belleville Area Independent 734 699-9020
152 Main St Ste 9 Belleville (48111) ***(G-1480)***
Belleville Hookah Lounge, Van Buren Twp *Also called Belleville Lounge LLC* ***(G-17512)***
Belleville Lounge LLC 734 270-4977
9612 Belleville Rd Van Buren Twp (48111) ***(G-17512)***
Bellevue Proc Met Prep Inc 313 921-1931
5143 Bellevue St Detroit (48211) ***(G-4050)***
Bellevue Processing, Chesterfield *Also called Pfg Enterprises Inc* ***(G-2924)***
Bellinger Packing 989 838-2274
1557 E Wilson Rd Ashley (48806) ***(G-741)***
Bellmore Logging 906 498-2528
N15312 M3 Rd Hermansville (49847) ***(G-7860)***
Bells Brewery Inc 906 233-5002
3525 Airport Rd Escanaba (49829) ***(G-5060)***
Bells Brewery Inc 269 382-1402
355 E Kalamazoo Ave Kalamazoo (49007) ***(G-9134)***
Belmont Engineered Plas LLC 616 785-6279
5801 Safety Dr Ne Belmont (49306) ***(G-1501)***
Belmont Equipment Company, Madison Heights *Also called Cleary Developments Inc* ***(G-10689)***
Belmont Plastics Solutions LLC 616 340-3147
8211 Graphic Dr Ne Belmont (49306) ***(G-1502)***
Belocal, Mason *Also called N2 Publications* ***(G-11146)***
Belt-Tech USA Inc 450 372-5826
200 Ottawa Ave Nw Ste 900 Grand Rapids (49503) ***(G-6498)***
Beltone Skoric Hearng Aid Cntr 906 379-0606
240 W Portage Ave Sault Sainte Marie (49783) ***(G-15087)***
Beltone Skoric Hearng Aid Cntr 906 553-4660
3600 Ludington St Escanaba (49829) ***(G-5061)***
Belwith Products LLC 616 247-4000
3100 Broadway Ave Sw Grandville (49418) ***(G-7367)***
Bench Works, Clinton Township *Also called Benchwork Inc* ***(G-3182)***
Benchmark Coating Systems LLC 517 782-4061
2075 W Stadium Blvd Ann Arbor (48106) ***(G-399)***
Benchmark Inc 734 285-0900
4660 13th St Wyandotte (48192) ***(G-18812)***
Benchmark Manufacturing 231 375-8172
856 E Broadway Ave Norton Shores (49444) ***(G-12278)***
Benchwork Inc 586 464-6699
34100 Kelly Rd Clinton Township (48035) ***(G-3182)***
Benco Manufacturing, Troy *Also called Dieomatic Incorporated* ***(G-17061)***
Benecor Inc 248 437-4437
400 S Fenway Dr Fenton (48430) ***(G-5457)***
Benesh Corporation (PA) 734 244-4143
1910 N Telegraph Rd Monroe (48162) ***(G-11532)***
Benjamin Moore Authorized Ret, Muskegon *Also called Port City Paints Mfg Inc* ***(G-11895)***
Benjamin Moore Authorized Ret, Portage *Also called Rollie Williams Paint Spot* ***(G-13600)***
Benlee Inc (PA) 586 791-1830
30383 Ecorse Rd Romulus (48174) ***(G-14257)***
Benmar Communications LLC 313 593-0690
1 Parklane Blvd Ste 1105e Dearborn (48126) ***(G-3813)***
Benmark Advertising, Flint *Also called Barrys Sign Company* ***(G-5651)***
Benmill LLC 616 243-7555
3522 Lousma Dr Se Grand Rapids (49548) ***(G-6499)***
Bennett Funeral Coaches Inc 616 538-8100
584 76th St Sw B Byron Center (49315) ***(G-2259)***
Bennett Pump Company, Norton Shores *Also called Bpc Acquisition Company* ***(G-12345)***
Bennett Sawmill 231 734-5733
4161 90th Ave Evart (49631) ***(G-5121)***
Bennett Steel LLC 616 401-5271
1239 Randolph Ave Sw Grand Rapids (49507) ***(G-6500)***
Bennett Wood Specialties Inc 616 772-6683
109 N Carlton St Zeeland (49464) ***(G-18996)***
Benny Gage Inc 734 455-3080
4875 Product Dr Ste A Wixom (48393) ***(G-18620)***
Benson Distribution Inc 269 344-5529
5792 Stoney Brook Rd Kalamazoo (49009) ***(G-9135)***
Bentek, Reed City *Also called BCT-2017 Inc* ***(G-13789)***
Benteler Almnium Systems Mich, Holland *Also called Benteler Auto Holland Inc* ***(G-7974)***
Benteler Auto Holland Inc 616 396-6591
533 Ottawa Ave Holland (49423) ***(G-7974)***
Benteler Automotive Corp 616 247-3936
2650 N Opdyke Rd Ste B Auburn Hills (48326) ***(G-810)***
Benteler Automotive Corp 616 245-4607
3721 Hagen Dr Se Grand Rapids (49548) ***(G-6501)***
Benteler Automotive Corp (HQ) 248 364-7190
2650 N Opdyke Rd Ste B Auburn Hills (48326) ***(G-811)***
Benteler Steel & Tube, Auburn Hills *Also called Benteler Automotive Corp* ***(G-810)***
Bentley Industries 810 625-0400
1105 University Ave Flint (48504) ***(G-5654)***
Bentley Mfg LLC 810 621-3616
804 Mack Ct Lennon (48449) ***(G-9992)***
Bently Sand & Gravel 810 629-6172
9220 Bennett Lake Rd Fenton (48430) ***(G-5458)***
Benton Chassix Harbor 248 728-8700
1320 Paw Paw Ave Benton Harbor (49022) ***(G-1534)***
Benton Harbor Awning & Tent 800 272-2187
2275 M 139 Benton Harbor (49022) ***(G-1535)***
Benton Harbor Heat Treating, Benton Harbor *Also called Benton Harbor LLC* ***(G-1536)***
Benton Harbor LLC 269 925-6581
800 S Fair Ave Benton Harbor (49022) ***(G-1536)***
Bentzer Enterprises 269 663-2289
26601 May St Edwardsburg (49112) ***(G-4999)***
Bentzer Incorporated 269 663-3649
69953 Section St Edwardsburg (49112) ***(G-5000)***
Benzie Manufacturing LLC 231 631-0498
401 Parkview Ln Frankfort (49635) ***(G-5875)***
Benzie Printing 231 714-7565
9780 Innwood W Interlochen (49643) ***(G-8679)***
Berci Printing Services Inc 248 350-0206
22400 Telegraph Rd Ste B Southfield (48033) ***(G-15506)***
Berg Marketing Group 314 457-9400
560 Kirts Blvd Ste 114 Troy (48084) ***(G-16973)***
Berg Tool Inc 586 646-7100
56253 Precision Dr Chesterfield (48051) ***(G-2850)***
Berger LLC 734 414-0402
44160 Plymouth Oaks Blvd Plymouth (48170) ***(G-13135)***
Berghof Group North Amer Inc 313 720-6884
1500 W Big Beavr Rd 2nd Troy (48084) ***(G-16974)***
Berkley Frosty Freeze Inc 248 336-2634
2415 Coolidge Hwy Berkley (48072) ***(G-1622)***
Berkley Industries Inc (PA) 989 656-2171
9938 Pigeon Rd Bay Port (48720) ***(G-1413)***
Berkley Pharmacy LLC 586 573-8300
28577 Schoenherr Rd Warren (48088) ***(G-17731)***
Berkley Screw Machine Pdts Inc 248 853-0044
2100 Royce Haley Dr Rochester Hills (48309) ***(G-13962)***
Berkshire & Associates Inc 734 719-1822
5840 N Canton Center Rd Canton (48187) ***(G-2440)***
Berlin Holdings LLC 517 523-2444
4445 S Pittsford Rd Pittsford (49271) ***(G-13067)***
Berline Group Inc 248 203-0492
423 N Main St Ste 300 Royal Oak (48067) ***(G-14516)***
Bermar Associates Inc 248 589-2460
433 Minnesota Dr Troy (48083) ***(G-16975)***
Bermaxx LLC 248 299-3600
2960 Technology Dr Rochester Hills (48309) ***(G-13963)***
Bermont Gage & Automation Inc 586 296-1103
34500 Klein Rd Fraser (48026) ***(G-5903)***
Bermont Technologies, Fraser *Also called Bermont Gage & Automation Inc* ***(G-5903)***
Bernal LLC 248 299-3600
2960 Technology Dr Rochester Hills (48309) ***(G-13964)***
Bernal Products, Bruce Twp *Also called Ronald R Wellington* ***(G-2180)***
Berne Enterprises Inc 989 453-3235
7190 Berne Rd Pigeon (48755) ***(G-13036)***
Bernier Cast Metals Inc 989 754-7571
2626 Hess Ave Saginaw (48601) ***(G-14615)***

ALPHABETIC SECTION

Bernthal Packing Inc 989 652-2648
9378 Junction Rd Frankenmuth (48734) *(G-5859)*

Berrien Custom Cab & Design, Berrien Springs Also called Berrien Custom Cabinet Inc *(G-1638)*

Berrien Custom Cabinet Inc 269 473-3404
4231 E Snow Rd Berrien Springs (49103) *(G-1638)*

Berrien Metal Products Inc 269 695-5000
460 Post Rd Ste A Buchanan (49107) *(G-2189)*

Berry & Associates Inc 734 426-3787
2434 Bishop Cir E Dexter (48130) *(G-4727)*

Berry Global Inc 269 435-2425
700 Centreville St Constantine (49042) *(G-3663)*

Berry Global Inc 616 772-4635
200 N Franklin St Zeeland (49464) *(G-18997)*

Berry Sns-Rbbeh Islmic Slghtrh 313 259-6925
2496 Orleans St Detroit (48207) *(G-4051)*

Bert Hazekamp & Son Inc 231 773-8302
3933 S Brooks Rd Muskegon (49444) *(G-11778)*

Berthiaume Slaughter House 989 879-4921
719 Jane St Pinconning (48650) *(G-13059)*

Bertoldi Oil Service Inc 906 774-1707
N2395 Cemetary Ln Iron Mountain (49801) *(G-8717)*

Bespro Pattern Inc 586 268-6970
31301 Mally Dr Madison Heights (48071) *(G-10681)*

Besse Forest Products Inc 906 353-7193
16522 Westland Dr Baraga (49908) *(G-1135)*

Bessenberg Bindery Corporation 734 996-9696
215 N 5th Ave Ann Arbor (48104) *(G-400)*

Besser Company (PA) 989 354-4111
801 Johnson St Alpena (49707) *(G-284)*

Besser Company USA 616 399-5215
201 W Washington Ave # 202 Zeeland (49464) *(G-18998)*

Besser Lithibar, Zeeland Also called Besser Company USA *(G-18998)*

Bessey Tool & Die Inc 616 887-8820
617 10 Mile Rd Nw Sparta (49345) *(G-15760)*

Bessinger Pickle Co Inc 989 876-8008
537 N Court St Au Gres (48703) *(G-756)*

Best Alloys, Warren Also called Best Block Company *(G-17732)*

Best Barricade Sysytem Inc 989 778-1482
314 State Park Dr Bay City (48706) *(G-1332)*

Best Binding LLC 734 459-7785
41230 Joy Rd Plymouth (48170) *(G-13136)*

Best Block Company (PA) 586 772-7000
22001 Groesbeck Hwy Warren (48089) *(G-17732)*

Best Buy Bones Inc 810 631-6971
7426 N Dort Hwy Mount Morris (48458) *(G-11668)*

Best Concrete & Supply Inc 734 283-7055
17200 Dix Toledo Hwy Brownstown (48193) *(G-2143)*

Best Granite and Marble Inc 313 247-3909
11080 E 9 Mile Rd Warren (48089) *(G-17733)*

Best Harvest 888 947-6226
4115 7 Mile Rd Bay City (48706) *(G-1333)*

Best Impressions Inc 313 839-9000
32680 Newman Fraser (48026) *(G-5904)*

Best Industrial Group Inc 586 826-8800
7256 Murthum Ave Warren (48092) *(G-17734)*

Best Metal Products Co Inc 616 942-7141
3570 Raleigh Dr Se Grand Rapids (49512) *(G-6502)*

Best Mfg Tooling Solutions 616 877-5149
4190 Pro Line Ct Dorr (49323) *(G-4767)*

Best Mfg Tooling Solutions Ltd 616 877-0504
1158 Morren Ct Wayland (49348) *(G-18190)*

Best Netwrk Design & Assoc LLC 313 680-2047
18249 Wyoming St Detroit (48221) *(G-4052)*

Best Portable Sign 616 291-2911
4932 Stauffer Ave Se Grand Rapids (49508) *(G-6503)*

Best Products Inc 313 538-7414
14208 Sarasota Redford (48239) *(G-13719)*

Best Rate Dumpster Rental Inc 248 391-5956
256 Marrin Ortonville (48462) *(G-12742)*

Best Self Storage 810 227-7050
7286 Grand River Rd Brighton (48114) *(G-1951)*

Best Tool & Engineering Co 586 792-4119
34730 Nova Dr Clinton Township (48035) *(G-3183)*

Best-Block Co 313 933-8676
14210 W Chicago St Detroit (48228) *(G-4053)*

Bestop Inc 586 268-0602
5555 Gatewood Dr Sterling Heights (48310) *(G-15945)*

Beswick Corporation 248 589-0562
2591 Elliott Dr Troy (48083) *(G-16976)*

Bethany House Publishers 616 676-9185
6030 Fulton St E Ada (49301) *(G-11)*

Betko Manufacturing LLC 734 854-1148
2993 Lennox Ct Lambertville (48144) *(G-9650)*

Better Built Gates Canvas LLC 616 818-9103
315 19 Mile Rd Ne Cedar Springs (49319) *(G-2642)*

Better Life Cleaning Products, Grand Rapids Also called Bissell Better Life LLC *(G-6510)*

Better Made Potato Chips, Detroit Also called Better Made Snack Foods Inc *(G-4054)*

Better Made Snack Foods Inc 313 925-4774
10148 Gratiot Ave Detroit (48213) *(G-4054)*

Better-Bilt Cabinet Co 586 469-0080
99 Cass Ave Mount Clemens (48043) *(G-11630)*

Better-Form, Ferndale Also called David Epstein Inc *(G-5539)*

Betterlife 248 889-3245
1935 Oakland Highland (48356) *(G-7883)*

Between The Lines, Farmington Hills Also called Pride Source Corporation *(G-5352)*

Betz Castings, Grand Rapids Also called Betz Industries Inc *(G-6504)*

Betz Contracting and Machining, Climax Also called Betz Contracting Inc *(G-3134)*

Betz Contracting Inc 269 746-3320
320 N Main St Climax (49034) *(G-3134)*

Betz Industries Inc 616 453-4429
2121 Bristol Ave Nw Grand Rapids (49504) *(G-6504)*

Beverlin Manufacturing, Grand Rapids Also called Specialty Tube LLC *(G-7214)*

Bewitching Stitchng Embroidery 810 289-3978
4051 Starville Rd China (48054) *(G-2969)*

Beyond Embroidery 616 726-7000
2013 E Wyndham Hill Dr Ne # 102 Grand Rapids (49505) *(G-6505)*

BF Franchising 313 565-2713
1825 N Martha St Dearborn (48128) *(G-3814)*

Bgm Electronic Services LLC 586 997-7090
815 N Opdyke Rd Ste 200 Auburn Hills (48326) *(G-812)*

Bh Polymers, Saint Clair Also called Pier One Polymers Incorporated *(G-14839)*

Bi-Rite Office Products Inc 586 751-1410
3681 E 12 Mile Rd Warren (48092) *(G-17735)*

Bianco Inc 313 682-2612
9805 Fairfield St Livonia (48150) *(G-10137)*

BIBLE DOCTRINES PUBLICATIONS, Comstock Park Also called Bible Doctrines To Live By Inc *(G-3590)*

Bible Doctrines To Live By Inc 616 453-0493
895 W River Center Dr Ne Comstock Park (49321) *(G-3590)*

Bichler Gravel & Concrete Co 906 786-0343
6851 County 426 M.5 Rd Escanaba (49829) *(G-5062)*

Bico Michigan Inc (HQ) 616 453-2400
99 Steele St Nw Grand Rapids (49534) *(G-6506)*

Bico Steel Service Centers, Grand Rapids Also called Bico Michigan Inc *(G-6506)*

Bielomatik Inc 248 446-9910
300 Eagle Pond Dr Apt 435 Commerce Township (48390) *(G-3515)*

Bielomatik USA Inc 248 446-9910
300 Eagle Pond Dr Apt 435 Commerce Township (48390) *(G-3516)*

Bier Barrel Distillery LLC 616 633-8601
5295 West River Dr Ne # 200 Comstock Park (49321) *(G-3591)*

Bier Distillery Company 616 633-8601
6263 Egypt Valley Ave Ne Rockford (49341) *(G-14157)*

Bieri Digital Hearing Center, Saginaw Also called Bieri Hearing Instruments Inc *(G-14616)*

Bieri Hearing Instruments Inc (PA) 989 793-2701
2650 Mccarty Rd Saginaw (48603) *(G-14616)*

Biewer Forest Management LLC 231 825-2855
6400 W Gerwoude Dr Mc Bain (49657) *(G-11177)*

Biewer of Lansing LLC 810 326-3930
812 S Riverside Ave Saint Clair (48079) *(G-14814)*

Biewer Sawmill, Mc Bain Also called John A Biewer Lumber Company *(G-11183)*

Biewer Sawmill Inc 231 825-2855
6251 W Gerwoude Dr Mc Bain (49657) *(G-11178)*

Biewer Sawmill Winona Inc 810 329-4789
812 S Riverside Ave Saint Clair (48079) *(G-14815)*

Biewer Sawmill-Lake City LLC 231 839-7646
1560 W Houghton Lake Rd Lake City (49651) *(G-9544)*

Big 3 Precision Products Inc 313 846-6601
10611 Haggerty St Dearborn (48126) *(G-3815)*

Big Bore Signs LLC 313 701-5900
6335 Reinhard Dr Dexter (48130) *(G-4728)*

Big Boy Restaurant Management, Southfield Also called Big Boy Restaurants Intl LLC *(G-15507)*

Big Boy Restaurants Intl LLC (PA) 586 759-6000
26300 Telg Rd Ste 101 Southfield (48033) *(G-15507)*

Big Boy Restaurants Intl LLC 586 263-6220
16880 Hall Rd Clinton Township (48038) *(G-3184)*

Big D LLC 248 787-2724
26038 Grand River Ave Redford (48240) *(G-13720)*

Big Dipper Dough Co Inc 231 883-6035
5109 Heritage Way Traverse City (49685) *(G-16620)*

Big Dog Marine LLC 248 705-2875
2986 White Oak Bch Highland (48356) *(G-7884)*

Big Dome Holdings Inc 616 735-6228
3044 Wilson Dr Nw Grand Rapids (49534) *(G-6507)*

Big Dutchman Inc (HQ) 616 392-5981
3900 John F Donnelly Dr Holland (49424) *(G-7975)*

Big Foot Manufacturing Co 231 775-5588
1480 Potthoff St Cadillac (49601) *(G-2315)*

Big Green Tomato LLC 269 282-1593
478 Main St Battle Creek (49014) *(G-1194)*

Big Lttle Wines Traverse Cy MI 231 714-4854
4519 S Elm Valley Rd Suttons Bay (49682) *(G-16338)*

Big Maple Press 231 313-4059
3933 Blue Water Rd Traverse City (49686) *(G-16621)*

Big Mikes Welding 269 420-8017
169 Van Buren St E Battle Creek (49017) *(G-1195)*

Big O Smokehouse Inc ... 616 891-5555
9740 Cherry Valley Ave Se Caledonia (49316) *(G-2368)*

Big PDQ, Brighton Also called PDQ Ink Inc *(G-2048)*

Big Rapids Printing ... 231 796-8588
2801 Oak Industrial Dr Ne Grand Rapids (49505) *(G-6508)*

Big Rapids Products Inc (PA) ... 231 796-3593
1313 Maple St Big Rapids (49307) *(G-1669)*

Big Rapids Tool & Engineering, Big Rapids Also called Big Rapids Products Inc *(G-1669)*

Big Ridge Forest Products, Onaway Also called Bruning Forest Products *(G-12697)*

Bigdaddybeauty.com, Warren Also called Smo International Inc *(G-18015)*

Bigos Precast ... 517 223-5000
555 E Van Riper Rd Fowlerville (48836) *(G-5835)*

Bigsignscom ... 800 790-7611
22 S Harbor Dr Unit 101 Grand Haven (49417) *(G-6279)*

Bihl+wiedemann Inc ... 616 345-0680
5570 Wilson Ave Sw Ste E Wyoming (49418) *(G-18852)*

Biker Bobs Hrly-Dvidson Motown, Taylor Also called Motown Harley-Davidson Inc *(G-16451)*

Bilar Tool & Die ... 248 740-3400
24700 Mound Rd Warren (48091) *(G-17736)*

Bilco Tool Corporation ... 586 574-9300
30076 Dequindre Rd Warren (48092) *(G-17737)*

Bill Carr Signs Inc ... 810 232-1569
719 W 12th St Flint (48503) *(G-5655)*

Bill Daup Signs Inc ... 810 235-4080
7389 Ponderosa Dr Swartz Creek (48473) *(G-16351)*

Billco Acquisition LLC ... 616 928-0637
1373 Lincoln Ave Holland (49423) *(G-7976)*

Billco Products, Holland Also called Billco Acquisition LLC *(G-7976)*

Bills Custom Fab Inc ... 989 772-5817
1836 Gover Pkwy Mount Pleasant (48858) *(G-11687)*

Bills Logging Inc ... 989 546-7164
2482 Delano Rd Comins (48619) *(G-3503)*

Bills Welding ... 989 330-1014
136 Cottage Dr Prudenville (48651) *(G-13656)*

Billsby Lumber Company, Harrison Also called Sabertooth Enterprises LLC *(G-7681)*

Bingham Boat Works Ltd ... 906 225-0050
58 Middle Island Point Rd Marquette (49855) *(G-11007)*

Binks Coca-Cola Bottling Co (PA) ... 906 786-4144
3001 Danforth Rd Escanaba (49829) *(G-5063)*

Binks Coca-Cola Bottling Co ... 906 774-3202
617 Industrial Dr Iron Mountain (49801) *(G-8718)*

Binsfeld Engineering Inc ... 231 334-4383
4571 Mcfarlane Rd Maple City (49664) *(G-10940)*

Binson-Becker Inc ... 888 246-7667
26834 Lawrence Center Line (48015) *(G-2680)*

Binsons Orthtic Prsthtics Svcs, Center Line Also called Binson-Becker Inc *(G-2680)*

Bio Cmmunication Solutions LLC ... 616 502-0238
15526 Linn Ct Spring Lake (49456) *(G-15805)*

Bio Kleen Products Inc ... 269 567-9400
810 Lake St Kalamazoo (49001) *(G-9136)*

Bio Source Naturals LLC ... 877 577-8223
26594 Romine Rd Bldg B New Boston (48164) *(G-12002)*

Bio-Vac Inc ... 248 350-2150
21316 Bridge St Southfield (48033) *(G-15508)*

Biobest USA Inc (HQ) ... 734 626-5693
11700 Mtr Arpt Ctr Dr # 110 Romulus (48174) *(G-14258)*

Biocomm.solutions, Spring Lake Also called Bio Cmmunication Solutions LLC *(G-15805)*

Biocomsolutions LLC ... 616 502-0238
15526 Linn Ct Spring Lake (49456) *(G-15806)*

Bioflex Inc ... 734 327-2946
6111 Jackson Rd Ste 200 Ann Arbor (48103) *(G-401)*

Biologcal Mdiation Systems LLC ... 970 221-5949
200 Industrial Dr Hillsdale (49242) *(G-7925)*

Biolyte Laboratories LLC ... 616 350-9055
310 Northern Dr Nw Grand Rapids (49534) *(G-6509)*

Biolyte Labs, Grand Rapids Also called Biolyte Laboratories LLC *(G-6509)*

Bioplstic Plymers Cmpsites LLC ... 517 349-2970
4275 Conifer Cir Okemos (48864) *(G-12660)*

Biopolymer Innovations LLC ... 517 432-3044
16647 Chandler Rd East Lansing (48823) *(G-4887)*

Biopro Inc ... 810 982-7777
2929 Lapeer Rd Port Huron (48060) *(G-13458)*

Biosan Laboratories Inc ... 586 755-8970
1950 Tobsal Ct Warren (48091) *(G-17738)*

Biosolutions LLC ... 616 846-1210
1800 Industrial Dr Ste F Grand Haven (49417) *(G-6280)*

Biotec Incorporated ... 616 772-2133
652 E Main Ave Zeeland (49464) *(G-18999)*

Bipco, Pontiac Also called Eastern Oil Company *(G-13364)*

Birch Point Woodworks ... 906 322-8761
5586 W Birch Point Loop Brimley (49715) *(G-2100)*

Birclar Electric and Elec LLC ... 734 941-7400
12060 Wayne Rd Romulus (48174) *(G-14259)*

Bird Lofts & Stuff Woodworking ... 248 882-1242
9211 Blondell Ave White Lake (48386) *(G-18451)*

Birds Eye Foods Inc ... 269 561-8211
100 Sherman Rd Fennville (49408) *(G-5434)*

Birds-Eye Creations Inc ... 906 337-5095
86 Staton Ave Mohawk (49950) *(G-11517)*

Birdsall Tool & Gage Co ... 248 474-5150
24735 Crestview Ct Farmington Hills (48335) *(G-5181)*

Birkhold Pattern Company Inc ... 269 467-8705
22921 S River Rd Centreville (49032) *(G-2696)*

Birks Works Environmental LLC ... 313 891-1310
19719 Mount Elliott St Detroit (48234) *(G-4055)*

Birlon Group LLC ... 313 551-5341
3801 Inkster Rd Ste 2 Inkster (48141) *(G-8659)*

Birlon Sacs, Inkster Also called Birlon Group LLC *(G-8659)*

Birmingham Benders Co ... 313 435-4200
1271 W Maple Rd Clawson (48017) *(G-3088)*

Birmingham Jewelry Inc ... 586 939-5100
34756 Dequindre Rd Sterling Heights (48310) *(G-15946)*

Birmingham Royal Oak Tent Awng, Royal Oak Also called Royal Oak & Birmingham Tent *(G-14578)*

Bisbee Infrared Services Inc ... 517 787-4620
569 Wildwood Ave Unit 2 Jackson (49201) *(G-8823)*

Biscayne and Associates Inc ... 248 304-0600
2515 Charms Rd Milford (48381) *(G-11455)*

Bischoff Enterprises LLC ... 734 856-8490
5732 St Anthony Rd Ottawa Lake (49267) *(G-12804)*

Bisnett Insurance ... 734 214-2676
7035 Jo Mar Dr Whitmore Lake (48189) *(G-18521)*

Bissell Better Life LLC ... 800 237-7691
2345 Walker Ave Nw Grand Rapids (49544) *(G-6510)*

Bissell Homecare Inc (HQ) ... 800 237-7691
2345 Walker Ave Nw Grand Rapids (49544) *(G-6511)*

Bitzenburger Machine & Tool ... 517 627-8433
13060 Lawson Rd Grand Ledge (48837) *(G-6386)*

Bivins Graphics ... 616 453-2211
808 Carpenter Ave Nw Grand Rapids (49504) *(G-6512)*

Bizcard Xpress ... 248 288-4800
229 N Alice Ave Rochester (48307) *(G-13893)*

Bjb Enterprises ... 248 737-0760
3915 Lone Pine Rd Apt 100 West Bloomfield (48323) *(G-18264)*

Bjg, Wixom Also called Brown Jig Grinding Co *(G-18626)*

BKM Fuels LLC ... 269 342-9576
5566 Gull Rd Kalamazoo (49048) *(G-9137)*

BLAack&co LLC ... 313 971-1857
17312 Alta Vista Dr Southfield (48075) *(G-15509)*

Blaaco, Southfield Also called BLAack&co LLC *(G-15509)*

Blac Detroit, Detroit Also called African Amercn Parent Pubg Inc *(G-3989)*

Blac Inc ... 313 690-3372
6200 2nd Ave Detroit (48202) *(G-4056)*

Black & Decker (us) Inc ... 410 716-3900
3040 28th St Se Grand Rapids (49512) *(G-6513)*

Black & Decker Corporation ... 248 597-5000
30475 Stephenson Hwy Madison Heights (48071) *(G-10682)*

Black Barn Vinyrd & Winery LLC ... 517 569-2164
10605 Churchill Rd Rives Junction (49277) *(G-13885)*

Black Bottom Brewing Co Inc ... 313 205-5493
1055 Trumbull St Detroit (48216) *(G-4057)*

Black Box Corporation ... 248 743-1320
1287 Rankin Dr Troy (48083) *(G-16977)*

Black Box Corporation ... 616 246-1320
8180 Broadmoor Ave Se A Caledonia (49316) *(G-2369)*

Black Label Customs LLC ... 231 924-8044
11833 S Fitzgerald Ave Grant (49327) *(G-7427)*

Black Owl Distillery LLC ... 616 901-9003
4717 Broadmoor Ave Se F Grand Rapids (49512) *(G-6514)*

Black River Manufacturing Inc (PA) ... 810 982-9812
2625 20th St Port Huron (48060) *(G-13459)*

Black River Manufacturing Inc ... 810 982-9812
2401 20th St Port Huron (48060) *(G-13460)*

Black River Pallet Company ... 616 772-6211
410 E Roosevelt Ave Zeeland (49464) *(G-19000)*

Black River Sanding Gravel, Cheboygan Also called 1johnson Erling *(G-2779)*

Black Ski Weekend LLC ... 313 879-7150
7650 Cooley Lk Rd Ste 955 West Bloomfield (48324) *(G-18265)*

Black Star Farms LLC (PA) ... 231 271-4970
10844 E Revold Rd Suttons Bay (49682) *(G-16339)*

Black Swamp Percussion LLC ... 800 557-0988
11114 James St Zeeland (49464) *(G-19001)*

Blackberry Publications ... 313 627-1520
3915 11th St Ecorse (48229) *(G-4980)*

Blackgirlperception LLC ... 313 398-4275
14635 Penrod St Detroit (48223) *(G-4058)*

Blackledge Tool Inc ... 989 865-8393
305 Entrepreneur Dr Saint Charles (48655) *(G-14801)*

Blackline Bear LLC ... 616 291-1521
5000 Hakes Dr Ste 200 Norton Shores (49441) *(G-12279)*

Blackmore Co Inc ... 734 483-8661
10800 Blackmore Ave Belleville (48111) *(G-1481)*

Blackrocks Brewery LLC ... 906 273-1333
950 W Washington St Marquette (49855) *(G-11008)*

Blackrocks Brewery LLC (PA) ... 906 360-6674
424 N 3rd St Marquette (49855) *(G-11009)*

ALPHABETIC SECTION
Bobbys Mobile Service LLC

Blacksmith Shop LLC 616 754-4719
809 Callaghan St Greenville (48838) ***(G-7477)***

Blade Excavating Inc 810 287-6457
2910 Wilton Pl Flint (48506) ***(G-5656)***

Blade Industrial Products Inc 248 773-7400
29289 Lorie Ln Wixom (48393) ***(G-18621)***

Blades Enterprises LLC 734 449-4479
47570 Avante Dr Wixom (48393) ***(G-18622)***

Blain Machining Inc 616 877-0426
1115 142nd Ave Ste 1 Wayland (49348) ***(G-18191)***

Blake's Orchard & Cider Mill, Armada *Also called Blakes Orchard Inc* ***(G-732)***

Blakes Orchard Inc (PA) 586 784-5343
17985 Armada Center Rd Armada (48005) ***(G-732)***

Blanck Canvas Photography LLC 248 342-4935
7022 Oakhurst Ridge Rd Clarkston (48348) ***(G-3019)***

Blank Slate Creamery LLC 734 218-3242
4090 Lori Lynn Ln Whitmore Lake (48189) ***(G-18522)***

Blarney Castle Inc (PA) 231 864-3111
12218 West St Bear Lake (49614) ***(G-1416)***

Blarney Castle Oil, Bear Lake *Also called Blarney Castle Inc* ***(G-1416)***

Blast of The Past Corp 734 772-4394
34860 Stellwagen St Wayne (48184) ***(G-18217)***

Ble Book Publishing, Grosse Pointe Woods *Also called Little Blue Book Inc* ***(G-7570)***

Bleistahl N Amer Ltd Partnr 269 719-8585
190 Clark Rd Battle Creek (49037) ***(G-1196)***

Blendco LLC 269 350-2914
5713 Venture Park Dr Kalamazoo (49009) ***(G-9138)***

Blevins Screw Products Inc 810 744-1820
1838 Remell St Flint (48503) ***(G-5657)***

Blind Bull LLC 616 516-4881
7420 Watermark Dr Allendale (49401) ***(G-215)***

Blind Spot and More LLC 616 828-6495
725 84th St Sw Byron Center (49315) ***(G-2260)***

Blind Xpress, Livonia *Also called Elsie Inc* ***(G-10196)***

Blinds and Designs Inc 770 971-5524
29988 Anthony Dr Wixom (48393) ***(G-18623)***

Bliss & Vinegar LLC 616 970-0732
888 Forest Hill Ave Se Grand Rapids (49546) ***(G-6515)***

Bliss Munitions Equipment 269 953-6655
1004 E State St Hastings (49058) ***(G-7782)***

Blissfield, Blissfield *Also called BMC Global LLC* ***(G-1762)***

Blissfield Div, Blissfield *Also called Maxitrol Company* ***(G-1769)***

Blissfield Manufacturing Co (PA) 517 486-2121
626 Depot St Blissfield (49228) ***(G-1761)***

Blockmatic Company, Niles *Also called Blockmatic Inc* ***(G-12113)***

Blockmatic Inc 269 683-1655
2519 S 17th St Niles (49120) ***(G-12113)***

Bloem LLC (PA) 616 622-6344
3301 Hudson Trail Dr Hudsonville (49426) ***(G-8571)***

Bloem Living, Hudsonville *Also called Bloem LLC* ***(G-8571)***

Bloodline Rich LLC 734 719-1650
18941 Alstead St Grosse Pointe Woods (48236) ***(G-7564)***

Bloom Industries LLC 616 890-8029
726 Hastings St Ste A Traverse City (49686) ***(G-16622)***

Bloom Industries LLC (PA) 616 453-2946
2218 Ashcreek Ct Nw Grand Rapids (49534) ***(G-6516)***

Bloomberry 586 212-9510
6189 Pleasant St East China (48054) ***(G-4856)***

Blossom Berry 517 775-6978
44325 W 12 Mile Rd H-172 Novi (48377) ***(G-12374)***

Blough Hardwoods Inc 616 693-2174
9975 W Clarksville Rd Clarksville (48815) ***(G-3078)***

Blough Inc 616 897-8407
9885 Centerline Rd Lowell (49331) ***(G-10496)***

Blts Wearable Art Inc 517 669-9659
1541 W Round Lake Rd Dewitt (48820) ***(G-4706)***

Blubridge, Howell *Also called Miccus Inc* ***(G-8480)***

Blue Circle Cement 313 842-4600
9333 Dearborn St Detroit (48209) ***(G-4059)***

Blue Collar Winery LLC 419 344-4715
6112 Wilcox Rd Dundee (48131) ***(G-4810)***

Blue Cube Holding LLC (HQ) 989 636-1000
2030 Dow Ctr Midland (48674) ***(G-11323)***

Blue De-Signs LLC 248 808-2583
4605 Briarwood Ave Royal Oak (48073) ***(G-14517)***

Blue Fire Manufacturing LLC 248 714-7166
5405 Perry Dr Waterford (48329) ***(G-18104)***

Blue Flash Supply Co, Grosse Pointe Woods *Also called Continntal Bldg Svcs of Cncnna* ***(G-7566)***

Blue Grill Foods, Milford *Also called Dimitri Mansour* ***(G-11462)***

Blue Lagoon 248 515-1363
3217 Shadydale Ct West Bloomfield (48323) ***(G-18266)***

Blue Lion Fitness, Ann Arbor *Also called Vanroth LLC* ***(G-709)***

Blue Pony LLC 616 291-5554
3479 8th Ave Hudsonville (49426) ***(G-8572)***

Blue Print Studio 616 283-2893
26 Holly Ct Holland (49423) ***(G-7977)***

Blue Ribbon Linen and Mat Svcs, Muskegon *Also called Apparelmaster-Muskegon Inc* ***(G-11772)***

Blue Shamrock Publishing Inc 269 687-7097
2585 Portage Rd Niles (49120) ***(G-12114)***

Blue Thumb Distributing Inc 989 921-3474
2650 Schust Rd Saginaw (48603) ***(G-14617)***

Blue Water Boring LLC 586 421-2100
46522 Erb Dr Macomb (48042) ***(G-10581)***

Blue Water Cabinetry AMP 231 246-2293
4845 Airline Rd Ste 4 Muskegon (49444) ***(G-11779)***

Blue Water Fabricators Inc 586 307-3550
21482 Carlo Dr Clinton Township (48038) ***(G-3185)***

Blue Water Manufacturing Inc 810 364-6170
1765 Michigan Ave Marysville (48040) ***(G-11082)***

Blue Water Printing Co Inc 810 664-0643
655 Mccormick Dr Ste B Lapeer (48446) ***(G-9914)***

Bluefire Industries LLC 269 235-9779
16757 Fort Custer Dr Augusta (49012) ***(G-1091)***

Bluewater Tech Group Inc 248 356-4399
37900 Interchange Dr Farmington Hills (48335) ***(G-5182)***

Bluewater Tech Group Inc (HQ) 248 356-4399
30303 Beck Rd Wixom (48393) ***(G-18624)***

Bluewater Tech Group Inc 231 885-2600
6305 W 115 Mesick (49668) ***(G-11269)***

Bluewater Tech Group Inc 616 656-9380
4245 44th St Se Ste 1 Grand Rapids (49512) ***(G-6517)***

Bluewater Thermal Solutions 269 925-6581
800 S Fair Ave Benton Harbor (49022) ***(G-1537)***

Bluewater Thermal Solutions 989 753-7770
2240 Veterans Mem Pkwy Saginaw (48601) ***(G-14618)***

Bluewater Visual Services, Wixom *Also called Bluewater Tech Group Inc* ***(G-18624)***

Blusys, Clinton Township *Also called Axis Tms Corp* ***(G-3179)***

Bmax USA LLC 248 794-4176
100 Engelwood Dr Ste B Lake Orion (48359) ***(G-9587)***

BMC Bil-Mac Company, Grandville *Also called BMC Bil-Mac Corporation* ***(G-7368)***

BMC Bil-Mac Corporation 616 538-1930
2995 44th St Sw Grandville (49418) ***(G-7368)***

BMC Global LLC 517 486-2121
626 Depot St Blissfield (49228) ***(G-1762)***

BMC Laboratory Casework, Muskegon *Also called Bmc/Industrial Eductl Svcs Inc* ***(G-11780)***

BMC Software Inc 248 888-4600
27555 Executive Dr # 155 Farmington Hills (48331) ***(G-5183)***

Bmc/Industrial Eductl Svcs Inc 231 733-1206
2831 Maffett St Muskegon (49444) ***(G-11780)***

Bme Inc 810 937-2974
3763 Lapeer Rd Ste E Port Huron (48060) ***(G-13461)***

Bms Enterprise LLC 281 516-9100
6334 Timberwood S West Bloomfield (48322) ***(G-18267)***

Bms Great Lakes LLC 248 390-1598
4577 S Lapeer Rd Ste G Lake Orion (48359) ***(G-9588)***

Bmt Aerospace Usa Inc 586 285-7700
18559 Malyn Blvd Fraser (48026) ***(G-5905)***

Bmu International LLC 248 342-4032
6230 Ascension St Clarkston (48348) ***(G-3020)***

Bnb Welding & Fabrication Inc 810 820-1508
3140 E Hemphill Rd Burton (48529) ***(G-2227)***

BNP Media Inc (PA) 248 362-3700
2401 W Big Beavr Rd # 700 Troy (48084) ***(G-16978)***

Bnw West Side Scrnprinting LLC 616 717-1082
2219 Holliday Dr Sw Wyoming (49519) ***(G-18853)***

Boa Software LLC 517 540-0681
2541 Birchwood Dr Howell (48855) ***(G-8430)***

Board For Student Publications 734 418-4115
420 Maynard St Ann Arbor (48109) ***(G-402)***

Board of Commissioners, Grand Rapids *Also called Kent County* ***(G-6887)***

Boars Belly 231 722-2627
333 W Western Ave Muskegon (49440) ***(G-11781)***

Boars Head Provisions Co Inc 941 955-0994
284 Roost Ave Holland (49424) ***(G-7978)***

Boat Customs Trailers LLC 517 712-3512
3678 68th St Se Caledonia (49316) ***(G-2370)***

Boat Guard Inc 989 424-1490
3577 N West Branch Dr Gladwin (48624) ***(G-6189)***

Boattown Woodshop 586 703-0538
108 S Wilson Blvd Mount Clemens (48043) ***(G-11631)***

Bob Allison Enterprises 248 540-8467
6560 Red Maple Ln Bloomfield Hills (48301) ***(G-1804)***

Bob Evans Farms Inc 517 437-3349
200 N Wolcott St Hillsdale (49242) ***(G-7926)***

Bob G Machining LLC 586 285-1400
44345 N Groesbeck Hwy Clinton Township (48036) ***(G-3186)***

Bob Jutila Logging 906 296-0753
55658 Traprock Valley Rd Lake Linden (49945) ***(G-9567)***

Bob Maxey Ford Howell Inc 517 545-5700
2798 E Grand River Ave Howell (48843) ***(G-8431)***

Bob-O-Link Associates LLC (PA) 616 891-6939
570 Market Ave Sw Grand Rapids (49503) ***(G-6518)***

Bobbys Mobile Service LLC 517 206-6026
1188 Herbert J Ave Jackson (49202) ***(G-8824)***

ALPHABETIC

Bobcat Oil & Gas Inc (PA)....989 426-4375
901 E Cedar Ave Gladwin (48624) ***(G-6190)***
Bobier Tool Supply Inc....810 732-4030
G4163 Corunna Rd Flint (48532) ***(G-5658)***
Bobs Welding & Fabricating....810 324-2592
5375 Kilgore Rd Kenockee (48006) ***(G-9423)***
Boch Publishing LLC....734 718-2973
41620 Pheasant Creek Dr Canton (48188) ***(G-2441)***
Boda Corporation....906 353-7320
Us 41 Chassell (49916) ***(G-2776)***
Body Contour Ventures LLC....248 579-6772
34405 W 12 Mile Rd # 200 Farmington Hills (48331) ***(G-5184)***
Body Exotics....231 753-8590
6649 Boone Rd Ste 207 Traverse City (49685) ***(G-16623)***
Body Faders, Mount Clemens *Also called Wickedglow Industries Inc* ***(G-11663)***
Body Language Scented Candles....989 906-0354
1303 S Center Rd Saginaw (48638) ***(G-14619)***
Bodycote Thermal Proc Inc....616 399-6880
3270 John F Donnelly Dr Holland (49424) ***(G-7979)***
Bodycote Thermal Proc Inc....616 245-0465
3700 Eastern Ave Se Grand Rapids (49508) ***(G-6519)***
Bodycote Thermal Proc Inc....734 623-3436
31889 Industrial Rd Livonia (48150) ***(G-10138)***
Bodycote Thermal Proc Inc....734 451-0338
8580 N Haggerty Rd Canton (48187) ***(G-2442)***
Bodycote Thermal Proc Inc....734 427-6814
31888 Glendale St Livonia (48150) ***(G-10139)***
Boeing Company....248 258-7191
6001 N Adams Rd Ste 105 Bloomfield Hills (48304) ***(G-1805)***
Boesch Built LLC....248 318-2136
1730 W Wardlow Rd Highland (48357) ***(G-7885)***
Boese Equipment Co, Saginaw *Also called Gregory M Boese* ***(G-14659)***
Bogen Concrete Inc....269 651-6751
26959 Bogen Rd Sturgis (49091) ***(G-16281)***
Bohning Company Ltd (PA)....231 229-4247
7361 N 7 Mile Rd Lake City (49651) ***(G-9545)***
Bohr Manufacturing LLC....734 261-3010
23206 Commerce Dr Farmington Hills (48335) ***(G-5185)***
Bokhara Pet Care Centers (PA)....231 264-6667
11535 S Elk Lake Rd Elk Rapids (49629) ***(G-5021)***
Bokhara's Grooming, Elk Rapids *Also called Bokhara Pet Care Centers* ***(G-5021)***
Bokum Tool Company, Madison Heights *Also called Tooling Solutions Group LLC* ***(G-10844)***
Bold Ammo & Guns Inc....616 826-0913
5083 Natchez Ct Ne Rockford (49341) ***(G-14158)***
Bold Companies Inc....231 773-8026
2291 Olthoff St Muskegon (49444) ***(G-11782)***
Bold Endeavors LLC....616 389-3902
17 Division Ave S Ste 100 Grand Rapids (49503) ***(G-6520)***
Bold Furniture, Muskegon *Also called Bold Companies Inc* ***(G-11782)***
Bold Services, Rockford *Also called Bold Ammo & Guns Inc* ***(G-14158)***
Bolden Industries Inc....248 387-9489
19231 Bretton Dr Detroit (48223) ***(G-4060)***
Boldsocks, Grand Rapids *Also called Bold Endeavors LLC* ***(G-6520)***
Bollhoff....313 506-0150
820 Kirts Blvd Spc 500 Troy (48084) ***(G-16979)***
Bollhoff Rivnut....248 269-0475
800 Kirts Blvd Ste 500 Troy (48084) ***(G-16980)***
Bolman Die Services Inc....810 919-2262
7523 19 Mile Rd Sterling Heights (48314) ***(G-15947)***
Bolyea Industries....586 293-8600
33847 Doreka Fraser (48026) ***(G-5906)***
Bomark Industries LLc....248 879-9577
1803 Smallbrook Dr Troy (48085) ***(G-16981)***
Bomaur Quality Plastics Inc....810 629-9701
10388 Jayne Valley Ln Fenton (48430) ***(G-5459)***
Bonal International Inc (PA)....248 582-0900
1300 N Campbell Rd Ste A Royal Oak (48067) ***(G-14518)***
Bonal Technologies Inc....248 582-0900
1300 N Campbell Rd Royal Oak (48067) ***(G-14519)***
Bond Bailey and Smith Company....313 496-0177
2707 W Fort St Detroit (48216) ***(G-4061)***
Bond Manufacturing LLC....313 671-0799
17910 Van Dyke St Detroit (48234) ***(G-4062)***
Bond Street Software....616 847-8377
820 Monroe Ave Nw Grand Rapids (49503) ***(G-6521)***
Bond, Bailey & Smith Machining, Detroit *Also called Bond Bailey and Smith Company* ***(G-4061)***
Bonnell Aluminum (niles) LLC....269 697-6063
2005 Mayflower Rd Niles (49120) ***(G-12115)***
Bonsal American Inc....248 338-0335
2280 Auburn Rd Auburn Hills (48326) ***(G-813)***
Bonsal American Inc....734 753-4413
36506 Sibley Rd New Boston (48164) ***(G-12003)***
Bonsan American, New Boston *Also called Bonsal American Inc* ***(G-12003)***
Bontaz Centre Usa Inc....248 588-8113
1099 Chicago Rd Troy (48083) ***(G-16982)***
Bonwrx Ltd....517 481-2924
924 Terminal Rd Lansing (48906) ***(G-9675)***
Bookcomp Inc....616 774-9700
6124 Belmont Ave Ne Belmont (49306) ***(G-1503)***
Bookwear, Honor *Also called Field Crafts Inc* ***(G-8359)***
Boomer Company (PA)....313 832-5050
1940 E Forest Ave Detroit (48207) ***(G-4063)***
Boomer Construction Materials, Detroit *Also called Boomer Company* ***(G-4063)***
Boomerang Amusements....586 323-3327
46600 Vineyard Ave Shelby Township (48317) ***(G-15178)***
Boomerang Enterprises Inc....269 547-9715
49759 Wentworth Dr Mattawan (49071) ***(G-11163)***
Boomerang Exhibits....315 525-6973
3223 Kraft Ave Se Grand Rapids (49512) ***(G-6522)***
Boomerang Retro & Relics....906 362-7876
100 W Washington St Marquette (49855) ***(G-11010)***
Boomerangs Gift Gallery....248 228-0314
161 W Nepessing St Lapeer (48446) ***(G-9915)***
Booms Stone Company....313 531-3000
12275 Dixie Redford (48239) ***(G-13721)***
Boone Express....248 583-7080
3920 S Hadley Rd Ortonville (48462) ***(G-12743)***
Boones Candle Co....248 444-0621
125 Liza Ln Commerce Township (48382) ***(G-3517)***
Boones Welding & Fabricating....517 782-7461
1309 Westlane St Jackson (49203) ***(G-8825)***
Boos Products Inc....734 498-2207
20416 Kaiser Rd Gregory (48137) ***(G-7513)***
Boostbutton LLC....734 223-0813
9340 Wildwood Lake Dr Whitmore Lake (48189) ***(G-18523)***
Booth Newspaper....517 487-8888
108 S Washington Sq Ste 1 Lansing (48933) ***(G-9814)***
Bopp-Busch Manufacturing Co (PA)....989 876-7121
545 E Huron Rd Au Gres (48703) ***(G-757)***
Bopp-Busch Manufacturing Co....989 876-7924
205 N Mackinaw St Au Gres (48703) ***(G-758)***
Bopp-Busch Plant 2, Au Gres *Also called Bopp-Busch Manufacturing Co* ***(G-758)***
Boral Building Products Inc (HQ)....800 521-8486
29797 Beck Rd Wixom (48393) ***(G-18625)***
Borchers Sheet Metal....260 413-0632
6521 Bradenwood Dr Hudsonville (49426) ***(G-8573)***
Border City Tool and Mfg Co....586 758-5574
19211 Tyrone St Harper Woods (48225) ***(G-7664)***
Border Line Rich Apparel LLC....866 959-3003
15437 Lkside Vlg Dr Unit Clinton Township (48038) ***(G-3187)***
Border Line Rich Clothing LLC....586 267-5251
21396 Cass Ave Clinton Township (48036) ***(G-3188)***
Bordrin Motor Corporation Inc....877 507-3267
14925 W 11 Mile Rd Oak Park (48237) ***(G-12595)***
Boretti Div, Farmington Hills *Also called Enertrols Inc* ***(G-5234)***
Borg Warner Automotive, Cadillac *Also called Borgwarner Thermal Systems Inc* ***(G-2317)***
Borgia Die & Engineering Inc....616 677-3595
14750 Raymer Cir Marne (49435) ***(G-10990)***
Borgman Tool & Engineering LLC....231 733-4133
2912 Hamilton Rd Muskegon (49445) ***(G-11783)***
Borgwarner Arden LLC....248 754-9200
3850 Hamlin Rd Auburn Hills (48326) ***(G-814)***
Borgwarner Automotive, Marshall *Also called Borgwarner Thermal Systems Inc* ***(G-11053)***
Borgwarner Global Holding LLC (HQ)....248 754-9200
3850 Hamlin Rd Auburn Hills (48326) ***(G-815)***
Borgwarner Inc....248 371-0040
3800 Automation Ave # 100 Auburn Hills (48326) ***(G-816)***
Borgwarner Inc....231 779-7500
1100 Wright St Cadillac (49601) ***(G-2316)***
Borgwarner Inc (PA)....248 754-9200
3850 Hamlin Rd Auburn Hills (48326) ***(G-817)***
Borgwarner Inc....248 754-9600
3800 Automation Ave Auburn Hills (48326) ***(G-818)***
Borgwarner Inc....248 754-9200
3850 Hamlin Rd Auburn Hills (48326) ***(G-819)***
Borgwarner Intl Svcs LLC....248 813-2000
3000 University Dr Auburn Hills (48326) ***(G-820)***
Borgwarner Inv Holdg Inc (HQ)....248 754-9200
3850 Hamlin Rd Auburn Hills (48326) ***(G-821)***
Borgwarner Jersey Holdings LLC (HQ)....248 754-9200
3850 Hamlin Rd Auburn Hills (48326) ***(G-822)***
Borgwarner Pds (usa) Inc (HQ)....248 754-9600
3850 Hamlin Rd Auburn Hills (48326) ***(G-823)***
Borgwarner Pds Anderson LLC....248 641-3045
5455 Corporate Dr Ste 116 Troy (48098) ***(G-16983)***
Borgwarner Powdered Metals Inc (PA)....734 261-5322
32059 Schoolcraft Rd Livonia (48150) ***(G-10140)***
Borgwarner Tech Svcs LLC....248 754-9200
3000 University Dr Auburn Hills (48326) ***(G-824)***
Borgwarner Thermal Systems Inc (HQ)....269 781-1228
1507 S Kalamazoo Ave Marshall (49068) ***(G-11053)***
Borgwarner Thermal Systems Inc....231 779-7500
1100 Wright St Cadillac (49601) ***(G-2317)***
Borgwarner Transm Pdts LLC....248 754-9200
3850 Hamlin Rd Auburn Hills (48326) ***(G-825)***
Borgwarner Transm Systems LLC (HQ)....248 754-9200
3850 Hamlin Rd Auburn Hills (48326) ***(G-826)***

Borgwarner US Holding LLC (HQ) 248 754-9200
3850 Hamlin Rd Auburn Hills (48326) ***(G-827)***
Borgwarner USA Corporation 248 813-2000
3000 University Dr Auburn Hills (48326) ***(G-828)***
Borgwrner Emssions Systems LLC (HQ) 248 754-9200
3850 Hamlin Rd Auburn Hills (48326) ***(G-829)***
Borgwrner Emssons Systems Mich (HQ) 248 754-9600
3800 Automation Ave # 200 Auburn Hills (48326) ***(G-830)***
Borgwrner Prplsion Systems LLC (HQ) 248 707-5224
3000 University Dr Auburn Hills (48326) ***(G-831)***
Borgwrner Prplsion Systems LLC 248 813-2000
3000 University Dr Auburn Hills (48326) ***(G-832)***
Borgwrner Prplsion Systems LLC 248 813-2000
5725 Innovation Dr Troy (48098) ***(G-16984)***
Borgwrner Trbo Emssion Systems, Auburn Hills *Also called Borgwrner Emssons Systems Mich* ***(G-830)***
Boride Engineered Abrasives, Traverse City *Also called Botsg Inc* ***(G-16625)***
Borisch Mfg, Grand Rapids *Also called Amphenol Borisch Tech Inc* ***(G-6458)***
Borite Manufacturing Corp 248 588-7260
31711 Sherman Ave Madison Heights (48071) ***(G-10683)***
Borneman & Peterson Inc 810 744-1890
1810 Remell St Flint (48503) ***(G-5659)***
Boropharm Inc (PA) 248 348-5776
39555 Orchard Hill Pl # 600 Novi (48375) ***(G-12375)***
Boropharm Inc 517 455-7847
2800 Plymouth Rd Bldg 40 Ann Arbor (48109) ***(G-403)***
Borries Mkg Systems Partnr 734 761-9549
3744 Plaza Dr Ste 1c Ann Arbor (48108) ***(G-404)***
Borroughs LLC (PA) 269 342-0161
3002 N Burdick St Kalamazoo (49004) ***(G-9139)***
Bos Automotive Products Inc (HQ) 248 289-6072
2956 Waterview Dr Rochester Hills (48309) ***(G-13965)***
BOS Field Machining Inc 517 204-1688
1750 Maywood Rd Houghton Lake (48629) ***(G-8394)***
Bos Manufacturing LLC (PA) 231 398-3328
237 Renaissance Dr Manistee (49660) ***(G-10895)***
Bosal Industries-Georgia Inc 734 547-7038
1476 Seaver Way Bldg C Ypsilanti (48197) ***(G-18926)***
Bosal Industries-Georgia Inc 734 547-7023
1476 Seaver Way Bldg B Ypsilanti (48197) ***(G-18927)***
Bosal Industries-Georgia Inc (HQ) 734 547-7022
1476 Seaver Way Bldg A Ypsilanti (48197) ***(G-18928)***
Bosal International North Amer, Ypsilanti *Also called Bosal Industries-Georgia Inc* ***(G-18928)***
Bosanic Lwrnce Sons Tmber Pdts 906 341-5609
1840n W Kendall Rd Manistique (49854) ***(G-10917)***
Bosch, Ira *Also called Sejasmi Industries Inc* ***(G-8713)***
Bosch Auto Svc Solutions Inc (HQ) 586 574-2332
28635 Mound Rd Warren (48092) ***(G-17739)***
Bosch Auto Svc Solutions Inc 586 574-1820
5775 Enterprise Ct Warren (48092) ***(G-17740)***
Bosch Chassis St Joseph Plant, Saint Joseph *Also called Robert Bosch LLC* ***(G-14957)***
Bosco's Pizza Co., Warren *Also called Artisan Bread Co LLC* ***(G-17714)***
Boskage Commerce Publications 269 673-7242
510 E Milham Ave Portage (49002) ***(G-13547)***
Boss Electro Static Inc 616 575-0577
3974 Linden Ave Se Wyoming (49548) ***(G-18854)***
Boss Outdoors LLC 269 465-3631
3385 Livingston Rd Bridgman (49106) ***(G-1922)***
Boss Shotshell Mfg., Bridgman *Also called DLM Holding Group LLC* ***(G-1925)***
Boss Shotshells, Bridgman *Also called Boss Outdoors LLC* ***(G-1922)***
Bostik Inc 269 781-8246
205 W Oliver Dr Marshall (49068) ***(G-11054)***
Boston Bioscience Inc 617 515-5336
2710 Oliver Rd Royal Oak (48073) ***(G-14520)***
Bostontec Inc (PA) 989 496-9510
2700 James Savage Rd Midland (48642) ***(G-11324)***
Bostwick Enterprises Inc (PA) 231 946-8613
3575 Veterans Dr Traverse City (49684) ***(G-16624)***
Botsg Inc 231 929-2121
2615 Aero Park Dr Traverse City (49686) ***(G-16625)***
Bottling Group Inc 517 545-2624
755 Mcpherson Park Dr Howell (48843) ***(G-8432)***
Bouchey and Sons Inc 989 588-4118
750 Kapplinger Dr Farwell (48622) ***(G-5421)***
Boulding Filtration Co LLC 313 300-2388
11900 E Mcnichols Rd Detroit (48205) ***(G-4064)***
Bourdo Logging 269 623-4981
5794 Mullen Ridge Dr Delton (49046) ***(G-3962)***
Bourne Industries Inc 989 743-3461
491 S Comstock St Corunna (48817) ***(G-3705)***
Bourque H James & Assoc Inc 906 635-9191
3060 W M 28 Brimley (49715) ***(G-2101)***
Bovvy Mkt LLC 313 706-7922
14377 Warwick St Detroit (48223) ***(G-4065)***
Bowditch, Lawrence *Also called Rhino Products Inc* ***(G-9984)***
Bower Tool & Manufacturing Inc 734 522-0444
27481 Schoolcraft Rd Livonia (48150) ***(G-10141)***
Bowers Aluminum 269 251-8625
1401 Shiga Dr Springfield (49037) ***(G-15862)***
Bowers Harbor Vinyrd & Winery 231 223-7615
2896 Bowers Harbor Rd Traverse City (49686) ***(G-16626)***
Bowling Enterprises Inc 231 864-2653
9091 Chief Rd Kaleva (49645) ***(G-9376)***
Bowling Hydroseeding, Kaleva *Also called Bowling Enterprises Inc* ***(G-9376)***
Bowman Enterprises Inc 269 720-1946
1905 Lakeview Dr Portage (49002) ***(G-13548)***
Bowman Printing Inc 810 982-8202
600 Huron Ave Port Huron (48060) ***(G-13462)***
Bowman Welding and Fabrication 231 580-6438
23855 19 Mile Rd Big Rapids (49307) ***(G-1670)***
Bowtie Catering LLC 313 989-3952
23123 Normandy Ave Eastpointe (48021) ***(G-4928)***
Boxer Equipment/Morbark Inc 989 866-2381
8507 S Winn Rd Winn (48896) ***(G-18589)***
Boyd, Grand Rapids *Also called Action Fabricators Inc* ***(G-6423)***
Boyer Glassworks Inc 231 526-6359
207 State St Harbor Springs (49740) ***(G-7642)***
Boyers Meat Processing Inc 734 495-1342
4125 Barr Rd Canton (48188) ***(G-2443)***
Boyers Tool and Die Inc 517 782-7869
1729 W Ganson St Jackson (49202) ***(G-8826)***
Boyne Area Wldg & Fabrication 231 582-6078
1095 Dam Rd Boyne City (49712) ***(G-1883)***
Boyne City Division, Big Rapids *Also called Federal Screw Works* ***(G-1673)***
Boyne City Gazette 231 582-2799
5 W Main St Unit 7 Boyne City (49712) ***(G-1884)***
Boyne Machine Company Inc 616 669-7178
2169 Pine Ridge Dr Sw A Jenison (49428) ***(G-9047)***
Bozz Lashez LLC 734 799-7020
9790 Andover Dr Van Buren Twp (48111) ***(G-17513)***
Bozzer Brothers Inc 989 732-9684
1252 Krys Rd Gaylord (49735) ***(G-6120)***
BP, Hamtramck *Also called Seven Mile and Grnd River Fuel* ***(G-7613)***
BP Gas/ JB Fuel 517 531-3400
107 W Main St Parma (49269) ***(G-12936)***
BP Lubricants USA Inc 231 689-0002
201 N Webster St White Cloud (49349) ***(G-18439)***
BP Pack Inc 612 594-0839
3007 Akins Ln Bellaire (49615) ***(G-1472)***
Bpc Acquisition Company 231 798-1310
1218 E Pontaluna Rd Norton Shores (49456) ***(G-12345)***
Bpg International Fin Co LLC (PA) 616 855-1480
4760 Fulton St E Ste 201 Ada (49301) ***(G-12)***
Bpi Holdings International Inc 815 363-9000
1101 Technology Dr Ann Arbor (48108) ***(G-405)***
Bpv Environmental, Byron Center *Also called Bpv LLC* ***(G-2261)***
Bpv LLC 616 281-4502
511 76th St Sw Byron Center (49315) ***(G-2261)***
BR Safety Products Inc 734 582-4499
1255 S Mill St Plymouth (48170) ***(G-13137)***
Bracelet Shack 312 656-9191
5193 Frankwill Ave Clarkston (48346) ***(G-3021)***
Bracy & Associates Ltd 616 298-8120
965 N Baywood Dr Holland (49424) ***(G-7980)***
Bradeen Specialties LLC 269 349-0276
3450 Claxton St Kalamazoo (49048) ***(G-9140)***
Bradford Company (PA) 616 399-3000
13500 Quincy St Holland (49424) ***(G-7981)***
Bradford Packaging, Holland *Also called Bradford Company* ***(G-7981)***
Bradford Printing Inc 517 887-0044
1020 E Jolly Rd Lansing (48910) ***(G-9815)***
Bradford-White Corporation 269 795-3364
200 Lafayette St Middleville (49333) ***(G-11303)***
Bradhart Products Inc 248 437-3746
7747 Lochlin Dr Brighton (48116) ***(G-1952)***
Bradley Allen Interiors Inc 989 689-6770
6788 N Swede Rd Rhodes (48652) ***(G-13822)***
Bradley Jacob Printing LLC 248 953-9010
1356 Marina Pointe Blvd Lake Orion (48362) ***(G-9589)***
Bradley-Thompson Tool Company 248 352-1466
22108 W 8 Mile Rd Southfield (48033) ***(G-15510)***
Brady Worldwide Inc 248 650-1952
632 Rewold Dr Rochester (48307) ***(G-13894)***
Bradys Fence Company Inc 313 492-8804
11093 Armstrong Rd South Rockwood (48179) ***(G-15463)***
Braiq Inc 858 729-4116
2000 Brush St Ste 201 Detroit (48226) ***(G-4066)***
Brake Roller Co Inc 269 965-2371
1125 Watkins Rd Battle Creek (49015) ***(G-1197)***
Brake Team 313 914-6000
19803 E 9 Mile Rd Saint Clair Shores (48080) ***(G-14849)***
Bralyn Inc 231 865-3186
259 N 3rd Ave Fruitport (49415) ***(G-6061)***
Brambles Woodwork LLC 616 446-9118
6344 Dunbarton St Se Ada (49301) ***(G-13)***
Bramco Containers Inc 906 428-2855
824 Clark Dr Gladstone (49837) ***(G-6174)***

ALPHABETIC

Bramin Enterprises 313 960-1528
2218 Ford St Detroit (48238) *(G-4067)*
Branch Office, Pontiac Also called Erae AMS USA Manufacturing LLC *(G-13369)*
Branch West Concrete Products 989 345-0794
3350 Rau Rd West Branch (48661) *(G-18326)*
Brand Logoed Barware 517 763-1044
203 Mac Ave East Lansing (48823) *(G-4888)*
Brandnburg Tech Div Dtroit His, Sterling Heights Also called Detroit Hoist & Crane Co L L C *(G-15982)*
Brandon Bernard Collection LLC 888 611-7011
24444 W 7 Mile Rd Detroit (48219) *(G-4068)*
Brandons Defense 517 669-5272
12583 Ro Dic Don Dr Dewitt (48820) *(G-4707)*
Brandt Manufacturing Inc 517 851-7000
4974 Bird Dr Stockbridge (49285) *(G-16272)*
Branson Ultrasonics Corp 586 276-0150
6590 Sims Dr Sterling Heights (48313) *(G-15948)*
Brapos LLC 248 677-6700
4271 Stoddard Rd West Bloomfield (48323) *(G-18268)*
Brasco International Inc 313 393-0393
32400 Industrial Dr Madison Heights (48071) *(G-10684)*
Brass Craft Mfg Co, Novi Also called Brasscraft Manufacturing Co *(G-12376)*
Brass Kings Inc 248 674-1860
11725 N Hilbrand Rd Manton (49663) *(G-10930)*
Brasscraft Manufacturing Co (HQ) 248 305-6000
39600 Orchard Hill Pl Novi (48375) *(G-12376)*
Brauer Clamps USA 586 427-5304
25269 Mound Rd Warren (48091) *(G-17741)*
Braund Manufacturing Co, Battle Creek Also called Barker Manufacturing Co *(G-1190)*
Brawn Mixer Inc 616 399-5600
12838 Stainless Dr Holland (49424) *(G-7982)*
Brazeway LLC (PA) 517 265-2121
2711 E Maumee St Adrian (49221) *(G-54)*
BRC, Battle Creek Also called Brake Roller Co Inc *(G-1197)*
BRC Automotive Engrg & Sls Off, Auburn Hills Also called BRC Rubber & Plastics Inc *(G-833)*
BRC Rubber & Plastics Inc 248 745-9200
1091 Centre Rd Ste 210 Auburn Hills (48326) *(G-833)*
Brd Printing Inc 517 372-0268
912 W Saint Joseph St Lansing (48915) *(G-9816)*
Bread of Life Bakery & Cafe 906 663-4005
105 N Sophie St Bessemer (49911) *(G-1647)*
Break Mold LLC 269 359-0822
1601 W Centre Ave # 104 Portage (49024) *(G-13549)*
Break-A-Beam 586 758-7790
25257 Mound Rd Warren (48091) *(G-17742)*
Breakaway Media Marketing LLC 734 787-3382
44004 Harris Rd Belleville (48111) *(G-1482)*
Breasco LLC 734 961-9020
3840 Carpenter Rd Ypsilanti (48197) *(G-18929)*
Breck Graphics Incorporated (PA) 616 248-4110
3983 Linden Ave Se Grand Rapids (49548) *(G-6523)*
Breckers ABC Tool Company Inc 586 779-1122
15919 E 12 Mile Rd Roseville (48066) *(G-14381)*
Breco LLC 517 317-2211
57 Cole St Quincy (49082) *(G-13664)*
Brede Inc 313 273-1079
378 S Cranbrook Rd Bloomfield Hills (48301) *(G-1806)*
Breesport Holdings Inc 248 685-9500
1235 Holden Ave Milford (48381) *(G-11456)*
Breitburn Operating LP 989 348-8459
8892 W 7 Mile Rd Grayling (49738) *(G-7457)*
Breiten Box & Packaging Co Inc 586 469-0800
42828 Executive Dr Harrison Township (48045) *(G-7690)*
Breiten Lumber, Sandusky Also called Stoutenburg Inc *(G-15068)*
Brembo 517 568-4398
6259 30 Mile Rd Homer (49245) *(G-8345)*
Brembo North America Inc 517 568-4398
5851 30 Mile Rd Homer (49245) *(G-8346)*
Brembo North America Inc (HQ) 734 416-1275
47765 Halyard Dr Plymouth (48170) *(G-13138)*
Brembo North America Inc 517 568-3301
29991 E M 60 Homer (49245) *(G-8347)*
Brembo North America Homer Inc 517 568-4398
29991 E M 60 Homer (49245) *(G-8348)*
Brembo Racing, Plymouth Also called Brembo North America Inc *(G-13138)*
Bremen Corp 574 546-4238
300 N Alloy Dr Fenton (48430) *(G-5460)*
Bremer Authentic Ingredients 616 772-9100
420 100th Ave Zeeland (49464) *(G-19002)*
Bremer Prosthetic Design Inc (PA) 810 733-3375
3487 S Linden Rd Ste U Flint (48507) *(G-5660)*
Bremer Prosthetics LLC 989 249-9400
3995 Fashion Square Blvd # 1 Saginaw (48603) *(G-14620)*
Brent Bastian Logging Inc 906 482-6378
54215 Salo Rd Hancock (49930) *(G-7616)*
Brenton Consulting LLC 248 342-6590
21820 Garfield Rd Northville (48167) *(G-12198)*

Bretton Square Industries 517 346-9607
812 E Jolly Rd Ste 216 Lansing (48910) *(G-9817)*
Bretts Printing Service 517 482-2256
2435 S Rundle Ave 39 Lansing (48910) *(G-9818)*
Brew Detroit LLC 313 974-7366
1401 Abbott St Detroit (48216) *(G-4069)*
Brewers City Dock Inc 616 396-6563
24 Pine Ave Holland (49423) *(G-7983)*
Brewery, Grand Rapids Also called Speciation Artisan Ales LLC *(G-7215)*
Brewery Vivant, Grand Rapids Also called One Beer At A Time LLC *(G-7059)*
Brewing Company, Midland Also called Midland Brewing Co LLC *(G-11391)*
Brewing World, Warren Also called Kuhnhenn Brewing Co LLC *(G-17898)*
Brews Brothers III Inc 228 255-5548
510 Crescent Dr Dearborn (48124) *(G-3816)*
Brewts LLC 616 291-1117
1260 100th St Sw Ste 2 Byron Center (49315) *(G-2262)*
Brian A Broomfield 989 309-0709
14776 10th Ave Remus (49340) *(G-13814)*
Brian M Fowler Pipe Organs 517 485-3748
215 Dexter Rd Eaton Rapids (48827) *(G-4956)*
Brians Foods LLC 248 739-5280
21444 Bridge St Southfield (48033) *(G-15511)*
Brickers Box Board Inc 734 981-0828
2200 N Canton Center Rd # 120 Canton (48187) *(G-2444)*
Brico Welding & Fab Inc 586 948-8881
27057 Morelli Dr Chesterfield (48051) *(G-2851)*
Bridal Nook, Clio Also called Genesee County Herald Inc *(G-3399)*
Bridge Organics Company 269 649-4200
311 W Washington St Vicksburg (49097) *(G-17600)*
Bridge Street Design & Mktg, Southfield Also called Grigg Graphic Services Inc *(G-15585)*
Bridge Tool and Die LLC 231 269-3200
125 S Industrial Dr Buckley (49620) *(G-2205)*
Bridgeport Manufacturing Inc 989 777-4314
6689 Dixie Hwy Bridgeport (48722) *(G-1915)*
Bridgewater Industries 810 228-3963
4023 W Pierson Rd Flint (48504) *(G-5661)*
Bridgewater Interiors LLC (HQ) 313 842-3300
4617 W Fort St Detroit (48209) *(G-4070)*
Bridgewater Interiors LLC 586 753-3072
7500 Tank Ave Warren (48092) *(G-17743)*
Bridgville Plastics Inc 269 465-6516
7380 Jericho Rd Stevensville (49127) *(G-16241)*
Briggs Contracting 989 687-7331
62 E Saginaw Rd Sanford (48657) *(G-15072)*
Briggs Industries Inc 586 749-5191
54145 Bates Rd Chesterfield (48051) *(G-2852)*
Briggs Mold & Die Inc 517 784-6908
414 N Jackson St 97-12 Jackson (49201) *(G-8827)*
Bright Star Sign Inc 313 933-4460
13300 Foley St Detroit (48227) *(G-4071)*
Bright Technologies, Wayland Also called Sebright Products Inc *(G-18206)*
Brighter Sign Age 248 719-5389
22700 Stephens St Saint Clair Shores (48080) *(G-14850)*
Brighter Smile By Tierra LLC 248 278-3117
4291 17th St Detroit (48208) *(G-4072)*
Brightformat Inc 616 247-1161
5300 Corprte Grv Dr Se Grand Rapids (49512) *(G-6524)*
Brightly Twisted 313 303-1364
1418 Michigan Ave Detroit (48216) *(G-4073)*
Brighton Laboratories Inc 810 225-9520
11871 Grand River Rd Brighton (48116) *(G-1953)*
Brighton Technical Center, Brighton Also called Bwi North America Inc *(G-1957)*
Brilar LLC 248 547-6439
13200 Northend Ave Oak Park (48237) *(G-12596)*
Brill Company Inc 231 843-2430
715 S James St Ludington (49431) *(G-10528)*
Brilliance Audio, Grand Haven Also called Brilliance Publishing Inc *(G-6281)*
Brilliance Publishing Inc 616 846-5256
1704 Eaton Dr Grand Haven (49417) *(G-6281)*
Brilliant Industries LLC 616 954-9209
4864 Glen Meadow Ct Se Grand Rapids (49546) *(G-6525)*
Brindley Lumber & Pallet Co 989 345-3497
1971 State Rd Lupton (48635) *(G-10561)*
Brindley Pallets, Lupton Also called Brindley Lumber & Pallet Co *(G-10561)*
Brine, Warren Also called Warrior Sports Inc *(G-18063)*
Brinks Family Creamery LLC 231 826-0099
3560 E Mulder Rd Mc Bain (49657) *(G-11179)*
Brinston Acquisition LLC 248 269-1000
840 W Long Lake Rd Troy (48098) *(G-16985)*
Brintley Enterprises 248 991-4086
8660 Rosemont Ave Detroit (48228) *(G-4074)*
Brio Device LLC 734 945-5728
2104 Georgetown Blvd Ann Arbor (48105) *(G-406)*
Bristol Manufacturing Inc 810 658-9510
4416 N State Rd Davison (48423) *(G-3774)*
Bristol Steel & Conveyor Corp 810 658-9510
4416 N State Rd Davison (48423) *(G-3775)*
Bristol-Myers Squibb Company 248 528-2476
2460 Waltham Dr Troy (48085) *(G-16986)*

Brite Products, Detroit *Also called Smith Wa Inc* ***(G-4598)***
British Carburetors LLC........616 920-0203
1556 Philadelphia Ave Se Grand Rapids (49507) ***(G-6526)***
British Cnvrtng Sltns Nrth AME........281 764-6651
259 E Michigan Ave # 305 Kalamazoo (49007) ***(G-9141)***
Britt Manufacturing........810 982-9720
2600 20th St Port Huron (48060) ***(G-13463)***
Britt Mfg........810 966-0223
5150 Lakeshore Rd Fort Gratiot (48059) ***(G-5818)***
Britten Inc........231 941-8200
2322 Cass Rd Traverse City (49684) ***(G-16627)***
Britten Banners LLC........231 941-8200
2322 Cass Rd Traverse City (49684) ***(G-16628)***
Britten Metalworks LLC........231 421-1615
1661 Northern Star Dr Traverse City (49696) ***(G-16629)***
Britten Woodworks Inc........231 275-5457
2322 Cass Rd Traverse City (49684) ***(G-16630)***
Broaching Industries Inc........586 949-3775
25755 Dhondt Ct Chesterfield (48051) ***(G-2853)***
Broadside Press........313 736-5338
20117 Monica St Detroit (48221) ***(G-4075)***
Broadsword Solutions Corp........248 341-3367
3795 Dorothy Ln Waterford (48329) ***(G-18105)***
Broadteq Incorporated........248 794-9323
5119 Highland Rd Ste 386 Waterford (48327) ***(G-18106)***
Broadway, Manchester *Also called Enkon LLC* ***(G-10883)***
Broadway Embroidery........248 838-8074
24 N Broadway St Lake Orion (48362) ***(G-9590)***
Brockie Fabricating & Wldg LLC........517 750-7500
1027 Hurst Rd Jackson (49201) ***(G-8828)***
Brollytime Inc........312 854-7606
306 S Washington Ave # 400 Royal Oak (48067) ***(G-14521)***
Bron Machine Inc........616 392-5320
821 Productions Pl Holland (49423) ***(G-7984)***
Bronco Printing Company........248 544-1120
21841 Dequindre Rd Hazel Park (48030) ***(G-7821)***
Bronner Christmas Decorations, Frankenmuth *Also called Bronner Display Sign Advg Inc* ***(G-5860)***
Bronner Display Sign Advg Inc........989 652-9931
25 Christmas Ln Frankenmuth (48734) ***(G-5860)***
Brookfield Inc........616 997-9663
8041 Leonard St Coopersville (49404) ***(G-3681)***
Brooklyn Products Intl........517 592-2185
171 Wamplers Lake Rd Brooklyn (49230) ***(G-2122)***
Brooklyn Special Tees........623 521-3230
11455 Brighton Hwy Brooklyn (49230) ***(G-2123)***
Brooks & Perkins Inc........231 775-2229
8051 E 34 Rd Cadillac (49601) ***(G-2318)***
Brooks Manufacturing........231 832-4961
8457 E 64th St Chase (49623) ***(G-2775)***
Brooks Meter Devices, Novi *Also called Brooks Utility Products Group* ***(G-12377)***
Brooks Utility Products Group, Novi *Also called Ekstrom Industries Inc* ***(G-12412)***
Brooks Utility Products Group (PA)........248 477-0250
43045 W 9 Mile Rd Novi (48375) ***(G-12377)***
Brophy Engraving Co Inc........313 871-2333
626 Harper Ave Detroit (48202) ***(G-4076)***
Brose Harmon Road........248 339-4702
1650 Harmon Rd Auburn Hills (48326) ***(G-834)***
Brose New Boston Inc........248 340-1100
1107 Centre Rd Auburn Hills (48326) ***(G-835)***
Brose New Boston Inc........248 339-4000
3933 Automation Ave Auburn Hills (48326) ***(G-836)***
Brose New Boston Inc (HQ)........248 339-4021
23400 Bell Rd New Boston (48164) ***(G-12004)***
Brose North America Inc (HQ)........248 339-4000
3933 Automation Ave Auburn Hills (48326) ***(G-837)***
Brose North America Inc........734 753-4902
23400 Bell Rd New Boston (48164) ***(G-12005)***
Brother Industrial Equipment, Ann Arbor *Also called Catylist Inc* ***(G-416)***
Brother Mike Pubg & Mus Co LLC........313 506-8866
4886 Beacon Hill Dr Bloomfield Hills (48301) ***(G-1807)***
Brothers Baking, Jackson *Also called Dawn Food Products Inc* ***(G-8862)***
Brothers Baking Company........269 663-8591
27260 Max St Edwardsburg (49112) ***(G-5001)***
Brothers In Arms Mfg LLC........989 464-9615
509 Lockwood St Alpena (49707) ***(G-285)***
Brothers Industrials Inc........248 794-5080
38844 Steeple Chase # 27101 Farmington Hills (48331) ***(G-5186)***
Brothers Mead 3 LLC........269 883-6241
19915 Capital Ave Ne # 208 Battle Creek (49017) ***(G-1198)***
Browe Inc........248 877-3800
36359 Harper Ave Clinton Township (48035) ***(G-3189)***
Brown & Sharpe Precision Ctr, Novi *Also called Hexagon Mfg Intelligence Inc* ***(G-12433)***
Brown Forman........248 464-2011
1030 N Crooks Rd Ste B Clawson (48017) ***(G-3089)***
Brown House Publishing........248 470-4690
2263 Timberridge Dr West Bloomfield (48324) ***(G-18269)***
Brown Jig Grinding Co........248 349-7744
28005 Oakland Oaks Ct Wixom (48393) ***(G-18626)***
Brown Mch Group Intrmdate Hldn (HQ)........989 435-7741
330 N Ross St Beaverton (48612) ***(G-1424)***
Brown-Campbell Company (PA)........586 884-2180
11800 Investment Dr Shelby Township (48315) ***(G-15179)***
Brown-Campbell Steel, Shelby Township *Also called Brown-Campbell Company* ***(G-15179)***
Browndog Creamery LLC........248 361-3759
118 E Main St Northville (48167) ***(G-12199)***
Brownie Signs LLC........248 437-0800
8791 Earhart Rd South Lyon (48178) ***(G-15428)***
Brownlee Group LLC........512 202-0568
23333 Quinn Rd Clinton Township (48035) ***(G-3190)***
Brownwood Acres Foods Inc........231 599-3101
4819 Us 31 Eastport (49627) ***(G-4949)***
Bruce Inc........517 371-5205
108 S Washington Sq Lansing (48933) ***(G-9819)***
Bruce Kane Enterprises LLC (PA)........410 727-0637
28200 Orchard Lake Rd # 107 Farmington Hills (48334) ***(G-5187)***
Bruce Weld Edwards LLC........248 693-6222
1520 S Lapeer Rd Ste 211 Lake Orion (48360) ***(G-9591)***
Brugola Oeb Indstriale USA Inc........734 468-0009
45555 Port St Plymouth (48170) ***(G-13139)***
Brun Laboratories Inc........616 456-1114
1120 Monroe Ave Nw # 180 Grand Rapids (49503) ***(G-6527)***
Bruning Forest Products........989 733-2880
16854 5 Mile Hwy Onaway (49765) ***(G-12697)***
Bruno Wojcik........989 785-5555
12270 E Shore Atlanta (49709) ***(G-744)***
Brunswick Bowling Products, Muskegon *Also called Bbp Investment Holdings LLC* ***(G-11777)***
Brunswick Bowling Products LLC (HQ)........231 725-4966
525 W Laketon Ave Muskegon (49441) ***(G-11784)***
Brunswick Indoor Recreation........231 725-4764
525 W Laketon Ave Muskegon (49441) ***(G-11785)***
Brunt Associates Inc........248 960-8295
47689 Avante Dr Wixom (48393) ***(G-18627)***
Brusarosco, Port Huron *Also called Afx Industries LLC* ***(G-13432)***
Brute Industries, Escanaba *Also called Race Ramps LLC* ***(G-5094)***
Brutsche Concrete Products Co (PA)........269 963-1554
15150 6 1/2 Mile Rd Battle Creek (49014) ***(G-1199)***
Bry Mac Inc........231 799-2211
865 E Porter Rd Norton Shores (49441) ***(G-12280)***
Bryan K Sergent........231 670-2106
19383 10 Mile Rd Stanwood (49346) ***(G-15903)***
Brydges Group LLC........734 649-6635
4950 W Dickman Rd Ste C Battle Creek (49037) ***(G-1200)***
Bryllan LLC........248 442-7620
12501 Grand River Rd Brighton (48116) ***(G-1954)***
Brys Winery Lc........231 223-8446
3309 Blue Water Rd Traverse City (49686) ***(G-16631)***
BS Bars........734 358-3832
4175 Whitmore Lake Rd Ann Arbor (48105) ***(G-407)***
BT Aerospace, Southfield *Also called Bradley-Thompson Tool Company* ***(G-15510)***
BT Engineering LLC........734 417-2218
223 River St Spring Lake (49456) ***(G-15807)***
Bti Measurement Tstg Svcs LLC (PA)........734 769-2100
7035 Jomar Dr Whitmore Lake (48189) ***(G-18524)***
Bti Measurement Tstg Svcs LLC........734 769-2100
2800 Zeeb Rd Dockk Dexter (48130) ***(G-4729)***
Bti Precision Measurement Tstg, Whitmore Lake *Also called Balance Technology Inc* ***(G-18520)***
Btm National Holdings LLC........616 794-0100
1114 S Bridge St Belding (48809) ***(G-1441)***
Btmc Holdings Inc (PA)........616 794-0100
1114 S Bridge St Belding (48809) ***(G-1442)***
Buchanan Global Inc........269 635-5270
2121 W Chicago Rd Ste C Niles (49120) ***(G-12116)***
Buchanan Metal Forming Inc (PA)........269 695-3836
103 W Smith St Buchanan (49107) ***(G-2190)***
Bucher Hydraulics Inc (HQ)........616 458-1306
1363 Michigan St Ne Grand Rapids (49503) ***(G-6528)***
Bucher Hydraulics Inc........231 652-2773
201 Cooperative Center Dr Newaygo (49337) ***(G-12078)***
Buck Pole Archery Deerranch, Marion *Also called Pollington Machine Tool Inc* ***(G-10976)***
Buck Stop Lure Company Inc........989 762-5091
3600 N Grow Rd Stanton (48888) ***(G-15899)***
Buck-N-Ham Machines Inc (HQ)........231 587-5322
413 Dale Ave Mancelona (49659) ***(G-10867)***
Buck-Spica Equipment Ltd........269 792-2251
631 W Cherry St Wayland (49348) ***(G-18192)***
Buckeye Terminals LLC........616 842-2450
17806 N Shore Rd Ferrysburg (49409) ***(G-5601)***
Buckeys Contracting & Service........989 835-9512
707 Jefferson Ave Midland (48640) ***(G-11325)***
Buckingham Tool Corp........734 591-2333
11915 Market St Livonia (48150) ***(G-10142)***
Bucklin Township Candles LLC........248 403-0600
111 Walnut St River Rouge (48218) ***(G-13852)***
Bucks Cement Inc........810 233-4141
4299 Fenton Rd Burton (48529) ***(G-2228)***

ALPHABETIC

(PA)=Parent Co (HQ)=Headquarters (DH)=Div Headquarters
2022 Harris Michigan Industrial Directory
949

Bucks Sports Products Inc 763 229-1331
7721 Lake Bluff 19.4 Rd Gladstone (49837) ***(G-6175)***
Budd Magnetic Products Inc 248 353-2533
22525 Telegraph Rd Southfield (48033) ***(G-15512)***
Buddies Foods LLC 586 776-4036
17445 Malyn Blvd Fraser (48026) ***(G-5907)***
Budget Europe Travel Service 734 668-0529
2557 Meade Ct Ann Arbor (48105) ***(G-408)***
Budget Print Center, Grand Rapids *Also called Cascade Prtg & Graphics Inc* ***(G-6556)***
Budget Printing Center, East Lansing *Also called Aalpha Tinadawn Inc* ***(G-4884)***
Buffoli North America Corp 616 610-4362
4508 128th Ave Holland (49424) ***(G-7985)***
Bugay Logging 906 428-2125
8409 N P.11 Dr Gladstone (49837) ***(G-6176)***
Buhler Technologies LLC 248 652-1546
1030 W Hamlin Rd Rochester Hills (48309) ***(G-13966)***
Buhlerprince Inc (HQ) 616 394-8248
670 Windcrest Dr Holland (49423) ***(G-7986)***
Builders Iron Inc 616 647-9288
7770 Venture Ave Nw Sparta (49345) ***(G-15761)***
Builders Plbg Sup Traverse Cy 800 466-5160
1610 W South Airport Rd Traverse City (49686) ***(G-16632)***
Built Systems LLC 616 834-5099
11511 James St Holland (49424) ***(G-7987)***
Buiter Tool & Die Inc 616 455-7410
8187 Division Ave S Grand Rapids (49548) ***(G-6529)***
Bulk AG Innovations LLC 269 925-0900
1007 Nickerson Ave Benton Harbor (49022) ***(G-1538)***
Bull Hn Info Systems Inc 616 942-7126
2620 Horizon Dr Se D1 Grand Rapids (49546) ***(G-6530)***
Bulldog Fabricating Corp 734 761-3111
50 Enterprise Dr Ann Arbor (48103) ***(G-409)***
Bulldog Factory Service, Madison Heights *Also called Santanna Tool & Design LLC* ***(G-10824)***
Bulldog Innovative Mfg LLC 517 223-2500
925 Garden Ln Fowlerville (48836) ***(G-5836)***
Bulldog Welding 248 342-1189
4785 Ormond Rd Davisburg (48350) ***(G-3761)***
Bulletin Moon 734 453-9985
44315 Plymouth Oaks Blvd Plymouth (48170) ***(G-13140)***
Bulletin of Concerned Asi 231 228-7116
3693 S Bay Bluffs Dr Cedar (49621) ***(G-2636)***
Bulletsafe Bulletproof Vests 248 457-6877
352 Oliver Dr Troy (48084) ***(G-16987)***
Bulls-Eye Wire & Cable Inc 810 245-8600
1498 N Saginaw St Ste 4 Lapeer (48446) ***(G-9916)***
Bullseye Power 231 788-5209
2134 Northwoods Ave Muskegon (49442) ***(G-11786)***
Bulman Products Inc 616 363-4416
1650 Mcreynolds Ave Nw Grand Rapids (49504) ***(G-6531)***
Bulmann Dock & Lift, Boyne City *Also called Bulmann Enterprises Inc* ***(G-1885)***
Bulmann Enterprises Inc 231 549-5020
175 Magnet Dr Boyne City (49712) ***(G-1885)***
Bundeze LLC 248 343-9179
9717 Cottontail St West Olive (49460) ***(G-18348)***
Bundy Corporation 517 439-1132
200 Arch Ave Hillsdale (49242) ***(G-7927)***
Bundy Tubing Division, Auburn Hills *Also called TI Group Auto Systems LLC* ***(G-1056)***
Bunker & Sons Sawmill LLC 989 983-2715
119 Alexander Rd Vanderbilt (49795) ***(G-17568)***
Bunting Bearings LLC 269 345-8691
4252 E Kilgore Rd Portage (49002) ***(G-13550)***
Bunting Sand & Gravel Products 989 345-2373
3247 Cook Rd West Branch (48661) ***(G-18327)***
Burch Tank & Truck Inc 989 495-0342
4200 James Savage Rd Midland (48642) ***(G-11326)***
Burch Tank & Truck Inc (PA) 989 772-6266
2113 Enterprise Dr Mount Pleasant (48858) ***(G-11688)***
Burch Truck and Trailer Parts, Midland *Also called Burch Tank & Truck Inc* ***(G-11326)***
Burch Truck and Trailer Parts, Mount Pleasant *Also called Burch Tank & Truck Inc* ***(G-11688)***
Burco Inc 616 453-7771
2936 S Wilson Ct Nw Grand Rapids (49534) ***(G-6532)***
Burgaflex North America LLC 810 714-3285
1101 Copper Ave Fenton (48430) ***(G-5461)***
Burgaflex North America Inc 810 584-7296
8186 Industrial Park Dr Grand Blanc (48439) ***(G-6237)***
Burge Chemical Products, Grand Rapids *Also called Burge Incorporated* ***(G-6533)***
Burge Incorporated 616 791-2214
2751 Westbrook Dr Nw Grand Rapids (49504) ***(G-6533)***
Burger Iron Co 330 794-1716
99 Steele St Nw Grand Rapids (49534) ***(G-6534)***
Burhani Labs Inc 313 212-3842
18254 Livernois Ave Detroit (48221) ***(G-4077)***
Burkard Industries Inc 586 791-6520
35300 Kelly Rd Clinton Township (48035) ***(G-3191)***
Burke E Porter Machinery Co (PA) 616 234-1200
730 Plymouth Ave Ne Grand Rapids (49505) ***(G-6535)***
Burke Porter Group, Ada *Also called Bpg International Fin Co LLC* ***(G-12)***
Burke Porter Machinery Co, Grand Rapids *Also called Burke E Porter Machinery Co* ***(G-6535)***
Burkett Signs Corp 269 746-4285
15886 E Michigan Ave Climax (49034) ***(G-3135)***
Burkholder Excavating Inc 269 426-4227
4898 Weechik Rd Sawyer (49125) ***(G-15107)***
Burkk Inc 616 365-0354
4455 Airwest Dr Se Grand Rapids (49512) ***(G-6536)***
Burkland Inc (PA) 810 636-2233
6520 S State Rd Goodrich (48438) ***(G-6222)***
Burlingame Industries Inc 616 682-5691
6757 Cascade Rd Se Grand Rapids (49546) ***(G-6537)***
Burlwoodbox 734 662-7274
3735 N Territorial Rd E Ann Arbor (48105) ***(G-410)***
Burly Oak Builders Inc 734 368-4912
9980 Dexter Chelsea Rd Dexter (48130) ***(G-4730)***
Burners Inc 248 676-9141
4901 Mccarthy Dr Milford (48381) ***(G-11457)***
Burnette Foods Inc (PA) 231 264-8116
701 S Us Highway 31 Elk Rapids (49629) ***(G-5022)***
Burnette Foods Inc 269 621-3181
87171 County Road 687 Hartford (49057) ***(G-7762)***
Burnette Foods Inc 231 536-2284
200 State St East Jordan (49727) ***(G-4860)***
Burnette Foods Inc 231 861-2151
4856 1st St New ERA (49446) ***(G-12026)***
Burnette Foods Inc 231 223-4282
2955 Kroupa Rd Traverse City (49686) ***(G-16633)***
Burnham & Northern Inc 517 279-7501
169 Industrial Ave Coldwater (49036) ***(G-3422)***
Burnrite Pellet Corporation 989 429-1067
2495 E Rock Rd Clare (48617) ***(G-2974)***
Burnside Acquisition LLC (PA) 616 243-2800
1060 Kenosha Indus Dr Se Grand Rapids (49508) ***(G-6538)***
Burnside Acquisition LLC 231 798-3394
6830 Grand Haven Rd Norton Shores (49456) ***(G-12346)***
Burnside Industries LLC 231 798-3394
6830 Grand Haven Rd Norton Shores (49456) ***(G-12347)***
Burr Bench, Chelsea *Also called Abrasive Finishing Inc* ***(G-2801)***
Burr Engineering & Dev Co (PA) 269 966-3122
1125 Watkins Rd Battle Creek (49015) ***(G-1201)***
Burr Oak Tool, Sturgis *Also called Burr Oak Tool Inc* ***(G-16282)***
Burr Oak Tool Inc (PA) 269 651-9393
405 W South St Sturgis (49091) ***(G-16282)***
Burrell Tri-County Vaults Inc 734 483-2024
1106 E Michigan Ave Ypsilanti (48198) ***(G-18930)***
Burrone Family Vineyards 989 379-3786
212 Pinebrook Dr Lachine (49753) ***(G-9531)***
Burrow Industries Inc 734 847-1842
7380 Express Rd Temperance (48182) ***(G-16529)***
Burst Led 248 321-6262
29412 Windmill Ct Farmington Hills (48334) ***(G-5188)***
Burt Moeke & Son Hardwoods 231 587-5388
2509 Valley Rd Mancelona (49659) ***(G-10868)***
Burton Industries Inc 906 932-5970
1260 Wall St Ironwood (49938) ***(G-8758)***
Burton Industries Inc 906 932-5970
1260 Wall St Ironwood (49938) ***(G-8759)***
Burton Press Co Inc 248 853-0212
2156 Avon Industrial Dr Rochester Hills (48309) ***(G-13967)***
Busch Industries Inc 616 957-3737
900 East Paris Ave Se # 304 Grand Rapids (49546) ***(G-6539)***
Busch Machine Tool Supply LLC 989 798-4794
7251 Midland Rd Freeland (48623) ***(G-6019)***
Busche Alum Tchnlgies Franklin, Southfield *Also called Shipston Aluminum Tech Ind Inc* ***(G-15701)***
Busche Aluminum Technologies, Fruitport *Also called Shipston Alum Tech Mich Inc* ***(G-6070)***
Busche Aluminum Technologies, Southfield *Also called Shipston Alum Tech Intl Inc* ***(G-15699)***
Busche Performance Group, Southfield *Also called Busche Southfield Inc* ***(G-15513)***
Busche Southfield Inc 248 357-5180
26290 W 8 Mile Rd Southfield (48033) ***(G-15513)***
Bush Concrete Products Inc 231 733-1904
3584 Airline Rd Norton Shores (49444) ***(G-12281)***
Bush Polishing Buffing LLC 989 855-2248
5624 E Charles Rd Ionia (48846) ***(G-8687)***
Bushings Inc 248 650-0603
1967 Rochester Indus Dr Rochester Hills (48309) ***(G-13968)***
Business Cards Plus Inc 269 327-7727
8785 Portage Indus Dr Portage (49024) ***(G-13551)***
Business Connect L3c 833 229-6753
2146 Division Ave S Grand Rapids (49507) ***(G-6540)***
Business Connect World, Grand Rapids *Also called Business Connect L3c* ***(G-6540)***
Business Design Solutions Inc (PA) 248 672-8007
17360 W 12 Mile Rd # 201 Southfield (48076) ***(G-15514)***
Business Direct Review 269 373-7100
401 S Burdick St Kalamazoo (49007) ***(G-9142)***

ALPHABETIC SECTION

Business News 231 929-7919
129 E Front St Unit 200 Traverse City (49684) *(G-16634)*
Business News Publishing 248 362-3700
2401 W Big Beavr Rd # 70 Troy (48084) *(G-16988)*
Business Press Inc 248 652-8855
917 N Main St Rochester (48307) *(G-13895)*
Business Review, Kalamazoo *Also called Business Direct Review (G-9142)*
Business Signs of America 810 814-3987
14250 North Rd Fenton (48430) *(G-5462)*
Business Software Services, Jenison *Also called Nu-Wool Co Inc (G-9065)*
Business To Business, Monroe *Also called Monroe Environmental Corp (G-11562)*
Buskirk Lumber Company 616 765-5103
319 Oak St Freeport (49325) *(G-6032)*
Busscher Septic Tank Company, Holland *Also called Busscher Septic Tank Service (G-7988)*
Busscher Septic Tank Service 616 392-9653
11305 E Lakewood Blvd Holland (49424) *(G-7988)*
Busted Bra Shop LLC 313 288-0449
15 E Kirby St Ste A Detroit (48202) *(G-4078)*
Bustedtees LLC 989 448-3179
1782 Orourke Blvd Gaylord (49735) *(G-6121)*
Buster Mathis Foundation 616 843-4433
4409 Carol Ave Sw Wyoming (49519) *(G-18855)*
Busy Bees EMB & Gifts LLC 989 261-7446
3018 Log Cabin Trl Sheridan (48884) *(G-15381)*
Butler Mill Service Company 313 429-2486
8800 Dix St Detroit (48209) *(G-4079)*
Butler Plastics Company 810 765-8811
766 Degurse Ave Marine City (48039) *(G-10956)*
Butter Cobbler & Things LLC 810 391-8432
714 Natures Cove Ct Wixom (48393) *(G-18628)*
Butterball Farms Inc 616 243-0105
1435 Buchanan Ave Sw Grand Rapids (49507) *(G-6541)*
Buttered Body Essentials LLC 313 687-3847
676 Lothrop Rd Detroit (48202) *(G-4080)*
Buy Best Manufacturing LLC 248 875-2491
988 Rickett Rd Ste B Brighton (48116) *(G-1955)*
Buyers Development Group LLC (PA) 734 677-0009
4095 Stone School Rd Ann Arbor (48108) *(G-411)*
Buyers Guide, Sandusky *Also called Great Northern Publishing Inc (G-15059)*
Buyers Guide 616 897-9261
105 N Broadway St Lowell (49331) *(G-10497)*
Buyers Guide 231 722-3784
1781 5th St Ste 1 Muskegon (49441) *(G-11787)*
BV Technology LLC 616 558-1746
7855 Sandy Hollow Dr Se Alto (49302) *(G-329)*
Bva Inc 248 348-4920
29222 Trident Indus Blvd New Hudson (48165) *(G-12044)*
BVA OILS, New Hudson *Also called Bva Inc (G-12044)*
Bwa Receivables Corporation 248 754-9200
3850 Hamlin Rd Auburn Hills (48326) *(G-838)*
Bwb LLC 231 439-9200
33469 W 14 Mile Rd Ste 10 Farmington Hills (48331) *(G-5189)*
Bwi Chassis Dynamics NA Inc (HQ) 937 455-5308
12501 Grand River Rd Brighton (48116) *(G-1956)*
Bwi North America Inc 810 494-4584
12501 Grand River Rd Brighton (48116) *(G-1957)*
Bwjs Printing LLC 248 678-3610
12610 Riad St Detroit (48224) *(G-4081)*
Byers Manufacturing, Lawton *Also called Amjs Incorporated (G-9987)*
Byers, D C Company, Grand Rapids *Also called DC Byers Co/Grand Rapids Inc (G-6635)*
Byk USA Inc 203 265-2086
2932 Waterview Dr Rochester Hills (48309) *(G-13969)*
Byrne Elec Specialists Inc (PA) 616 866-3461
320 Byrne Industrial Dr Rockford (49341) *(G-14159)*
Byrne Elec Specialists Inc 616 866-3461
725 Byrne Industrial Dr Rockford (49341) *(G-14160)*
Byrne Tool & Die Inc 616 866-4479
316 Byrne Industrial Dr Rockford (49341) *(G-14161)*
Byrnes Manufacturing Co LLC 810 664-3686
870 Whitney Dr Lapeer (48446) *(G-9917)*
Byrnes Tool Co Inc 810 664-3686
870 Whitney Dr Lapeer (48446) *(G-9918)*
Byron Manufacturing, Flint *Also called Engineered Products Company (G-5696)*
C & A Wholesale Inc 248 302-3555
18942 Hayes St Detroit (48205) *(G-4082)*
C & A Wood Products Inc 313 365-8400
17434 Cliff St Detroit (48212) *(G-4083)*
C & C Enterprises Inc 989 772-5095
1106 Packard Rd Mount Pleasant (48858) *(G-11689)*
C & C Machine Tool Inc 248 693-3347
1584 Oneida Trl Lake Orion (48362) *(G-9592)*
C & C Manufacturing Inc 586 268-3650
35605 Stanley Dr Sterling Heights (48312) *(G-15949)*
C & C Sports Inc 810 227-7068
8090 Grand River Rd Brighton (48114) *(G-1958)*
C & D Enterprises Inc 248 373-0011
G4349 S Dort Hwy Burton (48529) *(G-2229)*
C & D Gage Inc 517 548-7049
8736 Glen Haven Dr Howell (48843) *(G-8433)*
C & D Tool & Die Company Inc 248 922-5937
12395 Shaffer Rd Davisburg (48350) *(G-3762)*
C & G News Inc 586 498-8000
13650 E 11 Mile Rd Warren (48089) *(G-17744)*
C & G Publishing Inc 586 498-8000
13650 E 11 Mile Rd Warren (48089) *(G-17745)*
C & H Stamping Inc 517 750-3600
205 Obrien Rd Jackson (49201) *(G-8829)*
C & J Fabrication Inc 586 791-6269
34885 Groesbeck Hwy Clinton Township (48035) *(G-3192)*
C & J Pallets Inc 517 263-7415
2368 E Us Highway 223 Adrian (49221) *(G-55)*
C & J Steel Processing, Detroit *Also called Scotten Steel Processing Inc (G-4585)*
C & K Box Company Inc 517 784-1779
423 Barrett Ave Jackson (49202) *(G-8830)*
C & K Hardwoods LLC 269 231-0048
7325 Elm Valley Rd Three Oaks (49128) *(G-16554)*
C & M Coatings Inc 616 842-1925
1730 Airpark Dr Ste C Grand Haven (49417) *(G-6282)*
C & M Manufacturing Corp Inc 586 749-3455
30207 Commerce Blvd Chesterfield (48051) *(G-2854)*
C & M Manufacturing Inc 517 279-0013
129 Industrial Ave Coldwater (49036) *(G-3423)*
C & M Tool LLC 734 944-3355
1235 Industrial Dr Ste 7 Saline (48176) *(G-15006)*
C & N Manufacturing Inc 586 293-9150
33722 James J Pompo Dr Fraser (48026) *(G-5908)*
C & R Tool Die 231 584-3588
4643 Alba Hwy Alba (49611) *(G-113)*
C & S Automated Systems LLC 586 265-1416
31784 Groesbeck Hwy Fraser (48026) *(G-5909)*
C & S Machine Products Inc (PA) 269 695-6859
2929 Saratore Dr Niles (49120) *(G-12117)*
C & S Machine Products Inc 269 695-6859
248 Post Rd Buchanan (49107) *(G-2191)*
C & S Millwork Inc 586 465-6470
44163 N Groesbeck Hwy Clinton Township (48036) *(G-3193)*
C & S Security Inc 989 821-5759
138 Argus Ct Roscommon (48653) *(G-14347)*
C & T Fabrication LLC 616 678-5133
90 Spring St Kent City (49330) *(G-9428)*
C A P S, Livonia *Also called Central Admxture Phrm Svcs Inc (G-10151)*
C and M Construction 989 213-1955
5463 Van Wagnen Rd Vassar (48768) *(G-17578)*
C and N Press WD Enhncents LLC 810 712-7771
2375 Bacon Ave Berkley (48072) *(G-1623)*
C D C Logging 906 524-6369
17311 Kent St Lanse (49946) *(G-9656)*
C D Tool and Gage 616 682-1111
3223 3 Mile Rd Nw Grand Rapids (49534) *(G-6542)*
C E B Tooling Inc 269 489-2251
335 S 2nd St Burr Oak (49030) *(G-2211)*
C E C Controls Company Inc (HQ) 586 779-0222
14555 Barber Ave Warren (48088) *(G-17746)*
C E C Controls Company Inc 248 926-5701
50208 Pontiac Trl Wixom (48393) *(G-18629)*
C E S Industries Inc 734 425-0522
12751 Inkster Rd Livonia (48150) *(G-10143)*
C F Burger Creamery Co 313 584-4040
8101 Greenfield Rd Detroit (48228) *(G-4084)*
C F Long & Sons Inc 248 624-1562
1555 E West Maple Rd Walled Lake (48390) *(G-17665)*
C F S, Fenton *Also called Classfcation Flotation Systems (G-5464)*
C G Witvoet & Sons Company 616 534-6677
356 Crown St Sw Grand Rapids (49548) *(G-6543)*
C H Industries Inc 586 997-1717
50699 Central Indus Dr Shelby Township (48315) *(G-15180)*
C H M Graphics & Litho Inc 586 777-4550
23519 Little Mack Ave Saint Clair Shores (48080) *(G-14851)*
C I F, Edmore *Also called Campbell Industrial Force LLC (G-4990)*
C I I Ltd 248 585-9905
354 Indusco Ct Troy (48083) *(G-16989)*
C J Graphics Inc 906 774-8636
121 S Carpenter Ave Kingsford (49802) *(G-9506)*
C L Design Inc 248 474-4220
20739 Sunnydale St Farmington Hills (48336) *(G-5190)*
C L Mailing Printing 248 471-3330
24980 Creekside Dr Farmington Hills (48336) *(G-5191)*
C L Rieckhoff Company Inc (PA) 734 946-8220
26265 Northline Rd Taylor (48180) *(G-16388)*
C M I, Fenton *Also called Cmi-Schneible Group (G-5465)*
C N C Machining, Cassopolis *Also called Franks Products (G-2628)*
C P I Inc 810 664-8686
1449 Bowers Rd Lapeer (48446) *(G-9919)*
C P R, Troy *Also called Control Power-Reliance LLC (G-17026)*
C P S, Clinton Township *Also called Complete Prototype Svcs Inc (G-3207)*
C R B Crane & Service Co (PA) 586 757-1222
3751 E 10 Mile Rd Warren (48091) *(G-17747)*
C R I, New Haven *Also called Centerless Rebuilders Inc (G-12030)*

C R Stitching........734 449-2633
7870 Kearney Rd Whitmore Lake (48189) ***(G-18525)***
C R Stitching........313 538-1660
26150 5 Mile Rd 1c Redford (48239) ***(G-13722)***
C R T & Associates Inc........231 946-1680
806 Hastings St Ste H Traverse City (49686) ***(G-16635)***
C S A, Grand Rapids *Also called Contract Source & Assembly Inc* ***(G-6599)***
C S L Inc........248 549-4434
1323 E 11 Mile Rd Royal Oak (48067) ***(G-14522)***
C S M, Allendale *Also called Constructive Sheet Metal Inc* ***(G-217)***
C S M Manufacturing Corp (PA)........248 471-0700
24650 N Industrial Dr Farmington Hills (48335) ***(G-5192)***
C S Mobile Welding LLC........517 543-2339
516 N Washington St Charlotte (48813) ***(G-2737)***
C T & T Inc........248 623-9422
5619 Dixie Hwy Waterford (48329) ***(G-18107)***
C T I, Sterling Heights *Also called Control Technique Incorporated* ***(G-15970)***
C T L Enterprises Inc........616 392-1159
832 Productions Pl Holland (49423) ***(G-7989)***
C T Machining Inc........586 772-0320
23108 Edgewater St Saint Clair Shores (48082) ***(G-14852)***
C Thorrez Industries Inc (PA)........517 750-3160
4909 W Michigan Ave Jackson (49201) ***(G-8831)***
C W A Manufacturing Co Inc........810 686-3030
7406 N Dort Hwy Mount Morris (48458) ***(G-11669)***
C W Enterprises Inc........810 385-9100
4137 24th Ave Fort Gratiot (48059) ***(G-5819)***
C W Industries........586 465-4157
27999 Hambeltonian Dr Chesterfield (48047) ***(G-2855)***
C W Marsh Company (PA)........231 722-3781
1385 Hudson St Muskegon (49441) ***(G-11788)***
C&C Forklift........313 729-2850
15060 Michael St Taylor (48180) ***(G-16389)***
C&D Pallets Inc........517 285-5228
13777 S Jones Rd Eagle (48822) ***(G-4851)***
C&E Welding........248 990-3191
920 Cloverdale Dr Royal Oak (48067) ***(G-14523)***
C&O Sportswear, Mount Pleasant *Also called Express Sportswear Inc* ***(G-11697)***
C&P Hoover LLC........248 887-2400
1100 S Milford Rd Ste 100 Highland (48357) ***(G-7886)***
C-Plastics Inc........616 837-7396
12463 Cleveland St Nunica (49448) ***(G-12577)***
C.A.R.S., Rochester Hills *Also called Canadian Amrcn Rstoration Sups* ***(G-13970)***
C.H. Industries, Shelby Township *Also called C H Industries Inc* ***(G-15180)***
C.P., Flat Rock *Also called Single Source Inc* ***(G-5630)***
C/W South Inc........810 767-2806
1220 N Center Rd Burton (48509) ***(G-2230)***
C2 Group The, Grand Rapids *Also called Argus Technologies LLC* ***(G-6469)***
C2 Imaging LLC........248 743-2903
1725 John R Rd Troy (48083) ***(G-16990)***
C2dx Inc........269 409-0068
555 E Eliza St Ste A Schoolcraft (49087) ***(G-15112)***
C3 Industries Inc........248 255-1283
2082 S State St Ann Arbor (48104) ***(G-412)***
CA Picard Inc........269 962-2231
305 Hill Brady Rd Battle Creek (49037) ***(G-1202)***
CA Picard Surface Engrg Inc........440 366-5400
305 Hill Brady Rd Battle Creek (49037) ***(G-1203)***
Cabco, Grand Rapids *Also called Calumet Abrasives Co Inc* ***(G-6545)***
Cabell Publishing LLC........906 361-6828
467 Lakewood Ln Marquette (49855) ***(G-11011)***
Cabin-N-Woods LLC........248 828-4138
657 Trinway Dr Troy (48085) ***(G-16991)***
Cabinet Finishers........248 635-7584
21002 Orchard Lake Rd Farmington Hills (48336) ***(G-5193)***
Cabinet Headquarters LLC........231 286-3207
3522 Airline Rd Norton Shores (49444) ***(G-12282)***
Cabinet Install Shop........586 946-0500
50515 Metzen Dr Chesterfield (48051) ***(G-2856)***
Cabinet One Inc........248 625-9440
4571 White Lake Ct Clarkston (48346) ***(G-3022)***
Cabinets By H & K Inc........313 903-8500
1111 Inkster Rd Inkster (48141) ***(G-8660)***
Cabinets By Robert Inc........231 947-3261
2774 Garfield Rd N Ste C Traverse City (49686) ***(G-16636)***
Cabinets Cuntertops Direct LLC........616 238-6608
1225 Baldwin St Jenison (49428) ***(G-9048)***
Cabinets Express........810 494-0511
9325 Maltby Rd Brighton (48116) ***(G-1959)***
Cabinetworks Group Mich LLC (PA)........734 205-4600
4600 Arrowhead Dr Ann Arbor (48105) ***(G-413)***
Cablcon, Troy *Also called Quad Electronics Inc* ***(G-17323)***
Cad CAM, Metamora *Also called Aurora Cad CAM Inc* ***(G-11276)***
Cad CAM Services Inc........616 554-5222
4017 Brockton Dr Se Grand Rapids (49512) ***(G-6544)***
Cadillac Casting Inc (PA)........231 779-9600
1500 4th Ave Cadillac (49601) ***(G-2319)***
Cadillac Culvert Inc........231 775-3761
5305 M 115 Cadillac (49601) ***(G-2320)***
Cadillac Engineered Plas Inc........231 775-2900
1550 Leeson Ave Cadillac (49601) ***(G-2321)***
Cadillac Fabrication Inc (PA)........231 775-7386
1340 Marty Paul St Cadillac (49601) ***(G-2322)***
Cadillac Oil Company........313 365-6200
13650 Helen St Detroit (48212) ***(G-4085)***
Cadillac Plating Corporation........586 771-9191
23849 Groesbeck Hwy Warren (48089) ***(G-17748)***
Cadillac Printing Company........231 775-2488
214 S Mitchell St Cadillac (49601) ***(G-2323)***
Cadillac Products Inc (PA)........248 813-8200
5800 Crooks Rd Ste 100 Troy (48098) ***(G-16992)***
Cadillac Products Inc........989 766-2294
4858 Williams Rd Rogers City (49779) ***(G-14208)***
Cadillac Products Inc........586 774-1700
29784 Little Mack Ave Roseville (48066) ***(G-14382)***
Cadillac Products Auto Co, Roseville *Also called Cadillac Products Inc* ***(G-14382)***
Cadillac Products Packaging Co (PA)........248 879-5000
5800 Crooks Rd Troy (48098) ***(G-16993)***
Cadillac Prsentation Solutions........248 288-9777
1195 Equity Dr Troy (48084) ***(G-16994)***
Cadillac Tool and Die Inc........231 775-9007
1011 6th St Cadillac (49601) ***(G-2324)***
Cadillac Winery, Bay City *Also called Evergreen Winery LLC* ***(G-1353)***
Cadon Plating & Coatings LLC........734 282-8100
3715 11th St Wyandotte (48192) ***(G-18813)***
Caea Auto Elctrnic Systems USA (HQ)........586 649-9036
30500 Van Dyke Ave Ste 20 Warren (48093) ***(G-17749)***
Caflor Industries LLC........734 604-1168
2375 Parkwood Ypsilanti (48198) ***(G-18931)***
Caillau Usa Inc........248 446-1900
7000 Kensington Rd Brighton (48116) ***(G-1960)***
Cain Brothers Logging Inc........906 345-9252
1001 County Road 510 Negaunee (49866) ***(G-11964)***
Cake Connection Tc LLC........231 943-3531
5730 Cherry Blossom Dr Traverse City (49685) ***(G-16637)***
Cake Flour........231 571-3054
1811 W Norton Ave Norton Shores (49441) ***(G-12283)***
Cal Chemical Manufacturing Co........586 778-7006
605 Shore Club Dr Saint Clair Shores (48080) ***(G-14853)***
Cal Grinding Inc (PA)........906 786-8749
1401 N 26th St Stop 16 Escanaba (49829) ***(G-5064)***
Cal Manufacturing Company Inc........269 649-2942
5500 E V Ave Vicksburg (49097) ***(G-17601)***
Cal-Chlor Corp........231 843-1147
5379 W 6th St Ludington (49431) ***(G-10529)***
Calcomco Inc (PA)........313 885-9228
5544 S Red Pine Cir Kalamazoo (49009) ***(G-9143)***
Calder Bros Dairy Inc........313 381-8858
1020 Southfield Rd Lincoln Park (48146) ***(G-10044)***
Calderwood Enterprises, Trout Creek *Also called Calderwood WD Pdts & Svcs LLC* ***(G-16897)***
Calderwood WD Pdts & Svcs LLC........906 852-3232
9968 Calderwood Rd Trout Creek (49967) ***(G-16897)***
Caldwell Gasket Company, Grand Rapids *Also called N-K Sealing Technologies LLC* ***(G-7035)***
Caledonia Cmnty Sawmill LLC........616 891-8561
8298 96th St Se Alto (49302) ***(G-330)***
Calhoun Communications Inc (PA)........517 629-0041
125 E Cass St Albion (49224) ***(G-118)***
Calhoun County Med Care Fcilty........269 962-5458
1150 Michigan Ave E Battle Creek (49014) ***(G-1204)***
Calhoun Foundry Company Inc........517 568-4415
506 S Clay St Homer (49245) ***(G-8349)***
Caliber Industries LLC........586 774-6775
100 Shafer Dr Romeo (48065) ***(G-14221)***
Caliber Metals Inc........586 465-7650
36870 Green St New Baltimore (48047) ***(G-11979)***
Caligirlbooks LLC........415 361-1533
45841 Heather Ridge Dr Macomb (48044) ***(G-10582)***
Callahan Supply LLC........231 878-9023
10429 W Watergate Rd Cadillac (49601) ***(G-2325)***
Calm Welding........417 358-8131
18388 M 86 Three Rivers (49093) ***(G-16568)***
Calumet Abrasives Co Inc........219 844-2695
3890 Buchanan Ave Sw Grand Rapids (49548) ***(G-6545)***
Calumet Machine, Calumet *Also called Mq Operating Company* ***(G-2412)***
Calvin Lutz Farm, Kaleva *Also called Fruit Haven Nursery Inc* ***(G-9379)***
CAM Packaging LLC........989 426-1200
705 Weaver Ct Gladwin (48624) ***(G-6191)***
CAM Publishing Inc........248 848-3148
38800 Country Club Dr Farmington Hills (48331) ***(G-5194)***
Camaco, Farmington Hills *Also called P & C Group I Inc* ***(G-5341)***
Camaco LLC (HQ)........248 442-6800
37000 W Twlve Mile Rd Ste Farmington Hills (48331) ***(G-5195)***
Cambria Tool and Machine Inc........517 437-3500
121 Mechanic Rd Hillsdale (49242) ***(G-7928)***
Cambric Corporation........801 415-7300
41050 W 11 Mile Rd Novi (48375) ***(G-12378)***

Cambridge Financial Services 248 840-6650
5435 Corporate Dr Ste 250 Troy (48098) ***(G-16995)***
Cambridge Sharpe Inc 248 613-5562
8325 N Rushton Rd South Lyon (48178) ***(G-15429)***
Cambro Products Inc 586 468-8847
41135 Irwin Dr Harrison Township (48045) ***(G-7691)***
Cambron Engineering Inc 989 684-5890
3800 Wilder Rd Bay City (48706) ***(G-1334)***
Camcar LLC (HQ) 586 254-3900
6125 18 Mile Rd Sterling Heights (48314) ***(G-15950)***
Camcar Plastics Inc 231 726-5000
1732 Glade St Muskegon (49441) ***(G-11789)***
Camden Publications, Camden *Also called Campub Inc* ***(G-2419)***
Camdex Inc 248 528-2300
2330 Alger Dr Troy (48083) ***(G-16996)***
Cameron Kirk Forest Pdts Inc 989 426-3439
1467 S Shearer Rd Gladwin (48624) ***(G-6192)***
Cameron S Roat 810 620-7628
4065 Manor Dr 190443 Burton (48519) ***(G-2231)***
Cameron Tool Corporation 517 487-3671
1800 Bassett St Lansing (48915) ***(G-9820)***
Camerons of Jackson LLC 517 531-3400
107 W Main St Parma (49269) ***(G-12937)***
Cammand Machining LLC 586 752-0366
101 Shafer Dr Romeo (48065) ***(G-14222)***
Cammenga & Associates LLC 313 914-7160
2011 Bailey St Dearborn (48124) ***(G-3817)***
Camoplast 517 278-8567
25 Concept Dr Coldwater (49036) ***(G-3424)***
Campaign-Stickers.com, Grand Rapids *Also called Middleton Printing Inc* ***(G-7004)***
Campbell & Shaw Steel Inc 810 364-5100
1705 Michigan Ave Marysville (48040) ***(G-11083)***
Campbell and Co Publishing LLC 810 320-0224
4340 Greenview Cir Fort Gratiot (48059) ***(G-5820)***
Campbell Inc Press Repair 517 371-1034
925 River St Lansing (48912) ***(G-9821)***
Campbell Industrial Force LLC 989 427-0011
1380 Industrial Park Dr Edmore (48829) ***(G-4990)***
Campbell Soup Company 313 295-6884
21740 Trlley Indus Dr D Taylor (48180) ***(G-16390)***
Campbell Soup Company 248 336-8486
1220 E 9 Mile Rd Ferndale (48220) ***(G-5532)***
Campub Inc (HQ) 517 368-0365
331 E Bell St Camden (49232) ***(G-2419)***
Camryn Fabrication LLC 586 949-0818
50625 Richard W Blvd Chesterfield (48051) ***(G-2857)***
Camryn Industries LLC (HQ) 248 663-5850
21624 Melrose Ave Southfield (48075) ***(G-15515)***
Camshaft Acquisition Inc 517 787-2040
717 Woodworth Rd Jackson (49202) ***(G-8832)***
Camshaft Machine Company, Jackson *Also called Camshaft Acquisition Inc* ***(G-8832)***
Camshaft Machine Company LLC (PA) 517 787-2040
717 Woodworth Rd Jackson (49202) ***(G-8833)***
Can You Handlebar LLC 248 821-2171
239 Church St Mount Clemens (48043) ***(G-11632)***
Can-AM Metallurgical, Detroit *Also called American Metallurgical Svcs* ***(G-4013)***
Canadian Amrcn Rstoration Sups (PA) 248 853-8900
2600 Bond St Rochester Hills (48309) ***(G-13970)***
Canadian Harvest LP (HQ) 952 835-6429
16369 Us Highway 131 S Schoolcraft (49087) ***(G-15113)***
Canam Undrwter Hockey Gear LLC 906 399-7857
7660 Perkins 30.5 Rd Rapid River (49878) ***(G-13682)***
Candle Factory Grand Traverse 231 946-2280
301 W Grandview Pkwy Traverse City (49684) ***(G-16638)***
Candle Knight Light 248 291-5483
10332 W 9 Mile Rd Oak Park (48237) ***(G-12597)***
Candle Wick 248 547-2987
175 W 9 Mile Rd Ferndale (48220) ***(G-5533)***
Candlelite Publishing LLC 248 841-8925
1438 Oakbrook E Rochester Hills (48307) ***(G-13971)***
Candles By Cottonwood 734 344-2339
3567 Bluebush Rd Monroe (48162) ***(G-11533)***
Candles By Jugg 313 732-1349
21712 Donald Ave Eastpointe (48021) ***(G-4929)***
Candles By Lori LLC 734 474-6314
390 E Castlebury Cir Saline (48176) ***(G-15007)***
Caniff Electric Supply 586 221-1663
75 S Rose St Mount Clemens (48043) ***(G-11633)***
Cannon Machine Inc 616 363-4014
1641 Davis Ave Nw Grand Rapids (49504) ***(G-6546)***
Cannon Vibrator Div, Edmore *Also called Edmore Tool & Grinding Inc* ***(G-4992)***
Cannon-Muskegon Corporation 231 755-1681
2875 Lincoln St Norton Shores (49441) ***(G-12284)***
Cannonsburg Wood Products Inc 616 866-4459
10251 Northland Dr Ne Rockford (49341) ***(G-14162)***
Cant Products, Pontiac *Also called Oak Way Manufacturing Inc* ***(G-13404)***
Canton Embroidery LLC 734 216-3374
3901 Bestech Rd Ste 800 Ypsilanti (48197) ***(G-18932)***
Canton Manufacturing, Canton *Also called Twb Company LLC* ***(G-2536)***
Canton Renewables LLC 248 380-3920
46280 Dylan Dr Ste 200 Novi (48377) ***(G-12379)***
Cantrick Kip Co 248 644-7622
774 Lakeside Dr Birmingham (48009) ***(G-1719)***
Canusa LLC 906 259-0800
2510 Ashmun St Sault Sainte Marie (49783) ***(G-15088)***
Canusa Inc 906 446-3327
502 2nd St Gwinn (49841) ***(G-7583)***
Canusa Wood Products, Gwinn *Also called Canusa Inc* ***(G-7583)***
Canvas Innovations LLC 616 393-4400
11276 E Lakewood Blvd Holland (49424) ***(G-7990)***
Canvas Shoppe Inc 810 733-1841
3198 One Half S Dye Rd Flint (48507) ***(G-5662)***
Canvas Townhomes Allendale 616 499-2680
10295 48th Ave Allendale (49401) ***(G-216)***
Canyouhandlebar LLC 313 354-5851
3031 Glenview Ave Royal Oak (48073) ***(G-14524)***
Cap Collet & Tool Co Inc 734 283-4040
4082 6th St Wyandotte (48192) ***(G-18814)***
Capacity House Publishing 586 209-3924
18121 E 8 Mile Rd Eastpointe (48021) ***(G-4930)***
Capco Automovite 248 616-8888
82 Park Dr Troy (48083) ***(G-16997)***
Capital Assets Resources LLC 248 252-7854
17253 Magnolia Pkwy Southfield (48075) ***(G-15516)***
Capital Billing Systems Inc 248 478-7298
33533 W 12 Mile Rd # 131 Farmington Hills (48331) ***(G-5196)***
Capital City Blue Print Inc 517 482-5431
1110 Center St Lansing (48906) ***(G-9676)***
Capital City Reprographics, Lansing *Also called Capital City Blue Print Inc* ***(G-9676)***
Capital Equipment Clare LLC (PA) 517 669-5533
12263 S Us Highway 27 Dewitt (48820) ***(G-4708)***
Capital Imaging Inc 517 482-2292
2521 E Michigan Ave Lansing (48912) ***(G-9822)***
Capital Induction Inc 586 322-1444
6505 Diplomat Dr Sterling Heights (48314) ***(G-15951)***
Capital Software Inc Michigan 517 324-9100
4660 S Hagadorn Rd # 100 East Lansing (48823) ***(G-4889)***
Capital Stamping & Machine Inc (PA) 248 471-0700
24650 N Industrial Dr Farmington Hills (48335) ***(G-5197)***
Capital Steel & Builders Sup 517 694-0451
3897 Holt Rd Holt (48842) ***(G-8304)***
Capital Welding Inc 248 355-0410
20101 Hoover St Detroit (48205) ***(G-4086)***
Capitol Bedding Co Inc 615 370-7000
2238 N Grand River Ave Lansing (48906) ***(G-9677)***
Capler Mfg 586 264-7851
6664 Sterling Dr N Sterling Heights (48312) ***(G-15952)***
Capnesity Inc 317 401-6766
1778 Imlay City Rd Lapeer (48446) ***(G-9920)***
Caprice Brands LLC 989 745-1286
31183 Schoolcraft Rd Livonia (48150) ***(G-10144)***
Capsonic Automotive Inc 248 754-1100
3121 University Dr # 120 Auburn Hills (48326) ***(G-839)***
Car Pak 248 280-1401
1250 Allen Dr Troy (48083) ***(G-16998)***
Car Pak Manufacturing Co 480 625-3655
1401 Axtell Dr Troy (48084) ***(G-16999)***
Car Quest Machine Shop 989 686-3111
3616 Wilder Rd Bay City (48706) ***(G-1335)***
Car Shop, Escanaba *Also called Escanaba and Lk Superior RR Co* ***(G-5070)***
Car-Min-Vu Farm 517 749-9112
2965 E Howell Rd Webberville (48892) ***(G-18243)***
Caraco Pharma Inc 313 871-8400
1150 Elijah Mccoy Dr Detroit (48202) ***(G-4087)***
Caraustar Cstm Packg Group Inc 616 247-0330
1957 Beverly Ave Sw Grand Rapids (49519) ***(G-6547)***
Caravan Technologies Inc 313 632-8545
3033 Bourke St Detroit (48238) ***(G-4088)***
Carb-A-Tron Tool Co 517 782-2249
4615 S Jackson Rd Jackson (49201) ***(G-8834)***
Carbide Form Master Inc 248 625-9373
10565 Dixie Hwy Davisburg (48350) ***(G-3763)***
Carbide Savers 248 388-1572
41960 Joy Rd Plymouth (48170) ***(G-13141)***
Carbide Surface Company (PA) 586 465-6110
44336 Reynolds Dr Clinton Township (48036) ***(G-3194)***
Carbide Technologies Inc 586 296-5200
18101 Malyn Blvd Fraser (48026) ***(G-5910)***
Carboline Company 734 525-2824
32820 Capitol St Livonia (48150) ***(G-10145)***
Carbon Green Bioenergy LLC 616 374-4000
7795 Saddlebag Lake Rd Lake Odessa (48849) ***(G-9573)***
Carbon Impact Inc 231 929-8152
2628 Garfield Rd N Ste 38 Traverse City (49686) ***(G-16639)***
Carbon Tool & Manufacturing 734 422-0380
12735 Inkster Rd Livonia (48150) ***(G-10146)***
Carbone of America 989 894-2911
900 Harrison St Bay City (48708) ***(G-1336)***

ALPHABETIC

Carbonless 365 .... 810 969-4014
   349 Mccormick Dr Lapeer (48446) *(G-9921)*
Carco Inc 313 925-1053
   10333 Shoemaker St Detroit (48213) *(G-4089)*
Carcostics Tech Ctr N Amer Inc 248 251-1737
   1400 Durant Dr Howell (48843) *(G-8434)*
Carcoustics Usa Inc 517 548-6700
   1400 Durant Dr Howell (48843) *(G-8435)*
Cardan Robotics, Portage Also called Gys Tech LLC *(G-13563)*
Cardboard Prophets 517 512-1267
   5472 Oak Hills Dr Eaton Rapids (48827) *(G-4957)*
Cardboard Robot Visuals LLC 231 577-8710
   10199 Samson Woods Dr Buckley (49620) *(G-2206)*
Cardell Automotive, Auburn Hills Also called Cardell Corporation *(G-840)*
Cardell Corporation 248 371-9700
   2025 Taylor Rd Auburn Hills (48326) *(G-840)*
Cardiac Assist Holdings LLC 781 727-1391
   46701 Commerce Center Dr Plymouth (48170) *(G-13142)*
Cardinal Custom Designs Inc 586 296-2060
   31469 Utica Rd Fraser (48026) *(G-5911)*
Cardinal Economic Sand Finance 734 926-6989
   315 2nd St Apt 504 Ann Arbor (48103) *(G-414)*
Cardinal Fabricating Inc 517 655-2155
   3394 Corwin Rd Williamston (48895) *(G-18570)*
Cardinal Group Industries Corp 517 437-6000
   266 Industrial Dr Hillsdale (49242) *(G-7929)*
Cardinal Machine Co 810 686-1190
   860 Tacoma Ct Clio (48420) *(G-3394)*
Cardinal Rule Press, Novi Also called Maria Dismondy Inc *(G-12471)*
Cards of Wood Inc 616 887-8680
   7754 Pine Island Ct Ne Belmont (49306) *(G-1504)*
Cards4heroescom LLC 877 640-8206
   3093 N Tipsico Lake Rd Hartland (48353) *(G-7767)*
Carefluence, Grand Blanc Also called Comet Information Systems LLC *(G-6238)*
Cargill Incorporated 608 868-5150
   1510 Hathaway St Owosso (48867) *(G-12825)*
Cargill Incorporated 810 329-2736
   916 S Riverside Ave Saint Clair (48079) *(G-14816)*
Cargill Americas Inc 810 989-7689
   31029 Comcast Dr Ste 100 New Haven (48048) *(G-12029)*
Cargo King Manufacturing Inc 269 483-9900
   600 S Miller Rd White Pigeon (49099) *(G-18473)*
Carhartt Inc (PA) 313 271-8460
   5750 Mercury Dr Dearborn (48126) *(G-3818)*
Carhartt Inc 517 282-4193
   128 Spring Meadows Ln Dewitt (48820) *(G-4709)*
Caribbean Adventure LLC 269 441-5675
   5420 Beckley Rd Ste 244 Battle Creek (49015) *(G-1205)*
Carl Zeiss Nts LLC 248 486-7600
   6826 Kensington Rd Brighton (48116) *(G-1961)*
Carlee Woodworking 734 660-0491
   15777 Twin Ponds Pinckney (48169) *(G-13044)*
Carlesimo Products Inc 248 474-0415
   29800 W 8 Mile Rd Farmington Hills (48336) *(G-5198)*
Carlex Glass America LLC 248 824-8800
   1209 E Big Beaver Rd Troy (48083) *(G-17000)*
Carlo John Inc 586 254-3800
   12345 23 Mile Rd Shelby Township (48315) *(G-15181)*
Carlon Meter Inc 616 842-0420
   1710 Eaton Dr Grand Haven (49417) *(G-6283)*
Carlson 248 824-7600
   1950 Austin Dr Troy (48083) *(G-17001)*
Carlson Enterprises Inc 248 656-1442
   922 S Rochester Rd Rochester Hills (48307) *(G-13972)*
Carlson Metal Products Inc 248 528-1931
   2335 Alger Dr Troy (48083) *(G-17002)*
Carlson Technology Inc 248 476-0013
   30945 8 Mile Rd Livonia (48152) *(G-10147)*
Carlton Sgnature Pub Relations 248 387-9849
   553 Pingree Ct Waterford (48327) *(G-18108)*
Carlton, Robert Hanger Company, Zeeland Also called Bennett Wood Specialties Inc *(G-18996)*
Carmac Tool LLC 586 649-7245
   22969 Rasch Dr Clinton Township (48035) *(G-3195)*
Carmel Township 888 805-6182
   661 Beech Hwy Charlotte (48813) *(G-2738)*
Carmens Screen Printing & EMB 248 535-4161
   3451 Indianwood Rd Lake Orion (48362) *(G-9593)*
Carmeuse Lime Inc 906 484-2201
   5093 E M 134 Cedarville (49719) *(G-2668)*
Carmeuse Lime Inc 313 849-9268
   25 Marion Ave River Rouge (48218) *(G-13853)*
Carmeuse Lime & Stone, River Rouge Also called Carmeuse Lime Inc *(G-13853)*
Carmeuse Lime & Stone, Rogers City Also called O-N Minerals Michigan Company *(G-14214)*
Carmeuse Lime & Stone, Cedarville Also called O-N Minerals Michigan Company *(G-2673)*
Caro Carbide Corporation 248 588-4252
   553 Robbins Dr Troy (48083) *(G-17003)*
Caro Test Center, Caro Also called TI Group Auto Systems LLC *(G-2581)*

Carol Packing House 989 673-2688
   1131 Weeden Rd Caro (48723) *(G-2566)*
Carolyns Publication 810 787-4114
   909 Carton St Flint (48505) *(G-5663)*
Carom L Embroidery 231 690-0571
   612 N Lakeshore Dr Ludington (49431) *(G-10530)*
Carpathians Manufacturing 248 291-6232
   1250 Rankin Dr Ste B Troy (48083) *(G-17004)*
Carpe Candle 734 837-3053
   11633 N Shore Dr Whitmore Lake (48189) *(G-18526)*
Carpenters Cabinets 989 777-1070
   5066 Dixie Hwy Saginaw (48601) *(G-14621)*
Carpenters Friend Woodworking 231 218-2736
   3189 El Shaddai Ln Interlochen (49643) *(G-8680)*
Carpet Crafters, Grand Rapids Also called James E Sullivan & Associates *(G-6860)*
Carquest Auto Parts, Bay City Also called General Parts Inc *(G-1360)*
Carr Brothers and Sons Inc 517 629-3549
   14555 Elm Row Rd Albion (49224) *(G-119)*
Carr Brothers and Sons Inc (PA) 517 531-3358
   13613 E Erie Rd Albion (49224) *(G-120)*
Carr Engineering 248 447-4109
   21557 Telegraph Rd Southfield (48033) *(G-15517)*
Carriage Town Press 810 410-5113
   703 Mason St Flint (48503) *(G-5664)*
Carrier & Gable Inc (PA) 248 477-8700
   24110 Research Dr Farmington Hills (48335) *(G-5199)*
Carrigan Graphics Inc 734 455-6550
   7994 N Lilley Rd Canton (48187) *(G-2445)*
Carrington Precious Metals LLC 517 323-9154
   4616 N Grand River Ave # 8 Lansing (48906) *(G-9678)*
Carroll Tool and Die Co 586 949-7670
   46650 Erb Dr Macomb (48042) *(G-10583)*
Carrollton Concrete Mix Inc 989 753-7737
   2924 Carrollton Rd Saginaw (48604) *(G-14622)*
Carrollton Paving Co 989 752-7139
   2924 Carrollton Rd Saginaw (48604) *(G-14623)*
Carrom Company, Ludington Also called Merdel Game Manufacturing Co *(G-10544)*
Carry Manufacturing Inc 989 672-2779
   1360 Prospect Ave Caro (48723) *(G-2567)*
Carry Pump Co., Caro Also called Carry Manufacturing Inc *(G-2567)*
Carry-All Products Inc 616 399-8080
   4498 128th Ave Holland (49424) *(G-7991)*
Carson Wood Specialties Inc 269 465-6091
   7526 Jericho Rd Stevensville (49127) *(G-16242)*
Carstill Wagon Pub/Toasty Toes 734 325-7542
   750 W Huron River Dr # 2 Van Buren Twp (48111) *(G-17514)*
Carter Creations 800 710-8055
   847 Sumpter Rd Van Buren Twp (48111) *(G-17515)*
Carter Fuel Systems LLC 248 371-8392
   3255 W Hamlin Rd Rochester Hills (48309) *(G-13973)*
Carter Industries Inc 510 324-6700
   906 James St Adrian (49221) *(G-56)*
Carter Products Company Inc 616 647-3380
   2871 Northridge Dr Nw Grand Rapids (49544) *(G-6548)*
Carter's Children's Store, Grand Rapids Also called Carters Inc *(G-6549)*
Carters Inc 616 647-9452
   3390 Alpine Ave Nw Grand Rapids (49544) *(G-6549)*
Carters Imagewear & Awards 231 881-9324
   300 W Mitchell St Petoskey (49770) *(G-12992)*
Cartex Corporation (HQ) 610 759-1650
   1515 Equity Dr 100 Troy (48084) *(G-17005)*
Cartex Corporation 734 857-5961
   15573 Oakwood Dr Romulus (48174) *(G-14260)*
Cartidge World 810 229-5599
   9864 E Grand River Ave Brighton (48116) *(G-1962)*
Cartridges Are US, Ithaca Also called Cau Acquisition Company LLC *(G-8787)*
Casa D'Oro, Troy Also called Pure & Simple Solutions LLC *(G-17320)*
Casadei Steel, Sterling Heights Also called Casadei Structural Steel Inc *(G-15953)*
Casadei Structural Steel Inc 586 698-2898
   40675 Mound Rd Sterling Heights (48310) *(G-15953)*
Casalbi Company Inc 517 782-0345
   540 Wayne St Jackson (49202) *(G-8835)*
Cascade Cart Solutions, Grand Rapids Also called Cascade Engineering Inc *(G-6552)*
Cascade Die Casting Group Inc (HQ) 616 281-1774
   7441 Division Ave S A1 Grand Rapids (49548) *(G-6550)*
Cascade Die Casting Group Inc 616 887-1771
   9983 Sparta Ave Nw Sparta (49345) *(G-15762)*
Cascade Die Casting Group Inc 616 455-4010
   7750 Division Ave S Grand Rapids (49548) *(G-6551)*
Cascade Die Casting/Mid-State, Grand Rapids Also called Cascade Die Casting Group Inc *(G-6551)*
Cascade Engineering Inc (PA) 616 975-4800
   3400 Innovation Ct Se Grand Rapids (49512) *(G-6552)*
Cascade Engineering Inc 616 975-4767
   3739 Patterson Ave Se Grand Rapids (49512) *(G-6553)*
Cascade Engineering Inc 616 975-4965
   4950 37th St Se Grand Rapids (49512) *(G-6554)*
Cascade Equipment Company 734 697-7870
   43412 N Interstate 94 Ser Van Buren Twp (48111) *(G-17516)*

ALPHABETIC SECTION

Cascade Manufacturing, Grand Haven *Also called Lakeshore Fittings Inc (G-6328)*
Cascade Paper Converters LLC 616 974-9165
  4935 Starr St Se Grand Rapids (49546) *(G-6555)*
Cascade Prtg & Graphics Inc 616 222-2937
  6504 28th St Se Ste A Grand Rapids (49546) *(G-6556)*
Cascade Rental Centers, Grand Rapids *Also called Decc Company Inc (G-6638)*
Cascades Enviropac HPM LLC 616 243-4870
  236 Stevens St Sw Grand Rapids (49507) *(G-6557)*
Casco Products Corporation 248 957-0400
  25921 Meadowbrook Rd Novi (48375) *(G-12380)*
Case Island Glass LLC 810 252-1704
  1120 Beach St Flint (48502) *(G-5665)*
Case Quality Upkeep LLC 231 233-8013
  3237 Jefferson Rd Pentwater (49449) *(G-12971)*
Case Systems Inc 989 496-9510
  2700 James Savage Rd Midland (48642) *(G-11327)*
Case Tool Inc 734 261-2227
  12589 Farmington Rd Livonia (48150) *(G-10148)*
Case Welding & Fabrication Inc 517 278-2729
  235 N Angola Rd Coldwater (49036) *(G-3425)*
Case-Free Inc 616 245-3136
  240 32nd St Se Grand Rapids (49548) *(G-6558)*
Casemer Tool & Machine Inc 248 628-4807
  2765 Metamora Rd Oxford (48371) *(G-12880)*
Caseville Village Government 989 856-4407
  6685 Clay St Caseville (48725) *(G-2603)*
Caseway Industrial Products, Bay City *Also called Highland Industrial Inc (G-1365)*
Casper Corporation 248 442-9000
  24081 Research Dr Farmington Hills (48335) *(G-5200)*
Cass, Detroit *Also called Custom Archtctral Shtmtl Spcls (G-4113)*
Cass City Chronicle Inc 989 872-2010
  6550 Main St Cass City (48726) *(G-2612)*
Cass Polymers (HQ) 517 543-7510
  815 W Shepherd St Ste 2 Charlotte (48813) *(G-2739)*
Cass River Trader East, Vassar *Also called Tuscola County Advertiser Inc (G-17583)*
Casselman Logging 231 885-1040
  23400 13 Mile Rd Mesick (49668) *(G-11270)*
Cast Coatings Inc (PA) 269 545-8373
  203 W Southeastern St Galien (49113) *(G-6087)*
Castano Plastics Inc 248 624-3724
  2337 Solano Dr Wolverine Lake (48390) *(G-18796)*
Castel Leasing, Three Rivers *Also called Progressive Paper Corp (G-16582)*
Caster Concepts Inc 517 629-2456
  214 E Michigan Ave Albion (49224) *(G-121)*
Caster Concepts Inc (PA) 888 781-1470
  16000 E Michigan Ave Albion (49224) *(G-122)*
Castine Communications Inc 248 477-1600
  22658 Brookdale St Farmington (48336) *(G-5134)*
Casting Industries Inc 586 776-5700
  315 Whiting St Saint Clair (48079) *(G-14817)*
Castino Corporation (PA) 734 941-7200
  16777 Wahrman St Romulus (48174) *(G-14261)*
Castle Remedies Inc 734 973-8990
  2345 S Huron Pkwy Ste 1 Ann Arbor (48104) *(G-415)*
Castleton Village Center Inc 616 247-8100
  3580 Rgr B Chaffee Mem Dr Grand Rapids (49548) *(G-6559)*
Casual Ptio Furn Rfnishing Inc 586 254-1900
  7851 Haverhill Ct N Canton (48187) *(G-2446)*
Catapult Business Services, Holland *Also called Trendway Svcs Organization LLC (G-8227)*
Catem North America, Novi *Also called Purem Novi Inc (G-12519)*
Catherine Pawlowski 248 698-3614
  301 Hurondale Dr White Lake (48386) *(G-18452)*
Catholic Weekly, Saginaw *Also called GLS Diocesan Reports (G-14653)*
CATI Armor LLC 269 788-4322
  435 Packard Hwy Ste C Charlotte (48813) *(G-2740)*
Catl USA, Rochester Hills *Also called Contemporary Amperex Tech USA (G-13984)*
Cattlemans Fresh Mt & Fish Mkt, Taylor *Also called Cattlemans Meat Company (G-16391)*
Cattlemans Meat Company 734 287-8260
  11400 Telegraph Rd Taylor (48180) *(G-16391)*
Catylist Inc 734 973-3185
  2360 E Stadium Blvd # 16 Ann Arbor (48104) *(G-416)*
Cau Acquisition Company LLC (PA) 989 875-8133
  100 Raycraft Dr Ithaca (48847) *(G-8787)*
Cav Tool Company 248 349-7860
  22605 Heslip Dr Novi (48375) *(G-12381)*
Caveman Pallets LLC 616 675-7270
  2382 Van Dyke St Conklin (49403) *(G-3660)*
Cayman Chemical Company Inc (PA) 734 971-3335
  1180 E Ellsworth Rd Ann Arbor (48108) *(G-417)*
CB Fabricating & Service 586 758-4980
  25215 Hoover Rd Warren (48089) *(G-17750)*
CB Industrial LLC 248 264-9800
  55397 Lyon Industrial Dr New Hudson (48165) *(G-12045)*
CB Marcellus Metalcasters Inc 269 646-0202
  214 E Read St Marcellus (49067) *(G-10946)*
Cbark Manufacturing Inc 810 922-3092
  4812 Lore Dr Waterford (48329) *(G-18109)*
Cbbn Restoration LLc 231 220-9892
  967 E Commerce Dr Bldg 1 Traverse City (49685) *(G-16640)*

Cbd With B Wellness Ltd Lblty 248 595-3583
  21731 Bournemouth St Harper Woods (48225) *(G-7665)*
Cbk Warehouse & Distribution, Clarkston *Also called Chase Plastic Services Inc (G-3023)*
Cbm LLC 800 487-2323
  2395 S Huron Pkwy Ste 200 Ann Arbor (48104) *(G-418)*
Cbp Fabrication Inc 313 653-4220
  12700 Mansfield St Detroit (48227) *(G-4090)*
Cbr Industries, Traverse City *Also called Cabinets By Robert Inc (G-16636)*
CBS, Bruce Twp *Also called Arctic Solutions Inc (G-2163)*
CBS Enterprises LLC 248 335-6702
  938 Featherstone St Pontiac (48342) *(G-13352)*
CBS Tool Inc 586 566-5945
  51601 Oro Dr Shelby Township (48315) *(G-15182)*
CC Embroidery Vinyl Designs 517 996-6030
  1435 E Mason St Dansville (48819) *(G-3755)*
CC Industries LLC 269 426-3342
  13550 Three Oaks Rd Sawyer (49125) *(G-15108)*
Ccd Holdings, Holland *Also called Eco - Composites LLC (G-8022)*
CCI, Mecosta *Also called Chrouch Communications Inc (G-11190)*
CCI Arnheim Inc 906 353-6330
  14935 Arnheim Baraga (49908) *(G-1136)*
CCI Companies, Wixom *Also called Covenant Cpitl Investments Inc (G-18637)*
CD Tool & Gage 616 682-1111
  6490 Fulton St E Ada (49301) *(G-14)*
Cdgjl Inc (PA) 517 787-2100
  1900 Wellworth Jackson (49203) *(G-8836)*
CDK Enterprises LLC 586 296-9300
  16601 E 13 Mile Rd Fraser (48026) *(G-5912)*
CDM Machine Co 313 538-9100
  23009 Lake Ravines Dr Southfield (48033) *(G-15518)*
Cdp Diamond Products Inc 734 591-1041
  11919 Globe St Livonia (48150) *(G-10149)*
Cdp Environmental Inc 586 776-7890
  16517 Eastland St Roseville (48066) *(G-14383)*
Cdr Pigments & Dispersions, Livonia *Also called Flint Group US LLC (G-10211)*
Cds Specialty Coatings LLC 313 300-8997
  4015 16th St Ecorse (48229) *(G-4981)*
Ce II Holdings Inc 248 305-7700
  12866 Sutherland Rd Brighton (48116) *(G-1963)*
Cedar Log Lbr Millersburg Inc 989 733-2676
  6019 Millersburg Rd Millersburg (49759) *(G-11497)*
Cedar Mobile Home Service Inc 616 696-1580
  4720 Russell St Cedar Springs (49319) *(G-2643)*
Cedar Ridge Custom Wdwkg LLC 248 425-0185
  500 S Glaspie St Ste B Oxford (48371) *(G-12881)*
Cedar Springs Castings, Cedar Springs *Also called Steeltech Ltd (G-2663)*
Cedar Springs Post Inc 616 696-3655
  36 E Maple Cedar Springs (49319) *(G-2644)*
Cedar Springs Post Newspaper, Cedar Springs *Also called Cedar Springs Post Inc (G-2644)*
Cedar Springs Sales & Graphix, Cedar Springs *Also called Cedar Springs Sales LLC (G-2645)*
Cedar Springs Sales LLC 616 696-2111
  2571 20 Mile Rd Ne Cedar Springs (49319) *(G-2645)*
CEDARVILLE MARINE, Cedarville *Also called Floatation Docking Inc (G-2669)*
Ceeflow Inc 231 526-5579
  5334 S Lake Shore Dr Harbor Springs (49740) *(G-7643)*
Cei, Manchester *Also called CEi Composite Materials LLC (G-10882)*
CEi Composite Materials LLC 734 212-3006
  800 E Duncan St Manchester (48158) *(G-10882)*
Ceiling Scenes, Warren *Also called Applied Visual Concepts LLC (G-17709)*
Cel Plastics Inc 231 777-3941
  1985 E Laketon Ave Muskegon (49442) *(G-11790)*
Celanese Americas LLC 248 377-2700
  1195 Centre Rd Auburn Hills (48326) *(G-841)*
Celani Printing Co 810 395-1609
  126 N Main St Capac (48014) *(G-2546)*
Celano Precision Mfg Inc 734 748-1744
  30016 Richland St Livonia (48150) *(G-10150)*
Celebrations 906 482-4946
  110 E Quincy St Hancock (49930) *(G-7617)*
Celebrations Bridal & Formal, Hancock *Also called Celebrations (G-7617)*
Celerity Systems N Amer Inc 248 994-7696
  28175 Haggerty Rd Novi (48377) *(G-12382)*
Celia Corporation (PA) 616 887-7387
  309 S Union St Sparta (49345) *(G-15763)*
Celia Deboer 269 279-9102
  14791 Hoffman Rd Three Rivers (49093) *(G-16569)*
Cell Safe, Spring Lake *Also called Biocomsolutions LLC (G-15806)*
Cell-Con, Rochester Hills *Also called Cellular Concepts Co Inc (G-13974)*
Cellar 849 Winery 734 254-0275
  849 Penniman Ave Ste 101 Plymouth (48170) *(G-13143)*
Cello-Foil Products Inc (PA) 229 435-4777
  155 Brook St Battle Creek (49037) *(G-1206)*
Cellular Concepts Co Inc 313 371-4800
  3667 Merriweather Ln Rochester Hills (48306) *(G-13974)*
Cellulose Mtl Solutions LLC 616 669-2990
  2472 Port Sheldon St Jenison (49428) *(G-9049)*

Celsee Inc...866 748-1448
100 Phoenix Dr Ste 321 Ann Arbor (48108) ***(G-419)***

Cemex Cement Inc...231 547-9971
1600 Bells Bay Rd Charlevoix (49720) ***(G-2712)***

Centech Inc...517 546-9185
1325 Grand Oaks Dr Howell (48843) ***(G-8436)***

Centen AG Inc, Midland *Also called Centen AG LLC* ***(G-11328)***

Centen AG LLC (HQ)...989 636-1000
2030 Dow Ctr Midland (48674) ***(G-11328)***

Centennial Coatings LLC...616 748-9410
371 N Centennial St Zeeland (49464) ***(G-19003)***

Centennial Technologies Inc...989 752-6167
1335 Agricola Dr Saginaw (48604) ***(G-14624)***

Center Cupcakes...248 302-6503
6271 Bromley Ct West Bloomfield (48322) ***(G-18270)***

Center For Qlty Trning Intl LL...586 212-9524
50485 Utica Dr Shelby Township (48315) ***(G-15183)***

Center Line Gage Inc...810 387-4300
110 Commerce Dr Brockway (48097) ***(G-2106)***

Center Machine & Tool LLC...517 748-2500
150 Factory Rd Michigan Center (49254) ***(G-11291)***

Center Mass Inc...734 207-8934
6845 Woonsocket St Canton (48187) ***(G-2447)***

Center of World Woodshop Inc...269 469-5687
4102 Hanover Rd Three Oaks (49128) ***(G-16555)***

Centerless Grinder Repair Div, Roseville *Also called Aero Grinding Inc* ***(G-14371)***

Centerless Rebuilders Inc (PA)...586 749-6529
57877 Main St New Haven (48048) ***(G-12030)***

Centerline Engineering Inc...616 735-2506
940 7 Mile Rd Nw Comstock Park (49321) ***(G-3592)***

Centracore LLC...586 776-5700
315 Whiting St Saint Clair (48079) ***(G-14818)***

Centracore De Mexico LLC...586 776-5700
315 Whiting St Saint Clair (48079) ***(G-14819)***

Central Admxture Phrm Svcs Inc...734 953-6760
37497 Schoolcraft Rd Livonia (48150) ***(G-10151)***

Central Asphalt Inc...989 772-0720
900 S Bradley St Mount Pleasant (48858) ***(G-11690)***

Central Concrete Products Inc...810 659-7488
4067 Commerce Dr Flushing (48433) ***(G-5804)***

Central Conveyor Company LLC (HQ)...248 446-0118
52800 Pontiac Trl Wixom (48393) ***(G-18630)***

Central Elevator Co Inc (PA)...269 329-0705
18 Baur Ln Vicksburg (49097) ***(G-17602)***

Central Gear Inc...800 589-1602
540 Ajax Dr Madison Heights (48071) ***(G-10685)***

Central Industrial Corporation...616 784-9612
2916 Walkent Dr Nw Grand Rapids (49544) ***(G-6560)***

Central Industrial Mfg Inc...231 347-5920
1211 W Conway Rd Harbor Springs (49740) ***(G-7644)***

Central Industrial Packaging, Grand Rapids *Also called Central Industrial Corporation* ***(G-6560)***

Central Lake Armor Express Inc...231 544-6090
7915 Cameron St Central Lake (49622) ***(G-2691)***

Central Metalizing & Machine, Saginaw *Also called Treib Inc* ***(G-14778)***

Central Mich Knwrth Lnsing LLC...517 394-7000
2556 Alamo Dr Lansing (48911) ***(G-9823)***

Central Mich Knwrth Sginaw LLC...989 754-4500
3046 Commerce Centre Dr Saginaw (48601) ***(G-14625)***

Central Mich Met Fbrcation LLC...989 875-9172
4476 W Saint Charles Rd Ithaca (48847) ***(G-8788)***

Central Michigan Crematory...269 963-1554
151506 One Half Mile Rd Battle Creek (49014) ***(G-1207)***

Central Michigan Engravers...517 485-5865
412 W Gier St Lansing (48906) ***(G-9679)***

Central Michigan Tank Rental...989 681-5963
9701 Gruett Rd Saint Louis (48880) ***(G-14989)***

Central Michigan University...989 774-3216
160 Combined Svcs Bldg Mount Pleasant (48859) ***(G-11691)***

Central On Line Data Systems...586 939-7000
34200 Mound Rd Sterling Heights (48310) ***(G-15954)***

Central Screw Products Company...313 893-9100
1070 Maplelawn Dr Troy (48084) ***(G-17006)***

Central Vac International, Dollar Bay *Also called Young Manufacturing Inc* ***(G-4766)***

Central Wood and Strapping...231 743-2800
7300 18 Mile Rd Marion (49665) ***(G-10971)***

Centro Division, Detroit *Also called Hackett Brass Foundry Co* ***(G-4291)***

Centrum Force Fabrication LLC...517 857-4774
3425 Stone School Rd Ann Arbor (48108) ***(G-420)***

Centurn Machine & Tool Inc...231 947-4773
5588 S French Rd Cedar (49621) ***(G-2637)***

Century Inc (PA)...231 947-6400
2410 W Aero Park Ct Traverse City (49686) ***(G-16641)***

Century Inc...231 946-7500
2410 W Aero Park Ct Traverse City (49686) ***(G-16642)***

Century Foundry Inc...231 733-1572
339 W Hovey Ave Muskegon (49444) ***(G-11791)***

Century Fuel Products...734 728-0300
51225 Martz Rd Van Buren Twp (48111) ***(G-17517)***

Century Instrument Company...734 427-0340
11865 Mayfield St Livonia (48150) ***(G-10152)***

Century Lanes Inc...616 392-7086
478 E 16th St Holland (49423) ***(G-7992)***

Century Plastics LLC...586 697-5752
51102 Quadrate Dr Macomb (48042) ***(G-10584)***

Century Plastics LLC (HQ)...586 566-3900
15030 23 Mile Rd Shelby Township (48315) ***(G-15184)***

Century Qual Products...734 728-0300
51225 Martz Rd Van Buren Twp (48111) ***(G-17518)***

Century Roll Inc...810 743-5065
G4463 S Dort Hwy Ste C Burton (48529) ***(G-2232)***

Century Tool & Gage LLC...810 629-0784
200 S Alloy Dr Fenton (48430) ***(G-5463)***

Century Tool Welding Inc...586 758-3330
32873 Groesbeck Hwy Fraser (48026) ***(G-5913)***

Century Truss...248 486-4000
17199 N Laurel Park Dr # 402 Livonia (48152) ***(G-10153)***

Century-Sun Metal Treating, Traverse City *Also called Century Inc* ***(G-16641)***

Cequent Performance Group, Plymouth *Also called Horizon Global Americas Inc* ***(G-13191)***

Cequent Uk Ltd...734 656-3000
47912 Halyard Dr Ste 100 Plymouth (48170) ***(G-13144)***

Ceratizit Usa Inc...586 759-2280
11355 Stephens Rd Warren (48089) ***(G-17751)***

Cerco Inc (PA)...734 362-8664
27301 Fort St Brownstown Twp (48183) ***(G-2153)***

Cerephex Corporation...517 719-0414
3001 Miller Rd Bancroft (48414) ***(G-1126)***

Cerny Industries LLC...231 929-2140
1645 Park Dr Traverse City (49686) ***(G-16643)***

Certainteed Gypsum Inc...906 524-6101
200 S Main St Lanse (49946) ***(G-9657)***

Certainteed LLC...517 787-8898
701 E Washington Ave Jackson (49203) ***(G-8837)***

Certainteed LLC...517 787-1737
803 Belden Rd Jackson (49203) ***(G-8838)***

Certified Metal Products Inc...586 598-1000
22802 Morelli Dr Clinton Township (48036) ***(G-3196)***

Certified Reducer Rbldrs Inc...248 585-0883
6480 Sims Dr Sterling Heights (48313) ***(G-15955)***

Certified Sheet Metal, Muskegon *Also called East Muskegon Roofg Shtmtl Co* ***(G-11806)***

Cerutti Bernal, Rochester Hills *Also called Bernal LLC* ***(G-13964)***

Cerva Screen Printing...616 272-2635
3125 Rypens Dr Nw Grand Rapids (49504) ***(G-6561)***

Cesere Enterprises Inc...989 799-3350
2614 State St Saginaw (48602) ***(G-14626)***

Cetusa, Grand Rapids *Also called Council For Edctl Trvl US Amer* ***(G-6609)***

CF Components Inc...248 670-2974
16231 Nola Dr Livonia (48154) ***(G-10154)***

CF Manufacturing LLC...231 409-9468
3028 Keystone Rd N Traverse City (49686) ***(G-16644)***

CF Plastic Fabricating Inc...586 954-1296
41590 Production Dr Harrison Township (48045) ***(G-7692)***

Cfb Michigan Inc...269 663-8855
27450 May St Edwardsburg (49112) ***(G-5002)***

CFC, Grand Rapids *Also called Contract Flavors Inc* ***(G-6598)***

Cfe Racing Products Inc...586 773-6310
16834 Chesterfield Ave Eastpointe (48021) ***(G-4931)***

Cff Inc...517 242-6903
570 Limewood Dr Apt E Battle Creek (49017) ***(G-1208)***

Cfh Inc...734 947-9574
12550 Universal Dr Taylor (48180) ***(G-16392)***

Cft Company, Milford *Also called Breesport Holdings Inc* ***(G-11456)***

Cg Automation, Comstock Park *Also called CG Automation & Fixture Inc* ***(G-3593)***

CG Automation & Fixture Inc...616 785-5400
5352 Rusche Dr Nw Comstock Park (49321) ***(G-3593)***

Cg Cabinet Wholesale...269 459-6833
6033 S Westnedge Ave Portage (49002) ***(G-13552)***

Cg Cabinets Wholesale...248 583-9666
30776 John R Rd Madison Heights (48071) ***(G-10686)***

Cg Detroit...248 553-0202
26970 Haggerty Rd Ste 200 Farmington Hills (48331) ***(G-5201)***

Cg Liquidation Incorporated...586 803-1000
12020 Shelby Tech Dr Shelby Township (48315) ***(G-15185)***

Cg Liquidation Incorporated (HQ)...586 575-9800
2111 Walter P Reuther Dr Warren (48091) ***(G-17752)***

Cg Logging...906 322-1018
11375 W Irish Line Rd Brimley (49715) ***(G-2102)***

Cg Plastics Inc...616 785-1900
5349 Rusche Dr Nw Comstock Park (49321) ***(G-3594)***

Cgc Water, Hartland *Also called Village & Cntry Wtr Trtmnt Inc* ***(G-7773)***

Chad S Signs and Shirts...248 821-3087
9430 Tiger Run Trl Davison (48423) ***(G-3776)***

Chadko LLC...616 402-9207
725 Taylor Ave Ste B Grand Haven (49417) ***(G-6284)***

Chain Industries Inc (PA)...248 348-7722
51035 Grand River Ave Wixom (48393) ***(G-18631)***

Chain-Sys Corporation (PA)...517 627-1173
8530 Ember Glen Pass Lansing (48917) ***(G-9757)***

Chair City Supply, Sterling Heights *Also called Richelieu America Ltd* ***(G-16151)***
Chaldean News LLC.......248 996-8360
30850 Telg Rd Ste 220 Bingham Farms (48025) ***(G-1693)***
Chalker Tool & Gauge Inc.......586 977-8660
35425 Beattie Dr Sterling Heights (48312) ***(G-15956)***
Challenge Machinery Company (PA).......231 799-8484
6125 Norton Center Dr Norton Shores (49441) ***(G-12285)***
Challenge Manufacturing.......616 735-6500
3079 3 Mile Rd Nw Walker (49534) ***(G-17632)***
Challenge Mfg Company.......616 735-6500
6375 W Grand River Ave Lansing (48906) ***(G-9680)***
Challenge Mfg Company.......616 735-6530
3200 Fruit Ridge Ave Nw Walker (49544) ***(G-17633)***
Challenge Mfg Company LLC.......616 735-6500
2969 3 Mile Rd Nw Walker (49534) ***(G-17634)***
Challenge Mfg Company LLC (PA).......616 735-6500
3200 Fruit Ridge Ave Nw Walker (49544) ***(G-17635)***
Challenge Mfg Company LLC.......616 735-6500
3200 Fruit Ridge Ave Nw Grand Rapids (49544) ***(G-6562)***
Challenge Mfg Company LLC.......616 396-2079
1401 Washington Ave Holland (49423) ***(G-7993)***
Challenge Mfg Holdings LLC.......616 735-6500
3200 Fruit Ridge Ave Nw Grand Rapids (49544) ***(G-6563)***
Challenge Packaging Division, Dearborn *Also called E C Moore Company* ***(G-3832)***
Challenger Communications LLC.......517 680-0125
704 N Clark St Albion (49224) ***(G-123)***
Challenger Manufacturing LLC.......248 930-9920
20733 Sunnydale St Farmington Hills (48336) ***(G-5202)***
Chambers Enterprises II LLC.......810 688-3750
6595 Bernie Kohler Dr North Branch (48461) ***(G-12177)***
Chambers Industrial Tech Inc.......616 249-8190
2220 Byron Center Ave Sw Wyoming (49519) ***(G-18856)***
Chambers Ottawa Inc.......231 238-2122
2064 Campbell Rd Cheboygan (49721) ***(G-2781)***
Chames LLC.......616 363-0000
163 Ann St Ne Ste 1 Grand Rapids (49505) ***(G-6564)***
Champagne Grinding & Mfg Co.......734 459-1759
8600 Ronda Dr Canton (48187) ***(G-2448)***
Champion Alloys, Lake Odessa *Also called Franklin Metal Trading Corp* ***(G-9575)***
Champion Bus Inc.......810 724-1753
331 Graham Rd Imlay City (48444) ***(G-8628)***
Champion Charter Sls & Svc Inc.......906 779-2300
180 Traders Mine Rd Iron Mountain (49801) ***(G-8719)***
Champion Die Incorporated.......616 784-2397
5510 West River Dr Ne Comstock Park (49321) ***(G-3595)***
Champion Foods LLC.......734 753-3663
23900 Bell Rd New Boston (48164) ***(G-12006)***
Champion Fortune Corporation.......989 422-6130
387 S Harrison Rd Houghton Lake (48629) ***(G-8395)***
Champion Gasket & Rubber Inc.......248 624-6140
3225 Haggerty Hwy Commerce Township (48390) ***(G-3518)***
Champion Home Builders Inc (HQ).......248 614-8200
755 W Big Beavr Rd # 1000 Troy (48084) ***(G-17007)***
Champion Laboratories Inc.......586 247-9044
51180 Celeste Shelby Township (48315) ***(G-15186)***
Champion Plastics Inc.......248 373-8995
1892 Taylor Rd Auburn Hills (48326) ***(G-842)***
Champion Screen Printers.......616 881-0760
7355 Clyde Park Ave Sw Byron Center (49315) ***(G-2263)***
Champion Screw Mch Engrg Inc (PA).......248 624-4545
30419 Beck Rd Wixom (48393) ***(G-18632)***
Champlain Specialty Metals Inc.......269 926-7241
2235 Dewey Ave Benton Harbor (49022) ***(G-1539)***
Chandas Engineering Inc.......313 582-8666
4800 Curtis St Dearborn (48126) ***(G-3819)***
Chandelier & More LLC.......248 214-1525
209 E Washington Ave Jackson (49201) ***(G-8839)***
Changan US R&D Center, Plymouth *Also called Changan US RES & Dev Ctr Inc* ***(G-13145)***
Changan US RES & Dev Ctr Inc.......734 259-6440
47799 Halyard Dr Ste 77 Plymouth (48170) ***(G-13145)***
Change Dynamix Inc.......248 671-6700
4327 Delemere Ct Royal Oak (48073) ***(G-14525)***
Change Parts Incorporated.......231 845-5107
185 S Jebavy Dr Ludington (49431) ***(G-10531)***
Changeover Integration LLC.......231 845-5320
787 S Pere Marquette Hwy Ludington (49431) ***(G-10532)***
Changstar Industries LLC.......248 446-1811
12364 Nantucket Dr South Lyon (48178) ***(G-15430)***
Chaosium Inc.......734 972-9551
3450 Wooddale Ct Ann Arbor (48104) ***(G-421)***
Chaotic Cotton Company LLC.......810 624-6153
16133 Softwater Lake Dr Linden (48451) ***(G-10060)***
Charboneau Inc.......989 293-1773
4361 Oakridge Rd Bay City (48706) ***(G-1337)***
Chardam Gear Company Inc.......586 795-8900
40805 Mound Rd Sterling Heights (48310) ***(G-15957)***
Charidimos Inc.......248 827-7733
23100 Telegraph Rd Southfield (48033) ***(G-15519)***
Charles A Specialties LLC.......231 946-3389
2694 Garfield Rd N Ste 28 Traverse City (49686) ***(G-16645)***
Charles Bowman & Company.......616 786-4000
3328 John F Donnelly Dr Holland (49424) ***(G-7994)***
Charles Group Inc (PA).......336 882-0186
7441 Div Ave S Ste A1 Grand Rapids (49548) ***(G-6565)***
Charles Lange.......989 777-0110
5763 Dixie Hwy Saginaw (48601) ***(G-14627)***
Charles Phipps and Sons Ltd.......810 359-7141
6951 Lakeshore Rd Lexington (48450) ***(G-10027)***
Charleston Mill Services, Dearborn *Also called Edw C Levy Co* ***(G-3835)***
Charlevoix Courier, The, Petoskey *Also called Northern Michigan Review Inc* ***(G-13009)***
Charlevoix Screen Masters Inc.......231 547-5111
12512 Taylor Rd Charlevoix (49720) ***(G-2713)***
Charlotte Anodizing Pdts Inc.......517 543-1911
591 Packard Hwy Charlotte (48813) ***(G-2741)***
Charlotte Cabinets Inc.......517 543-1522
629 W Seminary St Charlotte (48813) ***(G-2742)***
Charter Communication.......989 634-1093
2877 Miller Rd Bancroft (48414) ***(G-1127)***
Charter Communication.......810 515-8418
4370 Miller Rd Flint (48507) ***(G-5666)***
Charter Communication.......810 360-2748
8180 Grand River Rd Brighton (48114) ***(G-1964)***
Charter House Holdings LLC.......616 399-6000
200 N Franklin St Ste B Zeeland (49464) ***(G-19004)***
Charter Inds Extrusions LLC (PA).......616 245-3388
3900 S Greenbrooke Dr Se Kentwood (49512) ***(G-9448)***
Chase Nedrow Manufacturing Inc.......248 669-9886
150 Landrow Dr Wixom (48393) ***(G-18633)***
Chase Plastic Services Inc.......616 246-7190
1115 Cadillac Dr Se Grand Rapids (49506) ***(G-6566)***
Chase Plastic Services Inc (PA).......248 620-2120
6467 Waldon Center Dr # 200 Clarkston (48346) ***(G-3023)***
Chassis Brakes Intl USA (PA).......248 957-9997
34500 Grand River Ave Farmington (48335) ***(G-5135)***
Chassis Co. of Michigan, LLC, Port Huron *Also called Aludyne East Michigan LLC* ***(G-13437)***
Chassis Shop Prfmce Pdts Inc.......231 873-3640
1931 N 24th Ave Mears (49436) ***(G-11189)***
Chassix - Dmi Montague, Montague *Also called Aludyne Montague LLC* ***(G-11594)***
Chassix Blackstone Operat.......586 782-7311
23300 Blackstone Ave Warren (48089) ***(G-17753)***
Chassix Holdings Inc.......248 728-8700
300 Galleria Ofc Ctr Southfield (48034) ***(G-15520)***
Chateau Aronautique Winery LLC.......517 569-2132
101 Chief Dr Jackson (49201) ***(G-8840)***
Chateau Chantal, Traverse City *Also called Chateau Operations Ltd* ***(G-16647)***
Chateau Grand Travers Ltd.......231 223-7355
12239 Center Rd Traverse City (49686) ***(G-16646)***
Chateau Grand Traverse, Traverse City *Also called OKeefe Centre Ltd* ***(G-16779)***
Chateau Operations Ltd.......231 223-4110
15900 Rue De Vin Traverse City (49686) ***(G-16647)***
Chatman Walker Publishing LLC.......586 604-7534
22456 Glen Oak Dr Clinton Township (48035) ***(G-3197)***
Chaubrei Gardens, Richland *Also called Eileen Smeltzer* ***(G-13824)***
Cheal Woodworking, Toivola *Also called Thomas Cheal* ***(G-16593)***
Cheap Electric Contractors Co.......734 205-9591
2424 E Stadium Blvd Ann Arbor (48104) ***(G-422)***
Cheap Electric Contractors Co.......734 452-1964
16999 S Laurel Park Dr Livonia (48154) ***(G-10155)***
Cheap Electric Contractors Co.......734 205-9596
3205 Boardwalk St Ann Arbor (48108) ***(G-423)***
Cheap Electric Contractors Co.......734 286-9165
12269 Dix Toledo Rd Southgate (48195) ***(G-15749)***
Cheap Fast Prints LLC.......517 490-0864
3309 Jerree St Lansing (48911) ***(G-9824)***
Cheap Recently Acquired Pdts.......616 272-4212
2405 Porter St Sw Wyoming (49519) ***(G-18857)***
Cheboygan Cement Products Inc (PA).......231 627-5631
702 Lafayette Ave Cheboygan (49721) ***(G-2782)***
Cheboygan Cement Products Inc.......989 742-4107
800 E Progress St Hillman (49746) ***(G-7911)***
Cheboygan Cement Products Inc.......989 356-5156
400 Commerce Dr Alpena (49707) ***(G-286)***
Cheboygan Cnty Hbtat For Hmnit.......231 597-4663
9385 N Straits Hwy Cheboygan (49721) ***(G-2783)***
Cheboygan Harbor Marine, Cheboygan *Also called J B Lunds & Sons Inc* ***(G-2788)***
Cheboygan Tribune, Cheboygan *Also called Shoppers Fair Inc* ***(G-2799)***
Check Technology Solutions LLC.......248 680-2323
1800 Stephenson Hwy Troy (48083) ***(G-17008)***
Cheeba Hut Smoke Shop LLC.......586 213-5156
50189 Gratiot Ave Chesterfield (48051) ***(G-2858)***
Cheese Lady LLC.......231 728-3000
808 Terrace St Muskegon (49440) ***(G-11792)***
Cheese Lady Muskegon, The, Muskegon *Also called Cheese Lady LLC* ***(G-11792)***
Cheese Lady The, Traverse City *Also called Reilchz Inc* ***(G-16819)***
Cheesecake and Ecetera LLC.......734 335-8757
12335 Stark Rd Livonia (48150) ***(G-10156)***
Cheesecake Ecetera, Livonia *Also called Cheesecake and Ecetera LLC* ***(G-10156)***

Cheeze Kurls LLC...616 784-6095
2915 Walkent Dr Nw Grand Rapids (49544) ***(G-6567)***
Chefshell Catering, Port Huron *Also called Jabars Complements LLC* ***(G-13489)***
Chelsea Grinding Company...517 796-0343
2417 Vinsetta Blvd Royal Oak (48073) ***(G-14526)***
Chelsea Milling Company (PA)...734 475-1361
201 W North St Chelsea (48118) ***(G-2806)***
Chelsea Milling Company...269 781-2823
310 W Oliver Dr Marshall (49068) ***(G-11055)***
Chelsea Tool Inc...734 475-9679
20401 W Old Us Highway 12 # 4 Chelsea (48118) ***(G-2807)***
Chelsea Vlg Candles & Gifts...734 385-6588
12110 Silver Lake Hwy Brooklyn (49230) ***(G-2124)***
Chelsea-Megan Holding Inc...248 307-9160
1121 Rochester Rd Troy (48083) ***(G-17009)***
Chem Link Inc...269 679-4440
353 E Lyons St Schoolcraft (49087) ***(G-15114)***
Chem Station...517 371-8068
911 Center St Lansing (48906) ***(G-9681)***
Chem-Trend Holding Inc...517 545-7980
1445 Mcpherson Park Dr Howell (48843) ***(G-8437)***
Chem-Trend Limited Partnership (HQ)...517 546-4520
1445 Mcpherson Park Dr Howell (48843) ***(G-8438)***
Chem-Trend Limited Partnership...517 546-4520
3205 E Grand River Ave Howell (48843) ***(G-8439)***
Chemcast, Troy *Also called US Farathane Holdings Corp* ***(G-17415)***
Chemetall Americas, Jackson *Also called Chemetall US Inc* ***(G-8841)***
Chemetall US Inc...517 787-4846
1100 Technology Dr Jackson (49201) ***(G-8841)***
Chemical Process Inds LLC...248 547-5200
25428 John R Rd Madison Heights (48071) ***(G-10687)***
Chemical Processing Inc...313 925-3400
25428 John R Rd Madison Heights (48071) ***(G-10688)***
Chemical Specialties, Caledonia *Also called Helen Inc* ***(G-2378)***
Chemico Mays, Southfield *Also called Chemico Systems Inc* ***(G-15521)***
Chemico Systems Inc (PA)...248 723-3263
25200 Telg Rd Ste 120 Southfield (48034) ***(G-15521)***
Chemico Systems Inc...586 986-2343
6250 Chicago Rd Warren (48092) ***(G-17754)***
Chemloc Inc...989 465-6541
4996 N Dickenson Rd Coleman (48618) ***(G-3462)***
Chemprotect, Sterling Heights *Also called Atotech Usa LLC* ***(G-15936)***
Chemsol, Livonia *Also called Quantum Chemical LLC* ***(G-10379)***
Chemtool Incorporated...734 439-7010
415 Squires Dr Milan (48160) ***(G-11432)***
Chemtrade Chemicals US LLC...313 842-5222
800 Marion Ave Detroit (48218) ***(G-4091)***
Cherry Bend Tool & Die...231 947-3046
Hoxie Rd Cedar (49621) ***(G-2638)***
Cherry Blossom...231 342-3635
8365 Park Rd Williamsburg (49690) ***(G-18552)***
Cherry Central Cooperative Inc (PA)...231 946-1860
1771 N Us Highway 31 S Traverse City (49685) ***(G-16648)***
Cherry Central Cooperative Inc...231 861-2141
168 Lincoln St Shelby (49455) ***(G-15149)***
Cherry Cone LLC...231 944-1036
240 E Front St Traverse City (49684) ***(G-16649)***
Cherry Creek Post Co, Evart *Also called Cherry Creek Post LLC* ***(G-5122)***
Cherry Creek Post LLC...231 734-2466
5882 7 Mile Rd Evart (49631) ***(G-5122)***
Cherry Growers Inc (PA)...231 276-9241
401 S Old Woodward Ave # 340 Birmingham (48009) ***(G-1720)***
Cherry Growers Inc...231 947-2502
9440 S Center Hwy Traverse City (49684) ***(G-16650)***
Cherry Growers Plant 2, Traverse City *Also called Cherry Growers Inc* ***(G-16650)***
Cherry Hut Products LLC (PA)...231 882-4431
1046 Michigan Ave Benzonia (49616) ***(G-1613)***
Cherry Oak Landscaping LLC...517 339-2881
16400 Upton Rd East Lansing (48823) ***(G-4890)***
Cherry Republic Inc (PA)...231 334-3150
6026 S Lake St Glen Arbor (49636) ***(G-6209)***
Cherryflex Inc...888 947-4047
2811 Cass Rd Ste C1 Traverse City (49684) ***(G-16651)***
Chesterfield Engines Inc...586 949-5777
52420 Gratiot Ave Chesterfield (48051) ***(G-2859)***
Chesterfield Engines Nic, Chesterfield *Also called Chesterfield Engines Inc* ***(G-2859)***
Chewys Gourmet Kitchen LLC...313 757-2595
2939 Russell St Detroit (48207) ***(G-4092)***
CHI Co/Tabor Hill Winery (PA)...269 422-1161
185 Mount Tabor Rd Buchanan (49107) ***(G-2192)***
Chicago Blow Pipe Company...773 533-6100
405 Lakewood Ln Marquette (49855) ***(G-11012)***
Chicago Miniature Optoelectron, Troy *Also called Chicl LLC* ***(G-17010)***
Chicago Tribune Company LLC...734 464-6500
19500 Victor Pkwy Ste 100 Livonia (48152) ***(G-10157)***
Chicl LLC...859 294-5590
1708 Northwood Dr Troy (48084) ***(G-17010)***
Chieftain Coating LLC...586 791-1866
35300 Kelly Rd Clinton Township (48035) ***(G-3198)***
Chiipss...248 345-6112
10229 Joseph Campau St Detroit (48212) ***(G-4093)***
Child Evngelism Fellowship Inc...269 461-6953
7463 Elm St Berrien Center (49102) ***(G-1635)***
Childrens Bible Hour Inc...616 647-4500
2060 43rd St Se Grand Rapids (49508) ***(G-6568)***
Chip Enterprises Sole Member, Fowlerville *Also called IEC Fabrication LLC* ***(G-5842)***
Chip Systems International...269 626-8000
10953 Norscott St Scotts (49088) ***(G-15130)***
Chippewa Development Inc...269 685-2646
960 Industrial Pkwy Plainwell (49080) ***(G-13071)***
Chippewa Farm Supply LLC...989 471-5523
6701 N Us Highway 23 Spruce (48762) ***(G-15885)***
Chippewa Plastics, Evart *Also called Rkaa Business LLC* ***(G-5127)***
Chippewa Stone & Gravel Inc...231 867-5757
15240 110th Ave Rodney (49342) ***(G-14206)***
Chivis Sportsman Cases...231 834-1162
1192 E 112th St Grant (49327) ***(G-7428)***
Chocolate Vault Llc...517 688-3388
8475 Chicago Rd Horton (49246) ***(G-8372)***
Choctaw-Kaul Distribution Co, Detroit *Also called Kaul Glove and Mfg Co* ***(G-4353)***
Choice Corporation...586 783-5600
44383 Reynolds Dr Clinton Township (48036) ***(G-3199)***
Choice Mold Components, Clinton Township *Also called Choice Corporation* ***(G-3199)***
Choice Mold Components Inc...586 783-5600
44383 Reynolds Dr Clinton Township (48036) ***(G-3200)***
Choice Publications Inc...989 732-8160
112 E 6th St Gaylord (49735) ***(G-6122)***
Chor Industries Inc...248 585-3323
500 Robbins Dr Troy (48083) ***(G-17011)***
Chosen Tees LLC...313 766-4550
25122 Donald Redford (48239) ***(G-13723)***
Chouteau Fuels Company LLC...734 302-4800
414 S Main St Ste 600 Ann Arbor (48104) ***(G-424)***
Chp Consulting, Birmingham *Also called Alfa Financial Software Inc* ***(G-1717)***
CHR W LLC...989 755-4000
2795 Harrison St Saginaw (48604) ***(G-14628)***
Chris Brown Industries LLC...734 323-5651
21415 Civic Center Dr # 300 Southfield (48076) ***(G-15522)***
Chris Faulknor...231 645-1970
5 W Main St Unit 7 Boyne City (49712) ***(G-1886)***
Chris Muma Forest Products...989 426-5916
1154 W 1st St Gladwin (48624) ***(G-6193)***
Christensen Fiberglass LLC...616 738-1219
126 Aniline Ave N Holland (49424) ***(G-7995)***
Christian Oil Company...269 673-2218
2589 30th St Allegan (49010) ***(G-151)***
Christian Schools Intl...616 957-1070
2969 Pririe St Sw Ste 102 Grandville (49418) ***(G-7369)***
Christian Unity Press Inc...810 732-1831
5195 Exchange Dr Ste A Flint (48507) ***(G-5667)***
Christianson Industries Inc...269 663-8502
27328 May St Edwardsburg (49112) ***(G-5003)***
Christman Screenprint Inc...800 962-9330
2851 W Dickman Rd Springfield (49037) ***(G-15863)***
Christy Vault Company Inc...415 994-1378
3669 Bridgehampton Dr Ne Grand Rapids (49546) ***(G-6569)***
Chromatech Inc (PA)...734 451-1230
7723 Market Dr Canton (48187) ***(G-2449)***
Chromatic Graphics Inc...616 393-0034
654 E Lakewood Blvd Holland (49424) ***(G-7996)***
Chrome Craft Corporation...313 868-2444
5663 E 9 Mile Rd Warren (48091) ***(G-17755)***
Chronotech Swiss LLC...818 415-5039
5367 Hauser Way West Bloomfield (48323) ***(G-18271)***
Chrouch Communications Inc...231 972-0339
6644 9 Mile Rd Mecosta (49332) ***(G-11190)***
Chrysan Industries Inc (PA)...734 451-5411
14707 Keel St Plymouth (48170) ***(G-13146)***
Chrysler & Koppin Company...313 491-7100
868 Lakeland Ct Grosse Pointe (48230) ***(G-7527)***
Chrysler Engine Plant 2, Detroit *Also called FCA US LLC* ***(G-4229)***
Chrysler Group LLC...586 977-4900
7150 Metropolitan Pkwy Sterling Heights (48312) ***(G-15958)***
Chrysler International Sales, Sterling Heights *Also called FCA US LLC* ***(G-16011)***
Chrysler Sterling Test Center, Sterling Heights *Also called Chrysler Group LLC* ***(G-15958)***
Chrysler Twinsburg Stamping, Auburn Hills *Also called FCA US LLC* ***(G-894)***
Cht USA Inc (HQ)...269 445-0847
805 Wolfe Ave Cassopolis (49031) ***(G-2626)***
Chuck and Dave's Salsa, Fraser *Also called Buddies Foods LLC* ***(G-5907)***
Chunk Nibbles, Troy *Also called Otb Enterprises LLC* ***(G-17293)***
Ci Lighting LLC...248 997-4415
2083 Pontiac Rd Auburn Hills (48326) ***(G-843)***
CIE Automotive Usa Inc (HQ)...734 793-5320
15030 23 Mile Rd Shelby Township (48315) ***(G-15187)***
Cie Newcor Mtg Owosso, Owosso *Also called Machine Tool & Gear Inc* ***(G-12839)***
Cie Newcor RGI, Clifford *Also called Machine Tool & Gear Inc* ***(G-3132)***
Cie USA, Shelby Township *Also called Century Plastics LLC* ***(G-15184)***

Cig Jan Products Ltd 616 698-9070
  3300 Hanna Lk Indus Dr Se Caledonia (49316) *(G-2371)*
Cignet LLC (PA) 586 307-3790
  24601 Capital Blvd Clinton Township (48036) *(G-3201)*
Cignys, Saginaw *Also called Saginaw Products Corporation* *(G-14750)*
Cignys Bridgeport, Saginaw *Also called Charles Lange* *(G-14627)*
Cignys Inc 989 753-1411
  68 Williamson St Saginaw (48601) *(G-14629)*
Cignys-Shields, Saginaw *Also called Saginaw Products Corporation* *(G-14748)*
Cima Energy LP 231 941-0633
  125 S Park St Ste 450 Traverse City (49684) *(G-16652)*
Cincinnati Tyrolit Inc 513 458-8121
  4636 Regency Dr Shelby Township (48316) *(G-15188)*
Cinnabar Engineering Inc 810 648-2444
  116 Orval St Sandusky (48471) *(G-15057)*
Cipa Usa Inc (PA) 810 982-3555
  3350 Griswold Rd Port Huron (48060) *(G-13464)*
Circle C Mold & Plas Group Inc 269 496-5515
  55664 Parkville Rd Mendon (49072) *(G-11216)*
Circle Engineering Inc 586 978-8120
  5495 Gatewood Dr Sterling Heights (48310) *(G-15959)*
Circle K Service Corporation 989 496-0511
  4300 James Savage Rd Midland (48642) *(G-11329)*
Circle S Products Inc (PA) 734 675-2960
  16415 Carter Rd Woodhaven (48183) *(G-18798)*
Circlebuilder .com, Franklin *Also called Circlebuilder Software LLC* *(G-5882)*
Circlebuilder Software LLC 248 770-3191
  24811 Franklin Park Dr Franklin (48025) *(G-5882)*
Circles Way To Go Around Inc 313 384-1193
  43508 Rivergate Dr Clinton Township (48038) *(G-3202)*
Circuit Controls Corporation 231 347-0760
  2277 M 119 Petoskey (49770) *(G-12993)*
Circuits of Sound 313 886-5599
  840 Shoreham Rd Grosse Pointe Woods (48236) *(G-7565)*
Circus Procession LLC 616 834-8048
  622 Graafschap Rd Holland (49423) *(G-7997)*
Cirko LLC 586 504-1313
  54080 Birchfield Dr E Shelby Township (48316) *(G-15189)*
Cisco Systems Inc 800 553-6387
  200 Renaissance Ctr Detroit (48243) *(G-4094)*
Citation Berlin, Southfield *Also called Grede Wscnsn Subsidiaries LLC* *(G-15583)*
Citation Camden Cast Ctr LLC 248 727-1800
  20750 Civic Center Dr # 100 Southfield (48076) *(G-15523)*
Citizen Newspaper, The, Ortonville *Also called Sherman Publications Inc* *(G-12752)*
Citizens LLC 517 541-1449
  421 N Cochran Ave Charlotte (48813) *(G-2743)*
City Animation Co (PA) 248 589-0600
  57 Park Dr Troy (48083) *(G-17012)*
City Animation Co. 989 743-3458
  1013 N Shiawassee St Corunna (48817) *(G-3706)*
City Auto Glass Co (PA) 616 842-3235
  295 N Beechtree St Grand Haven (49417) *(G-6285)*
City of East Jordan 231 536-2561
  218 N Lake St East Jordan (49727) *(G-4861)*
City of Greenville 616 754-0100
  415 S Lafayette St Greenville (48838) *(G-7478)*
City of Saginaw 989 759-1670
  1741 S Jefferson Ave Saginaw (48601) *(G-14630)*
City Press Inc 800 867-2626
  30 Rissman Ln Ortonville (48462) *(G-12744)*
City Sign Company, Pontiac *Also called Wenz & Gibbens Enterprises* *(G-13424)*
CJ Chemicals LLC 888 274-1044
  3469 E Grand River Ave # 112 Howell (48843) *(G-8440)*
Cj's Smoked Spc Dom Game Proc, Hesperia *Also called Lowry Joanellen* *(G-7870)*
Cjg LLC 734 793-1400
  31800 Industrial Rd Livonia (48150) *(G-10158)*
CK Technologies 616 836-6384
  3360 Allen St Hudsonville (49426) *(G-8574)*
Ckc Industries Inc 248 667-6286
  24824 Ross Dr Redford (48239) *(G-13724)*
Ckd USA Corporation 248 740-7004
  675 E Big Beaver Rd Troy (48083) *(G-17013)*
Ckna, Southfield *Also called Marelli North America Inc* *(G-15644)*
Clair Sawyer 906 228-8242
  1225 W Washington St Marquette (49855) *(G-11013)*
Claire Aldin Publications 313 702-4028
  20813 Wkfield Way Apt 203 Southfield (48076) *(G-15524)*
Clamp Industries Incorporated 248 335-8131
  342 Irwin Ave Pontiac (48341) *(G-13353)*
Clamptech LLC 989 832-8027
  106 S Walnut St Ste 1 Bay City (48706) *(G-1338)*
Clancy Crushed Concrete, Roseville *Also called Clancy Excavating Co* *(G-14384)*
Clancy Excavating Co 586 294-2900
  29950 Little Mack Ave Roseville (48066) *(G-14384)*
Clare Bedding Mfg Co 906 789-9902
  433 Stephenson Ave Escanaba (49829) *(G-5065)*
Clare County Cleaver Inc 989 539-7496
  183 W Main St Harrison (48625) *(G-7675)*

Clare County Review 989 386-4414
  105 W 4th St Ste 1 Clare (48617) *(G-2975)*
Clare Print & Pulp 989 386-3497
  409 N Mcewan St Clare (48617) *(G-2976)*
Clarence McNamara Logging, Newberry *Also called McNamara & Mcnamara* *(G-12093)*
Clarey Custom Frmng & Art LLC 989 415-4152
  437 River Rd Bay City (48706) *(G-1339)*
Clarience Technologies LLC (HQ) 716 665-6214
  20600 Civic Center Dr Southfield (48076) *(G-15525)*
Clarion Corporation America 248 991-3100
  31440 Northwestern Hwy Farmington Hills (48334) *(G-5203)*
Clarion Group, Farmington Hills *Also called Clarion Corporation America* *(G-5203)*
Clarion Technologies Inc (PA) 616 698-7277
  238 S River Ave Fl 2 Holland (49423) *(G-7998)*
Clarion Technologies Inc 616 754-1199
  501 S Cedar St Greenville (48838) *(G-7479)*
Clarios LLC 734 995-3016
  1935 S Industrial Hwy Ann Arbor (48104) *(G-425)*
Clarity Comm Advisors Inc 248 327-4390
  2 Corporate Dr Ste 250 Southfield (48076) *(G-15526)*
Clarity Voice, Southfield *Also called Clarity Comm Advisors Inc* *(G-15526)*
Clark Brothers Instrument Co 586 781-7000
  56680 Mound Rd Shelby Township (48316) *(G-15190)*
Clark Engineering Co (PA) 989 723-7930
  1470 Mcmillan Rd Owosso (48867) *(G-12826)*
Clark Granco Inc 616 794-2600
  7298 Storey Rd Belding (48809) *(G-1443)*
Clark Instrument Inc 248 669-3100
  46590 Ryan Ct Novi (48377) *(G-12383)*
Clark Manufacturing Company 231 946-5110
  2485 Aero Park Dr Traverse City (49686) *(G-16653)*
Clark Perforating Company Inc 734 439-1170
  15875 Allen Rd Milan (48160) *(G-11433)*
Clark-Mxr Inc 734 426-2803
  7300 Huron River Dr Ste 1 Dexter (48130) *(G-4731)*
Clarklake Machine Incorporated 517 529-9454
  9451 S Meridian Rd Clarklake (49234) *(G-3003)*
Clarkson Controls & Eqp Co 248 380-9915
  42572 Cherry Hill Rd Novi (48375) *(G-12384)*
Clarkston Carbide Tool & Mch (PA) 248 625-3182
  1959 Viola Dr Ortonville (48462) *(G-12745)*
Clarkston Control Products 248 394-1430
  4809 Crestview Dr Clarkston (48348) *(G-3024)*
Clarkston Courts LLC 248 383-8444
  6110 Dixie Hwy Clarkston (48346) *(G-3025)*
Classfcation Flotation Systems 810 714-5200
  235 Industrial Way Fenton (48430) *(G-5464)*
Classic Boat Decks LLC 586 465-3606
  31469 N River Rd Harrison Township (48045) *(G-7693)*
Classic Cabinets Interiors LLC (PA) 517 423-2600
  118 W Chicago Blvd Tecumseh (49286) *(G-16491)*
Classic Car Port & Canopies 586 759-5490
  11800 E 9 Mile Rd Warren (48089) *(G-17756)*
Classic Container Corporation 734 853-3000
  32432 Capitol St Livonia (48150) *(G-10159)*
Classic Design, Troy *Also called Classic Systems LLC* *(G-17015)*
Classic Design Concepts LLC 248 504-5202
  53194 Pontiac Trl Milford (48381) *(G-11458)*
Classic Die Inc 616 454-3760
  610 Plymouth Ave Ne Grand Rapids (49505) *(G-6570)*
Classic Glass Battle Creek Inc 269 968-2791
  21472 Bedford Rd N Battle Creek (49017) *(G-1209)*
Classic Gutter Systems LLC 269 665-2700
  155 Mccollum Galesburg (49053) *(G-6074)*
Classic Images Embroidery 616 844-1702
  15774 Ronny Rd Grand Haven (49417) *(G-6286)*
Classic Instruments Inc 231 582-0461
  826 Moll Dr Boyne City (49712) *(G-1887)*
Classic Log Homes Incorporated 989 821-6118
  7340 Hillcrest Rd Higgins Lake (48627) *(G-7876)*
Classic Metal Finishing Inc 517 990-0011
  2500 W Argyle St Jackson (49202) *(G-8842)*
Classic Mfg 616 651-2921
  21900 Us Highway 12 Sturgis (49091) *(G-16283)*
Classic Plating Inc 313 532-1440
  12600 Farley Redford (48239) *(G-13725)*
Classic Precision, LLC, Wixom *Also called CP Acquisition LLC* *(G-18638)*
Classic Stitch 586 737-7767
  42450 Van Dyke Ave Sterling Heights (48314) *(G-15960)*
Classic Stone MBL & Gran Inc 248 588-1599
  2340 Alger Dr Troy (48083) *(G-17014)*
Classic Systems LLC 248 588-2738
  2400 Stephenson Hwy Troy (48083) *(G-17015)*
Classic Tool & Boring Inc 586 795-8967
  5970 Wall St Sterling Heights (48312) *(G-15961)*
Classic Turning Inc (PA) 517 764-1335
  3000 E South St Jackson (49201) *(G-8843)*
Classic Welding Inc 586 758-2400
  21500 Ryan Rd Warren (48091) *(G-17757)*

Classy Threadz 989 479-9595
  1529 Eppenbrock Rd Harbor Beach (48441) *(G-7629)*
Clausing Industrial Inc 269 345-7155
  3963 Emerald Dr Kalamazoo (49001) *(G-9144)*
Clausing Industrial Inc (PA) 269 345-7155
  3963 Emerald Dr Kalamazoo (49001) *(G-9145)*
Clausing Industrial Svc Ctr, Kalamazoo Also called Clausing Industrial Inc *(G-9144)*
Clawson Container Company (PA) 248 625-8700
  4545 Clawson Tank Dr Clarkston (48346) *(G-3026)*
Clawson Custom Woodwork LLC 248 515-5336
  295 Broadacre Ave Clawson (48017) *(G-3090)*
Clawson Tank, Clarkston Also called Steel Tank & Fabricating Co *(G-3069)*
Clawson Tank Company (PA) 248 625-8700
  4701 White Lake Rd Clarkston (48346) *(G-3027)*
Clay & Graham Inc 989 354-5292
  4770 Werth Rd Alpena (49707) *(G-287)*
Claytec, East Lansing Also called Inpore Technologies Inc *(G-4897)*
Cldd LLC 517 748-9326
  1255 Falahee Rd Jackson (49203) *(G-8844)*
Clean Air Technology Inc 734 459-6320
  41105 Capital Dr Canton (48187) *(G-2450)*
Clean Cut Divison, Auburn Hills Also called Rite Mark Stamp Company *(G-1021)*
Clean Harbors Envmtl Svcs Inc 231 258-8014
  4030 Columbus Dr Ne Kalkaska (49646) *(G-9385)*
Clean Planet Foods, Taylor Also called Great Fresh Foods Co LLC *(G-16422)*
Clean Rooms International Inc 616 452-8700
  4939 Starr St Se Grand Rapids (49546) *(G-6571)*
Clean Tech Inc 734 529-2475
  500 Dunham St Dundee (48131) *(G-4811)*
Clean Tech Inc 734 529-2475
  500 Dunham St Dundee (48131) *(G-4812)*
Clean Tech Inc (HQ) 734 455-3600
  41605 Ann Arbor Rd E Plymouth (48170) *(G-13147)*
Cleaning Solutions Inc 616 243-0555
  1250 Ramona St Se Grand Rapids (49507) *(G-6572)*
Cleaning Up Detroit City LLC 517 715-7010
  4369 W Euclid St Detroit (48204) *(G-4095)*
Clear Cut Water Jet Machining 616 534-9119
  4515 Patterson Ave Se Grand Rapids (49512) *(G-6573)*
Clear Estimates Inc 734 368-9951
  1509 Granger Ave Ann Arbor (48104) *(G-426)*
Clear Image Devices LLC 734 645-6459
  3930 N Michael Rd Ann Arbor (48103) *(G-427)*
Cleardot Info, Inkster Also called Donbar LLC *(G-8662)*
Clearform 616 656-5359
  5220 68th St Se Ste 8 Caledonia (49316) *(G-2372)*
Clearview Lighting LLC 248 709-8707
  31572 Mayfair Ln Beverly Hills (48025) *(G-1662)*
Clearwater Paper - Menominee, Menominee Also called Menominee Acquisition Corp *(G-11246)*
Clearwater Treatment Systems 517 688-9316
  4700 Industrial Dr Clarklake (49234) *(G-3004)*
Cleary Developments Inc (PA) 248 588-7011
  32055 Edward Ave Madison Heights (48071) *(G-10689)*
Cleary Developments Inc 248 588-6614
  32033 Edward Ave Madison Heights (48071) *(G-10690)*
Clemco Printing Inc 989 269-8364
  116 Scott St Bad Axe (48413) *(G-1099)*
Clemens Welcome Center 517 278-2500
  285 N Michigan Ave Coldwater (49036) *(G-3426)*
Cleveland L&W Inc 440 882-5195
  17757 Woodland Dr New Boston (48164) *(G-12007)*
Cleveland Tramrail Systems, Sterling Heights Also called Versa Handling Co *(G-16222)*
Cleveland-Cliffs Inc 906 475-3547
  101 Tilden Mine Rd Ishpeming (49849) *(G-8775)*
Cleveland-Cliffs Steel Corp 313 317-8900
  14661 Rotunda Dr Dearborn (48120) *(G-3820)*
Cleveland-Cliffs Steel Corp 800 532-8857
  4001 Miller Rd Ste 12 Dearborn (48120) *(G-3821)*
Click Care LLC 989 792-1544
  2650 Mcleod Dr N Saginaw (48604) *(G-14631)*
Cliff Keen Athletic, Ann Arbor Also called Cliff Keen Wrestling Pdts Inc *(G-428)*
Cliff Keen Wrestling Pdts Inc 734 975-8800
  4480 Varsity Dr Ste B Ann Arbor (48108) *(G-428)*
Cliffs Sand & Gravel Inc 989 422-3463
  1128 Federal Ave Houghton Lake (48629) *(G-8396)*
Clinton Machine Inc 989 834-2235
  1300 S Main St Ovid (48866) *(G-12813)*
Clinton River Medical Pdts LLC 248 289-1825
  1025 Doris Rd Auburn Hills (48326) *(G-844)*
Clio Massena LLC 248 477-5148
  28214 Beck Rd Wixom (48393) *(G-18634)*
Clipper Belt Lacer Company 616 459-3196
  1995 Oak Industrial Dr Ne Grand Rapids (49505) *(G-6574)*
Clips & Clamps Industries, Plymouth Also called Consolidated Clips Clamps Inc *(G-13149)*
Clips Coupons of Ann Arbo 248 437-9294
  9477 Silverside South Lyon (48178) *(G-15431)*
Clm Vibetech Inc 269 344-3878
  7025 E K Ave Kalamazoo (49048) *(G-9146)*

Clossons Manufacturing LLC 269 363-4261
  3783 S Pipestone Rd Sodus (49126) *(G-15393)*
Cloud 9 Pipe Tobacco Inc 313 522-1957
  33878 Dequindre Rd Sterling Heights (48310) *(G-15962)*
Cloud Apps Consulting LLC 616 528-0528
  1406 Laurel Ave Se Grand Rapids (49506) *(G-6575)*
Cloud White Publishing 248 684-6460
  262 Noble St Milford (48381) *(G-11459)*
Cloudface LLC 248 756-1688
  996 Grace St Northville (48167) *(G-12200)*
Clover Industries Inc 231 929-1660
  1424 International Dr Traverse City (49686) *(G-16654)*
Cloyes-Renold, Royal Oak Also called AAM Pwder Metal Components Inc *(G-14501)*
Clyde Union (holdings) Inc 269 966-4600
  4600 W Dickman Rd Battle Creek (49037) *(G-1210)*
Clydes Frame & Wheel Service 248 338-0323
  725 Cesar E Chavez Ave Pontiac (48340) *(G-13354)*
Clymer Manufacturing Company 248 853-5555
  1605 W Hamlin Rd Rochester Hills (48309) *(G-13975)*
CM Book, Ann Arbor Also called Cushing-Malloy Inc *(G-440)*
CMA Engineering Center, Brighton Also called Torque 2020 CMA Acqstion LLC D *(G-2083)*
CMC, Niles Also called Custom Marine Carpet *(G-12122)*
CMC Plastyk LLC 989 588-4468
  176 E Ludington Dr Farwell (48622) *(G-5422)*
Cme Plastics 517 456-7722
  903 Industrial Dr Tecumseh (49286) *(G-16492)*
Cmg America Inc 810 686-3064
  11424 N Saginaw Rd Clio (48420) *(G-3395)*
Cmi-Schneible Group (HQ) 810 354-0404
  3061 W Thompson Rd Ste 1 Fenton (48430) *(G-5465)*
Cmm Optic, Troy Also called Contour Metrological & Mfg Inc *(G-17025)*
Cmn Fabrication Inc 586 294-1941
  32580 Kelly Rd Roseville (48066) *(G-14385)*
Cmp Acquisitions LLC 888 519-2286
  25501 Glendale Redford (48239) *(G-13726)*
CMS, Grand Rapids Also called Frost Incorporated *(G-6722)*
CMS, Jenison Also called Cellulose Mtl Solutions LLC *(G-9049)*
CMS Conveyor Maint & Sup Div, Grand Rapids Also called Frost Incorporated *(G-6724)*
CMS Enterprises Company (HQ) 517 788-0550
  1 Energy Plaza Dr Jackson (49201) *(G-8845)*
Cmu 989 774-7143
  802 Industrial Dr Mount Pleasant (48858) *(G-11692)*
Cmu University Press, Mount Pleasant Also called Central Michigan University *(G-11691)*
CNB International Inc 269 948-3300
  1004 S East St Hastings (49058) *(G-7783)*
Cnc, Jackson Also called Classic Turning Inc *(G-8843)*
CNC MACHINING, Auburn Hills Also called Paravis Industries Inc *(G-993)*
CNC Products LLC 269 684-5500
  2126 S 11th St Niles (49120) *(G-12118)*
CNc Products Acquisition Inc 269 684-5500
  2126 S 11th St Niles (49120) *(G-12119)*
Cnc Prototype of Michigan 586 218-3291
  101 W Big Beavr Rd # 1400 Troy (48084) *(G-17016)*
Cnc Tooling Solutions LLC 248 890-5625
  1211 Rosewood St Ferndale (48220) *(G-5534)*
Cnd Products LLC 616 361-1000
  1642 Broadway Ave Nw 3n Grand Rapids (49504) *(G-6576)*
Cni Enterprises Inc 248 581-0200
  29333 Stephenson Hwy Madison Heights (48071) *(G-10691)*
Cni Plastics LLC 517 541-4960
  400 Parkland Dr Charlotte (48813) *(G-2744)*
Cni-Owosso LLC 248 586-3300
  1451 E Lincoln Ave Madison Heights (48071) *(G-10692)*
Co-Op Machine & Tool, Durand Also called B & M Machine & Tool Company *(G-4839)*
Co-Pipe Products Inc 734 287-1000
  20501 Goddard Rd Taylor (48180) *(G-16393)*
Co2 Central, Albion Also called Ernie Romanco *(G-125)*
Coach House Iron Inc 616 785-8967
  1005 9 Mile Rd Nw Ste 1 Sparta (49345) *(G-15764)*
Coast To Coast Cabinets LLC (PA) 517 719-0118
  2398 Jolly Rd Ste 300 Okemos (48864) *(G-12661)*
Coastal Concierge 269 639-1515
  1210 Phoenix St Ste 9 South Haven (49090) *(G-15402)*
Coastal Container Corporation 616 355-9800
  1201 Industrial Ave Holland (49423) *(G-7999)*
Coastal Energy, Holland Also called Coastal Container Corporation *(G-7999)*
Coastline Manufacturing LLC 231 798-1700
  6215 Norton Center Dr Norton Shores (49441) *(G-12286)*
Coat It Inc of Detroit 313 869-8500
  15400 Woodrow Wilson St Detroit (48238) *(G-4096)*
Coatings By Pcd Inc 616 952-0032
  2825 17 Mile Rd Ste C Kent City (49330) *(G-9429)*
Coatings Plus Inc 616 451-2427
  675 Chestnut St Sw Grand Rapids (49503) *(G-6577)*
Cobalt Friction Tech LLC 734 930-6902
  330 Meadow Creek Dr Ann Arbor (48105) *(G-429)*
Cobalt Friction Technologies 734 274-3030
  4595 Platt Rd Ann Arbor (48108) *(G-430)*

Cobblestone Cabinets.....248 398-3700
3311 12 Mile Rd Berkley (48072) *(G-1624)*
Cobblestone Press.....989 832-0166
4516 Washington St Midland (48642) *(G-11330)*
Cobham McRlctrnic Slutions Inc (HQ).....734 426-1230
310 Dino Dr Ann Arbor (48103) *(G-431)*
Cobra Aero LLC.....517 437-9100
240 Uran St Hillsdale (49242) *(G-7930)*
Cobra Enterprises, Madison Heights *Also called Cobra Patterns & Models Inc (G-10694)*
Cobra Enterprises Inc.....248 588-2669
32303 Howard Ave Madison Heights (48071) *(G-10693)*
Cobra Maufacturing.....248 585-1606
1147 Rankin Dr Troy (48083) *(G-17017)*
Cobra Patterns & Models Inc.....248 588-2669
32303 Howard Ave Madison Heights (48071) *(G-10694)*
Cobra Torches Inc.....248 499-8122
180 Engelwood Dr Ste J Lake Orion (48359) *(G-9594)*
Cobrex Ltd.....734 429-9758
5880 Braun Rd Saline (48176) *(G-15008)*
Coca-Cola, Hancock *Also called Hancock Bottling Co Inc (G-7618)*
Coca-Cola Bottling Co.....313 868-2167
12225 Oakland Pkwy Highland Park (48203) *(G-7902)*
Coca-Cola Company.....269 657-3171
38279 W Red Arrow Hwy Paw Paw (49079) *(G-12943)*
Coca-Cola Refreshments USA Inc.....616 913-0400
1208 Butterworth St Sw Grand Rapids (49504) *(G-6578)*
Coca-Cola Refreshments USA Inc.....231 947-4150
1031 Hastings St Traverse City (49686) *(G-16655)*
Coca-Cola Refreshments USA Inc.....616 458-4536
1440 Butterworth St Sw Grand Rapids (49504) *(G-6579)*
Coca-Cola Refreshments USA Inc.....269 657-8538
38279 W Red Arrow Hwy Paw Paw (49079) *(G-12944)*
Coca-Cola Refreshments USA Inc.....313 897-5000
26777 Halsted Rd Farmington Hills (48331) *(G-5204)*
Cochran Corporation.....517 857-2211
120 Mill St Springport (49284) *(G-15879)*
Code Blue Corporation.....616 392-8296
259 Hedcor St Ste 1 Holland (49423) *(G-8000)*
Code Systems Inc.....248 307-3884
2365 Pontiac Rd Frnt Auburn Hills (48326) *(G-845)*
Codo Machine & Tool Inc.....517 789-5113
1418 Lewis St Jackson (49203) *(G-8846)*
Cody Kresta Vineyard & Winery.....269 668-3800
45727 27th St Mattawan (49071) *(G-11164)*
Coeus LLC.....248 564-1958
1605 S Telegraph Rd Bloomfield Hills (48302) *(G-1808)*
Coffee Beanery Ltd (HQ).....810 733-1020
3429 Pierson Pl Flushing (48433) *(G-5805)*
Coffman Electrical Eqp Co.....616 452-8708
3300 Jefferson Ave Se Grand Rapids (49548) *(G-6580)*
Cog Marketers Ltd.....989 224-4117
3026 W M 21 Saint Johns (48879) *(G-14897)*
Cog Marketers Ltd.....434 455-3209
302 W Sectionline Rd Ashley (48806) *(G-742)*
Cog Marketers Ltd.....989 224-4117
3055 W M 21 Saint Johns (48879) *(G-14898)*
Cognisys Inc.....231 943-2425
459 Hughes Dr Traverse City (49696) *(G-16656)*
Cogsdill Tool Products Inc.....734 744-4500
11757 Globe St Livonia (48150) *(G-10160)*
Cohda Wireless America LLC.....248 513-2105
3135 S State St Ste 102 Ann Arbor (48108) *(G-432)*
Coil Anodizing, Muskegon *Also called Lorin Industries Inc (G-11861)*
Coil Drilling Technologies Inc.....989 773-6504
2362 Northway Dr Mount Pleasant (48858) *(G-11693)*
Coit Avenue Gravel Co Inc.....616 363-7777
4772 Coit Ave Ne Grand Rapids (49525) *(G-6581)*
Coke Bottle.....810 424-3352
2515 Lapeer Rd Flint (48503) *(G-5668)*
Colcha Linens Inc.....313 355-8300
14555 Jib St Plymouth (48170) *(G-13148)*
Cold Forming Technology Inc.....586 254-4600
44476 Phoenix Dr Sterling Heights (48314) *(G-15963)*
Cold Heading Co (HQ).....586 497-7000
21777 Hoover Rd Warren (48089) *(G-17758)*
Cold Heading Co.....586 497-7016
22155 Hoover Rd Warren (48089) *(G-17759)*
Cold Saw Precision, Williamsburg *Also called Thomas A Despres Inc (G-18565)*
Cold Stone Creamery, Washington *Also called WG Sweis Investments LLC (G-18091)*
Cold Stone Creamery.....313 886-4020
16823 Kercheval Ave Grosse Pointe Park (48230) *(G-7550)*
Coldwater Plant, Coldwater *Also called Exo-S US LLC (G-3433)*
Coldwater Veneer Inc (PA).....517 278-5676
548 Race St Coldwater (49036) *(G-3427)*
Coldwter Sintered Met Pdts Inc.....517 278-8750
300 Race St Coldwater (49036) *(G-3428)*
Cole Carbide Industries Inc (PA).....248 276-1278
4930 S Lapeer Rd Lake Orion (48359) *(G-9595)*
Cole Carbide Industries Inc.....989 872-4348
6880 Cass City Rd Cass City (48726) *(G-2613)*
Cole Carter Inc.....269 626-8891
8713 38th St S Scotts (49088) *(G-15131)*
Cole King Foods.....313 872-0220
40 Clairmount St Detroit (48202) *(G-4097)*
Cole King LLC.....248 276-1278
4930 S Lapeer Rd Orion (48359) *(G-12725)*
Cole Tooling Systems Inc.....586 573-9450
4930 S Lapeer Rd Lake Orion (48359) *(G-9596)*
Cole Tooling Systems Inc.....586 558-9450
34841 Mound Rd Ste 224 Sterling Heights (48310) *(G-15964)*
Cole Wagner Cabinetry.....248 642-5330
735 Forest Ave Birmingham (48009) *(G-1721)*
Cole Wagner Cabinetry.....248 852-2406
2511 Leach Rd Rochester Hills (48309) *(G-13976)*
Coleman Bowman & Associates.....248 642-8221
3535 Wooddale Ct Bloomfield Hills (48301) *(G-1809)*
Coleman Machine Inc (PA).....906 863-1113
N1597 Us Highway 41 Menominee (49858) *(G-11229)*
Coleman Racing Products, Menominee *Also called Coleman Machine Inc (G-11229)*
Coleman Specialty Products, Bloomfield Hills *Also called Coleman Bowman & Associates (G-1809)*
Coles Custom Con Coatings LLC.....231 651-0709
367 Spring Valley St Beulah (49617) *(G-1653)*
Coles Machine Service Inc.....810 658-5373
201 W Rising St Davison (48423) *(G-3777)*
Coles Quality Foods Inc.....231 722-1651
1188 Lakeshore Dr Muskegon (49441) *(G-11793)*
Coles Quality Foods Inc (PA).....231 722-1651
4079 Park East Ct Se A Grand Rapids (49546) *(G-6582)*
Colfran Industrial Sales Inc.....734 595-8920
38127 Ecorse Rd Romulus (48174) *(G-14262)*
Collagecom LLC.....248 971-0538
1471 Lynwood Ln White Lake (48383) *(G-18453)*
Collectors Zone.....517 788-8498
1425 Wildwood Ave Jackson (49202) *(G-8847)*
College Park Industries Inc.....586 294-7950
27955 College Park Dr Warren (48088) *(G-17760)*
Collier Enterprise III.....269 503-3402
1510 Sunnyfield Rd Sturgis (49091) *(G-16284)*
Collins Brothers Sawmill Inc.....906 524-5511
17579 Watters St Lanse (49946) *(G-9658)*
Collins Caviar Company.....269 469-4576
9595 Union Pier Rd Union Pier (49129) *(G-17499)*
Coloma Frozen Foods Inc (PA).....269 849-0500
4145 Coloma Rd Coloma (49038) *(G-3475)*
Colombo Beverage Chase Systems, Davisburg *Also called Colombo Sales & Engrg Inc (G-3764)*
Colombo Sales & Engrg Inc.....248 547-2820
10421 Enterprise Dr Ste A Davisburg (48350) *(G-3764)*
Colombo Sales and Engrg Inc.....248 547-2820
17108 S Hemlock Rd Oakley (48649) *(G-12654)*
Colonial Bushings Inc.....586 954-3880
44336 Reynolds Dr Clinton Township (48036) *(G-3203)*
Colonial Chemical Corp.....517 789-8161
720 E Mansion St Jackson (49203) *(G-8848)*
Colonial Engineering Inc (PA).....269 323-2495
6400 Corporate Ave Portage (49002) *(G-13553)*
Colonial Group, Clinton Township *Also called Colonial Mold Inc (G-3204)*
Colonial Group, Shelby Township *Also called Colonial Plastics Incorporated (G-15191)*
Colonial Manufacturing LLC.....269 926-1000
1246 E Empire Ave Benton Harbor (49022) *(G-1540)*
Colonial Mold Inc.....586 469-4944
44479 Reynolds Dr Clinton Township (48036) *(G-3204)*
Colonial Packaging, Grand Rapids *Also called Advance Packaging Acquisition (G-6432)*
Colonial Plastics Incorporated.....586 469-4944
51734 Filomena Dr Shelby Township (48315) *(G-15191)*
Colonial Tool Sales & Svc LLC.....734 946-2733
12344 Delta St Taylor (48180) *(G-16394)*
Color Coat Plating Company.....248 744-0445
355 W Girard Ave Madison Heights (48071) *(G-10695)*
Color Connection.....248 351-0920
29487 Northwestern Hwy Southfield (48034) *(G-15527)*
Color Detroit Publishing LLC.....313 974-9000
321 Lonesome Oak Dr Rochester Hills (48306) *(G-13977)*
Color Express Printing Inc.....734 213-4980
625 State Cir Ste 1 Ann Arbor (48108) *(G-433)*
Color Factory.....810 577-2974
8034 N Mckinley Rd Flushing (48433) *(G-5806)*
Color House Graphics Inc.....616 241-1916
3505 Eastern Ave Se Grand Rapids (49508) *(G-6583)*
Color Source Graphics Inc.....248 458-2040
1925 W Maple Rd Ste A Troy (48084) *(G-17018)*
Colorado Pavers & Walls Inc.....517 881-1704
3328 Torrey Rd Flint (48507) *(G-5669)*
Colorhub LLC.....616 333-4411
4950 Kraft Ave Se Grand Rapids (49512) *(G-6584)*
Colorized Prints, Mount Morris *Also called Daniel Ward (G-11670)*
Colorpoint Print.com, Troy *Also called Corporate Electronic Sty Inc (G-17030)*

Colors & Effects USA LLC (HQ)....973 245-6000
3000 Town Ctr Ste 2400 Southfield (48075) ***(G-15528)***
Colors & Effects USA LLC....248 304-5753
24710 W 11 Mile Rd Southfield (48034) ***(G-15529)***
Colortech Graphics Inc....586 779-7800
28700 Hayes Rd Roseville (48066) ***(G-14386)***
Colorworx, Macomb *Also called Admore Inc* ***(G-10571)***
Colson Casters....269 944-6063
2024 Hawthorne Ave Saint Joseph (49085) ***(G-14924)***
Colt - 7 Corporation....586 792-9050
34859 Groesbeck Hwy Clinton Township (48035) ***(G-3205)***
Columbia Marking Tools Inc....586 949-8400
27430 Luckino Dr Chesterfield (48047) ***(G-2860)***
Columbus Oil & Gas LLC....810 385-9140
6436 Lakeshore Rd Burtchville (48059) ***(G-2218)***
Columbus Printing Inc....614 534-0266
4920 Starr St Se Grand Rapids (49546) ***(G-6585)***
Columbus Tree The, Ithaca *Also called Stage Stop* ***(G-8795)***
Colwell Industries Inc....248 841-1254
1780 N Livernois Rd Rochester Hills (48306) ***(G-13978)***
Comau LLC (HQ)....248 353-8888
21000 Telegraph Rd Southfield (48033) ***(G-15530)***
Comau LLC....248 219-0756
21175 Telegraph Rd Southfield (48033) ***(G-15531)***
Comau Pico, Southfield *Also called Comau LLC* ***(G-15530)***
Combine International Inc (PA)....248 585-9900
354 Indusco Ct Troy (48083) ***(G-17019)***
Combustion Research Corp....248 852-3611
2516 Leach Rd Rochester Hills (48309) ***(G-13979)***
Comec USA....810 299-3000
7202 Whitmore Lake Rd Brighton (48116) ***(G-1965)***
Comet Energy Services LLC....231 933-3600
954 Business Park Dr Traverse City (49686) ***(G-16657)***
Comet Information Systems LLC....248 686-2600
8359 Office Park Dr Grand Blanc (48439) ***(G-6238)***
Comfoot Shoes, Kalamazoo *Also called Fernand Corporation* ***(G-9185)***
Comfort Mattress Co....586 293-4000
30450 Little Mack Ave Roseville (48066) ***(G-14387)***
Comfort-Aire, Jackson *Also called Cdgjl Inc* ***(G-8836)***
Comma, Plymouth *Also called Plymouth-Canton Cmnty Crier* ***(G-13268)***
Command Electronics Inc....269 679-4011
15670 Morris Indus Dr Schoolcraft (49087) ***(G-15115)***
Command Publishing LLC....734 776-2692
43311 Joy Rd Ste 201 Canton (48187) ***(G-2451)***
Commando Lock Company, Troy *Also called Solidbody Technology Company* ***(G-17359)***
Commando Lock Company LLC....248 709-7901
395 Elmwood Dr Troy (48083) ***(G-17020)***
Commercial Blueprint Inc....517 372-8360
3125 Pinetree Rd Ste B Lansing (48911) ***(G-9825)***
Commercial Coating Systems LLC....616 490-6242
11760 Forestwood Dr Ne Cedar Springs (49319) ***(G-2646)***
Commercial Fabricating & Engrg (PA)....248 887-1595
1395 Energy Way Highland (48357) ***(G-7887)***
Commercial Graphics Company....517 278-2159
205 W Garfield Ave Coldwater (49036) ***(G-3429)***
Commercial Graphics Inc....586 726-8150
42704 Mound Rd Sterling Heights (48314) ***(G-15965)***
Commercial Group Inc (PA)....313 931-6100
12801 Universal Dr Taylor (48180) ***(G-16395)***
Commercial Group Lifting Pdts, Taylor *Also called Commercial Group Inc* ***(G-16395)***
Commercial Indus A Sltions LLC....269 373-8797
6830 E Michigan Ave Kalamazoo (49048) ***(G-9147)***
Commercial Mfg & Assembly Inc....616 847-9980
17087 Hayes St Grand Haven (49417) ***(G-6287)***
Commercial Painting Services, Quincy *Also called CPS LLC* ***(G-13666)***
Commercial Steel Treating Corp (PA)....248 588-3300
31440 Stephenson Hwy Madison Heights (48071) ***(G-10696)***
Commercial Tool & Die Inc....616 785-8100
5351 Rusche Dr Nw Comstock Park (49321) ***(G-3596)***
Commercial Tool Group, Comstock Park *Also called Commercial Tool & Die Inc* ***(G-3596)***
Commercial Trck Transf Signs....586 754-7100
4133 E 10 Mile Rd Warren (48091) ***(G-17761)***
Commercial Welding Company Inc....269 782-5252
316 Cass Ave Dowagiac (49047) ***(G-4778)***
Commercial Works....269 795-2060
200 Lafayette St Middleville (49333) ***(G-11304)***
Common Earth Press LLC....313 407-2919
10000 Nadine Ave Huntington Woods (48070) ***(G-8620)***
Common Sensors LLC....248 722-8556
27520 W 8 Mile Rd Farmington Hills (48336) ***(G-5205)***
Commonwealth Associates Inc (PA)....517 788-3000
2700 W Argyle St Jackson (49202) ***(G-8849)***
Commonwealth Service Sls Corp....313 581-8050
1715 W Hamlin Rd Rochester Hills (48309) ***(G-13980)***
Commonwealth Sewing Company....313 319-2417
1314 Holden St Detroit (48202) ***(G-4098)***
Communications Dept, Sault Sainte Marie *Also called Sault Tribe News* ***(G-15099)***
Community Access Center....269 343-2211
359 S Kalamazoo Mall # 300 Kalamazoo (49007) ***(G-9148)***
Community Mntal Hlth Auth Clnt....517 323-9558
3200 Remy Dr Lansing (48906) ***(G-9682)***
Community Publishing & Mktg....866 822-0101
26955 Northline Rd Taylor (48180) ***(G-16396)***
Community Shoppers Guide Inc....269 694-9431
117 N Farmer St Otsego (49078) ***(G-12784)***
Compac, Burton *Also called Compak Inc* ***(G-2233)***
Compac Specialties Inc....616 786-9100
13444 Barry St Holland (49424) ***(G-8001)***
Compact PCI Systems, Saint Clair Shores *Also called Opensystems Publishing LLC* ***(G-14876)***
Compak Inc....989 288-3199
1220 N Center Rd Burton (48509) ***(G-2233)***
Companions' Cuisine, Saginaw *Also called Mkr Fabricating Inc* ***(G-14703)***
Company Products Inc....586 757-6160
11800 Commerce St Warren (48089) ***(G-17762)***
Compass Interiors LLC....231 348-5353
300 E Mitchell St Petoskey (49770) ***(G-12994)***
Compatible Laser Products Inc....810 629-0459
1045 Grant St Fenton (48430) ***(G-5466)***
Competitive Cmpt Info Tech Inc....732 829-9699
100 Maincentre Ste 1 Northville (48167) ***(G-12201)***
Competitive Edge Designs Inc....616 257-0565
4506 R B Chaffee Mem Dr S Grand Rapids (49548) ***(G-6586)***
Competitive Edge Wood Spc Inc....616 842-1063
711 E Savidge Spring Mi 4 Muskegon (49441) ***(G-11794)***
Complete Auto-Mation Inc....248 693-0500
1776d W Clarkston Rd Lake Orion (48362) ***(G-9597)***
Complete Automation CMF....269 343-0500
4301 Manchester Rd Ste A Kalamazoo (49001) ***(G-9149)***
Complete Companies, Lake Orion *Also called Complete Filtration Inc* ***(G-9598)***
Complete Cutting Tl & Mfg Inc....248 662-9811
47577 Avante Dr Wixom (48393) ***(G-18635)***
Complete Data Products Inc (PA)....248 651-8602
5755 New King Dr Ste 210 Troy (48098) ***(G-17021)***
Complete Dsign Automtn Systems (PA)....734 424-2789
2117 Bishop Cir E Dexter (48130) ***(G-4732)***
Complete Filtration Inc....248 693-0500
1776d W Clarkston Rd Lake Orion (48362) ***(G-9598)***
Complete Health System....810 720-3891
5084 Vlla Lnde Pkwy Ste 7 Flint (48532) ***(G-5670)***
Complete HM Advg Mdia Prmtnal....586 254-9555
15018 Technology Dr Shelby Township (48315) ***(G-15192)***
Complete Kitchen Design LLC....586 790-2800
33827 Harper Ave Clinton Township (48035) ***(G-3206)***
Complete Metal Finishing Inc....269 343-0500
4301 Manchester Rd Ste A Kalamazoo (49001) ***(G-9150)***
Complete Metalcraft LLC....248 952-8002
184 W Wardlow Rd Highland (48357) ***(G-7888)***
Complete Packaging Inc....734 241-2794
633 Detroit Ave Monroe (48162) ***(G-11534)***
Complete Prototype Svcs Inc (PA)....586 690-8897
44783 Morley Dr Clinton Township (48036) ***(G-3207)***
Complete Services LLC....248 470-8247
32401 8 Mile Rd Livonia (48152) ***(G-10161)***
Complete Source Inc....616 285-9110
4455 44th St Se Grand Rapids (49512) ***(G-6587)***
Complete Surface Technologies....586 493-5800
21338 Carlo Dr Clinton Township (48038) ***(G-3208)***
Complete Truck and Trailer....989 732-9000
184 Meecher Rd Gaylord (49735) ***(G-6123)***
Complex Steel & Wire Corp....734 326-1600
36254 Annapolis St Wayne (48184) ***(G-18218)***
Complex Tool & Machine Inc....248 625-0664
6460 Sashabaw Rd Clarkston (48346) ***(G-3028)***
Component Engrg Solutions LLC....616 514-1343
1740 Chicago Dr Sw Grand Rapids (49519) ***(G-6588)***
Component Solutions LLC....906 863-2682
2219 10th Ave Menominee (49858) ***(G-11230)***
Composite Builders LLC....616 377-7767
430 W 18th St Holland (49423) ***(G-8002)***
Composite Forgings Ltd Partnr....313 496-1226
2300 W Jefferson Ave Detroit (48216) ***(G-4099)***
Composite Techniques Inc....616 878-9795
3345 Brook Trl Se Grand Rapids (49508) ***(G-6589)***
Compositech....269 908-7846
683 Lincoln Lake Ave Se Lowell (49331) ***(G-10498)***
Compound Technology, Troy *Also called Chelsea-Megan Holding Inc* ***(G-17009)***
Compressor Industries LLC....313 389-2800
17162 Francis St Melvindale (48122) ***(G-11197)***
Compressor Technologies Inc....616 949-7000
4420 40th St Se Grand Rapids (49512) ***(G-6590)***
Comptek Inc....248 477-5215
37450 Enterprise Ct Farmington Hills (48331) ***(G-5206)***
Compton Press Industries LLC....248 473-8210
23079 Commerce Dr Farmington Hills (48335) ***(G-5207)***
Compudyne Inc....906 360-9081
925 W Washington St # 104 Marquette (49855) ***(G-11014)***
Compunetics Incorporated....248 524-6376
2500 Rochester Ct Troy (48083) ***(G-17022)***

Compunetics Systems Inc 248 531-0015
3235 Fulham Dr Rochester Hills (48309) **(G-13981)**
Computer Assistanc, Grand Blanc *Also called Innovative Programming Systems* **(G-6249)**
Computer Decisions Intl Inc 248 473-5900
22260 Haggerty Rd Ste 300 Northville (48167) **(G-12202)**
Computer Mail Services Inc (PA) 248 352-6700
44648 Mound Rd Sterling Heights (48314) **(G-15966)**
Computer Operated Mfg 989 686-1333
1710 Lewis St Bay City (48706) **(G-1340)**
Computer Sciences Corp 734 761-8513
1947 S Industrial Hwy Ann Arbor (48104) **(G-434)**
Computer Sciences Corporation 586 825-5043
6000 17 Mile Rd Sterling Heights (48313) **(G-15967)**
Computerized SEC Systems Inc (HQ) 248 837-3700
31750 Sherman Ave Madison Heights (48071) **(G-10697)**
Compuware Corporation (HQ) 313 227-7300
1 Campus Martius Fl 4 Detroit (48226) **(G-4100)**
Comstar Automotive USA LLC 517 266-2445
900 Industrial Dr Tecumseh (49286) **(G-16493)**
Comtrex, Rochester Hills *Also called Ssb Holdings Inc* **(G-14117)**
Comtronics 517 750-3160
4909 W Michigan Ave Jackson (49201) **(G-8850)**
Con-De Manufacturing Inc 269 651-3756
26436 Us Highway 12 Sturgis (49091) **(G-16285)**
Conagra Brands Inc 810 724-2715
415 S Blacks Corners Rd Imlay City (48444) **(G-8629)**
Conagra Brands Inc 402 240-8210
4551 Squires Rd Quincy (49082) **(G-13665)**
Conagra Brands Inc 616 392-2359
147 E 6th St Holland (49423) **(G-8003)**
Conair North America 814 437-6861
503 S Mercer St Pinconning (48650) **(G-13060)**
Conant Gardeners 313 863-2624
18621 San Juan Dr Detroit (48221) **(G-4101)**
Concen Grinding Inc (HQ) 517 787-8172
2620 Saradan Dr Jackson (49202) **(G-8851)**
Concentric Industries Inc 734 848-5133
720 La Voy Rd Erie (48133) **(G-5046)**
Concentric Labs Inc 517 969-3038
715 Hall Blvd Mason (48854) **(G-11119)**
Concentric Medical Inc 269 385-2600
2825 Airview Blvd Portage (49002) **(G-13554)**
Concentric Mfg Svcs LLC 989 506-8636
6755 W Shore Dr Weidman (48893) **(G-18250)**
Concepp Technologies 734 324-6750
1609 Biddle Ave Wyandotte (48192) **(G-18815)**
Concept Alloys Inc 734 449-9680
11234 Lemen Rd Whitmore Lake (48189) **(G-18527)**
Concept Circuits Corporation 248 852-5200
1854 Star Batt Dr Rochester Hills (48309) **(G-13982)**
Concept Metal Machining LLC 616 647-9200
5320 6 Mile Ct Nw Comstock Park (49321) **(G-3597)**
Concept Metal Products Inc (PA) 231 799-3202
16928 148th Ave Spring Lake (49456) **(G-15808)**
Concept Metals Group, Spring Lake *Also called Concept Metal Products Inc* **(G-15808)**
Concept Molds Inc 269 679-2100
12273 N Us Highway 131 Schoolcraft (49087) **(G-15116)**
Concept Technology Inc (PA) 248 765-0100
144 Wimbleton Dr Birmingham (48009) **(G-1722)**
Concept Tool & Die Inc 616 875-4600
9371 Henry Ct Zeeland (49464) **(G-19005)**
Concept Tooling Systems Inc 616 301-6906
555 Plymouth Ave Ne Grand Rapids (49505) **(G-6591)**
Concord Editorial & Design LLC 616 868-0148
5583 Bancroft Ave Se Alto (49302) **(G-331)**
Concord Industrial Corporation 248 646-9225
36400 Woodward Ave # 110 Bloomfield Hills (48304) **(G-1810)**
Concord Tool and Mfg Inc 586 465-6537
118 N Groesbeck Hwy Ste E Mount Clemens (48043) **(G-11634)**
Concordant Publishing Concern 810 798-3563
6800 Hough Rd Almont (48003) **(G-257)**
Concorde Inc 248 391-8177
4200 N Atlantic Blvd Auburn Hills (48326) **(G-846)**
Concrete Manufacturing Inc 586 777-3320
29100 Groesbeck Hwy Roseville (48066) **(G-14388)**
Concrete Step Co 810 789-3061
G5491 Clio Rd Flint (48504) **(G-5671)**
Concrete Store 231 577-3433
8181 E 34 Rd Cadillac (49601) **(G-2326)**
Condat Corporation 734 944-4994
250 S Industrial Dr Saline (48176) **(G-15009)**
Cone Drive Gearing Solutions, Traverse City *Also called Cone Drive Operations Inc* **(G-16658)**
Cone Drive Operations Inc (HQ) 231 946-8410
240 E Twelfth St Traverse City (49684) **(G-16658)**
Conform Automotive, Bingham Farms *Also called Dti Molded Products Inc* **(G-1695)**
Conform Automotive LLC 248 647-0400
51258 Quadrate Dr Macomb (48042) **(G-10585)**
Conform Automotive LLC 248 647-0400
5505 52nd St Sw Grand Rapids (49512) **(G-6592)**
Conform Automotive LLC 517 322-0711
5421 W Mount Hope Hwy E Lansing (48917) **(G-9758)**
Conform Automotive LLC (PA) 248 647-0400
32500 Telg Rd Ste 207 Bingham Farms (48025) **(G-1694)**
Conform Group, Bingham Farms *Also called Conform Automotive LLC* **(G-1694)**
Conformance Coatings Prototype 810 364-4333
2321 Busha Hwy Marysville (48040) **(G-11084)**
Conical Cutting Tools Inc 616 531-8500
3890 Buchanan Ave Sw Grand Rapids (49548) **(G-6593)**
Conical Tool Company, Grand Rapids *Also called Conical Cutting Tools Inc* **(G-6593)**
Conine Publishing Inc (HQ) 231 723-3592
75 Maple St Manistee (49660) **(G-10896)**
Conley Composites LLC 918 299-5051
4855 Broadmoor Ave Se Grand Rapids (49512) **(G-6594)**
Conley Manufacturing Inc 586 262-4484
51559 Oro Dr Shelby Township (48315) **(G-15193)**
Connect With Us LLC 586 262-4359
4311 Kingmont Dr Shelby Township (48317) **(G-15194)**
Connection Service Company 269 926-2658
1377 M 139 Benton Harbor (49022) **(G-1541)**
Connell Limited Partnership 989 875-5135
255 Industrial Pkwy Ithaca (48847) **(G-8789)**
Connells Restoration & Sealan 269 370-0805
16011 Hoffman St Vandalia (49095) **(G-17565)**
Conner Engineering LLC 586 465-9590
21200 Carlo Dr Clinton Township (48038) **(G-3209)**
Conner Steel Products (PA) 248 852-5110
2295 Star Ct Rochester Hills (48309) **(G-13983)**
Connexion Inc 248 453-5177
40 W Howard St Ste 404 Pontiac (48342) **(G-13355)**
Connolly 248 683-7985
5805 Pontiac Lake Rd Waterford (48327) **(G-18110)**
Connor Sports Flooring LLC 906 822-7311
251 Industrial Park Rd Amasa (49903) **(G-338)**
Conquest Manufacturing LLC 586 576-7600
28408 Lorna Ave Warren (48092) **(G-17763)**
Conquest Scents 810 653-2759
8399 E Bristol Rd Davison (48423) **(G-3778)**
Conrad Machine Company 231 893-7455
1525 Warner St Whitehall (49461) **(G-18492)**
Conros, Melvindale *Also called Lepages 2000 Inc* **(G-11203)**
Consider Magazine 734 769-0500
1429 Hill St Ann Arbor (48104) **(G-435)**
Considine Sales & Marketing 248 889-7887
611 S Milford Rd Highland (48357) **(G-7889)**
Consistacom Inc 906 482-7653
47420 State Highway M26 # 2 Houghton (49931) **(G-8381)**
Consoldted Dcment Slutions LLC 586 293-8100
17601 Malyn Blvd Fraser (48026) **(G-5914)**
Consoldted Rsource Imaging LLC 616 735-2080
2943 S Wilson Ct Nw Grand Rapids (49534) **(G-6595)**
Consolidated Clips Clamps Inc 734 455-0880
15050 Keel St Plymouth (48170) **(G-13149)**
Consolidated Computing Svcs 989 906-0467
2001 S Farragut St Bay City (48708) **(G-1341)**
Consolidated Metal Pdts Inc 616 538-1000
3831 Clay Ave Sw Grand Rapids (49548) **(G-6596)**
Consort Corporation (PA) 269 388-4532
2129 Portage St Kalamazoo (49001) **(G-9151)**
Consort Display Group, Kalamazoo *Also called Consort Corporation* **(G-9151)**
Constellium Automotive USA LLC (HQ) 734 879-9700
6331 Schooner St Van Buren Twp (48111) **(G-17519)**
Constine Inc 989 723-6043
2625 W M 21 Owosso (48867) **(G-12827)**
Construction Diamond Products, Livonia *Also called Cdp Diamond Products Inc* **(G-10149)**
Construction Retail Svcs Inc 586 469-2289
38555 Moravian Dr Clinton Township (48036) **(G-3210)**
Constructive Sheet Metal Inc 616 245-5306
11670 46th Ave Allendale (49401) **(G-217)**
Consulting Engineering, Norton Shores *Also called Soils and Structures Inc* **(G-12333)**
Consumers Concrete Corp 616 243-3651
1505 Burlingame Ave Sw Wyoming (49509) **(G-18858)**
Consumers Concrete Corp 269 384-0977
3809 E Michigan Ave Kalamazoo (49048) **(G-9152)**
Consumers Concrete Corporation (PA) 269 342-0136
3506 Lovers Ln Kalamazoo (49001) **(G-9153)**
Consumers Concrete Corporation 800 643-4235
465 12th St Plainwell (49080) **(G-13072)**
Consumers Concrete Corporation 231 777-3981
4450 Evanston Ave Muskegon (49442) **(G-11795)**
Consumers Concrete Corporation 269 792-9009
3316 12th St Wayland (49348) **(G-18193)**
Consumers Concrete Corporation 231 924-6131
4550 W 72nd St Fremont (49412) **(G-6037)**
Consumers Concrete Corporation 269 925-3109
1800 Yore Ave Benton Harbor (49022) **(G-1542)**
Consumers Concrete Corporation 517 784-9108
3342 Page Ave Jackson (49203) **(G-8852)**
Consumers Concrete Corporation 517 267-8428
1367 Lake Lansing Rd Lansing (48912) **(G-9826)**

Consumers Concrete Corporation....616 827-0063
8257 S Division Ave Byron Center (49315) ***(G-2264)***
Consumers Concrete Corporation....269 342-5983
700 Nazareth Rd Kalamazoo (49048) ***(G-9154)***
Consumers Concrete Corporation....269 965-2321
1020 Raymond Rd N Battle Creek (49014) ***(G-1211)***
Consumers Concrete Corporation....616 392-6190
4312 M 40 Holland (49423) ***(G-8004)***
Consumers Concrete Corporation....269 684-8760
1523 Lake St Niles (49120) ***(G-12120)***
Consumers Concrete Corporation....231 894-2705
2259 Holton Whitehall Rd Whitehall (49461) ***(G-18493)***
Consumers Concrete Products, Kalamazoo *Also called Consumers Concrete Corporation* ***(G-9153)***
Container Specialties Inc....989 728-4231
3540 Darton Rd Hale (48739) ***(G-7588)***
Contamination Control, Livonia *Also called Acorn Industries Inc* ***(G-10100)***
Contech (us) Inc....616 459-4139
314 Straight Ave Sw Grand Rapids (49504) ***(G-6597)***
Contech Engnered Solutions LLC....517 676-3000
661 Jerico Dr Mason (48854) ***(G-11120)***
Contemporary Amperex Tech USA....248 289-6200
2114 Austin Ave Rochester Hills (48309) ***(G-13984)***
Contemporary Bride, Shelby Township *Also called R S C Productions* ***(G-15313)***
Contemporary Industries Inc (PA)....248 478-8850
24037 Research Dr Farmington Hills (48335) ***(G-5208)***
Contessa Wine Cellars....269 468-5534
3235 Friday Rd Coloma (49038) ***(G-3476)***
Conteur Publishing LLC....248 602-9749
37382 Catherine Marie Dr Sterling Heights (48312) ***(G-15968)***
Context Furniture L L C....248 200-0724
1054 W Lewiston Ave Ferndale (48220) ***(G-5535)***
Continent Wines Inc....248 467-7383
7457 Deerview Ct Clarkston (48348) ***(G-3029)***
Continental Aluminum LLC....248 437-1001
29201 Milford Rd New Hudson (48165) ***(G-12046)***
Continental Auto Systems Inc....248 253-2969
2400 Executive Hills Dr Auburn Hills (48326) ***(G-847)***
Continental Auto Systems Inc....248 874-2597
2400 Executive Hills Dr Auburn Hills (48326) ***(G-848)***
Continental Auto Systems Inc....906 248-6700
9301 S M 221 Brimley (49715) ***(G-2103)***
Continental Auto Systems Inc....248 874-1801
2400 Executive Hills Dr Auburn Hills (48326) ***(G-849)***
Continental Auto Systems Inc....248 267-9408
4685 Investment Dr Troy (48098) ***(G-17023)***
Continental Carbide Ltd Inc....586 463-9577
23545 Reynolds Ct Clinton Township (48036) ***(G-3211)***
Continental Crane & Service....586 294-7900
33681 Groesbeck Hwy Fraser (48026) ***(G-5915)***
Continental Dar Facilities LLC....616 837-7641
999 W Randall St Coopersville (49404) ***(G-3682)***
Continental Diamond, Brighton *Also called La Gold Mine Inc* ***(G-2018)***
Continental Midland LLC....734 367-7032
33200 Capitol St Livonia (48150) ***(G-10162)***
Continental Plastics Co....586 294-4600
50900 Birch Rd Shelby Township (48315) ***(G-15195)***
Continntal Auto Systems US Inc....248 764-6400
4685 Investment Dr Troy (48098) ***(G-17024)***
Continntal Bldg Svcs of Cncnna....313 336-8543
580 Cook Rd Grosse Pointe Woods (48236) ***(G-7566)***
Continntal Strl Plas Hldngs Co, Auburn Hills *Also called Teijin Auto Tech NA Hldngs Cor.* ***(G-1048)***
Continntal Strl Plas Mnchster, Manchester *Also called Teijin Auto Tech Mnchester LLC* ***(G-10890)***
Contour Engineering Inc....989 828-6526
2305 E Coe Rd Shepherd (48883) ***(G-15376)***
Contour Machining Inc....734 525-4877
11837 Brookfield St Livonia (48150) ***(G-10163)***
Contour Metrological & Mfg Inc (PA)....248 273-1111
488 Oliver Dr Troy (48084) ***(G-17025)***
Contour Mold Corporation....810 245-4070
1830 N Lapeer Rd Lapeer (48446) ***(G-9922)***
Contour Tool & Engineering Inc....616 772-6360
2425 104th Ave Zeeland (49464) ***(G-19006)***
Contour Tool and Machine Inc....517 787-6806
2393 Research Dr Jackson (49203) ***(G-8853)***
Contract Flavors Inc....616 454-5950
3855 Linden Ave Se Grand Rapids (49548) ***(G-6598)***
Contract Furn Solutions Inc....734 941-2750
25069 Pine Ridge Dr Brownstown (48134) ***(G-2144)***
Contract People Corporation....248 304-9900
29444 Northwestern Hwy Southfield (48034) ***(G-15532)***
Contract Source & Assembly Inc....616 897-2186
5230 33rd St Se Grand Rapids (49512) ***(G-6599)***
Contract Welding and Fabg Inc....734 699-5561
385 Sumpter Rd Van Buren Twp (48111) ***(G-17520)***
Contractors Fence Service....313 592-1300
14900 Telegraph Rd Detroit (48239) ***(G-4102)***
Contractors Steel Company....616 531-4000
2768 Dormax St Sw Grand Rapids (49519) ***(G-6600)***
Contribute A Verse Publishing....616 447-2271
2862 Leelanau Dr Ne Grand Rapids (49525) ***(G-6601)***
Control Dekk LLC....616 828-4862
4035 Oak Valley Ct Sw Wyoming (49519) ***(G-18859)***
Control Electronics....734 941-5008
29231 Northline Rd Romulus (48174) ***(G-14263)***
Control Gaging Inc....734 668-6750
847 Avis Dr Ann Arbor (48108) ***(G-436)***
Control One Inc....586 979-6106
6460 Sims Dr Ste A Sterling Heights (48313) ***(G-15969)***
Control Pak International, Fenton *Also called Energy Control Solutions Inc* ***(G-5472)***
Control Power-Reliance LLC (HQ)....248 583-1020
310 Executive Dr 314 Troy (48083) ***(G-17026)***
Control Solutions Inc....616 247-9422
5805 Weller Ct Sw Ste A Wyoming (49509) ***(G-18860)***
Control Technique Incorporated....586 997-3200
41200 Technology Park Dr Sterling Heights (48314) ***(G-15970)***
Controlled Magnetics Inc....734 449-7225
10766 Plaza Dr Whitmore Lake (48189) ***(G-18528)***
Controlled Plating Tech Inc....616 243-6622
1100 Godfrey Ave Sw Grand Rapids (49503) ***(G-6602)***
Controlled Power Company (PA)....248 528-3700
1955 Stephenson Hwy Ste G Troy (48083) ***(G-17027)***
Controlled Turning Inc....517 782-0517
1607 S Gorham St Jackson (49203) ***(G-8854)***
Controller Security Systems, Eastpointe *Also called Controller Systems Corporation* ***(G-4932)***
Controller Systems Corporation....586 772-6100
21363 Gratiot Ave Eastpointe (48021) ***(G-4932)***
Controls For Industries Inc....517 468-3385
5279 Royce Rd Webberville (48892) ***(G-18244)***
Conventional Graphics Inc....231 943-4301
11682 Us Highway 31 Interlochen (49643) ***(G-8681)***
Convergence Technologies, Holland *Also called Ghsp Inc* ***(G-8050)***
Convergent Solutions LLC....616 490-8747
4343 S Montcalm Ave Lowell (49331) ***(G-10499)***
Convex Mold Inc....586 978-0808
35360 Beattie Dr Sterling Heights (48312) ***(G-15971)***
Conveyor Components, Croswell *Also called Material Control Inc* ***(G-3732)***
Conveyor Concepts Michigan LLC....616 997-5200
743 Main St Coopersville (49404) ***(G-3683)***
Conveyor Systems, Alpena *Also called Csi Service Parts Corp* ***(G-289)***
Conway Detroit Corporation....586 552-8413
28070 Hayes Rd Roseville (48066) ***(G-14389)***
Conway Products Corporation....616 698-2601
4150 East Paris Ave Se # 1 Grand Rapids (49512) ***(G-6603)***
Conway Publications....517 424-1614
9390 Newburg Ct Tecumseh (49286) ***(G-16494)***
Conway-Cleveland Corp (PA)....616 458-0056
2320 Oak Industrial Dr Ne Grand Rapids (49505) ***(G-6604)***
Cook Industries Inc....586 754-4070
23515 Pinewood St Warren (48091) ***(G-17764)***
Cook Sign Plus....586 254-7000
48534 Van Dyke Ave Shelby Township (48317) ***(G-15196)***
Cookie Bouquet, Rochester Hills *Also called Carlson Enterprises Inc* ***(G-13972)***
Cookie Music Ent LLC....209 851-6633
19400 Syracuse St Detroit (48234) ***(G-4103)***
Cooks Blacksmith Welding Inc....231 796-6819
402 Bjornson St Big Rapids (49307) ***(G-1671)***
Cool Artesian Water, Crystal Falls *Also called Crystal Falls Springs Inc* ***(G-3741)***
Cool Products Division, Ann Arbor *Also called Tecumseh Products Company LLC* ***(G-679)***
Coolant Chillers, Lansing *Also called Fluid Chillers Inc* ***(G-9837)***
Cooler King LLC....248 789-3699
35500 Central City Pkwy Westland (48185) ***(G-18361)***
Cooper & Cooper Sales Inc....810 327-6247
851 W Pointe Port Huron (48060) ***(G-13465)***
Cooper Foundry Inc....269 343-2808
8216 Douglas Ave Kalamazoo (49009) ***(G-9155)***
Cooper Genomics....313 579-9650
705 S Main St Plymouth (48170) ***(G-13150)***
Cooper Publishing Group LLC....231 933-9958
251 Knollwood Dr Traverse City (49686) ***(G-16659)***
Cooper Rolland....734 482-8705
5546 Grayfield Cir Ypsilanti (48197) ***(G-18933)***
COOPER STANDARD, Northville *Also called Cooper-Standard Holdings Inc* ***(G-12207)***
Cooper-Standard Auto OH LLC....248 596-5900
40300 Traditions Dr Northville (48168) ***(G-12203)***
Cooper-Standard Automotive Inc (HQ)....248 596-5900
40300 Traditions Dr Northville (48168) ***(G-12204)***
Cooper-Standard Automotive Inc....734 542-6300
11820 Globe St Livonia (48150) ***(G-10164)***
Cooper-Standard Automotive Inc....248 630-7262
2545 N Opdyke Rd Ste 102 Auburn Hills (48326) ***(G-850)***
Cooper-Standard Automotive Inc....989 848-2272
2799 E Miller Rd Fairview (48621) ***(G-5129)***
Cooper-Standard Fhs LLC....248 596-5900
40300 Traditions Dr Northville (48168) ***(G-12205)***

Cooper-Standard Foundation Inc 248 596-5900
40300 Traditions Dr Northville (48168) *(G-12206)*
Cooper-Standard Holdings Inc (PA) 248 596-5900
40300 Traditions Dr Northville (48168) *(G-12207)*
Cooper-Stndard Indus Spclty Gr (HQ) 330 339-3373
40300 Traditions Dr Northville (48168) *(G-12208)*
Cooper-Stndard Indus Spclty Gr (HQ) 248 596-5900
40300 Traditions Dr Northville (48168) *(G-12209)*
Coopersville Observer Inc 616 997-5049
1374 W Randall St Coopersville (49404) *(G-3684)*
Copeland-Gibson Products Corp 248 740-4400
1025 E Maple Rd Troy (48083) *(G-17028)*
Copilot Printing 248 797-0150
3754 Tyler Ave Berkley (48072) *(G-1625)*
Coplas Inc 586 739-8940
6700 18 1/2 Mile Rd Sterling Heights (48314) *(G-15972)*
Coplas-Tiercon, Sterling Heights *Also called Coplas Inc* *(G-15972)*
Copper Kettle Distilling Co 989 366-4412
939 W Houghton Lake Dr Prudenville (48651) *(G-13657)*
Coppercraft Distillery LLC 616 796-8274
196 120th Ave Holland (49424) *(G-8005)*
Coppertec Inc 313 278-0139
2424 Beech Daly Rd Inkster (48141) *(G-8661)*
Copperwood Resources Inc 906 229-3115
310 E Us Highway 2 Wakefield (49968) *(G-17618)*
Copy Cat Sign & Print, Marysville *Also called Van Kehrberg Vern* *(G-11111)*
Copy Central Inc 231 941-2298
314 E Eighth St Traverse City (49684) *(G-16660)*
Copy Connection LLC 734 425-3150
6500 Nollar Rd Whitmore Lake (48189) *(G-18529)*
Copy Copy Center, Warren *Also called Bi-Rite Office Products Inc* *(G-17735)*
Copyrite Printing Inc 586 774-0006
30503 Gratiot Ave Roseville (48066) *(G-14390)*
Copytwo Inc 734 665-9200
611 Church St Ann Arbor (48104) *(G-437)*
Cor Health, Flushing *Also called Vets Access LLC* *(G-5815)*
Cor-Met Inc 810 227-0004
12500 Grand River Rd Brighton (48116) *(G-1966)*
Corban Industries Inc 248 393-2720
4590 Joslyn Rd Orion (48359) *(G-12726)*
Core Electric Company Inc (PA) 313 382-7140
25125 Outer Dr Melvindale (48122) *(G-11198)*
Core Energy LLC 231 946-2419
1011 Noteware Dr Traverse City (49686) *(G-16661)*
Core Energy and Automation LLC 248 830-0476
35245 Schoolcraft Rd Livonia (48150) *(G-10165)*
Core Lite Industries LLC 616 481-3940
8901 Cedar Lake Dr Jenison (49428) *(G-9050)*
Core Technology Corporation 517 627-1521
11518 Millstone Dr Grand Ledge (48837) *(G-6387)*
Core-Lite Industries LLC 616 843-5993
13354 Greenleaf Ln Grand Haven (49417) *(G-6288)*
Core-Lite Industries LLC 616 822-7587
13750 172nd Ave Ste A Grand Haven (49417) *(G-6289)*
Coreled Systems LLC 734 516-2060
31478 Industrial Rd # 400 Livonia (48150) *(G-10166)*
Corey 313 565-8501
3125 Walnut St Dearborn (48124) *(G-3822)*
Corey's Bootery, Kalamazoo *Also called Kalamazoo Orthotics & Dbtc* *(G-9244)*
Corian By Solicor Industries, Livonia *Also called Sol-I-Cor Industries* *(G-10413)*
Corium Inc 616 656-4563
4558 50th St Se Grand Rapids (49512) *(G-6605)*
Corium Inc (HQ) 650 298-8255
4558 50th St Se Grand Rapids (49512) *(G-6606)*
Corky's Bar and Restaurant, Taylor *Also called Hancock Enterprises Inc* *(G-16424)*
Corlett-Turner Co 616 772-9082
2500 104th Ave Zeeland (49464) *(G-19007)*
Corlett-Turner Co 616 772-9082
1060 Kn O Sha Indus Dr Se Grand Rapids (49508) *(G-6607)*
Corlin Company 616 842-7093
1640 Marion Ave Grand Haven (49417) *(G-6290)*
Corls Kiln 989 673-4925
2978 W Deckerville Rd Caro (48723) *(G-2568)*
Cornbelt Beef Corporation 313 237-0087
14150 Ludlow Pl Oak Park (48237) *(G-12598)*
Cornelius Systems Inc (PA) 248 545-5558
1302 Anderson Rd Clawson (48017) *(G-3091)*
Cornell Publications LLC 810 225-3075
11075 Shadywood Dr Brighton (48114) *(G-1967)*
Corner Brewery LLC 734 480-2739
720 Norris St Ypsilanti (48198) *(G-18934)*
Corners Limited (PA) 269 353-8311
628 S 8th St Kalamazoo (49009) *(G-9156)*
Cornerstone Fabg & Cnstr Inc (PA) 989 642-5241
667 Watson Rd Hemlock (48626) *(G-7850)*
Cornerstone Furniture Inc 269 795-3379
1035 E State St Hastings (49058) *(G-7784)*
Cornhole America, Cedar Springs *Also called Sly Fox Prints LLC* *(G-2661)*
Cornhole Stop LLC 704 728-1550
6050 Sundance Trl Brighton (48116) *(G-1968)*
Cornillie Concrete, Cadillac *Also called Lc Materials LLC* *(G-2342)*
Cornillie Concrete, Farmington Hills *Also called Bwb LLC* *(G-5189)*
Cornillie Concrete 231 439-9200
710 W Conway Rd Harbor Springs (49740) *(G-7645)*
Corning Incorporated 248 680-4701
50 W Big Beavr Rd Ste 225 Troy (48084) *(G-17029)*
Corporate, Northville *Also called Spiders Software Solutions LLC* *(G-12262)*
Corporate Electronic Sty Inc 248 583-7070
2708 American Dr Troy (48083) *(G-17030)*
Corr Pack In 248 348-4188
9833 5 Mile Rd Northville (48168) *(G-12210)*
Corr-Fac Corporation 989 358-7050
4040 Us Highway 23 N Alpena (49707) *(G-288)*
Correct Compression Inc 231 864-2101
11903 Chippewa Hwy Bear Lake (49614) *(G-1417)*
Corrigan Enterprises Inc 810 229-6323
775 N 2nd St Brighton (48116) *(G-1969)*
Corrugated Pratt 734 853-3030
32432 Capitol St Livonia (48150) *(G-10167)*
Corrugating Division, Grand Rapids *Also called Pratt Industries Inc* *(G-7096)*
Corsair Engineering Inc (PA) 810 233-0440
3020 Airpark Dr S Flint (48507) *(G-5672)*
Corsair Engineering Inc 810 234-3664
2702 N Dort Hwy Flint (48506) *(G-5673)*
Corson Fabricating LLC 810 326-0532
1701 Sinclair St Ste B Saint Clair (48079) *(G-14820)*
Cortar Laser and Fab LLC 248 446-1110
12828 Emerson Dr Brighton (48116) *(G-1970)*
Corteva Agriscience LLC 989 479-3245
305 N Huron Ave Harbor Beach (48441) *(G-7630)*
Corunna Mills Feed LLC 989 743-3110
417 S Shiawassee St Corunna (48817) *(G-3707)*
Corvac Composites LLC 616 281-2430
4450 36th St Se Grand Rapids (49512) *(G-6608)*
Corvac Composites LLC (HQ) 616 281-4028
4450 36th St Se Kentwood (49512) *(G-9449)*
Corvette Central, Sawyer *Also called CC Industries LLC* *(G-15108)*
Cosella Dorken Products Inc 888 433-5824
1795 Chase Dr Rochester (48307) *(G-13896)*
Cosma Body Assembly Michigan, New Hudson *Also called Magna Services America Inc* *(G-12061)*
Cosma Casting Michigan, Battle Creek *Also called Dieomatic Incorporated* *(G-1219)*
Cosma Engineering, Troy *Also called Vehma International Amer Inc* *(G-17434)*
Cosma Engineering, Troy *Also called Cosma International Amer Inc* *(G-17031)*
Cosma Engineering, Troy *Also called Vehma International Amer Inc* *(G-17436)*
Cosma International Amer Inc (HQ) 248 631-1100
750 Tower Dr Troy (48098) *(G-17031)*
Cosner Ice Company Inc 812 279-8930
1755 Yeager St Port Huron (48060) *(G-13466)*
Costello Machine LLC 586 749-0136
56358 Precision Dr Chesterfield (48051) *(G-2861)*
Cotson Fabricating Inc 248 589-2758
5971 Product Dr Sterling Heights (48312) *(G-15973)*
Cotton Concepts Printing LLC 313 444-3857
1220 Longfellow St Detroit (48202) *(G-4104)*
Cougar Cutting Tools Inc 586 469-1310
23529 Reynolds Ct Clinton Township (48036) *(G-3212)*
Council For Edctl Trvl US Amer 949 940-1140
678 Front Ave Nw Ste 91a Grand Rapids (49504) *(G-6609)*
Counter Point Furniture Pdts, Spring Lake *Also called Jsj Corporation* *(G-15828)*
Counter Reaction LLC 248 624-7900
46915 Liberty Dr Wixom (48393) *(G-18636)*
Counterpoint By Hlf 734 699-7100
44001 Van Born Rd Van Buren Twp (48111) *(G-17521)*
Country Candles 231 327-2730
2832 S Laurel Dr White Cloud (49349) *(G-18440)*
Country Choice Inc 616 241-6043
2511 Ancient Dr Sw Wyoming (49519) *(G-18861)*
Country Custom Cabinets 937 354-2163
57440 Butcher Rd Lawrence (49064) *(G-9981)*
Country Dairy Inc (PA) 231 861-4636
3476 S 80th Ave New ERA (49446) *(G-12027)*
Country Fresh LLC 734 261-7980
28795 Goddard Rd Ste 204 Romulus (48174) *(G-14264)*
Country Home Creations Inc 810 244-7348
5132 Richfield Rd Flint (48506) *(G-5674)*
Country Mill Farms LLC 517 543-1019
4648 Otto Rd Charlotte (48813) *(G-2745)*
Country Register of Mich Inc 989 793-4211
3790 Manistee St Saginaw (48603) *(G-14632)*
Country Schoolhouse Kingsford 906 828-1971
600 East Blvd Kingsford (49802) *(G-9507)*
Country Side Sawmill 989 352-7198
7682 N Greenville Rd Lakeview (48850) *(G-9640)*
Countryside Foods LLC (HQ) 586 447-3500
26661 Bunert Rd Warren (48089) *(G-17765)*

A L P H A B E T I C

Countryside Quality Meats LLC 517 741-4275
1184 Adolph Rd Union City (49094) ***(G-17491)***
Counts Investment Group LLC 313 613-6866
18635 Ohio St Detroit (48221) ***(G-4105)***
County Journal Inc 517 543-1099
241 S Cochran Ave Ste 1 Charlotte (48813) ***(G-2746)***
County Line Pallet 231 834-8416
2031 22 Mile Rd Kent City (49330) ***(G-9430)***
County of Muskegon 231 744-3580
1563 Scenic Dr Muskegon (49445) ***(G-11796)***
County of St Clair 810 982-4111
1221 Pine Grove Ave Port Huron (48060) ***(G-13467)***
Court-Side Inc 269 948-2811
122 W Mill St Hastings (49058) ***(G-7785)***
Covalent Medical Inc 734 604-0688
4750 S State Rd Ann Arbor (48108) ***(G-438)***
Covenant Cpitl Investments Inc 248 477-4230
49175 West Rd Wixom (48393) ***(G-18637)***
Coventry Creations Inc (PA) 248 547-2987
195 W 9 Mile Rd Ferndale (48220) ***(G-5536)***
Coventry Creations Inc 248 545-8360
930 E Lewiston Ave Ferndale (48220) ***(G-5537)***
Coventry Industries LLC 248 761-8462
313 E Sherman St Holly (48442) ***(G-8263)***
Coveris 269 964-1130
155 Brook St Battle Creek (49037) ***(G-1212)***
Covestro LLC 248 475-7700
2401 E Walton Blvd Auburn Hills (48326) ***(G-851)***
Covia Solutions Inc 800 255-7263
400 Riverview Dr Ste 302 Benton Harbor (49022) ***(G-1543)***
Covisint Corporation (HQ) 248 483-2000
26533 Evergreen Rd # 500 Southfield (48076) ***(G-15533)***
Cox Brothers Machining Inc 517 796-4662
2300 E Ganson St Jackson (49202) ***(G-8855)***
Cox Industries Inc (PA) 586 749-6650
30800 26 Mile Rd Chesterfield (48051) ***(G-2862)***
Cox Machine LLC 269 953-5446
2823 Cass Rd Ste F1 Traverse City (49684) ***(G-16662)***
Coxen Enterprises Inc 248 486-3800
12785 Emerson Dr Brighton (48116) ***(G-1971)***
Coxline Inc 269 345-1132
2829 N Burdick St Kalamazoo (49004) ***(G-9157)***
Coy Laboratory Products Inc 734 433-9296
14500 Coy Dr Grass Lake (49240) ***(G-7436)***
Coye's Canvas & Awnings, Grand Rapids *Also called Case-Free Inc* ***(G-6558)***
Coye's Canvas and Awning, Grand Rapids *Also called Cut Once LLC* ***(G-6624)***
Cozart Producers 810 736-1046
3130 Mcclure Ave Flint (48506) ***(G-5675)***
Cozy Cup Coffee Company Llc 989 984-7619
4083 Denise Ct Oscoda (48750) ***(G-12755)***
CP Acquisition LLC 248 349-8811
28016 Oakland Oaks Ct Wixom (48393) ***(G-18638)***
CPI Creative Products, Holland *Also called Creative Products Intl* ***(G-8007)***
Cpj Company Inc 616 784-6355
3739 Laramie Dr Ne Comstock Park (49321) ***(G-3598)***
CPM Acquisition Corp 231 947-6400
2412 W Aero Park Ct Traverse City (49686) ***(G-16663)***
CPM Acquisition Corp 231 947-6400
2412 W Aero Park Ct Traverse City (49686) ***(G-16664)***
CPM Century Extrusion, Traverse City *Also called CPM Acquisition Corp* ***(G-16664)***
CPM Services Group Inc 248 624-5100
47924 West Rd Wixom (48393) ***(G-18639)***
Cpr Inc 734 459-7251
44029 S Umberland Cir Canton (48187) ***(G-2452)***
CPR III Inc 248 652-2900
380 South St Rochester (48307) ***(G-13897)***
Cpr Racing, Troy *Also called Creative Performance Racg LLC* ***(G-17032)***
CPS LLC 517 639-1464
11 E Chicago St Quincy (49082) ***(G-13666)***
Cq Simple LLC 989 492-7068
5103 Eastman Ave Ste 125 Midland (48640) ***(G-11331)***
Cr Forge LLC 231 924-2033
1914 S Comstock Ave Fremont (49412) ***(G-6038)***
Cracker Publishing LLC 248 429-9098
28339 Beck Rd Ste F6 Wixom (48393) ***(G-18640)***
Craft Electric 517 529-7164
245 Hyde Rd Clarklake (49234) ***(G-3005)***
Craft Industries Inc 586 726-4300
13231 23 Mile Rd Shelby Township (48315) ***(G-15197)***
Craft Precision Inc 269 679-5121
610 E Eliza St Schoolcraft (49087) ***(G-15117)***
Craft Press Printing Inc 269 683-9694
312 Bell Rd Niles (49120) ***(G-12121)***
Craft Room, Union City *Also called Millworks Engineering Inc* ***(G-17496)***
Craft Steel Products Inc 616 935-7575
16885 148th Ave Spring Lake (49456) ***(G-15809)***
Craftwood Industries Inc 616 796-1209
2530 Kamar Dr Holland (49424) ***(G-8006)***
Craig Assembly Inc 810 326-1374
1111 Fred W Moore Hwy Saint Clair (48079) ***(G-14821)***
Craig EDM, Farmington Hills *Also called C L Design Inc* ***(G-5190)***
Craigs Signs 810 667-7446
1498 N Saginaw St Ste 2 Lapeer (48446) ***(G-9923)***
Crain Communications Inc (PA) 313 446-6000
1155 Gratiot Ave Detroit (48207) ***(G-4106)***
Crain Family Bible 734 673-8620
11399 Saddlebrook Cir Pinckney (48169) ***(G-13045)***
Cramblits Welding LLC 906 932-3773
1215 Wall St Ironwood (49938) ***(G-8760)***
Crandall Precision Inc 231 775-7101
615 5th St Cadillac (49601) ***(G-2327)***
Crandell Bros Trucking Co 517 543-2930
800 Island Hwy Charlotte (48813) ***(G-2747)***
Crane 1 Services Inc 586 468-0909
42827 Irwin Dr Harrison Township (48045) ***(G-7694)***
Crane Pro Services, Novi *Also called Konecranes Inc* ***(G-12454)***
Crane Technologies Group Inc 248 652-8700
1954 Rochester Indus Dr Rochester Hills (48309) ***(G-13985)***
Crankshaft Craftsman Inc 313 366-0140
1960 W West Maple Rd Commerce Township (48390) ***(G-3519)***
Crankshaft Machine Company (HQ) 517 787-3791
314 N Jackson St Jackson (49201) ***(G-8856)***
Crash Tool Inc 517 552-0250
1225 Fendt Dr Howell (48843) ***(G-8441)***
Crawford Associates Inc 248 549-9494
4526 Fernlee Ave Royal Oak (48073) ***(G-14527)***
Crawford County Avalanche 989 348-6811
108 E Michigan Ave Grayling (49738) ***(G-7458)***
Crawford Forest Products 989 742-3855
705 E Progress St Hillman (49746) ***(G-7912)***
Crazy Metals LLC 810 730-9489
6279 Porter Rd Grand Blanc (48439) ***(G-6239)***
Crazy Red Head Publishing 248 862-6096
3900 Walnut Lake Rd West Bloomfield (48323) ***(G-18272)***
Crb Crane Services Inc (PA) 517 552-5699
1194 Austin Ct Howell (48843) ***(G-8442)***
CRC Industries Inc 313 883-6977
14650 Dequindre St Detroit (48212) ***(G-4107)***
Cream Cup Dairy 231 889-4158
7377 Feldhak Rd Kaleva (49645) ***(G-9377)***
Creation Highway 307 220-7309
160 Canfield St Milan (48160) ***(G-11434)***
Creative Automation Solutions 313 790-4848
34552 Dover Ave Livonia (48150) ***(G-10168)***
Creative Characters Inc 231 544-6084
7924 Cameron St Central Lake (49622) ***(G-2692)***
Creative Cntrls Hndcpped Drvin, Madison Heights *Also called Creative Controls Inc* ***(G-10698)***
Creative Composites Inc 906 474-9941
7637 Us Highway 2 Rapid River (49878) ***(G-13683)***
Creative Controls Inc 248 577-9800
32217 Stephenson Hwy Madison Heights (48071) ***(G-10698)***
Creative Designs & Signs Inc 248 334-5580
146 Cesar E Chavez Ave Pontiac (48342) ***(G-13356)***
Creative Embossing 248 851-1302
6730 E Dartmoor Rd West Bloomfield (48322) ***(G-18273)***
Creative Engineering Inc 734 996-5900
7621 E Joy Rd Ann Arbor (48105) ***(G-439)***
Creative Eyeball Agency 517 398-8008
11 E Chicago St Quincy (49082) ***(G-13667)***
Creative Foam Cmpsite Systems 810 629-4149
6401 Taylor Dr Flint (48507) ***(G-5676)***
Creative Foam Corporation (PA) 810 629-4149
300 N Alloy Dr Fenton (48430) ***(G-5467)***
Creative Foam Corporation 269 782-3483
55210 Rudy Rd Dowagiac (49047) ***(G-4779)***
Creative Foam Corporation 810 714-0140
555 N Fenway Dr Fenton (48430) ***(G-5468)***
Creative Form Corp 810 714-5860
1100 Copper Ave Fenton (48430) ***(G-5469)***
Creative Graphic Concepts, Royal Oak *Also called Crawford Associates Inc* ***(G-14527)***
Creative Graphics Inc 517 784-0391
430 N Mechanic St Jackson (49201) ***(G-8857)***
Creative Health Products, Ann Arbor *Also called Creative Engineering Inc* ***(G-439)***
Creative Image & Printing LLC 586 222-4288
34841 Mound Rd Ste 291 Sterling Heights (48310) ***(G-15974)***
Creative Kids Publication, Bruce Twp *Also called Your Hometown Shopper LLC* ***(G-2187)***
Creative Loop 231 629-8228
21241 Northland Dr Paris (49338) ***(G-12932)***
Creative Machine Company 248 669-4230
50140 Pontiac Trl Wixom (48393) ***(G-18641)***
Creative Machining Inc 616 772-2328
2620 Remico St Sw Wyoming (49519) ***(G-18862)***
Creative Performance Racg LLC 248 250-6187
120 Birchwood Dr Troy (48083) ***(G-17032)***
Creative Power Systems Inc 313 961-2460
1921 10th St Detroit (48216) ***(G-4108)***
Creative Print Crew LLC 248 629-9404
1119 Rochester Rd Troy (48083) ***(G-17033)***

ALPHABETIC SECTION
Csquared Innovations Inc

Creative Printing & Graphics...810 235-8815
430 S Dort Hwy Flint (48503) ***(G-5677)***
Creative Printing Solutions...616 931-1040
201 W Washington Ave # 66 Zeeland (49464) ***(G-19008)***
Creative Products Intl...616 335-3333
A-4699 61st St Unit H Holland (49423) ***(G-8007)***
Creative Repair Solutions LLC...586 615-1517
51821 Industrial Dr Macomb (48042) ***(G-10586)***
Creative Solutions Group Inc (PA)...248 288-9700
1250 N Crooks Rd Clawson (48017) ***(G-3092)***
Creative Solutions Group Inc...734 425-2257
12285 Dixie Redford (48239) ***(G-13727)***
Creative Steel Rule Dies Inc...630 307-8880
4157 Stafford Ave Sw Grand Rapids (49548) ***(G-6610)***
Creative Stitching...248 210-9584
1155 Purdy Ln Howell (48843) ***(G-8443)***
Creative Store Fixtures, Warren *Also called Frank Terlecki Company Inc* ***(G-17818)***
Creative Surfaces Inc...586 226-2950
20500 Hall Rd Clinton Township (48038) ***(G-3213)***
Creative Techniques Inc...248 373-3050
200 Northpointe Dr Orion (48359) ***(G-12727)***
Creative Visions Publishing Co...248 545-3528
14280 Elgin St Oak Park (48237) ***(G-12599)***
Creative Woodworks, Plymouth *Also called Donald K Stappert* ***(G-13161)***
Creativitees Studio...586 565-2213
54470 Aurora Park Shelby Township (48316) ***(G-15198)***
Creek Diesel Services Inc...800 974-4600
3748 Water Leaf Ct Ne Grand Rapids (49525) ***(G-6611)***
Creek Plastics LLC...517 423-1003
638 W Maumee St Adrian (49221) ***(G-57)***
Creekside Lumber...231 924-1934
3810 W 72nd St Newaygo (49337) ***(G-12079)***
Creform Corporation...248 926-2555
29795 Hudson Dr Novi (48377) ***(G-12385)***
Creme Curls Bakery Inc...616 669-6230
5292 Lawndale Ave Hudsonville (49426) ***(G-8575)***
Crescent Casting Inc...248 541-1052
8720 Northend Ave Oak Park (48237) ***(G-12600)***
Crescent Div Key Gas Cmponents, Allegan *Also called Key Gas Components Inc* ***(G-163)***
Crescent Machining Inc...248 541-7010
8720 Northend Ave Oak Park (48237) ***(G-12601)***
Crescent Manufacturing Company...517 486-2670
368 Sherman St Blissfield (49228) ***(G-1763)***
Crescent Pattern Company...248 541-1052
8720 Northend Ave Oak Park (48237) ***(G-12602)***
Crescive Die and Tool Inc...734 482-0303
905 Woodland Dr Saline (48176) ***(G-15010)***
Crest Boats, Owosso *Also called Maurell Products Inc* ***(G-12841)***
Crest Marine LLC...989 725-5188
2710 S M 52 Owosso (48867) ***(G-12828)***
Crete Dry-Mix & Supply Co...616 784-5790
20 N Park St Comstock Park (49321) ***(G-3599)***
Crew Family Rest & Bky LLC...269 337-9800
3810 E Cork St Kalamazoo (49001) ***(G-9158)***
Crew, The, Kalamazoo *Also called Crew Family Rest & Bky LLC* ***(G-9158)***
Crewbotiq LLC...248 939-4229
755 W Big Beaver Rd # 2020 Troy (48084) ***(G-17034)***
Crg Directories, Eaton Rapids *Also called Total Local Acquisitions LLC* ***(G-4974)***
Crg Directories, Eaton Rapids *Also called Adtek Graphics Inc* ***(G-4950)***
Crimson Craft Co, Fenton *Also called Melissa Fowler* ***(G-5491)***
Crippen Manufacturing Company...989 681-4323
400 Woodside Dr Saint Louis (48880) ***(G-14990)***
Crk Ltd...586 779-5240
23205 Gratiot Ave Eastpointe (48021) ***(G-4933)***
Crl Inc...906 428-3710
623 Rains Dr Gladstone (49837) ***(G-6177)***
Crm Inc...231 947-0304
495 W South Airport Rd Traverse City (49686) ***(G-16665)***
Crop Marks Printing...616 356-5555
128 Coldbrook St Ne Grand Rapids (49503) ***(G-6612)***
Cross Chemical Company, Westland *Also called Cross Technologies Group Inc* ***(G-18362)***
Cross Country Oilfld Svcs Inc...337 366-3840
4833 Linda Ln Metamora (48455) ***(G-11278)***
Cross Paths Corp...616 248-5371
955 Ken O Sha Ind Park Dr Grand Rapids (49508) ***(G-6613)***
Cross Technologies Group Inc...734 895-8084
1210 Manufacturers Dr Westland (48186) ***(G-18362)***
Crossbrook LLC...616 772-5921
3255 Production Ct Unit B Zeeland (49464) ***(G-19009)***
Crosscon Industries LLC...248 852-5888
2889 Bond St Rochester Hills (48309) ***(G-13986)***
Crossroads Industries Inc...989 732-1233
2464 Silver Fox Trl Gaylord (49735) ***(G-6124)***
Crow & Moss Chocolate, Petoskey *Also called Crow and Moss LLC* ***(G-12995)***
Crow and Moss LLC...231 838-9875
1601 Standish Ave Unit 3 Petoskey (49770) ***(G-12995)***
Crow Forge...269 948-5346
2563 N Charlton Park Rd Hastings (49058) ***(G-7786)***

Crown Boring Industries LLC...586 447-3900
15985 Sturgeon St Roseville (48066) ***(G-14391)***
Crown Coat, Grand Rapids *Also called Wealthy Street Corporation* ***(G-7326)***
Crown Equipment Corporation...616 530-3000
903 Lynch Dr Ste 103 Traverse City (49686) ***(G-16666)***
Crown Equipment Corporation...616 530-3000
4131 Roger Chaffee Mem Se Grand Rapids (49548) ***(G-6614)***
Crown Group Co...313 922-8433
15794 Nicolai Ave Eastpointe (48021) ***(G-4934)***
Crown Group Co (HQ)...586 575-9800
5875 New King Ct Troy (48098) ***(G-17035)***
Crown Group Detroit Plant, Eastpointe *Also called Crown Group Co* ***(G-4934)***
Crown Group, The, Shelby Township *Also called Cg Liquidation Incorporated* ***(G-15185)***
Crown Heating Inc...248 352-1688
24521 W Mcnichols Rd Detroit (48219) ***(G-4109)***
Crown Industrial Services Inc (PA)...734 483-7270
2480 Airport Dr Ypsilanti (48198) ***(G-18935)***
Crown Industrial Services Inc...734 483-7270
924 Minion St Ypsilanti (48198) ***(G-18936)***
Crown Industrial Services Inc...517 905-5300
2080 Brooklyn Rd Jackson (49203) ***(G-8858)***
Crown Lift Trucks, Traverse City *Also called Crown Equipment Corporation* ***(G-16666)***
Crown Lift Trucks, Grand Rapids *Also called Crown Equipment Corporation* ***(G-6614)***
Crown Manufacturing LLC...616 295-7018
6262 N Moe Rd Middleville (49333) ***(G-11305)***
Crown Steel Rail Co (PA)...248 593-7100
6347 Northfield Rd West Bloomfield (48322) ***(G-18274)***
Crown Tumbling, Ypsilanti *Also called Crown Industrial Services Inc* ***(G-18935)***
Crowne Group LLC...734 855-4512
17199 N Laurel Park Dr # 322 Livonia (48152) ***(G-10169)***
Croze Nest Cooperage LLC...616 805-9132
316 Collindale Ave Sw Grand Rapids (49534) ***(G-6615)***
Croze Nest Oak Barrels, Grand Rapids *Also called Croze Nest Cooperage LLC* ***(G-6615)***
Crumbl Cookies Grand Rapids, Grand Rapids *Also called Actt Management LLC* ***(G-6425)***
Cruse Hardwood Lumber Inc...517 688-4891
2499 Cole St Birmingham (48009) ***(G-1723)***
Crushing Hearts and Black...224 234-9677
25515 Hillsdale Dr Novi (48374) ***(G-12386)***
Cruux LLC...248 515-8411
4897 River Bank Ct Troy (48085) ***(G-17036)***
Crystal Cut Tool Inc...734 946-0099
10360 Harrison Romulus (48174) ***(G-14265)***
Crystal Falls Springs Inc...906 875-3191
346 Rock Crusher Rd Crystal Falls (49920) ***(G-3741)***
Crystal Ice Resource LLC...616 560-8102
6054 S Moorland Rd Ravenna (49451) ***(G-13688)***
Crystal Lk Aprtmnts Fmly Ltd P (PA)...586 731-3500
2001 Crystal Lake Dr Shelby Township (48316) ***(G-15199)***
Crystal Machine & Tool Inc...586 552-1503
21986 Schmeman Ave Warren (48089) ***(G-17766)***
Crystal Vista Vineyard LLC...231 269-4165
10911 Heuser Hwy Thompsonville (49683) ***(G-16553)***
Cs Express Inc...248 425-1726
2181 Siboney Ct Rochester Hills (48309) ***(G-13987)***
Cs Intermediate Holdco 1 LLC...248 596-5900
40300 Traditions Dr Northville (48168) ***(G-12211)***
Cs Manufacturing Inc...616 696-2772
299 W Cherry St Cedar Springs (49319) ***(G-2647)***
Cs Tool Engineering Inc...616 696-0940
251 W Cherry St Cedar Springs (49319) ***(G-2648)***
Cs Vendetta Pub LLC...616 422-7555
2330 Valleywood Dr Se K5 Grand Rapids (49546) ***(G-6616)***
Cs X Press Inc...586 864-3360
5621 Toronto Dr Sterling Heights (48314) ***(G-15975)***
Csa Services Inc...248 596-6184
39550 Orchard Hill Pl Novi (48375) ***(G-12387)***
CSB Industries LLC...231 651-9484
90 S Haze Rd Beulah (49617) ***(G-1654)***
Cse Morse Inc...269 962-5548
17 Race Ct Battle Creek (49017) ***(G-1213)***
Csg Storage Facility, Redford *Also called Creative Solutions Group Inc* ***(G-13727)***
Csh Incorporated...989 723-8985
2151 W M 21 Ste A Owosso (48867) ***(G-12829)***
Csi Emergency Apparatus LLC...989 348-2877
2332 Dupont St Grayling (49738) ***(G-7459)***
Csi Service Parts Corp...989 358-7199
1995 Hamilton Rd Alpena (49707) ***(G-289)***
CSM Cold Heading, Farmington Hills *Also called C S M Manufacturing Corp* ***(G-5192)***
CSM Products Inc...248 836-4995
1920 Opdyke Ct Ste 200 Auburn Hills (48326) ***(G-852)***
Csn Manufacturing Inc...616 364-0027
1750 Elizabeth Ave Nw Grand Rapids (49504) ***(G-6617)***
CSP Holding Corp (HQ)...248 237-7800
255 Rex Blvd Auburn Hills (48326) ***(G-853)***
CSP Holding Corp...248 724-4410
1200 Harmon Rd Auburn Hills (48326) ***(G-854)***
CSP Truck, Troy *Also called Central Screw Products Company* ***(G-17006)***
Csquared Innovations Inc...734 998-8330
45145 W 12 Mile Rd Novi (48377) ***(G-12388)***

ALPHABETIC

CST, Zeeland *Also called Spurt Industries LLC* ***(G-19080)***
CT Automotive, Livonia *Also called Ims/Chinatool Jv LLC* ***(G-10247)***
CT Custom Collision LLC......313 912-9776
8330 Pinehurst St Detroit (48204) ***(G-4110)***
CTA Acoustics Inc (HQ)......248 544-2580
25211 Dequindre Rd Madison Heights (48071) ***(G-10699)***
Ctc Acquisition Company LLC......616 884-7100
825 Northland Dr Ne Rockford (49341) ***(G-14163)***
CTC Distribution Inc (PA)......313 486-2225
20200 E 9 Mile Rd Saint Clair Shores (48080) ***(G-14854)***
Ctc Fabricators LLC......586 242-8809
8797 Stone Rd Clay (48001) ***(G-3118)***
Ctcm Auburn Hills, Auburn Hills *Also called Borgwrner Prplsion Systems LLC* ***(G-832)***
Cte Publishing LLC......313 338-4335
18451 Rosemont Ave Detroit (48219) ***(G-4111)***
CTI, Grand Rapids *Also called Compressor Technologies Inc* ***(G-6590)***
Ctmf Inc......734 482-3086
924 Minion St Ypsilanti (48198) ***(G-18937)***
Ctmi Group Inc......248 542-1615
29800 Stephenson Hwy Madison Heights (48071) ***(G-10700)***
CTS Manufacturing Inc......586 465-4594
44760 Trinity Dr Clinton Township (48038) ***(G-3214)***
CTS Welding......269 521-4481
39065 County Road 388 Bloomingdale (49026) ***(G-1876)***
Cuadvantage Mktg Solutions, Saginaw *Also called Reimold Printing Corporation* ***(G-14736)***
Cubbie Publications......248 852-5297
590 Lehigh Rd Rochester Hills (48307) ***(G-13988)***
Cube Tracker LLC......269 436-1270
46980 86th Ave Decatur (49045) ***(G-3945)***
Cucina Moda - Birmingham LLC (PA)......248 792-2285
1700 Stutz Dr Ste 37 Troy (48084) ***(G-17037)***
Cujographyx LLC......248 318-6407
18812 Glenmore Redford (48240) ***(G-13728)***
Cul-Mac Industries Inc......734 728-9700
3720 Venoy Rd Wayne (48184) ***(G-18219)***
Cultivation Station Inc......313 383-1766
6540 Allen Rd Allen Park (48101) ***(G-191)***
Cultured Love LLC......703 362-5991
2752 Meadow Dr Zeeland (49464) ***(G-19010)***
Culver J Manufacturing Company......248 541-0297
520 Forest Ave Royal Oak (48067) ***(G-14528)***
Cumberland Furniture, Grand Rapids *Also called S F Gilmore Inc* ***(G-7175)***
Cummings-Moore Graphite Co......313 841-1615
1646 N Green St Detroit (48209) ***(G-4112)***
Cummins Bridgeway, New Hudson *Also called K & S Property Inc* ***(G-12059)***
Cummins Bridgeway Grove Cy LLC......614 604-6000
21810 Clessie Ct New Hudson (48165) ***(G-12047)***
Cummins Inc......586 469-2010
43575 N Gratiot Ave Clinton Township (48036) ***(G-3215)***
Cummins Inc......616 538-2250
3715 Clay Ave Sw Grand Rapids (49548) ***(G-6618)***
Cummins Inc......989 752-5200
722 N Outer Dr Saginaw (48601) ***(G-14633)***
Cummins Inc......313 843-6200
3760 Wyoming St Dearborn (48120) ***(G-3823)***
Cummins Inc......248 573-1900
54250 Grand River Ave New Hudson (48165) ***(G-12048)***
Cummins Inc......906 774-2424
1901 N Stephenson Ave Iron Mountain (49801) ***(G-8720)***
Cummins Inc......248 573-1600
21810 Clessie Ct New Hudson (48165) ***(G-12049)***
Cummins Label Company......269 345-3386
2230 Glendenning Rd Kalamazoo (49001) ***(G-9159)***
Cummins Npower LLC......906 475-8800
75 Us Hwy 41 N Negaunee (49866) ***(G-11965)***
Cunningham Industries LLC......734 225-1044
13814 Cameron Ave Southgate (48195) ***(G-15750)***
Cup Acquisition LLC (PA)......616 735-4410
2535 Waldorf Ct Nw Grand Rapids (49544) ***(G-6619)***
Cupcakes and Kisses......248 382-5314
108 S Saginaw St Holly (48442) ***(G-8264)***
Curb Apparel LLC......248 548-2324
13340 Victoria Ave Huntington Woods (48070) ***(G-8621)***
Curbco Inc......810 232-2121
3145 S Dye Rd Flint (48507) ***(G-5678)***
Curbell Plastics Inc......734 513-0531
28455 Schoolcraft Rd # 5 Livonia (48150) ***(G-10170)***
Curbs & Damper Products Inc......586 776-7890
16525 Eastland St Roseville (48066) ***(G-14392)***
Curbs and Dampers, Roseville *Also called Cdp Environmental Inc* ***(G-14383)***
Curry Fresh Inc......734 262-0560
2874 Washtenaw Rd Ypsilanti (48197) ***(G-18938)***
Curtis Country Connection LLC......517 368-5542
338 E Bell St Camden (49232) ***(G-2420)***
Curtis Metal Finishing Co......248 588-3300
31440 Stephenson Hwy Madison Heights (48071) ***(G-10701)***
Curtis Printing Inc......810 230-6711
2171 Lodge Rd Flint (48532) ***(G-5679)***
Curtiss-Wright Surface Tech......734 728-8600
30100 Cypress Rd Romulus (48174) ***(G-14266)***
Cusack Music LLC......616 546-8888
514 Lincoln Ave Holland (49423) ***(G-8008)***
Cushing-Malloy Inc......734 663-8554
1350 N Main St Ann Arbor (48104) ***(G-440)***
Cushion Lrry Trphies Engrv LLC......517 332-1667
300 N Clippert St Ste 14 Lansing (48912) ***(G-9827)***
Cusolar Industries Inc......586 949-3880
28161 Kehrig St Chesterfield (48047) ***(G-2863)***
Custard Corner Inc......734 771-4396
2972 W Jefferson Ave Grosse Ile (48138) ***(G-7517)***
Custer Tool & Mfg LLC......734 854-5943
7714 Secor Rd Lambertville (48144) ***(G-9651)***
Custom Architectural Products......616 748-1905
430 100th Ave Zeeland (49464) ***(G-19011)***
Custom Archtctral Shtmtl Spcls......313 571-2277
5641 Conner St Detroit (48213) ***(G-4113)***
Custom Blend Feeds Inc......810 798-3265
77500 Brown Rd Bruce Twp (48065) ***(G-2165)***
Custom Built Brush Company......269 463-3171
7390 Dan Smith Rd Watervliet (49098) ***(G-18179)***
Custom Built Holsters LLC......517 825-9856
517 Crest Ln Jonesville (49250) ***(G-9086)***
Custom Cabinets & More......517 285-7286
3476 Mcconnell Hwy Charlotte (48813) ***(G-2748)***
Custom Cabinets & More LLC......734 231-9086
22752 Donnelly Ave Brownstown (48193) ***(G-2145)***
Custom Caseworks, Grand Rapids *Also called Ufp Sauk Rapids LLC* ***(G-7292)***
Custom Coating Tech Inc......734 442-4074
24341 Brest Taylor (48180) ***(G-16397)***
Custom Coating Technologies......734 244-3610
26601 W Huron River Dr Flat Rock (48134) ***(G-5617)***
Custom Components Corporation......616 523-1111
1111 E Main St Ionia Ionia (48846) ***(G-8688)***
Custom Components Truss Co......810 744-0771
3109 E Bristol Rd Burton (48529) ***(G-2234)***
Custom Counters By Handorn, Grand Rapids *Also called Handorn Inc* ***(G-6801)***
Custom Crafters......269 763-9180
7889 S Ionia Rd Bellevue (49021) ***(G-1497)***
Custom Craftsmen Woodworking......616 638-4768
17915 Mohawk Dr Spring Lake (49456) ***(G-15810)***
Custom Design Inc......269 323-8561
4481 Commercial Ave Portage (49002) ***(G-13555)***
Custom Design & Manufacturing......989 754-9962
3673 Carrollton Rd Carrollton (48724) ***(G-2587)***
Custom Design Components Inc......231 937-6166
19569 W Edgar Rd Howard City (49329) ***(G-8408)***
Custom Door Parts......616 949-5000
8177 Clyde Park Ave Sw Byron Center (49315) ***(G-2265)***
Custom Electric Mfg LLC......248 305-7700
48941 West Rd Wixom (48393) ***(G-18642)***
Custom Embroidery Plus LLC (PA)......989 227-9432
304 N Lansing St Saint Johns (48879) ***(G-14899)***
Custom Engineering & Design......248 680-1435
3448 Rowland Ct Troy (48083) ***(G-17038)***
Custom Fab Inc......586 755-7260
24440 Gibson Dr Warren (48089) ***(G-17767)***
Custom Fireplace Doors Inc......248 673-3121
3809 Lakewood Dr Waterford (48329) ***(G-18111)***
Custom Foods Inc......989 249-8061
634 Kendrick St Saginaw (48602) ***(G-14634)***
Custom Gears Inc......616 243-2723
3761 Linden Ave Se Ste B Grand Rapids (49548) ***(G-6620)***
Custom Giant LLC......313 799-2085
22721 Nottingham Ln Southfield (48033) ***(G-15534)***
Custom Interiors of Toledo......419 865-3090
7979 Whiteford Rd Ottawa Lake (49267) ***(G-12805)***
Custom Line Cabinets......810 459-0414
482 Mulberry Dr Commerce Township (48390) ***(G-3520)***
Custom Lining and Molding, Kalamazoo *Also called Clm Vibetech Inc* ***(G-9146)***
Custom Machining By Farley......616 896-8469
2792 24th Ave Hudsonville (49426) ***(G-8576)***
Custom Marine and Mch Servic......989 732-5455
1440 Beaver Dam Rd Gaylord (49735) ***(G-6125)***
Custom Marine Carpet......269 684-1922
423 N 9th St Niles (49120) ***(G-12122)***
Custom Metal Products Corp......734 591-2500
12283 Levan Rd Livonia (48150) ***(G-10171)***
Custom Metal Works Inc......810 420-0390
316 S Belle River Ave # 11 Marine City (48039) ***(G-10957)***
Custom Molds......574 326-7576
1325 Rolling Ridge Ln Sturgis (49091) ***(G-16286)***
Custom Powder and Fabricators......616 915-9995
2100 Nelson Ave Se Grand Rapids (49507) ***(G-6621)***
Custom Powder Coating LLC......616 454-9730
1601 Madison Ave Se Ste 1 Grand Rapids (49507) ***(G-6622)***
Custom Printers Inc......616 454-9224
2801 Oak Industrial Dr Ne Grand Rapids (49505) ***(G-6623)***

Custom Printing......248 509-7134
1659 Rochester Rd Troy (48083) *(G-17039)*
Custom Printing of Michigan......248 585-9222
1659 Rochester Rd Troy (48083) *(G-17040)*
Custom Pro Products Inc......734 558-2070
31550 Gossett Dr Ste B Rockwood (48173) *(G-14198)*
Custom Products Inc......269 983-9500
180 Kerth St Saint Joseph (49085) *(G-14925)*
Custom Profile, Grand Rapids *Also called Cup Acquisition LLC (G-6619)*
Custom Ptint Ink LLC......586 799-2465
14943 E 9 Mile Rd Eastpointe (48021) *(G-4935)*
Custom Service & Design Inc (PA)......248 340-9005
1259 Doris Rd Ste B Auburn Hills (48326) *(G-855)*
Custom Service Printers Inc......231 726-3297
916 E Keating Ave Muskegon (49442) *(G-11797)*
Custom Signs By Huntley......810 399-8185
1416 Ida St Flint (48503) *(G-5680)*
Custom Threads and Sports LLC......248 391-0088
260 Engelwood Dr Ste A Lake Orion (48359) *(G-9599)*
Custom Tool & Die Service Inc......616 662-1068
5090 40th Ave Ste A Hudsonville (49426) *(G-8577)*
Custom Tool and Die Co......269 465-9130
7059 Red Arrow Hwy Stevensville (49127) *(G-16243)*
Custom Tooling Systems Inc......616 748-9880
3331 80th Ave Zeeland (49464) *(G-19012)*
Custom Trends Printing LLc......586 563-3946
8475 Farnum Ave Warren (48093) *(G-17768)*
Custom Valve Concepts Inc......248 597-8999
31651 Research Park Dr Madison Heights (48071) *(G-10702)*
Custom Verticals Unlimited......734 522-1615
14621 Ludlow St Oak Park (48237) *(G-12603)*
Custom Vinyl Prints......810 841-4301
9001 Smiths Creek Rd Wales (48027) *(G-17626)*
Custom Welding......586 243-6298
4175 S Baldwin Rd Lake Orion (48359) *(G-9600)*
Custom Wheel Solutions......248 547-9587
482 Rivard Blvd Grosse Pointe (48230) *(G-7528)*
Custom Wood Products, Burton *Also called Custom Components Truss Co (G-2234)*
Custom Woodwork & Rmdlg LLC......586 778-9224
23579 Lauren Ave Warren (48089) *(G-17769)*
Custom Workroom, Huntington Woods *Also called Lorne Hanley (G-8622)*
Custombilt of Toledo, Ottawa Lake *Also called Custom Interiors of Toledo (G-12805)*
Customcat, Detroit *Also called Mylockercom LLC (G-4473)*
Customer Metal Fabrication Inc (PA)......906 774-3216
W8762 Lakeview Dr Iron Mountain (49801) *(G-8721)*
Custometal Products, Saint Joseph *Also called Custom Products Inc (G-14925)*
Cut All Water Jet Cutting Inc......734 946-7880
25944 Northline Rd Taylor (48180) *(G-16398)*
Cut Once LLC......616 245-3136
240 32nd St Se Grand Rapids (49548) *(G-6624)*
Cut-Rite EDM Services LLC......586 566-0100
51445 Oro Dr Shelby Township (48315) *(G-15200)*
Cute N Classy Collection LLC......313 279-8217
13311 Hurston Foster Ln Detroit (48215) *(G-4114)*
Cutex Inc......734 953-8908
12496 Globe St Livonia (48150) *(G-10172)*
Cutting Edge Poly......269 953-2866
175 S M 37 Hwy Hastings (49058) *(G-7787)*
Cutting Edge Technologies Inc......616 738-0800
13305 New Holland St B Holland (49424) *(G-8009)*
Cvk Ink, West Bloomfield *Also called Cvk Publishing Inc (G-18275)*
Cvk Publishing Inc......248 877-6384
6689 Orchard Lake Rd # 324 West Bloomfield (48322) *(G-18275)*
Cw Champion Welding Alloys LLC......906 296-9633
52705 State Highway M26 Lake Linden (49945) *(G-9568)*
Cw Creative Welding Inc......586 294-1050
33360 Groesbeck Hwy Fraser (48026) *(G-5916)*
CWk International Corp......616 396-2063
2221 Sunset Bluff Dr Holland (49424) *(G-8010)*
Cyber Data Lock, Detroit *Also called Paragon Vciso Group LLC (G-4507)*
Cyberlogic Technologies Inc......248 631-2200
755 W Big Beavr Rd # 2020 Troy (48084) *(G-17041)*
Cyclone International, Holland *Also called Big Dutchman Inc (G-7975)*
Cyclone Manufacturing Inc......269 782-9670
56850 Woodhouse Dr Dowagiac (49047) *(G-4780)*
Cygnet Financial Freedom House, Waterford *Also called Cygnet Financial Planning Inc (G-18112)*
Cygnet Financial Planning Inc......248 673-2900
4139 W Walton Blvd Ste D Waterford (48329) *(G-18112)*
Cygnus Inc......231 347-5404
829 Charlevoix Ave Petoskey (49770) *(G-12996)*
Cypress Computer Systems Inc......810 245-2300
1778 Imlay City Rd Lapeer (48446) *(G-9924)*
Cypress Industries Inc......269 381-2160
3535 Bronson Blvd Kalamazoo (49008) *(G-9160)*
Cyprium Induction LLC......586 884-4982
42770 Mound Rd Sterling Heights (48314) *(G-15976)*
Cyrus Forest Products......269 751-6535
4234 127th Ave Allegan (49010) *(G-152)*
Cytec Industries Inc......269 349-6677
3115 Miller Rd Kalamazoo (49001) *(G-9161)*
Cytk Corp......313 288-9360
111 S Lafayette St # 880 South Lyon (48178) *(G-15432)*
Cz Industries Inc......248 475-4415
1929-1939 N Opdyke Rd Ste Auburn Hills (48326) *(G-856)*
D Mac Industries Inc......734 536-7754
31492 Glendale St Livonia (48150) *(G-10173)*
D & A Welding & Fabg LLC......313 220-2277
19169 Northrop St Detroit (48219) *(G-4115)*
D & B Heat Transfer Pdts Inc......616 827-0028
8031 Division Ave S Ste C Grand Rapids (49548) *(G-6625)*
D & B Metal Finishing......586 725-6056
34537 Shorewood St Chesterfield (48047) *(G-2864)*
D & C Investment Group Inc (PA)......734 994-0591
5840 Interface Dr Ann Arbor (48103) *(G-441)*
D & D Building Inc......616 248-7908
3959 Linden Ave Se Grand Rapids (49548) *(G-6626)*
D & D Business Machines Inc......616 364-8446
3545 Brandau Dr Ne Grand Rapids (49525) *(G-6627)*
D & D Driers Timber Product......906 224-7251
115 E Old Us 2 Wakefield (49968) *(G-17619)*
D & D Fabrications Inc......810 798-2491
8005 Tiffany Dr Almont (48003) *(G-258)*
D & D Investments Equipment, Fenton *Also called Burgaflex North America LLC (G-5461)*
D & D Printing, Kalamazoo *Also called Dekoff & Sons Inc (G-9165)*
D & D Printing Co......616 454-7710
342 Market Ave Sw Unit 1 Grand Rapids (49503) *(G-6628)*
D & D Production Inc......248 334-2112
2500 Williams Dr Waterford (48328) *(G-18113)*
D & D Retaining Walls Inc......260 341-8496
1481 Crystal Lake Rd Whitehall (49461) *(G-18494)*
D & D Tool Inc......616 772-2416
218 E Harrison Ave Zeeland (49464) *(G-19013)*
D & F Corporation......586 254-5300
42455 Merrill Rd Sterling Heights (48314) *(G-15977)*
D & F Mold LLC......269 465-6633
8088 Jericho Rd Bridgman (49106) *(G-1923)*
D & J Mfg & Machining......231 830-9522
507 W Hovey Ave Muskegon (49444) *(G-11798)*
D & J Precision Machine Svcs......269 673-4010
611 N Eastern Ave Allegan (49010) *(G-153)*
D & L Tooling Inc......517 369-5655
675 W Central Rd Bronson (49028) *(G-2110)*
D & L Water Control Inc......734 455-6982
7534 Baron Dr Canton (48187) *(G-2453)*
D & M Cabinet Shop Inc......989 479-9271
5230 Purdy Rd Ruth (48470) *(G-14597)*
D & M Silkscreening......517 694-4199
4202 Charlar Dr Ste 3 Holt (48842) *(G-8305)*
D & M Truck Top Co Inc......248 792-7972
2354 Dorchester Dr N # 108 Troy (48084) *(G-17042)*
D & N Bending Corp (PA)......586 752-5511
150 Shafer Dr Romeo (48065) *(G-14223)*
D & N Casting, Romeo *Also called D & N Bending Corp (G-14223)*
D & N Gage Inc......586 336-2110
161 E Pond Dr Romeo (48065) *(G-14224)*
D & R Fabrication Inc......616 794-1130
200 Gooding St Belding (48809) *(G-1444)*
D & S Engine Specialist Inc......248 583-9240
875 N Rochester Rd Clawson (48017) *(G-3093)*
D & W Awning and Window Co......810 742-0340
8068 E Court St Davison (48423) *(G-3779)*
D & W Management Company Inc......586 758-2284
23660 Sherwood Ave Warren (48091) *(G-17770)*
D & W Square LLC......313 493-4970
8932 Coyle St Detroit (48228) *(G-4116)*
D A C Industries Inc......616 235-0140
600 11th St Nw Grand Rapids (49504) *(G-6629)*
D and D Welding......810 824-3622
6111 Eastwood Dr Burtchville (48059) *(G-2219)*
D and WP Rints LLC......313 646-6571
16315 Grand River Ave Detroit (48227) *(G-4117)*
D B International LLC......616 796-0679
650 Riley St Ste C Holland (49424) *(G-8011)*
D D Quality Servicing......517 709-3705
1596 Witherspoon Way Holt (48842) *(G-8306)*
D E Rogers & Assoc., Waterford *Also called Donald E Rogers Associates (G-18116)*
D Fab, Madison Heights *Also called Design Fabrications Inc (G-10705)*
D Find Corporation......248 641-2858
1955 Rolling Woods Dr Troy (48098) *(G-17043)*
D H P, Grand Rapids *Also called Discovery House Publishers (G-6651)*
D H Tool & Die, Commerce Township *Also called Heinzmann D Tool & Die Inc (G-3535)*
D J and G Enterprise Inc......231 258-9925
402 E Dresden St Kalkaska (49646) *(G-9386)*
D J McQuestion & Sons Inc......231 768-4403
17708 18 Mile Rd Leroy (49655) *(G-10005)*
D J Rotunda Associates Inc......586 772-3350
2634 Peterboro Ct West Bloomfield (48323) *(G-18276)*

ALPHABETIC

D J S Systems Inc 517 568-4444
801 S Hillsdale St Homer (49245) *(G-8350)*

D K Enterprises Inc 586 756-7350
21942 Dequindre Rd Warren (48091) *(G-17771)*

D L R Manufacturing Inc 734 394-0690
44205 Yost Rd Van Buren Twp (48111) *(G-17522)*

D L W Publishing Co 313 593-4554
7739 Brace St Detroit (48228) *(G-4118)*

D M C International Inc 586 465-1112
42470 Executive Dr Harrison Township (48045) *(G-7695)*

D M J Corp 810 239-9071
3910 Fenton Rd Ste 15 Flint (48507) *(G-5681)*

D M P E 269 428-5070
5790 Saint Joseph Ave Stevensville (49127) *(G-16244)*

D M Tool & Fab Inc 586 726-8390
6101 18 1/2 Mile Rd Sterling Heights (48314) *(G-15978)*

D N D Business Machines, Grand Rapids Also called A A A Mailing & Packg Sups LLC *(G-6408)*

D O W Asphalt Paving LLC 810 743-2633
10421 Calkins Rd Swartz Creek (48473) *(G-16352)*

D P Equipment Co 517 368-5266
10700 S Edon Rd Camden (49232) *(G-2421)*

D R W Systems 989 874-4663
4484 N Van Dyke Rd Filion (48432) *(G-5612)*

D S C Services Inc (PA) 734 241-9500
1510 E 1st St Monroe (48161) *(G-11535)*

D S N Satellites, Mason Also called Digital Success Network *(G-11130)*

D Sharp Masonry 313 292-2375
6360 Mcguire St Taylor (48180) *(G-16399)*

D Sign LLC 616 392-3841
511 Chicago Dr Holland (49423) *(G-8012)*

D T Fowler Mfg Co Inc (PA) 810 245-9336
101 N Mapleleaf Rd Lapeer (48446) *(G-9925)*

D T M 1 Inc 248 889-9210
1450 N Milford Rd Ste 101 Highland (48357) *(G-7890)*

D T R Sign Co LLC 616 889-8927
6315 Thornapple Valley Dr Hastings (49058) *(G-7788)*

D W Hines Manufacturing Corp 586 775-1200
21887 Schoenherr Rd Warren (48089) *(G-17772)*

D W Machine Inc 517 787-9929
2501 Precision St Jackson (49202) *(G-8859)*

D&D Defense LLC 248 255-8765
10827 B Dr N Ceresco (49033) *(G-2703)*

D&D Planning Design Mllwk LLC 586 754-6500
8646 E 9 Mile Rd Warren (48089) *(G-17773)*

D&E Incorporated 313 673-3284
20542 Oldham Rd Southfield (48076) *(G-15535)*

D&G Equipment, Williamston Also called Hutson Inc *(G-18573)*

D&Js Plastics LLC 616 745-5798
2322 Edson Dr Hudsonville (49426) *(G-8578)*

D&L Logging 231 709-5477
6703 Summit City Rd Kingsley (49649) *(G-9522)*

D&M Metal Products Company 616 784-0601
4994 West River Dr Ne Comstock Park (49321) *(G-3600)*

D&W Fine Pack LLC 866 296-2020
1191 Wolfson Ct Gladwin (48624) *(G-6194)*

D' Printer Inc-Shop, Tecumseh Also called DPrinter Inc *(G-16499)*

D'Angelico Strings, Springfield Also called GHS Corporation *(G-15868)*

D-M-E USA Inc 616 754-4601
1117 E Fairplains St Greenville (48838) *(G-7480)*

D-Mark Inc 586 949-3610
130 N Groesbeck Hwy Mount Clemens (48043) *(G-11635)*

D-N-S Industries Inc 586 465-2444
44805 Trinity Dr Clinton Township (48038) *(G-3216)*

D-Sign, Holland Also called D Sign LLC *(G-8012)*

D.A. Stuart Company, Detroit Also called Quaker Houghton Pa Inc *(G-4545)*

D2 Ink Inc 248 590-7076
37933 Glengrove Dr Farmington Hills (48331) *(G-5209)*

D2 Print Inc 248 229-7633
31211 Stephenson Hwy # 10 Madison Heights (48071) *(G-10703)*

D3w Industries Inc 248 798-0703
22865 Heslip Dr Novi (48375) *(G-12389)*

D4 Apparel LLC 586 207-1841
60480 Kunstman Rd Ray (48096) *(G-13698)*

Dablon Vineyards LLC 269 422-2846
111 W Shawnee Rd Baroda (49101) *(G-1159)*

Dac Inc 313 388-4342
2930 S Dartmouth St Detroit (48217) *(G-4119)*

Daca Div, Romulus Also called United Brass Manufacturers Inc *(G-14334)*

Daco Hand Controllers Inc 248 982-3266
24404 Catherine Industria Novi (48375) *(G-12390)*

Dad and Sons Farming LLC 517 719-2048
790 S Shaytown Rd Vermontville (49096) *(G-17587)*

Dadco Inc (PA) 734 207-1100
43850 Plymouth Oaks Blvd Plymouth (48170) *(G-13151)*

Dadco Inc 616 785-2888
848 W River Center Dr Ne C Comstock Park (49321) *(G-3601)*

Daddy DZ Granola Co 616 374-0020
619 6th Ave Lake Odessa (48849) *(G-9574)*

Dads Panels Inc 810 245-1871
2142 Imlay City Rd Lapeer (48446) *(G-9926)*

Dag Ltd LLC 586 276-9310
34400 Mound Rd Sterling Heights (48310) *(G-15979)*

Dag R&D 248 444-0575
1677 Melody Ln Milford (48380) *(G-11460)*

Dag Technology Inc 586 276-9310
10168 N Holly Rd Grand Blanc (48439) *(G-6240)*

Dagenham Millworks LLC 616 698-8883
4525 Airwest Dr Se Grand Rapids (49512) *(G-6630)*

Dager Systems, Chesterfield Also called Kimastle Corporation *(G-2902)*

Dagher Signs 313 729-9555
22476 Telegraph Rd Southfield (48033) *(G-15536)*

Daiek Door Sytem, Troy Also called Daiek Products Inc *(G-17044)*

Daiek Products Inc 248 816-1360
1725 Blaney Dr Troy (48084) *(G-17044)*

Daifuku North America Holdg Co (HQ) 248 553-1000
30100 Cabot Dr Novi (48377) *(G-12391)*

Daily Bill 989 631-2068
610 W Saint Andrews Rd Midland (48640) *(G-11332)*

Daily Contracts LLC 734 676-0903
7779 Grays Dr Grosse Ile (48138) *(G-7518)*

Daily De-Lish 616 450-9562
1235 Thrnpple River Dr Se Ada (49301) *(G-15)*

Daily Gardener LLC 734 754-6527
5211 Pontiac Trl Ann Arbor (48105) *(G-442)*

Daily News 616 754-9301
109 N Lafayette St Greenville (48838) *(G-7481)*

Daily Oakland Press (HQ) 248 332-8181
38500 Woodward Ave # 100 Bloomfield Hills (48304) *(G-1811)*

Daily Oakland Press 248 332-8181
58 W Huron St Pontiac (48342) *(G-13357)*

Daily Recycling of Michigan 734 654-9800
201 Matlin Rd Carleton (48117) *(G-2550)*

Daily Reporter 517 278-2318
15 W Pearl St Coldwater (49036) *(G-3430)*

Daily Telegram, The, Adrian Also called Gatehouse Media LLC *(G-69)*

Daimay North America Auto Inc (HQ) 313 533-9680
24400 Plymouth Rd Redford (48239) *(G-13729)*

Dairy Doo, Sears Also called Morgan Composting Inc *(G-15137)*

Dairy Farmers America Inc 517 265-5045
1336 E Maumee St Adrian (49221) *(G-58)*

Daisy Chain Online 330 259-6457
4999 Crabapple Ct West Bloomfield (48324) *(G-18277)*

Dajaco Ind Inc 586 949-1590
49715 Leona Dr Chesterfield (48051) *(G-2865)*

Dajaco Industries Inc 586 949-1590
49715 Leona Dr Chesterfield (48051) *(G-2866)*

Dakkota Integrated Systems LLC (PA) 517 694-6500
123 Brighton Lake Rd # 202 Brighton (48116) *(G-1972)*

Dakkota Integrated Systems LLC 517 321-3064
16130 Grove Rd Lansing (48906) *(G-9683)*

Dakkota Integrated Systems LLC 517 694-6500
1420 E 10 Mile Rd Ste 200 Hazel Park (48030) *(G-7822)*

Dakkota Integrated Systems LLC 517 694-6500
4147 Keller Rd Holt (48842) *(G-8307)*

Dakkota Lighting Tech LLC (HQ) 517 694-2823
4147 Keller Rd Holt (48842) *(G-8308)*

Dakoda Love Manufacturing 616 840-0804
1701 Clyde Park Ave Sw # 3 Wyoming (49509) *(G-18863)*

Dakota Aerospace LLC 787 403-3564
10116 Kress Rd Pinckney (48169) *(G-13046)*

Dal-Tile Corporation 248 471-7150
24640 Drake Rd Farmington Hills (48335) *(G-5210)*

Dale Prentice, Oak Park Also called Engineered Resources Inc *(G-12611)*

Dale Routley Logging 231 861-2596
1870 N 100th Ave Hart (49420) *(G-7750)*

Daler Inc 989 752-1582
1115 W Genesee Ave Saginaw (48602) *(G-14635)*

Dales LLC 734 444-4620
348 Cty Center St Lapeer (48446) *(G-9927)*

Dallas Design Inc 810 238-4546
3432 S Saginaw St Flint (48503) *(G-5682)*

Dallas Industries, Troy Also called Advanced Feedlines LLC *(G-16908)*

Dalton Armond Publishers Inc 517 351-8520
2867 Jolly Rd Okemos (48864) *(G-12662)*

Dalton Industries LLC 248 673-0755
2800 Alliance Ste B Waterford (48328) *(G-18114)*

Dama Tool & Gauge Company 616 842-9631
6175 Norton Center Dr Norton Shores (49441) *(G-12287)*

Damar Machinery Co 616 453-4655
3389 3 Mile Rd Nw Grand Rapids (49534) *(G-6631)*

Damar Tool Manufacturing, Romulus Also called Millennium Technology II Inc *(G-14306)*

Damick Enterprises 248 652-7500
1801 Rochester Indus Ct Rochester Hills (48309) *(G-13989)*

Damionisha 823 Cosmetics LLC 586 557-9893
19705 Binder St Detroit (48234) *(G-4120)*

Damonds Mobile Welding 313 932-4135
36 Ridge St Ecorse (48229) *(G-4982)*

Dana 419 887-3000
6938 Elm Valley Dr # 101 Kalamazoo (49009) ***(G-9162)***
Dana & Sean Roberds 989 382-7564
53 E Marion Ave Barryton (49305) ***(G-1172)***
Dana Driveshaft Mfg LLC 248 623-2185
4440 N Atlantic Blvd Auburn Hills (48326) ***(G-857)***
Dana Incorporated 734 629-1200
27870 Cabot Dr Novi (48377) ***(G-12392)***
Dana Incorporated 269 567-1537
6938 Elm Valley Dr # 101 Kalamazoo (49009) ***(G-9163)***
Dana Limited 586 467-1600
28201 Van Dyke Ave Warren (48093) ***(G-17774)***
Dana Limited 810 329-2500
2020 Christian B Haas Dr Saint Clair (48079) ***(G-14822)***
Dana Off-Hghway Components LLC 586 467-1600
3040 S Dye Rd Flint (48507) ***(G-5683)***
Dana Thermal Products LLC 810 329-2500
2020 Christian B Haas Dr Saint Clair (48079) ***(G-14823)***
Dana Thermal Products LLC 810 329-2500
2020 Christian B Haas Dr Saint Clair (48079) ***(G-14824)***
Dana Trading, Grand Rapids *Also called Foremost Graphics LLC* ***(G-6715)***
Dancorp Inc 269 663-5566
27496 Max St Edwardsburg (49112) ***(G-5004)***
Dandy Delights 248 496-8523
2460 Lakena Rd West Bloomfield (48324) ***(G-18278)***
Dane Systems LLC 269 465-3263
7275 Red Arrow Hwy Stevensville (49127) ***(G-16245)***
Daneks Goodtime Ice Co Inc 989 725-5920
210 N Gould St Owosso (48867) ***(G-12830)***
Daniel D Slater 989 833-7135
10361 W Van Buren Rd Riverdale (48877) ***(G-13863)***
Daniel Olson 269 816-1838
12646 Born St Jones (49061) ***(G-9083)***
Daniel Pruitoff 616 392-1371
271 E 26th St Holland (49423) ***(G-8013)***
Daniel Snderson Cstm Cabinetry 231 421-5743
5148 Stonefield Dr Traverse City (49684) ***(G-16667)***
Daniel Ward 810 965-6535
7352 N Tort Hi W Y Ste 2 Mount Morris (48458) ***(G-11670)***
Danjos Foods Inc 517 543-2260
594 Tirrell Rd Charlotte (48813) ***(G-2749)***
Danka 616 249-8199
4489 Byron Center Ave Sw B Wyoming (49519) ***(G-18864)***
Danly IEM 800 243-2659
4300 40th St Se Grand Rapids (49512) ***(G-6632)***
Danlyn Controls Inc 586 773-6797
25090 Terra Industrial Dr Chesterfield (48051) ***(G-2867)***
Danmar Products Inc (PA) 734 761-1990
221 Jackson Industrial Dr Ann Arbor (48103) ***(G-443)***
Danmark Graphics LLC 616 675-7499
153 N Main St Casnovia (49318) ***(G-2606)***
Danny K Bundy 231 590-6924
2630 E 16 1/2 Rd Manton (49663) ***(G-10931)***
Dans Concrete LLC 517 242-0754
9202 Riverside Dr Grand Ledge (48837) ***(G-6388)***
Dapco Industries, Dexter *Also called Dexter Automatic Products Co* ***(G-4734)***
Darby Metal Treating Inc 269 204-6504
892 Wakefield Plainwell (49080) ***(G-13073)***
Darby Ready Mix Concrete Co 517 547-7004
U.S 12 & Herold Hwy Addison (49220) ***(G-43)***
Darby Ready Mix-Dundee LLC 734 529-7100
7801 N Ann Arbor Rd Dundee (48131) ***(G-4813)***
Darbyreadymix.com, Addison *Also called Darby Ready Mix Concrete Co* ***(G-43)***
Dare Auto Inc 734 228-6243
47548 Halyard Dr Ste B Plymouth (48170) ***(G-13152)***
Dare Products Inc 269 965-2307
860 Betterly Rd Springfield (49037) ***(G-15864)***
Daring Company 248 340-0741
180 Engelwood Dr Ste B Orion (48359) ***(G-12728)***
Dark Star Publishing 810 858-1135
34633 Cedar Rdg Richmond (48062) ***(G-13835)***
Darkhorse Brewing Company, The, Marshall *Also called Mor-Dall Enterprises Inc* ***(G-11071)***
Darkhorse Cargo Inc 269 464-2620
500 S Miller Rd White Pigeon (49099) ***(G-18474)***
Darla Nagel 810 624-9043
7080 Stanley Rd Flushing (48433) ***(G-5807)***
Darling Ingredients Inc 989 752-4340
340 Tyler St Carrollton (48724) ***(G-2588)***
Darling Ingredients Inc 517 279-9731
600 Jay St Coldwater (49036) ***(G-3431)***
Darling Ingredients Inc 269 751-0560
5900 Old Allegan Rd Hamilton (49419) ***(G-7597)***
Darrell A Curtice 231 745-9890
669 E Roosevelt Rd Bitely (49309) ***(G-1758)***
Darrell R Hanson 810 364-7892
579 Michigan Ave Marysville (48040) ***(G-11085)***
Darren McCaffery Stucco 321 303-0988
10329 E 20 Rd Manton (49663) ***(G-10932)***
Darson Corporation 313 875-7781
10610 Galaxie Ave Ferndale (48220) ***(G-5538)***

Dart Container Corp California 517 244-6408
500 Hogsback Rd Mason (48854) ***(G-11121)***
Dart Container Corp Florida (PA) 800 248-5960
500 Hogsback Rd Mason (48854) ***(G-11122)***
Dart Container Corp Georgia (PA) 517 676-3800
500 Hogsback Rd Mason (48854) ***(G-11123)***
Dart Container Corp Kentucky (PA) 517 676-3800
500 Hogsback Rd Mason (48854) ***(G-11124)***
Dart Container Corporation 517 327-0613
16637 Corporate Avi Dr Lansing (48906) ***(G-9684)***
Dart Container Corporation 517 676-3800
710 Hogsback Rd Bldg 9 Mason (48854) ***(G-11125)***
Dart Container Corporation (PA) 517 676-3800
500 Hogsback Rd Mason (48854) ***(G-11126)***
Dart Container Michigan LLC 248 669-3767
46918 Liberty Dr Wixom (48393) ***(G-18643)***
Dart Container Michigan LLC 517 244-6249
3120 W Howell Rd Mason (48854) ***(G-11127)***
Dart Container Michigan LLC 888 327-8001
3120 Sovereign Dr Ste 4b Lansing (48911) ***(G-9828)***
Dart Container Michigan LLC (HQ) 800 248-5960
500 Hogsback Rd Mason (48854) ***(G-11128)***
Dart Container Michigan LLC 517 694-9455
2148 Depot St Holt (48842) ***(G-8309)***
Dart Container Michigan LLC 517 676-3803
432 Hogsback Rd Mason (48854) ***(G-11129)***
Dart Energy Corporation 231 885-1665
23862 13 Mile Rd Mesick (49668) ***(G-11271)***
Dart Machinery Ltd 248 362-1188
2097 Bart Ave Warren (48091) ***(G-17775)***
Dart Polymers, Mason *Also called Dart Container Corp Kentucky* ***(G-11124)***
Darwin Sneller 989 977-3718
8677 Kilmanagh Rd Sebewaing (48759) ***(G-15139)***
Daryls Use Truck Sales, Pigeon *Also called Thumb Truck and Trailer Co* ***(G-13041)***
Das Group Inc 248 670-2718
2417 Vinsetta Blvd Royal Oak (48073) ***(G-14529)***
DAS Technologies Inc 269 657-0541
138 Ampey Rd Paw Paw (49079) ***(G-12945)***
Dassault Systmes Americas Corp 248 267-9696
900 N Squirrel Rd Ste 100 Auburn Hills (48326) ***(G-858)***
Data Acquisition Ctrl Systems 248 437-6096
7965 Kensington Ct Ste A2 Brighton (48116) ***(G-1973)***
Data Center, Dearborn *Also called Active Solutions Group Inc* ***(G-3805)***
Data Cover .com, Pontiac *Also called Mis Associates Inc* ***(G-13398)***
Data Mail Services Inc 248 588-2415
747 E Whitcomb Ave Madison Heights (48071) ***(G-10704)***
Data Pro Inc 269 685-9214
108 S Main St Ste B Plainwell (49080) ***(G-13074)***
Data Reproductions Corporation 248 371-3700
4545 Glenmeade Ln Auburn Hills (48326) ***(G-859)***
Datacover Inc 844 875-4076
1735 Highwood W Pontiac (48340) ***(G-13358)***
Datacover Inc 248 391-2163
1070 W Silverbell Rd Lake Orion (48359) ***(G-9601)***
Datalyzer International Inc 248 960-3535
29445 Beck Rd Ste A207 Wixom (48393) ***(G-18644)***
Datamartz LLC 248 202-1559
2232 S Main St Ann Arbor (48103) ***(G-444)***
Datamatic Processing Inc (PA) 517 882-4401
5545 Enterprise Dr Lansing (48911) ***(G-9829)***
Dataspeed Inc (PA) 248 243-8889
2736 Research Dr Rochester Hills (48309) ***(G-13990)***
Datec, Portage *Also called Dynamic Auto Test Engineering* ***(G-13556)***
Datum Industries LLC 616 977-1995
4740 44th St Se Grand Rapids (49512) ***(G-6633)***
Datum Precision Machine Inc 586 790-1120
35235 Automation Dr Clinton Township (48035) ***(G-3217)***
Daughtery Group Inc 313 452-7918
16892 Parkside St Detroit (48221) ***(G-4121)***
Daughtry Nwspapers Investments 269 683-2100
217 N 4th St Niles (49120) ***(G-12123)***
Daulinas LLC 313 258-0958
13877 Bringard Dr Detroit (48205) ***(G-4122)***
Davalor Mold, Chesterfield *Also called Oth Consultants Inc* ***(G-2920)***
Davalor Mold Company LLC 586 598-0100
46480 Continental Dr Chesterfield (48047) ***(G-2868)***
Davco Manufacturing LLC 734 429-5665
1600 Woodland Dr Saline (48176) ***(G-15011)***
Davco Technology LLC 734 429-5665
1600 Woodland Dr Saline (48176) ***(G-15012)***
Dave Brand 269 651-4693
26541 Us 12 Sturgis (49091) ***(G-16287)***
Dave Lewishcky Fantsy Camp 248 328-0891
2040 Ranch Rd Holly (48442) ***(G-8265)***
Dave Ray & Associates, Orion *Also called George Instrument Company* ***(G-12731)***
Daves Concrete Products Inc 269 624-4100
79811 M 40 Lawton (49065) ***(G-9988)***
Daves Diamond Inc 248 693-2482
416 S Broadway St Lake Orion (48362) ***(G-9602)***

ALPHABETIC

Daves Printing 989 355-1204
2600 State St Saginaw (48602) *(G-14636)*
David Brown Union Pumps Co Pay 269 966-4702
4600 W Dickman Rd Battle Creek (49037) *(G-1214)*
David Epstein Inc 248 542-0802
1135 E 9 Mile Rd Ferndale (48220) *(G-5539)*
David Gauss Logging 517 851-8102
4635 Cooper Rd Stockbridge (49285) *(G-16273)*
David Hirn Cabinets and Contg 906 428-1935
1319 Delta Ave Gladstone (49837) *(G-6178)*
David Jenks 810 793-7340
5955 Chapman Rd North Branch (48461) *(G-12178)*
David Kimberly Door Company 248 652-8833
394 South St Ste B Rochester (48307) *(G-13898)*
David Lee Naturals 248 328-1131
113 Battle Aly Holly (48442) *(G-8266)*
David Newman Logging 906 201-1125
14673 Bellaire Rd Baraga (49908) *(G-1137)*
David R Lacharite Lmsw 517 347-0988
4747 Okemos Rd Okemos (48864) *(G-12663)*
Davids Heating & Cooling Inc 586 601-5108
17000 Cedarcroft Pl Southfield (48076) *(G-15537)*
Davis Dental Laboratory 616 261-9191
5830 Crossroads Cmmrce Wyoming (49519) *(G-18865)*
Davis Iron Works Inc 248 624-5960
1166 Benstein Rd Commerce Township (48390) *(G-3521)*
Davis Steel Rule Die 269 492-9908
2222 Glendenning Rd 9b Kalamazoo (49001) *(G-9164)*
Davismade Inc 810 743-5262
4400 S Saginaw St # 1470 Flint (48507) *(G-5684)*
Davison-Rite Products Co 734 513-0505
2736 Havenwood Dr White Lake (48383) *(G-18454)*
Davon Manufacturing 616 745-8453
3625 80th Ave Zeeland (49464) *(G-19014)*
Davon Manufacturing Company 616 896-7888
3531 Perry St Hudsonville (49426) *(G-8579)*
Dawlen Corporation 517 787-2200
2029 Micor Dr Jackson (49203) *(G-8860)*
Dawn Equipment Company Inc 517 789-4500
2021 Micor Dr Jackson (49203) *(G-8861)*
Dawn Food Products, Jackson Also called Dawn Equipment Company Inc *(G-8861)*
Dawn Food Products Inc 517 789-4400
3333 Sargent Rd Jackson (49201) *(G-8862)*
Dawn Food Products Inc 800 654-4843
2885 Clydon Ave Sw Grand Rapids (49519) *(G-6634)*
Dawn Food Products Inc (HQ) 517 789-4400
3333 Sargent Rd Jackson (49201) *(G-8863)*
Dawn Foods Inc (PA) 517 789-4400
3333 Sargent Rd Jackson (49201) *(G-8864)*
Dawn Foods International Corp 517 789-4400
3333 Sargent Rd Jackson (49201) *(G-8865)*
Dawson Grinding, Grand Haven Also called Grand Haven Steel Products Inc *(G-6306)*
Dawson Manufacturing Company (PA) 269 925-0100
1042 N Crystal Ave Benton Harbor (49022) *(G-1544)*
Dawson Manufacturing Company 269 925-0100
1042 N Crystal Ave Benton Harbor (49022) *(G-1545)*
Dawson Mfg Co Morganfield 269 639-4229
400 Aylworth Ave South Haven (49090) *(G-15403)*
Dawzye Excavation Inc 906 786-5276
7575 Rays M.7 Cir 7m Gladstone (49837) *(G-6179)*
Day International Inc (HQ) 734 781-4600
17177 N Laurel Park Dr # 30 Livonia (48152) *(G-10174)*
Dayco LLC (PA) 248 404-6500
1650 Research Dr Ste 100 Troy (48083) *(G-17045)*
Dayco Incorporated (HQ) 248 404-6500
1650 Research Dr Ste 100 Troy (48083) *(G-17046)*
Dayco Products LLC 989 775-0689
1799 Gover Pkwy Mount Pleasant (48858) *(G-11694)*
Dayco Products LLC 248 404-6506
1650 Research Dr Ste 100 Troy (48083) *(G-17047)*
Dayco Products LLC 517 439-0689
215 Industrial Dr Hillsdale (49242) *(G-7931)*
Dayco Products LLC (HQ) 248 404-6500
1650 Research Dr Ste 100 Troy (48083) *(G-17048)*
Dayco Products LLC 248 404-6537
16000 Common Rd Roseville (48066) *(G-14393)*
Dayco Products LLC 248 404-6500
16000 Common Rd Roseville (48066) *(G-14394)*
Dayton Lamina Corp 231 533-8646
3650 S Derenzy Rd Bellaire (49615) *(G-1473)*
Dayton Precision Services, Carleton Also called Rvm Company of Toledo *(G-2562)*
DB Communications Inc 800 692-8200
32922 Brookside Cir Livonia (48152) *(G-10175)*
Dbusiness 313 929-0090
5750 New King Dr Ste 100 Troy (48098) *(G-17049)*
DC Byers Co/Grand Rapids Inc (PA) 616 538-7300
5946 Clay Ave Sw Grand Rapids (49548) *(G-6635)*
Dcd Idid Enterprise LLC 517 424-0577
610 S Maumee St Tecumseh (49286) *(G-16495)*
DCI Aerotech, Detroit Also called Detroit Chrome Inc *(G-4140)*

Dcl Inc (PA) 231 547-5600
8660 Ance Rd Charlevoix (49720) *(G-2714)*
Dcp Midstream LLC 936 615-5189
2510 Busha Hwy Marysville (48040) *(G-11086)*
Dcr Services & Cnstr Inc (PA) 313 297-6544
2200 Hunt St Ste 487 Detroit (48207) *(G-4123)*
DD Parker Enterprises Inc 734 241-6898
1402 W 7th St Monroe (48161) *(G-11536)*
Ddks Industries LLC 586 323-5909
14954 Technology Dr Shelby Township (48315) *(G-15201)*
Ddm, Clinton Township Also called Diamond Die and Mold Company *(G-3221)*
Ddp Hillsdale Shipping, Hillsdale Also called Ddp Spclty Elctrnic Mtls US LL *(G-7932)*
Ddp Saginaw Shipping, Midland Also called Ddp Spclty Elctrnic Mtls US In *(G-11334)*
Ddp Spclty Elctrnic Mtls US 9 .... 989 496-6000
2200 W Salzburg Rd Midland (48686) *(G-11333)*
Ddp Spclty Elctrnic Mtls US In 989 708-6737
3800 S Saginaw Rd Gate177 Midland (48640) *(G-11334)*
Ddp Spclty Elctrnic Mtls US LL 517 439-4440
190 Uran St Hillsdale (49242) *(G-7932)*
Ddp Spclty Elctrnic Mtls US LL 989 636-9953
3400 S Saginaw Rd Midland (48640) *(G-11335)*
Ddr Heating Inc (PA) 269 673-2145
700 Grand St Allegan (49010) *(G-154)*
De Antigua, Holland Also called Prime Wood Products Inc *(G-8170)*
De Klomp Wden Shoe Delft Fctry, Holland Also called Veldheer Tulip Garden Inc *(G-8235)*
De Luxe Die Set Inc 810 227-2556
5939 Ford Ct Brighton (48116) *(G-1974)*
De Vru Printing Co 616 452-5451
1446 Eastern Ave Se Grand Rapids (49507) *(G-6636)*
De Witt Products Co 313 554-0575
5860 Plumer St Detroit (48209) *(G-4124)*
De-Sta-Co, Auburn Hills Also called Dover Energy Inc *(G-866)*
De-Sta-Co Cylinders Inc 248 836-6700
15 Corporate Dr Auburn Hills (48326) *(G-860)*
Deadline Detroit 248 219-5985
66 Winder St Apt 443 Detroit (48201) *(G-4125)*
Deadline Detroit 586 863-8397
615 Griswold St Lbby 7 Detroit (48226) *(G-4126)*
Deadline Detroit 202 309-5555
15 E Kirby St Apt 526 Detroit (48202) *(G-4127)*
Dealer Aid Enterprises 313 331-5800
8200 E Jefferson Ave # 60 Detroit (48214) *(G-4128)*
Dean Richard Woodworking 586 764-6586
2655 Orchard Lake Rd Sylvan Lake (48320) *(G-16360)*
Deans Ice Cream Inc 269 685-6641
307 N Sherwood Ave Plainwell (49080) *(G-13075)*
Dearborn Lithograph Inc 734 464-4242
12380 Globe St Livonia (48150) *(G-10176)*
Dearborn Mid West Conveyor Co 313 273-2804
19440 Glendale St Detroit (48223) *(G-4129)*
Dearborn Mid-West Company LLC (PA) 734 288-4400
20334 Superior Rd Taylor (48180) *(G-16400)*
Dearborn Offset Printing Inc 313 561-1173
1946 Monroe St Dearborn (48124) *(G-3824)*
Dearborn Total Auto Svc Ctr 313 291-6300
23416 Van Born Rd Dearborn Heights (48125) *(G-3922)*
Dearborn Water Department, Dearborn Also called Water Department *(G-3915)*
Dearborn Works, Dearborn Also called Cleveland-Cliffs Steel Corp *(G-3820)*
Dearborne Cummins 313 843-6200
3760 Wyoming St Dearborn (48120) *(G-3825)*
Debbink and Sons Inc 231 845-6421
1010 Conrad Industrial Dr Ludington (49431) *(G-10533)*
Debi Designs 989 832-9598
2801 Saint Marys Dr Midland (48640) *(G-11336)*
Debron Industrial Elec LLC 248 588-7220
591 Executive Dr Troy (48083) *(G-17050)*
Deburring Company 734 542-9800
12690 Newburgh Rd Livonia (48150) *(G-10177)*
Decade Products LLC (PA) 616 975-4965
3400 Innovation Ct Se Grand Rapids (49512) *(G-6637)*
Decatur Republican, Decatur Also called Moormann Printing Inc *(G-3950)*
Decatur Wood Products Inc 269 657-6041
79201 M 51 Decatur (49045) *(G-3946)*
Decc Company Inc 616 245-0431
1266 Wallen Ave Sw Grand Rapids (49507) *(G-6638)*
Decca Pattern Co Inc 586 775-8450
29778 Little Mack Ave Roseville (48066) *(G-14395)*
Decker Gear Inc (PA) 810 388-1500
1500 Glendale St Saint Clair (48079) *(G-14825)*
Decker Manufacturing Corp (PA) 517 629-3955
703 N Clark St Albion (49224) *(G-124)*
Deckorators, White Pigeon Also called Maine Ornamental LLC *(G-18482)*
Deckorators Inc 616 365-4201
68956 Us Highway 131 White Pigeon (49099) *(G-18475)*
Declarks Landscaping Inc 586 752-7200
13800 33 Mile Rd Bruce Twp (48065) *(G-2166)*
Deco Engineering Inc 989 761-7521
9900 Main St Clifford (48727) *(G-3131)*
Deco Finishes, Pontiac Also called Akzo Nobel Coatings Inc *(G-13347)*

Decoma Admark, Troy *Also called Magna Exteriors America Inc* ***(G-17220)***
Decor Group International Inc....248 307-2430
3748 Sunset Blvd Orchard Lake (48324) ***(G-12716)***
Decorative Concrete By John....616 862-7152
5000 Fruit Ridge Ave Nw Grand Rapids (49544) ***(G-6639)***
Decorative Finishes Division....616 450-4918
13 Mcconnell St Sw Grand Rapids (49503) ***(G-6640)***
Decorative Panels Intl Inc....989 354-2121
416 Ford Ave Alpena (49707) ***(G-290)***
Decoties Inc....906 285-1286
807 Spring St Bessemer (49911) ***(G-1648)***
Dedoes Industries LLC (PA)....248 624-7710
1060 W West Maple Rd Walled Lake (48390) ***(G-17666)***
Dee-Blast Corporation (PA)....269 428-2400
5992 Oelke Park St Stevensville (49127) ***(G-16246)***
Deep Wood Press....231 587-0506
121 Cedar River Dr Bellaire (49615) ***(G-1474)***
Deerings Jerky Co LLC....231 590-5687
2015 Sandy Dr Interlochen (49643) ***(G-8682)***
Defense Component Detroit LLC....248 393-2300
1597 Atlantic Blvd Auburn Hills (48326) ***(G-861)***
Defense Components America LLC....248 789-1578
30955 Northwestern Hwy Farmington Hills (48334) ***(G-5211)***
Defiance Group, The, Westland *Also called Gt Technologies Inc* ***(G-18378)***
Deford Engine....989 872-3640
65 N Crawford Rd Deford (48729) ***(G-3960)***
Deforest & Bloom Septic Tanks....231 544-3599
7994 Houghton Rd Central Lake (49622) ***(G-2693)***
Degele Manufacturing Inc....586 949-3550
25700 Dhondt Ct Chesterfield (48051) ***(G-2869)***
Degrasyn Biosciences LLC....713 582-3395
4476 Boulder Pond Dr Ann Arbor (48108) ***(G-445)***
Dehaan Forest Products Inc....906 883-3417
25367 Mud Creek Rd Mass City (49948) ***(G-11161)***
Dehring Mold E-D-M....269 683-5970
1450 Jerome St Niles (49120) ***(G-12124)***
Dejon Cabinetry Inc....586 468-8611
44310 N Groesbeck Hwy Clinton Township (48036) ***(G-3218)***
Deka Batteries & Cables, Sterling Heights *Also called East Penn Manufacturing Co* ***(G-16001)***
Dekes Concrete Inc....810 686-5570
6653 Andersonville Rd Clarkston (48346) ***(G-3030)***
Dekker Bookbinding, Grand Rapids *Also called John H Dekker & Sons Inc* ***(G-6872)***
Dekoff & Sons Inc....269 344-5816
2531 Azo Dr Kalamazoo (49048) ***(G-9165)***
Delaco Steel Corporation (PA)....313 491-1200
8111 Tireman Ave Ste 1 Dearborn (48126) ***(G-3826)***
Deland Manufacturing Inc....586 323-2350
50674 Central Indus Dr Shelby Township (48315) ***(G-15202)***
Delaware Dynamics Michigan LLC....586 997-1717
50699 Central Indus Dr Shelby Township (48315) ***(G-15203)***
Delco Elec Overseas Corp (HQ)....248 813-2000
5820 Innovation Dr Troy (48098) ***(G-17051)***
Delfab Inc....906 428-9570
103 N 12th St Gladstone (49837) ***(G-6180)***
Delfield Company LLC....989 773-7981
980 S Isabella Rd Mount Pleasant (48858) ***(G-11695)***
Delfingen Industry, Rochester Hills *Also called Delfingen Us-Holding Inc* ***(G-13993)***
Delfingen Us Inc (HQ)....716 215-0300
3985 W Hamlin Rd Rochester Hills (48309) ***(G-13991)***
Delfingen Us-Central Amer Inc....248 230-3500
3985 W Hamlin Rd Rochester Hills (48309) ***(G-13992)***
Delfingen Us-Holding Inc (HQ)....248 230-3500
3985 W Hamlin Rd Rochester Hills (48309) ***(G-13993)***
Delicate Creations Inc....313 406-6268
25623 Pennie St Dearborn Heights (48125) ***(G-3923)***
Dell Marking Systems....248 481-2119
938 Featherstone St Pontiac (48342) ***(G-13359)***
Dell Marking Systems Inc....248 547-7750
6841 N Rochester Rd # 250 Rochester Hills (48306) ***(G-13994)***
Delmas Typesetting....734 662-8899
461 Hilldale Dr Ann Arbor (48105) ***(G-446)***
Delorean Aerospace LLC....248 752-2380
2779 Amberly Rd Bloomfield Hills (48301) ***(G-1812)***
Delorean Associates Inc....248 646-1930
2779 Amberly Rd Bloomfield Hills (48301) ***(G-1813)***
Delphi, Troy *Also called Aptiv Services 3 (us) LLC* ***(G-16946)***
Delphi, Auburn Hills *Also called Aptiv Corporation* ***(G-794)***
Delphi, Troy *Also called Aptiv Services Us LLC* ***(G-16948)***
Delphi, Troy *Also called Dph LLC* ***(G-17065)***
Delphi....248 813-2000
5725 Innovation Dr Troy (48098) ***(G-17052)***
Delphi Automotive Systems....248 813-2000
5820 Innovation Dr Troy (48098) ***(G-17053)***
Delphi Corp....313 996-3429
5800 Mercury Dr Dearborn (48126) ***(G-3827)***
Delphi Customer Tech Ctr Mich, Auburn Hills *Also called Aptiv Services Us LLC* ***(G-795)***
Delphi Powertrain Corporation, Auburn Hills *Also called Borgwarner USA Corporation* ***(G-828)***
Delphi Pwertrain Intl Svcs LLC, Auburn Hills *Also called Borgwarner Intl Svcs LLC* ***(G-820)***
Delphi Pwrtrain Tech Gen Prtnr....248 813-2000
5820 Innovation Dr Troy (48098) ***(G-17054)***
Delphi World Headquarters....248 813-3045
5725 Innovation Dr Troy (48098) ***(G-17055)***
Delphinus Medical Technologies....248 522-9600
45525 Grand River Ave Novi (48374) ***(G-12393)***
Delta 6 LLC....248 778-6414
20341 Parker St Livonia (48152) ***(G-10178)***
Delta Containers Inc (PA)....810 742-2730
1400 Eddy St Bay City (48708) ***(G-1342)***
Delta Gear Inc....734 525-8000
36251 Schoolcraft Rd Livonia (48150) ***(G-10179)***
Delta Iron Works Inc....313 579-1445
558 Lincoln Rd Grosse Pointe (48230) ***(G-7529)***
Delta Machining Inc....269 683-7775
2361 Reum Rd Niles (49120) ***(G-12125)***
Delta Manufacturing, Escanaba *Also called Hj Manufacturing Inc* ***(G-5076)***
Delta Optical Supply Inc....248 628-3977
496 Harwood Ct Oxford (48371) ***(G-12882)***
Delta Packaging International....517 321-6548
3463 Millwood Rd Lansing (48906) ***(G-9685)***
Delta Paving Inc....810 232-0220
4186 Holiday Dr Flint (48507) ***(G-5685)***
Delta Polymers Co (PA)....586 795-2900
6685 Sterling Dr N Sterling Heights (48312) ***(G-15980)***
Delta Precision Inc....248 585-2344
33214 Janet Fraser (48026) ***(G-5917)***
Delta Rail Division, Holly *Also called Delta Tube & Fabricating Corp* ***(G-8268)***
Delta Research Corporation....734 261-6400
32971 Capitol St Livonia (48150) ***(G-10180)***
Delta Six, Livonia *Also called Delta 6 LLC* ***(G-10178)***
Delta Sports Service & EMB....517 482-6565
1611 N Grand River Ave # 2 Lansing (48906) ***(G-9686)***
Delta Steel Inc....989 752-5129
1410 Webber St Saginaw (48601) ***(G-14637)***
Delta Technologies, LLC, Auburn Hills *Also called USF Delta Tooling LLC* ***(G-1075)***
Delta Tube & Fabricating Corp....810 239-0154
2610 N Dort Hwy Flint (48506) ***(G-5686)***
Delta Tube & Fabricating Corp (PA)....248 634-8267
4149 Grange Hall Rd Holly (48442) ***(G-8267)***
Delta Tube & Fabricating Corp....248 634-8267
4149 Grange Hall Rd Holly (48442) ***(G-8268)***
Delta Tube & Fabrication....810 233-0440
3020 Airpark Dr S Bldg A Flint (48507) ***(G-5687)***
Delta Welding Services....906 786-4348
411413 75th Rd Escanaba (49829) ***(G-5066)***
Deluxe Data Printers, Madison Heights *Also called Total Business Systems Inc* ***(G-10845)***
Deluxe Frame Company Inc....248 373-8811
2275 N Opdyke Rd Ste D Auburn Hills (48326) ***(G-862)***
Deluxe Technologies LLC....586 294-2340
34537 Bennett Fraser (48026) ***(G-5918)***
Demaria Building Company Inc....248 486-2598
53655 Grand River Ave New Hudson (48165) ***(G-12050)***
Demeester Wood Products Inc....616 677-5995
15527 32nd Ave Coopersville (49404) ***(G-3685)***
Demmak Industries LLC....586 884-6441
12475 31 Mile Rd Ste B Washington (48095) ***(G-18079)***
Demmem Enterprises LLC....810 564-9500
4268 W Vienna Rd Clio (48420) ***(G-3396)***
Demmer Corporation (HQ)....517 321-3600
4520 N Grand River Ave Lansing (48906) ***(G-9687)***
Demmer Investments Inc (PA)....517 321-3600
4520 N Grand River Ave Lansing (48906) ***(G-9688)***
Denali Incorporated....517 574-0047
11600 Maxfield Blvd Hartland (48353) ***(G-7768)***
Denali Lighting LLC....586 731-0399
50178 Van Dyke Ave Shelby Township (48317) ***(G-15204)***
Denarco Inc....269 435-8404
301 Industrial Park Dr Constantine (49042) ***(G-3664)***
Dendritech Inc....989 496-1152
3110 Schuette Rd Midland (48642) ***(G-11337)***
Dendritic Nanotechnologies Inc....989 774-3096
1515 Commerce Dr Ste C Midland (48642) ***(G-11338)***
Denesczuk Firebrick Company, Riverview *Also called Dfc Inc* ***(G-13870)***
Denim & Roses Childrens CL LLC....313 363-0387
16709 Rosemont Ave Detroit (48219) ***(G-4130)***
Denim City LLC....313 270-2942
15846 Murray Hill St Detroit (48227) ***(G-4131)***
Denlin Industries Inc....586 303-5209
371 Mill Pond Ln Milford (48381) ***(G-11461)***
Dennco LLC....866 977-4467
418 Ashmun St Ste E Sault Sainte Marie (49783) ***(G-15089)***
Dennison Automatics LLC....616 837-7063
12301 Cleveland St Ste A Nunica (49448) ***(G-12578)***
Denny Davis....989 785-3433
12090 Dennis St Atlanta (49709) ***(G-745)***

ALPHABETIC

Denny Grice Inc 269 279-6113
702 Webber Ave Three Rivers (49093) *(G-16570)*

Denova, Ann Arbor *Also called Cabinetworks Group Mich LLC (G-413)*

Denso Air Systems Michigan Inc (HQ) 269 962-9676
300 Fritz Keiper Blvd Battle Creek (49037) *(G-1215)*

Denso International Amer Inc 248 359-4177
8652 Haggerty Rd Ste 220 Van Buren Twp (48111) *(G-17523)*

Denso International Amer Inc (HQ) 248 350-7500
24777 Denso Dr Southfield (48033) *(G-15538)*

Denso Manufacturing Mich Inc (HQ) 269 965-3322
1 Denso Rd Battle Creek (49037) *(G-1216)*

Denso Manufacturing NC Inc 269 441-2040
500 Fritz Keiper Blvd Battle Creek (49037) *(G-1217)*

Denso Sales Michigan Inc 269 965-3322
1 Denso Rd Battle Creek (49037) *(G-1218)*

Dental Art Laboratories Inc 517 485-2200
1721 N Grand River Ave # 1 Lansing (48906) *(G-9689)*

Dental Consultants Inc 734 663-6777
3100 W Liberty Rd Ann Arbor (48103) *(G-447)*

Denton Atd Inc 734 451-7878
47460 Galleon Dr Plymouth (48170) *(G-13153)*

Denton Bobeldyk 616 669-2076
2711 Thrush Dr Jenison (49428) *(G-9051)*

Denudts Portable Welding 517 605-5154
12152 Wegner Rd Riga (49276) *(G-13848)*

Dependable Gage & Tool Co 248 545-2100
15321 W 11 Mile Rd Oak Park (48237) *(G-12604)*

Deperez Contracting LLC 947 224-1999
4192 31st St Detroit (48210) *(G-4132)*

Depierre Industries Inc 517 263-5781
1408 E Church St Adrian (49221) *(G-59)*

Depor Industries Inc (HQ) 248 362-3900
1902 Northwood Dr Troy (48084) *(G-17056)*

Depottey Acquisition Inc 616 846-4150
401 N Griffin St Grand Haven (49417) *(G-6291)*

Deppe Mold & Tooling Inc 616 530-1331
2814 Franklin Ave Sw Grandville (49418) *(G-7370)*

Derby Fabg Solutions LLC 616 866-1650
687 Byrne Industrial Dr Rockford (49341) *(G-14164)*

Derby Hats By Rachelle 248 489-0971
35945 Fredericksburg Rd Farmington Hills (48331) *(G-5212)*

Derk Pieter Co Inc 616 554-7777
4513 Broadmoor Ave Se A Grand Rapids (49512) *(G-6641)*

Deru Extracts LLC 734 497-2963
12915 Sumpter Rd Carleton (48117) *(G-2551)*

Deshler Group Inc (PA) 734 525-9100
34450 Industrial Rd Livonia (48150) *(G-10181)*

Design & Test Technology Inc 734 665-4111
2430 Scio Rd Dexter (48130) *(G-4733)*

Design & Test Technology Inc (PA) 734 665-4316
3744 Plaza Dr Ste 2 Ann Arbor (48108) *(G-448)*

Design Converting Inc 616 942-7780
3470 Raleigh Dr Se Grand Rapids (49512) *(G-6642)*

Design Design Inc (PA) 866 935-2648
19 La Grave Ave Se Grand Rapids (49503) *(G-6643)*

Design Fabrications Inc 248 597-0988
1100 E Mandoline Ave A Madison Heights (48071) *(G-10705)*

Design Manufacturing LLC 616 647-2229
1700 Northridge Dr Nw Walker (49544) *(G-17636)*

Design Metal Inc 248 547-4170
10841 Capital St Oak Park (48237) *(G-12605)*

Design Services Unlimited Inc 586 463-3225
25754 Dhondt Ct Chesterfield (48051) *(G-2870)*

Design Usa Inc 734 233-8677
14680 Jib St Plymouth (48170) *(G-13154)*

Designer Window Fashions 734 421-1600
436 N Center St Northville (48167) *(G-12212)*

Designers Sheet Metal Inc 269 429-4133
205 Palladium Dr Saint Joseph (49085) *(G-14926)*

Designotype Printers Inc 906 482-2424
22950 Airpark Blvd Laurium (49913) *(G-9979)*

Designs By D LLC 313 629-3617
107 Geneva St Highland Park (48203) *(G-7903)*

Designs In Stones, Muskegon *Also called Muskegon Monument & Stone Co (G-11882)*

Designs N Signs LLC 248 789-8797
28020 Groesbeck Hwy Roseville (48066) *(G-14396)*

Designs Unlimited, West Bloomfield *Also called Janice Morse Inc (G-18293)*

Designshirtscom Inc 734 414-7604
14777 Keel St Plymouth (48170) *(G-13155)*

Designtech Custom Interiors 989 695-6306
8570 Carter Rd Freeland (48623) *(G-6020)*

Deslatae 313 820-4321
5522 Bluehill St Detroit (48224) *(G-4133)*

Desrochers Brothers Inc 906 353-6346
107 3rd St Baraga (49908) *(G-1138)*

Destaco Industries, Auburn Hills *Also called Dover Energy Inc (G-865)*

Destiny Plastics Incorporated 810 622-0018
2121 Stoutenberg Deckerville (48427) *(G-3953)*

Destiny River, Wyoming *Also called Viking Spas Inc (G-18917)*

Detail Precision Products Inc 248 544-3390
1480 E 9 Mile Rd Ferndale (48220) *(G-5540)*

Detail Production Company Inc 248 544-3390
1480 E 9 Mile Rd Ferndale (48220) *(G-5541)*

Detail Standard Company, Roseville *Also called Paradigm Engineering Inc (G-14458)*

Detail Technologies LLC 616 261-1313
5900 Crssrds Cmmrce Pkwy Wyoming (49519) *(G-18866)*

Detmar Corporation 313 831-1155
2001 W Alexandrine St Detroit (48208) *(G-4134)*

Detroit Abrasives Company 989 725-2405
1500 W Oliver St Owosso (48867) *(G-12831)*

Detroit Abrasives Company (PA) 734 475-1651
11910 Dexter Chelsea Rd Chelsea (48118) *(G-2808)*

Detroit Architectural Metal, Redford *Also called Cmp Acquisitions LLC (G-13726)*

Detroit Asphalt Paving Company, Troy *Also called Ajax Materials Corporation (G-16912)*

Detroit Auto Specialties Inc 248 496-3856
6960 Orchard Lake Rd # 301 West Bloomfield (48322) *(G-18279)*

Detroit Axle, Ferndale *Also called Axle of Dearborn Inc (G-5529)*

Detroit Bikes LLC (PA) 313 646-4109
13639 Elmira St Detroit (48227) *(G-4135)*

Detroit Blow Pipe & Shtmtl 313 365-8970
7495 E Davison St Detroit (48212) *(G-4136)*

Detroit Boiler Company (PA) 313 921-7060
2931 Beaufait St Detroit (48207) *(G-4137)*

Detroit Boring & Mch Co LLC 586 604-6506
42818 Mound Rd Sterling Heights (48314) *(G-15981)*

Detroit Bubble Tea Company 248 239-1131
22821 Woodward Ave Ferndale (48220) *(G-5542)*

Detroit Bullet Works, Wixom *Also called Tactical Simplicity LLC (G-18765)*

Detroit Business Centercom Inc 313 255-4300
18461 W Mcnichols Rd Detroit (48219) *(G-4138)*

Detroit Chassis LLC 313 571-2100
6501 Lynch Rd Detroit (48234) *(G-4139)*

Detroit Chrome Inc 313 341-9478
7515 Lyndon St Detroit (48238) *(G-4140)*

Detroit City Distillery LLC 313 338-3760
2462 Riopelle St Detroit (48207) *(G-4141)*

Detroit CLB Prtg Hse Craftsmen 734 953-9729
9820 Seltzer St Livonia (48150) *(G-10182)*

Detroit Coil, Troy *Also called Ross Decco Company (G-17337)*

Detroit Coil Co 248 658-1543
2435 Hilton Rd Ferndale (48220) *(G-5543)*

Detroit Cornice & Slate Co Inc 248 398-7690
1315 Academy St Ferndale (48220) *(G-5544)*

Detroit Couture 734 237-6826
17390 W 8 Mile Rd Southfield (48075) *(G-15539)*

Detroit Cover, Romulus *Also called John Johnson Company (G-14291)*

Detroit Cstm Trck Trailor LLC 734 925-2233
33234 Beechwood St Westland (48185) *(G-18363)*

Detroit Custom Chassis LLC 313 571-2100
6501 Lynch Rd Detroit (48234) *(G-4142)*

Detroit Custom Services Inc (PA) 586 465-3631
150 N Groesbeck Hwy Mount Clemens (48043) *(G-11636)*

Detroit Cycle Pub LLC 231 286-5257
16089 Diamante Dr Macomb (48044) *(G-10587)*

Detroit Denim Company LLC 313 626-9216
109 Eason St Highland Park (48203) *(G-7904)*

Detroit Denim LLC 313 351-1040
12811 Hillview St Detroit (48227) *(G-4143)*

Detroit Diameters Inc 248 669-2330
45380 W Park Dr Novi (48377) *(G-12394)*

Detroit Diesel Corporation (HQ) 313 592-5000
13400 W Outer Dr Detroit (48239) *(G-4144)*

Detroit Diesel Corporation 313 592-8256
12200 Telegraph Rd Redford (48239) *(G-13730)*

Detroit Diesel USA, Detroit *Also called Detroit Diesel Corporation (G-4144)*

Detroit Dumpster Inc 313 466-3174
8701 Grinnell St Detroit (48213) *(G-4145)*

Detroit Edge Tool Company (PA) 313 366-4120
6570 E Nevada St Detroit (48234) *(G-4146)*

Detroit Edge Tool Company 586 776-3727
28370 Groesbeck Hwy Roseville (48066) *(G-14397)*

Detroit Edge Tool Company 586 776-1598
28370 Groesbeck Hwy Roseville (48066) *(G-14398)*

Detroit Elevator Company 248 591-7484
2121 Burdette St Ste A Ferndale (48220) *(G-5545)*

Detroit Fd Entrprnrship Acdemy 248 894-8941
4444 2nd Ave Detroit (48201) *(G-4147)*

Detroit Fine Products LLC 877 294-5826
2615 Wolcott St Ste E Ferndale (48220) *(G-5546)*

Detroit Flame Hardening Co 586 484-1726
35674 Shook Ln Clinton Township (48035) *(G-3219)*

DETROIT FOOD ACADEMY, Detroit *Also called Detroit Fd Entrprnrship Acdemy (G-4147)*

Detroit Free Press, Saginaw *Also called Detroit Newspaper Partnr LP (G-14638)*

Detroit Free Press Inc (HQ) 313 222-2300
160 W Fort St Fl 1 Detroit (48226) *(G-4148)*

Detroit Frends Potato Chip LLC 313 924-0085
8230 E Forest Ave Detroit (48214) *(G-4149)*

Detroit Fudge Company Inc....734 369-8573
2251 W Liberty St Ann Arbor (48103) *(G-449)*
Detroit Gear & Axle Facility, Detroit *Also called American Axle & Mfg Inc (G-4010)*
Detroit Grooming Company LLC, Ferndale *Also called Detroit Fine Products LLC (G-5546)*
Detroit Hitch Co....248 379-0071
651 N Rochester Rd Clawson (48017) *(G-3094)*
Detroit Hoist & Crane Co L L C....586 268-2600
6650 Sterling Dr N Sterling Heights (48312) *(G-15982)*
Detroit Impression Company Inc....313 921-9077
1351 Three Mile Dr Grosse Pointe Park (48230) *(G-7551)*
Detroit Jewish New, Farmington Hills *Also called Renaissance Media LLC (G-5367)*
Detroit Jewish News Ltd Partnr (PA)....248 354-6060
32255 Northwestern Hwy Farmington Hills (48334) *(G-5213)*
Detroit Laser Co LLC....313 338-9494
24770 Crestview Ct Farmington Hills (48335) *(G-5214)*
Detroit Legal News Company (PA)....313 961-6000
2001 W Lafayette Blvd Detroit (48216) *(G-4150)*
Detroit Legal News Pubg LLC....248 577-6100
1409 Allen Dr Ste B Troy (48083) *(G-17057)*
Detroit Legal News Pubg LLC....734 477-0201
2301 Platt Rd Ste 300 Ann Arbor (48104) *(G-450)*
Detroit Litho Inc....313 993-6186
8200 W Outer Dr Detroit (48219) *(G-4151)*
Detroit Marking Products Corp....313 838-9760
8201 Ronda Dr Canton (48187) *(G-2454)*
Detroit Materials Inc....248 924-5436
33225 Grand River Ave Farmington (48336) *(G-5136)*
Detroit Media Partnership, Detroit *Also called Detroit Newspaper Partnr LP (G-4155)*
Detroit Metal Elements LLC....313 300-9057
23334 Schoenherr Rd Warren (48089) *(G-17776)*
Detroit Mfg Systems LLC (PA)....313 243-0700
12701 Suthfield Rd Bldg A Detroit (48223) *(G-4152)*
Detroit Mini Safe Co, Carleton *Also called A & L Metal Products (G-2549)*
Detroit Name Plate Etching Inc....248 543-5200
10610 Galaxie Ave Ferndale (48220) *(G-5547)*
Detroit News Inc....313 222-6400
600 W Fort St Detroit (48226) *(G-4153)*
Detroit News Inc....313 222-6400
6200 Metropolitan Pkwy Sterling Heights (48312) *(G-15983)*
Detroit News Inc....313 222-6400
615 W Lafayette Blvd Detroit (48226) *(G-4154)*
Detroit News, The, Detroit *Also called Detroit News Inc (G-4153)*
Detroit News, The, Detroit *Also called Detroit Free Press Inc (G-4148)*
Detroit News, The, Sterling Heights *Also called Detroit News Inc (G-15983)*
Detroit News, The, Detroit *Also called Detroit News Inc (G-4154)*
Detroit Newspaper Partnr LP....989 752-3023
2654 N Outer Dr Ste 4 Saginaw (48601) *(G-14638)*
Detroit Newspaper Partnr LP....586 826-7187
6200 Metropolitan Pkwy Sterling Heights (48312) *(G-15984)*
Detroit Newspaper Partnr LP (HQ)....313 222-2300
160 W Fort St Detroit (48226) *(G-4155)*
Detroit Newspaper Partnr LP....313 222-6400
600 W Fort St Detroit (48226) *(G-4156)*
Detroit Nipple Works Inc (PA)....313 872-6370
6530 Beaubien St Detroit (48202) *(G-4157)*
Detroit Office & Warehouse, Detroit *Also called FCA US LLC (G-4230)*
Detroit Original Winery....248 924-2920
44464 Larchwood Dr Northville (48168) *(G-12213)*
Detroit Peanuts LLC....313 826-4327
1515 W Lafayette Blvd Detroit (48216) *(G-4158)*
Detroit Plate Fabricators Inc....313 921-7020
2931 Beaufait St Detroit (48207) *(G-4159)*
Detroit Popcorn Company, Redford *Also called Farber Concessions Inc (G-13733)*
Detroit Popcorn Company, Redford *Also called We Pop Corn LLC (G-13786)*
Detroit Printed Products....586 226-3860
42121 Brianna Dr Clinton Township (48038) *(G-3220)*
Detroit Qulty Brush Mfg Co Inc....734 525-5660
32165 Schoolcraft Rd Livonia (48150) *(G-10183)*
Detroit Radiator, Taylor *Also called Heavy Duty Radiator LLC (G-16426)*
Detroit Radiator Corporation....800 525-0011
26111 Northline Rd Taylor (48180) *(G-16401)*
Detroit Ready Mix Concrete....313 931-7043
9189 Central St Detroit (48204) *(G-4160)*
Detroit Recker Sales, Southfield *Also called Hydro King Incorporated (G-15596)*
Detroit Recycled Concrete Co (PA)....248 553-0600
39525 W 13 Mile Rd # 300 Novi (48377) *(G-12395)*
Detroit Recycled Concrete Co....313 934-7677
14294 Meyers Rd Detroit (48227) *(G-4161)*
Detroit Renewable Energy LLC....313 972-5700
541 Madison St Detroit (48226) *(G-4162)*
Detroit Rvrtown Brwing Cmpay L....313 877-9205
237 Joseph Campau St Detroit (48207) *(G-4163)*
Detroit Sales Office, West Bloomfield *Also called Phillips-Medisize LLC (G-18305)*
Detroit Salt Company LC (HQ)....313 554-0456
12841 Sanders St Detroit (48217) *(G-4164)*
Detroit Savings LLC....313 971-5696
1509 Chateaufort Pl Detroit (48207) *(G-4165)*
Detroit Sewn Inc....248 722-8407
67 N Saginaw St Pontiac (48342) *(G-13360)*
Detroit Sign Factory LLC....313 782-4667
2900 E Jefferson Ave B4 Detroit (48207) *(G-4166)*
Detroit Signs LLC....313 345-5858
2648 E Jefferson Ave B Detroit (48207) *(G-4167)*
Detroit Sls & Engrg Ctr Div of, Farmington Hills *Also called Akwel Cadillac Usa Inc (G-5166)*
Detroit Sock & Stocking Co LLC....313 409-8735
1465 Lakepointe St Grosse Pointe Park (48230) *(G-7552)*
Detroit Steel Group Inc....248 298-2900
916 S Washington Ave Royal Oak (48067) *(G-14530)*
Detroit Steel Treating Company....248 334-7436
1631 Highwood E Pontiac (48340) *(G-13361)*
Detroit Stoker Company....734 241-9500
1510 E 1st St Monroe (48161) *(G-11537)*
Detroit Tarpaulin Repr Sp Inc....734 955-8200
6760 Metro Plex Dr Romulus (48174) *(G-14267)*
Detroit Tech Innovation LLC....734 259-4168
25036 W 6 Mile Rd Redford (48240) *(G-13731)*
Detroit Testing Machine Co....248 669-3100
46590 Ryan Ct Novi (48377) *(G-12396)*
Detroit Thermal, Detroit *Also called Detroit Renewable Energy LLC (G-4162)*
Detroit Torch....248 499-8122
1555 W Hamlin Rd Rochester Hills (48309) *(G-13995)*
Detroit Torch Company, Lake Orion *Also called Cobra Torches Inc (G-9594)*
Detroit Tube Products LLC....313 841-0300
300 S Junction St Detroit (48209) *(G-4168)*
Detroit Tubing Mill Inc....313 491-8823
12301 Hubbell St Detroit (48227) *(G-4169)*
Detroit Tubular Rivet Inc (PA)....734 282-7979
1213 Grove St Wyandotte (48192) *(G-18816)*
Detroit Washer & Specials, West Bloomfield *Also called Mh Industries Ltd (G-18298)*
Detroit Wilbert Vault Corp....313 862-1616
20514 Woodingham Dr Detroit (48221) *(G-4170)*
Detroit Wire Rope Splcing Corp....248 585-1063
31623 Stephenson Hwy Madison Heights (48071) *(G-10706)*
Detroit Wlbert Crmtion Svcs LL....248 853-0559
70 S Squirrel Rd Auburn Hills (48326) *(G-863)*
Detroit Woodworking, Saint Clair Shores *Also called Elite Woodworking LLC (G-14856)*
Detroit Wrecker Sales Llc....313 835-8700
19303 W Davison St Detroit (48223) *(G-4171)*
Detroit's Own, Livonia *Also called McKae Group LLC (G-10307)*
Detroits Very Own CL Co LLC....313 614-1033
15517 Appoline St Detroit (48227) *(G-4172)*
Detronic Industries Inc (PA)....586 977-5660
35800 Beattie Dr Sterling Heights (48312) *(G-15985)*
Deuwave LLC....888 238-9283
200 S Wing St Northville (48167) *(G-12214)*
Development Office, Plymouth *Also called Toledo Molding & Die Inc (G-13317)*
Developmental Services Inc....313 653-1185
13621 Park Grove St Detroit (48205) *(G-4173)*
Devereaux Saw Mill Inc....989 593-2552
2872 N Hubbardston Rd Pewamo (48873) *(G-13027)*
Dewent Redi-Mix LLC....616 457-2100
1601 Chicago Dr Jenison (49428) *(G-9052)*
Deweys Lumberville Inc....313 885-0960
757 Notre Dame St Grosse Pointe (48230) *(G-7530)*
Dewitt Packaging Corporation....616 698-0210
5080 Kraft Ave Se Grand Rapids (49512) *(G-6644)*
Dewitts Radiator LLC....517 548-0600
1275 Grand Oaks Dr Howell (48843) *(G-8444)*
Dewsbury Manufactruing Company, Trenton *Also called Rick Wykle LLC (G-16891)*
Dewsbury Manufacturing Company....734 839-6376
3022 Strohm Ave Trenton (48183) *(G-16887)*
Dewys Manufacturing Inc (PA)....616 677-5281
15300 8th Ave Marne (49435) *(G-10991)*
Dexko Global Inc (HQ)....248 533-0029
39555 Orchard Hill Pl Novi (48375) *(G-12397)*
Dexsys, Lansing *Also called Norplas Industries Inc (G-9781)*
Dextech, Dexter *Also called Dexter Fastener Tech Inc (G-4736)*
Dexter Automatic Products Co....734 426-8900
2500 Bishop Cir E Dexter (48130) *(G-4734)*
Dexter Cabinet Works Inc....734 426-5035
1084 Baker Rd Dexter (48130) *(G-4735)*
Dexter Cider Mill Inc....734 475-6419
4885 Kalmbach Rd Chelsea (48118) *(G-2809)*
Dexter Fastener Tech Inc (PA)....734 426-0311
2110 Bishop Cir E Dexter (48130) *(G-4736)*
Dexter Fastener Tech Inc....734 426-5200
2103 Bishop Cir W Dexter (48130) *(G-4737)*
Dexter Manufacturing Inc....734 475-8046
20401 W Old Us Highway 12 # 1 Chelsea (48118) *(G-2810)*
Dexter Print & Stitch....734 580-2181
3170 Baker Rd Dexter (48130) *(G-4738)*
Dexter Research Center Inc....734 426-3921
7300 Huron River Dr Ste 2 Dexter (48130) *(G-4739)*
Dexter Stamping Company LLC....517 750-3414
1013 Thorrez Rd Jackson (49201) *(G-8866)*

ALPHABETIC

Dfc Inc.....734 285-6749
17651 Yorkshire Dr Riverview (48193) *(G-13870)*
DFI, Clinton Township *Also called Diversified Fabricators Inc (G-3225)*
DForte Inc.....269 657-6996
57440 County Road 671 Paw Paw (49079) *(G-12946)*
Dg Brewing Company LLC.....616 427-3242
5530 Clemwood Ct Se Ada (49301) *(G-16)*
DGa Printing Inc.....586 979-2244
567 Robbins Dr Troy (48083) *(G-17058)*
Dgh Enterprises Inc (PA).....269 925-0657
1225 Milton St Benton Harbor (49022) *(G-1546)*
Dgh Enterprises Inc.....269 925-0657
1225 Milton St Benton Harbor (49022) *(G-1547)*
Dgp Inc.....989 635-7531
3260 Fenner St Marlette (48453) *(G-10980)*
DH Custom Fabrication.....517 264-8045
1209 E Beecher St Adrian (49221) *(G-60)*
DH Custom Fabrication.....517 366-9067
2314 Treat St Adrian (49221) *(G-61)*
Dhake Industries Inc.....734 420-0101
15169 Northville Rd Plymouth (48170) *(G-13156)*
Dhs Inc.....313 724-6566
1925 Elsmere St Detroit (48209) *(G-4174)*
Dhs/Cbp.....586 954-2214
41130 Castle Ave Selfridge Angb (48045) *(G-15147)*
Di Square America Inc.....248 374-5051
39555 Orchard Hill Pl Novi (48375) *(G-12398)*
DI Tee Pee LLC.....906 493-6929
38336 S Glen Cove Rd Drummond Island (49726) *(G-4800)*
Di-Anodic Finishing Corp.....616 454-0470
736 Ottawa Ave Nw 38 Grand Rapids (49503) *(G-6645)*
Di-Coat Corporation.....248 349-1211
42900 W 9 Mile Rd Novi (48375) *(G-12399)*
Diack, Beulah *Also called Auric Enterprises Inc (G-1652)*
Diagknowstics Tutoring.....877 382-1133
44165 Vassar St Canton (48188) *(G-2455)*
Diagnostic Instruments Inc.....586 731-6000
6540 Burroughs Ave Sterling Heights (48314) *(G-15986)*
Diagnostic Systems Assoc Inc.....269 544-9000
6190 Technology Ave Kalamazoo (49009) *(G-9166)*
Dial Tent & Awning Co.....989 793-0741
5330 Davis Rd Saginaw (48604) *(G-14639)*
Dialogue, Grand Rapids *Also called Intaglio LLC (G-6848)*
Diamond Alternatives LLC.....734 755-1505
11602 Finzel Rd Carleton (48117) *(G-2552)*
Diamond Automation Ltd.....734 838-7138
32235 Industrial Rd Livonia (48150) *(G-10184)*
Diamond Boutique.....313 451-4217
3200 Greenfield Rd # 300 Dearborn (48120) *(G-3828)*
Diamond Broach Company.....586 757-5131
3560 E 10 Mile Rd Warren (48091) *(G-17777)*
Diamond Chrome Plating Inc.....517 546-0150
604 S Michigan Ave Howell (48843) *(G-8445)*
Diamond Die and Mold Company.....586 791-0700
35401 Groesbeck Hwy Clinton Township (48035) *(G-3221)*
Diamond Electric.....734 995-5525
455 E Eisenhower Pkwy # 200 Ann Arbor (48108) *(G-451)*
Diamond Electric Mfg Corp.....734 995-5525
23065 Commerce Dr Farmington Hills (48335) *(G-5215)*
Diamond Graphics Inc.....269 345-1164
2328 Lake St Kalamazoo (49048) *(G-9167)*
Diamond Moba Americas Inc.....248 476-7100
23400 Haggerty Rd Farmington Hills (48335) *(G-5216)*
Diamond Power Specialty Co.....734 429-8527
1779 Oakview Dr Ann Arbor (48108) *(G-452)*
Diamond Press Solutions LLC.....269 945-1997
1611 S Hanover St Hastings (49058) *(G-7789)*
Diamond Racing Products.....586 792-6620
35075 Automation Dr Clinton Township (48035) *(G-3222)*
Diamond Racing Products Inc.....586 792-6620
23003 Diamond Dr Clinton Township (48035) *(G-3223)*
Diamond Recyclers, Carleton *Also called Diamond Alternatives LLC (G-2552)*
Diamond Sign.....586 519-4296
7067 Continental Ave Warren (48091) *(G-17778)*
Diamond Standard Mch Co LLC.....248 805-7144
199 Dogwood Dr Oakland (48363) *(G-12652)*
Diamond Systems, Farmington Hills *Also called Diamond Moba Americas Inc (G-5216)*
Diamond Tool Manufacturing.....616 895-4007
6075 Taylor St Hudsonville (49426) *(G-8580)*
Diamond Tool Manufacturing Inc.....734 416-1900
14540 Jib St Plymouth (48170) *(G-13157)*
Diamondback Abrasive Co, Commerce Township *Also called Diamondback Corp (G-3522)*
Diamondback Corp.....248 960-8260
3141 Old Farm Ln Commerce Township (48390) *(G-3522)*
Diamondbck-Drectional Drlg LLC.....231 943-3000
2122 S M 37 Traverse City (49685) *(G-16668)*
Dianamic Abrasive Products.....248 280-1185
2566 Industrial Row Dr Troy (48084) *(G-17059)*
Dias Holding Inc.....313 928-1254
16630 Southfield Rd Allen Park (48101) *(G-192)*
Diazem Corp.....989 832-3612
1406 E Pine St Midland (48640) *(G-11339)*
Dibbleville Woodwork Co.....810 750-1139
12272 N Fenton Rd Ste 3 Fenton (48430) *(G-5470)*
Dicastal North America Inc (HQ).....616 619-7500
1 Dicastal Dr Greenville (48838) *(G-7482)*
Dice Corporation.....989 891-2800
1410 S Valley Center Dr Bay City (48706) *(G-1343)*
Dick and Jane Baking Co LLC.....248 519-2418
755 W Big Beaver Rd # 2020 Troy (48084) *(G-17060)*
Dickinson Homes Inc (PA).....906 774-5800
1500 W Breitung Ave Kingsford (49802) *(G-9508)*
Dicks Signs.....810 987-9002
2560 40th St Port Huron (48060) *(G-13468)*
Dico Manufacturing LLC.....586 731-3008
48605 Structural Dr Chesterfield (48051) *(G-2871)*
Die Cad Group.....937 243-8327
8595 Byron Commerce Dr Sw Byron Center (49315) *(G-2266)*
Die Cast Press Mfg Co Inc (PA).....269 657-6060
56480 Kasper Dr Paw Paw (49079) *(G-12947)*
Die Services International LLC.....734 699-3400
45000 Van Born Rd Van Buren Twp (48111) *(G-17524)*
Die Stampco Inc.....989 893-7790
1301 N Lincoln St Bay City (48708) *(G-1344)*
Die Tech Services Inc.....616 363-6604
2457 Waldorf Ct Nw Walker (49544) *(G-17637)*
Die-Matic Tool and Die Inc.....616 531-0060
4309 Aldrich Ave Sw Wyoming (49509) *(G-18867)*
Die-Matic USA LLC.....616 531-0060
4309 Aldrich Ave Sw Wyoming (49509) *(G-18868)*
Die-Mold-Automation Component.....313 581-6510
14300 Henn St Ste A Dearborn (48126) *(G-3829)*
Die-Namic Inc.....734 710-3200
7565 Haggerty Rd Van Buren Twp (48111) *(G-17525)*
Die-Namic Tool & Design Llc.....517 787-4900
147 Hobart St Jackson (49202) *(G-8867)*
Die-Namic Tool Corp.....616 954-7882
4541 Patterson Ave Se Grand Rapids (49512) *(G-6646)*
Die-Tech and Engineering Inc.....616 530-9030
4620 Herman Ave Sw Grand Rapids (49509) *(G-6647)*
Die-Verse Solutions LLC.....616 914-9427
1174 Comstock St Marne (49435) *(G-10992)*
Diebotics, Comstock Park *Also called Preferred Tool & Die Co Inc (G-3638)*
Diecutting Service Inc.....734 426-0290
2415 Bishop Cir W Dexter (48130) *(G-4740)*
Diehl Inc.....517 265-5045
1336 E Maumee St Adrian (49221) *(G-62)*
Dieomatic Incorporated.....269 966-4900
10 Clark Rd Battle Creek (49037) *(G-1219)*
Dieomatic Incorporated (HQ).....319 668-2031
750 Twer Dr Mail Code 700 Troy (48098) *(G-17061)*
Dies and Fixtures Mold Corp.....269 465-6633
8088 Jericho Rd Bridgman (49106) *(G-1924)*
Diesel Performance Products.....586 726-7478
7459 Flickinger Dr Shelby Township (48317) *(G-15205)*
Dietech, Norton Shores *Also called Bry Mac Inc (G-12280)*
Dietech NA, Roseville *Also called Dietech North America LLC (G-14399)*
Dietech North America LLC.....586 771-8580
16630 Eastland St Roseville (48066) *(G-14399)*
Dietech Tool & Mfg Inc.....810 724-0505
385 Industrial Dr Imlay City (48444) *(G-8630)*
Dietert Foundry Testing Eqp (PA).....313 491-4680
9190 Roselawn St Detroit (48204) *(G-4175)*
Diez Group LLC (PA).....734 675-1700
25325 Hall Rd Woodhaven (48183) *(G-18799)*
Different By Design Inc.....248 588-4840
38611 Cedarbrook Ct Farmington Hills (48331) *(G-5217)*
Different Music Group Ent LLC.....313 980-6159
42389 Clinton Place Dr Clinton Township (48038) *(G-3224)*
Digested Organics LLC.....844 934-4378
23745 Research Dr Farmington Hills (48335) *(G-5218)*
Diggypod Inc.....734 429-3307
301 Industrial Dr Tecumseh (49286) *(G-16496)*
Digigraphx Co.....586 755-1130
24722 Forterra Dr Warren (48089) *(G-17779)*
DIGILIANT, Okemos *Also called Digilink Technology Inc (G-12664)*
Digilink Technology Inc.....517 381-8888
5100 Marsh Rd Ste E3 Okemos (48864) *(G-12664)*
Digimax Business Corporation.....313 255-4300
18461 W Mcnichols Rd Detroit (48219) *(G-4176)*
Digimax Copy Store, Detroit *Also called Detroit Business Centercom Inc (G-4138)*
Digiscroll Press.....214 846-1826
2320 Rolling Meadow Dr Ne Belmont (49306) *(G-1505)*
Digital Die Solutions Inc.....734 542-2222
13281 Merriman Rd Livonia (48150) *(G-10185)*
Digital Fabrication Inc.....616 794-2848
7251 Whites Bridge Rd Belding (48809) *(G-1445)*
Digital Imaging Group Inc.....269 686-8744
504 Eastern Ave Allegan (49010) *(G-155)*

Digital Impact Design Inc...269 337-4200
403 Balch St Kalamazoo (49001) ***(G-9168)***
Digital Performance Tech...877 983-4230
3221 W Big Beaver Rd Troy (48084) ***(G-17062)***
Digital Print Specialties...248 545-5888
6538 Russell St Detroit (48211) ***(G-4177)***
Digital Printing & Graphics...586 566-9499
50711 Wing Dr Shelby Township (48315) ***(G-15206)***
Digital Printing Solutions LLC...586 566-4910
48688 Eagle Butte Ct Shelby Township (48315) ***(G-15207)***
Digital Success Network...517 244-0771
205 S Cedar St Mason (48854) ***(G-11130)***
Digital Tool & Die Inc...616 532-8020
2606 Sanford Ave Sw Grandville (49418) ***(G-7371)***
Digital Xpress...248 325-9061
5262 Potomac Run E West Bloomfield (48322) ***(G-18280)***
Digitaleo Corporation...248 250-9205
755 W Big Beaver Rd Troy (48084) ***(G-17063)***
Digitally Assured...734 730-8800
1320 Warner St Ypsilanti (48197) ***(G-18939)***
Digitrace Limited, Wayland *Also called Digitrace Machine Works Ltd* ***(G-18194)***
Digitrace Machine Works Ltd...616 877-4818
1158 Morren Ct Wayland (49348) ***(G-18194)***
Dihydro Services Inc...586 978-0900
40833 Brentwood Dr Sterling Heights (48310) ***(G-15987)***
Dijet Incorporated (HQ)...734 454-9100
45807 Helm St Plymouth (48170) ***(G-13158)***
Dikar Tool Company Inc...248 348-0010
22635 Heslip Dr Novi (48375) ***(G-12400)***
Dillion Renee Entities...989 443-0654
600 Baker St Lansing (48910) ***(G-9830)***
Dillon Forest Products, Republic *Also called Dillon Forest Products Inc* ***(G-13820)***
Dillon Forest Products Inc...906 869-4671
2666 State Highway M95 Republic (49879) ***(G-13820)***
Dimaggio Jseph A Mstr Gldsmith, Grosse Pointe Woods *Also called Joseph A Dimaggio* ***(G-7569)***
Dimension Graphics Inc...616 245-1447
800 Burton St Se Grand Rapids (49507) ***(G-6648)***
Dimension Machine Tech LLC...586 649-4747
18815 Kelly Ct Bloomfield Hills (48304) ***(G-1814)***
Dimension Products Corporation...616 842-6050
13746 172nd Ave Grand Haven (49417) ***(G-6292)***
Dimitri Mansour...248 684-4545
426 N Main St Milford (48381) ***(G-11462)***
Dimond Machinery Company Inc...269 945-5908
922 N M 37 Hwy Hastings (49058) ***(G-7790)***
Dimplex Thermal Solutions Inc (HQ)...269 349-6800
2625 Emerald Dr Kalamazoo (49001) ***(G-9169)***
Dina Mia Kitchens Inc...906 265-9082
751 N 4th Ave Iron River (49935) ***(G-8740)***
Dino S Dumpsters LLC...989 225-5635
900 Harry S Truman Pkwy Bay City (48706) ***(G-1345)***
Diocesan Publications (PA)...616 878-5200
1050 74th St Sw Byron Center (49315) ***(G-2267)***
Diocese of Lansing...517 484-4449
1500 W Saginaw St Ste 2 Lansing (48915) ***(G-9831)***
Diop Collection LLC...313 522-6029
16145 Ferguson St Detroit (48235) ***(G-4178)***
Diplomat Spclty Phrm Flint LLC...810 768-9000
4100 S Saginaw St Flint (48507) ***(G-5688)***
Dipsol Chemicals, Livonia *Also called Dipsol of America Inc* ***(G-10186)***
Dipsol of America Inc...734 367-0530
34005 Schoolcraft Rd Livonia (48150) ***(G-10186)***
Direct Aim Media LLC...800 817-7101
1778 Grand Ct Ne Grand Rapids (49525) ***(G-6649)***
Directional Drilling Contrs, Traverse City *Also called Diamondbck-Drectional Drlg LLC* ***(G-16668)***
Directv Dish Doctor...989 983-3214
11803 Dunham Rd Vanderbilt (49795) ***(G-17569)***
Dirkes Industries, Saint Clair *Also called Reeling Systems LLC* ***(G-14841)***
Dirksen Screw Products Co (PA)...586 247-5400
14490 23 Mile Rd Shelby Township (48315) ***(G-15208)***
Discount Jewelry Center Inc...734 266-8200
8339 N Wayne Rd Westland (48185) ***(G-18364)***
Discount Pallets...616 453-5455
4580 Airwest Dr Se Grand Rapids (49512) ***(G-6650)***
Discount Restaurant & Supply...574 370-9574
2035 28th St Sw Wyoming (49519) ***(G-18869)***
Discount Vitamin Store, Jackson *Also called Trulife Inc* ***(G-9026)***
Discover Your Mobility Inc...866 868-9694
32 E 10 Mile Rd Hazel Park (48030) ***(G-7823)***
Discovery Gold Corp...269 429-7002
4472 Winding Ln Stevensville (49127) ***(G-16247)***
Discovery House Publishers...616 942-9218
3000 Kraft Ave Se Grand Rapids (49512) ***(G-6651)***
Discovery Map...231 421-1466
958 Shamrock Ln Traverse City (49696) ***(G-16669)***
Discraft Inc...248 624-2250
51000 Grand River Ave Wixom (48393) ***(G-18645)***
Dispense Technologies LLC...248 486-6244
7036 Kensington Rd Brighton (48116) ***(G-1975)***
Display Cses By Grndpas Cbnets...586 506-2222
55750 Danube Ave Macomb (48042) ***(G-10588)***
Display Pack Inc (PA)...616 451-3061
650 West St Cedar Springs (49319) ***(G-2649)***
Display Pack Disc Vdh Inc...616 451-3061
650 West St Cedar Springs (49319) ***(G-2650)***
Dissrad Inc...586 463-8722
195 Grand Ave Mount Clemens (48043) ***(G-11637)***
Distilled Kalamazoo LLC...269 993-2859
3903 Devonshire Ave Kalamazoo (49006) ***(G-9170)***
Distillery 9 LLC...517 990-2929
8040 Apple Creek Ct Whitmore Lake (48189) ***(G-18530)***
Distinctive Appliances Distrg...248 380-2007
51155 Grand River Ave Wixom (48393) ***(G-18646)***
Distinctive Machine Corp...616 433-4111
300 Byrne Industrial Dr B Rockford (49341) ***(G-14165)***
Distinctive Machining, Zeeland *Also called Distinctive Mfg Group LLC* ***(G-19015)***
Distinctive Mfg Group LLC...616 953-8999
759 Construction Ct Ste 2 Zeeland (49464) ***(G-19015)***
Distyll Graphics, Adrian *Also called Adrian Steel Company* ***(G-50)***
Div Edw C Levy Co, Wixom *Also called Lyon Sand & Gravel Co* ***(G-18701)***
Diva Publications...517 887-8271
4018 Seaway Dr Lansing (48911) ***(G-9832)***
Diverse Manufacturing Soltion...517 423-6691
805 S Maumee St Tecumseh (49286) ***(G-16497)***
Diversfied Chem Tchnlgies Oprt...313 867-5444
15477 Woodrow Wilson St Detroit (48238) ***(G-4179)***
Diversfied Prcurement Svcs LLC...248 821-1147
1530 Farrow St Ferndale (48220) ***(G-5548)***
Diversfied Tchncal Systems Inc...248 513-6050
25881 Meadowbrook Rd Novi (48375) ***(G-12401)***
Diversified Chemical Tech Inc (PA)...313 867-5444
15477 Woodrow Wilson St Detroit (48238) ***(G-4180)***
Diversified Davitco LLC...248 681-9197
2569 Dixie Hwy Waterford (48328) ***(G-18115)***
Diversified E D M Inc...248 547-2320
1019 E 10 Mile Rd Madison Heights (48071) ***(G-10707)***
Diversified Engrg & Plas LLC...517 789-8118
1801 Wildwood Ave Jackson (49202) ***(G-8868)***
Diversified Fabricators Inc...586 868-1000
21482 Carlo Dr Clinton Township (48038) ***(G-3225)***
Diversified Machine Inc...231 894-9562
5353 Wilcox St Montague (49437) ***(G-11595)***
Diversified Mech Svcs Inc...616 785-2735
844 W River Center Dr Ne Comstock Park (49321) ***(G-3602)***
Diversified Metal Fabricators...248 541-0500
2351 Hilton Rd Ferndale (48220) ***(G-5549)***
Diversified Metal Products Inc...989 448-7120
1489 Oorouk Blvd Gaylord (49735) ***(G-6126)***
Diversified Mfg & Assembly LLC (PA)...586 272-2431
5545 Bridgewood Dr Sterling Heights (48310) ***(G-15988)***
Diversified Pdts & Svcs LLC...616 836-6600
500 E 8th St Holland (49423) ***(G-8014)***
Diversified Precision Pdts Inc...517 750-2310
6999 Spring Arbor Rd Spring Arbor (49283) ***(G-15790)***
Diversified Prof Rlty Svcs...313 215-1840
950 E 9 Mile Rd Hazel Park (48030) ***(G-7824)***
Diversified Prof Svcs Group, Hazel Park *Also called Diversified Prof Rlty Svcs* ***(G-7824)***
Diversified Services Tech, Romulus *Also called Dst Industries Inc* ***(G-14268)***
Diversified Tool & Engineering...734 692-1260
10340 Ruthmere Ave Grosse Ile (48138) ***(G-7519)***
Diversified Tooling Group Inc...248 837-5828
31240 Stephenson Hwy Madison Heights (48071) ***(G-10708)***
Diversified Tube LLC...313 790-7348
21056 Bridge St Southfield (48033) ***(G-15540)***
Diversified Welding & Fabg...616 738-0400
12813 Riley St Holland (49424) ***(G-8015)***
Diversiform LLC...989 278-9605
4656 Sunset St Oscoda (48750) ***(G-12756)***
Diversitak Inc...313 869-8500
15477 Woodrow Wilson St Detroit (48238) ***(G-4181)***
Divine Dessert...313 278-3322
25930 Ford Rd Dearborn Heights (48127) ***(G-3924)***
Divino Intl Wine & Spirit LLC...586 770-9409
2707 Aldrin Dr Lake Orion (48360) ***(G-9603)***
Division 6 Fbrction Instlltion...586 200-3030
27450 Gloede Dr Warren (48088) ***(G-17780)***
Division Oglebay Norton Co, Rogers City *Also called O-N Minerals Michigan Company* ***(G-14215)***
Division P, Marysville *Also called ZF Axle Drives Marysville LLC* ***(G-11114)***
Division Six, Warren *Also called Division 6 Fbrction Instlltion* ***(G-17780)***
Division Z, Northville *Also called ZF North America Inc* ***(G-12272)***
Dixon & Ryan Corporation...248 549-4000
4343 Normandy Ct Ste A Royal Oak (48073) ***(G-14531)***
Dj Customs LLC...810 358-0236
5238 Attica Rd Attica (48412) ***(G-752)***

A L P H A B E T I C

Djc Products Inc 586 992-1352
  56700 Mound Rd Shelby Township (48316) *(G-15209)*
Djd Mfg LLC 586 359-2090
  29970 Calahan Rd Roseville (48066) *(G-14400)*
DJL Logging Inc 231 590-2012
  5905 N Brown Rd Manton (49663) *(G-10933)*
Djw Enterprises Inc 414 791-6192
  324 N Light Lake Rd Crystal Falls (49920) *(G-3742)*
DK Concepts LLC 586 222-5255
  13943 Amanda Dr Sterling Heights (48313) *(G-15989)*
Dki, Hemlock Also called Douglas King Industries Inc *(G-7851)*
Dko Intl 248 926-9115
  39500 W 14 Mile Rd Commerce Township (48390) *(G-3523)*
Dl Engineering & Tech Inc 248 852-6900
  1749 W Hamlin Rd Rochester Hills (48309) *(G-13996)*
Dlh Rollform LLC 586 231-0507
  8990 Marquette Rd Wales (48027) *(G-17627)*
Dlh World LLC 313 915-0274
  2517 Hazelwood St Detroit (48206) *(G-4182)*
Dlhbowles Inc 248 569-0652
  20755 Greenfield Rd # 806 Southfield (48075) *(G-15541)*
DLM Holding Group LLC 269 465-3631
  3385 Livingston Rd Bridgman (49106) *(G-1925)*
Dln Publications LLC 248 410-7337
  22041 Shadybrook Dr Novi (48375) *(G-12402)*
Dlr Logistics Inc 248 499-2368
  2735 S Wagner Rd Unit 6a Ann Arbor (48103) *(G-453)*
Dm Vault Forms 989 275-4797
  10713 Johnson Rd Roscommon (48653) *(G-14348)*
Dm3d Technology LLC 248 409-7900
  2350 Pontiac Rd Auburn Hills (48326) *(G-864)*
Dma, Sterling Heights Also called Diversified Mfg & Assembly LLC *(G-15988)*
DMC Service Group 313 526-2431
  11111 Sturgis St Detroit (48234) *(G-4183)*
Dme Company LLC (HQ) 248 398-6000
  29111 Stephenson Hwy Madison Heights (48071) *(G-10709)*
Dmi Automotive Inc 517 548-1414
  1200 Durant Dr Howell (48843) *(G-8446)*
Dmi Edon, LLC, Southfield Also called Aludyne Mexico LLC *(G-15480)*
Dmi Sheet Metal LLC 517 242-6005
  740 Taylor Ave Ste A Grand Haven (49417) *(G-6293)*
Dmmi, Battle Creek Also called Denso Manufacturing Mich Inc *(G-1216)*
Dmp Sign Company 248 996-9281
  20732 Negaunee St Southfield (48033) *(G-15542)*
DMS Electric Apparatus Service 269 349-7000
  630 Gibson St Kalamazoo (49007) *(G-9171)*
DMS Mnufacturing Solutions Inc 517 423-6691
  800 S Maumee St Tecumseh (49286) *(G-16498)*
Dn Plastics Corporation 616 942-6060
  1415 Steele Ave Sw Ste 2 Grand Rapids (49507) *(G-6652)*
Dn-Lawrence Industries Inc 269 552-4999
  423 Walbridge St Kalamazoo (49007) *(G-9172)*
Dna Software Inc 734 222-9080
  46701 Commerce Center Dr Plymouth (48170) *(G-13159)*
Dnl Fabrication LLC 586 872-2656
  28514 Hayes Rd Roseville (48066) *(G-14401)*
DNR Inc 734 722-4000
  45759 Helm St Plymouth (48170) *(G-13160)*
DNR Inc (PA) 734 722-4000
  38475 Webb Dr Westland (48185) *(G-18365)*
Do & Co Detroit Inc (PA) 424 288-9025
  5 Detroit Metro Airport Detroit (48242) *(G-4184)*
Do It Best, Port Huron Also called Port Huron Building Supply Co *(G-13519)*
Do It Best, Portage Also called Nelson Hardware *(G-13587)*
Do It Best, Rose City Also called Masons Lumber & Hardware Inc *(G-14365)*
Do Rite Tool Inc 734 522-7510
  2800 Van Amberg Rd Brighton (48114) *(G-1976)*
Do-All Plastic Inc 313 824-6565
  1265 Terminal St Detroit (48214) *(G-4185)*
Do-It Corporation 269 637-1121
  1201 Blue Star Mem Hwy South Haven (49090) *(G-15404)*
Doan Companies, Ypsilanti Also called Doan Construction Co *(G-18940)*
Doan Construction Co (PA) 734 971-4678
  3670 Carpenter Rd Ypsilanti (48197) *(G-18940)*
Dobb Printing Inc 231 722-1060
  2431 Harvey St Muskegon (49442) *(G-11799)*
Dobday Manufacturing Co Inc 586 254-6777
  42750 Merrill Rd Sterling Heights (48314) *(G-15990)*
Dobson Heavy Haul Inc Division, Bay City Also called Dobson Industrial Inc *(G-1346)*
Dobson Industrial Inc (PA) 800 298-6063
  3660 N Euclid Ave Bay City (48706) *(G-1346)*
Doc Popcorn 734 250-8133
  23000 Eureka Rd Taylor (48180) *(G-16402)*
Dock Foundry Company 269 278-1765
  429 4th St Three Rivers (49093) *(G-16571)*
Dockside Canvas Co Inc 586 463-1231
  29939 S River Rd Harrison Township (48045) *(G-7696)*
Dockside Imports, Marquette Also called Wattsson & Wattsson Jewelers *(G-11049)*

Docnetwork Inc 734 619-8300
  5430 Data Ct Ste 250 Ann Arbor (48108) *(G-454)*
Dodge West Joe Nickel 810 691-2133
  2219 E Farrand Rd Clio (48420) *(G-3397)*
Doerken Corporation 517 522-4600
  11200 Cedar Knoll Dr Grass Lake (49240) *(G-7437)*
Dog Might LLC 734 679-0646
  303 Metty Dr Ann Arbor (48103) *(G-455)*
Dolav, Grand Rapids Also called Decade Products LLC *(G-6637)*
Dole Packaged Food Company, Decatur Also called Dole Packaged Foods LLC *(G-3947)*
Dole Packaged Foods LLC 269 423-6375
  101 W Bronson St Decatur (49045) *(G-3947)*
Doll Face Chef LLC 248 495-8280
  41000 Woodward Ave # 350 Bloomfield Hills (48304) *(G-1815)*
Dollar Bill Copying, Ann Arbor Also called Copytwo Inc *(G-437)*
Dollars From Scents 847 650-0317
  5190 S Scenic Dr New ERA (49446) *(G-12028)*
Dollars Sense 231 369-3610
  7850 Scotch Blf Sw Fife Lake (49633) *(G-5605)*
Dolphin Dumpsters LLC 734 272-8981
  30650 River Gln Farmington Hills (48336) *(G-5219)*
Dolphin Manufacturing Inc 734 946-6322
  12650 Universal Dr Taylor (48180) *(G-16403)*
Doltek Enterprises Inc 616 837-7828
  11335 Apple Dr Nunica (49448) *(G-12579)*
Domart Inc 616 285-9177
  3923 28th St Se Grand Rapids (49512) *(G-6653)*
Dome Production LLC 517 787-9178
  1415 W Argyle St Ste B Jackson (49202) *(G-8869)*
Domer Industries LLC 269 226-4000
  3434 S Burdick St Kalamazoo (49001) *(G-9173)*
Domestic Forge & Forming Inc 586 749-9559
  57760 Main St Ste 2 New Haven (48048) *(G-12031)*
Domico Med-Device LLC 810 750-5300
  14241 N Fenton Rd Fenton (48430) *(G-5471)*
Dominion Tech Group Inc 586 773-3303
  15736 Sturgeon St Roseville (48066) *(G-14402)*
Dominos Pizza LLC (HQ) 734 930-3030
  30 Frank Lloyd Wright Dr Ann Arbor (48105) *(G-456)*
Domnmar Manufacturing Group, Detroit Also called Gerald Harris *(G-4261)*
Domtar Eddy Specialty Papers, Port Huron Also called E B Eddy Paper Inc *(G-13473)*
Domtar Gypsum, Port Huron Also called Domtar Industries LLC *(G-13469)*
Domtar Industries LLC 810 982-0191
  1700 Washington Ave Port Huron (48060) *(G-13469)*
Don Duff Rebuilding 734 522-7700
  31130 Industrial Rd Livonia (48150) *(G-10187)*
Don Machalk Sons Fencing Corp 906 753-4002
  N7396 Us Highway 41 Ingalls (49848) *(G-8657)*
Don Marcos Tortillas, Southfield Also called Mexican Food Specialties Inc *(G-15656)*
Don Sawmill Inc 989 733-2780
  17131 Twin School Hwy Onaway (49765) *(G-12698)*
Don Theyken 734 996-8359
  1319 Algonac St Ann Arbor (48103) *(G-457)*
Don Yohe Enterprises Inc 586 784-5556
  74054 Church St Armada (48005) *(G-733)*
Donald E Rogers Associates 248 673-9878
  2627 Williams Dr Waterford (48328) *(G-18116)*
Donald K Stappert 734 459-0004
  6400 Curtis Rd Plymouth (48170) *(G-13161)*
Donald Lll Sons Logging 231 420-3800
  260 Townline Rd Pellston (49769) *(G-12967)*
Donald Schilstra 616 534-1897
  1452 Trentwood St Sw Grand Rapids (49509) *(G-6654)*
Donalyn Enterprises Inc 517 546-9798
  907 Fowler St Howell (48843) *(G-8447)*
Donato Woodworks 586 899-7430
  7287 Henry Center Line (48015) *(G-2681)*
Donbar LLC 313 784-3519
  4224 John Daly St Inkster (48141) *(G-8662)*
Done Right Engraving Inc 248 332-3133
  119 N Saginaw St Pontiac (48342) *(G-13362)*
Done Right Enterprises, Pontiac Also called Done Right Engraving Inc *(G-13362)*
Dongah America Inc 734 946-7940
  24500 Northline Rd Taylor (48180) *(G-16404)*
Donley Computer Services LLC 231 750-1774
  166 N Causeway St Muskegon (49445) *(G-11800)*
Donnelly Corp 231 652-8425
  700 S Industrial Dr Newaygo (49337) *(G-12080)*
Dons Quality Tools LLC 248 701-5154
  2560 Tyrone St Flint (48504) *(G-5689)*
Dontech Solutions LLC 248 789-3086
  4755 Treasure Lake Dr Howell (48843) *(G-8448)*
Door County White Fish, Stephenson Also called Ruleau Brothers Inc *(G-15911)*
Door SEC Solutions of Mich 616 301-1991
  6757 Cascade Rd Se 304 Grand Rapids (49546) *(G-6655)*
Doors & Drawers, Dexter Also called Rose Corporation *(G-4753)*
Doors4, Portage Also called Eliason Corporation *(G-13557)*
Doorstep Printing LLC 248 470-9567
  7300 W 7 Mile Rd Detroit (48221) *(G-4186)*

ALPHABETIC SECTION
Dpr Manufacturing & Svcs Inc

Dorden & Company Inc 313 834-7910
7446 Central St Detroit (48210) ***(G-4187)***

Dorden Squeegees, Detroit *Also called Dorden & Company Inc* ***(G-4187)***

Dorel Home Furnishings Inc 269 782-8661
202 Spaulding St Dowagiac (49047) ***(G-4781)***

Dornbos Printing Impressions, Saginaw *Also called Weighman Enterprises Inc* ***(G-14792)***

Dornbos Sign Inc 517 543-4000
619 W Harris St Charlotte (48813) ***(G-2750)***

Dorothy Dawson Food Products 517 788-9830
251 W Euclid Ave Jackson (49203) ***(G-8870)***

Dorr Industries, Byron Center *Also called Tg Manufacturing LLC* ***(G-2296)***

Dorris Company 586 293-5260
17430 Malyn Blvd Fraser (48026) ***(G-5919)***

DOT Bridge Inc 248 921-7363
25905 Cobblers Ln South Lyon (48178) ***(G-15433)***

DOT Sign 248 760-8236
31158 Woodland St Wixom (48393) ***(G-18647)***

Dotmine Day Planners, Ann Arbor *Also called Edward and Cole Inc* ***(G-467)***

Double B'S Steel and Mfg, Wheeler *Also called Patch Works Farms Inc* ***(G-18436)***

Double Check Tools Service 231 947-1632
6937 M 72 E Williamsburg (49690) ***(G-18553)***

Double Eagle Defense LLC (PA) 313 562-5550
25205 Trowbridge St Dearborn (48124) ***(G-3830)***

Double Eagle Steel Coating Co 313 203-9800
3000 Miller Rd Dearborn (48120) ***(G-3831)***

Double Gun Journal 231 536-7439
5014 Rockery School Rd East Jordan (49727) ***(G-4862)***

Double H Mfg Inc 734 729-3450
6171 Commerce Dr Westland (48185) ***(G-18366)***

Double Otis Inc 616 878-3998
1415 Division Ave S Grand Rapids (49507) ***(G-6656)***

Double Six Sports Complex 989 762-5342
4860 N Sheridan Rd Stanton (48888) ***(G-15900)***

Doubleo O Supply & Craftsmen, Grand Rapids *Also called Double Otis Inc* ***(G-6656)***

Doug Anderson Logging 906 337-3707
54586 Oikarinen Rd Calumet (49913) ***(G-2409)***

Doug Murdicks Fudge Inc 231 938-2330
4500 N Us Highway 31 N Traverse City (49686) ***(G-16670)***

Doug Wirt Enterprises Inc 989 684-5777
400 Martin St Bay City (48706) ***(G-1347)***

Dougco Industries LLC 313 808-1689
5119 Cadillac Ave Detroit (48213) ***(G-4188)***

Dough & Spice Inc 586 756-6100
2150 E 10 Mile Rd Warren (48091) ***(G-17781)***

Dough Masters 248 585-0600
23412 Dequindre Rd Warren (48091) ***(G-17782)***

Doughnut World, Grand Rapids *Also called Roskam Baking Company* ***(G-7169)***

Douglas Autotech Corporation (HQ) 517 369-2315
300 Albers Rd Bronson (49028) ***(G-2111)***

Douglas Corp 517 767-4112
103 S Main St Tekonsha (49092) ***(G-16522)***

Douglas Dynamics LLC 414 362-3890
531 Ajax Dr Madison Heights (48071) ***(G-10710)***

Douglas Gage Inc 586 727-2089
69681 Lowe Plank Rd Richmond (48062) ***(G-13836)***

Douglas Innovation LLC 586 596-3641
1389 Wheaton Dr Ste 300 Troy (48083) ***(G-17064)***

Douglas King Industries Inc 989 642-2865
16425 Northern Pintail Dr Hemlock (48626) ***(G-7851)***

Douglas Marine Corporation 269 857-1764
6780 Enterprise Dr Douglas (49406) ***(G-4772)***

Douglas Milton Lamp Co 888 738-3332
208 Kensington Cir Battle Creek (49015) ***(G-1220)***

Douglas Stamping Company 248 542-3940
25531 Dequindre Rd Madison Heights (48071) ***(G-10711)***

Douglas Steel Fabricating Corp 517 322-2050
1312 S Waverly Rd Lansing (48917) ***(G-9759)***

Douglas Water Conditioning (PA) 248 363-8383
7234 Cooley Lake Rd Waterford (48327) ***(G-18117)***

Douglas West Company Inc 734 676-8882
9177 Groh Rd Bldg 43 Grosse Ile (48138) ***(G-7520)***

Douthitt Corporation (PA) 313 259-1565
245 Adair St Detroit (48207) ***(G-4189)***

Douthitt Corporation 313 259-1565
277 Adair St Detroit (48207) ***(G-4190)***

Dover Energy Inc 248 836-6750
15 Corporate Dr Auburn Hills (48326) ***(G-865)***

Dover Energy Inc (HQ) 248 836-6700
691 N Squirrel Rd Ste 250 Auburn Hills (48326) ***(G-866)***

Dover Pmps Prcess Sltons Sgmen 616 241-1611
1809 Century Ave Sw Grand Rapids (49503) ***(G-6657)***

Dovetails Inc 248 674-8777
5600 Williams Lake Rd B Waterford (48329) ***(G-18118)***

Dow Agrosciences LLC 989 636-4400
433 Bldg Midland (48674) ***(G-11340)***

Dow Chemical Company (HQ) 989 636-1000
2211 H H Dow Way Midland (48642) ***(G-11341)***

Dow Chemical Company 231 845-4285
1600 S Madison St Ludington (49431) ***(G-10534)***

Dow Chemical Company 989 636-1000
2511 S Saginaw Rd Midland (48640) ***(G-11342)***

Dow Chemical Company 989 636-4406
1801 Larkin Center Dr Midland (48642) ***(G-11343)***

Dow Chemical Company 517 439-4400
195 Uran St Hillsdale (49242) ***(G-7933)***

Dow Chemical Company 810 966-9816
3381 Woodview Clyde (48049) ***(G-3412)***

Dow Chemical Company 989 636-1000
2511 E Patrick Rd Midland (48642) ***(G-11344)***

Dow Chemical Company 989 636-1000
S Saginaw Bldg 304 Midland (48667) ***(G-11345)***

Dow Chemical Company 989 636-5430
2050 Abbott Rd Midland (48674) ***(G-11346)***

Dow Chemical Company 989 636-1000
2030 Willard H Dow Center Midland (48674) ***(G-11347)***

Dow Chemical Company 989 695-2584
M B S Intl Hngr 5 Freeland (48623) ***(G-6021)***

Dow Chemical Company 989 832-1000
2040 Dow Ctr Midland (48674) ***(G-11348)***

Dow Chemical Company 989 636-0540
1320 Waldo Ave Ste 300 Midland (48642) ***(G-11349)***

Dow Chemical Company 989 638-6441
Gpc Building Midland (48667) ***(G-11350)***

Dow Chemical Company 925 432-5000
2030 Dow Ctr Midland (48674) ***(G-11351)***

Dow Chemical Company 989 636-5409
3700 James Savage Rd Midland (48642) ***(G-11352)***

Dow Corning, Auburn *Also called Dow Silicones Corporation* ***(G-765)***

Dow Corning Corporation 989 839-2808
1404 Peppermill Cir Midland (48642) ***(G-11353)***

Dow Inc (PA) 989 636-1000
2211 H H Dow Way Midland (48642) ***(G-11354)***

Dow International Holdings Co (HQ) 989 636-1000
2030 Dow Ctr Midland (48674) ***(G-11355)***

Dow Silicones Corporation (HQ) 989 496-4000
2200 W Salzburg Rd Auburn (48611) ***(G-765)***

Dow Silicones Corporation 800 248-2481
1635 N Gleaner Rd Hemlock (48626) ***(G-7852)***

Dow Silicones Corporation 989 895-3397
1 E Main St Bay City (48708) ***(G-1348)***

Dowagiac Daily News, Niles *Also called Daughtry Nwspapers Investments* ***(G-12123)***

Dowaksa Carbon Wrap, Midland *Also called Dowaksa Usa LLC* ***(G-11356)***

Dowaksa Usa LLC (PA) 989 600-8610
3720 James Savage Rd Midland (48642) ***(G-11356)***

Dowd Brothers Forest Products, Alger *Also called Dowd Brothers Forestry* ***(G-137)***

Dowd Brothers Forestry 989 345-7459
2718 School Rd Alger (48610) ***(G-137)***

Dowding Industries 319 294-9094
503 Marilin Ave Eaton Rapids (48827) ***(G-4958)***

Dowding Industries Inc (PA) 517 663-5455
449 Marilin Ave Eaton Rapids (48827) ***(G-4959)***

Dowding Industries Inc 517 663-5455
502 Marilin Ave Eaton Rapids (48827) ***(G-4960)***

Dowding Machining LLC 517 663-5455
503 Marilin Ave Eaton Rapids (48827) ***(G-4961)***

Dowding Tool Products LLC 517 541-2795
8950 Narrow Lake Rd Springport (49284) ***(G-15880)***

Down & Associates, Howell *Also called Down Home Inc* ***(G-8449)***

Down Home Inc (PA) 517 545-5955
110 W Grand River Ave Howell (48843) ***(G-8449)***

Down Inc 616 241-3922
635 Evergreen St Se Grand Rapids (49507) ***(G-6658)***

Downey's & Design, Waterford *Also called Downeys Potato Chips-Waterford* ***(G-18119)***

Downeys Potato Chips-Waterford 248 673-3636
4709 Highland Rd Waterford (48328) ***(G-18119)***

Downriver Boatworks Ltd 313 335-4288
1428 Rose Ave Lincoln Park (48146) ***(G-10045)***

Downriver Creative Woodworking 313 274-4090
4631 Parkside Blvd Allen Park (48101) ***(G-193)***

Downriver Crushed Concrete 734 283-1833
20538 Pennsylvania Rd Taylor (48180) ***(G-16405)***

Downriver Deburring Inc 313 388-2640
20248 Lorne St Taylor (48180) ***(G-16406)***

Dowsett Spring Company 269 782-2138
27071 Marcellus Hwy Dowagiac (49047) ***(G-4782)***

Doyle Forest Products Inc 231 832-5586
21364 Meceola Rd Paris (49338) ***(G-12933)***

Doylen Albring Jr 989 427-2919
3873 E Edgar Rd Edmore (48829) ***(G-4991)***

Dph LLC 248 813-2000
5820 Innovation Dr Troy (48098) ***(G-17065)***

Dph-Das Global (holdings) LLC 248 813-2000
5820 Innovation Dr Troy (48098) ***(G-17066)***

Dph-Das LLC 248 813-2000
5820 Innovation Dr Troy (48098) ***(G-17067)***

Dpi In Mold Applications, Grand Rapids *Also called Hanson Inc* ***(G-6802)***

Dpr Manufacturing & Svcs Inc 586 757-1421
23675 Mound Rd Warren (48091) ***(G-17783)***

ALPHABETIC

(PA)=Parent Co (HQ)=Headquarters (DH)=Div Headquarters
2022 Harris Michigan Industrial Directory
979

DPrinter Inc 517 423-6554
   6197 N Adrian Hwy Tecumseh (49286) *(G-16499)*
Dqb Industries, Livonia Also called Detroit Qulty Brush Mfg Co Inc *(G-10183)*
Dr and Hl Mold and Mch Inc 989 672-2192
   3266 Leix Rd Caro (48723) *(G-2569)*
Dr Forklift 734 968-6576
   9870 Finnegan Dr Brighton (48116) *(G-1977)*
Dr Pepper Snapple Group, Cadillac Also called Keurig Dr Pepper Inc *(G-2339)*
Dr Pepper Snapple Group 616 393-5800
   777 Brooks Ave Holland (49423) *(G-8016)*
Dr Schneider Auto Systems Inc 270 858-5400
   716 Advance St Ste A Brighton (48116) *(G-1978)*
Dr. John's Candies, Comstock Park Also called Sugar Free Specialties LLC *(G-3646)*
Draco Mfg Inc 248 585-0320
   629 Minnesota Dr Troy (48083) *(G-17068)*
Drag Finishing Tech LLC (PA) 616 785-0400
   835 W River Center Dr Ne # 1 Comstock Park (49321) *(G-3603)*
Dragon Acquisition Intermediat 248 692-4367
   39555 Orchard Hill Pl # 52 Novi (48375) *(G-12403)*
Dragon Acquisition Parent Inc (PA) 248 692-4367
   39555 Orchard Hill Pl # 52 Novi (48375) *(G-12404)*
Dragon Bleu USA, Bloomfield Hills Also called RGI Brands LLC *(G-1856)*
Drake Enterprises Inc 586 783-3009
   24800 Capital Blvd Clinton Township (48036) *(G-3226)*
Drake Publishing 269 963-4810
   664 Minges Rd E Battle Creek (49015) *(G-1221)*
Drano, Saint Clair Shores Also called CTC Distribution Inc *(G-14854)*
Drapery Workroom 269 463-5633
   5864 N County Line Rd Watervliet (49098) *(G-18180)*
Draths Corporation 517 349-0668
   236 Crystal Ct Howell (48843) *(G-8450)*
Draught Horse Group LLC 231 631-5218
   57721 Grand River Ave New Hudson (48165) *(G-12051)*
Drayton Iron & Metal Inc (PA) 248 673-1269
   5229 Williams Lake Rd Waterford (48329) *(G-18120)*
Drayton Plains Tool Company, Saline Also called Mmi Engineered Solutions Inc *(G-15028)*
Dreal Inc 248 813-2000
   5820 Innovation Dr Troy (48098) *(G-17069)*
Dream Catchers Publishing LLC 313 575-3933
   17165 Rutherford St Detroit (48235) *(G-4191)*
Dream Clean Trucking Service 313 285-4029
   24661 Huron River Dr New Boston (48164) *(G-12008)*
Dream Custom Cabinets 586 718-4812
   33314 Duncan Fraser (48026) *(G-5920)*
Dreambuilder Publications 989 465-1583
   104 E Adams St Coleman (48618) *(G-3463)*
Dreamweaver Lure Company Inc 231 843-3652
   5712 Brookwood Pl Ludington (49431) *(G-10535)*
Dresco Machining & Fabrication, Bay City Also called Graphite Electrodes Ltd *(G-1362)*
Drew Technologies Inc (HQ) 734 222-5228
   3915 Res Pk Dr Ste A10 Ann Arbor (48108) *(G-458)*
Dri-Design Inc 616 355-2970
   12480 Superior Ct Ste 1 Holland (49424) *(G-8017)*
Drink Branders LLC 231 668-4121
   1015 Noteware Dr Traverse City (49686) *(G-16671)*
Drip Therapi LLC 586 488-1256
   14202 Lakeside Blvd N 1a Shelby Township (48315) *(G-15210)*
Drive Medical 404 349-0280
   1446 S 35th St Galesburg (49053) *(G-6075)*
Drive System Integration Inc 248 568-7750
   32600 Westlady Dr Beverly Hills (48025) *(G-1663)*
Driven Designs Inc 616 794-9977
   1135 S Bridge St Belding (48809) *(G-1446)*
Driven Fabrication 248 491-4940
   29585 Costello Dr New Hudson (48165) *(G-12052)*
Driven-4 LLC 269 281-7567
   3515 Lakeshore Dr Ste 1 Saint Joseph (49085) *(G-14927)*
Drought, Berkley Also called Panther James LLC *(G-1634)*
Drs C3 & Aviation Company 248 588-0365
   900 E Whitcomb Ave Madison Heights (48071) *(G-10712)*
Drs Technical Services, Madison Heights Also called Drs C3 & Aviation Company *(G-10712)*
Drummond Dolemite, Drummond Island Also called Osborne Materials Company *(G-4803)*
Drummond Press Inc 248 834-7007
   143 Northpointe Dr Lake Orion (48359) *(G-9604)*
Drushal Fabricating LLC 517 539-5921
   3900 Francis St Jackson (49203) *(G-8871)*
Drw Systems Carbide LLC 810 392-3526
   12618 Masters Rd Riley (48041) *(G-13849)*
Dry Coolers Inc (PA) 248 969-3400
   575 S Glaspie St Oxford (48371) *(G-12883)*
Dryden Mold Services Inc 810 614-8621
   2988 Walker Rd Dryden (48428) *(G-4804)*
Dryden Steel LLC 586 777-7600
   5585 North St Bldg D Dryden (48428) *(G-4805)*
DRYE Custom Pallets Inc 313 381-2681
   19400 Allen Rd Melvindale (48122) *(G-11199)*
Ds Automotion LLC 248 370-8950
   691 N Squirrel Rd 119 Auburn Hills (48326) *(G-867)*

Ds Mold LLC 616 794-1639
   807 Edna St Belding (48809) *(G-1447)*
Ds Sales Inc 248 960-6411
   46903 West Rd Wixom (48393) *(G-18648)*
DSC Laboratories Inc 800 492-5988
   1979 Latimer Dr Muskegon (49442) *(G-11801)*
Dse Industries LLC 313 530-6668
   51315 Regency Center Dr Macomb (48042) *(G-10589)*
DSM Engineering Materials Inc 616 667-2643
   7784 Steele Ave Jenison (49428) *(G-9053)*
DSM Engineering Plastics Inc 608 477-0157
   203 W Big Beaver Rd Troy (48084) *(G-17070)*
Dss Valve Products Inc 269 340-7303
   1800 Mayflower Rd Niles (49120) *(G-12126)*
Dst Industries Inc (HQ) 734 941-0300
   34364 Goddard Rd Romulus (48174) *(G-14268)*
Dst Industries Inc 734 941-0300
   11900 Tecumseh Clinton Rd Clinton (49236) *(G-3136)*
DSU, Chesterfield Also called Design Services Unlimited Inc *(G-2870)*
Dsw Holdings Inc (PA) 313 567-4500
   400 Renaissance Ctr Ste Detroit (48243) *(G-4192)*
Dt Manufacturing Company, Highland Also called Dt Manufacturing One LLC *(G-7891)*
Dt Manufacturing One LLC 248 889-9210
   1450 N Milford Rd Ste 101 Highland (48357) *(G-7891)*
DTE Energy Company (PA) 313 235-4000
   1 Energy Plz Detroit (48226) *(G-4193)*
DTE Energy Resources Inc (HQ) 734 302-4800
   414 S Main St Ste 600 Ann Arbor (48104) *(G-459)*
DTE Energy Trust II 313 235-8822
   2000 2nd Ave Detroit (48226) *(G-4194)*
DTE Energy Ventures Inc (HQ) 313 235-8000
   1 Energy Plz Detroit (48226) *(G-4195)*
DTE Gas & Oil Company 231 995-4000
   10691 E Carter Rd Ste 201 Traverse City (49684) *(G-16672)*
DTe Hankin Inc 734 279-1831
   399 E Center St Petersburg (49270) *(G-12983)*
Dti, Redford Also called Detroit Tech Innovation LLC *(G-13731)*
Dti Molded Products Inc (HQ) 248 647-0400
   32500 Telg Rd Ste 207 Bingham Farms (48025) *(G-1695)*
Dti Plastic Products, Macomb Also called Conform Automotive LLC *(G-10585)*
Dtm Inc 734 944-1109
   1283 Industrial Dr Saline (48176) *(G-15013)*
Dtown Grillz LLC 734 624-9657
   21700 Greenfield Rd # 348 Oak Park (48237) *(G-12606)*
DTR Logistics, Taylor Also called Dongah America Inc *(G-16404)*
Dts Enterprises Inc 231 599-3123
   9910 N Us Highway 31 Ellsworth (49729) *(G-5035)*
Du Val Industries LLC 586 737-2710
   6410 19 Mile Rd Sterling Heights (48314) *(G-15991)*
Duall Division 989 725-8184
   1172 S M 13 Lennon (48449) *(G-9993)*
Duane F Proehl Inc 906 474-6630
   11064 T.65 Rd Rapid River (49878) *(G-13684)*
Duberville Logging 906 586-6267
   W16683 Sandtown Rd Curtis (49820) *(G-3750)*
Dubetsky K9 Academy LLC 586 997-1717
   50699 Central Indus Dr Shelby Township (48315) *(G-15211)*
Dubois Production Services Inc 616 785-0088
   30 N Park St Ne Comstock Park (49321) *(G-3604)*
Duff Brush LLC 906 863-3319
   630 7th St Menominee (49858) *(G-11231)*
Dufferin Aggregates 734 529-2411
   6211 N Ann Arbor Rd Dundee (48131) *(G-4814)*
Duggan Manufacturing LLC 586 254-7400
   50150 Ryan Rd Shelby Township (48317) *(G-15212)*
Duggans Limited LLC 586 254-7400
   50150 Ryan Rd Ste 15 Shelby Township (48317) *(G-15213)*
Dugrees Sand and Gravel 906 295-1569
   W6017 Us Highway 2 Hermansville (49847) *(G-7861)*
Duke De Jong Inc 734 403-1708
   12680 Delta St Taylor (48180) *(G-16407)*
Dumas Concepts In Building Inc (PA) 313 895-2555
   8711 Epworth St Detroit (48204) *(G-4196)*
Dumbarton Tool Inc 231 775-4342
   151 Clay Dr Cadillac (49601) *(G-2328)*
Dun Mor Design, Troy Also called Dun Mor Embroidery & Designs *(G-17071)*
Dun Mor Embroidery & Designs 248 577-1155
   360 E Maple Rd Ste O Troy (48083) *(G-17071)*
Dun-Rite Machine Co 616 688-5266
   4526 Adams St Zeeland (49464) *(G-19016)*
Dundee Castings Company 734 529-2455
   500 Ypsilanti St Dundee (48131) *(G-4815)*
Dundee Manufacturing Co Inc 734 529-2540
   107 Fairchild Dr Dundee (48131) *(G-4816)*
Dundee Plant, Dundee Also called Holcim (us) Inc *(G-4824)*
Dundee Products Company 734 529-2441
   14490 Stowell Rd Dundee (48131) *(G-4817)*
Dunhams Athleisure Corporation 248 658-1382
   32101 John R Rd Madison Heights (48071) *(G-10713)*

Dunkin Donuts & Baskin-Robbins 989 835-8412
5000 Foxcroft Dr Midland (48642) ***(G-11357)***
Dunkley International Inc 269 343-5583
1910 Lake St Kalamazoo (49001) ***(G-9174)***
Dunlop Dreams Candles 231 633-4064
1112 Rose St Traverse City (49686) ***(G-16673)***
Dunn Beverage Intl LLC 269 420-1547
95 Minges Rd N Battle Creek (49015) ***(G-1222)***
Dunn Paper Inc 810 984-5521
144 1st St Menominee (49858) ***(G-11232)***
Dunn Paper Inc (HQ) 810 984-5521
218 Riverview St Port Huron (48060) ***(G-13470)***
Dunn Paper - Wiggins LLC 810 984-5521
218 Riverview St Port Huron (48060) ***(G-13471)***
Dunn Paper Holdings Inc (PA) 810 984-5521
218 Riverview St Port Huron (48060) ***(G-13472)***
Dunnage Engineering Inc (PA) 810 229-9501
721 Advance St Brighton (48116) ***(G-1979)***
Dunne-Rite Performance Inc 616 828-0908
26063 Newport Ave Warren (48089) ***(G-17784)***
Dunns Welding Inc 248 356-3866
22930 Lahser Rd Southfield (48033) ***(G-15543)***
Duo Gard Industries Inc 734 459-9166
1317 Sheridan St Plymouth (48170) ***(G-13162)***
Duo Robotic Solutions Inc 586 883-7559
50570 Wing Dr Shelby Township (48315) ***(G-15214)***
Duo Security Inc 866 768-4247
130 S 1st St Ste 100 Ann Arbor (48104) ***(G-460)***
Duo Security LLC (HQ) 734 330-2673
123 N Ashley St Ste 200 Ann Arbor (48104) ***(G-461)***
Duo-Form Acquisition Corp 269 663-8525
69836 Kraus Rd Edwardsburg (49112) ***(G-5005)***
Duo-Form Plastics, Edwardsburg *Also called Duo-Form Acquisition Corp* ***(G-5005)***
Duo-Gard Industries Inc 734 207-9700
40442 Koppernick Rd Canton (48187) ***(G-2456)***
Dupearl Technology LLC 248 390-9609
120 Hadsell Dr Bloomfield Hills (48302) ***(G-1816)***
Duperon Corporation 800 383-8479
1200 Leon Scott Ct Saginaw (48601) ***(G-14640)***
Duplicast Corporation 586 756-5900
44648 Mound Rd 202 Sterling Heights (48314) ***(G-15992)***
Dupont 651 767-2527
3100 James Savage Rd Midland (48642) ***(G-11358)***
Dupont Office and Self St 206 471-3700
1710 Birchview Dr Kewadin (49648) ***(G-9486)***
Dupont Performance Materials, Auburn Hills *Also called E I Du Pont De Nemours & Co* ***(G-872)***
Duquaine Incorporated 906 228-7290
1744 Presque Isle Ave Marquette (49855) ***(G-11015)***
Dura Automotive - Global Fwdg, Auburn Hills *Also called Global Automotive Systems LLC* ***(G-915)***
Dura Automotive Systems, Auburn Hills *Also called Dus Operating Inc* ***(G-869)***
Dura Automotive Systems, Auburn Hills *Also called Dura Operating LLC* ***(G-868)***
Dura Automotive Systems, Fremont *Also called Dus Operating Inc* ***(G-6039)***
Dura Global Technologies Inc 248 299-7500
2791 Research Dr Rochester Hills (48309) ***(G-13997)***
Dura Hog Inc 586 825-0066
33637 Sterling Ponds Blvd Sterling Heights (48312) ***(G-15993)***
Dura Mold Inc 269 465-3301
3390 W Linco Rd Stevensville (49127) ***(G-16248)***
Dura Operating LLC (PA) 248 299-7500
1780 Pond Run Auburn Hills (48326) ***(G-868)***
Dura Pack, Taylor *Also called Dura-Pack Inc* ***(G-16408)***
Dura Shifter LLC 248 299-7500
2791 Research Dr Rochester Hills (48309) ***(G-13998)***
Dura Sill Corporation 248 348-2490
22500 Heslip Dr Novi (48375) ***(G-12405)***
Dura Thread Gage Inc 248 545-2890
971 E 10 Mile Rd Madison Heights (48071) ***(G-10714)***
Dura-Pack Inc 313 299-9600
7641 Holland Rd Taylor (48180) ***(G-16408)***
Duraflex Coatings LLC 586 855-1087
8589 Mary Ann Ave Shelby Township (48317) ***(G-15215)***
Durakon Industries Inc (HQ) 608 742-5301
2101 N Lapeer Rd Lapeer (48446) ***(G-9928)***
Duramet Corporation 586 759-2280
11350 Stephens Rd Warren (48089) ***(G-17785)***
Duramic Abrasive Products Inc 586 755-7220
24135 Gibson Dr Warren (48089) ***(G-17786)***
Duratran Company, The, Spring Lake *Also called New Rules Marketing Inc* ***(G-15839)***
Durez Corporation (HQ) 248 313-7000
46820 Magellan Dr Ste C Novi (48377) ***(G-12406)***
Duro-Last Inc (PA) 800 248-0280
525 E Morley Dr Saginaw (48601) ***(G-14641)***
Duro-Last Inc 800 248-0280
525 W Morley Dr Saginaw (48601) ***(G-14642)***
Duro-Last Roofing, Saginaw *Also called Duro-Last Inc* ***(G-14641)***
Durr Inc (HQ) 734 459-6800
26801 Northwestern Hwy Southfield (48033) ***(G-15544)***
Durr Systems Inc (HQ) 248 450-2000
26801 Northwestern Hwy Southfield (48033) ***(G-15545)***
Durr Systems Inc 248 745-8500
26801 Northwestern Hwy Southfield (48033) ***(G-15546)***
Dus Operating Inc (HQ) 248 299-7500
1780 Pond Run Auburn Hills (48326) ***(G-869)***
Dus Operating Inc 231 924-0930
502 Connie Ave Fremont (49412) ***(G-6039)***
Duscha Management LLC 352 247-2113
4614 N 2nd St Luna Pier (48157) ***(G-10560)***
Dusevoir Acquisitions LLC 313 562-5550
1609 White Blossom Ln Howell (48843) ***(G-8451)***
Dusevoir Metal Products, Howell *Also called Dusevoir Acquisitions LLC* ***(G-8451)***
Dust & Ashes Publications 231 722-6657
8940 Sorrento Ridge Dr Se Byron Center (49315) ***(G-2268)***
Dust Control & Loading Systems, Charlevoix *Also called Dcl Inc* ***(G-2714)***
Dutchmans Welding & Repair 989 584-6861
6161 County Line Rd Carson City (48811) ***(G-2592)***
DVine Cookies 248 417-7850
4467 Stony River Dr Bloomfield Hills (48301) ***(G-1817)***
Dvs Technology America Inc 734 656-2080
44099 Plymouth Oaks Blvd Plymouth (48170) ***(G-13163)***
Dw-National Standard-Niles LLC 269 683-8100
1631 Lake St Niles (49120) ***(G-12127)***
Dwayne Thomleys Redneck 906 353-7376
16172 Bellaire Rd Baraga (49908) ***(G-1139)***
Dwm Holdings Inc 586 541-0013
23171 Groesbeck Hwy Warren (48089) ***(G-17787)***
Dyemurex Inc 586 447-2509
26670 Belleair St Roseville (48066) ***(G-14403)***
Dyers Sawmill Inc 231 768-4438
17688 15 Mile Rd Leroy (49655) ***(G-10006)***
Dyna Plate Inc 616 452-6763
344 Mart St Sw Grand Rapids (49548) ***(G-6659)***
Dyna Sales & Service LLC 231 734-4433
8440 State Rd Millington (48746) ***(G-11499)***
Dyna- Bignell Products LLC 989 418-5050
201 W 3rd St Clare (48617) ***(G-2977)***
Dyna-Con, Norton Shores *Also called Dynamic Conveyor Corporation* ***(G-12288)***
Dynaflex, Romulus *Also called Cartex Corporation* ***(G-14260)***
Dynamic Auto Test Engineering 269 342-1334
1017 W Kilgore Rd Portage (49024) ***(G-13556)***
Dynamic Color Publications 248 553-3115
32905 W 12 Mile Rd # 210 Farmington Hills (48334) ***(G-5220)***
Dynamic Conveyor Corporation 231 798-0014
5980 Grand Haven Rd Norton Shores (49441) ***(G-12288)***
Dynamic Corporation 248 338-1100
2193 Executive Hills Dr Auburn Hills (48326) ***(G-870)***
Dynamic Corporation (PA) 616 399-2200
2565 Van Ommen Dr Holland (49424) ***(G-8018)***
Dynamic Development Inc 231 723-8318
314 W Parkdale Ave Manistee (49660) ***(G-10897)***
Dynamic Energy Tech LLC 248 212-5904
22181 Morton St Oak Park (48237) ***(G-12607)***
Dynamic Exploration Inc 231 723-7879
314 E Parkdale Ave Manistee (49660) ***(G-10898)***
Dynamic Jig Grinding Corp 248 589-3110
985 Troy Ct Troy (48083) ***(G-17072)***
Dynamic Manufacturing LLC 989 644-8109
5059 W Weidman Rd Weidman (48893) ***(G-18251)***
Dynamic Metal Treating, Canton *Also called Morning Star Land Company LLC* ***(G-2498)***
Dynamic Metals Group LLC 586 790-5615
260 E Brown St Ste 280 Birmingham (48009) ***(G-1724)***
Dynamic Metrology Services, Holland *Also called Dynamic Corporation* ***(G-8018)***
Dynamic Mtal Treating Intl Inc 734 459-8022
7784 Ronda Dr Canton (48187) ***(G-2457)***
Dynamic Plastics Inc 586 749-6100
29831 Commerce Blvd Chesterfield (48051) ***(G-2872)***
Dynamic Precision Tool & Mfg, Troy *Also called Dynamic Jig Grinding Corp* ***(G-17072)***
Dynamic Print & Imaging 586 738-4367
2107 Koper Dr Sterling Heights (48310) ***(G-15994)***
Dynamic Prototype Operations, Auburn Hills *Also called Dynamic Corporation* ***(G-870)***
Dynamic Robotic Solutions Inc 248 829-2800
1255 Harmon Rd Auburn Hills (48326) ***(G-871)***
Dynamic Staffing Solutions (PA) 616 399-5220
2565 Van Ommen Dr Holland (49424) ***(G-8019)***
Dynamic Supply Solutions Inc 248 987-2205
56 Sunningdale Dr Grosse Pointe Shores (48236) ***(G-7561)***
Dynamic Surface Technologies, Canton *Also called Dynamic Mtal Treating Intl Inc* ***(G-2457)***
Dynamic Wood Products Inc 616 897-8114
9385 Potters Rd Saranac (48881) ***(G-15077)***
Dynamic Wood Solutions 616 935-7727
18518 Trimble Ct Spring Lake (49456) ***(G-15811)***
Dynamite Machining Inc 586 247-8230
51149 Filomena Dr Shelby Township (48315) ***(G-15216)***
Dynapath Systems Inc., Livonia *Also called Hal International Inc* ***(G-10233)***
Dynas Products, Millington *Also called Dyna Sales & Service LLC* ***(G-11499)***
Dynasty Fab LLC 586 623-0227
51195 Regency Center Dr Macomb (48042) ***(G-10590)***

ALPHABETIC

Dynasty Mechanical Inc 313 506-5504
   18445 Greenlawn St Detroit (48221) *(G-4197)*

Dynatect Manufacturing In 231 947-4124
   2101 Precision Dr Traverse City (49686) *(G-16674)*

Dynetics Inc 248 619-1681
   1100 Owendale Dr Troy (48083) *(G-17073)*

Dynics Inc 734 677-6100
   620 Technology Dr Ann Arbor (48108) *(G-462)*

Dynotech Driveshafts, Peck Also called Ametek Inc *(G-12960)*

Dyson Service Center 248 808-6952
   1969 W Maple Rd Troy (48084) *(G-17074)*

Dyson Service Center 248 960-0052
   50160 Pontiac Trl Unit 1 Wixom (48393) *(G-18649)*

Dytron Corporation 586 296-9600
   17000 Masonic Fraser (48026) *(G-5921)*

E & B Machine Co, Otsego Also called Vanmeer Corporation *(G-12802)*

E & C Manufacturing LLC 248 330-0400
   2125 Butterfield Dr # 200 Troy (48084) *(G-17075)*

E & D Engineering Systems LLC 989 246-0770
   890 Industrial Dr Gladwin (48624) *(G-6195)*

E & D Machine Company Inc 248 473-0255
   32777 Chesley Dr Farmington (48336) *(G-5137)*

E & E Custom Products LLC 586 978-3377
   7200 Miller Dr Warren (48092) *(G-17788)*

E & E Manufacturing Co Inc (PA) 734 451-7600
   300 400 Indus Drv Plymouth (48170) *(G-13164)*

E & E Manufacturing Co Inc 734 451-7600
   200 Industrial Dr Plymouth (48170) *(G-13165)*

E & E Manufacturing Co Inc 248 616-1300
   701 S Main St Clawson (48017) *(G-3095)*

E & E Special Products LLC 586 978-3377
   7200 Miller Dr Warren (48092) *(G-17789)*

E & M Cores Inc 989 386-9223
   9805 S Athey Ave Clare (48617) *(G-2978)*

E & R Bindery Service Inc 734 464-7954
   37477 Schoolcraft Rd Livonia (48150) *(G-10188)*

E & S Graphics Inc 989 875-2828
   300 Industrial Pkwy Ithaca (48847) *(G-8790)*

E A Wood Inc (PA) 989 739-9118
   6718 Loud Dr Oscoda (48750) *(G-12757)*

E and K Arts and More 855 285-0320
   71 N Saginaw St Pontiac (48342) *(G-13363)*

E and M Cores, Clare Also called E & M Cores Inc *(G-2978)*

E and P Form Tool Company Inc 734 261-3530
   31759 Block St Ste A Garden City (48135) *(G-6093)*

E B Eddy Paper Inc 810 982-0191
   1700 Washington Ave Port Huron (48060) *(G-13473)*

E B I Inc 810 227-8180
   10454 Grand River Rd Brighton (48116) *(G-1980)*

E C Moore Company (PA) 313 581-7878
   13325 Leonard St Dearborn (48126) *(G-3832)*

E Coat Division, Grand Haven Also called Seaver Finishing Inc *(G-6358)*

E D C O Publishing Inc 248 690-9184
   990 S Baldwin Rd Clarkston (48348) *(G-3031)*

E D M Shuttle Inc 586 468-9880
   44695 Enterprise Dr Clinton Township (48038) *(G-3227)*

E D M Specialties Inc 248 344-4080
   26111 Lannys Rd Novi (48375) *(G-12407)*

E F D, Madison Heights Also called Efd Induction Inc *(G-10717)*

E H Inc 269 673-6456
   2870 116th Ave Allegan (49010) *(G-156)*

E H Tulgestka & Sons Inc 989 734-2129
   1160 Hwy F 21 S Rogers City (49779) *(G-14209)*

E I Du Pont De Nemours & Co 302 999-6566
   1250 Harmon Rd Auburn Hills (48326) *(G-872)*

E J I W, Oak Park Also called Ej Usa Inc *(G-12610)*

E J M Ball Screw LLC 989 893-7674
   209 Morton St Bay City (48706) *(G-1349)*

E L Nickell Co 269 435-2475
   385 Centreville St Constantine (49042) *(G-3665)*

E Leet Woodworking 269 664-5203
   10175 3 Mile Rd Plainwell (49080) *(G-13076)*

E M I Construction Products 616 392-7207
   526 E 64th St Holland (49423) *(G-8020)*

E M P, Escanaba Also called Engineered Machined Pdts Inc *(G-5069)*

E M P Manufacturing Corp 586 949-8277
   28190 23 Mile Rd Chesterfield (48051) *(G-2873)*

E M Smokers Inc 586 207-1172
   14052 Patterson Dr Shelby Township (48315) *(G-15217)*

E P I, Clinton Township Also called Electroplating Industries Inc *(G-3230)*

E Q R 2 Inc 586 731-3483
   44479 Phoenix Dr Sterling Heights (48314) *(G-15995)*

E R Tool Company Inc 586 757-1159
   3720 E 10 Mile Rd Ste A Warren (48091) *(G-17790)*

E S I Industries 231 256-9245
   10 S Highland Dr Lake Leelanau (49653) *(G-9559)*

E Smart Fuels America Inc 248 687-8003
   1001 Brush St Detroit (48226) *(G-4198)*

E T A, Troy Also called Engineering Tech Assoc Inc *(G-17091)*

E Tech Plastics, Marysville Also called Rak-O-Nizer LLC *(G-11098)*

E U P Woods Shavings 906 495-1141
   16816 S Hugginn St Kincheloe (49788) *(G-9501)*

E Z Logic Data Systems Inc 248 817-8800
   31455 Northwestern Hwy Farmington Hills (48334) *(G-5221)*

E&S Sales LLC 586 212-6018
   36252 Tindell Dr Sterling Heights (48312) *(G-15996)*

E-Con LLC 248 766-9000
   320 Martin St Ste 60 Birmingham (48009) *(G-1725)*

E-Course Machinery, Detroit Also called Ivan Doverspike *(G-4328)*

E-Light LLC 734 427-0600
   3144 Martin Rd Commerce Township (48390) *(G-3524)*

E-Procurement Services LLC 248 630-7200
   691 N Squirrel Rd Ste 220 Auburn Hills (48326) *(G-873)*

E-Snap Publications LLC 708 740-0910
   23211 Woodward Ave Ferndale (48220) *(G-5550)*

E-T-M Enterprises I Inc (PA) 517 627-8461
   920 N Clinton St Grand Ledge (48837) *(G-6389)*

E-Z Burr Tool, Livonia Also called Cogsdill Tool Products Inc *(G-10160)*

E-Zee Set Wood Products Inc 248 398-0090
   21650 Coolidge Hwy Oak Park (48237) *(G-12608)*

E.a Graphics, Sterling Heights Also called Ethnic Artwork Inc *(G-16006)*

Eab Fabrication Inc 517 639-7080
   150 S Main St Quincy (49082) *(G-13668)*

Eab Fabrication Inc (PA) 517 639-7080
   64 Cole St Quincy (49082) *(G-13669)*

Eagile Incorporated 616 243-1200
   1880 Turner Ave Nw Ste A Grand Rapids (49504) *(G-6660)*

Eagle Alum Prmnt Mold Cstngs I 231 788-4884
   2134 Northwoods Ave Muskegon (49442) *(G-11802)*

Eagle Cnc Technology, Muskegon Also called Eagle T M C Technologies *(G-11804)*

Eagle Creek Mfg & Sales 989 643-7521
   6753 S Steel Rd Saint Charles (48655) *(G-14802)*

Eagle Design & Technology Inc 616 748-1022
   55 E Roosevelt Ave Zeeland (49464) *(G-19017)*

Eagle Engineering & Supply Co 989 356-4526
   101 N Industrial Hwy Alpena (49707) *(G-291)*

Eagle Exploration Inc 231 252-4624
   4287 S M 37 Grawn (49637) *(G-7450)*

Eagle Fasteners Inc 248 577-1441
   185 Park Dr Troy (48083) *(G-17076)*

Eagle Grafix 989 624-4638
   10525 S Block Rd Birch Run (48415) *(G-1706)*

Eagle Graphic and Design Inc 248 668-0344
   317 N Pontiac Trl Walled Lake (48390) *(G-17667)*

Eagle Graphics and Design 248 618-0000
   2040 Airport Rd Waterford (48327) *(G-18121)*

Eagle Group II Ltd 616 754-7777
   8384 Peck Rd Greenville (48838) *(G-7483)*

Eagle Indus Group Federal LLC 616 863-8623
   555 Plymouth Ave Ne Grand Rapids (49505) *(G-6661)*

Eagle Industrial Group Inc 616 647-9904
   847 W River Center Dr Ne Comstock Park (49321) *(G-3605)*

Eagle Industries Inc 248 624-4266
   51135 Century Ct Wixom (48393) *(G-18650)*

Eagle Industries Inc (PA) 248 624-4266
   30926 Century Dr Wixom (48393) *(G-18651)*

Eagle Machine Products Company 586 268-2460
   35440 Stanley Dr Sterling Heights (48312) *(G-15997)*

Eagle Machine Tool Corporation 231 798-8473
   6060 Grand Haven Rd Norton Shores (49441) *(G-12289)*

Eagle Manufacturing Corp 586 323-0303
   52113 Shelby Pkwy Shelby Township (48315) *(G-15218)*

Eagle Masking Fabrication Inc 586 992-3080
   6633 Diplomat Dr Sterling Heights (48314) *(G-15998)*

Eagle Mine LLC 906 339-7000
   4547 County Road 601 Champion (49814) *(G-2704)*

Eagle Powder Coating 517 784-2556
   2218 E High St Ste C Jackson (49203) *(G-8872)*

Eagle Precision Cast Parts Inc 231 788-3318
   5112 Evanston Ave Muskegon (49442) *(G-11803)*

Eagle Press Repairs & Ser 419 539-7206
   2025 E Gier Rd Adrian (49221) *(G-63)*

Eagle Quest International Ltd 616 850-2630
   17863 170th Ave Ste 201 Spring Lake (49456) *(G-15812)*

Eagle Ridge Paper Ltd 248 376-9503
   15355 Oakwood Dr Romulus (48174) *(G-14269)*

Eagle T M C Technologies 231 766-3914
   2357 Whitehall Rd Muskegon (49445) *(G-11804)*

Eagle Thread Verifier LLC 586 764-8218
   40631 Firesteel Dr Sterling Heights (48313) *(G-15999)*

Eagle Tool, Iron Mountain Also called Laydon Enterprises Inc *(G-8724)*

Eagle Tool Group LLC 586 997-0800
   42724 Mound Rd Sterling Heights (48314) *(G-16000)*

Eagleburgmann Industries LP 989 486-1571
   1821 Austin St Midland (48642) *(G-11359)*

Eaglematic, Shelby Township Also called Eagle Manufacturing Corp *(G-15218)*

Eakas Corp 815 488-1879
   40000 Grand River Ave # 4 Novi (48375) *(G-12408)*

Earl Daup Signs 810 767-2020
6060 Birch Rd Flint (48507) *(G-5690)*
Earl St John Forest Products 906 497-5667
N16226 Birch St Spalding (49886) *(G-15759)*
Earle Press Inc 231 773-2111
2140 Latimer Dr Muskegon (49442) *(G-11805)*
Earle Press Printing, Muskegon *Also called Earle Press Inc (G-11805)*
Earthbound Inc 616 774-0096
1116 Plnfeld Ave Ne Ste 2 Grand Rapids (49503) *(G-6662)*
Earthtronics Inc 231 332-1188
800 E Ellis Rd Ste 574 Norton Shores (49441) *(G-12290)*
Earthwerks LLC 800 275-7943
319 S 2nd St Grand Haven (49417) *(G-6294)*
Earthworm Cstngs Unlimited LLC 248 882-3329
1179 Sylvertis Dr Waterford (48328) *(G-18122)*
Easco-Sparcatron, Mount Clemens *Also called Liquid Drive Corporation (G-11647)*
Easi, Troy *Also called Actalent Services LLC (G-16905)*
East - Lind Heat Treat Inc 248 585-1415
32045 Dequindre Rd Madison Heights (48071) *(G-10715)*
East Branch Forest Products 906 852-3315
5160 E Hwy 28 Kenton (49967) *(G-9439)*
East Coast Finishers 844 366-9966
30300 Nwestern Hwy # 113 Farmington Hills (48334) *(G-5222)*
East Jordan Ironworks Inc 517 566-7211
7300 W Grand Ledge Hwy Sunfield (48890) *(G-16334)*
East Jordan Sandblasting, East Jordan *Also called Northwest Fabrication Inc (G-4878)*
East Kingsford Iron & Metal Co, Iron Mountain *Also called Schneider Iron & Metal Inc (G-8732)*
East Michigan Lumber, Sterling *Also called Maple Ridge Hardwoods Inc (G-15913)*
East Muskegon Roofg Shtmtl Co (PA) 231 744-2461
1665 Holton Rd Muskegon (49445) *(G-11806)*
East Penn Manufacturing, Lansing *Also called Wonch Battery Company (G-9904)*
East Penn Manufacturing Co 586 979-5300
6023 Progress Dr Sterling Heights (48312) *(G-16001)*
East River Machine & Tool Inc 231 767-1701
1701 Wierengo Dr Muskegon (49442) *(G-11807)*
East Side Gear, Warren *Also called Bauer Precision Tool Co (G-17728)*
East Side Locksmith, Mount Clemens *Also called Weber Security Group Inc (G-11662)*
Eastern Michigan Industries 586 757-4140
23850 Ryan Rd Warren (48091) *(G-17791)*
Eastern Oil Company (PA) 248 333-1333
590 S Paddock St Pontiac (48341) *(G-13364)*
Eastern Power and Lighting 248 739-0908
5758 Hubbell St Dearborn Heights (48127) *(G-3925)*
Eastern Upper Pnsula WD Shvngs, Kincheloe *Also called Eup Wood Shavings Inc (G-9502)*
Eastport Group Inc 989 732-0030
9301 M 32 E Johannesburg (49751) *(G-9081)*
Eastside Coatings 313 936-1000
25614 Jefferson Ave Saint Clair Shores (48081) *(G-14855)*
Eastside Spot Inc 906 226-9431
129 E Hewitt Ave Marquette (49855) *(G-11016)*
Easy Dock Corp 231 750-5052
3823 W Giles Rd Muskegon (49445) *(G-11808)*
Easy Printing Center, Saginaw *Also called Tsunami Inc (G-14780)*
Easy Scrub LLC 586 565-1777
16629 Bettmar St Roseville (48066) *(G-14404)*
Eaton Aeroquip LLC 949 452-9575
300 S East Ave Jackson (49203) *(G-8873)*
Eaton Aerospace LLC 517 787-8121
300 S East Ave Jackson (49203) *(G-8874)*
Eaton Aerospace LLC 616 949-1090
3675 Patterson Ave Se Grand Rapids (49512) *(G-6663)*
Eaton Corporation 269 781-0200
19218 B Dr S Marshall (49068) *(G-11056)*
Eaton Corporation 248 226-6347
26201 Northwestern Hwy Southfield (48076) *(G-15547)*
Eaton Corporation 586 228-2029
19700 Hall Rd Ste B Clinton Township (48038) *(G-3228)*
Eaton Corporation 269 342-3000
13100 E Michigan Ave Galesburg (49053) *(G-6076)*
Eaton Corporation 517 789-1148
2425 W Michigan Ave Jackson (49202) *(G-8875)*
Eaton Corporation 517 787-8121
4743 Venture Dr Ann Arbor (48108) *(G-463)*
Eaton Corporation 269 342-3000
13100 E Michigan Ave Galesburg (49053) *(G-6077)*
Eaton Corporation 248 226-6200
26101 Northwestern Hwy Southfield (48076) *(G-15548)*
Eaton Detroit Spring Svc Co 313 963-3839
1555 Michigan Ave Detroit (48216) *(G-4199)*
Eaton Fuller Reman Center, Galesburg *Also called Eaton Corporation (G-6077)*
Eaton Industries Inc (PA) 734 428-0000
254 S Wagner Rd Ann Arbor (48103) *(G-464)*
Eaton Inoac Company (HQ) 248 226-6200
26101 Northwestern Hwy Southfield (48076) *(G-15549)*
Eaton Steel Bar Company, Oak Park *Also called Eaton Steel Corporation (G-12609)*
Eaton Steel Corporation (PA) 248 398-3434
10221 Capital St Oak Park (48237) *(G-12609)*
Eaton Steel Corporation 248 398-3434
38901 Amrhein Rd Livonia (48150) *(G-10189)*
Ebels Equipment LLC 231 826-3334
490 E Prosper Rd Falmouth (49632) *(G-5132)*
Ebels Hardware Inc 231 826-3334
490 E Prosper Rd Falmouth (49632) *(G-5133)*
Eberhard and Father Signworks 989 892-5566
108 Woodside Ave Essexville (48732) *(G-5113)*
Eberspecher Contrls N Amer Inc 248 994-7010
2035 Charles Orndorf Dr Brighton (48116) *(G-1981)*
Ebinger Manufacturing Company 248 486-8880
7869 Kensington Rd Brighton (48116) *(G-1982)*
Ebling & Son Inc 616 532-8400
4484 Rger B Chffee Mem Dr Kentwood (49548) *(G-9450)*
Ebling & Son Blacksmith, Kentwood *Also called Ebling & Son Inc (G-9450)*
Ebonex Corporation (PA) 313 388-0063
18400 Rialto St Melvindale (48122) *(G-11200)*
Ebw Electronics Inc 616 786-0575
13110 Ransom St Holland (49424) *(G-8021)*
Ebwe, Holland *Also called Ebw Electronics Inc (G-8021)*
Eca Educational Services Div, Commerce Township *Also called Eca Educational Services Inc (G-3525)*
Eca Educational Services Inc 248 669-7170
1981 Dallavo Dr Commerce Township (48390) *(G-3525)*
Eca Enterprises LLC 313 828-4098
1712 Heatherwood Dr # 102 Inkster (48141) *(G-8663)*
Ecco Tool Co Inc 248 349-0840
42525 W 11 Mile Rd Novi (48375) *(G-12409)*
Echo Engrg & Prod Sups Inc 734 241-9622
725 Ternes Dr Monroe (48162) *(G-11538)*
Echo Etching, Grand Rapids *Also called Grand River Interiors Inc (G-6777)*
Echo Quality Grinding Inc 231 544-6637
3166 Muckle Rd Central Lake (49622) *(G-2694)*
ECJ Processing 248 540-2336
17379 Park Ln Southfield (48076) *(G-15550)*
Eckert Mfg Co 517 521-4905
3820 Nicholson Rd Fowlerville (48836) *(G-5837)*
Eckhart USA, Clay *Also called Auto Craft Tool & Die Co (G-3116)*
Eclectic Metal Arts LLC 248 251-5924
20225 Livernois Ave Detroit (48221) *(G-4200)*
Eclipse Print Emporium Inc 248 477-8337
32753 8 Mile Rd Livonia (48152) *(G-10190)*
Eclipse Print Services 517 304-2151
46980 Liberty Dr Wixom (48393) *(G-18652)*
Eclipse Tanning, Brighton *Also called Horn Corp (G-2009)*
Eclipse Tanning, Troy *Also called Horn Corporation (G-17151)*
Eclipse Tool & Die Inc 616 877-3717
4713 Circuit Ct Ste A Wayland (49348) *(G-18195)*
ECM Manufacturing Inc 810 736-0299
4301 Western Rd Flint (48506) *(G-5691)*
ECM Specialties Inc 810 736-0299
4301 Western Rd Flint (48506) *(G-5692)*
Eco - Composites LLC 616 395-8902
845 Allen Dr Holland (49423) *(G-8022)*
Eco Bio Plastics Midland Inc 989 496-1934
4037 S Saginaw Rd Midland (48640) *(G-11360)*
Eco Brushes and Fibers 231 683-9202
2658 Heights Ravenna Rd Muskegon (49444) *(G-11809)*
Eco Brushes and Fibers S.A.s, Muskegon *Also called Eco Brushes and Fibers (G-11809)*
Eco Paper 248 652-3601
1150 W Hamlin Rd Rochester Hills (48309) *(G-13999)*
Eco Sign Solutions LLC 734 276-8585
37 Enterprise Dr Ann Arbor (48103) *(G-465)*
Eco Tax Group Inc 313 422-1300
24901 Northwestern Hwy # 409 Southfield (48075) *(G-15551)*
Ecoclean Inc (HQ) 248 450-2000
26801 Northwestern Hwy Southfield (48033) *(G-15552)*
Ecolab Inc 248 697-0202
28550 Cabot Dr Ste 100 Novi (48377) *(G-12410)*
Ecolo-Tech Inc 248 541-1100
1743 E 10 Mile Rd Madison Heights (48071) *(G-10716)*
Ecology Coatings 248 370-9900
2701 Cmbridge Ct Ste 100 Auburn Hills (48326) *(G-874)*
Econ Global Services, Birmingham *Also called E-Con LLC (G-1725)*
Econ-O-Line Abrasive Products 616 846-4150
401 N Griffin St Grand Haven (49417) *(G-6295)*
Econo Print Inc 734 878-5806
10312 Dexter Pinckney Rd Pinckney (48169) *(G-13047)*
Econoline Abrasive Products, Grand Haven *Also called Depottey Acquisition Inc (G-6291)*
Economy Printing, Kalamazoo *Also called River Run Press Inc (G-9320)*
Ecoprint Services LLC 616 254-8019
549 Ottawa Ave Nw Ste 103 Grand Rapids (49503) *(G-6664)*
Ecoquest Intl Independent 734 854-6080
10950 Strasburg Rd Erie (48133) *(G-5047)*
Ecorse McHy Sls & Rbldrs Inc 313 383-2100
4621 13th St Wyandotte (48192) *(G-18817)*
Ecorse Precision Products, Wyandotte *Also called Ecorse McHy Sls & Rbldrs Inc (G-18817)*

ALPHABETIC

Ecovia Renewables Inc ...248 953-0594
600 Suth Wagner Rd Ste 15 Ann Arbor (48103) *(G-466)*
Ed Cumings Inc ...810 736-0130
2305 Branch Rd Flint (48506) *(G-5693)*
Edco Media, Clarkston *Also called E D C O Publishing Inc (G-3031)*
Eddies Quick Stop Inc ...313 712-1818
5517 Middlesex St Dearborn (48126) *(G-3833)*
Ede Co ...586 756-7555
26969 Ryan Rd Warren (48091) *(G-17792)*
Eden Foods Inc (PA) ...517 456-7424
701 Tecumseh Rd Clinton (49236) *(G-3137)*
Eden Foods Inc ...313 921-2053
9104 Culver St Detroit (48213) *(G-4201)*
Eden Organic Pasta Company, Detroit *Also called Eden Foods Inc (G-4201)*
Edens Political ...313 277-0700
360 Devonshire St Dearborn (48124) *(G-3834)*
Edge Fitnes Training Hdqtr LLC ...989 486-9870
1403 Washington St # 26 Midland (48640) *(G-11361)*
Edge Industries Inc ...616 453-5458
2887 3 Mile Rd Nw Grand Rapids (49534) *(G-6665)*
Edge-Sweets Company, Grand Rapids *Also called Edge Industries Inc (G-6665)*
Edgemarc Energy Holdings LLC (PA) ...724 749-8466
401 S Old Woodward Ave # 340 Birmingham (48009) *(G-1726)*
Edgemen Screen Printing ...586 465-6820
19757 15 Mile Rd Clinton Township (48035) *(G-3229)*
Edgewater Apartments ...517 663-8123
223 N Main St Eaton Rapids (48827) *(G-4962)*
Edgewell Personal Care Company ...866 462-8669
12103 Delta St Taylor (48180) *(G-16409)*
EDM Inc ...586 933-3187
1900 Stephenson Hwy # 100 Troy (48083) *(G-17077)*
EDM Wire Tek ...810 235-5344
4155 Holiday Dr Flint (48507) *(G-5694)*
Edmar Manufacturing Inc ...616 392-7218
526 E 64th St Holland (49423) *(G-8023)*
Edmore Tool & Grinding Inc ...989 427-3790
4255 E Hward Cy Edmore Rd Edmore (48829) *(G-4992)*
Edon Controls Inc ...248 280-0420
2891 Industrial Row Dr Troy (48084) *(G-17078)*
EDP Company, Livonia *Also called Electronic Design & Packg Co (G-10194)*
Edrich Products Inc ...586 296-3350
33672 Doreka Fraser (48026) *(G-5922)*
EDS Enterprises, Flint *Also called Earl Daup Signs (G-5690)*
EDS Industries ...989 274-2551
1543 W Hamlin Rd Rochester Hills (48309) *(G-14000)*
Edston Plastics Company ...734 941-3750
8730 Riverside Dr Brighton (48116) *(G-1983)*
Edstrom Prototype LLC ...616 566-4361
356 Roosevelt Ave Holland (49424) *(G-8024)*
Edt Welding & Fabrication LLC ...978 257-4700
5952 Iosco Mountain Rd Gregory (48137) *(G-7514)*
Edw C Levy Co (PA) ...313 429-2200
9300 Dix Dearborn (48120) *(G-3835)*
Edw C Levy Co ...248 334-4302
2470 Auburn Rd Auburn Hills (48326) *(G-875)*
Edw C Levy Co ...248 349-8600
27575 Wixom Rd Novi (48374) *(G-12411)*
Edw C Levy Co ...313 843-7200
8800 Dix St Detroit (48209) *(G-4202)*
Edw C Levy Co ...248 634-0879
16255 Tindall Rd Davisburg (48350) *(G-3765)*
Edward and Cole Inc ...734 996-9074
5540 Tanglewood Dr Ann Arbor (48105) *(G-467)*
Edward E Yates ...517 467-4961
8573 M 50 Onsted (49265) *(G-12705)*
Edwards Industrial Sales Inc ...517 887-6100
5646 Commerce St Ste D Lansing (48911) *(G-9833)*
Edwards Machine & Tool Co, Jackson *Also called Edwards Machining Inc (G-8876)*
Edwards Machinery and Repa ...616 422-2584
2064 W Snow Rd Baroda (49101) *(G-1160)*
Edwards Machining Inc ...517 782-2568
2335 Research Dr Jackson (49203) *(G-8876)*
Edwards Publications In ...864 882-3272
344 N State St Caro (48723) *(G-2570)*
Edwards Sign & Screen Printing ...989 725-2988
1585 S M 52 Owosso (48867) *(G-12832)*
Ees Coke Battery LLC ...313 235-4000
414 S Main St Ste 600 Ann Arbor (48104) *(G-468)*
Efd Induction Inc ...248 658-0700
31511 Dequindre Rd Madison Heights (48071) *(G-10717)*
Efesto LLC ...734 913-0428
3400 Woodhill Cir Superior Township (48198) *(G-16336)*
Efficiency Production, Mason *Also called Arcosa Epi LLC (G-11116)*
Efficiency Shoring and Supply, Mason *Also called Fw Shoring Company (G-11133)*
Efi Custom Injection Molding, Troy *Also called Eagle Fasteners Inc (G-17076)*
Eflex Sytems, Rochester Hills *Also called Elite Engineering Inc (G-14003)*
Eftec North America LLC (HQ) ...248 585-2200
20219 Northline Rd Taylor (48180) *(G-16410)*
Egeler Industrial Services, Livonia *Also called Eis Inc (G-10192)*
Egemin Automation Inc ...616 393-0101
11818 James St Holland (49424) *(G-8025)*
Egemin Group, Inc., Holland *Also called Egemin Automation Inc (G-8025)*
Eggers Excavating LLC ...989 695-5205
7832 Kochville Rd Ste 1 Freeland (48623) *(G-6022)*
Egt Printing Solutions LLC ...248 583-2500
32031 Townley St Madison Heights (48071) *(G-10718)*
Ehc Inc (PA) ...313 259-2266
3150 Livernois Rd Ste 170 Troy (48083) *(G-17079)*
Eid Real Estates LLC ...717 471-5996
533 Slumber Ln Rochester Hills (48307) *(G-14001)*
Eidemller Prcsion McHining Inc ...248 669-2660
4998 Mccarthy Dr Milford (48381) *(G-11463)*
Eifel Mold & Engineering Inc ...586 296-9640
31071 Fraser Dr Fraser (48026) *(G-5923)*
Eight Mile Signs ...248 762-3889
30845 8 Mile Rd Livonia (48152) *(G-10191)*
Eiklae Products ...734 671-0752
10286 Boucher Rd Grosse Ile (48138) *(G-7521)*
Eikos Holdings Inc ...248 280-0300
2613 Industrial Row Dr Troy (48084) *(G-17080)*
Eileen Smeltzer ...269 629-8056
8227 N 30th St Richland (49083) *(G-13824)*
Eiler Brothers Inc ...517 784-0970
2201 Brooklyn Rd Jackson (49203) *(G-8877)*
Eimo Americas, Vicksburg *Also called Eimo Technologies Inc (G-17603)*
Eimo Technologies Inc (HQ) ...269 649-0545
14320 Portage Rd Vicksburg (49097) *(G-17603)*
Eis Inc ...734 266-6500
31478 Industrial Rd # 100 Livonia (48150) *(G-10192)*
Eissmann Auto Port Huron LLC (HQ) ...810 216-6300
2440 20th St Port Huron (48060) *(G-13474)*
Eissmann Auto Port Huron LLC ...248 829-4990
2655 Product Dr Rochester Hills (48309) *(G-14002)*
Ej Americas LLC (HQ) ...231 536-2261
301 Spring St East Jordan (49727) *(G-4863)*
Ej Ardmore Inc ...231 536-2261
301 Spring St East Jordan (49727) *(G-4864)*
Ej Asia-Pacific Inc (HQ) ...231 536-2261
301 Spring St East Jordan (49727) *(G-4865)*
Ej Co ...231 536-4527
5000 Airport Rd East Jordan (49727) *(G-4866)*
Ej Europe LLC (HQ) ...231 536-2261
301 Spring St East Jordan (49727) *(G-4867)*
Ej Group Inc (PA) ...231 536-2261
301 Spring St East Jordan (49727) *(G-4868)*
Ej Timber Producers Inc ...231 544-9866
972 Toby Rd East Jordan (49727) *(G-4869)*
Ej Usa Inc (HQ) ...800 874-4100
301 Spring St East Jordan (49727) *(G-4870)*
Ej Usa Inc ...248 546-2004
13001 Northend Ave Oak Park (48237) *(G-12610)*
Ej Usa Inc ...616 538-2040
5075 Clyde Park Ave Sw Wyoming (49509) *(G-18870)*
Ej Usa Inc ...231 536-2261
5000 Airport Rd East Jordan (49727) *(G-4871)*
Ejw Contract Inc ...616 293-5181
7930 Forest Creek Ct Whitmore Lake (48189) *(G-18531)*
Eklund Holdings Inc (PA) ...231 777-2537
1800 E Keating Ave Muskegon (49442) *(G-11810)*
Ekstrom Industries Inc ...248 477-0040
43045 W 9 Mile Rd Novi (48375) *(G-12412)*
El 903 Element LLC ...517 655-3492
139 W Lake Lansing Rd # 21 East Lansing (48823) *(G-4891)*
El Acapulco Tamales, Burt *Also called Villanuevo Soledad (G-2216)*
El Informador LLC ...616 272-1092
2000 28th St Sw Ste 4 Wyoming (49519) *(G-18871)*
El Paso LLC ...231 587-0704
8616 Anr Storage Rd Ne Mancelona (49659) *(G-10869)*
El Sol Custom Lighting ...269 281-0435
3909 Stonegate Park Saint Joseph (49085) *(G-14928)*
El Vocero Hispano Inc ...616 246-6023
2818 Vineland Ave Se Grand Rapids (49508) *(G-6666)*
El-Milagro of Michigan Inc (PA) ...616 452-6625
1846 Clyde Park Ave Sw Grand Rapids (49509) *(G-6667)*
Elan Designs Inc ...248 682-3000
238 S Telegraph Rd Pontiac (48341) *(G-13365)*
Elaree FABrication&welding ...517 505-5998
4531 Meridian Rd Williamston (48895) *(G-18571)*
Elba Inc ...248 288-6098
1925 W Maple Rd Ste B Troy (48084) *(G-17081)*
ELBA LABORATORIES, Troy *Also called Elba Inc (G-17081)*
Elco Enterprises Inc ...517 782-8040
5750 Marathon Dr Ste B Jackson (49201) *(G-8878)*
Elco Machine Enterprises, Taylor *Also called Micro Fixtures Inc (G-16446)*
Eldean Company ...616 335-5843
2223 S Shore Dr Macatawa (49434) *(G-10566)*
Eldean Shipyard & Yacht Sales, Macatawa *Also called Eldean Company (G-10566)*
Eldean Yacht Basin Ltd (PA) ...616 786-2205
1862 Ottawa Beach Rd Holland (49424) *(G-8026)*

Eldec LLC ...248 364-4750
3355 Bald Mountain Rd # 30 Auburn Hills (48326) ***(G-876)***
Elden Cylinder Testing Inc ...734 946-6900
9465 Inkster Rd Taylor (48180) ***(G-16411)***
Elden Industries Corp ...734 946-6900
9465 Inkster Rd Taylor (48180) ***(G-16412)***
Elder Creek Sign Design ...517 857-4252
28354 W Dr N Springport (49284) ***(G-15881)***
Elderberry Steam Engines ...989 245-0652
5215 Pheasant Run Dr # 5 Saginaw (48638) ***(G-14643)***
Eldon Publishing LLC ...810 648-5282
43 S Elk St Sandusky (48471) ***(G-15058)***
Eldor Automotive N Amer Inc ...248 878-9193
100 W Big Beavr Rd # 200 Troy (48084) ***(G-17082)***
Electra Cable & Communication ...586 754-3479
24846 Forterra Dr Warren (48089) ***(G-17793)***
Electra-Tec Inc ...269 694-6652
567 W M 89 Hwy Otsego (49078) ***(G-12785)***
Electric Beach Tanning Co ...313 423-6539
15797 Mack Ave Grosse Pointe Park (48224) ***(G-7553)***
Electric Contractors Company ...734 205-9594
1501 Briarwood Cir Ann Arbor (48108) ***(G-469)***
Electric Equipment Company ...269 925-3266
401 Klock Rd Benton Harbor (49022) ***(G-1548)***
Electric Eye Cafe ...734 369-6904
811 N Main St Ann Arbor (48104) ***(G-470)***
Electric Last Mile Inc ...888 825-9111
1055 W Square Lake Rd Troy (48098) ***(G-17083)***
Electric Last Mile Solutions, Troy *Also called Electric Last Mile Inc* ***(G-17083)***
Electric Motor & Contg Co ...313 871-3775
7273 Flamingo St Clay (48001) ***(G-3119)***
Electric Soul Tattoo and Fine ...616 930-3113
876 Grandville Ave Sw Grand Rapids (49503) ***(G-6668)***
Electric Steam Generator, Buchanan *Also called Optimystic Enterprises Inc* ***(G-2200)***
Electrical Product Sales Inc ...248 583-6100
2611 Elliott Dr Troy (48083) ***(G-17084)***
Electro ARC Manufacturing Co ...734 483-4233
2055 N Lima Center Rd A Dexter (48130) ***(G-4741)***
Electro Chemical Finishing Co ...616 531-1250
379 44th St Sw Grand Rapids (49548) ***(G-6669)***
Electro Chemical Finishing Co (PA) ...616 531-0670
2973 Dormax St Sw Grandville (49418) ***(G-7372)***
Electro Diamond Tools, Oxford *Also called Superior Abrasive Products* ***(G-12921)***
Electro Optics Mfg Inc ...734 283-3000
4459 13th St Wyandotte (48192) ***(G-18818)***
Electro Tech, Otsego *Also called Impert Industries Inc* ***(G-12788)***
Electro-Heat, Allegan *Also called Ddr Heating Inc* ***(G-154)***
Electro-Matic Company, Farmington Hills *Also called Electro-Matic Products Inc* ***(G-5224)***
Electro-Matic Integrated Inc ...248 478-1182
23410 Industrial Park Ct Farmington Hills (48335) ***(G-5223)***
Electro-Matic Products Inc (HQ) ...248 478-1182
23409 Industrial Park Ct Farmington Hills (48335) ***(G-5224)***
Electro-Matic Ventures Inc (PA) ...248 478-1182
23409 Industrial Park Ct Farmington Hills (48335) ***(G-5225)***
Electro-Matic Visual Inc ...248 478-1182
23660 Industrial Park Dr Farmington Hills (48335) ***(G-5226)***
Electro-Optics Technology Inc (PA) ...231 935-4044
3340 Parkland Ct Traverse City (49686) ***(G-16675)***
Electro-Plating Service Inc ...248 541-0035
945 E 10 Mile Rd Madison Heights (48071) ***(G-10719)***
Electrocom Midwest Sales Inc (PA) ...248 449-2643
32500 Concord Dr Ste 298 Madison Heights (48071) ***(G-10720)***
Electrocraft Michigan Inc ...603 516-1297
1705 Woodland Dr Saline (48176) ***(G-15014)***
Electrodynamics Inc ...734 422-5420
31091 Schoolcraft Rd Livonia (48150) ***(G-10193)***
Electroheat Technologies LLC ...810 798-2400
691 N Squirrel Rd Ste 247 Auburn Hills (48326) ***(G-877)***
Electrojet Inc ...734 272-4709
50164 Pontiac Trl Unit 5 Wixom (48393) ***(G-18653)***
Electrolabs Inc ...586 294-4150
18503 E 14 Mile Rd Fraser (48026) ***(G-5924)***
Electrolux Professional Inc ...248 338-4320
214 S Telegraph Rd Pontiac (48341) ***(G-13366)***
Electronic Design & Packg Co ...734 591-9176
36704 Commerce St Livonia (48150) ***(G-10194)***
Electronics For Imaging Inc ...734 641-3062
1260 James L Hart Pkwy Ypsilanti (48197) ***(G-18941)***
Electronics Tech Center, Grand Haven *Also called Ghsp Inc* ***(G-6301)***
Electroplating Industries Inc ...586 469-2390
21410 Carlo Dr Clinton Township (48038) ***(G-3230)***
Eleetus, Ottawa Lake *Also called Yakkertech Limited* ***(G-12812)***
Elegant Glassworks ...734 845-1901
8636 Roundhill Ct Saline (48176) ***(G-15015)***
Elegant Invitations, Plymouth *Also called Artcraft Printing Corporation* ***(G-13126)***
Elegant Wood Craftsmanship ...231 742-0706
1260 W Polk Rd Hart (49420) ***(G-7751)***
Elegant Woodworking ...248 363-3804
3711 Ellisia Rd Commerce Township (48382) ***(G-3526)***
Element 22 Coml Group LLC ...269 910-6739
2425 S 11th St Ste D Kalamazoo (49009) ***(G-9175)***
Element 80 Engraving LLC ...616 318-7407
519 Macomb Ave Nw Grand Rapids (49534) ***(G-6670)***
Element Facility Services ...734 895-8716
6094 2nd St Romulus (48174) ***(G-14270)***
Element Services LLC ...517 672-1005
3650 Norton Rd Howell (48843) ***(G-8452)***
Elemental Artistry LLC ...616 326-1758
957 Leonard St Nw Grand Rapids (49504) ***(G-6671)***
Elenbaas Hardwood Incorporated ...269 343-7791
3751 Alvan Rd Kalamazoo (49001) ***(G-9176)***
Elenz Inc (PA) ...989 732-7233
1829 Calkins Dr Gaylord (49735) ***(G-6127)***
Elenz Inc ...989 732-7233
1455 Dickerson Rd Gaylord (49735) ***(G-6128)***
Elevated Technologies Inc ...616 288-9817
817 Ottawa Ave Nw Grand Rapids (49503) ***(G-6672)***
Elevator Concepts Ltd ...734 246-4700
18720 Krause St Riverview (48193) ***(G-13871)***
Eleven Mile Trck Frame Axle In ...248 399-7536
1750 E 11 Mile Rd Madison Heights (48071) ***(G-10721)***
Eleven Mile Truck Collision Co, Madison Heights *Also called Eleven Mile Trck Frame Axle In* ***(G-10721)***
Eliason Corporation (HQ) ...269 327-7003
9229 Shaver Rd Portage (49024) ***(G-13557)***
Eliason Corporation ...269 621-2100
County Rd Cr 65 1/2 Hartford (49057) ***(G-7763)***
Elite Bus Svcs Exec Stffing In ...734 956-4550
2510 S Telg Rd Ste L280 Bloomfield Hills (48302) ***(G-1818)***
Elite Canvas LLC ...231 343-7649
294 Pine St Fruitport (49415) ***(G-6062)***
Elite Defense LLC ...734 424-9955
1332 Anderson Rd Clawson (48017) ***(G-3096)***
Elite Dog and Pet Supply LLC ...947 900-1101
24100 Sthfeld Rd Ste 110c Southfield (48075) ***(G-15553)***
Elite Engineering Inc ...517 304-3254
210 W Tienken Rd Rochester Hills (48306) ***(G-14003)***
Elite Industrial Mfg LLC ...616 377-7769
12764 Greenly St Ste 40 Holland (49424) ***(G-8027)***
Elite Machining LLC ...517 784-0986
3832 Thorncrest Dr Jackson (49203) ***(G-8879)***
Elite Manufacturing Tech LLC ...586 846-2055
33670 Lipke St Clinton Township (48035) ***(G-3231)***
Elite Medical Molding, Shelby Township *Also called Elite Mold & Engineering Inc* ***(G-15219)***
Elite Metal Manufacturing LLC ...734 718-0061
32473 Schoolcraft Rd Livonia (48150) ***(G-10195)***
Elite Mold & Engineering Inc ...586 314-4000
51548 Filomena Dr Shelby Township (48315) ***(G-15219)***
Elite Plastic Products Inc ...586 247-5800
51354 Filomena Dr Shelby Township (48315) ***(G-15220)***
Elite Prcsion McHining Tooling ...269 383-9714
3816 Miller Rd Kalamazoo (49001) ***(G-9177)***
Elite Sign Company ...906 481-7446
125 Howard St Big Rapids (49307) ***(G-1672)***
Elite Tooling L.L.C., Kalamazoo *Also called Elite Prcsion McHining Tooling* ***(G-9177)***
Elite Woodworking LLC ...586 204-5882
22960 W Industrial Dr Saint Clair Shores (48080) ***(G-14856)***
Elk Brewing ...616 214-8172
400 Dodge Rd Ne Comstock Park (49321) ***(G-3606)***
Elk Lake Tool Co ...231 264-5616
203 Ec Loomis Dr Elk Rapids (49629) ***(G-5023)***
Elk Rapids Engineering Inc ...231 264-5661
210 Industrial Park Dr Elk Rapids (49629) ***(G-5024)***
Elk Software LLC ...800 658-3420
28345 Beck Rd Ste 103 Wixom (48393) ***(G-18654)***
Elkay Fastening Systems, Kalamazoo *Also called Elkay Industries Inc* ***(G-9178)***
Elkay Industries Inc ...269 381-4266
1804 Reed Ave Kalamazoo (49001) ***(G-9178)***
Elkhart Plastics - 08, White Pigeon *Also called Elkhart Plastics LLC* ***(G-18476)***
Elkhart Plastics LLC ...269 464-4107
605 Sol Morris Ave White Pigeon (49099) ***(G-18476)***
Elkins Machine & Tool Co Inc (PA) ...734 941-0266
27510 Northline Rd Romulus (48174) ***(G-14271)***
Ell Tron Manufacturing Co (PA) ...989 983-3181
11893 Old 27 Hwy N Vanderbilt (49795) ***(G-17570)***
Ellenbaum Truck Sales, Sebewaing *Also called Trucksforsalecom* ***(G-15145)***
Elliott Group International, Auburn Hills *Also called Elliott Tape Inc* ***(G-878)***
Elliott Tape Inc (PA) ...248 475-2000
1882 Pond Run Auburn Hills (48326) ***(G-878)***
Ellis Infinity LLC ...313 570-0840
1545 Clay St Unit 6 Detroit (48211) ***(G-4203)***
Ellsworth Cutting Tools Ltd ...586 598-6040
25190 Terra Industrial Dr Chesterfield (48051) ***(G-2874)***
Ellsworth, Belinda, Pinckney *Also called Step Into Success Inc* ***(G-13057)***
Elm International Inc (PA) ...517 332-4900
4360 Hagadorn Rd Okemos (48864) ***(G-12665)***
Elmer's, White Cloud *Also called M 37 Concrete Products Inc* ***(G-18446)***

Elmers Construction Engrg, Traverse City *Also called Elmers Crane and Dozer Inc* ***(G-16676)***

Elmers Crane and Dozer Inc (PA) ... 231 943-3443
3600 Rennie School Rd Traverse City (49685) ***(G-16676)***

Elmers Crane and Dozer Inc ... 231 943-3443
781 N Mission Rd Mount Pleasant (48858) ***(G-11696)***

Elmet North America Inc ... 517 664-9011
4103 Grand Oak Dr B102 Lansing (48911) ***(G-9834)***

Elmhirst Industries Inc ... 586 731-8663
7630 19 Mile Rd Sterling Heights (48314) ***(G-16002)***

Elmo Manufacturing Co Inc ... 734 995-5966
98 Valhalla Dr 950 Ann Arbor (48103) ***(G-471)***

Elmont District Library ... 810 798-3100
213 W Saint Clair St Almont (48003) ***(G-259)***

Elmwood Manufacturing Company ... 313 571-1777
3925 Beaufait St Detroit (48207) ***(G-4204)***

Elopak Inc ... 248 486-4600
46962 Liberty Dr Wixom (48393) ***(G-18655)***

Elringklinger Auto Mfg Inc (HQ) ... 248 727-6600
23300 Northwestern Hwy Southfield (48075) ***(G-15554)***

Elringklinger Auto Mfg Inc ... 248 727-6600
23300 Northwestern Hwy Southfield (48075) ***(G-15555)***

Elringklinger North Amer Inc, Southfield *Also called Elringklinger Auto Mfg Inc* ***(G-15554)***

Elringklinger North Amer Inc ... 734 738-1800
47912 Halyard Dr Ste 111 Plymouth (48170) ***(G-13166)***

Elsa Enterprises Inc ... 248 816-1454
2800 W Big Beaver Rd # 124 Troy (48084) ***(G-17085)***

Elsie Inc ... 734 421-8844
12752 Stark Rd Ste 1 Livonia (48150) ***(G-10196)***

Elsie Publishing Institute (PA) ... 517 371-5257
500 W Ionia St Lansing (48933) ***(G-9835)***

Elston Enterprises Inc ... 313 561-8000
22250 Ford Rd Dearborn Heights (48127) ***(G-3926)***

Eltek Inc ... 616 363-6397
6688 Wildwood Creek Dr Ne Belmont (49306) ***(G-1506)***

Elucidation Fabrication ... 586 612-4601
3921 32nd St Port Huron (48060) ***(G-13475)***

Elumigen LLC ... 855 912-0477
820 Kirts Blvd Ste 300 Troy (48084) ***(G-17086)***

Em A Give Break Safety ... 231 263-6625
6502 M 37 Kingsley (49649) ***(G-9523)***

Emabond Solutions LLC ... 248 481-8048
1797 Atlantic Blvd Auburn Hills (48326) ***(G-879)***

Emack Manufacturing ... 616 241-3040
1012 Ken O Sha Ind Pk Dr Grand Rapids (49508) ***(G-6673)***

Emaculate Enterprises LLC ... 313 805-0654
18300 Van Dyke St Detroit (48234) ***(G-4205)***

Emag LLC (HQ) ... 248 477-7440
38800 Grand River Ave Farmington Hills (48335) ***(G-5227)***

Emag Technologies Inc ... 734 996-3624
775 Technology Dr Ste 300 Ann Arbor (48108) ***(G-472)***

Emag USA Corporation ... 248 477-7440
38800 Grand River Ave Farmington Hills (48335) ***(G-5228)***

Ematrix Energy Systems Inc ... 248 797-2149
21520 Bridge St Southfield (48033) ***(G-15556)***

Ematrix Energy Systems Inc ... 248 629-9111
4425 Fernlee Ave Royal Oak (48073) ***(G-14532)***

Embers Ballscrew Repair ... 586 216-8444
10200 Grinnell St Detroit (48213) ***(G-4206)***

Embest, Romulus *Also called Country Fresh LLC* ***(G-14264)***

Embrace Premium Vodka LLC ... 616 617-5602
515 Ferris St Ypsilanti (48197) ***(G-18942)***

Embracelets ... 616 719-3545
1422 Margaret Ave Se Grand Rapids (49507) ***(G-6674)***

Embroid ME, Traverse City *Also called Top Shells Embroidery LLC* ***(G-16863)***

Embroider It LLC ... 248 538-9965
6785 Candlewood Trl West Bloomfield (48322) ***(G-18281)***

Embroidery & Much More LLC ... 586 771-3832
27419 Harper Ave Saint Clair Shores (48081) ***(G-14857)***

Embroidery House Inc ... 616 669-6400
2688 Edward St Jenison (49428) ***(G-9054)***

Embroidery Hutch ... 810 459-8728
10248 Beacon Ct Grand Blanc (48439) ***(G-6241)***

Embroidery Shoppe LLC ... 734 595-7612
39017 Cherry Hill Rd Westland (48186) ***(G-18367)***

Embroidery Wearhouse ... 906 228-5818
2112 Us Highway 41 W # 3 Marquette (49855) ***(G-11017)***

Embroidme Grand Rapids ... 616 974-1033
6161 28th St Se Ste 3 Grand Rapids (49546) ***(G-6675)***

EMC Corporation ... 248 957-5800
36555 Corporate Dr # 200 Farmington Hills (48331) ***(G-5229)***

EMC Educational Services LLC ... 616 460-3345
1953 Kinney Ave Nw Walker (49534) ***(G-17638)***

EMC Welding & Fabrication Inc ... 231 788-4172
4966 Evanston Ave Muskegon (49442) ***(G-11811)***

Emco Chemical Inc ... 313 894-7650
4470 Lawton St Detroit (48208) ***(G-4207)***

Emcon Technologies, Auburn Hills *Also called Faurecia Emssons Ctrl Tech USA* ***(G-887)***

Emcor Inc ... 989 667-0652
5154 Alliance Dr Bay City (48706) ***(G-1350)***

EMD Wire Tek ... 810 235-5344
4155 Holiday Dr Flint (48507) ***(G-5695)***

Emerald Bioagriculture Corp ... 517 882-7370
4211 Okemos Rd Ste 20 Okemos (48864) ***(G-12666)***

Emerald Graphics, Grand Rapids *Also called Kennedy Acquisition Inc* ***(G-6884)***

Emerald Graphics Inc ... 616 871-3020
4949 W Greenbrooke Dr Se Grand Rapids (49512) ***(G-6676)***

Emerald Growth Partners LLC ... 248 756-0286
41900 Executive Dr Harrison Township (48045) ***(G-7697)***

Emerald Spa, Grand Rapids *Also called Conway Products Corporation* ***(G-6603)***

Emerald Tool Inc ... 231 799-9193
6305 Norton Center Dr Norton Shores (49441) ***(G-12291)***

Emergency Services LLC ... 231 727-7400
1660 Dodson Dr Muskegon (49442) ***(G-11812)***

Emergency Technology Inc (PA) ... 616 896-7100
3900 Central Pkwy Hudsonville (49426) ***(G-8581)***

Emergent Biodef Oper Lnsng LLC ... 517 327-1500
3500 N Martin Luther King Lansing (48906) ***(G-9690)***

Emergent Biosolutions Inc ... 517 327-1500
3500 N Mar L King Jr Blvd Lansing (48906) ***(G-9691)***

Emergent Technologies Co, Vicksburg *Also called Ronningen Research and Dev Co* ***(G-17611)***

Emerging Advanced Products LLC ... 734 942-1060
39555 Intrstate 94 S Svc Belleville (48111) ***(G-1483)***

Emerson Electric Co ... 616 846-3950
15399 Hofma Dr Grand Haven (49417) ***(G-6296)***

Emerson Electric Co ... 586 268-3104
6590 Sims Dr Sterling Heights (48313) ***(G-16003)***

Emerson Electric Co ... 734 420-0832
15024 Robinwood Dr Plymouth (48170) ***(G-13167)***

Emerson Geophysical LLC ... 231 943-1400
3819 4 Mile Rd N Traverse City (49686) ***(G-16677)***

Emerson Prcess MGT Pwr Wtr Slt ... 313 874-0860
3031 W Grand Blvd Ste 423 Detroit (48202) ***(G-4208)***

Emery Design & Woodwork LLC ... 734 709-1687
8277 Tower Rd South Lyon (48178) ***(G-15434)***

Emesa Foods Company ... 248 982-3908
29790 Palmer Ct Farmington Hills (48336) ***(G-5230)***

Emesa Foods Company LLC ... 248 982-3908
13430 Huron St Taylor (48180) ***(G-16413)***

Emhart Industries, Chesterfield *Also called Emhart Teknologies LLC* ***(G-2875)***

Emhart Teknologies LLC ... 586 949-0440
50501 E Russell Schmidt B Chesterfield (48051) ***(G-2875)***

Emhart Teknologies LLC ... 800 783-6427
49201 Gratiot Ave Chesterfield (48051) ***(G-2876)***

Emhart Teknologies LLC ... 248 677-9693
2500 Meijer Dr Troy (48084) ***(G-17087)***

Emhart Teknologies LLC ... 800 783-6427
2400 Meijer Dr Bldg 2 Troy (48084) ***(G-17088)***

Emhart Teknologies LLC ... 800 783-6427
2500 Meijer Dr Troy (48084) ***(G-17089)***

EMI Construction Products, Holland *Also called Edmar Manufacturing Inc* ***(G-8023)***

Emitted Energy Inc (PA) ... 855 752-3347
6559 Diplomat Dr Sterling Heights (48314) ***(G-16004)***

Emm Inc ... 248 478-1182
23409 Industrial Park Ct Farmington Hills (48335) ***(G-5231)***

Emma Sogoian Inc ... 248 549-8690
4336 Normandy Ct Royal Oak (48073) ***(G-14533)***

Emmie Die and Engineering Corp ... 810 346-2914
7254 Maple Valley Rd Brown City (48416) ***(G-2136)***

Emp Advanced Development LLC ... 906 789-7497
2701 N 30th St Escanaba (49829) ***(G-5067)***

Emp Racing Inc ... 906 786-8404
2701 N 30th St Escanaba (49829) ***(G-5068)***

Empatheticbot LLC ... 810 938-3168
301 Roosevelt St Canton (48188) ***(G-2458)***

Empire Forest Products Company, Plainwell *Also called Chippewa Development Inc* ***(G-13071)***

Empire Hardchrome ... 810 392-3122
33450 Bordman Rd Richmond (48062) ***(G-13837)***

Empire Iron Mining Partnership ... 906 475-3600
Empire Mine Rd Palmer (49871) ***(G-12930)***

Empire Machine & Conveyors Inc ... 989 541-2060
5111 S Durand Rd Durand (48429) ***(G-4841)***

Empire Machine Company ... 269 684-3713
350 Palladium Dr Saint Joseph (49085) ***(G-14929)***

Empire Molded Plastics, Benton Harbor *Also called Colonial Manufacturing LLC* ***(G-1540)***

Empire Moulding and Milwork, Zeeland *Also called Novo Distribution LLC* ***(G-19061)***

Empire Printing ... 248 547-9223
28535 Orchard Lake Rd # 400 Farmington Hills (48334) ***(G-5232)***

Empire Sports, Oak Park *Also called Noir Sportswear Corp* ***(G-12634)***

Empire Tool Co ... 734 283-8600
4261 13th St Wyandotte (48192) ***(G-18819)***

Empirical Bioscience Inc ... 877 479-9949
2007 Eastcastle Dr Se Grand Rapids (49508) ***(G-6677)***

Empower Financials Inc ... 734 747-9393
4343 Concourse Dr Ste 140 Ann Arbor (48108) ***(G-473)***

EMR Corp ... 810 376-4710
3473 Main St Deckerville (48427) ***(G-3954)***

Ems Equipment Management Svcs, Southgate *Also called Abtech Installation & Svc Inc* ***(G-15747)***
Ems Grand Rapids, Grand Rapids *Also called Grand Rapids Elc Mtr Svcs LLC* ***(G-6756)***
Ems Parts Div 517 319-5306
16800 Industrial Pkwy Lansing (48906) ***(G-9692)***
Emssons Faurecia Ctrl Systems 248 724-5100
2800 High Meadow Cir Auburn Hills (48326) ***(G-880)***
En Novative Technologies, Dexter *Also called QEd Envmtl Systems Inc* ***(G-4751)***
Ena North America Corporation 248 926-0011
51150 Century Ct Wixom (48393) ***(G-18656)***
Enagon LLC 269 455-5110
3381 Blue Star Hwy Saugatuck (49453) ***(G-15083)***
Enamelite Industries, Grand Rapids *Also called Mdm Enterprises Inc* ***(G-6974)***
Encore Commercial Products Inc 248 354-4090
37525 Interchange Dr Farmington Hills (48335) ***(G-5233)***
Encore Music Publishers 231 432-8322
399 W Harbour Ridge Ct Maple City (49664) ***(G-10941)***
Encore Publications 269 488-3143
117 W Cedar St Ste A Kalamazoo (49007) ***(G-9179)***
End Grain Woodwork 248 420-3228
32819 W Chicago St Livonia (48150) ***(G-10197)***
End Product Results LLC 586 585-1210
27115 Gratiot Ave Ste B Roseville (48066) ***(G-14405)***
Endless Engravings 517 962-4293
319 S Maurice Ave Jackson (49203) ***(G-8880)***
Endless Possibilities Inc 248 262-7443
1169 S I 75 Business Loop Grayling (49738) ***(G-7460)***
Endoscopic Solutions 248 625-4055
5701 Bow Pointe Dr Clarkston (48346) ***(G-3032)***
Endra Life Sciences Inc 734 335-0468
3600 Green Ct Ste 350 Ann Arbor (48105) ***(G-474)***
Endura Coatings, Sterling Heights *Also called Stechschulte/Wegerly AG LLC* ***(G-16190)***
Endura-Veyor Inc 989 358-7060
3490 Us Highway 23 N Alpena (49707) ***(G-292)***
Endurance Carbide, Saginaw *Also called M Curry Corporation* ***(G-14685)***
Ener-TEC Inc 517 741-5015
306 Railroad St Union City (49094) ***(G-17492)***
Ener2 LLC 248 842-2662
7685 Athlone Dr Brighton (48116) ***(G-1984)***
Enerco Corporation (PA) 517 627-1669
317 N Bridge St Grand Ledge (48837) ***(G-6390)***
Energy Acquisition 616 350-9129
2992 28th St Sw Grandville (49418) ***(G-7373)***
Energy Acquisition Corp 517 339-0249
2385 Delhi Commerce Dr # 5 Holt (48842) ***(G-8310)***
Energy Control Solutions Inc 810 735-2800
11494 Delmar Dr Ste 100 Fenton (48430) ***(G-5472)***
Energy Design Svc Systems LLC 810 227-3377
7050 Jo Mar Dr Whitmore Lake (48189) ***(G-18532)***
Energy Development Assoc LLC 313 354-2644
15201 Century Dr Dearborn (48120) ***(G-3836)***
Energy Efficient Ltg LLC Eel 586 214-5557
3297 Wdview Lk Rd Ste 200 West Bloomfield (48323) ***(G-18282)***
Energy Exploration 248 579-6531
40411 Oakwood Dr Novi (48375) ***(G-12413)***
Energy Products Inc 248 866-5622
315 Indusco Ct Troy (48083) ***(G-17090)***
Energy Products Inc (PA) 248 545-7700
1551 E Lincoln Ave # 101 Madison Heights (48071) ***(G-10722)***
Energy Products & Services, Rochester *Also called US Energia LLC* ***(G-13936)***
Energy Products Service Dept, Troy *Also called Energy Products Inc* ***(G-17090)***
Energy Steel & Supply Co 810 538-4990
1785 Northfield Dr Rochester Hills (48309) ***(G-14004)***
Energy Suppliers LLC 269 342-9482
2813 W Main St Kalamazoo (49006) ***(G-9180)***
Enersave LLC 616 785-1800
3716 Dykstra Dr Nw Grand Rapids (49544) ***(G-6678)***
Enertech Corporation 231 832-5587
210 S Division St Hersey (49639) ***(G-7866)***
Enertemp Inc 616 243-2752
3961 Eastern Ave Se Grand Rapids (49508) ***(G-6679)***
Enertrols Inc 734 595-4500
23435 Industrial Park Dr Farmington Hills (48335) ***(G-5234)***
Eng Advance Technology Dev Ctr, Auburn Hills *Also called American Axle & Mfg Inc* ***(G-782)***
Engai 313 605-8220
27056 Pinewood Dr Apt 203 Wixom (48393) ***(G-18657)***
Engine Parts Grinding, Grand Haven *Also called Engine Power Components Inc* ***(G-6297)***
Engine Power Components Inc 616 846-0110
1333 Fulton Ave Grand Haven (49417) ***(G-6297)***
Engineered Alum Fabricators, Ferndale *Also called Engineered Alum Fabricators Co* ***(G-5551)***
Engineered Alum Fabricators Co 248 582-3430
1530 Farrow St Ferndale (48220) ***(G-5551)***
Engineered Concepts Inc 574 333-9110
67990 Milmc Ln Cassopolis (49031) ***(G-2627)***
Engineered Heat Treat Inc 248 588-5141
31271 Stephenson Hwy Madison Heights (48071) ***(G-10723)***
Engineered Machined Pdts Inc (PA) 906 786-8404
3111 N 28th St Escanaba (49829) ***(G-5069)***
Engineered Plastic Components, Farmington Hills *Also called Aees Power Systems Ltd Partnr* ***(G-5160)***
Engineered Plastic Components, Allen Park *Also called Aees Power Systems Ltd Partnr* ***(G-187)***
Engineered Plastic Pdts Mfg, Ypsilanti *Also called Engineered Plastic Products* ***(G-18943)***
Engineered Plastic Products (PA) 734 439-0310
699 James L Hart Pkwy Ypsilanti (48197) ***(G-18943)***
Engineered Polymer Products 269 461-6955
7988 W Eureka Rd Eau Claire (49111) ***(G-4976)***
Engineered Prfmce Coatings Inc 616 988-7927
4881 Kendrick St Se Grand Rapids (49512) ***(G-6680)***
Engineered Prfmce Mtls Co LLC 734 904-4023
11228 Lemen Rd Ste A Whitmore Lake (48189) ***(G-18533)***
Engineered Products Company (PA) 810 767-2050
601 Kelso St Flint (48506) ***(G-5696)***
Engineered Resources Inc 248 399-5500
26511 Harding St Oak Park (48237) ***(G-12611)***
Engineered Tooling Systems Inc 616 647-5063
2780 Courier Dr Nw Grand Rapids (49534) ***(G-6681)***
Engineered Tools Corp 989 673-8733
2710 W Caro Rd Caro (48723) ***(G-2571)***
Engineering, Rochester Hills *Also called Dataspeed Inc* ***(G-13990)***
Engineering and Mfg Svcs, Westland *Also called High-Star Corporation* ***(G-18381)***
Engineering Graphics Inc 517 485-5828
16333 S Us Highway 27 Lansing (48906) ***(G-9693)***
Engineering Reproduction Inc (PA) 313 366-3390
13550 Conant St Detroit (48212) ***(G-4209)***
Engineering Service of America 248 357-3800
21556 Telegraph Rd Southfield (48033) ***(G-15557)***
Engineering Systems Intl, Southfield *Also called Engineering Service of America* ***(G-15557)***
Engineering Tech Assoc Inc (PA) 248 729-3010
5445 Corporate Dr Ste 300 Troy (48098) ***(G-17091)***
Enginered Combustn Systems LLC 248 549-1703
4240 Delemere Ct Royal Oak (48073) ***(G-14534)***
Enginred Plstic Components Inc 810 326-1650
2015 S Range Rd Saint Clair (48079) ***(G-14826)***
Enginred Plstic Components Inc 248 825-4508
100 W Big Beavr Rd # 200 Troy (48084) ***(G-17092)***
Enginred Plstic Components Inc 810 326-1650
2000 Christian B Haas Dr Saint Clair (48079) ***(G-14827)***
Enginred Plstic Components Inc 586 336-9500
187 E Pond Dr Romeo (48065) ***(G-14225)***
Enginred Plstic Components Inc 810 326-3010
2015 S Range Rd Saint Clair (48079) ***(G-14828)***
Engrave A Remembrance Inc 586 772-7480
28555 Flanders Ave Warren (48088) ***(G-17794)***
Engraved Memories 586 703-7983
54989 Sherwood Ln Shelby Township (48315) ***(G-15221)***
Engraving Connection, Plymouth *Also called Rex M Tubbs* ***(G-13281)***
Engtechnik Inc (PA) 734 667-4237
40615 Koppernick Rd # 2 Canton (48187) ***(G-2459)***
Enhanced MSC, Madison Heights *Also called Martin Fluid Power Company* ***(G-10776)***
Enhanceher Collection LLC 313 279-7308
1420 Washington Blvd # 301 Detroit (48226) ***(G-4210)***
Enkon LLC 937 890-5678
10521 Mi State Road 52 Manchester (48158) ***(G-10883)***
Enmark Tool Company 586 293-2797
18100 Cross Fraser (48026) ***(G-5925)***
Enovapremier LLC 517 541-3200
403 Parkland Dr Charlotte (48813) ***(G-2751)***
Enovate It 248 721-8104
1250 Woodward Hts Ferndale (48220) ***(G-5552)***
Enprotech Industrial Tech LLC 517 372-0950
16740 16800 Indus Pkwy Lansing (48906) ***(G-9694)***
Enprotech Industrial Tech LLC 216 883-3220
16800 Industrial Pkwy Lansing (48906) ***(G-9695)***
Enrinity Supplements Inc 734 322-4966
6480 Commerce Dr Westland (48185) ***(G-18368)***
Ensign Emblem Ltd (PA) 231 946-7703
1746 Keane Dr Traverse City (49696) ***(G-16678)***
Ensign Equipment Inc 616 738-9000
12523 Superior Ct Holland (49424) ***(G-8028)***
Ensign Publishing House 734 369-3983
2830 Pebble Creek Dr Ann Arbor (48108) ***(G-475)***
Ensign Technical Services, Traverse City *Also called Ensign Emblem Ltd* ***(G-16678)***
Ensley Sand & Gravel, Sand Lake *Also called R & C Redi-Mix Inc* ***(G-15051)***
Enstrom Helicopter Corporation 906 863-1200
2209 22nd St Menominee (49858) ***(G-11233)***
Ensure Technologies Inc 734 547-1600
135 S Prospect St Ste 100 Ypsilanti (48198) ***(G-18944)***
Enterprise Hinge Inc 269 857-2111
6779 Enterprise Dr Douglas (49406) ***(G-4773)***
Enterprise Plastics LLC 586 665-1030
51354 Filomena Dr Shelby Township (48315) ***(G-15222)***
Enterprise Tool & Die LLC 616 538-0920
4270 White St Sw Grandville (49418) ***(G-7374)***

ALPHABETIC

Enterprise Tool and Gear Inc (PA)....989 269-9797
635 Liberty St Bad Axe (48413) *(G-1100)*
Entertainment, Troy *Also called HSP Epi Acquisition LLC (G-17156)*
Entertainment Publications Inc....248 404-1000
1401 Crooks Rd Ste 150 Troy (48084) *(G-17093)*
Entire Rprdction Imging Sltion, Clawson *Also called American Reprographics Co LLC (G-3086)*
Entrepreneur Solutions LLC....248 660-2858
20235 Wybridge St Apt 201 Clinton Township (48036) *(G-3232)*
Entrepreneurial Pursuits....248 829-6903
2727 Product Dr Rochester Hills (48309) *(G-14005)*
Entron Computer Systems Inc....248 349-8898
44554 Chedworth Ct Northville (48167) *(G-12215)*
Enuf Haircare and Lashes LLC....586 354-1798
4085 Hereford St Detroit (48224) *(G-4211)*
Envirnmntal Pllet Slutions Inc....616 283-1784
9500 Henry Ct Ste 350 Zeeland (49464) *(G-19018)*
Enviro Industries Inc....906 492-3402
11874 N Whitefish Pt Rd Paradise (49768) *(G-12931)*
Enviro-Brite Solutions LLC....989 387-2758
4150 Arrow St Oscoda (48750) *(G-12758)*
Envirodrone Inc....226 344-5614
440 Burroughs St Detroit (48202) *(G-4212)*
Envirodyne Technologies Inc....269 342-1918
7574 E Michigan Ave Kalamazoo (49048) *(G-9181)*
Envirolite LLC (PA)....248 792-3184
1700 W Big Beavr Rd # 150 Troy (48084) *(G-17094)*
Envirolite LLC....888 222-2191
421 Race St Coldwater (49036) *(G-3432)*
Environ Manufacturing Inc....616 644-6846
972 Graham Lake Ter Battle Creek (49014) *(G-1223)*
Environmental Catalysts LLC....248 813-2000
5820 Innovation Dr Troy (48098) *(G-17095)*
Environmental Safe Oil Change, Wixom *Also called Esoc Inc (G-18658)*
Envirotronics, Grand Rapids *Also called Weiss Technik North Amer Inc (G-7329)*
Envision Engineering LLC....616 897-0599
12650 Envision Dr Se Lowell (49331) *(G-10500)*
Envision Machine & Mfg, Holland *Also called Envision Machine and Mfg LLC (G-8029)*
Envision Machine and Mfg LLC....616 953-8580
741 Waverly Ct Holland (49423) *(G-8029)*
Envisiontec US LLC....313 436-4300
15162 S Commerce Dr Dearborn (48120) *(G-3837)*
Eoi Pioneer Inc....626 823-5639
110 Research Pkwy Dundee (48131) *(G-4818)*
Eon Project....313 717-5976
14875 Penrod St Detroit (48223) *(G-4213)*
Eot, Traverse City *Also called Electro-Optics Technology Inc (G-16675)*
Eotech Inc....734 741-8868
1201 E Ellsworth Rd Ann Arbor (48108) *(G-476)*
Eotech LLC....248 971-4027
1201 E Ellsworth Rd Ann Arbor (48108) *(G-477)*
Eovations LLC (HQ)....989 671-1460
12629 Whisper Ridge Dr Freeland (48623) *(G-6023)*
Eovations LLC....616 361-7136
2801 E Beltline Ave Ne Grand Rapids (49525) *(G-6682)*
Epath Logic Inc....313 375-5375
418 N Main St 200 Royal Oak (48067) *(G-14535)*
EPC Columbia, Saint Clair *Also called Enginred Plstic Components Inc (G-14826)*
Epc-Columbia Inc....810 326-1650
2000 Christian B Haas Dr Saint Clair (48079) *(G-14829)*
Epcon, Rochester Hills *Also called F I D Corporation (G-14008)*
Epi Market, Battle Creek *Also called Epi Printers Inc (G-1226)*
Epi Marketing Services, Battle Creek *Also called Epi Printers Inc (G-1224)*
Epi Marketing Services, Battle Creek *Also called Epi Printers Inc (G-1228)*
Epi Printers Inc (PA)....800 562-9733
5404 Wayne Rd Battle Creek (49037) *(G-1224)*
Epi Printers Inc....269 968-2221
61 Clark Rd Battle Creek (49037) *(G-1225)*
Epi Printers Inc....269 968-2221
5350 W Dickman Rd Battle Creek (49037) *(G-1226)*
Epi Printers Inc....269 964-4600
4956 Wayne Rd Battle Creek (49037) *(G-1227)*
Epi Printers Inc....734 261-9400
13305 Wayne Rd Livonia (48150) *(G-10198)*
Epi Printers Inc....269 964-6744
65 Clark Rd Battle Creek (49037) *(G-1228)*
Epic Equipment & Engrg Inc....586 314-0020
52301 Shelby Pkwy Shelby Township (48315) *(G-15223)*
Epic Fine Arts Company Inc (HQ)....313 274-7400
21001 Van Born Rd Taylor (48180) *(G-16414)*
Epic Machine Inc....810 629-9400
201 Industrial Way Ste A Fenton (48430) *(G-5473)*
Epicure By Mills, The, Birmingham *Also called Mills Phrm & Apothecary LLC (G-1737)*
Epiphany Studios Ltd....248 745-3786
770 Orchard Lake Rd Pontiac (48341) *(G-13367)*
EPM, Whitmore Lake *Also called Engineered Prfmce Mtls Co LLC (G-18533)*
Epoch Robotics....616 820-3369
13365 Tyler St Holland (49424) *(G-8030)*
Eponds.com, Saginaw *Also called Blue Thumb Distributing Inc (G-14617)*
Epoxi-Pro, Rochester Hills *Also called Simiron Inc (G-14112)*
Eppinger Mfg Co....313 582-3205
6340 Schaefer Rd Dearborn (48126) *(G-3838)*
Epredia, Kalamazoo *Also called Thermo Fisher Scientific Inc (G-9356)*
Eps Industries Inc....616 844-9220
585 Second St Ferrysburg (49409) *(G-5602)*
Eptech Inc....586 254-2722
51483 Quadrate Dr Ste C Macomb (48042) *(G-10591)*
Eq Resource Recovery Inc (HQ)....734 727-5500
36345 Van Born Rd Romulus (48174) *(G-14272)*
Eqi Ltd....616 850-2630
5797 Harvey St Norton Shores (49444) *(G-12292)*
Eqi, Ltd., Spring Lake *Also called Eagle Quest International Ltd (G-15812)*
Equitable Engineering Co Inc....248 689-9700
1840 Austin Dr Troy (48083) *(G-17096)*
Equivalent Base Co....586 759-2030
4175 E 10 Mile Rd Warren (48091) *(G-17795)*
Equus Magnificus....651 407-0023
526 S Lamkin Rd Harbor Springs (49740) *(G-7646)*
Er Simons, Auburn *Also called Ittner Bean & Grain Inc (G-766)*
ERA Tool & Engineering Co....734 464-7788
28175 Wingfield Way Farmington Hills (48331) *(G-5235)*
Erae AMS America Corp....419 386-8876
2011 Centerpoint Pkwy Pontiac (48341) *(G-13368)*
Erae AMS USA Manufacturing LLC....314 600-3434
2011 Centerpoint Pkwy Pontiac (48341) *(G-13369)*
Erbsloeh Alum Solutions Inc....269 323-2565
6565 S Sprinkle Rd Portage (49002) *(G-13558)*
Erdman Machine Co....231 894-1010
8529 Silver Creek Rd Whitehall (49461) *(G-18495)*
Eric Henry Woodworks....248 613-5696
9496 Cedargrove Rd Clarkston (48348) *(G-3033)*
Eric Rogers LLC....517 543-7126
1101 Lipsey Dr Charlotte (48813) *(G-2752)*
Erich Jaeger USA Inc....734 404-5940
17199 N Laurel Park Dr # 10 Livonia (48152) *(G-10199)*
Erickson Logging Inc....906 481-4021
40734 Lower Pike Rd Chassell (49916) *(G-2777)*
Erickson Lumber & True Value....906 524-6295
17752 Us Hwy 41 Lanse (49946) *(G-9659)*
Erie Custom Signs, Saginaw *Also called Erie Marking Inc (G-14644)*
Erie Marking Inc....989 754-8360
1017 S Wheeler St Saginaw (48602) *(G-14644)*
Erie Technologies, Ottawa Lake *Also called F&B Technologies (G-12806)*
Erin Industries Inc (PA)....248 669-2050
902 N Pontiac Trl Walled Lake (48390) *(G-17668)*
Erla's Food Center, Cass City *Also called Erlas Inc (G-2614)*
Erlas Inc....989 872-2191
6233 Church St Cass City (48726) *(G-2614)*
Ernest Inds Acquisition LLC....734 459-8881
14601 Keel St Plymouth (48170) *(G-13168)*
Ernest Industries Acquisition, (PA)....734 595-9500
39133 Webb Dr Westland (48185) *(G-18369)*
Ernest Industries Company, Westland *Also called Ernest Industries Acquisition, (G-18369)*
Ernest Industries Company, Plymouth *Also called Ernest Inds Acquisition LLC (G-13168)*
Ernie Romanco....517 531-3686
661 N Concord Rd Albion (49224) *(G-125)*
Ernst Benz Company LLC....248 203-2323
177 S Old Woodward Ave Birmingham (48009) *(G-1727)*
Ervin Amasteel, Ann Arbor *Also called Ervin Industries Inc (G-478)*
Ervin Development Center, Tecumseh *Also called Ervin Industries Inc (G-16500)*
Ervin Industries Inc....517 265-6118
915 Tabor St Adrian (49221) *(G-64)*
Ervin Industries Inc (PA)....734 769-4600
3893 Research Park Dr Ann Arbor (48108) *(G-478)*
Ervin Industries Inc....517 423-5477
200 Industrial Dr Tecumseh (49286) *(G-16500)*
Ervins Group LLC (PA)....248 203-2000
550 Hulet Dr Ste 103 Bloomfield Hills (48302) *(G-1819)*
Ervott Tool Co LLC....616 842-3688
13951 132nd Ave Grand Haven (49417) *(G-6298)*
Erwin Quarder Inc....616 575-1600
5101 Kraft Ave Se Ste B Grand Rapids (49512) *(G-6683)*
Escanaba and Lk Superior RR Co....906 786-9399
1401 N 26th St Bldg 20 Escanaba (49829) *(G-5070)*
Escanaba Paper Company, Escanaba *Also called Verso Corporation (G-5105)*
Esco Co Ltd Partnership....231 726-3106
2406 Roberts St Muskegon (49444) *(G-11813)*
Esco Company LLC....231 726-3106
2330 East Paris Ave Se Grand Rapids (49546) *(G-6684)*
Esco Group Inc (PA)....616 453-5458
2887 3 Mile Rd Nw Grand Rapids (49534) *(G-6685)*
Ese LLc....810 538-1000
3344 John Conley Dr Lapeer (48446) *(G-9929)*
Esgar Products, Van Buren Twp *Also called Kage Group LLC (G-17532)*
Esirpal Inc....586 337-7848
55549 Danube Ave Macomb (48042) *(G-10592)*

Esl Supplies LLC 517 525-7877
600 N College Rd Mason (48854) ***(G-11131)***
Esmies Cabinet 269 921-1578
1565 N Teakwood Dr Stevensville (49127) ***(G-16249)***
Esoc Inc 248 624-7992
48553 West Rd Wixom (48393) ***(G-18658)***
ESP, Detroit *Also called Essential Screen Printing LLC* ***(G-4215)***
Espar Inc 248 994-7010
43700 Gen Mar Ste 3 Novi (48375) ***(G-12414)***
Espec Corp 616 896-6100
4141 Central Pkwy Hudsonville (49426) ***(G-8582)***
Esperion Therapeutics Inc 734 887-3903
3891 Ranchero Dr Ste 150 Ann Arbor (48108) ***(G-479)***
Espinoza Bros 313 468-7775
2397 Stair St Detroit (48209) ***(G-4214)***
Esr 989 619-7160
2225 E Tait Rd Harrisville (48740) ***(G-7742)***
Ess Tec Inc 616 394-0230
3347 128th Ave Holland (49424) ***(G-8031)***
Essen Bioscience, Ann Arbor *Also called Essen Instruments Inc* ***(G-480)***
Essen Instruments Inc (HQ) 734 769-1600
300 W Morgan Rd Ann Arbor (48108) ***(G-480)***
Essential Photo Gear 502 244-2888
5782 Church Hwy Rogers City (49779) ***(G-14210)***
Essential Screen Printing LLC 313 300-6411
2630 Orleans St Detroit (48207) ***(G-4215)***
Est Tools America Inc 810 824-3323
10138 Radiance Dr Ira (48023) ***(G-8695)***
Esterline Mmtron Input Cmpnnts, Frankenmuth *Also called Memtron Technologies Co* ***(G-5869)***
Esto Connectors, Kalamazoo *Also called Corners Limited* ***(G-9156)***
Esv Precision LLC 810 441-0953
1353 N Van Dyke Rd Imlay City (48444) ***(G-8631)***
Esyntrk Industries LLC 248 730-0640
4250 Pine Ln Orchard Lake (48323) ***(G-12717)***
Esys Automation LLC (HQ) 248 484-9927
1000 Brown Rd Auburn Hills (48326) ***(G-881)***
Esys Automation LLC 284 484-9724
1500 Highwood E Pontiac (48340) ***(G-13370)***
Esys Automation LLC 248 484-9702
6701 Center Dr Sterling Heights (48312) ***(G-16005)***
Etcs Inc 586 268-4870
21275 Mullin Ave Warren (48089) ***(G-17796)***
Eternabond Inc 847 540-0600
4401 Page Ave Michigan Center (49254) ***(G-11292)***
Eteron Inc 248 478-2900
23944 Freeway Park Dr Farmington Hills (48335) ***(G-5236)***
Ether LLC 248 795-8830
4950 Hummer Lake Rd Ortonville (48462) ***(G-12746)***
Ethnic Artwork Inc 586 726-1400
42111 Van Ave Sterling Heights (48314) ***(G-16006)***
Ethnicemedia LLC 248 762-8904
338 Thistle Ln Troy (48098) ***(G-17097)***
Ethnicemeida, Troy *Also called Ethnicemedia LLC* ***(G-17097)***
Ethyl, Southfield *Also called Afton Chemical Corporation* ***(G-15471)***
Ethylene LLC 616 554-3464
4855 Broadmoor Ave Se Kentwood (49512) ***(G-9451)***
Etna Distributors LLC 810 232-4760
2395 Lapeer Rd Flint (48503) ***(G-5697)***
Eto Magnetic Corp (HQ) 616 957-2570
5925 Patterson Ave Se Grand Rapids (49512) ***(G-6686)***
Ets Exco Tooling Solutions, Chesterfield *Also called Exco Extrusion Dies Inc* ***(G-2877)***
Etx Inc (HQ) 989 463-1151
2000 Michigan Ave Alma (48801) ***(G-240)***
Etx Holdings Inc (HQ) 989 463-1151
2000 Michigan Ave Alma (48801) ***(G-241)***
Euclid Coating Systems Inc 989 922-4789
3494 N Euclid Ave Bay City (48706) ***(G-1351)***
Euclid Industries Inc (PA) 989 686-8920
1655 Tech Dr Bay City (48706) ***(G-1352)***
Euclid Machine & Mfg Co 734 941-1080
29030 Northline Rd Romulus (48174) ***(G-14273)***
Euclid Manufacturing Co Inc 734 397-6300
1500 E Euclid St Detroit (48211) ***(G-4216)***
Eugene 313 217-9297
22116 Grand River Ave Detroit (48219) ***(G-4217)***
Euko Design-Signs Inc 248 478-1330
24849 Hathaway St Farmington Hills (48335) ***(G-5237)***
Euko Signs, Farmington Hills *Also called Euko Design-Signs Inc* ***(G-5237)***
Eup Wood Shavings Inc 586 943-7199
16888 S Hugginin St Kincheloe (49788) ***(G-9502)***
Eureka Welding Alloys Inc 248 588-0001
2000 E Avis Dr Madison Heights (48071) ***(G-10724)***
Euridium Solutions LLC 248 535-7005
55 E Long Lake Rd Ste 243 Troy (48085) ***(G-17098)***
Euro-Craft Interiors Inc 586 254-9130
6611 Diplomat Dr Sterling Heights (48314) ***(G-16007)***
European Cabinet Mfg Co 586 445-8909
30665 Groesbeck Hwy Roseville (48066) ***(G-14406)***
European Skin Care & Cosmetics, Southfield *Also called Mineral Cosmetics Inc* ***(G-15659)***
Eutectic Engineering Co Inc 313 892-2248
817 Rock Spring Rd Bloomfield Hills (48304) ***(G-1820)***
Ev Anywhere LLC 313 653-9870
3011 W Grand Blvd # 1800 Detroit (48202) ***(G-4218)***
Evans Coatings L L C 248 583-9890
1330 Souter Dr Troy (48083) ***(G-17099)***
Evans Holding Company, Troy *Also called Ehc Inc* ***(G-17079)***
Evans Industries Inc (HQ) 313 259-2266
3150 Livernois Rd Ste 170 Troy (48083) ***(G-17100)***
Evans Industries Inc 313 272-8200
12402 Hubbell St Detroit (48227) ***(G-4219)***
Evans Tempcon Delaware LLC 616 361-2681
3260 Eagle Park Dr Ne Ne100 Grand Rapids (49525) ***(G-6687)***
Evans Tool & Engineering Inc 616 791-6333
4287 3 Mile Rd Nw Grand Rapids (49534) ***(G-6688)***
Eve Salonspa 269 327-4811
7117 S Westnedge Ave 3b Portage (49002) ***(G-13559)***
Even Weight Brush LLC 906 863-3319
603 6th St Menominee (49858) ***(G-11234)***
Even-Cut Abrasive Company 216 881-9595
3890 Buchanan Ave Sw Grand Rapids (49548) ***(G-6689)***
Evenheat Kiln Inc 989 856-2281
6949 Legion Rd Caseville (48725) ***(G-2604)***
Evening News 734 242-1100
20 W 1st St Monroe (48161) ***(G-11539)***
Events To Envy 248 841-8400
113 E University Dr Ste 5 Rochester (48307) ***(G-13899)***
Ever-Flex Inc 313 389-2060
1490 John A Papalas Dr Lincoln Park (48146) ***(G-10046)***
Everblades Inc 906 483-0174
46104 State Highway M26 Atlantic Mine (49905) ***(G-749)***
Everest Energy Fund L L C 586 445-2300
30078 Schoenherr Rd # 150 Warren (48088) ***(G-17797)***
Everest Expedition LLC 616 392-1848
199 E 17th St Holland (49423) ***(G-8032)***
Everest Manufacturing Inc 313 401-2608
23800 Research Dr Farmington Hills (48335) ***(G-5238)***
Everfresh Beverages Inc 586 755-9500
6600 E 9 Mile Rd Warren (48091) ***(G-17798)***
Evergreen Grease Service Inc 517 264-9913
1445 Enterprise Ave Adrian (49221) ***(G-65)***
Evergreen Winery LLC 989 392-2044
3835 Huszan Dr Bay City (48706) ***(G-1353)***
Eversharp Tools Inc 810 824-3323
10138 Radiance Dr Ira (48023) ***(G-8696)***
Everson Tool & Machine Ltd 906 932-3440
620 Easy St Ironwood (49938) ***(G-8761)***
Everything Edbl Trats For Stne 313 725-0118
6008 Scotten St Detroit (48210) ***(G-4220)***
Evia Learning Inc 616 393-8803
720 E 8th St Ste 4 Holland (49423) ***(G-8033)***
Eview 360 LLC 248 306-5191
39255 Country Club Dr B Farmington Hills (48331) ***(G-5239)***
Evolution Tool Inc 810 664-5500
587 Mccormick Dr Lapeer (48446) ***(G-9930)***
Evolve Longboards USA LLC 616 915-3876
1959 Will Ave Nw Grand Rapids (49504) ***(G-6690)***
Evoqua Water Technologies LLC 616 772-9011
2155 112th Ave Holland (49424) ***(G-8034)***
Evosys North America Corp 248 973-1703
1091 Centre Rd Ste 140 Auburn Hills (48326) ***(G-882)***
Ewc Woodhaven Inc 734 552-3731
26747 Kirkway Cir Woodhaven (48183) ***(G-18800)***
Ewellix USA LLC 586 752-0060
69900 Powell Rd Armada (48005) ***(G-734)***
Ews Legacy LLC (PA) 248 853-6363
2119 Austin Ave Rochester Hills (48309) ***(G-14006)***
Ex Soli LLC (PA) 800 525-2431
3680 Stadium Park Way Kalamazoo (49009) ***(G-9182)***
Exact Fabrication 248 240-4506
8990 Pontiac Trl South Lyon (48178) ***(G-15435)***
Exatec LLC 248 926-4200
31220 Oak Creek Dr Wixom (48393) ***(G-18659)***
Excalibur Crossbow Inc 810 937-5864
2929 Lapeer Rd Port Huron (48060) ***(G-13476)***
Excavation, Manistique *Also called Joseph Lakosky Logging* ***(G-10920)***
Excel Circuits LLC 248 373-0700
2601 Lapeer Rd Auburn Hills (48326) ***(G-883)***
Excel Graphics 248 442-9390
31647 8 Mile Rd Livonia (48152) ***(G-10200)***
Excel Machinery Intl Corp 810 348-9162
13479 Neal Rd Davisburg (48350) ***(G-3766)***
Excel Real Estate Holdings LLC 919 250-1973
28011 Grand Oaks Ct Wixom (48393) ***(G-18660)***
Excelda Mfg Holdg LLC 517 223-8000
900 Garden Ln Fowlerville (48836) ***(G-5838)***
Excell Machine & Tool Co LLC 231 728-1210
1084 E Hackley Ave Muskegon (49444) ***(G-11814)***

ALPHABETIC

Excell Manufacturing Inc ...989 496-0473
3258 Patterson Rd Bay City (48706) **(G-1354)**
Excell Paving Plus, Coldwater *Also called RWS & Associates LLC* **(G-3451)**
Excellence Lawn Landscape ...810 623-9742
10379 Greenbrier Brighton (48114) **(G-1985)**
Excellence Manufacturing Inc ...616 456-9928
629 Ionia Ave Sw Grand Rapids (49503) **(G-6691)**
Excellent Designs Swimwear ...586 977-9140
5751 E 13 Mile Rd Warren (48092) **(G-17799)**
Exceptional Product Sales LLC ...586 286-3240
13425 19 Mile Rd Ste 300 Sterling Heights (48313) **(G-16008)**
Exclusive Brands LLC ...734 210-0107
38701 7 Mile Rd Ste 160 Livonia (48152) **(G-10201)**
Exclusive Heating & Coolg Comp ...248 219-9528
7725 W Mcnichols Rd Detroit (48221) **(G-4221)**
Exclusive Imagery Inc ...248 436-2999
1505 E 11 Mile Rd Royal Oak (48067) **(G-14536)**
Exclusive Provisioning Center, Livonia *Also called Exclusive Brands LLC* **(G-10201)**
Exco Extrusion Dies Inc ...586 749-5400
56617 N Bay Dr Chesterfield (48051) **(G-2877)**
Exco USA ...586 749-5400
56617 N Bay Dr Chesterfield (48051) **(G-2878)**
Excrution Painting, Garden City *Also called International Extrusions Inc* **(G-6102)**
Executive Operations LLC ...313 312-0653
8391 Mallard Xing Brighton (48116) **(G-1986)**
Exel Industries Group, Plymouth *Also called Sames Kremlin Inc* **(G-13292)**
Exfil, Livonia *Also called Air Filter & Equipment Inc* **(G-10106)**
Exide Technologies LLC ...248 853-5000
2750 Auburn Rd Auburn Hills (48326) **(G-884)**
Exie Smith Publications LLC ...248 360-2917
1829 Union Lake Rd Commerce Township (48382) **(G-3527)**
Exlterra Inc ...248 268-2336
618 E 10 Mile Rd Hazel Park (48030) **(G-7825)**
Exo-S US LLC ...248 614-9707
1500 W Big Beaver Rd 101c Troy (48084) **(G-17101)**
Exo-S US LLC ...517 278-8567
25 Concept Dr Coldwater (49036) **(G-3433)**
Exodus Pressure Control ...231 258-8001
110 W Park Dr Kalkaska (49646) **(G-9387)**
Exone Americas LLC (HQ) ...248 740-1580
2341 Alger Dr Troy (48083) **(G-17102)**
Exotic Automation & Supply, New Hudson *Also called Exotic Rubber & Plastics Corp* **(G-12053)**
Exotic Rubber & Plastics Corp (PA) ...248 477-2122
53500 Grand River Ave New Hudson (48165) **(G-12053)**
Expan Inc (PA) ...586 725-0405
51513 Industrial Dr New Baltimore (48047) **(G-11980)**
Expectancy Learning LLC ...866 829-9533
3152 Peregrine Dr Ne # 110 Grand Rapids (49525) **(G-6692)**
Expedite Freight LLC ...313 502-7572
19320 Braile St Detroit (48219) **(G-4222)**
Expediting, Detroit *Also called One Source Trucking LLC* **(G-4499)**
Experi-Metal Inc ...586 977-7800
6385 Wall St Sterling Heights (48312) **(G-16009)**
Experienced Concepts Inc ...586 752-4200
15400 Chets Way St Armada (48005) **(G-735)**
Experimac Macomb ...586 884-6292
15715 Hall Rd Macomb (48044) **(G-10593)**
Expernced Prcsion McHining Inc ...989 635-2299
2720 Lamotte St Marlette (48453) **(G-10981)**
Expert Coating Company Inc ...616 453-8261
2855 Marlin Ct Nw Grand Rapids (49534) **(G-6693)**
Expert Machine & Tool Inc ...810 984-2323
2424 Lapeer Rd Port Huron (48060) **(G-13477)**
Exponent, The, Brooklyn *Also called Schepeler Corporation* **(G-2132)**
Export Corporation ...810 227-6153
6060 Whitmore Lake Rd Brighton (48116) **(G-1987)**
Express Care of South Lyon ...248 437-6919
501 S Lafayette St South Lyon (48178) **(G-15436)**
Express Cnc & Fabrication LLC ...517 937-8760
3041 North Adams Rd Jonesville (49250) **(G-9087)**
Express Coat Corporation ...586 773-2682
27350 Gloede Dr Warren (48088) **(G-17800)**
Express Expediting ...313 347-9975
20614 Washtenaw St Harper Woods (48225) **(G-7666)**
Express Press Inc ...269 684-2080
201 E Main St Niles (49120) **(G-12128)**
Express Publications Inc ...231 947-8787
135 W State St Traverse City (49684) **(G-16679)**
Express Sportswear Inc ...989 773-7515
1530 S Mission St Mount Pleasant (48858) **(G-11697)**
Express Welding Inc ...906 786-8808
2525 14th Ave N Escanaba (49829) **(G-5071)**
Expressign Design ...734 747-7444
2239 W Liberty St Ann Arbor (48103) **(G-481)**
Expressive Window Fashions ...269 663-8833
69351 M 62 Edwardsburg (49112) **(G-5006)**
Exquise Inc ...248 220-9048
2512 W Grand Blvd Detroit (48208) **(G-4223)**
Extang Corporation ...734 677-0444
5400 S State Rd Ann Arbor (48108) **(G-482)**
Extol Inc (PA) ...616 741-0231
651 Case Karsten Dr Zeeland (49464) **(G-19019)**
Extract ...269 362-4879
7303 Cuesta Way Dr Ne Rockford (49341) **(G-14166)**
Extreem Laser Dynamics, Traverse City *Also called Rare Earth Hardwoods Inc* **(G-16817)**
Extreme Fitness Gym, Saint Louis *Also called 4 Seasons Gym LLC* **(G-14983)**
Extreme Machine Inc ...810 231-0521
10125 Industrial Dr Whitmore Lake (48189) **(G-18534)**
Extreme Machine Inc ...810 231-0521
10068 Industrial Dr Whitmore Lake (48189) **(G-18535)**
Extreme Machine Inc (PA) ...810 231-0521
10034 Industrial Dr Whitmore Lake (48189) **(G-18536)**
Extreme Precision Screw Pdts ...810 744-1980
1838 Remell St Flint (48503) **(G-5698)**
Extreme Screen Prints ...616 889-8305
3723 Burlingame Ave Sw Grand Rapids (49509) **(G-6694)**
Extreme Screenprints ...616 889-8305
3030 Sangra Ave Sw Grandville (49418) **(G-7375)**
Extreme Signs Inc ...586 846-3251
34853 S Gratiot Ave Clinton Township (48035) **(G-3233)**
Extreme Tool and Engrg Inc (PA) ...906 229-9100
999 Production Dr Wakefield (49968) **(G-17620)**
Extreme Tool and Engrg Inc ...906 229-9100
703 Chippawa Dr Wakefield (49968) **(G-17621)**
Extreme Wire EDM Service Inc ...616 249-3901
3636 Busch Dr Sw Grandville (49418) **(G-7376)**
Extrude Hone LLC ...616 647-9050
2882 Northridge Dr Nw Grand Rapids (49544) **(G-6695)**
Extruded Aluminum, Belding *Also called Belding McHy & Eqp Lsg Corp* **(G-1439)**
Extruded Aluminum Corporation ...616 794-0300
7200 Industrial Dr Belding (48809) **(G-1448)**
Extrunet America Inc ...517 301-4504
903 Industrial Dr Tecumseh (49286) **(G-16501)**
Extrusion Punch & Tool Company ...248 689-3300
1977 Rochester Indus Dr Rochester Hills (48309) **(G-14007)**
Extrusions Division Inc ...616 247-3611
201 Cottage Grove St Se Grand Rapids (49507) **(G-6696)**
Eye 2 Eye Contact ...313 378-7883
723 River Park Vlg Blvd Northville (48167) **(G-12216)**
Eyes Media, Traverse City *Also called Business News* **(G-16634)**
Eyewear Detroit Company ...248 396-2214
6466 Shappie Rd Clarkston (48348) **(G-3034)**
Eyry of Eagle Publish ...734 623-0337
625 Liberty Pointe Dr Ann Arbor (48103) **(G-483)**
EZ Fuel Inc ...810 744-4452
1330 E Atherton Rd Flint (48507) **(G-5699)**
EZ Logic, Farmington Hills *Also called E Z Logic Data Systems Inc* **(G-5221)**
EZ Vent LLC ...616 874-2787
8235 Belding Rd Ne Rockford (49341) **(G-14167)**
Ezbake Technologies LLC ...817 430-1621
7244 Driftwood Dr Fenton (48430) **(G-5474)**
Eze Prints A Div Allied ...616 281-2406
517 32nd St Se Grand Rapids (49548) **(G-6697)**
Ezm LLC ...248 861-2602
730 Welch Rd Commerce Township (48390) **(G-3528)**
F & A Enterprises of Michigan ...906 228-3222
519 N Lakeshore Blvd Marquette (49855) **(G-11018)**
F & A Fabricating, Battle Creek *Also called Hdn F&A Inc* **(G-1236)**
F & F Mold Inc ...517 287-5866
5931 Knowles Rd North Adams (49262) **(G-12176)**
F & G Tool Company ...734 261-0022
11863 Brookfield St Livonia (48150) **(G-10202)**
F & H Manufacturing Co Inc ...517 783-2311
149 W Porter St Jackson (49202) **(G-8881)**
F & M Gas ...313 292-2519
22422 Wick Rd Taylor (48180) **(G-16415)**
F & S Diversified Products Inc ...248 409-0960
4260 Giddings Rd Auburn Hills (48326) **(G-885)**
F & S Tool & Gauge Co Inc ...517 787-2661
1027 E South St Jackson (49203) **(G-8882)**
F A A, Farmington Hills *Also called Fujikura Automotive Amer LLC* **(G-5247)**
F and R Associates ...734 316-7763
745 Woodland Dr Saline (48176) **(G-15016)**
F C & A, Allegan *Also called Fabricted Cmpnnts Assmblies In* **(G-157)**
F C Simpson Lime Co ...810 367-3510
1293 Wadhams Rd Kimball (48074) **(G-9492)**
F F Industries ...313 291-7600
7620 Telegraph Rd Taylor (48180) **(G-16416)**
F G Cheney Limestone Co ...269 763-9541
9400 Sand Rd Bellevue (49021) **(G-1498)**
F H C, Wyoming *Also called Fhc Holding Company* **(G-18872)**
F I D Corporation ...248 373-7005
3424 Charlwood Dr Rochester Hills (48306) **(G-14008)**
F J Lucido & Associates (PA) ...586 574-3577
29400 Van Dyke Ave Warren (48093) **(G-17801)**
F J Manufacturing Co ...248 583-4777
32329 Milton Ave Madison Heights (48071) **(G-10725)**

F L M, Clinton Township *Also called Five Lakes Manufacturing Inc* ***(G-3239)***
F M T Products Inc.....517 568-3373
140 W Main St Homer (49245) ***(G-8351)***
F P Horak Company (PA).....989 892-6505
1311 Straits Dr Bay City (48706) ***(G-1355)***
F P Rosback Co.....269 983-2582
125 Hawthorne Ave Saint Joseph (49085) ***(G-14930)***
F T I, Litchfield *Also called Finishing Touch Inc* ***(G-10077)***
F&B Technologies.....734 856-2118
6875 Memorial Hwy Ottawa Lake (49267) ***(G-12806)***
F2 Industries LLC.....616 610-0894
11129 Autumn Dr Zeeland (49464) ***(G-19020)***
Faac Incorporated.....734 761-5836
1195 Oak Valley Dr Ann Arbor (48108) ***(G-484)***
Faac Incorporated (HQ).....734 761-5836
1229 Oak Valley Dr Ann Arbor (48108) ***(G-485)***
Fab Concepts.....586 466-6411
52826 Turnberry Dr Chesterfield (48051) ***(G-2879)***
Fab Masters Company Inc.....269 646-5315
51787 M 40 Marcellus (49067) ***(G-10947)***
Fab-All Manufacturing Inc.....248 585-6700
645 Executive Dr Troy (48083) ***(G-17103)***
Fab-Alloy Company.....517 787-4313
1163 E Morrell St Jackson (49203) ***(G-8883)***
Fab Jet Services LLC.....586 463-9622
44335 Macomb Indus Dr Clinton Township (48036) ***(G-3234)***
Fab-Lite Inc.....231 398-8280
330 Washington St Manistee (49660) ***(G-10899)***
Fab-N-Weld Sheetmetal.....269 471-7453
4445 E Shawnee Rd Berrien Springs (49103) ***(G-1639)***
Fabco Automotive, Livonia *Also called R Cushman & Associates Inc* ***(G-10381)***
Fabiano Bros Dev - Wscnsin LLC.....989 509-0200
1885 Bevanda Ct Bay City (48706) ***(G-1356)***
Fabri-Kal Corporation.....269 385-5050
4141 Manchester Rd Kalamazoo (49001) ***(G-9183)***
Fabri-Tech Inc (PA).....616 662-0150
6719 Pine Ridge Ct Sw Jenison (49428) ***(G-9055)***
Fabric Patch Ltd.....906 932-5260
100 W Mcleod Ave Ironwood (49938) ***(G-8762)***
Fabricated Customs.....517 488-7273
2767 Carnoustie Dr Okemos (48864) ***(G-12667)***
Fabrication Concepts LLC.....517 750-4742
347 E Main St Spring Arbor (49283) ***(G-15791)***
Fabrication Plus.....231 730-9374
4300 Fruitvale Rd Montague (49437) ***(G-11596)***
Fabrication Specialties Inc.....313 891-7181
9600 Melissa Ln Davisburg (48350) ***(G-3767)***
Fabrications Plus Inc.....269 749-3050
7898 Marshall Rd Olivet (49076) ***(G-12693)***
Fabrications Unlimited Inc (PA).....313 567-9616
45757 Cornwall St Shelby Township (48317) ***(G-15224)***
Fabrications Unlimited Inc.....313 567-9616
4651 Beaufait St Detroit (48207) ***(G-4224)***
Fabricted Cmpnnts Assmblies In.....269 673-7100
603 N Eastern Ave Allegan (49010) ***(G-157)***
Fabrilaser Mfg LLC.....269 789-9490
1308 S Kalamazoo Ave Marshall (49068) ***(G-11057)***
Fabtec Enterprises Inc.....616 878-9288
8538 Centre Indus Dr Sw Byron Center (49315) ***(G-2269)***
Fabtronic Inc.....586 786-6114
51685 Industrial Dr Macomb (48042) ***(G-10594)***
Fabulous Printing Inc.....734 422-5555
15076 Middlebelt Rd Livonia (48154) ***(G-10203)***
Fabx Industries Inc (PA).....616 225-1724
715 Callaghan St Greenville (48838) ***(G-7484)***
Facements, Walker *Also called Vista Manufacturing Inc* ***(G-17656)***
Facet Business Communications.....248 912-0800
22777 Heslip Dr Novi (48375) ***(G-12415)***
Fahl Forest Products Inc.....231 587-5388
2509 Valley Rd Mancelona (49659) ***(G-10870)***
Fair & Square Pallet & Lbr Co.....989 727-3949
5700 Ratz Rd Hubbard Lake (49747) ***(G-8546)***
Fair Industries LLC.....248 740-7841
3260 Talbot Dr Troy (48083) ***(G-17104)***
Fairfax Prints Ltd.....517 321-5590
4918 Delta River Dr Lansing (48906) ***(G-9696)***
Fairfield Investment Co.....734 427-4141
32738 Barkley St Livonia (48154) ***(G-10204)***
Fairlane Co.....586 294-6100
33792 Doreka Fraser (48026) ***(G-5926)***
Fairlane Gear Inc.....734 459-2440
8182 N Canton Center Rd Canton (48187) ***(G-2460)***
Fairmont Sign Company (PA).....313 368-4000
3750 E Outer Dr Detroit (48234) ***(G-4225)***
Fairview Farms.....269 449-0500
6735 S Scottdale Rd Berrien Springs (49103) ***(G-1640)***
Fairview Sawmill Inc.....989 848-5238
1901 Kneeland Rd Fairview (48621) ***(G-5130)***
Fairway Optical Inc.....231 744-6168
4490 W Giles Rd Muskegon (49445) ***(G-11815)***

Fairway Products Division, Hillsdale *Also called Acme Mills Company* ***(G-7919)***
Faith Alive Christn Resources (PA).....800 333-8300
1700 28th St Se Grand Rapids (49508) ***(G-6698)***
Faith Plastics LLC.....269 646-2294
239 E Main St Marcellus (49067) ***(G-10948)***
Faith Publishing Service.....517 853-7600
1500 E Saginaw St Ofc C Lansing (48906) ***(G-9697)***
Falcon Asphalt Repair Eqp, Freeland *Also called Mmgg Inc* ***(G-6026)***
Falcon Consulting Services LLC.....989 262-9325
112 1/2 W Chisholm St A Alpena (49707) ***(G-293)***
Falcon Corporation.....616 842-7071
14510 Cleveland St Spring Lake (49456) ***(G-15813)***
Falcon Global LLC.....734 302-3025
1630 Timber Trl Ann Arbor (48103) ***(G-486)***
Falcon Industry Inc.....586 468-7010
44660 Macomb Indus Dr Clinton Township (48036) ***(G-3235)***
Falcon Lakeside Mfg Inc.....269 429-6193
4999 Advance Way Stevensville (49127) ***(G-16250)***
Falcon Motorsports Inc.....248 328-2222
255 Elm St Holly (48442) ***(G-8269)***
Falcon Network Services Inc.....248 726-0577
200 E Big Beaver Rd Troy (48083) ***(G-17105)***
Falcon Printing Inc.....616 676-3737
6360 Fulton St E Ada (49301) ***(G-17)***
Falcon Promotional Tools, Ada *Also called Falcon Printing Inc* ***(G-17)***
Falcon Rme, Midland *Also called Falcon Road Maint Eqp LLC* ***(G-11362)***
Falcon Road Maint Eqp LLC.....989 495-9332
2000 Austin St Midland (48642) ***(G-11362)***
Falcon Stamping Inc.....517 540-6197
1201 Fendt Dr Howell (48843) ***(G-8453)***
Falcon Tool & Die, Spring Lake *Also called Falcon Corporation* ***(G-15813)***
Falcon Trucking Company (PA).....313 843-7200
9300 Dix Dearborn (48120) ***(G-3839)***
Falcon Trucking Company.....989 656-2831
8785 Ribble Rd Bay Port (48720) ***(G-1414)***
Falcon Trucking Company.....248 634-9471
16240 Tindall Rd Davisburg (48350) ***(G-3768)***
Falk Panel, Grand Rapids *Also called Falk Production LLC* ***(G-6699)***
Falk Production LLC.....616 540-1053
1782 Northridge Dr Nw Grand Rapids (49544) ***(G-6699)***
Fallen Oaks Cabinet Shop Inc.....586 463-4454
302 Robbins Dr Troy (48083) ***(G-17106)***
Family Machinists.....734 340-1848
20456 Lexington Redford (48240) ***(G-13732)***
Family Safety Products Inc.....616 530-6540
2879 Remico St Sw Grandville (49418) ***(G-7377)***
Family Tradition Wdwkg Plans.....989 871-6688
8728 State Rd Millington (48746) ***(G-11500)***
Family Trdtons Tree Stands LLC.....517 543-3926
202 Morrell St Charlotte (48813) ***(G-2753)***
Familygradegravel Yahoocom.....517 202-4121
924 Chickasaw Dr Mason (48854) ***(G-11132)***
Fannon Products LLC (PA).....810 794-2000
5318 Pointe Tremble Rd Algonac (48001) ***(G-141)***
Fantastic Sams Hair Salon.....713 861-2500
29341 John R Rd Madison Heights (48071) ***(G-10726)***
Fanuc America Corporation (HQ).....248 377-7000
3900 W Hamlin Rd Rochester Hills (48309) ***(G-14009)***
Far Associates Inc.....734 282-1881
11801 Longsdorf St Riverview (48193) ***(G-13872)***
Farago & Associates LLC.....248 546-7070
30600 Northwestern Hwy # 105 Farmington Hills (48334) ***(G-5240)***
Farber Concessions Inc.....313 387-1600
14950 Telegraph Rd Redford (48239) ***(G-13733)***
Farm Crest Foods, Pigeon *Also called Active Feed Company* ***(G-13034)***
Farmers Egg Cooperative.....517 649-8957
1300 W Mount Hope Hwy Charlotte (48813) ***(G-2754)***
Farmhouse Woodworking LLC.....269 350-0582
8540 Ruggles Rd Baroda (49101) ***(G-1161)***
Farmington Cabinet Company.....248 476-2666
30795 8 Mile Rd Livonia (48152) ***(G-10205)***
Farnell Contracting Inc.....810 714-3421
3355 Lahring Rd Linden (48451) ***(G-10061)***
Faro Screen Process Inc.....734 207-8400
41805 Koppernick Rd Canton (48187) ***(G-2461)***
Farr & Faron Associates Inc.....810 229-7730
136 E Grand River Ave 3 Brighton (48116) ***(G-1988)***
Fast Cash.....269 966-0079
641 Capital Ave Sw Battle Creek (49015) ***(G-1229)***
Fast Tech Mfg Inc.....586 783-1741
41601 Irwin Dr Harrison Township (48045) ***(G-7698)***
Fastball LLC.....810 955-8510
4302 Charter Oaks Dr Davison (48423) ***(G-3780)***
Fastco Industries Inc (PA).....616 453-5428
2685 Mullins Ct Nw Grand Rapids (49534) ***(G-6700)***
Fastco Industries Inc.....616 389-1390
2700 Courier Dr Nw Grand Rapids (49534) ***(G-6701)***
Fastco Industries Inc.....616 453-5428
2759 Mullins Ave Grand Rapids (49534) ***(G-6702)***

A L P H A B E T I C

Fastener Advance PDT Co Ltd....734 428-8070
750 Hogan Rd Manchester (48158) ***(G-10884)***
Fastener Coatings Inc....269 279-5134
1111 River St Three Rivers (49093) ***(G-16572)***
Fastime Racing Engines & Parts....734 947-1600
12254 Universal Dr Taylor (48180) ***(G-16417)***
Fastsigns, Kalamazoo *Also called Digital Impact Design Inc* ***(G-9168)***
Fastsigns, Brighton *Also called Scarlet Spartan Inc* ***(G-2068)***
Fastsigns, Sterling Heights *Also called Sterling Creative Team Inc* ***(G-16191)***
Fastsigns, Ann Arbor *Also called Kore Group Inc* ***(G-542)***
Fastsigns....313 345-5858
2648 E Jefferson Ave # 1 Detroit (48207) ***(G-4226)***
Fastsigns....616 377-7491
6374 Eaglewood Dr Hudsonville (49426) ***(G-8583)***
Fastsigns....248 372-9554
22554 Telegraph Rd Southfield (48033) ***(G-15558)***
Fastsigns....248 488-9010
27615 Halsted Rd Farmington Hills (48331) ***(G-5241)***
Fastsigns - 381501, Monroe *Also called Hoppenjans Inc* ***(G-11548)***
Fastsigns International Inc....231 941-0300
1420 Trade Center Dr Traverse City (49696) ***(G-16680)***
Fata Aluminum LLC (PA)....248 802-9853
260 Engelwood Dr Orion (48359) ***(G-12729)***
Fata Automation Inc (PA)....248 724-7660
2333 E Walton Blvd Auburn Hills (48326) ***(G-886)***
Fathom Drones Inc....586 216-7047
401 Hall St Sw Ste 213 Grand Rapids (49503) ***(G-6703)***
Faucher Industries....248 515-4772
1005 Troy Ct Troy (48083) ***(G-17107)***
Faucher Industries....586 434-5115
5971 Product Dr Sterling Heights (48312) ***(G-16010)***
Faulkner Fabricators Inc....269 473-3073
10106 N Tudor Rd Berrien Springs (49103) ***(G-1641)***
Faulkner Tech Inc....517 857-4241
239 S Cochran Ave Charlotte (48813) ***(G-2755)***
Faurecia Auto Seating LLC....248 563-9241
13000 Oakland Park Blvd Highland Park (48203) ***(G-7905)***
Faurecia Auto Seating LLC....248 563-9241
12900 Oakland Park Blvd Highland Park (48203) ***(G-7906)***
Faurecia Emssons Ctrl Tech USA (HQ)....248 724-5100
2800 High Meadow Cir Auburn Hills (48326) ***(G-887)***
Faurecia Emssons Ctrl Tech USA....734 947-1688
24850 Northline Rd Taylor (48180) ***(G-16418)***
Faurecia Exhaust Systems LLC....248 409-3500
2500 Executive Hills Dr Auburn Hills (48326) ***(G-888)***
Faurecia Interior Systems Inc (HQ)....248 724-5100
2800 High Meadow Cir Auburn Hills (48326) ***(G-889)***
Faurecia Intr Systems Sline LL....734 429-0030
7700 E Michigan Ave Saline (48176) ***(G-15017)***
Faurecia North America, Auburn Hills *Also called Faurecia Interior Systems Inc* ***(G-889)***
Faurecia North America Inc....248 288-1000
2800 High Meadow Cir Auburn Hills (48326) ***(G-890)***
Faurecia USA Holdings Inc (HQ)....248 724-5100
2800 High Meadow Cir Auburn Hills (48326) ***(G-891)***
Favi Entertainment, Washington Township *Also called Yakel Enterprises LLC* ***(G-18097)***
Faygo Beverages Inc (HQ)....313 925-1600
3579 Gratiot Ave Detroit (48207) ***(G-4227)***
Fbe Associates Inc....989 894-2785
513 N Madison Ave Ste 101 Bay City (48708) ***(G-1357)***
FCA Intrntional Operations LLC....800 334-9200
1000 Chrysler Dr Auburn Hills (48326) ***(G-892)***
FCA North America Holdings LLC (HQ)....248 512-2950
1000 Chrysler Dr Auburn Hills (48326) ***(G-893)***
FCA US LLC....248 512-2950
1000 Chrysler Dr Auburn Hills (48326) ***(G-894)***
FCA US LLC....586 468-2891
151 Lafayette St Mount Clemens (48043) ***(G-11638)***
FCA US LLC....313 369-7312
3675 E Outer Dr Detroit (48234) ***(G-4228)***
FCA US LLC....734 478-5658
5800 N Ann Arbor Rd Dundee (48131) ***(G-4819)***
FCA US LLC....313 957-7000
4500 Saint Jean St Detroit (48214) ***(G-4229)***
FCA US LLC....586 978-0067
38111 Van Dyke Ave Sterling Heights (48312) ***(G-16011)***
FCA US LLC....586 497-2500
21500 Mound Rd Warren (48091) ***(G-17802)***
FCA US LLC....800 334-9200
12501 Chrysler Dr Detroit (48203) ***(G-4230)***
FCA US LLC....734 422-0557
37200 Amrhein Rd Livonia (48150) ***(G-10206)***
FCA US LLC (HQ)....248 576-5741
1000 Chrysler Dr Auburn Hills (48326) ***(G-895)***
FCA US LLC....248 576-5741
6565 E 8 Mile Rd Warren (48091) ***(G-17803)***
Fcaus Dundee Engine Plant....734 529-9256
5800 N Ann Arbor Rd Dundee (48131) ***(G-4820)***
Fcx Performance Inc (PA)....734 654-2201
845 Monroe St Carleton (48117) ***(G-2553)***
FD Lake Company....616 241-5639
3313 Lousma Dr Se Grand Rapids (49548) ***(G-6704)***
Fdi Group, Novi *Also called Startech Software Systems Inc* ***(G-12542)***
Feb Inc....231 759-0911
2333 Henry St Muskegon (49441) ***(G-11816)***
Fec Inc....586 580-2622
51341 Celeste Shelby Township (48315) ***(G-15225)***
FEC Automation Systems, Shelby Township *Also called Fec Inc* ***(G-15225)***
Federal Broach & Mch Co LLC....989 539-7420
1961 Sullivan Dr Harrison (48625) ***(G-7676)***
Federal Group Usa Inc....248 545-5000
21126 Bridge St Southfield (48033) ***(G-15559)***
Federal Group, The, Southfield *Also called Federal Group Usa Inc* ***(G-15559)***
Federal Heath Sign Company LLC....248 656-8000
1806 Rochester Indl Dr Rochester Hills (48309) ***(G-14010)***
Federal Industrial Services....313 533-9888
12980 Inkster Rd Redford (48239) ***(G-13734)***
Federal Industrial Svcs Inc (PA)....586 427-6383
11223 E 8 Mile Rd Warren (48089) ***(G-17804)***
Federal Mgul Wrldwide Aftrmrke, Southfield *Also called Federal-Mogul Corporation* ***(G-15561)***
Federal Screw Works (PA)....734 941-4211
34846 Goddard Rd Romulus (48174) ***(G-14274)***
Federal Screw Works....734 941-4211
34846 Goddard Rd Romulus (48174) ***(G-14275)***
Federal Screw Works....734 941-4211
400 N Dekraft Ave Big Rapids (49307) ***(G-1673)***
Federal Screw Works....231 796-7664
400 N Dekraft Ave Big Rapids (49307) ***(G-1674)***
Federal Screw Works....231 922-9500
2270 Traversefield Dr Traverse City (49686) ***(G-16681)***
Federal Screw Works....810 227-7712
77 Advance St Brighton (48116) ***(G-1989)***
Federal-Mogul Chassis LLC (HQ)....248 354-7700
27300 W 11 Mile Rd # 100 Southfield (48034) ***(G-15560)***
Federal-Mogul Corporation (HQ)....248 354-7700
26555 Northwestern Hwy Southfield (48033) ***(G-15561)***
Federal-Mogul Ignition LLC (HQ)....248 354-7700
26555 Northwestern Hwy Southfield (48033) ***(G-15562)***
Federal-Mogul Motorparts, Southfield *Also called Federal-Mogul Chassis LLC* ***(G-15560)***
Federal-Mogul Motorparts LLC (HQ)....248 354-7700
27300 W 11 Mile Rd # 100 Southfield (48034) ***(G-15563)***
Federal-Mogul Piston Rings Inc (HQ)....248 354-7700
26555 Northwestern Hwy Southfield (48033) ***(G-15564)***
Federal-Mogul Powertrain LLC....616 754-5681
510 E Grove St Greenville (48838) ***(G-7485)***
Federal-Mogul Powertrain LLC (HQ)....248 354-7700
27300 W 11 Mile Rd # 100 Southfield (48034) ***(G-15565)***
Federal-Mogul Products US LLC (HQ)....248 354-7700
26555 Northwestern Hwy Southfield (48033) ***(G-15566)***
Federal-Mogul Valve Train Inte (HQ)....248 354-7700
27300 W 11 Mile Rd Southfield (48034) ***(G-15567)***
Federal-Mogul World Wide Inc (HQ)....248 354-7700
26555 Northwestern Hwy Southfield (48033) ***(G-15568)***
Federl-Mgul Dutch Holdings Inc....248 354-7700
26555 Northwestern Hwy Southfield (48033) ***(G-15569)***
Fedex Office & Print Svcs Inc....734 761-4539
505 E Liberty St Ste 400 Ann Arbor (48104) ***(G-487)***
Fedex Office & Print Svcs Inc....517 332-5855
626 Michigan Ave East Lansing (48823) ***(G-4892)***
Fedex Office & Print Svcs Inc....248 651-2679
133 S Main St Rochester (48307) ***(G-13900)***
Feed - Lease Corp....248 377-0000
2750 Paldan Dr Auburn Hills (48326) ***(G-896)***
Fega Tool & Gage Company....586 469-4400
44837 Macomb Indus Dr Clinton Township (48036) ***(G-3236)***
Feleo Mfg Strategies LLC....517 795-1193
4115 Felters Rd Michigan Center (49254) ***(G-11293)***
Fema Corporation of Michigan....269 323-1369
1716 Vanderbilt Ave Portage (49024) ***(G-13560)***
Femur Buyer Inc....517 694-2300
1489 Cedar St Holt (48842) ***(G-8311)***
Fendt Builders Supply Inc (PA)....248 474-3211
22005 Gill Rd Farmington Hills (48335) ***(G-5242)***
Fendt Builders Supply Inc....734 663-4277
3285 W Liberty Rd Ann Arbor (48103) ***(G-488)***
Fenixx Technologies LLC....586 254-6000
17009 Masonic Fraser (48026) ***(G-5927)***
Fenixx Technologies LLC....586 254-6000
6633 Diplomat Dr Sterling Heights (48314) ***(G-16012)***
Fenn Valley Vineyards Inc (PA)....269 561-2396
6130 122nd Ave Fennville (49408) ***(G-5435)***
Fenton Concrete Inc....810 629-0783
10513 Old Us 23 Fenton (48430) ***(G-5475)***
Fenton Corporation (PA)....810 629-2858
3236 Owen Rd Fenton (48430) ***(G-5476)***
Fenton Memorials & Vaults Inc....810 629-2858
3236 Owen Rd Fenton (48430) ***(G-5477)***
Fenton Radiator & Garage Inc....810 629-0923
1542 N Leroy St Ste 4 Fenton (48430) ***(G-5478)***

ALPHABETIC SECTION

Fenton Systems Inc 810 636-6318
7160 S State Rd Ste B Goodrich (48438) *(G-6223)*
Fenway Business Unit, Fenton *Also called Creative Foam Corporation* *(G-5468)*
Fergin & Associates Inc 906 477-0040
Pk N9263 Kraus Rd Engadine (49827) *(G-5043)*
Ferguson Block Co Inc 810 653-2812
5430 N State Rd Davison (48423) *(G-3781)*
Ferguson Enterprises LLC 616 803-7521
3900 44th St Se Kentwood (49512) *(G-9452)*
Ferguson Enterprises LLC 989 790-2220
3944 Fortune Blvd Saginaw (48603) *(G-14645)*
Ferguson Enterprises LLC 269 383-1200
2900 Millcork St Kalamazoo (49001) *(G-9184)*
Ferguson Enterprises LLC 586 459-4491
24425 Schoenherr Rd Warren (48089) *(G-17805)*
Ferguson Steel Inc 810 984-3918
3755 N River Rd Fort Gratiot (48059) *(G-5821)*
Ferguson Waterworks, Kentwood *Also called Ferguson Enterprises LLC* *(G-9452)*
Ferguson Waterworks, Kalamazoo *Also called Ferguson Enterprises LLC* *(G-9184)*
Fernand Corporation 231 882-9622
326 W Kalamazoo Ave # 105 Kalamazoo (49007) *(G-9185)*
Fernco Inc (PA) 810 503-9000
300 S Dayton St Davison (48423) *(G-3782)*
Fernco Joint Sealer Company, Davison *Also called Fernco Inc* *(G-3782)*
Ferndale Contract Mfg, Ferndale *Also called Ferndale Laboratories Inc* *(G-5553)*
Ferndale Laboratories Inc (HQ) 248 548-0900
780 W 8 Mile Rd Ferndale (48220) *(G-5553)*
Ferndale Pharma Group Inc (PA) 248 548-0900
780 W 8 Mile Rd Ferndale (48220) *(G-5554)*
Ferrante Manufacturing Co 313 571-1111
6626 Gratiot Ave Detroit (48207) *(G-4231)*
Ferrees Tools Inc 269 965-0511
1477 Michigan Ave E Battle Creek (49014) *(G-1230)*
Ferris Wheel Innovation Center 810 213-4720
615 S Saginaw St Flint (48502) *(G-5700)*
Ferro Fab LLC 586 791-3561
23309 Quinn Rd Clinton Township (48035) *(G-3237)*
Ferro Industries Inc 586 792-6001
35200 Union Lake Rd Harrison Township (48045) *(G-7699)*
Ferrous Cal Co., Gibraltar *Also called Hycal Corp* *(G-6171)*
Festida Foods, Grand Rapids *Also called Great Lkes Fstida Holdings Inc* *(G-6789)*
Fettes Manufacturing Co 586 939-8500
35855 Stanley Dr Sterling Heights (48312) *(G-16013)*
Fev Test Systems Inc 248 373-6000
4554 Glenmeade Ln Auburn Hills (48326) *(G-897)*
Fgm Solutions, Marysville *Also called Flow Gas Misture Solutions Inc* *(G-11087)*
Fhc Holding Company (PA) 616 538-3231
2509 29th St Sw Wyoming (49519) *(G-18872)*
Fhi Family of Companies, Hastings *Also called Flexfab Horizons Intl Inc* *(G-7791)*
FI, Lansing *Also called Friedland Industries Inc* *(G-9701)*
FI Publishing 248 282-9905
3883 Telegraph Rd Bloomfield Hills (48302) *(G-1821)*
Fiamm Technologies, Cadillac *Also called Cadillac Engineered Plas Inc* *(G-2321)*
Fiamm Technologies LLC (HQ) 248 427-3200
23880 Industrial Park Dr Farmington Hills (48335) *(G-5243)*
Fiat Chrysler Automobiles, Auburn Hills *Also called FCA US LLC* *(G-895)*
Fiber By-Products Corp (PA) 269 483-0066
70721 Us Highway 131 White Pigeon (49099) *(G-18477)*
Fiber-Char Corporation 989 356-5501
3336 Piper Rd Alpena (49707) *(G-294)*
Fiberglass Technology Inds Inc 740 335-9400
1637 Marty Paul St Cadillac (49601) *(G-2329)*
Fibers of Kalamazoo Inc 269 344-3122
436 W Willard St Ste A Kalamazoo (49007) *(G-9186)*
Fibre Converters Inc (PA) 269 279-1700
1 Industrial Park Dr Constantine (49042) *(G-3666)*
Fibrek Inc 906 864-9125
701 4th Ave Menominee (49858) *(G-11235)*
Fibrek Recycling US Inc (HQ) 906 863-8137
701 4th Ave Menominee (49858) *(G-11236)*
Fibrek US Inc 906 864-9125
701 4th Ave Menominee (49858) *(G-11237)*
Fibro Laepple Technology Inc 248 591-4494
33286 Sterling Ponds Blvd Sterling Heights (48312) *(G-16014)*
Ficosa North America Corp (HQ) 248 307-2230
30890 Stephenson Hwy Madison Heights (48071) *(G-10727)*
Fidia Co 248 680-0700
3098 Research Dr Rochester Hills (48309) *(G-14011)*
Fido & Stitch 616 288-7992
820 Monroe Ave Nw Grand Rapids (49503) *(G-6705)*
Fido Enterprises Inc 586 790-8200
34692 Nova Dr Clinton Township (48035) *(G-3238)*
Field Crafts Inc (PA) 231 325-1122
9930 Honor Hwy Honor (49640) *(G-8359)*
Field Tech Services Inc 989 786-7046
3860 County Road 491 Lewiston (49756) *(G-10019)*
Fieldstone Hard Cider 248 923-1742
388 South St Rochester (48307) *(G-13901)*

Fife Pearce Electric Company 313 369-2560
20201 Sherwood St Detroit (48234) *(G-4232)*
Fifth Box Industries LLC 734 323-6388
292 Ely Dr N Northville (48167) *(G-12217)*
Figment Screen Printing 269 858-9998
307 West St Three Rivers (49093) *(G-16573)*
Filcon Inc 989 386-2986
528 Pioneer Pkwy Clare (48617) *(G-2979)*
Filler Specialties Inc 616 772-9235
440 100th Ave Zeeland (49464) *(G-19021)*
Filter Plus Inc 734 475-7403
2442 Mckinley Rd Chelsea (48118) *(G-2811)*
Filtration Machine 810 845-0536
10049 N Hunt Ct Davison (48423) *(G-3783)*
Filtrona Porous Technologies, Saint Charles *Also called Porex Technologies Corp* *(G-14807)*
Finazzo Tool & Die LLC 586 598-5806
56335 Precision Dr Chesterfield (48051) *(G-2880)*
Finch Sand & Gravel LLC 734 439-1044
10980 N Platt Rd Milan (48160) *(G-11435)*
Fine Art Metalwork, Ironwood *Also called Cramblits Welding LLC* *(G-8760)*
Fine Arts 269 695-6263
108 W Roe St Buchanan (49107) *(G-2193)*
Fine Manufacturing & Tool Co, Oscoda *Also called Migatron Precision Products* *(G-12765)*
Fineeye Color Solutions Inc 616 988-6119
1218 Tall Tree Ln Muskegon (49445) *(G-11817)*
Fini Finish Metal Finishing 586 758-0050
24657 Mound Rd Warren (48091) *(G-17806)*
Finish Line Fabricating LLC 269 686-8400
779 38th St Allegan (49010) *(G-158)*
Finishers Unlimited Monroe Inc 734 243-3502
757 S Telegraph Rd Monroe (48161) *(G-11540)*
Finishing Services Inc 734 484-1700
877 Ann St Ypsilanti (48197) *(G-18945)*
Finishing Technologies Inc 616 794-4001
7125 Whites Bridge Rd Belding (48809) *(G-1449)*
Finishing Touch Inc 517 542-5581
191 Simpson Dr Litchfield (49252) *(G-10077)*
Finishing Touches By Odell 231 947-3080
7138 Lake Leelanau Dr Traverse City (49684) *(G-16682)*
Finkl Steel- Composite, Detroit *Also called Composite Forgings Ltd Partnr* *(G-4099)*
Finn Directional Inc 231 944-0923
6775 W Pine Dr Roscommon (48653) *(G-14349)*
Fintech, Belding *Also called Finishing Technologies Inc* *(G-1449)*
Fintex LLC 734 946-3100
8900 Inkster Rd Romulus (48174) *(G-14276)*
Fiore Construction 517 404-0000
936 Pingree Rd Howell (48843) *(G-8454)*
Fire Acadamy, Wayne *Also called Backdraft Brewing Company* *(G-18215)*
Fire Equipment Company 313 891-3164
20100 John R St Detroit (48203) *(G-4233)*
Fire Fabrication & Supply, Spring Arbor *Also called Fabrication Concepts LLC* *(G-15791)*
Fire Fly 586 601-8792
35837 Deville Dr Sterling Heights (48312) *(G-16015)*
Fire Safety Displays Co 313 274-7888
20422 Van Born Rd Dearborn Heights (48125) *(G-3927)*
Fire Sfety Prtction Pdts / Svc, Detroit *Also called Exquise Inc* *(G-4223)*
Fire-Kote, Grand Rapids *Also called Mpd Welding - Grand Rapids Inc* *(G-7031)*
Fire-Pit Pellets, Kingsley *Also called Michael Chris Storms* *(G-9525)*
Fire-Rite Inc 313 273-3730
13801 Lyndon St Detroit (48227) *(G-4234)*
Firebolt Group Inc (PA) 248 624-8880
28059 Center Oaks Ct Wixom (48393) *(G-18661)*
Firebolt Igniting Brand Prfmce, Wixom *Also called Firebolt Group Inc* *(G-18661)*
Fireboy-Xintex Inc (HQ) 616 735-9380
O-379 Lake Michigan Dr Nw Grand Rapids (49534) *(G-6706)*
Firefish Topco LLC (PA) 248 299-7500
1780 Pond Run Auburn Hills (48326) *(G-898)*
Firehouse Woodworks LLC 616 285-2300
1945 Kalamazoo Ave Se Grand Rapids (49507) *(G-6707)*
Fireright Controls, Grand Haven *Also called Warner Instruments* *(G-6379)*
Fireside Coffee Company Inc 810 635-9196
3239 S Elms Rd Swartz Creek (48473) *(G-16353)*
Firewater Lighting LLC 616 570-0088
7929 Fitzsimmons Ct Se Alto (49302) *(G-332)*
First Class Tire Shredders Inc 810 639-4466
7302 W Vienna Rd Clio (48420) *(G-3398)*
First Impression Prtg Howell, Howell *Also called Donalyn Enterprises Inc* *(G-8447)*
First Optometry Lab 248 546-1300
195 Ajax Dr Madison Heights (48071) *(G-10728)*
First Place Manufacturing LLC 231 798-1694
6234 Norton Center Dr Norton Shores (49441) *(G-12293)*
First Response Med Sups LLC 313 731-2554
2020 N Lafayette St Dearborn (48128) *(G-3840)*
First Technology Safety System, Farmington Hills *Also called Humantics Innvtive Sltions Inc* *(G-5264)*
First Wilson Inc 586 935-2687
54036 Birchfield Dr W Shelby Township (48316) *(G-15226)*

Firstronic LLC 616 456-9220
  1655 Michigan St Ne Grand Rapids (49503) *(G-6708)*
Fischell Machinery LLC 517 445-2828
  6122 Whaley Hwy Clayton (49235) *(G-3129)*
Fischer America Inc 248 276-1940
  1084 Doris Rd Auburn Hills (48326) *(G-899)*
Fischer Automotive Systems, Auburn Hills Also called *Fischer America Inc (G-899)*
Fischer Tanks LLC 231 362-8265
  13884 Rengo Ave Kaleva (49645) *(G-9378)*
Fischer Tool & Die Corp (PA) 734 847-4788
  7155 Industrial Dr Ste A Temperance (48182) *(G-16530)*
Fish On Sports Inc 231 342-5231
  11838 Us Highway 31 Interlochen (49643) *(G-8683)*
Fishall Lures 231 821-9020
  5850 Holton Duck Lake Rd Twin Lake (49457) *(G-17467)*
Fisher & Company Incorporated (PA) 586 746-2000
  33300 Fisher Dr Saint Clair Shores (48082) *(G-14858)*
Fisher & Company Incorporated 248 280-0808
  1625 W Maple Rd Troy (48084) *(G-17108)*
Fisher & Company Incorporated 248 280-0808
  1625 W Maple Rd Troy (48084) *(G-17109)*
Fisher & Company Incorporated 586 746-2280
  33200 Fisher Dr Saint Clair Shores (48082) *(G-14859)*
Fisher & Company Incorporated 586 746-2000
  6550 Progress Dr Sterling Heights (48312) *(G-16016)*
Fisher & Company Incorporated 586 746-2101
  1625 W Marble Rd Troy (48084) *(G-17110)*
Fisher Cnstr Aggregates Inc 989 539-6431
  900 S Bradley St Mount Pleasant (48858) *(G-11698)*
Fisher Dynamics, Saint Clair Shores Also called *Fisher & Company Incorporated (G-14858)*
Fisher Dynamics Corporation 586 746-2000
  33300 Fisher Dr Saint Clair Shores (48082) *(G-14860)*
Fisher Dynamics Metal Forming, Sterling Heights Also called *Fisher & Company Incorporated (G-16016)*
Fisher Kellering Co 586 749-6616
  30500 Commerce Blvd Chesterfield (48051) *(G-2881)*
Fisher McCall Oil Gas 616 318-9155
  18640 Mack Ave Ste 1133 Grosse Pointe Farms (48236) *(G-7535)*
Fisher Redi Mix Concrete 989 723-1622
  599 Oakwood Ave Owosso (48867) *(G-12833)*
Fisher Safety Structures, Saint Clair Shores Also called *Fisher & Company Incorporated (G-14859)*
Fisher Sand and Gravel Company 989 835-7187
  3403 Contractors Dr Midland (48642) *(G-11363)*
Fisher Scientific Intl LLC 734 622-0413
  110 Miller Ave Ste 200 Ann Arbor (48104) *(G-489)*
Fisher-Baker Corporation 810 765-3548
  420 S Water St Marine City (48039) *(G-10958)*
Fishes & Loaves Food Pantry 517 759-4421
  410 E Maumee St Adrian (49221) *(G-66)*
Fishkorn Publishing LLC 734 624-2211
  22811 Braydon Ct Novi (48374) *(G-12416)*
Fisk Precision Tech LLC 616 514-1415
  3403 Lousma Dr Se Wyoming (49548) *(G-18873)*
Fisk Wood Products, Kent City Also called *County Line Pallet (G-9430)*
FisII Media LLC 646 492-8533
  2950 W Square Lake Rd Troy (48098) *(G-17111)*
Fit Fuel By Kt LLC 517 643-8827
  16400 Upton Rd Lot 227 East Lansing (48823) *(G-4893)*
Fitness Finders Inc 517 750-1500
  1007 Hurst Rd Jackson (49201) *(G-8884)*
Fitz Manufacturing Inc 248 589-1780
  324 Robbins Dr Troy (48083) *(G-17112)*
Fitz-Rite Products Inc 248 528-8440
  1122 Naughton Dr Troy (48083) *(G-17113)*
Fitz-Rite Products LLC 248 360-3730
  4228 Pioneer Dr Commerce Township (48390) *(G-3529)*
Fitzgerald Finishing, Detroit Also called *Flexible Controls Corporation (G-4237)*
Fitzgerald Finishing LLC 313 368-3630
  17450 Filer St Detroit (48212) *(G-4235)*
Fitzpatrick Manufacturing, Sterling Heights Also called *Dura Hog Inc (G-15993)*
Five Count Publishing LLC 616 308-6148
  16543 Lake Shore Dr Gowen (49326) *(G-6229)*
Five Lakes Manufacturing Inc 586 463-4123
  24400 Capital Blvd Clinton Township (48036) *(G-3239)*
Five Peaks Technology LLC 231 830-8099
  700 Terrace Point Dr # 200 Muskegon (49440) *(G-11818)*
Five Star Industries Inc 586 786-0500
  51550 Hayes Rd Macomb (48042) *(G-10595)*
Five Star Manufacturing Inc 815 723-2245
  2430 E Walton Blvd Auburn Hills (48326) *(G-900)*
Five Star Products, Troy Also called *Fsp Inc (G-17123)*
Five Star Window Coatings, Grand Rapids Also called *Chames LLC (G-6564)*
Five-Way Switch Music 269 425-2843
  9478 Huntington Rd Battle Creek (49017) *(G-1231)*
Fives Cinetic Corp (HQ) 248 477-0800
  23400 Halsted Rd Farmington Hills (48335) *(G-5244)*
Fixall Electric Motor Service 616 454-6863
  737 Butterworth St Sw Grand Rapids (49504) *(G-6709)*

Fixture Max Inc 517 376-6421
  327 Catrell Dr Howell (48843) *(G-8455)*
Fixtureworks LLC 586 294-6100
  33792 Doreka Fraser (48026) *(G-5928)*
Fjr Industrial Sales Inc 616 427-3776
  4282 Brockton Dr Se Ste D Kentwood (49512) *(G-9453)*
Fk Fuel Inc 313 383-6005
  1312 Fort St Lincoln Park (48146) *(G-10047)*
Fka Distributing Co LLC (PA) 248 863-3000
  3000 N Pontiac Trl Commerce Township (48390) *(G-3530)*
FL Tool Holders LLC 734 591-0134
  36010 Industrial Rd Livonia (48150) *(G-10207)*
Flagg Distribution LLC 248 926-0510
  48155 West Rd Ste 6 Wixom (48393) *(G-18662)*
Flagler Corporation 586 749-6300
  56513 Precision Dr Chesterfield (48051) *(G-2882)*
Flairwood, Norton Shores Also called *Fwi Inc (G-12294)*
Flambeau Inc (PA) 248 364-3357
  2701 Cambridge Ct Ste 515 Auburn Hills (48326) *(G-901)*
Flamingo Label Co 586 469-9587
  21428 Carlo Dr Clinton Township (48038) *(G-3240)*
Flamm Pickle and Packaging Co 269 461-6916
  4502 Hipps Hollow Rd Eau Claire (49111) *(G-4977)*
Flanders Industries Inc 906 863-4491
  3010 10th St Menominee (49858) *(G-11238)*
Flannery Machine & Tool Inc 231 587-5076
  8420 S Us Highway 131 Mancelona (49659) *(G-10871)*
Flare Fittings Incorporated 269 344-7600
  2980 Interstate Pkwy Kalamazoo (49048) *(G-9187)*
Flaretite Inc 810 750-4140
  7723 Kensington Ct Brighton (48116) *(G-1990)*
Flashes Advertising & News, Charlotte Also called *County Journal Inc (G-2746)*
Flashes Publishers Inc 269 673-2141
  54 W 8th St Holland (49423) *(G-8035)*
Flashplays Live LLC 978 888-3935
  412 Hamilton Pl Ann Arbor (48104) *(G-490)*
Flashpoint Sign LLC 734 231-3361
  18073 Ray St Riverview (48193) *(G-13873)*
Flat Iron LLC (PA) 248 268-1668
  27251 Gratiot Ave Roseville (48066) *(G-14407)*
Flat Rock, Flat Rock Also called *Bar Processing Corporation (G-5616)*
Flat Rock Metal Inc 734 782-4454
  26601 W Huron River Dr Flat Rock (48134) *(G-5618)*
Flat-To-Form Metal Spc Inc 231 924-1288
  9577 W 40th St Fremont (49412) *(G-6040)*
Flatlander Signs 810 867-2207
  10427 Potter Rd Flushing (48433) *(G-5808)*
Flatrock Metal Bar and Proc, Flat Rock Also called *Flat Rock Metal Inc (G-5618)*
Flatrock Tire 734 783-0100
  24599 Gibraltar Rd Flat Rock (48134) *(G-5619)*
Flaunt It Sportswear 616 696-9084
  34 N Main Ste B Cedar Springs (49319) *(G-2651)*
Flavored Group LLC 517 775-4371
  437 Lentz Ct Lansing (48917) *(G-9760)*
Flavors & Fragrances, Northville Also called *Northville Laboratories Inc (G-12246)*
Flavorsum LLC (PA) 800 525-2431
  3680 Stadium Pkwy Kalamazoo (49009) *(G-9188)*
Flea, Traverse City Also called *Mopega LLC (G-16764)*
Fleet Engineers, Muskegon Also called *Access Works Inc (G-11761)*
Fleet Fuel Company LLC 586 939-7000
  12225 Stephens Rd Warren (48089) *(G-17807)*
Fleet Truck Service, Roseville Also called *NBC Truck Equipment Inc (G-14452)*
Fleetwood Tool & Gage Inc 734 326-6737
  39050 Webb Ct Westland (48185) *(G-18370)*
Flex Building Systems LLC 586 803-6000
  42400 Merrill Rd Sterling Heights (48314) *(G-16017)*
Flex Cable, Howard City Also called *Northern Cable & Automtn LLC (G-8413)*
Flex Manufacturing Inc 586 469-1076
  44805 Trinity Dr Clinton Township (48038) *(G-3241)*
Flex Slotter Inc 586 756-6444
  3462 E 10 Mile Rd Warren (48091) *(G-17808)*
Flex-N-Gate LLC 586 759-8900
  5663 E 9 Mile Rd Warren (48091) *(G-17809)*
Flex-N-Gate Battle Creek LLC 269 962-2982
  10250 F Dr N Battle Creek (49014) *(G-1232)*
Flex-N-Gate Corporation 586 773-0800
  26269 Groesbeck Hwy Warren (48089) *(G-17810)*
Flex-N-Gate Detroit LLC 586 759-8092
  9201 Saint Cyril St Detroit (48213) *(G-4236)*
Flex-N-Gate Forming Tech, Warren Also called *Flex-N-Gate Corporation (G-17810)*
Flex-N-Gate Knshan Hldings LLC (HQ) 586 759-8900
  5663 E 9 Mile Rd Warren (48091) *(G-17811)*
Flex-N-Gate LLC 616 222-3296
  3075 Breton Rd Se Grand Rapids (49512) *(G-6710)*
Flex-N-Gate Michigan LLC 586 759-8900
  5663 E 9 Mile Rd Warren (48091) *(G-17812)*
Flex-N-Gate Shelby LLC 586 251-2300
  52674 Shelby Pkwy Shelby Township (48315) *(G-15227)*

Flex-N-Gate Stamping LLC (HQ) 586 759-8900
5663 E 9 Mile Rd Warren (48091) *(G-17813)*
Flex-N-Gate Troy LLC 586 759-8900
1400 Rochester Rd Troy (48083) *(G-17114)*
Flexco, Walker *Also called Flexible Steel Lacing Company (G-17639)*
Flexdex Inc 810 522-9009
10421 Citation Dr Ste 900 Brighton (48116) *(G-1991)*
Flexdex Surgical, Brighton *Also called Flexdex Inc (G-1991)*
Flexfab LLC 269 945-3533
5333 33rd St Se Grand Rapids (49512) *(G-6711)*
Flexfab De Mexico, Hastings *Also called Flexfab LLC (G-7792)*
Flexfab Horizons Intl Inc (PA) 269 945-4700
102 Cook Rd Hastings (49058) *(G-7791)*
Flexfab LLC (HQ) 800 331-0003
1699 W M 43 Hwy Hastings (49058) *(G-7792)*
Flexi Display Marketing Inc 800 875-1725
2156 Maplehurst Dr Commerce Township (48390) *(G-3531)*
Flexible Controls Corporation 313 368-3630
17450 Filer St Detroit (48212) *(G-4237)*
Flexible Metal Inc 810 231-1300
7495 E M 36 Hamburg (48139) *(G-7591)*
Flexible Steel Lacing Company 616 459-3196
1854 Northbridge Dr Nw Walker (49544) *(G-17639)*
Flexpost Inc 616 928-0829
2236 112th Ave Ste 80 Holland (49424) *(G-8036)*
Flextronics Automotive USA Inc (HQ) 248 853-5724
323 Skeels St Coopersville (49404) *(G-3686)*
Flight Mold & Engineering Inc 810 329-2900
1940 Fred W Moore Hwy Saint Clair (48079) *(G-14830)*
Flint Aic, Livonia *Also called Flint CPS Inks North Amer LLC (G-10208)*
Flint Boxmakers Inc 810 743-0400
G 2490 E Bristol Rd Burton (48529) *(G-2235)*
Flint CPS Inks North Amer LLC (HQ) 734 781-4600
17177 N Laurel Park Dr # 30 Livonia (48152) *(G-10208)*
Flint Group Pckg Inks N Amer C (HQ) 734 781-4600
17177 N Laurel Park Dr # 30 Livonia (48152) *(G-10209)*
Flint Group Pckg Inks N Amer H (PA) 734 781-4600
17177 N Laurel Park Dr # 30 Livonia (48152) *(G-10210)*
Flint Group US LLC (HQ) 734 781-4600
17177 N Laurel Park Dr # 30 Livonia (48152) *(G-10211)*
Flint Hydrostatics Inc (HQ) 901 794-2462
48175 Gratiot Ave Chesterfield (48051) *(G-2883)*
Flint Ink Receivables Corp 734 781-4600
17177 N Laurel Park Dr # 300 Livonia (48152) *(G-10212)*
Flint Journal, The, Flint *Also called Herald Newspapers Company Inc (G-5714)*
Flint Lime Industries Inc 313 843-6050
327 S Fordson St Detroit (48217) *(G-4238)*
Flint Optical Company Inc 810 235-4607
518 S Saginaw St Flint (48502) *(G-5701)*
Flint Packaging Systems Div, Bay City *Also called Delta Containers Inc (G-1342)*
Flint Stool & Chair Co Inc 810 235-7001
1517 N Dort Hwy Flint (48506) *(G-5702)*
Flipsnack LLC 650 741-1328
2701 Troy Center Dr # 255 Troy (48084) *(G-17115)*
Floatation Docking Inc (PA) 906 484-3422
160 Hodeck St Cedarville (49719) *(G-2669)*
Flodraulic Group Incorporated 734 326-5400
375 Manufacturers Dr Westland (48186) *(G-18371)*
Floodwell Print Studio 231 943-2930
903 Woodmere Ave Traverse City (49686) *(G-16683)*
Floorcovering Engineers LLC 616 299-1007
2489 Maplevalley Dr Se Grand Rapids (49512) *(G-6712)*
Flor TEC Inc 616 897-3122
4475 Causeway Dr Ne Lowell (49331) *(G-10501)*
Floracraft Corporation (PA) 231 845-5127
1 Longfellow Pl Ludington (49431) *(G-10536)*
Florance Turning Company Inc 248 347-0068
44862 Aspen Ridge Dr Northville (48168) *(G-12218)*
Florheat Company 517 272-4441
3130 Sovereign Dr Lansing (48911) *(G-9836)*
Florida Coca-Cola Bottling Co 906 495-2261
4760 W Curtis St Kincheloe (49788) *(G-9503)*
Florida Machine & Casting Co 561 655-3771
926 N Lake St Boyne City (49712) *(G-1888)*
Florida Production Engrg Inc 248 588-4870
550 Stephenson Hwy # 360 Troy (48083) *(G-17116)*
Florkeys Conveyor Service 810 772-1930
21810 Schmeman Ave Warren (48089) *(G-17814)*
Flotronics Automation Inc 248 625-8890
2704 Paldan Dr Auburn Hills (48326) *(G-902)*
Flour Shop Bakery & Pizza, The, Stevensville *Also called Klaus Nixdorf (G-16256)*
Flow Ezy Filters Inc 734 665-8777
147 Enterprise Dr Ann Arbor (48103) *(G-491)*
Flow Gas Misture Solutions Inc 810 488-1492
110 Huron Blvd Ste A Marysville (48040) *(G-11087)*
Flow-Rite Controls Ltd 616 583-1700
960 74th St Sw Byron Center (49315) *(G-2270)*
Flowcor LLC (PA) 616 554-1100
4855 Broadmoor Ave Se Kentwood (49512) *(G-9454)*
Flowing Well Publications 231 622-8630
510 Jennings Ave Petoskey (49770) *(G-12997)*
Flowserve US Inc 269 381-2650
2100 Factory St Kalamazoo (49001) *(G-9189)*
Flowserve US Inc 989 496-3897
2420 Schuette Rd Midland (48642) *(G-11364)*
Flowtek Inc 231 734-3415
206 E Park Dr Kalkaska (49646) *(G-9388)*
Flue Sentinel LLC 586 739-4373
8123 Janis St Shelby Township (48317) *(G-15228)*
Fluid Automation Inc 248 669-3717
49175 West Rd Wixom (48393) *(G-18663)*
Fluid Chillers Inc (PA) 517 484-9190
2730 Alpha Access St Lansing (48910) *(G-9837)*
Fluid Hutchinson Management (HQ) 248 679-1327
3201 Cross Creek Pkwy Auburn Hills (48326) *(G-903)*
Fluid Systems Division, Marysville *Also called TI Group Auto Systems LLC (G-11108)*
Fluid Systems Engineering Inc 586 790-8880
18855 E 14 Mile Rd Clinton Township (48035) *(G-3242)*
Fluid-Bag LLC 513 310-9550
3463 Millwood Rd Lansing (48906) *(G-9698)*
Fluidtherm Corp Michigan 989 344-1500
7730 Old 27 N Frederic (49733) *(G-6015)*
Fluir Creative LLC 734 494-0308
15223 Farmington Rd Livonia (48154) *(G-10213)*
Fluresh LLC (PA) 616 600-0420
1213 Phillips Ave Sw Grand Rapids (49507) *(G-6713)*
Fluresh LLC 616 600-0420
1751 W Beecher Rd Adrian (49221) *(G-67)*
Fluxtrol Inc 248 393-2000
1388 Atlantic Blvd Auburn Hills (48326) *(G-904)*
Flying Otter Winery LLC 517 424-7107
3402 Chase Rd Adrian (49221) *(G-68)*
Flying Pig Coatings LLC 616 947-1118
3529 3 Mile Rd Nw Grand Rapids (49534) *(G-6714)*
FM International LLC (HQ) 248 354-7700
26555 Northwestern Hwy Southfield (48033) *(G-15570)*
FM Research Management LLC 906 360-5833
1958 Eben Trenary Rd Trenary (49891) *(G-16884)*
Fmmb LLC 313 372-7420
4786 Bellevue St Detroit (48207) *(G-4239)*
Fms Lansing LLC (HQ) 781 699-9000
920 Winter St Lansing (48901) *(G-9838)*
Foam Factory Incorporated 586 739-7449
17500 23 Mile Rd Ste A Macomb (48044) *(G-10596)*
Foam-It, Grand Rapids *Also called Innovative Cleaning Eqp Inc (G-6845)*
Foampartner Americas Inc 248 243-3100
2923 Technology Dr Rochester Hills (48309) *(G-14012)*
Focal Point Metal Fab LLC 616 844-7670
17354 Teunis Dr Spring Lake (49456) *(G-15814)*
Focus 1, Plymouth *Also called Hatteras Inc (G-13183)*
Focus Cleaning LLC 734 883-9560
609 Calder Ave Ypsilanti (48198) *(G-18946)*
Focus Hope Logistics, Detroit *Also called Hope Focus Companies Inc (G-4308)*
Focus Hope Manufacturing, Detroit *Also called Hope Focus (G-4306)*
Focus Marketing 616 355-4362
2495 112th Ave Ste 8 Holland (49424) *(G-8037)*
Fogelsonger Vault Co Inc 989 684-0262
210 Ausable State Rd Bay City (48706) *(G-1358)*
Foggy Mountain Woodworks 231 675-1757
6959 Thumb Lake Rd Boyne Falls (49713) *(G-1907)*
Folk Sign Studio LLC 734 883-8259
5215 Moechel Rd Stockbridge (49285) *(G-16274)*
Foltz Screen Printing 989 772-3947
2094 S Isabella Rd Mount Pleasant (48858) *(G-11699)*
Fomcore LLC 231 366-4791
1770 E Keating Ave Muskegon (49442) *(G-11819)*
Fontaine Chateau 231 256-0000
2290 S French Rd Lake Leelanau (49653) *(G-9560)*
Fontana Forest Products, Detroit *Also called Michigan Box Company (G-4444)*
Fontijne Grotnes Inc 269 262-4700
30257 Redfield St Niles (49120) *(G-12129)*
Fonts About Inc 248 767-7504
143 Cadycentre 130 Northville (48167) *(G-12219)*
Food For Thought Inc 231 326-5444
7738 N Long Lake Rd Traverse City (49685) *(G-16684)*
Food Truck Shop, The, Westland *Also called Detroit Cstm Trck Trailor LLC (G-18363)*
Foodtools Consolidated Inc 269 637-9969
190 Veterans Blvd South Haven (49090) *(G-15405)*
For The Love of Cupcakes 906 399-3004
5835 F Rd Bark River (49807) *(G-1154)*
Forbes Sanitation & Excavation 231 723-2311
1878 E Parkdale Ave Manistee (49660) *(G-10900)*
Forche Rd Welding 517 920-3473
10187 Forche Rd Blissfield (49228) *(G-1764)*
Ford Global Technologies LLC (HQ) 313 312-3000
30600 Telg Rd Ste 2345 Bingham Farms (48025) *(G-1696)*
Ford Investment Entps Corp 973 764-8783
1 American Rd Dearborn (48126) *(G-3841)*

ALPHABETIC

(PA)=Parent Co (HQ)=Headquarters (DH)=Div Headquarters
2022 Harris Michigan Industrial Directory
995

Ford Motor Company (PA) 313 322-3000
1 American Rd Dearborn (48126) ***(G-3842)***
Ford Motor Company 313 446-5945
300 Renaissance Ctr Detroit (48243) ***(G-4240)***
Ford Motor Company 734 484-8626
10300 Textile Rd Ypsilanti (48197) ***(G-18947)***
Ford Motor Company 313 594-0050
3001 Miller Rd Dearborn (48120) ***(G-3843)***
Ford Motor Company 313 322-7715
21175 Oakwood Blvd Dearborn (48124) ***(G-3844)***
Ford Motor Company 734 523-3000
36200 Plymouth Rd Livonia (48150) ***(G-10214)***
Ford Motor Company 313 594-4090
1555 Fairlane Dr Ste 100 Allen Park (48101) ***(G-194)***
Ford Motor Company 910 381-7998
21001 Van Born Rd Taylor (48180) ***(G-16419)***
Ford Motor Company 734 782-7800
1 International Dr Flat Rock (48134) ***(G-5620)***
Ford Motor Company 734 241-2498
3200 E Elm Ave Monroe (48162) ***(G-11541)***
Ford Motor Company 734 523-3000
11871 Middlebelt Rd Livonia (48150) ***(G-10215)***
Ford Motor Company 734 942-6248
24999 Pennsylvania Rd Brownstown (48174) ***(G-2146)***
Fordsell Machine Products Co 586 751-4700
30400 Ryan Rd Warren (48092) ***(G-17815)***
Fordson Health Care, Lincoln Park *Also called Wright & Filippis LLC* ***(G-10058)***
Forefront Control Systems LLC 616 796-3495
4314 136th Ave Ste 200 Holland (49424) ***(G-8038)***
Foremost Graphics LLC 616 453-4747
2921 Wilson Dr Nw Grand Rapids (49534) ***(G-6715)***
Forerunner 3d Printing 231 722-1144
411 64th Ave N Coopersville (49404) ***(G-3687)***
Forerunner Press LLC 248 677-3272
29300 Woodward Ave # 101 Royal Oak (48073) ***(G-14537)***
Foresee Session Replay Inc 800 621-2850
2500 Green Rd Ste 400 Ann Arbor (48105) ***(G-492)***
Foresight Group Inc (PA) 517 485-5700
2822 N Mrtn Lther King Jr Lansing (48906) ***(G-9699)***
Forest Blake Products Inc 231 879-3913
10723 Shippy Rd Sw Fife Lake (49633) ***(G-5606)***
Forest Corullo Products Corp 906 667-0275
300 S Massie Ave Bessemer (49911) ***(G-1649)***
Forest Elders Products Inc 616 866-9317
10367 Northland Dr Ne Rockford (49341) ***(G-14168)***
Forest Grove Power Eqp LLC 616 896-8344
3188 32nd Ave Hudsonville (49426) ***(G-8584)***
Forest View Lanes LLC 734 847-4915
2345 W Dean Rd Temperance (48182) ***(G-16531)***
Forestry Management Svcs Inc 517 456-7431
430 Division St Clinton (49236) ***(G-3138)***
Forever Young Publishers 574 276-1805
2674 Korn St Niles (49120) ***(G-12130)***
Foreward Logistics LLC 877 488-9724
25900 Grnfeld Rd Ste 326 Oak Park (48237) ***(G-12612)***
Foreword Magazine Inc 231 933-3699
425 Boardman Ave Traverse City (49684) ***(G-16685)***
Foreword Magazine Inc 231 933-3699
413 E Eighth St Traverse City (49686) ***(G-16686)***
Foreword Reviews 231 933-5397
425 Boardman Ave Traverse City (49684) ***(G-16687)***
Forge Die & Tool Corp 248 477-0020
31800 W 8 Mile Rd Farmington Hills (48336) ***(G-5245)***
Forge Div Midwest Tl & Cutly, Kalkaska *Also called Midwest Tool and Cutlery Co* ***(G-9398)***
Forge Industries Lc 616 402-7887
4191 88th Ave Zeeland (49464) ***(G-19022)***
Forge Precision Company 248 477-0020
31800 W 8 Mile Rd Farmington Hills (48336) ***(G-5246)***
Forge Tech Inc 989 685-3443
464 E Industrial Dr Rose City (48654) ***(G-14363)***
Forged Tubular 313 843-4870
9339 W Fort St Detroit (48209) ***(G-4241)***
Forged Tubular Products Inc (PA) 313 843-6720
9339 W Fort St Detroit (48209) ***(G-4242)***
Forgetek, Sterling Heights *Also called Rucci Forged Wheels Inc* ***(G-16161)***
Forging Holdings LLC (HQ) 313 758-2000
1 Dauch Dr Detroit (48211) ***(G-4243)***
Forkardt Inc 231 995-8300
2155 Traversefield Dr Traverse City (49686) ***(G-16688)***
Forkardt North America, Traverse City *Also called Forkardt Inc* ***(G-16688)***
Forklift Parts Group 248 792-7132
2601 Fox Chase Dr Troy (48098) ***(G-17117)***
Form All Tool Company 231 894-6303
803 S Mears Ave Whitehall (49461) ***(G-18496)***
Form G Tech Co 248 583-3610
1291 Rochester Rd Troy (48083) ***(G-17118)***
Forma-Kool Manufacturing Inc 586 949-4813
46880 Continental Dr Chesterfield (48047) ***(G-2884)***
Formax Manufacturing Corp 616 456-5458
168 Wealthy St Sw Grand Rapids (49503) ***(G-6716)***
Formax Precision Gear Inc 586 323-9067
6047 18 Mile Rd Sterling Heights (48314) ***(G-16018)***
Formed Solutions Inc 616 395-5455
1900 Lamar Ct Holland (49423) ***(G-8039)***
Former Company LLC 248 202-0473
2920 E Jefferson Ave Detroit (48207) ***(G-4244)***
Formex International Div, Port Huron *Also called Tapex American Corporation* ***(G-13531)***
Formfab LLC 248 844-3676
3044 Research Dr Rochester Hills (48309) ***(G-14013)***
Forming Technologies LLC 231 777-7030
1885 E Laketon Ave Muskegon (49442) ***(G-11820)***
Formrite Inc 517 521-1373
2060 Elm Rd Webberville (48892) ***(G-18245)***
Forms Trac Enterprises Inc 248 524-0006
37827 Brookwood Dr Sterling Heights (48312) ***(G-16019)***
Formsprag LLC 586 758-5000
23601 Hoover Rd Warren (48089) ***(G-17816)***
Formtech Inds Holdings LLC 248 597-3800
2727 W 14 Mile Rd Royal Oak (48073) ***(G-14538)***
Formula One Tool & Engineering 810 794-3617
6052 Pointe Tremble Rd Algonac (48001) ***(G-142)***
Forrest Brothers Inc (PA) 989 356-4011
1272 Millbocker Rd Gaylord (49735) ***(G-6129)***
Forrest Company 269 384-6120
7877 N 12th St Kalamazoo (49009) ***(G-9190)***
Forsons Inc 517 787-4562
139 S Mechanic St Jackson (49201) ***(G-8885)***
Forsports, Fort Gratiot *Also called Nobby Inc* ***(G-5822)***
Forst-Usa Incorporated 586 759-9380
23640 Hoover Rd Warren (48089) ***(G-17817)***
Forsters and Sons Oil Change 248 618-6860
4773 Dixie Hwy Waterford (48329) ***(G-18123)***
Forsyth Millwork and Farms 810 266-4000
15315 Duffield Rd Byron (48418) ***(G-2253)***
Fort Grtiot Cbnets Counter LLC 810 364-1924
3390 Ravenswood Rd Port Huron (48060) ***(G-13478)***
Forte Industries Mill Inc 906 753-6256
N8076 Us Highway 41 Stephenson (49887) ***(G-15907)***
Fortech Products Inc 248 446-9500
7600 Kensington Ct Brighton (48116) ***(G-1992)***
Fortis Energy Services Inc (PA) 248 283-7100
3001 W Big Beaver Rd # 525 Troy (48084) ***(G-17119)***
Fortis Sltions Group Centl LLC (PA) 248 437-5200
28505 Automation Blvd Wixom (48393) ***(G-18664)***
Fortress Manufacturing Inc 269 925-1336
2255 Pipestone Rd Benton Harbor (49022) ***(G-1549)***
Fortress Stblztion Systems LLC 616 355-1421
184 W 64th St Holland (49423) ***(G-8040)***
Fortune Tool & Machine Inc 248 669-9119
29650 Beck Rd Wixom (48393) ***(G-18665)***
Forty Eight Forty Solutions 713 332-6145
31750 Enterprise Dr Livonia (48150) ***(G-10216)***
Forum and Link Inc 313 945-5465
12740 W Wrren Ave Ste 100 Dearborn (48126) ***(G-3845)***
Forward Inking Design & Print 231 714-8646
404 Hughes Dr Traverse City (49696) ***(G-16689)***
Forward Metal Craft Inc 616 459-6051
329 Summer Ave Nw Grand Rapids (49504) ***(G-6717)***
Forzza Corporation 616 884-6121
915 Grand Rapids St Middleville (49333) ***(G-11306)***
Fosters Ventures LLC 248 519-7446
1371 Souter Dr Troy (48083) ***(G-17120)***
Foundations Press Inc 517 625-3052
308 N Madison St Perry (48872) ***(G-12977)***
Four Leaf Brewing, Farwell *Also called James Joy LLC* ***(G-5424)***
Four Lkes Spcial Assssment Dst 989 941-3005
233 E Larkin St Ste 2 Midland (48640) ***(G-11365)***
Four Seasons Mobile Press 616 902-6233
417 Morse St Ionia (48846) ***(G-8689)***
Four Seasons Publishing Inc 906 341-5200
212 Walnut St Manistique (49854) ***(G-10918)***
Four Star Rubber Inc 810 632-3335
3185 Old Farm Ln Commerce Township (48390) ***(G-3532)***
Four Star Tooling & Engrg Inc 586 264-4090
40550 Brentwood Dr Sterling Heights (48310) ***(G-16020)***
Four Way Industries Inc 248 588-5421
855 N Rochester Rd Clawson (48017) ***(G-3097)***
Four Way Pallet Service 734 782-5914
3988 Will Carleton Rd Flat Rock (48134) ***(G-5621)***
Four-Slide Technology Inc 586 755-7778
33946 Doreka Fraser (48026) ***(G-5929)***
Four-Way Tool and Die Inc (PA) 248 585-8255
239 Indusco Ct Troy (48083) ***(G-17121)***
Fournier Enterprises Inc 586 323-9160
17 N Rose St Ste A Mount Clemens (48043) ***(G-11639)***
Fourslides Inc 313 564-5600
50801 E Rssell Schmidt Bl Chesterfield (48051) ***(G-2885)***
Fourth Ave Birkenstock 734 663-1644
209 N 4th Ave Ann Arbor (48104) ***(G-493)***

Fourth Seacoast Publishing Co 586 779-5570
25300 Little Mack Ave Saint Clair Shores (48081) ***(G-14861)***

Fourway Machinery Sales Co 517 782-9371
3215 Gregory Rd Jackson (49202) ***(G-8886)***

Foust Electro Mold Inc 517 439-1062
277 Industrial Dr Hillsdale (49242) ***(G-7934)***

Fowler Organ Co, Eaton Rapids *Also called Brian M Fowler Pipe Organs* ***(G-4956)***

Fowlerville Feed & Pet Sups 517 223-9115
120 Hale St Fowlerville (48836) ***(G-5839)***

Fowlerville Machine Tool Inc 517 223-8871
5010 W Grand River Rd Fowlerville (48836) ***(G-5840)***

Fowlerville News & Views 517 223-8760
206 E Grand River Ave Fowlerville (48836) ***(G-5841)***

Fox Aluminum Products Inc 248 399-4288
1355 E Woodward Hts Blvd Hazel Park (48030) ***(G-7826)***

Fox Fire Glass LLC 248 332-2442
3071 W Thompson Rd Fenton (48430) ***(G-5479)***

Fox Mfg Co 586 468-1421
32535 S River Rd Harrison Township (48045) ***(G-7700)***

Foxys Leotards 616 949-1847
4540 East Paris Ave Se A Grand Rapids (49512) ***(G-6718)***

Fpe, Troy *Also called Florida Production Engrg Inc* ***(G-17116)***

Fpt Schlafer 313 925-8200
1950 Medbury St Detroit (48211) ***(G-4245)***

Fra-Wod Company Inc 586 254-4450
44035 Phoenix Dr Sterling Heights (48314) ***(G-16021)***

Fraco Products Ltd 248 667-9260
5225 Renshaw Dr Troy (48085) ***(G-17122)***

Fragrance Outlet Inc 517 552-9545
1475 N Burkhart Rd E115 Howell (48855) ***(G-8456)***

Fram Group Limited, Rochester Hills *Also called Fram Group Operations LLC* ***(G-14014)***

Fram Group Operations LLC (HQ) 800 890-2075
3255 W Hamlin Rd Rochester Hills (48309) ***(G-14014)***

Framar, Clinton Township *Also called SRS Manufacturing Inc* ***(G-3362)***

Framon Mfg Co Inc (PA) 989 354-5623
1201 W Chisholm St Alpena (49707) ***(G-295)***

Franchino Mold & Engrg Co 517 321-5609
5867 W Grand River Ave Lansing (48906) ***(G-9700)***

Frandale Sub Shop 616 446-6311
11250 Kistler Dr Unit 5 Allendale (49401) ***(G-218)***

Frank Condon Inc 517 849-2505
250 Industrial Dr Hillsdale (49242) ***(G-7935)***

Frank Industries Inc 810 346-3234
4467 Vine St Brown City (48416) ***(G-2137)***

Frank Terlecki Company Inc 586 759-5770
4129 Kendall Rd Warren (48091) ***(G-17818)***

Franke Salisbury Virginia 231 775-7014
11894 S Mackinaw Trl Cadillac (49601) ***(G-2330)***

Franke Septic Tank Service, Cadillac *Also called Franke Salisbury Virginia* ***(G-2330)***

Frankenmuth Brewery LLC 989 262-8300
425 S Main St Frankenmuth (48734) ***(G-5861)***

Frankenmuth Industrial Svcs 989 652-3322
310 List St Frankenmuth (48734) ***(G-5862)***

Frankenmuth News LLC 989 652-3246
527 N Franklin St Ste A Frankenmuth (48734) ***(G-5863)***

Frankenmuth Printing, Davison *Also called Riegle Press Inc* ***(G-3795)***

Frankenmuth Welding & Fabg 989 754-9457
4765 E Holland Rd Saginaw (48601) ***(G-14646)***

Frankfort Manufacturing Inc 231 352-7551
1105 Main St Frankfort (49635) ***(G-5876)***

Franklin Electric Corporation 248 442-8000
32606 Industrial Rd Garden City (48135) ***(G-6094)***

Franklin Fastener Company 313 537-8900
12701 Beech Daly Rd Redford (48239) ***(G-13735)***

Franklin Iron & Metal Co Inc (PA) 269 968-6111
120 South Ave Battle Creek (49014) ***(G-1233)***

Franklin Metal Trading Corp 616 374-7171
609 Tupper Lake St Lake Odessa (48849) ***(G-9575)***

Franklin Plastics, Battle Creek *Also called Franklin Iron & Metal Co Inc* ***(G-1233)***

Franklin Press Inc 616 538-5320
2426 28th St Sw Grand Rapids (49519) ***(G-6719)***

Franks Performance Development, Pittsford *Also called Reeds Equipment LLC* ***(G-13068)***

Franks Products 269 350-7366
66796 N Shore Dr Cassopolis (49031) ***(G-2628)***

Fraser Fab and Machine Inc 248 852-9050
1696 Star Batt Dr Rochester Hills (48309) ***(G-14015)***

Fraser Grinding Co (PA) 586 293-6060
34235 Riviera Fraser (48026) ***(G-5930)***

Fraser Mfg Facility, Fraser *Also called Hhi Formtech LLC* ***(G-5935)***

Fraser Tool & Gauge LLC 313 882-9192
1352 Harvard Rd Grosse Pointe Park (48230) ***(G-7554)***

Frazeli Prints, Lansing *Also called Fairfax Prints Ltd* ***(G-9696)***

Freal Fuel Inc 248 790-7202
28230 23 Mile Rd Chesterfield (48051) ***(G-2886)***

Fred Oswalts Pins Unltd 269 342-1387
2610 Hill An Brook Dr Portage (49024) ***(G-13561)***

Fred's Rubber Stamp Shop, Marquette *Also called F & A Enterprises of Michigan* ***(G-11018)***

Freds Jerky Products 517 202-1908
436 Pleasant St Charlotte (48813) ***(G-2756)***

Free Rnge Ntrals Dog Trats Inc 586 737-0797
44648 Mound Rd Sterling Heights (48314) ***(G-16022)***

Free State Boring Inc 248 821-8860
5425 Perry Dr Ste 105 Waterford (48329) ***(G-18124)***

Freedom Technologies Corp (PA) 810 227-3737
10559 Citation Dr Ste 205 Brighton (48116) ***(G-1993)***

Freedom Tool & Mfg Co 231 788-2898
1741 S Wolf Lake Rd Muskegon (49442) ***(G-11821)***

Freelands Country Upolstery 269 330-2416
4054 Osborne Rd Delton (49046) ***(G-3963)***

Freeport Milling 616 765-8421
223 Division St Freeport (49325) ***(G-6033)***

Freer Tool & Die Inc 586 463-3200
44675 Morley Dr Clinton Township (48036) ***(G-3243)***

Freer Tool & Die Inc 586 741-5274
44675 Morley Dr Clinton Township (48036) ***(G-3244)***

Freer Tool & Supply, Clinton Township *Also called Freer Tool & Die Inc* ***(G-3244)***

Freer Tool and Supply, Clinton Township *Also called Freer Tool & Die Inc* ***(G-3243)***

Freescale Semiconductor Inc 248 324-3260
28125 Cabot Dr Ste 100 Novi (48377) ***(G-12417)***

Freeway, Hart *Also called Oceanas Herald-Journal Inc* ***(G-7759)***

Freiborne Industries Inc 248 333-2490
15 W Silverdome Indus Par Pontiac (48342) ***(G-13371)***

Fremont Community Digester LLC 248 735-6684
23955 Novi Rd Novi (48375) ***(G-12418)***

Fremont Generate Digester LLC 231 924-9401
1634 Locust St Fremont (49412) ***(G-6041)***

Fremont Regional Digester, Fremont *Also called Fremont Generate Digester LLC* ***(G-6041)***

French Paper Company 269 683-1100
100 French St Niles (49120) ***(G-12131)***

French Press Knits LLC 810 623-0650
10631 Oakhill St Fenton (48430) ***(G-5480)***

French Road Cellars LLC 231 256-0680
2300 S French Rd Lake Leelanau (49653) ***(G-9561)***

French Valley Vineyard L L C 231 228-2616
3655 S French Rd Cedar (49621) ***(G-2639)***

Frenchys Skirting Inc 734 721-3013
34111 Michigan Ave Wayne (48184) ***(G-18220)***

Frequency Finders LLC 734 660-3357
793 3rd Ave Pontiac (48340) ***(G-13372)***

Fresh Baked Prints 888 327-4137
13807 W 9 Mile Rd Oak Park (48237) ***(G-12613)***

Fresh Coast Candles 616 405-8518
6445 146th Ave Holland (49423) ***(G-8041)***

Fresh Heir LLC 313 312-4492
23994 Earl Ct Farmington (48335) ***(G-5138)***

Fresh Start Cmnty Initiative 941 225-9693
535 Griswold St 111-19 Detroit (48226) ***(G-4246)***

Fresh Tracks, Lansing *Also called Seelye Group Ltd* ***(G-9894)***

Fresh Water Buyer II LLC 517 914-8284
5260 S Clinton Trl Eaton Rapids (48827) ***(G-4963)***

Freshwater Communications, Battle Creek *Also called Caribbean Adventure LLC* ***(G-1205)***

Freshwater Digital 616 682-5470
4585 40th St Se Kentwood (49512) ***(G-9455)***

Freshwter Dgtal Mdia Prtners L 616 446-1771
4585 40th St Se Kentwood (49512) ***(G-9456)***

Fretty Media LLC 231 894-8055
201 W Obell St Whitehall (49461) ***(G-18497)***

Freudenberg N Amer Ltd Partnr (HQ) 734 354-5505
47774 W Anchor Ct Plymouth (48170) ***(G-13169)***

Freudenberg-Nok General Partnr (HQ) 734 451-0020
47774 W Anchor Ct Plymouth (48170) ***(G-13170)***

Freudenberg-Nok General Partnr 734 451-0020
47805 Galleon Dr Plymouth (48170) ***(G-13171)***

Freudenberg-Nok Sealing Tech, Plymouth *Also called Freudenberg-Nok General Partnr* ***(G-13170)***

Freudnberg Btry Pwr Systems LL 989 698-3329
2700 S Saginaw Rd Midland (48640) ***(G-11366)***

Fricia Enterprises Inc 586 977-1900
6070 18 Mile Rd Sterling Heights (48314) ***(G-16023)***

Friction Coating Corporation 586 731-0990
44833 Centre Ct Clinton Township (48038) ***(G-3245)***

Friction Control LLC 586 741-8493
35360 Forton Ct Clinton Township (48035) ***(G-3246)***

Friedland Industries Inc 517 482-3000
405 E Maple St Lansing (48906) ***(G-9701)***

Friends of Liz Brater 734 547-1953
8205 Starling Ct Ypsilanti (48197) ***(G-18948)***

Friendship Industries Inc (PA) 586 323-0033
6520 Arrow Dr Sterling Heights (48314) ***(G-16024)***

Friendship Industries Inc 586 997-1325
6521 Arrow Dr Sterling Heights (48314) ***(G-16025)***

Frimo Inc (HQ) 248 668-3160
50685 Century Ct Wixom (48393) ***(G-18666)***

Friscos Mechanical & Fabg 517 719-3933
3932 Berry Ridge Dr Holt (48842) ***(G-8312)***

Frito-Lay North America Inc 989 754-0435
100 S Outer Dr Saginaw (48601) ***(G-14647)***

Fritz Advertising Company, Spring Arbor *Also called R J Designers Inc* ***(G-15797)***

Fritz Enterprises 313 841-9460
255 Marion Ave Detroit (48218) ***(G-4247)***
Fritz Enterprises (HQ) 734 283-7272
1650 W Jefferson Ave Trenton (48183) ***(G-16888)***
Fritz Products, Detroit *Also called Fritz Enterprises* ***(G-4247)***
Fritz Products Inc, Trenton *Also called Fritz Enterprises* ***(G-16888)***
From Log Up LLC 989 728-0611
1872 M 65 Hale (48739) ***(G-7589)***
From Photos To Canvas Prints 248 760-4694
492 Buttercup Dr Rochester Hills (48307) ***(G-14016)***
Front Line Services Inc 989 695-6633
8588 Carter Rd Freeland (48623) ***(G-6024)***
Frontier Medical Devices Inc 906 232-1200
512 4th St Gwinn (49841) ***(G-7584)***
Frontier Rnwable Resources LLC (PA) 906 228-7960
210 N Front St Ste 1 Marquette (49855) ***(G-11019)***
Frontier Technology Inc 269 673-9464
2489 118th Ave Allegan (49010) ***(G-159)***
Frontlines Publishing 616 887-6256
72 Ransom Ave Ne Ofc Grand Rapids (49503) ***(G-6720)***
Frost Division, Fraser *Also called Hi-Craft Engineering Inc* ***(G-5936)***
Frost Inc (PA) 616 785-9030
2020 Bristol Ave Nw Grand Rapids (49504) ***(G-6721)***
Frost Incorporated (HQ) 616 453-7781
2020 Bristol Ave Nw Grand Rapids (49504) ***(G-6722)***
Frost Incorporated 616 453-7781
2020 Bristol Ave Nw Grand Rapids (49504) ***(G-6723)***
Frost Incorporated 616 785-9030
2020 Bristol Ave Nw Grand Rapids (49504) ***(G-6724)***
Frost Links (PA) 616 785-9030
2020 Bristol Ave Nw Grand Rapids (49504) ***(G-6725)***
Frosty Cove 231 343-6643
2133 Lakeshore Dr Muskegon (49441) ***(G-11822)***
Frostys Ice Cream Machine Retn 616 886-1418
2080 Ottawa Beach Rd Holland (49424) ***(G-8042)***
Froude Inc 248 579-4295
41123 Jo Dr Ste A Novi (48375) ***(G-12419)***
Froyo Pinckney LLC 248 310-4465
3282 Swarthout Rd Pinckney (48169) ***(G-13048)***
Fruit Fro Yo 517 580-3967
5100 Marsh Rd Okemos (48864) ***(G-12668)***
Fruit Haven Nursery Inc 231 889-9973
8576 Chief Rd Kaleva (49645) ***(G-9379)***
Frushour Publishers 248 701-2548
4871 Curtis Ln Clarkston (48346) ***(G-3035)***
Fry Krisp Company, The, Jackson *Also called Fry Krisp Food Products Inc* ***(G-8887)***
Fry Krisp Food Products Inc 517 784-8531
3514 Wayland Dr Jackson (49202) ***(G-8887)***
Frye Printing Company Inc (PA) 517 456-4124
11801 Tecumseh Clinton Rd Clinton (49236) ***(G-3139)***
FSI Label Company 586 776-4110
6227 136th Ave Holland (49424) ***(G-8043)***
Fsp Inc 248 585-0760
1270 Rankin Dr Ste B Troy (48083) ***(G-17123)***
FTC LLC 313 622-1583
27611 Sloan St Novi (48374) ***(G-12420)***
Fte Automotive North Amer Inc 248 340-1262
4100 N Atlantic Blvd Auburn Hills (48326) ***(G-905)***
Fte Automotive USA Inc 248 209-8239
12700 Oakland Park Blvd Highland Park (48203) ***(G-7907)***
Fudge and Frosting 517 763-2040
333 S Washington Sq Lansing (48933) ***(G-9839)***
Fudge Business Forms Inc 248 299-3666
2251 Star Ct Rochester Hills (48309) ***(G-14017)***
Fuel Cell System Mfg LLC 313 319-5571
20001 Brownstown Ctr Dr Brownstown Township (48183) ***(G-2152)***
Fuel of Parma, Parma *Also called Camerons of Jackson LLC* ***(G-12937)***
Fuel Source LLC 313 506-0448
29112 E River Rd Grosse Ile (48138) ***(G-7522)***
Fuel Systems, Troy *Also called TI Group Auto Systems LLC* ***(G-17391)***
Fuel Tobacco Stop 810 487-2040
226 E Main St Flushing (48433) ***(G-5809)***
Fug Inc 269 781-8036
315 Woolley Dr Marshall (49068) ***(G-11058)***
Fujikura Automotive Amer LLC (HQ) 248 957-0130
27555 Executive Dr # 150 Farmington Hills (48331) ***(G-5247)***
Fulcrum Industries Inc 888 818-5121
4849 Barden Ct Se Grand Rapids (49512) ***(G-6726)***
Full of Scents 734 972-6542
47845 Milan Ct Northville (48167) ***(G-12220)***
Full Spectrum Solutions Inc (PA) 517 783-3800
2021 Wellworth Jackson (49203) ***(G-8888)***
Full Spectrum Stained GL Inc 269 432-2610
31323 W Colon Rd Colon (49040) ***(G-3487)***
Full Spectrum Tech Inc 810 225-4760
6457 Brighton Rd Brighton (48116) ***(G-1994)***
Full Upholstery LLC 248 760-3985
900 Cesar E Chavez Ave Pontiac (48340) ***(G-13373)***
Fuller Printing 989 304-0230
2688 E Stanton Rd Stanton (48888) ***(G-15901)***
Fullerton Tool Company Inc (PA) 989 799-4550
121 Perry St Saginaw (48602) ***(G-14648)***
Fully Promoted 616 285-8009
6161 28th St Se Ste 2 Grand Rapids (49546) ***(G-6727)***
Fultz Manufacturing Inc 231 947-5801
1631 Park Dr Ste A Traverse City (49686) ***(G-16690)***
Fun Foods, Muskegon *Also called L & P LLC* ***(G-11854)***
Fun Learning Company LLC 269 362-0651
21341 Fairfield Dr Macomb (48044) ***(G-10597)***
Function Inc 570 317-0737
6610 Patterson Ave Se Caledonia (49316) ***(G-2373)***
Function of Beauty, Caledonia *Also called Function Inc* ***(G-2373)***
Functional Fluidics Inc 410 493-8322
440 Burroughs St Ste 641 Detroit (48202) ***(G-4248)***
Functional Hand Strength, Plymouth *Also called Thunderdome Media LLC* ***(G-13314)***
Fuoss Bros, Owosso *Also called Fuoss Gravel Company* ***(G-12834)***
Fuoss Gravel Company 989 725-2084
777 Busha Rd Owosso (48867) ***(G-12834)***
Fur Brained Ideas 248 830-0764
1405 Brys Dr Grosse Pointe Woods (48236) ***(G-7567)***
Furnaces Ovens & Baths Inc 248 625-7400
195 Campbell St River Rouge (48218) ***(G-13854)***
Furniture City Glass Corp 616 784-5500
1012 Ken O Sha Ind Pk Dr Grand Rapids (49508) ***(G-6728)***
Furniture Partners LLC 616 355-3051
199 E 17th St Holland (49423) ***(G-8044)***
Fusion Design Group Ltd 269 469-8226
30 N Brton St New Bffalo New Buffalo (49117) ***(G-12023)***
Fusion Flexo LLC (PA) 269 685-5827
6330 Canterwood Dr Richland (49083) ***(G-13825)***
Fusion Flexo LLC 269 685-5827
156 10th St Plainwell (49080) ***(G-13077)***
Fusion Mfg Solutions LLC 734 224-7216
7193 Sulier Dr Temperance (48182) ***(G-16532)***
Futuramic Tool & Engrg Co (PA) 586 758-2200
24680 Gibson D Warren (48089) ***(G-17819)***
Future Industries Inc 616 844-0772
1729 Airpark Dr Grand Haven (49417) ***(G-6299)***
Future Mill Inc 586 754-8088
25450 Ryan Rd Warren (48091) ***(G-17820)***
Future Mold Corporation 989 588-9948
215 S Webber St Farwell (48622) ***(G-5423)***
Future Reproductions Inc 248 350-2060
21477 Bridge St Ste L Southfield (48033) ***(G-15571)***
Future Tool and Machine Inc 734 946-2100
28900 Goddard Rd Romulus (48174) ***(G-14277)***
Future Vision, Saginaw *Also called Michigan Satellite* ***(G-14698)***
Futuris Automotive, Oak Park *Also called Futuris Global Holdings LLC* ***(G-12615)***
Futuris Automotive, Madison Heights *Also called Cni Enterprises Inc* ***(G-10691)***
Futuris Automotive, Madison Heights *Also called Cni-Owosso LLC* ***(G-10692)***
Futuris Automotive, Charlotte *Also called Cni Plastics LLC* ***(G-2744)***
Futuris Automotive (ca) LLC 510 771-2300
49200 Halyard Dr Plymouth (48170) ***(G-13172)***
Futuris Automotive (us) Inc (HQ) 248 439-7800
14925 W 11 Mile Rd Oak Park (48237) ***(G-12614)***
Futuris Global Holdings LLC (HQ) 248 439-7800
14925 W 11 Mile Rd Oak Park (48237) ***(G-12615)***
Futuristic Artwear Inc 248 680-0200
787 Majestic Rochester Hills (48306) ***(G-14018)***
Futuristic Furnishings, Farmington Hills *Also called Millennm-The Inside Sltion Inc* ***(G-5323)***
Fuzen Software Inc 248 504-6870
22260 Haggerty Rd Ste 285 Northville (48167) ***(G-12221)***
Fuzzybutz 269 983-9663
306 State St Ste A Saint Joseph (49085) ***(G-14931)***
Fw Shoring Company (PA) 517 676-8800
685 Hull Rd Mason (48854) ***(G-11133)***
Fwi Inc 231 798-8324
6230 Norton Center Dr Norton Shores (49441) ***(G-12294)***
Fxi Novi 248 994-0630
28700 Cabot Dr Novi (48377) ***(G-12421)***
Fyke Washed Sand Gravel 248 547-4714
3500 11 Mile Rd Ste D Berkley (48072) ***(G-1626)***
Fzb Technology, Plymouth *Also called Dare Auto Inc* ***(G-13152)***
G & C Carports 616 678-4308
1324 17 Mile Rd Kent City (49330) ***(G-9431)***
G & D Wood Products Inc 517 254-4463
12860 Hillsdale Rd Camden (49232) ***(G-2422)***
G & F Tool Products 517 663-3646
7127 E 5 Point Hwy Eaton Rapids (48827) ***(G-4964)***
G & G Die and Engineering Inc 586 716-8099
6091 Corporate Dr Ira (48023) ***(G-8697)***
G & G Metal Products Inc 248 625-8099
9575 Rattalee Lake Rd Clarkston (48348) ***(G-3036)***
G & G Steel Fabricating Co 586 979-4112
31154 Dequindre Rd Warren (48092) ***(G-17821)***
G & G Wood & Supply Inc 586 293-0450
29920 Little Mack Ave Roseville (48066) ***(G-14408)***
G & H Producers, Midland *Also called Oil City Venture Inc* ***(G-11399)***

G & L Mfg Inc 810 724-4101
2 Mountain Dr Imlay City (48444) *(G-8632)*
G & L Powerup Inc 586 200-2169
31044 Gratiot Ave Roseville (48066) *(G-14409)*
G & L Tool Inc 734 728-1990
5874 E Executive Dr Westland (48185) *(G-18372)*
G & L Tool & Die, Westland *Also called G & L Tool Inc (G-18372)*
G & R Machine Tool Inc 734 641-6560
20410 Superior Rd Taylor (48180) *(G-16420)*
G & S Logging LLC 989 876-6596
2215 Edmonds Rd Turner (48765) *(G-17463)*
G & T Industries Inc (PA) 616 452-8611
1001 76th St Sw Byron Center (49315) *(G-2271)*
G & W Display Fixtures Inc 517 369-7110
300 Mill St Bronson (49028) *(G-2112)*
G & W Machine Co 616 363-4435
2107 Merlin St Ne Grand Rapids (49525) *(G-6729)*
G A Machine Company Inc 313 836-5646
8851 Mark Twain St Detroit (48228) *(G-4249)*
G A Richards Company (PA) 616 243-2800
1060 Ken O Sha Ind Pk Dr Grand Rapids (49508) *(G-6730)*
G A Richards Company 616 850-8528
701 E Savidge St Spring Lake (49456) *(G-15815)*
G and R Laser Solutions Inc 734 748-6603
42035 Addison Ave Canton (48187) *(G-2462)*
G B Wolfgram and Sons Inc 231 238-4638
6083 River St Indian River (49749) *(G-8652)*
G Defense Company B 616 202-4500
823 Ottawa Ave Nw Grand Rapids (49503) *(G-6731)*
G F Inc 231 946-5330
1032 Woodmere Ave Ste B Traverse City (49686) *(G-16691)*
G G & D Inc 248 623-1212
5911 Dixie Hwy Clarkston (48346) *(G-3037)*
G I, Jackson *Also called Great Lakes Industry Inc (G-8895)*
G L Nelson Inc 630 682-5958
290 Patrick Dr Indian River (49749) *(G-8653)*
G M Paris Bakery Inc 734 425-2060
28418 Joy Rd Livonia (48150) *(G-10217)*
G M S, Coldwater *Also called Groholski Mfg Solutions LLC (G-3436)*
G P Dura 248 299-7500
2791 Research Dr Rochester Hills (48309) *(G-14019)*
G P Manufacturing Inc 269 695-1202
16689 Bakertown Rd Buchanan (49107) *(G-2194)*
G P Reeves Inc 616 399-8893
4551 Holland Ave Holland (49424) *(G-8045)*
G P Technologies, Sterling Heights *Also called Genix LLC (G-16029)*
G P Woodworking L L C 313 600-9414
2382 Woodvale Trl Brighton (48114) *(G-1995)*
G S I, Grand Rapids *Also called Graphic Specialties Inc (G-6783)*
G T Gundrilling Inc 586 992-3301
51195 Regency Center Dr Macomb (48042) *(G-10598)*
G T Jerseys LLC 248 588-3231
997 Rochester Rd Ste C Troy (48083) *(G-17124)*
G Tech Sales LLC 586 803-9393
6601 Burroughs Ave Sterling Heights (48314) *(G-16026)*
G W I Engineering Division, Grand Rapids *Also called New 9 Inc (G-7040)*
G&G Industries Inc 586 726-6000
50665 Corporate Dr Shelby Township (48315) *(G-15229)*
G&J Products & Services 734 522-2984
8219 Roselawn St Westland (48185) *(G-18373)*
G-E-M, White Lake *Also called Generl-Lctrical-Mechanical Inc (G-18456)*
G-Force Tooling LLC (PA) 517 541-2747
1325 Island Hwy Charlotte (48813) *(G-2757)*
G-M Graphics, Newaygo *Also called G-M Wood Products Inc (G-12081)*
G-M Wood Products Inc (PA) 231 652-2201
531 S Clay St Newaygo (49337) *(G-12081)*
G. A. Rchards - Corlett Turner, Grand Rapids *Also called Corlett-Turner Co (G-6607)*
G.A. Rchrds Indstrial Oprtions, Norton Shores *Also called Burnside Industries LLC (G-12347)*
G5 Outdoors LLC (PA) 866 456-8836
34775 Potter St Memphis (48041) *(G-11212)*
GA Dalbeck Logging LLC 906 364-3300
205 N County Road 519 Wakefield (49968) *(G-17622)*
Gabriel Ride Control LLC 248 247-7600
39300 Country Club Dr Farmington Hills (48331) *(G-5248)*
Gac 269 639-3010
1301 M 43 South Haven (49090) *(G-15406)*
Gaco Sourcing LLC 248 633-2656
2254 Cole St Birmingham (48009) *(G-1728)*
Gadget Factory LLC 517 449-1444
5157 Aurelius Rd Lansing (48911) *(G-9840)*
Gaffey & Associates, Holt *Also called Shayleslie Corporation (G-8332)*
Gage Bilt Inc 586 226-1500
44766 Centre Ct Clinton Township (48038) *(G-3247)*
Gage Company 269 965-4279
4550 Wayne Rd Springfield (49037) *(G-15865)*
Gage Corporation (PA) 248 541-3824
821 Wanda St Ste 1 Ferndale (48220) *(G-5555)*
Gage Eagle Spline Inc 586 776-7240
2357 E 9 Mile Rd Warren (48091) *(G-17822)*
Gage Global Services Inc (PA) 248 541-3824
821 Wanda St Ste 2 Ferndale (48220) *(G-5556)*
Gage Numerical Inc 231 328-4426
900 S 7 Mile Rd Lake City (49651) *(G-9546)*
Gage Pattern & Model Inc 248 361-6609
32070 Townley St Madison Heights (48071) *(G-10729)*
Gage Printing, Springfield *Also called Gage Company (G-15865)*
Gage Products Company, Ferndale *Also called Gage Global Services Inc (G-5556)*
Gage Products Company 248 541-3824
625 Wanda St Ferndale (48220) *(G-5557)*
Gage Rite Products Inc 248 588-7796
356 Executive Dr Troy (48083) *(G-17125)*
Gags and Games Inc (HQ) 734 591-1717
35901 Veronica St Livonia (48150) *(G-10218)*
Gainors Meat Packing Inc 989 269-8161
317 N Port Crescent St Bad Axe (48413) *(G-1101)*
Gaishin Manufacturing 269 459-6996
330 W Mosel Ave Kalamazoo (49004) *(G-9191)*
Gaishin Manufacturing Inc 269 934-9340
240 Urbandale Ave Benton Harbor (49022) *(G-1550)*
GAL Gage Co 269 465-5750
2953 Hinchman Rd Bridgman (49106) *(G-1926)*
Galaxy Pipe Tobacco, Sterling Heights *Also called Cloud 9 Pipe Tobacco Inc (G-15962)*
Galco Industrial Elec Inc 248 542-9090
1001 Lincoln St Madison Heights (48071) *(G-10730)*
Gale Briggs Inc (PA) 517 543-1320
311 State St Charlotte (48813) *(G-2758)*
Gallagher Fire Equipment Co 248 477-1540
30895 8 Mile Rd Livonia (48152) *(G-10219)*
Gallagher-Kaiser Corporation (PA) 313 368-3100
777 Chicago Rd Ste 1 Troy (48083) *(G-17126)*
Gallant Inc 616 772-1880
600 E Riley St Zeeland (49464) *(G-19023)*
Gambles Redi-Mix Inc 989 539-6460
1415 N Clare Ave Harrison (48625) *(G-7677)*
Gamco Inc 269 683-4280
3001 S 11th St Niles (49120) *(G-12132)*
Gampco, Hillsdale *Also called General Automatic Mch Pdts Co (G-7936)*
Gan Systems Corp 248 609-7643
2723 S State St Ste 150 Ann Arbor (48104) *(G-494)*
Ganas LLC 313 646-9966
7400 E Davison St Detroit (48212) *(G-4250)*
Gannett National Newspaper Sls, Troy *Also called Indiana Newspapers LLC (G-17164)*
Gannett Stllite Info Ntwrk Inc 734 229-1150
601 Rogell Dr Detroit (48242) *(G-4251)*
Gannons General Contract 734 429-5859
9216 Yorkshire Dr Saline (48176) *(G-15018)*
Gantec Inc 989 631-9300
777 E Isabella Rd Midland (48640) *(G-11367)*
Gap, Romulus *Also called Global Automotive Products Inc (G-14278)*
Gar-Ber, Novi *Also called General Filters Inc (G-12423)*
Gar-V Manufacturing Inc 269 279-5134
1111 River St Three Rivers (49093) *(G-16574)*
Garage Grus Fdrl-Mgul Mtrparts 800 325-8886
24477 W 10 Mile Rd Southfield (48033) *(G-15572)*
Garants Office Sups & Prtg Inc 989 356-3930
117 W Washington Ave Alpena (49707) *(G-296)*
Garbage Man LLC 810 225-3001
5441 Ethel St Brighton (48116) *(G-1996)*
Garbarino Industries LLC 586 215-5479
24100 Capital Blvd Clinton Township (48036) *(G-3248)*
Garcia Company 248 459-0952
10255 Fish Lake Rd Holly (48442) *(G-8270)*
Garden City Products Inc 269 684-6264
833 Carberry Rd Niles (49120) *(G-12133)*
Garden Fresh Gourmet LLC (HQ) 866 725-7239
1220 E 9 Mile Rd Ferndale (48220) *(G-5558)*
Garden of Edyn 517 410-9931
4075 Holt Rd Lot 248 Holt (48842) *(G-8313)*
Gardner Denver Mp Pumps, Fraser *Also called M P Pumps Inc (G-5959)*
Gardner Signs Inc 248 689-9100
1087 Naughton Dr Troy (48083) *(G-17127)*
Garneau Baits LLC 616 676-0186
9575 Conservation St Ne Ada (49301) *(G-18)*
Garrett Motion Inc (PA) 734 359-5901
47548 Halyard Dr Plymouth (48170) *(G-13173)*
Garrisons Hitch Center Inc 810 239-5728
1050 Meida St Flint (48532) *(G-5703)*
Gary Cork Incorporated (PA) 231 946-1061
806 S Garfield Ave Ste B Traverse City (49686) *(G-16692)*
Gary L Melchi Inc 810 231-0262
11275 Merrill Rd Whitmore Lake (48189) *(G-18537)*
Gary Nankervis Logging 906 524-7735
14210 Bayview Dr Lanse (49946) *(G-9660)*
Gary's Custom Meat Processing, Union *Also called Garys Custom Meats (G-17487)*
Garys Custom Meats 269 641-5683
16237 Mason St Union (49130) *(G-17487)*

ALPHABETIC

(PA)=Parent Co (HQ)=Headquarters (DH)=Div Headquarters
2022 Harris Michigan
Industrial Directory
999

Garys Polishing 810 621-4137
10720 E Lennon Rd Lennon (48449) ***(G-9994)***
Gas Control Systems, Sparta *Also called Storage Control Systems Inc* ***(G-15783)***
Gas Recovery Systems LLC 248 305-7774
10611 5 Mile Rd Northville (48168) ***(G-12222)***
Gasbarre Products Inc 734 425-5165
12953 Farmington Rd Livonia (48150) ***(G-10220)***
Gasket Holdings Inc 248 354-7700
26555 Northwestern Hwy Southfield (48033) ***(G-15573)***
Gast Cabinet Co 269 422-1587
8836 Stvnsvlle Broda Rd L Baroda (49101) ***(G-1162)***
Gast Manufacturing Inc (HQ) 269 926-6171
2300 M 139 Benton Harbor (49022) ***(G-1551)***
Gast Manufacturing Inc 269 926-6171
2550 Meadowbrook Rd Benton Harbor (49022) ***(G-1552)***
Gatco Incorporated 734 453-2295
42330 Ann Arbor Rd E Plymouth (48170) ***(G-13174)***
Gatehouse Media LLC 517 265-5111
133 N Winter St Adrian (49221) ***(G-69)***
Gatehouse Media LLC 269 651-5407
209 John St Sturgis (49091) ***(G-16288)***
Gatehouse Publishing, Coldwater *Also called Daily Reporter* ***(G-3430)***
Gates Corporation 248 260-2300
2975 Waterview Dr Rochester Hills (48309) ***(G-14020)***
Gateway Engineering Inc 616 284-1425
6534 Clay Ave Sw Grand Rapids (49548) ***(G-6732)***
Gatherall Bindery Inc 248 669-6850
15085 E 11 Mile Rd Roseville (48066) ***(G-14410)***
Gatherall Bindery Inc 248 669-6850
15085 E 11 Mile Rd Roseville (48066) ***(G-14411)***
Gathering Place of White Lake 248 379-9582
825 Oxbow Lake Rd White Lake (48386) ***(G-18455)***
Gator Grafix & Signs 269 362-2039
13747 N Red Bud Trl Buchanan (49107) ***(G-2195)***
Gaty 313 381-2853
8989 Fox Ave Allen Park (48101) ***(G-195)***
Gaus 517 764-6178
3123 Catalpa Dr Jackson (49203) ***(G-8889)***
Gayles Chocolates Limited 248 398-0001
417 S Washington Ave Royal Oak (48067) ***(G-14539)***
Gaylord Mch & Fabrication LLC 989 732-0817
2758 Dickerson Rd Gaylord (49735) ***(G-6130)***
Gazelle Prototype LLC 616 844-1820
18683 Trimble Ct Spring Lake (49456) ***(G-15816)***
Gazelle Publishing 734 529-2688
112 Park Pl Ste 3 Dundee (48131) ***(G-4821)***
Gazette Newspapers Inc 248 524-4868
6966 Crooks Rd Ste 22 Troy (48098) ***(G-17128)***
Gb Dynamics Inc 313 400-3570
1620 Kearney St Port Huron (48060) ***(G-13479)***
Gb Sportz 734 604-8919
5277 Jackson Rd Ann Arbor (48103) ***(G-495)***
Gbl Group The, Southfield *Also called George Brown Legacy Group* ***(G-15574)***
Gc Boring Inc 313 937-2320
12570 Inkster Rd Redford (48239) ***(G-13736)***
Gch Machinery Division, Warren *Also called Grinders Clearinghouse Inc* ***(G-17840)***
Gch Tool Group Inc 586 777-6250
13265 E 8 Mile Rd Warren (48089) ***(G-17823)***
GCI, Coldwater *Also called Gokoh Coldwater Incorporated* ***(G-3434)***
GCI Water Solutions LLC 312 928-9992
5202 Dale St Midland (48642) ***(G-11368)***
Gd Enterprises LLC 248 486-9800
7974 Lochlin Dr Ste B4 Brighton (48116) ***(G-1997)***
Gd Enterprises LLC 248 207-1366
6496 Milford Rd Holly (48442) ***(G-8271)***
Gdc Worldwide 248 348-4189
9833 5 Mile Rd Northville (48168) ***(G-12223)***
GE Aviation, Muskegon *Also called Johnson Technology Inc* ***(G-11846)***
GE Aviation Muskegon, Muskegon *Also called Johnson Technology Inc* ***(G-11847)***
GE Aviation Systems LLC 616 241-7000
3290 Patterson Ave Se Grand Rapids (49512) ***(G-6733)***
GE Aviation Systems LLC 616 224-6480
3290 Patterson Ave Se Grand Rapids (49512) ***(G-6734)***
GE Edison Works, Grand Rapids *Also called GE Aviation Systems LLC* ***(G-6734)***
Gear Gear Inc 517 861-7757
129 Bell St Ypsilanti (48197) ***(G-18949)***
Gear Master Inc 810 798-9254
7481 Research Dr Almont (48003) ***(G-260)***
Geartec Inc 810 987-4700
1105 24th St Port Huron (48060) ***(G-13480)***
Geckobrands LLC 561 704-8400
2950 Prrie St Sw Ste 1000 Grandville (49418) ***(G-7378)***
Gedia Michigan LLC 248 392-9090
269 Kay Industrial Dr Orion (48359) ***(G-12730)***
Gedia Michigan LLC (PA) 248 392-9090
315 W Silverbell Rd # 180 Lake Orion (48359) ***(G-9605)***
Gee & Missler Inc 734 284-1224
744 Vinewood St Wyandotte (48192) ***(G-18820)***
Geeks and Gurus Inc 313 549-2796
24305 Broadview St Farmington Hills (48336) ***(G-5249)***
Geeks of Detroit LLC 734 576-2363
282 Newport St Ste 1a Detroit (48215) ***(G-4252)***
Geelhoed Performance 616 837-6666
2400 Turner Ave Nw Ste E Grand Rapids (49544) ***(G-6735)***
Geerpres Inc 231 773-3211
1780 Harvey St Muskegon (49442) ***(G-11823)***
Gehring Corporation 248 478-8060
24800 Drake Rd Farmington Hills (48335) ***(G-5250)***
Gehring Honing Machs 248 478-8061
24800 Drake Rd Farmington Hills (48335) ***(G-5251)***
Geiger EDM Inc 517 369-9752
898 W Chicago Rd Bronson (49028) ***(G-2113)***
Geisler Company 313 255-1450
30295 Schoolcraft Rd Livonia (48150) ***(G-10221)***
Geislinger Corporation 269 441-7000
200 Geislinger Dr Battle Creek (49037) ***(G-1234)***
Gelman Sciences Inc 734 665-0651
674 S Wagner Rd Ann Arbor (48103) ***(G-496)***
Gem Asset Acquisition LLC 248 338-0335
2280 Auburn Rd Auburn Hills (48326) ***(G-906)***
Gem Gallery, Ann Arbor *Also called Abracadabra Jewelry* ***(G-345)***
Gem Industries & Fold A Cover, Caledonia *Also called Gem Industries Inc* ***(G-2374)***
Gem Industries Inc 616 656-9779
4045 Korona Ct Se Caledonia (49316) ***(G-2374)***
Gem Plastics Inc 616 538-5966
2533 Thornwood St Sw Grand Rapids (49519) ***(G-6736)***
Gema, Dundee *Also called Global Engine Mfg Aliance LLC* ***(G-4822)***
Gemini Corporation 616 459-4545
401 Hall St Sw Ste 331a Grand Rapids (49503) ***(G-6737)***
Gemini Group Inc (PA) 989 269-6272
175 Thompson Rd Ste A Bad Axe (48413) ***(G-1102)***
Gemini Group ME & T 989 553-5685
727 Skinner St Bad Axe (48413) ***(G-1103)***
Gemini Group Services Inc 248 435-7271
175 Thompson Rd Ste A Bad Axe (48413) ***(G-1104)***
Gemini Plastics, Ubly *Also called Pepro Enterprises Inc* ***(G-17480)***
Gemini Plastics, Clawson *Also called Pepro Enterprises Inc* ***(G-3103)***
Gemini Plastics Inc 989 658-8557
4385 Garfield St Ubly (48475) ***(G-17476)***
Gemini Plastics De Mexico Inc 989 658-8557
4385 Garfield St Ubly (48475) ***(G-17477)***
Gemini Precision Machining Inc (HQ) 989 269-9702
700 E Soper Rd Bad Axe (48413) ***(G-1105)***
Gemini Publications, Grand Rapids *Also called Gemini Corporation* ***(G-6737)***
Gemo Hopkins Usa Inc 734 330-1271
2900 Auburn Ct Auburn Hills (48326) ***(G-907)***
Gemseal Pvement Pdts - Detroit, Auburn Hills *Also called Gem Asset Acquisition LLC* ***(G-906)***
Gen3 Defense and Aerospace LLC 616 345-8031
285 Dodge Ct Ste E Comstock Park (49321) ***(G-3607)***
Genco Alliance LLC 269 216-5500
630 Gibson St Kalamazoo (49007) ***(G-9192)***
Gene Brow & Sons Inc 906 635-0859
2754 W 20th St Sault Sainte Marie (49783) ***(G-15090)***
Gene Codes Forensics Inc 734 769-7249
525 Avis Dr Ste 8 Ann Arbor (48108) ***(G-497)***
Genentech Inc 650 225-1000
362 Kirksway Ln Lake Orion (48362) ***(G-9606)***
General Aire 866 476-5101
43800 Grand River Ave Novi (48375) ***(G-12422)***
General Automatic Mch Pdts Co 517 437-6000
266 Industrial Dr Hillsdale (49242) ***(G-7936)***
General Broach & Engrg Inc 586 726-4300
5750 New King Dr Ste 200 Troy (48098) ***(G-17129)***
General Broach Company (HQ) 517 458-7555
307 Salisbury St Morenci (49256) ***(G-11611)***
General Broach Company 517 458-7555
555 W Main St Ste C Morenci (49256) ***(G-11612)***
General Chemical Corporation 248 587-5600
12336 Emerson Dr Brighton (48116) ***(G-1998)***
General Coach America Inc (HQ) 810 724-6474
275 Graham Rd Imlay City (48444) ***(G-8633)***
General Die & Engineering Inc (PA) 616 698-6961
6500 Clay Ave Sw Grand Rapids (49548) ***(G-6738)***
General Dynamics Corporation 615 427-5768
25435 Brest Taylor (48180) ***(G-16421)***
General Dynamics Mission 530 271-2500
2909 Waterview Dr Rochester Hills (48309) ***(G-14021)***
General Dynmics Advnced Info S, Ypsilanti *Also called General Dynmics Mssion Systems* ***(G-18951)***
General Dynmics Globl Imging T (HQ) 248 293-2929
2909 Waterview Dr Rochester Hills (48309) ***(G-14022)***
General Dynmics Mssion Systems 734 480-5000
1200 Joe Hall Dr Ypsilanti (48197) ***(G-18950)***
General Dynmics Mssion Systems 734 480-5000
1200 Joe Hall Dr Ypsilanti (48197) ***(G-18951)***

ALPHABETIC SECTION George Koch Sons LLC

General Electric Company 734 728-1472
38303 Michigan Ave Wayne (48184) ***(G-18221)***
General Electric Company 734 727-4619
1 Village Center Dr Wayne (48184) ***(G-18222)***
General Electric Company 616 676-0870
7575 Fulton St E 74-1a Ada (49355) ***(G-19)***
General Filters Inc (PA) 248 476-5100
43800 Grand River Ave Novi (48375) ***(G-12423)***
General Formulations, Sparta *Also called Celia Corporation* ***(G-15763)***
General Hardwood Co, Detroit *Also called Northern Millwork Co* ***(G-4490)***
General Hardwood Company (PA) 313 365-7733
7201 E Mcnichols Rd Detroit (48212) ***(G-4253)***
General Inspection LLC 248 625-0529
10585 Enterprise Dr Davisburg (48350) ***(G-3769)***
General Machine & Boring Inc 810 220-1203
5983 Ford Ct Brighton (48116) ***(G-1999)***
General Machine Service Inc 989 752-5161
494 E Morley Dr Saginaw (48601) ***(G-14649)***
General Machine Services 269 695-2244
807 W 4th St Buchanan (49107) ***(G-2196)***
General Media LLC 586 541-0075
24114 Harper Ave Saint Clair Shores (48080) ***(G-14862)***
General Mill Supply Company 248 668-0800
50690 General Mill Dr Wixom (48393) ***(G-18667)***
General Mills Inc 231 832-3285
128 E Slosson Ave Reed City (49677) ***(G-13790)***
General Mills Inc 763 764-7600
6805 Beatrice Dr Kalamazoo (49009) ***(G-9193)***
General Mills Inc 269 337-0288
3800 Midlink Dr Kalamazoo (49048) ***(G-9194)***
General Motors China LLC (HQ) 313 556-5000
300 Renaissance Ctr L1 Detroit (48243) ***(G-4254)***
General Motors Company 248 249-6347
20001 Brownstown Ctr Dr Brownstown (48183) ***(G-2147)***
General Motors Company 989 757-1576
1629 N Washington Ave Saginaw (48601) ***(G-14650)***
General Motors Company 586 218-9240
7015 Edward Cole Blvd Warren (48093) ***(G-17824)***
General Motors Company (PA) 313 667-1500
300 Renaissance Ctr L1 Detroit (48243) ***(G-4255)***
General Motors Holdings LLC (HQ) 313 667-1500
300 Renaissance Ctr L1 Detroit (48243) ***(G-4256)***
General Motors LLC 810 234-2710
G-2238 W Bristol Rd Flint (48553) ***(G-5704)***
General Motors LLC 989 894-7210
1001 Woodside Ave Bay City (48708) ***(G-1359)***
General Motors LLC 989 757-0528
3900 N Towerline Rd Saginaw (48601) ***(G-14651)***
General Motors LLC 810 234-2710
2238 W Bristol Rd Flint (48507) ***(G-5705)***
General Motors LLC 586 342-2728
6200 19 Mile Rd Sterling Heights (48314) ***(G-16027)***
General Motors LLC 517 885-6669
4400 W Mount Hope Hwy Lansing (48917) ***(G-9761)***
General Motors LLC 810 635-5281
6060 W Bristol Rd Swartz Creek (48473) ***(G-16354)***
General Motors LLC 586 441-8483
28720 Lorna Ave Warren (48092) ***(G-17825)***
General Motors LLC 734 481-3555
50000 Ecorse Rd Van Buren Twp (48111) ***(G-17526)***
General Motors LLC 313 408-3987
3000 University Dr Fl 2 Auburn Hills (48326) ***(G-908)***
General Motors LLC 313 972-6000
2500 E Grand Blvd Detroit (48211) ***(G-4257)***
General Motors LLC 810 236-1970
425 S Stevenson St Flint (48503) ***(G-5706)***
General Motors LLC 248 874-1737
895 Joslyn Ave Pontiac (48340) ***(G-13374)***
General Motors LLC (HQ) 313 665-4919
300 Renaissance Ctr L1 Detroit (48243) ***(G-4258)***
General Motors LLC 313 972-6000
2500 E Grand Blvd Detroit (48211) ***(G-4259)***
General Motors LLC 248 857-3500
1251 Joslyn Ave Pontiac (48340) ***(G-13375)***
General Motors LLC 313 556-5000
2500 E Grand Motors Blvd Detroit (48211) ***(G-4260)***
General Mtrs Cmpnents Holdings, Detroit *Also called GM Components Holdings LLC* ***(G-4265)***
General Parts Inc 989 686-3114
3616 Wilder Rd Bay City (48706) ***(G-1360)***
General Plymers Thrmplstic Mtl 800 920-8033
6841 N Rochester Rd Stdio1 Rochester Hills (48306) ***(G-14023)***
General Processing Systems Inc 630 554-7804
12838 Stainless Dr Holland (49424) ***(G-8046)***
General Scientific Corporation 734 996-9200
77 Enterprise Dr Ann Arbor (48103) ***(G-498)***
General Structures Inc 586 774-6105
23171 Groesbeck Hwy Warren (48089) ***(G-17826)***
General Tactical Vehicles LLC 586 825-7242
38500 Mound Rd Sterling Heights (48310) ***(G-16028)***
General Tape Label Liquidating 248 437-5200
28505 Automation Blvd Wixom (48393) ***(G-18668)***
General Technology Inc 269 751-7516
4521 48th St Holland (49423) ***(G-8047)***
Generation Press Inc 616 392-4405
10861 Paw Paw Dr Holland (49424) ***(G-8048)***
Generation Tool Inc 734 641-6937
307 Manufacturers Dr Westland (48186) ***(G-18374)***
Generl-Lctrical-Mechanical Inc 248 698-1110
10415 Highland Rd White Lake (48386) ***(G-18456)***
Genesee County Herald Inc 810 686-3840
10098 N Dort Hwy Clio (48420) ***(G-3399)***
Genesee Cut Stone & Marble Co (PA) 810 743-1800
5276 S Saginaw Rd Grand Blanc (48507) ***(G-6242)***
Genesee Group Inc 810 235-6120
1102 N Averill Ave Flint (48506) ***(G-5707)***
Genesee Packaging, Flint *Also called Genesee Group Inc* ***(G-5707)***
Genesee Valley Vault Inc 810 629-3909
10510 N Holly Rd Holly (48442) ***(G-8272)***
Genesis Casket Company, Mason *Also called Genesis International LLC* ***(G-11134)***
Genesis Graphics Inc 906 786-4913
1823 7th Ave N Ste 7 Escanaba (49829) ***(G-5072)***
Genesis Innovation Group LLC 616 294-1026
13827 Port Sheldon St Holland (49424) ***(G-8049)***
Genesis International LLC 317 777-6700
200 E Kipp Rd Mason (48854) ***(G-11134)***
Genesis Sand and Gravel Inc 313 587-8530
6689 Orchard Lake Rd # 219 West Bloomfield (48322) ***(G-18283)***
Genesis Seating Inc (HQ) 616 954-1040
3445 East Paris Ave Se Grand Rapids (49512) ***(G-6739)***
Genesis Seating 0519, Grand Rapids *Also called Genesis Seating Inc* ***(G-6739)***
Genesis Service Associates LLC 734 994-3900
3255 Central St Apt 1 Dexter (48130) ***(G-4742)***
Genex Window Inc 586 754-2917
23110 Sherwood Ave Warren (48091) ***(G-17827)***
Genix LLC 248 761-3030
3151 Walnut Lake Rd West Bloomfield (48323) ***(G-18284)***
Genix LLC (PA) 248 419-0231
43665 Utica Rd Sterling Heights (48314) ***(G-16029)***
Genoak Materials Inc (PA) 248 634-8276
14300 Shields Rd Holly (48442) ***(G-8273)***
Genomeweb, Detroit *Also called Crain Communications Inc* ***(G-4106)***
Genomic Diagnostics Na Inc 734 730-8399
2890 Carptr Rd Ste 2000 Ann Arbor (48108) ***(G-499)***
Genova-Minnesota Inc 810 744-4500
7034 E Court St Davison (48423) ***(G-3784)***
Genstone LLC 517 902-4730
1273 Evergreen Trl Adrian (49221) ***(G-70)***
Gentex Corporation (PA) 616 772-1800
600 N Centennial St Zeeland (49464) ***(G-19024)***
Gentex Corporation 616 772-1800
9001 Riley St Zeeland (49464) ***(G-19025)***
Gentex Corporation 616 772-1800
58 E Riley St Zeeland (49464) ***(G-19026)***
Gentex Corporation 616 772-1800
675 N State St Zeeland (49464) ***(G-19027)***
Gentex Corporation 616 392-7195
10985 Chicago Dr Zeeland (49464) ***(G-19028)***
Gentex Corporation 616 772-1800
310 E Riley St Zeeland (49464) ***(G-19029)***
Gentherm Incorporated (PA) 248 504-0500
21680 Haggerty Rd Ste 101 Northville (48167) ***(G-12224)***
Gentile Packaging Machinery Co 734 429-1177
8300 Boettner Rd Saline (48176) ***(G-15019)***
Gentle Machine Tool & Die 734 699-2013
13600 Martinsville Rd Van Buren Twp (48111) ***(G-17527)***
Gentleman, Detroit *Also called Former Company LLC* ***(G-4244)***
Gentry Services of Alabama 248 321-6368
31943 Red Run Dr Warren (48093) ***(G-17828)***
Gentz Aero, Warren *Also called MB Aerospace Warren LLC* ***(G-17920)***
Gentz Industry 586 772-2501
14132 E 10 Mile Rd Warren (48089) ***(G-17829)***
Genus Inc 810 580-9197
767 Grand Marais St Grosse Pointe Park (48230) ***(G-7555)***
Genx Corporation 269 341-4242
2911 Emerald Dr Kalamazoo (49001) ***(G-9195)***
Geofabrica Inc 810 728-2468
2900 Auburn Ct Auburn Hills (48326) ***(G-909)***
Geoffrey Manufacturing Inc 734 479-4030
20080 Trentwood Ct Brownstown Twp (48183) ***(G-2154)***
Geolean USA LLC 313 859-9780
11998 Merriman Rd Livonia (48150) ***(G-10222)***
Geomembrane Research 231 943-2266
1567 W South Airport Rd Traverse City (49686) ***(G-16693)***
George Brown Legacy Group 313 770-9928
23375 Riverside Dr Southfield (48033) ***(G-15574)***
George Instrument Company (PA) 248 280-1111
220 Engelwood Dr Ste D Orion (48359) ***(G-12731)***
George Koch Sons LLC 248 237-1100
2745 Bond St Rochester Hills (48309) ***(G-14024)***

ALPHABETIC

George Moses Co.....810 227-1575
110 E North St Brighton (48116) ***(G-2000)***
George P Johnson Company (HQ).....248 475-2500
3600 Giddings Rd Auburn Hills (48326) ***(G-910)***
George W Trapp Co (PA).....313 531-7180
15000 Fox Redford (48239) ***(G-13737)***
George Washburn.....269 694-2930
515 S Wilmott St Otsego (49078) ***(G-12786)***
Georgia-Pacific LLC.....734 439-2441
951 County St Milan (48160) ***(G-11436)***
Georgia-Pacific LLC.....989 725-5191
465 S Delaney Rd Owosso (48867) ***(G-12835)***
Georgia-Pacific LLC.....989 348-7275
4113 W 4 Mile Rd Grayling (49738) ***(G-7461)***
Geotech Environmental Eqp Inc.....517 655-5616
1099 W Grnd Riv 6 Williamston (48895) ***(G-18572)***
Gerald Harris.....985 774-0261
14846 Dexter Ave Detroit (48238) ***(G-4261)***
Gerber Products Company.....231 928-2076
405 State St Fremont (49412) ***(G-6042)***
Gerber Products Company.....231 928-2000
445 State St Fremont (49413) ***(G-6043)***
Gerbers Home Made Sweets.....231 348-3743
8218 Pincherry Rd Charlevoix (49720) ***(G-2715)***
Gerdau Macsteel Inc.....517 764-0311
3100 Brooklyn Rd Jackson (49203) ***(G-8890)***
Gerdau Macsteel Inc.....734 243-2446
3000 E Front St Monroe (48161) ***(G-11542)***
Gerdau Macsteel Inc.....734 243-2446
3000 E Front St Monroe (48161) ***(G-11543)***
Gerdau Macsteel Inc (HQ).....517 782-0415
5591 Morrill Rd Jackson (49201) ***(G-8891)***
Gerdau McSteel Atmsphere Annli (HQ).....517 782-0415
209 W Mount Hope Ave # 1 Lansing (48910) ***(G-9841)***
Gerdau McSteel Atmsphere Annli.....517 482-1374
1801 Bassett St Lansing (48915) ***(G-9842)***
Gerdau Special Steel N Amer, Monroe *Also called Gerdau Macsteel Inc* ***(G-11542)***
Germack Nut Co, Detroit *Also called Nutco Inc* ***(G-4494)***
German/American Newspaper Age, Warren *Also called Wochen-Post* ***(G-18069)***
Gerref Industries Inc.....616 794-3110
206 N York St Belding (48809) ***(G-1450)***
Gestamp Alabama LLC.....810 245-3100
100 E Fair St Lapeer (48446) ***(G-9931)***
Gestamp Mason LLC.....517 244-8800
200 E Kipp Rd Mason (48854) ***(G-11135)***
Gestamp North America Inc (HQ).....248 743-3400
2701 Troy Center Dr # 150 Troy (48084) ***(G-17130)***
Gestamp North America Plant, Lapeer *Also called Gestamp Alabama LLC* ***(G-9931)***
Gestamp Washtenaw LLC.....734 593-9036
5800 Sibley Rd Chelsea (48118) ***(G-2812)***
Get Customized.....586 909-3881
3055 Crooks Rd Rochester Hills (48309) ***(G-14025)***
Get In Game Marketing LLC.....231 846-1976
2322 Cass Rd Traverse City (49684) ***(G-16694)***
Gfg Dynamation, Ann Arbor *Also called Gfg Instrumentation Inc* ***(G-500)***
Gfg Instrumentation Inc.....734 769-0573
1194 Oak Valley Dr Ste 20 Ann Arbor (48108) ***(G-500)***
Gfl Envronmental Real Property (PA).....888 877-4996
26999 Central Park Blvd # 200 Southfield (48076) ***(G-15575)***
Gfm LLC (HQ).....586 859-4587
29685 Calahan Rd Roseville (48066) ***(G-14412)***
Gh Imaging, Muskegon *Also called Graphics Hse Spt Prmotions Inc* ***(G-11828)***
Ghf Corp.....269 968-3351
2813 Wilbur St Springfield (49037) ***(G-15866)***
Ghi Electronics LLC.....248 397-8856
501 E Whitcomb Ave Madison Heights (48071) ***(G-10731)***
Ghost Island Brewery.....219 242-4800
17656 Us Highway 12 New Buffalo (49117) ***(G-12024)***
Ghs Corporation.....269 968-3351
2813 Wilbur St Springfield (49037) ***(G-15867)***
GHS Corporation (PA).....800 388-4447
2813 Wilbur St Springfield (49037) ***(G-15868)***
Ghs Strings, Springfield *Also called Ghs Corporation* ***(G-15867)***
Ghsp, Grand Haven *Also called Jsj Corporation* ***(G-6323)***
Ghsp Inc (HQ).....616 842-5500
701 S Waverly Rd Ste 100 Holland (49423) ***(G-8050)***
Ghsp Inc.....248 588-5095
1250 S Beechtree St Grand Haven (49417) ***(G-6300)***
Ghsp Inc.....231 873-3300
1500 Industrial Park Dr Hart (49420) ***(G-7752)***
Ghsp Inc.....248 581-0890
1250 S Beechtree St Grand Haven (49417) ***(G-6301)***
Ghsp Hart Plant, Hart *Also called Ghsp Inc* ***(G-7752)***
Gl Millworks Inc.....734 451-1100
14970 Cleat St Plymouth (48170) ***(G-13175)***
Gibbies Deer Processing.....231 924-6042
215 Jerrette Ave Fremont (49412) ***(G-6044)***
Gibbys Transport LLC.....269 838-2794
719 E Woodlawn Ave Hastings (49058) ***(G-7793)***
Gibraltar Inc.....616 748-4857
421 N Centennial St Zeeland (49464) ***(G-19030)***
Gibraltar National Corporation.....248 634-8257
14311 Cmi Dr Holly (48442) ***(G-8274)***
Gic LLC.....231 237-7000
12575 Us Highway 31 N Charlevoix (49720) ***(G-2716)***
Gic Thermo Dynamics, Charlevoix *Also called Gic LLC* ***(G-2716)***
Gielow Pickles Inc (PA).....810 359-7680
5260 Main St Lexington (48450) ***(G-10028)***
Gifts Engraved Inc.....248 321-8900
1526 Butternut Ave Royal Oak (48073) ***(G-14540)***
Giguere Logging Inc.....906 786-3975
3200 5th Ave S Escanaba (49829) ***(G-5073)***
Gil-Mar Manufacturing Co (PA).....248 640-4303
7925 Ronda Dr Canton (48187) ***(G-2463)***
Gil-Mar Manufacturing Co.....734 422-1925
12841 Stark Rd Livonia (48150) ***(G-10223)***
Gil-Mar Manufacturing Co.....734 459-4803
7777 Ronda Dr Canton (48187) ***(G-2464)***
Gilbert & Riplo Company, Ravenna *Also called Griptrac Inc* ***(G-13689)***
Gilbert's Chocolates, Jackson *Also called W2 Inc* ***(G-9032)***
Gilchrist Premium Lumber Pdts (PA).....989 826-8300
1284 Mapes Rd Mio (48647) ***(G-11507)***
Gildner's Concrete Products, Alpena *Also called Cheboygan Cement Products Inc* ***(G-286)***
Gill Corporation (HQ).....616 453-4491
5271 Plainfield Ave Ne Grand Rapids (49525) ***(G-6740)***
Gill Holding Company Inc (HQ).....616 559-2700
5271 Plainfield Ave Ne Grand Rapids (49525) ***(G-6741)***
Gill Industries Inc (HQ).....616 559-2700
5271 Plainfield Ave Ne Grand Rapids (49525) ***(G-6742)***
Gill Industries Inc.....616 559-2700
5271 Plainfield Ave Nw Grand Rapids (49525) ***(G-6743)***
Gill Manufacturing, Grand Rapids *Also called Gill Industries Inc* ***(G-6743)***
Gilligan Steele Tastings LLC.....269 808-3455
432 E Paterson St Kalamazoo (49007) ***(G-9196)***
Gillisons Var Fabrication Inc (PA).....231 882-5921
3033 Benzie Hwy Benzonia (49616) ***(G-1614)***
Gilmore Logistics LLC.....586 488-9895
1461 Crescent St Inkster (48141) ***(G-8664)***
Gilners Concrete, Hillman *Also called Cheboygan Cement Products Inc* ***(G-7911)***
Gilsbach Fabricating LLC.....734 379-9169
19484 Homestead Ln Gibraltar (48173) ***(G-6170)***
Ginger Tree Press.....269 779-5780
3609 Olney Rd Kalamazoo (49006) ***(G-9197)***
Ginkgotree Inc.....734 707-7191
1555 Broadway St Ste 300 Detroit (48226) ***(G-4262)***
Ginsan Liquidating Company LLC.....616 791-8100
3611 3 Mile Rd Nw Grand Rapids (49534) ***(G-6744)***
Gionl LLC.....313 957-9247
15601 Schoolcraft St Detroit (48227) ***(G-4263)***
Giovannis Apptzing Fd Pdts Inc.....773 960-1945
37775 Division Rd Richmond (48062) ***(G-13838)***
Gipson Fabrications.....616 245-7331
2151 Chicago Dr Sw Wyoming (49519) ***(G-18874)***
Gissing North America LLC (HQ).....248 647-0400
32500 Telegraph Rd Ste 20 Bingham Farms (48025) ***(G-1697)***
Give Thanks Bakery, Rochester *Also called Paladin Baking Company LLC* ***(G-13919)***
Give-Em A Brake Safety LLC.....616 531-8705
2610 Sanford Ave Sw Grandville (49418) ***(G-7379)***
Giving Press.....702 302-2039
324 E Exchange St Spring Lake (49456) ***(G-15817)***
Gj Prey Coml & Indus Pntg Cov.....248 250-4792
710 N Crooks Rd Clawson (48017) ***(G-3098)***
Gjm Property LLC.....248 592-7323
8834 E 34 Rd Ste 131 Boon (49618) ***(G-1881)***
GKN Automotive, Auburn Hills *Also called GKN Driveline North Amer Inc* ***(G-911)***
GKN Driveline North Amer Inc (HQ).....248 296-7000
2200 N Opdyke Rd Auburn Hills (48326) ***(G-911)***
GKN North America Inc.....248 296-7200
2200 N Opdyke Rd Auburn Hills (48326) ***(G-912)***
GKN North America Services Inc.....248 377-1200
3300 University Dr Auburn Hills (48326) ***(G-913)***
GKN Powder Metallurgy, Auburn Hills *Also called GKN Sinter Metals LLC* ***(G-914)***
GKN Sinter Metals LLC (HQ).....248 883-4500
1670 Opdyke Ct Auburn Hills (48326) ***(G-914)***
Gladiator Quality Sorting LLC.....734 578-1950
43220 Oakbrook Ct Canton (48187) ***(G-2465)***
Gladstone Metals, Gladstone *Also called Vanaire Inc* ***(G-6187)***
Gladstone Printing, Lansing *Also called Millbrook Press Works* ***(G-9777)***
Gladwin County Newspapers LLC.....989 426-9411
700 E Cedar Ave Gladwin (48624) ***(G-6196)***
Gladwin Machine Inc.....989 426-8753
535 S M 18 Gladwin (48624) ***(G-6197)***
Gladwin Metal Processing Inc.....989 426-9038
795 E Maple St Gladwin (48624) ***(G-6198)***
Gladwin Tank Manufacturing Inc.....989 426-4768
207 Industrial Park Ave Gladwin (48624) ***(G-6199)***
Glamour Girl Hair LLC.....313 204-4143
1300 E Lafayette St # 1103 Detroit (48207) ***(G-4264)***

Glass Recyclers Ltd 313 584-3434
  6465 Wyoming St Dearborn (48126) *(G-3846)*
Glassicart Decorative Glwr 231 739-5956
  3128 7th St Muskegon (48444) *(G-11824)*
Glassline Incorporated 734 453-2728
  199 W Ann Arbor Trl Plymouth (48170) *(G-13176)*
Glassmaster Controls Co Inc 269 382-2010
  831 Cobb Ave Kalamazoo (49007) *(G-9198)*
Glassource, Grand Haven *Also called City Auto Glass Co (G-6285)*
Glastender Inc (PA) 989 752-4275
  5400 N Michigan Rd Saginaw (48604) *(G-14652)*
Glastron LLC 800 354-3141
  925 Frisbie St Cadillac (49601) *(G-2331)*
Glaxosmithkline LLC 989 450-9859
  1331 S Dehmel Rd Frankenmuth (48734) *(G-5864)*
Glaxosmithkline LLC 989 928-6535
  875 Island Lake Dr Oxford (48371) *(G-12884)*
Glaxosmithkline LLC 989 280-1225
  2518 Abbott Rd Apt V11 Midland (48642) *(G-11369)*
Glaxosmithkline LLC 248 561-3022
  721 Parkman Dr Bloomfield Hills (48304) *(G-1822)*
Glcc Co 269 657-3167
  39149 W Red Arrow Hwy Paw Paw (49079) *(G-12948)*
Gld Holdings Inc 616 877-4288
  4560 Division Moline (49335) *(G-11518)*
Gle Solar Energy, Saint Joseph *Also called Great Lakes Electric LLC (G-14932)*
Gleason Holbrook Mfg Co 586 749-5519
  22401 28 Mile Rd Ray (48096) *(G-13699)*
Gleason Race Cars 231 882-2336
  8244 Love Rd Benzonia (49616) *(G-1615)*
Glenn Knochel 989 684-7869
  2152 E Beaver Rd Kawkawlin (48631) *(G-9415)*
Glenn Vineyards LLC 269 330-2350
  2128 62nd St Fennville (49408) *(G-5436)*
Glide Bearings & Seal Systems, Alto *Also called Mssb LLC (G-337)*
Global Advanced Products LLC 586 749-6800
  30707 Commerce Blvd Chesterfield (48051) *(G-2887)*
Global Auditing Solutions, Farmington Hills *Also called Norman A Lewis (G-5334)*
Global Automotive Products Inc 734 589-6179
  38100 Jay Kay Dr Romulus (48174) *(G-14278)*
Global Automotive Systems, Roseville *Also called Global Rollforming Systems LLC (G-14413)*
Global Automotive Systems LLC (PA) 248 299-7500
  1780 Pond Run Auburn Hills (48326) *(G-915)*
Global Battery Solutions LLC 800 456-4265
  581 Ottawa Ave Ste 100 Holland (49423) *(G-8051)*
Global Builder Supply, Ottawa Lake *Also called Pure Liberty Manufacturing LLC (G-12811)*
Global Chesterfield, Chesterfield *Also called Global Enterprise Limited (G-2888)*
Global CNC Industries Ltd 734 464-1920
  15150 Cleat St Plymouth (48170) *(G-13177)*
Global Components LLC 586 755-9134
  4175 E 10 Mile Rd Warren (48091) *(G-17830)*
Global Connections & More LLC 248 990-2266
  19335 Fitzgerald St Livonia (48152) *(G-10224)*
Global Digital Printing 734 244-5010
  20 W 1st St Monroe (48161) *(G-11544)*
Global Draught Service 810 844-6888
  418 Pearl St Pinckney (48169) *(G-13049)*
Global Electronics Limited 248 353-0100
  2075 Franklin Rd Bloomfield Hills (48302) *(G-1823)*
Global Engine Mfg Aliance LLC 734 529-9888
  5800 N Ann Arbor Rd Dundee (48131) *(G-4822)*
Global Engineering Inc 586 566-0423
  50685 Rizzo Dr Shelby Township (48315) *(G-15230)*
Global Enterprise Limited 586 948-4100
  50450 E Rssell Schmidt Bl Chesterfield (48051) *(G-2888)*
Global Enterprises, Huntington Woods *Also called Polymerica Limited Company (G-8623)*
Global Fleet Sales LLC 248 327-6483
  24725 W 12 Mile Rd # 114 Southfield (48034) *(G-15576)*
Global Fmi LLC 810 964-5555
  17195 Silver Pkwy Ste 111 Fenton (48430) *(G-5481)*
Global Green Corporation 734 560-1743
  5068 Plymouth Rd Ste 3 Ann Arbor (48105) *(G-501)*
Global Impact Group LLC 248 895-9900
  9082 S Saginaw Rd Grand Blanc (48439) *(G-6243)*
Global Industries Inc 248 357-7211
  25925 Telg Rd Ste 145 Southfield (48033) *(G-15577)*
Global Information Systems Inc 248 223-9800
  17177 N Laurel Park Dr # 446 Livonia (48152) *(G-10225)*
Global Lift Corp 989 269-5900
  1330 Pigeon Rd Bad Axe (48413) *(G-1106)*
Global Logistics Services, Warren *Also called GLS Industries LLC (G-17831)*
Global Manufacturing Inds (PA) 513 271-2180
  128 W Calgary Dr Hastings (49058) *(G-7794)*
Global Mfg & Assembly Corp 517 789-8116
  1801 Wildwood Ave Jackson (49202) *(G-8892)*
Global Plastic Systems, Chesterfield *Also called Grace Production Services LLC (G-2889)*
Global Pump Company LLC (PA) 810 653-4828
  10162 E Coldwater Rd Davison (48423) *(G-3785)*

Global Restaurant Group Inc 313 271-2777
  13250 Rotunda Dr Dearborn (48120) *(G-3847)*
Global Retool Group Amer LLC 248 289-5820
  7290 Kensington Rd Brighton (48116) *(G-2001)*
Global Rollforming Systems LLC 586 218-5100
  15500 E 12 Mile Rd Roseville (48066) *(G-14413)*
Global Silks Gifts N Crafts, Ortonville *Also called Sheri Boston (G-12751)*
Global Strgc Sup Solutions LLC 734 525-9100
  34450 Industrial Rd Livonia (48150) *(G-10226)*
Global Supply Integrator LLC 586 484-0734
  10145 Creekwood Trl Davisburg (48350) *(G-3770)*
Global Technologies, Spring Lake *Also called Oleco Inc (G-15841)*
Global Technology Ventures Inc (PA) 248 324-3707
  37408 Hills Tech Dr Farmington Hills (48331) *(G-5252)*
Global Thread Gage Inc 313 438-6789
  25302 Trowbridge St Dearborn (48124) *(G-3848)*
Global Tooling Systems LLC 586 726-0500
  16445 23 Mile Rd Macomb (48042) *(G-10599)*
Global Vehicle Works, Grand Blanc *Also called Global Impact Group LLC (G-6243)*
Global Warming Salsa 248 882-3266
  6900 Teluride Dr White Lake (48383) *(G-18457)*
Global Wholesale & Marketing 248 910-8302
  6566 Burroughs Ave Sterling Heights (48314) *(G-16030)*
Globaltech Ventures, Farmington Hills *Also called Global Technology Ventures Inc (G-5252)*
Globe Industries Incorporated 906 932-3540
  121 Mill St Ironwood (49938) *(G-8763)*
Globe Printing & Specialties 906 485-1033
  200 W Division St Ishpeming (49849) *(G-8776)*
Globe Sand & Gravel, Ironwood *Also called Globe Industries Incorporated (G-8763)*
Globe Tech LLC 734 656-2200
  40300 Plymouth Rd Plymouth (48170) *(G-13178)*
Globe Tech Manufactured Pdts, Plymouth *Also called Globe Tech LLC (G-13178)*
Globe Technologies Corporation 989 846-9591
  1109 W Cedar St Standish (48658) *(G-15888)*
Globe Tumbling Barrel Eqp, Jackson *Also called Casalbi Company Inc (G-8835)*
Glocatch, Westland *Also called Home Chef Ltd (G-18384)*
Glov Enterprises LLC 517 423-9700
  412 S Maumee St Tecumseh (49286) *(G-16502)*
Glove Coaters Incorporated 517 741-8402
  8380 M 60 Union City (49094) *(G-17493)*
Glr, Roseville *Also called Great Lakes Paper Stock Corp (G-14416)*
GLS Diocesan Reports (PA) 989 793-7661
  1520 Court St Saginaw (48602) *(G-14653)*
GLS Enterprises Inc 616 243-2574
  960 W Rver Ctr Dr Ne Ste Comstock Park (49321) *(G-3608)*
GLS Industries LLC (PA) 586 255-9221
  7111 E 11 Mile Rd Warren (48092) *(G-17831)*
GLS Industries LLC 586 255-9221
  8333 E 11 Mile Rd Warren (48093) *(G-17832)*
GLS Promotional Specialties, Comstock Park *Also called GLS Enterprises Inc (G-3608)*
Glt Packaging, Grand Rapids *Also called Great Lakes-Triad Plastic (G-6788)*
Glw Finishing 616 395-0112
  741 Waverly Ct Holland (49423) *(G-8052)*
Glycon Corp 517 423-8356
  912 Industrial Dr Tecumseh (49286) *(G-16503)*
Glynn, Mark, Builder, Traverse City *Also called G F Inc (G-16691)*
GM, Canton *Also called Gil-Mar Manufacturing Co (G-2463)*
GM Bassett Pattern Inc 248 477-6454
  31162 W 8 Mile Rd Farmington Hills (48336) *(G-5253)*
GM Components Holdings LLC (HQ) 870 594-0351
  300 Renaissance Ctr Detroit (48243) *(G-4265)*
GM Defense LLC (HQ) 313 462-8782
  300 Renaissance Ctr Fl 24 Detroit (48243) *(G-4266)*
GM Defense LLC 586 359-8880
  3300 General Motors Rd # 32 Milford (48380) *(G-11464)*
GM Division Plant, Mason *Also called Lear Corporation (G-11141)*
GM Gdls Defense Group LLC (HQ) 586 825-4000
  38500 Mound Rd Sterling Heights (48310) *(G-16031)*
GM Laam Holdings LLC (HQ) 313 556-5000
  300 Renaissance Ctr Detroit (48243) *(G-4267)*
GM Orion Assembly 248 377-5260
  4555 Giddings Rd Lake Orion (48359) *(G-9607)*
GM Powertrain-Romulus Engine 734 595-5203
  36880 Ecorse Rd Romulus (48174) *(G-14279)*
GMA Industries Inc 734 595-7300
  38127 Ecorse Rd Romulus (48174) *(G-14280)*
GMC (general Motors) 517 265-4222
  1450 E Beecher St Adrian (49221) *(G-71)*
Gmd Industries Inc 616 245-1215
  1464 28th St Se Grand Rapids (49508) *(G-6745)*
GME, Union City *Also called Trinity Industries Inc (G-17498)*
GMI, Chelsea *Also called Greene Manufacturing Inc (G-2813)*
GMI Composites Inc 231 755-1611
  1355 W Sherman Blvd Muskegon (49441) *(G-11825)*
GMI Packaging Co (PA) 734 972-7389
  1371 Centennial Ln Ann Arbor (48103) *(G-502)*
Gmr Quality Stone, Sterling Heights *Also called Gmr Stone Products LLC (G-16032)*

Gmr Stone Products LLC 586 739-2700
36955 Metro Ct Sterling Heights (48312) *(G-16032)*
Gms Industries, Buchanan Also called General Machine Services *(G-2196)*
Gnap LLC (PA) 616 583-5000
9000 Byron Commerce Dr Sw Byron Center (49315) *(G-2272)*
Gnass Masonry LLC 616 530-3214
6612 Sunfield Dr Sw Byron Center (49315) *(G-2273)*
Gns America Co., Holland Also called Gns Holland Inc *(G-8053)*
Gns Canton LLC (HQ) 734 927-9520
7261 Commerce Blvd Canton (48187) *(G-2466)*
Gns Holland Inc 616 796-0433
13341 Quincy St Holland (49424) *(G-8053)*
Gns North America Inc (PA) 616 796-0433
13341 Quincy St Holland (49424) *(G-8054)*
Gnu Software Development Inc 586 778-9182
14156 E 11 Mile Rd Warren (48089) *(G-17833)*
Go Beyond Healthy LLC 407 255-0314
2290 Christine Ct Se Grand Rapids (49546) *(G-6746)*
Go Cat Feather Toys 517 543-7519
605 W Lovett St Charlotte (48813) *(G-2759)*
Go Frac LLC 817 731-0301
7000 Calmont Ave Ste 310 Detroit (48207) *(G-4268)*
Go Office.com, Grand Rapids Also called Mobile Office Vehicle Inc *(G-7016)*
Go Power Systems, Novi Also called Froude Inc *(G-12419)*
Godfrey & Wing Inc 330 562-1440
2240 Veterans Mem Pkwy Saginaw (48601) *(G-14654)*
Godin Tool Inc 231 946-2210
466 Hughes Dr Traverse City (49696) *(G-16695)*
Goetz Craft Printers Inc 734 973-7604
121 Paula Dr Brooklyn (49230) *(G-2125)*
Gofrac, Detroit Also called Go Frac LLC *(G-4268)*
Gogettaz Clothing Company LLC 630 800-3279
17314 Bonstelle Ave Southfield (48075) *(G-15578)*
Gogosqueez, Grawn Also called Materne North America Corp *(G-7452)*
Gokoh Coldwater Incorporated 517 279-1080
100 Concept Dr Coldwater (49036) *(G-3434)*
Gold Bond, National City Also called Ng Operations LLC *(G-11960)*
Gold Bond Building Pdts LLC 989 756-2741
2375 S National City Rd National City (48748) *(G-11959)*
Gold Coast Ice Makers LLC 231 845-2745
3785 W Us Highway 10 Ludington (49431) *(G-10537)*
Gold Coast Icemakers, Ludington Also called Gold Coast Ice Makers LLC *(G-10537)*
Golde Auburn Hills LLC (HQ) 248 606-1912
4000 Pinnacle Ct Auburn Hills (48326) *(G-916)*
Golden Apple 231 477-5366
336 River St Manistee (49660) *(G-10901)*
Golden Dental Solutions, Eastpointe Also called Visual Chimera *(G-4948)*
Golden Dental Solutions, Roseville Also called End Product Results LLC *(G-14405)*
Golden Eagle Pallets LLC 616 233-0970
1701 Clyde Park Ave Sw # 8 Wyoming (49509) *(G-18875)*
Golden Fashion 616 288-9465
1949 Eastern Ave Se Grand Rapids (49507) *(G-6747)*
Golden Pointe Awning & Sign Co, Detroit Also called Golden Pointe Inc *(G-4269)*
Golden Pointe Inc 313 581-8284
16050 W Warren Ave Detroit (48228) *(G-4269)*
Golden Refrigerant, Livonia Also called Cjg LLC *(G-10158)*
Golden Satchel LLC 248 636-0550
402 Palmerston St River Rouge (48218) *(G-13855)*
Golden Sign Co 313 580-4094
841 Farmdale St Ferndale (48220) *(G-5559)*
Goldendent, Roseville Also called Avo Dental Supplies LLC *(G-14378)*
Golf Store 517 347-8733
1492 W Grand River Ave Okemos (48864) *(G-12669)*
Golich Glass 248 667-9084
7796 Boardwalk Rd Brighton (48116) *(G-2002)*
Gollnick Tool Co 586 755-0100
24300 Marmon Ave Warren (48089) *(G-17834)*
Gombar Corp 989 793-9427
5645 State St Ste B Saginaw (48603) *(G-14655)*
Gongwer News Service Inc 517 482-3500
101 S Wash Sq Ste 540 Lansing (48933) *(G-9843)*
Gonzalez Group Jonesville LLC 517 849-9908
3980 Beck Rd Jonesville (49250) *(G-9088)*
Gonzalez Jr Pallets LLC 616 885-0201
1601 Madison St Sw Grand Rapids (49507) *(G-6748)*
Gonzalez Universal Pallets LLC 616 243-5524
955 Godfrey Ave Sw Grand Rapids (49503) *(G-6749)*
Good Do Up Skateboards 248 301-5188
440 Rosario Ln White Lake (48386) *(G-18458)*
Good God Printing 313 694-2985
4215 Miracles Blvd Detroit (48201) *(G-4270)*
Good Harbor Vineyards Winery 231 632-0703
34 S Manitou Trl Lake Leelanau (49653) *(G-9562)*
Good Juice, Detroit Also called Super Fluids LLC *(G-4615)*
Good Life Naturals LLC 616 207-9230
6555 Alden Nash Ave Se Alto (49302) *(G-333)*
Good Neighbor Organic 231 386-5636
9825 E Engles Rd Northport (49670) *(G-12187)*

Good Parts 248 656-7643
140 W Hamlin Rd Rochester Hills (48307) *(G-14026)*
Good Sense Coffee LLC 810 355-2349
7931 State St Brighton (48116) *(G-2003)*
Goodale Enterprises LLC (PA) 616 453-7690
21 Fennessey St Sw Grand Rapids (49534) *(G-6750)*
Goodells Equestrian Center 586 615-8535
8820 Sparling Rd Wales (48027) *(G-17628)*
Goodpack 248 458-0041
2820 W Maple Rd Ste 128 Troy (48084) *(G-17131)*
Goodrich Brothers Inc (PA) 989 593-2104
11409 E Blwter Hwy Pewamo Pewamo (48873) *(G-13028)*
Goodrich Brothers Inc 989 224-4944
3060 County Farm Rd Saint Johns (48879) *(G-14900)*
Goodwill Cadillac Transition H, Cadillac Also called Goodwill Inds Nthrn Mich Inc *(G-2332)*
Goodwill Inds Nthrn Mich Inc 231 779-1311
901 N Mitchell St Ste 15 Cadillac (49601) *(G-2332)*
Goodwill Inds Nthrn Mich Inc 231 779-1361
610 S Mitchell St Cadillac (49601) *(G-2333)*
Goodwill Inds Nthrn Mich Inc 231 922-4890
1329 S Division St Traverse City (49684) *(G-16696)*
Goodwill Inn, Traverse City Also called Goodwill Inds Nthrn Mich Inc *(G-16696)*
Goodwill Resale Store, Cadillac Also called Goodwill Inds Nthrn Mich Inc *(G-2333)*
Goodyear Tire & Rubber Company 248 336-0135
29444 Woodward Ave Royal Oak (48073) *(G-14541)*
Gopher Scope Manufacturing 248 667-4025
29563 Costello Dr New Hudson (48165) *(G-12054)*
Gorang Industries Inc 248 651-9010
305 South St Rochester (48307) *(G-13902)*
Gordinier Electronics Corp 586 778-0426
16380 E 13 Mile Rd Roseville (48066) *(G-14414)*
Gordon Metal Products Inc 586 445-0960
8101 Lyndon St Detroit (48238) *(G-4271)*
Gordon Woodwork LLC 734 612-3586
13909 Rawsonville Rd Belleville (48111) *(G-1484)*
Gosen Tool & Machine Inc 989 777-6493
2054 Brettrager Dr Saginaw (48601) *(G-14656)*
Gossamer Press LLC 616 363-4608
940 Knapp St Ne Grand Rapids (49505) *(G-6751)*
Gotts Transit Mix Inc 734 439-1528
605 S Platt Rd Milan (48160) *(G-11437)*
Gougeon Holding Co (PA) 989 684-7286
100 Patterson Ave Bay City (48706) *(G-1361)*
Govro-Nelson Co 810 329-4727
1132 Ladd Rd Commerce Township (48390) *(G-3533)*
Gower Corporation 989 249-5938
2840 Universal Dr Saginaw (48603) *(G-14657)*
GP Strategies C/O Transpak, Sterling Heights Also called Transpak Inc *(G-16209)*
Gpbc Inc 734 741-7325
120 W Washington St Ste 1 Ann Arbor (48104) *(G-503)*
Gpi-X LLC 616 453-4170
11310 1st Ave Nw Grand Rapids (49534) *(G-6752)*
Gr Psp LLC 616 785-1070
3593 Alpine Ave Nw Grand Rapids (49544) *(G-6753)*
Gr Tooling & Automation Inc 616 299-1521
3670 Mill Creek Dr Ne Comstock Park (49321) *(G-3609)*
Gr X Manufacturing 616 541-7420
7000 Dtton Indus Pk Dr Se Caledonia (49316) *(G-2375)*
Grabber Inc 616 940-1914
365 84th St Sw Ste 4 Byron Center (49315) *(G-2274)*
Grabill Windows & Doors LLC 810 798-2817
7463 Research Dr Almont (48003) *(G-261)*
Grace Contracting Services LLC 906 630-4680
25688 County Road 98 Mc Millan (49853) *(G-11188)*
Grace Engineering Corp (PA) 810 392-2181
34775 Potter St Memphis (48041) *(G-11213)*
Grace Engineering Corp 810 392-2181
11501 Lambs Rd Riley (48041) *(G-13850)*
Grace Metal Prods Inc 231 264-8133
6322 Yuba Rd Williamsburg (49690) *(G-18554)*
Grace Metal Products Inc 231 264-8133
115 Ames St Elk Rapids (49629) *(G-5025)*
Grace Production Services LLC 810 643-8070
52100 Sierra Dr Chesterfield (48047) *(G-2889)*
Grace USA, Elk Rapids Also called Grace Metal Products Inc *(G-5025)*
Graceland Fruit Inc 231 352-7181
1123 Main St Frankfort (49635) *(G-5877)*
Graf Acres LLC 517 851-8693
4230 Swan Rd Stockbridge (49285) *(G-16275)*
Grafaktri Inc 734 665-0717
1200 N Main St Ann Arbor (48104) *(G-504)*
Graham Medical Tech LLC 586 677-9600
16137 Leone Dr Macomb (48042) *(G-10600)*
Grahams Printing Company Inc 313 925-1188
8620 Gratiot Ave Detroit (48213) *(G-4272)*
Grain and Cattle Farm, Morenci Also called Triple K Farms Inc *(G-11617)*
Grakon LLC 734 462-1201
19500 Victor Pkwy Ste 325 Livonia (48152) *(G-10227)*
Grakon Michigan, Livonia Also called Grakon LLC *(G-10227)*

Gram, Grand Rapids *Also called Grand River Aseptic Mfg Inc* ***(G-6776)***
Gramedica, Macomb *Also called Graham Medical Tech LLC* ***(G-10600)***
Graminex LLC (PA)....989 797-5502
95 Midland Rd Saginaw (48638) ***(G-14658)***
Gramma N Stitches....810 664-8606
1664 Daley Rd Lapeer (48446) ***(G-9932)***
Grand Apps LLC....517 927-5140
13150 Lawson Rd Grand Ledge (48837) ***(G-6391)***
Grand Blanc Cement Pdts Inc (PA)....810 694-7500
10709 Center Rd Grand Blanc (48439) ***(G-6244)***
Grand Blanc Printing Inc....810 694-1155
9449 Holly Rd Grand Blanc (48439) ***(G-6245)***
Grand Blanc Processing LLC....810 694-6000
10151 Gainey Rd Holly (48442) ***(G-8275)***
Grand Haven Custom Molding LLC....616 935-3160
1500 S Beechtree St Grand Haven (49417) ***(G-6302)***
Grand Haven Gasket Company....616 842-7682
1701 Eaton Dr Grand Haven (49417) ***(G-6303)***
Grand Haven Nursery Products, Grand Haven *Also called West Michigan Molding Inc* ***(G-6382)***
Grand Haven Powder Coating Inc....616 850-8822
1710 Airpark Dr Grand Haven (49417) ***(G-6304)***
Grand Haven Publishing Corp....616 842-6400
101 N 3rd St Grand Haven (49417) ***(G-6305)***
Grand Haven Steel Products Inc....616 842-2740
1627 Marion Ave Grand Haven (49417) ***(G-6306)***
Grand Haven Tribune, Grand Haven *Also called Grand Haven Publishing Corp* ***(G-6305)***
Grand Industries Inc....616 846-7120
1700 Airpark Dr Grand Haven (49417) ***(G-6307)***
Grand Occasions....248 622-7144
6904 Covington Ct West Bloomfield (48322) ***(G-18285)***
Grand Power Systems, Grand Haven *Also called Gti Power Acquisition LLC* ***(G-6310)***
Grand Rapids Carvers Inc....616 538-0022
4465 Rger B Chffee Mem Dr Grand Rapids (49548) ***(G-6754)***
Grand Rapids Chair Company....616 774-0561
1250 84th St Sw Byron Center (49315) ***(G-2275)***
Grand Rapids Controls Company, Rockford *Also called Ctc Acquisition Company LLC* ***(G-14163)***
Grand Rapids Custom Tooling....616 836-0274
232 E Roosevelt Ave Zeeland (49464) ***(G-19031)***
Grand Rapids Elc Mtr Svc LLC....616 243-8866
1057 Cottage Grove St Se Grand Rapids (49507) ***(G-6755)***
Grand Rapids Elc Mtr Svcs LLC....616 243-8866
1057 Cottage Grove St Se Grand Rapids (49507) ***(G-6756)***
Grand Rapids Embroidery....616 451-2827
4223 Valley Side Dr Ne Grand Rapids (49525) ***(G-6757)***
Grand Rapids Graphix....616 359-2383
3853 Llewellyn Ct Sw Wyoming (49519) ***(G-18876)***
Grand Rapids Graphix LLC....616 359-2383
1360 Canary Grass Dr Se Grand Rapids (49508) ***(G-6758)***
Grand Rapids Graphix LLC....616 359-2383
3371 68th St Se Ste 1 Caledonia (49316) ***(G-2376)***
Grand Rapids Gravel Company (PA)....616 538-9000
2700 28th St Sw Grand Rapids (49519) ***(G-6759)***
Grand Rapids Gravel Company....616 538-9000
3800 7 Mile Rd Ne Belmont (49306) ***(G-1507)***
Grand Rapids Gravel Company....616 538-9000
13180 Quincy St Holland (49424) ***(G-8055)***
Grand Rapids Gravel Company....231 777-2777
1780 S Sheridan Dr Muskegon (49442) ***(G-11826)***
Grand Rapids Label Company....616 459-8134
2351 Oak Industrial Dr Ne Grand Rapids (49505) ***(G-6760)***
Grand Rapids Legal News, Ada *Also called West Michigan Printing Inc* ***(G-41)***
Grand Rapids Legal News....616 454-9293
1430 Monroe Ave Nw # 140 Grand Rapids (49505) ***(G-6761)***
Grand Rapids Letter Service....616 459-4711
315 Fuller Ave Ne Grand Rapids (49503) ***(G-6762)***
Grand Rapids Machine Repair....616 248-4760
3710 Linden Ave Se Grand Rapids (49548) ***(G-6763)***
Grand Rapids Machine Repr Inc....616 245-9102
4000 Eastern Ave Se Grand Rapids (49508) ***(G-6764)***
Grand Rapids Metaltek Inc....616 791-2373
2860 Marlin Ct Nw Grand Rapids (49534) ***(G-6765)***
Grand Rapids Polsg & Buffing....616 241-2233
3000 Hillcroft Ave Sw Grand Rapids (49548) ***(G-6766)***
Grand Rapids Press Inc....616 459-1400
3102 Walker Ridge Dr Nw Grand Rapids (49544) ***(G-6767)***
Grand Rapids Printing Ink Co (PA)....616 241-5681
4920 Starr St Se Grand Rapids (49546) ***(G-6768)***
Grand Rapids Salsa....616 780-1801
1301 Benjamin Ave Se Grand Rapids (49506) ***(G-6769)***
Grand Rapids Stripping Co....616 361-0794
1933 Will Ave Nw Grand Rapids (49504) ***(G-6770)***
Grand Rapids Technologies Inc....616 245-7700
3133 Madison Ave Se Ste B Grand Rapids (49548) ***(G-6771)***
Grand Rapids Times Inc....616 245-8737
2016 Eastern Ave Se Grand Rapids (49507) ***(G-6772)***
Grand Rapids Wood Works....616 690-2889
3818 Bruce Dr Sw Grandville (49418) ***(G-7380)***
Grand Rapids Woodworking....616 780-7137
3993 Roger B Chaffee Mem Grand Rapids (49548) ***(G-6773)***
Grand Rapids Woodworking LLC....616 301-8719
247 Dickinson St Se Grand Rapids (49507) ***(G-6774)***
Grand River Aseptic Mfg....616 678-2400
524 Butterworth St Sw Grand Rapids (49504) ***(G-6775)***
Grand River Aseptic Mfg Inc (PA)....616 678-2400
140 Front Ave Sw Grand Rapids (49504) ***(G-6776)***
Grand River Brewery, Jackson *Also called Veritas Vineyard LLC* ***(G-9030)***
Grand River Interiors Inc....616 454-2800
974 Front Ave Nw Ste 2 Grand Rapids (49504) ***(G-6777)***
Grand River Polishing Co Corp....616 846-1420
19191 174th Ave Spring Lake (49456) ***(G-15818)***
Grand Rpids Wilbert Burial Vlt....616 453-9429
2500 3 Mile Rd Nw Grand Rapids (49534) ***(G-6778)***
Grand Strategy LLC....269 637-8330
15038 73rd St South Haven (49090) ***(G-15407)***
Grand Traverse Assembly Inc....231 588-2406
7161 Essex Rd Ellsworth (49729) ***(G-5036)***
Grand Traverse Canvas Works....231 947-3140
3975 3 Mile Rd N Traverse City (49686) ***(G-16697)***
Grand Traverse Container, Traverse City *Also called Grand Traverse Reels Inc* ***(G-16700)***
Grand Traverse Continuous Inc....231 941-5400
1661 Park Dr Traverse City (49686) ***(G-16698)***
Grand Traverse Crane, Traverse City *Also called L & C Enterprises Inc* ***(G-16736)***
Grand Traverse Dist Tasting Rm....269 254-8113
224 E Michigan Ave Kalamazoo (49007) ***(G-9199)***
Grand Traverse Forging & Steel, Traverse City *Also called Great Lakes Forge Inc* ***(G-16704)***
Grand Traverse Machine Co....231 946-8006
1247 Boon St Traverse City (49686) ***(G-16699)***
Grand Traverse Pallet, Ellsworth *Also called Grand Traverse Assembly Inc* ***(G-5036)***
Grand Traverse Reels Inc....231 946-1057
1050 Business Park Dr Traverse City (49686) ***(G-16700)***
Grand Traverse Stamping Co....231 929-4215
1677 Park Dr Traverse City (49686) ***(G-16701)***
Grand Traverse Tool Inc....231 929-4743
396 Hughes Dr Traverse City (49696) ***(G-16702)***
Grand Traverse Vineyards, Traverse City *Also called Chateau Grand Travers Ltd* ***(G-16646)***
Grand Valley State University....847 744-0508
1 Campus Dr Allendale (49401) ***(G-219)***
Grand Valley Wood Products Inc....616 475-5890
4030 Eastern Ave Se Grand Rapids (49508) ***(G-6779)***
Grandads Sweet Tea LLC....313 320-4446
26532 Joe Dr Warren (48091) ***(G-17835)***
Grandkids Edcted Motivated Gem....313 539-7330
18626 Wexford St Detroit (48234) ***(G-4273)***
Grandpapas Inc....313 891-6830
6500 E Davison St Detroit (48212) ***(G-4274)***
Grandville Industries Inc....616 538-0920
4270 White St Sw Grandville (49418) ***(G-7381)***
Grandville Printing Co....616 534-8647
4719 Ivanrest Ave Sw Grandville (49418) ***(G-7382)***
Grandville Tractor Svcs LLC....616 530-2030
3408 Busch Dr Sw Ste E Grandville (49418) ***(G-7383)***
Granite City Inc....248 478-0033
31693 8 Mile Rd Livonia (48152) ***(G-10228)***
Granite Precision Tool Corp....248 299-8317
2257 Star Ct Rochester Hills (48309) ***(G-14027)***
Graniteonecom Inc....616 452-8372
639 Hoyt St Se Grand Rapids (49507) ***(G-6780)***
Granola Project Llc....919 219-7158
38233 Hyman St Westland (48186) ***(G-18375)***
Grant Industries, Clinton Township *Also called Press-Way Inc* ***(G-3325)***
Grant Industries Incorporated (PA)....586 293-9200
33415 Groesbeck Hwy Fraser (48026) ***(G-5931)***
Grape Harbor, Traverse City *Also called Peninsula Cellars* ***(G-16787)***
Grapentin Specialties Inc....810 724-0636
5599 Bowers Rd Imlay City (48444) ***(G-8634)***
Graph-ADS Printing Inc....989 779-6000
711 W Pickard St Ste I Mount Pleasant (48858) ***(G-11700)***
Graph-X Signs....734 420-0906
45650 Mast St Plymouth (48170) ***(G-13179)***
Graphic Art Service & Supply....810 229-4700
1343 Rickett Rd Brighton (48116) ***(G-2004)***
Graphic Arts Service & Sup Inc (PA)....616 698-9300
3933 S Greenbrooke Dr Se Grand Rapids (49512) ***(G-6781)***
Graphic Enterprises Inc....248 616-4900
1200 E Avis Dr Madison Heights (48071) ***(G-10732)***
Graphic Gear Inc....734 283-3864
3018 Fort St Lincoln Park (48146) ***(G-10048)***
Graphic Impressions Inc....616 455-0303
6621 Division Ave S Grand Rapids (49548) ***(G-6782)***
Graphic Packaging Intl LLC....269 343-6104
1421 N Pitcher St Kalamazoo (49007) ***(G-9200)***
Graphic Packaging Intl LLC....269 651-2365
305 W South St Sturgis (49091) ***(G-16289)***
Graphic Resource Group Inc....248 588-6100
528 Robbins Dr Troy (48083) ***(G-17132)***

ALPHABETIC

Graphic Specialties Inc (PA)......616 247-0060
2350 Brton Indus Pk Dr Se Grand Rapids (49508) ***(G-6783)***
Graphic Visions Inc......248 347-3355
455 E Cady St Northville (48167) ***(G-12225)***
Graphicolor Exhibits, Livonia *Also called Graphicolor Systems Inc* ***(G-10229)***
Graphicolor Systems Inc......248 347-0271
12788 Currie Ct Livonia (48150) ***(G-10229)***
Graphics & Printing Co Inc......269 381-1482
5356 N Riverview Dr Kalamazoo (49004) ***(G-9201)***
Graphics 3 Inc......517 278-2159
205 W Garfield Ave Coldwater (49036) ***(G-3435)***
Graphics Arts Service & Supply, Brighton *Also called Graphic Art Service & Supply* ***(G-2004)***
Graphics Depot Inc......248 383-5055
7625 Highland Rd Waterford (48327) ***(G-18125)***
Graphics East Inc......586 598-1500
16005 Sturgeon St Roseville (48066) ***(G-14415)***
Graphics Embossed Images Inc......616 791-0404
1975 Waldorf St Nw Ste A Grand Rapids (49544) ***(G-6784)***
Graphics House Printing, Muskegon *Also called Graphics House Publishing* ***(G-11827)***
Graphics House Publishing......231 739-4004
2632 Peck St Muskegon (49444) ***(G-11827)***
Graphics Hse Spt Prmotions Inc (PA)......231 739-4004
444 Irwin Ave Muskegon (49442) ***(G-11828)***
Graphics Hse Spt Prmotions Inc......231 733-1877
444 Irwin Ave Muskegon (49442) ***(G-11829)***
Graphics Unlimited Inc......231 773-2696
1279 Porter Rd Norton Shores (49441) ***(G-12295)***
Graphicus Signs & Designs......231 652-9160
477 S Industrial Dr Newaygo (49337) ***(G-12082)***
Graphite Electrodes Ltd......989 893-3635
1311 N Sherman St Bay City (48708) ***(G-1362)***
Graphite Engineering & Sls Co......616 754-5671
712 Industrial Park Dr Greenville (48838) ***(G-7486)***
Graphite Machining Inc......810 678-2227
4141 S Oak St Metamora (48455) ***(G-11279)***
Graphite Products Corp......248 548-7800
1797 E 10 Mile Rd Madison Heights (48071) ***(G-10733)***
Graphix 2 Go Inc......269 969-7321
7200 Tower Rd Battle Creek (49014) ***(G-1235)***
Graphix Gurus......616 217-6470
550 W Main Ave Zeeland (49464) ***(G-19032)***
Graphix Signs & Embroidery......616 396-0009
11223 E Lakewood Blvd Holland (49424) ***(G-8056)***
Grapho LLC......734 223-2144
2410 Foxway Dr Ann Arbor (48105) ***(G-505)***
Graphx Shop......248 678-5432
3089 Orchard Lake Rd Keego Harbor (48320) ***(G-9421)***
Grasel Graphics Inc......989 652-5151
9710 Junction Rd Frankenmuth (48734) ***(G-5865)***
Grass Lake Community Pharmacy......517 522-4100
116 E Michigan Ave Grass Lake (49240) ***(G-7438)***
Grasshopper Signs Graphics LLC......248 946-8475
24655 Halsted Rd Farmington Hills (48335) ***(G-5254)***
Gratefulthreadembroider......231 855-1340
661 N Wythe St Pentwater (49449) ***(G-12972)***
Gratiot County Herald, Ithaca *Also called Macdonald Publications Inc* ***(G-8793)***
Grav Co LLC......269 651-5467
400 Norwood St Sturgis (49091) ***(G-16290)***
Gravel Capital Brewing LLC......248 895-8399
14 N Washington St Oxford (48371) ***(G-12885)***
Gravel Flow Inc (PA)......269 651-5467
400 Norwood St Sturgis (49091) ***(G-16291)***
Graveldinger Graphix......248 535-8074
1360 Merkle St Ortonville (48462) ***(G-12747)***
Gravelle Woods......616 617-7712
7000 4 Mile Rd Ne Ada (49301) ***(G-20)***
Gravikor Inc......734 302-3200
401 W Morgan Rd Ann Arbor (48108) ***(G-506)***
Gravity Software LLC......844 464-7284
300 Rverfront Dr Unit 22a Detroit (48226) ***(G-4275)***
Gray & Company (HQ)......231 873-5628
3325 W Polk Rd Hart (49420) ***(G-7753)***
Gray Bros Stamping & Mch Inc......269 483-7615
424 W Chicago Rd White Pigeon (49099) ***(G-18478)***
Gray Brothers Mfg Inc......269 483-7615
424 W Chicago Rd White Pigeon (49099) ***(G-18479)***
Gray Skies Distillery......616 437-1119
700 Ottawa Ave Nw Grand Rapids (49503) ***(G-6785)***
Grayling Outdoor Products Inc......989 348-2956
2075 Industrial Dr Grayling (49738) ***(G-7462)***
Graywolf Printing, Birmingham *Also called Alpha Data Business Forms Inc* ***(G-1718)***
Grazing Fields, Charlotte *Also called Farmers Egg Cooperative* ***(G-2754)***
Great American Base Company......734 722-7700
5697 E Executive Dr Westland (48185) ***(G-18376)***
Great American Publishing Co......616 887-9008
75 Applewood Dr Ste A Sparta (49345) ***(G-15765)***
Great Atlantic News LLC......517 784-7163
2571 Saradan Dr Jackson (49202) ***(G-8893)***
Great Deals Magazine, Portage *Also called Bowman Enterprises Inc* ***(G-13548)***
Great Fresh Foods Co LLC......734 904-0731
21740 Trolley Industrial Taylor (48180) ***(G-16422)***
Great Harvest Bread Co......586 566-9500
48923 Hayes Rd Shelby Township (48315) ***(G-15231)***
Great Lake Foam Technologies......517 563-8030
104 W Main St Hanover (49241) ***(G-7624)***
Great Lake Woods Inc......616 399-3300
3303 John F Donnelly Dr Holland (49424) ***(G-8057)***
Great Lakes Aero Products......810 235-1402
915 Kearsley Park Blvd Flint (48503) ***(G-5708)***
Great Lakes Aggregates LLC (PA)......734 379-0311
5699 Ready Rd South Rockwood (48179) ***(G-15464)***
Great Lakes Allied LLC......231 924-5794
87 N Benson St White Cloud (49349) ***(G-18441)***
Great Lakes American, Spring Lake *Also called Great Lakes Cordage Inc* ***(G-15819)***
Great Lakes Bath & Body Inc......231 421-9160
110 E Front St Traverse City (49684) ***(G-16703)***
Great Lakes Bindery Inc......616 245-5264
3741 Linden Ave Se Grand Rapids (49548) ***(G-6786)***
Great Lakes Castings LLC (HQ)......231 843-2501
800 N Washington Ave Ludington (49431) ***(G-10538)***
Great Lakes Castings LLC......616 399-9710
12970 Ransom St Holland (49424) ***(G-8058)***
Great Lakes Chemical Serv......269 353-1841
125 N Leja Dr Vicksburg (49097) ***(G-17604)***
Great Lakes Chemical Services......269 372-6886
616 W Centre Ave Portage (49024) ***(G-13562)***
Great Lakes Coach, Muskegon *Also called Emergency Services LLC* ***(G-11812)***
Great Lakes Coating, Benton Harbor *Also called Arnt Asphalt Sealing Inc* ***(G-1530)***
Great Lakes Coca-Cola Dist LLC......989 895-8537
2500 Broadway St Bay City (48708) ***(G-1363)***
Great Lakes Coca-Cola Dist LLC......906 475-7003
201 Summit St 53 Negaunee (49866) ***(G-11966)***
Great Lakes Coca-Cola Dist LLC......517 322-2349
3300 S Creyts Rd Lansing (48917) ***(G-9762)***
Great Lakes Coca-Cola Dist LLC......734 397-2700
100 Coca Cola Dr Belleville (48111) ***(G-1485)***
Great Lakes Compression Inc......989 786-3788
3690 County Road 491 Lewiston (49756) ***(G-10020)***
Great Lakes Contracting Inc......616 846-8888
14370 172nd Ave Grand Haven (49417) ***(G-6308)***
Great Lakes Cordage Inc......616 842-4455
17045 148th Ave Spring Lake (49456) ***(G-15819)***
Great Lakes Crystal Tech Inc......517 249-4395
4942 Dawn Ave Ste 118 East Lansing (48823) ***(G-4894)***
Great Lakes Custom Embroidery......734 844-7347
1356 N Beck Rd Canton (48187) ***(G-2467)***
Great Lakes Custom Metalworks......231 818-5888
9656 N M 33 Hwy Cheboygan (49721) ***(G-2784)***
Great Lakes Cylinders LLC......248 437-4141
57075 Pontiac Trl New Hudson (48165) ***(G-12055)***
Great Lakes Diagnostics Inc......248 307-9494
1713 Larchwood Dr Ste B Troy (48083) ***(G-17133)***
Great Lakes Die Cast, Muskegon *Also called New Gldc LLC* ***(G-11884)***
Great Lakes Die Cast, Muskegon *Also called New Gldc LLC* ***(G-11885)***
Great Lakes Dock & Door LLC......313 368-6300
19345 John R St Detroit (48203) ***(G-4276)***
Great Lakes Draperies, Holland *Also called Window Designs Inc* ***(G-8250)***
Great Lakes Drone Company LLC......317 430-5291
2618 W John Beers Rd Stevensville (49127) ***(G-16251)***
Great Lakes Electric LLC......269 408-8276
1776 Hilltop Rd Saint Joseph (49085) ***(G-14932)***
Great Lakes Epoxy Coatings LLC......810 820-7073
1469 Casto Blvd Burton (48509) ***(G-2236)***
Great Lakes Exploration Inc......906 352-4024
414 10th Ave Ste 1 Menominee (49858) ***(G-11239)***
Great Lakes Feedscrews, Tecumseh *Also called Glycon Corp* ***(G-16503)***
Great Lakes Filter, Bloomfield Hills *Also called Acme Mills Company* ***(G-1791)***
Great Lakes Fine Cabinetry......906 493-5780
844 E 3 Mile Rd Sault Sainte Marie (49783) ***(G-15091)***
Great Lakes Finishing Inc......231 733-9566
510 W Hackley Ave Muskegon (49444) ***(G-11830)***
Great Lakes Fluid Power, Kalkaska *Also called Great Lakes Hydra Corporation* ***(G-9389)***
Great Lakes Food Center LLC......248 397-8166
32102 Howard Ave Madison Heights (48071) ***(G-10734)***
Great Lakes Forge Inc......231 947-4931
2465 N Aero Park Ct Traverse City (49686) ***(G-16704)***
Great Lakes Gages LLC......810 797-8300
3689 Hadley Rd Metamora (48455) ***(G-11280)***
Great Lakes Gauge Company......989 652-6136
6950 Junction Rd Bridgeport (48722) ***(G-1916)***
Great Lakes Graphics Inc......517 783-5500
209 E Washington Ave # 355 Jackson (49201) ***(G-8894)***
Great Lakes Grilling Co......616 791-8600
2685 Northridge Dr Nw C Grand Rapids (49544) ***(G-6787)***
Great Lakes Hydra Corporation......231 258-4338
410 E Dresden St Kalkaska (49646) ***(G-9389)***
Great Lakes Industry Inc......517 784-3153
1927 Wildwood Ave Jackson (49202) ***(G-8895)***

Great Lakes Infotronics Inc (PA)..........248 476-2500
22300 Haggerty Rd 100 Northville (48167) **(G-12226)**
Great Lakes Insulspan, Blissfield *Also called Midwest Panel Systems Inc* **(G-1770)**
Great Lakes Jig & Fixture..........269 795-4349
11310 Bowens Mill Rd Middleville (49333) **(G-11307)**
Great Lakes Label LLC..........616 647-9880
910 Metzgar Dr Nw Comstock Park (49321) **(G-3610)**
Great Lakes Laser Dynamics Inc..........616 892-7070
4881 Allen Park Dr Allendale (49401) **(G-220)**
Great Lakes Laser Services..........248 584-1828
147 E 10 Mile Rd Madison Heights (48071) **(G-10735)**
Great Lakes Lift Inc..........989 673-2109
1382 E Caro Rd Caro (48723) **(G-2572)**
Great Lakes Log & Firewd Co..........231 206-4073
11405 Russell Rd Twin Lake (49457) **(G-17468)**
Great Lakes Lube-Tech, Portage *Also called Lube-Tech Inc* **(G-13580)**
Great Lakes Mechanical Corp (PA)..........313 581-1400
3800 Maple St Dearborn (48126) **(G-3849)**
Great Lakes Metal Fabricating, Niles *Also called Great Lakes Precision Machine* **(G-12134)**
Great Lakes Metal Fabrication..........248 218-0540
13500 Wayne Rd Livonia (48150) **(G-10230)**
Great Lakes Metal Finshg LLC..........517 764-1335
3000 E South St Jackson (49201) **(G-8896)**
Great Lakes Metal Stamping Inc..........269 465-4415
4607 Rambo Rd Bridgman (49106) **(G-1927)**
Great Lakes Metal Works..........269 789-2342
819 Industrial Rd Marshall (49068) **(G-11059)**
Great Lakes Mobile Welding..........406 890-5757
276 E Finerty Rd West Branch (48661) **(G-18328)**
Great Lakes Ncw LLC..........616 355-2626
386 Bay Park Dr Ste 10 Holland (49424) **(G-8059)**
Great Lakes Neon..........517 582-7451
9861 W Grand River Hwy Grand Ledge (48837) **(G-6392)**
Great Lakes Nursery Soils Inc..........231 788-2770
680 S Maple Island Rd Muskegon (49442) **(G-11831)**
Great Lakes Packing Co..........231 264-5561
6556 Quarterline Rd Kewadin (49648) **(G-9487)**
Great Lakes Pallet Inc..........989 883-9220
714 N Beck St Sebewaing (48759) **(G-15140)**
Great Lakes Paper Stock Corp..........586 779-1310
30835 Groesbeck Hwy Roseville (48066) **(G-14416)**
Great Lakes Photo Inc..........586 784-5446
29080 Armada Ridge Rd Richmond (48062) **(G-13839)**
Great Lakes Plastics Division, Troy *Also called Evans Industries Inc* **(G-17100)**
Great Lakes Post LLC..........248 941-1349
12466 Scenic View Ct Milford (48380) **(G-11465)**
Great Lakes Pot Pies LLC..........248 266-1160
460 Laurelwood Ct Bloomfield Hills (48302) **(G-1824)**
Great Lakes Powder Coating LLC..........248 522-6222
1020 Decker Rd Walled Lake (48390) **(G-17669)**
Great Lakes Precision Machine..........269 695-4580
1760 Foundation Dr Niles (49120) **(G-12134)**
Great Lakes Prtg Solutions Inc..........231 799-6000
5163 Robert Hunter Dr Norton Shores (49441) **(G-12296)**
Great Lakes Publishing Inc..........517 647-4444
212 Kent St Ste 6 Portland (48875) **(G-13638)**
Great Lakes Pulp & Fibre, Menominee *Also called Fibrek Recycling US Inc* **(G-11236)**
Great Lakes Pwr Generation LLC..........231 492-3764
112 N Brand St Elk Rapids (49629) **(G-5026)**
Great Lakes Right of Way LLC..........616 263-9898
1177 17 Mile Rd Ne Cedar Springs (49319) **(G-2652)**
Great Lakes Rubber Co..........248 624-5710
30573 Anderson Ct Wixom (48393) **(G-18669)**
Great Lakes Sand & Gravel LLC..........616 374-3169
7940 Woodland Rd Lake Odessa (48849) **(G-9576)**
Great Lakes Spt Publications..........734 507-0241
3588 Plymouth Rd Ann Arbor (48105) **(G-507)**
Great Lakes Stainless Inc..........231 943-7648
1305 Stepke Ct Traverse City (49685) **(G-16705)**
Great Lakes Stair & Case Co..........269 465-3777
9155 Gast Rd Bridgman (49106) **(G-1928)**
Great Lakes Tech & Mfg LLC..........810 593-0257
201 S Alloy Dr Ste C Fenton (48430) **(G-5482)**
Great Lakes Technologies..........734 362-8217
17900 Parke Ln Grosse Ile (48138) **(G-7523)**
Great Lakes Tire LLC..........586 939-7000
12225 Stephens Rd Warren (48089) **(G-17836)**
Great Lakes Tissue Company..........231 627-0200
437 S Main St Cheboygan (49721) **(G-2785)**
Great Lakes Toll Services..........616 847-1868
17354 Teunis Dr Ste D Spring Lake (49456) **(G-15820)**
Great Lakes Tool LLC..........586 759-5253
24027 Ryan Rd Warren (48091) **(G-17837)**
Great Lakes Towers LLC..........734 682-4000
111 Borchert Park Dr Monroe (48161) **(G-11545)**
Great Lakes Treatment Corp..........517 566-8008
5630 E Eaton Hwy Sunfield (48890) **(G-16335)**
Great Lakes Trim Inc..........231 267-3000
6183 S Railway Cmn Williamsburg (49690) **(G-18555)**
Great Lakes Waterjet Laser LLC..........517 629-9900
1101 Industrial Blvd Albion (49224) **(G-126)**
Great Lakes Weld LLC..........231 943-4180
889 S East Silver Lake Rd Traverse City (49685) **(G-16706)**
Great Lakes Welding Co..........810 689-8182
8117 State Rd Burtchville (48059) **(G-2220)**
Great Lakes Wellhead Inc (PA)..........231 943-9100
4243 S M 37 Grawn (49637) **(G-7451)**
Great Lakes Wine & Spirits LLC (PA)..........313 278-5400
373 Victor St Highland Park (48203) **(G-7908)**
Great Lakes Wood Products..........906 228-3737
434 Us Highway 41 E Negaunee (49866) **(G-11967)**
Great Lakes Woodworking Co Inc..........313 892-8500
11345 Mound Rd Detroit (48212) **(G-4277)**
Great Lakes Woodworking LLC..........248 550-1991
3361 Aspen Dr Apt 6304 Orion (48359) **(G-12732)**
Great Lakes X-Cel, Niles *Also called N & K Fulbright LLC* **(G-12149)**
Great Lakes-Triad Plastic (PA)..........616 241-6441
3939 36th St Se Grand Rapids (49512) **(G-6788)**
Great Legs Wnery Brwry Dist LL..........616 298-7600
2478 Nuttall Ct Holland (49424) **(G-8060)**
Great Lkes Finshg Svcs Detroit, Pontiac *Also called Kent Upholstery Inc* **(G-13392)**
Great Lkes Fstida Holdings Inc..........616 241-0400
219 Canton St Sw Ste A Grand Rapids (49507) **(G-6789)**
Great Lkes Htg Colg Rfrgn Shtm, Dearborn *Also called Great Lakes Mechanical Corp* **(G-3849)**
Great Lkes Indus Frnc Svcs Inc..........586 323-9200
6780 19 1/2 Mile Rd Sterling Heights (48314) **(G-16033)**
Great Lkes Tex Restoration LLC..........989 448-8600
651 Expressway Ct Gaylord (49735) **(G-6131)**
Great North Woodworks..........231 622-6200
1131 Emmet St Petoskey (49770) **(G-12998)**
Great Northern Lumber Mich LLC..........989 736-6192
507 W Traverse Bay Rd Lincoln (48742) **(G-10034)**
Great Northern Publishing Inc..........810 648-4000
356 E Sanilac Rd Sandusky (48471) **(G-15059)**
Great Northern Quiver Co LLC..........269 838-5437
8635 Thornapple Lake Rd Nashville (49073) **(G-11954)**
Great Openings, Ludington *Also called Metalworks Inc* **(G-10546)**
Great Put On Inc..........810 733-8021
3240 W Pasadena Ave Flint (48504) **(G-5709)**
Great Put On Inc..........810 771-4174
12235 S Saginaw St Grand Blanc (48439) **(G-6246)**
Greatech Integration USA Inc..........734 673-5985
47119 Cartier Ct Wixom (48393) **(G-18670)**
Greater Lansing Bus Monthly..........517 203-0123
221 W Saginaw St Lansing (48933) **(G-9844)**
Greater Lansing Orthotic Clini..........517 337-0856
200 N Homer St Ste A Lansing (48912) **(G-9845)**
Greatlakespowertoolscom..........231 733-6200
4841 Airline Rd Muskegon (49444) **(G-11832)**
Grede Holdings LLC (HQ)..........248 440-9500
20750 Civic Center Dr # 100 Southfield (48076) **(G-15579)**
Grede II LLC (HQ)..........248 440-9500
20750 Civic Center Dr # 100 Southfield (48076) **(G-15580)**
Grede LLC..........906 774-7250
801 S Carpenter Ave Kingsford (49802) **(G-9509)**
Grede LLC (HQ)..........248 440-9500
20750 Civic Center Dr # 100 Southfield (48076) **(G-15581)**
Grede Omaha LLC..........248 727-1800
20750 Civic Center Dr # 100 Southfield (48076) **(G-15582)**
Grede Wscnsin Subsidiaries LLC (HQ)..........248 727-1800
20750 Civic Center Dr # 100 Southfield (48076) **(G-15583)**
Green Age Organics, Washington *Also called Green Age Products & Svcs LLC* **(G-18080)**
Green Age Products & Svcs LLC..........586 207-5724
64155 Van Dyke Rd Ste 238 Washington (48095) **(G-18080)**
Green Bay Packaging Inc..........269 552-1000
5350 E N Ave Kalamazoo (49048) **(G-9202)**
Green Day Management LLC..........313 652-1390
607 Shelby St Ste 700-100 Detroit (48226) **(G-4278)**
Green Door Distilling Co LLC..........269 207-2298
429 E North St Kalamazoo (49007) **(G-9203)**
Green Dreamzz LLC..........313 377-2926
8587 Northlawn St Detroit (48204) **(G-4279)**
Green Fuels Llc..........734 735-6802
715 Indian Trail Rd Carleton (48117) **(G-2554)**
Green Gables Saw Mill..........989 386-7846
5605 E Surrey Rd Clare (48617) **(G-2980)**
Green Industries Inc..........248 446-8900
48145 West Rd Wixom (48393) **(G-18671)**
Green Ink Works..........616 254-7350
3637 Clyde Park Ave Sw # 2 Wyoming (49509) **(G-18877)**
Green Link Inc..........269 216-9229
5519 E Cork St Ste A Kalamazoo (49048) **(G-9204)**
Green Manufacturing Inc..........517 458-1500
9650 Packard Rd Morenci (49256) **(G-11613)**
Green Oak Tool and Svcs Inc..........586 531-2255
9449 Maltby Rd Brighton (48116) **(G-2005)**
Green Peak Industries LLC..........517 408-0178
10070 Harvest Park Dimondale (48821) **(G-4763)**

ALPHABETIC

Green Plastics LLC   **ALPHABETIC SECTION**

Green Plastics LLC 616 295-2718
   13370 Barry St Ste A Holland (49424) *(G-8061)*
Green Polymeric Materials Inc 313 933-7390
   6031 Joy Rd Detroit (48204) *(G-4280)*
Green Room Michigan LLC 248 289-3288
   32000 Northwestern Hwy Farmington Hills (48334) *(G-5255)*
Green Sign Man 269 370-0554
   311 S North St Otsego (49078) *(G-12787)*
Greenbrook Tms Neurohealth Ctr 855 940-4867
   4136 Legacy Pkwy Ste 110 Lansing (48911) *(G-9846)*
Greendale Screw Pdts Co Inc 586 759-8100
   11500 Hupp Ave Warren (48089) *(G-17838)*
Greene Group Industries, Port Huron Also called Greene Manufacturing Tech LLC *(G-13481)*
Greene Manufacturing Inc 734 428-8304
   3985 S Fletcher Rd Chelsea (48118) *(G-2813)*
Greene Manufacturing Tech LLC 810 982-9720
   2600 20th St Port Huron (48060) *(G-13481)*
Greene Metal Products Inc (PA) 586 465-6800
   24500 Capital Blvd Clinton Township (48036) *(G-3249)*
Greenfeld Homemade Egg Noodles, Detroit Also called Greenfield Noodle Specialty Co *(G-4281)*
Greenfield Cabinetry Inc 586 759-3300
   23811 Ryan Rd Warren (48091) *(G-17839)*
Greenfield Noodle Specialty Co 313 873-2212
   600 Custer St Detroit (48202) *(G-4281)*
Greenforces LLC 906 231-7769
   600 E Lkeshore Dr Ste 111 Houghton (49931) *(G-8382)*
Greenglow Products LLC 248 827-1451
   21170 Bridge St Southfield (48033) *(G-15584)*
Greenia Custom Woodworking Inc 989 868-9790
   2380 W Vassar Rd Reese (48757) *(G-13806)*
Greening Incorporated (PA) 313 366-7160
   19465 Mount Elliott St Detroit (48234) *(G-4282)*
Greening Associates Inc 313 366-7160
   19465 Mount Elliott St Detroit (48234) *(G-4283)*
Greening Testing Laboratories, Detroit Also called Greening Associates Inc *(G-4283)*
Greenlight Home Inspection Svc 313 885-5616
   23340 Westbury St Saint Clair Shores (48080) *(G-14863)*
Greenman's Printing & Imaging, Farmington Hills Also called Jomark Inc *(G-5275)*
Greenmans Speedy Printing 248 478-2600
   30650 W 8 Mile Rd Farmington Hills (48336) *(G-5256)*
Greenmark Biomedical Inc 517 336-4665
   3815 Tech Blvd Ste 1055 Lansing (48910) *(G-9847)*
Greenseed LLC 313 295-0100
   26980 Trolley Indus Dr Taylor (48180) *(G-16423)*
Greenville Cabinet Distri 616 225-2424
   1323 Callaghan St Greenville (48838) *(G-7487)*
Greenville Tool & Die Co 616 754-5693
   1215 S Lafayette St Greenville (48838) *(G-7488)*
Greenville Trck Wldg Sups LLC (PA) 616 754-6120
   201 W Greenville West Dr Greenville (48838) *(G-7489)*
Greenville Truck and Welding, Greenville Also called Greenville Trck Wldg Sups LLC *(G-7489)*
Greenville Ventr Partners LLC 616 303-2400
   6501 Fitzner Rd Greenville (48838) *(G-7490)*
Greenwell Machine Shop Inc 231 347-3346
   1048 Emmet St Petoskey (49770) *(G-12999)*
Greg Linska Sales Inc 248 765-6354
   2987 Hill Dr Troy (48085) *(G-17134)*
Greg Socha 269 344-1204
   5611 King Hwy Kalamazoo (49048) *(G-9205)*
Gregg Publishing Co 906 789-1139
   413 S 7th St Escanaba (49829) *(G-5074)*
Greggs Wood Duck Boxes 989 770-5204
   3240 Fergus Rd Burt (48417) *(G-2215)*
Gregory M Boese 989 754-2990
   2929 River St Saginaw (48601) *(G-14659)*
Gregs Dockside Marine Svc LLC 810 874-8250
   6311 Benoit Rd Clay (48001) *(G-3120)*
Greif, Grand Rapids Also called Cascade Paper Converters LLC *(G-6555)*
Greif Inc 586 415-0000
   20101 Cornillie Dr Roseville (48066) *(G-14417)*
Greko Print & Imaging Inc 734 453-0341
   260 Ann Arbor Rd W Plymouth (48170) *(G-13180)*
Grenell Manufacturing LLC 616 304-1593
   400 Lake Dr Lakeview (48850) *(G-9641)*
Gresham Driving Aids Inc (PA) 248 624-1533
   30800 S Wixom Rd Wixom (48393) *(G-18672)*
Grey Wolfe Publishing LLC 248 914-4027
   23565 Old Orchard Trl Bingham Farms (48025) *(G-1698)*
Greystone Imaging LLC 616 742-3810
   5510 33rd St Se Ste 1 Grand Rapids (49512) *(G-6790)*
Greystone Medical LLC 248 955-3069
   7433 Pine Creek Trl Ste B Waterford (48327) *(G-18126)*
Grg, Brighton Also called Global Retool Group Amer LLC *(G-2001)*
Grg, Troy Also called Graphic Resource Group Inc *(G-17132)*
Griff & Son Tree Service Inc 989 735-5160
   2921 Lakeshore Dr Glennie (48737) *(G-6212)*

Griffen Fab Works LLC 616 890-0621
   10195 S Kent Dr Sw Byron Center (49315) *(G-2276)*
Griffin Tool Inc 269 429-4077
   2951 Johnson Rd Stevensville (49127) *(G-16252)*
Griffon Inc 231 788-4630
   820 S Broton Rd Muskegon (49442) *(G-11833)*
Grigg Graphic Services Inc 248 356-5005
   20982 Bridge St Southfield (48033) *(G-15585)*
Grills To Go At Bannasch Wldg, Lansing Also called Bannasch Welding Inc *(G-9674)*
Grimbac Division, Ann Arbor Also called TGI Direct Inc *(G-685)*
Grimm Industries LLC 810 335-3188
   50661 Jefferson Ave Apt 3 New Baltimore (48047) *(G-11981)*
Grind Repair, Roseville Also called Aero Grinding Inc *(G-14372)*
Grind-All Precision Tool Co 586 954-3430
   21300 Carlo Dr Clinton Township (48038) *(G-3250)*
Grinders Clearinghouse Inc (PA) 586 771-1500
   13301 E 8 Mile Rd Warren (48089) *(G-17840)*
Grinding Products Company Inc 586 757-2118
   11084 E 9 Mile Rd Warren (48089) *(G-17841)*
Grinding Specialists Inc 734 729-1775
   38310 Abruzzi Dr Westland (48185) *(G-18377)*
Grindmaster Eqp & Mchs USA LLC 517 455-3675
   6539 Westland Way Ste 13 Lansing (48917) *(G-9763)*
Grip Studios 248 757-0796
   743 Wing St Rear Bldg Plymouth (48170) *(G-13181)*
Grippe Machining and Mfg Co 586 778-3150
   15642 Common Rd Roseville (48066) *(G-14418)*
Griptrac Inc 231 853-2284
   4865 S Ravenna Rd Ravenna (49451) *(G-13689)*
Griswold Tool and Die Inc 517 741-7433
   204 Railroad St Union City (49094) *(G-17494)*
Grit Manufacturing LLC 517 285-5277
   7646 Skegemog Point Rd Williamsburg (49690) *(G-18556)*
Grizzly Peak Brewing Company, Ann Arbor Also called Gpbc Inc *(G-503)*
Grlabel, Grand Rapids Also called Grand Rapids Label Company *(G-6760)*
Grm Automation Inc 616 559-2700
   5271 Plainfield Ave Ne Grand Rapids (49525) *(G-6791)*
Grm Corporation (PA) 989 453-2322
   39 N Caseville Rd Pigeon (48755) *(G-13037)*
Grm Corporation 989 453-2322
   7375 Crescent Beach Rd Pigeon (48755) *(G-13038)*
Groholski Mfg Solutions LLC 517 278-9339
   127 Industrial Ave Coldwater (49036) *(G-3436)*
Gross Machine Shop 989 587-4021
   319 E Main St Westphalia (48894) *(G-18434)*
Gross Ventures Inc 231 767-1301
   6172 Valduga Dr Sw Ste B Byron Center (49315) *(G-2277)*
Grosse Pointe News, Grosse Pointe Park Also called Anteebo Publishers Inc *(G-7546)*
Grosse Pointe News 734 674-0131
   1167 Longfellow Dr Canton (48187) *(G-2468)*
Grosse Tool and Machine Co 586 773-6770
   23080 Groesbeck Hwy Warren (48089) *(G-17842)*
Grossel Tool Co 586 294-3660
   34190 Doreka Fraser (48026) *(G-5932)*
Ground Effects LLC (HQ) 810 250-5560
   3435 Vanslyke Rd Flint (48507) *(G-5710)*
Ground Effects LLC 810 250-5560
   2501 Lippincott Blvd Flint (48507) *(G-5711)*
Group 7500 Inc 313 875-9026
   7500 Oakland St Detroit (48211) *(G-4284)*
Group B Industries II Inc 734 941-6640
   15399 Oakwood Dr Romulus (48174) *(G-14281)*
Group Infotech Inc 517 336-7110
   3101 Tech Blvd Ste E Lansing (48910) *(G-9848)*
Group Tour Magazines, Holland Also called Shoreline Creations Ltd *(G-8192)*
Groupe Stahl, Saint Clair Shores Also called Stahls Inc *(G-14887)*
Grouper Wild LLC (HQ) 248 299-7500
   1780 Pond Run Auburn Hills (48326) *(G-917)*
Grouper Wild LLC 269 665-4261
   9000 E Michigan Ave Galesburg (49053) *(G-6078)*
Grow Show, The, Ann Arbor Also called Buyers Development Group LLC *(G-411)*
Growgeneration Michigan Corp (HQ) 248 473-0450
   5711 Enterprise Dr Lansing (48911) *(G-9849)*
GRS&s, Grand Rapids Also called Gill Corporation *(G-6740)*
Grt Avionics Inc 616 245-7700
   3133 Madison Ave Se Ste B Wyoming (49548) *(G-18878)*
Gruber Supplies & Accessories, Southfield Also called Marshall-Gruber Company LLC *(G-15647)*
Grupo Antolin Michigan Inc (HQ) 989 635-5055
   6300 Euclid St Marlette (48453) *(G-10982)*
Grupo Antolin North Amer Inc (HQ) 248 373-1749
   1700 Atlantic Blvd Auburn Hills (48326) *(G-918)*
Grupo Antolin Primera Auto Sys (HQ) 734 495-9180
   47440 Mi Ave Ste 150 Canton (48188) *(G-2469)*
Grupo Antolin Wayne, Canton Also called Grupo Antolin Primera Auto Sys *(G-2469)*
Grupo Resilient Intl Inc (PA) 810 410-8177
   15091 Poberezny Ct Linden (48451) *(G-10062)*

ALPHABETIC SECTION
H L F Furniture Incorporated

Grw Technologies Inc....616 575-8119
4460 44th St Se Ste B Grand Rapids (49512) ***(G-6792)***
GRX Manufacturing....616 570-0832
3800 36th St Se Grand Rapids (49512) ***(G-6793)***
Gs3, Livonia *Also called Global Strgc Sup Solutions LLC* ***(G-10226)***
Gsa Direct Supply LLC....313 739-6375
12908 W 7 Mile Rd Detroit (48235) ***(G-4285)***
Gsb & Associates Inc....770 424-1886
3680 Stadium Pkwy Kalamazoo (49009) ***(G-9206)***
GSC Riii - Grede LLC....248 440-9500
20750 Civic Center Dr # 100 Southfield (48076) ***(G-15586)***
Gst Autoleather Holdco Corp....248 436-2300
2920 Waterview Dr Rochester Hills (48309) ***(G-14028)***
Gt Performance Coatings LLC....248 627-5905
1342 S Ortonville Rd Ortonville (48462) ***(G-12748)***
Gt Plastics & Equipment LLC....616 678-7445
13425 Peach Ridge Ave Kent City (49330) ***(G-9432)***
Gt Plastics Incorporated....989 739-7803
4681 Industrial Row Oscoda (48750) ***(G-12759)***
GT Solutions LLC....616 259-0700
31 E 8th St Ste 310 Holland (49423) ***(G-8062)***
Gt Technologies Inc (HQ)....734 467-8371
5859 E Executive Dr Westland (48185) ***(G-18378)***
Gti Liquidating Inc (PA)....616 842-5430
1500 Marion Ave Grand Haven (49417) ***(G-6309)***
Gti Power Acquisition LLC (PA)....616 842-5430
1500 Marion Ave Grand Haven (49417) ***(G-6310)***
GTM Steamer Service Inc....989 732-7678
647 Poplar Dr Gaylord (49735) ***(G-6132)***
Guardhat Inc....248 281-6089
20300 Civic Center Dr # 1103 Southfield (48076) ***(G-15587)***
Guardian Automotive Trim, Warren *Also called Srg Global Automotive LLC* ***(G-18024)***
Guardian Fabrication LLC (HQ)....248 340-1800
2300 Harmon Rd Auburn Hills (48326) ***(G-919)***
Guardian Fabrication Inc....248 340-1800
2300 Harmon Rd Auburn Hills (48326) ***(G-920)***
Guardian Fiberglass, Albion *Also called Knauf Insulation Inc* ***(G-128)***
Guardian Glass LLC....248 340-1800
2300 Harmon Rd Auburn Hills (48326) ***(G-921)***
Guardian Industries LLC....517 629-9464
1000 E North St Albion (49224) ***(G-127)***
Guardian Industries LLC....734 654-4285
14600 Romine Rd Carleton (48117) ***(G-2555)***
Guardian Industries LLC (HQ)....248 340-1800
2300 Harmon Rd Auburn Hills (48326) ***(G-922)***
Guardian Industries LLC....734 654-1111
14511 Romine Rd Carleton (48117) ***(G-2556)***
Guardian Manufacturing Corp....734 591-1454
12193 Levan Rd Livonia (48150) ***(G-10231)***
Guardian Science & Tech Ctr, Carleton *Also called Guardian Industries LLC* ***(G-2556)***
Gudel Inc....734 214-0000
4881 Runway Blvd Ann Arbor (48108) ***(G-508)***
Gudho USA Inc....616 682-7814
138 Deer Run Dr Ne Ada (49301) ***(G-21)***
Guelph Tool Sales Inc....586 755-3333
24150 Gibson Dr Warren (48089) ***(G-17843)***
Guerne Precision Machining....231 834-7417
13761 Bailey Rd Bailey (49303) ***(G-1119)***
Guernsey Dairy Stores Inc....248 349-1466
21300 Novi Rd Northville (48167) ***(G-12227)***
Guernsey Farms Dairy, Northville *Also called Guernsey Dairy Stores Inc* ***(G-12227)***
Guess Inc....517 546-2933
1475 N Burkhart Rd B100 Howell (48855) ***(G-8457)***
Guess Factory Store 185, Howell *Also called Guess Inc* ***(G-8457)***
Guest Publications LLC....231 651-9281
3804 Morningside Dr Traverse City (49684) ***(G-16707)***
Guhring Inc....262 784-6730
24975 Trans X Rd Novi (48375) ***(G-12424)***
Guhring-Michigan, Novi *Also called Guhring Inc* ***(G-12424)***
Guiding Our Destiny Ministry....313 212-9063
14811 Greenfield Rd A4 Detroit (48227) ***(G-4286)***
Guidobono Concrete Inc....810 229-2666
7474 Whitmore Lake Rd Brighton (48116) ***(G-2006)***
Guile & Son Inc....517 376-2116
11951 Rathbon Rd Byron (48418) ***(G-2254)***
Guilford of Maine Marketing Co....616 554-2250
5300 Corprte Grv Dr Se # 200 Grand Rapids (49512) ***(G-6794)***
Guilford Performance Textiles....910 794-5810
21557 Telegraph Rd Southfield (48033) ***(G-15588)***
Guo Ji Tooling Systems LLC....616 301-6906
555 Plymouth Ave Ne Grand Rapids (49505) ***(G-6795)***
Gustafson Smoked Fish....906 292-5424
W4467 Us 2 Moran (49760) ***(G-11609)***
Gustos Quality Systems....231 409-0219
11655 Gusto Dr Fife Lake (49633) ***(G-5607)***
Guyoung Tech Usa Inc (HQ)....248 746-4261
26555 Evergreen Rd # 1515 Southfield (48076) ***(G-15589)***
Guys You Are Real Heroes Pubg....248 682-2537
5047 Shenandoah Ct West Bloomfield (48323) ***(G-18286)***
Guzman Woodworks....313 436-1912
2740 Honorah St Detroit (48209) ***(G-4287)***
Gvb Group-La Fiesta LLC....231 843-7600
8155 Cook St Montague (49437) ***(G-11597)***
Gvd Industries LLC....616 836-4067
217 E 24th St Ste 140 Holland (49423) ***(G-8063)***
Gvd Industries LLC....616 298-7243
373 Highbanks Ct Holland (49424) ***(G-8064)***
Gvn Group Corp (PA)....248 340-0342
486 S Opdyke Rd Pontiac (48341) ***(G-13376)***
Gw Fishing Lures Inc....989 684-6431
3476 Killarney Beach Rd Bay City (48706) ***(G-1364)***
Gwen Frostic Prints, Benzonia *Also called Presscraft Papers Inc* ***(G-1616)***
Gwinnett Plastics Inc....765 215-6593
2233 Mapleton St Ne Grand Rapids (49505) ***(G-6796)***
Gws Tool LLC....616 971-4700
3987 Brockton Dr Se Grand Rapids (49512) ***(G-6797)***
Gyb LLC....586 218-3222
31065 Ryan Rd Warren (48092) ***(G-17844)***
Gyms Sawmill....989 826-8299
931 W Kittle Rd Mio (48647) ***(G-11508)***
Gypsy Vodka, Bingham Farms *Also called High Five Spirits LLC* ***(G-1699)***
Gyro Powder Coating Inc....616 846-2580
1624 Marion Ave Grand Haven (49417) ***(G-6311)***
Gys Tech LLC....269 385-2600
2825 Airview Blvd Portage (49002) ***(G-13563)***
H & A Pharmacy II LLC....313 995-4552
2379 S Venoy Rd Westland (48186) ***(G-18379)***
H & B Machining LLC....810 986-2423
4392 Musson Rd Howell (48855) ***(G-8458)***
H & G Tool Company....586 573-7040
30700 Ryan Rd Warren (48092) ***(G-17845)***
H & H Powdercoating Inc....810 750-1800
300 S Fenway Dr Fenton (48430) ***(G-5483)***
H & H Publications, Fowlerville *Also called Fowlerville News & Views* ***(G-5841)***
H & H Welding & Repair LLC....517 676-1800
700 Acme Dr Mason (48854) ***(G-11136)***
H & J Mfg Consulting Svcs Corp....734 941-8314
15771 S Huron River Dr Romulus (48174) ***(G-14282)***
H & J Printing....734 344-9447
22411 Silver Creek Ln Rockwood (48173) ***(G-14199)***
H & K Machine Company Inc....269 756-7339
7451 Us Highway 12 Three Oaks (49128) ***(G-16556)***
H & L Advantage Inc....616 532-1012
3500 Busch Dr Sw Grandville (49418) ***(G-7384)***
H & L Manufacturing Co....269 795-5000
900 E Main St Middleville (49333) ***(G-11308)***
H & L Tool & Engineering Inc....586 755-2806
23701 Blackstone Ave Warren (48089) ***(G-17846)***
H & L Tool Company Inc....248 585-7474
32701 Dequindre Rd Madison Heights (48071) ***(G-10736)***
H & M Machining, Roseville *Also called Rocksteady Manufacturing LLC* ***(G-14472)***
H & M Machining Inc....586 778-5028
29625 Parkway Roseville (48066) ***(G-14419)***
H & M Pallet LLC....231 821-8800
9148 S 200th Ave Holton (49425) ***(G-8338)***
H & M Vibro, Grandville *Also called Midwest Vibro Inc* ***(G-7401)***
H & M Welding and Fabricating....517 764-3630
3600 Page Ave Jackson (49203) ***(G-8897)***
H & R Electrical Contrs LLC....517 669-2102
10588 S Us Highway 27 Dewitt (48820) ***(G-4710)***
H & R Enterprises, Hillsdale *Also called Ron Watkins* ***(G-7946)***
H & R Industries Inc (PA)....616 247-1165
3020 Stafford Ave Sw Grand Rapids (49548) ***(G-6798)***
H & R Wood Specialties Inc....269 628-2181
20783 County Road 653 Gobles (49055) ***(G-6217)***
H & S Mold Inc....989 732-3566
1640 Orourke Blvd Gaylord (49735) ***(G-6133)***
H A Eckhart & Associates Inc....517 321-7700
16185 National Pkwy Lansing (48906) ***(G-9702)***
H A King Co Inc (PA)....248 280-0006
5038 Leafdale Blvd Royal Oak (48073) ***(G-14542)***
H and M Lube DBA Jlube....231 929-1197
529 W Fourteenth St Traverse City (49684) ***(G-16708)***
H B D M Inc....269 273-1976
1149 Millard St Three Rivers (49093) ***(G-16575)***
H C Starck Inc....517 279-9511
460 Jay St Coldwater (49036) ***(G-3437)***
H E L P Printers Inc....734 847-0554
9673 Lewis Ave Temperance (48182) ***(G-16533)***
H E Lyons Inc....517 467-2232
10125 W Us Highway 223 Adrian (49221) ***(G-72)***
H E Morse Co....616 396-4604
455 Douglas Ave Holland (49424) ***(G-8065)***
H G Geiger Manufacturing Co....517 369-7357
416 Mill St Bronson (49028) ***(G-2114)***
H H Barnum Co....248 486-5982
12865 Silver Lake Rd Brighton (48116) ***(G-2007)***
H L F Furniture Incorporated....734 697-3000
44001 Van Born Rd Van Buren Twp (48111) ***(G-17528)***

ALPHABETIC

H M Day Signs Inc 231 946-7132
233 E Twelfth St Traverse City (49684) ***(G-16709)***
H M Products Inc 313 875-5148
1435 E Milwaukee St Detroit (48211) ***(G-4288)***
H M T, Rochester Hills *Also called Hot Melt Technologies Inc* ***(G-14034)***
H M White, Detroit *Also called Hmw Contracting LLC* ***(G-4302)***
H O Trerice Co Inc 248 399-8000
12950 W 8 Mile Rd Oak Park (48237) ***(G-12616)***
H P P 248 307-4263
1200 E Avis Dr Madison Heights (48071) ***(G-10737)***
H S Die & Engineering Inc 616 453-5451
2640 Mullins Ct Nw Grand Rapids (49534) ***(G-6799)***
H S Express, Rochester Hills *Also called HS Inc* ***(G-14035)***
H W Jencks Incorporated 231 352-4422
1339 Elm St Frankfort (49635) ***(G-5878)***
H W Motor Homes Inc 734 394-2000
5390 Belleville Rd Canton (48188) ***(G-2470)***
H-O-H Water Technology Inc 248 669-6667
1013 Rig St Commerce Township (48390) ***(G-3534)***
HA Automotive Systems Inc (HQ) 248 781-0001
1300 Coolidge Hwy Troy (48084) ***(G-17135)***
Haarala Ceramic Tile & Marble 734 422-1168
30765 Westfield St Livonia (48150) ***(G-10232)***
Haartz Corporation 248 646-8200
40950 Woodward Ave # 150 Bloomfield Hills (48304) ***(G-1825)***
Haas Food Services, Negaunee *Also called Stephen Haas* ***(G-11975)***
Haas Group International LLC 810 236-0032
G3100 Van Slyke Rd Flint (48551) ***(G-5712)***
Hacht Sales, Southfield *Also called Prestige Pet Products Inc* ***(G-15680)***
Hacienda Mexican Foods LLC (PA) 313 895-8823
6100 Buchanan St Detroit (48210) ***(G-4289)***
Hacker Machine Inc 517 569-3348
11200 Broughwell Rd Rives Junction (49277) ***(G-13886)***
Hackett Brass Foundry Co (PA) 313 822-1214
1200 Lillibridge St Detroit (48214) ***(G-4290)***
Hackett Brass Foundry Co 313 331-6005
45 Saint Jean St Detroit (48214) ***(G-4291)***
Hackley Health Ventures Inc (HQ) 231 728-5720
1675 Leahy St Ste 101 Muskegon (49442) ***(G-11834)***
Hackley Hearing Center, Muskegon *Also called Hackley Health Ventures Inc* ***(G-11834)***
Hacks Key Shop Inc 517 485-9488
1109 River St Lansing (48912) ***(G-9850)***
Hadley Products Corporation (HQ) 616 530-1717
2851 Prairie St Sw Ste A Grandville (49418) ***(G-7385)***
Haerter Stamping LLC 616 871-9400
3840 Model Ct Se Kentwood (49512) ***(G-9457)***
Hagen Cement Products Inc 269 483-9641
17149 Us Highway 12 White Pigeon (49099) ***(G-18480)***
Hager Wood Preserving LLC 616 248-0905
1211 Judd Ave Sw Wyoming (49509) ***(G-18879)***
Haighs Maple Syrup & Sups LLC 517 202-6975
11756 Scipio Hwy Vermontville (49096) ***(G-17588)***
Hair Vault LLC 586 649-8218
1098 Ann Arbor Rd W Ste 5 Plymouth (48170) ***(G-13182)***
Hajjar Plating, Detroit *Also called Micro Platers Sales Inc* ***(G-4454)***
Hak Inc (PA) 231 587-5322
413 Dale Ave Mancelona (49659) ***(G-10872)***
Hal International Inc 248 488-0440
34155 Industrial Rd Livonia (48150) ***(G-10233)***
Haldex Brake Products Corp 616 827-9641
5801 Weller Ct Sw Ste D Wyoming (49509) ***(G-18880)***
Hale Manufacturing Inc 231 529-6271
6235 Cupp Rd Alanson (49706) ***(G-111)***
Hall Mat, Gladwin *Also called William R Hall Kimberly* ***(G-6208)***
Hall Wood Creations 248 645-0983
15766 Birwood Ave Beverly Hills (48025) ***(G-1664)***
Halliday Sand & Gravel Inc 989 422-3463
1128 Federal Ave Houghton Lake (48629) ***(G-8397)***
Hallmark Tool and Gage Co Inc 248 669-4010
51200 Pontiac Trl Wixom (48393) ***(G-18673)***
Hallstrom Company 906 439-5439
M-94 W Eben Junction (49825) ***(G-4978)***
Haltermann Carless Us Inc 248 422-6548
901 Wilshire Dr Ste 570 Troy (48084) ***(G-17136)***
Hamaton Inc 248 308-3856
47815 West Rd Ste D-109 Wixom (48393) ***(G-18674)***
Hamblin Company 517 423-7491
40900 Woodward Ave # 111 Bloomfield Hills (48304) ***(G-1826)***
Hambones Wood Works 313 304-5590
4323 E Newport Rd Newport (48166) ***(G-12102)***
Hamilton Block & Ready Mix Co 269 751-5129
4510 132nd Ave Hamilton (49419) ***(G-7598)***
Hamilton Electric Co 989 799-6291
3175 Pierce Rd Saginaw (48604) ***(G-14660)***
Hamilton Engineering Inc 734 419-0200
34000 Autry St Livonia (48150) ***(G-10234)***
Hamilton Harley-Davidson 269 651-3424
68951 White School Rd Us-12 Sturgis (49091) ***(G-16292)***
Hamilton Industrial Products 269 751-5153
4555 134th Ave Hamilton (49419) ***(G-7599)***
Hamilton Ranch Trucking, Mc Bain *Also called Lee Hamilton Gary Jr* ***(G-11184)***
Hamilton Steel Fabrications 269 751-8757
3290 Lincoln Rd Hamilton (49419) ***(G-7600)***
Hamiltons Custom Stairs 810 686-5698
3024 Ridgelawn Dr Clio (48420) ***(G-3400)***
Hamlin Tool & Machine Co Inc 248 651-6302
1671 E Hamlin Rd Rochester Hills (48307) ***(G-14029)***
Hammar's Welding, Kimball *Also called Hammars Contracting LLC* ***(G-9493)***
Hammars Contracting LLC 810 367-3037
1177 Wadhams Rd Kimball (48074) ***(G-9493)***
Hammerhead Industries 574 277-8911
1325 Airport Rd Niles (49120) ***(G-12135)***
Hammond Machinery Inc 269 345-7151
1600 Douglas Ave Kalamazoo (49007) ***(G-9207)***
Hammond Publishing Company 810 686-8879
G7166 N Saginaw St Mount Morris (48458) ***(G-11671)***
Hammound Roto-Finish, Kalamazoo *Also called Kalamazoo Company* ***(G-9237)***
Hamp 989 366-5341
126 Winding Dr Houghton Lake (48629) ***(G-8398)***
Hampshire Chemical Corp 989 636-1000
2211 H H Dow Way Midland (48642) ***(G-11370)***
Hampton Block & Supply, Oxford *Also called Hampton Block Co* ***(G-12886)***
Hampton Block Co 248 628-1333
465 Tanview Dr Oxford (48371) ***(G-12886)***
Hampton Company Inc 517 765-2222
12709 M 60 E Burlington (49029) ***(G-2209)***
Hamtech Inc 231 796-3917
1916 Industrial Dr N Big Rapids (49307) ***(G-1675)***
Hamtramck Review Inc 313 874-2100
3020 Caniff St Detroit (48212) ***(G-4292)***
Hanchett Manufacturing Inc 231 796-7678
20000 19 Mile Rd Big Rapids (49307) ***(G-1676)***
Hancock Bottling Co Inc 906 482-3701
1800 Birch St Hancock (49930) ***(G-7618)***
Hancock Enterprises Inc 734 287-8840
20655 Northline Rd Taylor (48180) ***(G-16424)***
Hand 2 Hand Whl & Dist LLC 313 574-2861
11942 Roxbury St Detroit (48224) ***(G-4293)***
Hand Cast Covers 810 225-7770
425 Mystic Meadows Ct Howell (48843) ***(G-8459)***
Handicap Sign Inc 616 454-9416
1142 Wealthy St Se Grand Rapids (49506) ***(G-6800)***
Handley Industries Inc 517 787-8821
2101 Brooklyn Rd Jackson (49203) ***(G-8898)***
Handorn Inc 616 241-6181
636 Crofton St Se Grand Rapids (49507) ***(G-6801)***
Hands That Heal 517 740-6930
1144 Herbert J Ave Jackson (49202) ***(G-8899)***
Handy Bindery Co Inc 586 469-2240
23170 Giacoma Ct Clinton Township (48036) ***(G-3251)***
Handy Home, Monroe *Also called Backyard Products LLC* ***(G-11526)***
Handy Wacks Corporation (PA) 616 887-8268
100 E Averill St Sparta (49345) ***(G-15766)***
Handy Wacks Corporation 616 887-8268
100 E Averill St Sparta (49345) ***(G-15767)***
Hang On Express 231 271-0202
316 N Saint Joseph St Suttons Bay (49682) ***(G-16340)***
Hanger Prsthetcs & Ortho Inc 517 394-5850
4424 S Pennsylvania Ave Lansing (48910) ***(G-9851)***
Hanho America Co Ltd 248 422-6921
100 E Big Beaver Rd # 845 Troy (48083) ***(G-17137)***
Hank Thorn Co 248 348-7800
29164 Wall St Wixom (48393) ***(G-18675)***
Hankerds Sportswear Basic TS 989 725-2979
116 W Exchange St Owosso (48867) ***(G-12836)***
Hankins & Assoc, Petersburg *Also called DTe Hankin Inc* ***(G-12983)***
Hanlo Gauges & Engineering Co 734 422-4224
34403 Glendale St Livonia (48150) ***(G-10235)***
Hanon Printing Company 248 541-9099
34 Cambridge Blvd Pleasant Ridge (48069) ***(G-13105)***
Hanon Systems Usa LLC (HQ) 248 907-8000
39600 Lewis Dr Novi (48377) ***(G-12425)***
Hanse Environmental Inc (PA) 269 673-8638
235 Hubbard St Allegan (49010) ***(G-160)***
Hansen Towing and Recovery, Grand Rapids *Also called Brilliant Industries LLC* ***(G-6525)***
Hanson Cold Storage LLC (HQ) 269 982-1390
440 Renaissance Dr Saint Joseph (49085) ***(G-14933)***
Hanson Inc 616 451-3061
1340 Monroe Ave Nw Grand Rapids (49505) ***(G-6802)***
Hanson International Inc (PA) 269 429-5555
440 Renaissance Dr Saint Joseph (49085) ***(G-14934)***
Hanson International Inc 269 429-5555
3500 Hollywood Rd Saint Joseph (49085) ***(G-14935)***
Hanson Lehigh Inc 989 233-5343
3820 Serr Rd Corunna (48817) ***(G-3708)***
Hanson Logistics, Saint Joseph *Also called Hanson Cold Storage LLC* ***(G-14933)***
Hanson Mold Division, Saint Joseph *Also called Hanson International Inc* ***(G-14934)***

Hanwha Advanced Mtls Amer LLC 810 629-2496
1530 E Front St Monroe (48161) ***(G-11546)***
Hanwha Azdel Inc 810 629-2496
2200 Centerwood Dr Warren (48091) ***(G-17847)***
Hanwha L&C Alabama, Monroe *Also called Hanwha Advanced Mtls Amer LLC* ***(G-11546)***
Haosen Automation N Amer Inc 248 556-6398
691 N Squirrel Rd Ste 288 Auburn Hills (48326) ***(G-923)***
Hapman 269 382-8257
5944 E N Ave Kalamazoo (49048) ***(G-9208)***
Happy Bums 616 987-3159
201 Montcalm Ave Se Lowell (49331) ***(G-10502)***
Happy Candy 248 629-9819
2325 John B Ave Warren (48091) ***(G-17848)***
Happy Howies Inc 313 537-7200
15510 Dale St Detroit (48223) ***(G-4294)***
Harada Industry America Inc (HQ) 248 374-2587
22925 Venture Dr Novi (48375) ***(G-12426)***
Harbinger Laser 269 445-1499
708 Sherman Ln Cassopolis (49031) ***(G-2629)***
Harbisonwalker Intl Inc 231 689-6641
1301 E 8th St White Cloud (49349) ***(G-18442)***
Harbor Beach Times 989 479-3605
123 N 1st St Harbor Beach (48441) ***(G-7631)***
Harbor Deburring & Finshg Co, Grand Haven *Also called V & V Inc* ***(G-6377)***
Harbor Foam Inc 616 855-8150
2950 Pririe St Sw Ste 300 Grandville (49418) ***(G-7386)***
Harbor Graphics, Benton Harbor *Also called Vomela Specialty Company* ***(G-1600)***
Harbor Green Solutions LLC 269 352-0265
900 Davis Dr Benton Harbor (49022) ***(G-1553)***
Harbor Industries Inc (PA) 616 842-5330
14130 172nd Ave Grand Haven (49417) ***(G-6312)***
Harbor Industries Inc 231 547-3280
100 Harbor View Ln Charlevoix (49720) ***(G-2717)***
Harbor Industries Inc 616 842-5330
107 Airport Dr Charlevoix (49720) ***(G-2718)***
Harbor Industries Inc 616 842-5330
14170 172nd Ave Grand Haven (49417) ***(G-6313)***
Harbor Isle Plastics LLC 269 465-6004
2337 W Marquette Woods Rd Stevensville (49127) ***(G-16253)***
Harbor Kitchen & Bath LLC 231 624-8060
987 S Forestlane Dr Traverse City (49686) ***(G-16710)***
Harbor Light Newspaper, Harbor Springs *Also called North Country Publishing Corp* ***(G-7653)***
Harbor Master Ltd 616 669-3170
3127 Highland Blvd Hudsonville (49426) ***(G-8585)***
Harbor Packaging, Benton Harbor *Also called Jomar Inc* ***(G-1560)***
Harbor Packaging 616 494-9913
342 E 40th St Holland (49423) ***(G-8066)***
Harbor Retail, Grand Haven *Also called Harbor Industries Inc* ***(G-6312)***
Harbor Screw Machine Products 269 925-5855
430 Cass St Benton Harbor (49022) ***(G-1554)***
Harbor Software Intl Inc 231 347-8866
231 State St Ste 5 Petoskey (49770) ***(G-13000)***
Harbor Sprng Vnyrds Winery LLC 231 242-4062
5699 S Lake Shore Dr Harbor Springs (49740) ***(G-7647)***
Harbor Tool and Machine 989 479-6708
225 Hunter Industrial Dr Harbor Beach (48441) ***(G-7632)***
Harborfront Interiors Inc 231 777-3838
2300 Black Creek Rd Muskegon (49444) ***(G-11835)***
Harborlite, Vicksburg *Also called Imerys Perlite Usa Inc* ***(G-17605)***
Harbrook Tool Inc 248 477-8040
40391 Grand River Ave Novi (48375) ***(G-12427)***
Hard Milling Solutions Inc 586 286-2300
107 Peyerk Ct Bruce Twp (48065) ***(G-2167)***
Hardcrete Inc 989 644-5543
3610 N Rolland Rd Weidman (48893) ***(G-18252)***
Harding Energy Inc 231 798-7033
725 Taylor Ave Ste A Grand Haven (49417) ***(G-6314)***
Hardware Exchange Inc 440 449-8006
3854 Broadmoor Ave Se # 101 Grand Rapids (49512) ***(G-6803)***
Hardwood Solutions, Chelsea *Also called Precision Hrdwood Rsources Inc* ***(G-2824)***
Hardwoods of Michigan, Clinton *Also called Forestry Management Svcs Inc* ***(G-3138)***
Hardwoods Prtg & Advg Servic, Jenison *Also called R & R Harwood Inc* ***(G-9069)***
Hardy & Sons Sign Service Inc 586 779-8018
22340 Harper Ave Saint Clair Shores (48080) ***(G-14864)***
Hardy-Reed Tool & Die Co Inc 517 547-7107
16269 Manitou Beach Rd Manitou Beach (49253) ***(G-10927)***
Harley Attachments, Dexter *Also called Sweepster Attachments LLC* ***(G-4757)***
Harlo Corporation (PA) 616 538-0550
4210 Ferry St Sw Grandville (49418) ***(G-7387)***
Harlo Products Corporation (HQ) 616 538-0550
4210 Ferry St Sw Grandville (49418) ***(G-7388)***
Harloff Manufacturing Co LLC 269 655-1097
828 Duo Tang Rd Unit A Paw Paw (49079) ***(G-12949)***
Harlow Sheet Metal LLC 734 996-1509
5140 Park Rd Ann Arbor (48103) ***(G-509)***
Harman Becker Auto Systems Inc (HQ) 248 785-2361
39001 W 12 Mile Rd Farmington Hills (48331) ***(G-5257)***
Harman Becker Auto Systems Inc 248 703-3010
30001 Cabot Dr Novi (48377) ***(G-12428)***
Harman Builders, Union *Also called Harman Lumber & Supply Inc* ***(G-17488)***
Harman Consumer Group, Farmington Hills *Also called Harman Becker Auto Systems Inc* ***(G-5257)***
Harman Corporation (PA) 248 651-4477
360 South St Rochester (48307) ***(G-13903)***
Harman Lumber & Supply Inc 269 641-5424
15479 Us Highway 12 Ste 7 Union (49130) ***(G-17488)***
Harmon Sign Inc (PA) 248 348-8150
28054 Center Oaks Ct A Wixom (48393) ***(G-18676)***
Harmonie International LLC 248 737-9933
30201 Orchard Lake Rd Farmington Hills (48334) ***(G-5258)***
Harnel Company, Grand Rapids *Also called Zayna LLC* ***(G-7356)***
Harold G Schaevitz Inds LLC 248 636-1515
42690 Woodward Ave # 200 Bloomfield Hills (48304) ***(G-1827)***
Harold K Schultz 517 279-9764
15 W Pearl St Coldwater (49036) ***(G-3438)***
Harp Column LLC 215 564-3232
304 E Central Ave Zeeland (49464) ***(G-19033)***
Harper Arrington Pubg LLC 313 282-6751
18701 Grand River Ave # 105 Detroit (48223) ***(G-4295)***
Harper Dermatology PC 586 776-7546
21 Stillmeadow Ln Grosse Pointe Shores (48236) ***(G-7562)***
Harper Machine Tool Inc 586 756-0140
21410 Ryan Rd Warren (48091) ***(G-17849)***
Harpercollins Christn Pubg Inc 616 698-3230
3900 Sparks Dr Se Grand Rapids (49546) ***(G-6804)***
Harrells LLC 248 446-8070
53410 Grand River Ave New Hudson (48165) ***(G-12056)***
Harrington Construction Co 269 543-4251
6720 124th Ave Fennville (49408) ***(G-5437)***
Harris Obrien Woodworks 616 292-2613
7000 Dtton Indus Pk Dr Se Caledonia (49316) ***(G-2377)***
Harris Rebar, Lansing *Also called Ambassador Steel Corporation* ***(G-9804)***
Harris Sheet Metal Co 989 496-3080
3313 S Saginaw Rd Midland (48640) ***(G-11371)***
Harrison Industries 231 881-4704
7223 Lightfoot Rd Harbor Springs (49740) ***(G-7648)***
Harrison Packing Co Inc (PA) 269 381-3837
3420 Stadium Pkwy Kalamazoo (49009) ***(G-9209)***
Harrison Steel LLC 586 247-1230
50390 Utica Dr Shelby Township (48315) ***(G-15232)***
Harroun Enterprises Inc 810 629-9885
1111 Fenway Cir Fenton (48430) ***(G-5484)***
Harry & Assoc LLC 248 446-8820
11432 Hammerstone Dr South Lyon (48178) ***(G-15437)***
Harrys Meme LLC 248 977-0168
41679 Magnolia Ct Novi (48377) ***(G-12429)***
Harrys Steering Gear Repair 586 677-5580
52197 Sawmill Creek Dr Macomb (48042) ***(G-10601)***
Hart & Cooley LLC (HQ) 616 656-8200
5030 Corp Exch Blvd Se Grand Rapids (49512) ***(G-6805)***
Hart Acquisition Company LLC 313 537-0490
12700 Marion Redford (48239) ***(G-13738)***
Hart Concrete LLC 231 873-2183
540 Maple St Spring Lake (49456) ***(G-15821)***
Hart Enterprises USA Inc 616 887-0400
400 Apple Jack Ct Sparta (49345) ***(G-15768)***
Hart Fabrication Inc 517 924-1109
912 Beckwith Shr Quincy (49082) ***(G-13670)***
Hart Freeze Pack LIC 231 873-2175
835 S Griswold St Hart (49420) ***(G-7754)***
Hart Industries LLC 313 588-1837
43718 Utica Rd Sterling Heights (48314) ***(G-16034)***
Hart Precision Products Inc 313 537-0490
12700 Marion Redford (48239) ***(G-13739)***
Harvard Clothing Company 517 542-2986
411 Marshall St Litchfield (49252) ***(G-10078)***
Harvest Energy Inc 269 838-4595
2820 Division Ave S Grand Rapids (49548) ***(G-6806)***
Harvest Indus & Trade Co LLC 636 675-6430
455 E Cady St Northville (48167) ***(G-12228)***
Harvest Oak Manufaturing 517 781-4016
804 N Matteson St Bronson (49028) ***(G-2115)***
Harvest Time Partners Inc 269 254-8999
6842 Shallowford Way Portage (49024) ***(G-13564)***
Harvey Industries LLC 734 405-2430
17177 N Laurel Park Dr # 243 Livonia (48152) ***(G-10236)***
Harvey Pattern Works Inc 906 774-4285
410 North Blvd Kingsford (49802) ***(G-9510)***
Harvey S Freeman 248 852-2222
4159 Ladysmith St West Bloomfield (48323) ***(G-18287)***
Harveys Commodities LLC 616 920-1805
729 W Main St Carson City (48811) ***(G-2593)***
Harwood Hritg Gold Maple Syrup, Charlevoix *Also called Parsons Centennial Farm LLC* ***(G-2727)***
Hashems of Dearborn Heights 313 278-2000
26509 Ford Rd Dearborn Heights (48127) ***(G-3928)***

Haskell Office — ALPHABETIC SECTION

Haskell Office 616 988-0880
　3770 Hagen Dr Se Wyoming (49548) *(G-18881)*
Hassan Sons Spcial HM Svcs LLC 313 558-1031
　27631 Michigan Ave Inkster (48141) *(G-8665)*
Hastings Equipment, Grand Rapids *Also called Hel Inc* *(G-6808)*
Hastings Fiber Glass Pdts Inc 269 945-9541
　1301 W Green St Hastings (49058) *(G-7795)*
Hastings Manufacturing Company 269 945-2491
　325 N Hanover St Hastings (49058) *(G-7796)*
Hatch Stamping Co 734 475-6507
　190 W Main St Spring Arbor (49283) *(G-15792)*
Hatch Stamping Company LLC (HQ) 734 475-8628
　635 E Industrial Dr Chelsea (48118) *(G-2814)*
Hatchback Publishing 810 394-8612
　7138 Ridgeview Dr Genesee (48437) *(G-6168)*
Hatfield Elc Indus Apprtus Rep, Kalamazoo *Also called Heco Inc* *(G-9210)*
Hatfield Enterprises 616 677-5215
　15627 24th Ave Marne (49435) *(G-10993)*
Hatman, Kalamazoo *Also called Kalamazoo Mfg Corp Globl* *(G-9243)*
Hatteras Inc 734 525-5500
　13200 N Haggerty Rd # 160 Plymouth (48170) *(G-13183)*
Hattiegirl Ice Cream Foods LLC 877 444-3738
　16159 Wyoming St Detroit (48221) *(G-4296)*
Haulin Oats Inc 248 225-1672
　18090 Buckhannon St Roseville (48066) *(G-14420)*
Hausbeck Pickle Company (PA) 989 754-4721
　1626 Hess Ave Saginaw (48601) *(G-14661)*
Haven Innovation Inc 616 935-1040
　1705 Eaton Dr Grand Haven (49417) *(G-6315)*
Haven Manufacturing Company 616 842-1260
　13720 172nd Ave Grand Haven (49417) *(G-6316)*
Havercroft Tool & Die Inc 989 724-5913
　5002 Main St Greenbush (48738) *(G-7472)*
Havers Heritage 517 423-3455
　7500 Clinton Macon Rd Clinton (49236) *(G-3140)*
Haviland Contoured Plastics 616 361-6691
　2168 Avastar Pkwy Nw Walker (49544) *(G-17640)*
Havis Inc 734 414-0699
　47099 Five Mile Rd Plymouth (48170) *(G-13184)*
Hawk Design Inc 989 781-1152
　7760 Gratiot Rd Saginaw (48609) *(G-14662)*
Hawk Tool and Machine Inc 248 349-0121
　29183 Lorie Ln Wixom (48393) *(G-18677)*
Hawkshadow Publishing Company 586 979-5046
　34481 Heartsworth Ln Sterling Heights (48312) *(G-16035)*
Haworth Inc (HQ) 616 393-3000
　1 Haworth Ctr Holland (49423) *(G-8067)*
Haworth Hong Kong LLC (PA) 616 393-3484
　1 Haworth Ctr Gladstone (49837) *(G-6181)*
Haworth International Ltd (PA) 616 393-3000
　1 Haworth Ctr Holland (49423) *(G-8068)*
Hawtal Whiting 248 262-2020
　41155 Technology Park Dr Sterling Heights (48314) *(G-16036)*
Hawthorne Metal Products Co 248 549-1375
　4336 Coolidge Hwy Royal Oak (48073) *(G-14543)*
Hayden - McNeil LLC 734 455-7900
　14903 Pilot Dr Plymouth (48170) *(G-13185)*
Hayden Neitzke LLC 989 875-2440
　2035 S Warner Rd Sumner (48889) *(G-16331)*
Hayes Lemmerz International, Novi *Also called Maxion Wheels LLC* *(G-12476)*
Hayes Lemmerz Intl Import LLC 734 737-5000
　39500 Orchard Hill Pl # 50 Novi (48375) *(G-12430)*
Hayes Lemmerz Intl-Commrcl Hwy, Novi *Also called Maxion Wheels Akron LLC* *(G-12475)*
Hayes Lmmerz Intrntnl-Grgia LL 734 737-5000
　39500 Orchard Hill Pl # 50 Novi (48375) *(G-12431)*
Hayes Manufacturing Inc 231 879-3372
　6875 Us Highway 131 Fife Lake (49633) *(G-5608)*
Hayes-Albion Corporation 517 629-2141
　1999 Wildwood Ave Jackson (49202) *(G-8900)*
Haynie and Hess Realty Co LLC 586 296-2750
　33670 Riviera Fraser (48026) *(G-5933)*
Hazekamps Wholesale Meat Co, Muskegon *Also called Bert Hazekamp & Son Inc* *(G-11778)*
Hazeltree Woodworking 517 320-2954
　16191 N Dr S Marshall (49068) *(G-11060)*
HB Carbide Company 989 786-4223
　4210 Doyle Lewiston (49756) *(G-10021)*
HB Fuller Co 248 585-2200
　20219 Northline Rd Taylor (48180) *(G-16425)*
HB Manufacturing LLC 586 703-5269
　49333 Mackinaw Ct Shelby Township (48315) *(G-15233)*
HB Stubbs Company LLC 586 574-9700
　27027 Mound Rd Warren (48092) *(G-17850)*
Hbeat Medical, Plymouth *Also called Cardiac Assist Holdings LLC* *(G-13142)*
Hbm Inc 248 350-8300
　26555 Evergreen Rd # 700 Southfield (48076) *(G-15590)*
Hbpo North America Inc 248 823-7076
　700 Tower Dr Troy (48098) *(G-17138)*
Hci, Warren *Also called Hydronic Components Inc* *(G-17858)*
Hci, Pigeon *Also called Huron Casting Inc* *(G-13039)*

HD Hudson Manufacturing Co (PA) 800 977-8661
　1000 Foreman St Lowell (49331) *(G-10503)*
Hd Selcating Pav Solutions LLC 248 241-6526
　8205 Valleyview Dr Clarkston (48348) *(G-3038)*
Hdn F&A Inc 269 965-3268
　104 Arbor St Battle Creek (49015) *(G-1236)*
Hdt Automotive Solutions LLC (HQ) 810 359-5344
　38701 7 Mile Rd Ste 2 Livonia (48152) *(G-10237)*
Head Over Heels 248 435-2954
　164 E Maple Rd Ste G Troy (48083) *(G-17139)*
Header Products, Rose City *Also called Atf Inc* *(G-14362)*
Header Products, Romulus *Also called Michigan ATF Holdings, LLC* *(G-14305)*
Headqrter Strlng Hts Oprations 765 654-0477
　6125 18 Mile Rd Sterling Heights (48314) *(G-16037)*
Heals & Herbs LLC 888 604-1474
　29255 Franklin Hills Dr Southfield (48034) *(G-15591)*
Health Enhancement Systems Inc (PA) 989 839-0852
　800 Cambridge St Ste 101 Midland (48642) *(G-11372)*
Healthcare Drble Med Eqpmnts L 734 975-6668
　2911 Carpenter Rd Ann Arbor (48108) *(G-510)*
Healthcare Inds Mtls Site, Hemlock *Also called Dow Silicones Corporation* *(G-7852)*
Healthcare Medical Supply, Ann Arbor *Also called Healthcare Drble Med Eqpmnts L* *(G-510)*
Healthcure LLC 313 743-2331
　6501 Lynch Rd Detroit (48234) *(G-4297)*
Hear Clear Inc 734 525-8467
　311 Castlebury Dr Saline (48176) *(G-15020)*
Hear USA 734 525-3900
　31160 5 Mile Rd Livonia (48154) *(G-10238)*
Hearing Health Science Inc 734 476-9490
　2723 S State St Ste 150 Ann Arbor (48104) *(G-511)*
Heart of The Vnyrd Wnry/Bd/Brk, Baroda *Also called R C M S Inc* *(G-1169)*
Heart Sync Inc 734 213-5530
　4401 Varsity Dr Ste D Ann Arbor (48108) *(G-512)*
Heart Truss & Engineering Corp 517 372-0850
　1830 N Grand River Ave Lansing (48906) *(G-9703)*
Heart-N-Home, Owosso *Also called Hearth-N-Home Inc* *(G-12837)*
Hearth & Vine 231 944-1297
　10844 E Revold Rd Suttons Bay (49682) *(G-16341)*
Hearth-N-Home Inc (PA) 517 625-5586
　6990 W M 21 Owosso (48867) *(G-12837)*
Hearthwoods At Home, Lakeside *Also called Hearthwoods Ltd Inc* *(G-9639)*
Hearthwoods Ltd Inc 269 469-5551
　15310 Red Arrow Hwy Lakeside (49116) *(G-9639)*
Heartland Machine & Engrg LLC 616 437-1641
　4200 Legion Dr Mason (48854) *(G-11137)*
Heartland Steel Products LLC (PA) 810 364-7421
　2420 Wills St Marysville (48040) *(G-11088)*
Heartwood Mills LLC 888 829-5909
　4740 Skop Rd Ste A Boyne Falls (49713) *(G-1908)*
Heat Controller LLC 517 787-2100
　1900 Wellworth Jackson (49203) *(G-8901)*
Heat Treating Svcs Corp Amer (PA) 248 858-2230
　217 Central Ave Pontiac (48341) *(G-13377)*
Heat Treating Svcs Corp Amer 248 332-1510
　915 Cesar E Chavez Ave Pontiac (48340) *(G-13378)*
Heat Treating Svcs Corp Amer 248 253-9560
　2501 Williams Dr Waterford (48328) *(G-18127)*
Heath Manufacturing Company (HQ) 616 997-8181
　140 Mill St Ste A Coopersville (49404) *(G-3688)*
Heath Ultra Products, Coopersville *Also called Heath Manufacturing Company* *(G-3688)*
Heating Induction Services Inc 586 791-3160
　24483 Sorrentino Ct Clinton Township (48035) *(G-3252)*
Heating Treating Services, Waterford *Also called Heat Treating Svcs Corp Amer* *(G-18127)*
Heatsinkusa LLC 800 901-2395
　801 Industrial Park Dr Greenville (48838) *(G-7491)*
Heaven Is My Home, Cedar Springs *Also called Quality Guest Publishing Inc* *(G-2660)*
Heaven Scent Candle Co & Decor 810 374-6279
　10067 N State Rd Unit B Otisville (48463) *(G-12781)*
Heavenly Vineyards LLC 616 710-2751
　14155 Olin Lakes Dr Cedar Springs (49319) *(G-2653)*
Heavy Duty Radiator LLC 800 525-0011
　26111 Northline Rd Taylor (48180) *(G-16426)*
Heb Development LLC (PA) 616 363-3825
　1946 Turner Ave Nw Grand Rapids (49504) *(G-6807)*
Heck Industries Incorporated 810 632-5400
　1498 Old Us 23 Hwy Hartland (48353) *(G-7769)*
Heco Inc (PA) 269 381-7200
　3509 S Burdick St Kalamazoo (49001) *(G-9210)*
Heed Industries 906 233-7192
　2520 1st Ave S Escanaba (49829) *(G-5075)*
Hegenscheidt-Mfd Corporation 586 274-4900
　6255 Center Dr Sterling Heights (48312) *(G-16038)*
Hehr Michigan Division, Chesaning *Also called Lippert Components Mfg Inc* *(G-2829)*
HEI, Howell *Also called Highland Engineering Inc* *(G-8460)*
Heiden Lumber & Fencing, Stephenson *Also called Terry Heiden* *(G-15912)*
Heidtman Logging Inc 906 249-3914
　748 County Road 550 Marquette (49855) *(G-11020)*

ALPHABETIC SECTION

Heinzmann D Tool & Die Inc ... 248 363-5115
4335 Pineview Dr Commerce Township (48390) *(G-3535)*
Hekman Furniture Company (HQ) ... 616 748-2660
860 E Main Ave Zeeland (49464) *(G-19034)*
Hel Inc ... 616 774-9032
450 Market Ave Sw Grand Rapids (49503) *(G-6808)*
Helen Inc ... 616 698-8102
6450 Hanna Lake Ave Se Caledonia (49316) *(G-2378)*
Helian Technologies LLC ... 248 535-6545
5974 Windemere Ln Shelby Township (48316) *(G-15234)*
Helical Lap & Manufacturing Co (HQ) ... 586 307-8322
121 Madison Ave Mount Clemens (48043) *(G-11640)*
Helion Industries LLC ... 618 303-0214
9860 Stadium Dr Kalamazoo (49009) *(G-9211)*
Helios Solar LLC ... 269 343-5581
248 W Michigan Ave Kalamazoo (49007) *(G-9212)*
Helium Home Base LLC ... 734 895-3608
2600 Nichols Ct Westland (48186) *(G-18380)*
Helium Studio ... 734 725-3811
3127 S Wayne Rd Wayne (48184) *(G-18223)*
Helix Steel, Ann Arbor Also called Polytorx LLC *(G-614)*
Heller Inc ... 248 288-5000
1225 Equity Dr Troy (48084) *(G-17140)*
Hello Life Inc (PA) ... 616 808-3290
4655 Patterson Ave Se C Grand Rapids (49512) *(G-6809)*
Hello Vino ... 231 350-7138
122 N Bridge St Bellaire (49615) *(G-1475)*
Helm Incorporated (HQ) ... 734 468-3700
47911 Halyard Dr Plymouth (48170) *(G-13186)*
Help-U-Sell RE Big Rapids ... 231 796-3966
412 S State St Ofc A Big Rapids (49307) *(G-1677)*
Helping Hands Therapy ... 313 492-6007
23999 Northwestern Hwy Southfield (48075) *(G-15592)*
Helping Hearts Helping Hands ... 248 980-5090
285 Mill St Constantine (49042) *(G-3667)*
Hemco Machine Co Inc ... 586 264-8911
6785 Chicago Rd Warren (48092) *(G-17851)*
Hemingway Screw Products Inc ... 313 383-7300
17840 Dix Rd Melvindale (48122) *(G-11201)*
Hemlock Semiconductor LLC ... 989 301-5000
12334 Geddes Rd Hemlock (48626) *(G-7853)*
Hemlock Smcndctor Oprtions LLC ... 989 301-5000
12334 Geddes Rd Hemlock (48626) *(G-7854)*
Hemp Global Products Inc ... 616 617-6476
503 Essenburg Dr Holland (49424) *(G-8069)*
Henkel Surface Technologies, Madison Heights Also called Henkel US Operations Corp *(G-10739)*
Henkel Surface Technologies ... 248 307-0240
31200 Stephenson Hwy Madison Heights (48071) *(G-10738)*
Henkel US Operations Corp ... 586 759-5555
23343 Sherwood Ave Warren (48091) *(G-17852)*
Henkel US Operations Corp ... 248 588-1082
32100 Stephenson Hwy Madison Heights (48071) *(G-10739)*
Henniges Auto Holdings Inc (HQ) ... 248 340-4100
2750 High Meadow Cir Auburn Hills (48326) *(G-924)*
Henniges Auto Sling Systems N (HQ) ... 248 340-4100
2750 High Meadow Cir Auburn Hills (48326) *(G-925)*
Henniges Automotive N Amer Inc (HQ) ... 248 340-4100
2750 High Meadow Cir Auburn Hills (48326) *(G-926)*
Hennigs Automobiles, Auburn Hills Also called Henniges Auto Holdings Inc *(G-924)*
Henrob Corporation (HQ) ... 248 493-3800
30000 S Hill Rd New Hudson (48165) *(G-12057)*
Henry Bath LLC ... 410 633-7055
6725 Daly Rd Unit 250662 West Bloomfield (48325) *(G-18288)*
Henry Plambeck ... 586 463-3410
40962 Production Dr Harrison Township (48045) *(G-7701)*
Henry Stephens Memorial Lib, Almont Also called Elmont District Library *(G-259)*
Henshaw Inc ... 586 752-0700
70890 Powell Rd Armada (48005) *(G-736)*
Hensley Mfg Inc ... 810 653-3226
1097 S State Rd Ste 3 Davison (48423) *(G-3786)*
Henze Industries, Troy Also called Henze Stamping & Mfg Co *(G-17141)*
Henze Stamping & Mfg Co (PA) ... 248 588-5620
754 W Maple Rd Troy (48084) *(G-17141)*
Hephaestus Holdings LLC (HQ) ... 248 479-2700
39475 W 13 Mile Rd # 105 Novi (48377) *(G-12432)*
Herald Bi-County Inc ... 517 448-2201
115 S Church St Hudson (49247) *(G-8550)*
Herald Newspapers Company Inc ... 269 345-3511
6825 Beatrice Dr Ste C Kalamazoo (49009) *(G-9213)*
Herald Newspapers Company Inc ... 231 722-3161
379 W Western Ave Ste 100 Muskegon (49440) *(G-11836)*
Herald Newspapers Company Inc ... 616 222-5400
3102 Walker Ridge Dr Nw Grand Rapids (49544) *(G-6810)*
Herald Newspapers Company Inc ... 734 926-4510
704 Airport Blvd Ste 6 Ann Arbor (48108) *(G-513)*
Herald Newspapers Company Inc ... 989 752-7171
540 S Saginaw St 3 Flint (48502) *(G-5713)*
Herald Newspapers Company Inc ... 810 766-6100
540 S Saginaw St Ste 101 Flint (48502) *(G-5714)*
Herald Newspapers Company Inc ... 517 787-2300
1750 S Cooper St Jackson (49203) *(G-8902)*
Herald Newspapers Company Inc ... 734 834-6376
3102 Walker Ridge Dr Nw Grand Rapids (49544) *(G-6811)*
Herald Newspapers Company Inc ... 989 895-8551
540 S Saginaw St Ste 101 Flint (48502) *(G-5715)*
Herald Newspapers Company Inc ... 269 388-8501
401 S Burdick St Kalamazoo (49007) *(G-9214)*
Herald Palladium, The, Saint Joseph Also called Paxton Media Group LLC *(G-14953)*
Herald Publishing Company ... 517 423-2174
110 E Logan St Tecumseh (49286) *(G-16504)*
Herald Publishing Company LLC ... 734 623-2500
111 N Ashley St Ste 100 Ann Arbor (48104) *(G-514)*
Herald Publishing Company LLC (HQ) ... 616 222-5400
3102 Walker Ridge Dr Nw Walker (49544) *(G-17641)*
Hercules Drawn Steel Div, Livonia Also called Eaton Steel Corporation *(G-10189)*
Hercules Electric Mobility Inc ... 734 666-8078
2875 E Grand Blvd Detroit (48202) *(G-4298)*
Hercules Electric Vehicles, Detroit Also called Hercules Electric Mobility Inc *(G-4298)*
Hercules LLC ... 269 388-8676
5325 Autumn Glen St Kalamazoo (49009) *(G-9215)*
Hercules Machine TI & Die LLC ... 586 778-4120
33901 James J Pompo Dr Fraser (48026) *(G-5934)*
Herfert Chiropractic Software, Eastpointe Also called Herfert Software *(G-4936)*
Herfert Software ... 586 776-2880
15700 E 9 Mile Rd Eastpointe (48021) *(G-4936)*
Heritage ... 734 414-0343
1405 Gold Smith Plymouth (48170) *(G-13187)*
Heritage Forestry LLC ... 231 689-5721
3729 N Evergreen Dr White Cloud (49349) *(G-18443)*
Heritage Guitar Inc ... 269 385-5721
225 Parsons St Ste 286 Kalamazoo (49007) *(G-9216)*
Heritage Mfg Inc ... 586 949-7446
49787 Leona Dr Chesterfield (48051) *(G-2890)*
Heritage Newspaper, Belleville Also called View Newspaper *(G-1494)*
Heritage Newspapers ... 586 783-0300
28 W Huron St Pontiac (48342) *(G-13379)*
Heritage Press, Caro Also called Tuscola County Advertiser Inc *(G-2584)*
Heritage Resources Inc ... 616 554-9888
6490 68th St Se Caledonia (49316) *(G-2379)*
Heritage Wdwrks Grnd Rpids LLC ... 616 780-9499
318 Paris Ave Se Grand Rapids (49503) *(G-6812)*
Heritage Woodworking ... 734 753-3368
22272 Bell Rd New Boston (48164) *(G-12009)*
Herkules Equipment Corporation ... 248 960-7100
2760 Ridgeway Ct Commerce Township (48390) *(G-3536)*
Herman Hillbillies Farm LLC ... 906 201-0760
18194 Lahti Rd Lanse (49946) *(G-9661)*
Herman Hills Sugar Bush, Lanse Also called Herman Hillbillies Farm LLC *(G-9661)*
Hermans Boy ... 616 866-2900
220 Northland Dr Ne Rockford (49341) *(G-14169)*
Hermiz Publishing In ... 586 212-4490
3567 Du Pon Dr Sterling Heights (48310) *(G-16039)*
Herrmann Aerospace ... 810 695-1758
5202 Moceri Ln Grand Blanc (48439) *(G-6247)*
Hess Asphalt Pav Sand Cnstr Co ... 810 984-4466
6330 Lapeer Rd Clyde (48049) *(G-3413)*
Hess Printing ... 734 285-4377
201 Elm St Apt A Wyandotte (48192) *(G-18821)*
Hestia Inc ... 616 296-0533
650 Airport Pl Norton Shores (49441) *(G-12297)*
Hexagon Enterprises Inc ... 248 583-0550
256 Minnesota Dr Troy (48083) *(G-17142)*
Hexagon Mfg Intelligence Inc ... 248 662-1740
46444 Hexagon Way Novi (48377) *(G-12433)*
Hexagon Mfg Intelligence Inc ... 248 449-9400
46444 Hexagon Way Novi (48377) *(G-12434)*
Hexarmor, Grand Rapids Also called Performance Fabrics Inc *(G-7079)*
Hexon Corporation ... 248 585-7585
26050 Orchard Lake Rd # 10 Farmington Hills (48334) *(G-5259)*
Heyboer Transformers Inc (PA) ... 616 842-5830
17382 Hayes St Grand Haven (49417) *(G-6317)*
Heys Fabrication and Mch Co ... 616 247-0065
3059 Hillcroft Ave Sw Wyoming (49548) *(G-18882)*
Hf, Madison Heights Also called Howard Finishing LLC *(G-10742)*
Hgc Westshore LLC ... 616 796-1218
3440 Windquest Dr Holland (49424) *(G-8070)*
Hha, Troy Also called Hanho America Co Ltd *(G-17137)*
Hhi Forging LLC (HQ) ... 248 284-2900
2727 W 14 Mile Rd Royal Oak (48073) *(G-14544)*
Hhi Formtech LLC ... 586 415-2000
18450 15 Mile Rd Fraser (48026) *(G-5935)*
Hhi Formtech LLC ... 248 597-3800
2727 W 14 Mile Rd Royal Oak (48073) *(G-14545)*
Hhi Formtech Industries LLC ... 248 597-3800
2727 W 14 Mile Rd Royal Oak (48073) *(G-14546)*
Hhi Funding II LLC ... 313 758-2000
1 Dauch Dr Detroit (48211) *(G-4299)*

Hhi Holdings LLC (HQ)....313 758-2000
1 Dauch Dr Detroit (48211) *(G-4300)*
Hhj Holdings Limited (PA)....248 652-9716
1957 Crooks Rd A Troy (48084) *(G-17143)*
Hhsi, Ann Arbor *Also called Hearing Health Science Inc (G-511)*
HI TEC Stainless Inc....269 543-4205
6790 124th Ave Fennville (49408) *(G-5438)*
HI Tech Mechanical Svcs LLC....734 847-1831
7070 Crabb Rd Temperance (48182) *(G-16534)*
Hi-Craft Engineering Inc....586 293-0551
33105 Kelly Rd Ste B Fraser (48026) *(G-5936)*
Hi-Lex, Litchfield *Also called Tsk of America Inc (G-10086)*
Hi-Lex America Incorporated (HQ)....269 968-0781
5200 Wayne Rd Battle Creek (49037) *(G-1237)*
Hi-Lex America Incorporated....248 844-0096
2911 Research Dr Rochester Hills (48309) *(G-14030)*
Hi-Lex America Incorporated....517 542-2955
152 Simpson Dr Litchfield (49252) *(G-10079)*
Hi-Lex Automotive Centre, Rochester Hills *Also called Hi-Lex America Incorporated (G-14030)*
HI-Lex Controls Incorporated....517 448-2752
15780 Steger Indus Dr Hudson (49247) *(G-8551)*
Hi-Lex Controls Incorporated (HQ)....517 542-2955
152 Simpson Dr Litchfield (49252) *(G-10080)*
Hi-Lites Graphic Inc (PA)....231 924-0630
1212 Locust St Fremont (49412) *(G-6045)*
Hi-Lites Shoppers Guide, Fremont *Also called Hi-Lites Graphic Inc (G-6045)*
Hi-Tech Coatings Inc (PA)....586 759-3559
24600 Industrial Hwy Warren (48089) *(G-17853)*
Hi-Tech Fasteners LLC....231 689-6000
1341 E Pine Hill Ave White Cloud (49349) *(G-18444)*
HI-Tech Flexible Products Inc....517 783-5911
2000 Townley St Jackson (49203) *(G-8903)*
Hi-Tech Furnace Systems Inc....586 566-0600
13179 W Star Dr Shelby Township (48315) *(G-15235)*
Hi-Tech Industries, Farmington *Also called Sam Brown Sales LLC (G-5147)*
Hi-Tech Mold & Engineering Inc....248 844-0722
1758 Northfield Dr Rochester Hills (48309) *(G-14031)*
Hi-Tech Mold & Engineering Inc (PA)....248 852-6600
2775 Commerce Dr Rochester Hills (48309) *(G-14032)*
Hi-Tech Optical Inc....989 799-9390
3139 Christy Way S Saginaw (48603) *(G-14663)*
Hi-Tech Plastics, Hudsonville *Also called Royal Technologies Corporation (G-8607)*
Hi-Tech Steel Treating Inc....800 835-8294
2720 Roberts St Saginaw (48601) *(G-14664)*
Hi-Tech/Fpa Inc....616 942-0076
4585 40th St Se Grand Rapids (49512) *(G-6813)*
Hi-Trac Industries Inc....810 625-7193
5161 Harp Dr Linden (48451) *(G-10063)*
Hibiskus Biopharma Inc....616 234-2841
4717 Campus Dr Ste 100 Kalamazoo (49008) *(G-9217)*
Hibshman Screw Mch Pdts Inc....269 641-7525
69351 Union Rd S Union (49130) *(G-17489)*
Hice and Summey Inc (PA)....269 651-6217
404 Union St Bronson (49028) *(G-2116)*
Hickmans Woodworking LLC....616 678-4180
2875 18 Mile Rd Kent City (49330) *(G-9433)*
Hicks Plastics Company Inc (HQ)....586 786-5640
51308 Industrial Dr Macomb (48042) *(G-10602)*
Hidden Lake Cabinet Trim....586 246-9119
5254 Heath Ave Clarkston (48346) *(G-3039)*
Hig Recovery Fund Inc....269 435-8414
485 Florence Rd Constantine (49042) *(G-3668)*
Higgins and Associates Inc....989 772-8853
735 S Mission Rd Mount Pleasant (48858) *(G-11701)*
Higgins Corp....269 365-7744
219 Old Stage Rd Roscommon (48653) *(G-14350)*
Higgins Lake Family Campground....989 821-6891
37012 Charter Oaks Blvd Clinton Township (48036) *(G-3253)*
Higgins Marine Metals LLC....616 990-2732
8717 Riley St Zeeland (49464) *(G-19035)*
High Effcncy Pwr Solutions Inc....800 833-7094
11060 Hi Tech Dr Whitmore Lake (48189) *(G-18538)*
High End Signs Svc & Lighting....248 596-9301
40213 Tonabee Ct Sterling Heights (48313) *(G-16040)*
High Five Spirits LLC....248 217-6057
32960 Bingham Rd Bingham Farms (48025) *(G-1699)*
High Frequency Healing Co LLC....313 938-9711
17349 Stoepel St Detroit (48221) *(G-4301)*
High Grade Concrete Pdts Co, Muskegon *Also called M 37 Concrete Products Inc (G-11863)*
High Grade Concrete Pdts Co....616 842-8630
540 Maple St Spring Lake (49456) *(G-15822)*
High Grade Materials Company....616 554-8828
6869 E Paris Ave Se Caledonia (49316) *(G-2380)*
High Grade Materials Company (PA)....616 754-5545
9266 Snows Lake Rd Greenville (48838) *(G-7492)*
High Grade Materials Company....269 926-6900
1915 Yore Ave Benton Harbor (49022) *(G-1555)*
High Grade Materials Company....269 349-8222
2700 E Cork St Kalamazoo (49001) *(G-9218)*
High Grade Materials Company....616 677-1271
10561 Linden Dr Nw Grand Rapids (49534) *(G-6814)*
High Grade Materials Company....517 374-1029
1800 Turner St Lansing (48906) *(G-9704)*
High Grade Materials Company....989 365-3010
3261 W Fleck Rd Six Lakes (48886) *(G-15388)*
High Grade Materials Company....616 696-9540
16180 Northland Dr Sand Lake (49343) *(G-15048)*
High Impact Solutions Inc....248 473-9804
20793 Farmington Rd # 13 Farmington Hills (48336) *(G-5260)*
High Life Farms, Chesaning *Also called Vb Chesaning LLC (G-2831)*
High Point Group....810 543-0448
1284 Rochester Rd Lakeville (48367) *(G-9647)*
High Prfmce Met Finshg Inc....269 327-8897
1821 Vanderbilt Ave Portage (49024) *(G-13565)*
High Q Lighting Inc....616 396-3591
11439 E Lakewood Blvd Holland (49424) *(G-8071)*
High Rize Candles....616 818-9527
136 41st St Sw Wyoming (49548) *(G-18883)*
High Tech Insulators Inc....734 525-9030
34483 Glendale St Livonia (48150) *(G-10239)*
High Touch Healthcare LLC....248 513-2425
29307 Douglas Dr Novi (48377) *(G-12435)*
High Winds Graphix....313 363-3434
15108 Kercheval Ave Grosse Pointe Park (48230) *(G-7556)*
High-Po-Chlor Inc....734 942-1500
1181 Freesia Ct Ann Arbor (48105) *(G-515)*
High-Star Corporation....734 743-1503
6171 Commerce Dr Westland (48185) *(G-18381)*
High-Tech Inds of Holland....616 399-5430
3269 John F Donnelly Dr Holland (49424) *(G-8072)*
High-Tech Industries, Holland *Also called Hti Associates LLC (G-8089)*
Higher Image Signs & Wraps LLC....989 964-0443
2905 Mccarty Rd Saginaw (48603) *(G-14665)*
Highland Engineering Inc....517 548-4372
1153 Grand Oaks Dr Howell (48843) *(G-8460)*
Highland Hills Maple Syrup LLC....231 920-1589
10380 S Dickerson Rd Mc Bain (49657) *(G-11180)*
Highland Industrial Inc....989 391-9992
3487 Highland Dr Bay City (48706) *(G-1365)*
Highland Machine Design Inc....248 669-6150
3125 Old Farm Ln Commerce Township (48390) *(G-3537)*
Highland Manufacturing Inc....248 585-8040
339 E Whitcomb Ave Madison Heights (48071) *(G-10740)*
Highland Supply Inc....248 714-8355
1415 Enterprise Dr Highland (48357) *(G-7892)*
Highland Tank & Mfg Co....248 795-2000
4701 White Lake Rd Clarkston (48346) *(G-3040)*
Highlander Graphics LLC....734 449-9733
75 Aprill Dr Ann Arbor (48103) *(G-516)*
Highlight Industries Inc....616 531-2464
2694 Prairie St Sw Wyoming (49519) *(G-18884)*
Highpoint Finshg Solutions Inc....616 772-4425
541 E Roosevelt Ave Zeeland (49464) *(G-19036)*
Hightech Signs, Grand Rapids *Also called Castleton Village Center Inc (G-6559)*
Highwood Die & Engineering Inc....248 338-1807
1353 Highwood Blvd Pontiac (48340) *(G-13380)*
Hikking Production Embroidery, Ypsilanti *Also called Imagillation Inc (G-18954)*
Hil-Man Automation LLC....616 741-9099
260 E Roosevelt Ave Zeeland (49464) *(G-19037)*
Hilco Fixture Finders LLC....616 453-1300
1345 Monroe Ave Nw # 321 Grand Rapids (49505) *(G-6815)*
Hilco Industrial Plastics LLC....616 554-8833
3260 Hnna Lk Ind Pk Dr Se Caledonia (49316) *(G-2381)*
Hilco Industrial Plastics LLC....616 554-8833
3260 Hanna Lake Ind Park Caledonia (49316) *(G-2382)*
Hilco Technologies, Caledonia *Also called Hilco Industrial Plastics LLC (G-2381)*
Hilgraeve Inc....734 243-0576
115 E Elm Ave Monroe (48162) *(G-11547)*
Hilite Industries Inc....248 475-4580
250 Kay Industrial Dr Lake Orion (48359) *(G-9608)*
Hilite International, Whitehall *Also called Acutex Inc (G-18489)*
Hill Bros Orchards, Grand Rapids *Also called Hill Brothers (G-6816)*
Hill Brothers....616 784-2767
6159 Peach Ridge Ave Nw Grand Rapids (49544) *(G-6816)*
Hill Machine Works LLC....586 238-2897
33950 Riviera Fraser (48026) *(G-5937)*
Hill Machinery Co....616 940-2800
4585 Danvers Dr Se Grand Rapids (49512) *(G-6817)*
Hill Screw Machine Products....734 427-8237
8463 Hugh St Westland (48185) *(G-18382)*
Hills Crate Mill Inc....616 761-3555
3851 Hoyt Rd Belding (48809) *(G-1451)*
Hills-Mccanna LLC....616 554-9308
4855 Broadmoor Ave Se Kentwood (49512) *(G-9458)*
Hillsdale Pallet LLC....517 254-4777
1242 E Montgomery Rd Hillsdale (49242) *(G-7937)*

Hillsdale Terminal, Hillsdale *Also called Frank Condon Inc* ***(G-7935)***
Hillshire Brands Company.....616 875-8131
8300 96th Ave Zeeland (49464) ***(G-19038)***
Hillshire Brands Company.....231 947-2100
2314 Sybrant Rd Traverse City (49684) ***(G-16711)***
Hillside Finsihing, Belding *Also called West Mich Auto Stl & Engrg Inc* ***(G-1464)***
Hilton Screeners Inc.....810 653-0711
210 N Main St Davison (48423) ***(G-3787)***
Hincka Logging LLC.....989 766-8893
6464 Lake Augusta Hwy Posen (49776) ***(G-13643)***
Hines Corporation (PA).....231 799-6240
1218 E Pontaluna Rd Ste B Norton Shores (49456) ***(G-12348)***
Hines Industries Inc (PA).....734 769-2300
240 Metty Dr Ste A Ann Arbor (48103) ***(G-517)***
Hippies Chippies Inc.....616 259-2133
2322 Lake Michigan Dr Nw Grand Rapids (49504) ***(G-6818)***
Hippiwic Candles.....586 488-8931
21090 Elroy Ave Warren (48089) ***(G-17854)***
Hirose Electric USA Inc.....734 542-9963
37727 Prof Ctr Dr Ste 100 Livonia (48154) ***(G-10240)***
Hirotec America Inc (HQ).....248 836-5100
3000 High Meadow Cir Auburn Hills (48326) ***(G-927)***
Hirschmann Auto N Amer LLC.....248 495-2677
2927 Waterview Dr Rochester Hills (48309) ***(G-14033)***
Hirschmann Car Comm Inc.....248 373-7150
1183 Centre Rd Auburn Hills (48326) ***(G-928)***
Hirschmann Electronics, Auburn Hills *Also called Hirschmann Car Comm Inc* ***(G-928)***
Hirzel Canning Company.....419 360-3220
6363 Livernois Rd Troy (48098) ***(G-17144)***
His Stamping Division, Manchester *Also called American Engnred Cmponents Inc* ***(G-10881)***
Hispanic Visions, Saginaw *Also called Verdoni Productions Inc* ***(G-14790)***
Historic Denver Inc.....989 354-2121
416 Ford Ave Alpena (49707) ***(G-297)***
Hitachi America Ltd.....248 477-5400
34500 Grand River Ave Farmington Hills (48335) ***(G-5261)***
Hite Tool Co Inc.....734 422-1777
32127 Block St Ste 200 Garden City (48135) ***(G-6095)***
Hitec Sensor Developments Inc.....313 506-2460
47460 Galleon Dr Plymouth (48170) ***(G-13188)***
Hj Manufacturing Inc.....906 233-1500
3707 19th Ave N Escanaba (49829) ***(G-5076)***
HL Manufacturing Inc.....586 731-2800
45399 Utica Park Blvd Utica (48315) ***(G-17502)***
Hl Outdoors.....989 422-3264
308 Huron St Houghton Lake (48629) ***(G-8399)***
Hlc Industries Inc.....810 477-9600
38880 Grand River Ave Farmington Hills (48335) ***(G-5262)***
Hme Inc.....616 534-1463
1950 Byron Center Ave Sw Wyoming (49519) ***(G-18885)***
Hme Ahrens-Fox, Wyoming *Also called Hme Inc* ***(G-18885)***
Hmg Agency.....989 443-3819
4352 Bay Rd Ste 131 Saginaw (48603) ***(G-14666)***
Hmi, Rives Junction *Also called Hacker Machine Inc* ***(G-13886)***
Hmi Hardwoods LLC.....517 456-7431
430 Division St Clinton (49236) ***(G-3141)***
Hmr Fabrication Unlimited Inc.....586 569-4288
33830 Riviera Fraser (48026) ***(G-5938)***
HMS Mfg Co (PA).....248 689-3232
1230 E Big Beaver Rd Troy (48083) ***(G-17145)***
HMS Mfg Co.....248 740-7040
1863 Long Pointe Dr Bloomfield Hills (48302) ***(G-1828)***
HMS Products Co.....248 689-8120
1200 E Big Beaver Rd Troy (48083) ***(G-17146)***
Hmw Contracting LLC.....313 531-8477
12855 Burt Rd Detroit (48223) ***(G-4302)***
Hoag & Sons Book Bindery Inc.....517 857-2033
145 N Main St Eaton Rapids (48827) ***(G-4965)***
Hobart Brothers LLC.....231 933-1234
1631 International Dr Traverse City (49686) ***(G-16712)***
Hobe Inc.....231 845-5196
292 N Stiles Rd Ludington (49431) ***(G-10539)***
Hochstetler Sawmill.....269 467-7018
24700 Walters Rd Centreville (49032) ***(G-2697)***
Hockey Weekly, Farmington *Also called Castine Communications Inc* ***(G-5134)***
Hodges & Irvine Inc.....810 329-4787
1900 Sinclair St Saint Clair (48079) ***(G-14831)***
Hodgkiss & Douma, Charlevoix *Also called Bdk Group Northern Mich Inc* ***(G-2711)***
Hoechst Celanese, Auburn Hills *Also called Celanese Americas LLC* ***(G-841)***
Hoeganaes Corporation.....248 435-6764
304 Mount Vernon Blvd Royal Oak (48073) ***(G-14547)***
Hoff Engineering Co Inc (PA).....248 969-8272
475 S Glaspie St Oxford (48371) ***(G-12887)***
Hoffmann Die Cast LLC.....269 983-1102
229 Kerth St Saint Joseph (49085) ***(G-14936)***
Hoffmann Filter Corporation (PA).....248 486-8430
7627 Kensington Ct Brighton (48116) ***(G-2008)***
Hog Forging LLC.....248 765-7180
1629 Banbury St Birmingham (48009) ***(G-1729)***
Hogge Crochet.....313 808-1302
200 W 2nd St Unit 951 Royal Oak (48068) ***(G-14548)***
Hogle Sales & Mfg LLC.....517 592-1980
208 Irwin St Brooklyn (49230) ***(G-2126)***
Hohmann & Barnard Inc.....765 420-7940
909 Abbot Rd Ste 2b East Lansing (48823) ***(G-4895)***
Holbrook Racing Engines.....734 762-4315
31831 Schoolcraft Rd Livonia (48150) ***(G-10241)***
Holcim (us) Inc.....734 529-2411
6211 N Ann Arbor Rd Dundee (48131) ***(G-4823)***
Holcim (us) Inc.....734 529-4600
15215 Day Rd Dundee (48131) ***(G-4824)***
Holcim (us) Inc.....989 755-7515
900 N Adams St Saginaw (48604) ***(G-14667)***
Hold It Products Corporation.....248 624-1195
1900 Easy St Commerce Township (48390) ***(G-3538)***
Hold-It Inc.....810 984-4213
2301 16th St Port Huron (48060) ***(G-13482)***
Holder Corporation.....517 484-5453
2538 W Main St Lansing (48917) ***(G-9764)***
Hole Chief, Schoolcraft *Also called New Concept Products Inc* ***(G-15125)***
Hole Industries Incorporated.....517 548-4229
600 Chukker Cv Howell (48843) ***(G-8461)***
Holiday Distributing Co.....517 782-7146
3990 Francis St Jackson (49203) ***(G-8904)***
Holiday Rmbler Recrtl Vhcl CLB.....616 847-0582
18134 N Fruitport Rd Spring Lake (49456) ***(G-15823)***
Holland Alloys Inc.....616 396-6444
534 Chicago Dr Holland (49423) ***(G-8073)***
Holland Automotive Machine, Holland *Also called Daniel Pruitoff* ***(G-8013)***
Holland Awning Co., Zeeland *Also called Ifr Inc* ***(G-19043)***
Holland Bar Stool Company.....616 399-5530
12839 Corporate Circle Pl Holland (49424) ***(G-8074)***
Holland Bowl Mill.....616 396-6513
120 James St Holland (49424) ***(G-8075)***
Holland Community Hosp Aux Inc.....616 355-3926
854 Wshington Ave Ste 330 Holland (49423) ***(G-8076)***
Holland Custom Signs.....616 566-4783
4047 56th St Holland (49423) ***(G-8077)***
Holland Electric Motor Co.....616 392-1115
11598 E Lakewood Blvd B Holland (49424) ***(G-8078)***
Holland Honey Cake Co., Holland *Also called Holland Bar Stool Company* ***(G-8074)***
Holland House Candles Inc (PA).....800 238-8467
16656 Riley St Holland (49424) ***(G-8079)***
Holland Intrchnge Drv Dist Ctr, Holland *Also called Perrigo Company* ***(G-8164)***
Holland Litho Printing Service, Zeeland *Also called Holland Litho Service Inc* ***(G-19039)***
Holland Litho Service Inc.....616 392-4644
10972 Chicago Dr Zeeland (49464) ***(G-19039)***
Holland Pallet Repair Inc.....616 875-8642
13370 Barry St Ste A Holland (49424) ***(G-8080)***
Holland Panel Products Inc.....616 392-1826
615 E 40th St Holland (49423) ***(G-8081)***
Holland Pattern Co (PA).....616 396-6348
534 Chicago Dr Holland (49423) ***(G-8082)***
Holland Plastics Corporation (PA).....616 844-2505
14000 172nd Ave Grand Haven (49417) ***(G-6318)***
Holland Printing Center Inc (PA).....616 786-3101
4314 136th Ave Ste 100 Holland (49424) ***(G-8083)***
Holland Screen Print Inc.....616 396-7630
4665 44th St Holland (49423) ***(G-8084)***
Holland Stitchcraft Inc.....616 399-3868
13163 Reflections Dr Holland (49424) ***(G-8085)***
Holland Transplanter Co Inc.....616 392-3579
510 E 16th St Holland (49423) ***(G-8086)***
Holland Transport Services LLC.....313 605-3103
57958 Rosecrest St New Haven (48048) ***(G-12032)***
Holland Vision Systems Inc.....616 494-9974
11301 James St Holland (49424) ***(G-8087)***
Holli Forest Products.....906 486-9352
900 Cooper Lake Rd Ishpeming (49849) ***(G-8777)***
Hollingsworth Container LLC.....313 768-1400
14225 W Warren Ave Dearborn (48126) ***(G-3850)***
Hollow Hill Woodworks.....906 493-6913
33486 S Center St Drummond Island (49726) ***(G-4801)***
Holloway Equipment Co Inc.....810 748-9577
4856 Middle Channel Dr Harsens Island (48028) ***(G-7749)***
Holly Sand & Gravel, Davisburg *Also called Falcon Trucking Company* ***(G-3768)***
Hollywood Dry Cleaners.....734 922-2630
5999 N Wayne Rd Westland (48185) ***(G-18383)***
Holmquist Feed Mill.....906 446-3325
232 N Main St Trenary (49891) ***(G-16885)***
Holo-Source Corporation.....734 427-1530
11700 Belden Ct Livonia (48150) ***(G-10242)***
Holsinger Manufacturing Corp.....989 684-3101
2922 S Huron Rd Kawkawlin (48631) ***(G-9416)***
Holt Products Company.....517 927-4198
4200 Legion Dr Mason (48854) ***(G-11138)***
Holy Art Framing.....248 634-8190
201 S Saginaw St Holly (48442) ***(G-8276)***

ALPHABETIC

Holz Enterprises Inc 810 392-2840
37994 Weber Rd Richmond (48062) *(G-13840)*
Homag Machinery North Amer Inc 616 254-8181
4577 Patterson Ave Se Grand Rapids (49512) *(G-6819)*
Home & Garden Concepts, Bloomfield Hills Also called Delorean Associates Inc *(G-1813)*
Home Bakery 248 651-4830
300 S Main St Rochester (48307) *(G-13904)*
Home Chef Ltd 734 468-2544
39005 Webb Dr Westland (48185) *(G-18384)*
Home City Ice Company 734 955-9094
15475 Oakwood Dr Romulus (48174) *(G-14283)*
Home Elements, Traverse City Also called Candle Factory Grand Traverse *(G-16638)*
Home Inspection Protection 906 370-6704
25599 Pt Mills Estates Rd Hancock (49930) *(G-7619)*
Home Style Co 989 871-3654
8400 Caine Rd Millington (48746) *(G-11501)*
Home Style Foods Inc 313 874-3250
5163 Edwin St Detroit (48212) *(G-4303)*
Home Winery Supply LLC 734 529-3296
208 Main St Dundee (48131) *(G-4825)*
Homedics, Commerce Township Also called Fka Distributing Co LLC *(G-3530)*
Homedics Group Canada, Commerce Township Also called Homedics Usa LLC *(G-3539)*
Homedics Usa LLC (HQ) 248 863-3000
3000 N Pontiac Trl Commerce Township (48390) *(G-3539)*
Homer Concrete Products, Imlay City Also called Imlay City Concrete Inc *(G-8636)*
Homer Index 517 568-4646
122 E Main St Homer (49245) *(G-8352)*
Homes Bracelet 231 499-9402
516 E Eighth St Traverse City (49686) *(G-16713)*
Homes Bracelet LLC 231 463-9808
807 Airport Access Rd Ste Traverse City (49686) *(G-16714)*
Homes For Sale, Pontiac Also called 21st Century Newspapers Inc *(G-13343)*
Homespun Furniture Inc 734 284-6277
18540 Fort St Riverview (48193) *(G-13874)*
Homestead Elements LLC 248 560-7122
3984 Cabaret Trl W Saginaw (48603) *(G-14668)*
Homestead Foundry, Coleman Also called Homestead Tool and Machine *(G-3465)*
Homestead Graphics Design Inc 906 353-6741
516 S Superior Ave Baraga (49908) *(G-1140)*
Homestead Products Inc 989 465-6182
2618 Coolidge Rd Coleman (48618) *(G-3464)*
Homestead Tool and Machine 989 465-6182
2618 Coolidge Rd Coleman (48618) *(G-3465)*
Hometown America LLC 810 686-7020
2197 E Mount Morris Rd Mount Morris (48458) *(G-11672)*
Hometown Publishing Inc 989 834-2264
200 S Main St Ovid (48866) *(G-12814)*
Homeworks 810 533-2030
28024 Nieman St Saint Clair Shores (48081) *(G-14865)*
Hommel Movomatic, Rochester Hills Also called Jenoptik Automotive N Amer LLC *(G-14043)*
Honee Bear Canning Co, Lawton Also called Packers Canning Co Inc *(G-9989)*
Honey Creek Woodworks 616 706-2539
8321 Conservation St Ne Ada (49301) *(G-22)*
Honey Tree 734 697-1000
9624 Belleville Rd Van Buren Twp (48111) *(G-17529)*
Honeybees Custom Tees 248 421-0817
334 Union St Milford (48381) *(G-11466)*
Honeywell 248 362-7154
234 E Maple Rd Troy (48083) *(G-17147)*
Honeywell Authorized Dealer, Marquette Also called Duquaine Incorporated *(G-11015)*
Honeywell Authorized Dealer, Battle Creek Also called Cse Morse Inc *(G-1213)*
Honeywell Authorized Dealer, Temperance Also called HI Tech Mechanical Svcs LLC *(G-16534)*
Honeywell Authorized Dealer, Kalamazoo Also called Kalamazoo Mechanical Inc *(G-9241)*
Honeywell International Inc 989 792-8707
5153 Hampton Pl Saginaw (48604) *(G-14669)*
Honeywell International Inc 231 582-5686
375 N Lake St Boyne City (49712) *(G-1889)*
Honeywell International Inc 586 777-7870
31807 Utica Rd Fraser (48026) *(G-5939)*
Honeywell International Inc 734 392-5501
47548 Halyard Dr Plymouth (48170) *(G-13189)*
Honeyworks LLC 313 575-0871
17410 Northlawn St Detroit (48221) *(G-4304)*
Honhart Mid-Nite Black Co 248 588-1515
501 Stephenson Hwy Troy (48083) *(G-17148)*
Hooper Printing LLC 616 897-6719
2125 Bowes Rd Lowell (49331) *(G-10504)*
Hoosier Tank and Manufacturing 269 683-2550
2190 Industrial Dr Niles (49120) *(G-12136)*
Hoover Treated Wood Pdts Inc 313 365-4200
7500 E Davison St Detroit (48212) *(G-4305)*
Hoover Universal Inc (HQ) 734 454-0994
49200 Halyard Dr Plymouth (48170) *(G-13190)*
Hope Focus 313 494-4500
1400 Oakman Blvd Detroit (48238) *(G-4306)*
Hope Focus (PA) 313 494-5500
1400 Oakman Blvd Detroit (48238) *(G-4307)*

Hope Focus Companies Inc (HQ) 313 494-5500
1200 Oakman Blvd Detroit (48238) *(G-4308)*
Hope Global of Detroit, Detroit Also called Rtlf-Hope LLC *(G-4573)*
Hope Network West Michigan 231 775-3425
1610 Corwin St Cadillac (49601) *(G-2334)*
Hope Network West Michigan 231 796-4801
21685 Northland Dr Paris (49338) *(G-12934)*
Hopeful Harvest Foods Inc 248 967-1500
21800 Greenfield Rd Oak Park (48237) *(G-12617)*
Hoppenjans Inc 734 344-5304
1339 N Telegraph Rd Monroe (48162) *(G-11548)*
Horak Company, The, Bay City Also called F P Horak Company *(G-1355)*
Horiba Automotive Test Systems 248 689-9000
2890 John R Rd Troy (48083) *(G-17149)*
Horiba Instruments Inc 734 213-6555
5900 Hines Dr Ann Arbor (48108) *(G-518)*
Horiba Instruments Inc 866 540-2715
5449 Research Dr Canton (48188) *(G-2471)*
Horiba Instruments Inc 734 487-8300
5449 Research Dr Canton (48188) *(G-2472)*
Horiba Instruments Inc 248 689-9000
2890 John R Rd Troy (48083) *(G-17150)*
Horizon Bros Painting Corp 810 632-3362
1053 Kendra Ln Howell (48843) *(G-8462)*
Horizon Die Company 248 590-2966
30100 Telegraph Rd # 236 Bingham Farms (48025) *(G-1700)*
Horizon Global Americas, Plymouth Also called Cequent Uk Ltd *(G-13144)*
Horizon Global Americas Inc (HQ) 734 656-3000
47912 Halyard Dr Ste 100 Plymouth (48170) *(G-13191)*
Horizon Global Corporation (PA) 734 656-3000
47912 Halyard Dr Ste 100 Plymouth (48170) *(G-13192)*
Horizon Intl Group LLC 734 341-9336
1411 Westboro Birmingham (48009) *(G-1730)*
Horizontal Lift Technologies 231 421-9696
1503 Garfield Rd N Traverse City (49696) *(G-16715)*
Hormel Foods Corporation 616 454-0418
801 Broadway Ave Nw Grand Rapids (49504) *(G-6820)*
Horn Corp 248 358-8883
2169 Corlett Rd Brighton (48114) *(G-2009)*
Horn Corporation 248 583-7789
1263 Rochester Rd Troy (48083) *(G-17151)*
Hornshaw Wood Works LLC 616 566-0720
15774 Ransom St Holland (49424) *(G-8088)*
Horse Creek Candles LLC 517 962-1476
2429 Smiley Way Jackson (49203) *(G-8905)*
Horstman Inc 586 737-2100
44215 Phoenix Dr Sterling Heights (48314) *(G-16041)*
Hosco Inc (PA) 248 912-1750
28026 Oakland Oaks Ct Wixom (48393) *(G-18678)*
Hosco Fittings LLC 248 912-1750
28026 Oakland Oaks Ct Wixom (48393) *(G-18679)*
Hosford & Co Inc 734 769-5660
1204 N Main St Ann Arbor (48104) *(G-519)*
Hosmer 248 541-9829
90 W Guthrie Ave Madison Heights (48071) *(G-10741)*
Hostess Cake ITT Contntl Bkg 231 775-4629
838 N Mitchell St Cadillac (49601) *(G-2335)*
Hot Logic LLC 616 935-1040
1705 Eaton Dr Grand Haven (49417) *(G-6319)*
Hot Melt Technologies Inc 248 853-2011
1723 W Hamlin Rd Rochester Hills (48309) *(G-14034)*
Hot Prints Inc 989 627-6463
103 N Clinton Ave Saint Johns (48879) *(G-14901)*
Hot Rod Holdings Inc 517 424-0577
610 S Maumee St Tecumseh (49286) *(G-16505)*
Hot Rods Bbq Services 989 375-2191
2726 Hartsell Rd Elkton (48731) *(G-5031)*
Hot Tool Cutter Grinding Co 586 790-4867
33545 Groesbeck Hwy Fraser (48026) *(G-5940)*
Hot Tubs, Lansing Also called Hotwater Works Inc *(G-9852)*
Hotfab LLC 586 489-7989
13118 E 9 Mile Rd Warren (48089) *(G-17855)*
Hotset Corp 269 964-0271
1045 Harts Lake Rd Battle Creek (49037) *(G-1238)*
Hotwater Works Inc (PA) 517 364-8827
2116 E Michigan Ave Lansing (48912) *(G-9852)*
Hougen Manufacturing Inc 810 635-7111
3001 Hougen Dr Swartz Creek (48473) *(G-16355)*
Houghton Cmnty Brdcstg Corp 906 482-7700
313 E Montezuma Ave Houghton (49931) *(G-8383)*
Houghton Lake Resorter Inc 989 366-5341
4049 W Houghton Lake Dr Houghton Lake (48629) *(G-8400)*
Hour Detroit Magazine, Troy Also called Hour Media LLC *(G-17152)*
Hour Media LLC (PA) 248 691-1800
5750 New King Dr Ste 100 Troy (48098) *(G-17152)*
Hour Media Group LLC 248 691-1800
5750 New King Dr Ste 100 Troy (48098) *(G-17153)*
House of Flavors Inc (HQ) 231 845-7369
110 N William St Ludington (49431) *(G-10540)*

House of Hero LLC 248 260-8300
7335 Deep Run Apt 513 Bloomfield Hills (48301) *(G-1829)*
House of Marley LLC 248 863-3000
3000 N Pontiac Trl Commerce Township (48390) *(G-3540)*
House of Marley Canada, Commerce Township *Also called House of Marley LLC (G-3540)*
Houseart LLC 248 651-8124
386 South St Rochester (48307) *(G-13905)*
Housey Phrm RES Labs LLC 248 663-7000
16800 W 12 Mile Rd Southfield (48076) *(G-15593)*
Housler Sawmill Inc 231 824-6353
222 E 16 Rd Mesick (49668) *(G-11272)*
Houston Flame Hardening Co 713 926-8017
35674 Shook Ln Clinton Township (48035) *(G-3254)*
Hovertechnics LLC 269 461-3934
1520 Townline Rd Bldg A Benton Harbor (49022) *(G-1556)*
Howa USA Holdings Inc (HQ) 248 715-4000
25125 Regency Dr Novi (48375) *(G-12436)*
Howard Energy Co Inc (PA) 231 995-7850
125 S Park St Ste 250 Traverse City (49684) *(G-16716)*
Howard Finishing LLC (PA) 248 588-9050
32565 Dequindre Rd Madison Heights (48071) *(G-10742)*
Howard Miller Company (PA) 616 772-9131
860 E Main Ave Zeeland (49464) *(G-19040)*
Howard Structural Steel Inc 989 752-3000
807 Veterans Mem Pkwy Saginaw (48601) *(G-14670)*
Howe Racing Enterprises Inc 989 435-7080
3195 Lyle Rd Beaverton (48612) *(G-1425)*
Howe US Inc 616 419-2226
401 Hall St Sw Ste 458 Grand Rapids (49503) *(G-6821)*
Howell Engine Developments Inc 810 765-5100
6201 Industrial Way Cottrellville (48039) *(G-3720)*
Howell Gear Company LLC 517 273-5202
1045 Durant Dr Howell (48843) *(G-8463)*
Howell Machine Products Inc 517 546-0580
6265 Grand River Rd # 100 Brighton (48114) *(G-2010)*
Howell Penncraft Inc 517 548-2250
3333 W Grand River Ave Howell (48855) *(G-8464)*
Howell Tool Service Inc 517 548-1114
5818 Sterling Dr Howell (48843) *(G-8465)*
Howells Mainstreet Winery 517 545-9463
201 W Grand River Ave Howell (48843) *(G-8466)*
Howey Tree Baler Corporation 231 328-4321
6069 E Gaukel Rd Merritt (49667) *(G-11266)*
Howies Hockey Incorporated 616 643-0594
3445 36th St Se Ste B Grand Rapids (49512) *(G-6822)*
Howies Hockey Tape, Grand Rapids *Also called Howies Hockey Incorporated (G-6822)*
Howmedica Osteonics Corp 269 389-8959
1901 Romence Road Pkwy Portage (49002) *(G-13566)*
Howmet Aerospace Inc 231 981-3002
3850 White Lake Dr Whitehall (49461) *(G-18498)*
Howmet Aerospace Inc 231 894-7290
1500 Warner St Whitehall (49461) *(G-18499)*
Howmet Aerospace Inc 231 894-5686
1 Misco Dr Whitehall (49461) *(G-18500)*
Howmet Corporation (HQ) 231 894-5686
1 Misco Dr Whitehall (49461) *(G-18501)*
Howmet Corporation 231 894-7183
555 Benston Rd Whitehall (49461) *(G-18502)*
Howmet Corporation 231 981-3269
1600 Warner St Whitehall (49461) *(G-18503)*
Howmet Corporation 231 894-5686
555 Benston Rd Whitehall (49461) *(G-18504)*
Howmet Corporation 231 894-5686
1 Misco Dr Whitehall (49461) *(G-18505)*
Howmet Holdings Corporation (HQ) 231 894-5686
1 Misco Dr Whitehall (49461) *(G-18506)*
Hoyt & Company LLC 810 624-4445
12555 N Saginaw Rd Clio (48420) *(G-3401)*
Hp Inc 650 857-1501
7335 Westshire Dr Ste 101 Lansing (48917) *(G-9765)*
Hp Inc 248 614-6600
560 Kirts Blvd Ste 120 Troy (48084) *(G-17154)*
HP Pelzer Auto Systems Inc (HQ) 248 280-1010
1175 Crooks Rd Troy (48084) *(G-17155)*
HP Pelzer Auto Systems Inc 810 987-4444
2415 Dove St Port Huron (48060) *(G-13483)*
HP Pelzer Automotive Systems 810 987-0725
2630 Dove St Port Huron (48060) *(G-13484)*
Hpc Holdings Inc (PA) 248 634-9361
111 Rosette St Holly (48442) *(G-8277)*
Hpc Holdings Inc 810 714-9213
1101 Copper Ave Fenton (48430) *(G-5485)*
Hpi 989 465-6141
2618 Coolidge Rd Coleman (48618) *(G-3466)*
Hpi Products Inc 248 773-7460
640 Griswold St Ste 200 Northville (48167) *(G-12229)*
HPS Fabrications Inc 734 282-2285
4410 13th St Wyandotte (48192) *(G-18822)*
HR Technologies Inc 248 284-1170
32500 N Avis Dr Madison Heights (48071) *(G-10743)*
HRF Exploration & Prod LLC 989 732-6950
990 S Wisconsin Ave Gaylord (49735) *(G-6134)*
Hrsflow, Byron Center *Also called Inglass Usa Inc (G-2278)*
HS Inc (PA) 616 453-5451
O-215 Lake Michigan Dr Nw Grand Rapids (49534) *(G-6823)*
HS Inc 248 373-4048
1720 Star Batt Dr Rochester Hills (48309) *(G-14035)*
HSP Epi Acquisition LLC (PA) 248 404-1520
1401 Crooks Rd Ste 150 Troy (48084) *(G-17156)*
Hss Industries Inc 231 946-6101
2464 Cass Rd Traverse City (49684) *(G-16717)*
Ht Computing Services 313 563-0087
23253 Edward St Dearborn (48128) *(G-3851)*
Htc Products, Ira *Also called Htc Sales Corporation (G-8698)*
Htc Sales Corporation 800 624-2027
6560 Bethuy Rd Ira (48023) *(G-8698)*
Hti Associates LLC 616 399-5430
3269 John F Donnelly Dr Holland (49424) *(G-8089)*
Hti Cybernetics 586 826-8346
40033 Mitchell Dr Sterling Heights (48313) *(G-16042)*
Hti Cybernetics Inc (PA) 586 826-8346
40033 Mitchell Dr Sterling Heights (48313) *(G-16043)*
Hti Usa Inc 248 358-5533
33106 W 8 Mile Rd Farmington (48336) *(G-5139)*
Httm LLC 616 820-2500
300 E 48th St Holland (49423) *(G-8090)*
Hubble Enterprises Inc 616 676-4485
7807 Ashwood Dr Se Ada (49301) *(G-23)*
Hubert Group, Fraser *Also called Sharp Die & Mold Co (G-5993)*
Hubscher & Son Inc (PA) 989 773-5369
1101 N Franklin Ave Mount Pleasant (48858) *(G-11702)*
Hubscher & Son Inc 989 875-2151
8189 W Washington Rd Sumner (48889) *(G-16332)*
Hudson Industries Inc 313 777-5622
34543 Sandpebble Dr Sterling Heights (48310) *(G-16044)*
Hudson Post Gazette 517 448-2611
113 S Market St Hudson (49247) *(G-8552)*
Hudsonville Products LLC 616 836-1904
1735 Elizabeth Ave Nw Grand Rapids (49504) *(G-6824)*
Huebner E W & Son Mfg Co Inc 734 427-2600
12871 Farmington Rd Livonia (48150) *(G-10243)*
Huf North America Automoti 248 213-4605
24860 Hathaway St Farmington Hills (48335) *(G-5263)*
Huff Machine & Tool Co Inc 231 734-3291
5469 85th Ave Evart (49631) *(G-5123)*
Hug-A-Plug Inc 810 626-1224
2332 Pine Hollow Trl Brighton (48114) *(G-2011)*
Hughes Electronics Pdts Corp (PA) 734 427-8310
34467 Industrial Rd Livonia (48150) *(G-10244)*
Hughes Network Systems LLC 301 428-5500
24000 Northwestern Hwy Southfield (48075) *(G-15594)*
Hugo Benzing LLC 248 264-6478
29233 Haas Rd Wixom (48393) *(G-18680)*
Hugo Brothers Pallet Mfg 989 684-5564
2474 River Rd Kawkawlin (48631) *(G-9417)*
Huhtamaki Inc 989 633-8900
5760 W Shaffer Rd Coleman (48618) *(G-3467)*
Huhtamaki Plastics, Coleman *Also called Huhtamaki Inc (G-3467)*
Huizenga & Sons Inc 616 772-6241
10075 Gordon St Zeeland (49464) *(G-19041)*
Huizenga Gravel Company Inc (PA) 616 772-6241
10075 Gordon St Zeeland (49464) *(G-19042)*
Huizenga Redi-Mix, Zeeland *Also called Huizenga & Sons Inc (G-19041)*
Hulet Body Co Inc 313 931-6000
19700 Meadowbrook Rd Northville (48167) *(G-12230)*
Human Synergistics Inc 734 459-1030
39819 Plymouth Rd Plymouth (48170) *(G-13193)*
Humantics Innvtive Sltions Inc (HQ) 734 451-7878
23300 Haggerty Rd Farmington Hills (48335) *(G-5264)*
Hummus & Co 313 769-5557
23117 Outer Dr Allen Park (48101) *(G-196)*
Hummus Goodness LLC 248 229-9606
295 Henley St Birmingham (48009) *(G-1731)*
Humphrey Companies LLC (PA) 616 530-1717
2851 Prairie St Sw Grandville (49418) *(G-7389)*
Hunt & Noyer LLC 517 914-6259
14861 W Eleven Mile Rd Berkley (48072) *(G-1627)*
Hunt & Noyer Woodworks, Berkley *Also called Hunt & Noyer LLC (G-1627)*
Hunt Hoppough Custom Crafted 616 794-3455
700 Reed St Belding (48809) *(G-1452)*
Hunters Jewelry Repair Ctr Inc 313 892-7621
20250 Packard St Detroit (48234) *(G-4309)*
Huntington Foam LLC 661 225-9951
1323 Moore St Greenville (48838) *(G-7493)*
Huntler Industries Inc 586 566-7684
51532 Schoenherr Rd Shelby Township (48315) *(G-15236)*
Huntsman Advnced Mtls Amrcas L 517 351-5900
4917 Dawn Ave East Lansing (48823) *(G-4896)*
Huntsman Corporation 248 322-8682
2190 Exec Dr Blvd Auburn Hills (48326) *(G-929)*

A L P H A B E T I C

Huntsman Polyurethanes, Auburn Hills *Also called Huntsman-Cooper LLC* ***(G-930)***
Huntsman-Cooper LLC 248 322-7300
2190 Executive Hills Dr Auburn Hills (48326) ***(G-930)***
Hurless Machine Shop Inc 269 945-9362
2450 Lower Lake Rd Hastings (49058) ***(G-7797)***
Huron Advertising Company Inc 734 483-2000
663 S Mansfield St Ypsilanti (48197) ***(G-18952)***
Huron Casting Inc (PA) 989 453-3933
7050 Hartley St Pigeon (48755) ***(G-13039)***
Huron Daily Tribune, The, Bad Axe *Also called Huron Publishing Company Inc* ***(G-1107)***
Huron Glass Block 586 598-6900
46562 Erb Dr Macomb (48042) ***(G-10603)***
Huron High School 734 782-2441
12431 Longsdorf St Riverview (48193) ***(G-13875)***
Huron Inc (HQ) 810 359-5344
6554 Lakeshore Rd Lexington (48450) ***(G-10029)***
Huron Industries Inc 810 984-4213
2301 16th St Port Huron (48060) ***(G-13485)***
Huron Publishing Company Inc (HQ) 989 269-6461
211 N Heisterman St Bad Axe (48413) ***(G-1107)***
Huron Quality Mfg Inc 989 736-8121
481 State St Lincoln (48742) ***(G-10035)***
Huron Sign Co, Ypsilanti *Also called Huron Advertising Company Inc* ***(G-18952)***
Huron Soap Candle Company 810 989-5952
313 Huron Ave Port Huron (48060) ***(G-13486)***
Huron Tool & Engineering Co (HQ) 989 269-9927
635 Liberty St Bad Axe (48413) ***(G-1108)***
Huron Tool & Gage Co Inc 313 381-1900
28005 Oakland Oaks Ct Wixom (48393) ***(G-18681)***
Huron Township Plant, New Boston *Also called Plastic Omnium Auto Inrgy USA* ***(G-12018)***
Huron Valley Steel Corporation (PA) 734 479-3500
1650 W Jefferson Ave Trenton (48183) ***(G-16889)***
Huron Vlleys Hrse Blnket Hdqtr 248 859-2398
28525 Beck Rd Unit 102 Wixom (48393) ***(G-18682)***
Hurricane Machine Inc 313 383-8614
1815 Southfield Rd Lincoln Park (48146) ***(G-10049)***
Hush Puppies Retail LLC 231 937-1004
214 Washburn St Howard City (49329) ***(G-8409)***
Husite Engineering Co Inc 248 588-0337
44831 N Groesbeck Hwy Clinton Township (48036) ***(G-3255)***
Husky Envelope Products Inc (PA) 248 624-7070
1225 E West Maple Rd Walled Lake (48390) ***(G-17670)***
Husky LLC 586 774-6148
28100 Hayes Rd Roseville (48066) ***(G-14421)***
Husky Precision, Roseville *Also called Husky LLC* ***(G-14421)***
Hussmann Corporation 248 668-0790
46974 Liberty Dr Wixom (48393) ***(G-18683)***
Hutchinson Corporation (HQ) 616 459-4541
460 Fuller Ave Ne Grand Rapids (49503) ***(G-6825)***
Hutchinson Fts, Inc., Auburn Hills *Also called Fluid Hutchinson Management* ***(G-903)***
Hutchinson Seal Corporation 248 375-4190
3201 Cross Creek Pkwy Auburn Hills (48326) ***(G-931)***
Hutchinson Seal De Mexico, Auburn Hills *Also called Hutchinson Seal Corporation* ***(G-931)***
Hutchinson Sealing Systems Inc (HQ) 248 375-3720
3201 Cross Creek Pkwy Auburn Hills (48326) ***(G-932)***
Hutchinson SNC, Auburn Hills *Also called Hutchinson Sealing Systems Inc* ***(G-932)***
Hutchnson Antvbrtion Systems I (HQ) 616 459-4541
460 Fuller Ave Ne Grand Rapids (49503) ***(G-6826)***
Hutchnson Antvbrtion Systems I 231 775-9737
600 7th St Cadillac (49601) ***(G-2336)***
Hutchnson Auto Anti Vbrtion Sy, Grand Rapids *Also called Hutchnson Antvbrtion Systems I* ***(G-6826)***
Hutson Inc 517 655-4606
2 Industrial Park Dr Williamston (48895) ***(G-18573)***
Huxl Denim 248 595-8480
16500 N Park Dr Apt 1914 Southfield (48075) ***(G-15595)***
Huys Industries 734 895-3067
28421 Highland Rd Romulus (48174) ***(G-14284)***
Hvac, Plymouth *Also called Mjs Investing LLC* ***(G-13246)***
Hy Capacity Inc 616 558-5690
7567 Brighton Rd Brighton (48116) ***(G-2012)***
Hy-Ko Products Company LLC 330 467-7446
9031 Shaver Rd Portage (49024) ***(G-13567)***
Hy-Test Inc 616 866-5500
9341 Courtland Dr Ne Rockford (49351) ***(G-14170)***
Hy-Vac Technologies, Detroit *Also called Mjc Industries Inc* ***(G-4461)***
Hycal Corp 216 671-6161
27800 W Jefferson Ave Gibraltar (48173) ***(G-6171)***
Hycorr LLC 269 381-6349
3654 Midlink Dr Kalamazoo (49048) ***(G-9219)***
Hyde Spring and Wire Company 313 272-2201
14341 Schaefer Hwy Detroit (48227) ***(G-4310)***
Hydra-Lock Corporation 586 783-5007
25000 Joy Blvd Mount Clemens (48043) ***(G-11641)***
Hydra-Tech Inc 586 232-4479
1483 Quadrate Dr Ste C Macomb (48042) ***(G-10604)***
Hydraulex Global, Chesterfield *Also called Hydraulex Intl Holdings Inc* ***(G-2891)***
Hydraulex Intl Holdings Inc (PA) 914 682-2700
48175 Gratiot Ave Chesterfield (48051) ***(G-2891)***
Hydraulic Press Service 586 859-7099
4175 22 Mile Rd Shelby Township (48317) ***(G-15237)***
Hydraulic Pump Division, Otsego *Also called Parker-Hannifin Corporation* ***(G-12796)***
Hydraulic Systems Technology 248 656-5810
1156 Whispering Knoll Ln Rochester Hills (48306) ***(G-14036)***
Hydraulic Tubes & Fittings LLC 810 660-8088
434 Mccormick Dr Lapeer (48446) ***(G-9933)***
Hydro Abrasive Products LLC 313 456-9410
21750 Schoenherr Rd Warren (48089) ***(G-17856)***
Hydro Chem Laboratories Inc 248 348-1737
1565 Switzerland Dr Commerce Township (48382) ***(G-3541)***
Hydro Extrusion North Amer LLC 269 349-6626
5575 N Riverview Dr Kalamazoo (49004) ***(G-9220)***
Hydro Giant 4 Inc 248 661-0034
7480 Haggerty Rd West Bloomfield (48322) ***(G-18289)***
Hydro King Incorporated 313 835-8700
21384 Mcclung Ave Southfield (48075) ***(G-15596)***
Hydro Pros Indoor Garden Sup, Chesterfield *Also called Zerilli & Sesi LLC* ***(G-2967)***
Hydro-Abrasive Products LLC 734 459-1544
45507 Denise Dr Plymouth (48170) ***(G-13194)***
Hydro-Chem Systems Inc 616 531-6420
6605 Broadmoor Ave Se Caledonia (49316) ***(G-2383)***
Hydro-Craft Inc 248 652-8100
1821 Rochester Indus Ct Rochester Hills (48309) ***(G-14037)***
Hydro-Logic Inc 586 757-7477
24832 Romano St Warren (48091) ***(G-17857)***
Hydrochem LLC 313 841-5800
987 W Hurd Rd Monroe (48162) ***(G-11549)***
Hydrochempsc, Monroe *Also called Hydrochem LLC* ***(G-11549)***
Hydrochempsc, Detroit *Also called PSC Industrial Outsourcing LP* ***(G-4540)***
Hydrodynamics International 517 887-2007
5711 Enterprise Dr Lansing (48911) ***(G-9853)***
Hydrolake Inc 231 825-2233
420 S Roth St Ste A Reed City (49677) ***(G-13791)***
Hydrolake Inc (HQ) 231 825-2233
6151 W Gerwoude Dr Mc Bain (49657) ***(G-11181)***
Hydrolake Inc 231 825-2233
6151 W Gerwoude Dr Mc Bain (49657) ***(G-11182)***
Hydrolake Leasing, Mc Bain *Also called Hydrolake Inc* ***(G-11182)***
Hydronic Components Inc 586 268-1640
7243 Miller Dr Ste 200 Warren (48092) ***(G-17858)***
Hygiene of Sweden USA LLC 248 760-3241
2681 Orchard Lake Rd E Sylvan Lake (48320) ***(G-16361)***
Hygratek LLC 847 962-6180
333 Jackson Plz Ann Arbor (48103) ***(G-520)***
Hylite Tool & Machine Inc 586 465-7878
44685 Macomb Indus Dr Clinton Township (48036) ***(G-3256)***
Hypo-Systems, Ann Arbor *Also called High-Po-Chlor Inc* ***(G-515)***
Hyponex Corporation 810 724-2875
332 Graham Rd Imlay City (48444) ***(G-8635)***
Hytech Spring and Machine, Plainwell *Also called Tokusen Hytech Inc* ***(G-13100)***
Hytech Spring and Machine Co, Plainwell *Also called Magiera Holdings Inc* ***(G-13082)***
Hytech Spring and Machine Co., Plainwell *Also called Tokusen Hytech Inc* ***(G-13099)***
Hytrol Manufacturing Inc 734 261-8030
4005 Morrill Rd Jackson (49201) ***(G-8906)***
I & D Manufacturing LLC 517 852-9215
6895 Marshall Rd Nashville (49073) ***(G-11955)***
I & G Tool Co Inc 586 777-7690
7270 Starville Rd Cottrellville (48039) ***(G-3721)***
I & K Distributors, Warren *Also called Countryside Foods LLC* ***(G-17765)***
I B P Inc 248 588-4710
9295 Allen Rd Clarkston (48348) ***(G-3041)***
I C R, Warren *Also called Lorna Icr LLC* ***(G-17907)***
I C S Corporation America Inc 616 554-9300
4675 Talon Ct Se Grand Rapids (49512) ***(G-6827)***
I D Medical Systems Inc 616 698-0535
3954 44th St Se Grand Rapids (49512) ***(G-6828)***
I D Merch 734 237-4111
153 Merriman Rd Garden City (48135) ***(G-6096)***
I D Pro Embroidery LLC 734 847-6650
1287 W Sterns Rd Temperance (48182) ***(G-16535)***
I Do Signs 616 604-0431
312 S 2nd St Grand Haven (49417) ***(G-6320)***
I E & E Industries Inc (PA) 248 544-8181
111 E 10 Mile Rd Madison Heights (48071) ***(G-10744)***
I E T, Auburn Hills *Also called Industrial Exprmental Tech LLC* ***(G-938)***
I F I, Sterling Heights *Also called Industrial Frnc Interiors Inc* ***(G-16048)***
I M A, Detroit *Also called Integrated Mfg & Assembly LLC* ***(G-4322)***
I M F, Cottrellville *Also called Industrial Mtal Fbricators LLC* ***(G-3722)***
I M I, Spring Lake *Also called Industrial Mtal Idntfction Inc* ***(G-15824)***
I M I, Washington *Also called Innovative Mold Inc* ***(G-18081)***
I M P, Oxford *Also called Industrial Machine Pdts Inc* ***(G-12889)***
I Pallet LLC 586 625-2238
3187 Kilborne Dr Sterling Heights (48310) ***(G-16045)***

I Parth Inc 248 548-9722
2206 Burdette St Ferndale (48220) ***(G-5560)***
I S P Coatings Corp 586 752-5020
130 E Pond Dr Romeo (48065) ***(G-14226)***
I S Two 616 396-5634
262 E 26th St Holland (49423) ***(G-8091)***
I T W Workholding, Traverse City *Also called Illinois Tool Works Inc* ***(G-16719)***
I Way Software, Troy *Also called Information Builders Inc* ***(G-17166)***
I-9 Advantage 800 724-8546
101 W Big Beaver Rd 14 Troy (48084) ***(G-17157)***
I-94 Enterprises 269 945-3185
2195 Tamarack Cove Dr Hastings (49058) ***(G-7798)***
I-Drink Products Inc 734 531-6324
727 W Ellsworth Rd Ste 15 Ann Arbor (48108) ***(G-521)***
I.D.A., Warren *Also called Independent Die Association* ***(G-17861)***
I.E. Communications, Detroit *Also called Industrial Elc Co Detroit Inc* ***(G-4315)***
I.M. Branded, Troy *Also called Automotive Media LLC* ***(G-16966)***
I.S.I. Automation Products, Saline *Also called Norgren Automtn Solutions LLC* ***(G-15030)***
I.S.T., Okemos *Also called Instrumented Sensor Tech Inc* ***(G-12670)***
I.V.C. Industrial, Grand Haven *Also called PPG Industries Inc* ***(G-6346)***
I2 International Dev LLC 616 534-8100
2905 Wilson Ave Sw # 200 Grandville (49418) ***(G-7390)***
IAC Creative LLC 248 455-7000
27777 Franklin Rd # 2000 Southfield (48034) ***(G-15597)***
IAC Group, Southfield *Also called Interntnal Auto Cmpnnts Group* ***(G-15606)***
IAC Mexico Holdings Inc (HQ) 248 455-7000
27777 Franklin Rd # 2000 Southfield (48034) ***(G-15598)***
IAC Plymouth LLC 734 207-7000
47785 W Anchor Ct Plymouth (48170) ***(G-13195)***
Iaec Corporation 586 354-5996
21641 34 Mile Rd Armada (48005) ***(G-737)***
Ianna Fab Inc 586 739-2410
5575 22 Mile Rd Shelby Township (48317) ***(G-15238)***
Iannuzzi Millwork Inc 586 285-1000
33877 Doreka Fraser (48026) ***(G-5941)***
IBC North America Inc (HQ) 248 625-8700
4545 Clawson Tank Dr Clarkston (48346) ***(G-3042)***
IBC Precision Inc 248 373-8202
2715 Paldan Dr Auburn Hills (48326) ***(G-933)***
Ibidltd-Blue Green Energy (PA) 909 547-5160
6659 Schaefer Rd Ste 110 Dearborn (48126) ***(G-3852)***
IBM, Midland *Also called International Bus Mchs Corp* ***(G-11375)***
Ice Makers, Port Huron *Also called Northern Pure Ice Co L L C* ***(G-13510)***
Ice Tools, Chesterfield *Also called Indexable Cutter Engineering* ***(G-2892)***
Iceberg Enterprises LLC 269 651-9488
1505 W Chicago Rd Sturgis (49091) ***(G-16293)***
Icmp Inc 269 445-0847
805 Wolfe Ave Cassopolis (49031) ***(G-2630)***
Icon Choppers 616 292-0536
1538 Beechwood Dr Jenison (49428) ***(G-9056)***
Icon Industries Inc 616 241-1877
1522 Madison Ave Se Grand Rapids (49507) ***(G-6829)***
Icon Integrated Solutions, Lansing *Also called Superior Machine & Tool Inc* ***(G-9793)***
Icon Shelter Systems, Holland *Also called Icon Shelters Inc* ***(G-8092)***
Icon Shelters Inc 616 396-0919
1455 Lincoln Ave Holland (49423) ***(G-8092)***
Icon Sign & Design Inc 517 372-1104
3308 W Saint Joseph St Lansing (48917) ***(G-9766)***
Icon Signs Inc 906 401-0162
250 Us Highway 41 E Negaunee (49866) ***(G-11968)***
Ics Filtration Products, Grand Rapids *Also called I C S Corporation America Inc* ***(G-6827)***
Ict Industries 586 727-2677
68001 Lowe Plank Rd Lenox (48050) ***(G-9998)***
ID Enterprises 248 442-4849
24333 Indoplex Cir Farmington Hills (48335) ***(G-5265)***
ID Systems Inc 231 799-8760
676 E Ellis Rd Norton Shores (49441) ***(G-12298)***
Ida D Byler 810 672-9355
4169 Moore Rd Cass City (48726) ***(G-2615)***
Idc Industries Inc 586 427-4321
18901 15 Mile Rd Clinton Township (48035) ***(G-3257)***
Idea Mia LLC 248 891-8939
18513 San Quentin Dr Lathrup Village (48076) ***(G-9976)***
Idea MNP Com LLC 269 459-8955
505 E Kalamazoo Ave Kalamazoo (49007) ***(G-9221)***
Idea Signs Visually 269 779-9163
1110 Engleman Ave Kalamazoo (49048) ***(G-9222)***
Ideal Fabricators Inc 734 422-5320
30579 Schoolcraft Rd Livonia (48150) ***(G-10245)***
Ideal Heated Knives Inc 248 437-1510
57007 Pontiac Trl New Hudson (48165) ***(G-12058)***
Ideal Machine Tool Tech LLC 248 320-4729
675 E Big Beaver Rd # 105 Troy (48083) ***(G-17158)***
Ideal Millwork Enterprises LLC 248 461-6460
5724 Williams Lake Rd A Waterford (48329) ***(G-18128)***
Ideal Printing 616 453-5556
2059 Lake Michigan Dr Nw Grand Rapids (49504) ***(G-6830)***
Ideal Printing Company (PA) 616 454-9224
2801 Oak Industrial Dr Ne Grand Rapids (49505) ***(G-6831)***
Ideal Shield LLC 866 825-8659
2525 Clark St Detroit (48209) ***(G-4311)***
Ideal Steel & Bldrs Sups LLC 313 849-0000
2525 Clark St Detroit (48209) ***(G-4312)***
Ideal Tool Inc 989 893-8336
1707 Marquette St Bay City (48706) ***(G-1366)***
Ideal Wholesale Inc 989 873-5850
3430 Henderson Lake Rd Prescott (48756) ***(G-13651)***
Ideation Inc 734 761-4360
3389 Breckland Ct Ann Arbor (48108) ***(G-522)***
Ideation International Inc 248 737-8854
32000 Northwestern Hwy # 145 Farmington Hills (48334) ***(G-5266)***
Idel LLC 231 929-3195
1315 Woodmere Ave Traverse City (49686) ***(G-16718)***
Idemitsu Chemicals USA Corp 248 355-0666
3000 Town Ctr Ste 2820 Southfield (48075) ***(G-15599)***
Idemitsu Lubricants Amer Corp 248 355-0666
3000 Town Ctr Ste 2820 Southfield (48075) ***(G-15600)***
Identicom, Farmington Hills *Also called Grasshopper Signs Graphics LLC* ***(G-5254)***
Identicom Sign Solutions LLC 248 344-9590
24657 Halsted Rd Farmington Hills (48335) ***(G-5267)***
Identify Inc 313 802-2015
25163 Dequindre Rd Madison Heights (48071) ***(G-10745)***
Ididit, Tecumseh *Also called Hot Rod Holdings Inc* ***(G-16505)***
Ididit, LLC, Tecumseh *Also called Dcd Idid Enterprise LLC* ***(G-16495)***
Idp Inc 248 352-0044
21300 W 8 Mile Rd Southfield (48075) ***(G-15601)***
IDS, Hudsonville *Also called Innovtive Dsplay Solutions LLC* ***(G-8586)***
IDS, Shelby Township *Also called Intergrted Dspnse Slutions LLC* ***(G-15239)***
IDS, Roseville *Also called Industrial Duct Systems Inc* ***(G-14422)***
IDS, Sterling Heights *Also called Innovtive Design Solutions Inc* ***(G-16049)***
IEC Fabrication LLC 810 623-1546
144 National Park Dr Fowlerville (48836) ***(G-5842)***
IEC N.A., Fowlerville *Also called Invention Evolution Comp LLC* ***(G-5843)***
Ied Inc 231 728-9154
1938 Sanford St Muskegon (49441) ***(G-11837)***
IEM, Hope *Also called International Engrg & Mfg Inc* ***(G-8361)***
Ieq Industries 616 902-1865
730 Lincoln Lake Ave Se Lowell (49331) ***(G-10505)***
Ies-Synergy Inc 586 206-4410
330 E Maple Rd Ste U Troy (48083) ***(G-17159)***
Iet, Southfield *Also called Industrial Exprmental Tech LLC* ***(G-15604)***
If and or But Publishing 269 274-6102
33 Broad St N Battle Creek (49017) ***(G-1239)***
Ifca International Inc (PA) 616 531-1840
3520 Fairlanes Ave Sw Grandville (49418) ***(G-7391)***
Ifm, Roseville *Also called Iron Fetish Metalworks Inc* ***(G-14426)***
Ifm Efector 800 441-8246
39340 Country Club Dr Farmington Hills (48331) ***(G-5268)***
Ifr Inc 616 772-2052
10875 Chicago Dr Zeeland (49464) ***(G-19043)***
IGA Abrasives LLC 616 243-5566
3011 Hillcroft Ave Sw Grand Rapids (49548) ***(G-6832)***
Igan Mich Publishing LLC 248 877-4649
7025 Dandison Blvd West Bloomfield (48324) ***(G-18290)***
Iha Vsclar Endvsclar Spcalists 734 712-8150
5325 Elliott Dr Ste 104 Ypsilanti (48197) ***(G-18953)***
Ihc Inc 313 535-3210
12400 Burt Rd Detroit (48228) ***(G-4313)***
Ihi Detroit Turbo Engrg Ctr 947 777-4976
39575 Lewis Dr Ste 100 Novi (48377) ***(G-12437)***
Ihs Inc 616 464-4224
2851 Charlevoix Dr Se # 314 Grand Rapids (49546) ***(G-6833)***
Il Adrian LLC W2fuel 517 920-4863
1571 W Beecher Rd Adrian (49221) ***(G-73)***
Il Enterprises Inc 734 285-6030
555 Grove St Wyandotte (48192) ***(G-18823)***
Il Stanley Co Inc (HQ) 269 660-7777
1500 Hill Brady Rd Battle Creek (49037) ***(G-1240)***
Ilg-Dss Technologies LLC 586 725 5300
6100 Bethuy Rd Ira (48023) ***(G-8699)***
IKEA Chip LLC 877 218-9931
2609 Crooks Rd Ste 235 Troy (48084) ***(G-17160)***
Ikes Welding Shop and Mfg 989 892-2783
50 N Finn Rd Munger (48747) ***(G-11751)***
Illinois Tool Works Inc 231 258-5521
111 W Park Dr Kalkaska (49646) ***(G-9390)***
Illinois Tool Works Inc 231 947-5755
2155 Traversefield Dr Traverse City (49686) ***(G-16719)***
Illinois Tool Works Inc 616 772-1910
500 N Fairview Rd Zeeland (49464) ***(G-19044)***
Illinois Tool Works Inc 231 947-5755
2155 Traversefield Dr Traverse City (49686) ***(G-16720)***
Illinois Tool Works Inc 248 969-4248
2425 N Lapeer Rd Oxford (48371) ***(G-12888)***
Illinois Tool Works Inc 248 589-2500
100 Kirts Blvd Troy (48084) ***(G-17161)***

ALPHABETIC

(PA)=Parent Co (HQ)=Headquarters (DH)=Div Headquarters
2022 Harris Michigan
Industrial Directory
1019

Illmatik Industries 714 767-1296
 50 Valley Ave Nw Grand Rapids (49504) *(G-6834)*
Illumination Machines LLC 856 685-7403
 2830 Steamboat Springs Dr Rochester Hills (48309) *(G-14038)*
Illusion Signs & Graphic Inc 313 443-0567
 14241 Michigan Ave Dearborn (48126) *(G-3853)*
Ilmor Engineering Inc (PA) 734 456-3600
 43939 Plymouth Oaks Blvd Plymouth (48170) *(G-13196)*
Ilmor High Performance Marine, Plymouth Also called *Ilmor Engineering Inc* *(G-13196)*
Ilumigreen Corp 616 318-3087
 6259 Norton Center Dr Norton Shores (49441) *(G-12299)*
Im, Rochester Hills Also called *Illumination Machines LLC* *(G-14038)*
Im A Beer Hound 517 331-0528
 602 N Grace St Lansing (48917) *(G-9767)*
Imagamerica, Sterling Heights Also called *E Q R 2 Inc* *(G-15995)*
Image Factory Inc 989 732-2712
 870 N Center Ave Gaylord (49735) *(G-6135)*
Image Machine & Tool Inc 586 466-3400
 34501 Bennett Fraser (48026) *(G-5942)*
Image Printing Inc 248 585-4080
 1902 Crooks Rd Royal Oak (48073) *(G-14549)*
Image Projections Inc 810 629-0700
 1470 Torrey Rd Fenton (48430) *(G-5486)*
Image360-Plymouth, Plymouth Also called *Sgo Corporate Center LLC* *(G-13296)*
Imagecraft 517 750-0077
 100 Robinson Rd Jackson (49203) *(G-8907)*
Imagemaster LLC (PA) 734 821-2500
 1182 Oak Valley Dr Ann Arbor (48108) *(G-523)*
Imagemaster Printing, Ann Arbor Also called *Imagemaster LLC* *(G-523)*
Images 2 Print 616 383-1121
 486 E Division St Sparta (49345) *(G-15769)*
Images Unlimited LLC 248 608-8685
 361 South St Ste A Rochester (48307) *(G-13906)*
Images2printcom 616 821-7143
 1094 11 Mile Rd Ne Comstock Park (49321) *(G-3611)*
Imagesoft 919 462-8505
 100 Morningside Dr Se Grand Rapids (49506) *(G-6835)*
Imagillation Inc 734 481-0140
 133 W Michigan Ave Ste 2 Ypsilanti (48197) *(G-18954)*
IMC, Escanaba Also called *Independent Machine Co Inc* *(G-5077)*
IMC Dataworks LLC 248 356-4311
 525 Avis Dr Ste 14 Ann Arbor (48108) *(G-524)*
IMC Products Inc 231 759-3430
 2743 Henry St 130 Muskegon (49441) *(G-11838)*
Imcs, Holland Also called *International Material Co* *(G-8097)*
Imeco Inc 906 774-0202
 1401 Carpenter Ave Iron Mountain (49801) *(G-8722)*
Imerys Perlite Usa Inc 269 649-1352
 1950 E W Ave Vicksburg (49097) *(G-17605)*
Imet, Jackson Also called *Intern Metals and Energy* *(G-8909)*
IMI, Auburn Hills Also called *Industrial Model Inc* *(G-939)*
Imlay City Concrete Inc (PA) 810 724-3905
 205 S Cedar St Imlay City (48444) *(G-8636)*
Imlay City Molded Pdts Corp 810 721-9100
 593 S Cedar St Imlay City (48444) *(G-8637)*
Imm Inc 989 344-7662
 758 Isenhauer Rd Grayling (49738) *(G-7463)*
Immuno Concepts NA Ltd 734 464-0701
 17199 N Laurel Park Dr # 320 Livonia (48152) *(G-10246)*
Immunospec, Livonia Also called *Sigma Diagnostics Inc* *(G-10407)*
Impact Fab Inc 616 399-9970
 3440 John F Donnelly Dr Holland (49424) *(G-8093)*
Impact Label Corporation (PA) 269 381-4280
 8875 Krum Ave Galesburg (49053) *(G-6079)*
Impact Operations LLC 616 642-9570
 8808 Grand River Ave Saranac (48881) *(G-15078)*
Impeccable Machining Inc 734 844-3855
 42600 Executive Dr Unit 3 Canton (48188) *(G-2473)*
Impeccable Machining Inc 734 844-3855
 1021 Manufacturers Dr Westland (48186) *(G-18385)*
Impel Industries Inc 586 254-5800
 44494 Phoenix Dr Sterling Heights (48314) *(G-16046)*
Imperial Clinical RES Svcs Inc 616 784-0100
 3100 Walkent Dr Nw Grand Rapids (49544) *(G-6836)*
Imperial Graphics, Grand Rapids Also called *Imperial Clinical RES Svcs Inc* *(G-6836)*
Imperial Laser Inc 616 735-9315
 11473 1st Ave Nw Grand Rapids (49534) *(G-6837)*
Imperial Metal Products Co 616 452-1700
 835 Hall St Sw Grand Rapids (49503) *(G-6838)*
Imperial Plastics Mfg, North Branch Also called *Johnson Walker & Assoc LLC* *(G-12179)*
Imperial Press Inc 734 728-5430
 36024 W Michigan Ave Wayne (48184) *(G-18224)*
Impert Industries Inc 269 694-2727
 557 Lincoln Rd Otsego (49078) *(G-12788)*
Impres Engineering Svcs LLC 616 796-8976
 147 Douglas Ave Holland (49424) *(G-8094)*
Impression Center Co 248 989-8080
 224 Minnesota Dr Troy (48083) *(G-17162)*
Impressions Custom Graphics 989 429-0079
 4195 N Clare Ave Harrison (48625) *(G-7678)*
Impressions Promotional Group 313 299-3140
 20449 Ecorse Rd Taylor (48180) *(G-16427)*
Impressions Specialty Advg, Taylor Also called *Monograms & More Inc* *(G-16449)*
Impressive Auto Care LLC 734 306-4880
 8428 Wahrman St Romulus (48174) *(G-14285)*
Imprint House LLC 810 985-8203
 1113 Military St Port Huron (48060) *(G-13487)*
Imra America Inc (HQ) 734 669-7377
 1044 Woodridge Ave Ann Arbor (48105) *(G-525)*
IMS, Pontiac Also called *Integrated Marketing Svcs LLC* *(G-13381)*
IMS, Norton Shores Also called *Ioperations Inc* *(G-12301)*
IMS, Clare Also called *Integrity Machine Services* *(G-2981)*
Ims/Chinatool Jv LLC (PA) 734 466-5151
 17199 N Laurel Park Dr # 412 Livonia (48152) *(G-10247)*
Imservice, South Lyon Also called *International Machining Svc* *(G-15440)*
IMT, Northville Also called *Innovative Machine Technology* *(G-12231)*
Imtt, Troy Also called *Ideal Machine Tool Tech LLC* *(G-17158)*
In Know Inc 734 827-9711
 723 W Madison St Apt 9 Ann Arbor (48103) *(G-526)*
In The Stars Candles 231 590-7407
 226 E Eleventh St Traverse City (49684) *(G-16721)*
In The Zone Sports Camps 616 889-5571
 260 Langlois Dr Se Grand Rapids (49546) *(G-6839)*
In-Depth Editions LLC 616 566-6009
 1134 Goodwood Ct Holland (49424) *(G-8095)*
In-Tronics, Sterling Heights Also called *Aero Embedded Technologies Inc* *(G-15925)*
Inalfa Holding Inc 248 371-3060
 1370 Pacific Dr Auburn Hills (48326) *(G-934)*
Inalfa Roof Systems Inc (HQ) 248 371-3060
 1370 Pacific Dr Auburn Hills (48326) *(G-935)*
Inalfa Roof Systems Inc 586 758-6620
 12500 E 9 Mile Rd Warren (48089) *(G-17859)*
Inalfa-Hollandia, Auburn Hills Also called *Inalfa Roof Systems Inc* *(G-935)*
Inalfa/Ssi Roof Systems LLC 586 758-6620
 12500 E 9 Mile Rd Warren (48089) *(G-17860)*
Inateg LLC 734 276-3899
 34081 La Moyne St Livonia (48154) *(G-10248)*
Incoe Corporation (PA) 248 616-0220
 2850 High Meadow Cir Auburn Hills (48326) *(G-936)*
Incoe International Inc (HQ) 248 616-0220
 2850 High Meadow Cir Auburn Hills (48326) *(G-937)*
Income Waxcom 616 457-4277
 7702 Harold Ave Jenison (49428) *(G-9057)*
Increase Enterprises LLC 616 550-8553
 1940 Fruitwood Dr Nw Grand Rapids (49504) *(G-6840)*
Indelco Plastics Corporation 616 452-7077
 3322 Lousma Dr Se Grand Rapids (49548) *(G-6841)*
Independent Dairy Inc (PA) 734 241-6016
 126 N Telegraph Rd Monroe (48162) *(G-11550)*
Independent Die Association 586 773-9000
 14689 E 11 Mile Rd Warren (48088) *(G-17861)*
Independent Die Cutting Inc 616 452-3197
 1265 Godfrey Ave Sw Grand Rapids (49503) *(G-6842)*
Independent Engineering Co, West Bloomfield Also called *Harvey S Freeman* *(G-18287)*
Independent Machine Co Inc 906 428-4524
 2501 Danforth Rd Escanaba (49829) *(G-5077)*
Independent Mfg Solutions Corp 248 960-3550
 46918 Liberty Dr Wixom (48393) *(G-18684)*
Independent Newspapers Inc (HQ) 586 469-4510
 100 Macomb Daily Dr Mount Clemens (48043) *(G-11642)*
Independent Newspapers, The, Dundee Also called *Gazelle Publishing* *(G-4821)*
Independent Tool and Mfg Co 269 521-4811
 661 44th St Allegan (49010) *(G-161)*
Indepndent Advsor Nwsppr Group 989 723-1118
 1907 W M 21 Owosso (48867) *(G-12838)*
Indepndnce Tling Solutions LLC 586 274-2300
 1200 Rochester Rd Troy (48083) *(G-17163)*
Index Prints 248 327-6621
 25901 W 10 Mile Rd Southfield (48033) *(G-15602)*
Indexable Cutter Engineering 586 598-1540
 50525 Metzen Dr Chesterfield (48051) *(G-2892)*
Indian River Custom Log Homes, Indian River Also called *G B Wolfgram and Sons Inc* *(G-8652)*
Indian Summer, Belding Also called *Mizkan America Inc* *(G-1457)*
Indian Summer Cooperative Inc 231 873-7504
 409 Wood St Hart (49420) *(G-7755)*
Indian Summer Cooperative Inc (PA) 231 845-6248
 3958 W Chauvez Rd Ste 1 Ludington (49431) *(G-10541)*
Indiana Newspapers LLC 248 680-9905
 340 E Big Beaver Rd Ste 1 Troy (48083) *(G-17164)*
Indicon LLC (PA) 586 274-0505
 6125 Center Dr Sterling Heights (48312) *(G-16047)*
Indispensable Health, Grass Lake Also called *Grass Lake Community Pharmacy* *(G-7438)*
Indocomp Systems Inc 810 678-3990
 3383 S Lapeer Rd Metamora (48455) *(G-11281)*

Indratech LLC ... 502 381-5798
2482 Wickfield Rd West Bloomfield (48323) *(G-18291)*
Indratech LLC (PA) ... 248 377-1877
1212 E Maple Rd Troy (48083) *(G-17165)*
Indril, Kalkaska *Also called Beckman Production Svcs Inc (G-9384)*
Induction Engineering Inc ... 586 716-4700
51517 Industrial Dr New Baltimore (48047) *(G-11982)*
Induction Processing Inc ... 586 756-5101
24872 Gibson Dr Warren (48089) *(G-17862)*
Induction Services Inc ... 586 754-1640
24800 Mound Rd Warren (48091) *(G-17863)*
Indus Technologies Inc ... 630 915-8034
1922 Savannah Ln Ypsilanti (48198) *(G-18955)*
Industrial Assemblies Inc ... 231 865-6500
3130 Farr Rd Fruitport (49415) *(G-6063)*
Industrial Atomated Design LLC ... 810 648-9200
245 S Stoutenburg Rd Sandusky (48471) *(G-15060)*
Industrial Automation LLC (PA) ... 248 598-5900
2968 Waterview Dr Rochester Hills (48309) *(G-14039)*
Industrial Bag & Spc Inc ... 248 559-5550
17800 Northland Park Ct # 107 Southfield (48075) *(G-15603)*
Industrial Building Panels, Clarkston *Also called I B P Inc (G-3041)*
Industrial Computer & Controls ... 734 697-4152
43774 Bemis Rd Van Buren Twp (48111) *(G-17530)*
Industrial Container Inc ... 313 923-8778
6671 French Rd Detroit (48213) *(G-4314)*
Industrial Control Systems LLC ... 269 689-3241
70380 M 66 Sturgis (49091) *(G-16294)*
Industrial Converting Inc ... 586 757-8820
21650 Hoover Rd Warren (48089) *(G-17864)*
Industrial Dsign Innvtions Div, Dearborn *Also called Big 3 Precision Products Inc (G-3815)*
Industrial Duct Systems Inc ... 586 498-3993
30015 Groesbeck Hwy Roseville (48066) *(G-14422)*
Industrial Elc Co Detroit Inc ... 313 872-1133
275 E Milwaukee St Detroit (48202) *(G-4315)*
Industrial Engineering Service ... 616 794-1330
215 E High St Belding (48809) *(G-1453)*
Industrial Engnrng Service, Belding *Also called Industrial Engineering Service (G-1453)*
Industrial Exprmental Tech LLC ... 248 371-8000
3199 Lapeer Rd Auburn Hills (48326) *(G-938)*
Industrial Exprmental Tech LLC ... 248 948-1100
21556 Telegraph Rd Southfield (48033) *(G-15604)*
Industrial Extrusion Belting, Cassopolis *Also called Stephen A James (G-2634)*
Industrial Fabg Systems Inc ... 248 685-7373
4965 Technical Dr Milford (48381) *(G-11467)*
Industrial Fabric Products Inc ... 269 932-4440
4133 M 139 Saint Joseph (49085) *(G-14937)*
Industrial Fabricating Inc ... 734 676-2710
28233 Fort St Brownstown Twp (48183) *(G-2155)*
Industrial Fabrication LLC ... 269 465-5960
9550 Mathieu St Bridgman (49106) *(G-1929)*
Industrial Frnc Interiors Inc ... 586 977-9600
35160 Stanley Dr Sterling Heights (48312) *(G-16048)*
Industrial Imprntng & Die Ctng ... 586 778-9470
15291 E 10 Mile Rd Eastpointe (48021) *(G-4937)*
Industrial Innovations Inc ... 616 249-1525
2936 Dormax St Sw Grandville (49418) *(G-7392)*
Industrial Kinetics Inc ... 586 212-3894
36661 Haley Dr New Baltimore (48047) *(G-11983)*
Industrial Machine Pdts Inc ... 248 628-3621
32 Louck St Oxford (48371) *(G-12889)*
Industrial Machining Services, Zeeland *Also called PI Optima Inc (G-19068)*
Industrial Magnetics Inc (PA) ... 231 582-3100
1385 S M 75 Boyne City (49712) *(G-1890)*
Industrial Marking Products ... 517 699-2160
1415 Grovenburg Rd Holt (48842) *(G-8314)*
Industrial Metal Coating Co, Sterling Heights *Also called Fricia Enterprises Inc (G-16023)*
Industrial Metal Finishing Co, Sterling Heights *Also called Oliver Industries Inc (G-16120)*
Industrial Model Inc ... 586 254-0450
2170 Pontiac Rd Auburn Hills (48326) *(G-939)*
Industrial Mtal Fbricators LLC ... 810 765-8960
2700 Plank Rd Cottrellville (48039) *(G-3722)*
Industrial Mtal Idntfction Inc ... 616 847-0060
17796 North Shore Dr Spring Lake (49456) *(G-15824)*
Industrial Packaging Corp (PA) ... 248 677-0084
3060 11 Mile Rd Berkley (48072) *(G-1628)*
Industrial Plant Svcs Nat LLC ... 586 221-9017
51410 Milano Dr Ste 110 Macomb (48042) *(G-10605)*
Industrial Powder Coating, Caledonia *Also called RKP Consulting Inc (G-2397)*
Industrial Processing, Auburn Hills *Also called Autotech Engrg R&D USA Inc (G-808)*
Industrial Resin Recycling, Fowlerville *Also called Ravago Americas LLC (G-5853)*
Industrial Service Tech Inc ... 616 247-1033
3286 Kentland Ct Se Grand Rapids (49548) *(G-6843)*
Industrial Services Group ... 269 945-5291
683 Lincoln Lake Ave Se Lowell (49331) *(G-10506)*
Industrial Sew Innvtion Ctr Is ... 313 870-1898
5800 Cass Ave Ste 43 Detroit (48202) *(G-4316)*
Industrial Stamping & Mfg Co ... 586 772-8430
16590 E 13 Mile Rd Roseville (48066) *(G-14423)*
Industrial Steel Treating Co ... 517 787-6312
613 Carroll Ave Jackson (49202) *(G-8908)*
Industrial System Services, Casco *Also called Magnetic Chuck Services Co Inc (G-2600)*
Industrial Temperature Control (PA) ... 734 451-8740
7282 N Haggerty Rd Canton (48187) *(G-2474)*
Industrial Woodworking Corp ... 616 741-9663
9380 Pentatech Dr Zeeland (49464) *(G-19045)*
Industries Indy Bear ... 248 446-1435
883 Hidden Creek Dr South Lyon (48178) *(G-15438)*
Industries Unlimited Inc ... 586 949-4300
49739 Leona Dr Chesterfield (48051) *(G-2893)*
Infection Prevention Tech LLC ... 248 340-8800
1245 E Grand Blanc Rd Grand Blanc (48439) *(G-6248)*
Infinicoat LLC ... 810 721-9631
593 S Lake Pleasant Rd Attica (48412) *(G-753)*
Infinity Controls & Engrg Inc ... 248 397-8267
3039 Cedar Key Dr Lake Orion (48360) *(G-9609)*
Infinity Recycling LLC ... 248 939-2563
44057 N Groesbeck Hwy Clinton Township (48036) *(G-3258)*
Infinity Transportation, Clinton Township *Also called Infinity Recycling LLC (G-3258)*
Inflatable Industries ... 517 505-0700
9510 Burt Rd Birch Run (48415) *(G-1707)*
Inflatable Marine Products Inc ... 616 723-8140
9485 N Reed Rd Ste C Howard City (49329) *(G-8410)*
Infoguys Inc ... 517 482-2125
910 W Ottawa St Lansing (48915) *(G-9854)*
Infonorm Inc ... 248 276-9027
4820 Joslyn Rd Lake Orion (48359) *(G-9610)*
Infor (us) LLC ... 616 258-3311
3040 Charlevoix Dr Se # 200 Grand Rapids (49546) *(G-6844)*
Informa Business Media Inc ... 248 357-0800
3000 Town Ctr Ste 2750 Southfield (48075) *(G-15605)*
Information Builders Inc ... 248 641-8820
1301 W Long Lake Rd # 150 Troy (48098) *(G-17166)*
Information Stn Specialists ... 616 772-2300
3368 88th Ave Zeeland (49464) *(G-19046)*
Infotel ... 313 879-0820
105 E Bethune St Detroit (48202) *(G-4317)*
Infra Corporation ... 248 623-0400
5454 Dixie Hwy Waterford (48329) *(G-18129)*
Infrared Telemetrics Inc ... 906 482-0012
1780 Birch St Hancock (49930) *(G-7620)*
Infusco Coffee Roasters LLC ... 269 213-5282
5846 Sawyer Rd Sawyer (49125) *(G-15109)*
Infusion Cosmetics, Livonia *Also called Infusion Tanning Products LLC (G-10249)*
Infusion Tanning Products LLC ... 734 422-9826
30969 5 Mile Rd Livonia (48154) *(G-10249)*
Ingersoll CM Systems LLC ... 989 495-5000
3505 Centennial Dr Midland (48642) *(G-11373)*
Ingersoll Prod Systems LLC ... 248 585-9130
1000 John R Rd Ste 108 Troy (48083) *(G-17167)*
Ingham Tool LLC ... 734 929-2390
6155 Jackson Rd Ste B Ann Arbor (48103) *(G-527)*
Inglass Usa Inc (HQ) ... 616 228-6900
920 74th St Sw Byron Center (49315) *(G-2278)*
Inhe Manufacturing LLC ... 616 863-2222
904 Chicago Dr Jenison (49428) *(G-9058)*
Initial Attraction ... 269 341-4444
3021 Oakland Dr Ste A Kalamazoo (49008) *(G-9223)*
Ink Chemistry Screen Printing ... 810 429-9095
4019 Baldwin Rd Holly (48442) *(G-8278)*
Ink Frenzy ... 734 562-2621
420 N Main St Ste 400 Chelsea (48118) *(G-2815)*
Ink On Paper Printing, Livonia *Also called E & R Bindery Service Inc (G-10188)*
Ink-Refills-Ink.com, Vicksburg *Also called Printer Ink Warehousecom LLC (G-17610)*
Inkorporate ... 734 261-4657
6841 Middlebelt Rd Garden City (48135) *(G-6097)*
Inkpressions ... 248 956-7974
3175 Martin Rd Commerce Township (48390) *(G-3542)*
Inkpressions LLC ... 248 461-2555
3175 Martin Rd Commerce Township (48390) *(G-3543)*
Inkster Fuel & Food Inc ... 313 565-8230
1021 Inkster Rd Inkster (48141) *(G-8666)*
Inkwell Screen Printing ... 586 292-4050
289 South St Ste B Rochester (48307) *(G-13907)*
Inland Craft Products, Madison Heights *Also called ABI International (G-10656)*
Inland Diamond Products Co ... 248 585-1762
32051 Howard Ave Madison Heights (48071) *(G-10746)*
Inland Lakes Machine Inc ... 231 775-6543
314 Haynes St Cadillac (49601) *(G-2337)*
Inland Management Inc (HQ) ... 313 899-3014
4086 Michigan Ave Detroit (48210) *(G-4318)*
Inland Press, Detroit *Also called Detroit Legal News Company (G-4150)*
Inland Vapor of Michigan LLC (PA) ... 734 237-4389
33447 Ford Rd Garden City (48135) *(G-6098)*
Inland Vapor of Michigan LLC ... 734 738-6312
125 N Haggerty Rd Canton (48187) *(G-2475)*
Inmatech Inc ... 734 717-8247
1600 Huron Pkwy Ann Arbor (48109) *(G-528)*

ALPHABETIC

Inn Settle & Suites 214 606-3531
1275 Us Highway 41 W Marquette (49855) ***(G-11021)***
Innkeeper LLC 734 743-1707
4902 Dewitt Rd Ste 104 Canton (48188) ***(G-2476)***
Innotec Corp (PA) 616 772-5959
441 E Roosevelt Ave Zeeland (49464) ***(G-19047)***
Innotec Automation, Zeeland *Also called Innotec Corp* ***(G-19047)***
Innovate Industries Inc 586 558-8990
5600 Enterprise Ct Warren (48092) ***(G-17865)***
Innovated Portable Weldin 586 322-4442
5221 Lois Ct Casco (48064) ***(G-2598)***
Innovation Fab Inc 586 752-3092
77909 Pearl Dr Bruce Twp (48065) ***(G-2168)***
Innovation Machining Corp 269 683-3343
1461 S 3rd St Niles (49120) ***(G-12137)***
Innovation Tech LLC 248 797-2686
29020 S Wixom Rd Wixom (48393) ***(G-18685)***
Innovation Unlimited LLC 574 635-1064
1409 4th St Bay City (48708) ***(G-1367)***
Innovative Apparel Printing 989 395-1204
1921 Wood St Saginaw (48602) ***(G-14671)***
Innovative Cleaning Eqp Inc 616 656-9225
3833 Soundtech Ct Se Grand Rapids (49512) ***(G-6845)***
Innovative Drone Services LLC 313 333-6956
875 S Grove St Ypsilanti (48198) ***(G-18956)***
Innovative Engineering Mich 517 977-0460
712 Terminal Rd Lansing (48906) ***(G-9705)***
Innovative Fab Inc 269 782-9154
29160 Middle Crossing Rd Dowagiac (49047) ***(G-4783)***
Innovative Fabrication LLC 734 789-9099
23851 Vreeland Rd Flat Rock (48134) ***(G-5622)***
Innovative Firewood Products, Alpena *Also called Speedy Blaze Inc* ***(G-318)***
Innovative Fluids LLC 734 241-5699
415 Squires Dr Milan (48160) ***(G-11438)***
Innovative Groups Inc 313 309-7064
400 Renaissance Ctr # 2600 Detroit (48243) ***(G-4319)***
Innovative Iron Inc 616 248-4250
3370 Jefferson Ave Se Grand Rapids (49548) ***(G-6846)***
Innovative Leather Tech LLC 734 953-1100
36255 Michigan Ave Wayne (48184) ***(G-18225)***
Innovative Machine Technology 248 348-1630
7591 Chubb Rd Northville (48168) ***(G-12231)***
Innovative Machines Inc 616 669-1649
1811 Chicago Dr Jenison (49428) ***(G-9059)***
Innovative Material Handling 586 291-3694
18820 Woodward Ave Detroit (48203) ***(G-4320)***
Innovative Mfg Technologi 810 941-4675
10086 Smiths Creek Rd Wales (48027) ***(G-17629)***
Innovative Mold Inc 586 752-2996
12500 31 Mile Rd Washington (48095) ***(G-18081)***
Innovative Packg Solutions LLC 517 213-3169
2075 Dean Ave Ste 2 Holt (48842) ***(G-8315)***
Innovative Pdts Unlimited Inc 269 684-5050
2120 Industrial Dr Niles (49120) ***(G-12138)***
Innovative Pharmaceuticals LLC 248 789-0999
2250 Gnoa Bus Pk Dr Ste 1 Brighton (48114) ***(G-2013)***
Innovative Polymers Inc 989 224-9500
208 Kuntz St Saint Johns (48879) ***(G-14902)***
Innovative Programming Systems 810 695-9332
8210 S Saginaw St Ste 1 Grand Blanc (48439) ***(G-6249)***
Innovative Sftwr Solutions Ltd 616 785-0745
4300 Plnfeld Ave Ne Ste H Grand Rapids (49525) ***(G-6847)***
Innovative Sheet Metals LLC 231 788-5751
1681 S Wolf Lake Rd Muskegon (49442) ***(G-11839)***
Innovative Solutions Tech Inc 734 335-6665
41158 Koppernick Rd Canton (48187) ***(G-2477)***
Innovative Support Svcs Inc 248 585-3600
1270 Souter Dr Troy (48083) ***(G-17168)***
Innovative Surface Works 734 261-3010
23206 Commerce Dr Farmington Hills (48335) ***(G-5269)***
Innovative Thermal Systems LLC 586 920-2900
21400 Hoover Rd Warren (48089) ***(G-17866)***
Innovative Tool Inc 586 329-4922
28195 Kehrig St Chesterfield (48047) ***(G-2894)***
Innovative Tool and Design Inc 248 542-1831
10725 Capital St Oak Park (48237) ***(G-12618)***
Innovative Weld Solutions LLC 937 545-7695
1022 Miners Run Rochester (48306) ***(G-13908)***
Innovative Woodworking 269 926-9663
2227 Plaza Dr Benton Harbor (49022) ***(G-1557)***
Innovative Woodworking 616 638-1139
748 E Bard Rd Muskegon (49445) ***(G-11840)***
Innovative Works Inc 586 329-1557
28323 Anchor Dr Chesterfield (48047) ***(G-2895)***
Innovtive Design Solutions Inc 248 583-1010
6801 15 Mile Rd Sterling Heights (48312) ***(G-16049)***
Innovtive Dsplay Solutions LLC 616 896-6080
4256 Corp Exch Dr Ste A Hudsonville (49426) ***(G-8586)***
Innovtive Polymers Rampf Group, Saint Johns *Also called Innovative Polymers Inc* ***(G-14902)***
Innovtive Srgcal Solutions LLC 248 595-0420
50461 Pontiac Trl Wixom (48393) ***(G-18686)***
Inoac Automotive, Farmington Hills *Also called Inoac Interior Systems LLC* ***(G-5270)***
Inoac Interior Systems LLC (HQ) 248 488-7610
22670 Haggerty Rd Ste 150 Farmington Hills (48335) ***(G-5270)***
Inoac Usa Inc (HQ) 248 619-7031
1515 Equity Dr Ste 200 Troy (48084) ***(G-17169)***
Inora Technologies Inc (PA) 734 302-7488
525 Avis Dr Ste 11 Ann Arbor (48108) ***(G-529)***
Inovatech Automation Inc 586 210-9010
16105 Leone Dr Macomb (48042) ***(G-10606)***
Inovation Services LLC 586 932-7653
3750 Seminole St Detroit (48214) ***(G-4321)***
Inovision Inc 248 299-1915
2610 Bond St Rochester Hills (48309) ***(G-14040)***
Inovision Sftwr Solutions Inc (PA) 586 598-8750
50561 Chesterfield Rd Chesterfield (48051) ***(G-2896)***
Inpore Technologies Inc 517 481-2270
5901 E Sleepy Hollow Ln East Lansing (48823) ***(G-4897)***
Inrad, Kentwood *Also called Rls Interventional Inc* ***(G-9476)***
Inscribd LLC 231 445-9104
6050 Carey Rd Cheboygan (49721) ***(G-2786)***
Insealator, Holly *Also called Bars Products Inc* ***(G-8262)***
Inside English 586 801-4351
16272 Pine Ridge Dr N Fraser (48026) ***(G-5943)***
Inspection Control Company, Lake City *Also called Gage Numerical Inc* ***(G-9546)***
Instacoat Premium Product 877 552-6724
5920 N Huron Ave Oscoda (48750) ***(G-12760)***
Instacoat Premium Products LLC (PA) 586 770-1773
5920 N Huron Ave Oscoda (48750) ***(G-12761)***
Instacote Inc 734 847-5260
160 La Voy Rd Ste C Erie (48133) ***(G-5048)***
Installations Inc 313 532-9000
25257 W 8 Mile Rd Redford (48240) ***(G-13740)***
Installers Glass Block 586 463-1214
6177 Trailside Dr Washington (48094) ***(G-18082)***
Instant Car Credit Inc 231 922-8180
3650 N Us Highway 31 S Traverse City (49684) ***(G-16722)***
Instant Copy Center, Flint *Also called Irwin Enterprises Inc* ***(G-5716)***
Instant Framer 231 947-8908
322 S Union St Traverse City (49684) ***(G-16723)***
Instantwhip Detroit Inc 734 379-9474
31607 Gossett Dr Rockwood (48173) ***(G-14200)***
Instaset Plastics Company LLC 586 725-0229
10101 Marine City Hwy Anchorville (48004) ***(G-339)***
Institute Adv of Prosthetics, Lansing *Also called Hanger Prsthetcs & Ortho Inc* ***(G-9851)***
Instrument and Valve Services 734 459-0375
14789 Keel St Plymouth (48170) ***(G-13197)***
Instrumented Sensor Tech Inc 517 349-8487
4704 Moore St Okemos (48864) ***(G-12670)***
Insty-Prints, Plymouth *Also called Alliance Franchise Brands LLC* ***(G-13122)***
Insty-Prints, Jackson *Also called Forsons Inc* ***(G-8885)***
Insty-Prints, Lansing *Also called Bruce Inc* ***(G-9819)***
Instyle Cabinets LLC 248 589-0300
4300 Rochester Rd Royal Oak (48073) ***(G-14550)***
Insulation Wholesale Supply 269 968-9746
11280 Michigan Ave E Battle Creek (49014) ***(G-1241)***
Insulspan, Blissfield *Also called Pfb Manufacturing LLC* ***(G-1773)***
Intaglio LLC 616 243-3300
3106 3 Mile Rd Nw Grand Rapids (49534) ***(G-6848)***
Intaglio Associates In Design, Auburn Hills *Also called George P Johnson Company* ***(G-910)***
Intec Automated Controls Inc 586 532-8881
44440 Phoenix Dr Sterling Heights (48314) ***(G-16050)***
Integra Mold Inc 269 327-4337
10746 S Westnedge Ave Portage (49002) ***(G-13568)***
Integrated Building Solutions 616 889-3070
13609 Larner Rd Chesaning (48616) ***(G-2828)***
Integrated Conveyor Ltd 231 747-6430
301 W Laketon Ave Muskegon (49441) ***(G-11841)***
Integrated Industries Inc 586 790-1550
33670 Lipke St Clinton Township (48035) ***(G-3259)***
Integrated Interiors Inc 586 756-4840
21221 Hoover Rd Warren (48089) ***(G-17867)***
Integrated Marketing Svcs LLC 248 625-7444
125 E Columbia Ave Pontiac (48340) ***(G-13381)***
Integrated Metal Tech Inc 616 844-3032
17155 Van Wagoner Rd Spring Lake (49456) ***(G-15825)***
Integrated Mfg & Assembly LLC (PA) 734 530-5600
6501 E Nevada St Detroit (48234) ***(G-4322)***
Integrated Practice Service 248 646-7009
111 S Lafayette St # 609 South Lyon (48178) ***(G-15439)***
Integrated Security Corp 248 624-0700
46755 Magellan Dr Novi (48377) ***(G-12438)***
Integrated Sensing Systems 734 604-4301
1240 Severn Ct Ann Arbor (48105) ***(G-530)***
Integrated Sensing Systems Inc (PA) 734 547-9896
391 Airport Industrial Dr Ypsilanti (48198) ***(G-18957)***
Integrated Terminals, Woodhaven *Also called Diez Group LLC* ***(G-18799)***

Integricoat Inc 616 935-7878
16928 148th Ave Spring Lake (49456) *(G-15826)*
Integrity Beverage Inc 248 348-1010
28004 Center Oaks Ct # 206 Wixom (48393) *(G-18687)*
Integrity Design & Mfg LLC 248 628-6927
3285 Metamora Rd Ste A Oxford (48371) *(G-12890)*
Integrity Door LLC 616 896-8077
3010 143rd Ave Dorr (49323) *(G-4768)*
Integrity Fab & Machine Inc 989 481-3200
150 Enterprise Dr Breckenridge (48615) *(G-1911)*
Integrity Force Products, Negaunee *Also called Robbins Inc (G-11973)*
Integrity Forest Products LLC 513 871-8988
844 E M28 Kenton (49967) *(G-9440)*
Integrity Machine Services 989 386-0216
5615 S Clare Ave Clare (48617) *(G-2981)*
Integrity Marketing Products 734 522-5050
5905 Middlebelt Rd Garden City (48135) *(G-6099)*
Integrity Municipal Service 858 218-3750
500 E Washington Ave Zeeland (49464) *(G-19048)*
Integrity Printing, Clare *Also called Ktr Printing Inc (G-2984)*
Integrity Sltons Feld Svcs Inc 517 481-4724
401 Republic Ave Alma (48801) *(G-242)*
Integrity Spray Foam LLC 231 631-6084
3601 Bluff Rd Traverse City (49686) *(G-16724)*
Integrity Trailers, Nunica *Also called Jrm Industries Inc (G-12581)*
Integrted Database Systems Inc 989 546-4512
2625 Denison Dr A Mount Pleasant (48858) *(G-11703)*
Integrted Systems Group Div of, Sparta *Also called Speedrack Products Group Ltd (G-15782)*
Intellibee Inc 313 586-4122
400 Renaissance Ctr # 2600 Detroit (48243) *(G-4323)*
Intellichem LLC 810 765-4075
887 Chartier Marine City (48039) *(G-10959)*
Intelligent Document Solutions, Madison Heights *Also called Data Mail Services Inc (G-10704)*
Intelligent Document Solutions, Madison Heights *Also called Lasertec Inc (G-10769)*
Intelligent Dynamics LLC 313 727-9920
456 Berkley St Dearborn (48124) *(G-3854)*
Intellitech Systems Inc 586 219-3737
303 Evaline Dr Troy (48085) *(G-17170)*
Inter City Neon Inc 586 754-6020
23920 Amber Ave Warren (48089) *(G-17868)*
Inter Dyne Systems, Norton Shores *Also called ID Systems Inc (G-12298)*
Inter State Foods Inc (PA) 517 372-5500
5133 W Grand River Ave Lansing (48906) *(G-9706)*
Inter-Lakes Bases Inc 586 294-8120
17480 Malyn Blvd Fraser (48026) *(G-5944)*
Inter-Pack Corporation (PA) 734 242-7755
399 Detroit Ave Monroe (48162) *(G-11551)*
Inter-Power Corporation (PA) 810 798-9201
3578 Van Dyke Rd Almont (48003) *(G-262)*
Interact Websites Inc 800 515-9672
3526 E Curtis Rd Midland (48642) *(G-11374)*
Interactive Aerial Inc 231 645-6007
2662 Cass Rd Ste B Traverse City (49684) *(G-16725)*
Interactrv, Midland *Also called Interact Websites Inc (G-11374)*
Interclean Equipment LLC (PA) 734 961-3300
709 James L Hart Pkwy Ypsilanti (48197) *(G-18958)*
Interdyne Inc 517 849-2281
530 Industrial Pkwy Jonesville (49250) *(G-9089)*
Interfibe Corporation (PA) 269 327-6141
16369 Us Highway 131 S Schoolcraft (49087) *(G-15118)*
Intergrted Dspnse Slutions LLC 586 554-7404
14310 Industrial Ctr Dr Shelby Township (48315) *(G-15239)*
Interior Concepts Corporation 616 842-5550
18525 Trimble Ct Spring Lake (49456) *(G-15827)*
Interior Spc of Holland 616 396-5634
262 E 26th St Holland (49423) *(G-8096)*
Interkal LLC (HQ) 269 349-1521
5981 E Cork St Kalamazoo (49048) *(G-9224)*
Interlock Design 616 784-5901
5830 Comstock Park Dr Nw Comstock Park (49321) *(G-3612)*
Intermet Systems, Grand Rapids *Also called International Met Systems Inc (G-6850)*
Intern Metals and Energy (PA) 248 765-7747
522 Hupp Ave Jackson (49203) *(G-8909)*
Internal Grinding Abrasives 616 243-5566
3011 Hillcroft Ave Sw Grand Rapids (49548) *(G-6849)*
International Abrasives Inc 586 778-8490
27980 Groesbeck Hwy Roseville (48066) *(G-14424)*
International Assn Lions Clubs 989 644-6562
1100 El Camino Grande Weidman (48893) *(G-18253)*
International Auto Components 248 755-3928
750 Chicago Rd Troy (48083) *(G-17171)*
International Bus Mchs Corp 989 832-6000
2125 Ridgewood Dr Midland (48642) *(G-11375)*
International Casting Corp (PA) 586 293-8220
37087 Green St New Baltimore (48047) *(G-11984)*
International Casting Corp 586 293-8220
28178 Hayes Rd Roseville (48066) *(G-14425)*
International Door Inc 248 547-7240
8001 Ronda Dr Canton (48187) *(G-2478)*
International Engrg & Mfg Inc 989 689-4911
6054 N Meridian Rd Hope (48628) *(G-8361)*
International Extrusion 734 427-1934
32841 Parklane St Ste 6 Garden City (48135) *(G-6100)*
International Extrusions 734 956-6841
32416 Industrial Rd Garden City (48135) *(G-6101)*
International Extrusions Inc (PA) 734 427-8700
5800 Venoy Rd Garden City (48135) *(G-6102)*
International Hardcoat, Detroit *Also called Ihc Inc (G-4313)*
International Isocyanate Inst 989 878-0336
1232 Holyrood St Midland (48640) *(G-11376)*
International Machine Too 810 588-9591
8460 Ronda Dr Canton (48187) *(G-2479)*
International Machinery 248 619-9999
225 Elmwood Dr Troy (48083) *(G-17172)*
International Machining Svc 248 486-3600
12622 10 Mile Rd South Lyon (48178) *(G-15440)*
International Master Pdts Corp (PA) 231 894-5651
9751 Us Hhwy 31 Montague (49437) *(G-11598)*
International Material Co 616 355-2800
510 E 40th St Holland (49423) *(G-8097)*
International Mch Tl Svcs LLC 734 667-2233
4028 Hartland Rd Hartland (48353) *(G-7770)*
International Met Systems Inc 616 971-1005
4767 Broadmoor Ave Se # 7 Grand Rapids (49512) *(G-6850)*
International Mfg & Assembly, Royal Oak *Also called Manufcturing Assembly Intl LLC (G-14559)*
International Minute Press, Warren *Also called JMS Printing Svc LLC (G-17887)*
International Mold 586 727-7898
1618 Palms Rd Columbus (48063) *(G-3498)*
International Mold Corporation (PA) 586 783-6890
23224 Giacoma Ct Clinton Township (48036) *(G-3260)*
International Noodle Co Inc 248 583-2479
32811 Groveland St Madison Heights (48071) *(G-10747)*
International Paint Stripping (PA) 734 942-0500
15300 Oakwood Dr Romulus (48174) *(G-14286)*
International Paint Stripping 734 942-0500
15326 Oakwood Dr Romulus (48174) *(G-14287)*
International Paper Company 269 273-8461
1321 3rd St Three Rivers (49093) *(G-16576)*
International Robot Support 586 783-8000
56 Macomb Pl Mount Clemens (48043) *(G-11643)*
International Smart Tan Netwrk 517 841-4920
3101 Page Ave Jackson (49203) *(G-8910)*
International Sports Timing, Grand Rapids *Also called Industrial Service Tech Inc (G-6843)*
International Temperature Ctrl 989 876-8075
2415 E Huron Rd Au Gres (48703) *(G-759)*
International Wheel & Tire Inc (PA) 248 298-0207
23255 Commerce Dr Farmington Hills (48335) *(G-5271)*
International Wood Inds Inc 800 598-9663
2801 E Beltline Ave Ne Grand Rapids (49525) *(G-6851)*
Internet Publishing Inc 248 438-8192
42733 Faulkner Dr Novi (48377) *(G-12439)*
Interntnal Auto Cmpnnts Group, Southfield *Also called IAC Creative LLC (G-15597)*
Interntnal Auto Cmpnnts Group 989 620-7649
1965 Williams Rd Alma (48801) *(G-243)*
Interntnal Auto Cmpnnts Group 734 456-2800
47785 W Anchor Ct Plymouth (48170) *(G-13198)*
Interntnal Auto Cmpnnts Group 586 795-7800
6600 15 Mile Rd Sterling Heights (48312) *(G-16051)*
Interntnal Auto Cmpnnts Group 810 987-8500
1905 Beard St Port Huron (48060) *(G-13488)*
Interntnal Auto Cmpnnts Group 231 734-9000
601 W 7th St Evart (49631) *(G-5124)*
Interntnal Auto Cmpnnts Group (HQ) 248 455-7000
27777 Franklin Rd # 2000 Southfield (48034) *(G-15606)*
Interntnal Def Fabrication LLC 810 643-1198
1460 Imlay City Rd T4 Lapeer (48446) *(G-9934)*
Interntnal Hrvest Ventures LLC 248 387-9944
30936 Industrial Rd Livonia (48150) *(G-10250)*
Interntnal Mnute Press Clawson 248 629-4220
640 W 14 Mile Rd Clawson (48017) *(G-3099)*
Interntnal Prcast Slutions LLC 313 843-0073
60 Haltiner St River Rouge (48218) *(G-13856)*
Interplai Inc (PA) 734 274-4628
330 E Liberty St Ann Arbor (48104) *(G-531)*
Interpower Induction Svcs Inc 586 296-7697
34197 Doreka Fraser (48026) *(G-5945)*
Interpro Technology Inc 248 650-8695
722 W University Dr Rochester (48307) *(G-13909)*
Intersrce Recovery Systems Inc (PA) 269 375-5100
1470 S 8th St Kalamazoo (49009) *(G-9225)*
Intertec Systems LLC (HQ) 248 488-7610
22670 Haggerty Rd Ste 150 Farmington Hills (48335) *(G-5272)*
Inteva - Troy Engineering Ctr, Troy *Also called Inteva Products LLC (G-17173)*
Inteva Adrian, Adrian *Also called Inteva Products LLC (G-74)*

ALPHABETIC

Inteva Products LLC | **ALPHABETIC SECTION**

Inteva Products LLC 517 266-8030
  1450 E Beecher St Adrian (49221) *(G-74)*
Inteva Products LLC 248 655-8886
  2305 Crooks Rd Troy (48084) *(G-17173)*
Inteva Products LLC (HQ) 248 655-8886
  1401 Crooks Rd Troy (48084) *(G-17174)*
Inteva Products Usa LLC 248 655-8886
  1401 Crooks Rd Troy (48084) *(G-17175)*
Intheknow313 LLC 248 445-1953
  2165 White Ave Lincoln Park (48146) *(G-10050)*
Intier Automotive Seating, Novi Also called Magna Seating America Inc *(G-12469)*
Intl Giuseppes Oils & Vinegars 586 698-2754
  38033 Opatik Ct Sterling Hts (48312) *(G-16236)*
Intra Business LLC 269 262-0863
  70600 Batchelor Dr Niles (49120) *(G-12139)*
Intra Corporation (PA) 734 326-7030
  885 Manufacturers Dr Westland (48186) *(G-18386)*
Intramode LLC 313 964-6990
  1420 Brdwy St Detroit (48226) *(G-4324)*
Intrepid Plastics Mfg Inc 616 901-5718
  7675 Howard Cy Edmore Rd Lakeview (48850) *(G-9642)*
Intric Grouting Solutions LLC 855 801-7453
  1159 Electric Ave Wayland (49348) *(G-18196)*
Intricate Grinding Mch Spc Inc 231 798-2154
  1081 S Gateway Blvd Norton Shores (49441) *(G-12300)*
Intrinsic4d LLC (PA) 248 469-8811
  30800 Telg Rd Ste 4775 Bingham Farms (48025) *(G-1701)*
Intuitive Technology Inc 602 249-5750
  3223 Boulder Ct Dexter (48130) *(G-4743)*
Invecast Corporation 586 755-4050
  25737 Sherwood Ave Warren (48091) *(G-17869)*
Invention Evolution Comp LLC 517 219-0180
  144 National Park Dr Fowlerville (48836) *(G-5843)*
Inverness Dairy Inc 231 627-4655
  1631 Woiderski Rd Cheboygan (49721) *(G-2787)*
Invertech Inc 734 944-4400
  1404 Industrial Dr Ste 1 Saline (48176) *(G-15021)*
Invest Buy Own LLC 248 467-2048
  1933 Forest View Ct Commerce Township (48390) *(G-3544)*
Invest Positive LLC 313 205-9815
  26213 Summerdale Dr Southfield (48033) *(G-15607)*
Invis Inc 517 279-7585
  702 E Chicago Rd Coldwater (49036) *(G-3439)*
Invitations By Design 269 342-8551
  223 S Kalamazoo Mall Kalamazoo (49007) *(G-9226)*
Invo Spline Inc (PA) 586 757-8840
  2357 E 9 Mile Rd Warren (48091) *(G-17870)*
Inzi Controls Detroit LLC 334 282-4237
  2950 Technology Dr Rochester Hills (48309) *(G-14041)*
Iochpe Holdings LLC (HQ) 734 737-5000
  39500 Orchard Hill Pl # 500 Novi (48375) *(G-12440)*
Ionbond LLC (HQ) 248 398-9100
  1823 E Whitcomb Ave Madison Heights (48071) *(G-10748)*
Ionia County Shoppers Guide, Saranac Also called Advertiser Publishing Co Inc *(G-15076)*
Ionxhealth Inc 616 808-3290
  4635 40th St Se Grand Rapids (49512) *(G-6852)*
Ioperations Inc 616 607-9751
  1269 E Mt Grfeld Rd Ste D Norton Shores (49441) *(G-12301)*
Iorio Gelato Kentwood LLC 517 927-9928
  4455 Breton Rd Se Grand Rapids (49508) *(G-6853)*
Iosco News County Herald, East Tawas Also called Iosco News Press Publishing Co *(G-4917)*
Iosco News Press Publishing Co (HQ) 989 739-2054
  311 S State St Oscoda (48750) *(G-12762)*
Iosco News Press Publishing Co 989 362-3456
  110 W State St East Tawas (48730) *(G-4917)*
Ipax Atlantic LLC 313 933-4211
  8301 Lyndon St Detroit (48238) *(G-4325)*
Ipax Cleanogel Inc 313 933-4211
  8301 Lyndon St Detroit (48238) *(G-4326)*
IPC Communication Services, Saint Joseph Also called Journal Disposition Corp *(G-14938)*
Ipg Photonics Corporation 248 863-5001
  46695 Magellan Dr Novi (48377) *(G-12441)*
Ipg Phtnics - Mdwest Oprations, Novi Also called Ipg Photonics Corporation *(G-12441)*
Ipp Logistic LLC 248 330-5379
  29155 Northwestern Hwy Southfield (48034) *(G-15608)*
Ipr Automation Sohner Plastic, Dexter Also called Sohner Plastics LLC *(G-4756)*
Ips Assembly Corp 734 391-0080
  12077 Merriman Rd Livonia (48150) *(G-10251)*
Iq Manufacturing LLC 586 634-7185
  1180 Centre Rd Auburn Hills (48326) *(G-940)*
Ir Telemetrics, Hancock Also called Infrared Telemetrics Inc *(G-7620)*
Irene Industries LLC 757 696-3969
  866 Grandview Dr Commerce Township (48390) *(G-3545)*
Iridium Manufacturing, Washington Also called Demmak Industries LLC *(G-18079)*
Iris Design & Print Inc 313 277-0505
  24730 Michigan Ave Dearborn (48124) *(G-3855)*
Irish Boat Shop Inc 231 547-9967
  13000 Stover Rd Charlevoix (49720) *(G-2719)*

Iriso USA Inc (HQ) 248 324-9780
  34405 W 12 Mile Rd # 237 Farmington Hills (48331) *(G-5273)*
Iron Capital of America Co 586 771-5840
  21550 Groesbeck Hwy Warren (48089) *(G-17871)*
Iron Clad Welding LLC 810 304-1180
  11076 Norman Rd Brockway (48097) *(G-2107)*
Iron Eagle Logging 269 945-9617
  317 E High St Hastings (49058) *(G-7799)*
Iron Fetish Metalworks Inc 586 776-8311
  30233 Groesbeck Hwy Roseville (48066) *(G-14426)*
Iron Heart Canning Company LLC 231 675-1839
  3630 Sutter Ln Kewadin (49648) *(G-9488)*
Iron Pot Soups, Ypsilanti Also called Advancing Bus Solutions LLC *(G-18923)*
Iron River Mfg Co Inc 906 265-5121
  3390 Us Highway 2 Iron River (49935) *(G-8741)*
Ironmann Industries 810 695-9177
  407 Hadley St Holly (48442) *(G-8279)*
Ironwood Consulting LLC 616 916-9111
  507 Rock Hollow Dr Ne Rockford (49341) *(G-14171)*
Ironwood Plastics Inc (HQ) 906 932-5025
  1235 Wall St Ironwood (49938) *(G-8764)*
Ironwood Testing & Design Div, Ironwood Also called Ruppe Manufacturing Company *(G-8771)*
Iroquois Assembly Systems Inc 586 771-5734
  23220 Pinewood St Warren (48091) *(G-17872)*
Iroquois Hoods, Byron Center Also called Gross Ventures Inc *(G-2277)*
Iroquois Industries Inc (PA) 586 771-5734
  25101 Groesbeck Hwy Warren (48089) *(G-17873)*
Iroquois Industries Inc 586 465-1023
  7177 Marine City Hwy Cottrellville (48039) *(G-3723)*
Iroquois Industries Inc 586 353-1410
  23750 Regency Park Dr Warren (48089) *(G-17874)*
Irvin Acquisition LLC (HQ) 248 451-4100
  2600 Centerpoint Pkwy Pontiac (48341) *(G-13382)*
Irvin Automotive Products LLC (HQ) 248 451-4100
  2600 Centerpoint Pkwy Pontiac (48341) *(G-13383)*
Irwin Enterprises Inc 810 732-0770
  3030 W Pasadena Ave Flint (48504) *(G-5716)*
Irwin Seating Holding Company (PA) 616 574-7400
  3251 Fruit Ridge Ave Nw Grand Rapids (49544) *(G-6854)*
Is Field Services, Alma Also called Integrity Sltons Feld Svcs Inc *(G-242)*
Iscuplt LLC 313 728-7982
  9440 Oak St Taylor (48180) *(G-16428)*
Isingularis Inc 248 347-0742
  45619 Addington Ln Novi (48374) *(G-12442)*
Island Machine and Engrg LLC 810 765-8228
  847 Degurse Ave Marine City (48039) *(G-10960)*
Island Sun Times Inc 810 230-1735
  5152 Commerce Rd Flint (48507) *(G-5717)*
ISS, Zeeland Also called Information Stn Specialists *(G-19046)*
ISS, Troy Also called Innovative Support Svcs Inc *(G-17168)*
Issys, Ypsilanti Also called Integrated Sensing Systems Inc *(G-18957)*
Ist, Jackson Also called Industrial Steel Treating Co *(G-8908)*
It Service, Canton Also called Automated Media Inc *(G-2438)*
Itac Software Inc 248 450-2446
  26801 Northwestern Hwy Southfield (48033) *(G-15609)*
Italian BTR Bread Sticks Bky 313 893-4945
  4241 E Mcnichols Rd Detroit (48212) *(G-4327)*
Italian Tribune 586 783-3260
  45445 Mound Rd Shelby Township (48317) *(G-15240)*
Itc Incorporated (PA) 616 396-1355
  3030 Corp Grove Dr Ste A Hudsonville (49426) *(G-8587)*
Iteg, Pinconning Also called Conair North America *(G-13060)*
Iterotext, Bloomfield Also called AAA Language Services *(G-1780)*
Ithaca Manufacturing Corp 989 875-4949
  1210 Avenue A Ithaca (48847) *(G-8791)*
ITM, Warren Also called FCA US LLC *(G-17803)*
Its Yours 517 676-7003
  306 S Cedar St Mason (48854) *(G-11139)*
ITT Gage Inc 231 766-2155
  3253 Whitehall Rd Muskegon (49445) *(G-11842)*
ITT Industries Holdings Inc 248 863-2153
  46785 Magellan Dr Novi (48377) *(G-12443)*
ITT Koni America, LLC, Novi Also called ITT Motion Tech Amer LLC *(G-12444)*
ITT Motion Tech Amer LLC 248 863-2161
  46785 Magellan Dr Novi (48377) *(G-12444)*
ITT Motion Technologies LLC 248 863-2161
  46785 Magellan Dr Novi (48377) *(G-12445)*
Ittner Bean & Grain Inc (PA) 989 662-4461
  301 Park Ave Auburn (48611) *(G-766)*
ITW Dahti Seating 616 866-1323
  206 Byrne Industrial Dr Rockford (49341) *(G-14172)*
Ivan Doverspike 313 579-3000
  9501 Conner St Detroit (48213) *(G-4328)*
Ivory Industries Inc 313 821-3291
  2253 Burns St Detroit (48214) *(G-4329)*
Ivy Snow LLC 248 842-1242
  4110 Commonwealth St Detroit (48208) *(G-4330)*

Iwis Engine Systems LP 248 247-3178
340 E Big Beaver Rd # 155 Troy (48083) *(G-17176)*
Ix Innovations LLC ....
4488 Jackson Rd Ste 6 Ann Arbor (48103) *(G-532)*
IXL Graphics 313 350-2800
6000 Pardee Rd Taylor (48180) *(G-16429)*
IXL Machine Shop Inc 616 392-9803
117 W 7th St Holland (49423) *(G-8098)*
Iza Design and Manufacturing, Sterling Heights *Also called Precision Laser & Mfg LLC* *(G-16131)*
Izzy, Grand Haven *Also called Jsj Furniture Corporation* *(G-6326)*
J & B Precision Inc 313 565-3431
5886 Pelham Rd Taylor (48180) *(G-16430)*
J & B Products Ltd 989 792-6119
2201 S Michigan Ave Saginaw (48602) *(G-14672)*
J & E Appliance Company Inc 248 642-9191
30170 Stellamar St Beverly Hills (48025) *(G-1665)*
J & E Manufacturing Company 586 777-5614
16470 E 13 Mile Rd Roseville (48066) *(G-14427)*
J & G Pallets Inc (PA) 313 921-0222
2971 Bellevue St Detroit (48207) *(G-4331)*
J & J Engineering and Machine 616 554-3302
3265 68th St Se Caledonia (49316) *(G-2384)*
J & J Industries Inc 517 784-3586
260 W Euclid Ave Jackson (49203) *(G-8911)*
J & J Laminate Connection Inc 810 227-1824
10603 Grand River Rd Brighton (48116) *(G-2014)*
J & J Machine Ltd 231 773-4100
3011 S Milliron Rd Muskegon (49444) *(G-11843)*
J & J Metal Products Inc 586 792-2680
34145 Groesbeck Hwy Clinton Township (48035) *(G-3261)*
J & J Sheet Metal, Clinton Township *Also called J & J Metal Products Inc* *(G-3261)*
J & J Spring Co Inc 586 566-7600
14100 23 Mile Rd Shelby Township (48315) *(G-15241)*
J & J Spring Enterprises LLC 586 566-7600
14100 23 Mile Rd Shelby Township (48315) *(G-15242)*
J & J Transport LLC 231 582-6083
4556 Lakeshore Rd Boyne City (49712) *(G-1891)*
J & J United Industries LLC 734 443-3737
39111 6 Mile Rd Livonia (48152) *(G-10252)*
J & K Industries LLC 586 948-2747
28003 Graham Dr Chesterfield (48047) *(G-2897)*
J & K Spratt Enterprises Inc 517 439-5010
256 Industrial Dr Hillsdale (49242) *(G-7938)*
J & L Manufacturing Co Inc (PA) 269 789-1507
1507 George Brown Dr Marshall (49068) *(G-11061)*
J & L Mfg Co (PA) 586 445-9530
23334 Schoenherr Rd Warren (48089) *(G-17875)*
J & L Turning Inc 810 765-5755
5664 River Rd East China (48054) *(G-4857)*
J & M Machine Products Inc 231 755-1622
1821 Manor Dr Norton Shores (49441) *(G-12302)*
J & M Products and Service LLC 517 263-3082
615 N Scott St Adrian (49221) *(G-75)*
J & R Tool Inc 989 662-0026
4575 Garfield Rd Auburn (48611) *(G-767)*
J & S Livonia Inc 734 793-9000
12658 Richfield Ct Livonia (48150) *(G-10253)*
J & T Machining Inc 616 897-6744
681 Lincoln Lake Ave Se Lowell (49331) *(G-10507)*
J & W Machine & Tool, Mount Pleasant *Also called J & W Machine Inc* *(G-11704)*
J & W Machine Inc 989 773-9951
315 E Pickard St Mount Pleasant (48858) *(G-11704)*
J & Z Distribution Co LLC 925 828-6260
15846 Golfview Dr Riverview (48193) *(G-13876)*
J A S Veneer & Lumber Inc 906 635-0710
1300 W 12th St Sault Sainte Marie (49783) *(G-15092)*
J America, Fowlerville *Also called J America Licensed Pdts Inc* *(G-5844)*
J America Licensed Pdts Inc (PA) 517 655-8800
445 E Van Riper Rd Fowlerville (48836) *(G-5844)*
J and K Lumber Inc 906 265-9130
100 Homer Rd Iron River (49935) *(G-8742)*
J and L Custom Services 269 641-7800
66252 Rainbow Rd Vandalia (49095) *(G-17566)*
J and N Fabrications Inc 586 751-6350
30130 Ryan Rd Warren (48092) *(G-17876)*
J and W Dolphin LLC 267 686-3713
385 Bishop Woods Rd Marquette (49855) *(G-11022)*
J B Cutting Inc 586 468-4765
171 Grand Ave Mount Clemens (48043) *(G-11644)*
J B Dough Co 269 944-4160
5600 E Napier Ave Benton Harbor (49022) *(G-1558)*
J B Express LLC 313 903-4601
8614 Appleton St Dearborn Heights (48127) *(G-3929)*
J B Lunds & Sons Inc 231 627-9070
707 Cleveland Ave Cheboygan (49721) *(G-2788)*
J B M Technology 269 344-5716
4155 S 9th St Kalamazoo (49009) *(G-9227)*
J C Gibbons Mfg Inc 734 266-5544
35055 Glendale St Livonia (48150) *(G-10254)*
J C Manufacturing Company 586 757-2713
23900 Ryan Rd Warren (48091) *(G-17877)*
J C S, Essexville *Also called JCs Tool & Mfg Co Inc* *(G-5114)*
J Carey Logging Inc 906 542-3420
Sawyer Lake Rd Channing (49815) *(G-2706)*
J D Russell Company 586 254-8500
44865 Utica Rd Utica (48317) *(G-17503)*
J David Inc 888 274-0669
2626 Elliott Dr A Troy (48083) *(G-17177)*
J E Enterprises 586 463-5129
38154 Willowmere St Harrison Township (48045) *(G-7702)*
J E Myles Inc (PA) 248 583-1020
310 Executive Dr Troy (48083) *(G-17178)*
J E Wood Co 248 585-5711
395 W Girard Ave Madison Heights (48071) *(G-10749)*
J E Wood Comp, Warren *Also called Stanhope Tool Inc* *(G-18027)*
J F McCaughin Co (HQ) 231 759-7304
2817 Mccracken St Norton Shores (49441) *(G-12303)*
J G Kern Enterprises Inc 586 531-9472
44044 Merrill Rd Sterling Heights (48314) *(G-16052)*
J G Welding & Maintenance Inc 586 758-0150
7059 Lindsey Rd China (48054) *(G-2970)*
J H Bennett and Company Inc (PA) 248 596-5100
22975 Venture Dr Novi (48375) *(G-12446)*
J H P Inc (PA) 248 588-0110
32401 Stephenson Hwy Madison Heights (48071) *(G-10750)*
J Hansen-Balk Stl Treating Co 616 458-1414
1230 Monroe Ave Nw Grand Rapids (49505) *(G-6855)*
J House LLC 313 220-4449
71 Lake Shore Rd Grosse Pointe Farms (48236) *(G-7536)*
J I B Properties LLC 313 382-3234
17100 Francis St Melvindale (48122) *(G-11202)*
J J Pattern & Castings Inc (PA) 248 543-7119
1780 E 11 Mile Rd Madison Heights (48071) *(G-10751)*
J J Steel Inc 269 964-0474
2000 Ottawa Trl Battle Creek (49037) *(G-1242)*
J J Wohlferts Custom Furniture 989 593-3283
10691 W M 21 Fowler (48835) *(G-5829)*
J Kaltz & Co 616 942-6070
3987 Brockton Dr Se Ste C Grand Rapids (49512) *(G-6856)*
J L Becker Acquisition LLC 734 656-2000
41150 Joy Rd Plymouth (48170) *(G-13199)*
J L International Inc (PA) 734 941-0300
34364 Goddard Rd Romulus (48174) *(G-14288)*
J L Milling Inc 269 679-5769
15262 Industrial Dr Schoolcraft (49087) *(G-15119)*
J L Schroth Co 586 759-4240
24074 Gibson Dr Warren (48089) *(G-17878)*
J M Kusch Inc 989 684-8820
3530 Wheeler Rd Bay City (48706) *(G-1368)*
J M L Contracting & Sales Inc 586 756-4133
5649 E 8 Mile Rd Warren (48091) *(G-17879)*
J M Longyear Heirs Inc (PA) 906 228-7960
210 N Front St Ste 1 Marquette (49855) *(G-11023)*
J M Mold & Engineering 586 783-3300
44910 Vic Wertz Dr Clinton Township (48036) *(G-3262)*
J M Mold Technologies Inc 586 773-6664
25185 Easy St Warren (48089) *(G-17880)*
J Mark Systems Inc 616 784-6005
3696 Northridge Dr Nw # 10 Grand Rapids (49544) *(G-6857)*
J N B Machinery LLC 517 223-0725
9119 W Grand River Rd Fowlerville (48836) *(G-5845)*
J Naylor LLC 248 227-8250
4072 Greensboro Dr Troy (48085) *(G-17179)*
J O Well Service, Mount Pleasant *Also called JO Well Service and Tstg Inc* *(G-11705)*
J R C Inc (PA) 810 648-4000
356 E Sanilac Rd Sandusky (48471) *(G-15061)*
J Rettenmaier USA LP 269 323-1588
1615 Vanderbilt Ave Portage (49024) *(G-13569)*
J Rettenmaier USA LP (HQ) 269 679-2340
16369 Us Highway 131 S Schoolcraft (49087) *(G-15120)*
J Sterling Industries LLC 269 492-6922
6825 Beatrice Dr Ste A Kalamazoo (49009) *(G-9228)*
J Sterling Industries Ltd 269 492-6920
6825 Beatrice Dr Kalamazoo (49009) *(G-9229)*
J T Express Ltd 810 724-6471
4200 Van Dyke Rd Brown City (48416) *(G-2138)*
J T Products, Burton *Also called Tyrone Tool Company Inc* *(G-2249)*
J W Briney Products, Clarkston *Also called Complex Tool & Machine Inc* *(G-3028)*
J W Froehlich Inc 586 580-0025
7305 19 Mile Rd Sterling Heights (48314) *(G-16053)*
J W Holdings Inc 616 530-9889
2530 Thornwood St Sw B Grand Rapids (49519) *(G-6858)*
J W Manchester Company Inc 810 632-5409
3552 Hartland Rd Ste 201 Hartland (48353) *(G-7771)*
J&B Pharmacy Services Inc 888 611-2941
50496 Pontiac Trl Ste 15 Wixom (48393) *(G-18688)*
J&C Industries 734 479-0069
20129 Coachwood Rd Riverview (48193) *(G-13877)*

ALPHABETIC

J&D Industries LLC 734 430-6582
4611 Pointe Aux Peaux Newport (48166) *(G-12103)*

J&J Custom Print Services 616 581-0545
8436 Cascade St Commerce Township (48382) *(G-3546)*

J&J Freon Removal 586 264-6379
32344 Newcastle Dr Warren (48093) *(G-17881)*

J&M Group Industrial Svcs Inc 248 957-0006
6354 Swartout Rd Clay (48001) *(G-3121)*

J&N Custom Woodworking 517 726-0290
2396 N Pease Rd Vermontville (49096) *(G-17589)*

J&S Fab, Lewiston *Also called Jack & Sons Welding & Fabg LLC (G-10022)*

J&S Homemade Candles 517 885-1983
5608 Appleton Ave Apt 31 Lansing (48911) *(G-9855)*

J&S Technologies Inc 616 837-7080
16952 Woodlane Nunica (49448) *(G-12580)*

J-Ad Graphics Inc (PA) 800 870-7085
1351 N M 43 Hwy Hastings (49058) *(G-7800)*

J-Ad Graphics Inc 269 965-3955
1001 Columbia Ave E Battle Creek (49014) *(G-1243)*

J-Ad Graphics Inc 269 945-9554
514 S Kalamazoo Ave Marshall (49068) *(G-11062)*

J. L. Becker Co., Plymouth *Also called J L Becker Acquisition LLC (G-13199)*

J. Lewis Cooper Co., Highland Park *Also called Great Lakes Wine & Spirits LLC (G-7908)*

J.L. McHael Hayk Kyyan Jwelers, Bloomfield *Also called Kayayan Hayk Jewelry Mfg Co (G-1782)*

J2 Licensing Inc (PA) 586 307-3400
351 Executive Dr Troy (48083) *(G-17180)*

Ja Sportswear & Printing LLC 248 706-1213
4382 Foxpointe Dr West Bloomfield (48323) *(G-18292)*

Jaan Technolgies, Sterling Heights *Also called Baird Investments LLC (G-15943)*

Jaaz Management LLC 248 957-9197
40440 Grand River Ave C Novi (48375) *(G-12447)*

Jabars Complements LLC 810 966-8371
2639 24th St Port Huron (48060) *(G-13489)*

Jabil Circuit Michigan Inc 248 292-6000
3800 Giddings Rd Auburn Hills (48326) *(G-941)*

Jabil Inc 248 292-6000
3800 Giddings Rd Auburn Hills (48326) *(G-942)*

JAC Custom Pouches Inc 269 782-3190
56525 Woodhouse Dr Dowagiac (49047) *(G-4784)*

Jac Holding Corporation (HQ) 248 874-1800
3937 Campus Dr Pontiac (48341) *(G-13384)*

Jac Mfg Inc 269 679-3301
12611 N Us Highway 131 Schoolcraft (49087) *(G-15121)*

Jac Products Inc 734 944-8844
151 S Industrial Dr Saline (48176) *(G-15022)*

Jac Products Inc 248 874-1800
3937 Campus Dr Pontiac (48341) *(G-13385)*

Jac Products Inc 586 254-1534
12000 Shelby Tech Dr Shelby Township (48315) *(G-15243)*

Jack & Sons Welding & Fabg LLC 248 302-6496
4402 Judy Ave Lewiston (49756) *(G-10022)*

Jack Batdorss (PA) 231 796-4831
22405 18 Mile Rd Big Rapids (49307) *(G-1678)*

Jack Batdorss 231 723-3592
75 Maple St Manistee (49660) *(G-10902)*

Jack Millikin Inc 989 348-8411
4680 W N Down River Rd Grayling (49738) *(G-7464)*

Jack Ripper & Associates Inc 734 453-7333
14708 Keel St Plymouth (48170) *(G-13200)*

Jack Weaver Corp 517 263-6500
343 Lawrence Ave Adrian (49221) *(G-76)*

Jack-Post Corporation 269 695-7000
800 E 3rd St Buchanan (49107) *(G-2197)*

Jackieswoodworks 616 914-2961
753 Ross Rd Norton Shores (49441) *(G-12304)*

Jackpine Business Center, Manistee *Also called Jackpine Press Incorporated (G-10903)*

Jackpine Press Incorporated (PA) 231 723-8344
76 Filer St Manistee (49660) *(G-10903)*

Jackson Archtctral Met Fbrctor 517 782-8884
1421 S Cooper St Jackson (49203) *(G-8912)*

Jackson Canvas Company 517 768-8459
2100 Brooklyn Rd Jackson (49203) *(G-8913)*

Jackson Citizen Patriot, Jackson *Also called Herald Newspapers Company Inc (G-8902)*

Jackson Flexible Products, Jackson *Also called Jfp Acquisition LLC (G-8920)*

Jackson Grinding Co Inc 517 782-8080
1300 Bagley Ave Jackson (49203) *(G-8914)*

Jackson Industrial Coating Svc 517 782-8169
3600 Scheele Dr Ste A Jackson (49202) *(G-8915)*

Jackson Oven Supply Inc 517 784-9660
3507 Wayland Dr Jackson (49202) *(G-8916)*

Jackson Pandrol Inc 231 843-3431
200 S Jackson Rd Ludington (49431) *(G-10542)*

Jackson Precision Inds Inc 517 782-8103
1900 Cooper St Jackson (49202) *(G-8917)*

Jackson Tumble Finish Corp 517 787-0368
1801 Mitchell St Jackson (49203) *(G-8918)*

Jackson Typesetting Company, Jackson *Also called Jtc Inc (G-8925)*

Jacksons Industrial Mfg 616 531-1820
4310 Willow Lane Dr Ne Grand Rapids (49525) *(G-6859)*

Jacobsen Industries Inc 734 591-6111
12173 Market St Livonia (48150) *(G-10255)*

Jacobson Logging Inc 906 246-3497
W4193 Lantz Dr Felch (49831) *(G-5431)*

Jacquart Fabric Products Inc 906 932-1339
1238 Wall St Ironwood (49938) *(G-8765)*

Jade Mfg Inc 734 942-1462
36535 Grant St Romulus (48174) *(G-14289)*

Jade Pharmaceuticals Entp LLC 248 716-8333
32229 Schoolcraft Rd Livonia (48150) *(G-10256)*

Jade Scientific Inc (PA) 734 207-3775
39103 Warren Rd Westland (48185) *(G-18387)*

Jade Tool Inc 231 946-7710
891 Duell Rd Traverse City (49686) *(G-16726)*

Jag Enterprises Inc 586 784-4231
51915 Gratiot Ave Chesterfield (48051) *(G-2898)*

Jaimes Cupcake Haven 586 596-6809
26142 Fairfield Ave Warren (48089) *(G-17882)*

Jaimes Industries, Livonia *Also called J & S Livonia Inc (G-10253)*

Jaimes Liquidation Inc 248 356-8600
19270 W 8 Mile Rd Southfield (48075) *(G-15610)*

Jaimes Trusses and Wall Panels 734 462-6100
12658 Richfield Ct Livonia (48150) *(G-10257)*

Jakeway, Greenville *Also called Belding Bleacher Erectors Inc (G-7476)*

Jam Enterprises 313 417-9200
16349 E Warren Ave Detroit (48224) *(G-4332)*

Jam Tire Inc 586 772-2900
36031 Groesbeck Hwy Clinton Township (48035) *(G-3263)*

Jamcat Candles LLC 313 319-3125
1029 Audubon Rd Grosse Pointe Park (48230) *(G-7557)*

Jamco Manufacturing Inc 248 852-1988
2960 Auburn Ct Auburn Hills (48326) *(G-943)*

James Ave Catering 517 655-4532
1311 James Ave Williamston (48895) *(G-18574)*

James E Sullivan & Associates 616 453-0345
4617 Sundial Dr Ne Grand Rapids (49525) *(G-6860)*

James Glove & Supply 810 733-5780
3422 W Pasadena Ave Flint (48504) *(G-5718)*

James Gordon Marsh 517 372-8685
1714 Lindbergh Dr Lansing (48910) *(G-9856)*

James Joy LLC 989 317-6629
412 N Mcewan St Farwell (48622) *(G-5424)*

James L Barnett 231 544-8118
2759 Finkton Rd East Jordan (49727) *(G-4872)*

James L Miller 989 539-5540
2500 Major Mountain Rd Harrison (48625) *(G-7679)*

James Pollard Logging 906 884-6744
37294 Tikka Rd Ontonagon (49953) *(G-12709)*

James R Goff Logging 231 420-3455
11328 Huffman Lake Rd Vanderbilt (49795) *(G-17571)*

James Spicer Inc 906 265-2385
1571 W Adams St Iron River (49935) *(G-8743)*

James Steel & Tube Company (HQ) 248 547-4200
29774 Stephenson Hwy Madison Heights (48071) *(G-10752)*

James W Liess Co Inc 248 547-9160
3410 Baroque Ct Rochester Hills (48306) *(G-14042)*

Jamesway Tool and Die Inc 616 396-3731
401 120th Ave Holland (49424) *(G-8099)*

Jamie Byrnes 248 872-2513
1775 Chateau Rd Commerce Township (48382) *(G-3547)*

Jamison Industries Inc 734 946-3088
12669 Delta St Taylor (48180) *(G-16431)*

Jampot, Eagle Harbor *Also called Society of Saint John Inc (G-4853)*

Jams Media LLC 810 664-0811
1521 Imlay City Rd Lapeer (48446) *(G-9935)*

Jan Fan, Rochester Hills *Also called Entrepreneurial Pursuits (G-14005)*

Jandron Il 906 225-9600
605 Couty Rd Hq Marquette (49855) *(G-11024)*

Jandys Home 616 446-7013
6330 Snow Ave Se Alto (49302) *(G-334)*

Janelle Peterson 616 447-9070
5274 Plainfield Ave Ne Grand Rapids (49525) *(G-6861)*

Janesville LLC 269 964-5400
2500 Logistics Dr Battle Creek (49037) *(G-1244)*

Janesville LLC (HQ) 248 948-1811
29200 Northwestern Hwy # 400 Southfield (48034) *(G-15611)*

Janesville Acoustics, Southfield *Also called Janesville LLC (G-15611)*

Janet and Company Inc 248 887-2050
1385 Clyde Rd Highland (48357) *(G-7893)*

Janet Kelly 231 775-2313
110 W River St Cadillac (49601) *(G-2338)*

Janice Morse Inc 248 624-7300
3160 Haggerty Rd Ste N West Bloomfield (48323) *(G-18293)*

Janitorial, Flint *Also called Lockett Enterprises LLC (G-5725)*

Jansen Industries Inc 517 788-6800
2400 Enterprise St Jackson (49203) *(G-8919)*

Jant Group LLC 616 863-6600
8111 Belmont Ave Ne Belmont (49306) *(G-1508)*

Jantec Incorporated 231 941-4339
1777 Northern Star Dr Traverse City (49696) *(G-16727)*
Janutol Printing Co Inc 313 526-6196
9920 Conner St Detroit (48213) *(G-4333)*
Japhil Inc 616 455-0260
7475 Division Ave S Grand Rapids (49548) *(G-6862)*
Jar-ME LLC 313 319-7765
16801 Grand River Ave # 2 Detroit (48227) *(G-4334)*
Jarmans Pure Maple Syrup LLC 231 818-5315
6856 Jarman Rd Cheboygan (49721) *(G-2789)*
Jaroche Brothers Inc 231 525-8100
4250 Secord Rd Wolverine (49799) *(G-18795)*
Jarvis Concrete Products Inc 269 463-3000
7584 Red Arrow Hwy Watervliet (49098) *(G-18181)*
Jarvis Saw Mill Inc 231 861-2078
1570 S 112th Ave Shelby (49455) *(G-15150)*
Jarvis Sawmill, Shelby *Also called Jarvis Saw Mill Inc (G-15150)*
Jasco International LLC (PA) 313 841-5000
7140 W Fort St Detroit (48209) *(G-4335)*
Jaslin Assembly Inc 248 528-3024
4537 Harold Dr Troy (48085) *(G-17181)*
Jason Breneman & Son Logging 269 432-1378
26940 Kirby Rd Mendon (49072) *(G-11217)*
Jason Laponsie 906 440-3567
8453 Old Brimley Grade Rd Brimley (49715) *(G-2104)*
Jason Lutke 231 824-6655
615 Rw Harris Dr Manton (49663) *(G-10934)*
Jasons Apple Service & Sls LLC 586 530-4908
48858 Park Place Dr Macomb (48044) *(G-10607)*
Jasper Weller LLC 616 249-8596
5960 Burlingame Ave Sw Wyoming (49509) *(G-18886)*
Jasper Weller LLC (HQ) 616 724-2000
1500 Gezon Pkwy Sw Wyoming (49509) *(G-18887)*
Jaspers Sugar Bush LLC 906 639-2588
W1867 County Road 374 Carney (49812) *(G-2563)*
Java Manufacturing Inc 616 784-3873
4760 West River Dr Ne Comstock Park (49321) *(G-3613)*
Jax Services LLC 586 703-3212
25343 Masch Ave Warren (48091) *(G-17883)*
Jay & Kay Manufacturing LLC (PA) 810 679-2333
72 Louise St Croswell (48422) *(G-3730)*
Jay & Kay Manufacturing LLC 810 679-3079
141 E Sanborn Ave Croswell (48422) *(G-3731)*
Jay Cee Sales & Rivet Inc 248 478-2150
32861 Chesley Dr Farmington (48336) *(G-5140)*
Jay Enn, Troy *Also called Jay/Enn Corporation (G-17182)*
Jay Industries Inc 313 240-7535
7455 Fox Hill Ln Northville (48168) *(G-12232)*
Jay Titanium Sports LLC 616 502-5945
6692 Grand Haven Rd Norton Shores (49456) *(G-12349)*
Jay/Enn Corporation 248 588-2393
33943 Dequindre Rd Troy (48083) *(G-17182)*
Jayda Gale Distilling Inc 269 397-1132
152 S Main St Wayland (49348) *(G-18197)*
Jays Famous Fd Hotdogs & More 313 648-7225
18020 Bradford St Detroit (48205) *(G-4336)*
Jaytec LLC 734 713-4500
620 S Platt Rd Milan (48160) *(G-11439)*
Jaytec LLC 734 397-6300
5800 Sibley Rd Chelsea (48118) *(G-2816)*
Jaytec LLC (HQ) 517 451-8272
17757 Woodland Dr New Boston (48164) *(G-12010)*
JB Autotech LLC 734 838-3963
32235 Industrial Rd Livonia (48150) *(G-10258)*
JB Machinery LLC 419 727-1772
11118 Thompson Hwy Blissfield (49228) *(G-1765)*
JB Products Inc 248 549-1900
143 Indusco Ct Troy (48083) *(G-17183)*
JB Whiskey Creek 269 965-4052
3905 W Dickman Rd Springfield (49037) *(G-15869)*
Jbj Products and Machinery 517 655-4734
1432 E Grand River Rd Williamston (48895) *(G-18575)*
Jbl Enterprises 616 530-8647
3535 Wentworth Dr Sw Grand Rapids (49519) *(G-6863)*
Jbl Systems Inc 586 802-6700
51935 Filomena Dr Shelby Township (48315) *(G-15244)*
Jbr Associates 586 693-5666
36950 Dequindre Rd Sterling Heights (48310) *(G-16054)*
Jbr Junk Removal LLC 248 818-3471
34841 Mound Rd Ste 314 Sterling Heights (48310) *(G-16055)*
Jbs Coating 231 366-7159
3158 Farr Rd Fruitport (49415) *(G-6064)*
Jbs Packerland Inc 269 685-6886
11 11th St Plainwell (49080) *(G-13078)*
Jbs Plainwell Inc 269 685-6886
11 11th St Plainwell (49080) *(G-13079)*
Jbs Sheet Metal Inc 231 777-2802
2226 S Getty St Muskegon (49444) *(G-11844)*
Jbt Bottling LLC 269 377-4905
8322 Waterwood Dr Kalamazoo (49048) *(G-9230)*
JC and Associates 616 401-5798
1904 Leonard St Nw Grand Rapids (49504) *(G-6864)*
JC Metal Fabricating Inc 231 629-0425
21831 9 Mile Rd Reed City (49677) *(G-13792)*
Jci Jones Chemicals Inc 734 283-0677
18000 Payne Ave Wyandotte (48192) *(G-18824)*
Jcim Mexico Holdings LLC 734 254-3100
45000 Helm St Ste 200 Plymouth (48170) *(G-13201)*
Jcp LLC 989 754-7496
1422 S 25th St Saginaw (48601) *(G-14673)*
Jcr Fabrication LLC 906 235-2683
23642 W State Highway M64 Ontonagon (49953) *(G-12710)*
Jcr Industries Inc 616 364-4856
2471 Pineview Dr Ne Grand Rapids (49525) *(G-6865)*
JCs Tool & Mfg Co Inc 989 892-8975
193 N Powell Rd Essexville (48732) *(G-5114)*
Jcu International Inc 248 313-6630
51004 Century Ct Wixom (48393) *(G-18689)*
JD Edwards MGT Group Inc 586 727-4039
4200 Bethuy Rd Casco (48064) *(G-2599)*
JD Group Inc 248 735-9999
26600 Heyn Dr Novi (48374) *(G-12448)*
JD Hemp Inc 248 549-0095
31930 Woodward Ave Royal Oak (48073) *(G-14551)*
JD Machine 906 233-7420
6614 N.75 Dr Escanaba (49829) *(G-5078)*
JD Metalworks Inc 989 386-3231
635 Industrial Dr Clare (48617) *(G-2982)*
JD Plating Company Inc (PA) 248 547-5200
25428 John R Rd Madison Heights (48071) *(G-10753)*
Jda Software Group Inc 734 741-4205
900 Victors Way Ste 360 Ann Arbor (48108) *(G-533)*
Jdi Technologies, Auburn Hills *Also called Jo-Dan International Inc (G-944)*
Jdl Enterprises Inc 586 977-8863
7200 Miller Dr Warren (48092) *(G-17884)*
Jdti, Holland *Also called Amneon Acquisitions LLC (G-7965)*
Je Machining LLC 616 340-1786
1045 Comstock St Marne (49435) *(G-10994)*
Jean Smith Designs 616 942-9212
2704 Boston St Se Grand Rapids (49506) *(G-6866)*
Jeanies LLC 313 412-8760
918 Oak St Wyandotte (48192) *(G-18825)*
Jedco Inc (PA) 616 459-5161
1615 Broadway Ave Nw Grand Rapids (49504) *(G-6867)*
Jedtco Corp 734 326-3010
5899 E Executive Dr Westland (48185) *(G-18388)*
Jef-Scot Metal Industries 231 582-0452
926 N Lake St Boyne City (49712) *(G-1892)*
Jeff Schaller Transport Inc 810 724-7640
2835 N Van Dyke Rd Imlay City (48444) *(G-8638)*
Jefferson Iron Works Inc 248 542-3554
2441 Wolcott St Ferndale (48220) *(G-5561)*
Jeffery Lucas 231 797-5152
10975 E Old M 63 Luther (49656) *(G-10563)*
Jeffrey S Zimmer 810 385-0726
6117 Wildrose Ln Burtchville (48059) *(G-2221)*
Jeffrey Scheiber 248 207-7036
285 Biddle Ave Wyandotte (48192) *(G-18826)*
Jelaga Inc 517 263-5190
371 Miles Dr Adrian (49221) *(G-77)*
Jeld-Wen Inc 616 554-3551
4100 Korona Ct Se Caledonia (49316) *(G-2385)*
Jeld-Wen Inc 616 531-5440
4200 Roger B Chaffee Se Grand Rapids (49548) *(G-6868)*
Jem Computers Inc 586 783-3400
23537 Lakepointe Dr Clinton Township (48036) *(G-3264)*
Jem Tech Group, Clinton Township *Also called Jem Computers Inc (G-3264)*
Jemar Tool Inc 586 726-6960
3523 Highland Dr Hudsonville (49426) *(G-8588)*
Jemms-Cascade Inc 248 526-8100
238 Executive Dr Troy (48083) *(G-17184)*
Jems of Litchfield Inc 517 542-5367
174 Simpson Dr Litchfield (49252) *(G-10081)*
Jenda Controls Inc 248 656-0090
363 South St Apt B Rochester (48307) *(G-13910)*
Jene Holly Designs Inc 586 954-0255
39876 Shoreline Dr Harrison Township (48045) *(G-7703)*
Jenkins Group Inc 231 933-4954
1129 Woodmere Ave Ste B Traverse City (49686) *(G-16728)*
Jenoptik Automotive N Amer LLC 248 853-5888
1500 W Hamlin Rd Rochester Hills (48309) *(G-14043)*
Jensen Bridge & Supply Company (PA) 810 648-3000
400 Stoney Creek Dr Sandusky (48471) *(G-15062)*
Jentees Custom Logo Gear, Traverse City *Also called Jentees Custom Screen Prtg LLC (G-16729)*
Jentees Custom Screen Prtg LLC 231 929-3610
515 Wellington St Traverse City (49686) *(G-16729)*
Jep Industries LLC 734 844-3506
1965 Oakview Dr Canton (48187) *(G-2480)*

A L P H A B E T I C

Jer-Den Plastics Inc (PA)....989 681-4303
750 Woodside Dr Saint Louis (48880) *(G-14991)*
Jered LLC....906 776-1800
821 East Blvd Iron Mountain (49802) *(G-8723)*
Jerky Stock LLc....616 481-2329
3220 Dawes Ave Se Grand Rapids (49508) *(G-6869)*
Jerome Miller Lumber Co (PA)....231 745-3694
7027 S James Rd Baldwin (49304) *(G-1122)*
Jerome Miller Lumber Co....231 745-3694
Baldwin Rd Baldwin (49304) *(G-1123)*
Jerrys Pallets....734 242-1577
232 E Hurd Rd Monroe (48162) *(G-11552)*
Jerrys Quality Quick Print....248 354-1313
28810 Northwestern Hwy Southfield (48034) *(G-15612)*
Jerrys Welding Inc....231 853-6494
11210 Ellis Rd Ravenna (49451) *(G-13690)*
Jershon Inc....231 861-2900
980 Industrial Park Dr Shelby (49455) *(G-15151)*
Jervis B Webb Company (HQ)....248 553-1000
30100 Cabot Dr Novi (48377) *(G-12449)*
Jerz Machine Tool Corporation....269 782-3535
415 E Prairie Ronde St Dowagiac (49047) *(G-4785)*
Jess Enterprises LLC....517 546-5818
5776 E Grand River Ave Howell (48843) *(G-8467)*
Jesse James Logging....906 395-6819
16938 Dynamite Hill Rd Lanse (49946) *(G-9662)*
Jessup Systems, Rochester Hills *Also called George Koch Sons LLC (G-14024)*
Jet Box Co Inc....248 362-1260
1822 Thunderbird Troy (48084) *(G-17185)*
Jet Fuel....231 767-9566
2177 S Mill Iron Rd Muskegon (49442) *(G-11845)*
Jet Gage & Tool Inc....586 294-3770
31265 Kendall Fraser (48026) *(G-5946)*
Jet Industries Inc....734 641-0900
38379 Abruzzi Dr Westland (48185) *(G-18389)*
Jet Speed Printing Company....989 224-6475
313 N Clinton Ave Saint Johns (48879) *(G-14903)*
Jet Subsurface Rod Pumps Corp....989 732-7513
450 Sides Dr Gaylord (49735) *(G-6136)*
Jetco Federal Supply, Grand Rapids *Also called Jetco Packaging Solutions LLC (G-6870)*
Jetco Packaging Solutions LLC....616 588-2492
5575 Kraft Ave Se Ste 100 Grand Rapids (49512) *(G-6870)*
Jetco Signs....269 420-0202
302 Capital Ave Sw Battle Creek (49037) *(G-1245)*
Jetech Inc....269 965-6311
555 Industrial Park Dr Battle Creek (49037) *(G-1246)*
Jetpack Industries LLC....248 689-5083
3848 Darleen Ct Troy (48084) *(G-17186)*
Jets Glove Manufacturing, Brighton *Also called Ebinger Manufacturing Company (G-1982)*
Jewel Albright Cohen Pubg LLC....248 672-8889
4885 Oak Hill Dr Waterford (48329) *(G-18130)*
Jewish News, The, Farmington Hills *Also called Detroit Jewish News Ltd Partnr (G-5213)*
Jex Manufacturing Inc....586 463-4274
41 Eldredge St Mount Clemens (48043) *(G-11645)*
JF Hubert Enterprises Inc (PA)....586 293-8660
34480 Commerce Fraser (48026) *(G-5947)*
Jfd North, Holland *Also called Magna Mirrors America Inc (G-8135)*
Jfp Acquisition LLC....517 787-8877
7765 Clinton Rd Jackson (49201) *(G-8920)*
JG Distributing Inc....906 225-0882
120 Morgan Meadows Rd Marquette (49855) *(G-11025)*
Jga Press/Jackson Gates Assoc....313 957-0200
1115 W Boston Blvd Detroit (48202) *(G-4337)*
Jgr Plastics LLC....810 990-1957
2040 International Way Port Huron (48060) *(G-13490)*
Jgs Machining LLC....810 329-4210
4455 Davis Rd Saint Clair (48079) *(G-14832)*
Jgs Manufacturing LLC....248 376-1659
20300 Farmington Rd Livonia (48152) *(G-10259)*
Jh Packaging, Allegan *Also called Digital Imaging Group Inc (G-155)*
Jhs Grinding LLC....586 427-6006
24700 Mound Rd Warren (48091) *(G-17885)*
Jic Metalworks....989 390-2077
1442 W Kittle Rd Mio (48647) *(G-11509)*
Jier North America Inc....734 404-6683
14975 Cleat St Plymouth (48170) *(G-13202)*
Jiffy Mix....734 475-1361
201 W North St Chelsea (48118) *(G-2817)*
Jiffy Print....269 692-3128
381 W Allegan St Ste C Otsego (49078) *(G-12789)*
Jim Bennett....517 323-9061
2607 Lafayette Ave Lansing (48906) *(G-9707)*
Jim Detweiler....269 467-7728
64177 Rommel Rd Sturgis (49091) *(G-16295)*
Jim Schnabelt, Dexter *Also called Siko Products Inc (G-4754)*
Jimdi Plastics, Allendale *Also called Antara Systems LLC (G-214)*
Jimdi Receivables Inc....616 895-7766
5375 Edgeway Dr Allendale (49401) *(G-221)*
Jing-Jin Electric N Amer LLC....248 554-7247
34700 Grand River Ave Farmington Hills (48335) *(G-5274)*
Jireh Metal Products Inc (PA)....616 531-7581
3635 Nardin St Sw Grandville (49418) *(G-7393)*
Jirgens Modern Tool Corp....269 381-5588
3536 Gembrit Cir Kalamazoo (49001) *(G-9231)*
JIT....248 799-9210
21145 Virginia St Southfield (48076) *(G-15613)*
JIT Steel Corp....313 491-3212
8111 Tireman Ave Ste 1 Dearborn (48126) *(G-3856)*
JJ Jinkleheimer & Co Inc....517 546-4345
2705 E Grand River Ave Howell (48843) *(G-8468)*
JK Machining Inc....269 344-0870
5955 W D Ave Kalamazoo (49009) *(G-9232)*
Jk Manufacturing Co....231 258-2638
520 E Dresden St Kalkaska (49646) *(G-9391)*
Jk Outdoors LLC....906 863-2932
N1180 Country Side Ln P 2 Menominee (49858) *(G-11240)*
JKL Hardwoods Inc....906 265-9130
1101 Homer Rd Iron River (49935) *(G-8744)*
Jl Dumpsters LLC....313 258-0767
24133 Elwell Rd Belleville (48111) *(G-1486)*
JL Geisler Sign Company....586 574-1800
1017 Naughton Dr Troy (48083) *(G-17187)*
Jlc Print and Ship Inc....517 544-0404
156 W Michigan Ave Jackson (49201) *(G-8921)*
Jlm Elec....989 486-3788
1854 Smith Ct Midland (48640) *(G-11377)*
Jlm Manufacturing....586 447-3500
14299 Frazho Rd Warren (48089) *(G-17886)*
Jlm Whlsale S/Verett Dukes Inc....800 522-2940
3095 Mullins Ct Oxford (48371) *(G-12891)*
Jlr Printing Inc....734 728-0250
7559 Merriman Rd Romulus (48174) *(G-14290)*
JM Longyear LLC....906 228-7960
210 N Front St Ste 1 Marquette (49855) *(G-11026)*
Jma Manufacturing, New Haven *Also called Jma Tool Company Inc (G-12033)*
Jma Tool Company Inc....586 270-6706
58233 Gratiot Ave New Haven (48048) *(G-12033)*
Jmc Custom Cabinetry....989 345-0475
960 W Houghton Ave West Branch (48661) *(G-18329)*
JMJ Inc....269 948-2828
1029 Enterprise Dr Hastings (49058) *(G-7801)*
JMS of Holland Inc....616 796-2727
1010 Productions Ct Holland (49423) *(G-8100)*
JMS Printing Svc LLC....734 414-6203
14147 Edison Dr Warren (48088) *(G-17887)*
Jn Newman Construction LLC....269 968-1290
2869 W Dickman Rd Springfield (49037) *(G-15870)*
Jn Press....517 708-0300
110 E Cesar E Chavez Ave Lansing (48906) *(G-9708)*
JNB Machining Company Inc (PA)....517 223-0725
9119 W Grand River Rd Fowlerville (48836) *(G-5846)*
Jns Sawmill....989 352-5430
4991 N Satterlee Rd Coral (49322) *(G-3699)*
JO Well Service and Tstg Inc....989 772-4221
6825 Lea Pick Dr Mount Pleasant (48858) *(G-11705)*
Jo-Ad Industries Inc....248 588-4810
31465 Stephenson Hwy Madison Heights (48071) *(G-10754)*
Jo-Dan International Inc (PA)....248 340-0300
2704 Paldan Dr Auburn Hills (48326) *(G-944)*
Jo-Mar Enterprises Inc....313 365-9200
7489 E Davison St Detroit (48212) *(G-4338)*
Jo-Mar Industries Inc....248 588-9625
2876 Elliott Dr Troy (48083) *(G-17188)*
Joan Arnoudse....616 364-9075
2499 Omega Dr Ne Grand Rapids (49525) *(G-6871)*
Job Shop Ink Inc....517 372-3900
2321 W Main St Lansing (48917) *(G-9768)*
Jobs Inc....810 714-0522
14829 Philomene Blvd Allen Park (48101) *(G-197)*
Jodon Engineering Assoc Inc....734 761-4044
62 Enterprise Dr Ann Arbor (48103) *(G-534)*
Joe Beam Woodworking....269 873-0160
6000 Red Arrow Hwy Stevensville (49127) *(G-16254)*
Joe Bosanic Forest Products....906 341-2037
1808 Nw Kendall Rd Manistique (49854) *(G-10919)*
Joe Davis Crushing Inc....586 757-3612
42101 Bobjean St Sterling Heights (48314) *(G-16056)*
Joe S Handyman Service....616 642-6038
8194 Morrison Lake Gdns Saranac (48881) *(G-15079)*
Joes Tables LLC....989 846-4970
2700 W Huron Rd Standish (48658) *(G-15889)*
Joes Trailer Manufacturing....734 261-0050
13374 Farmington Rd Ste A Livonia (48150) *(G-10260)*
Joggle Tool & Die Co Inc....586 792-7477
24424 Kolleen Ln Clinton Township (48035) *(G-3265)*
Jogue Inc....248 349-1501
100 Rural Hill St Northville (48167) *(G-12233)*
Jogue Inc (PA)....734 207-0100
14731 Helm Ct Plymouth (48170) *(G-13203)*

Jogue Inc 313 921-4802
6349 E Palmer St Detroit (48211) *(G-4339)*
Johan Van De Weerd Co Inc 517 542-3817
916 Anderson Rd Litchfield (49252) *(G-10082)*
John A Biewer Co of Illinois 810 326-3930
812 S Riverside Ave Saint Clair (48079) *(G-14833)*
John A Biewer Lumber Company 231 839-7646
1560 W Houghton Lake Rd Lake City (49651) *(G-9547)*
John A Biewer Lumber Company (PA) 810 329-4789
812 S Riverside Ave Saint Clair (48079) *(G-14834)*
John A Biewer Lumber Company 231 825-2855
6251 W Gerwoude Dr Mc Bain (49657) *(G-11183)*
John A Van Den Bosch Co (PA) 616 848-2000
4511 Holland Ave Holland (49424) *(G-8101)*
John Allen Enterprises 734 426-2507
4281 Climbing Way Ann Arbor (48103) *(G-535)*
John Crane Inc 989 496-9292
3300 Centennial Dr Midland (48642) *(G-11378)*
John Crowley Inc (PA) 517 782-0491
703 S Cooper St Jackson (49203) *(G-8922)*
John Deere Authorized Dealer, Gaylord *Also called Lappans of Gaylord Inc (G-6142)*
John Fuller Logging 517 304-3298
6318 Nicholson Rd Fowlerville (48836) *(G-5847)*
John H Dekker & Sons Inc 616 257-4120
2941 Clydon Ave Sw Grand Rapids (49519) *(G-6872)*
John Henry, Lansing *Also called MPS Hrl LLC (G-9718)*
John Johnson Company 313 496-0600
15500 Oakwood Dr Romulus (48174) *(G-14291)*
John L Hinkle Holding Co Inc 269 344-3640
1206 E Crosstown Pkwy Kalamazoo (49001) *(G-9233)*
John Lamantia Corporation 269 428-8100
4825 Roosevelt Rd Stevensville (49127) *(G-16255)*
John Ostrander Company, Madison Heights *Also called Ostrander Company Inc (G-10793)*
John R Sand & Gravel Co Inc 810 678-3715
1717 E Dryden Rd Metamora (48455) *(G-11282)*
John Sams Tool Co 586 776-3560
14478 E 9 Mile Rd Warren (48089) *(G-17888)*
John T Stoliker Enterprises 586 727-1402
9353 Gratiot Ave Columbus (48063) *(G-3499)*
John Vuk & Son Inc 906 524-6074
Vuk Rd Lanse (49946) *(G-9663)*
John Zellar Jr Forest Products, Germfask *Also called Zellar Forest Products (G-6169)*
Johnico LLC 248 895-7820
400 Monroe St Ste 480 Detroit (48226) *(G-4340)*
Johnny Meyers Trucking, Middleton *Also called Meyers John (G-11298)*
Johnnyamp Mobile Welding Svcs 269 338-8013
2706 Territorial Rd Benton Harbor (49022) *(G-1559)*
Johns Small Engine and Outdoo 517 523-1060
6560 Reading Rd E Osseo (49266) *(G-12775)*
Johnson & Berry Mfg Inc 906 524-6433
15442 Roth Rd Lanse (49946) *(G-9664)*
Johnson Carbide Products, Saginaw *Also called Jcp LLC (G-14673)*
Johnson Cntrls-Bttle Creek Vnt, Plymouth *Also called Hoover Universal Inc (G-13190)*
Johnson Contrls Authorized Dlr, Saginaw *Also called Ferguson Enterprises LLC (G-14645)*
Johnson Contrls Authorized Dlr, Detroit *Also called Young Supply Company (G-4699)*
Johnson Controls, Warren *Also called Adient (G-17692)*
Johnson Controls, Ann Arbor *Also called Clarios LLC (G-425)*
Johnson Controls Inc 734 254-5000
49200 Halyard Dr Plymouth (48170) *(G-13204)*
Johnson Controls Inc 313 842-3300
4617 W Fort St Detroit (48209) *(G-4341)*
Johnson Controls Inc 734 254-7200
47700 Halyard Dr Plymouth (48170) *(G-13205)*
Johnson Controls Inc 313 842-3479
41873 Ecorse Rd Van Buren Twp (48111) *(G-17531)*
Johnson Controls Inc 616 394-6818
88 E 48th St Holland (49423) *(G-8102)*
Johnson Controls Inc 616 392-5151
1 Prince Ctr Holland (49423) *(G-8103)*
Johnson Controls Inc 586 826-8845
6111 Sterling Dr N Sterling Heights (48312) *(G-16057)*
Johnson Controls Inc 248 276-6000
2875 High Meadow Cir Auburn Hills (48326) *(G-945)*
Johnson Electric N Amer Inc (HQ) 734 392-5300
47660 Halyard Dr Plymouth (48170) *(G-13206)*
Johnson Lifters, Taylor *Also called Specialty Eng Components LLC (G-16477)*
Johnson Matthey North Amer Inc 734 946-9856
12600 Universal Dr Taylor (48180) *(G-16432)*
Johnson Multimedia Group LLC 989 753-1151
506 Salzburg Ave Bay City (48706) *(G-1369)*
Johnson Precision Mold & Engrg 269 651-2553
1001 Haines Blvd Sturgis (49091) *(G-16296)*
Johnson Sign Company Inc 517 784-3720
2240 Lansing Ave Jackson (49202) *(G-8923)*
Johnson Sign Mint Cnslting LLC 231 796-8880
5555 E 13 Mile Rd Paris (49338) *(G-12935)*
Johnson Systems Inc 616 455-1900
7835 100th St Se Caledonia (49316) *(G-2386)*
Johnson Technology Inc 231 777-2685
2034 Latimer Dr Muskegon (49442) *(G-11846)*
Johnson Technology Inc 231 777-2685
6060 Norton Center Dr Norton Shores (49441) *(G-12305)*
Johnson Technology Inc (HQ) 231 777-2685
2034 Latimer Dr Muskegon (49442) *(G-11847)*
Johnson Walker & Assoc LLC 810 688-1600
4337 Mill St North Branch (48461) *(G-12179)*
Johnson-Clark Printers Inc 231 947-6898
1224 Centre St Traverse City (49686) *(G-16730)*
Johnsons Fabrication and Wldg 616 607-2202
740 Taylor Ave Grand Haven (49417) *(G-6321)*
Johnston Boiler Company 616 842-5050
300 Pine St Ferrysburg (49409) *(G-5603)*
Johnston Printing & Offset 906 786-1493
711 Ludington St Escanaba (49829) *(G-5079)*
Joint Clutch & Gear Svc Inc (PA) 734 641-7575
30200 Cypress Rd Romulus (48174) *(G-14292)*
Joint Production Tech Inc (PA) 586 786-0080
15381 Hallmark Ct Macomb (48042) *(G-10608)*
Joleado, Hudsonville *Also called Blue Pony LLC (G-8572)*
Jolico/J-B Tool Inc 586 739-5555
4325 22 Mile Rd Shelby Township (48317) *(G-15245)*
Jolicor Manufacturing Services 586 323-5090
13357 W Star Dr Shelby Township (48315) *(G-15246)*
Jolman & Jolman Enterprises 231 744-4500
1384 Linden Dr Muskegon (49445) *(G-11848)*
Jomar Inc 269 925-2222
1090 S Crystal Ave Benton Harbor (49022) *(G-1560)*
Jomar Performance Products LLC 248 322-3080
211 N Cass Ave Pontiac (48342) *(G-13386)*
Jomark Inc 248 478-2600
30650 W 8 Mile Rd Farmington Hills (48336) *(G-5275)*
Jomat Industries Ltd 586 336-1801
131 Mclean Bruce Twp (48065) *(G-2169)*
Jomesa North America Inc 248 457-0023
2095 E Big Beaver Rd Troy (48083) *(G-17189)*
Jon Bee Distribution LLC 248 846-0491
247 Ridgemont Dr Pontiac (48340) *(G-13387)*
Jon F Canty, Warren *Also called Mica TEC Inc (G-17928)*
Jon Morris 269 967-2862
914 Jones St Marshall (49068) *(G-11063)*
Jonathan Showalter 269 496-7001
20960 M 60 Mendon (49072) *(G-11218)*
Jonathan Stevens Mattress Co (PA) 616 243-4342
3800 Division Ave S Grand Rapids (49548) *(G-6873)*
Jones & Hollands Inc 810 364-6400
1777 Busha Hwy Marysville (48040) *(G-11089)*
Jones Chemical Inc 734 283-0677
18000 Payne St Riverview (48193) *(G-13878)*
Jones Electric Company 231 726-5001
1965 Sanford St Muskegon (49441) *(G-11849)*
Jones Equipment Rental, Marysville *Also called Jones & Hollands Inc (G-11089)*
Jones Mfg & Sup Co Inc 616 877-4442
1177 Electric Ave Moline (49335) *(G-11519)*
Jones Music Co 313 521-6471
18982 Runyon St Detroit (48234) *(G-4342)*
Jones Precision Jig Grinding 248 549-4866
4520 Fernlee Ave Royal Oak (48073) *(G-14552)*
Jones Ray Well Servicing Inc 989 832-8071
172 N 11 Mile Rd Midland (48640) *(G-11379)*
Jonesville Tool and Mfg, Jonesville *Also called Jt Manufacturing Inc (G-9090)*
Joplins Salsa 419 787-8195
1565 Harvest Ln Ypsilanti (48198) *(G-18959)*
Jordan Advertising Inc 989 792-7446
321 Lyon St Saginaw (48602) *(G-14674)*
Jordan Barnett 734 243-9565
2549 Reinhardt Rd Monroe (48162) *(G-11553)*
Jordan Exploration Co LLC 231 935-4220
1503 Garfield Rd N Traverse City (49696) *(G-16731)*
Jordan Manufacturing Company 616 794-0900
308 Reed St Belding (48809) *(G-1454)*
Jordan Tool Corporation 586 755-6700
11801 Commerce St Warren (48089) *(G-17889)*
Jordan Valley Concrete Service 231 536-7701
126 Garner Rd East Jordan (49727) *(G-4873)*
Jordan Valley Glassworks 231 536-0539
209 State St East Jordan (49727) *(G-4874)*
Jorgensen's Supermarket, Greenville *Also called Jorgensens Inc (G-7494)*
Jorgensens Inc 989 831-8338
1325 W Washington St Greenville (48838) *(G-7494)*
Josefs French Pastry Shop Co 313 881-5710
21150 Mack Ave Grosse Pointe Woods (48236) *(G-7568)*
Joseph A Dimaggio 313 881-5353
19876 Mack Ave Grosse Pointe Woods (48236) *(G-7569)*
Joseph D Eckenswiller 586 784-8542
27759 Bordman Rd Riley (48041) *(G-13851)*
Joseph Lakosky Logging 906 573-2783
10502w Government Rd Manistique (49854) *(G-10920)*

ALPHABETIC

(PA)=Parent Co (HQ)=Headquarters (DH)=Div Headquarters
2022 Harris Michigan Industrial Directory
1029

Joseph M Hoffman Inc (PA)...586 774-8500
16560 Industrial St Roseville (48066) ***(G-14428)***
Joseph Miller...231 821-2430
7781 Brickyard Rd Holton (49425) ***(G-8339)***
Joseph Scott Falbe...269 282-1597
459 Orchard Ln Battle Creek (49015) ***(G-1247)***
Jost International Corp (HQ)...616 846-7700
1770 Hayes St Grand Haven (49417) ***(G-6322)***
Jostens Inc...734 308-3879
4670 Fulton St E Ste 202 Ada (49301) ***(G-24)***
Journal Disposition Corp...269 428-2054
2180 Maiden Ln Saint Joseph (49085) ***(G-14938)***
Journals Unlimited, Bay City *Also called 4-Health Inc* ***(G-1313)***
Journeyman Distillery LLC...269 820-2050
109 Generation Dr Three Oaks (49128) ***(G-16557)***
Joy Carpet Cleaning LLC...734 656-8827
28948 York St Inkster (48141) ***(G-8667)***
Joy Industries Inc...248 334-4062
117 Turk St Pontiac (48341) ***(G-13388)***
Joy of Moldings LLC...248 543-9754
1574 Eaton Rd Berkley (48072) ***(G-1629)***
Joyce Mims...616 469-5016
9691 Community Hall Rd Union Pier (49129) ***(G-17500)***
Joyson Sfety Systems Acqstion...248 373-8040
2500 Innovation Dr Auburn Hills (48326) ***(G-946)***
Joyson Sfety Systems Acqstion (HQ)...248 373-8040
2025 Harmon Rd Auburn Hills (48326) ***(G-947)***
JP Castings Inc...517 857-3660
211 Mill St Springport (49284) ***(G-15882)***
JP Skidmore LLC...906 424-4127
W5634 Evergreen Road No 3 Menominee (49858) ***(G-11241)***
Jpg Resources Food Mfg, Battle Creek *Also called Snackwerks of Michigan LLC* ***(G-1296)***
JPS Mfg Inc...586 415-8702
17640 15 Mile Rd Fraser (48026) ***(G-5948)***
Jpt, Macomb *Also called Joint Production Tech Inc* ***(G-10608)***
Jr Automation, Holland *Also called JR Automation Tech LLC* ***(G-8104)***
JR Automation Tech LLC (HQ)...616 399-2168
13365 Tyler St Holland (49424) ***(G-8104)***
Jr Automation Technologies, Holland *Also called Jr Technology Group LLC* ***(G-8105)***
Jr Automation Technologies, Stevensville *Also called Dane Systems LLC* ***(G-16245)***
Jr Technology Group LLC (HQ)...616 399-2168
13365 Tyler St Holland (49424) ***(G-8105)***
Jra-Sign Supplies...800 447-7365
14708 Keel St Plymouth (48170) ***(G-13207)***
Jrb Enterprises, Oscoda *Also called Oscoda Plastics Inc* ***(G-12767)***
JRC Fabricating Sales and Mfg...734 459-6711
8539 Ronda Dr Canton (48187) ***(G-2481)***
Jrd, Oak Park *Also called Just Right Duplications LLC* ***(G-12619)***
Jrj Energy Services LLC...231 823-2171
7302 Northland Dr Stanwood (49346) ***(G-15904)***
Jrm Industries Inc...616 837-9758
12409 Cleveland St Nunica (49448) ***(G-12581)***
JS Original Silkscreens LLC...586 779-5456
18132 E 10 Mile Rd Eastpointe (48021) ***(G-4938)***
Js Printing...734 266-3350
30777 Schoolcraft Rd Livonia (48150) ***(G-10261)***
Jsj Corporation...616 842-5500
1250 S Beechtree St Grand Haven (49417) ***(G-6323)***
Jsj Corporation (PA)...616 842-6350
700 Robbins Rd Grand Haven (49417) ***(G-6324)***
Jsj Corporation...231 873-3300
1500 Industrial Park Dr Hart (49420) ***(G-7756)***
Jsj Corporation...616 847-7000
17237 Van Wagoner Rd Spring Lake (49456) ***(G-15828)***
Jsj DC Holdings Inc...616 842-7110
724 Robbins Rd Grand Haven (49417) ***(G-6325)***
Jsj Furniture Corporation (HQ)...616 847-6534
700 Robbins Rd Grand Haven (49417) ***(G-6326)***
Jsk Specialties...616 218-2416
11007 Chicago Dr Ste 34 Zeeland (49464) ***(G-19049)***
Jsp International LLC...517 748-5200
4335 County Farm Rd Jackson (49201) ***(G-8924)***
Jsp International LLC...248 397-3200
1443 E 12 Mile Rd Madison Heights (48071) ***(G-10755)***
Jsp International LLC...724 477-5100
13889 W Chicago St Detroit (48228) ***(G-4343)***
Jss - Macomb LLC...586 709-6305
11858 Forest Glen Ln Shelby Township (48315) ***(G-15247)***
JST Sales America Inc...248 324-1957
37879 Interchange Dr Farmington Hills (48335) ***(G-5276)***
Jt Bakers...989 424-5102
127 W 4th St Ste 2 Clare (48617) ***(G-2983)***
Jt General Industries LLC...517 712-8481
2837 E Grand River Ave Howell (48843) ***(G-8469)***
Jt Manufacturing Inc...517 849-2923
540 Industrial Pkwy Jonesville (49250) ***(G-9090)***
Jtc Inc...517 784-0576
1820 W Ganson St Jackson (49202) ***(G-8925)***
Jtekt Automotive N Amer Inc...734 454-1500
47771 Halyard Dr Plymouth (48170) ***(G-13208)***
Jtekt Toyoda Americas Corp...847 506-2415
51300 Pontiac Trl Wixom (48393) ***(G-18690)***
Juanita L Signs...269 429-7248
1101 Wedgewood Rd Saint Joseph (49085) ***(G-14939)***
Judah Scents...810 219-9956
1825 Rockcreek Ln Flint (48507) ***(G-5719)***
Julian Brothers Inc...248 588-0280
540 S Rochester Rd Clawson (48017) ***(G-3100)***
Julie Opticians, Flint *Also called Flint Optical Company Inc* ***(G-5701)***
Jumpin Johnnys Inc...989 832-0160
1309 W Reardon St Apt 2 Midland (48640) ***(G-11380)***
Jungnitsch Bros Logging...989 233-8091
15250 W Townline Rd Saint Charles (48655) ***(G-14803)***
Junk Man LLC...248 459-7359
111 Vernon Dr Pontiac (48342) ***(G-13389)***
Junkless Foods Inc...616 560-7895
6749 S Westnedge Ave K Portage (49002) ***(G-13570)***
Jupiter Manufacturing...989 551-0519
8661 Sand Beach Rd Harbor Beach (48441) ***(G-7633)***
Jus Kutz LLC...248 882-5462
1213 Colony Ln Pontiac (48340) ***(G-13390)***
Just Adorable Crocheting...586 746-7137
17443 Kingsbrooke Cir # 103 Clinton Township (48038) ***(G-3266)***
Just Cover It Up...734 247-4729
34754 Lynn Dr Romulus (48174) ***(G-14293)***
Just Girls LLC...248 952-1967
6907 Orchard Lake Rd Troy (48098) ***(G-17190)***
Just Press Play...248 470-7797
19175 Auburndale St Livonia (48152) ***(G-10262)***
Just Right Duplications LLC...313 655-3555
25900 Greenfield Rd # 326 Oak Park (48237) ***(G-12619)***
Just Rite Bracket...248 477-0592
21565 Verdun St Farmington Hills (48336) ***(G-5277)***
Just Signs Sometimes T-Shirts...616 401-1215
101 Fuller Ave Ne Grand Rapids (49503) ***(G-6874)***
Just Wear It...734 458-4015
33650 5 Mile Rd Livonia (48154) ***(G-10263)***
Just Wing It Inc...248 549-9338
31681 Dequindre Rd Madison Heights (48071) ***(G-10756)***
Just Write Invites LLC...248 797-7844
30409 Mirlon Dr Farmington Hills (48331) ***(G-5278)***
Just-In Time Auto Dtailing LLC...248 590-0085
17356 W 12 Mile Rd Ste 20 Southfield (48076) ***(G-15614)***
Justgirls Boutique, Troy *Also called Just Girls LLC* ***(G-17190)***
Justice...517 780-4035
1850 W Michigan Ave # 774 Jackson (49202) ***(G-8926)***
Justice...616 531-4534
3700 Rvrtwn Pkwy Sw # 2144 Grandville (49418) ***(G-7394)***
Justinscstmgatesandwoodworking...906 748-1999
5381 Bunker Rd Mason (48854) ***(G-11140)***
Juvenex Inc...248 436-2866
26222 Telegraph Rd Southfield (48033) ***(G-15615)***
Jvdw, Litchfield *Also called Johan Van De Weerd Co Inc* ***(G-10082)***
Jvis - USA, Shelby Township *Also called Jvis International LLC* ***(G-15249)***
Jvis - Usa LLC (PA)...586 884-5700
52048 Shelby Pkwy Shelby Township (48315) ***(G-15248)***
Jvis - Usa LLC...586 803-6056
34501 Harper Ave Clinton Township (48035) ***(G-3267)***
Jvis International LLC (HQ)...586 739-9542
52048 Shelby Pkwy Shelby Township (48315) ***(G-15249)***
Jvis Manufacturing LLC...586 405-1950
34501 Harper Ave Clinton Township (48035) ***(G-3268)***
Jvis Masonic, Shelby Township *Also called Jvis - Usa LLC* ***(G-15248)***
Jvis USA LLC - Harper, Clinton Township *Also called Jvis - Usa LLC* ***(G-3267)***
Jvis-Teresa, Shelby Township *Also called Tnj Manufacturing LLC* ***(G-15353)***
Jvrf Unified Inc...248 973-2006
13854 Lakeside Cir 503-O Sterling Heights (48313) ***(G-16058)***
JW Liess Machine Shop...248 219-0444
20475 Woodingham Dr Detroit (48221) ***(G-4344)***
Jwg Industries...734 881-0312
30762 Ford Rd Garden City (48135) ***(G-6103)***
K & D Wholesale & Embroidery, Prescott *Also called Ideal Wholesale Inc* ***(G-13651)***
K & E Tackle Inc...269 945-4496
2530 Barber Rd Hastings (49058) ***(G-7802)***
K & F Electronic Inc...586 294-8720
33041 Groesbeck Hwy Fraser (48026) ***(G-5949)***
K & K Die Inc...586 268-8812
40700 Enterprise Dr Sterling Heights (48314) ***(G-16059)***
K & K Mfg Inc...616 784-4286
951 9 Mile Rd Nw Sparta (49345) ***(G-15770)***
K & K Motorsports, Sault Sainte Marie *Also called K & K Racing LLC* ***(G-15093)***
K & K Racing LLC...906 322-1276
1877 Timber Wolf Ln Sault Sainte Marie (49783) ***(G-15093)***
K & K Tannery LLC...517 849-9720
561 Industrial Pkwy Jonesville (49250) ***(G-9091)***
K & K Tool & Die, Fraser *Also called Koch Limited* ***(G-5952)***

K & L Manufacturing Ltd....734 475-1009
4720 Clear Lake Shore Dr Grass Lake (49240) ***(G-7439)***
K & L Sheet Metal LLC....269 965-0027
131 Grand Trunk Ave Ste C Battle Creek (49037) ***(G-1248)***
K & M Industrial LLC....906 420-8770
80 Delta Ave Gladstone (49837) ***(G-6182)***
K & M Machine-Fabricating Inc....269 445-2495
20745 M 60 Cassopolis (49031) ***(G-2631)***
K & N Transport LLC....313 384-0037
10780 Duprey St Detroit (48224) ***(G-4345)***
K & S Automation LLC....248 861-2123
275 S Glaspie St Oxford (48371) ***(G-12892)***
K & S Printing Centers Inc....734 482-1680
4860 Greenway Ct Ann Arbor (48103) ***(G-536)***
K & S Property Inc (PA)....248 573-1600
21810 Clessie Ct New Hudson (48165) ***(G-12059)***
K & T Tool and Die Inc....616 884-5900
7805 Childsdale Ave Ne Rockford (49341) ***(G-14173)***
K & W Manufacturing Co Inc....517 369-9708
555 W Chicago Rd Bronson (49028) ***(G-2117)***
K & Y Manufacturing LLC....734 414-7000
41880 Koppernick Rd Canton (48187) ***(G-2482)***
K A L Enterprises, Shelby Township *Also called Diesel Performance Products* ***(G-15205)***
K and A Publishing Co LLC....734 743-1541
18085 Forrer St Detroit (48235) ***(G-4346)***
K and J Absorbent Products LLC....517 486-3110
10009 E Us Highway 223 Blissfield (49228) ***(G-1766)***
K and J Lighting....586 625-2001
28041 Ginley St Roseville (48066) ***(G-14429)***
K and K Machine Tools Inc....586 463-1177
22393 Starks Dr Clinton Township (48036) ***(G-3269)***
K and S 39 Corporation....734 883-3868
8933 Ringneck Dr Ypsilanti (48197) ***(G-18960)***
K and W Landfill Inc....906 883-3504
11877 State Highway M38 Ontonagon (49953) ***(G-12711)***
K C M Inc....616 245-8599
1010 Chicago Dr Sw Grand Rapids (49509) ***(G-6875)***
K G S Screen Process Inc....313 794-2777
12650 Burt Rd Detroit (48223) ***(G-4347)***
K M I, Battle Creek *Also called Kmi Cleaning Solutions Inc* ***(G-1263)***
K M S Company....616 994-7000
5072 Lakeshore Dr Holland (49424) ***(G-8106)***
K P, Flushing *Also called King Par LLC* ***(G-5810)***
K S S, Auburn Hills *Also called Key Sfety Rstraint Systems Inc* ***(G-953)***
K S S, Auburn Hills *Also called Key Safety Systems Inc* ***(G-951)***
K Two Welding....810 858-3072
1307 Oak St Port Huron (48060) ***(G-13491)***
K&A Machine and Tool Inc....517 750-9244
4821 W Michigan Ave Jackson (49201) ***(G-8927)***
K&F Electronics, Fraser *Also called K & F Electronic Inc* ***(G-5949)***
K&G Welding LLC....810 887-0560
2515 Elmwood St Port Huron (48060) ***(G-13492)***
K&H Supply of Lansing Inc (PA)....517 482-7600
3503 W Saint Joseph St Lansing (48917) ***(G-9769)***
K&K Stamping Company....586 443-7900
23015 W Industrial Dr Saint Clair Shores (48080) ***(G-14866)***
K&S Consultants LLC....269 240-7767
404 River St Buchanan (49107) ***(G-2198)***
K&S Custom Embroidery LLC....734 709-2689
44234 Ardmore St Canton (48188) ***(G-2483)***
K&S Fuel Ventures....248 360-0055
519 W Commerce Rd Commerce Township (48382) ***(G-3548)***
K&W Tool and Machine Inc....616 754-7540
1216 Shearer Rd Ste A Greenville (48838) ***(G-7495)***
K-B Tool Corporation....586 795-9003
5985 Wall St Sterling Heights (48312) ***(G-16060)***
K-Bur Enterprises Inc....616 447-7446
5120 Plainfield Ave Ne Grand Rapids (49525) ***(G-6876)***
K-C Welding Supply Inc....989 893-6509
1309 Main St Essexville (48732) ***(G-5115)***
K-Mar Structures LLC....231 924-3895
7960 Meinert Rd Fremont (49412) ***(G-6046)***
K-O Products Company, Benton Harbor *Also called Dgh Enterprises Inc* ***(G-1546)***
K-R Metal Engineers Corp....989 892-1901
815 S Henry St Bay City (48706) ***(G-1370)***
K-Space Associates Inc....734 426-7977
2182 Bishop Cir E Dexter (48130) ***(G-4744)***
K-TEC Systems Inc (PA)....248 414-4100
2615 Wolcott St Ferndale (48220) ***(G-5562)***
K-Tel Corporation....517 543-6174
518 W Lovett St Ste 1 Charlotte (48813) ***(G-2760)***
K-Tool Corporation Michigan (PA)....863 603-0777
45225 Five Mile Rd Plymouth (48170) ***(G-13209)***
K-Tool International, Plymouth *Also called K-Tool Corporation Michigan* ***(G-13209)***
K-Two Inc....269 961-2000
1 Kellogg Sq Battle Creek (49017) ***(G-1249)***
K-Value Insulation LLC....248 688-5816
4956 Butler Dr Troy (48085) ***(G-17191)***
K.I.S.M., Wixom *Also called Kennedy Industries Inc* ***(G-18691)***
K2 Stoneworks LLC....989 790-3250
5195 Dixie Hwy Saginaw (48601) ***(G-14675)***
Ka-Wood Gear & Machine Co....248 585-8870
32500 Industrial Dr Madison Heights (48071) ***(G-10757)***
Kace Logistics LLC (PA)....734 946-8600
862 Will Carleton Rd Carleton (48117) ***(G-2557)***
Kadant Johnson LLC (HQ)....269 278-1715
805 Wood St Three Rivers (49093) ***(G-16577)***
Kae Organics LLC....248 832-0403
6514 Greenview Ave Detroit (48228) ***(G-4348)***
Kaechele Publications Inc....269 673-5534
241 Hubbard St Allegan (49010) ***(G-162)***
Kage Group LLC....734 604-5052
13835 Basswood Cir Van Buren Twp (48111) ***(G-17532)***
Kah....734 727-0478
38700 Webb Dr Westland (48185) ***(G-18390)***
Kaines West Michigan Co, Ludington *Also called West Michigan Wire Co* ***(G-10556)***
Kaiser Aluminum Corporation....269 488-0957
5205 Midlink Dr Kalamazoo (49048) ***(G-9234)***
Kaiser Aluminum Fab Pdts LLC....269 250-8400
5205 Kaiser Dr Kalamazoo (49048) ***(G-9235)***
Kaiser Optical Systems Inc (HQ)....734 665-8083
371 Parkland Plz Ann Arbor (48103) ***(G-537)***
Kalamazoo Candle Company....269 532-9816
5111 E MI Ave Ste A15 Kalamazoo (49048) ***(G-9236)***
Kalamazoo Chuck Mfg Svc Ctr Co....269 679-2325
11825 S Shaver Rd Schoolcraft (49087) ***(G-15122)***
Kalamazoo Company (PA)....269 345-7151
1600 Douglas Ave Kalamazoo (49007) ***(G-9237)***
Kalamazoo Electric Motor Inc....269 345-7802
414 Mills St Kalamazoo (49001) ***(G-9238)***
Kalamazoo Electropolishing Co, Vicksburg *Also called Kepco Inc* ***(G-17607)***
Kalamazoo Engrg & Mfg LLC....269 569-5205
2525 Miller Rd Kalamazoo (49001) ***(G-9239)***
Kalamazoo Fabricating, Kalamazoo *Also called Envirodyne Technologies Inc* ***(G-9181)***
Kalamazoo Gazette, Kalamazoo *Also called Herald Newspapers Company Inc* ***(G-9213)***
Kalamazoo Gazette, Kalamazoo *Also called Herald Newspapers Company Inc* ***(G-9214)***
Kalamazoo Holdings Inc (PA)....269 349-9711
3713 W Main St Kalamazoo (49006) ***(G-9240)***
Kalamazoo Machine Tool Co Inc....269 321-8860
6700 Quality Way Portage (49002) ***(G-13571)***
Kalamazoo Meadery, Kalamazoo *Also called American Brewers Inc* ***(G-9113)***
Kalamazoo Mechanical Inc....269 343-5351
5507 E Cork St Kalamazoo (49048) ***(G-9241)***
Kalamazoo Metal Finishers Inc....269 382-1611
2019 Glendenning Rd Kalamazoo (49001) ***(G-9242)***
Kalamazoo Metal Muncher Inc....269 492-0268
3428 E B Ave Plainwell (49080) ***(G-13080)***
Kalamazoo Mfg Corp Globl (PA)....269 382-8200
5944 E N Ave Kalamazoo (49048) ***(G-9243)***
Kalamazoo Orthotics & Dbtc....269 349-2247
1016 E Cork St Kalamazoo (49001) ***(G-9244)***
Kalamazoo Packaging Systems....616 534-2600
900 47th St Sw Ste I Grand Rapids (49509) ***(G-6877)***
Kalamazoo Packg Systems LLC....616 534-2600
900 47th St Sw Ste J Wyoming (49509) ***(G-18888)***
Kalamazoo Photo Comp Svcs....269 345-3706
701 Commerce Ln Kalamazoo (49004) ***(G-9245)***
Kalamazoo Prtg & Promotions....269 818-1122
533 Whitcomb St Kalamazoo (49008) ***(G-9246)***
Kalamazoo Regalia Inc....269 344-4299
728 W Michigan Ave Kalamazoo (49007) ***(G-9247)***
Kalamazoo Sportswear Inc....269 344-4242
728 W Michigan Ave Kalamazoo (49007) ***(G-9248)***
Kalamazoo Stillhouse....269 352-0250
618 E Michigan Ave Kalamazoo (49007) ***(G-9249)***
Kalamazoo Stripping Derusting....269 323-1340
3921 E Centre Ave Portage (49002) ***(G-13572)***
Kalazack, Kalamazoo *Also called Kalamazoo Holdings Inc* ***(G-9240)***
Kalb & Associates Inc....586 949-2735
50271 E Rssell Schmidt Bl Chesterfield (48051) ***(G-2899)***
Kaliniak Design LLC....616 675-3850
13984 Eagle Ridge Dr Kent City (49330) ***(G-9434)***
Kalkaska Screw Products Inc....231 258-2560
775 Rabourn Rd Ne Kalkaska (49646) ***(G-9392)***
Kaller Gas Springs, Fraser *Also called Barnes Group Inc* ***(G-5900)***
Kalsec Inc (HQ)....269 349-9711
3713 W Main St Kalamazoo (49006) ***(G-9250)***
Kaltec Scientific Inc....248 349-8100
22425 Heslip Dr Novi (48375) ***(G-12450)***
Kam Plastics Corp....616 355-5900
935 E 40th St Holland (49423) ***(G-8107)***
Kamax Inc (HQ)....248 879-0200
1606 Star Batt Dr Rochester Hills (48309) ***(G-14044)***
Kamax Inc....810 272-2090
1805 Bowers Rd Lapeer (48446) ***(G-9936)***
Kamax Inc....810 664-7741
1194 Roods Lake Rd Lapeer (48446) ***(G-9937)***

ALPHABETIC

Kamex Molded Products LLC (PA) 616 355-5900
611 Ottawa Ave Holland (49423) *(G-8108)*
Kamps Inc 313 381-2681
19001 Glendale St Detroit (48223) *(G-4349)*
Kamps Inc (HQ) 616 453-9676
2900 Peach Ridge Ave Nw Grand Rapids (49534) *(G-6878)*
Kamps Inc 517 645-2800
4400 Shance Hwy Potterville (48876) *(G-13646)*
Kamps Inc 734 281-3300
20310 Pennsylvania Rd Taylor (48180) *(G-16433)*
Kamps Inc 269 683-6372
2193 Industrial Dr Ste B Niles (49120) *(G-12140)*
Kamps Inc 269 342-8113
1122 E Crosstown Pkwy Kalamazoo (49001) *(G-9251)*
Kamps Pallets, Detroit Also called Kamps Inc *(G-4349)*
Kamps Wood Resources, Grand Rapids Also called Kamps Inc *(G-6878)*
Kandle Shack, The, Maple Rapids Also called Kymora Kandles LLC *(G-10945)*
Kanerva Forest Products Inc 906 356-6061
15096 Autumn Ln Rock (49880) *(G-14150)*
Kansmackers Manufacturing Co 248 249-6666
312 W Willow St Lansing (48906) *(G-9709)*
Kap Building Services Inc 888 622-0527
6220 Commerce Dr Westland (48185) *(G-18391)*
Kapex Manufacturing LLC 989 928-4993
3130 Christy Way N Ste 3 Saginaw (48603) *(G-14676)*
Kappen Saw Mill 989 872-4410
4518 Hurds Corner Rd Cass City (48726) *(G-2616)*
Kar Enterprises, Brighton Also called Welk-Ko Fabricators Inc *(G-2096)*
Kar Nut Products Company LLC 248 588-1903
1200 E 14 Mile Rd Ste A Madison Heights (48071) *(G-10758)*
Kar's Nuts, Madison Heights Also called Kar Nut Products Company LLC *(G-10758)*
Kar-Bones Inc 313 582-5551
8350 John Kronk St Detroit (48210) *(G-4350)*
Karemor Inc 517 323-3042
5242 W Saginaw Hwy Lansing (48917) *(G-9770)*
Karen Spranger 719 359-4047
7520 Hudson Ave Warren (48091) *(G-17890)*
Karges Furniture Co, Grand Rapids Also called Kindel Furniture Company LLC *(G-6896)*
Karjo Trucking Inc 248 597-3700
1890 E Maple Rd Troy (48083) *(G-17192)*
Karmann Manufacturing LLC 734 582-5900
14967 Pilot Dr Plymouth (48170) *(G-13210)*
Karona, Caledonia Also called Jeld-Wen Inc *(G-2385)*
Karps Kitchens & Baths Inc 989 732-7676
10683 Old Us Highway 27 S Gaylord (49735) *(G-6137)*
Karr Spring Company (PA) 616 394-1277
966 Brooks Ave Holland (49423) *(G-8109)*
Karr Unlimited Inc 231 652-9045
515 S Division St Newaygo (49337) *(G-12083)*
Karttunen Logging 906 884-4312
29015 W State Highway M64 Ontonagon (49953) *(G-12712)*
Kash St James LLC 248 571-1160
4016 29th St Detroit (48210) *(G-4351)*
Kasper Industries Inc 989 705-1177
356 Expressway Ct Gaylord (49735) *(G-6138)*
Kasper Machine Co (HQ) 248 547-3150
29275 Stephenson Hwy Madison Heights (48071) *(G-10759)*
Kasson Sand & Gravel Co Inc 231 228-5455
10282 S Pierce Rd Maple City (49664) *(G-10942)*
Kassouni Manufacturing Inc 616 794-0989
815 S Front St Belding (48809) *(G-1455)*
Kasten Machinery Inc 269 945-1999
1611 S Hanover St Ste 107 Hastings (49058) *(G-7803)*
Kasza Sugar Bush 231 742-1930
2500 W Buchanan Rd Shelby (49455) *(G-15152)*
Katai Machine Shop 269 465-6051
8632 Jericho Rd Bridgman (49106) *(G-1930)*
Katarina Naturals 517 333-6880
2000 Merritt Rd East Lansing (48823) *(G-4898)*
Katcon Global Usa Inc (HQ) 248 239-1362
2965 Lapeer Rd Auburn Hills (48326) *(G-948)*
Katcon USA, Auburn Hills Also called Katcon Global Usa Inc *(G-948)*
Katech Inc 586 791-4120
24324 Sorrentino Ct Clinton Township (48035) *(G-3270)*
Katech Performance, Clinton Township Also called Katech Inc *(G-3270)*
Kath Khemicals LLC 586 275-2646
6050 19 Mile Rd Sterling Heights (48314) *(G-16061)*
Kathrein Automotive N Amer Inc 248 230-2951
1760 Opdyke Ct Auburn Hills (48326) *(G-949)*
Kathrein Automotive USA, Auburn Hills Also called Kathrein Automotive N Amer Inc *(G-949)*
Katrina Love-Jones LLC 248 779-6017
12068 Littlefield St Detroit (48227) *(G-4352)*
Katts Candles & More 269 281-6805
2666 Lincoln Ave Saint Joseph (49085) *(G-14940)*
Kaufman Cstm Shtmtl Fbrction L 906 932-2130
400 W Aurora St Ironwood (49938) *(G-8766)*
Kaufman Enterprises Inc (PA) 269 324-0040
6054 Lovers Ln Portage (49002) *(G-13573)*

Kaul Glove and Mfg Co (PA) 313 894-9494
3540 Vinewood St Detroit (48208) *(G-4353)*
Kautex Detroit, Detroit Also called Kautex Inc *(G-4354)*
Kautex Inc 231 739-2704
1085 W Sherman Blvd Muskegon (49441) *(G-11850)*
Kautex Inc 313 633-2254
2627 Clark St Detroit (48210) *(G-4354)*
Kautex Inc (HQ) 248 616-5100
800 Tower Dr Ste 200 Troy (48098) *(G-17193)*
Kautex Inc 248 616-0327
32201 N Avis Dr Madison Heights (48071) *(G-10760)*
Kawasaki Prcision McHy USA Inc 616 975-3100
3838 Broadmoor Ave Se Grand Rapids (49512) *(G-6879)*
Kawkawlin Church Furn Mfg Co, Midland Also called Kawkawlin Manufacturing Co *(G-11381)*
Kawkawlin Manufacturing Co (PA) 989 684-5470
2707 Highbrook Dr Midland (48642) *(G-11381)*
Kay Automotive Graphics, Lake Orion Also called Kay Screen Printing Inc *(G-9611)*
Kay Manufacturing Company 269 408-8344
3491 S Lakeshore Dr Saint Joseph (49085) *(G-14941)*
Kay Screen Printing Inc (HQ) 248 377-4999
57 Kay Industrial Dr Lake Orion (48359) *(G-9611)*
Kayayan Hayk Jewelry Mfg Co (PA) 248 626-3060
869 W Long Lake Rd Bloomfield (48302) *(G-1782)*
Kaycee Lux LLC 248 461-7117
32031 Middlebelt Rd Farmington Hills (48334) *(G-5279)*
Kaydon Corporation (HQ) 734 747-7025
2723 S State St Ste 300 Ann Arbor (48104) *(G-538)*
Kaydon Corporation 231 755-3741
2860 Mccracken St Norton Shores (49441) *(G-12306)*
Kayler Mold & Engineering Inc 586 739-0699
35620 Beattie Dr Sterling Heights (48312) *(G-16062)*
Kays Glrous Bked Gds Dist LLC 248 830-1717
5 Lantern Ln Pontiac (48340) *(G-13391)*
KB Property Holdings LLC 269 344-0870
5955 W D Ave Kalamazoo (49009) *(G-9252)*
KB Stamping Inc 616 866-5917
8110 Graphic Dr Ne Belmont (49306) *(G-1509)*
Kba Defense 586 552-9268
409 Race St Lakeville (48367) *(G-9648)*
Kbd Properties, Manitou Beach Also called Hardy-Reed Tool & Die Co Inc *(G-10927)*
Kbe Hoist, New Baltimore Also called Kbe Precision Products LLC *(G-11985)*
Kbe Precision Products LLC 586 725-4200
51537 Industrial Dr New Baltimore (48047) *(G-11985)*
Kbs Welding Service 231 263-7164
5546 Weaver Rd Kingsley (49649) *(G-9524)*
KC Jones Brazing Inc 586 755-4900
2845 E 10 Mile Rd Warren (48091) *(G-17891)*
KC Jones Plating Co (PA) 586 755-4900
2845 E 10 Mile Rd Warren (48091) *(G-17892)*
KC Jones Plating Co 248 399-8500
321 W 10 Mile Rd Hazel Park (48030) *(G-7827)*
Kci Prentis Building 313 578-4400
110 E Warren Ave Detroit (48201) *(G-4355)*
Kci Printsource, Grand Rapids Also called Kent Communications Inc *(G-6886)*
Kd Essentials LLC 248 632-7180
23551 Geneva St Oak Park (48237) *(G-12620)*
Kdf Fluid Treatment Inc 269 273-3300
1500 Kdf Dr Three Rivers (49093) *(G-16578)*
Kdk Downhole Tooling LC 231 590-3137
6671 M 72 E Williamsburg (49690) *(G-18557)*
Kds Controls, Grand Haven Also called Ghsp Inc *(G-6300)*
Keane Saunders & Associates 616 954-7088
6350 Cascade Pointe Dr Se Grand Rapids (49546) *(G-6880)*
Kearsley Lake Terrace LLC 810 736-7000
3400 Benmark Pl Ofc Flint (48506) *(G-5720)*
Keays Family Truckin 231 838-6430
1658 Ashley Ln Gaylord (49735) *(G-6139)*
Kecy Corporation 517 448-8954
4111 Munson Hwy Hudson (49247) *(G-8553)*
Kecy Metal Technologies, Hudson Also called ARC Metal Stamping LLC *(G-8548)*
Kecy Products Inc 517 448-8954
4111 Munson Hwy Hudson (49247) *(G-8554)*
Keebler Company (HQ) 269 961-2000
1 Kellogg Sq Battle Creek (49017) *(G-1250)*
Keebler Company 231 445-0335
10364 Neuman Rd Cheboygan (49721) *(G-2790)*
Keeler-Glasgow Company Inc 269 621-2415
80444 County Road 687 Hartford (49057) *(G-7764)*
Keen Point International Inc 248 340-8732
1377 Atlantic Blvd Auburn Hills (48326) *(G-950)*
Keetz Kloset Kollection LLC 313 878-1032
9461 Wayburn St Detroit (48224) *(G-4356)*
Keg Guys, Grand Rapids Also called Quiktap LLC *(G-7132)*
Keglove LLC 616 610-7289
6403 Sand Castle Vw Holland (49423) *(G-8110)*
Kehrig Manufacturing Company 586 949-9610
28151 William P Rosso Hwy Chesterfield (48047) *(G-2900)*
Kehrig Steel Inc 586 716-9700
9279 Marine City Hwy Ira (48023) *(G-8700)*

Keith Falan 231 834-7358
14097 S Mason Dr Grant (49327) *(G-7429)*
Keizer-Morris Intl Inc 810 688-1234
6561 Bernie Kohler Dr North Branch (48461) *(G-12180)*
Kel Graphics, Cadillac *Also called Janet Kelly* *(G-2338)*
Kelder LLC 231 757-3000
979 W 1st St Scottville (49454) *(G-15135)*
Keller Sports-Optics 248 894-0960
35797 Smithfield Rd Farmington (48335) *(G-5141)*
Keller Tool Ltd (PA) 734 425-4500
12701 Inkster Rd Livonia (48150) *(G-10264)*
Kelley Laboratories Inc 231 861-6257
617 Industrial Park Dr Shelby (49455) *(G-15153)*
Kelley Machining Inc 231 861-0951
647 Industrial Park Dr Shelby (49455) *(G-15154)*
Kellogg (thailand) Limited 269 969-8937
1 Kellogg Sq Battle Creek (49017) *(G-1251)*
Kellogg Asia Marketing Inc (HQ) 269 961-2000
1 Kellogg Sq Battle Creek (49017) *(G-1252)*
Kellogg Chile Inc 269 961-2000
1 Kellogg Sq Battle Creek (49017) *(G-1253)*
Kellogg Co, Battle Creek *Also called Austin Quality Sales Company* *(G-1187)*
Kellogg Company 269 961-2000
2 Hamblin Ave E Battle Creek (49017) *(G-1254)*
Kellogg Company 810 653-5625
2166 Oak Shade Dr Davison (48423) *(G-3788)*
Kellogg Company (PA) 269 961-2000
1 Kellogg Sq Battle Creek (49017) *(G-1255)*
Kellogg Company 269 961-9387
235 Potter St Mulliken (48861) *(G-11749)*
Kellogg Company 269 964-8525
70 Michigan Ave W Ste 750 Battle Creek (49017) *(G-1256)*
Kellogg Company 269 969-8107
235 Porter St Battle Creek (49014) *(G-1257)*
Kellogg Company 269 961-6693
3300 Rger B Chffee Mem Dr Wyoming (49548) *(G-18889)*
Kellogg Company 269 961-2000
2 E Hammond Ave Battle Creek (49014) *(G-1258)*
Kellogg Company 616 247-4841
310 28th St Se Grand Rapids (49548) *(G-6881)*
Kellogg Company 269 961-6693
Financial Service Ctr Battle Creek (49014) *(G-1259)*
Kellogg Crankshaft Co 517 788-9200
3524 Wayland Dr Jackson (49202) *(G-8928)*
Kellogg North America Company (HQ) 269 961-2000
1 Kellogg Sq Battle Creek (49017) *(G-1260)*
Kellogg USA Inc (HQ) 269 961-2000
1 Kellogg Sq Battle Creek (49017) *(G-1261)*
Kellogg USA Inc 269 961-2000
425 Porter St Battle Creek (49014) *(G-1262)*
Kelloggs Corporation 616 219-6100
5300 Patterson Ave Se Grand Rapids (49512) *(G-6882)*
Kells Sawmill Inc 906 753-2778
N8780 County Road 577 Stephenson (49887) *(G-15908)*
Kelly Oil & Gas Inc 231 929-0591
303 S Union St Ofc C Traverse City (49684) *(G-16732)*
Kellys Recycling Service Inc 313 389-7870
14800 Castleton St Detroit (48227) *(G-4357)*
Kelm Acubar, Benton Harbor *Also called Acubar Inc* *(G-1526)*
Kelm Acubar Company, Benton Harbor *Also called Kelm Acubar Lc* *(G-1561)*
Kelm Acubar Lc (PA) 269 927-3000
1055 N Shore Dr Benton Harbor (49022) *(G-1561)*
Kelm Acubar Lc 269 925-2007
1055 N Shore Dr Benton Harbor (49022) *(G-1562)*
Kelsheimer Industries LLC 810 701-9455
318 E State St Corunna (48817) *(G-3709)*
Keltrol Enterprises Inc 734 697-3011
35 Main St Ste 102 Belleville (48111) *(G-1487)*
Kemai (usa) Chemical Co Ltd 248 924-2225
48948 Freestone Dr Northville (48168) *(G-12234)*
Kemin Industries Inc 248 869-3080
14925 Galleon Ct Plymouth (48170) *(G-13211)*
Kemkraft Engineering Inc 734 414-6500
47650 Clipper St Plymouth (48170) *(G-13212)*
Kemnitz Fine Candies 734 453-0480
896 W Ann Arbor Trl Plymouth (48170) *(G-13213)*
Kemnitz Fine Candies & Gifts, Plymouth *Also called Kemnitz Fine Candies* *(G-13213)*
Ken Budowick Fabricating LLC 586 263-1318
42781 Heydenreich Rd Clinton Township (48038) *(G-3271)*
Ken Gorsline Welding (PA) 269 649-0650
2210 E Vw Ave Vicksburg (49097) *(G-17606)*
Ken Luneack Construction Inc (PA) 989 681-5774
721 E Washington St Saint Louis (48880) *(G-14992)*
Ken Measel Supply Inc 810 798-3293
6343 Hayfield Ln Almont (48003) *(G-263)*
Ken Rodenhouse Door & Window 616 784-3365
5120 West River Dr Ne Comstock Park (49321) *(G-3614)*
Kencoat Comp 586 754-1400
24500 Capital Blvd Clinton Township (48036) *(G-3272)*
Kendall & Company Inc 810 733-7330
1624 Lambden Rd Flint (48532) *(G-5721)*
Kendall Printing, Flint *Also called Kendall & Company Inc* *(G-5721)*
Kendor Steel Rule Die Inc 586 293-7111
31275 Fraser Dr Fraser (48026) *(G-5950)*
Kendrick Plastics Inc 616 975-4000
5050 Kendrick St Se Grand Rapids (49512) *(G-6883)*
Kenewell Group 810 714-4290
3031 W Thompson Rd Fenton (48430) *(G-5487)*
Kenkraft Industrial Weldi 269 543-3153
6889 120th Ave Fennville (49408) *(G-5439)*
Kennametal Inc 231 946-2100
2879 Aero Park Dr Traverse City (49686) *(G-16733)*
Kennedy Acquisition Inc (PA) 616 871-3020
4949 W Greenbrooke Dr Se Grand Rapids (49512) *(G-6884)*
Kennedy Game Calls LLC 269 870-5001
8375 W C Ave Kalamazoo (49009) *(G-9253)*
Kennedy Industries Inc 248 684-1200
4925 Holtz Dr Wixom (48393) *(G-18691)*
Kennedy Sales Inc 586 228-9390
19683 Tanglewood Cir Clinton Township (48038) *(G-3273)*
Kenneth A Gould 231 828-4705
2790 W Raymond Rd Twin Lake (49457) *(G-17469)*
Kenneth David Kent 906 475-7036
521 Cherry St Negaunee (49866) *(G-11969)*
Kenny G Mfg & Sls LLC 313 218-6297
27275 Ritter Blvd Brownstown (48134) *(G-2148)*
Kenny Machining, Shepherd *Also called Paul Jeffrey Kenny* *(G-15378)*
Kenona Industries LLC 616 735-6228
3044 Wilson Dr Nw Grand Rapids (49534) *(G-6885)*
Kenowa Industries Inc (PA) 616 392-7080
11405 E Lakewood Blvd Holland (49424) *(G-8111)*
Kenowa Industries Inc 517 322-0311
2924 Sanders Rd Lansing (48917) *(G-9771)*
Kenrie Inc 616 494-3200
500 E 8th St Ste 1100 Holland (49423) *(G-8112)*
Kens Carburetor Service Inc 517 627-1417
13828 Hartel Rd Grand Ledge (48837) *(G-6393)*
Kens Redi Mix Inc 810 687-6000
14406 N Saginaw Rd Clio (48420) *(G-3402)*
Kens Redi Mix Inc (PA) 810 636-2630
8016 S State Rd Goodrich (48438) *(G-6224)*
Kent City Plastics LLC 616 678-4900
90 Spring St Ste B Kent City (49330) *(G-9435)*
Kent Commerce Center, Grand Rapids *Also called Ace Vending Service Inc* *(G-6422)*
Kent Communications Inc 616 957-2120
3901 East Paris Ave Se Grand Rapids (49512) *(G-6886)*
Kent County 616 632-7580
300 Monroe Ave Nw Grand Rapids (49503) *(G-6887)*
Kent Design & Manufacturing, Grand Rapids *Also called Benmill LLC* *(G-6499)*
Kent Door & Specialty Inc 616 534-9691
2535 28th St Sw Grand Rapids (49519) *(G-6888)*
Kent Door Supply, Grand Rapids *Also called Kent Door & Specialty Inc* *(G-6888)*
Kent Foundry Company 616 754-1100
1413 Callaghan St Greenville (48838) *(G-7496)*
Kent Manufacturing Company 616 454-9495
2200 Oak Industrial Dr Ne Grand Rapids (49505) *(G-6889)*
Kent Quality Foods Inc 616 459-4595
3426 Quincy St Hudsonville (49426) *(G-8589)*
Kent Tool and Die Inc 586 949-6600
50605 Richard W Blvd Chesterfield (48051) *(G-2901)*
Kent Upholstery Inc 248 332-7260
408 Auburn Ave Pontiac (48342) *(G-13392)*
Kent Welding Inc 616 363-4414
1915 Sterling Ave Nw Grand Rapids (49504) *(G-6890)*
Kentucky Trailer Technologies, Wixom *Also called Trailer Tech Holdings LLC* *(G-18776)*
Kentwater Tool & Mfg Co 616 784-7171
5516 West River Dr Ne Comstock Park (49321) *(G-3615)*
Kentwood Fuel Inc 616 455-2387
1980 44th St Se Kentwood (49508) *(G-9459)*
Kentwood Manufacturing Co 616 698-6370
6172 Valduga Dr Sw Ste F Byron Center (49315) *(G-2279)*
Kentwood Packaging Corporation 616 698-9000
2102 Avastar Pkwy Nw Walker (49544) *(G-17642)*
Kentwood Powder Coat Inc 616 698-8181
3900 Swank Dr Se Grand Rapids (49512) *(G-6891)*
Kenwal Pickling LLC 313 739-1040
8223 W Warren Ave Dearborn (48126) *(G-3857)*
Kenyon Specialties Inc 810 686-3190
1153 Liberty St Clio (48420) *(G-3403)*
Kenyon Tj & Associates Inc 231 544-1144
902 Green Acres St Bellaire (49615) *(G-1476)*
Keo Cutters Inc 586 771-2050
25040 Easy St Warren (48089) *(G-17893)*
Kepco Inc 269 649-5800
145 N Leja Dr Vicksburg (49097) *(G-17607)*
Kerkau Manufacturing, Bay City *Also called Baldauf Enterprises Inc* *(G-1325)*
Kerkau Manufacturing Company, Bay City *Also called Baldauf Enterprises Inc* *(G-1324)*

ALPHABETIC

Kerkstra Mechanical LLC..........616 532-6100
4345 44th St Se Ste C Grand Rapids (49512) ***(G-6892)***
Kerkstra Precast LLC..........616 457-4920
3373 Busch Dr Sw Grandville (49418) ***(G-7395)***
Kern Auto Sales and Svc LLC..........734 475-2722
1630 S Main St Chelsea (48118) ***(G-2818)***
Kern Industries Inc..........248 349-4866
43000 W 10 Mile Rd Frnt Novi (48375) ***(G-12451)***
Kern-Liebers Pieron Inc..........248 427-1100
24505 Indoplex Cir Farmington Hills (48335) ***(G-5280)***
Kernel Bennys..........989 928-3950
701 Mill St Frankenmuth (48734) ***(G-5866)***
Kernel Burner..........989 792-2808
6171 Tittabawassee Rd Saginaw (48603) ***(G-14677)***
Kerns Sausages Inc..........989 652-2684
110 W Jefferson St Frankenmuth (48734) ***(G-5867)***
Kerns Wood Works LLC..........734 368-1951
49946 W Huron River Dr Van Buren Twp (48111) ***(G-17533)***
Kerosene Fragrances..........810 292-5772
1613 Court St Port Huron (48060) ***(G-13493)***
Kerr Corporation..........734 946-7800
28200 Wick Rd Romulus (48174) ***(G-14294)***
Kerr Industries of Michigan..........586 578-9383
24649 Mound Rd Warren (48091) ***(G-17894)***
Kerr Manufacturing, Romulus *Also called Kerr Corporation* ***(G-14294)***
Kerr Pump and Supply Inc..........248 543-3880
12880 Cloverdale St Oak Park (48237) ***(G-12621)***
Kerr Screw Products Co Inc..........248 589-2200
32069 Milton Ave Madison Heights (48071) ***(G-10761)***
Kerry Foods..........616 871-9940
4444 52nd St Se Grand Rapids (49512) ***(G-6893)***
Kerry Inc..........616 871-9940
4444 52nd St Detroit (48210) ***(G-4358)***
Kerry J McNeely..........734 776-1928
15810 Harrison St Livonia (48154) ***(G-10265)***
Kerry's Pallets, Livonia *Also called Kerry J McNeely* ***(G-10265)***
Keska LLC..........616 283-7056
87 Chriscraft Ln Holland (49424) ***(G-8113)***
Kessebohmer Ergonomie Amer Inc..........616 202-1239
3900 Linden Ave Se Grand Rapids (49548) ***(G-6894)***
Ketchum Machine Corporated..........616 765-5101
219 Oak St Freeport (49325) ***(G-6034)***
Keur Industries Acquisition Co, Spring Lake *Also called Multi-Lab LLC* ***(G-15838)***
Keurig Dr Pepper Inc..........231 775-7393
1481 Potthoff St Cadillac (49601) ***(G-2339)***
Keurig Dr Pepper Inc..........313 937-3500
12201 Beech Daly Rd Detroit (48239) ***(G-4359)***
Keviar Candles..........248 325-4087
16400 N Park Dr Apt 306 Southfield (48075) ***(G-15616)***
Kevin Larkin Inc..........248 736-8203
2611 Woodbourne Dr Waterford (48329) ***(G-18131)***
Kevin Wheat & Assoc Ltd..........517 349-0101
4990 Marsh Rd Okemos (48864) ***(G-12671)***
Keweenaw Bay Indian Community..........906 524-5757
16429 Bear Town Rd Baraga (49908) ***(G-1141)***
Key Casting Company Inc (PA)..........269 426-3800
13145 Red Arrow Hwy Sawyer (49125) ***(G-15110)***
Key Energy Services Inc..........231 258-9637
4030 Columbus Dr Ne Kalkaska (49646) ***(G-9393)***
Key Gas Components Inc..........269 673-2151
1303 Lincoln Rd Allegan (49010) ***(G-163)***
Key Plastics, Grand Rapids *Also called Novares US LLC* ***(G-7051)***
Key Plastics LLC..........248 449-6100
44191 Plymouth Oaks Blvd Plymouth (48170) ***(G-13214)***
Key Safety Systems Inc (HQ)..........248 373-8040
2025 Harmon Rd Auburn Hills (48326) ***(G-951)***
Key Safety Systems Inc..........586 726-3905
2025 Harmon Rd Auburn Hills (48326) ***(G-952)***
Key Sfety Rstraint Systems Inc (HQ)..........586 726-3800
2025 Harmon Rd Auburn Hills (48326) ***(G-953)***
Keyes-Davis Company..........269 962-7505
74 14th St N Springfield (49037) ***(G-15871)***
Keykert, Wixom *Also called Kiekert Usa Inc* ***(G-18693)***
KEYS FOR KIDS MINISTRIES, Grand Rapids *Also called Childrens Bible Hour Inc* ***(G-6568)***
Keys N More..........248 260-1967
2985 Crooks Rd Rochester Hills (48309) ***(G-14045)***
Keys Plus In 15 Minute..........248 581-0112
27050 John R Rd Madison Heights (48071) ***(G-10762)***
Keystone Cable Corporation..........313 924-9720
8200 Lynch Rd Detroit (48234) ***(G-4360)***
Keystone Manufacturing..........248 796-2546
100 E Cicotte St River Rouge (48218) ***(G-13857)***
Keystone Manufacturing LLC..........269 343-4108
6387 Technology Ave Ste B Kalamazoo (49009) ***(G-9254)***
Keystone Universal, Melvindale *Also called Ebonex Corporation* ***(G-11200)***
Kft, Gaylord *Also called Keays Family Truckin* ***(G-6139)***
Kgf Enterprise Inc..........586 430-4182
2141 Werner Rd Columbus (48063) ***(G-3500)***
Khalsa Metal Products Inc..........616 791-4794
3142 Broadmoor Ave Se Kentwood (49512) ***(G-9460)***
Kharon Industries..........810 630-6355
7445 Grove St Swartz Creek (48473) ***(G-16356)***
Khearma Group LLC..........248 513-5763
8301 Saint Aubin St Detroit (48211) ***(G-4361)***
Kibby Welding LLC..........231 258-8838
2695 M 66 Se Kalkaska (49646) ***(G-9394)***
Kidde Safety..........800 880-6788
39550 W 13 Mile Rd # 101 Novi (48377) ***(G-12452)***
Kidder Machine Company..........231 775-9271
702 8th St Cadillac (49601) ***(G-2340)***
Kids World News Too..........517 202-1808
555 E Downie St Alma (48801) ***(G-244)***
Kiekert Usa Inc..........248 960-4100
50695 Varsity Ct Wixom (48393) ***(G-18692)***
Kiekert Usa Inc (HQ)..........248 960-4100
46941 Liberty Dr Wixom (48393) ***(G-18693)***
Kiilunen Mfg Group Inc..........906 337-2433
25280 Renaissance Rd Calumet (49913) ***(G-2410)***
Kilgore Industries, Buchanan *Also called K&S Consultants LLC* ***(G-2198)***
Killer Paint Ball..........248 491-0088
509 S Lafayette St South Lyon (48178) ***(G-15441)***
Kiln Kreations..........989 435-3296
5366 M 18 Beaverton (48612) ***(G-1426)***
Kilobar Compacting Mich LLC..........989 460-1981
3916 Traxler Ct Ste C Bay City (48706) ***(G-1371)***
Kilwins Chocolate Kitchen, Petoskey *Also called Kilwins Qulty Confections Inc* ***(G-13001)***
Kilwins Qulty Confections Inc (PA)..........231 347-3800
1050 Bay View Rd Petoskey (49770) ***(G-13001)***
Kimastle Corporation..........586 949-2355
28291 Kehrig St Chesterfield (48047) ***(G-2902)***
Kimball's Brand Source, Port Huron *Also called P and K Graphics Inc* ***(G-13513)***
Kimberly Led Lighting, Clarkston *Also called Kimberly Lighting LLC* ***(G-3043)***
Kimberly Lighting LLC..........888 480-0070
5827 Terex Clarkston (48346) ***(G-3043)***
Kimberly-Clark Corporation..........586 949-1649
21346 Summerfield Dr Macomb (48044) ***(G-10609)***
Kimberly-Clark Corporation..........810 985-1830
2609 Electric Ave Ste C Port Huron (48060) ***(G-13494)***
Kimble Auto and Rv LLC..........517 227-5089
132 W Chicago Rd Coldwater (49036) ***(G-3440)***
Kimbow Inc..........616 774-4680
901 Metzgar Dr Nw Comstock Park (49321) ***(G-3616)***
Kimprint Inc..........734 459-2960
14875 Galleon Ct Plymouth (48170) ***(G-13215)***
Kims Mart Inc..........313 592-4929
20240 W 7 Mile Rd Detroit (48219) ***(G-4362)***
Kind Crumbs LLC..........616 881-6388
4751 3 Mile Rd Nw Ste I Grand Rapids (49534) ***(G-6895)***
Kindel Furniture Company LLC (PA)..........616 243-3676
4047 Eastern Ave Se Grand Rapids (49508) ***(G-6896)***
Kinder Company Inc..........810 240-3065
7070 N Saginaw Rd Mount Morris (48458) ***(G-11673)***
Kinder Products Unlimited LLC..........586 557-3453
6471 Metro Pkwy Sterling Heights (48312) ***(G-16063)***
Kinetic Wave Power LLC..........989 839-9757
2861 N Tupelo Dr Midland (48642) ***(G-11382)***
King Centerless Grinding Co, Madison Heights *Also called Ctmi Group Inc* ***(G-10700)***
King Coil, Roseville *Also called Comfort Mattress Co* ***(G-14387)***
King Milling Company..........616 897-9264
115 S Broadway St Lowell (49331) ***(G-10508)***
King Par LLC..........810 732-2470
5140 Flushing Rd Flushing (48433) ***(G-5810)***
King Steel Corporation (PA)..........800 638-2530
5225 E Cook Rd Ste K Grand Blanc (48439) ***(G-6250)***
King Steel Fasteners Inc..........810 721-0300
1800 Metamora Rd Oxford (48371) ***(G-12893)***
King Tool & Die Inc..........517 265-2741
971 Division St Adrian (49221) ***(G-78)***
King-Hughes Fasteners, Oxford *Also called King Steel Fasteners Inc* ***(G-12893)***
Kingdom Building Merchandise..........313 334-3866
20230 Ardmore St Detroit (48235) ***(G-4363)***
Kingdom Cartridge Inc..........734 564-1590
11704 Morgan Ave Plymouth (48170) ***(G-13216)***
Kingdom Geekdom LLC..........517 610-5016
81 S Wolcott St Hillsdale (49242) ***(G-7939)***
Kings Self Defense LLC..........910 890-4322
6769 Bent Grass Dr Se Grand Rapids (49508) ***(G-6897)***
Kings Time Printing Press LLC..........734 426-8169
4245 Hawthorn Pl Ann Arbor (48103) ***(G-539)***
Kingsford Broach & Tool Inc..........906 774-4917
2200 Maule Dr Kingsford (49802) ***(G-9511)***
Kingston Educational Software..........248 895-4803
38452 Lynwood Ct Farmington Hills (48331) ***(G-5281)***
Kingston Prperty Advisers Corp..........248 825-9657
25742 Schoolcraft Redford (48239) ***(G-13741)***
Kinne Plastics Inc..........989 435-4373
5381 Roehrs Rd Fl 435437 Beaverton (48612) ***(G-1427)***

Kinney Tool and Die Inc 616 997-0901
1300 W Randall St Coopersville (49404) ***(G-3689)***
Kinross Fab & Machine Inc 906 495-1900
17422 S Dolan St Kincheloe (49788) ***(G-9504)***
Kirby Grinding, Roseville *Also called Detroit Edge Tool Company* ***(G-14398)***
Kirby Metal Corporation 810 743-3360
4072 Flint Asphalt Dr Burton (48529) ***(G-2237)***
Kirby Steel, Burton *Also called Kirby Metal Corporation* ***(G-2237)***
Kirchhoff Auto Tecumseh Inc (HQ) 517 423-2400
1200 E Chicago Blvd Tecumseh (49286) ***(G-16506)***
Kirchhoff Automotive Companies, Tecumseh *Also called Van-Rob USA Holdings* ***(G-16521)***
Kirchhoff Automotive USA Inc 248 247-3740
2600 Bellingham Dr # 400 Troy (48083) ***(G-17194)***
Kirk Enterprises Inc 248 357-5070
20905 Telegraph Rd Southfield (48033) ***(G-15617)***
Kirks Automotive Incorporated (PA) 313 933-7030
9330 Roselawn St Detroit (48204) ***(G-4364)***
Kirmin Die & Tool Inc 734 722-9210
36360 Ecorse Rd Romulus (48174) ***(G-14295)***
Kirtland Products LLC 231 582-7505
1 Altair Dr Boyne City (49712) ***(G-1893)***
Kiser Industrial Mfg Co 269 934-9220
1860 Yore Ave Benton Harbor (49022) ***(G-1563)***
Kismet Strategic Sourcing Part 269 932-4990
717 Sint Jseph Dr Ste 270 Saint Joseph (49085) ***(G-14942)***
Kissco Publishing, Okemos *Also called Kissman Consulting LLC* ***(G-12672)***
Kissman Consulting LLC 517 256-1077
2109 Hamilton Rd Ste 113 Okemos (48864) ***(G-12672)***
Kistler Automotive, Farmington Hills *Also called Kistler Instrument Corp* ***(G-5282)***
Kistler Instrument Corp 248 489-1090
39205 Country Club Dr C20 Farmington Hills (48331) ***(G-5282)***
Kistler Instrument Corporation (HQ) 248 668-6900
30280 Hudson Dr Novi (48377) ***(G-12453)***
Kitchen Joy 616 682-7327
887 Bailey Park Dr Ne Grand Rapids (49525) ***(G-6898)***
Kitchen Supply Co, Jackson *Also called Royal Cabinet Inc* ***(G-8999)***
Kitty Condo LLC 419 690-9063
17197 N Laurel Park Dr # 40 Livonia (48152) ***(G-10266)***
Kjm Specialty Welding LLC 734 626-2442
15669 Scott St Southgate (48195) ***(G-15751)***
Kk Logging 906 524-6047
16234 Skanee Rd Lanse (49946) ***(G-9665)***
Kksp Precision Machining LLC 810 329-4731
650 Hathaway St East China (48054) ***(G-4858)***
Kl Companies Inc 231 332-1700
1790 Sun Dolphin Rd Muskegon (49444) ***(G-11851)***
Kl Outdoor, Rochester Hills *Also called Ameriform Acquisition Co LLC* ***(G-13947)***
Klann 313 565-4135
1439 S Telegraph Rd Dearborn (48124) ***(G-3858)***
Klassic Tool Crib, Romulus *Also called Plum Brothers LLC* ***(G-14321)***
Klaus Nixdorf 269 429-3259
1727 W John Beers Rd Stevensville (49127) ***(G-16256)***
KLC Enterprises Inc 989 753-0496
4765 E Holland Rd Saginaw (48601) ***(G-14678)***
Kleiberit Adhesives USA Inc 248 709-9308
4305 Beverly Ct Royal Oak (48073) ***(G-14553)***
Klein Bros Fence & Stakes LLC 248 684-6919
2400 E Buno Rd Milford (48381) ***(G-11468)***
Kleins 3d Prtg Solutions LLC 586 212-9763
15330 Cambridge Dr Fraser (48026) ***(G-5951)***
Klingler Consulting & Mfg 810 765-3700
837 Degurse Ave Marine City (48039) ***(G-10961)***
Klise Manufacturing Company 616 459-4283
11450 3rd Ave Nw Grand Rapids (49534) ***(G-6899)***
Kloeffler, Wm Industries, Marine City *Also called Wm Kloeffler Industries Inc* ***(G-10969)***
Klopp Group LLC 877 256-4528
3535 Bay Rd Ste 3 Saginaw (48603) ***(G-14679)***
Km and I 248 792-2782
3155 W Big Beaver Rd # 111 Troy (48084) ***(G-17195)***
Km International, North Branch *Also called Keizer-Morris Intl Inc* ***(G-12180)***
Kmak Inc 517 784-8800
1232 S West Ave Jackson (49203) ***(G-8929)***
Kmg Prestige, Wayland *Also called Sawmill Estates* ***(G-18205)***
Kmi, Belding *Also called Kassouni Manufacturing Inc* ***(G-1455)***
Kmi Cleaning Solutions Inc 269 964-2557
157 Beadle Lake Rd Battle Creek (49014) ***(G-1263)***
Kmj Global Inc 240 594-5050
1137 S Adams Rd Birmingham (48009) ***(G-1732)***
Kmk Machining 231 629-8068
10842 Northland Dr Big Rapids (49307) ***(G-1679)***
Knape & Vogt Manufacturing Co (HQ) 616 459-3311
2700 Oak Industrial Dr Ne Grand Rapids (49505) ***(G-6900)***
Knape Industries Inc 616 866-1651
10701 Northland Dr Ne Rockford (49341) ***(G-14174)***
Knapp Manufacturing Inc 517 279-9538
555 Hillside Dr Coldwater (49036) ***(G-3441)***
Knapp Printing Services Inc 616 754-9159
6540 S Greenville Rd Greenville (48838) ***(G-7497)***
Knappen Milling Company 269 731-4141
110 S Water St Augusta (49012) ***(G-1092)***
Knauf Insulation Inc 517 630-2000
1000 E North St Albion (49224) ***(G-128)***
Knickerbocker 616 345-5642
417 Bridge St Nw Grand Rapids (49504) ***(G-6901)***
Knickerbocker Baking Inc 248 541-2110
26040 Pinehurst Dr Madison Heights (48071) ***(G-10763)***
Knight Tonya 313 255-3434
17390 W 8 Mile Rd Southfield (48075) ***(G-15618)***
Knight Carbide Inc 586 598-4888
48665 Structural Dr Chesterfield (48051) ***(G-2903)***
Knight Global, Auburn Hills *Also called Knight Industries Inc* ***(G-954)***
Knight Industries Inc 248 377-4950
2705 Commerce Pkwy Auburn Hills (48326) ***(G-954)***
Knights Glass Block Windows, Southfield *Also called Knight Tonya* ***(G-15618)***
Knit and Crochet 4 Charity 248 224-4965
32545 Greenbriar Ave Warren (48092) ***(G-17895)***
Knoedler Manufacturers Inc 269 969-7722
7185 Tower Rd Battle Creek (49014) ***(G-1264)***
Knouse Foods Cooperative Inc 269 657-5524
815 S Kalamazoo St Paw Paw (49079) ***(G-12950)***
Knowlton Enterprises Inc (PA) 810 987-7100
1755 Yeager St Port Huron (48060) ***(G-13495)***
Knpc Holdco LLC (PA) 248 588-1903
1200 E 14 Mile Rd Madison Heights (48071) ***(G-10764)***
Knust Masonry 231 322-2587
6092 Aarwood Rd Nw Rapid City (49676) ***(G-13681)***
Ko Industries 248 882-6888
748 Rachelle St White Lake (48386) ***(G-18459)***
Ko Products, Benton Harbor *Also called Dgh Enterprises Inc* ***(G-1547)***
Koch Limited 586 296-3103
34230 Riviera Fraser (48026) ***(G-5952)***
Kodiak Manufacturing Co Inc 248 335-5552
51920 Woodward Ave Ste B Pontiac (48342) ***(G-13393)***
Koegel Meats Inc (PA) 810 238-3685
3400 W Bristol Rd Flint (48507) ***(G-5722)***
Koehler Industries Inc 269 934-9670
1520 Townline Rd Benton Harbor (49022) ***(G-1564)***
Koenig Fuel & Supply Co 313 368-1870
5501 Cogswell Rd Wayne (48184) ***(G-18226)***
Koetje Wood Products Inc 616 393-9191
11743 Greenway Dr Holland (49424) ***(G-8114)***
Koeze Company (PA) 616 724-2601
2555 Burlingame Ave Sw Grand Rapids (49509) ***(G-6902)***
Koeze Direct, Grand Rapids *Also called Koeze Company* ***(G-6902)***
Kolco Industries Inc 248 486-1690
10078 Colonial Indus Dr South Lyon (48178) ***(G-15442)***
Kolenda Technologies LLC 616 299-0126
2544 Garfield Ave Nw Grand Rapids (49544) ***(G-6903)***
Kolene Corporation (PA) 313 273-9220
12890 Westwood St Detroit (48223) ***(G-4365)***
Kolene Corporation 586 771-1200
30435 Groesbeck Hwy Roseville (48066) ***(G-14430)***
Kolossos Printing Inc (PA) 734 994-5400
2055 W Stadium Blvd Ann Arbor (48103) ***(G-540)***
Kolossos Printing Inc 734 741-1600
301 E Liberty St Ann Arbor (48104) ***(G-541)***
Koltec Div, Coldwater *Also called Vachon Industries Inc* ***(G-3460)***
Komarnicki Tool & Die Company 586 776-9300
29650 Parkway Roseville (48066) ***(G-14431)***
Kommar Industries 231 334-3475
6137 Bay Ln Glen Arbor (49636) ***(G-6210)***
Konecranes Inc 248 380-2626
43050 W 10 Mile Rd Novi (48375) ***(G-12454)***
Konecranes Inc 269 323-1222
865 Lenox Ave Ste A Portage (49024) ***(G-13574)***
Kongsberg Automotive, Novi *Also called Kongsberg Holding III Inc* ***(G-12457)***
Kongsberg Automotive Inc (HQ) 248 468-1300
27275 Haggerty Rd Ste 610 Novi (48377) ***(G-12455)***
Kongsberg Holding I Inc (PA) 248 468-1300
27275 Haggerty Rd Ste 610 Novi (48377) ***(G-12456)***
Kongsberg Holding III Inc (HQ) 248 468-1300
27275 Haggerty Rd Ste 610 Novi (48377) ***(G-12457)***
Kongsberg Intr Systems I Inc, Novi *Also called Kongsberg Intr Systems II LLC* ***(G-12458)***
Kongsberg Intr Systems II LLC (HQ) 956 465-4541
27275 Haggerty Rd Ste 610 Novi (48377) ***(G-12458)***
Konrad Technologies Inc (HQ) 248 489-1200
27300 Haggerty Rd F-10 Farmington Hills (48331) ***(G-5283)***
Konrad Technologies USA, Farmington Hills *Also called Konrad Technologies Inc* ***(G-5283)***
Konwinski Kabnets Inc 989 773-2906
1900 Gover Pkwy Mount Pleasant (48858) ***(G-11706)***
Kooiker Tool & Die Inc 616 554-3630
3259 68th St Se Caledonia (49316) ***(G-2387)***
Koolblast, Chelsea *Also called Advanced Industries Inc* ***(G-2802)***
Kopach Filters LLC 906 863-8611
N3840 R 2 Ln Wallace (49893) ***(G-17660)***
Koppel A Color Image, Grandville *Also called A Koppel Color Image Company* ***(G-7360)***

ALPHABETIC

Koppel Tool & Engineering LLC — ALPHABETIC SECTION

Koppel Tool & Engineering LLC 616 638-2611
  1099 N Gateway Blvd Norton Shores (49441) *(G-12307)*
Koppert Biological Systems Inc 734 641-3763
  1502 N Old Us 23 Howell (48843) *(G-8470)*
Kor-Cast Products, Troy *Also called Korcast Products Incorporated (G-17196)*
Korcast Products Incorporated (PA) 248 740-2340
  1725 Larchwood Dr Troy (48083) *(G-17196)*
Korcast Products Incorporated 248 740-2340
  1725 Larchwood Dr Troy (48083) *(G-17197)*
Kord Industrial Inc 248 374-8900
  47845 Anna Ct Wixom (48393) *(G-18694)*
Kore Inc 616 785-5900
  5263 6 Mile Ct Nw Comstock Park (49321) *(G-3617)*
Kore Group Inc (PA) 734 677-1500
  3500 Washtenaw Ave Ann Arbor (48104) *(G-542)*
Korens 248 817-5188
  1685 W Hamlin Rd Rochester Hills (48309) *(G-14046)*
Korstone, Madison Heights *Also called KS Liquidating LLC (G-10765)*
Korten Quality Inc 586 752-6255
  69069 Powell Rd Bruce Twp (48065) *(G-2170)*
Koski Log Homes, Ontonagon *Also called Koskis Log Homes Inc (G-12713)*
Koski Welding Inc 906 353-7588
  13529 Old 41 Rd Baraga (49908) *(G-1142)*
Koskis Log Homes Inc 906 884-4937
  35993 Us Highway 45 Ontonagon (49953) *(G-12713)*
Kostal Group, Rochester Hills *Also called Kostal Kontakt Systeme Inc (G-14047)*
Kostal Kontakt Systeme Inc 248 284-7600
  1350 W Hamlin Rd Rochester Hills (48309) *(G-14047)*
Kostal North America, Troy *Also called Kostal of America Inc (G-17198)*
Kostal of America Inc 248 284-6500
  350 Stephenson Hwy Troy (48083) *(G-17198)*
Kostamo Logging 906 353-6171
  10408 Kostamo Rd Pelkie (49958) *(G-12964)*
Kotocorp (usa) Inc (HQ) 269 349-1521
  5981 E Cork St Kalamazoo (49048) *(G-9255)*
Kotzian Tool Inc 231 861-5377
  6971 W Shelby Rd Shelby (49455) *(G-15155)*
Kowalski Companies Inc (PA) 313 873-8200
  2270 Holbrook St Detroit (48212) *(G-4366)*
Kowloon Noodle Company, Battle Creek *Also called New Moon Noodle Incorporated (G-1278)*
Koyo Corp 269 962-9676
  300 Fritz Keiper Blvd Battle Creek (49037) *(G-1265)*
Kp Sogoian, Royal Oak *Also called Kyrie Enterprises LLC (G-14555)*
Kpc Graphics, Kalamazoo *Also called Kalamazoo Photo Comp Svcs (G-9245)*
Kpl Custom Woodworking LLC 313 530-5507
  31040 Industrial Rd Livonia (48150) *(G-10267)*
Kpmf Usa Inc 248 377-4999
  67 Kay Industrial Dr Lake Orion (48359) *(G-9612)*
Kraft Foods, Grand Rapids *Also called Kraft Heinz Foods Company (G-6904)*
Kraft Heinz Foods Company 616 396-6557
  431 W 16th St Holland (49423) *(G-8115)*
Kraft Heinz Foods Company 616 447-0481
  3950 Sparks Dr Se Grand Rapids (49546) *(G-6904)*
Kraft Maid Cabinetry 734 205-4600
  4600 Arrowhead Dr Ann Arbor (48105) *(G-543)*
Kraft Outdoor Svc 517 404-8023
  6320 W Grand River Rd Fowlerville (48836) *(G-5848)*
Kraft Power Corporation 989 748-4040
  2852 D And M Dr Gaylord (49735) *(G-6140)*
Kraft-Wrap Inc 586 755-2050
  21650 Hoover Rd Warren (48089) *(G-17896)*
Kraftbrau Brewery Inc 269 384-0288
  402 E Kalamazoo Ave Kalamazoo (49007) *(G-9256)*
Krafts & Thingz 810 689-2457
  51382 Village Edge N Chesterfield (48047) *(G-2904)*
Kraftube Inc 231 832-5562
  925 E Church Ave Reed City (49677) *(G-13793)*
Kraig Biocraft Labs Inc 734 619-8066
  2723 S State St Ste 150 Ann Arbor (48104) *(G-544)*
Kramer International Inc 586 726-4300
  5750 New King Dr Ste 200 Troy (48098) *(G-17199)*
Krams Enterprises Inc 248 415-8500
  30400 Telg Rd Ste 200 Bingham Farms (48025) *(G-1702)*
Krane, Menominee *Also called Plutchak Fab (G-11256)*
Kraus & Co, Monroe *Also called Paul C Doerr (G-11568)*
Kraus Fire Equipment Inc 810 744-4780
  G4080 S Dort Hwy Burton (48529) *(G-2238)*
Krause Welding Inc 231 773-4443
  4350 Evanston Ave Muskegon (49442) *(G-11852)*
Krauter Forest Products LLC 815 317-6561
  21224 Sylvan Rd Reed City (49677) *(G-13794)*
Kreations Inc 313 255-1230
  15340 Dale St Detroit (48223) *(G-4367)*
Krebs Tool Inc 734 697-8611
  611 Savage Rd Van Buren Twp (48111) *(G-17534)*
Kregel Inc (PA) 616 531-7707
  4014 Chicago Dr Sw Grandville (49418) *(G-7396)*

Kregel Parable Christn Stores, Grandville *Also called Kregel Inc (G-7396)*
Kremin Inc 989 790-5147
  235 Keystone Way Frankenmuth (48734) *(G-5868)*
Krh Industries, LLC, Sterling Heights *Also called B & B Holdings Groesbeck LLC (G-15940)*
Krieger Craftsmen Inc 616 735-9200
  2758 3 Mile Rd Nw Grand Rapids (49534) *(G-6905)*
Kriewall Enterprises Inc 586 336-0600
  140 Shafer Dr Romeo (48065) *(G-14227)*
Kring Pizza Inc 586 792-0049
  35415 Jefferson Ave Harrison Township (48045) *(G-7704)*
Kringer Industrial Corporation 519 818-3509
  24435 Forterra Dr Warren (48089) *(G-17897)*
Kriseler Welding Inc 989 624-9266
  11877 Maple Rd Birch Run (48415) *(G-1708)*
Krista Messer 734 459-1952
  50619 Colchester Ct Canton (48187) *(G-2484)*
Kristus Inc 269 321-3330
  8370 Greenfield Shores Dr Scotts (49088) *(G-15132)*
Krmc LLC 734 955-9311
  27456 Northline Rd Romulus (48174) *(G-14296)*
Kronos Inc 248 357-5604
  20750 Civic Center Dr # 380 Southfield (48076) *(G-15619)*
Krontz General Machine & Tool 269 651-5882
  412 W Congress St Sturgis (49091) *(G-16297)*
Kropp Woodworking Inc 586 463-2300
  154 S Rose St Mount Clemens (48043) *(G-11646)*
Kropp Woodworking Inc 586 997-3000
  6812 19 1/2 Mile Rd Sterling Heights (48314) *(G-16064)*
Kross Kraft LLC 616 399-9167
  4731 N 168th Ave Holland (49424) *(G-8116)*
Krt Precision Tool & Mfg Co 517 783-5715
  1300 Mitchell St Jackson (49203) *(G-8930)*
Kruger Plastic Products LLC 269 545-3311
  117 S Grant St Galien (49113) *(G-6088)*
Krumb Satcher Cookies, Battle Creek *Also called Krumb Snatcher Cookie Co LLC (G-1266)*
Krumb Snatcher Cookie Co LLC 313 408-6802
  92 Review Ave Battle Creek (49037) *(G-1266)*
Krumbsnatcher Cookies, Detroit *Also called Krumbsnatcher Enterprises LLC (G-4368)*
Krumbsnatcher Enterprises LLC 313 408-6802
  11000 W Mcnic Detroit (48235) *(G-4368)*
Krumrie Saw Mill Services 269 838-9060
  1986 Us Highway 12 Galien (49113) *(G-6089)*
Krupp Industries LLC 734 261-0410
  37050 Plymouth Rd Livonia (48150) *(G-10268)*
Krupp Industries LLC (PA) 616 475-5905
  2735 West River Dr Nw Walker (49544) *(G-17643)*
Krush Industries Inc 248 238-2296
  12729 Universal Dr Taylor (48180) *(G-16434)*
Kryptane Systems, Gwinn *Also called Argonics Inc (G-7581)*
Krysak Industries LLC 312 848-1952
  30515 Fairfax St Southfield (48076) *(G-15620)*
Krzysiak Family Restaurant 989 894-5531
  1605 Michigan Ave Bay City (48708) *(G-1372)*
Krzysiak's House, Bay City *Also called Krzysiak Family Restaurant (G-1372)*
KS Liquidating LLC 248 577-8220
  32031 Howard Ave Madison Heights (48071) *(G-10765)*
Ksb Dubric Inc 616 784-6355
  3737 Laramie Dr Ne Comstock Park (49321) *(G-3618)*
Ksr Industrial Corporation 248 213-7208
  26261 Evergreen Rd # 415 Southfield (48076) *(G-15621)*
Ktc Industries LLC 989 838-0388
  100 N Park St Traverse City (49684) *(G-16734)*
Ktd Print 248 670-4200
  120 E Hudson Ave Royal Oak (48067) *(G-14554)*
Ktna, Novi *Also called Treves N Kotobukiya Amer Inc (G-12558)*
Ktr Dental Lab & Pdts LLC 248 224-9158
  17040 W 12 Mile Rd # 150 Southfield (48076) *(G-15622)*
Ktr Printing Inc 989 386-9740
  801 Industrial Dr Clare (48617) *(G-2984)*
Ktwo Welding 810 216-6087
  3390 Ravenswood Rd Port Huron (48060) *(G-13496)*
Ktx America Inc 734 737-0100
  31651 Schoolcraft Rd Livonia (48150) *(G-10269)*
Kubica Corp 248 344-7750
  22575 Heslip Dr Novi (48375) *(G-12459)*
Kubisch Sausage, Auburn Hills *Also called Mello Meats Inc (G-972)*
Kuhlman Casting Co Inc 248 853-2382
  20415 Woodingham Dr Detroit (48221) *(G-4369)*
Kuhlman Concrete, Monroe *Also called Kuhlman Corporation (G-11554)*
Kuhlman Corporation 734 241-8692
  15370 S Dixie Hwy Monroe (48161) *(G-11554)*
Kuhnhenn Brewing Co LLC (PA) 586 979-8361
  5951 Chicago Rd Warren (48092) *(G-17898)*
Kuhnhenn Brewing Co LLC 586 231-0249
  3600 Groes Beck Hwy Clinton Township (48035) *(G-3274)*
Kuka Aerospace, Sterling Heights *Also called Kuka Systems North America LLC (G-16066)*
Kuka Assembly and Test Corp (HQ) 989 220-3088
  5675 Dixie Hwy Saginaw (48601) *(G-14680)*

Kuka Assembly and Test Corp 810 593-0350
255 S Fenway Dr Fenton (48430) *(G-5488)*
Kuka Omnimove, Shelby Township *Also called Kuka Robotics Corporation (G-15250)*
Kuka Robotics, Sterling Heights *Also called Kuka US Holdings Company LLC (G-16067)*
Kuka Robotics Corporation 586 795-2000
51870 Shelby Pkwy Shelby Township (48315) *(G-15250)*
Kuka Systems North America LLC 586 795-2000
7408 Metropolitan Pkwy Sterling Heights (48312) *(G-16065)*
Kuka Systems North America LLC (HQ) 586 795-2000
6600 Center Dr Sterling Heights (48312) *(G-16066)*
Kuka Systems North America LLC 586 726-4300
13231 23 Mile Rd Shelby Township (48315) *(G-15251)*
Kuka US Holdings Company LLC (HQ) 586 795-2000
6600 Center Dr Sterling Heights (48312) *(G-16067)*
Kulick Enterprises Inc 734 283-6999
4082 Biddle Ave Wyandotte (48192) *(G-18827)*
Kumanu Inc 734 822-6673
535 W William St Ste 4n Ann Arbor (48103) *(G-545)*
Kunststoff Tchnik Schrer Trier 734 944-5080
3150 Livernois Rd Ste 275 Troy (48083) *(G-17200)*
Kuntz Tool & Die, Grand Blanc *Also called Rdc Machine Inc (G-6260)*
Kunzman & Associates West 269 663-8978
18555 Warner Rd Decatur (49045) *(G-3948)*
Kurabe America Corporation 248 939-5803
37735 Interchange Dr Farmington Hills (48335) *(G-5284)*
Kure Products Distribution Inc 248 330-3933
37460 Hills Tech Dr Farmington Hills (48331) *(G-5285)*
Kurek Tool Inc 989 777-5300
4735 Dixie Hwy Saginaw (48601) *(G-14681)*
Kurrent Welding Inc 734 753-9197
18488 Wahrman Rd New Boston (48164) *(G-12011)*
Kurt Dubowski 231 796-0055
14472 Mckinley Rd Big Rapids (49307) *(G-1680)*
Kurt Machine Tool Co Inc 586 296-5070
33910 Riviera Fraser (48026) *(G-5953)*
Kurtis Kitchen & Bath Centers, Livonia *Also called Kurtis Mfg & Distrg Corp (G-10270)*
Kurtis Mfg & Distrg Corp (PA) 734 522-7600
12500 Merriman Rd Livonia (48150) *(G-10270)*
Kurtz Gravel Company Inc (HQ) 810 787-6543
33469 W 14 Mile Rd Ste 10 Farmington Hills (48331) *(G-5286)*
Kustom Creations Inc 586 997-4141
6665 Burroughs Ave Sterling Heights (48314) *(G-16068)*
Kustom Kaps, Temperance *Also called Royal Stewart Enterprises (G-16548)*
Kustom Welding LLC 231 823-2912
9770 185th Ave Stanwood (49346) *(G-15905)*
Kut-Rite Manufacturing Company, Romulus *Also called Krmc LLC (G-14296)*
Kuzimski Enterprises Inc 989 422-5377
9100 Knapp Rd Houghton Lake (48629) *(G-8401)*
Kva Engineering Inc 616 745-7483
2161 200th Ave Morley (49336) *(G-11620)*
Kva Inc 269 982-2888
2095 Niles Rd Saint Joseph (49085) *(G-14943)*
Kvga Publishing 517 545-0841
804 Spring St Howell (48843) *(G-8471)*
Kwik Paint Products, Detroit *Also called R B L Plastics Incorporated (G-4550)*
Kwik Print Plus, Ludington *Also called Worten Copy Center Inc (G-10558)*
Kwik-Site Corporation 734 326-1500
5555 Treadwell St Wayne (48184) *(G-18227)*
Kwikie Inc 231 946-9942
700 Boon St Traverse City (49686) *(G-16735)*
Kwk Industries Inc 269 423-6213
56040 Territorial Rd Decatur (49045) *(G-3949)*
KY Holdings, Rochester *Also called Trans Industries Plastics LLC (G-13934)*
Kyklos Holdings Inc (HQ) 313 758-2000
1 Dauch Dr Detroit (48211) *(G-4370)*
Kyler Industries Inc 616 392-1042
192 E 48th St Holland (49423) *(G-8117)*
Kymora Kandles LLC 517 667-6067
306 E Union St Maple Rapids (48853) *(G-10945)*
Kyocera Unimerco Tooling Inc 734 944-4433
6620 State Rd Saline (48176) *(G-15023)*
Kyosi Electronics America Inc 248 773-3690
39555 Orchard Hill Pl # 165 Novi (48375) *(G-12460)*
Kyowa-Dmller Prcsion Machining, Milford *Also called Eidemller Prcsion McHining Inc (G-11463)*
Kyrie Enterprises LLC 248 549-8690
4336 Normandy Ct Royal Oak (48073) *(G-14555)*
Kysor Industrial Corporation 231 779-7500
1100 Wright St Cadillac (49601) *(G-2341)*
Kyungshin Cable Intl Corp 248 679-7578
19500 Victor Pkwy Ste 120 Livonia (48152) *(G-10271)*
L & C Enterprises Inc 231 943-7787
3876 Blair Townhall Rd Traverse City (49685) *(G-16736)*
L & H Diversified Mfg USA LLC 586 615-4873
51559 Oro Dr Shelby Township (48315) *(G-15252)*
L & J Enterprises Inc 586 995-4153
3181 Wynns Mill Ct Metamora (48455) *(G-11283)*
L & J Omnico Agv, Clinton Township *Also called Omnico Agv LLC (G-3315)*
L & J Products K Huntington 810 919-3550
9954 Weber St Brighton (48116) *(G-2015)*
L & L Pattern Inc 231 733-2646
2401 Park St Muskegon (49444) *(G-11853)*
L & L Products Inc (HQ) 586 336-1600
160 Mclean Bruce Twp (48065) *(G-2171)*
L & L Products Inc 586 752-6681
160 Mclean Bruce Twp (48065) *(G-2172)*
L & L Products Inc 586 336-1600
159 Mclean Bruce Twp (48065) *(G-2173)*
L & M Hardwood & Skids LLC 734 281-3043
15361 Goddard Rd Southgate (48195) *(G-15752)*
L & M Machining & Mfg Inc 586 498-7110
14200 E 10 Mile Rd Warren (48089) *(G-17899)*
L & M Mfg Inc 989 689-4010
6016 N Meridian Rd Hope (48628) *(G-8362)*
L & M Woodworking LLC 404 391-3868
2062 Easy Ct Oxford (48370) *(G-12894)*
L & P LLC 231 733-1415
2376 Dels Dr Muskegon (49444) *(G-11854)*
L & R Centerless Grinding 734 397-3031
5701 S Sheldon Rd Canton (48188) *(G-2485)*
L & R Grinding, Canton *Also called Merchants Industries Inc (G-2494)*
L & R Limited LLC 910 308-7278
1801 N Opdyke Rd Auburn Hills (48326) *(G-955)*
L & S Products LLC 517 238-4645
294 Block Rd Coldwater (49036) *(G-3442)*
L & S Transit Mix Concrete Co 989 354-5363
500 Tuttle St Alpena (49707) *(G-298)*
L & W Inc 734 397-8085
6771 Haggerty Rd Van Buren Twp (48111) *(G-17535)*
L & W Inc 517 486-6321
11505 E Us Highway 223 Blissfield (49228) *(G-1767)*
L & W Inc 734 529-7290
5461 Circle Seven Dr Dundee (48131) *(G-4826)*
L & W Inc (HQ) 734 397-6300
17757 Woodland Dr New Boston (48164) *(G-12012)*
L & W Inc 734 397-2212
6201 Haggerty Rd Van Buren Twp (48111) *(G-17536)*
L & W Inc 616 394-9665
808 E 32nd St Holland (49423) *(G-8118)*
L & W Inc 517 627-7333
13112 Oneida Rd Grand Ledge (48837) *(G-6394)*
L & W Engineering, New Boston *Also called L & W Inc (G-12012)*
L & W Engineering Co, Holland *Also called L & W Inc (G-8118)*
L & W Engineering Co Plant 2, Van Buren Twp *Also called L & W Inc (G-17536)*
L & W Mexico LLC (HQ) 734 397-6300
6301 Haggerty Rd Van Buren Twp (48111) *(G-17537)*
L & W, Engineering, Grand Ledge *Also called L & W Inc (G-6394)*
L A Burnhart Inc (PA) 810 227-4567
2095 Euler Rd Brighton (48114) *(G-2016)*
L A Martin Company 313 581-3444
14400 Henn St Dearborn (48126) *(G-3859)*
L A S Leasing Inc 734 727-5148
36253 Michigan Ave Wayne (48184) *(G-18228)*
L Barge & Associates Inc 248 582-3430
1530 Farrow St Ferndale (48220) *(G-5563)*
L C Redi Mix, Kalkaska *Also called Srm Concrete LLC (G-9404)*
L D J Inc 906 524-6194
202 N Main St Lanse (49946) *(G-9666)*
L D S Sheet Metal Inc 313 892-2624
21831 Schoenherr Rd Warren (48089) *(G-17900)*
L E Jones Company 906 863-1043
1200 34th Ave Menominee (49858) *(G-11242)*
L E Q Inc 248 257-5466
5600 Williams Lake Rd B Waterford (48329) *(G-18132)*
L F M Enterprises Inc 586 792-7220
33256 Kelly Rd Clinton Township (48035) *(G-3275)*
L I S Manufacturing Inc 734 525-3070
15223 Farmington Rd Ste 8 Livonia (48154) *(G-10272)*
L L C, Midland *Also called S and P Drctnal Boring Svc LLC (G-11412)*
L Lewallen Co Inc 586 792-9930
22900 Interstate Dr Clinton Township (48035) *(G-3276)*
L M Gear Company Division, Chesterfield *Also called Anderson-Cook Inc (G-2844)*
L M Group, Sterling Heights *Also called Luckmarr Plastics Inc (G-16077)*
L M I, Fenton *Also called Linear Measurement Instrs Corp (G-5489)*
L N T Inc 248 347-6006
24300 Catherne Ind Dr # 405 Novi (48375) *(G-12461)*
L Perrigo Company (HQ) 269 673-8451
515 Eastern Ave Allegan (49010) *(G-164)*
L Perrigo Company 269 673-7962
300 Water St Allegan (49010) *(G-165)*
L Perrigo Company 616 738-0150
13295 Reflections Dr Holland (49424) *(G-8119)*
L Perrigo Company 269 673-7962
809 Airway Dr Allegan (49010) *(G-166)*
L Perrigo Company 269 673-1608
500 Eastern Ave Allegan (49010) *(G-167)*

ALPHABETIC

L Perrigo Company 248 687-1036
101 W Big Beaver Rd Troy (48084) ***(G-17201)***
L R Oliver and Company Inc 810 765-1000
7445 Mayer Rd Cottrellville (48039) ***(G-3724)***
L S Machining Inc 248 583-7277
1250 Rankin Dr Ste E Troy (48083) ***(G-17202)***
L T C Roll & Engineering Co (PA) 586 465-1023
23500 John Gorsuch Dr Clinton Township (48036) ***(G-3277)***
L T C Roll & Engineering Co 586 465-1023
31140 Kendall Fraser (48026) ***(G-5954)***
L T C Solutions Inc 586 323-2071
50150 Shelby Rd Shelby Township (48317) ***(G-15253)***
L T W, Lawrence *Also called Lanphear Tool Works Inc* ***(G-9982)***
L& L Products, Bruce Twp *Also called Zephyros Inc* ***(G-2188)***
L&L Printing Inc 586 263-0060
42120 Garfield Rd Clinton Township (48038) ***(G-3278)***
L&W Engineering Co Plant 1, Van Buren Twp *Also called L & W Inc* ***(G-17535)***
L&W Products 248 661-3889
34150 Old Timber Ct Farmington Hills (48331) ***(G-5287)***
L'Anse Sentinel, Lanse *Also called L D J Inc* ***(G-9666)***
L-3 Combat Propulsion Systems, Muskegon *Also called Renk America LLC* ***(G-11907)***
L3 Aviation Products Inc (HQ) 616 949-6600
5353 52nd St Se Grand Rapids (49512) ***(G-6906)***
L3 Commnctons Avionics Systems, Grand Rapids *Also called L3 Aviation Products Inc* ***(G-6906)***
L3 Technologies Inc 734 741-8868
1201 E Ellsworth Rd Ann Arbor (48108) ***(G-546)***
L4 Manufacturing LLC 810 217-3407
6377 Wildflower Ln Brighton (48116) ***(G-2017)***
La Azteca Foods LLC 313 413-2014
3748 W Jefferson Ave Ecorse (48229) ***(G-4983)***
LA East Inc 269 476-7170
62702 Woodland Dr Vandalia (49095) ***(G-17567)***
La Familia Stop 'n' Shop, Grand Rapids *Also called Agenda 2020 Inc* ***(G-6438)***
La Fata Cabinets, Shelby Township *Also called Lafata Cabinet Shop* ***(G-15255)***
La Fiesta Chip Company, Montague *Also called Gvb Group-La Fiesta LLC* ***(G-11597)***
La Gold Mine Inc 517 540-1050
425 W Main St Brighton (48116) ***(G-2018)***
La Jalisciense Inc (PA) 313 237-0008
31048 Applewood Ln Farmington Hills (48331) ***(G-5288)***
La Rosa Refrigeration & Eqp Co 313 368-6620
19191 Filer St Detroit (48234) ***(G-4371)***
La Solucion Corp 313 893-9760
19930 Conner St Detroit (48234) ***(G-4372)***
La-Z-Boy, Monroe *Also called Lzb Manufacturing Inc* ***(G-11559)***
La-Z-Boy Casegoods Inc (HQ) 734 242-1444
1 Lazboy Dr Monroe (48162) ***(G-11555)***
La-Z-Boy Global Limited 734 241-2438
1 Lazboy Dr Monroe (48162) ***(G-11556)***
La-Z-Boy Greensboro, Inc., Monroe *Also called La-Z-Boy Casegoods Inc* ***(G-11555)***
La-Z-Boy Incorporated (PA) 734 242-1444
1 Lazboy Dr Monroe (48162) ***(G-11557)***
Lab Link Testing LLC 419 283-6387
711 W 13 Mile Rd Madison Heights (48071) ***(G-10766)***
Lab Tool and Engineering Corp 517 750-4131
7755 King Rd Spring Arbor (49283) ***(G-15793)***
Label Motorsports LLC 616 288-7710
4920 Fulton St E Ste 3 Ada (49301) ***(G-25)***
Label Tech Inc 586 247-6444
51322 Oro Dr Shelby Township (48315) ***(G-15254)***
Labeled Lucky Brand Inc 517 962-1729
38701 Valley View Dr Romulus (48174) ***(G-14297)***
Labor Aiding Systems Corp 517 768-7478
3101 Hart Rd Jackson (49201) ***(G-8931)***
Labor Education and Res Prj 313 842-6262
7435 Michigan Ave Detroit (48210) ***(G-4373)***
Labor Notes, Detroit *Also called Labor Education and Res Prj* ***(G-4373)***
Labor World, Fraser *Also called A B Rusgo Inc* ***(G-5886)***
Labortrio Elttrofisico USA Inc 248 340-7040
40 Engelwood Dr Ste H Lake Orion (48359) ***(G-9613)***
Labtech Corporation 313 862-1737
7707 Lyndon St Detroit (48238) ***(G-4374)***
Lach Diamond 616 698-0101
4350 Airwest Dr Se Ofc A Grand Rapids (49512) ***(G-6907)***
Lachman & Company, Southfield *Also called Lachman Enterprises Inc* ***(G-15623)***
Lachman Enterprises Inc 248 948-9944
20955 Telegraph Rd Southfield (48033) ***(G-15623)***
Lacks Enterprises Inc (PA) 616 949-6570
5460 Cascade Rd Se Grand Rapids (49546) ***(G-6908)***
Lacks Exterior Systems LLC (HQ) 616 949-6570
5460 Cascade Rd Se Grand Rapids (49546) ***(G-6909)***
Lacks Exterior Systems LLC 616 949-6570
5010 52nd St Se Grand Rapids (49512) ***(G-6910)***
Lacks Exterior Systems LLC 248 351-0555
39500 Mackenzie Dr # 500 Novi (48377) ***(G-12462)***
Lacks Exterior Systems LLC 616 949-6570
5711 Kraft Ave Se Grand Rapids (49512) ***(G-6911)***
Lacks Exterior Systems LLC 616 554-7805
4655 Patterson Ave Se Kentwood (49512) ***(G-9461)***
Lacks Exterior Systems LLC 616 949-6570
5801 Kraft Ave Se Grand Rapids (49512) ***(G-6912)***
Lacks Exterior Systems LLC 616 949-6570
4315 52nd St Se Grand Rapids (49512) ***(G-6913)***
Lacks Exterior Systems LLC 616 949-6570
3703 Patterson Sw Grand Rapids (49512) ***(G-6914)***
Lacks Exterior Systems LLC 616 554-7180
3703 Patterson Ave Se Kentwood (49512) ***(G-9462)***
Lacks Industries Inc 616 698-6890
4260 Airwest Dr Se Grand Rapids (49512) ***(G-6915)***
Lacks Industries Inc 616 698-3600
4375 52nd St Se Grand Rapids (49512) ***(G-6916)***
Lacks Industries Inc 616 554-7135
4655 Patterson Ave Se Kentwood (49512) ***(G-9463)***
Lacks Industries Inc 616 698-6854
4090 Barden Dr Grand Rapids (49512) ***(G-6917)***
Lacks Industries Inc 616 698-9852
4260 Airlane Dr Se Grand Rapids (49512) ***(G-6918)***
Lacks Industries Inc 616 554-7134
3505 Kraft Ave Se Grand Rapids (49512) ***(G-6919)***
Lacks Industries Inc 616 698-2776
4275 Airwest Dr Se Grand Rapids (49512) ***(G-6920)***
Lacks Industries Inc 616 656-2910
4365 52nd St Se Grand Rapids (49512) ***(G-6921)***
Lacks Trim Systems, Grand Rapids *Also called Lacks Exterior Systems LLC* ***(G-6909)***
Lacks Trim Systems, Grand Rapids *Also called Lacks Industries Inc* ***(G-6917)***
Lacks Trim Systems, Kentwood *Also called Lacks Exterior Systems LLC* ***(G-9462)***
Lacks Wheel Trim Systems, Kentwood *Also called Lacks Industries Inc* ***(G-9463)***
Lacks Wheel Trim Systems, Grand Rapids *Also called Lacks Industries Inc* ***(G-6919)***
Lacks Wheel Trim Systems LLC 248 351-0555
39500 Mackenzie Dr # 500 Novi (48377) ***(G-12463)***
Lacks Wheel Trim Systems LLC (PA) 616 949-6570
5460 Cascade Rd Se Grand Rapids (49546) ***(G-6922)***
Laco Inc 231 929-3300
1561 Laitner Dr Traverse City (49696) ***(G-16737)***
Lacy Tool Company Inc 248 476-5250
40375 Grand River Ave Novi (48375) ***(G-12464)***
Ladder Carolina Company Inc 734 482-5946
12 E Forest Ave Ypsilanti (48198) ***(G-18961)***
Laddertech LLC 248 437-7100
7081 Dan Mcguire Dr Brighton (48116) ***(G-2019)***
Laduke Corporation 248 414-6600
10311 Capital St Oak Park (48237) ***(G-12622)***
Laduke Roofing, Oak Park *Also called Laduke Corporation* ***(G-12622)***
Lady Jane Gourmet Seed Co., Metamora *Also called L & J Enterprises Inc* ***(G-11283)***
Lady Lazarus LLC 810 441-9115
22801 Woodward Ave Ferndale (48220) ***(G-5564)***
Lafarge North America Inc 989 399-1005
1701 N 1st St Saginaw (48601) ***(G-14682)***
Lafarge North America Inc 989 894-0157
1500 Main St Essexville (48732) ***(G-5116)***
Lafarge North America Inc 989 595-3820
11351 E Grand Lake Rd Presque Isle (49777) ***(G-13654)***
Lafarge North America Inc 269 983-6333
200 Upton Dr Saint Joseph (49085) ***(G-14944)***
Lafarge North America Inc 216 566-0545
1500 Main St Essexville (48732) ***(G-5117)***
Lafarge North America Inc 703 480-3600
6211 N Ann Arbor Rd Dundee (48131) ***(G-4827)***
Lafarge North America Inc 231 726-3291
1047 7th St Muskegon (49441) ***(G-11855)***
Lafarge North America Inc 989 354-4171
1435 Ford Ave Alpena (49707) ***(G-299)***
Lafarge North America Inc 313 842-9258
1301 Springwells Ct Detroit (48209) ***(G-4375)***
Lafargeholcim, Essexville *Also called Lafarge North America Inc* ***(G-5116)***
Lafarghlcim Acm Nwco Tx-La LLC 972 837-2462
6211 N Ann Arbor Rd Dundee (48131) ***(G-4828)***
Lafata Cabinet Shop (PA) 586 247-6536
50905 Hayes Rd Shelby Township (48315) ***(G-15255)***
Laforce LLC 248 588-5601
289 Robbins Dr Troy (48083) ***(G-17203)***
Lafrontera Tortillas Inc 734 231-1701
32845 Cleveland St Rockwood (48173) ***(G-14201)***
Lahti Fabrication Inc 989 343-0420
2574 School Rd Alger (48610) ***(G-138)***
Laidco Sales Inc 231 832-1327
4753 175th Ave Hersey (49639) ***(G-7867)***
Laingsburg Screw Inc 517 651-2757
9805 Round Lake Rd Laingsburg (48848) ***(G-9536)***
Lairds Custom Cabinetry Inc 810 494-5164
11371 Eagle Way Brighton (48114) ***(G-2020)***
Lake City Forge, Lake City *Also called Lc Manufacturing LLC* ***(G-9548)***
Lake City Redi Mix, Traverse City *Also called Srm Concrete LLC* ***(G-16839)***
Lake County Star, Big Rapids *Also called Pgi Holdings Inc* ***(G-1683)***
Lake Design and Mfg Co 616 794-0290
7280 Storcy Rd Belding (40809) ***(G-1456)***

Lake Effect Alpacas 616 836-7906
4266 60th St Holland (49423) *(G-8120)*
Lake Effect Embroidery LLC 616 502-7844
9896 Basswood Dr West Olive (49460) *(G-18349)*
Lake Erie Med Surgical Sup Inc (PA) 734 847-3847
7560 Lewis Ave Temperance (48182) *(G-16536)*
Lake Fabricators Inc 269 651-1935
1000 N Clay St Sturgis (49091) *(G-16298)*
Lake House Publishing LLC 231 377-2017
6377 Cottage Rd Bellaire (49615) *(G-1477)*
Lake Michigan Candles LLC 231 766-0412
5282 Bittersweet Dr Muskegon (49445) *(G-11856)*
Lake Michigan Mailers Inc (PA) 269 383-9333
3777 Sky King Blvd Kalamazoo (49009) *(G-9257)*
Lake Michigan Vintners LLC 269 326-7195
8972 First St Baroda (49101) *(G-1163)*
Lake Michigan Wire LLC 616 786-9200
4211 Hallacy Dr Holland (49424) *(G-8121)*
Lake Orion Concrete Orna Pdts 248 693-8683
62 W Scripps Rd Lake Orion (48360) *(G-9614)*
Lake Shore Services Inc 734 285-7007
4354 Biddle Ave Wyandotte (48192) *(G-18828)*
Lake Shore Systems Inc (PA) 906 774-1500
2141 Woodward Ave Kingsford (49802) *(G-9512)*
Lake Shore Systems Inc 906 265-5414
1520 W Adams St Iron River (49935) *(G-8745)*
Lake State Cleaning Inc 314 961-7939
154 East St Oxford (48371) *(G-12895)*
Lake Superior Press Inc 906 228-7450
802 S Lake St Marquette (49855) *(G-11027)*
Lake Superior Soap Co, Waterford *Also called Kevin Larkin Inc* *(G-18131)*
Lakeland Elec Mtr Svcs Inc 616 647-0331
3810 Mill Creek Dr Ne Comstock Park (49321) *(G-3619)*
Lakeland Finishing Corporation 616 949-8001
5400 36th St Se Grand Rapids (49512) *(G-6923)*
Lakeland Mills Inc 989 427-5133
1 Lakeland Pl Edmore (48829) *(G-4993)*
Lakeland Pallets Inc (PA) 616 949-9515
3801 Kraft Ave Se Grand Rapids (49512) *(G-6924)*
Lakeland Paper Corporation (PA) 269 651-5474
68345 Edgewater Beach Rd White Pigeon (49099) *(G-18481)*
Lakepoint Elec 586 983-2510
56812 Mound Rd Shelby Township (48316) *(G-15256)*
Lakeshore Cement Products 989 739-9341
5251 N Us Highway 23 Oscoda (48750) *(G-12763)*
Lakeshore Custom Powdr Coating 616 296-9330
411 N Griffin St Grand Haven (49417) *(G-6327)*
Lakeshore Die Cast Inc 269 422-1523
8829 Stvnsville Baroda Rd Baroda (49101) *(G-1164)*
Lakeshore Fabrication LLC 231 740-5861
8435 Sternberg Rd Nunica (49448) *(G-12582)*
Lakeshore Fittings Inc 616 846-5090
1865 Industrial Park Dr Grand Haven (49417) *(G-6328)*
Lakeshore Global, Detroit *Also called Lgc Global Inc* *(G-4395)*
Lakeshore Graphics 810 359-2087
7047 Lakeshore Rd Lexington (48450) *(G-10030)*
Lakeshore Marble Company Inc 269 429-8241
4410 N Roosevelt Rd Stevensville (49127) *(G-16257)*
Lakeshore Mold and Die LLC 269 429-6764
2355 W Marquette Woods Rd Stevensville (49127) *(G-16258)*
Lakeshore Paints & Coating 616 831-6990
761 Baylis St Sw Grand Rapids (49503) *(G-6925)*
Lakeshore Publishing 616 846-0620
109 S Buchanan St Spring Lake (49456) *(G-15829)*
Lakeshore Vision & Robotics 616 394-9201
11007 Chicago Dr Zeeland (49464) *(G-19050)*
Lakeside Aggregate LLC (PA) 616 837-5858
16861 120th Ave Nunica (49448) *(G-12583)*
Lakeside Building Products 248 349-3500
9189 Central St Detroit (48204) *(G-4376)*
Lakeside Canvas & Upholstery 231 755-2514
3200 Lakeshore Dr Muskegon (49441) *(G-11857)*
Lakeside Cstm Cbinets Bldg LLC 269 718-7960
24088 Findley Rd Sturgis (49091) *(G-16299)*
Lakeside Custom Printing LLC 517 936-5904
11581 Bradley Dr Jerome (49249) *(G-9078)*
Lakeside Manufacturing Co 269 429-6193
4999 Advance Way Stevensville (49127) *(G-16259)*
Lakeside Mechanical Contrs 616 786-0211
1741 Forest Cove Trl Allegan (49010) *(G-168)*
Lakeside Property Services 863 455-9038
14250 Ottawa Creek Ln Holland (49424) *(G-8122)*
Lakeside Software LLC 248 686-1700
201 S Main St Ste 200 Ann Arbor (48104) *(G-547)*
Lakeside Spring LLC 616 847-2706
2615 Temple St Muskegon (49444) *(G-11858)*
Laketon Truss Inc 231 798-3467
1527 Scranton Dr Norton Shores (49441) *(G-12308)*
Lakeview Cabinetry 810 650-1420
5674 Lakeview Dr Port Hope (48468) *(G-13429)*
Lakeview Publishing Company 586 443-5913
26824 Koerber St Saint Clair Shores (48081) *(G-14867)*
Lakeview Quality Tool Inc 989 732-6417
696 Alpine Rd Gaylord (49735) *(G-6141)*
Lakewood Machine Products Co 734 654-6677
12429 Maxwell Rd Carleton (48117) *(G-2558)*
Lakewood Organics LLC (PA) 231 861-6333
3104 W Baseline Rd Shelby (49455) *(G-15156)*
Lam Industries 734 266-1404
12985 Wayne Rd Livonia (48150) *(G-10273)*
Lamacs Inc 248 643-9210
360 E Maple Rd Ste I Troy (48083) *(G-17204)*
Lamantia Machine Company, Stevensville *Also called John Lamantia Corporation* *(G-16255)*
Lamay Woodworking 734 421-6032
36713 Richland St Livonia (48150) *(G-10274)*
Lambert Industries, Centreville *Also called Wayne Allen Lambert* *(G-2701)*
Lambert Industries Inc 734 668-6864
69 Enterprise Dr Ann Arbor (48103) *(G-548)*
Lamina Inc 248 489-9122
38505 Country Club Dr # 100 Farmington Hills (48331) *(G-5289)*
Laminin Medical Products Inc 616 871-3390
3760 East Paris Ave Se Grand Rapids (49512) *(G-6926)*
Lamon Group Inc 616 710-3169
889 76th St Sw Unit 1 Byron Center (49315) *(G-2280)*
Lamons 989 488-4580
807 Pershing St Midland (48640) *(G-11383)*
Lamour Printing Co 734 241-6006
123 E Front St Monroe (48161) *(G-11558)*
Lampco Industries of MI Inc 517 783-3414
1635 Losey Ave Jackson (49203) *(G-8932)*
Lancast Urethane Inc 517 485-6070
1132 Ladd Rd Commerce Township (48390) *(G-3549)*
Lance Industries LLC 248 549-1968
1260 Kempar Ave Madison Heights (48071) *(G-10767)*
Lance Safford Welding LLC 989 464-7841
230 S County St Hillman (49746) *(G-7913)*
Lancer Tool Co 248 380-8830
29289 Lorie Ln Wixom (48393) *(G-18695)*
Land & Homes Inc 616 534-5792
1701 Porter St Sw Ste 6 Grand Rapids (49519) *(G-6927)*
Land and Sea Group, Northville *Also called Competitive Cmpt Info Tech Inc* *(G-12201)*
Land Enterprises Inc 248 398-7276
26641 Townley St Madison Heights (48071) *(G-10768)*
Land Quilts, Crystal Falls *Also called Magiglide Inc* *(G-3743)*
Land Star Inc 313 834-2366
14284 Meyers Rd Detroit (48227) *(G-4377)*
Landahl Packaging Systems, Burton *Also called Flint Boxmakers Inc* *(G-2235)*
Landers Drafting Inc 906 228-8690
105 Garfield Ave Marquette (49855) *(G-11028)*
Landis Machine Shop, Romulus *Also called Lewkowicz Corporation* *(G-14298)*
Landman 231 946-4678
602 W Tenth St Traverse City (49684) *(G-16738)*
Landmesser Tools Company Inc 248 682-4689
960 S Cass Lake Rd Waterford (48328) *(G-18133)*
Landra Prsthtics Orthotics Inc 586 294-7188
29840 Harper Ave Saint Clair Shores (48082) *(G-14868)*
Landra Prsthtics Orthotics Inc (PA) 734 281-8144
14725 Northline Rd Southgate (48195) *(G-15753)*
Landscape Stone Supply Inc 616 953-2028
5960 136th Ave Holland (49424) *(G-8123)*
Lane Automotive Inc 269 463-4113
8300 Lane Dr Watervliet (49098) *(G-18182)*
Lane Soft Water 269 673-3272
132 Grand St Allegan (49010) *(G-169)*
Lane Tool 248 528-1606
1940 S Livernois Rd Rochester Hills (48307) *(G-14048)*
Lane Tool and Mfg Corp 248 528-1606
1940 S Livernois Rd Rochester Hills (48307) *(G-14049)*
Lang Tool Company 989 435-9864
2520 Glidden Rd Beaverton (48612) *(G-1428)*
Langenberg Machine Pdts Inc 517 485-9450
1234 S Holmes St Lansing (48912) *(G-9857)*
Langes Beef & Bull Inc 989 756-2941
6750 Plant Rd Whittemore (48770) *(G-18550)*
Langley Powder Coating 989 739-5203
4025 Arrow St Oscoda (48750) *(G-12764)*
Langs Inc 248 634-6048
5469 Jacobs Dr Holly (48442) *(G-8280)*
Lannis Fence Systems, Jackson *Also called Midway Strl Pipe & Sup Inc* *(G-8961)*
Lanphear Tool Works Inc 269 674-8877
311 S Paw Paw St Lawrence (49064) *(G-9982)*
Lansing Athletics 517 327-8828
5572 W Saginaw Hwy Lansing (48917) *(G-9772)*
Lansing Eastside Gateway 517 894-6125
615 E Kalamazoo St Lansing (48912) *(G-9858)*
Lansing Forge Inc (HQ) 517 882-2056
5232 Aurelius Rd Lansing (48911) *(G-9859)*
Lansing Fuel Ventures Inc 517 371-1198
601 W Saginaw St Lansing (48933) *(G-9860)*

ALPHABETIC

Lansing Holding Company Inc (PA)...517 882-2056
5232 Aurelius Rd Lansing (48911) ***(G-9861)***
Lansing Ice and Fuel Company (PA)...517 372-3850
911 Center St Lansing (48906) ***(G-9710)***
Lansing Labor News Inc...517 484-7408
16910 Black Walnut Ln East Lansing (48823) ***(G-4899)***
Lansing Nwsppers In Edcatn Inc...517 377-1000
300 S Wash Sq Ste 300 # 300 Lansing (48933) ***(G-9862)***
Lansing Plating Company...517 485-6915
1303 Case St Lansing (48906) ***(G-9711)***
Lanzen Incorporated (PA)...586 771-7070
100 Peyerk Ct Bruce Twp (48065) ***(G-2174)***
Lanzen Incorporated...231 587-8200
611 N East Limits St Mancelona (49659) ***(G-10873)***
Lanzen Fabricating, Bruce Twp *Also called Lanzen Incorporated* ***(G-2174)***
Lanzen-Mancelona, Mancelona *Also called Lanzen Incorporated* ***(G-10873)***
Lanzen-Petoskey LLC...231 881-9602
126 Fulton St Petoskey (49770) ***(G-13002)***
Lapeer Div, Lapeer *Also called Kamax Inc* ***(G-9936)***
Lapeer Fuel Ventures Inc...810 664-8770
252 S Main St Lapeer (48446) ***(G-9938)***
Lapeer Industries Inc (PA)...810 538-0589
14100 23 Mile Rd Shelby Township (48315) ***(G-15257)***
Lapeer Manufacturing Company, Lapeer *Also called Souris Enterprises Inc* ***(G-9961)***
Lapeer Plating & Plastics Inc...810 667-4240
395 Demille Rd Lapeer (48446) ***(G-9939)***
Lapine Metal Products Inc...269 388-5900
5232 Azo Ct Kalamazoo (49048) ***(G-9258)***
Lapointe Cedar Products Inc...906 753-4072
N7247 17.75 Ln Ingalls (49848) ***(G-8658)***
Laporte Industries, Clinton Township *Also called L F M Enterprises Inc* ***(G-3275)***
Lappans of Gaylord Inc...989 732-3274
4085 Old Us Highway 27 S Gaylord (49735) ***(G-6142)***
Larkhite Development System...616 457-6722
1501 Port Sheldon St Jenison (49428) ***(G-9060)***
Larry's Taxidermy Studio, Pleasant Lake *Also called Larrys Taxidermy Inc* ***(G-13103)***
Larrys Tarpaulin Shop LLC...313 563-2292
3452 Beech Daly Rd Inkster (48141) ***(G-8668)***
Larrys Taxidermy Inc...517 769-6104
8640 N Meridian Rd Pleasant Lake (49272) ***(G-13103)***
Larsen Graphics Inc...989 823-3000
1065 E Huron Ave Vassar (48768) ***(G-17579)***
Larsen Service Inc...810 374-6132
11018 Clar Eve Dr Otisville (48463) ***(G-12782)***
Larson Tactical Arms...906 204-8228
914 N Main St Ishpeming (49849) ***(G-8778)***
Larson-Juhl US LLC...734 416-3302
47584 Galleon Dr Plymouth (48170) ***(G-13217)***
Las Brazas Tortillas...616 886-0737
3416 Crystal Valley Ct Holland (49424) ***(G-8124)***
Las Tortugas Pallet Co...313 283-3279
1583 Austin Ave Lincoln Park (48146) ***(G-10051)***
Laser Access Inc...616 459-5496
3691 Northridge Dr Nw # 1 Grand Rapids (49544) ***(G-6928)***
Laser Blast, Plymouth *Also called Advanced Avionics Inc* ***(G-13119)***
Laser Connection LLC...989 662-4022
947 W Midland Rd Auburn (48611) ***(G-768)***
Laser Craft LLC...248 340-8922
151 Premier Dr Lake Orion (48359) ***(G-9615)***
Laser Cutting Co...586 468-5300
42300 Executive Dr Harrison Township (48045) ***(G-7705)***
Laser Dynamics, Auburn Hills *Also called Art Laser Inc* ***(G-798)***
Laser Fab Inc...586 415-8090
33901 Riviera Fraser (48026) ***(G-5955)***
Laser Marking Technologies LLC...989 673-6690
1101 W Sanilac Rd Caro (48723) ***(G-2573)***
Laser Mechanisms Inc (PA)...248 474-9480
25325 Regency Dr Novi (48375) ***(G-12465)***
Laser Mfg Inc...313 292-2299
9965 Lapham Way Plymouth (48170) ***(G-13218)***
Laser North Inc...906 353-6090
455 N Superior Ave Baraga (49908) ***(G-1143)***
Laser North Inc (PA)...906 353-6090
442 N Superior Ave Baraga (49908) ***(G-1144)***
Laser Printer Technologies Inc...231 941-5273
1379 Trade Center Dr Traverse City (49696) ***(G-16739)***
Laser Product Development LLC...800 765-4424
24340 Sherwood Center Line (48015) ***(G-2682)***
Laser Re-Nu LLC...248 630-1454
239 Voorheis St Pontiac (48341) ***(G-13394)***
Laser Shield, Milford *Also called Noir Laser Company LLC* ***(G-11478)***
Laser Specialists Inc...586 294-8830
17921 Malyn Blvd Plant 1 1 Plant Fraser (48026) ***(G-5956)***
Laser-Dynamics, Allendale *Also called Great Lakes Laser Dynamics Inc* ***(G-220)***
Lasercutting Services Inc...616 975-2000
4101 40th St Se Ste 7 Grand Rapids (49512) ***(G-6929)***
Laserline Inc...248 826-5041
46025 Port St Plymouth (48170) ***(G-13219)***
Lasers Plus LLC...734 926-1030
4421 Hyacinth Holt (48842) ***(G-8316)***
Lasers Resource Inc...616 554-5555
5555 Glnwood Hlls Pkwy Se Grand Rapids (49512) ***(G-6930)***
Lasers Unlimited Inc...616 977-2668
4600 36th St Se Grand Rapids (49512) ***(G-6931)***
Lasertec Inc...586 274-4500
747 E Whitcomb Ave Madison Heights (48071) ***(G-10769)***
Lasl Inc...586 331-2600
74100 Van Dyke Rd Bruce Twp (48065) ***(G-2175)***
Lastek Industries LLC...586 739-6666
50515 Corporate Dr Shelby Township (48315) ***(G-15258)***
Latin American Industries LLC...616 301-1878
3120 Kn O Sha Indus Ct Se Grand Rapids (49508) ***(G-6932)***
Latino Press Inc...313 361-3000
6301 Michigan Ave Detroit (48210) ***(G-4378)***
Latitude Recycling Inc...586 243-5153
60451 Kunstman Rd Ray (48096) ***(G-13700)***
Lattimore Material...972 837-2462
6211 N Ann Arbor Rd Dundee (48131) ***(G-4829)***
Laughabits LLC...248 990-3011
9301 Dwight St Detroit (48214) ***(G-4379)***
Laughing Needles EMB LLC...231 720-5789
6471 Holton Duck Lake Rd Holton (49425) ***(G-8340)***
Lauren Zinn...734 996-3524
918 Bath St Ann Arbor (48103) ***(G-549)***
Lavalier Corp...248 616-8880
900 Rochester Rd Troy (48083) ***(G-17205)***
Lavanway Sign Co Inc...248 356-1600
22124 Telegraph Rd Southfield (48033) ***(G-15624)***
Lavern Beechy...269 651-5095
65022 Balk Rd Sturgis (49091) ***(G-16300)***
Law Enforcement Development Co...734 656-4100
47801 W Anchor Ct Plymouth (48170) ***(G-13220)***
Law Enforcement Supply Inc...616 895-7875
10920 64th Ave Allendale (49401) ***(G-222)***
Law Offices Towana Tate PC...248 560-7250
30300 Northwestern Hwy Farmington Hills (48334) ***(G-5290)***
Lawrence Co, Houghton *Also called Lawrence J Julio LLC* ***(G-8384)***
Lawrence Industries Inc...269 664-4614
329 Highland Ct Plainwell (49080) ***(G-13081)***
Lawrence J Julio LLC...906 483-4781
47212 Main St Houghton (49931) ***(G-8384)***
Lawrence Plastics LLC...248 475-0186
6338 Sashabaw Rd Clarkston (48346) ***(G-3044)***
Lawrence Surface Tech Inc...248 609-9001
1895 Crooks Rd Troy (48084) ***(G-17206)***
Laws & Ponies Logging Show...269 838-3942
6805 Pine Lake Rd Delton (49046) ***(G-3964)***
Lawson Manufacturing Inc...248 624-1818
920 Ladd Rd Walled Lake (48390) ***(G-17671)***
Lawson Printers Inc...269 965-0525
685 Columbia Ave W Battle Creek (49015) ***(G-1267)***
Lawsons Logging...517 567-0025
5251 E Territorial Rd Camden (49232) ***(G-2423)***
Lawton Plant, Lawton *Also called Welch Foods Inc A Cooperative* ***(G-9990)***
Lawton Ridge Winery LLC...269 372-9463
8456 Stadium Dr Kalamazoo (49009) ***(G-9259)***
Lay Manufacturing Inc...313 369-1627
31614 Iroquois Dr Warren (48088) ***(G-17901)***
LAY Precision Machine Inc...989 726-5022
620 Parkway Dr West Branch (48661) ***(G-18330)***
Laydon Enterprises Inc (PA)...906 774-4633
101 Woodward Ave Iron Mountain (49802) ***(G-8724)***
Laylin Welding Inc...269 782-2910
501 E Prairie Ronde St Dowagiac (49047) ***(G-4786)***
Layline Oil and Gas LLC...231 743-2452
135 E Main St Marion (49665) ***(G-10972)***
Lazer Graphics...269 926-1066
1101 Pipestone Rd Benton Harbor (49022) ***(G-1565)***
Lazer Images, Livonia *Also called Fairfield Investment Co* ***(G-10204)***
Lazy Ballerina Winery LLC (PA)...269 363-6218
315 State St Saint Joseph (49085) ***(G-14945)***
Lazy Ballerina Winery LLC...269 759-8486
4209 Lake St Bridgman (49106) ***(G-1931)***
Lbv Sales LLC...616 874-9390
5669 Rolling Highlands Dr Belmont (49306) ***(G-1510)***
Lc Manufacturing LLC (PA)...231 839-7102
4150 N Wolcott Rd Lake City (49651) ***(G-9548)***
Lc Manufacturing LLC...734 753-3990
36485 S Huron Rd New Boston (48164) ***(G-12013)***
Lc Materials, Big Rapids *Also called Srm Concrete LLC* ***(G-1688)***
Lc Materials LLC (HQ)...231 946-5600
805 W 13th St Cadillac (49601) ***(G-2342)***
Lc Materials LLC...817 835-4100
710 W Conway Rd Harbor Springs (49740) ***(G-7649)***
Lc Materials LLC...231 946-5600
17443 Pleasanton Hwy Bear Lake (49614) ***(G-1418)***
Lc Redi Mix, Reed City *Also called Srm Concrete LLC* ***(G-13799)***

ALPHABETIC SECTION

Lca International Publishing 313 908-4583
   5218 Royal Vale Ln Dearborn (48126) *(G-3860)*

Lca Mold & Engineering Inc 269 651-1193
   1200 W Lafayette St Sturgis (49091) *(G-16301)*

Lcss Worldwide, Washington *Also called Low Cost Surcing Solutions LLC (G-18084)*

LDB Plastics Inc 586 566-9698
   50845 Rizzo Dr Shelby Township (48315) *(G-15259)*

LDM Technologies Inc 248 858-2800
   2500 Executive Hills Dr Auburn Hills (48326) *(G-956)*

Le Forges Pipe & Fab Inc 734 482-2100
   64 Wiard Rd Ypsilanti (48198) *(G-18962)*

Le Host LLC 248 546-4247
   305 W 9 Mile Rd Ferndale (48220) *(G-5565)*

Le USA Walker Scientific, Lake Orion *Also called Labortrio Elttrofisico USA Inc (G-9613)*

LE Warren Inc 517 784-8701
   1600 S Jackson St Jackson (49203) *(G-8933)*

Le'tush, Croswell *Also called Renes Inc (G-3735)*

Le-Q Fabricators Ltd 906 246-3402
   W4106 M 69 Felch (49831) *(G-5432)*

Lead Screws International Inc 262 786-1500
   2101 Precision Dr Traverse City (49686) *(G-16740)*

Leader Corporation (PA) 586 566-7114
   51644 Filomena Dr Shelby Township (48315) *(G-15260)*

Leader Printing and Design Inc 313 565-0061
   25034 W Warren St Dearborn Heights (48127) *(G-3930)*

Leader Publications LLC (PA) 269 683-2100
   217 N 4th St Niles (49120) *(G-12141)*

Leader Tool Company - HB Inc 989 479-3281
   630 N Huron Ave Harbor Beach (48441) *(G-7634)*

Leadership Group LLC 586 251-2090
   14225 Southgate Dr Sterling Heights (48313) *(G-16069)*

Leading Edge Engineering Inc 586 786-0382
   14498 Oakwood Dr Shelby Township (48315) *(G-15261)*

Lean Factory America LLC 513 297-3086
   816 E 3rd St Buchanan (49107) *(G-2199)*

Leann Kelley Enterprises LLC 505 270-5687
   5030 136th Ave Hamilton (49419) *(G-7601)*

Leanne Sowa 616 225-8858
   10855 Sandy Oak Trl Cedar Springs (49319) *(G-2654)*

Leapers Inc (PA) 734 542-1500
   32700 Capitol St Livonia (48150) *(G-10275)*

Lear Automotive Mfg LLC 248 447-1603
   6555 E Davison St Detroit (48212) *(G-4380)*

Lear Automotive Mfg LLC 248 447-1603
   6555 E Davidson St Detroit (48212) *(G-4381)*

Lear Corp Eeds and Interiors (HQ) 248 447-1500
   21557 Telegraph Rd Southfield (48033) *(G-15625)*

Lear Corporation 313 731-0840
   6501 E Nevada St Detroit (48234) *(G-4382)*

Lear Corporation 313 852-7800
   21557 Telg Rd Ste 300 Southfield (48033) *(G-15626)*

Lear Corporation 313 965-0507
   119 State St Detroit (48226) *(G-4383)*

Lear Corporation 989 588-6181
   505 Hoover St Farwell (48622) *(G-5425)*

Lear Corporation 248 447-1500
   454 North St Mason (48854) *(G-11141)*

Lear Corporation 248 447-1500
   21700 Telegraph Rd Southfield (48033) *(G-15627)*

Lear Corporation 248 299-7100
   3000 Research Dr Rochester Hills (48309) *(G-14050)*

Lear Corporation 248 447-1563
   9501 Conner St Detroit (48213) *(G-4384)*

Lear Corporation 989 275-5794
   10161 N Roscommon Rd Roscommon (48653) *(G-14351)*

Lear Corporation (PA) 248 447-1500
   21557 Telegraph Rd Southfield (48033) *(G-15628)*

Lear Corporation 231 947-0160
   710 Carver St Traverse City (49686) *(G-16741)*

Lear Corporation 248 853-3122
   2930 W Auburn Rd Rochester Hills (48309) *(G-14051)*

Lear Corporation 313 731-0833
   902 E Hamilton Ave Flint (48550) *(G-5723)*

Lear European Operations Corp 248 447-1500
   21557 Telegraph Rd Southfield (48033) *(G-15629)*

Lear Global Technology Corp Uk (HQ) 248 447-1500
   21557 Telegraph Rd Southfield (48033) *(G-15630)*

Lear Ima Detroit, Detroit *Also called Lear Corporation (G-4382)*

Lear Mexican Seating Corp (HQ) 248 447-1500
   21557 Telegraph Rd Southfield (48033) *(G-15631)*

Lear Operations Corporation (HQ) 248 447-1500
   21557 Telegraph Rd Southfield (48033) *(G-15632)*

Lear Trim LP (PA) 248 447-1500
   21557 Telegraph Rd Southfield (48033) *(G-15633)*

Lease Management Inc (PA) 989 773-5948
   503 Industrial Dr Mount Pleasant (48858) *(G-11707)*

Leather Lore 269 548-7160
   475 W Randall St Coopersville (49404) *(G-3690)*

Leather Unlimited, Detroit *Also called Reed Sportswear Mfg Co (G-4561)*

Leathercrafts By Bear 616 453-8308
   751 Brownwood Ave Nw Grand Rapids (49504) *(G-6933)*

Lebalab Inc 519 542-4236
   35 Ash Dr Kimball (48074) *(G-9494)*

Lebanon Baking Company, Detroit *Also called Sophias Bakery Inc (G-4599)*

Leblond Lathe Service, Bruce Twp *Also called Willenborg Associates Inc (G-2186)*

Lebutt Publishing LLC 248 756-1613
   5922 Strawberry Cir Commerce Township (48382) *(G-3550)*

Leco Corporation (PA) 269 983-5531
   3000 Lakeview Ave Saint Joseph (49085) *(G-14946)*

Leco Corporation 269 985-5496
   Hilltop Rd Saint Joseph (49085) *(G-14947)*

Lecreuset 248 209-7025
   4000 Baldwin Rd Auburn Hills (48326) *(G-957)*

Lectra Tool Company, Howell *Also called Jess Enterprises LLC (G-8467)*

Lectronix Inc (PA) 517 492-1900
   5858 Enterprise Dr Lansing (48911) *(G-9863)*

Led Source Detroit 586 983-9905
   6095 15 Mile Rd Sterling Heights (48312) *(G-16070)*

Ledco-Chargeguard, Plymouth *Also called Law Enforcement Development Co (G-13220)*

Ledges Sign Company 517 925-1139
   136 N Clinton St Grand Ledge (48837) *(G-6395)*

Ledgestone, Wixom *Also called Northern Mich Aggregates LLC (G-18722)*

Lee Cleaners Inc 517 351-5655
   2843 E Grnd Rvr Ave # 140 East Lansing (48823) *(G-4900)*

Lee Hamilton Gary Jr 231 884-9600
   10695 W Geers Rd Mc Bain (49657) *(G-11184)*

Lee Manufacturing Inc 231 865-3359
   6406 Airline Rd Fruitport (49415) *(G-6065)*

Lee Printing & Graphics, Norton Shores *Also called Micrgraphics Printing Inc (G-12311)*

Lee Printing Company 586 463-1564
   21222 Cass Ave Clinton Township (48036) *(G-3279)*

Lee Spring Company LLC 586 296-9850
   34137 Doreka Fraser (48026) *(G-5957)*

Lee Stevens Machinery Inc 248 926-8400
   49650 Martin Dr Wixom (48393) *(G-18696)*

Lee-Cobb Company 269 553-0873
   415 W Maple St Kalamazoo (49001) *(G-9260)*

Leeann Plastics Inc 269 489-5035
   300 Halfway Rd Burr Oak (49030) *(G-2212)*

Leedy Manufacturing Co LLC 616 245-0517
   210 Hall St Sw Grand Rapids (49507) *(G-6934)*

Leelanau Enterprise Inc 231 256-9827
   7200 E Duck Lake Rd Lake Leelanau (49653) *(G-9563)*

Leelanau Industries Inc 231 947-0372
   6052 E Traverse Hwy Traverse City (49684) *(G-16742)*

Leelanau Prints 231 386-7616
   6411 N Overlook Rd Northport (49670) *(G-12188)*

Leelanau Redi-Mix Inc 231 228-5005
   12488 S Newman Rd Maple City (49664) *(G-10943)*

Leelanau Redi-Mix & Gravel, Maple City *Also called Leelanau Redi-Mix Inc (G-10943)*

Leelanau Wine Cellars Ltd (PA) 231 386-5201
   7161 N West Bay Shore Dr Northport (49670) *(G-12189)*

Leelanau Woodworking 231 946-4437
   9995 E Lincoln Rd Traverse City (49684) *(G-16743)*

Leep Logging Inc 517 852-1540
   8445 Guy Rd Nashville (49073) *(G-11956)*

Lees Ready Mix Inc 989 734-7666
   3232 Birchwood Dr Rogers City (49779) *(G-14211)*

Leeward Tool Inc 586 754-7200
   23781 Blackstone Ave Warren (48089) *(G-17902)*

Left Foot Charley 231 995-0500
   806 Reads Run Traverse City (49685) *(G-16744)*

Lefty Love LLC 248 795-3858
   17144 Plainview Ave Detroit (48219) *(G-4385)*

Legacy Barricades Inc 616 656-9600
   4320 Airwest Dr Se Ste B Grand Rapids (49512) *(G-6935)*

Legacy Canvas & Upholstery LLC 231 578-9972
   2066 Poplar Ct Muskegon (49445) *(G-11859)*

Legacy Design Studio LLC 248 710-3219
   1010 W Hamlin Rd Rochester Hills (48309) *(G-14052)*

Legacy Distillers Inc 231 933-0631
   10691 E Carter Rd Ste 101 Traverse City (49684) *(G-16745)*

Legacy Metal Fabricating LLC 616 258-8406
   21 N Park St Nw Grand Rapids (49544) *(G-6936)*

Legacy Metal Services Inc 810 721-7775
   2073 S Almont Ave Imlay City (48444) *(G-8639)*

Legacy Precision Molds Inc 616 532-6536
   4668 Spartan Indus Dr Sw Grandville (49418) *(G-7397)*

Legacy Tool LLC 231 335-8983
   9023 S Baldwin Ave Newaygo (49337) *(G-12084)*

Legal Art Works, Bingham Farms *Also called Intrinsic4d LLC (G-1701)*

Legend Lllys Pet Grming Ret Sp 734 346-6030
   3479 S Bassett St Detroit (48217) *(G-4386)*

Legend Sign Company 616 447-7446
   5120 Plainfield Ave Ne Grand Rapids (49525) *(G-6937)*

Legendary Fabrication Wldg LLC 989 872-9353
   8260 Van Dyke Rd Cass City (48726) *(G-2617)*

Legendary Millwork Inc 248 588-5663
2655 Elliott Dr Troy (48083) ***(G-17207)***
Legends Game Call Co 517 499-6962
100 North St Napoleon (49261) ***(G-11953)***
Leggett & Platt Incorporated 417 358-8131
1333 Gratiot Ave Detroit (48207) ***(G-4387)***
Leggett Platt Components Inc 616 784-7000
7701 Venture Ave Nw Sparta (49345) ***(G-15771)***
Lehman Publishingcom 810 395-4535
15997 Hough Rd Allenton (48002) ***(G-230)***
Lehost Hair & Wigs, Ferndale *Also called Le Host LLC* ***(G-5565)***
Leica Geo Systems Gr LLC 616 949-7430
6330 28th St Se Grand Rapids (49546) ***(G-6938)***
Leif Distribution LLC 517 481-2122
3529 3 Mile Rd Nw Grand Rapids (49534) ***(G-6939)***
Leif Led, Grand Rapids *Also called Leif Distribution LLC* ***(G-6939)***
Leighs Garden Winery Inc 906 553-7799
209 S 12th St Escanaba (49829) ***(G-5080)***
Leitelt Iron Works, Grand Rapids *Also called Padnos Leitelt Inc* ***(G-7067)***
Leitz Tooling Systems LP 616 698-7010
4301 East Paris Ave Se Grand Rapids (49512) ***(G-6940)***
Leitz Tooling Systems LP 616 698-7010
4301 East Paris Ave Se Grand Rapids (49512) ***(G-6941)***
Lej Investments LLC 616 452-3707
2950 Pririe St Sw Ste 900 Grandville (49418) ***(G-7398)***
Lejanae Designs LLC 248 621-3677
26747 Stanford Dr E Southfield (48033) ***(G-15634)***
Lematic Inc 517 787-3301
2410 W Main St Jackson (49203) ***(G-8934)***
Lemforder Corp 734 416-6200
15811 Centennial Dr Northville (48168) ***(G-12235)***
Lemica Corporation 313 839-2150
11201 Manning St Detroit (48234) ***(G-4388)***
Lemon Creek Farm, Berrien Springs *Also called Lemon Creek Winery Ltd* ***(G-1643)***
Lemon Creek Fruit Farm 269 471-1321
533 E Lemon Creek Rd Berrien Springs (49103) ***(G-1642)***
Lemon Creek Winery Ltd (PA) 269 471-1321
533 E Lemon Creek Rd Berrien Springs (49103) ***(G-1643)***
Len-Way Machine & Tool, Hamilton *Also called Lenway Machine Company Inc* ***(G-7602)***
Lenawee Industrial Pnt Sup Inc (PA) 734 729-8080
5645 Cogswell Rd Wayne (48184) ***(G-18229)***
Lenawee Tool & Automation Inc 517 458-7222
807 Gorham St Morenci (49256) ***(G-11614)***
Lenderink Inc 616 887-8257
1267 House St Ne Belmont (49306) ***(G-1511)***
Lenderink Family Tree Farms, Belmont *Also called Lenderink Inc* ***(G-1511)***
Lenox Block Club Assn 313 823-0941
1136 Lenox St Detroit (48215) ***(G-4389)***
Lenox Inc 586 727-1488
65601 Gratiot Ave Lenox (48050) ***(G-9999)***
Lenox Pharmacy LLC 313 971-5928
36267 26 Mile Rd Ste 1 Lenox (48048) ***(G-10000)***
Lenox Septic Tanks, Lenox *Also called Lenox Inc* ***(G-9999)***
Lenscrafters, Okemos *Also called Luxottica of America Inc* ***(G-12673)***
Lenway Machine Company Inc 269 751-5183
3165 60th St Hamilton (49419) ***(G-7602)***
Leon Automotive Interiors, Holland *Also called Leon Interiors Inc* ***(G-8125)***
Leon Interiors Inc (HQ) 616 422-7557
88 E 48th St Holland (49423) ***(G-8125)***
Leonard & Randy Inc 734 287-9500
20555 Northline Rd Taylor (48180) ***(G-16435)***
Leonard Fountain Spc Inc 313 891-4141
4601 Nancy St Detroit (48212) ***(G-4390)***
Leonard J Hill Logging Co 906 337-3435
30980 Woodbush Rd Calumet (49913) ***(G-2411)***
Leonard Machine Tool Systems 586 757-8040
22800 Hoover Rd Warren (48089) ***(G-17903)***
Leonard's Syrups, Detroit *Also called Leonard Fountain Spc Inc* ***(G-4390)***
Leonards Newcorp Inc 313 366-9300
17350 Ryan Rd Detroit (48212) ***(G-4391)***
Leoni Wiring Systems Inc 586 782-4444
2800 Livernois Rd Ste 600 Troy (48083) ***(G-17208)***
Lepages 2000 Inc 416 357-0041
18765 Seaway Dr Melvindale (48122) ***(G-11203)***
Leprino Foods Company 989 967-3635
311 N Sheridan Ave Remus (49340) ***(G-13815)***
Leprino Foods Company 616 895-5800
4700 Rich St Allendale (49401) ***(G-223)***
Leroy Tool & Die Inc 231 768-4336
17951 180th Ave Leroy (49655) ***(G-10007)***
Leroy Worden 231 325-3837
1944 N Marshall Rd Beulah (49617) ***(G-1655)***
Les Cheneaux Distillers Inc 906 748-0505
172 S Meridian St Cedarville (49719) ***(G-2670)***
Lesco Design & Mfg Co Inc 248 596-9301
28243 Beck Rd Ste B1 Wixom (48393) ***(G-18697)***
Lesley Elizabeth Inc 810 667-0706
449 Mccormick Dr Lapeer (48446) ***(G-9940)***
Lesley Elizabeth Inc (PA) 810 667-0706
877 Whitney Dr Lapeer (48446) ***(G-9941)***
Lesnau Printing Company 586 795-9200
6025 Wall St Sterling Heights (48312) ***(G-16071)***
Less Pay Pallets Inc 586 649-3800
36750 Jefferson Ave Harrison Township (48045) ***(G-7706)***
Lesso Kitchen and Bath 517 662-3230
2075 W Beecher Rd Adrian (49221) ***(G-79)***
Lesson Rooms 248 677-1341
309 N Main St Royal Oak (48067) ***(G-14556)***
Lester Detterbeck Enterprises, Iron River *Also called Iron River Mfg Co Inc* ***(G-8741)***
Lester Detterbeck Entps Ltd (PA) 906 265-5121
3390 Us Highway 2 Iron River (49935) ***(G-8746)***
Let Love Rule 734 749-7435
21391 Russell St Rockwood (48173) ***(G-14202)***
Letherer Truss Inc (PA) 989 386-4999
851 Industrial Dr Clare (48617) ***(G-2985)***
Letica Corporation (HQ) 248 652-0557
52585 Dequindre Rd Rochester Hills (48307) ***(G-14053)***
Letnan Industries Inc 586 726-1155
6520 Arrow Dr Sterling Heights (48314) ***(G-16072)***
Lettering Inc 248 223-9700
13324 Farmington Rd Livonia (48150) ***(G-10276)***
Lettering Inc of Michigan 248 223-9700
13324 Farmington Rd Livonia (48150) ***(G-10277)***
Letts Industries Inc (PA) 313 579-1100
1111 Bellevue St Detroit (48207) ***(G-4392)***
Leutz Enterprise Inc 906 228-5887
1200 Wright St Ste 4 Marquette (49855) ***(G-11029)***
Levannes Inc 269 327-4484
8840 Portage Indus Dr Portage (49024) ***(G-13575)***
Level 6 231 755-7000
1991 Lakeshore Dr Unit B Muskegon (49441) ***(G-11860)***
Level Eleven LLC 313 662-2000
1520 Woodward Ave Fl 3 Detroit (48226) ***(G-4393)***
Levi Ohman Micah 612 251-1293
320 W College Ave Apt 1 Marquette (49855) ***(G-11030)***
Leviathan Defense Group 419 575-7792
7720 N Dixie Hwy Newport (48166) ***(G-12104)***
Levy Environmental Services Co 313 429-2272
9300 Dix Dearborn (48120) ***(G-3861)***
Levy Indiana Slag Co (HQ) 313 843-7200
9300 Dix Dearborn (48120) ***(G-3862)***
Levy Machining LLC 517 563-2013
11901 Strait Rd Hanover (49241) ***(G-7625)***
Lewis Metals LLC 231 468-3435
850 Arbutus Dr Cadillac (49601) ***(G-2343)***
Lewis Welding Inc 616 452-9226
274 Mart St Sw Wyoming (49548) ***(G-18890)***
Lewiston Forest Products, Saint Charles *Also called Michigan Pallet Inc* ***(G-14805)***
Lewiston Sand & Gravel Inc 989 786-2742
5122 County Road 612 Lewiston (49756) ***(G-10023)***
Lewkowicz Corporation 734 941-0411
36425 Grant St Romulus (48174) ***(G-14298)***
Lewmar Custom Designs Inc 586 677-5135
56588 Scotland Blvd Shelby Township (48316) ***(G-15262)***
Lexalite, Charlevoix *Also called Alp Lighting Ceiling Pdts Inc* ***(G-2709)***
Lexamar Corporation 231 582-3163
100 Lexamar Dr Boyne City (49712) ***(G-1894)***
Lexatronics LLC 734 878-6237
9768 Cedar Lake Rd Pinckney (48169) ***(G-13050)***
Lexmark International Inc 248 352-0616
2 Towne Sq Ste 150 Southfield (48076) ***(G-15635)***
Lg Chem Battery Co, Holland *Also called Lg Energy Solution Mich Inc* ***(G-8126)***
Lg Chem Michigan Inc Tech Ctr, Troy *Also called Lg Energy Solution Mich Inc* ***(G-17212)***
Lg Elctrnics Vhcl Cmpnnts USA (HQ) 248 268-5851
1400 E 10 Mile Rd Ste 100 Hazel Park (48030) ***(G-7828)***
Lg Electronics USA Inc 248 268-5100
1835 Technology Dr Troy (48083) ***(G-17209)***
Lg Electronics Vehicle Compone 248 268-5851
1835 Technology Dr Bldg E Troy (48083) ***(G-17210)***
Lg Energy Solution Mich Inc 248 291-2385
3221 W Big Beaver Rd Troy (48084) ***(G-17211)***
Lg Energy Solution Mich Inc 248 307-1800
1857 Technology Dr Troy (48083) ***(G-17212)***
Lg Energy Solution Mich Inc 616 494-7153
1400 E 10 Mile Rd Ste 100 Hazel Park (48030) ***(G-7829)***
Lg Energy Solution Mich Inc 616 494-7100
12850 E 9 Mile Rd Warren (48089) ***(G-17904)***
Lg Energy Solution Mich Inc 616 494-7100
10885 Textile Rd Belleville (48111) ***(G-1488)***
Lg Energy Solution Mich Inc (HQ) 616 494-7100
1 Lg Way Holland (49423) ***(G-8126)***
Lg Essentials LLC 313 312-3813
8541 Birwood St Detroit (48204) ***(G-4394)***
Lga Retail Inc 248 910-1918
22770 Spy Glass Hill Dr South Lyon (48178) ***(G-15443)***
Lgb USA Inc (HQ) 586 777-4542
15585 Sturgeon St Roseville (48066) ***(G-14432)***

Lgc Global Inc ... 313 989-4141
7310 Woodward Ave 500a Detroit (48202) ***(G-4395)***
Lgc Global Energy Fm Llc ... 313 989-4141
7310 Woodward Ave 500a Detroit (48202) ***(G-4396)***
Lgi International, Auburn Hills *Also called F & S Diversified Products Inc* ***(G-885)***
Liberty 3d Technologies, Saint Joseph *Also called Liberty Steel Fabricating Inc* ***(G-14948)***
Liberty Advisors Inc ... 269 679-3281
11811 S Shaver Rd Schoolcraft (49087) ***(G-15123)***
Liberty Automotive Tech LLC ... 269 487-8114
4554 128th Ave Holland (49424) ***(G-8127)***
Liberty Bell Powdr Coating LLC ... 586 557-6328
1408 Enterprise Dr Highland (48357) ***(G-7894)***
Liberty Burnishing Co ... 313 366-7878
18401 Sherwood St Detroit (48234) ***(G-4397)***
Liberty Cast Products, Sterling Heights *Also called Sterling Metal Works LLC* ***(G-16193)***
Liberty Dairy Company ... 800 632-5552
302 N River St Evart (49631) ***(G-5125)***
Liberty Embroidery ... 269 419-0327
257 Wagon Wheel Ln Battle Creek (49017) ***(G-1268)***
Liberty Fabricators Inc ... 810 877-7117
2229 W Hill Rd Flint (48507) ***(G-5724)***
Liberty Manufacturing Company ... 269 327-0997
8631 Portage Indus Dr Portage (49024) ***(G-13576)***
Liberty Molds, Portage *Also called Liberty Manufacturing Company* ***(G-13576)***
Liberty Plastics Inc ... 616 994-7033
13170 Ransom St Holland (49424) ***(G-8128)***
Liberty Powder Coating, Highland *Also called Liberty Bell Powdr Coating LLC* ***(G-7894)***
Liberty Products Inc ... 231 853-2323
3073 Mortimer St Ravenna (49451) ***(G-13691)***
Liberty Research Co Inc ... 734 508-6237
291 Squires Dr Milan (48160) ***(G-11440)***
Liberty Spring Lapeer Inc ... 418 248-7781
3056 Davison Rd Lapeer (48446) ***(G-9942)***
Liberty Steel Fabricating Inc ... 269 556-9792
350 Palladium Dr Saint Joseph (49085) ***(G-14948)***
Liberty Tool Inc ... 586 726-2449
44404 Phoenix Dr Sterling Heights (48314) ***(G-16073)***
Liberty Transit Mix LLC ... 586 254-2212
7520 23 Mile Rd Shelby Township (48316) ***(G-15263)***
Liberty Turned Components LLC (PA) ... 734 508-6237
291 Squires Dr Milan (48160) ***(G-11441)***
Libertys High Prfmce Pdts Inc ... 586 469-1140
41775 Production Dr Harrison Township (48045) ***(G-7707)***
Libra Industries Inc Michigan (PA) ... 517 787-5675
1435 N Blackstone St Jackson (49202) ***(G-8935)***
Libra Manufacturing, Tecumseh *Also called Libra Precision Machining Inc* ***(G-16507)***
Libra Precision Machining Inc ... 517 423-1365
5353 N Rogers Hwy Tecumseh (49286) ***(G-16507)***
Liebherr Aerospace Saline Inc ... 734 429-7225
1465 Woodland Dr Saline (48176) ***(G-15024)***
Liebner Enterprises LLC ... 231 331-3076
1160 E State St Unit C Cheboygan (49721) ***(G-2791)***
Liedel Power Cleaning ... 734 848-2827
2850 Luna Pier Rd Erie (48133) ***(G-5049)***
Life Otreach Ctr Houghton Cnty ... 906 482-8681
300b Quincy St Hancock (49930) ***(G-7621)***
Lifesafer ... 888 294-7002
730 W Washington St Marquette (49855) ***(G-11031)***
Lifestyle Kitchen Studio ... 616 454-2563
222 Fulton St E Grand Rapids (49503) ***(G-6942)***
Lifetime Company ... 248 862-2578
2275 Cameo Lake Ct Bloomfield Hills (48302) ***(G-1830)***
Light Corp Inc (PA) ... 616 842-5100
14800 172nd Ave Grand Haven (49417) ***(G-6329)***
Light Metal Forming Corp ... 248 851-3984
4397 Stony River Dr Bloomfield Hills (48301) ***(G-1831)***
Light Metals Corporation ... 616 538-3030
2740 Prairie St Sw Wyoming (49519) ***(G-18891)***
Light Speed Usa LLC ... 616 308-0054
1971 E Beltlin Ave Ne 106-130 Grand Rapids (49525) ***(G-6943)***
Light-Rx, Farmington Hills *Also called Body Contour Ventures LLC* ***(G-5184)***
Lightguide Inc ... 248 374-8000
48443 Alpha Dr Wixom (48393) ***(G-18698)***
Lighthouse Cards and Gifts, Detroit *Also called Lighthouse Direct Buy LLC* ***(G-4398)***
Lighthouse Direct Buy LLC ... 313 340-1850
16143 Wyoming St Detroit (48221) ***(G-4398)***
Lighthouse Elec Protection LLC ... 586 932-2690
7314 19 Mile Rd Sterling Heights (48314) ***(G-16074)***
Lighting Enterprises Inc ... 313 693-9504
16706 Telegraph Rd Detroit (48219) ***(G-4399)***
Lighting One, Shelby Township *Also called Denali Lighting LLC* ***(G-15204)***
Lighting Printing ... 989 792-2793
2511 Busch Rd Birch Run (48415) ***(G-1709)***
Lightning Litho Inc ... 517 394-2995
5731 Enterprise Dr Lansing (48911) ***(G-9864)***
Lightning Machine Holland LLC ... 616 786-9280
128 Manufacturers Dr Holland (49424) ***(G-8129)***
Lightning Technologies Inc (PA) ... 248 572-6700
2171 Xcelsior Dr Oxford (48371) ***(G-12896)***
Lightworks Magazine Inc ... 248 626-8026
6966 Holiday Dr Bloomfield (48301) ***(G-1783)***
Lillian Fuel Inc ... 734 439-8505
1200 Dexter St Milan (48160) ***(G-11442)***
Lily Products Michigan Inc ... 616 245-9193
2070 Calvin Ave Se Grand Rapids (49507) ***(G-6944)***
Limbright Consulting Inc ... 810 227-5510
51100 Grand River Ave Wixom (48393) ***(G-18699)***
Lime Gypsum Products ... 989 867-4611
3425 Britt Rd Turner (48765) ***(G-17464)***
Limelite Printing LLC ... 313 839-7321
15285 Cedargrove St Detroit (48205) ***(G-4400)***
Limited Lblty Co Colormemink ... 313 707-3366
23211 Lorraine Blvd # 101 Brownstown Twp (48183) ***(G-2156)***
Limo-Reid Inc ... 517 447-4164
420 Carey St Deerfield (49238) ***(G-3957)***
Lin Adam Fuel Inc ... 313 733-6631
13330 Linwood St Detroit (48238) ***(G-4401)***
Linak US Inc ... 502 413-0387
678 Front Ave Nw Ste 175 Grand Rapids (49504) ***(G-6945)***
Linamar Holding Nevada Inc (HQ) ... 248 477-6240
32233 8 Mile Rd Livonia (48152) ***(G-10278)***
Lincoln Forge, Brownstown *Also called Lincoln Park Die & Tool Co* ***(G-2149)***
Lincoln Industries (PA) ... 989 736-6421
202 S Second St Lincoln (48742) ***(G-10036)***
Lincoln Park Boring Co ... 734 946-8300
28089 Wick Rd Romulus (48174) ***(G-14299)***
Lincoln Park Die & Tool Co ... 734 285-1680
18325 Dix Toledo Hwy Brownstown (48193) ***(G-2149)***
Lincoln Park Fuel, Lincoln Park *Also called Fk Fuel Inc* ***(G-10047)***
Lincoln Precision Carbide Inc ... 989 736-8113
600 S 2nd St Lincoln (48742) ***(G-10037)***
Lincoln Service LLC (PA) ... 734 793-0083
11862 Brookfield St Livonia (48150) ***(G-10279)***
Lincoln Tool Co Inc ... 989 736-8711
3140 E M 72 Harrisville (48740) ***(G-7743)***
Lincoln Welding Company ... 313 292-2299
4445 Brogan Rd Stockbridge (49285) ***(G-16276)***
Linda Mia Inc (PA) ... 906 265-9082
751 N 4th Ave Iron River (49935) ***(G-8747)***
Lindas Woodcrafts & Cabinets ... 989 734-2903
3350 W Heythaler Hwy Rogers City (49779) ***(G-14212)***
Lindberg Fluid Power Division, Jackson *Also called Crankshaft Machine Company* ***(G-8856)***
Lindberg Hydraulic Systems ... 517 787-3791
314 N Jackson St Jackson (49201) ***(G-8936)***
Lindberg/Mph, Riverside *Also called Tps LLC* ***(G-13866)***
Linde Gas & Equipment Inc ... 734 282-3830
2025 Eureka Rd Wyandotte (48192) ***(G-18829)***
Linde Gas & Equipment Inc ... 630 857-6460
21421 Hilltop St Ste 1 Southfield (48033) ***(G-15636)***
Linde Gas North America, Southfield *Also called Linde Gas & Equipment Inc* ***(G-15636)***
Linde Inc ... 269 317-7225
1578 36th Ave Hudsonville (49426) ***(G-8590)***
Linden Art Glass ... 734 459-5060
580 Forest Ave Ste 2a Plymouth (48170) ***(G-13221)***
Lindsay Nettell Inc ... 906 482-3549
47301 Janovosky Rd Atlantic Mine (49905) ***(G-750)***
Lindy Press Inc ... 231 937-6169
9794 Locust Ave Howard City (49329) ***(G-8411)***
Line Precision Inc ... 248 474-5280
31666 W 8 Mile Rd Farmington Hills (48336) ***(G-5291)***
Line-X of Grand Rapids, Wyoming *Also called 4d Industries Inc* ***(G-18847)***
Line-X of Livonia ... 734 237-3115
35043 Plymouth Rd Livonia (48150) ***(G-10280)***
Line-X of Waterford ... 248 270-8848
6650 Highland Rd Ste 101 Waterford (48327) ***(G-18134)***
Linear AMS, Livonia *Also called Linear Mold & Engineering LLC* ***(G-10282)***
Linear AMS, Livonia *Also called Linear Mold & Engineering LLC* ***(G-10283)***
Linear Measurement Instrs Corp ... 810 714-5811
101 N Alloy Dr Ste B Fenton (48430) ***(G-5489)***
Linear Mold & Engineering LLC ... 734 744-4548
34435 Glendale St Livonia (48150) ***(G-10281)***
Linear Mold & Engineering LLC (PA) ... 734 422-6060
12163 Globe St Livonia (48150) ***(G-10282)***
Linear Mold & Engineering LLC ... 734 422-6060
35450 Industrial Rd Livonia (48150) ***(G-10283)***
Linear Motion LLC ... 989 759-8300
628 N Hamilton St Saginaw (48602) ***(G-14683)***
Link Engineering Company, Plymouth *Also called Link Manufacturing Inc* ***(G-13223)***
Link Engineering Company, Ottawa Lake *Also called Link Manufacturing Inc* ***(G-12807)***
Link Engineering Company, Plymouth *Also called Link Group Inc* ***(G-13222)***
Link Group Inc (PA) ... 734 453-0800
43855 Plymouth Oaks Blvd Plymouth (48170) ***(G-13222)***
Link Industries, Indian River *Also called Link Manufacturing Inc* ***(G-8654)***
Link Manufacturing Inc (HQ) ... 734 453-0800
43855 Plymouth Oaks Blvd Plymouth (48170) ***(G-13223)***
Link Manufacturing Inc ... 231 238-8741
2208 S Straits Hwy Indian River (49749) ***(G-8654)***

ALPHABETIC

Link Manufacturing Inc 734 387-1001
8000 Yankee Rd Ste 105 Ottawa Lake (49267) ***(G-12807)***
Link Mechanical Solutions LLC 734 744-5616
11970 Mayfield St Livonia (48150) ***(G-10284)***
Link Tech Inc 269 427-8297
59648 M 43 Bangor (49013) ***(G-1129)***
Link Technology Inc 269 324-8212
4100 E Milham Ave Portage (49002) ***(G-13577)***
Link Tool & Mfg Co LLC 734 710-0010
39115 Warren Rd Westland (48185) ***(G-18392)***
Linked Live Inc 248 345-5993
30550 Brush St Madison Heights (48071) ***(G-10770)***
Linktool Group, Westland *Also called Link Tool & Mfg Co LLC* ***(G-18392)***
Linn Energy 989 786-7592
4890 Airport Rd Lewiston (49756) ***(G-10024)***
Lintech Global Inc 248 553-8033
34119 W 12 Mile Rd # 200 Farmington Hills (48331) ***(G-5292)***
Linwood Tool Co Inc 989 697-4403
229 S Huron Rd Linwood (48634) ***(G-10074)***
Lion Labs Ltd 248 231-0753
4800 N Grand River Ave Lansing (48906) ***(G-9712)***
Lions Pride Pressure Wshg LLC 989 251-5577
140 W Willow St Perry (48872) ***(G-12978)***
Lipp America Tank Systems LLC 616 201-6761
4246 Kalamazoo Ave Se Grand Rapids (49508) ***(G-6946)***
Lippert Components Inc 586 275-2107
6801 15 Mile Rd Sterling Heights (48312) ***(G-16075)***
Lippert Components Mfg Inc 989 845-3061
1103 Pearl St Chesaning (48616) ***(G-2829)***
Lipstick Jodi LLC 616 430-5389
13638 Starflower Ln Cedar Springs (49319) ***(G-2655)***
Liquid Drive Corporation 248 634-5382
18 1st St Mount Clemens (48043) ***(G-11647)***
Liquid Dustlayer Inc 231 723-3750
3320 Grant Hwy Manistee (49660) ***(G-10904)***
Liquid Manufacturing LLC 810 220-2802
305 Westwood Ave Ann Arbor (48103) ***(G-550)***
Liquid Otc LLC 248 214-7771
3250 Old Farm Ln Ste 1 Commerce Township (48390) ***(G-3551)***
Liquidgoldconcept Inc 734 926-9197
3858 Bestech Rd Ste C Ypsilanti (48197) ***(G-18963)***
Lisa Bain 313 389-9661
9636 Chatham Ave Allen Park (48101) ***(G-198)***
Lisi Automotive Hl Vol Inc 734 266-6958
11813 Hubbard St Livonia (48150) ***(G-10285)***
Lisi Automotive Hl Vol Inc (HQ) 734 266-6900
12955 Inkster Rd Livonia (48150) ***(G-10286)***
Lite Bright Welding 269 208-5698
5993 16 Mile Rd Ne Cedar Springs (49319) ***(G-2656)***
Lite Load Services LLC 269 751-6037
3866 40th St Hamilton (49419) ***(G-7603)***
Lite N Go Inc 248 414-7540
5410 Argyle St Dearborn (48126) ***(G-3863)***
Litebrake Tech LLC 906 523-2007
406 2nd St Houghton (49931) ***(G-8385)***
Litehouse Inc 616 897-5911
1400 Foreman St Lowell (49331) ***(G-10509)***
Literari Bookstore, Ann Arbor *Also called Literati LLC* ***(G-551)***
Literati LLC 909 921-5242
124 E Washington St Ann Arbor (48104) ***(G-551)***
Lites Alternative Inc 989 685-3476
2643 S M 33 Rose City (48654) ***(G-14364)***
Litesalternative, Rose City *Also called Lites Alternative Inc* ***(G-14364)***
Litetek, Plymouth *Also called Autosystems America Inc* ***(G-13129)***
Litho Photo Enterprises LLC 313 717-6615
6000 Pardee Rd Taylor (48180) ***(G-16436)***
Litho Printers Inc 269 651-7309
620 N Centerville Rd Sturgis (49091) ***(G-16302)***
Litho Printing Service Inc 586 772-6067
21541 Gratiot Ave Eastpointe (48021) ***(G-4939)***
Litho-Graphics Printing Pdts 586 775-1670
19361 E 10 Mile Rd Roseville (48066) ***(G-14433)***
Lithotech 269 471-6027
212 Harrigan Hall Berrien Springs (49104) ***(G-1644)***
Litsenberger Print Shop 906 482-3903
224 Shelden Ave Houghton (49931) ***(G-8386)***
Little Bay Concrete Products 906 428-9859
119 N 9th St Gladstone (49837) ***(G-6183)***
Little Bird Press LLC 616 676-9052
8550 Vergennes St Se Ada (49301) ***(G-26)***
Little Blue Book Inc 313 469-0052
19803 Mack Ave Grosse Pointe Woods (48236) ***(G-7570)***
Little Buildings Inc 586 752-7100
161 Shafer Dr Romeo (48065) ***(G-14228)***
Little Legends Creations LLC 313 828-7292
17431 Juliana Ave Eastpointe (48021) ***(G-4940)***
Little Man Winery 269 637-2229
7143 107th Ave South Haven (49090) ***(G-15408)***
Little Spoke Big Wheel Pubg 313 779-9327
20880 Duns Scotus St Southfield (48075) ***(G-15637)***

Littlite, Whitmore Lake *Also called A E C Inc* ***(G-18515)***
Liturgical Commission, Lansing *Also called Diocese of Lansing* ***(G-9831)***
Livbig LLC 888 519-8290
1821 Vanderbilt Ave Ste A Portage (49024) ***(G-13578)***
Live Edge Detroit 248 909-2259
241 Park Dr Troy (48083) ***(G-17213)***
Live Track Productions Inc 313 704-2224
848 Manistique St Detroit (48215) ***(G-4402)***
Liver Transplant/Univ of Mich 734 936-7670
1500 E Medical Center Dr Ann Arbor (48109) ***(G-552)***
Livermore Software Tech LLC 925 449-2500
1740 W Big Beavr Rd # 100 Troy (48084) ***(G-17214)***
Liveroof LLC 616 842-1392
14109 Cleveland St Nunica (49448) ***(G-12584)***
Livespace LLC 616 929-0191
4995 Starr St Se Grand Rapids (49546) ***(G-6947)***
Living Hope Books & More, Fenton *Also called Mott Media LLC* ***(G-5492)***
Living On Etch 810 229-7955
6132 Briggs Lake Dr Brighton (48116) ***(G-2021)***
Living Quarters 616 874-6160
14179 Meta Dr Coral (49322) ***(G-3700)***
Living Word International Inc 989 832-7547
2010 N Stark Rd Midland (48642) ***(G-11384)***
Livingston County Concrete Inc 810 632-3030
550 N Old Us Highway 23 Brighton (48114) ***(G-2022)***
Livingston Lakes Live Bait & T, Brighton *Also called My Tec-Tronics LLC* ***(G-2038)***
Livingston Machine Inc 517 546-4253
7445 Schrepfer Rd Howell (48855) ***(G-8472)***
Livingston Stairway 517 546-7132
2521 Bowen Rd Howell (48855) ***(G-8473)***
Livonia Automatic Incorporated 734 591-0321
12650 Newburgh Rd Livonia (48150) ***(G-10287)***
Livonia Magnetics Co Inc 734 397-8844
23801 Industrial Park Dr # 210 Farmington Hills (48335) ***(G-5293)***
Livonia Observer 734 525-4657
8928 Virginia St Livonia (48150) ***(G-10288)***
Livonia Trophy & Screen Prtg 734 464-9191
38065 Ann Arbor Rd Livonia (48150) ***(G-10289)***
Lj Disposal, Marne *Also called Log Jam Forest Products Inc* ***(G-10995)***
Lj/Hah Holdings Corporation (HQ) 248 340-4100
2750 High Meadow Cir Auburn Hills (48326) ***(G-958)***
Ljs Kitchens & Interiors Ltd 989 773-2132
1105 N Mission St Mount Pleasant (48858) ***(G-11708)***
LL Becker Publications 248 366-9037
11375 Brigham Ln White Lake (48386) ***(G-18460)***
LLC Ash Stevens (HQ) 734 282-3370
18655 Krause St Riverview (48193) ***(G-13879)***
LLC Helton Brothers 517 927-6941
30958 Industrial Rd Ste A Livonia (48150) ***(G-10290)***
LLC Stahl Cross 810 688-2505
110 N Saginaw St Lapeer (48446) ***(G-9943)***
Llink Technologies LLC 586 336-9370
3953 Burnsline Rd Brown City (48416) ***(G-2139)***
Llomen Inc 269 345-3555
5346 Ivanhoe Ct Portage (49002) ***(G-13579)***
Llowds Retail Construction, Clinton Township *Also called Construction Retail Svcs Inc* ***(G-3210)***
Lloyd Flanders Industries, Menominee *Also called Flanders Industries Inc* ***(G-11238)***
Lloyd Johnson Livestock Inc 906 786-4878
3697 18th Rd Escanaba (49829) ***(G-5081)***
Lloyd Miller & Sons Inc 517 223-3112
3695 E M 21 Corunna (48817) ***(G-3710)***
Lloyd Tool & Mfg Corp 810 694-3519
5505 Chatham Ln Grand Blanc (48439) ***(G-6251)***
Lloyd Waters & Associates (PA) 734 525-2777
33180 Industrial Rd Ste A Livonia (48150) ***(G-10291)***
Lloyds Cabinet Shop Inc 989 879-3015
1947 N Huron Rd Pinconning (48650) ***(G-13061)***
LMC, Wyoming *Also called Light Metals Corporation* ***(G-18891)***
LMI Technologies Inc 248 298-2839
29488 Woodward Ave # 331 Royal Oak (48073) ***(G-14557)***
Lmm Group Inc 269 276-9909
443 E D Ave Kalamazoo (49009) ***(G-9261)***
Lmp Worldwide Inc 248 669-6103
51135 Pontiac Trl Wixom (48393) ***(G-18700)***
LMS, Midland *Also called Aptargroup Inc* ***(G-11322)***
Lna Solutions Inc 734 677-2305
3924a Varsity Dr Ste A Ann Arbor (48108) ***(G-553)***
Loadmaster Corporation 906 563-9226
100 E 9th Ave Norway (49870) ***(G-12353)***
Lobo Signs Inc 231 941-7739
322 E Welch Ct Traverse City (49686) ***(G-16746)***
Loc Performance Products Inc 734 453-2300
33852 Sterling Ponds Blvd Sterling Heights (48312) ***(G-16076)***
Loc Performance Products LLC (PA) 734 453-2300
13505 N Haggerty Rd Plymouth (48170) ***(G-13224)***
Loc Performance Products LLC 734 453-2300
1600 N Larch St Lansing (48906) ***(G-9713)***

Loc Performance Products LLC 734 453-2300
290 Mccormick Dr Lapeer (48446) *(G-9944)*
Local Bsket Case LLC - Rckford 616 884-0749
65 Courtland St Rockford (49341) *(G-14175)*
Local Grind 269 623-5777
117 S Grove St Delton (49046) *(G-3965)*
Local Logic Media 517 914-2486
123 Marietta Rd Spring Arbor (49283) *(G-15794)*
Local Media Group Inc 313 885-2612
9 Alger Pl Detroit (48230) *(G-4403)*
Lochinvar LLC 734 454-4480
45900 Port St Plymouth (48170) *(G-13225)*
Lock and Load Corp 800 975-9658
3390 16 Mile Rd Marion (49665) *(G-10973)*
Lockett Enterprises LLC 810 407-6644
607 E 2nd Ave Ste 30 Flint (48502) *(G-5725)*
Locpac Inc 734 453-2300
13505 N Haggerty Rd Plymouth (48170) *(G-13226)*
Lodal Inc 906 779-1700
620 N Hooper St Kingsford (49802) *(G-9513)*
Loduca Woodworks LLC 734 626-2525
37151 Willow Ln Clinton Township (48036) *(G-3280)*
Loftis Alumi-TEC Inc 616 846-1990
13888 172nd Ave Grand Haven (49417) *(G-6330)*
Loftis Machine Company 616 846-1990
13888 172nd Ave Grand Haven (49417) *(G-6331)*
Loftis Manufacturing Inc 855 564-8665
30103 Commerce Blvd Chesterfield (48051) *(G-2905)*
Log Cabin Lumber, Riverdale *Also called Daniel D Slater (G-13863)*
Log Home Specialty 231 943-9410
903 Hammond Pl S Traverse City (49686) *(G-16747)*
Log Jam Forest Products Inc 616 677-2560
15342 24th Ave Marne (49435) *(G-10995)*
Logan Brothers Printing Inc 517 485-3771
13544 Blackwood Dr Dewitt (48820) *(G-4711)*
Logan Diesel Incorporated 517 589-8811
4567 Churchill Rd Leslie (49251) *(G-10014)*
Logan Tool and Engineering 586 755-3555
23919 Blackstone Ave Warren (48089) *(G-17905)*
Loggers Brewing Co 989 401-3085
1215 S River Rd Saginaw (48609) *(G-14684)*
Logging-In Com Inc 248 466-0708
32770 Grand River Ave # 2 Farmington Hills (48336) *(G-5294)*
Logging-Incom LLC 248 662-7864
37085 Grand River Ave # 3 Farmington Hills (48335) *(G-5295)*
Logic Quantum LLC 734 930-0009
2929 Plymouth Rd Ste 207 Ann Arbor (48105) *(G-554)*
Logical Digital Audio Video 734 572-0022
4602 Central Blvd Ann Arbor (48108) *(G-555)*
Logistics Insight Corp 810 424-0511
3311 Torrey Rd Flint (48507) *(G-5726)*
Logistics On The Go Inc 248 750-6654
142 N Lafayette Blvd Warren (48091) *(G-17906)*
Logofit LLC 810 715-1980
3202 Lapeer Rd Flint (48503) *(G-5727)*
Logos and Letters 248 795-2093
6525 Dixie Hwy Clarkston (48346) *(G-3045)*
Logospot 616 785-7170
8200 Graphic Dr Ne Belmont (49306) *(G-1512)*
Lol, Commerce Township *Also called Liquid Otc LLC (G-3551)*
Lomar Machine & Tool Co 517 563-8136
5931 Coats Rd Horton (49246) *(G-8373)*
Lomar Machine & Tool Co 517 750-4089
7755 King Rd Spring Arbor (49283) *(G-15795)*
Lomar Machine & Tool Co (PA) 517 563-8136
135 Main St Horton (49246) *(G-8374)*
Lomar Machine & Tool Co 517 563-8136
7595 Moscow Rd Horton (49246) *(G-8375)*
Lomar Machine & Tool Co 517 563-8800
7595 Moscow Rd Horton (49246) *(G-8376)*
Lone Wolf Archery, Glennie *Also called Lone Wolf Custom Bows (G-6213)*
Lone Wolf Custom Bows 989 735-3358
3893 Gray St Glennie (48737) *(G-6213)*
Lonero Engineering Co Inc 248 689-9120
2050 Stephenson Hwy Troy (48083) *(G-17215)*
Loneys Alpaca Junction 231 229-4530
3109 N 7 Mile Rd Lake City (49651) *(G-9549)*
Loneys Welding & Excvtg Inc 231 328-4408
6735 E Houghton Lake Rd Merritt (49667) *(G-11267)*
Long Manufacturing, Saint Clair *Also called Dana Thermal Products LLC (G-14824)*
Long Road Distillers LLC 616 356-1770
537 Leonard St Nw Ste A Grand Rapids (49504) *(G-6948)*
Longshot Golf Inc 586 764-9847
60750 Stonecrest Dr Washington (48094) *(G-18083)*
Longson International Corp 734 657-8719
3336 Woodhill Cir Superior Township (48198) *(G-16337)*
Longstreet Group LLC 517 278-4487
720 E Chicago Rd Coldwater (49036) *(G-3443)*
LONGSTREET LIVING, Coldwater *Also called Longstreet Group LLC (G-3443)*

Looking Aft Publications 231 759-8581
409 Mill Pond Rd Whitehall (49461) *(G-18507)*
Lookingbus, Saline *Also called Svn Inc (G-15042)*
Looksharp Marketing, Paw Paw *Also called Sporting Image Inc (G-12956)*
Loonar Stn Two The 2 or 2nd 419 720-1222
6656 Lewis Ave Ste 5 Temperance (48182) *(G-16537)*
Looney Baker of Livonia Inc 734 425-8569
13931 Farmington Rd Livonia (48154) *(G-10292)*
Loope Enterprises Inc 269 639-1567
73475 8th Ave South Haven (49090) *(G-15409)*
Loose Plastics Inc 989 246-1880
1016 E 1st St Gladwin (48624) *(G-6200)*
Lopez Reproductions Inc 313 386-4526
645 Griswold St Ste 27 Detroit (48226) *(G-4404)*
Lor Manufacturing Co Inc 989 644-2581
7131 W Drew Rd Weidman (48893) *(G-18254)*
Lor Products Inc 989 382-9020
2962 16 Mile Rd Remus (49340) *(G-13816)*
Lorann Oils Inc 517 882-0215
4518 Aurelius Rd Lansing (48910) *(G-9865)*
Lorbec Metals - Usa Ltd 810 736-0961
3415 Western Rd Flint (48506) *(G-5728)*
Lorenzo White 313 943-3667
20029 Cooley St Detroit (48219) *(G-4405)*
Lorin Industries Inc (PA) 231 722-1631
1960 Roberts St Muskegon (49442) *(G-11861)*
Lorna Icr LLC 586 582-1500
28601 Lorna Ave Warren (48092) *(G-17907)*
Lorne Hanley 248 547-9865
10085 Lincoln Dr Huntington Woods (48070) *(G-8622)*
Los Cuarto Amigos 989 984-0200
1626 E Us 23 East Tawas (48730) *(G-4918)*
Loshaw Bros Inc 989 732-7263
231 Meecher Rd Gaylord (49735) *(G-6143)*
Lost Cellars Inc 734 626-0969
745 High Pines Trl Boyne City (49712) *(G-1895)*
Lotis Technologies Inc 248 340-6065
100 Engelwood Dr Ste F Orion (48359) *(G-12733)*
Lotte U S A, Battle Creek *Also called Lotte USA Incorporated (G-1269)*
Lotte USA Incorporated 269 963-6664
5243 Wayne Rd Battle Creek (49037) *(G-1269)*
Lottery Info 734 326-0097
8432 Hannan Rd Wayne (48184) *(G-18230)*
Lotus Corporation 616 494-0112
100 Aniline Ave N Ste 180 Holland (49424) *(G-8130)*
Lotus International Company 734 245-0140
6880 Commerce Blvd Canton (48187) *(G-2486)*
Lotus Technologies LLC 313 550-1889
1420 Washington Blvd # 301 Detroit (48226) *(G-4406)*
Lou Jack City Publishing LLC 404 863-7124
1603 Lawrence St Detroit (48206) *(G-4407)*
Louca Mold & Arospc Machining, Auburn Hills *Also called Louca Mold Arspc Machining Inc (G-959)*
Louca Mold Arspc Machining Inc (PA) 248 391-1616
1925 Taylor Rd Auburn Hills (48326) *(G-959)*
Loud N Clear Extracts LLC 312 320-4970
18201 Cleveland Ave Galien (49113) *(G-6090)*
Loudon Steel Inc 989 871-9353
8208 Ellis Rd Millington (48746) *(G-11502)*
Louies Meats Inc 231 946-4811
2040 Cass Rd Traverse City (49684) *(G-16748)*
Louis J Wickings 989 823-8765
4740 Waltan Rd Vassar (48768) *(G-17580)*
Louis Padnos Iron and Metal Co 517 372-6600
1900 W Willow St Lansing (48917) *(G-9773)*
Louisiana-Pacific Corporation 906 293-3265
7299 N County Road 403 Newberry (49868) *(G-12092)*
Love Machinery Inc 734 427-0824
36232 Lawrence Dr Livonia (48150) *(G-10293)*
Love Publicity 313 288-8342
277 Gratiot Ave Ste 600 Detroit (48226) *(G-4408)*
Loven Spoonful 517 522-3953
119 E Main St Grass Lake (49240) *(G-7440)*
Low Cost Surcing Solutions LLC 248 535-7721
57253 Willow Way Ct Washington (48094) *(G-18084)*
Low Impact Logging Inc 906 250-5117
3172 Us Highway 2 Iron River (49935) *(G-8748)*
Low Mar, Horton *Also called Lomar Machine & Tool Co (G-8376)*
Lowell Engineering, Alto *Also called Magna Mirrors North Amer LLC (G-336)*
Lowell Litho, Lowell *Also called Buyers Guide (G-10497)*
Lowery Corporation (PA) 616 554-5200
5555 Glnwood Hlls Pkwy Se Grand Rapids (49512) *(G-6949)*
Lowing Products LLC 616 530-7440
1500 Whiting St Sw Wyoming (49509) *(G-18892)*
Lowry Joanellen 231 873-2323
7833 Lincoln St Hesperia (49421) *(G-7870)*
Lowry Holding Company Inc (PA) 810 229-7200
9420 Maltby Rd Brighton (48116) *(G-2023)*
Lowry Solutions, Brighton *Also called Lowry Holding Company Inc (G-2023)*

Loyalty 1977 Ink 313 759-1006
18528 Margareta St Detroit (48219) **(G-4409)**
LP Industries Ltd 313 834-4847
15366 Coyle St Detroit (48227) **(G-4410)**
LP Products (PA) 989 465-0287
6680 M 18 Coleman (48618) **(G-3468)**
Lps-2 Inc 313 538-0181
24755 5 Mile Rd Ste 100 Redford (48239) **(G-13742)**
Lrs Inc 734 416-5050
9448 Northern Ave Plymouth (48170) **(G-13227)**
Ls Precision Tool & Die Inc 269 963-9910
140 Jacaranda Dr Battle Creek (49015) **(G-1270)**
Lsd Investments Inc 248 333-9085
2350 Franklin Rd Ste 115 Bloomfield Hills (48302) **(G-1832)**
LSI, Fraser *Also called Laser Specialists Inc* **(G-5956)**
Lsjd Publications LLC 843 576-9040
324 E Spruce St Sault Sainte Marie (49783) **(G-15094)**
LSm Systems Engineering Inc 248 674-4967
4670 Hatchery Rd Waterford (48329) **(G-18135)**
Lspedia LLC 248 320-1909
6230 Orchard Lake Rd # 280 West Bloomfield (48322) **(G-18294)**
Lsr Incorporated 734 455-6530
11050 N Beck Rd Plymouth (48170) **(G-13228)**
Lst Lighting, Shelby Township *Also called Lumasmart Technology Intl Inc* **(G-15265)**
Lt Global, Grand Rapids *Also called Lub-Tech Inc* **(G-6950)**
Ltc, Milan *Also called Liberty Turned Components LLC* **(G-11441)**
Ltek Industries Inc 734 747-6105
2298 S Industrial Hwy Ann Arbor (48104) **(G-556)**
Lub-Tech Inc 616 299-3540
470 Market Ave Sw Unit 13 Grand Rapids (49503) **(G-6950)**
Lube - Power Inc 586 247-6500
50146 Utica Dr Shelby Township (48315) **(G-15264)**
Lube-Tech Inc 269 329-1269
3960 Arbutus Trl Portage (49024) **(G-13580)**
Lubecon Systems Inc 231 689-0002
201 N Webster St White Cloud (49349) **(G-18445)**
Luberda Wood Products Inc 989 876-4334
1188 E Huron Rd Omer (48749) **(G-12696)**
Lubetronics, White Cloud *Also called Lubecon Systems Inc* **(G-18445)**
Lubo Inc 248 632-1185
32250 Howard Ave Madison Heights (48071) **(G-10771)**
Lubo Usa Inc 810 244-5826
32250 Howard Ave Madison Heights (48071) **(G-10772)**
Lubrizol Corporation 989 496-3780
2300 James Savage Rd Midland (48642) **(G-11385)**
Lucas Logging 906 246-3629
W1564 State Highway M69 Bark River (49807) **(G-1155)**
Lucasvarity Inc 517 223-8330
500 E Van Riper Rd Fowlerville (48836) **(G-5849)**
Lucerne Forging Inc 248 674-7210
40 Corporate Dr Auburn Hills (48326) **(G-960)**
Lucido, F J & Associates, Warren *Also called F J Lucido & Associates* **(G-17801)**
Luckmarr Plastics Inc 586 978-8498
35735 Stanley Dr Sterling Heights (48312) **(G-16077)**
Lucky Bird Candle Co 734 272-7338
139 Van Buren St Chelsea (48118) **(G-2819)**
Lucky Girl Brwing - Cross Rads 630 723-4285
34016 M 43 Paw Paw (49079) **(G-12951)**
Lucky Press LLC 614 309-0048
4929 Turfway Trl Harbor Springs (49740) **(G-7650)**
Ludhaven Sugarvush 906 647-2400
8726 E Sawmill Point Rd Barbeau (49710) **(G-1152)**
Ludington Concrete Products, Ludington *Also called Hobe Inc* **(G-10539)**
Ludington Daily News Inc 231 845-5181
202 N Rath Ave Ludington (49431) **(G-10543)**
Ludvanwall Inc 616 842-4500
19156 174th Ave Spring Lake (49456) **(G-15830)**
Ludwick's Sour Cream Donuts, Grand Rapids *Also called Ludwicks Frozen Donuts Inc* **(G-6951)**
Ludwicks Frozen Donuts Inc 616 453-6880
3217 3 Mile Rd Nw Grand Rapids (49534) **(G-6951)**
Luebke & Vogt Corporation 248 449-3232
25903 Meadowbrook Rd Novi (48375) **(G-12466)**
Luhu LLC 320 469-3162
540 Glenmoor Rd East Lansing (48823) **(G-4901)**
Luke Legacy Publications LLC 313 363-5949
1098 Ann Arbor Rd W Plymouth (48170) **(G-13229)**
Lululemon USA Inc 586 690-6001
17360 Hall Rd Ste 183 Clinton Township (48038) **(G-3281)**
Luma Laser and Medi Spa 248 817-5499
1920 S Telegraph Rd Bloomfield Hills (48302) **(G-1833)**
Lumasmart Technology Intl Inc 586 232-4125
51560 Celeste Shelby Township (48315) **(G-15265)**
Lumbee Custom Painting LLC 586 296-5083
31725 Fraser Dr Fraser (48026) **(G-5958)**
Lumber & Truss Inc 810 664-7290
162 S Saginaw St Lapeer (48446) **(G-9945)**
Lumber Jack Hardwoods Inc (PA) 906 863-7090
N2509 O1 Dr Menominee (49858) **(G-11243)**
Lumberjack Logging LLC 616 799-4657
4778 Whitefish Woods Dr Pierson (49339) **(G-13033)**
Lumberjack Shack Inc 810 724-7230
7230 Webster Rd Imlay City (48444) **(G-8640)**
Lumbertown, Holt *Also called Pageant Homes Inc* **(G-8324)**
Lumbertown Portable Sawmill 231 206-4600
1650 Madison St Muskegon (49442) **(G-11862)**
Lumco Manufacturing Company 810 724-0582
2027 Mitchell Lake Rd Lum (48412) **(G-10559)**
Lumecon LLC 248 505-1090
23107 Commerce Dr Farmington Hills (48335) **(G-5296)**
Lumen North America Inc 248 289-6100
2850 Commerce Dr Rochester Hills (48309) **(G-14054)**
Lumenflow Corp 269 795-9007
15346 Leonard Rd Spring Lake (49456) **(G-15831)**
Lumerica Corporation 248 543-8085
21400 Hoover Rd Warren (48089) **(G-17908)**
Lumichron Inc 616 245-8888
2215 29th St Se Ste B4 Grand Rapids (49508) **(G-6952)**
Lumileds LLC 248 553-9080
34119 W 12 Mile Rd Ste 10 Farmington Hills (48331) **(G-5297)**
Lummi Customs Lc 702 713-8428
707 Cherry St Linden (48451) **(G-10064)**
Luna Optoeletronics 734 864-5611
2925 Boardwalk St Ann Arbor (48104) **(G-557)**
Lunar Industries, Clinton Township *Also called Roth-Williams Industries Inc* **(G-3342)**
Lupa R A and Sons Repair 810 346-3579
3580 Willis Rd Marlette (48453) **(G-10983)**
Lupaul Industries Inc (PA) 517 783-3223
310 E Steel St Saint Johns (48879) **(G-14904)**
Lusciously Silked LLC 313 878-7058
1550 Cherboneau Pl # 204 Detroit (48207) **(G-4411)**
Lush 586 228-1594
17370 Hall Rd Clinton Township (48038) **(G-3282)**
Lutco Inc 231 972-5566
8800 Midstate Dr Mecosta (49332) **(G-11191)**
Lutke Forest Products, Manton *Also called Jason Lutke* **(G-10934)**
Lutke Hydraulics 231 824-9505
606 R W Harris Dr Manton (49663) **(G-10935)**
Lutke Welding LLC 231 590-6565
7419 N 45 Rd Manton (49663) **(G-10936)**
Luttmann Precision Mold Inc 269 651-1193
1200 W Lafayette St Sturgis (49091) **(G-16303)**
Luxottica of America Inc 517 349-0784
1982 W Grand River Ave # 815 Okemos (48864) **(G-12673)**
Luxottica of America Inc 989 624-8958
8825 Market Place Dr # 340 Birch Run (48415) **(G-1710)**
Luxury Bath Systems 586 264-2561
31239 Mound Rd Warren (48092) **(G-17909)**
Luxury Richland LLc 269 222-7979
1444 Michigan St Ne Ste 5 Grand Rapids (49503) **(G-6953)**
Lv Metals Inc 734 654-8081
2094 Ready Rd Carleton (48117) **(G-2559)**
Lvc Technologies Inc 248 373-3778
2200 S State Rd Davison (48423) **(G-3789)**
Lwhs Ltd 616 452-5300
1001 40th St Se Grand Rapids (49508) **(G-6954)**
Lws - Design Center Detroit, Troy *Also called Leoni Wiring Systems Inc* **(G-17208)**
Lxr Biotech LLC 248 860-4246
2983 Waterview Dr Rochester Hills (48309) **(G-14055)**
Lxr Biotech LLC (PA) 248 860-4246
4225 N Atlantic Blvd Auburn Hills (48326) **(G-961)**
Lydall Performance Mtls US Inc 248 596-2800
22260 Haggerty Rd Ste 200 Northville (48167) **(G-12236)**
Lydall Sealing Solutions Inc 248 596-2800
22260 Haggerty Rd Ste 200 Northville (48167) **(G-12237)**
Lyle Industries 989 435-7717
4144 Lyle Rd Beaverton (48612) **(G-1429)**
Lyle Jamieson Wood Turning 231 947-2348
285 Lauri Wil Ln Traverse City (49696) **(G-16749)**
Lymtal International Inc (PA) 248 373-8100
4150 S Lapeer Rd Orion (48359) **(G-12734)**
Lyncs Metal Fabrication 616 813-2071
12490 64th St Se Alto (49302) **(G-335)**
Lyndon Fabricators Inc 313 937-3640
12478 Beech Daly Rd Detroit (48239) **(G-4412)**
Lynn Shaler Fine Prints LLC 248 644-5148
4621 Kensington Rd Bloomfield Hills (48304) **(G-1834)**
Lyon Hide Leather Goods LLC 517 997-6067
106 W Lovett St Charlotte (48813) **(G-2761)**
Lyon Manufacturing Inc 734 359-3000
7121 N Haggerty Rd Canton (48187) **(G-2487)**
Lyon Sand & Gravel Co (PA) 313 843-7200
9300 Dix Dearborn (48120) **(G-3864)**
Lyon Sand & Gravel Co 248 348-8511
51455 W 12 Mile Rd Wixom (48393) **(G-18701)**
Lyonnais Inc 616 868-6625
3760 Snow Ave Se Lowell (49331) **(G-10510)**
Lyons Graphics and Tees 586 770-9630
59860 Cynthia Dr New Haven (48048) **(G-12034)**

Lyons Industries Inc (PA)....269 782-3404
30000 M 62 W Dowagiac (49047) *(G-4787)*
Lyons Tool & Engineering Inc....586 200-3003
13720 E 9 Mile Rd Warren (48089) *(G-17910)*
Lyons Tool and Mfg Corp....248 344-9644
47840 Anna Ct Wixom (48393) *(G-18702)*
Lyte Poles Incorporated....586 771-4610
24874 Groesbeck Hwy Warren (48089) *(G-17911)*
Lzb Manufacturing Inc (HQ)....734 242-1444
1 Lazboy Dr Monroe (48162) *(G-11559)*
M & A Machining Inc....269 342-0026
1523 N Burdick St Kalamazoo (49007) *(G-9262)*
M & B Welding Inc....989 635-8017
6411 Euclid St Marlette (48453) *(G-10984)*
M & E Plastics LLC....989 875-4191
205 Industrial Pkwy Ithaca (48847) *(G-8792)*
M & F Machine & Tool Inc....734 847-0571
6555 S Dixie Hwy Erie (48133) *(G-5050)*
M & J Entp Grnd Rapids LLC....616 485-9775
5304 Alpine Ave Nw Comstock Park (49321) *(G-3620)*
M & J Forest Products, Wolverine *Also called Jaroche Brothers Inc (G-18795)*
M & J Graphics Enterprises Inc....734 542-8800
36060 Industrial Rd Livonia (48150) *(G-10294)*
M & J Manufacturing Inc....586 778-6322
22711 Morelli Dr Clinton Township (48036) *(G-3283)*
M & K Cabinets LLC....313 744-2755
20424 Ann Arbor Trl Dearborn Heights (48127) *(G-3931)*
M & M Automatic Products Inc....517 782-0577
420 Ingham St Jackson (49201) *(G-8937)*
M & M Irish Enterprises Inc....248 644-0666
34164 Woodward Ave Birmingham (48009) *(G-1733)*
M & M Machining Inc....586 997-9910
42876 Mound Rd Sterling Heights (48314) *(G-16078)*
M & M Services Inc....248 619-9861
1844 Woodslee Dr Troy (48083) *(G-17216)*
M & M Thread & Assembly Inc....248 583-9696
42716 Mound Rd Sterling Heights (48314) *(G-16079)*
M & M Turning Co....586 791-7188
19000 15 Mile Rd Clinton Township (48035) *(G-3284)*
M & M Typewriter Service Inc....734 995-4033
251 Collingwood St Ann Arbor (48103) *(G-558)*
M & N Controls Inc....734 850-2127
7180 Sulier Dr Temperance (48182) *(G-16538)*
M & R Machine Company....313 277-1570
5900 N Telegraph Rd Dearborn Heights (48127) *(G-3932)*
M & R Printing Inc....248 543-8080
26430 W 7 Mile Rd Redford (48240) *(G-13743)*
M & S Extrusions, Imlay City *Also called Vintech Industries Inc (G-8650)*
M & W Manufacturing Co LLC....586 741-8897
46409 Continental Dr Chesterfield (48047) *(G-2906)*
M & W Tubing, Chesterfield *Also called M & W Manufacturing Co LLC (G-2906)*
M 37 Concrete Products Inc (PA)....231 733-8247
767 E Sherman Blvd Muskegon (49444) *(G-11863)*
M 37 Concrete Products Inc....231 689-1785
1231 E 16th St M White Cloud (49349) *(G-18446)*
M A C, Wixom *Also called Mac Valves Inc (G-18705)*
M A S Information Age Tech....248 352-0162
23132 Lake Ravines Dr Southfield (48033) *(G-15638)*
M and A Castings Ltd....517 879-2222
3603 N Huron Rd Pinconning (48650) *(G-13062)*
M and A Fuels....313 397-7141
13601 Plymouth Rd Detroit (48227) *(G-4413)*
M and G Laminated Products....517 784-4974
507 W Michigan Ave Jackson (49201) *(G-8938)*
M and L Fabrication LLC....616 259-7754
3408 Busch Dr Sw Ste D Grandville (49418) *(G-7399)*
M Antonik....248 236-0333
690 Golf Villa Dr Oxford (48371) *(G-12897)*
M B A Printing, Comstock Park *Also called MBA Printing Inc (G-3623)*
M B Jewelry Design & Mfg, Bloomfield *Also called Bednarsh Mrris Jwly Design Mfg (G-1781)*
M Beard Solutions LLC....734 441-0660
3200 Greenfield Rd # 300 Dearborn (48120) *(G-3865)*
M Beshara Inc....248 542-9220
10020 Capital St Oak Park (48237) *(G-12623)*
M C, Grand Rapids *Also called Metal Components LLC (G-6978)*
M C Carbide Tool Co....248 486-9590
28565 Automation Blvd Wixom (48393) *(G-18703)*
M C M Fixture Company Inc....248 547-9280
21306 John R Rd Hazel Park (48030) *(G-7830)*
M C M Stainless Fabricating, Hazel Park *Also called M C M Fixture Company Inc (G-7830)*
M C Molds Inc....517 655-5481
125 Industrial Park Dr Williamston (48895) *(G-18576)*
M C Ward Inc....810 982-9720
4100 Griswold Rd Port Huron (48060) *(G-13497)*
M Curry Corporation....989 777-7950
4475 Marlea Dr Saginaw (48601) *(G-14685)*
M D Hubbard Spring Co Inc....248 628-2528
595 S Lapeer Rd Oxford (48371) *(G-12898)*
M D I, Edwardsburg *Also called Mercury Displacement Inds Inc (G-5009)*
M Forche Farms Inc....517 447-3488
1080 S Piotter Hwy Blissfield (49228) *(G-1768)*
M Industries LLC....616 745-4279
6060 Sagebrook Dr Ne Ada (49301) *(G-27)*
M J Day Machine Tool Company....313 730-1200
19231 Van Born Rd Allen Park (48101) *(G-199)*
M J Diamonds, Dearborn *Also called Michels Inc (G-3872)*
M J Mechanical Inc....989 865-9633
11787 Prior Rd Saint Charles (48655) *(G-14804)*
M K Eaton Services LLC....608 852-3118
11036 Woodland Ridge Ct South Lyon (48178) *(G-15444)*
M M Custom Canvas Shrink....734 658-0497
5402 Reuter St Dearborn (48126) *(G-3866)*
M M R LLC....734 502-5239
31831 Schoolcraft Rd Livonia (48150) *(G-10295)*
M P D, Auburn Hills *Also called Multi-Precision Detail Inc (G-978)*
M P D Welding Inc (PA)....248 340-0330
4200 S Lapeer Rd Orion (48359) *(G-12735)*
M P I Coating, Riverview *Also called Materials Processing Inc (G-13880)*
M P I International Inc (PA)....608 764-5416
2129 Austin Ave Rochester Hills (48309) *(G-14056)*
M P Jackson LLC....517 782-0391
1824 River St Jackson (49202) *(G-8939)*
M P Pumps Inc....586 293-8240
34800 Bennett Fraser (48026) *(G-5959)*
M Print....248 550-4405
33707 Pondview Cir Livonia (48152) *(G-10296)*
M Print Dance Company....616 575-9969
3782 29th St Se Kentwood (49512) *(G-9464)*
M R A, Litchfield *Also called Michigan Rebuild & Automtn Inc (G-10083)*
M S Machining Systems Inc (PA)....517 546-1170
5833 Fisher Rd Howell (48855) *(G-8474)*
M S Manufacturing Inc....586 463-2788
44431 Reynolds Dr Clinton Township (48036) *(G-3285)*
M T E, Flint *Also called Monroe Truck Equipment Inc (G-5736)*
M T S, Plymouth *Also called Miller Technical Services Inc (G-13243)*
M T S Chenault LLC....269 861-0053
665 Pipestone St Benton Harbor (49022) *(G-1566)*
M Three Manufacturing LLC....810 824-4734
71 Ash Dr Kimball (48074) *(G-9495)*
M&D Dumpsters LLC....616 299-0234
6117 Polk St Hudsonville (49426) *(G-8591)*
M&I Machine Inc....269 849-3624
5040 M 63 N Coloma (49038) *(G-3477)*
M&M Polishing Inc....269 468-4407
320 Park St Coloma (49038) *(G-3478)*
M-22 Challenge....231 392-2212
121 E Front St Ste 104 Traverse City (49684) *(G-16750)*
M-36 Coffee Roasters LLC....734 449-8910
10815 Plaza Dr Whitmore Lake (48189) *(G-18539)*
M-52 Sand & Gravel LLC....734 453-3695
8483 Ann Arbor Rd W Plymouth (48170) *(G-13230)*
M-57 Aggregate Company....810 639-7516
170 W State St Montrose (48457) *(G-11605)*
M-A Metals Inc....989 268-5080
7470 N Crystal Rd Vestaburg (48891) *(G-17594)*
M-B-M Manufacturing Inc....231 924-9614
9576 W 40th St Fremont (49412) *(G-6047)*
M-Industries LLC....616 682-4642
6352 Fulton St E Ada (49301) *(G-28)*
M-R Products Inc (PA)....231 378-2251
16612 Russo Dr Copemish (49625) *(G-3698)*
M-Seal Products Co LLC....313 884-6147
55 Fairford Rd Grosse Pointe Shores (48236) *(G-7563)*
M-Tek Inc....248 553-1581
29065 Cabot Dr 300 Novi (48377) *(G-12467)*
M.M.F.T., Roseville *Also called Mercury Metal Forming Tech LLC (G-14440)*
M.R. Village Pizzeria, Middleton *Also called Shady Nook Farms (G-11300)*
M1 Plant, Grand Rapids *Also called Roskam Baking Company (G-7167)*
M10 Group Holding Company (PA)....248 356-4399
24050 Northwestern Hwy Southfield (48075) *(G-15639)*
M2 Plant, Grand Rapids *Also called Roskam Baking Company (G-7168)*
M2 Scientifics LLC....616 379-9080
4850 Allen Park Dr Ste 2 Allendale (49401) *(G-224)*
M4 CIC LLC....734 436-8507
719 W Ellsworth Rd Ste 1a Ann Arbor (48108) *(G-559)*
MA MA La Rosa Foods Inc....734 946-7878
12100 Universal Dr Taylor (48180) *(G-16437)*
Mabco, Madison Heights *Also called Michigan Auto Bending Corp (G-10781)*
Mac Enterprises Inc (PA)....313 846-4567
11940 Hieber Rd Manchester (48158) *(G-10885)*
Mac Lean Fasteners, Royal Oak *Also called Mac Lean-Fogg Company (G-14558)*
Mac Lean-Fogg Company....248 280-0880
3200 W 14 Mile Rd Royal Oak (48073) *(G-14558)*
Mac Material Acquisition Co....248 685-8393
1197 Craven Dr Highland (48356) *(G-7895)*
Mac Valve Asia Inc (HQ)....248 624-7700
30569 Beck Rd Wixom (48393) *(G-18704)*

ALPHABETIC

Mac Valves Inc (PA) 248 624-7700
30569 Beck Rd Wixom (48393) *(G-18705)*

Mac Valves Inc 734 529-5099
5555 N Ann Arbor Rd Dundee (48131) *(G-4830)*

Mac-Mold Base Inc 586 752-1956
14921 32 Mile Rd Bruce Twp (48065) *(G-2176)*

Mac-Tech Tooling Corporation 248 743-1400
1874 Larchwood Dr Troy (48083) *(G-17217)*

Macarthur Corp (PA) 810 606-1777
3190 Tri Park Dr Grand Blanc (48439) *(G-6252)*

Macarthur Corp 810 744-1380
3202 Lapeer Rd Flint (48503) *(G-5729)*

Macatawa Bay Boat Works, Saugatuck Also called N D R Enterprises Inc *(G-15084)*

Macauto Usa Inc 248 556-5256
2654 Elliott Dr Troy (48083) *(G-17218)*

Macb Woodworking LLC 734 645-8990
3036 Dhu Varren Ct Ann Arbor (48105) *(G-560)*

Macdermid Incorporated 248 399-3553
1221 Farrow St Ferndale (48220) *(G-5566)*

Macdermid Incorporated 248 437-8161
29111 Milford Rd New Hudson (48165) *(G-12060)*

Macdermid Ferndale Facility, Ferndale Also called Macdermid Incorporated *(G-5566)*

Macdonald Publications Inc 989 875-4151
123 N Main St Ithaca (48847) *(G-8793)*

Mach II Enterprises Inc 248 347-8822
200 S Main St Ste A Northville (48167) *(G-12238)*

Mach II Tax Service, Northville Also called Mach II Enterprises Inc *(G-12238)*

Machine Center, The, Albion Also called Caster Concepts Inc *(G-121)*

Machine Control Technology 517 655-3506
4033 Vanneter Rd Williamston (48895) *(G-18577)*

Machine Division, Romulus Also called United Brass Manufacturers Inc *(G-14335)*

Machine Guard & Cover Co 616 392-8188
6187 136th Ave Holland (49424) *(G-8131)*

Machine Shop, Whitmore Lake Also called Michigan Cnc Tool Inc *(G-18541)*

Machine Shop, Holland Also called Impres Engineering Svcs LLC *(G-8094)*

Machine Shop Beer Company LLC 810 577-4202
14194 Landings Way Fenton (48430) *(G-5490)*

Machine Shop Services LLC 616 396-4898
4211 Hallacy Dr Holland (49424) *(G-8132)*

Machine Star LLC 616 245-6400
4674 Clay Ave Sw Ste D Grand Rapids (49548) *(G-6955)*

Machine Tool & Gear Inc 989 723-5486
401 S Chestnut St Owosso (48867) *(G-12839)*

Machine Tool & Gear Inc 989 761-7521
9900 Main St Clifford (48727) *(G-3132)*

Machine Tool & Gear Inc (HQ) 989 743-3936
1021 N Shiawassee St Corunna (48817) *(G-3711)*

Machined Solutions 517 759-4075
360 Mulzer Ave Adrian (49221) *(G-80)*

Machinery Prts Specialists LLC 989 662-7810
4533d Garfield Rd Auburn (48611) *(G-769)*

Machining & Fabricating Inc 586 773-9288
30546 Groesbeck Hwy Roseville (48066) *(G-14434)*

Machining Speci 248 589-4070
1619 Donna Ave Madison Heights (48071) *(G-10773)*

Machining Specialists Inc Mich 517 881-2863
2712 N Saginaw St Ofc Flint (48505) *(G-5730)*

Machining Specialties, Madison Heights Also called Central Gear Inc *(G-10685)*

Machining Technologies LLC 248 379-4201
9635 Davisburg Rd Clarkston (48348) *(G-3046)*

Maci, Parma Also called Michigan Auto Comprsr Inc *(G-12938)*

Mack Andrew & Son Brush Co 517 849-9272
216 E Chicago St Jonesville (49250) *(G-9092)*

Mack Industries Michigan Inc 248 620-7400
8265 White Lake Rd White Lake (48386) *(G-18461)*

Mack Oil Corporation 231 590-5903
7721 Outer Dr S Traverse City (49685) *(G-16751)*

Mack's Ear Plugs, Warren Also called McKeon Products Inc *(G-17922)*

Mackellar Screenworks, Dimondale Also called Trikala Inc *(G-4765)*

Mackenzie Company 231 335-1997
1600 Clay St Detroit (48211) *(G-4414)*

Mackenzies Bakery (PA) 269 343-8440
1319 Grand Ave Kalamazoo (49006) *(G-9263)*

Maclean Master LLC 734 414-0500
12271 Globe St Livonia (48150) *(G-10297)*

Maclean Royal Oak LLC 248 840-0880
23400 Haggerty Rd Farmington Hills (48335) *(G-5298)*

Macmichigan Inc 248 613-6372
43422 W Oaks Dr Novi (48377) *(G-12468)*

Maco Tool & Engineering Inc 989 224-6723
210 Spring St Saint Johns (48879) *(G-14905)*

Macom Technology Solutions Inc 734 864-5664
2925 Boardwalk St Ann Arbor (48104) *(G-561)*

Macomb 4x4 LLC 586 744-0335
28145 Kehrig St Chesterfield (48047) *(G-2907)*

Macomb Business Forms Inc 586 790-8500
34895 Groesbeck Hwy Clinton Township (48035) *(G-3286)*

Macomb County Cougars 586 231-5543
21673 Laurel St Clinton Township (48035) *(G-3287)*

Macomb Daily, Sterling Heights Also called 21st Century Newspapers Inc *(G-15915)*

Macomb Marketing Media, Clinton Township Also called Macomb Printing Inc *(G-3288)*

Macomb North Clinton Advisor 586 731-1000
48075 Van Dyke Ave Shelby Township (48317) *(G-15266)*

Macomb Printing Inc 586 463-2301
44272 N Groesbeck Hwy Clinton Township (48036) *(G-3288)*

Macomb Products LLC 586 855-0223
20103 Ballantrae Dr Macomb (48044) *(G-10610)*

Macomb Residential Opprtnts 586 231-0363
15780 17 Mile Rd Clinton Township (48038) *(G-3289)*

Macomb Sheet Metal Inc 586 790-4600
35195 Forton Ct Clinton Township (48035) *(G-3290)*

Macomb Signs & Graphics 586 350-9789
46566 Erb Dr Macomb (48042) *(G-10611)*

Macomb Smoked Meats LLC 313 842-2375
2450 Wyoming St Dearborn (48120) *(G-3867)*

Macomb Stairs Inc 586 226-2800
51032 Oro Dr Shelby Township (48315) *(G-15267)*

Macomb Tube Fabricating Co 586 445-6770
13403 E 9 Mile Rd Warren (48089) *(G-17912)*

Macs Marina Motorsports 248 486-8300
546 Mcmunn St South Lyon (48178) *(G-15445)*

Macsteel Monroe, Monroe Also called Gerdau Macsteel Inc *(G-11543)*

Mad Dog Software 248 940-2963
34100 Woodward Ave Birmingham (48009) *(G-1734)*

Madain Postal Services LLC 586 323-3573
43755 Saint Julian Ct Sterling Heights (48314) *(G-16080)*

Madar Metal Fabricating LLC 517 267-9610
3310 Ranger Rd Lansing (48906) *(G-9714)*

Madden Enterprises Inc 734 284-5330
3557 Fort St Wyandotte (48192) *(G-18830)*

Maddox Industries Inc 517 369-8665
900 W Chicago Rd Bronson (49028) *(G-2118)*

Madison Electric Company (PA) 586 825-0200
31855 Van Dyke Ave Warren (48093) *(G-17913)*

Madison Electric Company 586 294-8300
17930 E 14 Mile Rd Fraser (48026) *(G-5960)*

Madison Electronics, Warren Also called Madison Electric Company *(G-17913)*

Madison Machine Company 517 265-8532
801 Johnson St Alpena (49707) *(G-300)*

Madison Street Holdings LLC 517 252-2031
1408 E Church St Adrian (49221) *(G-81)*

Maeder Bros Inc 989 644-2235
5016 W Weidman Rd Weidman (48893) *(G-18255)*

Maeder Bros Qlty WD Pllets Inc 989 644-3500
5180 W Weidman Rd Weidman (48893) *(G-18256)*

Maeder Bros Saw Mill, Weidman Also called Maeder Bros Inc *(G-18255)*

Maes Tool & Die Co Inc 517 750-3131
1074 Toro Dr Jackson (49201) *(G-8940)*

Mag Automotive LLC (HQ) 586 446-7000
6015 Center Dr Sterling Heights (48312) *(G-16081)*

Mag Automotive LLC 586 446-7000
2555 20th St Port Huron (48060) *(G-13498)*

Mag Machine Tool 734 281-1700
14127 Middle Gibralter Rd Gibralter (48173) *(G-6172)*

Mag-Powertrain 586 446-7000
6015 Center Dr Sterling Heights (48312) *(G-16082)*

Mag-TEC Casting Corporation 517 789-8505
2411 Research Dr Jackson (49203) *(G-8941)*

Magazines In Motion Inc 248 310-7647
35451 Valley Crk Farmington Hills (48335) *(G-5299)*

Magic Pop Popcorn, Colon Also called Whm Investments Inc *(G-3492)*

Magic Treatz LLC 248 989-9956
24245 Coolidge Hwy Oak Park (48237) *(G-12624)*

Magiera Holdings Inc 269 685-1768
950 Lincoln Pkwy Plainwell (49080) *(G-13082)*

Magiglide Inc 906 822-7321
257 Industrial Park Rd Crystal Falls (49920) *(G-3743)*

Magline Inc (PA) 800 624-5463
1205 W Cedar St Standish (48658) *(G-15890)*

Magline Inc 800 624-5463
1205 W Cedar St Standish (48658) *(G-15891)*

Magline International LLC 989 512-1000
1205 W Cedar St Standish (48658) *(G-15892)*

Magna 616 786-7403
3401 128th Ave Holland (49424) *(G-8133)*

Magna Car Top Systems Amer Inc (HQ) 248 836-4500
456 Wimpole Dr Rochester Hills (48309) *(G-14057)*

Magna Donnelly Corp 616 844-8257
1800 Hayes St Grand Haven (49417) *(G-6332)*

Magna E-Car USA LLC 248 606-0600
10410 N Holly Rd Holly (48442) *(G-8281)*

Magna Elc Vhcl Strctres - Mich, Saint Clair Also called Magna Services America Inc *(G-14835)*

Magna Electronics Inc 810 606-8683
10345 N Holly Rd Holly (48442) *(G-8282)*

Magna Electronics Inc 810 606-0444
1465 Combermere Dr Troy (48083) *(G-17219)*

Magna Electronics Inc (HQ) 248 729-2643
2050 Auburn Rd Auburn Hills (48326) *(G-962)*
Magna Electronics Inc 248 606-0606
2050 Auburn Rd Auburn Hills (48326) *(G-963)*
Magna Electronics Tech Inc (HQ) 810 606-0145
10410 N Holly Rd Holly (48442) *(G-8283)*
Magna Engineered Glass, Grand Rapids Also called Magna Mirrors America Inc *(G-6956)*
Magna Exteriors & Interiors, Warren Also called Magna Modular Systems LLC *(G-17914)*
Magna Exteriors America Inc (HQ) 248 631-1100
750 Tower Dr Troy (48098) *(G-17220)*
Magna Extrors Intrors Amer Inc 248 729-2400
750 Tower Dr Troy (48098) *(G-17221)*
Magna International Amer Inc (HQ) 248 729-2400
750 Twer Dr Mail Code 700 Troy (48084) *(G-17222)*
Magna Mirrors America Inc (HQ) 616 786-7000
5085 Kraft Ave Se Grand Rapids (49512) *(G-6956)*
Magna Mirrors America Inc. 616 786-7300
414 E 40th St Holland (49423) *(G-8134)*
Magna Mirrors America Inc 616 942-0163
579 S Industrial Dr Newaygo (49337) *(G-12085)*
Magna Mirrors America Inc 616 738-0115
3601 John F Donnelly Dr Holland (49424) *(G-8135)*
Magna Mirrors America Inc. 616 786-7000
1800 Hayes St Grand Haven (49417) *(G-6333)*
Magna Mirrors America Inc. 616 786-7000
3401 128th Ave Holland (49424) *(G-8136)*
Magna Mirrors America Inc. 616 786-7772
3501 John F Donnelly Dr Holland (49424) *(G-8137)*
Magna Mirrors America Inc 231 652-4450
700 S Industrial Dr Newaygo (49337) *(G-12086)*
Magna Mirrors Newaygo Division, Newaygo Also called Magna Mirrors America Inc *(G-12085)*
Magna Mirrors North Amer LLC (HQ) 616 868-6122
6151 Bancroft Ave Se Alto (49302) *(G-336)*
Magna Modular Systems LLC 586 279-2000
14253 Frazho Rd Warren (48089) *(G-17914)*
Magna Powertrain America Inc 517 316-1013
3140 Spanish Oak Dr Lansing (48911) *(G-9866)*
Magna Powertrain America Inc (HQ) 248 597-7811
1870 Technology Dr Troy (48083) *(G-17223)*
Magna Powertrain Lansing, Lansing Also called Mpt Lansing LLC *(G-9872)*
Magna Powertrain Usa Inc (HQ) 248 680-4900
1870 Technology Dr Troy (48083) *(G-17224)*
Magna Powertrain Usa Inc 248 524-1397
1875 Research Dr Troy (48083) *(G-17225)*
Magna Powertrain Usa Inc 248 680-4900
1870 Technology Dr Troy (48083) *(G-17226)*
Magna Sealing & Glass Systems, Holland Also called Magna Mirrors America Inc *(G-8137)*
Magna Seating America Inc 248 243-7158
3800 Lapeer Rd Auburn Hills (48326) *(G-964)*
Magna Seating America Inc (HQ) 248 567-4000
30020 Cabot Dr Novi (48377) *(G-12469)*
Magna Seating America Inc 313 422-6000
12800 Oakland Pkwy Detroit (48203) *(G-4415)*
Magna Seating America Inc 586 816-1400
6200 26 Mile Rd Shelby Township (48316) *(G-15268)*
Magna Seating Auburn Hills, Auburn Hills Also called Magna Seating America Inc *(G-964)*
Magna Seating Detriot, Detroit Also called Magna Seating America Inc *(G-4415)*
Magna Services America Inc 248 617-3200
54725 Grand River Ave New Hudson (48165) *(G-12061)*
Magna Services America Inc 816 602-5872
1811 S Range Rd Saint Clair (48079) *(G-14835)*
Magna Steyr LLC 248 740-0214
1965 Research Dr Ste 100 Troy (48083) *(G-17227)*
Magna Steyr North America, Troy Also called Magna Steyr LLC *(G-17227)*
Magnatron NC Pattern and Mfg 810 522-7520
325 Roosevelt St Howell (48843) *(G-8475)*
Magnecor Australia Limited 248 471-9505
24581 Crestview Ct Farmington Hills (48335) *(G-5300)*
Magnesium Products America Inc (HQ) 734 416-8600
47805 Galleon Dr Plymouth (48170) *(G-13231)*
Magneti Marelli, Southfield Also called Marelli Holding USA LLC *(G-15643)*
Magneti Marelli Tennessee LLC 248 418-3000
26555 Northwestern Hwy Southfield (48033) *(G-15640)*
Magneti Mrlli Cfap Suspensions, Troy Also called Marelli Tennessee USA LLC *(G-17236)*
Magnetic Chuck Services Co Inc 586 822-9441
9391 Lindsey Rd Casco (48064) *(G-2600)*
Magnetic Michigan 734 922-7068
101 N Main St Ann Arbor (48104) *(G-562)*
Magnetic Products Inc 248 887-5600
683 Town Center Dr Highland (48356) *(G-7896)*
Magnetic Systems International 231 582-9600
3890 Charlevoix Rd Petoskey (49770) *(G-13003)*
Magnetic Systems Intl Inc 231 582-9600
1095 Dam Rd Boyne City (49712) *(G-1896)*
Magnetool Inc 248 588-5400
505 Elmwood Dr Troy (48083) *(G-17228)*
Magni Group Inc (PA) 248 647-4500
390 Park St Ste 300 Birmingham (48009) *(G-1735)*

Magni-Industries Inc (HQ) 313 843-7855
2771 Hammond St Detroit (48209) *(G-4416)*
Magnicote, Troy Also called Depor Industries Inc *(G-17056)*
Magnum Fabricating 734 484-5800
1754 E Michigan Ave Ypsilanti (48198) *(G-18964)*
Magnum Induction Inc 586 716-4700
51517 Industrial Dr New Baltimore (48047) *(G-11986)*
Magnum Manufacturing, Westland Also called Moderno Industrial LLC *(G-18397)*
Magnum Powder Coating Inc 616 785-3155
5500 West River Dr Ne Comstock Park (49321) *(G-3621)*
Magnum Tool Inc 586 716-8075
51620 Birch St New Baltimore (48047) *(G-11987)*
Magnum Toolscom LLC 734 595-4600
30690 Cypress Rd Romulus (48174) *(G-14300)*
Magnus Precision Tool LLC 586 285-2500
34082 James J Pompo Dr Fraser (48026) *(G-5961)*
Magnus Software Inc 517 294-0315
3883 Hogback Rd Fowlerville (48836) *(G-5850)*
Mahale, Troy Also called Hbpo North America Inc *(G-17138)*
Maher Group LLC 616 863-6046
575 Byrne Industrial Dr Rockford (49341) *(G-14176)*
Mahindra Automotive N Amer Mfg, Auburn Hills Also called Mahindra N Amrcn Tchncal Ctr I *(G-965)*
Mahindra Genze, Auburn Hills Also called Mahindra Tractor Assembly Inc *(G-966)*
Mahindra Genze, Ann Arbor Also called Mahindra Tractor Assembly Inc *(G-563)*
Mahindra N Amercn Technical 248 268-6600
1322 Rankin Dr Troy (48083) *(G-17229)*
Mahindra N Amrcn Tchncal Ctr I (HQ) 248 268-6600
275 Rex Blvd Auburn Hills (48326) *(G-965)*
Mahindra Tractor Assembly Inc (HQ) 650 779-5180
275 Rex Blvd Auburn Hills (48326) *(G-966)*
Mahindra Tractor Assembly Inc 734 274-2239
1901 E Ellsworth Rd Ann Arbor (48108) *(G-563)*
Mahle Inc 248 305-8200
23030 Mahle Dr Farmington Hills (48335) *(G-5301)*
Mahle Aftermarket Inc 717 840-0678
916 W State St Ste B Saint Johns (48879) *(G-14906)*
Mahle Aftermarket Inc (HQ) 248 347-9700
23030 Mahle Dr Farmington (48335) *(G-5142)*
Mahle Behr Dayton LLc 937 369-2900
2700 Daley Dr Troy (48083) *(G-17230)*
Mahle Behr Industy America Lp 616 647-3490
5858 Safety Dr Ne Belmont (49306) *(G-1513)*
Mahle Behr Mfg MGT Inc 248 735-3623
2700 Daley Dr Troy (48083) *(G-17231)*
Mahle Behr USA Inc 336 768-3429
1350 Eisenhower Pl Ann Arbor (48108) *(G-564)*
Mahle Behr USA Inc (HQ) 248 743-3700
2700 Daley Dr Troy (48083) *(G-17232)*
Mahle Behr USA Inc 248 735-3623
5820 Innovation Dr Troy (48098) *(G-17233)*
Mahle Behr USA Inc (HQ) 248 743-3700
2700 Daley Dr Troy (48083) *(G-17234)*
Mahle Eng Components USA Inc (HQ) 989 224-2384
916 W State St Saint Johns (48879) *(G-14907)*
Mahle Eng Components USA Inc 248 305-8200
23030 Haggerty Rd Farmington Hills (48335) *(G-5302)*
Mahle Industries Incorporated (HQ) 248 305-8200
23030 Mahle Dr Farmington Hills (48335) *(G-5303)*
Mahle Industries Incorporated (HQ) 248 305-8200
23030 Mahle Dr Farmington Hills (48335) *(G-5304)*
Mahle Industries Incorporated 248 305-8200
1883 E Laketon Ave Muskegon (49442) *(G-11864)*
Mahle Industries Incorporated 248 473-6511
23030 Haggerty Rd Farmington Hills (48335) *(G-5305)*
Mahle Manufacturing MGT Inc (HQ) 248 735-3623
23030 Mahle Dr Farmington Hills (48335) *(G-5306)*
Mahle Powertrain LLC (HQ) 248 305-8200
23030 Mahle Dr Farmington Hills (48335) *(G-5307)*
Mahle Service Solutions, Saint Johns Also called Mahle Aftermarket Inc *(G-14906)*
Mahnke Machine Inc 231 775-0581
1551 Filmore Ave Ste A Cadillac (49601) *(G-2344)*
Main & Company 517 789-7183
2700 Cooper St Jackson (49201) *(G-8942)*
Main Street Spectacles LLC 231 429-7234
310 E Euclid St Mc Bain (49657) *(G-11185)*
Maine Ornamental LLC 800 556-8449
68956 Us Highway 131 White Pigeon (49099) *(G-18482)*
Majeske Machine Inc 319 273-8905
44650 Pinetree Dr Plymouth (48170) *(G-13232)*
Majestic Formed Plastics 269 663-2870
69815 Brizendine St Edwardsburg (49112) *(G-5007)*
Majestic Industries Inc 586 786-9100
15378 Hallmark Ct Macomb (48042) *(G-10612)*
Majestic Pattern Company Inc 313 892-5800
20400 Sherwood St Detroit (48234) *(G-4417)*
Majestic Sonrise Alpacas 616 848-7414
1189 Sorrento Ct Holland (49423) *(G-8138)*

Majik Graphics Inc ... 586 792-8055
19751 15 Mile Rd Clinton Township (48035) *(G-3291)*
Major Industries Ltd ... 810 985-9372
521 Michigan St Port Huron (48060) *(G-13499)*
Major One Electronics LLC ... 313 652-3723
18284 Ardmore St Detroit (48235) *(G-4418)*
Major Powdered Metal Tech, Livonia *Also called Gasbarre Products Inc (G-10220)*
Major Products, Allen Park *Also called Riviera Industries Inc (G-203)*
Mak Press & Machinery Co ... 734 266-3044
29322 Hemlock Dr Farmington Hills (48336) *(G-5308)*
MAKARIOS DECOR, Byron Center *Also called Shop Makarios LLC (G-2295)*
Make It Mine Dsign EMB Screen ... 989 448-8678
147 W Main St Gaylord (49735) *(G-6144)*
Make It Yours ... 517 990-6799
6982 Surrey Ln Jackson (49201) *(G-8943)*
Maker Works ... 734 222-4911
3765 Plaza Dr Ann Arbor (48108) *(G-565)*
Makkedah Mt Proc & Bulk Fd Str ... 231 873-2113
1813 N 136th Ave Hart (49420) *(G-7757)*
MAKS INCORPORATED ... 248 733-9771
1150 Rankin Dr Troy (48083) *(G-17235)*
Malabar Manufacturing Inc ... 517 448-2155
4255 Munson Hwy Hudson (49247) *(G-8555)*
Malach Group Plutonium Paint ... 248 827-4844
21170 Bridge St Southfield (48033) *(G-15641)*
Malachi Printing LLC ... 517 395-4813
69936 Elkhart Rd Edwardsburg (49112) *(G-5008)*
Maleports Sault Prtg Co Inc ... 906 632-3369
314 Osborn Blvd Sault Sainte Marie (49783) *(G-15095)*
Malibu Skateboards LLC ... 616 243-3154
917 Pinecrest Ave Se Grand Rapids (49506) *(G-6957)*
Mall City Aluminum Inc ... 269 349-5088
850 E Crosstown Pkwy Kalamazoo (49001) *(G-9264)*
Mall City Containers, Inc., Kalamazoo *Also called McC Kalamazoo Inc (G-9267)*
Mall Tooling & Engineering ... 586 463-6520
150 Grand Ave Mount Clemens (48043) *(G-11648)*
Malmac Tool and Fixture Inc ... 517 448-8244
4255 Munson Hwy Hudson (49247) *(G-8556)*
Mamemarquees LLC ... 586 322-2215
55711 Broughton Rd Macomb (48042) *(G-10613)*
Mammoth, Holland *Also called Nortek Air Solutions LLC (G-8156)*
Mammoth Distilling LLC ... 773 841-4242
1554 N East Torch Lake Dr Central Lake (49622) *(G-2695)*
Man Store, The, Livonia *Also called Gags and Games Inc (G-10218)*
Man U TEC Inc ... 586 262-4085
6522 Diplomat Dr Sterling Heights (48314) *(G-16083)*
Management Training Inn ... 734 439-1546
555 S Platt Rd Milan (48160) *(G-11443)*
Manchester Industries Inc VA ... 269 496-2715
26920 M 60 Mendon (49072) *(G-11219)*
Maness Petroleum Corp ... 989 773-5475
1425 S Mission Rd Mount Pleasant (48858) *(G-11709)*
Manhattan Container, Romulus *Also called Packaging Specialties Inc (G-14315)*
Manigg Enterprises Inc (PA) ... 989 356-4986
1010 Us Highway 23 N Alpena (49707) *(G-301)*
Manistee News Advocate ... 231 723-3592
75 Maple St Manistee (49660) *(G-10905)*
Manistee Wldg & Piping Svc Inc (PA) ... 231 723-2551
325 Oak Grove St Manistee (49660) *(G-10906)*
Manistique Machine, Negaunee *Also called U P Fabricating Co Inc (G-11976)*
Manistique Pioneer Tribune, Manistique *Also called Four Seasons Publishing Inc (G-10918)*
Manistique Rentals Inc ... 906 341-6955
415 Chippewa Ave Manistique (49854) *(G-10921)*
Manitou Boats, Lansing *Also called Triton Industries Inc (G-9745)*
Manitwoc Fdsrvice Cmpanies LLC ... 989 773-7981
980 S Isabella Rd Mount Pleasant (48858) *(G-11710)*
Manly Innovations LLC ... 734 548-0200
19735 Deerfield Ct Chelsea (48118) *(G-2820)*
Mann + Hummel Inc (HQ) ... 269 329-3900
6400 S Sprinkle Rd Portage (49002) *(G-13581)*
Mann + Hummel Usa Inc ... 248 857-8501
3411 Ctr Park Plz Kalamazoo (49048) *(G-9265)*
Mann + Hummel Usa Inc (HQ) ... 269 329-3900
6400 S Sprinkle Rd Portage (49002) *(G-13582)*
Mann Metal Finishing Inc ... 269 621-6359
200 Prospect St Hartford (49057) *(G-7765)*
Mannetron ... 269 962-3475
74 Leonard Wood Rd Battle Creek (49037) *(G-1271)*
Mannetron Animatronics, Battle Creek *Also called Mannetron (G-1271)*
Mannhummel, Portage *Also called Mann + Hummel Usa Inc (G-13582)*
Manning Enterprises Inc ... 269 657-2346
45872 30th St Paw Paw (49079) *(G-12952)*
Mannino Tile & Marble Inc ... 586 978-3390
38790 Hartwell Dr Sterling Heights (48312) *(G-16084)*
Mannix RE Holdings LLC ... 231 972-0088
8965 Midstate Dr Mecosta (49332) *(G-11192)*
Manor Industries Inc ... 586 463-4604
24400 Maplehurst Dr Clinton Township (48036) *(G-3292)*
Manos Authentic LLC ... 800 242-2796
22599 15 Mile Rd Clinton Township (48035) *(G-3293)*
Manray Press LLC ... 734 558-0580
1788 Oak St Wyandotte (48192) *(G-18831)*
Manrisa ... 248 364-4415
2965 Lapeer Rd Auburn Hills (48326) *(G-967)*
Mansa Denim Company ... 313 384-3929
607 Shelby St Ste 700 Detroit (48226) *(G-4419)*
Manta Group LLC ... 248 325-8264
35 W Huron St Ste 10 Pontiac (48342) *(G-13395)*
Manthei Inc ... 231 347-4672
3996 Charlevoix Rd Petoskey (49770) *(G-13004)*
Manthei Development Corp ... 231 347-6282
3996 Charlevoix Rd Petoskey (49770) *(G-13005)*
Manthei Veneer, Petoskey *Also called Manthei Inc (G-13004)*
Mantissa Industries Inc ... 517 694-2260
2362 Jarco Dr Holt (48842) *(G-8317)*
Manufacturers / Mch Bldrs Svcs ... 734 748-3706
13035 Wayne Rd Livonia (48150) *(G-10298)*
Manufacturers Hardware Company ... 313 892-6650
17641 Filer St Detroit (48212) *(G-4420)*
Manufacturers Services Inds (PA) ... 906 493-6685
40014 S Cream City Pt Rd Drummond Island (49726) *(G-4802)*
Manufacturers Solutions LLC ... 616 894-2964
108 N Irving St Greenville (48838) *(G-7498)*
Manufacturing, Spring Lake *Also called Meta Tool Technologies LLC (G-15834)*
Manufacturing, Chesterfield *Also called Ellsworth Cutting Tools Ltd (G-2874)*
Manufacturing & Indus Tech Inc ... 248 522-6959
30445 Northwestern Hwy Farmington Hills (48334) *(G-5309)*
Manufacturing Associates Inc ... 248 421-4943
39201 Amrhein Rd Livonia (48150) *(G-10299)*
Manufacturing Center, Sterling Heights *Also called Proto Gage Inc (G-16136)*
Manufacturing Ctrl Systems Inc ... 248 853-7400
1928 Star Batt Dr Ste C Rochester Hills (48309) *(G-14058)*
Manufacturing Dynamics Co ... 248 670-0264
1642 E 11 Mile Rd Madison Heights (48071) *(G-10774)*
Manufacturing Hero ... 269 271-0031
10619 Chancellor St Portage (49002) *(G-13583)*
Manufacturing Options ... 989 430-6770
455 E Bradford Rd Midland (48640) *(G-11386)*
Manufacturing Products & Svcs ... 734 927-1964
260 Ann Arbor Rd W Plymouth (48170) *(G-13233)*
Manufax Inc ... 231 929-3226
1324 Barlow St Ste D Traverse City (49686) *(G-16752)*
Manufctring Partners Group LLC ... 517 749-4050
1639 Horton Lake Rd Lapeer (48446) *(G-9946)*
Manufctring Solutions Tech LLC ... 734 744-5050
1975 Alpha St Commerce Township (48382) *(G-3552)*
Manufcturing Assembly Intl LLC (PA) ... 248 549-4700
2521 Torquay Ave Royal Oak (48073) *(G-14559)*
Manus Tool Inc ... 989 724-7171
510 S 3rd St Harrisville (48740) *(G-7744)*
Manutec, Sterling Heights *Also called Man U TEC Inc (G-16083)*
Map To Elopak Precision ... 417 467-7419
1200 Benstein Rd Commerce Township (48390) *(G-3553)*
Mapal Inc (HQ) ... 810 364-8020
4032 Dove Rd Port Huron (48060) *(G-13500)*
Mapco Manufacturing, Canton *Also called Merchants Automatic Pdts Inc (G-2493)*
Maple Industries, New Hudson *Also called TEC Industries Inc (G-12072)*
Maple Island Log Homes Inc (PA) ... 231 821-2151
2387 Bayne Rd Twin Lake (49457) *(G-17470)*
Maple Lane Ag-Bag, Kawkawlin *Also called Glenn Knochel (G-9415)*
Maple Leaf Press Inc ... 616 846-8844
1215 S Beechtree St Grand Haven (49417) *(G-6334)*
Maple Leaf Woodworking ... 616 262-9754
8863 Lake View Dr Orleans (48865) *(G-12740)*
Maple Mold Technologies, Rochester Hills *Also called Precision Masters Inc (G-14087)*
Maple Mold Technologies, Auburn Hills *Also called Precision Masters Inc (G-1003)*
Maple Press LLC ... 248 733-9669
31211 Stephenson Hwy # 10 Madison Heights (48071) *(G-10775)*
Maple Ridge Companies Inc ... 989 356-4807
9528 S Bolton Rd Posen (49776) *(G-13644)*
Maple Ridge Hardwoods Inc ... 989 873-5305
2270 Dobler Rd Sterling (48659) *(G-15913)*
Maple Row Sugarhouse, Jones *Also called Daniel Olson (G-9083)*
Maple Valley Pallet Co ... 231 228-6641
9285 S Nash Rd Maple City (49664) *(G-10944)*
Maple Valley Plastics LLC ... 810 346-3040
4119 Main St Brown City (48416) *(G-2140)*
Maple Valley Truss Co ... 989 389-4267
4287 E West Branch Rd Prudenville (48651) *(G-13658)*
Maples Sawmill Inc ... 906 484-3926
2736 Chard Rd Hessel (49745) *(G-7874)*
Maquet Monthly ... 906 226-6500
810 N 3rd St Marquette (49855) *(G-11032)*
Mar Cor Purification Inc ... 248 373-7844
180 Engelwood Dr Ste D Lake Orion (48359) *(G-9616)*
Mar-Med Inc ... 616 454-3000
333 Fuller Ave Ne Grand Rapids (49503) *(G-6958)*

Mar-Vo Mineral Company Inc 517 523-2669
115 E Bacon St Hillsdale (49242) *(G-7940)*
Marada Industries 586 264-4908
54725 Grand River Ave New Hudson (48165) *(G-12062)*
Marana Group, Kalamazoo *Also called Lake Michigan Mailers Inc (G-9257)*
Marathon Oil, Flushing *Also called Fuel Tobacco Stop (G-5809)*
Marathon Weld Group LLC 517 782-8040
5750 Marathon Dr Jackson (49201) *(G-8944)*
Marbelite Corp 248 348-1900
22500 Heslip Dr Novi (48375) *(G-12470)*
Marbels Outdoors, Gladstone *Also called Crl Inc (G-6177)*
Marblecast Kitchens & Baths, Oak Park *Also called Marblecast of Michigan Inc (G-12625)*
Marblecast of Michigan Inc 248 398-0600
14831 W 11 Mile Rd Oak Park (48237) *(G-12625)*
Marc Molina 810 701-3587
10122 E Stanley Rd Davison (48423) *(G-3790)*
Marc Schrreiber & Company LLC 734 222-9930
1389 King George Blvd Ann Arbor (48104) *(G-566)*
Marceau Enterprises Inc 586 697-8100
11517 Laurel Woods Dr Washington (48094) *(G-18085)*
Marcella Manifolds 248 259-6696
4625 S Milford Rd Milford (48381) *(G-11469)*
Marcellus Metalcasters Inc 269 646-0202
214 E Read St Marcellus (49067) *(G-10949)*
March Coatings Inc (PA) 810 229-6464
160 Summit St Brighton (48116) *(G-2024)*
Marcie Electric Inc 248 486-1200
8190 Boardwalk Rd Ste B Brighton (48116) *(G-2025)*
Marcon Technologies LLC 269 279-1701
1 Industrial Park Dr Constantine (49042) *(G-3669)*
Mardan Fabrication Inc 586 466-6401
41001 Production Dr Harrison Township (48045) *(G-7708)*
Marelli Automotive Ltg LLC (HQ) 248 418-3000
26555 Northwestern Hwy Southfield (48033) *(G-15642)*
Marelli Automotive Ltg LLC 248 418-3000
5600 Bow Pointe Dr Clarkston (48346) *(G-3047)*
Marelli Holding USA LLC (HQ) 248 418-3000
26555 Northwestern Hwy Southfield (48033) *(G-15643)*
Marelli North America Inc (HQ) 931 684-4490
26555 Northwestern Hwy Southfield (48033) *(G-15644)*
Marelli North America Inc 248 403-2033
26555 Northwestern Hwy Southfield (48033) *(G-15645)*
Marelli Tennessee USA LLC 248 418-3000
26555 Northwestern Hwy Southfield (48033) *(G-15646)*
Marelli Tennessee USA LLC 248 680-8872
1389 Wheaton Dr Troy (48083) *(G-17236)*
Marfood USA 313 292-4100
21655 Trolley Indus Dr Taylor (48180) *(G-16438)*
Margate Industries Inc 810 387-4300
129 N Main St Yale (48097) *(G-18919)*
Marhar Snowboards LLC 616 432-3104
5693 Airline Rd Fruitport (49415) *(G-6066)*
Mari Villa Vineyards 231 935-4513
8175 Center Rd Traverse City (49686) *(G-16753)*
Maria Dismondy Inc 248 302-1800
1181 West Lake Dr Novi (48377) *(G-12471)*
Mariah Industries Inc (PA) 248 237-0404
1407 Allen Dr Ste E Troy (48083) *(G-17237)*
Marias Italian Bakery Inc 734 981-1200
115 N Haggerty Rd Canton (48187) *(G-2488)*
Marie Minnie Bakers Inc 734 522-1100
12301 Farmington Rd Livonia (48150) *(G-10300)*
Marilyn's Needlework, Grand Rapids *Also called Stoney Creek Collection Inc (G-7227)*
Marimba Auto LLC 734 398-9000
41150 Van Born Rd Canton (48188) *(G-2489)*
Marine Automated Doc System 989 539-9010
2900 Doc Dr Harrison (48625) *(G-7680)*
Marine Industries Inc 989 635-3644
2900 Boyne Rd Marlette (48453) *(G-10985)*
Marine Machining and Mfg 586 791-8800
33475 Giftos Dr Clinton Township (48035) *(G-3294)*
Marine Propulsion LLC 248 396-2353
6897 Chimney Hill Dr # 207 West Bloomfield (48322) *(G-18295)*
Mario Anthony Tabone 734 667-2946
379 Red Ryder Dr Plymouth (48170) *(G-13234)*
Marion Pallet 231 743-6124
7414 20 Mile Rd Marion (49665) *(G-10974)*
Marisa Manufacturing Inc 586 754-3000
26020 Sherwood Ave Warren (48091) *(G-17915)*
Marix Specialty Welding Co 586 754-9685
3822 Kiefer Ave Warren (48091) *(G-17916)*
Marjeannes Creations 810 798-7278
7346 Hollow Corners Rd Almont (48003) *(G-264)*
Marjo Plastics Company Inc 734 455-4130
1081 Cherry Plymouth (48170) *(G-13235)*
Mark 4 Automotive, Troy *Also called Dayco Products LLC (G-17047)*
Mark A Nelson 989 305-5769
332 Oneil Rd Lupton (48635) *(G-10562)*
Mark Adler Homes 586 850-0630
401 S Old Woodward Ave # 3 Birmingham (48009) *(G-1736)*
Mark Barclay Ministries, Midland *Also called Living Word International Inc (G-11384)*
Mark Beem 231 510-8122
861 N Green Rd Lake City (49651) *(G-9550)*
Mark Carbide Co 248 545-0606
1830 Brinston Dr Troy (48083) *(G-17238)*
Mark Eaton Sales and Mfg 517 741-5000
8480 M 60 Union City (49094) *(G-17495)*
Mark Four CAM Inc 586 204-5906
22926 W Industrial Dr Saint Clair Shores (48080) *(G-14869)*
Mark Griessel 810 378-6060
7068 Jordan Rd Melvin (48454) *(G-11195)*
Mark II Enterprises, Northville *Also called Northville Stitching Post (G-12247)*
Mark Land Industries Inc 313 615-0503
5433 Miller Rd Dearborn (48126) *(G-3868)*
Mark Maker Company Inc (PA) 616 538-6980
4157 Stafford Ave Sw Grand Rapids (49548) *(G-6959)*
Mark Mold and Engineering 989 687-9786
773 W Beamish Rd Sanford (48657) *(G-15073)*
Mark MSA 586 716-5941
35632 Hamer St New Baltimore (48047) *(G-11988)*
Mark One Corporation 989 732-2427
517 Alpine Rd Gaylord (49735) *(G-6145)*
Mark Precision Tool and Engrg, Commerce Township *Also called Mark Tool & Die Company Inc (G-3554)*
Mark Schwager Inc 248 275-1978
13170 W Star Dr Shelby Township (48315) *(G-15269)*
Mark Tool & Die Company Inc 248 363-1567
4360 Haggerty Hwy Commerce Township (48390) *(G-3554)*
Mark-Pack Inc (PA) 616 837-5400
776 Main St Coopersville (49404) *(G-3691)*
Markdom of America Inc (PA) 716 681-8306
2285 S Michigan Rd Eaton Rapids (48827) *(G-4966)*
Marked Tool Inc 616 669-3201
2934 Highland Blvd Hudsonville (49426) *(G-8592)*
Markerboard People Inc 517 372-1666
2227 Spikes Ln Unit 1 Lansing (48906) *(G-9715)*
Market Place Pet Supplies, South Lyon *Also called Harry & Assoc LLC (G-15437)*
Marketeer, The, Brighton *Also called George Moses Co (G-2000)*
Marketing Displays Inc 248 553-1900
38271 W 12 Mile Rd Farmington Hills (48331) *(G-5310)*
Marketing Displays Intl, Farmington Hills *Also called Marketing Displays Inc (G-5310)*
Marketing Impact, Flint *Also called Printcomm Inc (G-5749)*
Marketing VI Group Inc 989 793-3933
4414 Bay Rd Ste 1 Saginaw (48603) *(G-14686)*
Marketlab Inc 866 237-3722
6850 Southbelt Dr Se Caledonia (49316) *(G-2388)*
Marketplus Software Inc (PA) 269 968-4240
2821 Wilbur St Springfield (49037) *(G-15872)*
Markham Peat Corp 800 851-7230
9475 Jefferson Rd Lakeview (48850) *(G-9643)*
Marking Machine Co 517 767-4155
286 Spires Pkwy Tekonsha (49092) *(G-16523)*
Markit Products 616 458-7881
2430 Turner Ave Nw Ste D Grand Rapids (49544) *(G-6960)*
Marland Clutch, Warren *Also called Formsprag LLC (G-17816)*
Marley Precision Inc (HQ) 269 963-7374
455 Fritz Keiper Blvd Battle Creek (49037) *(G-1272)*
Maro Precision Tool Company 734 261-3100
5041 Pheasant Cv West Bloomfield (48323) *(G-18296)*
Marquee Engraving Inc 810 686-7550
600 S Mill St Ste A Clio (48420) *(G-3404)*
Marquette Castings LLC 248 798-8035
123 W 5th St Royal Oak (48067) *(G-14560)*
Marquette Distillery 906 869-4933
844 W Bluff St Marquette (49855) *(G-11033)*
Marquette Fence Company Inc 906 249-8000
1446 State Highway M28 E Marquette (49855) *(G-11034)*
Marquette Machining & Fabg, Marquette *Also called Clair Sawyer (G-11013)*
Marquette Maple Company, Marquette *Also called Levi Ohman Micah (G-11030)*
Marquis Industries Inc 616 842-2810
17310 Teunis Dr Spring Lake (49456) *(G-15832)*
Marquis Wood Works 810 488-9406
8793 Lakeshore Rd Burtchville (48059) *(G-2222)*
Marrel Corporation 616 863-9155
4750 14 Mile Rd Ne Rockford (49341) *(G-14177)*
Marrone Michigan Manufactoring 269 427-0300
700 Industrial Park Rd Bangor (49013) *(G-1130)*
Marrs Discount Furniture 989 720-5436
1544 E M 21 Owosso (48867) *(G-12840)*
Marsack Sand & Gravel Inc 586 293-4414
20900 E 14 Mile Rd Roseville (48066) *(G-14435)*
Marsh Brothers Inc 517 869-2653
9800 Youngs Rd Quincy (49082) *(G-13671)*
Marsh Industrial Services Inc 231 258-4870
135 E Mile Rd Kalkaska (49646) *(G-9395)*
Marsh Plating Corporation (PA) 734 483-5767
103 N Grove St Ypsilanti (48198) *(G-18965)*
Marsh Welding, Kalkaska *Also called Marsh Industrial Services Inc (G-9395)*

ALPHABETIC

Marshal E Hyman and Associates 248 643-0642
3250 W Big Beavr Rd # 529 Troy (48084) ***(G-17239)***
Marshall Bldg Components Corp 269 781-4236
1605 Brooks Dr Marshall (49068) ***(G-11064)***
Marshall Brass Co, Marshall *Also called S H Leggitt Company* ***(G-11073)***
Marshall Excelsior Co (HQ) 269 789-6700
1506 George Brown Dr Marshall (49068) ***(G-11065)***
Marshall Floral Products 517 787-7620
710 Wildwood Ave Jackson (49201) ***(G-8945)***
Marshall Gas Controls Inc 269 781-3901
450 Leggitt Rd Marshall (49068) ***(G-11066)***
Marshall Metal Products Inc 269 781-3924
1006 E Michigan Ave Marshall (49068) ***(G-11067)***
Marshall Middleby Holding LLC 906 863-4401
5600 13th St Menominee (49858) ***(G-11244)***
Marshall Plastic Film, Martin *Also called Mpf Acquisitions Inc* ***(G-11080)***
Marshall Ryerson Co 616 299-1751
7440 Lime Hollow Dr Se Grand Rapids (49546) ***(G-6961)***
Marshall Tool Service Inc 989 777-3137
2700 Iowa Ave Saginaw (48601) ***(G-14687)***
Marshall's Fudge, Mackinaw City *Also called Marshalls Trail Inc* ***(G-10568)***
Marshall-Gruber Company LLC (HQ) 248 353-4100
26776 W 12 Mile Rd Ste 20 Southfield (48034) ***(G-15647)***
Marshalls Crossing 810 639-4740
12050 Trident Blvd Montrose (48457) ***(G-11606)***
Marshalls Trail Inc 231 436-5082
308 E Central Ave Mackinaw City (49701) ***(G-10568)***
Martec Land Services Inc 231 929-3971
3335 S Arprt Rd W Ste A5 Traverse City (49684) ***(G-16754)***
Martel Tool Corporation 313 278-2420
5831 Pelham Rd Allen Park (48101) ***(G-200)***
Marten Models & Molds Inc 586 293-2260
18291 Mike C Ct Fraser (48026) ***(G-5962)***
Martens Logging 616 675-5473
2335 Canada Rd Casnovia (49318) ***(G-2607)***
Martin and Hattie Rasche Inc 616 245-1223
3353 Eastern Ave Se Grand Rapids (49508) ***(G-6962)***
Martin Bros Mill Fndry Sup Co 269 927-1355
289 Hinkley St Benton Harbor (49022) ***(G-1567)***
Martin Fluid Power Company (PA) 248 585-8170
900 E Whitcomb Ave Madison Heights (48071) ***(G-10776)***
Martin Mretta Magnesia Spc LLC 231 723-2577
1800 E Lake Rd Manistee (49660) ***(G-10907)***
Martin Powder Coating 517 625-4220
124 W Third St Perry (48872) ***(G-12979)***
Martin Products Company Inc 269 651-1721
66635 M 66 N Sturgis (49091) ***(G-16304)***
Martin Saw & Tool Inc (PA) 906 863-6812
1212 19th Ave Menominee (49858) ***(G-11245)***
Martin Tool & Machine Inc 586 775-1800
29739 Groesbeck Hwy Roseville (48066) ***(G-14436)***
Martinrea Featherstone, Auburn Hills *Also called Martinrea Jonesville LLC* ***(G-968)***
Martinrea Hot Stampings Inc 859 509-3031
14401 Frazho Rd Warren (48089) ***(G-17917)***
Martinrea Industries Inc (HQ) 734 428-2400
10501 Mi State Road 52 Manchester (48158) ***(G-10886)***
Martinrea Industries Inc 231 832-5504
603 E Church Ave Reed City (49677) ***(G-13795)***
Martinrea Jonesville LLC (HQ) 517 849-2195
260 Gaige St Jonesville (49250) ***(G-9093)***
Martinrea Jonesville LLC 248 630-7730
2325 Featherstone Rd Auburn Hills (48326) ***(G-968)***
Martinrea Metal Industries Inc (HQ) 248 392-9700
2100 N Opdyke Rd Auburn Hills (48326) ***(G-969)***
Marvel Industries, Greenville *Also called Northland Corporation* ***(G-7502)***
Marvin Nelson Forest Products 906 384-6700
9868 County 426 E Rd Cornell (49818) ***(G-3701)***
Marwood International, Detroit *Also called Tranor Industries LLC* ***(G-4643)***
Mary Palaszek Dr 616 453-2255
1636 Leonard St Nw Grand Rapids (49504) ***(G-6963)***
Marysville Hydrocarbons LLC 586 445-2300
30078 Schoenherr Rd # 150 Warren (48088) ***(G-17918)***
Marysville Hydrocarbons LLC (HQ) 586 445-2300
2510 Busha Hwy Marysville (48040) ***(G-11090)***
Mas Inc 231 894-0409
2100 Cogswell Dr Whitehall (49461) ***(G-18508)***
Masco Building Products Corp (HQ) 313 274-7400
17450 College Pkwy Livonia (48152) ***(G-10301)***
Masco Cabinetry LLC 517 263-0771
5353 W Us Highway 223 Adrian (49221) ***(G-82)***
Masco Corporation (PA) 313 274-7400
17450 College Pkwy Livonia (48152) ***(G-10302)***
Masco Corporation of Indiana 810 664-8501
211 Mccormick Dr Lapeer (48446) ***(G-9947)***
Masco De Puerto Rico Inc 313 274-7400
21001 Van Born Rd Taylor (48180) ***(G-16439)***
Masco Services Inc 313 274-7400
17450 College Pkwy Livonia (48152) ***(G-10303)***
Mask Makers LLC 313 790-1784
23769 Point O Woods Ct South Lyon (48178) ***(G-15446)***
Maslin Corporation (PA) 586 777-7500
20304 Harper Ave Harper Woods (48225) ***(G-7667)***
Maslo Fabrication LLC 616 298-7700
155 Manufacturers Dr Holland (49424) ***(G-8139)***
Mason Forge & Die Inc 517 676-2992
841 Hull Rd Mason (48854) ***(G-11142)***
Mason Specialty Forge, Mason *Also called Mason Forge & Die Inc* ***(G-11142)***
Mason Tackle Company 810 631-4571
11273 Center St Otisville (48463) ***(G-12783)***
Masonite International Corp 517 545-5811
5665 Sterling Dr Howell (48843) ***(G-8476)***
Masons Lumber & Hardware Inc 989 685-3999
2493 S M 33 Rose City (48654) ***(G-14365)***
Maspac International, Novi *Also called Clarkson Controls & Eqp Co* ***(G-12384)***
Mass Mountain Technologies 855 722-7900
3341 Ashton Rd Se Grand Rapids (49546) ***(G-6964)***
Massee Products Ltd 269 684-8255
2612 N 5th St Niles (49120) ***(G-12142)***
Massie Mfg Inc 906 353-6381
445 N Superior Ave Baraga (49908) ***(G-1145)***
Massive Mineral Mix LLC 517 857-4544
21110 29 1/2 Mile Rd Springport (49284) ***(G-15883)***
Massobrio Precision Products, Kimball *Also called Mpp Corp* ***(G-9496)***
Mast Mini Barns, Fremont *Also called K-Mar Structures LLC* ***(G-6046)***
Mast Mini Barns LLC 231 924-3895
7680 Meinert Rd Holton (49425) ***(G-8341)***
Master Automatic, Livonia *Also called Maclean Master LLC* ***(G-10297)***
Master Coat LLC 734 405-2340
6120 Commerce Dr Westland (48185) ***(G-18393)***
Master Craft Extrusion Tls Inc 231 386-5149
771 N Mill St Northport (49670) ***(G-12190)***
Master Finish Co 877 590-5819
2100 Nelson Ave Se Grand Rapids (49507) ***(G-6965)***
Master Jig Grinding & Gage Co 248 380-8515
28005 Oakland Oaks Ct Wixom (48393) ***(G-18706)***
Master Machine & Tool Co Inc 586 469-4243
23414 Reynolds Ct Clinton Township (48036) ***(G-3295)***
Master Machining Inc 248 509-7185
1960 Thunderbird Troy (48084) ***(G-17240)***
Master Mfg Inc 248 628-9400
3287 Metamora Rd Oxford (48371) ***(G-12899)***
Master Mix Company 734 487-7870
612 S Mansfield St Ypsilanti (48197) ***(G-18966)***
Master Model & Fixture Inc 586 532-1153
51731 Oro Dr Shelby Township (48315) ***(G-15270)***
Master Precision Molds, Greenville *Also called Master Precision Products Inc* ***(G-7499)***
Master Precision Products Inc 616 754-5483
1212 E Fairplains St Greenville (48838) ***(G-7499)***
Master Precision Tool Corp 586 739-3240
7362 19 Mile Rd Sterling Heights (48314) ***(G-16085)***
Master Tag, Montague *Also called International Master Pdts Corp* ***(G-11598)***
Master Woodworks 269 240-3262
2916 Veronica Ct Saint Joseph (49085) ***(G-14949)***
Masterbilt Products Corp 269 749-4841
719 N Main St Olivet (49076) ***(G-12694)***
Masterline Design & Mfg 586 463-5888
41580 Production Dr Harrison Township (48045) ***(G-7709)***
Mastermix, Ypsilanti *Also called Master Mix Company* ***(G-18966)***
Masters Millwork LLC 248 987-4511
30700 Stephenson Hwy Madison Heights (48071) ***(G-10777)***
Masters Publishing 586 323-2723
42126 Bobjean St Sterling Heights (48314) ***(G-16086)***
Masters Tool & Die Inc 989 777-2450
4485 Marlea Dr Saginaw (48601) ***(G-14688)***
Mastery Technologies Inc 248 888-8420
41214 Bridge St Novi (48375) ***(G-12472)***
Matcor Automotive Michigan Inc 616 527-4050
401 S Steele St Ionia (48846) ***(G-8690)***
Matech Lighting Systems, Holland *Also called GT Solutions LLC* ***(G-8062)***
Matelski Lumber Company 231 549-2780
2617 M 75 S Boyne Falls (49713) ***(G-1909)***
Material Cnversion Systems Div, Fenton *Also called Atlas Technologies LLC* ***(G-5451)***
Material Control Inc (PA) 630 892-4274
130 Seltzer Rd Croswell (48422) ***(G-3732)***
Material Difference Tech LLC 888 818-1283
51195 Regency Center Dr Macomb (48042) ***(G-10614)***
Material Handling Tech Inc 586 725-5546
9023 Marine City Hwy B Ira (48023) ***(G-8701)***
Material Hdlg Techniques Inc 616 890-1475
2782 134th Ave Hopkins (49328) ***(G-8366)***
Material Sciences Corporation (PA) 734 207-4444
6855 Commerce Blvd Canton (48187) ***(G-2490)***
Material Transfer and Stor Inc 269 673-2125
1214 Lincoln Rd Allegan (49010) ***(G-170)***
Materialise Usa LLC 734 259-6445
44650 Helm Ct Plymouth (48170) ***(G-13236)***
Materials Group LLC 616 863-6046
575 Byrne Industrial Dr Rockford (49341) ***(G-14178)***

Materials Processing Inc 734 282-1888
17423 Jefferson Riverview (48193) *(G-13880)*
Materne North America Corp 231 346-6600
6331 Us Highway 31 Grawn (49637) *(G-7452)*
Matheson 586 498-8315
26415 Gratiot Ave Roseville (48066) *(G-14437)*
Mathew Parmelee 248 894-5955
707 W Hamlin Rd Rochester Hills (48307) *(G-14059)*
Mathson Group Inc 248 821-5478
1737 Thunderbird Troy (48084) *(G-17241)*
Matney Models 734 848-8195
10765 Victory Rd Erie (48133) *(G-5051)*
Matrix Construction Pdts LLC 720 961-5454
1760 Harbour View Dr Marquette (49855) *(G-11035)*
Matrix Controls Group Inc 248 380-7600
28287 Beck Rd Ste D16 Wixom (48393) *(G-18707)*
Matrix Engineering and Sls Inc 734 981-7321
44330 Duchess Dr Canton (48187) *(G-2491)*
Matrix Engineering Inc 810 231-0212
8830 Whitmore Lake Rd Brighton (48116) *(G-2026)*
Matrix Manufacturing Inc 616 532-6000
862 47th St Sw Ste B2 Grand Rapids (49509) *(G-6966)*
Matrix Mtlcraft LLP A Ltd Prtn (PA) 248 724-1800
68 S Squirrel Rd Auburn Hills (48326) *(G-970)*
Matrix Mtlcraft LLP A Ltd Prtn 586 469-9611
15721 Leone Dr Macomb (48042) *(G-10615)*
Matrix North Amercn Cnstr Inc 734 847-4605
6945 Crabb Rd Temperance (48182) *(G-16539)*
Matrix Printing & Mailing, Grand Rapids *Also called Graphic Impressions Inc (G-6782)*
Matt and Dave LLC 734 439-1988
4706 N Ann Arbor Rd Dundee (48131) *(G-4831)*
Matteson Manufacturing Inc 231 779-2898
1480 Potthoff St Cadillac (49601) *(G-2345)*
Matthews Mill Inc 989 257-3271
6400 E County Line Rd South Branch (48761) *(G-15396)*
Matthews Plating Inc 517 784-3535
405 N Mechanic St Jackson (49201) *(G-8946)*
Mattress Mart, Waterford *Also called Midwest Quality Bedding Inc (G-18138)*
Mattress Wholesale 248 968-2200
14510 W 8 Mile Rd Oak Park (48237) *(G-12626)*
Mattson Tool & Die Corp 616 447-9012
4174 5 Mile Rd Ne Grand Rapids (49525) *(G-6967)*
Maufacturing, Holland *Also called Global Battery Solutions LLC (G-8051)*
Maurell Products Inc 989 725-5188
2710 S M 52 Owosso (48867) *(G-12841)*
Maurer Meat Processors Inc 989 658-8185
4075 Purdy Rd Ubly (48475) *(G-17478)*
Mauser 248 795-2330
4750 Clawson Tank Dr Clarkston (48346) *(G-3048)*
Maven Drive LLC 313 667-1541
300 Renaissance Ctr Detroit (48243) *(G-4421)*
Maverick Building Systems LLC 248 366-9410
3190 Walnut Lake Rd Commerce Township (48390) *(G-3555)*
Maverick Exploration Prod Inc 231 929-3923
3301 Veterans Dr Ste 107 Traverse City (49684) *(G-16755)*
Maverick Machine Tool 269 789-1617
101 E Oliver Dr Marshall (49068) *(G-11068)*
Maw Ventures Inc 231 798-8324
6230 Norton Center Dr Norton Shores (49441) *(G-12309)*
Max Casting Company Inc 269 925-8081
116 Paw Paw Ave Benton Harbor (49022) *(G-1568)*
Max Manufacturing 517 990-9180
205 Watts Rd Jackson (49203) *(G-8947)*
Max2 LLC 269 468-3452
1440 Territorial Rd Benton Harbor (49022) *(G-1569)*
Max3 LLC 269 925-2044
360 Urbandale Ave Benton Harbor (49022) *(G-1570)*
Maxable Inc 517 592-5638
202 Sherman St Brooklyn (49230) *(G-2127)*
Maxair Trampoline 616 929-0882
5161 Woodfield Ct Ne # 1 Grand Rapids (49525) *(G-6968)*
Maxal Hobart Brothers, Traverse City *Also called Hobart Brothers LLC (G-16712)*
Maxi-Grip, Warren *Also called Rens LLC (G-17996)*
Maxim Integrated Products Inc 408 601-1000
10355 Citation Dr Ste 100 Brighton (48116) *(G-2027)*
Maximtrak, Farmington Hills *Also called Routeone Holdings LLC (G-5373)*
Maximum Manufacturing LLC 810 272-0804
4581 S Lapeer Rd Ste E Lake Orion (48359) *(G-9617)*
Maximum Mold Inc 269 468-6291
1440 Territorial Rd Benton Harbor (49022) *(G-1571)*
Maximum Oilfield Service Inc 989 731-0099
7929 Alba Hwy Elmira (49730) *(G-5039)*
Maxion Fumagalli Auto USA 734 737-5000
39500 Orchard Hill Pl Novi (48375) *(G-12473)*
Maxion Import LLC 734 737-5000
39500 Orchard Hill Pl # 500 Novi (48375) *(G-12474)*
Maxion Wheels Akron LLC 330 794-2310
39500 Orchard Hill Pl Novi (48375) *(G-12475)*
Maxion Wheels LLC (HQ) 734 737-5000
39500 Orchard Hill Pl # 50 Novi (48375) *(G-12476)*
Maxion Wheels USA LLC (HQ) 734 737-5000
39500 Orchard Hill Pl # 500 Novi (48375) *(G-12477)*
Maxitrol Company 517 486-2820
235 Sugar St Blissfield (49228) *(G-1769)*
Maxitrol Company 269 432-3291
1000 E State St Colon (49040) *(G-3488)*
Maxitrol Company (PA) 248 356-1400
23555 Telegraph Rd Southfield (48033) *(G-15648)*
Maxpow International LLC 734 578-5369
37570 Avondale St Westland (48186) *(G-18394)*
Maxs Concrete Inc 231 972-7558
15323 75th Ave Mecosta (49332) *(G-11193)*
Maxum LLC 248 726-7110
600 Oliver Dr Rochester Hills (48309) *(G-14060)*
Maxxar 248 675-1040
28033 Center Oaks Ct Wixom (48393) *(G-18708)*
Maxxlite Led Signs 248 397-5769
44731 Woodward Ave Pontiac (48341) *(G-13396)*
May Mobility Inc 312 869-2711
650 Avis Dr Ste 100 Ann Arbor (48108) *(G-567)*
May Venture Inc 248 481-3890
4713 S Baldwin Rd Lake Orion (48359) *(G-9618)*
May-Day Window Manufacturing 989 348-2809
403 N Wilcox Bridge Rd Grayling (49738) *(G-7465)*
Maya Gage Co., Farmington Hills *Also called Maya Jig Grinding & Gage Co (G-5311)*
Maya Jig Grinding & Gage Co 248 471-0820
20770 Parker St Farmington Hills (48336) *(G-5311)*
Maya Plastics Inc 586 997-6000
13179 W Star Dr Shelby Township (48315) *(G-15271)*
Mayco International LLC 586 803-6000
34501 Harper Ave Clinton Township (48035) *(G-3296)*
Mayco International LLC 586 803-6000
1020 Doris Rd Auburn Hills (48326) *(G-971)*
Mayco International LLC 586 803-6000
27027 Mound Rd Warren (48092) *(G-17919)*
Mayco International LLC (PA) 586 803-6000
42400 Merrill Rd Sterling Heights (48314) *(G-16087)*
Mayco Plastics, Sterling Heights *Also called Stonebridge Industries Inc (G-16195)*
Mayco Tool 616 785-7350
5880 Comstock Park Dr Nw Comstock Park (49321) *(G-3622)*
Mayer Alloys Corporation (PA) 248 399-2233
10711 Northend Ave Ferndale (48220) *(G-5567)*
Mayer Tool & Engineering Inc 269 651-1428
1404 N Centerville Rd Sturgis (49091) *(G-16305)*
Mayfair Accessories Inc 989 732-8400
1639 Calkins Dr Gaylord (49735) *(G-6146)*
Mayfair Golf Accessories 989 732-8400
1639 Calkins Dr Gaylord (49735) *(G-6147)*
Mayfair Plastics Inc 989 732-2441
845 Dickerson Rd Gaylord (49735) *(G-6148)*
Maygrove Awning Co., Livonia *Also called American Roll Shutter Awng Co (G-10116)*
Maynard L Maclean L C 586 949-0471
50855 E Russell Schmidt Chesterfield (48051) *(G-2908)*
Mayne McKenney 248 709-5250
26300 Northwestern Hwy # 300 Southfield (48076) *(G-15649)*
Mayne-Mc Kenney Inc 248 258-0300
100 W Long Lake Rd # 220 Bloomfield Hills (48304) *(G-1835)*
Mayo Welding & Fabricating Co 248 435-2730
5061 Delemere Ave Royal Oak (48073) *(G-14561)*
Mayrose Sign and Mktg Co LLC 616 837-1884
4035 Hayes St Coopersville (49404) *(G-3692)*
Mayser Usa Inc 734 858-1290
6200 Schooner St Van Buren Twp (48111) *(G-17538)*
Maytag Appliances, Benton Harbor *Also called Maytag Corporation (G-1572)*
Maytag Corporation (HQ) 269 923-5000
2000 N M 63 Benton Harbor (49022) *(G-1572)*
Mayville Engineering Co Inc 616 878-5235
990 84th St Sw Byron Center (49315) *(G-2281)*
Mayville Engineering Co Inc 989 748-6031
1444 Alexander Rd Vanderbilt (49795) *(G-17572)*
Mayville Engineering Co Inc 616 877-2073
4714 Circuit Ct Wayland (49348) *(G-18198)*
Mayville Engineering Co Inc 989 983-3911
8276 Yuill Rd Vanderbilt (49795) *(G-17573)*
Mazzella Lifting Tech Inc 734 953-7300
12671 Richfield Ct Livonia (48150) *(G-10304)*
Mazzella Lifting Tech Inc 248 585-1063
31623 Stephenson Hwy Madison Heights (48071) *(G-10778)*
MB, Capac *Also called Miller Broach Inc (G-2547)*
MB Aerospace Holdings III Corp 586 977-9200
38111 Commerce Dr Sterling Heights (48312) *(G-16088)*
MB Aerospace Sterling Hts Inc 586 977-9200
38111 Commerce Dr Sterling Heights (48312) *(G-16089)*
MB Aerospace Warren LLC 586 772-2500
25250 Easy St Warren (48089) *(G-17920)*
MB Fluid Services LLC 616 392-7036
11372 E Lakewood Blvd Holland (49424) *(G-8140)*
MB Liquidating Corporation 810 638-5388
7162 Sheridan Rd Flushing (48433) *(G-5811)*

ALPHABETIC

MB Woodworks and Co 231 452-6321
77 W State Rd Newaygo (49337) *(G-12087)*

MBA Printing Inc 616 243-1600
90 Windflower St Ne Comstock Park (49321) *(G-3623)*

Mbcd Inc 517 484-4426
1520 E Malcolm X St Lansing (48912) *(G-9867)*

Mbm Fabricators Co Inc 734 941-0100
36333 Northline Rd Romulus (48174) *(G-14301)*

Mbs, Jackson Also called Modern Builders Supply Inc *(G-8968)*

Mbwwproducts Inc 616 464-1650
825 Buchanan Ave Sw Grand Rapids (49507) *(G-6969)*

Mc Creadie Sales, Midland Also called MHR Investments Inc *(G-11388)*

Mc Donald Computer Corporation 248 350-9290
21411 Civic Center Dr # 100 Southfield (48076) *(G-15650)*

Mc Guire Mill & Lumber 989 735-3851
4499 Ford Rd Glennie (48737) *(G-6214)*

Mc Guire Spring Corporation 517 546-7311
6135 Grand River Rd Brighton (48114) *(G-2028)*

Mc Nally Elevator Company (PA) 269 381-1860
223 W Ransom St Kalamazoo (49007) *(G-9266)*

Mc Pherson Industrial Corp 586 752-5555
120 E Pond Dr Romeo (48065) *(G-14229)*

Mc Pherson Plastics Inc 269 694-9487
1347 E M 89 89 M Otsego (49078) *(G-12790)*

Mc REA Corporation 734 420-2116
40422 Cove Ct Plymouth (48170) *(G-13237)*

McBf, Warren Also called Melody Digiglio *(G-17923)*

McC Kalamazoo Inc (HQ) 269 381-2706
2710 N Pitcher St Kalamazoo (49004) *(G-9267)*

McCallum Fabricating LLC 586 784-5555
13927 Hough Rd Allenton (48002) *(G-231)*

McCarthy Group Incorporated (PA) 616 977-2900
5505 52nd St Se Grand Rapids (49512) *(G-6970)*

McClure Metals Group Inc 616 957-5955
6161 28th St Se Ste 5 Grand Rapids (49546) *(G-6971)*

McClure Tables Inc (PA) 616 662-5974
6661 Roger Dr Ste C Jenison (49428) *(G-9061)*

McClures Pickles LLC 248 837-9323
8201 Saint Aubin St Detroit (48211) *(G-4422)*

McClures Pickles LLC 248 837-9323
212 Royal Ave Royal Oak (48073) *(G-14562)*

McCoig Materials LLC 734 414-6179
40500 Ann Arbor Rd E # 20 Plymouth (48170) *(G-13238)*

McConnell & Scully Inc (PA) 517 568-4104
146 W Main St Homer (49245) *(G-8353)*

McCormick & Company Inc 586 558-8424
28660 Dequindre Rd Warren (48092) *(G-17921)*

McCoy Craftsman LLC 616 634-7455
1642 Broadway Ave Nw Grand Rapids (49504) *(G-6972)*

McCoy's Care Transportation, Benton Harbor Also called Serena Hines *(G-1583)*

McCray Press 989 792-8681
2710 State St Saginaw (48602) *(G-14689)*

McCrea Controls Inc 248 544-1366
2193 Oxford Rd Berkley (48072) *(G-1630)*

McCullys Wldg Fabrication LLC 231 499-3842
3916 E Old State Rd East Jordan (49727) *(G-4875)*

McDivitt Road Facility, Jackson Also called Advance Turning and Mfg Inc *(G-8803)*

McDonald Acquisitions LLC 616 878-7800
8074 Clyde Park Ave Sw Byron Center (49315) *(G-2282)*

McDonald Enterprises Inc 734 464-4664
36650 Plymouth Rd Livonia (48150) *(G-10305)*

McDonald Modular Solutions, Milford Also called 4d Building Inc *(G-11452)*

McDonald Wholesale Distributor 313 273-2870
19536 W Davison St Detroit (48223) *(G-4423)*

McDonalds 248 851-7310
655 N Lapeer Rd Oxford (48371) *(G-12900)*

McElroy Metal Mill Inc 269 781-8313
311 W Oliver Dr Marshall (49068) *(G-11069)*

McElroys Automotive Svc LLC 248 427-0501
30863 W 10 Mile Rd Farmington Hills (48336) *(G-5312)*

McEsson Drug Company, Livonia Also called McKesson Corporation *(G-10308)*

McG Plastics Inc 989 667-4349
3661 N Euclid Ave Bay City (48706) *(G-1373)*

McGean-Rohco Inc 216 441-4900
38521 Schoolcraft Rd Livonia (48150) *(G-10306)*

McGraw Hill Co 616 802-3000
3195 Wilson Dr Nw Grand Rapids (49534) *(G-6973)*

McIntyres Soft Water Svc Ltd 810 735-5778
1014 N Bridge St Linden (48451) *(G-10065)*

McKae Group LLC 313 564-5100
15356 Middlebelt Rd Livonia (48154) *(G-10307)*

McKay Press Inc 989 631-2360
7600 W Wackerly St Midland (48642) *(G-11387)*

McKechnie Tooling and Engrg, Roseville Also called McKechnie Vhcl Cmpnnts USA Inc *(G-14438)*

McKechnie Vhcl Cmpnnts USA Inc 218 894-1218
27087 Gratiot Ave 2 Roseville (48066) *(G-14438)*

McKechnie Vhcl Cmpnnts USA Inc (HQ) 586 491-2600
27087 Gratiot Ave Fl 2 Roseville (48066) *(G-14439)*

McKenna Enterprises Inc 248 375-3388
3128 Walton Blvd Rochester Hills (48309) *(G-14061)*

McKeon Products Inc (PA) 586 427-7560
25460 Guenther Warren (48091) *(G-17922)*

McKesson Corporation 734 953-2523
38220 Plymouth Rd Livonia (48150) *(G-10308)*

McKesson Pharmacy Systems LLC 800 521-1758
30933 Schoolcraft Rd Livonia (48150) *(G-10309)*

McL Jasco Inc 313 294-7414
7140 W Fort St Detroit (48209) *(G-4424)*

McL Jasco International, Detroit Also called McL Jasco Inc *(G-4424)*

McLanahan Corporation 517 614-2007
227 Chesterfield Pkwy East Lansing (48823) *(G-4902)*

McLaren Inc 989 720-4328
2170 W M 21 Owosso (48867) *(G-12842)*

McLaren Engineering, Livonia Also called Linamar Holding Nevada Inc *(G-10278)*

McLaren Plumbing Htg & Coolg, Owosso Also called McLaren Inc *(G-12842)*

McM, Novi Also called Michigan Custom Machines Inc *(G-12480)*

McM Disposal LLC 616 656-4049
978 64th St Sw Byron Center (49315) *(G-2283)*

McMackon Mktg ADM Pubg Svcs LL 734 878-3198
8407 Old Mill Dr Pinckney (48169) *(G-13051)*

McManus Software Development 810 231-6589
5171 Lisch Dr Whitmore Lake (48189) *(G-18540)*

MCN Oil & Gas, Traverse City Also called DTE Gas & Oil Company *(G-16672)*

McNamara & Mcnamara 906 293-5281
13123 State Highway M123 Newberry (49868) *(G-12093)*

McNaughton & Gunn Inc (PA) 734 429-5411
960 Woodland Dr Saline (48176) *(G-15025)*

McNaughton-Mckay Electric Co (PA) 248 399-7500
1357 E Lincoln Ave Madison Heights (48071) *(G-10779)*

McNees Manufacturing Inc 616 675-7480
750 Canada Rd Bailey (49303) *(G-1120)*

McNichols Conveyor Company 248 357-6077
21411 Civic Center Dr # 204 Southfield (48076) *(G-15651)*

McNichols Polsg & Anodizing (PA) 313 538-3470
12139 Woodbine Redford (48239) *(G-13744)*

McNichols Polsg & Anodizing 313 538-3470
12139 Wormer Redford (48239) *(G-13745)*

MCO, Mount Clemens Also called J B Cutting Inc *(G-11644)*

McPp-Detroit, Warren Also called Mitsubishi Chemical Amer Inc *(G-17932)*

MCS Consultants Inc 810 229-4222
1347 Rickett Rd Brighton (48116) *(G-2029)*

MCS Custom Design, Westland Also called Mikes Cabinet Shop Inc *(G-18396)*

MCS Industries Inc 517 568-4161
124 W Platt St Homer (49245) *(G-8354)*

MD Hiller Corp 877 751-9010
2021 Monroe St Ste 103 Dearborn (48124) *(G-3869)*

MD Investors Corporation (HQ) 734 207-6200
1 Dauch Dr Detroit (48211) *(G-4425)*

Mdc Contracting LLC 231 547-6595
5481 Us Highway 31 S Charlevoix (49720) *(G-2720)*

Mdla Inc 248 643-0807
2862 W Maple Rd Troy (48084) *(G-17242)*

Mdm Enterprises Inc 616 452-1591
3829 Rger B Chffee Mem Dr Grand Rapids (49548) *(G-6974)*

Mead Johnson & Company LLC 616 748-7100
725 E Main Ave Zeeland (49464) *(G-19051)*

Mead Westvaco Paper Div 906 233-2362
1800 20th Ave N Escanaba (49829) *(G-5082)*

Meal and More Incorporated 517 625-3186
130 W 3rd Ave Morrice (48857) *(G-11625)*

Mean Erectors Inc 989 737-3285
1928 Wilson Ave Saginaw (48638) *(G-14690)*

Means Inds - Southfield MI Off, Southfield Also called Means Industries Inc *(G-15652)*

Means Industries Inc (HQ) 989 754-1433
3715 E Washington Rd Saginaw (48601) *(G-14691)*

Means Industries Inc 989 754-0312
1811 S Jefferson Ave Saginaw (48601) *(G-14692)*

Means Industries Inc 586 826-8500
7026 Sterling Ponds Ct Sterling Heights (48312) *(G-16090)*

Means Industries Inc 989 754-1433
Oakland Cmmons Ii 20750 C Southfield (48034) *(G-15652)*

Means Industries Inc 989 754-3300
1860 S Jefferson Ave Saginaw (48601) *(G-14693)*

Means Trnsform Pdts - StrIng H, Sterling Heights Also called Means Industries Inc *(G-16090)*

Mec 989 983-3911
8276 Mill St Vanderbilt (49795) *(G-17574)*

Meca Systeme USA 616 294-1439
11846 Greenway Dr Holland (49424) *(G-8141)*

Meca-Systeme Usa Inc 616 843-5566
101 Washington Ave Grand Haven (49417) *(G-6335)*

Meccom Corporation 313 895-4900
5945 Martin St Detroit (48210) *(G-4426)*

Meccom Industrial Products Co 586 463-2828
22760 Macomb Indus Dr Clinton Township (48036) *(G-3297)*

Mechancal Sup A Div Nthrn McHn 906 789-0355
1701 N 26th St Escanaba (49029) *(G-5083)*

Mechanic Evltion Crtfction For 231 734-3483
1620 70th Ave Evart (49631) ***(G-5126)***
Mechanical Engineer, Troy *Also called Tata Autocomp Systems Limited* ***(G-17385)***
Mechanical Fabricators Inc 810 765-8853
770 Degurse Ave Marine City (48039) ***(G-10962)***
Mechanical Products Co, Jackson *Also called Mp Hollywood LLC* ***(G-8970)***
Mechanical Sheet Metal Co 734 284-1006
723 Walnut St Wyandotte (48192) ***(G-18832)***
Mechanical Transplanter Co LLC 616 396-8738
1150 Central Ave Holland (49423) ***(G-8142)***
Mectron Engineering Co Inc 734 944-8777
400 S Industrial Dr Saline (48176) ***(G-15026)***
Med Michigan Holdings LLC (PA) 888 891-1200
40600 Ann Arbor Rd E Plymouth (48170) ***(G-13239)***
Med-Kas Hydraulics Inc 248 585-3220
1805 Brinston Dr Troy (48083) ***(G-17243)***
Med-Tek, Suttons Bay *Also called Tilco Inc* ***(G-16346)***
Medalist 269 789-4653
117 E Michigan Ave Marshall (49068) ***(G-11070)***
Medallion Instrmnttion Systems 616 847-3700
17150 Hickory St Spring Lake (49456) ***(G-15833)***
Medbio LLC (PA) 616 245-0214
5346 36th St Se Grand Rapids (49512) ***(G-6975)***
Media Solutions Inc 313 831-3152
4715 Woodward Ave Fl 2 Detroit (48201) ***(G-4427)***
Media Tecnologies, Eaton Rapids *Also called Hoag & Sons Book Bindery Inc* ***(G-4965)***
Mediatechnologies, Shelby *Also called Silver Street Incorporated* ***(G-15160)***
Medical ACC & Reseach Co, Zeeland *Also called Artisan Medical Displays LLC* ***(G-18993)***
Medical Engineering & Dev 517 563-2352
4910 Dancer Rd Horton (49246) ***(G-8377)***
Medical Infrmtics Slutions LLC 248 851-3124
7285 Cathedral Dr Bloomfield Hills (48301) ***(G-1836)***
Medical Laser Group, Oxford *Also called Medical Laser Resources LLC* ***(G-12901)***
Medical Laser Resources LLC 248 628-8120
610 Gallagher Ct Oxford (48371) ***(G-12901)***
Medical Product Manufacturer, Ann Arbor *Also called Tissue Seal LLC* ***(G-692)***
Medical Systems Resource Group 248 476-5400
26105 Orchard Lake Rd Farmington Hills (48334) ***(G-5313)***
Medimage Inc 734 665-5400
331 Metty Dr Ste 1 Ann Arbor (48103) ***(G-568)***
Medsker Electric Inc 248 855-3383
28650 Grand River Ave Farmington Hills (48336) ***(G-5314)***
Medtest Holdings Inc 866 540-2715
5449 Research Dr Canton (48188) ***(G-2492)***
Medtronic Inc 616 643-5200
620 Watson St Sw Grand Rapids (49504) ***(G-6976)***
Medtronic Usa Inc 248 449-5027
39555 Orchard Hill Pl # 500 Novi (48375) ***(G-12478)***
Medwin Publishers LLC 248 247-6042
2609 Crooks Rd Ste 229 Troy (48084) ***(G-17244)***
Meech Road Ltd 734 255-9119
367 E South St Mason (48854) ***(G-11143)***
Meeders Dim & Lbr Pdts Co 231 587-8611
7810 S M 88 Hwy Mancelona (49659) ***(G-10874)***
Meeders Lumber Co 231 587-8611
7810 S M 88 Hwy Mancelona (49659) ***(G-10875)***
Meezherati Industries LLC 734 931-0466
2037 Collingwood St Detroit (48206) ***(G-4428)***
MEGA Precast Inc 586 477-5959
14670 23 Mile Rd Shelby Township (48315) ***(G-15272)***
Mega Printing Inc 248 624-6065
1600 W West Maple Rd D Walled Lake (48390) ***(G-17672)***
Mega Screen Corp 517 849-7057
549 Industrial Pkwy Jonesville (49250) ***(G-9094)***
Mega Wall Inc 616 647-4190
5340 6 Mile Ct Nw Comstock Park (49321) ***(G-3624)***
Megapixel Ideas LLC 616 307-5220
5880 Egypt Valley Ave Ne Belmont (49306) ***(G-1514)***
Megaplast North America, Shelby Township *Also called Moller Group North America Inc* ***(G-15284)***
Megapro Marketing Usa Inc 866 522-3652
2710 S 3rd St Niles (49120) ***(G-12143)***
Megee Print Document Solutions, Kalamazoo *Also called Megee Printing Inc* ***(G-9268)***
Megee Printing Inc 269 344-3226
509 Mills St Kalamazoo (49001) ***(G-9268)***
Meggitt 989 759-8327
628 N Hamilton St Saginaw (48602) ***(G-14694)***
Meghan March LLC 231 740-8114
3385 Verna Ave Muskegon (49442) ***(G-11865)***
Meh Logging Co, Nashville *Also called Mike Hughes* ***(G-11957)***
Mehring Books Inc 248 967-2924
25900 Greenfield Rd # 258 Oak Park (48237) ***(G-12627)***
Meiden America Inc 734 459-1781
15800 Centennial Dr Northville (48168) ***(G-12239)***
Meiers Signs Inc 906 786-3424
1717 N Lincoln Rd Escanaba (49829) ***(G-5084)***
Meijer Inc 269 556-2400
5019 Red Arrow Hwy Stevensville (49127) ***(G-16260)***
Mejenta Systems Inc 248 434-2583
30233 Southfield Rd # 113 Southfield (48076) ***(G-15653)***
Mel Media Group, Taylor *Also called Mel Printing Co Inc* ***(G-16440)***
Mel Printing Co Inc 313 928-5440
6000 Pardee Rd Taylor (48180) ***(G-16440)***
Melange Computer Services Inc 517 321-8434
808 Century Blvd Ste 100 Lansing (48917) ***(G-9774)***
Meliss Company Inc 248 398-1970
5020 White Lake Rd Clarkston (48346) ***(G-3049)***
Melissa Fowler 818 447-9903
1020 N Lemen St Fenton (48430) ***(G-5491)***
Melix Services Inc 248 387-9303
2359 Livernois Rd Ste 300 Hamtramck (48212) ***(G-7612)***
Mellemas Cut Stone 616 984-2493
16610 Findley Dr Sand Lake (49343) ***(G-15049)***
Melling Automotive Products, Jackson *Also called Melling Tool Co* ***(G-8951)***
Melling Do Brasil LLC 517 787-8172
2620 Saradan Dr Jackson (49202) ***(G-8948)***
Melling Industries Inc 517 787-8172
2620 Saradan Dr Jackson (49202) ***(G-8949)***
Melling Manufacturing Inc 517 750-3580
4901 James Mcdevitt St Jackson (49201) ***(G-8950)***
Melling Pattern and Prototype, Battle Creek *Also called A C Foundry Incorporated* ***(G-1175)***
Melling Products North LLC 989 588-6147
333 Grace St Farwell (48622) ***(G-5426)***
Melling Tool Co (PA) 517 787-8172
2620 Saradan Dr Jackson (49202) ***(G-8951)***
Melling Tool Co 517 787-8172
3700 Scheele Dr Jackson (49202) ***(G-8952)***
Melling Tool J4, Jackson *Also called Melling Tool Co* ***(G-8952)***
Mello Meats Inc (PA) 800 852-5019
270 Rex Blvd Auburn Hills (48326) ***(G-972)***
Melody Digiglio 586 754-4405
8088 E 9 Mile Rd Warren (48089) ***(G-17923)***
Melody Farms LLC 734 261-7980
31770 Enterprise Dr Livonia (48150) ***(G-10310)***
Meltex, Benton Harbor *Also called Martin Bros Mill Fndry Sup Co* ***(G-1567)***
Melttools LLC 269 978-0968
7849 S Sprinkle Rd Portage (49002) ***(G-13584)***
Memcon North America LLC 269 281-0478
6000 Red Arrow Hwy Unit I Stevensville (49127) ***(G-16261)***
Memories Manor 810 329-2800
5011 Davis Rd Saint Clair (48079) ***(G-14836)***
Memories Xpress 248 582-1836
29777 Stephenson Hwy Madison Heights (48071) ***(G-10780)***
Memtech Inc (PA) 734 455-8550
9033 General Dr Plymouth (48170) ***(G-13240)***
Memtron Technologies Co 989 652-2656
530 N Franklin St Frankenmuth (48734) ***(G-5869)***
Men of Steel Inc 989 635-4866
2920 Municipal Dr Marlette (48453) ***(G-10986)***
Menchies Frozen Yogurt, Lake Orion *Also called May Venture Inc* ***(G-9618)***
Mendenhall Associates Inc 734 741-4710
1500 Cedar Bend Dr Ann Arbor (48105) ***(G-569)***
Mendota Mantels LLC 651 271-7544
E6638 Maple Creek Rd Ironwood (49938) ***(G-8767)***
Mennel Milling Co of Mich Inc 269 782-5175
301 S Mill St Dowagiac (49047) ***(G-4788)***
Menominee Acquisition Corp 906 863-5595
144 1st St Menominee (49858) ***(G-11246)***
Menominee Carbide Cutting Tls, Menominee *Also called Menominee Saw and Supply Co* ***(G-11248)***
Menominee City of Michigan 906 863-3050
1301 5th Ave Menominee (49858) ***(G-11247)***
Menominee Cnty Jurnl Print Sp 906 753-2296
S322 Menominee St Stephenson (49887) ***(G-15909)***
Menominee Saw and Supply Co (PA) 906 863-2609
900 16th St Menominee (49858) ***(G-11248)***
Menominee Saw and Supply Co 906 863-8998
2134 13th St Menominee (49858) ***(G-11249)***
Menomnee Rver Lbr Dmnsions LLC 906 863-2682
2219 10th Ave Menominee (49858) ***(G-11250)***
Mensch Manufacturing LLC 269 945-5300
2333 S M 37 Hwy Hastings (49058) ***(G-7804)***
Mensch Mfg Mar Div Inc 269 945-5300
2499 S M 37 Hwy Hastings (49058) ***(G-7805)***
Mentor Enterprises Inc 269 483-7675
70431 M 103 White Pigeon (49099) ***(G-18483)***
Menu Pulse Inc 989 708-1207
1901 Kollen St Saginaw (48602) ***(G-14695)***
Merc-O-Tronic Instruments Corp 586 894-9529
215 Branch St Almont (48003) ***(G-265)***
Mercedes-Benz Extra LLC 205 747-8006
36455 Corp Dr Ste 175 Farmington Hills (48331) ***(G-5315)***
Merchandising Productions 616 676-6000
7575 Fulton St E Ada (49356) ***(G-29)***
Merchant Holdings Inc 906 786-7120
440 N 10th St Escanaba (49829) ***(G-5085)***

ALPHABETIC

Merchants Automatic Pdts Inc 734 829-0020
5740 S Beck Rd Canton (48188) *(G-2493)*
Merchants Industries Inc 734 397-3031
5715 S Sheldon Rd Canton (48188) *(G-2494)*
Merchants Metals LLC 810 227-3036
830 Grand Oaks Dr Howell (48843) *(G-8477)*
Mercury Displacement Inds Inc 269 663-8574
25028 Us 12 E Edwardsburg (49112) *(G-5009)*
Mercury Manufacturing Company 734 285-5150
1212 Grove St Wyandotte (48192) *(G-18833)*
Mercury Metal Forming Tech LLC 586 778-4444
29440 Calahan Rd Roseville (48066) *(G-14440)*
Mercury Products Corp 586 749-6800
30707 Commerce Blvd Chesterfield (48051) *(G-2909)*
Mercury Stamping Div, Saint Johns *Also called Lupaul Industries Inc (G-14904)*
Mercy Health Partners (HQ) 231 728-4032
1675 Leahy St Ste 101 Muskegon (49442) *(G-11866)*
Mercy Health Partners 231 672-4886
1560 E Sherman Blvd # 145 Muskegon (49444) *(G-11867)*
Merdel Game Manufacturing Co 231 845-1263
218 E Dowland St Ludington (49431) *(G-10544)*
Meredith Lea Sand Gravel 517 930-3662
6703 Lansing Rd Charlotte (48813) *(G-2762)*
Meridian Energy Corporation 517 339-8444
6009 Marsh Rd Haslett (48840) *(G-7775)*
Meridian Industries 248 526-0444
2500 Rochester Ct Troy (48083) *(G-17245)*
Meridian Lightweight Tech, Plymouth *Also called Magnesium Products America Inc (G-13231)*
Meridian Lightweight Tech Inc 248 663-8100
47805 Galleon Dr Ste B Plymouth (48170) *(G-13241)*
Meridian Mechatronics LLC 517 447-4587
120 W Keegan St Deerfield (49238) *(G-3958)*
Meridian Screen Prtg & Design, Okemos *Also called Meridian Screen Prtg & Design (G-12674)*
Meridian Screen Prtg & Design 517 351-2525
3362 Hulett Rd Okemos (48864) *(G-12674)*
Meridian Weekly, The, Ovid *Also called Hometown Publishing Inc (G-12814)*
Meridianrx LLC 855 323-4580
1 Campus Martius Ste 750 Detroit (48226) *(G-4429)*
Merillat Industries LLC 517 263-0269
5353 W Us Highway 223 Adrian (49221) *(G-83)*
Merillat LP (HQ) 517 263-0771
5353 W Us Highway 223 Adrian (49221) *(G-84)*
Meritor Inc (PA) 248 435-1000
2135 W Maple Rd Troy (48084) *(G-17246)*
Meritor Heavy Vhcl Systems LLC (HQ) 248 435-1000
2135 W Maple Rd Troy (48084) *(G-17247)*
Meritor Industrial Pdts LLC (HQ) 888 725-9355
2135 W Maple Rd Troy (48084) *(G-17248)*
Meritor Intl Holdings LLC (HQ) 248 435-1000
2135 W Maple Rd Troy (48084) *(G-17249)*
Meritor Specialty Products LLC 517 545-5800
1045 Durant Dr Howell (48843) *(G-8478)*
Meritor Specialty Products LLC (HQ) 248 435-1000
2135 W Maple Rd Troy (48084) *(G-17250)*
Meritt Tool & Die 517 726-1452
2354 N Pease Rd Vermontville (49096) *(G-17590)*
Merlin Simulation Inc 703 560-7203
2135 Bishop Cir E Ste 6 Dexter (48130) *(G-4745)*
Merrifield McHy Solutions Inc 248 494-7335
5430 Gatewood Dr Sterling Heights (48310) *(G-16091)*
Merrill Aviation & Defense, Saginaw *Also called Merrill Technologies Group (G-14696)*
Merrill Fabricators, Alma *Also called Merrill Technologies Group Inc (G-246)*
Merrill Institute Inc 989 462-0330
520 Republic Ave Alma (48801) *(G-245)*
Merrill Technologies Group 989 921-1490
1023 S Wheeler St Saginaw (48602) *(G-14696)*
Merrill Technologies Group Inc (PA) 989 791-6676
400 Florence St Saginaw (48602) *(G-14697)*
Merrill Technologies Group Inc 989 462-0330
520 Republic Ave Alma (48801) *(G-246)*
Merrill Technologies Group Inc 989 643-7981
21659 Gratiot Rd Merrill (48637) *(G-11263)*
Merrill Tool & Machine, Merrill *Also called Merrill Technologies Group Inc (G-11263)*
Merrill Tool Holding Company, Saginaw *Also called Merrill Technologies Group Inc (G-14697)*
Merriman Products Inc 517 787-1825
1302 W Ganson St Jackson (49202) *(G-8953)*
Merritt Energy 231 723-6587
4000 Fisk Rd Manistee (49660) *(G-10908)*
Merritt Press Inc 517 394-0118
6534 Aurelius Rd Lansing (48911) *(G-9868)*
Merritt Raceway LLC 231 590-4431
7300 N Maple Valley Rd Ne Mancelona (49659) *(G-10876)*
Mersen 989 894-2911
900 Harrison St Bay City (48708) *(G-1374)*
Mersen USA Bay City-MI LLC, Bay City *Also called Mersen USA Gs Corp (G-1375)*
Mersen USA Gs - Greenville, Greenville *Also called Mersen USA Gs Corp (G-7500)*
Mersen USA Gs - Greenville, Greenville *Also called Mersen USA Gs Corp (G-7501)*
Mersen USA Gs Corp 616 754-5671
712 Industrial Park Dr Greenville (48838) *(G-7500)*
Mersen USA Gs Corp 989 894-2911
900 Harrison St Bay City (48708) *(G-1375)*
Mersen USA Gs Corp 616 754-5671
712 Industrial Park Dr Greenville (48838) *(G-7501)*
Mesa Corporation 517 669-5656
1000 E Geneva Dr Dewitt (48820) *(G-4712)*
Mesick Mold Co 231 885-1304
4901 Industrial Dr Mesick (49668) *(G-11273)*
Messenger Printing & Copy Svc 616 669-5620
5300 Plaza Ave Hudsonville (49426) *(G-8593)*
Messenger Printing Service Inc 313 381-0300
20136 Ecorse Rd Taylor (48180) *(G-16441)*
Messersmith Manufacturing Inc 906 466-9010
2612 F Rd Bark River (49807) *(G-1156)*
Messina Concrete Inc 734 783-1020
14675 Telegraph Rd Flat Rock (48134) *(G-5623)*
Met Inc 231 845-1737
640 S Pere Marquette Hwy Ludington (49431) *(G-10545)*
Met-L-Tec LLC (PA) 734 847-7004
7310 Express Rd Temperance (48182) *(G-16540)*
Met-Pro Technologies LLC 989 725-8184
1172 S M 13 Lennon (48449) *(G-9995)*
Meta Tool Technologies LLC 616 295-2115
17024 Taft Rd Spring Lake (49456) *(G-15834)*
Meta4mat LLC 616 214-7418
320 Dodge Rd Ne Ste B Comstock Park (49321) *(G-3625)*
Metabolic Solutions Dev Co LLC 269 343-6732
3133 Orchard Vista Dr Se Grand Rapids (49546) *(G-6977)*
Metal Arc Inc 231 865-3111
3792 E Ellis Rd Muskegon (49444) *(G-11868)*
Metal Components LLC (PA) 616 252-1900
3281 Roger B Grand Rapids (49548) *(G-6978)*
Metal Components LLC 616 252-1900
3281 Rger B Chffee Mem Dr Grand Rapids (49548) *(G-6979)*
Metal Components Inc 616 389-2400
2000 Chicago Dr Sw Wyoming (49519) *(G-18893)*
Metal Craft Impression Die, Livonia *Also called Metalcraft Impression Die Co (G-10311)*
Metal Design Manufacturing LLC 313 893-9810
17891 Ryan Rd Detroit (48212) *(G-4430)*
Metal Dynamics Detroit 313 841-1800
3100 Lonyo St Detroit (48209) *(G-4431)*
Metal Fab Tool & Machine, Mio *Also called Metalfab Tool & Machine Inc (G-11511)*
Metal Fabrication, Blissfield *Also called Adaptive Metal Works LLC (G-1760)*
Metal Fbrication Machining Div, Fennville *Also called Harrington Construction Co (G-5437)*
Metal Finishing Technology 231 733-9736
2652 Hoyt St Muskegon (49444) *(G-11869)*
Metal Flow Corporation 616 392-7976
11694 James St Holland (49424) *(G-8143)*
Metal Forge, Commerce Township *Also called SPX Corporation (G-3574)*
Metal Forming & Coining Corp 586 731-2003
51810 Danview Tech Ct Shelby Township (48315) *(G-15273)*
Metal Forming Technology Inc 586 949-4586
48630 Structural Dr Chesterfield (48051) *(G-2910)*
Metal Improvement Company LLC 734 728-8600
30100 Cypress Rd Romulus (48174) *(G-14302)*
Metal Mart USA Inc 586 977-5820
31164 Dequindre Rd Warren (48092) *(G-17924)*
Metal Master Welding LLC 810 706-0476
3857 Hollow Corners Rd Dryden (48428) *(G-4806)*
Metal Mates Inc (PA) 248 646-9831
20135 Elwood St Beverly Hills (48025) *(G-1666)*
Metal Mechanics Inc 269 679-2525
350 S 14th St Schoolcraft (49087) *(G-15124)*
Metal Merchants of Michigan 248 293-0621
2691 Leach Rd Rochester Hills (48309) *(G-14062)*
Metal Plus LLC 616 459-7587
3711 Dykstra Dr Nw Grand Rapids (49544) *(G-6980)*
Metal Prep Technology Inc 313 843-2890
621 Nightingale St Dearborn (48128) *(G-3870)*
Metal Punch Corporation 231 775-8391
907 Saunders St Cadillac (49601) *(G-2346)*
Metal Quest Inc 989 733-2011
11739 M68-33 Hwy Onaway (49765) *(G-12699)*
Metal Sales Manufacturing Corp 989 686-5879
5209 Mackinaw Rd Bay City (48706) *(G-1376)*
Metal Spinning Specialists 810 743-6797
3217 Eastgate St Burton (48519) *(G-2239)*
Metal Standard Corp 616 396-6356
286 Hedcor St Holland (49423) *(G-8144)*
Metal Stmping Spport Group LLC, Romeo *Also called Nidec Chs LLC (G-14230)*
Metal Tech Products Inc 313 533-5277
15720 Dale St Detroit (48223) *(G-4432)*
Metal Worxs Inc 586 484-9355
7374 Flamingo St Clay (48001) *(G-3122)*
Metalbuilt LLC 586 786-9106
50171 E Rssell Schmidt Bl Chesterfield (48051) *(G-2911)*

Metalcraft Cutting Tools LLC 586 243-5591
37060 Garfield Rd Ste T-4 Clinton Township (48036) *(G-3298)*
Metalcraft Impression Die Co 734 513-8058
11914 Brookfield St Livonia (48150) *(G-10311)*
Metaldyne, Detroit *Also called MD Investors Corporation (G-4425)*
Metaldyne LLC (HQ) 734 207-6200
1 Dauch Dr Detroit (48211) *(G-4433)*
Metaldyne Prfmce Group Inc (HQ) 248 727-1800
1 Towne Sq Ste 550 Southfield (48076) *(G-15654)*
Metaldyne Pwrtrain Cmpnnts Inc (HQ) 313 758-2000
1 Dauch Dr Detroit (48211) *(G-4434)*
Metaldyne Tblar Components LLC (HQ) 248 727-1800
1 Towne Sq Ste 550 Southfield (48076) *(G-15655)*
Metalfab Inc (PA) 313 381-7579
6900 Chase Rd Dearborn (48126) *(G-3871)*
Metalfab Manufacturing Inc 989 826-2301
378 Booth Rd Mio (48647) *(G-11510)*
Metalfab Tool & Machine Inc 989 826-6044
55 W Kittle Rd Mio (48647) *(G-11511)*
Metalform Industries LLC 248 462-0056
52830 Tuscany Grv Shelby Township (48315) *(G-15274)*
Metalform LLC 517 569-3313
2223 Rives Eaton Rd Jackson (49201) *(G-8954)*
Metallurgical High Vacuum Corp 269 543-4291
6708 124th Ave Fennville (49408) *(G-5440)*
Metallurgical Processing Co., Warren *Also called Metallurgical Processing LLC (G-17925)*
Metallurgical Processing LLC 586 758-3100
23075 Warner Ave Warren (48091) *(G-17925)*
Metalmite Corporation 248 651-9415
194 S Elizabeth St Rochester (48307) *(G-13911)*
Metals Preservation Group LLC 586 944-2720
23010 E Industrial Dr Saint Clair Shores (48080) *(G-14870)*
Metalsa SA De Cv, Sterling Heights *Also called Metalsa Structural Pdts Inc (G-16092)*
Metalsa Structural Pdts Inc 248 669-3704
40117 Mitchell Dr Sterling Heights (48313) *(G-16092)*
Metalsa Structural Pdts Inc (HQ) 248 669-3704
29575 Hudson Dr Novi (48377) *(G-12479)*
Metaltec Steel Abrasive Co (HQ) 734 459-7900
41155 Joy Rd Canton (48187) *(G-2495)*
Metalution Tool Die 616 355-9700
60 W 64th St Holland (49423) *(G-8145)*
Metalworking Industries of MI 248 538-0680
27750 Stansbury Blvd # 100 Farmington Hills (48334) *(G-5316)*
Metalworking Lubricants Co (PA) 248 332-3500
25 W Silverdome Indus Par Pontiac (48342) *(G-13397)*
Metalworks Inc (PA) 231 845-5136
902 4th St Ludington (49431) *(G-10546)*
Metaris Hydraulics 586 949-4240
48175 Gratiot Ave Chesterfield (48051) *(G-2912)*
Metavation LLC (HQ) 248 351-1000
900 Wilshire Dr Ste 270 Troy (48084) *(G-17251)*
Meteor Web Marketing Inc 734 822-4999
3438 E Ellsworth Rd Ste A Ann Arbor (48108) *(G-570)*
Meter Devices Company Inc 330 455-0301
23847 Industrial Park Dr Farmington Hills (48335) *(G-5317)*
Meter USA LLC 810 388-9373
1765 Michigan Ave Marysville (48040) *(G-11091)*
Method Tool, Saint Charles *Also called MTI Precision Machining Inc (G-14806)*
Methodica Technologies LLC (PA) 312 622-7697
100 W Big Beavr Rd # 200 Troy (48084) *(G-17252)*
Methods Machine Tools Inc 248 624-8601
50531 Varsity Ct Wixom (48393) *(G-18709)*
Methods Prtable Machining Wldg 989 413-5022
9607 Price Rd Laingsburg (48848) *(G-9537)*
Metra Inc 248 543-3500
24211 John R Rd Hazel Park (48030) *(G-7831)*
Metrex Research LLC 734 947-6700
28210 Wick Rd Romulus (48174) *(G-14303)*
Metric Hydrulic Components LLC 586 786-6990
13870 Cavaliere Dr Shelby Township (48315) *(G-15275)*
Metric Manufacturing Co Inc 616 897-5959
1001 Foreman St Lowell (49331) *(G-10511)*
Metric Precision Tool LLC 734 946-8114
12222 Universal Dr Taylor (48180) *(G-16442)*
Metric Tool Company Inc 313 369-9610
17144 Mount Elliott St Detroit (48212) *(G-4435)*
Metrie Inc 313 299-1860
27025 Trolley Indus Dr Taylor (48180) *(G-16443)*
Metro Broach Inc 586 758-2340
2160 E 9 Mile Rd Warren (48091) *(G-17926)*
Metro Cast Corporation 734 728-0210
6170 Commerce Dr Westland (48185) *(G-18395)*
Metro Detroit Printing LLC 734 469-7174
12892 Farmington Rd Livonia (48150) *(G-10312)*
Metro Detroit Screen Prtg LLC 586 337-5167
14416 Towering Oaks Dr Shelby Township (48315) *(G-15276)*
Metro Duct Inc 517 783-2646
485 E South St Jackson (49203) *(G-8955)*
Metro Elevator, Grand Rapids *Also called Elevated Technologies Inc (G-6672)*
Metro Engrg of Grnd Rapids 616 458-2823
845 Ottawa Ave Nw Grand Rapids (49503) *(G-6981)*
Metro Graphic Arts Inc 616 245-2271
900 40th St Se Grand Rapids (49508) *(G-6982)*
Metro Machine Works Inc 734 941-4571
11977 Harrison Romulus (48174) *(G-14304)*
Metro Medical Eqp Mfg Inc 734 522-8400
38415 Schoolcraft Rd Livonia (48150) *(G-10313)*
Metro Parent Media Group, Ferndale *Also called All Kids Cnsdred Pubg Group In (G-5521)*
Metro Piping Inc 313 872-4330
1500b Trombly St Detroit (48211) *(G-4436)*
Metro Powder Coating 313 744-7134
18434 Fitzpatrick St Detroit (48228) *(G-4437)*
Metro Printing Service Inc 248 545-4444
1950 Barrett Dr Troy (48084) *(G-17253)*
Metro Prints Inc 586 979-9690
5580 Gatewood Dr Ste 103 Sterling Heights (48310) *(G-16093)*
Metro Promotional Specialties, Troy *Also called Metro Printing Service Inc (G-17253)*
Metro Rebar Inc 248 851-5894
4275 Middlebelt Rd West Bloomfield (48323) *(G-18297)*
Metro Sign Fabricators Inc 586 493-0502
43984 N Groesbeck Hwy Clinton Township (48036) *(G-3299)*
Metro Stamping & Mfg Co 313 538-6464
26955 Fullerton Redford (48239) *(G-13746)*
Metro Technologies Ltd 248 528-9240
1462 E Big Beaver Rd Troy (48083) *(G-17254)*
Metro-Fabricating LLC 989 667-8100
1650 Tech Dr Bay City (48706) *(G-1377)*
Metroastyling 586 991-6854
5400 18 Mile Rd Sterling Heights (48314) *(G-16094)*
Metronom US, Ann Arbor *Also called Inora Technologies Inc (G-529)*
Metropolitan Alloys Corp 313 366-4443
17385 Ryan Rd Detroit (48212) *(G-4438)*
Metropolitan Baking Company 313 875-7246
8579 Lumpkin St Detroit (48212) *(G-4439)*
Metropolitan Indus Lithography 269 323-9333
1116 W Centre Ave Portage (49024) *(G-13585)*
Metropoulos Amplification Inc 810 614-3905
10460 N Holly Rd Holly (48442) *(G-8284)*
Mettek LLC 616 895-2033
11480 53rd Ave Ste B Allendale (49401) *(G-225)*
Metter Flooring LLC 517 914-2004
2531 W Territorial Rd Rives Junction (49277) *(G-13887)*
Metter Flooring and Cnstr, Rives Junction *Also called Metter Flooring LLC (G-13887)*
Mettes Printery Inc 734 261-6262
27454 Plymouth Rd Livonia (48150) *(G-10314)*
Mettle Craft Manufacturing LLC 586 306-8962
3223 15 Mile Rd Sterling Heights (48310) *(G-16095)*
Metzeler Auto Profile Systems, Auburn Hills *Also called Henniges Auto Sling Systems N (G-925)*
Metzgar Conveyor Co 616 784-0930
5801 Clay Ave Sw Ste A Grand Rapids (49548) *(G-6983)*
Metzger Sawmill 269 963-3022
3100 W Halbert Rd Battle Creek (49017) *(G-1273)*
Mexamerica Foods LLC 814 781-1447
219 Canton St Sw Ste A Grand Rapids (49507) *(G-6984)*
Mexican Food Specialties Inc 734 779-2370
21084 Bridge St Southfield (48033) *(G-15656)*
Mexico Express 313 843-6717
7611 W Vernor Hwy Detroit (48209) *(G-4440)*
Mextor Disposable LLC 313 921-6860
607 Shelby St Ste 700 Detroit (48226) *(G-4441)*
Meyers Boat Company Inc 517 265-9821
343 Lawrence Ave Adrian (49221) *(G-85)*
Meyers John 989 236-5400
5752 Cleveland Rd Middleton (48856) *(G-11298)*
MFC Netform Inc 586 731-2003
51810 Danview Tech Ct Shelby Township (48315) *(G-15277)*
Mfg United LLC 313 928-1802
17025 Clarann St Melvindale (48122) *(G-11204)*
Mfp Automation Engineering Inc 616 538-5700
4404 Central Pkwy Hudsonville (49426) *(G-8594)*
Mfr Enterprises Inc 517 285-9555
623 N Rosemary St Lansing (48917) *(G-9775)*
Mfr Enterprises LLC 248 965-3220
1223 Chicago Rd Troy (48083) *(G-17255)*
Mg Welding Inc 586 405-2909
76380 Andrews Rd Richmond (48062) *(G-13841)*
MGM Industries Inc 248 561-7558
2192 Oakshire Ave Berkley (48072) *(G-1631)*
MGR Molds Inc 586 254-6020
6450 Cotter Ave Sterling Heights (48314) *(G-16096)*
Mgs Horticultural USA Inc 248 661-4378
9900 Mount Elliott St Detroit (48211) *(G-4442)*
Mh Industries Ltd 734 261-2600
8101 Lyndon St Detroit (48238) *(G-4443)*
Mh Industries Ltd 734 261-7560
6960 Orchard Lake Rd # 301 West Bloomfield (48322) *(G-18298)*
Mh Publishing LLC 313 881-3724
166 Hillcrest Ln Grosse Pointe Farms (48236) *(G-7537)*

ALPHABETIC

(PA)=Parent Co (HQ)=Headquarters (DH)=Div Headquarters
2022 Harris Michigan Industrial Directory
1057

Mhr Inc 616 394-0191
78 Veterans Dr Holland (49423) *(G-8146)*
MHR Investments Inc 989 832-5395
601 S Saginaw Rd Midland (48640) *(G-11388)*
MHS Conveyor Corp 231 798-4547
1300 E Mount Garfield Rd Norton Shores (49441) *(G-12310)*
MI Classical Press 734 747-6337
2377 Timbercrest Ct Ann Arbor (48105) *(G-571)*
MI Custom Signs LLC 734 946-7446
20109 Northline Rd Taylor (48180) *(G-16444)*
MI Dynaco, Kingston Also called Midynaco LLC *(G-9526)*
MI Frozen Food LLC 231 357-4334
33 Lake St Manistee (49660) *(G-10909)*
MI Probation, Ionia Also called Uniprax LLC *(G-8692)*
MI Soy Candle Company LLC 586 350-7654
27550 Liberty Dr Warren (48092) *(G-17927)*
Mi-Tech Tooling Inc 989 912-2440
6215 Garfield Ave Cass City (48726) *(G-2618)*
Miba Hydramechanica Corp 586 264-3094
6625 Cobb Dr Sterling Heights (48312) *(G-16097)*
Mibiz, Norton Shores Also called News One Inc *(G-12316)*
Mica Crafters Inc 517 548-2924
3845 W Grand River Ave Howell (48855) *(G-8479)*
Mica TEC Inc 586 758-4404
21325 Hoover Rd Warren (48089) *(G-17928)*
Miccus Inc 616 604-4449
3336 Lakewood Shores Dr Howell (48843) *(G-8480)*
Michael Anderson 231 652-5717
4933 E Croton Dr Newaygo (49337) *(G-12088)*
Michael Chris Storms 231 263-7516
1401 W Center Rd Kingsley (49649) *(G-9525)*
Michael E Nipke LLC 616 350-0200
51 Monroe Center St Nw # 201 Grand Rapids (49503) *(G-6985)*
Michael Engineering Ltd 989 772-4073
5625 Venture Way Mount Pleasant (48858) *(G-11711)*
Michael John LLC 734 560-9268
9840 Mayfield St Livonia (48150) *(G-10315)*
Michael Kors 616 730-7071
350 84th St Sw Ste 700 Byron Center (49315) *(G-2284)*
Michael Niederpruem 231 935-0241
880 Lake Dr Ne Kalkaska (49646) *(G-9396)*
Michael Schafer and Associates, Wixom Also called Midwest Sales Associates Inc *(G-18710)*
Michael-Stephens Company 248 583-7767
1206 E Maple Rd Troy (48083) *(G-17256)*
Michaelene's Gourmet Granola, Clarkston Also called Michaelenes Inc *(G-3050)*
Michaelenes Inc 248 625-0156
7415 Deer Forest Ct Clarkston (48348) *(G-3050)*
Michalski Enterprises Inc 517 703-0777
16733 Industrial Pkwy Lansing (48906) *(G-9716)*
Michcor Container Inc 616 452-7089
1151 Sheldon Ave Se Grand Rapids (49507) *(G-6986)*
Michelle's Restaurant, Harper Woods Also called Sweetheart Bakery of Michigan *(G-7673)*
Michels Inc (PA) 313 441-3620
18900 Michigan Ave K103 Dearborn (48126) *(G-3872)*
Michiana Aggregate Inc 269 695-7669
3265 W Us Highway 12 Niles (49120) *(G-12144)*
Michiana Corrugated Pdts Co 269 651-5225
110 N Franks Ave Sturgis (49091) *(G-16306)*
Michiana Forklift 269 663-2700
69735 Brizendine St Edwardsburg (49112) *(G-5010)*
Michiana Rtational Molding LLC 574 849-7077
950 Industrial Park Dr Constantine (49042) *(G-3670)*
Michigan -Bsed Frdman Dscndnts 810 820-3017
2406 Thom St Flint (48506) *(G-5731)*
Michigan Acdemy Fmly Physcians 517 347-0098
2164 Commons Pkwy Okemos (48864) *(G-12675)*
Michigan AG Services Inc 616 374-8803
3587 W Tupper Lake Rd Lake Odessa (48849) *(G-9577)*
Michigan Aggr Sand/Gravel Haul 231 258-8237
765 Rabourn Rd Ne Kalkaska (49646) *(G-9397)*
Michigan Aggregates Corp 517 688-4414
996 E Chicago Rd Jerome (49249) *(G-9079)*
Michigan ATF Holdings LLC (HQ) 734 941-2220
11850 Wayne Rd Romulus (48174) *(G-14305)*
Michigan Auto Bending Corp 248 528-1150
1700 E 14 Mile Rd Madison Heights (48071) *(G-10781)*
Michigan Auto Comprsr Inc (HQ) 517 796-3200
2400 N Dearing Rd Parma (49269) *(G-12938)*
Michigan Baking Co., Detroit Also called Metropolitan Baking Company *(G-4439)*
Michigan Biodiesel LLC 269 427-0804
2813 W Main St Kalamazoo (49006) *(G-9269)*
Michigan Biofuels, Kalamazoo Also called Energy Suppliers LLC *(G-9180)*
Michigan Box Company (PA) 313 873-9500
1910 Trombly St Detroit (48211) *(G-4444)*
Michigan Brand Inc 989 395-4345
320 Heinlein Strasse Frankenmuth (48734) *(G-5870)*
Michigan Brass Division, Spring Lake Also called Marquis Industries Inc *(G-15832)*
Michigan Brush Mfg Co 313 834-1070
7446 Central St Detroit (48210) *(G-4445)*

Michigan Btlg & Cstm Pack Co 313 846-1717
13940 Tireman St Detroit (48228) *(G-4446)*
Michigan Carbide Company Inc 586 264-8780
1263 Souter Dr Troy (48083) *(G-17257)*
Michigan Carton Paper Boy 269 963-4004
79 Fountain St E Battle Creek (49017) *(G-1274)*
Michigan Celery Promotion Coop 616 669-1250
5009 40th Ave Hudsonville (49426) *(G-8595)*
Michigan Chese Prtein Pdts LLC 517 403-5247
10015 Wisner Hwy Tipton (49287) *(G-16591)*
Michigan Chimneys 810 640-7961
9341 Neff Rd Clio (48420) *(G-3405)*
Michigan Chronicle Pubg Co 313 963-5522
1452 Randolph St Ste 400 Detroit (48226) *(G-4447)*
Michigan Church Supply Co Inc (PA) 810 686-8877
7166 N Saginaw Rd Mount Morris (48458) *(G-11674)*
Michigan Cnc Tool Inc 734 449-9590
11710 Green Oak Indus Dr Whitmore Lake (48189) *(G-18541)*
Michigan Coating Products Inc 616 456-8800
3761 Eastern Ave Se Grand Rapids (49508) *(G-6987)*
Michigan Crane Parts & Svc Co, Rochester Hills Also called Crane Technologies Group Inc *(G-13985)*
Michigan Crushed Concrete Inc 313 534-1500
25012 Plymouth Rd Detroit (48239) *(G-4448)*
Michigan Custom Machines Inc 248 347-7900
22750 Heslip Dr Novi (48375) *(G-12480)*
Michigan Dessert Corporation 248 544-4574
10750 Capital St Oak Park (48237) *(G-12628)*
Michigan Die Casting LLC 269 471-7715
51241 M 51 N Dowagiac (49047) *(G-4789)*
Michigan Diversfd Holdings Inc 248 280-0450
700 E Whitcomb Ave Madison Heights (48071) *(G-10782)*
Michigan Diversified Metals 517 223-7730
144 Veterans Dr Fowlerville (48836) *(G-5851)*
Michigan Drill, Troy Also called Republic Drill/Apt Corp *(G-17330)*
Michigan Dutch Barns Inc 616 693-2754
9811 Thompson Rd Lake Odessa (48849) *(G-9578)*
Michigan East Side Sales LLC 989 354-6867
4220 Us Highway 23 S Alpena (49707) *(G-302)*
Michigan Envelope Inc 616 554-3404
6650 Clay Ave Sw Grand Rapids (49548) *(G-6988)*
Michigan Ethanol, LLC, Caro Also called Poet Biorefining - Caro LLC *(G-2577)*
Michigan Fab and Engrg LLC 248 297-5268
12700 Mansfield St Detroit (48227) *(G-4449)*
Michigan Farm Cheese Dairy 231 462-3301
4295 E Millerton Rd Fountain (49410) *(G-5827)*
Michigan Farm To Freezer, Manistee Also called MI Frozen Food LLC *(G-10909)*
Michigan Fire Estinguishers, Detroit Also called Fire Equipment Company *(G-4233)*
Michigan Flame Hardening, Detroit Also called Detroit Edge Tool Company *(G-4146)*
Michigan Foam Products Inc 616 452-9611
1820 Chicago Dr Sw Grand Rapids (49519) *(G-6989)*
Michigan For Vaccine Choice 586 294-3074
22615 Francis St Saint Clair Shores (48082) *(G-14871)*
Michigan Forge Company LLC 815 758-6400
2807 S Martin L Kng Jr Bl Lansing (48910) *(G-9869)*
Michigan Freeze Pack, Hart Also called Hart Freeze Pack LIC *(G-7754)*
Michigan Front Page LLC 313 963-5522
479 Ledyard St Detroit (48201) *(G-4450)*
Michigan Fuels 313 886-7110
20700 Mack Ave Grosse Pointe Woods (48236) *(G-7571)*
Michigan Gear & Engineering, Gregory Also called Boos Products Inc *(G-7513)*
Michigan General Grinding LLC 616 454-5089
328 Winter Ave Nw Grand Rapids (49504) *(G-6990)*
Michigan Glass Lined Storage, Lake Odessa Also called Michigan AG Services Inc *(G-9577)*
Michigan Graphic Arts 517 278-4120
131 N Angola Rd Coldwater (49036) *(G-3444)*
Michigan Graphics & Awards, Berkley Also called Michigan Plaques & Awards Inc *(G-1632)*
Michigan Graphics & Signs 989 224-1936
1110 E Steel Rd Saint Johns (48879) *(G-14908)*
Michigan Grower Products Inc 269 665-7071
251 Mccollum Galesburg (49053) *(G-6080)*
Michigan Gypsum Co 989 792-8734
6105 Jefferson Ave Midland (48640) *(G-11389)*
Michigan Herbal Remedies LLC (PA) 616 818-0823
904 Chicago Dr Jenison (49428) *(G-9062)*
Michigan Highway Signs Inc (PA) 810 695-7529
5182 S Saginaw Rd Grand Blanc (48507) *(G-6253)*
Michigan Hooks & Bullets Mag, Cadillac Also called Triple S Publications LLC *(G-2362)*
Michigan Hrdwood Vneer Lbr Div, Munising Also called Timber Products Co Ltd Partnr *(G-11755)*
Michigan Indus Met Pdts Inc 616 786-3922
1674 S Getty St Muskegon (49442) *(G-11870)*
Michigan Industrial Finishes 248 553-7014
29463 Shenandoah Dr Farmington Hills (48331) *(G-5318)*
Michigan Industrial Tools, Grand Rapids Also called Tekton Inc *(G-7251)*
Michigan Industrial Trim Inc (PA) 734 947-0344
12400 Universal Dr Taylor (48180) *(G-16445)*

Michigan Instruments LLC 616 554-9696
  4717 Talon Ct Se Grand Rapids (49512) *(G-6991)*
Michigan Interlock LLC 248 481-9743
  2911 Pontiac Lake Rd A Waterford (48328) *(G-18136)*
Michigan Journal, The, Dearborn *Also called Univesity Michigan-Dearborn (G-3906)*
Michigan Kitchen Distributors, Marshall *Also called W S Townsend Company (G-11078)*
Michigan Kitchen Distributors, Lansing *Also called W S Townsend Company (G-9903)*
Michigan Ladder Company LLC 734 482-5946
  12 E Forest Ave Ypsilanti (48198) *(G-18967)*
Michigan Laser Mfg LLC 810 623-2783
  718 Advance St Brighton (48116) *(G-2030)*
Michigan Lasercut, Grand Rapids *Also called Lasercutting Services Inc (G-6929)*
Michigan Legal Publishing Ltd 877 525-1990
  2885 Sanford Ave Sw Grandville (49418) *(G-7400)*
Michigan Lightning Protection 866 712-4071
  2401 O Brien Rd Sw Grand Rapids (49534) *(G-6992)*
Michigan Lumber & Wood Fiber I 989 848-2100
  4776 N Abbe Rd Comins (48619) *(G-3504)*
Michigan Machining Inc 810 686-6655
  3322 E Mount Morris Rd Mount Morris (48458) *(G-11675)*
Michigan Maple Block Company 231 347-4170
  1420 Standish Ave Petoskey (49770) *(G-13006)*
Michigan Maps Inc 231 264-6800
  104 Dexter St Elk Rapids (49629) *(G-5027)*
Michigan Masonry Materials, Detroit *Also called Land Star Inc (G-4377)*
Michigan Med Innovations LLC 616 682-4848
  481 Pettis Ave Se Ada (49301) *(G-30)*
Michigan Medical Society, East Lansing *Also called Michigan State Medical Society (G-4904)*
Michigan Metal Coatings Co 810 966-9240
  2015 Dove St Port Huron (48060) *(G-13501)*
Michigan Metal Fabricators 586 754-0421
  24575 Hoover Rd Warren (48089) *(G-17929)*
Michigan Metal Tech Inc 586 598-7800
  50250 E Russell Schmidt Chesterfield (48051) *(G-2913)*
Michigan Metals and Mfg Inc 248 910-7674
  29100 Northwestern Hwy Southfield (48034) *(G-15657)*
Michigan Metro Times Inc 313 961-4060
  1100 Woodward Hts Ferndale (48220) *(G-5568)*
Michigan Milk Producers Assn (PA) 248 474-6672
  41310 Bridge St Novi (48375) *(G-12481)*
Michigan Milk Producers Assn 989 834-2221
  431 W Williams St Ovid (48866) *(G-12815)*
Michigan Milk Producers Assn 269 435-2835
  125 Depot St Constantine (49042) *(G-3671)*
Michigan Mobile Welding Co 810 569-0229
  8173 Silver Lake Rd Linden (48451) *(G-10066)*
Michigan Modular Service, Kalkaska *Also called Patton Welding Inc (G-9401)*
Michigan Mold Inc 269 468-4407
  500 Washington St Coloma (49038) *(G-3479)*
Michigan Motor Exchange, Detroit *Also called Navarre Inc (G-4478)*
Michigan Oil and Gas Assn 517 487-0480
  124 W Allegan St Ste 1610 Lansing (48933) *(G-9870)*
Michigan Ornamental Ir & Fabg 616 899-2441
  219 Roosevelt St Conklin (49403) *(G-3661)*
Michigan Packaging Company (HQ) 517 676-8700
  700 Eden Rd Mason (48854) *(G-11144)*
Michigan Pallet Inc (PA) 989 865-9915
  1225 N Saginaw St Saint Charles (48655) *(G-14805)*
Michigan Paper Die Inc 313 873-0404
  632 Harper Ave Detroit (48202) *(G-4451)*
Michigan Pattern Works Inc 616 245-9259
  872 Grandville Ave Sw Grand Rapids (49503) *(G-6993)*
Michigan Paving and Mtls Co 517 787-4200
  1600 N Elm Ave Jackson (49202) *(G-8956)*
Michigan Paving and Mtls Co (HQ) 734 397-2050
  2575 S Haggerty Rd # 100 Canton (48188) *(G-2496)*
Michigan Paving and Mtls Co 734 485-1717
  1785 Rawsonville Rd Van Buren Twp (48111) *(G-17539)*
Michigan Paving and Mtls Co 989 463-1323
  1950 Williams Rd Alma (48801) *(G-247)*
Michigan Peaceworks 734 262-4283
  911 N University Ave Ann Arbor (48109) *(G-572)*
Michigan Peaceworks 734 232-3079
  1009 Greene St Ann Arbor (48109) *(G-573)*
Michigan Peaceworks 734 764-1717
  412 Maynard St Ann Arbor (48109) *(G-574)*
Michigan Peak Company, Sandusky *Also called Bay-Houston Towing Company (G-15056)*
Michigan Pipe Company, Grand Ledge *Also called Michigan Poly Pipe Inc (G-6396)*
Michigan Plaques & Awards Inc 248 398-6400
  3742 12 Mile Rd Berkley (48072) *(G-1632)*
Michigan Plating LLC 248 544-3500
  21733 Dequindre Rd Hazel Park (48030) *(G-7832)*
Michigan Poly Pipe Inc 517 709-8100
  10242 W Grand River Hwy Grand Ledge (48837) *(G-6396)*
Michigan Polymer Reclaim Inc 989 227-0497
  107 E Walker Rd Saint Johns (48879) *(G-14909)*
Michigan Power Cleaning, Kalamazoo *Also called Becktold Enterprises Inc (G-9133)*
Michigan Prcsion Swiss Prts In 810 329-2270
  2145 Wadhams Rd Saint Clair (48079) *(G-14837)*

Michigan Precision TI & Engrg, Dowagiac *Also called Michigan Precision TI & Engrg (G-4790)*
Michigan Precision TI & Engrg 269 783-1300
  613 Rudy Rd Dowagiac (49047) *(G-4790)*
Michigan Printer Service, Ann Arbor *Also called M & M Typewriter Service Inc (G-558)*
Michigan Printing Impressions, Shelby Township *Also called Peg-Master Business Forms Inc (G-15298)*
Michigan Prod Machining Inc (PA) 586 228-9700
  16700 23 Mile Rd Macomb (48044) *(G-10616)*
Michigan Protein Inc 877 869-0630
  15030 Stout Ave Ne Cedar Springs (49319) *(G-2657)*
Michigan Pump, Melvindale *Also called Core Electric Company Inc (G-11198)*
Michigan Pure Ice Co LLC 231 420-9896
  126 N Straits Hwy Indian River (49749) *(G-8655)*
Michigan Rebuild & Automtn Inc 517 542-6000
  7460 Herring Rd Litchfield (49252) *(G-10083)*
Michigan Reef Development 989 288-2172
  8252 E Lansing Rd Durand (48429) *(G-4842)*
Michigan Rod Products Inc (PA) 517 552-9812
  1326 Grand Oaks Dr Howell (48843) *(G-8481)*
Michigan Roll Form Inc (PA) 248 669-3700
  1132 Ladd Rd Commerce Township (48390) *(G-3556)*
Michigan Roller Inc 269 651-2304
  1113 N Clay St Sturgis (49091) *(G-16307)*
Michigan Satellite 989 792-6666
  3215 Christy Way S Saginaw (48603) *(G-14698)*
Michigan Sawmill Sales LLC 810 625-3848
  8392 Argentine Rd Linden (48451) *(G-10067)*
Michigan Scientific Corp (PA) 248 685-3939
  321 E Huron St Milford (48381) *(G-11470)*
Michigan Scientific Corp 231 547-5511
  8500 Ance Rd Charlevoix (49720) *(G-2721)*
Michigan Screen Printing 810 687-5550
  204 S Railway St Clio (48420) *(G-3406)*
Michigan Shippers Supply Inc (PA) 616 935-6680
  17369 Taft Rd Spring Lake (49456) *(G-15835)*
Michigan Sign Supplies, Lansing *Also called Alpine Sign and Prtg Sup Inc (G-9754)*
Michigan Signs Inc 734 662-1503
  5527 Gallery Park Dr Ann Arbor (48103) *(G-575)*
Michigan Slotting Company Inc 586 772-1270
  22214 Schoenherr Rd Warren (48089) *(G-17930)*
Michigan Snowmobiler Inc 231 536-2371
  200 Main St Ste B East Jordan (49727) *(G-4876)*
Michigan Soft Water of Centr 517 339-0722
  2075 E M 78 East Lansing (48823) *(G-4903)*
Michigan Soy Products Company 248 544-7742
  1213 N Main St Royal Oak (48067) *(G-14563)*
Michigan Spline Gage Co Inc 248 544-7303
  1626 E 9 Mile Rd Hazel Park (48030) *(G-7833)*
Michigan Spring & Stamping LLC (HQ) 231 755-1691
  2700 Wickham Dr Muskegon (49441) *(G-11871)*
Michigan State Medical Society (PA) 517 337-1351
  120 W Saginaw St East Lansing (48823) *(G-4904)*
Michigan State Univ Press 517 355-9543
  Manly Mles Bldg 1405 S Hr East Lansing (48823) *(G-4905)*
Michigan State University 517 353-9310
  220 Service Rd East Lansing (48824) *(G-4906)*
Michigan State University Pape, East Lansing *Also called State News Inc (G-4909)*
Michigan Steel and Trim Inc 517 647-4555
  349 N Water St Portland (48875) *(G-13639)*
Michigan Steel Fabricators Inc 810 785-1478
  5225 Energy Dr Flint (48505) *(G-5732)*
Michigan Steel Finishing Co 313 838-3925
  12850 Mansfield St Detroit (48227) *(G-4452)*
Michigan Steel Spring Company, Detroit *Also called Michigan Steel Finishing Co (G-4452)*
Michigan Sugar Beet Growers, Bay City *Also called Michigan Sugar Company (G-1379)*
Michigan Sugar Company 989 673-3126
  725 S Almer St Caro (48723) *(G-2574)*
Michigan Sugar Company 989 686-0161
  107 Mcgraw St Bay City (48708) *(G-1378)*
Michigan Sugar Company 989 883-3200
  763 N Beck St Sebewaing (48759) *(G-15141)*
Michigan Sugar Company 810 679-2241
  159 S Howard Ave Croswell (48422) *(G-3733)*
Michigan Sugar Company (PA) 989 686-0161
  122 Uptown Dr Unit 300 Bay City (48708) *(G-1379)*
Michigan Sugar Company 989 673-2223
  819 Peninsular St Caro (48723) *(G-2575)*
Michigan Tile and Marble Co (PA) 313 931-1700
  9317 Freeland St Detroit (48228) *(G-4453)*
Michigan Timber Sawmill LLC 989 266-2417
  21909 County Road 624 Hillman (49746) *(G-7914)*
Michigan Tool & Gauge Inc 517 548-4604
  1010 Packard Dr Howell (48843) *(G-8482)*
Michigan Tool Works LLC 269 651-5139
  618 N Centerville Rd Sturgis (49091) *(G-16308)*
Michigan Tooling Solutions LLC 616 681-2210
  8226 Vinton Ave Nw Sparta (49345) *(G-15772)*

Michigan Trkey Prdcers Coop In (PA)...616 245-2221
1100 Hall St Sw Grand Rapids (49503) ***(G-6994)***
Michigan Trkey Prdcers Coop In...616 245-2221
2140 Chicago Dr Sw Wyoming (49519) ***(G-18894)***
Michigan Tube Swgers Fbrctors (PA)...734 847-3875
7100 Industrial Dr Temperance (48182) ***(G-16541)***
Michigan Turkey Producers...616 875-1838
9983 Polk St Zeeland (49464) ***(G-19052)***
Michigan Turkey Producers LLC...616 243-4186
1100 Hall St Grand Rapids (49501) ***(G-6995)***
Michigan Veal Inc...616 669-6688
3007 Van Buren St Hudsonville (49426) ***(G-8596)***
Michigan Vehicle Solutions LLC...734 720-7649
16600 Fort St Southgate (48195) ***(G-15754)***
Michigan Wheel Corp...616 647-1078
2685 Northridge Dr Nw E Grand Rapids (49544) ***(G-6996)***
Michigan Wheel Marine, Grand Rapids *Also called Michigan Wheel Operations LLC* ***(G-6997)***
Michigan Wheel Operations LLC (HQ)...616 452-6941
1501 Buchanan Ave Sw Grand Rapids (49507) ***(G-6997)***
Michigan Wholesale Prtg Inc...248 350-8230
24653 Halsted Rd Farmington Hills (48335) ***(G-5319)***
Michigan Wine Trail...231 944-5220
2561 East Crown Dr Traverse City (49685) ***(G-16756)***
Michigan Wire EDM Services...616 742-0940
1246 Scribner Ave Nw Grand Rapids (49504) ***(G-6998)***
Michigan Wireline Service...989 772-5075
4854 E River Rd Mount Pleasant (48858) ***(G-11712)***
Michigan Wood Fibers Llc...616 875-2241
9426 Henry Ct Zeeland (49464) ***(G-19053)***
Michigan Wood Fuels LLC...616 355-4955
1125 Industrial Ave Holland (49423) ***(G-8147)***
Michigan Wood Pellet LLC...989 348-4100
2211 Industrial Dr Grayling (49738) ***(G-7466)***
Michigan Woodwork...517 204-4394
1234 Christian Way Mason (48854) ***(G-11145)***
Michiganensian...734 418-4115
420 Maynard St Ann Arbor (48109) ***(G-576)***
Michigrain Distillery...517 580-8624
523 E Shiawassee St Lansing (48912) ***(G-9871)***
Michiwest Energy Inc...989 772-2107
1425 S Mission Rd Ste 2 Mount Pleasant (48858) ***(G-11713)***
Mico Industries Inc (PA)...616 245-6426
2929 32nd St Se Ste 8 Grand Rapids (49512) ***(G-6999)***
Mico Industries Inc...616 245-6426
2725 Prairie St Sw Grand Rapids (49519) ***(G-7000)***
Mico Industries Inc...616 514-1143
219 Canton St Sw Ste B Grand Rapids (49507) ***(G-7001)***
Micrgraphics Printing Inc (PA)...231 739-6575
2637 Emerson Blvd Norton Shores (49441) ***(G-12311)***
Micro Belmont, Byron Center *Also called Micro Engineering Inc* ***(G-2285)***
Micro EDM Co LLC...989 872-4306
6172 Main St Cass City (48726) ***(G-2619)***
Micro Engineering Inc...616 534-9681
257 Sorrento Dr Se Byron Center (49315) ***(G-2285)***
Micro Fixtures Inc...313 382-9781
20448 Lorne St Taylor (48180) ***(G-16446)***
Micro Focus Software Inc...248 353-8010
26677 W 12 Mile Rd Ste 1 Southfield (48034) ***(G-15658)***
Micro Form Inc...517 750-3660
180 Teft Rd Spring Arbor (49283) ***(G-15796)***
Micro Gauge Inc...248 446-3720
7350 Kensington Rd Brighton (48116) ***(G-2031)***
Micro Gind, Hazel Park *Also called Micro Grind Co Inc* ***(G-7834)***
Micro Grind Co Inc...248 398-9770
1648 E 9 Mile Rd Hazel Park (48030) ***(G-7834)***
Micro Logic...248 432-7209
4710 Rolling Ridge Rd West Bloomfield (48323) ***(G-18299)***
Micro Manufacturing Inc...616 554-9200
6900 Dtton Indus Pk Dr Se Caledonia (49316) ***(G-2389)***
Micro Platers Sales Inc...313 865-2293
221 Victor St Detroit (48203) ***(G-4454)***
Micro Precision Molds Inc...269 344-2044
3915 Ravine Rd Kalamazoo (49006) ***(G-9270)***
Micro Rim Corporation...313 865-1090
221 Victor St Detroit (48203) ***(G-4455)***
Microcide Inc...248 526-9663
2209 Niagara Dr Troy (48083) ***(G-17258)***
Microdental Laboratories Inc (PA)...877 711-8778
500 Stephenson Hwy Troy (48083) ***(G-17259)***
Microform Tool Company Inc...586 776-4840
20601 Stephens St Saint Clair Shores (48080) ***(G-14872)***
Microforms Inc...586 939-7900
30706 Georgetown Dr Beverly Hills (48025) ***(G-1667)***
Microgauge Machining Inc...248 446-3720
7350 Kensington Rd Brighton (48116) ***(G-2032)***
Micromatic Screw Products Inc...517 787-3666
825 Carroll Ave Jackson (49202) ***(G-8957)***
Micromet Corp...231 885-1047
3790 Burning Tree Dr Bloomfield Hills (48302) ***(G-1837)***
Micron Holdings Inc...616 698-0707
4436 Broadmoor Ave Se Kentwood (49512) ***(G-9465)***
Micron Mfg Company...616 453-5486
1722 Kloet St Nw Grand Rapids (49504) ***(G-7002)***
Micron Precision Machining Inc (PA)...989 759-1030
225 E Morley Dr Saginaw (48601) ***(G-14699)***
Microphoto Incorporated...586 772-1999
30499 Edison Dr Roseville (48066) ***(G-14441)***
Microprecision Cleaning...586 997-6960
6145 Wall St Sterling Heights (48312) ***(G-16098)***
Microsoft Corporation...248 205-5990
2800 W Big Beaver Rd Troy (48084) ***(G-17260)***
Microtech Machine Company...517 750-4422
4801 W Michigan Ave Jackson (49201) ***(G-8958)***
Microtemp Fluid Systems LLC...248 703-5056
23900 Haggerty Rd Farmington Hills (48335) ***(G-5320)***
Microworld Technologies Inc...248 470-1119
39555 Orchard Hill Pl # 60 Novi (48375) ***(G-12482)***
Microx Labs Inc...248 318-3548
565 Foxhall Ct Bloomfield Hills (48304) ***(G-1838)***
Mid America Building Pdts Div, Wixom *Also called Tapco Holdings Inc* ***(G-18766)***
Mid America Commodities LLC...810 936-0108
7420 Majestic Woods Dr Linden (48451) ***(G-10068)***
Mid American AEL LLC...810 229-5483
1375 Rickett Rd Brighton (48116) ***(G-2033)***
Mid Cost Grass Choppers...985 445-7155
5381 Frankwill Ave Clarkston (48346) ***(G-3051)***
Mid McHgan Feed Ingrdients LLC...989 236-5014
4585 5 Garfield Rd Middleton (48856) ***(G-11299)***
Mid McHigan Indus Coatings LLC...989 441-1277
5059 W Weidman Rd Weidman (48893) ***(G-18257)***
Mid Michigan Industries, Clare *Also called Mid-Michigan Industries Inc* ***(G-2986)***
Mid Michigan Logging...231 229-4501
9620 N Nelson Rd Lake City (49651) ***(G-9551)***
Mid Michigan Pipe Inc...989 772-5664
977 Ada Place Dr Se Ste A Grand Rapids (49546) ***(G-7003)***
Mid Michigan Repair Service...989 835-6014
3344 N Sturgeon Rd Midland (48642) ***(G-11390)***
Mid Michigan Wood Specialites...989 855-3667
1370 Divine Hwy Lyons (48851) ***(G-10564)***
Mid State Oil Tools Inc (PA)...989 773-4114
1934 Commercial Dr Mount Pleasant (48858) ***(G-11714)***
Mid West Pallet...810 919-3072
2206 E Parkwood Ave Burton (48529) ***(G-2240)***
Mid-America Machining Inc...517 592-4945
11530 Brooklyn Rd Brooklyn (49230) ***(G-2128)***
Mid-Michigan Blinds...810 225-8488
7041 Grand River Rd # 250 Brighton (48114) ***(G-2034)***
Mid-Michigan Industries Inc (PA)...989 773-6918
2426 Parkway Dr Mount Pleasant (48858) ***(G-11715)***
Mid-Michigan Industries Inc...989 386-7707
790 Industrial Dr Clare (48617) ***(G-2986)***
Mid-Michigan Mailing & Prtg, Burton *Also called Cameron S Roat* ***(G-2231)***
Mid-Michigan Screen Printing...989 624-9827
11917 Conquest St Birch Run (48415) ***(G-1711)***
Mid-Michigan Truss Components, Saginaw *Also called CHR W LLC* ***(G-14628)***
Mid-State Plating Co Inc...810 767-1622
602 Kelso St Flint (48506) ***(G-5733)***
Mid-State Printing Inc...989 875-4163
145 Industrial Pkwy Ithaca (48847) ***(G-8794)***
Mid-States Bolt & Screw Co...989 732-3265
1069 Orourke Blvd Gaylord (49735) ***(G-6149)***
Mid-Tech Inc...734 426-4327
175 Dino Dr Ann Arbor (48103) ***(G-577)***
Mid-West Behavioral Associates...517 267-5502
1148 Runaway Bay Dr 1a Lansing (48917) ***(G-9776)***
Mid-West Innovators Inc...989 358-7147
3810 Us Highway 23 N Alpena (49707) ***(G-303)***
Mid-West Instrument Company, Sterling Heights *Also called Astra Associates Inc* ***(G-15935)***
Mid-West Mfg., Alpena *Also called Mid-West Innovators Inc* ***(G-303)***
Mid-West Screw Products Co...734 591-1800
11975 Globe St Livonia (48150) ***(G-10316)***
Mid-West Spring & Stamping Inc...231 777-2707
1935 E Laketon Ave Muskegon (49442) ***(G-11872)***
Mid-West Spring Mfg Co...231 777-2707
1935 E Laketon Ave Muskegon (49442) ***(G-11873)***
Mid-West Waltham Abrasives Co...517 725-7161
510 S Washington St Owosso (48867) ***(G-12843)***
Mid-West Wire Products Inc...248 548-3200
1109 Brompton Rd Rochester Hills (48309) ***(G-14063)***
Midas Foods International, Oak Park *Also called Michigan Dessert Corporation* ***(G-12628)***
Midas Muffler, Taylor *Also called Anh Enterprises LLC* ***(G-16379)***
Midbrook Inc (PA)...800 966-9274
2621 E Kimmel Rd Jackson (49201) ***(G-8959)***
Midbrook LLC...800 966-9274
1300 Falahee Rd Ste 51 Jackson (49203) ***(G-8960)***
Midco 2 Inc...517 467-2222
11703 Pentecost Hwy Onsted (49265) ***(G-12706)***
Middlebury Trailers, Vandalia *Also called LA East Inc* ***(G-17567)***

Middleby Corporation 906 863-4401
5600 13th St Menominee (49858) *(G-11251)*
Middleton Printing Inc 616 247-8742
200 32nd St Se Ste A Grand Rapids (49548) *(G-7004)*
Middleton Well Drilling 989 465-1078
3890 W Mcnally Rd Coleman (48618) *(G-3469)*
Middleville Tool & Die Co Inc 269 795-3646
1900 Patterson Rd Middleville (49333) *(G-11309)*
Midland Brewing Co LLC 989 259-7210
5011 N Saginaw Rd Midland (48642) *(G-11391)*
Midland Cmpnding Cnsulting Inc 989 495-9367
3802 James Savage Rd Midland (48642) *(G-11392)*
Midland Daily News, Midland Also called Midland Publishing Company *(G-11394)*
Midland Glass Bonding Facility, Midland Also called Ddp Spclty Elctrnic Mtls US LL *(G-11335)*
Midland Iron Works Inc 989 832-3041
57 W Chippewa River Rd Midland (48640) *(G-11393)*
Midland Publishing Company 989 835-7171
124 S Mcdonald St Midland (48640) *(G-11394)*
Midland Silicon Company LLC 248 674-3736
3840 Island Park Dr Waterford (48329) *(G-18137)*
Midnight Logging LLC 202 521-1484
7588 E 112th St Howard City (49329) *(G-8412)*
Midnight Scoop, South Lyon Also called Mykin Inc *(G-15448)*
Midori Auto Leather N Amer Inc (PA) 248 305-6437
40000 Grand River Ave # 206 Novi (48375) *(G-12483)*
Midstates Industrial Group Inc 586 307-3414
21299 Carlo Dr Clinton Township (48038) *(G-3300)*
Midway Group LLC 586 264-5380
6227 Metropolitan Pkwy Sterling Heights (48312) *(G-16099)*
Midway Machine Tech Inc 616 772-0808
555 N State St Zeeland (49464) *(G-19054)*
Midway Products Group Inc (PA) 734 241-7242
1 Lyman E Hoyt Dr Monroe (48161) *(G-11560)*
Midway Rotary Die Solutions, Williamston Also called Seeley Inc *(G-18582)*
Midway Strl Pipe & Sup Inc (PA) 517 787-1350
1611 Clara St Jackson (49203) *(G-8961)*
Midwest Acorn Nut Company (PA) 800 422-6887
256 Minnesota Dr Troy (48083) *(G-17261)*
Midwest Air Products Co Inc 231 941-5865
281 Hughes Dr Traverse City (49696) *(G-16757)*
Midwest Aquatics Group Inc 734 426-4155
8930 Dexter Pinckney Rd Pinckney (48169) *(G-13052)*
Midwest Brake Bond Co 586 775-3000
26255 Groesbeck Hwy Warren (48089) *(G-17931)*
Midwest Build Center LLC 989 672-1388
1750 Speirs Rd Ste 1 Caro (48723) *(G-2576)*
Midwest Bus Corporation (PA) 989 723-5241
1940 W Stewart St Owosso (48867) *(G-12844)*
Midwest Cabinet Counters 248 586-4260
650 E Mandoline Ave Madison Heights (48071) *(G-10783)*
Midwest Circuits, Ferndale Also called I Parth Inc *(G-5560)*
Midwest Custom Embroidery Co 269 381-7660
621 E North St Kalamazoo (49007) *(G-9271)*
Midwest Die Corp 269 422-2171
9220 First St Baroda (49101) *(G-1165)*
Midwest Direct Transport Inc 616 698-8900
1144 73rd St Sw Ste A Byron Center (49315) *(G-2286)*
Midwest Diversified Products, Ferndale Also called L Barge & Associates Inc *(G-5563)*
Midwest Fabricating Inc 734 921-3914
26465 Northline Rd Taylor (48180) *(G-16447)*
Midwest Fbrglas Fbricators Inc 810 765-7445
1796 S Parker St Marine City (48039) *(G-10963)*
Midwest Fire Protection, Sturgis Also called Con-De Manufacturing Inc *(G-16285)*
Midwest Flex Systems Inc 810 424-0060
415 Sb Chavez Dr Flint (48503) *(G-5734)*
Midwest Forklift Parts LLC 248 830-5982
456 Sunset Blvd Oxford (48371) *(G-12902)*
Midwest Fruit Package Co., Benton Harbor Also called Mpc Company Inc *(G-1576)*
Midwest Gear & Tool Inc 586 779-1300
15700 Common Rd Roseville (48066) *(G-14442)*
Midwest Graphics & Awards Inc 734 424-3700
2135 Bishop Cir E Ste 8 Dexter (48130) *(G-4746)*
Midwest Grinding 734 395-1033
14222 Cone Rd Maybee (48159) *(G-11170)*
Midwest Heat Treat Inc 616 395-9763
2127 112th Ave Holland (49424) *(G-8148)*
Midwest II Inc 734 856-5200
6194 Section Rd Ottawa Lake (49267) *(G-12808)*
Midwest International Wines, Macomb Also called Andretta & Associates Inc *(G-10577)*
Midwest Machining Inc 616 837-0165
526 Omalley Dr Coopersville (49404) *(G-3693)*
Midwest Marketing Inc 989 793-9393
105 Lyon St Saginaw (48602) *(G-14700)*
MIDWEST MEDIA MANAGEMENT DIV, Grand Rapids Also called Rbc Ministries *(G-7142)*
Midwest Mold Services Inc 586 888-8800
29900 Hayes Rd Roseville (48066) *(G-14443)*
Midwest Pallet, Holland Also called Midwest Heat Treat Inc *(G-8148)*

Midwest Panel Systems Inc 517 486-4844
9012 E Us Highway 223 Blissfield (49228) *(G-1770)*
Midwest Plastic Engineering 269 651-5223
1501 Progress St Sturgis (49091) *(G-16309)*
Midwest Plating Company Inc 616 451-2007
613 North Ave Ne Grand Rapids (49503) *(G-7005)*
Midwest Product Spc Inc 231 767-9942
2190 Aurora Dr Muskegon (49442) *(G-11874)*
Midwest Products Finshg Co Inc 734 856-5200
6194 Section Rd Ottawa Lake (49267) *(G-12809)*
Midwest Quality Bedding Inc 614 504-5971
1384 Glenview Dr Waterford (48327) *(G-18138)*
Midwest Resin Inc 586 803-3417
15320 Common Rd Roseville (48066) *(G-14444)*
Midwest Rubber Company (PA) 810 376-2085
3525 Range Line Rd Deckerville (48427) *(G-3955)*
Midwest Safety Products Inc 616 554-5155
4929 East Paris Ave Se Grand Rapids (49512) *(G-7006)*
Midwest Sales Associates Inc 248 348-9600
29445 Beck Rd Ste A103 Wixom (48393) *(G-18710)*
Midwest Seating Solutions Inc 616 222-0636
2234 Burning Tree Dr Se Grand Rapids (49546) *(G-7007)*
Midwest Sign Install Inc 616 862-7568
2900 Barry St Hudsonville (49426) *(G-8597)*
Midwest Stainless Fabricating 248 476-4502
32433 8 Mile Rd Livonia (48152) *(G-10317)*
Midwest Steel Inc (PA) 313 873-2220
2525 E Grand Blvd Detroit (48211) *(G-4456)*
Midwest Steel Carports Inc (PA) 877 235-5210
13479 S Mason Dr Grant (49327) *(G-7430)*
Midwest Timber Inc 269 663-5315
190 Kraus Rd Edwardsburg (49112) *(G-5011)*
Midwest Timer Service Inc 269 849-2800
4815 M63 N Benton Harbor (49022) *(G-1573)*
Midwest Tool & Die Inc 616 863-8187
7970 Childsdale Ave Ne Rockford (49341) *(G-14179)*
Midwest Tool and Cutlery Co (PA) 269 651-2476
1210 Progress St Sturgis (49091) *(G-16310)*
Midwest Tool and Cutlery Co 231 258-2341
222 Seeley Rd Ne Kalkaska (49646) *(G-9398)*
Midwest Tractor & Equipment Co 231 269-4100
10736 N M 37 Buckley (49620) *(G-2207)*
Midwest Transportation Inc 313 615-7282
7020 Plainfield St Dearborn Heights (48127) *(G-3933)*
Midwest Tube Fabricators Inc 586 264-9898
36845 Metro Ct Sterling Heights (48312) *(G-16100)*
Midwest Vibro Inc 616 532-7670
3715 28th St Sw Grandville (49418) *(G-7401)*
Midwest Wall Company LLC 517 881-3701
13753 Cottonwood Dr Dewitt (48820) *(G-4713)*
Midynaco LLC 989 550-8552
3719 Ross St Kingston (48741) *(G-9526)*
Miedema Realty Inc 616 538-4800
4072 Chicago Dr Sw Ste 3 Grandville (49418) *(G-7402)*
Mien Company Inc 616 818-1970
2547 3 Mile Rd Nw Ste F Grand Rapids (49534) *(G-7008)*
Mif Custom Coatings, Farmington Hills Also called Michigan Industrial Finishes *(G-5318)*
Mig Molding LLC 810 660-8435
3778 Van Dyke Rd Almont (48003) *(G-266)*
Mig Molding LLC 810 724-7400
611 Industrial Park Dr Imlay City (48444) *(G-8641)*
Migatron Precision Products (PA) 989 739-1439
4296 E River Rd Oscoda (48750) *(G-12765)*
Mighty Co 616 822-1013
50 Louis St Nw 520 Hudsonville (49426) *(G-8598)*
Mighty In The Midwest, Hudsonville Also called Mighty Co *(G-8598)*
MII Disposition Inc 616 554-9696
4717 Talon Ct Se Grand Rapids (49512) *(G-7009)*
Mika Tool & Die Inc 989 662-6979
5127 Garfield Rd Auburn (48611) *(G-770)*
Mikan Corporation 734 944-9447
1271 Industrial Dr Ste 3 Saline (48176) *(G-15027)*
Mike Haas, Detroit Also called Carco Inc *(G-4089)*
Mike Hughes 269 377-3578
6054 Marshall Rd Nashville (49073) *(G-11957)*
Mike Vaughn Custom Sports Inc 248 969-8956
550 S Glaspie St Oxford (48371) *(G-12903)*
Mikes Cabinet Shop Inc 734 722-1800
37100 Enterprise Dr Westland (48186) *(G-18396)*
Mikes Meat Processing 269 468-6173
5135 N Coloma Rd Coloma (49038) *(G-3480)*
Mikes Steamer Service Inc 231 258-8500
11825 Russell Ridge Rd Williamsburg (49690) *(G-18558)*
Milacron LLC 517 424-8981
5550 S Occidental Rd Tecumseh (49286) *(G-16508)*
Milair, Sterling Heights Also called Horstman Inc *(G-16041)*
Milan Burial Vault Inc 734 439-1538
10475 N Ann Arbor Rd Milan (48160) *(G-11444)*
Milan Cast Metal Corporation 734 439-0510
13905 N Sanford Rd Milan (48160) *(G-11445)*

Milan Metal Systems LLC   **ALPHABETIC SECTION**

Milan Metal Systems LLC 734 439-1546
   555 S Platt Rd Milan (48160) *(G-11446)*
Milan Metal Worx LLC 734 369-7115
   16779 Ida West Rd Petersburg (49270) *(G-12984)*
Milan Screw Products Inc 734 439-2431
   291 Squires Dr Milan (48160) *(G-11447)*
Milan Vault, Milan Also called Milan Burial Vault Inc *(G-11444)*
Milano Bakery Inc 313 833-3500
   3500 Russell St Detroit (48207) *(G-4457)*
Milcare Inc (HQ) 616 654-8000
   855 E Main Ave Zeeland (49464) *(G-19055)*
Milfab Systems LLC 248 391-8100
   2388 Canoe Circle Dr Lake Orion (48360) *(G-9619)*
Milford Jewelers Inc 248 676-0721
   441 N Main St Milford (48381) *(G-11471)*
Milford Redi-Mix Company 248 684-1465
   800 Concrete Dr Milford (48381) *(G-11472)*
Milford Sand & Gravel, Detroit Also called Edw C Levy Co *(G-4202)*
Military Apparel Co 810 637-1542
   2664 Military St Port Huron (48060) *(G-13502)*
Military Vtrans Affirs Mich De 231 775-7222
   415 Haynes St Cadillac (49601) *(G-2347)*
Miljevich Corporation 906 224-2651
   511 Putnam St Wakefield (49968) *(G-17623)*
Miljoco Corp (PA) 586 777-4280
   200 Elizabeth St Mount Clemens (48043) *(G-11649)*
Mill Assist Services Inc 269 692-3211
   141 N Farmer St Otsego (49078) *(G-12791)*
Mill Creek Fabrication LLC 616 419-4857
   5402 Rusche Dr Nw Comstock Park (49321) *(G-3626)*
Mill Creek Industries, Lexington Also called Patton Tool and Die Inc *(G-10031)*
Mill Steel Co (PA) 616 949-6700
   2905 Lucerne Dr Se # 100 Grand Rapids (49546) *(G-7010)*
Mill Town Woodworks, Bay City Also called A & B Display Systems Inc *(G-1314)*
Millbrook Press Works 517 323-2111
   517 S Waverly Rd Lansing (48917) *(G-9777)*
Millendo Transactionsub Inc 734 845-9300
   301 N Main St Ste 100 Ann Arbor (48104) *(G-578)*
Millenia, White Lake Also called Ashley Garcia *(G-18450)*
Millennium Adhesive Products (PA) 800 248-4010
   4401 Page Ave Michigan Center (49254) *(G-11294)*
Millennium Cabinetry 248 477-4420
   24748 Crestview Ct Farmington Hills (48335) *(G-5321)*
Millennium Filters, Farmington Hills Also called Millennium Planet LLC *(G-5322)*
Millennium Machining & Asm, Auburn Hills Also called TI Fluid Systems *(G-1053)*
Millennium Mold & Tool Inc 586 791-1711
   35225 Automation Dr Clinton Township (48035) *(G-3301)*
Millennium Planet LLC 248 835-2331
   27300 Haggerty Rd Ste F28 Farmington Hills (48331) *(G-5322)*
Millennium Screw Machine Inc 734 525-5235
   13311 Stark Rd Livonia (48150) *(G-10318)*
Millennium Steering LLC 989 872-8823
   6285 Garfield Ave Cass City (48726) *(G-2620)*
Millennium Technology II Inc 734 479-4440
   28888 Goddard Rd Ste 200 Romulus (48174) *(G-14306)*
Millennm-The Inside Sltion Inc 248 645-9005
   24748 Crestview Ct Farmington Hills (48335) *(G-5323)*
Miller Broach Inc 810 395-8810
   14510 Bryce Rd Capac (48014) *(G-2547)*
Miller Designworks LLC 313 562-4000
   3001 S Gulley Rd Ste D Dearborn (48124) *(G-3873)*
Miller Energy Company, Traverse City Also called Summit Petroleum Company LLC *(G-16845)*
Miller Energy Inc 269 352-5960
   277 S Rose St Ste 3300 Kalamazoo (49007) *(G-9272)*
Miller Exploration Company (PA) 231 941-0004
   3104 Logan Valley Rd Traverse City (49684) *(G-16758)*
Miller Industrial Products Inc 517 783-2756
   801 Water St Jackson (49203) *(G-8962)*
Miller Investment Company LLC 231 933-3233
   10850 E Traverse Hwy # 5595 Traverse City (49684) *(G-16759)*
Miller Machine & Technologies, Jackson Also called Miller Tool & Die Co *(G-8963)*
Miller Machine Inc 734 455-5333
   41250 Joy Rd Plymouth (48170) *(G-13242)*
Miller Mold Co 989 793-8881
   690 Wren Rd Frankenmuth (48734) *(G-5871)*
Miller Prod & Machining Inc 810 395-8810
   14510 Bryce Rd Capac (48014) *(G-2548)*
Miller Products & Supply Co 906 774-1243
   1801 N Stephenson Ave Iron Mountain (49801) *(G-8725)*
Miller Sand & Gravel Company 269 672-5601
   1466 120th Ave Hopkins (49328) *(G-8367)*
Miller Technical Services Inc 734 207-3159
   47801 W Anchor Ct Plymouth (48170) *(G-13243)*
Miller Tool & Die Co 517 782-0347
   829 Belden Rd Jackson (49203) *(G-8963)*
Miller Tool Die Co 734 738-1970
   47801 W Anchor Ct Plymouth (48170) *(G-13244)*
Miller Transit Mix, Richmond Also called Mirkwood Properties Inc *(G-13842)*

Millerknoll Inc (PA) 616 654-3000
   855 E Main Ave Zeeland (49464) *(G-19056)*
Millerknoll Inc 616 453-5995
   2915 Stonewood St Nw Grand Rapids (49504) *(G-7011)*
Millerknoll Inc 616 949-3660
   5460 44th St Se Grand Rapids (49512) *(G-7012)*
Millers Custom Boat Top Inc 586 468-5533
   41700 Conger Bay Dr Harrison Township (48045) *(G-7710)*
Millers Redi-Mix Inc 989 587-6511
   6218 S Wright Rd Fowler (48835) *(G-5830)*
Millers Shoe Parlor Inc 517 783-1258
   103 W Michigan Ave Jackson (49201) *(G-8964)*
Millers Woodworking 989 386-8110
   3378 E Beaverton Rd Clare (48617) *(G-2987)*
Milliken and Company, Southfield Also called Morris Associates Inc *(G-15662)*
Milliken Millwork Inc (HQ) 586 264-0950
   6361 Sterling Dr N Sterling Heights (48312) *(G-16101)*
Milliman Communications Inc (PA) 517 327-8407
   4601 W Saginaw Hwy Apt 2 Lansing (48917) *(G-9778)*
Mills Phrm & Apothecary LLC 248 633-2872
   1740 W Maple Rd Birmingham (48009) *(G-1737)*
Millstar, Lake Orion Also called Cole Tooling Systems Inc *(G-9596)*
Millwork Design Group LLC 248 472-2178
   414 Union St Apt 202 Milford (48381) *(G-11473)*
Millworks Engineering Inc 517 741-5511
   584 W Girard Rd Union City (49094) *(G-17496)*
Milo Boring & Machining Inc 586 293-8611
   34275 Riviera Fraser (48026) *(G-5963)*
Milo Range Training Systems, Ann Arbor Also called Faac Incorporated *(G-485)*
Milsco LLC 517 787-3650
   2313 Brooklyn Rd Jackson (49203) *(G-8965)*
Milton Manufacturing Inc 313 366-2450
   301 E Grixdale Detroit (48203) *(G-4458)*
Miltons Cabinet Shop Inc 269 473-2743
   10331 Us Highway 31 Berrien Springs (49103) *(G-1645)*
Mindchip Industries LLC 313 355-2447
   22684 Starling Dr Brownstown (48183) *(G-2150)*
Mineral Cosmetics Inc 248 542-7733
   21314 Hilltop St Southfield (48033) *(G-15659)*
Mineral Visions Inc 800 255-7263
   3840 Livingston Rd Bridgman (49106) *(G-1932)*
Minerals Processing Corp 906 352-4024
   414 10th Ave Menominee (49858) *(G-11252)*
Minerick Logging Inc 906 542-3583
   N10670 State Highway M95 Sagola (49881) *(G-14798)*
Mini Storage of Manton 231 645-6727
   656 R W Harris Dr Manton (49663) *(G-10937)*
Mini-Mix Inc 586 792-2260
   33600 Kelly Rd Clinton Township (48035) *(G-3302)*
Miniature Custom Mfg LLC 269 998-1277
   170 N Leja Dr Vicksburg (49097) *(G-17608)*
Mining Jrnl Bsness Offc-Dtrial 906 228-2500
   249 W Washington St Marquette (49855) *(G-11036)*
Minland Machine Inc 269 641-7998
   19801 Old 205 Edwardsburg (49112) *(G-5012)*
Minor Creations Incorporated 517 347-2900
   693 W Grand River Ave Okemos (48864) *(G-12676)*
Mint Steel Forge Inc 248 276-9000
   162 Northpointe Dr Lake Orion (48359) *(G-9620)*
Minth Group US Holding Inc (HQ) 248 848-8530
   51331 Pontiac Trl Wixom (48393) *(G-18711)*
Minth North America Inc 248 259-7468
   51331 Pontiac Trl Wixom (48393) *(G-18712)*
Mintmesh Inc 888 874-3644
   400 Renaissance Ctr # 2600 Detroit (48243) *(G-4459)*
Minute Maid Co 269 657-3171
   38279 W Red Arrow Hwy Paw Paw (49079) *(G-12953)*
Minuteman Metal Works Inc 989 269-8342
   1600 Patterson St Bad Axe (48413) *(G-1109)*
Miracle Petroleum LLC 231 946-8090
   2780 Garfield Rd N Traverse City (49686) *(G-16760)*
Miracle Sign 313 663-0145
   2526 Oakwood Blvd Melvindale (48122) *(G-11205)*
Mirkwood Properties Inc 586 727-3363
   35555 Division Rd Richmond (48062) *(G-13842)*
Mirrage Ltd 734 697-6447
   8300 Belleville Rd Van Buren Twp (48111) *(G-17540)*
Mirs News, Lansing Also called Infoguys Inc *(G-9854)*
Mirus Industries Inc 616 402-3256
   736 Woodlawn Ave Grand Haven (49417) *(G-6336)*
Mis Associates Inc 844 225-8156
   1735 Highwood W Pontiac (48340) *(G-13398)*
Mis Controls Inc 586 339-3900
   2890 Technology Dr Rochester Hills (48309) *(G-14064)*
Misc Products 586 263-3300
   16730 Enterprise Dr Macomb (48044) *(G-10617)*
Mishigama Brewing Company 734 547-5840
   124 Pearl St Ypsilanti (48197) *(G-18968)*
Miss Print Rocks 517 639-8785
   13 E Chicago St Quincy (49082) *(G-13672)*

Missaukee Molded Rubber Inc 231 839-5309
6400 W Blue Rd Lake City (49651) ***(G-9552)***
Mission Pathways LLC 734 260-9411
3445 W Delhi Rd Ann Arbor (48103) ***(G-579)***
Mission Point Press 231 421-9513
2554 Chandler Rd Traverse City (49696) ***(G-16761)***
Mistequay Group Ltd 989 752-7700
1212 N Niagara St Saginaw (48602) ***(G-14701)***
Mistequay Group Ltd 989 846-1000
1015 W Cedar St Standish (48658) ***(G-15893)***
Mistequay Group Ltd (PA) 989 752-7700
1156 N Niagara St Saginaw (48602) ***(G-14702)***
Mistequay NDT Center, Saginaw *Also called Mistequay Group Ltd* ***(G-14702)***
Mit, Farmington Hills *Also called Manufacturing & Indus Tech Inc* ***(G-5309)***
Mitchart Inc 989 835-3964
2611 Schuette Rd Ste A Midland (48642) ***(G-11395)***
Mitchell Coates 231 582-5878
5293 Korthase Rd Boyne City (49712) ***(G-1897)***
Mitchell Equipment Corporation 734 529-3400
5275 N Ann Arbor Rd Dundee (48131) ***(G-4832)***
Mitchell Graphics Inc (PA) 231 347-4635
2363 Mitchell Park Dr Petoskey (49770) ***(G-13007)***
Mitchell Rail Gear, Dundee *Also called Mitchell Equipment Corporation* ***(G-4832)***
Mitchs Slots 586 739-5157
41751 Marold Dr Sterling Heights (48314) ***(G-16102)***
Mitsubishi Chemical Amer Inc 586 755-1660
24060 Hoover Rd Warren (48089) ***(G-17932)***
Mitsubishi Elc Auto Amer Inc 734 453-6200
15603 Centennial Dr Northville (48168) ***(G-12240)***
Mitsubishi Electric Us Inc 734 453-6200
15603 Centennial Dr Northville (48168) ***(G-12241)***
Mitsubishi Steel Mfg Co Ltd 248 502-8000
2040 Crooks Rd Ste A Troy (48084) ***(G-17262)***
Mitten Fruit Company LLC 269 585-8541
3680 Stadium Pkwy Kalamazoo (49009) ***(G-9273)***
Mitten Fruit Company, The, Kalamazoo *Also called Mitten Fruit Company LLC* ***(G-9273)***
Mitten Made Woodcrafts LLC 616 430-2762
3215 Lake Michigan Dr Nw Grand Rapids (49534) ***(G-7013)***
Mitten Spray Foam Insul LLC 616 250-8355
4010 Milan Ave Sw Wyoming (49509) ***(G-18895)***
Mittler Supply 616 451-3055
1000 Scribner Ave Nw Grand Rapids (49504) ***(G-7014)***
Miwi, Jackson *Also called Crown Industrial Services Inc* ***(G-8858)***
Mix Head Repair, Holland *Also called Mhr Inc* ***(G-8146)***
Mix Masters Inc 616 490-8520
530 76th St Sw Ste 400 Byron Center (49315) ***(G-2287)***
Miyachi Unitek Corp 616 676-2634
1382 Glen Ellyn Dr Se Grand Rapids (49546) ***(G-7015)***
Mizjayzbraidz LLC 313 799-7756
6115 Auburn St Detroit (48228) ***(G-4460)***
Mizkan America Inc 616 794-0226
700 Kiddville St Belding (48809) ***(G-1457)***
Mizkan America Inc 616 794-3670
702 Kiddville St Belding (48809) ***(G-1458)***
Mj Cabinet Designs 734 354-9633
9475 Red Maple Dr Plymouth (48170) ***(G-13245)***
Mj Creative Printing LLC 248 891-1117
19566 Hardy St Livonia (48152) ***(G-10319)***
Mj Global Services, Sterling Heights *Also called Mycdbdmk Services LLC* ***(G-16110)***
Mj Industries LLC 586 200-3903
28540 Utica Rd Roseville (48066) ***(G-14445)***
Mj Mechanical Services, Saint Charles *Also called M J Mechanical Inc* ***(G-14804)***
Mj Mfg Co 810 744-3840
2441 E Bristol Rd Burton (48529) ***(G-2241)***
Mj Print & Imaging 734 216-6273
4501 Jacob Rd Grass Lake (49240) ***(G-7441)***
Mj-Hick Inc 989 345-7610
2367 S M 76 West Branch (48661) ***(G-18331)***
MJB Stairs LLC 586 822-9559
56728 Mound Rd Shelby Township (48316) ***(G-15278)***
Mjbcustomwoodworking 989 695-2737
8850 N Orr Rd Freeland (48623) ***(G-6025)***
Mjc Industries Inc 313 838-2800
15701 Glendale St Detroit (48227) ***(G-4461)***
Mjc Tool & Machine Co Inc 586 790-4766
35806 Groesbeck Hwy Clinton Township (48035) ***(G-3303)***
Mjs Investing LLC 734 455-6500
41170 Joy Rd Plymouth (48170) ***(G-13246)***
Mjs Publishing Group 734 391-7370
41500 Bellridge Blvd Van Buren Twp (48111) ***(G-17541)***
MK Chambers Company (PA) 810 688-3750
2251 Johnson Mill Rd North Branch (48461) ***(G-12181)***
Mkg, Clarkston *Also called Mobile Knowledge Group LLC* ***(G-3052)***
MKP Enterprises Inc 248 809-2525
19785 W 12 Mile Rd 338 Southfield (48076) ***(G-15660)***
Mkr Fabricating Inc 989 753-8100
810 N Towerline Rd Saginaw (48601) ***(G-14703)***
Mlc Manufacturing 616 846-6990
18784 174th Ave Spring Lake (49456) ***(G-15836)***
Mlc of Wakefield Inc 906 224-1120
893 Cemetery Rd Wakefield (49968) ***(G-17624)***
Mlc Window Co Inc (PA) 586 731-3500
2001 Crystal Lake Dr Shelby Township (48316) ***(G-15279)***
Mlcwindows & Doors, Shelby Township *Also called Mlc Window Co Inc* ***(G-15279)***
Mle, Holland *Also called Graphix Signs & Embroidery* ***(G-8056)***
Mlh Services LLC 313 768-4403
11310 Kenmoor St Detroit (48205) ***(G-4462)***
Mlive Com 517 768-4984
214 S Jackson St Jackson (49201) ***(G-8966)***
Mlive Media Group 212 286-2860
111 N Ashley St Ste 100 Ann Arbor (48104) ***(G-580)***
Mlivecom 231 725-6343
981 3rd St Muskegon (49440) ***(G-11875)***
Mlp Mfg Inc 616 842-8767
18630 Trimble Ct Spring Lake (49456) ***(G-15837)***
MLS Automotive Incorporated 844 453-3669
27280 Haggerty Rd Ste C-9 Farmington Hills (48331) ***(G-5324)***
MLS Signs Inc 586 948-0200
50617 Plaza Dr Macomb (48042) ***(G-10618)***
Mmbs, Livonia *Also called Manufacturers / Mch Bldrs Svcs* ***(G-10298)***
Mmgg Inc 989 324-7319
2600 Salzburg Rd Freeland (48623) ***(G-6026)***
Mmi Companies LLC 248 528-1680
1094 Naughton Dr Troy (48083) ***(G-17263)***
Mmi Door, Sterling Heights *Also called Milliken Millwork Inc* ***(G-16101)***
Mmi Engineered Solutions Inc (HQ) 734 429-4664
1715 Woodland Dr Saline (48176) ***(G-15028)***
Mmi Engineered Solutions Inc 734 429-5130
12700 Stephens Rd Warren (48089) ***(G-17933)***
MMI OF CENTRAL MICHIGAN, Mount Pleasant *Also called Mid-Michigan Industries Inc* ***(G-11715)***
Mmp Molded Magnesium Pdts LLC 517 789-8505
2336 E High St Jackson (49203) ***(G-8967)***
Mmsp, Birch Run *Also called Mid-Michigan Screen Printing* ***(G-1711)***
MNP Corporation (PA) 586 254-1320
44225 Utica Rd Utica (48317) ***(G-17504)***
Mobex Global, Southfield *Also called Shipston Group US Inc* ***(G-15702)***
Mobex Global, Southfield *Also called Shipston Alum Tech Intl LLC* ***(G-15700)***
Mobile Installations, Holland *Also called Carry-All Products Inc* ***(G-7991)***
Mobile Knowledge Group LLC (PA) 248 625-3327
5750 Bella Rosa Blvd # 100 Clarkston (48348) ***(G-3052)***
Mobile Office Vehicle Inc 616 971-0080
4053 Brockton Dr Se Ste A Grand Rapids (49512) ***(G-7016)***
Mobile Pallet Service Inc (PA) 269 792-4200
858 S Main St Wayland (49348) ***(G-18199)***
Mobility Accessories LLC 734 262-3760
7610 Salem Woods Dr Northville (48168) ***(G-12242)***
Mobility Howell Products 586 558-8308
11374 Common Rd Warren (48093) ***(G-17934)***
Mobility Innovations LLC 586 843-3816
51277 Celeste Shelby Township (48315) ***(G-15280)***
Mobility Products and Design, Shelby Township *Also called Veigel North America LLC* ***(G-15364)***
Mobility Trnsp Svcs Inc 734 453-6452
42000 Koppernick Rd A3 Canton (48187) ***(G-2497)***
Mobilitytrans, Canton *Also called Mobility Trnsp Svcs Inc* ***(G-2497)***
Mobilitytrans LLC 734 262-3760
12633 Inkster Rd Livonia (48150) ***(G-10320)***
Mobimogul Inc 313 575-2795
29193 Northwestern Hwy Southfield (48034) ***(G-15661)***
Mod Interiors Inc 586 725-8227
9301 Marine City Hwy Ira (48023) ***(G-8702)***
Mod Signs Inc 616 455-0260
7475 Division Ave S Grand Rapids (49548) ***(G-7017)***
Moda Manufacturing LLC 586 204-5120
39255 Country Club Dr B1 Farmington Hills (48331) ***(G-5325)***
Model Pattern Company Inc 616 878-9710
8499 Centre Indus Dr Sw Byron Center (49315) ***(G-2288)***
Model Printing Service Inc 989 356-0834
829 W Chisholm St Alpena (49707) ***(G-304)***
Model-Matic Inc 248 528-1680
1094 Naughton Dr Troy (48083) ***(G-17264)***
Models & Tools Inc 586 580-6900
51400 Bellestri Ct Shelby Township (48315) ***(G-15281)***
Modern Builders 989 773-1405
1534 S Wise Rd Mount Pleasant (48858) ***(G-11716)***
Modern Builders Supply Inc 517 787-3633
2401 Brooklyn Rd Jackson (49203) ***(G-8968)***
Modern CAM and Tool Co 734 946-9800
27272 Wick Rd Taylor (48180) ***(G-16448)***
Modern Concrete Products, Flint *Also called Modern Industries Inc* ***(G-5735)***
Modern Craft Winery LLC 989 876-4948
211 E Huron Rd Au Gres (48703) ***(G-760)***
Modern Engrg Solutions LLC 616 835-2711
4985 52nd St Se Grand Rapids (49512) ***(G-7018)***
Modern Fur Dressing LLC 517 589-5575
801 Rice St Leslie (49251) ***(G-10015)***

ALPHABETIC

Modern Hard Chrome Service Co 586 445-0330
376 Chalfonte Ave Grosse Pointe Farms (48236) ***(G-7538)***
Modern Industries Inc 810 767-3330
3275 W Pasadena Ave Flint (48504) ***(G-5735)***
Modern Kitchen & Bath, Troy *Also called Korcast Products Incorporated* ***(G-17197)***
Modern Machine Co 989 895-8563
1111 S Water St Bay City (48708) ***(G-1380)***
Modern Machine Tool Co 517 788-9120
2005 Losey Ave Jackson (49203) ***(G-8969)***
Modern Machining Inc 269 964-4415
415 Upton Ave Battle Creek (49037) ***(G-1275)***
Modern Metal Processing Corp 517 655-4402
3448 Corwin Rd Williamston (48895) ***(G-18578)***
Modern Metalcraft Inc 989 835-3716
2033 Roxbury Ct Midland (48642) ***(G-11396)***
Modern Millwork Inc 248 347-4777
29020 S Wixom Rd Ste 100 Wixom (48393) ***(G-18713)***
Modern Monogram 248 792-6266
805 S Pemberton Rd Bloomfield Hills (48302) ***(G-1839)***
Modern Neon Sign Co Inc 269 349-8636
1219 E Vine St Kalamazoo (49001) ***(G-9274)***
Modern Plastics Technology LLC 810 966-3376
2043 International Way Port Huron (48060) ***(G-13503)***
Modern Tech Machining LLC 810 531-7992
808 Gratiot Blvd Marysville (48040) ***(G-11092)***
Modern Tool and Tapping Inc 586 777-5144
33517 Kelly Rd Fraser (48026) ***(G-5964)***
Modern Woodsmith LLC 906 387-5577
E9998 State Highway M28 Wetmore (49895) ***(G-18435)***
Moderne Slate Inc 231 584-3499
8333 County Road 571 Ne Mancelona (49659) ***(G-10877)***
Moderno Industrial LLC 734 727-0560
39140 Webb Dr Westland (48185) ***(G-18397)***
Modified Gear and Spline Inc 313 893-3511
18300 Mount Elliott St Detroit (48234) ***(G-4463)***
Modified Technologies Inc 586 725-0448
6500 Bethuy Rd Ira (48023) ***(G-8703)***
Modineer Co LLC (PA) 269 683-2550
2190 Industrial Dr Niles (49120) ***(G-12145)***
Modineer Co LLC 269 683-2550
2121 W Chicago Rd Niles (49120) ***(G-12146)***
Modineer Co LLC 269 684-3138
1501 S 3rd St Niles (49120) ***(G-12147)***
Modineer Coatings Division 269 925-0702
2200 E Empire Ave Benton Harbor (49022) ***(G-1574)***
Modineer P-K Tool LLC 269 683-2550
2190 Industrial Dr Niles (49120) ***(G-12148)***
Modular Data Systems Inc 586 739-5870
53089 Bellamine Dr Shelby Township (48316) ***(G-15282)***
Modular Systems Inc 231 865-3167
169 Park St Fruitport (49415) ***(G-6067)***
Modulated Metals Inc 586 749-8400
56409 Precision Dr Chesterfield (48051) ***(G-2914)***
Moehrle Inc 734 761-2000
4305 Pontiac Trl Ann Arbor (48105) ***(G-581)***
Moeke Foresty 231 631-9600
710 Hull St Boyne City (49712) ***(G-1898)***
Moeller Aerospace Tech Inc 231 347-9575
8725 Moeller Dr Harbor Springs (49740) ***(G-7651)***
Moeller Manufacturing Co, Grand Rapids *Also called Moeller Mfg Company LLC* ***(G-7019)***
Moeller Mfg Company LLC 616 285-5012
3757 Broadmoor Ave Se Grand Rapids (49512) ***(G-7019)***
Mogultech LLC 734 944-5053
1454 Judd Rd Saline (48176) ***(G-15029)***
Moheco Products Company 734 855-4194
34410 Rosati Ave Livonia (48150) ***(G-10321)***
Mohr Engineering Inc 810 227-4598
1351 Rickett Rd Brighton (48116) ***(G-2035)***
Moiron Branch 0918, Sparta *Also called Leggett Platt Components Inc* ***(G-15771)***
Mokasoft LLC 517 703-0237
4468 Oakwood Dr Okemos (48864) ***(G-12677)***
Mol Belting Company, Grand Rapids *Also called Mol Belting Systems Inc* ***(G-7020)***
Mol Belting Systems Inc 616 453-2484
2532 Waldorf Ct Nw Grand Rapids (49544) ***(G-7020)***
Mol-Son Inc 269 668-3377
53196 N Main St Mattawan (49071) ***(G-11165)***
Mold Masters Co 810 245-4100
1455 Imlay City Rd Lapeer (48446) ***(G-9948)***
Mold Matter 231 933-6653
1650 Barlow St Traverse City (49686) ***(G-16762)***
Mold Specialties Inc 586 247-4660
51232 Oro Dr Shelby Township (48315) ***(G-15283)***
Mold Tech Michigan, Fraser *Also called Standex International Corp* ***(G-6000)***
Mold Tooling Systems Inc 616 735-6653
4315 3 Mile Rd Nw Grand Rapids (49534) ***(G-7021)***
Mold-Rite LLC (PA) 586 296-3970
33830 Riviera Fraser (48026) ***(G-5965)***
Molded Materials 734 927-1989
14555 Jib St Plymouth (48170) ***(G-13247)***
Molded Plastic Industries Inc 517 694-7434
2382 Jarco Dr Holt (48842) ***(G-8318)***
Molded Plastics & Tooling 517 268-0849
2200 Depot St Holt (48842) ***(G-8319)***
Moldex Crank Shaft Inc 313 561-7676
12255 Wormer Redford (48239) ***(G-13747)***
Moldex3d Northern America Inc (HQ) 248 946-4570
27725 Stansbury Blvd # 1 Farmington Hills (48334) ***(G-5326)***
Molding Concepts Inc 586 264-6990
6700 Sims Dr Sterling Heights (48313) ***(G-16103)***
Molding Solutions Inc (PA) 616 847-6822
1734 Airpark Dr Ste F Grand Haven (49417) ***(G-6337)***
Moller Group North America Inc (HQ) 586 532-0860
13877 Teresa Dr Shelby Township (48315) ***(G-15284)***
Mollers North America Inc 616 942-6504
5215 52nd St Se Grand Rapids (49512) ***(G-7022)***
Mollertech LLC 586 615-9154
51280 Regency Center Dr Macomb (48042) ***(G-10619)***
Mollewood Export Inc 248 624-1885
46921 Enterprise Ct Wixom (48393) ***(G-18714)***
Mom & ME Embroidery 231 590-0256
12412 Milarch Rd Bear Lake (49614) ***(G-1419)***
Mom of Shire Apothecary LLC 734 751-9443
30550 Pierce St Garden City (48135) ***(G-6104)***
Momentum Industries Inc 989 681-5735
100 Woodside Dr Saint Louis (48880) ***(G-14993)***
Monarch Electric Apparatus Svc, Melvindale *Also called Monarch Electric Service Co* ***(G-11206)***
Monarch Electric Service Co 313 388-7800
18800 Meginnity St Melvindale (48122) ***(G-11206)***
Monarch Metal Mfg Inc 616 247-0412
3303 Union Ave Se Grand Rapids (49548) ***(G-7023)***
Monarch Millwork Inc (PA) 989 348-8292
2211 Industrial Dr Grayling (49738) ***(G-7467)***
Monarch Powder Coating Inc 231 798-1422
5906 Grand Haven Rd Norton Shores (49441) ***(G-12312)***
Monarch Print and Mail LLC 734 620-8378
1461 Selma St Westland (48186) ***(G-18398)***
Monarch Welding & Engrg Inc 231 733-7222
519 W Hackley Ave Muskegon (49444) ***(G-11876)***
Mondrella Process Systems LLC 616 281-9836
2049 Innwood Dr Se Grand Rapids (49508) ***(G-7024)***
Monnier, Clay *Also called Nu-ERA Holdings Inc* ***(G-3123)***
Mono Ceramics Inc 269 925-0212
2235 Pipestone Rd Benton Harbor (49022) ***(G-1575)***
Monogram Etc 989 743-5999
231 N Shiawassee St Corunna (48817) ***(G-3712)***
Monogram Goods Naples LLC 231 526-7700
261 E Main St Harbor Springs (49740) ***(G-7652)***
Monogram Lady 313 649-2160
1841 Lancaster St Grosse Pointe Woods (48236) ***(G-7572)***
Monogram Market LLC 517 455-9083
1161 Clark Cors Dewitt (48820) ***(G-4714)***
Monograms & More Inc 313 299-3140
20449 Ecorse Rd Taylor (48180) ***(G-16449)***
Monroe LLC 616 942-9820
4490 44th St Se Ste A Grand Rapids (49512) ***(G-7025)***
Monroe Atellos 19 .... 734 682-3467
830 S Monroe St Monroe (48161) ***(G-11561)***
Monroe Environmental Corp 734 242-2420
810 W Front St Monroe (48161) ***(G-11562)***
Monroe Evening News 734 242-1100
20 W 1st St Monroe (48161) ***(G-11563)***
Monroe Fuel Company LLC 734 302-4824
414 S Main St Ste 600 Ann Arbor (48104) ***(G-582)***
Monroe Inc 616 284-3358
4490 44th St Se Ste A Grand Rapids (49512) ***(G-7026)***
Monroe Machinining LLC 734 457-2088
300 Detroit Ave Monroe (48162) ***(G-11564)***
Monroe Mold, Monroe *Also called DD Parker Enterprises Inc* ***(G-11536)***
Monroe Publishing Company (HQ) 734 242-1100
20 W 1st St Monroe (48161) ***(G-11565)***
Monroe Sattler LLC 586 725-1140
6024 Corporate Dr Ira (48023) ***(G-8704)***
Monroe Sp Inc 517 374-6544
437 Lentz Ct Lansing (48917) ***(G-9779)***
Monroe Success Vlc 734 682-3720
1000 S Monroe St Monroe (48161) ***(G-11566)***
Monroe Truck and Auto ACC, Muskegon *Also called Monroes Custom Campers Inc* ***(G-11877)***
Monroe Truck Equipment Inc (PA) 810 238-4603
2400 Reo Dr Flint (48507) ***(G-5736)***
Monroes Custom Campers Inc 231 773-0005
2915 E Apple Ave Muskegon (49442) ***(G-11877)***
Monsanto Company 269 483-1300
67760 Us 31 Constantine (49042) ***(G-3672)***
Montague Latch Company 810 687-4242
2000 W Dodge Rd Clio (48420) ***(G-3407)***
Montague Metal Products Inc 231 893-0547
4101 Fruitvale Rd Montague (49437) ***(G-11599)***

Montague Tool, Clio *Also called Montague Latch Company* ***(G-3407)***
Montague Tool and Mfg Co..........810 686-0000
11533 Liberty St Ste 3 Clio (48420) ***(G-3408)***
Montaplast North America Inc..........248 353-5553
1849 Pond Run Auburn Hills (48326) ***(G-973)***
Montcalm Aggregates Inc..........989 772-7038
2201 Commerce St Ste 4 Mount Pleasant (48858) ***(G-11717)***
Monte Package Company LLC..........269 849-1722
3752 Riverside Rd Riverside (49084) ***(G-13864)***
Montina Manufacturing Inc..........616 846-1080
13740 172nd Ave Grand Haven (49417) ***(G-6338)***
Montmorency County Tribune, Atlanta *Also called Montmorency Press Inc* ***(G-746)***
Montmorency Press Inc..........989 785-4214
12625 State 33 N Atlanta (49709) ***(G-746)***
Montronix Inc..........734 213-6500
3820 Packard St Ste 110 Ann Arbor (48108) ***(G-583)***
Montrose Trailers Inc..........810 639-7431
180 Ruth St Montrose (48457) ***(G-11607)***
Moo-Ville Inc..........517 852-9003
5875 S M 66 Hwy Nashville (49073) ***(G-11958)***
Moo-Ville Creamery, Nashville *Also called Moo-Ville Inc* ***(G-11958)***
Moody Bible Inst of Chicago..........616 772-7300
3764 84th Ave Zeeland (49464) ***(G-19057)***
Moog Fcs, Plymouth *Also called Moog Inc* ***(G-13248)***
Moog Inc..........734 738-5862
47495 Clipper St Plymouth (48170) ***(G-13248)***
Moomers Homemade Ice Cream LLC..........231 941-4122
7263 N Long Lake Rd Traverse City (49685) ***(G-16763)***
Moon River Soap Co LLC..........248 930-9467
339 East St Ste 100 Rochester (48307) ***(G-13912)***
Moon Roof Corporation America (PA)..........586 772-8730
28117 Groesbeck Hwy Roseville (48066) ***(G-14446)***
Moon Roof Corporation America..........586 552-1901
30750 Edison Dr Roseville (48066) ***(G-14447)***
Moonlight Graphics Inc..........616 243-3166
3144 Broadmoor Ave Se Grand Rapids (49512) ***(G-7027)***
Moore Brothers Electrical Co..........810 232-2148
2602 Leith St Flint (48506) ***(G-5737)***
Moore Flame Cutting Co..........586 978-1090
1022 Top View Rd Bloomfield Hills (48304) ***(G-1840)***
Moore Ingredients Ltd..........513 881-7144
1717 Douglas Ave Kalamazoo (49007) ***(G-9275)***
Moore Production Tool Spc, Farmington *Also called Moore Production Tool Spc* ***(G-5143)***
Moore Production Tool Spc..........248 476-1200
37531 Grand River Ave Farmington (48335) ***(G-5143)***
Moore Signs Investments Inc..........586 783-9339
5220 Rail View Ct Apt 245 Shelby Township (48316) ***(G-15285)***
Mooreco Inc..........616 451-7800
549 Ionia Ave Sw Grand Rapids (49503) ***(G-7028)***
Moormann Printing Inc..........269 423-2411
121 S Phelps St Decatur (49045) ***(G-3950)***
Moose Mfg & Machining LLC..........586 765-4686
440 Burroughs St Ste 692 Detroit (48202) ***(G-4464)***
Mopec, Madison Heights *Also called Mp Acquisition LLC* ***(G-10784)***
Mopega LLC..........231 631-2580
238 E Front St Traverse City (49684) ***(G-16764)***
Mophie LLC..........269 743-1340
6244 Technology Ave Kalamazoo (49009) ***(G-9276)***
Mor-Dall Enterprises Inc..........269 558-4915
511 S Kalamazoo Ave Marshall (49068) ***(G-11071)***
Moraine Vineyards LLC..........269 422-1309
111 E Shawnee Rd Baroda (49101) ***(G-1166)***
Moran Iron Works Inc..........989 733-2011
11739 M68-33 Hwy Onaway (49765) ***(G-12700)***
Morbark LLC (HQ)..........989 866-2381
8507 S Winn Rd Winn (48896) ***(G-18590)***
More Signature Cakes LLC..........248 266-0504
5065 Livernois Rd Troy (48098) ***(G-17265)***
Moreys Logo..........989 772-4492
3357 E River Rd Mount Pleasant (48858) ***(G-11718)***
Morgan Composting Inc (PA)..........231 734-2451
4353 Us Highway 10 Sears (49679) ***(G-15137)***
Morgan Composting Inc..........231 734-2790
4281 Us Highway 10 Sears (49679) ***(G-15138)***
Morgan Farm and Gardens, Sears *Also called Morgan Composting Inc* ***(G-15138)***
Morgan Machining LLC..........248 293-3277
2760 Auburn Rd Auburn Hills (48326) ***(G-974)***
Morgan Olson LLC (HQ)..........269 659-0200
1801 S Nottawa St Sturgis (49091) ***(G-16311)***
Morgan Sofa Co..........347 262-5995
2501 Russell St Ste 400 Detroit (48207) ***(G-4465)***
Morgold Inc..........269 445-3844
18409 Quaker St Cassopolis (49031) ***(G-2632)***
Morin Boats..........989 686-7353
377 State Park Dr Bay City (48706) ***(G-1381)***
Morkin and Sowards Inc..........734 729-4242
38058 Van Born Rd Wayne (48184) ***(G-18231)***
Morley Brands LLC..........586 468-4300
23770 Hall Rd Clinton Township (48036) ***(G-3304)***
Morning Star..........989 755-2660
306 E Remington St Saginaw (48601) ***(G-14704)***
Morning Star Land Company LLC..........734 459-8022
7857 Ronda Dr Canton (48187) ***(G-2498)***
Morning Star Publishing Co..........989 463-6071
311 E Superior St Ste A Alma (48801) ***(G-248)***
Morning Star Publishing Co (HQ)..........989 779-6000
311 E Superior St Ste A Alma (48801) ***(G-249)***
Morning Star Publishing Co..........989 779-6000
311 E Superior St Ste A Alma (48801) ***(G-250)***
Morning Star Publishing Co..........989 732-5125
48 W Huron St Pontiac (48342) ***(G-13399)***
Morrell Incorporated (PA)..........248 373-1600
3333 Bald Mountain Rd Auburn Hills (48326) ***(G-975)***
Morren Mold & Machine Inc..........616 892-7474
10345 60th Ave Allendale (49401) ***(G-226)***
Morris Associates Inc..........248 355-9055
24007 Telegraph Rd Southfield (48033) ***(G-15662)***
Morris Excavating Inc..........269 483-7773
69067 S Kalamazoo St White Pigeon (49099) ***(G-18484)***
Morris Kall Incorporated..........815 528-8665
2005 Wetton Ave Marquette (49855) ***(G-11037)***
Morrison Indust Ries North..........248 859-4864
46480 Magellan Dr Novi (48377) ***(G-12484)***
Morrow Foundry..........231 582-0452
926 N Lake St Boyne City (49712) ***(G-1899)***
Morse Concrete & Excavating..........989 826-3975
106 S Vine St Mio (48647) ***(G-11512)***
Morse-Hemco, Holland *Also called H E Morse Co* ***(G-8065)***
Morstar Inc..........248 605-3291
12868 Farmington Rd Livonia (48150) ***(G-10322)***
Morton Buildings Inc..........616 696-4747
59924 S Us Highway 131 Three Rivers (49093) ***(G-16579)***
Morton Industries LLC..........616 453-7121
1125 Covell Ave Nw Grand Rapids (49504) ***(G-7029)***
Morton Salt Inc..........231 398-0758
180 6th St Manistee (49660) ***(G-10910)***
Moser Racing Inc..........248 348-6502
43641 Serenity Dr Northville (48167) ***(G-12243)***
Mosiac Potash Hersey LLC..........231 832-3755
1395 135th Ave Hersey (49639) ***(G-7868)***
Mosley..........734 654-2969
9628 Lazy Oak Dr Carleton (48117) ***(G-2560)***
Moss Audio Corporation..........616 451-9933
561 Century Ave Sw Grand Rapids (49503) ***(G-7030)***
Moss Telecommunications Svcs, Grand Rapids *Also called Moss Audio Corporation* ***(G-7030)***
Motan Inc..........269 685-1050
320 Acorn St Plainwell (49080) ***(G-13083)***
Motawi Tileworks Inc..........734 213-0017
170 Enterprise Dr Ann Arbor (48103) ***(G-584)***
Mote Enterprises Inc..........248 613-3413
57446 River Oaks Dr New Haven (48048) ***(G-12035)***
Motembo Fine Foods LLC..........800 692-4814
2853 Jolly Rd Ste 3 Okemos (48864) ***(G-12678)***
Motembo Foods, Okemos *Also called Motembo Fine Foods LLC* ***(G-12678)***
Motion Dynamics Corporation..........231 865-7400
5621 Airline Rd Fruitport (49415) ***(G-6068)***
Motion Industries Inc..........989 771-0200
1646 Champagne Dr N Saginaw (48604) ***(G-14705)***
Motion Machine Company..........810 664-9901
524 Mccormick Dr Lapeer (48446) ***(G-9949)***
Motion Systems Incorporated..........586 774-5666
21335 Schoenherr Rd Warren (48089) ***(G-17935)***
Motor City Aerospace..........616 916-5473
10500 Harvard Ave Ne Rockford (49341) ***(G-14180)***
Motor City Bending & Rolling..........313 368-4400
17655 Filer St Detroit (48212) ***(G-4466)***
Motor City Carburetor..........586 443-8048
19907 Maxine St Saint Clair Shores (48080) ***(G-14873)***
Motor City Designs LLC..........313 686-1025
6659 Schaefer Rd Ste 1078 Dearborn (48126) ***(G-3874)***
Motor City Electric Tech Inc..........313 921-5300
9440 Grinnell St Detroit (48213) ***(G-4467)***
Motor City Home Inc..........248 562-7296
4537 Wagon Wheel Dr Bloomfield Hills (48301) ***(G-1841)***
Motor City Manufacturing Ltd..........586 731-1086
23440 Woodward Ave Ferndale (48220) ***(G-5569)***
Motor City Metal Fab Inc..........734 345-1001
24340 Northline Rd Taylor (48180) ***(G-16450)***
Motor City Naturals LLC..........313 329-4071
24201 Hoover Rd Warren (48089) ***(G-17936)***
Motor City Products, Flint *Also called U S Speedo Inc* ***(G-5787)***
Motor City Quick Lube One Inc..........734 367-6457
11900 Middlebelt Rd Ste A Livonia (48150) ***(G-10323)***
Motor City Racks Inc..........519 776-9153
24445 Forterra Dr Warren (48089) ***(G-17937)***
Motor City Signs LLC..........810 867-2207
10427 Potter Rd Flushing (48433) ***(G-5812)***

A
L
P
H
A
B
E
T
I
C

(PA)=Parent Co (HQ)=Headquarters (DH)=Div Headquarters

Motor City Stampings Inc (PA)...586 949-8420
47783 Gratiot Ave Chesterfield (48051) ***(G-2915)***
Motor City Wash Works Inc...248 313-0272
48285 Frank St Wixom (48393) ***(G-18715)***
Motor Control Incorporated...313 389-4000
17100 Francis St Melvindale (48122) ***(G-11207)***
Motor Parts Inc of Michigan...248 852-1522
2751 Commerce Dr Rochester Hills (48309) ***(G-14065)***
Motor Products Corporation (HQ)...989 725-5151
201 S Delaney Rd Owosso (48867) ***(G-12845)***
Motor State Distributing, Watervliet *Also called Lane Automotive Inc* ***(G-18182)***
Motor Tool Manufacturing Co...734 425-3300
14710 Flamingo St Livonia (48154) ***(G-10324)***
Motorola Solutions Inc...517 321-6655
6500 Centurion Dr Ste 250 Lansing (48917) ***(G-9780)***
Motors Online LLC...989 723-8985
503 S Shiawassee St Corunna (48817) ***(G-3713)***
Motown Harley-Davidson Inc...734 947-4647
14100 Telegraph Rd Taylor (48180) ***(G-16451)***
Mott Media LLC (PA)...810 714-4280
1130 Fenway Cir Fenton (48430) ***(G-5492)***
Mottes Materials Inc...906 265-9955
4084 Us Highway 2 Iron River (49935) ***(G-8749)***
Motto Cedar Products Inc...906 753-4892
Us Hwy 41 & County Rd 360 Daggett (49821) ***(G-3753)***
Motus Holdings LLC (HQ)...616 422-7557
88 E 48th St Holland (49423) ***(G-8149)***
Motus Integrated Technologies, Holland *Also called Motus LLC* ***(G-8150)***
Motus LLC (HQ)...616 422-7557
88 E 48th St Holland (49423) ***(G-8150)***
Motwon Sign Company LLC...313 580-4094
428 E Harry Ave Hazel Park (48030) ***(G-7835)***
Mound Steel & Supply Inc...248 852-6630
1450 Rochester Rd Troy (48083) ***(G-17266)***
Mount Clemens Orthopedic Appls...586 463-3600
24432 Crocker Blvd Clinton Township (48036) ***(G-3305)***
Mount Clmens Orthopaedic Appls, Clinton Township *Also called Mount Clemens Orthopedic Appls* ***(G-3305)***
Mount Mfg LLC...231 487-2118
200 Echelon Dr Ste C Negaunee (49866) ***(G-11970)***
Mount-N-Repair...248 647-8670
205 Pierce St Ste 101 Birmingham (48009) ***(G-1738)***
Mount-N-Repair Silver Jewelry, Birmingham *Also called Mount-N-Repair* ***(G-1738)***
Mountain Machine LLC...734 480-2200
7850 Rawsonville Rd Van Buren Twp (48111) ***(G-17542)***
Mountain Town Stn Brew Pub LLC...989 775-2337
506 W Broadway St Mount Pleasant (48858) ***(G-11719)***
Mountain Town Stn Brewing Co &, Mount Pleasant *Also called Mountain Town Stn Brew Pub LLC* ***(G-11719)***
Movellus Circuits Inc (PA)...877 321-7667
206 E Huron St Ann Arbor (48104) ***(G-585)***
Moving & Shipping Solutions...231 824-4190
3485 N Brown Rd Manton (49663) ***(G-10938)***
Moyer Wldg & Fabrication LLC...734 243-1212
13685 Dunlap Rd La Salle (48145) ***(G-9528)***
Moyle Lumber, Houghton *Also called Thomas J Moyle Jr Incorporated* ***(G-8393)***
Mp Acquisition LLC (PA)...800 362-8491
800 Tech Row Madison Heights (48071) ***(G-10784)***
Mp Components, Byron Center *Also called Model Pattern Company Inc* ***(G-2288)***
Mp Hollywood LLC (PA)...517 782-0391
1824 River St Jackson (49202) ***(G-8970)***
Mp Tool & Engineering Company...586 772-7730
15850 Common Rd Roseville (48066) ***(G-14448)***
Mp-Tec Inc...734 367-1284
32920 Capitol St Livonia (48150) ***(G-10325)***
Mp6 LLC...231 409-7530
2488 Cass Rd Traverse City (49684) ***(G-16765)***
Mpc...313 297-6386
1001 S Oakwood Detroit (48217) ***(G-4468)***
Mpc Company Inc...269 927-3371
1891 Territorial Rd Benton Harbor (49022) ***(G-1576)***
Mpd Welding - Grand Rapids Inc...616 248-9353
1903 Clyde Park Ave Sw Grand Rapids (49509) ***(G-7031)***
Mpd Welding Center, Orion *Also called M P D Welding Inc* ***(G-12735)***
Mpf Acquisitions Inc...269 672-5511
904 E Allegan St Martin (49070) ***(G-11080)***
Mpg, Southfield *Also called Metaldyne Prfmce Group Inc* ***(G-15654)***
Mpg Inc (PA)...734 207-6200
47659 Halyard Dr Plymouth (48170) ***(G-13249)***
Mpg Holdco I Inc...734 207-6200
47659 Halyard Dr Plymouth (48170) ***(G-13250)***
Mpi, Highland *Also called Magnetic Products Inc* ***(G-7896)***
Mpi, Holt *Also called Molded Plastic Industries Inc* ***(G-8318)***
Mpi Engineered Tech LLC...248 237-3007
901 Tower Dr Ste 315 Troy (48098) ***(G-17267)***
Mpi Plastics...201 502-1534
51315 Regency Center Dr Macomb (48042) ***(G-10620)***
Mpi Products Holdings LLC (HQ)...248 237-3007
2129 Austin Ave Rochester Hills (48309) ***(G-14066)***
Mpi Products LLC...248 237-3007
2129 Austin Ave Rochester Hills (48309) ***(G-14067)***
Mpm, Macomb *Also called Michigan Prod Machining Inc* ***(G-10616)***
Mpp Corp...810 364-2939
82 Airport Dr Kimball (48074) ***(G-9496)***
Mpr, Visitmpr, Saint Johns *Also called Michigan Polymer Reclaim Inc* ***(G-14909)***
Mpress Deisghns LLC...313 627-9727
19030 Veronica Ave Eastpointe (48021) ***(G-4941)***
MPS, Saint Clair *Also called Michigan Prcsion Swiss Prts In* ***(G-14837)***
MPS Holdco Inc (HQ)...517 886-2526
5800 W Grand River Ave Lansing (48906) ***(G-9717)***
MPS Holdings, Lansing *Also called MPS Holdco Inc* ***(G-9717)***
MPS Holland, Holland *Also called Steketee-Van Huis Inc* ***(G-8202)***
MPS Hrl LLC...800 748-0517
5800 W Grand River Ave Lansing (48906) ***(G-9718)***
MPS Lansing Inc (HQ)...517 323-9000
5800 W Grand River Ave Lansing (48906) ***(G-9719)***
MPS Trading Group LLC...313 841-7588
38755 Hills Tech Dr Farmington Hills (48331) ***(G-5327)***
MPS/Ih LLC...517 323-9001
5800 W Grand River Ave Lansing (48906) ***(G-9720)***
Mpt Driveline Systems...248 680-3786
1870 Technology Dr Troy (48083) ***(G-17268)***
Mpt Lansing LLC...517 316-1013
3140 Spanish Oak Dr Ste A Lansing (48911) ***(G-9872)***
Mq Operating Company...906 337-1515
416 6th St Calumet (49913) ***(G-2412)***
Mr Axle...231 788-4624
6336 E Apple Ave Muskegon (49442) ***(G-11878)***
Mr Chain, Copemish *Also called M-R Products Inc* ***(G-3698)***
Mr Chips Inc (HQ)...989 879-3555
2628 N Huron Rd Pinconning (48650) ***(G-13063)***
Mr Cs Custom Tees...989 965-2222
151 Lind Ave Clarksville (48815) ***(G-3079)***
Mr E Machine LLC...810 407-0319
2445 E Bay Ridge Dr Au Gres (48703) ***(G-761)***
Mr ES Eatery LLC...313 502-9256
33742 Elford Dr Sterling Heights (48312) ***(G-16104)***
Mr Everything LLC (PA)...248 301-2580
15994 Sumner Redford (48239) ***(G-13748)***
Mr Lube Inc...313 615-6161
6915 Airport Hwy Wyandotte (48192) ***(G-18834)***
Mr McGooz Products Inc...313 693-4003
18911 W 7 Mile Rd Detroit (48219) ***(G-4469)***
Mr Peel Inc...734 266-2022
33975 Autry St Livonia (48150) ***(G-10326)***
Mr Sogs Creatures...901 413-0291
29700 Citation Cir # 14205 Farmington Hills (48331) ***(G-5328)***
MRC Indsutries...586 204-5241
30700 Edison Dr Roseville (48066) ***(G-14449)***
MRC Industries...269 552-5586
1606 S Burdick St Kalamazoo (49001) ***(G-9277)***
MRC Industries Inc (PA)...269 343-0747
2538 S 26th St Kalamazoo (49048) ***(G-9278)***
MRC Manufacturing, Roseville *Also called Moon Roof Corporation America* ***(G-14446)***
Mrd Aerospace...586 468-1196
37729 Elmlane Harrison Township (48045) ***(G-7711)***
Mrj Sign Company LLC...248 521-2431
256 Narrin St Ortonville (48462) ***(G-12749)***
MRM Ida Products Co Inc...313 834-0200
8385 Lyndon St Detroit (48238) ***(G-4470)***
Ms Chip Inc...586 296-9850
34137 Doreka Fraser (48026) ***(G-5966)***
Ms International Holdings LLC...443 210-1446
7205 Sterling Ponds Ct Sterling Heights (48312) ***(G-16105)***
Ms Plastic Welders LLC...517 223-1059
1101 Highview Dr Webberville (48892) ***(G-18246)***
MSC Blinds & Shades Inc...269 489-5188
1241 W Chicago Rd Bronson (49028) ***(G-2119)***
MSC Canton, Canton *Also called Material Sciences Corporation* ***(G-2490)***
Mscsoftware Corporation...734 994-3800
50 W Big Beavr Rd Ste 430 Troy (48084) ***(G-17269)***
Mscsoftware Corporation...734 994-3800
201 Depot St Ste 100 Ann Arbor (48104) ***(G-586)***
Msd Stamping, Livonia *Also called Amanda Manufacturing LLC* ***(G-10113)***
Mse...586 264-4120
40809 Brentwood Dr Sterling Heights (48310) ***(G-16106)***
MSE Fabrication LLC...586 991-6138
6624 Burroughs Ave Sterling Heights (48314) ***(G-16107)***
Mshiikenh Rnwble Resources LLC...231 818-9353
8585 Swan Pointe Dr Cheboygan (49721) ***(G-2792)***
MSI, Boyne City *Also called Magnetic Systems Intl Inc* ***(G-1896)***
MSI, Drummond Island *Also called Manufacturers Services Inds* ***(G-4802)***
MSI Machine Tool Parts Inc...248 589-0515
1619 Donna Ave Madison Heights (48071) ***(G-10785)***
Msinc...248 275-1978
50463 Wing Dr Shelby Township (48315) ***(G-15286)***

Msmac Designs LLC 313 521-6289
11069 Nashville St Detroit (48205) **(G-4471)**
Msnow, Plainwell *Also called Plastisnow LLC* **(G-13090)**
MSP Industries Corporation 248 628-4150
45 W Oakwood Rd Oxford (48371) **(G-12904)**
Msr-Pallets & Packaging LLC 810 360-0425
1000 Lily Pond Dr Brighton (48116) **(G-2036)**
Mssb LLC 616 868-9730
6090 Alden Nash Ave Se Alto (49302) **(G-337)**
Mssc Inc (HQ) 248 502-8000
2040 Crooks Rd Ste A Troy (48084) **(G-17270)**
Mstation, Kalamazoo *Also called Mophie LLC* **(G-9276)**
MSU Bakers, East Lansing *Also called Michigan State University* **(G-4906)**
Msw Print and Imaging 734 544-1626
3901 Bestech Rd Ypsilanti (48197) **(G-18969)**
Msx International Inc 248 585-6654
30031 Stephenson Hwy Madison Heights (48071) **(G-10786)**
Mt Clemens Glass & Mirror Co 586 465-1733
1231 S Gratiot Ave Clinton Township (48036) **(G-3306)**
Mt Pleasant Buyers Guide 989 779-6000
711 W Pickard St Ste A Mount Pleasant (48858) **(G-11720)**
Mt Pleasant Centl Con Pdts Co 989 772-3695
900 S Bradley St Ste A Mount Pleasant (48858) **(G-11721)**
Mt. Clemens Crane, Harrison Township *Also called Crane 1 Services Inc* **(G-7694)**
Mtg, Corunna *Also called Machine Tool & Gear Inc* **(G-3711)**
MTI Precision Machining Inc 989 865-9880
11980 Beaver Rd Saint Charles (48655) **(G-14806)**
MTI-Saline, Saline *Also called Crescive Die and Tool Inc* **(G-15010)**
Mtm Machine Inc 586 443-5703
35310 Stanley Dr Sterling Heights (48312) **(G-16108)**
MTS, Benton Harbor *Also called Midwest Timer Service Inc* **(G-1573)**
MTS Burgess LLC 734 847-2937
1244 W Dean Rd Temperance (48182) **(G-16542)**
MTS Seating, Temperance *Also called Michigan Tube Swgers Fbrctors* **(G-16541)**
Mtu America Inc 248 560-8298
19771 Brownstown Ctr Dr Brownstown (48183) **(G-2151)**
Mtw Industries Inc 989 317-3301
706 W Pickard St Mount Pleasant (48858) **(G-11722)**
Mtw Performance & Fab 989 317-3301
706 W Pickard St Mount Pleasant (48858) **(G-11723)**
Mubea Inc 248 393-9600
1701 Harmon Rd Auburn Hills (48326) **(G-976)**
Mud Quick Change Tooling, Greenville *Also called D-M-E USA Inc* **(G-7480)**
Mueller Brass Co (HQ) 810 987-7770
2199 Lapeer Ave Port Huron (48060) **(G-13504)**
Mueller Brass Co 616 794-1200
302 Ashfield St Belding (48809) **(G-1459)**
Mueller Brass Co 810 987-7770
2199 Lapeer Ave Port Huron (48060) **(G-13505)**
Mueller Brass Forging Co Inc 810 987-7770
2199 Lapeer Ave Port Huron (48060) **(G-13506)**
Mueller Brass Products, Port Huron *Also called Mueller Brass Co* **(G-13504)**
Mueller Brass Products, Belding *Also called Mueller Brass Co* **(G-1459)**
Mueller Impacts Company Inc 810 364-3700
2409 Wills St Marysville (48040) **(G-11093)**
Mueller Industrial Realty Co 810 987-7770
2199 Lapeer Ave Port Huron (48060) **(G-13507)**
Mueller Industries Inc 248 446-3720
7350 Kensington Rd Brighton (48116) **(G-2037)**
Mug Shots Burgers and Brews 616 895-2337
4633 Lake Michigan Dr Allendale (49401) **(G-227)**
Muhleck Enterprises Inc 517 333-0713
2863 Jolly Rd Okemos (48864) **(G-12679)**
Mull-It-Over Products LLC 616 730-2162
4275 White St Sw Grandville (49418) **(G-7403)**
Multi McHning Capabilities Inc 734 955-5592
27482 Northline Rd # 100 Romulus (48174) **(G-14307)**
Multi Packg Solutions Intl Ltd 517 323-9000
5800 W Grand River Ave Lansing (48906) **(G-9721)**
Multi Precision Intl LLC 248 373-3330
2635 Paldan Dr Auburn Hills (48326) **(G-977)**
Multi Steel Services 734 261-6201
17159 Loveland St Livonia (48152) **(G-10327)**
Multi Tech Precision Inc 616 514-1415
3403 Lousma Dr Se Grand Rapids (49548) **(G-7032)**
Multi Tech Systems, Troy *Also called MAKS INCORPORATED* **(G-17235)**
Multi-Form Plastics Inc 586 786-4229
51315 Regency Center Dr Macomb (48042) **(G-10621)**
Multi-Lab LLC 616 846-6990
18784 174th Ave Spring Lake (49456) **(G-15838)**
Multi-Precision Detail Inc 248 373-3330
2635 Paldan Dr Auburn Hills (48326) **(G-978)**
Multiax International Inc 616 534-4530
3000 Remico St Sw Grandville (49418) **(G-7404)**
Multiform Plastics Inc 586 726-2688
6594 Diplomat Dr Sterling Heights (48314) **(G-16109)**
Multiform Studios LLC 248 437-5964
12012 Doane Rd South Lyon (48178) **(G-15447)**
Multimatic Michigan LLC 517 962-7190
2400 Enterprise St Jackson (49203) **(G-8971)**
Munimula Inc 517 605-5343
548 Squires Rd Quincy (49082) **(G-13673)**
Munn Manufacturing Company 616 765-3067
312 County Line Rd Freeport (49325) **(G-6035)**
Munro Printing 586 773-9579
16145 E 10 Mile Rd Eastpointe (48021) **(G-4942)**
Murdick's Fudge Kitchen, Mackinac Island *Also called Original Murdicks Fudge Co* **(G-10567)**
Murleys Marine 586 725-7446
8174 Dixie Hwy Ira (48023) **(G-8705)**
Murphy Software Company, Roseville *Also called Paul Murphy Plastics Co* **(G-14460)**
Murphys Bits, Davison *Also called Murphys Water Well Bits* **(G-3791)**
Murphys Water Well Bits (PA) 810 658-1554
3340 S State Rd Davison (48423) **(G-3791)**
Murray Equipment Company Inc (PA) 313 869-4444
6737 E 8 Mile Rd Warren (48091) **(G-17938)**
Murray Grinding Inc 313 295-6030
5441 Sylvia St Dearborn Heights (48125) **(G-3934)**
Murrays Worldwide Inc 248 691-9156
21841 Wyoming St Ste 1 Oak Park (48237) **(G-12629)**
Murtech Energy Services LLC 810 653-5681
3097 Aberdeen Ct Port Huron (48060) **(G-13508)**
Musashi Auto Parts Mich Inc 269 965-0057
195 Brydges Dr Battle Creek (49037) **(G-1276)**
Music 313 854-3606
2647 Crane St Detroit (48214) **(G-4472)**
Music Box 517 539-5069
300 W North St Jackson (49202) **(G-8972)**
Musical Sneakers Incorporated (PA) 888 410-7050
2885 Snford Ave Sw 3533 Grandville (49418) **(G-7405)**
Musicalia Press 734 433-1289
226 South St Chelsea (48118) **(G-2821)**
Muskegon Awning & Fabrication, Muskegon *Also called Feb Inc* **(G-11816)**
Muskegon Awning & Mfg Co 231 759-0911
2333 Henry St Muskegon (49441) **(G-11879)**
Muskegon Brake & Distrg Co LLC (PA) 231 733-0874
848 E Broadway Ave Norton Shores (49444) **(G-12313)**
Muskegon Brake & Parts, Norton Shores *Also called Muskegon Brake & Distrg Co LLC* **(G-12313)**
Muskegon Charter Township Fire 231 329-3068
265 N Mararebecah Ln Muskegon (49442) **(G-11880)**
Muskegon Chronicle, Muskegon *Also called Herald Newspapers Company Inc* **(G-11836)**
Muskegon Development Company 989 772-4900
1425 S Mission Rd Ste 1 Mount Pleasant (48858) **(G-11724)**
Muskegon Formulation Plant, Muskegon *Also called Bayer Cropscience LP* **(G-11776)**
Muskegon Gas and Fuel, Muskegon *Also called Jet Fuel* **(G-11845)**
Muskegon Heights Water Filter 231 780-3415
2323 Seminole Rd Norton Shores (49441) **(G-12314)**
Muskegon Industrial Finishng 231 733-7663
2000 Sanford St Muskegon (49444) **(G-11881)**
Muskegon Monument & Stone Co 231 722-2730
1396 Pine St Muskegon (49442) **(G-11882)**
Muskegon Pioneer County Park, Muskegon *Also called County of Muskegon* **(G-11796)**
Muskegon Tools LLC 231 788-4633
5142 Evanston Ave Muskegon (49442) **(G-11883)**
Mustang Aeronautics Inc 248 649-6818
1990 Heide Dr Troy (48084) **(G-17271)**
Mv Metal Pdts & Solutions LLC 269 462-4010
51241 M 51 N Dowagiac (49047) **(G-4791)**
Mv Metal Pdts & Solutions LLC (PA) 269 471-7715
3585 Bellflower Dr Portage (49024) **(G-13586)**
Mvc, Roseville *Also called McKechnie Vhcl Cmpnnts USA Inc* **(G-14439)**
Mvc Holdings LLC (PA) 586 491-2600
27087 Gratiot Ave Fl 2 Roseville (48066) **(G-14450)**
Mvm7 LLC 989 317-3901
210 W Pickard St Mount Pleasant (48858) **(G-11725)**
Mvp Sports Store 517 764-5165
5000 Ann Arbor Rd Jackson (49201) **(G-8973)**
Mw Minerals 517 294-6709
3157 Loss Trl Milford (48380) **(G-11474)**
Mwa Company, Owosso *Also called Mid-West Waltham Abrasives Co* **(G-12843)**
MWC (michigan) LLC 575 791-9559
1640 Technical Dr Saint Johns (48879) **(G-14910)**
My Dream Dress Brdal Salon LLC 248 327-6049
19471 W 10 Mile Rd Southfield (48075) **(G-15663)**
My Electrician Grand Rapids 616 208-4113
19 Jordan St Sw Grand Rapids (49548) **(G-7033)**
MY GREEN FEELS, Traverse City *Also called Selestial Soap LLC* **(G-16828)**
My Little Prints 248 613-8439
26645 Normandy Rd Franklin (48025) **(G-5883)**
My Metal Medium 231 590-4051
5774 N M 37 Mesick (49668) **(G-11274)**
My Permit Pal Inc 248 432-2699
5030 Meadowbrook Dr West Bloomfield (48322) **(G-18300)**
My Print Works MI 269 344-3226
509 Mills St Kalamazoo (49001) **(G-9279)**

My Secret Bundles LLC 586 610-2804
42491 Clinton Place Dr Clinton Township (48038) *(G-3307)*
My Tec-Tronics LLC 586 218-0118
10894 Grand River Rd Brighton (48116) *(G-2038)*
My-Can LLC 989 288-7779
989 N Saginaw St Durand (48429) *(G-4843)*
Mycdbdmk Services LLC 586 994-7910
35251 Malibu Dr Sterling Heights (48312) *(G-16110)*
Myco Enterprises Inc (PA) 248 348-3806
3608 Dukeshire Hwy Royal Oak (48073) *(G-14564)*
Mycrona Inc 734 453-9348
14777 Keel St Plymouth (48170) *(G-13251)*
Mykin Inc 248 667-8030
10056 Colonial Indus Dr South Lyon (48178) *(G-15448)*
Myles Group, Troy *Also called J E Myles Inc (G-17178)*
Mylockercom LLC 877 898-3366
1300 Rosa Parks Blvd Detroit (48216) *(G-4473)*
Myrtle Industries Inc 517 784-8579
1810 E High St Ste 2 Jackson (49203) *(G-8974)*
Mz. Tilly Sunday ACC Bra Plug, Westland *Also called Sundai Imports Inc (G-18419)*
N & K Fulbright LLC 269 695-4580
1760 Foundation Dr Niles (49120) *(G-12149)*
N & S Customs 269 651-8237
66315 Austrian Ln Sturgis (49091) *(G-16312)*
N A Actuaplast Inc 734 744-4010
31690 Glendale St Livonia (48150) *(G-10328)*
N A Sodecia Inc 586 879-8969
24331 Sherwood Center Line (48015) *(G-2683)*
N A Visscher-Caravelle Inc 248 851-9800
2525 S Telg Rd Ste 302 Bloomfield Hills (48302) *(G-1842)*
N C Brighton Machine Corp 810 227-6190
7300 Whitmore Lake Rd Brighton (48116) *(G-2039)*
N D C Contracting, Petoskey *Also called Manthei Development Corp (G-13005)*
N D R Enterprises Inc 269 857-4556
297 S Maple St Saugatuck (49453) *(G-15084)*
N F P Inc 989 631-0009
7550 Eastman Ave Midland (48642) *(G-11397)*
N Forcer, Dearborn *Also called Die-Mold-Automation Component (G-3829)*
N G S G I Natural Gas Ser 989 786-3788
3690 County Road 491 Lewiston (49756) *(G-10025)*
N I S, Troy *Also called National Industrial Sup Co Inc (G-17273)*
N O C Industries, Cadillac *Also called Hope Network West Michigan (G-2334)*
N Pack Ship Center 906 863-4095
1045 10th St Menominee (49858) *(G-11253)*
N S International Ltd (HQ) 248 251-1600
600 Wilshire Dr Troy (48084) *(G-17272)*
N S S Industries, Canton *Also called Nss Technologies Inc (G-2502)*
N-K Manufacturing Tech LLC (PA) 616 248-3200
1134 Freeman Ave Sw Grand Rapids (49503) *(G-7034)*
N-K Sealing Technologies LLC (PA) 616 248-3200
1134 Freeman Ave Sw Grand Rapids (49503) *(G-7035)*
N-P Grinding Inc 586 756-6262
3700 E 10 Mile Rd Warren (48091) *(G-17939)*
N. C. I., Rochester Hills *Also called Northville Circuits Inc (G-14073)*
N/C Production & Grinding Inc 586 731-2150
43758 Merrill Rd Sterling Heights (48314) *(G-16111)*
N2 Publications 517 488-2607
77 Lake Ridge Dr Mason (48854) *(G-11146)*
N2 Publishing, Farmington Hills *Also called D2 Ink Inc (G-5209)*
Naams LLC 586 285-5684
25141 Easy St Warren (48089) *(G-17940)*
Nabco Inc (HQ) 231 832-2001
660 Commerce Dr Reed City (49677) *(G-13796)*
Nabtesco Motion Control Inc 248 553-3020
23976 Freeway Park Dr Farmington Hills (48335) *(G-5329)*
Nacs USA Inc (HQ) 800 253-9000
8181 Logistics Dr Zeeland (49464) *(G-19058)*
Nadex of America Corporation (PA) 248 477-3900
24775 Crestview Ct Farmington Hills (48335) *(G-5330)*
Nafa Printing LLC 734 338-2103
37000 Industrial Rd Livonia (48150) *(G-10329)*
Nafta Benchmarking Center 248 335-0366
2500 Centerpoint Pkwy Pontiac (48341) *(G-13400)*
Nagel Meat Processing 517 568-5035
3265 22 Mile Rd Homer (49245) *(G-8355)*
Nagel Paper Inc 810 644-7043
6437 Lennon Rd Swartz Creek (48473) *(G-16357)*
Nagel Precision Inc 734 426-5650
288 Dino Dr Ann Arbor (48103) *(G-587)*
Nagel Precision Inc 248 380-4052
22025 Arbor Ln Novi (48375) *(G-12485)*
Nagle Paving Company (PA) 248 553-0600
39525 W 13 Mile Rd # 300 Novi (48377) *(G-12486)*
Nagle Paving Company 734 591-1484
36780 Amrhein Rd Livonia (48150) *(G-10330)*
Nail Time 313 837-3871
8862 Greenfield Rd Detroit (48228) *(G-4474)*
Nakagawa Special Stl Amer Inc 248 449-6050
42400 Grand River Ave # 102 Novi (48375) *(G-12487)*
Naked Fuel Juice Bar 248 325-9735
6718 Orchard Lake Rd West Bloomfield (48322) *(G-18301)*
Naked Shirt Custom Prtg LLC 269 625-7235
33246 Us 12 Burr Oak (49030) *(G-2213)*
Nalcor LLC (PA) 248 541-1140
1365 Jarvis St Ferndale (48220) *(G-5570)*
Nalpac Enterprises, Ferndale *Also called Nalcor LLC (G-5570)*
Nano Innovations LLC 906 231-2101
22151 Ridge Rd Houghton (49931) *(G-8387)*
Nano Magic Holdings Inc (PA) 844 273-6462
31601 Research Park Dr Madison Heights (48071) *(G-10787)*
Nano Materials & Processes Inc 248 529-3873
659 Heritage Dr Milford (48381) *(G-11475)*
Nano-Tex, Bloomfield Hills *Also called Nanotex LLC (G-1843)*
Nanocerox Inc (PA) 734 741-9522
712 State Cir Ann Arbor (48108) *(G-588)*
Nanomag LLC 734 261-2800
13753 Otterson Ct Livonia (48150) *(G-10331)*
Nanoplas, Grandville *Also called Lej Investments LLC (G-7398)*
Nanorete Inc 517 336-4680
3815 Tech Blvd Ste 1050 Lansing (48910) *(G-9873)*
Nanosynthons LLC 989 317-3737
1200 N Fancher Ave Mount Pleasant (48858) *(G-11726)*
Nanosystems Inc 734 274-0020
3588 Plymouth Rd Ann Arbor (48105) *(G-589)*
Nanotex LLC (HQ) 248 855-6000
38500 Woodward Ave # 201 Bloomfield Hills (48304) *(G-1843)*
NAPA, Ludington *Also called 751 Parts Company Inc (G-10524)*
Napco, South Haven *Also called National Appliance Parts Co (G-15410)*
Napolitano Bakery, Saginaw *Also called Cesere Enterprises Inc (G-14626)*
Narburgh & Tidd LLC 734 281-1959
18835 Krause St Riverview (48193) *(G-13881)*
Nartron, Reed City *Also called Uusi LLC (G-13803)*
Nash Car Trailer Corporation 269 673-5776
1305 Lincoln Rd Allegan (49010) *(G-171)*
Nash Products Inc 269 323-2980
5750 E S Ave Vicksburg (49097) *(G-17609)*
Nass Controls, New Baltimore *Also called Nass Corporation (G-11989)*
Nass Corporation 586 725-6610
51509 Birch St New Baltimore (48047) *(G-11989)*
Nate Ronald 269 424-3777
50317 W Lakeshore Dr Dowagiac (49047) *(G-4792)*
Nates Custom Welding 574 303-2254
1101 Carberry Rd Niles (49120) *(G-12150)*
Nathan Shetler 269 521-4554
44815 County Rd Ste 388 Bloomingdale (49026) *(G-1877)*
Nathaniel Rose Wine 989 302-3297
10417 E Bingham Rd Traverse City (49684) *(G-16766)*
Nation Wide Fuel Inc 734 721-7110
6341 Barrie St Dearborn (48126) *(G-3875)*
National Advnced Mblity Cnsrti 734 205-5920
455 E Eisenhower Pkwy # 27 Ann Arbor (48108) *(G-590)*
National Aircraft Service Inc 517 423-7589
9133 Tecumseh Clinton Hwy Tecumseh (49286) *(G-16509)*
National Ambucs Inc 231 798-4244
708 Mapleway Dr Norton Shores (49441) *(G-12315)*
National Appliance Parts Co 269 639-1469
900 Indiana Ave South Haven (49090) *(G-15410)*
National Asphalt Products, Shelby Township *Also called Carlo John Inc (G-15181)*
National Bakery 313 891-7803
736 E State Fair Detroit (48203) *(G-4475)*
National Block Company 734 721-4050
39000 Ford Rd Westland (48185) *(G-18399)*
National Bronze Mfg Co, Roseville *Also called Conway Detroit Corporation (G-14389)*
National Bulk Equipment Inc (PA) 616 399-2220
12838 Stainless Dr Holland (49424) *(G-8151)*
National Carbon Tech LLC 651 330-4063
513 4th St Gwinn (49841) *(G-7585)*
National Case Corp 586 803-3245
13220 W Star Dr Shelby Township (48315) *(G-15287)*
National Case Corporation 586 726-1710
42710 Mound Rd Sterling Heights (48314) *(G-16112)*
National Chemical & Oil, Oak Park *Also called Ncoc Inc (G-12632)*
National Chili, Roseville *Also called National Coney Island Chili Co (G-14451)*
National Composites LLC (PA) 989 723-8997
401 S Delaney Rd Owosso (48867) *(G-12846)*
National Coney Island Chili Co 313 365-5611
27947 Groesbeck Hwy Roseville (48066) *(G-14451)*
National Control Systems Inc 810 231-2901
10737 Hamburg Rd Hamburg (48139) *(G-7592)*
National Crane & Hoist Service 248 789-4535
1630 Noble Rd Leonard (48367) *(G-10002)*
National Credit Corporation (PA) 734 459-8100
7091 Orchard Lake Rd # 300 West Bloomfield (48322) *(G-18302)*
National Discount X-Ray Supply, Ann Arbor *Also called Associated Metals Inc (G-384)*
National Element Inc 248 486-1810
7939 Lochlin Dr Brighton (48116) *(G-2040)*
National Flag Football, Bloomfield Hills *Also called B4 Sports Inc (G-1802)*

National Fleet Service LLC 313 923-1799
10100 Grinnell St Detroit (48213) ***(G-4476)***

National Fuels Inc 734 895-7836
40401 Michigan Ave Canton (48188) ***(G-2499)***

National Galvanizing LP 734 243-1882
1500 Telb St Monroe (48162) ***(G-11567)***

National Indus Sp Coatings LLC 989 894-8538
2600 N West River Rd Sanford (48657) ***(G-15074)***

National Industrial Sup Co Inc 248 588-1828
1201 Rochester Rd Troy (48083) ***(G-17273)***

National Innovation Center 248 414-3913
26431 Raine St Oak Park (48237) ***(G-12630)***

National Instruments Corp 734 464-2310
20255 Victor Pkwy Ste 195 Livonia (48152) ***(G-10332)***

National Intgrated Systems Inc 734 927-3030
29241 Beck Rd Wixom (48393) ***(G-18716)***

National Manufacturing Inc 586 755-8983
25426 Ryan Rd Warren (48091) ***(G-17941)***

National Metal Sales Inc 734 942-3000
27400 Northline Rd Romulus (48174) ***(G-14308)***

National Millwork Inc 248 307-1299
32350 Howard Ave Madison Heights (48071) ***(G-10788)***

National Nail Corp (PA) 616 538-8000
2964 Clydon Ave Sw Grand Rapids (49519) ***(G-7036)***

National Ordanace Auto Mfg LLC 248 853-8822
2900 Auburn Ct Auburn Hills (48326) ***(G-979)***

National Ordnance Auto Mfg LLC 248 853-8822
2900 Auburn Ct Auburn Hills (48326) ***(G-980)***

National Packaging Corporation 248 652-3600
1150 W Hamlin Rd Rochester Hills (48309) ***(G-14068)***

National Pattern Inc 989 755-6274
5900 Sherman Rd Saginaw (48604) ***(G-14706)***

National Piling Products Inc 855 801-7453
1159 Electric Ave Ste B Wayland (49348) ***(G-18200)***

National Plastek Inc 616 698-9559
7050 Dtton Indus Pk Dr Se Caledonia (49316) ***(G-2390)***

National Precast Strl Inc 586 294-6430
14670 23 Mile Rd Shelby Township (48315) ***(G-15288)***

National Printing Services 616 813-0758
5360 Pine Slope Dr Sw Wyoming (49519) ***(G-18896)***

National Product Co 269 344-3640
1206 E Crosstown Pkwy Kalamazoo (49001) ***(G-9280)***

National Ready-Mix, Westland *Also called National Block Company* ***(G-18399)***

National Roofg & Shtmtl Co Inc 989 964-0557
200 Lee St Saginaw (48602) ***(G-14707)***

National Sign & Signal Co 269 963-2817
301 Armstrong Rd Battle Creek (49037) ***(G-1277)***

National Soap Company Inc 248 545-8180
1911 Bellaire Ave Royal Oak (48067) ***(G-14565)***

National Television Book Co, Troy *Also called Ntvb Media Inc* ***(G-17282)***

National Time and Signal Corp 248 291-5867
21800 Wyoming St Oak Park (48237) ***(G-12631)***

National Tool & Die Welding 734 522-0072
13340 Merriman Rd Livonia (48150) ***(G-10333)***

National Wholesale Prtg Corp 734 416-8400
41290 Joy Rd Plymouth (48170) ***(G-13252)***

National Zinc Processors Inc 269 926-1161
1256 Milton St Benton Harbor (49022) ***(G-1577)***

National-Standard LLC (HQ) 269 683-9902
1631 Lake St Niles (49120) ***(G-12151)***

Nationwide Communications LLC 517 990-1223
5263 Thames Ct Jackson (49201) ***(G-8975)***

Nationwide Design Inc 586 254-5493
6605 Burroughs Ave Sterling Heights (48314) ***(G-16113)***

Nationwide Intelligence, Saginaw *Also called Nationwide Network Inc* ***(G-14708)***

Nationwide Laser Technologies 248 488-0155
27600 Farmington Rd B1 Farmington Hills (48334) ***(G-5331)***

Nationwide Network Inc (PA) 989 793-0123
3401 Peale Dr Saginaw (48602) ***(G-14708)***

Nationwide Toner Cartridge, Farmington Hills *Also called Nationwide Laser Technologies* ***(G-5331)***

Native Detroiter Pubg Inc 313 822-1958
8200 E Jefferson Ave # 1204 Detroit (48214) ***(G-4477)***

Native Green LLC 248 365-4200
180 Engelwood Dr Ste A Orion (48359) ***(G-12736)***

Natural Aggregate, Wixom *Also called American Aggregates Mich Inc* ***(G-18607)***

Natural Aggregates Corporation (PA) 248 685-1502
3362 Muir Rd Milford (48380) ***(G-11476)***

Natural American Foods LLC (PA) 517 467-2065
10464 Bryan Hwy Onsted (49265) ***(G-12707)***

Natural Gas Cmprssion Systems (PA) 231 941-0107
2480 Aero Park Dr Traverse City (49686) ***(G-16767)***

Natural Hlth Essntial Oils LLC 906 495-5404
6307 W Kallio Rd Kinross (49752) ***(G-9527)***

Natural Therapeutics LLC 734 604-7313
401 W Morgan Rd Ann Arbor (48108) ***(G-591)***

Natural Way Cheese 989 935-9380
6060 E Beaverton Rd Clare (48617) ***(G-2988)***

Nature Patch Soaps 734 847-3759
2300 W Dean Rd Temperance (48182) ***(G-16543)***

Natures Best Top Soil Compost 810 657-9528
640 Old 51 Carsonville (48419) ***(G-2596)***

Nautical Knots 231 206-0400
301 N Harbor Dr Ste 12 Grand Haven (49417) ***(G-6339)***

Nauticraft 810 356-2942
3120 Levalley Rd Columbiaville (48421) ***(G-3494)***

Nava Solar LLC 734 707-8260
504 S Fancher St Mount Pleasant (48858) ***(G-11727)***

Navarre Inc 313 892-7300
3500 E 8 Mile Rd Detroit (48234) ***(G-4478)***

Navigator Wireline Service Inc 989 275-9112
609 S 5th St Roscommon (48653) ***(G-14352)***

Navistar Defense LLC 248 680-7505
1675 E Whitcomb Ave Madison Heights (48071) ***(G-10789)***

Navitas Advnced Sltons Group L (HQ) 734 913-8176
4880 Venture Dr Ann Arbor (48108) ***(G-592)***

Navtech LLC 248 427-1080
47906 West Rd Wixom (48393) ***(G-18717)***

Nb Cement Co 313 278-8299
4203 Merrick St Dearborn Heights (48125) ***(G-3935)***

Nb Media Solutions LLC 616 724-7175
6907 Cascade Rd Se Grand Rapids (49546) ***(G-7037)***

NBC Truck Equipment Inc (PA) 586 774-4900
28130 Groesbeck Hwy Roseville (48066) ***(G-14452)***

Nbhx Trim USA Corporation 616 785-9400
3056 Wlker Ridge Ct Ste D Walker (49544) ***(G-17644)***

Nbhx Trim USA Corporation (HQ) 616 785-9400
1020 7 Mile Rd Nw Comstock Park (49321) ***(G-3627)***

Nci Mfg Inc 248 380-4151
12665 Richfield Ct Livonia (48150) ***(G-10334)***

Ncoc Inc 248 548-5950
21251 Meyers Rd Oak Park (48237) ***(G-12632)***

Ncp Coatings Inc (PA) 269 683-3377
225 Fort St Niles (49120) ***(G-12152)***

ND Industries Inc (PA) 248 288-0000
1000 N Crooks Rd Clawson (48017) ***(G-3101)***

ND Technologies, Clawson *Also called ND Industries Inc* ***(G-3101)***

Ndex 248 432-9000
31440 Northwestern Hwy Farmington Hills (48334) ***(G-5332)***

Ndsay Nettell Logging 906 482-3549
47301 Janovosky Rd Atlantic Mine (49905) ***(G-751)***

Neapco Drivelines LLC 734 447-1316
6735 Haggerty Rd Van Buren Twp (48111) ***(G-17543)***

Neapco Drivelines LLC (HQ) 734 447-1300
6735 Haggerty Rd Van Buren Twp (48111) ***(G-17544)***

Neapco Holdings LLC (HQ) 248 699-6500
38900 Hills Tech Dr Farmington Hills (48331) ***(G-5333)***

Nears Logging 989 390-4951
11391 Billman Rd Roscommon (48653) ***(G-14353)***

Nedrow Refractories Co 248 669-2500
150 Landrow Dr Wixom (48393) ***(G-18718)***

Needles N Pins Inc 734 459-0625
754 S Main St Plymouth (48170) ***(G-13253)***

Neenah Paper Inc 906 387-2700
501 E Munising Ave Munising (49862) ***(G-11752)***

Neetz Printing Inc 989 684-4620
700 S Euclid Ave Bay City (48706) ***(G-1382)***

Nefco, Jonesville *Also called North East Fabrication Co Inc* ***(G-9095)***

Negal Paving, Detroit *Also called Detroit Recycled Concrete Co* ***(G-4161)***

Neighborhood Artisans Inc 313 865-5373
85 Oakman Blvd Detroit (48203) ***(G-4479)***

Nel Group Inc (PA) 734 730-9164
655 Fairfield Ct Ann Arbor (48108) ***(G-593)***

Nelms Technologies Inc 734 955-6500
15385 Pine Romulus (48174) ***(G-14309)***

Nelson Company 517 788-6117
654 Hupp Ave Jackson (49203) ***(G-8976)***

Nelson Farms 989 560-1303
7530 Madison Rd Elwell (48832) ***(G-5041)***

Nelson Hardware 269 327-3583
9029 Portage Rd Portage (49002) ***(G-13587)***

Nelson Iron Works Inc 313 925-5355
6350 Benham St Detroit (48211) ***(G-4480)***

Nelson Manufacturing Inc 810 648-0065
1240 W Sanilac Rd Ste A Sandusky (48471) ***(G-15063)***

Nelson Paint Co of Mich Inc (PA) 906 774-5566
1 Nelson Dr Kingsford (49802) ***(G-9514)***

Nelson Paint Company Ala Inc (PA) 906 774-5566
1 Nelson Dr Kingsford (49802) ***(G-9515)***

Nelson Paint Company Mich Inc 906 774-5566
1 Nelson Dr Iron Mountain (49802) ***(G-8726)***

Nelson Rapids Co Inc 616 691-8041
11834 Old Belding Rd Ne Belding (48809) ***(G-1460)***

Nelson Specialties Company 269 983-1878
1389 Norman Rd Saint Joseph (49085) ***(G-14950)***

Nelson Steel Products Inc 616 396-1515
410 E 48th St Holland (49423) ***(G-8152)***

Nelson Technologies, Kingsford *Also called Nelson Paint Co of Mich Inc* ***(G-9514)***

Nelsonite Chemical Pdts Inc 616 456-7098
2320 Oak Industrial Dr Ne Grand Rapids (49505) ***(G-7038)***

Nelsons Saw Mill Inc 231 829-5220
8482 N Raymond Rd Tustin (49688) ***(G-17466)***
Nemak International Inc 248 350-3999
2 Towne Sq Ste 300 Southfield (48076) ***(G-15664)***
Nematron, Ann Arbor *Also called D & C Investment Group Inc* ***(G-441)***
Nemo Capital Partners LLC 855 944-2995
28819 Franklin Rd Ste 130 Southfield (48034) ***(G-15665)***
Neo Manufacturing Inc 269 503-7630
21900 Us Highway 12 Sturgis (49091) ***(G-16313)***
Neo Trailers, Sturgis *Also called Neo Manufacturing Inc* ***(G-16313)***
Neogen Corporation (PA) 517 372-9200
620 Lesher Pl Lansing (48912) ***(G-9874)***
Neogen Corporation 800 327-5487
2620 S Cleveland Ave # 100 Saint Joseph (49085) ***(G-14951)***
Neon Roehler Services LLC 248 895-8705
4508 Rohr Rd Lake Orion (48359) ***(G-9621)***
Neopost Mailing Equipment, Grand Rapids *Also called D & D Business Machines Inc* ***(G-6627)***
Neotech Industries Inc 248 681-6667
1034 Meadowcrest Dr Waterford (48327) ***(G-18139)***
Nephew Fabrication Inc 616 875-2121
10752 Polk St Zeeland (49464) ***(G-19059)***
Nepko Lake Nursery, Escanaba *Also called Plum Creek Timber Company Inc* ***(G-5090)***
Neptech Inc 810 225-2222
2000 E Highland Rd Highland (48356) ***(G-7897)***
Neptix 248 520-6181
915 E Maple Rd Birmingham (48009) ***(G-1739)***
Neptune Candles LLC 231 947-0554
6360 Herkner Rd Traverse City (49685) ***(G-16768)***
Neptune Chemical Pump Company (HQ) 215 699-8700
1809 Century Ave Sw Grand Rapids (49503) ***(G-7039)***
Neptune Coating Services 616 403-9034
10996 Campanel Dr Zeeland (49464) ***(G-19060)***
Neptune Mixer, Grand Rapids *Also called Neptune Chemical Pump Company* ***(G-7039)***
Nesco Tool & Fixture LLC 517 618-7052
530 Fowler St Howell (48843) ***(G-8483)***
Nestle Infant Nutrition, Fremont *Also called Gerber Products Company* ***(G-6043)***
Nestle Purina Petcare Company 888 202-4554
600 Executive Dr Troy (48083) ***(G-17274)***
Nestle Usa Inc 231 928-2000
445 State St Fremont (49413) ***(G-6048)***
Nestle Usa Inc 989 755-7940
222 E Morley Dr Saginaw (48601) ***(G-14709)***
Netcon Enterprises Inc 248 673-7855
5085 Williams Lake Rd A Waterford (48329) ***(G-18140)***
Netshape International LLC 616 846-8700
1900 Hayes St Grand Haven (49417) ***(G-6340)***
Nettleton Wood Products Inc 906 297-5791
34882 S Mcadams Rd De Tour Village (49725) ***(G-3802)***
Netwave 586 263-4469
20539 Country Side Dr Macomb (48044) ***(G-10622)***
Network Sign Company Inc 517 548-1232
10958 Silver Lake Hwy Brooklyn (49230) ***(G-2129)***
Networks Enterprises Inc 248 446-8590
57450 Travis Rd New Hudson (48165) ***(G-12063)***
Neumann Enterprises Inc 906 293-8122
1011 Newberry Ave Newberry (49868) ***(G-12094)***
Neumeier Logging Inc 906 786-5242
700 Stephenson Ave Escanaba (49829) ***(G-5086)***
Neuvokas Corporation 906 934-2661
32066 Rd Ahmeek (49901) ***(G-109)***
Nevill Supply Incorporated 989 386-4522
8415 S Eberhart Ave Clare (48617) ***(G-2989)***
Nevis Energy, Traverse City *Also called Phoenix Technology Svcs USA* ***(G-16790)***
New 11 Inc 616 494-9370
1886 Russel Ct Holland (49423) ***(G-8153)***
New 9 Inc 616 459-8274
1411 Michigan St Ne Grand Rapids (49503) ***(G-7040)***
New Age Coatings 248 217-1842
415 N Cass Ave Pontiac (48342) ***(G-13401)***
New Alexandria Press 248 529-3108
2870 Eric Dr White Lake (48383) ***(G-18462)***
New Boston Candle Company 734 782-5809
21941 Merriman Rd New Boston (48164) ***(G-12014)***
New Boston Forge, New Boston *Also called Lc Manufacturing LLC* ***(G-12013)***
New Boston Rtm Inc 734 753-9956
19155 Shook Rd New Boston (48164) ***(G-12015)***
New Center News, Warren *Also called Springer Publishing Co Inc* ***(G-18023)***
New Center Stamping Inc 313 872-3500
950 E Milwaukee St Detroit (48211) ***(G-4481)***
New Classics Press LLC 616 975-9070
2400 Ridgecroft Ave Se Grand Rapids (49546) ***(G-7041)***
New Concept Products Inc 269 679-5970
277 E Lyons St Schoolcraft (49087) ***(G-15125)***
New Concepts Software Inc 586 776-2855
28490 Bohn St Roseville (48066) ***(G-14453)***
New Delray Baking Co, Taylor *Also called Rainbow Pizza Inc* ***(G-16465)***
New Dimension Laser Inc 586 415-6041
29540 Calahan Rd Roseville (48066) ***(G-14454)***
New Electric 586 580-2405
34000 Mound Rd Sterling Heights (48310) ***(G-16114)***
New Genesis Enterprise Inc 313 220-0365
37774 Willow Ln Apt S2 Westland (48185) ***(G-18400)***
New Gldc LLC 989 879-4009
1940 Henry St Muskegon (49441) ***(G-11884)***
New Gldc LLC 231 726-4002
701 W Laketon Ave Muskegon (49441) ***(G-11885)***
New Harper Seasoning Inc 734 767-6290
12715 Harper Ave Detroit (48213) ***(G-4482)***
New Holland Brewery 616 202-7200
427 Bridge St Nw Grand Rapids (49504) ***(G-7042)***
New Holland Brewing Co LLC 616 355-2941
684 Commerce Ct Holland (49424) ***(G-8154)***
New Hudson Corporation (PA) 248 437-3970
57077 Pontiac Trl New Hudson (48165) ***(G-12064)***
New Image Dental P C 586 727-1100
35000 Division Rd Ste 4 Richmond (48062) ***(G-13843)***
New Key Pet LLC 734 716-5357
440 Lenox Dr Canton (48188) ***(G-2500)***
New Layer Customs LLC 313 358-3629
330 E Maple Rd Ste A Troy (48083) ***(G-17275)***
New Life Cop Brass Mint Free M 586 725-3286
9984 Marine City Hwy Casco (48064) ***(G-2601)***
New Line Inc 586 228-4820
15164 Commercial Dr Shelby Township (48315) ***(G-15289)***
New Line Laminate Design, Shelby Township *Also called New Line Inc* ***(G-15289)***
New Martha Washington Bakery 313 872-1988
10335 Joseph Campau St Detroit (48212) ***(G-4483)***
New Meridian, Clinton *Also called Eden Foods Inc* ***(G-3137)***
New Method Steel Stamps Inc 586 293-0200
17801 Helro Fraser (48026) ***(G-5967)***
New Monitor 248 439-1863
23082 Reynolds Ave Hazel Park (48030) ***(G-7836)***
New Moon Noodle Incorporated 269 962-8820
909 Stanley Dr Battle Creek (49037) ***(G-1278)***
New Pioneer Ceramics LLC 248 200-9893
3097 Lincolnview St Auburn Hills (48326) ***(G-981)***
New Port Fuel Stop 734 586-1401
8733 Swan Creek Rd Newport (48166) ***(G-12105)***
New Product Development LLC 616 399-6253
785 Mary Ave Holland (49424) ***(G-8155)***
New Rules Marketing Inc 800 962-3119
540 Oak St Spring Lake (49456) ***(G-15839)***
New Technologies Tool & Mfg 810 694-5426
4380 E Baldwin Rd Grand Blanc (48439) ***(G-6254)***
New Unison Corporation 248 544-9500
1601 Wanda St Ferndale (48220) ***(G-5571)***
New Venture Foundry, Hillsdale *Also called Paragon Metals LLC* ***(G-7941)***
New Vintage Usa Inc 248 259-4964
21840 Wyoming Pl Ste 1 Oak Park (48237) ***(G-12633)***
New Wake Inc 800 957-5606
7873 Mooring Ct Hudsonville (49426) ***(G-8599)***
New World Etching N Amer Ve 586 296-8082
33870 Riviera Fraser (48026) ***(G-5968)***
New World Systems, Troy *Also called Brinston Acquisition LLC* ***(G-16985)***
New Yasmeen Bakery, Dearborn *Also called New Yasmeen Detroit Inc* ***(G-3876)***
New Yasmeen Detroit Inc 313 582-6035
13900 W Warren Ave Dearborn (48126) ***(G-3876)***
New York Bagel Baking Co (PA) 248 548-2580
23316 Woodward Ave Ferndale (48220) ***(G-5572)***
New-Matic Industries Inc 586 415-9801
31256 Fraser Dr Fraser (48026) ***(G-5969)***
Newark Gravel Company 810 796-3072
4290 Calkins Rd Dryden (48428) ***(G-4807)***
Newark Morning Ledger Co 517 487-8888
217 N Sycamore St Lansing (48933) ***(G-9875)***
Neway Manufacturing, Troy *Also called City Animation Co* ***(G-17012)***
Neway Manufacturing, Corunna *Also called City Animation Co* ***(G-3706)***
Neway Manufacturing Inc 989 743-3458
1013 N Shiawassee St Corunna (48817) ***(G-3714)***
Newberry Bottling Co Inc (PA) 906 293-5189
80 N Newberry Ave Newberry (49868) ***(G-12095)***
Newberry News Inc 906 293-8401
316 Newberry Ave Newberry (49868) ***(G-12096)***
Newberry Redi-Mix Inc (PA) 906 293-5178
307 E Victory Way Newberry (49868) ***(G-12097)***
Newberry Wood Enterprises Inc 906 293-3131
7300 N County Road 403 Newberry (49868) ***(G-12098)***
Newco Industries LLC 517 542-0105
900 Anderson Rd Litchfield (49252) ***(G-10084)***
Newcor Inc (HQ) 248 537-0014
1021 N Shiawassee St Corunna (48817) ***(G-3715)***
Newcor, Deco Division, Clifford *Also called Deco Engineering Inc* ***(G-3131)***
Newcraft Cabinetry 269 220-5440
700 1/2 Hatfield Ave Kalamazoo (49001) ***(G-9281)***
Newell Brands Inc 734 284-2528
20033 Eureka Rd Taylor (48180) ***(G-16452)***

Newkirk and Associates Inc ... 616 863-9899
9767 Shaw Creek Ct Ne Rockford (49341) *(G-14181)*
Newman Construction, Springfield *Also called Jn Newman Construction LLC (G-15870)*
News Group, The, Jackson *Also called Great Atlantic News LLC (G-8893)*
News One Inc ... 231 798-4669
4080 Oak Hollow Ct Norton Shores (49441) *(G-12316)*
Newsweb, Greenville *Also called Stafford Media Inc (G-7505)*
Newtech 3 Inc ... 248 912-0807
28373 Beck Rd Ste H7 Wixom (48393) *(G-18719)*
Nex Solutions, Litchfield *Also called Newco Industries LLC (G-10084)*
Nexiq Technologies Inc ... 248 293-8200
2950 Waterview Dr Rochester Hills (48309) *(G-14069)*
Next Chapter Mfg Corp ... 616 773-1200
4221 Edinburgh Dr Se Grand Rapids (49546) *(G-7043)*
Next In Line Publishing LLc ... 248 954-1280
14063 Harrison St Livonia (48154) *(G-10335)*
Next Level Die Cutting LLC ... 888 819-9959
6778 18th Ave Jenison (49428) *(G-9063)*
Next Level Manufacturing LLC (PA) ... 269 397-1220
6778 18th Ave Jenison (49428) *(G-9064)*
Next Level Manufacturing LLC ... 616 965-1913
5405 Pine Island Dr Ne Comstock Park (49321) *(G-3628)*
Next Level Media Inc ... 248 762-7043
15989 Addison St Southfield (48075) *(G-15666)*
Next Level Sandbag, East Jordan *Also called Next-Level Sandbag LLC (G-4877)*
Next Tool LLC ... 734 405-7079
41200 Coca Cola Dr Belleville (48111) *(G-1489)*
Next-Level Sandbag LLC ... 231 350-6738
2831 S M 66 East Jordan (49727) *(G-4877)*
Nexteer - Plant 6, Saginaw *Also called Nexteer Automotive Corporation (G-14714)*
Nexteer - Plant 6 E-Bike, Saginaw *Also called Nexteer Automotive Corporation (G-14718)*
Nexteer - Saginaw Plant 1, Saginaw *Also called Nexteer Automotive Corporation (G-14719)*
Nexteer - Saginaw Plant 3, Saginaw *Also called Nexteer Automotive Corporation (G-14716)*
Nexteer - Saginaw Plant 4, Saginaw *Also called Nexteer Automotive Corporation (G-14715)*
Nexteer - Saginaw Plant 5, Saginaw *Also called Nexteer Automotive Corporation (G-14713)*
Nexteer - Saginaw Plant 7, Saginaw *Also called Nexteer Automotive Corporation (G-14712)*
Nexteer Automotive Corporation ... 989 757-5000
3900 E Holland Rd Saginaw (48601) *(G-14710)*
Nexteer Automotive Corporation ... 989 754-1920
2975 Nodular Dr Saginaw (48601) *(G-14711)*
Nexteer Automotive Corporation ... 989 757-5000
3900 E Holland Rd Saginaw (48601) *(G-14712)*
Nexteer Automotive Corporation ... 989 757-5000
3900 E Holland Rd Saginaw (48601) *(G-14713)*
Nexteer Automotive Corporation ... 989 757-5000
3900 E Holland Rd Saginaw (48601) *(G-14714)*
Nexteer Automotive Corporation ... 989 757-5000
3900 E Holland Rd Saginaw (48601) *(G-14715)*
Nexteer Automotive Corporation ... 989 757-5000
3900 E Holland Rd Saginaw (48601) *(G-14716)*
Nexteer Automotive Corporation ... 989 757-5000
3900 E Holland Rd Saginaw (48601) *(G-14717)*
Nexteer Automotive Corporation ... 989 757-5000
3900 E Holland Rd Saginaw (48601) *(G-14718)*
Nexteer Automotive Corporation ... 989 757-5000
3900 E Holland Rd Saginaw (48601) *(G-14719)*
Nexteer Automotive Corporation ... 989 757-5000
5153 Hess Rd Saginaw (48601) *(G-14720)*
Nexteer Automotive Corporation (HQ) ... 248 340-8200
1272 Doris Rd Auburn Hills (48326) *(G-982)*
Nexteer Automotive Group Ltd ... 989 757-5000
3900 E Holland Rd Saginaw (48601) *(G-14721)*
Nexteer Saginaw, Saginaw *Also called Nexteer Automotive Corporation (G-14710)*
Nextek Power Systems Inc (PA) ... 313 887-1321
461 Burroughs St Detroit (48202) *(G-4484)*
Nexthermal Corporation ... 269 964-0271
1045 Harts Lake Rd Battle Creek (49037) *(G-1279)*
Ng Operations LLC ... 989 756-2741
2375 S National City Rd National City (48748) *(G-11960)*
NGK Spark Plug Mfg USA Inc (HQ) ... 248 926-6900
46929 Magellan Wixom (48393) *(G-18720)*
NGK Spark Plugs USA, Wixom *Also called NGK Spark Plug Mfg USA Inc (G-18720)*
Ngu Industries LLC ... 313 283-9570
918 Dix Hwy Lincoln Park (48146) *(G-10052)*
Niagara Cutter LLC ... 248 528-5220
2805 Bellingham Dr Troy (48083) *(G-17276)*
Niagara Machine, Hastings *Also called CNB International Inc (G-7783)*
Nicholas E Kappel ... 810 404-9486
1335 W Frenchline Rd Sandusky (48471) *(G-15064)*
Nicholas Wine Sampling Room, Cheboygan *Also called Nicholass Black River Vineyar (G-2793)*
Nicholass Black River Vineyar (PA) ... 231 625-9060
6209 N Black River Rd Cheboygan (49721) *(G-2793)*
Nicholson Terminal & Dock Co (PA) ... 313 842-4300
380 E Great Lakes St River Rouge (48218) *(G-13858)*
Nicholson's, Ann Arbor *Also called Power Sports Ann Arbor LLC (G-617)*
Nickels Boat Works Inc ... 810 767-4050
1871 Tower St Flint (48503) *(G-5738)*
Nickels Logging ... 906 563-5880
1108 Railroad Ave Norway (49870) *(G-12354)*
Nicole Lennox Lmt ... 248 509-4433
3093 Sashabaw Rd Ste A Waterford (48329) *(G-18141)*
Nicolet Sign & Construction, Iron River *Also called Nicolet Sign & Design (G-8750)*
Nicolet Sign & Design ... 906 265-5220
612 W Adams St Iron River (49935) *(G-8750)*
Nidec Chs LLC ... 586 777-7440
100 Shafer Dr Romeo (48065) *(G-14230)*
Nidec Indl Automation USA ... 203 735-6367
41200 Technology Park Dr Sterling Heights (48314) *(G-16115)*
Nidec Motors & Actuators (usa) ... 248 340-9977
1800 Opdyke Ct Auburn Hills (48326) *(G-983)*
Nieboer Electric Inc ... 231 924-0960
502 E Main St Fremont (49412) *(G-6049)*
Nieboers Pit Stop ... 616 997-2026
288 Main St Coopersville (49404) *(G-3694)*
Niereschers Print ... 248 736-4501
411 Nuttal Br Oxford (48371) *(G-12905)*
Nihil Ultra Corporation ... 413 723-3218
55 E Long Lake Rd Troy (48085) *(G-17277)*
Nike Inc ... 616 583-0754
350 84th St Sw Ste 300 Byron Center (49315) *(G-2289)*
Nikkis Printing & More LLC ... 313 532-0281
20291 Kentfield St Detroit (48219) *(G-4485)*
Nikolic Industries Inc ... 586 254-4810
43252 Merrill Rd Sterling Heights (48314) *(G-16116)*
Nikon Metrology Inc (HQ) ... 810 220-4360
12701 Grand River Rd Brighton (48116) *(G-2041)*
Nikon Metrology Inc ... 810 220-4347
12589 Grand River Rd Brighton (48116) *(G-2042)*
Nil-Cor LLC ... 616 554-3100
4855 Broadmoor Ave Se Kentwood (49512) *(G-9466)*
Niles Aluminum Products Inc ... 269 683-1191
1434 S 9th St Niles (49120) *(G-12153)*
Niles Daily Star, Niles *Also called Leader Publications LLC (G-12141)*
Niles Machine & Tool Company ... 269 684-2594
2124 S 11th St Niles (49120) *(G-12154)*
Niles Precision Company ... 269 683-0585
1308 Fort St Niles (49120) *(G-12155)*
Nims Precision Machining Inc ... 248 446-1053
9493 Pontiac Trl South Lyon (48178) *(G-15449)*
Ninja Pants Press LLC ... 248 669-6577
1980 Blue Stone Ln Commerce Township (48390) *(G-3557)*
Ninja Tees N More ... 248 541-2547
505 W 9 Mile Rd Ste B Hazel Park (48030) *(G-7837)*
Niowave Inc ... 517 999-3475
1012 N Walnut St Lansing (48906) *(G-9722)*
Nipguards LLC ... 734 544-4490
2232 S Main St Ste 361 Ann Arbor (48103) *(G-594)*
Nippa Sauna Stoves LLC ... 231 882-7707
8862 Us Highway 31 Beulah (49617) *(G-1656)*
Nippon Paint Auto Americas Inc ... 248 365-1100
901 Wilshire Dr 105 Troy (48084) *(G-17278)*
Nisshinbo Automotive Mfg Inc ... 586 997-1000
6100 19 Mile Rd Sterling Heights (48314) *(G-16117)*
Nitelights of SE Michigan ... 248 684-4664
2675 Fini Dr Milford (48380) *(G-11477)*
Nitrex Inc (HQ) ... 517 676-6370
822 Kim Dr Mason (48854) *(G-11147)*
Nitro Steel, Jackson *Also called Gerdau Macsteel Inc (G-8891)*
Nitro-Vac Heat Treat Inc ... 586 754-4350
23080 Dequindre Rd Warren (48091) *(G-17942)*
Nits Solutions Inc ... 248 231-2267
40850 Grand River Ave # 100 Novi (48375) *(G-12488)*
Nitto Inc ... 732 276-1039
36663 Van Born Rd Ste 360 Romulus (48174) *(G-14310)*
Nitto Inc ... 734 729-7800
36663 Van Born Rd Ste 360 Romulus (48174) *(G-14311)*
Nitto Inc ... 248 449-2300
45880 Dylan Dr Novi (48377) *(G-12489)*
Nitto Denko, Novi *Also called Nitto Inc (G-12489)*
Nitto Denko Automotive, Romulus *Also called Nitto Inc (G-14311)*
Nitto Seiko Co Ltd ... 248 588-0133
1301 Rankin Dr Troy (48083) *(G-17279)*
Nitz Valve Hardware Inc ... 989 883-9500
8610 Unionville Rd Sebewaing (48759) *(G-15142)*
Nivers Sand Gravel ... 231 743-6126
19937 M 115 Marion (49665) *(G-10975)*
Nje Enterprises LLC ... 313 963-3600
400 Renaissance Ctr Lbby Detroit (48243) *(G-4486)*
Njt Enterprises LLC, Clinton Township *Also called Mayco International LLC (G-3296)*
Njt Enterprises LLC, Auburn Hills *Also called Mayco International LLC (G-971)*
Njt Enterprises LLC, Sterling Heights *Also called Mayco International LLC (G-16087)*
Nk Dockside Service & Repair ... 906 420-0777
1014 8th Ave S Escanaba (49829) *(G-5087)*

ALPHABETIC

Nmp Inc 231 798-8851
6170 Norton Center Dr Norton Shores (49441) *(G-12317)*

Nn Inc 616 698-0707
4180 40th St Se Kentwood (49512) *(G-9467)*

Nn Inc 269 591-6951
4180 40th St Se Grand Rapids (49512) *(G-7044)*

No Limit Wireless-Michigan Inc 313 285-8402
6236 Michigan Ave Detroit (48210) *(G-4487)*

Noack Ventures LLC 248 583-0311
1407 Allen Dr Ste G Troy (48083) *(G-17280)*

Nobby Inc 810 984-3300
3950 Pine Grove Ave Fort Gratiot (48059) *(G-5822)*

Nobilis Pipe Company 248 470-5692
30850 Collingdale Dr Novi (48377) *(G-12490)*

Noble Films Corporation 616 977-3770
967 Spaulding Ave Se B1 Ada (49301) *(G-31)*

Noble Forestry Inc 989 866-6495
5012 Taylor Rd Blanchard (49310) *(G-1759)*

Noble Industries 616 245-7400
6850 N Solomon Rd Middleville (49333) *(G-11310)*

Noble Polymers LLC 616 975-4800
4855 37th St Se Grand Rapids (49512) *(G-7045)*

Nodel-Co 248 543-1325
2615 Wolcott St Ferndale (48220) *(G-5573)*

Nof Metal Coatings North Amer 248 617-3033
55860 Grand River Ave New Hudson (48165) *(G-12065)*

Noir Laser Company LLC 800 521-9746
4975 Technical Dr Milford (48381) *(G-11478)*

Noir Manufacturing, South Lyon *Also called Noir Medical Technologies LLC* *(G-15450)*

Noir Manufacturing Co, Milford *Also called Noir Medical Technologies LLC* *(G-11479)*

Noir Medical Technologies LLC (PA) 734 769-5565
4975 Technical Dr Milford (48381) *(G-11479)*

Noir Medical Technologies LLC 248 486-3760
10125 Colonial Indus Dr South Lyon (48178) *(G-15450)*

Noir Sportswear Corp 248 607-3615
13181 W 10 Mile Rd Oak Park (48237) *(G-12634)*

Noisefighters, Lowell *Also called Obsolete LLC* *(G-10512)*

Noisemeters Inc 248 840-6559
3233 Coolidge Hwy Berkley (48072) *(G-1633)*

Nolans Top Tin Inc 586 899-3421
8428 Republic Ave Warren (48089) *(G-17943)*

Nomad Cidery LLC 231 313-8627
2500 Kroupa Rd Traverse City (49686) *(G-16769)*

Non-Ferrous Cast Alloys Inc 231 799-0550
1146 N Gateway Blvd Norton Shores (49441) *(G-12318)*

Noora Health 402 981-0421
18833 Whispering Trl Traverse City (49686) *(G-16770)*

Nopras Technologies Inc 248 486-6684
13513 Windmoor Dr South Lyon (48178) *(G-15451)*

Nor-Cote Inc 586 756-1200
11425 Timken Ave Warren (48089) *(G-17944)*

Nor-Dic Tool Company Inc 734 326-3610
6577 Beverly Plz Romulus (48174) *(G-14312)*

Norbord Panels USA Inc 248 608-0387
410 W University Dr # 210 Rochester (48307) *(G-13913)*

Norbrook Plating Inc 586 755-4110
11400 E 9 Mile Rd Warren (48089) *(G-17945)*

Norbrook Plating Inc 313 369-9304
19230 Mount Elliott St Detroit (48234) *(G-4488)*

Norcross Viscosity Controls 586 336-0700
12427 31 Mile Rd Washington (48095) *(G-18086)*

Nord Publications Inc 734 455-5271
8115 Tillotson Ct Canton (48187) *(G-2501)*

NORDIC HOT TUBS, Grand Rapids *Also called Nordic Products Inc* *(G-7046)*

Nordic Products Inc 616 940-4036
4655 Patterson Ave Se B Grand Rapids (49512) *(G-7046)*

Nordson Corporation 734 459-8600
28775 Beck Rd Wixom (48393) *(G-18721)*

Norgren Automtn Solutions LLC (HQ) 734 429-4989
1325 Woodland Dr Saline (48176) *(G-15030)*

Norgren Automtn Solutions LLC 586 463-3000
2871 Bond St Rochester Hills (48309) *(G-14070)*

Norma Americas, Auburn Hills *Also called Norma Michigan Inc* *(G-984)*

Norma Group Craig Assembly 810 326-1374
1219 Fred Moore Hwy Saint Clair (48079) *(G-14838)*

Norma Michigan Inc (HQ) 248 373-4300
2430 E Walton Blvd Auburn Hills (48326) *(G-984)*

Norma Michigan Inc 248 373-4300
325 W Silverbell Rd Lake Orion (48359) *(G-9622)*

Normac Incorporated 248 349-2644
720 Baseline Rd Northville (48167) *(G-12244)*

Norman A Lewis 248 219-5736
27268 Pembridge Ln Farmington Hills (48331) *(G-5334)*

Norman Township 231 848-4495
17201 6th St Wellston (49689) *(G-18258)*

Norman Township Fire Dept, Wellston *Also called Norman Township* *(G-18258)*

Normic Industries Inc 231 947-8860
1733 Park Dr Traverse City (49686) *(G-16771)*

Norplas Industries Inc 517 999-1400
5589 W Mount Hope Hwy Lansing (48917) *(G-9781)*

Norris Graphics Inc 586 447-0646
33251 S Gratiot Ave Clinton Township (48035) *(G-3308)*

Nortech LLC 248 446-7575
30163 Research Dr New Hudson (48165) *(G-12066)*

Nortek Inc 616 719-5588
2547 3 Mile Rd Nw Ste A Grand Rapids (49534) *(G-7047)*

Nortek Air Solutions LLC 616 738-7148
4433 Holland Ave Holland (49424) *(G-8156)*

North Amer Fuel Systems Rmnfct 616 541-1100
4232 Brockton Dr Se Grand Rapids (49512) *(G-7048)*

North American Asphalt 586 754-0014
11720 Susan Ave Warren (48093) *(G-17946)*

North American Assembly LLC 248 335-6702
4325 Giddings Rd Auburn Hills (48326) *(G-985)*

North American Color Inc 269 323-0552
5960 S Sprinkle Rd Portage (49002) *(G-13588)*

North American Controls Inc 586 532-7140
13955 Teresa Dr Shelby Township (48315) *(G-15290)*

North American Forest Products (HQ) 269 663-8500
27263 May St Edwardsburg (49112) *(G-5013)*

North American Forest Products 269 663-8500
69708 Kraus Rd Edwardsburg (49112) *(G-5014)*

North American Graphics Inc 586 486-1110
24487 Gibson Dr Warren (48089) *(G-17947)*

North American Machine & Engrg, Shelby Township *Also called North American Mch & Engrg Co* *(G-15291)*

North American Mch & Engrg Co 586 726-6700
13290 W Star Dr Shelby Township (48315) *(G-15291)*

North American Mold LLC (PA) 248 335-6702
4345 Giddings Rd Auburn Hills (48326) *(G-986)*

North American Oss Operations, Washington *Also called ZF Active Safety & Elec US LLC* *(G-18093)*

North Amrcn Frest Pdts Lqdtion, Edwardsburg *Also called North Amrcn Mlding Lqdtion LLC* *(G-5015)*

North Amrcn Mlding Lqdtion LLC (HQ) 269 663-5300
70151 April St Edwardsburg (49112) *(G-5015)*

North Arrow Log Homes Inc 906 484-5524
5943 N 3 Mile Rd Pickford (49774) *(G-13031)*

North Attleboro Taps, Cheboygan *Also called Precision Threading Corp* *(G-2796)*

North Branch Machining & Engrg 989 795-2324
9318 Beech St Fostoria (48435) *(G-5825)*

North Central Machine, Houghton Lake *Also called Kuzimski Enterprises Inc* *(G-8401)*

North Central Welding Co 989 275-8054
402 Southline Rd Roscommon (48653) *(G-14354)*

North Coast Golf Company LLC 810 547-4900
3968 Jack Pine Ln Port Huron (48060) *(G-13509)*

North Coast Paper & Packg LLC 586 648-7600
51514 Industrial Dr New Baltimore (48047) *(G-11990)*

North Coast Studios Inc 586 359-6630
29181 Calahan Rd Roseville (48066) *(G-14455)*

North Country Power Generation 231 499-3951
121 Ames St Elk Rapids (49629) *(G-5028)*

North Country Publishing Corp 231 526-2191
211 E 3rd St Harbor Springs (49740) *(G-7653)*

North Country Sun Inc 906 932-3530
216 E Aurora St Ste 4 Ironwood (49938) *(G-8768)*

North East Fabrication Co Inc 517 849-8090
113 Deal Pkwy Jonesville (49250) *(G-9095)*

North Kent Base LLC 616 636-4300
109 N 3rd St Sand Lake (49343) *(G-15050)*

North Land Septic Tank Service, East Jordan *Also called Jordan Valley Concrete Service* *(G-4873)*

North Peak Brewing Company, Traverse City *Also called Schelde Enterprises Inc* *(G-16825)*

North Pier Brewing Company LLC 312 545-0446
3266 Estates Dr Saint Joseph (49085) *(G-14952)*

North Post Inc 906 482-5210
120 Quincy St Hancock (49930) *(G-7622)*

North Sails Group LLC 586 776-1330
22600 Greater Mack Ave Saint Clair Shores (48080) *(G-14874)*

North Sails-Detroit, Saint Clair Shores *Also called North Sails Group LLC* *(G-14874)*

North Shore Machine Works Inc 616 842-8360
595 W 2nd Spring Lake (49456) *(G-15840)*

North Shore Mfg Corp 269 849-2551
4706 M 63 N Coloma (49038) *(G-3481)*

North Star Candle Company LLC 248 430-4321
2030 Dacosta St Dearborn (48128) *(G-3877)*

North State Sales 989 681-2806
6298 N State Rd Saint Louis (48880) *(G-14994)*

North Woods Industrial 616 784-2840
3644 Mill Creek Dr Ne Comstock Park (49321) *(G-3629)*

North Woods Sign Shop 231 843-3956
5111 W Us Highway 10 # 4 Ludington (49431) *(G-10547)*

North-East Gage Inc 586 792-6790
33398 Kelly Rd Clinton Township (48035) *(G-3309)*

Northamerican Reproduction 734 421-6800
34943 6 Mile Rd Livonia (48152) *(G-10336)*

Northbound Industries LLC 661 510-8537
469 Arms Ct Rochester Hills (48307) *(G-14071)*

Northeastern Products Corp 906 265-6241
85 Brady Ave Caspian (49915) (G-2608)
Northern A 1 Services Inc 231 258-9961
3947 Us Highway 131 Ne Kalkaska (49646) (G-9399)
Northern Blind Co 616 299-9399
1511 Indian Lakes Rd Ne Sparta (49345) (G-15773)
Northern Building Components, Bloomingdale *Also called Nathan Shetler* (G-1877)
Northern Cable & Automtn LLC (PA) 231 937-8000
5822 Henkel Rd Howard City (49329) (G-8413)
Northern Canvas & Upholstery 989 735-2150
7995 State Rd Glennie (48737) (G-6215)
Northern Chain Specialties 231 889-3151
7329 Chief Rd Kaleva (49645) (G-9380)
Northern Coatings & Chem Co 906 863-2641
705 6th Ave Menominee (49858) (G-11254)
Northern Concrete Pipe Inc 517 645-2777
5281 Lansing Rd Charlotte (48813) (G-2763)
Northern Concrete Pipe Inc (PA) 989 892-3545
401 Kelton St Bay City (48706) (G-1383)
Northern Design Services Inc 231 258-9900
424 E Dresden St Kalkaska (49646) (G-9400)
Northern Express Publications, Traverse City *Also called Express Publications Inc* (G-16679)
Northern Fab & Machine LLC 906 863-8506
5601 13th St Menominee (49858) (G-11255)
Northern Hardwoods 906 487-6400
6946 County Road 392 Newberry (49868) (G-12099)
Northern Hardwoods Oper Co LLC 860 632-3505
45807 Hwy M 26 South Range (49963) (G-15461)
Northern Industrial Mfg Corp 586 468-2790
41000 Executive Dr Harrison Township (48045) (G-7712)
Northern Industrial Wood Inc 989 736-6192
507 State St Lincoln (48742) (G-10038)
Northern Label Inc 231 854-6301
265 S Division St Hesperia (49421) (G-7871)
Northern Laser Creations 517 581-7699
6482 Moreland Rd Jonesville (49250) (G-9096)
Northern Lkes Safood Meats LLC 313 368-4234
12301 Conant St Detroit (48212) (G-4489)
Northern Log Homes, West Branch *Also called Northern Michigan Log Homes* (G-18332)
Northern Logistics LLC 989 386-2389
805 Industrial Dr Clare (48617) (G-2990)
Northern Machine Tool Company 231 755-1603
761 Alberta Ave Norton Shores (49441) (G-12319)
Northern Machining & Repr Inc 906 786-0526
1701 N 26th St Escanaba (49829) (G-5088)
Northern Metalcraft Inc 586 997-9630
50490 Corporate Dr Shelby Township (48315) (G-15292)
Northern Mich Aggregates LLC 989 354-3502
51445 W12 Mile Rd Wixom (48393) (G-18722)
Northern Mich Endocrine Pllc 989 281-1125
103 Misty Meadow Ct Roscommon (48653) (G-14355)
Northern Mich Hardwoods Inc 231 347-4575
5151 Manthei Rd Petoskey (49770) (G-13008)
Northern Mich Mmrals Monuments 231 290-2333
2754 Old Mackinaw Rd Cheboygan (49721) (G-2794)
Northern Mich Supportive Hsing 231 929-1309
250 E Front St Traverse City (49684) (G-16772)
Northern Mich Wdding Offciants 231 938-1683
4617 Bartlett Rd Williamsburg (49690) (G-18559)
Northern Mich Wldlife Art Fram 989 340-1272
12595 Long Rapids Rd Lachine (49753) (G-9532)
Northern Michigan Glass LLC 231 941-0050
1101 Hammond Rd W Traverse City (49686) (G-16773)
Northern Michigan Leather 231 675-4712
6779 Bay Shore West Dr Charlevoix (49720) (G-2722)
Northern Michigan Log Homes 989 345-7463
1968 Lost Lake Trl West Branch (48661) (G-18332)
Northern Michigan Prop Sp LLC 231 275-7173
20080 Maple St Lake Ann (49650) (G-9542)
Northern Michigan Publishing 231 946-7878
2438 Potter Rd E Traverse City (49696) (G-16774)
Northern Michigan Review Inc (PA) 231 547-6558
2058 S Otsego Ave Gaylord (49735) (G-6150)
Northern Michigan Review Inc 231 547-6558
319 State St Petoskey (49770) (G-13009)
Northern Michigan Sawmill 231 409-1314
4593 Hampshire Dr Williamsburg (49690) (G-18560)
Northern Michigan Veneers Inc 906 428-1082
710 Rains Dr Gladstone (49837) (G-6184)
Northern Millwork Co 313 365-7733
7201 E Mcnichols Rd Detroit (48212) (G-4490)
Northern Mold 231 629-1342
21051 Dewey Rd Howard City (49329) (G-8414)
Northern Oak Brewery Inc 248 634-7515
806 N Saginaw St Holly (48442) (G-8285)
Northern Outdoor Woodworks LLC 231 275-1181
8581 Bent Pine Dr Lake Ann (49650) (G-9543)
Northern Packaging Mi Inc 734 692-4700
27665 Elba Dr Grosse Ile (48138) (G-7524)
Northern Pallet 989 386-7556
4915 E Colonville Rd Clare (48617) (G-2991)
Northern Plastics Inc 586 979-7737
6137 Product Dr Sterling Heights (48312) (G-16118)
Northern Precision Inc 989 736-6322
601 S Lake St Lincoln (48742) (G-10039)
Northern Precision Pdts Inc 231 768-4435
4790 Mackinaw Trl Leroy (49655) (G-10008)
Northern Processes & Sales LLC 248 669-3918
49700 Martin Dr Wixom (48393) (G-18723)
Northern Processing 989 734-9007
286 W Huron Ave Rogers City (49779) (G-14213)
Northern Products of Wisconsin 715 589-4417
W8969 Frei Dr Iron Mountain (49801) (G-8727)
Northern Promotions, Lachine *Also called Northern Mich Wldlife Art Fram* (G-9532)
Northern Pure Ice Co L L C 989 344-2088
1755 Yeager St Port Huron (48060) (G-13510)
Northern Rfractories Insul Div, Brownstown Twp *Also called Cerco Inc* (G-2153)
Northern Sand & Gravel, Sault Sainte Marie *Also called Van Sloten Enterprises Inc* (G-15102)
Northern Screen Printing & EMB, Escanaba *Also called SM & AM Enterprise Inc* (G-5100)
Northern Sierra Corporation 989 777-4784
5450 East Rd Saginaw (48601) (G-14722)
Northern Sign Co 248 333-7733
2181 E Walton Blvd # 100 Auburn Hills (48326) (G-987)
Northern Staircase Co Inc 248 836-0652
630 Cesar E Chavez Ave Pontiac (48342) (G-13402)
Northern Stampings Inc (PA) 586 598-6969
1853 Rochester Indus Ct Rochester Hills (48309) (G-14072)
Northern Star, Pontiac *Also called Morning Star Publishing Co* (G-13399)
Northern Tank LLC 989 386-2389
805 Industrial Dr Clare (48617) (G-2992)
Northern Tank Truck Service 989 732-7531
10764 Old Us Highway 27 S Gaylord (49735) (G-6151)
Northern Tire Inc 906 486-4463
1880 Us Highway 41 W Ishpeming (49849) (G-8779)
Northern Tool & Engineering, Baraga *Also called Laser North Inc* (G-1144)
Northern Trading Group LLC 248 885-8750
284 W Maple Rd Birmingham (48009) (G-1740)
Northern Wings Repair Inc (PA) 906 477-6176
6679 County Road 392 Newberry (49868) (G-12100)
Northern Woodcrafters 989 348-2553
8449 W Hulbert Rd Frederic (49733) (G-6016)
Northfield Manufacturing Inc 734 729-2890
38549 Webb Dr Westland (48185) (G-18401)
Northfork Readi Mix Inc 906 341-3445
5665w Us Highway 2 Manistique (49854) (G-10922)
Northland Ad-Liner, West Branch *Also called Ogemaw County Herald Inc* (G-18333)
Northland Castings Corporation 231 873-4974
4130 W Tyler Rd Hart (49420) (G-7758)
Northland Corporation 616 754-5601
1260 E Van Deinse St Greenville (48838) (G-7502)
Northland Corporation (HQ) 616 754-5601
1260 E Van Deinse St Greenville (48838) (G-7503)
Northland Publishers Inc 906 265-9927
801 W Adams St Iron River (49935) (G-8751)
Northland Refrigeration, Greenville *Also called Northland Corporation* (G-7503)
Northland Tool & Die Inc 616 866-4451
10399 Northland Dr Ne Rockford (49341) (G-14182)
Northline Express, Roscommon *Also called Ace Consulting & MGT Inc* (G-14346)
Northrop Grmmn Spce & Mssn Sys 734 266-2600
12025 Tech Center Dr Livonia (48150) (G-10337)
Northshore Pontoon 517 547-8877
3985 Munson Hwy Hudson (49247) (G-8557)
Northside Noodle Company 906 779-2181
609 Vulcan St Iron Mountain (49801) (G-8728)
Northstar Metalcraft 248 858-8484
35 W Silverdome Indus Par Pontiac (48342) (G-13403)
Northstar Sourcing LLC 313 782-4749
1399 Combermere Dr Troy (48083) (G-17281)
Northstar Wholesale 517 545-2379
5818 Sterling Dr Howell (48843) (G-8484)
Northville Cider Mill Inc 248 349-3181
714 Baseline Rd Northville (48167) (G-12245)
Northville Circuits Inc 248 853-3232
1679 W Hamlin Rd Rochester Hills (48309) (G-14073)
Northville Laboratories, Northville *Also called Jogue Inc* (G-12233)
Northville Laboratories, Plymouth *Also called Jogue Inc* (G-13203)
Northville Laboratories Inc 248 349-1500
100 Rural Hill St Northville (48167) (G-12246)
Northville Stitching Post 248 347-7622
200 S Main St Ste A Northville (48167) (G-12247)
Northville Winery 248 320-6507
630 Baseline Rd Northville (48167) (G-12248)
Northwest Canvas 231 676-1757
5195 Us Highway 31 S Charlevoix (49720) (G-2723)
Northwest Confections Mich LLC 971 666-8282
525 S Court St Ste 110 Lapeer (48446) (G-9950)

ALPHABETIC

Northwest Fabrication Inc 231 536-3229
450 Griffin Rd East Jordan (49727) *(G-4878)*
Northwest Hardwoods Inc 989 786-6100
3293 County Road 491 Lewiston (49756) *(G-10026)*
Northwest Market 517 787-5005
7051 Standish Rd Jackson (49201) *(G-8977)*
Northwest Metal Products Inc 616 453-0556
2055 Walker Ct Nw Grand Rapids (49544) *(G-7049)*
Northwest Orthotics-Prosthetic 248 477-1443
39830 Grand River Ave B1d Novi (48375) *(G-12491)*
Northwest Paint Pros 231 944-3446
1620 Andrew Pl Traverse City (49686) *(G-16775)*
Northwest Pattern Company 248 477-7070
29473 Medbury St Farmington Hills (48336) *(G-5335)*
Northwest Tool & Machine Inc 517 750-1332
1014 Hurst Rd Jackson (49201) *(G-8978)*
Northwods Prperty Holdings LLC 231 334-3000
6053 S Glen Lake Rd Glen Arbor (49636) *(G-6211)*
Northwood Lumber 989 826-1751
937 W Kittle Rd Mio (48647) *(G-11513)*
Northwood Signs Inc 231 843-3956
5111 W Us Highway 10 # 4 Ludington (49431) *(G-10548)*
Northwoods Hardware, Glen Arbor *Also called Northwods Prperty Holdings LLC (G-6211)*
Northwoods Manufacturing Inc 906 779-2370
850 East Blvd Kingsford (49802) *(G-9516)*
Northwoods Trading Post, Hancock *Also called North Post Inc (G-7622)*
Norton Equipment Corporation (PA) 517 486-2113
203 E Adrian St Blissfield (49228) *(G-1771)*
Norton Tool & Gage LLC 231 750-9789
4442 Hickory Ln Norton Shores (49441) *(G-12320)*
Nortronic Company 313 893-3730
20210 Sherwood St Detroit (48234) *(G-4491)*
Norway Granite Marble, Norway *Also called Steinbrecher Stone Corp (G-12357)*
Notes From Man Cave LLC 586 604-1997
3680 Seminole St Detroit (48214) *(G-4492)*
Notions Marketing Intl Corp 616 243-8424
517 Crofton St Se Grand Rapids (49507) *(G-7050)*
Nova Industries Inc 586 294-9182
34180 Klein Rd Fraser (48026) *(G-5970)*
Nova International LLC 269 381-6779
9110 Portage Rd Portage (49002) *(G-13589)*
Nova Steel, Portage *Also called Nova International LLC (G-13589)*
Nova-Tron Controls Corp 989 358-6126
111 S Second Ave Alpena (49707) *(G-305)*
Novacare Prosthetics Orthotics, Southfield *Also called P & O Services Inc (G-15670)*
Novaceuticals LLC 248 309-3402
3201 University Dr # 250 Auburn Hills (48326) *(G-988)*
Novares Corporation US Inc (HQ) 248 449-6100
19575 Victor Pkwy Ste 400 Livonia (48152) *(G-10338)*
Novares Group, Livonia *Also called Novares US LLC (G-10339)*
Novares US Eng Components Inc 248 799-8949
29200 Northwestern Hwy Southfield (48034) *(G-15667)*
Novares US LLC (HQ) 248 449-6100
19575 Victor Pkwy Ste 400 Livonia (48152) *(G-10339)*
Novares US LLC 517 546-1900
1301 Mcpherson Park Dr Howell (48843) *(G-8485)*
Novares US LLC 616 554-3555
5375 Intl Pkwy Se Grand Rapids (49512) *(G-7051)*
Novastar Solutionscom LLC 734 453-8003
35200 Plymouth Rd Livonia (48150) *(G-10340)*
Novation Analytics LLC 313 910-3280
300 E Long Lake Rd # 200 Bloomfield Hills (48304) *(G-1844)*
Novavax Inc 248 656-5336
870 Parkdale Rd Rochester (48307) *(G-13914)*
Novel Publicity LLC 248 563-6637
5087 Canyon Oaks Dr Brighton (48114) *(G-2043)*
Novelis Corporation 248 668-5111
39550 W 13 Mile Rd # 150 Novi (48377) *(G-12492)*
Novell, Southfield *Also called Micro Focus Software Inc (G-15658)*
Novelty House 248 583-9900
1400 E Avis Dr Ste B Madison Heights (48071) *(G-10790)*
Novex Tool Division, Brighton *Also called Federal Screw Works (G-1989)*
Novi Crushed Concrete LLC 248 305-6020
46900 W 12 Mile Rd Novi (48377) *(G-12493)*
Novi Manufacturing Co 248 476-4350
25555 Seeley Rd Novi (48375) *(G-12494)*
Novi Matic Valves, Redford *Also called Novi Tool & Machine Company (G-13749)*
Novi Precision Products Inc 810 227-1024
11777 Grand River Rd Brighton (48116) *(G-2044)*
Novi Spring Inc 248 486-4220
7735 Boardwalk Rd Brighton (48116) *(G-2045)*
Novi Tool & Machine Company 313 532-0900
12202 Woodbine Redford (48239) *(G-13749)*
Novo Building Products, Zeeland *Also called Nacs USA Inc (G-19058)*
Novo Distribution LLC (HQ) 616 772-7272
8181 Logistics Dr Zeeland (49464) *(G-19061)*
Novus Corporation 248 545-8600
3077 Chard Ave Warren (48092) *(G-17948)*
Nowak Cabinets Inc 231 264-8603
11744 S Us Highway 31 Williamsburg (49690) *(G-18561)*
Nowak Machine Products, Norton Shores *Also called Nmp Inc (G-12317)*
Npi 248 478-0010
23910 Freeway Park Dr Farmington Hills (48335) *(G-5336)*
Npi Wireless (PA) 231 922-9273
3054 Cass Rd Traverse City (49684) *(G-16776)*
Npo Synergy Donor Management, Southfield *Also called Mejenta Systems Inc (G-15653)*
Npworld Co 586 826-9702
14235 Valusek Dr Sterling Heights (48312) *(G-16119)*
Nr Racing LLC 248 767-0421
1960 W West Maple Rd # 200 Commerce Township (48390) *(G-3558)*
Nse Property Group LLC 313 605-1646
1732 S Deacon St Detroit (48217) *(G-4493)*
Nsi, Rochester Hills *Also called Northern Stampings Inc (G-14072)*
NSK Americas Inc (HQ) 734 913-7500
4200 Goss Rd Ann Arbor (48105) *(G-595)*
NSK Steering Systems Amer Inc (HQ) 734 913-7500
4200 Goss Rd Ann Arbor (48105) *(G-596)*
Nss Technologies Inc (HQ) 734 459-9500
8680 N Haggerty Rd Canton (48187) *(G-2502)*
Nssa Hq, Ann Arbor *Also called NSK Steering Systems Amer Inc (G-596)*
Nt Fabricating Inc 586 566-7280
15061 Technology Dr Shelby Township (48315) *(G-15293)*
Ntf Filter, Oscoda *Also called Ntf Manufacturing Usa LLC (G-12766)*
Ntf Manufacturing Usa LLC 989 739-8560
4691 Industrial Row Oscoda (48750) *(G-12766)*
Ntvb Media Inc (PA) 248 583-4190
213 Park Dr Troy (48083) *(G-17282)*
Nu Art Designs Sign Fabg, Traverse City *Also called Lobo Signs Inc (G-16746)*
Nu Con Corporation 734 525-0770
34100 Industrial Rd Livonia (48150) *(G-10341)*
Nu Tek Sales Parts Inc 616 258-0631
2051 Harvey St Muskegon (49442) *(G-11886)*
Nu-Core, Inkster *Also called Coppertec Inc (G-8661)*
Nu-Core Inc 231 547-2600
8833 Gibbons Dr Charlevoix (49720) *(G-2724)*
Nu-ERA Holdings Inc (PA) 810 794-4935
2034 Fruit St Clay (48001) *(G-3123)*
Nu-ERA Holdings Inc 248 477-2288
32613 Folsom Rd Farmington Hills (48336) *(G-5337)*
Nu-Ice Age Inc 517 990-0665
9700 Myers Rd Clarklake (49234) *(G-3006)*
Nu-Pak Solutions Inc 231 755-1662
2850 Lincoln St Norton Shores (49441) *(G-12321)*
Nu-Tech North Inc 231 347-1992
445 E Mitchell St Ste 6 Petoskey (49770) *(G-13010)*
Nu-Tran LLC 616 350-9575
2947 Buchanan Ave Sw Wyoming (49548) *(G-18897)*
Nu-Vu Food Service Systems, Menominee *Also called Marshall Middleby Holding LLC (G-11244)*
Nu-Way Stove Inc 989 733-8792
6566 Rainey Lake Rd Onaway (49765) *(G-12701)*
Nu-Wool Co Inc 800 748-0128
2472 Port Sheldon St Jenison (49428) *(G-9065)*
Nubill Corporation 248 246-7640
4815 Delemere Ave Royal Oak (48073) *(G-14566)*
Nubreed Nutrition Inc 734 272-7395
318 John R Rd Ste 310 Troy (48083) *(G-17283)*
Nucast LLC 313 532-4610
11745 Woodbine Redford (48239) *(G-13750)*
Nucraft Furniture Company 616 784-6016
5151 West River Dr Ne Comstock Park (49321) *(G-3630)*
Nucraft Metal Products, Roscommon *Also called North Central Welding Co (G-14354)*
Nugent Sand Company Inc 231 755-1686
2925 Lincoln St Norton Shores (49441) *(G-12322)*
Nugentec Oilfield Chem LLC 517 518-2712
1105 Grand Oaks Dr Howell (48843) *(G-8486)*
Nuko Precision LLC 734 464-6856
35455 Schoolcraft Rd Livonia (48150) *(G-10342)*
Null Taphouse 734 792-9124
2319 Bishop Cir E Dexter (48130) *(G-4747)*
Numatics, Sandusky *Also called Asco LP (G-15054)*
Nustep LLC 734 769-3939
5111 Venture Dr Ste 1 Ann Arbor (48108) *(G-597)*
Nutco Inc (PA) 800 872-4006
2140 Wilkins St Detroit (48207) *(G-4494)*
Nutek Abrasives, LLC, Novi *Also called Nutek Industries LLC (G-12495)*
Nutek Industries LLC 800 637-9194
42900 W 9 Mile Rd Novi (48375) *(G-12495)*
Nutrien AG Solutions Inc 989 842-1185
8263 N Ransom Rd Breckenridge (48615) *(G-1912)*
Nuts & Coffee Gallery 313 581-3212
13041 W Warren Ave Dearborn (48126) *(G-3878)*
Nuvar Inc 616 394-5779
895 E 40th St Holland (49423) *(G-8157)*
Nuvosun Inc 408 514-6200
2040 Abbott Rd Midland (48674) *(G-11398)*

ALPHABETIC SECTION — Odor Gone Inc

Nuwave Technology Partners LLC 616 942-7520
  4079 Park East Ct Se B Grand Rapids (49546) *(G-7052)*
Nuway Tool 616 452-4366
  3365 36th St Se Grand Rapids (49512) *(G-7053)*
NV Labs Inc 248 358-9022
  20777 East St Southfield (48033) *(G-15668)*
Nvent Thermal LLC 248 273-3359
  900 Wilshire Dr Ste 150 Troy (48084) *(G-17284)*
Nyatex Chemical Company 517 546-4046
  2112 Industrial Dr Howell (48843) *(G-8487)*
Nylok LLC (PA) 586 786-0100
  15260 Hallmark Ct Macomb (48042) *(G-10623)*
Nyloncraft of Michigan LLC 517 849-9911
  1640 E Chicago Rd Jonesville (49250) *(G-9097)*
Nylube Products Company LLC (PA) 248 852-6500
  2299 Star Ct Rochester Hills (48309) *(G-14074)*
Nylube Products Div, Rochester Hills *Also called Nylube Products Company LLC (G-14074)*
Nyman Industries LLC 702 290-9433
  1458 Wayburn St Grosse Pointe (48230) *(G-7531)*
Nyx LLC (PA) 734 462-2385
  36111 Schoolcraft Rd Livonia (48150) *(G-10343)*
Nyx LLC 734 467-7200
  1000 Manufacturers Dr Westland (48186) *(G-18402)*
Nyx LLC 734 261-4324
  28100 Plymouth Rd Livonia (48150) *(G-10344)*
Nyx LLC 734 421-3850
  30111 Schoolcraft Rd Livonia (48150) *(G-10345)*
Nyx LLC 734 464-0800
  38700 Plymouth Rd Livonia (48150) *(G-10346)*
Nyx LLC 734 261-7535
  28350 Plymouth Rd Livonia (48150) *(G-10347)*
Nyx Livonia Plant II, Livonia *Also called Nyx LLC (G-10347)*
Nyx LLC 734 462-2385
  36930 Industrial Rd Livonia (48150) *(G-10348)*
Nyx Newburgh, Livonia *Also called Nyx LLC (G-10348)*
Nyx Plymouth, Livonia *Also called Nyx LLC (G-10346)*
Nyx Technologies, Livonia *Also called Nyx LLC (G-10343)*
O & S Tool and Machine Inc 248 926-8045
  50400 Dennis Ct Unit B Wixom (48393) *(G-18724)*
O and P Sparton 517 220-4960
  2947 Eyde Pkwy East Lansing (48823) *(G-4907)*
O D L, Zeeland *Also called Odl Incorporated (G-19062)*
O E M Company Inc 810 985-9070
  3495 24th St Port Huron (48060) *(G-13511)*
O Flex Group Inc 248 505-0322
  5780 Garnet Cir Clarkston (48348) *(G-3053)*
O I K Industries Inc 269 382-1210
  7882 Douglas Ave Kalamazoo (49009) *(G-9282)*
O Keller Tool Engrg Co LLC 734 425-4500
  12701 Inkster Rd Livonia (48150) *(G-10349)*
O N Minerals 906 484-2201
  5093 E M 134 Cedarville (49719) *(G-2671)*
O R T, Erie *Also called Ort Tool & Die Corporation (G-5052)*
O-N Minerals Michigan Company 906 484-2201
  5093 E M 134 Cedarville (49719) *(G-2672)*
O-N Minerals Michigan Company 989 734-2131
  1035 Calcite Rd Rogers City (49779) *(G-14214)*
O-N Minerals Michigan Company 906 484-2201
  5093 E M 134 Cedarville (49719) *(G-2673)*
O-N Minerals Michigan Company (PA) 989 734-2131
  1035 Calcite Rd Rogers City (49779) *(G-14215)*
O. Keller Tool Engineering Co., Livonia *Also called Keller Tool Ltd (G-10264)*
O2/Specialty Mfg Holdings LLC (PA) 248 554-4228
  40900 Woodward Ave # 130 Bloomfield Hills (48304) *(G-1845)*
O2totes Llc 734 730-4472
  20315 E 9 Mile Rd Saint Clair Shores (48080) *(G-14875)*
Oak Division, Mount Pleasant *Also called Refrigeration Research Inc (G-11736)*
Oak Leaf Publishing Inc 248 547-7103
  24731 Parklawn St Oak Park (48237) *(G-12635)*
Oak Mountain Industries 734 941-7000
  14770 5 M Center Dr Romulus (48174) *(G-14313)*
Oak North Manufacturing Inc 906 475-7992
  114 Us Highway 41 E Negaunee (49866) *(G-11971)*
Oak Press Solutions Inc 269 651-8513
  504 Wade Rd Sturgis (49091) *(G-16314)*
Oak Tree Cabinet & Woodworking, Reese *Also called Rohloff Builders Inc (G-13808)*
Oak Way Manufacturing Inc 248 335-9476
  556 N Saginaw St Pontiac (48342) *(G-13404)*
Oakes Carton Company, Kalamazoo *Also called S & C Industries Inc (G-9326)*
Oakland Automation LLC 248 589-3350
  13017 Newburgh Rd Livonia (48150) *(G-10350)*
Oakland Bolt & Nut Co LLC 313 659-1677
  8977 Lyndon St Detroit (48238) *(G-4495)*
Oakland Engineering Filtration, Pontiac *Also called United Fbrcnts Strainrite Corp (G-13422)*
Oakland Machine Company 248 674-2201
  4865 Highland Rd Ste G Waterford (48328) *(G-18142)*
Oakland Orthopedic Appls Inc (PA) 989 893-7544
  515 Mulholland St Bay City (48708) *(G-1384)*

OAKLAND POST, Rochester *Also called Oakland Sail Inc (G-13915)*
Oakland Sail Inc 248 370-4268
  61 Oakland Ctr Rochester (48309) *(G-13915)*
Oakland Sand & Gravel, Dearborn *Also called Lyon Sand & Gravel Co (G-3864)*
Oakland Stamping LLC (HQ) 734 397-6300
  1200 Woodland St Detroit (48211) *(G-4496)*
Oakland Stamping LLC 248 340-2520
  4555 Giddings Rd Lake Orion (48359) *(G-9623)*
Oakland Tactical Supply LLC 810 991-1436
  1818 N Old Us 23 Howell (48843) *(G-8488)*
Oakland Welding Industries 586 949-4090
  28162 23 Mile Rd Chesterfield (48051) *(G-2916)*
Oakley Inds Sub Assmbly Div In, Flint *Also called Oakley Sub Assembly Inc (G-5740)*
Oakley Inds Sub Assmbly Div In 586 754-5555
  25295 Guenther Ste 200 Warren (48091) *(G-17949)*
Oakley Inds Sub Assmbly Div In (PA) 810 720-4444
  4333 Matthew Flint (48507) *(G-5739)*
Oakley Inds Sub Assmbly Div In 586 754-5555
  25295 Guenther Rear Rear Warren (48091) *(G-17950)*
Oakley Industries Inc (PA) 586 791-3194
  35166 Automation Dr Clinton Township (48035) *(G-3310)*
Oakley Industries Inc 586 792-1261
  35224 Automation Dr Clinton Township (48035) *(G-3311)*
Oakley Sub Assembly Inc 810 720-4444
  4333 Matthew Flint (48507) *(G-5740)*
Oakley Sub Assembly Intl Inc 810 720-4444
  4333 Matthew Flint (48507) *(G-5741)*
Oakridge Supermarket, Royal Oak *Also called Raleigh & Ron Corporation (G-14571)*
Oaks Concrete Products Inc 248 684-5004
  51744 Pontiac Trl Wixom (48393) *(G-18725)*
Oakwood Energy Management Inc (HQ) 734 947-7700
  9755 Inkster Rd Taylor (48180) *(G-16453)*
Oakwood Expansion, Taylor *Also called Oakwood Energy Management Inc (G-16453)*
Oakwood Group, The, Dearborn *Also called Oakwood Metal Fabricating Co (G-3879)*
Oakwood Metal Fabricating Co (PA) 313 561-7740
  1100 Oakwood Blvd Dearborn (48124) *(G-3879)*
Oakwood Metal Fabricating Co 734 947-7740
  9755 Inkster Rd Taylor (48180) *(G-16454)*
Oakwood Sports Inc (PA) 517 321-6852
  1025 Clark Rd Lansing (48917) *(G-9782)*
Oakwood Veneer Company 248 720-0288
  1830 Stephenson Hwy Ste A Troy (48083) *(G-17285)*
Oasys LLC 414 529-3922
  5920 Enterprise Dr Lansing (48911) *(G-9876)*
Obdpros LLC 734 274-5315
  45564 Baldwin Ct Canton (48187) *(G-2503)*
Obep, Deerfield *Also called OBrien Engineered Products (G-3959)*
Obertron Electronic Mfg Inc 734 428-0722
  10098 Mi State Road 52 Manchester (48158) *(G-10887)*
Oblut Limited 810 241-4029
  4511 Ennismore Dr Clarkston (48346) *(G-3054)*
Obr Control Systems Inc 248 672-3339
  32233 8 Mile Rd Livonia (48152) *(G-10351)*
OBrien Engineered Products 517 447-3602
  420 Carey St Deerfield (49238) *(G-3959)*
OBrien Harris Woodworks Llc 616 248-0779
  1125 41st St Se Ste A Grand Rapids (49508) *(G-7054)*
Obsolete LLC 616 843-0351
  11901 Fulton St E Ste 1 Lowell (49331) *(G-10512)*
Oc Tees 248 858-9191
  180 N Saginaw St Pontiac (48342) *(G-13405)*
OCC Systems, Ferndale *Also called Overhead Conveyor Company (G-5574)*
Occasions (PA) 517 694-6437
  3575 Scholar Ln Holt (48842) *(G-8320)*
Oceana Foods, Shelby *Also called Cherry Central Cooperative Inc (G-15149)*
Oceana Foods Inc 231 861-2141
  168 Lincoln St Shelby (49455) *(G-15157)*
Oceana Forest Products Inc 231 861-6115
  2033 Loop Rd Shelby (49455) *(G-15158)*
Oceanas Herald-Journal Inc 231 873-5602
  123 S State St Hart (49420) *(G-7759)*
Octet Industries LLC 225 302-0541
  3471 Richmond Ct Ann Arbor (48105) *(G-598)*
Ocuphire Pharma Inc (PA) 248 681-9815
  37000 Grand River Ave # 1 Farmington Hills (48335) *(G-5338)*
Oden Sanitation LLC 248 513-5763
  25666 Carl St Roseville (48066) *(G-14456)*
Odin Defense Industries Inc 248 434-5072
  2145 Crooks Rd Ste 210 Troy (48084) *(G-17286)*
Odin International Inc 262 569-7171
  N9448 Manistique Lakes Rd Curtis (49820) *(G-3751)*
Odl Incorporated (PA) 616 772-9111
  215 E Roosevelt Ave Zeeland (49464) *(G-19062)*
Odl Incorporated 616 772-9111
  100 Mulder Rd Zeeland (49464) *(G-19063)*
Odonnells Docks 269 244-1446
  12097 M 60 Jones (49061) *(G-9084)*
Odor Gone Inc 888 636-7292
  2849 Air Park Dr Zeeland (49464) *(G-19064)*

(PA)=Parent Co (HQ)=Headquarters (DH)=Div Headquarters

Odyssey Electronics Inc....734 421-8340
12886 Fairlane St Livonia (48150) ***(G-10352)***
Odyssey Industries LLC....248 814-8800
3020 Indianwood Rd Lake Orion (48362) ***(G-9624)***
Odyssey Tool LLC....586 468-6696
22373 Starks Dr Clinton Township (48036) ***(G-3312)***
OEM Wheels....248 556-9993
20416 Harper Ave Harper Woods (48225) ***(G-7668)***
Oerlikon Blzers Cating USA Inc....248 409-5900
199 Kay Industrial Dr Lake Orion (48359) ***(G-9625)***
Oerlikon Blzers Cating USA Inc....989 463-6268
7800 N Alger Rd Alma (48801) ***(G-251)***
Oerlikon Blzers Cating USA Inc....586 465-0412
42728 Executive Dr Harrison Township (48045) ***(G-7713)***
Oerlikon Metco (us) Inc....248 288-0027
1972 Meijer Dr Troy (48084) ***(G-17287)***
Oex, Troy *Also called Office Express Inc* ***(G-17288)***
Off Site Manufacturing Tech, Chesterfield *Also called Offsite Manufacturing Inc* ***(G-2918)***
Off Site Mfg Tech Inc (PA)....586 598-3110
50350 E Rssell Schmidt Bl Chesterfield (48051) ***(G-2917)***
Office Connection Inc (PA)....248 871-2003
37676 Enterprise Ct Farmington Hills (48331) ***(G-5339)***
Office Design & Furn LLC....734 217-2717
710 Webb St Jackson (49202) ***(G-8979)***
Office Express Inc....248 307-1850
1280 E Big Beaver Rd A Troy (48083) ***(G-17288)***
Office Services Division, Lansing *Also called Technology MGT & Budgt Dept* ***(G-9899)***
Office Station Enterprises Inc....616 633-3339
4370 Chicago Dr Sw Ste B Grandville (49418) ***(G-7406)***
Office Ways, Jackson *Also called Office Design & Furn LLC* ***(G-8979)***
Official Brand Limited....734 224-9942
3347 Heritage Pkwy Dearborn (48124) ***(G-3880)***
Official Media Solutions, Dearborn *Also called Official Brand Limited* ***(G-3880)***
Offsite Manufacturing Inc....586 598-8850
750 Structural Dr Chesterfield (48051) ***(G-2918)***
Oflow-Rite Controls Ltd....616 583-1700
960 74th St Sw Byron Center (49315) ***(G-2290)***
Og Technologies Inc....734 973-7500
4480 Varsity Dr Ste G Ann Arbor (48108) ***(G-599)***
Ogden Newspapers Inc....906 497-5652
W3985 2nd St Powers (49874) ***(G-13649)***
Ogden Newspapers Virginia LLC....906 228-8920
249 W Washington St Marquette (49855) ***(G-11038)***
Ogemaw County Herald Inc (PA)....989 345-0044
215 W Houghton Ave West Branch (48661) ***(G-18333)***
Ogilvie Manufacturing Company....810 793-6598
2445 Henry Rd Lapeer (48446) ***(G-9951)***
Ogura Corporation....586 749-1900
631 Ajax Dr Madison Heights (48071) ***(G-10791)***
Ogura Corporation....586 749-1900
55025 Gratiot Ave Chesterfield (48051) ***(G-2919)***
OH So Cheesy LLC....616 835-1249
435 Ionia Ave Sw Grand Rapids (49503) ***(G-7055)***
Oil Chem Inc....810 235-3040
711 W 12th St Flint (48503) ***(G-5742)***
Oil City Venture Inc....989 832-8071
172 N 11 Mile Rd Midland (48640) ***(G-11399)***
OIL Energy Corp (PA)....231 933-3600
954 Businemi Pk Dr Ste 5 Traverse City (49686) ***(G-16777)***
Oil Exchange 6 Inc....734 641-4310
140 Middlebelt Rd Inkster (48141) ***(G-8669)***
Oil Field Investments Limited, Traverse City *Also called Comet Energy Services LLC* ***(G-16657)***
Oil Patch Machine & Tool, Mount Pleasant *Also called Oilpatch Machine Tool Inc* ***(G-11728)***
Oiles America Corporation....734 414-7400
44099 Plymouth Oaks Blvd Plymouth (48170) ***(G-13254)***
Oilgear Company (HQ)....231 929-1660
1424 International Dr Traverse City (49686) ***(G-16778)***
Oilpatch Machine Tool Inc....989 772-0637
6773 E Pickard Rd Mount Pleasant (48858) ***(G-11728)***
Oils and Elements LLC....989 450-4081
1211 N Williams St Bay City (48706) ***(G-1385)***
OKeefe Centre Ltd (PA)....231 223-7355
12239 Center Rd Traverse City (49686) ***(G-16779)***
Oktober LLC....231 750-1998
5 Colfax St Ne Grand Rapids (49505) ***(G-7056)***
Okuno International Corp....248 536-2727
40000 Grant Rver Ave Ste Novi (48375) ***(G-12496)***
Old Dura Inc (PA)....248 299-7500
1780 Pond Run Auburn Hills (48326) ***(G-989)***
Old Mission Gazette....231 590-4715
12875 Bluff Rd Traverse City (49686) ***(G-16780)***
Old Mission Multigrain LLC....231 366-4121
1515 Chimney Ridge Dr Traverse City (49686) ***(G-16781)***
Old Orchard Brands LLC....616 887-1745
1991 12 Mile Rd Nw Sparta (49345) ***(G-15774)***
Old Sawmill Woodworking Co....248 366-6245
4552 Newcroft St Commerce Township (48382) ***(G-3559)***
Old Woodward Cellar....248 792-5452
912 S Old Woodward Ave # 2 Birmingham (48009) ***(G-1741)***
Old World Olive Press....734 667-2755
467 Forest Ave Plymouth (48170) ***(G-13255)***
Old Xembedded LLC....734 975-0577
3915 Res Pk Dr Ste A8 Ann Arbor (48108) ***(G-600)***
Oldcastle Buildingenvelope Inc....616 896-8341
4257 30th St Burnips (49314) ***(G-2210)***
Oldcastle Buildingenvelope Inc....734 947-9670
26471 Nrthline Cmmerce Dr Taylor (48180) ***(G-16455)***
Oleco Inc (PA)....616 842-6790
18683 Trimble Ct Spring Lake (49456) ***(G-15841)***
Oliver Carbide Products, Cottrellville *Also called L R Oliver and Company Inc* ***(G-3724)***
Oliver Healthcare Packaging Co (HQ)....616 456-7711
445 6th St Nw Grand Rapids (49504) ***(G-7057)***
Oliver Industries Inc....586 977-7750
6070 18 Mile Rd Sterling Heights (48314) ***(G-16120)***
Oliver of Adrian Inc....517 263-2132
1111 E Beecher St Adrian (49221) ***(G-86)***
Oliver Packaging and Eqp Co....616 356-2950
3236 Wilson Dr Nw Walker (49534) ***(G-17645)***
Oliver Racing Parts, Charlevoix *Also called Baldwin Precision Inc* ***(G-2710)***
Olivet Machine Tool Engrg Co....269 749-2671
423 N Main St Olivet (49076) ***(G-12695)***
Olympian Tool LLC....989 224-4817
604 N Us Highway 27 Saint Johns (48879) ***(G-14911)***
Olympus Group....616 965-2671
1685 Viewpond Dr Se Kentwood (49508) ***(G-9468)***
Omaha Automation Inc....313 557-3565
8301 Saint Aubin St Detroit (48211) ***(G-4497)***
Omaha Plant, Southfield *Also called Grede Omaha LLC* ***(G-15582)***
Omara Sprung Floors Inc....810 743-8281
3130 Eugene St Burton (48519) ***(G-2242)***
Omax Tool Products Inc....517 768-0300
68500 Hawkins Ln Ray (48096) ***(G-13701)***
Omc Archtrim....517 482-9411
810 E Mount Hope Ave Lansing (48910) ***(G-9877)***
Omega Industries Michigan LLC....616 460-0500
3744 Linden Ave Se Grand Rapids (49548) ***(G-7058)***
Omega Plastic Inc....816 246-3115
24401 Capital Blvd Clinton Township (48036) ***(G-3313)***
Omega Plastics Inc....586 954-2100
24401 Capital Blvd Clinton Township (48036) ***(G-3314)***
Omimex Energy Inc....231 845-7358
4854 W Angling Rd Ludington (49431) ***(G-10549)***
Omimex Energy Inc....517 628-2820
3505 W Barnes Rd Mason (48854) ***(G-11148)***
Omni Die & Engineering, Holland *Also called Karr Spring Company* ***(G-8109)***
Omni Ergonomics, Saint Johns *Also called Omni Technical Services Inc* ***(G-14912)***
Omni Metalcraft Corp (PA)....989 354-4075
4040 Us Highway 23 N Alpena (49707) ***(G-306)***
Omni Technical Services Inc....989 227-8900
203 E Tolles Dr Saint Johns (48879) ***(G-14912)***
Omni United (usa) Inc (HQ)....855 906-6646
9900 Two Lakes Trl Charlevoix (49720) ***(G-2725)***
Omnico Agv LLC....586 268-7700
44538 Macomb Indus Dr Clinton Township (48036) ***(G-3315)***
Omnilink Communications Corp....517 336-1800
3101 Technology Blvd Lansing (48910) ***(G-9878)***
Omo Enterprises LLC....248 392-6397
19646 Brady Redford (48240) ***(G-13751)***
Omron Automotive Electronics....248 893-0200
29185 Cabot Dr Novi (48377) ***(G-12497)***
Omt Veyhl....616 738-6688
4430 136th Ave Ste 3 Holland (49424) ***(G-8158)***
Omteco, Olivet *Also called Olivet Machine Tool Engrg Co* ***(G-12695)***
Omtron Inc....248 673-3896
2560 Silverside Rd Waterford (48328) ***(G-18143)***
On Base Food Group LLC....248 672-7659
146 W Maple Rd Birmingham (48009) ***(G-1742)***
On Sight Armory, Niles *Also called Performance Machining Inc* ***(G-12158)***
On Site Car Wash and Detail....313 350-8357
2744 W Davison Detroit (48238) ***(G-4498)***
On The Level Woodworking....269 429-4570
4712 Jamestown Dr Stevensville (49127) ***(G-16262)***
On The Mark Inc....989 317-8033
801 Industrial Dr Mount Pleasant (48858) ***(G-11729)***
On The Side Sign Dsign Grphics....810 266-7446
15216 Murray Rd Byron (48418) ***(G-2255)***
On-The-Spot-engraving, Holt *Also called Applause Inc* ***(G-8303)***
Oncofusion Therapeutics Inc....248 361-3341
120 W Main St Ste 300 Northville (48167) ***(G-12249)***
Oncourse Inc....231 946-1259
10660 E Carter Rd Traverse City (49684) ***(G-16782)***
One Beer At A Time LLC....616 719-1604
925 Cherry St Se Ste 1-2 Grand Rapids (49506) ***(G-7059)***
One Plus Boats Inc....586 493-9900
36301 Jefferson Ave Harrison Township (48045) ***(G-7714)***

One Source Trucking LLC 855 999-7723
20185 Washburn St Detroit (48221) ***(G-4499)***
One Stop Embroidery 248 799-8662
29207 Northwestern Hwy Southfield (48034) ***(G-15669)***
One Stop Sign Services 810 358-1962
3731 Ravenswood Rd Marysville (48040) ***(G-11094)***
One Stop Store 15, Flint *Also called D M J Corp* ***(G-5681)***
One Tree Research Group LLC 616 466-4880
8510 Grand River Dr Se Ada (49301) ***(G-32)***
One-Way Tool & Die Inc 248 477-2964
32845 8 Mile Rd Livonia (48152) ***(G-10353)***
One.ai, Novi *Also called Our Next Energy Inc* ***(G-12500)***
Oneida Tool Corporation 313 537-0770
12700 Inkster Rd Redford (48239) ***(G-13752)***
Oneiric Systems Inc (PA) 248 554-3090
31711 Sherman Ave Madison Heights (48071) ***(G-10792)***
Onesian Enterprises Inc 313 382-5875
10520 Balfour Ave Allen Park (48101) ***(G-201)***
Onestream Software Corp 248 841-1356
425 S Main St Ste 203 Rochester (48307) ***(G-13916)***
Onestream Software LLC (PA) 248 342-1541
362 South St Rochester (48307) ***(G-13917)***
Onion Crock of Michigan Inc 616 458-2922
1221 Mcreynolds Ave Nw Grand Rapids (49504) ***(G-7060)***
Online Engineering Inc 906 341-0090
400 N Cedar St Manistique (49854) ***(G-10923)***
Online Publications Inc 248 879-2133
55 E Long Lake Rd Troy (48085) ***(G-17289)***
Only Tool Co 734 552-8876
26360 Bell Rd New Boston (48164) ***(G-12016)***
Onodi Tool & Engineering Co 313 386-6682
19150 Meginnity St Melvindale (48122) ***(G-11208)***
Onstar LLC 313 300-0106
300 Renaissance Ctr Detroit (48243) ***(G-4500)***
Ontario Die Company America (HQ) 810 987-5060
1671 5th St Marysville (48040) ***(G-11095)***
Ontonagon Herald Co Inc 906 884-2826
326 River St Ontonagon (49953) ***(G-12714)***
Onyx Manufacturing Inc 248 687-8611
1663 Star Batt Dr Rochester Hills (48309) ***(G-14075)***
Opco Lubrication Systems Inc 231 924-6160
9569 W 40th St Fremont (49412) ***(G-6050)***
Openalpr Software Solutions L 800 935-1699
324 Annison Dr Commerce Township (48382) ***(G-3560)***
Openings Inc 248 623-6899
6145 Delfield Dr Waterford (48329) ***(G-18144)***
Opensystems Publishing LLC (PA) 586 415-6500
30233 Jefferson Ave Saint Clair Shores (48082) ***(G-14876)***
Operator Specialty Company Inc 616 675-5050
2547 3 Mile Rd Nw Grand Rapids (49534) ***(G-7061)***
Opio LLc 313 433-1098
3 Parklane Blvd Dearborn (48126) ***(G-3881)***
Oplogic, Clawson *Also called Wilson Technologies Inc* ***(G-3112)***
Ops Solutions LLC (PA) 248 374-8000
48443 Alpha Dr Ste 175 Wixom (48393) ***(G-18726)***
Optec Inc 616 897-9351
199 Smith St Lowell (49331) ***(G-10513)***
Opteos Inc 734 929-3333
775 Technology Dr Ste 200 Ann Arbor (48108) ***(G-601)***
Opti 02 LLC 517 381-9831
2174 Butternut Dr Okemos (48864) ***(G-12680)***
Opti Temp Inc 231 946-2931
1500 International Dr Traverse City (49686) ***(G-16783)***
Optic Edge Corporation 231 547-6090
6279 Us Highway 31 S Charlevoix (49720) ***(G-2726)***
Optilogic, Ann Arbor *Also called Optonomy Inc* ***(G-602)***
Optimal Electric Vehicles LLC 734 414-7933
47802 W Anchor Ct Plymouth (48170) ***(G-13256)***
Optimems Technology Inc 248 660-0380
43422 W Oaks Dr Ste 183 Novi (48377) ***(G-12498)***
Optimizerx Corporation (PA) 248 651-6568
400 Water St Ste 200 Rochester (48307) ***(G-13918)***
Optimystic Enterprises Inc 269 695-7741
600 S Oak St Buchanan (49107) ***(G-2200)***
Option Energy LLC 269 329-4317
102 E River Rd Traverse City (49696) ***(G-16784)***
Options 248 855-6151
32696 Ravine Dr Franklin (48025) ***(G-5884)***
Options Cabinetry Inc 248 669-0000
2121 Easy St Commerce Township (48390) ***(G-3561)***
Optisource LLC 616 554-9048
310 Dodge Rd Ne Ste A Comstock Park (49321) ***(G-3631)***
Opto Solutions Inc 269 254-9716
140 E Bridge St Plainwell (49080) ***(G-13084)***
Optonomy Inc 734 604-6472
303 Detroit St Ste 1 Ann Arbor (48104) ***(G-602)***
Optrand Inc 734 451-3480
46155 Five Mile Rd Plymouth (48170) ***(G-13257)***
Opus Packaging, Caledonia *Also called Action Packaging LLC* ***(G-2366)***
Opus Packaging - Kalamazoo LLC 800 643-6721
2710 N Pitcher St Kalamazoo (49004) ***(G-9283)***
Opus Packaging Group Inc (PA) 616 871-5200
6995 Southbelt Dr Se Caledonia (49316) ***(G-2391)***
Opus Products LLC 586 202-1870
120 Londonderry Ln Oakland Twp (48306) ***(G-12653)***
Oracle America Inc 989 495-0465
2200 Salzburg St Midland (48640) ***(G-11400)***
Oracle Brewing Company LLC 989 401-7446
1411 W Pine River Rd Breckenridge (48615) ***(G-1913)***
Oracle Corporation 248 393-2498
3216 Hickory Dr Orion (48359) ***(G-12737)***
Oracle Systems Corporation 248 614-5139
1365 N Fairview Ln Rochester Hills (48306) ***(G-14076)***
Oracle Systems Corporation 248 816-8050
3290 W Big Beavr Rd # 30 Troy (48084) ***(G-17290)***
Orange October Publishing Co 231 828-1039
2719 Duff Rd Twin Lake (49457) ***(G-17471)***
Orangebox Us Inc 616 988-8624
4595 Broadmoor Ave Se # 120 Grand Rapids (49512) ***(G-7062)***
Orbion Space Technology Inc 906 362-2509
101 W Lakeshore Dr Ste 4 Houghton (49931) ***(G-8388)***
Orbis Corporation 248 616-3232
999 Chicago Rd Troy (48083) ***(G-17291)***
Orbit Technology Inc 906 776-7248
100 W Brown St Iron Mountain (49801) ***(G-8729)***
Orbitform Group, Jackson *Also called Smsg LLC* ***(G-9011)***
Orbitform Group LLC 800 957-4838
1600 Executive Dr Jackson (49203) ***(G-8980)***
Orchid Connecticut, Holt *Also called Orchid Orthpd Sltons Organ Inc* ***(G-8322)***
Orchid Lansing, Holt *Also called Orchid Orthpd Solutions LLC* ***(G-8323)***
Orchid Macdee LLC 734 475-9165
13800 Luick Dr Chelsea (48118) ***(G-2822)***
Orchid MPS Holdings LLC 517 694-2300
1489 Cedar St Holt (48842) ***(G-8321)***
Orchid Orthopedic Solutions, Holt *Also called Tulip US Holdings Inc* ***(G-8336)***
Orchid Orthopedic Solutions, Holt *Also called Femur Buyer Inc* ***(G-8311)***
Orchid Orthopedic Solutions 517 694-2300
1365 N Cedar Rd Mason (48854) ***(G-11149)***
Orchid Orthpd Sltons Organ Inc 203 877-3341
1489 Cedar St Holt (48842) ***(G-8322)***
Orchid Orthpd Solutions LLC 989 746-0780
6688 Dixie Hwy Bridgeport (48722) ***(G-1917)***
Orchid Orthpd Solutions LLC (HQ) 517 694-2300
1489 Cedar St Holt (48842) ***(G-8323)***
Ore Dock Brewing Company LLC 906 228-8888
114 W Spring St Marquette (49855) ***(G-11039)***
Oreos Wldg & Fabrication LLC 989 529-0815
2681 Ringle Rd Akron (48701) ***(G-110)***
Original Footwear Company 231 796-5828
1005 Baldwin St Big Rapids (49307) ***(G-1681)***
Original Footwear Mfg, Big Rapids *Also called Original Footwear Mfg BR Inc* ***(G-1682)***
Original Footwear Mfg BR Inc 231 796-5828
1005 Baldwin St Big Rapids (49307) ***(G-1682)***
Original Murdicks Fudge Co (PA) 906 847-3530
7363 Main St Mackinac Island (49757) ***(G-10567)***
Original Stay Cool Cap, The, Detroit *Also called Brintley Enterprises* ***(G-4074)***
Orin Jewelers Inc (PA) 734 422-7030
29317 Ford Rd Garden City (48135) ***(G-6105)***
Orion Bus Accnting Sltions LLC 248 893-1060
1611 Ford Ave Wyandotte (48192) ***(G-18835)***
Orion Hunting Products LLC 906 563-1230
N2615 Valley View Rd Norway (49870) ***(G-12355)***
Orion Machine Inc 231 728-1229
392 Irwin Ave Muskegon (49442) ***(G-11887)***
Orion Manufacturing Inc 616 527-5994
480 Apple Tree Dr Ionia (48846) ***(G-8691)***
Orion Test Systems Inc 248 373-9097
4260 Giddings Rd Auburn Hills (48326) ***(G-990)***
Orion Test Systems & Engrg, Auburn Hills *Also called Orion Test Systems Inc* ***(G-990)***
Orlandi Gear Company Inc 586 285-9900
17755 Masonic Fraser (48026) ***(G-5971)***
Ornamental Mouldings LLC 616 748-0188
8181 Logistics Dr Zeeland (49464) ***(G-19065)***
Oronoko Iron Works Inc 269 326-7045
9243 First St Baroda (49101) ***(G-1167)***
Orotex Corporation 248 773-8630
22475 Venture Dr Novi (48375) ***(G-12499)***
Orr Lumber, North Branch *Also called Production Threaded Parts Co* ***(G-12183)***
Orri Corp 248 618-1104
5385 Perry Dr Waterford (48329) ***(G-18145)***
Orsco Inc 314 679-4200
69900 Powell Rd Armada (48005) ***(G-738)***
Ort Tool & Die Corporation (PA) 419 242-9553
6555 S Dixie Hwy Erie (48133) ***(G-5052)***
Ortho-Clinical Diagnostics Inc 248 797-8087
2128 Lancer Dr Troy (48084) ***(G-17292)***
Orthopaedic Associates Mich, Grand Rapids *Also called Orthopaedic Associates Mich* ***(G-7063)***

ALPHABETIC

Orthopaedic Associates Mich (PA) 616 459-7101
4665 44th St Se Ste A190 Grand Rapids (49512) ***(G-7063)***
Orthopedic Network News, Ann Arbor *Also called Mendenhall Associates Inc* ***(G-569)***
Orthotic Shop Inc 800 309-0412
14200 Industrial Ctr Dr Shelby Township (48315) ***(G-15294)***
Orthotics & Prosthetics Center, Ann Arbor *Also called Regents of The University Mich* ***(G-638)***
Orthotics and Prosthetics, Muskegon *Also called Mercy Health Partners* ***(G-11867)***
Orthotool LLC (PA) 734 455-8103
50325 Ann Arbor Rd W Plymouth (48170) ***(G-13258)***
Orwood Precision Pdts Caratron, Fraser *Also called Bmt Aerospace Usa Inc* ***(G-5905)***
Os Holdings LLc (HQ) 734 397-6300
17757 Woodland Dr New Boston (48164) ***(G-12017)***
Osborne Concrete Co 734 941-3008
37500 Northline Rd Romulus (48174) ***(G-14314)***
Osborne Materials Company 906 493-5211
23311 E Haul Rd Drummond Island (49726) ***(G-4803)***
Osborne Transformer Corp 586 218-6900
33258 Groesbeck Hwy Fraser (48026) ***(G-5972)***
Oscar's Printing, Saint Joseph *Also called Tuteur Inc* ***(G-14966)***
Osco, Grand Rapids *Also called Operator Specialty Company Inc* ***(G-7061)***
Osco Inc 248 852-7310
2937 Waterview Dr Rochester Hills (48309) ***(G-14077)***
Oscoda Plastics Inc 989 739-6900
525 W Morley Dr Saginaw (48601) ***(G-14723)***
Oscoda Plastics Inc (PA) 989 739-6900
5585 N Huron Ave Oscoda (48750) ***(G-12767)***
Oscoda Press, Oscoda *Also called Iosco News Press Publishing Co* ***(G-12762)***
Oshino Lamps America Ltd 262 226-8620
47550 Avante Dr Wixom (48393) ***(G-18727)***
Oshkosh Defense LLC 586 576-8301
27600 Donald Ct Warren (48092) ***(G-17951)***
Osowet Collections Inc 313 844-8171
5809 Bluehill St Detroit (48224) ***(G-4501)***
Ossineke Industries Inc 989 471-2197
10401 Piper Rd Ossineke (49766) ***(G-12778)***
Oster Manufacturing Company 989 729-1160
1535 N Hickory Rd Owosso (48867) ***(G-12847)***
Oster Pipe Threaders, Owosso *Also called Superior Threading Inc* ***(G-12859)***
Ostrander Company Inc 248 646-6680
1200 W 12 Mile Rd Madison Heights (48071) ***(G-10793)***
Ot Dynamics LLC 734 984-7022
27100 Hall Rd Flat Rock (48134) ***(G-5624)***
Otb Enterprises LLC 248 266-5568
1407 Allen Dr Ste A Troy (48083) ***(G-17293)***
Oth Consultants Inc 586 598-0100
46480 Continental Dr Chesterfield (48047) ***(G-2920)***
Otr Performance Inc 586 799-4375
51619 Industrial Dr Macomb (48042) ***(G-10624)***
Otsego Crane & Hoist LLC 269 672-7222
1677 116th Ave Otsego (49078) ***(G-12792)***
Otsego Paper, Otsego *Also called United States Gypsum Company* ***(G-12801)***
Otsego Paper Inc 269 692-6141
320 N Farmer St Otsego (49078) ***(G-12793)***
Ottawa County Window Clg LLC 248 878-5377
520 Gordon St Ste 2 Zeeland (49464) ***(G-19066)***
Ottawa Forest Products Inc 906 932-9701
1243 Wall St Ironwood (49938) ***(G-8769)***
Ottawa Tool & Machine LLC 616 677-1743
2188 Leonard St Nw Grand Rapids (49534) ***(G-7064)***
Otto Bock, Rochester Hills *Also called Foampartner Americas Inc* ***(G-14012)***
Our Next Energy Inc 408 623-1896
29050 Cabot Dr Novi (48377) ***(G-12500)***
Out On A Limb Playhouses 616 502-4251
13104 116th Ave Grand Haven (49417) ***(G-6341)***
Outdoor Lines LLC 616 844-7351
13334 Hidden Creek Dr Grand Haven (49417) ***(G-6342)***
Outerwears Inc 269 679-3301
12611 N Us Highway 131 Schoolcraft (49087) ***(G-15126)***
Ovascience Inc 617 351-2590
301 N Main St Ste 100 Ann Arbor (48104) ***(G-603)***
Over Top Steel Coating LLC 616 647-9140
931 W River Center Dr Ne B Comstock Park (49321) ***(G-3632)***
Overhead Conveyer, Ferndale *Also called Structural Equipment Co* ***(G-5587)***
Overhead Conveyor Company (PA) 248 547-3800
1330 Hilton Rd Ferndale (48220) ***(G-5574)***
Overhead Door Company Alpena 989 354-8316
2550 Us Highway 23 S Alpena (49707) ***(G-307)***
Overkill Research & Dev Labs 517 768-8155
2010 Micor Dr Jackson (49203) ***(G-8981)***
Overseas Auto Parts Inc 734 427-4840
32400 Plymouth Rd Livonia (48150) ***(G-10354)***
Overstreet Management, Benton Harbor *Also called Overstreet Property MGT Co* ***(G-1578)***
Overstreet Property MGT Co 269 281-3880
1852 Commonwealth Rd Benton Harbor (49022) ***(G-1578)***
Ovidon Manufacturing LLC 517 548-4005
1200 Grand Oaks Dr Howell (48843) ***(G-8489)***
Ovshinsky Technologies LLC 248 752-2344
2550 S Telg Rd Ste 106 Bloomfield Hills (48302) ***(G-1846)***
Owens Building Co Inc 989 835-1293
1928 N Stark Rd Midland (48642) ***(G-11401)***
Owens Cabinet & Trim, Midland *Also called Owens Building Co Inc* ***(G-11401)***
Owens Classic International, Saint Joseph *Also called Worldwide Marketing Svcs Inc* ***(G-14981)***
Owens Products Inc 269 651-2300
1107 Progress St Sturgis (49091) ***(G-16315)***
Owl Leasing, Springfield *Also called Marketplus Software Inc* ***(G-15872)***
Owl Wineries 586 229-7217
28087 Gratiot Ave Roseville (48066) ***(G-14457)***
Owntheplay Inc 248 514-0352
1401 Vermont St Ste 180 Detroit (48216) ***(G-4502)***
Owosso Country Club Pro Shop 989 723-1470
4200 N Chipman Rd Owosso (48867) ***(G-12848)***
Owosso Fabrication and Design, Owosso *Also called Transit Bus Rebuilders Inc* ***(G-12863)***
Owosso Graphic Arts Inc 989 725-7112
151 N Delaney Rd Owosso (48867) ***(G-12849)***
Owosso Ready Mix Co 989 723-1295
441 Cleveland Ave Owosso (48867) ***(G-12850)***
Owosso Soft Trim, Saint Louis *Also called American Soft Trim Inc* ***(G-14984)***
Ox Engineered Products LLC (PA) 248 289-9950
22260 Haggerty Rd Ste 365 Northville (48167) ***(G-12250)***
Ox Engineered Products LLC 269 435-2425
700 Centreville St Constantine (49042) ***(G-3673)***
Ox Paperboard Michigan LLC 800 345-8881
700 Centreville St Constantine (49042) ***(G-3674)***
Oxbow Machine Products Inc (PA) 734 422-7730
12743 Merriman Rd Livonia (48150) ***(G-10355)***
Oxford Biomedical Research Inc (PA) 248 852-8815
4600 Gardner Rd Metamora (48455) ***(G-11284)***
Oxford Brands LLC 248 408-4020
318 N Lapeer Rd Ste A Oxford (48371) ***(G-12906)***
Oxford Forge Inc 248 628-1303
2300 Xcelsior Dr Oxford (48371) ***(G-12907)***
Oxford Leader, Oxford *Also called Sherman Publications Inc* ***(G-12916)***
Oxford Manufacturing Facility, Oxford *Also called MSP Industries Corporation* ***(G-12904)***
Oxford Woodworks 248 736-3090
9536 S West Bay Shore Dr Traverse City (49684) ***(G-16785)***
Oxid 248 474-9817
24730 Crestview Ct Farmington Hills (48335) ***(G-5340)***
Oxid Corporation 248 474-9817
25325 Regency Dr Novi (48375) ***(G-12501)***
Oxmaster Inc (PA) 810 987-7600
1105 24th St Port Huron (48060) ***(G-13512)***
Oxus America Inc 248 475-0925
2046 Brown Rd Auburn Hills (48326) ***(G-991)***
Oxygenplus LLC 586 221-9112
15760 19 Mile Rd Ste E Clinton Township (48038) ***(G-3316)***
Ozinga Bros Inc 269 469-2515
825 S Whittaker St New Buffalo (49117) ***(G-12025)***
P & A Conveyor Sales Inc 734 285-7970
18999 Quarry St Riverview (48193) ***(G-13882)***
P & C Group I Inc (PA) 248 442-6800
37000 W 12 Mile Rd Ste 10 Farmington Hills (48331) ***(G-5341)***
P & G Technologies Inc 248 399-3135
6503 19 1/2 Mile Rd Sterling Heights (48314) ***(G-16121)***
P & K Technologies Inc 586 336-9545
111 Shafer Dr Romeo (48065) ***(G-14231)***
P & M Industries Inc 517 223-1000
5901 Weller Rd Gregory (48137) ***(G-7515)***
P & O Services Inc 248 809-3072
24293 Telg Rd Ste 140 Southfield (48033) ***(G-15670)***
P & P Manufacturing Co Inc 810 667-2712
260 Mccormick Dr Lapeer (48446) ***(G-9952)***
P A Products, Livonia *Also called PA Products Inc* ***(G-10357)***
P and K Graphics Inc 810 984-1575
945 Lapeer Ave Port Huron (48060) ***(G-13513)***
P C S Companies Inc 616 754-2229
1251 Callaghan St Greenville (48838) ***(G-7504)***
P D E Systems Inc 586 725-3330
37230 26 Mile Rd Chesterfield (48047) ***(G-2921)***
P D P LLC 616 437-9618
2675 Chicago Dr Sw Wyoming (49519) ***(G-18898)***
P D Q Press Inc 586 725-1888
7752 Dixie Hwy Ira (48023) ***(G-8706)***
P E T S, Auburn Hills *Also called Plastic Engrg Tchncal Svcs Inc* ***(G-998)***
P G K Enterprises LLC 248 535-4411
23450 Telegraph Rd Southfield (48033) ***(G-15671)***
P G S Inc 248 526-3800
1600 E Big Beaver Rd Troy (48083) ***(G-17294)***
P I W Corporation 989 448-2501
1492 Orourke Blvd Gaylord (49735) ***(G-6152)***
P J Printing 269 673-3372
633 114th Ave Ste 5 Allegan (49010) ***(G-172)***
P J Wallbank Springs Inc 810 987-2992
2121 Beard St Port Huron (48060) ***(G-13514)***

ALPHABETIC SECTION

P L Optima Inc 616 828-8377
2734 84th Ave Zeeland (49464) *(G-19067)*
P L Schmitt Crbide Tooling LLC 313 706-5756
8865 Seymour Rd Grass Lake (49240) *(G-7442)*
P M R Industries Inc 810 989-5020
2311 16th St Port Huron (48060) *(G-13515)*
P M Z Technology Inc 248 471-0447
33302 7 Mile Rd Livonia (48152) *(G-10356)*
P R Machining & Prototype Inc 586 468-7146
39 N Rose St Ste A Mount Clemens (48043) *(G-11650)*
P T M Corporation (PA) 586 725-2211
6560 Bethuy Rd Ira (48023) *(G-8707)*
P T M Corporation 586 725-2733
6520 Bethuy Rd Ira (48023) *(G-8708)*
P T T, Fraser *Also called Product and Tooling Tech Inc* *(G-5980)*
P W P, Pentwater *Also called Windy Lake LLC* *(G-12975)*
P X Tool Co 248 585-9330
32354 Edward Ave Madison Heights (48071) *(G-10794)*
P&K Socks LLC 586 295-5427
244 Mckinley Ave Grosse Pointe Farms (48236) *(G-7539)*
P&L Development & Mfg LLC 989 739-5203
4025 Arrow St Oscoda (48750) *(G-12768)*
P&L Development and Mfg, Oscoda *Also called P&L Development & Mfg LLC* *(G-12768)*
P.A.w Hardwood Flooring & Sups, Kalamazoo *Also called PAW Enterprises LLC* *(G-9290)*
P2r Metal Fabrication Inc 586 606-5266
49620 Hayes Rd Macomb (48044) *(G-10625)*
PA Products Inc 734 421-1060
33709 Schoolcraft Rd Livonia (48150) *(G-10357)*
Pac-Cnc Inc 616 288-3389
4045 Remembrance Rd Nw Grand Rapids (49534) *(G-7065)*
Pace Industries LLC 231 777-3941
2121 Latimer Dr Muskegon (49442) *(G-11888)*
Pace Industries LLC 231 773-4491
1868 Port City Blvd Muskegon (49442) *(G-11889)*
Pace Industries LLC 231 777-3941
1985 E Laketon Ave Muskegon (49442) *(G-11890)*
Pace Industries LLC 231 777-3941
711 E Porter Rd Norton Shores (49441) *(G-12323)*
Pace Industries LLC 231 777-5615
2350 Black Creek Rd Muskegon (49444) *(G-11891)*
Pace Software Systems Inc 586 727-3189
5345 Meldrum Rd Casco (48064) *(G-2602)*
Pacific Door & Trim 619 887-1786
20125 Balfour St Harper Woods (48225) *(G-7669)*
Pacific Engineering Corp 248 359-7823
39555 Orchard Hill Pl Novi (48375) *(G-12502)*
Pacific Epoxy Polymers Inc 616 949-1634
3450 Charlevoix Dr Se Grand Rapids (49546) *(G-7066)*
Pacific Industrial Dev Corp (PA) 734 930-9292
4788 Runway Blvd Ann Arbor (48108) *(G-604)*
Pacific Industrial Furnace Div, Wixom *Also called Afc-Holcroft LLC* *(G-18598)*
Pacific Industries Inc 810 360-9141
11768 Freedom Dr Whitmore Lake (48189) *(G-18542)*
Pacific Oil Resources Inc 734 397-1120
44141 Yost Rd Van Buren Twp (48111) *(G-17545)*
Pacific Stamex Clg Systems Inc 231 773-1330
2259 S Sheridan Dr Muskegon (49442) *(G-11892)*
Pacific Tool & Engineering Ltd (PA) 586 737-2710
6410 19 Mile Rd Sterling Heights (48314) *(G-16122)*
Package Design & Mfg Inc (PA) 248 486-4390
12424 Emerson Dr Brighton (48116) *(G-2046)*
Packaging Corporation America 616 530-5700
3251 Chicago Dr Sw Grandville (49418) *(G-7407)*
Packaging Corporation America 734 453-6262
936 N Sheldon Rd Plymouth (48170) *(G-13259)*
Packaging Corporation America 734 266-1877
28330 Plymouth Rd Livonia (48150) *(G-10358)*
Packaging Corporation America 269 567-7340
809 Harrison St Kalamazoo (49007) *(G-9284)*
Packaging Corporation America 231 723-1442
2246 Udell St Filer City (49634) *(G-5610)*
Packaging Corporation America 989 427-2130
1106 Industrial Park Dr Edmore (48829) *(G-4994)*
Packaging Corporation America 989 427-5129
1106 Industrial Park Dr Edmore (48829) *(G-4995)*
Packaging Engineering LLC 248 437-9444
7138 Kensington Rd Brighton (48116) *(G-2047)*
Packaging Engineering-Brighton, Brighton *Also called Packaging Engineering LLC* *(G-2047)*
Packaging Specialties Inc (HQ) 586 473-6703
8111 Middlebelt Rd Romulus (48174) *(G-14315)*
Packard Farms LLC 989 386-3816
6584 S Brand Ave Clare (48617) *(G-2993)*
Packers Canning Co Inc 269 624-4681
72100 M 40 Lawton (49065) *(G-9989)*
Packys Pet Supplies LLC 989 422-5484
9437 E Houghton Lake Dr Houghton Lake (48629) *(G-8402)*
Paddle Hard Distributing LLC 513 309-1192
118 E Michigan Ave Grayling (49738) *(G-7468)*

Paddle King Inc 989 235-6776
7110 S Crystal Rd Carson City (48811) *(G-2594)*
Paddlesports Warehouse Inc 231 757-9051
467 W Us Highway 10 31 Scottville (49454) *(G-15136)*
Paddletek LLC 269 340-5967
1990 S 11th St Ste 3 Niles (49120) *(G-12156)*
Padnos Leitelt Inc 616 363-3817
2301 Turner Ave Nw Grand Rapids (49544) *(G-7067)*
Pafnow, Southfield *Also called Process Analytics Factory LLC* *(G-15684)*
Pag, Troy *Also called Product Assembly Group LLC* *(G-17317)*
Page Litho Inc 313 885-8555
7 Wellington Pl Grosse Pointe (48230) *(G-7532)*
Page One Inc 810 724-0254
594 N Almont Ave Imlay City (48444) *(G-8642)*
Page Pallet & Lumber, Camden *Also called G & D Wood Products Inc* *(G-2422)*
Pageant Homes Inc 517 694-0431
4000 Holt Rd Holt (48842) *(G-8324)*
Pagekicker Corporation 734 646-6277
1521 Martha Ave Ann Arbor (48103) *(G-605)*
Pages In Time, Grand Rapids *Also called Janelle Peterson* *(G-6861)*
Pageworks, Grand Rapids *Also called Custom Printers Inc* *(G-6623)*
Paice Technologies LLC 248 376-1115
5843 Bravo Ct Orchard Lake (48324) *(G-12718)*
Paich Railworks Inc 734 397-2424
41275 Van Born Rd Van Buren Twp (48111) *(G-17546)*
Paine Press LLC 231 645-1970
209 S Lake St Boyne City (49712) *(G-1900)*
Painexx Corporation 313 863-1200
18307 James Couzens Fwy Detroit (48235) *(G-4503)*
Painless Printing 517 812-6852
4796 Trumble Rd Jackson (49201) *(G-8982)*
Paint Finishing Div, Belding *Also called Belco Industries Inc* *(G-1437)*
Paint Work Incorporated 586 759-6640
2088 Riggs Ave Warren (48091) *(G-17952)*
Paint Your Masterpiece 231 622-8824
110 Williams St Petoskey (49770) *(G-13011)*
Pak Mail Center of America 248 543-3097
23211 Woodward Ave Ferndale (48220) *(G-5575)*
Pak-Rite Industries Inc 313 388-6400
4270 High St Ecorse (48229) *(G-4984)*
Pak-Rite Michigan, Wixom *Also called Mollewood Export Inc* *(G-18714)*
Pal-TEC Inc 906 788-4229
14 Ln W5886 Wallace (49893) *(G-17661)*
Paladin Attachments, Dexter *Also called Paladin Brands Group Inc* *(G-4748)*
Paladin Baking Company LLC 248 601-1542
225 S Main St Rochester (48307) *(G-13919)*
Paladin Brands Group Inc (HQ) 319 378-3696
2800 Zeeb Rd Dexter (48130) *(G-4748)*
Paladin Ind Inc 616 698-7495
4990 W Greenbrooke Dr Se Grand Rapids (49512) *(G-7068)*
Paladino Publications 586 759-2795
24454 Curie St Warren (48091) *(G-17953)*
Palazzolo's Gelato, Fennville *Also called PGI of Saugatuck Inc* *(G-5441)*
Palfam Industries Inc 248 922-0590
1959 Viola Dr Ortonville (48462) *(G-12750)*
Paliot Solutions LLC (PA) 616 648-5939
41100 Plymouth Rd Plymouth (48170) *(G-13260)*
Pall Life Sciences, Ann Arbor *Also called Gelman Sciences Inc* *(G-496)*
Pallet Man 269 274-8825
555 Upton Ave Springfield (49037) *(G-15873)*
Pallet Pros LLC 586 864-3353
8233 Sterling Center Line (48015) *(G-2684)*
Palm Sweets LLC 586 554-7979
3605 15 Mile Rd Sterling Heights (48310) *(G-16123)*
Palm Sweets Bakery & Cafe, Sterling Heights *Also called Palm Sweets LLC* *(G-16123)*
Palmer Distributors Inc 586 772-4225
33525 Groesbeck Hwy Fraser (48026) *(G-5973)*
Palmer Engineering Inc 517 321-3600
3525 Capitol City Blvd Lansing (48906) *(G-9723)*
Palmer Envelope Co 269 965-1336
309 Fritz Keiper Blvd Battle Creek (49037) *(G-1280)*
Palmer Paint Products Inc 248 588-4500
1291 Rochester Rd Troy (48083) *(G-17295)*
Palmer Printing Co, Detroit *Also called Zak Brothers Printing LLC* *(G-4700)*
Palmer Promotional Products, Fraser *Also called Palmer Distributors Inc* *(G-5973)*
Palo Alto Manufacturing LLC 248 266-3669
2700 Auburn Ct Auburn Hills (48326) *(G-992)*
Pancheck LLC 989 288-6886
221 N Saginaw St Durand (48429) *(G-4844)*
Panda King Express 616 796-3286
520 Butternut Dr Ste 30 Holland (49424) *(G-8159)*
Pandia Industries LLC 269 386-2110
160 Palmer Ave Colon (49040) *(G-3489)*
Panel Pro LLC 734 427-1691
16809 Ryan Rd Livonia (48154) *(G-10359)*
Panel Processing New Jersey 856 317-1998
1030 Devere Dr Alpena (49707) *(G-308)*

Panel Processing Oregon Inc (HQ)........989 356-9007
1030 Devere Dr Alpena (49707) ***(G-309)***
Panel Processing Texas Inc........903 586-2423
1030 Devere Dr Alpena (49707) ***(G-310)***
Panelcraft Inc........734 646-2173
8205 Ronda Dr Canton (48187) ***(G-2504)***
Pangea Made Inc (PA)........248 436-2300
2920 Waterview Dr Rochester Hills (48309) ***(G-14078)***
Panoplate Lithographics Inc........269 343-4644
101 N Riverview Dr Kalamazoo (49004) ***(G-9285)***
Panter Master Controls Inc........810 687-5600
3060 S Dye Rd Ste A Flint (48507) ***(G-5743)***
Panther James LLC........248 850-7522
2070 11 Mile Rd Berkley (48072) ***(G-1634)***
Panther Publishing........586 202-9814
5341 Northwood Rd Grand Blanc (48439) ***(G-6255)***
Pantless Jams LLC........419 283-8470
6937 Maplewood Dr Temperance (48182) ***(G-16544)***
Papa Joes Grmet Mkt Hnry Ford........248 609-5670
2799 W Grand Blvd Detroit (48202) ***(G-4504)***
Paper and Print Usa LLC........616 940-8311
3400 Raleigh Dr Se Grand Rapids (49512) ***(G-7069)***
Paper Chase American Dream LLC........248 819-0939
7174 Mackenzie St Detroit (48204) ***(G-4505)***
Paper Image Printing Centres, Holt *Also called Printing Centre Inc* ***(G-8326)***
Paper Machine Service Inds (PA)........989 695-2646
3075 Shattuck Rd Ste 801 Saginaw (48603) ***(G-14724)***
Paper Petal Press........248 935-5193
6847 Saline Dr Waterford (48329) ***(G-18146)***
Paper Press........248 438-6238
7335 Woodlore Dr West Bloomfield (48323) ***(G-18303)***
Pappas Cutlery-Grinding Inc........800 521-0888
575 E Milwaukee St Detroit (48202) ***(G-4506)***
Par Excellence Publication........989 345-8305
2548 Caribou Trl West Branch (48661) ***(G-18334)***
Par Pharmaceutical, Rochester *Also called Par Sterile Products LLC* ***(G-13920)***
Par Sterile Products LLC........248 651-9081
870 Parkdale Rd Rochester (48307) ***(G-13920)***
Paradigm Conveyor LLC........616 667-4040
15342 24th Ave Marne (49435) ***(G-10996)***
Paradigm Engineering Inc........586 776-5910
16470 E 13 Mile Rd Roseville (48066) ***(G-14458)***
Paragon D&E, Grand Rapids *Also called Paragon Die & Engineering Co* ***(G-7070)***
Paragon Die & Engineering Co (PA)........616 949-2220
5225 33rd St Se Grand Rapids (49512) ***(G-7070)***
Paragon Leather Inc USA........269 323-9483
10210 Shaver Rd Ste A Portage (49024) ***(G-13590)***
Paragon Manufacturing Corp........810 629-4100
2046 W Thompson Rd Fenton (48430) ***(G-5493)***
Paragon Metals LLC (PA)........517 639-4629
3010 Mechanic Rd Hillsdale (49242) ***(G-7941)***
Paragon Model and Tool Inc........248 960-1223
46934 Magellan Wixom (48393) ***(G-18728)***
Paragon Model Shop Inc........616 693-3224
10083 Thompson Rd Freeport (49325) ***(G-6036)***
Paragon Molds Corporation........586 294-7630
33997 Riviera Fraser (48026) ***(G-5974)***
Paragon Ready Mix Inc (PA)........586 731-8000
48000 Hixson Ave Shelby Township (48317) ***(G-15295)***
Paragon Ready Mix Inc........248 623-0100
4389 Lessing Waterford (48329) ***(G-18147)***
Paragon Tempered Glass LLC (HQ)........269 684-5060
1830 Terminal Rd Niles (49120) ***(G-12157)***
Paragon Tool, Wixom *Also called Paragon Model and Tool Inc* ***(G-18728)***
Paragon Tool Company........734 326-1702
36130 Ecorse Rd Romulus (48174) ***(G-14316)***
Paragon Vciso Group LLC........248 895-9866
16777 Avon Ave Detroit (48219) ***(G-4507)***
Parallax Printing LLC........248 397-5156
2615 Wolcott St Ferndale (48220) ***(G-5576)***
Parameter Driven Software Inc (PA)........248 553-6410
32605 W 12 Mile Rd # 275 Farmington Hills (48334) ***(G-5342)***
Paramont Machine Co LLC........330 339-3489
2810 N Burdick St Kalamazoo (49004) ***(G-9286)***
Paramount Baking Company........313 690-4844
29790 Little Mack Ave Roseville (48066) ***(G-14459)***
Paramount Coffee Co., Lansing *Also called Inter State Foods Inc* ***(G-9706)***
Paramount Industrial Machining........248 543-2100
15255 W 11 Mile Rd Oak Park (48237) ***(G-12636)***
Paramount Signs LLC........734 548-1721
15145 Prospect St Dearborn (48126) ***(G-3882)***
Paramount Solutions Inc........586 914-0708
59285 Elizabeth Ln Ray (48096) ***(G-13702)***
Paramount Technologies Inc (PA)........248 960-0909
3636 Christy Way W Saginaw (48603) ***(G-14725)***
Paramount Tool and Die Inc........616 677-0000
1245 Comstock St Marne (49435) ***(G-10997)***
Paravis Industries Inc........248 393-2300
1597 Atlantic Blvd Auburn Hills (48326) ***(G-993)***
Pardon Inc........906 428-3494
3510 State Highway M35 Gladstone (49837) ***(G-6185)***
Paris North Hardwood Lumber........231 584-2500
542 Tobias Rd Elmira (49730) ***(G-5040)***
Pariseaus Printing Inc........810 653-8420
218 Mill St Davison (48423) ***(G-3792)***
Parish Publications........248 613-2384
63 Barden Ct Bloomfield Hills (48304) ***(G-1847)***
Parjana Distribution LLC........313 915-5418
21455 Melrose Ave Ste 22 Southfield (48075) ***(G-15672)***
Park Street Machine Inc........231 739-9165
2201 Park St Muskegon (49444) ***(G-11893)***
Parkedale Pharmaceuticals Inc........248 650-6400
1200 Parkdale Rd Rochester (48307) ***(G-13921)***
Parker & Associates........269 694-6709
338 W Franklin St Otsego (49078) ***(G-12794)***
Parker Engineering Amer Co Ltd........734 326-7630
38147 Abruzzi Dr Westland (48185) ***(G-18403)***
Parker Excvtg Grav & Recycle........616 784-1681
295 Hayes Rd Nw Comstock Park (49321) ***(G-3633)***
Parker Fluid Syst Connectors........989 352-7264
8790 Tamarack Rd Lakeview (48850) ***(G-9644)***
Parker HSD........269 384-3915
2220 Palmer Ave Kalamazoo (49001) ***(G-9287)***
Parker Machine & Engineering........734 692-4600
25028 Research Way Woodhaven (48183) ***(G-18801)***
Parker Pattern Inc........586 466-5900
195 Malow St Mount Clemens (48043) ***(G-11651)***
Parker Property Dev Inc........616 842-6118
12589 104th Ave Grand Haven (49417) ***(G-6343)***
Parker Tooling & Design Inc........616 791-1080
2563 3 Mile Rd Nw Grand Rapids (49534) ***(G-7071)***
Parker's Hilltop Brewery, Clarkston *Also called Clarkston Courts LLC* ***(G-3025)***
Parker-Hannifin Corporation........269 384-3459
2220 Palmer Ave Kalamazoo (49001) ***(G-9288)***
Parker-Hannifin Corporation........269 694-9411
300 Parker Dr Otsego (49078) ***(G-12795)***
Parker-Hannifin Corporation........269 629-5000
8676 M 89 Richland (49083) ***(G-13826)***
Parker-Hannifin Corporation........269 692-6254
100 Parker Dr Otsego (49078) ***(G-12796)***
Parker-Hannifin Corporation........330 253-5239
601 S Wilmott St Otsego (49078) ***(G-12797)***
Parker-Hannifin Corporation........269 384-3400
2220 Palmer Ave Kalamazoo (49001) ***(G-9289)***
Parkside Speedy Print Inc........810 985-8484
1319 Military St Port Huron (48060) ***(G-13516)***
Parkway Contract Group, Livonia *Also called Parkway Drapery & Uphl Co Inc* ***(G-10360)***
Parkway Drapery & Uphl Co Inc........734 779-1300
12784 Currie Ct Livonia (48150) ***(G-10360)***
Parkway Elc Communications LLC (PA)........616 392-2788
11952 James St Ste A Holland (49424) ***(G-8160)***
Parma Diversified Technologies, Rochester Hills *Also called Mathew Parmelee* ***(G-14059)***
Parma Tube Corp........269 651-2351
1008 Progress St Sturgis (49091) ***(G-16316)***
Parmalat Grand Rapids, Grand Rapids *Also called Agropur Inc* ***(G-6439)***
Parousia Plastics Inc........989 832-4054
2412 Judith Ct Midland (48642) ***(G-11402)***
Parry Precision Inc........248 585-1234
845 E Mandoline Ave Madison Heights (48071) ***(G-10795)***
Parshallville Cider Mill........810 629-9079
8507 Parshallville Rd Fenton (48430) ***(G-5494)***
Parson Adhesives Inc (PA)........248 299-5585
3345 W Auburn Rd Ste 107 Rochester Hills (48309) ***(G-14079)***
Parsons Centennial Farm LLC........231 547-2038
61 Parsons Rd Charlevoix (49720) ***(G-2727)***
Parsons Industrial Maintenance........734 236-4163
876 Indian Trail Rd Carleton (48117) ***(G-2561)***
Parton & Preble Inc........586 773-6000
23507 Groesbeck Hwy Warren (48089) ***(G-17954)***
Partridge Pointe Press LLC........248 321-0475
2470 Strawberry Frm St Ne Belmont (49306) ***(G-1515)***
Parts Finishing Group, Detroit *Also called Bellevue Proc Met Prep Inc* ***(G-4050)***
Parts Finishing Group Inc........586 755-4053
13251 Stephens Rd Warren (48089) ***(G-17955)***
Party Time Ice Co, Port Huron *Also called Knowlton Enterprises Inc* ***(G-13495)***
Parvox Technology........231 924-4366
531 Chippewa Dr Fremont (49412) ***(G-6051)***
Parvox Technology........231 924-4366
14 W Main St Fremont (49412) ***(G-6052)***
Paschal Burial Vault Svc LLC........517 448-8868
431 School St Hudson (49247) ***(G-8558)***
Paschal Burial Vaults, Hudson *Also called Paschal Burial Vault Svc LLC* ***(G-8558)***
Paslin Company........586 755-1693
23655 Hoover Rd Warren (48089) ***(G-17956)***
Paslin Company (HQ)........586 758-0200
25303 Ryan Rd Warren (48091) ***(G-17957)***
Paslin Company........248 953-8419
52550 Shelby Pkwy Shelby Township (48315) ***(G-15296)***

Paslin Company..586 755-3606
  3400 E 10 Mile Rd Warren (48091) *(G-17958)*
Paslin Controls Group, Warren Also called Paslin Company *(G-17958)*
Passenger Inc..323 556-5400
  1940 Olympia Dr Howell (48843) *(G-8490)*
Passivebolt Inc...734 972-0306
  2723 S State St Unit 1 Ann Arbor (48104) *(G-606)*
Passport Health of Michigan, Farmington Hills Also called Bruce Kane Enterprises LLC *(G-5187)*
Pasty Oven Inc (PA)...906 774-2328
  W7279 Us Highway 2 Quinnesec (49876) *(G-13676)*
Pat Ro Publishing...248 553-4935
  32364 Nottingwood St Farmington Hills (48334) *(G-5343)*
Patch Master Services, Sterling Heights Also called Rite Way Asphalt Inc *(G-16154)*
Patch Works Farms Inc......................................989 430-3610
  9710 E Monroe Rd Wheeler (48662) *(G-18436)*
Patchwood Products Inc (PA)............................989 742-2605
  14797 State St Hillman (49746) *(G-7915)*
Patchwood Products Inc....................................989 742-2605
  105 Stagecoach Dr Lachine (49753) *(G-9533)*
Patco Air Tool Inc..248 648-8830
  100 Engelwood Dr Ste G Orion (48359) *(G-12738)*
Patent Lcnsing Clringhouse LLC.......................248 299-7500
  2791 Research Dr Rochester Hills (48309) *(G-14080)*
Paterek Mold & Engineering...............................586 784-8030
  74081 Church St Armada (48005) *(G-739)*
Pathway Publishers, Bloomingdale Also called Pathway Publishing Corporation *(G-1878)*
Pathway Publishing Corporation (HQ)..............269 521-3025
  43632 County Road 390 Bloomingdale (49026) *(G-1878)*
Patio Land Mfg Inc...586 758-5660
  8407 E 9 Mile Rd Warren (48089) *(G-17959)*
Patmai Company Inc...586 294-0370
  31425 Fraser Dr Fraser (48026) *(G-5975)*
Patrick Carbide Die LLC....................................517 546-5646
  840 Victory Dr Ste 200 Howell (48843) *(G-8491)*
Patrick D Duffy..989 828-5467
  306 N 4th St Shepherd (48883) *(G-15377)*
Patrick Newland Logging Ltd.............................906 524-2255
  14738 Pequaming Rd Lanse (49946) *(G-9667)*
Patriot Bars Mfg LLC...248 342-3319
  51568 Stern Ln Chesterfield (48051) *(G-2922)*
Patriot Pyrotechnics..989 831-7788
  5735 S Townhall Rd B Sheridan (48884) *(G-15382)*
Patriot Sensors & Contrls Corp..........................810 378-5511
  6380 Brockway Rd Peck (48466) *(G-12962)*
Patriot Sensors & Contrls Corp (HQ).................248 435-0700
  6380 Brockway Rd Peck (48466) *(G-12963)*
Patriot Solar Group LLC....................................517 629-9292
  708 Valhalla Dr Albion (49224) *(G-129)*
Patriot Solutions LLC..616 240-8164
  5575 Kraft Ave Se Ste 100 Grand Rapids (49512) *(G-7072)*
Patriot Tool Inc..313 299-1400
  5310 Bayham St Dearborn Heights (48125) *(G-3936)*
Patten Monument Company (PA)......................616 785-4141
  3980 West River Dr Ne Comstock Park (49321) *(G-3634)*
Pattern Monument, Comstock Park Also called Patten Monument Company *(G-3634)*
Patterson Precision Mfg Inc...............................231 733-1913
  1188 E Broadway Ave Norton Shores (49444) *(G-12324)*
Patton Tool and Die Inc.....................................810 359-5336
  7185 Baker Rd Lexington (48450) *(G-10031)*
Patton Welding, Kalkaska Also called D J and G Enterprise Inc *(G-9386)*
Patton Welding Inc..231 258-9925
  402 E Dresden St Kalkaska (49646) *(G-9401)*
Patty Raymond..517 256-6673
  15680 S Niles Rd Eagle (48822) *(G-4852)*
Paul C Doerr...734 242-2058
  407 E Front St Monroe (48161) *(G-11568)*
Paul Horn and Associates.................................248 682-8490
  2525 Sylvan Shores Dr Waterford (48328) *(G-18148)*
Paul Jeffrey Kenny..989 828-6109
  1345 E Pleasant Valley Rd Shepherd (48883) *(G-15378)*
Paul Murphy Plastics Co (PA)............................586 774-4880
  15301 E 11 Mile Rd Roseville (48066) *(G-14460)*
Paul W Reed DDS...231 347-4145
  414 Petoskey St Petoskey (49770) *(G-13012)*
Paul W Reed DDS Ms, Petoskey Also called Paul W Reed DDS *(G-13012)*
Paulstra C R C-Cadillac Div, Cadillac Also called Hutchnson Antvbrtion Systems I *(G-2336)*
Paumac Tubing LLC (PA)...................................810 985-9400
  315 Cuttle Rd Marysville (48040) *(G-11096)*
Pauri Retail Store LLC.......................................415 980-1525
  2785 E Grand Blvd # 312 Detroit (48211) *(G-4508)*
Pavco MCR...734 464-2220
  38521 Schoolcraft Rd Livonia (48150) *(G-10361)*
PAW Enterprises LLC..269 329-1865
  3308 Covington Rd Ste 1 Kalamazoo (49001) *(G-9290)*
Paw Paw Everlast Label Company....................269 657-4921
  37837 Peters Dr Paw Paw (49079) *(G-12954)*
Paw Paw Flashes, Paw Paw Also called Vineyard Press Inc *(G-12959)*
Paw Paw Fuel Stop..269 657-7357
  60902 M 51 Paw Paw (49079) *(G-12955)*
Paw Print Creations LLC...................................810 577-0410
  7484 Braymont St Mount Morris (48458) *(G-11676)*
Paw Print Gardens..616 791-4758
  601 Kinney Ave Nw Grand Rapids (49534) *(G-7073)*
Paws Workholding, Clio Also called Montague Tool and Mfg Co *(G-3408)*
Paxton Countertops, Lansing Also called Paxton Products Inc *(G-9783)*
Paxton Media Group LLC..................................269 429-2400
  3450 Hollywood Rd Saint Joseph (49085) *(G-14953)*
Paxton Products Inc..517 627-3688
  1340 S Waverly Rd Lansing (48917) *(G-9783)*
Payne & Dolan Inc...989 731-0700
  1029 Gornick Ave Ste 105 Gaylord (49735) *(G-6153)*
Pazzel Inc...616 291-0257
  100 Stevens St Sw Grand Rapids (49507) *(G-7074)*
Pbg Michigan LLC...989 345-2595
  610 Parkway Dr West Branch (48661) *(G-18335)*
PBM Nutritionals LLC..269 673-8451
  515 Eastern Ave Allegan (49010) *(G-173)*
PC Complete Inc...248 545-4211
  742 Livernois St Ferndale (48220) *(G-5577)*
PC Solutions...517 787-9934
  1200 S West Ave Jackson (49203) *(G-8983)*
PC Solutions of Michigan, Jackson Also called PC Solutions *(G-8983)*
PC Techs On Wheels..734 262-4424
  8418 Brooke Park Dr # 111 Canton (48187) *(G-2505)*
PCA, Livonia Also called Packaging Corporation America *(G-10358)*
PCA, Kalamazoo Also called Packaging Corporation America *(G-9284)*
PCA Grandville, Grandville Also called Packaging Corporation America *(G-7407)*
PCA/Edmore 321, Edmore Also called Packaging Corporation America *(G-4995)*
PCA/Edmore 321a, Edmore Also called Packaging Corporation America *(G-4994)*
PCA/Filer City 640, Filer City Also called Packaging Corporation America *(G-5610)*
Pcb Load & Torque Inc......................................248 471-0065
  24350 Indoplex Cir Farmington Hills (48335) *(G-5344)*
Pcb Piezotronics Inc..888 684-0014
  4000 Grand River Blvd Novi (48375) *(G-12503)*
Pcb Piezotronics Inc..716 684-0001
  24350 Indoplex Cir Farmington Hills (48335) *(G-5345)*
PCI, Melvindale Also called Piping Components Inc *(G-11209)*
PCI Industries Inc..248 542-2570
  21717 Republic Ave Oak Park (48237) *(G-12637)*
PCI Procal Inc...989 358-7070
  3810 Us Highway 23 N Alpena (49707) *(G-311)*
Pcm US Steering Holding LLC..........................313 556-5000
  1272 Doris Rd Auburn Hills (48326) *(G-994)*
Pcmi Manufacturing Integration, Shelby Township Also called Prototype Cast Mfg Inc *(G-15311)*
PCS Company (HQ)..586 294-7780
  34488 Doreka Fraser (48026) *(G-5976)*
Pcs Outdoors..989 569-3480
  5911 Mission St Oscoda (48750) *(G-12769)*
Pcs Pharmaceuticals LLC.................................248 289-7054
  41000 Woodward Ave # 350 Bloomfield Hills (48304) *(G-1848)*
Pcs Pharmacy, Bloomfield Hills Also called Pcs Pharmaceuticals LLC *(G-1848)*
Pct Security Inc...888 567-3287
  34668 Nova Dr Clinton Township (48035) *(G-3317)*
PDC (PA)..269 651-9975
  69701 White St Sturgis (49091) *(G-16317)*
Pdf Mfg Inc..517 522-8431
  11000 Cedar Knoll Dr Grass Lake (49240) *(G-7443)*
Pdl LLC...810 844-3209
  8767 Bergin Rd Howell (48843) *(G-8492)*
PDM, Brighton Also called Package Design & Mfg Inc *(G-2046)*
PDM Industries Inc..231 943-9601
  1124 Stepke Ct Traverse City (49685) *(G-16786)*
PDQ Ink Inc...810 229-2989
  7475 Grand River Rd Brighton (48114) *(G-2048)*
Pds Plastics Inc...616 896-1109
  3297 140th Ave Dorr (49323) *(G-4769)*
Peacekeeper Cnc, Auburn Hills Also called Defense Component Detroit LLC *(G-861)*
Peacock Industries Inc......................................231 745-4609
  254 S M 37 Baldwin (49304) *(G-1124)*
Peacocks Eco Log & Sawmill LLC.....................231 250-3462
  14823 4 Mile Rd Morley (49336) *(G-11621)*
Peak Edm Inc..248 380-0871
  28221 Beck Rd Ste A2 Wixom (48393) *(G-18729)*
Peak Industries Co Inc......................................313 846-8666
  5320 Oakman Blvd Dearborn (48126) *(G-3883)*
Peak Manufacturing Inc.....................................517 769-6900
  11855 Bunkerhill Rd Pleasant Lake (49272) *(G-13104)*
Peake Asphalt Inc..586 254-4567
  48181 Ryan Rd Shelby Township (48317) *(G-15297)*
Peaker Services, Brighton Also called PSI Holding Company *(G-2057)*
Peaker Services Inc...248 437-4174
  8080 Kensington Ct Brighton (48116) *(G-2049)*
Peaktronics Inc..248 542-5640
  1363 Anderson Rd Ste A Clawson (48017) *(G-3102)*

Peanut Shop Inc 517 374-0008
117 S Washington Sq Ste 1 Lansing (48933) ***(G-9879)***
Pearce Plastics LLC 231 519-5994
4898 W 80th St Fremont (49412) ***(G-6053)***
Pearson Auto Service Inc 313 538-6870
20800 W 7 Mile Rd Detroit (48219) ***(G-4509)***
Pearson Industries LLC 740 584-9080
18205 Marx St Detroit (48203) ***(G-4510)***
Pearson Precast Concrete Pdts 517 486-4060
7951 E Us Highway 223 Blissfield (49228) ***(G-1772)***
Pearson Software Company 313 878-2687
21124 Schoolcraft Apt B1 Detroit (48223) ***(G-4511)***
Pease Packing, Scotts *Also called Cole Carter Inc* ***(G-15131)***
Pebco Sales, Clinton Township *Also called Meccom Industrial Products Co* ***(G-3297)***
PEC of America, Novi *Also called Pacific Engineering Corp* ***(G-12502)***
PEC of America Corporation (HQ) 248 675-3130
39555 Orchard Hill Pl # 220 Novi (48375) ***(G-12504)***
Peck Engineering Inc 313 534-2950
12660 Farley Redford (48239) ***(G-13753)***
Peckham Vocational Inds Inc (PA) 517 316-4000
3510 Capitol City Blvd Lansing (48906) ***(G-9724)***
Peckham Vocational Inds Inc 517 316-4478
2511 N Mrtn Lthr Kng Jr B Lansing (48906) ***(G-9725)***
Pedmic Converting Inc 810 679-9600
7241 Wildcat Rd Croswell (48422) ***(G-3734)***
Pedri Mold Inc 586 598-0882
46429 Continental Dr Chesterfield (48047) ***(G-2923)***
Peerless Canvas Products Inc 269 429-0600
2355 Niles Rd Saint Joseph (49085) ***(G-14954)***
Peerless Gage 734 261-3000
39645 Muirfield Ln Northville (48168) ***(G-12251)***
Peerless Mtal Pwders Abrsive L 313 841-5400
131 S Military St Detroit (48209) ***(G-4512)***
Peerless Mtal Pwders Abrsive L 313 841-5400
6307 W Fort St Detroit (48209) ***(G-4513)***
Peerless Quality Products 313 933-7525
7707 Lyndon St Detroit (48238) ***(G-4514)***
Peerless Steel Company 616 530-6695
3280 Century Center St Sw Grandville (49418) ***(G-7408)***
Peerless Tooling Components, Madison Heights *Also called P X Tool Co* ***(G-10794)***
Peerless Waste Solutions LLC 616 355-2800
510 E 40th St Holland (49423) ***(G-8161)***
Peg-Master Business Forms Inc 586 566-8694
15018 Technology Dr Shelby Township (48315) ***(G-15298)***
Pegasus Industries 810 356-5579
2759 Watchhill Dr Lapeer (48446) ***(G-9953)***
Pegasus Industries Inc 313 937-0770
12380 Beech Daly Rd Redford (48239) ***(G-13754)***
Pegasus Mold & Die Inc 517 423-2009
415 E Russell Rd Tecumseh (49286) ***(G-16510)***
Pegasus Tool LLC 313 255-5900
12680 Farley Detroit (48239) ***(G-4515)***
Pelhams Construction LLC 517 549-8276
10800 Concord Rd Jonesville (49250) ***(G-9098)***
Peloton Inc 269 694-9702
124 E Allegan St Otsego (49078) ***(G-12798)***
Pelzer 248 250-6161
2878 Roundtree Dr Troy (48083) ***(G-17296)***
Pen, Madison Heights *Also called Nano Magic Holdings Inc* ***(G-10787)***
Penchura LLC 810 229-6245
889 S Old Us 23 Brighton (48114) ***(G-2050)***
Pencil Pushers LLC 248 252-7839
2570 Maplecrest Dr Waterford (48329) ***(G-18149)***
Pender Boatworks LLC 269 207-0627
15226 Marshfield Rd Hickory Corners (49060) ***(G-7875)***
Penguin Juice Co (PA) 734 467-6991
39002 Webb Ct Westland (48185) ***(G-18404)***
Penguin LLC 269 651-9488
1855 W Chicago Rd Sturgis (49091) ***(G-16318)***
Penguin-Iceberg Enterprises, Sturgis *Also called Penguin LLC* ***(G-16318)***
Peninslar Oil Gas Cmpny-Mchgan 616 676-2090
3196 Kraft Ave Se Ste 305 Grand Rapids (49512) ***(G-7075)***
Peninsula Cellars 231 223-4050
2464 Kroupa Rd Traverse City (49686) ***(G-16787)***
Peninsula Plastics Company Inc (PA) 248 852-3731
2800 Auburn Ct Auburn Hills (48326) ***(G-995)***
Peninsula Powder Coating Inc 906 353-7234
128 Hemlock St Baraga (49908) ***(G-1146)***
Peninsula Prestress Company, Wyoming *Also called P D P LLC* ***(G-18898)***
Peninsula Products Inc 906 296-9801
54385 Cemetery Rd Lake Linden (49945) ***(G-9569)***
Peninsular Inc 586 775-7211
27650 Groesbeck Hwy Roseville (48066) ***(G-14461)***
Peninsular Cylinder Company, Roseville *Also called Peninsular Inc* ***(G-14461)***
Peninsular Technologies LLC 616 676-9811
3196 Kraft Ave Se Ste 305 Grand Rapids (49512) ***(G-7076)***
Penka Cutter Grinding, Madison Heights *Also called Penka Tool Corporation* ***(G-10796)***
Penka Tool Corporation 248 543-3940
1717 E 10 Mile Rd Madison Heights (48071) ***(G-10796)***
Penn Automotive Inc 734 595-3000
7845 Middlebelt Rd # 200 Romulus (48174) ***(G-14317)***
Penn Automotive Inc (HQ) 248 599-3700
5331 Dixie Hwy Waterford (48329) ***(G-18150)***
Penn Engineering & Mfg Corp 313 299-8500
5331 Dixie Hwy Waterford (48329) ***(G-18151)***
Penn Engineering & Mfg Corp 586 731-3560
5331 Dixie Hwy Waterford (48329) ***(G-18152)***
Penn Sign 814 932-7181
10160 Miriam St Romulus (48174) ***(G-14318)***
Pennisular Packaging LLC 313 304-4724
13505 N Haggerty Rd Plymouth (48170) ***(G-13261)***
Penny Saver, Three Rivers *Also called Three Rivers Commercial News* ***(G-16588)***
Penrose Therapeutix LLC 847 370-0303
46701 Commerce Center Dr Plymouth (48170) ***(G-13262)***
Penske Company LLC (HQ) 248 648-2000
2555 S Telegraph Rd Bloomfield Hills (48302) ***(G-1849)***
Penstone Inc 734 379-3160
31605 Gossett Dr Rockwood (48173) ***(G-14203)***
Pentagon Mold Co 269 496-7072
21015 M 60 Mendon (49072) ***(G-11220)***
Pentamere Winery 517 423-9000
131 E Chicago Blvd Ste 1 Tecumseh (49286) ***(G-16511)***
Pentar Stamping Inc 517 782-0700
1821 Wildwood Ave Jackson (49202) ***(G-8984)***
Pentech Industries Inc 586 445-1070
15645 Sturgeon St Roseville (48066) ***(G-14462)***
Pentel Tool & Die Inc 734 782-9500
26531 King Rd Romulus (48174) ***(G-14319)***
Pentier Group Inc 810 664-7997
587 S Court St Ste 300 Lapeer (48446) ***(G-9954)***
Penzo America Inc 248 723-0802
6335 Thorncrest Dr Bloomfield Hills (48301) ***(G-1850)***
Pepin-Ireco Inc 906 486-4473
9045 County Road 476 Ishpeming (49849) ***(G-8780)***
Pepperidge Farm Incorporated 734 953-6729
29115 8 Mile Rd Livonia (48152) ***(G-10362)***
Pepperidge Farm Thrift Store, Livonia *Also called Pepperidge Farm Incorporated* ***(G-10362)***
Pepperlee Paper Company 313 949-5917
722 Glen Cir Rochester Hills (48307) ***(G-14081)***
Pepro Enterprises Inc 989 658-3200
2147 Leppek Rd Ubly (48475) ***(G-17479)***
Pepro Enterprises Inc (HQ) 989 658-3200
4385 Garfield St Ubly (48475) ***(G-17480)***
Pepro Enterprises Inc 248 435-7271
53 W Maple Rd Clawson (48017) ***(G-3103)***
Pepsi 231 627-2290
6303 N Straits Hwy Cheboygan (49721) ***(G-2795)***
Pepsi Beverages Co 989 754-0435
100 S Outer Dr Saginaw (48601) ***(G-14726)***
Pepsi Bottling Group 810 966-8060
2111 Wadhams Rd Kimball (48074) ***(G-9497)***
Pepsi Bottling Group 517 546-2777
404 Mason Rd Howell (48843) ***(G-8493)***
Pepsi Co Wixom 248 305-3500
625 E Main St Milan (48160) ***(G-11448)***
Pepsi Cola Botling Co Houghton 906 482-0161
309 E Sharon Ave Houghton (49931) ***(G-8389)***
Pepsi-Cola Metro Btlg Co Inc 517 321-0231
4900 W Grand River Ave Lansing (48906) ***(G-9726)***
Pepsi-Cola Metro Btlg Co Inc 248 335-3528
960 Featherstone St Pontiac (48342) ***(G-13406)***
Pepsi-Cola Metro Btlg Co Inc 989 345-2595
610 Parkway Dr West Branch (48661) ***(G-18336)***
Pepsi-Cola Metro Btlg Co Inc 231 946-0452
4248 Cherri Pepsi Way Traverse City (49685) ***(G-16788)***
Pepsi-Cola Metro Btlg Co Inc 989 755-1020
736 N Outer Dr Saginaw (48601) ***(G-14727)***
Pepsi-Cola Metro Btlg Co Inc 517 546-2777
725 Mcpherson St Howell (48843) ***(G-8494)***
Pepsi-Cola Metro Btlg Co Inc 269 226-6400
2725 E Kilgore Rd Kalamazoo (49001) ***(G-9291)***
Pepsi-Cola Metro Btlg Co Inc 810 232-3925
6200g Taylor Dr Flint (48507) ***(G-5744)***
Pepsi-Cola Metro Btlg Co Inc 616 285-8200
3700 Kraft Ave Se Grand Rapids (49512) ***(G-7077)***
Pepsi-Cola Metro Btlg Co Inc 989 772-3158
919 Industrial Dr Mount Pleasant (48858) ***(G-11730)***
Pepsi-Cola Metro Btlg Co Inc 517 279-8436
101 Treat Dr Coldwater (49036) ***(G-3445)***
Pepsi-Cola Metro Btlg Co Inc 810 987-2181
2111 Wadhams Rd Kimball (48074) ***(G-9498)***
Pepsi-Cola Metro Btlg Co Inc 313 832-0910
1555 Mack Ave Detroit (48207) ***(G-4516)***
Pepsi-Cola Metro Btlg Co Inc 231 798-1274
4900 Paul Ct Norton Shores (49441) ***(G-12325)***
Pepsi-New Bern-Howell-151 ....517 546-7542
755 Mcpherson Park Dr Howell (48843) ***(G-8495)***
Pepsico, Milan *Also called Pepsi Co Wixom* ***(G-11448)***
Pepsico, Kimball *Also called Pepsi Bottling Group* ***(G-9497)***

Pepsico, Howell *Also called Pepsi-New Bern-Howell-151* ***(G-8495)***
Pepsico, Cheboygan *Also called Pepsi* ***(G-2795)***
Pepsico, Howell *Also called Pepsi Bottling Group* ***(G-8493)***
Pepsico, Houghton *Also called Pepsi Cola Botling Co Houghton* ***(G-8389)***
Pepsico Inc....734 374-9841
12862 Reeck Rd Southgate (48195) ***(G-15755)***
Pepsico Inc....586 276-4102
6600 17 Mile Rd Sterling Heights (48313) ***(G-16124)***
Pepsicola, Newberry *Also called Newberry Bottling Co Inc* ***(G-12095)***
Perceptive Controls Inc....269 685-3040
140 E Bridge St Plainwell (49080) ***(G-13085)***
Perceptive Industries Inc....269 204-6768
951 Industrial Pkwy Plainwell (49080) ***(G-13086)***
Perceptron Inc (HQ)....734 414-6100
47827 Halyard Dr Plymouth (48170) ***(G-13263)***
Peregrine Manufacturing, Michigan Center *Also called Feleo Mfg Strategies LLC* ***(G-11293)***
Peregrine Wood Products, Muskegon *Also called Quality Pallet Inc* ***(G-11901)***
Perennial Software....734 414-0760
45185 Joy Rd Ste 102 Canton (48187) ***(G-2506)***
Perfect Dish LLC....734 272-9871
21867 Kings Pte Blvd Taylor (48180) ***(G-16456)***
Perfect Expressions....248 640-1287
3643 W Maple Rd Bloomfield Hills (48301) ***(G-1851)***
Perfect Eyes Optical....248 275-7861
15292 E 8 Mile Rd Detroit (48205) ***(G-4517)***
Perfect Fit Brdal Tuxedos Prom, Clio *Also called Demmem Enterprises LLC* ***(G-3396)***
Perfect Signs....231 233-3721
338 4th St Manistee (49660) ***(G-10911)***
Perfect Stitch Inc....407 797-5527
3422 W Wilson Rd Clio (48420) ***(G-3409)***
Perfect Sync Inc....231 947-9300
1902 Penbroke Dr Traverse City (49696) ***(G-16789)***
Perfected Grave Vault Co....616 243-3375
2500 3 Mile Rd Nw Grand Rapids (49534) ***(G-7078)***
Perfection Industries Inc (PA)....313 272-4040
18571 Weaver St Detroit (48228) ***(G-4518)***
Perfection Sprinkler Company....734 761-5110
2077 S State St Ann Arbor (48104) ***(G-607)***
Perfecto Industries Inc (PA)....989 732-2941
1567 Calkins Dr Gaylord (49735) ***(G-6154)***
Perforated Tubes Inc....616 942-4550
4850 Fulton St E Ada (49301) ***(G-33)***
Perform3-D LLC....734 604-4100
411 Huronview Blvd # 200 Ann Arbor (48103) ***(G-608)***
Performance Fabrics Inc....616 459-4144
640 Leffingwell Ave Ne Grand Rapids (49505) ***(G-7079)***
Performance Fuels Systems Inc....248 202-1789
3108 Newport Ct Troy (48084) ***(G-17297)***
Performance Machinery LLC....586 698-2508
5430 Gatewood Dr Sterling Heights (48310) ***(G-16125)***
Performance Machining Inc....269 683-4370
919 Michigan St Niles (49120) ***(G-12158)***
Performance Plus, Prudenville *Also called Viking Oil LLC* ***(G-13659)***
Performance Print and Mktg....517 896-9682
1907 Burkley Rd Williamston (48895) ***(G-18579)***
Performance Sailing Inc....586 790-7500
24227 Sorrentino Ct Clinton Township (48035) ***(G-3318)***
Performance Springs Inc....248 486-3372
57575 Travis Rd New Hudson (48165) ***(G-12067)***
Performance Systematix LLC (HQ)....616 949-9090
5569 33rd St Se Grand Rapids (49512) ***(G-7080)***
Performcoat of Michigan LLC....269 282-7030
319 Mcintyre Ln Springfield (49037) ***(G-15874)***
Performnce Assmbly Sltions LLC....734 466-6380
28190 Plymouth Rd Livonia (48150) ***(G-10363)***
Performnce Dcutting Finshg LLC....616 245-3636
955 Godfrey Ave Sw Grand Rapids (49503) ***(G-7081)***
Perigee Manufacturing Co Inc....313 933-4420
7519 Intervale St Detroit (48238) ***(G-4519)***
Periscope Playschool....989 875-4409
3676 N Bagley Rd Alma (48801) ***(G-252)***
Permacoat Inc....313 388-7798
14868 Champaign Rd Allen Park (48101) ***(G-202)***
Permaloc Aluminum Edging, Holland *Also called Permaloc Corporation* ***(G-8162)***
Permaloc Corporation....616 399-9600
13505 Barry St Holland (49424) ***(G-8162)***
Perman Industries LLC....586 991-5600
51523 Celeste Shelby Township (48315) ***(G-15299)***
Permawick Company Inc (PA)....248 433-3500
255 E Brown St Ste 100 Birmingham (48009) ***(G-1743)***
Perpetual Measurement Inc....248 343-2952
3185 Seebaldt Ave Waterford (48329) ***(G-18153)***
Perras Holster Sales LLC....248 467-4254
57680 Deere Ct South Lyon (48178) ***(G-15452)***
Perrigo Brnded Phrmcticals Inc, Allegan *Also called PMI Branded Pharmaceuticals* ***(G-179)***
Perrigo China Bus Trustee LLC....269 673-8451
515 Eastern Ave Allegan (49010) ***(G-174)***
Perrigo Company....269 686-1973
900 Industrial Dr Allegan (49010) ***(G-175)***
Perrigo Company (HQ)....269 673-8451
515 Eastern Ave Allegan (49010) ***(G-176)***
Perrigo Company....616 396-0941
3896 58th St Holland (49423) ***(G-8163)***
Perrigo Company....269 686-1782
796 Interchange Dr Holland (49423) ***(G-8164)***
Perrigo Company....269 673-7962
515 Eastern Ave Allegan (49010) ***(G-177)***
Perrigo Grand Rapids Mfg, Grand Rapids *Also called Ranir LLC* ***(G-7139)***
Perrigo Logistics Center, Allegan *Also called Perrigo Company* ***(G-175)***
Perrigo New York Inc....269 673-8451
515 Eastern Ave Allegan (49010) ***(G-178)***
Perrigo Printing Inc....616 454-6761
3852 44th St Se Grand Rapids (49512) ***(G-7082)***
Perrin Screen Printing Inc....616 785-9900
5320 Rusche Dr Nw Comstock Park (49321) ***(G-3635)***
Perrin Souvenir Distrs Inc....616 785-9700
5320 Rusche Dr Nw Comstock Park (49321) ***(G-3636)***
Perrone Vineyards....231 330-1493
6715 N Us Highway 31 Levering (49755) ***(G-10016)***
Perry Creek Woodworking Inc....989 848-2125
211 E Kneeland Rd Mio (48647) ***(G-11514)***
Perry Tool Company Inc....734 283-7393
12329 Hale St Riverview (48193) ***(G-13883)***
Persico Usa Inc....248 299-5100
50450 Wing Dr Shelby Township (48315) ***(G-15300)***
Personal Graphics....231 347-6347
270 Creekside Dr Petoskey (49770) ***(G-13013)***
Personal Power Press Inc....989 239-8628
5225 3 Mile Rd Bay City (48706) ***(G-1386)***
Personal Touch....313 354-4255
8481 Stahelin Ave Detroit (48228) ***(G-4520)***
Personal Tuch By AP Imprssions, Livonia *Also called AP Impressions Inc* ***(G-10121)***
Persons Inc....989 734-3835
285 S Bradley Hwy Ste 2 Rogers City (49779) ***(G-14216)***
Perspective Enterprises Inc....269 327-0869
7829 S Sprinkle Rd Ste A Portage (49002) ***(G-13591)***
Perspective Software....248 308-2418
143 Cdycntre 86nrthvl 86 Northville Northville (48167) ***(G-12252)***
Perspectives Cabinetry, Troy *Also called Perspectives Custom Cabinetry* ***(G-17298)***
Perspectives Custom Cabinetry....248 288-4100
1401 Axtell Dr Troy (48084) ***(G-17298)***
Pesti Manufacturing Company....586 920-2731
25211 Mound Rd Warren (48091) ***(G-17960)***
Pet Patrol of Macomb-Oakland....586 675-2451
25155 Rosenbusch Blvd Warren (48089) ***(G-17961)***
Pet Supplies Plus....616 554-3600
6159 Kalamazoo Ave Se Grand Rapids (49508) ***(G-7083)***
Pet Treats Plus....313 533-1701
14141 Marion Redford (48239) ***(G-13755)***
Petal Pushers By Liz LLC....616 481-9513
5535 Division Ave N Comstock Park (49321) ***(G-3637)***
Pete Pullum Company Inc....313 837-9440
15330 Castleton St Detroit (48227) ***(G-4521)***
Peter Dehaan Publishing Inc....616 284-1305
2386 Outback Dr Hudsonville (49426) ***(G-8600)***
Peter-Lacke Usa LLC (HQ)....248 588-9400
865 Stephenson Hwy Troy (48083) ***(G-17299)***
Peterman Concrete Co, Portage *Also called Peterman Mobile Concrete Inc* ***(G-13592)***
Peterman Mobile Concrete Inc (PA)....269 324-1211
333 Peterman Ln Portage (49002) ***(G-13592)***
Peters Sand and Gravel Inc....906 595-7223
W7276 Hiawatha Trl Naubinway (49762) ***(G-11961)***
Petersen Products Inc....248 446-0500
7915 Kensington Ct Brighton (48116) ***(G-2051)***
Peterson American Corporation (HQ)....248 799-5400
21200 Telegraph Rd Southfield (48033) ***(G-15673)***
Peterson American Corporation....248 799-5410
3285 Martin Rd Ste N106 Commerce Township (48390) ***(G-3562)***
Peterson American Corporation....269 279-7421
16805 Heimbach Rd Three Rivers (49093) ***(G-16580)***
Peterson Farms Inc....231 861-6333
3104 W Baseline Rd Shelby (49455) ***(G-15159)***
Peterson Jig & Fixture Inc (PA)....616 866-8296
301 Rockford Park Dr Ne Rockford (49341) ***(G-14183)***
Peterson Publishing Inc....906 387-3282
339 Alger St Marquette (49855) ***(G-11040)***
Peterson Spring....248 799-5400
679 E Mandoline Ave Madison Heights (48071) ***(G-10797)***
Peterson Spring Cima, Three Rivers *Also called Peterson American Corporation* ***(G-16580)***
Peterson Spring-Tech Pdts Ctr, Southfield *Also called Peterson American Corporation* ***(G-15673)***
Petnet Solutions Inc....865 218-2000
3601 W 13 Mile Rd Royal Oak (48073) ***(G-14567)***
Petoskey Frms Vnyrd Winery LLC....231 290-9463
3720 Atkins Rd Petoskey (49770) ***(G-13014)***
Petoskey News Review, Gaylord *Also called Northern Michigan Review Inc* ***(G-6150)***
Petoskey Plastics Inc (PA)....231 347-2602
1 Petoskey St Petoskey (49770) ***(G-13015)***

ALPHABETIC

Petoskey Plastics Inc — 231 347-2602
4226 Us Hwy 31 Petoskey (49770) *(G-13016)*

Petra Electronic Mfg Inc — 616 877-1991
3440 Windquest Dr Holland (49424) *(G-8165)*

Petroleum Resources Inc (PA) — 586 752-7856
134 W Saint Clair St Romeo (48065) *(G-14232)*

Petronis Industries, Wixom *Also called Squires Industries Inc* *(G-18756)*

Pets Supplys Plus, Grand Rapids *Also called Sk Enterprises Inc* *(G-7201)*

Petschke Manufacturing Company — 586 463-0841
187 Hubbard St Mount Clemens (48043) *(G-11652)*

Petter Investments Inc — 269 637-1997
233 Veterans Blvd South Haven (49090) *(G-15411)*

Pettibone Parts and Mch Svc, Baraga *Also called Pettibone/Traverse Lift LLC* *(G-1147)*

Pettibone/Traverse Lift LLC (HQ) — 906 353-4800
1100 S Superior Ave Baraga (49908) *(G-1147)*

Petty Machine & Tool Inc — 517 782-9355
4035 Morrill Rd Jackson (49201) *(G-8985)*

Petzpaws LLC — 313 414-9894
4448 Rolling Pine Dr West Bloomfield (48323) *(G-18304)*

PEWABIC POTTERY, Detroit *Also called Pewabic Society Inc* *(G-4522)*

Pewabic Society Inc — 313 626-2000
10125 E Jefferson Ave Detroit (48214) *(G-4522)*

Pezco Industries Inc — 248 589-1140
380 E Mandoline Ave Madison Heights (48071) *(G-10798)*

Pfb Manufacturing LLC — 517 486-4844
9012 E Us Highway 223 Blissfield (49228) *(G-1773)*

Pfg Enterprises Inc (PA) — 586 755-1053
50271 E Rssell Smith Blvd Chesterfield (48051) *(G-2924)*

Pfizer Inc — 248 867-9067
7064 Oak Meadows Dr Clarkston (48348) *(G-3055)*

Pfizer Inc — 734 679-7368
18141 Meridian Rd Grosse Ile (48138) *(G-7525)*

Pfizer Inc — 734 671-9315
3495 Margarette Dr Trenton (48183) *(G-16890)*

Pfizer Inc — 269 833-5143
7171 Portage Rd Kalamazoo (49001) *(G-9292)*

Pfizer Inc — 269 833-2358
7000 Portage Rd Kalamazoo (49001) *(G-9293)*

Pfs, Taylor *Also called Precision Framing Systems Inc* *(G-16458)*

Pfs - Pnt Fnal Assmbly Systems, Southfield *Also called Durr Systems Inc* *(G-15545)*

Pft Industries, Romulus *Also called J L International Inc* *(G-14288)*

Pgf Technology Group Inc — 248 852-2800
2993 Technology Dr Rochester Hills (48309) *(G-14082)*

Pgi Holdings Inc (HQ) — 231 796-4831
115 N Michigan Ave Big Rapids (49307) *(G-1683)*

Pgi Holdings Inc — 231 937-4740
115 N Michigan Ave Big Rapids (49307) *(G-1684)*

PGI of Saugatuck Inc — 800 443-5286
413 3rd St Fennville (49408) *(G-5441)*

Pgm Products Inc — 586 757-4400
21034 Ryan Rd Warren (48091) *(G-17962)*

Pgp Corp (PA) — 313 291-7500
7925 Beech Daly Rd Taylor (48180) *(G-16457)*

Pgw, Rochester Hills *Also called Pittsburgh Glass Works LLC* *(G-14084)*

Phadia US Inc (HQ) — 269 492-1940
4169 Commercial Ave Portage (49002) *(G-13593)*

Phalanx Press — 517 213-9393
4832 W Kalamo Hwy Charlotte (48813) *(G-2764)*

Pharmaceutical Specialties LLC — 269 382-6402
1541 N 30th St Galesburg (49053) *(G-6081)*

Pharmacia & Upjohn Company LLC — 908 901-8000
7000 Portage Rd Kalamazoo (49001) *(G-9294)*

Pharmspec, Galesburg *Also called Pharmaceutical Specialties LLC* *(G-6081)*

Phase III Graphics Inc (PA) — 616 949-9290
255 Colrain St Sw Ste 1 Grand Rapids (49548) *(G-7084)*

Phelps Services — 231 942-8044
8466 N 7 Mile Rd Lake City (49651) *(G-9553)*

Phenomics Health Inc — 410 336-2404
1600 Huron Pkwy Fl 2 Ann Arbor (48109) *(G-609)*

Phenosynthesis LLC, Grand Rapids *Also called Light Speed Usa LLC* *(G-6943)*

Pherotech, Grand Rapids *Also called Contech (us) Inc* *(G-6597)*

Phg Aviation LLC — 231 526-7380
380 Franklin Park Ste 1 Harbor Springs (49740) *(G-7654)*

Phiber Printing LLC — 248 471-9435
19437 Bainbridge Ave Livonia (48152) *(G-10364)*

Phil Brown Welding Corporation — 616 784-3046
4689 8 Mile Rd Conklin (49403) *(G-3662)*

Phil Elenbaas Millwork Inc — 231 526-8399
341 Franklin Park Harbor Springs (49740) *(G-7655)*

Phil Elenbaas Millwork Inc (PA) — 616 791-1616
3000 Wilson Dr Nw Grand Rapids (49534) *(G-7085)*

Philips Automotive Ltg N Amer, Farmington Hills *Also called Philips North America LLC* *(G-5346)*

Philips Machining Company — 616 997-7777
80 Mason Dr Coopersville (49404) *(G-3695)*

Philips North America LLC — 248 553-9080
34119 W 12 Mile Rd Ste 10 Farmington Hills (48331) *(G-5346)*

Phillips Bros Screw Pdts Co — 517 882-0279
2909 S Martin Luther King Lansing (48910) *(G-9880)*

Phillips Enterprises Inc — 586 615-6208
51245 Filomena Dr Shelby Township (48315) *(G-15301)*

Phillips Service Inds Inc (PA) — 734 853-5000
1800 Landsdowne Rd Ann Arbor (48105) *(G-610)*

Phillips-Medisize LLC — 248 592-2144
5706 Stonington Ct West Bloomfield (48322) *(G-18305)*

Phoenix Cmposite Solutions LLC — 989 739-7108
5911 Mission St Oscoda (48750) *(G-12770)*

Phoenix Color, Chelsea *Also called Al Corp* *(G-2804)*

Phoenix Dental Inc — 810 750-2328
3452 W Thompson Rd Fenton (48430) *(G-5495)*

Phoenix Fixtures LLC (az) — 616 847-0895
16910 148th Ave Spring Lake (49456) *(G-15842)*

Phoenix Imaging Inc (PA) — 248 476-4200
29865 6 Mile Rd Livonia (48152) *(G-10365)*

Phoenix Imaging Machine Vision, Livonia *Also called Phoenix Imaging Inc* *(G-10365)*

Phoenix Induction Corporation — 248 486-7377
10132 Colonial Indus Dr South Lyon (48178) *(G-15453)*

Phoenix Innovate, Troy *Also called Phoenix Press Incorporated* *(G-17300)*

Phoenix Intergration Inc — 586 484-8196
26200 Town Center Dr # 150 Novi (48375) *(G-12505)*

Phoenix Operating Company Inc — 231 929-7171
4480b Mount Hope Rd Williamsburg (49690) *(G-18562)*

Phoenix Packaging, Chesterfield *Also called Anchor Bay Packaging Corp* *(G-2842)*

Phoenix Press Incorporated — 248 435-8040
1775 Bellingham Dr Troy (48083) *(G-17300)*

Phoenix Safety Systems, Troy *Also called Phoenix Wire Cloth Inc* *(G-17301)*

Phoenix Technology Svcs USA — 231 995-0100
327 E Welch Ct Ste A Traverse City (49686) *(G-16790)*

Phoenix Trailer & Body Company — 248 360-7184
4751 Juniper Dr Commerce Township (48382) *(G-3563)*

Phoenix Wire Cloth Inc — 248 585-6350
585 Stephenson Hwy Troy (48083) *(G-17301)*

Phone Guide, Petoskey *Also called Review Directories Inc* *(G-13020)*

Photo Offset Inc — 906 786-5800
109 S Lincoln Rd Escanaba (49829) *(G-5089)*

Photo Systems Inc (PA) — 734 424-9625
7200 Huron River Dr Ste B Dexter (48130) *(G-4749)*

Photo-Offset Printing, Escanaba *Also called Photo Offset Inc* *(G-5089)*

Photo-Tron Corp — 248 852-5200
1854 Star Batt Dr Rochester Hills (48309) *(G-14083)*

Photodon LLC — 847 377-1185
1517 Nthrn Star Dr Ste A Traverse City (49696) *(G-16791)*

Photographic Support Inc — 586 264-9957
6210 Product Dr Sterling Heights (48312) *(G-16126)*

Photonics Products Grou — 616 301-7800
4375 Donkers Ct Se Grand Rapids (49512) *(G-7086)*

Phototron, Rochester Hills *Also called Concept Circuits Corporation* *(G-13982)*

Physicians Compounding Phrm — 248 758-9100
1900 S Telg Rd Ste 102 Bloomfield Hills (48302) *(G-1852)*

PI Optima Inc — 616 772-2138
2734 84th Ave Zeeland (49464) *(G-19068)*

PI Optima Manufacturing LLC — 616 931-9750
2734 84th Ave Zeeland (49464) *(G-19069)*

Pic-Turn, Detroit *Also called Tri-Vision LLC* *(G-4644)*

Pick Energy Savings LLC — 248 343-8354
3625 Tara Dr Highland (48356) *(G-7898)*

Pickle Print & Marketing LLC — 231 668-4148
525 W Fourteenth St D Traverse City (49684) *(G-16792)*

Pickled Door LLC — 616 916-6836
503 S Shore Dr Caledonia (49316) *(G-2392)*

Picko Ferrum Fabricating LLC — 810 626-7086
10800 Featherly Dr Hamburg (48139) *(G-7593)*

Pico, Southfield *Also called Comau LLC* *(G-15531)*

Picpatch LLC — 248 670-2681
2488 Pearson Rd Milford (48380) *(G-11480)*

Picwood USA, Kalamazoo *Also called Picwood USA LLC* *(G-9295)*

Picwood USA LLC — 844 802-1599
2002 Charles Ave Kalamazoo (49048) *(G-9295)*

Pidc, Ann Arbor *Also called Pacific Industrial Dev Corp* *(G-604)*

Piedmont Concrete Inc — 248 474-7740
29934 W 8 Mile Rd Farmington Hills (48336) *(G-5347)*

Piedmont Heat Treating, Lansing *Also called Al-Fe Heat Treating LLC* *(G-9802)*

Pier One Polymers Incorporated — 810 326-1456
2011 Christian B Haas Dr Saint Clair (48079) *(G-14839)*

Pier Pressure Custom Boats — 231 723-0124
14051 Lakeside Ave Bear Lake (49614) *(G-1420)*

Pierburg Pump Tech US LLC — 864 688-1322
975 S Opdyke Rd Ste 100 Auburn Hills (48326) *(G-996)*

Pierburg Us LLC — 864 688-1322
975 S Opdyke Rd Ste 100 Auburn Hills (48326) *(G-997)*

Pierce Engineers Inc — 517 321-5051
5122 N Grand River Ave # 1 Lansing (48906) *(G-9727)*

Pierce Personal Defense LLC — 269 664-6960
12320 Crum Rd Plainwell (49080) *(G-13087)*

Piercetek Inc 586 757-0379
13201 Stephens Rd Warren (48089) ***(G-17963)***
Pierian Press Inc 734 434-4074
3196 Maple Dr Ypsilanti (48197) ***(G-18970)***
Pierino Frozen Foods Inc 313 928-0950
1695 Southfield Rd Lincoln Park (48146) ***(G-10053)***
Pietrzyk Foods LLC 313 614-9393
1429 Gratiot Ave Ste 109 Detroit (48207) ***(G-4523)***
Pietrzyk Pierogi, Detroit *Also called Pietrzyk Foods LLC* ***(G-4523)***
Pifers Airmotive Inc 248 674-0909
11080 Bendix Dr Goodrich (48438) ***(G-6225)***
Pigeon River Publishing LLC 616 528-4027
5566 Coral Way Haslett (48840) ***(G-7776)***
Pilkington Glass - Niles, Niles *Also called Pilkington North America Inc* ***(G-12159)***
Pilkington North America Inc 989 754-2956
1400 Weiss St Saginaw (48602) ***(G-14728)***
Pilkington North America Inc 248 542-8300
1920 Bellaire Ave Royal Oak (48067) ***(G-14568)***
Pilkington North America Inc 269 687-2100
2121 W Chicago Rd Ste E Niles (49120) ***(G-12159)***
Pillar Induction 586 254-8470
30100 Stephenson Hwy Madison Heights (48071) ***(G-10799)***
Pillar Manufacturing Inc 269 628-5605
35620 County Road 388 Gobles (49055) ***(G-6218)***
Pilz Automtn Safety Ltd Partnr (HQ) 734 354-0272
7150 Commerce Blvd Canton (48187) ***(G-2507)***
Pin Point Welding Inc 586 598-7382
50505 Metzen Dr Chesterfield (48051) ***(G-2925)***
Pinckney Automatic & Mfg 734 878-3430
6128 Cedar Lake Rd Pinckney (48169) ***(G-13053)***
Pinconning Metals Inc 989 879-3144
1140 E Cody Estey Rd Pinconning (48650) ***(G-13064)***
Pine Creek Log Home 231 848-4436
14746 Pine Lake Rd Wellston (49689) ***(G-18259)***
Pine Needle People LLC 517 242-4752
934 Clark St Ste 4 Lansing (48906) ***(G-9728)***
Pine River Inc 231 758-3400
5339 M 66 N Charlevoix (49720) ***(G-2728)***
Pine Tech Inc (PA) 989 426-0006
14941 Cleat St Plymouth (48170) ***(G-13264)***
Pingree Detroit, Detroit *Also called Pingree Mfg L3c* ***(G-4524)***
Pingree Mfg L3c 313 444-8428
15707 Livernois Ave Detroit (48238) ***(G-4524)***
Pink Diamond LLC 586 298-7863
35131 Brittany Park St Harrison Township (48045) ***(G-7715)***
Pink Pallet LLC 586 873-2982
4176 Knollwood Dr Grand Blanc (48439) ***(G-6256)***
Pink Pin Lady LLC 586 731-1532
47768 Barclay Ct Shelby Township (48317) ***(G-15302)***
Pinkney Hill Meat Co 616 897-4921
3577 Pinckney Rd Saranac (48881) ***(G-15080)***
Pinnacle Cabinet Company Inc 989 772-3866
1121 N Fancher Ave Mount Pleasant (48858) ***(G-11731)***
Pinnacle Energy LLC 248 623-6091
5071 Timber Ridge Trl Clarkston (48346) ***(G-3056)***
Pinnacle Engineering Co Inc 734 428-7039
18700 English Rd Manchester (48158) ***(G-10888)***
Pinnacle Foods Group LLC 810 724-6144
415 S Blacks Corners Rd Imlay City (48444) ***(G-8643)***
Pinnacle Mold & Machine Inc 616 892-9018
9900 Lake Michigan Dr West Olive (49460) ***(G-18350)***
Pinnacle Printing & Promotions, Redford *Also called Rar Group Inc* ***(G-13761)***
Pinnacle Technology Group 734 568-6600
7076 Schnipke Dr Ottawa Lake (49267) ***(G-12810)***
Pinnacle Tool Incorporated 616 257-2700
1150 Gezon Pkwy Sw Wyoming (49509) ***(G-18899)***
Pinsmedalscoins LLC 312 771-2973
733 Cleveland St Lansing (48906) ***(G-9729)***
Pinstripe Publishing LLC 734 276-0554
3629 Greenook Blvd Ann Arbor (48103) ***(G-611)***
Pinto Products & Company, Kalamazoo *Also called Arete Products & Mfg LLC* ***(G-9119)***
Pinto Products Inc 269 383-0015
2525 Miller Rd Kalamazoo (49001) ***(G-9296)***
Piolax Corporation 734 668-6005
47075 Five Mile Rd Plymouth (48170) ***(G-13265)***
Pioneer Automotive Inc 586 758-7730
6425 19 Mile Rd Sterling Heights (48314) ***(G-16127)***
Pioneer Broach Midwest Inc 231 768-5800
13957 Pioneer Ave Leroy (49655) ***(G-10009)***
Pioneer Cabinetry Inc 810 658-2075
301 W Rising St Ste 2 Davison (48423) ***(G-3793)***
Pioneer Die Sets, Byron Center *Also called Pioneer Steel Corporation* ***(G-2291)***
Pioneer Foundry Company Inc 517 782-9469
606 Water St Jackson (49203) ***(G-8986)***
Pioneer Group, The, Manistee *Also called Jack Batdorss* ***(G-10902)***
Pioneer Machine and Tech Inc 248 546-4451
1167 E 10 Mile Rd Madison Heights (48071) ***(G-10800)***
Pioneer Meats LLC 248 862-1988
915 E Maple Rd Birmingham (48009) ***(G-1744)***
Pioneer Metal Finishing LLC 877 721-1100
13251 Stephens Rd Warren (48089) ***(G-17964)***
Pioneer Metal Finishing LLC 734 384-9000
525 Ternes Dr Monroe (48162) ***(G-11569)***
Pioneer Metal Finishing LLC 877 721-1100
13251 Stephens Rd Warren (48089) ***(G-17965)***
Pioneer Michigan Broach Co 231 768-5800
13957 Pioneer Ave Leroy (49655) ***(G-10010)***
Pioneer Molded Products Inc 616 977-4172
5505 52nd St Se Grand Rapids (49512) ***(G-7087)***
Pioneer Molding, Warren *Also called Pioneer Plastics Inc* ***(G-17966)***
Pioneer Oil Tools Inc 989 644-6999
5179 W Weidman Rd Mount Pleasant (48858) ***(G-11732)***
Pioneer Plastics Inc 586 262-0159
35871 Mound Rd 201 Sterling Heights (48310) ***(G-16128)***
Pioneer Plastics Inc (PA) 586 262-0159
2295 Bart Ave Warren (48091) ***(G-17966)***
Pioneer Pole Buildings N Inc 989 386-2570
7400 S Clare Ave Clare (48617) ***(G-2994)***
Pioneer Press, Big Rapids *Also called Jack Batdorss* ***(G-1678)***
Pioneer Press Printing (PA) 231 864-2404
12326 Virginia St Bear Lake (49614) ***(G-1421)***
Pioneer Steel Corporation (PA) 313 933-9400
7447 Intervale St Detroit (48238) ***(G-4525)***
Pioneer Steel Corporation 616 878-5800
8700 Byron Commerce Dr Sw Byron Center (49315) ***(G-2291)***
Pioneer Surgical Tech Inc (HQ) 906 226-9909
375 River Park Cir Marquette (49855) ***(G-11041)***
Pioneer Technologies Corp 702 806-3152
7998 W 90th St Fremont (49412) ***(G-6054)***
Pipe Fabricators Inc 269 345-8657
1018 Staples Ave Kalamazoo (49007) ***(G-9297)***
Pipeline Packaging 248 743-0248
1421 Piedmont Dr Troy (48083) ***(G-17302)***
Piper Industries Inc 586 771-5100
15930 Common Rd Roseville (48066) ***(G-14463)***
Piping Components Inc 313 382-6400
4205 Oakwood Blvd Melvindale (48122) ***(G-11209)***
Piping Plover Prints 231 929-0261
817 Parsons Rd Traverse City (49686) ***(G-16793)***
Pipp MBL Stor Systems Hldg Cor 616 735-9100
2966 Wilson Dr Nw Walker (49534) ***(G-17646)***
Pippa Custom Design Printing 734 552-1598
22025 King Rd Woodhaven (48183) ***(G-18802)***
Pira International, Lansing *Also called Pira Testing LLC* ***(G-9784)***
Pira Testing LLC 517 574-4297
6539 Westland Way Ste 24 Lansing (48917) ***(G-9784)***
Piramal Pharma Solutions, Riverview *Also called LLC Ash Stevens* ***(G-13879)***
Piranha Hose Products Inc 231 779-4390
2500 Weigel St Cadillac (49601) ***(G-2348)***
Pisces Fish Machinery Inc (PA) 906 789-1636
7036 Us Highway 2 41 M35 Gladstone (49837) ***(G-6186)***
Piston Automotive LLC (HQ) 313 541-8674
12723 Telegraph Rd Ste 1 Redford (48239) ***(G-13756)***
Piston Automotive LLC 313 541-8789
4015 Michigan Ave Detroit (48210) ***(G-4526)***
Piston Automotive LLC 313 541-8789
8500 Haggerty Rd Van Buren Twp (48111) ***(G-17547)***
Piston Group LLC (PA) 248 226-3976
3000 Town Ctr Ste 3250 Southfield (48075) ***(G-15674)***
Piston Modules LLC 313 897-1540
4015 Michigan Ave Detroit (48210) ***(G-4527)***
Pitchford Bertie 517 627-1151
7821 W Grand River Hwy Grand Ledge (48837) ***(G-6397)***
Pitchfords Auto Parts & Svc, Grand Ledge *Also called Pitchford Bertie* ***(G-6397)***
Pitney Bowes Inc 203 356-5000
23594 Prescott Ln W South Lyon (48178) ***(G-15454)***
Pitney Bowes Inc 517 393-4101
1545 Keystone Ave Lansing (48911) ***(G-9881)***
Pitney Bowes Inc 616 285-9590
4460 44th St Se Ste D Grand Rapids (49512) ***(G-7088)***
Pitss America LLC 248 740-0935
570 Kirts Blvd Ste 207 Troy (48084) ***(G-17303)***
Pitstop Engineering, Livonia *Also called Carlson Technology Inc* ***(G-10147)***
Pittsburgh Glass Works LLC 248 371-1700
3255 W Hamlin Rd Rochester Hills (48309) ***(G-14084)***
Pittsburgh Glass Works LLC 734 727-5001
1515 S Newburgh Rd Unit B Westland (48186) ***(G-18405)***
Pittsfield of Indiana, Ann Arbor *Also called Pittsfield Products Inc* ***(G-612)***
Pittsfield Products Inc (PA) 734 665-3771
5741 Jackson Rd Ann Arbor (48103) ***(G-612)***
Pivot Materials LLC 248 982-7970
1741 Chief Okemos Cir Okemos (48864) ***(G-12681)***
Piwarski Brothers Logging Inc 906 265-2914
941 Gibbs City Rd Iron River (49935) ***(G-8752)***
Pixel Rush Printing 248 231-4642
264 Gibson St South Lyon (48178) ***(G-15455)***
Pizza Crust Company Inc 517 482-3368
728 E Cesar E Chavez Ave Lansing (48906) ***(G-9730)***

ALPHABETIC

Pk Fabricating Inc 248 398-4500
1975 Hilton Rd Ferndale (48220) ***(G-5578)***

Pk Global Logistics, Pontiac *Also called Manta Group LLC* ***(G-13395)***

Pkc Group, Farmington Hills *Also called Aees Inc* ***(G-5159)***

Pkc Group USA Inc (HQ) 248 489-4700
36555 Corp Dr Ste 300 Farmington Hills (48331) ***(G-5348)***

PL Schmitt Crbide Toling LLC 517 522-6891
133 Drake St Grass Lake (49240) ***(G-7444)***

Plainview Industries LLC 517 652-1466
416 N Washington St Charlotte (48813) ***(G-2765)***

Plainwell Ice Cream Co 269 685-8586
621 E Bridge St Plainwell (49080) ***(G-13088)***

Plamondon Oil Co Inc 231 256-9261
525 W Main St Lake Leelanau (49653) ***(G-9564)***

Plamondons Welding/Fab LLC 231 632-0406
10200 E Cherry Bend Rd Traverse City (49684) ***(G-16794)***

Planet Neon, Wixom *Also called Harmon Sign Inc* ***(G-18676)***

Planewave Instruments Inc 310 639-1662
1375 N Main St Ste 1 Adrian (49221) ***(G-87)***

Planning & Zoning Center Inc 517 886-0555
715 N Cedar St Ste 2 Lansing (48906) ***(G-9731)***

Planning & Zoning News, Lansing *Also called Planning & Zoning Center Inc* ***(G-9731)***

Plant 1, Portage *Also called Summit Polymers Inc* ***(G-13624)***

Plant 2, Shelby Township *Also called Schwab Industries Inc* ***(G-15325)***

Plant 2, Chesterfield *Also called Prototech Laser Inc* ***(G-2933)***

Plant 2, Mendon *Also called Th Plastics Inc* ***(G-11223)***

Plant 4, Blissfield *Also called L & W Inc* ***(G-1767)***

Plant Df 734 397-0397
41133 Van Born Rd Ste 205 Van Buren Twp (48111) ***(G-17548)***

Plant Products, Detroit *Also called Mgs Horticultural USA Inc* ***(G-4442)***

Plantet Dogs, Birmingham *Also called On Base Food Group LLC* ***(G-1742)***

Plas-Labs Incorporated 517 372-7178
401 E North St Ste 1 Lansing (48906) ***(G-9732)***

Plas-TEC Inc 248 853-7777
1926 Northfield Dr Rochester Hills (48309) ***(G-14085)***

Plas-Tech Mold and Design Inc 269 225-1223
946 Industrial Pkwy Plainwell (49080) ***(G-13089)***

Plasan Carbon Composites Inc 616 965-9450
47000 Liberty Dr Wixom (48393) ***(G-18730)***

Plasan Carbon Composites Inc (HQ) 616 965-9450
3195 Wilson Dr Nw Walker (49534) ***(G-17647)***

Plasan North America Inc 616 559-0032
3195 Wilson Dr Nw Walker (49534) ***(G-17648)***

Plasan Us Inc (PA) 616 559-0032
3195 Wilson Dr Nw Walker (49534) ***(G-17649)***

Plascon 231 421-3119
250 E Front St Ste 317 Traverse City (49684) ***(G-16795)***

Plascon Inc 231 935-1580
2375 Traversefield Dr Traverse City (49686) ***(G-16796)***

Plascon Films Inc 231 935-1580
2375 Traversefield Dr Traverse City (49686) ***(G-16797)***

Plascore Inc 616 772-1220
581 E Roosevelt Ave Zeeland (49464) ***(G-19070)***

Plascore Inc 616 772-1220
500a E Roosevelt Ave Zeeland (49464) ***(G-19071)***

Plasma Biolife Services L P 616 667-0264
6331 Kenowa Ave Sw Grandville (49418) ***(G-7409)***

Plasma-Tec Inc 616 455-2593
455 Douglas Ave Holland (49424) ***(G-8166)***

Plason Scraping Co Inc 248 588-7280
32825 Dequindre Rd Madison Heights (48071) ***(G-10801)***

Plasport Inc 231 935-1580
2375 Traversefield Dr Traverse City (49686) ***(G-16798)***

Plast-O-Foam LLC 586 307-3790
24601 Capital Blvd Clinton Township (48036) ***(G-3319)***

Plastatech Engineering Ltd (PA) 989 754-6500
725 E Morley Dr Saginaw (48601) ***(G-14729)***

Plastech, Detroit *Also called Yanfeng US Auto Intr Systems I* ***(G-4697)***

Plastechs of Michigan LLC 734 429-3129
1270 Barnes Ct Saline (48176) ***(G-15031)***

Plasteel Corporation 313 562-5400
26970 Princeton St Inkster (48141) ***(G-8670)***

Plastgage Cstm Fabrication LLC 517 817-0719
250 W Monroe St Jackson (49202) ***(G-8987)***

Plasti - Paint Inc (PA) 989 285-2280
801 Woodside Dr Saint Louis (48880) ***(G-14995)***

Plasti-Co Equipment Co, Wixom *Also called Limbright Consulting Inc* ***(G-18699)***

Plasti-Fab Inc 248 543-1415
2305 Hilton Rd Ferndale (48220) ***(G-5579)***

Plastic Dress-Up Service Inc 586 727-7878
2735 20th St Port Huron (48060) ***(G-13517)***

Plastic Engrg Tchncal Svcs Inc 248 373-0800
4141 Luella Ln Auburn Hills (48326) ***(G-998)***

Plastic Mold Technology Inc (PA) 616 698-9810
4201 Broadmoor Ave Se Kentwood (49512) ***(G-9469)***

Plastic Mold Technology Inc 616 698-9810
3870 Model Ct Se Grand Rapids (49512) ***(G-7089)***

Plastic Molding Development 586 739-4500
42400 Yearego Dr Sterling Heights (48314) ***(G-16129)***

Plastic Omnium Inc 248 458-0772
2710 Bellingham Dr # 400 Troy (48083) ***(G-17304)***

Plastic Omnium Auto Inrgy USA 248 743-5700
2585 W Maple Rd Troy (48084) ***(G-17305)***

Plastic Omnium Auto Inrgy USA 734 753-1350
36000 Bruelle Ave New Boston (48164) ***(G-12018)***

Plastic Omnium Auto Inrgy USA (HQ) 248 743-5700
2710 Bellingham Dr Troy (48083) ***(G-17306)***

Plastic Omnium Auto Inrgy USA 517 265-1100
1549 W Beecher Rd Adrian (49221) ***(G-88)***

Plastic Plaque Inc 810 982-9591
1635 Poplar St Port Huron (48060) ***(G-13518)***

Plastic Plate LLC (HQ) 616 455-5240
3500 Raleigh Dr Se Grand Rapids (49512) ***(G-7090)***

Plastic Plate LLC 616 698-3678
5675 Kraft Ave Se Kentwood (49512) ***(G-9470)***

Plastic Plate LLC 616 455-5288
5357 52nd St Se Ste B Grand Rapids (49512) ***(G-7091)***

Plastic Plate LLC 616 949-6570
3505 Kraft Ave Se Kentwood (49512) ***(G-9471)***

Plastic Service Centers Inc 586 307-3900
21445 Carlo Dr Clinton Township (48038) ***(G-3320)***

Plastic Solutions LLC 231 824-7350
1300 Stepke Ct Traverse City (49685) ***(G-16799)***

Plastic Tool Company American, Brighton *Also called Unified Industries Inc* ***(G-2087)***

Plastic Trends Inc 586 232-4167
56400 Mound Rd Shelby Township (48316) ***(G-15303)***

Plastic Trim Inc 937 429-1100
905 Cedar St Tawas City (48763) ***(G-16365)***

Plastic Trim International Inc 989 362-4419
905 Cedar St Tawas City (48763) ***(G-16366)***

Plastic Trim International Inc (HQ) 248 259-7468
935 Aulerich Rd East Tawas (48730) ***(G-4919)***

Plastic Trim International Inc 989 362-4419
935 Aulerich Rd East Tawas (48730) ***(G-4920)***

Plastic-Plate Inc 616 698-2030
5460 Cascade Rd Se Grand Rapids (49546) ***(G-7092)***

Plastico Industries Inc (PA) 616 304-6289
320 W Main St Carson City (48811) ***(G-2595)***

Plasticore Inc 877 573-3090
200 Renaissance Ctr # 2682 Detroit (48243) ***(G-4528)***

Plasticos Inc 586 493-1908
21445 Carlo Dr Ste B Clinton Township (48038) ***(G-3321)***

Plasticrafts Inc 313 532-1900
25675 W 8 Mile Rd Redford (48240) ***(G-13757)***

Plastics By Design Inc 269 646-3388
13300 Shannon St Marcellus (49067) ***(G-10950)***

Plastics In Paint 248 520-7177
7251 Ida Ter Waterford (48329) ***(G-18154)***

Plastics Plus Inc (PA) 800 975-8694
4237 N Atlantic Blvd Auburn Hills (48326) ***(G-999)***

Plastics Recycling Tech Inc 248 486-1449
1145 Sutton St Howell (48843) ***(G-8496)***

Plastipak Holdings Inc 209 681-9919
44564 Twyckingham Ln Canton (48187) ***(G-2508)***

Plastipak Holdings Inc (PA) 734 455-3600
41605 Ann Arbor Rd E Plymouth (48170) ***(G-13266)***

Plastipak Packaging Inc 734 326-6184
1351 N Hix Rd Westland (48185) ***(G-18406)***

Plastipak Packaging Inc 734 467-7519
36445 Van Born Rd Ste 200 Romulus (48174) ***(G-14320)***

Plastisnow LLC 414 397-1233
200 Prince St Plainwell (49080) ***(G-13090)***

Plastomer Corporation 734 464-0700
37819 Schoolcraft Rd Livonia (48150) ***(G-10366)***

Platemate, Clarklake *Also called Your Home Town USA Inc* ***(G-3010)***

Platform Computing Inc 248 359-7825
2000 Town Ctr Ste 1900 Southfield (48075) ***(G-15675)***

Platformsh Inc 734 707-9124
106 S Main St Ste 4 Brooklyn (49230) ***(G-2130)***

Plating Products Consulta 586 755-7210
27318 Dover Ave Warren (48088) ***(G-17967)***

Plating Specialties Inc (PA) 248 547-8660
1625 E 10 Mile Rd Madison Heights (48071) ***(G-10802)***

Plating Specialties Inc 248 547-8660
1675 E 10 Mile Rd Madison Heights (48071) ***(G-10803)***

Plating Systems and Tech Inc 517 783-4776
317 N Mechanic St Jackson (49201) ***(G-8988)***

Plating Technologies 586 756-1825
21225 Mullin Ave Warren (48089) ***(G-17968)***

Platt Mounts - Usa Inc 586 202-2920
100 Engelwood Dr Ste D Lake Orion (48359) ***(G-9626)***

Play Wright LLC 616 784-5437
8162 Rockford Pnes Ne Rockford (49341) ***(G-14184)***

Plead Arms LLC 248 563-1822
1093 Badder Dr Ste A Troy (48083) ***(G-17307)***

Pleasant Graphics Inc 989 773-7777
6835 Lea Pick Dr Mount Pleasant (48858) ***(G-11733)***

ALPHABETIC SECTION
Porter Steel & Welding Company

Pleasant Valley Packing LLC 517 278-2500
572 Newton Rd Coldwater (49036) ***(G-3446)***
Plesh Industries, Brighton *Also called Allor Manufacturing Inc* ***(G-1943)***
Plesh Industries Inc (PA) 716 873-4916
12534 Emerson Dr Brighton (48116) ***(G-2052)***
Plexicase Inc 616 246-6400
2431 Clyde Park Ave Sw Wyoming (49509) ***(G-18900)***
Plexus Cards 231 652-5355
382 W Barton St Newaygo (49337) ***(G-12089)***
Pliant Plastics Corp (PA) 616 844-0300
17000 Taft Rd Spring Lake (49456) ***(G-15843)***
Pliant Plastics Corp 616 844-3215
17024 Taft Rd Spring Lake (49456) ***(G-15844)***
Plow Point Brewing Co 734 562-9102
6447 Stillwater Dr Chelsea (48118) ***(G-2823)***
Plt Express Transportation LLC 248 809-3241
17348 W 12 Mile Rd Ste 20 Southfield (48076) ***(G-15676)***
Plugs To Panels Electrical LLC 248 318-5915
1471 Crest Rd Howell (48843) ***(G-8497)***
Plum Brothers LLC 734 947-8100
9350 Harrison Romulus (48174) ***(G-14321)***
Plum Creek Timber Company Inc 715 453-7952
2831 N Lincoln Rd Escanaba (49829) ***(G-5090)***
Plush Apparel Cstm Impressions, Ferndale *Also called Troy Haygood* ***(G-5589)***
Plush Products Mfg LLC 586 871-8082
3140 Nokomis Trl Clyde (48049) ***(G-3414)***
Pluskate Boarding Company 248 426-0899
33335 Grand River Ave Farmington (48336) ***(G-5144)***
Plutchak Fab 906 864-4650
N1715 Us Highway 41 Menominee (49858) ***(G-11256)***
Ply-Forms Incorporated 989 686-5681
4684 Fraser Rd Bay City (48706) ***(G-1387)***
Plymouth Brazing Inc 734 453-6274
6140 N Hix Rd Westland (48185) ***(G-18407)***
Plymouth Garage LLC 734 459-3667
33943 Plymouth Rd Livonia (48150) ***(G-10367)***
Plymouth Plating Works Inc 734 453-1560
42200 Joy Rd Plymouth (48170) ***(G-13267)***
Plymouth Technology Inc 248 537-0081
2700 Bond St Rochester Hills (48309) ***(G-14086)***
Plymouth-Canton Cmnty Crier (PA) 734 453-6900
821 Penniman Ave Plymouth (48170) ***(G-13268)***
PM Power Group Inc 906 885-7100
29639 Willow Rd White Pine (49971) ***(G-18487)***
Pmd Automotive LLC 248 732-7554
40 W Pike St Pontiac (48342) ***(G-13407)***
PME - Croswell, Warren *Also called Proper Polymers - Warren LLC* ***(G-17984)***
PMI Branded Pharmaceuticals 269 673-8451
515 Eastern Ave Allegan (49010) ***(G-179)***
Pmmco, Warren *Also called Progressive Metal Mfg Co* ***(G-17978)***
Pneumatic Feed Service, Romeo *Also called Caliber Industries LLC* ***(G-14221)***
Poco Inc 313 220-6752
4850 S Sheldon Rd Canton (48188) ***(G-2509)***
Poet Biorefining - Caro LLC 989 672-1222
1551 Empire Dr Caro (48723) ***(G-2577)***
Poetry Factory Ltd 586 296-3125
34028 James J Pompo Dr Fraser (48026) ***(G-5977)***
Pohl's Cstm Cnter Tops Cbnetry, Fowler *Also called Pohls Custom Counter Tops* ***(G-5831)***
Pohls Custom Counter Tops 989 593-2174
12185 W Colony Rd Fowler (48835) ***(G-5831)***
Point A Organization 313 971-4625
12091 Cloverlawn St Detroit (48204) ***(G-4529)***
Pointe Printing Inc 313 821-0030
1103 Balfour St Grosse Pointe Park (48230) ***(G-7558)***
Pointe Scientific, Canton *Also called Horiba Instruments Inc* ***(G-2472)***
Polaris Engineering Inc 586 296-1603
17540 15 Mile Rd Fraser (48026) ***(G-5978)***
Poligon, Holland *Also called Porter Corp* ***(G-8167)***
Polk Gas Producer LLC 734 913-2970
414 S Main St Ste 600 Ann Arbor (48104) ***(G-613)***
Pollard Brewing 734 207-3886
43636 Hanover Ct Canton (48187) ***(G-2510)***
Pollington Machine Tool Inc 231 743-2003
20669 30th Ave Marion (49665) ***(G-10976)***
Pollums Natural Resources 810 245-7268
732 S Elba Rd Lapeer (48446) ***(G-9955)***
Pollution Control Services, Kalkaska *Also called Northern A 1 Services Inc* ***(G-9399)***
Polly Products, Mulliken *Also called Alr Products Inc* ***(G-11748)***
Polsorb Sales, Sterling Heights *Also called Global Wholesale & Marketing* ***(G-16030)***
Poly Flex Products Inc (PA) 734 458-4194
23093 Commerce Dr Farmington Hills (48335) ***(G-5349)***
Poly Tech Industries Inc 248 589-9950
395 W Lincoln Ave Ste B Madison Heights (48071) ***(G-10804)***
Polycem LLC 231 799-1040
1271 Judson Rd Norton Shores (49456) ***(G-12350)***
Polymer Inc (PA) 248 353-3035
24671 Telegraph Rd Southfield (48033) ***(G-15677)***
Polymer Process Dev LLC 586 464-6400
11969 Shelby Tech Dr Shelby Township (48315) ***(G-15304)***
Polymer Products Group Inc 989 723-9510
3670 N M 52 Owosso (48867) ***(G-12851)***
Polymerica Limited Company (PA) 248 542-2000
26909 Woodward Ave Huntington Woods (48070) ***(G-8623)***
Polyply Composites LLC 616 842-6330
1540 Marion Ave Grand Haven (49417) ***(G-6344)***
Polytec Foha Inc (HQ) 586 978-9386
7020 Murthum Ave Warren (48092) ***(G-17969)***
Polytek Michigan Inc 734 782-0378
24601 Vreeland Rd Ste 2 Flat Rock (48134) ***(G-5625)***
Polytorx LLC (HQ) 734 322-2114
2300 Washtenaw Ave # 200 Ann Arbor (48104) ***(G-614)***
Polyvalve LLC 616 554-1100
4855 Broadmoor Ave Se Kentwood (49512) ***(G-9472)***
Polyworks USA Training Center 216 226-1617
41700 Gardenbrook Rd Novi (48375) ***(G-12506)***
Pomeroy Forest Products Inc 906 474-6780
9577 Ee.25 Rd Rapid River (49878) ***(G-13685)***
Poncraft Door Co Inc 248 373-6060
2005 Pontiac Rd Auburn Hills (48326) ***(G-1000)***
Pond Biologics LLC 800 527-9420
56828 Mound Rd Shelby Township (48316) ***(G-15305)***
Ponder Industrial 989 391-4575
3780 N Euclid Ave Bay City (48706) ***(G-1388)***
Ponder Industrial Incorporated 989 684-9841
287 S River Rd Bay City (48708) ***(G-1389)***
Pontiac Coil Inc (PA) 248 922-1100
5800 Moody Dr Clarkston (48348) ***(G-3057)***
Pontiac Electric Motor Works 248 332-4622
224 W Sheffield Ave Pontiac (48340) ***(G-13408)***
Pontiac Properties LLC 248 639-4360
28 N Saginaw St Pontiac (48342) ***(G-13409)***
Pontoon Rentals 906 387-2685
1330 Commercial St Munising (49862) ***(G-11753)***
Pooles Meat Processing 989 846-6348
3084 Grove Street Rd Standish (48658) ***(G-15894)***
Poor Boy Woodworks Inc 989 799-9440
3075 Shattuck Rd Saginaw (48603) ***(G-14730)***
Pop Daddy Popcorn LLC 734 550-9900
11234 Lemen Industrial Dr C Whitmore Lake (48189) ***(G-18543)***
Popcorn Press Inc 248 588-4444
32400 Edward Ave Ste A Madison Heights (48071) ***(G-10805)***
Popped Kernel 586 295-4977
14107 Silent Woods Dr Shelby Township (48315) ***(G-15306)***
Poppin Top Hat LLC 313 427-0400
1376 Broadway St Detroit (48226) ***(G-4530)***
Poppyseed Press LLC 616 450-8521
105 Oswego St Nw Grand Rapids (49504) ***(G-7093)***
Porcupine Press Inc 906 439-5111
3720 Munising St E Chatham (49816) ***(G-2778)***
Porex Technologies Corp 989 865-8200
5301 S Graham Rd Saint Charles (48655) ***(G-14807)***
Porite USA Co Ltd 248 597-9988
1295 Combermere Dr Troy (48083) ***(G-17308)***
Porky Press, Chatham *Also called Porcupine Press Inc* ***(G-2778)***
Port Austin Level & Tl Mfg Co 989 738-5291
130 Arthur St Port Austin (48467) ***(G-13428)***
Port City Castings, Norton Shores *Also called Pace Industries LLC* ***(G-12323)***
Port City Custom Plastics, Muskegon *Also called Pace Industries LLC* ***(G-11889)***
Port City Custom Plastics, Muskegon *Also called Cel Plastics Inc* ***(G-11790)***
Port City Die Cast, Muskegon *Also called Pace Industries LLC* ***(G-11888)***
Port City Industrial Finishing 231 726-4288
1867 Huizenga St Muskegon (49442) ***(G-11894)***
Port City Metal Products, Muskegon *Also called Pace Industries LLC* ***(G-11891)***
Port City Paints Mfg Inc 231 726-5911
1250 9th St Muskegon (49440) ***(G-11895)***
Port City Redi-Mix, Grand Rapids *Also called Grand Rapids Gravel Company* ***(G-6759)***
Port City Redi-Mix Co, Muskegon *Also called Grand Rapids Gravel Company* ***(G-11826)***
Port Cy Archtctral Signage LLC 231 739-3463
2350 S Getty St Muskegon (49444) ***(G-11896)***
Port Huron Building Supply Co 810 987-2666
3555 Electric Ave Port Huron (48060) ***(G-13519)***
Port Huron Medical Assoc 810 982-0100
3825 24th Ave Fort Gratiot (48059) ***(G-5823)***
Portable Factory 586 883-6843
20600 Stephens St Saint Clair Shores (48080) ***(G-14877)***
Portage Paper Co Inc 616 345-7131
401 E Alcott St Kalamazoo (49001) ***(G-9298)***
Portage Printing, Portage *Also called Metropolitan Indus Lithography* ***(G-13585)***
Portage Wire Systems Inc 231 889-4215
4853 Joseph Rd Onekama (49675) ***(G-12703)***
Portage Yacht Club, Pinckney *Also called Midwest Aquatics Group Inc* ***(G-13052)***
Portal Architects, Ann Arbor *Also called Skysync Inc* ***(G-655)***
Portenga Manufacturing Company 616 846-2691
220 5th St Ferrysburg (49409) ***(G-5604)***
Porter Corp 616 399-1963
4240 136th Ave Holland (49424) ***(G-8167)***
Porter Steel & Welding Company 231 733-4495
831 E Hovey Ave Muskegon (49444) ***(G-11897)***

ALPHABETIC

Porters Orchards Farm Market...810 636-7156
12160 Hegel Rd Goodrich (48438) *(G-6226)*
Portland Plastics Co...517 647-4115
3 Industrial Dr Portland (48875) *(G-13640)*
Pos Complete, Ferndale *Also called PC Complete Inc (G-5577)*
Posa-Cut Corporation...248 474-5620
23600 Haggerty Rd Farmington Hills (48335) *(G-5350)*
Poseidon Industries Inc...586 949-3550
25700 Dhondt Ct Chesterfield (48051) *(G-2926)*
Positech Inc...616 949-4024
4134 36th St Se Grand Rapids (49512) *(G-7094)*
Positive Tool & Engineering Co...313 532-1674
26025 W 7 Mile Rd Redford (48240) *(G-13758)*
Possibilities For Change LLC...810 333-1347
674 S Wagner Rd Ann Arbor (48103) *(G-615)*
Post Foods LLC...269 966-1000
275 Cliff St Battle Creek (49014) *(G-1281)*
Post Hardwoods Inc...269 751-2221
3544 38th St Hamilton (49419) *(G-7604)*
Post Production Solutions LLC...734 428-7000
110 Division St Ste 1 Manchester (48158) *(G-10889)*
Postal Savers, Flint *Also called Postal Savings Direct Mktg (G-5745)*
Postal Savings Direct Mktg...810 238-8866
1035 Ann Arbor St Flint (48503) *(G-5745)*
Postema Sign Co, Grand Rapids *Also called Japhil Inc (G-6862)*
Postema Signs & Graphics, Grand Rapids *Also called Mod Signs Inc (G-7017)*
Postguard, Farmington Hills *Also called Encore Commercial Products Inc (G-5233)*
Posthaste Electronics LLC...616 794-9977
1135 S Bridge St Belding (48809) *(G-1461)*
Postma Brothers Maple Syrup...906 478-3051
10702 W Ploegstra Rd Rudyard (49780) *(G-14594)*
PostNet, Jackson *Also called Jlc Print and Ship Inc (G-8921)*
Powco Inc...269 646-5385
56165 Moorlag Rd Marcellus (49067) *(G-10951)*
Powder Coating Services, Greenville *Also called P C S Companies Inc (G-7504)*
Powder Cote II Inc (PA)...586 463-7040
50 N Rose St Mount Clemens (48043) *(G-11653)*
Powder Cote II Inc...586 463-7040
60 N Rose St Mount Clemens (48043) *(G-11654)*
Powder It Inc...586 949-0395
46070 Edgewater St Chesterfield (48047) *(G-2927)*
Powell Fabrication & Mfg LLC...989 681-2158
740 E Monroe Rd Saint Louis (48880) *(G-14996)*
Power Capes...313 454-1492
34029 Schoolcraft Rd Livonia (48150) *(G-10368)*
Power Cleaning Systems Inc...248 347-7727
28294 Beck Rd Wixom (48393) *(G-18731)*
Power Cleaning Systems Inc...248 347-7727
46085 Grand River Ave Novi (48374) *(G-12507)*
Power Components, Plymouth *Also called Dadco Inc (G-13151)*
Power Control Systems Inc...517 339-1442
2861 Jolly Rd Ste C Okemos (48864) *(G-12682)*
Power Controllers LLC...248 888-9896
23900 Freeway Park Dr Farmington Hills (48335) *(G-5351)*
Power Cool Systems Inc...317 852-4193
2111 Euler Rd Brighton (48114) *(G-2053)*
Power Industries Corp...586 783-3818
41901 Irwin Dr Harrison Township (48045) *(G-7716)*
Power Manufacturing, Holland *Also called New 11 Inc (G-8153)*
Power Marine LLC...586 344-1192
38303 Mast St Harrison Township (48045) *(G-7717)*
Power Precision Industries Inc...586 997-0600
43545 Utica Rd Sterling Heights (48314) *(G-16130)*
Power Process Engrg Co Inc...248 473-8450
24300 Catherne Ind Dr # 403 Novi (48375) *(G-12508)*
Power Process Piping Inc (PA)...734 451-0130
45780 Port St Plymouth (48170) *(G-13269)*
Power Property Solutions LLC...734 306-0299
34516 John St Wayne (48184) *(G-18232)*
Power Rank Inc...650 387-2336
2390 Adare Rd Ann Arbor (48104) *(G-616)*
Power Solutions International, Madison Heights *Also called Powertrain Integration LLC (G-10806)*
Power Sports Ann Arbor LLC...734 585-3300
4405 Jackson Rd Ann Arbor (48103) *(G-617)*
Power Wheels Pro...248 686-2035
4895 Highland Rd Ste D Waterford (48328) *(G-18155)*
Power Without Wires, Detroit *Also called Creative Power Systems Inc (G-4108)*
Power-Brite of Michigan Inc...734 591-7911
12053 Levan Rd Livonia (48150) *(G-10369)*
Powerlase Photonics Inc...248 305-2963
26800 Meadowbrook Rd # 113 Novi (48377) *(G-12509)*
Powermat Inc...616 259-4867
2885 Sanford Ave Sw # 40939 Grandville (49418) *(G-7410)*
Powers Printing, Powers *Also called Ogden Newspapers Inc (G-13649)*
Powerscreen of Michigan LLC...586 690-7224
36639 Groesbeck Hwy Clinton Township (48035) *(G-3322)*
Powerscreen USA LLC...989 288-3121
212 S Oak St Durand (48429) *(G-4845)*
Powerstroke Printing...734 740-7616
3019 S Wayne Rd Wayne (48184) *(G-18233)*
Powerthru Inc...734 583-5004
11825 Mayfield St Livonia (48150) *(G-10370)*
Powerthru Inc...734 853-5004
11825 Mayfield St Livonia (48150) *(G-10371)*
Powertrain Integration LLC...248 577-0010
32505 Industrial Dr Madison Heights (48071) *(G-10806)*
Powertran Corporation...248 399-4300
1605 Bonner St Ferndale (48220) *(G-5580)*
Ppc Design, Novi *Also called Programmed Products Corp (G-12517)*
PPG 5622, Novi *Also called PPG Industries Inc (G-12510)*
PPG 5624, Shelby Township *Also called PPG Industries Inc (G-15307)*
PPG 5625, Southfield *Also called PPG Industries Inc (G-15678)*
PPG 5628, Warren *Also called PPG Industries Inc (G-17970)*
PPG 5629, Waterford *Also called PPG Industries Inc (G-18156)*
PPG 5637, Clarkston *Also called PPG Industries Inc (G-3058)*
PPG 9356, Jackson *Also called PPG Industries Inc (G-8989)*
PPG Automotive, Flint *Also called PPG Industries Inc (G-5746)*
PPG Coating Services, Troy *Also called Crown Group Co (G-17035)*
PPG Industrial Coatings...616 844-4391
14295 172nd Ave Grand Haven (49417) *(G-6345)*
PPG Industries Inc...248 640-4174
54197 Myrica Dr Macomb (48042) *(G-10626)*
PPG Industries Inc...833 279-7021
1224 E Pontaluna Rd Norton Shores (49456) *(G-12351)*
PPG Industries Inc...810 767-8030
3601 James P Cole Blvd Flint (48505) *(G-5746)*
PPG Industries Inc...616 846-4400
1855 Industrial Park Dr Grand Haven (49417) *(G-6346)*
PPG Industries Inc...248 625-7282
5860 Sashabaw Rd Clarkston (48346) *(G-3058)*
PPG Industries Inc...517 784-6138
167 W North St Jackson (49202) *(G-8989)*
PPG Industries Inc...248 478-1300
40400 Grand River Ave C Novi (48375) *(G-12510)*
PPG Industries Inc...586 566-3789
13651 23 Mile Rd Shelby Township (48315) *(G-15307)*
PPG Industries Inc...248 357-4817
23361 Telegraph Rd Southfield (48033) *(G-15678)*
PPG Industries Inc...734 287-2110
23361 Telegraph Rd Southfield (48033) *(G-15679)*
PPG Industries Inc...586 755-2011
13344 E 11 Mile Rd Warren (48089) *(G-17970)*
PPG Industries Inc...248 683-8052
497 Elizabeth Lake Rd Waterford (48328) *(G-18156)*
PPG Industries Inc...248 641-2000
5875 New King Ct Troy (48098) *(G-17309)*
Ppi, Flint *Also called Premiere Packaging Inc (G-5748)*
Ppi LLC (PA)...586 772-7736
23514 Groesbeck Hwy Warren (48089) *(G-17971)*
Ppi Aerospace, Warren *Also called Ppi LLC (G-17971)*
PR Plastic Welding Service...734 355-3341
2553 Clivedon Rd Howell (48843) *(G-8498)*
PR Solo Cup Inc...517 244-2837
500 Hogsback Rd Mason (48854) *(G-11150)*
Pr39 Industries LLC...248 481-8512
2005 Pontiac Rd Auburn Hills (48326) *(G-1001)*
Pr39 Industries LLC...248 866-1445
1681 Maddy Ln Keego Harbor (48320) *(G-9422)*
PRA Company (PA)...989 846-1029
1415 W Cedar St Standish (48658) *(G-15895)*
Prab Inc (HQ)...269 382-8200
5801 E N Ave Kalamazoo (49048) *(G-9299)*
Prab Inc...269 382-8200
5801 E N Ave Kalamazoo (49048) *(G-9300)*
Prab Inc...269 343-1675
5944 E N Ave Kalamazoo (49048) *(G-9301)*
Prab and Hapman, Kalamazoo *Also called Prab Inc (G-9299)*
Practical Paper Inc...616 887-1723
98 E Division St Sparta Cedar Springs (49319) *(G-2658)*
Practical Power...866 385-2961
202 South St Rochester (48307) *(G-13922)*
Practice Management Tech...231 352-9844
541 Lake St Frankfort (49635) *(G-5879)*
Praet Tool & Engineering Inc...586 677-3800
51214 Industrial Dr Macomb (48042) *(G-10627)*
Prairie Pride Carrier, Troy *Also called Sadia Enterprises Inc (G-17340)*
Prairie Wood Products Inc...269 659-1163
506 Prairie St Sturgis (49091) *(G-16319)*
Praise Sign Company...616 439-0315
3404 Busch Dr Sw Ste F Grandville (49418) *(G-7411)*
Prakken Publications Inc...734 975-2800
2851 Boardwalk St Ann Arbor (48104) *(G-618)*
Prankster Press LLC...616 550-3099
1492 Gratiot Ave Detroit (48207) *(G-4531)*

Pratt & Whitney Autoair Inc (HQ) 517 393-4040
5640 Enterprise Dr Lansing (48911) **(G-9882)**
Pratt & Whitney Autoair Inc 517 348-1416
1781 Holloway Dr Holt (48842) **(G-8325)**
Pratt (bell Packaging) Inc 616 452-2111
2000 Beverly Ave Sw Grand Rapids (49519) **(G-7095)**
Pratt Burnerd America, Kalamazoo *Also called Clausing Industrial Inc* **(G-9145)**
Pratt Classic Container Inc 734 525-0410
32432 Capitol St Livonia (48150) **(G-10372)**
Pratt Industries Inc 269 465-7676
11365 Red Arrow Hwy Bridgman (49106) **(G-1933)**
Pratt Industries Inc 616 452-2111
2000 Beverly Ave Sw Grand Rapids (49519) **(G-7096)**
Pratt Industries Inc 734 853-3000
32432 Capitol St Livonia (48150) **(G-10373)**
Praxair, Hudsonville *Also called Linde Inc* **(G-8590)**
Praxair, Wyandotte *Also called Linde Gas & Equipment Inc* **(G-18829)**
PRC Commercial Services LLC 313 445-1760
3011 Syracuse St Dearborn (48124) **(G-3884)**
Pre-Cut Patterns 616 392-4415
26 W 6th St Holland (49423) **(G-8168)**
Preacher Industries 248 881-6590
5387 Touraine Dr White Lake (48383) **(G-18463)**
Precise Cnc Routing Inc 616 538-8608
2605 Thornwood St Sw A Grand Rapids (49519) **(G-7097)**
Precise Finishing Systems Inc (PA) 517 552-9200
1650 N Burkhart Rd Howell (48855) **(G-8499)**
Precise Machine & Tool Co 517 787-7699
2921 Wildwood Ave Ste A Jackson (49202) **(G-8990)**
Precise Machining Inc 231 937-7957
17279 Almy Rd Howard City (49329) **(G-8415)**
Precise McHining Unlimited LLC 517 524-3104
505 Spring Arbor Rd Concord (49237) **(G-3654)**
Precise Metal Components Inc 734 769-0790
91 Enterprise Dr Ste A Ann Arbor (48103) **(G-619)**
Precise Power Systems LLC 734 550-9505
10520 Plaza Dr Whitmore Lake (48189) **(G-18544)**
Precise Tool & Cutter Inc 248 684-8480
51143 Pontiac Trl Wixom (48393) **(G-18732)**
Precision Advanced Machining 586 463-3900
24400 Maplehurst Dr Clinton Township (48036) **(G-3323)**
Precision Aerospace Corp 616 243-8112
5300 Corporate Grv Grand Rapids (49512) **(G-7098)**
Precision Automotive Mch Sp 616 534-6946
2320 Chicago Dr Sw Wyoming (49519) **(G-18901)**
Precision Boring and Machine 248 371-9140
2238 E Walton Blvd Auburn Hills (48326) **(G-1002)**
Precision Castparts Corp 586 690-8659
46192 Rocker Dr Macomb (48044) **(G-10628)**
Precision Coatings Inc (PA) 248 363-8361
8120 Goldie St Commerce Township (48390) **(G-3564)**
Precision Components 248 588-5650
324 Robbins Dr Troy (48083) **(G-17310)**
Precision Controls Company 734 663-3104
107 Enterprise Dr Ann Arbor (48103) **(G-620)**
Precision Devices Inc 734 439-2462
606 County St Milan (48160) **(G-11449)**
Precision Dial Co 269 375-5601
7240 W Kl Ave Kalamazoo (49009) **(G-9302)**
Precision Die and Machine Co 810 329-2861
1400 S Carney Dr Saint Clair (48079) **(G-14840)**
Precision Die Cast Inc 586 463-1800
65 Gaffield Dr Kimball (48074) **(G-9499)**
Precision Edge Srgcal Pdts LLC 231 459-4304
1448 Lexamar Dr Boyne City (49712) **(G-1901)**
Precision Edge Srgcal Pdts LLC (PA) 906 632-5600
415 W 12th Ave Sault Sainte Marie (49783) **(G-15096)**
Precision Embroidery 248 684-1359
12632 Fleetwood Ct Milford (48380) **(G-11481)**
Precision Extraction Corp 855 420-0020
2468 Industrial Row Dr Troy (48084) **(G-17311)**
Precision Extraction Solutions, Troy *Also called Precision Extraction Corp* **(G-17311)**
Precision Finishing Co Inc 616 245-2255
1010 Chicago Dr Sw Grand Rapids (49509) **(G-7099)**
Precision Forestry 989 619-1016
4285 S County Line Rd Onaway (49765) **(G-12702)**
Precision Framing Systems Inc 704 588-6680
21001 Van Born Rd Taylor (48180) **(G-16458)**
Precision Gage, Hillsdale *Also called J & K Spratt Enterprises Inc* **(G-7938)**
Precision Global Systems, Troy *Also called P G S Inc* **(G-17294)**
Precision Guides LLC 517 536-7234
151 Factory Rd Michigan Center (49254) **(G-11295)**
Precision Heat Treating Co 269 382-4660
660 Gull Rd Kalamazoo (49007) **(G-9303)**
Precision Hone & Tool Inc 313 493-9760
13600 Evergreen Rd Detroit (48223) **(G-4532)**
Precision Honing 586 757-0304
16627 Eastland St Roseville (48066) **(G-14464)**
Precision Hrdwood Rsources Inc 734 475-0144
680 E Industrial Dr Chelsea (48118) **(G-2824)**
Precision Industries Inc 810 239-5816
3002 E Court St Flint (48506) **(G-5747)**
Precision Jig & Fixture, Rockford *Also called Peterson Jig & Fixture Inc* **(G-14183)**
Precision Jig & Fixture Inc 616 696-2595
4030 Cedar Coml Dr Ne Cedar Springs (49319) **(G-2659)**
Precision Jig Grinding Inc 989 865-7953
165 Entrepreneur Dr Saint Charles (48655) **(G-14808)**
Precision Karting Tech LLC 248 924-3272
28718 Wall St Wixom (48393) **(G-18733)**
Precision Label Inc 616 534-9935
4181 Spartan Indus Dr Sw Grandville (49418) **(G-7412)**
Precision Laser & Mfg LLC 519 733-8422
5690 18 Mile Rd Sterling Heights (48314) **(G-16131)**
Precision Machine & Engrg, Grand Rapids *Also called Premach Engineering Ltd* **(G-7101)**
Precision Machining 248 669-2660
4998 Mccarthy Dr Milford (48381) **(G-11482)**
Precision Machining Company 810 688-8674
6637 Bernie Kohler Dr North Branch (48461) **(G-12182)**
Precision Manufacturing Svcs 734 995-3505
3738 W Liberty Rd Ann Arbor (48103) **(G-621)**
Precision Masking Inc 734 848-4200
721 La Voy Rd Erie (48133) **(G-5053)**
Precision Masters Inc (PA) 248 853-0308
1985 Northfield Dr Rochester Hills (48309) **(G-14087)**
Precision Masters Inc 248 648-8071
2441 N Opdyke Rd Auburn Hills (48326) **(G-1003)**
Precision Measurement Co 734 995-0041
885 Oakdale Rd Ann Arbor (48105) **(G-622)**
Precision Metal Finishing, Jackson *Also called Classic Metal Finishing Inc* **(G-8842)**
Precision Metals Plus Inc 269 342-6330
7574 E Mich Ave Kalamazoo Kalamazoo (49048) **(G-9304)**
Precision Metrology Inspection, Flint *Also called Bobier Tool Supply Inc* **(G-5658)**
Precision Micro Mill 269 290-3603
210 Commerce St Wayland (49348) **(G-18201)**
Precision Mold Machining Svcs 586 774-2330
13143 E 9 Mile Rd Warren (48089) **(G-17972)**
Precision Mtl Hdlg Eqp LLC (HQ) 313 789-8101
26700 Princeton St Inkster (48141) **(G-8671)**
Precision Mtl Hdlg Eqp LLC 734 351-7350
36663 Van Born Rd Ste 350 Romulus (48174) **(G-14322)**
Precision Optical Mfg, Auburn Hills *Also called The Pom Group Inc* **(G-1051)**
Precision Packing Corporation 586 756-8700
2145 Centerwood Dr Warren (48091) **(G-17973)**
Precision Pallet LLC 252 943-5193
17195 Beck Rd Charlevoix (49720) **(G-2729)**
Precision Parts Holdings Inc 248 853-9010
2129 Austin Ave Rochester Hills (48309) **(G-14088)**
Precision Plastic, Saline *Also called Windsor Mold Inc* **(G-15045)**
Precision Plus 906 553-7900
6911 County 426 M.5 Rd Escanaba (49829) **(G-5091)**
Precision Poly LLC, Grand Rapids *Also called Spire Michigan Acquisition LLC* **(G-7220)**
Precision Polymer Mfg Inc 269 344-2044
3915 Ravine Rd Kalamazoo (49006) **(G-9305)**
Precision Print Label 248 853-9007
2140 Avon Industrial Dr Rochester Hills (48309) **(G-14089)**
Precision Printer Services Inc 269 384-5725
9185 Portage Indus Dr Portage (49024) **(G-13594)**
Precision Prototype & Mfg Inc 517 663-4114
500 Marilin Ave Eaton Rapids (48827) **(G-4967)**
Precision Race Services Inc 248 634-4010
16749 Dixie Hwy Ste 9 Davisburg (48350) **(G-3771)**
Precision Sealant 616 667-9447
8855 Cedar Lake Dr Jenison (49428) **(G-9066)**
Precision Speed Equipment Inc 269 651-4303
1400 W Lafayette St Sturgis (49091) **(G-16320)**
Precision Spindle Service Co 248 544-0100
836 Woodward Hts Ferndale (48220) **(G-5581)**
Precision Stamping Co Inc 517 546-5656
1244 Grand Oaks Dr Howell (48843) **(G-8500)**
Precision Threading Corp 231 627-3133
1306 Higgins Dr Cheboygan (49721) **(G-2796)**
Precision Tool Inc 517 726-1060
519 Allegan Rd Vermontville (49096) **(G-17591)**
Precision Tool & Machine Inc 989 291-3365
154 E Condensery Rd Sheridan (48884) **(G-15383)**
Precision Tool & Mold LLC 906 932-3440
620 Easy St Ironwood (49938) **(G-8770)**
Precision Tool Company Inc 231 733-0811
2839 Henry St Muskegon (49441) **(G-11898)**
Precision Torque Control Inc 989 495-9330
220 Arrow Cv Midland (48642) **(G-11403)**
Precision Welding N Fab 810 931-6853
10500 Rolston Rd Byron (48418) **(G-2256)**
Precision Wire EDM Service 616 453-4360
3180 3 Mile Rd Nw Grand Rapids (49534) **(G-7100)**
Precision Wire Forms Inc (PA) 269 279-0053
1100 W Broadway St Three Rivers (49093) **(G-16581)**
Precision Wldg & Mch Repr LLC 989 309-0699
5301 S Birch Dr Barryton (49305) **(G-1173)**

Precisioncraft Co — 586 954-9510
44395 Reynolds Dr Clinton Township (48036) *(G-3324)*

Predator Products Company — 231 799-8300
4030 Chilton Dr Norton Shores (49441) *(G-12326)*

Preferred Avionics Instrs LLC — 800 521-5130
3679 Bowen Rd Howell (48855) *(G-8501)*

Preferred Engineering, Rochester Also called CPR III Inc *(G-13897)*

Preferred Flooring MI LLC — 616 279-2162
2853 3 Mile Rd Nw Ste B Walker (49534) *(G-17650)*

Preferred Industries Inc — 810 364-4090
11 Ash Dr Kimball (48074) *(G-9500)*

Preferred Machine LLC — 616 272-6334
6673 Pine Ridge Ct Sw C Jenison (49428) *(G-9067)*

Preferred Packg Solutions Inc — 734 844-9092
27000 Wick Rd Taylor (48180) *(G-16459)*

Preferred Plastics Inc (PA) — 269 685-5873
800 E Bridge St Plainwell (49080) *(G-13091)*

Preferred Printing Inc (PA) — 269 782-5488
304 E Division St Dowagiac (49047) *(G-4793)*

Preferred Products Inc — 248 255-0200
1200 Benstein Rd Commerce Township (48390) *(G-3565)*

Preferred Screen Printing, Commerce Township Also called Preferred Products Inc *(G-3565)*

Preferred Tool & Die Co Inc — 616 784-6789
5400 West River Dr Ne Comstock Park (49321) *(G-3638)*

Preferred Welding LLC — 616 294-1068
4552 136th Ave Holland (49424) *(G-8169)*

Pregnancy Resource Center, Grand Rapids Also called Frontlines Publishing *(G-6720)*

Prehab Technologies LLC — 734 368-9983
103 E Liberty St Ste 201 Ann Arbor (48104) *(G-623)*

Prell's Sawmill, Hawks Also called Prells Saw Mill Inc *(G-7815)*

Prells Saw Mill Inc — 989 734-2939
8571 F-21 Hwy Hawks (49743) *(G-7815)*

Premach Engineering Ltd — 616 247-3750
750 Curve St Sw Grand Rapids (49503) *(G-7101)*

Premier Casing Crews Inc — 989 775-7436
5580 Venture Way Mount Pleasant (48858) *(G-11734)*

Premier Corrugated Inc — 517 629-5700
916 Burstein Dr Albion (49224) *(G-130)*

Premier Custom Trailers LLC — 877 327-0888
12394 N Us Highway 131 Schoolcraft (49087) *(G-15127)*

Premier Finishing Inc — 616 785-3070
3180 Fruit Ridge Ave Nw Grand Rapids (49544) *(G-7102)*

Premier Industries, Monroe Also called Thomas L Snarey & Assoc Inc *(G-11582)*

Premier International, Wixom Also called Ds Sales Inc *(G-18648)*

Premier Kitchen Cabinetry Inc — 248 375-0124
587 Castlebar Dr Rochester Hills (48309) *(G-14090)*

Premier Malt Products Inc — 586 443-3355
25760 Groesbeck Hwy # 103 Warren (48089) *(G-17974)*

Premier Pallet Inc — 269 483-8000
11097 Us Highway 12 White Pigeon (49099) *(G-18485)*

Premier Panel Company — 734 427-1700
12300 Merriman Rd Livonia (48150) *(G-10374)*

Premier Passivation Services — 269 432-2244
1244 Blossom Rd Colon (49040) *(G-3490)*

Premier Plastic Resins Inc — 248 766-7578
189 W Clarkston Rd Ste 14 Lake Orion (48362) *(G-9627)*

Premier Printin — 248 924-3211
28389 Beck Rd Wixom (48393) *(G-18734)*

Premier Promotions, Saint Joseph Also called Twin City Engraving Company *(G-14968)*

Premier Prototype Inc — 586 323-6114
7775 18 1/2 Mile Rd Sterling Heights (48314) *(G-16132)*

Premier Signs Plus Inc — 248 633-5598
24514 Terra Del Mar Dr Novi (48374) *(G-12511)*

Premier Tooling Systems, Grand Blanc Also called Selmuro Ltd *(G-6263)*

Premiere Packaging Inc (PA) — 810 239-7650
6220 Lehman Dr Flint (48507) *(G-5748)*

Premiere Tool & Die Cast — 269 782-3030
6146 W Main St Ste C Kalamazoo (49009) *(G-9306)*

Premium Air Systems Inc — 248 680-8800
1051 Naughton Dr Troy (48083) *(G-17312)*

Premium Machine & Tool Inc — 989 855-3326
207 Water St Lyons (48851) *(G-10565)*

Premium Sund Slutions Amer LLC (PA) — 734 259-6142
44099 Plymouth Oaks Blvd Plymouth (48170) *(G-13270)*

Prenovo, Ann Arbor Also called Prehab Technologies LLC *(G-623)*

Prepress Services, Traverse City Also called Johnson-Clark Printers Inc *(G-16730)*

Prescott Inc — 517 515-0007
2821 W Willow St Lansing (48917) *(G-9785)*

Presque Isle Newspapers Inc — 989 734-2105
104 S 3rd St Rogers City (49779) *(G-14217)*

Press On Juice — 231 409-9971
305 Knollwood Dr Traverse City (49686) *(G-16800)*

Press Play — 231 753-2841
3134 Voss Dr Traverse City (49685) *(G-16801)*

Press Play LLC — 248 802-3837
2123 Willot Rd Auburn Hills (48326) *(G-1004)*

Press Room Eqp Sls & Svc Co — 248 334-1880
244 W Sheffield Ave Pontiac (48340) *(G-13410)*

Press-Way Inc — 586 790-3324
19101 15 Mile Rd Clinton Township (48035) *(G-3325)*

Pressburg LLC — 269 873-0775
6526 N 2nd St Kalamazoo (49009) *(G-9307)*

Presscraft Papers Inc — 231 882-5505
5140 River Rd Benzonia (49616) *(G-1616)*

Pressure Releases Corporation (PA) — 616 531-8116
2035 Porter St Sw Grand Rapids (49519) *(G-7103)*

Pressure Vessel Service Inc (PA) — 313 921-1200
10900 Harper Ave Detroit (48213) *(G-4533)*

Prestige Advance, Madison Heights Also called Prestige Engrg Rsrces Tech Inc *(G-10808)*

Prestige Advanced Inc — 586 868-4000
30031 Stephenson Hwy Madison Heights (48071) *(G-10807)*

Prestige Coating Solutions — 248 402-3732
4955 Cromwell Rd Sterling Heights (48310) *(G-16133)*

Prestige Engrg Rsrces Tech Inc — 586 573-3070
30031 Stephenson Hwy Madison Heights (48071) *(G-10808)*

Prestige Engrg Rsrces Tech Inc — 586 777-1820
26155 Groesbeck Hwy Warren (48089) *(G-17975)*

Prestige Machining — 248 879-1028
5651 Houghten Dr Troy (48098) *(G-17313)*

Prestige Pet Products Inc — 248 615-1526
30410 Balewood St Southfield (48076) *(G-15680)*

Prestige Powder Coating — 616 401-0250
2811 84th St Se Caledonia (49316) *(G-2393)*

Prestige Printing Inc — 616 532-5133
4437 Eastern Ave Se Ste 1 Grand Rapids (49508) *(G-7104)*

Prestige Stamping LLC — 586 773-2700
23513 Groesbeck Hwy Warren (48089) *(G-17976)*

Prestolite Electric LLC (HQ) — 248 313-3807
30120 Hudson Dr Novi (48377) *(G-12512)*

Prestolite Electric Holding — 248 313-3807
30120 Hudson Dr Novi (48377) *(G-12513)*

Prestolite Electric Inc (HQ) — 866 463-7078
30120 Hudson Dr Novi (48377) *(G-12514)*

Prestolite International Holdg, Novi Also called Prestolite Electric Holding *(G-12513)*

Prestolite Wire LLC (HQ) — 248 355-4422
26677 W 12 Mile Rd Southfield (48034) *(G-15681)*

Prestressed Group — 313 962-9189
60 Haltiner St River Rouge (48218) *(G-13859)*

Preusser Jewelers — 616 458-1425
125 Ottawa Ave Nw Ste 195 Grand Rapids (49503) *(G-7105)*

Preyde LLC — 517 333-1600
303 W Saginaw St Ste C-3 Lansing (48933) *(G-9883)*

Prf Manufacturing USA Inc — 586 218-3055
15232 Common Rd Roseville (48066) *(G-14465)*

Price Industries LLC — 313 706-9862
3301 Lincoln St Dearborn (48124) *(G-3885)*

Price Koch Industries — 616 871-0263
5041 68th St Se Caledonia (49316) *(G-2394)*

Priceless Dtils Auto Cncrge LL — 313 701-6851
1093 Foxboro Troy (48083) *(G-17314)*

Pride Printing Inc — 906 228-8182
2847 Us Highway 41 W Marquette (49855) *(G-11042)*

Pride Source Corporation — 734 293-7200
33608 Edmonton St Farmington Hills (48335) *(G-5352)*

Pridgeon & Clay Inc (PA) — 616 241-5675
50 Cottage Grove St Sw Grand Rapids (49507) *(G-7106)*

Prima Technologies Inc — 586 759-0250
24837 Sherwood Center Line (48015) *(G-2685)*

Prima Wldg & Experimental Inc — 586 415-8873
31000 Fraser Dr Fraser (48026) *(G-5979)*

Primary Tool & Cutter Grinding — 248 588-1530
32388 Edward Ave Madison Heights (48071) *(G-10809)*

Prime Assemblies Inc — 906 875-6420
2525 Us Highway 2 Crystal Falls (49920) *(G-3744)*

Prime Cuts of Jackson LLC — 517 768-8090
1821 Horton Rd Jackson (49203) *(G-8991)*

Prime Industries Inc — 734 946-8588
12350 Universal Dr Taylor (48180) *(G-16460)*

Prime Land Farm — 989 550-6120
7442 Toppin Rd Harbor Beach (48441) *(G-7635)*

Prime Mold LLC — 586 221-2512
44645 Macomb Indus Dr Clinton Township (48036) *(G-3326)*

Prime Pdiatrics Adolescent PLC — 281 259-5785
2291 Lake Ridge Dr Grand Blanc (48439) *(G-6257)*

Prime Products Inc — 616 531-8970
2755 Remico St Sw Grand Rapids (49519) *(G-7107)*

Prime Technologies, Novi Also called Kubica Corp *(G-12459)*

Prime Wheel Corporation — 248 207-4739
6250 N Haggerty Rd Canton (48187) *(G-2511)*

Prime Wood Products Inc (PA) — 616 399-4700
308 N River Ave Holland (49424) *(G-8170)*

Primera Pathways, Zeeland Also called Primera Plastics Inc *(G-19072)*

Primera Plastics Inc (PA) — 616 748-6248
3424 Production Ct Zeeland (49464) *(G-19072)*

Primeway Inc — 248 583-6922
4250 Normandy Ct Royal Oak (48073) *(G-14569)*

Primo Crafts — 248 373-3229
1304 University Dr Pontiac (48342) *(G-13411)*

ALPHABETIC SECTION

Primo Tool & Manufacturing 231 592-5262
   20070 19 Mile Rd Big Rapids (49307) (G-1685)
Primore Inc (PA) 517 263-2220
   2300 W Beecher Rd Adrian (49221) (G-89)
Princessa Designs Inc 616 285-6868
   743 W Woodmeade Ct Se Ada (49301) (G-34)
Pringles Manufacturing Company 731 421-3148
   1 Kellogg Sq Battle Creek (49017) (G-1282)
Prins Bethesda LLC 269 903-2237
   3026 Witters Ct Portage (49024) (G-13595)
Print 4 U Promotional Prtg LLC 313 575-1080
   8211 Chatham Redford (48239) (G-13759)
Print All 586 430-4383
   69347 N Main St Richmond (48062) (G-13844)
Print and Save Now 989 352-8171
   518 E Forest St Edmore (48829) (G-4996)
Print Express Office Products, Saginaw Also called Hawk Design Inc (G-14662)
Print Haus 616 786-4030
   295 120th Ave Ste 10 Holland (49424) (G-8171)
Print House Inc 248 473-1414
   23014 Commerce Dr Farmington Hills (48335) (G-5353)
Print Julep 614 937-5114
   5345 Sunnycrest Dr West Bloomfield (48323) (G-18306)
Print Masters Inc 248 548-7100
   26039 Dequindre Rd Madison Heights (48071) (G-10810)
Print Masters Printing Co, Madison Heights Also called Print Masters Inc (G-10810)
Print Metro, Cedar Springs Also called Practical Paper Inc (G-2658)
Print Metro Inc 616 887-1723
   98 E Division St Sparta (49345) (G-15775)
Print n go 989 362-6041
   1769 E Us 23 East Tawas (48730) (G-4921)
Print Plus Inc 586 888-8000
   28324 Elmdale St Saint Clair Shores (48081) (G-14878)
Print Rapids LLC 616 202-6508
   4254 Central Pkwy Hudsonville (49426) (G-8601)
Print Room 231 489-8181
   208 W Mitchell St Ste 1 Petoskey (49770) (G-13017)
Print Shop 313 499-8444
   18000 Vernier Rd Ste 626 Harper Woods (48225) (G-7670)
Print Shop 231 347-2000
   324 Michigan St Petoskey (49770) (G-13018)
Print Shop 4u LLC 810 721-7500
   110 N Almont Ave Imlay City (48444) (G-8644)
Print Shop, The, Imlay City Also called Print Shop 4u LLC (G-8644)
Print Shop, The, Houghton Also called Litsenberger Print Shop (G-8386)
Print Shop, The, Saginaw Also called Gombar Corp (G-14655)
Print Shop, The, Clarkston Also called G G & D Inc (G-3037)
Print Shop, The, Kalkaska Also called Michael Niederpruem (G-9396)
Print Xpress 313 886-6850
   20373 Mack Ave Grosse Pointe Woods (48236) (G-7573)
Print Zone 313 278-0800
   23936 Michigan Ave Dearborn (48124) (G-3886)
Print-Tech Inc 734 996-2345
   6800 Jackson Rd Ann Arbor (48103) (G-624)
Printastic LLC 248 761-5697
   46555 Humboldt Dr Ste 200 Novi (48377) (G-12515)
Printcomm Inc (PA) 810 239-5763
   3040 S Dye Rd Flint (48507) (G-5749)
Printed Impressions Inc 248 473-5333
   32210 W 8 Mile Rd Farmington Hills (48336) (G-5354)
Printed Memories 248 388-7788
   730 Globe Rd Waterford (48328) (G-18157)
Printek Inc (PA) 269 925-3200
   3515 Lakeshore Dr Ste 1 Saint Joseph (49085) (G-14955)
Printer Ink Warehousecom LLC 269 649-5492
   109 E Prairie St Vicksburg (49097) (G-17610)
Printery Inc 616 396-4655
   79 Clover St Holland (49423) (G-8172)
Printex Printing & Graphics 269 629-0122
   8988 E D Ave Richland (49083) (G-13827)
Printing Buying Service 586 907-2011
   28108 Roy St Saint Clair Shores (48081) (G-14879)
Printing Buying Services, Saint Clair Shores Also called Printing Buying Service (G-14879)
Printing By Marc 248 355-0848
   26074 Summerdale Dr Southfield (48033) (G-15682)
Printing Centre Inc 517 694-2400
   1900 Cedar St Holt (48842) (G-8326)
Printing Consolidation Co LLC (PA) 616 233-3161
   190 Monroe Ave Nw Ste 600 Grand Rapids (49503) (G-7108)
Printing Industries of Mich 248 946-5895
   41300 Beacon Rd Novi (48375) (G-12516)
Printing King 517 367-7066
   735 E Hazel St Lansing (48912) (G-9884)
Printing Lounge The, Sault Sainte Marie Also called Dennco LLC (G-15089)
Printing Place, The, Traverse City Also called Copy Central Inc (G-16660)
Printing Plus Inc 734 482-1680
   989 James L Hart Pkwy Ypsilanti (48197) (G-18971)
Printing Productions Ink, Grand Rapids Also called Shawnieboy Enterprises Inc (G-7191)

Printing Productions Ink 616 871-9292
   4183 40th St Se Grand Rapids (49512) (G-7109)
Printing Services 269 321-9826
   7419 S Sprinkle Rd Portage (49002) (G-13596)
Printing Services Inc 734 944-1404
   1283 Industrial Dr Saline (48176) (G-15032)
Printing Systems Inc 734 946-5111
   12005 Beech Daly Rd Taylor (48180) (G-16461)
Printing Xpress AMP Promo 586 915-9043
   1755 Livernois Rd Troy (48083) (G-17315)
Printlink Shrt Run Bus Frms In 269 965-1336
   309 Fritz Keiper Blvd Battle Creek (49037) (G-1283)
Printmasters, Cadillac Also called William C Fox Enterprises Inc (G-2364)
Printmill Inc 269 382-0428
   4001 Portage St Kalamazoo (49001) (G-9308)
Printwell Acquisition Co Inc 734 941-6300
   26975 Northline Rd Taylor (48180) (G-16462)
Printwell Printing, Taylor Also called Printwell Acquisition Co Inc (G-16462)
Printxpress Inc 313 846-1644
   7120 Chase Rd Dearborn (48126) (G-3887)
Priorat Importers Corporation 248 217-4608
   815 Baldwin Ave Royal Oak (48067) (G-14570)
Priority One Emergency Inc 734 398-5900
   5755 Belleville Rd Canton (48188) (G-2512)
Priority Waste LLC 586 228-1200
   42822 Garfield Rd Clinton Township (48038) (G-3327)
Prism, Port Huron Also called Jgr Plastics LLC (G-13490)
Prism Plastics Inc (HQ) 810 292-6300
   52111 Sierra Dr Chesterfield (48047) (G-2928)
Prism Plastics Inc 810 292-6300
   50581 Sabrina Dr Shelby Township (48315) (G-15308)
Prism Printing 586 786-1250
   51168 Milano Dr Macomb (48042) (G-10629)
Prism Publications Inc 231 941-8174
   125 S Park St Ste 155 Traverse City (49684) (G-16802)
Pritech Corporation 248 488-9120
   46036 Michigan Ave # 188 Canton (48188) (G-2513)
Private Life Corp 248 922-9800
   4353 S Meadow Dr Waterford (48329) (G-18158)
Prk Holdings Inc 231 728-1155
   1485 S Getty St Muskegon (49442) (G-11899)
Pro - Tech Graphics Ltd 586 791-6363
   34851 Groesbeck Hwy Clinton Township (48035) (G-3328)
Pro ADS America 586 219-6040
   19106 Alexa Dr Walled Lake (48390) (G-17673)
Pro Body, Holland Also called Autoform Development Inc (G-7966)
Pro Coatings Inc 616 887-8808
   233 1/2 Prospect St Sparta (49345) (G-15776)
Pro Floor Service 517 663-5012
   11636 Columbia Hwy Eaton Rapids (48827) (G-4968)
Pro Gear Printing LLC 734 386-1105
   48161 Park Lane Ct Canton (48187) (G-2514)
Pro Image Design 231 322-8052
   331 W South Airport Rd Traverse City (49686) (G-16803)
Pro King Trucking Inc 909 800-7885
   3241 Doris St Detroit (48238) (G-4534)
Pro Kitchen Software, Grand Rapids Also called Real View LLC (G-7143)
Pro Lighting Group Inc 810 229-5600
   716 Advance St Ste A Brighton (48116) (G-2054)
Pro Linez of Ann Arbor 734 755-7309
   10236 Gilcyn St Temperance (48182) (G-16545)
Pro Pet L L C 248 930-2880
   2313 Garfield St Ferndale (48220) (G-5582)
Pro Polymers Inc 734 222-8820
   4974 Bird Dr Stockbridge (49285) (G-16277)
Pro Precision Inc 586 247-6160
   14178 Randall Dr Sterling Heights (48313) (G-16134)
Pro Release Inc 810 512-4120
   420 S Water St 275 Marine City (48039) (G-10964)
Pro Sealants 616 318-6067
   3683 Maplebrook Dr Nw Grand Rapids (49534) (G-7110)
Pro Shop The/P S Graphics 517 448-8490
   309 W Main St Hudson (49247) (G-8559)
Pro Shot Basketball Inc 877 968-3865
   407 Hadley St Holly (48442) (G-8286)
Pro Sign and Awning Inc 313 581-9333
   17627 W Warren Ave Detroit (48228) (G-4535)
Pro Slot Ltd 616 897-6000
   12 W Main St Hartford (49057) (G-7766)
Pro Source Manufacturing Inc 616 607-2990
   12880 N Cedar Dr Grand Haven (49417) (G-6347)
Pro Stamp Plus LLC 616 447-2988
   1988 Alpine Ave Nw Grand Rapids (49504) (G-7111)
Pro Tool & Die LLC 586 840-7040
   25777 Dhondt Ct Chesterfield (48051) (G-2929)
Pro Tool LLC 616 850-0556
   14714 Indian Trails Dr Grand Haven (49417) (G-6348)
Pro-Built Mfg 989 354-1321
   820 Long Lake Ave Alpena (49707) (G-312)

(PA)=Parent Co (HQ)=Headquarters (DH)=Div Headquarters

Pro-CAM Services LLC 616 748-4200
323 E Roosevelt Ave Zeeland (49464) ***(G-19073)***
Pro-Face America LLC (HQ) 734 477-0600
1050 Highland Dr Ste D Ann Arbor (48108) ***(G-625)***
Pro-Finish Powder Coating Inc 616 245-7550
1000 Kn O Sha Indus Dr Se Grand Rapids (49508) ***(G-7112)***
Pro-Line Doors LLC 586 765-1657
24415 Maplehurst Dr Clinton Township (48036) ***(G-3329)***
Pro-Motion Tech Group LLC 248 668-3100
29755 Beck Rd Wixom (48393) ***(G-18735)***
Pro-Powersports 734 457-0829
7779 Townway Dr Monroe (48161) ***(G-11570)***
Pro-Soil Site Services Inc 517 267-8767
3323 N East St Lansing (48906) ***(G-9733)***
Pro-Tech Group LLC 888 221-1505
21555 Melrose Ave Ste 24 Southfield (48075) ***(G-15683)***
Pro-Tech Machine Inc 810 743-1854
3085 Joyce St Burton (48529) ***(G-2243)***
Pro-Vision Solutions LLC 616 583-1520
8625 Byron Commerce Dr Sw Byron Center (49315) ***(G-2292)***
Pro-Vision Video Systems, Byron Center *Also called Pro-Vision Solutions LLC* ***(G-2292)***
Pro-Weld, Chesterfield *Also called Camryn Fabrication LLC* ***(G-2857)***
Probe-TEC 765 252-0257
48454 Harbor Dr Chesterfield (48047) ***(G-2930)***
Probus Technical Services Inc 876 226-5692
2424 Crooks Rd Apt 21 Troy (48084) ***(G-17316)***
Procal, Alpena *Also called Punching Concepts Inc* ***(G-313)***
Process Analytics Factory LLC (HQ) 929 350-4053
2000 Town Ctr Ste 1800 Southfield (48075) ***(G-15684)***
Process Partners Inc 616 875-2156
3770 Chicago Dr Hudsonville (49426) ***(G-8602)***
Process Systems Inc (HQ) 586 757-5711
23633 Pinewood St Warren (48091) ***(G-17977)***
Process Technology & Controls, Novi *Also called Venture Technology Groups Inc* ***(G-12566)***
Procolrcopy A Div Prclor Group 248 458-2040
1581 W Hamlin Rd Rochester Hills (48309) ***(G-14091)***
Procore Drones LLC 850 774-0604
19091 W Spring Lake Rd Spring Lake (49456) ***(G-15845)***
Proctor Logging Inc 231 775-3820
298 Bramblewood Cadillac (49601) ***(G-2349)***
Product and Tooling Tech Inc 586 293-1810
33957 Riviera Fraser (48026) ***(G-5980)***
Product Assembly Group LLC 586 549-8601
1080 Naughton Dr Troy (48083) ***(G-17317)***
Product Saver, Holland *Also called General Processing Systems Inc* ***(G-8046)***
Production Accessories Co 313 366-1500
123 E Golden Gate Detroit (48203) ***(G-4536)***
Production Dev Systems LLC 810 648-2111
245 Campbell Rd Sandusky (48471) ***(G-15065)***
Production Fabricators Inc 231 777-3822
1608 Creston St Muskegon (49442) ***(G-11900)***
Production Industries II Inc 231 352-7500
3535 Rennie School Rd Traverse City (49685) ***(G-16804)***
Production Machining of Alma 989 463-1495
6595 N Jerome Rd Alma (48801) ***(G-253)***
Production Saw & Machine Co 517 529-4014
9091 S Meridian Rd Clarklake (49234) ***(G-3007)***
Production Spring LLC 248 583-0036
1151 Allen Dr Troy (48083) ***(G-17318)***
Production Threaded Parts Co 810 688-3186
6829 Lincoln St North Branch (48461) ***(G-12183)***
Production Tooling Inc 269 668-6789
23650 French Rd Mattawan (49071) ***(G-11166)***
Production Tube Company Inc 313 259-3990
481 Beaufait St Detroit (48207) ***(G-4537)***
Production, Publishing, Detroit *Also called Osowet Collections Inc* ***(G-4501)***
Productivity Technologies (PA) 810 714-0200
3100 Copper Ave Fenton (48430) ***(G-5496)***
Profab, Muskegon *Also called Production Fabricators Inc* ***(G-11900)***
Proface America, Ann Arbor *Also called Pro-Face America LLC* ***(G-625)***
Professional Fabricating Inc 616 531-1240
902 47th St Sw Ste A Grand Rapids (49509) ***(G-7113)***
Professional Fabricating & Mfg, Grand Rapids *Also called Professional Fabricating Inc* ***(G-7113)***
Professional Hearing Services 517 439-1610
1231 Hudson Rd Hillsdale (49242) ***(G-7942)***
Professional Metal Finishers 616 365-2620
2474 Turner Ave Nw Ste 4 Grand Rapids (49544) ***(G-7114)***
Professional Metal Works Inc 517 351-7411
8109 Old M 78 Haslett (48840) ***(G-7777)***
Proficient Machine & Tool, Byron Center *Also called McDonald Acquisitions LLC* ***(G-2282)***
Proficient Machining Inc 616 453-9496
3455 3 Mile Rd Nw Grand Rapids (49534) ***(G-7115)***
Proficient Products Inc 586 977-8630
6283 Millett Ave Sterling Heights (48312) ***(G-16135)***
Profil System Inc 248 536-2130
5331 Dixie Hwy Waterford (48329) ***(G-18159)***
Profile Films, Grand Rapids *Also called Profile Industrial Packg Corp* ***(G-7116)***
Profile Gear Inc 810 324-2731
4777 Brott Rd North Street (48049) ***(G-12186)***
Profile Inc 517 224-8012
345 Wright Indus Pkwy Potterville (48876) ***(G-13647)***
Profile Industrial Packg Corp 616 245-7260
1976 Avastar Pkwy Nw Grand Rapids (49544) ***(G-7116)***
Profile Mfg Inc 586 598-0007
50790 Richard W Blvd Chesterfield (48051) ***(G-2931)***
Profile Steel and Wire, Waterford *Also called Penn Automotive Inc* ***(G-18150)***
Proforma, Williamston *Also called Performance Print and Mktg* ***(G-18579)***
Proforma Pltnum Prtg Prmotions 248 341-3814
143 W Tacoma St Clawson (48017) ***(G-3104)***
Programmed Products Corp 248 348-7755
44311 Grand River Ave Novi (48375) ***(G-12517)***
Progress Custom Screen Prtg, Ferndale *Also called Progress Custom Screen Prtg* ***(G-5583)***
Progress Custom Screen Prtg 248 982-4247
364 Hilton Rd Ferndale (48220) ***(G-5583)***
Progress Machine & Tool Inc 231 798-3410
1155 Judson Rd Norton Shores (49456) ***(G-12352)***
Progress Printers Inc 231 947-5311
1445 Woodmere Ave Traverse City (49686) ***(G-16805)***
Progressive Cutter Grinding Co 586 580-2367
14207 Rick Dr Shelby Township (48315) ***(G-15309)***
Progressive Dynamics Inc 269 781-4241
507 Industrial Rd Marshall (49068) ***(G-11072)***
Progressive Finishing Inc 586 949-6961
50800 E Rssell Schmidt Bl Chesterfield (48051) ***(G-2932)***
Progressive Graphics 269 945-9249
115 S Jefferson St Hastings (49058) ***(G-7806)***
Progressive Manufacturing LLC 231 924-9975
425 Connie Ave Fremont (49412) ***(G-6055)***
Progressive Metal Mfg Co (PA) 248 546-2827
3100 E 10 Mile Rd Warren (48091) ***(G-17978)***
Progressive Panel Systems Inc 616 748-1384
8095 Riley St Zeeland (49464) ***(G-19074)***
Progressive Paper Corp 269 279-6320
1111 3rd St Three Rivers (49093) ***(G-16582)***
Progressive Printing, Plymouth *Also called Kimprint Inc* ***(G-13215)***
Progressive Prtg & Graphics 269 965-8909
148 Columbia Ave E Battle Creek (49015) ***(G-1284)***
Progressive Surface Inc (PA) 616 957-0871
4695 Danvers Dr Se Grand Rapids (49512) ***(G-7117)***
Progressive Surface Inc 616 957-0871
4671 Danvers Dr Se Grand Rapids (49512) ***(G-7118)***
Project Die and Mold Inc 616 862-8689
228 Wesley St Se Grand Rapids (49548) ***(G-7119)***
Project Echo LLC (PA) 248 971-4027
1332 Anderson Rd Clawson (48017) ***(G-3105)***
Prolighting, Brighton *Also called Pro Lighting Group Inc* ***(G-2054)***
Promac North America Corp 248 817-2346
1395 Wheaton Dr Ste 200 Troy (48083) ***(G-17319)***
Promax Engineering LLC 734 979-0888
6035 E Executive Dr Westland (48185) ***(G-18408)***
Promess Inc (PA) 810 229-9334
11429 Grand River Rd Brighton (48116) ***(G-2055)***
Promess Dimensions, Brighton *Also called Promess Inc* ***(G-2055)***
Promess Incorporated 810 229-9334
11475 Grand River Rd Brighton (48116) ***(G-2056)***
Promethient Inc 231 525-0500
2382 Cass Rd Traverse City (49684) ***(G-16806)***
Promogarden.com, Holland *Also called Walters Seed Co LLC* ***(G-8241)***
Promoquip Inc 989 287-6211
223 W North St Lakeview (48850) ***(G-9645)***
Prompt Pattern, Warren *Also called Equivalent Base Co* ***(G-17795)***
Prompt Pattern Inc 586 759-2030
4175 E 10 Mile Rd Warren (48091) ***(G-17979)***
Prompt Plastics 586 307-8525
5524 E 10 Mile Rd Warren (48091) ***(G-17980)***
Prong Horn 616 456-1903
6757 Cascade Rd Se # 164 Grand Rapids (49546) ***(G-7120)***
Pronghorn Imprinting Co, Grand Rapids *Also called Prong Horn* ***(G-7120)***
Pronto Printing 586 215-9670
46755 Partridge Creek Dr Macomb (48044) ***(G-10630)***
Prontoprinting LLC 313 622-7565
17145 Plainview Ave Detroit (48219) ***(G-4538)***
Proos Manufacturing LLC 616 454-5622
2555 Oak Industrial Dr Ne Ae Grand Rapids (49505) ***(G-7121)***
Prop Art Studio Inc 313 824-2200
112 E Grand Blvd Detroit (48207) ***(G-4539)***
Proper Arospc & Machining LLC 586 779-8787
13870 E 11 Mile Rd Warren (48089) ***(G-17981)***
Proper Group International Inc 586 552-5267
14575 E 11 Mile Rd Warren (48088) ***(G-17982)***
Proper Group International LLC (PA) 586 779-8787
13870 E 11 Mile Rd Warren (48089) ***(G-17983)***
Proper Polymers, Warren *Also called Proper Group International Inc* ***(G-17982)***
Proper Polymers - Warren LLC (PA) 586 552-5267
13870 E 11 Mile Rd Warren (48089) ***(G-17984)***
Proper Polymers Pulaski, Warren *Also called Proper Polymers- Tennessee Inc* ***(G-17985)***

Proper Polymers- Tennessee Inc 586 779-8787
13870 E 11 Mile Rd Warren (48089) ***(G-17985)***
Proper Polymers-Pulaski LLC 931 371-3147
13870 E 11 Mile Rd Warren (48089) ***(G-17986)***
Proper Tooling, Warren *Also called Proper Group International LLC* ***(G-17983)***
Prophotonix Limited 586 778-1100
15935 Sturgeon St Roseville (48066) ***(G-14466)***
Propride Inc 810 695-1127
8538 Old Plank Rd Grand Blanc (48439) ***(G-6258)***
Propride Inc 810 962-0219
8137 Embury Rd Unit 7 Grand Blanc (48439) ***(G-6259)***
Proquest Outdoor Solutions Inc 734 761-4700
789 E Eisenhower Pkwy Ann Arbor (48108) ***(G-626)***
Proservice Machine Ltd 734 317-7266
10835 Telegraph Rd Erie (48133) ***(G-5054)***
Prospectors LLC 616 634-8260
5035 W Greenbrooke Dr Se # 2 Grand Rapids (49512) ***(G-7122)***
Prospectors Cold Brew Coffee, Grand Rapids *Also called Prospectors LLC* ***(G-7122)***
Prosper-Tech Machine & Tl LLC 586 727-8800
69160 Skinner Dr Richmond (48062) ***(G-13845)***
Prosthetic & Implant Dentistry 248 254-3945
31396 Northwestern Hwy Farmington Hills (48334) ***(G-5355)***
Prosthetic Center Inc 517 372-7007
7343 Dupre Ave Dimondale (48821) ***(G-4764)***
Prosys Industries Inc 734 207-3710
7666 Market Dr Canton (48187) ***(G-2515)***
Protean Electric Inc 248 504-4940
1700 Harmon Rd Ste 3 Auburn Hills (48326) ***(G-1005)***
Protean Holdings Corp (PA) 248 504-4940
1700 Harmon Rd Ste 3 Auburn Hills (48326) ***(G-1006)***
Protective Coating Associates, Bronson *Also called Hice and Summey Inc* ***(G-2116)***
Protective Land & Sea Systems, Chesterfield *Also called SL Holdings Inc* ***(G-2948)***
Protein Cheesecake Company 248 495-3258
454 Romeo Rd Unit 213 Rochester (48307) ***(G-13923)***
Protein Procurement Svcs Inc (PA) 248 738-7970
1750 S Telg Rd Ste 310 Bloomfield Hills (48302) ***(G-1853)***
Proto Crafts Inc (PA) 810 376-3665
4740 Shabbona Rd Deckerville (48427) ***(G-3956)***
Proto Gage Inc 586 978-2783
5972 Product Dr Sterling Heights (48312) ***(G-16136)***
Proto Manufacturing Inc 734 946-0974
12350 Universal Dr Taylor (48180) ***(G-16463)***
Proto Shapes Inc 517 278-3947
125 Industrial Ave Coldwater (49036) ***(G-3447)***
Proto-CAM Inc 616 454-9810
1009 Ottawa Ave Nw Grand Rapids (49503) ***(G-7123)***
Proto-Cast Inc 313 565-5400
2699 John Daly St Inkster (48141) ***(G-8672)***
Proto-Form Engineering Inc 586 727-9803
10312 Gratiot Ave Columbus (48063) ***(G-3501)***
Proto-TEC Inc 616 772-9511
260 N Church St Zeeland (49464) ***(G-19075)***
Proto-Tek Manufacturing Inc 586 772-2663
16094 Common Rd Roseville (48066) ***(G-14467)***
Protocon Rm, Sterling Heights *Also called Midway Group LLC* ***(G-16099)***
Protodesign Inc 586 739-4340
50495 Corporate Dr Ste 10 Shelby Township (48315) ***(G-15310)***
Protojet LLC 810 956-8000
17850 E 14 Mile Rd Fraser (48026) ***(G-5981)***
Protomatic Inc 734 426-3655
2125 Bishop Cir W Dexter (48130) ***(G-4750)***
Prototech Laser Inc 586 948-3032
46340 Continental Dr Chesterfield (48047) ***(G-2933)***
Prototech Laser Inc (PA) 586 598-6900
46340 Continental Dr Chesterfield (48047) ***(G-2934)***
Prototype Cast Mfg Inc (PA) 586 739-0180
51752 Danview Tech Ct Shelby Township (48315) ***(G-15311)***
Prototype Cast Mfg Inc 586 615-8524
42872 Mound Rd Sterling Heights (48314) ***(G-16137)***
Prototypes Plus Inc 269 751-7141
3537 Lincoln Rd Hamilton (49419) ***(G-7605)***
Protxs Inc (PA) 989 255-3836
7974 Parkside Ct Jenison (49428) ***(G-9068)***
Provemont Hill Vineyard 231 256-8839
150 S French Rd Lake Leelanau (49653) ***(G-9565)***
Providence Worldwide LLC 313 586-4144
39005 Webb Dr Westland (48185) ***(G-18409)***
Provision Cnc LLC 616 309-4545
1704 Kingsland Dr Byron Center (49315) ***(G-2293)***
Provisions Print LLC 248 214-1766
196 Oakmont Auburn Hills (48326) ***(G-1007)***
Prs & PIP Ftrs L 506 .... 906 789-9784
2601 N 30th St Escanaba (49829) ***(G-5092)***
Prs Judd 734 470-6162
1035 Judd Rd Saline (48176) ***(G-15033)***
Prs Manufacturing Inc 616 784-4409
3745 Dykstra Dr Nw Grand Rapids (49544) ***(G-7124)***
PS & T, Jackson *Also called Plating Systems and Tech Inc* ***(G-8988)***
Psa Courier C 810 234-8770
109 Welch Blvd Flint (48503) ***(G-5750)***
PSC Industrial Outsourcing LP 313 824-5859
515 Lycaste St Detroit (48214) ***(G-4540)***
PSI, Ann Arbor *Also called Phillips Service Inds Inc* ***(G-610)***
PSI Automotive Support Group, Sterling Heights *Also called Photographic Support Inc* ***(G-16126)***
PSI Holding Company (PA) 248 437-4174
8080 Kensington Ct Brighton (48116) ***(G-2057)***
PSI Hydraulics 734 261-4160
14492 N Sheldon Rd # 374 Plymouth (48170) ***(G-13271)***
PSI Labs 734 369-6273
3970 Varsity Dr Ann Arbor (48108) ***(G-627)***
PSI Marine Inc 989 695-2646
5690 Hackett Rd Saginaw (48603) ***(G-14731)***
PSI Repair Services Inc (HQ) 734 853-5000
11900 Mayfield St Livonia (48150) ***(G-10375)***
PSI Satellite, Alger *Also called Zk Enterprises Inc* ***(G-140)***
PSI Semicon Services, Livonia *Also called PSI Repair Services Inc* ***(G-10375)***
Pss, Plymouth *Also called Premium Sund Slutions Amer LLC* ***(G-13270)***
Pt Tech Stamping Inc 586 293-1810
33222 Groesbeck Hwy Fraser (48026) ***(G-5982)***
Pt Woody, Mount Clemens *Also called Auto-Tech Plastics Inc* ***(G-11628)***
PT&t Precise Machining LLC 517 748-9325
325 Watts Rd Jackson (49203) ***(G-8992)***
PT&t Properties, Jackson *Also called PT&t Precise Machining LLC* ***(G-8992)***
Pti Engineered Plastics Inc 586 263-5100
50900 Corporate Dr Macomb (48044) ***(G-10631)***
Pti International, Wixom *Also called Minth North America Inc* ***(G-18712)***
Pti Qlity Cntnment Sltions LLC (PA) 313 365-3999
18615 Sherwood St Detroit (48234) ***(G-4541)***
PTL Engineering Inc 810 664-2310
3333 John Conley Dr # 2 Lapeer (48446) ***(G-9956)***
Ptm-Electronics Inc 248 987-4446
39205 Country Club Dr C40 Farmington Hills (48331) ***(G-5356)***
Publishing Systems Inc 248 852-0185
3740 Warwick Dr Rochester Hills (48309) ***(G-14092)***
Publishing Xpress 248 582-1834
29777 Stephenson Hwy Madison Heights (48071) ***(G-10811)***
Puck Hogs Pro Shop Inc 419 540-1388
562 Heather Ln Grosse Pointe Woods (48236) ***(G-7574)***
Puff Baby LLC 734 620-9991
6250 Middlebelt Rd Garden City (48135) ***(G-6106)***
Pull-Buoy Inc 586 997-0900
6515 Cotter Ave Sterling Heights (48314) ***(G-16138)***
Pullman Company (HQ) 734 243-8000
1 International Dr Monroe (48161) ***(G-11571)***
Pulverdryer Usa Inc 269 552-5290
139 Vanbruggen St Galesburg (49053) ***(G-6082)***
Pummill Print Services Lc 616 785-7960
960 W Rver Ctr Dr Ne Ste Comstock Park (49321) ***(G-3639)***
Pump House 616 647-5481
2090 Celebration Dr Ne # 120 Grand Rapids (49525) ***(G-7125)***
Punati Chemical Corp 248 276-0101
1160 N Opdyke Rd Auburn Hills (48326) ***(G-1008)***
Punch Tech 810 364-4811
2701 Busha Hwy Marysville (48040) ***(G-11097)***
Punchcraft McHning Tooling LLC 586 573-4840
30500 Ryan Rd Warren (48092) ***(G-17987)***
Punching Concepts Inc 989 358-7070
3810 Us Highway 23 N Alpena (49707) ***(G-313)***
Punkin Dsign Seds Orgnlity LLC 313 347-8488
633 Burlingame St Detroit (48202) ***(G-4542)***
Punktual Printing Inc 734 664-8045
8045 N Middlebelt Rd Westland (48185) ***(G-18410)***
Pure & Simple Solutions LLC 248 398-4600
1187 Souter Dr Troy (48083) ***(G-17320)***
Pure Green Pharmaceuticals Inc 248 515-0097
4761 Tara Ct West Bloomfield (48323) ***(G-18307)***
Pure Herbs Ltd 586 446-8200
33410 Sterling Ponds Blvd Sterling Heights (48312) ***(G-16139)***
Pure Liberty Manufacturing LLC 734 224-0333
7075 Schnipke Dr Ottawa Lake (49267) ***(G-12811)***
Pure Luxe LLC 248 987-8734
22541 Maywood Ct Farmington Hills (48335) ***(G-5357)***
Pure Products International In 989 471-1104
11925 Us Highway 23 S Ossineke (49766) ***(G-12779)***
Pure Pulp Products Inc 269 385-5050
600 Plastics Pl Kalamazoo (49001) ***(G-9309)***
Pureflex Inc 616 554-1100
4855 Broadmoor Ave Se Kentwood (49512) ***(G-9473)***
Purem Novi Inc 248 778-5231
43700 Gen Mar Novi (48375) ***(G-12518)***
Purem Novi Inc (HQ) 248 994-7010
29101 Haggerty Rd Novi (48377) ***(G-12519)***
Purem Novi Inc 248 632-2731
30220 Oak Creek Dr Wixom (48393) ***(G-18736)***
Purem Novi Inc 810 225-4582
2035 Orndorf Dr Brighton (48116) ***(G-2058)***
Purescription Grade LLC 313 410-5686
5364 W Doherty Dr West Bloomfield (48323) ***(G-18308)***

ALPHABETIC

Purforms Inc 616 897-3000
   615 Chatham St Ste 1 Lowell (49331) *(G-10514)*
Purina Mills LLC 517 322-0200
   5620 Millett Hwy Lansing (48917) *(G-9786)*
Puritan Automation LLC 248 668-1114
   28389 Beck Rd Ste J2 Wixom (48393) *(G-18737)*
Puritan Magnetics Inc 248 628-3808
   533 S Lapeer Rd Ste C Oxford (48371) *(G-12908)*
Purity Cylinder Gases Inc 517 321-9555
   1035 Mak Tech Dr Ste A Lansing (48906) *(G-9734)*
Purity Foods Inc 517 448-7440
   417 S Meridian Rd Hudson (49247) *(G-8560)*
Puroclean Restoration Services, Washington Also called Marceau Enterprises Inc *(G-18085)*
Purus Candles 586 876-7800
   36346 Saint Clair Dr New Baltimore (48047) *(G-11991)*
Pushard Welding LLC 269 760-9611
   25222 Red Arrow Hwy Mattawan (49071) *(G-11167)*
Pushman Manufacturing Co Inc 810 629-9688
   1044 Grant St Fenton (48430) *(G-5497)*
Putnam Cabinetry 248 442-0118
   29233 Scotten St Farmington Hills (48336) *(G-5358)*
Putnam Machine Products Inc 517 278-2364
   35 Cecil Dr Coldwater (49036) *(G-3448)*
Puzzle Escape 313 645-6405
   18727 Grandville Ave Detroit (48219) *(G-4543)*
Puzzleman Toys, The, Saline Also called Shields Classic Toys *(G-15039)*
Pvh Corp 989 624-5575
   8925 Market Place Dr # 450 Birch Run (48415) *(G-1712)*
Pvh Corp 989 345-7939
   2990 Cook Rd Ste 104 West Branch (48661) *(G-18337)*
Pvh Corp 989 624-5651
   12245 S Beyer Rd Ste A060 Birch Run (48415) *(G-1713)*
PVS Chemicals, Detroit Also called Pressure Vessel Service Inc *(G-4533)*
Pwv Studios Ltd 616 361-5659
   1650 Broadway Ave Nw Grand Rapids (49504) *(G-7126)*
Px2 Holdings LLC 855 420-0020
   2468 Industrial Row Dr Troy (48084) *(G-17321)*
Pyper Products Corporation, Battle Creek Also called Systex Products Corporation *(G-1304)*
Pyramid Paving and Contg Co (PA) 989 895-5861
   600 N Jefferson St Bay City (48708) *(G-1390)*
Pyramid Paving Co, Bay City Also called Pyramid Paving and Contg Co *(G-1390)*
Pyrinas LLC 810 422-7535
   10574 Waterford Rd Traverse City (49684) *(G-16807)*
Pyro Service Company 248 547-2552
   25812 John R Rd Madison Heights (48071) *(G-10812)*
Pyxis Technologies LLC 734 414-0261
   45911 Port St Plymouth (48170) *(G-13272)*
Q B E, Rochester Hills Also called Quality Business Engraving *(G-14094)*
Q C I, Ann Arbor Also called Quad City Innovations LLC *(G-629)*
Q M E Inc 269 422-2137
   9070 First St Baroda (49101) *(G-1168)*
Q P S Printing, Ypsilanti Also called Printing Plus Inc *(G-18971)*
Q S I, Saint Johns Also called Quest Software LLC *(G-14913)*
Q Sage Inc 989 775-2424
   2150 Jbs Trl Mount Pleasant (48858) *(G-11735)*
Q-Photonics LLC 734 477-0133
   3830 Packard St Ste 170 Ann Arbor (48108) *(G-628)*
Qad Inc 248 324-9890
   27555 Executive Dr # 155 Farmington Hills (48331) *(G-5359)*
Qc American LLC 734 961-0300
   575 S Mansfield St Ypsilanti (48197) *(G-18972)*
Qc Tech LLC 248 597-3984
   1605 E Avis Dr Madison Heights (48071) *(G-10813)*
Qcd, Fraser Also called Quantum Custom Designs LLC *(G-5984)*
Qcq Design & Fab Inc 810 735-4033
   5887 Deerfield Indus Dr Linden (48451) *(G-10069)*
Qcr Tech, Madison Heights Also called Qc Tech LLC *(G-10813)*
Qdc Plastics, Lansing Also called Quality Dairy Company *(G-9886)*
Qe, Walker Also called Quality Edge Inc *(G-17651)*
QEd Envmtl Systems Inc (HQ) 734 995-2547
   2355 Bishop Cir W Dexter (48130) *(G-4751)*
Qfc 248 786-0272
   1134 E Big Beaver Rd Troy (48083) *(G-17322)*
Qfd Recycling 810 733-2335
   4450 Linden Creek Pkwy Flint (48507) *(G-5751)*
Qg LLC 989 496-3333
   1700 James Savage Rd Midland (48642) *(G-11404)*
Qmi Group Inc 248 589-0505
   1645 E Avis Dr Madison Heights (48071) *(G-10814)*
Qnx Software Systems 248 513-3412
   25849 Meadowbrook Rd Novi (48375) *(G-12520)*
Qp Acquisition 2 Inc 248 594-7432
   2000 Town Ctr Ste 2450 Southfield (48075) *(G-15685)*
Qpi Precast and Supply, Kalamazoo Also called Quality Precast Inc *(G-9310)*
Qps Printing, Ann Arbor Also called K & S Printing Centers Inc *(G-536)*
Qquest Corporation 313 441-0022
   5119 Highland Rd Ste 397 Waterford (48327) *(G-18160)*

Qrp Inc (PA) 989 496-2955
   94 Ashman Cir Midland (48640) *(G-11405)*
Qrp Inc 989 496-2955
   3000 James Savage Rd Midland (48642) *(G-11406)*
Qsdg Manufacturing LLC 231 941-1222
   1576 International Dr Traverse City (49686) *(G-16808)*
Qsr Outdoor Products Inc 989 354-0777
   600 W Campbell St Alpena (49707) *(G-314)*
Qsti, Coldwater Also called Quality Spring/Togo Inc *(G-3449)*
Qsv Pharma LLC 269 324-2358
   3585 Bellflower Dr Portage (49024) *(G-13597)*
Qt Glamour Collection LLC 248 605-5507
   14182 Collingham Dr Detroit (48205) *(G-4544)*
Qts, Muskegon Also called Quality Tool & Stamping Co Inc *(G-11902)*
Quad City Innovations LLC 513 200-6980
   600 S Wagner Rd Ann Arbor (48103) *(G-629)*
Quad Electronics Inc (HQ) 800 969-9220
   359 Robbins Dr Troy (48083) *(G-17323)*
Quad Precision Tool Co Inc 248 608-2400
   1763 W Hamlin Rd Rochester Hills (48309) *(G-14093)*
Quad/Graphics Inc 248 637-9950
   3250 W Big Beavr Rd # 12 Troy (48084) *(G-17324)*
Quaker Houghton Pa Inc 313 273-7374
   9100 Freeland St Detroit (48228) *(G-4545)*
Quaker Houghton Pa Inc 248 641-3231
   17177 N Laurel Park Dr # 21 Livonia (48152) *(G-10376)*
Quaker Houghton Pa Inc 248 265-7745
   5750 New King Dr 350 Troy (48098) *(G-17325)*
Quali Tone Corporation 269 426-3664
   13092 Red Arrow Hwy Sawyer (49125) *(G-15111)*
Quali Tone Pwdr Cating Sndblst, Sawyer Also called Quali Tone Corporation *(G-15111)*
Qualite Inc 517 439-4316
   215 W Mechanic St Hillsdale (49242) *(G-7943)*
Qualite Sports Lighting, Hillsdale Also called Qualite Inc *(G-7943)*
Quality Alum Acquisition LLC 734 783-0990
   14544 Telegraph Rd Ste 1 Flat Rock (48134) *(G-5626)*
Quality Alum Acquisition LLC (PA) 800 550-1667
   429 S Michigan Ave Hastings (49058) *(G-7807)*
Quality Assured Plastics Inc 269 674-3888
   1200 Crandall Pkwy Lawrence (49064) *(G-9983)*
Quality Awning Shops Inc 517 882-2491
   4512 S Martin Luther King Lansing (48910) *(G-9885)*
Quality Bending Threading Inc 313 898-5100
   5100 Stanton St Detroit (48208) *(G-4546)*
Quality Business Engraving 248 852-5123
   2167 1/2 W Avon Rd Rochester Hills (48309) *(G-14094)*
Quality Cable Assembly LLC 248 236-9915
   465 S Glaspie St Ste A Oxford (48371) *(G-12909)*
Quality Care Products LLC 734 847-3847
   7560 Lewis Ave Temperance (48182) *(G-16546)*
Quality Cavity Inc 248 344-9995
   3958 Napier Rd Canton (48187) *(G-2516)*
Quality Chaser Co Div, Romeo Also called Mc Pherson Industrial Corp *(G-14229)*
Quality Clutches Inc 734 782-0783
   3966 Dauncy Rd Flat Rock (48134) *(G-5627)*
Quality Coatings 517 294-0394
   5323 Meadowlawn Rd Fowlerville (48836) *(G-5852)*
Quality Craft Fabricators LLC 586 353-2104
   24631 Gibson Dr Warren (48089) *(G-17988)*
Quality Craft Woodworking 248 343-6358
   1711 Pinewood Milford (48381) *(G-11483)*
Quality Customs Cons LLC 313 564-9327
   4134 Spruce St Inkster (48141) *(G-8673)*
Quality Dairy Company 517 319-4302
   111 W Mount Hope Ave 3a Lansing (48910) *(G-9886)*
Quality Dairy Company 517 367-2400
   1400 S Washington Ave Lansing (48910) *(G-9887)*
Quality Decals & Signs 517 441-1200
   7340 E Nye Hwy Eaton Rapids (48827) *(G-4969)*
Quality Dial Inc 231 947-1071
   404 Hughes Dr Traverse City (49696) *(G-16809)*
Quality Door & More Inc 989 317-8314
   135 Miles Pkwy Coleman (48618) *(G-3470)*
Quality Draft Systems LLC 616 259-9852
   3876 East Paris Ave Se # 16 Grand Rapids (49512) *(G-7127)*
Quality Edge Inc (HQ) 616 735-3833
   2712 Walkent Dr Nw Walker (49544) *(G-17651)*
Quality Engineering Company 248 351-9000
   30194 S Wixom Rd Wixom (48393) *(G-18738)*
Quality Filters Inc 734 668-0211
   7215 Jackson Rd Ste 3 Ann Arbor (48103) *(G-630)*
Quality Finishing Systems 231 834-9131
   333 W 136th St Grant (49327) *(G-7431)*
Quality First Fire Alarm 810 736-4911
   4286 Pheasant Dr Flint (48506) *(G-5752)*
Quality First Systems Inc 248 922-4780
   10301 Enterprise Dr Davisburg (48350) *(G-3772)*
Quality Grinding Inc 586 293-3780
   33950 Riviera Fraser (48026) *(G-5983)*

Quality Guest Publishing Inc 616 894-1111
12920 Algoma Ave Ne Cedar Springs (49319) ***(G-2660)***
Quality Industries Inc 517 439-1591
215 W Mechanic St Hillsdale (49242) ***(G-7944)***
Quality Inspections Inc 586 323-6135
7563 19 Mile Rd Sterling Heights (48314) ***(G-16140)***
Quality Liquid Feeds Inc 616 784-2930
5715 Comstock Park Dr Nw Comstock Park (49321) ***(G-3640)***
Quality Lock & Door, Detroit *Also called Lorenzo White* ***(G-4405)***
Quality Lube Express Inc 586 421-0600
50900 Donner Rd Chesterfield (48047) ***(G-2935)***
Quality Machine & Automation 616 399-4415
184 Manufacturers Dr Holland (49424) ***(G-8173)***
Quality Metal Detectors 734 624-8462
14253 Longtin St Southgate (48195) ***(G-15756)***
Quality Metal Fabricating 616 901-5510
1324 Burke Ave Ne Grand Rapids (49505) ***(G-7128)***
Quality Metalcraft Inc (HQ) 734 261-6700
28101 Schoolcraft Rd Livonia (48150) ***(G-10377)***
Quality Metalcraft Inc 734 261-6700
12001 Farmington Rd Livonia (48150) ***(G-10378)***
Quality Model & Pattern Co 616 791-1156
2663 Elmridge Dr Nw Grand Rapids (49534) ***(G-7129)***
Quality Mold and Engineering, Baroda *Also called Q M E Inc* ***(G-1168)***
Quality Pallet Inc 231 788-5161
7220 Hall Rd Muskegon (49442) ***(G-11901)***
Quality Pallets LLC 231 825-8361
9773 S Burkett Rd Mc Bain (49657) ***(G-11186)***
Quality Pipe Products Inc 734 606-5100
17275 Huron River Dr New Boston (48164) ***(G-12019)***
Quality Precast Inc 269 342-0539
7800 Adobe Kalamazoo (49009) ***(G-9310)***
Quality Precast Con Pdts LLC 269 342-0539
3815 N Westnedge Ave Kalamazoo (49004) ***(G-9311)***
Quality Precision Inc 313 254-9141
5171 Miller Rd Dearborn (48126) ***(G-3888)***
Quality Press 248 541-0753
144 Roth Blvd Clawson (48017) ***(G-3106)***
Quality Printing & Graphics 616 949-3400
3109 Broadmoor Ave Se Grand Rapids (49512) ***(G-7130)***
Quality Sandblasting, Grandville *Also called Apex Rack and Coating Co* ***(G-7365)***
Quality Socks, Fraser *Also called Soyad Brothers Textile Corp* ***(G-5994)***
Quality Spring/Togo Inc 517 278-2391
355 Jay St Coldwater (49036) ***(G-3449)***
Quality Stainless Mfg Co 248 546-4141
1150 E 11 Mile Rd Madison Heights (48071) ***(G-10815)***
Quality Stainless MGF 248 866-6219
2820 Island Point Dr Metamora (48455) ***(G-11285)***
Quality Steel Fabg & Erct 989 672-2873
2990 E Dayton Rd Caro (48723) ***(G-2578)***
Quality Steel Products Inc 248 684-0555
4978 Technical Dr Milford (48381) ***(G-11484)***
Quality Time Components 231 947-1071
343 Hughes Dr Traverse City (49696) ***(G-16810)***
Quality Tool & Gear Inc 734 266-1500
12693 Marlin Dr Redford (48239) ***(G-13760)***
Quality Tool & Stamping Co Inc 231 733-2538
541 E Sherman Blvd Muskegon (49444) ***(G-11902)***
Quality Tool and Die LLC 248 707-0060
934 Broadacre Ave Clawson (48017) ***(G-3107)***
Quality Transparent Bag Inc (PA) 989 893-3561
110 Mcgraw St Bay City (48708) ***(G-1391)***
Quality Way Products LLC 248 634-2401
407 Hadley St Holly (48442) ***(G-8287)***
Quality Wood Products Inc 989 658-2160
3399 Bay Cy Frestville Rd Ubly (48475) ***(G-17481)***
Quanenergy Systems Inc 248 859-5587
2655 E Oakley Park Rd # 105 Commerce Township (48390) ***(G-3566)***
Quanta Containers LLC (PA) 734 282-3044
15801 Huron St Taylor (48180) ***(G-16464)***
Quantam Solutions LLC 248 395-2200
18877 W 10 Mile Rd Ste 10 Southfield (48075) ***(G-15686)***
Quantum Chemical LLC 734 429-0033
12944 Farmington Rd Livonia (48150) ***(G-10379)***
Quantum Compliance Systems 734 930-0009
2111 Golfside Rd Ste B Ypsilanti (48197) ***(G-18973)***
Quantum Composites Inc 989 922-3863
1310 S Valley Center Dr Bay City (48706) ***(G-1392)***
Quantum Custom Designs LLC 989 293-7372
33771 Groesbeck Hwy Fraser (48026) ***(G-5984)***
Quantum Data Analytics Inc 248 894-7442
1411 Pembroke Dr Rochester Hills (48307) ***(G-14095)***
Quantum Difference Corp 810 845-8765
5321 Gateway Ctr Flint (48507) ***(G-5753)***
Quantum Digital Group LLC 888 408-3199
1681 Harmon Rd Auburn Hills (48326) ***(G-1009)***
Quantum Digital Ventures LLC 248 292-5686
24680 Mound Rd Warren (48091) ***(G-17989)***
Quantum Graphics Inc 586 566-5656
50720 Corporate Dr Shelby Township (48315) ***(G-15312)***
Quantum Life LLC 248 634-2784
3013 Oak Dr Holly (48442) ***(G-8288)***
Quantum Manufacturing 248 690-9410
2990 Lapeer Rd Auburn Hills (48326) ***(G-1010)***
Quantum Mold & Engineering LLC 586 276-0100
6300 Sterling Dr N Sterling Heights (48312) ***(G-16141)***
Quantum Opus LLC 517 680-0011
22500 Devron Ct Novi (48374) ***(G-12521)***
Quantum Sails Design Group LLC (PA) 231 941-1222
1576 International Dr Traverse City (49686) ***(G-16811)***
Quantum Ventures LLC 248 325-8380
18055 Fish Lake Rd Holly (48442) ***(G-8289)***
Quantum Whatever LLC 734 546-4353
9250 Macey Rd Willis (48191) ***(G-18587)***
Quarry Ridge Stone Inc 616 827-8244
555 Ste B Sw Byron Center (49315) ***(G-2294)***
Quarrystone Inc 906 786-0343
6851 County 426 M.5 Rd Escanaba (49829) ***(G-5093)***
Quarter To 5, Sault Sainte Marie *Also called Canusa LLC* ***(G-15088)***
Quarters LLC 313 510-5555
1415 Sheridan St Plymouth (48170) ***(G-13273)***
Quarters Vending LLC 313 510-5555
3174 Old Farm Ln Commerce Township (48390) ***(G-3567)***
Quasar Industries Inc (PA) 248 844-7190
1911 Northfield Dr Rochester Hills (48309) ***(G-14096)***
Quasar Industries Inc 248 852-0300
2687 Commerce Dr Rochester Hills (48309) ***(G-14097)***
Quasar Prototype and Tool Co., Ira *Also called P T M Corporation* ***(G-8707)***
Quest - IV Incorporated 734 847-5487
7116 Summerfield Rd Lambertville (48144) ***(G-9652)***
Quest Industries Inc 810 245-4535
3309 John Conley Dr Lapeer (48446) ***(G-9957)***
Quest Precision LLC 616 288-6101
7462 Las Palmas Dr Ne Rockford (49341) ***(G-14185)***
Quest Software LLC 800 541-2593
106 W Tolles Dr Saint Johns (48879) ***(G-14913)***
Questor Partners Fund II LP (PA) 248 593-1930
101 Southfield Rd 2 Birmingham (48009) ***(G-1745)***
Questron Packaging LLC 313 657-1630
7650 W Chicago Detroit (48204) ***(G-4547)***
Questyme Usa Inc 832 912-4994
26878 Wembley Ct Farmington Hills (48331) ***(G-5360)***
Quick and Reliable Printing, Midland *Also called Qrp Inc* ***(G-11405)***
Quick Beverages, Southfield *Also called Viva Beverages LLC* ***(G-15739)***
Quick Caller, The, Saint Clair Shores *Also called Fourth Seacoast Publishing Co* ***(G-14861)***
Quick Draw Tarpaulin Systems 313 561-0554
26125 Trowbridge St Inkster (48141) ***(G-8674)***
Quick Draw Tarpaulin Systems (PA) 313 945-0766
10200 Ford Rd Dearborn (48126) ***(G-3889)***
Quick Print, Adrian *Also called Quickprint of Adrian Inc* ***(G-90)***
Quick Printing Company Inc 616 241-0506
2642 Division Ave S Grand Rapids (49507) ***(G-7131)***
Quick Reliable Printing, Midland *Also called Qrp Inc* ***(G-11406)***
Quickmitt Inc 517 849-2141
2400 E Chicago Rd Jonesville (49250) ***(G-9099)***
Quickprint of Adrian Inc 517 263-2290
142 N Main St Adrian (49221) ***(G-90)***
Quickrete, Walker *Also called Quikrete Companies LLC* ***(G-17652)***
Quicktrophy LLC 906 228-2604
446 E Crescent St Marquette (49855) ***(G-11043)***
Quiet Concepts, Oak Park *Also called PCI Industries Inc* ***(G-12637)***
Quiet Moose, Petoskey *Also called Compass Interiors LLC* ***(G-12994)***
Quigley Co 989 983-3911
8276 Mill St Vanderbilt (49795) ***(G-17575)***
Quigley Industries Inc (HQ) 248 426-8600
38880 Grand River Ave Farmington Hills (48335) ***(G-5361)***
Quigley Lumber Inc 989 257-5116
5874 Heath Rd South Branch (48761) ***(G-15397)***
Quigley Manufacturing Inc (PA) 248 426-8600
38880 Grand River Ave Farmington Hills (48335) ***(G-5362)***
Quikrete Companies LLC 616 784-5790
20 N Park St Nw Walker (49544) ***(G-17652)***
Quikrete Detroit 313 491-3500
8951 Schaefer Hwy Ste 4 Detroit (48228) ***(G-4548)***
Quikrete Gibraltar National, Holly *Also called Gibraltar National Corporation* ***(G-8274)***
Quiktap LLC 855 784-5827
702 Hall St Sw Grand Rapids (49503) ***(G-7132)***
Quinco Tool 313 353-1340
21000 Hubbell St Oak Park (48237) ***(G-12638)***
Quincy Street Inc 616 399-3330
13350 Quincy St Holland (49424) ***(G-8174)***
Quincy Woodwrights LLC (PA) 808 397-0818
408 E Montezuma Ave Houghton (49931) ***(G-8390)***
Quirkroberts Publishing Ltd 248 879-2598
6219 Seminole Dr Troy (48085) ***(G-17326)***
Quirky 3d Printing 810 247-6732
5794 Hibbard Rd Corunna (48817) ***(G-3716)***
Qwik Tool & Mfg Inc 231 739-8849
480 W Hume Ave Muskegon (49444) ***(G-11903)***

R & A Tool & Engineering Co....734 981-2000
39127 Ford Rd Westland (48185) ***(G-18411)***
R & B EDM Inc....810 714-5050
1065 Grant St Fenton (48430) ***(G-5498)***
R & B Electronics Inc (PA)....906 632-1542
1520 Industrial Park Dr Sault Sainte Marie (49783) ***(G-15097)***
R & B Industries Inc....734 462-9478
12055 Globe St Livonia (48150) ***(G-10380)***
R & B Plastics Machinery LLC....734 429-9421
1605 Woodland Dr Saline (48176) ***(G-15034)***
R & C Redi-Mix Inc....616 636-5650
11991 Elm St Sand Lake (49343) ***(G-15051)***
R & D Cnc Machining Inc....269 751-4171
3506 Lincoln Rd Hamilton (49419) ***(G-7606)***
R & D Enterprises Inc....248 349-7077
46900 Port St Plymouth (48170) ***(G-13274)***
R & D Machine and Tool Inc....231 798-8500
6059 Norton Center Dr Norton Shores (49441) ***(G-12327)***
R & D Screw Products Inc....517 546-2380
810 Fowler St Howell (48843) ***(G-8502)***
R & DS Manufacturing LLC....586 716-9900
51690 Birch St New Baltimore (48047) ***(G-11992)***
R & H Machine Products, Three Rivers *Also called Denny Grice Inc* ***(G-16570)***
R & J Manufacturing Company....248 669-2460
3200 Martin Rd Commerce Township (48390) ***(G-3568)***
R & K Woodworking....734 741-3664
413 Browning Dr Howell (48843) ***(G-8503)***
R & L Color Graphics Inc....313 345-3838
18709 Meyers Rd Detroit (48235) ***(G-4549)***
R & L Machine Products Inc....734 992-2574
15995 S Huron River Dr Romulus (48174) ***(G-14323)***
R & M Machine Inc....586 754-8447
23895 Regency Park Dr Warren (48089) ***(G-17990)***
R & M Machine Tool Inc....989 695-6601
7920 Webster Rd Freeland (48623) ***(G-6027)***
R & M Manufacturing Company....269 683-9550
2424 N 5th St Niles (49120) ***(G-12160)***
R & N Lumber....989 848-5553
1388 Caldwell Rd Mio (48647) ***(G-11515)***
R & R Broach Inc....586 779-2227
21391 Carlo Dr Clinton Township (48038) ***(G-3330)***
R & R Harwood Inc....616 669-6400
2688 Edward St Jenison (49428) ***(G-9069)***
R & R Ready-Mix Inc (PA)....989 753-3862
6050 Melbourne Rd Saginaw (48604) ***(G-14732)***
R & R Ready-Mix Inc....989 892-9313
1601 W Youngs Ditch Rd Bay City (48708) ***(G-1393)***
R & S Cutter Grind Inc....989 791-3100
2870 Universal Dr Saginaw (48603) ***(G-14733)***
R & S Propeller Inc....616 636-8202
212 S 3rd St Sand Lake (49343) ***(G-15052)***
R & S Propeller Repair, Sand Lake *Also called R & S Propeller Inc* ***(G-15052)***
R & S Tool & Die Inc....989 673-8511
545 Columbia St Ste B Caro (48723) ***(G-2579)***
R & T Tooling....586 218-7644
26725 Groveland St Roseville (48066) ***(G-14468)***
R A Miller Industries Inc (PA)....888 845-9450
14500 168th Ave Grand Haven (49417) ***(G-6349)***
R A Townsend Company....989 498-7000
2845 Mccarty Rd Saginaw (48603) ***(G-14734)***
R and J Dumpsters LLC....248 863-8579
5886 Lange Rd Howell (48843) ***(G-8504)***
R and T Sporting Clays Inc....586 215-9861
37853 Elmlane Harrison Township (48045) ***(G-7718)***
R and T West Michigan Inc....616 698-9931
6955 E Paris Indus Ct Se Caledonia (49316) ***(G-2395)***
R Andrews Pallet Co Inc....616 677-3270
1035 Comstock St Marne (49435) ***(G-10998)***
R B Christian Inc (PA)....269 963-9327
525 24th St N Battle Creek (49037) ***(G-1285)***
R B L Plastics Incorporated....313 873-8800
6040 Russell St Detroit (48211) ***(G-4550)***
R C Grinding and Tool Company....586 949-4373
49669 Leona Dr Chesterfield (48051) ***(G-2936)***
R C M S Inc....269 422-1617
10981 Hills Rd Baroda (49101) ***(G-1169)***
R C Plastics Inc....517 523-2112
4790 Hudson Rd Osseo (49266) ***(G-12776)***
R Chamberlin Woodworking....269 377-7232
229 Woodward Ave Kalamazoo (49007) ***(G-9312)***
R Concepts Incorporated....810 632-4857
10083 Bergin Rd Howell (48843) ***(G-8505)***
R Cushman & Associates Inc....248 477-9900
12623 Newburgh Rd Livonia (48150) ***(G-10381)***
R D M Enterprises Co Inc....810 985-4721
4045 Griswold Rd Port Huron (48060) ***(G-13520)***
R D Tool & Mfg, Erie *Also called Concentric Industries Inc* ***(G-5046)***
R E B Tool Inc....734 397-9116
5910 Belleville Rd Van Buren Twp (48111) ***(G-17549)***
R E Cap Inc....231 864-3959
8100 11 Mile Rd Bear Lake (49614) ***(G-1422)***
R E D Industries Inc....248 542-2211
1671 E 9 Mile Rd Hazel Park (48030) ***(G-7838)***
R E Gallaher Corp....586 725-3333
9601 Marine City Hwy Ira (48023) ***(G-8709)***
R E Glancy Inc (PA)....989 362-0997
124 W M 55 Tawas City (48763) ***(G-16367)***
R E R Software Inc....586 744-0881
345 Diversion St Ste 206 Rochester Hills (48307) ***(G-14098)***
R F M Incorporated....810 229-4567
2001 Orndorf Dr Brighton (48116) ***(G-2059)***
R G Ray Corporation....248 373-4300
2430 E Walton Blvd Auburn Hills (48326) ***(G-1011)***
R Gari Sign and Display Inc....810 355-1245
10098 Imus Rd Pinckney (48169) ***(G-13054)***
R Gari Sign Studio Inc....810 355-1245
9043 Buckhorn Ln Brighton (48116) ***(G-2060)***
R H & Company Inc....269 345-7814
4510 W Kl Ave Kalamazoo (49006) ***(G-9313)***
R H Cross Enterprises Inc....269 488-4009
6080 Corporate Ave Portage (49002) ***(G-13598)***
R H Huhtala Aggregates Inc....906 524-7758
18154 Us Highway 41 Lanse (49946) ***(G-9668)***
R H K Technology Inc....248 577-5426
1233 Chicago Rd Troy (48083) ***(G-17327)***
R H M Rubber & Manufacturing....248 624-8277
203 Bernstadt St Novi (48377) ***(G-12522)***
R House Industries LLC....616 890-7125
929 Alpine Commerce Park Grand Rapids (49544) ***(G-7133)***
R J Chemical Manufacturing LLC....810 252-8425
920 Tacoma Ct Clio (48420) ***(G-3410)***
R J Designers Inc....517 750-1990
8032 Spring Arbor Rd Spring Arbor (49283) ***(G-15797)***
R J Flood Professional Co....269 930-3608
2691 Orchard Ln Stevensville (49127) ***(G-16263)***
R J M, Jackson *Also called R J Michaels Inc* ***(G-8993)***
R J Manufacturing....810 610-0205
4196 S Irish Rd Davison (48423) ***(G-3794)***
R J Manufacturing Incorporated....906 779-9151
110 Forest Gtwy Crystal Falls (49920) ***(G-3745)***
R J Marshall Company (PA)....248 353-4100
26776 W 12 Mile Rd # 201 Southfield (48034) ***(G-15687)***
R J Michaels Inc....517 783-2637
515 S West Ave Jackson (49203) ***(G-8993)***
R J S, Birmingham *Also called R J S Tool & Gage Co* ***(G-1746)***
R J S Tool & Gage Co....248 642-8620
1081 S Eton St Birmingham (48009) ***(G-1746)***
R J Woodworking Inc....231 766-2511
3108 Whitehall Rd Muskegon (49445) ***(G-11904)***
R JS Printing Inc....773 936-7825
1001 2nd St Kalamazoo (49001) ***(G-9314)***
R K C Corporation....231 627-9131
600 Riggs Dr Cheboygan (49721) ***(G-2797)***
R K Parts, Detroit *Also called Kirks Automotive Incorporated* ***(G-4364)***
R L Adams Plastics Inc....616 261-4400
5955 Crossroads Commerce Grand Rapids (49519) ***(G-7134)***
R L Canvas....989 837-6352
3429 Rivercrest Ct Midland (48640) ***(G-11407)***
R L M Industries Inc....248 628-5103
100 Hummer Lake Rd Oxford (48371) ***(G-12910)***
R L Schmitt Company Inc....734 525-9310
34506 Glendale St Livonia (48150) ***(G-10382)***
R M I, Madison Heights *Also called Rotary Multiforms Inc* ***(G-10819)***
R M Wright Company Inc (PA)....248 476-9800
23910 Freeway Park Dr Farmington Hills (48335) ***(G-5363)***
R M Young Company....231 946-3980
2801 Aero Park Dr Traverse City (49686) ***(G-16812)***
R N B Machine & Tool Inc....616 784-6868
5200 West River Dr Ne Comstock Park (49321) ***(G-3641)***
R N E Business Enterprises (PA)....313 963-3600
400 Renaissance Ctr Lbby Detroit (48243) ***(G-4551)***
R N Fink Manufacturing Co....517 655-4351
1530 Noble Rd Williamston (48895) ***(G-18580)***
R P T Cincinnati Inc....313 382-5880
1636 John A Papalas Dr Lincoln Park (48146) ***(G-10054)***
R R Donnelley & Sons Company....248 583-2500
32031 Townley St Madison Heights (48071) ***(G-10816)***
R S C Productions....586 532-9200
7811 24 Mile Rd Shelby Township (48316) ***(G-15313)***
R S L Tool LLC....616 786-2880
13417 New Hlland St Ste 2 Holland (49424) ***(G-8175)***
R Smith and Sons, Allegan *Also called Southwest Gravel Inc* ***(G-182)***
R T C Enviro Fab Inc....517 596-2987
9043 M 106 Munith (49259) ***(G-11757)***
R T Gordon Inc....586 294-6100
33792 Doreka Fraser (48026) ***(G-5985)***
R T London Company (PA)....616 364-4800
1642 Broadway Ave Nw # 1 Grand Rapids (49504) ***(G-7135)***

R V Wolverine 989 426-9241
1088 N M 18 Gladwin (48624) ***(G-6201)***
R W Fernstrum & Company 906 863-5553
1716 11th Ave Menominee (49858) ***(G-11257)***
R W Patterson Printing Co 269 925-2177
1550 Territorial Rd Benton Harbor (49022) ***(G-1579)***
R W Summers Co 231 946-7923
90 E River Rd Traverse City (49696) ***(G-16813)***
R Wl Sign Co, Kalamazoo *Also called Rwl Sign Co LLC* ***(G-9323)***
R&H Logging Inc 906 241-7248
11435 Sa Rd Cornell (49818) ***(G-3702)***
R&R Tool & Gage, Mount Clemens *Also called Rebecca Eiben* ***(G-11656)***
R+r Mfg/Eng Inc 586 758-4420
21448 Mullin Ave Warren (48089) ***(G-17991)***
R-Bo Co Inc 616 748-9733
150 W Washington Ave Zeeland (49464) ***(G-19076)***
R.T. Baldwin Hardwood Floors, Hudsonville *Also called Rt Baldwin Enterprises Inc* ***(G-8610)***
R5 Construxtion Inc 855 480-7663
4695 N M 37 Hwy Ste C Middleville (49333) ***(G-11311)***
Ra Prcsion Grnding Mtlwrks Inc 586 783-7776
40801 Irwin Dr Harrison Township (48045) ***(G-7719)***
Rabaut Printing Co, Shelby Township *Also called Complete HM Advg Mdia Prmtnal* ***(G-15192)***
Race Fuel Candles LLC 616 889-1674
10455 Country Aire Dr Ne Rockford (49341) ***(G-14186)***
Race Graphics Plus 989 465-9117
10751 E Rosebush Rd Coleman (48618) ***(G-3471)***
Race Ramps LLC 866 464-2788
2003 23rd Ave N Ste A Escanaba (49829) ***(G-5094)***
Racelogic USA Corporation 248 994-9050
27260 Haggerty Rd Ste A2 Farmington Hills (48331) ***(G-5364)***
Rack & Pinion Inc 517 563-8872
7595 Moscow Rd Horton (49246) ***(G-8378)***
Rack Engineering Division, Alpena *Also called Corr-Fac Corporation* ***(G-288)***
Radar Mexican Investments LLC 586 779-0300
27101 Groesbeck Hwy Warren (48089) ***(G-17992)***
Radar Tool & Manufacturing Co 586 759-2800
22800 Hoover Rd Warren (48089) ***(G-17993)***
Radiant Electric Sign Corp 313 835-1400
14500 Schoolcraft St Detroit (48227) ***(G-4552)***
Radical Plants LLC 586 243-8128
25967 Little Mack Ave Saint Clair Shores (48081) ***(G-14880)***
Radio Advertising Bureau Inc 248 514-7048
28175 Haggerty Rd Novi (48377) ***(G-12523)***
Radiolgical Fabrication Design 810 632-6000
10187 Bergin Rd Howell (48843) ***(G-8506)***
Radius LLC 248 685-0773
4922 Technical Dr Milford (48381) ***(G-11485)***
Radley Corp of Grand Rapids, Grand Rapids *Also called Radley Corporation* ***(G-7136)***
Radley Corporation 616 554-9060
4595 Broadmoor Ave Se # 115 Grand Rapids (49512) ***(G-7136)***
Radtke Farms, Berrien Springs *Also called Fairview Farms* ***(G-1640)***
Rae Precision Products Inc 810 987-9170
1327 Cedar St Port Huron (48060) ***(G-13521)***
Raenell Press LLC 616 534-8890
3637 Clyde Park Ave Sw # 6 Grand Rapids (49509) ***(G-7137)***
Rafalski CPA 248 689-1685
1607 E Big Beaver Rd # 103 Troy (48083) ***(G-17328)***
Rainbow Hollow Press 231 825-2962
16695 115th Ave Rodney (49342) ***(G-14207)***
Rainbow Pizza Inc 734 246-4250
14702 Allen Rd Taylor (48180) ***(G-16465)***
Rainbow Seamless Systems Inc (PA) 231 933-8888
4107 Manor Wood Dr S Traverse City (49685) ***(G-16814)***
Rainbow Tape & Label Inc 734 941-6090
11600 Wayne Rd Romulus (48174) ***(G-14324)***
Rainbow Wrap 586 949-3976
46440 Jefferson Ave Chesterfield (48047) ***(G-2937)***
Rak Welding 231 651-0732
7739 Valley Rd Honor (49640) ***(G-8360)***
Rak-O-Nizer LLC 810 444-9807
1718 Colorado St Marysville (48040) ***(G-11098)***
Ralco Industries Inc (PA) 248 853-3200
1025 Doris Rd Auburn Hills (48326) ***(G-1012)***
Ralco Industries Inc 248 853-3200
1025 Doris Rd Auburn Hills (48326) ***(G-1013)***
Ralco Industries Inc 248 853-3200
2860 Auburn Ct Auburn Hills (48326) ***(G-1014)***
Raleigh & Ron Corporation (PA) 248 280-2820
2560 Crooks Rd Royal Oak (48073) ***(G-14571)***
Ralrube Inc 734 429-0033
8423 Boettner Rd Saline (48176) ***(G-15035)***
Ram Die Corp 616 647-2855
2980 3 Mile Rd Nw Grand Rapids (49534) ***(G-7138)***
Ram Electronics, Fruitport *Also called Bralyn Inc* ***(G-6061)***
Ram Electronics Inc 231 865-3186
259 N 3rd Ave Fruitport (49415) ***(G-6069)***
Ram Meter Inc (HQ) 248 362-0990
1815 Bellaire Ave Ste B Royal Oak (48067) ***(G-14572)***
Ram-Pak Industries LLC 616 334-1443
2629 Prairie St Sw Ste E Wyoming (49519) ***(G-18902)***
Ramco, Jenison *Also called Tannewitz Inc* ***(G-9073)***
Ramer Products Inc 269 409-8583
400 Post Rd Buchanan (49107) ***(G-2201)***
Rami, Grand Haven *Also called R A Miller Industries Inc* ***(G-6349)***
Rampant Media LLC 231 218-0401
206 E Ninth St Traverse City (49684) ***(G-16815)***
Ramparts LLC 616 656-2250
4855 Broadmoor Ave Se Kentwood (49512) ***(G-9474)***
Ramtec Corp 586 752-9270
409 E Saint Clair St Romeo (48065) ***(G-14233)***
Ramzak Woodworking 734 595-8155
37109 Gilchrist St Westland (48186) ***(G-18412)***
Ran-Mark Co 231 873-5103
2978 E Hazel Rd Hart (49420) ***(G-7760)***
Ranch Production LLC 231 869-2050
3908 W Hogan Rd Pentwater (49449) ***(G-12973)***
Rand L Industries Inc 989 657-5175
2046 Partridge St Alpena (49707) ***(G-315)***
Rand Worldwide Subsidiary Inc 616 261-8183
4445 Wilson Ave Sw Ste 4 Grandville (49418) ***(G-7413)***
Randall Foods Inc 517 767-3247
401 S Main St Tekonsha (49092) ***(G-16524)***
Randalls Bakery 906 224-5401
505 Sunday Lake St Wakefield (49968) ***(G-17625)***
Randy & Sandy Davis 248 887-7124
557 Harvey Lake Rd Highland (48356) ***(G-7899)***
RANDY'S CATERING, Pontiac *Also called Unique Food Management Inc* ***(G-13421)***
Randys Lawn Care Services LLC 313 447-9536
3392 S Ethel St Detroit (48217) ***(G-4553)***
Randys Seal Coat 231 342-8031
7182 Cherry Ln Traverse City (49685) ***(G-16816)***
Ranger Die, Coopersville *Also called Kinney Tool and Die Inc* ***(G-3689)***
Ranger Tool & Die Co 989 754-1403
317 S Westervelt Rd Saginaw (48604) ***(G-14735)***
Rani Nutra Foods, Ann Arbor *Also called Ranis Granola* ***(G-631)***
Ranir LLC 616 957-7790
4470 44th St Se Ste B Kentwood (49512) ***(G-9475)***
Ranir LLC (HQ) 616 698-8880
4701 East Paris Ave Se Grand Rapids (49512) ***(G-7139)***
Ranir Global Holdings LLC 616 698-8880
4701 East Paris Ave Se Grand Rapids (49512) ***(G-7140)***
Ranis Granola 734 223-2995
3604 Platt Rd Ann Arbor (48108) ***(G-631)***
Rankam Metal Products 586 799-4259
48582 Van Dyke Ave Shelby Township (48317) ***(G-15314)***
Rankin Biomedical Corporation 248 625-4104
14515 Mackey Rd Holly (48442) ***(G-8290)***
Rap Electronics & Machines 616 846-1437
13353 Green St Grand Haven (49417) ***(G-6350)***
Rap Products Inc 989 893-5583
500 Germania St Bay City (48706) ***(G-1394)***
Rapa Electric Inc 269 673-3157
1173 Lincoln Rd Allegan (49010) ***(G-180)***
Rapid Coating Solutions Llc 586 255-7142
6559 Diplomat Dr Sterling Heights (48314) ***(G-16142)***
Rapid Engineering LLC (PA) 616 784-0500
1100 7 Mile Rd Nw Comstock Park (49321) ***(G-3642)***
Rapid Graphics Inc 269 925-7087
2185 M 139 Benton Harbor (49022) ***(G-1580)***
Rapid Printing, Benton Harbor *Also called Rapid Graphics Inc* ***(G-1580)***
Rapid River Loghome, Rapid River *Also called Rapid River Rustic Inc* ***(G-13686)***
Rapid River Rustic Inc (PA) 906 474-6404
9211 County 511 22 And Rapid River (49878) ***(G-13686)***
Rapid-Packaging Corporation 616 949-0950
5151 52nd St Se Grand Rapids (49512) ***(G-7141)***
Rapid-Veyor, Hudsonville *Also called Rapidtek LLC* ***(G-8603)***
Rapids Tool & Engineering 517 663-8721
10618 Petrieville Hwy Eaton Rapids (48827) ***(G-4970)***
Rapids Tool & Engnrng, Eaton Rapids *Also called Rapids Tool & Engineering* ***(G-4970)***
Rapidtek LLC 616 662-0954
3825 Central Pkwy Ste A Hudsonville (49426) ***(G-8603)***
Rapp & Son Inc (PA) 734 283-1000
3767 11th St Wyandotte (48192) ***(G-18836)***
Raq LLC 313 473-7271
392 S Sanford St Pontiac (48342) ***(G-13412)***
Rar Group Inc 248 353-2266
19994 Lennane Redford (48240) ***(G-13761)***
Rare Bird Holdings LLC 616 335-9463
849 Allen Dr Holland (49423) ***(G-8176)***
Rare Earth Hardwoods Inc 231 946-0043
5800 Denali Dr Traverse City (49684) ***(G-16817)***
Rare Tool Inc 517 423-5000
300 E Russell Rd Tecumseh (49286) ***(G-16512)***
Rassey Industries Inc 586 803-9500
50375 Central Indus Dr Shelby Township (48315) ***(G-15315)***
Rassini Chassis Systems LLC 419 485-1524
14500 N Beck Rd Plymouth (48170) ***(G-13275)***

ALPHABETIC

Rathco Safety Supply Inc 269 323-0153
6742 Lovers Ln Portage (49002) ***(G-13599)***
Ratio Machining Inc 313 531-5155
12214 Woodbine Redford (48239) ***(G-13762)***
Rattle Top Precision Assembly 231 937-5333
6342 Henkel Rd Howard City (49329) ***(G-8416)***
Rattunde Corporation (PA) 616 940-3340
5080 Beltway Dr Se Caledonia (49316) ***(G-2396)***
Ravago Americas 810 225-0029
7280 Forest Way Brighton (48116) ***(G-2061)***
Ravago Americas LLC 517 548-4140
705 E Van Riper Rd Fowlerville (48836) ***(G-5853)***
Raval USA Inc 248 260-4050
1939 Northfield Dr Rochester Hills (48309) ***(G-14099)***
Rave Computer Association Inc 586 939-8230
7171 Sterling Ponds Ct Sterling Heights (48312) ***(G-16143)***
Raven Acquisition LLC 734 254-5000
428 Cogshall St Holly (48442) ***(G-8291)***
Raven Engineering Inc 248 969-9450
725 S Glaspie St Oxford (48371) ***(G-12911)***
Ravenna Casting Center Inc 231 853-0300
3800 Adams Rd Ravenna (49451) ***(G-13692)***
Ravenna Hydraulics, Ravenna *Also called Ravenna Pattern & Mfg* ***(G-13693)***
Ravenna Pattern & Mfg 231 853-2264
13101 Apple Ave Ravenna (49451) ***(G-13693)***
Ravenna Sealcoating Inc 231 766-0571
1120 S Mill Iron Rd Muskegon (49442) ***(G-11905)***
Ravenwood 231 421-5682
503 Devonshire Ct Traverse City (49686) ***(G-16818)***
Ravishing Wreaths 248 613-6210
3404 Watersedge Dr Brighton (48114) ***(G-2062)***
Ray Printing Company Inc 517 787-4130
201 Brookley Ave Jackson (49202) ***(G-8994)***
Ray Scott Industries Inc 248 535-2528
3921 32nd St Port Huron (48060) ***(G-13522)***
Ray's Big Game Processing, Brown City *Also called Rays Game* ***(G-2141)***
Raybend, Rochester *Also called Sales Driven Services LLC* ***(G-13926)***
Raybend, Kalamazoo *Also called Sales Driven Ltd Liability Co* ***(G-9327)***
Rayce Americas Inc 248 537-3159
2600 Auburn Rd Ste 120 Auburn Hills (48326) ***(G-1015)***
Raychris 734 404-5485
9278 General Dr Plymouth (48170) ***(G-13276)***
Rayco Manufacturing Inc 586 795-2884
5520 Bridgewood Dr Sterling Heights (48310) ***(G-16144)***
Rayconnect Inc 248 265-4000
2350 Austin Ave Ste 100 Rochester Hills (48309) ***(G-14100)***
Raydiance, West Bloomfield *Also called Tru-Fit International Inc* ***(G-18319)***
Rays Game 810 346-2628
4101 Maple St Brown City (48416) ***(G-2141)***
Rays Ice Cream Co Inc 248 549-5256
4233 Coolidge Hwy Royal Oak (48073) ***(G-14573)***
Rays Pure Mple Syrup Pdts LLC 269 601-7694
14399 S 47th St Fulton (49052) ***(G-6072)***
Raze It Printing Inc 248 366-8691
1784 Heron View Ct West Bloomfield (48324) ***(G-18309)***
Raze-It Printing 248 543-3813
24221 John R Rd Hazel Park (48030) ***(G-7839)***
RB Christian Ironworks LLC 269 963-2222
298 Hamblin Ave W Battle Creek (49037) ***(G-1286)***
RB Construction Company (PA) 586 264-9478
249 Cass Ave Mount Clemens (48043) ***(G-11655)***
RB Oil Enterprises LLC 734 354-0700
Plymouth Mi Plymouth (48170) ***(G-13277)***
RB&w Detroit 234 380-8544
30100 Stephenson Hwy Madison Heights (48071) ***(G-10817)***
Rbc Enterprises Inc (PA) 313 491-3350
12301 Hubbell St Detroit (48227) ***(G-4554)***
Rbc Ministries (PA) 616 942-6770
3000 Kraft Ave Se Grand Rapids (49512) ***(G-7142)***
Rbd Creative 313 259-5507
705 S Main St Ste 220 Plymouth (48170) ***(G-13278)***
Rbl Products Inc 313 873-8806
6040 Russell St Detroit (48211) ***(G-4555)***
Rbm Chemical Company LLC 248 766-1974
4108 Oak Tree Cir Rochester (48306) ***(G-13924)***
Rbt Mfg LLC 800 691-8204
9033 General Dr Plymouth (48170) ***(G-13279)***
RC Cabinetry 734 513-2677
11140 Karen St Livonia (48150) ***(G-10383)***
RC Metal Products Inc 616 696-1694
4365 21 Mile Rd Sand Lake (49343) ***(G-15053)***
Rcd Quality Coatings 313 575-8125
15534 Dixie Redford (48239) ***(G-13763)***
RCO Aerospace Products LLC 586 774-8400
15725 E 12 Mile Rd Roseville (48066) ***(G-14469)***
Rcs Services Company LLC 989 732-7999
10850 Hetherton Rd Johannesburg (49751) ***(G-9082)***
Rdc, Grand Rapids *Also called Ram Die Corp* ***(G-7138)***
Rdc Machine Inc 810 695-5587
11891 Shell Bark Ln Grand Blanc (48439) ***(G-6260)***
Rdi Switching Technologies 951 699-8919
1130 Elmwood Dr Ann Arbor (48104) ***(G-632)***
Rdr Books, Muskegon *Also called Roger D Rapoport* ***(G-11910)***
Rdz Racing Incorporated 517 468-3254
9642 Sober Rd Fowlerville (48836) ***(G-5854)***
Re-Sol LLC 248 270-7777
1771 Harmon Rd Ste 150 Auburn Hills (48326) ***(G-1016)***
Ready Boring & Tooling, Farmington Hills *Also called Ready Molds Inc* ***(G-5365)***
Ready Molds Inc (PA) 248 474-4007
32645 Folsom Rd Farmington Hills (48336) ***(G-5365)***
Real Estate Book, Farmington Hills *Also called Dynamic Color Publications* ***(G-5220)***
Real Estate One Inc 248 851-2600
3100 Old Farm Ln Ste 10 Commerce Township (48390) ***(G-3569)***
Real Estate One Licensing Co, Commerce Township *Also called Real Estate One Inc* ***(G-3569)***
Real Green Systems Inc (HQ) 888 345-2154
4375 Pineview Dr Commerce Township (48390) ***(G-3570)***
Real Ink Publishing LLC 313 766-1344
48450 Denton Rd Apt 103 Van Buren Twp (48111) ***(G-17550)***
Real Steel Manufacturing LLC 231 457-4673
304 W Delano Ave Muskegon (49444) ***(G-11906)***
Real Time Diagnostics, Warren *Also called Tambra Investments Inc* ***(G-18035)***
Real Times Media LLC (PA) 313 963-8100
1452 Randolph St Ste 400 Detroit (48226) ***(G-4556)***
Real View LLC 616 524-5243
2505 East Paris Ave Se # 140 Grand Rapids (49546) ***(G-7143)***
Realm 313 706-4401
34950 Van Born Rd Wayne (48184) ***(G-18234)***
Realryteshop, Detroit *Also called Eugene* ***(G-4217)***
Ream Logistics Dlvry Svcs LLC 877 246-7857
419 Nevada Belleville (48111) ***(G-1490)***
Rearden Development Corp 616 464-4434
5960 Tahoe Dr Se Ste 103 Grand Rapids (49546) ***(G-7144)***
Reau Manufacturing Co 734 823-5603
100 Research Pkwy Dundee (48131) ***(G-4833)***
REB Research & Consulting Co 248 545-0155
12851 Capital St Oak Park (48237) ***(G-12639)***
REB Tool Company, Van Buren Twp *Also called R E B Tool Inc* ***(G-17549)***
Rebeats (PA) 989 463-4757
219 Prospect Ave Alma (48801) ***(G-254)***
Rebecca Eiben 586 231-0548
191 Grand Ave Mount Clemens (48043) ***(G-11656)***
Rebel Nell L3c 716 640-4267
4731 Grand River Ave Detroit (48208) ***(G-4557)***
Rebo Lighting & Elec LLC 734 213-4159
3990 Research Park Dr Ann Arbor (48108) ***(G-633)***
Reborn Wear 313 680-6806
31967 Groat Blvd Rockwood (48173) ***(G-14204)***
Rec Boat Holdings LLC (HQ) 231 779-2616
925 Frisbie St Cadillac (49601) ***(G-2350)***
Recardo North America Inc 248 364-3818
49200 Halyard Dr Plymouth (48170) ***(G-13280)***
Recaro Automotive North Amer (HQ) 586 210-2600
24801 Capital Blvd Clinton Township (48036) ***(G-3331)***
Recaro North America Inc 734 254-4704
24801 Capital Blvd Clinton Township (48036) ***(G-3332)***
Recco Products Inc 269 792-2243
702 S Main St Wayland (49348) ***(G-18202)***
Recollections Co 989 734-0566
7956 F-21 Hwy Hawks (49743) ***(G-7816)***
Recon Fishing Systems Inc 989 358-2923
1504 S Second Ave Alpena (49707) ***(G-316)***
Recon Technologies LLC 616 241-1877
1522 Madison Ave Se Grand Rapids (49507) ***(G-7145)***
Reconserve of Michigan Inc 269 965-0427
170 Angell St Battle Creek (49037) ***(G-1287)***
Recovere LLC 269 370-3165
3261 E B Ave Plainwell (49080) ***(G-13092)***
Recticel Foam Corporation (HQ) 248 241-9100
5600 Bow Pointe Dr Clarkston (48346) ***(G-3059)***
Recursive LLC 904 449-2386
14595 Jamesway Ave Holland (49424) ***(G-8177)***
Recycled Paperboard Pdts Corp 313 579-6608
10400 Devine St Detroit (48213) ***(G-4558)***
Recycled Polymetric Materials 313 957-6373
15477 Woodrow Wilson St Detroit (48238) ***(G-4559)***
Recycledlps Com 810 623-4498
6320 Superior Dr Brighton (48116) ***(G-2063)***
Recycletech Products Inc 517 649-2243
12 Charlotte St Mulliken (48861) ***(G-11750)***
Recycling Concepts W Mich Inc 616 942-8888
5015 52nd St Se Grand Rapids (49512) ***(G-7146)***
Recycling Fluid Technologies 269 788-0488
4039 Columbia Ave W Battle Creek (49015) ***(G-1288)***
Recycling Rizzo Services LLC 248 541-4020
414 E Hudson Ave Royal Oak (48067) ***(G-14574)***
Red Barn Maps 906 346-2226
410 Avenue A Gwinn (49841) ***(G-7586)***

Red Carpet Capital Inc 248 952-8583
3514 Arrowvale Dr Orchard Lake (48324) *(G-12719)*
Red Door Digital, Detroit *Also called Group 7500 Inc (G-4284)*
Red Falcon Press 248 439-0432
123 W Sunnybrook Dr Royal Oak (48073) *(G-14575)*
Red Hat Inc 978 392-2459
315 W Huron St Ann Arbor (48103) *(G-634)*
Red Headed Honey LLC 707 616-4278
14900 Woodbridge Rd Camden (49232) *(G-2424)*
Red Laser Inc 517 540-1300
51200 Pontiac Trl 3b Wixom (48393) *(G-18739)*
Red Rose Flooring Shop, Sturgis *Also called Dave Brand (G-16287)*
Red Spot Westland Inc 734 729-1913
550 Edwin St Westland (48186) *(G-18413)*
RED Stamp Inc 616 878-7771
3800 Patterson Ave Se Grand Rapids (49512) *(G-7147)*
Red Tin Boat 734 239-3796
4081 Thornoaks Dr Ann Arbor (48104) *(G-635)*
Red Wing Bags, Holland *Also called Rj Corp (G-8181)*
Redbird WD Pdts Bldwin Twnship 989 362-7670
776 Aulerich Rd East Tawas (48730) *(G-4922)*
Redbud Roots Lab I LLC 312 656-3823
215 Post Rd Buchanan (49107) *(G-2202)*
Redeem Power Services 248 679-5277
43422 W Oaks Dr Ste 178 Novi (48377) *(G-12524)*
Redi-Crete, Negaunee *Also called Rudy Goupille & Sons Inc (G-11974)*
Redi-Rock International LLC 866 222-8400
2940 Parkview Dr Petoskey (49770) *(G-13019)*
Redline Fabrications 810 984-5621
4752 Walker Rd Clyde (48049) *(G-3415)*
Redline Manufacturing, Kalamazoo *Also called Greg Socha (G-9205)*
Redtail Software 231 587-0720
1414 Plum Valley Rd Ne Mancelona (49659) *(G-10878)*
Redviking, Plymouth *Also called Superior Controls Inc (G-13306)*
Reed City Group LLC 231 832-7500
603 E Church Ave Reed City (49677) *(G-13797)*
Reed Fuel LLC 574 520-3101
1445 S 3rd St Niles (49120) *(G-12161)*
Reed Sportswear Mfg Co (PA) 313 963-7980
1601 W Lafayette Blvd Detroit (48216) *(G-4560)*
Reed Sportswear Mfg Co 313 963-7980
1601 W Lafayette Blvd Detroit (48216) *(G-4561)*
Reed Yacht Sales LLC (PA) 419 304-4405
11840 Toledo Beach Rd La Salle (48145) *(G-9529)*
Reed Yacht Sales LLC 616 842-8899
1333 Madison St Blgd A St Grand Haven (49417) *(G-6351)*
Reeds Equipment LLC 517 567-4415
10815 S Pittsford Rd Pittsford (49271) *(G-13068)*
Reef Tool & Gage Co 586 468-3000
44800 Macomb Indus Dr Clinton Township (48036) *(G-3333)*
Reeling Systems LLC 810 364-3900
5323 Gratiot Ave Saint Clair (48079) *(G-14841)*
Reemarkable Eyes LLC 313 461-3006
18121 E 8 Mile Rd 321a Eastpointe (48021) *(G-4943)*
Reemco Incorporated 734 522-8988
11801 Belden Ct Livonia (48150) *(G-10384)*
Reese Business Group LLC 246 216-2605
29236 Fieldstone Farmington Hills (48334) *(G-5366)*
Reese Inspection Services LLC 248 481-3598
3321 Lapeer Rd W Auburn Hills (48326) *(G-1017)*
Reeves Plastics LLC 616 997-0777
507 Omalley Dr Coopersville (49404) *(G-3696)*
Refab Metal Fabrication LLC 616 842-9705
1811 Hayes St Ste D Grand Haven (49417) *(G-6352)*
Refinery Corporation America 877 881-0336
20008 Kelly Rd Harper Woods (48225) *(G-7671)*
Reflective Art Inc 616 452-0712
2662 Prairie St Sw Wyoming (49519) *(G-18903)*
Reforma, Southfield *Also called NV Labs Inc (G-15668)*
Refreshment Product Svcs Inc 906 475-7003
201 Summit St Bldg 53 Negaunee (49866) *(G-11972)*
Refrigeration Concepts Inc 616 785-7335
5959 Comstock Park Dr Nw Comstock Park (49321) *(G-3643)*
Refrigeration Research Inc (PA) 810 227-1151
525 N 5th St Brighton (48116) *(G-2064)*
Refrigeration Research Inc 989 773-7540
2174 Commerce St Mount Pleasant (48858) *(G-11736)*
Refrigeration Sales Inc 517 784-8579
1810 E High St Ste 2 Jackson (49203) *(G-8995)*
Reg Publishers LLC 616 889-4232
2191 Walker Ridge Rd Hopkins (49328) *(G-8368)*
Regal Finishing Co Inc 269 849-2963
3927 Bessemer Rd Coloma (49038) *(G-3482)*
Regency Construction Corp 586 741-8000
35240 Forton Ct Clinton Township (48035) *(G-3334)*
Regency Dki, Clinton Township *Also called Regency Construction Corp (G-3334)*
Regency Plastics - Ubly Inc (HQ) 989 658-8504
4147 N Ubly Rd Ubly (48475) *(G-17482)*
Regener-Eyes LLC 248 207-4641
330 E Liberty St Ll Ann Arbor (48104) *(G-636)*
Regents of The University Mich 734 936-0435
3003 S State St Spc 1272 Ann Arbor (48109) *(G-637)*
Regents of The University Mich 734 973-2400
2850 S Industrial Hwy # 400 Ann Arbor (48104) *(G-638)*
Reger Manufacturing Company 586 293-5096
31375 Fraser Dr Fraser (48026) *(G-5986)*
Rehau Incorporated 269 651-7845
1110 N Clay St Sturgis (49091) *(G-16321)*
Rehmann Industries Inc 810 748-7793
23051 Roseberry Ave Warren (48089) *(G-17994)*
Reid Manufacturing, Fremont *Also called White River Knife and Tool (G-6057)*
Reif Carbide Tool Co Inc 586 754-1890
11055 E 9 Mile Rd Warren (48089) *(G-17995)*
Reilchz Inc 231 421-9600
600 W Front St Traverse City (49684) *(G-16819)*
Reilly & Associates Inc 248 605-9393
7754 Parkcrest Cir Clarkston (48348) *(G-3060)*
Reimold Printing Corporation 989 799-0784
5171 Blackbeak Dr Saginaw (48604) *(G-14736)*
Reinhart Industries, Livonia *Also called SB Investments LLC (G-10400)*
Reis Custom Cabinets 586 791-4925
1398 S Bradford Rd Reese (48757) *(G-13807)*
Rejoice International Corp 855 345-5575
21800 Haggerty Rd Ste 203 Northville (48167) *(G-12253)*
Rekey Luxury Homes LLC 586 747-0342
637 E Big Beaver Rd # 103 Troy (48083) *(G-17329)*
Reklein Plastics Incorporated 586 739-8850
42130 Mound Rd Sterling Heights (48314) *(G-16145)*
Rekmakker Millwork Inc 616 546-3680
6035 145th Ave Holland (49423) *(G-8178)*
Reko International Holdings (HQ) 519 737-6974
6001 N Adams Rd Ste 251 Bloomfield Hills (48304) *(G-1854)*
Rel Inc 906 337-3018
57640 11th St Calumet (49913) *(G-2413)*
Relationship Examiner 256 653-7374
604 S Saint Joseph Ave Niles (49120) *(G-12162)*
Reliable Architectural Mtls Co, Detroit *Also called Reliable Glass Company (G-4562)*
Reliable Glass Company 313 924-9750
9751 Erwin St Detroit (48213) *(G-4562)*
Reliable Reasonable Tl Svc LLC 586 630-6016
21356 Carlo Dr Clinton Township (48038) *(G-3335)*
Reliable Sales Co 248 969-0943
660 Lakes Edge Dr Oxford (48371) *(G-12912)*
Reliable Sign Service Inc 586 465-6829
26701 Ponchartrain St Harrison Township (48045) *(G-7720)*
Reliance Electric Machine Co 810 232-3355
2601 Leith St Flint (48506) *(G-5754)*
Reliance Finishing Co 616 241-4436
1236 Judd Ave Sw Grand Rapids (49509) *(G-7148)*
Reliance Metal Products Inc 734 641-3334
38289 Abruzzi Dr Westland (48185) *(G-18414)*
Reliance Plastisol Coating Co 616 245-2297
1240 Judd Ave Sw Grand Rapids (49509) *(G-7149)*
Reliance Rubber Industries Inc 734 641-4100
38230 N Executive Dr Westland (48185) *(G-18415)*
Reliance Spray Mask Co Inc 616 784-3664
2825 Northridge Dr Nw Grand Rapids (49544) *(G-7150)*
Reliant Industries Inc 586 275-0479
6119 15 Mile Rd Sterling Heights (48312) *(G-16146)*
Religious Communications LLC 313 822-3361
5590 Coplin St Detroit (48213) *(G-4563)*
Remacon Compressors Inc 313 842-8219
7939 Mcgraw St Detroit (48210) *(G-4564)*
Reminder Shopping Guide Inc 269 427-7474
416 Railroad St Bangor (49013) *(G-1131)*
Reminder, The, Hastings *Also called J-Ad Graphics Inc (G-7800)*
Remnant Publications Inc 517 279-1304
649 E Chicago Rd Ste B Coldwater (49036) *(G-3450)*
Remote Tank Monitors, Saginaw *Also called Advance Tech Solutions LLC (G-14601)*
Rempco Acquisition Inc 231 775-0108
251 Bell Ave Cadillac (49601) *(G-2351)*
Remy Girls 313 397-2870
19445 Livernois Ave Detroit (48221) *(G-4565)*
Remy International Inc 765 778-6499
60558 Pennington Way Rochester (48306) *(G-13925)*
Renaissance Media LLC 248 354-6060
32255 Northwestern Hwy # 205 Farmington Hills (48334) *(G-5367)*
Renas Fudge Shops Inc 586 293-0600
31181 Kendall Fraser (48026) *(G-5987)*
Rendon & Sons Machining Inc 269 628-2200
21870 M 40 Gobles (49055) *(G-6219)*
Renegade Cstm Screen Prtg LLC 313 475-8489
2091 Thomas St Lincoln Park (48146) *(G-10055)*
Renegade Screen Printing 248 632-0207
141 Fisher Ct Clawson (48017) *(G-3108)*
Renes Inc 810 294-5008
3131 Mortimer Line Rd Croswell (48422) *(G-3735)*
Renew Valve & Machine Co., Carleton *Also called Fcx Performance Inc (G-2553)*

Renewable World Energies LLC 906 828-0808
1001 Stephenson St Ste C Norway (49870) ***(G-12356)***
Renk America LLC 231 724-2666
76 S Getty St Muskegon (49442) ***(G-11907)***
Renosol Seating, Farwell *Also called Lear Corporation* ***(G-5425)***
Rens LLC 586 756-6777
24871 Gibson Dr Warren (48089) ***(G-17996)***
Renucell 888 400-6032
41 Washington Ave Ste 345 Grand Haven (49417) ***(G-6353)***
REO Fab LLC (PA) 810 969-4667
1567 Imlay City Rd Ste A Lapeer (48446) ***(G-9958)***
REO Hydraulic & Mfg Inc 313 891-2244
18475 Sherwood St Detroit (48234) ***(G-4566)***
REO Hydro-Pierce Inc 313 891-2244
18475 Sherwood St Detroit (48234) ***(G-4567)***
Rep Innovations Inc 734 744-6968
34435 Glendale St Livonia (48150) ***(G-10385)***
Repair Industries Michigan Inc 313 365-5300
6501 E Mcnichols Rd Detroit (48212) ***(G-4568)***
Repairers of The Brach Mskegon 231 375-0990
1124 Williams St Muskegon (49442) ***(G-11908)***
Repcolite Decorating Center, Holland *Also called Repcolite Paints Inc* ***(G-8179)***
Repcolite Paints Inc (PA) 616 396-5213
473 W 17th St Holland (49423) ***(G-8179)***
Replacement Brush Tables, Plymouth *Also called Rbt Mfg LLC* ***(G-13279)***
Replacement West Glass 248 974-4635
32401 8 Mile Rd Livonia (48152) ***(G-10386)***
Reply Inc (HQ) 248 686-2481
691 N Squirrel Rd Ste 202 Auburn Hills (48326) ***(G-1018)***
Reporter & Shoppers Guide, Iron River *Also called Northland Publishers Inc* ***(G-8751)***
Reporter Papers Inc 734 429-5428
106 W Michigan Ave Saline (48176) ***(G-15036)***
Reproductions Resource, Saint Clair Shores *Also called Print Plus Inc* ***(G-14878)***
Reprographics One, Livonia *Also called M & J Graphics Enterprises Inc* ***(G-10294)***
Republic Die & Tool Co 734 699-3400
45000 Van Born Rd Van Buren Twp (48111) ***(G-17551)***
Republic Drill/Apt Corp 248 689-5050
1863 Larchwood Dr Troy (48083) ***(G-17330)***
Republic Roller Corporation 269 273-9591
205 S Us Highway 131 Three Rivers (49093) ***(G-16583)***
Request Foods Inc (PA) 616 786-0900
3460 John F Donnelly Dr Holland (49424) ***(G-8180)***
Resa Power LLC 763 784-4040
50613 Varsity Ct Wixom (48393) ***(G-18740)***
Rescar Inc 517 486-3130
11440 Cemetery Rd Blissfield (49228) ***(G-1774)***
Resco Pet Products, Commerce Township *Also called Tecla Company Inc* ***(G-3576)***
Research and Development Off, Escanaba *Also called Emp Advanced Development LLC* ***(G-5067)***
Research Tool Corporation 989 834-2246
1401 S Main St Ovid (48866) ***(G-12816)***
Resetar Equipment Inc 313 291-0500
26950 Van Born Rd Dearborn Heights (48125) ***(G-3937)***
Resin Services, Sterling Heights *Also called Reklein Plastics Incorporated* ***(G-16145)***
Resin Services Inc 586 254-6770
5959 18 1/2 Mile Rd Sterling Heights (48314) ***(G-16147)***
Resins Unlimited LLC 586 725-6873
52438 Silent Ridge Dr Chesterfield (48051) ***(G-2938)***
Resistnce Wldg Mch Accssory LL 269 428-4770
255 Palladium Dr Saint Joseph (49085) ***(G-14956)***
Reska Spline Gage Inc 586 778-4000
29171 Calahan Rd Roseville (48066) ***(G-14470)***
Resolute Forest Products, Menominee *Also called Fibrek Inc* ***(G-11235)***
Resolute FP US Inc 877 547-2737
701 4th Ave Menominee (49858) ***(G-11258)***
Resource Rcovery Solutions Inc 248 454-3442
100 W Sheffield Ave Pontiac (48340) ***(G-13413)***
Resourcemfg 810 937-5058
203 Huron Ave Port Huron (48060) ***(G-13523)***
Response Welding Inc 586 795-8090
40785 Brentwood Dr Sterling Heights (48310) ***(G-16148)***
Restraint Systems Division, Auburn Hills *Also called Joyson Sfety Systems Acqstion* ***(G-946)***
Restricted Area LLC 419 975-8109
15410 Young St Detroit (48205) ***(G-4569)***
Resurgo LLC 313 559-2325
786 W Grand Blvd Detroit (48216) ***(G-4570)***
Retail, Clinton Township *Also called Border Line Rich Clothing LLC* ***(G-3188)***
Retail Sign Systems, Belmont *Also called Jant Group LLC* ***(G-1508)***
Retro Enterprises Inc 269 435-8583
1045 Parkview St Constantine (49042) ***(G-3675)***
Retro-A-Go-go LLC 734 476-0300
214 S Michigan Ave Howell (48843) ***(G-8507)***
Retrosense Therapeutics LLC 734 369-9333
330 E Liberty St Ll Ann Arbor (48104) ***(G-639)***
Returnable Packaging Corp 586 206-8050
1917 S Riveerhill Dr Clinton Township (48038) ***(G-3336)***
Reuland Electric Co 517 546-4400
4500 E Grand River Ave Howell (48843) ***(G-8508)***
Reurink Roof Maint & Coating 269 795-2337
12795 Jackson Rd Middleville (49333) ***(G-11312)***
Reutter LLC (HQ) 248 466-0652
2723 S State St Ste 150 Ann Arbor (48104) ***(G-640)***
Revak Precision Grinding Inc 313 388-2626
20188 Lorne St Taylor (48180) ***(G-16466)***
Reveal Publishing LLC 248 798-3440
2749 Pendleton Dr Bloomfield Hills (48304) ***(G-1855)***
Revere Plastics Systems LLC 586 415-4823
18401 Malyn Blvd Fraser (48026) ***(G-5988)***
Revere Plastics Systems LLC (HQ) 833 300-4043
39555 Orchard Hill Pl # 155 Novi (48375) ***(G-12525)***
Review Directories Inc 231 347-8606
311 E Mitchell St Petoskey (49770) ***(G-13020)***
Revolutions Signs Designs LLC 248 439-0727
2429 N Connecticut Ave Royal Oak (48073) ***(G-14576)***
Revstone Industries LLC 248 351-1000
900 Wilshire Dr Ste 270 Troy (48084) ***(G-17331)***
Revstone Industries LLC 248 351-8800
2000 Town Ctr Ste 2100 Southfield (48075) ***(G-15688)***
Revue Holding Company 616 608-6170
2422 Burton St Se Grand Rapids (49546) ***(G-7151)***
Revue Magazine, Grand Rapids *Also called Revue Holding Company* ***(G-7151)***
Revwires LLC 269 683-8100
1631 Lake St Niles (49120) ***(G-12163)***
Rew Industries Inc 586 803-1150
51572 Danview Tech Ct Shelby Township (48315) ***(G-15316)***
Rewardpal Inc 800 377-6099
43422 W Oaks Dr Novi (48377) ***(G-12526)***
Rex M Tubbs 734 459-3180
1205 S Main St Plymouth (48170) ***(G-13281)***
Rex Materials Inc (PA) 517 223-3787
1600 Brewer Rd Howell (48855) ***(G-8509)***
Rexair Holdings Inc 248 643-7222
2600 W Big Beavr Rd # 555 Troy (48084) ***(G-17332)***
Reyers Advertising, Spring Lake *Also called Reyers Company Inc* ***(G-15846)***
Reyers Company Inc 616 414-5530
700 E Savidge St Spring Lake (49456) ***(G-15846)***
Reynolda Mfg Solutions Inc 336 699-4204
30419 Beck Rd Wixom (48393) ***(G-18741)***
Reynolds Cntrless Grinding LLC 313 418-5109
26730 W Davison Redford (48239) ***(G-13764)***
Reynolds Water Conditioning Co 248 888-5000
24545 Hathaway St Farmington Hills (48335) ***(G-5368)***
Rezoop LLC 248 952-8070
1270 Romney Rd Bloomfield (48304) ***(G-1784)***
Rf Design, Howell *Also called Radiolgical Fabrication Design* ***(G-8506)***
Rf System Lab, Traverse City *Also called Seneca Enterprises LLC* ***(G-16829)***
Rfc Woodworks 810 357-9072
1003 Jenks Blvd Kalamazoo (49006) ***(G-9315)***
Rfm Manufacturing 810 522-6922
2001 Orndorf Dr Brighton (48116) ***(G-2065)***
RGI Brands LLC (PA) 312 253-7400
3950 Wabeek Lake Dr E Bloomfield Hills (48302) ***(G-1856)***
Rgils Vineyard, Farmington Hills *Also called Virgils Vineyard LLC* ***(G-5411)***
Rgm New Ventures Inc (PA) 248 624-5050
48230 West Rd Wixom (48393) ***(G-18742)***
Rh Spies Group, Sterling Heights *Also called Letnan Industries Inc* ***(G-16072)***
Rhe-Tech LLC 517 223-4874
9201 W Grand River Rd Fowlerville (48836) ***(G-5855)***
Rhe-Tech LLC 734 769-3558
1550 E N Territorial Rd Whitmore Lake (48189) ***(G-18545)***
Rhema Products Inc 313 561-6800
24141 Ann Arbor Trl Ste 5 Dearborn Heights (48127) ***(G-3938)***
Rhinevault Olsen Machine & Tl 989 753-4363
2533 Carrollton Rd Saginaw (48604) ***(G-14737)***
Rhino Linings of Grand Rapids 616 361-9786
1520 Rupert St Ne Grand Rapids (49525) ***(G-7152)***
Rhino Products Inc 269 674-8309
57100 48th Ave Lawrence (49064) ***(G-9984)***
Rhino Seed & Landscape Sup LLC (PA) 800 482-3130
1093 129th Ave Wayland (49348) ***(G-18203)***
Rhino Strapping Products Inc 734 442-4040
24341 Brest Taylor (48180) ***(G-16467)***
Rhm Fluid Power, Westland *Also called Flodraulic Group Incorporated* ***(G-18371)***
Rhodes Welding Inc 248 568-0857
1206 W Selfridge Blvd Clawson (48017) ***(G-3109)***
Rhombus Energy Solutions Inc 313 406-3292
15201 Century Dr Dearborn (48120) ***(G-3890)***
Rhys World Publishing LLC 248 974-7408
18579 Innsbrook Dr Apt 2 Northville (48168) ***(G-12254)***
Ricardo Defense Inc 805 882-1884
35860 Beattie Dr Sterling Heights (48312) ***(G-16149)***
Rice Juice Company Inc 906 774-1733
873 Evergreen Ct Iron Mountain (49802) ***(G-8730)***
Rich Mars Mobile Spa LLC 734 210-2797
13464 Garfield Redford (48239) ***(G-13765)***
Rich-Wall Custom Cabine 734 237-4934
28243 Plymouth Rd Livonia (48150) ***(G-10387)***

Richard Bennett & Associates 313 831-4262
470 Brainard St Detroit (48201) ***(G-4571)***
Richard D Matzke 517 320-0964
1844 Ferndale Dr Hillsdale (49242) ***(G-7945)***
Richard L Martin Construction, Higgins Lake *Also called Classic Log Homes Incorporated* ***(G-7876)***
Richard Larabee 248 827-7755
22132 W 9 Mile Rd Southfield (48033) ***(G-15689)***
Richard Reproductions, Southfield *Also called Richard Larabee* ***(G-15689)***
Richard Teachworht 231 527-8227
17270 Kent Ave Morley (49336) ***(G-11622)***
Richard Tool & Die Corporation 248 486-0900
29700 Wk Smith Dr New Hudson (48165) ***(G-12068)***
Richard-Allan Scientific Co (HQ) 269 544-5600
4481 Campus Dr Kalamazoo (49008) ***(G-9316)***
Richards Printing 906 786-3540
718 Ludington St Escanaba (49829) ***(G-5095)***
Richards Quality Bedding Co 616 363-0070
3443 Manderley Dr Ne Grand Rapids (49525) ***(G-7153)***
Richardson Acqstions Group Inc 248 624-2272
961 Decker Rd Walled Lake (48390) ***(G-17674)***
Richcoat LLC 586 978-1311
40573 Brentwood Dr Sterling Heights (48310) ***(G-16150)***
Richelieu America Ltd (HQ) 586 264-1240
7021 Sterling Ponds Ct Sterling Heights (48312) ***(G-16151)***
Richfield Industries, Flint *Also called Transportation Tech Group Inc* ***(G-5781)***
Richland Machine & Pump Co 269 629-4344
9854 M 89 Richland (49083) ***(G-13828)***
Richmond Instrs & Systems Inc 586 954-3770
21392 Carlo Dr Clinton Township (48038) ***(G-3337)***
Richmond Millwork Inc 586 727-6747
10134 Radiance Dr Ira (48023) ***(G-8710)***
Richmond Steel Inc 586 948-4700
50570 E Rssell Schmidt Bl Chesterfield (48051) ***(G-2939)***
Richmonds Steel Inc 989 453-7010
6767 Pigeon Rd Pigeon (48755) ***(G-13040)***
Richter Precision Inc 586 465-0500
17741 Malyn Blvd Fraser (48026) ***(G-5989)***
Richter Sawmill 231 829-3071
20408 18 Mile Rd Leroy (49655) ***(G-10011)***
Richwood Industries Inc (PA) 616 243-2700
2700 Buchanan Ave Sw Grand Rapids (49548) ***(G-7154)***
Rick Owen & Jason Vogel Partnr 734 417-3401
10475 N Territorial Rd Dexter (48130) ***(G-4752)***
Rick Wykle LLC 734 839-6376
3022 Strohm Ave Trenton (48183) ***(G-16891)***
Rick's Deer Processing, Eaton Rapids *Also called Ricks Meat Processing LLC* ***(G-4971)***
Ricks Meat Processing LLC 517 628-2263
3320 Onondaga Rd Eaton Rapids (48827) ***(G-4971)***
Rico Technologies 248 896-0110
50250 Dennis Ct Wixom (48393) ***(G-18743)***
Ride Control LLC (HQ) 248 247-7600
39300 Country Club Dr Farmington Hills (48331) ***(G-5369)***
Rider Report Magazine 248 854-8460
3906 Baldwin Rd Auburn Hills (48321) ***(G-1019)***
Rider Type & Design 989 839-0015
3600 E Mary Jane Dr Midland (48642) ***(G-11408)***
Ridge Cider 231 674-2040
351 W 136th St Grant (49327) ***(G-7432)***
Ridge Locomotive 989 714-4671
9961 Buck Rd Freeland (48623) ***(G-6028)***
Ridge Pointe Publishing LLC 586 948-4660
23962 Pointe Dr Macomb (48042) ***(G-10632)***
Ridgefield Company LLC 888 226-8665
2601 Elmridge Dr Nw Grand Rapids (49534) ***(G-7155)***
Ridgeview Industries Inc 616 453-8636
2727 3 Mile Rd Nw Grand Rapids (49534) ***(G-7156)***
Ridgeview Industries Inc 616 414-6500
16933 144th Ave Nunica (49448) ***(G-12585)***
Ridgeview Industries Inc (PA) 616 453-8636
3093 Northridge Dr Nw Grand Rapids (49544) ***(G-7157)***
Ridgewood Stoves LLC 989 488-3397
1293 170th Ave Hersey (49639) ***(G-7869)***
Ridgid Slotting LLC 616 847-0332
12046 120th Ave Grand Haven (49417) ***(G-6354)***
Riedel USA Inc 734 595-9820
2625 Emerald Dr Kalamazoo (49001) ***(G-9317)***
Riedel USA Inc 734 595-9820
2315 Cambridge Dr Kalamazoo (49001) ***(G-9318)***
Riegle Press Inc (PA) 810 653-9631
1282 N Gale Rd Davison (48423) ***(G-3795)***
Rieke-Arminak Corp 248 631-5450
39400 Woodward Ave # 130 Bloomfield Hills (48304) ***(G-1857)***
Rieth-Riley Cnstr Co Inc 231 263-2100
4435 S M 37 Grawn (49637) ***(G-7453)***
Rieth-Riley Cnstr Co Inc 616 248-0920
2100 Chicago Dr Sw Wyoming (49519) ***(G-18904)***
Rigaku Innovative Tech Inc 248 232-6400
1900 Taylor Rd Auburn Hills (48326) ***(G-1020)***
Right Brain Brewery 231 922-9662
1837 Carlisle Rd Traverse City (49696) ***(G-16820)***
Rilas & Rogers LLC 937 901-4228
44440 Meadowcreek Ln Canton (48187) ***(G-2517)***
Rim Custom Racks, Detroit *Also called Repair Industries Michigan Inc* ***(G-4568)***
Rima Manufacturing Company (PA) 517 448-8921
3850 Munson Hwy Hudson (49247) ***(G-8561)***
Ring Screw LLC 810 695-0800
4146 Baldwin Rd Holly (48442) ***(G-8292)***
Ring Screw LLC (HQ) 586 997-5600
6125 18 Mile Rd Sterling Heights (48314) ***(G-16152)***
Ringmaster Software Corp 802 383-1050
631 E Big Beaver Rd # 109 Troy (48083) ***(G-17333)***
Ringmasters Mfg LLC 734 729-6110
36502 Van Born Rd Wayne (48184) ***(G-18235)***
Ripe Harvest Foods LLC 630 863-2440
24291 Veterans Mem Hwy Hillman (49746) ***(G-7916)***
Rippa Products Inc 906 337-0010
25256 Renaissance Rd Calumet (49913) ***(G-2414)***
Ripper Ventures LLC 248 808-2325
14708 Keel St Plymouth (48170) ***(G-13282)***
Ripple Science Corporation 919 451-0241
303 Detroit St Ste 100 Ann Arbor (48104) ***(G-641)***
Riprap 734 945-0892
407 N Oak St Durand (48429) ***(G-4846)***
Rise Beyond LLC 734 203-0644
7825 Newbury Dr Ypsilanti (48197) ***(G-18974)***
Rise Health LLC 616 451-2775
555 3 Mile Rd Nw Grand Rapids (49544) ***(G-7158)***
Rise Machine Company Inc 989 772-2151
905 N Kinney Ave Mount Pleasant (48858) ***(G-11737)***
Rite Machine Products Inc 586 465-9393
44795 Enterprise Dr Clinton Township (48038) ***(G-3338)***
Rite Mark Stamp Company 248 391-7600
4141 N Atlantic Blvd Auburn Hills (48326) ***(G-1021)***
Rite Tool Company Inc 586 264-1900
36740 Metro Ct Sterling Heights (48312) ***(G-16153)***
Rite Way Asphalt Inc 586 264-1020
6699 16 Mile Rd Ste B Sterling Heights (48312) ***(G-16154)***
Rite Way Printing 734 721-2746
5821 Essex St Romulus (48174) ***(G-14325)***
Ritsema Prcision Machining Inc 269 344-8882
3221 Redmond Ave Kalamazoo (49001) ***(G-9319)***
Ritz Craft Corp of Michigan, Jonesville *Also called Ritz-Craft Corp PA Inc* ***(G-9100)***
Ritz-Craft Corp PA Inc 517 849-7425
118 Deal Pkwy Jonesville (49250) ***(G-9100)***
Rival Shop 248 461-6281
3526 Sashabaw Rd Ste B Waterford (48329) ***(G-18161)***
Rivas Inc (PA) 586 566-0326
12146 Monsbrook Dr Sterling Heights (48312) ***(G-16155)***
Riveer Environmental, The, South Haven *Also called Petter Investments Inc* ***(G-15411)***
River Bend Driving Range, Harrison Township *Also called J E Enterprises* ***(G-7702)***
River City Metal Products Inc (PA) 616 235-3746
655 Godfrey Ave Sw Ste 5 Grand Rapids (49503) ***(G-7159)***
River City Steel Svc 616 301-7227
2989 Chicago Dr Sw Grandville (49418) ***(G-7414)***
River Raisin Publications 517 486-2400
121 Newspaper St Blissfield (49228) ***(G-1775)***
River Run Press Inc 269 349-7603
600 Shoppers Ln Kalamazoo (49004) ***(G-9320)***
River Valley Machine Inc 269 673-8070
600 N Eastern Ave Allegan (49010) ***(G-181)***
River Valley Shopper, Big Rapids *Also called Pgi Holdings Inc* ***(G-1684)***
Riverbend Timber Framing Inc 517 486-3629
9012 E Us Highway 223 Blissfield (49228) ***(G-1776)***
Riverbend Woodworing 231 869-4965
1293 W Adams Rd Pentwater (49449) ***(G-12974)***
Rivercity Rollform Inc 231 799-9550
1130 E Mount Garfield Rd Norton Shores (49441) ***(G-12328)***
Riverfront Cycle Inc 517 482-8585
507 E Shiawassee St Lansing (48912) ***(G-9888)***
Riverhill Publications & Prtg 586 468-6011
8850 Dixie Hwy Ira (48023) ***(G-8711)***
Riveridge Cider Co LLC 616 887-6873
9000 Fruit Ridge Ave Nw Sparta (49345) ***(G-15777)***
Riverside Cnc LLC 616 246-6000
3331 Lousma Dr Se Wyoming (49548) ***(G-18905)***
Riverside Defense Training LLC 231 825-2895
5360 S Dickerson Rd Lake City (49651) ***(G-9554)***
Riverside Electric Service Inc 269 849-1222
3864 Riverside Rd Riverside (49084) ***(G-13865)***
Riverside Energy Michigan LLC 231 995-4000
10691 E Carter Rd Ste 201 Traverse City (49684) ***(G-16821)***
Riverside Grinding Co, Jackson *Also called Alro Riverside LLC* ***(G-8813)***
Riverside Plastic Co 231 937-7333
138 Washburn St Howard City (49329) ***(G-8417)***
Riverside Prtg of Grnd Rapids 616 458-8011
1375 Monroe Ave Nw Grand Rapids (49505) ***(G-7160)***
Riverside Screw Mch Pdts Inc 269 962-5449
52 Edison St S Battle Creek (49014) ***(G-1289)***

ALPHABETIC

Riverside Spline & Gear Inc................810 765-8302
1390 S Parker St Marine City (48039) *(G-10965)*
Riverside Tank & Mfg Corp................810 329-7143
1230 Clinton Ave Saint Clair (48079) *(G-14842)*
Riverside Tool................586 980-7630
37909 Sunnybrook St Harrison Township (48045) *(G-7721)*
Riverside Vans Inc................269 432-3212
57951 Farrand Rd Colon (49040) *(G-3491)*
Riverview Products Inc................616 866-1305
201 Byrne Industrial Dr Rockford (49341) *(G-14187)*
Rives Manufacturing Inc................517 569-3380
4000 Rives Eaton Rd Rives Junction (49277) *(G-13888)*
Rivian Automotive Inc (PA)................734 855-4350
13250 N Haggerty Rd Plymouth (48170) *(G-13283)*
Rivian Automotive Inc................408 483-1987
41100 Plymouth Rd 4ne Plymouth (48170) *(G-13284)*
Rivian Automotive LLC (HQ)................734 855-4350
13250 N Haggerty Rd Plymouth (48170) *(G-13285)*
Riviera Industries Inc................313 381-5500
16038 Southfield Rd Allen Park (48101) *(G-203)*
Rivmax Manufacturing Inc................517 784-2556
2218 E High St Ste C Jackson (49203) *(G-8996)*
Rivore Metals LLC (PA)................800 248-1250
850 Stephenson Hwy # 308 Troy (48083) *(G-17334)*
Rizk National Industries Inc................586 757-4700
24422 Ryan Rd Warren (48091) *(G-17997)*
Rizzo Environmental Services, Southfield Also called Gfl Environmental Real Property *(G-15575)*
Rizzo Packaging Inc................269 685-5808
930 Lincoln Pkwy Plainwell (49080) *(G-13093)*
Rj Acquisition Corp Rj USA................586 268-2300
5585 Gatewood Dr Sterling Heights (48310) *(G-16156)*
Rj Corp................616 396-0552
2127 112th Ave Holland (49424) *(G-8181)*
Rjg Technologies Inc (PA)................231 947-3111
3111 Park Dr Traverse City (49686) *(G-16822)*
RJL Sciences Inc................800 528-4513
33939 Harper Ave Clinton Township (48035) *(G-3339)*
Rjl Systems, Clinton Township Also called RJL Sciences Inc *(G-3339)*
Rk Boring Inc................734 542-7920
35425 Schoolcraft Rd Livonia (48150) *(G-10388)*
RK Wojan Inc................231 347-1160
6336 Us Highway 31 N Charlevoix (49720) *(G-2730)*
Rka Design Build................269 362-5558
11337 Coveney Rd Buchanan (49107) *(G-2203)*
Rkaa Business LLC................231 734-5517
5843 100th Ave Evart (49631) *(G-5127)*
RKP Consulting Inc................616 698-0300
3286 Hnna Lk Ind Pk Dr Se Caledonia (49316) *(G-2397)*
Rl Flo-Master, Lowell Also called Root-Lowell Manufacturing Co *(G-10515)*
Rlh Industries Inc................989 732-0493
1574 Calkins Dr Gaylord (49735) *(G-6155)*
Rls Interventional Inc................616 301-7800
4375 Donkers Ct Se Kentwood (49512) *(G-9476)*
Rm Machine & Mold................734 721-8800
30399 Ecorse Rd Romulus (48174) *(G-14326)*
Rmg Family Sugar Bush Inc................906 478-3038
11866 W Thompson Rd Rudyard (49780) *(G-14595)*
Rmg Maple Products Inc................906 478-3038
11866 W Thompson Rd Rudyard (49780) *(G-14596)*
Rml Industries LLC................616 935-3839
14500 168th Ave Grand Haven (49417) *(G-6355)*
Rmt Acquisition Company LLC (PA)................248 353-4229
45755 Five Mile Rd Plymouth (48170) *(G-13286)*
Rmt Woodworth, Plymouth Also called Rmt Acquisition Company LLC *(G-13286)*
Rmt Woodworth, Plymouth Also called Savanna Inc *(G-13294)*
Rmt Woodworth Heat Treating, Southfield Also called Savanna Inc *(G-15695)*
Rnd Engineering LLC................734 328-8277
46036 Michigan Ave # 201 Canton (48188) *(G-2518)*
Rnj Services Inc................906 786-0585
2003 23rd Ave N Ste A Escanaba (49829) *(G-5096)*
Road To Freedom................810 775-0992
211 N 1st St Brighton (48116) *(G-2066)*
Roaring River Press................248 342-2281
57760 Main St Ste 1 New Haven (48048) *(G-12036)*
Rob Enterprises Inc................269 685-5827
156 10th St Plainwell (49080) *(G-13094)*
Robal Tech LLC................248 436-8105
415 W 11 Mile Rd Madison Heights (48071) *(G-10818)*
Robb Machine Tool Co................616 532-6642
4301 Clyde Park Ave Sw Grand Rapids (49509) *(G-7161)*
Robbie Dean Press LLC................734 973-9511
2910 E Eisenhower Pkwy Ann Arbor (48108) *(G-642)*
Robbie DS LLC................989 992-0153
3175 Shattuck Arms Blvd Saginaw (48603) *(G-14738)*
Robbins Inc................513 619-5936
844 Highway M 28 Negaunee (49866) *(G-11973)*
Robbins Publishing Group Inc................734 260-3258
945 N Lake Angelus Rd Lake Angelus (48326) *(G-9539)*

Robe Aerospace................231 933-9355
895 N Keystone Rd Traverse City (49696) *(G-16823)*
Robert & Son Black Ox Special................586 778-7633
30665 Edison Dr Roseville (48066) *(G-14471)*
Robert Anderson................586 552-5648
31384 Harper Ave Saint Clair Shores (48082) *(G-14881)*
Robert Bosch Btry Systems LLC (HQ)................248 620-5700
38000 Hills Tech Dr Farmington Hills (48331) *(G-5370)*
Robert Bosch Fuel Systems LLC................616 554-6500
4700 S Broadmoor Ste 100 Kentwood (49512) *(G-9477)*
Robert Bosch GMBH, Farmington Hills Also called Robert Bosch LLC *(G-5371)*
Robert Bosch LLC (HQ)................248 876-1000
38000 Hills Tech Dr Farmington Hills (48331) *(G-5371)*
Robert Bosch LLC................734 302-2000
3021 Miller Rd Ann Arbor (48103) *(G-643)*
Robert Bosch LLC................248 921-9054
Novi Res Pk 27275 Hggrty Novi (48377) *(G-12527)*
Robert Bosch LLC................734 979-3000
15000 N Haggerty Rd Plymouth (48170) *(G-13287)*
Robert Bosch LLC................734 979-3412
39765 Five Mile Rd Plymouth (48170) *(G-13288)*
Robert Bosch LLC................269 429-3221
3737 Red Arrow Hwy Saint Joseph (49085) *(G-14957)*
Robert Carmichael................248 576-5741
1000 Chrysler Dr Auburn Hills (48326) *(G-1022)*
Robert Craig Logging LLC................906 287-0906
210 W Avenue C Newberry (49868) *(G-12101)*
Robert Crawford & Son Logging................989 379-2712
15490 Green Farm Rd Lachine (49753) *(G-9534)*
Robert E Nelson & Son................810 664-6091
4375 W Oregon Rd Lapeer (48446) *(G-9959)*
Robert Gentz Forest Pdts Inc (PA)................231 398-9194
9644 Guenthardt Rd Manistee (49660) *(G-10912)*
Roberts Movable Walls Inc................269 626-0227
9611 32nd St S Scotts (49088) *(G-15133)*
Roberts Sinto Corporation (HQ)................517 371-2460
3001 W Main St Lansing (48917) *(G-9787)*
Roberts Tool Company................517 423-6691
800 S Maumee St Tecumseh (49286) *(G-16513)*
Robiccon Inc................734 425-7080
27521 Schoolcraft Rd Livonia (48150) *(G-10389)*
Robinson Industries Inc................989 465-6111
3051 W Curtis Rd Coleman (48618) *(G-3472)*
Robinson Solutions U.S. , Inc., Okemos Also called Rvi Management Inc *(G-12684)*
Roblaw Industries, Taylor Also called AJM Packaging Corporation *(G-16375)*
Robmar Plastics Inc................989 386-9600
1385 E Maple Rd Clare (48617) *(G-2995)*
Robmar Precision Mfg Inc................734 326-2664
38189 Abruzzi Dr Westland (48185) *(G-18416)*
Robo-Fence LLC................586 232-3909
33646 Lipke St Clinton Township (48035) *(G-3340)*
Robogistics LLC................409 234-1033
100 Industrial Dr Adrian (49221) *(G-91)*
Robot Space, The, Lapeer Also called Cypress Computer Systems Inc *(G-9924)*
Robot Systems and Engineering, Wixom Also called Innovation Tech LLC *(G-18685)*
Robotic System Integration, Wixom Also called Allfi Robotics Inc *(G-18604)*
Robovent Products Group Inc (HQ)................586 698-1800
37900 Mound Rd Sterling Heights (48310) *(G-16157)*
Robroy Enclosures Inc................616 794-0700
505 W Maple St Belding (48809) *(G-1462)*
Rochester Fudge Company LLC................248 402-3444
1101 Hickory Hill Dr Rochester Hills (48309) *(G-14101)*
Rochester Gear Inc (HQ)................989 659-2899
9900 Main St Clifford (48727) *(G-3133)*
Rochester Grinding, Rochester Hills Also called Special Mold Engineering Inc *(G-14116)*
Rochester Hills Facility, Rochester Hills Also called Lear Corporation *(G-14051)*
Rochester Machine Products................586 466-6190
41530 Production Dr Harrison Township (48045) *(G-7722)*
Rochester Pallet................248 266-1094
2641 W Auburn Rd Rochester Hills (48309) *(G-14102)*
Rochester Petroleum Inc................507 533-9156
33477 Woodward Ave # 800 Birmingham (48009) *(G-1747)*
Rochester Sports LLC................248 608-6000
1900 S Rochester Rd Rochester Hills (48307) *(G-14103)*
Rochester Welding Company Inc................248 628-0801
2793 Metamora Rd Oxford (48371) *(G-12913)*
Rock Construction, Bloomfield Hills Also called Rock Industries Inc *(G-1858)*
Rock Industries Inc (PA)................248 338-2800
6125 Old Orchard Dr Bloomfield Hills (48301) *(G-1858)*
Rock Products, Saginaw Also called Rock Redi Mix LLC *(G-14739)*
Rock Products, The, Carrollton Also called Rock Redi-Mix Inc *(G-2589)*
Rock Redi Mix LLC................989 754-5861
5606 N Westervelt Rd Saginaw (48604) *(G-14739)*
Rock Redi-Mix Inc................989 752-0795
2820 Carrollton Rd Carrollton (48724) *(G-2589)*
Rock River Fabrications Inc................616 281-5769
7670 Caterpillar Ct Sw Grand Rapids (49548) *(G-7162)*
Rock Tool & Machine Co Inc................734 455-9840
45145 Five Mile Rd Plymouth (48170) *(G-13289)*

Rocket Copy Print Ship Inc 248 336-3636
605 S Washington Ave Royal Oak (48067) *(G-14577)*
Rocket Fuel, Troy *Also called Sizmek Dsp Inc (G-17355)*
Rocketplane Global Inc 734 476-2888
3036 W Willow St Lansing (48917) *(G-9788)*
Rockford Carving Co, Marine City *Also called Klingler Consulting & Mfg (G-10961)*
Rockford Contract Mfg 616 304-3837
198 Rollingwood Dr Rockford (49341) *(G-14188)*
Rockford Molding & Trim 616 874-8997
8317 Woodcrest Dr Ne Rockford (49341) *(G-14189)*
Rockman & Sons Publishing LLC 810 750-6011
240 N Fenway Dr Fenton (48430) *(G-5499)*
Rockman Communications Inc 810 433-6800
256 N Fenway Dr Fenton (48430) *(G-5500)*
Rockstar Digital Inc 888 808-5868
6520 Cotter Ave Sterling Heights (48314) *(G-16158)*
Rockstar Group, Sterling Heights *Also called Rockstar Digital Inc (G-16158)*
Rocksteady Manufacturing LLC 586 778-5028
29625 Parkway Roseville (48066) *(G-14472)*
Rocktech Systems LLC 586 330-9031
50250 E Russell Schmidt Chesterfield (48051) *(G-2940)*
Rockwell Automation Inc 248 696-1200
1441 W Long Lake Rd # 150 Troy (48098) *(G-17335)*
Rockwell Automation Inc 248 435-2574
2135 W Maple Rd Troy (48084) *(G-17336)*
Rockwell Automation Inc 269 792-9137
1121 133rd Ave Wayland (49348) *(G-18204)*
Rockwell Medical Inc (PA) 248 960-9009
30142 S Wixom Rd Wixom (48393) *(G-18744)*
Rockwell Team Sports, Mount Morris *Also called Kinder Company Inc (G-11673)*
Rockwood Quarry LLC (PA) 734 783-7415
5699 Ready Rd South Rockwood (48179) *(G-15465)*
Rockwood Quarry LLC 734 783-7400
7500 Reaume Rd Newport (48166) *(G-12106)*
Rocky Mountain Chocolate, Troy *Also called Elsa Enterprises Inc (G-17085)*
Rocky Mtn Choclat Fctry Inc 810 606-8550
12821 S Saginaw St Grand Blanc (48439) *(G-6261)*
Rocky Mtn Choclat Fctry Inc 989 624-4784
8825 Market Place Dr # 425 Birch Run (48415) *(G-1714)*
Rocky Top Farm's, Ellsworth *Also called Thomas Cooper (G-5037)*
Rocon LLC 248 542-9635
1755 E 9 Mile Rd Hazel Park (48030) *(G-7840)*
Rod Chomper Inc 616 392-9677
4249 58th St Holland (49423) *(G-8182)*
Rodan Tool & Mold LLC 248 926-9200
3185 Old Farm Ln Commerce Township (48390) *(G-3571)*
Rodenhouse Door & Window, Comstock Park *Also called Ken Rodenhouse Door & Window (G-3614)*
Rodenhouse Inc 616 454-3100
130 Graham St Sw Grand Rapids (49503) *(G-7163)*
Rodney E Harter 231 796-6734
12880 190th Ave Big Rapids (49307) *(G-1686)*
Rodzina Industries Inc 810 235-2341
3518 Fenton Rd Flint (48507) *(G-5755)*
Roe LLC 231 755-5043
1446 Randolph Ave Muskegon (49441) *(G-11909)*
Roe Publishing Department 517 522-3598
2535 Grey Tower Rd Jackson (49201) *(G-8997)*
Roesch Manufacturing, Tecumseh *Also called Roesch Maufacturing Co LLC (G-16514)*
Roesch Maufacturing Co LLC 517 424-6300
904 Industrial Dr Tecumseh (49286) *(G-16514)*
Rofin-Sinar Technologies LLC (HQ) 734 416-0206
40984 Concept Dr Plymouth (48170) *(G-13290)*
Roger Bazuin & Sons Inc 231 825-2889
8750 W Stoney Corners Rd Mc Bain (49657) *(G-11187)*
Roger D Rapoport 231 755-6665
1487 Glen Ave Muskegon (49441) *(G-11910)*
Roger Mix Storage 231 352-9762
1218 Elm St Frankfort (49635) *(G-5880)*
Roger Randall Bakery, Wakefield *Also called Randalls Bakery (G-17625)*
Roger Zatkoff Company (PA) 248 478-2400
23230 Industrial Park Dr Farmington Hills (48335) *(G-5372)*
Rogers Athletic 989 386-7393
495 Pioneer Pkwy Clare (48617) *(G-2996)*
Rogers Athletic Company Inc 800 457-5337
3760 W Ludington Dr Farwell (48622) *(G-5427)*
Rogers Beef Farms 906 632-1584
6917 S Nicolet Rd Sault Sainte Marie (49783) *(G-15098)*
Rogers Foam Automotive Corp (HQ) 810 820-6323
501 W Kearsley St Flint (48503) *(G-5756)*
Rogers Printing Inc 231 853-2244
3350 Main St Ravenna (49451) *(G-13694)*
Rogue Industrial Service, Atlanta *Also called Bruno Wojcik (G-744)*
Rogue Welding Service LLC 616 648-9723
5787 Hilltop Dr Middleville (49333) *(G-11313)*
Rohloff Builders Inc 989 868-3191
9916 Saginaw St Reese (48757) *(G-13808)*
Rohm and Monsanto PLC 313 886-1966
31408 Harper Ave Saint Clair Shores (48082) *(G-14882)*
Rohm Haas Dnmark Invstmnts LLC 989 636-1463
2030 Dow Ctr Midland (48674) *(G-11409)*
Rohmann Iron Works Inc 810 233-5611
201 Kelso St Flint (48506) *(G-5757)*
Rohr Woodworking 248 363-9743
2813 Bay Dr West Bloomfield (48324) *(G-18310)*
Roi Rich Oles Industries LLC 616 610-7050
4464 Lincoln Ave Saint Joseph (49085) *(G-14958)*
Rokan Corp 810 735-9170
5929 Deerfield Indus Dr Linden (48451) *(G-10070)*
Rol Group, Holland *Also called Rol Usa Inc (G-8183)*
Rol Usa Inc 616 499-8484
694 E 40th St Holland (49423) *(G-8183)*
Roll It Up Inc 248 735-8900
19414 Gerald St Northville (48167) *(G-12255)*
Roll Rite Corporation 989 345-3434
650 Indl Pk Ave Gladwin (48624) *(G-6202)*
Roll Rite Group Holdings, Gladwin *Also called Roll-Rite LLC (G-6204)*
Roll Rite Group Holdings LLC (HQ) 989 345-3434
650 Industrial Dr Gladwin (48624) *(G-6203)*
Roll Tech Inc 517 283-3811
104 Enterprise St Reading (49274) *(G-13704)*
Roll-Rite LLC (HQ) 989 345-3434
650 Industrial Dr Gladwin (48624) *(G-6204)*
Rolled Alloys Inc (PA) 734 847-0561
125 W Sterns Rd Temperance (48182) *(G-16547)*
Rolleigh Inc 517 283-3811
104 Enterprise St Reading (49274) *(G-13705)*
Rollie Williams Paint Spot 269 321-3174
4570 Commercial Ave Portage (49002) *(G-13600)*
Rolls Royce Power Systems, Novi *Also called Rolls-Royce Solutions Amer Inc (G-12528)*
Rolls-Royce Solutions Amer Inc 734 261-0309
30946 Industrial Rd Livonia (48150) *(G-10390)*
Rolls-Royce Solutions Amer Inc (HQ) 248 560-8000
39525 Mackenzie Dr Novi (48377) *(G-12528)*
Rollstock Inc 616 803-5370
3680 44th St Se Ste 100a Grand Rapids (49512) *(G-7164)*
Rolston Hockey Academy LLC 248 450-5300
13950 Oak Park Blvd Oak Park (48237) *(G-12640)*
Roma Tool Inc 248 218-1889
50 Northpointe Dr Lake Orion (48359) *(G-9628)*
Roman Engineering 231 238-7644
1715 E M 68 Hwy Afton (49705) *(G-107)*
Romeo Mold Technologies Inc 586 336-1245
121 Mclean Bruce Twp (48065) *(G-2177)*
Romeo North, Bruce Twp *Also called L & L Products Inc (G-2172)*
Romeo Printing Company Inc 586 752-9003
225 N Main St Romeo (48065) *(G-14234)*
Romeo South, Bruce Twp *Also called L & L Products Inc (G-2173)*
Romeo Technologies Inc 586 336-5015
101 Mclean Bruce Twp (48065) *(G-2178)*
Romeo-Rim Inc 586 336-5800
74000 Van Dyke Rd Bruce Twp (48065) *(G-2179)*
Romulus Division, Romulus *Also called Penn Automotive Inc (G-14317)*
Romulus Nut Division, Romulus *Also called Federal Screw Works (G-14275)*
Ron Pair Enterprises Inc 231 547-4000
105 Stover Rd Charlevoix (49720) *(G-2731)*
Ron Watkins 517 439-5451
4080 State Rd Hillsdale (49242) *(G-7946)*
Ronal Industries Inc 248 616-9691
6615 19 Mile Rd Sterling Heights (48314) *(G-16159)*
Ronald R Wellington 586 488-3087
141 Mclean Bruce Twp (48065) *(G-2180)*
Ronningen Research and Dev Co 269 649-0520
6700 E Yz Ave Vicksburg (49097) *(G-17611)*
Rook Metering Equipment, Mount Pleasant *Also called Michael Engineering Ltd (G-11711)*
Rooms of Grand Rapids LLC 616 260-1452
17971 N Fruitport Rd Spring Lake (49456) *(G-15847)*
Roost Oil Company, Coldwater *Also called Warner Oil Company (G-3461)*
Root Spring Scraper Co 269 382-2025
527 W North St Kalamazoo (49007) *(G-9321)*
Root-Lowell Manufacturing Co 616 897-9211
1000 Foreman St Lowell (49331) *(G-10515)*
Rooto Corporation 517 546-8330
3505 W Grand River Ave Howell (48855) *(G-8510)*
Roots Industries 231 779-2865
870 Holly Rd Cadillac (49601) *(G-2352)*
Rosary Workshop 906 788-4846
5209 W 16 5 Ln Stephenson (49887) *(G-15910)*
Rosati Specialties LLC 586 783-3866
24300 Capital Blvd Clinton Township (48036) *(G-3341)*
Rose Acres Pallets LLC 989 268-3074
4769 N Bollinger Rd Vestaburg (48891) *(G-17595)*
Rose Acres Tallets 989 268-3074
9932 E Kendaville Rd Vestaburg (48891) *(G-17596)*
Rose Computer Consulting, Bloomfield Hills *Also called Rose Mobile Computer Repr LLC (G-1859)*
Rose Corporation 734 426-0005
2467 Bishop Cir E Dexter (48130) *(G-4753)*

ALPHABETIC

Rose Denim — ALPHABETIC SECTION

Rose Denim 517 694-3020
  2301 Tiffany Ln Holt (48842) *(G-8327)*

Rose Embroidery LLC 616 245-9191
  1118 Burton St Sw Wyoming (49509) *(G-18906)*

Rose Laila 989 598-0950
  420 Hancock St Saginaw (48602) *(G-14740)*

Rose Medical, Grand Rapids Also called Rose Technologies Company *(G-7165)*

Rose Mobile Computer Repr LLC 248 653-0865
  4881 Old Post Ct Bloomfield Hills (48301) *(G-1859)*

Rose Nail 313 271-8804
  3565 Fairlane Dr Allen Park (48101) *(G-204)*

Rose Technologies Company 616 233-3000
  1440 Front Ave Nw Grand Rapids (49504) *(G-7165)*

Rose Tool & Die Inc 989 343-1015
  640 S Valley St West Branch (48661) *(G-18338)*

Rosedale Products Inc (PA) 734 665-8201
  3730 W Liberty Rd Ann Arbor (48103) *(G-644)*

Rosemary Felice 517 861-7434
  335 Norlynn Dr Howell (48843) *(G-8511)*

Rosenthal Logging 231 348-8168
  577 Blanchard Rd Petoskey (49770) *(G-13021)*

Roses Susies Feather 989 689-6570
  7191 Middle Rd Hope (48628) *(G-8363)*

Roskam Baking Company (PA) 616 574-5757
  4880 Corp Exch Blvd Se Grand Rapids (49512) *(G-7166)*

Roskam Baking Company 616 419-1863
  5565 Broadmoor Ave Se Kentwood (49512) *(G-9478)*

Roskam Baking Company 616 574-5757
  3225 32nd St Se Grand Rapids (49512) *(G-7167)*

Roskam Baking Company 616 574-5757
  3035 32nd St Se Grand Rapids (49512) *(G-7168)*

Roskam Baking Company 616 554-9160
  4855 52nd St Se Grand Rapids (49512) *(G-7169)*

Roskam Baking Company 616 574-5757
  5353 Broadmoor Ave Se Grand Rapids (49512) *(G-7170)*

Rosler Metal Finishing USA LLC (PA) 269 441-3000
  1551 Denso Rd Battle Creek (49037) *(G-1290)*

Ross Cabinets II Inc 586 752-7750
  50169 Hayes Rd Shelby Township (48315) *(G-15317)*

Ross Decco Company 248 764-1845
  1250 Stephenson Hwy Troy (48083) *(G-17337)*

Ross Design & Engineering Inc (PA) 517 547-6033
  14445 E Chicago Rd Cement City (49233) *(G-2676)*

Ross Joseph 269 424-5448
  93264 Wolf Dr Dowagiac (49047) *(G-4794)*

Ross Pallet Co 810 966-4945
  3360 Petit St Port Huron (48060) *(G-13524)*

Rosta USA Corp 269 841-5448
  797 Ferguson Dr Benton Harbor (49022) *(G-1581)*

Rotary Multiforms Inc 586 558-7960
  1340 E 11 Mile Rd Madison Heights (48071) *(G-10819)*

Rotary Valve Systems LLC 517 780-4002
  807 Airport Rd Jackson (49202) *(G-8998)*

Rotational Levitation Levi, Bay City Also called Twm Technology LLC *(G-1407)*

Roth Fabricating Inc 517 458-7541
  9600 Skyline Dr Morenci (49256) *(G-11615)*

Roth-Williams Industries Inc 586 792-0090
  34335 Groesbeck Hwy Clinton Township (48035) *(G-3342)*

Rothbury Farms, Grand Rapids Also called Advanced Food Technologies Inc *(G-6434)*

Rothbury Farms Inc 616 574-5757
  3061 Shaffer Ave Se Grand Rapids (49512) *(G-7171)*

Rothig Forest Products Inc 231 266-8292
  3600 N M 37 Irons (49644) *(G-8757)*

Roto Flo, Rochester Hills Also called U S Equipment Co *(G-14134)*

Roto-Plastics Corporation 517 263-8981
  1001 Division St Adrian (49221) *(G-92)*

Rottman Manufacturing Group 586 693-5676
  35566 Mound Rd Sterling Heights (48310) *(G-16160)*

Rouch Enterprises, Farmington Also called Roush Manufacturing Inc *(G-5146)*

Rough Road Trucking LLC 231 645-3355
  775 Prairie Ln Sw Kalkaska (49646) *(G-9402)*

Rouhan Signs LLC 406 202-2369
  23667 Atikwa Trl Howard City (49329) *(G-8418)*

Round Lake Sand & Gravel Inc 517 467-4458
  8707 Round Lake Hwy Addison (49220) *(G-44)*

Roura Acquisition Inc (PA) 586 790-6100
  35355 Forton Ct Clinton Township (48035) *(G-3343)*

Roura Material Handling, Clinton Township Also called Roura Acquisition Inc *(G-3343)*

Roush Enterprises Inc 734 779-7006
  12447 Levan Rd Livonia (48150) *(G-10391)*

Roush Enterprises Inc 313 294-8200
  16630 Southfield Rd Allen Park (48101) *(G-205)*

Roush Enterprises Inc (PA) 734 805-4400
  34300 W 9 Mile Rd Farmington (48335) *(G-5145)*

Roush Industries Inc 734 779-7016
  36580 Commerce St Livonia (48150) *(G-10392)*

Roush Industries Inc 734 779-7013
  11874 Market St Livonia (48150) *(G-10393)*

Roush Industries Inc 734 779-7000
  12447 Levan Rd Bldg 6 Livonia (48150) *(G-10394)*

Roush Industries Inc 313 937-8603
  12100 Inkster Rd Redford (48239) *(G-13766)*

Roush Manufacturing Inc 734 805-4400
  34300 W 9 Mile Rd Farmington (48335) *(G-5146)*

Roush Manufacturing Inc (HQ) 734 779-7006
  12447 Levan Rd Livonia (48150) *(G-10395)*

Roussin M & Ubelhor R Inc 586 783-6015
  41903 Irwin Dr Harrison Township (48045) *(G-7723)*

Route 66 Pennzoil 313 382-8888
  20121 Ecorse Rd Taylor (48180) *(G-16468)*

Routeone Holdings LLC (HQ) 800 282-6308
  31500 Northwestern Hwy # 300 Farmington Hills (48334) *(G-5373)*

Rowe Custom Cabinetry 517 526-1413
  815 Kent St Portland (48875) *(G-13641)*

Rowerdink Inc 734 487-1911
  252 Airport Industrial Dr Ypsilanti (48198) *(G-18975)*

Rowland Mold & Machine Inc 616 875-5400
  9395 Henry Ct Zeeland (49464) *(G-19077)*

Rowland Plastics LLC 616 875-5400
  9395 Henry Ct Zeeland (49464) *(G-19078)*

Rowsey Construction & Dev LLC 313 675-2464
  607 Shelby St Ste 722 Detroit (48226) *(G-4572)*

Rowster Coffee Inc 616 780-7777
  100 Stevens St Sw Grand Rapids (49507) *(G-7172)*

Roxbury Creek LLC 989 731-2062
  207 Arrowhead Trl Gaylord (49735) *(G-6156)*

Roy A Hutchins Company 248 437-3470
  57455 Travis Rd New Hudson (48165) *(G-12069)*

Royal Accoutrements Inc 517 347-7983
  172 W Sherwood Rd Okemos (48864) *(G-12683)*

Royal ARC Crane Service, Flat Rock Also called Royal ARC Welding Company *(G-5628)*

Royal ARC Inc 586 758-0718
  520 Sheffield Dr Madison Heights (48071) *(G-10820)*

Royal ARC Welding Company (PA) 734 789-9099
  23851 Vreeland Rd Flat Rock (48134) *(G-5628)*

Royal Building Products, Shelby Township Also called Plastic Trends Inc *(G-15303)*

Royal Cabinet Inc 517 787-2940
  3900 Francis St Jackson (49203) *(G-8999)*

Royal Cabinets 313 541-1190
  15730 Telegraph Rd Redford (48239) *(G-13767)*

Royal Coffee Maker, Okemos Also called Royal Accoutrements Inc *(G-12683)*

Royal Container Inc 248 967-0910
  21100 Hubbell St Oak Park (48237) *(G-12641)*

Royal Crest Inc 248 399-2476
  14851 W 11 Mile Rd Oak Park (48237) *(G-12642)*

Royal Design, Madison Heights Also called J H P Inc *(G-10750)*

Royal Design & Manufacturing 248 588-0110
  32401 Stephenson Hwy Madison Heights (48071) *(G-10821)*

Royal Enterprizes 269 429-5878
  1394 Linden Dr Saint Joseph (49085) *(G-14959)*

Royal Flex-N-Gate Oak LLC 248 549-3800
  5663 E 9 Mile Rd Warren (48091) *(G-17998)*

Royal Food Foods, Madison Heights Also called Great Lakes Food Center LLC *(G-10734)*

Royal Lux Magazine 248 602-6565
  25055 Champlaign Dr Southfield (48034) *(G-15690)*

Royal Oak & Birmingham Tent (PA) 248 542-5552
  2625 W 14 Mile Rd Royal Oak (48073) *(G-14578)*

Royal Oak Industries Inc 248 628-2830
  700 S Glaspie St Oxford (48371) *(G-12914)*

Royal Oak Name Plate Company 586 774-8500
  16560 Industrial St Roseville (48066) *(G-14473)*

Royal Oak Products Company, Troy Also called Gage Rite Products Inc *(G-17125)*

Royal Oak Recycling, Royal Oak Also called V & M Corporation *(G-14588)*

Royal Oak Recycling, Royal Oak Also called Recycling Rizzo Services LLC *(G-14574)*

Royal Pallets Inc 616 261-2884
  3570 Viaduct St Sw Grandville (49418) *(G-7415)*

Royal Plastics LLC 616 669-3393
  3765 Quincy St Hudsonville (49426) *(G-8604)*

Royal Publishing 810 768-3057
  5608 Maplebrook Ln Flint (48507) *(G-5758)*

Royal Stewart Enterprises 734 224-7994
  7355 Lewis Ave Ste B Temperance (48182) *(G-16548)*

Royal Stone LLC 248 343-6282
  3014 Dietz Rd Williamston (48895) *(G-18581)*

Royal Technologies Corporation 616 669-3393
  3614 Quincy St Hudsonville (49426) *(G-8605)*

Royal Technologies Corporation 616 667-4102
  3133 Highland Blvd Hudsonville (49426) *(G-8606)*

Royal Technologies Corporation (PA) 616 669-3393
  3765 Quincy St Hudsonville (49426) *(G-8607)*

Royal Technologies Corporation 616 667-4102
  3712 Quincy St Hudsonville (49426) *(G-8608)*

Royal Technologies Corporation 616 669-3393
  2905 Corporate Grove Dr Hudsonville (49426) *(G-8609)*

Royaltees Golf LLC 517 783-5911
  2000 Townley St Jackson (49203) *(G-9000)*

Royce Corporation 586 758-1500
  23042 Sherwood Ave Warren (48091) *(G-17999)*

Royce Rolls Ringer Company 616 361-9266
16 Riverview Ter Ne Grand Rapids (49505) ***(G-7173)***
Rpb Safety, Royal Oak *Also called Abretec Group LLC* ***(G-14503)***
RPC Company 989 752-3618
1708 N Michigan Ave Saginaw (48602) ***(G-14741)***
Rpd Manufacturing LLC 248 760-4796
3171 Rolling Green Ct Milford (48380) ***(G-11486)***
RPS Tool and Engineering Inc (PA) 586 298-6590
16149 Common Rd Roseville (48066) ***(G-14474)***
RR, Bruce Twp *Also called Romeo-Rim Inc* ***(G-2179)***
RR Donnelley 248 588-2941
32021 Edward Ave Madison Heights (48071) ***(G-10822)***
Rrr Training & Publishing 906 396-9546
1040 E Grant St Iron Mountain (49801) ***(G-8731)***
Rs Products LLC 801 722-9746
53416 Christy Dr Chesterfield (48051) ***(G-2941)***
Rs Technologies Ltd 248 888-8260
25286 Witherspoon St Farmington Hills (48335) ***(G-5374)***
Rsb Transmissions Na Inc (HQ) 517 568-4171
24425 W M 60 Homer (49245) ***(G-8356)***
RSI 586 566-7716
14026 Simone Dr Shelby Township (48315) ***(G-15318)***
RSI Global Sourcing LLC 734 604-2448
43630 Wendingo Ct Novi (48375) ***(G-12529)***
RSI of West Michigan LLC 231 728-1155
1485 S Getty St Muskegon (49442) ***(G-11911)***
Rsls Corp 248 726-0675
51084 Filomena Dr Shelby Township (48315) ***(G-15319)***
RSM & Associates Co 517 750-9330
4107 W Michigan Ave Jackson (49202) ***(G-9001)***
RSM Auto Co., Jackson *Also called RSM & Associates Co* ***(G-9001)***
RSR Industries, Ann Arbor *Also called RSR Sales Inc* ***(G-645)***
RSR Sales Inc 734 668-8166
232 Haeussler Ct Ann Arbor (48103) ***(G-645)***
Rss Baker LLC 616 844-5429
11118 Us 31 Grand Haven (49417) ***(G-6356)***
Rt Baldwin Enterprises Inc 616 669-1626
4322 Cent Pkwy Ste A Hudsonville (49426) ***(G-8610)***
Rt London, Grand Rapids *Also called R T London Company* ***(G-7135)***
Rt Manufacturing Inc 906 233-9158
2522 14th Ave N Escanaba (49829) ***(G-5097)***
Rt Swanson Inc 517 627-4955
1030 Tulip St Grand Ledge (48837) ***(G-6398)***
Rta Industries LLC 269 327-2916
7086 Sandpiper St Portage (49024) ***(G-13601)***
Rta Water Treatment, Athens *Also called Teachout and Associates Inc* ***(G-743)***
RTD Manufacturing Inc 517 783-1550
1150 S Elm Ave Jackson (49203) ***(G-9002)***
Rtg Products Inc 734 323-8916
15924 Centralia Redford (48239) ***(G-13768)***
Rti Products LLC 269 684-9960
1451 Lake St Niles (49120) ***(G-12164)***
Rti Surgical, Marquette *Also called Pioneer Surgical Tech Inc* ***(G-11041)***
Rtlf-Hope LLC 313 538-1700
1401 Abbott St Detroit (48216) ***(G-4573)***
Rto Auto Repair Service 586 779-9450
28837 Bunert Rd Warren (48088) ***(G-18000)***
Rtr Alpha Inc 248 377-4060
2285 N Opdyke Rd Ste G Auburn Hills (48326) ***(G-1023)***
RTS Cutting Tools Inc 586 954-1900
24100 Capital Blvd Clinton Township (48036) ***(G-3344)***
Rubbair LLC 269 327-7003
9229 Shaver Rd Portage (49024) ***(G-13602)***
Rubber & Plastics Co (PA) 248 370-0700
3650 Lapeer Rd Auburn Hills (48326) ***(G-1024)***
Rubber Enterprises Inc 810 724-9200
2093 Reek Rd Imlay City (48444) ***(G-8645)***
Rubber Rope Products Company 906 358-4133
25760 Old Hwy 2e 2 E Watersmeet (49969) ***(G-18178)***
Rubber Round-Up, Hastings *Also called Mensch Mfg Mar Div Inc* ***(G-7805)***
Rubber Stamps Unlimited Inc 734 451-7300
334 S Harvey St Ste 1 Plymouth (48170) ***(G-13291)***
Rubber Tucker LLC 586 216-7071
41491 Mary Kay Dr Clinton Township (48038) ***(G-3345)***
Ruby Sand & Gravel 810 364-6100
6601 Imlay City Rd Clyde (48049) ***(G-3416)***
Rucci Forged Wheels Inc (PA) 248 577-3500
2003 E 14 Mile Rd Sterling Heights (48310) ***(G-16161)***
Rudy Goupille & Sons Inc 906 475-9816
117 Midway Dr Negaunee (49866) ***(G-11974)***
Rudys Sock Drive 313 409-1778
7615 Weddel St Taylor (48180) ***(G-16469)***
Ruelle Industries Inc 248 618-0333
5756 Knob Hill Cir Clarkston (48348) ***(G-3061)***
Ruess Winchester Inc 989 725-5809
705 Mcmillan Rd Owosso (48867) ***(G-12852)***
Ruf International Mfg Corp 954 448-3454
8020 Shrigley Rd Charlevoix (49720) ***(G-2732)***
Ruff Life LLC 231 347-1214
309 Howard St Petoskey (49770) ***(G-13022)***
Ruff Love Pet LLC 734 351-6289
10914 Grams Rd Maybee (48159) ***(G-11171)***
Rugged Liner Inc 989 725-8354
200 Universal Dr Owosso (48867) ***(G-12853)***
Ruleau Brothers Inc (PA) 906 753-4767
W521 Stephenson S Dr Stephenson (49887) ***(G-15911)***
Rumler Brothers Inc 517 437-2990
72 W Carleton Rd Hillsdale (49242) ***(G-7947)***
Runguards, Ann Arbor *Also called Nipguards LLC* ***(G-594)***
Runnin Gears, Harrison *Also called James L Miller* ***(G-7679)***
Ruppe Manufacturing Company (PA) 906 932-3540
100 Mill St Ironwood (49938) ***(G-8771)***
Rusas Printing Co Inc 313 952-2977
26770 Grand River Ave Redford (48240) ***(G-13769)***
Rush Air Inc 810 694-5763
200 Quality Way Holly (48442) ***(G-8293)***
Rush Machining Inc 248 583-0550
256 Minnesota Dr Troy (48083) ***(G-17338)***
Rush Print and Pack 989 835-5161
1515 Commerce Dr Ste D Midland (48642) ***(G-11410)***
Rush Technologies, Holly *Also called Rush Air Inc* ***(G-8293)***
Rusnak Tool & Mfg LLC 734 362-8656
22452 Devonshire St Woodhaven (48183) ***(G-18803)***
Russ Parke Awnings, Warren *Also called Patio Land Mfg Inc* ***(G-17959)***
Russell Farms Inc 269 349-6120
5616 N Riverview Dr Kalamazoo (49004) ***(G-9322)***
Russell R Peters Co LLC 989 732-0660
1370 Pineview St Gaylord (49735) ***(G-6157)***
Russells Technical Pdts Inc 616 392-3161
1883 Russel Ct Holland (49423) ***(G-8184)***
Russo Bros Inc 906 485-5250
1710 Us Highway 41 W Ishpeming (49849) ***(G-8781)***
Russos Bakery Inc 586 791-7320
35160 Forton Ct Clinton Township (48035) ***(G-3346)***
Rustop Technologies LLC (PA) 517 223-5098
4831 W Grand River Ave Howell (48855) ***(G-8512)***
Ruth Drain Tile Inc 989 864-3406
4551 Ruth Rd Ruth (48470) ***(G-14598)***
Rutherford & Associates Inc 616 392-5000
1009 Productions Ct Holland (49423) ***(G-8185)***
Rvi Management Inc 580 531-5826
2152 Commons Pkwy Ste A Okemos (48864) ***(G-12684)***
Rvm Company of Toledo 734 654-2201
845 Monroe St Carleton (48117) ***(G-2562)***
Rwc Inc (PA) 989 684-4030
2105 S Euclid Ave Bay City (48706) ***(G-1395)***
Rwi Manufacturing, Owosso *Also called Ruess Winchester Inc* ***(G-12852)***
Rwl Sign Co LLC 269 372-3629
6185 W Kl Ave Kalamazoo (49009) ***(G-9323)***
RWS & Associates LLC 517 278-3134
305 W Chicago Rd Coldwater (49036) ***(G-3451)***
Rx Optical Laboratories Inc (PA) 269 342-5958
1825 S Park St Kalamazoo (49001) ***(G-9324)***
Rx Optical Laboratories Inc 269 349-7627
5349 W Main St Ofc Kalamazoo (49009) ***(G-9325)***
Rx Optical Laboratories Inc 269 965-5106
65 Columbia Ave E Battle Creek (49015) ***(G-1291)***
Rx-Rite Optical Co 586 293-8888
32925 Groesbeck Hwy Fraser (48026) ***(G-5990)***
Ryan Daup 810 240-6016
11294 Grand Oak Dr Apt 3 Grand Blanc (48439) ***(G-6262)***
Ryan Polishing Corporation 248 548-6832
10709 Capital St Oak Park (48237) ***(G-12643)***
Ryans Equipment Inc 989 427-2829
111 Quicksilver Ln Edmore (48829) ***(G-4997)***
Ryder Integrated Logistics Inc 517 492-4446
2901 S Canal Rd Lansing (48917) ***(G-9789)***
Rydin & Associates, Clinton Township *Also called Rydin and Associates Inc* ***(G-3347)***
Rydin and Associates Inc 586 783-9772
44604 Macomb Indus Dr Clinton Township (48036) ***(G-3347)***
Ryson Tube Inc 810 227-4567
2095 Euler Rd Brighton (48114) ***(G-2067)***
Rytam Technolgy, Rochester Hills *Also called Dl Engineering & Tech Inc* ***(G-13996)***
S & C Industries Inc 269 381-6022
5575 Collingwood Ave Kalamazoo (49004) ***(G-9326)***
S & C Plastic Coating, Grand Rapids *Also called Simmons Crtrght Plstic Ctngs L* ***(G-7200)***
S & C Tool & Manufacturing 313 378-1003
30954 Industrial Rd Ste A Livonia (48150) ***(G-10396)***
S & G Erection Company 517 546-9240
2055 N Lima Center Dr Howell (48843) ***(G-8513)***
S & G Prototype Inc 586 716-3600
51540 Industrial Dr New Baltimore (48047) ***(G-11993)***
S & J Inc 248 299-0822
1860 Star Batt Dr Rochester Hills (48309) ***(G-14104)***
S & K Tool & Die Company Inc 269 345-2174
4401 Environmental Dr Portage (49002) ***(G-13603)***

ALPHABETIC

S & L Machine Products Inc 248 543-6633
30250 Stephenson Hwy Madison Heights (48071) ***(G-10823)***
S & L Tool Inc 734 464-4200
11833 Brookfield St Livonia (48150) ***(G-10397)***
S & M Logging LLC 231 830-7317
2131 Debaker Rd Muskegon (49442) ***(G-11912)***
S & M Machining Company 248 348-0310
47590 Avante Dr Wixom (48393) ***(G-18745)***
S & N Graphic Solutions LLC 734 495-3314
1818 Stonebridge Way Canton (48188) ***(G-2519)***
S & N Machine & Fabricating 231 894-2658
7989 S Michigan Ave Rothbury (49452) ***(G-14498)***
S & P Fabricating Inc 586 421-1950
25201 Terra Industrial Dr A Chesterfield (48051) ***(G-2942)***
S & S Die Co 517 272-1100
2727 Lyons Ave Lansing (48910) ***(G-9889)***
S & S Forest Products 906 892-8268
905 W Munising Ave Munising (49862) ***(G-11754)***
S & S Machine Tool Repair LLC 616 877-4930
1664 144th Ave Dorr (49323) ***(G-4770)***
S & S Mold & Tool, Grand Junction *Also called Sollman & Son Mold & Tool* ***(G-6383)***
S & S Mowing Inc 906 466-9009
1460 15.5 Rd Bark River (49807) ***(G-1157)***
S & S Specialties, Dorr *Also called S & S Machine Tool Repair LLC* ***(G-4770)***
S & S Tool Inc 616 458-3219
2522 Bristol Ave Nw Grand Rapids (49544) ***(G-7174)***
S & S Tube Inc 989 656-7211
9938 Pigeon Rd Bay Port (48720) ***(G-1415)***
S & W Holdings Ltd (PA) 248 723-2870
114 S Old Woodward Ave Birmingham (48009) ***(G-1748)***
S A R Company LLC 248 979-7590
31074 Seneca Ln Novi (48377) ***(G-12530)***
S A S 586 725-6381
33614 Lakeview St Chesterfield (48047) ***(G-2943)***
S A Trinseo 989 636-5409
3700 James Savage Rd Midland (48642) ***(G-11411)***
S and L Associates 616 608-6583
4341 Applewood Ct Sw Grandville (49418) ***(G-7416)***
S and N Products Inc 810 542-9635
3001 Canada Ct Lake Orion (48360) ***(G-9629)***
S and P Drctnal Boring Svc LLC 989 832-7716
801 W Meadowbrook Dr Midland (48640) ***(G-11412)***
S and S Welding 989 588-6916
1011 Florence Dr Farwell (48622) ***(G-5428)***
S B C Holdings Inc 313 446-2000
300 River Place Dr # 5000 Detroit (48207) ***(G-4574)***
S C Johnson & Son Inc 248 822-2174
3001 W Big Beavr Rd # 40 Troy (48084) ***(G-17339)***
S C Johnson & Son Inc 989 667-0211
4867 Wilder Rd Bay City (48706) ***(G-1396)***
S C Johnson Wax, Troy *Also called S C Johnson & Son Inc* ***(G-17339)***
S C Johnson Wax, Bay City *Also called S C Johnson & Son Inc* ***(G-1396)***
S C S, Ann Arbor *Also called Strategic Computer Solutions* ***(G-667)***
S F Gilmore Inc 616 475-5100
321 Terminal St Sw Grand Rapids (49548) ***(G-7175)***
S F R Precision Turning Inc 517 709-3367
29431 Lorie Ln Wixom (48393) ***(G-18746)***
S F S Carbide Tool 989 777-3890
4480 Marlea Dr Saginaw (48601) ***(G-14742)***
S G Publications Inc (PA) 517 676-5100
140 E Ash St Mason (48854) ***(G-11151)***
S H A, Wixom *Also called Semicndctor Hybrid Assmbly Inc* ***(G-18751)***
S H Leggitt Company 269 781-3901
450 Leggitt Rd Marshall (49068) ***(G-11073)***
S Hasan Publishing LLC 734 858-8800
3655 Henry St Inkster (48141) ***(G-8675)***
S K D L P 517 849-2166
260 Gaige St Jonesville (49250) ***(G-9101)***
S L H Metals Inc 989 743-3467
229 Sleeseman Dr Corunna (48817) ***(G-3717)***
S M W, Holland *Also called SMW Tooling Inc* ***(G-8198)***
S Main Company LLC 248 960-1540
50489 Pontiac Trl Wixom (48393) ***(G-18747)***
S N D Steel Fabrication Inc 586 997-1500
11611 Park Ct Shelby Township (48315) ***(G-15320)***
S P Kish Industries Inc 517 543-2650
600 W Seminary St Charlotte (48813) ***(G-2766)***
S P P D, Fenton *Also called Creative Foam Corporation* ***(G-5467)***
S R P Inc 517 784-3153
1927 Wildwood Ave Jackson (49202) ***(G-9003)***
S S Graphics Inc 734 246-4420
4176 6th St Wyandotte (48192) ***(G-18837)***
S Sheree Collection LLC 616 930-1416
432 Storrs St Se Grand Rapids (49507) ***(G-7176)***
S T A Inc 248 328-5000
4150 Grange Hall Rd Holly (48442) ***(G-8294)***
S T I, Waterford *Also called Safety Technology Intl Inc* ***(G-18163)***
S T M, Holland *Also called Stm Mfg Inc* ***(G-8204)***

S Wood Enterprises LLC 989 673-8150
1549 E Deckerville Rd Caro (48723) ***(G-2580)***
S& A Fuel LLC 313 945-6555
10005 W Warren Ave Dearborn (48126) ***(G-3891)***
S&G Group LLC 616 719-3124
3876 East Paris Ave Se # 8 Grand Rapids (49512) ***(G-7177)***
S&M Logging LLC 231 821-0588
6141 16th St Twin Lake (49457) ***(G-17472)***
S&N Fabricating, Rothbury *Also called S & N Machine & Fabricating* ***(G-14498)***
S-3 Engineering Inc 734 996-2303
95 Enterprise Dr Ann Arbor (48103) ***(G-646)***
S1 Plant, Grand Rapids *Also called Roskam Baking Company* ***(G-7170)***
S2 Games LLC 269 344-8020
950 Trade Centre Way # 200 Portage (49002) ***(G-13604)***
SA Automotive Ltd (PA) 517 521-4205
1307 Highview Dr Webberville (48892) ***(G-18247)***
SA Automotive Ltd LLC 989 723-0425
751 S Delaney Rd Owosso (48867) ***(G-12854)***
SA Industries 2 Inc 248 391-5705
651 Beck St Jonesville (49250) ***(G-9102)***
SA Industries 2 Inc (PA) 248 693-9100
1081 Indianwood Rd Lake Orion (48362) ***(G-9630)***
SA Sport, Lansing *Also called Spieth Anderson USA Lc* ***(G-9739)***
Saa Tech Inc 313 933-4960
7420 Intervale St Detroit (48238) ***(G-4575)***
Saagara LLC 734 658-4693
709 W Ellsworth Rd # 200 Ann Arbor (48108) ***(G-647)***
Saarsteel Incorporated 248 608-0849
445 S Livernois Rd # 222 Rochester Hills (48307) ***(G-14105)***
Saba Software Inc 248 228-7300
26999 Centrl Pk Blvd # 210 Southfield (48076) ***(G-15691)***
Sabertooth Enterprises LLC 989 539-9842
2725 Larch Rd Harrison (48625) ***(G-7681)***
Sabo Creative 616 842-7226
16402 Lannin Ln Spring Lake (49456) ***(G-15848)***
Sabre Manufacturing 269 945-4120
2324 S M 37 Hwy Hastings (49058) ***(G-7808)***
Sabre-TEC Inc 586 949-5386
48705 Structural Dr Chesterfield (48051) ***(G-2944)***
Sac Legacy Company LLC 517 750-2903
635 E Industrial Dr Chelsea (48118) ***(G-2825)***
Sac Plastics Inc 616 846-0820
17259 Hickory St Spring Lake (49456) ***(G-15849)***
Saddle Up Magazine 810 714-9000
8415 Hogan Rd Fenton (48430) ***(G-5501)***
Sadia Enterprises Inc 248 854-4666
3373 Rochester Rd Troy (48083) ***(G-17340)***
Sadie Oil LLC 517 675-1325
12635 Red Pine Ln Perry (48872) ***(G-12980)***
Saegertown Manufacturing Inc 517 281-9789
1175 Callaway Ct Howell (48843) ***(G-8514)***
Saf-Air Products Inc 734 522-8360
32839 Manor Park Garden City (48135) ***(G-6107)***
Saf-Holland Inc (HQ) 231 773-3271
1950 Industrial Blvd Muskegon (49442) ***(G-11913)***
Saf-Holland Inc 616 396-6501
430 W 18th St Holland (49423) ***(G-8186)***
Saf-Holland USA, Muskegon *Also called Saf-Holland Inc* ***(G-11913)***
Safari Circuits Inc (PA) 269 694-9471
411 Washington St Otsego (49078) ***(G-12799)***
Safari Meats Llc 313 539-3367
24570 Oneida Blvd Oak Park (48237) ***(G-12644)***
Safari Signs 231 727-9200
771 Access Hwy Muskegon (49442) ***(G-11914)***
Safe N Simple LLC 248 875-0840
5827 Terex Clarkston (48346) ***(G-3062)***
Safety Decals, Ludington *Also called Tyes Inc* ***(G-10553)***
Safety Technology Holdings Inc (PA) 415 983-2706
23300 Haggerty Rd Farmington Hills (48335) ***(G-5375)***
Safety Technology Intl, Waterford *Also called Safety Technology Intl Inc* ***(G-18162)***
Safety Technology Intl Inc (PA) 248 673-9898
2306 Airport Rd Waterford (48327) ***(G-18162)***
Safety Technology Intl Inc 248 673-9898
3777 Airport Rd Waterford (48329) ***(G-18163)***
Safety-Kleen Systems Inc 989 753-3261
3899 Wolf Rd Saginaw (48601) ***(G-14743)***
Saffe Furniture Corp 231 329-1790
200 Viridian Dr Muskegon (49440) ***(G-11915)***
Safie Specialty Foods Co Inc 586 598-8282
25565 Terra Industrial Dr Chesterfield (48051) ***(G-2945)***
Saflok, Madison Heights *Also called Computerized SEC Systems Inc* ***(G-10697)***
Safran Group, The, Beverly Hills *Also called Microforms Inc* ***(G-1667)***
Safran Printing Company Inc 586 939-7600
30706 Georgetown Dr Beverly Hills (48025) ***(G-1668)***
Sag USA, Detroit *Also called Sakthi Auto Group USA Inc* ***(G-4578)***
Sage Automotive Interiors Inc 248 355-9055
24007 Telegraph Rd Southfield (48033) ***(G-15692)***
Sage Control Ordnance Inc 989 739-2200
3455 Kings Corner Rd Oscoda (48750) ***(G-12771)***

ALPHABETIC SECTION

Sage Direct Inc 616 940-8311
  3400 Raleigh Dr Se Grand Rapids (49512) *(G-7178)*
Sage International Limited 989 739-7000
  3455 Kings Corner Rd Oscoda (48750) *(G-12772)*
Sage Tool & Engineering 517 625-7817
  10980 S M 52 Perry (48872) *(G-12981)*
Saginaw, Saginaw Also called Bluewater Thermal Solutions *(G-14618)*
Saginaw Asphalt Paving Co 989 755-8147
  2981 Carrollton Rd Carrollton (48724) *(G-2590)*
Saginaw Bay Plastics Inc 989 686-7860
  2768 S Huron Rd Kawkawlin (48631) *(G-9418)*
Saginaw Bearing Company 989 752-3169
  1400 Agricola Dr Saginaw (48604) *(G-14744)*
Saginaw Control & Engrg Inc (PA) 989 799-6871
  95 Midland Rd Saginaw (48638) *(G-14745)*
Saginaw Industries LLC 989 752-5514
  1622 Champagne Dr N Saginaw (48604) *(G-14746)*
Saginaw Knitting Mills Inc 989 695-2481
  8788 Carter Rd Freeland (48623) *(G-6029)*
Saginaw Machine Systems Inc 989 753-8465
  800 N Hamilton St Saginaw (48602) *(G-14747)*
Saginaw News, Flint Also called Herald Newspapers Company Inc *(G-5713)*
Saginaw Products Corporation (PA) 989 753-1411
  68 Williamson St Saginaw (48601) *(G-14748)*
Saginaw Products Corporation 989 753-1411
  5763 Dixie Hwy Saginaw (48601) *(G-14749)*
Saginaw Products Corporation 989 753-1411
  1320 S Graham Rd Saginaw (48609) *(G-14750)*
Saginaw Rock Products Co 989 754-6589
  5606 N Westervelt Rd Saginaw (48604) *(G-14751)*
Saginaw Valley Inst Mtls Inc 989 496-2307
  4800 James Savage Rd Midland (48642) *(G-11413)*
Saginaw Vly Rehabilitation Ctr, Saginaw Also called Svrc Industries Inc *(G-14768)*
Sagola Hardwoods Inc 906 542-7200
  N10640 State Highway M95 Sagola (49881) *(G-14799)*
Saia Fabricating, Sumner Also called Hayden Neitzke LLC *(G-16331)*
Saint Johns Computer Machining, Saint Johns Also called St Johns Computer Machining *(G-14916)*
Saint Julian Winery 248 951-2113
  506 W 14 Mile Rd Troy (48083) *(G-17341)*
Saint Laurent Brothers, Bay City Also called St Laurent Brothers Inc *(G-1405)*
Saint-Gobain Prfmce Plas Corp 989 435-9533
  3910 Terry Dianne St Beaverton (48612) *(G-1430)*
Saint-Gobain Prfmce Plas Corp 231 264-0101
  11590 S Us Highway 31 Williamsburg (49690) *(G-18563)*
Saint-Gobain Prfmce Plas Corp 989 435-9533
  3910 Industrial Dr Beaverton (48612) *(G-1431)*
Saint-Gobain Prfmce Plas Corp 586 884-9237
  51424 Van Dyke Ave Shelby Township (48316) *(G-15321)*
Saja Natural Herbs 313 769-6411
  10820 W Warren Ave Dearborn (48126) *(G-3892)*
Sakaiya Company America Ltd 517 521-5633
  901 Highview Dr Webberville (48892) *(G-18248)*
Sakor Technologies Inc 989 720-2700
  1900 Krouse Rd Owosso (48867) *(G-12855)*
Sakthi Auto Group USA Inc 313 551-6001
  100 American Way St Detroit (48209) *(G-4576)*
Sakthi Auto Group USA Inc 248 292-9328
  201 S Waterman St Detroit (48209) *(G-4577)*
Sakthi Auto Group USA Inc (PA) 313 652-5254
  6401 W Fort St Detroit (48209) *(G-4578)*
Salad Specialist LLC 734 325-4032
  46036 Michigan Ave # 135 Canton (48188) *(G-2520)*
Salco Engineering and Mfg Inc 517 789-9010
  2030 Micor Dr Jackson (49203) *(G-9004)*
Saldet Sales and Services Inc 586 469-4312
  44810 Vic Wertz Dr Clinton Township (48036) *(G-3348)*
Saleen 248 499-5333
  777 Enterprise Dr Ste 100 Pontiac (48341) *(G-13414)*
Saleen Special Vehicles Inc 909 978-6700
  1225 E Maple Rd Troy (48083) *(G-17342)*
Salem Tool Company 248 349-2632
  7811 Salem Rd Northville (48168) *(G-12256)*
Salem/Savard Industries LLC 313 931-6880
  8561 W Chicago Detroit (48204) *(G-4579)*
Salenbien Welding Service Inc 734 529-3280
  460 Roosevelt St Dundee (48131) *(G-4834)*
Salerno Tool Works Inc 586 755-5000
  21034 Ryan Rd Warren (48091) *(G-18001)*
Sales & Engineering Inc 734 525-9030
  32920 Industrial Rd Livonia (48150) *(G-10398)*
Sales Driven Ltd Liability Co 269 254-8497
  2723 Kersten Ct Kalamazoo (49048) *(G-9327)*
Sales Driven Services LLC 586 854-9494
  3128 Walt Blvd Ste 216 Rochester (48309) *(G-13926)*
Sales Mfg 810 597-7707
  1113 University Ave Flint (48504) *(G-5759)*
Salesman Inc 517 592-5886
  129 S Main St Brooklyn (49230) *(G-2131)*

Salesman Inc (PA) 517 783-4080
  1101 Greenwood Ave Jackson (49203) *(G-9005)*
Salesman Publications, Jackson Also called Salesman Inc *(G-9005)*
Salespage Technologies LLC (PA) 269 567-7400
  600 E Michigan Ave # 103 Kalamazoo (49007) *(G-9328)*
Salient Sign Studio 248 532-0013
  8720 W 9 Mile Rd Oak Park (48237) *(G-12645)*
Saline Lectronics Inc 734 944-2120
  710 N Maple Rd Saline (48176) *(G-15037)*
Saline Manufacturing Inc 586 294-4701
  15890 Sturgeon Ct Roseville (48066) *(G-14475)*
Salk Communications Inc 248 342-7109
  40 W Howard St Ste 204 Pontiac (48342) *(G-13415)*
Salk Sound, Pontiac Also called Salk Communications Inc *(G-13415)*
Salt Brewing Company LLC 517 446-0375
  519 W Ionia St Lansing (48933) *(G-9890)*
Salter Labs, Grand Rapids Also called Salter Medical Holdings Corp *(G-7180)*
Salter Labs LLC (HQ) 847 739-3224
  2710 Northridge Dr Nw A Grand Rapids (49544) *(G-7179)*
Salter Medical Holdings Corp 800 421-0024
  2710 Northridge Dr Nw A Grand Rapids (49544) *(G-7180)*
Salvo Tool & Engineering Co (PA) 810 346-2727
  3948 Burnsline Rd Brown City (48416) *(G-2142)*
Sam, Clinton Township Also called Synergy Additive Mfg LLC *(G-3369)*
Sam Brown Sales LLC (HQ) 248 358-2626
  33106 W 8 Mile Rd Farmington (48336) *(G-5147)*
Samco Industries LLC 586 447-3900
  15985 Sturgeon St Roseville (48066) *(G-14476)*
Sames Kremlin Inc (HQ) 734 979-0100
  45001 Five Mile Rd Plymouth (48170) *(G-13292)*
Sames Kremlin Inc 734 979-0100
  45001 Five Mile Rd Plymouth (48170) *(G-13293)*
Samhita Press 248 747-7792
  33803 Bartola Dr Sterling Heights (48312) *(G-16162)*
Sampling Bag Technologies LLC 734 525-8600
  27491 Schoolcraft Rd Livonia (48150) *(G-10399)*
Sampson Tool Incorporated 248 651-3313
  383 South St Rochester (48307) *(G-13927)*
Sams Suit Fctry & Alteration 248 424-8666
  25040 Southfield Rd Southfield (48075) *(G-15693)*
Sams Welding Inc 313 350-5010
  6903 Hartwell St Dearborn (48126) *(G-3893)*
Samsung Sdi America Inc (HQ) 408 544-4470
  4121 N Atlantic Blvd Auburn Hills (48326) *(G-1025)*
Samvardhana Mtherson Reflectec, Marysville Also called SMR Automotive Systems USA Inc *(G-11102)*
Sand Products Corporation 906 292-5432
  W5021 Us Hwy 2 Moran (49760) *(G-11610)*
Sandbox Solutions Inc 248 349-7010
  1001 Doheny Dr Northville (48167) *(G-12257)*
Sande-Wells Company 248 276-9313
  1554 Charter Oak Dr Rochester Hills (48309) *(G-14106)*
Sanders Candy LLC (HQ) 800 651-7263
  23770 Hall Rd Clinton Township (48036) *(G-3349)*
Sanders Information Publishing 248 669-0991
  41606 Kenilworth Ln Novi (48377) *(G-12531)*
Sanderson Insulation 269 496-7660
  840 Avery Dr Mendon (49072) *(G-11221)*
Sandhill Crane Vineyards LLC 517 764-0679
  4724 Walz Rd Jackson (49201) *(G-9006)*
Sandkey Publishing LLC 248 475-3662
  2060 Hickory Trail Dr Rochester Hills (48309) *(G-14107)*
Sandlot Sports 989 835-9696
  2900 Universal Dr Saginaw (48603) *(G-14752)*
Sandlot Sports (PA) 989 391-9684
  600 N Euclid Ave Bay City (48706) *(G-1397)*
Sandman Inc 248 652-3432
  5877 Livernois Rd Ste 103 Troy (48098) *(G-17343)*
Sandusky Concrete & Supply 810 648-2627
  376 E Sanilac Rd Sandusky (48471) *(G-15066)*
Sandvik Inc 989 345-6138
  510 Griffin Rd West Branch (48661) *(G-18339)*
Sandvik Inc 269 926-7241
  2235 Dewey Ave Benton Harbor (49022) *(G-1582)*
Sandys Contracting 810 629-2259
  10464 Circle J Ct Fenton (48430) *(G-5502)*
Sanford Customs LLC 586 722-7274
  7355 Heather Heath West Bloomfield (48322) *(G-18311)*
Sanhua Automotive Usa Inc (HQ) 248 244-8870
  3729 Auburn Rd Auburn Hills (48326) *(G-1026)*
Sani Zeevi 248 546-4489
  14131 Ludlow Pl Oak Park (48237) *(G-12646)*
Sanilac Drain and Tile Co 810 648-4100
  61 Orval St Sandusky (48471) *(G-15067)*
Sanilac Steel Inc 989 635-2992
  2487 S Van Dyke Rd Marlette (48453) *(G-10987)*
Saninocencio Logging 269 945-3567
  2900 Roush Rd Hastings (49058) *(G-7809)*
Saniones LLC 833 726-4111
  2660 Auburn Rd Ste 700 Auburn Hills (48326) *(G-1027)*

Sanitation Strategies LLC 517 268-3303
1798 Holloway Dr Ste A Holt (48842) ***(G-8328)***
Sanitor Mfg Co 269 327-3001
1221 W Centre Ave Portage (49024) ***(G-13605)***
Sankuer Composite Tech Inc 586 264-1880
36850 Metro Ct Sterling Heights (48312) ***(G-16163)***
Santanna Tool & Design LLC 248 541-3500
25880 Commerce Dr Madison Heights (48071) ***(G-10824)***
Santti Brothers Inc 906 355-2347
26339 Ford Rd Watton (49970) ***(G-18185)***
Sanvik Mtls Tech Strip Pdts Di, Benton Harbor *Also called Sandvik Inc* ***(G-1582)***
Sanyo Machine America Corp 248 651-5911
950 S Rochester Rd Rochester Hills (48307) ***(G-14108)***
Sapa Transmission Inc 954 608-0125
51901 Shelby Pkwy Shelby Township (48315) ***(G-15322)***
Sappington Crude Oil Inc 989 345-1052
123 N 6th St West Branch (48661) ***(G-18340)***
Saranac Tank Inc 616 642-9481
100 W Main St Saranac (48881) ***(G-15081)***
Sargam International Inc 310 855-9694
3751 Finch Dr Troy (48084) ***(G-17344)***
Sargent Sand Co 989 792-8734
6105 Jefferson Ave Midland (48640) ***(G-11414)***
Sarns Industries Inc 586 463-5829
41451 Irwin Dr Harrison Twp (48045) ***(G-7739)***
Sarns Machine, Harrison Twp *Also called Sarns Industries Inc* ***(G-7739)***
Sas Automotive Systems, Sterling Heights *Also called Sas Automotive Usa Inc* ***(G-16164)***
Sas Automotive Usa Inc (HQ) 248 606-1152
42555 Merrill Rd Sterling Heights (48314) ***(G-16164)***
Sas Global Corporation (PA) 248 414-4470
21601 Mullin Ave Warren (48089) ***(G-18002)***
Sas Global Corporation 248 414-4470
21601 Mullin Ave Warren (48089) ***(G-18003)***
Sashabaw Bead Co 248 969-1353
2730 S Sashabaw Rd Oxford (48371) ***(G-12915)***
Sat Plating, Troy *Also called Surface Activation Tech LLC* ***(G-17381)***
Satellite Controls 313 532-6848
13446 Crosley Redford (48239) ***(G-13770)***
Satin Petals LLC 248 905-3866
15599 Agnew Pl Southfield (48075) ***(G-15694)***
Sattler Inc 586 725-1140
6024 Corporate Dr Ira (48023) ***(G-8712)***
Sattler Ira, Ira *Also called Monroe Sattler LLC* ***(G-8704)***
Saturn Electronics Corp 734 941-8100
28450 Northline Rd Romulus (48174) ***(G-14327)***
Saturn Flex Systems Inc 734 532-4093
27642 Northline Rd Romulus (48174) ***(G-14328)***
Saugatuck Brewing Company Inc 269 857-7222
2948 Blue Star Hwy Douglas (49406) ***(G-4774)***
Sault Tribe News 906 632-6398
531 Ashmun St Sault Sainte Marie (49783) ***(G-15099)***
Saurs Custom Woodworking 906 288-3202
7400 Autumn Blaze Trl Toivola (49965) ***(G-16592)***
Sauter North America Inc 734 207-0900
1116 Centre Rd Auburn Hills (48326) ***(G-1028)***
Savage Seamoss LLC 313 288-6899
16250 Stansbury St Detroit (48235) ***(G-4580)***
Savair, Chesterfield *Also called Aro Welding Technologies Inc* ***(G-2847)***
Savanna Inc 734 254-0566
45755 Five Mile Rd Plymouth (48170) ***(G-13294)***
Savanna Inc (PA) 248 353-8180
20941 East St Southfield (48033) ***(G-15695)***
Savard Corporation 313 931-6880
8561 W Chicago Detroit (48204) ***(G-4581)***
Save On Everything LLC (PA) 248 362-9119
1000 W Maple Rd Ste 200 Troy (48084) ***(G-17345)***
Save On Printing 586 202-4469
38062 Douglas Dr Sterling Heights (48310) ***(G-16165)***
Savers Wholesale Printing, Madison Heights *Also called Just Wing It Inc* ***(G-10756)***
Savory Foods, Grand Rapids *Also called Baking Company LLC* ***(G-6493)***
Savory Foods Inc 616 241-2583
900 Hynes Ave Sw Ofc Grand Rapids (49507) ***(G-7181)***
Savoy Energy, Traverse City *Also called Savoy Exploration Inc* ***(G-16824)***
Savoy Exploration Inc 231 941-9552
920 Hastings St Ste A Traverse City (49686) ***(G-16824)***
Savs Welding Services Inc 313 841-3430
11811 Pleasant St Detroit (48217) ***(G-4582)***
Saw Tubergen Service Inc 616 534-0701
5252 Division Ave S Grand Rapids (49548) ***(G-7182)***
Sawdust and Lace 517 331-4535
3532 Delta River Dr Lansing (48906) ***(G-9735)***
Sawdust Bin Inc 906 932-5518
629 W Cloverland Dr Ste 5 Ironwood (49938) ***(G-8772)***
Sawing Logz LLC 586 883-5649
28634 Milton Ave Warren (48092) ***(G-18004)***
Sawmill Bill Lumber Inc 231 275-3000
18657 Us Highway 31 Interlochen (49643) ***(G-8684)***
Sawmill Estates 269 792-7500
1185 Eagle Dr Wayland (49348) ***(G-18205)***
Sawtelle Industries LLC 248 645-1869
1158 Ardmoor Dr Bloomfield Hills (48301) ***(G-1860)***
Sawyer Logging LLC 989 942-6324
4523 S M 76 West Branch (48661) ***(G-18341)***
Saylor-Beall Manufacturing Co 989 224-2371
400 N Kibbee St Saint Johns (48879) ***(G-14914)***
SB Investments LLC 734 462-9478
12055 Globe St Livonia (48150) ***(G-10400)***
Sb Tools LLC 313 729-2759
9827 Sil St Taylor (48180) ***(G-16470)***
Sbf Enterprises, Kalamazoo *Also called Specialty Business Forms Inc* ***(G-9340)***
Sbhpp, Novi *Also called Bakelite N Sumitomo Amer Inc* ***(G-12373)***
Sboy LLC 313 350-0496
1938 Franklin St Ste 106 Detroit (48207) ***(G-4583)***
SBR Printing USA Inc 810 388-9441
2101 Cypress St Port Huron (48060) ***(G-13525)***
SBS Corp 248 844-8200
2700 Auburn Ct Auburn Hills (48326) ***(G-1029)***
Sbsi Software Inc (PA) 248 567-3044
23570 Haggerty Rd Farmington Hills (48335) ***(G-5376)***
Sbti Company 586 726-5756
50600 Corporate Dr Shelby Township (48315) ***(G-15323)***
Sbz Corporation 248 649-1166
3001 W Big Beaver Rd # 402 Troy (48084) ***(G-17346)***
SC Custom Display Inc 616 940-0563
3010 Shaffer Ave Se Ste 1 Kentwood (49512) ***(G-9479)***
SC Johnson & Son 989 667-0235
4867 Wilder Rd Bay City (48706) ***(G-1398)***
SC Thread Cutting Tools Inc 248 365-4044
1920 Opdyke Ct Ste 200 Auburn Hills (48326) ***(G-1030)***
SC Tools, Auburn Hills *Also called SC Thread Cutting Tools Inc* ***(G-1030)***
Scaff-All Inc 888 204-9990
7269 Cardinal St Clay (48001) ***(G-3124)***
Scapegoat Press Inc 586 439-8381
1112 Mollno St Wyandotte (48192) ***(G-18838)***
Scarlet Spartan Inc 810 224-5700
533 W Grand River Ave Brighton (48116) ***(G-2068)***
Scavolini By Cucina Moda, Troy *Also called Cucina Moda - Birmingham LLC* ***(G-17037)***
SCC Plastics Inc 231 759-8820
1869 Lindberg Dr Norton Shores (49441) ***(G-12329)***
SCE, Saginaw *Also called Saginaw Control & Engrg Inc* ***(G-14745)***
Scenario Systems Ltd 586 532-1320
50466 Rizzo Dr Shelby Township (48315) ***(G-15324)***
Scentmatchers LLC 231 878-9918
514 Camp Ten Rd Gaylord (49735) ***(G-6158)***
Schad Boiler Setting Company 313 273-2235
15240 Castleton St Detroit (48227) ***(G-4584)***
Schad Refractory Cnstr Co, Detroit *Also called Schad Boiler Setting Company* ***(G-4584)***
Schaefer Screw Products Co 734 522-0020
32832 Indl Rd Garden City (48135) ***(G-6108)***
Schaeffler Group USA Inc 810 360-0294
4574 Windswept Dr Milford (48380) ***(G-11487)***
Schaenzle Tool and Die Inc 248 656-0596
1785 E Hamlin Rd Rochester Hills (48307) ***(G-14109)***
Schafer Hardwood Flooring Co 989 732-8800
10695 Macon Hwy Tecumseh (49286) ***(G-16515)***
Schafers Elevator Co 517 263-7202
4105 Country Club Rd Adrian (49221) ***(G-93)***
Schaffer Woodworks, Tecumseh *Also called Schafer Hardwood Flooring Co* ***(G-16515)***
Schaller Corporation (PA) 586 949-6000
49495 Gratiot Ave Chesterfield (48051) ***(G-2946)***
Schaller Group, Chesterfield *Also called Schaller Corporation* ***(G-2946)***
Schaller Tool & Die Co 586 949-5500
49505 Gratiot Ave Chesterfield (48051) ***(G-2947)***
Schap Specialty Machine Inc (PA) 616 846-6530
17309 Taft Rd Ste A Spring Lake (49456) ***(G-15850)***
Schawk, Battle Creek *Also called Sgk LLC* ***(G-1292)***
Schawk Inc (PA) 269 381-3820
2325 N Burdick St Kalamazoo (49007) ***(G-9329)***
Scheels Concrete Inc 734 782-1464
33146 Grennada St Livonia (48154) ***(G-10401)***
Schelde Enterprises Inc 231 941-7325
400 W Front St Traverse City (49684) ***(G-16825)***
Schepeler Corporation 517 592-6811
160 S Main St Brooklyn (49230) ***(G-2132)***
Scherdel Sales & Tech Inc (HQ) 231 777-7774
3440 E Laketon Ave Muskegon (49442) ***(G-11916)***
Schienke Electric & Mch Svcs I, Bruce Twp *Also called Schienke Products Inc* ***(G-2181)***
Schienke Products Inc 586 752-5454
120 Mclean Bruce Twp (48065) ***(G-2181)***
Schindler Elevator Corporation 517 272-1234
3135 Pinetree Rd Ste 2b Lansing (48911) ***(G-9891)***
Schindler Software LLC 574 360-9045
1415 Stonecreek Dr Niles (49120) ***(G-12165)***
Schlafer Iron & Steel Co, Detroit *Also called Fpt Schlafer* ***(G-4245)***
Schleben Forest Products Inc 989 734-2858
3302 S Ward Branch Rd Rogers City (49779) ***(G-14218)***

ALPHABETIC SECTION

Schleben Rhinold Forest Pdts, Rogers City Also called Schleben Forest Products Inc (G-14218)
Schlegel 248 344-0997
  17732 Rolling Woods Cir Northville (48168) (G-12258)
Schmald Tool & Die Inc (PA) 810 743-1600
  G4206 S Saginaw St Burton (48529) (G-2244)
Schmaltz Hsptlity Westland LLC 734 728-6170
  6400 Telg Rd Ste 2000 Bloomfield Hills (48301) (G-1861)
Schmidt Grinding 269 649-4604
  202 E Raymond St Vicksburg (49097) (G-17612)
Schmitz Foam Products LLC 517 781-6615
  188 Treat Dr Coldwater (49036) (G-3452)
Schmude Oil Inc 231 947-4410
  2150 Ste B S Airport Rd W Traverse City (49684) (G-16826)
Schneider Electric Usa Inc 810 733-9400
  4110 Pier North Blvd D Flint (48504) (G-5760)
Schneider Iron & Metal Inc 906 774-0644
  100 E Superior St Iron Mountain (49801) (G-8732)
Schneider National Inc 810 636-2220
  10316 Gale Rd Goodrich (48438) (G-6227)
Schneider Sheet Metal Sup Inc 517 694-7661
  6836 Aurelius Rd Lansing (48911) (G-9892)
Schnitzelstein Baking Co 616 988-2316
  1305 Fulton St E Grand Rapids (49503) (G-7183)
School of Rock Canton 734 845-7448
  5810 N Sheldon Rd Canton (48187) (G-2521)
Schott Saw Co 269 782-3203
  54813 M 51 N Dowagiac (49047) (G-4795)
Schrader Bellows, Otsego Also called Parker-Hannifin Corporation (G-12797)
Schrader Steel Fabg Svcs, Niles Also called Schrader Stoves of Michiana (G-12166)
Schrader Stoves of Michiana 269 684-4494
  801 N 8th St Niles (49120) (G-12166)
Schramms Mead 248 439-5000
  327 W 9 Mile Rd Ferndale (48220) (G-5584)
Schrams Custom Woodworking 989 335-0847
  1179 E Ritchie Rd Lincoln (48742) (G-10040)
Schreiber Foods Inc 616 538-3822
  5252 Clay Ave Sw Grand Rapids (49548) (G-7184)
Schreur Printing, Holland Also called Generation Press Inc (G-8048)
Schrier Plastics Corp 616 669-7174
  2019 Pine Ridge Dr Sw Jenison (49428) (G-9070)
Schroth Enterprises Inc 586 939-0770
  40736 Brentwood Dr Sterling Heights (48310) (G-16166)
Schroth Enterprises Inc 586 759-4240
  95 Tonnacour Pl Grosse Pointe Farms (48236) (G-7540)
Schuette Farms 989 550-0563
  2679 N Elkton Rd Elkton (48731) (G-5032)
Schuler Hydroforming, Canton Also called Schuler Incorporated (G-2522)
Schuler Incorporated (HQ) 734 207-7200
  7145 Commerce Blvd Canton (48187) (G-2522)
Schultz Logging 906 863-5719
  4109 14th St Menominee (49858) (G-11259)
Schultz Motors, Dundee Also called Matt and Dave LLC (G-4831)
Schunk Oil Field Service Inc 517 676-8900
  4161 Legion Dr Mason (48854) (G-11152)
Schutte Corporation 517 782-3600
  4055 Morrill Rd Jackson (49201) (G-9007)
Schwab Industries Inc 586 566-8090
  50750 Rizzo Dr Shelby Township (48315) (G-15325)
Schwab Industries Inc (PA) 586 566-8090
  50850 Rizzo Dr Shelby Township (48315) (G-15326)
Schwartz Blast & Paint, Cheboygan Also called Schwartz Boiler Shop Inc (G-2798)
Schwartz Boiler Shop Inc 231 627-2556
  850 Lahaie Rd Cheboygan (49721) (G-2798)
Schwartz Industries Inc 586 759-1777
  6909 E 11 Mile Rd Warren (48092) (G-18005)
Schwartz Machine Co 586 756-2300
  4441 E 8 Mile Rd Warren (48091) (G-18006)
Schwartz Manufacturing 517 552-3100
  1045 Durant Dr Howell (48843) (G-8515)
Schwarzerobitec Inc 616 278-3971
  3566 Roger B Chaffee Mem Grand Rapids (49548) (G-7185)
Schwintek Inc 269 445-9999
  310 Ranger Rd Cassopolis (49031) (G-2633)
SCI Consulting, Sterling Heights Also called Standard Components LLC (G-16189)
Sciaccess Publishers 616 676-7012
  3039 Ledgestone Pl Ne Grand Rapids (49525) (G-7186)
Scic LLC (PA) 800 248-5960
  500 Hogsback Rd Mason (48854) (G-11153)
Sciemetric Inc (HQ) 248 509-2209
  1670 Star Batt Dr Rochester Hills (48309) (G-14110)
Sciencekitwarehousecom 800 992-8338
  1981 Dallavo Dr Commerce Township (48390) (G-3572)
Scientemp Corp 517 263-6020
  3565 S Adrian Hwy Adrian (49221) (G-94)
Scientific Notebook Company 269 429-8285
  3295 W Linco Rd Stevensville (49127) (G-16264)
Scitex LLC 517 694-7449
  2046 Depot St Bldg B Holt (48842) (G-8329)
Scitex LLC 517 694-7449
  3982 Holt Rd Holt (48842) (G-8330)
Scitex Trick Titanium LLC 517 349-3736
  4251 Hulett Rd Okemos (48864) (G-12685)
Scodeller Construction Inc 248 374-1102
  51722 Grand River Ave Wixom (48393) (G-18748)
Scorpion Reloads LLC 586 214-3843
  34054 James J Pompo Dr Fraser (48026) (G-5991)
Scotco Woodworking 586 749-9805
  23793 28 Mile Rd Ray (48096) (G-13703)
Scott & ITOH Machine Company 248 585-5385
  31690 Stephenson Hwy Madison Heights (48071) (G-10825)
Scott Group Custom Carpets LLC (PA) 616 954-3200
  3232 Kraft Ave Se Ste A Grand Rapids (49512) (G-7187)
Scott Group Studio, Grand Rapids Also called Scott Group Custom Carpets LLC (G-7187)
Scott Iron Works Inc 248 548-2822
  24529 John R Rd Hazel Park (48030) (G-7841)
Scott Johnson Forest Pdts Co 906 482-3978
  43850 Superior Rd Houghton (49931) (G-8391)
Scott Machine Inc 517 787-6616
  4025 Morrill Rd Jackson (49201) (G-9008)
Scott Philip Custom Wdwkg LLC 616 723-9074
  5865 Egypt Valley Ave Ne Belmont (49306) (G-1516)
Scott's Wood Products, Roscommon Also called Scotts Enterprises Inc (G-14356)
Scott-Systems, Clay Also called Scaff-All Inc (G-3124)
Scotten Steel Processing Inc 313 897-8837
  3545 Scotten St Detroit (48210) (G-4585)
Scotts Company LLC 586 254-6849
  6575 Arrow Dr Sterling Heights (48314) (G-16167)
Scotts Enterprises Inc 989 275-5011
  554 W Federal Hwy Roscommon (48653) (G-14356)
Scotts Signs 616 532-2034
  3386 Olivet St Sw Grandville (49418) (G-7417)
Scranton Machine Inc 517 437-6000
  266 Industrial Dr Hillsdale (49242) (G-7948)
Scrapaloo 269 623-7310
  6590 S M 43 Hwy Delton (49046) (G-3966)*
Scrappy Chic 248 426-9020
  33523 8 Mile Rd Ste C1 Livonia (48152) (G-10402)
Screen Graphics Co Inc 231 238-4499
  5859 S Straits Hwy Indian River (49749) (G-8656)
Screen Ideas Inc 616 458-5119
  3257 Union Ave Se Grand Rapids (49548) (G-7188)
Screen Print Department 616 235-2200
  1181 Taylor Ave N Grand Rapids (49503) (G-7189)
Screen Works, Novi Also called Ar2 Engineering LLC (G-12364)
Scriblical Vibez Publishing 313 544-3042
  6800 Central City Pkwy Westland (48185) (G-18417)
Scrubs Myway LLC 616 201-8366
  13976 Johnson St Grand Haven (49417) (G-6357)
Scs Embedded Tech LLC 248 615-4441
  25893 Meadowbrook Rd Novi (48375) (G-12532)
Scs Fasteners LLC 586 563-0865
  23205 Gratiot Ave Eastpointe (48021) (G-4944)
Scw Industries LLC 616 656-5959
  5134 S Pennsylvania Ave Lansing (48911) (G-9893)
SD Oil Enterprises Inc 248 688-1419
  28851 Hoover Rd Warren (48093) (G-18007)
SDrol Metals Inc 734 753-3410
  36211 S Huron Rd New Boston (48164) (G-12020)
SDS LLC 231 492-5996
  537 W Fourteenth St Traverse City (49684) (G-16827)
SE Tools, Lapeer Also called Shaws Enterprises Inc (G-9960)
Se-Kure Domes & Mirrors Inc 269 651-9351
  1139 Haines Blvd Sturgis (49091) (G-16322)
Sea Fare Foods Inc 313 568-0223
  2127 Brewster St Detroit (48207) (G-4586)
Sea Wolf, Howard City Also called Inflatable Marine Products Inc (G-8410)
Seaberg Pontoon Rentals, Munising Also called Pontoon Rentals (G-11753)
Seabrook Plastics, Norton Shores Also called SCC Plastics Inc (G-12329)
Seagate Plastics Company 517 547-8123
  320 S Steer St Addison (49220) (G-45)
Seal Bowling Balls LLC 248 707-6482
  5422 Bristol Parke Dr Clarkston (48348) (G-3063)
Seal Right Services Inc 231 357-5595
  141 W Wexford Ave Buckley (49620) (G-2208)
Seal Support Systems Inc (HQ) 918 258-6484
  141 Shafer Dr Romeo (48065) (G-14235)
Sealex Inc 231 348-5020
  8850 Moeller Dr Harbor Springs (49740) (G-7656)
Sealmaster/Michigan, Plymouth Also called Laser Mfg Inc (G-13218)
Sealmaster/Michigan 313 779-8415
  9965 Lapham Way Plymouth (48170) (G-13295)
Sean Michael Brines 517 404-5481
  11539 Owosso Rd Fowlerville (48836) (G-5856)
Searchlight Safety LLC 313 333-9200
  15500 Old Dixon Rd Dundee (48131) (G-4835)
Searles Construction Inc (PA) 989 224-3297
  1213 N Us 127 Saint Johns (48879) (G-14915)

(PA)=Parent Co (HQ)=Headquarters (DH)=Div Headquarters

Seaver Finishing, Grand Haven *Also called Seaver-Smith Inc* ***(G-6360)***
Seaver Finishing Inc......616 844-4360
16900 Hayes St Grand Haven (49417) ***(G-6358)***
Seaver Industrial Finishing Co......616 842-8560
1645 Marion Ave Grand Haven (49417) ***(G-6359)***
Seaver-Smith Inc (PA)......616 842-8560
1645 Marion Ave Grand Haven (49417) ***(G-6360)***
Sebawaing Flow Control, Sebewaing *Also called Sebewaing Tool and Engrg Co* ***(G-15144)***
Sebewaing Concrete Pdts Inc......989 883-3860
8552 Unionville Rd Sebewaing (48759) ***(G-15143)***
Sebewaing Tool and Engrg Co......989 883-2000
415 Union St Sebewaing (48759) ***(G-15144)***
Sebright Machining Inc......616 399-0445
613 Commerce Ct Holland (49424) ***(G-8187)***
Sebright Products Inc (PA)......269 793-7183
127 N Water St Hopkins (49328) ***(G-8369)***
Sebright Products Inc......269 792-6229
2631 12th St Wayland (49348) ***(G-18206)***
Sebro Plastics Inc (HQ)......248 348-4121
29200 Wall St Wixom (48393) ***(G-18749)***
Seco Holding Co Inc......248 528-5200
2805 Bellingham Dr Troy (48083) ***(G-17347)***
Secord Solutions LLC......734 363-8887
240 Southfield Rd Ecorse (48229) ***(G-4985)***
Secure Crossing RES & Dev Inc......248 535-3800
1122 Mason St Dearborn (48124) ***(G-3894)***
Securecom Inc......989 837-4005
3079 E Commercial Dr Midland (48642) ***(G-11415)***
Securit Metal Products Co......269 782-7076
55905 92nd Ave Dowagiac (49047) ***(G-4796)***
Security Countermeasures Tech......248 237-6263
37637 5 Mile Rd Livonia (48154) ***(G-10403)***
Security Steelcraft Corp......231 733-1101
2636 Sanford St Muskegon (49444) ***(G-11917)***
Sedco Inc......517 263-2220
2304 W Beecher Rd Adrian (49221) ***(G-95)***
Sedco Directional Drilling......231 258-5318
4030 Columbus Dr Ne Kalkaska (49646) ***(G-9403)***
Sedco Division Primore, Inc., Adrian *Also called Primore Inc* ***(G-89)***
See Our Designs......866 431-0025
924 E 12 Mile Rd Royal Oak (48073) ***(G-14579)***
Seeking......586 489-2524
18518 Country Club Dr Macomb (48042) ***(G-10633)***
Seeley Inc......517 655-5631
811 Progress Ct Williamston (48895) ***(G-18582)***
Seelye Group Ltd......517 267-2001
912 E Michigan Ave Lansing (48912) ***(G-9894)***
Seg Automotive North Amer LLC (HQ)......248 465-2602
27275 Haggerty Rd Ste 420 Novi (48377) ***(G-12533)***
SEI, Gwinn *Also called Superior Extrusion Inc* ***(G-7587)***
Seifert City-Wide Printing Co......248 477-9525
30789 Shiawassee Rd # 12 Farmington (48336) ***(G-5148)***
Sejasmi Industries Inc......586 725-5300
6100 Bethuy Rd Ira (48023) ***(G-8713)***
Sekisui America Corporation......517 279-7587
17 Allen Ave Coldwater (49036) ***(G-3453)***
Sekisui Kydex LLC......616 394-3810
1305 Lincoln Ave Holland (49423) ***(G-8188)***
Sekisui Plastics US A Inc......248 308-3000
28345 Beck Rd Ste 406 Wixom (48393) ***(G-18750)***
Sekisui Voltek LLC (HQ)......800 225-0668
17 Allen Ave Coldwater (49036) ***(G-3454)***
Sekisui Voltek LLC......517 279-7587
17 Allen Ave Coldwater (49036) ***(G-3455)***
Select Building Supplies, Holland *Also called American Classic Homes Inc* ***(G-7964)***
Select Cut Logging LLC......231 690-6085
20962 Hoxeyville Rd Wellston (49689) ***(G-18260)***
Select Dental Equipment LLC......734 667-1194
47118 N Pointe Dr Canton (48187) ***(G-2523)***
Select Distributors LLC......586 510-4647
2324 Morrissey Ave Warren (48091) ***(G-18008)***
Select Graphics Corporation......586 755-7700
24024 Gibson Dr Warren (48089) ***(G-18009)***
Select Hinges, Kalamazoo *Also called Select Products Limited* ***(G-9330)***
Select Millwork......269 685-2646
960 Industrial Pkwy Plainwell (49080) ***(G-13095)***
Select Products Limited......269 323-4433
3258 Stadium Dr Kalamazoo (49008) ***(G-9330)***
Select Steel Fabricators Inc......248 945-9582
23281 Telegraph Rd Southfield (48033) ***(G-15696)***
Select Tool and Die Inc......269 422-2812
9170 First St Baroda (49101) ***(G-1170)***
Selective Industries Inc......810 765-4666
6100 King Rd Marine City (48039) ***(G-10966)***
Selector Spline Products Co......586 254-4020
6576 Diplomat Dr Sterling Heights (48314) ***(G-16168)***
Selestial Soap LLC......231 944-1978
345 W Airport Rd Traverse City (49686) ***(G-16828)***
Self Lube, Coopersville *Also called Midwest Machining Inc* ***(G-3693)***
Selfridge Plating Inc......586 469-3141
42081 Irwin Dr Harrison Township (48045) ***(G-7724)***
Selfridge Technologies, Harrison Township *Also called Selfridge Plating Inc* ***(G-7724)***
Selkey Fabricators LLC......906 353-7104
13170 Lindblom Rd Baraga (49908) ***(G-1148)***
Selkirk Corporation (HQ)......616 656-8200
5030 Corp Exch Blvd Se Grand Rapids (49512) ***(G-7190)***
Selmuro Ltd......810 603-2117
3111 Tri Park Dr Grand Blanc (48439) ***(G-6263)***
Semicndctor Hybrid Assmbly Inc......248 668-9050
49113 Wixom Tech Dr Wixom (48393) ***(G-18751)***
Semisource Corporation......734 331-2104
1116 Arthurs Ct Pinckney (48169) ***(G-13055)***
Semperian Collection Center, Detroit *Also called Ally Servicing LLC* ***(G-4003)***
Semtron Inc......810 732-9080
6465 Corunna Rd Flint (48532) ***(G-5761)***
Seneca Enterprises LLC......231 943-1171
1745 Barlow St Traverse City (49686) ***(G-16829)***
Senica LLC......248 426-2200
24293 Telg Rd Ste 218 Southfield (48033) ***(G-15697)***
Sensatnal Smlls From Mesha LLC......734 905-1058
570 Kansas Ave Ypsilanti (48198) ***(G-18976)***
Senscomp Inc......734 953-4783
36704 Commerce St Livonia (48150) ***(G-10404)***
Sensible Technologies, Livonia *Also called Bell and Howell LLC* ***(G-10136)***
Sensible Vision Inc......734 478-1130
40376 Wilderness Dunes Ln Covert (49043) ***(G-3725)***
Sensient Flavors LLC......989 479-3211
79 State St Harbor Beach (48441) ***(G-7636)***
Sensient Technologies Corp......989 479-3211
79 State St Harbor Beach (48441) ***(G-7637)***
Sensigma LLC......734 998-8328
3660 Plaza Dr Ann Arbor (48108) ***(G-648)***
Sensitile Systems LLC......313 872-6314
1735 Holmes Rd Ypsilanti (48198) ***(G-18977)***
Sensor Connection, The, Bloomfield Hills *Also called Harold G Schaevitz Inds LLC* ***(G-1827)***
Sensor Manufacturing Company......248 474-7300
40750 Grand River Ave Novi (48375) ***(G-12534)***
Sensordata Technologies Inc......586 739-4254
50207 Hayes Rd Shelby Township (48315) ***(G-15327)***
Senstronic Inc......586 466-4108
44990 Vic Wertz Dr Ste A Clinton Township (48036) ***(G-3350)***
Sensual Scents......586 306-4233
11242 Saar Dr Sterling Heights (48314) ***(G-16169)***
Sensus......517 230-1529
1612 Snyder Rd East Lansing (48823) ***(G-4908)***
Sentio, Wixom *Also called Innovtive Srgcal Solutions LLC* ***(G-18686)***
Seoul International Inc......586 275-2494
40622 Mound Rd Sterling Heights (48310) ***(G-16170)***
Sephora Inside Jcpenney......810 385-9800
4400 24th Ave Fort Gratiot (48059) ***(G-5824)***
Sephora Inside Jcpenney......517 323-4000
5304 W Saginaw Hwy Lansing (48917) ***(G-9790)***
Sepracor Inc......508 481-6700
49928 Parkside Dr Northville (48168) ***(G-12259)***
Sequoia Molding......586 463-4400
820 Lakeland St Grosse Pointe (48230) ***(G-7533)***
Sequoia Tool Inc......586 463-4400
44831 N Groesbeck Hwy Clinton Township (48036) ***(G-3351)***
SER Inc......586 725-0192
51529 Birch St New Baltimore (48047) ***(G-11994)***
Serapid Inc......586 274-0774
34100 Mound Rd Sterling Heights (48310) ***(G-16171)***
Serapid Scenic Technologies, Sterling Heights *Also called Serapid Inc* ***(G-16171)***
Serena Hines (PA)......269 252-0895
668 E High St Benton Harbor (49022) ***(G-1583)***
Serendipity Woods......269 217-8197
7175 Vail Dr Kalamazoo (49009) ***(G-9331)***
Serenity Woodworking LLC......734 812-5429
61155 Serene Ct South Lyon (48178) ***(G-15456)***
Serenus Johnson Portables LLC......800 605-0693
1928 N Stark Rd Midland (48642) ***(G-11416)***
Serniuk Software......248 668-3826
818 Wolverine Dr Wolverine Lake (48390) ***(G-18797)***
Serra Spring & Mfg LLC......586 932-2202
7515 19 Mile Rd Sterling Heights (48314) ***(G-16172)***
Serv-A-Pure, Bay City *Also called Servapure Company* ***(G-1399)***
Servapure Company......989 892-7745
5215 Mackinaw Rd Bay City (48706) ***(G-1399)***
Service Control Inc......248 478-1133
2852 Amberwood Trl Howell (48855) ***(G-8516)***
Service Diamond Tool Company......248 669-3100
46590 Ryan Ct Novi (48377) ***(G-12535)***
Service Extrusion Die Co Inc......616 784-6933
3648 Mill Creek Dr Ne Comstock Park (49321) ***(G-3644)***
Service File Sharpening, Saginaw *Also called S F S Carbide Tool* ***(G-14742)***
Service Iron Works Inc......248 446-9750
245 S Mill St South Lyon (48178) ***(G-15457)***
Service Physical Testers Div, Novi *Also called Service Diamond Tool Company* ***(G-12535)***

Service Steel Co - Detroit, Detroit *Also called Van Pelt Corporation* ***(G-4662)***
Service Steel Company, Sterling Heights *Also called Van Pelt Corporation* ***(G-16221)***
Service Tectonics Inc...517 263-0758
2827 Treat St Adrian (49221) ***(G-96)***
Services To Enhance Potential (PA)...313 278-3040
2941 S Gulley Rd Dearborn (48124) ***(G-3895)***
Serviscreen Inc...616 669-1640
1765 Chicago Dr Jenison (49428) ***(G-9071)***
Servo Innovations LLC...269 792-9279
2560 Patterson Rd Wayland (49348) ***(G-18207)***
Servotech Industries Inc (PA)...734 697-5555
25580 Brest Taylor (48180) ***(G-16471)***
Sesco Inc...313 843-7710
7800 Dix St Detroit (48209) ***(G-4587)***
Sesco Products Group Inc...586 979-4400
40549 Brentwood Dr Sterling Heights (48310) ***(G-16173)***
Sesko Incorporated, Detroit *Also called Sesco Inc* ***(G-4587)***
Set Duct Manufacturing LLC...313 491-4380
7800 Intervale St Detroit (48238) ***(G-4588)***
Set Enterprises Inc (PA)...586 573-3600
29488 Woodward Ave 296 Royal Oak (48073) ***(G-14580)***
Set Enterprises of Mi Inc (HQ)...586 573-3600
38600 Van Dyke Ave # 325 Sterling Heights (48312) ***(G-16174)***
Set Liquidation Inc (PA)...517 694-2300
1489 Cedar St Holt (48842) ***(G-8331)***
Set Steel - Ford, New Boston *Also called SDrol Metals Inc* ***(G-12020)***
Seven Mile and Grnd River Fuel...313 535-3000
5099 Fredro St Hamtramck (48212) ***(G-7613)***
Seven-Up of Detroit, Detroit *Also called Keurig Dr Pepper Inc* ***(G-4359)***
Severance Tool Industries Inc (PA)...989 777-5500
3790 Orange St Saginaw (48601) ***(G-14753)***
Severance Tool Industries Inc...989 777-5500
2150 Iowa Ave Saginaw (48601) ***(G-14754)***
Sew Saintly...586 773-8480
2245 Wadhams Rd Saint Clair (48079) ***(G-14843)***
Sewphisticated Stitching...269 428-4402
1349 Nelson Rd Saint Joseph (49085) ***(G-14960)***
Sextant Advisor Group Inc...248 650-8280
431 6th St Rochester (48307) ***(G-13928)***
Seybert's Billiard Supply, Coldwater *Also called Invis Inc* ***(G-3439)***
SF Holdings Group Inc (HQ)...800 248-5960
500 Hogsback Rd Mason (48854) ***(G-11154)***
SFE, Portage *Also called Stainless Fabg & Engrg Inc* ***(G-13610)***
Sfi Acquisition Inc...248 471-1500
30550 W 8 Mile Rd Farmington Hills (48336) ***(G-5377)***
Sfm LLC...248 719-0212
43587 Prestwick Cir S Northville (48168) ***(G-12260)***
Sfs LLC...734 947-4377
12621 Universal Dr Taylor (48180) ***(G-16472)***
SGC Industries Inc...586 293-5260
17430 Malyn Blvd Fraser (48026) ***(G-5992)***
Sgk LLC...269 381-3820
70 Michigan Ave W Ste 400 Battle Creek (49017) ***(G-1292)***
Sgl Carbon Group, Shelby Township *Also called Sgl Technic LLC* ***(G-15328)***
Sgl Technic LLC...248 540-9508
2156 Willow Cir Shelby Township (48316) ***(G-15328)***
Sgm Transformer LLC...734 922-2400
210 Little Lake Dr Ste 9 Ann Arbor (48103) ***(G-649)***
Sgo Corporate Center LLC (PA)...248 596-8626
47581 Galleon Dr Plymouth (48170) ***(G-13296)***
SGS Wood Works LLC...239 564-8449
3702 Meadow Ln Saline (48176) ***(G-15038)***
Shadko Enterprises Inc...248 816-1712
1701 Lexington Dr Troy (48084) ***(G-17348)***
Shadowood Technology Inc...810 358-2569
4221 Meadow Pond Ln Metamora (48455) ***(G-11286)***
Shadvin Industries LLC...509 263-7128
401 Harvard St Bay City (48708) ***(G-1400)***
Shady Lane Cellars, Suttons Bay *Also called Shady Lane Orchards Inc* ***(G-16342)***
Shady Lane Orchards Inc...231 935-1620
9580 E Shady Ln Suttons Bay (49682) ***(G-16342)***
Shady Nook Farms (PA)...989 236-7240
129 S Newton St Middleton (48856) ***(G-11300)***
Shafer Bros Inc...517 629-4800
29150 C Dr N Albion (49224) ***(G-131)***
Shafer Brothers, Albion *Also called Shafer Redi-Mix Inc* ***(G-132)***
Shafer Redi-Mix Inc (PA)...517 629-4800
29150 C Dr N Albion (49224) ***(G-132)***
Shafer Redi-Mix Inc...517 764-0517
5405 E Michigan Ave Jackson (49201) ***(G-9009)***
Shaftmasters...313 383-6347
1668 John A Papalas Dr Lincoln Park (48146) ***(G-10056)***
Shais Ldscpg Snow Plowing LLC...248 234-3663
995 N Pontiac Trl Walled Lake (48390) ***(G-17675)***
Shakes and Cakes LLC...313 707-0923
13806 Woodward Ave Highland Park (48203) ***(G-7909)***
Shalco Systems, Lansing *Also called Roberts Sinto Corporation* ***(G-9787)***
Shamco Inc...906 265-5065
4128 Us Highway 2 Iron River (49935) ***(G-8753)***
Shamco Lumber Inc...906 265-5065
4128 Us Highway 2 Iron River (49935) ***(G-8754)***
Shamion Brothers...906 265-5065
4128 Us Highway 2 Iron River (49935) ***(G-8755)***
Shamrock Fabricating Inc...810 744-0677
2347 E Bristol Rd Burton (48529) ***(G-2245)***
Shamrock Industries LLC...616 566-6214
15720 Ryan Dr Holland (49424) ***(G-8189)***
Shamrock Publications...269 459-1099
10711 Portage Rd Portage (49002) ***(G-13606)***
Shamrock Publishing...313 881-1721
1523 N Renaud Rd Grosse Pointe Woods (48236) ***(G-7575)***
Shane Group LLC (HQ)...517 439-4316
215 W Mechanic St Hillsdale (49242) ***(G-7949)***
Shannon Distribution Center, Madison Heights *Also called Shannon Precision Fastener LLC* ***(G-10826)***
Shannon Distribution Center, Madison Heights *Also called Shannon Precision Fastener LLC* ***(G-10827)***
Shannon Precision Fastener LLC...248 658-3015
800 E 14 Mile Rd Madison Heights (48071) ***(G-10826)***
Shannon Precision Fastener LLC...248 589-9670
4425 Purks Rd Auburn Hills (48326) ***(G-1031)***
Shannon Precision Fastener LLC (PA)...248 589-9670
31600 Stephenson Hwy Madison Heights (48071) ***(G-10827)***
Shape Corp (PA)...616 846-8700
1900 Hayes St Grand Haven (49417) ***(G-6361)***
Shape Corp...616 846-8700
17155 Van Wagoner Rd Spring Lake (49456) ***(G-15851)***
Shape Corp...616 846-8700
16344 Comstock St Grand Haven (49417) ***(G-6362)***
Shape Process Automation, Auburn Hills *Also called Dynamic Robotic Solutions Inc* ***(G-871)***
Shared Vision LLC (PA)...586 759-1777
6909 E 11 Mile Rd Warren (48092) ***(G-18010)***
Sharedbook Inc...734 302-6500
4750 Venture Dr Ste 400 Ann Arbor (48108) ***(G-650)***
Sharewell, Grosse Ile *Also called Douglas West Company Inc* ***(G-7520)***
Shark Tool & Die Inc...586 749-7400
9412 Gratiot Ave Columbus (48063) ***(G-3502)***
Sharp Die & Mold Co...586 293-8660
34480 Commerce Fraser (48026) ***(G-5993)***
Sharp Industries Incorporated...810 229-6305
5975 Ford Ct Brighton (48116) ***(G-2069)***
Sharp Model Co (PA)...586 752-3099
70745 Powell Rd Bruce Twp (48065) ***(G-2182)***
Sharp Tooling and Assembly, Fraser *Also called JF Hubert Enterprises Inc* ***(G-5947)***
Sharp Tooling Solutions, Bruce Twp *Also called Sharp Model Co* ***(G-2182)***
Sharpco Wldg & Fabrication LLC...989 915-0556
26 Consumers Energy Pkwy Clare (48617) ***(G-2997)***
Sharpertek, Pontiac *Also called Gvn Group Corp* ***(G-13376)***
Shatila Food Products Inc (PA)...313 934-1520
8505 W Warren Ave Dearborn (48126) ***(G-3896)***
Shaw & Slavsky Inc (PA)...313 834-3990
13821 Elmira St Detroit (48227) ***(G-4589)***
Shaw & Slavsky Inc...313 834-3990
13639 Elmira St Detroit (48227) ***(G-4590)***
Shaw Design, Detroit *Also called Shaw & Slavsky Inc* ***(G-4590)***
Shaw Design Group, Detroit *Also called Shaw & Slavsky Inc* ***(G-4589)***
Shaw Industries Detroit Rdc...800 469-9516
41133 Van Born Rd Ste 205 Van Buren Twp (48111) ***(G-17552)***
Shaw's Pharmacy, Durand *Also called Pancheck LLC* ***(G-4844)***
Shawmut LLC...810 987-2222
2770 Dove St Port Huron (48060) ***(G-13526)***
Shawmut Mills, Port Huron *Also called Shawmut LLC* ***(G-13526)***
Shawn Muma...989 426-9505
2315 Dassay Rd Gladwin (48624) ***(G-6205)***
Shawn Muma Logging...989 426-6852
2315 Dassay Rd Gladwin (48624) ***(G-6206)***
Shawnieboy Enterprises Inc...616 871-9292
4183 40th St Se Grand Rapids (49512) ***(G-7191)***
Shaws Enterprises Inc...810 664-2981
415 Howard St Lapeer (48446) ***(G-9960)***
Shay Water Co Inc...989 755-3221
320 W Bristol St Saginaw (48602) ***(G-14755)***
Shayleslie Corporation...517 694-4115
2385 Delhi Commerce Dr # 1 Holt (48842) ***(G-8332)***
Shayn Allen Marquetry...586 991-0445
14009 Simone Dr Shelby Township (48315) ***(G-15329)***
Sheer Madness Drap & Blinds...248 379-2145
21014 Vesper Dr Macomb (48044) ***(G-10634)***
Sheet Metal Workers Local...231 590-1112
3912 Blair Townhall Rd Traverse City (49685) ***(G-16830)***
Sheffler Manufacturing LLC...248 409-0966
6338 Sashabaw Rd Clarkston (48346) ***(G-3064)***
Sheffler Mfg Intl Lgistics LLC...248 409-0960
6338 Sashabaw Rd Clarkston (48346) ***(G-3065)***
Shefit, Hudsonville *Also called Xrs Holdings Inc* ***(G-8619)***
Shefit Operating Company LLC...616 209-7003
4400 Central Pkwy Hudsonville (49426) ***(G-8611)***

ALPHABETIC

Sheila J Eaton Phd PC 586 215-1035
12200 E 13 Mile Rd Ste 11 Warren (48093) ***(G-18011)***
Shelby Antolin Inc 734 395-0328
52888 Shelby Pkwy Shelby Township (48315) ***(G-15330)***
Shelby Auto Trim Inc 586 939-9090
40430 Mound Rd Sterling Heights (48310) ***(G-16175)***
Shelby Foam Systems, Shelby Township *Also called Magna Seating America Inc* ***(G-15268)***
Shelby Industries Inc 586 884-4421
15002 Technology Dr Shelby Township (48315) ***(G-15331)***
Shelby Signarama Township 586 843-3702
51053 Celeste Shelby Township (48315) ***(G-15332)***
Shelby Trim Auto Uphl Cnvrtibl, Sterling Heights *Also called Shelby Auto Trim Inc* ***(G-16175)***
Shelby Utica News, The, Warren *Also called C & G News Inc* ***(G-17744)***
Sheler Corporation 586 979-8560
37885 Commerce Dr Sterling Heights (48312) ***(G-16176)***
Shelf Genie, Rochester *Also called Shelfgenie Southeastern Mich* ***(G-13929)***
Shelfgenie Southeastern Mich 248 805-1834
523 Wilcox St Rochester (48307) ***(G-13929)***
Shell Lubricants 313 354-1187
245 Marion Ave River Rouge (48218) ***(G-13860)***
Shellback Manufacturing Co 248 544-4600
1320 E Elza Ave Hazel Park (48030) ***(G-7842)***
Shellcast Inc 231 893-8245
5230 Industrial Park Rd Montague (49437) ***(G-11600)***
Shelter Carpet Specialties 616 475-4944
2025 Calvin Ave Se Grand Rapids (49507) ***(G-7192)***
Shelti Inc 989 893-1739
3020 N Water St Bay City (48708) ***(G-1401)***
Shelton Technology LLC 248 816-1585
4201 Frostwood Ct Troy (48098) ***(G-17349)***
Shepherd Hardware Products Inc 269 756-3830
6961 Us Highway 12 Three Oaks (49128) ***(G-16558)***
Shepherd Jnes Pblcations Press 313 221-3000
17140 Maryland St Southfield (48075) ***(G-15698)***
Shepherd Speciality Papers Inc (PA) 269 629-8001
10211 M 89 Ste 230 Richland (49083) ***(G-13829)***
Sheptime Music 586 806-9058
27035 Lorraine Ave Warren (48093) ***(G-18012)***
Sheren Plumbing & Heating Inc 231 943-7916
3801 Rennie School Rd Traverse City (49685) ***(G-16831)***
Sheri Boston 248 627-9576
1119 Briar Ridge Ln Ortonville (48462) ***(G-12751)***
Sheridan Books Inc (HQ) 734 475-9145
613 E Industrial Dr Chelsea (48118) ***(G-2826)***
Sheridan Pubg Grnd Rapids Inc 616 957-5100
5100 33rd St Se Grand Rapids (49512) ***(G-7193)***
Sherman Dairy Bar, Holland *Also called Sherman Dairy Products Co Inc* ***(G-8190)***
Sherman Dairy Products Co Inc 269 637-8251
345 E 48th St Ste 200 Holland (49423) ***(G-8190)***
Sherman Publications Inc (PA) 248 628-4801
666 S Lapeer Rd Oxford (48371) ***(G-12916)***
Sherman Publications Inc 248 627-4332
12 South St Ortonville (48462) ***(G-12752)***
Sherwood Enterprises, Livonia *Also called Geisler Company* ***(G-10221)***
Sherwood Furniture, West Bloomfield *Also called Sherwood Studios Inc* ***(G-18312)***
Sherwood Manufacturing Corp 231 386-5132
922 N Mill St Northport (49670) ***(G-12191)***
Sherwood Prototype Inc 313 883-3880
124 Victor St Highland Park (48203) ***(G-7910)***
Sherwood Studios Inc (PA) 248 855-1600
6644 Orchard Lake Rd West Bloomfield (48322) ***(G-18312)***
Sheski Logging 906 786-1886
2875 18th Rd Escanaba (49829) ***(G-5098)***
Shiawassee County 9/12 Comm 989 288-5049
512 N Marquette St Durand (48429) ***(G-4847)***
Shiawassee County Independent, Owosso *Also called Indepndent Advsor Nwsppr Group* ***(G-12838)***
Shiawssee Rhbilitation Program, Owosso *Also called Svrc Industries Inc* ***(G-12860)***
Shield Material Handling Inc 248 418-0986
4280 N Atlantic Blvd Auburn Hills (48326) ***(G-1032)***
Shields & Shields Enterprises 269 345-7744
4302 S Westnedge Ave Kalamazoo (49008) ***(G-9332)***
Shields Acquisition Co Inc (PA) 734 782-4454
26601 W Huron River Dr Flat Rock (48134) ***(G-5629)***
Shields Classic Toys 888 806-2632
1400 E Michigan Ave Ste F Saline (48176) ***(G-15039)***
Shift Roasting Company LLC 734 915-3666
9304 Warner Rd Saline (48176) ***(G-15040)***
Shiloh Inds Hot Stamping LLC, Auburn Hills *Also called Grouper Wild LLC* ***(G-917)***
Shiloh Inds Hot Stamping LLC, Galesburg *Also called Grouper Wild LLC* ***(G-6078)***
Shimp Sand & Gravel LLC 517 369-1632
822 Snow Prairie Rd Bronson (49028) ***(G-2120)***
Shinola/Detroit LLC (PA) 888 304-2534
485 W Milwaukee St Detroit (48202) ***(G-4591)***
Shinwon USA Inc 734 469-2550
12147 Globe St Livonia (48150) ***(G-10405)***
Shipping Container Corporation 313 937-2411
26000 Capitol Redford (48239) ***(G-13771)***
Shipston Alum Tech Intl Inc (HQ) 317 738-0282
22122 Telegraph Rd Southfield (48033) ***(G-15699)***
Shipston Alum Tech Intl LLC (HQ) 317 738-0282
22122 Telegraph Rd Southfield (48033) ***(G-15700)***
Shipston Alum Tech Mich Inc 616 842-3500
14638 Apple Dr Fruitport (49415) ***(G-6070)***
Shipston Aluminum Tech Ind Inc 317 738-0282
22122 Telegraph Rd Southfield (48033) ***(G-15701)***
Shipston Group US Inc (PA) 248 372-9018
22122 Telegraph Rd Southfield (48033) ***(G-15702)***
Shirt Razor LLC 810 623-7116
126 E Grand River Ave Brighton (48116) ***(G-2070)***
Shirt Traveler 800 403-4117
6005 Miller Rd Ste 7 Swartz Creek (48473) ***(G-16358)***
Shirt Works 989 448-8889
1196 Energy Dr Gaylord (49735) ***(G-6159)***
Shively Corp 269 683-9503
2604 S 11th St Niles (49120) ***(G-12167)***
Shock-Tek LLC 313 886-0530
23336 Robert John St Saint Clair Shores (48080) ***(G-14883)***
Shoe Shop 231 739-2174
3324 Glade St Muskegon (49444) ***(G-11918)***
Shooks Asphalt Paving Co Inc (PA) 989 236-7740
3588 W Cleveland Rd Perrinton (48871) ***(G-12976)***
Shop IV Sbusid Inv Grede LLC 248 440-9515
20750 Civic Center Dr # 100 Southfield (48076) ***(G-15703)***
Shop Makarios LLC 800 479-0032
4390 104th St Sw Byron Center (49315) ***(G-2295)***
Shopper's Guide, Coldwater *Also called Harold K Schultz* ***(G-3438)***
Shoppers Fair Inc 231 627-7144
308 N Main St Cheboygan (49721) ***(G-2799)***
Shorecrest Enterprises Inc 586 948-9226
33251 S Gratiot Ave Clinton Township (48035) ***(G-3352)***
Shoreline Container LLC (PA) 616 399-2088
4450 136th Ave Holland (49424) ***(G-8191)***
Shoreline Container and Packg, Holland *Also called Shoreline Container LLC* ***(G-8191)***
Shoreline Creations Ltd (PA) 616 393-2077
2465 112th Ave Holland (49424) ***(G-8192)***
Shoreline Fruit LLC (PA) 231 941-4336
10106 Us Highway 31 N Williamsburg (49690) ***(G-18564)***
Shoreline Manufacturing LLC 616 834-1503
11867 Greenway Dr Holland (49424) ***(G-8193)***
Shoreline Manufacturing LLC 616 834-1503
155 Manufacturers Dr Holland (49424) ***(G-8194)***
Shoreline Media, Ludington *Also called Ludington Daily News Inc* ***(G-10543)***
Shoreline Mold & Engrg LLC 269 926-2223
1530 Townline Rd Benton Harbor (49022) ***(G-1584)***
Shoreline Mtal Fabricators Inc 231 722-4443
1880 Park St Muskegon (49441) ***(G-11919)***
Shoreline Recycling & Supply 231 722-6081
259 Ottawa St Muskegon (49442) ***(G-11920)***
Shores Cremation & Burial 616 395-3630
11939 James St Holland (49424) ***(G-8195)***
Shores Engineering Co Inc 586 792-2748
34632 Nova Dr Clinton Township (48035) ***(G-3353)***
Shores Tool and Mfg, Harrison Township *Also called Roussin M & Ubelhor R Inc* ***(G-7723)***
Short Books Inc 231 796-2167
955 Godfrey Ave Sw Grand Rapids (49503) ***(G-7194)***
Short Iron Fabrication 231 375-8825
2861 S Milliron Rd Muskegon (49444) ***(G-11921)***
Shoulder Innovations Inc 616 294-1026
1535 Steele Ave Sw Ste B Grand Rapids (49507) ***(G-7195)***
Shouldice Indus Mfrs Cntrs Inc 269 962-5579
182 Elm St Battle Creek (49014) ***(G-1293)***
Shouse Tool Inc 810 629-0391
290 N Alloy Dr Fenton (48430) ***(G-5503)***
Shred-Pac Inc 269 793-7978
2982 22nd St Hopkins (49328) ***(G-8370)***
Shurco LLC 616 366-2367
7192 Bridge Town Ln Se Caledonia (49316) ***(G-2398)***
Shure Star LLC 248 365-4382
2498 Commercial Dr Auburn Hills (48326) ***(G-1033)***
Shutterbooth 734 680-6067
4972 S Ridgeside Cir Ann Arbor (48105) ***(G-651)***
Shutterbooth 586 747-4110
2441 Burleigh St West Bloomfield (48324) ***(G-18313)***
Shwayder Company 248 645-9511
2335 E Lincoln St Birmingham (48009) ***(G-1749)***
Shyft Group Inc (PA) 517 543-6400
41280 Bridge St Novi (48375) ***(G-12536)***
Shyft Group Inc 517 543-6400
1541 Reynolds Rd Charlotte (48813) ***(G-2767)***
Shyft Group Inc 517 543-6400
1549 Mikesell St Charlotte (48813) ***(G-2768)***
Shyft Group Usa Inc (HQ) 517 543-6400
1000 Reynolds Rd Charlotte (48813) ***(G-2769)***
Sidekick Device 231 894-6905
7426 Wiczer Dr Whitehall (49461) ***(G-18509)***
Sideline Signatures, Traverse City *Also called Britten Banners LLC* ***(G-16628)***

ALPHABETIC SECTION

Sidley Diamond Tool Company (PA) 734 261-7970
32320 Ford Rd Garden City (48135) *(G-6109)*
Siemens Industry Inc 248 307-3400
777 Chicago Rd Troy (48083) *(G-17350)*
Siemens Industry Software Inc 313 317-6100
1555 Fairlane Dr Ste 300 Allen Park (48101) *(G-206)*
Siemens Industry Software Inc 734 953-2700
38695 7 Mile Rd Ste 300 Livonia (48152) *(G-10406)*
Siemens Industry Software Inc 734 994-7300
2600 Green Rd Ste 100 Ann Arbor (48105) *(G-652)*
Sierra Plastics Inc 989 269-6272
175 Thompson Rd Ste A Bad Axe (48413) *(G-1110)*
Sigma Diagnostics Inc 734 744-4846
14155 Farmington Rd Ste D Livonia (48154) *(G-10407)*
Sigma International Inc (PA) 248 230-9681
36800 Plymouth Rd Livonia (48150) *(G-10408)*
Sigma Luminous LLC 866 755-3563
23000 W Industrial Dr B Saint Clair Shores (48080) *(G-14884)*
Sigma Machine Inc 269 806-5679
3358 Center Park Pl Kalamazoo (49048) *(G-9333)*
Sigma Tool Mfg Inc 586 792-3300
35280 Forton Ct Clinton Township (48035) *(G-3354)*
Sigma Wireless LLC 313 423-2629
8063 Coyle St Detroit (48228) *(G-4592)*
Sign & Graphics Operations LLC 248 596-8626
47585 Galleon Dr Plymouth (48170) *(G-13297)*
Sign & Vinyl Graphix Express 586 838-4741
34423 Richard O Dr Sterling Heights (48310) *(G-16177)*
Sign A Rama 517 489-4314
2189 W Grand River Ave Okemos (48864) *(G-12686)*
Sign A Rama 517 489-4314
15851 S Us Highway 27 Lansing (48906) *(G-9736)*
Sign A Rama Inc 810 494-7446
5050 S Old Us Highway 23 # 200 Brighton (48114) *(G-2071)*
Sign and Banner World 248 957-1240
31178 Grand River Ave Farmington (48336) *(G-5149)*
Sign and Design 231 348-9256
427 Creekside Dr Petoskey (49770) *(G-13023)*
Sign Art Inc (PA) 269 381-3012
5757 E Cork St Kalamazoo (49048) *(G-9334)*
Sign Cabinets Inc 231 725-7187
2000 9th St Muskegon (49444) *(G-11922)*
Sign Center, Kalamazoo Also called Sign On Inc *(G-9338)*
Sign Center of Kalamazoo Inc 269 381-6869
711 Portage St Kalamazoo (49001) *(G-9335)*
Sign City Inc 269 375-1385
7178 Stadium Dr Kalamazoo (49009) *(G-9336)*
Sign Concepts Corporation 248 680-8970
1119 Wheaton Dr Troy (48083) *(G-17351)*
Sign Division 269 548-8978
1923 Pipestone Rd Benton Harbor (49022) *(G-1585)*
Sign Fabricators Inc 586 468-7360
38140 Circle Dr Harrison Township (48045) *(G-7725)*
Sign Graphix 248 241-6531
8457 Andersonville Rd Clarkston (48346) *(G-3066)*
Sign Image Inc 989 781-5229
8155 Gratiot Rd Saginaw (48609) *(G-14756)*
Sign Impressions Inc 269 382-5152
3929 Ravine Rd Kalamazoo (49006) *(G-9337)*
Sign of The Loon Gifts Inc 231 436-5155
311 W Central Ave Mackinaw City (49701) *(G-10569)*
Sign On Inc 269 381-6869
711 Portage St Kalamazoo (49001) *(G-9338)*
Sign Pal 989 755-7773
2301 N Michigan Ave Saginaw (48602) *(G-14757)*
Sign Pros LLC 313 310-1010
5671 Berwyn St Dearborn Heights (48127) *(G-3939)*
Sign Screen 231 942-2273
450 S Mackinaw Trl Cadillac (49601) *(G-2353)*
Sign Screen Inc 810 239-1100
408 S Center Rd Flint (48506) *(G-5762)*
Sign Shop, The, Kalamazoo Also called Shields & Shields Enterprises *(G-9332)*
Sign Solutions, Marquette Also called Landers Drafting Inc *(G-11028)*
Sign Studio Inc 214 526-6940
11450 Stephens Rd Warren (48089) *(G-18013)*
Sign Stuff Inc 734 458-1055
13604 Merriman Rd Livonia (48150) *(G-10409)*
Sign Up Inc 906 789-7446
1300 Ludington St Escanaba (49829) *(G-5099)*
Sign Up Schumann Outdoor Arts, Escanaba Also called Sign Up Inc *(G-5099)*
Sign With Sally C LLC 586 612-5100
10051 Saint John Dr Algonac (48001) *(G-143)*
Sign Works Inc 517 546-3620
5380 E Grand River Ave Howell (48843) *(G-8517)*
Sign-A-Rama, Brighton Also called Sign A Rama Inc *(G-2071)*
Sign-A-Rama, Okemos Also called Sign A Rama *(G-12686)*
Sign-A-Rama, Lansing Also called Sign A Rama *(G-9736)*
Sign-A-Rama, Grand Rapids Also called K-Bur Enterprises Inc *(G-6876)*
Sign-A-Rama, Flint Also called Stnj LLC *(G-5770)*

Sign-A-Rama 586 792-7446
36886 Harper Ave Clinton Township (48035) *(G-3355)*
Sign-A-Rama Inc 734 522-6661
6641 Middlebelt Rd Garden City (48135) *(G-6110)*
Sign-On Connect 313 539-3246
296 Lothrop Rd Grosse Pointe Farms (48236) *(G-7541)*
Signa Group Inc 231 845-5101
5175 W 6th St Ludington (49431) *(G-10550)*
Signal 7 Wines LLC 616 581-8900
1425 Pontiac Trl Ann Arbor (48105) *(G-653)*
Signal Conditioning Solutions, Novi Also called Scs Embedded Tech LLC *(G-12532)*
Signal Medical Corporation (PA) 810 364-7070
400 Pyramid Dr Ste 2 Marysville (48040) *(G-11099)*
Signal-Return Inc 313 567-8970
1345 Division St Ste 102 Detroit (48207) *(G-4593)*
Signalx Technologies LLC 248 935-4237
41100 Plymouth Rd Ste 3 Plymouth (48170) *(G-13298)*
Signarama Farmington 248 957-1240
31178 Grand River Ave Farmington (48336) *(G-5150)*
Signarama Troy Metro Detroit, Troy Also called Signproco Inc *(G-17352)*
Signature Designs Inc 248 426-9735
24357 Indoplex Cir Farmington Hills (48335) *(G-5378)*
Signature Truck Systems LLC 810 564-2294
13460 N Saginaw Rd Clio (48420) *(G-3411)*
Signature Wall Solutions Inc 616 366-4242
1928 N Stark Rd Midland (48642) *(G-11417)*
Signcomp LLC 616 784-0405
3032 Walker Ridge Dr Nw Grand Rapids (49544) *(G-7196)*
Signcrafters Inc 231 773-3343
2325 Black Creek Rd Muskegon (49444) *(G-11923)*
Signing Savvy LLC 517 455-7663
2025 Central Park Dr # 1009 Okemos (48805) *(G-12687)*
Signmakers Ltd 616 455-4220
7290 Division Ave S Ste A Grand Rapids (49548) *(G-7197)*
Signmeupcom Inc 312 343-1263
1285 N Telegraph Rd Monroe (48162) *(G-11572)*
Signoutfitters.com, Wyandotte Also called S S Graphics Inc *(G-18837)*
Signplicity Sign Systems Inc 231 943-3800
1555 S M 37 Traverse City (49685) *(G-16832)*
Signproco Inc 248 585-6880
1017 Naughton Dr Troy (48083) *(G-17352)*
Signs & Designs Inc 269 968-8909
17 32nd St N Battle Creek (49015) *(G-1294)*
Signs & Laser Engraving 248 577-6191
1221 E 14 Mile Rd Troy (48083) *(G-17353)*
Signs & More, Troy Also called Fosters Ventures LLC *(G-17120)*
Signs & Wonders LLC 618 694-4960
1378 Lacosta Dr Dewitt (48820) *(G-4715)*
Signs and More 810 820-9955
3295 S Linden Rd Flint (48507) *(G-5763)*
Signs By Crannie Inc (PA) 810 487-0000
4145 Market Pl Flint (48507) *(G-5764)*
Signs By Rhonda LLC 248 408-0552
39911 Day Dr Clinton Township (48038) *(G-3356)*
Signs By Tmrrow - Rchster Hlls 248 299-9229
1976 Star Batt Dr Rochester Hills (48309) *(G-14111)*
Signs By Tomorrow, Clinton Township Also called Norris Graphics Inc *(G-3308)*
Signs By Tomorrow, Plymouth Also called Sign & Graphics Operations LLC *(G-13297)*
Signs By Tomorrow, Clinton Township Also called Shorecrest Enterprises Inc *(G-3352)*
Signs By Tomorrow, Royal Oak Also called JD Hemp Inc *(G-14551)*
Signs By Tomorrow 616 647-7446
5657 Marlin Ave Hudsonville (49426) *(G-8612)*
Signs By Tomorrow 734 522-8440
33611 Plymouth Rd Livonia (48150) *(G-10410)*
Signs By Tomorrow 248 478-5600
40400 Grand River Ave H Novi (48375) *(G-12537)*
Signs Direct LLC 810 732-5067
2259 Wicklow South Dr Davison (48423) *(G-3796)*
Signs In LLC 248 939-7446
34705 W 12 Mile Rd Farmington Hills (48331) *(G-5379)*
Signs Letters & Graphics Inc 231 536-7929
4095 Jonathon Dr East Jordan (49727) *(G-4879)*
Signs Now, Negaunee Also called 5 Pyn Inc *(G-11962)*
Signs Now, Holland Also called C T L Enterprises Inc *(G-7989)*
Signs Now, Traverse City Also called Auxier & Associates LLC *(G-16608)*
Signs of Love Inc 586 413-1269
38490 Ammerst Dr Clinton Township (48038) *(G-3357)*
Signs of Prosperity LLC 248 488-9010
27615 Halsted Rd Farmington Hills (48331) *(G-5380)*
Signs Plus (PA) 810 987-7446
1604 Stone St Port Huron (48060) *(G-13527)*
Signs That Scream 616 698-6284
6570 Millstream Loop Se Caledonia (49316) *(G-2399)*
Signs With Design, Rockford Also called AC Design LLC *(G-14151)*
Signs365com LLC 800 265-8830
51245 Filomena Dr Shelby Township (48315) *(G-15333)*
Signtech, Grand Rapids Also called Signcomp LLC *(G-7196)*

Signtext Incorporated 248 442-9080
24333 Indoplex Cir Farmington Hills (48335) ***(G-5381)***
Signtext 2, Farmington Hills *Also called Signtext Incorporated* ***(G-5381)***
Signworks of Michigan Inc (PA) 616 954-2554
4612 44th St Se Grand Rapids (49512) ***(G-7198)***
Sigvaris Inc 616 741-4281
13055 Riley St Ste 30 Holland (49424) ***(G-8196)***
Sika Advanced Resins US, Madison Heights *Also called Sika Auto Eaton Rapids Inc* ***(G-10828)***
Sika Auto Eaton Rapids Inc (HQ) 248 588-2270
30800 Stephenson Hwy Madison Heights (48071) ***(G-10828)***
Sika Corporation 248 577-0020
30800 Stephenson Hwy Madison Heights (48071) ***(G-10829)***
Sika Industry, Madison Heights *Also called Sika Corporation* ***(G-10829)***
Siko Products Inc 734 426-3476
2155 Bishop Cir E Dexter (48130) ***(G-4754)***
Silbond Corporation 517 436-3171
9901 Sand Creek Hwy Weston (49289) ***(G-18433)***
Silent Call Communications, Waterford *Also called Silent Call Corporation* ***(G-18164)***
Silent Call Corporation 248 673-7353
5095 Williams Lake Rd Waterford (48329) ***(G-18164)***
Silent Observer, Greenville *Also called City of Greenville* ***(G-7478)***
Silent Observer 269 966-3550
20 Division St N Battle Creek (49014) ***(G-1295)***
Siler Precision Machine Inc 989 643-7793
136 E Saginaw St Merrill (48637) ***(G-11264)***
Siliconature Corporation 312 987-1848
4255 68th St Se Caledonia (49316) ***(G-2400)***
Silicones Rd Center, Ann Arbor *Also called Wacker Chemical Corporation* ***(G-712)***
Silikids Inc 866 789-7454
153 1/2 E Front St Ste B Traverse City (49684) ***(G-16833)***
Silk Reflections 313 292-1150
22018 Haig St Taylor (48180) ***(G-16473)***
Silk Screenstuff 517 543-7716
2860 S Cochran Rd Charlotte (48813) ***(G-2770)***
Silkroute Global Inc 248 854-3409
950 Stephenson Hwy Troy (48083) ***(G-17354)***
Sill Farms & Market Inc 269 674-3755
50241 Red Arrow Hwy Lawrence (49064) ***(G-9985)***
Silver Creek Cabinets 989 387-0858
1775 Chappel Dam Rd Gladwin (48624) ***(G-6207)***
Silver Creek Manufacturing Inc 231 798-3003
696 Airport Pl Norton Shores (49441) ***(G-12330)***
Silver Slate LLC 248 486-3989
4964 Technical Dr Milford (48381) ***(G-11488)***
Silver Street Incorporated 231 861-2194
892 Industrial Park Dr Shelby (49455) ***(G-15160)***
Silver Tortoise Sound Lab, Ann Arbor *Also called Logical Digital Audio Video* ***(G-555)***
Silverglide Surgical Tech,, Portage *Also called Link Technology Inc* ***(G-13577)***
Silversmith Inc 989 732-8988
1370 Millbocker Rd Gaylord (49735) ***(G-6160)***
Silvery Sawmill, Elmira *Also called Paris North Hardwood Lumber* ***(G-5040)***
Simco Automotive Trim 800 372-3172
51362 Quadrate Dr Macomb (48042) ***(G-10635)***
Simco Automotive Trim Inc 616 608-9818
3831 Patterson Ave Se Grand Rapids (49512) ***(G-7199)***
Simerics Inc 248 513-3200
39500 Orchard Hill Pl # 190 Novi (48375) ***(G-12538)***
Simerson Inc 989 233-1420
6088 Caro Rd Vassar (48768) ***(G-17581)***
Simi Air 517 401-0284
120 E Congress St Morenci (49256) ***(G-11616)***
Simiron Inc 248 585-7500
3000 Research Dr Rochester Hills (48309) ***(G-14112)***
Simmons Crtrght Plstic Ctngs L 616 365-0045
2701a West River Dr Nw Grand Rapids (49544) ***(G-7200)***
Simolex Rubber Corporation 734 453-4500
14505 Keel St Plymouth (48170) ***(G-13299)***
Simonds Industries, Big Rapids *Also called Simonds International LLC* ***(G-1687)***
Simonds International LLC 231 527-2322
120 E Pere Marquette St Big Rapids (49307) ***(G-1687)***
Simpatico Coffee, Holland *Also called Two Cups Coffee Co LLC* ***(G-8232)***
Simplicabinets, Wixom *Also called Belash Inc* ***(G-18619)***
Simplicity Engineering Company 989 288-3121
212 S Oak St Durand (48429) ***(G-4848)***
Simplify Inventions LLC 248 960-1700
38955 Hills Tech Dr Farmington Hills (48331) ***(G-5382)***
Simply Cabinets 810 923-8792
29200 Lyon Oaks Dr Wixom (48393) ***(G-18752)***
Simply Custom 734 558-4051
1732 Eureka Rd Wyandotte (48192) ***(G-18839)***
Simply Divine Baking LLC 313 903-2881
25162 Coral Gables St Southfield (48033) ***(G-15704)***
Simply Green Outdoor Svcs LLC 734 385-6190
1535 Baker Rd Dexter (48130) ***(G-4755)***
Simply Suzanne LLC 917 364-4549
200 River Place Dr Apt 10 Detroit (48207) ***(G-4594)***
Simply Woodworking LLC 586 405-1080
1352 Maryland St Grosse Pointe Park (48230) ***(G-7559)***
Simply Zara S Treats LLC 313 327-5002
19928 Lindsay St Detroit (48235) ***(G-4595)***
Simpson Industrial Svcs LLC 810 392-2717
9020 Green Rd Wales (48027) ***(G-17630)***
Simpsons Enterprises Inc 269 279-7237
55255 Franklin Dr Three Rivers (49093) ***(G-16584)***
Sims Software II Inc 586 491-0058
44668 Morley Dr Clinton Township (48036) ***(G-3358)***
Sinclair Designs & Engrg LLC 877 517-0311
1104 Industrial Blvd Albion (49224) ***(G-133)***
Sindelar Fine Woodworking Co 269 663-8841
69953 Section St Edwardsburg (49112) ***(G-5016)***
Sine Systems Corporation (HQ) 586 465-3131
44724 Morley Dr Clinton Township (48036) ***(G-3359)***
Singh Automation LLC 269 267-6078
7804 S Sprinkle Rd Portage (49002) ***(G-13607)***
Single Shot Rifle Journal, Marquette *Also called Assra* ***(G-11005)***
Single Source Inc 765 825-4111
27100 Hall Rd Flat Rock (48134) ***(G-5630)***
Single Vision Solution Inc 586 464-1522
118 Cass Ave Mount Clemens (48043) ***(G-11657)***
Sink Rite Die Company 586 268-0000
6170 Wall St Sterling Heights (48312) ***(G-16178)***
Sintel Inc 616 842-6960
18437 171st Ave Spring Lake (49456) ***(G-15852)***
Sinto America Inc (HQ) 517 371-2460
3001 W Main St Lansing (48917) ***(G-9791)***
Sir Speedy, Royal Oak *Also called C S L Inc* ***(G-14522)***
Sir Speedy, Sterling Heights *Also called T J K Inc* ***(G-16199)***
Sir Speedy, Port Huron *Also called Bowman Printing Inc* ***(G-13462)***
Sir Speedy, Harper Woods *Also called Maslin Corporation* ***(G-7667)***
Sir Speedy, Saginaw *Also called Marketing VI Group Inc* ***(G-14686)***
Sir Speedy, Grand Rapids *Also called Derk Pieter Co Inc* ***(G-6641)***
Sirionlabs Inc 313 300-0588
1129 Yorkshire Rd Grosse Pointe Park (48230) ***(G-7560)***
Sista Roles Cuisine LLC 313 588-1142
3905 Bewick St Detroit (48214) ***(G-4596)***
Sisters In Inc 269 857-4085
3467 Blue Star Hwy Saugatuck (49453) ***(G-15085)***
Sisu Mouthguards, Saline *Also called Akervall Technologies Inc* ***(G-14999)***
Sitronic North America Corp 248 939-5910
2000 Town Ctr Ste 1800 Southfield (48075) ***(G-15705)***
Six Collection LLC 313 516-9999
19179 Kenosha St Harper Woods (48225) ***(G-7672)***
Six Lugs LLC 231 275-0600
19718 Platte River Jct Interlochen (49643) ***(G-8685)***
Sizmek Dsp Inc 313 516-4482
101 W Big Beaver Rd Troy (48084) ***(G-17355)***
Sizzl LLC 201 454-1938
721 S Forest Ave Apt 309 Ann Arbor (48104) ***(G-654)***
Sk Enterprises Inc 616 785-1070
3593 Alpine Ave Nw Grand Rapids (49544) ***(G-7201)***
Skamp Industries Inc 269 731-2666
5255 Bronson Blvd Portage (49024) ***(G-13608)***
Skater Boats, Douglas *Also called Douglas Marine Corporation* ***(G-4772)***
Skechers Factory Outlet 235, Birch Run *Also called Skechers USA Inc* ***(G-1715)***
Skechers USA Inc 989 624-9336
12240 S Beyer Rd Birch Run (48415) ***(G-1715)***
SKF USA Inc 810 231-2400
9961 Hamburg Rd Brighton (48116) ***(G-2072)***
Skg International Inc 248 620-4139
7550 Deerhill Dr Clarkston (48346) ***(G-3067)***
Skidmore, Benton Harbor *Also called Vent-Rite Valve Corp* ***(G-1598)***
Skill-Craft Company Inc 586 716-4300
10125 Radiance Dr Ira (48023) ***(G-8714)***
Skilled Manufacturing Inc (PA) 231 941-0290
3680 Cass Rd Traverse City (49684) ***(G-16834)***
Skin Bar VII LLC 313 397-9919
18951 Livernois Ave Detroit (48221) ***(G-4597)***
Skinny Kid Race Cars 248 668-1040
3170 E Oakley Park Rd A Commerce Township (48390) ***(G-3573)***
Skinny Petes LLc 906 369-1431
700 Calumet St Lake Linden (49945) ***(G-9570)***
Skip Printing and Dup Co 586 779-2640
28032 Groesbeck Hwy Roseville (48066) ***(G-14477)***
Skip Printing Co., Roseville *Also called Skip Printing and Dup Co* ***(G-14477)***
Skokie Castings LLC 248 727-1800
20750 Civic Center Dr # 100 Southfield (48076) ***(G-15706)***
Skop Powder Coating 231 881-9909
2469 N Us Highway 31 Petoskey (49770) ***(G-13024)***
Skoric Hearing Aid Center LLC 248 961-4329
5462 State St Saginaw (48603) ***(G-14758)***
Sks Industries Inc (PA) 517 546-1117
1551 N Burkhart Rd Howell (48855) ***(G-8518)***
SKW Automation Inc 517 563-8288
6422 Hanover Rd Ste 105 Hanover (49241) ***(G-7626)***

Sky Electric Northern Michigan, Traverse City *Also called William Shaw Inc* ***(G-16880)***
Sky Industries...810 614-6044
5007 Lonsberry Rd Columbiaville (48421) ***(G-3495)***
Skyapple LLC...248 588-5990
32501 Dequindre Rd Madison Heights (48071) ***(G-10830)***
Skyblade Fan Company...586 806-5107
24501 Hoover Rd Warren (48089) ***(G-18014)***
Skyline Champion Corporation (PA)...248 614-8211
755 W Big Beavr Rd # 100 Troy (48084) ***(G-17356)***
Skyline Fall Protection, Allendale *Also called Skyline Window Cleaning Inc* ***(G-228)***
Skyline Screen Printing & EMB, Madison Heights *Also called Authority Customwear Ltd* ***(G-10676)***
Skyline Window Cleaning Inc...616 895-4143
8528 Lake Michigan Dr Allendale (49401) ***(G-228)***
Skysync Inc...734 822-6858
30 Parkland Plz Ste B Ann Arbor (48103) ***(G-655)***
Skywalker Drone Solutions LLC...248 342-6747
335 Ridgemont Rd Oxford (48370) ***(G-12917)***
Skyway Precision Inc (PA)...734 454-3550
41225 Plymouth Rd Plymouth (48170) ***(G-13300)***
Skyworks LLC...972 284-9093
15461 Bay Hill Dr Northville (48168) ***(G-12261)***
SL America Corporation...586 731-8511
4375 Giddings Rd Auburn Hills (48326) ***(G-1034)***
SL Holdings Inc...586 949-0912
50625 Richard W Blvd Chesterfield (48051) ***(G-2948)***
SL Wheels Inc...734 744-8500
38701 7 Mile Rd Ste 155 Livonia (48152) ***(G-10411)***
Slades Printing Company Inc...248 334-6257
2697 Costa Mesa Rd Waterford (48329) ***(G-18165)***
Slater Tools Inc...586 465-5000
44725 Trinity Dr Clinton Township (48038) ***(G-3360)***
Slaughter Instrument Company...269 428-7471
4356 N Roosevelt Rd Stevensville (49127) ***(G-16265)***
Slaughterhouse Collective LLC...248 259-5257
1604 Jewell St Ferndale (48220) ***(G-5585)***
Slayer Outdoor Products...517 726-0221
435 Packard Hwy Ste A Charlotte (48813) ***(G-2771)***
SLC Meter LLC...248 625-0667
595 Bradford St Pontiac (48341) ***(G-13416)***
Sled Shed Enterprises LLC...517 783-5136
1150 S Elm Ave Jackson (49203) ***(G-9010)***
Sleeping Bear Apiaries Ltd...231 882-4456
971 S Pioneer Rd Beulah (49617) ***(G-1657)***
Sleeping Bear Farms, Beulah *Also called Sleeping Bear Apiaries Ltd* ***(G-1657)***
Sleeping Bear Press, Ann Arbor *Also called Cbm LLC* ***(G-418)***
Slick Shirts Screen Printing...517 371-3600
805 Vine St Lansing (48912) ***(G-9895)***
Sliding Systems Inc...517 339-1455
8080 E Old M Haslett (48840) ***(G-7778)***
Slik Metal Fabrication LLC...586 344-5621
55390 Rhine Ave Macomb (48042) ***(G-10636)***
Slip Defense Inc...248 366-4423
10279 Lakeside Dr White Lake (48386) ***(G-18464)***
Slipnot, Detroit *Also called Traction Tech Holdings LLC* ***(G-4642)***
SLM Solutions Na Inc...248 243-5400
48561 Alpha Dr Ste 300 Wixom (48393) ***(G-18753)***
Sloan Transportation Pdts Inc...616 395-5600
534 E 48th St Holland (49423) ***(G-8197)***
Sloan Transportation Products, Holland *Also called Tramec Sloan LLC* ***(G-8224)***
Sloan Valve Company...248 446-5300
30075 Research Dr New Hudson (48165) ***(G-12070)***
Slotbrokers LLC...231 929-7568
1625 Lake Dr Traverse City (49685) ***(G-16835)***
Slotting Ingram & Machine...248 478-2430
32175 Industrial Rd Livonia (48150) ***(G-10412)***
Slpt Global Pump Group, Rochester Hills *Also called Slw Automotive Inc* ***(G-14113)***
Slsi, Freeland *Also called Front Line Services Inc* ***(G-6024)***
Sludgehammer Group Ltd...231 348-5866
4772 Us Highway 131 Petoskey (49770) ***(G-13025)***
Slw Automotive Inc (HQ)...248 464-6200
1955 W Hamlin Rd Rochester Hills (48309) ***(G-14113)***
Sly Fox Prints LLC (PA)...616 900-9677
1321 17 Mile Rd Ne Cedar Springs (49319) ***(G-2661)***
SM & AM Enterprise Inc...906 786-0373
1001 Ludington St Escanaba (49829) ***(G-5100)***
SM Andia Sealcoating LLC...586 997-9752
52711 Brenton Shelby Township (48316) ***(G-15334)***
Smart Automation Systems Inc (PA)...248 651-5911
950 S Rochester Rd Rochester Hills (48307) ***(G-14114)***
Smart Diet Scale LLC...586 383-6734
75903 Peters Dr Bruce Twp (48065) ***(G-2183)***
Smart Label Solutions LLC...800 996-7343
1100 Durant Dr Howell (48843) ***(G-8519)***
Smart Power Systems Inc...231 832-5525
5000 N Us 131 Reed City (49677) ***(G-13798)***
Smart Swatter LLC...989 763-2626
3229 Valleyview Trl Harbor Springs (49740) ***(G-7657)***
Smart USA Inc...248 214-1022
777 E Eisenhower Pkwy # 10 Ann Arbor (48108) ***(G-656)***
Smart Vision Lights LLC...231 722-1199
5113 Robert Hunter Dr Norton Shores (49441) ***(G-12331)***
Smartcoast LLC...231 571-2020
3200 Broadmoor Ave Se Grand Rapids (49512) ***(G-7202)***
Smarteye Corporation...248 853-4495
2637 Bond St Rochester Hills (48309) ***(G-14115)***
Smartpat PLC...248 854-2233
1785 Bradford Rd Birmingham (48009) ***(G-1750)***
Sme Holdings LLC...586 254-5310
6750 19 Mile Rd Sterling Heights (48314) ***(G-16179)***
Smede-Son Steel and Sup Co Inc (PA)...313 937-8300
12584 Inkster Rd Redford (48239) ***(G-13772)***
Smeko Inc...586 254-5310
6750 19 Mile Rd Sterling Heights (48314) ***(G-16180)***
Smeltzer Companies Inc...231 882-4421
6032 Joyfield Rd Frankfort (49635) ***(G-5881)***
Smeltzer Orchard Company, Frankfort *Also called Smeltzer Companies Inc* ***(G-5881)***
SMI American Inc...313 438-0096
6835 Monroe Blvd Taylor (48180) ***(G-16474)***
SMI Automotive, Traverse City *Also called Skilled Manufacturing Inc* ***(G-16834)***
SMI Evaporative Systems, Midland *Also called Snow Machines Incorporated* ***(G-11418)***
Smigelski Properties LLC...989 255-6252
712 N Second Ave Alpena (49707) ***(G-317)***
Smith & Sons Meat Proc Inc...989 772-6048
5080 E Broadway Rd Mount Pleasant (48858) ***(G-11738)***
Smith - Sons ME...989 772-6048
5080 E Broadway Rd Mount Pleasant (48858) ***(G-11739)***
Smith and Nephew...616 288-6153
3 Leonard St Ne Grand Rapids (49503) ***(G-7203)***
Smith Bros. Tool Company, Shelby Township *Also called Sbti Company* ***(G-15323)***
Smith Brothers Tool Company...586 726-5756
50600 Corporate Dr Shelby Township (48315) ***(G-15335)***
Smith Castings Inc...906 774-4956
Ford Plant Iron Mountain (49802) ***(G-8733)***
Smith Castings Incorporated...906 774-4956
601 N Balsam St Kingsford (49802) ***(G-9517)***
Smith Concrete Products...989 875-4687
3282 S Crapo Rd North Star (48862) ***(G-12185)***
Smith Dumpsters...616 675-9399
13546 Kenowa Ave Kent City (49330) ***(G-9436)***
Smith Logging LLC...616 558-0729
2717 134th Ave Hopkins (49328) ***(G-8371)***
Smith Manufacturing Co Inc...269 925-8155
1636 Red Arrow Hwy Benton Harbor (49022) ***(G-1586)***
Smith Meat Packing Inc...810 985-5900
2043 International Way Port Huron (48060) ***(G-13528)***
Smith Metal LLC...269 731-5211
211 S Webster St Augusta (49012) ***(G-1093)***
Smith Metal Turning Inc...269 731-5211
211 S Webster St Augusta (49012) ***(G-1094)***
Smith Metal Turning Service, Augusta *Also called Smith Metal Turning Inc* ***(G-1094)***
Smith Processor Products, Berkley *Also called American Information Services* ***(G-1620)***
Smith Wa Inc...313 883-6977
14650 Dequindre St Detroit (48212) ***(G-4598)***
Smith Welding...989 306-0154
9750 County Road 489 Atlanta (49709) ***(G-747)***
Smiths Machine & Grinding Inc...269 665-4231
203 E Battle Creek St Galesburg (49053) ***(G-6083)***
Smj Inc...248 343-6244
1151 Stone Barn Milford (48380) ***(G-11489)***
Smm Printing Inc...989 893-8788
1914 3rd St Bay City (48708) ***(G-1402)***
Smo International Inc...248 275-1091
31745 Mound Rd Warren (48092) ***(G-18015)***
Smoke-Free Kids Inc...989 772-4063
3780 Saint Andrews Dr Mount Pleasant (48858) ***(G-11740)***
Smooth Logics, Holland *Also called Solid Logic LLC* ***(G-8200)***
Smoothies...231 498-2374
11937 Stone Circle Dr Kewadin (49648) ***(G-9489)***
Smoracy LLC...989 561-2270
6750 W Millbrook Rd Remus (49340) ***(G-13817)***
Smp, Sturgis *Also called Sturgis Molded Products Co* ***(G-16324)***
SMR Atmtive Mrror Intl USA Inc (HQ)...810 364-4141
1855 Busha Hwy Marysville (48040) ***(G-11100)***
SMR Atmtive Tech Hldngs USA PR (HQ)...810 364-4141
1855 Busha Hwy Marysville (48040) ***(G-11101)***
SMR Automotive Systems USA Inc...810 937-2456
2611 16th St Port Huron (48060) ***(G-13529)***
SMR Automotive Systems USA Inc (HQ)...810 364-4141
1855 Busha Hwy Marysville (48040) ***(G-11102)***
SMS, Saginaw *Also called Saginaw Machine Systems Inc* ***(G-14747)***
SMS Elotherm North America LLC...586 469-8324
13129 23 Mile Rd Shelby Township (48315) ***(G-15336)***
SMS Group, Saginaw *Also called SMS Holding Co Inc* ***(G-14759)***
SMS Group Inc...734 246-8230
15200 Huron St Taylor (48180) ***(G-16475)***

ALPHABETIC

SMS Holding Co Inc (PA)...989 753-8465
800 N Hamilton St Saginaw (48602) *(G-14759)*
SMS Technical Service LLC...313 322-4890
4001 Miller Rd Dearborn (48120) *(G-3897)*
SMS Technical Services...586 445-0330
12880 E 9 Mile Rd Warren (48089) *(G-18016)*
Smsg LLC (PA)...517 787-9447
1600 Executive Dr Jackson (49203) *(G-9011)*
Smullen Fire App Sales & Svcs...517 546-8898
3680 W Grand River Ave Howell (48855) *(G-8520)*
Smw Mfg Inc (HQ)...517 596-3300
8707 Samuel Barton Dr Van Buren Twp (48111) *(G-17553)*
Smw Mfg Inc...517 596-3300
25575 Brest Taylor (48180) *(G-16476)*
Smw Mfg Inc...517 596-3300
41200 Coca Cola Dr Belleville (48111) *(G-1491)*
SMW Tooling Inc...616 355-9822
11781 Greenway Dr Holland (49424) *(G-8198)*
Snackwerks of Michigan LLC...269 719-8282
180 Goodale Ave E Battle Creek (49037) *(G-1296)*
Snake Island, Detroit *Also called Zemis 5 LLC (G-4703)*
Snap Display Frames...616 846-7747
101 Washington Ave Grand Haven (49417) *(G-6363)*
Snap Jaws Manufacturing Inc...248 588-1099
33215 Dequindre Rd Troy (48083) *(G-17357)*
Snap Quickprint, Traverse City *Also called Gary Cork Incorporated (G-16692)*
Snavely Gordon A Atty Reserv...248 760-0617
3240 Pine Lake Rd West Bloomfield (48324) *(G-18314)*
Snd Manufacturing LLC...313 996-5088
23000 Arlington St Dearborn (48128) *(G-3898)*
Sniffer Robotics LLC...855 476-4333
330 E Liberty St Fl 4 Ann Arbor (48104) *(G-657)*
Snook Inc...231 799-3333
6430 Norton Center Dr Norton Shores (49441) *(G-12332)*
Snow Machines Incorporated (PA)...989 631-6091
1512 Rockwell Dr Midland (48642) *(G-11418)*
Snyder Corporation...586 726-4300
13231 23 Mile Rd Shelby Township (48315) *(G-15337)*
Snyder Plastics Inc...989 684-8355
1707 Lewis St Bay City (48706) *(G-1403)*
Soaring Concepts Aerospace LLC...574 286-9670
3001 W Airport Rd Hastings (49058) *(G-7810)*
Sobaks Pharmacy Inc (PA)...989 725-2785
112 W Exchange St Owosso (48867) *(G-12856)*
Soccer World's, Rochester Hills *Also called Rochester Sports LLC (G-14103)*
Society of Saint John Inc...906 289-4484
6559 State Highway M26 Eagle Harbor (49950) *(G-4853)*
Sock Hop LLC...248 689-2683
371 Scottsdale Dr Troy (48084) *(G-17358)*
Socks & Associates Development...231 421-5150
516 Hidden Ridge Dr Traverse City (49686) *(G-16836)*
Socks Direct USA LLC...248 535-7590
5400 Crispin Way Rd West Bloomfield (48323) *(G-18315)*
Socks Kick LLC...231 222-2402
117 S Lake St East Jordan (49727) *(G-4880)*
Sodecia Auto Detroit Corp...586 759-2200
15260 Common Rd Roseville (48066) *(G-14478)*
Sodecia Auto Detroit Corp (HQ)...586 759-2200
24331 Sherwood Center Line (48015) *(G-2686)*
Sodecia Group, Center Line *Also called N A Sodecia Inc (G-2683)*
Sodecia USA, Center Line *Also called Sodecia Auto Detroit Corp (G-2686)*
Sodius Corporation...248 270-2950
418 N Main St Ste 200 Royal Oak (48067) *(G-14581)*
Sodus Hard Chrome Inc...269 925-2077
3085 Yore Ave Sodus (49126) *(G-15394)*
Sofia Rose Industries Inc...810 278-4907
9100 Island Dr Clay (48001) *(G-3125)*
Softaire Diffusers Inc...810 730-1668
4198 Neal Ct Linden (48451) *(G-10071)*
Software Advantage Consulting...586 264-5632
8814 Pemberton Dr Sterling Heights (48312) *(G-16181)*
Software Assoc Inc...248 477-6112
35560 Grand River Ave Farmington (48335) *(G-5151)*
Software Bots Inc...734 730-6526
2200 N Canton Center Rd # 220 Canton (48187) *(G-2524)*
Software Finesse LLC (PA)...248 737-8990
31224 Mulfordton St # 200 Farmington Hills (48334) *(G-5383)*
Sohner Plastics LLC...734 222-4847
7275 Joy Rd Ste D Dexter (48130) *(G-4756)*
Soils and Structures Inc...800 933-3959
6480 Grand Haven Rd Norton Shores (49441) *(G-12333)*
Sol-I-Cor Industries...248 476-0670
30795 8 Mile Rd Livonia (48152) *(G-10413)*
Solaire Medical Storage LLC...888 435-2256
1239 Comstock St Marne (49435) *(G-10999)*
Solar Control Systems...734 671-6899
8463 Thorntree Dr Grosse Ile (48138) *(G-7526)*
Solar EZ Inc...989 773-3347
5340 E Jordan Rd Mount Pleasant (48858) *(G-11741)*
Solar Flare Bar...269 830-0499
250 Wahwahtaysee Way Battle Creek (49015) *(G-1297)*
Solar Research Division, Brighton *Also called Refrigeration Research Inc (G-2064)*
Solar Street Lights Usa LLC...269 983-6361
169 Manufacturers Dr # 1 Holland (49424) *(G-8199)*
Solar Tonic LLC (PA)...734 368-0215
2232 S Main St Ste 364 Ann Arbor (48103) *(G-658)*
Solarfall Industries LLC...269 274-6108
16331 Blue Teal Trl Hemlock (48626) *(G-7855)*
Solaronics Inc...248 651-5333
3720 Lapeer Rd Auburn Hills (48326) *(G-1035)*
Sole Industries LLC...586 322-5492
5253 Suncreek Ct Washington Township (48094) *(G-18096)*
Soleo Health Inc...248 513-8687
26800 Meadowbrook Rd # 119 Novi (48377) *(G-12539)*
Soli-Bond Inc (PA)...989 684-9611
2377 2 Mile Rd Bay City (48706) *(G-1404)*
Solid Epoxy Coatings LLC...248 785-7313
2975 Ford Rd White Lake (48383) *(G-18465)*
Solid Logic LLC...616 738-8922
3455 John F Donnelly Dr Holland (49424) *(G-8200)*
Solid Manufacturing Inc...517 522-5895
125 W Michigan Ave Grass Lake (49240) *(G-7445)*
Solidbody Technology Company...248 709-7901
395 Elmwood Dr Troy (48083) *(G-17359)*
Solidica Inc...734 222-4680
5840 Interface Dr Ste 200 Ann Arbor (48103) *(G-659)*
Solidthinking Inc...248 526-1920
1820 E Big Beaver Rd Troy (48083) *(G-17360)*
Sollman & Son Mold & Tool...269 236-6700
254 58th St Grand Junction (49056) *(G-6383)*
Solo Cup, Mason *Also called SF Holdings Group Inc (G-11154)*
Solo Cup Company LLC (HQ)...800 248-5960
500 Hogsback Rd Mason (48854) *(G-11155)*
Solo Cup Operating Corporation (HQ)...800 248-5960
500 Hogsback Rd Mason (48854) *(G-11156)*
Solohill Engineering Inc...734 973-2956
4370 Varsity Dr Ste B Ann Arbor (48108) *(G-660)*
Soltis Plastics Corp...248 698-1440
10479 Highland Rd White Lake (48386) *(G-18466)*
Solutia Inc...734 676-4400
5100 W Jefferson Ave Trenton (48183) *(G-16892)*
Solution Steel Treating LLC...586 247-9250
51689 Oro Dr Shelby Township (48315) *(G-15338)*
Solutions For Industry Inc...517 448-8608
13240 Egypt Rd Hudson (49247) *(G-8562)*
Solutions In Stone Inc...734 453-4444
41980 Ann Arbor Rd E Plymouth (48170) *(G-13301)*
Solutionsnowbiz...269 321-5062
8675 Portage Rd Ste 7 Portage (49002) *(G-13609)*
Somanetics...248 689-3050
1653 E Maple Rd Troy (48083) *(G-17361)*
Somerset Cleaners, Troy *Also called Mdla Inc (G-17242)*
Somerset Collection Ltd Partnr...248 827-4600
2801 W Big Beaver Rd Troy (48084) *(G-17362)*
Sommer Co., Warren *Also called Midwest Brake Bond Co (G-17931)*
Sommers Marine, Harrison Township *Also called Arthur R Sommers (G-7689)*
Somoco Inc...231 946-0200
13685 S West Bay Shore Dr Traverse City (49684) *(G-16837)*
Sonic Alert, Troy *Also called R H K Technology Inc (G-17327)*
Sonima Corp...302 450-6452
325 W Silverbell Rd # 250 Lake Orion (48359) *(G-9631)*
Sonoco Products Company...586 978-0808
35360 Beattie Dr Sterling Heights (48312) *(G-16182)*
Sonoco Products Company...269 408-0182
500 Renaissance Dr 102d Saint Joseph (49085) *(G-14961)*
Sonoco Prtective Solutions Inc...989 723-3720
123 N Chipman St Owosso (48867) *(G-12857)*
Sonrize LLC...586 329-3225
48051 Book Ct Chesterfield (48047) *(G-2949)*
Sonus Engineered Solutions LLC...586 427-3838
23031 Sherwood Ave Warren (48091) *(G-18017)*
SOO Welding Inc...906 632-8241
934 E Portage Ave Sault Sainte Marie (49783) *(G-15100)*
Soper Manufacturing Company...269 429-5245
3638 Bacon School Rd Saint Joseph (49085) *(G-14962)*
Sophias Bakery Inc...313 582-6992
8421 Michigan Ave Detroit (48210) *(G-4599)*
Sophias Textiles & Furn Inc...586 759-6231
24170 Sherwood Center Line (48015) *(G-2687)*
Soroc Products Inc...810 743-2660
4349 S Dort Hwy Burton (48529) *(G-2246)*
Sort-Tek Insptn Systems Inc...248 273-5200
1784 Larchwood Dr Troy (48083) *(G-17363)*
SOS Engineering Inc...616 846-5767
1901 Hayes St Grand Haven (49417) *(G-6364)*
SOS Well Services LLC...586 580-2576
51330 Oro Dr Shelby Township (48315) *(G-15339)*
Soul of The City Classics Socc, Wyoming *Also called Buster Mathis Foundation (G-18855)*

Sound Productions Entrmt......989 386-2221
1601 E Maple Rd Clare (48617) ***(G-2998)***
Sound-Off Signal, Hudsonville *Also called Emergency Technology Inc* ***(G-8581)***
Soundcase, Clare *Also called Sound Productions Entrmt* ***(G-2998)***
Soupcan Inc......269 381-2101
9406 E K Ave Ste 5 Galesburg (49053) ***(G-6084)***
Source 1 Cnc LLC......734 269-3381
7007 Todd Rd Ida (48140) ***(G-8624)***
Source Capital Backyard LLC......734 242-6900
1000 Ternes Dr Monroe (48162) ***(G-11573)***
Source One Digital LLC......231 759-3160
1137 N Gateway Blvd Norton Shores (49441) ***(G-12334)***
Source One Dist Svcs Inc......248 399-5060
900 Tech Row Madison Heights (48071) ***(G-10831)***
Source Point Press......269 501-3690
3603 Orchard Dr Midland (48640) ***(G-11419)***
Source Vending, Lansing *Also called Kansmackers Manufacturing Co* ***(G-9709)***
Sourcehub LLC......800 246-1844
1875 Stephenson Hwy Troy (48083) ***(G-17364)***
Sourceone Imaging LLC......616 452-2001
4500 Broadmoor Ave Se Grand Rapids (49512) ***(G-7204)***
Souris Enterprises Inc......810 664-2964
2045 N Lapeer Rd Lapeer (48446) ***(G-9961)***
Soutec Div of Andritz Bricmont......248 305-2955
26800 Meadowbrook Rd # 113 Novi (48377) ***(G-12540)***
South / Win LLC......734 525-9000
11800 Sears St Livonia (48150) ***(G-10414)***
South Bay Superabrasives, Saint Clair Shores *Also called South Bay Supply LLC* ***(G-14885)***
South Bay Supply LLC......313 882-8090
21250 Harper Ave Ste 1 Saint Clair Shores (48080) ***(G-14885)***
South Flint Gravel Inc......810 232-8911
6090 Belford Rd Holly (48442) ***(G-8295)***
South Haven Coil Inc (HQ)......269 637-5201
05585 Blue Star Mem Hwy South Haven (49090) ***(G-15412)***
South Haven Finishing Inc......269 637-2047
1610 Stieve Dr South Haven (49090) ***(G-15413)***
South Haven Packaging, South Haven *Also called Loope Enterprises Inc* ***(G-15409)***
South Haven Packaging Inc......269 639-1567
73475 8th Ave South Haven (49090) ***(G-15414)***
South Haven Tribune......269 637-1104
308 Kalamazoo St South Haven (49090) ***(G-15415)***
South Hill Sand and Gravel (PA)......248 828-1726
5877 Livernois Rd Ste 103 Troy (48098) ***(G-17365)***
South Hill Sand and Gravel......248 685-7020
4303 S Hill Rd Milford (48381) ***(G-11490)***
South Lyon Bb Inc......248 437-8000
21775 Pontiac Trl South Lyon (48178) ***(G-15458)***
South Park Sales & Mfg Inc......313 381-7579
6900 Chase Rd Dearborn (48126) ***(G-3899)***
South Park Welding Sups LLC (PA)......810 364-6521
50 Gratiot Blvd Marysville (48040) ***(G-11103)***
South Pointe Radiator......734 941-1460
30026 Beverly Rd Romulus (48174) ***(G-14329)***
South Range Bottling Works Inc......906 370-2295
23 Champion St South Range (49963) ***(G-15462)***
South Shore Tool & Die Inc......269 925-9660
2460 Meadowbrook Rd Benton Harbor (49022) ***(G-1587)***
Southast Berrien Cnty Landfill......269 695-2500
1540 Mayflower Rd Niles (49120) ***(G-12168)***
Southeastern Packaging, Mason *Also called Michigan Packaging Company* ***(G-11144)***
Southern Auto Wholesalers Inc......248 335-5555
597 N Saginaw St Pontiac (48342) ***(G-13417)***
Southfield Signs & Lighting, Southfield *Also called Bbj Graphics Inc* ***(G-15504)***
Southstern Mich Accsory Ctr 2......248 519-9848
1755 Maplelawn Dr Troy (48084) ***(G-17366)***
Southwest Broach......714 356-2967
311 E Harris St Cadillac (49601) ***(G-2354)***
Southwest Gravel Inc......269 673-4665
3641 108th Ave Allegan (49010) ***(G-182)***
Southwest Mich Innovation Ctr......269 353-1823
4717 Campus Dr Ste 100 Kalamazoo (49008) ***(G-9339)***
Southwestern Foam Tech Inc (HQ)......616 726-1677
1700 Alpine Ave Nw Grand Rapids (49504) ***(G-7205)***
Southwestern Industries Inc......517 667-0466
3124 Cobblestone Rdg Tecumseh (49286) ***(G-16516)***
Southwestern Mich Dust Ctrl......269 521-7638
110 E Spring St Bloomingdale (49026) ***(G-1879)***
Soy D-Lights & Scentsations......989 728-5947
7731 Hillsdale Dr Hale (48739) ***(G-7590)***
Soyad Brothers Textile Corp......586 755-5700
34272 Doreka Fraser (48026) ***(G-5994)***
Sp Industries, Hopkins *Also called Shred-Pac Inc* ***(G-8370)***
Spacerak, Marysville *Also called Heartland Steel Products LLC* ***(G-11088)***
Spagnuolo George & Sons......810 229-4424
9903 Loch Lomond Dr Brighton (48114) ***(G-2073)***
Spalding......734 414-1567
7298 Green Meadow Ln Canton (48187) ***(G-2525)***
Span America Detroit Inc......734 957-1600
41775 Ecorse Rd Ste 100 Van Buren Twp (48111) ***(G-17554)***
Spancrete Great Lakes, Grandville *Also called Kerkstra Precast LLC* ***(G-7395)***
Spare Die Inc......734 522-2508
30948 Industrial Rd Livonia (48150) ***(G-10415)***
Spare Key Winery LLC......231 250-7442
6872 Upper Bay Shore Rd Charlevoix (49720) ***(G-2733)***
Sparkling Woodsby LLC......313 724-0455
700 Claremont St Dearborn (48124) ***(G-3900)***
Sparks Belting Company Inc......800 451-4537
5005 Kraft Ave Se Ste A Grand Rapids (49512) ***(G-7206)***
Sparks Belting Company Inc (HQ)......616 949-2750
5005 Kraft Ave Se Grand Rapids (49512) ***(G-7207)***
Sparks Exhbits Envrnments Corp......248 291-0007
600 E 11 Mile Rd Royal Oak (48067) ***(G-14582)***
Sparta Outlets......616 887-6010
470 E Division St Sparta (49345) ***(G-15778)***
Sparta Sheet Metal Inc......616 784-9035
2200 Bristol Ave Nw Grand Rapids (49544) ***(G-7208)***
Sparta Wash & Storage LLC......616 887-1034
510 S State St Sparta (49345) ***(G-15779)***
Spartan Barricading......313 292-2488
27730 Ecorse Rd Romulus (48174) ***(G-14330)***
Spartan Carbide Inc......586 285-9786
34110 Riviera Fraser (48026) ***(G-5995)***
Spartan Central Kitchen......616 878-8940
463 44th St Se Grand Rapids (49548) ***(G-7209)***
Spartan Chassis, Charlotte *Also called Spartan Motors Chassis Inc* ***(G-2772)***
Spartan Corner, East Lansing *Also called Student Book Store Inc* ***(G-4910)***
Spartan Flag Company Inc......231 386-5150
323 S Shabwasung St Northport (49670) ***(G-12192)***
Spartan Graphics Inc......616 887-1073
200 Applewood Dr Sparta (49345) ***(G-15780)***
Spartan Grinding Inc......586 774-1970
28186 Hayes Rd Roseville (48066) ***(G-14479)***
Spartan Industries, Benton Harbor *Also called Anbren Inc* ***(G-1529)***
Spartan Metal Fab LLC......517 322-9050
4905 N Grand River Ave Lansing (48906) ***(G-9737)***
Spartan Motors, Charlotte *Also called Shyft Group Inc* ***(G-2767)***
Spartan Motors Chassis Inc......517 543-6400
1541 Reynolds Rd Charlotte (48813) ***(G-2772)***
Spartan Pallet LLC......586 291-8898
22387 Starks Dr Clinton Township (48036) ***(G-3361)***
Spartan PMI, Wixom *Also called Spartan Prcision Machining Inc* ***(G-18754)***
Spartan Prcision Machining Inc......248 344-0101
29431 Lorie Ln Wixom (48393) ***(G-18754)***
Spartan Printing Inc......517 372-6910
15551 S Us Highway 27 Lansing (48906) ***(G-9738)***
Spartan Steel Coating LLC......734 289-5400
3300 Wolverine Monroe (48162) ***(G-11574)***
Spartan Tool LLC (HQ)......815 539-7411
1618 Terminal Rd Niles (49120) ***(G-12169)***
Spartan Tool Sales Inc......586 268-1556
13715 Heritage Rd Sterling Heights (48312) ***(G-16183)***
Spartan Village LLC......661 724-6438
5742 Bordeau Rd Standish (48658) ***(G-15896)***
Spartans Finishing LLC......517 528-5510
8060 Old M 78 Haslett (48840) ***(G-7779)***
Spatz Bakery Inc......989 755-5551
1120 State St Saginaw (48602) ***(G-14760)***
Spaulding Machine Co Inc......989 777-0694
5366 East Rd Saginaw (48601) ***(G-14761)***
Spaulding Mfg Inc......989 777-4550
5366 East Rd Saginaw (48601) ***(G-14762)***
SPD America LLC......734 709-7624
195 E Hamburg St Pinckney (48169) ***(G-13056)***
Spec Abrasives and Finishing......231 722-1926
543 W Southern Ave Muskegon (49441) ***(G-11924)***
Spec Abrassive, Muskegon *Also called Spec Abrasives and Finishing* ***(G-11924)***
Spec Check, Shelby Township *Also called Spec Technologies Inc* ***(G-15340)***
Spec Corporation......517 529-4105
4701 Industrial Dr Clarklake (49234) ***(G-3008)***
Spec International Inc......616 248-9116
739 Cottage Grove St Se Grand Rapids (49507) ***(G-7210)***
Spec International Inc (PA)......616 248-3022
840 Cottage Grove St Se Grand Rapids (49507) ***(G-7211)***
Spec Technologies Inc......586 726-0000
51455 Schoenherr Rd Shelby Township (48315) ***(G-15340)***
Spec Tool Company (PA)......888 887-1717
389 E Div St Sparta (49345) ***(G-15781)***
Special Div, Westland *Also called Thermal One Inc* ***(G-18421)***
Special Drill and Reamer Corp......248 588-5333
408 E 14 Mile Rd Madison Heights (48071) ***(G-10832)***
Special Fabricators Inc......248 588-6717
31649 Stephenson Hwy Madison Heights (48071) ***(G-10833)***
Special Mold Engineering Inc (PA)......248 652-6600
1900 Production Dr Rochester Hills (48309) ***(G-14116)***
Special Projects Engineering......517 676-8525
2072 Tomlinson Rd Mason (48854) ***(G-11157)***
Special Projects Inc......734 455-7130
45901 Helm St Plymouth (48170) ***(G-13302)***

ALPHABETIC

Special T Custom Products ALPHABETIC SECTION

Special T Custom Products....810 654-9602
1492 Newcastle Dr Davison (48423) *(G-3797)*
Special Tool & Engineering Inc (PA)....586 285-5900
33910 James J Pompo Dr Fraser (48026) *(G-5996)*
Special Tooling Service, Inc., Commerce Township *Also called Fitz-Rite Products Inc (G-3529)*
Special Welding Services, Saginaw *Also called Sws - Trimac Inc (G-14771)*
Special-Lite Inc....800 821-6531
860 S Williams St Decatur (49045) *(G-3951)*
Special-Lite Inc - Benton....269 423-7068
1394 E Empire Ave Benton Harbor (49022) *(G-1588)*
Speciality Grinding Co., Grand Rapids *Also called Graphic Arts Service & Sup Inc (G-6781)*
Specialty Business Forms Inc....269 345-0828
815 E Crosstown Pkwy Kalamazoo (49001) *(G-9340)*
Specialty Castings, Springport *Also called JP Castings Inc (G-15882)*
Specialty Coatings Inc (PA)....586 294-8343
33835 Kelly Rd Fraser (48026) *(G-5997)*
Specialty Eng Components LLC (PA)....734 955-6500
25940 Northline Rd Taylor (48180) *(G-16477)*
Specialty Engine Components....734 955-6500
15385 Pine Romulus (48174) *(G-14331)*
Specialty Fabrication, Taylor *Also called Cfh Inc (G-16392)*
Specialty Fabrication Services, Taylor *Also called Sfs LLC (G-16472)*
Specialty Hardwood Moldings....734 847-3997
1244 W Dean Rd Temperance (48182) *(G-16549)*
Specialty Manufacturing Inc....989 790-9011
2210 Midland Rd Saginaw (48603) *(G-14763)*
Specialty Metal Fabricators....616 698-9020
6975 Dtton Indus Pk Dr Se Caledonia (49316) *(G-2401)*
Specialty Pdts & Polymers Inc....269 684-5931
2100 Progressive Dr Niles (49120) *(G-12170)*
Specialty Steel Treating Inc....586 293-5355
31610 W 8 Mile Rd Farmington Hills (48336) *(G-5384)*
Specialty Steel Treating Inc (PA)....586 293-5355
34501 Commerce Fraser (48026) *(G-5998)*
Specialty Tool & Mold Inc....616 531-3870
4542 Rger B Chffee Mem Dr Grand Rapids (49548) *(G-7212)*
Specialty Tooling Systems Inc....616 784-2353
4315 3 Mile Rd Nw Grand Rapids (49534) *(G-7213)*
Specialty Tube LLC....616 949-5990
3515 Raleigh Dr Se Grand Rapids (49512) *(G-7214)*
Specialty Tube Solutions....989 848-0880
339 E Miller Rd Mio (48647) *(G-11516)*
Specialty Welding....517 627-5566
12703 Melody Rd Grand Ledge (48837) *(G-6399)*
Speciation Artisan Ales LLC....616 279-3929
928 Wealthy St Se Grand Rapids (49506) *(G-7215)*
Specifications Service Company....248 353-0244
5444 Saint Martins Ct Bloomfield (48302) *(G-1785)*
Specified A Sltons Hldings LLC (HQ)....616 784-0500
1100 7 Mile Rd Nw Comstock Park (49321) *(G-3645)*
Specilty Adhesives Coating Inc....269 345-3801
3334 N Pitcher St Kalamazoo (49004) *(G-9341)*
Specilty Vhcl Acquisition Corp....586 446-4701
6115 E 13 Mile Rd Warren (48092) *(G-18018)*
Specs Office Supply, Bloomfield *Also called Specifications Service Company (G-1785)*
Spectra Link....313 417-3723
21885 River Rd Grosse Pointe Woods (48236) *(G-7576)*
Spectra Lmp LLC (PA)....313 571-2100
6501 Lynch Rd Detroit (48234) *(G-4600)*
Spectrum Automation Company....734 522-2160
34447 Schoolcraft Rd Livonia (48150) *(G-10416)*
Spectrum Cubic, Grand Rapids *Also called Spectrum Industries Inc (G-7216)*
Spectrum Cubic Inc (PA)....616 451-0784
5265 Kellogg Woods Dr Se Kentwood (49548) *(G-9480)*
Spectrum E-Coat, Inc., Belding *Also called Wealthy Street Corporation (G-1463)*
Spectrum Graphics, Grand Rapids *Also called Wolverine Printing Company LLC (G-7347)*
Spectrum Illumination Co Inc....231 894-4590
5114 Industrial Park Rd Montague (49437) *(G-11601)*
Spectrum Industries Inc (PA)....616 451-0784
700 Wealthy St Sw Grand Rapids (49504) *(G-7216)*
Spectrum Map Publishing Inc....517 655-5641
795 Progress Ct Williamston (48895) *(G-18583)*
Spectrum Metal Products Inc....734 595-7600
38289 Abruzzi Dr Westland (48185) *(G-18418)*
Spectrum Neon Company....313 366-7333
1280 Kempar Ave Madison Heights (48071) *(G-10834)*
Spectrum Printers Inc....517 423-5735
400 E Russell Rd Ste 1 Tecumseh (49286) *(G-16517)*
Spectrum Signs & Designs, Dearborn *Also called Miller Designworks LLC (G-3873)*
Spectrum Wireless (usa) Inc....586 693-7525
27601 Little Mack Ave Saint Clair Shores (48081) *(G-14886)*
Speed Cinch Inc....269 646-2016
22724 96th Ave Marcellus (49067) *(G-10952)*
Speedline, Livonia *Also called SL Wheels Inc (G-10411)*
Speedrack Products Group Ltd....517 639-8781
42 Cole St Quincy (49082) *(G-13674)*
Speedrack Products Group Ltd (PA)....616 887-0002
7903 Venture Ave Nw Sparta (49345) *(G-15782)*
Speedreducer.com, Detroit *Also called B & H Machine Sales Inc (G-4039)*
Speedway LLC....231 775-8101
2010 N Mitchell St Cadillac (49601) *(G-2355)*
Speedway Superamerica 3570, Cadillac *Also called Speedway LLC (G-2355)*
Speedy Blaze Inc....989 340-2028
307 S Third Ave Alpena (49707) *(G-318)*
Spen-Tech Machine Engrg Corp....810 275-6800
2851 James P Cole Blvd Flint (48505) *(G-5765)*
Spence Industries Inc....586 758-3800
23888 Dequindre Rd Warren (48091) *(G-18019)*
Spencer Farms and Timber LLC....810 459-4487
2585 Shadlow Trl Se Ada (49301) *(G-35)*
Spencer Manufacturing Inc....269 637-9459
165 Veterans Dr South Haven (49090) *(G-15416)*
Spencer Plastics Inc....231 942-7100
2300 Gary E Schwach St Cadillac (49601) *(G-2356)*
Spencer Tool....877 956-6868
2800 Birch Grove Ct Oxford (48370) *(G-12918)*
Spencer Tool....248 628-3677
3100 Adventure Ln Oxford (48371) *(G-12919)*
Spencer Zdanowitz Inc....517 841-9380
120 S Dwight St Jackson (49203) *(G-9012)*
Spes Publishing Co LLC....734 741-1241
3977 S Michael Rd Ann Arbor (48103) *(G-661)*
Speyside Real Estate LLC....248 354-7700
26555 Northwestern Hwy Southfield (48033) *(G-15707)*
SPI Blow Molding LLC....269 849-3200
3930 Bessemer Rd Coloma (49038) *(G-3483)*
SPI LLC....586 566-5870
51370 Celeste Shelby Township (48315) *(G-15341)*
Spicer Heavy Axle & Brake Inc....269 567-1000
6938 Elm Valley Dr Kalamazoo (49009) *(G-9342)*
Spicer's, Iron River *Also called James Spicer Inc (G-8743)*
Spicers Boat Cy Hughton Lk Inc....989 366-8384
4165 W Houghton Lake Dr Houghton Lake (48629) *(G-8403)*
Spiders Software Solutions LLC....248 305-3225
49831 Parkside Dr Northville (48168) *(G-12262)*
Spieth Anderson USA Lc....817 536-3366
3327 Ranger Rd Lansing (48906) *(G-9739)*
Spiffys Slay Station LLC....313 401-8906
18529 Anglin St Detroit (48234) *(G-4601)*
Spillson Ltd....734 384-0284
878 Regents Park Dr Monroe (48161) *(G-11575)*
Spin Lo Angler....231 882-6450
6450 Bixler Rd Beulah (49617) *(G-1658)*
Spina Electric Company....586 771-8080
26801 Groesbeck Hwy Warren (48089) *(G-18020)*
Spina Wind LLC....586 771-8080
26801 Groesbeck Hwy Warren (48089) *(G-18021)*
Spindel Corp Specialized....616 554-2200
4517 Broadmoor Ave Se Grand Rapids (49512) *(G-7217)*
Spindel Electronics, Grand Rapids *Also called Spindel Corp Specialized (G-7217)*
Spindle Grinding Service Inc....517 629-9334
826 Jupiter Dr Albion (49224) *(G-134)*
Spinform Inc....810 767-4660
1848 Tower St Flint (48503) *(G-5766)*
Spinnaker Corp....616 956-7677
554 Prestwick Ave Se Grand Rapids (49546) *(G-7218)*
Spinnaker Forms Systems Corp....616 956-7677
6812 Old 28th St Se Ste L Grand Rapids (49546) *(G-7219)*
Spiral Industries Inc....810 632-6300
1572 N Old Hwy Us23 Howell (48843) *(G-8521)*
Spiral-Matic Inc....248 486-5080
7772 Park Pl Brighton (48116) *(G-2074)*
Spiratex Company....734 289-4800
1916 Frenchtown Ctr Dr Monroe (48162) *(G-11576)*
Spire Integrated Systems Inc....248 544-0072
2786 Industrial Row Dr Troy (48084) *(G-17367)*
Spire Michigan Acquisition LLC....616 458-4924
2500 Oak Industrial Dr Ne Grand Rapids (49505) *(G-7220)*
Spirit Industries Inc....517 371-7840
2900 7th Ave Lansing (48906) *(G-9740)*
Spirit of Livingston Inc....517 545-8831
3280 W Grand River Ave Howell (48855) *(G-8522)*
Spirit Publishing LLC....231 399-1538
7977 S Shoreside Dr Traverse City (49684) *(G-16838)*
Spirit Shoppe, Kalamazoo *Also called R H & Company Inc (G-9313)*
Spirits of Detroit, The, Detroit *Also called Detroit City Distillery LLC (G-4141)*
Spitting Image Pblications LLC....989 498-9459
1902 Ottawa St Saginaw (48602) *(G-14764)*
Splash of Vinyl....616 723-0311
3257 Larue St Sw Grandville (49418) *(G-7418)*
Spline Specialist Inc....586 731-4569
7346 19 Mile Rd Sterling Heights (48314) *(G-16184)*
Split Second Defense LLC....586 709-1385
34024 James J Pompo Dr Fraser (48026) *(G-5999)*
Spm Industries Inc....586 758-1100
2455 E 10 Mile Rd Warren (48091) *(G-18022)*

Spoiler Wing King...810 733-9464
5042 Exchange Dr Flint (48507) ***(G-5767)***
Spoonful Press...313 862-6579
16617 Muirland St Detroit (48221) ***(G-4602)***
Sportcap, Farmington Hills *Also called American Silk Screen & EMB* ***(G-5169)***
Sporting Image Inc...269 657-5646
37174 W Red Arrow Hwy Paw Paw (49079) ***(G-12956)***
Sports Ink Screen Prtg EMB LLC...231 723-5696
316 W Parkdale Ave Manistee (49660) ***(G-10913)***
Sports Junction (PA)...989 791-5900
5605 State St Saginaw (48603) ***(G-14765)***
Sports Resorts International...989 725-8354
200 Universal Dr Owosso (48867) ***(G-12858)***
Sports Stop...517 676-2199
124 W Ash St Mason (48854) ***(G-11158)***
Sports Stop Sportswear, Mason *Also called Sports Stop* ***(G-11158)***
Sportswear Specialties Inc...734 416-9941
7930 N Lilley Rd Canton (48187) ***(G-2526)***
Spot Design LLC...734 997-0866
275 Metty Dr Ann Arbor (48103) ***(G-662)***
Spot Imaging Solutions, Sterling Heights *Also called Diagnostic Instruments Inc* ***(G-15986)***
Spot On Machine Shop...616 283-9830
2119 W Maple Ct Zeeland (49464) ***(G-19079)***
Spotlight Couture LLC...313 768-5305
23663 Irving St Taylor (48180) ***(G-16478)***
Spotlight Media LLC...269 808-4473
1704 Whites Rd Kalamazoo (49008) ***(G-9343)***
Spotted Cow...517 265-6188
1336 N Main St Adrian (49221) ***(G-97)***
Spray Booth Products Inc...313 766-4400
26211 W 7 Mile Rd Redford (48240) ***(G-13773)***
Spray Foam Fabrication LLC...517 745-7885
3627 Pickett Rd Parma (49269) ***(G-12939)***
Spray Metal Mold Technology...269 781-7151
200 Woolley Dr Marshall (49068) ***(G-11074)***
Spray Right, Grandville *Also called Industrial Innovations Inc* ***(G-7392)***
Sprayerusa Inc...800 253-4642
13495 Crestwood Dr Lowell (49331) ***(G-10516)***
Spraying Systems Co...248 473-1331
39340 Country Club Dr # 100 Farmington Hills (48331) ***(G-5385)***
Spraytek Inc (HQ)...248 546-3551
2535 Wolcott St Ferndale (48220) ***(G-5586)***
Sprik Custom Woodworks LLC...616 826-0858
13139 Sikkema Dr Grand Haven (49417) ***(G-6365)***
Spring Air Co...616 459-8234
630 Myrtle St Nw Grand Rapids (49504) ***(G-7221)***
Spring Arbor Coatings, LLC, Chelsea *Also called Sac Legacy Company LLC* ***(G-2825)***
Spring Design and Mfg Inc...586 566-9741
14105 Industrial Ctr Dr D Shelby Township (48315) ***(G-15342)***
Spring Dynamics Inc...810 798-2622
7378 Research Dr Almont (48003) ***(G-267)***
Spring Saginaw Company...989 624-9333
11008 Dixie Hwy Birch Run (48415) ***(G-1716)***
Springdale Automatics Inc...517 523-2424
7201 Hudson Rd Osseo (49266) ***(G-12777)***
Springer Machine...616 531-9816
4785 Stafford Ave Sw Wyoming (49548) ***(G-18907)***
Springer Prsthtic Orthtic Svcs (PA)...517 337-0300
200 N Homer St Lansing (48912) ***(G-9896)***
Springer Publishing Co Inc (PA)...586 939-6800
31201 Chicago Rd S A101 Warren (48093) ***(G-18023)***
Springfield Industries LLC...248 601-1445
609 Folk Ct Imlay City (48444) ***(G-8646)***
Springfield Machine and Tl Inc...269 968-8223
257 30th St N Springfield (49037) ***(G-15875)***
Sprouting Sunflowers LLC...248 982-2406
17530 Rainbow Dr Lathrup Village (48076) ***(G-9977)***
Spry Sign & Graphics Co LLC...517 524-7685
12123 Spring Arbor Rd Concord (49237) ***(G-3655)***
Spunky Duck Press...269 365-7285
802 N Main St Plainwell (49080) ***(G-13096)***
Spurt Industries...248 956-7643
2041 Charms Rd Wixom (48393) ***(G-18755)***
Spurt Industries LLC...616 688-5575
5204 Adams St Zeeland (49464) ***(G-19080)***
SPX Corporation...248 669-5100
3160 Dallavo Ct Commerce Township (48390) ***(G-3574)***
SPX Flow Us LLC...269 966-4782
4600 W Dickman Rd Battle Creek (49037) ***(G-1298)***
Square M LLC...720 988-5836
42150 Mound Rd Sterling Heights (48314) ***(G-16185)***
Squires Industries Inc...248 449-6092
29181 Beck Rd Wixom (48393) ***(G-18756)***
Sr Injection Molding Inc...586 260-2360
41565 Production Dr Harrison Township (48045) ***(G-7726)***
Sra Industries...586 251-2000
14938 Technology Dr Shelby Township (48315) ***(G-15343)***
Srg Global Inc...586 757-7800
12620 Delta St Taylor (48180) ***(G-16479)***
Srg Global LLC (HQ)...248 509-1100
800 Stephenson Hwy Troy (48083) ***(G-17368)***
Srg Global Automotive LLC (HQ)...586 757-7800
23751 Amber Ave Warren (48089) ***(G-18024)***
Srg Global Automotive LLC...586 757-7800
35555 Mound Rd Sterling Heights (48310) ***(G-16186)***
Srg Global Coatings LLC (HQ)...248 509-1100
800 Stephenson Hwy Troy (48083) ***(G-17369)***
Srg Global Coatings, Inc., Troy *Also called Srg Global Coatings LLC* ***(G-17369)***
SRI Delaware Holdings LLC (HQ)...248 489-9300
39675 Mackenzie Dr # 400 Novi (48377) ***(G-12541)***
Srm Concrete LLC...231 796-8685
15151 Old Millpond Rd Big Rapids (49307) ***(G-1688)***
Srm Concrete LLC...989 422-4202
9142 Knapp Rd Houghton Lake (48629) ***(G-8404)***
Srm Concrete LLC...231 943-4818
3165 S M 37 Traverse City (49685) ***(G-16839)***
Srm Concrete LLC...231 839-4319
1317 W Sanborn Rd Lake City (49651) ***(G-9555)***
Srm Concrete LLC...231 775-9301
8183 E 34 Rd Cadillac (49601) ***(G-2357)***
Srm Concrete LLC...231 258-8633
500 M 72 Kalkaska (49646) ***(G-9404)***
Srm Concrete LLC...231 832-5460
955 E Church Ave Reed City (49677) ***(G-13799)***
Srm Concrete LLC...989 344-0235
3881 W 4 Mile Rd Grayling (49738) ***(G-7469)***
SRP Software...231 779-3602
9372 E 50 Rd Cadillac (49601) ***(G-2358)***
SRS Fiberglass Products LLC...231 747-6839
1041 E Keating Ave Muskegon (49442) ***(G-11925)***
SRS Manufacturing Inc...586 792-5693
18840 Kelly Ct Clinton Township (48035) ***(G-3362)***
Srw Inc...989 732-8884
10691 E Carter Rd Ste 201 Traverse City (49684) ***(G-16840)***
Srw Inc (PA)...989 269-8528
175 Thompson Rd Ste A Bad Axe (48413) ***(G-1111)***
Ss Custom Market...269 816-1311
405 S Constantine St Three Rivers (49093) ***(G-16585)***
Ss Stripping...586 268-5799
36870 Metro Ct Sterling Heights (48312) ***(G-16187)***
SS&e Metalcraft, Grand Rapids *Also called Steel Supply & Engineering Co* ***(G-7223)***
Ssa Consumer Brands Inc...734 430-0565
455 E Eisenhower Pkwy # 30 Ann Arbor (48108) ***(G-663)***
Ssa Global, Grand Rapids *Also called Infor (us) LLC* ***(G-6844)***
Ssb Holdings Inc...586 755-1660
2619 Bond St Rochester Hills (48309) ***(G-14117)***
Ssi Electronics Inc...616 866-8880
8080 Graphic Dr Ne Belmont (49306) ***(G-1517)***
Ssi Technology Inc...248 582-0600
35715 Stanley Dr Sterling Heights (48312) ***(G-16188)***
SSS Spring & Wire, Grand Rapids *Also called Stump Schlele Somappa Sprng* ***(G-7230)***
St Ambrose Cellars...231 383-4262
971 S Pioneer Rd Beulah (49617) ***(G-1659)***
St Charles Hardwood Michigan...989 865-9299
10500 Mckeighan Rd Saint Charles (48655) ***(G-14809)***
St Clair Packaging Inc...810 364-4230
2121 Busha Hwy Marysville (48040) ***(G-11104)***
St Clair Steel Corporation...586 758-4356
27720 College Park Dr Warren (48088) ***(G-18025)***
St Evans Inc...269 663-6100
27383 May St Edwardsburg (49112) ***(G-5017)***
St Ignace News...906 643-9150
359 Reagon St Saint Ignace (49781) ***(G-14895)***
St Joe Tool Co...269 426-4300
11521 Red Arrow Hwy Bridgman (49106) ***(G-1934)***
St John...313 576-8212
4100 John R St Detroit (48201) ***(G-4603)***
St Johns Computer Machining...989 224-7664
501 E Steel St Saint Johns (48879) ***(G-14916)***
St Johns Reminder, Alma *Also called Morning Star Publishing Co* ***(G-250)***
St Julian Wine Company Inc (PA)...269 657-5568
716 S Kalamazoo St Paw Paw (49079) ***(G-12957)***
St Julian Wine Company Inc...734 529-3700
700 Freedom Ct Dundee (48131) ***(G-4836)***
St Julian Wine Company Inc...989 652-3281
127 S Main St Frankenmuth (48734) ***(G-5872)***
St Julian Winery...616 263-9087
4425 14 Mile Rd Ne Rockford (49341) ***(G-14190)***
St Laurent Brothers Inc...989 893-7522
1101 N Water St Bay City (48708) ***(G-1405)***
St Marys Cement Inc (us)...269 679-5253
640 South St Schoolcraft (49087) ***(G-15128)***
St Onge Masonry LLC...248 709-8161
4200 N Squirrel Rd Auburn Hills (48326) ***(G-1036)***
St Pierre Inc...248 620-2755
9649 Northwest Ct Clarkston (48346) ***(G-3068)***
St Regis Culvert Inc (PA)...517 543-3430
202 Morrell St Charlotte (48813) ***(G-2773)***

ALPHABETIC

St USA Holding Corp (PA)....517 278-7144
491 W Garfield Ave Coldwater (49036) ***(G-3456)***
St USA Holding Corp....800 637-3303
575 Race St Coldwater (49036) ***(G-3457)***
St. Clair Paper & Supply, Marysville *Also called St Clair Packaging Inc* ***(G-11104)***
Stable ARC, Novi *Also called RSI Global Sourcing LLC* ***(G-12529)***
Stackpole International, Auburn Hills *Also called Stackpole Pwrtrn Intl USA LLC* ***(G-1037)***
Stackpole Pwrtrn Intl USA LLC....248 481-4600
3201 University Dr # 350 Auburn Hills (48326) ***(G-1037)***
Stadium Bleachers LLC....810 245-6258
3597 Lippincott Rd Lapeer (48446) ***(G-9962)***
Stafford Media Inc (PA)....616 754-9301
109 N Lafayette St Greenville (48838) ***(G-7505)***
Stafford Media Inc....616 754-1178
1005 E Fairplains St Greenville (48838) ***(G-7506)***
Stage 5 Coatings, Wayne *Also called Lenawee Industrial Pnt Sup Inc* ***(G-18229)***
Stage Right, Clare *Also called Stageright Corporation* ***(G-2999)***
Stage Stop....989 838-4039
5348 Us 127 S Ithaca (48847) ***(G-8795)***
Stageright Corporation (PA)....989 386-7393
495 Pioneer Pkwy Clare (48617) ***(G-2999)***
Stagg Machine Products Inc....231 775-2355
11711 W Cadillac Rd Cadillac (49601) ***(G-2359)***
Stahlin Enclosures, Belding *Also called Robroy Enclosures Inc* ***(G-1462)***
Stahls Inc (PA)....800 478-2457
25901 Jefferson Ave Saint Clair Shores (48081) ***(G-14887)***
Stained Glass and Gifts....810 736-6766
4290 N Genesee Rd Flint (48506) ***(G-5768)***
Stainless Concepts LLC....616 427-6682
221 E Washington Ave # 4 Zeeland (49464) ***(G-19081)***
Stainless Fabg & Engrg Inc....269 329-6142
9718 Portage Rd Portage (49002) ***(G-13610)***
Stair Specialist Inc....269 420-0486
2257 Columbia Ave W Battle Creek (49015) ***(G-1299)***
Stamatopolos & Sons....734 369-2995
869 W Eisenhower Pkwy Ann Arbor (48103) ***(G-664)***
Stamp-Rite Incorporated....517 487-5071
2822 N Mrtn Lther King Jr Lansing (48906) ***(G-9741)***
Stampede Die & Engineering, Wayland *Also called Stampede Die Corp* ***(G-18208)***
Stampede Die Corp....616 877-0100
1142 Electric Ave Wayland (49348) ***(G-18208)***
Stamping Plant....734 467-0008
37500 Van Born Rd Wayne (48184) ***(G-18236)***
Stamping Support Group....734 727-0605
4935 Hannan Rd Wayne (48184) ***(G-18237)***
Stamprite Supersine, Lansing *Also called Stamp-Rite Incorporated* ***(G-9741)***
Stan Sax Corp (PA)....248 683-9199
10900 Harper Ave Detroit (48213) ***(G-4604)***
Stanco Metal Products Inc (PA)....616 842-5000
2101 168th Ave Grand Haven (49417) ***(G-6366)***
Stanco Metal Products Company, Grand Haven *Also called Stanco Metal Products Inc* ***(G-6366)***
Standale Lumber and Supply Co....616 530-8200
2971 Franklin Ave Sw Grandville (49418) ***(G-7419)***
Standale Smoothie LLC....810 691-9625
1028 N Leroy St Fenton (48430) ***(G-5504)***
Standard Automation LLC....248 227-6964
3939 W Hamlin Rd Rochester Hills (48309) ***(G-14118)***
Standard Coating Inc....248 297-6650
32565 Dequindre Rd Madison Heights (48071) ***(G-10835)***
Standard Components LLC....586 323-9700
44208 Phoenix Dr Sterling Heights (48314) ***(G-16189)***
Standard Die International Inc (PA)....800 838-5464
12980 Wayne Rd Livonia (48150) ***(G-10417)***
Standard Electric Company....906 774-4455
701 Valsam St Kingsford (49802) ***(G-9518)***
Standard Plaque Incorporated....313 383-7233
17271 Francis St Melvindale (48122) ***(G-11210)***
Standard Printing....734 483-0339
120 E Cross St Ypsilanti (48198) ***(G-18978)***
Standard Printing of Warren....586 771-3770
13647 E 10 Mile Rd Warren (48089) ***(G-18026)***
Standard Provision LLC....989 354-4975
1505 Greenhaven Ln Alpena (49707) ***(G-319)***
Standard Register....616 987-3128
43 Kendra Ct Lowell (49331) ***(G-10517)***
Standard Scale & Supply Co (PA)....313 255-6700
25421 Glendale Detroit (48239) ***(G-4605)***
Standard Spring, Royal Oak *Also called American Industrial Gauge Inc* ***(G-14507)***
Standard Tool & Die Inc....269 465-6004
2950 Johnson Rd Stevensville (49127) ***(G-16266)***
Standex International Corp....586 296-5500
34497 Kelly Rd Fraser (48026) ***(G-6000)***
Standfast Industries Inc....248 380-3223
13570 Wayne Rd Livonia (48150) ***(G-10418)***
Standing Company....989 746-9100
5848 Dixie Hwy Saginaw (48601) ***(G-14766)***
Standing Dani, Flint *Also called Davismade Inc* ***(G-5684)***
Standing Wheelchair Company, Saginaw *Also called Standing Company* ***(G-14766)***
Standish Magline, Standish *Also called Magline Inc* ***(G-15891)***
Stanek Rack Company, Detroit *Also called Fmmb LLC* ***(G-4239)***
Stange Company, Grand Rapids *Also called Terryberry Company LLC* ***(G-7254)***
Stanhope Tool Inc....248 585-5711
2357 E 9 Mile Rd Warren (48091) ***(G-18027)***
Stanisci Design and Mfg Inc....248 572-6880
700 S Glaspie St Oxford (48371) ***(G-12920)***
Stanley Elc Holdg Amer Inc (HQ)....269 660-7777
1500 Hill Brady Rd Battle Creek (49037) ***(G-1300)***
Stanley Electric Sales America....248 471-1300
37000 Grand River Ave Farmington Hills (48335) ***(G-5386)***
Stanley Engineered Fastening, Chesterfield *Also called Emhart Teknologies LLC* ***(G-2876)***
STANLEY ENGINEERED FASTENING, Troy *Also called Emhart Teknologies LLC* ***(G-17087)***
Stanley Engineered Fastening, Troy *Also called Emhart Teknologies LLC* ***(G-17088)***
Stansley Industries Inc....810 515-1919
4171 Holiday Dr Flint (48507) ***(G-5769)***
Stansley Mineral Resources Inc....517 456-6310
13500 Allen Rd Clinton (49236) ***(G-3142)***
Stant USA Corp....765 827-8104
1955 Enterprise Dr Rochester Hills (48309) ***(G-14119)***
Stapels Manufacturing LLC....248 577-5570
2612 Elliott Dr Troy (48083) ***(G-17370)***
Star Board ATT Tev, Grand Haven *Also called Star Board Multi Media Inc* ***(G-6367)***
Star Board Multi Media Inc....616 296-0823
41 Washington Ave Ste 395 Grand Haven (49417) ***(G-6367)***
Star Buyers Guide....989 366-8341
4772 W Houghton Lake Dr Houghton Lake (48629) ***(G-8405)***
Star Crane Hist Svc of Klmazoo....269 321-8882
8722 Portage Indus Dr Portage (49024) ***(G-13611)***
Star Cutter Co (PA)....248 474-8200
23461 Industrial Park Dr Farmington Hills (48335) ***(G-5387)***
Star Cutter Company, Farmington Hills *Also called Star Cutter Co* ***(G-5387)***
Star Cutter Company Inc....248 474-8200
980 Aulerich Rd East Tawas (48730) ***(G-4923)***
Star Design Metro Detroit LLC....734 740-0189
32401 8 Mile Rd Ste 1-1 Livonia (48152) ***(G-10419)***
Star Ink and Thread....989 823-3660
221 N Water St Vassar (48768) ***(G-17582)***
Star Line Commercial Printing....810 733-1152
6122 W Pierson Rd Unit 5 Flushing (48433) ***(G-5813)***
Star Lite International LLC, Oak Park *Also called Sani Zeevi* ***(G-12646)***
Star of West Milling Company (PA)....989 652-9971
121 E Tuscola St Frankenmuth (48734) ***(G-5873)***
Star Paper Converters....313 254-9833
100 Labadie St Ecorse (48229) ***(G-4986)***
Star Paper Converters Inc....313 963-5200
1717 17th St Detroit (48216) ***(G-4606)***
Star Paper Products, Detroit *Also called Star Paper Converters Inc* ***(G-4606)***
Star Publication, Gaylord *Also called Upper Michigan Newspapers LLC* ***(G-6165)***
Star Ringmaster....734 641-7147
1261 S Lotz Rd Canton (48188) ***(G-2527)***
Star Shade Cutter Co....269 983-2403
2028 Washington Ave Saint Joseph (49085) ***(G-14963)***
Star Su Company LLC....248 474-8200
23461 Industrial Park Dr Farmington Hills (48335) ***(G-5388)***
Star Textile Inc....888 527-5700
1000 Tech Row Madison Heights (48071) ***(G-10836)***
Starbuck Machining Inc....616 399-9720
13413 New Holland St Holland (49424) ***(G-8201)***
Stardock Systems Inc (PA)....734 927-0677
15090 N Beck Rd Ste 300 Plymouth (48170) ***(G-13303)***
Starlight Technologies Inc....248 250-9607
2055 Applewood Dr Troy (48085) ***(G-17371)***
Starlite Coatings, Canton *Also called Innovative Solutions Tech Inc* ***(G-2477)***
Starlite Tool & Die Welding....313 533-3462
12091 Woodbine Detroit (48239) ***(G-4607)***
Starr Puff Factory, Grand Rapids *Also called Roskam Baking Company* ***(G-7166)***
Startec Training Institute....313 808-7013
20021 Carrie St Detroit (48234) ***(G-4608)***
Startech Software Systems Inc....248 344-2266
39500 High Pointe Blvd # 400 Novi (48375) ***(G-12542)***
Startech-Solutions LLC....248 419-0650
6689 Orchard Lake Rd # 267 West Bloomfield (48322) ***(G-18316)***
Startech-Solutions LLC....248 419-0650
26300 Telg Rd Ste 101 Southfield (48033) ***(G-15708)***
Starwood Homes....734 340-2326
1998 White Oak Ln Ypsilanti (48198) ***(G-18979)***
State Building Product Inc....586 772-8878
21751 Schmeman Ave Warren (48089) ***(G-18028)***
State Fabricators, Farmington Hills *Also called Sfi Acquisition Inc* ***(G-5377)***
State Heat Treating Company....616 243-0178
520 32nd St Se Grand Rapids (49548) ***(G-7222)***
State News Inc....517 295-1680
435 E Grand River Ave # 100 East Lansing (48823) ***(G-4909)***
State Tool & Manufacturing Co (PA)....269 927-3153
1650 E Empire Ave Benton Harbor (49022) ***(G-1589)***

State Wide Grinding Co 586 778-5700
27980 Groesbeck Hwy Roseville (48066) *(G-14480)*
Statewide Boring and Mch Inc 734 397-5950
6401 Haggerty Rd Van Buren Twp (48111) *(G-17555)*
Static Controls Corp 248 926-4400
30460 S Wixom Rd Wixom (48393) *(G-18757)*
Statistical Processed Products (PA) 586 792-6900
35409 Groesbeck Hwy Clinton Township (48035) *(G-3363)*
Status Transportation, Grand Rapids *Also called Pressure Releases Corporation (G-7103)*
Steadfast Engineered Pdts LLC 616 846-4747
775 Woodlawn Ave Grand Haven (49417) *(G-6368)*
Steadfast Lab 248 242-2291
22018 John R Rd Hazel Park (48030) *(G-7843)*
Steadfast Tool & Machine Inc 989 856-8127
6601 Limerick Rd Caseville (48725) *(G-2605)*
Steal Leading and Drum Company, Warren *Also called St Clair Steel Corporation (G-18025)*
Stealth Medical Technologies, Holt *Also called Set Liquidation Inc (G-8331)*
Stec Usa Inc (PA) 248 307-1440
31900 Sherman Ave Madison Heights (48071) *(G-10837)*
Stechschulte/Wegerly AG LLC 586 739-0101
42250 Yearego Dr Sterling Heights (48314) *(G-16190)*
Stedman Corp 269 629-5930
10301 M 89 Richland (49083) *(G-13830)*
Steel 21 LLC 616 884-2121
11786 White Creek Ave Ne Cedar Springs (49319) *(G-2662)*
STEEL AND WIRE, Utica *Also called MNP Corporation (G-17504)*
Steel Appeal 231 326-6116
12100 S Plowman Rd Empire (49630) *(G-5042)*
Steel Craft Inc 989 358-7196
1086 Hamilton Rd Alpena (49707) *(G-320)*
Steel Craft Technologies Inc 616 866-4400
8057 Graphic Dr Ne Belmont (49306) *(G-1518)*
Steel Fab, Flint *Also called Wpw Inc (G-5796)*
Steel Forming Systems, Grand Haven *Also called Trainer Metal Forming Co Inc (G-6371)*
Steel Industries Inc 734 427-8550
41790 Broquet Dr Northville (48167) *(G-12263)*
Steel Industries Inc 313 535-8505
12600 Beech Daly Rd Redford (48239) *(G-13774)*
Steel Master LLC 810 771-4943
8018 Embury Rd Grand Blanc (48439) *(G-6264)*
Steel Mill Components Inc 586 920-2595
22522 Hoover Rd Warren (48089) *(G-18029)*
Steel Mill Components Inc (PA) 313 386-0893
17000 Ecorse Rd Allen Park (48101) *(G-207)*
Steel Plus Solutions, Grand Rapids *Also called Mill Steel Co (G-7010)*
Steel Products, Homer *Also called MCS Industries Inc (G-8354)*
Steel Skinz Graphics, Howell *Also called Steel Skinz LLC (G-8523)*
Steel Skinz LLC 517 545-9955
4836 Pinckney Rd Howell (48843) *(G-8523)*
Steel Supply & Engineering Co (PA) 616 452-3281
2020 Newark Ave Se Grand Rapids (49507) *(G-7223)*
Steel Tank & Fabricating Co (PA) 248 625-8700
4701 White Lake Rd Clarkston (48346) *(G-3069)*
Steel Tank & Fabricating Co 231 587-8412
9517 Lake St Mancelona (49659) *(G-10879)*
Steel Tool & Engineering Co 734 692-8580
28005 Fort St Brownstown Twp (48183) *(G-2157)*
Steel-Fab Wilson & Machine 989 773-6046
1219 N Mission St Mount Pleasant (48858) *(G-11742)*
Steelcase Inc (PA) 616 247-2710
901 44th St Se Grand Rapids (49508) *(G-7224)*
Steelcraft Tool Co Inc 734 522-7130
12930 Wayne Rd Livonia (48150) *(G-10420)*
Steele Supply Co 269 983-0920
3413 Hill St Saint Joseph (49085) *(G-14964)*
Steelhead Industries LLC 989 506-7416
121 E Broadway St Mount Pleasant (48858) *(G-11743)*
Steeltech Ltd (PA) 616 243-7920
1251 Phillips Ave Sw Grand Rapids (49507) *(G-7225)*
Steeltech Ltd 616 696-1130
69 Maple Cedar Springs (49319) *(G-2663)*
Steelworks Inc 734 692-3020
2335 Toledo St Trenton (48183) *(G-16893)*
Steenson Enterprises 248 628-0036
4444 Forest St Leonard (48367) *(G-10003)*
Steeplechase Tool & Die Inc 989 352-5544
9307 Howard Cy Edmore Rd Lakeview (48850) *(G-9646)*
Steering Solutions - Plant 3 .... 989 757-5000
3900 E Holland Rd Saginaw (48601) *(G-14767)*
Stegman Tool Co Inc 248 588-4634
1985 Ring Dr Troy (48083) *(G-17372)*
Stegner Controls LLC 248 904-0400
3333 Bald Mountain Rd Auburn Hills (48326) *(G-1038)*
Steigers Timber Operations 906 667-0266
401 S Tamarack Ave Bessemer (49911) *(G-1650)*
Steinbauer Performance LLC 704 587-0856
22790 Fosdick St Dowagiac (49047) *(G-4797)*
Steinbrecher Stone Corp (PA) 906 563-5852
N1443 Forest Dr Norway (49870) *(G-12357)*
Steiner Associates 734 422-5188
15735 Norwich St Livonia (48154) *(G-10421)*
Steiner Tractor Parts Inc 810 621-3000
1660 S M 13 Lennon (48449) *(G-9996)*
Steinke-Fenton Fabricators 517 782-8174
1355 Page Ave Jackson (49203) *(G-9013)*
Steketee-Van Huis Inc 616 392-2326
13 W 4th St Holland (49423) *(G-8202)*
Stella-Maris, Pellston *Also called Vte Inc (G-12968)*
Stellar Computer Services LLC 989 732-7153
633 Crestwood Dr Gaylord (49735) *(G-6161)*
Stellar Forge Products Inc (PA) 313 535-7631
6651 Timber Ridge Dr Bloomfield Hills (48301) *(G-1862)*
Stellar Materials Intl LLC 561 504-3924
777 Eight Mile Rd Whitmore Lake (48189) *(G-18546)*
Stellar Plastics Fabg LLC 313 527-7337
14121 Gratiot Ave Detroit (48205) *(G-4609)*
Stelmatic Industries Inc 586 949-0160
50575 Richard W Blvd Chesterfield (48051) *(G-2950)*
Stemco Kaiser, Millington *Also called Stemco Products Inc (G-11503)*
Stemco Products Inc 888 854-6474
4641 Industrial Dr Millington (48746) *(G-11503)*
Step, Dearborn *Also called Services To Enhance Potential (G-3895)*
Step Into Success Inc 734 426-1075
9940 Sunrise Dr Pinckney (48169) *(G-13057)*
Stephanies Unlimited Creat LLC 616 379-5392
6613 Center Industrial Dr Jenison (49428) *(G-9072)*
Stephen A James 269 641-5879
68730 Calvin Center Rd Cassopolis (49031) *(G-2634)*
Stephen Haas 906 475-4826
96 Croix St Apt 6 Negaunee (49866) *(G-11975)*
Stephen Rex Fetterley Jr 269 215-2035
2550 W Cloverdale Rd Delton (49046) *(G-3967)*
Stephens Fence Supply, Grand Rapids *Also called Stephens Pipe & Steel LLC (G-7226)*
Stephens Pipe & Steel LLC 616 248-3433
3400 Rger B Chffee Mem Dr Grand Rapids (49548) *(G-7226)*
Steplen Coatings LLC 810 653-6418
2234 S Irish Rd Davison (48423) *(G-3798)*
Stepscreen Printing 734 770-5009
656 Saint Marys Ave Monroe (48162) *(G-11577)*
Sterling, Shelby Township *Also called SPI LLC (G-15341)*
Sterling Contracting, Farmington Hills *Also called Sterling Millwork Inc (G-5389)*
Sterling Creative Team Inc 586 978-0100
34238 Van Dyke Ave Ste A Sterling Heights (48312) *(G-16191)*
Sterling Diagnostics Inc 586 979-2141
36645 Metro Ct Sterling Heights (48312) *(G-16192)*
Sterling Die & Engineering Inc 586 677-0707
15767 Claire Ct Macomb (48042) *(G-10637)*
Sterling Edge Inc 248 438-6034
50230 Dennis Ct Wixom (48393) *(G-18758)*
Sterling Manufacturing & Engrg, Sterling Heights *Also called Sme Holdings LLC (G-16179)*
Sterling Metal Works LLC 586 977-9577
35705 Beattie Dr Sterling Heights (48312) *(G-16193)*
Sterling Millwork Inc 248 427-1400
24000 Research Dr Farmington Hills (48335) *(G-5389)*
Sterling Performance Inc 248 685-7811
54420 Pontiac Trl Milford (48381) *(G-11491)*
Sterling Printing & Graphics, Troy *Also called DGa Printing Inc (G-17058)*
Sterling Prmeasure Systems Inc 586 254-5310
6750 19 Mile Rd Sterling Heights (48314) *(G-16194)*
Sterling Prod Machining LLC 586 493-0633
42522 Executive Dr Harrison Township (48045) *(G-7727)*
Sterling Security LLC 248 809-9309
21700 Northwestern Hwy Southfield (48075) *(G-15709)*
Sterling Truck and Wstn Star (HQ) 313 592-4200
13400 W Outer Dr Redford (48239) *(G-13775)*
Sterling Trucking, Redford *Also called Sterling Truck and Wstn Star (G-13775)*
Steve Tonkovich 810 348-4046
3109 Lansdowne Rd Waterford (48329) *(G-18166)*
Steven Crandell 231 582-7445
10436 Burnett Rd Charlevoix (49720) *(G-2734)*
Steven J Devlin 734 439-1325
268 S Platt St Milan (48160) *(G-11450)*
Steven Schadler, Saint Joseph *Also called Neogen Corporation (G-14951)*
Stevens Custom Fabrication 989 340-1184
928 Lockwood St Alpena (49707) *(G-321)*
Stevens Custom Fabrication 989 340-1184
615 W Campbell St Alpena (49707) *(G-322)*
Stevenson Building and Sup Co 734 856-3931
8197 Secor Rd Lambertville (48144) *(G-9653)*
Steves Backroom LLC 313 527-7240
13250 Rotunda Dr Dearborn (48120) *(G-3901)*
Steves Custom Signs Inc 734 662-5964
4676 Freedom Dr Ann Arbor (48108) *(G-665)*
Steves Machine Shop LLC 248 563-1662
2119 Garry Dr Troy (48083) *(G-17373)*
Stewart Components, Escanaba *Also called Emp Racing Inc (G-5068)*
Stewart General Incorporated 616 318-4971
16991 Birchview Dr Nunica (49448) *(G-12586)*

ALPHABETIC

Stewart Industries LLC 269 660-9290
150 Mcquiston Dr Battle Creek (49037) ***(G-1301)***
Stewart Knives LLC 906 789-1801
6911 County 426 M.5 Rd Escanaba (49829) ***(G-5101)***
Stewart Manufacturing LLC 906 498-7600
N16415 Earle Dr Hermansville (49847) ***(G-7862)***
Stewart Printing Company Inc 734 283-8440
2715 Fort St Wyandotte (48192) ***(G-18840)***
Stewart Steel Specialties 248 477-0680
20755 Whitlock St Farmington Hills (48336) ***(G-5390)***
Stewart Sutherland Inc 269 649-0530
5411 E V Ave Vicksburg (49097) ***(G-17613)***
Stickerchef LLC 231 622-9900
141 Joseph St Saint Ignace (49781) ***(G-14896)***
Stickmann Baeckerei 269 205-2444
11332 W M 179 Hwy Middleville (49333) ***(G-11314)***
Stilson Die-Draulic, Roseville *Also called Prophotonix Limited* ***(G-14466)***
Stilson Products LLC 586 778-1100
28400 Groesbeck Hwy Roseville (48066) ***(G-14481)***
Stimmel Construction LLC (PA) 734 263-8949
32176 Chester St Garden City (48135) ***(G-6111)***
Stinkn Pretty LLC 517 694-8659
1624 Gunn Rd Holt (48842) ***(G-8333)***
Stirnemann Tool & Mch Co Inc 248 435-4040
1457 N Main St Clawson (48017) ***(G-3110)***
Stitch Alley Customs 616 377-7082
11140 Watertower Ct # 140 Holland (49424) ***(G-8203)***
Stitch Inventions 248 698-7773
8953 Haymarket St White Lake (48386) ***(G-18467)***
Stitch Kustoms 248 622-4563
304 N Johnson St Pontiac (48341) ***(G-13418)***
Stitch N Lyds Embroidery 231 675-1916
13929 Phelps Rd Charlevoix (49720) ***(G-2735)***
Stitched Now 586 460-6175
18600 Eureka St Detroit (48234) ***(G-4610)***
Stitches and Steel 248 330-6302
8600 Timberline Trl Harrison (48625) ***(G-7682)***
Stm Mfg Inc (PA) 616 392-4656
494 E 64th St Holland (49423) ***(G-8204)***
Stm Power Inc (PA) 734 214-1448
275 Metty Dr Ann Arbor (48103) ***(G-666)***
Stm Powersports, Waterford *Also called Supreme Tool & Machine Inc* ***(G-18168)***
Stnj LLC (PA) 810 230-6445
4297 Miller Rd Flint (48507) ***(G-5770)***
Stockbridge Manufacturing Co 517 851-7865
4859 E Main St Stockbridge (49285) ***(G-16278)***
Stoked & Bearded LLC 248 513-2927
42533 Clinton Place Dr Clinton Township (48038) ***(G-3364)***
Stokes Automation 248 573-5277
7478 Fox Hill Ln Northville (48168) ***(G-12264)***
Stokes Steel Treating Company 810 235-3573
624 Kelso St Flint (48506) ***(G-5771)***
Stokosa Prosthetic Clinic, Okemos *Also called American Prosthetic Institute* ***(G-12655)***
Stone Circle Bakehouse LLC 517 881-0603
3647 Willoughby Rd Holt (48842) ***(G-8334)***
Stone For You 248 651-9940
111 W 2nd St Ste A Rochester (48307) ***(G-13930)***
Stone House Bread LLC (PA) 231 933-8864
4200 Us Highway 31 S Traverse City (49685) ***(G-16841)***
Stone House Bread Inc 231 933-8864
4200 Us Highway 31 S Traverse City (49685) ***(G-16842)***
Stone Plastics and Mfg Inc 616 748-9740
8245 Riley St Ste 100 Zeeland (49464) ***(G-19082)***
Stone Shop Inc 248 852-4700
2920 Wright St Port Huron (48060) ***(G-13530)***
Stone Soap Company Inc 248 706-1000
2000 Pontiac Dr Sylvan Lake (48320) ***(G-16362)***
Stonebrdge Technical Entps Ltd 810 750-0040
14165 N Fenton Rd 102c Fenton (48430) ***(G-5505)***
Stonebridge Industries Inc 586 323-0348
42400 Merrill Rd Sterling Heights (48314) ***(G-16195)***
Stonebridge Technical Services, Fenton *Also called Stonebrdge Technical Entps Ltd* ***(G-5505)***
Stoneco Inc 734 587-7125
6837 Scofield Rd Maybee (48159) ***(G-11172)***
Stoneco of Michigan Inc 734 236-6538
7250 Reaume Rd Newport (48166) ***(G-12107)***
Stoneco of Michigan Inc (PA) 734 241-8966
15203 S Telegraph Rd Monroe (48161) ***(G-11578)***
Stonecrafters Inc 517 529-4990
4807 Industrial Dr Clarklake (49234) ***(G-3009)***
Stoned Like Willy LLC 833 378-6633
26677 W 12 Mile Rd Southfield (48034) ***(G-15710)***
Stonehedge Farm 231 536-2779
2246 Pesek Rd East Jordan (49727) ***(G-4881)***
Stoneridge Inc (PA) 248 489-9300
39675 Mackenzie Dr # 400 Novi (48377) ***(G-12543)***
Stoneridge Inc 781 830-0340
39675 Mackenzie Dr # 400 Novi (48377) ***(G-12544)***
Stoneridge Control Devices Inc 248 489-9300
39675 Mackenzie Dr # 400 Novi (48377) ***(G-12545)***
Stoneway Marble Granite & Tile, Grand Haven *Also called Parker Property Dev Inc* ***(G-6343)***
Stoney Acres Winery 989 356-1041
4268 Truckey Rd Alpena (49707) ***(G-323)***
Stoney Creek Collection Inc 616 363-4858
4336 Plnfeld Ave Ne Ste H Grand Rapids (49525) ***(G-7227)***
Stoney Creek Tmber Qrter Hrses 517 677-9661
810 Lester Rd Reading (49274) ***(G-13706)***
Stoney Crest Regrind Service 989 777-7190
6243 Dixie Hwy Bridgeport (48722) ***(G-1918)***
Stoney Ridge Vineyards LLC 616 540-4318
2255 Indian Lakes Rd Kent City (49330) ***(G-9437)***
Stony Creek Essential Oils 989 227-5500
6718 W Centerline Rd Saint Johns (48879) ***(G-14917)***
Stony Lake Corporation 734 944-9426
5115 Saline Waterworks Rd Saline (48176) ***(G-15041)***
Stop & Go No 10 Inc 734 281-7500
13785 Allen Rd Southgate (48195) ***(G-15757)***
Stop & Go Transportation LLC 313 346-7114
13425 Amberglen Dr Washington (48094) ***(G-18087)***
Stoppa Signs & Engraving LLC 616 532-0230
3540 Raven Ave Sw Wyoming (49509) ***(G-18908)***
Storage Control Systems Inc (PA) 616 887-7994
100 Applewood Dr Sparta (49345) ***(G-15783)***
Storch Magnetics, Livonia *Also called Storch Products Company Inc* ***(G-10422)***
Storch Products Company Inc 734 591-2200
11827 Globe St Livonia (48150) ***(G-10422)***
Stork Industries Cbd LLC 248 513-1778
1699 Traditional Dr Commerce Township (48390) ***(G-3575)***
Storm Seal Co Inc 248 689-1900
1687 Hillman Dr Troy (48083) ***(G-17374)***
Stoutenburg Inc 810 648-4400
121 Campbell Rd Sandusky (48471) ***(G-15068)***
Stovall Drilling, Grand Rapids *Also called Stovall Well Drilling Co* ***(G-7228)***
Stovall Well Drilling Co 616 364-4144
2132 4 Mile Rd Ne Grand Rapids (49525) ***(G-7228)***
Stow Company (PA) 616 399-3311
130 Central Ave Ste 400 Holland (49423) ***(G-8205)***
Str Company 517 206-6058
6442 Wooster Rd Grass Lake (49240) ***(G-7446)***
Straight Line Design 616 296-0920
18055 174th Ave Spring Lake (49456) ***(G-15853)***
Strait Astrid 269 672-4110
4139 1/2 W Joy Rd Shelbyville (49344) ***(G-15374)***
Straitoplane Inc 616 997-2211
7193 Arthur St Coopersville (49404) ***(G-3697)***
Straits Area Printing Corp 231 627-5647
313 Lafayette Ave Cheboygan (49721) ***(G-2800)***
Straits Corporation (PA) 989 684-5088
616 Oak St Tawas City (48763) ***(G-16368)***
Straits Operations Company 989 684-5088
616 Oak St Tawas City (48763) ***(G-16369)***
Straits Service Corporation 989 684-5088
616 Oak St Tawas City (48763) ***(G-16370)***
Straits Steel and Wire Company (HQ) 231 843-3416
902 N Rowe St Ste 100 Ludington (49431) ***(G-10551)***
Straits Wood Treating Inc (HQ) 989 684-5088
616 Oak St Tawas City (48763) ***(G-16371)***
Strata Design, Traverse City *Also called Cerny Industries LLC* ***(G-16643)***
Strategic Computer Solutions 248 888-0666
2625 Shefman Ter Ste 200 Ann Arbor (48105) ***(G-667)***
Stratford-Cambridge Group Co (PA) 734 404-6047
801 W Ann Arbor Trl # 235 Plymouth (48170) ***(G-13304)***
Stratford-Cambridge Group, The, Plymouth *Also called Stratford-Cambridge Group Co* ***(G-13304)***
Strattec Power Access LLC (HQ) 248 649-9742
2998 Dutton Rd Auburn Hills (48326) ***(G-1039)***
Strattec Security Corporation 248 649-9742
2998 Dutton Rd Auburn Hills (48326) ***(G-1040)***
Strauss Tool Inc 989 743-4741
410 S Shiawassee St Corunna (48817) ***(G-3718)***
Street Denim & Co 313 837-1200
15530 Grand River Ave Detroit (48227) ***(G-4611)***
Strema Sales Corp 248 645-0626
31000 Telg Rd Ste 240 Bingham Farms (48025) ***(G-1703)***
Stretchy Screens 989 780-1624
5969 Pidge Rdg Se Caledonia (49316) ***(G-2402)***
Stride Inc 616 309-1600
678 Front Ave Nw Grand Rapids (49504) ***(G-7229)***
Stridepost, Ann Arbor *Also called AK Rewards LLC* ***(G-358)***
Strider Software Inc 906 863-7798
1605 7th St Menominee (49858) ***(G-11260)***
Striker Tools LLC 248 990-7767
210 Park St Manitou Beach (49253) ***(G-10928)***
Strive O&P, Sterling Heights *Also called Strive Orthtics Prsthetics LLC* ***(G-16196)***
Strive Orthtics Prsthetics LLC 586 803-4325
41400 Dequindre Rd # 105 Sterling Heights (48314) ***(G-16196)***

Stroh Companies Inc (PA)...313 446-2000
300 River Place Dr # 5000 Detroit (48207) *(G-4612)*
Strohs...734 285-5480
3162 Biddle Ave Wyandotte (48192) *(G-18841)*
Stromberg-Carlson Products Inc...231 947-8600
2323 Traversefield Dr Traverse City (49686) *(G-16843)*
Strong Steel Products LLC...313 267-3300
6464 Strong St Detroit (48211) *(G-4613)*
Strongs Woodworking...989 350-9113
76 Magee Rd N Boyne Falls (49713) *(G-1910)*
Stroyko Construction Group Inc...281 240-3332
5879 Seville Cir Orchard Lake (48324) *(G-12720)*
Structural Concepts Corp (PA)...231 798-8888
888 E Porter Rd Norton Shores (49441) *(G-12335)*
Structural Equipment Co...248 547-3800
1330 Hilton Rd Ferndale (48220) *(G-5587)*
Structural Plastics Inc...810 953-9400
3401 Chief Holly (48442) *(G-8296)*
Structural Standards Inc...616 813-1798
465 Apple Jack Ct Sparta (49345) *(G-15784)*
Stryker Australia LLC (HQ)...269 385-2600
2825 Airview Blvd Portage (49002) *(G-13612)*
Stryker Communications Inc (HQ)...972 410-7000
2825 Airview Blvd Portage (49002) *(G-13613)*
Stryker Corporation...269 389-3741
6300 S Sprinkle Rd Portage (49002) *(G-13614)*
Stryker Corporation (PA)...269 385-2600
2825 Airview Blvd Portage (49002) *(G-13615)*
Stryker Corporation...248 374-6352
27275 Haggerty Rd Ste 680 Novi (48377) *(G-12546)*
Stryker Corporation...269 389-2300
1901 Romence Road Pkwy Portage (49002) *(G-13616)*
Stryker Customs Brokers LLC...269 389-2300
1901 Romence Road Pkwy Portage (49002) *(G-13617)*
Stryker Far East Inc (HQ)...269 385-2600
2825 Airview Blvd Portage (49002) *(G-13618)*
Stryker Instruments, Portage *Also called Stryker Sales LLC* *(G-13621)*
Stryker Prfmce Solutions LLC...269 385-2600
2825 Airview Blvd Portage (49002) *(G-13619)*
Stryker Sales LLC...269 324-5346
750 Trade Cntre Way Ste 2 Portage (49002) *(G-13620)*
Stryker Sales LLC...269 323-1027
1941 Stryker Way Portage (49002) *(G-13621)*
STS, Mio *Also called Specialty Tube Solutions* *(G-11516)*
STS, Grand Rapids *Also called Specialty Tooling Systems Inc* *(G-7213)*
Stt Usa Inc...248 522-9655
47815 West Rd Ste D-101 Wixom (48393) *(G-18759)*
Stuarts of Novi...248 615-2955
41390 W 10 Mile Rd Novi (48375) *(G-12547)*
Stud Boy Traction, Ravenna *Also called Liberty Products Inc* *(G-13691)*
Student Book Store Inc...517 351-6768
103 E Grand River Ave East Lansing (48823) *(G-4910)*
Studio 626, Marysville *Also called Thorpe Printing Services Inc* *(G-11107)*
Studio One Midwest Inc...269 962-3475
74 Leonard Wood Rd Battle Creek (49037) *(G-1302)*
Studiocraft, Kentwood *Also called SC Custom Display Inc* *(G-9479)*
Studtmans Stuff (PA)...269 673-3126
422 N Cedar St Allegan (49010) *(G-183)*
Stuff A Pal...734 646-3775
14401 Cone Rd Maybee (48159) *(G-11173)*
Stump Schlele Somappa Sprng...616 361-2791
5161 Woodfield Ct Ne Grand Rapids (49525) *(G-7230)*
Stumpp Schuele Somappa USA Inc...616 361-2791
5161 Woodfield Ct Ne Grand Rapids (49525) *(G-7231)*
Sturak Brothers Inc...269 345-2929
2450 S Sprinkle Rd Kalamazoo (49001) *(G-9344)*
Sturdy Grinding Machining Inc...586 463-8880
58600 Rosell Rd New Haven (48048) *(G-12037)*
Sturgeon Controls, Roseville *Also called Dominion Tech Group Inc* *(G-14402)*
Sturgis Electric Motor Service...269 651-2955
703 N Centerville Rd Sturgis (49091) *(G-16323)*
Sturgis Molded Products Co...269 651-9381
70343 Clark Rd Sturgis (49091) *(G-16324)*
Sturgis Tool and Die Inc...269 651-5435
817 Broadus St Sturgis (49091) *(G-16325)*
Stus Welding & Fabrication...616 392-8459
4249 58th St Holland (49423) *(G-8206)*
Style Craft Prototype Inc...248 619-9048
1820 Brinston Dr Troy (48083) *(G-17375)*
Stylecraft Printing & Graphics, Canton *Also called Stylecraft Printing Co* *(G-2528)*
Stylecraft Printing Co (PA)...734 455-5500
8472 Ronda Dr Canton (48187) *(G-2528)*
Stylerite Label Corporation (PA)...248 853-7977
2140 Avon Industrial Dr Rochester Hills (48309) *(G-14120)*
Styroloution...734 676-3616
4906 Jackson St Trenton (48183) *(G-16894)*
Styrolution...248 320-7230
29247 Glencastle Ct Farmington Hills (48336) *(G-5391)*
Styx & Twigs LLC...231 245-6083
20912 Almy Rd Howard City (49329) *(G-8419)*
Su-Dan Company (PA)...248 651-6035
190 Northpointe Dr Lake Orion (48359) *(G-9632)*
Su-Dan Company...248 754-1430
4693 Gallagher Rd Rochester (48306) *(G-13931)*
Su-Dan Plastics Inc...248 651-6035
4693 Gallagher Rd Rochester (48306) *(G-13932)*
Su-Dan Plastics Inc (PA)...248 651-6035
190 Northpointe Dr Lake Orion (48359) *(G-9633)*
Su-Dan Plastics Inc...248 651-6035
1949 Rochester Indus Dr Rochester Hills (48309) *(G-14121)*
Su-Tec Inc...248 852-4711
1852 Star Batt Dr Rochester Hills (48309) *(G-14122)*
Subassembly Plus Inc...616 395-2075
11359 James St Holland (49424) *(G-8207)*
Sublime Prints...231 335-7799
283 Munn St Hesperia (49421) *(G-7872)*
Submerge Camera, Portage *Also called Livbig LLC* *(G-13578)*
Subterranean Press...810 232-1489
913 Beard St Flint (48503) *(G-5772)*
Suburban Industries Inc...734 676-6141
28093 Fort St Brownstown Twp (48183) *(G-2158)*
Subway Restaurant...248 625-5739
7743 Sashabaw Rd Ste B Clarkston (48348) *(G-3070)*
Success By Design Inc...800 327-0057
3741 Linden Ave Se Wyoming (49548) *(G-18909)*
Sudan, Lake Orion *Also called Su-Dan Company* *(G-9632)*
Sues Scented Soy Candles...989 642-3352
2991 Laporte Rd Hemlock (48626) *(G-7856)*
Suez Water Indiana LLC...734 379-3855
34001 W Jefferson Ave Rockwood (48173) *(G-14205)*
Sugar Berry...517 321-0177
5451 W Saginaw Hwy Lansing (48917) *(G-9792)*
Sugar Free Specialties LLC (PA)...616 734-6999
5320 West River Dr Ne Comstock Park (49321) *(G-3646)*
Sugar Kissed Cupcakes LLC...231 421-9156
127 E Front St Traverse City (49684) *(G-16844)*
Sugar Sugar Cotton Candy Co...248 847-0070
3300 S Center Rd Burton (48519) *(G-2247)*
Sugru Inc...877 990-9888
38120 Amrhein Rd Livonia (48150) *(G-10423)*
Suite Spa Manufacturing LLC...616 560-2713
464 Stanton Farms Dr Caledonia (49316) *(G-2403)*
Suiter Industries Inc...989 277-1554
1931 Devonshire Ave Lansing (48910) *(G-9897)*
Sulfo-Technologies LLC...248 307-9150
32300 Howard Ave Madison Heights (48071) *(G-10838)*
Sulugu Corporation USA Inc...478 714-0325
448 Oakdale St Se Grand Rapids (49507) *(G-7232)*
Sumika Polymers North Amer LLC (HQ)...248 284-4797
27555 Executive Dr # 300 Farmington Hills (48331) *(G-5392)*
Sumitomo Chemical America Inc...248 284-4797
45525 Grand River Ave # 200 Novi (48374) *(G-12548)*
Sumitomo Electric Carbide Inc...734 451-0200
26800 Meadowbrook Rd # 120 Novi (48377) *(G-12549)*
Summers Rd Gravel, Almont *Also called Summers Road Gravel & Dev LLC* *(G-268)*
Summers Road Gravel & Dev LLC...810 798-8533
3620 Van Dyke Rd Almont (48003) *(G-268)*
Summit Cutting Tool and Mfg In...248 624-3949
2069 Devonshire Dr Wixom (48393) *(G-18760)*
Summit Industrial Services LLC...248 762-0982
107 S Vista Auburn Hills (48326) *(G-1041)*
Summit Petroleum Company LLC...231 942-8134
102 W Front St Ste 200 Traverse City (49684) *(G-16845)*
Summit Plastic Molding Inc...586 262-4500
51340 Celeste Shelby Township (48315) *(G-15344)*
Summit Plastic Molding II Inc (PA)...586 262-4500
51340 Celeste Shelby Township (48315) *(G-15345)*
Summit Polymers Inc (PA)...269 324-9330
6715 S Sprinkle Rd Portage (49002) *(G-13622)*
Summit Polymers Inc...269 324-9320
6615 S Sprinkle Rd Portage (49002) *(G-13623)*
Summit Polymers Inc...269 324-9330
5858 E N Ave Kalamazoo (49048) *(G-9345)*
Summit Polymers Inc...269 323-1301
4750 Executive Dr Portage (49002) *(G-13624)*
Summit Polymers Inc...269 651-1643
1211 Progress St Sturgis (49091) *(G-16326)*
Summit Polymers Inc...269 649-4900
115 S Leja Dr Vicksburg (49097) *(G-17614)*
Summit Services Inc...586 977-8300
51340 Celeste Shelby Township (48315) *(G-15346)*
Summit Tooling & Mfg Inc...231 856-7037
451 N Cass St Morley (49336) *(G-11623)*
Summit Training Source Inc (PA)...800 842-0466
4170 Embassy Dr Se Grand Rapids (49546) *(G-7233)*
Summit Truss, Holton *Also called Joseph Miller* *(G-8339)*
Summit-Reed City Inc...989 433-5716
4147 E Monroe St Rosebush (48878) *(G-14367)*

ALPHABETIC

Sun Chemical Corporation 513 681-5950
5025 Evanston Ave Muskegon (49442) *(G-11926)*
Sun Chemical Corporation 231 788-2371
5025 Evanston Ave Muskegon (49442) *(G-11927)*
Sun Coast Coverings LLC 734 947-1230
26395 Northline Commrc Dr Taylor (48180) *(G-16480)*
Sun Coating Co, Plymouth *Also called Sun Plastics Coating Company (G-13305)*
Sun Communities Inc (PA) 248 208-2500
27777 Franklin Rd Ste 200 Southfield (48034) *(G-15711)*
Sun Daily 248 842-2925
4226 Cherry Hill Dr Orchard Lake (48323) *(G-12721)*
Sun Gro Horticulture Dist Inc 517 639-3115
1150 E Chicago Rd Quincy (49082) *(G-13675)*
Sun Pharmaceutical Inds Inc 248 346-7302
29714 Orion Ct Farmington Hills (48334) *(G-5393)*
Sun Plastics Coating Company 734 453-0822
42105 Postiff Ave Plymouth (48170) *(G-13305)*
Sun Ray Sign Group Inc 616 392-2824
376 Roost Ave Holland (49424) *(G-8208)*
Sun Steel Treating Inc 877 471-0844
550 N Mill St South Lyon (48178) *(G-15459)*
Sun Tool Company 313 837-2442
18505 Weaver St Detroit (48228) *(G-4614)*
Sun-Tec Corp (PA) 248 669-3100
46590 Ryan Ct Novi (48377) *(G-12550)*
Sunbeam, Livonia *Also called American Household Inc (G-10114)*
Sunburst Shutters 248 674-4600
5499 Perry Dr Ste M Waterford (48329) *(G-18167)*
Sundai Imports Inc 877 517-7788
36500 Ford Rd Ste 241 Westland (48185) *(G-18419)*
Sundance Beverage Company, Warren *Also called Sundance Beverages Inc (G-18030)*
Sundance Beverages Inc 586 755-9470
6600 E 9 Mile Rd Warren (48091) *(G-18030)*
Sundog Construction Heaters, Birmingham *Also called U S Distributing Inc (G-1755)*
Sunera Technologies Inc (PA) 248 434-0808
631 E Big Beaver Rd # 105 Troy (48083) *(G-17376)*
Suneratech, Troy *Also called Sunera Technologies Inc (G-17376)*
Sunglass Hut 4711, Birch Run *Also called Luxottica of America Inc (G-1710)*
Sungwoo Hitech Co Ltd 248 561-0604
3221 W Big Beavr Rd # 30 Troy (48084) *(G-17377)*
Sunhill America LLC (PA) 616 249-3600
5300 Broadmoor Ave Se B Grand Rapids (49512) *(G-7234)*
Sunmed Holdings LLC (PA) 616 259-8400
2710 Northridge Dr Nw Grand Rapids (49544) *(G-7235)*
Sunningdale Tech Inc (HQ) 248 526-0517
100 W Big Beaver Rd Troy (48084) *(G-17378)*
Sunopta Ingredients Inc 502 587-7999
16369 Us Highway 131 S Schoolcraft (49087) *(G-15129)*
Sunraise Inc 810 359-7301
6547 Lakeshore Rd Lexington (48450) *(G-10032)*
Sunrise Fiberglass LLC 651 462-5313
1732 Crooks Rd Troy (48084) *(G-17379)*
Sunrise Print Cmmnications Inc 989 345-4475
118 W Houghton Ave West Branch (48661) *(G-18342)*
Sunrise Tool Products Inc 989 724-6688
604 S 3rd St Harrisville (48740) *(G-7745)*
Sunsation Boats, Clay *Also called Sunsation Products Inc (G-3126)*
Sunsation Products Inc 810 794-4888
9666 Kretz Dr Clay (48001) *(G-3126)*
Sunset Coast Publishing LLC 574 440-3228
25526 Joelle Ct Edwardsburg (49112) *(G-5018)*
Sunset Enterprises Inc (PA) 269 373-6440
633 W Michigan Ave Kalamazoo (49007) *(G-9346)*
Sunset Sportswear Inc 248 437-7611
676 Shady Maple Dr Wixom (48393) *(G-18761)*
Sunset Valley Creamatory, Bay City *Also called Fogelsonger Vault Co Inc (G-1358)*
Sunshine Meadery LLC 231 215-7956
50 W Englewood Ave Ste B Twin Lake (49457) *(G-17473)*
Sunstone Granite & Marble Co, Grand Rapids *Also called Grand Valley Wood Products Inc (G-6779)*
Suntech Industrials LLC 734 678-5922
5137 Colonial Ct Ann Arbor (48108) *(G-668)*
Super Book, Portage *Also called Llomen Inc (G-13579)*
Super Fluids LLC 313 409-6522
8838 3rd St Detroit (48202) *(G-4615)*
Super Steel Treating Inc 586 755-9140
6227 Rinke Ave Warren (48091) *(G-18031)*
Super Woman Productions Pubg L 313 491-6819
8539 Meyers Rd Detroit (48228) *(G-4616)*
Superabrasives Inc 248 348-7670
28047 Grand Oaks Ct Wixom (48393) *(G-18762)*
Superalloy North America LLC 810 252-1552
31000 Telg Rd Ste 280 Bingham Farms (48025) *(G-1704)*
Superb Machine Repair Inc (PA) 586 749-8800
59180 Havenridge Rd New Haven (48048) *(G-12038)*
Superfly Manufacturing Co 313 454-1492
31505 Grand River Ave 7c Farmington (48336) *(G-5152)*
Superior Abrasive Products 248 969-4090
85 S Glaspie St Ste A Oxford (48371) *(G-12921)*
Superior Attachment Inc 906 864-1708
N3522 Us Highway 41 Menominee (49858) *(G-11261)*
Superior Auto Glass of Mich 989 366-9691
7006 W Houghton Lake Dr Houghton Lake (48629) *(G-8406)*
Superior Automotive Eqp Inc 231 829-9902
18153 150th Ave Leroy (49655) *(G-10012)*
Superior Block Company Inc 906 482-2731
100 Isle Royale St Houghton (49931) *(G-8392)*
Superior Brass & Alum Cast Co 517 351-7534
4893 Dawn Ave East Lansing (48823) *(G-4911)*
Superior Cam Inc 248 588-1100
31240 Stephenson Hwy Madison Heights (48071) *(G-10839)*
Superior Cedar Products Inc 906 639-2132
N285 Us 41 S Carney (49812) *(G-2564)*
Superior Collision Inc 231 946-4983
9419 Westwood Dr Traverse City (49685) *(G-16846)*
Superior Controls Inc 734 454-0500
46247 Five Mile Rd Plymouth (48170) *(G-13306)*
Superior Cutter Grinding Inc 586 781-2365
54631 Franklin Dr Shelby Township (48316) *(G-15347)*
Superior Cutting Service Inc 616 796-0114
4740 136th Ave Holland (49424) *(G-8209)*
Superior Design & Mfg 810 678-3950
4180 Pleasant St Metamora (48455) *(G-11287)*
Superior Distribution Svcs LLC 616 453-6358
4001 3 Mile Rd Nw Grand Rapids (49534) *(G-7236)*
Superior Elc Mtr Sls & Svc, Marquette *Also called Superior Elc Mtr Sls & Svc Inc (G-11044)*
Superior Elc Mtr Sls & Svc Inc 906 226-9051
1740 Presque Isle Ave Marquette (49855) *(G-11044)*
Superior Equipment & Supply Co 906 774-1789
1515 S Stephenson Ave Iron Mountain (49801) *(G-8734)*
Superior Equipment LLC 269 388-2871
7008 E N Ave Kalamazoo (49048) *(G-9347)*
Superior Extrusion Inc 906 346-7308
118 Avenue G Gwinn (49841) *(G-7587)*
Superior Fabricating Inc 989 354-8877
320 N Eleventh Ave Alpena (49707) *(G-324)*
Superior Fabrication Co LLC 906 495-5634
17499 S Dolan St Bldg 434 Kincheloe (49788) *(G-9505)*
Superior Fixture & Tooling LLC 616 828-1566
425 36th St Se Grand Rapids (49548) *(G-7237)*
Superior Fluid Systems 734 246-4550
7804 Beech Daly Rd Taylor (48180) *(G-16481)*
Superior Fuels LLC 586 738-6851
6833 Kingsley St Dearborn (48126) *(G-3902)*
Superior Furniture Company, Grand Rapids *Also called Van Zee Acquisitions Inc (G-7305)*
Superior Growers Supply, Lansing *Also called Growgeneration Michigan Corp (G-9849)*
Superior Heat Treat LLC 586 792-9500
36125 Groesbeck Hwy Clinton Township (48035) *(G-3365)*
Superior Hockey LLC (PA) 906 225-9008
401 E Fair Ave Marquette (49855) *(G-11045)*
Superior Imaging, Kalamazoo *Also called Superior Typesetting Service (G-9349)*
Superior Imaging Services Inc 269 382-0428
4001 Portage St Kalamazoo (49001) *(G-9348)*
Superior Industries Intl Inc (PA) 248 352-7300
26600 Telg Rd Ste 400 Southfield (48033) *(G-15712)*
Superior Industries N Amer LLC 248 352-7300
26600 Telegraph Rd # 400 Southfield (48033) *(G-15713)*
Superior Information Tech LLC 734 666-9963
38701 7 Mile Rd Ste 285 Livonia (48152) *(G-10424)*
Superior Inspection Svc 231 258-9400
1864 Prough Rd Sw Kalkaska (49646) *(G-9405)*
Superior Machine & Tool Inc 800 822-9524
1301 Sunset Ave Lansing (48917) *(G-9793)*
Superior Machining Inc 248 446-9451
55378 Lyon Industrial Dr New Hudson (48165) *(G-12071)*
Superior Manufacturing Corp (PA) 313 935-1550
431 Stephenson Hwy Troy (48083) *(G-17380)*
Superior Mar & Envmtl Svcs LLC 906 253-9448
3779 S Riverside Dr Sault Sainte Marie (49783) *(G-15101)*
Superior Materials LLC 734 941-2479
39001 W Huron River Dr Romulus (48174) *(G-14332)*
Superior Materials LLC (PA) 248 788-8000
30701 W 10 Mile Rd Farmington Hills (48336) *(G-5394)*
Superior Materials Holdings 586 468-3544
40 Floral Ave Mount Clemens (48043) *(G-11658)*
Superior Materials Inc (PA) 248 788-8000
585 Stewart Ave Farmington Hills (48333) *(G-5395)*
Superior Mold Services Inc 586 264-9570
6100 15 Mile Rd Sterling Heights (48312) *(G-16197)*
Superior Monuments Co (PA) 231 728-2211
354 Ottawa St Muskegon (49442) *(G-11928)*
Superior Mtal Finshg Rustproof 313 893-1050
3510 E Mcnichols Rd Detroit (48212) *(G-4617)*
Superior Mtls Holdings LLC 248 788-8000
30701 W 10 Mile Rd Farmington Hills (48336) *(G-5396)*
Superior Polymer Products, Calumet *Also called Kiilunen Mfg Group Inc (G-2410)*
Superior Polyolefin Films Inc 248 334-8074
465 Fox River Dr Bloomfield Hills (48304) *(G-1863)*

Superior Products Mfg Inc....810 679-4479
124 Louise St Croswell (48422) *(G-3736)*
Superior Receipt Book Co Inc....269 467-8265
215 S Clark St Centreville (49032) *(G-2698)*
Superior Roll LLC....734 279-1831
399 E Center St Petersburg (49270) *(G-12985)*
Superior Roll & Turning, Petersburg *Also called Superior Roll LLC (G-12985)*
Superior Spindle Services LLC....734 946-4646
25377 Brest Taylor (48180) *(G-16482)*
Superior Steel Components Inc (PA)....616 866-4759
180 Monroe Ave Nw Ste 2r Grand Rapids (49503) *(G-7238)*
Superior Stitch....734 347-1956
14724 W Dunbar Rd Petersburg (49270) *(G-12986)*
Superior Suppliers Network LLC....906 284-1561
1307 Harrison Ave Crystal Falls (49920) *(G-3746)*
Superior Text LLC....866 482-8762
151 Airport Industrial Dr Ypsilanti (48198) *(G-18980)*
Superior Threading Inc....989 729-1160
1535 N Hickory Rd Owosso (48867) *(G-12859)*
Superior Tool & Fabg LLC....906 353-7588
13529 Old 41 Rd Keweenaw Bay (49908) *(G-9490)*
Superior Typesetting Service....269 382-0428
4001 Portage St Kalamazoo (49001) *(G-9349)*
Superior USA LLC....586 786-4261
16089 Leone Dr Macomb (48042) *(G-10638)*
Superior Vault Co....989 643-4200
345 E Mahoney Merrill (48637) *(G-11265)*
Superior Washing and Pain....616 293-5347
1033 Lincoln Lk Lowell (49331) *(G-10518)*
Superior Waterjet Service, Chesterfield *Also called American Brake and Clutch Inc (G-2838)*
Superior Welding & Mfg Inc....906 498-7616
5704 Old Us 2 Rd 43 Hermansville (49847) *(G-7863)*
Supermarket Liquidation, Grand Rapids *Also called Hilco Fixture Finders LLC (G-6815)*
Supersine Company....313 892-6200
27634 Rackham Dr Lathrup Village (48076) *(G-9978)*
Superstroke Golf, Wixom *Also called Technique Golf LLC (G-18769)*
Supertramp Cstm Trmpline LLC D....616 634-2010
5161 Woodfield Ct Ne # 1 Grand Rapids (49525) *(G-7239)*
Supplement Group Inc....248 588-2055
32787 Stephenson Hwy Madison Heights (48071) *(G-10840)*
Supplements Geeks, Novi *Also called Jaaz Management LLC (G-12447)*
Supply Line International LLC....248 242-7140
42350 Grand River Ave Novi (48375) *(G-12551)*
Supply Pro....810 239-8658
5402 Hill 23 Dr Flint (48507) *(G-5773)*
Supported Intelligence LLC....517 908-4420
1555 Watertower Pl # 300 East Lansing (48823) *(G-4912)*
Supreme Bakery & Deli, Detroit *Also called Supreme Baking Company (G-4618)*
Supreme Baking Company....313 894-0222
5401 Proctor St Detroit (48210) *(G-4618)*
Supreme Casting Inc....269 465-5757
3389 W Linco Rd Stevensville (49127) *(G-16267)*
Supreme Domestic Intl Sls Corp....616 842-6550
18686 172nd Ave Spring Lake (49456) *(G-15854)*
Supreme Gear Co (PA)....586 775-6325
17430 Malyn Bvld Fraser (48026) *(G-6001)*
Supreme Industries LLC....586 725-2500
6015 Corporate Dr Ira (48023) *(G-8715)*
Supreme Machined Pdts Co Inc (PA)....616 842-6550
18686 172nd Ave Spring Lake (49456) *(G-15855)*
Supreme Media Blasting and Pow....586 792-7705
36427 Groesbeck Hwy Clinton Township (48035) *(G-3366)*
Supreme Tool & Machine Inc....248 673-8408
5409 Perry Dr Waterford (48329) *(G-18168)*
Sur-Form LLC....586 221-1950
50320 E Rssell Schmidt Bl Chesterfield (48051) *(G-2951)*
Sure -Loc Edging-Wolverine Tls, Holland *Also called Sure-Loc Aluminum Edging Inc (G-8210)*
Sure Alloy Steel, Warren *Also called Sas Global Corporation (G-18003)*
Sure Conveyors Inc....248 926-2100
48155 West Rd Ste 6 Wixom (48393) *(G-18763)*
Sure Flow Products LLC....248 380-3569
28265 Beck Rd Ste C11 Wixom (48393) *(G-18764)*
Sure Solutions Corporation....248 674-7210
40 Corporate Dr Auburn Hills (48326) *(G-1042)*
Sure-Flo Fittings, Ann Arbor *Also called Perfection Sprinkler Company (G-607)*
Sure-Loc Aluminum Edging Inc....616 392-3209
310 E 64th St Holland (49423) *(G-8210)*
Sure-Plating Rack Co, Southfield *Also called Sure-Weld & Plating Rack Co (G-15714)*
Sure-Weld & Plating Rack Co (PA)....248 304-9430
21680 W 8 Mile Rd Southfield (48075) *(G-15714)*
Surefil, Kentwood *Also called Abaco Partners LLC (G-9441)*
Surefit Parts LLC....586 416-9150
50400 Patricia St Chesterfield (48051) *(G-2952)*
Surface Activation Tech LLC....248 273-0037
1837 Thunderbird Troy (48084) *(G-17381)*
Surface Coatings Co....248 977-9478
3695 Merritt Lake Dr Metamora (48455) *(G-11288)*
Surface Coatings Company, Auburn Hills *Also called Bonsal American Inc (G-813)*
Surface Expressions LLC....231 843-8282
904 1st St Ludington (49431) *(G-10552)*
Surface Induction Tech....248 881-2481
51200 Milano Dr Ste C Macomb (48042) *(G-10639)*
Surface Mausoleum Company Inc....989 864-3460
1799 Main St Minden City (48456) *(G-11506)*
Surfaceprep, Byron Center *Also called Gnap LLC (G-2272)*
Surfalloy, Troy *Also called Alloying Surfaces Inc (G-16927)*
Surgitech Surgical Svcs Inc....248 593-0797
1477 Schooner Cv Highland (48356) *(G-7900)*
Surplus Coatings, Kent City *Also called Coatings By Pcd Inc (G-9429)*
Surrey USA LLC....800 248-5960
500 Hogsback Rd Mason (48854) *(G-11159)*
Suse Linux, Southfield *Also called Suse LLC (G-15715)*
Suse LLC....248 353-8010
26677 W 12 Mile Rd Ste 1 Southfield (48034) *(G-15715)*
Suspa Incorporated (HQ)....616 241-4200
3970 Rger B Chffee Mem Dr Grand Rapids (49548) *(G-7240)*
Sutherland Felt Co, Madison Heights *Also called Michigan Diversfd Holdings Inc (G-10782)*
Suttons Bay Ciders....734 646-3196
10530 E Hilltop Rd Suttons Bay (49682) *(G-16343)*
Suttons Bay Tasting Room, Suttons Bay *Also called Black Star Farms LLC (G-16339)*
Sv Logging LLC....715 360-0035
102 Mattson Rd Iron River (49935) *(G-8756)*
Svf Bloomingdale Inc....269 521-3026
43073 County Road 388 Bloomingdale (49026) *(G-1880)*
Svk Media and Publishing LLC....616 379-4001
5480 Alberta Dr Ste 1 Hudsonville (49426) *(G-8613)*
Svn Inc....734 707-7131
6763 Heatheridge Dr Saline (48176) *(G-15042)*
Svrc Industries Inc (PA)....989 280-3038
203 S Washington Ave Saginaw (48607) *(G-14768)*
Svrc Industries Inc....989 723-8205
2009 Corunna Ave Owosso (48867) *(G-12860)*
Swain Company Inc....989 773-3700
220 E Ludington Dr Farwell (48622) *(G-5429)*
Swain Meter Company....989 773-3700
220 E Ludington Dr Farwell (48622) *(G-5430)*
Swan Creek Candle, Dundee *Also called Ambrosia Inc (G-4809)*
Swanson Grading & Brining Inc....231 853-2289
11561 Heights Ravenna Rd Ravenna (49451) *(G-13695)*
Swanson Pickle Co Inc....231 853-2289
11561 Heights Ravenna Rd Ravenna (49451) *(G-13696)*
Swansons Excavating Inc....989 873-4419
2733 Greenwood Rd Prescott (48756) *(G-13652)*
Swarovski....248 344-2922
27500 Novi Rd Novi (48377) *(G-12552)*
Swarovski North America Ltd....586 226-4420
17410 Hall Rd Ste 175 Clinton Township (48038) *(G-3367)*
Swartzmiller Lumber Company (PA)....989 845-6625
802 W Broad St Chesaning (48616) *(G-2830)*
Swat Environmental Inc (PA)....517 322-2999
2607 Eaton Rapids Rd Lansing (48911) *(G-9898)*
Sweed Dreams LLC....313 704-6694
27552 Schoolcraft Rd Livonia (48150) *(G-10425)*
Sweeney Metalworking LLC....989 401-6531
4450 Marlea Dr Saginaw (48601) *(G-14769)*
Sweepster Attachments LLC....734 996-9116
2800 Zeeb Rd Dexter (48130) *(G-4757)*
Sweet & Sweeter Inc....586 977-9338
4059 17 Mile Rd Sterling Heights (48310) *(G-16198)*
Sweet & Sweeter By Linda, Sterling Heights *Also called Sweet & Sweeter Inc (G-16198)*
Sweet Creations....989 327-1157
1375 Lathrup Ave Saginaw (48638) *(G-14770)*
Sweet Earth....248 850-8031
313 S Main St Royal Oak (48067) *(G-14583)*
Sweet Harvest Foods, Onsted *Also called Natural American Foods LLC (G-12707)*
Sweet Manufacturing Inc....269 344-2086
3421 S Burdick St Kalamazoo (49001) *(G-9350)*
Sweet Mellisas Cupcakes....616 889-3998
4413 Causeway Dr Ne Lowell (49331) *(G-10519)*
Sweet N Sporty Tees....313 693-9793
20410 W 7 Mile Rd Detroit (48219) *(G-4619)*
Sweet Sugas LLC....313 444-8570
35598 Ashton Ct Clinton Township (48035) *(G-3368)*
Sweet Tmpttons Ice Cream Prlor....616 842-8108
1003 S Beacon Blvd Grand Haven (49417) *(G-6369)*
Sweetest Taboo LLC....313 575-4642
14091 Mark Twain St Detroit (48227) *(G-4620)*
Sweetheart Bakery Inc (PA)....313 839-6330
19200 Kelly Rd Detroit (48225) *(G-4621)*
Sweetheart Bakery of Michigan....586 795-1660
19200 Kelly Rd Harper Woods (48225) *(G-7673)*
Sweetheart Corp....847 405-2100
500 Hogsback Rd Mason (48854) *(G-11160)*
Sweetie Pie Pantry (PA)....517 669-9300
108 N Bridge St Dewitt (48820) *(G-4716)*

A L P H A B E T I C

Sweetwater Brew LLC 616 805-5077
1760 44th St Sw Wyoming (49519) ***(G-18910)***
Sweetwaters Donut Mill 269 979-1944
2807 Capital Ave Sw Battle Creek (49015) ***(G-1303)***
Sweney-Kern Manufacturing, Saginaw *Also called Midwest Marketing Inc* ***(G-14700)***
Swift Biosciences Inc 734 330-2568
674 S Wagner Rd Ste 100 Ann Arbor (48103) ***(G-669)***
Swift Printing and Comm, Grand Rapids *Also called Swift Printing Co* ***(G-7241)***
Swift Printing Co 616 459-4263
404 Bridge St Nw Grand Rapids (49504) ***(G-7241)***
Swiftwall Solutions, Midland *Also called Signature Wall Solutions Inc* ***(G-11417)***
Swing-Lo Suspended Scaffold Co 269 764-8989
75609 County Road 376 Covert (49043) ***(G-3726)***
Swing-Lo System, Covert *Also called Swing-Lo Suspended Scaffold Co* ***(G-3726)***
Swirlberry 734 779-0830
17382 Haggerty Rd Livonia (48152) ***(G-10426)***
Swiss American Screw Pdts Inc 734 397-1600
5740 S Sheldon Rd Canton (48188) ***(G-2529)***
Swiss Industries Inc 517 437-3682
305 Arch Ave Hillsdale (49242) ***(G-7950)***
Swiss Precision Machining Inc 586 677-7558
54370 Oconee Dr Macomb (48042) ***(G-10640)***
Swivl - Eze Marine 616 897-9241
1016 N Monroe St Lowell (49331) ***(G-10520)***
Swoboda Inc 616 554-6161
4108 52nd St Se Grand Rapids (49512) ***(G-7242)***
Sws - Trimac Inc 989 791-4595
5225 Davis Rd Saginaw (48604) ***(G-14771)***
Sxs Gear 810 265-7219
6075 Birch Rd Flint (48507) ***(G-5774)***
Sy Fuel Inc 313 531-5894
27360 Grand River Ave Redford (48240) ***(G-13776)***
Sybron Dental Specialti 734 947-6927
28210 Wick Rd Romulus (48174) ***(G-14333)***
Syd Enterprises 517 719-2740
3850 E Grand River Ave Howell (48843) ***(G-8524)***
Sylvania Minerals, South Rockwood *Also called Great Lakes Aggregates LLC* ***(G-15464)***
Symbiosis International, Okemos *Also called Umakanth Consultants Inc* ***(G-12691)***
Symbiote Inc 616 772-1790
300 N Centennial St Zeeland (49464) ***(G-19083)***
Symonds Machine Co Inc 269 782-8051
414 West St Dowagiac (49047) ***(G-4798)***
Symorex Ltd 734 971-6000
3728 Plaza Dr Ste 3 Ann Arbor (48108) ***(G-670)***
Symphony Cabinetry LLC 231 421-5421
811 S Garfield Ave Traverse City (49686) ***(G-16847)***
Sync Technologies Inc (PA) 313 963-5353
2727 2nd Ave Ste 107 Detroit (48201) ***(G-4622)***
Synchron Laser Service Inc 248 486-0402
41303 Concept Dr Plymouth (48170) ***(G-13307)***
Synchronous Manufacturing Inc 517 764-6930
4050 Page Ave Michigan Center (49254) ***(G-11296)***
Syncon Inc 313 914-4481
31001 Schoolcraft Rd Livonia (48150) ***(G-10427)***
Syndevco Inc 248 356-2839
24205 Telegraph Rd Southfield (48033) ***(G-15716)***
Synergy Additive Mfg LLC (HQ) 248 719-2194
22792 Macomb Indus Dr Clinton Township (48036) ***(G-3369)***
Synergy Prototype Stamping LLC (PA) 586 961-6109
22778 Macomb Indus Dr Clinton Township (48036) ***(G-3370)***
Synod of Great Lakes 616 698-7071
4500 60th St Se Grand Rapids (49512) ***(G-7243)***
Syntech Plant, Sturgis *Also called Summit Polymers Inc* ***(G-16326)***
Syscom Technologies Inc 231 946-1411
3124 Logan Valley Rd Traverse City (49684) ***(G-16848)***
System 2/90 Inc 616 656-4310
5350 Corprte Grv Dr Se Grand Rapids (49512) ***(G-7244)***
System Components Inc 269 637-2191
1635 Stieve Dr South Haven (49090) ***(G-15417)***
System Controls Inc 734 427-0440
35245 Schoolcraft Rd Livonia (48150) ***(G-10428)***
Systems Control, Howell *Also called Service Control Inc* ***(G-8516)***
Systems Control Inc 906 774-0440
3201 E Industrial Dr Iron Mountain (49801) ***(G-8735)***
Systems Design & Installation 269 543-4204
2091 66th St Fennville (49408) ***(G-5442)***
Systems Duplicating Co Inc 248 585-7590
358 Robbins Dr Troy (48083) ***(G-17382)***
Systex Products Corporation (HQ) 269 964-8800
300 Buckner Rd Battle Creek (49037) ***(G-1304)***
Systrand Manufacturing Corp (PA) 734 479-8100
19050 Allen Rd Brownstown Twp (48183) ***(G-2159)***
Systrand Prsta Eng Systems LLC 734 479-8100
19050 Allen Rd Ste 200 Brownstown Twp (48183) ***(G-2160)***
Szymanowski Electric LLC 612 928-8370
784 105th Ave Plainwell (49080) ***(G-13097)***
T & C Tool & Sales Inc 586 677-8390
60950 Van Dyke Rd Washington (48094) ***(G-18088)***
T & J Uphl Sp & Marathon Svc, Moran *Also called Gustafson Smoked Fish* ***(G-11609)***
T & K Industries Inc 586 212-9100
18057 Gaylord Ct Clinton Township (48035) ***(G-3371)***
T & K Woodworks 734 868-0028
1983 W Stein Rd La Salle (48145) ***(G-9530)***
T & L Products 989 868-4428
2586 S Bradleyville Rd Reese (48757) ***(G-13809)***
T & L Transport Inc 313 350-1535
13801 Westbrook Rd Plymouth (48170) ***(G-13308)***
T & M Homes 989 239-4699
1018 Lindsay Dr Saginaw (48602) ***(G-14772)***
T & M Machining Inc 586 294-5781
18110 E 14 Mile Rd Fraser (48026) ***(G-6002)***
T & T Tools Inc 800 521-6893
4470 128th Ave Holland (49424) ***(G-8211)***
T & W Tool & Die Corporation 248 548-5400
21770 Wyoming Pl Oak Park (48237) ***(G-12647)***
T - Shirt Printing Plus Inc 269 383-3666
8608 W Main St Ste B Kalamazoo (49009) ***(G-9351)***
T 4 Manufacturing 616 952-0020
390 Wynwood Kent City (49330) ***(G-9438)***
T and A Welding 269 228-1268
21660 Mason St Edwardsburg (49112) ***(G-5019)***
T and RC Anvas Awning LLC 810 230-1740
2153 Lodge Rd Flint (48532) ***(G-5775)***
T and T Tools, Holland *Also called T & T Tools Inc* ***(G-8211)***
T C H Industries Incorporated (HQ) 616 942-0505
7441 Div Ave S Ste A1 Grand Rapids (49548) ***(G-7245)***
T C V S, Ann Arbor *Also called Terumo Crdvscular Systems Corp* ***(G-683)***
T D I C, Sterling Heights *Also called TD Industrial Coverings Inc* ***(G-16202)***
T D Vinette Company 906 786-1884
1212 N 19th St Escanaba (49829) ***(G-5102)***
T E C Boring 586 443-5437
15645 Sturgeon St Roseville (48066) ***(G-14482)***
T E L, Ann Arbor *Also called Thalner Electronic Labs Inc* ***(G-686)***
T E Technology Inc 231 929-3966
1590 Keane Dr Traverse City (49696) ***(G-16849)***
T F Boyer Industries Inc 248 674-8420
5489 Perry Dr Ste C Waterford (48329) ***(G-18169)***
T J K Inc 586 731-9639
39370 Bella Vista Dr Sterling Heights (48313) ***(G-16199)***
T J Northwoods Services LLC 906 250-3509
120 N Daisy St Ishpeming (49849) ***(G-8782)***
T K Industries Inc 586 242-5969
53586 Applewood Dr Shelby Township (48315) ***(G-15348)***
T L V Inc 989 773-4362
5747 W Isabella Rd Mount Pleasant (48858) ***(G-11744)***
T M Shea Products Inc 800 992-5233
1950 Austin Dr Troy (48083) ***(G-17383)***
T M Smith Tool Intl Corp (PA) 586 468-1465
360 Hubbard St Mount Clemens (48043) ***(G-11659)***
T M Wood Products Mfg Inc 586 427-2364
24301 Hoover Rd Warren (48089) ***(G-18032)***
T Q Machining Inc 231 726-5914
450 W Hackley Ave Muskegon (49444) ***(G-11929)***
T R S Fieldbus Systems Inc 586 826-9696
666 Baldwin Ct Birmingham (48009) ***(G-1751)***
T S M Foods LLC 313 262-6556
1241 Woodward Ave Detroit (48226) ***(G-4623)***
T Shirt Guy 586 944-5900
31368 Beechwood Dr Warren (48088) ***(G-18033)***
T Shirt Shop 810 285-8857
G5082 N Saginaw St Flint (48505) ***(G-5776)***
T W S Wldg & Cstm Fabrication, Kalkaska *Also called Todds Welding Service Inc* ***(G-9408)***
T Wigley Inc 313 831-6881
1537 Hale St Detroit (48207) ***(G-4624)***
T&K Machine 989 836-0811
1486 N M 76 Alger (48610) ***(G-139)***
T-Print USA 269 751-4603
3410 136th Ave Hamilton (49419) ***(G-7607)***
T-Tool Company, Livonia *Also called Rep Innovations Inc* ***(G-10385)***
T/D Village Winery LLC 586 752-5510
134 W Saint Clair St Romeo (48065) ***(G-14236)***
T4 Software 313 610-3297
26300 Ford Rd Dearborn Heights (48127) ***(G-3940)***
Ta Delaware Inc (PA) 248 675-6000
17672 N Lrel Pk Dr Ste 40 Novi (48377) ***(G-12553)***
TA Systems Inc 248 656-5150
1842 Rochester Indus Dr Rochester Hills (48309) ***(G-14123)***
Tabletting Inc 616 957-0281
4201 Danvers Ct Se Grand Rapids (49512) ***(G-7246)***
Tabone Vineyards LLC 734 354-7271
14916 Peninsula Dr Traverse City (49686) ***(G-16850)***
Tabor Hill Winery & Restaurant, Buchanan *Also called CHI Co/Tabor Hill Winery* ***(G-2192)***
Tabs Floor Covering LLC 616 846-1684
17370 Woodland Ln Nunica (49448) ***(G-12587)***
TAC Manufacturing Inc (HQ) 517 789-7000
4111 County Farm Rd Jackson (49201) ***(G-9014)***
Tachi-S Engineering USA Inc (HQ) 248 478-5050
23227 Commerce Dr Farmington Hills (48335) ***(G-5397)***

ALPHABETIC SECTION Tecart Industries Inc

Tachyon Corporation 586 598-4320
48705 Gratiot Ave Chesterfield (48051) ***(G-2953)***

Tack Electronics Inc 616 698-0960
5030 Kraft Ave Se Ste A Grand Rapids (49512) ***(G-7247)***

Tactical Simplicity LLC 248 410-4523
2817 Beck Rd Ste E-16 Wixom (48393) ***(G-18765)***

Tad, Grand Rapids *Also called Trece Adhesive Division* ***(G-7272)***

Tade Publishing Group, Troy *Also called Timothy J Tade Inc* ***(G-17392)***

Tadey Frank R Radian Tool Co 586 754-7422
23823 Blackstone Ave Warren (48089) ***(G-18034)***

Tafcor Inc 269 471-2351
9918 N Tudor Rd Berrien Springs (49103) ***(G-1646)***

Tags R Us LLC 248 880-4062
920 Lake Jason Dr White Lake (48386) ***(G-18468)***

Tai Consulting, Franklin *Also called Talbot & Associates Inc* ***(G-5885)***

Tait Grinding Service Inc 248 437-5100
1940 Olympia Dr Howell (48843) ***(G-8525)***

Taiz Fuel Inc 313 485-2972
4630 S Beech Daly St Dearborn Heights (48125) ***(G-3941)***

Tajco North America Inc 248 418-7550
2851 High Meadow Cir # 19 Auburn Hills (48326) ***(G-1043)***

Takata Americas (HQ) 336 547-1600
2500 Takata Dr Ste 300 Auburn Hills (48326) ***(G-1044)***

Take Care Natural Products 989 280-3947
3645 Cooklin Rd Cass City (48726) ***(G-2621)***

Take Us-4-Granite Inc 586 803-1305
13000 23 Mile Rd Shelby Township (48315) ***(G-15349)***

Take-A-Label Inc 616 837-9300
16900 Power Dr Nunica (49448) ***(G-12588)***

Talbot & Associates Inc 248 723-9700
30400 Telg Rd Ste 479 Franklin (48025) ***(G-5885)***

Talco Industries 989 269-6260
705 E Woodworth St Bad Axe (48413) ***(G-1112)***

Talent Industries Inc 313 531-4700
12950 Inkster Rd Redford (48239) ***(G-13777)***

Taletyano Press 517 381-1960
4107 Breakwater Dr Okemos (48864) ***(G-12688)***

Talisman 616 458-1391
2033 Oak Industrial Dr Ne Grand Rapids (49505) ***(G-7248)***

Talkin Tackle LLC 517 474-6241
205 S Sandstone Rd Jackson (49201) ***(G-9015)***

Tall City LLC 248 854-0713
3386 Countryside Cir Auburn Hills (48326) ***(G-1045)***

Tall Pauls Pickles LLC 734 476-2424
4488 Jackson Rd Ann Arbor (48103) ***(G-671)***

Tallon Printing 517 721-1307
1715 W Grand River Ave Okemos (48864) ***(G-12689)***

Tallulahs Satchels 231 775-4082
615 White Pine Dr Cadillac (49601) ***(G-2360)***

Talon LLC 313 392-1000
350 Talon Centre Dr Detroit (48207) ***(G-4625)***

Tamara Tool Inc 269 273-1463
1234 William R Monroe Blv Three Rivers (49093) ***(G-16586)***

Tambra Investments Inc 866 662-7897
23247 Pinewood St Warren (48091) ***(G-18035)***

Tamsco Inc 586 415-1500
43175 W Kirkwood Dr Clinton Township (48038) ***(G-3372)***

Tandem Ciders Inc 231 271-0050
2055 N Setterbo Rd Suttons Bay (49682) ***(G-16344)***

Tandis LLC 248 345-3448
6357 Branford Dr West Bloomfield (48322) ***(G-18317)***

Tangico, Pontiac *Also called Connexion Inc* ***(G-13355)***

Tanis Custom Grills, Grand Rapids *Also called Klise Manufacturing Company* ***(G-6899)***

Tanis Technologies LLC 616 796-2712
645 Commerce Ct Ste 10 Holland (49424) ***(G-8212)***

Tank Truck Service & Sales Inc 989 731-4887
1981 Engel Ave Gaylord (49735) ***(G-6162)***

Tank Truck Service & Sales Inc (PA) 586 757-6500
25150 Dequindre Rd Warren (48091) ***(G-18036)***

Tannewitz Inc 616 457-5999
794 Chicago Dr Jenison (49428) ***(G-9073)***

Tanning Trends, Jackson *Also called International Smart Tan Netwrk* ***(G-8910)***

Tapco Group, The, Wixom *Also called Boral Building Products Inc* ***(G-18625)***

Tapco Holdings Inc (HQ) 248 668-6400
29797 Beck Rd Wixom (48393) ***(G-18766)***

Tapemaster, Troy *Also called Lavalier Corp* ***(G-17205)***

Taper-Line Inc (PA) 586 775-5960
23426 Reynolds Ct Clinton Township (48036) ***(G-3373)***

Tapestry Inc 616 538-5802
3700 Rvrtwn Pkwy Sw Grandville (49418) ***(G-7420)***

Tapestry Inc 631 724-8066
14000 Lakeside Cir Sterling Heights (48313) ***(G-16200)***

Tapex American Corporation 810 987-4722
2626 20th St Port Huron (48060) ***(G-13531)***

Tapoos LLC 619 319-4872
21813 Hunter Cir S Taylor (48180) ***(G-16483)***

Tara Industries Inc (PA) 248 477-6520
30105 8 Mile Rd Livonia (48152) ***(G-10429)***

Target Construction Inc 616 866-7728
3850 Russell St Cedar Springs (49319) ***(G-2664)***

Target Mold Corporation 231 798-3535
4088 Treeline Dr Norton Shores (49441) ***(G-12336)***

Tarifa, Almont *Also called Inter-Power Corporation* ***(G-262)***

Tarpon Automation & Design Co 586 774-8020
44785 Macomb Indus Dr Clinton Township (48036) ***(G-3374)***

Tarpon Industries Inc 810 364-7421
2420 Wills St Marysville (48040) ***(G-11105)***

Tarps Now, Saint Joseph *Also called Industrial Fabric Products Inc* ***(G-14937)***

Tarrs Tree Service Inc 248 528-3313
2009 Milverton Dr Troy (48083) ***(G-17384)***

Tartan Industries Inc 810 387-4255
2 1st St Yale (48097) ***(G-18920)***

Tarus Products Inc (PA) 586 977-1400
38100 Commerce Dr Sterling Heights (48312) ***(G-16201)***

Tassier Boat Works Inc 906 484-2573
1011 S Islington Rd Cedarville (49719) ***(G-2674)***

Tata Autocomp Systems Limited 248 680-4608
200 E Big Beaver Rd # 145 Troy (48083) ***(G-17385)***

TAW Plastics LLC (PA) 616 302-0954
1118 S Edgewood St Greenville (48838) ***(G-7507)***

Tawas Plating Company 989 362-2011
510 Industrial Ave Tawas City (48763) ***(G-16372)***

Tawas Powder Coating Inc 989 362-2011
510 Industrial Ave Tawas City (48763) ***(G-16373)***

Tawas Tool Co Inc (HQ) 989 362-6121
756 Aulerich Rd East Tawas (48730) ***(G-4924)***

Tawas Tool Co Inc 989 362-0414
980 Aulerich Rd East Tawas (48730) ***(G-4925)***

Tawas Tools Plant 2, East Tawas *Also called Tawas Tool Co Inc* ***(G-4925)***

Taylor Communications Inc 248 304-4800
24800 Denso Dr Ste 140 Southfield (48033) ***(G-15717)***

Taylor Company, The, Grand Rapids *Also called Van Zee Corporation* ***(G-7306)***

Taylor Controls Inc 269 637-8521
10529 Blue Star Mem Hwy South Haven (49090) ***(G-15418)***

Taylor Freezer Michigan Inc 616 453-0531
2111 Walker Ct Nw Grand Rapids (49544) ***(G-7249)***

Taylor Hills Compost Facility 734 991-3902
16300 Racho Blvd Taylor (48180) ***(G-16484)***

Taylor Machine Products Inc 734 287-3550
176 S Harvey St Plymouth (48170) ***(G-13309)***

Taylor Screw Products Company 734 697-8018
16894 Haggerty Rd Van Buren Twp (48111) ***(G-17556)***

Taylor Supply Company, The, Detroit *Also called Detroit Nipple Works Inc* ***(G-4157)***

Taylor Turning Inc 248 960-7920
29632 West Tech Dr Wixom (48393) ***(G-18767)***

Tazz Broach and Machine Inc 586 296-7755
41565 Production Dr Harrison Township (48045) ***(G-7728)***

Tbf Graphics, Saginaw *Also called Turner Business Forms Inc* ***(G-14782)***

Tbl Fabrications Inc 586 294-2087
28178 Hayes Rd Roseville (48066) ***(G-14483)***

Tc Office Express 231 929-3549
3311 S Airport Rd W Traverse City (49684) ***(G-16851)***

TCH Supply Inc 517 545-4900
895 Grand Oaks Dr Howell (48843) ***(G-8526)***

Tcwc LLC (HQ) 231 922-8292
201 E Fourteenth St Traverse City (49684) ***(G-16852)***

TD Industrial Coverings Inc 586 731-2080
6220 18 1/2 Mile Rd Sterling Heights (48314) ***(G-16202)***

Tdw Custom Apparel & More LLC 248 934-0312
20466 Kentucky St Detroit (48221) ***(G-4626)***

Teachout and Associates Inc 269 729-4440
1887 M 66 Athens (49011) ***(G-743)***

Team Acquistions, Kalkaska *Also called Team Spooling Services LLC* ***(G-9407)***

Team Breadwinner LLC 313 460-0152
14414 Mansfield St Detroit (48227) ***(G-4627)***

Team Pharma 269 344-8326
2022 Fulford St Kalamazoo (49001) ***(G-9352)***

Team Services LLC 231 258-9130
1587 Enterprise Dr Kalkaska (49646) ***(G-9406)***

Team Spooling Services LLC 231 258-9130
209 E Park Dr Kalkaska (49646) ***(G-9407)***

Team Sports Covers LLC 269 207-0241
123 Ellen St Union City (49094) ***(G-17497)***

Teamtech Motorsports Safety 989 792-4880
6285 Bay Rd Ste 7 Saginaw (48604) ***(G-14773)***

Tebis America Inc 248 524-0430
400 E Big Beaver Rd # 300 Troy (48083) ***(G-17386)***

TEC Industries Inc 248 446-9560
55309 Lyon Industrial Dr New Hudson (48165) ***(G-12072)***

TEC Welding Sales Incorporated 248 969-7490
3202 Adventure Ln Oxford (48371) ***(G-12922)***

TEC-3 Prototypes Inc 810 678-8909
4321 Blood Rd Metamora (48455) ***(G-11289)***

Tec-Option Inc 517 486-6055
334 Sherman St Blissfield (49228) ***(G-1777)***

Tecart Industries Inc 248 624-8880
28059 Center Oaks Ct Wixom (48393) ***(G-18768)***

ALPHABETIC

Tecat Performance Systems LLC 248 615-9862
  705 Technology Dr Ann Arbor (48108) *(G-672)*
Tech Electric Co LLC 586 697-5095
  16177 Leone Dr Macomb (48042) *(G-10641)*
Tech Enterprises, Saint Clair Shores Also called Technology Network Svcs Inc *(G-14888)*
Tech Forms Metal Ltd 616 956-0430
  2437 Coit Ave Ne Grand Rapids (49505) *(G-7250)*
Tech Group, Wayne Also called Cul-Mac Industries Inc *(G-18219)*
Tech Group Grand Rapids Inc 616 490-2197
  3116 N Wilson Ct Nw Walker (49534) *(G-17653)*
Tech Tool Company Inc 313 836-4131
  18235 Weaver St Detroit (48228) *(G-4628)*
Tech Tool Supply LLC 734 207-7700
  9060 General Dr Plymouth (48170) *(G-13310)*
Tech Tooling Specialties Inc 517 782-8898
  1708 Cooper St Jackson (49202) *(G-9016)*
Tech World LLC 616 901-2611
  2515 5th St Shelbyville (49344) *(G-15375)*
Tech-Source International Inc 231 652-9100
  1000 S Industrial Dr Newaygo (49337) *(G-12090)*
Techncal Audio Video Solutions 810 899-5546
  5695 Whispering Oaks Dr Howell (48855) *(G-8527)*
Techni CAM and Manufacturing 734 261-6477
  30633 Schoolcraft Rd A Livonia (48150) *(G-10430)*
Techni Sand Inc 269 465-5833
  400 Riverview Dr Benton Harbor (49022) *(G-1590)*
Technical Air Products LLC 616 863-9115
  8069 Belmont Ave Ne Belmont (49306) *(G-1519)*
Technical Auto Parts, Battle Creek Also called Musashi Auto Parts Mich Inc *(G-1276)*
Technical Center, Portage Also called Summit Polymers Inc *(G-13622)*
Technical Enterprises LLC 313 333-1438
  16519 Lawton St Detroit (48221) *(G-4629)*
Technical Environmental Svcs 810 229-6323
  775 N 2nd St Brighton (48116) *(G-2075)*
Technical Illustration Corp 313 982-9660
  46177 Windridge Ln Canton (48188) *(G-2530)*
Technical Machining Welding 269 463-3738
  3008 N County Line Rd Watervliet (49098) *(G-18183)*
Technical Manufacturers Inc 989 846-6885
  4767 S Huron Rd Standish (48658) *(G-15897)*
Technical Rotary Services Inc 586 772-6755
  14020 Hovey Ave Warren (48089) *(G-18037)*
Technical Stamping Inc 586 948-3285
  50600 E Russell Schmidt Chesterfield (48051) *(G-2954)*
Technichem 810 744-3770
  4289 E Coldwater Rd Flint (48506) *(G-5777)*
Technickel Inc 269 926-8505
  1200 S Crystal Ave Benton Harbor (49022) *(G-1591)*
Technimold Inc 906 284-1921
  501 W Railroad Caspian (49915) *(G-2609)*
Techniplas LLC 517 849-9911
  1640 E Chicago Rd Jonesville (49250) *(G-9103)*
Technique Inc 517 789-8988
  1500 Technology Dr Jackson (49201) *(G-9017)*
Technique Golf LLC 586 758-7807
  29706 West Tech Dr Wixom (48393) *(G-18769)*
Technisand Inc 269 465-5833
  400 Riverview Dr Ste 300 Benton Harbor (49022) *(G-1592)*
Techno-Coat Inc 616 396-6446
  861 E 40th St Holland (49423) *(G-8213)*
Technology & Manufacturing Inc 248 755-1444
  3190 Pine Cone Ct Milford (48381) *(G-11492)*
Technology MGT & Budget Dept 517 322-1897
  7461 Crowner Dr Lansing (48913) *(G-9899)*
Technology Network Svcs Inc (PA) 586 294-7771
  31375 Harper Ave Saint Clair Shores (48082) *(G-14888)*
Technology Plus Trailers Inc 734 928-0001
  7780 Ronda Dr Canton (48187) *(G-2531)*
Technotrim Inc 734 254-5000
  49200 Halyard Dr Plymouth (48170) *(G-13311)*
Technova Corporation 517 485-1402
  3927 Dobie Rd Okemos (48864) *(G-12690)*
Tecla Company Inc (PA) 248 624-8200
  1250 Ladd Rd Commerce Township (48390) *(G-3576)*
Tecniq Inc 269 629-4440
  9100 E Michigan Ave Galesburg (49053) *(G-6085)*
Tecnoma LLC 248 354-8888
  26400 Lahser Rd Ste 310 Southfield (48033) *(G-15718)*
Tecnoma Industries, Southfield Also called Tecnoma LLC *(G-15718)*
Tecomet Inc 517 882-4311
  5212 Aurelius Rd Lansing (48911) *(G-9900)*
Tecra Systems Inc (PA) 248 888-1116
  6005 E Executive Dr Westland (48185) *(G-18420)*
Tectonics Industries LLC (PA) 248 597-1600
  1681 Harmon Rd Auburn Hills (48326) *(G-1046)*
Tectum Holdings Inc (HQ) 734 677-0444
  5400 Data Ct Ann Arbor (48108) *(G-673)*
Tectum Holdings Inc 734 926-2362
  4670 Runway Blvd Ann Arbor (48108) *(G-674)*

Tecumseh Compressor Co LLC 662 566-2231
  5683 Hines Dr Ann Arbor (48108) *(G-675)*
Tecumseh Compressor Company 734 585-9500
  1136 Oak Valley Dr Ann Arbor (48108) *(G-676)*
Tecumseh Division, Tecumseh Also called Tecumseh Packg Solutions Inc *(G-16518)*
Tecumseh Herald, Tecumseh Also called Herald Publishing Company *(G-16504)*
Tecumseh Packg Solutions Inc (PA) 517 423-2126
  707 S Evans St Tecumseh (49286) *(G-16518)*
Tecumseh Products Company LLC (HQ) 734 585-9500
  5683 Hines Dr Ann Arbor (48108) *(G-677)*
Tecumseh Products Company LLC 734 585-9500
  1136 Oak Valley Dr Ann Arbor (48108) *(G-678)*
Tecumseh Products Company LLC 734 585-9500
  5683 Hines Dr Ann Arbor (48108) *(G-679)*
Tecumseh Products Holdings LLC (HQ) 734 585-9500
  5683 Hines Dr Ann Arbor (48108) *(G-680)*
Ted Senk Tooling Inc 989 725-6067
  1117 E Henderson Rd Owosso (48867) *(G-12861)*
Tedson Industries Inc 248 588-9230
  1408 Allen Dr Troy (48083) *(G-17387)*
Tee 810 231-2764
  7673 Athlone Dr Brighton (48116) *(G-2076)*
Tee - The Extra Effort LLC 734 891-4789
  333 E Parent Ave Unit 42 Royal Oak (48067) *(G-14584)*
Tee Pal LLC 231 563-3770
  7099 Oakshore Dr Twin Lake (49457) *(G-17474)*
Tee Quilters 248 336-9779
  3308 Inman St Ferndale (48220) *(G-5588)*
Teeq Spirits Inc 866 877-1840
  43311 Joy Rd Ste 273 Canton (48187) *(G-2532)*
Teesnitch Screen Printing 734 667-1636
  8215 Ronda Dr Canton (48187) *(G-2533)*
Teijin Advan Compo Ameri Inc 248 365-6600
  1200 Harmon Rd Auburn Hills (48326) *(G-1047)*
Teijin Auto Tech Mnchester LLC 734 428-8301
  17951 W Austin Rd Manchester (48158) *(G-10890)*
Teijin Auto Tech NA Hldngs Cor (HQ) 248 237-7800
  255 Rex Blvd Auburn Hills (48326) *(G-1048)*
Teijin Automotive Tech Inc (HQ) 248 237-7800
  255 Rex Blvd Auburn Hills (48326) *(G-1049)*
Tekkra Systems Inc 517 568-4121
  300 S Elm St Homer (49245) *(G-8357)*
Teknikut Corporation 586 778-7150
  46036 Michigan Ave Canton (48188) *(G-2534)*
Teksid Aluminum North Amer Inc (HQ) 248 304-4001
  2 Towne Sq Ste 300 Southfield (48076) *(G-15719)*
Teksid Inc 734 846-5492
  36524 Grand River Ave B-1 Farmington (48335) *(G-5153)*
Tekton Inc 616 243-2443
  3707 Rger B Chffee Mem Dr Grand Rapids (49548) *(G-7251)*
Tel-X Corporation 734 425-2225
  32400 Ford Rd Garden City (48135) *(G-6112)*
Telco Tools 616 296-0253
  510 Elm St Spring Lake (49456) *(G-15856)*
Telescopic Seating Systems LLC 616 566-9232
  190 E 8th St Unit 1556 Holland (49422) *(G-8214)*
Telescopic Seating Systems LLC (PA) 855 713-0118
  335 N Griffin St Grand Haven (49417) *(G-6370)*
Telespector Corporation 248 373-5400
  1460 N Opdyke Rd Auburn Hills (48326) *(G-1050)*
Tellurex Corporation (PA) 231 947-0110
  1462 International Dr Traverse City (49686) *(G-16853)*
Telmar Manufacturing Company 810 577-7050
  2121 W Thompson Rd Fenton (48430) *(G-5506)*
Telo 810 845-8051
  707 Hickory St Fenton (48430) *(G-5507)*
Telsonic Ultrasonics Inc (HQ) 586 802-0033
  14120 Industrial Ctr Dr Shelby Township (48315) *(G-15350)*
Tem-Press Division, Saint Joseph Also called Leco Corporation *(G-14946)*
Temcor Systems Inc 810 229-0006
  1341 Rickett Rd Brighton (48116) *(G-2077)*
Temp Rite Steel Treating Inc 586 469-3071
  42386 Executive Dr Harrison Township (48045) *(G-7729)*
Temper Inc 616 293-1349
  12333 Luyk Dr Ne Cedar Springs (49319) *(G-2665)*
Temperance Distilling Company 734 847-5262
  177 Reed Dr Temperance (48182) *(G-16550)*
Temperance Fuel Stop Inc 734 206-2676
  2110 Anita Ave Grosse Pointe Woods (48236) *(G-7577)*
Temperance Printing 419 290-6846
  3363 Hemmingway Ln Lambertville (48144) *(G-9654)*
Temperform LLC 248 349-5230
  25425 Trans X Rd Novi (48375) *(G-12554)*
Temperform Corp 248 851-9611
  1975 Tuckaway Dr Bloomfield Hills (48302) *(G-1864)*
Tempo Vino Winery Kalamazoo 269 342-9463
  260 E Michigan Ave Kalamazoo (49007) *(G-9353)*
Temprel Inc 231 582-6585
  206 Industrial Parkway Dr Boyne City (49712) *(G-1902)*

Tempro Industries Inc ... 734 451-5900
47808 Galleon Dr Plymouth (48170) ***(G-13312)***
Ten X Plastics LLC ... 616 813-3037
610 Maryland Ave Ne Ste A Grand Rapids (49505) ***(G-7252)***
Tengam Engineering Inc ... 269 694-9466
545 Washington St Otsego (49078) ***(G-12800)***
Tenibac-Graphion Inc (HQ) ... 586 792-0150
35155 Automation Dr Clinton Township (48035) ***(G-3375)***
Tennant & Associates Inc ... 248 643-6140
1700 Stutz Dr Ste 61 Troy (48084) ***(G-17388)***
Tennant Commercial ... 616 994-4000
12875 Ransom St Holland (49424) ***(G-8215)***
Tennant Company ... 616 994-4000
12875 Ransom St Holland (49424) ***(G-8216)***
Tenneco Automotive Oper Co ... 248 849-1258
15701 Technology Dr Northville (48168) ***(G-12265)***
Tenneco Automotive Oper Co Inc ... 517 522-5520
3901 Willis Rd Grass Lake (49240) ***(G-7447)***
Tenneco Automotive Oper Co Inc ... 734 243-8000
4722 Grand Riv Lansing (48906) ***(G-9742)***
Tenneco Automotive Oper Co Inc ... 734 243-8039
13910 Lake Dr Monroe (48161) ***(G-11579)***
Tenneco Automotive Oper Co Inc ... 269 781-1350
904 Industrial Rd Marshall (49068) ***(G-11075)***
Tenneco Automotive Oper Co Inc ... 517 542-5511
929 Anderson Rd Litchfield (49252) ***(G-10085)***
Tenneco Automotive Oper Co Inc ... 517 522-5525
2701 N Dettman Rd Jackson (49201) ***(G-9018)***
Tenneco Automotive Oper Co Inc ... 734 243-4615
1 International Dr Monroe (48161) ***(G-11580)***
Tenneco Automotive Oper Co Inc ... 734 243-8000
1 International Dr Monroe (48161) ***(G-11581)***
Tenneco Clean Air US Inc ... 517 253-8902
4722 N Grand River Ave Lansing (48906) ***(G-9743)***
Tenneco Inc ... 734 254-1122
44099 Plymouth Oaks Blvd Plymouth (48170) ***(G-13313)***
Tenneco Inc ... 248 354-7700
26555 Northwestern Hwy Southfield (48033) ***(G-15720)***
Tenneco Inc ... 248 886-0900
7151 Astro Dr N Waterford (48327) ***(G-18170)***
Tennessee Fabricators LLC ... 615 793-4444
35900 Mound Rd Sterling Heights (48310) ***(G-16203)***
Tentcraft LLC ... 800 950-4553
2662 Cass Rd Traverse City (49684) ***(G-16854)***
Tepel Brothers, Troy *Also called C2 Imaging LLC* ***(G-16990)***
Tepso Gen-X Plastics LLC ... 248 869-2130
28525 Beck Rd Unit 111 Wixom (48393) ***(G-18770)***
Tequionbrookins LLC ... 313 290-0303
21460 Glenmorra St Southfield (48076) ***(G-15721)***
Ter Molen & Hart Inc ... 616 458-4832
3056 Eastern Ave Se Ste C Grand Rapids (49508) ***(G-7253)***
Teradyne Inc ... 313 425-3900
1800 Fairlane Dr Ste 200 Allen Park (48101) ***(G-208)***
Teradyne Diagnostic Solutions, Allen Park *Also called Teradyne Inc* ***(G-208)***
Terametrix LLC ... 540 769-8430
2725 S Industrial Hwy # 100 Ann Arbor (48104) ***(G-681)***
Terex Canica, Durand *Also called Terex Corporation* ***(G-4849)***
Terex Corporation ... 360 993-0515
212 S Oak St Durand (48429) ***(G-4849)***
Terex Simplicity, Durand *Also called Simplicity Engineering Company* ***(G-4848)***
Terex Simplicity, Durand *Also called Powerscreen USA LLC* ***(G-4845)***
Terra Caloric LLC ... 989 356-2113
3336 Piper Rd Alpena (49707) ***(G-325)***
Terra Green Ceramics Inc ... 810 742-4611
1307 N Belsay Rd Burton (48509) ***(G-2248)***
Terrace Hill Vineyards ... 269 428-2168
1464 Silverbrook Ln Saint Joseph (49085) ***(G-14965)***
Terratrike, Grand Rapids *Also called Wiz Wheelz Inc* ***(G-7342)***
Terrell Manufacturing Svcs Inc ... 231 788-2000
7245 Hall Rd Muskegon (49442) ***(G-11930)***
Terry Butler Prints LLC ... 734 255-8592
2281 Manchester Rd Ann Arbor (48104) ***(G-682)***
Terry Heiden ... 906 753-6248
N8745 Us Highway 41 Stephenson (49887) ***(G-15912)***
Terry Tool & Die Co ... 517 750-1771
1080 Toro Dr Jackson (49201) ***(G-9019)***
Terryberry Company LLC (PA) ... 616 458-1391
2033 Oak Industrial Dr Ne Grand Rapids (49505) ***(G-7254)***
Terumo Crdvscular Systems Corp (HQ) ... 734 663-4145
6200 Jackson Rd Ann Arbor (48103) ***(G-683)***
Terumo Heart Incorporated ... 734 663-4145
6190 Jackson Rd Ann Arbor (48103) ***(G-684)***
Tes America LLC ... 616 786-5353
215 Central Ave 250 Holland (49423) ***(G-8217)***
TEs Filer Cy Stn Ltd Partnr ... 231 723-6573
700 Mee St Filer City (49634) ***(G-5611)***
Tesa Plant Sparta LLC ... 616 887-1757
324 S Union St Sparta (49345) ***(G-15785)***
Tesa Tape Inc ... 616 785-6970
2945 Walkent Ct Nw Walker (49544) ***(G-17654)***
Tesa Tape Inc ... 616 887-3107
324 S Union St Sparta (49345) ***(G-15786)***
Tesca Usa Inc ... 586 991-0744
2638 Bond St Rochester Hills (48309) ***(G-14124)***
Tesla Inc ... 248 205-3206
2850 W Big Beaver Rd Troy (48084) ***(G-17389)***
Tesla Machine & Tool Ltd ... 586 441-2402
5415 E 8 Mile Rd Warren (48091) ***(G-18038)***
Tesla Motors, Troy *Also called Tesla Inc* ***(G-17389)***
Teslir LLC ... 248 644-5500
100 W Long Lake Rd # 102 Bloomfield Hills (48304) ***(G-1865)***
Tesma Instruments LLC ... 517 940-1362
8770 Giovanni Ct Howell (48855) ***(G-8528)***
Tessonics Corp ... 248 885-8335
2019 Hazel St Birmingham (48009) ***(G-1752)***
Test Products Incorporated ... 586 997-9600
41255 Technology Park Dr Sterling Heights (48314) ***(G-16204)***
Testek LLC ... 248 573-4980
28320 Lakeview Dr Wixom (48393) ***(G-18771)***
Testron Incorporated ... 734 513-6820
34153 Industrial Rd Livonia (48150) ***(G-10431)***
Tetra Corporation ... 401 529-1630
1606 Hults Dr Eaton Rapids (48827) ***(G-4972)***
Tetradyn Ltd ... 202 415-7295
9833 E Cherry Bend Rd Traverse City (49684) ***(G-16855)***
Texas Corners Brewing Company, Kalamazoo *Also called Apple Blossom Winery LLC* ***(G-9114)***
Texas Transformer, Grand Haven *Also called Gti Liquidating Inc* ***(G-6309)***
Textile Fabrication & Dist Inc ... 586 566-9100
120 Grove Park St Mount Clemens (48043) ***(G-11660)***
Textiss USA ... 310 909-6062
61245 S Us Highway 131 Three Rivers (49093) ***(G-16587)***
Textron Inc ... 248 545-2035
25225 Dequindre Rd Madison Heights (48071) ***(G-10841)***
Texwood Industries ... 517 266-4739
5353 W Us Highway 223 Adrian (49221) ***(G-98)***
Tf Entertainment LLC ... 424 303-3407
16800 Birwood St Detroit (48221) ***(G-4630)***
Tfi Inc ... 231 728-2310
2620 Park St Muskegon (49444) ***(G-11931)***
Tg Fluid Systems USA Corp ... 810 220-6161
100 Brighton Interior Dr Brighton (48116) ***(G-2078)***
Tg Fluid Systems USA Corporati ... 248 486-8950
7854 Lochlin Dr Brighton (48116) ***(G-2079)***
Tg Manufacturing LLC ... 616 842-1503
4720 44th St Se Ste B Grand Rapids (49512) ***(G-7255)***
Tg Manufacturing LLC (PA) ... 616 935-7575
8197 Clyde Park Ave Sw Byron Center (49315) ***(G-2296)***
Tg North America, Brighton *Also called Tg Fluid Systems USA Corp* ***(G-2078)***
TGI Direct Inc (PA) ... 810 239-5553
5365 Hill 23 Dr Flint (48507) ***(G-5778)***
TGI Direct Inc ... 810 239-5553
1225 Rosewood St Ann Arbor (48104) ***(G-685)***
Tgw Systems Inc (HQ) ... 616 888-2595
3001 Orchard Vista Dr Se # 3 Grand Rapids (49546) ***(G-7256)***
Th Plastics Inc (PA) ... 269 496-8495
106 E Main St Mendon (49072) ***(G-11222)***
Th Plastics Inc ... 269 496-8495
106 E Main St Mendon (49072) ***(G-11223)***
Thai Paradize LLC ... 248 331-7355
47516 Pontiac Trl Wixom (48393) ***(G-18772)***
Thai Summit America Corp (HQ) ... 517 548-4900
1480 Mcpherson Park Dr Howell (48843) ***(G-8529)***
Thalner Electronic Labs Inc ... 734 761-4506
7235 Jackson Rd Ann Arbor (48103) ***(G-686)***
That French Place ... 231 437-6037
212 Bridge St Charlevoix (49720) ***(G-2736)***
Thayne Art Mart, Battle Creek *Also called W W Thayne Advertising Cons* ***(G-1309)***
The Daily Tribune, Mount Clemens *Also called Independent Newspapers Inc* ***(G-11642)***
The Envelope Printery Inc (PA) ... 734 398-7700
8979 Samuel Barton Dr Van Buren Twp (48111) ***(G-17557)***
The Gluten Free Bar, The, Grand Rapids *Also called West Thomas Partners LLC* ***(G-7336)***
The Mix ... 269 382-1300
2804 W Michigan Ave Kalamazoo (49006) ***(G-9354)***
The Pom Group Inc ... 248 409-7900
2350 Pontiac Rd Auburn Hills (48326) ***(G-1051)***
The Shopping Guide, Mason *Also called S G Publications Inc* ***(G-11151)***
The Sign Chap Inc ... 248 585-6880
31211 Stephenson Hwy # 100 Madison Heights (48071) ***(G-10842)***
The Signwriter, Kalamazoo *Also called Sunset Enterprises Inc* ***(G-9346)***
The South Main Company, Wixom *Also called S Main Company LLC* ***(G-18747)***
The Spott ... 269 459-6462
550 E Cork St Kalamazoo (49001) ***(G-9355)***
The Sun ... 800 878-6397
214 S Jackson St Jackson (49201) ***(G-9020)***
Therapeutic Health Choices LLC ... 989 459-2020
903 N Euclid Ave Bay City (48706) ***(G-1406)***
Therm Technology Corp ... 616 530-6540
2879 Remico St Sw Grandville (49418) ***(G-7421)***

ALPHABETIC

Therm-O-Disc Incorporated...231 799-4100
851 E Porter Rd Norton Shores (49441) *(G-12337)*
Therm-O-Disc Midwest Inc...231 799-4100
851 E Porter Rd Norton Shores (49441) *(G-12338)*
Therma-Tech Engineering Inc...313 537-5330
24900 Capitol Redford (48239) *(G-13778)*
Thermaglas Corporation...517 754-7461
1930 S 23rd St Saginaw (48601) *(G-14774)*
Thermal Designs & Manufacturng...586 773-5231
16660 E 13 Mile Rd Roseville (48066) *(G-14484)*
Thermal Designs & Mfg...248 476-2978
41069 Vincenti Ct Novi (48375) *(G-12555)*
Thermal One Inc (PA)...734 721-8500
39026 Webb Ct Westland (48185) *(G-18421)*
Thermal Products, Saint Clair *Also called Dana Limited (G-14822)*
Thermal Solutions Mfg (PA)...734 655-7145
35255 Glendale St Livonia (48150) *(G-10432)*
Thermal Wave Imaging Inc...248 414-3730
25175 Dequindre Rd Madison Heights (48071) *(G-10843)*
Thermalfab Products Inc...517 486-2073
10005 E Us Highway 223 Blissfield (49228) *(G-1778)*
Thermbond Refractory Solutions...561 330-9300
777 Eight Mile Rd Whitmore Lake (48189) *(G-18547)*
Thermfrmer Parts Suppliers LLC...989 435-3800
3818 Terry Dianne St Beaverton (48612) *(G-1432)*
Thermo Arl US Inc...313 336-3901
15300 Rotunda Dr Ste 301 Dearborn (48120) *(G-3903)*
Thermo Fisher Scientific Inc...231 932-0242
6270 S West Bay Shore Dr Traverse City (49684) *(G-16856)*
Thermo Fisher Scientific Inc...800 346-4364
4169 Commercial Ave Portage (49002) *(G-13625)*
Thermo Fisher Scientific Inc...269 544-5600
4481 Campus Dr Kalamazoo (49008) *(G-9356)*
Thermo Fisher Scientific Inc...734 662-4117
2868 W Delhi Rd Ann Arbor (48103) *(G-687)*
Thermo Flex LLC...734 458-4194
23093 Commerce Dr Farmington Hills (48335) *(G-5398)*
Thermo Pressed Laminates, Alpena *Also called Panel Processing Oregon Inc (G-309)*
Thermo Vac Inc...248 969-0300
201 W Oakwood Rd Oxford (48371) *(G-12923)*
Thermo-Shield Window Mfg, Alpena *Also called Overhead Door Company Alpena (G-307)*
Thermoforming Tech Group LLC (HQ)...989 435-7741
330 N Ross St Beaverton (48612) *(G-1433)*
Thermoforms Inc...616 974-0055
4374 Donkers Ct Se Kentwood (49512) *(G-9481)*
Thermotron Industries Inc...616 928-9044
875 Brooks Ave Holland (49423) *(G-8218)*
Thermotron Industries Inc (HQ)...616 392-1491
291 Kollen Park Dr Holland (49423) *(G-8219)*
Thesnowmobilestore.com, Gladstone *Also called Bucks Sports Products Inc (G-6175)*
Thetford Corporation (HQ)...734 769-6000
7101 Jackson Rd Ann Arbor (48103) *(G-688)*
Theut Concrete Products Inc...810 679-3376
138 E Harrington Rd Croswell (48422) *(G-3737)*
Theut Products Inc...810 364-7132
1444 Gratiot Blvd Marysville (48040) *(G-11106)*
Theut Products Inc...810 765-9321
1910 S Parker St Marine City (48039) *(G-10967)*
Theut Products Inc...586 949-1300
47875 Gratiot Ave Chesterfield (48051) *(G-2955)*
Thi Equipment, Grand Rapids *Also called Thierica Equipment Corporation (G-7259)*
Thielenhaus Microfinish Corp...248 349-9450
42925 W 9 Mile Rd Novi (48375) *(G-12556)*
Thierica Inc (HQ)...616 458-1538
900 Clancy Ave Ne Grand Rapids (49503) *(G-7257)*
Thierica Controls Inc...616 956-5500
4400 Donkers Ct Se Grand Rapids (49512) *(G-7258)*
Thierica Display Products, Grand Rapids *Also called Thierica Inc (G-7257)*
Thierica Equipment Corporation (HQ)...616 453-6570
3147 N Wilson Ct Nw Grand Rapids (49534) *(G-7259)*
Think Chromatic...248 719-2058
3934 West River Dr Ne Comstock Park (49321) *(G-3647)*
Think Club Publication...248 651-3106
4353 Stonewood Ct Rochester (48306) *(G-13933)*
Think NA, Dearborn *Also called Think North America Inc (G-3904)*
Think North America Inc (PA)...313 565-6781
22226 Garrison St Dearborn (48124) *(G-3904)*
Think Social Media...810 360-0170
209 W Main St Brighton (48116) *(G-2080)*
Thk Rhythm Auto Mich Corp...517 647-4121
902 Lyons Rd Portland (48875) *(G-13642)*
Thm Publishing Detroit LLC...586 232-3037
6303 26 Mile Rd Washington (48094) *(G-18089)*
Thomas A Despres Inc...313 633-9648
4229 Williamston Ct Williamsburg (49690) *(G-18565)*
Thomas and Milliken Mllwk Inc (PA)...231 386-7236
931 N Mill St Northport (49670) *(G-12193)*
Thomas Cake Shop, Troy *Also called More Signature Cakes LLC (G-17265)*
Thomas Cheal...906 288-3487
40240 Aspen Rd Toivola (49965) *(G-16593)*
Thomas Construction, Belding *Also called Hunt Hoppough Custom Crafted (G-1452)*
Thomas Cooper...231 599-2251
11486 Essex Rd Ellsworth (49729) *(G-5037)*
Thomas Dale Noble & Noble, Blanchard *Also called Noble Forestry Inc (G-1759)*
Thomas Engineering...248 620-7916
9647 Rattalee Lake Rd Clarkston (48348) *(G-3071)*
Thomas Industrial Rolls Inc...313 584-9696
8526 Brandt St Dearborn (48126) *(G-3905)*
Thomas J Moyle Jr Incorporated (PA)...906 482-3000
46702 Hwy M 26 Houghton (49931) *(G-8393)*
Thomas L Snarey & Assoc Inc (PA)...734 241-8474
513 N Dixie Hwy Monroe (48162) *(G-11582)*
Thomas Porchea Collection LLC...313 693-6308
18628 Greeley St Detroit (48203) *(G-4631)*
Thomas-Ward Systems LLC...734 929-0644
314 Pauline Blvd Ann Arbor (48103) *(G-689)*
Thompson Art Glass Inc...810 225-8766
6815 Grand River Rd Brighton (48114) *(G-2081)*
Thompson Custom Woodworking...616 446-1058
1635 Acacia Dr Nw Grand Rapids (49504) *(G-7260)*
Thompson Fabrication Inds, Muskegon *Also called Tfi Inc (G-11931)*
Thompson Glass Co, Howell *Also called Thompson John (G-8530)*
Thompson I.g, Fenton *Also called Tig Entity LLC (G-5508)*
Thompson John...810 225-8780
5345 Crooked Lake Rd Howell (48843) *(G-8530)*
Thompson Surgical Instrs Inc...231 922-0177
10170 E Cherry Bend Rd Traverse City (49684) *(G-16857)*
Thompson Surgical Instrs Inc...231 922-5169
10341 E Cherry Bend Rd Traverse City (49684) *(G-16858)*
Thompson Surgical Instrs Inc...231 922-5169
10321 E Cherry Bend Rd Traverse City (49684) *(G-16859)*
Thompson Well Drilling...616 754-5032
12944 Lincoln Lake Ave Gowen (49326) *(G-6230)*
Thomson Aerospace & Defense, Saginaw *Also called Linear Motion LLC (G-14683)*
Thomson Plastics Inc...517 545-5026
3970 Parsons Rd Howell (48855) *(G-8531)*
Thomson-Shore Inc...734 426-3939
7300 Joy Rd Dexter (48130) *(G-4758)*
Thor Industries Inc...810 724-6474
331 Graham Rd Imlay City (48444) *(G-8647)*
Thor Tool and Machine LLC...248 628-3185
401 E Elmwood Lakeville (48367) *(G-9649)*
Thoratec LLC...734 827-7422
6190 Jackson Rd Ann Arbor (48103) *(G-690)*
Thoreson-Mc Cosh Inc...248 362-0960
2600 Regency Dr Lake Orion (48359) *(G-9634)*
Thorn Apple Brewing Company...616 288-6907
6262 28th St Se Grand Rapids (49546) *(G-7261)*
Thorn Creek Lumber LLC...231 832-1600
9676 S Hawkins Rd Reed City (49677) *(G-13800)*
Thorpe Printing Services Inc...810 364-6222
604 Busha Hwy Marysville (48040) *(G-11107)*
Thortarp, Curtis *Also called Odin International Inc (G-3751)*
Thought Prvoking Tees Prtg LLC...313 673-6632
19409 Revere St Detroit (48234) *(G-4632)*
Thread Grinding Service Inc...248 474-5350
32420 W 8 Mile Rd Farmington Hills (48336) *(G-5399)*
Thread West - Michigan...231 755-5229
1701 W Sherman Blvd Ste 4 Norton Shores (49441) *(G-12339)*
Thread-Craft Inc...586 323-1116
43643 Utica Rd Sterling Heights (48314) *(G-16205)*
Threaded Products Co...586 727-3435
68750 Oak St Richmond (48062) *(G-13846)*
Threads, Traverse City *Also called Get In Game Marketing LLC (G-16694)*
Threads By Bb...989 401-7525
6285 Bay Rd Ste 4 Saginaw (48604) *(G-14775)*
Threads Invisable...248 516-5051
31535 W 13 Mile Rd Farmington Hills (48334) *(G-5400)*
Three 60 Roto LLC...517 545-3600
741 Victory Dr Howell (48843) *(G-8532)*
Three Fires Wine...231 620-9463
5046 S West Bay Shore Dr Suttons Bay (49682) *(G-16345)*
Three M Tool & Machine Inc...248 363-0982
8135 Richardson Rd Commerce Township (48390) *(G-3577)*
Three Oaks Engraving & Engrg...269 469-2124
14381 Three Oaks Rd Three Oaks (49128) *(G-16559)*
Three Rivers Commercial News...269 279-7488
124 N Main St Three Rivers (49093) *(G-16588)*
Three Rivers Driveline Fcilty, Three Rivers *Also called American Axle & Mfg Inc (G-16562)*
Three Roses Woodwork...248 763-1837
439 N Main St Romeo (48065) *(G-14237)*
Three Sheep and A Mill LLC, Grand Rapids *Also called Three Sheep LLC (G-7262)*
Three Sheep LLC (PA)...616 215-1848
625 Kenmoor Ave Se Grand Rapids (49546) *(G-7262)*
Three-Dimensional Services Inc...248 852-1333
2547 Product Dr Rochester Hills (48309) *(G-14125)*

Thumb Bioenergy LLC 810 404-2466
155 Orval St Sandusky (48471) *(G-15069)*
Thumb Blanket 989 269-9918
55 Westland Dr Bad Axe (48413) *(G-1113)*
Thumb Plastics Inc 989 269-9791
400 Liberty St Bad Axe (48413) *(G-1114)*
Thumb Tool & Engineering Co 989 269-9731
354 Liberty St Bad Axe (48413) *(G-1115)*
Thumb Truck and Trailer Co 989 453-3133
8305 Geiger Rd Pigeon (48755) *(G-13041)*
Thumbprint News 810 794-2300
8061 Marsh Rd Clay (48001) *(G-3127)*
Thunder Bay Concrete Products, Alpena *Also called Clay & Graham Inc (G-287)*
Thunder Bay Pattern Works Inc 586 783-1126
44345 Macomb Indus Dr Clinton Township (48036) *(G-3376)*
Thunder Bay Press Inc 517 694-3205
2325 Jarco Dr Holt (48842) *(G-8335)*
Thunder Bay Press Michigan LLC 989 701-2430
4503 S M 76 West Branch (48661) *(G-18343)*
Thunder Bay Winery 989 358-9463
109 N Second Ave Ste 101 Alpena (49707) *(G-326)*
Thunder Technologies LLC 248 844-4875
1618 Star Batt Dr Rochester Hills (48309) *(G-14126)*
Thunderdome Media LLC 800 978-0206
6218 Valleyfield Dr Plymouth (48170) *(G-13314)*
Thyssenkrupp Bilstein Amer Inc 248 530-2900
3155 W Big Beavr Rd # 26 Troy (48084) *(G-17390)*
Thyssenkrupp Materials NA Inc (HQ) 248 233-5600
22355 W 11 Mile Rd Southfield (48033) *(G-15722)*
Thyssenkrupp Steel Svcs Trdg, Southfield *Also called Thyssenkrupp Materials NA Inc (G-15722)*
Thyssenkrupp System Engrg (HQ) 248 340-8000
901 Doris Rd Auburn Hills (48326) *(G-1052)*
TI Automotive Systems, Chesterfield *Also called TI Group Auto Systems LLC (G-2956)*
TI Fluid Systems 586 948-6036
30600 Commerce Blvd New Haven (48048) *(G-12039)*
TI Fluid Systems 248 393-4525
1700 Harmon Rd Ste 2 Auburn Hills (48326) *(G-1053)*
TI Fluid Systems LLC (HQ) 248 494-5000
2020 Taylor Rd Auburn Hills (48326) *(G-1054)*
TI Group Auto Systems LLC (HQ) 248 296-8000
2020 Taylor Rd Auburn Hills (48326) *(G-1055)*
TI Group Auto Systems LLC 859 235-5420
2020 Taylor Rd Auburn Hills (48326) *(G-1056)*
TI Group Auto Systems LLC 989 672-1200
630 Columbia St Caro (48723) *(G-2581)*
TI Group Auto Systems LLC 989 673-7727
630 Columbia St Caro (48723) *(G-2582)*
TI Group Auto Systems LLC 248 475-4663
1227 Centre Rd Auburn Hills (48326) *(G-1057)*
TI Group Auto Systems LLC 248 494-5000
100 W Big Beaver Rd Troy (48084) *(G-17391)*
TI Group Auto Systems LLC 810 364-3277
184 Gratiot Blvd Marysville (48040) *(G-11108)*
TI Group Auto Systems LLC 586 948-6006
30600 Commerce Blvd Chesterfield (48051) *(G-2956)*
Ti-Coating Inc 586 726-1900
50500 Corporate Dr Shelby Township (48315) *(G-15351)*
Tianhai Electric N Amer Inc (HQ) 248 987-2100
70 E Silverdome Indus Par Pontiac (48342) *(G-13419)*
Tiara Yachts Inc (PA) 616 392-7163
725 E 40th St Holland (49423) *(G-8220)*
Tiara Yachts Inc 616 335-3594
2081 Lakeway Dr Holland (49423) *(G-8221)*
Ticglobal, Canton *Also called Technical Illustration Corp (G-2530)*
Ticket Avengers Inc 248 635-3279
28599 Wauketa Ave Warren (48092) *(G-18039)*
Tico Titanium Inc 248 446-0400
52900 Grand River Ave New Hudson (48165) *(G-12073)*
Ticona Polymers Inc 248 377-6868
2600 N Opdyke Rd Auburn Hills (48326) *(G-1058)*
Tide Rings LLC 586 206-3142
14150 Hough Rd Allenton (48002) *(G-232)*
Tideslide Mooring Products, Saginaw *Also called PSI Marine Inc (G-14731)*
Tidy Mro Enterprises LLC 734 649-1122
520 Wolverine St Manchester (48158) *(G-10891)*
Tig Entity LLC 810 629-9558
3196 W Thompson Rd Fenton (48430) *(G-5508)*
Tiger Neuroscience LLC 872 903-1904
200 Viridian Dr Muskegon (49440) *(G-11932)*
Tigmaster Co 800 824-4830
9283 First St Baroda (49101) *(G-1171)*
Tigner Printing Inc 989 465-6916
221 E Railway St Coleman (48618) *(G-3473)*
Tijer Inc 586 741-0308
44326 Macomb Indus Dr Clinton Township (48036) *(G-3377)*
Tilco Inc 248 644-0901
1719 S Apple Ct Suttons Bay (49682) *(G-16346)*
Tilden Mine, Ishpeming *Also called Tilden Mining Company LC (G-8783)*
Tilden Mining Company LC 906 475-3400
2 Miles S Of Ishpeming Ishpeming (49849) *(G-8783)*
Tile By Bill & Sondra 616 554-5413
6873 Rosecrest Dr Se Caledonia (49316) *(G-2404)*
Tile Craft Inc (PA) 231 929-7207
1430 Trade Center Dr Traverse City (49696) *(G-16860)*
Tile Installation, Sterling Heights *Also called Mannino Tile & Marble Inc (G-16084)*
Tiller Tool and Die Inc 517 458-6602
551 Industrial Pkwy Jonesville (49250) *(G-9104)*
Tillerman Jfp LLC (PA) 616 443-8346
10451 W Garbow Rd Middleville (49333) *(G-11315)*
Tillman Manufacturing Com 248 802-8430
27067 Lincolnshire Dr Southfield (48034) *(G-15723)*
Tim's Cabinet Shop, Pinconning *Also called Tims Cabinet Inc (G-13065)*
Timber Coast Woodworks 231 287-3042
17501 Reitsma Ln Spring Lake (49456) *(G-15857)*
Timber Pdts Mich Ltd Partnr (PA) 906 779-2000
104 E B St Iron Mountain (49801) *(G-8736)*
Timber Products Co Ltd Partnr 906 452-6221
Hwy M 28 E Munising (49862) *(G-11755)*
Timberland Forestry 906 387-4350
E6971 Wildwood Rd Munising (49862) *(G-11756)*
Timberline Logging Inc 989 731-2794
855 Dickerson Rd Gaylord (49735) *(G-6163)*
Timberstone Cstm Woodworks LLC 810 227-6404
4119 Buno Rd Brighton (48114) *(G-2082)*
Timbertech Inc 231 348-2750
8796 Moeller Dr Harbor Springs (49740) *(G-7658)*
Timberview Woodworking 517 726-0321
6201 Brick Hwy Vermontville (49096) *(G-17592)*
Timberwolf Furnace Co 231 924-6654
12727 Van Wagoner Ave Grant (49327) *(G-7433)*
Time For Blinds Inc 248 363-9174
9633 Highland Rd White Lake (48386) *(G-18469)*
Time Machines Unlimited, Ellsworth *Also called Dts Enterprises Inc (G-5035)*
Time Traveling DJS 517 402-0976
615 S Main St Eaton Rapids (48827) *(G-4973)*
Timeless Picture Framing 231 233-2221
6161 E Millerton Rd Fountain (49410) *(G-5828)*
Timers Enterprises LLC 517 617-3092
871 Brown Rd Reading (49274) *(G-13707)*
Times and Titles 616 828-5640
396 Pettis Ave Se Ste 200 Ada (49301) *(G-36)*
Times Herald Company (HQ) 810 985-7171
1411 3rd St Ste E Port Huron (48060) *(G-13532)*
Times Indicator Publications 231 924-4400
44 W Main St Fremont (49412) *(G-6056)*
Timothy J Tade Inc (PA) 248 552-8583
4798 Butler Dr Troy (48085) *(G-17392)*
Timothy Michael Goodwin 586 322-3312
80080 Robert St Memphis (48041) *(G-11214)*
Tims Cabinet Inc 989 846-9831
5309 S Huron Rd Pinconning (48650) *(G-13065)*
Tims Custom Cabinets LLC 248 912-4154
525 W Oakley Park Rd Commerce Township (48390) *(G-3578)*
Tin Can Dewitt 517 624-2078
13175 Schavey Rd Dewitt (48820) *(G-4717)*
Tindall Packaging Inc 269 649-1163
9718 Portage Rd Portage (49002) *(G-13626)*
Tinilite World Inc 734 334-0839
2591 Carmel St Ann Arbor (48104) *(G-691)*
Tip of Mitt Welding LLC 231 582-2977
3058 Glenwood Beach Dr Boyne City (49712) *(G-1903)*
Tip Top Drilling LLC 616 291-8006
8274 Alpine Ave Sparta (49345) *(G-15787)*
Tip Top Gravel Co Inc 616 897-8342
9741 Fulton St E Ada (49301) *(G-37)*
Tip Top Screw Manufacturi 989 739-5157
725 W Morley Dr Saginaw (48601) *(G-14776)*
Tip-Top Screw Mfg Inc 989 739-5157
4183 Forest St Oscoda (48750) *(G-12773)*
Tipaloy Inc 313 875-5145
1435 E Milwaukee St Detroit (48211) *(G-4633)*
Tiq Woodworking LLC 616 206-9369
11900 Nash Hwy Clarksville (48815) *(G-3080)*
Tire Wholesalers Company 269 349-9401
3883 Emerald Dr Kalamazoo (49001) *(G-9357)*
Tischco Signs 231 755-5529
2107 Henry St Ste 1 Muskegon (49441) *(G-11933)*
Tischco Signs & Service, Muskegon *Also called Tischco Signs (G-11933)*
Tissue Seal LLC 734 213-5530
4401 Varsity Dr Ste D Ann Arbor (48108) *(G-692)*
Titan Coatings International, Detroit *Also called Titan Sales International LLC (G-4634)*
Titan Global Oil Services Inc 248 594-5983
401 S Old Woodward Ave # 308 Birmingham (48009) *(G-1753)*
Titan Pharmaceutical McHy Inc 248 220-7421
50649 Central Indus Dr Shelby Township (48315) *(G-15352)*
Titan Sales International LLC 313 469-7105
1497 E Grand Blvd Detroit (48211) *(G-4634)*

ALPHABETIC

(PA)=Parent Co (HQ)=Headquarters (DH)=Div Headquarters
2022 Harris Michigan Industrial Directory
1131

Titan Sprinkler LLC 517 540-1851
1987 Sundance Rdg Howell (48843) ***(G-8533)***
Titan Tool & Die Inc 231 799-8680
6435 Schamber Dr Norton Shores (49444) ***(G-12340)***
Titanium Building Co Inc 586 634-8580
53355 Fairchild Rd Macomb (48042) ***(G-10642)***
Titanium Elite MTS Global LLC 616 262-5222
9112 Elm Rd Clarksville (48815) ***(G-3081)***
Titanium Industries 734 335-2808
14555 Jib St Plymouth (48170) ***(G-13315)***
Titanium Operations LLC 616 717-0218
5199 Mountain Ridge Dr Ne Ada (49301) ***(G-38)***
Titanium Sports LLC 734 818-0904
13705 Stowell Rd Dundee (48131) ***(G-4837)***
Titus Welding Company 248 476-9366
20750 Sunnydale St Farmington Hills (48336) ***(G-5401)***
Tj Pant LLC 419 215-8434
25993 Us Highway 12 Sturgis (49091) ***(G-16327)***
Tk Elevator Corporation 616 942-4710
5169 Northland Dr Ne Grand Rapids (49525) ***(G-7263)***
Tk Enterprises Inc 989 865-9915
1225 N Saginaw St Saint Charles (48655) ***(G-14810)***
Tk Holdings, Auburn Hills *Also called Takata Americas* ***(G-1044)***
Tk Holdings Inc 517 545-9535
1199 Austin Ct Howell (48843) ***(G-8534)***
Tk Mexico Inc 248 373-8040
2500 Innovation Dr Auburn Hills (48326) ***(G-1059)***
Tk Mold & Engineering Inc 586 752-5840
131 Shafer Dr Romeo (48065) ***(G-14238)***
Tks Industrial Company (HQ) 248 786-5000
901 Tower Dr Ste 300 Troy (48098) ***(G-17393)***
Tlr Coatings 269 870-3083
6275 26th St S Scotts (49088) ***(G-15134)***
Tls Productions Inc 810 220-8577
78 Jackson Plz Ann Arbor (48103) ***(G-693)***
TMC Furniture Inc 734 622-0080
119 E Ann St Ann Arbor (48104) ***(G-694)***
TMC Furniture Inc (PA) 734 622-0080
4525 Airwest Dr Se Kentwood (49512) ***(G-9482)***
TMC Group Inc 248 819-6063
26 Elm Park Blvd Pleasant Ridge (48069) ***(G-13106)***
Tmd Machining Inc 269 685-3091
751 Wakefield Plainwell (49080) ***(G-13098)***
Tmg, Rockford *Also called Materials Group LLC* ***(G-14178)***
TMI Climate Solutions Inc (HQ) 810 694-5763
200 Quality Way Holly (48442) ***(G-8297)***
TMJ Manufacturing LLC 248 987-7857
26842 Haggerty Rd Farmington Hills (48331) ***(G-5402)***
Tms International LLC 734 241-3007
3000 E Front St Monroe (48161) ***(G-11583)***
Tms International LLC 517 764-5123
3100 Brooklyn Rd Jackson (49203) ***(G-9021)***
Tms International LLC 313 378-6502
1 Quality Dr Ecorse (48229) ***(G-4987)***
Tms International LLC 734 241-3007
3000 E Front St Monroe (48161) ***(G-11584)***
Tmt Investment Company 248 616-8880
900 Rochester Rd Troy (48083) ***(G-17394)***
Tnj Manufacturing LLC 586 251-1900
13877 Teresa Dr Shelby Township (48315) ***(G-15353)***
Tnr Machine Inc 269 623-2827
2050 W Dowling Rd Dowling (49050) ***(G-4799)***
TNT Marble and Stone Inc 248 887-8237
1240 Bogie Lake Rd Hartland (48353) ***(G-7772)***
TNT Pipe and Tube LLC 419 466-1144
640 Lavoy Rd Erie (48133) ***(G-5055)***
TNT-Edm Inc 734 459-1700
47689 E Anchor Ct Plymouth (48170) ***(G-13316)***
To Willow Harbor Vineyard 269 369-3900
3223 Kaiser Rd Three Oaks (49128) ***(G-16560)***
To Z A Manufacturing 734 782-3911
24685 Telegraph Rd Flat Rock (48134) ***(G-5631)***
Toastmasters International 810 385-5477
6415 State Rd Burtchville (48059) ***(G-2223)***
Toastmasters International 517 651-6507
6687 Westview Dr Laingsburg (48848) ***(G-9538)***
Toda America Incorporated 269 962-0353
4750 W Dickman Rd Battle Creek (49037) ***(G-1305)***
Today Publications, Indian River *Also called G L Nelson Inc* ***(G-8653)***
Todd R Larocque Home Imprv, Freeland *Also called Todd R Lrcque Pntg Wllcvring L* ***(G-6030)***
Todd R Lrcque Pntg Wllcvring L 989 252-9424
8521 Pierce Rd Freeland (48623) ***(G-6030)***
Todds Welding Service Inc 231 587-9969
8604 Us 131 N Kalkaska (49646) ***(G-9408)***
Toefco Engineering Inc 269 683-0188
1220 N 14th St Niles (49120) ***(G-12171)***
Toefco Engnred Coating Systems, Niles *Also called Toefco Engineering Inc* ***(G-12171)***
Togreencleancom 269 428-4812
4791 S Cedar Trl Stevensville (49127) ***(G-16268)***
Tokai Rika Group, Battle Creek *Also called Trmi Inc* ***(G-1307)***
Tokusen Hytech Inc 269 685-1768
950 Lincoln Pkwy Plainwell (49080) ***(G-13099)***
Tokusen Hytech Inc 269 658-1768
950 Lincoln Pkwy Plainwell (49080) ***(G-13100)***
Toledo Molding & Die Inc 734 233-6338
47912 Halyard Dr Plymouth (48170) ***(G-13317)***
Toledo Press Industries Inc 734 727-0605
4935 Hannan Rd Wayne (48184) ***(G-18238)***
Tolerance Tool & Engineering 313 592-4011
20541 Glendale St Detroit (48223) ***(G-4635)***
Tom Clisch Logging Inc 906 338-2900
Hwy 134700 Pelkie (49958) ***(G-12965)***
Tom's Sign, Rochester Hills *Also called Toms Sign Service* ***(G-14127)***
Toman Industries Inc 734 289-1393
1652 E Hurd Rd Monroe (48162) ***(G-11585)***
Tomar Inc 313 382-2293
3827 16th St Ecorse (48229) ***(G-4988)***
Tomas Plastics Inc 734 455-4706
42600 Cherry Hill Rd # 308 Canton (48187) ***(G-2535)***
Tomas Plastics Inc 734 455-4706
9833 Tennyson Dr Plymouth (48170) ***(G-13318)***
Tomco Fabricating & Engrg Inc 248 669-2900
50853 Century Ct Wixom (48393) ***(G-18773)***
Tomkins Products Inc 313 894-2222
1040 W Grand Blvd Detroit (48208) ***(G-4636)***
Tommark Lansing, Lansing *Also called 2 Brothers Holdings LLC* ***(G-9797)***
Tommie Inc 313 377-2931
24801 5 Mile Rd Ste 26 Redford (48239) ***(G-13779)***
Tommy Joe Reed 989 291-5768
6551 S Townhall Rd Sheridan (48884) ***(G-15384)***
Tompkins Products Inc (PA) 313 894-2222
1040 W Grand Blvd Detroit (48208) ***(G-4637)***
Toms Sign Service 248 852-3550
2926 Grant Rd Rochester Hills (48309) ***(G-14127)***
Toms World of Wood 517 264-2836
105 Sand Creek Hwy Adrian (49221) ***(G-99)***
Tomukun Noodle Bar 734 995-8668
505 E Liberty St Ste 200 Ann Arbor (48104) ***(G-695)***
Ton-Tex Corporation (PA) 616 957-3200
4029 E Grv Unit 7 Greenville (48838) ***(G-7508)***
Ton-Tex Corporation 616 957-3200
4245 44th St Se Ste 1 Grand Rapids (49512) ***(G-7264)***
Tony S Die Machine Company 586 773-7379
24358 Groesbeck Hwy Warren (48089) ***(G-18040)***
Tool & Die, Clinton Township *Also called Synergy Prototype Stamping LLC* ***(G-3370)***
Tool and Die, Muskegon *Also called Freedom Tool & Mfg Co* ***(G-11821)***
Tool Company Inc 586 598-1519
48707 Gratiot Ave Chesterfield (48051) ***(G-2957)***
Tool Craft, Lansing *Also called Michalski Enterprises Inc* ***(G-9716)***
Tool House Inc 248 481-7092
1080 Centre Rd Ste C Auburn Hills (48326) ***(G-1060)***
Tool North Inc 231 941-1150
2475 N Aero Park Ct Traverse City (49686) ***(G-16861)***
Tool Organisations Service, Lapeer *Also called Dads Panels Inc* ***(G-9926)***
Tool Service Company Inc 586 296-2500
34150 Riviera Fraser (48026) ***(G-6003)***
Tool-Craft Industries Inc 248 549-0077
6101 Product Dr Sterling Heights (48312) ***(G-16206)***
Toolco Inc 734 453-9911
47709 Galleon Dr Plymouth (48170) ***(G-13319)***
Tooling & Equipment Intl Corp 734 522-1422
12550 Tech Center Dr Livonia (48150) ***(G-10433)***
Tooling Cncepts Design Not Inc 810 444-9807
3921 32nd St Port Huron (48060) ***(G-13533)***
Tooling Solutions Group LLC 248 585-0222
32301 Dequindre Rd Madison Heights (48071) ***(G-10844)***
Tooling Solutions Plus, Port Huron *Also called Tooling Cncepts Design Not Inc* ***(G-13533)***
Tooling Systems Enterprises, Grand Rapids *Also called Tooling Systems Group Inc* ***(G-7265)***
Tooling Systems Group Inc (PA) 616 863-8623
555 Plymouth Ave Ne Grand Rapids (49505) ***(G-7265)***
Tooling Tech Group, Macomb *Also called Tooling Technology LLC* ***(G-10643)***
Tooling Technology LLC (PA) 937 381-9211
51223 Quadrate Dr Macomb (48042) ***(G-10643)***
Toolpak Solutions LLC 586 646-5655
53689 Dorner Lake Dr New Baltimore (48051) ***(G-11995)***
Tooltech Machinery Inc (PA) 248 628-1813
625 S Glaspie St Oxford (48371) ***(G-12924)***
Top Craft Tool Inc 586 461-4600
33674 Giftos Dr Clinton Township (48035) ***(G-3378)***
Top Deck Systems Inc 586 263-1550
48247 Milonas Dr Shelby Township (48315) ***(G-15354)***
Top Fabricators 313 563-7126
6390 Pelham Rd Taylor (48180) ***(G-16485)***
Top Notch Cookies & Cakes Inc 734 467-9550
1849 Knolson St Westland (48185) ***(G-18422)***
Top Notch Printing LLC 248 268-3257
24055 Dequindre Rd Hazel Park (48030) ***(G-7844)***
Top of Line Crane Service LLC 231 267-5326
6925 M 72 E Williamsburg (49690) ***(G-18566)***

Top OMichigan Reclaimers Inc 989 705-7983
620 E Main St Gaylord (49735) ***(G-6164)***
Top Quality Cleaning LLC 810 493-4211
2718 Mallery St Flint (48504) ***(G-5779)***
Top Quality Records, Flint *Also called Top Quality Cleaning LLC* ***(G-5779)***
Top Shelf Embroidery LLC 231 932-0688
1567 W South Arprt Rd # 3 Traverse City (49686) ***(G-16862)***
Top Shelf Painter Inc 586 465-0867
34400 Klein Rd Fraser (48026) ***(G-6004)***
Top Shells Embroidery LLC 231 932-0688
1525 S Div St Ste 106 Traverse City (49684) ***(G-16863)***
Top Shop Inc 517 323-9085
2526 N Grand River Ave Lansing (48906) ***(G-9744)***
Topas Advanced Polymes Inc 859 746-6447
27240 Haggerty Rd E-20 Farmington Hills (48331) ***(G-5403)***
Topduck Products LLC 517 322-3202
203 E Tolles Dr Saint Johns (48879) ***(G-14918)***
Tops-In-Quality Inc 810 364-7150
148 Huron Blvd Marysville (48040) ***(G-11109)***
Topsydekennel LLC 313 655-5804
16709 Rosemont Ave Detroit (48219) ***(G-4638)***
Toray Resin Company 248 269-8800
2800 Livernois Rd D115 Troy (48083) ***(G-17395)***
Torenzo Inc 313 732-7874
6632 Telegraph Rd Ste 122 Bloomfield Hills (48301) ***(G-1866)***
Toreson Industries Inc 818 261-7249
410 Biltmore St Inkster (48141) ***(G-8676)***
Torqstorm Superchargers 616 706-5580
2909 Buchanan Ave Sw Wyoming (49548) ***(G-18911)***
Torque 2020 CMA Acqstion LLC D 810 229-2534
7015 Fieldcrest Dr Brighton (48116) ***(G-2083)***
Torsion Control Products Inc 248 537-1900
1900 Northfield Dr Rochester Hills (48309) ***(G-14128)***
Tortillas Tita LLC 734 756-7646
3763 Commerce Ct Wayne (48184) ***(G-18239)***
Toshiba America Electronic 248 347-2608
48679 Alpha Dr Ste 120 Wixom (48393) ***(G-18774)***
Total Business Systems Inc (PA) 248 307-1076
30800 Montpelier Dr Madison Heights (48071) ***(G-10845)***
Total Chips Company Inc 989 866-2610
11285 S Winn Rd Shepherd (48883) ***(G-15379)***
Total Door An Openings, Waterford *Also called Openings Inc* ***(G-18144)***
Total Door II Inc 866 781-2069
6145 Delfield Dr Waterford (48329) ***(G-18171)***
Total Flow Products Inc 248 588-4490
1197 Rochester Rd Ste N Troy (48083) ***(G-17396)***
Total Grinding Solutions LLC 586 541-5300
13265 E 8 Mile Rd Warren (48089) ***(G-18041)***
Total Innovative Mfg LLC 616 399-9903
13395 Tyler St Holland (49424) ***(G-8222)***
Total Lee Sports Inc 989 772-6121
714 W Pickard St Mount Pleasant (48858) ***(G-11745)***
Total Life Changes LLC (PA) 810 471-3812
6094 Corporate Dr Ira (48023) ***(G-8716)***
Total Local Acquisitions LLC 517 663-2405
117 E Knight St Eaton Rapids (48827) ***(G-4974)***
Total Molding Solutions Inc 517 424-5900
416 E Cummins St Tecumseh (49286) ***(G-16519)***
Total Packaging Solutions LLC 248 519-2376
615 Griswold St Ste 700 Detroit (48226) ***(G-4639)***
Total Plastics International, Kalamazoo *Also called Total Plastics Resources LLC* ***(G-9358)***
Total Plastics Resources LLC (HQ) 269 344-0009
2810 N Burdick St Ste A Kalamazoo (49004) ***(G-9358)***
Total Plastics Resources LLC 248 299-9500
1661 Northfield Dr Rochester Hills (48309) ***(G-14129)***
Total Quality Machining Inc 231 767-1825
2620 Park St Muskegon (49444) ***(G-11934)***
Total Repair Express MI LLC 248 690-9410
2990 Lapeer Rd Auburn Hills (48326) ***(G-1061)***
Total Source Led Inc 313 575-8889
3914 Mckinley St Dearborn Heights (48125) ***(G-3942)***
Total Tennis LLC 248 594-1749
2519 W Maple Rd Bloomfield Hills (48301) ***(G-1867)***
Total Tooling Concepts Inc 616 785-8402
4870 West River Dr Ne A Comstock Park (49321) ***(G-3648)***
Total Toxicology Labs LLC 248 352-7171
24525 Southfield Rd Southfield (48075) ***(G-15724)***
Total Vinyl Products Inc 734 485-7280
10750 Hi Tech Dr Ste B Whitmore Lake (48189) ***(G-18548)***
Totd, Grand Rapids *Also called Treat of Day LLC* ***(G-7271)***
Totle Inc 248 645-1111
260 E Brown St Ste 200 Birmingham (48009) ***(G-1754)***
TOUCH REVOLUTION, Holland *Also called Tpk America LLC* ***(G-8223)***
Touch World Inc 248 539-3700
31500 W 13 Mile Rd # 101 Farmington Hills (48334) ***(G-5404)***
Touched By Cupids 313 704-6334
10725 Mckinney St Detroit (48224) ***(G-4640)***
Touchstone Distributing Inc 517 669-8200
103 S Bridge St Ste B Dewitt (48820) ***(G-4718)***
Touchstone Pottery, Dewitt *Also called Touchstone Distributing Inc* ***(G-4718)***
Touchstone Systems & Svcs Inc 616 532-0060
1817 Porter St Sw Wyoming (49519) ***(G-18912)***
Tough Coatings, Sturgis *Also called Collier Enterprise III* ***(G-16284)***
Tough Weld Fabrication 810 937-2038
1486 Michigan Rd Port Huron (48060) ***(G-13534)***
Tourist Printing 231 733-5687
2632 Peck St Muskegon (49444) ***(G-11935)***
Tow-Line Trailer Sales, Saginaw *Also called Tow-Line Trailers* ***(G-14777)***
Tow-Line Trailers 989 752-0055
4854 E Holland Rd Saginaw (48601) ***(G-14777)***
Tower Acquisition Co II LLC 248 675-6000
17672 N Laurel Park Dr Livonia (48152) ***(G-10434)***
Tower Atmtive Oprtons USA I LL 989 375-2201
81 Drettman St Elkton (48731) ***(G-5033)***
Tower Atmtive Oprtons USA I LL (HQ) 734 397-6300
17757 Woodland Dr New Boston (48164) ***(G-12021)***
Tower Atmtive Oprtons USA I LL 616 802-1600
4695 44th St Se Ste B175 Grand Rapids (49512) ***(G-7266)***
Tower Atmtive Oprtons USA I LL 586 465-5158
44850 N Groesbeck Hwy Clinton Township (48036) ***(G-3379)***
Tower Atmtive Oprtons USA I LL 734 414-3100
43955 Plymouth Oaks Blvd Plymouth (48170) ***(G-13320)***
Tower Atmtive Oprtons USA II L (HQ) 248 675-6000
17672 N Laurel Park Dr 400e Livonia (48152) ***(G-10435)***
Tower Atmtive Oprtons USA III (HQ) 248 675-6000
17672 N Laurel Park Dr Livonia (48152) ***(G-10436)***
Tower Auto Holdings II A LLC 248 675-6000
17672 N Laurel Park Dr 400e Livonia (48152) ***(G-10437)***
Tower Auto Holdings USA LLC (HQ) 248 675-6000
17672 N Laurel Park Dr # 40 Livonia (48152) ***(G-10438)***
Tower Defense & Aerospace LLC 248 675-6000
17672 N Laurel Park Dr Livonia (48152) ***(G-10439)***
Tower International, Livonia *Also called Tower Auto Holdings USA LLC* ***(G-10438)***
Tower International, Novi *Also called Ta Delaware Inc* ***(G-12553)***
Tower International Inc 616 802-1600
4695 44th St Se Ste B175 Grand Rapids (49512) ***(G-7267)***
Tower International Inc (HQ) 248 675-6000
17672 N Laurel Park Dr 400e Livonia (48152) ***(G-10440)***
Tower Laboratories Ltd 860 767-2127
5163 Robert Hunter Dr Norton Shores (49441) ***(G-12341)***
Tower Laboratories Ltd 231 893-1472
8060 Whitbeck Rd Montague (49437) ***(G-11602)***
Tower Tag & Label LLC 269 927-1065
1300 E Empire Ave Benton Harbor (49022) ***(G-1593)***
Towing & Equipment Magazine 248 601-1385
1700 W Hamlin Rd Ste 100 Rochester Hills (48309) ***(G-14130)***
Town Crier, Saint Ignace *Also called St Ignace News* ***(G-14895)***
Toyo Seat USA Corporation (HQ) 810 724-0300
2155 S Almont Ave Imlay City (48444) ***(G-8648)***
Toyoda Gosei North Amer Corp (HQ) 248 280-2100
1400 Stephenson Hwy Troy (48083) ***(G-17397)***
Toyota Industries Elctc Sys N 248 489-7700
28700 Cabot Dr Ste 100 Novi (48377) ***(G-12557)***
TP Logos LLC 810 956-9484
707 Lomasney Ln Marysville (48040) ***(G-11110)***
Tpa Inc 248 302-9131
1360 Oakman Blvd Detroit (48238) ***(G-4641)***
Tpi Industries LLC 810 987-2222
2770 Dove St Port Huron (48060) ***(G-13535)***
Tpi Powder Metallurgy Inc (PA) 989 865-9921
12030 Beaver Rd Saint Charles (48655) ***(G-14811)***
Tpk America LLC 616 786-5300
215 Central Ave Ste 200 Holland (49423) ***(G-8223)***
Tps, Beaverton *Also called Thermfrmer Parts Suppliers LLC* ***(G-1432)***
Tps LLC 269 849-2700
3827 Riverside Rd Riverside (49084) ***(G-13866)***
TR Timber Co 989 345-5350
502 E State Rd West Branch (48661) ***(G-18344)***
Trace Zero Inc 248 289-1277
2740 Auburn Ct Auburn Hills (48326) ***(G-1062)***
Trackcore Inc 616 632-2222
25 Commerce Ave Sw # 200 Grand Rapids (49503) ***(G-7268)***
Tractech Inc (HQ) 248 226-6800
26201 Northwestern Hwy Southfield (48076) ***(G-15725)***
Traction Tech Holdings LLC 313 923-0400
2545 Beaufait St Detroit (48207) ***(G-4642)***
Trade Specific Solutions LLC 734 752-7124
13092 Superior St Southgate (48195) ***(G-15758)***
Trademark Die & Engineering 616 863-6660
8060 Graphic Dr Ne Unit 1 Belmont (49306) ***(G-1520)***
Traffic & Safety, Wixom *Also called Traffic Sfety Ctrl Systems Inc* ***(G-18775)***
Traffic Engineering, Saginaw *Also called City of Saginaw* ***(G-14630)***
Traffic Sfety Ctrl Systems Inc 248 348-0570
48584 Downing St Wixom (48393) ***(G-18775)***
Traffic Signs Inc 269 964-7511
341 Helmer Rd N Springfield (49037) ***(G-15876)***
Trailer Tech Holdings LLC 248 960-9700
48282 Frank St Wixom (48393) ***(G-18776)***
Trailer Tech One, Plymouth *Also called Trailer Tech Repair Inc* ***(G-13321)***

Trailer Tech Repair Inc 734 354-6680
13101 Eckles Rd Plymouth (48170) *(G-13321)*
Trainer Metal Forming Co Inc 616 844-9982
14080 172nd Ave Grand Haven (49417) *(G-6371)*
Trainingmask LLC 888 407-7555
1140 Plett Rd Cadillac (49601) *(G-2361)*
Tram Inc (HQ) 734 254-8500
47200 Port St Plymouth (48170) *(G-13322)*
Tram Inc 269 966-0100
100 Hill Brady Rd Battle Creek (49037) *(G-1306)*
Tramar Industries 313 387-3600
12693 Marlin Dr Redford (48239) *(G-13780)*
Tramec Sloan LLC (HQ) 616 395-5600
534 E 48th St Holland (49423) *(G-8224)*
Tramm Tech Inc 989 723-2944
807 S Delaney Rd Owosso (48867) *(G-12862)*
Trane Inc 616 222-3750
5805 Weller Ct Sw Ste C Wyoming (49509) *(G-18913)*
Trane Technologies Company LLC 248 398-6200
29555 Stephenson Hwy Madison Heights (48071) *(G-10846)*
Trane US Inc 800 245-3964
5335 Hill 23 Dr Flint (48507) *(G-5780)*
Trane US Inc 734 367-0700
33725 Schoolcraft Rd Livonia (48150) *(G-10441)*
Trane US Inc 734 452-2000
37001 Industrial Rd Livonia (48150) *(G-10442)*
Trane US Inc 616 971-1400
5005 Corporate Exchange B Grand Rapids (49512) *(G-7269)*
Tranor Industries LLC 313 733-4888
19365 Sherwood St Detroit (48234) *(G-4643)*
Tranquil Systems Intl LLC 800 631-0212
528 Pioneer Pkwy Clare (48617) *(G-3000)*
Trans Industries Plastics LLC (PA) 248 310-0008
414 East St Rochester (48307) *(G-13934)*
Trans Parts Plus Inc 734 427-6844
32816 Manor Park Garden City (48135) *(G-6113)*
Trans Tube Inc 248 334-5720
34 W Sheffield Ave Pontiac (48340) *(G-13420)*
Trans-Matic Mfg Co Inc (PA) 616 820-2500
300 E 48th St Holland (49423) *(G-8225)*
Transet, Grand Rapids *Also called Northwest Metal Products Inc (G-7049)*
Transfer Tool Products, Grand Haven *Also called Transfer Tool Systems LLC (G-6372)*
Transfer Tool Systems LLC 616 846-8510
14444 168th Ave Grand Haven (49417) *(G-6372)*
Transfigure Print Co 810 404-4569
1020 Sibley St Nw Grand Rapids (49504) *(G-7270)*
Transform Automotive LLC 586 826-8500
52400 Shelby Pkwy Shelby Township (48315) *(G-15355)*
Transform Automotive LLC 586 826-8500
33596 Sterling Ponds Blvd Sterling Heights (48312) *(G-16207)*
Transform Automotive LLC (HQ) 586 826-8500
7026 Sterling Ponds Ct Sterling Heights (48312) *(G-16208)*
Transglobal Design & Mfg LLC (PA) 734 525-2651
1020 Doris Rd Auburn Hills (48326) *(G-1063)*
Transign LLC 248 623-6400
281 Collier Rd Auburn Hills (48326) *(G-1064)*
Transit Bus Rebuilders Inc 989 277-3645
500 Smith Ave Owosso (48867) *(G-12863)*
Transnav Holdings Inc (PA) 586 716-5600
35105 Cricklewood Blvd New Baltimore (48047) *(G-11996)*
Transnav Technologies Inc (HQ) 888 249-9955
35105 Cricklewood Blvd New Baltimore (48047) *(G-11997)*
Transology Associates 517 694-8645
2915 Crestwood Dr East Lansing (48823) *(G-4913)*
Transpak Inc 586 264-2064
34400 Mound Rd Sterling Heights (48310) *(G-16209)*
Transport Trailers Co 269 543-4405
2166 68th St Fennville (49408) *(G-5443)*
Transportation Tech Group Inc (PA) 810 233-0440
3020 Airpark Dr S Flint (48507) *(G-5781)*
Transtar Autobody Tech LLC 810 220-3000
2040 Heiserman Dr Brighton (48114) *(G-2084)*
Travel Information Services 989 275-8042
101 E Federal Hwy Roscommon (48653) *(G-14357)*
Traverse Bay Canvas Inc 231 347-3001
787 W Conway Rd Harbor Springs (49740) *(G-7659)*
Traverse Bay Manufacturing Inc 231 264-8111
8980 Cairn Hwy Elk Rapids (49629) *(G-5029)*
Traverse City Pie Company LLC 231 929-7437
2911 Garfield Rd N Traverse City (49686) *(G-16864)*
Traverse City Print & Copy, Traverse City *Also called Kwikie Inc (G-16735)*
Traverse City Products LLC 231 946-4414
501 Hughes Dr Traverse City (49696) *(G-16865)*
Traverse City Record-Eagle, Traverse City *Also called Traverse Cy Record- Eagle Inc (G-16866)*
Traverse Cy Record- Eagle Inc 231 946-2000
120 W Front St Traverse City (49684) *(G-16866)*
Traverse Nthrn Michigans Mag, Traverse City *Also called Prism Publications Inc (G-16802)*
Travis Creek Tooling 269 685-2000
923 Industrial Pkwy Plainwell (49080) *(G-13101)*
Travis Fulmore LLC 810 701-6981
413 Garland St Flint (48503) *(G-5782)*
Treasure Enterprise LLC 810 233-7128
1161 N Ballenger Hwy # 7 Flint (48504) *(G-5783)*
Treat of Day LLC 616 706-1717
2540 Ridgemoor Dr Se Grand Rapids (49512) *(G-7271)*
Trece Adhesive Division 918 785-3061
314 Straight Ave Sw Grand Rapids (49504) *(G-7272)*
Tree Cutting Stump Grinding 231 856-9021
2245 Brady Lake Dr Morley (49336) *(G-11624)*
Tree House Software Inc 503 208-6171
1750 Fulmer St Ann Arbor (48103) *(G-696)*
Tree Line Maple Syrup 616 889-6016
7220 Baumhoff Ave Nw Grand Rapids (49544) *(G-7273)*
Tree Tech 248 543-2166
820 S Washington Ave Royal Oak (48067) *(G-14585)*
Tregets Tool & Engineering Co 517 782-0044
1021 Airport Rd Jackson (49202) *(G-9022)*
Treib Inc (PA) 989 752-4821
850 S Outer Dr Saginaw (48601) *(G-14778)*
Trelan Manufacturing 989 561-2280
498 8 Mile Rd Remus (49340) *(G-13818)*
Trellborg Sling Sltions US Inc 269 639-4217
1042 N Crystal Ave Benton Harbor (49022) *(G-1594)*
Trellborg Sling Sltions US Inc 734 354-1250
15701 Centennial Dr Northville (48168) *(G-12266)*
Trellborg Sling Sltions US Inc 810 655-3900
2111 W Thompson Rd Fenton (48430) *(G-5509)*
Trelleborg Automotive, Northville *Also called Vibracoustic Usa Inc (G-12269)*
Trelleborg Automotive, South Haven *Also called Vibracoustic Usa Inc (G-15422)*
Trelleborg Automotive, Sandusky *Also called Vibracoustic Usa Inc (G-15070)*
Trelleborg Corporation (HQ) 269 639-9891
200 Veterans Blvd Ste 3 South Haven (49090) *(G-15419)*
Trelleborg Sealing Solutions 231 264-0087
222 Industrial Park Dr Elk Rapids (49629) *(G-5030)*
Tremco Inc Sealex Mfg Pla 231 348-5020
8850 Moeller Dr Harbor Springs (49740) *(G-7660)*
Trenary Wood Products, Trenary *Also called Holmquist Feed Mill (G-16885)*
Trend Millwork LLC 313 383-6300
1300 John A Papalas Dr Lincoln Park (48146) *(G-10057)*
Trend Services Company 231 258-9951
311 Maple St Kalkaska (49646) *(G-9409)*
Trend Software LLC 616 452-8032
2935 Pioneer Club Rd Se Grand Rapids (49506) *(G-7274)*
Trendway Corporation (HQ) 616 399-3900
13467 Quincy St Holland (49424) *(G-8226)*
Trendway Svcs Organization LLC 616 994-5327
13467 Quincy St Holland (49424) *(G-8227)*
Trendwell Energy Corporation 616 866-5024
10 E Bridge St Ste 200 Rockford (49341) *(G-14191)*
Trenton Corporation (PA) 734 424-3600
7700 Jackson Rd Ann Arbor (48103) *(G-697)*
Trenton Forging Company 734 675-1620
5523 Hoover St Trenton (48183) *(G-16895)*
Trenton Jewelers Ltd 734 676-0188
2355 West Rd Trenton (48183) *(G-16896)*
Trestle Plastic Services LLC 616 262-5484
3393 Lincoln Rd Hamilton (49419) *(G-7608)*
Treves N Kotobukiya Amer Inc 248 513-4255
39500 Orchard Hill Pl # 110 Novi (48375) *(G-12558)*
Trexel Inc 248 687-1353
101 W Big Beaver Rd Troy (48084) *(G-17398)*
Tri City Record LLC 269 463-6397
138 N Main St Watervliet (49098) *(G-18184)*
Tri City Times, Imlay City *Also called Page One Inc (G-8642)*
Tri County Oil & Gas Co Inc 248 390-0682
54739 Pelican Ln Shelby Township (48315) *(G-15356)*
Tri County Precision Grinding 586 776-6600
21960 Schmeman Ave Warren (48089) *(G-18042)*
Tri County Sand & Stone Shop, Alden *Also called Tri County Sand and Stone Inc (G-136)*
Tri County Sand and Stone Inc 231 331-6549
5318 Bebb Rd Alden (49612) *(G-136)*
Tri K Cylinder Service Inc 269 965-3981
4539 Wayne Rd Springfield (49037) *(G-15877)*
Tri Matics Mfg Inc 586 469-3150
25500 Henry B Joy Blvd Harrison Township (48045) *(G-7730)*
Tri State Optical Inc 517 279-2701
350 Marshall St Ste B Coldwater (49036) *(G-3458)*
Tri Tech Tooling Inc 616 396-6000
11615 Greenway Dr Holland (49424) *(G-8228)*
Tri Vector Printing 734 748-7006
14792 Hubbard St Livonia (48154) *(G-10443)*
Tri-C Publications Inc 616 581-7967
2710 Hickorywood Ln Se Grand Rapids (49546) *(G-7275)*
Tri-City Aggregates Inc 248 634-8276
14300 Shields Rd Holly (48442) *(G-8298)*
Tri-City Repair Company 989 835-4784
6700 Middle Rd Hope (48628) *(G-8364)*
Tri-City Vinyl Inc 989 401-7992
640 E Morley Dr Saginaw (48601) *(G-14779)*

Tri-County Diversified Inds, Lansing *Also called Community Mntal Hlth Auth Clnt* ***(G-9682)***
Tri-County Equip-Sandusky, Sandusky *Also called Bader & Co* ***(G-15055)***
Tri-County Logging, Clinton *Also called Hmi Hardwoods LLC* ***(G-3141)***
Tri-County Precision Grinding, Warren *Also called Tri County Precision Grinding* ***(G-18042)***
Tri-County Times, Fenton *Also called Rockman Communications Inc* ***(G-5500)***
Tri-M-Mold Inc 269 465-3301
3390 W Linco Rd Stevensville (49127) ***(G-16269)***
Tri-Master Inc 248 541-1864
1616 W Houstonia Ave Royal Oak (48073) ***(G-14586)***
Tri-Matic Screw Products Co 517 548-6414
5684 E Highland Rd Howell (48843) ***(G-8535)***
Tri-Mation Industries Inc 269 668-4333
24778 Cole Ave Mattawan (49071) ***(G-11168)***
Tri-Power Manufacturing Inc 734 414-8084
9229 General Dr Ste B Plymouth (48170) ***(G-13323)***
Tri-Star Engineering, Sterling Heights *Also called Tri-Star Tooling LLC* ***(G-16210)***
Tri-Star Molding Inc 269 646-0062
51540 M 40 Marcellus (49067) ***(G-10953)***
Tri-Star Tool & Machine Co 734 729-5700
613 Manufacturers Dr Westland (48186) ***(G-18423)***
Tri-Star Tooling LLC 586 978-0435
35640 Beattie Dr Sterling Heights (48312) ***(G-16210)***
Tri-State Aluminum LLC (HQ) 231 722-7825
1060 E Keating Ave Muskegon (49442) ***(G-11936)***
Tri-State Cast Technologies Co (PA) 231 582-0452
926 N Lake St Boyne City (49712) ***(G-1904)***
Tri-State Technical Services 517 563-8743
9659 Grover Rd Hanover (49241) ***(G-7627)***
Tri-Tech Engineering Inc 734 283-3700
3663 11th St Wyandotte (48192) ***(G-18842)***
Tri-Tool Boring Machine Co 586 598-0036
46440 Continental Dr Chesterfield (48047) ***(G-2958)***
Tri-Vision LLC (PA) 313 526-6020
12326 E Mcnichols Rd Detroit (48205) ***(G-4644)***
Tri-Way Manufacturing Inc 586 776-0700
15363 E 12 Mile Rd Roseville (48066) ***(G-14485)***
Tri-Way Mold & Engineering, Roseville *Also called Tri-Way Manufacturing Inc* ***(G-14485)***
Triad Industrial Corp 989 358-7191
11656 Reimann Rd Atlanta (49709) ***(G-748)***
Triad Manufacturing Co Inc 248 583-9636
32020 Edward Ave Madison Heights (48071) ***(G-10847)***
Triad Process Equipment Inc 248 685-9938
4922 Technical Dr Milford (48381) ***(G-11493)***
Triangle Broach Company 313 838-2150
18404 Fitzpatrick St Detroit (48228) ***(G-4645)***
Triangle Grinding Company Inc 586 749-6540
57877 Main St New Haven (48048) ***(G-12040)***
Triangle Printing Inc 586 293-7530
30520 Gratiot Ave Roseville (48066) ***(G-14486)***
Triangle Product Distributors 970 609-9001
5750 Lakeshore Dr Holland (49424) ***(G-8229)***
Triangle Window Fashions Inc 616 538-9676
2625 Buchanan Ave Sw A Wyoming (49548) ***(G-18914)***
Trianon Industries Corporation 586 759-2200
24331 Sherwood Center Line (48015) ***(G-2688)***
Tribal Manufacturing Inc (PA) 269 781-3901
450 Leggitt Rd Marshall (49068) ***(G-11076)***
Tribar Manufacturing LLC 248 669-0077
30517 Anderson Ct Wixom (48393) ***(G-18777)***
Tribar Manufacturing LLC 248 374-5870
29883 Beck Rd Wixom (48393) ***(G-18778)***
Tribar Manufacturing LLC (HQ) 248 516-1600
2211 Grand Commerce Dr Howell (48855) ***(G-8536)***
Tribar Technologies Inc (PA) 248 516-1600
48668 Alpha Dr Wixom (48393) ***(G-18779)***
Tribune Recorder, Sandusky *Also called Eldon Publishing LLC* ***(G-15058)***
Tric Tool Ltd 616 395-1530
3760 John F Donnelly Dr Holland (49424) ***(G-8230)***
Trick Titanium, Holt *Also called Scitex LLC* ***(G-8330)***
Trick Titanium, Holt *Also called Scitex LLC* ***(G-8329)***
Trico Group Inc 800 388-7426
3255 W Hamlin Rd Rochester Hills (48309) ***(G-14131)***
Trico Incorporated 517 764-1780
7401 Foxworth Ct Jackson (49201) ***(G-9023)***
Trico Products Corporation (HQ) 248 371-1700
3255 W Hamlin Rd Rochester Hills (48309) ***(G-14132)***
Trident Lighting LLC 616 957-9500
2929 32nd St Se Grand Rapids (49512) ***(G-7276)***
Trident Mfg LLC 989 875-5145
301 Industrial Pkwy Ithaca (48847) ***(G-8796)***
Trig Tool Inc 248 543-2550
26657 Haverhill Dr Warren (48091) ***(G-18043)***
Trigon Metal Products, Livonia *Also called A&G Corporate Holdings LLC* ***(G-10094)***
Trigon Metal Products Inc 734 513-3488
12725 Inkster Rd Livonia (48150) ***(G-10444)***
Trigon Steel Components Inc 616 834-0506
1448 Lincoln Ave Holland (49423) ***(G-8231)***
Trijicon Inc (PA) 248 960-7700
49385 Shafer Ct Wixom (48393) ***(G-18780)***
Trikala Inc 517 646-8188
11546 Ransom Hwy Dimondale (48821) ***(G-4765)***
Trillacorpe Construction, Bingham Farms *Also called Trillacorpe/Bk LLC* ***(G-1705)***
Trillacorpe/Bk LLC 248 433-0585
30100 Telg Rd Ste 366 Bingham Farms (48025) ***(G-1705)***
Trim Die Manufacturer, Stevensville *Also called Custom Tool and Die Co* ***(G-16243)***
Trim Pac Inc 269 279-9498
315 7th Ave Three Rivers (49093) ***(G-16589)***
Trimas Company LLC (HQ) 248 631-5450
39400 Woodward Ave # 130 Bloomfield Hills (48304) ***(G-1868)***
Trimas Corporation 248 631-5451
315 E Eisenhower Pkwy Ann Arbor (48108) ***(G-698)***
Trimas Corporation (PA) 248 631-5450
38505 Woodward Ave # 200 Bloomfield Hills (48304) ***(G-1869)***
Trimet Industries Inc 231 929-9100
829 Duell Rd Traverse City (49686) ***(G-16867)***
Trims Unlimited LLC 810 724-3500
3863 Van Dyke Rd Almont (48003) ***(G-269)***
Trin Inc 260 587-9282
47200 Port St Plymouth (48170) ***(G-13324)***
Trin-Mac Company Inc 586 774-1900
24825 Little Mack Ave Saint Clair Shores (48080) ***(G-14889)***
Trinco, Fraser *Also called Trinity Tool Co* ***(G-6006)***
Trinity Equipment Co 231 719-1813
3918 Holton Rd Muskegon (49445) ***(G-11937)***
Trinity Holding Inc (PA) 517 787-3100
420 Ingham St Jackson (49201) ***(G-9024)***
Trinity Industries Inc 586 285-1692
33910 James J Pompo Dr Fraser (48026) ***(G-6005)***
Trinity Industries Inc 517 741-4300
594 M 60 Union City (49094) ***(G-17498)***
Trinity Tool Co 586 296-5900
34600 Commerce Fraser (48026) ***(G-6006)***
Trinseo LLC 248 340-0109
691 N Squirrel Rd Auburn Hills (48326) ***(G-1065)***
TRINSEO S.A., Midland *Also called S A Trinseo* ***(G-11411)***
Triple A Crochet LLC 248 534-0818
9271 Shamrock Ln Clarkston (48348) ***(G-3072)***
Triple C Geothermal Inc 517 282-7249
487 W Forest Ave Muskegon (49441) ***(G-11938)***
Triple Creek Shirts and More 269 273-5154
420 Grove St Constantine (49042) ***(G-3676)***
Triple E LLC 517 531-4481
8535 E Michigan Ave Parma (49269) ***(G-12940)***
Triple Inc 248 817-5151
2321 John R Rd Troy (48083) ***(G-17399)***
Triple K Farms Inc 517 458-9741
13648 Wabash Rd Morenci (49256) ***(G-11617)***
Triple R Precision Boring Co, West Bloomfield *Also called Maro Precision Tool Company* ***(G-18296)***
Triple S Publications LLC 231 775-6113
7416 S 33 Rd Cadillac (49601) ***(G-2362)***
Triple Tool 586 795-1785
40715 Brentwood Dr Sterling Heights (48310) ***(G-16211)***
Trison Tool and Machine Inc 248 628-8770
925 S Glaspie St Oxford (48371) ***(G-12925)***
Tristone Flowtech USA Inc (HQ) 248 560-1724
2000 Town Ctr Ste 660 Southfield (48075) ***(G-15726)***
Tritec Performance Solutions, Fenton *Also called Tts Oldco LLC* ***(G-5511)***
Triton 3d LLC 616 405-8662
904 36th St Se Ste B Grand Rapids (49508) ***(G-7277)***
Triton Global Sources Inc 734 668-7107
3914 Bestech Rd Ste C Ypsilanti (48197) ***(G-18981)***
Triton Industries Inc 517 322-3822
16020 S Lowell Rd Lansing (48906) ***(G-9745)***
Triumph Gear Systems - McOmb I 586 781-2800
15375 23 Mile Rd Macomb (48042) ***(G-10644)***
Triumph Publishing House Inc 248 423-1765
18000 W 9 Mile Rd Ste 520 Southfield (48075) ***(G-15727)***
Triunfar Industries Inc 313 790-5592
10813 Bouldercrest Dr South Lyon (48178) ***(G-15460)***
Triunfar Industries Inc I 248 993-9302
2375 Bevin Ct Commerce Township (48382) ***(G-3579)***
Trmi Inc 269 966-0800
100 Hill Brady Rd Battle Creek (49037) ***(G-1307)***
Trojan Heat Treat Inc 517 568-4403
809 S Byron St Homer (49245) ***(G-8358)***
Trojan Sand and Gravel LLC 517 712-5086
1771 Charlotte Landing Rd Springport (49284) ***(G-15884)***
Tronox Incorporated 231 328-4986
4176 N Dorr Rd Merritt (49667) ***(G-11268)***
Trophy Center West Michigan 231 893-1686
8060 Whitehall Rd Whitehall (49461) ***(G-18510)***
Trout Enterprises LLC 810 309-4289
1840 Groveland Ave Flint (48505) ***(G-5784)***
Troy Design & Manufacturing Co (HQ) 734 738-2300
14425 N Sheldon Rd Plymouth (48170) ***(G-13325)***
Troy Haygood 313 478-3308
2871 Hilton Rd Ferndale (48220) ***(G-5589)***

A L P H A B E T I C

Troy Industries Inc 586 739-7760
13300 W Star Dr Shelby Township (48315) *(G-15357)*
Troy Laboratories Inc 248 652-6000
440 South St Rochester (48307) *(G-13935)*
Troy Metal Fabricating LLC 248 506-6142
2341 Alger Dr Troy (48083) *(G-17400)*
Troy Millwork Inc 248 852-8383
1841 Northfield Dr Rochester Hills (48309) *(G-14133)*
Troy Puzzles LLC 248 828-3153
1339 Barton Way Dr Troy (48098) *(G-17401)*
Troy Somerset Gazette, Troy Also called Gazette Newspapers Inc *(G-17128)*
Troy Synchro Sharkettes 734 395-8899
1328 Rue Willette Blvd Ypsilanti (48198) *(G-18982)*
Troy Tube & Manufacturing Co 586 949-8700
50100 E Russell Schmidt B Chesterfield (48051) *(G-2959)*
Troys Welding Company 810 633-9388
2572 Marlette Rd Applegate (48401) *(G-727)*
Trp Enterprises Inc 810 329-4027
6267 Saint Clair Hwy East China (48054) *(G-4859)*
Trp Sand & Gravel, East China Also called Trp Enterprises Inc *(G-4859)*
Tru Blu Industries LLC 269 684-4989
1920 Industrial Dr Niles (49120) *(G-12172)*
Tru Color Printing 248 737-2041
5538 Abington West Bloomfield (48322) *(G-18318)*
Tru Custom Blends Inc 810 407-6207
2321 Branch Rd Flint (48506) *(G-5785)*
Tru Die Cast Corporation 269 426-3361
13066 California Rd New Troy (49119) *(G-12075)*
Tru Flo Carbide Inc 989 658-8515
3999 N Ubly Rd Ubly (48475) *(G-17483)*
Tru Line Co 313 215-1935
35562 Dove Trl Westland (48185) *(G-18424)*
Tru Point Corporation 313 897-9100
6707 W Warren Ave Detroit (48210) *(G-4646)*
Tru Tech Systems LLC (HQ) 586 469-2700
24550 N River Rd Mount Clemens (48043) *(G-11661)*
Tru-Bore Machine Tool Co Inc 734 729-9590
6262 E Executive Dr Westland (48185) *(G-18425)*
Tru-Coat Inc 810 785-3331
10428 Seymour Rd Montrose (48457) *(G-11608)*
Tru-Fit International Inc 248 855-8845
5799 W Maple Rd Ste 167 West Bloomfield (48322) *(G-18319)*
Tru-Line Metal Products Co, Livonia Also called Tru-Line Screw Products Inc *(G-10445)*
Tru-Line Screw Products Inc (PA) 734 261-8780
15223 Farmington Rd Ste 5 Livonia (48154) *(G-10445)*
Tru-Syzygy Inc 248 622-7211
1151 Sunset Hills Dr Lake Orion (48360) *(G-9635)*
Tru-Thread Co Inc 248 399-0255
1600 Hilton Rd Ferndale (48220) *(G-5590)*
Truans Candies Inc (PA) 313 281-0185
4251 Fleming Way Plymouth (48170) *(G-13326)*
Truarx Inc 248 538-7809
2000 Town Ctr Ste 2050 Southfield (48075) *(G-15728)*
Trucent Inc (PA) 734 426-9015
7400 Newman Blvd Dexter (48130) *(G-4759)*
Trucent Separation Tech LLC 734 426-9015
7400 Newman Blvd Dexter (48130) *(G-4760)*
Truck Trailer Transit Inc 313 516-7151
1400 Rochester Rd Troy (48083) *(G-17402)*
Truck Acquisition Inc (HQ) 877 875-4376
5400 Data Ct Ann Arbor (48108) *(G-699)*
Truck Hero Ann Arbor, Ann Arbor Also called Tectum Holdings Inc *(G-674)*
Truck Holdings Inc (PA) 877 875-4376
5400 Data Ct Ste 100 Ann Arbor (48108) *(G-700)*
Trucksforsalecom 989 883-3382
8440 Unionville Rd Sebewaing (48759) *(G-15145)*
Trudex One Inc 248 392-2036
2300 Old Plank Rd Milford (48381) *(G-11494)*
True Anlytics Mfg Slutions LLC 517 902-9700
5400 Douglas Rd Ida (48140) *(G-8625)*
True Die Inc 616 772-6360
2425 104th Ave Zeeland (49464) *(G-19084)*
True Fabrications & Machine 248 288-0140
1731 Thorncroft Dr Troy (48084) *(G-17403)*
True Industrial Corporation (PA) 586 771-3500
15300 E 12 Mile Rd Roseville (48066) *(G-14487)*
True Industries, Roseville Also called True Industrial Corporation *(G-14487)*
True Teknit Inc 616 656-5111
5300 Corprte Grv Dr Se Grand Rapids (49512) *(G-7278)*
True Tool Cnc Regrinding & Mfg 616 677-1751
14110 Ironwood Dr Nw Grand Rapids (49534) *(G-7279)*
True Value, Ludington Also called Ardy Inc *(G-10527)*
True Welding LLC 586 822-5398
16242 Bell Ave Eastpointe (48021) *(G-4945)*
Truemner Enterprises Inc 586 756-6470
25418 Ryan Rd Warren (48091) *(G-18044)*
Truform Machine Inc 517 782-8523
2510 Precision St Jackson (49202) *(G-9025)*
Truing Systems Inc 248 588-9060
1060 Chicago Rd Troy (48083) *(G-17404)*
Trulife Inc (HQ) 800 492-1088
2010 E High St Jackson (49203) *(G-9026)*
Truly Free LLC (PA) 231 252-4571
3175 Continental Dr Traverse City (49686) *(G-16868)*
Truly Tees & Co LLc 313 266-1819
6421 Vaughan St Detroit (48228) *(G-4647)*
Trumpf Inc 734 354-9770
47711 Clipper St Plymouth (48170) *(G-13327)*
Trusco, Grand Rapids Also called Ginsan Liquidating Company LLC *(G-6744)*
Truss Development 248 624-8100
1573 S Telegraph Rd Bloomfield Hills (48302) *(G-1870)*
Truss Technologies Inc 231 788-6330
404 S Maple Island Rd Muskegon (49442) *(G-11939)*
Trussway 713 691-6900
8450 Winona Dr Jenison (49428) *(G-9074)*
Trusted Tool Mfg Grand Haven 616 607-2023
1800 Industrial Dr Grand Haven (49417) *(G-6373)*
Trusted Tool Mfg Inc 810 750-6000
8075 Old Us 23 Fenton (48430) *(G-5510)*
Truth & Tidings 517 782-9798
2030 Jeffrey Ct Jackson (49203) *(G-9027)*
Truth Sand Contemplations 269 342-0369
5145 Morningside Dr Portage (49024) *(G-13627)*
Truth Traxx LLC 800 792-2239
3123 Stevenson St Flint (48504) *(G-5786)*
Trutron Corporation 248 583-9166
274 Executive Dr Troy (48083) *(G-17405)*
TRW Atomotive Holdg Mexico LLC 734 855-2600
12001 Tech Center Dr Livonia (48150) *(G-10446)*
TRW Automotive (Iv) Corp (HQ) 734 855-2600
12001 Tech Center Dr Livonia (48150) *(G-10447)*
TRW Automotive US LLC 248 426-3901
23855 Research Dr Farmington Hills (48335) *(G-5405)*
TRW East Inc 734 855-2600
12001 Tech Center Dr Livonia (48150) *(G-10448)*
TRW Occupant Safety Systems 586 752-1409
14761 32 Mile Rd Bruce Twp (48065) *(G-2184)*
TRW Odyssey Inc., Livonia Also called ZF String Active Safety US Inc *(G-10491)*
TRW Odyssey Mexico LLC 734 855-2600
12001 Tech Center Dr Livonia (48150) *(G-10449)*
TRW Oss, Romeo Also called ZF Passive Sfety Systems US In *(G-14241)*
TRW Parts & Service America, Farmington Hills Also called ZF Active Safety US Inc *(G-5418)*
TRW Safety Systems Mexico LLC 734 855-2600
12001 Tech Center Dr Livonia (48150) *(G-10450)*
Tryco Inc 734 953-6800
23800 Research Dr Farmington Hills (48335) *(G-5406)*
Trynex International LLC 248 586-3500
531 Ajax Dr Madison Heights (48071) *(G-10848)*
TS Carbide Inc 248 486-8330
3131 Ruler Dr Commerce Township (48390) *(G-3580)*
TS Enterprise Associates Inc 248 348-2963
110 W Main St Northville (48167) *(G-12267)*
TSC Group Inc 269 544-9966
226 N 28th St Springfield (49037) *(G-15878)*
Tsg Tooling Systems Group, Comstock Park Also called Advanced Tooling Systems Inc *(G-3586)*
Tsg Tooling Systems Group.com, Grand Rapids Also called Engineered Tooling Systems Inc *(G-6681)*
Tsk of America Inc (HQ) 517 542-2955
152 Simpson Dr Litchfield (49252) *(G-10086)*
Tsm Corporation 248 276-4700
1175 N Opdyke Rd Auburn Hills (48326) *(G-1066)*
Tsnap Services, Van Buren Twp Also called Anthony Castellani *(G-17509)*
TSS, Warren Also called TSS Inc *(G-18045)*
TSS Inc 586 427-0070
21000 Hoover Rd Warren (48089) *(G-18045)*
TST Tooling Software Tech LLC (PA) 248 922-9293
6547 Dixie Hwy Clarkston (48346) *(G-3073)*
Tsunami Inc 989 497-5200
6235 Gratiot Rd Saginaw (48638) *(G-14780)*
Tsw Technologies LLC 248 773-5026
25909 Meadowbrook Rd Novi (48375) *(G-12559)*
Ttadevelopment LLC 626 399-4225
11687 Yellowstone St Detroit (48204) *(G-4648)*
Ttg Automation, Temperance Also called Bel-Kur Inc *(G-16528)*
Tts Oldco LLC (HQ) 810 655-3900
2111 W Thompson Rd Fenton (48430) *(G-5511)*
Tu Way, Troy Also called Tuway American Group Inc *(G-17407)*
Tube City AK, Dearborn Also called Cleveland-Cliffs Steel Corp *(G-3821)*
Tube Fab/Roman Engrg Co Inc 231 238-9366
1715 Michigan 68 Afton Afton (49705) *(G-108)*
Tube Wright Inc (PA) 810 227-4567
2111 Euler Rd Brighton (48114) *(G-2085)*
Tube Wright Inc 734 449-9129
10781 Plaza Dr Whitmore Lake (48189) *(G-18549)*
Tube-Co Inc 586 775-0244
23094 Schoenherr Rd Warren (48089) *(G-18046)*

ALPHABETIC SECTION

Tubelite Inc (HQ) 800 866-2227
3056 Walker Ridge Dr Nw Walker (49544) *(G-17655)*
Tubelite Inc 800 866-2227
4878 Mackinaw Trl Reed City (49677) *(G-13801)*
Tubergen Cutting Tools, Grand Rapids Also called Saw Tubergen Service Inc *(G-7182)*
Tubesource Manufacturing Inc 248 543-4746
1600 E 9 Mile Rd Ferndale (48220) *(G-5591)*
Tubular Metal Systems LLC (HQ) 989 879-2611
401 E 5th St Pinconning (48650) *(G-13066)*
Tubular Products Division, Grand Rapids Also called Benteler Automotive Corp *(G-6501)*
Tuff Automation Inc 616 735-3939
2751 Courier Dr Nw Grand Rapids (49534) *(G-7280)*
Tuff Body Padding Company, Adrian Also called Roto-Plastics Corporation *(G-92)*
Tulip US Holdings Inc (PA) 517 694-2300
1489 Cedar St Holt (48842) *(G-8336)*
Tumacs Corporation 517 816-8141
7619 Northport Dr Lansing (48917) *(G-9794)*
Tumbl Trak, Mount Pleasant Also called T L V Inc *(G-11744)*
Tunkers Inc 734 744-5990
36200 Mound Rd Sterling Heights (48310) *(G-16212)*
Tunkers-Mastech, Sterling Heights Also called Tunkers Inc *(G-16212)*
Tunnel Vision Brewery, Harbor Springs Also called Harbor Sprng Vnyrds Winery LLC *(G-7647)*
Tunnel Vision Pipeline Svcs, Escanaba Also called Upper Peninsula Rubber Co Inc *(G-5104)*
Tuocai America LLC 248 346-5910
5700 Crooks Rd Ste 222 Troy (48098) *(G-17406)*
Tupes of Saginaw Inc 989 799-1550
845 Windrush Ct Unit 15 Saginaw (48609) *(G-14781)*
Turbine Tool & Gage Inc 734 427-2270
11901 Brookfield St Livonia (48150) *(G-10451)*
Turbo Grips, Chesterfield Also called 2-N-1 Grips Inc *(G-2833)*
Turbosocks Performance 586 864-3252
50765 Cedargrove Rd Shelby Township (48317) *(G-15358)*
Turn Key Automotive LLC 248 628-5556
2171 Xcelsior Dr Oxford (48371) *(G-12926)*
Turn Key Harness & Wire LLC 248 236-9915
2171 Xcelsior Dr Oxford (48371) *(G-12927)*
Turn Key/Redico, Oxford Also called Turn Key Automotive LLC *(G-12926)*
Turn Tech Inc 586 415-8090
33901 Riviera Fraser (48026) *(G-6007)*
Turner Business Forms Inc (PA) 989 752-5540
19 Slatestone Dr Saginaw (48603) *(G-14782)*
Turner Custom Woodworking 810 324-6254
4085 Kilgore Rd Kenockee (48006) *(G-9421)*
Turnkey Fabrication LLC 616 248-9116
840 Cottage Grove St Se Grand Rapids (49507) *(G-7281)*
Turpeinen Bros Inc 906 338-2870
12900 State Highway M38 Pelkie (49958) *(G-12966)*
Turris Italian Foods Inc (PA) 586 773-6010
16695 Common Rd Roseville (48066) *(G-14488)*
Turtle Racing LLC 517 918-3444
625 N East St Morenci (49256) *(G-11618)*
Tuscarora Inc -Vs 989 729-2780
123 N Chipman St Owosso (48867) *(G-12864)*
Tuscola County Advertiser Inc (PA) 989 673-3181
344 N State St Caro (48723) *(G-2583)*
Tuscola County Advertiser Inc 517 673-3181
344 N State St Caro (48723) *(G-2584)*
Tuscola County Advertiser Inc 989 823-8651
5881 Frankenmuth Rd Vassar (48768) *(G-17583)*
Tuscola Logging 517 231-2905
1138 Luce St Sw Grand Rapids (49534) *(G-7282)*
Tuteur Inc 269 983-1246
1721 Lakeshore Dr Saint Joseph (49085) *(G-14966)*
Tuttle Forest Products 906 283-3871
1964 W Hwy Us 2 Gulliver (49840) *(G-7578)*
Tuway American Group Inc 248 205-9999
3155 W Big Beavr Rd # 104 Troy (48084) *(G-17407)*
Tva Kane Inc (PA) 248 946-4670
45380 W 10 Mile Rd # 100 Novi (48375) *(G-12560)*
Tvb Inc 616 456-9629
544 Richmond St Nw Grand Rapids (49504) *(G-7283)*
Tvdn Group LLC 248 255-6402
1472 N Cranbrook Rd Bloomfield Hills (48301) *(G-1871)*
Twb Company LLC (HQ) 734 289-6400
1600 Nadeau Rd Monroe (48162) *(G-11586)*
Twb Company LLC 734 454-4000
7295 N Haggerty Rd Canton (48187) *(G-2536)*
Twb of Indiana Inc 734 289-6400
1600 Nadeau Rd Monroe (48162) *(G-11587)*
Tweddle Group Inc (PA) 586 307-3700
24700 Maplehurst Dr Clinton Township (48036) *(G-3380)*
Tweddle Group Inc 586 840-3275
2111 Woodward Ave 8f Detroit (48201) *(G-4649)*
Tweddle Litho Inc 586 795-0515
34000 Mound Rd Sterling Heights (48310) *(G-16213)*
Twig Power LLC 248 613-9652
40480 Grand River Ave J Novi (48375) *(G-12561)*

Twin Bay Dock and Products 231 943-8420
982 E Commerce Dr Ste B Traverse City (49685) *(G-16869)*
Twin Bay Medical, Williamsburg Also called Saint-Gobain Prfmce Plas Corp *(G-18563)*
Twin Cities Orthotic & Prosthe 269 428-2910
3538 Magnolia Ln Saint Joseph (49085) *(G-14967)*
Twin City Engraving Company 269 983-0601
2024 Washington Ave Ste 3 Saint Joseph (49085) *(G-14968)*
Twin City Foods Inc 616 374-4002
801 Lincoln St Lake Odessa (48849) *(G-9579)*
Twin Mold and Engineering LLC 586 532-8558
51738 Filomena Dr Shelby Township (48315) *(G-15359)*
Twin Pines, Detroit Also called C F Burger Creamery Co *(G-4084)*
Twinlab Holdings Inc 800 645-5626
3133 Orchard Vista Dr Se Grand Rapids (49546) *(G-7284)*
Twins Studio 248 676-8157
2435 Childs Lake Rd Milford (48381) *(G-11495)*
Twist 248 859-2169
6331 Haggerty Rd West Bloomfield (48322) *(G-18320)*
Twisted Scissor 248 620-2626
5907 Dixie Hwy Ste A Clarkston (48346) *(G-3074)*
Twm Technology LLC 989 684-7050
3490 E North Union Rd Bay City (48706) *(G-1407)*
Two Cups Coffee Co LLC 616 953-0534
490 Lincoln Ave Ste 10 Holland (49423) *(G-8232)*
Two James Spirits LLC 313 964-4800
2445 Michigan Ave Detroit (48216) *(G-4650)*
Two Mitts Inc (PA) 800 888-5054
600 Plastics Pl Kalamazoo (49001) *(G-9359)*
Two Tracks Bow Co 989 834-0588
8317 Welter Rd Ovid (48866) *(G-12817)*
Twosixnine Studios 269 365-6719
12140 Highview Shrs Vicksburg (49097) *(G-17615)*
Tws, Oxford Also called TEC Welding Sales Incorporated *(G-12922)*
Tyde Group Worldwide LLC 248 879-7656
5700 Crooks Rd Ste 207 Troy (48098) *(G-17408)*
Tyes Inc 888 219-6301
5236 W 1st St Ludington (49431) *(G-10553)*
Tygrus LLC 248 218-0347
1134 E Big Beaver Rd Troy (48083) *(G-17409)*
Tyler Technologies Inc 734 677-0550
525 Avis Dr Ste 3 Ann Arbor (48108) *(G-701)*
Tyrone Tool Company Inc 810 742-4762
3336 Associates Dr Burton (48529) *(G-2249)*
Tyson Foods Inc 231 922-3214
2314 Sybrant Rd Traverse City (49684) *(G-16870)*
Tyson Foods Inc 231 929-2456
845 Bertina Ln Traverse City (49696) *(G-16871)*
Tyson Foods /Hr 616 875-2311
8300 96th Ave Zeeland (49464) *(G-19085)*
Tyson Fresh Meats Inc 248 213-1000
26999 Central Park Blvd Southfield (48076) *(G-15729)*
Tzamco Inc (PA) 248 624-7710
1060 W West Maple Rd Walled Lake (48390) *(G-17676)*
U E I, Grand Rapids Also called Uei Inc *(G-7285)*
U K Sailmakers, Clinton Township Also called Performance Sailing Inc *(G-3318)*
U P Concrete Pipe, Escanaba Also called Upper Peninsula Con Pipe Co *(G-5103)*
U P Fabricating Co Inc (PA) 906 475-4400
120 Us Highway 41 E Ste A Negaunee (49866) *(G-11976)*
U P Fabricating Co Inc 906 341-2868
342 Elm St Manistique (49854) *(G-10924)*
U P Machine & Engineering Co 906 497-5278
N15930 Main St Powers (49874) *(G-13650)*
U P North Structures 989 654-2350
6300 Ward Rd Sterling (48659) *(G-15914)*
U S Baird Corporation 616 826-5013
8121 108th St Se Middleville (49333) *(G-11316)*
U S Distributing Inc 248 646-0550
2333 Cole St Birmingham (48009) *(G-1755)*
U S Engineering, Grand Rapids Also called J W Holdings Inc *(G-6858)*
U S Equipment Co (HQ) 313 526-8300
3667 Merriweather Ln Rochester Hills (48306) *(G-14134)*
U S Fabrication & Design LLC 248 919-2910
32890 Capitol St Livonia (48150) *(G-10452)*
U S Farathane Port Huron LLC 248 754-7000
2700 High Meadow Cir Auburn Hills (48326) *(G-1067)*
U S Graphite Inc (PA) 989 755-0441
1620 E Holland Ave Saginaw (48601) *(G-14783)*
U S Group Inc (PA) 313 372-7900
3667 Merriweather Ln Rochester Hills (48306) *(G-14135)*
U S Ice Corp 313 862-3344
10625 W 8 Mile Rd Detroit (48221) *(G-4651)*
U S Pattern Company Inc 586 727-2896
69150 Skinner Dr Richmond (48062) *(G-13847)*
U S Speedo Inc 810 244-0909
6050 Birch Rd Flint (48507) *(G-5787)*
U.P. Machine, Powers Also called U P Machine & Engineering Co *(G-13650)*
U.S. Frthane Corp Extrsion Gro, Auburn Hills Also called US Farathane Holdings Corp *(G-1073)*
U.S. Wire & Rope, Detroit Also called US Wire Rope Supply Inc *(G-4655)*

Uacj Auto Whitehall Inds Inc 231 845-5101
801 S Madison St Ludington (49431) *(G-10554)*
Uantum Lifecare, Holly *Also called Quantum Ventures LLC (G-8289)*
Ube Industries, Ann Arbor *Also called Ube Machinery Inc (G-702)*
Ube Machinery Inc 734 741-7000
5700 S State Rd Ann Arbor (48108) *(G-702)*
Uber Hair and Nails Llc 248 268-3227
990 W 8 Mile Rd Ferndale (48220) *(G-5592)*
Ubly Bean Knife Mfg Inc 231 723-3244
1388 Hill Rd Manistee (49660) *(G-10914)*
Uc Holdings Inc (PA) 248 728-8642
300 Galleria Officentre Southfield (48034) *(G-15730)*
Ucb Advertising 269 808-2411
12047 Oakridge Rd Plainwell (49080) *(G-13102)*
Uchiyama Mktg & Dev Amer LLC 248 859-3986
46805 Magellan Dr Novi (48377) *(G-12562)*
Uckele Health & Nutrition, Blissfield *Also called Uckele Health and Nutrition (G-1779)*
Uckele Health and Nutrition (PA) 800 248-0330
5600 Silberhorn Hwy Blissfield (49228) *(G-1779)*
Ucp, White Pigeon *Also called Deckorators Inc (G-18475)*
Uei Inc 616 361-6093
2771 West River Dr Nw Grand Rapids (49544) *(G-7285)*
Ufi Filters Usa Inc 248 376-0441
50 W Big Beavr Rd Ste 440 Troy (48084) *(G-17410)*
Ufi Filters Usa Inc 248 376-0441
50 W Big Beavr Rd Ste 440 Troy (48084) *(G-17411)*
Ufm, Hazel Park *Also called Universal Flow Monitors Inc (G-7845)*
Ufp Atlantic LLC 616 364-6161
2801 E Beltline Ave Ne Grand Rapids (49525) *(G-7286)*
Ufp Eastern Division Inc (HQ) 616 364-6161
2801 E Beltline Ave Ne Grand Rapids (49525) *(G-7287)*
Ufp Grand Rapids LLC 616 464-1650
825 Buchanan Ave Sw Grand Rapids (49507) *(G-7288)*
Ufp Industries Inc (PA) 616 364-6161
2801 E Beltline Ave Ne Grand Rapids (49525) *(G-7289)*
Ufp International LLC (HQ) 770 472-3050
2801 E Beltline Ave Ne Grand Rapids (49525) *(G-7290)*
Ufp Lansing LLC 517 325-5572
2801 E Beltline Ave Ne Grand Rapids (49525) *(G-7291)*
Ufp Lansing LLC 517 322-0025
2509 Snow Rd Lansing (48917) *(G-9795)*
Ufp Sauk Rapids LLC 320 259-5190
2801 E Beltline Ave Ne Grand Rapids (49525) *(G-7292)*
Ufp Southwest LLC 616 364-6161
2801 E Beltline Ave Ne Grand Rapids (49525) *(G-7293)*
Ufp Technologies, Grand Rapids *Also called Simco Automotive Trim Inc (G-7199)*
Ufp Technologies Inc 616 949-8100
3831 Patterson Ave Se Grand Rapids (49512) *(G-7294)*
Ufp West Central LLC 616 364-6161
2801 E Beltline Ave Ne Grand Rapids (49525) *(G-7295)*
Ugs, Troy *Also called United Global Sourcing Inc (G-17412)*
Uis Industries LLC 734 443-3737
39111 6 Mile Rd Livonia (48152) *(G-10453)*
Ukc Liquidating Inc (PA) 269 343-9020
100 E Kilgore Rd Portage (49002) *(G-13628)*
Ulb LLC 734 233-0961
28200 Lakeview Dr Wixom (48393) *(G-18781)*
Ultimate Bed, Menominee *Also called Anderson Manufacturing Co Inc (G-11226)*
Ultimate Graphic and Sign LLC 989 865-5200
8071 S Iva Rd Saint Charles (48655) *(G-14812)*
Ultimate Highway Solutions, Grand Haven *Also called Alternate Number Five Inc (G-6272)*
Ultimate Software Group Inc 616 682-9639
5990 Fulton St E Ste E Ada (49301) *(G-39)*
Ultimate Systems, Madison Heights *Also called Usi Inc (G-10854)*
Ultimate Tube Bender Part 810 599-7862
3245 Sandpoint Dr Brighton (48114) *(G-2086)*
Ultimation Industries LLC 586 771-1881
15935 Sturgeon St Roseville (48066) *(G-14489)*
Ultra Derm Systems, Saginaw *Also called J & B Products Ltd (G-14672)*
Ultra Fab & Machine Inc 248 628-7065
465 S Glaspie St Ste D Oxford (48371) *(G-12928)*
Ultra Forms Plus Inc 269 337-6000
301 Peekstock Rd Kalamazoo (49001) *(G-9360)*
Ultra Stitch Embroidery 586 498-5600
32475 Stephenson Hwy Madison Heights (48071) *(G-10849)*
Ultra Tool Grind Inc 989 471-5169
2616 Gehrke Rd Ossineke (49766) *(G-12780)*
Ultra-Dex Tooling Systems, Flushing *Also called MB Liquidating Corporation (G-5811)*
Ultra-Dex USA LLC 810 638-5388
7144 Sheridan Rd Flushing (48433) *(G-5814)*
Ultra-Grip International Div, Commerce Township *Also called Three M Tool & Machine Inc (G-3577)*
Ultra-Sonic Extrusion Dies Inc 586 791-8550
34863 Groesbeck Hwy Clinton Township (48035) *(G-3381)*
Ultra-Tech Printing Co 616 249-0500
5851 Crossrds Cmmrce Pkwy Wyoming (49519) *(G-18915)*
Ultra-Temp Corporation 810 794-4709
7270 Flamingo St Clay (48001) *(G-3128)*
Ultraform Industries Inc 586 752-4508
150 Peyerk Ct Bruce Twp (48065) *(G-2185)*
Ultralight Prosthetics Inc 313 538-8500
24781 5 Mile Rd Redford (48239) *(G-13781)*
Ultraseal America Inc 734 222-9478
4343 Concourse Dr Ste 340 Ann Arbor (48108) *(G-703)*
Um Orthotics Pros Cntr 734 764-3100
2500 Green Rd Ste 100 Ann Arbor (48105) *(G-704)*
Umakanth Consultants Inc 517 347-7500
3581 Cabaret Trl Okemos (48864) *(G-12691)*
Umi, Holland *Also called United Manufacturing Inc (G-8233)*
Umix Dissoultion Corp 586 446-9950
6050 15 Mile Rd Sterling Heights (48312) *(G-16214)*
Umlaut Product Solutions Inc 248 703-7724
1225 Spartan St Madison Heights (48071) *(G-10850)*
Uncle Johns Cider Mill Inc 989 224-3686
8614 N Us Highway 27 Saint Johns (48879) *(G-14919)*
Uncle Rays LLC (HQ) 313 834-0800
14245 Birwood St Detroit (48238) *(G-4652)*
Uncle Rons Woodworking 248 585-7837
611 W Girard Ave Madison Heights (48071) *(G-10851)*
Unco Automotive Products, Livonia *Also called Mid-West Screw Products Co (G-10316)*
Under Pressure Pwr Washers LLC 616 292-4289
885 Meyer Ln Marne (49435) *(G-11000)*
Under Stairs 586 781-6202
53715 Sprnghill Madows Dr Macomb (48042) *(G-10645)*
Undercar Products Group Inc 616 719-4571
4247 Eastern Ave Se Wyoming (49508) *(G-18916)*
Underground Printing, Ann Arbor *Also called A-1 Screenprinting LLC (G-342)*
Underground Shirts 734 274-5494
2248 S Main St Ann Arbor (48103) *(G-705)*
Understated Corrugated LLC 248 880-5767
635 Horton St Northville (48167) *(G-12268)*
UNI-Bond Brake, Ferndale *Also called Amanda Products LLC (G-5525)*
UNI-Vue Inc 248 564-3251
2424 Wolcott St Ferndale (48220) *(G-5593)*
Uniband Usa LLC 616 676-6011
2555 Oak Industrial Dr Ne Grand Rapids (49505) *(G-7296)*
Unicor, Norton Shores *Also called Dama Tool & Gauge Company (G-12287)*
Unicote Corporation 586 296-0700
33165 Groesbeck Hwy Fraser (48026) *(G-6008)*
Unifab Cages, Portage *Also called Unifab Corporation (G-13629)*
Unifab Corporation 269 382-2803
5260 Lovers Ln Portage (49002) *(G-13629)*
Unified Equipment Systems Inc 586 307-3770
42950 Walnut St Clinton Township (48036) *(G-3382)*
Unified Industries Inc (HQ) 517 546-3220
740 Advance St Brighton (48116) *(G-2087)*
Unified Scrning Crshing - MI L 888 464-9473
305 E Walker Rd Saint Johns (48879) *(G-14920)*
Unified Tool and Die Inc 517 768-8070
2010 Micor Dr Jackson (49203) *(G-9028)*
Unifilter Company, Novi *Also called Unifilter Inc (G-12563)*
Unifilter Inc 248 476-5100
43800 Grand River Ave Novi (48375) *(G-12563)*
Uniflex Inc 248 486-6000
7830 Lochlin Dr Brighton (48116) *(G-2088)*
Unilock Michigan Inc 248 437-7037
12591 Emerson Dr Brighton (48116) *(G-2089)*
Uniloy Inc (PA) 514 424-8900
5550 S Occidental Rd B Tecumseh (49286) *(G-16520)*
Unimerco Group A/S, Saline *Also called Kyocera Unimerco Tooling Inc (G-15023)*
Union Commissary LLC 248 795-2483
64 S Main St Clarkston (48346) *(G-3075)*
Union First Promotions, Grand Rapids *Also called Versatility Inc (G-7312)*
Union Kitchen, Clarkston *Also called Union Commissary LLC (G-3075)*
Union Oil Co 989 348-8459
8892 W 7 Mile Rd Grayling (49738) *(G-7470)*
Union Pallet & Cont Co Inc 517 279-4888
161 Race St Coldwater (49036) *(G-3459)*
Union Tank Car Company 989 615-3054
146 Building Dow Chemical Midland (48667) *(G-11420)*
Uniplas, Howell *Also called Plastics Recycling Tech Inc (G-8496)*
Uniprax LLC 616 522-3158
215 W Main St Ionia (48846) *(G-8692)*
Unique Connection Pubg Co 248 304-0030
26282 Summerdale Dr Southfield (48033) *(G-15731)*
Unique Embroidery 517 321-8647
4722 W Grand River Ave Lansing (48906) *(G-9746)*
Unique Fabricating Inc (PA) 248 853-2333
800 Standard Pkwy Auburn Hills (48326) *(G-1068)*
Unique Fabricating Na Inc (HQ) 248 853-2333
800 Standard Pkwy Auburn Hills (48326) *(G-1069)*
Unique Fabricating Na Inc 517 524-9010
13221 Allman Rd Concord (49237) *(G-3656)*
Unique Fabricating Na Inc 248 853-2333
2817 Bond St Rochester Hills (48309) *(G-14136)*
Unique Food Management Inc 248 738-9393
248 S Telegraph Rd Pontiac (48341) *(G-13421)*

Unique Hooka and Tobacco 586 883-7674
4086 17 Mile Rd Sterling Heights (48310) ***(G-16215)***
Unique Molded Foam Tech Inc 517 524-9010
13221 Allman Rd Concord (49237) ***(G-3657)***
Unique Reproductions Inc 248 788-2887
5470 Carol Run S West Bloomfield (48322) ***(G-18321)***
Unique Shape Fabricating, Clarkston *Also called Oblut Limited* ***(G-3054)***
Unique Tool & Mfg Co Inc 336 498-2614
100 Reed Dr Temperance (48182) ***(G-16551)***
Unique Truck Accessories, Sturgis *Also called Lake Fabricators Inc* ***(G-16298)***
Unique U Magazine LLC 586 696-1839
1221 Christine Ter Madison Heights (48071) ***(G-10852)***
Unique-Chardan Inc 419 636-6900
800 Standard Pkwy Auburn Hills (48326) ***(G-1070)***
Unique-Intasco Usa Inc 810 982-3360
800 Standard Pkwy Auburn Hills (48326) ***(G-1071)***
Unislat LLC 616 844-4211
13660 172nd Ave Grand Haven (49417) ***(G-6374)***
Unisorb Inc (HQ) 517 764-6060
4117 Felters Rd Ste A Michigan Center (49254) ***(G-11297)***
Unisorb Installation Tech, Michigan Center *Also called Unisorb Inc* ***(G-11297)***
Unist Inc (PA) 616 949-0853
4134 36th St Se Grand Rapids (49512) ***(G-7297)***
Unistrut Diversified Products, Wayne *Also called Unistrut International Corp* ***(G-18240)***
Unistrut International Corp 734 721-4040
4205 Elizabeth St Wayne (48184) ***(G-18240)***
Unit City Wigs LLC 313 264-8112
24836 Dale Ave Eastpointe (48021) ***(G-4946)***
Unit Step Company Inc 989 684-9361
3788 S Huron Rd Bay City (48706) ***(G-1408)***
United Abrasive Inc (PA) 906 563-9249
19100 Industrial Dr Vulcan (49892) ***(G-17616)***
United Brass Manufacturers Inc (PA) 734 941-0700
35030 Goddard Rd Romulus (48174) ***(G-14334)***
United Brass Manufacturers Inc 734 942-9224
39000 W Huron River Dr Romulus (48174) ***(G-14335)***
United Dowel Pin Mfg Co, Fraser *Also called United Sttes Scket Screw Mfg C* ***(G-6009)***
United Engineered Tooling 231 947-3650
1974 Cass Hartman Ct Traverse City (49685) ***(G-16872)***
United Fabricating Company 248 887-7289
160 N Saint John Rd Highland (48357) ***(G-7901)***
United Fabrications, Livonia *Also called J & J United Industries LLC* ***(G-10252)***
United Fbrcnts Strainrite Corp 800 487-3136
481 N Saginaw St Ste A Pontiac (48342) ***(G-13422)***
United Foam Products, Grand Rapids *Also called Ufp Technologies Inc* ***(G-7294)***
United For Srvval St Jsphs Rcy 269 983-3820
2215 Wilson Ct Saint Joseph (49085) ***(G-14969)***
United Global Sourcing Inc (PA) 248 952-5700
675 E Big Beaver Rd # 211 Troy (48083) ***(G-17412)***
United Kennel Club, Portage *Also called Ukc Liquidating Inc* ***(G-13628)***
United Lighting Standards Inc (PA) 586 774-5650
23171 Groesbeck Hwy Warren (48089) ***(G-18047)***
United Machining Inc (HQ) 586 323-4300
6300 18 1/2 Mile Rd Sterling Heights (48314) ***(G-16216)***
United Machining Inc 586 323-4300
51362 Quadrate Dr Macomb (48042) ***(G-10646)***
United Manufacturing Inc 616 738-8888
4150 Sunnyside Dr Holland (49424) ***(G-8233)***
United Metal Products, Detroit *Also called A & R Specialty Services Corp* ***(G-3971)***
United Metal Technology Inc 517 787-7940
144 W Monroe St Jackson (49202) ***(G-9029)***
United Mfg Netwrk Inc 586 321-7887
33717 Embassy St Chesterfield (48047) ***(G-2960)***
United Mill & Cabinet Company 734 482-1981
8842 Bunton Rd Willis (48191) ***(G-18588)***
United Paint & Chemical, Southfield *Also called Polymer Inc* ***(G-15677)***
United Paint and Chemical Corp 248 353-3035
24671 Telegraph Rd Southfield (48033) ***(G-15732)***
United Precision Pdts Co Inc 313 292-0100
25040 Van Born Rd Dearborn Heights (48125) ***(G-3943)***
United Resin Inc (PA) 800 521-4757
4359 Normandy Ct Royal Oak (48073) ***(G-14587)***
United Shield Intl LLC 231 933-1179
1462 International Dr Traverse City (49686) ***(G-16873)***
United Sign Co 616 642-0200
6983 Bluewater Hwy Saranac (48881) ***(G-15082)***
United States Gypsum Company 269 384-6335
320 N Farmer St Otsego (49078) ***(G-12801)***
United States Gypsum Company 313 624-4232
10090 W Jefferson Ave River Rouge (48218) ***(G-13861)***
United States Gypsum Company 313 842-4455
10090 W Jefferson Ave Detroit (48218) ***(G-4653)***
United States Ski Pole Company, Cheboygan *Also called Liebner Enterprises LLC* ***(G-2791)***
United Sttes Scket Screw Mfg C (PA) 586 469-8811
33891 Doreka Fraser (48026) ***(G-6009)***
United Systems 248 583-9670
525 Elmwood Dr Troy (48083) ***(G-17413)***
United Systems Group LLC (PA) 810 227-4567
2111 Euler Rd Brighton (48114) ***(G-2090)***
United Testing Systems 989 494-3664
15105 Restwood Dr Linden (48451) ***(G-10072)***
United Tool, Traverse City *Also called United Engineered Tooling* ***(G-16872)***
Universal / Devlieg Inc 989 752-3077
1270 Agricola Dr Saginaw (48604) ***(G-14784)***
Universal Brick System, Charlotte *Also called K-Tel Corporation* ***(G-2760)***
Universal Coating Inc 810 785-7555
5204 Energy Dr Flint (48505) ***(G-5788)***
Universal Coating Technology 616 847-6036
16891 Johnson St Ste A Grand Haven (49417) ***(G-6375)***
Universal Container Corp 248 543-2788
10750 Galaxie Ave Ferndale (48220) ***(G-5594)***
Universal Fabricators Inc 248 399-7565
25855 Commerce Dr Madison Heights (48071) ***(G-10853)***
Universal Flow Monitors Inc (PA) 248 542-9635
1755 E 9 Mile Rd Hazel Park (48030) ***(G-7845)***
Universal Forest Products, Grand Rapids *Also called Ufp Industries Inc* ***(G-7289)***
Universal Forest Products, Lansing *Also called Ufp Lansing LLC* ***(G-9795)***
Universal Forest Products, Grand Rapids *Also called Ufp Eastern Division Inc* ***(G-7287)***
Universal Handling Eqpt, Owosso *Also called Universal Hdlg Eqp Owosso LLC* ***(G-12865)***
Universal Hdlg Eqp Owosso LLC 989 720-1650
1650 Industrial Dr Owosso (48867) ***(G-12865)***
Universal Induction Inc 269 983-5543
207 Hawthorne Ave Ste 2 Saint Joseph (49085) ***(G-14970)***
Universal Induction Inc 269 925-9890
352 W Britain Ave Benton Harbor (49022) ***(G-1595)***
Universal Industries Inco 248 259-2674
16115 Violet Dr Macomb (48042) ***(G-10647)***
Universal Laundry Machinery, Westland *Also called Kah* ***(G-18390)***
Universal Led, Detroit *Also called Lighting Enterprises Inc* ***(G-4399)***
Universal Load Banks, Wixom *Also called Ulb LLC* ***(G-18781)***
Universal Magnetics Inc 231 937-5555
5555 N Amy School Rd Howard City (49329) ***(G-8420)***
Universal Manufacturing Co 586 463-2560
43900 N Groesbeck Hwy Clinton Township (48036) ***(G-3383)***
Universal Print 989 525-5055
2758 E Fisher Rd Bay City (48706) ***(G-1409)***
Universal Printing Company Inc 989 671-9409
1200 Woodside Ave Bay City (48708) ***(G-1410)***
Universal Products Inc 231 937-5555
210 Rockford Park Dr Ne Rockford (49341) ***(G-14192)***
Universal Pultrusion 269 423-7068
860 S Williams St Decatur (49045) ***(G-3952)***
Universal Sftwr Solutions Inc 810 653-5000
1334 S Irish Rd Davison (48423) ***(G-3799)***
Universal Sign Inc 616 554-9999
5001 Falcon View Ave Se Grand Rapids (49512) ***(G-7298)***
Universal Spiral Air, Walker *Also called Krupp Industries LLC* ***(G-17643)***
Universal Spiral Air Npp 616 475-5905
2735 West River Dr Nw Grand Rapids (49544) ***(G-7299)***
Universal Sprial Air, Livonia *Also called Krupp Industries LLC* ***(G-10268)***
Universal Stamping Inc 269 925-5300
1570 Townline Rd Benton Harbor (49022) ***(G-1596)***
Universal Tl Eqp & Contrls Inc 586 268-4380
42409 Van Dyke Ave Sterling Heights (48314) ***(G-16217)***
Universal Tool Inc 248 733-9800
552 Robbins Dr Troy (48083) ***(G-17414)***
Universal Tube Inc 248 853-5100
2607 Bond St Rochester Hills (48309) ***(G-14137)***
Universal Warranty Corpor 248 263-6900
300 Galleria Officentre Southfield (48034) ***(G-15733)***
Universal/Devlieg LLC 989 752-7700
1270 Agricola Dr Saginaw (48604) ***(G-14785)***
University Communications, Allendale *Also called Grand Valley State University* ***(G-219)***
University Michigan Software, Ann Arbor *Also called Regents of The University Mich* ***(G-637)***
University Plastics Inc 734 668-8773
7150 Jackson Rd Ann Arbor (48103) ***(G-706)***
Univesity Michigan-Dearborn 313 593-5428
4901 Evergreen Rd # 2130 Dearborn (48128) ***(G-3906)***
Unknown, Byron Center *Also called Nike Inc* ***(G-2289)***
Unlimited Marine Inc 248 249-0222
7775 Highland Rd White Lake (48383) ***(G-18470)***
Unypos Manufacturing Inc 810 701-8719
6203 Westview Dr Grand Blanc (48439) ***(G-6265)***
Unytrex Inc 810 796-9074
5901 Dryden Rd Dryden (48428) ***(G-4808)***
Up Catholic Newspaper 906 226-8821
347 Rock St Marquette (49855) ***(G-11046)***
UP Lure Company LLC 906 249-3526
209 Jean St Marquette (49855) ***(G-11047)***
Up North Sign LLC 231 838-6328
7726 Lake St Alanson (49706) ***(G-112)***
UP Seal-Coating 906 283-3433
2521w Quarry Rd Gulliver (49840) ***(G-7579)***
Up To Date Painting, Millington *Also called Home Style Co* ***(G-11501)***
UP Truck Center Inc 906 774-0098
4920 Menominee St Quinnesec (49876) ***(G-13677)***

ALPHABETIC

Upcycle Polymers LLC....248 446-8750
1145 Sutton St Howell (48843) *(G-8537)*
UPF Group PLC, Flint *Also called UPF Inc (G-5789)*
UPF Inc....810 768-0001
2851 James P Cole Blvd Flint (48505) *(G-5789)*
Upper Michigan Newspapers LLC....989 732-5125
1966 S Otsego Ave Gaylord (49735) *(G-6165)*
Upper Peninsula Con Pipe Co (PA)....906 786-0934
6480 Us Hwy 2 Escanaba (49829) *(G-5103)*
Upper Peninsula Rubber Co Inc....906 786-0460
2101 N 19th St Bldg B Escanaba (49829) *(G-5104)*
Upper Pnnsula Pbls Athors Assn....906 226-1543
126 Ridgewood Dr Marquette (49855) *(G-11048)*
Upperhand Tack Co LLC....906 424-0401
2950 Burkley Rd Williamston (48895) *(G-18584)*
UPS Store 093, Farmington *Also called Software Assoc Inc (G-5151)*
UPS Stores , The, Eastpointe *Also called Crk Ltd (G-4933)*
Upston Associates Inc....269 349-2782
5 Minges Ln Battle Creek (49015) *(G-1308)*
Upton Furnace Division, Roseville *Also called Kolene Corporation (G-14430)*
Urban Aging L3c....313 204-5140
1905 Hyde Park Rd Detroit (48207) *(G-4654)*
Urban Specialty Apparel Inc....248 395-9500
29540 Southfield Rd # 102 Southfield (48076) *(G-15734)*
Urgent Design and Mfg Inc....810 245-1300
2547 Product Dr Lapeer (48446) *(G-9963)*
Urgent Design and Mfg Inc....810 245-1300
3142 John Conley Dr Lapeer (48446) *(G-9964)*
Urgent Plastic Services Inc (PA)....248 852-8999
2777 Product Dr Rochester Hills (48309) *(G-14138)*
Urgent Tool and Machine Inc....616 288-5000
625 Chestnut St Sw Grand Rapids (49503) *(G-7300)*
URS Energy & Construction Inc....989 642-4190
12334 Geddes Rd Hemlock (48626) *(G-7857)*
US Boring Inc....586 756-7511
24895 Mound Rd Ste D Warren (48091) *(G-18048)*
US Energia LLC....248 669-1462
400 Water St Ste 250 Rochester (48307) *(G-13936)*
US Engine Production MI Inc....989 823-3800
555 E Huron Ave Vassar (48768) *(G-17584)*
US Farathane LLC....248 754-7000
2700 High Meadow Cir Auburn Hills (48326) *(G-1072)*
US Farathane Holdings Corp....586 726-1200
38000 Mound Rd Sterling Heights (48310) *(G-16218)*
US Farathane Holdings Corp (PA)....248 754-7000
2700 High Meadow Cir Auburn Hills (48326) *(G-1073)*
US Farathane Holdings Corp....586 978-2800
750 W Maple Rd Troy (48084) *(G-17415)*
US Farathane Holdings Corp....248 754-7000
2133 Petit St Port Huron (48060) *(G-13536)*
US Farathane Holdings Corp....248 754-7000
11650 Park Ct Bldg B Shelby Township (48315) *(G-15360)*
US Farathane Holdings Corp....248 754-7000
325 W Silverbell Rd # 220 Lake Orion (48359) *(G-9636)*
US Farathane Holdings Corp....586 991-6922
6543 Arrow Dr Sterling Heights (48314) *(G-16219)*
US Farathane Holdings Corp....780 246-1034
1350 Harmon Rd Auburn Hills (48326) *(G-1074)*
US Farathane Holdings Corp....586 978-2800
39200 Ford Rd Westland (48185) *(G-18426)*
US Farathane Holdings Corp....586 685-4000
42155 Merrill Rd Sterling Heights (48314) *(G-16220)*
US Farathane Holdings Corp....586 726-1200
11650 Park Ct Shelby Township (48315) *(G-15361)*
US Farathane Holdings Corp....248 754-7000
4872 S Lapeer Rd Orion (48359) *(G-12739)*
US Farathane Merrill Plant, Sterling Heights *Also called US Farathane Holdings Corp (G-16220)*
US Gbc Wm....616 691-1340
12199 Hart St Ne Greenville (48838) *(G-7509)*
US Green Energy Solutions LLC....810 955-2992
9532 Harrison St Livonia (48150) *(G-10454)*
US Gypsum Co....313 842-5800
10090 W Jefferson Ave River Rouge (48218) *(G-13862)*
US Jack Company....269 925-7777
1125 Industrial Ct Benton Harbor (49022) *(G-1597)*
US Metals LLC....586 915-2885
11675 E 8 Mile Rd Warren (48089) *(G-18049)*
US Mold LLC....586 719-7239
608 E 10 Mile Rd Hazel Park (48030) *(G-7846)*
US Printers....906 639-3100
W4763 Okwood Rd 30 Daggett (49821) *(G-3754)*
US RAC....248 505-0413
28995 Telegraph Rd Southfield (48034) *(G-15735)*
US Salon Supply LLC....616 365-5790
760 S Kalamazoo St Paw Paw (49079) *(G-12958)*
US Suburban Press....616 662-6420
4675 32nd Ave Ste B Hudsonville (49426) *(G-8614)*
US Tarp Inc....269 639-3010
1425 Kalamazoo St South Haven (49090) *(G-15420)*
US Trade LLC....800 676-0208
29145 Warren Rd Garden City (48135) *(G-6114)*
US Wire Rope Supply Inc....313 925-0444
6555 Sherwood St Detroit (48211) *(G-4655)*
Us-Bingo.com, Ann Arbor *Also called Meteor Web Marketing Inc (G-570)*
USA Brngs Sup LLC DBA JSB Grea....734 222-4177
210 Little Lake Dr Ann Arbor (48103) *(G-707)*
USA Carbide....248 817-5137
1395 Wheaton Dr Ste 500 Troy (48083) *(G-17416)*
USA Custom Cabinet Inc....313 945-9796
5404 Maple St Dearborn (48126) *(G-3907)*
USA Health LLC (PA)....248 846-0575
9 Edgerton Ln Dearborn (48120) *(G-3908)*
USA Hq Michigan, Plymouth *Also called Varroc Lighting Systems Inc (G-13329)*
USA Quality Metal Finshg LLC....269 427-9000
67131 56th St Lawrence (49064) *(G-9986)*
USA Sign Frame & Stake Inc....616 662-9100
2150 Center Industrial Ct Jenison (49428) *(G-9075)*
USA Summit Plas Silao 1 LLC....269 324-9330
6715 S Sprinkle Rd Portage (49002) *(G-13630)*
USA Switch Inc (PA)....248 960-8500
49030 Pontiac Trl Ste 100 Wixom (48393) *(G-18782)*
USA Today, Detroit *Also called Gannett Stllite Info Ntwrk Inc (G-4251)*
USA Today Advertising....248 680-6530
2800 Livernois Rd Ste 630 Troy (48083) *(G-17417)*
Used Car News, Saint Clair Shores *Also called General Media LLC (G-14862)*
USF Delta Tooling LLC (HQ)....248 391-6800
1350 Harmon Rd Auburn Hills (48326) *(G-1075)*
USF Westland LLC....248 754-7000
2700 High Meadow Cir Auburn Hills (48326) *(G-1076)*
Usher Enterprises Inc....313 834-7055
9000 Roselawn St Detroit (48204) *(G-4656)*
Usher Logging LLC....906 238-4261
4423 Cty Rd 557 Arnold (49819) *(G-740)*
Usher Logging LLC....906 238-4261
14443 Sa Rd Cornell (49818) *(G-3703)*
Usher Oil Company, Detroit *Also called Usher Enterprises Inc (G-4656)*
Usher Tool & Die Inc....616 583-9160
1015 84th St Sw Byron Center (49315) *(G-2297)*
Usi Inc....248 583-9337
31302 Stephenson Hwy A Madison Heights (48071) *(G-10854)*
Usimaki Logging Inc....920 869-4183
12347 Arvidson Rd Baraga (49908) *(G-1149)*
Usm Holdings LLC....313 758-2000
1 Dauch Dr Detroit (48211) *(G-4657)*
Usm Holdings LLC II....313 758-2000
1 Dauch Dr Detroit (48211) *(G-4658)*
Usmats Inc....810 765-4545
6347 King Rd Marine City (48039) *(G-10968)*
Usmfg Inc (HQ)....262 993-9197
601 Abbot Rd East Lansing (48823) *(G-4914)*
Usui International Corporation (HQ)....734 354-3626
44780 Helm St Plymouth (48170) *(G-13328)*
Utec, Sterling Heights *Also called Universal Tl Eqp & Contrls Inc (G-16217)*
Utica Aerospace Inc....586 598-9300
26950 23 Mile Rd Chesterfield (48051) *(G-2961)*
Utica Body & Assembly Inc (HQ)....586 726-4330
5750 New King Dr Ste 200 Troy (48098) *(G-17418)*
Utica Enterprises Inc (PA)....586 726-4300
5750 New King Dr Ste 200 Troy (48098) *(G-17419)*
Utica International Inc (HQ)....586 726-4330
5750 New King Dr Ste 200 Troy (48098) *(G-17420)*
Utica Laeser Systems, Troy *Also called Utica Enterprises Inc (G-17419)*
Utica Products Inc....586 726-4300
5750 New King Dr Ste 200 Troy (48098) *(G-17421)*
Utica Steel Inc....586 949-1900
48000 Structural Dr Chesterfield (48051) *(G-2962)*
Utica Washers....313 571-1568
3105 Beaufait St Detroit (48207) *(G-4659)*
Utilitec, Troy *Also called Ancor Information MGT LLC (G-16936)*
Utility Supply and Cnstr Co (PA)....231 832-2297
420 S Roth St Ste A Reed City (49677) *(G-13802)*
Uusi LLC....231 832-5513
5000 Old Us Highway 131 Reed City (49677) *(G-13803)*
Uv Angel, Grand Haven *Also called Uv Partners Inc (G-6376)*
Uv Partners Inc (PA)....888 277-2596
233 Washington Ave Grand Haven (49417) *(G-6376)*
Uva Mare Inc....858 848-4440
12489 24 Mile Rd Shelby Township (48315) *(G-15362)*
Uvsheltron Inc....888 877-7946
1601 Valdosta Cir Pontiac (48340) *(G-13423)*
V & M Corporation (PA)....248 591-6580
313 E Hudson Ave Royal Oak (48067) *(G-14588)*
V & S Detroit Galvanizing LLC....313 535-2600
12600 Arnold Redford (48239) *(G-13782)*
V & T Painting LLC....248 497-1494
29585 Gramercy Ct Farmington Hills (48336) *(G-5407)*
V & V Inc....616 842-8611
1703 Eaton Dr Grand Haven (49417) *(G-6377)*

ALPHABETIC SECTION — Van-Mark Products Corporation

V & V Industries Inc 248 624-7943
48553 West Rd Wixom (48393) *(G-18783)*

V and F Transformer 248 328-6288
10703 W Braemar Holly (48442) *(G-8299)*

V D B, Holland *Also called John A Van Den Bosch Co (G-8101)*

V E S T Inc 248 649-9550
3250 W Big Beaver Rd # 440 Troy (48084) *(G-17422)*

V S America Inc 248 585-6715
1000 John R Rd Ste 111 Troy (48083) *(G-17423)*

V-Line Precision Products, Walled Lake *Also called Richardson Acqstions Group Inc (G-17674)*

V.P.M., Eastpointe *Also called Valade Precision Machining Inc (G-4947)*

V2soft Inc (PA) 248 904-1702
300 Enterprise Ct Bloomfield Hills (48302) *(G-1872)*

Vac-Met Inc 586 264-8100
7236 Murthum Ave Warren (48092) *(G-18050)*

Vachon Industries Inc (PA) 517 278-2354
580 Race St Coldwater (49036) *(G-3460)*

Vaclovers Inc 616 246-1700
3611 3 Mile Rd Nw Grand Rapids (49534) *(G-7301)*

Vacuum Farm Tools, Grand Rapids *Also called Parker Tooling & Design Inc (G-7071)*

Vacuum Orna Metal Company Inc 734 941-9100
11380 Harrison Romulus (48174) *(G-14336)*

Vaive Wood Products Co 586 949-4900
24935 21 Mile Rd Macomb (48042) *(G-10648)*

Val Manufacturing Co LLC 248 765-8694
4112 Marywood Dr Troy (48085) *(G-17424)*

Valade Precision Machining Inc 586 771-7705
17155 Stephens Dr Eastpointe (48021) *(G-4947)*

Valassis Communications Inc (HQ) 734 591-3000
19975 Victor Pkwy Livonia (48152) *(G-10455)*

Valassis Communications Inc 734 432-8000
38905 6 Mile Rd Livonia (48152) *(G-10456)*

Valassis International Inc (HQ) 734 591-3000
19975 Victor Pkwy Livonia (48152) *(G-10457)*

Valentine Distilling 248 629-9951
161 Vester St Ferndale (48220) *(G-5595)*

Valentine Distilling Co 646 286-2690
965 Wanda St Ferndale (48220) *(G-5596)*

Valeo Inc 248 619-8300
150 Stephenson Hwy Troy (48083) *(G-17425)*

Valeo Friction Materials Inc (HQ) 248 619-8300
150 Stephenson Hwy Troy (48083) *(G-17426)*

Valeo Inc Eng Coolg Auto Div, Auburn Hills *Also called Valeo North America Inc (G-1077)*

Valeo Interior Controls, Troy *Also called Valeo Inc (G-17425)*

Valeo Kapec North America Inc 248 619-8710
150 Stephenson Hwy Troy (48083) *(G-17427)*

Valeo North America Inc 248 209-8253
4100 N Atlantic Blvd Auburn Hills (48326) *(G-1077)*

Valeo North America Inc 248 619-8300
150 Stephenson Hwy Troy (48083) *(G-17428)*

Valeo North America Inc (HQ) 248 619-8300
150 Stephenson Hwy Troy (48083) *(G-17429)*

Valeo North America Inc 313 883-8850
12240 Oakland Pkwy Detroit (48203) *(G-4660)*

Valeo Radar Systems Inc 248 340-3126
3000 University Dr Auburn Hills (48326) *(G-1078)*

Valeo Radar Systems Inc (HQ) 248 619-8300
150 Stephenson Hwy Troy (48083) *(G-17430)*

Valeo Service Center, Troy *Also called Valeo North America Inc (G-17428)*

Valeo Switches & Dete (HQ) 248 619-8300
150 Stephenson Hwy Troy (48083) *(G-17431)*

Valeo Wiper Systems, Troy *Also called Valeo Friction Materials Inc (G-17426)*

Valeo Wiper Systems, Troy *Also called Valeo North America Inc (G-17429)*

Valiant Specialties Inc 248 656-1001
301 Hacker St Unit 3 Rochester Hills (48307) *(G-14139)*

Valley City Plating Company, Grand Rapids *Also called Martin and Hattie Rasche Inc (G-6962)*

Valley City Sign Company 616 784-5711
5009 West River Dr Ne Comstock Park (49321) *(G-3649)*

Valley Enterprises, Ubly *Also called Pepro Enterprises Inc (G-17479)*

Valley Enterprises Ubly Inc 989 269-6272
4175 N Ubly Rd Ubly (48475) *(G-17484)*

Valley Enterprises Ubly Inc (HQ) 989 658-3200
2147 Leppek Rd Ubly (48475) *(G-17485)*

Valley Gear and Machine Inc 989 269-8177
514 Chickory St Bad Axe (48413) *(G-1116)*

Valley Glass Co Inc 989 790-9342
2424 Midland Rd Saginaw (48603) *(G-14786)*

Valley Group of Companies 989 799-9669
548 Shattuck Rd Ste B Saginaw (48604) *(G-14787)*

Valley Manufacturing 248 767-5078
28525 Beck Rd Unit 108 Wixom (48393) *(G-18784)*

Valley Publishing 989 671-1200
3100 Walker Ridge Dr Nw Grand Rapids (49544) *(G-7302)*

Valley Services, Saginaw *Also called Valley Group of Companies (G-14787)*

Valley Steel Company 989 799-2600
1322 King St Saginaw (48602) *(G-14788)*

Valley Trck Parts-Grand Rapids, Grand Rapids *Also called Valley Truck Parts Inc (G-7303)*

Valley Truck Parts Inc (PA) 616 241-5431
1900 Chicago Dr Sw Grand Rapids (49519) *(G-7303)*

Valley Ventures Mapping LLC 989 879-5023
2555 Pinconning Rd Rhodes (48652) *(G-13823)*

Valmec Inc 810 629-8750
12487 Thornbury Dr Fenton (48430) *(G-5512)*

Valtec LLC 810 724-5048
565 S Cedar St Imlay City (48444) *(G-8649)*

Valuable Services LLC 512 667-7490
9290 Lee Rd Ste 106 Brighton (48116) *(G-2091)*

Valves D S S, Niles *Also called Dss Valve Products Inc (G-12126)*

Vamp Company, Brownstown Twp *Also called Vamp Screw Products Company (G-2161)*

Vamp Screw Products Company 734 676-8020
28055 Fort St Brownstown Twp (48183) *(G-2161)*

Van Beeks Custom Wood Products 616 583-9002
7950 Clyde Park Ave Sw Byron Center (49315) *(G-2298)*

Van Boven Incorporated 734 665-7228
326 S State St Ann Arbor (48104) *(G-708)*

Van Boven Clothing, Ann Arbor *Also called Van Boven Incorporated (G-708)*

Van Buren Publishing LLC 734 740-8668
557 Main St Belleville (48111) *(G-1492)*

Van Buren Steel, Belleville *Also called Very Best Steel LLC (G-1493)*

Van Daeles Inc 734 587-7165
8830 Ida Maybee Rd Monroe (48162) *(G-11588)*

Van Dam Iron Works LLC 616 452-8627
1813 Chicago Dr Sw Grand Rapids (49519) *(G-7304)*

Van Dam Marine Co 231 582-2323
970 E Division St Boyne City (49712) *(G-1905)*

Van Dam Wood Craft, Boyne City *Also called Van Dam Marine Co (G-1905)*

Van Dellen Steel Inc 616 698-9950
6945 Dtton Indus Pk Dr Se Caledonia (49316) *(G-2405)*

Van Duinen Forest Products 231 328-4507
4680 E Houghton Lake Rd Lake City (49651) *(G-9556)*

Van Dyken Mechanical Inc 616 224-7030
4275 Spartan Indus Dr Sw Grandville (49418) *(G-7422)*

Van Eck Diesel Services, Grand Rapids *Also called Creek Diesel Services Inc (G-6611)*

Van Emon Bruce 269 467-7803
501 S Clark St Centreville (49032) *(G-2699)*

Van Enk Woodcrafters LLC 616 931-0090
500 E Washington Ave # 50 Zeeland (49464) *(G-19086)*

Van F Belknap Company, Wixom *Also called Hank Thorn Co (G-18675)*

Van Heusen, West Branch *Also called Pvh Corp (G-18337)*

Van Heusen, Birch Run *Also called Pvh Corp (G-1713)*

Van Horn Bros Inc (PA) 248 623-4830
3700 Airport Rd Waterford (48329) *(G-18172)*

Van Horn Bros Inc 248 623-6000
3770 Airport Rd Waterford (48329) *(G-18173)*

Van Horn Concrete, Waterford *Also called Van Horn Bros Inc (G-18172)*

Van Horn Concrete, Waterford *Also called Van Horn Bros Inc (G-18173)*

Van Industries Inc 248 398-6990
1285 Wordsworth St Ferndale (48220) *(G-5597)*

Van Kam Inc 231 744-2658
1316 Whitehall Rd Muskegon (49445) *(G-11940)*

Van Kehrberg Vern 810 364-1066
914 Gratiot Blvd Ste 3 Marysville (48040) *(G-11111)*

Van Loon Industries Inc 586 532-8530
51583 Filomena Dr Shelby Township (48315) *(G-15363)*

Van Machine Co 269 729-9540
131 2nd St East Leroy (49051) *(G-4915)*

Van Pelt Corporation (PA) 313 365-3600
36155 Mound Rd Sterling Heights (48310) *(G-16221)*

Van Pelt Corporation 313 733-0073
13700 Sherwood St Detroit (48212) *(G-4661)*

Van Pelt Corporation 313 365-6500
13700 Sherwood St Ste 1 Detroit (48212) *(G-4662)*

Van Pelt Industries, Spring Lake *Also called Avpi Limited (G-15804)*

Van Pelt Industries LLC 616 842-1200
720 Taylor Ave Grand Haven (49417) *(G-6378)*

Van Rob Lansing, Lansing *Also called Van-Rob Inc (G-9747)*

Van Ron Steel Services LLC 616 813-6907
1100 Comstock St Marne (49435) *(G-11001)*

Van S Fabrications Inc 810 679-2115
4446 Peck Rd Croswell (48422) *(G-3738)*

Van Sloten Enterprises Inc (PA) 906 635-5151
1320 W 3 Mile Rd Sault Sainte Marie (49783) *(G-15102)*

Van Straten Brothers Inc 906 353-6490
14908 Us Highway 41 Baraga (49908) *(G-1150)*

Van Zee Acquisitions Inc 616 855-7000
4047 Eastern Ave Se Grand Rapids (49508) *(G-7305)*

Van Zee Corporation 616 245-9000
4047 Eastern Ave Se Grand Rapids (49508) *(G-7306)*

Van's Fabrications, Croswell *Also called Van S Fabrications Inc (G-3738)*

Van-Dies Engineering Inc 586 293-1430
17525 Helro Fraser (48026) *(G-6010)*

Van-Mark Products Corporation 248 478-1200
24145 Industrial Park Dr Farmington Hills (48335) *(G-5408)*

Van-Rob Inc 517 657-2450
  16325 Felton Rd Lansing (48906) *(G-9747)*
Van-Rob USA Holdings (HQ) 517 423-2400
  1200 E Chicago Blvd Tecumseh (49286) *(G-16521)*
Vanaire Inc 906 428-4656
  840 Clark Dr Gladstone (49837) *(G-6187)*
Vancho Tool and Engineering, Sterling Heights Also called Vince Krstevski *(G-16224)*
Vanco Steel Inc 810 688-4333
  6573 Bernie Kohler Dr North Branch (48461) *(G-12184)*
Vandco Incorporated 906 482-1550
  200 Hancock St Hancock (49930) *(G-7623)*
Vandelay Services LLC 810 279-8550
  10051 E Highland Rd Howell (48843) *(G-8538)*
Vander Mill LLC 616 259-8828
  505 Ball Ave Ne Grand Rapids (49503) *(G-7307)*
Vander Wall Bros, Spring Lake Also called Ludvanwall Inc *(G-15830)*
Vandervest Electric Mtr & Fabg 231 843-6196
  5635 W Dewey Rd Ludington (49431) *(G-10555)*
Vanermen Smith Products Inc 517 575-6618
  319 E North St Lansing (48906) *(G-9748)*
Vanerum Stelter, Grand Rapids Also called Mooreco Inc *(G-7028)*
Vanex Mold Inc 616 662-4100
  2240 Pine Ridge Dr Sw Jenison (49428) *(G-9076)*
Vanguard Publications Inc 517 336-1600
  2807 Jolly Rd Ste 360 Okemos (48864) *(G-12692)*
Vanishing Point Lures 260 316-7768
  232 E Grant St Bronson (49028) *(G-2121)*
Vankam Trailer Sales & Mfg, Muskegon Also called Van Kam Inc *(G-11940)*
Vanmeer Corporation 269 694-6090
  1754 106th Ave Otsego (49078) *(G-12802)*
Vanroth LLC 734 929-5268
  401 S Maple Rd Ann Arbor (48103) *(G-709)*
Vans Pattern Corp 616 364-9483
  11970 24th Ave Marne (49435) *(G-11002)*
Vantage Plastics, Standish Also called Airpark Plastics LLC *(G-15886)*
Vantage Plastics, Standish Also called PRA Company *(G-15895)*
Vantage Point Mfg Inc 989 343-1070
  614 Parkway Dr West Branch (48661) *(G-18345)*
Varatech Inc 616 393-6408
  1141 Ambertrace Ln Apt 8 Holland (49424) *(G-8234)*
Varco Precision Products Co 313 538-4300
  26935 W 7 Mile Rd Redford (48240) *(G-13783)*
Vargas & Sons 989 754-4636
  125 S Park Ave Saginaw (48607) *(G-14789)*
Vari-Data Co., Galesburg Also called Impact Label Corporation *(G-6079)*
Variety Die & Stamping Co 734 426-4488
  2221 Bishop Cir E Dexter (48130) *(G-4761)*
Variety Foods Inc (PA) 586 268-4900
  7001 Chicago Rd Warren (48092) *(G-18051)*
Varn International Inc 734 781-4600
  17177 N Laurel Park Dr # 300 Livonia (48152) *(G-10458)*
Varners Pwr Coating & Sndblst 517 448-3425
  14935 Hemlock St Hudson (49247) *(G-8563)*
Varneys Fab & Weld LLC 231 865-6856
  5967 Maple Island Rd Nunica (49448) *(G-12589)*
Varroc Lighting Systems Inc (HQ) 734 446-4400
  47828 Halyard Dr Plymouth (48170) *(G-13329)*
Varsity Monthly Thumb 810 404-5297
  251 N State St Caro (48723) *(G-2585)*
Vast Production Services Inc 248 838-9680
  307 Robbins Dr Troy (48083) *(G-17432)*
Vaughan Industries Inc 313 935-2040
  8490 Lyndon St Detroit (48238) *(G-4663)*
Vaupell Midwest, Constantine Also called Vaupell Molding & Tooling Inc *(G-3677)*
Vaupell Molding & Tooling Inc 269 435-8414
  485 Florence Rd Constantine (49042) *(G-3677)*
Vb Chesaning LLC 989 323-2333
  624 Brady St Chesaning (48616) *(G-2831)*
Vci Inc (PA) 269 659-3676
  1500 Progress St Sturgis (49091) *(G-16328)*
Vconverter Corporation (PA) 248 388-0549
  43700 Gen Mar Novi (48375) *(G-12564)*
Vdl Steelweld Usa LLC 248 781-8141
  1095 Crooks Rd Ste 300 Troy (48084) *(G-17433)*
VDO Automotive, Auburn Hills Also called Continental Auto Systems Inc *(G-848)*
Vectech Pharmaceutical Cons (PA) 248 478-5820
  12501 Grand River Rd Brighton (48116) *(G-2092)*
Vector Distribution LLC 616 361-2021
  1642 Broadway Ave Nw Grand Rapids (49504) *(G-7308)*
Vector North America Inc 248 449-9290
  39500 Orchard Hill Pl Novi (48375) *(G-12565)*
Vectorall Manufacturing Inc 248 486-4570
  7675 Lochlin Dr Brighton (48116) *(G-2093)*
Veet Axelson Liberty Industry 586 776-3000
  14322 E 9 Mile Rd Warren (48089) *(G-18052)*
Veet Industries Inc 586 776-3000
  14322 E 9 Mile Rd Warren (48089) *(G-18053)*
Vegetable Growers News 616 887-9008
  343 S Union St Sparta (49345) *(G-15788)*

Vehicle Armor Systems, Wixom Also called 3M Technical Ceramics Inc *(G-18592)*
Vehicle Cy Wldg Fbrication LLC 810 836-2385
  2085 Diamond Ave Flint (48532) *(G-5790)*
Vehicle Research and Dev 586 504-1163
  3863 Van Dyke Rd Almont (48003) *(G-270)*
Vehicles, Southfield Also called Eaton Corporation *(G-15548)*
Vehma International Amer Inc 248 631-1100
  1807 E Maple Rd Troy (48083) *(G-17434)*
Vehma International Amer Inc 248 585-4800
  1230 Chicago Rd Troy (48083) *(G-17435)*
Vehma International Amer Inc (HQ) 248 631-2800
  750 Tower Dr 4000 Troy (48098) *(G-17436)*
Veigel North America LLC 586 843-3816
  51277 Celeste Shelby Township (48315) *(G-15364)*
Veit Tool & Gage Inc 810 658-4949
  303 S Dayton St Davison (48423) *(G-3800)*
Vel-Kal Manufacturing Inc 269 344-1204
  283 Vanbruggen St Galesburg (49053) *(G-6086)*
Vela Sciences, Pinckney Also called SPD America LLC *(G-13056)*
Velcro USA Inc 248 583-6060
  1210 Souter Dr Troy (48083) *(G-17437)*
Veldheer Tulip Garden Inc 616 399-1900
  12755 Quincy St Holland (49424) *(G-8235)*
Velesco Phrm Svcs Inc 734 545-0696
  28036 Oakland Oaks Ct Wixom (48393) *(G-18785)*
Velesco Phrm Svcs Inc (HQ) 734 274-9877
  46701 Commerce Center Dr Plymouth (48170) *(G-13330)*
Velocity USA, Grand Rapids Also called Velocity Worldwide Inc *(G-7309)*
Velocity Worldwide Inc 616 243-3400
  2280 29th St Se Grand Rapids (49508) *(G-7309)*
Veltri Tooling Company, Warren Also called Flex-N-Gate Michigan LLC *(G-17812)*
Venchurs Inc 517 263-8937
  800 Liberty St Adrian (49221) *(G-100)*
Venchurs Packaging, Adrian Also called Venchurs Inc *(G-100)*
Vendor Ventures, Detroit Also called Diop Collection LLC *(G-4178)*
Venetian Cabinets 586 580-3288
  14293 23 Mile Rd Shelby Township (48315) *(G-15365)*
Venntis Technologies LLC 616 395-8254
  1261 S Waverly Rd Holland (49423) *(G-8236)*
Vent-Rite Valve Corp 269 925-8812
  1875 Dewey Ave Benton Harbor (49022) *(G-1598)*
Ventcon Inc 313 336-4000
  500 Enterprise Dr Allen Park (48101) *(G-209)*
Ventech, Wixom Also called Puritan Automation LLC *(G-18737)*
Ventilation + Plus Eqp Inc 231 487-1156
  670 W Conway Rd 1 Harbor Springs (49740) *(G-7661)*
Ventower Industries, Monroe Also called Great Lakes Towers LLC *(G-11545)*
Ventra Evart LLC 231 734-9000
  601 W 7th St Evart (49631) *(G-5128)*
Ventra Fowlerville LLC 517 223-5900
  8887 W Grand River Rd Fowlerville (48836) *(G-5857)*
Ventra Grand Rapids 5 LLC 616 222-3296
  3075 Breton Rd Se Grand Rapids (49512) *(G-7310)*
Ventra Greenwich Holdings Corp 586 759-8900
  5663 E 9 Mile Rd Warren (48091) *(G-18054)*
Ventra Greenwich Tooling Co, Warren Also called Ventra Greenwich Holdings Corp *(G-18054)*
Ventra Ionia Main LLC (HQ) 616 597-3220
  14 Beardsley St Ionia (48846) *(G-8693)*
Ventra Plastics, Warren Also called Flex-N-Gate LLC *(G-17809)*
Ventuor LLC 248 790-8700
  336 W 1st St Ste 113 Flint (48502) *(G-5791)*
Ventura Aerospace LLC 734 357-0114
  51170 Grand River Ave A Wixom (48393) *(G-18786)*
Ventura Industries Inc 734 357-0114
  46301 Port St Plymouth (48170) *(G-13331)*
Ventura Manufacturing Inc 616 772-7405
  551 Case Karsten Dr Zeeland (49464) *(G-19087)*
Ventura Manufacturing Inc (PA) 616 772-7405
  471 E Roosevelt Ave # 100 Zeeland (49464) *(G-19088)*
Venture Grafix LLC 248 449-1330
  47757 West Rd Ste C-105 Wixom (48393) *(G-18787)*
Venture Label Inc 313 928-2545
  3380 Baseline Rd Detroit (48231) *(G-4664)*
Venture Manufacturing Inc 269 429-6337
  3542 Crestview Rd Saint Joseph (49085) *(G-14971)*
Venture Technology Groups Inc (PA) 248 473-8450
  24300 Catherine Industria Novi (48375) *(G-12566)*
Venture Tool & Metalizing 989 883-9121
  42 E Main St Sebewaing (48759) *(G-15146)*
Venture Woodworks 616 262-1930
  349 Scott Ave Nw Grand Rapids (49504) *(G-7311)*
Venturedyne Ltd 616 392-6550
  836 Brooks Ave Holland (49423) *(G-8237)*
Veoneer Inc (PA) 248 223-0600
  26360 American Dr Southfield (48034) *(G-15736)*
Veoneer Southfield, Southfield Also called Veoneer Us Inc *(G-15738)*

Veoneer Us Inc (HQ)....248 223-8074
26360 American Dr Southfield (48034) ***(G-15737)***
Veoneer Us Inc....248 223-0600
26360 American Dr Southfield (48034) ***(G-15738)***
Verbio North America Corp (PA)....866 306-4777
17199 N Laurel Park Dr # 409 Livonia (48152) ***(G-10459)***
Verdoni Productions Inc....989 790-0845
5090 Overhill Dr Saginaw (48603) ***(G-14790)***
Verduyn Tarps Detroit Inc....313 270-4890
19231 W Davison St Detroit (48223) ***(G-4665)***
Vergason Technology Inc....248 568-0120
1672 Stony Creek Dr Rochester (48307) ***(G-13937)***
Verimation Technology Inc....248 471-0000
23883 Industrial Park Dr Farmington Hills (48335) ***(G-5409)***
Verishow....212 913-0600
5640 W Maple Rd Ste 101 West Bloomfield (48322) ***(G-18322)***
Veritas USA Corporation....248 374-5019
39555 Orchard Hill Pl # 600 Novi (48375) ***(G-12567)***
Veritas Vineyard LLC (PA)....517 962-2427
117 W Louis Glick Hwy Jackson (49201) ***(G-9030)***
Verndale Products Inc....313 834-4190
8445 Lyndon St Detroit (48238) ***(G-4666)***
Verns Threedprinting....810 564-5184
3336 Leta Ave Burton (48529) ***(G-2250)***
Veronica K LLC....248 251-5144
24204 Lotus Dr Apt 101 Clinton Township (48036) ***(G-3384)***
Versa Handling Co (PA)....313 491-0500
35700 Stanley Dr Sterling Heights (48312) ***(G-16222)***
Versa Tech Technologies, Roseville *Also called Versi-Tech Incorporated* ***(G-14490)***
Versa-Craft Inc....586 465-5999
35117 Automation Dr Clinton Township (48035) ***(G-3385)***
Versacut Industries, Jonesville *Also called Tiller Tool and Die Inc* ***(G-9104)***
Versah LLC....844 711-5585
2000 Spring Arbor Rd B Jackson (49203) ***(G-9031)***
Versant Med Physics Rdtion SFE....888 316-3644
119 N Church St Ste 201 Kalamazoo (49007) ***(G-9361)***
Versatile Fabrication Co Inc....231 739-7115
2708 9th St Muskegon (49444) ***(G-11941)***
Versatile Stair System....269 983-5437
1111 Orchard Ave Saint Joseph (49085) ***(G-14972)***
Versatile Systems LLC....734 397-3957
8347 Ronda Dr Canton (48187) ***(G-2537)***
Versatility Inc....616 957-5555
2610 Berwyck Rd Se Grand Rapids (49506) ***(G-7312)***
Versatranz, Plymouth *Also called Designshirtscom Inc* ***(G-13155)***
Versatube Corporation....248 524-0299
4755 Rochester Rd Ste 200 Troy (48085) ***(G-17438)***
Verse Chocolate LLC....816 325-0208
180 E 40th St Ste 400 Holland (49423) ***(G-8238)***
Versi-Tech Incorporated....586 944-2230
29901 Calahan Rd Roseville (48066) ***(G-14490)***
Versicor LLC....734 306-9137
333 W 7th St Royal Oak (48067) ***(G-14589)***
Verso Corporation....906 786-1660
7100 County 426 M.5 Rd Escanaba (49829) ***(G-5105)***
Verso Paper Holding LLC....906 779-3200
W6791 Us Highway 2 Quinnesec (49876) ***(G-13678)***
Verso Quinnesec LLC....877 447-2737
W6791 Us Highway 2 Quinnesec (49876) ***(G-13679)***
Verso Quinnesec Rep LLC....906 779-3200
W6705 Us Highway 2 Quinnesec (49876) ***(G-13680)***
Verso Services Inc....734 368-0989
4676 Freedom Dr Ann Arbor (48108) ***(G-710)***
Verstar Group Inc (PA)....586 465-5033
50305 Patricia St Chesterfield (48051) ***(G-2963)***
Verstraete Conveyability Inc....800 798-0410
2889 Northridge Dr Nw Grand Rapids (49544) ***(G-7313)***
Vertellus Hlth Spclty Pdts LLC....616 772-2193
215 N Centennial St Zeeland (49464) ***(G-19089)***
Vertellus LLC....616 772-2193
215 N Centennial St Zeeland (49464) ***(G-19090)***
Vertellus Specialty Materials, Zeeland *Also called Vertellus Hlth Spclty Pdts LLC* ***(G-19089)***
Vertellus Zeeland, Zeeland *Also called Vertellus LLC* ***(G-19090)***
Vertex Industries Inc....248 838-1827
15080 N Commerce Dr Dearborn (48120) ***(G-3909)***
Vertex Steel Inc....248 684-4177
2175 Fyke Dr Milford (48381) ***(G-11496)***
Vertical Detroit....313 732-9463
1538 Centre St Detroit (48226) ***(G-4667)***
Vertical Machining Services....734 462-1800
37637 Schoolcraft Rd D Livonia (48150) ***(G-10460)***
Vertical Technologies LLC....586 619-0141
12901 Stephens Rd Warren (48089) ***(G-18055)***
Vertical Vics, Mount Clemens *Also called Detroit Custom Services Inc* ***(G-11636)***
Vertical Wrks Blinds & Drapery....586 992-2600
57597 Suffield Dr Washington (48094) ***(G-18090)***
Verticalscope USA Inc....248 220-1451
3290 W Big Beavr Rd # 500 Troy (48084) ***(G-17439)***
Vertigee Corporation....313 999-1020
1722 Wildwood Trl Saline (48176) ***(G-15043)***
Very Best Motors LLC....517 253-0707
5131 N Grand River Ave Lansing (48906) ***(G-9749)***
Very Best Steel LLC....734 697-8609
327 Davis St Belleville (48111) ***(G-1493)***
Veteran Liquids LLC....586 698-2100
318 Bourbon Ct Rochester Hills (48307) ***(G-14140)***
Veterans Utility Services LLC....888 878-4191
120 N Washington Sq # 300 Lansing (48933) ***(G-9901)***
Vetionx, Grand Rapids *Also called Ionxhealth Inc* ***(G-6852)***
Vetionx, Grand Rapids *Also called Hello Life Inc* ***(G-6809)***
Vets Access LLC....810 639-2222
1449 E Pierson Rd Ste B Flushing (48433) ***(G-5815)***
Vexa Group LLC....734 330-8858
52500 Grand River Ave Wixom (48393) ***(G-18788)***
Vg Kids....734 480-0667
815 W Michigan Ave Ypsilanti (48197) ***(G-18983)***
Vgage LLC....248 589-7455
13250 Northend Ave Oak Park (48237) ***(G-12648)***
Vgkids Inc....734 485-5128
884 Railroad St Ste C Ypsilanti (48197) ***(G-18984)***
Vhb-123 Corporation....248 623-4830
3770 Airport Rd Waterford (48329) ***(G-18174)***
Vi-Chem Corp....616 247-8501
55 Cottage Grove St Sw Grand Rapids (49507) ***(G-7314)***
Via-Tech Corp....989 358-7028
11715 M 32 W Lachine (49753) ***(G-9535)***
Viant Medical LLC....616 643-5200
620 Watson St Sw Grand Rapids (49504) ***(G-7315)***
Viaus Super Market....906 786-1950
1519 Sheridan Rd Escanaba (49829) ***(G-5106)***
Vibracoustic North America LP....248 410-5066
32605 W 12 Mile Rd # 350 Farmington Hills (48334) ***(G-5410)***
Vibracoustic North America LP (HQ)....269 637-2116
400 Aylworth Ave South Haven (49090) ***(G-15421)***
Vibracoustic Usa Inc....734 254-9140
15701 Centennial Dr Northville (48168) ***(G-12269)***
Vibracoustic Usa Inc (HQ)....269 637-2116
400 Aylworth Ave South Haven (49090) ***(G-15422)***
Vibracoustic Usa Inc....810 648-2100
180 Dawson St Sandusky (48471) ***(G-15070)***
Vibracoustic Usa Inc....810 648-2100
370 Industrial St Sandusky (48471) ***(G-15071)***
Vibration Controls Tech LLC....248 822-8010
2075 W Big Beaver Rd # 500 Troy (48084) ***(G-17440)***
Vibration Research Corporation....616 669-3028
1294 Chicago Dr Jenison (49428) ***(G-9077)***
Vickers Engineering Inc....269 756-9133
16860 Three Oaks Rd Three Oaks (49128) ***(G-16561)***
Vickers Engineering Inc....269 426-8545
3604 Glendora Rd New Troy (49119) ***(G-12076)***
Vickeryville Lumber Co LLC....989 261-3100
7042 S Vickeryville Rd Sheridan (48884) ***(G-15385)***
Vico Company....734 453-3777
41555 Ann Arbor Rd E Plymouth (48170) ***(G-13332)***
Vico Louisville LLC....502 245-1616
41555 Ann Arbor Rd E Plymouth (48170) ***(G-13333)***
Vico Products Co (PA)....734 453-3777
41555 Ann Arbor Rd E Plymouth (48170) ***(G-13334)***
Vicrodesigns Global LLC....616 307-3701
6026 Kalamazoo Ave Se Grand Rapids (49508) ***(G-7316)***
Victor Screw Products Co....269 489-2760
235 S 4th St Burr Oak (49030) ***(G-2214)***
Victora Usa Inc....810 798-0253
3776 Van Dyke Rd Almont (48003) ***(G-271)***
Victoria Tool & Machine Div, Warren *Also called Jordan Tool Corporation* ***(G-17889)***
Videka LLC....269 353-5536
4717 Campus Dr Ste 1500 Kalamazoo (49008) ***(G-9362)***
Video Service Center, Livonia *Also called P M Z Technology Inc* ***(G-10356)***
Vidon Plastics Inc....810 667-0634
3171 John Conley Dr Lapeer (48446) ***(G-9965)***
Vierson Boiler & Repair Co....616 949-0500
3700 Patterson Ave Se Grand Rapids (49512) ***(G-7317)***
Vieth Consulting LLC....517 622-3090
209 S Bridge St Grand Ledge (48837) ***(G-6400)***
View Newspaper....734 697-8255
159 Main St Belleville (48111) ***(G-1494)***
View Publication Co....734 461-1579
5892 New Meadow Dr Ypsilanti (48197) ***(G-18985)***
View, The, Belleville *Also called Action Ad Newspapers Inc* ***(G-1478)***
Vigel North America Inc (HQ)....734 947-9900
32375 Howard Ave Madison Heights (48071) ***(G-10855)***
Viking Corporation (HQ)....269 945-9501
210 Industrial Park Dr Hastings (49058) ***(G-7811)***
Viking Fabrication Svcs LLC (HQ)....269 945-9501
210 Industrial Park Dr Hastings (49058) ***(G-7812)***
Viking Group Inc....616 831-6448
210 Industrial Park Dr Hastings (49058) ***(G-7813)***
Viking Group Inc (HQ)....616 432-6800
5150 Beltway Dr Se Caledonia (49316) ***(G-2406)***

Viking Industries Inc 734 421-5416
6012 Hubbard St Garden City (48135) ***(G-6115)***
Viking Laser LLC (PA) 586 200-5369
29900 Parkway Roseville (48066) ***(G-14491)***
Viking Oil LLC 989 366-4772
55 W Houghton Lake Dr Prudenville (48651) ***(G-13659)***
Viking Sales Inc 810 227-2222
169 Summit St Brighton (48116) ***(G-2094)***
Viking Spas Inc 616 248-7800
2725 Prairie St Sw Wyoming (49519) ***(G-18917)***
Viking Technologies Inc 586 914-0819
25169 Dequindre Rd Madison Heights (48071) ***(G-10856)***
Viking Tool & Engineering Inc 231 893-0031
2780 Colby Rd Whitehall (49461) ***(G-18511)***
Viladon Corporation 248 548-0043
10411 Capital St Oak Park (48237) ***(G-12649)***
Viladon Laboratories, Oak Park *Also called Viladon Corporation* ***(G-12649)***
Village & Cntry Wtr Trtmnt Inc (PA) 810 632-7880
2875 Old Us 23 Hartland (48353) ***(G-7773)***
Village Automatics Inc 269 663-8521
69576 Section St Edwardsburg (49112) ***(G-5020)***
Village Cabinet Shoppe Inc 586 264-6464
37975 Commerce Dr Sterling Heights (48312) ***(G-16223)***
Village Press Inc 231 946-3712
2779 Aero Park Dr Traverse City (49686) ***(G-16874)***
Village Printing & Supply Inc 810 664-2270
349 Mccormick Dr Lapeer (48446) ***(G-9966)***
Village Shop Inc 231 946-3712
2779 Aero Park Dr Traverse City (49686) ***(G-16875)***
Villagebees 810 217-2962
1688 Indian Rd Lapeer (48446) ***(G-9967)***
Villanuevo Soledad 989 770-4309
2855 E Burt Rd Burt (48417) ***(G-2216)***
Vimax Publishing 248 563-2367
600 Ridge Rd Bloomfield Hills (48302) ***(G-1873)***
Vin-Lee-Ron Meat Packing LLC 574 353-1386
54501 Griffis Rd Cassopolis (49031) ***(G-2635)***
Vince Krstevski 586 739-7600
43450 Merrill Rd Sterling Heights (48314) ***(G-16224)***
Vine-N-Berry Wines 989 551-1616
3475 Stein Rd Bad Axe (48413) ***(G-1117)***
Vinette Boatworks, Escanaba *Also called T D Vinette Company* ***(G-5102)***
Vinewood Metalcraft Inc 734 946-8733
9501 Inkster Rd Taylor (48180) ***(G-16486)***
Vineyard 2121 LLC 269 429-0555
2121 Kerlikowske Rd Benton Harbor (49022) ***(G-1599)***
Vineyard On Plainfield 616 570-0659
3418 Plainfield Ave Ne Grand Rapids (49525) ***(G-7318)***
Vineyard Press Inc 269 657-5080
125 E Michigan Ave Paw Paw (49079) ***(G-12959)***
Vineyard Ventures LLC 517 420-4771
1104 N Fairview Ave Lansing (48912) ***(G-9902)***
Vinifera, Rochester *Also called American Vintners LLC* ***(G-13891)***
Vintage Views Press 616 475-7662
959 Ogden Ave Se Grand Rapids (49506) ***(G-7319)***
Vintech Industries Inc (PA) 810 724-7400
611 Industrial Park Dr Imlay City (48444) ***(G-8650)***
Vintners Cellar Winery of Kal 269 342-9463
260 E Michigan Ave Kalamazoo (49007) ***(G-9363)***
Vinyl Graphix Inc 586 774-1188
24731 Harper Ave Saint Clair Shores (48080) ***(G-14890)***
Vinyl Sash of Flint Inc (PA) 810 234-4831
5433 Fenton Rd G Grand Blanc (48507) ***(G-6266)***
Vinyl Spectrum 616 591-3410
4727 Clyde Park Ave Sw # 6 Wyoming (49509) ***(G-18918)***
Vinyl Tech Window Systems Inc 248 634-8900
405 Cogshall St Holly (48442) ***(G-8300)***
Viper Tool Company LLC 734 417-9974
1310 Iroquois Pl Ann Arbor (48104) ***(G-711)***
Vira Clean LLC 313 455-1020
5860 N Canton Center Rd # 3 Canton (48187) ***(G-2538)***
Virgils Vineyard LLC 248 719-2808
27044 Hampstead Blvd Farmington Hills (48331) ***(G-5411)***
Viron International Corp (PA) 254 773-9292
505 N Hintz Rd Owosso (48867) ***(G-12866)***
Virotech Biomaterials Inc 313 421-1648
8260 Dartmouth Dr Warren (48093) ***(G-18056)***
Virtec Manufacturing LLC 313 590-2367
28302 Hayes Rd Roseville (48066) ***(G-14492)***
Virtual Advantage LLc 877 772-6886
3290 W Big Beavr Rd # 310 Troy (48084) ***(G-17441)***
Virtual Technology Inc 248 528-6565
1345 Wheaton Dr Troy (48083) ***(G-17442)***
Virtue Cider 269 455-0526
2180 62nd St Fennville (49408) ***(G-5444)***
Virtuoso Custom Creations LLC 313 332-1299
1111 Bellevue St Unit 201 Detroit (48207) ***(G-4668)***
Viscount Equipment Co Inc 586 293-5900
24443 John R Rd Hazel Park (48030) ***(G-7847)***
Visiocorp Holding USA LLP 810 388-2403
1855 Busha Hwy Marysville (48040) ***(G-11112)***
Vision Air 989 202-4100
5187 W Houghton Lake Dr Houghton Lake (48629) ***(G-8407)***
Vision Fuels LLC 586 997-3286
51969 Van Dyke Ave Shelby Township (48316) ***(G-15366)***
Vision Global Industries 248 390-5805
16041 Leone Dr Macomb (48042) ***(G-10649)***
Vision Quest Embroidery LLC 517 375-1518
4900 Preston Rd Howell (48855) ***(G-8539)***
Vision Solutions Inc 810 695-9569
4417 Brighton Dr Grand Blanc (48439) ***(G-6267)***
Visionary Cabinetry and Design 248 850-7178
429 S Main St Clawson (48017) ***(G-3111)***
Visionary Landscaping, Shelby Township *Also called Huntler Industries Inc* ***(G-15236)***
Visionary Vitamin Co 734 788-5934
3205 Mckitrick St Melvindale (48122) ***(G-11211)***
Visioncraft 586 949-6540
28161 Kehrig St Chesterfield (48047) ***(G-2964)***
Visioneering Inc (PA) 248 622-5600
2055 Taylor Rd Auburn Hills (48326) ***(G-1079)***
Visioneering Inc 248 622-5600
17085 Masonic Fraser (48026) ***(G-6011)***
Visionit Supplies and Svcs Inc 313 664-5650
3031 W Grand Blvd Ste 600 Detroit (48202) ***(G-4669)***
Visions Car & Truck Acc 269 342-2962
8250 Douglas Ave Kalamazoo (49009) ***(G-9364)***
Visor Frames LLC 586 864-6058
6400 Sterling Dr N Ste B Sterling Heights (48312) ***(G-16225)***
Visotek Inc 734 427-4800
25325 Regency Dr Novi (48375) ***(G-12568)***
Vista Manufacturing Inc 616 719-5520
3110 Wilson Dr Nw Walker (49534) ***(G-17656)***
Vistaprint 260 615-0027
645 Griswold St Detroit (48226) ***(G-4670)***
Visteon Corporation 734 718-8927
45004 Lothrop Ct Canton (48188) ***(G-2539)***
Visteon Corporation (PA) 734 627-7384
1 Village Center Dr Van Buren Twp (48111) ***(G-17558)***
Visteon Electronics Corp 800 847-8366
1 Village Center Dr Van Buren Twp (48111) ***(G-17559)***
Visteon Global Electronics Inc (HQ) 800 847-8366
1 Village Center Dr Van Buren Twp (48111) ***(G-17560)***
Visteon International Business, Van Buren Twp *Also called Visteon Intl Holdings Inc* ***(G-17561)***
Visteon Intl Holdings Inc (HQ) 734 710-2000
1 Village Center Dr Van Buren Twp (48111) ***(G-17561)***
Visteon Systems LLC 313 755-9500
5500 Auto Club Dr Dearborn (48126) ***(G-3910)***
Visteon Systems LLC (HQ) 800 847-8366
1 Village Center Dr Van Buren Twp (48111) ***(G-17562)***
Visual Chimera 586 585-1210
23082 Saxony Ave Eastpointe (48021) ***(G-4948)***
Visual Precision Inc 248 546-7984
111 E 10 Mile Rd Madison Heights (48071) ***(G-10857)***
Visual Productions Inc 248 356-4399
6305 W M 115 Mesick (49668) ***(G-11275)***
Visual Workplace Byron Ctr Inc 616 583-9400
7381 Ardith Ct Sw Ste A Byron Center (49315) ***(G-2299)***
Visual Workplace LLC 616 583-9400
1300 Richfield Ct Sw Byron Center (49315) ***(G-2300)***
Vita Talalay 425 214-4732
2885 Sanford Ave Sw # 26440 Grandville (49418) ***(G-7423)***
Vital Concepts Inc 616 954-2890
5090 Kendrick Ct Se Grand Rapids (49512) ***(G-7320)***
Vital Signs Inc (PA) 313 491-2010
6753 Kings Mill Dr Canton (48187) ***(G-2540)***
Vitanorth USA LLC 734 595-4000
38309 Abruzzi Dr Westland (48185) ***(G-18427)***
Vitec LLC 313 633-2254
2801 Clark St Detroit (48210) ***(G-4671)***
Vitesco Technologies Usa LLC 313 583-5980
15001 N Commerce Dr Dearborn (48120) ***(G-3911)***
Vitesco Technologies Usa LLC (HQ) 248 209-4000
2400 Executive Hills Dr Auburn Hills (48326) ***(G-1080)***
Vitullo & Associates, Commerce Township *Also called Manufctring Solutions Tech LLC* ***(G-3552)***
Viva Beverages LLC 248 746-7044
27777 Franklin Rd # 1640 Southfield (48034) ***(G-15739)***
Viva Salon Nouvelle LLC 947 800-9115
16221 Grand River Ave Detroit (48227) ***(G-4672)***
Viva Zen Sales LLC 248 481-3605
1139 Centre Rd Auburn Hills (48326) ***(G-1081)***
Vivatar Inc 616 928-0750
935 E 40th St Holland (49423) ***(G-8239)***
Vivian Enterprises LLC 248 792-9925
29111 Telegraph Rd Southfield (48034) ***(G-15740)***
Vivica Miller LLC 313 434-3280
15466 Stansbury St Detroit (48227) ***(G-4673)***

Vivid Publishing....614 282-6479
1519 Stewart Rd Monroe (48162) *(G-11589)*
Vizcom Media, Grand Rapids *Also called Sourceone Imaging LLC (G-7204)*
Vn Industries Inc....616 540-2812
4635 40th St Se Grand Rapids (49512) *(G-7321)*
Vocational Strategies Inc....906 482-6142
23390 Airpark Blvd Calumet (49913) *(G-2415)*
Vochaska Engineering....269 637-5670
66935 County Road 388 South Haven (49090) *(G-15423)*
Voco America Inc....248 568-0964
280 Summer Shade Dr Howell (48843) *(G-8540)*
Vogel Engineering Inc....231 821-2125
6688 Maple Island Rd Holton (49425) *(G-8342)*
Voice Communications Corp (PA)....586 716-8100
6250 Metropolitan Pkwy Sterling Heights (48312) *(G-16226)*
Voice Newspapers, The, Sterling Heights *Also called Voice Communications Corp (G-16226)*
Voigt Schwtzer Galvanizers Inc....313 535-2600
12600 Arnold Redford (48239) *(G-13784)*
Voila Print Inc....866 942-1677
37000 Industrial Rd Livonia (48150) *(G-10461)*
Volcor Finishing Inc....616 527-5555
510 Apple Tree Dr Ionia (48846) *(G-8694)*
Volk Corporation....616 940-9900
455 E Cady St Northville (48167) *(G-12270)*
Volkswagen Auto Securitization, Auburn Hills *Also called Volkswagen Group America Inc (G-1082)*
Volkswagen Group, Auburn Hills *Also called Autombili Lamborghini Amer LLC (G-806)*
Volkswagen Group America Inc....248 754-5000
3800 Hamlin Rd Auburn Hills (48326) *(G-1082)*
Vollmer Ready-Mix Inc (PA)....989 453-2262
196 S Caseville Rd 204 Pigeon (48755) *(G-13042)*
Vollwerth & Co, Hancock *Also called Vandco Incorporated (G-7623)*
Volos Tube Form Inc....586 416-3600
50395 Corporate Dr Macomb (48044) *(G-10650)*
Vomela Specialty Company....269 927-6500
375 Urbandale Ave Benton Harbor (49022) *(G-1600)*
Von Weise LLC (HQ)....517 618-9763
402 Haven St Ste H Eaton Rapids (48827) *(G-4975)*
Voorheis Hausbeck Excavating....989 752-9666
2695 W Vassar Rd Reese (48757) *(G-13810)*
Vortec....616 292-2401
201 W Washington Ave # 110 Zeeland (49464) *(G-19091)*
Vortech Pharmaceutical Ltd....313 584-4088
6851 Chase Rd Dearborn (48126) *(G-3912)*
Vortek....248 767-2992
440 S Dexter St Pinckney (48169) *(G-13058)*
Vortex Industries Inc....855 867-8399
739 S Mill St Plymouth (48170) *(G-13335)*
Voss Steel, Taylor *Also called Pgp Corp (G-16457)*
Voxeljet America Inc....734 709-8237
41430 Haggerty Cir S Canton (48188) *(G-2541)*
Vp Demand Creation Services, Traverse City *Also called Village Press Inc (G-16874)*
VSI Archtectural Signs Systems, Canton *Also called Vital Signs Inc (G-2540)*
Vsp Logis Inc....734 957-9880
41873 Ecorse Rd Ste 200 Van Buren Twp (48111) *(G-17563)*
VSR Technologies Inc....734 425-7172
12270 Belden Ct Livonia (48150) *(G-10462)*
Vte Inc....231 539-8000
5437 Robinson Rd Pellston (49769) *(G-12968)*
Vtec Graphics Inc (PA)....734 953-9729
12487 Globe St Livonia (48150) *(G-10463)*
Vu Acquisitions LLC (PA)....248 269-0517
2151 Livernois Rd 200a Troy (48083) *(G-17443)*
Vu Manufacturing, Troy *Also called Vu Acquisitions LLC (G-17443)*
Vulcan Wood Products Inc....906 563-8995
N1549 Sturgeon Mill Rd Vulcan (49892) *(G-17617)*
Vvp Auto Glass Inc....734 727-5001
1515 S Newburgh Rd Westland (48186) *(G-18428)*
Vx-LLC....734 854-8700
8336 Monroe Rd Rm 201 Lambertville (48144) *(G-9655)*
W & S Development Inc....989 724-5463
4957 Main St Greenbush (48738) *(G-7473)*
W & W Tool and Die Inc....989 835-5522
1508 E Grove St Midland (48640) *(G-11421)*
W A Thomas Company....734 955-6500
25940 Northline Rd Taylor (48180) *(G-16487)*
W B Mason Co Inc....734 947-6370
25299 Brest Taylor (48180) *(G-16488)*
W Bay Cupcakes....231 632-2010
524 W Thirteenth St Traverse City (49684) *(G-16876)*
W G Benjey Inc (PA)....989 356-0016
2293 Werth Rd Alpena (49707) *(G-327)*
W G Benjey Inc....989 356-0027
108 E Herman St Alpena (49707) *(G-328)*
W G Benjey North, Alpena *Also called W G Benjey Inc (G-328)*
W H Green & Associates....616 682-5202
703 Cambridge Blvd Se Grand Rapids (49506) *(G-7322)*
W Industries, Livonia *Also called Tower Defense & Aerospace LLC (G-10439)*
W International LLC (PA)....248 577-0364
31720 Stephenson Hwy Madison Heights (48071) *(G-10858)*
W L Hamilton & Co....269 781-6941
325 Cherry St Marshall (49068) *(G-11077)*
W M H Fluidpower, Portage *Also called Wmh Fluidpower Inc (G-13634)*
W R Grace & Co-Conn....410 531-4000
1421 Kalamazoo St South Haven (49090) *(G-15424)*
W S Townsend Company (PA)....269 781-5131
106 E Oliver Dr Marshall (49068) *(G-11078)*
W S Townsend Company....517 393-7300
5320 S Pennsylvania Ave Lansing (48911) *(G-9903)*
W Soule & Co (PA)....269 324-7001
7125 S Sprinkle Rd Portage (49002) *(G-13631)*
W Soule & Co Service Group, Portage *Also called W Soule & Co (G-13631)*
W T & M Inc....313 533-7888
12635 Arnold Redford (48239) *(G-13785)*
W T Beresford Co....248 350-2900
26261 Evergreen Rd # 455 Southfield (48076) *(G-15741)*
W T C, Farmington Hills *Also called Nadex of America Corporation (G-5330)*
W T C, Farmington Hills *Also called Welding Technology Corp (G-5413)*
W T P, Coloma *Also called Witchcraft Tape Products Inc (G-3485)*
W Vbh....269 927-1527
78 W Wall St Benton Harbor (49022) *(G-1601)*
W W J Form Tool Company Inc....313 565-0015
26122 Michigan Ave Inkster (48141) *(G-8677)*
W W Thayne Advertising Cons....269 979-1411
4642 Capital Ave Sw Battle Creek (49015) *(G-1309)*
W W Williams Company LLC....313 584-6150
4000 Stecker St Dearborn (48126) *(G-3913)*
W-Lok Corporation....616 355-4015
861 Productions Pl Holland (49423) *(G-8240)*
W.A. Kates Company, The, Madison Heights *Also called Custom Valve Concepts Inc (G-10702)*
W.K. Kellogg Institute, Battle Creek *Also called Kellogg Company (G-1254)*
W2 Inc....517 764-3141
233 N Jackson St Jackson (49201) *(G-9032)*
W2fuel Adrian, Adrian *Also called Adrian Lva Biofuel LLC (G-48)*
W2fuel Adrian II, Adrian *Also called II Adrian LLC W2fuel (G-73)*
W2fuel Keokuk I, Adrian *Also called W2fuel LLC (G-101)*
W2fuel LLC (PA)....517 920-4868
1571 W Beecher Rd Adrian (49221) *(G-101)*
Waanders Concrete Co....269 673-6352
3169 Babylon Rd Allegan (49010) *(G-184)*
Wabco Air Comprsr Holdings Inc....248 260-9032
1220 Pacific Dr Auburn Hills (48326) *(G-1083)*
Wabco Expats Inc....248 260-9032
1220 Pacific Dr Auburn Hills (48326) *(G-1084)*
Wabco Group International Inc....248 260-9025
1220 Pacific Dr Auburn Hills (48326) *(G-1085)*
Wabco Holdings Inc (HQ)....248 260-9032
1220 Pacific Dr Auburn Hills (48326) *(G-1086)*
Waber Tool & Engineering Co....269 342-0765
1335 Ravine Rd Kalamazoo (49004) *(G-9365)*
Wachtel Tool & Broach Inc....586 758-0110
6676 Fred W Moore Hwy Saint Clair (48079) *(G-14844)*
Wacker Biochem Corporation....517 264-8500
3301 Sutton Rd Adrian (49221) *(G-102)*
Wacker Chemical Corporation (HQ)....517 264-8500
3301 Sutton Rd Adrian (49221) *(G-103)*
Wacker Chemical Corporation....734 882-4055
600 S Wagner Rd Ann Arbor (48103) *(G-712)*
Wacker Neuson Corporation....231 799-4500
1300 E Mount Garfield Rd Norton Shores (49441) *(G-12342)*
Wade Logging....231 463-0363
7108 W Sharon Rd Sw Fife Lake (49633) *(G-5609)*
Wade Printing & Publishing LLC....616 894-6350
2984 Gulliford Trl Lowell (49331) *(G-10521)*
Wagner Castings Company....248 952-2500
5445 Corporate Dr Ste 200 Troy (48098) *(G-17444)*
Wagon Automotive Inc....248 262-2020
28025 Oakland Oaks Ct Wixom (48393) *(G-18789)*
Wahmhoff Farms LLC....269 628-4308
11121 M 40 Gobles (49055) *(G-6220)*
Wahoo Composites LLC....734 424-0966
7190 Huron River Dr Dexter (48130) *(G-4762)*
Walbro LLC....989 872-2131
6242 Garfield Ave Cass City (48726) *(G-2622)*
Waldron's Exhaust, Centreville *Also called Waldrons Antique Exhaust (G-2700)*
Waldrons Antique Exhaust....269 467-7185
208 W Main St Centreville (49032) *(G-2700)*
Walker Printery Inc....248 548-5100
13351 Cloverdale St Oak Park (48237) *(G-12650)*
Walker Telecommunications....989 274-7384
1375 S Center Rd Saginaw (48638) *(G-14791)*
Walker Tool & Die Inc....616 453-5471
2411 Walker Ave Nw Grand Rapids (49544) *(G-7323)*
Walker Tool & Manufacturing, Redford *Also called W T & M Inc (G-13785)*

ALPHABETIC

Walker Wire (ispat) Inc....248 399-4800
42744 Mound Rd Sterling Heights (48314) ***(G-16227)***
Wall Co Incorporated (PA)....248 585-6400
101 W Girard Ave Madison Heights (48071) ***(G-10859)***
Wall Colmonoy Corporation (HQ)....248 585-6400
101 W Girard Ave Madison Heights (48071) ***(G-10860)***
Wall Pro Painting....248 632-8525
912 E 12 Mile Rd Royal Oak (48073) ***(G-14590)***
Wall Street Journal Gate A 20....734 941-4139
1 Detroit Metro Airport Detroit (48242) ***(G-4674)***
Wallace Publishing LLC....248 416-7259
1127 E Pearl Ave Hazel Park (48030) ***(G-7848)***
Wallace Stone Plant, Bay Port *Also called Falcon Trucking Company* ***(G-1414)***
Wallin Brothers Inc....734 525-7750
35270 Glendale St Ste 1 Livonia (48150) ***(G-10464)***
Wallis Diesel Welding....906 647-3245
479 W M 80 Sault Sainte Marie (49783) ***(G-15103)***
Walls Holding Company, Harbor Springs *Also called Central Industrial Mfg Inc* ***(G-7644)***
Wallside Inc....313 292-4400
27000 Trolley Indus Dr Taylor (48180) ***(G-16489)***
Wallside Window Factory, Taylor *Also called Wallside Inc* ***(G-16489)***
Walmart Inc....517 541-1481
1680 Packard Hwy Charlotte (48813) ***(G-2774)***
Waloon Lake Winery....231 622-8645
2505 Blackbird Rd Petoskey (49770) ***(G-13026)***
Walsworth Print Group, Saint Joseph *Also called Walsworth Publishing Co Inc* ***(G-14973)***
Walsworth Publishing Co Inc....269 428-2054
2180 Maiden Ln Saint Joseph (49085) ***(G-14973)***
Walter Jerome Lelo....989 274-8895
5795 Roedel Rd Bridgeport (48722) ***(G-1919)***
Walters Plumbing & Htg Sups, Battle Creek *Also called Walters Plumbing Company* ***(G-1310)***
Walters Plumbing Company....269 962-6253
189 20th St N Battle Creek (49015) ***(G-1310)***
Walters Seed Co LLC....616 355-7333
65 Veterans Dr Holland (49423) ***(G-8241)***
Walther Trowal LLC (HQ)....616 455-8940
6147 Valduga Dr Sw Ste A Byron Center (49315) ***(G-2301)***
Walther Trowal GMBH & Co KG....616 871-0031
4540 East Paris Ave Se Grand Rapids (49512) ***(G-7324)***
Walton Woodworking....248 730-2017
30680 Pierce St Southfield (48076) ***(G-15742)***
Waltz-Holst Blow Pipe Company....616 676-8119
230 Alta Dale Ave Se Ada (49301) ***(G-40)***
Wamu Fuel LLC....313 386-8700
17151 Middlebelt Rd Livonia (48152) ***(G-10465)***
Wandas Barium Cookie LLC....906 281-1788
25770 Elm St Calumet (49913) ***(G-2416)***
Wapc Holdings Inc....586 939-0770
40736 Brentwood Dr Sterling Heights (48310) ***(G-16228)***
Wara Construction Company LLC....248 299-2410
2927 Waterview Dr Rochester Hills (48309) ***(G-14141)***
Ward Lake Drilling Inc (HQ)....989 732-8499
685 E M 32 Ste 201 Gaylord (49735) ***(G-6166)***
Ward Lake Energy, Gaylord *Also called Ward Lake Drilling Inc* ***(G-6166)***
Ward-Williston Company (PA)....248 594-6622
36700 Woodward Ave # 101 Bloomfield (48304) ***(G-1786)***
Wardcraft Industries LLC....517 750-9100
1 Wardcraft Dr Spring Arbor (49283) ***(G-15798)***
Wardlaw Press LLC....313 806-4603
100 Hall Pl Grosse Pointe Farms (48236) ***(G-7542)***
Wards Automotive International, Southfield *Also called Informa Business Media Inc* ***(G-15605)***
Warfield Electric Company Inc....734 722-4044
5920 N Hix Rd Westland (48185) ***(G-18429)***
Warlock Lures....586 977-1606
4444 Reader Dr Warren (48092) ***(G-18057)***
Warm Rain Corporation (PA)....906 482-3750
51675 Industrial Dr Calumet (49913) ***(G-2417)***
Warmerscom....800 518-0938
365 84th St Sw Ste 4 Byron Center (49315) ***(G-2302)***
Warmilu LLC....855 927-6458
8186 Jackson Rd Ste C Ann Arbor (48103) ***(G-713)***
Warner Instruments....616 843-5342
1320 Fulton Ave Grand Haven (49417) ***(G-6379)***
Warner Oil Company....517 278-5844
400 Race St Coldwater (49036) ***(G-3461)***
Warner Power Acquisition LLC (HQ)....603 456-3111
1500 Marion Ave Grand Haven (49417) ***(G-6380)***
Warner Power Conversion LLC....603 456-3111
1500 Marion Ave Grand Haven (49417) ***(G-6381)***
Warner Software Co LLC....616 916-1182
3881 Yorkland Dr Nw Apt 8 Comstock Park (49321) ***(G-3650)***
Warren Abrasives Inc....586 772-0002
25800 Groesbeck Hwy Warren (48089) ***(G-18058)***
Warren Autometric Fasteners, Livonia *Also called Warren Screw Works Inc* ***(G-10466)***
Warren Broach & Machine Corp....586 254-7080
6541 Diplomat Dr Sterling Heights (48314) ***(G-16229)***
Warren Chassix....248 728-8700
300 Galleria Ofcntr Ste 5 Southfield (48034) ***(G-15743)***
Warren City Fuel....586 759-4759
134 N Silvery Ln Dearborn (48128) ***(G-3914)***
Warren Industrial Welding Co (PA)....586 756-0230
24275 Hoover Rd Warren (48089) ***(G-18059)***
Warren Industries Inc (PA)....586 741-0420
22805 Interstate Dr Clinton Township (48035) ***(G-3386)***
Warren Manufacturing....269 483-0603
68635 Suszek Rd White Pigeon (49099) ***(G-18486)***
Warren Manufacturing LLC....586 467-1600
28201 Van Dyke Ave Warren (48093) ***(G-18060)***
Warren Mfg Acquisition, Warren *Also called Warren Manufacturing LLC* ***(G-18060)***
Warren Mfg Facility, Warren *Also called Punchcraft McHning Tooling LLC* ***(G-17987)***
Warren Screw Products Inc....586 757-1280
13201 Stephens Rd Warren (48089) ***(G-18061)***
Warren Screw Works Inc....734 525-2920
13360 Wayne Rd Livonia (48150) ***(G-10466)***
Warren Steel Co....586 756-6600
21601 Hoover Rd Ste Ams Warren (48089) ***(G-18062)***
Warrior Sports Inc (HQ)....800 968-7845
32125 Hollingsworth Ave Warren (48092) ***(G-18063)***
Wartian Lock Company....586 777-2244
20525 E 9 Mile Rd Saint Clair Shores (48080) ***(G-14891)***
Wartrom Machine Systems Inc....586 469-1915
22786 Patmore Dr Clinton Township (48036) ***(G-3387)***
Warwick Mas & Equipment Co....810 966-3431
1621 Pine Grove Ave Port Huron (48060) ***(G-13537)***
Wasem Fruit Farm....734 482-2342
6580 Judd Rd Milan (48160) ***(G-11451)***
Washburn Woodwork & Cabinet, Otsego *Also called George Washburn* ***(G-12786)***
Washers Incorporated (PA)....734 523-1000
33375 Glendale St Livonia (48150) ***(G-10467)***
Washington Penn Plastic Co Inc....248 276-2275
3256 University Dr Ste 15 Auburn Hills (48326) ***(G-1087)***
Washington Street Printers LLC....734 240-5541
17 Washington St Monroe (48161) ***(G-11590)***
Washtenaw Communications Inc....734 662-7138
1510 Saunders Cres Ann Arbor (48103) ***(G-714)***
Washtenaw Legal News, Ann Arbor *Also called Detroit Legal News Pubg LLC* ***(G-450)***
Washtenaw Voice....734 677-5405
4800 E Huron River Dr Ann Arbor (48105) ***(G-715)***
Waste Management, Ontonagon *Also called K and W Landfill Inc* ***(G-12711)***
Waste Water Treatment, Menominee *Also called Menominee City of Michigan* ***(G-11247)***
Water Department....313 943-2307
2951 Greenfield Rd Dearborn (48120) ***(G-3915)***
Water Treatment, Linden *Also called McIntyres Soft Water Svc Ltd* ***(G-10065)***
Waterfall Jewelers, Waterford *Also called C T & T Inc* ***(G-18107)***
Waterford Today, Taylor *Also called Community Publishing & Mktg* ***(G-16396)***
Waterjetplus, Gaylord *Also called P I W Corporation* ***(G-6152)***
Waterloo Group Inc....248 840-6447
2865 Waterloo Dr Troy (48084) ***(G-17445)***
Waterman Tool & Machine Corp....989 823-8181
1032 E Huron Ave Vassar (48768) ***(G-17585)***
Waters Industries LLC....616 848-8050
4960 Lookout Trl Custer (49405) ***(G-3752)***
Watersong Publications....248 592-0109
29711 Sierra Pointe Cir Farmington Hills (48331) ***(G-5412)***
Watson Embroidery....313 459-5070
17395 Livernois Ave Detroit (48221) ***(G-4675)***
Wattsson & Wattsson Jewelers....906 228-5775
118 W Washington St # 100 Marquette (49855) ***(G-11049)***
Waub Ajijaak Press....248 802-8630
281 1st Ave Manistee (49660) ***(G-10915)***
Wave, Benton Harbor *Also called Worthington Armstrong Venture* ***(G-1611)***
Wave Music and Publishing....313 290-2193
12227 Findlay St Detroit (48205) ***(G-4676)***
Wave Tool LLC....989 912-2116
6215 Garfield Ave Cass City (48726) ***(G-2623)***
Wax Poetic....616 272-4693
1423 Lake Dr Se Grand Rapids (49506) ***(G-7325)***
Way Bakery (HQ)....517 787-6720
2100 Enterprise St Jackson (49203) ***(G-9033)***
Way2go Tech LLC....616 294-1301
425 142nd Ave Holland (49424) ***(G-8242)***
Wayne Allen Lambert....269 467-4624
231 N Clark St Centreville (49032) ***(G-2701)***
Wayne County Laboratory....734 285-5215
797 Central St Wyandotte (48192) ***(G-18843)***
Wayne Craft, Livonia *Also called Wayne-Craft Inc* ***(G-10468)***
Wayne Steel Tech, Farmington *Also called Detroit Materials Inc* ***(G-5136)***
Wayne Stmping Intrntnal- Sbsid, Detroit *Also called Milton Manufacturing Inc* ***(G-4458)***
Wayne Wire A Bag Cmponents Inc....231 258-9187
200 E Dresden St Kalkaska (49646) ***(G-9410)***
Wayne Wire Airbag Components, Kalkaska *Also called Wayne Wire Cloth Products Inc* ***(G-9411)***
Wayne Wire Cloth Products Inc....989 742-4591
221 Garfield St Hillman (49746) ***(G-7917)***

ALPHABETIC SECTION Wemco, Shelby Township

Wayne Wire Cloth Products Inc (PA) 231 258-9187
200 E Dresden St Kalkaska (49646) ***(G-9411)***
Wayne Wire Cloths, Bingham Farms *Also called Strema Sales Corp* ***(G-1703)***
Wayne-Craft Inc 734 421-8800
13525 Wayne Rd Livonia (48150) ***(G-10468)***
Waynes Portable Welding Svc 734 777-9888
5751 Labo Rd South Rockwood (48179) ***(G-15466)***
Wb, Roseville *Also called Wolverine Bronze Company* ***(G-14495)***
WB Pallets Inc 616 669-3000
4440 Chicago Dr Hudsonville (49426) ***(G-8615)***
Wcec, Shelby Township *Also called World Class Equipment Company* ***(G-15370)***
Wcg Design, Detroit *Also called Whiteside Consulting Group LLC* ***(G-4681)***
Wcscarts LLC (PA) 248 901-0965
900 Wilshire Dr Ste 202 Troy (48084) ***(G-17446)***
We Are Urban Technology LLC 313 779-4406
20325 Van Antwerp St Harper Woods (48225) ***(G-7674)***
We Haul Carz LLC 248 933-2246
6247 Eastbrooke West Bloomfield (48322) ***(G-18323)***
We Pop Corn LLC 313 387-1600
14950 Telegraph Rd Redford (48239) ***(G-13786)***
We're Rolling Pretzel Company, Howell *Also called Syd Enterprises* ***(G-8524)***
Wealth Club Nation LLC 323 695-1636
418 N Main St Ste 200 Royal Oak (48067) ***(G-14591)***
Wealthy Street Corporation 800 222-8116
2236 Crawford St Belding (48809) ***(G-1463)***
Wealthy Street Corporation (PA) 616 451-0784
700 Wealthy St Sw Grand Rapids (49504) ***(G-7326)***
Weather King of Indiana, Farmington *Also called Weather King Windows Doors Inc* ***(G-5154)***
Weather King Windows Doors Inc (PA) 313 933-1234
20775 Chesley Dr Farmington (48336) ***(G-5154)***
Weather King Windows Doors Inc 248 478-7788
20775 Chesley Dr Farmington (48336) ***(G-5155)***
Weather Pane Inc 810 798-8695
6209 Bordman Rd Almont (48003) ***(G-272)***
Weather Tight 989 817-2149
4521 Hamilton Dr Midland (48642) ***(G-11422)***
Weather-Rite LLC 612 338-1401
1100 7 Mile Rd Nw Comstock Park (49321) ***(G-3651)***
Weathergard Window Company Inc 248 967-8822
14350 W 8 Mile Rd Oak Park (48237) ***(G-12651)***
Weathergard Window Factory, Oak Park *Also called Weathergard Window Company Inc* ***(G-12651)***
Weatherproof Inc 517 764-1330
385 Watts Rd Jackson (49203) ***(G-9034)***
Weathervane Vinyards Inc 231 228-4800
6530 S Lake Shore Dr Cedar (49621) ***(G-2640)***
Weave Alloy Products Company, Sterling Heights *Also called Wapc Holdings Inc* ***(G-16228)***
Weaver Instructional Systems 616 942-2891
6161 28th St Se Ste 9 Grand Rapids (49546) ***(G-7327)***
Web Litho Inc 586 803-9000
560 John R Rd Rochester Hills (48307) ***(G-14142)***
Web Printing & Mktg Concepts 269 983-4646
4086 Red Arrow Hwy Saint Joseph (49085) ***(G-14974)***
Webasto Assembly, Rochester Hills *Also called Webasto Roof Systems Inc* ***(G-14145)***
Webasto Convertibles USA Inc (HQ) 734 582-5900
14988 Pilot Dr Plymouth (48170) ***(G-13336)***
Webasto Convertibles USA Inc 734 582-5900
2817 Bond St Rochester Hills (48309) ***(G-14143)***
Webasto Roof Systems Inc (HQ) 248 997-5100
2500 Executive Hills Dr Auburn Hills (48326) ***(G-1088)***
Webasto Roof Systems Inc 248 997-5100
14200 N Haggerty Rd Plymouth (48170) ***(G-13337)***
Webasto Roof Systems Inc 248 299-2000
2700 Product Dr Rochester Hills (48309) ***(G-14144)***
Webasto Roof Systems Inc 248 997-5100
2700 Product Dr Rochester Hills (48309) ***(G-14145)***
Webasto Roofing, Auburn Hills *Also called Webasto Roof Systems Inc* ***(G-1088)***
Webasto Sunroofs, Rochester Hills *Also called Webasto Roof Systems Inc* ***(G-14144)***
Webasto-Group, Plymouth *Also called Webasto Convertibles USA Inc* ***(G-13336)***
Webb Partners Inc 734 727-0560
39140 Webb Dr Westland (48185) ***(G-18430)***
Webber Woodworks LLC 517 896-8636
5544 Timothy Ln Bath (48808) ***(G-1174)***
Webcor Packaging Corporation (PA) 810 767-2806
1220 N Center Rd Burton (48509) ***(G-2251)***
Weber Automotive Corporation 248 393-5520
1750 Summit Dr Auburn Hills (48326) ***(G-1089)***
Weber Bros & White Metal Works 269 751-5193
4715 136th Ave Hamilton (49419) ***(G-7609)***
Weber Bros Sawmill Inc 989 644-2206
2862 N Winn Rd Mount Pleasant (48858) ***(G-11746)***
Weber Electric Mfg Co 586 323-9000
2465 23 Mile Rd Shelby Township (48316) ***(G-15367)***
Weber Precision Grinding Inc 616 842-1634
18438 171st Ave Spring Lake (49456) ***(G-15858)***
Weber Sand and Gravel Inc (PA) 248 373-0900
1401 E Silverbell Rd Lake Orion (48360) ***(G-9637)***
Weber Security Group Inc 586 582-0000
95 S Rose St Ste A Mount Clemens (48043) ***(G-11662)***
Weber Steel & Body, Vassar *Also called Weber Steel Inc* ***(G-17586)***
Weber Steel Inc 989 868-4162
3000 Bradford Rd Vassar (48768) ***(G-17586)***
Webers Woodwork LLC 989 798-7210
6316 Barnes Rd Millington (48746) ***(G-11504)***
Webster Cold Forge Co 313 554-4500
47652 Pine Creek Ct Northville (48168) ***(G-12271)***
Wec Group LLC 248 260-4252
1850 Northfield Dr Rochester Hills (48309) ***(G-14146)***
Weco International Inc 810 686-7221
235 S Seymour Rd Flushing (48433) ***(G-5816)***
Wedge Mill Tool Inc 248 486-6400
7771 Kensington Ct Brighton (48116) ***(G-2095)***
Wedin International Inc (PA) 231 779-8650
1111 6th Ave Cadillac (49601) ***(G-2363)***
Wedo Custom Screen Printing 616 965-7332
1077 Leonard St Ne Ste 1 Grand Rapids (49503) ***(G-7328)***
Wefa Cedar Inc 616 696-0873
104 W Beech St Cedar Springs (49319) ***(G-2666)***
Weiderman Motorsports 269 689-0264
28386 Witt Lake Rd Sturgis (49091) ***(G-16329)***
Weighman Enterprises Inc 989 755-2116
1131 E Genesee Ave Saginaw (48607) ***(G-14792)***
Weir Fabrication LLC 248 953-8363
35480 Mound Rd Sterling Heights (48310) ***(G-16230)***
Weiser Metal Products Inc 989 736-6055
3040 E Carbide Dr Harrisville (48740) ***(G-7746)***
Weiser Metal Products Inc 989 736-8151
3431 E M 72 Lincoln (48742) ***(G-10041)***
Weiss Technik North Amer Inc (HQ) 616 554-5020
3881 N Greenbrooke Dr Se Grand Rapids (49512) ***(G-7329)***
Welch Foods Inc A Cooperative 269 624-4141
400 Walker St Lawton (49065) ***(G-9990)***
Welchdry Inc 616 399-2711
4270 Sunnyside Dr Holland (49424) ***(G-8243)***
Weld-Aid Products, Detroit *Also called CRC Industries Inc* ***(G-4107)***
Weldall Corporation 989 375-2251
2295 Hartsell Rd Elkton (48731) ***(G-5034)***
Weldaloy Products Company 586 758-5550
24011 Hoover Rd Warren (48089) ***(G-18064)***
Weldcraft Inc 734 779-1303
11881 Belden Ct Livonia (48150) ***(G-10469)***
Welders & Presses Inc 586 948-4300
27295 Luckino Dr Chesterfield (48047) ***(G-2965)***
Welders and Presses, Chesterfield *Also called 1271 Associates Inc* ***(G-2832)***
Welding & Joining Tech LLC 734 926-9353
5439 Bristol Parke Dr Clarkston (48348) ***(G-3076)***
Welding Technology Corp 248 477-3900
24775 Crestview Ct Farmington Hills (48335) ***(G-5413)***
Welding Wizard 906 786-4745
6444 Marie L.45 Ln Escanaba (49829) ***(G-5107)***
Weldmet Industries Inc 586 773-0533
21799 Schmeman Ave Warren (48089) ***(G-18065)***
Weldore Manufacturing, Hazel Park *Also called Fox Aluminum Products Inc* ***(G-7826)***
Weldpower, Clarkston *Also called Welding & Joining Tech LLC* ***(G-3076)***
Welform Electrodes Inc 586 755-1184
2147 Kenney Ave Warren (48091) ***(G-18066)***
Welk-Ko Fabricators Inc 248 486-2598
53655 Grand River Ave New Hudson (48165) ***(G-12074)***
Welk-Ko Fabricators Inc (PA) 734 425-6840
11885 Mayfield St Livonia (48150) ***(G-10470)***
Welk-Ko Fabricators Inc 810 227-7500
11777 Grand River Rd Brighton (48116) ***(G-2096)***
Welker Cabinetry & Millwork 248 477-6600
12338 Stark Rd Livonia (48150) ***(G-10471)***
Weller Truck Parts, Wyoming *Also called Jasper Weller LLC* ***(G-18886)***
Weller Truck Parts, Wyoming *Also called Jasper Weller LLC* ***(G-18887)***
Wellington Fragrance 734 261-5531
33306 Glendale St Livonia (48150) ***(G-10472)***
Wellington-Almont LLC (HQ) 734 942-1060
39555 S Intrstate 94 Svc Belleville (48111) ***(G-1495)***
Wellmaster Consulting Inc 231 893-9266
2658 W Winston Rd Rothbury (49452) ***(G-14499)***
Wells Equipment Sales Inc 517 542-2376
534 Homer Rd Litchfield (49252) ***(G-10087)***
Wells Index Division, Muskegon *Also called A & D Run Off Inc* ***(G-11760)***
Wellsaw, Kalamazoo *Also called Coxline Inc* ***(G-9157)***
Wellsense USA Inc 888 335-0995
123 W Brown St Birmingham (48009) ***(G-1756)***
Wellwood Solutions LLC 734 368-0368
2198 Windmill Way Saline (48176) ***(G-15044)***
Welz Tool Mch & Boring Co Inc 734 425-3920
11952 Hubbard St Livonia (48150) ***(G-10473)***
Welzin Health Services LLC 313 953-8768
3218 20th St Wyandotte (48192) ***(G-18844)***
Wemco, Shelby Township *Also called Weber Electric Mfg Co* ***(G-15367)***

ALPHABETIC

Wende J Periard 989 770-4542
2717 E Birch Run Rd Burt (48417) *(G-2217)*
Wendling Sheet Metal Inc 989 753-5286
2633 Carrollton Rd Saginaw (48604) *(G-14793)*
Wendricks Truss Inc 906 635-8822
6142 S Mackinac Trl Sault Sainte Marie (49783) *(G-15104)*
Wendricks Truss Inc (PA) 906 498-7709
W5728 Old Us 2 Road No 43 Hermansville (49847) *(G-7864)*
Wendy Williamson 321 345-8297
1608 Sun Prairie Dr Saint Joseph (49085) *(G-14975)*
Wenstrom Dsign Fabrication LLC 269 760-2358
7525 N Woodbridge Ave Brohman (49312) *(G-2109)*
Wentzel Energy Partners LLC 817 713-3283
999 Tech Row Madison Heights (48071) *(G-10861)*
Wenz & Gibbens Enterprises 248 333-7938
101 E Walton Blvd Pontiac (48340) *(G-13424)*
Werkema Machine Company Inc 616 455-7650
7300 Division Ave S Grand Rapids (49548) *(G-7330)*
Wes Corp 231 536-2500
5900 Airport Rd East Jordan (49727) *(G-4882)*
Wes Stabeck Industries, Troy Also called Stapels Manufacturing LLC *(G-17370)*
Wesley Floor Care Company 313 978-4539
19483 Hartwell St Detroit (48235) *(G-4677)*
Weslope Industries Inc 248 320-7007
4822 Leafdale Blvd Royal Oak (48073) *(G-14592)*
Wesman Designs 616 669-3290
5489 32nd Ave Hudsonville (49426) *(G-8616)*
West Bay Exploration Company (PA) 231 946-3529
13685 S West Bay Shore Dr Traverse City (49684) *(G-16877)*
West Bay Geophysical Inc 231 946-3529
13685 S West Bay Shore Dr Traverse City (49684) *(G-16878)*
West Branch Wood Treating Inc 989 343-0066
3800 S M 30 West Branch (48661) *(G-18346)*
West Brothers LLC 734 457-0083
815 Scarlet Oak Dr Monroe (48162) *(G-11591)*
West Colony Graphic Inc 269 375-6625
2519 Summerdale Ave Kalamazoo (49004) *(G-9366)*
West Colony Printing, Kalamazoo Also called West Colony Graphic Inc *(G-9366)*
West Mich Auto Stl & Engrg Inc 616 560-8198
550 E Ellis Ave Belding (48809) *(G-1464)*
West Mich Awning, Holland Also called West Michigan Canvas Company *(G-8245)*
West Mich Cmnty Help Netwrk 231 727-5007
1877 Peck St Muskegon (49441) *(G-11942)*
West Mich Flcking Assembly LLC 269 639-1634
977 Ada Place Dr Se Grand Rapids (49546) *(G-7331)*
West Mich Off Interiors Inc 269 344-0768
3308 S Westnedge Ave Kalamazoo (49008) *(G-9367)*
West Mich Prcsion McHining Inc 616 791-1970
2500 Waldorf Ct Nw Grand Rapids (49544) *(G-7332)*
West Michigan Aerial LLc 269 998-4455
62422 M 40 Lawton (49065) *(G-9991)*
West Michigan Alpacas 616 990-0556
15747 Greenly St Holland (49424) *(G-8244)*
West Michigan Cabinet Supply 616 896-6990
4366 Central Pkwy Hudsonville (49426) *(G-8617)*
West Michigan Canvas Company 616 355-7855
11041 Paw Paw Dr Holland (49424) *(G-8245)*
West Michigan Cerakote, Grand Rapids Also called S&G Group LLC *(G-7177)*
West Michigan Coating LLC 616 647-9509
3150 Fruit Ridge Ave Nw Grand Rapids (49544) *(G-7333)*
West Michigan Compounding, Greenville Also called Wmc LLC *(G-7510)*
West Michigan Crematory Svc, Muskegon Also called Wilbert Burial Vault Company *(G-11946)*
West Michigan Fab Corp 616 794-3750
321 Root St 3ph Belding (48809) *(G-1465)*
West Michigan Fabrication 269 637-2415
860 68th St South Haven (49090) *(G-15425)*
West Michigan Forklift Inc 616 262-4949
4155 12th St Wayland (49348) *(G-18209)*
West Michigan Gage Inc 616 735-0585
4055 Rmmbrnce Rd Nw Ste 1 Walker (49534) *(G-17657)*
West Michigan GL Coatings Inc 616 970-4863
4047 Mission St Nw Grand Rapids (49534) *(G-7334)*
West Michigan Grinding Svc Inc 231 739-4245
1188 E Broadway Ave Norton Shores (49444) *(G-12343)*
West Michigan Medical 269 673-2141
595 Jenner Dr Allegan (49010) *(G-185)*
West Michigan Metals LLC 269 978-7021
1168 33rd St Allegan (49010) *(G-186)*
West Michigan Molding Inc 616 846-4950
1425 Aerial View Dr Grand Haven (49417) *(G-6382)*
West Michigan Nail & Wire Co, Grand Rapids Also called National Nail Corp *(G-7036)*
West Michigan Pedorthics, Muskegon Also called Shoe Shop *(G-11918)*
West Michigan Printing Inc 616 676-2190
513 Pine Land Dr Se Ada (49301) *(G-41)*
West Michigan Sawmill 616 693-0044
7760 Nash Hwy Clarksville (48815) *(G-3082)*
West Michigan Spline Inc 616 399-4078
156 Manufacturers Dr Holland (49424) *(G-8246)*

West Michigan Tag & Label Inc 616 235-0120
5300 Broadmoor Ave Se F Grand Rapids (49512) *(G-7335)*
West Michigan Tool & Die, Benton Harbor Also called Bulk AG Innovations LLC *(G-1538)*
West Michigan Tool & Die Co 269 925-0900
1007 Nickerson Ave Benton Harbor (49022) *(G-1602)*
West Michigan Truss Company, Muskegon Also called Truss Technologies Inc *(G-11939)*
West Michigan Welding LLC 231 578-3593
19195 112th Ave Nunica (49448) *(G-12590)*
West Michigan Wire Co 231 845-1281
211 E Dowland St Ludington (49431) *(G-10556)*
West Pharmaceutical, Walker Also called Tech Group Grand Rapids Inc *(G-17653)*
West River Machine, Niles Also called Shively Corp *(G-12167)*
West Shore Services Inc (PA) 616 895-4347
6620 Lake Michigan Dr Allendale (49401) *(G-229)*
West Side Flamehardening Inc 734 729-1665
38200 N Executive Dr Westland (48185) *(G-18431)*
West Side Mfg Fabrication Inc 248 380-6640
28776 Wall St Wixom (48393) *(G-18790)*
West System Inc 989 684-7286
102 Patterson Ave Bay City (48706) *(G-1411)*
West Thomas Partners LLC 616 430-7585
4053 Brockton Dr Se Ste A Grand Rapids (49512) *(G-7336)*
Westco Metalcraft Inc 734 425-0900
31846 Glendale St Livonia (48150) *(G-10474)*
Westcott Displays Inc (PA) 313 872-1200
450 Amsterdam St Detroit (48202) *(G-4678)*
Westcott Paper Products, Detroit Also called Westcott Displays Inc *(G-4678)*
Westech Corp 231 766-3914
2357 Whitehall Rd Muskegon (49445) *(G-11943)*
Westendorff Redi-Mix, Pewamo Also called Westendorff Transit Mix *(G-13029)*
Westendorff Transit Mix 989 593-2488
3344 N Hubbardston Rd Pewamo (48873) *(G-13029)*
Western Adhesive Inc 616 874-5869
6768 Kitson Dr Ne Rockford (49341) *(G-14193)*
Western Diversified, Mattawan Also called Mol-Son Inc *(G-11165)*
Western Diversified Plas LLC (PA) 269 668-3393
53150 N Main St Mattawan (49071) *(G-11169)*
Western Engineered Products 248 371-9259
540 N Lapeer Rd Ste 390 Lake Orion (48362) *(G-9638)*
Western Global, Troy Also called Western International Inc *(G-17447)*
Western International Inc 866 814-2470
1707 Northwood Dr Troy (48084) *(G-17447)*
Western Land Services Inc (PA) 231 843-8878
1100 Conrad Industrial Dr Ludington (49431) *(G-10557)*
Western Michigan Plastics 616 394-9269
5745 143rd Ave Holland (49423) *(G-8247)*
Western Pegasus Inc (PA) 616 393-9580
728 E 8th St Ste 3 Holland (49423) *(G-8248)*
Western Press, Troy Also called United Systems *(G-17413)*
Westgood Manufacturing Co (PA) 586 771-3970
15211 E 11 Mile Rd Roseville (48066) *(G-14493)*
Westmountain Software 734 776-3966
36702 Cherry Oak Dr Westland (48186) *(G-18432)*
Westool Corporation 734 847-2520
7383 Sulier Dr Temperance (48182) *(G-16552)*
Westport Fuel Systems US Inc 734 233-6850
14900 Galleon Ct Plymouth (48170) *(G-13338)*
Westport Innovations, Plymouth Also called Westport Fuel Systems US Inc *(G-13338)*
Westrock Rkt LLC 269 963-5511
177 Angell St Battle Creek (49037) *(G-1311)*
Westshore Design, Holland Also called Hgc Westshore LLC *(G-8070)*
Westshore Design, Holland Also called Cusack Music LLC *(G-8008)*
Westshore Testing, Holland Also called Parkway Elc Communications LLC *(G-8160)*
Westside Powder Coat LLC 734 729-1667
35777 Genron Ct Romulus (48174) *(G-14337)*
Westwood Lands Inc 906 475-9544
220 W Washington St # 220 Marquette (49855) *(G-11050)*
Wet N Rugged Sports, Galesburg Also called Soupcan Inc *(G-6084)*
Wetzel Tool & Engineering Inc 248 960-0430
46952 Liberty Dr Wixom (48393) *(G-18791)*
Weyerhaeuser Company 989 348-2881
4111 W 4 Mile Rd Grayling (49738) *(G-7471)*
Weyerhaeuser Company 906 524-2040
15800 Mead Rd Lanse (49946) *(G-9669)*
Weyv Inc 248 614-2400
1820 E Big Beaver Rd Troy (48083) *(G-17448)*
WG Sweis Investments LLC 313 477-8433
57155 Covington Dr Washington (48094) *(G-18091)*
Wgnb, Zeeland Also called Moody Bible Inst of Chicago *(G-19057)*
Wgs Global Services LC (PA) 810 239-4947
6350 Taylor Dr Flint (48507) *(G-5792)*
Wgs Global Services LC 810 694-3843
7075 Dort Hwy Grand Blanc (48439) *(G-6268)*
Wh Filtration Inc 248 633-4001
19 Clifford St Fl 8 Detroit (48226) *(G-4679)*
Wh Manufacturing Inc 616 534-7560
2606 Thornwood St Sw Grand Rapids (49519) *(G-7337)*

ALPHABETIC SECTION

Whaley Welding and Mechine LLC 810 835-5804
211 Industrial Way Fenton (48430) *(G-5513)*
What A Stitch 248 698-1104
10164 Elizabeth Lake Rd White Lake (48386) *(G-18471)*
Whats Scoop 616 662-6423
3667 Baldwin St Hudsonville (49426) *(G-8618)*
Whats Your Mix Menchies LLC 248 840-1668
2168 Scarboro Ct Shelby Township (48316) *(G-15368)*
Wheat Jewelers, Okemos *Also called Kevin Wheat & Assoc Ltd (G-12671)*
Wheatons Woodworking LLC 616 288-8159
1010 Solon Cedar Springs (49319) *(G-2667)*
Wheel Truing Brake Shoe Co, Rochester *Also called Gorang Industries Inc (G-13902)*
Wheelchair Barn 231 730-1647
2300 Barclay St Apt 1 Muskegon (49441) *(G-11944)*
Wheeler Insulation, Battle Creek *Also called Insulation Wholesale Supply (G-1241)*
Wheelers Wolf Lake Sawmill 231 745-7078
195 N M 37 # 137 Baldwin (49304) *(G-1125)*
Wheelhouse Graphix LLC 800 732-0815
445 Enterprise Ct Bloomfield Hills (48302) *(G-1874)*
Wheelock & Son Welding Shop 231 947-6557
9954 N Long Lake Rd Traverse City (49685) *(G-16879)*
Wheelock & Sons Welding, Traverse City *Also called Wheelock & Son Welding Shop (G-16879)*
Whimsical Fusions LLC 248 956-0952
2326 E 7 Mile Rd Detroit (48234) *(G-4680)*
Whipple Printing Inc 313 382-8033
17140 Ecorse Rd Allen Park (48101) *(G-210)*
Whirlpool Corporation (PA) 269 923-5000
2000 N M 63 Benton Harbor (49022) *(G-1603)*
Whirlpool Corporation 800 541-6390
553 Benson Rd Benton Harbor (49022) *(G-1604)*
Whirlpool Corporation 269 923-7441
500 Renaissance Dr # 102 Saint Joseph (49085) *(G-14976)*
Whirlpool Corporation 404 547-3194
2901 Lakeshore Dr Saint Joseph (49085) *(G-14977)*
Whirlpool Corporation 269 923-5000
600 W Main St Benton Harbor (49022) *(G-1605)*
Whirlpool Corporation 269 923-7400
1800 Paw Paw Ave Benton Harbor (49022) *(G-1606)*
Whirlpool Corporation 269 849-0907
3694 Kerlikowske Rd Coloma (49038) *(G-3484)*
Whirlpool Corporation 269 923-5000
750 Monte Rd Benton Harbor (49022) *(G-1607)*
Whirlpool Corporation 269 923-6057
303 Upton Dr Saint Joseph (49085) *(G-14978)*
Whirlpool Corporation 269 923-6486
151 Riverview Dr Benton Harbor (49022) *(G-1608)*
Whirlpool Corporation 269 923-5000
2000 N M 63 Benton Harbor (49022) *(G-1609)*
Whirlpool Corporation 269 923-3009
150 Hilltop Rd Mldrop 75 7590 Maildrop Benton Harbor (49022) *(G-1610)*
Whitaker Welding and Mech LLC 855 754-2548
69 N Hilton Park Rd Muskegon (49442) *(G-11945)*
Whitcomb and Sons Sign Co Inc 586 752-3576
315 E Lafayette St Romeo (48065) *(G-14239)*
Whitcomb Sign, Romeo *Also called Whitcomb and Sons Sign Co Inc (G-14239)*
White Automation & Tool Co 734 947-9822
28888 Goddard Rd Ste 100 Romulus (48174) *(G-14338)*
White Cloud Manufacturing Co (PA) 231 796-8603
123 N Dekraft Ave Big Rapids (49307) *(G-1689)*
White Cloud Mfg Co 231 689-6087
19 N Charles St White Cloud (49349) *(G-18447)*
White Dove Woodworks 734 717-6042
705 E Main St Manchester (48158) *(G-10892)*
White Engineering Inc 269 695-0825
3000 E Geyer Rd Niles (49120) *(G-12173)*
White Knight Fluid Hdlg Inc 435 783-6040
1077 Watson Rd Hemlock (48626) *(G-7858)*
White Knight Industries 269 823-4207
972 68th St South Haven (49090) *(G-15426)*
White Lake Beacon Inc 231 894-5356
432 E Spring St Whitehall (49461) *(G-18512)*
White Lake Excavating Inc 231 894-6918
2571 Holton Whitehall Rd Whitehall (49461) *(G-18513)*
White Lotus Farms Inc 734 904-1379
7217 W Liberty Rd Ann Arbor (48103) *(G-716)*
White Pallet Chair 989 424-8771
4961 E Colonville Rd Clare (48617) *(G-3001)*
White Pine Furniture LLC 269 366-4469
2002 Charles Ave Kalamazoo (49048) *(G-9368)*
White Pine Winery 269 281-0098
317 State St Saint Joseph (49085) *(G-14979)*
White River 231 894-9216
7386 Post Rd Montague (49437) *(G-11603)*
White River Knife and Tool 616 997-0026
515 Industrial Dr Fremont (49412) *(G-6057)*
White Tool & Engineering, Niles *Also called White Engineering Inc (G-12173)*
Whiteboard Depot, Rockford *Also called Newkirk and Associates Inc (G-14181)*

Whitefeather Creek Alpacas 517 368-5393
8274 Alvord Rd Montgomery (49255) *(G-11604)*
Whitehall Industries, Ludington *Also called Signa Group Inc (G-10550)*
Whitehall Products LLC 231 894-2688
1625 Warner St Whitehall (49461) *(G-18514)*
Whitehouse Logging & Hardwood, Manton *Also called Allen Whitehouse (G-10929)*
Whitens Kiln & Lumber Inc 906 498-2116
125801 Coney Rd Hermansville (49847) *(G-7865)*
Whites Bridge Tooling Inc 616 897-4151
1395 Bowes Rd Lowell (49331) *(G-10522)*
Whites Industrial Service 616 291-3706
5010 Abraham Dr Ne Lowell (49331) *(G-10523)*
Whitesell Frmed Components Inc 313 299-1178
5331 Dixie Hwy Waterford (48329) *(G-18175)*
Whiteside Consulting Group LLC 313 288-6598
19341 Stansbury St Detroit (48235) *(G-4681)*
Whitesville Mill Service Co, Detroit *Also called Butler Mill Service Company (G-4079)*
Whitlam Group Inc (PA) 586 757-5100
24800 Sherwood Center Line (48015) *(G-2689)*
Whitlock Business Systems Inc 248 548-1040
275 E 12 Mile Rd Madison Heights (48071) *(G-10862)*
Whitlock Distribution Svcs LLC 248 548-1040
275 E 12 Mile Rd Madison Heights (48071) *(G-10863)*
Whittaker Orgname Assoc Inc 616 786-2255
1889 Ottawa Beach Rd Holland (49424) *(G-8249)*
Whittaker Timber Corporation 989 872-3065
3623 Elmwood Rd Cass City (48726) *(G-2624)*
Whm Investments Inc 269 432-3251
29808 Brandt Rd Colon (49040) *(G-3492)*
WHOLESALE, Canton *Also called Advanced Magnet Source Corp (G-2430)*
Wholesale Proc Systems LLC 833 755-6696
4315 N Adrian Hwy Adrian (49221) *(G-104)*
Wholesale Weave Inc 800 762-2037
3130 E 8 Mile Rd Detroit (48234) *(G-4682)*
Wholesalemillworkcom 616 241-6011
4707 40th St Se Grand Rapids (49512) *(G-7338)*
Whos Who Publishing Co LLC 614 481-7300
1452 Randolph St Ste 400 Detroit (48226) *(G-4683)*
Wicked Wldg & Fabrication LLC 517 304-3709
8137 Embury Rd Unit 8 Grand Blanc (48439) *(G-6269)*
Wickedglow Industries Inc 586 776-4132
248 Nrthbound Gratiot Ave Mount Clemens (48043) *(G-11663)*
Wico Metal Products Company (PA) 586 755-9600
23500 Sherwood Ave Warren (48091) *(G-18067)*
Wico Metal Products Company 586 755-9600
24400 Sherwood Center Line (48015) *(G-2690)*
Wicwas Press 269 344-8027
1620 Miller Rd Kalamazoo (49001) *(G-9369)*
Wide Eyed 3d Printing 517 376-6612
5343 Edgewood Shores Dr Howell (48843) *(G-8541)*
Widell Industries Inc 989 742-4528
24601 Veterans Mem Hwy Hillman (49746) *(G-7918)*
Wiesen Edm Inc 616 208-0000
8634 Storey Rd Belding (48809) *(G-1466)*
Wiesen EDM Inc 616 794-9870
8630 Storey Rd Belding (48809) *(G-1467)*
Wiesen Powdercoating, Belding *Also called Wiesen Edm Inc (G-1466)*
Wieske Tool Inc 989 288-2648
202 S Hagle St Durand (48429) *(G-4850)*
Wikid Vinyl 313 585-7814
49862 Newark Dr Shelby Township (48315) *(G-15369)*
Wikoff Color Corporation 616 245-3930
3410 Jefferson Ave Se Grand Rapids (49548) *(G-7339)*
Wilbert Burial Vault Co, Traverse City *Also called Bostwick Enterprises Inc (G-16624)*
Wilbert Burial Vault Company (PA) 231 773-6631
1510 S Getty St Muskegon (49442) *(G-11946)*
Wilbert Burial Vault Company 231 773-6631
1546 S Getty St Muskegon (49442) *(G-11947)*
Wilbert Burial Vault Works 906 786-0261
609 S Carpenter Ave Kingsford (49802) *(G-9519)*
Wilbert Plastic Services, Troy *Also called Enginred Plstic Components Inc (G-17092)*
Wilbert Saginaw Vault Corp (PA) 989 753-3065
2810 Hess Ave Saginaw (48601) *(G-14794)*
Wilbur Products Inc 231 755-3805
950 W Broadway Ave Muskegon (49441) *(G-11948)*
Wild Flavors Inc 269 216-2603
1717 Douglas Ave Kalamazoo (49007) *(G-9370)*
Wild Manufacturing 586 719-2028
39201 Townhall St Harrison Township (48045) *(G-7731)*
Wildcat Buildings Inc 231 824-6406
656 Rw Hrris Indus Prk Dr Manton (49663) *(G-10939)*
Wilde Group, Muskegon *Also called Wilde Signs (G-11949)*
Wilde Signs 231 727-1200
771 Access Hwy Muskegon (49442) *(G-11949)*
Wilderness Treasures 906 647-4002
101 S M 129 Pickford (49774) *(G-13032)*
Wildfire Signs & Graphics 248 872-1998
1359 Somerville Dr Oxford (48371) *(G-12929)*

Wilfred Swartz & Swartz G 989 652-6322
11465 Holland Rd Reese (48757) **(G-13811)**
Wilkie Bros Conveyors Inc 810 364-4820
1765 Michigan Ave Ste 2 Marysville (48040) **(G-11113)**
Wilkie Brothers, Marysville *Also called American Metal Restoration* **(G-11081)**
Wilkinson Chemical Corporation 989 843-6163
8290 Lapeer Rd Mayville (48744) **(G-11174)**
Wilkinson Corporation 989 843-6163
8290 Lapeer Rd Mayville (48744) **(G-11175)**
Willbee Concrete Products Co 517 782-8246
2323 Brooklyn Rd Jackson (49203) **(G-9035)**
Willbee Transit-Mix Co Inc 517 782-9493
2323 Brooklyn Rd Jackson (49203) **(G-9036)**
Willc, Pontiac *Also called Williams International Co LLC* **(G-13425)**
Willenborg Associates Inc 810 724-5678
5801 34 Mile Rd Bruce Twp (48065) **(G-2186)**
William B Eerdmans Pubg Co 616 459-4591
4035 Park East Ct Se Grand Rapids (49546) **(G-7340)**
William Barnes 989 424-1849
508 Iroquois Ave Prudenville (48651) **(G-13660)**
William C Fox Enterprises Inc 231 775-2732
1215 N Mitchell St Cadillac (49601) **(G-2364)**
William F McGraw & Company, Riverview *Also called Narburgh & Tidd LLC* **(G-13881)**
William R Hall Kimberly 989 426-4605
4083 Cassidy Rd Gladwin (48624) **(G-6208)**
William S Wixtrom 906 376-8247
2131 County Road 601 Republic (49879) **(G-13821)**
William Shaw Inc 231 536-3569
402 Wadsworth St Traverse City (49684) **(G-16880)**
Williams Cheese Co 989 697-4492
998 N Huron Rd Linwood (48634) **(G-10075)**
Williams Diversified Inc 734 421-6100
13170 Merriman Rd Livonia (48150) **(G-10475)**
Williams Finishing Inc 734 421-6100
13170 Merriman Rd Livonia (48150) **(G-10476)**
Williams Form Engineering Corp (PA) 616 866-0815
8165 Graphic Dr Ne Belmont (49306) **(G-1521)**
Williams Gun Sight Company 800 530-9028
7389 Lapeer Rd Davison (48423) **(G-3801)**
Williams International Co LLC (PA) 248 624-5200
2000 Centerpoint Pkwy Pontiac (48341) **(G-13425)**
Williams Management Group LLC 248 506-7967
19745 Ralston St Detroit (48203) **(G-4684)**
Williams Milling & Moulding In 906 474-9222
10304 Bay Shore Dr Rapid River (49878) **(G-13687)**
Williams Parts & Supply Co 906 337-3813
701 Oak St Calumet (49913) **(G-2418)**
Williams Reddi Mix Inc 906 875-6952
1345 Us Highway 2 Crystal Falls (49920) **(G-3747)**
Williams Redi Mix 906 875-6839
170 Williams Rd Crystal Falls (49920) **(G-3748)**
Williams Tooling & Mfg 616 681-2093
1856 142nd Ave Dorr (49323) **(G-4771)**
Williams Welding Custom Metal 989 941-2901
2819 N Eastman Rd Midland (48642) **(G-11423)**
Williamston Products Inc (PA) 517 655-2131
845 Progress Ct Williamston (48895) **(G-18585)**
Williamston Products Inc 517 655-2273
1560 Noble Rd Williamston (48895) **(G-18586)**
Williamston Products Inc 989 723-0149
615 N Delany Rd Owosso (48867) **(G-12867)**
Willie N Eicher 269 432-3707
31534 Brandt Rd Colon (49040) **(G-3493)**
Willies Wicks 810 730-4176
1315 Kapp Ct Flushing (48433) **(G-5817)**
Willis Engine & Machining Svc 616 842-4366
19092 144th Ave Fruitport (49415) **(G-6071)**
Willoughby Press 989 723-3360
1407 Corunna Ave Owosso (48867) **(G-12868)**
Willow Mfg Inc 231 275-1026
11455 Us Highway 31 Interlochen (49643) **(G-8686)**
Willow Vineyards Inc 231 271-4810
10702 E Hilltop Rd Suttons Bay (49682) **(G-16347)**
Willsie Lumber Company 989 695-5094
9770 Pierce Rd Freeland (48623) **(G-6031)**
Wilson Technologies Inc 248 655-0005
851 W Maple Rd Clawson (48017) **(G-3112)**
Wilson-Garner Company 586 466-5880
40935 Production Dr Harrison Township (48045) **(G-7732)**
Wilsonart LLC 248 960-3388
50768 Varsity Ct Wixom (48393) **(G-18792)**
Winans Inc 810 744-1240
494 S Comstock St Corunna (48817) **(G-3719)**
Winans Electric Motor Repair, Corunna *Also called Winans Inc* **(G-3719)**
Winding Road Publishing Inc 248 545-8360
2355 Wolcott St Ferndale (48220) **(G-5598)**
Window Designs Inc (PA) 616 396-5295
753 Lincoln Ave Holland (49423) **(G-8250)**
Windshadow Farm & Dairy LLC 269 599-0467
24681 County Road 681 Bangor (49013) **(G-1132)**
Windsor Mold Inc 734 944-5080
1294 Beach Ct Saline (48176) **(G-15045)**
Windsor Mold Saline, Saline *Also called Windsor Mold USA Inc* **(G-15046)**
Windsor Mold USA Inc 734 944-5080
1294 Beach Ct Saline (48176) **(G-15046)**
Windy Lake LLC 877 869-6911
474 S Carroll St Pentwater (49449) **(G-12975)**
Wine and Canvas of Ann Arbor 734 277-9253
44730 Ford Rd Canton (48187) **(G-2542)**
Wine ND Canvas Grand Rapids 616 970-1082
2675 East Paris Ave Se # 3 Grand Rapids (49546) **(G-7341)**
Winery At Young Farms LLC 989 506-5142
8396 70th Ave Mecosta (49332) **(G-11194)**
Wines Printing Co 586 924-6229
41516 Schoenherr Rd Sterling Heights (48313) **(G-16231)**
Winford Engineering LLC 989 671-9721
4561 Garfield Rd Auburn (48611) **(G-771)**
Wing Pattern Inc 248 588-1121
42200 Mound Rd Sterling Heights (48314) **(G-16232)**
Wings Mfg Inc 585 873-3105
1550 Kingsley St Mount Clemens (48043) **(G-11664)**
Wings of Sturgis LLC 269 689-9326
71005 Miller Rd Sturgis (49091) **(G-16330)**
Winning Publications 269 342-8547
952 Vassar Dr Kalamazoo (49001) **(G-9371)**
Winsol Electronics LLC 810 767-2987
2000 N Saginaw St Flint (48505) **(G-5793)**
Winter 734 699-6825
13928 Kahla Dr Van Buren Twp (48111) **(G-17564)**
Winterset Woodworks LLC 248 207-8795
28310 Hayes Rd Roseville (48066) **(G-14494)**
Wirco Inc 586 267-1300
17001 19 Mile Rd Ste 1 Clinton Township (48038) **(G-3388)**
Wirco Manufacturing LLC 810 984-5576
2550 20th St Port Huron (48060) **(G-13538)**
Wirco Products Inc 810 984-5576
2550 20th St Port Huron (48060) **(G-13539)**
Wire Dynamics Inc 586 879-0321
18210 Malyn Blvd Fraser (48026) **(G-6012)**
Wire Fab Inc 313 893-8816
18055 Sherwood St Detroit (48234) **(G-4685)**
Wire Nets 248 669-5312
1873 Twin Sun Cir Commerce Township (48390) **(G-3581)**
Wire Wizard Welding Products, Jackson *Also called Elco Enterprises Inc* **(G-8878)**
Wired Technologies LLC 313 800-1611
31099 Schoolcraft Rd Livonia (48150) **(G-10477)**
Wireless Svcs Div Navy A Force, Taylor *Also called General Dynamics Corporation* **(G-16421)**
Wiric Corporation 248 598-5297
2781 Bond St Rochester Hills (48309) **(G-14147)**
Wirt Stone Dock, Bay City *Also called Doug Wirt Enterprises Inc* **(G-1347)**
Wirtz Manufacturing Co Inc (PA) 810 987-7600
1105 24th St Port Huron (48060) **(G-13540)**
Wismer Wood Works 616 262-9444
12125 Jordan Lake Rd Lake Odessa (48849) **(G-9580)**
Wisner Woodworking 231 924-5711
5015 S Wisner Ave Newaygo (49337) **(G-12091)**
Wit-O-Matic, Ortonville *Also called Palfam Industries Inc* **(G-12750)**
Wit-Son Carbide Tool Inc 231 536-2247
6490 Rogers Rd East Jordan (49727) **(G-4883)**
Wit-Son Quality Tool & Mfg LLC 989 335-4342
230 N Barlow Rd Harrisville (48740) **(G-7747)**
Witchcraft Tape Products Inc (PA) 269 468-3399
100 Klitchman Dr Coloma (49038) **(G-3485)**
Witco Inc 810 387-4231
6401 Bricker Rd Greenwood (48006) **(G-7512)**
Withers Corporation 586 758-2750
23801 Mound Rd Warren (48091) **(G-18068)**
Wittock Supply Company 810 721-8000
350 E 2nd St Imlay City (48444) **(G-8651)**
Witzenmann Usa LLC (HQ) 248 588-6033
1201 Stephenson Hwy Troy (48083) **(G-17449)**
Wixtrom Lumber Co, Republic *Also called William S Wixtrom* **(G-13821)**
Wiz Wheelz Inc 616 455-5988
4460 40th St Se Grand Rapids (49512) **(G-7342)**
Wizard Electronics, Rockford *Also called Rockford Contract Mfg* **(G-14188)**
Wkw Extrusion, Portage *Also called Erbsloeh Alum Solutions Inc* **(G-13558)**
Wkw Roof Rail Systems LLC 205 338-4242
6565 S Sprinkle Rd Portage (49002) **(G-13632)**
Wl Molding of Michigan LLC 269 327-3075
8212 Shaver Rd Portage (49024) **(G-13633)**
Wls Processing LLC 313 378-5743
6501 Mack Ave Detroit (48207) **(G-4686)**
Wlw Musical 248 956-3060
850 Ladd Rd Commerce Township (48390) **(G-3582)**
Wm Kloeffler Industries Inc 810 765-4068
6033 King Rd Marine City (48039) **(G-10969)**
WM Tube & Wire Forming Inc 231 830-9393
2724 9th St Muskegon (49444) **(G-11950)**

ALPHABETIC SECTION

Wmc LLC 616 560-4142
  1300 Moore St Greenville (48838) *(G-7510)*
Wmc Sales LLC 616 813-7237
  4455 Tiffany Ave Ne Ada (49301) *(G-42)*
Wmcs, Hudsonville *Also called West Michigan Cabinet Supply (G-8617)*
Wmgm, Norton Shores *Also called West Michigan Grinding Svc Inc (G-12343)*
Wmh Fluidpower Inc (PA) 269 327-7011
  6256 American Ave Portage (49002) *(G-13634)*
Wmt Properties Inc 248 486-6400
  7771 Kensington Ct Brighton (48116) *(G-2097)*
Wmtl, Grand Rapids *Also called West Michigan Tag & Label Inc (G-7335)*
Wnc of Grand Rapids 2 LLC 269 986-5066
  2675 East Paris Ave Se # 3 Grand Rapids (49546) *(G-7343)*
Wochen-Post 248 641-9944
  12200 E 13 Mile Rd Ste 14 Warren (48093) *(G-18069)*
Woco Tech Usa Inc 248 385-2854
  28970 Cabot Dr Ste 300 Novi (48377) *(G-12569)*
Woder Construction Inc 989 731-6371
  3661 Nowak Rd Gaylord (49735) *(G-6167)*
Wojo Associates, Commerce Township *Also called Highland Machine Design Inc (G-3537)*
Woldering Plastic Mold Tech, Grand Rapids *Also called Plastic Mold Technology Inc (G-7089)*
Wolfe Whistle 517 303-9197
  16140 S Lowell Rd Lansing (48906) *(G-9750)*
Wolverine Advanced Mtls LLC (HQ) 313 749-6100
  5850 Mercury Dr Ste 250 Dearborn (48126) *(G-3916)*
Wolverine Broach Co Inc (PA) 586 468-4445
  41200 Executive Dr Harrison Township (48045) *(G-7733)*
Wolverine Bronze Company (PA) 586 776-8180
  28178 Hayes Rd Roseville (48066) *(G-14495)*
Wolverine Carbide & Tool Inc 248 247-3888
  684 Robbins Dr Troy (48083) *(G-17450)*
Wolverine Carbide and Too 586 497-7000
  21777 Hoover Rd Warren (48089) *(G-18070)*
Wolverine Coil Spring Company 616 459-3504
  818 Front Ave Nw Grand Rapids (49504) *(G-7344)*
Wolverine Concrete Products 313 931-7189
  9189 Central St Detroit (48204) *(G-4687)*
Wolverine Crane & Service Inc (PA) 616 538-4870
  2557 Thornwood St Sw Grand Rapids (49519) *(G-7345)*
Wolverine Crane & Service Inc 734 467-9066
  30777 Beverly Rd Ste 150 Romulus (48174) *(G-14339)*
Wolverine Die Cast Ltd Prtnr O 586 757-1900
  30418 Saint Onge Cir Warren (48088) *(G-18071)*
Wolverine Gas and Oil Corp (PA) 616 458-1150
  1 Rivrfront Plz 55 Cmpau Grand Rapids (49503) *(G-7346)*
Wolverine Machine Products Co 248 634-9952
  319 Cogshall St Holly (48442) *(G-8301)*
Wolverine Metal Stamping Inc (PA) 269 429-6600
  3600 Tennis Ct Saint Joseph (49085) *(G-14980)*
Wolverine Packing Co (PA) 313 259-7500
  2535 Rivard St Detroit (48207) *(G-4688)*
Wolverine Plating Corporation 586 771-5000
  29456 Groesbeck Hwy Roseville (48066) *(G-14496)*
Wolverine Printing Company LLC 616 451-2075
  315 Grandville Ave Sw Grand Rapids (49503) *(G-7347)*
Wolverine Procurement Inc 616 866-9521
  175 S Main St Rockford (49341) *(G-14194)*
Wolverine Procurement Inc (HQ) 616 866-5500
  9341 Ne Courland Dr Rockford (49341) *(G-14195)*
Wolverine Production & Engrg 586 468-2890
  40960 Production Dr Harrison Township (48045) *(G-7734)*
Wolverine Products Inc 586 792-3740
  35220 Groesbeck Hwy Clinton Township (48035) *(G-3389)*
Wolverine Slipper Group Inc (HQ) 616 866-5500
  9341 Courtland Dr Ne Hb1141 Rockford (49351) *(G-14196)*
Wolverine Special Tool Inc 616 791-1027
  1857 Waldorf St Nw Grand Rapids (49544) *(G-7348)*
Wolverine Steel and Welding 517 524-7300
  13300 Spring Arbor Rd Concord (49237) *(G-3658)*
Wolverine Tool Co 810 664-2964
  2045 N Lapeer Rd Lapeer (48446) *(G-9968)*
Wolverine Trailers Inc 517 782-4950
  1500 Chanter Rd Jackson (49201) *(G-9037)*
Wolverine Water Trtmnt Systems, East Lansing *Also called Michigan Soft Water of Centr (G-4903)*
Wolverine Water Works Inc 248 673-4310
  2469 Airport Rd Waterford (48327) *(G-18176)*
Wolverine Waterworks, Waterford *Also called Wolverine Water Works Inc (G-18176)*
Wolverine World Wide Inc (PA) 616 866-5500
  9341 Courtland Dr Ne Rockford (49351) *(G-14197)*
Wolverine Worldwide, Rockford *Also called Wolverine Procurement Inc (G-14194)*
Wolvering Fur 313 961-0620
  2937 Russell St Detroit (48207) *(G-4689)*
Women Lifestyle Northshore, Muskegon *Also called Roe LLC (G-11909)*
Won-Door Corp 248 478-5757
  25629 Westmoreland Dr Farmington Hills (48336) *(G-5414)*
Wonch Battery Company 517 394-3600
  1521 Keystone Ave Lansing (48911) *(G-9904)*

Wonder Hostess Thrift Store, Cadillac *Also called Hostess Cake ITT Contntl Bkg (G-2335)*
Wonder Makers Environmental 269 382-4154
  2117 Lane Blvd Kalamazoo (49001) *(G-9372)*
Wonderland Graphics Inc 616 452-0712
  4030 Eastern Ave Se Grand Rapids (49508) *(G-7349)*
Wood Burn LLC 810 614-4204
  8106 Vassar Rd Millington (48746) *(G-11505)*
Wood Contracting LLC 989 479-6037
  265 Whitcomb St Harbor Beach (48441) *(G-7638)*
Wood Dowel & Dimension, Nunica *Also called Doltek Enterprises Inc (G-12579)*
Wood Graphics Signs, Greenville *Also called Woods Graphics (G-7511)*
Wood Haven Truss 231 821-0252
  7950 Brunswick Rd Holton (49425) *(G-8343)*
Wood Love Signs 586 322-6400
  21448 Sienna Dr Macomb (48044) *(G-10651)*
Wood Plus Cloth 231 421-8710
  144 Hall St Ste 101 Traverse City (49684) *(G-16881)*
Wood Shop Inc 231 582-9835
  111 N East St Boyne City (49712) *(G-1906)*
Wood Smiths Inc 269 372-6432
  1180 S 8th St Kalamazoo (49009) *(G-9373)*
Wood Tech Inc 616 455-0800
  670 76th St Sw Byron Center (49315) *(G-2303)*
Wood Wonders 313 461-2369
  23405 Sherwood Rd Belleville (48111) *(G-1496)*
Wood-Cutters Tooling Inc 616 257-7930
  4685 Spartan Indus Dr Sw Grandville (49418) *(G-7424)*
Woodard—Cm LLC 989 725-4265
  210 S Delaney Rd Owosso (48867) *(G-12869)*
Woodbridge Holdings Inc (HQ) 248 288-0100
  1515 Equity Dr Ste 100 Troy (48084) *(G-17451)*
Woodbridge Sales & Engrg Inc (HQ) 248 288-0100
  1515 Equity Dr Troy (48084) *(G-17452)*
Woodcraft Customs LLC 248 987-4473
  24790 Crestview Ct Farmington Hills (48335) *(G-5415)*
Woodcraft Industries, Marine City *Also called Usmats Inc (G-10968)*
Woodcrafters 517 741-7423
  855 Athens Rd Sherwood (49089) *(G-15387)*
Woodcrafters Custom Furniture, Sherwood *Also called Woodcrafters (G-15387)*
Woodcreek Customs 248 761-5652
  3111 Woodcreek Way Bloomfield Hills (48304) *(G-1875)*
Wooden Moon Studio 269 329-3229
  10334 Portage Rd Portage (49002) *(G-13635)*
Wooden Runabout Co 616 396-7248
  4261 58th St Holland (49423) *(G-8251)*
Woodhaven Log & Lumber, Mio *Also called Gilchrist Premium Lumber Pdts (G-11507)*
Woodhaven Log and Lumber 231 938-2200
  3504 Kirkland Ct Williamsburg (49690) *(G-18567)*
Woodie Manufacturing Inc 517 782-7663
  1400 Wildwood Ave Jackson (49202) *(G-9038)*
Woodland Creek Furniture Inc (PA) 231 258-2146
  546 M 72 E Kalkaska (49646) *(G-9412)*
Woodland Industries 989 686-6176
  112 S Huron Rd Kawkawlin (48631) *(G-9419)*
Woodland Park & Sales 810 229-2397
  7993 Grand River Rd Brighton (48114) *(G-2098)*
Woodland Paving Co (PA) 616 784-5220
  3566 Mill Creek Dr Ne Comstock Park (49321) *(G-3652)*
Woodland Pixie 503 330-8033
  404 S Mine St Bessemer (49911) *(G-1651)*
Woodmark Originals, Zeeland *Also called Hekman Furniture Company (G-19034)*
Woodrum Services LLC 616 827-1197
  1762 Rondo St Se Kentwood (49508) *(G-9483)*
Woods & Fields Community, Owosso *Also called Constine Inc (G-12827)*
Woods 2 G Logging LLC 248 469-7416
  7700 Golf Club Rd Howell (48843) *(G-8542)*
Woods Graphics 616 691-8025
  9180 Wabasis Ave Ne Greenville (48838) *(G-7511)*
Woodtech Builders Inc 906 932-8055
  219 E Frederick St Ironwood (49938) *(G-8773)*
Woodville Heights Enterprises 231 629-7750
  7147 6 Mile Rd Big Rapids (49307) *(G-1690)*
Woodward Energy Solutions LLC 888 967-4533
  719 Griswold St Ste 720 Detroit (48226) *(G-4690)*
Woodward Fst Inc 616 772-9171
  700 N Centennial St Zeeland (49464) *(G-19092)*
Woodward Printing Co, Troy *Also called Color Source Graphics Inc (G-17018)*
Woodways Inc 616 956-3070
  665 Construction Ct Zeeland (49464) *(G-19093)*
Woodways Custom Built, Grand Rapids *Also called Woodways Industries LLC (G-7350)*
Woodways Industries LLC (PA) 616 956-3070
  4265 28th St Se Ste A Grand Rapids (49512) *(G-7350)*
Woodworking Connection Inc 616 389-5481
  3763 N Spur Ct Wayland (49348) *(G-18210)*
Woodworks & Design Company 517 482-6665
  109 E South St Lansing (48910) *(G-9905)*
Woodworth Inc 810 820-6780
  4201 Pier North Blvd Flint (48504) *(G-5794)*

Woodworth Inc (PA) 248 481-2354
500 Centerpoint Pkwy N Pontiac (48341) *(G-13426)*
Woodworth Rassini Holding LLC (PA) 248 481-2354
500 Centerpoint Pkwy N Pontiac (48341) *(G-13427)*
Woody Hollow Candles 906 774-7839
507 Kent St Iron Mountain (49801) *(G-8737)*
Wooley Industries Inc 810 341-8823
3034 S Ballenger Hwy Flint (48507) *(G-5795)*
Woolly & Co LLC 248 480-4354
575 Stanley Blvd Birmingham (48009) *(G-1757)*
Woolly and Co, Birmingham *Also called Woolly & Co LLC (G-1757)*
Word Baron Inc 248 471-4080
315 E Eisenhower Pkwy # 2 Ann Arbor (48108) *(G-717)*
Worden Company, The, Holland *Also called Everest Expedition LLC (G-8032)*
Worden Farms, Beulah *Also called Leroy Worden (G-1655)*
Worden Group LLC 616 392-1848
199 E 17th St Holland (49423) *(G-8252)*
Work Apparel Division, Jackson *Also called Libra Industries Inc Michigan (G-8935)*
Workblades Inc 586 778-0060
21535 Groesbeck Hwy Warren (48089) *(G-18072)*
Workforce Payhub Inc 517 759-4026
104 E Maumee St Adrian (49221) *(G-105)*
Workforce Software LLC (PA) 734 542-4100
38705 7 Mile Rd Ste 300 Livonia (48152) *(G-10478)*
Workhorse Custom Chassis LLC (HQ) 248 588-5300
1675 E Whitcomb Ave Madison Heights (48071) *(G-10864)*
Workman Printing Inc 231 744-5500
1261 Holton Rd Muskegon (49445) *(G-11951)*
Workshop Detroit, Detroit *Also called Alo LLC (G-4004)*
World Class Equipment Company 586 331-2121
51515 Celeste Shelby Township (48315) *(G-15370)*
World Class Prototypes Inc 616 355-0200
400 Center St Holland (49423) *(G-8253)*
World Class Shopping Carts, Troy *Also called Wcscarts LLC (G-17446)*
World Class Steel & Proc Inc 586 585-1734
2673 American Dr Troy (48083) *(G-17453)*
World Corrugated Container Inc 517 629-9400
930 Elliott St Albion (49224) *(G-135)*
World Etching North America Ve, Fraser *Also called New World Etching N Amer Ve (G-5968)*
World Magnetics Company LLC 231 946-3800
810 Hastings St Traverse City (49686) *(G-16882)*
World of Cd-Rom 269 382-3766
4026 S Westnedge Ave D Kalamazoo (49008) *(G-9374)*
World of Cd-Rom , The, Kalamazoo *Also called World of Cd-Rom (G-9374)*
World of Pallets and Trucking 313 899-2000
3420 Lovett St Detroit (48210) *(G-4691)*
World Wide Cabinets Inc 248 683-2680
2655 Orchard Lake Rd # 101 Sylvan Lake (48320) *(G-16363)*
Worldcolor Midland, Midland *Also called Qg LLC (G-11404)*
Worldtek Industries LLC 734 494-5204
36310 Eureka Rd Romulus (48174) *(G-14340)*
Worldwide Marketing Svcs Inc 269 556-2000
1776 Hilltop Rd Saint Joseph (49085) *(G-14981)*
Worldwide Power Transm Div, Rochester Hills *Also called Gates Corporation (G-14020)*
Worswick Mold & Tool Inc 810 765-1700
6232 King Rd Marine City (48039) *(G-10970)*
Worten Copy Center Inc 231 845-7030
601 N Washington Ave Ludington (49431) *(G-10558)*
Worthington Armstrong Venture 269 934-6200
745 Enterprise Way Benton Harbor (49022) *(G-1611)*
Worthington Industries Inc 734 397-6187
5260 S Haggerty Rd Canton (48188) *(G-2543)*
Worthington Industries Inc 734 289-5416
3300 Wolverine Monroe (48162) *(G-11592)*
Worthington Steel of Michigan (HQ) 734 374-3260
11700 Worthington Dr Taylor (48180) *(G-16490)*
Wow Factor Tables and Events 248 550-5922
4337 E Grand River Ave Howell (48843) *(G-8543)*
Wow Products USA 989 672-1300
1111 S Colling Rd Caro (48723) *(G-2586)*
Wpi, Williamston *Also called Williamston Products Inc (G-18585)*
Wpw Inc 810 785-1478
5225 Energy Dr Flint (48505) *(G-5796)*
Wranosky & Sons Inc 586 336-9761
105 S Main St Romeo (48065) *(G-14240)*
Wraps N Signs 269 377-8488
8324 Shaver Rd Portage (49024) *(G-13636)*
Wreathinkingbykathie LLC 248 432-7312
29554 Colony Circle Dr Farmington Hills (48334) *(G-5416)*
Wright & Filippis Inc 313 832-5020
4201 Saint Antoine St Detroit (48201) *(G-4692)*
Wright & Filippis LLC 517 484-2624
1629 E Mich Ave Apt 101 Lansing (48912) *(G-9906)*
Wright & Filippis LLC 248 336-8460
23520 Woodward Ave Detroit (48220) *(G-3968)*
Wright & Filippis LLC 586 756-4020
13384 E 11 Mile Rd Warren (48089) *(G-18073)*
Wright & Filippis LLC 313 386-3330
4050 Fort St Lincoln Park (48146) *(G-10058)*

Wright Communications Inc 248 585-3838
1229 Chicago Rd Troy (48083) *(G-17454)*
Wright Plastic Products Co LLC 810 326-3000
2021 Christian B Haas Dr Saint Clair (48079) *(G-14845)*
Wright Plastic Products Co LLC (PA) 989 291-3211
201 E Condensery Rd Sheridan (48884) *(G-15386)*
Wright Time Foods LLc 810 835-9219
1414 S Graham Rd Flint (48532) *(G-5797)*
Wright Way Fabrication & Weldi 602 703-1393
W15383 Us Highway 2 Gould City (49838) *(G-6228)*
Wright-K Spare Parts and Svcs, Saginaw *Also called Wright-K Technology Inc (G-14795)*
Wright-K Technology Inc 989 752-2588
2025 E Genesee Ave Saginaw (48601) *(G-14795)*
Wrights Woodworks 989 295-7456
11735 Swan Creek Rd Saginaw (48609) *(G-14796)*
Write Idea 313 967-5881
613 Abbott St Ste 130e Detroit (48226) *(G-4693)*
Writers Bible LLc 734 286-7793
6037 4th St Romulus (48174) *(G-14341)*
Wrkco Inc 269 964-7181
4075 Columbia Ave W Battle Creek (49015) *(G-1312)*
Wrkco Inc 734 453-6700
11333 General Dr Plymouth (48170) *(G-13339)*
WSi Industrial Services Inc (PA) 734 942-9300
18555 Fort St Riverview (48193) *(G-13884)*
WUVS 103.7 THE BEAT, Muskegon *Also called West Mich Cmnty Help Netwrk (G-11942)*
Wyandotte Collet and Tool Inc 734 283-8055
4070 5th St Wyandotte (48192) *(G-18845)*
Wyatt Services Inc 586 264-8000
6425 Sims Dr Sterling Heights (48313) *(G-16233)*
Wyke Die & Engineering Inc 616 871-1175
4334 Brockton Dr Se Ste I Grand Rapids (49512) *(G-7351)*
Wyman-Gordon Forgings Inc 810 229-9550
7250 Whitmore Lake Rd Brighton (48116) *(G-2099)*
Wynalda International LLC 616 866-1561
8221 Graphic Dr Ne Belmont (49306) *(G-1522)*
Wynalda Litho Inc (PA) 616 866-1561
8221 Graphic Dr Ne Belmont (49306) *(G-1523)*
Wynalda Packaging, Belmont *Also called Wynalda Litho Inc (G-1523)*
Wyser Innovative Products LLC 616 583-9225
6157 Valduga Dr Sw Byron Center (49315) *(G-2304)*
Wysong, Midland *Also called N F P Inc (G-11397)*
Wysong Medical Corporation 989 631-0009
7550 Eastman Ave Midland (48642) *(G-11424)*
X L T Engineering Inc 989 684-4344
2595 S Huron Rd Kawkawlin (48631) *(G-9420)*
X-Bar Automation Inc 248 616-9890
961 Elmsford Dr Troy (48083) *(G-17455)*
X-Cel Industries Inc 248 226-6000
21121 Telegraph Rd Southfield (48033) *(G-15744)*
X-Edge Products Inc 866 591-9991
2727 Elmridge Dr Nw Grand Rapids (49534) *(G-7352)*
X-L Machine Co Inc 269 279-5128
20481 M 60 Three Rivers (49093) *(G-16590)*
X-Ray and Specialty Instrs Inc 734 485-6300
1980 E Michigan Ave Ypsilanti (48198) *(G-18986)*
X-Rite Company, The, Grand Rapids *Also called X-Rite Incorporated (G-7353)*
X-Rite Incorporated (HQ) 616 803-2100
4300 44th St Se Grand Rapids (49512) *(G-7353)*
X-Treme Graphics N Signs LLC 989 277-7517
13076 S State Rd Perry (48872) *(G-12982)*
X-Treme Printing Inc 810 232-3232
2638 Corunna Rd Flint (48503) *(G-5798)*
Xaerus Performance Fluids LLC 989 631-7871
2825 Schuette Rd Midland (48642) *(G-11425)*
Xalt Energy LLC (HQ) 989 486-8501
2700 S Saginaw Rd Midland (48640) *(G-11426)*
Xalt Energy LLC 816 525-1153
2700 S Saginaw Rd Midland (48640) *(G-11427)*
Xalt Energy Mi LLC 989 486-8501
2700 S Saginaw Rd Midland (48640) *(G-11428)*
Xc LLC 586 755-1660
24060 Hoover Rd Warren (48089) *(G-18074)*
Xcal Tools - Clare LLC 989 386-5376
314 E 4th St Clare (48617) *(G-3002)*
Xcell Software Inc 248 760-3160
3830 Benstein Rd Commerce Township (48382) *(G-3583)*
Xcentric Mold & Engrg LLC 586 598-4636
24541 Maplehurst Dr Clinton Township (48036) *(G-3390)*
Xenith LLC 866 888-2322
4333 W Fort St Detroit (48209) *(G-4694)*
Xg Sciences Inc 517 316-2038
2100 S Washington Ave Lansing (48910) *(G-9907)*
Xg Sciences Inc (PA) 517 703-1110
3101 Grand Oak Dr Lansing (48911) *(G-9908)*
Xileh Holding Inc (HQ) 248 340-4100
2750 High Meadow Cir Auburn Hills (48326) *(G-1090)*
Xl Engineering LLC 616 656-0324
6960 Hammond Ave Se Caledonia (49316) *(G-2407)*

XMCO Inc 586 558-8510
5501 Entp Ct Ste 400 Warren (48092) *(G-18075)*
Xoran Holdings LLC (PA) 734 418-5108
5210 S State Rd Ann Arbor (48108) *(G-718)*
Xoran Technologies LLC 734 663-7194
5210 S State Rd Ann Arbor (48108) *(G-719)*
Xplor Outside Box LLC 248 961-0536
31487 Pinto Dr Warren (48093) *(G-18076)*
Xplorer Motor Home Division, Brown City *Also called Frank Industries Inc (G-2137)*
Xpo Cnw Inc (HQ) 734 757-1444
2211 Old Earhart Rd Ann Arbor (48105) *(G-720)*
Xpress Packaging Solutions LLC 231 629-0463
11655 Park Ct Shelby Township (48315) *(G-15371)*
Xpress Printing, Saint Joseph *Also called Web Printing & Mktg Concepts (G-14974)*
Xrs Holdings Inc 616 209-7003
4400 Central Pkwy Hudsonville (49426) *(G-8619)*
Xsi, Ypsilanti *Also called X-Ray and Specialty Instrs Inc (G-18986)*
Xstream Tackle, Imlay City *Also called Grapentin Specialties Inc (G-8634)*
Xtol, Sterling Heights *Also called Hudson Industries Inc (G-16044)*
Xtra-Ordinary-You LLC 313 285-4472
4000 18th St Ecorse (48229) *(G-4989)*
Xtreme Mfg 906 353-8005
125 Main St Baraga (49908) *(G-1151)*
Xtreme Signs Inc 586 486-5068
27209 Van Dyke Ave Warren (48093) *(G-18077)*
Xxtar Associates LLC (PA) 888 946-6066
18100 Meyers Rd Ste L2 Detroit (48235) *(G-4695)*
Xyresic LLC 906 281-0021
4905 James Mcdevitt St Jackson (49201) *(G-9039)*
Xytek Industries Inc 313 838-6961
19431 W Davison St Detroit (48223) *(G-4696)*
XYZ McHine Tl Fabrications Inc 517 482-3668
2127 W Willow St Lansing (48917) *(G-9796)*
Y M C A Family Center 269 428-9622
3665 Hollywood Rd Saint Joseph (49085) *(G-14982)*
Y Not Candles 313 289-6299
5115 Michael St Dearborn Heights (48125) *(G-3944)*
Y Squared Inc (PA) 248 435-0301
5050b Leafdale Blvd Royal Oak (48073) *(G-14593)*
Yach Basin Marina, Holland *Also called Eldean Yacht Basin Ltd (G-8026)*
Yacks Dry Dock 989 689-6749
6227 N Meridian Rd Hope (48628) *(G-8365)*
Yakel Enterprises LLC 586 943-5885
8679 26 Mile Rd Ste 305 Washington Township (48094) *(G-18097)*
Yakkertech Limited 734 568-6162
8000 Yankee Rd Ste 350 Ottawa Lake (49267) *(G-12812)*
Yale Expositor 810 387-2300
21 S Main St Yale (48097) *(G-18921)*
Yale Steel Inc 810 387-2567
13334 Jeddo Rd Brockway (48097) *(G-2108)*
Yale Tool & Engraving Inc 734 459-7171
1471 Gold Smith Plymouth (48170) *(G-13340)*
Yamato International Corp 734 675-6055
22036 Commerce Dr Woodhaven (48183) *(G-18804)*
Yanfeng Auto Intr Systems, Holland *Also called Yanfeng US Auto Intr Systems I (G-8255)*
Yanfeng Automotive Interiors, Harrison Township *Also called Yanfeng US Auto Intr Systems I (G-7735)*
Yanfeng Global Auto Interiors, Holland *Also called Yanfeng US Auto Intr Systems I (G-8256)*
Yanfeng US Auto Intr Systems I 616 394-1567
915 E 32nd St Holland (49423) *(G-8254)*
Yanfeng US Auto Intr Systems I 734 254-5000
49200 Halyard Dr Plymouth (48170) *(G-13341)*
Yanfeng US Auto Intr Systems I (HQ) 248 319-7333
41935 W 12 Mile Rd Novi (48377) *(G-12570)*
Yanfeng US Auto Intr Systems I (HQ) 248 319-7333
41935 W 12 Mile Rd Novi (48377) *(G-12571)*
Yanfeng US Auto Intr Systems I 616 283-1349
1598 Washington Ave Holland (49423) *(G-8255)*
Yanfeng US Auto Intr Systems I 586 354-2101
42150 Executive Dr Harrison Township (48045) *(G-7735)*
Yanfeng US Auto Intr Systems I 616 392-5151
921 E 32nd St 69 Holland (49423) *(G-8256)*
Yanfeng US Auto Intr Systems I 734 289-4841
1833 Frenchtown Ctr Dr Monroe (48162) *(G-11593)*
Yanfeng US Auto Intr Systems I 313 259-3226
2931 E Jefferson Ave Detroit (48207) *(G-4697)*
Yanfeng US Auto Intr Systems I 734 946-0600
9800 Inkster Rd Romulus (48174) *(G-14342)*
Yanfeng US Auto Intr Systems I 810 987-2434
2133 Petit St Port Huron (48060) *(G-13541)*
Yanfeng US Automotive 616 394-1523
915 32nd St Tech Ctr Holland (49423) *(G-8257)*
Yanfeng US Automotive 517 721-0179
41935 W 12 Mile Rd Novi (48377) *(G-12572)*
Yanfeng USA Auto Trim Systems (HQ) 586 354-2101
42150 Executive Dr Harrison Township (48045) *(G-7736)*
Yankee Scrw Products Company 248 634-3011
212 Elm St Holly (48442) *(G-8302)*
Yapp USA Auto Systems Inc 248 817-5653
800 Kirts Blvd Troy (48084) *(G-17456)*
Yapp USA Auto Systems Inc 248 404-8696
36320 Eureka Rd Romulus (48174) *(G-14343)*
Yarbrough Precision Screws LLC 586 776-0752
17722 Rainbow Fraser (48026) *(G-6013)*
Yard & Home LLC 844 927-3466
2801 E Beltline Ave Nw Grand Rapids (49525) *(G-7354)*
Yard King, Cadillac *Also called Cadillac Fabrication Inc (G-2322)*
Yarema Die & Engineering Co (PA) 248 585-2830
300 Minnesota Dr Troy (48083) *(G-17457)*
Yaskawa America Inc 248 668-8800
2050 Austin Ave Rochester Hills (48309) *(G-14148)*
Yates Cider Mill Inc 248 651-8300
1990 E Avon Rd Rochester Hills (48307) *(G-14149)*
Yates Cylinders, Saint Clair Shores *Also called Yates Industries Inc (G-14892)*
Yates Forest Products Inc 989 739-8412
7110 Woodlea Rd Oscoda (48750) *(G-12774)*
Yates Industries Inc (PA) 586 778-7680
23050 E Industrial Dr Saint Clair Shores (48080) *(G-14892)*
Yazaki International Corp (HQ) 734 983-1000
6801 N Haggerty Rd 4707e Canton (48187) *(G-2544)*
Yell Sweets LLC 586 799-4560
14142 Lakeside Blvd N Shelby Township (48315) *(G-15372)*
Yello Dumpster 616 915-0506
1505 Steele Ave Sw Grand Rapids (49507) *(G-7355)*
Yellowstone Products Inc 616 299-7855
310 Dodge Rd Ne Ste C Comstock Park (49321) *(G-3653)*
Yen Group LLC 810 201-6457
2340 Dove St Port Huron (48060) *(G-13542)*
Yerington Brothers Inc 269 695-7669
3265 W Us Highway 12 Niles (49120) *(G-12174)*
Yeungs Lotus Express 248 380-3820
27500 Novi Rd Novi (48377) *(G-12573)*
YMCA, Saint Joseph *Also called Y M C A Family Center (G-14982)*
Yoe Industries Inc 586 791-7660
24451 Sorrentino Ct Clinton Township (48035) *(G-3391)*
Yogurtown Inc 313 908-9376
22231 Watsonia St Dearborn (48128) *(G-3917)*
Yooper Shirts Mqt 906 273-1837
503 N 3rd St Marquette (49855) *(G-11051)*
Yooper WD Wrks Restoration LLC 906 203-0056
312 Barbeau St Sault Sainte Marie (49783) *(G-15105)*
Yooper Winery LLC 906 361-0318
817 48th Ave Menominee (49858) *(G-11262)*
Yooper Wood Works & Designs, Sault Sainte Marie *Also called Yooper WD Wrks Restoration LLC (G-15105)*
Yoplait USA 231 832-3285
128 E Slosson Ave Reed City (49677) *(G-13804)*
Yore Creations LLC 313 463-8652
415 Brainard St Detroit (48201) *(G-4698)*
York Electric Inc (PA) 989 684-7460
611 Andre St Bay City (48706) *(G-1412)*
York Electric Inc 517 487-6400
1905 S Washington Ave Lansing (48910) *(G-9909)*
York Servo Motor Repair, Bay City *Also called York Electric Inc (G-1412)*
Yost Vises, Holland *Also called CWk International Corp (G-8010)*
Yost Vises LLC 616 396-2063
2221 Sunset Bluff Dr Holland (49424) *(G-8258)*
Young Cabinetry Inc 734 316-2896
1400 E Michigan Ave Saline (48176) *(G-15047)*
Young Diversified Industries 248 353-1867
21015 Bridge St Southfield (48033) *(G-15745)*
Young Ideas Enterprises, Troy *Also called Quirkroberts Publishing Ltd (G-17326)*
Young Manufacturing Inc 906 483-3851
23455 Hellman Ave Dollar Bay (49922) *(G-4766)*
Young Supply Company 313 875-3280
1177 W Baltimore St Detroit (48202) *(G-4699)*
Younggren Farm & Forest Inc 906 355-2272
34392 Younggren Rd Covington (49919) *(G-3727)*
Younggren Timber Company 906 355-2272
34392 Younggren Rd Covington (49919) *(G-3728)*
Youngtronics LLC 248 896-5790
49197 Wixom Tech Dr Ste A Wixom (48393) *(G-18793)*
Your Big Sign 248 881-9505
3440 Fenton Rd Hartland (48353) *(G-7774)*
Your Custom Image 989 621-2250
2021 E River Rd Mount Pleasant (48858) *(G-11747)*
Your Home Town USA Inc 517 529-9421
9301 Hyde Rd Clarklake (49234) *(G-3010)*
Your Hometown Shopper LLC 586 412-8500
11353 Covered Bridge Ln Bruce Twp (48065) *(G-2187)*
Your Personal Memoir LLC 248 629-0697
36 Oakdale Blvd Pleasant Ridge (48069) *(G-13107)*
Your Sign Lady LLC 586 741-8585
50322 Margaret Ave Macomb (48044) *(G-10652)*
Yoxheimer Tile Co 517 788-7542
919 E South St Jackson (49203) *(G-9040)*

ALPHABETIC

ALPHABETIC SECTION

Ypsinewscom 734 487-8109
   118 S Washington St Ypsilanti (48197) *(G-18987)*
Yti Office Express LLC 866 996-8952
   1280 E Big Beaver Rd A Troy (48083) *(G-17458)*
Z & A News 231 747-6232
   1239 W Giles Rd Muskegon (49445) *(G-11952)*
Z & R Electric Service Inc 906 774-0468
   619 Industrial Park Dr Iron Mountain (49801) *(G-8738)*
Z Mold & Engineering Inc 586 948-5000
   46390 Continental Dr Chesterfield (48047) *(G-2966)*
Z Technologies Corporation 313 937-0710
   26500 Capitol Redford (48239) *(G-13787)*
Z&G Auto Carriers LLC 586 819-1809
   34260 Pinewoods Cir # 203 Romulus (48174) *(G-14344)*
Z-Brite Metal Finishing Inc 269 422-2191
   6979 Stvnsville Baroda Rd Stevensville (49127) *(G-16270)*
Zajac Industries Inc 586 489-6746
   21319 Carlo Dr Clinton Township (48038) *(G-3392)*
Zajac Packaging, Clinton Township *Also called Zajac Industries Inc* *(G-3392)*
Zak Brothers Printing LLC 313 831-3216
   5480 Cass Ave Detroit (48202) *(G-4700)*
Zakoors 313 831-6969
   3909 Woodward Ave Detroit (48201) *(G-4701)*
Zalco Products LLC 586 354-0227
   23156 Hidden Creek Dr Macomb (48042) *(G-10653)*
Zander Colloids Lc 810 714-1623
   2040 W Thompson Rd Fenton (48430) *(G-5514)*
Zaremba & Co Inc 248 922-3300
   10590 Enterprise Dr Davisburg (48350) *(G-3773)*
Zatkoff Seals-Farmington, Farmington Hills *Also called Roger Zatkoff Company* *(G-5372)*
Zav-Tech Metal Finishing 269 422-2559
   6979 Stvnsville Baroda Rd Stevensville (49127) *(G-16271)*
Zayna LLC 616 452-4522
   1600 Marshall Ave Se Side Grand Rapids (49507) *(G-7356)*
Zcc USA Inc 734 997-3811
   3622 W Liberty Rd Ann Arbor (48103) *(G-721)*
Zccw, Ann Arbor *Also called Zhuzhou Cmntd Crbid Wrks USA* *(G-723)*
Zcs Interconnect LLC 616 399-8614
   138 W Washington Ave Zeeland (49464) *(G-19094)*
Zeeland Bio-Based Products LLC 616 748-1831
   2525 84th Ave Zeeland (49464) *(G-19095)*
Zeeland Farm Services Inc (PA) 616 772-9042
   2525 84th Ave Zeeland (49464) *(G-19096)*
Zeeland Farm Soya LLC 616 772-9042
   2525 84th Ave Zeeland (49464) *(G-19097)*
Zeeland Freight Services, Zeeland *Also called Zeeland Farm Services Inc* *(G-19096)*
Zeeland Print Shop Co 616 772-6636
   145 E Main Ave Zeeland (49464) *(G-19098)*
Zeeland Record Co 616 772-2131
   16 S Elm St Zeeland (49464) *(G-19099)*
Zeilinger Wool Co LLC 989 652-2920
   1130 Weiss St Frankenmuth (48734) *(G-5874)*
Zeiss Int 734 895-6004
   29295 Lyon Oaks Dr Wixom (48393) *(G-18794)*
Zeledyne Glass Corp 615 350-7500
   17333 Federal Dr Ste 230 Allen Park (48101) *(G-211)*
Zellar Forest Products 906 586-9817
   462 Lustila Rd Germfask (49836) *(G-6169)*
Zellars Group LLC 313 828-2309
   8615 Knodell St Detroit (48213) *(G-4702)*
Zellco Precision Inc 269 684-1720
   1710 E Main St Niles (49120) *(G-12175)*
Zemis 5 LLC 317 946-7015
   13207 Santa Clara St Detroit (48235) *(G-4703)*
Zenith Global LLC 517 546-7402
   1100 Sutton St Howell (48843) *(G-8544)*
Zephyros Inc (PA) 586 336-1600
   160 Mclean Bruce Twp (48065) *(G-2188)*
Zerilli & Sesi LLC 586 741-8805
   30504 23 Mile Rd Chesterfield (48047) *(G-2967)*
Zero Gage Division, Wixom *Also called Benny Gage Inc* *(G-18620)*
Zero Hour Parts, Ann Arbor *Also called Spot Design LLC* *(G-662)*
Zero Hour Parts 734 997-0866
   3765 Broadmoor Ave Se Kentwood (49512) *(G-9484)*
Zero Hour Production LLC 616 498-3545
   275 Metty Dr Ann Arbor (48103) *(G-722)*
ZF Active Safety & Elec US LLC 586 843-2100
   12025 Tech Center Dr Livonia (48150) *(G-10479)*
ZF Active Safety & Elec US LLC 248 478-7210
   24175 Research Dr Farmington Hills (48335) *(G-5417)*
ZF Active Safety & Elec US LLC 734 855-3631
   12075 Tech Center Dr Livonia (48150) *(G-10480)*
ZF Active Safety & Elec US LLC 586 232-7200
   4585 26 Mile Rd Washington (48094) *(G-18092)*
ZF Active Safety & Elec US LLC (HQ) 734 855-2600
   12001 Tech Center Dr Livonia (48150) *(G-10481)*
ZF Active Safety & Elec US LLC 586 232-7200
   4505 26 Mile Rd Washington (48094) *(G-18093)*
ZF Active Safety US Inc 906 248-3882
   21105 W M 28 Bldg 6 Brimley (49715) *(G-2105)*
ZF Active Safety US Inc 248 478-7210
   24175 Research Dr Farmington Hills (48335) *(G-5418)*
ZF Active Safety US Inc 956 491-9036
   1055 Packard Dr Howell (48843) *(G-8545)*
ZF Active Safety US Inc 517 223-8330
   500 E Van Riper Rd Fowlerville (48836) *(G-5858)*
ZF Active Safety US Inc (HQ) 734 812-6979
   12025 Tech Center Dr Livonia (48150) *(G-10482)*
ZF Active Safety US Inc 810 750-1036
   9475 Center Rd Fenton (48430) *(G-5515)*
ZF Active Safety US Inc 586 899-2807
   42315 R Mancini Dr Sterling Heights (48314) *(G-16234)*
ZF Active Safety US Inc 734 855-2470
   12200 Tech Center Dr Livonia (48150) *(G-10483)*
ZF Active Safety US Inc 248 863-2412
   2828 E Genesee Ave Saginaw (48601) *(G-14797)*
ZF Auto Holdings US Inc (HQ) 734 855-2600
   12001 Tech Center Dr Livonia (48150) *(G-10484)*
ZF Automotive JV US LLC (HQ) 734 855-2787
   12001 Tech Center Dr Livonia (48150) *(G-10485)*
ZF Automotive US Inc (HQ) 734 855-2600
   12001 Tech Center Dr Livonia (48150) *(G-10486)*
ZF Axle Drives Marysville LLC 810 989-8702
   2900 Busha Hwy Marysville (48040) *(G-11114)*
ZF Chassis Components LLC (HQ) 810 245-2000
   3300 John Conley Dr Lapeer (48446) *(G-9969)*
ZF Chassis Components LLC 810 245-2000
   3255 John Conley Dr Lapeer (48446) *(G-9970)*
ZF Chassis Components LLC 810 245-2000
   930 S Saginaw St Lapeer (48446) *(G-9971)*
ZF Friedrichshafen AG 734 855-2600
   12001 Tech Center Dr Livonia (48150) *(G-10487)*
ZF Lemforder Corp 810 245-7136
   3300 John Conley Dr Lapeer (48446) *(G-9972)*
ZF North America Inc (HQ) 734 416-6200
   15811 Centennial Dr Northville (48168) *(G-12272)*
ZF Passive Safety S Africa Inc 734 855-2600
   12001 Tech Center Dr Livonia (48150) *(G-10488)*
ZF Passive Safety US Inc (HQ) 734 855-2600
   12001 Tech Center Dr Livonia (48150) *(G-10489)*
ZF Passive Safety US Inc 586 232-7200
   4505 26 Mile Rd Washington (48094) *(G-18094)*
ZF Passive Sfety Systems US In 586 752-1409
   14761 E32 Mile Rd Romeo (48065) *(G-14241)*
ZF Passive Sfety Systems US In (HQ) 586 232-7200
   12001 Tech Center Dr Livonia (48150) *(G-10490)*
ZF Passive Sfety Systems US In 586 781-5511
   4505 26 Mile Rd Washington (48094) *(G-18095)*
ZF String Active Safety US Inc (HQ) 734 855-2600
   12001 Tech Center Dr Livonia (48150) *(G-10491)*
ZF TRW Auto Holdings Corp (HQ) 734 855-2600
   12001 Tech Center Dr Livonia (48150) *(G-10492)*
Zfs Creston LLC 616 748-1825
   2525 84th Ave Zeeland (49464) *(G-19100)*
Zfs Ithaca LLC (PA) 616 772-9042
   2525 84th Ave Zeeland (49464) *(G-19101)*
Zhi Publishing, Onsted *Also called Zonya Health International* *(G-12708)*
Zhongding Saling Parts USA Inc (HQ) 734 241-8870
   48600 Five Mile Rd Plymouth (48170) *(G-13342)*
Zhongli North America Inc 248 733-9300
   1511 E 14 Mile Rd Troy (48083) *(G-17459)*
Zhuzhou Cmntd Crbid Wrks USA 734 302-0125
   4651 Platt Rd Ann Arbor (48108) *(G-723)*
Ziebart International Corp (PA) 248 588-4100
   1290 E Maple Rd Troy (48083) *(G-17460)*
Ziel Optics Inc 734 994-9803
   7167 Jackson Rd Ann Arbor (48103) *(G-724)*
Zimbell House Publishing LLC 248 909-0143
   1093 Irwin Dr Waterford (48327) *(G-18177)*
Zimmer - Lieffring Inc (PA) 734 953-1630
   41370 Bridge St Novi (48375) *(G-12574)*
Zimmer Great Lakes, Novi *Also called Zimmer - Lieffring Inc* *(G-12574)*
Zimmer Marble Co Inc 517 787-1500
   1812 River St Jackson (49202) *(G-9041)*
Zimmermann Engineering Co Inc 248 358-0044
   24260 Telegraph Rd Southfield (48033) *(G-15746)*
Zinger Sheet Metal Inc 616 532-3121
   4005 Rger B Chffee Mem Dr Grand Rapids (49548) *(G-7357)*
Zingermans Bakehouse Inc 734 761-2095
   3711 Plaza Dr Ste 5 Ann Arbor (48108) *(G-725)*
Zink 586 781-5314
   5429 Vincent Trl Shelby Township (48316) *(G-15373)*
Zion Industries Inc 517 622-3409
   1180 Comet Ln Grand Ledge (48837) *(G-6401)*
Zip Cut, Kalamazoo *Also called Waber Tool & Engineering Co* *(G-9365)*
Zippers, Temperance *Also called Temperance Distilling Company* *(G-16550)*
Zk Enterprises Inc (PA) 989 728-4439
   2382 M 33 Alger (48610) *(G-140)*
Zkw Lighting Systems Usa Inc 248 509-7300
   100 W Big Beavr Rd # 300 Troy (48084) *(G-17461)*

Zodiac Enterprises LLC 810 640-7146
  1000 Church St Ste 1 Mount Morris (48458) *(G-11677)*
Zoe Health 616 485-1909
  5715 Christie Ave Se Kentwood (49508) *(G-9485)*
Zoet Poultry 269 751-2776
  4847 140th Ave Holland (49423) *(G-8259)*
Zoetis LLC 888 963-8471
  2605 E Kilgore Rd Kalamazoo (49001) *(G-9375)*
Zomedica Pharmaceuticals Inc (PA) 734 369-2555
  100 Phoenix Dr Ste 125 Ann Arbor (48108) *(G-726)*
Zondervan Corporation LLC (HQ) 616 698-6900
  3900 Sparks Dr Se Grand Rapids (49546) *(G-7358)*
Zondervan Publishing House, Grand Rapids *Also called Zondervan Corporation LLC (G-7358)*
Zonya Health International 517 467-6995
  7134 Donegal Dr Onsted (49265) *(G-12708)*
Zoomer Display LLC 616 734-0300
  522 Stocking Ave Nw Grand Rapids (49504) *(G-7359)*
Zoyes East Inc 248 584-3300
  1280 Hilton Rd Ferndale (48220) *(G-5599)*
Zsi-Foster Inc (HQ) 734 844-0055
  45065 Michigan Ave Canton (48188) *(G-2545)*
Zuckero & Sons Inc 586 772-3377
  27450 Groesbeck Hwy Roseville (48066) *(G-14497)*
Zulski Lumber Inc 231 539-8909
  2465 Zulski Rd Pellston (49769) *(G-12969)*
Zume It Inc 248 522-6868
  34405 W 12 Mile Rd # 137 Farmington Hills (48331) *(G-5419)*
Zunairah Fuels Inc 647 405-1606
  37109 Harper Ave Clinton Township (48036) *(G-3393)*
Zurn Industries LLC 313 864-2800
  7431 W 8 Mile Rd Detroit (48221) *(G-4704)*
Zygot Operations Limited 810 736-2900
  4301 Western Rd Flint (48506) *(G-5799)*
Zynp International Corp 734 947-1000
  27501 Hldbrndt Rd Ste 300 Romulus (48174) *(G-14345)*
Zyongyuan International, Romulus *Also called Zynp International Corp (G-14345)*

PRODUCT INDEX

• Product categories are listed in alphabetical order.

A

ABRASIVES
ABRASIVES: Aluminum Oxide Fused
ABRASIVES: Steel Shot
ABRASIVES: Synthetic
ABRASIVES: Tungsten Carbide
ABRASIVES: sandpaper
ACADEMIC TUTORING SVCS
ACADEMY
ACCELERATION INDICATORS & SYSTEM COMPONENTS: Aerospace
ACCELERATORS: Particle, High Voltage
ACCELEROMETERS
ACCOUNTING SVCS, NEC
ACIDS
ACIDS: Inorganic
ACIDS: Sulfuric, Oleum
ACOUSTICAL BOARD & TILE
ACRYLIC RESINS
ACTUATORS: Indl, NEC
ADDITIVE BASED PLASTIC MATERIALS: Plasticizers
ADHESIVES
ADHESIVES & SEALANTS
ADHESIVES & SEALANTS WHOLESALERS
ADHESIVES: Adhesives, plastic
ADHESIVES: Epoxy
ADULT DAYCARE CENTERS
ADVERTISING AGENCIES
ADVERTISING AGENCIES: Consultants
ADVERTISING COPY WRITING SVCS
ADVERTISING CURTAINS
ADVERTISING DISPLAY PRDTS
ADVERTISING MATERIAL DISTRIBUTION
ADVERTISING REPRESENTATIVES: Electronic Media
ADVERTISING REPRESENTATIVES: Newspaper
ADVERTISING REPRESENTATIVES: Printed Media
ADVERTISING SPECIALTIES, WHOLESALE
ADVERTISING SVCS, NEC
ADVERTISING SVCS: Billboards
ADVERTISING SVCS: Direct Mail
ADVERTISING SVCS: Display
ADVERTISING SVCS: Outdoor
ADVERTISING SVCS: Poster, Outdoor
AERIAL WORK PLATFORMS
AGENTS, BROKERS & BUREAUS: Personal Service
AGRICULTURAL CHEMICALS: Trace Elements
AGRICULTURAL EQPT: BARN, SILO, POULTRY, DAIRY/LIVESTOCK MACH
AGRICULTURAL EQPT: Clippers, Animal, Hand Or Electric
AGRICULTURAL EQPT: Fertilizng, Sprayng, Dustng/Irrigatn Mach
AGRICULTURAL EQPT: Grounds Mowing Eqpt
AGRICULTURAL EQPT: Harvesters, Fruit, Vegetable, Tobacco
AGRICULTURAL EQPT: Irrigation Eqpt, Self-Propelled
AGRICULTURAL EQPT: Storage Bins, Crop
AGRICULTURAL EQPT: Tractors, Farm
AGRICULTURAL EQPT: Transplanters
AGRICULTURAL LIMESTONE: Ground
AGRICULTURAL MACHINERY & EQPT: Wholesalers
AIR CLEANING SYSTEMS
AIR CONDITIONERS: Motor Vehicle
AIR CONDITIONING EQPT
AIR CONDITIONING UNITS: Complete, Domestic Or Indl
AIR MATTRESSES: Plastic
AIR POLLUTION CONTROL EQPT & SPLYS WHOLESALERS
AIR POLLUTION MEASURING SVCS
AIR PURIFICATION EQPT
AIRCRAFT & AEROSPACE FLIGHT INSTRUMENTS & GUIDANCE SYSTEMS
AIRCRAFT & HEAVY EQPT REPAIR SVCS
AIRCRAFT ASSEMBLY PLANTS
AIRCRAFT CONTROL SYSTEMS: Electronic Totalizing Counters
AIRCRAFT ENGINES & ENGINE PARTS: Cooling Systems
AIRCRAFT ENGINES & ENGINE PARTS: Mount Parts
AIRCRAFT ENGINES & ENGINE PARTS: Research & Development, Mfr
AIRCRAFT ENGINES & PARTS
AIRCRAFT EQPT & SPLYS WHOLESALERS
AIRCRAFT FLIGHT INSTRUMENTS
AIRCRAFT MAINTENANCE & REPAIR SVCS
AIRCRAFT PARTS & AUXILIARY EQPT: Assys, Subassemblies/Parts
AIRCRAFT PARTS & AUXILIARY EQPT: Countermeasure Dispensers
AIRCRAFT PARTS & AUXILIARY EQPT: Gears, Power Transmission
AIRCRAFT PARTS & AUXILIARY EQPT: Lighting/Landing Gear Assy
AIRCRAFT PARTS & AUXILIARY EQPT: Military Eqpt & Armament
AIRCRAFT PARTS & AUXILIARY EQPT: Pontoons
AIRCRAFT PARTS & EQPT, NEC
AIRCRAFT SERVICING & REPAIRING
AIRCRAFT TURBINES
AIRCRAFT: Airplanes, Fixed Or Rotary Wing
AIRCRAFT: Motorized
AIRCRAFT: Research & Development, Manufacturer
AIRPORTS, FLYING FIELDS & SVCS
ALARM SYSTEMS WHOLESALERS
ALARMS: Burglar
ALARMS: Fire
ALCOHOL: Ethyl & Ethanol
ALKALIES & CHLORINE
ALL-TERRAIN VEHICLE DEALERS
ALLOYS: Additive, Exc Copper Or Made In Blast Furnaces
ALTERNATORS & GENERATORS: Battery Charging
ALTERNATORS: Automotive
ALUMINUM
ALUMINUM PRDTS
ALUMINUM: Rolling & Drawing
AMMONIA & LIQUOR: Chemical Recovery Coke Oven
AMMUNITION: Cartridges Case, 30 mm & Below
AMMUNITION: Components
AMMUNITION: Shot, Steel
AMMUNITION: Small Arms
AMPLIFIERS
AMUSEMENT & RECREATION SVCS: Amusement Arcades
AMUSEMENT & RECREATION SVCS: Boating Club, Membership
AMUSEMENT & RECREATION SVCS: Recreation Center
AMUSEMENT & RECREATION SVCS: Ski Instruction
AMUSEMENT MACHINES: Coin Operated
AMUSEMENT PARK DEVICES & RIDES
AMUSEMENT PARK DEVICES & RIDES: Ferris Wheels
ANALGESICS
ANALYZERS: Coulometric, Exc Indl Process
ANALYZERS: Network
ANALYZERS: Respiratory
ANIMAL FEED & SUPPLEMENTS: Livestock & Poultry
ANIMAL FEED: Wholesalers
ANIMAL FOOD & SUPPLEMENTS: Alfalfa Or Alfalfa Meal
ANIMAL FOOD & SUPPLEMENTS: Bird Food, Prepared
ANIMAL FOOD & SUPPLEMENTS: Buttermilk Emulsion
ANIMAL FOOD & SUPPLEMENTS: Dog
ANIMAL FOOD & SUPPLEMENTS: Dog & Cat
ANIMAL FOOD & SUPPLEMENTS: Feed Premixes
ANIMAL FOOD & SUPPLEMENTS: Feed Supplements
ANIMAL FOOD & SUPPLEMENTS: Kelp Meal & Pellets
ANIMAL FOOD & SUPPLEMENTS: Livestock
ANIMAL FOOD & SUPPLEMENTS: Mineral feed supplements
ANIMAL FOOD & SUPPLEMENTS: Pet, Exc Dog & Cat, Dry
ANIMAL FOOD & SUPPLEMENTS: Poultry
ANIMAL FOOD & SUPPLEMENTS: Specialty, Mice & Other Pets
ANIMAL FOOD/SUPPLEMENTS: Feeds Fm Meat/Meat/Veg Combnd Meals
ANNEALING: Metal
ANODIZING SVC
ANTENNAS: Radar Or Communications
ANTENNAS: Receiving
ANTI-GLARE MATERIAL
ANTIBIOTICS
ANTIFREEZE
ANTIQUE REPAIR & RESTORATION SVCS, EXC FURNITURE & AUTOS
ANTIQUE SHOPS
APPAREL ACCESS STORES
APPAREL DESIGNERS: Commercial
APPLIANCE PARTS: Porcelain Enameled
APPLIANCES, HOUSEHOLD OR COIN OPERATED: Laundry Dryers
APPLIANCES, HOUSEHOLD: Kitchen, Major, Exc Refrigs & Stoves
APPLIANCES, HOUSEHOLD: Laundry Machines, Incl Coin-Operated
APPLIANCES, HOUSEHOLD: Refrigs, Mechanical & Absorption
APPLIANCES, HOUSEHOLD: Sewing Machines & Attchmnts, Domestic
APPLIANCES: Household, NEC
APPLIANCES: Household, Refrigerators & Freezers
APPLIANCES: Major, Cooking
APPLIANCES: Small, Electric
APPLICATIONS SOFTWARE PROGRAMMING
AQUARIUMS & ACCESS: Glass
AQUARIUMS & ACCESS: Plastic
ARCHITECTURAL SVCS
ARCHITECTURAL SVCS: Engineering
ARMATURE REPAIRING & REWINDING SVC
ARMOR PLATES
ARRESTERS & COILS: Lightning
ART & ORNAMENTAL WARE: Pottery
ART DESIGN SVCS
ART GALLERIES
ART GOODS & SPLYS WHOLESALERS
ARTISTS' MATERIALS: Boards, Drawing
ARTISTS' MATERIALS: Canvas Board
ARTS & CRAFTS SCHOOL
ARTWORK: Framed
ASBESTOS PRDTS: Friction Materials
ASBESTOS PRDTS: Pipe Covering, Heat Insulatng Matl, Exc Felt
ASBESTOS REMOVAL EQPT
ASPHALT & ASPHALT PRDTS
ASPHALT COATINGS & SEALERS
ASPHALT MINING & BITUMINOUS STONE QUARRYING SVCS
ASPHALT MIXTURES WHOLESALERS
ASPHALT PLANTS INCLUDING GRAVEL MIX TYPE
ASSEMBLING SVC: Plumbing Fixture Fittings, Plastic
ASSOCIATIONS: Business
ASSOCIATIONS: Engineering
ASSOCIATIONS: Manufacturers'
ASSOCIATIONS: Real Estate Management
ASSOCIATIONS: Trade
ATOMIZERS
AUCTION SVCS: Motor Vehicle
AUCTIONEERS: Fee Basis
AUDIO & VIDEO EQPT, EXC COMMERCIAL
AUDIO COMPONENTS
AUDIO ELECTRONIC SYSTEMS
AUDIO-VISUAL PROGRAM PRODUCTION SVCS
AUDIOLOGICAL EQPT: Electronic
AUTO & HOME SUPPLY STORES: Auto & Truck Eqpt & Parts
AUTO & HOME SUPPLY STORES: Auto Air Cond Eqpt, Sell/Install
AUTO & HOME SUPPLY STORES: Automotive Access
AUTO & HOME SUPPLY STORES: Automotive parts
AUTO & HOME SUPPLY STORES: Batteries, Automotive & Truck
AUTO & HOME SUPPLY STORES: Speed Shops, Incl Race Car Splys
AUTO & HOME SUPPLY STORES: Trailer Hitches, Automotive
AUTO & HOME SUPPLY STORES: Truck Eqpt & Parts
AUTO SPLYS & PARTS, NEW, WHSLE: Exhaust Sys, Mufflers, Etc
AUTOCLAVES: Laboratory
AUTOMATIC REGULATING CONTROL: Building Svcs Monitoring, Auto

PRODUCT INDEX

AUTOMATIC REGULATING CONTROLS: Appliance Regulators
AUTOMATIC REGULATING CONTROLS: Appliance, Exc Air-Cond/Refr
AUTOMATIC REGULATING CONTROLS: Energy Cutoff, Residtl/Comm
AUTOMATIC REGULATING CONTROLS: Float, Residential Or Comm
AUTOMATIC REGULATING CONTROLS: Gas Burner, Automatic
AUTOMATIC REGULATING CONTROLS: Hardware, Environmental Reg
AUTOMATIC REGULATING CONTROLS: Pneumatic Relays, Air-Cond
AUTOMATIC REGULATING CONTROLS: Refrig/Air-Cond Defrost
AUTOMATIC REGULATING CONTROLS: Thermocouples, Vacuum, Glass
AUTOMATIC REGULATING CONTROLS: Vapor Heating
AUTOMATIC REGULATING CTRLS: Damper, Pneumatic Or Electric
AUTOMATIC TELLER MACHINES
AUTOMATIC VENDING MACHINES: Mechanisms & Parts
AUTOMOBILE FINANCE LEASING
AUTOMOBILE RECOVERY SVCS
AUTOMOBILES & OTHER MOTOR VEHICLES WHOLESALERS
AUTOMOBILES: Midget, Power Driven
AUTOMOTIVE & TRUCK GENERAL REPAIR SVC
AUTOMOTIVE BATTERIES WHOLESALERS
AUTOMOTIVE BODY SHOP
AUTOMOTIVE BODY, PAINT & INTERIOR REPAIR & MAINTENANCE SVC
AUTOMOTIVE COLLISION SHOPS
AUTOMOTIVE CUSTOMIZING SVCS, NONFACTORY BASIS
AUTOMOTIVE EMISSIONS TESTING SVCS
AUTOMOTIVE GLASS REPLACEMENT SHOPS
AUTOMOTIVE PAINT SHOP
AUTOMOTIVE PARTS, ACCESS & SPLYS
AUTOMOTIVE PARTS: Plastic
AUTOMOTIVE PRDTS: Rubber
AUTOMOTIVE RADIATOR REPAIR SHOPS
AUTOMOTIVE REPAIR SHOPS: Diesel Engine Repair
AUTOMOTIVE REPAIR SHOPS: Electrical Svcs
AUTOMOTIVE REPAIR SHOPS: Engine Rebuilding
AUTOMOTIVE REPAIR SHOPS: Engine Repair
AUTOMOTIVE REPAIR SHOPS: Fuel System Repair
AUTOMOTIVE REPAIR SHOPS: Machine Shop
AUTOMOTIVE REPAIR SHOPS: Muffler Shop, Sale/Rpr/Installation
AUTOMOTIVE REPAIR SHOPS: Springs, Rebuilding & Repair
AUTOMOTIVE REPAIR SHOPS: Trailer Repair
AUTOMOTIVE REPAIR SHOPS: Truck Engine Repair, Exc Indl
AUTOMOTIVE REPAIR SVC
AUTOMOTIVE REPAIR SVCS, MISCELLANEOUS
AUTOMOTIVE SPLYS & PARTS, NEW, WHOL: Auto Servicing Eqpt
AUTOMOTIVE SPLYS & PARTS, NEW, WHOLESALE: Alternators
AUTOMOTIVE SPLYS & PARTS, NEW, WHOLESALE: Clutches
AUTOMOTIVE SPLYS & PARTS, NEW, WHOLESALE: Engines/Eng Parts
AUTOMOTIVE SPLYS & PARTS, NEW, WHOLESALE: Filters, Air & Oil
AUTOMOTIVE SPLYS & PARTS, NEW, WHOLESALE: Hardware
AUTOMOTIVE SPLYS & PARTS, NEW, WHOLESALE: Pumps, Oil & Gas
AUTOMOTIVE SPLYS & PARTS, NEW, WHOLESALE: Radiators
AUTOMOTIVE SPLYS & PARTS, NEW, WHOLESALE: Seat Belts
AUTOMOTIVE SPLYS & PARTS, NEW, WHOLESALE: Splys
AUTOMOTIVE SPLYS & PARTS, NEW, WHOLESALE: Stampings
AUTOMOTIVE SPLYS & PARTS, NEW, WHOLESALE: Tools & Eqpt
AUTOMOTIVE SPLYS & PARTS, NEW, WHOLESALE: Trailer Parts
AUTOMOTIVE SPLYS & PARTS, NEW, WHOLESALE: Trim
AUTOMOTIVE SPLYS & PARTS, USED, WHOLESALE
AUTOMOTIVE SPLYS & PARTS, USED, WHOLESALE: Access, NEC
AUTOMOTIVE SPLYS & PARTS, WHOLESALE, NEC
AUTOMOTIVE SPLYS, USED, WHOLESALE & RETAIL
AUTOMOTIVE SPLYS/PART, NEW, WHOL: Spring, Shock Absorb/Strut
AUTOMOTIVE SPLYS/PARTS, NEW, WHOL: Body Rpr/Paint Shop Splys
AUTOMOTIVE SVCS, EXC REP & CARWASHES: Do-It-Yourself Garages
AUTOMOTIVE SVCS, EXC REPAIR & CARWASHES: Customizing
AUTOMOTIVE SVCS, EXC REPAIR & CARWASHES: Insp & Diagnostic
AUTOMOTIVE SVCS, EXC REPAIR & CARWASHES: Lubrication
AUTOMOTIVE SVCS, EXC REPAIR & CARWASHES: Maintenance
AUTOMOTIVE SVCS, EXC REPAIR & CARWASHES: Road Svc
AUTOMOTIVE SVCS, EXC REPAIR & CARWASHES: Trailer Maintenance
AUTOMOTIVE SVCS, EXC REPAIR: Carwash, Automatic
AUTOMOTIVE SVCS, EXC REPAIR: Truck Wash
AUTOMOTIVE TOWING SVCS
AUTOMOTIVE UPHOLSTERY SHOPS
AUTOMOTIVE WELDING SVCS
AUTOMOTIVE: Bodies
AUTOMOTIVE: Seat Frames, Metal
AUTOMOTIVE: Seating
AUTOTRANSFORMERS: Electric
AWNINGS & CANOPIES
AWNINGS & CANOPIES: Awnings, Fabric, From Purchased Matls
AWNINGS & CANOPIES: Fabric
AWNINGS: Fiberglass
AWNINGS: Metal
AWNINGS: Wood
AXLES
AXLES: Rolled Or Forged, Made In Steel Mills

B

BABBITT (METAL)
BABY FORMULA
BACKFILLERS: Self-Propelled
BADGES, WHOLESALE
BADGES: Identification & Insignia
BAGS & CONTAINERS: Textile, Exc Sleeping
BAGS & SACKS: Shipping & Shopping
BAGS: Canvas
BAGS: Cement, Made From Purchased Materials
BAGS: Garment, Plastic Film, Made From Purchased Materials
BAGS: Paper
BAGS: Paper, Made From Purchased Materials
BAGS: Plastic
BAGS: Plastic & Pliofilm
BAGS: Plastic, Made From Purchased Materials
BAGS: Rubber Or Rubberized Fabric
BAGS: Shipping
BAGS: Textile
BAKERIES, COMMERCIAL: On Premises Baking Only
BAKERIES: On Premises Baking & Consumption
BAKERY FOR HOME SVC DELIVERY
BAKERY MACHINERY
BAKERY PRDTS: Bakery Prdts, Partially Cooked, Exc frozen
BAKERY PRDTS: Biscuits, Dry
BAKERY PRDTS: Bread, All Types, Fresh Or Frozen
BAKERY PRDTS: Buns, Bread Type, Fresh Or Frozen
BAKERY PRDTS: Cakes, Bakery, Exc Frozen
BAKERY PRDTS: Cakes, Bakery, Frozen
BAKERY PRDTS: Cones, Ice Cream
BAKERY PRDTS: Cookies
BAKERY PRDTS: Cookies & crackers
BAKERY PRDTS: Doughnuts, Exc Frozen
BAKERY PRDTS: Doughnuts, Frozen
BAKERY PRDTS: Dry
BAKERY PRDTS: Frozen
BAKERY PRDTS: Pastries, Exc Frozen
BAKERY PRDTS: Pies, Exc Frozen
BAKERY PRDTS: Pretzels
BAKERY PRDTS: Wholesalers
BAKERY: Wholesale Or Wholesale & Retail Combined
BALCONIES: Metal
BALERS
BALLASTS: Fluorescent
BALLOONS: Novelty & Toy
BALLOONS: Toy & Advertising, Rubber
BANNERS: Fabric
BANQUET HALL FACILITIES
BAR FIXTURES: Wood
BAR FIXTURES: Wood
BAR JOISTS & CONCRETE REINFORCING BARS: Fabricated
BARBECUE EQPT
BARGES BUILDING & REPAIR
BARRELS: Shipping, Metal
BARRETTES
BARRICADES: Metal
BARS & BAR SHAPES: Steel, Cold-Finished, Own Hot-Rolled
BARS & BAR SHAPES: Steel, Hot-Rolled
BARS, COLD FINISHED: Steel, From Purchased Hot-Rolled
BARS: Cargo, Stabilizing, Metal
BARS: Concrete Reinforcing, Fabricated Steel
BASES, BEVERAGE
BASKETS: Steel Wire
BATH SALTS
BATHROOM ACCESS & FITTINGS: Vitreous China & Earthenware
BATHROOM FIXTURES: Plastic
BATTERIES, EXC AUTOMOTIVE: Wholesalers
BATTERIES: Alkaline, Cell Storage
BATTERIES: Lead Acid, Storage
BATTERIES: Rechargeable
BATTERIES: Storage
BATTERIES: Wet
BATTERY CASES: Plastic Or Plastics Combination
BATTERY CHARGERS
BATTERY CHARGERS: Storage, Motor & Engine Generator Type
BATTERY CHARGING GENERATORS
BATTERY REPAIR & SVCS
BATTS & BATTING: Cotton
BAUXITE MINING
BEARINGS
BEARINGS & PARTS Ball
BEARINGS: Ball & Roller
BEARINGS: Roller & Parts
BEAUTY & BARBER SHOP EQPT
BEAUTY & BARBER SHOP EQPT & SPLYS WHOLESALERS
BEAUTY CONTEST PRODUCTION
BEAUTY SALONS
BED & BREAKFAST INNS
BEDDING & BEDSPRINGS STORES
BEDDING, BEDSPREADS, BLANKETS & SHEETS
BEDDING, BEDSPREADS, BLANKETS & SHEETS: Comforters & Quilts
BEDS & ACCESS STORES
BEDS: Hospital
BEER & ALE WHOLESALERS
BEER, WINE & LIQUOR STORES
BEER, WINE & LIQUOR STORES: Beer, Packaged
BEER, WINE & LIQUOR STORES: Wine
BEER, WINE & LIQUOR STORES: Wine & Beer
BELTING: Rubber
BELTS & BELT PRDTS
BELTS: Chain
BELTS: Conveyor, Made From Purchased Wire
BELTS: Seat, Automotive & Aircraft
BENCHES, WORK : Factory
BEVERAGE BASES & SYRUPS
BEVERAGE PRDTS: Brewers' Grain
BEVERAGE PRDTS: Malt Syrup
BEVERAGE STORES
BEVERAGE, NONALCOHOLIC: Iced Tea/Fruit Drink, Bottled/Canned
BEVERAGES, ALCOHOLIC: Ale
BEVERAGES, ALCOHOLIC: Applejack
BEVERAGES, ALCOHOLIC: Beer
BEVERAGES, ALCOHOLIC: Beer & Ale
BEVERAGES, ALCOHOLIC: Bourbon Whiskey
BEVERAGES, ALCOHOLIC: Distilled Liquors
BEVERAGES, ALCOHOLIC: Liquors, Malt
BEVERAGES, ALCOHOLIC: Rum
BEVERAGES, ALCOHOLIC: Vodka
BEVERAGES, ALCOHOLIC: Wine Coolers
BEVERAGES, ALCOHOLIC: Wines
BEVERAGES, MALT
BEVERAGES, NONALCOHOLIC: Bottled & canned soft drinks
BEVERAGES, NONALCOHOLIC: Carbonated

PRODUCT INDEX

BEVERAGES, NONALCOHOLIC: Carbonated, Canned & Bottled, Etc
BEVERAGES, NONALCOHOLIC: Cider
BEVERAGES, NONALCOHOLIC: Flavoring extracts & syrups, nec
BEVERAGES, NONALCOHOLIC: Fruit Drnks, Under 100% Juice, Can
BEVERAGES, NONALCOHOLIC: Soft Drinks, Canned & Bottled, Etc
BEVERAGES, NONALCOHOLIC: Tea, Iced, Bottled & Canned, Etc
BEVERAGES, WINE & DISTILLED ALCOHOLIC, WHOLESALE: Wine
BEVERAGES, WINE/DISTILLED ALCOHOLIC, WHOL: Cocktls, Premixed
BICYCLE SHOPS
BICYCLES WHOLESALERS
BICYCLES, PARTS & ACCESS
BILLING & BOOKKEEPING SVCS
BINDING SVC: Books & Manuals
BINS: Prefabricated, Metal Plate
BIOLOGICAL PRDTS: Exc Diagnostic
BIOLOGICAL PRDTS: Extracts
BIOLOGICAL PRDTS: Vaccines
BIOLOGICAL PRDTS: Vaccines & Immunizing
BIOLOGICAL PRDTS: Veterinary
BLACKSMITH SHOP
BLADES: Saw, Chain Type
BLANKBOOKS & LOOSELEAF BINDERS
BLANKBOOKS: Albums, Record
BLANKBOOKS: Receipt
BLANKBOOKS: Scrapbooks
BLANKETS, FROM PURCHASED MATERIALS
BLANKETS: Horse
BLASTING SVC: Sand, Metal Parts
BLINDS & SHADES: Vertical
BLINDS : Window
BLOCKS & BRICKS: Concrete
BLOCKS: Landscape Or Retaining Wall, Concrete
BLOCKS: Paving, Cut Stone
BLOCKS: Standard, Concrete Or Cinder
BLOWER FILTER UNITS: Furnace Blowers
BLOWERS & FANS
BLUEPRINTING SVCS
BOAT & BARGE COMPONENTS: Metal, Prefabricated
BOAT BUILDING & REPAIR
BOAT BUILDING & REPAIRING: Fiberglass
BOAT BUILDING & REPAIRING: Houseboats
BOAT BUILDING & REPAIRING: Kayaks
BOAT BUILDING & REPAIRING: Motorboats, Inboard Or Outboard
BOAT BUILDING & REPAIRING: Motorized
BOAT BUILDING & REPAIRING: Non-Motorized
BOAT BUILDING & REPAIRING: Pontoons, Exc Aircraft & Inflat
BOAT BUILDING & REPAIRING: Yachts
BOAT DEALERS
BOAT DEALERS: Canoe & Kayak
BOAT DEALERS: Inflatable
BOAT DEALERS: Kayaks
BOAT DEALERS: Marine Splys & Eqpt
BOAT DEALERS: Motor
BOAT DEALERS: Sailboats & Eqpt
BOAT LIFTS
BOAT REPAIR SVCS
BOAT YARD: Boat yards, storage & incidental repair
BOATS & OTHER MARINE EQPT: Plastic
BOATS: Plastic, Nonrigid
BODIES: Truck & Bus
BODY PARTS: Automobile, Stamped Metal
BOILER & HEATING REPAIR SVCS
BOILERS & BOILER SHOP WORK
BOILERS: Low-Pressure Heating, Steam Or Hot Water
BOLTS: Metal
BOLTS: Wooden, Hewn
BONDERIZING: Bonderizing, Metal Or Metal Prdts
BOOK STORES
BOOK STORES: College
BOOK STORES: Religious
BOOKS, WHOLESALE
BOOSTERS: Feeder Voltage, Electric
BOOTHS: Spray, Sheet Metal, Prefabricated
BOOTS: Men's
BORING MILL
BOTTLE CAPS & RESEALERS: Plastic

BOTTLED GAS DEALERS: Propane
BOTTLES: Plastic
BOUTIQUE STORES
BOWLING CENTERS
BOWLING EQPT & SPLYS
BOX & CARTON MANUFACTURING EQPT
BOXES & CRATES: Rectangular, Wood
BOXES & SHOOK: Nailed Wood
BOXES: Corrugated
BOXES: Filing, Paperboard Made From Purchased Materials
BOXES: Outlet, Electric Wiring Device
BOXES: Packing & Shipping, Metal
BOXES: Paperboard, Folding
BOXES: Paperboard, Set-Up
BOXES: Plastic
BOXES: Wooden
BRAKES & BRAKE PARTS
BRAKES: Bicycle, Friction Clutch & Other
BRAKES: Electromagnetic
BRAKES: Metal Forming
BRAKES: Press
BRASS & BRONZE PRDTS: Die-casted
BRASS FOUNDRY, NEC
BRAZING SVCS
BRAZING: Metal
BRIC-A-BRAC
BRICK, STONE & RELATED PRDTS WHOLESALERS
BRICKS & BLOCKS: Structural
BRICKS: Concrete
BRIDAL SHOPS
BROACHING MACHINES
BROADCASTING & COMMS EQPT: Antennas, Transmitting/Comms
BROADCASTING & COMMS EQPT: Trnsmttng TV Antennas/Grndng Eqpt
BROADCASTING & COMMUNICATIONS EQPT: Studio Eqpt, Radio & TV
BROKERS & DEALERS: Securities
BROKERS' SVCS
BROKERS: Automotive
BROKERS: Commodity Contracts
BROKERS: Food
BROKERS: Printing
BRONZE FOUNDRY, NEC
BROOMS
BROOMS & BRUSHES
BROOMS & BRUSHES: Household Or Indl
BROOMS & BRUSHES: Paintbrushes
BROOMS & BRUSHES: Street Sweeping, Hand Or Machine
BUCKLES & PARTS
BUFFING FOR THE TRADE
BUILDING & OFFICE CLEANING SVCS
BUILDING & STRUCTURAL WOOD MEMBERS
BUILDING CLEANING & MAINTENANCE SVCS
BUILDING COMPONENTS: Structural Steel
BUILDING ITEM REPAIR SVCS, MISCELLANEOUS
BUILDING MAINTENANCE SVCS, EXC REPAIRS
BUILDING PRDTS & MATERIALS DEALERS
BUILDING PRDTS: Concrete
BUILDING SCALES MODELS
BUILDINGS & COMPONENTS: Prefabricated Metal
BUILDINGS: Mobile, For Commercial Use
BUILDINGS: Portable
BUILDINGS: Prefabricated, Metal
BUILDINGS: Prefabricated, Plastic
BUILDINGS: Prefabricated, Wood
BUILDINGS: Prefabricated, Wood
BULLETPROOF VESTS
BUMPERS: Motor Vehicle
BURGLAR ALARM MAINTENANCE & MONITORING SVCS
BURIAL VAULTS: Concrete Or Precast Terrazzo
BURIAL VAULTS: Stone
BURNERS: Gas, Indl
BURNING: Metal
BUSHINGS & BEARINGS
BUSHINGS & BEARINGS: Brass, Exc Machined
BUSHINGS: Cast Steel, Exc Investment
BUSHINGS: Rubber
BUSINESS ACTIVITIES: Non-Commercial Site
BUSINESS FORMS WHOLESALERS
BUSINESS FORMS: Printed, Continuous
BUSINESS FORMS: Printed, Manifold
BUSINESS MACHINE REPAIR, ELECTRIC
BUSINESS SUPPORT SVCS
BUSINESS TRAINING SVCS

BUTTER WHOLESALERS
BUTYL RUBBER: Isoprene-Isoprene Rubbers

C

CABINETS & CASES: Show, Display & Storage, Exc Wood
CABINETS: Bathroom Vanities, Wood
CABINETS: Entertainment
CABINETS: Entertainment Units, Household, Wood
CABINETS: Factory
CABINETS: Filing, Wood
CABINETS: Kitchen, Wood
CABINETS: Office, Metal
CABINETS: Office, Wood
CABINETS: Radio & Television, Metal
CABINETS: Show, Display, Etc, Wood, Exc Refrigerated
CABLE & OTHER PAY TELEVISION DISTRIBUTION
CABLE & PAY TV SVCS: Satellite Master Antenna Sys/SMATV
CABLE WIRING SETS: Battery, Internal Combustion Engines
CABLE: Fiber Optic
CABLE: Noninsulated
CAFES
CAGES: Wire
CALCAREOUS TUFA: Crushed & Broken
CALCIUM META-PHOSPHATE
CALCULATING & ACCOUNTING EQPT
CALIBRATING SVCS, NEC
CAMERA & PHOTOGRAPHIC SPLYS STORES
CAMERAS & RELATED EQPT: Photographic
CAMPERS: Truck Mounted
CAMSHAFTS
CANDLE SHOPS
CANDLES
CANDY & CONFECTIONS: Candy Bars, Including Chocolate Covered
CANDY & CONFECTIONS: Chocolate Candy, Exc Solid Chocolate
CANDY & CONFECTIONS: Cough Drops, Exc Pharmaceutical Preps
CANDY & CONFECTIONS: Fruit & Fruit Peel
CANDY & CONFECTIONS: Fudge
CANDY, NUT & CONFECTIONERY STORE: Popcorn, Incl Caramel Corn
CANDY, NUT & CONFECTIONERY STORES: Candy
CANDY, NUT & CONFECTIONERY STORES: Nuts
CANDY, NUT & CONFECTIONERY STORES: Produced For Direct Sale
CANDY: Chocolate From Cacao Beans
CANDY: Hard
CANNED SPECIALTIES
CANS: Aluminum
CANS: Composite Foil-Fiber, Made From Purchased Materials
CANS: Metal
CANS: Tin
CANVAS PRDTS
CANVAS PRDTS: Air Cushions & Mattresses
CANVAS PRDTS: Boat Seats
CANVAS PRDTS: Convertible Tops, Car/Boat, Fm Purchased Mtrl
CAPACITORS: Fixed Or Variable
CAR WASH EQPT
CAR WASH EQPT & SPLYS WHOLESALERS
CARBIDES
CARBON & GRAPHITE PRDTS, NEC
CARBON SPECIALTIES Electrical Use
CARBURETORS
CARDS: Color
CARDS: Greeting
CARDS: Identification
CARPET & RUG CLEANING & REPAIRING PLANTS
CARPET & UPHOLSTERY CLEANING SVCS
CARPETS & RUGS: Tufted
CARPETS, RUGS & FLOOR COVERING
CARPETS: Textile Fiber
CARPORTS: Prefabricated Metal
CARS: Electric
CARTS: Grocery
CARVING SETS, STAINLESS STEEL
CASES, WOOD
CASES: Carrying
CASES: Carrying, Clothing & Apparel
CASES: Packing, Nailed Or Lock Corner, Wood
CASES: Shipping, Nailed Or Lock Corner, Wood
CASH REGISTER REPAIR SVCS
CASH REGISTERS & PARTS

PRODUCT INDEX

CASINGS: Sheet Metal
CASKETS & ACCESS
CASKETS WHOLESALERS
CAST STONE: Concrete
CASTERS
CASTINGS GRINDING: For The Trade
CASTINGS: Aerospace Investment, Ferrous
CASTINGS: Aerospace, Aluminum
CASTINGS: Aerospace, Nonferrous, Exc Aluminum
CASTINGS: Aluminum
CASTINGS: Brass, Bronze & Copper
CASTINGS: Brass, NEC Exc Die
CASTINGS: Bronze, NEC, Exc Die
CASTINGS: Commercial Investment, Ferrous
CASTINGS: Die, Aluminum
CASTINGS: Die, Copper & Copper Alloy
CASTINGS: Die, Lead & Zinc
CASTINGS: Die, Magnesium & Magnesium-Base Alloy
CASTINGS: Die, Nonferrous
CASTINGS: Die, Zinc
CASTINGS: Ductile
CASTINGS: Gray Iron
CASTINGS: Machinery, Aluminum
CASTINGS: Machinery, Copper Or Copper-Base Alloy
CASTINGS: Machinery, Nonferrous, Exc Die or Aluminum Copper
CASTINGS: Precision
CASTINGS: Steel
CASTINGS: Titanium
CASTINGS: Zinc
CATALOG & MAIL-ORDER HOUSES
CATALOG SALES
CATS, WHOLESALE
CEILING SYSTEMS: Luminous, Commercial
CEMENT & CONCRETE RELATED PRDTS & EQPT: Bituminous
CEMENT, EXC LINOLEUM & TILE
CEMENT: High Temperature, Refractory, Nonclay
CEMENT: Hydraulic
CEMENT: Magnesia
CEMENT: Masonry
CEMENT: Portland
CEMETERIES: Real Estate Operation
CEMETERY MEMORIAL DEALERS
CERAMIC FIBER
CERAMIC FLOOR & WALL TILE WHOLESALERS
CHAINS: Forged
CHANDELIERS: Commercial
CHARCOAL
CHASSIS: Motor Vehicle
CHEESE WHOLESALERS
CHEMICAL ELEMENTS
CHEMICAL PROCESSING MACHINERY & EQPT
CHEMICAL: Sodm Compnds/Salts, Inorg, Exc Rfnd Sodm Chloride
CHEMICALS & ALLIED PRDTS WHOLESALERS, NEC
CHEMICALS & ALLIED PRDTS, WHOL: Gases, Compressed/Liquefied
CHEMICALS & ALLIED PRDTS, WHOLESALE: Acids
CHEMICALS & ALLIED PRDTS, WHOLESALE: Alcohols
CHEMICALS & ALLIED PRDTS, WHOLESALE: Anti-Corrosion Prdts
CHEMICALS & ALLIED PRDTS, WHOLESALE: Aromatic
CHEMICALS & ALLIED PRDTS, WHOLESALE: Chemical Additives
CHEMICALS & ALLIED PRDTS, WHOLESALE: Chemicals, Indl
CHEMICALS & ALLIED PRDTS, WHOLESALE: Chemicals, Rustproofing
CHEMICALS & ALLIED PRDTS, WHOLESALE: Detergent/Soap
CHEMICALS & ALLIED PRDTS, WHOLESALE: Detergents
CHEMICALS & ALLIED PRDTS, WHOLESALE: Oil Additives
CHEMICALS & ALLIED PRDTS, WHOLESALE: Oxygen
CHEMICALS & ALLIED PRDTS, WHOLESALE: Plastics Prdts, NEC
CHEMICALS & ALLIED PRDTS, WHOLESALE: Plastics Sheets & Rods
CHEMICALS & ALLIED PRDTS, WHOLESALE: Polyurethane Prdts
CHEMICALS & ALLIED PRDTS, WHOLESALE: Resins, Plastics
CHEMICALS & ALLIED PRDTS, WHOLESALE: Rubber, Synthetic
CHEMICALS & ALLIED PRDTS, WHOLESALE: Spec Clean/Sanitation
CHEMICALS: Agricultural
CHEMICALS: Alcohols
CHEMICALS: Aluminum Compounds
CHEMICALS: Boron Compounds, Not From Mines, NEC
CHEMICALS: Brine
CHEMICALS: Calcium Chloride
CHEMICALS: Chromates & Bichromates
CHEMICALS: Fire Retardant
CHEMICALS: Fuel Tank Or Engine Cleaning
CHEMICALS: High Purity Grade, Organic
CHEMICALS: High Purity, Refined From Technical Grade
CHEMICALS: Inorganic, NEC
CHEMICALS: Medicinal
CHEMICALS: Medicinal, Organic, Uncompounded, Bulk
CHEMICALS: NEC
CHEMICALS: Nonmetallic Compounds
CHEMICALS: Organic, NEC
CHEMICALS: Phenol
CHEMICALS: Reagent Grade, Refined From Technical Grade
CHEMICALS: Silica Compounds
CHEMICALS: Tanning Agents, Synthetic Inorganic
CHEMICALS: Water Treatment
CHILD RESTRAINT SEATS, AUTOMOTIVE, WHOLESALE
CHILDBIRTH PREPARATION CLINIC
CHILDREN'S & INFANTS' CLOTHING STORES
CHILDREN'S WEAR STORES
CHIMNEYS & FITTINGS
CHLORINE
CHOCOLATE, EXC CANDY FROM BEANS: Chips, Powder, Block, Syrup
CHOCOLATE, EXC CANDY FROM PURCH CHOC: Chips, Powder, Block
CHRISTMAS NOVELTIES, WHOLESALE
CHRISTMAS TREE LIGHTING SETS: Electric
CHRISTMAS TREES: Artificial
CHUCKS
CHUTES: Metal Plate
CIGARETTE & CIGAR PRDTS & ACCESS
CIGARETTE FILTERS
CIGARETTE LIGHTERS
CIRCUIT BOARD REPAIR SVCS
CIRCUIT BOARDS, PRINTED: Television & Radio
CIRCUIT BREAKERS
CIRCUITS: Electronic
CLAMPS & COUPLINGS: Hose
CLAMPS: Metal
CLEANERS: Boiler Tube
CLEANING & DESCALING SVC: Metal Prdts
CLEANING COMPOUNDS: Rifle Bore
CLEANING EQPT: Blast, Dustless
CLEANING EQPT: Commercial
CLEANING EQPT: Dirt Sweeping Units, Indl
CLEANING EQPT: Floor Washing & Polishing, Commercial
CLEANING EQPT: High Pressure
CLEANING EQPT: Mop Wringers
CLEANING OR POLISHING PREPARATIONS, NEC
CLEANING PRDTS: Automobile Polish
CLEANING PRDTS: Bleaches, Household, Dry Or Liquid
CLEANING PRDTS: Degreasing Solvent
CLEANING PRDTS: Disinfectants, Household Or Indl Plant
CLEANING PRDTS: Drain Pipe Solvents Or Cleaners
CLEANING PRDTS: Dusting Cloths, Chemically Treated
CLEANING PRDTS: Floor Waxes
CLEANING PRDTS: Indl Plant Disinfectants Or Deodorants
CLEANING PRDTS: Laundry Preparations
CLEANING PRDTS: Metal Polish
CLEANING PRDTS: Polishing Preparations & Related Prdts
CLEANING PRDTS: Rug, Upholstery/Dry Clng Detergents/Spotters
CLEANING PRDTS: Sanitation Preparations
CLEANING PRDTS: Sanitation Preps, Disinfectants/Deodorants
CLEANING PRDTS: Specialty
CLEANING PRDTS: Window Cleaning Preparations
CLEANING SVCS
CLEANING SVCS: Industrial Or Commercial
CLIPS & FASTENERS, MADE FROM PURCHASED WIRE
CLOCKS
CLOSURES: Closures, Stamped Metal
CLOSURES: Plastic
CLOTHESPINS: Plastic
CLOTHING & ACCESS STORES
CLOTHING & ACCESS, WOMEN, CHILD & INFANT, WHSLE: Sportswear
CLOTHING & ACCESS, WOMEN, CHILD/INFANT, WHOLESALE: Child
CLOTHING & ACCESS, WOMEN, CHILDREN & INFANT, WHOL: Uniforms
CLOTHING & ACCESS, WOMEN, CHILDREN/INFANT, WHOL: Underwear
CLOTHING & ACCESS: Costumes, Theatrical
CLOTHING & ACCESS: Handicapped
CLOTHING & ACCESS: Handkerchiefs, Exc Paper
CLOTHING & ACCESS: Hospital Gowns
CLOTHING & ACCESS: Men's Miscellaneous Access
CLOTHING & ACCESS: Regalia
CLOTHING & ACCESS: Suspenders
CLOTHING & APPAREL STORES: Custom
CLOTHING & FURNISHINGS, MEN'S & BOYS', WHOLESALE: Caps
CLOTHING & FURNISHINGS, MEN'S & BOYS', WHOLESALE: Uniforms
CLOTHING & FURNISHINGS, MENS & BOYS, WHOL: Sportswear/Work
CLOTHING & FURNISHINGS, MENS & BOYS, WHOLESALE: Lined
CLOTHING STORES: Designer Apparel
CLOTHING STORES: Formal Wear
CLOTHING STORES: Hand Painted
CLOTHING STORES: Shirts, Custom Made
CLOTHING STORES: T-Shirts, Printed, Custom
CLOTHING STORES: Unisex
CLOTHING STORES: Work
CLOTHING: Access
CLOTHING: Access, Women's & Misses'
CLOTHING: Athletic & Sportswear, Men's & Boys'
CLOTHING: Athletic & Sportswear, Women's & Girls'
CLOTHING: Baker, Barber, Lab/Svc Ind Apparel, Washable, Men
CLOTHING: Blouses, Women's & Girls'
CLOTHING: Brassieres
CLOTHING: Children & Infants'
CLOTHING: Children's, Girls'
CLOTHING: Coats & Jackets, Leather & Sheep-Lined
CLOTHING: Coats & Suits, Men's & Boys'
CLOTHING: Costumes
CLOTHING: Culottes & Shorts, Children's
CLOTHING: Disposable
CLOTHING: Dresses
CLOTHING: Furs
CLOTHING: Gowns & Dresses, Wedding
CLOTHING: Hats & Caps, NEC
CLOTHING: Hats & Headwear, Knit
CLOTHING: Hosiery, Men's & Boys'
CLOTHING: Hospital, Men's
CLOTHING: Jackets, Field, Military
CLOTHING: Jeans, Men's & Boys'
CLOTHING: Jerseys, Knit
CLOTHING: Lounge, Bed & Leisurewear
CLOTHING: Men's & boy's clothing, nec
CLOTHING: Men's & boy's underwear & nightwear
CLOTHING: Neckwear
CLOTHING: Outerwear, Knit
CLOTHING: Outerwear, Lthr, Wool/Down-Filled, Men, Youth/Boy
CLOTHING: Outerwear, Women's & Misses' NEC
CLOTHING: Overalls & Coveralls
CLOTHING: Shirts
CLOTHING: Shirts, Dress, Men's & Boys'
CLOTHING: Socks
CLOTHING: Sportswear, Women's
CLOTHING: Sweatshirts & T-Shirts, Men's & Boys'
CLOTHING: Swimwear, Men's & Boys'
CLOTHING: Swimwear, Women's & Misses'
CLOTHING: T-Shirts & Tops, Knit
CLOTHING: Tights & Leg Warmers
CLOTHING: Uniforms, Firemen's, From Purchased Materials
CLOTHING: Uniforms, Men's & Boys'
CLOTHING: Uniforms, Team Athletic
CLOTHING: Vests, Sport, Suede, Leatherette, Etc, Mens & Boys
CLOTHING: Waterproof Outerwear
CLOTHING: Work, Men's
CLOTHS: Dust, Made From Purchased Materials
CLUTCHES OR BRAKES: Electromagnetic
CLUTCHES, EXC VEHICULAR
COAL GASIFICATION

PRODUCT INDEX

COAL MINING SERVICES
COAL MINING: Bituminous Coal & Lignite-Surface Mining
COATED OR PLATED PRDTS
COATING SVC
COATING SVC: Aluminum, Metal Prdts
COATING SVC: Electrodes
COATING SVC: Hot Dip, Metals Or Formed Prdts
COATING SVC: Metals & Formed Prdts
COATING SVC: Metals, With Plastic Or Resins
COATING SVC: Rust Preventative
COATING SVC: Silicon
COATINGS: Air Curing
COATINGS: Epoxy
COATINGS: Polyurethane
COFFEE SVCS
COIL WINDING SVC
COILS & TRANSFORMERS
COILS: Pipe
COKE: Petroleum & Coal Derivative
COLLETS
COLOR LAKES OR TONERS
COLORS: Pigments, Inorganic
COLORS: Pigments, Organic
COLUMNS: Concrete
COMMERCIAL & LITERARY WRITINGS
COMMERCIAL & OFFICE BUILDINGS RENOVATION & REPAIR
COMMERCIAL ART & GRAPHIC DESIGN SVCS
COMMERCIAL ART & ILLUSTRATION SVCS
COMMERCIAL CONTAINERS WHOLESALERS
COMMERCIAL EQPT WHOLESALERS, NEC
COMMERCIAL EQPT, WHOLESALE: Bakery Eqpt & Splys
COMMERCIAL EQPT, WHOLESALE: Coffee Brewing Eqpt & Splys
COMMERCIAL EQPT, WHOLESALE: Comm Cooking & Food Svc Eqpt
COMMERCIAL EQPT, WHOLESALE: Restaurant, NEC
COMMERCIAL EQPT, WHOLESALE: Scales, Exc Laboratory
COMMERCIAL EQPT, WHOLESALE: Store Fixtures & Display Eqpt
COMMERCIAL EQPT, WHOLESALE: Teaching Machines, Electronic
COMMERCIAL LAUNDRY EQPT
COMMERCIAL PRINTING & NEWSPAPER PUBLISHING COMBINED
COMMERCIAL REFRIGERATORS WHOLESALERS
COMMODITY CONTRACT TRADING COMPANIES
COMMODITY INSPECTION SVCS
COMMON SAND MINING
COMMUNICATIONS CARRIER: Wired
COMMUNICATIONS EQPT & SYSTEMS, NEC
COMMUNICATIONS EQPT REPAIR & MAINTENANCE
COMMUNICATIONS EQPT WHOLESALERS
COMMUNICATIONS SVCS
COMMUNICATIONS SVCS, NEC
COMMUNICATIONS SVCS: Cellular
COMMUNICATIONS SVCS: Data
COMMUNICATIONS SVCS: Electronic Mail
COMMUNICATIONS SVCS: Internet Connectivity Svcs
COMMUNICATIONS SVCS: Internet Host Svcs
COMMUNICATIONS SVCS: Telephone Or Video
COMMUNICATIONS SVCS: Telephone, Data
COMMUNITY DEVELOPMENT GROUPS
COMPACTORS: Trash & Garbage, Residential
COMPARATORS: Machinists
COMPARATORS: Optical
COMPASSES & ACCESS
COMPOST
COMPRESSORS: Air & Gas
COMPRESSORS: Air & Gas, Including Vacuum Pumps
COMPRESSORS: Refrigeration & Air Conditioning Eqpt
COMPRESSORS: Repairing
COMPRESSORS: Wholesalers
COMPUTER & COMPUTER SOFTWARE STORES
COMPUTER & COMPUTER SOFTWARE STORES: Peripheral Eqpt
COMPUTER & COMPUTER SOFTWARE STORES: Personal Computers
COMPUTER & COMPUTER SOFTWARE STORES: Printers & Plotters
COMPUTER & COMPUTER SOFTWARE STORES: Software & Access
COMPUTER & COMPUTER SOFTWARE STORES: Software, Bus/Non-Game
COMPUTER & COMPUTER SOFTWARE STORES: Software, Computer Game
COMPUTER & COMPUTER SOFTWARE STORES: Word Process Eqpt/Splys
COMPUTER & DATA PROCESSING EQPT REPAIR & MAINTENANCE
COMPUTER & OFFICE MACHINE MAINTENANCE & REPAIR
COMPUTER CALCULATING SVCS
COMPUTER FACILITIES MANAGEMENT SVCS
COMPUTER FORMS
COMPUTER GRAPHICS SVCS
COMPUTER INTERFACE EQPT: Indl Process
COMPUTER PERIPHERAL EQPT REPAIR & MAINTENANCE
COMPUTER PERIPHERAL EQPT, NEC
COMPUTER PERIPHERAL EQPT, WHOLESALE
COMPUTER PERIPHERAL EQPT: Graphic Displays, Exc Terminals
COMPUTER PERIPHERAL EQPT: Input Or Output
COMPUTER PLOTTERS
COMPUTER PROCESSING SVCS
COMPUTER PROGRAMMING SVCS
COMPUTER PROGRAMMING SVCS: Custom
COMPUTER RELATED MAINTENANCE SVCS
COMPUTER RELATED SVCS, NEC
COMPUTER SOFTWARE DEVELOPMENT
COMPUTER SOFTWARE DEVELOPMENT & APPLICATIONS
COMPUTER SOFTWARE SYSTEMS ANALYSIS & DESIGN: Custom
COMPUTER SOFTWARE WRITERS
COMPUTER STORAGE DEVICES, NEC
COMPUTER SYSTEMS ANALYSIS & DESIGN
COMPUTER TERMINALS
COMPUTER-AIDED DESIGN SYSTEMS SVCS
COMPUTER-AIDED ENGINEERING SYSTEMS SVCS
COMPUTER-AIDED MANUFACTURING SYSTEMS SVCS
COMPUTERS, NEC
COMPUTERS, NEC, WHOLESALE
COMPUTERS, PERIPHERALS & SOFTWARE, WHOLESALE: Printers
COMPUTERS, PERIPHERALS & SOFTWARE, WHOLESALE: Software
COMPUTERS: Mainframe
COMPUTERS: Mini
COMPUTERS: Personal
CONCENTRATES, DRINK
CONCRETE BUILDING PRDTS WHOLESALERS
CONCRETE CURING & HARDENING COMPOUNDS
CONCRETE MIXERS
CONCRETE PLANTS
CONCRETE PRDTS
CONCRETE PRDTS, PRECAST, NEC
CONCRETE REINFORCING MATERIAL
CONCRETE: Dry Mixture
CONCRETE: Ready-Mixed
CONDENSERS & CONDENSING UNITS: Air Conditioner
CONDENSERS: Heat Transfer Eqpt, Evaporative
CONDENSERS: Motors Or Generators
CONFECTIONERY PRDTS WHOLESALERS
CONFECTIONS & CANDY
CONNECTORS & TERMINALS: Electrical Device Uses
CONNECTORS: Electrical
CONNECTORS: Electronic
CONNECTORS: Power, Electric
CONSTRUCTION & MINING MACHINERY WHOLESALERS
CONSTRUCTION EQPT: Attachments
CONSTRUCTION EQPT: Attachments, Backhoe Mounted, Hyd Pwrd
CONSTRUCTION EQPT: Attachments, Snow Plow
CONSTRUCTION EQPT: Buckets, Excavating, Clamshell, Etc
CONSTRUCTION EQPT: Cranes
CONSTRUCTION EQPT: Finishers & Spreaders
CONSTRUCTION EQPT: Grinders, Stone, Portable
CONSTRUCTION EQPT: Mud Jacks
CONSTRUCTION EQPT: Roofing Eqpt
CONSTRUCTION EQPT: Subgraders
CONSTRUCTION EQPT: Tractors
CONSTRUCTION EQPT: Wellpoint Systems
CONSTRUCTION EQPT: Wrecker Hoists, Automobile
CONSTRUCTION MATERIALS, WHOL: Concrete/Cinder Bldg Prdts
CONSTRUCTION MATERIALS, WHOLESALE: Aggregate
CONSTRUCTION MATERIALS, WHOLESALE: Air Ducts, Sheet Metal
CONSTRUCTION MATERIALS, WHOLESALE: Architectural Metalwork
CONSTRUCTION MATERIALS, WHOLESALE: Awnings
CONSTRUCTION MATERIALS, WHOLESALE: Block, Concrete & Cinder
CONSTRUCTION MATERIALS, WHOLESALE: Brick, Exc Refractory
CONSTRUCTION MATERIALS, WHOLESALE: Building Stone
CONSTRUCTION MATERIALS, WHOLESALE: Building Stone, Granite
CONSTRUCTION MATERIALS, WHOLESALE: Building Stone, Marble
CONSTRUCTION MATERIALS, WHOLESALE: Building, Exterior
CONSTRUCTION MATERIALS, WHOLESALE: Building, Interior
CONSTRUCTION MATERIALS, WHOLESALE: Cement
CONSTRUCTION MATERIALS, WHOLESALE: Concrete Mixtures
CONSTRUCTION MATERIALS, WHOLESALE: Glass
CONSTRUCTION MATERIALS, WHOLESALE: Gravel
CONSTRUCTION MATERIALS, WHOLESALE: Insulation, Thermal
CONSTRUCTION MATERIALS, WHOLESALE: Limestone
CONSTRUCTION MATERIALS, WHOLESALE: Millwork
CONSTRUCTION MATERIALS, WHOLESALE: Pallets, Wood
CONSTRUCTION MATERIALS, WHOLESALE: Paving Materials
CONSTRUCTION MATERIALS, WHOLESALE: Prefabricated Structures
CONSTRUCTION MATERIALS, WHOLESALE: Roof, Asphalt/Sheet Metal
CONSTRUCTION MATERIALS, WHOLESALE: Roofing & Siding Material
CONSTRUCTION MATERIALS, WHOLESALE: Sand
CONSTRUCTION MATERIALS, WHOLESALE: Septic Tanks
CONSTRUCTION MATERIALS, WHOLESALE: Sewer Pipe, Clay
CONSTRUCTION MATERIALS, WHOLESALE: Siding, Exc Wood
CONSTRUCTION MATERIALS, WHOLESALE: Stone, Crushed Or Broken
CONSTRUCTION MATERIALS, WHOLESALE: Windows
CONSTRUCTION MATLS, WHOL: Lumber, Rough, Dressed/Finished
CONSTRUCTION MATLS, WHOLESALE: Struct Assy, Prefab, NonWood
CONSTRUCTION SAND MINING
CONSTRUCTION SITE PREPARATION SVCS
CONSTRUCTION: Agricultural Building
CONSTRUCTION: Apartment Building
CONSTRUCTION: Athletic & Recreation Facilities
CONSTRUCTION: Commercial & Institutional Building
CONSTRUCTION: Commercial & Office Building, New
CONSTRUCTION: Electric Power Line
CONSTRUCTION: Farm Building
CONSTRUCTION: Food Prdts Manufacturing or Packing Plant
CONSTRUCTION: Heavy
CONSTRUCTION: Heavy Highway & Street
CONSTRUCTION: Indl Building & Warehouse
CONSTRUCTION: Indl Buildings, New, NEC
CONSTRUCTION: Institutional Building
CONSTRUCTION: Natural Gas Compressor Station
CONSTRUCTION: Nonresidential Buildings, Custom
CONSTRUCTION: Parade Float
CONSTRUCTION: Parking Lot
CONSTRUCTION: Pipeline, NEC
CONSTRUCTION: Railroad & Subway
CONSTRUCTION: Refineries
CONSTRUCTION: Residential, Nec
CONSTRUCTION: Roads, Gravel or Dirt
CONSTRUCTION: Sewer Line
CONSTRUCTION: Silo, Agricultural
CONSTRUCTION: Single-Family Housing
CONSTRUCTION: Single-family Housing, New
CONSTRUCTION: Single-family Housing, Prefabricated
CONSTRUCTION: Street Surfacing & Paving
CONSTRUCTION: Swimming Pools
CONSTRUCTION: Telephone & Communication Line
CONSTRUCTION: Truck & Automobile Assembly Plant
CONSTRUCTION: Utility Line
CONSTRUCTION: Waste Water & Sewage Treatment Plant

PRODUCT INDEX

CONSTRUCTION: Water Main
CONSULTING SVC: Business, NEC
CONSULTING SVC: Chemical
CONSULTING SVC: Computer
CONSULTING SVC: Data Processing
CONSULTING SVC: Educational
CONSULTING SVC: Engineering
CONSULTING SVC: Financial Management
CONSULTING SVC: Human Resource
CONSULTING SVC: Management
CONSULTING SVC: Marketing Management
CONSULTING SVC: Online Technology
CONSULTING SVC: Productivity Improvement
CONSULTING SVC: Sales Management
CONSULTING SVC: Telecommunications
CONSULTING SVCS, BUSINESS: Communications
CONSULTING SVCS, BUSINESS: Environmental
CONSULTING SVCS, BUSINESS: Safety Training Svcs
CONSULTING SVCS, BUSINESS: Sys Engnrg, Exc Computer/Prof
CONSULTING SVCS, BUSINESS: Systems Analysis & Engineering
CONSULTING SVCS, BUSINESS: Systems Analysis Or Design
CONSULTING SVCS, BUSINESS: Test Development & Evaluation
CONSULTING SVCS: Oil
CONSULTING SVCS: Scientific
CONSUMER PURCHASING SVCS
CONTACT LENSES
CONTAINERS, GLASS: Cosmetic Jars
CONTAINERS: Air Cargo, Metal
CONTAINERS: Cargo, Wood
CONTAINERS: Cargo, Wood & Metal Combination
CONTAINERS: Cargo, Wood & Wood With Metal
CONTAINERS: Corrugated
CONTAINERS: Metal
CONTAINERS: Plastic
CONTAINERS: Plywood & Veneer, Wood
CONTAINERS: Sanitary, Food
CONTAINERS: Shipping & Mailing, Fiber
CONTAINERS: Shipping, Bombs, Metal Plate
CONTAINERS: Shipping, Metal, Milk, Fluid
CONTAINERS: Wood
CONTRACT DIVING SVC
CONTRACTOR: Dredging
CONTRACTOR: Rigging & Scaffolding
CONTRACTORS: Access Control System Eqpt
CONTRACTORS: Acoustical & Insulation Work
CONTRACTORS: Antenna Installation
CONTRACTORS: Asphalt
CONTRACTORS: Awning Installation
CONTRACTORS: Boiler & Furnace
CONTRACTORS: Boiler Maintenance Contractor
CONTRACTORS: Building Eqpt & Machinery Installation
CONTRACTORS: Building Front Installation, Metal
CONTRACTORS: Building Movers
CONTRACTORS: Building Sign Installation & Mntnce
CONTRACTORS: Building Site Preparation
CONTRACTORS: Carpentry Work
CONTRACTORS: Carpentry, Cabinet & Finish Work
CONTRACTORS: Carpentry, Cabinet Building & Installation
CONTRACTORS: Carpet Laying
CONTRACTORS: Closed Circuit Television Installation
CONTRACTORS: Closet Organizers, Installation & Design
CONTRACTORS: Coating, Caulking & Weather, Water & Fire
CONTRACTORS: Commercial & Office Building
CONTRACTORS: Concrete
CONTRACTORS: Concrete Repair
CONTRACTORS: Construction Caulking
CONTRACTORS: Construction Site Cleanup
CONTRACTORS: Countertop Installation
CONTRACTORS: Demolition, Building & Other Structures
CONTRACTORS: Directional Oil & Gas Well Drilling Svc
CONTRACTORS: Dock Eqpt Installation, Indl
CONTRACTORS: Drapery Track Installation
CONTRACTORS: Driveway
CONTRACTORS: Electric Power Systems
CONTRACTORS: Electrical
CONTRACTORS: Electronic Controls Installation
CONTRACTORS: Energy Management Control
CONTRACTORS: Erection & Dismantling, Poured Concrete Forms
CONTRACTORS: Excavating
CONTRACTORS: Excavating Slush Pits & Cellars Svcs
CONTRACTORS: Exterior Painting
CONTRACTORS: Exterior Wall System Installation
CONTRACTORS: Fence Construction
CONTRACTORS: Fire Detection & Burglar Alarm Systems
CONTRACTORS: Fire Sprinkler System Installation Svcs
CONTRACTORS: Floor Laying & Other Floor Work
CONTRACTORS: Flooring
CONTRACTORS: Foundation Building
CONTRACTORS: Gas Field Svcs, NEC
CONTRACTORS: Gasoline Condensation Removal Svcs
CONTRACTORS: General Electric
CONTRACTORS: Glass, Glazing & Tinting
CONTRACTORS: Gutters & Downspouts
CONTRACTORS: Heating Systems Repair & Maintenance Svc
CONTRACTORS: Highway & Street Construction, General
CONTRACTORS: Highway & Street Paving
CONTRACTORS: Highway & Street Resurfacing
CONTRACTORS: Home & Office Intrs Finish, Furnish/Remodel
CONTRACTORS: Hydraulic Eqpt Installation & Svcs
CONTRACTORS: Indl Building Renovation, Remodeling & Repair
CONTRACTORS: Insulation Installation, Building
CONTRACTORS: Kitchen & Bathroom Remodeling
CONTRACTORS: Kitchen Cabinet Installation
CONTRACTORS: Lighting Syst
CONTRACTORS: Lightweight Steel Framing Installation
CONTRACTORS: Machine Rigging & Moving
CONTRACTORS: Machinery Installation
CONTRACTORS: Masonry & Stonework
CONTRACTORS: Mechanical
CONTRACTORS: Oil & Gas Building, Repairing & Dismantling Svc
CONTRACTORS: Oil & Gas Field Geophysical Exploration Svcs
CONTRACTORS: Oil & Gas Well Casing Cement Svcs
CONTRACTORS: Oil & Gas Well Drilling Svc
CONTRACTORS: Oil & Gas Well Foundation Grading Svcs
CONTRACTORS: Oil & Gas Wells Svcs
CONTRACTORS: Oil Field Haulage Svcs
CONTRACTORS: Oil Field Lease Tanks: Erectg, Clng/Rprg Svcs
CONTRACTORS: Oil Field Pipe Testing Svcs
CONTRACTORS: Oil Sampling Svcs
CONTRACTORS: Oil/Gas Field Casing, Tube/Rod Running, Cut/Pull
CONTRACTORS: Oil/Gas Well Construction, Rpr/Dismantling Svcs
CONTRACTORS: On-Site Welding
CONTRACTORS: Ornamental Metal Work
CONTRACTORS: Painting & Wall Covering
CONTRACTORS: Painting, Commercial
CONTRACTORS: Painting, Commercial, Interior
CONTRACTORS: Painting, Indl
CONTRACTORS: Painting, Residential
CONTRACTORS: Parking Facility Eqpt Installation
CONTRACTORS: Parking Lot Maintenance
CONTRACTORS: Patio & Deck Construction & Repair
CONTRACTORS: Pipe & Boiler Insulating
CONTRACTORS: Plumbing
CONTRACTORS: Pollution Control Eqpt Installation
CONTRACTORS: Post Disaster Renovations
CONTRACTORS: Precast Concrete Struct Framing & Panel Placing
CONTRACTORS: Prefabricated Window & Door Installation
CONTRACTORS: Process Piping
CONTRACTORS: Pulpwood, Engaged In Cutting
CONTRACTORS: Refrigeration
CONTRACTORS: Resilient Floor Laying
CONTRACTORS: Rigging, Theatrical
CONTRACTORS: Roofing
CONTRACTORS: Roustabout Svcs
CONTRACTORS: Safety & Security Eqpt
CONTRACTORS: Sandblasting Svc, Building Exteriors
CONTRACTORS: Seismograph Survey Svcs
CONTRACTORS: Septic System
CONTRACTORS: Sheet Metal Work, NEC
CONTRACTORS: Sheet metal Work, Architectural
CONTRACTORS: Siding
CONTRACTORS: Single-family Home General Remodeling
CONTRACTORS: Skylight Installation
CONTRACTORS: Solar Energy Eqpt
CONTRACTORS: Special Trades, NEC
CONTRACTORS: Store Fixture Installation
CONTRACTORS: Store Front Construction
CONTRACTORS: Structural Iron Work, Structural
CONTRACTORS: Structural Steel Erection
CONTRACTORS: Stucco, Interior
CONTRACTORS: Svc Well Drilling Svcs
CONTRACTORS: Tile Installation, Ceramic
CONTRACTORS: Tuck Pointing & Restoration
CONTRACTORS: Underground Utilities
CONTRACTORS: Ventilation & Duct Work
CONTRACTORS: Wall Covering, Residential
CONTRACTORS: Warm Air Heating & Air Conditioning
CONTRACTORS: Water Intake Well Drilling Svc
CONTRACTORS: Water Well Drilling
CONTRACTORS: Waterproofing
CONTRACTORS: Well Acidizing Svcs
CONTRACTORS: Window Treatment Installation
CONTRACTORS: Wrecking & Demolition
CONTROL CIRCUIT DEVICES
CONTROL EQPT: Buses Or Trucks, Electric
CONTROL EQPT: Electric
CONTROL EQPT: Electric Buses & Locomotives
CONTROL EQPT: Noise
CONTROL PANELS: Electrical
CONTROLS & ACCESS: Indl, Electric
CONTROLS & ACCESS: Motor
CONTROLS: Air Flow, Refrigeration
CONTROLS: Automatic Temperature
CONTROLS: Crane & Hoist, Including Metal Mill
CONTROLS: Environmental
CONTROLS: Marine & Navy, Auxiliary
CONTROLS: Numerical
CONTROLS: Positioning, Electric
CONTROLS: Relay & Ind
CONTROLS: Resistance Welder
CONTROLS: Thermostats
CONTROLS: Voice
CONVENIENCE STORES
CONVENTION & TRADE SHOW SVCS
CONVERTERS: Data
CONVERTERS: Power, AC to DC
CONVERTERS: Rotary, Electrical
CONVERTERS: Torque, Exc Auto
CONVEYOR SYSTEMS
CONVEYOR SYSTEMS: Belt, General Indl Use
CONVEYOR SYSTEMS: Bucket Type
CONVEYOR SYSTEMS: Bulk Handling
CONVEYOR SYSTEMS: Pneumatic Tube
CONVEYOR SYSTEMS: Robotic
CONVEYORS & CONVEYING EQPT
CONVEYORS: Overhead
COOKING & FOOD WARMING EQPT: Commercial
COOKING & FOODWARMING EQPT: Coffee Brewing
COOKING & FOODWARMING EQPT: Commercial
COOKING EQPT, HOUSEHOLD: Convection Ovens, Incldg Portable
COOKING EQPT, HOUSEHOLD: Ranges, Gas
COOKING SCHOOL
COOKWARE, STONEWARE: Coarse Earthenware & Pottery
COOLERS & ICE CHESTS: Metal
COOLING TOWERS: Metal
COPPER ORE MILLING & PREPARATION
COPPER ORE MINING
COPPER: Cakes, Primary
COPPER: Rolling & Drawing
COPY MACHINES WHOLESALERS
CORD & TWINE
CORK & CORK PRDTS
CORK PRDTS, FABRICATED, WHOLESALE
CORRUGATED PRDTS: Boxes, Partition, Display Items, Sheet/Pad
COSMETIC PREPARATIONS
COSMETICS & TOILETRIES
COSMETOLOGIST
COSMETOLOGY & PERSONAL HYGIENE SALONS
COSTUME JEWELRY & NOVELTIES: Apparel, Exc Precious Metals
COSTUME JEWELRY & NOVELTIES: Bracelets, Exc Precious Metals
COSTUME JEWELRY & NOVELTIES: Exc Semi & Precious
COSTUME JEWELRY & NOVELTIES: Rosaries & Sm Religious Items
COUNTER & SINK TOPS
COUNTERS & COUNTING DEVICES
COUNTERS OR COUNTER DISPLAY CASES, EXC WOOD
COUNTERS OR COUNTER DISPLAY CASES, WOOD

PRODUCT INDEX

COUNTING DEVICES: Controls, Revolution & Timing
COUNTING DEVICES: Electromechanical
COUNTING DEVICES: Speedometers
COUNTING DEVICES: Vehicle Instruments
COUPLINGS, EXC PRESSURE & SOIL PIPE
COUPLINGS: Pipe
COUPLINGS: Shaft
COUPON REDEMPTION SVCS
COURIER SVCS: Ground
COURTS OF LAW: County Government
COVERS: Automobile Seat
COVERS: Automotive, Exc Seat & Tire
COVERS: Canvas
CRACKED CASTING REPAIR SVCS
CRANE & AERIAL LIFT SVCS
CRANES & MONORAIL SYSTEMS
CRANES: Indl Plant
CRANES: Overhead
CRANKSHAFTS & CAMSHAFTS: Machining
CRANKSHAFTS: Motor Vehicle
CRATES: Fruit, Wood Wirebound
CREDIT AGENCIES: Federal & Federally Sponsored
CREDIT CARD SVCS
CREDIT INST, SHORT-TERM BUSINESS: Accts Receiv & Coml Paper
CREDIT INST, SHORT-TERM BUSINESS: Financing Dealers
CREMATORIES
CROWNS & CLOSURES
CRUDE PETROLEUM & NATURAL GAS PRODUCTION
CRUDE PETROLEUM & NATURAL GAS PRODUCTION
CRUDE PETROLEUM PRODUCTION
CULTURE MEDIA
CULVERTS: Sheet Metal
CUPS & PLATES: Foamed Plastics
CUPS: Plastic Exc Polystyrene Foam
CURBING: Granite Or Stone
CURTAIN & DRAPERY FIXTURES: Poles, Rods & Rollers
CURTAINS & BEDDING: Knit
CURTAINS: Window, From Purchased Materials
CUSHIONS & PILLOWS
CUSHIONS & PILLOWS: Bed, From Purchased Materials
CUSTOM COMPOUNDING OF RUBBER MATERIALS
CUT STONE & STONE PRODUCTS
CUTLERY
CUTLERY WHOLESALERS
CUTOUTS: Cardboard, Die-Cut, Made From Purchased Materials
CUTTING SVC: Paperboard
CYCLIC CRUDES & INTERMEDIATES
CYLINDER & ACTUATORS: Fluid Power
CYLINDERS: Pressure
CYLINDERS: Pump

D

DAIRY EQPT
DAIRY PRDTS STORE: Cheese
DAIRY PRDTS STORE: Ice Cream, Packaged
DAIRY PRDTS STORES
DAIRY PRDTS WHOLESALERS: Fresh
DAIRY PRDTS: Butter
DAIRY PRDTS: Cheese
DAIRY PRDTS: Condensed Milk
DAIRY PRDTS: Cream Substitutes
DAIRY PRDTS: Dietary Supplements, Dairy & Non-Dairy Based
DAIRY PRDTS: Dried Milk
DAIRY PRDTS: Evaporated Milk
DAIRY PRDTS: Fermented & Cultured Milk Prdts
DAIRY PRDTS: Frozen Desserts & Novelties
DAIRY PRDTS: Ice Cream & Ice Milk
DAIRY PRDTS: Ice Cream, Bulk
DAIRY PRDTS: Ice Cream, Packaged, Molded, On Sticks, Etc.
DAIRY PRDTS: Milk, Chocolate
DAIRY PRDTS: Milk, Condensed & Evaporated
DAIRY PRDTS: Milk, Fluid
DAIRY PRDTS: Milk, Processed, Pasteurized, Homogenized/Btld
DAIRY PRDTS: Natural Cheese
DAIRY PRDTS: Powdered Milk
DAIRY PRDTS: Processed Cheese
DAIRY PRDTS: Spreads, Cheese
DAIRY PRDTS: Yogurt, Exc Frozen
DAIRY PRDTS: Yogurt, Frozen
DATA PROCESSING & PREPARATION SVCS

DATA PROCESSING SVCS
DECORATIVE WOOD & WOODWORK
DEFENSE SYSTEMS & EQPT
DEGREASING MACHINES
DEHUMIDIFIERS: Electric
DEHYDRATION EQPT
DELIVERY SVCS, BY VEHICLE
DENTAL EQPT
DENTAL EQPT & SPLYS
DENTAL EQPT & SPLYS: Cabinets
DENTAL EQPT & SPLYS: Compounds
DENTAL EQPT & SPLYS: Dental Materials
DENTAL EQPT & SPLYS: Enamels
DENTAL EQPT & SPLYS: Impression Materials
DENTAL EQPT & SPLYS: Metal
DENTAL EQPT & SPLYS: Teeth, Artificial, Exc In Dental Labs
DENTISTS' OFFICES & CLINICS
DERMATOLOGICALS
DESIGN SVCS, NEC
DESIGN SVCS: Commercial & Indl
DESIGN SVCS: Computer Integrated Systems
DESIGN SVCS: Hand Tools
DETECTION APPARATUS: Electronic/Magnetic Field, Light/Heat
DETECTION EQPT: Aeronautical Electronic Field
DETECTIVE & ARMORED CAR SERVICES
DEVELOPING & PRINTING: Motion Picture Film, Commercial
DIAGNOSTIC SUBSTANCES
DIAGNOSTIC SUBSTANCES OR AGENTS: Blood Derivative
DIAGNOSTIC SUBSTANCES OR AGENTS: In Vitro
DIAGNOSTIC SUBSTANCES OR AGENTS: Microbiology & Virology
DIAGNOSTIC SUBSTANCES OR AGENTS: Radioactive
DIAGNOSTIC SUBSTANCES OR AGENTS: Veterinary
DIAMOND SETTER SVCS
DIE CUTTING SVC: Paper
DIE SETS: Presses, Metal Stamping
DIES & TOOLS: Special
DIES: Cutting, Exc Metal
DIES: Extrusion
DIES: Plastic Forming
DIES: Steel Rule
DIFFERENTIAL ASSEMBLIES & PARTS
DIMENSION STONE: Buildings
DIODES: Light Emitting
DIRECT SELLING ESTABLISHMENTS, NEC
DIRECT SELLING ESTABLISHMENTS: Home Related Prdts
DIRECT SELLING ESTABLISHMENTS: Milk Delivery
DISC JOCKEYS
DISCOUNT DEPARTMENT STORES
DISHWASHING EQPT: Commercial
DISHWASHING EQPT: Household
DISINFECTING & PEST CONTROL SERVICES
DISINFECTING SVCS
DISK & DRUM DRIVES & COMPONENTS: Computers
DISK DRIVES: Computer
DISKS & DRUMS Magnetic
DISPENSING EQPT & PARTS, BEVERAGE: Fountain/Other Beverage
DISPLAY FIXTURES: Showcases, Wood, Exc Refrigerated
DISPLAY FIXTURES: Wood
DISPLAY ITEMS: Corrugated, Made From Purchased Materials
DISPLAY ITEMS: Solid Fiber, Made From Purchased Materials
DISPLAY LETTERING SVCS
DISPLAY STANDS: Merchandise, Exc Wood
DISTILLERS DRIED GRAIN & SOLUBLES
DISTRIBUTORS: Motor Vehicle Engine
DIVING EQPT STORES
DOCK EQPT & SPLYS, INDL
DOCK OPERATION SVCS, INCL BLDGS, FACILITIES, OPERS & MAINT
DOCKS: Floating, Wood
DOCKS: Prefabricated Metal
DOOR & WINDOW REPAIR SVCS
DOOR FRAMES: Wood
DOOR OPERATING SYSTEMS: Electric
DOORS & WINDOWS WHOLESALERS: All Materials
DOORS & WINDOWS: Screen & Storm
DOORS & WINDOWS: Storm, Metal
DOORS: Fiberglass
DOORS: Folding, Plastic Or Plastic Coated Fabric
DOORS: Garage, Overhead, Metal
DOORS: Garage, Overhead, Wood

DOORS: Glass
DOORS: Louver, Wood
DOORS: Rolling, Indl Building Or Warehouse, Metal
DOORS: Wooden
DOWELS & DOWEL RODS
DOWNSPOUTS: Sheet Metal
DRAFTING SPLYS WHOLESALERS
DRAFTING SVCS
DRAINAGE PRDTS: Concrete
DRAPERIES & CURTAINS
DRAPERIES & DRAPERY FABRICS, COTTON
DRAPERIES: Plastic & Textile, From Purchased Materials
DRAPERY & UPHOLSTERY STORES: Curtains
DRAPERY & UPHOLSTERY STORES: Draperies
DRAPES & DRAPERY FABRICS, FROM MANMADE FIBER
DRILL BITS
DRILLING MACHINERY & EQPT: Water Well
DRILLS & DRILLING EQPT: Mining
DRINK MIXES, NONALCOHOLIC: Cocktail
DRINKING PLACES: Alcoholic Beverages
DRINKING PLACES: Bars & Lounges
DRINKING PLACES: Beer Garden
DRINKING PLACES: Tavern
DRINKING PLACES: Wine Bar
DRIVE SHAFTS
DRIVES: High Speed Indl, Exc Hydrostatic
DRIVES: Hydrostatic
DRUG STORES
DRUG TESTING KITS: Blood & Urine
DRUGS & DRUG PROPRIETARIES, WHOL: Biologicals/Allied Prdts
DRUGS & DRUG PROPRIETARIES, WHOLESALE
DRUGS & DRUG PROPRIETARIES, WHOLESALE: Bandages
DRUGS & DRUG PROPRIETARIES, WHOLESALE: Medical Rubber Goods
DRUGS & DRUG PROPRIETARIES, WHOLESALE: Pharmaceuticals
DRUGS AFFECTING NEOPLASMS & ENDOCRINE SYSTEMS
DRUMS: Brake
DRUMS: Fiber
DUCTING: Metal Plate
DUCTS: Sheet Metal
DUMBWAITERS
DUMPSTERS: Garbage
DURABLE GOODS WHOLESALERS, NEC
DUST OR FUME COLLECTING EQPT: Indl
DYES & TINTS: Household
DYNAMOMETERS

E

EARTH SCIENCE SVCS
EATING PLACES
EDUCATIONAL SVCS
EDUCATIONAL SVCS, NONDEGREE GRANTING: Continuing Education
ELASTOMERS
ELECTRIC & OTHER SERVICES COMBINED
ELECTRIC MOTOR REPAIR SVCS
ELECTRIC POWER GENERATION: Fossil Fuel
ELECTRIC POWER, COGENERATED
ELECTRIC SERVICES
ELECTRIC SVCS, NEC: Power Generation
ELECTRICAL APPARATUS & EQPT WHOLESALERS
ELECTRICAL APPLIANCES, TELEVISIONS & RADIOS WHOLESALERS
ELECTRICAL CONSTRUCTION MATERIALS WHOLESALERS
ELECTRICAL CURRENT CARRYING WIRING DEVICES
ELECTRICAL DEVICE PARTS: Porcelain, Molded
ELECTRICAL DISCHARGE MACHINING, EDM
ELECTRICAL EQPT & SPLYS
ELECTRICAL EQPT FOR ENGINES
ELECTRICAL EQPT REPAIR & MAINTENANCE
ELECTRICAL EQPT REPAIR SVCS: High Voltage
ELECTRICAL EQPT: Automotive, NEC
ELECTRICAL GOODS, WHOLESALE: Alarms & Signaling Eqpt
ELECTRICAL GOODS, WHOLESALE: Batteries, Storage, Indl
ELECTRICAL GOODS, WHOLESALE: Circuit Breakers
ELECTRICAL GOODS, WHOLESALE: Electrical Appliances, Major
ELECTRICAL GOODS, WHOLESALE: Electrical Entertainment Eqpt

PRODUCT INDEX

ELECTRICAL GOODS, WHOLESALE: Electronic Parts
ELECTRICAL GOODS, WHOLESALE: Facsimile Or Fax Eqpt
ELECTRICAL GOODS, WHOLESALE: Generators
ELECTRICAL GOODS, WHOLESALE: Light Bulbs & Related Splys
ELECTRICAL GOODS, WHOLESALE: Lighting Fixtures, Comm & Indl
ELECTRICAL GOODS, WHOLESALE: Modems, Computer
ELECTRICAL GOODS, WHOLESALE: Motor Ctrls, Starters & Relays
ELECTRICAL GOODS, WHOLESALE: Motors
ELECTRICAL GOODS, WHOLESALE: Security Control Eqpt & Systems
ELECTRICAL GOODS, WHOLESALE: Signaling, Eqpt
ELECTRICAL GOODS, WHOLESALE: Switchboards
ELECTRICAL GOODS, WHOLESALE: Telephone Eqpt
ELECTRICAL GOODS, WHOLESALE: Transformers
ELECTRICAL GOODS, WHOLESALE: Wire & Cable
ELECTRICAL GOODS, WHOLESALE: Wire & Cable, Electronic
ELECTRICAL HOUSEHOLD APPLIANCE REPAIR
ELECTRICAL INDL APPARATUS, NEC
ELECTRICAL SPLYS
ELECTRICAL SUPPLIES: Porcelain
ELECTRODES: Indl Process
ELECTROMEDICAL EQPT
ELECTROMETALLURGICAL PRDTS
ELECTRON BEAM: Cutting, Forming, Welding
ELECTRONIC COMPONENTS
ELECTRONIC DEVICES: Solid State, NEC
ELECTRONIC EQPT REPAIR SVCS
ELECTRONIC LOADS & POWER SPLYS
ELECTRONIC PARTS & EQPT WHOLESALERS
ELECTRONIC SHOPPING
ELECTRONIC TRAINING DEVICES
ELECTROPLATING & PLATING SVC
ELEVATOR: Bean, Storage Only
ELEVATORS & EQPT
ELEVATORS WHOLESALERS
ELEVATORS: Installation & Conversion
ELEVATORS: Stair, Motor Powered
EMBLEMS: Embroidered
EMBOSSING SVC: Paper
EMBROIDERING & ART NEEDLEWORK FOR THE TRADE
EMBROIDERING SVC
EMBROIDERING SVC: Schiffli Machine
EMBROIDERY ADVERTISING SVCS
EMBROIDERY KITS
EMERGENCY ALARMS
EMPLOYEE LEASING SVCS
EMPLOYMENT AGENCY SVCS
EMPLOYMENT SVCS: Labor Contractors
ENAMELING SVC: Metal Prdts, Including Porcelain
ENCLOSURES: Electronic
ENCLOSURES: Screen
ENGINE PARTS & ACCESS: Internal Combustion
ENGINE REBUILDING: Diesel
ENGINE REBUILDING: Gas
ENGINEERING HELP SVCS
ENGINEERING SVCS
ENGINEERING SVCS: Acoustical
ENGINEERING SVCS: Aviation Or Aeronautical
ENGINEERING SVCS: Building Construction
ENGINEERING SVCS: Construction & Civil
ENGINEERING SVCS: Electrical Or Electronic
ENGINEERING SVCS: Industrial
ENGINEERING SVCS: Machine Tool Design
ENGINEERING SVCS: Marine
ENGINEERING SVCS: Mechanical
ENGINEERING SVCS: Pollution Control
ENGINEERING SVCS: Professional
ENGINEERING SVCS: Sanitary
ENGINEERING SVCS: Structural
ENGINES & ENGINE PARTS: Guided Missile
ENGINES: Diesel & Semi-Diesel Or Duel Fuel
ENGINES: Gasoline, NEC
ENGINES: Hydrojet, Marine
ENGINES: Internal Combustion, NEC
ENGINES: Marine
ENGINES: Steam
ENGRAVING SVC, NEC
ENGRAVING SVC: Jewelry & Personal Goods
ENGRAVING SVCS
ENTERTAINERS & ENTERTAINMENT GROUPS
ENTERTAINMENT SVCS

ENVELOPES
ENZYMES
EPOXY RESINS
EQUIPMENT: Pedestrian Traffic Control
EQUIPMENT: Rental & Leasing, NEC
ESCALATORS: Passenger & Freight
ETCHING & ENGRAVING SVC
ETHERS
ETHYLENE-PROPYLENE RUBBERS: EPDM Polymers
EXHAUST SYSTEMS: Eqpt & Parts
EXPANSION JOINTS: Rubber
EXPLOSIVES
EXPLOSIVES, EXC AMMO & FIREWORKS WHOLESALERS
EXTRACTS, FLAVORING
EYEGLASSES: Sunglasses
EYELASHES, ARTIFICIAL

F

FABRIC STORES
FABRICATED METAL PRODUCTS, NEC
FABRICS: Alpacas, Mohair, Woven
FABRICS: Apparel & Outerwear, Cotton
FABRICS: Automotive, From Manmade Fiber
FABRICS: Broadwoven, Cotton
FABRICS: Broadwoven, Synthetic Manmade Fiber & Silk
FABRICS: Broadwoven, Wool
FABRICS: Canvas
FABRICS: Chenilles, Tufted Textile
FABRICS: Coated Or Treated
FABRICS: Cords
FABRICS: Damasks, Cotton
FABRICS: Denims
FABRICS: Dress, From Manmade Fiber Or Silk
FABRICS: Fiberglass, Broadwoven
FABRICS: Furniture Denim
FABRICS: Laminated
FABRICS: Laundry, Cotton
FABRICS: Metallized
FABRICS: Nonwoven
FABRICS: Osnaburgs
FABRICS: Resin Or Plastic Coated
FABRICS: Rubberized
FABRICS: Satin
FABRICS: Scrub Cloths
FABRICS: Seat Cover, Automobile, Cotton
FABRICS: Shoe Laces, Exc Leather
FABRICS: Table Cover, Cotton
FABRICS: Tapestry, Cotton
FABRICS: Trimmings
FABRICS: Twills, Drills, Denims/Other Cotton Ribbed Fabrics
FABRICS: Upholstery, Cotton
FABRICS: Woven Wire, Made From Purchased Wire
FABRICS: Woven, Narrow Cotton, Wool, Silk
FACILITIES SUPPORT SVCS
FAMILY CLOTHING STORES
FANS, BLOWING: Indl Or Commercial
FANS, VENTILATING: Indl Or Commercial
FARM & GARDEN MACHINERY WHOLESALERS
FARM PRDTS, RAW MATERIALS, WHOLESALE: Skins
FARM SPLY STORES
FARM SPLYS WHOLESALERS
FARM SPLYS, WHOLESALE: Feed
FARM SPLYS, WHOLESALE: Fertilizers & Agricultural Chemicals
FARM SPLYS, WHOLESALE: Flower & Field Bulbs
FARM SPLYS, WHOLESALE: Garden Splys
FASTENERS WHOLESALERS
FASTENERS: Brads, Alum, Brass/Other Nonferrous Metal/Wire
FASTENERS: Metal
FASTENERS: Metal
FASTENERS: Notions, NEC
FASTENERS: Wire, Made From Purchased Wire
FAUCETS & SPIGOTS: Metal & Plastic
FELT, WHOLESALE
FELT: Acoustic
FENCES & FENCING MATERIALS
FENCES OR POSTS: Ornamental Iron Or Steel
FENCING DEALERS
FENCING MATERIALS: Docks & Other Outdoor Prdts, Wood
FENCING MATERIALS: Plastic
FENCING MATERIALS: Snow Fence, Wood
FENCING MATERIALS: Wood
FENCING: Chain Link
FENDERS: Automobile, Stamped Or Pressed Metal

FERTILIZER, AGRICULTURAL: Wholesalers
FERTILIZERS: NEC
FERTILIZERS: Phosphatic
FIBER & FIBER PRDTS: Acrylic
FIBER & FIBER PRDTS: Anidex
FIBER & FIBER PRDTS: Organic, Noncellulose
FIBER & FIBER PRDTS: Protein
FIBER & FIBER PRDTS: Synthetic Cellulosic
FIBERS: Carbon & Graphite
FIGURES, WAX
FILLERS & SEALERS: Wood
FILM & SHEET: Unsuppported Plastic
FILM DEVELOPING & PRINTING SVCS
FILM: Motion Picture
FILTER ELEMENTS: Fluid & Hydraulic Line
FILTERS
FILTERS & SOFTENERS: Water, Household
FILTERS & STRAINERS: Pipeline
FILTERS: Air
FILTERS: Air Intake, Internal Combustion Engine, Exc Auto
FILTERS: General Line, Indl
FILTERS: Motor Vehicle
FILTERS: Oil, Internal Combustion Engine, Exc Auto
FILTRATION DEVICES: Electronic
FINANCIAL INVESTMENT ADVICE
FINANCIAL SVCS
FINDINGS & TRIMMINGS: Fabric
FINDINGS & TRIMMINGS: Furniture, Fabric
FINGERPRINTING SVCS
FINISHING AGENTS: Leather
FIRE ALARM MAINTENANCE & MONITORING SVCS
FIRE ARMS, SMALL: Guns Or Gun Parts, 30 mm & Below
FIRE ARMS, SMALL: Pellet & BB guns
FIRE ARMS, SMALL: Shotguns Or Shotgun Parts, 30 mm & Below
FIRE CONTROL OR BOMBING EQPT: Electronic
FIRE EXTINGUISHER CHARGES
FIRE EXTINGUISHER SVC
FIRE EXTINGUISHERS, WHOLESALE
FIRE EXTINGUISHERS: Portable
FIRE OR BURGLARY RESISTIVE PRDTS
FIRE PROTECTION EQPT
FIRE PROTECTION SVCS: Contracted
FIREARMS: Large, Greater Than 30mm
FIREARMS: Small, 30mm or Less
FIREPLACE & CHIMNEY MATERIAL: Concrete
FIREPLACE EQPT & ACCESS
FIREWOOD, WHOLESALE
FIREWORKS
FISH & SEAFOOD PROCESSORS: Fresh Or Frozen
FISH FOOD
FISHING EQPT: Lures
FISHING EQPT: Nets & Seines
FITTINGS & ASSEMBLIES: Hose & Tube, Hydraulic Or Pneumatic
FITTINGS & SPECIALTIES: Steam
FITTINGS: Pipe
FITTINGS: Pipe, Fabricated
FIXTURES & EQPT: Kitchen, Metal, Exc Cast Aluminum
FIXTURES & EQPT: Kitchen, Porcelain Enameled
FIXTURES: Bank, Metal, Ornamental
FIXTURES: Cut Stone
FLAGS: Fabric
FLAKEBOARD
FLARES
FLAT GLASS: Antique
FLAT GLASS: Building
FLAT GLASS: Construction
FLAT GLASS: Plate, Polished & Rough
FLAT GLASS: Tempered
FLAT GLASS: Window, Clear & Colored
FLAVORS OR FLAVORING MATERIALS: Synthetic
FLOATING DRY DOCKS
FLOCKING METAL PRDTS
FLOOR CLEANING & MAINTENANCE EQPT: Household
FLOOR COVERING STORES
FLOOR COVERING STORES: Carpets
FLOOR COVERING: Plastic
FLOOR COVERINGS WHOLESALERS
FLOOR COVERINGS: Rubber
FLOOR COVERINGS: Textile Fiber
FLOORING & GRATINGS: Open, Construction Applications
FLOORING & SIDING: Metal
FLOORING: Baseboards, Wood
FLOORING: Hard Surface

PRODUCT INDEX

FLOORING: Hardwood
FLOORING: Rubber
FLOORING: Tile
FLORIST: Flowers, Fresh
FLORISTS
FLOWER ARRANGEMENTS: Artificial
FLOWER POTS Plastic
FLOWERS & FLORISTS' SPLYS WHOLESALERS
FLOWERS: Artificial & Preserved
FLUES & PIPES: Stove Or Furnace
FLUID METERS & COUNTING DEVICES
FLUID POWER PUMPS & MOTORS
FLUID POWER VALVES & HOSE FITTINGS
FLUXES
FLYSWATTERS
FOAM RUBBER
FOAMS & RUBBER, WHOLESALE
FOIL & LEAF: Metal
FOIL: Aluminum
FOOD CONTAMINATION TESTING OR SCREENING KITS
FOOD PRDTS, BREAKFAST: Cereal, Corn Flakes
FOOD PRDTS, BREAKFAST: Cereal, Granola & Muesli
FOOD PRDTS, CANNED OR FRESH PACK: Fruit Juices
FOOD PRDTS, CANNED OR FRESH PACK: Vegetable Juices
FOOD PRDTS, CANNED: Applesauce
FOOD PRDTS, CANNED: Barbecue Sauce
FOOD PRDTS, CANNED: Beans, Baked With Meat
FOOD PRDTS, CANNED: Chili
FOOD PRDTS, CANNED: Ethnic
FOOD PRDTS, CANNED: Fruit Juices, Concentrated
FOOD PRDTS, CANNED: Fruit Juices, Fresh
FOOD PRDTS, CANNED: Fruits
FOOD PRDTS, CANNED: Fruits
FOOD PRDTS, CANNED: Fruits & Fruit Prdts
FOOD PRDTS, CANNED: Jams, Including Imitation
FOOD PRDTS, CANNED: Jams, Jellies & Preserves
FOOD PRDTS, CANNED: Maraschino Cherries
FOOD PRDTS, CANNED: Soups
FOOD PRDTS, CANNED: Tomatoes
FOOD PRDTS, CONFECTIONERY, WHOLESALE: Candy
FOOD PRDTS, CONFECTIONERY, WHOLESALE: Nuts, Salted/Roasted
FOOD PRDTS, CONFECTIONERY, WHOLESALE: Snack Foods
FOOD PRDTS, CONFECTIONERY, WHOLESALE: Syrups, Fountain
FOOD PRDTS, DAIRY, WHOLESALE: Frozen Dairy Desserts
FOOD PRDTS, DAIRY, WHOLESALE: Milk & Cream, Fluid
FOOD PRDTS, FISH & SEAFOOD, WHOLESALE: Seafood
FOOD PRDTS, FISH & SEAFOOD: Fish, Salted
FOOD PRDTS, FISH & SEAFOOD: Fish, Smoked
FOOD PRDTS, FISH & SEAFOOD: Herring, Cured, NEC
FOOD PRDTS, FROZEN: Dinners, Packaged
FOOD PRDTS, FROZEN: Ethnic Foods, NEC
FOOD PRDTS, FROZEN: Fruits
FOOD PRDTS, FROZEN: Fruits & Vegetables
FOOD PRDTS, FROZEN: Fruits, Juices & Vegetables
FOOD PRDTS, FROZEN: NEC
FOOD PRDTS, FROZEN: Pizza
FOOD PRDTS, FROZEN: Snack Items
FOOD PRDTS, FROZEN: Vegetables, Exc Potato Prdts
FOOD PRDTS, FROZEN: Waffles
FOOD PRDTS, FRUITS & VEGETABLES, FRESH, WHOLESALE
FOOD PRDTS, FRUITS & VEGETABLES, FRESH, WHOLESALE: Fruits
FOOD PRDTS, FRUITS & VEGETABLES, FRESH, WHOLESALE: Vegetable
FOOD PRDTS, MEAT & MEAT PRDTS, WHOLESALE: Fresh
FOOD PRDTS, WHOLESALE: Beans, Field
FOOD PRDTS, WHOLESALE: Beverage Concentrates
FOOD PRDTS, WHOLESALE: Beverages, Exc Coffee & Tea
FOOD PRDTS, WHOLESALE: Coffee, Green Or Roasted
FOOD PRDTS, WHOLESALE: Diet
FOOD PRDTS, WHOLESALE: Dog Food
FOOD PRDTS, WHOLESALE: Grains
FOOD PRDTS, WHOLESALE: Juices
FOOD PRDTS, WHOLESALE: Natural & Organic
FOOD PRDTS, WHOLESALE: Oats
FOOD PRDTS, WHOLESALE: Pasta & Rice
FOOD PRDTS, WHOLESALE: Pizza Splys
FOOD PRDTS, WHOLESALE: Specialty
FOOD PRDTS, WHOLESALE: Spices & Seasonings
FOOD PRDTS, WHOLESALE: Tea
FOOD PRDTS, WHOLESALE: Wheat
FOOD PRDTS, WHOLESALE: Wine Makers' Eqpt & Splys
FOOD PRDTS: Animal & marine fats & oils
FOOD PRDTS: Box Lunches, For Sale Off Premises
FOOD PRDTS: Bread Crumbs, Exc Made In Bakeries
FOOD PRDTS: Breakfast Bars
FOOD PRDTS: Butter, Renovated & Processed
FOOD PRDTS: Cake Flour
FOOD PRDTS: Cereals
FOOD PRDTS: Chewing Gum Base
FOOD PRDTS: Chocolate Bars, Solid
FOOD PRDTS: Coconut Oil
FOOD PRDTS: Coffee
FOOD PRDTS: Coffee Roasting, Exc Wholesale Grocers
FOOD PRDTS: Corn Oil, Refined
FOOD PRDTS: Desserts, Ready-To-Mix
FOOD PRDTS: Dips, Exc Cheese & Sour Cream Based
FOOD PRDTS: Doughs & Batters From Purchased Flour
FOOD PRDTS: Doughs, Frozen Or Refrig From Purchased Flour
FOOD PRDTS: Dressings, Salad, Raw & Cooked Exc Dry Mixes
FOOD PRDTS: Dried & Dehydrated Fruits, Vegetables & Soup Mix
FOOD PRDTS: Edible Oil Prdts, Exc Corn Oil
FOOD PRDTS: Eggs, Processed
FOOD PRDTS: Emulsifiers
FOOD PRDTS: Flour
FOOD PRDTS: Flour & Other Grain Mill Products
FOOD PRDTS: Flour Mixes & Doughs
FOOD PRDTS: Freeze-Dried Coffee
FOOD PRDTS: Frosting Mixes, Dry, For Cakes, Cookies, Etc.
FOOD PRDTS: Fruit Juices
FOOD PRDTS: Fruits & Vegetables, Pickled
FOOD PRDTS: Fruits, Dried Or Dehydrated, Exc Freeze-Dried
FOOD PRDTS: Granola & Energy Bars, Nonchocolate
FOOD PRDTS: Honey
FOOD PRDTS: Horseradish, Exc Sauce
FOOD PRDTS: Ice, Blocks
FOOD PRDTS: Ice, Cubes
FOOD PRDTS: Instant Coffee
FOOD PRDTS: Macaroni, Noodles, Spaghetti, Pasta, Etc
FOOD PRDTS: Malt
FOOD PRDTS: Mixes, Doughnut From Purchased Flour
FOOD PRDTS: Mixes, Flour
FOOD PRDTS: Mixes, Salad Dressings, Dry
FOOD PRDTS: Nuts & Seeds
FOOD PRDTS: Oils & Fats, Marine
FOOD PRDTS: Olive Oil
FOOD PRDTS: Oriental Noodles
FOOD PRDTS: Pasta, Rice/Potatoes, Uncooked, Pkgd
FOOD PRDTS: Pasta, Uncooked, Packaged With Other Ingredients
FOOD PRDTS: Peanut Butter
FOOD PRDTS: Pickles, Vinegar
FOOD PRDTS: Pizza Doughs From Purchased Flour
FOOD PRDTS: Pizza, Refrigerated
FOOD PRDTS: Popcorn, Popped
FOOD PRDTS: Popcorn, Unpopped
FOOD PRDTS: Pork Rinds
FOOD PRDTS: Potato & Corn Chips & Similar Prdts
FOOD PRDTS: Potato Chips & Other Potato-Based Snacks
FOOD PRDTS: Potato Sticks
FOOD PRDTS: Preparations
FOOD PRDTS: Prepared Sauces, Exc Tomato Based
FOOD PRDTS: Raw cane sugar
FOOD PRDTS: Relishes, Fruit & Vegetable
FOOD PRDTS: Salads
FOOD PRDTS: Sandwiches
FOOD PRDTS: Sauerkraut, Bulk
FOOD PRDTS: Seasonings & Spices
FOOD PRDTS: Shortening & Solid Edible Fats
FOOD PRDTS: Soybean Oil, Refined, Exc Made In Mills
FOOD PRDTS: Soybean Protein Concentrates & Isolates
FOOD PRDTS: Spices, Including Ground
FOOD PRDTS: Sugar
FOOD PRDTS: Sugar, Beet
FOOD PRDTS: Sugar, Cane
FOOD PRDTS: Sugar, Granulated Sugar Beet
FOOD PRDTS: Sugar, Maple, Indl
FOOD PRDTS: Sugar, Refined Sugar Beet
FOOD PRDTS: Syrup, Maple
FOOD PRDTS: Tea
FOOD PRDTS: Tortilla Chips
FOOD PRDTS: Tortillas
FOOD PRDTS: Vegetable Oil Mills, NEC
FOOD PRDTS: Vinegar
FOOD PRDTS: Wheat Flour
FOOD PRDTS: Yeast
FOOD PRODUCTS MACHINERY
FOOD STORES: Convenience, Chain
FOOD STORES: Grocery, Independent
FOOD STORES: Supermarket, More Than 100K Sq Ft, Hypermrkt
FOOD STORES: Supermarkets, Independent
FOOD WARMING EQPT: Commercial
FOOTWEAR, WHOLESALE: Shoes
FOOTWEAR: Cut Stock
FORESTRY RELATED EQPT
FORGINGS
FORGINGS: Aluminum
FORGINGS: Automotive & Internal Combustion Engine
FORGINGS: Gear & Chain
FORGINGS: Iron & Steel
FORGINGS: Machinery, Ferrous
FORGINGS: Nonferrous
FORMS: Concrete, Sheet Metal
FOUNDRIES: Aluminum
FOUNDRIES: Brass, Bronze & Copper
FOUNDRIES: Gray & Ductile Iron
FOUNDRIES: Iron
FOUNDRIES: Nonferrous
FOUNDRIES: Steel
FOUNDRIES: Steel Investment
FOUNDRY MACHINERY & EQPT
FOUNDRY SAND MINING
FOUNTAIN PEN REPAIR SHOP
FRACTIONATION PRDTS OF CRUDE PETROLEUM, HYDROCARBONS, NEC
FRANCHISES, SELLING OR LICENSING
FREEZERS: Household
FREIGHT FORWARDING ARRANGEMENTS: Domestic
FREIGHT TRANSPORTATION ARRANGEMENTS
FREON
FRICTION MATERIAL, MADE FROM POWDERED METAL
FRUIT & VEGETABLE MARKETS
FRUIT STANDS OR MARKETS
FUEL ADDITIVES
FUEL CELLS: Solid State
FUEL OIL DEALERS
FUELS: Diesel
FUELS: Ethanol
FUELS: Gas, Liquefied
FUELS: Jet
FUELS: Kerosene
FUELS: Oil
FUNDRAISING SVCS
FUNGICIDES OR HERBICIDES
FUR APPAREL STORES
FUR: Apparel
FURNACE CASINGS: Sheet Metal
FURNACES & OVENS: Fuel-Fired
FURNACES & OVENS: Indl
FURNITURE & CABINET STORES: Cabinets, Custom Work
FURNITURE & CABINET STORES: Custom
FURNITURE & FIXTURES Factory
FURNITURE COMPONENTS: Porcelain Enameled
FURNITURE PARTS: Metal
FURNITURE REFINISHING SVCS
FURNITURE REPAIR & MAINTENANCE SVCS
FURNITURE STOCK & PARTS: Carvings, Wood
FURNITURE STOCK & PARTS: Dimension Stock, Hardwood
FURNITURE STOCK & PARTS: Hardwood
FURNITURE STOCK & PARTS: Turnings, Wood
FURNITURE STORES
FURNITURE STORES: Cabinets, Kitchen, Exc Custom Made
FURNITURE STORES: Custom Made, Exc Cabinets
FURNITURE STORES: Office
FURNITURE UPHOLSTERY REPAIR SVCS
FURNITURE WHOLESALERS
FURNITURE, HOUSEHOLD: Wholesalers
FURNITURE, MATTRESSES: Wholesalers
FURNITURE, OFFICE: Wholesalers
FURNITURE, WHOLESALE: Dressers
FURNITURE, WHOLESALE: Racks
FURNITURE, WHOLESALE: Theater Seats
FURNITURE: Altars & Pulpits
FURNITURE: Assembly Hall
FURNITURE: Bedroom, Wood

PRODUCT INDEX

FURNITURE: Benches, Office, Exc Wood
FURNITURE: Bookcases, Office, Wood
FURNITURE: Box Springs, Assembled
FURNITURE: Camp, Wood
FURNITURE: Chairs, Bentwood
FURNITURE: Chairs, Household Upholstered
FURNITURE: Chairs, Household, Metal
FURNITURE: Chairs, Office Exc Wood
FURNITURE: Church
FURNITURE: Console Tables, Wood
FURNITURE: Cut Stone
FURNITURE: Desks & Tables, Office, Exc Wood
FURNITURE: Desks, Wood
FURNITURE: Dining Room, Wood
FURNITURE: Dressers, Household, Wood
FURNITURE: Fiberglass & Plastic
FURNITURE: Foundations & Platforms
FURNITURE: Hotel
FURNITURE: Household, Metal
FURNITURE: Household, NEC
FURNITURE: Hydraulic Barber & Beauty Shop Chairs
FURNITURE: Institutional, Exc Wood
FURNITURE: Kitchen & Dining Room
FURNITURE: Laboratory
FURNITURE: Lawn & Garden, Metal
FURNITURE: Lawn, Wood
FURNITURE: Library
FURNITURE: Mattresses & Foundations
FURNITURE: Mattresses, Box & Bedsprings
FURNITURE: Mattresses, Innerspring Or Box Spring
FURNITURE: NEC
FURNITURE: Office Panel Systems, Exc Wood
FURNITURE: Office Panel Systems, Wood
FURNITURE: Office, Exc Wood
FURNITURE: Office, Wood
FURNITURE: Outdoor, Wood
FURNITURE: Pews, Church
FURNITURE: Picnic Tables Or Benches, Park
FURNITURE: Play Pens, Children's, Wood
FURNITURE: Restaurant
FURNITURE: School
FURNITURE: Stands & Chests, Exc Bedside Stands, Wood
FURNITURE: Storage Chests, Household, Wood
FURNITURE: Table Tops, Marble
FURNITURE: Tables & Table Tops, Wood
FURNITURE: Unfinished, Wood
FURNITURE: Upholstered
FURNITURE: Vehicle
FURRIERS
FUSES: Electric
Furs

G

GAMES & TOYS: Bingo Boards
GAMES & TOYS: Board Games, Children's & Adults'
GAMES & TOYS: Craft & Hobby Kits & Sets
GAMES & TOYS: Dolls, Exc Stuffed Toy Animals
GAMES & TOYS: Game Machines, Exc Coin-Operated
GAMES & TOYS: Kits, Science, Incl Microscopes/Chemistry Sets
GAMES & TOYS: Puzzles
GAMES & TOYS: Trains & Eqpt, Electric & Mechanical
GAMES & TOYS: Tricycles
GARBAGE DISPOSERS & COMPACTORS: Commercial
GAS & HYDROCARBON LIQUEFACTION FROM COAL
GAS & OIL FIELD EXPLORATION SVCS
GAS & OIL FIELD SVCS, NEC
GASES & LIQUIFIED PETROLEUM GASES
GASES: Acetylene
GASES: Carbon Dioxide
GASES: Helium
GASES: Indl
GASES: Neon
GASES: Oxygen
GASKET MATERIALS
GASKETS
GASKETS & SEALING DEVICES
GASOLINE FILLING STATIONS
GATES: Ornamental Metal
GAUGE BLOCKS
GAUGES
GEARS
GEARS & GEAR UNITS: Reduction, Exc Auto
GEARS: Power Transmission, Exc Auto

GEMSTONE & INDL DIAMOND MINING SVCS
GENERAL MERCHANDISE, NONDURABLE, WHOLESALE
GENERATION EQPT: Electronic
GENERATOR REPAIR SVCS
GENERATORS: Electric
GENERATORS: Ultrasonic
GENERATORS: Vehicles, Gas-Electric Or Oil-Electric
GIFT SHOP
GIFT, NOVELTY & SOUVENIR STORES: Gift Baskets
GIFT, NOVELTY & SOUVENIR STORES: Gifts & Novelties
GIFT, NOVELTY & SOUVENIR STORES: Party Favors
GIFTS & NOVELTIES: Wholesalers
GIFTWARE: Copper
GLASS FABRICATORS
GLASS PRDTS, FROM PURCHASED GLASS: Art
GLASS PRDTS, FROM PURCHASED GLASS: Glass Beads, Reflecting
GLASS PRDTS, FROM PURCHASED GLASS: Glassware
GLASS PRDTS, FROM PURCHASED GLASS: Insulating
GLASS PRDTS, FROM PURCHASED GLASS: Mirrored
GLASS PRDTS, FROM PURCHASED GLASS: Windshields
GLASS PRDTS, FROM PURCHD GLASS: Strengthened Or Reinforced
GLASS PRDTS, PRESSED OR BLOWN: Barware
GLASS PRDTS, PRESSED OR BLOWN: Bulbs, Electric Lights
GLASS PRDTS, PRESSED OR BLOWN: Glassware, Art Or Decorative
GLASS PRDTS, PRESSED OR BLOWN: Lighting Eqpt Parts
GLASS PRDTS, PRESSED OR BLOWN: Reflector, Lighting Eqpt
GLASS PRDTS, PRESSED OR BLOWN: Tubing
GLASS PRDTS, PRESSED/BLOWN: Glassware, Art, Decor/Novelty
GLASS PRDTS, PRESSED/BLOWN: Lenses, Lantern, Flshlght, Etc
GLASS PRDTS, PURCHASED GLASS: Insulating, Multiple-Glazed
GLASS PRDTS, PURCHSD GLASS: Ornamental, Cut, Engraved/Décor
GLASS STORE: Leaded Or Stained
GLASS STORES
GLASS, AUTOMOTIVE: Wholesalers
GLASS: Fiber
GLASS: Flat
GLASS: Insulating
GLASS: Optical
GLASS: Pressed & Blown, NEC
GLASS: Stained
GLASS: Tempered
GLASSWARE: Cut & Engraved
GLASSWARE: Indl
GLASSWARE: Laboratory
GLOBAL POSITIONING SYSTEMS & EQPT
GLOVES: Fabric
GLOVES: Leather, Work
GLUE
GOLD ORE MINING
GOLF EQPT
GOLF GOODS & EQPT
GOURMET FOOD STORES
GOVERNMENT, LEGISLATIVE BODIES: County Commissioner
GRANITE: Crushed & Broken
GRANITE: Cut & Shaped
GRANITE: Dimension
GRANITE: Dimension
GRAPHIC ARTS & RELATED DESIGN SVCS
GRAVE MARKERS: Concrete
GRAVEL MINING
GREASES & INEDIBLE FATS, RENDERED
GREASES: Lubricating
GREENHOUSES: Prefabricated Metal
GRILLS & GRILLWORK: Woven Wire, Made From Purchased Wire
GRINDING BALLS: Ceramic
GRINDING SVC: Precision, Commercial Or Indl
GRINDING SVCS: Ophthalmic Lens, Exc Prescription
GRINDS: Electric
GRIPS OR HANDLES: Rubber
GROCERIES WHOLESALERS, NEC
GROCERIES, GENERAL LINE WHOLESALERS
GROUTING EQPT: Concrete
GUARDS: Machine, Sheet Metal

GUIDED MISSILES & SPACE VEHICLES: Research & Development
GUIDED MISSILES/SPACE VEHICLE PARTS/AUX EQPT: Research/Devel
GUM & WOOD CHEMICALS
GUN PARTS MADE TO INDIVIDUAL ORDER
GUN SIGHTS: Optical
GUTTERS: Sheet Metal
GYPSUM MINING
GYPSUM PRDTS

H

HAIR & HAIR BASED PRDTS
HAIR ACCESS WHOLESALERS
HAIR CARE PRDTS
HAIR CURLERS: Beauty Shop
HAIRDRESSERS
HALL EFFECT DEVICES
HAMPERS: Laundry, Sheet Metal
HAND TOOLS, NEC: Wholesalers
HANDBAGS
HANDBAGS: Women's
HANDCUFFS & LEG IRONS
HANDLES: Wood
HANGERS: Garment, Plastic
HARDWARE
HARDWARE & BUILDING PRDTS: Plastic
HARDWARE & EQPT: Stage, Exc Lighting
HARDWARE STORES
HARDWARE STORES: Builders'
HARDWARE STORES: Door Locks & Lock Sets
HARDWARE STORES: Pumps & Pumping Eqpt
HARDWARE STORES: Tools
HARDWARE STORES: Tools, Power
HARDWARE WHOLESALERS
HARDWARE, WHOLESALE: Bolts
HARDWARE, WHOLESALE: Builders', NEC
HARDWARE, WHOLESALE: Casters & Glides
HARDWARE, WHOLESALE: Chains
HARDWARE, WHOLESALE: Rivets
HARDWARE, WHOLESALE: Screws
HARDWARE, WHOLESALE: Security Devices, Locks
HARDWARE, WHOLESALE: Staples
HARDWARE: Aircraft
HARDWARE: Builders'
HARDWARE: Cabinet
HARDWARE: Door Opening & Closing Devices, Exc Electrical
HARDWARE: Furniture
HARDWARE: Furniture, Builders' & Other Household
HARDWARE: Locking Systems, Security Cable
HARDWARE: Padlocks
HARDWARE: Rubber
HARNESS ASSEMBLIES: Cable & Wire
HARNESS WIRING SETS: Internal Combustion Engines
HARNESSES, HALTERS, SADDLERY & STRAPS
HARVESTING MACHINERY & EQPT WHOLESALERS
HEADPHONES: Radio
HEALTH & ALLIED SERVICES, NEC
HEALTH AIDS: Exercise Eqpt
HEALTH FOOD & SUPPLEMENT STORES
HEALTH PRACTITIONERS' OFFICES, NEC
HEALTH SCREENING SVCS
HEARING AIDS
HEAT EMISSION OPERATING APPARATUS
HEAT EXCHANGERS: After Or Inter Coolers Or Condensers, Etc
HEAT TREATING SALTS
HEAT TREATING: Metal
HEATERS: Room, Gas
HEATING & AIR CONDITIONING EQPT & SPLYS WHOLESALERS
HEATING & AIR CONDITIONING UNITS, COMBINATION
HEATING EQPT & SPLYS
HEATING EQPT: Complete
HEATING EQPT: Induction
HEATING SYSTEMS: Radiant, Indl Process
HEATING UNITS & DEVICES: Indl, Electric
HELICOPTERS
HELMETS: Athletic
HELP SUPPLY SERVICES
HERMETICS REPAIR SVCS
HIGHWAY & STREET MAINTENANCE SVCS
HITCHES: Trailer
HOBBY, TOY & GAME STORES: Arts & Crafts & Splys
HOBBY, TOY & GAME STORES: Toys & Games

PRODUCT INDEX

HOISTING SLINGS
HOISTS
HOISTS: Hand
HOLDERS, PAPER TOWEL, GROCERY BAG, ETC: Plastic
HOLDING COMPANIES: Investment, Exc Banks
HOLDING COMPANIES: Personal, Exc Banks
HOLDING COMPANIES: Public Utility
HOME CENTER STORES
HOME DELIVERY NEWSPAPER ROUTES
HOME ENTERTAINMENT EQPT: Electronic, NEC
HOME FURNISHINGS STORES, NEC
HOME FURNISHINGS WHOLESALERS
HOME HEALTH CARE SVCS
HOME IMPROVEMENT & RENOVATION CONTRACTOR AGENCY
HOMEBUILDERS & OTHER OPERATIVE BUILDERS
HOMEFURNISHING STORE: Bedding, Sheet, Blanket,Spread/Pillow
HOMEFURNISHING STORES: Closet organizers & shelving units
HOMEFURNISHING STORES: Lighting Fixtures
HOMEFURNISHING STORES: Vertical Blinds
HOMEFURNISHING STORES: Window Furnishings
HOMEFURNISHINGS, WHOLESALE: Blankets
HOMEFURNISHINGS, WHOLESALE: Blinds, Venetian
HOMEFURNISHINGS, WHOLESALE: Carpets
HOMEFURNISHINGS, WHOLESALE: Mirrors/Pictures, Framed/Unframd
HOMEFURNISHINGS, WHOLESALE: Pottery
HOMES, MODULAR: Wooden
HOMES: Log Cabins
HONES
HONING & LAPPING MACHINES
HOODS: Range, Sheet Metal
HOPPERS: Sheet Metal
HORNS: Marine, Compressed Air Or Steam
HORSE & PET ACCESSORIES: Textile
HORSESHOES
HOSE: Air Line Or Air Brake, Rubber Or Rubberized Fabric
HOSE: Automobile, Plastic
HOSE: Flexible Metal
HOSE: Plastic
HOSE: Pneumatic, Rubber Or Rubberized Fabric, NEC
HOSE: Rubber
HOSES & BELTING: Rubber & Plastic
HOSPITAL EQPT REPAIR SVCS
HOSPITALS: Medical & Surgical
HOSTELS
HOT TUBS
HOT TUBS: Plastic & Fiberglass
HOUSEHOLD APPLIANCE PARTS: Wholesalers
HOUSEHOLD APPLIANCE STORES
HOUSEHOLD APPLIANCE STORES: Electric Household, Major
HOUSEHOLD ARTICLES: Metal
HOUSEHOLD FURNISHINGS, NEC
HOUSEWARE STORES
HOUSEWARES, ELECTRIC, EXC COOKING APPLIANCES & UTENSILS
HOUSEWARES, ELECTRIC: Blankets
HOUSEWARES, ELECTRIC: Blenders
HOUSEWARES, ELECTRIC: Heaters, Sauna
HOUSEWARES, ELECTRIC: Heaters, Space
HOUSEWARES, ELECTRIC: Heating Units, Electric Appliances
HOUSEWARES, ELECTRIC: Humidifiers, Household
HOUSEWARES, ELECTRIC: Massage Machines, Exc Beauty/Barber
HOUSEWARES: Bowls, Wood
HOUSEWARES: Dishes, Plastic
HOUSEWARES: Dishes, Wooden
HOUSEWARES: Plates, Pressed/Molded Pulp, From Purchased Mtrl
HOUSING PROGRAMS ADMINISTRATION SVCS
HOUSINGS: Business Machine, Sheet Metal
HUB CAPS: Automobile, Stamped Metal
HUMIDIFIERS & DEHUMIDIFIERS
HUMIDIFYING EQPT, EXC PORTABLE
HYDRAULIC EQPT REPAIR SVC
HYDRAULIC FLUIDS: Synthetic Based
HYDROPONIC EQPT
Hard Rubber & Molded Rubber Prdts

I

ICE

ICE CREAM & ICES WHOLESALERS
ICE WHOLESALERS
IDENTIFICATION PLATES
IDENTIFICATION TAGS, EXC PAPER
IGNITION COILS: Automotive
IGNITION SYSTEMS: High Frequency
INCINERATORS
INDL & PERSONAL SVC PAPER WHOLESALERS
INDL & PERSONAL SVC PAPER, WHOL: Bags, Paper/Disp Plastic
INDL & PERSONAL SVC PAPER, WHOL: Boxes, Corrugtd/Solid Fiber
INDL & PERSONAL SVC PAPER, WHOL: Paper, Wrap/Coarse/Prdts
INDL & PERSONAL SVC PAPER, WHOLESALE: Press Sensitive Tape
INDL & PERSONAL SVC PAPER, WHOLESALE: Shipping Splys
INDL EQPT CLEANING SVCS
INDL EQPT SVCS
INDL MACHINERY & EQPT WHOLESALERS
INDL MACHINERY REPAIR & MAINTENANCE
INDL PATTERNS: Foundry Patternmaking
INDL PROCESS INSTRUMENTS: Control
INDL PROCESS INSTRUMENTS: Controllers, Process Variables
INDL PROCESS INSTRUMENTS: Data Loggers
INDL PROCESS INSTRUMENTS: Digital Display, Process Variables
INDL PROCESS INSTRUMENTS: Draft Gauges
INDL PROCESS INSTRUMENTS: Elements, Primary
INDL PROCESS INSTRUMENTS: Fluidic Devices, Circuit & Systems
INDL PROCESS INSTRUMENTS: Indl Flow & Measuring
INDL PROCESS INSTRUMENTS: Temperature
INDL PROCESS INSTRUMENTS: Water Quality Monitoring/Cntrl Sys
INDL SALTS WHOLESALERS
INDL SPLYS WHOLESALERS
INDL SPLYS, WHOL: Fasteners, Incl Nuts, Bolts, Screws, Etc
INDL SPLYS, WHOLESALE: Abrasives
INDL SPLYS, WHOLESALE: Abrasives & Adhesives
INDL SPLYS, WHOLESALE: Adhesives, Tape & Plasters
INDL SPLYS, WHOLESALE: Bearings
INDL SPLYS, WHOLESALE: Fasteners & Fastening Eqpt
INDL SPLYS, WHOLESALE: Filters, Indl
INDL SPLYS, WHOLESALE: Fittings
INDL SPLYS, WHOLESALE: Gaskets & Seals
INDL SPLYS, WHOLESALE: Glass Bottles
INDL SPLYS, WHOLESALE: Hydraulic & Pneumatic Pistons/Valves
INDL SPLYS, WHOLESALE: Mill Splys
INDL SPLYS, WHOLESALE: Plastic, Pallets
INDL SPLYS, WHOLESALE: Power Transmission, Eqpt & Apparatus
INDL SPLYS, WHOLESALE: Rubber Goods, Mechanical
INDL SPLYS, WHOLESALE: Seals
INDL SPLYS, WHOLESALE: Tools
INDL SPLYS, WHOLESALE: Tools, NEC
INDL SPLYS, WHOLESALE: Valves & Fittings
INDL TOOL GRINDING SVCS
INDUSTRIAL & COMMERCIAL EQPT INSPECTION SVCS
INFORMATION RETRIEVAL SERVICES
INFRARED OBJECT DETECTION EQPT
INGOT, EXTRUSION: Extrusion ingot, aluminum: rolling mills
INK OR WRITING FLUIDS
INK: Duplicating
INK: Printing
INNER TUBES: Truck Or Bus
INSECT LAMPS: Electric
INSECTICIDES & PESTICIDES
INSPECTION & TESTING SVCS
INSPECTION SVCS, TRANSPORTATION
INSTR, MEASURE & CONTROL: Gauge, Oil Pressure & Water Temp
INSTRUMENTS, LABORATORY: Spectrometers
INSTRUMENTS, MEASURING & CNTRL: Geophysical & Meteorological
INSTRUMENTS, MEASURING & CNTRL: Testing, Abrasion, Etc
INSTRUMENTS, MEASURING & CNTRLG: Aircraft & Motor Vehicle
INSTRUMENTS, MEASURING & CNTRLG: Fatigue Test, Indl, Mech

INSTRUMENTS, MEASURING & CNTRLG: Stress, Strain & Measure
INSTRUMENTS, MEASURING & CNTRLNG: Press & Vac Ind, Acft Eng
INSTRUMENTS, MEASURING & CONTROLLING: Gas Detectors
INSTRUMENTS, MEASURING & CONTROLLING: Weather Tracking
INSTRUMENTS, MEASURING/CNTRL: Gauging, Ultrasonic Thickness
INSTRUMENTS, MEASURING/CNTRLG: Fire Detect Sys, Non-Electric
INSTRUMENTS, MEASURING/CNTRLNG: Med Diagnostic Sys, Nuclear
INSTRUMENTS, OPTICAL: Lens Mounts
INSTRUMENTS, OPTICAL: Lenses, All Types Exc Ophthalmic
INSTRUMENTS, OPTICAL: Test & Inspection
INSTRUMENTS, SURGICAL & MEDICAL: Biopsy
INSTRUMENTS, SURGICAL & MEDICAL: Blood & Bone Work
INSTRUMENTS, SURGICAL & MEDICAL: Lasers, Ophthalmic
INSTRUMENTS, SURGICAL & MEDICAL: Lasers, Surgical
INSTRUMENTS, SURGICAL & MEDICAL: Plates & Screws, Bone
INSTRUMENTS, SURGICAL & MEDICAL: Skin Grafting
INSTRUMENTS: Ammeters, NEC
INSTRUMENTS: Analytical
INSTRUMENTS: Combustion Control, Indl
INSTRUMENTS: Differential Pressure, Indl
INSTRUMENTS: Endoscopic Eqpt, Electromedical
INSTRUMENTS: Flow, Indl Process
INSTRUMENTS: Frequency Meters, Electrical, Mech & Electronic
INSTRUMENTS: Indl Process Control
INSTRUMENTS: Infrared, Indl Process
INSTRUMENTS: Laser, Scientific & Engineering
INSTRUMENTS: Measurement, Indl Process
INSTRUMENTS: Measuring & Controlling
INSTRUMENTS: Measuring Electricity
INSTRUMENTS: Measuring, Current, NEC
INSTRUMENTS: Measuring, Electrical Energy
INSTRUMENTS: Measuring, Electrical Power
INSTRUMENTS: Medical & Surgical
INSTRUMENTS: Meteorological
INSTRUMENTS: Microwave Test
INSTRUMENTS: Photographic, Electronic
INSTRUMENTS: Power Measuring, Electrical
INSTRUMENTS: Pressure Measurement, Indl
INSTRUMENTS: Radio Frequency Measuring
INSTRUMENTS: Temperature Measurement, Indl
INSTRUMENTS: Test, Digital, Electronic & Electrical Circuits
INSTRUMENTS: Test, Electrical, Engine
INSTRUMENTS: Test, Electronic & Electric Measurement
INSTRUMENTS: Test, Electronic & Electrical Circuits
INSTRUMENTS: Testing, Semiconductor
INSTRUMENTS: Thermal Conductive, Indl
INSTRUMENTS: Thermal Property Measurement
INSTRUMENTS: Viscometer, Indl Process
INSULATING BOARD, CELLULAR FIBER
INSULATING COMPOUNDS
INSULATION & CUSHIONING FOAM: Polystyrene
INSULATION & ROOFING MATERIALS: Wood, Reconstituted
INSULATION MATERIALS WHOLESALERS
INSULATION: Fiberglass
INSULATORS & INSULATION MATERIALS: Electrical
INSURANCE ADVISORY SVCS
INSURANCE CARRIERS: Automobile
INSURANCE: Agents, Brokers & Service
INTERCOMMUNICATIONS SYSTEMS: Electric
INTERIOR DECORATING SVCS
INTERIOR DESIGN SVCS, NEC
INTERIOR DESIGNING SVCS
INTRAVENOUS SOLUTIONS
INVENTORY STOCKING SVCS
INVERTERS: Nonrotating Electrical
INVESTMENT FUNDS, NEC
INVESTORS, NEC
IRON & STEEL PRDTS: Hot-Rolled
IRON ORES
IRRIGATION SYSTEMS, NEC Water Distribution Or Sply Systems
ISOCYANATES

J

JACKS: Hydraulic

PRODUCT INDEX

JANITORIAL & CUSTODIAL SVCS
JANITORIAL EQPT & SPLYS WHOLESALERS
JAR RINGS: Rubber
JARS: Plastic
JEWELERS' FINDINGS & MATERIALS
JEWELERS' FINDINGS & MATERIALS: Castings
JEWELRY & PRECIOUS STONES WHOLESALERS
JEWELRY APPAREL
JEWELRY FINDINGS & LAPIDARY WORK
JEWELRY FINDINGS WHOLESALERS
JEWELRY REPAIR SVCS
JEWELRY STORES
JEWELRY STORES: Precious Stones & Precious Metals
JEWELRY, PRECIOUS METAL: Bracelets
JEWELRY, PRECIOUS METAL: Mountings & Trimmings
JEWELRY, PRECIOUS METAL: Rings, Finger
JEWELRY, WHOLESALE
JEWELRY: Decorative, Fashion & Costume
JEWELRY: Precious Metal
JIGS & FIXTURES
JIGS: Welding Positioners
JOB COUNSELING
JOB PRINTING & NEWSPAPER PUBLISHING COMBINED
JOB TRAINING & VOCATIONAL REHABILITATION SVCS
JOINTS OR FASTENINGS: Rail
JOINTS: Expansion
JOINTS: Expansion, Pipe
JOISTS: Fabricated Bar
JOISTS: Long-Span Series, Open Web Steel

K

KEYS: Machine
KILNS & FURNACES: Ceramic
KITCHEN CABINET STORES, EXC CUSTOM
KITCHEN CABINETS WHOLESALERS
KITCHEN TOOLS & UTENSILS WHOLESALERS
KITCHEN UTENSILS: Bakers' Eqpt, Wood
KITCHEN UTENSILS: Food Handling & Processing Prdts, Wood
KNIVES: Agricultural Or indl

L

LABELS: Paper, Made From Purchased Materials
LABOR RESOURCE SVCS
LABORATORIES, TESTING: Automobile Proving & Testing Ground
LABORATORIES, TESTING: Prdt Certification, Sfty/Performance
LABORATORIES, TESTING: Product Testing
LABORATORIES, TESTING: Product Testing, Safety/Performance
LABORATORIES: Biological Research
LABORATORIES: Biotechnology
LABORATORIES: Commercial Nonphysical Research
LABORATORIES: Dental
LABORATORIES: Dental, Artificial Teeth Production
LABORATORIES: Dental, Crown & Bridge Production
LABORATORIES: Electronic Research
LABORATORIES: Medical
LABORATORIES: Noncommercial Research
LABORATORIES: Physical Research, Commercial
LABORATORIES: Testing
LABORATORY APPARATUS & FURNITURE
LABORATORY APPARATUS, EXC HEATING & MEASURING
LABORATORY APPARATUS: Evaporation
LABORATORY APPARATUS: Granulators
LABORATORY APPARATUS: Microtomes
LABORATORY APPARATUS: Sample Preparation Apparatus
LABORATORY APPARATUS: Time Interval Measuring, Electric
LABORATORY CHEMICALS: Organic
LABORATORY EQPT, EXC MEDICAL: Wholesalers
LABORATORY EQPT: Centrifuges
LABORATORY EQPT: Clinical Instruments Exc Medical
LABORATORY EQPT: Incubators
LABORATORY EQPT: Sterilizers
LACQUERING SVC: Metal Prdts
LADDER & WORKSTAND COMBINATION ASSEMBLIES: Metal
LADDERS: Metal
LADDERS: Portable, Metal
LADDERS: Wood
LAMINATED PLASTICS: Plate, Sheet, Rod & Tubes
LAMINATING MATERIALS
LAMINATING SVCS

LAMP & LIGHT BULBS & TUBES
LAMP BULBS & TUBES, ELECTRIC: Electric Light
LAMP BULBS & TUBES, ELECTRIC: For Specialized Applications
LAMP BULBS & TUBES, ELECTRIC: Glow Lamp
LAMP BULBS & TUBES, ELECTRIC: Light, Complete
LAMP BULBS & TUBES, ELECTRIC: Vapor
LAMP BULBS & TUBES/PARTS, ELECTRIC: Generalized Applications
LAMP REPAIR & MOUNTING SVCS
LAMPS: Desk, Commercial
LAMPS: Table, Residential
LAMPS: Ultraviolet
LAND SUBDIVISION & DEVELOPMENT
LANGUAGE SCHOOLS
LASER SYSTEMS & EQPT
LASERS: Welding, Drilling & Cutting Eqpt
LATHES
LAUNDRY & GARMENT SVCS, NEC: Garment Making, Alter & Repair
LAUNDRY & GARMENT SVCS, NEC: Reweaving, Textiles
LAUNDRY EQPT: Commercial
LAUNDRY EQPT: Household
LAWN & GARDEN EQPT
LAWN & GARDEN EQPT: Blowers & Vacuums
LAWN & GARDEN EQPT: Edgers
LAWN & GARDEN EQPT: Grass Catchers, Lawn Mower
LAWN & GARDEN EQPT: Tractors & Eqpt
LAWN MOWER REPAIR SHOP
LEAD
LEAD & ZINC ORES
LEAD PENCILS & ART GOODS
LEASING & RENTAL SVCS: Cranes & Aerial Lift Eqpt
LEASING & RENTAL SVCS: Earth Moving Eqpt
LEASING & RENTAL: Computers & Eqpt
LEASING & RENTAL: Construction & Mining Eqpt
LEASING & RENTAL: Medical Machinery & Eqpt
LEASING & RENTAL: Mobile Home Sites
LEASING & RENTAL: Other Real Estate Property
LEASING & RENTAL: Trucks, Without Drivers
LEASING & RENTAL: Utility Trailers & RV's
LEASING: Passenger Car
LEASING: Shipping Container
LEATHER GOODS: Belting & Strapping
LEATHER GOODS: Embossed
LEATHER GOODS: Garments
LEATHER GOODS: Harnesses Or Harness Parts
LEATHER GOODS: Holsters
LEATHER GOODS: Money Holders
LEATHER GOODS: NEC
LEATHER GOODS: Personal
LEATHER GOODS: Straps
LEATHER TANNING & FINISHING
LEATHER: Cut
LEATHER: Die-cut
LEATHER: Equestrian Prdts
LEATHER: Handbag
LEATHER: Indl Prdts
LEATHER: Processed
LECTURING SVCS
LEGAL OFFICES & SVCS
LENS COATING: Ophthalmic
LICENSE TAGS: Automobile, Stamped Metal
LIGHT OIL CRUDE: From Chemical Recovery Coke Ovens
LIGHT SENSITIVE DEVICES
LIGHTING EQPT: Area & Sports Luminaries
LIGHTING EQPT: Motor Vehicle
LIGHTING EQPT: Motor Vehicle, Dome Lights
LIGHTING EQPT: Motor Vehicle, Headlights
LIGHTING EQPT: Motor Vehicle, NEC
LIGHTING EQPT: Motor Vehicle, Taillights
LIGHTING EQPT: Outdoor
LIGHTING EQPT: Reflectors, Metal, For Lighting Eqpt
LIGHTING EQPT: Searchlights
LIGHTING EQPT: Spotlights
LIGHTING FIXTURES WHOLESALERS
LIGHTING FIXTURES, NEC
LIGHTING FIXTURES: Fluorescent, Commercial
LIGHTING FIXTURES: Indl & Commercial
LIGHTING FIXTURES: Motor Vehicle
LIGHTING FIXTURES: Public
LIGHTING FIXTURES: Residential
LIGHTING FIXTURES: Residential, Electric
LIGHTING FIXTURES: Street
LIMESTONE & MARBLE: Dimension

LIMESTONE: Crushed & Broken
LIMESTONE: Dimension
LIMESTONE: Ground
LINEN SPLY SVC
LINEN SPLY SVC: Coat
LINEN SPLY SVC: Uniform
LINERS & COVERS: Fabric
LINERS & LINING
LINERS: Indl, Metal Plate
LIPSTICK
LITHOGRAPHIC PLATES
LOADS: Electronic
LOCK & KEY SVCS
LOCKS
LOCKSMITHS
LOG SPLITTERS
LOGGING
LOGGING CAMPS & CONTRACTORS
LOGGING: Fuel Wood Harvesting
LOGGING: Peeler Logs
LOGGING: Pulpwood Camp, Exc Pulp Mill At Same Site
LOGGING: Saw Logs
LOGGING: Skidding Logs
LOGGING: Stump Harvesting
LOGGING: Timber, Cut At Logging Camp
LOGGING: Wheel stock, Hewn
LOGGING: Wood Chips, Produced In The Field
LOGGING: Wooden Logs
LOGS: Gas, Fireplace
LOOSELEAF BINDERS
LOTIONS OR CREAMS: Face
LOTIONS: SHAVING
LOUDSPEAKERS
LUBRICANTS: Corrosion Preventive
LUBRICATING EQPT: Indl
LUBRICATING OIL & GREASE WHOLESALERS
LUBRICATION SYSTEMS & EQPT
LUGGAGE & LEATHER GOODS STORES: Leather, Exc Luggage & Shoes
LUMBER & BLDG MATLS DEALER, RET: Garage Doors, Sell/Install
LUMBER & BLDG MATLS DEALERS, RET: Energy Conservation Prdts
LUMBER & BLDG MATRLS DEALERS, RETAIL: Doors, Wood/Metal
LUMBER & BLDG MTRLS DEALERS, RET: Doors, Storm, Wood/Metal
LUMBER & BLDG MTRLS DEALERS, RET: Planing Mill Prdts/Lumber
LUMBER & BLDG MTRLS DEALERS, RET: Windows, Storm, Wood/Metal
LUMBER & BUILDING MATERIALS DEALER, RET: Door & Window Prdts
LUMBER & BUILDING MATERIALS DEALER, RET: Masonry Matls/Splys
LUMBER & BUILDING MATERIALS DEALERS, RETAIL: Brick
LUMBER & BUILDING MATERIALS DEALERS, RETAIL: Cement
LUMBER & BUILDING MATERIALS DEALERS, RETAIL: Countertops
LUMBER & BUILDING MATERIALS DEALERS, RETAIL: Modular Homes
LUMBER & BUILDING MATERIALS DEALERS, RETAIL: Paving Stones
LUMBER & BUILDING MATERIALS DEALERS, RETAIL: Sand & Gravel
LUMBER & BUILDING MATERIALS DEALERS, RETAIL: Siding
LUMBER & BUILDING MATERIALS RET DEALERS: Millwork & Lumber
LUMBER & BUILDING MATLS DEALERS, RET: Concrete/Cinder Block
LUMBER & BUILDING MTRLS DEALERS, RET: Insulation Mtrl, Bldg
LUMBER: Cants, Resawn
LUMBER: Dimension, Hardwood
LUMBER: Furniture Dimension Stock, Softwood
LUMBER: Hardwood Dimension
LUMBER: Hardwood Dimension & Flooring Mills
LUMBER: Kiln Dried
LUMBER: Panels, Plywood, Softwood
LUMBER: Plywood, Hardwood
LUMBER: Plywood, Hardwood or Hardwood Faced
LUMBER: Plywood, Prefinished, Hardwood
LUMBER: Plywood, Softwood

PRODUCT INDEX

LUMBER: Resawn, Small Dimension
LUMBER: Stacking Or Sticking
LUMBER: Treated
LUMBER: Veneer, Hardwood
LUNCHROOMS & CAFETERIAS

M

MACHINE PARTS: Stamped Or Pressed Metal
MACHINE SHOPS
MACHINE TOOL ACCESS: Arbors
MACHINE TOOL ACCESS: Boring Attachments
MACHINE TOOL ACCESS: Broaches
MACHINE TOOL ACCESS: Cams
MACHINE TOOL ACCESS: Cutting
MACHINE TOOL ACCESS: Diamond Cutting, For Turning, Etc
MACHINE TOOL ACCESS: Dies, Thread Cutting
MACHINE TOOL ACCESS: Dresser, Abrasive Wheel Or Other
MACHINE TOOL ACCESS: Dressing/Wheel Crushing Attach, Diamond
MACHINE TOOL ACCESS: Drill Bushings, Drilling Jig
MACHINE TOOL ACCESS: Drills
MACHINE TOOL ACCESS: End Mills
MACHINE TOOL ACCESS: Files
MACHINE TOOL ACCESS: Hobs
MACHINE TOOL ACCESS: Honing Heads
MACHINE TOOL ACCESS: Knives, Metalworking
MACHINE TOOL ACCESS: Machine Attachments & Access, Drilling
MACHINE TOOL ACCESS: Milling Machine Attachments
MACHINE TOOL ACCESS: Pushers
MACHINE TOOL ACCESS: Rotary Tables
MACHINE TOOL ACCESS: Shaping Tools
MACHINE TOOL ACCESS: Sockets
MACHINE TOOL ACCESS: Threading Tools
MACHINE TOOL ACCESS: Tool Holders
MACHINE TOOL ACCESS: Tools & Access
MACHINE TOOL ATTACHMENTS & ACCESS
MACHINE TOOLS & ACCESS
MACHINE TOOLS, METAL CUTTING: Brushing
MACHINE TOOLS, METAL CUTTING: Cutoff
MACHINE TOOLS, METAL CUTTING: Die Sinking
MACHINE TOOLS, METAL CUTTING: Drilling
MACHINE TOOLS, METAL CUTTING: Drilling & Boring
MACHINE TOOLS, METAL CUTTING: Electrochemical Milling
MACHINE TOOLS, METAL CUTTING: Electron-Discharge
MACHINE TOOLS, METAL CUTTING: Exotic, Including Explosive
MACHINE TOOLS, METAL CUTTING: Grind, Polish, Buff, Lapp
MACHINE TOOLS, METAL CUTTING: Home Workshop
MACHINE TOOLS, METAL CUTTING: Jig, Boring & Grinding
MACHINE TOOLS, METAL CUTTING: Lathes
MACHINE TOOLS, METAL CUTTING: Numerically Controlled
MACHINE TOOLS, METAL CUTTING: Pipe Cutting & Threading
MACHINE TOOLS, METAL CUTTING: Plasma Process
MACHINE TOOLS, METAL CUTTING: Regrinding, Crankshaft
MACHINE TOOLS, METAL CUTTING: Robot, Drilling, Cutting, Etc
MACHINE TOOLS, METAL CUTTING: Tool Replacement & Rpr Parts
MACHINE TOOLS, METAL CUTTING: Turret Lathes
MACHINE TOOLS, METAL CUTTING: Ultrasonic
MACHINE TOOLS, METAL CUTTING: Vertical Turning & Boring
MACHINE TOOLS, METAL FORMING: Beaders, Metal
MACHINE TOOLS, METAL FORMING: Bending
MACHINE TOOLS, METAL FORMING: Die Casting & Extruding
MACHINE TOOLS, METAL FORMING: Electroforming
MACHINE TOOLS, METAL FORMING: Forging Machinery & Hammers
MACHINE TOOLS, METAL FORMING: Gear Rolling
MACHINE TOOLS, METAL FORMING: Lathes, Spinning
MACHINE TOOLS, METAL FORMING: Magnetic Forming
MACHINE TOOLS, METAL FORMING: Marking
MACHINE TOOLS, METAL FORMING: Mechanical, Pneumatic Or Hyd
MACHINE TOOLS, METAL FORMING: Plasma Jet Spray
MACHINE TOOLS, METAL FORMING: Presses, Arbor
MACHINE TOOLS, METAL FORMING: Presses, Hyd & Pneumatic
MACHINE TOOLS, METAL FORMING: Punching & Shearing
MACHINE TOOLS, METAL FORMING: Rebuilt
MACHINE TOOLS, METAL FORMING: Robots, Pressing, Extrudg, Etc
MACHINE TOOLS, METAL FORMING: Spinning, Spline Rollg/Windg
MACHINE TOOLS, METAL FORMING: Spline Rolling
MACHINE TOOLS: Metal Cutting
MACHINE TOOLS: Metal Forming
MACHINERY & EQPT FINANCE LEASING
MACHINERY & EQPT, AGRICULTURAL, WHOL: Farm Eqpt Parts/Splys
MACHINERY & EQPT, AGRICULTURAL, WHOLESALE: Cultivating
MACHINERY & EQPT, AGRICULTURAL, WHOLESALE: Landscaping Eqpt
MACHINERY & EQPT, AGRICULTURAL, WHOLESALE: Livestock Eqpt
MACHINERY & EQPT, INDL, WHOL: Brewery Prdts Mfrg, Commercial
MACHINERY & EQPT, INDL, WHOL: Controlling Instruments/Access
MACHINERY & EQPT, INDL, WHOL: Environ Pollution Cntrl, Air
MACHINERY & EQPT, INDL, WHOL: Environ Pollution Cntrl, Water
MACHINERY & EQPT, INDL, WHOL: Meters, Consumption Registerng
MACHINERY & EQPT, INDL, WHOLESALE: Conveyor Systems
MACHINERY & EQPT, INDL, WHOLESALE: Cranes
MACHINERY & EQPT, INDL, WHOLESALE: Engines & Parts, Diesel
MACHINERY & EQPT, INDL, WHOLESALE: Engs & Parts, Air-Cooled
MACHINERY & EQPT, INDL, WHOLESALE: Food Manufacturing
MACHINERY & EQPT, INDL, WHOLESALE: Fuel Injection Systems
MACHINERY & EQPT, INDL, WHOLESALE: Hydraulic Systems
MACHINERY & EQPT, INDL, WHOLESALE: Indl Machine Parts
MACHINERY & EQPT, INDL, WHOLESALE: Instruments & Cntrl Eqpt
MACHINERY & EQPT, INDL, WHOLESALE: Lift Trucks & Parts
MACHINERY & EQPT, INDL, WHOLESALE: Machine Tools & Access
MACHINERY & EQPT, INDL, WHOLESALE: Machine Tools & Metalwork
MACHINERY & EQPT, INDL, WHOLESALE: Measure/Test, Electric
MACHINERY & EQPT, INDL, WHOLESALE: Metal Refining
MACHINERY & EQPT, INDL, WHOLESALE: Paint Spray
MACHINERY & EQPT, INDL, WHOLESALE: Petroleum Industry
MACHINERY & EQPT, INDL, WHOLESALE: Plastic Prdts Machinery
MACHINERY & EQPT, INDL, WHOLESALE: Pneumatic Tools
MACHINERY & EQPT, INDL, WHOLESALE: Processing & Packaging
MACHINERY & EQPT, INDL, WHOLESALE: Recycling
MACHINERY & EQPT, INDL, WHOLESALE: Robots
MACHINERY & EQPT, INDL, WHOLESALE: Safety Eqpt
MACHINERY & EQPT, INDL, WHOLESALE: Sawmill
MACHINERY & EQPT, INDL, WHOLESALE: Textile
MACHINERY & EQPT, INDL, WHOLESALE: Tool & Die Makers
MACHINERY & EQPT, INDL, WHOLESALE: Water Pumps
MACHINERY & EQPT, WHOLESALE: Blades, Graders, Scrapers, Etc
MACHINERY & EQPT, WHOLESALE: Construction & Mining, Ladders
MACHINERY & EQPT, WHOLESALE: Construction & Mining, Pavers
MACHINERY & EQPT, WHOLESALE: Construction, General
MACHINERY & EQPT, WHOLESALE: Logging & Forestry
MACHINERY & EQPT, WHOLESALE: Masonry
MACHINERY & EQPT, WHOLESALE: Oil Field Eqpt
MACHINERY & EQPT: Farm
MACHINERY & EQPT: Gas Producers, Generators/Other Rltd Eqpt
MACHINERY & EQPT: Liquid Automation
MACHINERY & EQPT: Metal Finishing, Plating Etc
MACHINERY & EQPT: Metal Pickling
MACHINERY & EQPT: Vibratory Parts Handling Eqpt
MACHINERY BASES
MACHINERY, EQPT & SUPPLIES: Parking Facility
MACHINERY, FOOD PRDTS: Cutting, Chopping, Grinding, Mixing
MACHINERY, FOOD PRDTS: Dairy & Milk
MACHINERY, FOOD PRDTS: Food Processing, Smokers
MACHINERY, FOOD PRDTS: Grinders, Commercial
MACHINERY, FOOD PRDTS: Juice Extractors, Fruit & Veg, Comm
MACHINERY, FOOD PRDTS: Ovens, Bakery
MACHINERY, FOOD PRDTS: Processing, Fish & Shellfish
MACHINERY, FOOD PRDTS: Roasting, Coffee, Peanut, Etc.
MACHINERY, FOOD PRDTS: Slicers, Commercial
MACHINERY, LUBRICATION: Automatic
MACHINERY, MAILING: Postage Meters
MACHINERY, METALWORKING: Assembly, Including Robotic
MACHINERY, METALWORKING: Coil Winding, For Springs
MACHINERY, METALWORKING: Coiling
MACHINERY, METALWORKING: Cutting & Slitting
MACHINERY, METALWORKING: Rotary Slitters, Metalworking
MACHINERY, OFFICE: Paper Handling
MACHINERY, PACKAGING: Carton Packing
MACHINERY, PACKAGING: Packing & Wrapping
MACHINERY, PACKAGING: Vacuum
MACHINERY, PACKAGING: Wrapping
MACHINERY, PAPER INDUSTRY: Coating & Finishing
MACHINERY, PAPER INDUSTRY: Converting, Die Cutting & Stampng
MACHINERY, PAPER INDUSTRY: Cutting
MACHINERY, PAPER INDUSTRY: Paper Mill, Plating, Etc
MACHINERY, PRINTING TRADES: Bookbinding Machinery
MACHINERY, PRINTING TRADES: Copy Holders
MACHINERY, PRINTING TRADES: Plates, Engravers' Metal
MACHINERY, PRINTING TRADES: Printing Trade Parts & Attchts
MACHINERY, PRINTING TRADES: Type & Type Making
MACHINERY, PRINTING TRADES: Type Casting, Founding/Melting
MACHINERY, SERVICING: Coin-Operated, Exc Dry Clean & Laundry
MACHINERY, SEWING: Sewing & Hat & Zipper Making
MACHINERY, TEXTILE: Bleaching
MACHINERY, TEXTILE: Embroidery
MACHINERY, TEXTILE: Heddles, Wire, For Loom Harnesses
MACHINERY, TEXTILE: Opening
MACHINERY, TEXTILE: Printing
MACHINERY, TEXTILE: Silk Screens
MACHINERY, TEXTILE: Thread Making Or Spinning
MACHINERY, WOODWORKING: Bandsaws
MACHINERY, WOODWORKING: Cabinet Makers'
MACHINERY, WOODWORKING: Furniture Makers
MACHINERY, WOODWORKING: Pattern Makers'
MACHINERY, WOODWORKING: Planers
MACHINERY/EQPT, INDL, WHOL: Cleaning, High Press, Sand/Steam
MACHINERY: Ammunition & Explosives Loading
MACHINERY: Assembly, Exc Metalworking
MACHINERY: Automotive Maintenance
MACHINERY: Automotive Related
MACHINERY: Blasting, Electrical
MACHINERY: Centrifugal
MACHINERY: Concrete Prdts
MACHINERY: Construction
MACHINERY: Custom
MACHINERY: Deburring
MACHINERY: Die Casting
MACHINERY: Dredging
MACHINERY: Drill Presses
MACHINERY: Electronic Component Making
MACHINERY: Electronic Teaching Aids
MACHINERY: Extruding
MACHINERY: Fiber Optics Strand Coating
MACHINERY: Folding
MACHINERY: Gear Cutting & Finishing
MACHINERY: General, Industrial, NEC
MACHINERY: Glass Cutting
MACHINERY: Glassmaking
MACHINERY: Grinding
MACHINERY: Ice Cream
MACHINERY: Ice Crushers
MACHINERY: Ice Making
MACHINERY: Ice Resurfacing
MACHINERY: Industrial, NEC
MACHINERY: Kilns

PRODUCT INDEX

MACHINERY: Labeling
MACHINERY: Lapping
MACHINERY: Marking, Metalworking
MACHINERY: Metalworking
MACHINERY: Milling
MACHINERY: Mining
MACHINERY: Ozone
MACHINERY: Packaging
MACHINERY: Paint Making
MACHINERY: Paper Industry Miscellaneous
MACHINERY: Pharmaciutical
MACHINERY: Photographic Reproduction
MACHINERY: Plastic Working
MACHINERY: Polishing & Buffing
MACHINERY: Printing Presses
MACHINERY: Recycling
MACHINERY: Riveting
MACHINERY: Road Construction & Maintenance
MACHINERY: Robots, Molding & Forming Plastics
MACHINERY: Rubber Working
MACHINERY: Saw & Sawing
MACHINERY: Screening Eqpt, Electric
MACHINERY: Semiconductor Manufacturing
MACHINERY: Separation Eqpt, Magnetic
MACHINERY: Service Industry, NEC
MACHINERY: Sheet Metal Working
MACHINERY: Snow Making
MACHINERY: Specialty
MACHINERY: Tapping
MACHINERY: Textile
MACHINERY: Thread Rolling
MACHINERY: Wire Drawing
MACHINERY: Woodworking
MACHINES: Forming, Sheet Metal
MACHINISTS' TOOLS & MACHINES: Measuring, Metalworking Type
MACHINISTS' TOOLS: Measuring, Precision
MACHINISTS' TOOLS: Precision
MAGAZINES, WHOLESALE
MAGNESIUM
MAGNETIC INK & OPTICAL SCANNING EQPT
MAGNETIC RESONANCE IMAGING DEVICES: Nonmedical
MAGNETIC SHIELDS, METAL
MAGNETIC TAPE, AUDIO: Prerecorded
MAGNETS: Ceramic
MAGNETS: Permanent
MAIL-ORDER HOUSE, NEC
MAIL-ORDER HOUSES: Computer Software
MAIL-ORDER HOUSES: Cosmetics & Perfumes
MAIL-ORDER HOUSES: Educational Splys & Eqpt
MAIL-ORDER HOUSES: Fitness & Sporting Goods
MAIL-ORDER HOUSES: Fruit
MAIL-ORDER HOUSES: Novelty Merchandise
MAIL-ORDER HOUSES: Tools & Hardware
MAILBOX RENTAL & RELATED SVCS
MAILING & MESSENGER SVCS
MAILING LIST: Compilers
MAILING SVCS, NEC
MANAGEMENT CONSULTING SVCS: Administrative
MANAGEMENT CONSULTING SVCS: Automation & Robotics
MANAGEMENT CONSULTING SVCS: Business
MANAGEMENT CONSULTING SVCS: Construction Project
MANAGEMENT CONSULTING SVCS: Hospital & Health
MANAGEMENT CONSULTING SVCS: Industrial
MANAGEMENT CONSULTING SVCS: Industrial & Labor
MANAGEMENT CONSULTING SVCS: Industrial Hygiene
MANAGEMENT CONSULTING SVCS: Industry Specialist
MANAGEMENT CONSULTING SVCS: Maintenance
MANAGEMENT CONSULTING SVCS: Management Engineering
MANAGEMENT CONSULTING SVCS: Manufacturing
MANAGEMENT CONSULTING SVCS: Quality Assurance
MANAGEMENT CONSULTING SVCS: Retail Trade Consultant
MANAGEMENT CONSULTING SVCS: Training & Development
MANAGEMENT SERVICES
MANAGEMENT SVCS, FACILITIES SUPPORT: Environ Remediation
MANAGEMENT SVCS: Administrative
MANAGEMENT SVCS: Business
MANAGEMENT SVCS: Construction
MANAGEMENT SVCS: Hospital
MANAGEMENT SVCS: Nursing & Personal Care Facility
MANAGEMENT SVCS: Restaurant

MANHOLES & COVERS: Metal
MANHOLES COVERS: Concrete
MANICURE PREPARATIONS
MANIFOLDS: Pipe, Fabricated From Purchased Pipe
MANNEQUINS
MANUFACTURED & MOBILE HOME DEALERS
MANUFACTURING INDUSTRIES, NEC
MAPS
MAPS & CHARTS, WHOLESALE
MARBLE, BUILDING: Cut & Shaped
MARINAS
MARINE BASIN OPERATIONS
MARINE CARGO HANDLING SVCS: Marine Terminal
MARINE ENGINE REPAIR SVCS
MARINE HARDWARE
MARINE PROPELLER REPAIR SVCS
MARINE RELATED EQPT
MARINE SPLY DEALERS
MARINE SPLYS WHOLESALERS
MARKERS
MARKETS: Meat & fish
MARKING DEVICES
MARKING DEVICES: Embossing Seals & Hand Stamps
MARKING DEVICES: Printing Dies, Marking Mach, Rubber/Plastic
MARKING DEVICES: Screens, Textile Printing
MARKING DEVICES: Seal Presses, Notary & Hand
MARKING DEVICES: Stationary Embossers, Personal
MASKS: Gas
MASQUERADE OR THEATRICAL COSTUMES STORES
MASSAGE MACHINES, ELECTRIC: Barber & Beauty Shops
MATERIAL GRINDING & PULVERIZING SVCS NEC
MATERIALS HANDLING EQPT WHOLESALERS
MATS, MATTING & PADS: Nonwoven
MATTRESS PROTECTORS: Rubber
MATTRESS STORES
MEAL DELIVERY PROGRAMS
MEAT & MEAT PRDTS WHOLESALERS
MEAT CUTTING & PACKING
MEAT MARKETS
MEAT PRDTS: Boxed Beef, From Slaughtered Meat
MEAT PRDTS: Canned Exc Baby Food, From Slaughtered Meat
MEAT PRDTS: Cooked Meats, From Purchased Meat
MEAT PRDTS: Corned Beef, From Purchased Meat
MEAT PRDTS: Cured, From Slaughtered Meat
MEAT PRDTS: Frankfurters, From Purchased Meat
MEAT PRDTS: Lamb, From Slaughtered Meat
MEAT PRDTS: Luncheon Meat, From Purchased Meat
MEAT PRDTS: Meat By-Prdts, From Slaughtered Meat
MEAT PRDTS: Pork, From Slaughtered Meat
MEAT PRDTS: Prepared Beef Prdts From Purchased Beef
MEAT PRDTS: Prepared Pork Prdts, From Purchased Meat
MEAT PRDTS: Sausages & Related Prdts, From Purchased Meat
MEAT PRDTS: Sausages, From Purchased Meat
MEAT PRDTS: Sausages, From Slaughtered Meat
MEAT PRDTS: Smoked
MEAT PRDTS: Snack Sticks, Incl Jerky, From Purchased Meat
MEAT PRDTS: Veal, From Slaughtered Meat
MEAT PROCESSED FROM PURCHASED CARCASSES
MEAT PROCESSING MACHINERY
MEATS, PACKAGED FROZEN: Wholesalers
MEDIA: Magnetic & Optical Recording
MEDICAL & HOSPITAL EQPT WHOLESALERS
MEDICAL & HOSPITAL SPLYS: Radiation Shielding Garments
MEDICAL & SURGICAL SPLYS: Abdominal Support, Braces/Trusses
MEDICAL & SURGICAL SPLYS: Absorbent Cotton, Sterilized
MEDICAL & SURGICAL SPLYS: Bandages & Dressings
MEDICAL & SURGICAL SPLYS: Belts, Surg, Sanitary & Corrective
MEDICAL & SURGICAL SPLYS: Braces, Orthopedic
MEDICAL & SURGICAL SPLYS: Canes, Orthopedic
MEDICAL & SURGICAL SPLYS: Clothing, Fire Resistant & Protect
MEDICAL & SURGICAL SPLYS: Cosmetic Restorations
MEDICAL & SURGICAL SPLYS: Crutches & Walkers
MEDICAL & SURGICAL SPLYS: Ear Plugs
MEDICAL & SURGICAL SPLYS: Foot Appliances, Orthopedic
MEDICAL & SURGICAL SPLYS: Limbs, Artificial
MEDICAL & SURGICAL SPLYS: Models, Anatomical
MEDICAL & SURGICAL SPLYS: Orthopedic Appliances

MEDICAL & SURGICAL SPLYS: Personal Safety Eqpt
MEDICAL & SURGICAL SPLYS: Prosthetic Appliances
MEDICAL & SURGICAL SPLYS: Respiratory Protect Eqpt, Personal
MEDICAL & SURGICAL SPLYS: Technical Aids, Handicapped
MEDICAL & SURGICAL SPLYS: Traction Apparatus
MEDICAL & SURGICAL SPLYS: Welders' Hoods
MEDICAL EQPT: Cardiographs
MEDICAL EQPT: Diagnostic
MEDICAL EQPT: Electromedical Apparatus
MEDICAL EQPT: Electrotherapeutic Apparatus
MEDICAL EQPT: Heart-Lung Machines, Exc Iron Lungs
MEDICAL EQPT: Laser Systems
MEDICAL EQPT: TENS Units/Transcutaneous Elec Nerve Stimulatr
MEDICAL EQPT: Ultrasonic Scanning Devices
MEDICAL HELP SVCS
MEDICAL SUNDRIES: Rubber
MEDICAL SVCS ORGANIZATION
MEDICAL, DENTAL & HOSP EQPT, WHOLESALE: X-ray Film & Splys
MEDICAL, DENTAL & HOSPITAL EQPT, WHOL: Hospital Eqpt & Splys
MEDICAL, DENTAL & HOSPITAL EQPT, WHOL: Hosptl Eqpt/Furniture
MEDICAL, DENTAL & HOSPITAL EQPT, WHOLESALE: Diagnostic, Med
MEDICAL, DENTAL & HOSPITAL EQPT, WHOLESALE: Hosp Furniture
MEDICAL, DENTAL & HOSPITAL EQPT, WHOLESALE: Med Eqpt & Splys
MEDICAL, DENTAL & HOSPITAL EQPT, WHOLESALE: Medical Lab
MEDICAL, DENTAL & HOSPITAL EQPT, WHOLESALE: Orthopedic
MEDICAL, DENTAL/HOSPITAL EQPT, WHOL: Tech Aids, Handicapped
MEMBERSHIP ORGANIZATIONS, BUSINESS: Growers' Association
MEMBERSHIP ORGANIZATIONS, NEC: Charitable
MEMBERSHIP ORGANIZATIONS, PROFESSIONAL: Health Association
MEMBERSHIP ORGANIZATIONS, REL: Covenant & Evangelical Church
MEMBERSHIP ORGANIZATIONS, RELIGIOUS: Catholic Church
MEMBERSHIP ORGANIZATIONS, RELIGIOUS: Reformed Church
MEMBERSHIP ORGS, CIVIC, SOCIAL & FRATERNAL: Protection
MEMBERSHIP SPORTS & RECREATION CLUBS
MEMORIES: Solid State
MEN'S & BOYS' CLOTHING ACCESS STORES
MEN'S & BOYS' CLOTHING STORES
MEN'S & BOYS' CLOTHING WHOLESALERS, NEC
MEN'S & BOYS' SPORTSWEAR CLOTHING STORES
MEN'S & BOYS' SPORTSWEAR WHOLESALERS
MEN'S & BOYS' UNDERWEAR WHOLESALERS
MEN'S & BOYS' WORK CLOTHING WHOLESALERS
MEN'S SUITS STORES
MERCHANDISING MACHINE OPERATORS: Vending
METAL & STEEL PRDTS: Abrasive
METAL COMPONENTS: Prefabricated
METAL CUTTING SVCS
METAL DETECTORS
METAL FABRICATORS: Architechtural
METAL FABRICATORS: Plate
METAL FABRICATORS: Sheet
METAL FABRICATORS: Structural, Ship
METAL FABRICATORS: Structural, Ship
METAL FINISHING SVCS
METAL MINING SVCS
METAL RESHAPING & REPLATING SVCS
METAL SERVICE CENTERS & OFFICES
METAL SLITTING & SHEARING
METAL SPINNING FOR THE TRADE
METAL STAMPING, FOR THE TRADE
METAL STAMPINGS: Ornamental
METAL STAMPINGS: Patterned
METAL STAMPINGS: Perforated
METAL TREATING COMPOUNDS
METALS SVC CENTERS & WHOL: Structural Shapes, Iron Or Steel
METALS SVC CENTERS & WHOLESALERS: Bars, Metal

PRODUCT INDEX

METALS SVC CENTERS & WHOLESALERS: Casting, Rough,Iron/Steel
METALS SVC CENTERS & WHOLESALERS: Copper
METALS SVC CENTERS & WHOLESALERS: Copper Prdts
METALS SVC CENTERS & WHOLESALERS: Ferroalloys
METALS SVC CENTERS & WHOLESALERS: Ferrous Metals
METALS SVC CENTERS & WHOLESALERS: Flat Prdts, Iron Or Steel
METALS SVC CENTERS & WHOLESALERS: Foundry Prdts
METALS SVC CENTERS & WHOLESALERS: Misc Nonferrous Prdts
METALS SVC CENTERS & WHOLESALERS: Pipe & Tubing, Steel
METALS SVC CENTERS & WHOLESALERS: Plates, Metal
METALS SVC CENTERS & WHOLESALERS: Rope, Wire, Exc Insulated
METALS SVC CENTERS & WHOLESALERS: Stampings, Metal
METALS SVC CENTERS & WHOLESALERS: Steel
METALS SVC CENTERS & WHOLESALERS: Zinc
METALS SVC CTRS & WHOLESALERS: Aluminum Bars, Rods, Etc
METALS: Precious NEC
METALS: Precious, Secondary
METALS: Primary Nonferrous, NEC
METALWORK: Miscellaneous
METALWORK: Ornamental
METEOROLOGIC TRACKING SYSTEMS
METERING DEVICES: Water Quality Monitoring & Control Systems
METERS: Liquid
METERS: Pyrometers, Indl Process
METERS: Solarimeters
MGMT CONSULTING SVCS: Matls, Incl Purch, Handle & Invntry
MGT SVCS, FACIL SUPPT: Base Maint Or Provide Personnel
MICA PRDTS
MICROCIRCUITS, INTEGRATED: Semiconductor
MICROFILM EQPT
MICROFILM EQPT WHOLESALERS
MICROFILM SVCS
MICROPHONES
MICROPROCESSORS
MICROSCOPES: Electron & Proton
MICROWAVE COMPONENTS
MILITARY GOODS & REGALIA STORES
MILITARY INSIGNIA, TEXTILE
MILLING: Chemical
MILLING: Corn Grits & Flakes, For Brewers' Use
MILLS: Ferrous & Nonferrous
MILLWORK
MINE DEVELOPMENT SVCS: Nonmetallic Minerals
MINERAL MINING: Nonmetallic
MINERAL PRODUCTS
MINERAL WOOL
MINERALS: Ground Or Otherwise Treated
MINERALS: Ground or Treated
MINING EXPLORATION & DEVELOPMENT SVCS
MINING MACHINERY & EQPT WHOLESALERS
MINING MACHINES & EQPT: Pellet Mills
MINING MACHINES & EQPT: Stamping Mill Machinery
MIRRORS: Motor Vehicle
MISCELLANEOUS FINANCIAL INVEST ACT: Oil/Gas Lease Brokers
MIXING EQPT
MIXTURES & BLOCKS: Asphalt Paving
MOBILE HOME REPAIR SVCS
MOBILE HOMES
MOBILE HOMES, EXC RECREATIONAL
MOBILE HOMES: Indl Or Commercial Use
MOBILE HOMES: Personal Or Private Use
MODELS
MODELS: Airplane, Exc Toy
MODELS: General, Exc Toy
MODULES: Solid State
MOLDED RUBBER PRDTS
MOLDING COMPOUNDS
MOLDING SAND MINING
MOLDINGS & TRIM: Metal, Exc Automobile
MOLDINGS & TRIM: Wood
MOLDINGS OR TRIM: Automobile, Stamped Metal
MOLDINGS: Picture Frame
MOLDS: Indl
MOLDS: Plastic Working & Foundry
MONASTERIES

MONUMENTS & GRAVE MARKERS, EXC TERRAZZO
MONUMENTS & GRAVE MARKERS, WHOLESALE
MONUMENTS: Cut Stone, Exc Finishing Or Lettering Only
MOPS: Floor & Dust
MOTEL: Franchised
MOTION PICTURE & VIDEO PRODUCTION SVCS
MOTOR & GENERATOR PARTS: Electric
MOTOR HOME DEALERS
MOTOR HOMES
MOTOR REBUILDING SVCS, EXC AUTOMOTIVE
MOTOR REPAIR SVCS
MOTOR SCOOTERS & PARTS
MOTOR VEHICLE ASSEMBLY, COMPLETE: Ambulances
MOTOR VEHICLE ASSEMBLY, COMPLETE: Autos, Incl Specialty
MOTOR VEHICLE ASSEMBLY, COMPLETE: Buses, All Types
MOTOR VEHICLE ASSEMBLY, COMPLETE: Cars, Armored
MOTOR VEHICLE ASSEMBLY, COMPLETE: Fire Department Vehicles
MOTOR VEHICLE ASSEMBLY, COMPLETE: Hearses
MOTOR VEHICLE ASSEMBLY, COMPLETE: Military Motor Vehicle
MOTOR VEHICLE ASSEMBLY, COMPLETE: Motor Homes, Self Containd
MOTOR VEHICLE ASSEMBLY, COMPLETE: Snow Plows
MOTOR VEHICLE ASSEMBLY, COMPLETE: Truck & Tractor Trucks
MOTOR VEHICLE ASSEMBLY, COMPLETE: Truck Tractors, Highway
MOTOR VEHICLE ASSEMBLY, COMPLETE: Trucks, Pickup
MOTOR VEHICLE ASSEMBLY, COMPLETE: Universal Carriers, Mil
MOTOR VEHICLE ASSEMBLY, COMPLETE: Wreckers, Tow Truck
MOTOR VEHICLE DEALERS: Automobiles, New & Used
MOTOR VEHICLE DEALERS: Cars, Used Only
MOTOR VEHICLE DEALERS: Pickups, New & Used
MOTOR VEHICLE DEALERS: Trucks, Tractors/Trailers, New & Used
MOTOR VEHICLE PARTS & ACCESS: Acceleration Eqpt
MOTOR VEHICLE PARTS & ACCESS: Air Conditioner Parts
MOTOR VEHICLE PARTS & ACCESS: Axel Housings & Shafts
MOTOR VEHICLE PARTS & ACCESS: Ball Joints
MOTOR VEHICLE PARTS & ACCESS: Bearings
MOTOR VEHICLE PARTS & ACCESS: Body Components & Frames
MOTOR VEHICLE PARTS & ACCESS: Brakes, Air
MOTOR VEHICLE PARTS & ACCESS: Cleaners, air
MOTOR VEHICLE PARTS & ACCESS: Clutches
MOTOR VEHICLE PARTS & ACCESS: Connecting Rods
MOTOR VEHICLE PARTS & ACCESS: Cylinder Heads
MOTOR VEHICLE PARTS & ACCESS: Defrosters
MOTOR VEHICLE PARTS & ACCESS: Directional Signals
MOTOR VEHICLE PARTS & ACCESS: Electrical Eqpt
MOTOR VEHICLE PARTS & ACCESS: Engines & Parts
MOTOR VEHICLE PARTS & ACCESS: Engs & Trans,Factory, Rebuilt
MOTOR VEHICLE PARTS & ACCESS: Frames
MOTOR VEHICLE PARTS & ACCESS: Fuel Pumps
MOTOR VEHICLE PARTS & ACCESS: Fuel Systems & Parts
MOTOR VEHICLE PARTS & ACCESS: Gas Tanks
MOTOR VEHICLE PARTS & ACCESS: Gears
MOTOR VEHICLE PARTS & ACCESS: Heaters
MOTOR VEHICLE PARTS & ACCESS: Horns
MOTOR VEHICLE PARTS & ACCESS: Instrument Board Assemblies
MOTOR VEHICLE PARTS & ACCESS: Manifolds
MOTOR VEHICLE PARTS & ACCESS: Mufflers, Exhaust
MOTOR VEHICLE PARTS & ACCESS: Oil Pumps
MOTOR VEHICLE PARTS & ACCESS: Pickup Truck Bed Liners
MOTOR VEHICLE PARTS & ACCESS: Power Steering Eqpt
MOTOR VEHICLE PARTS & ACCESS: Propane Conversion Eqpt
MOTOR VEHICLE PARTS & ACCESS: Pumps, Hydraulic Fluid Power
MOTOR VEHICLE PARTS & ACCESS: Rear Axel Housings
MOTOR VEHICLE PARTS & ACCESS: Thermostats
MOTOR VEHICLE PARTS & ACCESS: Tie Rods
MOTOR VEHICLE PARTS & ACCESS: Tops
MOTOR VEHICLE PARTS & ACCESS: Trailer Hitches
MOTOR VEHICLE PARTS & ACCESS: Transmission Housings Or Parts
MOTOR VEHICLE PARTS & ACCESS: Transmissions

MOTOR VEHICLE PARTS & ACCESS: Universal Joints
MOTOR VEHICLE PARTS & ACCESS: Water Pumps
MOTOR VEHICLE PARTS & ACCESS: Wheel rims
MOTOR VEHICLE PARTS & ACCESS: Wipers, Windshield
MOTOR VEHICLE PARTS & ACCESS: Wiring Harness Sets
MOTOR VEHICLE RADIOS WHOLESALERS
MOTOR VEHICLE SPLYS & PARTS WHOLESALERS: New
MOTOR VEHICLE SPLYS & PARTS WHOLESALERS: Used
MOTOR VEHICLE: Hardware
MOTOR VEHICLE: Radiators
MOTOR VEHICLE: Shock Absorbers
MOTOR VEHICLE: Steering Mechanisms
MOTOR VEHICLE: Wheels
MOTOR VEHICLES & CAR BODIES
MOTOR VEHICLES, WHOLESALE: Fire Trucks
MOTOR VEHICLES, WHOLESALE: Snowmobiles
MOTOR VEHICLES, WHOLESALE: Trailers for passenger vehicles
MOTOR VEHICLES, WHOLESALE: Trailers, Truck, New & Used
MOTOR VEHICLES, WHOLESALE: Truck bodies
MOTOR VEHICLES, WHOLESALE: Trucks, commercial
MOTORCYCLE & BICYCLE PARTS: Frames
MOTORCYCLE ACCESS
MOTORCYCLE DEALERS
MOTORCYCLE PARTS & ACCESS DEALERS
MOTORCYCLE REPAIR SHOPS
MOTORCYCLES & RELATED PARTS
MOTORS: Electric
MOTORS: Generators
MOTORS: Pneumatic
MOTORS: Starting, Automotive & Aircraft
MOUTHWASHES
MOWERS & ACCESSORIES
MUCILAGE
MUSEUMS
MUSIC BOXES
MUSIC BROADCASTING SVCS
MUSIC DISTRIBUTION APPARATUS
MUSIC RECORDING PRODUCER
MUSIC SCHOOLS
MUSICAL INSTRUMENT LESSONS
MUSICAL INSTRUMENTS & ACCESS: NEC
MUSICAL INSTRUMENTS & PARTS: String
MUSICAL INSTRUMENTS & SPLYS STORES
MUSICAL INSTRUMENTS & SPLYS STORES: String instruments
MUSICAL INSTRUMENTS/SPLYS STORE: Drums/Rltd Percussion Instr
MUSICAL INSTRUMENTS: Autophones/Organs W/Perfrtd Music Rolls
MUSICAL INSTRUMENTS: Fretted Instruments & Parts
MUSICAL INSTRUMENTS: Guitars & Parts, Electric & Acoustic
MUSICAL INSTRUMENTS: Organ Parts & Materials
MUSICAL INSTRUMENTS: Organs
MUSICAL INSTRUMENTS: Saxophones & Parts
MUSICAL INSTRUMENTS: Strings, Instrument
MUSICAL INSTRUMENTS: Violins & Parts

N

NAILS: Steel, Wire Or Cut
NAME PLATES: Engraved Or Etched
NAMEPLATES
NATURAL GAS COMPRESSING SVC, On-Site
NATURAL GAS DISTRIBUTION TO CONSUMERS
NATURAL GAS LIQUIDS PRODUCTION
NATURAL GAS LIQUIDS PRODUCTION
NATURAL GAS PRODUCTION
NATURAL GAS STORAGE SVCS
NATURAL GAS TRANSMISSION & DISTRIBUTION
NATURAL GASOLINE PRODUCTION
NAUTICAL REPAIR SVCS
NAVIGATIONAL SYSTEMS & INSTRUMENTS
NEIGHBORHOOD DEVELOPMENT GROUP
NETTING: Cargo
NEW & USED CAR DEALERS
NEWS DEALERS & NEWSSTANDS
NEWSPAPERS & PERIODICALS NEWS REPORTING SVCS
NEWSPAPERS, WHOLESALE
NICKEL ALLOY
NONCURRENT CARRYING WIRING DEVICES
NONDAIRY BASED FROZEN DESSERTS
NONFERROUS: Rolling & Drawing, NEC
NONMETALLIC MINERALS: Support Activities, Exc Fuels

PRODUCT INDEX

NOTEBOOKS, MADE FROM PURCHASED MATERIALS
NOTIONS: Fasteners, Glove
NOVELTIES
NOVELTIES: Plastic
NOZZLES & SPRINKLERS Lawn Hose
NOZZLES: Spray, Aerosol, Paint Or Insecticide
NURSERIES & LAWN & GARDEN SPLY STORE, RET: Lawn/Garden Splys
NURSERIES & LAWN & GARDEN SPLY STORES, RETAIL
NURSERIES & LAWN & GARDEN SPLY STORES, RETAIL: Fertilizer
NURSERIES & LAWN/GARDEN SPLY STORES, RET: Lawnmowers/Tractors
NURSERIES & LAWN/GARDEN SPLY STORES, RET: Garden Splys/Tools
NURSERIES/LAWN/GRDN SPLY STORE, RET: Nursery Stck, Seed/Bulb
NURSERY & GARDEN CENTERS
NURSERY STOCK, WHOLESALE
NURSING CARE FACILITIES: Skilled
NUTRITION SVCS
NUTS: Metal

O

OFFICE EQPT WHOLESALERS
OFFICE EQPT, WHOLESALE: Photocopy Machines
OFFICE MACHINES, NEC
OFFICE SPLY & STATIONERY STORES
OFFICE SPLY & STATIONERY STORES: Office Forms & Splys
OFFICE SPLYS, NEC, WHOLESALE
OFFICES & CLINICS OF DOCTORS OF MEDICINE: Dermatologist
OFFICES & CLINICS OF DOCTORS OF MEDICINE: Surgeon, Plastic
OFFICES & CLINICS OF DRS OF MED: Cardiologist & Vascular
OFFICES & CLINICS OF DRS OF MED: Health Maint Org Or HMO
OFFICES & CLINICS OF DRS OF MEDICINE: Physician, Orthopedic
OFFICES & CLINICS OF HEALTH PRACTITIONERS: Nutrition
OFFICES & CLINICS OF HEALTH PRACTITIONERS: Occu Therapist
OFFICES & CLINICS OF HEALTH PRACTITIONERS: Physical Therapy
OIL & GAS FIELD MACHINERY
OIL FIELD MACHINERY & EQPT
OIL FIELD SVCS, NEC
OILS & ESSENTIAL OILS
OILS & GREASES: Blended & Compounded
OILS & GREASES: Lubricating
OILS: Cutting
OILS: Essential
OILS: Lubricating
OILS: Lubricating
OILS: Magnetic Inspection Or Powder
OPERATOR: Apartment Buildings
OPERATOR: Nonresidential Buildings
OPHTHALMIC GOODS
OPHTHALMIC GOODS WHOLESALERS
OPHTHALMIC GOODS, NEC, WHOLESALE: Frames
OPHTHALMIC GOODS: Lenses, Ophthalmic
OPHTHALMIC GOODS: Protectors, Eye
OPHTHALMIC GOODS: Spectacles
OPTICAL GOODS STORES: Eyeglasses, Prescription
OPTICAL GOODS STORES: Opticians
OPTICAL INSTRUMENTS & APPARATUS
OPTICAL INSTRUMENTS & LENSES
OPTICAL SCANNING SVCS
OPTOMETRIC EQPT & SPLYS WHOLESALERS
OPTOMETRISTS' OFFICES
ORDNANCE
ORGAN TUNING & REPAIR SVCS
ORGANIZATIONS & UNIONS: Labor
ORGANIZATIONS: Medical Research
ORGANIZATIONS: Religious
ORGANIZATIONS: Research Institute
ORGANIZATIONS: Scientific Research Agency
ORGANIZERS, CLOSET & DRAWER Plastic
ORIENTED STRANDBOARD
OUTBOARD MOTOR DEALERS
OUTLETS: Electric, Convenience
OVENS: Infrared
OVENS: Paint Baking & Drying
OVENS: Smelting

P

PACKAGING & LABELING SVCS
PACKAGING MATERIALS, INDL: Wholesalers
PACKAGING MATERIALS, WHOLESALE
PACKAGING MATERIALS: Paper
PACKAGING MATERIALS: Paper, Coated Or Laminated
PACKAGING MATERIALS: Paper, Thermoplastic Coated
PACKAGING MATERIALS: Plastic Film, Coated Or Laminated
PACKAGING MATERIALS: Polystyrene Foam
PACKAGING: Blister Or Bubble Formed, Plastic
PACKING & CRATING SVC
PACKING & CRATING SVCS: Containerized Goods For Shipping
PACKING MATERIALS: Mechanical
PACKING SVCS: Shipping
PACKING: Metallic
PADDING: Foamed Plastics
PADS & PADDING: Insulator, Cordage
PADS: Athletic, Protective
PAILS: Shipping, Metal
PAINT & PAINTING SPLYS STORE
PAINT & PAINTING SPLYS STORE: Brushes, Rollers, Sprayers
PAINT STORE
PAINTING SVC: Metal Prdts
PAINTS & ADDITIVES
PAINTS & ALLIED PRODUCTS
PAINTS, VARNISHES & SPLYS WHOLESALERS
PAINTS, VARNISHES & SPLYS, WHOLESALE: Colors & Pigments
PAINTS, VARNISHES & SPLYS, WHOLESALE: Paints
PAINTS: Oil Or Alkyd Vehicle Or Water Thinned
PAINTS: Waterproof
PALLET REPAIR SVCS
PALLETIZERS & DEPALLETIZERS
PALLETS
PALLETS & SKIDS: Wood
PALLETS: Metal
PALLETS: Plastic
PALLETS: Wood & Metal Combination
PALLETS: Wooden
PANEL & DISTRIBUTION BOARDS & OTHER RELATED APPARATUS
PANEL & DISTRIBUTION BOARDS: Electric
PANELS, FLAT: Plastic
PANELS: Building, Metal
PANELS: Building, Plastic, NEC
PANELS: Building, Wood
PANELS: Switchboard, Slate
PANELS: Wood
PAPER & BOARD: Die-cut
PAPER CLIPS: Metal
PAPER CONVERTING
PAPER MANUFACTURERS: Exc Newsprint
PAPER PRDTS
PAPER PRDTS: Book Covers
PAPER PRDTS: Infant & Baby Prdts
PAPER PRDTS: Sanitary
PAPER PRDTS: Sanitary Tissue Paper
PAPER PRDTS: Toweling Tissue
PAPER: Adhesive
PAPER: Book
PAPER: Building, Insulating & Packaging
PAPER: Business Form
PAPER: Cardboard
PAPER: Coated & Laminated, NEC
PAPER: Newsprint
PAPER: Packaging
PAPER: Printer
PAPER: Waxed, Made From Purchased Materials
PAPER: Wrapping & Packaging
PAPERBOARD
PAPERBOARD CONVERTING
PAPERBOARD PRDTS: Coated & Treated Board
PAPERBOARD PRDTS: Food Board, Special
PAPERBOARD PRDTS: Packaging Board
PAPERBOARD: Boxboard
PAPERBOARD: Chipboard
PAPERBOARD: Coated
PARTICLEBOARD: Laminated, Plastic
PARTITIONS & FIXTURES: Except Wood
PARTITIONS: Solid Fiber, Made From Purchased Materials
PARTITIONS: Wood & Fixtures
PARTS: Metal
PARTY & SPECIAL EVENT PLANNING SVCS
PATTERNS: Indl
PAVING MATERIALS: Prefabricated, Concrete
PAWN SHOPS
PAYROLL SVCS
PEARLS, WHOLESALE
PEAT GRINDING SVCS
PEAT MINING SVCS
PENS & PENCILS: Mechanical, NEC
PERFORMANCE RIGHTS, PUBLISHING & LICENSING
PERFUMES
PERISCOPES
PERLITE: Processed
PERSONAL CREDIT INSTITUTION: Indl Loan Bank, Non Deposit
PERSONAL CREDIT INSTITUTIONS: Financing, Autos, Furniture
PESTICIDES
PESTICIDES WHOLESALERS
PET & PET SPLYS STORES
PET ACCESS: Collars, Leashes, Etc, Exc Leather
PET COLLARS, LEASHES, MUZZLES & HARNESSES: Leather
PET SPLYS
PETROLEUM & PETROLEUM PRDTS, WHOLESALE Fuel Oil
PETROLEUM BULK STATIONS & TERMINALS
PETROLEUM PRDTS WHOLESALERS
PHARMACEUTICAL PREPARATIONS: Adrenal
PHARMACEUTICAL PREPARATIONS: Druggists' Preparations
PHARMACEUTICAL PREPARATIONS: Emulsions
PHARMACEUTICAL PREPARATIONS: Medicines, Capsule Or Ampule
PHARMACEUTICAL PREPARATIONS: Powders
PHARMACEUTICAL PREPARATIONS: Proprietary Drug PRDTS
PHARMACEUTICAL PREPARATIONS: Solutions
PHARMACEUTICAL PREPARATIONS: Tablets
PHARMACEUTICALS
PHARMACEUTICALS: Medicinal & Botanical Prdts
PHARMACIES & DRUG STORES
PHOSPHORIC ACID ESTERS
PHOTO RECONNAISSANCE SYSTEMS
PHOTOCOPY MACHINE REPAIR SVCS
PHOTOCOPYING & DUPLICATING SVCS
PHOTOENGRAVING SVC
PHOTOGRAMMATIC MAPPING SVCS
PHOTOGRAPHIC EQPT & SPLY: Sound Recordg/Reprod Eqpt, Motion
PHOTOGRAPHIC EQPT & SPLYS
PHOTOGRAPHIC EQPT & SPLYS WHOLESALERS
PHOTOGRAPHIC EQPT & SPLYS: Cameras, Aerial
PHOTOGRAPHIC EQPT & SPLYS: Densitometers
PHOTOGRAPHIC EQPT & SPLYS: Printing Eqpt
PHOTOGRAPHIC EQPT & SPLYS: Printing Frames
PHOTOGRAPHIC EQPT & SPLYS: Sensitometers
PHOTOGRAPHIC EQPT & SPLYS: Toners, Prprd, Not Chem Plnts
PHOTOGRAPHIC EQPT & SPLYS: Trays, Printing & Processing
PHOTOGRAPHY SVCS: Commercial
PHOTOGRAPHY SVCS: Portrait Studios
PHOTOGRAPHY SVCS: School
PHOTOGRAPHY SVCS: Still Or Video
PHOTOGRAPHY: Aerial
PHOTOTYPESETTING SVC
PHOTOVOLTAIC Solid State
PHYSICAL FITNESS CENTERS
PHYSICIANS' OFFICES & CLINICS: Medical doctors
PICTURE FRAMES: Wood
PIECE GOODS & NOTIONS WHOLESALERS
PIECE GOODS, NOTIONS & DRY GOODS, WHOL: Textile Converters
PIECE GOODS, NOTIONS & OTHER DRY GOODS, WHOL: Flags/Banners
PIECE GOODS, NOTIONS/DRY GOODS, WHOL: Drapery Mtrl, Woven
PIECE GOODS, NOTIONS/DRY GOODS, WHOL: Silk Piece, Woven
PIGMENTS, INORGANIC: Bone Black
PILLOW FILLING MTRLS: Curled Hair, Cotton Waste, Moss
PILOT SVCS: Aviation

PRODUCT INDEX

PINS
PINS: Cotter
PINS: Dowel
PIPE & FITTING: Fabrication
PIPE & FITTINGS: Cast Iron
PIPE & FITTINGS: Pressure, Cast Iron
PIPE & TUBES: Copper & Copper Alloy
PIPE & TUBES: Seamless
PIPE FITTINGS: Plastic
PIPE JOINT COMPOUNDS
PIPE SECTIONS, FABRICATED FROM PURCHASED PIPE
PIPE, SEWER: Concrete
PIPE: Brass & Bronze
PIPE: Concrete
PIPE: Copper
PIPE: Plastic
PIPE: Sheet Metal
PIPELINE TERMINAL FACILITIES: Independent
PIPES & TUBES
PIPES & TUBES: Steel
PIPES & TUBES: Welded
PIPES: Steel & Iron
PIPES: Tobacco
PISTONS & PISTON RINGS
PLANING MILL, NEC
PLANING MILLS: Millwork
PLANTERS: Plastic
PLASTIC COLORING & FINISHING
PLASTIC PRDTS
PLASTIC WOOD
PLASTICS FILM & SHEET
PLASTICS FILM & SHEET: Polyethylene
PLASTICS FILM & SHEET: Vinyl
PLASTICS FINISHED PRDTS: Laminated
PLASTICS FOAM, WHOLESALE
PLASTICS MATERIAL & RESINS
PLASTICS MATERIALS, BASIC FORMS & SHAPES WHOLESALERS
PLASTICS PROCESSING
PLASTICS SHEET: Packing Materials
PLASTICS: Blow Molded
PLASTICS: Cast
PLASTICS: Extruded
PLASTICS: Finished Injection Molded
PLASTICS: Injection Molded
PLASTICS: Molded
PLASTICS: Polystyrene Foam
PLASTICS: Thermoformed
PLATE WORK: For Nuclear Industry
PLATE WORK: Metalworking Trade
PLATEMAKING SVC: Color Separations, For The Printing Trade
PLATEMAKING SVC: Gravure
PLATEMAKING SVC: Gravure, Plates Or Cylinders
PLATEMAKING SVC: Letterpress
PLATES
PLATES: Paper, Made From Purchased Materials
PLATES: Plastic Exc Polystyrene Foam
PLATES: Sheet & Strip, Exc Coated Prdts
PLATES: Steel
PLATES: Truss, Metal
PLATING & FINISHING SVC: Decorative, Formed Prdts
PLATING & POLISHING SVC
PLATING COMPOUNDS
PLATING SVC: Chromium, Metals Or Formed Prdts
PLATING SVC: Electro
PLATING SVC: NEC
PLAYGROUND EQPT
PLEATING & STITCHING SVC
PLUGS: Electric
PLUMBING & HEATING EQPT & SPLY, WHOL: Htg Eqpt/Panels, Solar
PLUMBING & HEATING EQPT & SPLY, WHOLESALE: Hydronic Htg Eqpt
PLUMBING & HEATING EQPT & SPLYS WHOLESALERS
PLUMBING & HEATING EQPT & SPLYS, WHOL: Plumbing Fitting/Sply
PLUMBING & HEATING EQPT & SPLYS, WHOL: Water Purif Eqpt
PLUMBING & HEATING EQPT & SPLYS, WHOLESALE: Brass/Fittings
PLUMBING & HEATING EQPT & SPLYS, WHOLESALE: Gas Burners
PLUMBING & HEATING EQPT & SPLYS, WHOLESALE: Sanitary Ware
PLUMBING & HEATING EQPT/SPLYS, WHOL: Boilers, Hot Water Htg
PLUMBING FIXTURES
PLUMBING FIXTURES: Brass, Incl Drain Cocks, Faucets/Spigots
PLUMBING FIXTURES: Plastic
POINT OF SALE DEVICES
POLISHING SVC: Metals Or Formed Prdts
POLYOXYMETHYLENE RESINS
POLYPROPYLENE RESINS
POLYSTYRENE RESINS
POLYURETHANE RESINS
POLYVINYL CHLORIDE RESINS
PONTOONS: Rubber
POPCORN & SUPPLIES WHOLESALERS
POSTAL EQPT: Locker Boxes, Exc Wood
POSTERS
POSTERS, WHOLESALE
POTPOURRI
POTTERY
POTTING SOILS
POULTRY & SMALL GAME SLAUGHTERING & PROCESSING
POWDER PUFFS & MITTS
POWDER: Metal
POWDER: Silver
POWER GENERATORS
POWER SPLY CONVERTERS: Static, Electronic Applications
POWER SUPPLIES: All Types, Static
POWER SUPPLIES: Transformer, Electronic Type
POWER TOOLS, HAND: Chain Saws, Portable
POWER TOOLS, HAND: Drills & Drilling Tools
POWER TOOLS, HAND: Drills, Port, Elec/Pneumatic, Exc Rock
POWER TOOLS, HAND: Guns, Pneumatic, Chip Removal
POWER TOOLS, HAND: Hammers, Portable, Elec/Pneumatic, Chip
POWER TRANSMISSION EQPT WHOLESALERS
POWER TRANSMISSION EQPT: Aircraft
POWER TRANSMISSION EQPT: Mechanical
PRECAST TERRAZZO OR CONCRETE PRDTS
PRECIOUS STONE MINING SVCS, NEC
PRERECORDED TAPE, CD & RECORD STORE: Record, Disc/Tape
PRERECORDED TAPE, COMPACT DISC & RECORD STORES: Records
PRESSES
PRIMARY METAL PRODUCTS
PRIMARY ROLLING MILL EQPT
PRINT CARTRIDGES: Laser & Other Computer Printers
PRINTED CIRCUIT BOARDS
PRINTERS & PLOTTERS
PRINTERS' SVCS: Folding, Collating, Etc
PRINTERS: Computer
PRINTERS: Magnetic Ink, Bar Code
PRINTING & BINDING: Books
PRINTING & BINDING: Pamphlets
PRINTING & BINDING: Textbooks
PRINTING & EMBOSSING: Plastic Fabric Articles
PRINTING & ENGRAVING: Invitation & Stationery
PRINTING & STAMPING: Fabric Articles
PRINTING & WRITING PAPER WHOLESALERS
PRINTING INKS WHOLESALERS
PRINTING MACHINERY
PRINTING MACHINERY, EQPT & SPLYS: Wholesalers
PRINTING, COMMERCIAL Newspapers, NEC
PRINTING, COMMERCIAL: Business Forms, NEC
PRINTING, COMMERCIAL: Catalogs, NEC
PRINTING, COMMERCIAL: Coupons, NEC
PRINTING, COMMERCIAL: Envelopes, NEC
PRINTING, COMMERCIAL: Imprinting
PRINTING, COMMERCIAL: Labels & Seals, NEC
PRINTING, COMMERCIAL: Letterpress & Screen
PRINTING, COMMERCIAL: Literature, Advertising, NEC
PRINTING, COMMERCIAL: Magazines, NEC
PRINTING, COMMERCIAL: Menus, NEC
PRINTING, COMMERCIAL: Periodicals, NEC
PRINTING, COMMERCIAL: Post Cards, Picture, NEC
PRINTING, COMMERCIAL: Promotional
PRINTING, COMMERCIAL: Publications
PRINTING, COMMERCIAL: Ready
PRINTING, COMMERCIAL: Screen
PRINTING, COMMERCIAL: Tags, NEC
PRINTING, COMMERCIAL: Tickets, NEC
PRINTING, LITHOGRAPHIC: Advertising Posters
PRINTING, LITHOGRAPHIC: Catalogs
PRINTING, LITHOGRAPHIC: Color
PRINTING, LITHOGRAPHIC: Decals
PRINTING, LITHOGRAPHIC: Forms & Cards, Business
PRINTING, LITHOGRAPHIC: Forms, Business
PRINTING, LITHOGRAPHIC: Newspapers
PRINTING, LITHOGRAPHIC: Offset & photolithographic printing
PRINTING, LITHOGRAPHIC: On Metal
PRINTING, LITHOGRAPHIC: Periodicals
PRINTING, LITHOGRAPHIC: Posters
PRINTING, LITHOGRAPHIC: Posters & Decals
PRINTING, LITHOGRAPHIC: Promotional
PRINTING, LITHOGRAPHIC: Tags
PRINTING, LITHOGRAPHIC: Wrappers & Seals
PRINTING: Books
PRINTING: Books
PRINTING: Broadwoven Fabrics. Cotton
PRINTING: Commercial, NEC
PRINTING: Flexographic
PRINTING: Gravure, Forms, Business
PRINTING: Gravure, Job
PRINTING: Gravure, Labels
PRINTING: Gravure, Rotogravure
PRINTING: Gravure, Stationery & Invitation
PRINTING: Gravure, Wrapper & Seal
PRINTING: Laser
PRINTING: Letterpress
PRINTING: Lithographic
PRINTING: Offset
PRINTING: Photo-Offset
PRINTING: Photolithographic
PRINTING: Rotary Photogravure
PRINTING: Screen, Broadwoven Fabrics, Cotton
PRINTING: Screen, Fabric
PRINTING: Screen, Manmade Fiber & Silk, Broadwoven Fabric
PRINTING: Thermography
PRIVATE INVESTIGATOR SVCS
PRODUCT ENDORSEMENT SVCS
PROFESSIONAL EQPT & SPLYS, WHOLESALE: Analytical Instruments
PROFESSIONAL EQPT & SPLYS, WHOLESALE: Optical Goods
PROFESSIONAL EQPT & SPLYS, WHOLESALE: Scientific & Engineerg
PROFESSIONAL INSTRUMENT REPAIR SVCS
PROFILE SHAPES: Unsupported Plastics
PROMOTERS OF SHOWS & EXHIBITIONS
PROMOTION SVCS
PROPELLERS: Ship, Cast Brass
PUBLIC FINANCE, TAX & MONETARY POLICY OFFICES, GOVT: State
PUBLIC FINANCE, TAXATION & MONETARY POLICY OFFICES
PUBLIC LIBRARY
PUBLIC RELATIONS & PUBLICITY SVCS
PUBLISHERS: Book
PUBLISHERS: Book Clubs, No Printing
PUBLISHERS: Books, No Printing
PUBLISHERS: Catalogs
PUBLISHERS: Comic Books, No Printing
PUBLISHERS: Directories, NEC
PUBLISHERS: Directories, Telephone
PUBLISHERS: Guides
PUBLISHERS: Magazines, No Printing
PUBLISHERS: Miscellaneous
PUBLISHERS: Music Book & Sheet Music
PUBLISHERS: Newsletter
PUBLISHERS: Newspaper
PUBLISHERS: Newspapers, No Printing
PUBLISHERS: Periodical, With Printing
PUBLISHERS: Periodicals, Magazines
PUBLISHERS: Periodicals, No Printing
PUBLISHERS: Posters
PUBLISHERS: Shopping News
PUBLISHERS: Technical Manuals
PUBLISHERS: Technical Manuals & Papers
PUBLISHERS: Telephone & Other Directory
PUBLISHERS: Textbooks, No Printing
PUBLISHERS: Trade journals, No Printing
PUBLISHING & BROADCASTING: Internet Only
PUBLISHING & PRINTING: Art Copy
PUBLISHING & PRINTING: Book Music
PUBLISHING & PRINTING: Books

PRODUCT INDEX

PUBLISHING & PRINTING: Comic Books
PUBLISHING & PRINTING: Directories, NEC
PUBLISHING & PRINTING: Directories, Telephone
PUBLISHING & PRINTING: Guides
PUBLISHING & PRINTING: Magazines: publishing & printing
PUBLISHING & PRINTING: Music, Book
PUBLISHING & PRINTING: Newsletters, Business Svc
PUBLISHING & PRINTING: Newspapers
PUBLISHING & PRINTING: Pamphlets
PUBLISHING & PRINTING: Posters
PUBLISHING & PRINTING: Shopping News
PUBLISHING & PRINTING: Textbooks
PUBLISHING & PRINTING: Trade Journals
PUBLISHING & PRINTING: Yearbooks
PULLEYS: Metal
PULLEYS: Power Transmission
PULP MILLS
PULP MILLS: Chemical & Semichemical Processing
PULP MILLS: Mechanical & Recycling Processing
PULVERIZED EARTH
PUMICE: Abrasives
PUMPS
PUMPS & PARTS: Indl
PUMPS & PUMPING EQPT REPAIR SVCS
PUMPS & PUMPING EQPT WHOLESALERS
PUMPS, HEAT: Electric
PUMPS: Domestic, Water Or Sump
PUMPS: Fluid Power
PUMPS: Gasoline, Measuring Or Dispensing
PUMPS: Hydraulic Power Transfer
PUMPS: Measuring & Dispensing
PUMPS: Oil Well & Field
PUMPS: Vacuum, Exc Laboratory
PUNCHES: Forming & Stamping
PUPPETS & MARIONETTES
PURIFICATION & DUST COLLECTION EQPT
PURSES: Women's

R

RACE CAR OWNERS
RACE TRACK OPERATION
RACETRACKS
RACEWAYS
RACKS: Display
RACKS: Garment, Exc Wood
RACKS: Pallet, Exc Wood
RACKS: Trash, Metal Rack
RADAR SYSTEMS & EQPT
RADIO & TELEVISION COMMUNICATIONS EQUIPMENT
RADIO & TELEVISION REPAIR
RADIO BROADCASTING & COMMUNICATIONS EQPT
RADIO BROADCASTING STATIONS
RADIO COMMUNICATIONS: Carrier Eqpt
RADIO PRODUCERS
RADIO RECEIVER NETWORKS
RADIO REPAIR & INSTALLATION SVCS
RADIO, TELEVISION & CONSUMER ELECTRONICS STORES: Eqpt, NEC
RADIO, TV & CONSUMER ELEC STORES: High Fidelity Stereo Eqpt
RADIO, TV & CONSUMER ELEC STORES: Radios, Receiver Type
RAIL & STRUCTURAL SHAPES: Aluminum rail & structural shapes
RAILINGS: Prefabricated, Metal
RAILROAD CAR RENTING & LEASING SVCS
RAILROAD CAR REPAIR SVCS
RAILROAD CARGO LOADING & UNLOADING SVCS
RAILROAD CROSSINGS: Steel Or Iron
RAILROAD EQPT
RAILROAD EQPT & SPLYS WHOLESALERS
RAILROAD EQPT: Brakes, Air & Vacuum
RAILROAD EQPT: Cars & Eqpt, Dining
RAILROAD EQPT: Cars & Eqpt, Train, Freight Or Passenger
RAILROAD EQPT: Cars, Rebuilt
RAILROAD EQPT: Street Cars & Eqpt
RAILROAD MAINTENANCE & REPAIR SVCS
RAILROAD RELATED EQPT
RAILROADS: Long Haul
RAILS: Steel Or Iron
RAMPS: Prefabricated Metal
RAZORS, RAZOR BLADES
REAL ESTATE AGENCIES & BROKERS
REAL ESTATE AGENCIES: Leasing & Rentals
REAL ESTATE AGENCIES: Residential

REAL ESTATE AGENTS & MANAGERS
REAL ESTATE INVESTMENT TRUSTS
REAL ESTATE LISTING SVCS
REAL ESTATE OPERATORS, EXC DEVELOPERS: Commercial/Indl Bldg
RECEIVERS: Radio Communications
RECLAIMED RUBBER: Reworked By Manufacturing Process
RECORD BLANKS: Phonographic
RECORDING & PLAYBACK HEADS: Magnetic
RECORDS & TAPES: Prerecorded
RECREATIONAL & SPORTING CAMPS
RECREATIONAL SPORTING EQPT REPAIR SVCS
RECREATIONAL VEHICLE DEALERS
RECREATIONAL VEHICLE REPAIRS
RECREATIONAL VEHICLE: Wholesalers
RECTIFIERS: Mercury Arc, Electrical
RECYCLING: Paper
REELS: Fiber, Textile, Made From Purchased Materials
REFINERS & SMELTERS: Aluminum
REFINERS & SMELTERS: Copper
REFINERS & SMELTERS: Gold, Secondary
REFINERS & SMELTERS: Nonferrous Metal
REFINERS & SMELTERS: Zinc, Primary, Including Zinc Residue
REFINERS & SMELTERS: Zinc, Secondary
REFINING LUBRICATING OILS & GREASES, NEC
REFINING: Petroleum
REFLECTIVE ROAD MARKERS, WHOLESALE
REFRACTORIES: Castable, Clay
REFRACTORIES: Cement
REFRACTORIES: Clay
REFRACTORIES: Graphite, Carbon Or Ceramic Bond
REFRACTORIES: Nonclay
REFRACTORIES: Tile & Brick, Exc Plastic
REFRIGERATION & HEATING EQUIPMENT
REFRIGERATION EQPT & SPLYS WHOLESALERS
REFRIGERATION EQPT & SPLYS, WHOLESALE: Beverage Coolers
REFRIGERATION EQPT & SPLYS, WHOLESALE: Ice Cream Cabinets
REFRIGERATION EQPT: Complete
REFRIGERATION REPAIR SVCS
REFRIGERATION SVC & REPAIR
REFUSE SYSTEMS
REGISTERS: Air, Metal
REGULATORS: Power
REGULATORS: Transmission & Distribution Voltage
REHABILITATION CENTER, OUTPATIENT TREATMENT
RELAYS & SWITCHES: Indl, Electric
RELAYS: Control Circuit, Ind
RELAYS: Electronic Usage
RELIGIOUS SPLYS WHOLESALERS
REMOVERS & CLEANERS
REMOVERS: Paint
RENTAL SVCS: Audio-Visual Eqpt & Sply
RENTAL SVCS: Bicycle
RENTAL SVCS: Business Machine & Electronic Eqpt
RENTAL SVCS: Invalid Splys
RENTAL SVCS: Oil Eqpt
RENTAL SVCS: Pleasure Boat
RENTAL SVCS: Pop-Up Camper
RENTAL SVCS: Propane Eqpt
RENTAL SVCS: Sign
RENTAL SVCS: Sound & Lighting Eqpt
RENTAL SVCS: Tent & Tarpaulin
RENTAL SVCS: Trailer
RENTAL SVCS: Tuxedo
RENTAL: Portable Toilet
REPAIR SERVICES, NEC
REPEATERS: Passive
RESEARCH, DEV & TESTING SVCS, COMM: Chem Lab, Exc Testing
RESEARCH, DEVELOPMENT & TEST SVCS, COMM: Research, Exc Lab
RESEARCH, DEVELOPMENT & TESTING SVCS, COMM: Natural Resource
RESEARCH, DEVELOPMENT & TESTING SVCS, COMM: Research Lab
RESEARCH, DEVELOPMENT & TESTING SVCS, COMMERCIAL: Business
RESEARCH, DEVELOPMENT & TESTING SVCS, COMMERCIAL: Food
RESEARCH, DEVELOPMENT & TESTING SVCS, COMMERCIAL: Medical

RESEARCH, DEVELOPMENT & TESTING SVCS, COMMERCIAL: Physical
RESEARCH, DEVELOPMENT SVCS, COMMERCIAL: Indl Lab
RESEARCH, DVLPT & TEST SVCS, COMM: Mkt Analysis or Research
RESEARCH, DVLPT & TESTING SVCS, COMM: Survey, Mktg
RESIDENTIAL REMODELERS
RESINS: Custom Compound Purchased
RESISTORS
RESPIRATORS
RESTAURANT EQPT REPAIR SVCS
RESTAURANT EQPT: Food Wagons
RESTAURANT EQPT: Sheet Metal
RESTAURANTS: Delicatessen
RESTAURANTS: Fast Food
RESTAURANTS:Full Svc, American
RESTAURANTS:Full Svc, Family
RESTAURANTS:Full Svc, Family, Chain
RESTAURANTS:Full Svc, Family, Independent
RESTAURANTS:Full Svc, Mexican
RESTAURANTS:Full Svc, Steak
RESTAURANTS:Limited Svc, Coffee Shop
RESTAURANTS:Limited Svc, Drive-In
RESTAURANTS:Limited Svc, Fast-Food, Independent
RESTAURANTS:Limited Svc, Ice Cream Stands Or Dairy Bars
RESTAURANTS:Limited Svc, Pizza
RESTAURANTS:Limited Svc, Pizzeria, Chain
RESTAURANTS:Limited Svc, Pizzeria, Independent
RESTAURANTS:Limited Svc, Sandwiches & Submarines Shop
RESTAURANTS:Limited Svc, Snack Shop
RESTAURANTS:Ltd Svc, Ice Cream, Soft Drink/Fountain Stands
RETAIL BAKERY: Bagels
RETAIL BAKERY: Bread
RETAIL BAKERY: Cakes
RETAIL BAKERY: Cookies
RETAIL BAKERY: Doughnuts
RETAIL BAKERY: Pastries
RETAIL BAKERY: Pretzels
RETAIL FIREPLACE STORES
RETAIL LUMBER YARDS
RETAIL STORES, NEC
RETAIL STORES: Alcoholic Beverage Making Eqpt & Splys
RETAIL STORES: Aquarium Splys
RETAIL STORES: Art & Architectural Splys
RETAIL STORES: Artificial Limbs
RETAIL STORES: Audio-Visual Eqpt & Splys
RETAIL STORES: Awnings
RETAIL STORES: Banners
RETAIL STORES: Batteries, Non-Automotive
RETAIL STORES: Business Machines & Eqpt
RETAIL STORES: Canvas Prdts
RETAIL STORES: Christmas Lights & Decorations
RETAIL STORES: Cleaning Eqpt & Splys
RETAIL STORES: Convalescent Eqpt & Splys
RETAIL STORES: Cosmetics
RETAIL STORES: Electronic Parts & Eqpt
RETAIL STORES: Farm Eqpt & Splys
RETAIL STORES: Farm Machinery, NEC
RETAIL STORES: Fire Extinguishers
RETAIL STORES: Flags
RETAIL STORES: Foam & Foam Prdts
RETAIL STORES: Hair Care Prdts
RETAIL STORES: Hearing Aids
RETAIL STORES: Hospital Eqpt & Splys
RETAIL STORES: Maps & Charts
RETAIL STORES: Medical Apparatus & Splys
RETAIL STORES: Mobile Telephones & Eqpt
RETAIL STORES: Monuments, Finished To Custom Order
RETAIL STORES: Motors, Electric
RETAIL STORES: Orthopedic & Prosthesis Applications
RETAIL STORES: Perfumes & Colognes
RETAIL STORES: Pet Splys
RETAIL STORES: Picture Frames, Ready Made
RETAIL STORES: Posters
RETAIL STORES: Religious Goods
RETAIL STORES: Rock & Stone Specimens
RETAIL STORES: Rubber Stamps
RETAIL STORES: Safety Splys & Eqpt
RETAIL STORES: Sales Barns
RETAIL STORES: Sauna Eqpt & Splys

PRODUCT INDEX

RETAIL STORES: Swimming Pools, Above Ground
RETAIL STORES: Technical Aids For The Handicapped
RETAIL STORES: Telephone Eqpt & Systems
RETAIL STORES: Water Purification Eqpt
RETAIL STORES: Welding Splys
RETORTS: Indl, Smelting, Etc
RETREADING MATERIALS: Tire
REUPHOLSTERY & FURNITURE REPAIR
REUPHOLSTERY SVCS
RHEOSTATS: Electronic
RIVETS: Metal
ROBOTS, SERVICES OR NOVELTY, WHOLESALE
ROBOTS: Assembly Line
ROBOTS: Indl Spraying, Painting, Etc
ROD & BAR Aluminum
RODS: Steel & Iron, Made In Steel Mills
RODS: Welding
ROLL FORMED SHAPES: Custom
ROLLING MACHINERY: Steel
ROLLING MILL MACHINERY
ROLLING MILL ROLLS: Cast Iron
ROLLS & BLANKETS, PRINTERS': Rubber Or Rubberized Fabric
ROLLS & ROLL COVERINGS: Rubber
ROOF DECKS
ROOFING GRANULES
ROOFING MATERIALS: Asphalt
ROOFING MATERIALS: Sheet Metal
ROOFING MEMBRANE: Rubber
ROOMING & BOARDING HOUSES: Furnished Room Rental
ROTORS: Motor
RUBBER
RUBBER PRDTS: Automotive, Mechanical
RUBBER PRDTS: Mechanical
RUBBER PRDTS: Reclaimed
RUBBER PRDTS: Silicone
RUBBER PRDTS: Sponge
RUBBER STAMP, WHOLESALE
RUBBER, CRUDE, WHOLESALE
RUST PROOFING SVC: Hot Dipping, Metals & Formed Prdts
RUST REMOVERS
RUST RESISTING

S

SAFES & VAULTS: Metal
SAFETY EQPT & SPLYS WHOLESALERS
SAILBOAT BUILDING & REPAIR
SAILS
SALES PROMOTION SVCS
SALT
SAND & GRAVEL
SAND LIME PRDTS
SAND MINING
SAND: Hygrade
SANDBLASTING EQPT
SANDBLASTING SVC: Building Exterior
SANDSTONE: Crushed & Broken
SANITARY SVCS: Refuse Collection & Disposal Svcs
SANITARY SVCS: Sanitary Landfill, Operation Of
SANITARY SVCS: Waste Materials, Recycling
SANITARY WARE: Metal
SANITATION CHEMICALS & CLEANING AGENTS
SASHES: Door Or Window, Metal
SATCHELS
SATELLITE COMMUNICATIONS EQPT
SATELLITES: Communications
SAUNA ROOMS: Prefabricated
SAW BLADES
SAWING & PLANING MILLS
SAWING & PLANING MILLS: Custom
SAWS & SAWING EQPT
SAWS: Portable
SCAFFOLDS: Mobile Or Stationary, Metal
SCALE REPAIR SVCS
SCALES & BALANCES, EXC LABORATORY
SCALES: Indl
SCALES: Truck
SCHOOL SPLYS, EXC BOOKS: Wholesalers
SCHOOLS: Elementary & Secondary
SCHOOLS: Vocational, NEC
SCIENTIFIC EQPT REPAIR SVCS
SCIENTIFIC INSTRUMENTS WHOLESALERS
SCRAP & WASTE MATERIALS, WHOLESALE: Ferrous Metal
SCRAP & WASTE MATERIALS, WHOLESALE: Metal

SCRAP & WASTE MATERIALS, WHOLESALE: Nonferrous Metals Scrap
SCRAP & WASTE MATERIALS, WHOLESALE: Oil
SCRAP & WASTE MATERIALS, WHOLESALE: Paper
SCRAP & WASTE MATERIALS, WHOLESALE: Plastics Scrap
SCRAP STEEL CUTTING
SCREENS: Woven Wire
SCREW MACHINE PRDTS
SCREW MACHINES
SCREWS: Metal
SEALANTS
SEALING COMPOUNDS: Sealing, synthetic rubber or plastic
SEALS: Hermetic
SEALS: Oil, Rubber
SEARCH & NAVIGATION SYSTEMS
SEAT BELTS: Automobile & Aircraft
SEATING: Bleacher, Portable
SEATING: Chairs, Table & Arm
SEATING: Stadium
SEATING: Transportation
SECRETARIAL & COURT REPORTING
SECURITY & COMMODITY EXCHANGES: Commodity, Contract
SECURITY CONTROL EQPT & SYSTEMS
SECURITY DEVICES
SECURITY EQPT STORES
SECURITY GUARD SVCS
SECURITY PROTECTIVE DEVICES MAINTENANCE & MONITORING SVCS
SECURITY SYSTEMS SERVICES
SEMICONDUCTOR & RELATED DEVICES: Read-Only Memory Or ROM
SEMICONDUCTOR CIRCUIT NETWORKS
SEMICONDUCTORS & RELATED DEVICES
SENSORS: Infrared, Solid State
SENSORS: Radiation
SENSORS: Temperature For Motor Windings
SEPTIC TANK CLEANING SVCS
SEPTIC TANKS: Concrete
SEWAGE & WATER TREATMENT EQPT
SEWAGE FACILITIES
SEWAGE TREATMENT SYSTEMS & EQPT
SEWER CLEANING EQPT: Power
SEWING CONTRACTORS
SEWING MACHINE STORES
SEWING, NEEDLEWORK & PIECE GOODS STORES: Sewing & Needlework
SEXTANTS
SHADES: Window
SHAFTS: Flexible
SHAPES & PILINGS, STRUCTURAL: Steel
SHAPES: Extruded, Aluminum, NEC
SHEET METAL SPECIALTIES, EXC STAMPED
SHEETS & STRIPS: Aluminum
SHEETS: Fabric, From Purchased Materials
SHEETS: Hard Rubber
SHELLAC
SHELTERED WORKSHOPS
SHELVES & SHELVING: Wood
SHELVING, MADE FROM PURCHASED WIRE
SHELVING: Office & Store, Exc Wood
SHIMS: Metal
SHIP BUILDING & REPAIRING: Cargo Vessels
SHIP BUILDING & REPAIRING: Rigging, Marine
SHIP BUILDING & REPAIRING: Transport Vessels, Troop
SHIPBUILDING & REPAIR
SHIPPING AGENTS
SHOE & BOOT ACCESS
SHOE MATERIALS: Counters
SHOE MATERIALS: Quarters
SHOE MATERIALS: Rands
SHOE STORES
SHOE STORES: Athletic
SHOE STORES: Custom
SHOE STORES: Custom & Orthopedic
SHOE STORES: Men's
SHOE STORES: Orthopedic
SHOES & BOOTS WHOLESALERS
SHOES: Athletic, Exc Rubber Or Plastic
SHOES: Canvas, Rubber Soled
SHOES: Men's
SHOES: Orthopedic, Children's
SHOES: Orthopedic, Men's
SHOES: Orthopedic, Women's

SHOES: Plastic Or Rubber
SHOES: Plastic Or Rubber Soles With Fabric Uppers
SHOES: Women's
SHOPPING CENTERS & MALLS
SHOT PEENING SVC
SHOWCASES & DISPLAY FIXTURES: Office & Store
SHREDDERS: Indl & Commercial
SHUTTERS, DOOR & WINDOW: Metal
SHUTTERS, DOOR & WINDOW: Plastic
SIDING & STRUCTURAL MATERIALS: Wood
SIDING MATERIALS
SIDING: Plastic
SIDING: Sheet Metal
SIGN LETTERING & PAINTING SVCS
SIGN PAINTING & LETTERING SHOP
SIGNALING APPARATUS: Electric
SIGNALS: Traffic Control, Electric
SIGNALS: Transportation
SIGNS & ADVERTISING SPECIALTIES
SIGNS & ADVERTISING SPECIALTIES: Artwork, Advertising
SIGNS & ADVERTISING SPECIALTIES: Letters For Signs, Metal
SIGNS & ADVERTISING SPECIALTIES: Novelties
SIGNS & ADVERTISING SPECIALTIES: Signs
SIGNS & ADVERTSG SPECIALTIES: Displays/Cutouts Window/Lobby
SIGNS, EXC ELECTRIC, WHOLESALE
SIGNS: Electrical
SIGNS: Neon
SILICON: Pure
SILICONE RESINS
SILICONES
SILK SCREEN DESIGN SVCS
SILLS: Concrete
SILVER ORE MINING
SILVER ORES PROCESSING
SILVERWARE & PLATED WARE
SIMULATORS: Flight
SIRENS: Vehicle, Marine, Indl & Warning
SKIDS: Wood
SKILL TRAINING CENTER
SKYLIGHTS
SLABS: Steel
SLAG PRDTS
SLAG: Crushed Or Ground
SLATE PRDTS
SLAUGHTERING & MEAT PACKING
SLINGS: Lifting, Made From Purchased Wire
SLINGS: Rope
SLIP RINGS
SLIPPERS: House
SMOKE DETECTORS
SMOKERS' SPLYS, WHOLESALE
SNOW PLOWING SVCS
SNOW REMOVAL EQPT: Residential
SNOWMOBILE DEALERS
SNOWMOBILES
SOAPS & DETERGENTS
SOAPS & DETERGENTS: Scouring Compounds
SOAPS & DETERGENTS: Textile
SOCKETS: Electric
SOFT DRINKS WHOLESALERS
SOFTWARE PUBLISHERS: Application
SOFTWARE PUBLISHERS: Business & Professional
SOFTWARE PUBLISHERS: Computer Utilities
SOFTWARE PUBLISHERS: Education
SOFTWARE PUBLISHERS: NEC
SOFTWARE PUBLISHERS: Operating Systems
SOFTWARE PUBLISHERS: Publisher's
SOFTWARE TRAINING, COMPUTER
SOLAR CELLS
SOLAR HEATING EQPT
SOLDERING EQPT: Electrical, Exc Handheld
SOLDERING EQPT: Irons Or Coppers
SOLENOIDS
SOLID CONTAINING UNITS: Concrete
SOLVENTS: Organic
SONAR SYSTEMS & EQPT
SOUND EQPT: Electric
SOUVENIRS, WHOLESALE
SOYBEAN PRDTS
SPACE PROPULSION UNITS & PARTS
SPACE VEHICLE EQPT
SPAS
SPEAKER SYSTEMS

PRODUCT INDEX

SPECIAL EVENTS DECORATION SVCS
SPECIALTY FOOD STORES, NEC
SPECIALTY FOOD STORES: Coffee
SPECIALTY FOOD STORES: Dietetic Foods
SPECIALTY FOOD STORES: Health & Dietetic Food
SPECIALTY OUTPATIENT CLINICS, NEC
SPECIALTY SAWMILL PRDTS
SPEED CHANGERS
SPICE & HERB STORES
SPIKES: Nonferrous Metal Or Wire
SPINDLES: Textile
SPONGES, ANIMAL, WHOLESALE
SPONGES: Plastic
SPOOLS: Indl
SPORTING & ATHLETIC GOODS: Arrows, Archery
SPORTING & ATHLETIC GOODS: Balls, Baseball, Football, Etc
SPORTING & ATHLETIC GOODS: Boomerangs
SPORTING & ATHLETIC GOODS: Bowling Alleys & Access
SPORTING & ATHLETIC GOODS: Bowling Balls
SPORTING & ATHLETIC GOODS: Bows, Archery
SPORTING & ATHLETIC GOODS: Camping Eqpt & Splys
SPORTING & ATHLETIC GOODS: Crossbows
SPORTING & ATHLETIC GOODS: Exercising Cycles
SPORTING & ATHLETIC GOODS: Fishing Bait, Artificial
SPORTING & ATHLETIC GOODS: Fishing Eqpt
SPORTING & ATHLETIC GOODS: Fishing Tackle, General
SPORTING & ATHLETIC GOODS: Football Eqpt & Splys, NEC
SPORTING & ATHLETIC GOODS: Game Calls
SPORTING & ATHLETIC GOODS: Gymnasium Eqpt
SPORTING & ATHLETIC GOODS: Hockey Eqpt & Splys, NEC
SPORTING & ATHLETIC GOODS: Hunting Eqpt
SPORTING & ATHLETIC GOODS: Masks, Hockey, Baseball, Etc
SPORTING & ATHLETIC GOODS: Protective Sporting Eqpt
SPORTING & ATHLETIC GOODS: Shafts, Golf Club
SPORTING & ATHLETIC GOODS: Shooting Eqpt & Splys, General
SPORTING & ATHLETIC GOODS: Shuffleboards & Shuffleboard Eqpt
SPORTING & ATHLETIC GOODS: Skateboards
SPORTING & ATHLETIC GOODS: Snow Skis
SPORTING & ATHLETIC GOODS: Strings, Tennis Racket
SPORTING & ATHLETIC GOODS: Targets, Archery & Rifle Shooting
SPORTING & ATHLETIC GOODS: Trampolines & Eqpt
SPORTING & ATHLETIC GOODS: Water Sports Eqpt
SPORTING & ATHLETIC GOODS: Winter Sports
SPORTING & RECREATIONAL GOODS & SPLYS WHOLESALERS
SPORTING & RECREATIONAL GOODS, WHOL: Sharpeners, Sporting
SPORTING & RECREATIONAL GOODS, WHOLESALE: Athletic Goods
SPORTING & RECREATIONAL GOODS, WHOLESALE: Boat Access & Part
SPORTING & RECREATIONAL GOODS, WHOLESALE: Canoes
SPORTING & RECREATIONAL GOODS, WHOLESALE: Fishing Tackle
SPORTING & RECREATIONAL GOODS, WHOLESALE: Golf & Skiing
SPORTING & RECREATIONAL GOODS, WHOLESALE: Gymnasium
SPORTING & RECREATIONAL GOODS, WHOLESALE: Hunting
SPORTING FIREARMS WHOLESALERS
SPORTING GOODS
SPORTING GOODS STORES, NEC
SPORTING GOODS STORES: Archery Splys
SPORTING GOODS STORES: Bait & Tackle
SPORTING GOODS STORES: Camping & Backpacking Eqpt
SPORTING GOODS STORES: Firearms
SPORTING GOODS STORES: Fishing Eqpt
SPORTING GOODS STORES: Hockey Eqpt, Exc Skates
SPORTING GOODS STORES: Playground Eqpt
SPORTING GOODS STORES: Skateboarding Eqpt
SPORTING GOODS STORES: Specialty Sport Splys, NEC
SPORTING GOODS STORES: Team sports Eqpt
SPORTING GOODS: Archery
SPORTING GOODS: Fishing Nets
SPORTS APPAREL STORES
SPORTS PROMOTION SVCS
SPOUTING: Plastic & Fiberglass Reinforced

SPRAYING & DUSTING EQPT
SPRAYING EQPT: Agricultural
SPRINGS: Automobile
SPRINGS: Clock, Precision
SPRINGS: Coiled Flat
SPRINGS: Cold Formed
SPRINGS: Instrument, Precision
SPRINGS: Leaf, Automobile, Locomotive, Etc
SPRINGS: Mechanical, Precision
SPRINGS: Precision
SPRINGS: Steel
SPRINGS: Torsion Bar
SPRINGS: Wire
SPRINKLER SYSTEMS: Field
SPRINKLING SYSTEMS: Fire Control
SPROCKETS: Power Transmission
STACKING MACHINES: Automatic
STADIUM EVENT OPERATOR SERVICES
STAFFING, EMPLOYMENT PLACEMENT
STAGE LIGHTING SYSTEMS
STAINLESS STEEL
STAINLESS STEEL WARE
STAINS: Wood
STAIRCASES & STAIRS, WOOD
STAMPINGS: Automotive
STAMPINGS: Metal
STANDS & RACKS: Engine, Metal
STARTERS & CONTROLLERS: Motor, Electric
STARTERS: Electric Motor
STARTERS: Motor
STATIONARY & OFFICE SPLYS, WHOLESALE: Carbon Paper
STATIONARY & OFFICE SPLYS, WHOLESALE: Inked Ribbons
STATIONARY & OFFICE SPLYS, WHOLESALE: Office Filing Splys
STATIONARY & OFFICE SPLYS WHOLESALERS
STATIONERY PRDTS
STATORS REWINDING SVCS
STEEL & ALLOYS: Tool & Die
STEEL FABRICATORS
STEEL MILLS
STEEL WOOL
STEEL, COLD-ROLLED: Flat Bright, From Purchased Hot-Rolled
STEEL, COLD-ROLLED: Strip NEC, From Purchased Hot-Rolled
STEEL, HOT-ROLLED: Sheet Or Strip
STEEL: Cold-Rolled
STEEL: Laminated
STEERING SYSTEMS & COMPONENTS
STENCILS
STERILIZERS, BARBER & BEAUTY SHOP
STITCHING SVCS: Custom
STOKERS: Mechanical, Domestic Or Indl
STONE: Crushed & Broken, NEC
STONE: Dimension, NEC
STONE: Quarrying & Processing, Own Stone Prdts
STOOLS: Factory
STORE FIXTURES: Exc Wood
STORE FIXTURES: Wood
STORES: Auto & Home Supply
STORES: Drapery & Upholstery
STOVES: Wood & Coal Burning
STRAIN GAGES: Solid State
STRAPS: Cotton Webbing
STRAPS: Spindle Banding
STRAWS: Drinking, Made From Purchased Materials
STRINGING BEADS
STRUCTURAL SUPPORT & BUILDING MATERIAL: Concrete
STUCCO
STUDIOS: Artists & Artists' Studios
STUDS & JOISTS: Sheet Metal
SUBPRESSES, METALWORKING
SUBSCRIPTION FULFILLMENT SVCS: Magazine, Newspaper, Etc
SUBSTANCE ABUSE COUNSELING
SUNDRIES & RELATED PRDTS: Medical & Laboratory, Rubber
SUNGLASSES, WHOLESALE
SUNROOFS: Motor Vehicle
SUPERMARKETS & OTHER GROCERY STORES
SURFACE ACTIVE AGENTS
SURFACE ACTIVE AGENTS: Emulsifiers, Exc Food & Pharmaceuticl

SURFACE ACTIVE AGENTS: Processing Assistants
SURFACE ACTIVE AGENTS: Textile Processing Assistants
SURFACERS: Concrete Grinding
SURGICAL APPLIANCES & SPLYS
SURGICAL APPLIANCES & SPLYS
SURGICAL EQPT: See Also Instruments
SURGICAL IMPLANTS
SURVEYING & MAPPING: Land Parcels
SUSPENSION SYSTEMS: Acoustical, Metal
SVC ESTABLISH EQPT, WHOLESALE: Carpet/Rug Clean Eqpt & Sply
SVC ESTABLISHMENT EQPT & SPLYS WHOLESALERS
SVC ESTABLISHMENT EQPT, WHOL: Cleaning & Maint Eqpt & Splys
SVC ESTABLISHMENT EQPT, WHOL: Concrete Burial Vaults & Boxes
SVC ESTABLISHMENT EQPT, WHOL: Funeral Director's Eqpt/Splys
SVC ESTABLISHMENT EQPT, WHOL: Laundry/Dry Cleaning Eqpt/Sply
SVC ESTABLISHMENT EQPT, WHOLESALE: Firefighting Eqpt
SVC ESTABLISHMENT EQPT, WHOLESALE: Shredders, Indl & Comm
SWEEPING COMPOUNDS
SWIMMING POOLS, EQPT & SPLYS: Wholesalers
SWITCHBOARDS & PARTS: Power
SWITCHES
SWITCHES: Electric Power
SWITCHES: Electronic
SWITCHES: Electronic Applications
SWITCHES: Solenoid
SWITCHGEAR & SWITCHBOARD APPARATUS
SYNCHROS
SYNTHETIC RESIN FINISHED PRDTS, NEC
SYRUPS, DRINK
SYSTEMS ENGINEERING: Computer Related
SYSTEMS INTEGRATION SVCS
SYSTEMS INTEGRATION SVCS: Local Area Network
SYSTEMS INTEGRATION SVCS: Office Computer Automation
SYSTEMS SOFTWARE DEVELOPMENT SVCS

T

TABLE OR COUNTERTOPS, PLASTIC LAMINATED
TABLES: Lift, Hydraulic
TAGS & LABELS: Paper
TAGS: Paper, Blank, Made From Purchased Paper
TALLOW: Animal
TANK COMPONENTS: Military, Specialized
TANK REPAIR & CLEANING SVCS
TANK REPAIR SVCS
TANKS & OTHER TRACKED VEHICLE CMPNTS
TANKS: Concrete
TANKS: Cryogenic, Metal
TANKS: For Tank Trucks, Metal Plate
TANKS: Fuel, Including Oil & Gas, Metal Plate
TANKS: Lined, Metal
TANKS: Plastic & Fiberglass
TANKS: Standard Or Custom Fabricated, Metal Plate
TANNERIES: Leather
TANNING SALONS
TAPE DRIVES
TAPES: Plastic Coated
TAPES: Pressure Sensitive
TAPS
TARPAULINS
TARPAULINS, WHOLESALE
TAX RETURN PREPARATION SVCS
TAXIDERMISTS
TECHNICAL WRITING SVCS
TELECOMMUNICATION EQPT REPAIR SVCS, EXC TELEPHONES
TELECOMMUNICATION SYSTEMS & EQPT
TELEGRAPH OR TELEPHONE CARRIER & REPEATER EQPT
TELEMARKETING BUREAUS
TELEMETERING EQPT
TELEPHONE EQPT: Modems
TELEPHONE EQPT: NEC
TELEPHONE SVCS
TELEPHONE: Fiber Optic Systems
TELEPHONE: Headsets
TELESCOPES
TELEVISION BROADCASTING STATIONS

PRODUCT INDEX

TELEVISION SETS
TELEVISION: Closed Circuit Eqpt
TEMPERING: Metal
TEMPORARY HELP SVCS
TEN PIN CENTERS
TENT REPAIR SHOP
TENTS: All Materials
TEST KITS: Pregnancy
TESTERS: Battery
TESTERS: Environmental
TESTERS: Hardness
TESTERS: Physical Property
TESTERS: Water, Exc Indl Process
TESTING SVCS
TEXTILE & APPAREL SVCS
TEXTILE FABRICATORS
TEXTILE FINISHING: Embossing, Cotton, Broadwoven
TEXTILE PRDTS: Hand Woven & Crocheted
TEXTILE: Finishing, Cotton Broadwoven
TEXTILE: Goods, NEC
TEXTILES
TEXTILES: Jute & Flax Prdts
TEXTILES: Linen Fabrics
TEXTILES: Mill Waste & Remnant
THEATRICAL LIGHTING SVCS
THEATRICAL PRODUCTION SVCS
THERMOCOUPLES
THERMOCOUPLES: Indl Process
THERMOELECTRIC DEVICES: Solid State
THERMOMETERS: Medical, Digital
THERMOPLASTIC MATERIALS
THERMOPLASTICS
THERMOSETTING MATERIALS
THREAD: Embroidery
THREAD: Hand Knitting
THREAD: Natural Fiber
TIES, FORM: Metal
TILE: Clay Refractory
TILE: Wall, Fiberboard
TIMBER PRDTS WHOLESALERS
TIMERS: Indl, Clockwork Mechanism Only
TIMING DEVICES: Cycle & Program Controllers
TIN
TIRE CORD & FABRIC
TIRE CORD & FABRIC: Cord, Rubber, Reinforcing
TIRE CORD & FABRIC: Steel
TIRE DEALERS
TIRE INFLATORS: Hand Or Compressor Operated
TIRE INNER-TUBES
TIRE RECAPPING & RETREADING
TIRES & INNER TUBES
TIRES & TUBES WHOLESALERS
TIRES & TUBES, WHOLESALE: Automotive
TIRES: Auto
TIRES: Cushion Or Solid Rubber
TITANIUM MILL PRDTS
TITLE ABSTRACT & SETTLEMENT OFFICES
TOBACCO LEAF PROCESSING
TOBACCO STORES & STANDS
TOBACCO: Chewing & Snuff
TOBACCO: Cigarettes
TOBACCO: Smoking
TOILET SEATS: Wood
TOILETRIES, COSMETICS & PERFUME STORES
TOILETRIES, WHOLESALE: Razor Blades
TOILETRIES, WHOLESALE: Toiletries
TOILETRIES, WHOLESALE: Toothbrushes, Exc Electric
TOILETS: Portable Chemical, Plastics
TOOL & DIE STEEL
TOOL REPAIR SVCS
TOOLS & EQPT: Used With Sporting Arms
TOOLS: Carpenters', Including Levels & Chisels, Exc Saws
TOOLS: Hand
TOOLS: Hand, Ironworkers'
TOOLS: Hand, Jewelers'
TOOLS: Hand, Power
TOOLS: Hand, Shovels Or Spades
TOOLS: Soldering
TOOTHBRUSHES: Exc Electric
TOUR OPERATORS
TOWELS: Linen & Linen & Cotton Mixtures
TOWERS, SECTIONS: Transmission, Radio & Television
TOWING & TUGBOAT SVC
TOWING BARS & SYSTEMS
TOWING SVCS: Marine

TOYS
TOYS & HOBBY GOODS & SPLYS, WHOLESALE: Arts/Crafts Eqpt/Sply
TOYS & HOBBY GOODS & SPLYS, WHOLESALE: Toys & Games
TOYS & HOBBY GOODS & SPLYS, WHOLESALE: Toys, NEC
TOYS, HOBBY GOODS & SPLYS WHOLESALERS
TOYS: Dolls, Stuffed Animals & Parts
TOYS: Rubber
TRADE SHOW ARRANGEMENT SVCS
TRAILERS & CHASSIS: Camping
TRAILERS & PARTS: Boat
TRAILERS & PARTS: Truck & Semi's
TRAILERS & TRAILER EQPT
TRAILERS: Bodies
TRAILERS: Bus, Tractor Type
TRAILERS: Demountable Cargo Containers
TRAILERS: House, Exc Permanent Dwellings
TRAILERS: Semitrailers, Missile Transportation
TRAILERS: Semitrailers, Truck Tractors
TRAILERS: Truck, Chassis
TRANSDUCERS: Electrical Properties
TRANSDUCERS: Pressure
TRANSFORMERS: Control
TRANSFORMERS: Distribution
TRANSFORMERS: Distribution, Electric
TRANSFORMERS: Doorbell, Electric
TRANSFORMERS: Electric
TRANSFORMERS: Fluorescent Lighting
TRANSFORMERS: Power Related
TRANSFORMERS: Rectifier
TRANSFORMERS: Voltage Regulating
TRANSLATION & INTERPRETATION SVCS
TRANSMISSIONS: Motor Vehicle
TRANSPORTATION BROKERS: Truck
TRANSPORTATION EPQT & SPLYS, WHOLESALE: Marine Crafts/Splys
TRANSPORTATION EPQT & SPLYS, WHOLESALE: Tanks & Tank Compnts
TRANSPORTATION EQUIPMENT, NEC
TRANSPORTATION SVCS, AIR, SCHEDULED: Helicopter Carriers
TRANSPORTATION SVCS: Rental, Local
TRANSPORTATION: Bus Transit Systems
TRANSPORTATION: Local Passenger, NEC
TRANSPORTATION: Transit Systems, NEC
TRAPS: Animal, Iron Or Steel
TRAPS: Stem
TRAVEL AGENCIES
TRAVEL TRAILER DEALERS
TRAVEL TRAILERS & CAMPERS
TRAYS: Plastic
TROPHIES, NEC
TROPHIES, WHOLESALE
TROPHIES: Metal, Exc Silver
TROPHY & PLAQUE STORES
TRUCK & BUS BODIES: Bus Bodies
TRUCK & BUS BODIES: Car Carrier
TRUCK & BUS BODIES: Cement Mixer
TRUCK & BUS BODIES: Garbage Or Refuse Truck
TRUCK & BUS BODIES: Motor Vehicle, Specialty
TRUCK & BUS BODIES: Truck Beds
TRUCK & BUS BODIES: Truck, Motor Vehicle
TRUCK & BUS BODIES: Van Bodies
TRUCK & FREIGHT TERMINALS & SUPPORT ACTIVITIES
TRUCK BODIES: Body Parts
TRUCK BODY SHOP
TRUCK GENERAL REPAIR SVC
TRUCK PAINTING & LETTERING SVCS
TRUCK PARTS & ACCESSORIES: Wholesalers
TRUCKING & HAULING SVCS: Animal & Farm Prdt
TRUCKING & HAULING SVCS: Contract Basis
TRUCKING & HAULING SVCS: Garbage, Collect/Transport Only
TRUCKING & HAULING SVCS: Lumber & Log, Local
TRUCKING & HAULING SVCS: Mail Carriers, Contract
TRUCKING & HAULING SVCS: Mobile Homes
TRUCKING & HAULING SVCS: Petroleum, Local
TRUCKING & HAULING SVCS: Steel, Local
TRUCKING & HAULING SVCS: Timber, Local
TRUCKING, DUMP
TRUCKING: Except Local
TRUCKING: Local, With Storage
TRUCKING: Local, Without Storage

TRUCKS & TRACTORS: Industrial
TRUCKS: Forklift
TRUCKS: Indl
TRUSSES & FRAMING: Prefabricated Metal
TRUSSES: Wood, Floor
TRUSSES: Wood, Roof
TUBE & PIPE MILL EQPT
TUBE & TUBING FABRICATORS
TUBES: Extruded Or Drawn, Aluminum
TUBES: Finned, For Heat Transfer
TUBES: Gas Or Vapor
TUBES: Paper
TUBES: Steel & Iron
TUBES: Wrought, Welded Or Lock Joint
TUBING: Copper
TUBING: Flexible, Metallic
TUBING: Plastic
TUBING: Rubber
TUBING: Seamless
TUMBLING
TUNGSTEN MILL PRDTS
TURBINE GENERATOR SET UNITS: Hydraulic, Complete
TURBINES & TURBINE GENERATOR SET UNITS, COMPLETE
TURBINES & TURBINE GENERATOR SETS
TURKEY PROCESSING & SLAUGHTERING
TURNKEY VENDORS: Computer Systems
TWINE PRDTS
TWINE: Binder & Baler
TYPESETTING SVC
TYPESETTING SVC: Computer

U

ULTRASONIC EQPT: Cleaning, Exc Med & Dental
UMBRELLAS & CANES
UNDERGROUND IRON ORE MINING
UNIFORM STORES
UNIVERSITY
UNSUPPORTED PLASTICS: Tile
UPHOLSTERY FILLING MATERIALS
UPHOLSTERY MATERIAL
USED CAR DEALERS
USED CLOTHING STORES
USED MERCHANDISE STORES
USED MERCHANDISE STORES: Office Furniture & Store Fixtures
UTILITY TRAILER DEALERS

V

VACUUM CLEANER REPAIR SVCS
VACUUM CLEANER STORES
VACUUM CLEANERS: Household
VACUUM CLEANERS: Indl Type
VACUUM CLEANERS: Wholesalers
VALVE REPAIR SVCS, INDL
VALVES
VALVES & PARTS: Gas, Indl
VALVES & PIPE FITTINGS
VALVES & REGULATORS: Pressure, Indl
VALVES: Aerosol, Metal
VALVES: Aircraft, Control, Hydraulic & Pneumatic
VALVES: Aircraft, Fluid Power
VALVES: Aircraft, Hydraulic
VALVES: Control, Automatic
VALVES: Engine
VALVES: Fluid Power, Control, Hydraulic & pneumatic
VALVES: Indl
VALVES: Regulating & Control, Automatic
VALVES: Regulating, Process Control
VALVES: Water Works
VAN CONVERSIONS
VAN CONVERSIONS
VEHICLE DRIVING SCHOOL
VEHICLES: All Terrain
VEHICLES: Recreational
VENDING MACHINE OPERATORS: Sandwich & Hot Food
VENDING MACHINES & PARTS
VENETIAN BLINDS & SHADES
VENTILATING EQPT: Metal
VENTILATING EQPT: Sheet Metal
VESSELS: Process, Indl, Metal Plate
VETERINARY PHARMACEUTICAL PREPARATIONS
VETERINARY PRDTS: Instruments & Apparatus
VIBRATORS: Concrete Construction
VIBRATORS: Interrupter

PRODUCT INDEX

VIDEO & AUDIO EQPT, WHOLESALE
VIDEO PRODUCTION SVCS
VIDEO REPAIR SVCS
VIDEO TAPE PRODUCTION SVCS
VINYL RESINS, NEC
VISES: Machine
VISUAL COMMUNICATIONS SYSTEMS
VITAMINS: Natural Or Synthetic, Uncompounded, Bulk
VITAMINS: Pharmaceutical Preparations
VOCATIONAL REHABILITATION AGENCY
VOCATIONAL TRAINING AGENCY

W

WALLPAPER STORE
WALLS: Curtain, Metal
WAREHOUSING & STORAGE FACILITIES, NEC
WAREHOUSING & STORAGE, REFRIGERATED: Cold Storage Or Refrig
WAREHOUSING & STORAGE, REFRIGERATED: Frozen Or Refrig Goods
WAREHOUSING & STORAGE: General
WAREHOUSING & STORAGE: General
WAREHOUSING & STORAGE: Liquid
WAREHOUSING & STORAGE: Miniwarehouse
WAREHOUSING & STORAGE: Self Storage
WAREHOUSING & STORAGE: Textile
WARM AIR HEATING & AC EQPT & SPLYS, WHOL: Dust Collecting
WARM AIR HEATING & AC EQPT & SPLYS, WHOLESALE Air Filters
WARM AIR HEATING & AC EQPT & SPLYS, WHOLESALE Furnaces, Elec
WARM AIR HEATING/AC EQPT/SPLYS, WHOL Dehumidifiers, Exc Port
WARM AIR HEATING/AC EQPT/SPLYS, WHOL Warm Air Htg Eqpt/Splys
WARRANTY INSURANCE: Automobile
WASHERS
WASHERS: Metal
WASHING MACHINES: Household
WATCH REPAIR SVCS
WATER HEATERS
WATER HEATERS WHOLESALERS EXCEPT ELECTRIC
WATER PURIFICATION EQPT: Household
WATER PURIFICATION PRDTS: Chlorination Tablets & Kits
WATER SOFTENER SVCS
WATER SOFTENING WHOLESALERS
WATER SPLY: Irrigation
WATER SUPPLY
WATER TREATMENT EQPT: Indl
WATER: Distilled
WATER: Mineral, Carbonated, Canned & Bottled, Etc
WATER: Pasteurized & Mineral, Bottled & Canned
WATER: Pasteurized, Canned & Bottled, Etc
WATERPROOFING COMPOUNDS
WAVEGUIDE STRUCTURES: Accelerating
WEATHER STRIP: Sponge Rubber
WEATHER VANES
WEB SEARCH PORTALS: Internet
WEDDING CONSULTING SVCS
WELDING & CUTTING APPARATUS & ACCESS, NEC
WELDING EQPT
WELDING EQPT & SPLYS WHOLESALERS
WELDING EQPT & SPLYS: Arc Welders, Transformer-Rectifier
WELDING EQPT & SPLYS: Electrodes
WELDING EQPT & SPLYS: Resistance, Electric
WELDING EQPT & SPLYS: Spot, Electric
WELDING EQPT & SPLYS: Wire, Bare & Coated
WELDING EQPT REPAIR SVCS
WELDING EQPT: Electric
WELDING EQPT: Electrical
WELDING MACHINES & EQPT: Ultrasonic
WELDING REPAIR SVC
WELDING SPLYS, EXC GASES: Wholesalers
WELDING TIPS: Heat Resistant, Metal
WELDMENTS
WET CORN MILLING
WHEEL BALANCING EQPT: Automotive
WHEELCHAIR LIFTS
WHEELCHAIRS
WHEELS
WHEELS & GRINDSTONES, EXC ARTIFICIAL: Abrasive
WHEELS & PARTS
WHEELS, GRINDING: Artificial
WHEELS: Abrasive
WHEELS: Buffing & Polishing
WHEELS: Disc, Wheelbarrow, Stroller, Etc, Stamped Metal
WHEELS: Iron & Steel, Locomotive & Car
WHISTLES
WICKER PRDTS
WICKING
WIGS & HAIRPIECES
WIGS, DOLL: Hair
WINCHES
WIND CHIMES
WINDINGS: Coil, Electronic
WINDMILLS: Electric Power Generation
WINDOW & DOOR FRAMES
WINDOW FRAMES & SASHES: Plastic
WINDOW FRAMES, MOLDING & TRIM: Vinyl
WINDOW FURNISHINGS WHOLESALERS
WINDOW SQUEEGEES
WINDOWS: Storm, Wood
WINDOWS: Wood
WINDSHIELD WIPER SYSTEMS
WINE & DISTILLED ALCOHOLIC BEVERAGES WHOLESALERS
WINE CELLARS, BONDED: Wine, Blended
WIRE
WIRE & CABLE: Aluminum
WIRE & CABLE: Nonferrous, Aircraft
WIRE & CABLE: Nonferrous, Automotive, Exc Ignition Sets
WIRE & CABLE: Nonferrous, Building
WIRE & WIRE PRDTS
WIRE CLOTH & WOVEN WIRE PRDTS, MADE FROM PURCHASED WIRE
WIRE CLOTH: Cylinder, Made From Purchased Wire
WIRE FABRIC: Welded Steel
WIRE FENCING & ACCESS WHOLESALERS
WIRE MATERIALS: Steel
WIRE PRDTS: Steel & Iron
WIRE WHOLESALERS
WIRE: Communication
WIRE: Magnet
WIRE: Mesh
WIRE: Nonferrous
WIRE: Steel, Insulated Or Armored
WIRE: Wire, Ferrous Or Iron
WOMEN'S & CHILDREN'S CLOTHING WHOLESALERS, NEC
WOMEN'S & GIRLS' SPORTSWEAR WHOLESALERS
WOMEN'S CLOTHING STORES
WOMEN'S SPORTSWEAR STORES
WOOD CARVINGS, WHOLESALE
WOOD CHIPS, PRODUCED AT THE MILL
WOOD FENCING WHOLESALERS
WOOD PRDTS
WOOD PRDTS: Applicators
WOOD PRDTS: Barrels & Barrel Parts
WOOD PRDTS: Barrels, Coopered
WOOD PRDTS: Beekeeping Splys
WOOD PRDTS: Brackets
WOOD PRDTS: Laundry
WOOD PRDTS: Mantels
WOOD PRDTS: Moldings, Unfinished & Prefinished
WOOD PRDTS: Mulch Or Sawdust
WOOD PRDTS: Mulch, Wood & Bark
WOOD PRDTS: Oars & Paddles
WOOD PRDTS: Outdoor, Structural
WOOD PRDTS: Paint Sticks
WOOD PRDTS: Poles
WOOD PRDTS: Shoe & Boot Prdts
WOOD PRDTS: Signboards
WOOD PRDTS: Survey Stakes
WOOD PRDTS: Trim
WOOD PRDTS: Veneer Work, Inlaid
WOOD PRODUCTS: Reconstituted
WOOD TREATING: Flooring, Block
WOOD TREATING: Structural Lumber & Timber
WOODWORK & TRIM: Interior & Ornamental
WOODWORK: Carved & Turned
WOODWORK: Interior & Ornamental, NEC
WOVEN WIRE PRDTS, NEC
WREATHS: Artificial
WRENCHES
WRITING FOR PUBLICATION SVCS

X

X-RAY EQPT & TUBES

Y

YARN : Crochet, Spun
YARN WHOLESALERS
YARN: Knitting, Spun
YARN: Manmade & Synthetic Fiber, Twisting Or Winding
YOGURT WHOLESALERS

Z

ZINC OINTMENT
ZINC ORE MINING

PRODUCT SECTION

Product category — **BOXES:** *Folding*
Edgar & Son Paperboard .... G 999 999-9999
    Yourtown *(G-11480)*
Ready Box Co .... E 999 999-9999
    Anytown *(G-7097)*
City

Indicates approximate employment figure
A = Over 500 employees, B = 251-500
C = 101-250, D = 51-100, E = 20-50
F = 10-19, G = 3-9
Business phone
Geographic Section entry number where full company information appears.

See footnotes for symbols and codes identification.
- Refer to the Industrial Product Index preceding this section to locate product headings.

ABRASIVES

3M Company .... E 313 372-4200
    Detroit *(G-3970)*
Abrasive Diamond Tool Company ..... E 248 588-4800
    Madison Heights *(G-10657)*
Abrasive Finishing Inc .... G 734 433-9236
    Chelsea *(G-2801)*
Abrasive Materials LLC .... G 517 437-4796
    Battle Creek *(G-1176)*
Auto Quip Inc .... F 810 364-3366
    Kimball *(G-9491)*
Belanger Inc .... D 248 349-7010
    Northville *(G-12197)*
Botsg Inc .... D 231 929-2121
    Traverse City *(G-16625)*
Cdp Diamond Products Inc .... E 734 591-1041
    Livonia *(G-10149)*
Crippen Manufacturing Company .... E 989 681-4323
    Saint Louis *(G-14990)*
Detroit Abrasives Company .... G 989 725-2405
    Owosso *(G-12831)*
Di-Coat Corporation .... E 248 349-1211
    Novi *(G-12399)*
Diamond Tool Manufacturing Inc .... E 734 416-1900
    Plymouth *(G-13157)*
Dianamic Abrasive Products .... F 248 280-1185
    Troy *(G-17059)*
E C Moore Company .... E 313 581-7878
    Dearborn *(G-3832)*
Ervin Industries Inc .... E 517 423-5477
    Tecumseh *(G-16500)*
Even-Cut Abrasive Company .... D 216 881-9595
    Grand Rapids *(G-6689)*
Ferro Industries Inc .... E 586 792-6001
    Harrison Township *(G-7699)*
Finishing Technologies Inc .... F 616 794-4001
    Belding *(G-1449)*
Hammond Machinery Inc .... D 269 345-7151
    Kalamazoo *(G-9207)*
Hydro Abrasive Products LLC .... G 313 456-9410
    Warren *(G-17856)*
Hydro-Abrasive Products LLC .... G 734 459-1544
    Plymouth *(G-13194)*
IGA Abrasives LLC .... E 616 243-5566
    Grand Rapids *(G-6832)*
International Abrasives Inc .... G 586 778-8490
    Roseville *(G-14424)*
Kalamazoo Company .... E 269 345-7151
    Kalamazoo *(G-9237)*
L R Oliver and Company Inc .... E 810 765-1000
    Cottrellville *(G-3724)*
Nutek Industries LLC .... F 800 637-9194
    Novi *(G-12495)*
Peerless Mtal Pwders Abrsive L .... G 313 841-5400
    Detroit *(G-4513)*
Sam Brown Sales LLC .... E 248 358-2626
    Farmington *(G-5147)*
Sandbox Solutions Inc .... C 248 349-7010
    Northville *(G-12257)*
Sidley Diamond Tool Company .... E 734 261-7970
    Garden City *(G-6109)*
South Bay Supply LLC .... G 313 882-8090
    Saint Clair Shores *(G-14885)*
Stan Sax Corp .... F 248 683-9199
    Detroit *(G-4604)*
Superabrasives Inc .... E 248 348-7670
    Wixom *(G-18762)*
Superior Abrasive Products .... F 248 969-4090
    Oxford *(G-12921)*
Trinity Tool Co .... E 586 296-5900
    Fraser *(G-6006)*
United Abrasive Inc .... F 906 563-9249
    Vulcan *(G-17616)*

ABRASIVES: Aluminum Oxide Fused

Detroit Abrasives Company .... G 734 475-1651
    Chelsea *(G-2808)*

ABRASIVES: Steel Shot

Beans Best LLC .... G 734 707-7378
    Ann Arbor *(G-397)*
Ervin Industries Inc .... D 517 265-6118
    Adrian *(G-64)*
Ervin Industries Inc .... E 734 769-4600
    Ann Arbor *(G-478)*
GMA Industries Inc .... E 734 595-7300
    Romulus *(G-14280)*
Metaltec Steel Abrasive Co .... E 734 459-7900
    Canton *(G-2495)*

ABRASIVES: Synthetic

D R W Systems .... G 989 874-4663
    Filion *(G-5612)*

ABRASIVES: Tungsten Carbide

Michigan Carbide Company Inc ...... F 586 264-8780
    Troy *(G-17257)*

ABRASIVES: sandpaper

Mid-West Waltham Abrasives Co .. E 517 725-7161
    Owosso *(G-12843)*

ACADEMIC TUTORING SVCS

Diagknowstics Tutoring .... G 877 382-1133
    Canton *(G-2455)*

ACADEMY

Detroit Fd Entrprnrship Acdemy ..... F 248 894-8941
    Detroit *(G-4147)*

ACCELERATION INDICATORS & SYSTEM COMPONENTS: Aerospace

Ascent Aerospace LLC .... A 586 726-0500
    Macomb *(G-10578)*
Beaver Aerospace & Defense Inc .. C 734 853-5003
    Livonia *(G-10133)*
Demmer Corporation .... C 517 321-3600
    Lansing *(G-9687)*
Elite Prcsion McHining Tooling .... G 269 383-9714
    Kalamazoo *(G-9177)*
Utica Aerospace Inc .... F 586 598-9300
    Chesterfield *(G-2961)*

ACCELERATORS: Particle, High Voltage

Niowave Inc .... G 517 999-3475
    Lansing *(G-9722)*

ACCELEROMETERS

Patriot Sensors & Contrls Corp ..... D 248 435-0700
    Peck *(G-12963)*

ACCOUNTING SVCS, NEC

Orion Bus Accnting Sltions LLC ..... G 248 893-1060
    Wyandotte *(G-18835)*

ACIDS

Trace Zero Inc .... F 248 289-1277
    Auburn Hills *(G-1062)*

ACIDS: Inorganic

Sterling Diagnostics Inc .... F 586 979-2141
    Sterling Heights *(G-16192)*

ACIDS: Sulfuric, Oleum

Pressure Vessel Service Inc .... E 313 921-1200
    Detroit *(G-4533)*

ACOUSTICAL BOARD & TILE

Gallant Inc .... F 616 772-1880
    Zeeland *(G-19023)*
Integrated Interiors Inc .... F 586 756-4840
    Warren *(G-17867)*

ACRYLIC RESINS

Allnex USA Inc .... D 269 385-1205
    Kalamazoo *(G-9109)*
Profile Industrial Packg Corp .... C 616 245-7260
    Grand Rapids *(G-7116)*

ACTUATORS: Indl, NEC

Acculift Inc .... G 313 382-5121
    Melvindale *(G-11196)*
Burr Engineering & Dev Co .... G 269 966-3122
    Battle Creek *(G-1201)*
Ctc Acquisition Company LLC .... C 616 884-7100
    Rockford *(G-14163)*
Meritor Inc .... C 248 435-1000
    Troy *(G-17246)*
Radius LLC .... G 248 685-0773
    Milford *(G-11485)*
Serapid Inc .... F 586 274-0774
    Sterling Heights *(G-16171)*
Stoneridge Inc .... A 248 489-9300
    Novi *(G-12543)*
Von Weise LLC .... G 517 618-9763
    Eaton Rapids *(G-4975)*

ADDITIVE BASED PLASTIC MATERIALS: Plasticizers

Sulfo-Technologies LLC .... G 248 307-9150
    Madison Heights *(G-10838)*

ADHESIVES

Action Fabricators Inc .... C 616 957-2032
    Grand Rapids *(G-6423)*
American Sealants Inc .... G 313 534-2500
    Detroit *(G-4014)*
Argent International Inc .... C 734 582-9800
    Plymouth *(G-13124)*
Chem Link Inc .... D 269 679-4440
    Schoolcraft *(G-15114)*
Covalent Medical Inc .... G 734 604-0688
    Ann Arbor *(G-438)*
Daring Company .... G 248 340-0741
    Orion *(G-12728)*
Diversitak Inc .... E 313 869-8500
    Detroit *(G-4181)*
Eternabond Inc .... G 847 540-0600
    Michigan Center *(G-11292)*
Kent Manufacturing Company .... D 616 454-9495
    Grand Rapids *(G-6889)*

ADHESIVES

Kleiberit Adhesives USA Inc ....G...... 248 709-9308
  Royal Oak *(G-14553)*
Lenderink Inc ....F...... 616 887-8257
  Belmont *(G-1511)*
Leonards Newcorp Inc ....F...... 313 366-9300
  Detroit *(G-4391)*
Master Mix Company ....G...... 734 487-7870
  Ypsilanti *(G-18966)*
Millennium Adhesive Products ....G...... 800 248-4010
  Michigan Center *(G-11294)*
Nyatex Chemical Company ....F...... 517 546-4046
  Howell *(G-8487)*
Parson Adhesives Inc ....G...... 248 299-5585
  Rochester Hills *(G-14079)*
Specilty Adhesives Coating Inc ....G...... 269 345-3801
  Kalamazoo *(G-9341)*
Stahls Inc ....E...... 800 478-2457
  Saint Clair Shores *(G-14887)*
Western Adhesive Inc ....F...... 616 874-5869
  Rockford *(G-14193)*

ADHESIVES & SEALANTS

A & B Display Systems Inc ....F...... 989 893-6642
  Bay City *(G-1314)*
Adco Products LLC ....C...... 517 841-7238
  Michigan Center *(G-11290)*
Alco Products LLC ....E...... 313 823-7500
  Detroit *(G-3996)*
Applied Molecules LLC ....G...... 810 355-1475
  Dexter *(G-4724)*
Bostik Inc ....G...... 269 781-8246
  Marshall *(G-11054)*
Cass Polymers ....E...... 517 543-7510
  Charlotte *(G-2739)*
Dow Chemical Company ....G...... 517 439-4400
  Hillsdale *(G-7933)*
Eftec North America LLC ....D...... 248 585-2200
  Taylor *(G-16410)*
Henniges Auto Holdings Inc ....B...... 248 340-4100
  Auburn Hills *(G-924)*
Henniges Auto Sling Systems N ....C...... 248 340-4100
  Auburn Hills *(G-925)*
Kiilunen Mfg Group Inc ....G...... 906 337-2433
  Calumet *(G-2410)*
L & L Products Inc ....B...... 586 752-6681
  Bruce Twp *(G-2172)*
Lj/Hah Holdings Corporation ....C...... 248 340-4100
  Auburn Hills *(G-958)*
Materials Processing Inc ....D...... 734 282-1888
  Riverview *(G-13880)*
Ncoc Inc ....E...... 248 548-5950
  Oak Park *(G-12632)*
ND Industries Inc ....C...... 248 288-0000
  Clawson *(G-3101)*
Portland Plastics Co ....F...... 517 647-4115
  Portland *(G-13640)*
Seal Support Systems Inc ....E...... 918 258-6484
  Romeo *(G-14235)*
Sealex Inc ....G...... 231 348-5020
  Harbor Springs *(G-7656)*
Sika Corporation ....D...... 248 577-0020
  Madison Heights *(G-10829)*
Transtar Autobody Tech LLC ....C...... 810 220-3000
  Brighton *(G-2084)*
Wall Colmonoy Corporation ....E...... 248 585-6400
  Madison Heights *(G-10860)*
Wilbur Products Inc ....F...... 231 755-5805
  Muskegon *(G-11948)*
Xileh Holding Inc ....G...... 248 340-4100
  Auburn Hills *(G-1090)*
Ziebart International Corp ....E...... 248 588-4100
  Troy *(G-17460)*

ADHESIVES & SEALANTS WHOLESALERS

Quantum Chemical LLC ....G...... 734 429-0033
  Livonia *(G-10379)*

ADHESIVES: Adhesives, plastic

Conley Composites LLC ....E...... 918 299-5051
  Grand Rapids *(G-6594)*
Highland Industrial Inc ....G...... 989 391-9992
  Bay City *(G-1365)*

ADHESIVES: Epoxy

West System Inc ....D...... 989 684-7286
  Bay City *(G-1411)*

ADULT DAYCARE CENTERS

Services To Enhance Potential ....G...... 313 278-3040
  Dearborn *(G-3895)*

ADVERTISING AGENCIES

All Seasons Agency Inc ....G...... 586 752-6381
  Bruce Twp *(G-2162)*
Bowman Enterprises Inc ....G...... 269 720-1946
  Portage *(G-13548)*
Fusion Design Group Ltd ....G...... 269 469-8226
  New Buffalo *(G-12023)*
Jack Batdorss ....F...... 231 723-3592
  Manistee *(G-10902)*
Kissman Consulting LLC ....G...... 517 256-1077
  Okemos *(G-12672)*
Pioneer Press Printing ....G...... 231 864-2404
  Bear Lake *(G-1421)*
Rtr Alpha Inc ....F...... 248 377-4060
  Auburn Hills *(G-1023)*
State News Inc ....D...... 517 295-1680
  East Lansing *(G-4909)*
Total Local Acquisitions LLC ....G...... 517 663-2405
  Eaton Rapids *(G-4974)*
Your Home Town USA Inc ....G...... 517 529-9421
  Clarklake *(G-3010)*
Your Hometown Shopper LLC ....F...... 586 412-8500
  Bruce Twp *(G-2187)*

ADVERTISING AGENCIES: Consultants

Ampm Inc ....E...... 989 837-8800
  Midland *(G-11321)*
Berline Group Inc ....E...... 248 203-0492
  Royal Oak *(G-14516)*
R J Michaels Inc ....E...... 517 783-2637
  Jackson *(G-8993)*
W W Thayne Advertising Cons ....F...... 269 979-1411
  Battle Creek *(G-1309)*

ADVERTISING COPY WRITING SVCS

State News Inc ....D...... 517 295-1680
  East Lansing *(G-4909)*

ADVERTISING CURTAINS

World Class Steel & Proc Inc ....G...... 586 585-1734
  Troy *(G-17453)*

ADVERTISING DISPLAY PRDTS

A & B Display Systems Inc ....F...... 989 893-6642
  Bay City *(G-1314)*
Altus Brands LLC ....F...... 231 421-3810
  Grawn *(G-7448)*
Charter House Holdings LLC ....C...... 616 399-6000
  Zeeland *(G-19004)*
Flexi Display Marketing Inc ....G...... 800 875-1725
  Commerce Township *(G-3531)*
Sizmek Dsp Inc ....E...... 313 516-4482
  Troy *(G-17355)*
Sparks Exhbits Envrnments Corp ....G...... 248 291-0007
  Royal Oak *(G-14582)*

ADVERTISING MATERIAL DISTRIBUTION

All Dealer Inventory LLC ....F...... 231 342-9823
  Lake Ann *(G-9541)*
MKP Enterprises Inc ....G...... 248 809-2525
  Southfield *(G-15660)*
Valassis Communications Inc ....A...... 734 591-3000
  Livonia *(G-10455)*
Valassis Communications Inc ....G...... 734 432-8000
  Livonia *(G-10456)*

ADVERTISING REPRESENTATIVES: Electronic Media

All Dealer Inventory LLC ....F...... 231 342-9823
  Lake Ann *(G-9541)*

ADVERTISING REPRESENTATIVES: Newspaper

Fowlerville News & Views ....G...... 517 223-8760
  Fowlerville *(G-5841)*
Herald Newspapers Company Inc ....G...... 989 752-7171
  Flint *(G-5713)*
Herald Newspapers Company Inc ....G...... 989 895-8551
  Flint *(G-5715)*

Maquet Monthly ....G...... 906 226-6500
  Marquette *(G-11032)*
Morning Star Publishing Co ....G...... 989 779-6000
  Alma *(G-250)*
Newark Morning Ledger Co ....D...... 517 487-8888
  Lansing *(G-9875)*
Tuscola County Advertiser Inc ....F...... 989 823-8651
  Vassar *(G-17583)*

ADVERTISING REPRESENTATIVES: Printed Media

Commercial Graphics Company ....G...... 517 278-2159
  Coldwater *(G-3429)*

ADVERTISING SPECIALTIES, WHOLESALE

Adco Specialties Inc ....G...... 616 452-6882
  Grand Rapids *(G-6430)*
Advertising Accents Inc ....G...... 313 937-3890
  Redford *(G-13711)*
Alex Delvecchio Entps Inc ....F...... 248 619-9600
  Troy *(G-16919)*
Armada Printwear Inc ....G...... 586 784-5553
  Armada *(G-730)*
Bay Supply & Marketing Inc ....G...... 231 943-3249
  Traverse City *(G-16616)*
Classic Images Embroidery ....G...... 616 844-1702
  Grand Haven *(G-6286)*
Dealer Aid Enterprises ....G...... 313 331-5800
  Detroit *(G-4128)*
Eclipse Print Emporium Inc ....G...... 248 477-8337
  Livonia *(G-10190)*
Edwards Sign & Screen Printing ....G...... 989 725-2988
  Owosso *(G-12832)*
Embroidery House Inc ....G...... 616 669-6400
  Jenison *(G-9054)*
Foresight Group Inc ....E...... 517 485-5700
  Lansing *(G-9699)*
GLS Enterprises Inc ....G...... 616 243-2574
  Comstock Park *(G-3608)*
Helm Incorporated ....G...... 734 468-3700
  Plymouth *(G-13186)*
Image Factory Inc ....G...... 989 732-2712
  Gaylord *(G-6135)*
Imprint House LLC ....G...... 810 985-8203
  Port Huron *(G-13487)*
Metro Printing Service Inc ....G...... 248 545-4444
  Troy *(G-17253)*
Monograms & More Inc ....E...... 313 299-3140
  Taylor *(G-16449)*
Pride Printing Inc ....G...... 906 228-8182
  Marquette *(G-11042)*
R & R Harwood Inc ....G...... 616 669-6400
  Jenison *(G-9069)*
Screen Ideas Inc ....G...... 616 458-5119
  Grand Rapids *(G-7188)*
Shayleslie Corporation ....G...... 517 694-4115
  Holt *(G-8332)*
Spinnaker Forms Systems Corp ....G...... 616 956-7677
  Grand Rapids *(G-7219)*
Tilco Inc ....G...... 248 644-0901
  Suttons Bay *(G-16346)*
Twin City Engraving Company ....G...... 269 983-0601
  Saint Joseph *(G-14968)*
Web Printing & Mktg Concepts ....G...... 269 983-4646
  Saint Joseph *(G-14974)*

ADVERTISING SVCS, NEC

Direct Aim Media LLC ....E...... 800 817-7101
  Grand Rapids *(G-6649)*
Kenewell Group ....G...... 810 714-4290
  Fenton *(G-5487)*

ADVERTISING SVCS: Billboards

Adams Outdoor Advg Ltd Partnr ....G...... 770 333-0399
  Lansing *(G-9670)*
Adams Outdoor Advg Ltd Partnr ....E...... 517 321-2121
  Lansing *(G-9671)*
R J Designers Inc ....G...... 517 750-1990
  Spring Arbor *(G-15797)*

ADVERTISING SVCS: Direct Mail

ADS Plus Printing LLC ....G...... 810 659-7190
  Flushing *(G-5800)*
Ancor Information MGT LLC ....D...... 248 740-8866
  Troy *(G-16936)*
Econo Print Inc ....G...... 734 878-5806
  Pinckney *(G-13047)*

PRODUCT SECTION

AIRCRAFT ASSEMBLY PLANTS

National Wholesale Prtg Corp .... G 734 416-8400
   Plymouth *(G-13252)*
P D Q Press Inc .... G 586 725-1888
   Ira *(G-8706)*
Print Masters Inc .... F 248 548-7100
   Madison Heights *(G-10810)*
Printwell Acquisition Co Inc .... D 734 941-6300
   Taylor *(G-16462)*
Ray Printing Company Inc .... F 517 787-4130
   Jackson *(G-8994)*
Real Green Systems Inc .... D 888 345-2154
   Commerce Township *(G-3570)*
Temperance Printing .... G 419 290-6846
   Lambertville *(G-9654)*
Valassis Communications Inc .... A 734 591-3000
   Livonia *(G-10455)*
Valassis Communications Inc .... G 734 432-8000
   Livonia *(G-10456)*

ADVERTISING SVCS: Display

A & B Display Systems Inc .... F 989 893-6642
   Bay City *(G-1314)*
Complete Source Inc .... G 616 285-9110
   Grand Rapids *(G-6587)*
Facet Business Communications .... F 248 912-0800
   Novi *(G-12415)*
Religious Communications LLC .... G 313 822-3361
   Detroit *(G-4563)*
Sign Image Inc .... F 989 781-5229
   Saginaw *(G-14756)*
Venture Grafix LLC .... G 248 449-1330
   Wixom *(G-18787)*

ADVERTISING SVCS: Outdoor

Graphic Resource Group Inc .... E 248 588-6100
   Troy *(G-17132)*
Steel Skinz LLC .... G 517 545-9955
   Howell *(G-8523)*

ADVERTISING SVCS: Poster, Outdoor

Bruce Inc .... G 517 371-5205
   Lansing *(G-9819)*

AERIAL WORK PLATFORMS

Great Lakes Exploration Inc .... G 906 352-4024
   Menominee *(G-11239)*
West Michigan Aerial LLc .... F 269 998-4455
   Lawton *(G-9991)*

AGENTS, BROKERS & BUREAUS: Personal Service

Rockwell Automation Inc .... G 248 696-1200
   Troy *(G-17335)*

AGRICULTURAL CHEMICALS: Trace Elements

Dow Agrosciences LLC .... E 989 636-4400
   Midland *(G-11340)*

AGRICULTURAL EQPT: BARN, SILO, POULTRY, DAIRY/LIVESTOCK MACH

Burly Oak Builders Inc .... G 734 368-4912
   Dexter *(G-4730)*
Packard Farms LLC .... E 989 386-3816
   Clare *(G-2993)*

AGRICULTURAL EQPT: Clippers, Animal, Hand Or Electric

Stuff A Pal .... G 734 646-3775
   Maybee *(G-11173)*

AGRICULTURAL EQPT: Fertilizng, Sprayng, Dustng/Irrigatn Mach

Logan Diesel Incorporated .... G 517 589-8811
   Leslie *(G-10014)*

AGRICULTURAL EQPT: Grounds Mowing Eqpt

Brilar LLC .... D 248 547-6439
   Oak Park *(G-12596)*
Overstreet Property MGT Co .... G 269 281-3880
   Benton Harbor *(G-1578)*

S & S Mowing Inc .... G 906 466-9009
   Bark River *(G-1157)*

AGRICULTURAL EQPT: Harvesters, Fruit, Vegetable, Tobacco

BEI International LLC .... F 616 204-8274
   Holland *(G-7973)*

AGRICULTURAL EQPT: Irrigation Eqpt, Self-Propelled

Triple K Farms Inc .... G 517 458-9741
   Morenci *(G-11617)*

AGRICULTURAL EQPT: Storage Bins, Crop

Glenn Knochel .... G 989 684-7869
   Kawkawlin *(G-9415)*

AGRICULTURAL EQPT: Tractors, Farm

Ebels Hardware Inc .... F 231 826-3334
   Falmouth *(G-5133)*
Mahindra Tractor Assembly Inc .... E 734 274-2239
   Ann Arbor *(G-563)*

AGRICULTURAL EQPT: Transplanters

Holland Transplanter Co Inc .... E 616 392-3579
   Holland *(G-8086)*
Liver Transplant/Univ of Mich .... G 734 936-7670
   Ann Arbor *(G-552)*
Mechanical Transplanter Co LLC .... E 616 396-8738
   Holland *(G-8142)*

AGRICULTURAL LIMESTONE: Ground

Trout Enterprises LLC .... G 810 309-4289
   Flint *(G-5784)*

AGRICULTURAL MACHINERY & EQPT: Wholesalers

Steiner Tractor Parts Inc .... E 810 621-3000
   Lennon *(G-9996)*

AIR CLEANING SYSTEMS

Clarkson Controls & Eqp Co .... G 248 380-9915
   Novi *(G-12384)*
Eagle Engineering & Supply Co .... E 989 356-4526
   Alpena *(G-291)*
Ecoquest Intl Independent .... G 734 854-6080
   Erie *(G-5047)*
Robovent Products Group Inc .... E 586 698-1800
   Sterling Heights *(G-16157)*
Technical Air Products LLC .... F 616 863-9115
   Belmont *(G-1519)*
Therma-Tech Engineering Inc .... E 313 537-5330
   Redford *(G-13778)*
Waltz-Holst Blow Pipe Company .... E 616 676-8119
   Ada *(G-40)*

AIR CONDITIONERS: Motor Vehicle

Air International (us) Inc .... D 248 391-7970
   Auburn Hills *(G-775)*
Espar Inc .... E 248 994-7010
   Novi *(G-12414)*
Evans Tempcon Delaware LLC .... G 616 361-2681
   Grand Rapids *(G-6687)*
Mahle Behr USA Inc .... C 248 743-3700
   Troy *(G-17232)*
Marelli North America Inc .... A 931 684-4490
   Southfield *(G-15644)*
Marelli North America Inc .... G 248 403-2033
   Southfield *(G-15645)*
Michigan Auto Comprsr Inc .... A 517 796-3200
   Parma *(G-12938)*
Therma-Tech Engineering Inc .... E 313 537-5330
   Redford *(G-13778)*

AIR CONDITIONING EQPT

Cdgjl Inc .... E 517 787-2100
   Jackson *(G-8836)*
Mjs Investing LLC .... E 734 455-6500
   Plymouth *(G-13246)*
Murtech Energy Services LLC .... G 810 653-5681
   Port Huron *(G-13508)*
Rush Air Inc .... F 810 694-5763
   Holly *(G-8293)*

Service Control Inc .... E 248 478-1133
   Howell *(G-8516)*
TI Fluid Systems LLC .... A 248 494-5000
   Auburn Hills *(G-1054)*

AIR CONDITIONING UNITS: Complete, Domestic Or Indl

Riedel USA Inc .... F 734 595-9820
   Kalamazoo *(G-9317)*
U S Distributing Inc .... E 248 646-0550
   Birmingham *(G-1755)*
Whirlpool Corporation .... G 269 923-5000
   Benton Harbor *(G-1609)*
Whirlpool Corporation .... A 269 923-5000
   Benton Harbor *(G-1603)*
Whirlpool Corporation .... G 269 923-5000
   Benton Harbor *(G-1605)*
Whirlpool Corporation .... C 269 849-0907
   Coloma *(G-3484)*
Whirlpool Corporation .... G 269 923-3009
   Benton Harbor *(G-1610)*

AIR MATTRESSES: Plastic

Denali Incorporated .... G 517 574-0047
   Hartland *(G-7768)*

AIR POLLUTION CONTROL EQPT & SPLYS WHOLESALERS

Robovent Products Group Inc .... E 586 698-1800
   Sterling Heights *(G-16157)*

AIR POLLUTION MEASURING SVCS

Advanced Recovery Tech Corp .... G 231 788-2911
   Nunica *(G-12575)*

AIR PURIFICATION EQPT

Advanced Air Technologies Inc .... G 989 743-5544
   Corunna *(G-3704)*
Cdgjl Inc .... E 517 787-2100
   Jackson *(G-8836)*
Gallagher-Kaiser Corporation .... D 313 368-3100
   Troy *(G-17126)*
Gelman Sciences Inc .... C 734 665-0651
   Ann Arbor *(G-496)*
Met-Pro Technologies LLC .... D 989 725-8184
   Lennon *(G-9995)*
Midwest Air Products Co Inc .... E 231 941-5865
   Traverse City *(G-16757)*
Tanis Technologies LLC .... G 616 796-2712
   Holland *(G-8212)*
Viron International Corp .... D 254 773-9292
   Owosso *(G-12866)*
Vision Air .... G 989 202-4100
   Houghton Lake *(G-8407)*

AIRCRAFT & AEROSPACE FLIGHT INSTRUMENTS & GUIDANCE SYSTEMS

General Dynamics Corporation .... G 615 427-5768
   Taylor *(G-16421)*
Gentz Industry .... G 586 772-2501
   Warren *(G-17829)*
Herrmann Aerospace .... G 810 695-1758
   Grand Blanc *(G-6247)*
Interactive Aerial Inc .... G 231 645-6007
   Traverse City *(G-16725)*
Phg Aviation LLC .... G 231 526-7380
   Harbor Springs *(G-7654)*
Preferred Avionics Instrs LLC .... E 800 521-5130
   Howell *(G-8501)*

AIRCRAFT & HEAVY EQPT REPAIR SVCS

Cascade Equipment Company .... G 734 697-7870
   Van Buren Twp *(G-17516)*
Grand Rapids Machine Repr Inc .... E 616 245-9102
   Grand Rapids *(G-6764)*
Liebherr Aerospace Saline Inc .... C 734 429-7225
   Saline *(G-15024)*

AIRCRAFT ASSEMBLY PLANTS

Ascent Aerospace Holdings LLC .... G 212 916-8142
   Macomb *(G-10579)*
Boeing Company .... G 248 258-7191
   Bloomfield Hills *(G-1805)*

AIRCRAFT ASSEMBLY PLANTS

C H Industries Inc .... F 586 997-1717
  Shelby Township (G-15180)
Dakota Aerospace LLC .... G 787 403-3564
  Pinckney (G-13046)
Delorean Aerospace LLC .... G 248 752-2380
  Bloomfield Hills (G-1812)
Eaton Aerospace LLC .... C 517 787-8121
  Jackson (G-8874)
Mrd Aerospace .... G 586 468-1196
  Harrison Township (G-7711)
Mustang Aeronautics Inc .... G 248 649-6818
  Troy (G-17271)
P2r Metal Fabrication Inc .... F 586 606-5266
  Macomb (G-10625)
Sika Corporation .... D 248 577-0020
  Madison Heights (G-10829)
Soaring Concepts Aerospace LLC .... F 574 286-9670
  Hastings (G-7810)
Textron Inc .... G 248 545-2035
  Madison Heights (G-10841)

AIRCRAFT CONTROL SYSTEMS: Electronic Totalizing Counters

GE Aviation Systems LLC .... E 616 224-6480
  Grand Rapids (G-6734)

AIRCRAFT ENGINES & ENGINE PARTS: Cooling Systems

Dry Coolers Inc .... E 248 969-3400
  Oxford (G-12883)
Stm Power Inc .... E 734 214-1448
  Ann Arbor (G-666)

AIRCRAFT ENGINES & ENGINE PARTS: Mount Parts

Rapp & Son Inc .... D 734 283-1000
  Wyandotte (G-18836)

AIRCRAFT ENGINES & ENGINE PARTS: Research & Development, Mfr

Eaton Corporation .... B 269 781-0200
  Marshall (G-11056)
Steven J Devlin .... G 734 439-1325
  Milan (G-11450)

AIRCRAFT ENGINES & PARTS

Advance Turning and Mfg Inc .... C 517 783-2713
  Jackson (G-8802)
Aerovision Aircraft Svcs LLC .... E 231 799-9000
  Norton Shores (G-12274)
Aerovision International LLC .... E 231 799-9000
  Norton Shores (G-12275)
Aircraft Precision Pdts Inc .... D 989 875-4186
  Ithaca (G-8785)
Approved Aircraft Accessories .... G 734 946-9000
  Romulus (G-14250)
AVI Inventory Services LLC .... E 231 799-9000
  Norton Shores (G-12277)
Barnes Group Inc .... A 517 393-5110
  Lansing (G-9812)
Dorris Company .... F 586 293-5260
  Fraser (G-5919)
Expernced Prcsion McHining Inc .... G 989 635-2299
  Marlette (G-10981)
Filtration Machine .... G 810 845-0536
  Davison (G-3783)
General Electric Company .... G 734 727-4619
  Wayne (G-18222)
Honeywell .... E 248 362-7154
  Troy (G-17147)
Honeywell International Inc .... G 989 792-8707
  Saginaw (G-14669)
Honeywell International Inc .... G 586 777-7870
  Fraser (G-5939)
Honeywell International Inc .... G 734 392-5501
  Plymouth (G-13189)
Johnson Technology Inc .... G 231 777-2685
  Muskegon (G-11846)
LAY Precision Machine Inc .... G 989 726-5022
  West Branch (G-18330)
Manufacturing & Indus Tech Inc .... G 248 522-6959
  Farmington Hills (G-10829)
MB Aerospace Warren LLC .... C 586 772-2500
  Warren (G-17920)
Merrill Technologies Group .... E 989 921-1490
  Saginaw (G-14696)

Merrill Technologies Group Inc .... D 989 791-6676
  Saginaw (G-14697)
Moeller Aerospace Tech Inc .... C 231 347-9575
  Harbor Springs (G-7651)
Niles Precision Company .... C 269 683-0585
  Niles (G-12155)
Nu Con Corporation .... E 734 525-0770
  Livonia (G-10341)
Pratt & Whitney Autoair Inc .... C 517 393-4040
  Lansing (G-9882)
Pratt & Whitney Autoair Inc .... E 517 348-1416
  Holt (G-8325)
SGC Industries Inc .... G 586 293-5260
  Fraser (G-5992)
Steel Tool & Engineering Co .... D 734 692-8580
  Brownstown Twp (G-2157)
Supreme Gear Co .... E 586 775-6325
  Fraser (G-6001)
Tidy Mro Enterprises LLC .... G 734 649-1122
  Manchester (G-10891)
United Precision Pdts Co Inc .... E 313 292-0100
  Dearborn Heights (G-3943)
Woodward Fst Inc .... C 616 772-9171
  Zeeland (G-19092)

AIRCRAFT EQPT & SPLYS WHOLESALERS

Great Lakes Aero Products .... F 810 235-1402
  Flint (G-5708)
Oshino Lamps America Ltd .... G 262 226-8620
  Wixom (G-18727)

AIRCRAFT FLIGHT INSTRUMENTS

Grand Rapids Machine Repr Inc .... E 616 245-9102
  Grand Rapids (G-6764)
L3 Aviation Products Inc .... B 616 949-6600
  Grand Rapids (G-6906)
Thierica Inc .... D 616 458-1538
  Grand Rapids (G-7257)

AIRCRAFT MAINTENANCE & REPAIR SVCS

Aerovision International LLC .... E 231 799-9000
  Norton Shores (G-12275)
Beaver Aerospace & Defense Inc .... C 734 853-5003
  Livonia (G-10133)
Northern Wings Repair Inc .... E 906 477-6176
  Newberry (G-12100)

AIRCRAFT PARTS & AUXILIARY EQPT: Assys, Subassemblies/Parts

Bradley-Thompson Tool Company .... E 248 352-1466
  Southfield (G-15510)
Phoenix Cmposite Solutions LLC .... C 989 739-7108
  Oscoda (G-12770)
Pifers Airmotive Inc .... G 248 674-0909
  Goodrich (G-6225)
R & B Electronics Inc .... D 906 632-1542
  Sault Sainte Marie (G-15097)
Ventura Aerospace LLC .... E 734 357-0114
  Wixom (G-18786)
Ventura Industries Inc .... F 734 357-0114
  Plymouth (G-13331)
Visioneering Inc .... E 248 622-5600
  Fraser (G-6011)

AIRCRAFT PARTS & AUXILIARY EQPT: Countermeasure Dispensers

Intergrted Dspnse Slutions LLC .... F 586 554-7404
  Shelby Township (G-15239)

AIRCRAFT PARTS & AUXILIARY EQPT: Gears, Power Transmission

Beaver Aerospace & Defense Inc .... C 734 853-5003
  Livonia (G-10133)
Bmt Aerospace Usa Inc .... D 586 285-7700
  Fraser (G-5905)
Dorris Company .... F 586 293-5260
  Fraser (G-5919)
Gear Master Inc .... F 810 798-9254
  Almont (G-260)
SGC Industries Inc .... G 586 293-5260
  Fraser (G-5992)
Triumph Gear Systems - McOmb I .... C 586 781-2800
  Macomb (G-10644)

AIRCRAFT PARTS & AUXILIARY EQPT: Lighting/Landing Gear Assy

Liebherr Aerospace Saline Inc .... C 734 429-7225
  Saline (G-15024)

AIRCRAFT PARTS & AUXILIARY EQPT: Military Eqpt & Armament

Dhs/Cbp .... G 586 954-2214
  Selfridge Angb (G-15147)
Eagle Industrial Group Inc .... E 616 647-9904
  Comstock Park (G-3605)
Lapeer Industries Inc .... C 810 538-0589
  Shelby Township (G-15257)
Military Vtrans Affirs Mich De .... C 231 775-7222
  Cadillac (G-2347)

AIRCRAFT PARTS & AUXILIARY EQPT: Pontoons

Pontoon Rentals .... G 906 387-2685
  Munising (G-11753)

AIRCRAFT PARTS & EQPT, NEC

AAR Corp .... F 231 779-4859
  Cadillac (G-2305)
Advanced Integration Tech LP .... G 586 749-5525
  Chesterfield (G-2837)
Aero Inspection & Tool LLC .... G 517 525-7373
  Leslie (G-10013)
Aero Train Corp .... G 810 230-8096
  Flint (G-5640)
Aerovision Aircraft Svcs LLC .... E 231 799-9000
  Norton Shores (G-12274)
Aerovision International LLC .... E 231 799-9000
  Norton Shores (G-12275)
Aircraft Precision Pdts Inc .... D 989 875-4186
  Ithaca (G-8785)
Aj Aircraft .... G 734 244-4015
  Monroe (G-11523)
American Aircraft Parts Mfg Co .... E 586 294-3300
  Clinton Township (G-3164)
AVI Inventory Services LLC .... E 231 799-9000
  Norton Shores (G-12277)
Chardam Gear Company Inc .... C 586 795-8900
  Sterling Heights (G-15957)
Detail Precision Products Inc .... E 248 544-3390
  Ferndale (G-5540)
Detroit Coil Co .... E 248 658-1543
  Ferndale (G-5543)
Dolphin Manufacturing Inc .... E 734 946-6322
  Taylor (G-16403)
Eaton Aeroquip LLC .... B 949 452-9575
  Jackson (G-8873)
Enstrom Helicopter Corporation .... C 906 863-1200
  Menominee (G-11233)
Extreme Precision Screw Pdts .... E 810 744-1980
  Flint (G-5698)
Fema Corporation of Michigan .... C 269 323-1369
  Portage (G-13560)
Flow-Rite Controls Ltd .... E 616 583-1700
  Byron Center (G-2270)
Grand Rapids Technologies Inc .... G 616 245-7700
  Grand Rapids (G-6771)
Hart Precision Products Inc .... E 313 537-0490
  Redford (G-13739)
Honeywell International Inc .... C 231 582-5686
  Boyne City (G-1889)
Hytrol Manufacturing Inc .... E 734 261-8030
  Jackson (G-8906)
Innovative Drone Services LLC .... G 313 333-6956
  Ypsilanti (G-18956)
Jedco Inc .... C 616 459-5161
  Grand Rapids (G-6867)
Liberty Tool Inc .... E 586 726-2449
  Sterling Heights (G-16073)
Linear Motion LLC .... C 989 759-8300
  Saginaw (G-14683)
Mas Inc .... F 231 894-0409
  Whitehall (G-18508)
Masterbilt Products Corp .... F 269 749-4841
  Olivet (G-12694)
Meggitt .... G 989 759-8327
  Saginaw (G-14694)
Melling Manufacturing Inc .... D 517 750-3580
  Jackson (G-8950)
Merrill Technologies Group .... E 989 921-1490
  Saginaw (G-14696)

PRODUCT SECTION

AMMUNITION: Shot, Steel

Moose Mfg & Machining LLC ....G........ 586 765-4686
  Detroit (G-4464)
Motor City Aerospace ....G........ 616 916-5473
  Rockford (G-14180)
National Aircraft Service Inc ....E........ 517 423-7589
  Tecumseh (G-16509)
Niles Precision Company ....C........ 269 683-0585
  Niles (G-12155)
Northern Wings Repair Inc ....E........ 906 477-6176
  Newberry (G-12100)
Nu Con Corporation ....E........ 734 525-0770
  Livonia (G-10341)
Odyssey Industries LLC ....C........ 248 814-8800
  Lake Orion (G-9624)
Parker-Hannifin Corporation ....B........ 269 384-3459
  Kalamazoo (G-9288)
Parker-Hannifin Corporation ....G........ 269 384-3400
  Kalamazoo (G-9289)
Prime Products Inc ....E........ 616 531-8970
  Grand Rapids (G-7107)
Saf-Air Products Inc ....G........ 734 522-8360
  Garden City (G-6107)
Scott Machine Inc ....E........ 517 787-6616
  Jackson (G-9008)
Teamtech Motorsports Safety ....G........ 989 792-4880
  Saginaw (G-14773)
United Precision Pdts Co Inc ....E........ 313 292-0100
  Dearborn Heights (G-3943)
Veet Industries Inc ....F........ 586 776-3000
  Warren (G-18053)
Wmh Fluidpower Inc ....F........ 269 327-7011
  Portage (G-13634)

AIRCRAFT SERVICING & REPAIRING

Liebherr Aerospace Saline Inc ....C........ 734 429-7225
  Saline (G-15024)

AIRCRAFT TURBINES

Johnson Technology Inc ....B........ 231 777-2685
  Norton Shores (G-12305)
Johnson Technology Inc ....B........ 231 777-2685
  Muskegon (G-11847)
Metro Machine Works Inc ....D........ 734 941-4571
  Romulus (G-14304)
Williams International Co LLC ....A........ 248 624-5200
  Pontiac (G-13425)

AIRCRAFT: Airplanes, Fixed Or Rotary Wing

Midwest Build Center LLC ....G........ 989 672-1388
  Caro (G-2576)

AIRCRAFT: Motorized

Great Lakes Drone Company LLC ....G........ 317 430-5291
  Stevensville (G-16251)
Procore Drones LLC ....G........ 850 774-0604
  Spring Lake (G-15845)
Skywalker Drone Solutions LLC ....G........ 248 342-6747
  Oxford (G-12917)

AIRCRAFT: Research & Development, Manufacturer

Temper Inc ....F........ 616 293-1349
  Cedar Springs (G-2665)

AIRPORTS, FLYING FIELDS & SVCS

Approved Aircraft Accessories ....G........ 734 946-9000
  Romulus (G-14250)

ALARM SYSTEMS WHOLESALERS

Dice Corporation ....E........ 989 891-2800
  Bay City (G-1343)

ALARMS: Burglar

Controller Systems Corporation ....E........ 586 772-6100
  Eastpointe (G-4932)
Safety Technology Intl Inc ....E........ 248 673-9898
  Waterford (G-18162)
Safety Technology Intl Inc ....E........ 248 673-9898
  Waterford (G-18163)

ALARMS: Fire

Gentex Corporation ....G........ 616 392-7195
  Zeeland (G-19028)

ALCOHOL: Ethyl & Ethanol

Carbon Green Bioenergy LLC ....E........ 616 374-4000
  Lake Odessa (G-9573)
Poet Biorefining - Caro LLC ....E........ 989 672-1222
  Caro (G-2577)

ALKALIES & CHLORINE

Dow Chemical Company ....A........ 989 636-1000
  Midland (G-11341)
Dow Chemical Company ....D........ 989 636-5409
  Midland (G-11352)
Jci Jones Chemicals Inc ....F........ 734 283-0677
  Wyandotte (G-18824)
Pittsburgh Glass Works LLC ....C........ 248 371-1700
  Rochester Hills (G-14084)
PPG Industries Inc ....F........ 248 641-2000
  Troy (G-17309)

ALL-TERRAIN VEHICLE DEALERS

Lumberjack Shack Inc ....G........ 810 724-7230
  Imlay City (G-8640)

ALLOYS: Additive, Exc Copper Or Made In Blast Furnaces

Alloying Surfaces Inc ....E........ 248 524-9200
  Troy (G-16927)
Cannon-Muskegon Corporation ....C........ 231 755-1681
  Norton Shores (G-12284)

ALTERNATORS & GENERATORS: Battery Charging

Arotech Corporation ....D........ 800 281-0356
  Ann Arbor (G-380)
Powermat Inc ....E........ 616 259-4867
  Grandville (G-7410)

ALTERNATORS: Automotive

Denso International Amer Inc ....G........ 248 359-4177
  Van Buren Twp (G-17523)
Don Duff Rebuilding ....G........ 734 522-7700
  Livonia (G-10187)
Prestolite Electric Inc ....F........ 866 463-7078
  Novi (G-12514)
Seg Automotive North Amer LLC ....E........ 248 465-2602
  Novi (G-12533)

ALUMINUM

Aleris International Inc ....F........ 517 279-9596
  Coldwater (G-3418)
Constellium Automotive USA LLC ....C........ 734 879-9700
  Van Buren Twp (G-17519)
Fritz Enterprises ....E........ 313 841-9460
  Detroit (G-4247)
General Motors LLC ....G........ 989 757-0528
  Saginaw (G-14651)
Howmet Aerospace Inc ....G........ 231 981-3002
  Whitehall (G-18498)
Howmet Aerospace Inc ....G........ 231 894-5686
  Whitehall (G-18500)
Kaiser Aluminum Fab Pdts LLC ....G........ 269 250-8400
  Kalamazoo (G-9235)
Nemak International Inc ....E........ 248 350-3999
  Southfield (G-15664)
Shipston Group US Inc ....E........ 248 372-9018
  Southfield (G-15702)
United Global Sourcing Inc ....F........ 248 952-5700
  Troy (G-17412)
Viking Industries Inc ....F........ 734 421-5416
  Garden City (G-6115)
Wayne-Craft Inc ....F........ 734 421-8800
  Livonia (G-10468)

ALUMINUM PRDTS

Air Conditioning Products Co ....E........ 734 326-0050
  Romulus (G-14247)
Aluminum Textures Inc ....E........ 616 538-3144
  Grandville (G-7364)
Arconic Corporation ....G........ 248 489-4900
  Farmington Hills (G-5172)
Austin Tube Products Inc ....F........ 231 745-2741
  Baldwin (G-1121)
Belding McHy & Eqp Lsg Corp ....C........ 616 794-0300
  Belding (G-1439)
Benteler Auto Holland Inc ....C........ 616 396-6591
  Holland (G-7974)
Bonnell Aluminum (niles) LLC ....C........ 269 697-6063
  Niles (G-12115)
Christianson Industries Inc ....E........ 269 663-8502
  Edwardsburg (G-5003)
D & W Awning and Window Co ....E........ 810 742-0340
  Davison (G-3779)
Erbsloeh Alum Solutions Inc ....B........ 269 323-2565
  Portage (G-13558)
Extruded Aluminum Corporation ....C........ 616 794-0300
  Belding (G-1448)
Flotronics Automation Inc ....E........ 248 625-8890
  Auburn Hills (G-902)
General Structures Inc ....F........ 586 774-6105
  Warren (G-17826)
Hancock Enterprises Inc ....D........ 734 287-8840
  Taylor (G-16424)
Heatsinkusa LLC ....G........ 800 901-2395
  Greenville (G-7491)
Hydro Extrusion North Amer LLC ....B........ 269 349-6626
  Kalamazoo (G-9220)
International Extrusion ....G........ 734 427-1934
  Garden City (G-6100)
International Extrusions ....F........ 734 956-6841
  Garden City (G-6101)
International Extrusions Inc ....C........ 734 427-8700
  Garden City (G-6102)
Kaiser Aluminum Corporation ....G........ 269 488-0957
  Kalamazoo (G-9234)
Light Metals Corporation ....B........ 616 538-3030
  Wyoming (G-18891)
Lippert Components Mfg Inc ....D........ 989 845-3061
  Chesaning (G-2829)
Loftis Alumi-TEC Inc ....G........ 616 846-1990
  Grand Haven (G-6330)
Lorin Industries Inc ....D........ 231 722-1631
  Muskegon (G-11861)
Marketing Displays Inc ....C........ 248 553-1900
  Farmington Hills (G-5310)
Mueller Brass Co ....C........ 810 987-7770
  Port Huron (G-13504)
Mueller Impacts Company Inc ....C........ 810 364-3700
  Marysville (G-11093)
Plascore Inc ....E........ 616 772-1220
  Zeeland (G-19070)
Quality Alum Acquisition LLC ....F........ 734 783-0990
  Flat Rock (G-5626)
Quality Alum Acquisition LLC ....D........ 800 550-1667
  Hastings (G-7807)
Quality Model & Pattern Co ....E........ 616 791-1156
  Grand Rapids (G-7129)
Special-Lite Inc ....C........ 800 821-6531
  Decatur (G-3951)
Superior Extrusion Inc ....C........ 906 346-7308
  Gwinn (G-7587)
Tubelite Inc ....C........ 800 866-2227
  Walker (G-17655)
Uacj Auto Whitehall Inds Inc ....D........ 231 845-5101
  Ludington (G-10554)
Ube Machinery Inc ....D........ 734 741-7000
  Ann Arbor (G-702)

ALUMINUM: Rolling & Drawing

AAR Manufacturing Inc ....E........ 231 779-8800
  Cadillac (G-2306)
General Structures Inc ....F........ 586 774-6105
  Warren (G-17826)

AMMONIA & LIQUOR: Chemical Recovery Coke Oven

America Wireless ....G........ 810 820-3273
  Flint (G-5644)

AMMUNITION: Cartridges Case, 30 mm & Below

Scorpion Reloads LLC ....G........ 586 214-3843
  Fraser (G-5991)

AMMUNITION: Components

Bliss Munitions Equipment ....G........ 269 953-6655
  Hastings (G-7782)

AMMUNITION: Shot, Steel

Boss Outdoors LLC ....G........ 269 465-3631
  Bridgman (G-1922)

AMMUNITION: Small Arms

Bold Ammo & Guns Inc ....G....... 616 826-0913
  Rockford *(G-14158)*
Brass Kings Inc..G....... 248 674-1860
  Manton *(G-10930)*
Kenneth David Kent ....G....... 906 475-7036
  Negaunee *(G-11969)*
Lairds Custom Cabinetry Inc ....G....... 810 494-5164
  Brighton *(G-2020)*
Oakland Tactical Supply LLC.......................G....... 810 991-1436
  Howell *(G-8488)*
On The Mark Inc ....G....... 989 317-8033
  Mount Pleasant *(G-11729)*
Sage Control Ordnance Inc.........................E....... 989 739-2200
  Oscoda *(G-12771)*
Tactical Simplicity LLC ....G....... 248 410-4523
  Wixom *(G-18765)*

AMPLIFIERS

Mitsubishi Elc Auto Amer Inc ....D....... 734 453-6200
  Northville *(G-12240)*

AMUSEMENT & RECREATION SVCS: Amusement Arcades

Century Lanes Inc..D....... 616 392-7086
  Holland *(G-7992)*

AMUSEMENT & RECREATION SVCS: Boating Club, Membership

Midwest Aquatics Group Inc.......................G....... 734 426-4155
  Pinckney *(G-13052)*

AMUSEMENT & RECREATION SVCS: Recreation Center

Y M C A Family Center ....G....... 269 428-9622
  Saint Joseph *(G-14982)*

AMUSEMENT & RECREATION SVCS: Ski Instruction

Plastisnow LLC ....G....... 414 397-1233
  Plainwell *(G-13090)*

AMUSEMENT MACHINES: Coin Operated

Slotbrokers LLC..G....... 231 929-7568
  Traverse City *(G-16835)*
Spec International Inc.................................F....... 616 248-3022
  Grand Rapids *(G-7211)*

AMUSEMENT PARK DEVICES & RIDES

Autosport Development LLC ....G....... 734 675-1620
  Trenton *(G-16886)*
Boomerang Amusements ....F....... 586 323-3327
  Shelby Township *(G-15178)*
Classic Turning Inc ....D....... 517 764-1335
  Jackson *(G-8843)*
Djc Products Inc...G....... 586 992-1352
  Shelby Township *(G-15209)*
Prestige Engrg Rsrces Tech Inc ....G....... 586 573-3070
  Madison Heights *(G-10808)*
S & M Machining Company ....G....... 248 348-0310
  Wixom *(G-18745)*
Tec-Option Inc ....F....... 517 486-6055
  Blissfield *(G-1777)*
TI Fluid Systems LLC ....A....... 248 494-5000
  Auburn Hills *(G-1054)*

AMUSEMENT PARK DEVICES & RIDES: Ferris Wheels

Ferris Wheel Innovation Center..................G....... 810 213-4720
  Flint *(G-5700)*

ANALGESICS

L Perrigo Company ....G....... 248 687-1036
  Troy *(G-17201)*
Perrigo China Bus Trustee LLC...................E....... 269 673-8451
  Allegan *(G-174)*
Perrigo Company ....A....... 269 673-8451
  Allegan *(G-176)*

ANALYZERS: Coulometric, Exc Indl Process

Neptech Inc...E....... 810 225-2222
  Highland *(G-7897)*

ANALYZERS: Network

Medical Infrmtics Slutions LLC ....G....... 248 851-3124
  Bloomfield Hills *(G-1836)*
Netwave ....G....... 586 263-4469
  Macomb *(G-10622)*
Syscom Technologies Inc ....G....... 231 946-1411
  Traverse City *(G-16848)*
Vexa Group LLC ....G....... 734 330-8858
  Wixom *(G-18788)*

ANALYZERS: Respiratory

Healthcare Drble Med Eqpmnts L...............G....... 734 975-6668
  Ann Arbor *(G-510)*

ANIMAL FEED & SUPPLEMENTS: Livestock & Poultry

Active Feed Company ....D....... 989 453-2472
  Pigeon *(G-13034)*
Belle Feeds ....G....... 269 628-1231
  Paw Paw *(G-12942)*
Cargill Incorporated ....F....... 608 868-5150
  Owosso *(G-12825)*
Custom Blend Feeds Inc ....G....... 810 798-3265
  Bruce Twp *(G-2165)*
Darling Ingredients Inc ....C....... 517 279-9731
  Coldwater *(G-3431)*
Darling Ingredients Inc ....G....... 269 751-0560
  Hamilton *(G-7597)*
Equus Magnificus ....G....... 651 407-0023
  Harbor Springs *(G-7646)*
Harveys Commodities LLC ....F....... 616 920-1805
  Carson City *(G-2593)*
Mid McHgan Feed Ingrdients LLC ....G....... 989 236-5014
  Middleton *(G-11299)*
N F P Inc ....G....... 989 631-0009
  Midland *(G-11397)*
Pet Treats Plus ....F....... 313 533-1701
  Redford *(G-13755)*
Purina Mills LLC ....E....... 517 322-0200
  Lansing *(G-9786)*
Reconserve of Michigan Inc ....G....... 269 965-0427
  Battle Creek *(G-1287)*

ANIMAL FEED: Wholesalers

Custom Blend Feeds Inc ....G....... 810 798-3265
  Bruce Twp *(G-2165)*
Holmquist Feed Mill ....G....... 906 446-3325
  Trenary *(G-16885)*
Purina Mills LLC ....E....... 517 322-0200
  Lansing *(G-9786)*

ANIMAL FOOD & SUPPLEMENTS: Alfalfa Or Alfalfa Meal

Darwin Sneller..G....... 989 977-3718
  Sebewaing *(G-15139)*
Prime Land Farm ....G....... 989 550-6120
  Harbor Beach *(G-7635)*

ANIMAL FOOD & SUPPLEMENTS: Bird Food, Prepared

Heath Manufacturing Company ....E....... 616 997-8181
  Coopersville *(G-3688)*
Markham Peat Corp ....F....... 800 851-7230
  Lakeview *(G-9643)*
Midwest Marketing Inc................................G....... 989 793-9393
  Saginaw *(G-14700)*

ANIMAL FOOD & SUPPLEMENTS: Buttermilk Emulsion

Jk Outdoors LLC ....G....... 906 863-2932
  Menominee *(G-11240)*

ANIMAL FOOD & SUPPLEMENTS: Dog

Free Rnge Ntrals Dog Trats Inc ....G....... 586 737-0797
  Sterling Heights *(G-16022)*
Happy Howies Inc ....G....... 313 537-7200
  Detroit *(G-4294)*
Videka LLC ....F....... 269 353-5536
  Kalamazoo *(G-9362)*

ANIMAL FOOD & SUPPLEMENTS: Dog & Cat

Wysong Medical Corporation ....F....... 989 631-0009
  Midland *(G-11424)*

Archer-Daniels-Midland Company ....G....... 517 647-4155
  Portland *(G-13637)*
Blendco LLC ....F....... 269 350-2914
  Kalamazoo *(G-9138)*
Nestle Purina Petcare Company ....E....... 888 202-4554
  Troy *(G-17274)*
Prestige Pet Products Inc ....G....... 248 615-1526
  Southfield *(G-15680)*
Pro Pet L L C ....G....... 248 930-2880
  Ferndale *(G-5582)*

ANIMAL FOOD & SUPPLEMENTS: Feed Premixes

Corunna Mills Feed LLC...............................G....... 989 743-3110
  Corunna *(G-3707)*

ANIMAL FOOD & SUPPLEMENTS: Feed Supplements

Kemin Industries Inc....................................F....... 248 869-3080
  Plymouth *(G-13211)*
Quality Liquid Feeds Inc ....G....... 616 784-2930
  Comstock Park *(G-3640)*

ANIMAL FOOD & SUPPLEMENTS: Kelp Meal & Pellets

Kilobar Compacting Mich LLC ....G....... 989 460-1981
  Bay City *(G-1371)*

ANIMAL FOOD & SUPPLEMENTS: Livestock

Holmquist Feed Mill ....G....... 906 446-3325
  Trenary *(G-16885)*
John A Van Den Bosch Co ....E....... 616 848-2000
  Holland *(G-8101)*
Meal and More Incorporated ....E....... 517 625-3186
  Morrice *(G-11625)*

ANIMAL FOOD & SUPPLEMENTS: Mineral feed supplements

Mar-Vo Mineral Company Inc ....G....... 517 523-2669
  Hillsdale *(G-7940)*

ANIMAL FOOD & SUPPLEMENTS: Pet, Exc Dog & Cat, Dry

Bake N Cakes LP ....G....... 517 337-2253
  Lansing *(G-9811)*
Elite Dog and Pet Supply LLC ....F....... 947 900-1101
  Southfield *(G-15553)*

ANIMAL FOOD & SUPPLEMENTS: Poultry

Chippewa Farm Supply LLC ....G....... 989 471-5523
  Spruce *(G-15885)*

ANIMAL FOOD & SUPPLEMENTS: Specialty, Mice & Other Pets

Wysong Medical Corporation ....F....... 989 631-0009
  Midland *(G-11424)*

ANIMAL FOOD/SUPPLEMENTS: Feeds Fm Meat/Meat/Veg Combnd Meals

Armada Grain Co ....E....... 586 784-5911
  Armada *(G-729)*

ANNEALING: Metal

Ajax Metal Processing Inc...........................C....... 586 497-7000
  Warren *(G-17695)*
Atmosphere Annealing LLC ....D....... 517 485-5090
  Lansing *(G-9808)*
Atmosphere Annealing LLC ....E....... 517 482-1374
  Lansing *(G-9809)*
Austemper Inc ....E....... 616 458-7061
  Grand Rapids *(G-6479)*
Cyprium Induction LLC ....G....... 586 884-4982
  Sterling Heights *(G-15976)*
Gerdau McSteel Atmsphere Annli ....F....... 517 782-0415
  Lansing *(G-9841)*
Hycal Corp..F....... 216 671-6161
  Gibraltar *(G-6171)*

PRODUCT SECTION — ART DESIGN SVCS

Mjc Industries Inc .... E 313 838-2800
  Detroit *(G-4461)*
Nor-Cote Inc ....E 586 756-1200
  Warren *(G-17944)*
Sun Steel Treating Inc ....D 877 471-0844
  South Lyon *(G-15459)*
Super Steel Treating Inc ....D 586 755-9140
  Warren *(G-18031)*
Western Engineered Products ....G 248 371-9259
  Lake Orion *(G-9638)*

ANODIZING SVC

Allan Tool & Machine Co Inc ....D 248 585-2910
  Troy *(G-16925)*
Almond Products Inc ....D 616 844-1813
  Spring Lake *(G-15802)*
Ano-Kal Company ....F 269 685-5743
  Plainwell *(G-13070)*
Bowers Aluminum ....G 269 251-8625
  Springfield *(G-15862)*
Changeover Integration LLC ....F 231 845-5320
  Ludington *(G-10532)*
Classic Metal Finishing Inc ....E 517 990-0011
  Jackson *(G-8842)*
Erbsloeh Alum Solutions Inc ....B 269 323-2565
  Portage *(G-13558)*
McNichols Polsg & Anodizing ....F 313 538-3470
  Redford *(G-13744)*
McNichols Polsg & Anodizing ....G 313 538-3470
  Redford *(G-13745)*
Professional Metal Finishers ....E 616 365-2620
  Grand Rapids *(G-7114)*

ANTENNAS: Radar Or Communications

R A Miller Industries Inc ....C 888 845-9450
  Grand Haven *(G-6349)*

ANTENNAS: Receiving

Accessories Wholesale Inc ....F 248 755-7465
  Pontiac *(G-13344)*
Dynamic Supply Solutions Inc ....G 248 987-2205
  Grosse Pointe Shores *(G-7561)*
Mobile Knowledge Group LLC ....G 248 625-3327
  Clarkston *(G-3052)*
Safari Circuits Inc ....C 269 694-9471
  Otsego *(G-12799)*

ANTI-GLARE MATERIAL

Rustop Technologies LLC ....E 517 223-5098
  Howell *(G-8512)*

ANTIBIOTICS

Aureogen Inc ....G 269 353-3805
  Kalamazoo *(G-9127)*

ANTIFREEZE

Recycling Fluid Technologies ....F 269 788-0488
  Battle Creek *(G-1288)*

ANTIQUE REPAIR & RESTORATION SVCS, EXC FURNITURE & AUTOS

A K Services Inc ....G 313 972-1010
  Detroit *(G-3972)*

ANTIQUE SHOPS

A K Services Inc ....G 313 972-1010
  Detroit *(G-3972)*

APPAREL ACCESS STORES

Border Line Rich Clothing LLC ....G 586 267-5251
  Clinton Township *(G-3188)*
Brintley Enterprises ....G 248 991-4086
  Detroit *(G-4074)*

APPAREL DESIGNERS: Commercial

Flavored Group LLC ....G 517 775-4471
  Lansing *(G-9760)*
Retro-A-Go-go LLC ....G 734 476-0300
  Howell *(G-8507)*

APPLIANCE PARTS: Porcelain Enameled

Lecreuset ....G 248 209-7025
  Auburn Hills *(G-957)*

Precision Stamping Co Inc ....E 517 546-5656
  Howell *(G-8500)*
Su-Dan Company ....D 248 651-6035
  Lake Orion *(G-9632)*

APPLIANCES, HOUSEHOLD OR COIN OPERATED: Laundry Dryers

Maytag Corporation ....C 269 923-5000
  Benton Harbor *(G-1572)*

APPLIANCES, HOUSEHOLD: Kitchen, Major, Exc Refrigs & Stoves

Cheap Recently Acquired Pdts ....G 616 272-4212
  Wyoming *(G-18857)*
Complete Kitchen Design LLC ....G 586 790-2800
  Clinton Township *(G-3206)*
J & E Appliance Company Inc ....G 248 642-9191
  Beverly Hills *(G-1665)*
Masco Building Products Corp ....G 313 274-7400
  Livonia *(G-10301)*
S A R Company LLC ....E 248 979-7590
  Novi *(G-12530)*

APPLIANCES, HOUSEHOLD: Laundry Machines, Incl Coin-Operated

Whirlpool Corporation ....G 269 923-7441
  Saint Joseph *(G-14976)*
Whirlpool Corporation ....C 269 849-0907
  Coloma *(G-3484)*
Whirlpool Corporation ....G 269 923-3009
  Benton Harbor *(G-1610)*

APPLIANCES, HOUSEHOLD: Refrigs, Mechanical & Absorption

Thetford Corporation ....C 734 769-6000
  Ann Arbor *(G-688)*
Whirlpool Corporation ....G 269 923-5000
  Benton Harbor *(G-1609)*
Whirlpool Corporation ....A 269 923-5000
  Benton Harbor *(G-1603)*
Whirlpool Corporation ....G 269 923-5000
  Benton Harbor *(G-1605)*
Whirlpool Corporation ....C 269 849-0907
  Coloma *(G-3484)*

APPLIANCES, HOUSEHOLD: Sewing Machines & Attchmnts, Domestic

Company Products Inc ....G 586 757-6160
  Warren *(G-17762)*

APPLIANCES: Household, NEC

Affordable Heat Llc ....G 517 673-0404
  Manitou Beach *(G-10926)*

APPLIANCES: Household, Refrigerators & Freezers

AGA Marvel ....G 616 754-5601
  Greenville *(G-7474)*
Flow Gas Misture Solutions Inc ....G 810 488-1492
  Marysville *(G-11087)*
Forma-Kool Manufacturing Inc ....E 586 949-4813
  Chesterfield *(G-2884)*
Maytag Corporation ....C 269 923-5000
  Benton Harbor *(G-1572)*
Scientemp Corp ....E 517 263-6020
  Adrian *(G-94)*
Whirlpool Corporation ....G 269 923-7400
  Benton Harbor *(G-1606)*

APPLIANCES: Major, Cooking

Delorean Associates Inc ....G 248 646-1930
  Bloomfield Hills *(G-1813)*

APPLIANCES: Small, Electric

E H Inc ....F 269 673-6456
  Allegan *(G-156)*
National Element Inc ....E 248 486-1810
  Brighton *(G-2040)*
Thoreson-Mc Cosh Inc ....E 248 362-0960
  Lake Orion *(G-9634)*

APPLICATIONS SOFTWARE PROGRAMMING

123go LLC ....G 734 773-0049
  Ann Arbor *(G-340)*
Adair Printing Company ....E 734 426-2822
  Dexter *(G-4721)*
Alfa Financial Software Inc ....D 855 680-7100
  Birmingham *(G-1717)*
Engtechnik Inc ....G 734 667-4237
  Canton *(G-2459)*
Ethnicemedia LLC ....G 248 762-8904
  Troy *(G-17097)*
Methodica Technologies LLC ....E 312 622-7697
  Troy *(G-17252)*
Real Green Systems Inc ....D 888 345-2154
  Commerce Township *(G-3570)*
Shadvin Industries LLC ....G 509 263-7128
  Bay City *(G-1400)*
Touch World Inc ....E 248 539-3700
  Farmington Hills *(G-5404)*

AQUARIUMS & ACCESS: Glass

Sciencekitwarhousecom ....G 800 992-8338
  Commerce Township *(G-3572)*

AQUARIUMS & ACCESS: Plastic

Blue Thumb Distributing Inc ....E 989 921-3474
  Saginaw *(G-14617)*
Rbl Products Inc ....F 313 873-8806
  Detroit *(G-4555)*

ARCHITECTURAL SVCS

Architectural Planners Inc ....E 248 674-1340
  Waterford *(G-18101)*
Eview 360 LLC ....E 248 306-5191
  Farmington Hills *(G-5239)*
Kreations Inc ....F 313 255-1230
  Detroit *(G-4367)*

ARCHITECTURAL SVCS: Engineering

Zoyes East Inc ....G 248 584-3300
  Ferndale *(G-5599)*

ARMATURE REPAIRING & REWINDING SVC

Heco Inc ....E 269 381-7200
  Kalamazoo *(G-9210)*
Industrial Elc Co Detroit Inc ....D 313 872-1133
  Detroit *(G-4315)*
Master Mfg Inc ....E 248 628-9400
  Oxford *(G-12899)*
McElroys Automotive Svc LLC ....G 248 427-0501
  Farmington Hills *(G-5312)*
Monarch Electric Service Co ....G 313 388-7800
  Melvindale *(G-11206)*
Rto Auto Repair Service ....G 586 779-9450
  Warren *(G-18000)*
Valley Truck Parts Inc ....D 616 241-5431
  Grand Rapids *(G-7303)*

ARMOR PLATES

Central Lake Armor Express Inc ....C 231 544-6090
  Central Lake *(G-2691)*

ARRESTERS & COILS: Lightning

Gary L Melchi Inc ....G 810 231-0262
  Whitmore Lake *(G-18537)*

ART & ORNAMENTAL WARE: Pottery

Make It Yours ....G 517 990-6799
  Jackson *(G-8943)*
Penzo America Inc ....G 248 723-0802
  Bloomfield Hills *(G-1850)*
Veldheer Tulip Garden Inc ....E 616 399-1900
  Holland *(G-8235)*

ART DESIGN SVCS

Alpha 21 LLC ....G 248 352-7330
  Southfield *(G-15476)*
Edwards Sign & Screen Printing ....G 989 725-2988
  Owosso *(G-12832)*
Valeo North America Inc ....E 248 619-8300
  Troy *(G-17428)*
Vinyl Graphix Inc ....G 586 774-1188
  Saint Clair Shores *(G-14890)*

Employee Codes: A=Over 500 employees, B=251-500
C=101-250, D=51-100, E=20-50, F=10-19, G=3-9

ART GALLERIES

ART GALLERIES
Art of Custom Framing Inc ....G....... 248 435-3726
  Troy *(G-16953)*
Electric Soul Tattoo and Fine ....G....... 616 930-3113
  Grand Rapids *(G-6668)*

ART GOODS & SPLYS WHOLESALERS
G-M Wood Products Inc ....D....... 231 652-2201
  Newaygo *(G-12081)*

ARTISTS' MATERIALS: Boards, Drawing
Markerboard People Inc ....E....... 517 372-1666
  Lansing *(G-9715)*

ARTISTS' MATERIALS: Canvas Board
E and K Arts and More ....G....... 855 285-0320
  Pontiac *(G-13363)*

ARTS & CRAFTS SCHOOL
Pewabic Society Inc ....E....... 313 626-2000
  Detroit *(G-4522)*

ARTWORK: Framed
Dandy Delights ....G....... 248 496-8523
  West Bloomfield *(G-18278)*
Leanne Sowa ....G....... 616 225-8858
  Cedar Springs *(G-2654)*
RecycledIps Com ....G....... 810 623-4498
  Brighton *(G-2063)*

ASBESTOS PRDTS: Friction Materials
Cobalt Friction Technologies ....F....... 734 274-3030
  Ann Arbor *(G-430)*

ASBESTOS PRDTS: Pipe Covering, Heat Insulatng Matl, Exc Felt
K-Value Insulation LLC ....G....... 248 688-5816
  Troy *(G-17191)*

ASBESTOS REMOVAL EQPT
Aerospace America Inc ....E....... 989 684-2121
  Bay City *(G-1319)*
Wonder Makers Environmental ....F....... 269 382-4154
  Kalamazoo *(G-9372)*

ASPHALT & ASPHALT PRDTS
Ajax Materials Corporation ....G....... 248 244-3300
  Troy *(G-16912)*
Ajax Paving Industries Inc ....C....... 248 244-3300
  Troy *(G-16913)*
Allied Asp Sealcoat & Repr LLC ....G....... 810 797-6080
  Flint *(G-5643)*
Angelos Crushed Concrete Inc ....G....... 586 756-1070
  Warren *(G-17706)*
Edw C Levy Co ....G....... 248 634-0879
  Davisburg *(G-3765)*
Edw C Levy Co ....B....... 313 429-2200
  Dearborn *(G-3835)*
Edw C Levy Co ....G....... 313 843-7200
  Detroit *(G-4202)*
Hess Asphalt Pav Sand Cnstr Co ......E....... 810 984-4466
  Clyde *(G-3413)*
Hhj Holdings Limited ....F....... 248 652-9716
  Troy *(G-17143)*
Nagle Paving Company ....F....... 248 553-0600
  Novi *(G-12486)*
Rite Way Asphalt Inc ....G....... 586 264-1020
  Sterling Heights *(G-16154)*
Saginaw Asphalt Paving Co ....D....... 989 755-8147
  Carrollton *(G-2590)*
Woodland Paving Co ....E....... 616 784-5220
  Comstock Park *(G-3652)*

ASPHALT COATINGS & SEALERS
Ameripave ....G....... 843 509-5502
  Romulus *(G-14248)*
Arnt Asphalt Sealing Inc ....D....... 269 927-1532
  Benton Harbor *(G-1530)*
Curbco Inc ....D....... 810 232-2121
  Flint *(G-5678)*
Detroit Cornice & Slate Co Inc ....E....... 248 398-7690
  Ferndale *(G-5544)*
Liveroof LLC ....E....... 616 842-1392
  Nunica *(G-12584)*
McElroy Metal Mill Inc ....D....... 269 781-8313
  Marshall *(G-11069)*
Michigan Paving and Mtls Co ....E....... 517 787-4200
  Jackson *(G-8956)*
Over Top Steel Coating LLC ....G....... 616 647-9140
  Comstock Park *(G-3632)*
Randys Seal Coat ....G....... 231 342-8031
  Traverse City *(G-16816)*
Ravenna Sealcoating Inc ....G....... 231 766-0571
  Muskegon *(G-11905)*
SM Andia Sealcoating LLC ....G....... 586 997-9752
  Shelby Township *(G-15334)*
UP Seal-Coating ....G....... 906 283-3433
  Gulliver *(G-7579)*

ASPHALT MINING & BITUMINOUS STONE QUARRYING SVCS
Eggers Excavating LLC ....F....... 989 695-5205
  Freeland *(G-6022)*
Mmgg Inc ....G....... 989 324-7319
  Freeland *(G-6026)*

ASPHALT MIXTURES WHOLESALERS
DLM Holding Group LLC ....G....... 269 465-3631
  Bridgman *(G-1925)*

ASPHALT PLANTS INCLUDING GRAVEL MIX TYPE
Bob-O-Link Associates LLC ....G....... 616 891-6939
  Grand Rapids *(G-6518)*
White Lake Excavating Inc ....E....... 231 894-6918
  Whitehall *(G-18513)*

ASSEMBLING SVC: Plumbing Fixture Fittings, Plastic
Fernco Inc ....C....... 810 503-9000
  Davison *(G-3782)*
Machine Guard & Cover Co ....G....... 616 392-8188
  Holland *(G-8131)*
Village & Cntry Wtr Trtmnt Inc ....F....... 810 632-7880
  Hartland *(G-7773)*

ASSOCIATIONS: Business
Grand Rapids Gravel Company ....E....... 616 538-9000
  Holland *(G-8055)*
Michigan Milk Producers Assn ....E....... 248 474-6672
  Novi *(G-12481)*

ASSOCIATIONS: Engineering
American Soc AG Blgcal Engners ....E....... 269 429-0300
  Saint Joseph *(G-14922)*

ASSOCIATIONS: Manufacturers'
Ram Electronics Inc ....F....... 231 865-3186
  Fruitport *(G-6069)*
SA Automotive Ltd LLC ....G....... 989 723-0425
  Owosso *(G-12854)*

ASSOCIATIONS: Real Estate Management
Mj-Hick Inc ....E....... 989 345-7610
  West Branch *(G-18331)*
Stroh Companies Inc ....G....... 313 446-2000
  Detroit *(G-4612)*

ASSOCIATIONS: Trade
Michigan Oil and Gas Assn ....G....... 517 487-0480
  Lansing *(G-9870)*

ATOMIZERS
Aftermarket Industries LLC ....G....... 810 229-3200
  Brighton *(G-1940)*
Airman Inc ....E....... 248 960-1354
  Brighton *(G-1941)*
American MSC Inc ....E....... 248 589-7770
  Troy *(G-16933)*
Benteler Automotive Corp ....C....... 248 364-7190
  Auburn Hills *(G-811)*
Burr Oak Tool Inc ....B....... 269 651-9393
  Sturgis *(G-16282)*
Busch Machine Tool Supply LLC .....G....... 989 798-4794
  Freeland *(G-6019)*

PRODUCT SECTION

Caflor Industries LLC ....G....... 734 604-1168
  Ypsilanti *(G-18931)*
Clover Industries Inc ....G....... 231 929-1660
  Traverse City *(G-16654)*
Division 6 Fbrction Instlltion ....F....... 586 200-3030
  Warren *(G-17780)*
Eagleburgmann Industries LP ....G....... 989 486-1571
  Midland *(G-11359)*
Ebinger Manufacturing Company .....F....... 248 486-8880
  Brighton *(G-1982)*
Emag LLC ....E....... 248 477-7440
  Farmington Hills *(G-5227)*
Emhart Teknologies LLC ....G....... 248 677-9693
  Troy *(G-17087)*
Esyntrk Industries LLC ....G....... 248 730-0640
  Orchard Lake *(G-12717)*
Faurecia Interior Systems Inc ....B....... 248 724-5100
  Auburn Hills *(G-889)*
Next Level Manufacturing LLC ....E....... 269 397-1220
  Jenison *(G-9064)*
Rayconnect Inc ....D....... 248 265-4000
  Rochester Hills *(G-14100)*
Rel Inc ....E....... 906 337-3018
  Calumet *(G-2413)*
Spring Air Co ....G....... 616 459-8234
  Grand Rapids *(G-7221)*
Timberwolf Furnace Co ....G....... 231 924-6654
  Grant *(G-7433)*
Venture Technology Groups Inc ......F....... 248 473-8450
  Novi *(G-12566)*
Vision Global Industries ....D....... 248 390-5805
  Macomb *(G-10649)*

AUCTION SVCS: Motor Vehicle
G Tech Sales LLC ....G....... 586 803-9393
  Sterling Heights *(G-16026)*

AUCTIONEERS: Fee Basis
Auction Masters ....G....... 586 576-7777
  Oak Park *(G-12593)*

AUDIO & VIDEO EQPT, EXC COMMERCIAL
BBC Communications Inc ....G....... 616 399-0432
  West Olive *(G-18347)*
Bluewater Tech Group Inc ....C....... 248 356-4399
  Wixom *(G-18624)*
Bluewater Tech Group Inc ....G....... 231 885-2600
  Mesick *(G-11269)*
Bluewater Tech Group Inc ....G....... 616 656-9380
  Grand Rapids *(G-6517)*
Charter Communication ....G....... 989 634-1093
  Bancroft *(G-1127)*
Charter Communication ....G....... 810 515-8418
  Flint *(G-5666)*
Charter Communication ....G....... 810 360-2748
  Brighton *(G-1964)*
Jeanies LLC ....G....... 313 412-8760
  Wyandotte *(G-18825)*
Lg Electronics USA Inc ....C....... 248 268-5100
  Troy *(G-17209)*
Logical Digital Audio Video ....G....... 734 572-0022
  Ann Arbor *(G-555)*
M10 Group Holding Company ....G....... 248 356-4399
  Southfield *(G-15639)*
Pro-Vision Solutions LLC ....D....... 616 583-1520
  Byron Center *(G-2292)*
Quantum Digital Group LLC ....G....... 888 408-3199
  Auburn Hills *(G-1009)*
Startech-Solutions LLC ....G....... 248 419-0650
  Southfield *(G-15708)*

AUDIO COMPONENTS
Clarion Corporation America ....E....... 248 991-3100
  Farmington Hills *(G-5203)*
Intaglio LLC ....E....... 616 243-3300
  Grand Rapids *(G-6848)*
Shinola/Detroit LLC ....C....... 888 304-2534
  Detroit *(G-4591)*

AUDIO ELECTRONIC SYSTEMS
Bluewater Tech Group Inc ....G....... 248 356-4399
  Farmington Hills *(G-5182)*
Cusack Music LLC ....E....... 616 546-8888
  Holland *(G-8008)*
Fast Cash ....G....... 269 966-0079
  Battle Creek *(G-1229)*
Mark MSA ....G....... 586 716-5941
  New Baltimore *(G-11988)*

Premium Sund Slutions Amer LLC .... G 734 259-6142
  Plymouth (G-13270)
Sargam International Inc .... F 310 855-9694
  Troy (G-17344)

AUDIO-VISUAL PROGRAM PRODUCTION SVCS

Best Netwrk Design & Assoc LLC .... E 313 680-2047
  Detroit (G-4052)
Verdoni Productions Inc .... G 989 790-0845
  Saginaw (G-14790)

AUDIOLOGICAL EQPT: Electronic

Bieri Hearing Instruments Inc .... G 989 793-2701
  Saginaw (G-14616)

AUTO & HOME SUPPLY STORES: Auto & Truck Eqpt & Parts

CC Industries LLC .... D 269 426-3342
  Sawyer (G-15108)
Horizon Global Corporation .... A 734 656-3000
  Plymouth (G-13192)
Joint Clutch & Gear Svc Inc .... E 734 641-7575
  Romulus (G-14292)
McElroys Automotive Svc LLC .... G 248 427-0501
  Farmington Hills (G-5312)
Nexteer Automotive Corporation .... B 989 757-5000
  Saginaw (G-14710)
Rto Auto Repair Service .... G 586 779-9450
  Warren (G-18000)
Ventra Evart LLC .... G 231 734-9000
  Evart (G-5128)

AUTO & HOME SUPPLY STORES: Auto Air Cond Eqpt, Sell/Install

Fenton Radiator & Garage Inc .... G 810 629-0923
  Fenton (G-5478)

AUTO & HOME SUPPLY STORES: Automotive Access

Alliance Automation LLC .... F 810 953-9539
  Flint (G-5642)
Auto-Masters Inc .... F 616 455-4510
  Grand Rapids (G-6480)

AUTO & HOME SUPPLY STORES: Automotive parts

751 Parts Company Inc .... F 231 845-1221
  Ludington (G-10524)
Afx Industries LLC .... G 810 966-4650
  Port Huron (G-13431)
Angstrom USA LLC .... E 313 295-0100
  Southfield (G-15488)
Axle of Dearborn Inc .... C 248 543-5995
  Ferndale (G-5529)
Canadian Amrcn Rstoration Sups .... E 248 853-8900
  Rochester Hills (G-13970)
Considine Sales & Marketing .... G 248 889-7887
  Highland (G-7889)
Ctc Fabricators LLC .... G 586 242-8809
  Clay (G-3118)
Dearborn Total Auto Svc Ctr .... F 313 291-6300
  Dearborn Heights (G-3922)
General Parts Inc .... G 989 686-3114
  Bay City (G-1360)
Hot Rod Holdings Inc .... E 517 424-0577
  Tecumseh (G-16505)
Howe Racing Enterprises Inc .... E 989 435-7080
  Beaverton (G-1425)
K & K Mfg Inc .... G 616 784-4286
  Sparta (G-15770)
Kurabe America Corporation .... F 248 939-5803
  Farmington Hills (G-5284)
Mark Land Industries Inc .... E 313 615-0503
  Dearborn (G-3868)
Mr Axle .... G 231 788-4624
  Muskegon (G-11878)
Nci Mfg Inc .... F 248 380-4151
  Livonia (G-10334)
Yanfeng US Auto Intr Systems I .... G 616 394-1567
  Holland (G-8254)

AUTO & HOME SUPPLY STORES: Batteries, Automotive & Truck

Batteries Plus .... G 269 925-7367
  Benton Harbor (G-1533)
G & L Powerup Inc .... G 586 200-2169
  Roseville (G-14409)
M & M Irish Enterprises Inc .... G 248 644-0666
  Birmingham (G-1733)

AUTO & HOME SUPPLY STORES: Speed Shops, Incl Race Car Splys

Lane Automotive Inc .... C 269 463-4113
  Watervliet (G-18182)

AUTO & HOME SUPPLY STORES: Trailer Hitches, Automotive

Erich Jaeger USA Inc .... G 734 404-5940
  Livonia (G-10199)

AUTO & HOME SUPPLY STORES: Truck Eqpt & Parts

Automotive Service Co .... F 517 784-6131
  Jackson (G-8818)
Carter Industries Inc .... D 510 324-6700
  Adrian (G-56)
Great Lakes Allied LLC .... G 231 924-5794
  White Cloud (G-18441)
Joes Trailer Manufacturing .... G 734 261-0050
  Livonia (G-10260)
UP Truck Center Inc .... E 906 774-0098
  Quinnesec (G-13677)

AUTO SPLYS & PARTS, NEW, WHSLE: Exhaust Sys, Mufflers, Etc

Technique Inc .... D 517 789-8988
  Jackson (G-9017)

AUTOCLAVES: Laboratory

Multi-Lab LLC .... F 616 846-6990
  Spring Lake (G-15838)

AUTOMATIC REGULATING CONTROL: Building Svcs Monitoring, Auto

Industrial Plant Svcs Nat LLC .... E 586 221-9017
  Macomb (G-10605)
Integrated Building Solutions .... F 616 889-3070
  Chesaning (G-2828)
Johnson Controls Inc .... D 248 276-6000
  Auburn Hills (G-945)
Sterling Security LLC .... E 248 809-9309
  Southfield (G-15709)

AUTOMATIC REGULATING CONTROLS: Appliance Regulators

System Controls Inc .... E 734 427-0440
  Livonia (G-10428)

AUTOMATIC REGULATING CONTROLS: Appliance, Exc Air-Cond/Refr

Precision Speed Equipment Inc .... C 269 651-4303
  Sturgis (G-16320)

AUTOMATIC REGULATING CONTROLS: Energy Cutoff, Residtl/Comm

Actalent Services LLC .... E 248 712-2750
  Troy (G-16905)
Energy Development Assoc LLC .... G 313 354-2644
  Dearborn (G-3836)
Kva Inc .... F 269 982-2888
  Saint Joseph (G-14943)
Rhombus Energy Solutions Inc .... G 313 406-3292
  Dearborn (G-3890)

AUTOMATIC REGULATING CONTROLS: Float, Residential Or Comm

Mercury Displacement Inds Inc .... D 269 663-8574
  Edwardsburg (G-5009)

AUTOMATIC REGULATING CONTROLS: Gas Burner, Automatic

Maxitrol Company .... G 269 432-3291
  Colon (G-3488)

AUTOMATIC REGULATING CONTROLS: Hardware, Environmental Reg

Swat Environmental Inc .... E 517 322-2999
  Lansing (G-9898)

AUTOMATIC REGULATING CONTROLS: Pneumatic Relays, Air-Cond

Edmore Tool & Grinding Inc .... F 989 427-3790
  Edmore (G-4992)

AUTOMATIC REGULATING CONTROLS: Refrig/Air-Cond Defrost

Therma-Tech Engineering Inc .... E 313 537-5330
  Redford (G-13778)

AUTOMATIC REGULATING CONTROLS: Thermocouples, Vacuum, Glass

Pyro Service Company .... G 248 547-2552
  Madison Heights (G-10812)

AUTOMATIC REGULATING CONTROLS: Vapor Heating

Inland Vapor of Michigan LLC .... D 734 237-4389
  Garden City (G-6098)

AUTOMATIC REGULATING CTRLS: Damper, Pneumatic Or Electric

Vibration Controls Tech LLC .... G 248 822-8010
  Troy (G-17440)

AUTOMATIC TELLER MACHINES

Atm International Services LLC .... E 734 524-9771
  Westland (G-18356)
Cornelius Systems Inc .... E 248 545-5558
  Clawson (G-3091)
Daler Inc .... G 989 752-1582
  Saginaw (G-14635)

AUTOMATIC VENDING MACHINES: Mechanisms & Parts

Kunzman & Associates West .... G 269 663-8978
  Decatur (G-3948)

AUTOMOBILE FINANCE LEASING

General Motors LLC .... A 313 972-6000
  Detroit (G-4257)

AUTOMOBILE RECOVERY SVCS

National Advnced Mblity Cnsrti .... G 734 205-5920
  Ann Arbor (G-590)

AUTOMOBILES & OTHER MOTOR VEHICLES WHOLESALERS

FCA Intrntional Operations LLC .... E 800 334-9200
  Auburn Hills (G-892)
General Motors LLC .... A 248 857-3500
  Pontiac (G-13375)
Global Fleet Sales LLC .... G 248 327-6483
  Southfield (G-15576)

AUTOMOBILES: Midget, Power Driven

RSM & Associates Co .... E 517 750-9330
  Jackson (G-9001)

AUTOMOTIVE & TRUCK GENERAL REPAIR SVC

Auto-Masters Inc .... F 616 455-4510
  Grand Rapids (G-6480)
Dearborn Total Auto Svc Ctr .... F 313 291-6300
  Dearborn Heights (G-3922)
Dts Enterprises Inc .... E 231 599-3123
  Ellsworth (G-5035)

AUTOMOTIVE & TRUCK GENERAL REPAIR SVC

Emergency Services LLC .... F 231 727-7400
  Muskegon *(G-11812)*
Fenton Radiator & Garage Inc .... G 810 629-0923
  Fenton *(G-5478)*
Front Line Services Inc .... F 989 695-6633
  Freeland *(G-6024)*
General Motors LLC .... G 734 481-3555
  Van Buren Twp *(G-17526)*
Harrys Steering Gear Repair .... G 586 677-5580
  Macomb *(G-10601)*
Hulet Body Co Inc .... F 313 931-6000
  Northville *(G-12230)*
Kirchhoff Automotive USA Inc .... F 248 247-3740
  Troy *(G-17194)*
Michigan Auto Bending Corp .... E 248 528-1150
  Madison Heights *(G-10781)*
Otr Performance Inc .... G 586 799-4375
  Macomb *(G-10624)*
Pitchford Bertie .... G 517 627-1151
  Grand Ledge *(G-6397)*
Techni CAM and Manufacturing .... F 734 261-6477
  Livonia *(G-10430)*

AUTOMOTIVE BATTERIES WHOLESALERS

Contemporary Amperex Tech USA .... G 248 289-6200
  Rochester Hills *(G-13984)*

AUTOMOTIVE BODY SHOP

Great Lakes Bath & Body Inc .... G 231 421-9160
  Traverse City *(G-16703)*
Superior Collision Inc .... G 231 946-4983
  Traverse City *(G-16846)*

AUTOMOTIVE BODY, PAINT & INTERIOR REPAIR & MAINTENANCE SVC

Autoform Development Inc .... F 616 392-4909
  Holland *(G-7966)*
Cartex Corporation .... D 734 857-5961
  Romulus *(G-14260)*
Lakeside Canvas & Upholstery .... G 231 755-2514
  Muskegon *(G-11857)*
Midwest Bus Corporation .... D 989 723-5241
  Owosso *(G-12844)*

AUTOMOTIVE COLLISION SHOPS

Eleven Mile Trck Frame Axle In .... E 248 399-7536
  Madison Heights *(G-10721)*

AUTOMOTIVE CUSTOMIZING SVCS, NONFACTORY BASIS

On The Side Sign Dsign Grphics .... G 810 266-7446
  Byron *(G-2255)*
Qp Acquisition 2 Inc .... A 248 594-7432
  Southfield *(G-15685)*

AUTOMOTIVE EMISSIONS TESTING SVCS

Diagnostic Systems Assoc Inc .... F 269 544-9000
  Kalamazoo *(G-9166)*
Intern Metals and Energy .... G 248 765-7747
  Jackson *(G-8909)*

AUTOMOTIVE GLASS REPLACEMENT SHOPS

Superior Auto Glass of Mich .... G 989 366-9691
  Houghton Lake *(G-8406)*

AUTOMOTIVE PAINT SHOP

Bdgn Corporation .... C 616 669-9040
  Hudsonville *(G-8570)*

AUTOMOTIVE PARTS, ACCESS & SPLYS

3d Polymers Inc .... F 248 588-5562
  Orchard Lake *(G-12715)*
751 Parts Company Inc .... F 231 845-1221
  Ludington *(G-10524)*
A I Flint LLC .... A 810 732-8760
  Flint *(G-5633)*
A&M Assembly and Machining LLC ...... E 313 369-9475
  Detroit *(G-3974)*
AAM Casting .... G 313 758-5968
  Southfield *(G-15469)*
AAM International Holdings Inc .... A 313 758-2000
  Detroit *(G-3976)*
AAM Mexico Holdings LLC .... D 313 758-2000
  Detroit *(G-3977)*
AAM Pwder Metal Components Inc ...... G 248 597-3800
  Royal Oak *(G-14501)*
AAM Travel Services LLC .... G 313 758-2000
  Detroit *(G-3978)*
Access Works Inc .... G 231 777-2537
  Muskegon *(G-11761)*
Accurate Automotive Engs Inc .... E 616 531-2050
  Grandville *(G-7361)*
Acutex Inc .... A 231 894-3200
  Whitehall *(G-18489)*
Adac Automotive Trim Inc .... E 616 957-0311
  Grand Rapids *(G-6426)*
Adac Plastics Inc .... E 616 957-0520
  Muskegon *(G-11763)*
Adac Plastics Inc .... E 616 957-0311
  Muskegon *(G-11764)*
Adient .... G 586 753-3072
  Warren *(G-17692)*
Adient US Entps Ltd Partnr .... G 734 254-5000
  Plymouth *(G-13115)*
Adient US LLC .... A 734 254-5000
  Plymouth *(G-13116)*
Adient US LLC .... B 734 254-5000
  Plymouth *(G-13117)*
Adient US LLC .... G 734 414-9215
  Plymouth *(G-13118)*
Adient US LLC .... G 510 771-2300
  Madison Heights *(G-10660)*
Adient US LLC .... E 269 968-3000
  Battle Creek *(G-1177)*
ADS Us Inc .... D 989 871-4550
  Millington *(G-11498)*
Advanced Assembly Products Inc .... G 248 543-2427
  Hazel Park *(G-7817)*
Advanced Auto Trends Inc .... E 248 628-4850
  Oxford *(G-12872)*
Advanced Auto Trends Inc .... E 248 628-6111
  Oxford *(G-12871)*
Advanced Vhcl Assemblies LLC .... A 248 299-7500
  Rochester Hills *(G-13944)*
Advantage Truck ACC Inc .... G 800 773-3110
  Ann Arbor *(G-356)*
ADW Industries Inc .... E 989 466-4742
  Alma *(G-233)*
Affinia Group Inc .... E 734 827-5400
  Ann Arbor *(G-357)*
Aftech Inc .... G 616 866-1650
  Grand Rapids *(G-6436)*
AGM Automotive Mexico LLC .... C 248 925-4152
  Farmington Hills *(G-5163)*
Agritek Industries Inc .... D 616 786-9200
  Holland *(G-7958)*
Air Lift Company .... E 517 322-2144
  Lansing *(G-9751)*
Airboss Flexible Products Co .... C 248 852-5500
  Auburn Hills *(G-776)*
Albion Automotive Limited .... G 313 758-2000
  Detroit *(G-3995)*
Allegan Tubular Products Inc .... D 269 673-6636
  Allegan *(G-146)*
Allison .... G 734 261-3735
  Garden City *(G-6092)*
Alma Products I LLC .... C 989 463-1151
  Alma *(G-237)*
Alpha Technology Corporation .... E 517 546-9700
  Howell *(G-8426)*
Aludyne Inc .... C 248 728-8700
  Southfield *(G-15478)*
Aludyne East Michigan LLC .... D 810 987-7633
  Port Huron *(G-13437)*
Aludyne International Inc .... C 248 728-8642
  Southfield *(G-15479)*
Aludyne Mexico LLC .... C 248 728-8642
  Southfield *(G-15480)*
Aludyne Montague LLC .... A 248 479-6455
  Montague *(G-11594)*
Aludyne North America Inc .... C 248 728-8642
  Southfield *(G-15481)*
Aludyne North America Inc .... C 248 728-8642
  Howell *(G-8427)*
Aludyne North America LLC .... D 248 728-8700
  Southfield *(G-15482)*
Aludyne North America LLC .... B 989 463-6966
  Alma *(G-238)*
Aludyne US LLC .... D 248 728-8700
  Southfield *(G-15483)*
Aludyne US LLC .... D 810 987-1112
  Port Huron *(G-13438)*
Aludyne West Michigan LLC .... E 248 728-8642
  Benton Harbor *(G-1528)*
Aludyne West Michigan LLC .... E 248 728-8642
  Stevensville *(G-16240)*
Amalgamated Uaw .... G 231 734-9286
  Evart *(G-5120)*
American Axle & Mfg Inc .... G 248 353-2155
  Southfield *(G-15485)*
American Axle & Mfg Inc .... G 248 475-3475
  Auburn Hills *(G-781)*
American Axle & Mfg Inc .... G 248 299-2900
  Rochester Hills *(G-13946)*
American Axle & Mfg Inc .... G 248 276-2328
  Auburn Hills *(G-782)*
American Axle Oxford .... G 248 361-6044
  Oxford *(G-12873)*
American Cooling Systems LLC .... E 616 954-0280
  Grand Rapids *(G-6452)*
American Lear .... F 616 252-3643
  Grand Rapids *(G-6453)*
American Mitsuba Corporation .... B 989 779-4962
  Mount Pleasant *(G-11679)*
American T-Mould LLC .... G 616 617-2422
  Grand Rapids *(G-6456)*
American Undercar .... F 989 235-1427
  Crystal *(G-3740)*
Anand Nvh North America Inc .... C 810 724-2400
  Imlay City *(G-8627)*
Android Indstrs-Dlta Township L .... D 517 322-0657
  Lansing *(G-9755)*
Android Industries-Wixom LLC .... F 248 255-5434
  Shelby Township *(G-15170)*
Android Industries-Wixom LLC .... E 248 732-0000
  Auburn Hills *(G-786)*
Angstrom Automotive Group LLC .... E 248 627-2871
  Ortonville *(G-12741)*
Anjun America Inc .... G 248 680-8825
  Auburn Hills *(G-787)*
Anrod Screen Cylinder Company .... E 989 872-2101
  Cass City *(G-2610)*
Antolin Interiors Usa Inc .... B 248 373-1749
  Auburn Hills *(G-789)*
Antolin Interiors Usa Inc .... A 517 548-0052
  Howell *(G-8429)*
Antolin Interiors Usa Inc .... D 248 567-4000
  Troy *(G-16938)*
Aptiv Corporation .... A 248 813-2000
  Troy *(G-16942)*
Aptiv Corporation .... C 248 724-5900
  Auburn Hills *(G-794)*
Aptiv Corporation .... A 248 813-3005
  Troy *(G-16943)*
Aptiv Intl Svcs Co LLC .... C 248 813-2000
  Troy *(G-16944)*
Aptiv Mexican Holdings US LLC .... C 248 813-2000
  Troy *(G-16945)*
Aptiv Services 3 (us) LLC .... C 248 813-2000
  Troy *(G-16946)*
Aptiv Services 5 Us LLC .... G 248 813-2000
  Troy *(G-16947)*
Aptiv Services Us LLC .... G 810 459-8809
  Auburn Hills *(G-795)*
Aptiv Services Us LLC .... G 248 724-5900
  Auburn Hills *(G-796)*
Aptiv Services Us LLC .... G 248 813-2000
  Hudsonville *(G-8567)*
Aptiv Services Us LLC .... G 330 373-7666
  Troy *(G-16948)*
Aptiv Services Us LLC .... G 248 813-2000
  Troy *(G-16949)*
Aptiv Trade MGT Svcs US LLC .... E 248 813-2000
  Troy *(G-16950)*
Arete Industries Inc .... F 231 582-4470
  Boyne City *(G-1882)*
Argent Tape & Label Inc .... G 734 582-9956
  Plymouth *(G-13125)*
Argo Ai LLC .... G 313 908-2447
  Allen Park *(G-190)*
Argonics Inc .... F 303 664-9467
  Gwinn *(G-7581)*
Artisans Cstm Mmory Mattresses .... F 989 793-3208
  Saginaw *(G-14605)*
Arvinmeritor Oe LLC .... G 248 435-1000
  Troy *(G-16957)*
Asmo Detroit Inc .... G 248 359-4440
  Novi *(G-12366)*
Asp Grede Acquisitionco LLC .... E 248 440-9515
  Southfield *(G-15493)*
Asp Hhi Acquisition Co Inc .... G 313 758-2000
  Detroit *(G-4030)*

Asp Hhi Holdings Inc A 248 597-3800
Royal Oak ***(G-14513)***

Aspra World Inc D 248 872-7030
Warren ***(G-17719)***

Atf Inc E 989 685-2468
Rose City ***(G-14362)***

Auria Albemarle LLC D 248 728-8000
Southfield ***(G-15495)***

Auria Solutions Intl Inc G 734 456-2800
Southfield ***(G-15496)***

Auria Solutions USA Inc A 248 728-8000
Southfield ***(G-15497)***

Auria St Clair LLC C 810 329-8400
Saint Clair ***(G-14813)***

Auto-Tech Plastics Inc G 586 783-0103
Mount Clemens ***(G-11628)***

Autocam Corp D 616 698-0707
Grand Rapids ***(G-6481)***

Autocam Corporation C 616 698-0707
Kentwood ***(G-9446)***

Autoform Development Inc F 616 392-4909
Holland ***(G-7966)***

Autoliv Asp Inc C 248 761-0081
Pontiac ***(G-13351)***

Autoliv Asp Inc C 248 475-9000
Auburn Hills ***(G-801)***

Autoliv Asp Inc C 248 475-9000
Auburn Hills ***(G-802)***

Autoliv Holding Inc B 248 475-9000
Auburn Hills ***(G-803)***

Automotive LLC C 248 712-1175
Southfield ***(G-15499)***

Automotive Exteriors LLC G 248 458-0702
Auburn Hills ***(G-807)***

Automotive International Svcs G 248 808-8112
Rochester Hills ***(G-13957)***

Autoneum North America Inc D 248 848-0100
Novi ***(G-12372)***

Autotech Engrg R&D USA Inc G 248 743-3400
Auburn Hills ***(G-808)***

Avl Powertrain Technologies G 734 414-9600
Plymouth ***(G-13132)***

Avl Properties Inc E 734 414-9600
Plymouth ***(G-13133)***

Avon Plastic Products Inc E 248 852-1000
Rochester Hills ***(G-13960)***

Bandit Utv Suspension G 586 419-9574
Columbus ***(G-3497)***

Barker Manufacturing Co E 269 965-2371
Battle Creek ***(G-1190)***

Barker Manufacturing Co F 269 965-2371
Battle Creek ***(G-1191)***

Bartec USA LLC E 586 685-1300
Sterling Heights ***(G-15944)***

Bdgn Corporation C 616 669-9040
Hudsonville ***(G-8570)***

BDS Company Inc F 517 279-2135
Coldwater ***(G-3421)***

Bearing Holdings LLC G 313 758-2000
Detroit ***(G-4046)***

Best Products Inc F 313 538-7414
Redford ***(G-13719)***

Bestop Inc F 586 268-0602
Sterling Heights ***(G-15945)***

Boesch Built LLC G 248 318-2136
Highland ***(G-7885)***

Boostbutton LLC G 734 223-0813
Whitmore Lake ***(G-18523)***

Borgwarner Arden LLC E 248 754-9200
Auburn Hills ***(G-814)***

Borgwarner Global Holding LLC A 248 754-9200
Auburn Hills ***(G-815)***

Borgwarner Inc G 248 371-0040
Auburn Hills ***(G-816)***

Borgwarner Inc G 231 779-7500
Cadillac ***(G-2316)***

Borgwarner Inc A 248 754-9200
Auburn Hills ***(G-817)***

Borgwarner Inc E 248 754-9600
Auburn Hills ***(G-818)***

Borgwarner Inc G 248 754-9200
Auburn Hills ***(G-819)***

Borgwarner Intl Svcs LLC F 248 813-2000
Auburn Hills ***(G-820)***

Borgwarner Inv Holdg Inc E 248 754-9200
Auburn Hills ***(G-821)***

Borgwarner Jersey Holdings LLC G 248 754-9200
Auburn Hills ***(G-822)***

Borgwarner Pds (usa) Inc B 248 754-9600
Auburn Hills ***(G-823)***

Borgwarner Pds Anderson LLC G 248 641-3045
Troy ***(G-16983)***

Borgwarner Tech Svcs LLC E 248 754-9200
Auburn Hills ***(G-824)***

Borgwarner Thermal Systems Inc C 269 781-1228
Marshall ***(G-11053)***

Borgwarner Transm Pdts LLC D 248 754-9200
Auburn Hills ***(G-825)***

Borgwarner US Holding LLC G 248 754-9200
Auburn Hills ***(G-827)***

Borgwarner USA Corporation E 248 813-2000
Auburn Hills ***(G-828)***

Borgwrner Emssions Systems LLC C 248 754-9200
Auburn Hills ***(G-829)***

Borgwrner Prplsion Systems LLC G 248 707-5224
Auburn Hills ***(G-831)***

Borgwrner Prplsion Systems LLC C 248 813-2000
Auburn Hills ***(G-832)***

Borgwrner Prplsion Systems LLC C 248 813-2000
Troy ***(G-16984)***

Bos Automotive Products Inc E 248 289-6072
Rochester Hills ***(G-13965)***

Bosch Auto Svc Solutions Inc D 586 574-2332
Warren ***(G-17739)***

Brake Team G 313 914-6000
Saint Clair Shores ***(G-14849)***

Brembo F 517 568-4398
Homer ***(G-8345)***

Brembo North America Inc D 734 416-1275
Plymouth ***(G-13138)***

Brose Harmon Road F 248 339-4702
Auburn Hills ***(G-834)***

Brose New Boston Inc G 248 340-1100
Auburn Hills ***(G-835)***

Brose New Boston Inc G 248 339-4000
Auburn Hills ***(G-836)***

Brose North America Inc C 248 339-4000
Auburn Hills ***(G-837)***

Brose North America Inc G 734 753-4902
New Boston ***(G-12005)***

Brugola Oeb Indstriale USA Inc F 734 468-0009
Plymouth ***(G-13139)***

Bullseye Power G 231 788-5209
Muskegon ***(G-11786)***

Burr Engineering & Dev Co G 269 966-3122
Battle Creek ***(G-1201)***

Bushings Inc F 248 650-0603
Rochester Hills ***(G-13968)***

Bwa Receivables Corporation G 248 754-9200
Auburn Hills ***(G-838)***

Bwi Chassis Dynamics NA Inc G 937 455-5308
Brighton ***(G-1956)***

Bwi North America Inc F 810 494-4584
Brighton ***(G-1957)***

C W A Manufacturing Co Inc E 810 686-3030
Mount Morris ***(G-11669)***

Cadillac Products Inc B 248 813-8200
Troy ***(G-16992)***

Cadillac Products Inc E 586 774-1700
Roseville ***(G-14382)***

Cadillac Products Inc F 989 766-2294
Rogers City ***(G-14208)***

Caea Auto Elctrnic Systems USA G 586 649-9036
Warren ***(G-17749)***

Cambridge Sharpe Inc F 248 613-5562
South Lyon ***(G-15429)***

Carr Engineering G 248 447-4109
Southfield ***(G-15517)***

Carter Industries Inc D 510 324-6700
Adrian ***(G-56)***

Cascade Engineering Inc G 616 975-4965
Grand Rapids ***(G-6554)***

Casco Products Corporation F 248 957-0400
Novi ***(G-12380)***

CC Industries LLC D 269 426-3342
Sawyer ***(G-15108)***

Century Qual Products G 734 728-0300
Van Buren Twp ***(G-17518)***

Chassix Blackstone Operat G 586 782-7311
Warren ***(G-17753)***

Check Technology Solutions LLC E 248 680-2323
Troy ***(G-17008)***

Chicago Blow Pipe Company F 773 533-6100
Marquette ***(G-11012)***

Cinnabar Engineering Inc F 810 648-2444
Sandusky ***(G-15057)***

Cipa Usa Inc E 810 982-3555
Port Huron ***(G-13464)***

Circuit Controls Corporation C 231 347-0760
Petoskey ***(G-12993)***

Citation Camden Cast Ctr LLC B 248 727-1800
Southfield ***(G-15523)***

Clio Massena LLC E 248 477-5148
Wixom ***(G-18634)***

Concen Grinding Inc G 517 787-8172
Jackson ***(G-8851)***

Concorde Inc F 248 391-8177
Auburn Hills ***(G-846)***

Conform Automotive LLC C 248 647-0400
Macomb ***(G-10585)***

Conform Automotive LLC F 248 647-0400
Grand Rapids ***(G-6592)***

Conform Automotive LLC D 517 322-0711
Lansing ***(G-9758)***

Conform Automotive LLC F 248 647-0400
Bingham Farms ***(G-1694)***

Continental Auto Systems Inc G 906 248-6700
Brimley ***(G-2103)***

Continental Auto Systems Inc G 248 267-9408
Troy ***(G-17023)***

Continntal Auto Systems US Inc D 248 764-6400
Troy ***(G-17024)***

Cooper-Standard Auto OH LLC G 248 596-5900
Northville ***(G-12203)***

Cooper-Standard Automotive Inc B 248 596-5900
Northville ***(G-12204)***

Cooper-Standard Automotive Inc D 734 542-6300
Livonia ***(G-10164)***

Cooper-Standard Fhs LLC C 248 596-5900
Northville ***(G-12205)***

Cooper-Standard Foundation Inc G 248 596-5900
Northville ***(G-12206)***

Cooper-Standard Holdings Inc G 248 596-5900
Northville ***(G-12207)***

Cosma International Amer Inc B 248 631-1100
Troy ***(G-17031)***

Creative Controls Inc E 248 577-9800
Madison Heights ***(G-10698)***

Crowne Group LLC G 734 855-4512
Livonia ***(G-10169)***

Cs Intermediate Holdco 1 LLC G 248 596-5900
Northville ***(G-12211)***

Csa Services Inc G 248 596-6184
Novi ***(G-12387)***

Cummins Inc G 248 573-1600
New Hudson ***(G-12049)***

Custom Pro Products Inc G 734 558-2070
Rockwood ***(G-14198)***

Custom Wheel Solutions G 248 547-9587
Grosse Pointe ***(G-7528)***

Daimay North America Auto Inc E 313 533-9680
Redford ***(G-13729)***

Dakkota Integrated Systems LLC G 517 694-6500
Holt ***(G-8307)***

Dana E 419 887-3000
Kalamazoo ***(G-9162)***

Dana Driveshaft Mfg LLC C 248 623-2185
Auburn Hills ***(G-857)***

Dana Incorporated C 269 567-1537
Kalamazoo ***(G-9163)***

Dana Limited G 586 467-1600
Warren ***(G-17774)***

Dana Limited G 810 329-2500
Saint Clair ***(G-14822)***

Dana Thermal Products LLC E 810 329-2500
Saint Clair ***(G-14823)***

Dana Thermal Products LLC E 810 329-2500
Saint Clair ***(G-14824)***

Davco Manufacturing LLC G 734 429-5665
Saline ***(G-15011)***

Dawson Manufacturing Company C 269 925-0100
Benton Harbor ***(G-1545)***

Dayco Products LLC G 989 775-0689
Mount Pleasant ***(G-11694)***

Dayco Products LLC G 517 439-0689
Hillsdale ***(G-7931)***

Dcd Idid Enterprise LLC E 517 424-0577
Tecumseh ***(G-16495)***

Dearborn Total Auto Svc Ctr F 313 291-6300
Dearborn Heights ***(G-3922)***

Dearborne Cummins F 313 843-6200
Dearborn ***(G-3825)***

Debron Industrial Elec LLC D 248 588-7220
Troy ***(G-17050)***

Delco Elec Overseas Corp C 248 813-2000
Troy ***(G-17051)***

Delphi E 248 813-2000
Troy ***(G-17052)***

Delphi Automotive Systems D 248 813-2000
Troy ***(G-17053)***

Employee Codes: A=Over 500 employees, B=251-500
C=101-250, D=51-100, E=20-50, F=10-19, G=3-9

2022 Harris Michigan
Industrial Directory

1189

Delphi Corp ....F.... 313 996-3429
Dearborn *(G-3827)*

Delphi Pwrtrain Tech Gen Prtnr ....E.... 248 813-2000
Troy *(G-17054)*

Delphi World Headquarters ....G.... 248 813-3045
Troy *(G-17055)*

Delta Gear Inc ....E.... 734 525-8000
Livonia *(G-10179)*

Delta Research Corporation ....E.... 734 261-6400
Livonia *(G-10180)*

Denso Sales Michigan Inc ....E.... 269 965-3322
Battle Creek *(G-1218)*

Design Usa Inc ....G.... 734 233-8677
Plymouth *(G-13154)*

Detroit Hitch Co ....F.... 248 379-0071
Clawson *(G-3094)*

Dgh Enterprises Inc ....E.... 269 925-0657
Benton Harbor *(G-1546)*

Dieomatic Incorporated ....F.... 269 966-4900
Battle Creek *(G-1219)*

Dieomatic Incorporated ....D.... 319 668-2031
Troy *(G-17061)*

Diesel Performance Products ....G.... 586 726-7478
Shelby Township *(G-15205)*

Diversified Machine Inc ....E.... 231 894-9562
Montague *(G-11595)*

Donnelly Corp ....G.... 231 652-8425
Newaygo *(G-12080)*

Dowding Industries Inc ....C.... 517 663-5455
Eaton Rapids *(G-4960)*

Dph LLC ....A.... 248 813-2000
Troy *(G-17065)*

Dph-Das Global (holdings) LLC ....C.... 248 813-2000
Troy *(G-17066)*

Dph-Das LLC ....C.... 248 813-2000
Troy *(G-17067)*

Dreal Inc ....F.... 248 813-2000
Troy *(G-17069)*

Dse Industries LLC ....G.... 313 530-6668
Macomb *(G-10589)*

Dst Industries Inc ....F.... 734 941-0300
Clinton *(G-3136)*

Dura Global Technologies Inc ....E.... 248 299-7500
Rochester Hills *(G-13997)*

Dura Shifter LLC ....F.... 248 299-7500
Rochester Hills *(G-13998)*

Durakon Industries Inc ....G.... 608 742-5301
Lapeer *(G-9928)*

Dus Operating Inc ....G.... 231 924-0930
Fremont *(G-6039)*

E & E Manufacturing Co Inc ....E.... 248 616-1300
Clawson *(G-3095)*

E-T-M Enterprises I Inc ....C.... 517 627-8461
Grand Ledge *(G-6389)*

Eagle Thread Verifier LLC ....G.... 586 764-8218
Sterling Heights *(G-15999)*

Eaton Corporation ....G.... 248 226-6200
Southfield *(G-15548)*

Eklund Holdings Inc ....C.... 231 777-2537
Muskegon *(G-11810)*

Elite Plastic Products Inc ....E.... 586 247-5800
Shelby Township *(G-15220)*

Elmwood Manufacturing Company ....G.... 313 571-1777
Detroit *(G-4204)*

Emma Sogoian Inc ....E.... 248 549-8690
Royal Oak *(G-14533)*

Emssons Faurecia Ctrl Systems ....G.... 248 724-5100
Auburn Hills *(G-880)*

Engineering Service of America ....D.... 248 357-3800
Southfield *(G-15557)*

Enovapremier LLC ....G.... 517 541-3200
Charlotte *(G-2751)*

Environmental Catalysts LLC ....F.... 248 813-2000
Troy *(G-17095)*

Ervins Group LLC ....E.... 248 203-2000
Bloomfield Hills *(G-1819)*

Erwin Quarder Inc ....D.... 616 575-1600
Grand Rapids *(G-6683)*

Etx Inc ....A.... 989 463-1151
Alma *(G-240)*

Etx Holdings Inc ....G.... 989 463-1151
Alma *(G-241)*

Euclid Industries Inc ....C.... 989 686-8920
Bay City *(G-1352)*

Excellence Manufacturing Inc ....E.... 616 456-9928
Grand Rapids *(G-6691)*

Expernced Prcsion McHining Inc ....G.... 989 635-2299
Marlette *(G-10981)*

Extang Corporation ....D.... 734 677-0444
Ann Arbor *(G-482)*

Fastime Racing Engines & Parts ....G.... 734 947-1600
Taylor *(G-16417)*

Faurecia Emssons Ctrl Tech USA ....B.... 734 947-1688
Taylor *(G-16418)*

Faurecia Exhaust Systems LLC ....E.... 248 409-3500
Auburn Hills *(G-888)*

Faurecia Intr Systems Sline LL ....G.... 734 429-0030
Saline *(G-15017)*

FCA North America Holdings LLC ....A.... 248 512-2950
Auburn Hills *(G-893)*

FCA US LLC ....B.... 734 478-5658
Dundee *(G-4819)*

FCA US LLC ....G.... 586 497-2500
Warren *(G-17802)*

Fcaus Dundee Engine Plant ....A.... 734 529-9256
Dundee *(G-4820)*

Federal Screw Works ....D.... 231 796-7664
Big Rapids *(G-1674)*

Federal-Mogul Chassis LLC ....F.... 248 354-7700
Southfield *(G-15560)*

Federal-Mogul Corporation ....E.... 248 354-7700
Southfield *(G-15561)*

Federal-Mogul Ignition LLC ....D.... 248 354-7700
Southfield *(G-15562)*

Federal-Mogul Motorparts LLC ....D.... 248 354-7700
Southfield *(G-15563)*

Federal-Mogul World Wide Inc ....D.... 248 354-7700
Southfield *(G-15568)*

Firefish Topco LLC ....D.... 248 299-7500
Auburn Hills *(G-898)*

Fisher & Company Incorporated ....G.... 248 280-0808
Troy *(G-17108)*

Fisher & Company Incorporated ....F.... 586 746-2280
Saint Clair Shores *(G-14859)*

Fisher & Company Incorporated ....F.... 586 746-2000
Sterling Heights *(G-16016)*

Fisher & Company Incorporated ....F.... 586 746-2101
Troy *(G-17110)*

Fisher Dynamics Corporation ....C.... 586 746-2000
Saint Clair Shores *(G-14860)*

Flex-N-Gate LLC ....C.... 586 759-8900
Warren *(G-17809)*

Flex-N-Gate Battle Creek LLC ....C.... 269 962-2982
Battle Creek *(G-1232)*

Flex-N-Gate Corporation ....G.... 586 773-0800
Warren *(G-17810)*

Flex-N-Gate Knshan Hldings LLC ....D.... 586 759-8900
Warren *(G-17811)*

Flextronics Automotive USA Inc ....D.... 248 853-5724
Coopersville *(G-3686)*

Ford Motor Company ....A.... 313 594-0050
Dearborn *(G-3843)*

Ford Motor Company ....F.... 734 523-3000
Livonia *(G-10214)*

Ford Motor Company ....F.... 313 594-4090
Allen Park *(G-194)*

Ford Motor Company ....A.... 313 322-3000
Dearborn *(G-3842)*

Ford Motor Company ....F.... 734 523-3000
Livonia *(G-10215)*

Ford Motor Company ....F.... 734 942-6248
Brownstown *(G-2146)*

Forged Tubular ....G.... 313 843-4870
Detroit *(G-4241)*

Forging Holdings LLC ....G.... 313 758-2000
Detroit *(G-4243)*

Formtech Inds Holdings LLC ....G.... 248 597-3800
Royal Oak *(G-14538)*

Fram Group Operations LLC ....G.... 800 890-2075
Rochester Hills *(G-14014)*

Frank Industries Inc ....E.... 810 346-3234
Brown City *(G-2137)*

Freudenberg N Amer Ltd Partnr ....G.... 734 354-5505
Plymouth *(G-13169)*

Freudenberg-Nok General Partnr ....C.... 734 451-0020
Plymouth *(G-13170)*

Fujikura Automotive Amer LLC ....E.... 248 957-0130
Farmington Hills *(G-5247)*

G P Dura ....F.... 248 299-7500
Rochester Hills *(G-14019)*

Gabriel Ride Control LLC ....E.... 248 247-7600
Farmington Hills *(G-5248)*

Gage Pattern & Model Inc ....D.... 248 361-6609
Madison Heights *(G-10729)*

Garage Grus Fdrl-Mgul Mtrparts ....F.... 800 325-8886
Southfield *(G-15572)*

Garrett Motion Inc ....A.... 734 359-5901
Plymouth *(G-13173)*

Gasket Holdings Inc ....G.... 248 354-7700
Southfield *(G-15573)*

Gates Corporation ....G.... 248 260-2300
Rochester Hills *(G-14020)*

General Motors China LLC ....G.... 313 556-5000
Detroit *(G-4254)*

General Motors Company ....F.... 248 249-6347
Brownstown *(G-2147)*

General Motors Company ....B.... 586 218-9240
Warren *(G-17824)*

General Motors Company ....A.... 313 667-1500
Detroit *(G-4255)*

General Motors Holdings LLC ....C.... 313 667-1500
Detroit *(G-4256)*

General Motors LLC ....G.... 810 635-5281
Swartz Creek *(G-16354)*

General Motors LLC ....G.... 734 481-3555
Van Buren Twp *(G-17526)*

General Motors LLC ....F.... 989 894-7210
Bay City *(G-1359)*

General Motors LLC ....F.... 586 342-2728
Sterling Heights *(G-16027)*

General Motors LLC ....F.... 517 885-6669
Lansing *(G-9761)*

General Motors LLC ....G.... 313 408-3987
Auburn Hills *(G-908)*

General Motors LLC ....A.... 313 972-6000
Detroit *(G-4257)*

General Motors LLC ....C.... 248 874-1737
Pontiac *(G-13374)*

General Motors LLC ....A.... 313 665-4919
Detroit *(G-4258)*

General Motors LLC ....A.... 313 556-5000
Detroit *(G-4260)*

Gentex Corporation ....C.... 616 772-1800
Zeeland *(G-19024)*

Gestamp Mason LLC ....B.... 517 244-8800
Mason *(G-11135)*

Gestamp North America Inc ....C.... 248 743-3400
Troy *(G-17130)*

Ghsp Inc ....B.... 616 842-5500
Holland *(G-8050)*

Ghsp Inc ....G.... 248 588-5095
Grand Haven *(G-6300)*

Ghsp Inc ....G.... 248 581-0890
Grand Haven *(G-6301)*

Ghsp Inc ....G.... 231 873-3300
Hart *(G-7752)*

Gissing North America LLC ....D.... 248 647-0400
Bingham Farms *(G-1697)*

Glassmaster Controls Co Inc ....E.... 269 382-2010
Kalamazoo *(G-9198)*

Global Automotive Systems LLC ....E.... 248 299-7500
Auburn Hills *(G-915)*

Global Fmi LLC ....D.... 810 964-5555
Fenton *(G-5481)*

Global Rollforming Systems LLC ....G.... 586 218-5100
Roseville *(G-14413)*

GM Components Holdings LLC ....C.... 870 594-0351
Detroit *(G-4265)*

GM Defense LLC ....C.... 313 462-8782
Detroit *(G-4266)*

GM Defense LLC ....E.... 586 359-8880
Milford *(G-11464)*

GM Laam Holdings LLC ....D.... 313 556-5000
Detroit *(G-4267)*

GMC (general Motors) ....G.... 517 265-4222
Adrian *(G-71)*

Grede Omaha LLC ....C.... 248 727-1800
Southfield *(G-15582)*

Ground Effects LLC ....C.... 810 250-5560
Flint *(G-5710)*

Ground Effects LLC ....B.... 810 250-5560
Flint *(G-5711)*

H & L Manufacturing Co ....C.... 269 795-5000
Middleville *(G-11308)*

Hadley Products Corporation ....C.... 616 530-1717
Grandville *(G-7385)*

Hamaton Inc ....F.... 248 308-3856
Wixom *(G-18674)*

Hamlin Tool & Machine Co Inc ....E.... 248 651-6302
Rochester Hills *(G-14029)*

Hanho America Co Ltd ....G.... 248 422-6921
Troy *(G-17137)*

Hanwha Advanced Mtls Amer LLC ....F.... 810 629-2496
Monroe *(G-11546)*

Harrys Steering Gear Repair ....G.... 586 677-5580
Macomb *(G-10601)*

Harvey S Freeman ....G.... 248 852-2222
West Bloomfield *(G-18287)*

Hayes Lmmerz Intrntnl-Grgia LL ....D.... 734 737-5000
Novi *(G-12431)*

PRODUCT SECTION — AUTOMOTIVE PARTS, ACCESS & SPLYS

Company	Code	Phone
Hayes-Albion Corporation Jackson (G-8900)	F	517 629-2141
Hdt Automotive Solutions LLC Livonia (G-10237)	G	810 359-5344
Heavy Duty Radiator LLC Taylor (G-16426)	E	800 525-0011
Henniges Auto Sling Systems N Auburn Hills (G-925)	C	248 340-4100
Hhi Formtech Fraser (G-5935)	E	586 415-2000
Hhi Formtech Industries LLC Royal Oak (G-14546)	D	248 597-3800
Hhi Funding II LLC Detroit (G-4299)	C	313 758-2000
Hhi Holdings LLC Detroit (G-4300)	G	313 758-2000
Hi-Lex America Incorporated Rochester Hills (G-14030)	B	248 844-0096
Hi-Lex Controls Incorporated Hudson (G-8551)	C	517 448-2752
Hitachi America Ltd Farmington Hills (G-5261)	G	248 477-5400
Hope Focus Detroit (G-4306)	E	313 494-4500
Hope Focus Detroit (G-4307)	C	313 494-5500
Hope Network West Michigan Paris (G-12934)	E	231 796-4801
Horizon Intl Group LLC Birmingham (G-1730)	G	734 341-9336
Howe Racing Enterprises Inc Beaverton (G-1425)	E	989 435-7080
HP Pelzer Auto Systems Inc Port Huron (G-13483)	B	810 987-4444
Huf North America Automoti Farmington Hills (G-5263)	G	248 213-4605
Humphrey Companies LLC Grandville (G-7389)	C	616 530-1717
Hydraulic Tubes & Fittings LLC Lapeer (G-9933)	E	810 660-8088
Hydro-Craft Inc Rochester Hills (G-14037)	G	248 652-8100
Ihi Detroit Turbo Engrg Ctr Novi (G-12437)	G	947 777-4976
IMC Products Inc Muskegon (G-11838)	F	231 759-3430
Inalfa Roof Systems Inc Warren (G-17859)	G	586 758-6620
Inoac Usa Inc Troy (G-17169)	E	248 619-7031
International Auto Components Troy (G-17171)	F	248 755-3928
Interntnal Auto Cmpnnts Group Alma (G-243)	C	989 620-7649
Interntnal Auto Cmpnnts Group Southfield (G-15606)	A	248 455-7000
Interntnal Auto Cmpnnts Group Port Huron (G-13488)	G	810 987-8500
Inteva Products LLC Troy (G-17173)	G	248 655-8886
Inteva Products LLC Troy (G-17174)	B	248 655-8886
Inteva Products Usa LLC Troy (G-17175)	C	248 655-8886
Inzi Controls Detroit LLC Rochester Hills (G-14041)	G	334 282-4237
Iochpe Holdings LLC Novi (G-12440)	D	734 737-5000
J G Kern Enterprises Inc Sterling Heights (G-16052)	D	586 531-9472
J L International Inc Romulus (G-14288)	C	734 941-0300
Jac Products Inc Shelby Township (G-15243)	G	586 254-1534
Jac Products Inc Pontiac (G-13385)	D	248 874-1800
Jay & Kay Manufacturing LLC Croswell (G-3730)	E	810 679-2333
Jay & Kay Manufacturing LLC Croswell (G-3731)	G	810 679-3079
Johnson Controls Inc Detroit (G-4341)	G	313 842-3300
Johnson Controls Inc Plymouth (G-13205)	G	734 254-7200
Johnson Controls Inc Holland (G-8102)	G	616 394-6818
Johnson Controls Inc Holland (G-8103)	G	616 392-5151
Joint Clutch & Gear Svc Inc Romulus (G-14292)	E	734 641-7575
Jomar Performance Products LLC Pontiac (G-13386)	G	248 322-3080
Jost International Corp Grand Haven (G-6322)	C	616 846-7700
Joyson Sfety Systems Acqstion Auburn Hills (G-946)	B	248 373-8040
Joyson Sfety Systems Acqstion Auburn Hills (G-947)	B	248 373-8040
Jsj Corporation Grand Haven (G-6323)	G	616 842-5500
Jtekt Automotive N Amer Inc Plymouth (G-13208)	A	734 454-1500
Kar-Bones Inc Detroit (G-4350)	G	313 582-5551
Katcon Global Usa Inc Auburn Hills (G-948)	D	248 239-1362
Kay Manufacturing Company Saint Joseph (G-14941)	E	269 408-8344
Kearsley Lake Terrace LLC Flint (G-5720)	G	810 736-7000
Kenona Industries LLC Grand Rapids (G-6885)	G	616 735-6228
Key Sfety Rstraint Systems Inc Auburn Hills (G-953)	A	586 726-3800
Kiekert Usa Inc Wixom (G-18692)	D	248 960-4100
Knoedler Manufacturers Inc Battle Creek (G-1264)	F	269 969-7722
Kongsberg Holding I Inc Novi (G-12456)	E	248 468-1300
Kongsberg Holding III Inc Novi (G-12457)	E	248 468-1300
Kongsberg Intr Systems II LLC Novi (G-12458)	D	956 465-4541
Kostal of America Inc Troy (G-17198)	C	248 284-6500
Ksr Industrial Corporation Southfield (G-15621)	G	248 213-7208
Kyklos Holdings Inc Detroit (G-4370)	G	313 758-2000
Kysor Industrial Corporation Cadillac (G-2341)	C	231 779-7500
L T C Roll & Engineering Co Fraser (G-5954)	F	586 465-1023
Lab Tool and Engineering Corp Spring Arbor (G-15793)	F	517 750-4131
Label Motorsports LLC Ada (G-25)	F	616 288-7710
Lacks Industries Inc Grand Rapids (G-6915)	C	616 698-6890
Lacks Industries Inc Grand Rapids (G-6921)	C	616 656-2910
Lakeland Finishing Corporation Grand Rapids (G-6923)	C	616 949-8001
Laserline Inc Plymouth (G-13219)	G	248 826-5041
LDM Technologies Inc Auburn Hills (G-956)	A	248 858-2800
Lear Corp Eeds and Interiors Southfield (G-15625)	G	248 447-1500
Lear Corporation Detroit (G-4382)	C	313 731-0840
Lear Corporation Southfield (G-15626)	G	313 852-7800
Lear Corporation Southfield (G-15627)	G	248 447-1500
Lear Corporation Rochester Hills (G-14050)	G	248 299-7100
Lear Corporation Traverse City (G-16741)	G	231 947-0160
Lear Mexican Seating Corp Southfield (G-15631)	G	248 447-1500
Lear Trim LP Southfield (G-15633)	C	248 447-1500
Leon Interiors Inc Holland (G-8125)	B	616 422-7557
Lippert Components Inc Sterling Heights (G-16075)	G	586 275-2107
Lippert Components Mfg Inc Chesaning (G-2829)	D	989 845-3061
Lj/Hah Holdings Corporation Auburn Hills (G-958)	C	248 340-4100
Longson International Corp Superior Township (G-16337)	G	734 657-8719
LSm Systems Engineering Inc Waterford (G-18135)	E	248 674-4967
M-Tek Inc Novi (G-12467)	F	248 553-1581
Mac Lean-Fogg Company Royal Oak (G-14558)	C	248 280-0880
Machine Tool & Gear Inc Clifford (G-3132)	B	989 761-7521
Machine Tool & Gear Inc Corunna (G-3711)	D	989 743-3936
Machinery Prts Specialists LLC Auburn (G-769)	G	989 662-7810
Magna Donnelly Corp Grand Haven (G-6332)	B	616 844-8257
Magna Electronics Tech Inc Holly (G-8283)	D	810 606-0145
Magna Extrors Intrors Amer Inc Troy (G-17221)	C	248 729-2400
Magna International Amer Inc Troy (G-17222)	B	248 729-2400
Magna Powertrain America Inc Lansing (G-9866)	G	517 316-1013
Magna Powertrain America Inc Troy (G-17223)	C	248 597-7811
Magna Powertrain Usa Inc Troy (G-17226)	E	248 680-4900
Magna Seating America Inc Auburn Hills (G-964)	D	248 243-7158
Magna Seating America Inc Novi (G-12469)	B	248 567-4000
Magna Seating America Inc Detroit (G-4415)	B	313 422-6000
Magna Seating America Inc Shelby Township (G-15268)	G	586 816-1400
Magna Services America Inc New Hudson (G-12061)	F	248 617-3200
Magna Services America Inc Saint Clair (G-14835)	D	816 602-5872
Magnesium Products America Inc Plymouth (G-13231)	B	734 416-8600
Magneti Marelli Tennessee LLC Southfield (G-15640)	A	248 418-3000
Mahle Inc Farmington Hills (G-5301)	E	248 305-8200
Mahle Aftermarket Inc Saint Johns (G-14906)	G	717 840-0678
Mahle Aftermarket Inc Farmington (G-5142)	D	248 347-9700
Mahle Behr USA Inc Ann Arbor (G-564)	G	336 768-3429
Mahle Behr USA Inc Troy (G-17233)	D	248 735-3623
Mahle Eng Components USA Inc Saint Johns (G-14907)	D	989 224-2384
Mahle Industries Incorporated Farmington Hills (G-5304)	G	248 305-8200
Mahle Industries Incorporated Farmington Hills (G-5305)	E	248 473-6511
Mahle Manufacturing MGT Inc Farmington Hills (G-5306)	G	248 735-3623
Mann + Hummel Usa Inc Kalamazoo (G-9265)	E	248 857-8501
Mann + Hummel Usa Inc Portage (G-13582)	F	269 329-3900
Marcella Manifolds Milford (G-11469)	F	248 259-6696
Marelli Holding USA LLC Southfield (G-15643)	A	248 418-3000
Mariah Industries Inc Troy (G-17237)	E	248 237-0404
Marley Precision Inc Battle Creek (G-1272)	G	269 963-7374
Martinrea Industries Inc Manchester (G-10886)	F	734 428-2400
Martinrea Metal Industries Inc Auburn Hills (G-969)	D	248 392-9700
Master Mfg Inc Oxford (G-12899)	E	248 628-9400
Maxable Inc Brooklyn (G-2127)	F	517 592-5638
Maxion Import LLC Novi (G-12474)	F	734 737-5000
Maxion Wheels Akron LLC Novi (G-12475)	C	330 794-2310
Mayne McKenney Southfield (G-15649)	G	248 709-5250
Mayne-Mc Kenney Inc Bloomfield Hills (G-1835)	E	248 258-0300
Mayser Usa Inc Van Buren Twp (G-17538)	D	734 858-1290
MD Investors Corporation Detroit (G-4425)	C	734 207-6200
Means Industries Inc Sterling Heights (G-16090)	F	586 826-8500
Means Industries Inc Southfield (G-15652)	F	989 754-1433

Employee Codes: A=Over 500 employees, B=251-500, C=101-250, D=51-100, E=20-50, F=10-19, G=3-9

AUTOMOTIVE PARTS, ACCESS & SPLYS — PRODUCT SECTION

Medallion Instrmnttion Systems ....C 616 847-3700
 Spring Lake *(G-15833)*
Melling Products North LLC ....D 989 588-6147
 Farwell *(G-5426)*
Meritor Industrial Pdts LLC ....G 888 725-9355
 Troy *(G-17248)*
Meritor Intl Holdings LLC ....G 248 435-1000
 Troy *(G-17249)*
Metaldyne LLC ....C 734 207-6200
 Detroit *(G-4433)*
Metaldyne Pwrtrain Cmpnnts Inc ......C 313 758-2000
 Detroit *(G-4434)*
Metalsa Structural Pdts Inc ....A 248 669-3704
 Sterling Heights *(G-16092)*
Metalsa Structural Pdts Inc ....D 248 669-3704
 Novi *(G-12479)*
Metavation LLC ....E 248 351-1000
 Troy *(G-17251)*
Michigan Auto Comprsr Inc ....A 517 796-3200
 Parma *(G-12938)*
Micron Holdings Inc ....A 616 698-0707
 Kentwood *(G-9465)*
Milan Metal Systems LLC ....C 734 439-1546
 Milan *(G-11446)*
Miller Industrial Products Inc ....E 517 783-2756
 Jackson *(G-8962)*
Mint Steel Forge Inc ....F 248 276-9000
 Lake Orion *(G-9620)*
Misc Products ....D 586 263-3300
 Macomb *(G-10617)*
Mistequay Group Ltd ....F 989 752-7700
 Saginaw *(G-14702)*
Mistequay Group Ltd ....E 989 846-1000
 Standish *(G-15893)*
Mj Mfg Co ....G 810 744-3840
 Burton *(G-2241)*
MNP Corporation ....A 586 254-1320
 Utica *(G-17504)*
Model-Matic Inc ....E 248 528-1680
 Troy *(G-17264)*
Montaplast North America Inc ....E 248 353-5553
 Auburn Hills *(G-973)*
Mpg Holdco I Inc ....G 734 207-6200
 Plymouth *(G-13250)*
Mpt Driveline Systems ....F 248 680-3786
 Troy *(G-17268)*
MSP Industries Corporation ....C 248 628-4150
 Oxford *(G-12904)*
Nafta Benchmarking Center ....G 248 335-0366
 Pontiac *(G-13400)*
National Fleet Service LLC ....E 313 923-1799
 Detroit *(G-4476)*
National Ordnance Auto Mfg LLC ......G 248 853-8822
 Auburn Hills *(G-980)*
Nationwide Design Inc ....F 586 254-5493
 Sterling Heights *(G-16113)*
Nbhx Trim USA Corporation ....F 616 785-9400
 Walker *(G-17644)*
Nbhx Trim USA Corporation ....B 616 785-9400
 Comstock Park *(G-3627)*
Neapco Holdings LLC ....C 248 699-6500
 Farmington Hills *(G-5333)*
Nexteer Automotive Corporation ....B 989 754-1920
 Saginaw *(G-14711)*
Nexteer Automotive Corporation ....C 989 757-5000
 Saginaw *(G-14714)*
Nexteer Automotive Corporation ....B 989 757-5000
 Saginaw *(G-14716)*
Nexteer Automotive Corporation ....D 989 757-5000
 Saginaw *(G-14717)*
Nexteer Automotive Corporation ....E 989 757-5000
 Saginaw *(G-14718)*
Nexteer Automotive Corporation ....A 248 340-8200
 Auburn Hills *(G-982)*
Nitrex Inc ....E 517 676-6370
 Mason *(G-11147)*
Nitto Inc ....D 732 276-1039
 Romulus *(G-14310)*
Nitto Inc ....F 734 729-7800
 Romulus *(G-14311)*
Nitto Inc ....D 248 449-2300
 Novi *(G-12489)*
Nodel-Co ....F 248 543-1325
 Ferndale *(G-5573)*
Norma Michigan Inc ....G 248 373-4300
 Lake Orion *(G-9622)*
Norma Michigan Inc ....C 248 373-4300
 Auburn Hills *(G-984)*
North Amer Fuel Systems Rmnfct .....C 616 541-1100
 Grand Rapids *(G-7048)*

Novares US LLC ....G 616 554-3555
 Grand Rapids *(G-7051)*
Nr Racing LLC ....G 248 767-0421
 Commerce Township *(G-3558)*
Nu Con Corporation ....E 734 525-0770
 Livonia *(G-10341)*
Nyx LLC ....D 734 261-4324
 Livonia *(G-10344)*
Nyx LLC ....D 734 261-7535
 Livonia *(G-10347)*
Nyx LLC ....C 734 462-2385
 Livonia *(G-10343)*
O Flex Group Inc ....G 248 505-0322
 Clarkston *(G-3053)*
Oakley Sub Assembly Intl Inc ....F 810 720-4444
 Flint *(G-5741)*
Obr Control Systems Inc ....G 248 672-3339
 Livonia *(G-10351)*
Offsite Manufacturing Inc ....G 586 598-8850
 Chesterfield *(G-2918)*
Ogura Corporation ....G 586 749-1900
 Madison Heights *(G-10791)*
Oiles America Corporation ....C 734 414-7400
 Plymouth *(G-13254)*
Orotex Corporation ....C 248 773-8630
 Novi *(G-12499)*
Oxford Forge Inc ....G 248 628-1303
 Oxford *(G-12907)*
P T M Corporation ....B 586 725-2211
 Ira *(G-8707)*
P T M Corporation ....G 586 725-2733
 Ira *(G-8708)*
Patent Lcnsing Clringhouse LLC ....F 248 299-7500
 Rochester Hills *(G-14080)*
PCI Procal Inc ....F 989 358-7070
 Alpena *(G-311)*
Pcm US Steering Holding LLC ....E 313 556-5000
 Auburn Hills *(G-994)*
Peckham Vocational Inds Inc ....D 517 316-4478
 Lansing *(G-9725)*
Pelzer ....G 248 250-6161
 Troy *(G-17296)*
Performnce Assmbly Sltions LLC .....E 734 466-6380
 Livonia *(G-10363)*
Piston Automotive LLC ....B 313 541-8674
 Redford *(G-13756)*
Piston Automotive LLC ....A 313 541-8789
 Detroit *(G-4526)*
Piston Automotive LLC ....D 313 541-8789
 Van Buren Twp *(G-17547)*
Piston Group LLC ....B 248 226-3976
 Southfield *(G-15674)*
Plasan Carbon Composites Inc ....D 616 965-9450
 Wixom *(G-18730)*
Plasan Carbon Composites Inc ....D 616 965-9450
 Walker *(G-17647)*
Plastic Omnium Auto Inrgy USA ....G 248 743-5700
 Troy *(G-17305)*
Plastic Omnium Auto Inrgy USA ....C 517 265-1100
 Adrian *(G-88)*
Plastic Plate LLC ....E 616 455-5240
 Grand Rapids *(G-7090)*
Plastic Plate LLC ....D 616 698-3678
 Kentwood *(G-9470)*
Plastic Plate LLC ....D 616 949-6570
 Kentwood *(G-9471)*
Pontiac Coil Inc ....C 248 922-1100
 Clarkston *(G-3057)*
Power Cool Systems Inc ....G 317 852-4193
 Brighton *(G-2053)*
Precision Karting Tech LLC ....G 248 924-3272
 Wixom *(G-18733)*
Prestige Engrg Rsrces Tech Inc ....F 586 777-1820
 Warren *(G-17975)*
Pridgeon & Clay Inc ....A 616 241-5675
 Grand Rapids *(G-7106)*
Product Assembly Group LLC ....G 586 549-8601
 Troy *(G-17317)*
Propride Inc ....G 810 695-1127
 Grand Blanc *(G-6258)*
Propride Inc ....G 810 962-0219
 Grand Blanc *(G-6259)*
Prototech Laser Inc ....F 586 948-3032
 Chesterfield *(G-2933)*
Prototypes Plus Inc ....G 269 751-7141
 Hamilton *(G-7605)*
Pullman Company ....F 734 243-8000
 Monroe *(G-11571)*
Purem Novi Inc ....C 248 778-5231
 Novi *(G-12518)*

Quality Customs Cons LLC ....F 313 564-9327
 Inkster *(G-8673)*
Quality Engineering Company ....F 248 351-9000
 Wixom *(G-18738)*
Quality Spring/Togo Inc ....C 517 278-2391
 Coldwater *(G-3449)*
Quality Steel Products Inc ....E 248 684-0555
 Milford *(G-11484)*
Ralco Industries Inc ....D 248 853-3200
 Auburn Hills *(G-1012)*
Ralco Industries Inc ....E 248 853-3200
 Auburn Hills *(G-1013)*
Rapp & Son Inc ....G 734 283-1000
 Wyandotte *(G-18836)*
Rassey Industries Inc ....E 586 803-9500
 Shelby Township *(G-15315)*
Ravenna Casting Center Inc ....G 231 853-0300
 Ravenna *(G-13692)*
Recardo North America Inc ....D 248 364-3818
 Plymouth *(G-13280)*
Regency Plastics - Ubly Inc ....D 989 658-8504
 Ubly *(G-17482)*
Remy International Inc ....G 765 778-6499
 Rochester *(G-13925)*
Rieke-Arminak Corp ....E 248 631-5450
 Bloomfield Hills *(G-1857)*
Rivas Inc ....D 586 566-0326
 Sterling Heights *(G-16155)*
Riverside Tank & Mfg Corp ....E 810 329-7143
 Saint Clair *(G-14842)*
Rivian Automotive LLC ....D 734 855-4350
 Plymouth *(G-13285)*
Robert Bosch LLC ....G 248 921-9054
 Novi *(G-12527)*
Robert Bosch LLC ....G 734 979-3412
 Plymouth *(G-13288)*
Roush Enterprises Inc ....A 734 779-7006
 Livonia *(G-10391)*
Roush Enterprises Inc ....A 313 294-8200
 Allen Park *(G-205)*
Roush Industries Inc ....G 734 779-7016
 Livonia *(G-10392)*
Roush Manufacturing Inc ....D 734 805-4400
 Farmington *(G-5146)*
Roush Manufacturing Inc ....C 734 779-7006
 Livonia *(G-10395)*
Royce Corporation ....G 586 758-1500
 Warren *(G-17999)*
Rugged Liner Inc ....E 989 725-8354
 Owosso *(G-12853)*
Ryder Integrated Logistics Inc ....F 517 492-4446
 Lansing *(G-9789)*
S H Leggitt Company ....B 269 781-3901
 Marshall *(G-11073)*
S K D L P ....G 517 849-2166
 Jonesville *(G-9101)*
SA Automotive Ltd LLC ....G 989 723-0425
 Owosso *(G-12854)*
Saf-Holland Inc ....G 616 396-6501
 Holland *(G-8186)*
Sam Brown Sales LLC ....E 248 358-2626
 Farmington *(G-5147)*
Sanhua Automotive Usa Inc ....G 248 244-8870
 Auburn Hills *(G-1026)*
Sas Automotive Usa Inc ....E 248 606-1152
 Sterling Heights *(G-16164)*
Schwab Industries Inc ....F 586 566-8090
 Shelby Township *(G-15325)*
Schwarzerobitec Inc ....G 616 278-3971
 Grand Rapids *(G-7185)*
Servotech Industries Inc ....G 734 697-5555
 Taylor *(G-16471)*
Sharp Model Co ....D 586 752-3099
 Bruce Twp *(G-2182)*
Shyft Group Inc ....A 517 543-6400
 Novi *(G-12536)*
Shyft Group Inc ....E 517 543-6400
 Charlotte *(G-2767)*
Sitronic North America Corp ....D 248 939-5910
 Southfield *(G-15705)*
Skilled Manufacturing Inc ....C 231 941-0290
 Traverse City *(G-16834)*
Skokie Castings LLC ....D 248 727-1800
 Southfield *(G-15706)*
SL America Corporation ....D 586 731-8511
 Auburn Hills *(G-1034)*
Smartpat PLC ....G 248 854-2233
 Birmingham *(G-1750)*
Sort-Tek Insptn Systems Inc ....G 248 273-5200
 Troy *(G-17363)*

Southstern Mich Accsory Ctr 2 ....E 248 519-9848
Troy ***(G-17366)***
Spectrum Cubic Inc ....D 616 451-0784
Kentwood ***(G-9480)***
Spicer Heavy Axle & Brake Inc ....G 269 567-1000
Kalamazoo ***(G-9342)***
Stackpole Pwrtrn Intl USA LLC ....G 248 481-4600
Auburn Hills ***(G-1037)***
Stant USA Corp ....C 765 827-8104
Rochester Hills ***(G-14119)***
Steering Solutions - Plant 3 ....F 989 757-5000
Saginaw ***(G-14767)***
Steinbauer Performance LLC ....G 704 587-0856
Dowagiac ***(G-4797)***
Strattec Security Corporation ....G 248 649-9742
Auburn Hills ***(G-1040)***
Stromberg-Carlson Products Inc ....F 231 947-8600
Traverse City ***(G-16843)***
Su-Dan Plastics Inc ....C 248 651-6035
Lake Orion ***(G-9633)***
Supply Line International LLC ....F 248 242-7140
Novi ***(G-12551)***
Swiss American Screw Pdts Inc ....E 734 397-1600
Canton ***(G-2529)***
Sxs Gear ....G 810 265-7219
Flint ***(G-5774)***
Synchronous Manufacturing Inc ....F 517 764-6930
Michigan Center ***(G-11296)***
Takata Americas ....A 336 547-1600
Auburn Hills ***(G-1044)***
Tata Autocomp Systems Limited ....G 248 680-4608
Troy ***(G-17385)***
Teamtech Motorsports Safety ....G 989 792-4880
Saginaw ***(G-14773)***
Teksid Aluminum North Amer Inc ....E 248 304-4001
Southfield ***(G-15719)***
Teksid Inc ....E 734 846-5492
Farmington ***(G-5153)***
Telmar Manufacturing Company ....G 810 577-7050
Fenton ***(G-5506)***
Tenneco Automotive Oper Co Inc ....C 517 522-5520
Grass Lake ***(G-7447)***
Tenneco Automotive Oper Co Inc ....G 517 522-5525
Jackson ***(G-9018)***
Tenneco Automotive Oper Co Inc ....F 734 243-4615
Monroe ***(G-11580)***
Tenneco Inc ....G 734 254-1122
Plymouth ***(G-13313)***
Tenneco Inc ....G 248 354-7700
Southfield ***(G-15720)***
Tenneco Inc ....G 248 886-0900
Waterford ***(G-18170)***
Tg Fluid Systems USA Corporati ....G 248 486-8950
Brighton ***(G-2079)***
Th Plastics Inc ....D 269 496-8495
Mendon ***(G-11223)***
Thermal Solutions Mfg ....D 734 655-7145
Livonia ***(G-10432)***
Thk Rhythm Auto Mich Corp ....B 517 647-4121
Portland ***(G-13642)***
TI Fluid Systems ....D 586 948-6036
New Haven ***(G-12039)***
TI Fluid Systems ....G 248 393-4525
Auburn Hills ***(G-1053)***
TI Group Auto Systems LLC ....G 989 672-1200
Caro ***(G-2581)***
TI Group Auto Systems LLC ....G 989 673-7727
Caro ***(G-2582)***
TI Group Auto Systems LLC ....G 810 364-3277
Marysville ***(G-11108)***
TI Group Auto Systems LLC ....G 586 948-6006
Chesterfield ***(G-2956)***
TI Group Auto Systems LLC ....G 859 235-5420
Auburn Hills ***(G-1056)***
TI Group Auto Systems LLC ....G 248 475-4663
Auburn Hills ***(G-1057)***
Tianhai Electric N Amer Inc ....D 248 987-2100
Pontiac ***(G-13419)***
Tomar Inc ....G 313 382-2293
Ecorse ***(G-4988)***
Torqstorm Superchargers ....G 616 706-5580
Wyoming ***(G-18911)***
Total Flow Products Inc ....G 248 588-4490
Troy ***(G-17396)***
Toyo Seat USA Corporation ....C 810 724-0300
Imlay City ***(G-8648)***
Tractech Inc ....E 248 226-6800
Southfield ***(G-15725)***
Tramec Sloan LLC ....E 616 395-5600
Holland ***(G-8224)***
Transform Automotive LLC ....G 586 826-8500
Shelby Township ***(G-15355)***
Transform Automotive LLC ....G 586 826-8500
Sterling Heights ***(G-16207)***
Transpak Inc ....E 586 264-2064
Sterling Heights ***(G-16209)***
Trident Lighting LLC ....D 616 957-9500
Grand Rapids ***(G-7276)***
Trimas Corporation ....B 248 631-5450
Bloomfield Hills ***(G-1869)***
Trin Inc ....E 260 587-9282
Plymouth ***(G-13324)***
Tristone Flowtech USA Inc ....E 248 560-1724
Southfield ***(G-15726)***
TRW Atomotive Holdg Mexico LLC ....D 734 855-2600
Livonia ***(G-10446)***
TRW East Inc ....D 734 855-2600
Livonia ***(G-10448)***
TRW Occupant Safety Systems ....G 586 752-1409
Bruce Twp ***(G-2184)***
TRW Odyssey Mexico LLC ....D 734 855-2600
Livonia ***(G-10449)***
TRW Safety Systems Mexico LLC ....G 734 855-2600
Livonia ***(G-10450)***
Ufp Technologies Inc ....D 616 949-8100
Grand Rapids ***(G-7294)***
Unifilter Inc ....F 248 476-5100
Novi ***(G-12563)***
Unique Fabricating Inc ....A 248 853-2333
Auburn Hills ***(G-1068)***
Unique-Chardan Inc ....D 419 636-6900
Auburn Hills ***(G-1070)***
United Machining Inc ....C 586 323-4300
Sterling Heights ***(G-16216)***
United Machining Inc ....G 586 323-4300
Macomb ***(G-10646)***
United Metal Technology Inc ....E 517 787-7940
Jackson ***(G-9029)***
US Engine Production MI Inc ....G 989 823-3800
Vassar ***(G-17584)***
US Farathane Holdings Corp ....E 586 991-6922
Sterling Heights ***(G-16219)***
Usm Holdings LLC ....F 313 758-2000
Detroit ***(G-4657)***
Usm Holdings LLC II ....F 313 758-2000
Detroit ***(G-4658)***
Usui International Corporation ....E 734 354-3626
Plymouth ***(G-13328)***
Valeo Inc ....A 248 619-8300
Troy ***(G-17425)***
Valeo North America Inc ....C 248 209-8253
Auburn Hills ***(G-1077)***
Valeo Switches & Dete ....E 248 619-8300
Troy ***(G-17431)***
Veet Industries Inc ....F 586 776-3000
Warren ***(G-18053)***
Vehicle Research and Dev ....G 586 504-1163
Almont ***(G-270)***
Vehma International Amer Inc ....C 248 631-1100
Troy ***(G-17434)***
Vehma International Amer Inc ....D 248 631-2800
Troy ***(G-17436)***
Vehma International Amer Inc ....D 248 585-4800
Troy ***(G-17435)***
Ventra Fowlerville LLC ....B 517 223-5900
Fowlerville ***(G-5857)***
Ventra Grand Rapids 5 LLC ....B 616 222-3296
Grand Rapids ***(G-7310)***
Veoneer Inc ....A 248 223-0600
Southfield ***(G-15736)***
Vibracoustic North America LP ....E 269 637-2116
South Haven ***(G-15421)***
Visiocorp Holding USA LLP ....G 810 388-2403
Marysville ***(G-11112)***
Visions Car & Truck Acc ....G 269 342-2962
Kalamazoo ***(G-9364)***
Visteon Corporation ....D 734 718-8927
Canton ***(G-2539)***
Visteon Electronics Corp ....D 800 847-8366
Van Buren Twp ***(G-17559)***
Visteon Global Electronics Inc ....G 800 847-8366
Van Buren Twp ***(G-17560)***
Vitesco Technologies Usa LLC ....C 313 583-5980
Dearborn ***(G-3911)***
Vitesco Technologies Usa LLC ....B 248 209-4000
Auburn Hills ***(G-1080)***
Vortek ....G 248 767-2992
Pinckney ***(G-13058)***
Vsp Logis Inc ....G 734 957-9880
Van Buren Twp ***(G-17563)***
Wabco Air Comprsr Holdings Inc ....F 248 260-9032
Auburn Hills ***(G-1083)***
Wagner Castings Company ....F 248 952-2500
Troy ***(G-17444)***
Walbro LLC ....D 989 872-2131
Cass City ***(G-2622)***
Waldrons Antique Exhaust ....G 269 467-7185
Centreville ***(G-2700)***
Walther Trowal GMBH & Co KG ....F 616 871-0031
Grand Rapids ***(G-7324)***
Warren Chassix ....F 248 728-8700
Southfield ***(G-15743)***
Warren Screw Products Inc ....C 586 757-1280
Warren ***(G-18061)***
Webasto Roof Systems Inc ....B 248 997-5100
Plymouth ***(G-13337)***
Webasto Roof Systems Inc ....B 248 299-2000
Rochester Hills ***(G-14144)***
Webasto Roof Systems Inc ....C 248 997-5100
Rochester Hills ***(G-14145)***
West Mich Auto Stl & Engrg Inc ....E 616 560-8198
Belding ***(G-1464)***
West Michigan Gage Inc ....F 616 735-0585
Walker ***(G-17657)***
Xileh Holding Inc ....G 248 340-4100
Auburn Hills ***(G-1090)***
Yanfeng US Auto Intr Systems I ....G 616 394-1567
Holland ***(G-8254)***
Yanfeng US Auto Intr Systems I ....G 734 254-5000
Plymouth ***(G-13341)***
Yanfeng US Auto Intr Systems I ....C 248 319-7333
Novi ***(G-12570)***
Yanfeng US Auto Intr Systems I ....D 248 319-7333
Novi ***(G-12571)***
Yanfeng US Auto Intr Systems I ....G 616 283-1349
Holland ***(G-8255)***
Yanfeng US Auto Intr Systems I ....G 586 354-2101
Harrison Township ***(G-7735)***
Yanfeng US Auto Intr Systems I ....G 616 392-5151
Holland ***(G-8256)***
Yanfeng US Auto Intr Systems I ....G 734 289-4841
Monroe ***(G-11593)***
Yanfeng US Auto Intr Systems I ....G 810 987-2434
Port Huron ***(G-13541)***
Young Diversified Industries ....G 248 353-1867
Southfield ***(G-15745)***
ZF Active Safety & Elec US LLC ....D 586 843-2100
Livonia ***(G-10479)***
ZF Active Safety & Elec US LLC ....B 248 478-7210
Farmington Hills ***(G-5417)***
ZF Active Safety US Inc ....G 906 248-3882
Brimley ***(G-2105)***
ZF Active Safety US Inc ....G 248 478-7210
Farmington Hills ***(G-5418)***
ZF Active Safety US Inc ....G 956 491-9036
Howell ***(G-8545)***
ZF Active Safety US Inc ....G 517 223-8330
Fowlerville ***(G-5858)***
ZF Active Safety US Inc ....G 810 750-1036
Fenton ***(G-5515)***
ZF Active Safety US Inc ....G 248 863-2412
Saginaw ***(G-14797)***
ZF Auto Holdings US Inc ....G 734 855-2600
Livonia ***(G-10484)***
ZF Axle Drives Marysville LLC ....B 810 989-8702
Marysville ***(G-11114)***
ZF Chassis Components LLC ....E 810 245-2000
Lapeer ***(G-9970)***
ZF Lemforder Corp ....F 810 245-7136
Lapeer ***(G-9972)***
ZF North America Inc ....B 734 416-6200
Northville ***(G-12272)***
ZF Passive Safety S Africa Inc ....E 734 855-2600
Livonia ***(G-10488)***
ZF Passive Safety US Inc ....B 734 855-2600
Livonia ***(G-10489)***
ZF Passive Safety US Inc ....G 586 232-7200
Washington ***(G-18094)***
ZF Passive Sfety Systems US In ....G 586 752-1409
Romeo ***(G-14241)***
ZF Passive Sfety Systems US In ....A 586 232-7200
Livonia ***(G-10490)***
ZF Passive Sfety Systems US In ....G 586 781-5511
Washington ***(G-18095)***
ZF String Active Safety US Inc ....G 734 855-2600
Livonia ***(G-10491)***
ZF TRW Auto Holdings Corp ....A 734 855-2600
Livonia ***(G-10492)***
Zynp International Corp ....E 734 947-1000
Romulus ***(G-14345)***

Employee Codes: A=Over 500 employees, B=251-500
C=101-250, D=51-100, E=20-50, F=10-19, G=3-9
2022 Harris Michigan
Industrial Directory
1193

AUTOMOTIVE PARTS: Plastic

Adduxi .... E 248 564-2000
Rochester Hills *(G-13942)*
Advanced Composite Tech Inc .... G 248 709-9097
Rochester *(G-13889)*
Aktis Engrg Solutions Inc .... G 313 450-2420
Southfield *(G-15474)*
Antolin St Clair LLC .... C 810 329-1045
China *(G-2968)*
Bdgn Corporation .... G 616 669-9040
Hudsonville *(G-8570)*
Blue Fire Manufacturing LLC .... E 248 714-7166
Waterford *(G-18104)*
Cadillac Products Inc .... F 989 766-2294
Rogers City *(G-14208)*
Capsonic Automotive Inc .... G 248 754-1100
Auburn Hills *(G-839)*
Carcostics Tech Ctr N Amer Inc .... G 248 251-1737
Howell *(G-8434)*
CIE Automotive Usa Inc .... D 734 793-5320
Shelby Township *(G-15187)*
Creative Repair Solutions LLC .... G 586 615-1517
Macomb *(G-10586)*
Crescent Machining Inc .... G 248 541-7010
Oak Park *(G-12601)*
Dag Technology Inc .... G 586 276-9310
Grand Blanc *(G-6240)*
Dana Incorporated .... G 734 629-1200
Novi *(G-12392)*
Dupearl Technology LLC .... G 248 390-9609
Bloomfield Hills *(G-1816)*
Enovapremier LLC .... G 517 541-3200
Charlotte *(G-2751)*
Fischer America Inc .... C 248 276-1940
Auburn Hills *(G-899)*
Flex-N-Gate Detroit LLC .... B 586 759-8092
Detroit *(G-4236)*
Flex-N-Gate Shelby LLC .... C 586 251-2300
Shelby Township *(G-15227)*
Global Automotive Products Inc .... F 734 589-6179
Romulus *(G-14278)*
IAC Mexico Holdings Inc .... A 248 455-7000
Southfield *(G-15598)*
IAC Plymouth LLC .... E 734 207-7000
Plymouth *(G-13195)*
Illinois Tool Works Inc .... G 248 589-2500
Troy *(G-17161)*
Ims/Chinatool Jv LLC .... F 734 466-5151
Livonia *(G-10247)*
Inoac Interior Systems LLC .... F 248 488-7610
Farmington Hills *(G-5270)*
Interntnal Auto Cmpnnts Group ..... G 734 456-2800
Plymouth *(G-13198)*
Interntnal Auto Cmpnnts Group ..... G 586 795-7800
Sterling Heights *(G-16051)*
Jvis - Usa LLC .... F 586 884-5700
Shelby Township *(G-15248)*
Jvis Manufacturing LLC .... C 586 405-1950
Clinton Township *(G-3268)*
Kyrie Enterprises LLC .... F 248 549-8690
Royal Oak *(G-14555)*
Lacks Exterior Systems LLC .... E 616 949-6570
Grand Rapids *(G-6911)*
Lacks Exterior Systems LLC .... C 616 949-6570
Grand Rapids *(G-6912)*
Lacks Exterior Systems LLC .... C 616 949-6570
Grand Rapids *(G-6913)*
Macauto Usa Inc .... E 248 556-5256
Troy *(G-17218)*
Machine Tool & Gear Inc .... B 989 761-7521
Clifford *(G-3132)*
Machine Tool & Gear Inc .... D 989 743-3936
Corunna *(G-3711)*
Markdom of America Inc .... G 716 681-8306
Eaton Rapids *(G-4966)*
Mathson Group Inc .... G 248 821-5478
Troy *(G-17241)*
McKechnie Vhcl Cmpnnts USA Inc .. F 586 491-2600
Roseville *(G-14439)*
Moon Roof Corporation America .... E 586 772-8730
Roseville *(G-14446)*
Mubea Inc .... G 248 393-9600
Auburn Hills *(G-976)*
Noble Polymers LLC .... F 616 975-4800
Grand Rapids *(G-7045)*
North American Assembly LLC ...... E 248 335-6702
Auburn Hills *(G-985)*
North American Mold LLC .... E 248 335-6702
Auburn Hills *(G-986)*
Novares Corporation US Inc .... C 248 449-6100
Livonia *(G-10338)*
Otr Performance Inc .... G 586 799-4375
Macomb *(G-10624)*
Pierburg Pump Tech US LLC .... D 864 688-1322
Auburn Hills *(G-996)*
Pioneer Plastics Inc .... E 586 262-0159
Warren *(G-17966)*
Plastic Plate LLC .... G 616 455-5288
Grand Rapids *(G-7091)*
Pmd Automotive LLC .... G 248 732-7554
Pontiac *(G-13407)*
Preferred Plastics Inc .... G 269 685-5873
Plainwell *(G-13091)*
Proper Group International LLC ..... G 586 779-8787
Warren *(G-17983)*
Rocktech Systems LLC .... E 586 330-9031
Chesterfield *(G-2940)*
SA Automotive Ltd .... C 517 521-4205
Webberville *(G-18247)*
Schwintek Inc .... G 269 445-9999
Cassopolis *(G-2633)*
Sheffler Mfg Intl Lgistics LLC .... E 248 409-0960
Clarkston *(G-3065)*
Svrc Industries Inc .... G 989 280-3038
Saginaw *(G-14768)*
Tecnoma LLC .... E 248 354-8888
Southfield *(G-15718)*
Tepso Gen-X Plastics LLC .... G 248 869-2130
Wixom *(G-18770)*
Thunder Bay Pattern Works Inc ..... F 586 783-1126
Clinton Township *(G-3376)*
Tnj Manufacturing LLC .... E 586 251-1900
Shelby Township *(G-15353)*
Toyoda Gosei North Amer Corp ..... C 248 280-2100
Troy *(G-17397)*
Tribar Technologies Inc .... E 248 516-1600
Wixom *(G-18779)*
Truck Acquisition Inc .... G 877 875-4376
Ann Arbor *(G-699)*
US Farathane Holdings Corp .... G 248 754-7000
Shelby Township *(G-15360)*
US Farathane Holdings Corp .... C 780 246-1034
Auburn Hills *(G-1074)*
Williamston Products Inc .... D 517 655-2131
Williamston *(G-18585)*
Williamston Products Inc .... C 517 655-2273
Williamston *(G-18586)*
Williamston Products Inc .... D 989 723-0149
Owosso *(G-12867)*
Woco Tech Usa Inc .... G 248 385-2854
Novi *(G-12569)*
Yapp USA Auto Systems Inc .... C 248 817-5653
Troy *(G-17456)*
Yapp USA Auto Systems Inc .... G 248 404-8696
Romulus *(G-14343)*

AUTOMOTIVE PRDTS: Rubber

Airboss Flexible Products Co .... C 248 852-5500
Auburn Hills *(G-776)*
Changan US RES & Dev Ctr Inc ...... G 734 259-6440
Plymouth *(G-13145)*
Evans Industries Inc .... G 313 259-2266
Troy *(G-17100)*
Henniges Auto Holdings Inc .... B 248 340-4100
Auburn Hills *(G-924)*
Hutchinson Sealing Systems Inc .... D 248 375-3720
Auburn Hills *(G-932)*
Inoac Interior Systems LLC .... F 248 488-7610
Farmington Hills *(G-5270)*
Korens .... G 248 817-5188
Rochester Hills *(G-14046)*
Northern Michigan Leather .... G 231 675-4712
Charlevoix *(G-2722)*
Northern Tire Inc .... F 906 486-4463
Ishpeming *(G-8779)*

AUTOMOTIVE RADIATOR REPAIR SHOPS

Fenton Radiator & Garage Inc .... G 810 629-0923
Fenton *(G-5478)*

AUTOMOTIVE REPAIR SHOPS: Diesel Engine Repair

Cummins Inc .... G 313 843-6200
Dearborn *(G-3823)*
Cummins Inc .... G 989 752-5200
Saginaw *(G-14633)*
Detroit Diesel Corporation .... A 313 592-5000
Detroit *(G-4144)*
Detroit Diesel Corporation .... F 313 592-8256
Redford *(G-13730)*

AUTOMOTIVE REPAIR SHOPS: Electrical Svcs

Creative Power Systems Inc .... F 313 961-2460
Detroit *(G-4108)*
Dearborn Total Auto Svc Ctr .... F 313 291-6300
Dearborn Heights *(G-3922)*
Precision Race Services Inc .... G 248 634-4010
Davisburg *(G-3771)*
Solutions For Industry Inc .... F 517 448-8608
Hudson *(G-8562)*

AUTOMOTIVE REPAIR SHOPS: Engine Rebuilding

Chesterfield Engines Inc .... G 586 949-5777
Chesterfield *(G-2859)*
D & S Engine Specialist Inc .... F 248 583-9240
Clawson *(G-3093)*
Daniel Pruitoff .... G 616 392-1371
Holland *(G-8013)*

AUTOMOTIVE REPAIR SHOPS: Engine Repair

Creek Diesel Services Inc .... F 800 974-4600
Grand Rapids *(G-6611)*
Kyrie Enterprises LLC .... F 248 549-8690
Royal Oak *(G-14555)*

AUTOMOTIVE REPAIR SHOPS: Fuel System Repair

Howell Engine Developments Inc .... F 810 765-5100
Cottrellville *(G-3720)*

AUTOMOTIVE REPAIR SHOPS: Machine Shop

Busche Southfield Inc .... C 248 357-5180
Southfield *(G-15513)*
Chesterfield Engines Inc .... G 586 949-5777
Chesterfield *(G-2859)*
Daniel Pruitoff .... G 616 392-1371
Holland *(G-8013)*
Experienced Concepts Inc .... F 586 752-4200
Armada *(G-735)*
General Parts Inc .... G 989 686-3114
Bay City *(G-1360)*
Midwest Fabricating Inc .... G 734 921-3914
Taylor *(G-16447)*
Mjc Tool & Machine Co Inc .... G 586 790-4766
Clinton Township *(G-3303)*
Mtm Machine Inc .... G 586 443-5703
Sterling Heights *(G-16108)*
New Concept Products Inc .... G 269 679-5970
Schoolcraft *(G-15125)*
Oilpatch Machine Tool Inc .... G 989 772-0637
Mount Pleasant *(G-11728)*
Peak Manufacturing Inc .... E 517 769-6900
Pleasant Lake *(G-13104)*
Pitchford Bertie .... G 517 627-1151
Grand Ledge *(G-6397)*
Three-Dimensional Services Inc ..... C 248 852-1333
Rochester Hills *(G-14125)*
Vochaska Engineering .... G 269 637-5670
South Haven *(G-15423)*

AUTOMOTIVE REPAIR SHOPS: Muffler Shop, Sale/Rpr/Installation

Dearborn Total Auto Svc Ctr .... F 313 291-6300
Dearborn Heights *(G-3922)*

AUTOMOTIVE REPAIR SHOPS: Springs, Rebuilding & Repair

Beattie Spring & Welding Svc .... G 810 239-9151
Flint *(G-5653)*

AUTOMOTIVE REPAIR SHOPS: Trailer Repair

A and D Design Electronics .... G 989 493-1884
Auburn *(G-762)*
Ajax Trailers Inc .... F 586 757-7676
Warren *(G-17696)*
D & W Management Company Inc .. F 586 758-2284
Warren *(G-17770)*

PRODUCT SECTION

AUTOMOTIVE SPLYS/PARTS, NEW, WHOL: Body Rpr/Paint Shop Splys

Lupa R A and Sons Repair ....G....... 810 346-3579
  Marlette (G-10983)
Transport Trailers Co ....G....... 269 543-4405
  Fennville (G-5443)

AUTOMOTIVE REPAIR SHOPS: Truck Engine Repair, Exc Indl

Midwest Tractor & Equipment Co..........F....... 231 269-4100
  Buckley (G-2207)

AUTOMOTIVE REPAIR SVC

Anh Enterprises LLC ....F....... 313 887-0800
  Taylor (G-16379)
Benlee Inc ....E....... 586 791-1830
  Romulus (G-14257)
Clydes Frame & Wheel Service ....F....... 248 338-0323
  Pontiac (G-13354)
Detroit Radiator Corporation ....C....... 800 525-0011
  Taylor (G-16401)
Energy Products Inc ....E....... 248 545-7700
  Madison Heights (G-10722)
Energy Products Inc ....E....... 248 866-5622
  Troy (G-17090)
Kern Auto Sales and Svc LLC ....F....... 734 475-2722
  Chelsea (G-2818)
Kustom Creations Inc ....G....... 586 997-4141
  Sterling Heights (G-16068)
Line-X of Livonia ....G....... 734 237-3115
  Livonia (G-10280)
Muskegon Brake & Distrg Co LLC ....E....... 231 733-0874
  Norton Shores (G-12313)
Valley Truck Parts Inc ....D....... 616 241-5431
  Grand Rapids (G-7303)

AUTOMOTIVE REPAIR SVCS, MISCELLANEOUS

RB Oil Enterprises LLC ....G....... 734 354-0700
  Plymouth (G-13277)

AUTOMOTIVE SPLYS & PARTS, NEW, WHOL: Auto Servicing Eqpt

Magna Mirrors America Inc ....G....... 616 786-7000
  Holland (G-8136)
Pti Qlity Cntnment Sltions LLC...............C....... 313 365-3999
  Detroit (G-4541)
Single Source Inc ....G....... 765 825-4111
  Flat Rock (G-5630)

AUTOMOTIVE SPLYS & PARTS, NEW, WHOLESALE: Alternators

Nabco Inc...E....... 231 832-2001
  Reed City (G-13796)

AUTOMOTIVE SPLYS & PARTS, NEW, WHOLESALE: Clutches

Ogura Corporation ....C....... 586 749-1900
  Chesterfield (G-2919)

AUTOMOTIVE SPLYS & PARTS, NEW, WHOLESALE: Engines/Eng Parts

GKN Driveline North Amer Inc ....B....... 248 296-7000
  Auburn Hills (G-911)
Illinois Tool Works Inc ....G....... 248 589-2500
  Troy (G-17161)

AUTOMOTIVE SPLYS & PARTS, NEW, WHOLESALE: Filters, Air & Oil

Unifilter Inc ....F....... 248 476-5100
  Novi (G-12563)

AUTOMOTIVE SPLYS & PARTS, NEW, WHOLESALE: Hardware

Ardy Inc...G....... 231 845-7318
  Ludington (G-10527)
Axle of Dearborn Inc ....C....... 248 543-5995
  Ferndale (G-5529)

AUTOMOTIVE SPLYS & PARTS, NEW, WHOLESALE: Pumps, Oil & Gas

Vortex Industries Inc............................F....... 855 867-8399
  Plymouth (G-13335)

AUTOMOTIVE SPLYS & PARTS, NEW, WHOLESALE: Radiators

D & B Heat Transfer Pdts Inc ....F....... 616 827-0028
  Grand Rapids (G-6625)

AUTOMOTIVE SPLYS & PARTS, NEW, WHOLESALE: Seat Belts

Craig Assembly Inc..............................C....... 810 326-1374
  Saint Clair (G-14821)

AUTOMOTIVE SPLYS & PARTS, NEW, WHOLESALE: Splys

Ziebart International Corp ....E....... 248 588-4100
  Troy (G-17460)

AUTOMOTIVE SPLYS & PARTS, NEW, WHOLESALE: Stampings

Matcor Automotive Michigan Inc............C....... 616 527-4050
  Ionia (G-8690)

AUTOMOTIVE SPLYS & PARTS, NEW, WHOLESALE: Tools & Eqpt

K-Tool Corporation Michigan ....D....... 863 603-0777
  Plymouth (G-13209)
Tooling Cncepts Design Not Inc ....F....... 810 444-9807
  Port Huron (G-13533)

AUTOMOTIVE SPLYS & PARTS, NEW, WHOLESALE: Trailer Parts

Erich Jaeger USA Inc...........................G....... 734 404-5940
  Livonia (G-10199)

AUTOMOTIVE SPLYS & PARTS, NEW, WHOLESALE: Trim

Detroit Tarpaulin Repr Sp Inc ....E....... 734 955-8200
  Romulus (G-14267)

AUTOMOTIVE SPLYS & PARTS, USED, WHOLESALE

D & D Fabrications Inc..........................G....... 810 798-2491
  Almont (G-258)
Mr Axle ....G....... 231 788-4624
  Muskegon (G-11878)
Valley Truck Parts Inc ....D....... 616 241-5431
  Grand Rapids (G-7303)

AUTOMOTIVE SPLYS & PARTS, USED, WHOLESALE: Access, NEC

Gemo Hopkins Usa Inc ....G....... 734 330-1271
  Auburn Hills (G-907)

AUTOMOTIVE SPLYS & PARTS, WHOLESALE, NEC

Alpha Technology Corporation ....E....... 517 546-9700
  Howell (G-8426)
American Furukawa Inc........................E....... 734 446-2200
  Plymouth (G-13123)
Asimco International Inc ....G....... 248 213-5200
  Southfield (G-15492)
Auto-Masters Inc..................................F....... 616 455-4510
  Grand Rapids (G-6480)
Canadian Amrcn Rstoration Sups..........E....... 248 853-8900
  Rochester Hills (G-13970)
Case Tool Inc ....G....... 734 261-2227
  Livonia (G-10148)
CC Industries LLC ....D....... 269 426-3342
  Sawyer (G-15108)
Cinnabar Engineering Inc ....G....... 810 648-2444
  Sandusky (G-15057)
Eagle Thread Verifier LLC ....G....... 586 764-8218
  Sterling Heights (G-15999)
Ena North America Corporation ....E....... 248 926-0011
  Wixom (G-18656)

Erin Industries Inc................................E....... 248 669-2050
  Walled Lake (G-17668)
Etx Holdings Inc...................................G....... 989 463-1151
  Alma (G-241)
F J Lucido & Associates ....E....... 586 574-3577
  Warren (G-17801)
F M T Products Inc..............................G....... 517 568-3373
  Homer (G-8351)
Faurecia Interior Systems Inc ....B....... 248 724-5100
  Auburn Hills (G-889)
Faurecia North America Inc ....E....... 248 288-1000
  Auburn Hills (G-890)
General Parts Inc ....G....... 989 686-3114
  Bay City (G-1360)
Henniges Automotive N Amer Inc ....C....... 248 340-4100
  Auburn Hills (G-926)
Horizon Intl Group LLC ....G....... 734 341-9336
  Birmingham (G-1730)
Hot Rod Holdings Inc...........................E....... 517 424-0577
  Tecumseh (G-16505)
HP Pelzer Auto Systems Inc ....B....... 810 987-4444
  Port Huron (G-13483)
K & K Mfg Inc......................................G....... 616 784-4286
  Sparta (G-15770)
Kirks Automotive Incorporated ....E....... 313 933-7030
  Detroit (G-4364)
Lane Automotive Inc.............................C....... 269 463-4113
  Watervliet (G-18182)
Mahle Behr Mfg MGT Inc ....E....... 248 735-3623
  Troy (G-17231)
N S International Ltd ....C....... 248 251-1600
  Troy (G-17272)
NSK Americas Inc................................C....... 734 913-7500
  Ann Arbor (G-595)
Oshino Lamps America Ltd ....G....... 262 226-8620
  Wixom (G-18727)
Piolax Corporation................................D....... 734 668-6005
  Plymouth (G-13265)
Polytec Foha Inc ....F....... 586 978-9386
  Warren (G-17969)
Quality Spring/Togo Inc........................G....... 517 278-2391
  Coldwater (G-3449)
Robert Bosch LLC ....G....... 248 876-1000
  Farmington Hills (G-5371)
Robert Bosch LLC ....G....... 248 921-9054
  Novi (G-12527)
Robert Bosch LLC ....G....... 734 979-3000
  Plymouth (G-13287)
Rowerdink Inc......................................G....... 734 487-1911
  Ypsilanti (G-18975)
Toledo Molding & Die Inc ....G....... 734 233-6338
  Plymouth (G-13317)
Toyo Seat USA Corporation..................C....... 810 724-0300
  Imlay City (G-8648)
Transpak Inc ....E....... 586 264-2064
  Sterling Heights (G-16209)
Valley Truck Parts Inc ....D....... 616 241-5431
  Grand Rapids (G-7303)
Van-Rob Inc...C....... 517 657-2450
  Lansing (G-9747)
Vectorall Manufacturing Inc ....E....... 248 486-4570
  Brighton (G-2093)
Woodbridge Sales & Engrg Inc ....C....... 248 288-0100
  Troy (G-17452)
Worldwide Marketing Svcs Inc ....F....... 269 556-2000
  Saint Joseph (G-14981)
Yazaki International Corp ....G....... 734 983-1000
  Canton (G-2544)
ZF North America Inc..........................B....... 734 416-6200
  Northville (G-12272)

AUTOMOTIVE SPLYS, USED, WHOLESALE & RETAIL

Innovation Unlimited LLC ....G....... 574 635-1064
  Bay City (G-1367)

AUTOMOTIVE SPLYS/PART, NEW, WHOL: Spring, Shock Absorb/Strut

Thyssenkrupp Bilstein Amer Inc ....A....... 248 530-2900
  Troy (G-17390)

AUTOMOTIVE SPLYS/PARTS, NEW, WHOL: Body Rpr/Paint Shop Splys

Reliance Spray Mask Co Inc ....F....... 616 784-3664
  Grand Rapids (G-7150)

Employee Codes: A=Over 500 employees, B=251-500
C=101-250, D=51-100, E=20-50, F=10-19, G=3-9

AUTOMOTIVE SVCS, EXC REP & CARWASHES: Do-It-Yourself Garages

AUTOMOTIVE SVCS, EXC REP & CARWASHES: Do-It-Yourself Garages

Bob Maxey Ford Howell Inc ....G..... 517 545-5700
  Howell *(G-8431)*

AUTOMOTIVE SVCS, EXC REPAIR & CARWASHES: Customizing

Priority One Emergency Inc ....G..... 734 398-5900
  Canton *(G-2512)*

AUTOMOTIVE SVCS, EXC REPAIR & CARWASHES: Insp & Diagnostic

Bosch Auto Svc Solutions Inc ....D..... 586 574-2332
  Warren *(G-17739)*
P G S Inc ....C..... 248 526-3800
  Troy *(G-17294)*
Spec Technologies Inc ....D..... 586 726-0000
  Shelby Township *(G-15340)*

AUTOMOTIVE SVCS, EXC REPAIR & CARWASHES: Lubrication

McElroys Automotive Svc LLC ....G..... 248 427-0501
  Farmington Hills *(G-5312)*
Rto Auto Repair Service ....G..... 586 779-9450
  Warren *(G-18000)*
Ziebart International Corp ....E..... 248 588-4100
  Troy *(G-17460)*

AUTOMOTIVE SVCS, EXC REPAIR & CARWASHES: Maintenance

Dynamic Auto Test Engineering ....G..... 269 342-1334
  Portage *(G-13556)*

AUTOMOTIVE SVCS, EXC REPAIR & CARWASHES: Road Svc

Michigan Paving and Mtls Co ....E..... 517 787-4200
  Jackson *(G-8956)*

AUTOMOTIVE SVCS, EXC REPAIR & CARWASHES: Trailer Maintenance

Premier Custom Trailers LLC ....F..... 877 327-0888
  Schoolcraft *(G-15127)*

AUTOMOTIVE SVCS, EXC REPAIR: Carwash, Automatic

Treib Inc ....F..... 989 752-4821
  Saginaw *(G-14778)*

AUTOMOTIVE SVCS, EXC REPAIR: Truck Wash

Interclean Equipment LLC ....E..... 734 961-3300
  Ypsilanti *(G-18958)*

AUTOMOTIVE TOWING SVCS

Brilliant Industries LLC ....G..... 616 954-9209
  Grand Rapids *(G-6525)*

AUTOMOTIVE UPHOLSTERY SHOPS

Dts Enterprises Inc ....E..... 231 599-3123
  Ellsworth *(G-5035)*
G&G Industries Inc ....E..... 586 726-6000
  Shelby Township *(G-15229)*
Lear Automotive Mfg LLC ....F..... 248 447-1603
  Detroit *(G-4380)*
Lear Automotive Mfg LLC ....F..... 248 447-1603
  Detroit *(G-4381)*
Shelby Auto Trim Inc ....E..... 586 939-9090
  Sterling Heights *(G-16175)*

AUTOMOTIVE WELDING SVCS

Angstrom Automotive Group LLC ....E..... 734 756-1164
  Southfield *(G-15487)*
Arcelrmttal Tlred Blnks Amrcas ....B..... 313 332-5300
  Detroit *(G-4024)*
Britten Metalworks LLC ....G..... 231 421-1615
  Traverse City *(G-16629)*
Classic Welding Inc ....F..... 586 758-2400
  Warren *(G-17757)*
Gustos Quality Systems ....G..... 231 409-0219
  Fife Lake *(G-5607)*
Hatch Stamping Company LLC ....C..... 734 475-8628
  Chelsea *(G-2814)*
Ianna Fab Inc ....G..... 586 739-2410
  Shelby Township *(G-15238)*
Joy Industries Inc ....F..... 248 334-4062
  Pontiac *(G-13388)*
Krause Welding Inc ....F..... 231 773-4443
  Muskegon *(G-11852)*
Mico Industries Inc ....D..... 616 245-6426
  Grand Rapids *(G-6999)*
Midwest Fabricating Inc ....G..... 734 921-3914
  Taylor *(G-16447)*
O E M Company Inc ....F..... 810 985-9070
  Port Huron *(G-13511)*
Response Welding Inc ....G..... 586 795-8090
  Sterling Heights *(G-16148)*
Technique Inc ....F..... 517 789-8988
  Jackson *(G-9017)*
UP Truck Center Inc ....E..... 906 774-0098
  Quinnesec *(G-13677)*
Virtec Manufacturing LLC ....F..... 313 590-2367
  Roseville *(G-14492)*

AUTOMOTIVE: Bodies

Bordrin Motor Corporation Inc ....F..... 877 507-3267
  Oak Park *(G-12595)*
Detroit Mfg Systems LLC ....D..... 313 243-0700
  Detroit *(G-4152)*
HP Pelzer Automotive Systems ....E..... 810 987-0725
  Port Huron *(G-13484)*
Quality Inspections Inc ....G..... 586 323-6135
  Sterling Heights *(G-16140)*
Special Projects Inc ....E..... 734 455-7130
  Plymouth *(G-13302)*
Very Best Motors LLC ....G..... 517 253-0707
  Lansing *(G-9749)*

AUTOMOTIVE: Seat Frames, Metal

Camaco LLC ....E..... 248 442-6800
  Farmington Hills *(G-5195)*
Nortech LLC ....E..... 248 446-7575
  New Hudson *(G-12066)*
P & C Group I Inc ....E..... 248 442-6800
  Farmington Hills *(G-5341)*

AUTOMOTIVE: Seating

Adient Inc ....A..... 734 254-5000
  Plymouth *(G-13114)*
American Metal Fab Inc ....D..... 269 279-5108
  Three Rivers *(G-16563)*
Bridgewater Interiors LLC ....A..... 586 753-3072
  Warren *(G-17743)*
Faurecia Auto Seating LLC ....B..... 248 563-9241
  Highland Park *(G-7905)*
Faurecia Auto Seating LLC ....C..... 248 563-9241
  Highland Park *(G-7906)*
Fisher & Company Incorporated ....B..... 586 746-2000
  Saint Clair Shores *(G-14858)*
Hoover Universal Inc ....E..... 734 454-0994
  Plymouth *(G-13190)*
Integrated Mfg & Assembly LLC ....B..... 734 530-5600
  Detroit *(G-4322)*
Lear Corporation ....B..... 248 447-1563
  Detroit *(G-4384)*
Lear Corporation ....B..... 248 447-1500
  Southfield *(G-15628)*
Lear European Operations Corp ....G..... 248 447-1500
  Southfield *(G-15629)*
Promax Engineering LLC ....C..... 734 979-0888
  Westland *(G-18408)*
Raven Acquisition LLC ....B..... 734 254-5000
  Holly *(G-8291)*
Recaro Automotive North Amer ....D..... 586 210-2600
  Clinton Township *(G-3331)*
Recaro North America Inc ....B..... 734 254-4704
  Clinton Township *(G-3332)*
Tachi-S Engineering USA Inc ....E..... 248 478-5050
  Farmington Hills *(G-5397)*
Toyo Seat USA Corporation ....C..... 810 724-0300
  Imlay City *(G-8648)*
Woodbridge Holdings Inc ....E..... 248 288-0100
  Troy *(G-17451)*
Yanfeng US Automotive ....G..... 616 394-1523
  Holland *(G-8257)*

AUTOTRANSFORMERS: Electric

Controlled Magnetics Inc ....F..... 734 449-7225
  Whitmore Lake *(G-18528)*
Gti Power Acquisition LLC ....C..... 616 842-5430
  Grand Haven *(G-6310)*
Rizk National Industries Inc ....F..... 586 757-4700
  Warren *(G-17997)*

AWNINGS & CANOPIES

Case-Free Inc ....G..... 616 245-3136
  Grand Rapids *(G-6558)*
D & W Awning and Window Co ....E..... 810 742-0340
  Davison *(G-3779)*

AWNINGS & CANOPIES: Awnings, Fabric, From Purchased Matls

American Roll Shutter Awng Co ....E..... 734 422-7110
  Livonia *(G-10116)*
Benton Harbor Awning & Tent ....E..... 800 272-2187
  Benton Harbor *(G-1535)*
Case-Free Inc ....G..... 616 245-3136
  Grand Rapids *(G-6558)*
Dial Tent & Awning Co ....F..... 989 793-0741
  Saginaw *(G-14639)*
Dockside Canvas Co Inc ....F..... 586 463-1231
  Harrison Township *(G-7696)*
Feb Inc ....F..... 231 759-0911
  Muskegon *(G-11816)*
Grand Traverse Canvas Works ....F..... 231 947-3140
  Traverse City *(G-16697)*
Holiday Distributing Co ....E..... 517 782-7146
  Jackson *(G-8904)*
Jackson Canvas Company ....E..... 517 768-8459
  Jackson *(G-8913)*
Jacquart Fabric Products Inc ....C..... 906 932-1339
  Ironwood *(G-8765)*
Muskegon Awning & Mfg Co ....E..... 231 759-0911
  Muskegon *(G-11879)*
Quality Awning Shops Inc ....G..... 517 882-2491
  Lansing *(G-9885)*
Royal Oak & Birmingham Tent ....F..... 248 542-5552
  Royal Oak *(G-14578)*
Traverse Bay Canvas Inc ....G..... 231 347-3001
  Harbor Springs *(G-7659)*

AWNINGS & CANOPIES: Fabric

Industrial Fabric Products Inc ....F..... 269 932-4440
  Saint Joseph *(G-14937)*

AWNINGS: Fiberglass

Case-Free Inc ....G..... 616 245-3136
  Grand Rapids *(G-6558)*
Golden Pointe Inc ....G..... 313 581-8284
  Detroit *(G-4269)*

AWNINGS: Metal

American Roll Shutter Awng Co ....E..... 734 422-7110
  Livonia *(G-10116)*
Patio Land Mfg Inc ....G..... 586 758-5660
  Warren *(G-17959)*

AWNINGS: Wood

Wayne-Craft Inc ....F..... 734 421-8800
  Livonia *(G-10468)*

AXLES

American Axle & Mfg Inc ....G..... 810 772-8778
  Detroit *(G-4010)*
American Axle & Mfg Inc ....A..... 269 278-0211
  Three Rivers *(G-16562)*
American Axle Mfg Holdings Inc ....A..... 313 758-2000
  Detroit *(G-4012)*
Grouper Wild LLC ....G..... 269 665-4261
  Galesburg *(G-6078)*
Meritor Specialty Products LLC ....A..... 248 435-1000
  Troy *(G-17250)*
Mr Axle ....G..... 231 788-4624
  Muskegon *(G-11878)*
Nexteer Automotive Corporation ....B..... 989 757-5000
  Saginaw *(G-14713)*
Nexteer Automotive Corporation ....B..... 989 757-5000
  Saginaw *(G-14715)*

PRODUCT SECTION

BAKERY FOR HOME SVC DELIVERY

AXLES: Rolled Or Forged, Made In Steel Mills
Axle of Dearborn Inc .... C 248 543-5995
  Ferndale (G-5529)

BABBITT (METAL)
Airtec Corporation .... E 313 892-7800
  Detroit (G-3991)

BABY FORMULA
Gerber Products Company .... E 231 928-2000
  Fremont (G-6043)

BACKFILLERS: Self-Propelled
Wacker Neuson Corporation .... F 231 799-4500
  Norton Shores (G-12342)

BADGES, WHOLESALE
Jbl Enterprises .... G 616 530-8647
  Grand Rapids (G-6863)

BADGES: Identification & Insignia
Brady Worldwide Inc .... G 248 650-1952
  Rochester (G-13894)
Rodzina Industries Inc .... G 810 235-2341
  Flint (G-5755)

BAGS & CONTAINERS: Textile, Exc Sleeping
Industrial Bag & Spc Inc .... F 248 559-5550
  Southfield (G-15603)
JAC Custom Pouches Inc .... E 269 782-3190
  Dowagiac (G-4784)

BAGS & SACKS: Shipping & Shopping
McKenna Enterprises Inc .... G 248 375-3388
  Rochester Hills (G-14061)

BAGS: Canvas
Birlon Group LLC .... G 313 551-5341
  Inkster (G-8659)
Foreward Logistics LLC .... G 877 488-9724
  Oak Park (G-12612)

BAGS: Cement, Made From Purchased Materials
Lisa Bain .... G 313 389-9661
  Allen Park (G-198)

BAGS: Garment, Plastic Film, Made From Purchased Materials
D&Js Plastics LLC .... F 616 745-5798
  Hudsonville (G-8578)

BAGS: Paper
Acme Mills Company .... E 517 437-8940
  Hillsdale (G-7919)
Concorde Inc .... F 248 391-8177
  Auburn Hills (G-846)

BAGS: Paper, Made From Purchased Materials
AJM Packaging Corporation .... D 313 291-6500
  Taylor (G-16375)
AJM Packaging Corporation .... D 248 901-0040
  Bloomfield Hills (G-1794)
AJM Packaging Corporation .... D 313 842-7530
  Detroit (G-3993)
Stewart Sutherland Inc .... C 269 649-0530
  Vicksburg (G-17613)

BAGS: Plastic
A-Pac Manufacturing Company .... E 616 791-7222
  Grand Rapids (G-6412)
Bioplstic Plymers Cmpsites LLC .... G 517 349-2970
  Okemos (G-12660)
Cadillac Products Inc .... F 989 766-2294
  Rogers City (G-14208)
Coveris .... C 269 964-1130
  Battle Creek (G-1212)

Idea Mia LLC .... G 248 891-8939
  Lathrup Village (G-9976)
Opus Packaging Group Inc .... D 616 871-5200
  Caledonia (G-2391)
Plasport Inc .... E 231 935-1580
  Traverse City (G-16798)

BAGS: Plastic & Pliofilm
Superior Polyolefin Films Inc .... G 248 334-8074
  Bloomfield Hills (G-1863)

BAGS: Plastic, Made From Purchased Materials
Cadillac Products Inc .... E 586 774-1700
  Roseville (G-14382)
Cadillac Products Inc .... B 248 813-8200
  Troy (G-16992)
Lbv Sales LLC .... G 616 874-9390
  Belmont (G-1510)
Quality Transparent Bag Inc .... F 989 893-3561
  Bay City (G-1391)

BAGS: Rubber Or Rubberized Fabric
Rubber Enterprises Inc .... G 810 724-9200
  Imlay City (G-8645)

BAGS: Shipping
Pak-Rite Industries Inc .... D 313 388-6400
  Ecorse (G-4984)

BAGS: Textile
Acme Mills Company .... E 517 437-8940
  Hillsdale (G-7919)
Lake State Cleaning Inc .... G 314 961-7939
  Oxford (G-12895)
Total Packaging Solutions LLC .... F 248 519-2376
  Detroit (G-4639)

BAKERIES, COMMERCIAL: On Premises Baking Only
Achatzs Hand Made Pie Co .... E 586 749-2882
  Chesterfield (G-2834)
Almar Orchards LLC .... F 810 659-6568
  Flushing (G-5801)
Amys Baking Company .... G 313 530-9694
  Bloomfield Hills (G-1797)
Apple Valley Natural Foods .... C 269 471-3234
  Berrien Springs (G-1637)
Big Boy Restaurants Intl LLC .... D 586 263-6220
  Clinton Township (G-3184)
Campbell Soup Company .... G 313 295-6884
  Taylor (G-16390)
Campbell Soup Company .... G 248 336-8486
  Ferndale (G-5532)
Carlson Enterprises Inc .... G 248 656-1442
  Rochester Hills (G-13972)
Coles Quality Foods Inc .... D 231 722-1651
  Muskegon (G-11793)
Country Mill Farms LLC .... G 517 543-1019
  Charlotte (G-2745)
Crew Family Rest & Bky LLC .... G 269 337-9800
  Kalamazoo (G-9158)
Cupcakes and Kisses .... G 248 382-5314
  Holly (G-8264)
For The Love of Cupcakes .... G 906 399-3004
  Bark River (G-1154)
G M Paris Bakery Inc .... G 734 425-2060
  Livonia (G-10217)
Great Harvest Bread Co .... F 586 566-9500
  Shelby Township (G-15231)
Home Bakery .... G 248 651-4830
  Rochester (G-13904)
Hostess Cake ITT Contntl Bkg .... G 231 775-4629
  Cadillac (G-2335)
Jaimes Cupcake Haven .... E 586 596-6809
  Warren (G-17882)
Jorgensens Inc .... E 989 831-8338
  Greenville (G-7494)
Josefs French Pastry Shop Co .... G 313 881-5710
  Grosse Pointe Woods (G-7568)
Julian Brothers Inc .... F 248 588-0280
  Clawson (G-3100)
Keebler Company .... B 269 961-2000
  Battle Creek (G-1250)
Klaus Nixdorf .... G 269 429-3259
  Stevensville (G-16256)

Looney Baker of Livonia Inc .... F 734 425-8569
  Livonia (G-10292)
Mackenzies Bakery .... E 269 343-8440
  Kalamazoo (G-9263)
Marias Italian Bakery Inc .... F 734 981-1200
  Canton (G-2488)
Marie Minnie Bakers Inc .... C 734 522-1100
  Livonia (G-10300)
New Yasmeen Detroit Inc .... F 313 582-6035
  Dearborn (G-3876)
New York Bagel Baking Co .... F 248 548-2580
  Ferndale (G-5572)
Rainbow Pizza Inc .... G 734 246-4250
  Taylor (G-16465)
Raleigh & Ron Corporation .... D 248 280-2820
  Royal Oak (G-14571)
Randalls Bakery .... G 906 224-5401
  Wakefield (G-17625)
Roskam Baking Company .... C 616 574-5757
  Grand Rapids (G-7166)
Roskam Baking Company .... B 616 419-1863
  Kentwood (G-9478)
Roskam Baking Company .... B 616 574-5757
  Grand Rapids (G-7167)
Roskam Baking Company .... B 616 574-5757
  Grand Rapids (G-7168)
Roskam Baking Company .... B 616 574-5757
  Grand Rapids (G-7170)
Rothbury Farms Inc .... E 616 574-5757
  Grand Rapids (G-7171)
Shatila Food Products Inc .... E 313 934-1520
  Dearborn (G-3896)
Simply Divine Baking LLC .... G 313 903-2881
  Southfield (G-15704)
Supreme Baking Company .... G 313 894-0222
  Detroit (G-4618)
Sweet Mellisas Cupcakes .... G 616 889-3998
  Lowell (G-10519)
Sweetheart Bakery Inc .... E 313 839-6330
  Detroit (G-4621)
Sweetheart Bakery of Michigan .... F 586 795-1660
  Harper Woods (G-7673)
Uncle Johns Cider Mill Inc .... E 989 224-3686
  Saint Johns (G-14919)
Vargas & Sons .... F 989 754-4636
  Saginaw (G-14789)
W Bay Cupcakes .... G 231 632-2010
  Traverse City (G-16876)
Walmart Inc .... F 517 541-1481
  Charlotte (G-2774)

BAKERIES: On Premises Baking & Consumption
Bake N Cakes LP .... G 517 337-2253
  Lansing (G-9811)
Bake Station Bakeries Mich Inc .... F 248 352-9000
  Southfield (G-15501)
Big Boy Restaurants Intl LLC .... D 586 263-6220
  Clinton Township (G-3184)
Campbell Soup Company .... G 313 295-6884
  Taylor (G-16390)
Campbell Soup Company .... G 248 336-8486
  Ferndale (G-5532)
New Martha Washington Bakery .... G 313 872-1988
  Detroit (G-4483)
Pepperidge Farm Incorporated .... F 734 953-6729
  Livonia (G-10362)
Rainbow Pizza Inc .... G 734 246-4250
  Taylor (G-16465)
Randalls Bakery .... G 906 224-5401
  Wakefield (G-17625)
Shatila Food Products Inc .... E 313 934-1520
  Dearborn (G-3896)
Stone House Bread Inc .... E 231 933-8864
  Traverse City (G-16842)
Supreme Baking Company .... G 313 894-0222
  Detroit (G-4618)
Sweetheart Bakery Inc .... E 313 839-6330
  Detroit (G-4621)
Sweetheart Bakery of Michigan .... F 586 795-1660
  Harper Woods (G-7673)
Top Notch Cookies & Cakes Inc .... G 734 467-9550
  Westland (G-18422)

BAKERY FOR HOME SVC DELIVERY
Butter Cobbler & Things LLC .... G 810 391-8432
  Wixom (G-18628)
Sweet Sugas LLC .... G 313 444-8570
  Clinton Township (G-3368)

Employee Codes: A=Over 500 employees, B=251-500
C=101-250, D=51-100, E=20-50, F=10-19, G=3-9

BAKERY FOR HOME SVC DELIVERY — PRODUCT SECTION

Wow Factor Tables and Events ....G...... 248 550-5922
  Howell (G-8543)
Yell Sweets LLC ....G...... 586 799-4560
  Shelby Township (G-15372)

BAKERY MACHINERY

Banner Engineering & Sales Inc ....F...... 989 755-0584
  Saginaw (G-14609)
Dawn Equipment Company Inc ....C...... 517 789-4500
  Jackson (G-8861)
Dawn Food Products Inc ....C...... 517 789-4400
  Jackson (G-8863)
Dawn Foods Inc ....C...... 517 789-4400
  Jackson (G-8864)
Lematic Inc ....D...... 517 787-3301
  Jackson (G-8934)
Oliver Packaging and Eqp Co ....D...... 616 356-2950
  Walker (G-17645)

BAKERY PRDTS: Bakery Prdts, Partially Cooked, Exc frozen

Dorothy Dawson Food Products ....E...... 517 788-9830
  Jackson (G-8870)

BAKERY PRDTS: Biscuits, Dry

Otb Enterprises LLC ....G...... 248 266-5568
  Troy (G-17293)

BAKERY PRDTS: Bread, All Types, Fresh Or Frozen

Aunt Millies Bakeries Inc ....E...... 734 528-1475
  Ypsilanti (G-18925)
Bay Bread Co ....G...... 231 922-8022
  Traverse City (G-16614)
Bread of Life Bakery & Cafe ....F...... 906 663-4005
  Bessemer (G-1647)
Darwin Sneller ....G...... 989 977-3718
  Sebewaing (G-15139)
Emesa Foods Company LLC ....G...... 248 982-3908
  Taylor (G-16413)
Haulin Oats Inc ....G...... 248 225-1672
  Roseville (G-14420)
Italian BTR Bread Sticks Bky ....G...... 313 893-4945
  Detroit (G-4327)
Knickerbocker Baking Inc ....D...... 248 541-2110
  Madison Heights (G-10763)
Metropolitan Baking Company ....D...... 313 875-7246
  Detroit (G-4439)
Milano Bakery Inc ....E...... 313 833-3500
  Detroit (G-4457)
Prime Land Farm ....G...... 989 550-6120
  Harbor Beach (G-7635)
Schnitzelstein Baking Co ....G...... 616 988-2316
  Grand Rapids (G-7183)
Schuette Farms ....G...... 989 550-0563
  Elkton (G-5032)
Zingermans Bakehouse Inc ....D...... 734 761-2095
  Ann Arbor (G-725)

BAKERY PRDTS: Buns, Bread Type, Fresh Or Frozen

Way Bakery ....C...... 517 787-6720
  Jackson (G-9033)
White Lotus Farms Inc ....G...... 734 904-1379
  Ann Arbor (G-716)

BAKERY PRDTS: Cakes, Bakery, Exc Frozen

Brothers Baking Company ....E...... 269 663-8591
  Edwardsburg (G-5001)
Cake Connection Tc LLC ....G...... 231 943-3531
  Traverse City (G-16637)
James Ave Catering ....G...... 517 655-4532
  Williamston (G-18574)
Magic Treatz LLC ....G...... 248 989-9956
  Oak Park (G-12624)
More Signature Cakes LLC ....G...... 248 266-0504
  Troy (G-17265)
Palm Sweets LLC ....G...... 586 554-7979
  Sterling Heights (G-16123)
Simply Zara S Treats LLC ....F...... 313 327-5002
  Detroit (G-4595)
Top Notch Cookies & Cakes Inc ......G...... 734 467-9550
  Westland (G-18422)

BAKERY PRDTS: Cakes, Bakery, Frozen

Dawn Foods Inc ....C...... 517 789-4400
  Jackson (G-8864)
Julian Brothers Inc ....F...... 248 588-0280
  Clawson (G-3100)
Sweet Creations ....G...... 989 327-1157
  Saginaw (G-14770)

BAKERY PRDTS: Cones, Ice Cream

Cherry Cone LLC ....G...... 231 944-1036
  Traverse City (G-16649)

BAKERY PRDTS: Cookies

Actt Management LLC ....E...... 616 803-8734
  Grand Rapids (G-6425)
Among Friends LLC ....F...... 734 997-9720
  Ann Arbor (G-365)
Cherry Republic Inc ....D...... 231 334-3150
  Glen Arbor (G-6209)
Keebler Company ....B...... 269 961-2000
  Battle Creek (G-1250)
Keebler Company ....C...... 231 445-0335
  Cheboygan (G-2790)
Kellogg Company ....A...... 269 961-2000
  Battle Creek (G-1255)
Kellogg North America Company .....C...... 269 961-2000
  Battle Creek (G-1260)
Krumbsnatcher Enterprises LLC ......F...... 313 408-6802
  Detroit (G-4368)
Lotte USA Incorporated ....F...... 269 963-6664
  Battle Creek (G-1269)
Pepperidge Farm Incorporated ....G...... 734 953-6729
  Livonia (G-10362)
Top Notch Cookies & Cakes Inc ......G...... 734 467-9550
  Westland (G-18422)

BAKERY PRDTS: Cookies & crackers

Campbell Soup Company ....G...... 313 295-6884
  Taylor (G-16390)
Campbell Soup Company ....G...... 248 336-8486
  Ferndale (G-5532)
Dick and Jane Baking Co LLC ....G...... 248 519-2418
  Troy (G-17060)
Krumb Snatcher Cookie Co LLC ......G...... 313 408-6802
  Battle Creek (G-1266)
Ludwicks Frozen Donuts Inc ....F...... 616 453-6880
  Grand Rapids (G-6951)
Marias Italian Bakery Inc ....F...... 734 981-1200
  Canton (G-2488)
Savory Foods Inc ....D...... 616 241-2583
  Grand Rapids (G-7181)
Shatila Food Products Inc ....E...... 313 934-1520
  Dearborn (G-3896)
Stone House Bread Inc ....G...... 231 933-8864
  Traverse City (G-16842)
Supreme Baking Company ....G...... 313 894-0222
  Detroit (G-4618)

BAKERY PRDTS: Doughnuts, Exc Frozen

Dunkin Donuts & Baskin-Robbins ....F...... 989 835-8412
  Midland (G-11357)
Sweetwaters Donut Mill ....G...... 269 979-1944
  Battle Creek (G-1303)

BAKERY PRDTS: Doughnuts, Frozen

Ludwicks Frozen Donuts Inc ....F...... 616 453-6880
  Grand Rapids (G-6951)

BAKERY PRDTS: Dry

Chewys Gourmet Kitchen LLC ....F...... 313 757-2595
  Detroit (G-4092)
DVine Cookies ....E...... 248 417-7850
  Bloomfield Hills (G-1817)
Kmj Global Inc ....G...... 240 594-5050
  Birmingham (G-1732)
Sweetie Pie Pantry ....F...... 517 669-9300
  Dewitt (G-4716)

BAKERY PRDTS: Frozen

Bakers Rhapsody ....G...... 269 767-1368
  Dowagiac (G-4777)
Marie Minnie Bakers Inc ....C...... 734 522-1100
  Livonia (G-10300)
Pepperidge Farm Incorporated ....G...... 734 953-6729
  Livonia (G-10362)

Savory Foods Inc ....D...... 616 241-2583
  Grand Rapids (G-7181)

BAKERY PRDTS: Pastries, Exc Frozen

Kellogg Company ....A...... 269 961-2000
  Battle Creek (G-1255)

BAKERY PRDTS: Pies, Exc Frozen

Great Lakes Pot Pies LLC ....G...... 248 266-1160
  Bloomfield Hills (G-1824)

BAKERY PRDTS: Pretzels

Artisan Bread Co LLC ....E...... 586 756-0100
  Warren (G-17714)
Bear Naked Inc ....F...... 203 662-1136
  Battle Creek (G-1193)
Frito-Lay North America Inc ....G...... 989 754-0435
  Saginaw (G-14647)
Karemor Inc ....G...... 517 323-3042
  Lansing (G-9770)
Nautical Knots ....G...... 231 206-0400
  Grand Haven (G-6339)
Syd Enterprises ....G...... 517 719-2740
  Howell (G-8524)

BAKERY PRDTS: Wholesalers

Beirut Bakery Inc ....F...... 313 533-4422
  Redford (G-13718)
Dick and Jane Baking Co LLC ....G...... 248 519-2418
  Troy (G-17060)
New Yasmeen Detroit Inc ....F...... 313 582-6035
  Dearborn (G-3876)
New York Bagel Baking Co ....F...... 248 548-2580
  Ferndale (G-5572)
Rothbury Farms Inc ....E...... 616 574-5757
  Grand Rapids (G-7171)
Shatila Food Products Inc ....E...... 313 934-1520
  Dearborn (G-3896)
Supreme Baking Company ....G...... 313 894-0222
  Detroit (G-4618)

BAKERY: Wholesale Or Wholesale & Retail Combined

A & D Distribution Inc ....F...... 248 378-1418
  Troy (G-16899)
All Around Beauty Shop LLC ....G...... 313 704-2494
  Garden City (G-6091)
Aunt Millies Bakeries ....G...... 989 356-6688
  Alpena (G-280)
Bake Station Bakeries Mich Inc ....F...... 248 352-9000
  Southfield (G-15501)
Bakewell Company ....G...... 269 459-8030
  Portage (G-13545)
Baking Company LLC ....E...... 616 241-2583
  Grand Rapids (G-6493)
Beirut Bakery Inc ....F...... 313 533-4422
  Redford (G-13718)
Chewys Gourmet Kitchen LLC ....F...... 313 757-2595
  Detroit (G-4092)
Coles Quality Foods Inc ....F...... 231 722-1651
  Grand Rapids (G-6582)
Creme Curls Bakery Inc ....C...... 616 669-6230
  Hudsonville (G-8575)
Dough Masters ....F...... 248 585-0600
  Warren (G-17782)
Emesa Foods Company ....G...... 248 982-3908
  Farmington Hills (G-5230)
Hand 2 Hand Whl & Dist LLC ....G...... 313 574-2861
  Detroit (G-4293)
Jt Bakers ....G...... 989 424-5102
  Clare (G-2983)
Kays Glrous Bked Gds Dist LLC .....G...... 248 830-1717
  Pontiac (G-13391)
Kind Crumbs LLC ....G...... 616 881-6388
  Grand Rapids (G-6895)
La Azteca Foods LLC ....G...... 313 413-2014
  Ecorse (G-4983)
Lg Essentials LLC ....G...... 313 312-3813
  Detroit (G-4394)
Maxpow International LLC ....G...... 734 578-5369
  Westland (G-18394)
Michigan State University ....G...... 517 353-9310
  East Lansing (G-4906)
National Bakery ....G...... 313 891-7803
  Detroit (G-4475)
New Martha Washington Bakery ......G...... 313 872-1988
  Detroit (G-4483)

PRODUCT SECTION

Old Mission Multigrain LLC ....G....... 231 366-4121
  Traverse City (G-16781)
Paladin Baking Company LLC ....F...... 248 601-1542
  Rochester (G-13919)
Ripe Harvest Foods LLC ....F...... 630 863-2440
  Hillman (G-7916)
Roskam Baking Company ....B...... 616 554-9160
  Grand Rapids (G-7169)
Russos Bakery Inc ....E...... 586 791-7320
  Clinton Township (G-3346)
Savory Foods Inc ....D...... 616 241-2583
  Grand Rapids (G-7181)
Shakes and Cakes LLC ....G....... 313 707-0923
  Highland Park (G-7909)
Skinny Petes LLc ....G....... 906 369-1431
  Lake Linden (G-9570)
Spatz Bakery Inc ....F...... 989 755-5551
  Saginaw (G-14760)
Stone Circle Bakehouse LLC ....G....... 517 881-0603
  Holt (G-8334)
Stone House Bread LLC ....E...... 231 933-8864
  Traverse City (G-16841)
Sweetest Taboo LLC ....G....... 313 575-4642
  Detroit (G-4620)
Telo ....G....... 810 845-8051
  Fenton (G-5507)
West Thomas Partners LLC ....E...... 616 430-7485
  Grand Rapids (G-7336)

BALCONIES: Metal

Stus Welding & Fabrication ....G....... 616 392-8459
  Holland (G-8206)

BALERS

Howey Tree Baler Corporation ....G....... 231 328-4321
  Merritt (G-11266)

BALLASTS: Fluorescent

Nextek Power Systems Inc ....G....... 313 887-1321
  Detroit (G-4484)

BALLOONS: Novelty & Toy

Lachman Enterprises Inc ....G....... 248 948-9944
  Southfield (G-15623)

BALLOONS: Toy & Advertising, Rubber

Gaco Sourcing LLC ....G....... 248 633-2656
  Birmingham (G-1728)

BANNERS: Fabric

Bannergalaxycom LLC ....G....... 231 941-8200
  Traverse City (G-16612)
Consort Corporation ....E...... 269 388-4532
  Kalamazoo (G-9151)
Engineering Reproduction Inc ....G....... 313 366-3390
  Detroit (G-4209)
Jack Ripper & Associates Inc ....G....... 734 453-7333
  Plymouth (G-13200)

BANQUET HALL FACILITIES

Forest View Lanes LLC ....E...... 734 847-4915
  Temperance (G-16531)

BAR FIXTURES: Wood

Ferrante Manufacturing Co ....E...... 313 571-1111
  Detroit (G-4231)

BAR FIXTURES: Wood

Glastender Inc ....B...... 989 752-4275
  Saginaw (G-14652)

BAR JOISTS & CONCRETE REINFORCING BARS: Fabricated

Ctc Fabricators LLC ....G....... 586 242-8809
  Clay (G-3118)

BARBECUE EQPT

American Household Inc ....G....... 601 296-5000
  Livonia (G-10114)

BARGES BUILDING & REPAIR

Arcosa Shoring Products Inc ....D...... 517 741-4300
  Union City (G-17490)

BARRELS: Shipping, Metal

Mauser ....E...... 248 795-2330
  Clarkston (G-3048)
Rap Products Inc ....G....... 989 893-5583
  Bay City (G-1394)

BARRETTES

Ann Barrette ....G....... 586 713-8145
  Clinton Township (G-3172)

BARRICADES: Metal

Avian Control Technologies LLC ....G....... 231 349-9050
  Stanwood (G-15902)
Best Barricade Sysytem Inc ....G....... 989 778-1482
  Bay City (G-1332)
Give-Em A Brake Safety LLC ....E...... 616 531-8705
  Grandville (G-7379)
Poco Inc ....E...... 313 220-6752
  Canton (G-2509)
Signature Wall Solutions Inc ....F...... 616 366-4242
  Midland (G-11417)
Spartan Barricading ....G....... 313 292-2488
  Romulus (G-14330)

BARS & BAR SHAPES: Steel, Cold-Finished, Own Hot-Rolled

Eaton Steel Corporation ....D...... 248 398-3434
  Oak Park (G-12609)
Eaton Steel Corporation ....D...... 248 398-3434
  Livonia (G-10189)
Gerdau Macsteel Inc ....B...... 517 764-0311
  Jackson (G-8890)
Gerdau Macsteel Inc ....B...... 734 243-2446
  Monroe (G-11543)
Gerdau Macsteel Inc ....E...... 517 782-0415
  Jackson (G-8891)

BARS & BAR SHAPES: Steel, Hot-Rolled

Gerdau Macsteel Inc ....A...... 734 243-2446
  Monroe (G-11542)

BARS, COLD FINISHED: Steel, From Purchased Hot-Rolled

BR Safety Products Inc ....G....... 734 582-4499
  Plymouth (G-13137)

BARS: Cargo, Stabilizing, Metal

Atf Inc ....E...... 989 685-2468
  Rose City (G-14362)
Friendship Industries Inc ....E...... 586 323-0033
  Sterling Heights (G-16024)
Lock and Load Corp ....G....... 800 975-9658
  Marion (G-10973)

BARS: Concrete Reinforcing, Fabricated Steel

Bowling Enterprises Inc ....G....... 231 864-2653
  Kaleva (G-9376)
Corson Fabricating LLC ....E...... 810 326-0532
  Saint Clair (G-14820)
Cotson Fabricating Inc ....E...... 248 589-2758
  Sterling Heights (G-15973)
D & D Fabrications Inc ....G....... 810 798-2491
  Almont (G-258)
Daughtery Group Inc ....G....... 313 452-7918
  Detroit (G-4121)
Econ-O-Line Abrasive Products ....F...... 616 846-4150
  Grand Haven (G-6295)
Global Lift Corp ....F...... 989 269-5900
  Bad Axe (G-1106)
Metro Rebar Inc ....G....... 248 851-5894
  West Bloomfield (G-18297)
N & K Fulbright LLC ....F...... 269 695-4580
  Niles (G-12149)
Tennessee Fabricators LLC ....G....... 615 793-4444
  Sterling Heights (G-16203)
Vanermen Smith Products Inc ....F...... 517 575-6618
  Lansing (G-9748)
Welk-Ko Fabricators Inc ....G....... 248 486-2598
  New Hudson (G-12074)

BASES, BEVERAGE

Sensient Technologies Corp ....G....... 989 479-3211
  Harbor Beach (G-7637)

BASKETS: Steel Wire

Transportation Tech Group Inc ....F...... 810 233-0440
  Flint (G-5781)

BATH SALTS

Bath Bombs By Lori ....G....... 734 890-3832
  Westland (G-18360)

BATHROOM ACCESS & FITTINGS: Vitreous China & Earthenware

Americast LLC ....G....... 989 681-4800
  Saint Louis (G-14985)
Cucina Moda - Birmingham LLC ....F...... 248 792-2285
  Troy (G-17037)
National Composites LLC ....E...... 989 723-8997
  Owosso (G-12846)
York Electric Inc ....G....... 517 487-6400
  Lansing (G-9909)

BATHROOM FIXTURES: Plastic

Lyons Industries Inc ....C...... 269 782-3404
  Dowagiac (G-4787)

BATTERIES, EXC AUTOMOTIVE: Wholesalers

A123 Systems LLC ....B...... 248 412-9249
  Novi (G-12359)
Alpine Power Systems Inc ....D...... 313 531-6600
  Redford (G-13713)
Batteries Plus ....G....... 269 925-7367
  Benton Harbor (G-1533)

BATTERIES: Alkaline, Cell Storage

Global Battery Solutions LLC ....E...... 800 456-4265
  Holland (G-8051)

BATTERIES: Lead Acid, Storage

Clarios LLC ....G....... 734 995-3016
  Ann Arbor (G-425)

BATTERIES: Rechargeable

A123 Systems LLC ....G....... 734 466-6521
  Livonia (G-10095)
Adana Voltaics LLC ....G....... 734 622-0193
  Ann Arbor (G-351)
Arotech Corporation ....D...... 800 281-0356
  Ann Arbor (G-380)
Ematrix Energy Systems Inc ....G....... 248 629-9111
  Royal Oak (G-14532)
G & L Powerup Inc ....G....... 586 200-2169
  Roseville (G-14409)
Lg Energy Solution Mich Inc ....C...... 616 494-7153
  Hazel Park (G-7829)

BATTERIES: Storage

A123 Systems LLC ....G....... 734 772-0600
  Romulus (G-14243)
A123 Systems LLC ....B...... 248 412-9249
  Novi (G-12359)
Advanced Battery Concepts LLC ....E...... 989 424-6645
  Clare (G-2972)
Akasol Inc ....E...... 248 259-7843
  Hazel Park (G-7818)
Alpine Power Systems Inc ....D...... 313 531-6600
  Redford (G-13713)
American Battery Solutions Inc ....C...... 248 462-6364
  Lake Orion (G-9585)
Batteries Plus ....G....... 269 925-7367
  Benton Harbor (G-1533)
Battery Center of America ....G....... 248 399-5999
  Ferndale (G-5531)
Contemporary Amperex Tech USA ....G....... 248 289-6200
  Rochester Hills (G-13984)
East Penn Manufacturing Co ....G....... 586 979-5300
  Sterling Heights (G-16001)
Ematrix Energy Systems Inc ....F...... 248 797-2149
  Southfield (G-15556)
Exide Technologies LLC ....G....... 248 853-5000
  Auburn Hills (G-884)
Harding Energy Inc ....E...... 231 798-7033
  Grand Haven (G-6314)
Httm LLC ....G....... 616 820-2500
  Holland (G-8090)

Employee Codes: A=Over 500 employees, B=251-500
C=101-250, D=51-100, E=20-50, F=10-19, G=3-9

BATTERIES: Storage

Innovative Weld Solutions LLC .... G 937 545-7695
  Rochester *(G-13908)*
Lg Energy Solution Mich Inc .... C 248 291-2385
  Troy *(G-17211)*
Lg Energy Solution Mich Inc .... C 248 307-1800
  Troy *(G-17212)*
Lg Energy Solution Mich Inc .... C 616 494-7100
  Belleville *(G-1488)*
Lg Energy Solution Mich Inc .... C 616 494-7100
  Holland *(G-8126)*
M & M Irish Enterprises Inc .... G 248 644-0666
  Birmingham *(G-1733)*
Navitas Advnced Sltons Group L .... G 734 913-8176
  Ann Arbor *(G-592)*
Our Next Energy Inc .... E 408 623-1896
  Novi *(G-12500)*
Redeem Power Services .... G 248 679-5277
  Novi *(G-12524)*
Robert Bosch Btry Systems LLC .... D 248 620-5700
  Farmington Hills *(G-5370)*
Rowerdink Inc .... G 734 487-1911
  Ypsilanti *(G-18975)*
TMC Group Inc .... C 248 819-6063
  Pleasant Ridge *(G-13106)*
Wonch Battery Company .... E 517 394-3600
  Lansing *(G-9904)*
Xalt Energy LLC .... F 989 486-8501
  Midland *(G-11426)*
Xalt Energy Mi LLC .... D 989 486-8501
  Midland *(G-11428)*

BATTERIES: Wet

G & L Powerup Inc .... G 586 200-2169
  Roseville *(G-14409)*
Mophie LLC .... B 269 743-1340
  Kalamazoo *(G-9276)*
Robert Bosch Btry Systems LLC .... D 248 620-5700
  Farmington Hills *(G-5370)*

BATTERY CASES: Plastic Or Plastics Combination

Akwel Cadillac Usa Inc .... G 248 848-9599
  Farmington Hills *(G-5166)*
D&Js Plastics LLC .... F 616 745-5798
  Hudsonville *(G-8578)*
US Farathane LLC .... C 248 754-7000
  Auburn Hills *(G-1072)*

BATTERY CHARGERS

Exide Technologies LLC .... G 248 853-5000
  Auburn Hills *(G-884)*

BATTERY CHARGERS: Storage, Motor & Engine Generator Type

Ies-Synergy Inc .... G 586 206-4410
  Troy *(G-17159)*

BATTERY CHARGING GENERATORS

Best Netwrk Design & Assoc LLC .... E 313 680-2047
  Detroit *(G-4052)*
Electrodynamics Inc .... G 734 422-5420
  Livonia *(G-10193)*
Freudnberg Btry Pwr Systems LL .... E 989 698-3329
  Midland *(G-11366)*
Lg Energy Solution Mich Inc .... C 616 494-7100
  Warren *(G-17904)*
Rizk National Industries Inc .... F 586 757-4700
  Warren *(G-17997)*

BATTERY REPAIR & SVCS

Alpine Power Systems Inc .... D 313 531-6600
  Redford *(G-13713)*
Energy Products Inc .... E 248 545-7700
  Madison Heights *(G-10722)*
Energy Products Inc .... G 248 866-5622
  Troy *(G-17090)*

BATTS & BATTING: Cotton

Zeilinger Wool Co LLC .... E 989 652-2920
  Frankenmuth *(G-5874)*

BAUXITE MINING

Howmet Aerospace Inc .... G 231 894-5686
  Whitehall *(G-18500)*

BEARINGS

Craft Steel Products Inc .... G 616 935-7575
  Spring Lake *(G-15809)*

BEARINGS & PARTS Ball

ABC Acquisition Company LLC .... E 734 335-4083
  Livonia *(G-10097)*

BEARINGS: Ball & Roller

Ewellix USA LLC .... C 586 752-0060
  Armada *(G-734)*
Frost Incorporated .... E 616 453-7781
  Grand Rapids *(G-6722)*
Independent Mfg Solutions Corp .... E 248 960-3550
  Wixom *(G-18684)*
Kaydon Corporation .... B 734 747-7025
  Ann Arbor *(G-538)*
Kaydon Corporation .... C 231 755-3741
  Norton Shores *(G-12306)*
Sunhill America LLC .... E 616 249-3600
  Grand Rapids *(G-7234)*
USA Brngs Sup LLC DBA JSB Grea .... G 734 222-4177
  Ann Arbor *(G-707)*

BEARINGS: Roller & Parts

Schaeffler Group USA Inc .... C 810 360-0294
  Milford *(G-11487)*

BEAUTY & BARBER SHOP EQPT

Aldez North America .... F 586 530-5314
  Clinton Township *(G-3161)*
B T I Industries .... F 586 532-8411
  Shelby Township *(G-15177)*
Bloom Industries LLC .... F 616 890-8029
  Traverse City *(G-16622)*
Brandt Manufacturing Inc .... F 517 851-7000
  Stockbridge *(G-16272)*
Coventry Industries LLC .... F 248 761-8462
  Holly *(G-8263)*
Crescent Manufacturing Company .... G 517 486-2670
  Blissfield *(G-1763)*
Innovative Thermal Systems LLC .... G 586 920-2900
  Warren *(G-17866)*
Intuitive Technology Inc .... E 602 249-5750
  Dexter *(G-4743)*
Jk Manufacturing Co .... F 231 258-2638
  Kalkaska *(G-9391)*
Jus Kutz LLC .... G 248 882-5462
  Pontiac *(G-13390)*
Karmann Manufacturing LLC .... E 734 582-5900
  Plymouth *(G-13210)*
Kims Mart Inc .... G 313 592-4929
  Detroit *(G-4362)*
Kriewall Enterprises Inc .... E 586 336-0600
  Romeo *(G-14227)*
Northbound Industries LLC .... G 661 510-8537
  Rochester Hills *(G-14071)*
Northwoods Manufacturing Inc .... D 906 779-2370
  Kingsford *(G-9516)*
Probus Technical Services Inc .... F 876 226-5692
  Troy *(G-17316)*
Qsdg Manufacturing LLC .... F 231 941-1222
  Traverse City *(G-16808)*
Rol Usa Inc .... G 616 499-8484
  Holland *(G-8183)*
Stewart Manufacturing LLC .... D 906 498-7600
  Hermansville *(G-7862)*
Telescopic Seating Systems LLC .... F 855 713-0118
  Grand Haven *(G-6370)*
US Salon Supply LLC .... F 616 365-5790
  Paw Paw *(G-12958)*
Vast Production Services Inc .... D 248 838-9680
  Troy *(G-17432)*
Waters Industries LLC .... G 616 848-8050
  Custer *(G-3752)*
Willow Mfg Inc .... G 231 275-1026
  Interlochen *(G-8686)*

BEAUTY & BARBER SHOP EQPT & SPLYS WHOLESALERS

US Salon Supply LLC .... F 616 365-5790
  Paw Paw *(G-12958)*

BEAUTY CONTEST PRODUCTION

Go Beyond Healthy LLC .... G 407 255-0314
  Grand Rapids *(G-6746)*

BEAUTY SALONS

Avissa Skin+body .... G 734 316-5556
  Ann Arbor *(G-389)*
Sweed Dreams LLC .... G 313 704-6694
  Livonia *(G-10425)*

BED & BREAKFAST INNS

Black Star Farms LLC .... F 231 271-4970
  Suttons Bay *(G-16339)*
Chateau Operations Ltd .... E 231 223-4110
  Traverse City *(G-16647)*
R C M S Inc .... G 269 422-1617
  Baroda *(G-1169)*

BEDDING & BEDSPRINGS STORES

Jonathan Stevens Mattress Co .... G 616 243-4342
  Grand Rapids *(G-6873)*

BEDDING, BEDSPREADS, BLANKETS & SHEETS

Colcha Linens Inc .... F 313 355-8300
  Plymouth *(G-13148)*
Grabber Inc .... E 616 940-1914
  Byron Center *(G-2274)*
Star Textile Inc .... E 888 527-5700
  Madison Heights *(G-10836)*

BEDDING, BEDSPREADS, BLANKETS & SHEETS: Comforters & Quilts

Down Inc .... E 616 241-3922
  Grand Rapids *(G-6658)*

BEDS & ACCESS STORES

Longstreet Group LLC .... F 517 278-4487
  Coldwater *(G-3443)*

BEDS: Hospital

Innovative Pdts Unlimited Inc .... G 269 684-5050
  Niles *(G-12138)*
Kci Prentis Building .... F 313 578-4400
  Detroit *(G-4355)*
Stryker Far East Inc .... A 269 385-2600
  Portage *(G-13618)*

BEER & ALE WHOLESALERS

Clarkston Courts LLC .... C 248 383-8444
  Clarkston *(G-3025)*
Oracle Brewing Company LLC .... F 989 401-7446
  Breckenridge *(G-1913)*
Thorn Apple Brewing Company .... G 616 288-6907
  Grand Rapids *(G-7261)*

BEER, WINE & LIQUOR STORES

Mpc Company Inc .... G 269 927-3371
  Benton Harbor *(G-1576)*
Two James Spirits LLC .... G 313 964-4800
  Detroit *(G-4650)*

BEER, WINE & LIQUOR STORES: Beer, Packaged

Brew Detroit LLC .... F 313 974-7366
  Detroit *(G-4069)*
Marias Italian Bakery Inc .... F 734 981-1200
  Canton *(G-2488)*
Mishigama Brewing Company .... G 734 547-5840
  Ypsilanti *(G-18968)*
Northwest Market .... F 517 787-5005
  Jackson *(G-8977)*
One Beer At A Time LLC .... E 616 719-1604
  Grand Rapids *(G-7059)*
Oracle Brewing Company LLC .... F 989 401-7446
  Breckenridge *(G-1913)*
Russo Bros Inc .... F 906 485-5250
  Ishpeming *(G-8781)*

BEER, WINE & LIQUOR STORES: Wine

Chateau Operations Ltd .... E 231 223-4110
  Traverse City *(G-16647)*
Fontaine Chateau 231 256-0000
  Lake Leelanau *(G-9560)*
Howells Mainstreet Winery .... G 517 545-9463
  Howell *(G-8466)*

PRODUCT SECTION

BEVERAGES, ALCOHOLIC: Distilled Liquors

Lemon Creek Winery Ltd .... E 269 471-1321
  Berrien Springs *(G-1643)*
Northville Cider Mill Inc .... F 248 349-3181
  Northville *(G-12245)*
Shady Lane Orchards Inc .... F 231 935-1620
  Suttons Bay *(G-16342)*
St Julian Wine Company Inc .... G 989 652-3281
  Frankenmuth *(G-5872)*
Winery At Young Farms LLC .... F 989 506-5142
  Mecosta *(G-11194)*

BEER, WINE & LIQUOR STORES: Wine & Beer

Veritas Vineyard LLC .... E 517 962-2427
  Jackson *(G-9030)*

BELTING: Rubber

Gates Corporation .... G 248 260-2300
  Rochester Hills *(G-14020)*
Mol Belting Systems Inc .... D 616 453-2484
  Grand Rapids *(G-7020)*
Sparks Belting Company Inc .... D 616 949-2750
  Grand Rapids *(G-7207)*

BELTS & BELT PRDTS

Outerwears Inc .... E 269 679-3301
  Schoolcraft *(G-15126)*

BELTS: Chain

Production Industries II Inc .... G 231 352-7500
  Traverse City *(G-16804)*

BELTS: Conveyor, Made From Purchased Wire

Lesco Design & Mfg Co Inc .... B 248 596-9301
  Wixom *(G-18697)*
Omni Technical Services Inc .... F 989 227-8900
  Saint Johns *(G-14912)*
Ton-Tex Corporation .... F 616 957-3200
  Greenville *(G-7508)*

BELTS: Seat, Automotive & Aircraft

Belt-Tech USA Inc .... C 450 372-5826
  Grand Rapids *(G-6498)*
Key Safety Systems Inc .... C 248 373-8040
  Auburn Hills *(G-951)*
Key Safety Systems Inc .... F 586 726-3905
  Auburn Hills *(G-952)*
Key Sfety Rstraint Systems Inc .... A 586 726-3800
  Auburn Hills *(G-953)*
Takata Americas .... A 336 547-1600
  Auburn Hills *(G-1044)*
Teamtech Motorsports Safety .... G 989 792-4880
  Saginaw *(G-14773)*
Tk Holdings Inc .... A 517 545-9535
  Howell *(G-8534)*

BENCHES, WORK : Factory

Benchwork Inc .... G 586 464-6699
  Clinton Township *(G-3182)*

BEVERAGE BASES & SYRUPS

Farber Concessions Inc .... E 313 387-1600
  Redford *(G-13733)*
Penguin Juice Co .... F 734 467-6991
  Westland *(G-18404)*

BEVERAGE PRDTS: Brewers' Grain

Kuhnhenn Brewing Co LLC .... F 586 979-8361
  Warren *(G-17898)*
Kuhnhenn Brewing Co LLC .... G 586 231-0429
  Clinton Township *(G-3274)*
One Beer At A Time LLC .... E 616 719-1604
  Grand Rapids *(G-7059)*

BEVERAGE PRDTS: Malt Syrup

Premier Malt Products Inc .... E 586 443-3355
  Warren *(G-17974)*

BEVERAGE STORES

Northville Cider Mill Inc .... F 248 349-3181
  Northville *(G-12245)*

Panther James LLC .... F 248 850-7522
  Berkley *(G-1634)*

BEVERAGE, NONALCOHOLIC: Iced Tea/Fruit Drink, Bottled/Canned

Ellis Infinity LLC .... G 313 570-0840
  Detroit *(G-4203)*

BEVERAGES, ALCOHOLIC: Ale

Clarkston Courts LLC .... C 248 383-8444
  Clarkston *(G-3025)*
Frankenmuth Brewery LLC .... E 989 262-8300
  Frankenmuth *(G-5861)*
Oracle Brewing Company LLC .... F 989 401-7446
  Breckenridge *(G-1913)*

BEVERAGES, ALCOHOLIC: Applejack

Mammoth Distilling LLC .... G 773 841-4242
  Central Lake *(G-2695)*

BEVERAGES, ALCOHOLIC: Beer

American Brewers Inc .... F 616 318-9230
  Kalamazoo *(G-9113)*
Atwater In Park .... G 313 344-5104
  Grosse Pointe Park *(G-7548)*
Backdraft Brewing Company .... F 734 722-7639
  Wayne *(G-18215)*
Beards Brewery LLC .... E 231 753-2221
  Petoskey *(G-12991)*
Bells Brewery Inc .... F 906 233-5002
  Escanaba *(G-5060)*
Bells Brewery Inc .... G 269 382-1402
  Kalamazoo *(G-9134)*
Black Bottom Brewing Co Inc .... G 313 205-5493
  Detroit *(G-4057)*
Blackrocks Brewery LLC .... G 906 273-1333
  Marquette *(G-11008)*
Blackrocks Brewery LLC .... G 906 360-6674
  Marquette *(G-11009)*
Brew Detroit LLC .... F 313 974-7366
  Detroit *(G-4069)*
Century Lanes Inc .... D 616 392-7086
  Holland *(G-7992)*
Corner Brewery LLC .... E 734 480-2739
  Ypsilanti *(G-18934)*
Eastside Spot Inc .... G 906 226-9431
  Marquette *(G-11016)*
Fabiano Bros Dev - Wscnsin LLC .... F 989 509-0200
  Bay City *(G-1356)*
Gpbc Inc .... F 734 741-7325
  Ann Arbor *(G-503)*
Gravel Capital Brewing LLC .... F 248 895-8399
  Oxford *(G-12885)*
Im A Beer Hound .... G 517 331-0528
  Lansing *(G-9767)*
James Joy LLC .... G 989 317-6629
  Farwell *(G-5424)*
Loggers Brewing Co .... G 989 401-3085
  Saginaw *(G-14684)*
Mor-Dall Enterprises Inc .... G 269 558-4915
  Marshall *(G-11071)*
Mountain Town Stn Brew Pub LLC .... D 989 775-2337
  Mount Pleasant *(G-11719)*
New Holland Brewing Co LLC .... C 616 355-2941
  Holland *(G-8154)*
Northern Oak Brewery Inc .... F 248 634-7515
  Holly *(G-8285)*
Ore Dock Brewing Company LLC .... F 906 228-8888
  Marquette *(G-11039)*
Paddle Hard Distributing LLC .... G 513 309-1192
  Grayling *(G-7468)*
S B C Holdings Inc .... F 313 446-2000
  Detroit *(G-4574)*
Salt Brewing Company LLC .... E 517 446-0375
  Lansing *(G-9890)*
Saugatuck Brewing Company Inc .... E 269 857-7222
  Douglas *(G-4774)*
Schelde Enterprises Inc .... G 231 941-7325
  Traverse City *(G-16825)*
Speciation Artisan Ales LLC .... G 616 279-3929
  Grand Rapids *(G-7215)*
Stony Lake Corporation .... G 734 944-9426
  Saline *(G-15041)*
Stroh Companies Inc .... G 313 446-2000
  Detroit *(G-4612)*

BEVERAGES, ALCOHOLIC: Beer & Ale

127 Brewing .... G 517 258-1346
  Jackson *(G-8797)*
Abaco Partners LLC .... C 616 532-1700
  Kentwood *(G-9441)*
Acoustic Tap Room .... G 231 714-5028
  Traverse City *(G-16596)*
Barkshanty Hops LLC .... G 810 300-8049
  Grosse Pointe Park *(G-7549)*
Detroit Cycle Pub LLC .... G 231 286-5257
  Macomb *(G-10587)*
Detroit Rvrtown Brwing Cmpay L .... C 313 877-9205
  Detroit *(G-4163)*
Dg Brewing Company LLC .... G 616 427-3242
  Ada *(G-16)*
Draught Horse Group LLC .... G 231 631-5218
  New Hudson *(G-12051)*
Elk Brewing .... G 616 214-8172
  Comstock Park *(G-3606)*
Ghost Island Brewery .... G 219 242-4800
  New Buffalo *(G-12024)*
Gilligan Steele Tastings LLC .... G 269 808-3455
  Kalamazoo *(G-9196)*
Global Draught Service .... G 810 844-6888
  Pinckney *(G-13049)*
Knickerbocker .... G 616 345-5642
  Grand Rapids *(G-6901)*
Kraftbrau Brewery Inc .... G 269 384-0288
  Kalamazoo *(G-9256)*
Lucky Girl Brwing - Cross Rads .... G 630 723-4285
  Paw Paw *(G-12951)*
M4 CIC LLC .... G 734 436-8507
  Ann Arbor *(G-559)*
Marquette Distillery .... G 906 869-4933
  Marquette *(G-11033)*
Mishigama Brewing Company .... G 734 547-5840
  Ypsilanti *(G-18968)*
Mug Shots Burgers and Brews .... G 616 895-2337
  Allendale *(G-227)*
New Holland Brewery .... F 616 202-7200
  Grand Rapids *(G-7042)*
North Pier Brewing Company LLC .... G 312 545-0446
  Saint Joseph *(G-14952)*
Null Taphouse .... G 734 792-9124
  Dexter *(G-4747)*
Plow Point Brewing Co .... G 734 562-9102
  Chelsea *(G-2823)*
Pollard Brewing .... G 734 207-3886
  Canton *(G-2510)*
Rare Bird Holdings LLC .... G 616 335-9463
  Holland *(G-8176)*
Sweetwater Brew LLC .... G 616 805-5077
  Wyoming *(G-18910)*
Thorn Apple Brewing Company .... G 616 288-6907
  Grand Rapids *(G-7261)*

BEVERAGES, ALCOHOLIC: Bourbon Whiskey

RGI Brands LLC .... F 312 253-7400
  Bloomfield Hills *(G-1856)*

BEVERAGES, ALCOHOLIC: Distilled Liquors

4 One 2 Distillery .... G 269 205-3223
  Wayland *(G-18186)*
Bier Barrel Distillery LLC .... G 616 633-8601
  Comstock Park *(G-3591)*
Bier Distillery Company .... G 616 633-8601
  Rockford *(G-14157)*
Brown Forman .... G 248 464-2011
  Clawson *(G-3089)*
Copper Kettle Distilling Co .... G 989 366-4412
  Prudenville *(G-13657)*
Detroit City Distillery LLC .... F 313 338-3760
  Detroit *(G-4141)*
Distilled Kalamazoo LLC .... G 269 993-2859
  Kalamazoo *(G-9170)*
Distillery 9 LLC .... G 517 990-2929
  Whitmore Lake *(G-18530)*
Grand Traverse Dist Tasting Rm .... G 269 254-8113
  Kalamazoo *(G-9199)*
Gray Skies Distillery .... F 616 437-1119
  Grand Rapids *(G-6785)*
Great Legs Wnery Brwry Dist LL .... G 616 298-7600
  Holland *(G-8060)*
Green Door Distilling Co LLC .... F 269 207-2298
  Kalamazoo *(G-9203)*
Jayda Gale Distilling Inc .... G 269 397-1132
  Wayland *(G-18197)*

Employee Codes: A=Over 500 employees, B=251-500
C=101-250, D=51-100, E=20-50, F=10-19, G=3-9

BEVERAGES, ALCOHOLIC: Distilled Liquors

Journeyman Distillery LLC .... G 269 820-2050
  Three Oaks *(G-16557)*
Kalamazoo Stillhouse .... G 269 352-0250
  Kalamazoo *(G-9249)*
Legacy Distillers Inc .... F 231 933-0631
  Traverse City *(G-16745)*
Les Cheneaux Distillers Inc .... E 906 748-0505
  Cedarville *(G-2670)*
Michigrain Distillery .... G 517 580-8624
  Lansing *(G-9871)*
Tcwc LLC .... E 231 922-8292
  Traverse City *(G-16852)*
Temperance Distilling Company .... F 734 847-5262
  Temperance *(G-16550)*
Two James Spirits LLC .... G 313 964-4800
  Detroit *(G-4650)*
Valentine Distilling Co .... G 646 286-2690
  Ferndale *(G-5596)*

BEVERAGES, ALCOHOLIC: Liquors, Malt

Apple Blossom Winery LLC .... G 269 668-3724
  Kalamazoo *(G-9114)*

BEVERAGES, ALCOHOLIC: Rum

Liquid Manufacturing LLC .... E 810 220-2802
  Ann Arbor *(G-550)*

BEVERAGES, ALCOHOLIC: Vodka

4 Detroiters Liquor LLC .... G 248 756-3678
  Farmington Hills *(G-5156)*
Embrace Premium Vodka LLC .... G 616 617-5602
  Ypsilanti *(G-18942)*
High Five Spirits LLC .... G 248 217-6057
  Bingham Farms *(G-1699)*
Valentine Distilling .... G 248 629-9951
  Ferndale *(G-5595)*

BEVERAGES, ALCOHOLIC: Wine Coolers

Caprice Brands LLC .... G 989 745-1286
  Livonia *(G-10144)*

BEVERAGES, ALCOHOLIC: Wines

12 Corners Vineyards .... G 269 926-7597
  Benton Harbor *(G-1524)*
45 North Vineyard & Winery .... F 231 271-1188
  Lake Leelanau *(G-9557)*
American Brewers Inc .... F 616 318-9230
  Kalamazoo *(G-9113)*
American Vintners LLC .... F 248 310-0575
  Rochester *(G-13891)*
Andretta & Associates Inc .... F 586 557-6226
  Macomb *(G-10577)*
B Nektar LLC .... F 313 744-6323
  Ferndale *(G-5530)*
Big Little Wines Traverse Cy MI ... G 231 714-4854
  Suttons Bay *(G-16338)*
Black Barn Vinyrd & Winery LLC . G 517 569-2164
  Rives Junction *(G-13885)*
Black Owl Distillery LLC .... G 616 901-9003
  Grand Rapids *(G-6514)*
Black Star Farms LLC .... F 231 271-4970
  Suttons Bay *(G-16339)*
Blue Collar Winery LLC .... G 419 344-4715
  Dundee *(G-4810)*
Bowers Harbor Vinyrd & Winery .. G 231 223-7615
  Traverse City *(G-16626)*
Brys Winery Lc .... G 231 223-8446
  Traverse City *(G-16631)*
Burrone Family Vineyards .... G 989 379-3786
  Lachine *(G-9531)*
Cellar 849 Winery .... G 734 254-0275
  Plymouth *(G-13143)*
Chateau Aronautique Winery LLC . G 517 569-2132
  Jackson *(G-8840)*
Chateau Grand Travers Ltd .... G 231 223-7355
  Traverse City *(G-16646)*
Chateau Operations Ltd .... E 231 223-4110
  Traverse City *(G-16647)*
CHI Co/Tabor Hill Winery .... D 269 422-1161
  Buchanan *(G-2192)*
Circus Procession LLC .... G 616 834-8048
  Holland *(G-7997)*
Cody Kresta Vineyard & Winery ... G 269 668-3800
  Mattawan *(G-11164)*
Contessa Wine Cellars .... G 269 468-5534
  Coloma *(G-3476)*
Continent Wines Inc .... G 248 467-7383
  Clarkston *(G-3029)*

Crystal Vista Vineyard LLC .... G 231 269-4165
  Thompsonville *(G-16553)*
Dablon Vineyards LLC .... G 269 422-2846
  Baroda *(G-1159)*
Detroit Original Winery .... G 248 924-2920
  Northville *(G-12213)*
Divino Intl Wine & Spirit LLC .... G 586 770-9409
  Lake Orion *(G-9603)*
Dunn Beverage Intl LLC .... G 269 420-1547
  Battle Creek *(G-1222)*
Fenn Valley Vineyards Inc .... F 269 561-2396
  Fennville *(G-5435)*
Fieldstone Hard Cider .... G 248 923-1742
  Rochester *(G-13901)*
Flying Otter Winery LLC .... G 517 424-7107
  Adrian *(G-68)*
Fontaine Chateau .... G 231 256-0000
  Lake Leelanau *(G-9560)*
French Road Cellars LLC .... G 231 256-0680
  Lake Leelanau *(G-9561)*
French Valley Vineyard L L C ...... G 231 228-2616
  Cedar *(G-2639)*
Glenn Vineyards LLC .... G 269 330-2350
  Fennville *(G-5436)*
Good Harbor Vineyards Winery ... G 231 632-0703
  Lake Leelanau *(G-9562)*
Good Neighbor Organic .... G 231 386-5636
  Northport *(G-12187)*
Harbor Sprng Vnyrds Winery LLC . G 231 242-4062
  Harbor Springs *(G-7647)*
Hearth & Vine .... G 231 944-1297
  Suttons Bay *(G-16341)*
Heavenly Vineyards LLC .... G 616 710-2751
  Cedar Springs *(G-2653)*
Hello Vino .... G 231 350-7138
  Bellaire *(G-1475)*
Home Winery Supply LLC .... G 734 529-3296
  Dundee *(G-4825)*
Howells Mainstreet Winery .... G 517 545-9463
  Howell *(G-8466)*
Lake Michigan Vintners LLC .... G 269 326-7195
  Baroda *(G-1163)*
Lawton Ridge Winery LLC .... G 269 372-9463
  Kalamazoo *(G-9259)*
Lazy Ballerina Winery LLC .... F 269 363-6218
  Saint Joseph *(G-14945)*
Lazy Ballerina Winery LLC .... F 269 759-8486
  Bridgman *(G-1931)*
Leelanau Wine Cellars Ltd .... F 231 386-5201
  Northport *(G-12189)*
Leighs Garden Winery Inc .... G 906 553-7799
  Escanaba *(G-5080)*
Lemon Creek Fruit Farm .... F 269 471-1321
  Berrien Springs *(G-1642)*
Lemon Creek Winery Ltd .... E 269 471-1321
  Berrien Springs *(G-1643)*
Little Man Winery .... G 269 637-2229
  South Haven *(G-15408)*
Lost Cellars Inc .... G 734 626-0969
  Boyne City *(G-1895)*
Mari Villa Vineyards .... F 231 935-4513
  Traverse City *(G-16753)*
Mario Anthony Tabone .... G 734 667-2946
  Plymouth *(G-13234)*
Michigan Wine Trail .... G 231 944-5220
  Traverse City *(G-16756)*
Modern Craft Winery LLC .... G 989 876-4948
  Au Gres *(G-760)*
Moraine Vineyards LLC .... G 269 422-1309
  Baroda *(G-1166)*
Nate Ronald .... G 269 424-3777
  Dowagiac *(G-4792)*
Nathaniel Rose Wine .... G 989 302-3297
  Traverse City *(G-16766)*
Nicholass Black River Vineyar .... G 231 625-9060
  Cheboygan *(G-2793)*
Nomad Cidery LLC .... G 231 313-8627
  Traverse City *(G-16769)*
Northville Winery .... G 248 320-6507
  Northville *(G-12248)*
OKeefe Centre Ltd .... G 231 223-7355
  Traverse City *(G-16779)*
Old Woodward Cellar .... G 248 792-5452
  Birmingham *(G-1741)*
Owl Wineries .... G 586 229-7217
  Roseville *(G-14457)*
Peninsula Cellars .... F 231 223-4050
  Traverse City *(G-16787)*
Pentamere Winery .... F 517 423-9000
  Tecumseh *(G-16511)*

Perrone Vineyards .... G 231 330-1493
  Levering *(G-10016)*
Petoskey Frms Vnyrd Winery LLC . G 231 290-9463
  Petoskey *(G-13014)*
Provemont Hill Vineyard .... G 231 256-8839
  Lake Leelanau *(G-9565)*
Saint Julian Winery .... G 248 951-2113
  Troy *(G-17341)*
Sandhill Crane Vineyards LLC .... G 517 764-0679
  Jackson *(G-9006)*
Schramms Mead .... G 248 439-5000
  Ferndale *(G-5584)*
Shady Lane Orchards Inc .... F 231 935-1620
  Suttons Bay *(G-16342)*
Signal 7 Wines LLC .... F 616 581-8900
  Ann Arbor *(G-653)*
Spare Key Winery LLC .... G 231 250-7442
  Charlevoix *(G-2733)*
Speciation Artisan Ales LLC .... G 616 279-3929
  Grand Rapids *(G-7215)*
St Ambrose Cellars .... G 231 383-4262
  Beulah *(G-1659)*
St Julian Wine Company Inc ...... G 734 529-3700
  Dundee *(G-4836)*
St Julian Wine Company Inc ...... E 269 657-5568
  Paw Paw *(G-12957)*
St Julian Winery .... G 616 263-9087
  Rockford *(G-14190)*
Stoney Acres Winery .... G 989 356-1041
  Alpena *(G-323)*
Stoney Ridge Vineyards LLC ...... G 616 540-4318
  Kent City *(G-9437)*
Sunshine Meadery LLC .... G 231 215-7956
  Twin Lake *(G-17473)*
Suttons Bay Ciders .... G 734 646-3196
  Suttons Bay *(G-16343)*
T/D Village Winery LLC .... G 586 752-5510
  Romeo *(G-14236)*
Tabone Vineyards LLC .... G 734 354-7271
  Traverse City *(G-16850)*
Tandem Ciders Inc .... G 231 271-0050
  Suttons Bay *(G-16344)*
Teeq Spirits Inc .... G 866 877-1840
  Canton *(G-2532)*
Tempo Vino Winery Kalamazoo ... G 269 342-9463
  Kalamazoo *(G-9353)*
Thunder Bay Winery .... G 989 358-9463
  Alpena *(G-326)*
To Willow Harbor Vineyard .... G 269 369-3900
  Three Oaks *(G-16560)*
Uva Mare Inc .... G 858 848-4440
  Shelby Township *(G-15362)*
Vander Mill LLC .... D 616 259-8828
  Grand Rapids *(G-7307)*
Veritas Vineyard LLC .... E 517 962-2427
  Jackson *(G-9030)*
Vine-N-Berry Wines .... G 989 551-1616
  Bad Axe *(G-1117)*
Vineyard On Plainfield .... G 616 570-0659
  Grand Rapids *(G-7318)*
Vineyard Ventures LLC .... G 517 420-4771
  Lansing *(G-9902)*
Vintners Cellar Winery of Kal ...... G 269 342-9463
  Kalamazoo *(G-9363)*
Virgils Vineyard LLC .... G 248 719-2808
  Farmington Hills *(G-5411)*
Virtue Cider .... F 269 455-0526
  Fennville *(G-5444)*
Waloon Lake Winery .... G 231 622-8645
  Petoskey *(G-13026)*
Weathervane Vinyards Inc .... G 231 228-4800
  Cedar *(G-2640)*
White Pine Winery .... G 269 281-0098
  Saint Joseph *(G-14979)*
Willow Vineyards Inc .... G 231 271-4810
  Suttons Bay *(G-16347)*
Winery At Young Farms LLC .... F 989 506-5142
  Mecosta *(G-11194)*
Yooper Winery LLC .... G 906 361-0318
  Menominee *(G-11262)*

BEVERAGES, MALT

Midland Brewing Co LLC .... G 989 259-7210
  Midland *(G-11391)*

BEVERAGES, NONALCOHOLIC: Bottled & canned soft drinks

Binks Coca-Cola Bottling Co .... E 906 786-4144
  Escanaba *(G-5063)*

Binks Coca-Cola Bottling Co ....F 906 774-3202
Iron Mountain *(G-8718)*
Bottling Group Inc ....G 517 545-2624
Howell *(G-8432)*
Coca-Cola Bottling Co ....F 313 868-2167
Highland Park *(G-7902)*
Coca-Cola Company ....G 269 657-3171
Paw Paw *(G-12943)*
Coca-Cola Refreshments USA Inc ....G 231 947-4150
Traverse City *(G-16655)*
Coca-Cola Refreshments USA Inc ....G 616 458-4536
Grand Rapids *(G-6579)*
Coca-Cola Refreshments USA Inc ....G 269 657-8538
Paw Paw *(G-12944)*
Coca-Cola Refreshments USA Inc ....G 313 897-5000
Farmington Hills *(G-5204)*
Coke Bottle ....G 810 424-3352
Flint *(G-5668)*
Florida Coca-Cola Bottling Co ....B 906 495-2261
Kincheloe *(G-9503)*
Great Lakes Coca-Cola Dist LLC ....F 989 895-8537
Bay City *(G-1363)*
Great Lakes Coca-Cola Dist LLC ....F 906 475-7003
Negaunee *(G-11966)*
Great Lakes Coca-Cola Dist LLC ....F 517 322-2349
Lansing *(G-9762)*
Great Lakes Coca-Cola Dist LLC ....F 734 397-2700
Belleville *(G-1485)*
Hancock Bottling Co Inc ....E 906 482-3701
Hancock *(G-7618)*
Hill Brothers ....G 616 784-2767
Grand Rapids *(G-6816)*
Jbt Bottling LLC ....G 269 377-4905
Kalamazoo *(G-9230)*
Jumpin Johnnys Inc ....G 989 832-0160
Midland *(G-11380)*
Liquid Manufacturing LLC ....E 810 220-2802
Ann Arbor *(G-550)*
Michigan Btlg & Cstm Pack Co ....D 313 846-1717
Detroit *(G-4446)*
Minute Maid Co ....G 269 657-3171
Paw Paw *(G-12953)*
Northville Cider Mill Inc ....F 248 349-3181
Northville *(G-12245)*
Pbg Michigan LLC ....G 989 345-2595
West Branch *(G-18335)*
Pepsi-Cola Metro Btlg Co Inc ....G 989 772-3158
Mount Pleasant *(G-11730)*
Select Distributors LLC ....F 586 510-4647
Warren *(G-18008)*
Simplify Inventions LLC ....D 248 960-1700
Farmington Hills *(G-5382)*
South Range Bottling Works Inc ....G 906 370-2295
South Range *(G-15462)*
St Julian Wine Company Inc ....G 989 652-3281
Frankenmuth *(G-5872)*
Wasem Fruit Farm ....G 734 482-2342
Milan *(G-11451)*

BEVERAGES, NONALCOHOLIC: Carbonated

Newberry Bottling Co Inc ....G 906 293-5189
Newberry *(G-12095)*
Pepsi ....G 231 627-2290
Cheboygan *(G-2795)*
Pepsi Beverages Co ....G 989 754-0435
Saginaw *(G-14726)*
Pepsi Bottling Group ....F 517 546-2777
Howell *(G-8493)*
Pepsi Co Wixom ....F 248 305-3500
Milan *(G-11448)*
Pepsi Cola Botling Co Houghton ....F 906 482-0161
Houghton *(G-8389)*
Pepsi-Cola Metro Btlg Co Inc ....G 517 321-0231
Lansing *(G-9726)*
Pepsi-Cola Metro Btlg Co Inc ....G 248 335-3528
Pontiac *(G-13406)*
Pepsi-Cola Metro Btlg Co Inc ....G 989 345-2595
West Branch *(G-18336)*
Pepsi-Cola Metro Btlg Co Inc ....G 231 946-0452
Traverse City *(G-16788)*
Pepsi-Cola Metro Btlg Co Inc ....G 989 755-1020
Saginaw *(G-14727)*
Pepsi-Cola Metro Btlg Co Inc ....G 517 546-2777
Howell *(G-8494)*
Pepsi-Cola Metro Btlg Co Inc ....G 269 226-6400
Kalamazoo *(G-9291)*
Pepsi-Cola Metro Btlg Co Inc ....G 616 285-8200
Grand Rapids *(G-7077)*
Pepsi-Cola Metro Btlg Co Inc ....G 313 832-0910
Detroit *(G-4516)*
Pepsi-New Bern-Howell-151 ....F 517 546-7542
Howell *(G-8495)*
Pepsico Inc ....F 734 374-9841
Southgate *(G-15755)*
Pepsico Inc ....G 586 276-4102
Sterling Heights *(G-16124)*

BEVERAGES, NONALCOHOLIC: Carbonated, Canned & Bottled, Etc

Global Restaurant Group Inc ....G 313 271-2777
Dearborn *(G-3847)*
Pepsi-Cola Metro Btlg Co Inc ....G 810 987-2181
Kimball *(G-9498)*
Viva Beverages LLC ....G 248 746-7044
Southfield *(G-15739)*

BEVERAGES, NONALCOHOLIC: Cider

Aseltine Cider Company Inc ....G 616 784-7676
Comstock Park *(G-3588)*
Blakes Orchard Inc ....G 586 784-5343
Armada *(G-732)*
Dexter Cider Mill Inc ....G 734 475-6419
Chelsea *(G-2809)*
Hill Brothers ....G 616 784-2767
Grand Rapids *(G-6816)*
Mizkan America Inc ....D 616 794-0226
Belding *(G-1457)*
Parshallville Cider Mill ....G 810 629-9079
Fenton *(G-5494)*
Porters Orchards Farm Market ....G 810 636-7156
Goodrich *(G-6226)*
Ridge Cider ....G 231 674-2040
Grant *(G-7432)*
Riveridge Cider Co LLC ....G 616 887-6873
Sparta *(G-15777)*
Uncle Johns Cider Mill Inc ....E 989 224-3686
Saint Johns *(G-14919)*
Yates Cider Mill Inc ....G 248 651-8300
Rochester Hills *(G-14149)*

BEVERAGES, NONALCOHOLIC: Flavoring extracts & syrups, nec

Coffee Beanery Ltd ....E 810 733-1020
Flushing *(G-5805)*
Flavorsum LLC ....E 800 525-2431
Kalamazoo *(G-9188)*
Jogue Inc ....G 248 349-1501
Northville *(G-12233)*
Kalsec Inc ....G 269 349-9711
Kalamazoo *(G-9250)*
Leroy Worden ....G 231 325-3837
Beulah *(G-1655)*
Lorann Oils Inc ....F 517 882-0215
Lansing *(G-9865)*
Moore Ingredients Ltd ....G 513 881-7144
Kalamazoo *(G-9275)*
Sensient Flavors LLC ....E 989 479-3211
Harbor Beach *(G-7636)*
Sunopta Ingredients Inc ....E 502 587-7999
Schoolcraft *(G-15129)*

BEVERAGES, NONALCOHOLIC: Fruit Drnks, Under 100% Juice, Can

Everfresh Beverages Inc ....D 586 755-9500
Warren *(G-17798)*
S B C Holdings Inc ....F 313 446-2000
Detroit *(G-4574)*
Stroh Companies Inc ....G 313 446-2000
Detroit *(G-4612)*
Sundance Beverages Inc ....D 586 755-9470
Warren *(G-18030)*

BEVERAGES, NONALCOHOLIC: Soft Drinks, Canned & Bottled, Etc

American Bottling Company ....F 810 564-1432
Mount Morris *(G-11667)*
American Bottling Company ....F 616 396-1281
Holland *(G-7962)*
American Bottling Company ....F 616 392-2124
Holland *(G-7963)*
American Bottling Company ....E 989 731-5392
Gaylord *(G-6118)*
American Bottling Company ....F 231 775-7393
Cadillac *(G-2312)*
American Bottling Company ....F 517 622-8605
Grand Ledge *(G-6384)*
Coca-Cola Refreshments USA Inc ....G 616 913-0400
Grand Rapids *(G-6578)*
Dr Pepper Snapple Group ....F 616 393-5800
Holland *(G-8016)*
Faygo Beverages Inc ....B 313 925-1600
Detroit *(G-4227)*
Keurig Dr Pepper Inc ....G 231 775-7393
Cadillac *(G-2339)*
Keurig Dr Pepper Inc ....G 313 937-3500
Detroit *(G-4359)*
Pepsi Bottling Group ....F 810 966-8060
Kimball *(G-9497)*
Pepsi-Cola Metro Btlg Co Inc ....G 810 232-3925
Flint *(G-5744)*
Pepsi-Cola Metro Btlg Co Inc ....G 517 279-8436
Coldwater *(G-3445)*
Pepsi-Cola Metro Btlg Co Inc ....G 231 798-1274
Norton Shores *(G-12325)*
Refreshment Product Svcs Inc ....G 906 475-7003
Negaunee *(G-11972)*

BEVERAGES, NONALCOHOLIC: Tea, Iced, Bottled & Canned, Etc

Detroit Bubble Tea Company ....G 248 239-1131
Ferndale *(G-5542)*
Grandads Sweet Tea LLC ....G 313 320-4446
Warren *(G-17835)*

BEVERAGES, WINE & DISTILLED ALCOHOLIC, WHOLESALE: Wine

Fontaine Chateau ....G 231 256-0000
Lake Leelanau *(G-9560)*
Great Lakes Wine & Spirits LLC ....C 313 278-5400
Highland Park *(G-7908)*

BEVERAGES, WINE/DISTILLED ALCOHOLIC, WHOL: Cocktls, Premixed

RGI Brands LLC ....F 312 253-7400
Bloomfield Hills *(G-1856)*

BICYCLE SHOPS

Assenmacher Lightweight Cycles ....G 810 635-7844
Swartz Creek *(G-16350)*
Detroit Bikes LLC ....G 313 646-4109
Detroit *(G-4135)*
Riverfront Cycle Inc ....G 517 482-8585
Lansing *(G-9888)*

BICYCLES WHOLESALERS

Shinola/Detroit LLC ....C 888 304-2534
Detroit *(G-4591)*

BICYCLES, PARTS & ACCESS

Aerospoke Incorporated ....G 248 685-9009
Brighton *(G-1939)*
Detroit Bikes LLC ....G 313 646-4109
Detroit *(G-4135)*
Shinola/Detroit LLC ....C 888 304-2534
Detroit *(G-4591)*
Velocity Worldwide Inc ....F 616 243-3400
Grand Rapids *(G-7309)*
Wiz Wheelz Inc ....E 616 455-5988
Grand Rapids *(G-7342)*

BILLING & BOOKKEEPING SVCS

Jax Services LLC ....G 586 703-3212
Warren *(G-17883)*
N F P Inc ....G 989 631-0009
Midland *(G-11397)*

BINDING SVC: Books & Manuals

A Koppel Color Image Company ....G 616 534-3600
Grandville *(G-7360)*
Afb Corporate Operations LLC ....E 248 669-1188
Plymouth *(G-13120)*
Aladdin Printing ....G 248 360-2842
Commerce Township *(G-3507)*
American Label & Tag Inc ....E 734 454-7600
Canton *(G-2433)*
Americas Finest Prtg Graphics ....G 586 296-1312
Fraser *(G-5893)*
Apb Inc ....G 248 528-2990
Troy *(G-16939)*

BINDING SVC: Books & Manuals

ASAP Printing Inc .... G 517 882-3500
  Okemos (G-12657)
Brd Printing Inc .... E 517 372-0268
  Lansing (G-9816)
Breck Graphics Incorporated .... E 616 248-4110
  Grand Rapids (G-6523)
Bronco Printing Company .... G 248 544-1120
  Hazel Park (G-7821)
Bruce Inc .... G 517 371-5205
  Lansing (G-9819)
Business Press Inc .... G 248 652-8855
  Rochester (G-13895)
Color Connection .... G 248 351-0920
  Southfield (G-15527)
Copy Central Inc .... G 231 941-2298
  Traverse City (G-16660)
Cushing-Malloy Inc .... E 734 663-8554
  Ann Arbor (G-440)
Custom Printers Inc .... D 616 454-9224
  Grand Rapids (G-6623)
De Vru Printing Co .... G 616 452-5451
  Grand Rapids (G-6636)
Derk Pieter Co Inc .... G 616 554-7777
  Grand Rapids (G-6641)
Dobb Printing Inc .... E 231 722-1060
  Muskegon (G-11799)
DPrinter Inc .... G 517 423-6554
  Tecumseh (G-16499)
Earle Press Inc .... E 231 773-2111
  Muskegon (G-11805)
Econo Print Inc .... G 734 878-5806
  Pinckney (G-13047)
F P Horak Company .... C 989 892-6505
  Bay City (G-1355)
Fedex Office & Print Svcs Inc .... F 734 761-4539
  Ann Arbor (G-487)
Fedex Office & Print Svcs Inc .... G 517 332-5855
  East Lansing (G-4892)
Foremost Graphics LLC .... D 616 453-4747
  Grand Rapids (G-6715)
Forsons Inc .... G 517 787-4562
  Jackson (G-8885)
Frye Printing Company Inc .... F 517 456-4124
  Clinton (G-3139)
Future Reproductions Inc .... F 248 350-2060
  Southfield (G-15571)
Gombar Corp .... G 989 793-9427
  Saginaw (G-14655)
Grand Blanc Printing Inc .... E 810 694-1155
  Grand Blanc (G-6245)
Graphic Impressions Inc .... G 616 455-0303
  Grand Rapids (G-6782)
Graphic Specialties Inc .... E 616 247-0060
  Grand Rapids (G-6783)
Hamblin Company .... E 517 423-7491
  Bloomfield Hills (G-1826)
Handy Bindery Co Inc .... E 586 469-2240
  Clinton Township (G-3251)
Hatteras Inc .... E 734 525-5500
  Plymouth (G-13183)
Hi-Lites Graphic Inc .... E 231 924-0630
  Fremont (G-6045)
Hodges & Irvine Inc .... F 810 329-4787
  Saint Clair (G-14831)
J-Ad Graphics Inc .... F 269 965-3955
  Battle Creek (G-1243)
J-Ad Graphics Inc .... D 800 870-7085
  Hastings (G-7800)
Kent Communications Inc .... D 616 957-2120
  Grand Rapids (G-6886)
Litsenberger Print Shop .... G 906 482-3903
  Houghton (G-8386)
Logan Brothers Printing Inc .... G 517 485-3771
  Dewitt (G-4711)
Macomb Printing Inc .... E 586 463-2301
  Clinton Township (G-3288)
Maleports Sault Prtg Co Inc .... F 906 632-3369
  Sault Sainte Marie (G-15095)
McNaughton & Gunn Inc .... C 734 429-5411
  Saline (G-15025)
Mel Printing Co Inc .... E 313 928-5440
  Taylor (G-16440)
Metropolitan Indus Lithography .... G 269 323-9333
  Portage (G-13585)
Micrgraphics Printing Inc .... F 231 739-6575
  Norton Shores (G-12311)
Mid-State Printing Inc .... F 989 875-4163
  Ithaca (G-8794)
Mitchell Graphics Inc .... E 231 347-4635
  Petoskey (G-13007)

Ogemaw County Herald Inc .... E 989 345-0044
  West Branch (G-18333)
Owosso Graphic Arts Inc .... E 989 725-7112
  Owosso (G-12849)
Parkside Speedy Print Inc .... G 810 985-8484
  Port Huron (G-13516)
Paul C Doerr .... G 734 242-2058
  Monroe (G-11568)
Phase III Graphics Inc .... G 616 949-9290
  Grand Rapids (G-7084)
Print-Tech Inc .... E 734 996-2345
  Ann Arbor (G-624)
Printcomm Inc .... D 810 239-5763
  Flint (G-5749)
Printery Inc .... E 616 396-4655
  Holland (G-8172)
Printing Plus Inc .... G 734 482-1680
  Ypsilanti (G-18971)
Printwell Acquisition Co Inc .... D 734 941-6300
  Taylor (G-16462)
Qrp Inc .... E 989 496-2955
  Midland (G-11406)
Qrp Inc .... E 989 496-2955
  Midland (G-11405)
R & R Harwood Inc .... G 616 669-6400
  Jenison (G-9069)
R W Patterson Printing Co .... D 269 925-2177
  Benton Harbor (G-1579)
Reyers Company Inc .... F 616 414-5530
  Spring Lake (G-15846)
Riegle Press Inc .... E 810 653-9631
  Davison (G-3795)
River Run Press Inc .... E 269 349-7603
  Kalamazoo (G-9320)
Spartan Graphics Inc .... D 616 887-1073
  Sparta (G-15780)
Spartan Printing Inc .... E 517 372-6910
  Lansing (G-9738)
Spectrum Printers Inc .... E 517 423-5735
  Tecumseh (G-16517)
T J K Inc .... E 586 731-9639
  Sterling Heights (G-16199)
Technology MGT & Budgt Dept .... E 517 322-1897
  Lansing (G-9899)
Thorpe Printing Services Inc .... G 810 364-6222
  Marysville (G-11107)
Tribar Manufacturing LLC .... E 248 669-0077
  Wixom (G-18777)
Turner Business Forms Inc .... E 989 752-5540
  Saginaw (G-14782)
Village Shop Inc .... E 231 946-3712
  Traverse City (G-16875)
Wolverine Printing Company LLC .... E 616 451-2075
  Grand Rapids (G-7347)

BINS: Prefabricated, Metal Plate

Contract Welding and Fabg Inc .... E 734 699-5561
  Van Buren Twp (G-17520)
L & W Inc .... G 734 397-2212
  Van Buren Twp (G-17536)
L & W Inc .... G 616 394-9665
  Holland (G-8118)

BIOLOGICAL PRDTS: Exc Diagnostic

Axonia Medical Inc .... E 269 615-6632
  Kalamazoo (G-9128)
Biosan Laboratories Inc .... F 586 755-8970
  Warren (G-17738)
Corium Inc .... C 650 298-8255
  Grand Rapids (G-6606)
Immuno Concepts NA Ltd .... E 734 464-0701
  Livonia (G-10246)
Koppert Biological Systems Inc .... E 734 641-3763
  Howell (G-8470)
Oxford Biomedical Research Inc .... G 248 852-8815
  Metamora (G-11284)
S and N Products Inc .... G 810 542-9635
  Lake Orion (G-9629)

BIOLOGICAL PRDTS: Extracts

Deru Extracts LLC .... G 734 497-2963
  Carleton (G-2551)
Extract .... G 269 362-4879
  Rockford (G-14166)
Loud N Clear Extracts LLC .... G 312 320-4970
  Galien (G-6090)

BIOLOGICAL PRDTS: Vaccines

Emergent Biodef Oper Lnsng LLC .... B 517 327-1500
  Lansing (G-9690)
Michigan For Vaccine Choice .... G 586 294-3074
  Saint Clair Shores (G-14871)

BIOLOGICAL PRDTS: Vaccines & Immunizing

Bruce Kane Enterprises LLC .... G 410 727-0637
  Farmington Hills (G-5187)
Novavax Inc .... G 248 656-5336
  Rochester (G-13914)

BIOLOGICAL PRDTS: Veterinary

Arbor Assays Inc .... F 734 677-1774
  Ann Arbor (G-373)
Neogen Corporation .... A 517 372-9200
  Lansing (G-9874)

BLACKSMITH SHOP

Cooks Blacksmith Welding Inc .... G 231 796-6819
  Big Rapids (G-1671)

BLADES: Saw, Chain Type

Saw Tubergen Service Inc .... G 616 534-0701
  Grand Rapids (G-7182)

BLANKBOOKS & LOOSELEAF BINDERS

Microforms Inc .... E 586 939-7900
  Beverly Hills (G-1667)

BLANKBOOKS: Albums, Record

Cookie Music Ent LLC .... G 209 851-6633
  Detroit (G-4103)
Top Quality Cleaning LLC .... F 810 493-4211
  Flint (G-5779)

BLANKBOOKS: Receipt

Superior Receipt Book Co Inc .... F 269 467-8265
  Centreville (G-2698)

BLANKBOOKS: Scrapbooks

Artful Scrapbooking & Rubber .... G 586 651-1577
  Washington (G-18078)
Gathering Place of White Lake .... G 248 379-9582
  White Lake (G-18455)
Janelle Peterson .... G 616 447-9070
  Grand Rapids (G-6861)
Memories Manor .... G 810 329-2800
  Saint Clair (G-14836)
Scrapaloo .... G 269 623-7310
  Delton (G-3966)
Scrappy Chic .... G 248 426-9020
  Livonia (G-10402)

BLANKETS, FROM PURCHASED MATERIALS

Cellulose Mtl Solutions LLC .... G 616 669-2990
  Jenison (G-9049)

BLANKETS: Horse

Huron Vlleys Hrse Blnket Hdqtr .... G 248 859-2398
  Wixom (G-18682)

BLASTING SVC: Sand, Metal Parts

Abrasive Solutions LLC .... G 517 592-2668
  Cement City (G-2675)
Beech & Rich Inc .... E 269 968-8012
  Springfield (G-15861)
Northwest Fabrication Inc .... G 231 536-3229
  East Jordan (G-4878)
Schwartz Boiler Shop Inc .... G 231 627-2556
  Cheboygan (G-2798)
Spec Abrasives and Finishing .... F 231 722-1926
  Muskegon (G-11924)
Supreme Media Blasting and Pow .... G 586 792-7705
  Clinton Township (G-3366)

BLINDS & SHADES: Vertical

A ME Vertical Incorporated .... G 248 720-0245
  Troy (G-16900)

PRODUCT SECTION — BOAT BUILDING & REPAIR

Custom Verticals Unlimited ....G....... 734 522-1615
Oak Park *(G-12603)*
Kyler Industries Inc ....G....... 616 392-1042
Holland *(G-8117)*
MSC Blinds & Shades Inc ....G....... 269 489-5188
Bronson *(G-2119)*
Sophias Textiles & Furn Inc ....F....... 586 759-6231
Center Line *(G-2687)*
Time For Blinds Inc ....G....... 248 363-9174
White Lake *(G-18469)*
Triangle Window Fashions Inc ....G....... 616 538-9676
Wyoming *(G-18914)*
Vertical Detroit ....G....... 313 732-9463
Detroit *(G-4667)*
Vertical Wrks Blinds & Drapery ....G....... 586 992-2600
Washington *(G-18090)*

BLINDS : Window

Advantage Blnds Shds Shtters L ....F....... 248 399-2154
 Royal Oak *(G-14504)*
Blind Bull LLC ....G....... 616 516-4881
 Allendale *(G-215)*
Blind Spot and More LLC ....G....... 616 828-6495
 Byron Center *(G-2260)*
Blinds and Designs Inc ....F....... 770 971-5524
 Wixom *(G-18623)*
Dave Brand ....G....... 269 651-4693
 Sturgis *(G-16287)*
Detroit Custom Services Inc ....E....... 586 465-3631
 Mount Clemens *(G-11636)*
Expressive Window Fashions ....G....... 269 663-8833
 Edwardsburg *(G-5006)*
Mid-Michigan Blinds ....G....... 810 225-8488
 Brighton *(G-2034)*
Parkway Drapery & Uphl Co Inc ....G....... 734 779-1300
 Livonia *(G-10360)*
Protein Cheesecake Company ....G....... 248 495-3258
 Rochester *(G-13923)*
Sheer Madness Drap & Blinds ....G....... 248 379-2145
 Macomb *(G-10634)*
Signature Designs Inc ....G....... 248 426-9735
 Farmington Hills *(G-5378)*
Sunburst Shutters ....G....... 248 674-4600
 Waterford *(G-18167)*

BLOCKS & BRICKS: Concrete

Carlesimo Products Inc ....E....... 248 474-0415
 Farmington Hills *(G-5198)*
Interlock Design ....F....... 616 784-5901
 Comstock Park *(G-3612)*
Kurtz Gravel Company Inc ....E....... 810 787-6543
 Farmington Hills *(G-5286)*
Lafarge North America Inc ....G....... 231 726-3291
 Muskegon *(G-11855)*
Miller Products & Supply Co ....F....... 906 774-1243
 Iron Mountain *(G-8725)*
St Marys Cement Inc (us) ....G....... 269 679-5253
 Schoolcraft *(G-15128)*
Swartzmiller Lumber Company ....G....... 989 845-6625
 Chesaning *(G-2830)*
Waanders Concrete Co ....F....... 269 673-6452
 Allegan *(G-184)*

BLOCKS: Landscape Or Retaining Wall, Concrete

Cherry Oak Landscaping LLC ....F....... 517 339-2881
 East Lansing *(G-4890)*
Declarks Landscaping Inc ....E....... 586 752-7200
 Bruce Twp *(G-2166)*
K-Tel Corporation ....F....... 517 543-6174
 Charlotte *(G-2760)*
Livingston County Concrete Inc ....E....... 810 632-3030
 Brighton *(G-2022)*
Simply Green Outdoor Svcs LLC ....G....... 734 385-6190
 Dexter *(G-4755)*
Zaremba & Co Inc ....G....... 248 922-3300
 Davisburg *(G-3773)*

BLOCKS: Paving, Cut Stone

Unilock Michigan Inc ....E....... 248 437-7037
 Brighton *(G-2089)*

BLOCKS: Standard, Concrete Or Cinder

Bark River Concrete Pdts Co ....G....... 906 466-9940
 Bark River *(G-1153)*
Best Block Company ....E....... 586 772-7000
 Warren *(G-17732)*
Branch West Concrete Products ....F....... 989 345-0794
 West Branch *(G-18326)*
Cheboygan Cement Products Inc ....E....... 231 627-5631
 Cheboygan *(G-2782)*
Clay & Graham Inc ....G....... 989 354-5292
 Alpena *(G-287)*
Consumers Concrete Corp ....C....... 616 243-3651
 Wyoming *(G-18858)*
Consumers Concrete Corp ....E....... 269 384-0977
 Kalamazoo *(G-9152)*
Consumers Concrete Corporation ....E....... 269 342-0136
 Kalamazoo *(G-9153)*
Consumers Concrete Corporation ....F....... 231 777-3981
 Muskegon *(G-11795)*
Fendt Builders Supply Inc ....F....... 734 663-4277
 Ann Arbor *(G-488)*
Fendt Builders Supply Inc ....E....... 248 474-3211
 Farmington Hills *(G-5242)*
Ferguson Block Co Inc ....E....... 810 653-2812
 Davison *(G-3781)*
Grand Blanc Cement Pdts Inc ....E....... 810 694-7500
 Grand Blanc *(G-6244)*
Hagen Cement Products Inc ....G....... 269 483-9641
 White Pigeon *(G-18480)*
Hampton Block Co ....G....... 248 628-1333
 Oxford *(G-12886)*
Hobe Inc ....G....... 231 845-5196
 Ludington *(G-10539)*
Lafarge North America Inc ....G....... 703 480-3600
 Dundee *(G-4827)*
Ludvanwall Inc ....E....... 616 842-4500
 Spring Lake *(G-15830)*
National Block Company ....E....... 734 721-4050
 Westland *(G-18399)*
Port Huron Building Supply Co ....F....... 810 987-2666
 Port Huron *(G-13519)*
Ruppe Manufacturing Company ....E....... 906 932-3540
 Ironwood *(G-8771)*
Superior Block Company Inc ....E....... 906 482-2731
 Houghton *(G-8392)*
Theut Concrete Products Inc ....F....... 810 679-3376
 Croswell *(G-3737)*

BLOWER FILTER UNITS: Furnace Blowers

Wh Filtration Inc ....G....... 248 633-4001
 Detroit *(G-4679)*

BLOWERS & FANS

AC Covers Inc ....F....... 313 541-7770
 Redford *(G-13710)*
Advance Products Corporation ....E....... 269 849-1000
 Benton Harbor *(G-1527)*
Anrod Screen Cylinder Company ....E....... 989 872-2101
 Cass City *(G-2610)*
Avl Test Systems Inc ....C....... 734 414-9600
 Plymouth *(G-13134)*
Borgwarner Thermal Systems Inc ....G....... 231 779-7500
 Cadillac *(G-2317)*
Chicago Blow Pipe Company ....F....... 773 533-6100
 Marquette *(G-11012)*
Clean Air Technology Inc ....E....... 734 459-6320
 Canton *(G-2450)*
Combustion Research Corp ....E....... 248 852-3611
 Rochester Hills *(G-13979)*
Compressor Technologies Inc ....F....... 616 949-7000
 Grand Rapids *(G-6590)*
Constructive Sheet Metal Inc ....E....... 616 245-5306
 Allendale *(G-217)*
Dcl Inc ....C....... 231 547-5600
 Charlevoix *(G-2714)*
Dexter Automatic Products Co ....C....... 734 426-8900
 Dexter *(G-4734)*
Forma-Kool Manufacturing Inc ....E....... 586 949-4813
 Chesterfield *(G-2884)*
General Aire ....G....... 866 476-5101
 Novi *(G-12422)*
Key Gas Components Inc ....E....... 269 673-2151
 Allegan *(G-163)*
Manrisa ....G....... 248 364-4415
 Auburn Hills *(G-967)*
Murtech Energy Services LLC ....G....... 810 653-5681
 Port Huron *(G-13508)*
Nortek Air Solutions LLC ....D....... 616 738-7148
 Holland *(G-8156)*
Parker-Hannifin Corporation ....B....... 269 629-5000
 Richland *(G-13826)*
Pittsfield Products Inc ....E....... 734 665-3771
 Ann Arbor *(G-612)*
Process Systems Inc ....E....... 586 757-5711
 Warren *(G-17977)*
Quality Filters Inc ....F....... 734 668-0211
 Ann Arbor *(G-630)*
Ronal Industries Inc ....F....... 248 616-9691
 Sterling Heights *(G-16159)*
Rosedale Products Inc ....D....... 734 665-8201
 Ann Arbor *(G-644)*
Salem/Savard Industries LLC ....F....... 313 931-6880
 Detroit *(G-4579)*
Wayne Wire Cloth Products Inc ....F....... 989 742-4591
 Hillman *(G-7917)*
West Mich Auto Stl & Engrg Inc ....E....... 616 560-8198
 Belding *(G-1464)*

BLUEPRINTING SVCS

American Reprographics Co LLC ....G....... 248 299-8900
 Clawson *(G-3086)*
Capital City Blue Print Inc ....G....... 517 482-5431
 Lansing *(G-9676)*
Capital Imaging Inc ....F....... 517 482-2292
 Lansing *(G-9822)*
Commercial Blueprint Inc ....E....... 517 372-8360
 Lansing *(G-9825)*
Copy Central Inc ....G....... 231 941-2298
 Traverse City *(G-16660)*
Daniel Ward ....G....... 810 965-6535
 Mount Morris *(G-11670)*
Engineering Reproduction Inc ....G....... 313 366-3390
 Detroit *(G-4209)*
PDQ Ink Inc ....E....... 810 229-2989
 Brighton *(G-2048)*

BOAT & BARGE COMPONENTS: Metal, Prefabricated

Bulldog Innovative Mfg LLC ....E....... 517 223-2500
 Fowlerville *(G-5836)*
K & M Industrial LLC ....G....... 906 420-8770
 Gladstone *(G-6182)*

BOAT BUILDING & REPAIR

A & B Tube Benders Inc ....F....... 586 773-0440
 Warren *(G-17678)*
Andersen Boat Works ....G....... 616 836-2502
 South Haven *(G-15399)*
Artisans Cstm Mmory Mattresses ....F....... 989 793-3208
 Saginaw *(G-14605)*
Barton Boatworks ....G....... 616 240-5562
 Holland *(G-7970)*
Bingham Boat Works Ltd ....G....... 906 225-0050
 Marquette *(G-11007)*
C & C Sports Inc ....E....... 810 227-7068
 Brighton *(G-1958)*
Downriver Boatworks Ltd ....G....... 313 335-4288
 Lincoln Park *(G-10045)*
Eldean Company ....E....... 616 335-5843
 Macatawa *(G-10566)*
Eldean Yacht Basin Ltd ....E....... 616 786-2205
 Holland *(G-8026)*
Geelhoed Performance ....G....... 616 837-6666
 Grand Rapids *(G-6735)*
Glastron LLC ....D....... 800 354-3141
 Cadillac *(G-2331)*
Gregs Dockside Marine Svc LLC ....G....... 810 874-8250
 Clay *(G-3120)*
Irish Boat Shop Inc ....E....... 231 547-9967
 Charlevoix *(G-2719)*
K and S 39 Corporation ....G....... 734 883-3868
 Ypsilanti *(G-18960)*
KI Companies Inc ....D....... 231 332-1700
 Muskegon *(G-11851)*
Marsh Brothers Inc ....F....... 517 869-2653
 Quincy *(G-13671)*
Max Manufacturing ....F....... 517 990-9180
 Jackson *(G-8947)*
Meyers Boat Company Inc ....E....... 517 265-9821
 Adrian *(G-85)*
Mid-Tech Inc ....G....... 734 426-4327
 Ann Arbor *(G-577)*
Midwest Aquatics Group Inc ....G....... 734 426-4155
 Pinckney *(G-13052)*
Morin Boats ....G....... 989 686-7353
 Bay City *(G-1381)*
N D R Enterprises Inc ....G....... 269 857-4556
 Saugatuck *(G-15084)*
Nauticraft ....G....... 810 356-2942
 Columbiaville *(G-3494)*
Northern Michigan Prop Sp LLC ....G....... 231 275-7173
 Lake Ann *(G-9542)*
Pender Boatworks LLC ....G....... 269 207-0627
 Hickory Corners *(G-7875)*

BOAT BUILDING & REPAIR

Pier Pressure Custom Boats ....G....... 231 723-0124
  Bear Lake *(G-1420)*
Rec Boat Holdings LLC ....B....... 231 779-2616
  Cadillac *(G-2350)*
Spicers Boat Cy Hughton Lk Inc ....E....... 989 366-8384
  Houghton Lake *(G-8403)*
Swivl - Eze Marine ....E....... 616 897-9241
  Lowell *(G-10520)*
T D Vinette Company ....G....... 906 786-1884
  Escanaba *(G-5102)*
Tassier Boat Works Inc ....G....... 906 484-2573
  Cedarville *(G-2674)*
Tiara Yachts Inc ....C....... 616 335-3594
  Holland *(G-8221)*
Unlimited Marine Inc ....G....... 248 249-0222
  White Lake *(G-18470)*
Van Dam Marine Co ....E....... 231 582-2323
  Boyne City *(G-1905)*
Wooden Runabout Co ....G....... 616 396-7248
  Holland *(G-8251)*

BOAT BUILDING & REPAIRING: Fiberglass

Northshore Pontoon ....G....... 517 547-8877
  Hudson *(G-8557)*
Sunsation Products Inc ....E....... 810 794-4888
  Clay *(G-3126)*
Tiara Yachts Inc ....A....... 616 392-7163
  Holland *(G-8220)*

BOAT BUILDING & REPAIRING: Houseboats

Maurell Products Inc ....E....... 989 725-5188
  Owosso *(G-12841)*

BOAT BUILDING & REPAIRING: Kayaks

Recon Fishing Systems Inc ....G....... 989 358-2923
  Alpena *(G-316)*

BOAT BUILDING & REPAIRING: Motorboats, Inboard Or Outboard

Douglas Marine Corporation ....E....... 269 857-1764
  Douglas *(G-4772)*
Sterling Performance Inc ....E....... 248 685-7811
  Milford *(G-11491)*

BOAT BUILDING & REPAIRING: Motorized

Murleys Marine ....G....... 586 725-7446
  Ira *(G-8705)*

BOAT BUILDING & REPAIRING: Non-Motorized

Ameriform Acquisition Co LLC ....B....... 231 733-2725
  Rochester Hills *(G-13947)*
Finishing Touches By Odell ....G....... 231 947-3080
  Traverse City *(G-16682)*
Macs Marina Motorsports ....F....... 248 486-8300
  South Lyon *(G-15445)*
Paddle King Inc ....F....... 989 235-6776
  Carson City *(G-2594)*
Rubber Rope Products Company ....G....... 906 358-4133
  Watersmeet *(G-18178)*

BOAT BUILDING & REPAIRING: Pontoons, Exc Aircraft & Inflat

American Pleasure Products Inc ....G....... 989 685-8484
  Rose City *(G-14360)*
Avalon & Tahoe Mfg Inc ....C....... 989 463-2112
  Alma *(G-239)*
Crest Marine LLC ....E....... 989 725-5188
  Owosso *(G-12828)*
Triton Industries Inc ....D....... 517 322-3822
  Lansing *(G-9745)*

BOAT BUILDING & REPAIRING: Yachts

Beardslee Investments Inc ....E....... 810 748-9951
  Harsens Island *(G-7748)*
Reed Yacht Sales LLC ....G....... 419 304-4405
  La Salle *(G-9529)*
Reed Yacht Sales LLC ....G....... 616 842-8899
  Grand Haven *(G-6351)*

BOAT DEALERS

Irish Boat Shop Inc ....E....... 231 547-9967
  Charlevoix *(G-2719)*

BOAT DEALERS: Canoe & Kayak

Paddlesports Warehouse Inc ....G....... 231 757-9051
  Scottville *(G-15136)*

BOAT DEALERS: Inflatable

Inflatable Marine Products Inc ....G....... 616 723-8140
  Howard City *(G-8410)*

BOAT DEALERS: Kayaks

Recon Fishing Systems Inc ....G....... 989 358-2923
  Alpena *(G-316)*

BOAT DEALERS: Marine Splys & Eqpt

Marine Propulsion LLC ....G....... 248 396-2353
  West Bloomfield *(G-18295)*
National Composites LLC ....E....... 989 723-8997
  Owosso *(G-12846)*
Tassier Boat Works Inc ....G....... 906 484-2573
  Cedarville *(G-2674)*

BOAT DEALERS: Motor

C & C Sports Inc ....E....... 810 227-7068
  Brighton *(G-1958)*
Northshore Pontoon ....G....... 517 547-8877
  Hudson *(G-8557)*
Rec Boat Holdings LLC ....B....... 231 779-2616
  Cadillac *(G-2350)*
Spicers Boat Cy Hughton Lk Inc ....E....... 989 366-8384
  Houghton Lake *(G-8403)*

BOAT DEALERS: Sailboats & Eqpt

Midwest Aquatics Group Inc ....E....... 734 426-4155
  Pinckney *(G-13052)*

BOAT LIFTS

Bulmann Enterprises Inc ....E....... 231 549-5020
  Boyne City *(G-1885)*
Great Lakes Lift Inc ....G....... 989 673-2109
  Caro *(G-2572)*
Harbor Master Ltd ....F....... 616 669-3170
  Hudsonville *(G-8585)*
L & M Mfg Inc ....G....... 989 689-4010
  Hope *(G-8362)*
Odonnells Docks ....G....... 269 244-1446
  Jones *(G-9084)*

BOAT REPAIR SVCS

Bingham Boat Works Ltd ....G....... 906 225-0050
  Marquette *(G-11007)*
Chesterfield Engines Inc ....G....... 586 949-5777
  Chesterfield *(G-2859)*
Tassier Boat Works Inc ....G....... 906 484-2573
  Cedarville *(G-2674)*

BOAT YARD: Boat yards, storage & incidental repair

Eldean Company ....E....... 616 335-5843
  Macatawa *(G-10566)*
Eldean Yacht Basin Ltd ....E....... 616 786-2205
  Holland *(G-8026)*
Irish Boat Shop Inc ....E....... 231 547-9967
  Charlevoix *(G-2719)*
Spicers Boat Cy Hughton Lk Inc ....E....... 989 366-8384
  Houghton Lake *(G-8403)*
T D Vinette Company ....G....... 906 786-1884
  Escanaba *(G-5102)*
Van Dam Marine Co ....E....... 231 582-2323
  Boyne City *(G-1905)*

BOATS & OTHER MARINE EQPT: Plastic

Inflatable Marine Products Inc ....G....... 616 723-8140
  Howard City *(G-8410)*
One Plus Boats Inc ....G....... 586 493-9900
  Harrison Township *(G-7714)*

BOATS: Plastic, Nonrigid

Meyers Boat Company Inc ....E....... 517 265-9821
  Adrian *(G-85)*

BODIES: Truck & Bus

AM General LLC ....B....... 734 523-8098
  Auburn Hills *(G-779)*

PRODUCT SECTION

Armada Rubber Manufacturing Co ......D....... 586 784-9135
  Armada *(G-731)*
Borgwarner Thermal Systems Inc ....G....... 231 779-7500
  Cadillac *(G-2317)*
Cameron Kirk Forest Pdts Inc ....G....... 989 426-3439
  Gladwin *(G-6192)*
Carter Industries Inc ....D....... 510 324-6700
  Adrian *(G-56)*
D & W Management Company Inc ......F....... 586 758-2284
  Warren *(G-17770)*
Dowding Industries Inc ....C....... 517 663-5455
  Eaton Rapids *(G-4960)*
Durakon Industries Inc ....G....... 608 742-5301
  Lapeer *(G-9928)*
E-T-M Enterprises I Inc ....C....... 517 627-8461
  Grand Ledge *(G-6389)*
Eleven Mile Trck Frame Axle In ....E....... 248 399-7536
  Madison Heights *(G-10721)*
Ford Motor Company ....A....... 313 322-3000
  Dearborn *(G-3842)*
Ford Motor Company ....G....... 313 322-7715
  Dearborn *(G-3844)*
Ford Motor Company ....F....... 910 381-7998
  Taylor *(G-16419)*
Ford Motor Company ....F....... 734 523-3000
  Livonia *(G-10215)*
Ford Motor Company ....F....... 734 942-6248
  Brownstown *(G-2146)*
Hme Inc ....C....... 616 534-1463
  Wyoming *(G-18885)*
Marsh Industrial Services Inc ....F....... 231 258-4870
  Kalkaska *(G-9395)*
Midwest Bus Corporation ....D....... 989 723-5241
  Owosso *(G-12844)*
Monroe Truck Equipment Inc ....C....... 810 238-4603
  Flint *(G-5736)*
NBC Truck Equipment Inc ....E....... 586 774-4900
  Roseville *(G-14452)*
Norma Michigan Inc ....C....... 248 373-4300
  Auburn Hills *(G-984)*
Norma Michigan Inc ....C....... 248 373-4300
  Lake Orion *(G-9622)*
Novi Manufacturing Co ....C....... 248 476-4350
  Novi *(G-12494)*
Optimal Electric Vehicles LLC ....E....... 734 414-7933
  Plymouth *(G-13256)*
Tractech Inc ....E....... 248 226-6800
  Southfield *(G-15725)*

BODY PARTS: Automobile, Stamped Metal

A G Simpson (usa) Inc ....G....... 586 268-4817
  Sterling Heights *(G-15918)*
A G Simpson (usa) Inc ....F....... 586 268-4817
  Sterling Heights *(G-15919)*
A G Simpson (usa) Inc ....G....... 586 825-9000
  Warren *(G-17682)*
A G Simpson (usa) Inc ....E....... 586 268-5844
  Sterling Heights *(G-15920)*
Aaron Incorporated ....G....... 586 791-0320
  Clinton Township *(G-3150)*
Aludyne US LLC ....D....... 810 987-1111
  Port Huron *(G-13438)*
Anderton Equity LLC ....G....... 248 430-6650
  Troy *(G-16937)*
Android Indstrs-Shreveport LLC ....E....... 248 454-0500
  Auburn Hills *(G-785)*
Anjun America Inc ....G....... 248 680-8825
  Auburn Hills *(G-787)*
Arcturian LLC ....G....... 313 643-5326
  Dearborn *(G-3810)*
Autokiniton US Holdings Inc ....C....... 734 397-6300
  New Boston *(G-12001)*
Automobili Lamborghini Amer LLC ......F....... 866 681-6276
  Auburn Hills *(G-806)*
Autowares Inc ....G....... 248 473-0928
  Farmington Hills *(G-5177)*
Avon Machining LLC ....D....... 586 884-2200
  Shelby Township *(G-15175)*
Avon Machining Holdings Inc ....G....... 586 884-2200
  Shelby Township *(G-15176)*
Bae Industries Inc ....C....... 586 754-3000
  Warren *(G-17725)*
Bae Industries Inc ....C....... 248 475-9600
  Auburn Hills *(G-809)*
Benesh Corporation ....F....... 734 244-4143
  Monroe *(G-11532)*
Challenge Mfg Company LLC ....C....... 616 735-6500
  Walker *(G-17634)*
Concord Tool and Mfg Inc ....C....... 586 465-6537
  Mount Clemens *(G-11634)*

PRODUCT SECTION

Cooper-Standard Automotive Inc ....G...... 248 630-7262
  Auburn Hills *(G-850)*
D T M 1 Inc ....E...... 248 889-9210
  Highland *(G-7890)*
Dajaco Industries Inc ....D...... 586 949-1590
  Chesterfield *(G-2866)*
Dayco Incorporated ....D...... 248 404-6500
  Troy *(G-17046)*
Dongah America Inc ....E...... 734 946-7940
  Taylor *(G-16404)*
Dunne-Rite Performance Inc ....F...... 616 828-0908
  Warren *(G-17784)*
Dynetics Inc ....G...... 248 619-1681
  Troy *(G-17073)*
F & S Diversified Products Inc ....F...... 248 409-0960
  Auburn Hills *(G-885)*
Ford Global Technologies LLC ....A...... 313 312-3000
  Bingham Farms *(G-1696)*
Gestamp Washtenaw LLC ....E...... 734 593-9036
  Chelsea *(G-2812)*
Gns Canton LLC ....C...... 734 927-9520
  Canton *(G-2466)*
Gns North America Inc ....G...... 616 796-0433
  Holland *(G-8054)*
Grant Industries Incorporated ....E...... 586 293-9200
  Fraser *(G-5931)*
Guelph Tool Sales Inc ....B...... 586 755-3333
  Warren *(G-17843)*
Hbpo North America Inc ....G...... 248 823-7076
  Troy *(G-17138)*
Invention Evolution Comp LLC ....E...... 517 219-0180
  Fowlerville *(G-5843)*
K&K Stamping Company ....E...... 586 443-7900
  Saint Clair Shores *(G-14866)*
Kecy Products Inc ....E...... 517 448-8954
  Hudson *(G-8554)*
Kirchhoff Auto Tecumseh Inc ....B...... 517 423-2400
  Tecumseh *(G-16506)*
Kirchhoff Automotive USA Inc ....F...... 248 247-3740
  Troy *(G-17194)*
Lacks Exterior Systems LLC ....F...... 616 554-7180
  Kentwood *(G-9462)*
Manufctrung Assembly Intl LLC ....F...... 248 549-4700
  Royal Oak *(G-14559)*
Martinrea Jonesville LLC ....A...... 517 849-2195
  Jonesville *(G-9093)*
Martinrea Jonesville LLC ....G...... 248 630-7730
  Auburn Hills *(G-968)*
Matcor Automotive Michigan Inc ....C...... 616 527-4050
  Ionia *(G-8690)*
Means Industries Inc ....E...... 989 754-3300
  Saginaw *(G-14693)*
Melling Products North LLC ....D...... 989 588-6147
  Farwell *(G-5426)*
Michigan Vehicle Solutions LLC ....F...... 734 720-7649
  Southgate *(G-15754)*
Microgauge Machining Inc ....G...... 248 446-3720
  Brighton *(G-2032)*
Minth North America Inc ....D...... 248 259-7468
  Wixom *(G-18712)*
Motor City Stampings Inc ....B...... 586 949-8420
  Chesterfield *(G-2915)*
Motus Holdings LLC ....G...... 616 422-7557
  Holland *(G-8149)*
Motus LLC ....C...... 616 422-7557
  Holland *(G-8150)*
N A Sodecia Inc ....B...... 586 879-8969
  Center Line *(G-2683)*
Pacific Engineering Corp ....G...... 248 359-7823
  Novi *(G-12502)*
Pinconning Metals Inc ....G...... 989 879-3144
  Pinconning *(G-13064)*
Plastic Trim International Inc ....B...... 248 259-7468
  East Tawas *(G-4919)*
Precision Stamping Co Inc ....E...... 517 546-5656
  Howell *(G-8500)*
Press-Way Inc ....E...... 586 790-3324
  Clinton Township *(G-3325)*
R D M Enterprises Co Inc ....G...... 810 985-4721
  Port Huron *(G-13520)*
Royal Flex-N-Gate Oak LLC ....B...... 248 549-3800
  Warren *(G-17998)*
Sales & Engineering Inc ....E...... 734 525-9030
  Livonia *(G-10398)*
Sodecia Auto Detroit Corp ....B...... 586 759-2200
  Roseville *(G-14478)*
Sodecia Auto Detroit Corp ....C...... 586 759-2200
  Center Line *(G-2686)*
Spoiler Wing King ....G...... 810 733-9464
  Flint *(G-5767)*
Su-Dan Company ....D...... 248 651-6035
  Lake Orion *(G-9632)*
Sungwoo Hitech Co Ltd ....G...... 248 561-0604
  Troy *(G-17377)*
Superior Cam Inc ....D...... 248 588-1100
  Madison Heights *(G-10839)*
Tajco North America Inc ....G...... 248 418-7550
  Auburn Hills *(G-1043)*
Tower Acquisition Co II LLC ....E...... 248 675-6000
  Livonia *(G-10434)*
Tower International Inc ....B...... 248 675-6000
  Livonia *(G-10440)*
Trexel Inc ....F...... 248 687-1353
  Troy *(G-17398)*
Tubular Metal Systems LLC ....C...... 989 879-2611
  Pinconning *(G-13066)*
Visor Frames LLC ....F...... 586 864-6058
  Sterling Heights *(G-16225)*
Wellington-Almont LLC ....D...... 734 942-1060
  Belleville *(G-1495)*
Wirco Products Inc ....F...... 810 984-5576
  Port Huron *(G-13539)*

BOILER & HEATING REPAIR SVCS

Mechanic Evltion Crtfction For ....G...... 231 734-3483
  Evart *(G-5126)*

BOILERS & BOILER SHOP WORK

Vierson Boiler & Repair Co ....F...... 616 949-0500
  Grand Rapids *(G-7317)*

BOILERS: Low-Pressure Heating, Steam Or Hot Water

Armstrong Hot Water Inc ....E...... 269 278-1413
  Three Rivers *(G-16566)*
Crown Heating Inc ....G...... 248 352-1688
  Detroit *(G-4109)*

BOLTS: Metal

A A Anchor Bolt Inc ....F...... 248 349-6565
  Northville *(G-12194)*
B & D Thread Rolling Inc ....D...... 734 728-7070
  Taylor *(G-16384)*
Cold Heading Co ....D...... 586 497-7000
  Warren *(G-17758)*
Cold Heading Co ....E...... 586 497-7016
  Warren *(G-17759)*
Connection Service Company ....E...... 269 926-2658
  Benton Harbor *(G-1541)*
Dexter Fastener Tech Inc ....C...... 734 426-0311
  Dexter *(G-4736)*
E M P Manufacturing Corp ....F...... 586 949-8277
  Chesterfield *(G-2873)*
Federal Screw Works ....D...... 231 796-7664
  Big Rapids *(G-1674)*
Federal Screw Works ....G...... 231 922-9500
  Traverse City *(G-16681)*
Federal Screw Works ....F...... 734 941-4211
  Romulus *(G-14274)*
Kamax Inc ....E...... 248 879-0200
  Rochester Hills *(G-14044)*
Kamax Inc ....C...... 810 272-2090
  Lapeer *(G-9936)*
Kamax Inc ....B...... 810 664-7741
  Lapeer *(G-9937)*
MNP Corporation ....A...... 586 254-1320
  Utica *(G-17504)*
Nss Technologies Inc ....E...... 734 459-9500
  Canton *(G-2502)*
Vico Products Co ....D...... 734 453-3777
  Plymouth *(G-13334)*
Wilson-Garner Company ....E...... 586 466-5880
  Harrison Township *(G-7732)*

BOLTS: Wooden, Hewn

Jaimes Trusses and Wall Panels ....G...... 734 462-6100
  Livonia *(G-10257)*

BONDERIZING: Bonderizing, Metal Or Metal Prdts

Ionbond LLC ....D...... 248 398-9100
  Madison Heights *(G-10748)*

BOWLING CENTERS

BOOK STORES

Baker Book House Company ....C...... 616 676-9185
  Ada *(G-10)*
Blackgirlperception LLC ....G...... 313 398-4275
  Detroit *(G-4058)*
Lighthouse Direct Buy LLC ....G...... 313 340-1850
  Detroit *(G-4398)*

BOOK STORES: College

Student Book Store Inc ....G...... 517 351-6768
  East Lansing *(G-4910)*

BOOK STORES: Religious

Diocese of Lansing ....G...... 517 484-4449
  Lansing *(G-9831)*

BOOKS, WHOLESALE

A B Publishing Inc ....G...... 989 875-4985
  Ithaca *(G-8784)*
Mott Media LLC ....G...... 810 714-4280
  Fenton *(G-5492)*
Superior Text LLC ....F...... 866 482-8762
  Ypsilanti *(G-18980)*

BOOSTERS: Feeder Voltage, Electric

Lvc Technologies Inc ....E...... 248 373-3778
  Davison *(G-3789)*

BOOTHS: Spray, Sheet Metal, Prefabricated

Custom Metal Works Inc ....G...... 810 420-0390
  Marine City *(G-10957)*
DMC Service Group ....G...... 313 526-2431
  Detroit *(G-4183)*
Gallagher-Kaiser Corporation ....D...... 313 368-3100
  Troy *(G-17126)*

BOOTS: Men's

Hy-Test Inc ....G...... 616 866-5500
  Rockford *(G-14170)*
Original Footwear Company ....B...... 231 796-5828
  Big Rapids *(G-1681)*

BORING MILL

ABC Boring Co Inc ....E...... 586 751-2580
  Warren *(G-17686)*
Fair Industries LLC ....F...... 248 740-7841
  Troy *(G-17104)*
Kasper Machine Co ....F...... 248 547-3150
  Madison Heights *(G-10759)*

BOTTLE CAPS & RESEALERS: Plastic

Berry Global Inc ....G...... 269 435-2425
  Constantine *(G-3663)*
Berry Global Inc ....G...... 616 772-4635
  Zeeland *(G-18997)*

BOTTLED GAS DEALERS: Propane

Van S Fabrications Inc ....G...... 810 679-2115
  Croswell *(G-3738)*

BOTTLES: Plastic

Inoac Usa Inc ....E...... 248 619-7031
  Troy *(G-17169)*
Novares US LLC ....G...... 616 554-3555
  Grand Rapids *(G-7051)*
Plastipak Packaging Inc ....G...... 734 326-6184
  Westland *(G-18406)*
Plastipak Packaging Inc ....F...... 734 467-7519
  Romulus *(G-14320)*
R N Fink Manufacturing Co ....E...... 517 655-4351
  Williamston *(G-18580)*

BOUTIQUE STORES

Diamond Boutique ....G...... 313 451-4217
  Dearborn *(G-3828)*

BOWLING CENTERS

Century Lanes Inc ....D...... 616 392-7086
  Holland *(G-7992)*

Employee Codes: A=Over 500 employees, B=251-500
C=101-250, D=51-100, E=20-50, F=10-19, G=3-9

BOWLING EQPT & SPLYS

BOWLING EQPT & SPLYS

2-N-1 Grips Inc	F	800 530-9878
Chesterfield *(G-2833)*		
Bbp Investment Holdings LLC	B	231 725-4966
Muskegon *(G-11777)*		
Brunswick Bowling Products LLC	B	231 725-4966
Muskegon *(G-11784)*		

BOX & CARTON MANUFACTURING EQPT

Pratt (bell Packaging) Inc	D	616 452-2111
Grand Rapids *(G-7095)*		

BOXES & CRATES: Rectangular, Wood

Action Wood Technologies Inc	E	586 468-2300
Clinton Township *(G-3155)*		
AS Property Management Inc	F	586 427-8000
Warren *(G-17716)*		
Diversified Pdts & Svcs LLC	G	616 836-6600
Holland *(G-8014)*		
Mollewood Export Inc	E	248 624-1885
Wixom *(G-18714)*		
Northern Packaging Mi Inc	F	734 692-4700
Grosse Ile *(G-7524)*		
Scotts Enterprises Inc	F	989 275-5011
Roscommon *(G-14356)*		

BOXES & SHOOK: Nailed Wood

Anbren Inc	G	269 944-5066
Benton Harbor *(G-1529)*		
Demeester Wood Products Inc	F	616 677-5995
Coopersville *(G-3685)*		
Diversified Pdts & Svcs LLC	G	616 836-6600
Holland *(G-8014)*		
Export Corporation	C	810 227-6153
Brighton *(G-1987)*		
Mollewood Export Inc	E	248 624-1885
Wixom *(G-18714)*		
Packaging Specialties Inc	E	586 473-6703
Romulus *(G-14315)*		
Scotts Enterprises Inc	F	989 275-5011
Roscommon *(G-14356)*		
Shields Classic Toys	G	888 806-2632
Saline *(G-15039)*		

BOXES: Corrugated

Aaa1 Box Division Container	G	269 983-1563
Saint Joseph *(G-14921)*		
Advance Packaging Acquisition	D	616 949-6610
Grand Rapids *(G-6432)*		
Advance Packaging Corporation	C	616 949-6610
Grand Rapids *(G-6433)*		
Aero Box Company	G	586 415-0000
Roseville *(G-14370)*		
All Packaging Solutions Inc	G	248 880-1548
Warren *(G-17697)*		
Alma Container Corporation	E	989 463-2106
Alma *(G-235)*		
Anchor Bay Packaging Corp	E	586 949-4040
Chesterfield *(G-2842)*		
Anchor Bay Packaging Corp	G	586 949-1500
Chesterfield *(G-2843)*		
Arvco Container Corporation	E	269 381-0900
Kalamazoo *(G-9123)*		
Arvco Container Corporation	E	269 381-0900
Kalamazoo *(G-9124)*		
Arvco Container Corporation	E	269 381-0900
Kalamazoo *(G-9125)*		
Arvco Container Corporation	E	231 876-0935
Cadillac *(G-2313)*		
Bay Corrugated Container Inc	C	734 243-5400
Monroe *(G-11530)*		
Bramco Containers Inc	G	906 428-2855
Gladstone *(G-6174)*		
Brickers Box Board Inc	G	734 981-0828
Canton *(G-2444)*		
C/W South Inc	E	810 767-2806
Burton *(G-2230)*		
Caraustar Cstm Packg Group Inc	D	616 247-0330
Grand Rapids *(G-6547)*		
Coastal Container Corporation	D	616 355-9800
Holland *(G-7999)*		
Corr Pack In	G	248 348-4188
Northville *(G-12210)*		
Corrugated Pratt	G	734 853-3030
Livonia *(G-10167)*		
Delta Containers Inc	C	810 742-2730
Bay City *(G-1342)*		
Dewitt Packaging Corporation	E	616 698-0210
Grand Rapids *(G-6644)*		
Flint Boxmakers Inc	G	810 743-0400
Burton *(G-2235)*		
Georgia-Pacific LLC	G	734 439-2441
Milan *(G-11436)*		
Georgia-Pacific LLC	G	989 725-5191
Owosso *(G-12835)*		
Grand Traverse Reels Inc	C	231 946-1057
Traverse City *(G-16700)*		
Great Lakes-Triad Plastic	D	616 241-6441
Grand Rapids *(G-6788)*		
Green Bay Packaging Inc	C	269 552-1000
Kalamazoo *(G-9202)*		
Industrial Packaging Corp	F	248 677-0084
Berkley *(G-1628)*		
Inter-Pack Corporation	E	734 242-7755
Monroe *(G-11551)*		
Jet Box Co Inc	F	248 362-1260
Troy *(G-17185)*		
Jetco Packaging Solutions Inc	F	616 588-2492
Grand Rapids *(G-6870)*		
Kentwood Packaging Corporation	D	616 698-9000
Walker *(G-17642)*		
Kraft-Wrap Inc	E	586 755-2050
Warren *(G-17896)*		
Loope Enterprises Inc	G	269 639-1567
South Haven *(G-15409)*		
McC Kalamazoo Inc	E	269 381-2706
Kalamazoo *(G-9267)*		
Michcor Container Inc	E	616 452-7089
Grand Rapids *(G-6986)*		
Michiana Corrugated Pdts Co	E	269 651-5225
Sturgis *(G-16306)*		
Michigan Box Company	D	313 873-9500
Detroit *(G-4444)*		
Michigan Packaging Company	D	517 676-8700
Mason *(G-11144)*		
Monte Package Company LLC	E	269 849-1722
Riverside *(G-13864)*		
Opus Packaging - Kalamazoo LLC	G	800 643-6721
Kalamazoo *(G-9283)*		
Opus Packaging Group Inc	D	616 871-5200
Caledonia *(G-2391)*		
Packaging Corporation America	G	616 530-5700
Grandville *(G-7407)*		
Packaging Corporation America	D	734 453-6262
Plymouth *(G-13259)*		
Packaging Corporation America	G	734 266-1877
Livonia *(G-10358)*		
Packaging Corporation America	G	269 567-7340
Kalamazoo *(G-9284)*		
Packaging Corporation America	B	231 723-1442
Filer City *(G-5610)*		
Packaging Corporation America	E	989 427-2130
Edmore *(G-4994)*		
Packaging Corporation America	E	989 427-5129
Edmore *(G-4995)*		
Packaging Specialties Inc	E	586 473-6703
Romulus *(G-14315)*		
Patriot Solutions LLC	E	616 240-8164
Grand Haven *(G-7072)*		
Pratt Industries Inc	G	616 452-2111
Grand Rapids *(G-7096)*		
Pratt Industries Inc	E	734 853-3000
Livonia *(G-10373)*		
Preferred Packg Solutions Inc	G	734 844-9092
Taylor *(G-16459)*		
Premier Corrugated Inc	C	517 629-5700
Albion *(G-130)*		
Royal Container Inc	E	248 967-0910
Oak Park *(G-12641)*		
S & C Industries Inc	E	269 381-6022
Kalamazoo *(G-9326)*		
Shipping Container Corporation	E	313 937-2411
Redford *(G-13771)*		
Shoreline Container LLC	C	616 399-2088
Holland *(G-8191)*		
South Haven Packaging Inc	C	269 639-1567
South Haven *(G-15414)*		
St Clair Packaging Inc	E	810 364-4230
Marysville *(G-11104)*		
Tecumseh Packg Solutions Inc	F	517 423-2126
Tecumseh *(G-16518)*		
Universal Container Corp	E	248 543-2788
Ferndale *(G-5594)*		
Webcor Packaging Corporation	E	810 767-2806
Burton *(G-2251)*		
Westrock Rkt LLC	G	269 963-5511
Battle Creek *(G-1311)*		
World Corrugated Container Inc	F	517 629-9400
Albion *(G-135)*		
Wrkco Inc	E	269 964-7181
Battle Creek *(G-1312)*		
Wrkco Inc	E	734 453-6700
Plymouth *(G-13339)*		

BOXES: Filing, Paperboard Made From Purchased Materials

Michigan Box Company	D	313 873-9500
Detroit *(G-4444)*		

BOXES: Outlet, Electric Wiring Device

Masco Building Products Corp	G	313 274-7400
Livonia *(G-10301)*		

BOXES: Packing & Shipping, Metal

Hollingsworth Container LLC	G	313 768-1400
Dearborn *(G-3850)*		
Pak Mail Center of America	G	248 543-3097
Ferndale *(G-5575)*		

BOXES: Paperboard, Folding

Caraustar Cstm Packg Group Inc	D	616 247-0330
Grand Rapids *(G-6547)*		
Complete Packaging Inc	D	734 241-2794
Monroe *(G-11534)*		
Graphic Packaging Intl LLC	D	269 651-2365
Sturgis *(G-16289)*		
Graphic Packaging Intl LLC	G	269 343-6104
Kalamazoo *(G-9200)*		
Michigan Carton Paper Boy	G	269 963-4004
Battle Creek *(G-1274)*		
Packaging Specialties Inc	E	586 473-6703
Romulus *(G-14315)*		
Rapid-Packaging Corporation	E	616 949-0950
Grand Rapids *(G-7141)*		
Steketee-Van Huis Inc	B	616 392-2326
Holland *(G-8202)*		
Wrkco Inc	E	269 964-7181
Battle Creek *(G-1312)*		
Wynalda International LLC	F	616 866-1561
Belmont *(G-1522)*		
Wynalda Litho Inc	C	616 866-1561
Belmont *(G-1523)*		

BOXES: Paperboard, Set-Up

Packaging Specialties Inc	E	586 473-6703
Romulus *(G-14315)*		

BOXES: Plastic

Datacover Inc	G	844 875-4076
Pontiac *(G-13358)*		
Handley Industries Inc	F	517 787-8821
Jackson *(G-8898)*		
National Case Corporation	G	586 726-1710
Sterling Heights *(G-16112)*		

BOXES: Wooden

Auto Pallets-Boxes Inc	F	248 559-7744
Lathrup Village *(G-9975)*		
C & K Box Company Inc	F	517 784-1779
Jackson *(G-8830)*		
Complete Packaging Inc	D	734 241-2794
Monroe *(G-11534)*		
Crossroads Industries Inc	E	989 732-1233
Gaylord *(G-6124)*		
Michigan Box Company	D	313 873-9500
Detroit *(G-4444)*		

BRAKES & BRAKE PARTS

Amanda Products LLC	E	248 547-3870
Ferndale *(G-5525)*		
Autocam Corporation	B	616 698-0707
Kentwood *(G-9444)*		
Bpi Holdings International Inc	G	815 363-9000
Ann Arbor *(G-405)*		
Brembo North America Inc	E	517 568-4398
Homer *(G-8346)*		
Cambro Products Inc	F	586 468-8847
Harrison Township *(G-7691)*		
Chassis Brakes Intl USA	G	248 957-9997
Farmington *(G-5135)*		
Litebrake Tech LLC	G	906 523-2007
Houghton *(G-8385)*		

PRODUCT SECTION — BUFFING FOR THE TRADE

Midwest Brake Bond Co .... E 586 775-3000
  Warren *(G-17931)*
Nisshinbo Automotive Mfg Inc .... E 586 997-1000
  Sterling Heights *(G-16117)*
Northrop Grmmn Spce & Mssn Sys .... A 734 266-2600
  Livonia *(G-10337)*
Old Dura Inc .... E 248 299-7500
  Auburn Hills *(G-989)*
Ricardo Defense Inc .... G 805 882-1884
  Sterling Heights *(G-16149)*
Robert Bosch LLC .... G 269 429-3221
  Saint Joseph *(G-14957)*
Robert Bosch LLC .... G 248 876-1000
  Farmington Hills *(G-5371)*
S & S Tube Inc .... E 989 656-7211
  Bay Port *(G-1415)*
Truck Trailer Transit Inc .... F 313 516-7151
  Troy *(G-17402)*
Vico Louisville LLC .... E 502 245-1616
  Plymouth *(G-13333)*
Wabco Expats Inc .... E 248 260-9032
  Auburn Hills *(G-1084)*
Wabco Holdings Inc .... A 248 260-9032
  Auburn Hills *(G-1086)*

BRAKES: Bicycle, Friction Clutch & Other

ITT Motion Tech Amer LLC .... F 248 863-2161
  Novi *(G-12444)*

BRAKES: Electromagnetic

Cusolar Industries Inc .... E 586 949-3880
  Chesterfield *(G-2863)*

BRAKES: Metal Forming

Brake Roller Co Inc .... F 269 965-2371
  Battle Creek *(G-1197)*

BRAKES: Press

Seg Automotive North Amer LLC .... E 248 465-2602
  Novi *(G-12533)*

BRASS & BRONZE PRDTS: Die-casted

Cooper Foundry Inc .... E 269 343-2808
  Kalamazoo *(G-9155)*
Evans Industries Inc .... G 313 259-2266
  Troy *(G-17100)*
Flare Fittings Incorporated .... E 269 344-7600
  Kalamazoo *(G-9187)*
Lubo Inc .... G 248 632-1185
  Madison Heights *(G-10771)*
Lubo Usa Inc .... G 810 244-5826
  Madison Heights *(G-10772)*
Wolverine Bronze Company .... D 586 776-8180
  Roseville *(G-14495)*

BRASS FOUNDRY, NEC

Ehc Inc .... G 313 259-2266
  Troy *(G-17079)*
Mueller Brass Co .... D 810 987-7770
  Port Huron *(G-13505)*
Non-Ferrous Cast Alloys Inc .... D 231 799-0550
  Norton Shores *(G-12318)*

BRAZING SVCS

Anderson Brazing Co Inc .... G 248 399-5155
  Madison Heights *(G-10669)*
D K Enterprises Inc .... G 586 756-7350
  Warren *(G-17771)*
KC Jones Brazing Inc .... G 586 755-4900
  Warren *(G-17891)*

BRAZING: Metal

Bell Induction Heating Inc .... G 734 697-0133
  Van Buren Twp *(G-17511)*
Bodycote Thermal Proc Inc .... G 734 623-3436
  Livonia *(G-10138)*
Bodycote Thermal Proc Inc .... G 734 451-0338
  Canton *(G-2442)*
Detroit Flame Hardening Co .... G 586 484-1726
  Clinton Township *(G-3219)*
Modern Metal Processing Corp .... G 517 655-4402
  Williamston *(G-18578)*
Nitro-Vac Heat Treat Inc .... F 586 754-4350
  Warren *(G-17942)*
Specialty Steel Treating Inc .... E 586 293-5355
  Fraser *(G-5998)*

Vac-Met Inc .... E 586 264-8100
  Warren *(G-18050)*
Wall Co Incorporated .... E 248 585-6400
  Madison Heights *(G-10859)*
West Side Flamehardening Inc .... F 734 729-1665
  Westland *(G-18431)*

BRIC-A-BRAC

Services To Enhance Potential .... G 313 278-3040
  Dearborn *(G-3895)*

BRICK, STONE & RELATED PRDTS WHOLESALERS

Hagen Cement Products Inc .... G 269 483-9641
  White Pigeon *(G-18480)*
Holcim (us) Inc .... D 734 529-2411
  Dundee *(G-4823)*
Lakeshore Cement Products .... G 989 739-9341
  Oscoda *(G-12763)*
Motawi Tileworks Inc .... E 734 213-0017
  Ann Arbor *(G-584)*
Newark Gravel Company .... F 810 796-3072
  Dryden *(G-4807)*
Willbee Transit-Mix Co Inc .... E 517 782-9493
  Jackson *(G-9036)*

BRICKS & BLOCKS: Structural

Heb Development LLC .... E 616 363-3825
  Grand Rapids *(G-6807)*

BRICKS: Concrete

Mbcd Inc .... E 517 484-4426
  Lansing *(G-9867)*

BRIDAL SHOPS

Celebrations .... G 906 482-4946
  Hancock *(G-7617)*
Genesee County Herald Inc .... F 810 686-3840
  Clio *(G-3399)*
Progressive Prtg & Graphics .... G 269 965-8909
  Battle Creek *(G-1284)*

BROACHING MACHINES

American Broach & Machine Co .... E 734 961-0300
  Ypsilanti *(G-18924)*
Apex Broaching Systems Inc .... F 586 758-2626
  Warren *(G-17708)*
Federal Broach & Mch Co LLC .... C 989 539-7420
  Harrison *(G-7676)*
Forst-Usa Incorporated .... G 586 759-9380
  Warren *(G-17817)*
General Broach & Engrg Inc .... C 586 726-4300
  Troy *(G-17129)*
General Broach Company .... G 517 458-7555
  Morenci *(G-11611)*

BROADCASTING & COMMS EQPT: Antennas, Transmitting/Comms

Amphenol T&M Antennas Inc .... G 847 478-5600
  Brighton *(G-1946)*
Harada Industry America Inc .... D 248 374-2587
  Novi *(G-12426)*
R A Miller Industries Inc .... C 888 845-9450
  Grand Haven *(G-6349)*

BROADCASTING & COMMS EQPT: Trnsmttng TV Antennas/Grndng Eqpt

Livbig LLC .... G 888 519-8290
  Portage *(G-13578)*

BROADCASTING & COMMUNICATIONS EQPT: Studio Eqpt, Radio & TV

Community Access Center .... F 269 343-2211
  Kalamazoo *(G-9148)*
Livespace LLC .... F 616 929-0191
  Grand Rapids *(G-6947)*

BROKERS & DEALERS: Securities

Batts Group Ltd .... G 616 956-3053
  Grand Rapids *(G-6496)*

BROKERS' SVCS

Cardinal Group Industries Corp .... F 517 437-6000
  Hillsdale *(G-7929)*
JD Edwards MGT Group Inc .... G 586 727-4039
  Casco *(G-2599)*
Novation Analytics LLC .... G 313 910-3280
  Bloomfield Hills *(G-1844)*

BROKERS: Automotive

Faurecia North America Inc .... F 248 288-1000
  Auburn Hills *(G-890)*

BROKERS: Commodity Contracts

Darling Ingredients Inc .... G 269 751-0560
  Hamilton *(G-7597)*

BROKERS: Food

Global Restaurant Group Inc .... G 313 271-2777
  Dearborn *(G-3847)*
Mexican Food Specialties Inc .... G 734 779-2370
  Southfield *(G-15656)*

BROKERS: Printing

Lloyd Waters & Associates .... G 734 525-2777
  Livonia *(G-10291)*

BRONZE FOUNDRY, NEC

White Cloud Mfg Co .... G 231 689-6087
  White Cloud *(G-18447)*

BROOMS

Sweepster Attachments LLC .... A 734 996-9116
  Dexter *(G-4757)*

BROOMS & BRUSHES

Duff Brush LLC .... G 906 863-3319
  Menominee *(G-11231)*
Even Weight Brush LLC .... G 906 863-3319
  Menominee *(G-11234)*
R J Manufacturing Incorporated .... G 906 779-9151
  Crystal Falls *(G-3745)*
Thierica Equipment Corporation .... E 616 453-6570
  Grand Rapids *(G-7259)*

BROOMS & BRUSHES: Household Or Indl

Brollytime Inc .... F 312 854-7606
  Royal Oak *(G-14521)*
Custom Built Brush Company .... F 269 463-3171
  Watervliet *(G-18179)*
Detroit Qulty Brush Mfg Co Inc .... D 734 525-5660
  Livonia *(G-10183)*
Laco Inc .... E 231 929-3300
  Traverse City *(G-16737)*
Michigan Brush Mfg Co .... E 313 834-1070
  Detroit *(G-4445)*
Rbt Mfg LLC .... F 800 691-8204
  Plymouth *(G-13279)*

BROOMS & BRUSHES: Paintbrushes

Mack Andrew & Son Brush Co .... G 517 849-9272
  Jonesville *(G-9092)*

BROOMS & BRUSHES: Street Sweeping, Hand Or Machine

Eco Brushes and Fibers .... G 231 683-9202
  Muskegon *(G-11809)*
Shais Ldscpg Snow Plowing LLC .... G 248 234-3663
  Walled Lake *(G-17675)*
Superior Equipment LLC .... G 269 388-2871
  Kalamazoo *(G-9347)*

BUCKLES & PARTS

Michigan ATF Holdings LLC .... D 734 941-2220
  Romulus *(G-14305)*
Rhino Strapping Products Inc .... F 734 442-4040
  Taylor *(G-16467)*

BUFFING FOR THE TRADE

A-W Custom Chrome Inc .... G 586 775-2040
  Eastpointe *(G-4926)*
B & K Buffing Inc .... G 734 941-2144
  Romulus *(G-14254)*

Employee Codes: A=Over 500 employees, B=251-500
C=101-250, D=51-100, E=20-50, F=10-19, G=3-9

BUFFING FOR THE TRADE / PRODUCT SECTION

Grand Rapids Polsg & Buffing ....E 616 241-2233
  Grand Rapids *(G-6766)*
Martin and Hattie Rasche Inc ....D 616 245-1223
  Grand Rapids *(G-6962)*
Patmai Company Inc ....F 586 294-0370
  Fraser *(G-5975)*
Ryan Polishing Corporation ....E 248 548-6832
  Oak Park *(G-12643)*

BUILDING & OFFICE CLEANING SVCS

Services To Enhance Potential ....G 313 278-3040
  Dearborn *(G-3895)*
Svrc Industries Inc ....E 989 280-3038
  Saginaw *(G-14768)*

BUILDING & STRUCTURAL WOOD MEMBERS

Bay Wood Homes Inc ....F 989 245-4156
  Fenton *(G-5456)*
Better-Bilt Cabinet Co ....G 586 469-0080
  Mount Clemens *(G-11630)*
Calderwood WD Pdts & Svcs LLC ....G 906 852-3232
  Trout Creek *(G-16897)*
Laketon Truss Inc ....G 231 798-3467
  Norton Shores *(G-12308)*
Midwest Panel Systems Inc ....F 517 486-4844
  Blissfield *(G-1770)*
North American Forest Products ....G 269 663-8500
  Edwardsburg *(G-5014)*
Rapid River Rustic Inc ....G 906 474-6404
  Rapid River *(G-13686)*
Riverbend Timber Framing Inc ....E 517 486-3629
  Blissfield *(G-1776)*
Truss Development ....G 248 624-8100
  Bloomfield Hills *(G-1870)*

BUILDING CLEANING & MAINTENANCE SVCS

Overstreet Property MGT Co ....G 269 281-3880
  Benton Harbor *(G-1578)*

BUILDING COMPONENTS: Structural Steel

Afco Manufacturing Corp ....F 248 634-4415
  Holly *(G-8260)*
Boomer Company ....E 313 832-5050
  Detroit *(G-4063)*
Bristol Steel & Conveyor Corp ....E 810 658-9510
  Davison *(G-3775)*
Busch Industries Inc ....G 616 957-3737
  Grand Rapids *(G-6539)*
Djd Mfg LLC ....G 586 359-2090
  Roseville *(G-14400)*
Eagle Engineering & Supply Co ....E 989 356-4526
  Alpena *(G-291)*
Howard Structural Steel Inc ....E 989 752-3000
  Saginaw *(G-14670)*
J & S Livonia Inc ....G 734 793-9000
  Livonia *(G-10253)*
Lna Solutions Inc ....F 734 677-2305
  Ann Arbor *(G-553)*
Mechanical Fabricators Inc ....E 810 765-8853
  Marine City *(G-10962)*
Midco 2 Inc ....G 517 467-2222
  Onsted *(G-12706)*
Nova International LLC ....E 269 381-6779
  Portage *(G-13589)*
Pk Fabricating Inc ....F 248 398-4500
  Ferndale *(G-5578)*
Rohmann Iron Works Inc ....E 810 233-5611
  Flint *(G-5757)*
Signa Group Inc ....B 231 845-5101
  Ludington *(G-10550)*
Steel Mill Components Inc ....G 313 386-0893
  Allen Park *(G-207)*
Tbl Fabrications Inc ....G 586 294-2087
  Roseville *(G-14483)*
Van Dellen Steel Inc ....E 616 698-9950
  Caledonia *(G-2405)*
Vci Inc ....G 269 659-3676
  Sturgis *(G-16328)*
Very Best Steel LLC ....G 734 697-8609
  Belleville *(G-1493)*

BUILDING ITEM REPAIR SVCS, MISCELLANEOUS

Colombo Sales & Engrg Inc ....F 248 547-2820
  Davisburg *(G-3764)*

BUILDING MAINTENANCE SVCS, EXC REPAIRS

Continnntal Bldg Svcs of Cncnna ....F 313 336-8543
  Grosse Pointe Woods *(G-7566)*

BUILDING PRDTS & MATERIALS DEALERS

Bozzer Brothers Inc ....G 989 732-9684
  Gaylord *(G-6120)*
Capital Steel & Builders Sup ....E 517 694-0451
  Holt *(G-8304)*
Daniel D Slater ....G 989 833-7135
  Riverdale *(G-13863)*
Deweys Lumberville Inc ....G 313 885-0960
  Grosse Pointe *(G-7530)*
Erickson Lumber & True Value ....G 906 524-6295
  Lanse *(G-9659)*
Fendt Builders Supply Inc ....F 734 663-4277
  Ann Arbor *(G-488)*
Fenton Concrete Inc ....G 810 629-0783
  Fenton *(G-5475)*
Jensen Bridge & Supply Company .....E 810 648-3000
  Sandusky *(G-15062)*
Land Star Inc ....G 313 834-2366
  Detroit *(G-4377)*
M 37 Concrete Products Inc ....G 231 689-1785
  White Cloud *(G-18446)*
Masons Lumber & Hardware Inc ....G 989 685-3999
  Rose City *(G-14365)*
Mc Guire Mill & Lumber ....G 989 735-3851
  Glennie *(G-6214)*
Motto Cedar Products Inc ....G 906 753-4892
  Daggett *(G-3753)*
Mound Steel & Supply Inc ....F 248 852-6630
  Troy *(G-17266)*
R B Christian Inc ....G 269 963-9327
  Battle Creek *(G-1285)*
Storm Seal Co Inc ....G 248 689-1900
  Troy *(G-17374)*
United Mill & Cabinet Company ....F 734 482-1981
  Willis *(G-18588)*
Yale Steel Inc ....G 810 387-2567
  Brockway *(G-2108)*

BUILDING PRDTS: Concrete

Bonsal American Inc ....E 734 753-4413
  New Boston *(G-12003)*
Ufp International LLC ....F 770 472-3050
  Grand Rapids *(G-7290)*

BUILDING SCALES MODELS

Sika Auto Eaton Rapids Inc ....F 248 588-2270
  Madison Heights *(G-10828)*

BUILDINGS & COMPONENTS: Prefabricated Metal

Biologcal Mdiation Systems LLC ....F 970 221-5949
  Hillsdale *(G-7925)*
Classic Car Port & Canopies ....F 586 759-5490
  Warren *(G-17756)*
Falk Production LLC ....F 616 540-1053
  Grand Rapids *(G-6699)*
Mast Mini Barns LLC ....G 231 924-3895
  Holton *(G-8341)*
McElroy Metal Mill Inc ....D 269 781-8313
  Marshall *(G-11069)*
Midwest Steel Carports Inc ....G 877 235-5210
  Grant *(G-7430)*
Mini Storage of Manton ....G 231 645-6727
  Manton *(G-10937)*
Morton Buildings Inc ....G 616 696-4747
  Three Rivers *(G-16579)*
Nathan Shetler ....F 269 521-4554
  Bloomingdale *(G-1877)*
Pioneer Pole Buildings N Inc ....F 989 386-2570
  Clare *(G-2994)*
Pro Tool & Die LLC ....G 586 840-7040
  Chesterfield *(G-2929)*
RB Construction Company ....E 586 264-9478
  Mount Clemens *(G-11655)*
Serenus Johnson Portables LLC ....F 800 605-0693
  Midland *(G-11416)*

Thoreson-Mc Cosh Inc ....E 248 362-0960
  Lake Orion *(G-9634)*

BUILDINGS: Mobile, For Commercial Use

CCI Arnheim Inc ....G 906 353-6330
  Baraga *(G-1136)*
Flex Building Systems LLC ....G 586 803-6000
  Sterling Heights *(G-16017)*

BUILDINGS: Portable

Brasco International Inc ....D 313 393-0393
  Madison Heights *(G-10684)*
Icon Shelters Inc ....E 616 396-0919
  Holland *(G-8092)*
Little Buildings Inc ....G 586 752-7100
  Romeo *(G-14228)*
Mark Adler Homes ....G 586 850-0630
  Birmingham *(G-1736)*
Wildcat Buildings Inc ....F 231 824-6406
  Manton *(G-10939)*

BUILDINGS: Prefabricated, Metal

Duo-Gard Industries Inc ....D 734 207-9700
  Canton *(G-2456)*
Gd Enterprises LLC ....G 248 207-1366
  Holly *(G-8271)*

BUILDINGS: Prefabricated, Plastic

Mollewood Export Inc ....E 248 624-1885
  Wixom *(G-18714)*

BUILDINGS: Prefabricated, Wood

/// 702 Cedar River Lbr Inc ....E 906 497-5365
  Powers *(G-13648)*
4d Building Inc ....F 248 799-7384
  Milford *(G-11452)*
Backyard Products LLC ....G 734 242-6900
  Monroe *(G-11526)*
Higgins Lake Family Campground .....G 989 821-6891
  Clinton Township *(G-3253)*
Home Inspection Protection ....G 906 370-6704
  Hancock *(G-7619)*
Little Buildings Inc ....G 586 752-7100
  Romeo *(G-14228)*
Maple Island Log Homes Inc ....D 231 821-2151
  Twin Lake *(G-17470)*
Pioneer Pole Buildings N Inc ....F 989 386-2570
  Clare *(G-2994)*
Premier Panel Company ....F 734 427-1700
  Livonia *(G-10374)*
Source Capital Backyard LLC ....F 734 242-6900
  Monroe *(G-11573)*
Starwood Homes ....G 734 340-2326
  Ypsilanti *(G-18979)*
T & M Homes ....G 989 239-4699
  Saginaw *(G-14772)*
Woodtech Builders Inc ....F 906 932-8055
  Ironwood *(G-8773)*

BUILDINGS: Prefabricated, Wood

Bay Wood Homes Inc ....F 989 245-4156
  Fenton *(G-5456)*
Michigan Dutch Barns Inc ....F 616 693-2754
  Lake Odessa *(G-9578)*
Pageant Homes Inc ....G 517 694-0431
  Holt *(G-8324)*
Skyline Champion Corporation ....A 248 614-8211
  Troy *(G-17356)*

BULLETPROOF VESTS

Bulletsafe Bulletproof Vests ....G 248 457-6877
  Troy *(G-16987)*
Central Lake Armor Express Inc ....C 231 544-6090
  Central Lake *(G-2691)*

BUMPERS: Motor Vehicle

Flex-N-Gate LLC ....G 616 222-3296
  Grand Rapids *(G-6710)*
Flex-N-Gate Michigan LLC ....D 586 759-8900
  Warren *(G-17812)*
Micro Rim Corporation ....F 313 865-1090
  Detroit *(G-4455)*
Norplas Industries Inc ....D 517 999-1400
  Lansing *(G-9781)*

BURGLAR ALARM MAINTENANCE & MONITORING SVCS

Sterling Security LLC .... E 248 809-9309
 Southfield (G-15709)

BURIAL VAULTS: Concrete Or Precast Terrazzo

Bostwick Enterprises Inc .... G 231 946-8613
 Traverse City (G-16624)
Brutsche Concrete Products Co .... F 269 963-1554
 Battle Creek (G-1199)
Burrell Tri-County Vaults Inc .... F 734 483-2024
 Ypsilanti (G-18930)
Central Michigan Crematory .... F 269 963-1554
 Battle Creek (G-1207)
Christy Vault Company Inc .... G 415 994-1378
 Grand Rapids (G-6569)
Detroit Wilbert Vault Corp .... E 313 862-1616
 Detroit (G-4170)
Detroit Wlbert Crmtion Svcs LL .... G 248 853-0559
 Auburn Hills (G-863)
Dm Vault Forms .... G 989 275-4797
 Roscommon (G-14348)
Fenton Memorials & Vaults Inc .... G 810 629-2858
 Fenton (G-5477)
Fogelsonger Vault Co Inc .... G 989 684-0262
 Bay City (G-1358)
Genesee Valley Vault Inc .... G 810 629-3909
 Holly (G-8272)
Grand Rpids Wilbert Burial Vlt .... E 616 453-9429
 Grand Rapids (G-6778)
Jarvis Concrete Products Inc .... G 269 463-3000
 Watervliet (G-18181)
Milan Burial Vault Inc .... E 734 439-1538
 Milan (G-11444)
Paschal Burial Vault Svc LLC .... G 517 448-8868
 Hudson (G-8558)
Peninsula Products Inc .... G 906 296-9801
 Lake Linden (G-9569)
Shores Cremation & Burial .... G 616 395-3630
 Holland (G-8195)
Smith Concrete Products .... G 989 875-4687
 North Star (G-12185)
Superior Vault Co .... G 989 643-4200
 Merrill (G-11265)
Surface Mausoleum Company Inc .... G 989 864-3460
 Minden City (G-11506)
Wilbert Burial Vault Company .... G 231 773-6931
 Muskegon (G-11946)
Wilbert Burial Vault Company .... G 231 773-6931
 Muskegon (G-11947)
Wilbert Burial Vault Works .... G 906 786-0261
 Kingsford (G-9519)
Wilbert Saginaw Vault Corp .... G 989 753-3065
 Saginaw (G-14794)
Willbee Concrete Products Co .... F 517 782-8246
 Jackson (G-9035)

BURIAL VAULTS: Stone

Pearson Precast Concrete Pdts .... G 517 486-4060
 Blissfield (G-1772)

BURNERS: Gas, Indl

Burners Inc .... G 248 676-9141
 Milford (G-11457)

BURNING: Metal

Induction Services Inc .... E 586 754-1640
 Warren (G-17863)
Steelworks Inc .... F 734 692-3020
 Trenton (G-16893)

BUSHINGS & BEARINGS

Federal-Mogul Powertrain LLC .... G 248 354-7700
 Southfield (G-15565)
Mssb LLC .... G 616 868-9730
 Alto (G-337)

BUSHINGS & BEARINGS: Brass, Exc Machined

Parker-Hannifin Corporation .... B 269 694-9411
 Otsego (G-12795)
Threaded Products Co .... E 586 727-3435
 Richmond (G-13846)

BUSHINGS: Cast Steel, Exc Investment

Axly Production Machining Inc .... G 989 269-2444
 Bad Axe (G-1096)

BUSHINGS: Rubber

Bushings Inc .... F 248 650-0603
 Rochester Hills (G-13968)

BUSINESS ACTIVITIES: Non-Commercial Site

Amrican Petro Inc .... G 313 520-8404
 Detroit (G-4017)
Angel Affects Candles LLC .... G 313 288-6899
 Detroit (G-4021)
Angels of Detroit LLC .... G 248 796-1079
 Redford (G-13714)
Bcs Creative LLC .... G 248 917-1660
 Davisburg (G-3760)
Bio Source Naturals LLC .... G 877 577-8223
 New Boston (G-12002)
Bloodline Rich LLC .... G 734 719-1650
 Grosse Pointe Woods (G-7564)
Boat Guard Inc .... G 989 424-1490
 Gladwin (G-6189)
Brenton Consulting LLC .... G 248 342-6590
 Northville (G-12198)
Bwjs Printing LLC .... G 248 678-3610
 Detroit (G-4081)
Caligirlbooks LLC .... G 415 361-1533
 Macomb (G-10582)
Center Mass Inc .... G 734 207-8934
 Canton (G-2447)
Circle S Products Inc .... G 734 675-2960
 Woodhaven (G-18798)
Collier Enterprise III .... G 269 503-3402
 Sturgis (G-16284)
Construction Retail Svcs Inc .... G 586 469-2289
 Clinton Township (G-3210)
Cruux LLC .... G 248 515-8411
 Troy (G-17036)
D&E Incorporated .... G 313 673-3284
 Southfield (G-15535)
Delta Optical Supply Inc .... G 248 628-3977
 Oxford (G-12882)
Djw Enterprises Inc .... G 414 791-6192
 Crystal Falls (G-3742)
Dse Industries LLC .... G 313 530-6668
 Macomb (G-10589)
Eco Brushes and Fibers .... G 231 683-9202
 Muskegon (G-11809)
Ecovia Renewables Inc .... G 248 953-0594
 Ann Arbor (G-466)
Elsie Publishing Institute .... F 517 371-5257
 Lansing (G-9835)
Embrace Premium Vodka LLC .... G 616 617-5602
 Ypsilanti (G-18942)
Ezbake Technologies LLC .... G 817 430-1621
 Fenton (G-5474)
Functional Fluidics Inc .... G 410 493-8322
 Detroit (G-4248)
Garbage Man LLC .... G 810 225-3001
 Brighton (G-1996)
Garden of Edyn .... G 517 410-9931
 Holt (G-8313)
Geartec Inc .... E 810 987-4700
 Port Huron (G-13480)
George Brown Legacy Group .... G 313 770-9928
 Southfield (G-15574)
Grace Contracting Services LLC .... G 906 630-4680
 Mc Millan (G-11188)
Grand Rapids Graphix .... G 616 359-2383
 Wyoming (G-18876)
Haulin Oats Inc .... G 248 225-1672
 Roseville (G-14420)
Hug-A-Plug Inc .... G 810 626-1224
 Brighton (G-2011)
Innovative Packg Solutions LLC .... G 517 213-3169
 Holt (G-8315)
Integrity Sltons Feld Svcs Inc .... E 517 481-4724
 Alma (G-242)
Intra Business LLC .... G 269 262-0863
 Niles (G-12139)
Jns Sawmill .... G 989 352-5430
 Coral (G-3699)
Jon Bee Distribution LLC .... G 248 846-0491
 Pontiac (G-13387)
Kash St James LLC .... G 248 571-1160
 Detroit (G-4351)
Kd Essentials LLC .... G 248 632-7180
 Oak Park (G-12620)
Kind Crumbs LLC .... G 616 881-6388
 Grand Rapids (G-6895)
Kringer Industrial Corporation .... F 519 818-3509
 Warren (G-17897)
Latitude Recycling Inc .... G 586 243-5153
 Ray (G-13700)
Live Track Productions Inc .... G 313 704-2224
 Detroit (G-4402)
Lotus Technologies LLC .... G 313 550-1889
 Detroit (G-4406)
Luhu LLC .... G 320 469-3162
 East Lansing (G-4901)
M-57 Aggregate Company .... G 810 639-7516
 Montrose (G-11605)
Mark Beem .... G 231 510-8122
 Lake City (G-9550)
National Ambucs Inc .... G 231 798-4244
 Norton Shores (G-12315)
Nb Media Solutions LLC .... G 616 724-7175
 Grand Rapids (G-7037)
Obdpros LLC .... G 734 274-5315
 Canton (G-2503)
Onyx Manufacturing Inc .... G 248 687-8611
 Rochester Hills (G-14075)
Pioneer Pole Buildings N Inc .... F 989 386-2570
 Clare (G-2994)
Premier Passivation Services .... G 269 432-2244
 Colon (G-3490)
Pro Gear Printing LLC .... G 734 386-1105
 Canton (G-2514)
S L H Metals Inc .... F 989 743-3467
 Corunna (G-3717)
Scentmatchers LLC .... G 231 878-9918
 Gaylord (G-6158)
Sheptime Music .... G 586 806-9058
 Warren (G-18012)
Sizzl LLC .... F 201 454-1938
 Ann Arbor (G-654)
Smart Diet Scale LLC .... G 586 383-6734
 Bruce Twp (G-2183)
Spiffys Slay Station LLC .... G 313 401-8906
 Detroit (G-4601)
Technical Enterprises LLC .... G 313 333-1438
 Detroit (G-4629)
Tequionbrookins LLC .... G 313 290-0303
 Southfield (G-15721)
True Analytics Mfg Slutions LLC .... G 517 902-9700
 Ida (G-8625)
Valmec Inc .... G 810 629-8750
 Fenton (G-5512)
Ventuor LLC .... G 248 790-8700
 Flint (G-5791)
Whiteside Consulting Group LLC .... G 313 288-6598
 Detroit (G-4681)
Winford Engineering LLC .... G 989 671-9721
 Auburn (G-771)
Z&G Auto Carriers LLC .... G 586 819-1809
 Romulus (G-14344)

BUSINESS FORMS WHOLESALERS

Alpha Data Business Forms Inc .... G 248 540-5930
 Birmingham (G-1718)
Complete Data Products Inc .... F 248 651-8602
 Troy (G-17021)
Earle Press Inc .... E 231 773-2111
 Muskegon (G-11805)
Kendall & Company Inc .... G 810 733-7330
 Flint (G-5721)
Lepages 2000 Inc .... G 416 357-0041
 Melvindale (G-11203)
Printcomm Inc .... D 810 239-5763
 Flint (G-5749)
Shayleslie Corporation .... G 517 694-4115
 Holt (G-8332)
Spinnaker Forms Systems Corp .... G 616 956-7677
 Grand Rapids (G-7219)
Turner Business Forms Inc .... E 989 752-5540
 Saginaw (G-14782)
Web Printing & Mktg Concepts .... G 269 983-4646
 Saint Joseph (G-14974)
Whitlock Business Systems Inc .... E 248 548-1040
 Madison Heights (G-10862)

BUSINESS FORMS: Printed, Continuous

Ultra Forms Plus Inc .... F 269 337-6000
 Kalamazoo (G-9360)

BUSINESS FORMS: Printed, Manifold

Alpha Data Business Forms Inc .... G 248 540-5930
  Birmingham *(G-1718)*
Business Press Inc .... G 248 652-8855
  Rochester *(G-13895)*
Earle Press Inc .... E 231 773-2111
  Muskegon *(G-11805)*
Forms Trac Enterprises Inc .... G 248 524-0006
  Sterling Heights *(G-16019)*
Frye Printing Company Inc .... F 517 456-4124
  Clinton *(G-3139)*
Grand Traverse Continuous Inc .... E 231 941-5400
  Traverse City *(G-16698)*
Imperial Clinical RES Svcs Inc .... C 616 784-0100
  Grand Rapids *(G-6836)*
Micrgraphics Printing Inc .... F 231 739-6575
  Norton Shores *(G-12311)*
Microforms Inc .... E 586 939-7900
  Beverly Hills *(G-1667)*
Peg-Master Business Forms Inc .... G 586 566-8694
  Shelby Township *(G-15298)*
Riegle Press Inc .... E 810 653-9631
  Davison *(G-3795)*
Spinnaker Corp .... G 616 956-7677
  Grand Rapids *(G-7218)*
Timbertech Inc .... F 231 348-2750
  Harbor Springs *(G-7658)*
Total Business Systems Inc .... F 248 307-1076
  Madison Heights *(G-10845)*
Whitlock Business Systems Inc .... E 248 548-1040
  Madison Heights *(G-10862)*

BUSINESS MACHINE REPAIR, ELECTRIC

Cornelius Systems Inc .... E 248 545-5558
  Clawson *(G-3091)*

BUSINESS SUPPORT SVCS

Ace & 1 Logistics LLC .... G 601 335-3625
  Shelby Township *(G-15163)*
Beamer Laser Marking .... D 810 471-3044
  Flushing *(G-5803)*
Bramin Enterprises .... G 313 960-1528
  Detroit *(G-4067)*
BV Technology LLC .... G 616 558-1746
  Alto *(G-329)*
Cherry Oak Landscaping LLC .... F 517 339-2881
  East Lansing *(G-4890)*
Delta 6 LLC .... G 248 778-6414
  Livonia *(G-10178)*
Ethnicemedia LLC .... G 248 762-8904
  Troy *(G-17097)*
Flashplays Live LLC .... G 978 888-3935
  Ann Arbor *(G-490)*
High Touch Healthcare LLC .... G 248 513-2425
  Novi *(G-12435)*
Holland Transport Services LLC .... G 313 605-3103
  New Haven *(G-12032)*
Kingsford Broach & Tool Inc .... E 906 774-4917
  Kingsford *(G-9511)*
Krumbsnatcher Enterprises LLC .... F 313 408-6802
  Detroit *(G-4368)*
M2 Scientifics LLC .... F 616 379-9080
  Allendale *(G-224)*
Striker Tools LLC .... G 248 990-7767
  Manitou Beach *(G-10928)*
Talkin Tackle LLC .... G 517 474-6241
  Jackson *(G-9015)*
US Green Energy Solutions LLC .... G 810 955-2992
  Livonia *(G-10454)*
Virotech Biomaterials Inc .... G 313 421-1648
  Warren *(G-18056)*

BUSINESS TRAINING SVCS

Siemens Industry Software Inc .... G 734 953-2700
  Livonia *(G-10406)*

BUTTER WHOLESALERS

Butterball Farms Inc .... C 616 243-0105
  Grand Rapids *(G-6541)*

BUTYL RUBBER: Isobutylene-Isoprene Rubbers

A-Line Products Corporation .... F 313 571-8300
  Detroit *(G-3975)*

CABINETS & CASES: Show, Display & Storage, Exc Wood

Impert Industries Inc .... G 269 694-2727
  Otsego *(G-12788)*
Structural Concepts Corp .... A 231 798-8888
  Norton Shores *(G-12335)*

CABINETS: Bathroom Vanities, Wood

Cabinet One Inc .... G 248 625-9440
  Clarkston *(G-3022)*
Crystal Lk Aprtmnts Fmly Ltd P .... E 586 731-3500
  Shelby Township *(G-15199)*
Designtech Custom Interiors .... G 989 695-6306
  Freeland *(G-6020)*
Gast Cabinet Co .... G 269 422-1587
  Baroda *(G-1162)*
Janice Morse Inc .... E 248 624-7300
  West Bloomfield *(G-18293)*
Masco Cabinetry LLC .... E 517 263-0771
  Adrian *(G-82)*
Masco Corporation .... A 313 274-7400
  Livonia *(G-10302)*
Owens Building Co Inc .... E 989 835-1293
  Midland *(G-11401)*
Perspectives Custom Cabinetry .... E 248 288-4100
  Troy *(G-17298)*
Pioneer Cabinetry Inc .... D 810 658-2075
  Davison *(G-3793)*

CABINETS: Entertainment

European Cabinet Mfg Co .... E 586 445-8909
  Roseville *(G-14406)*
George Washburn .... G 269 694-2930
  Otsego *(G-12786)*
Pazzel Inc .... G 616 291-0257
  Grand Rapids *(G-7074)*
Ross Cabinets II Inc .... F 586 752-7750
  Shelby Township *(G-15317)*
Sterling Millwork Inc .... D 248 427-1400
  Farmington Hills *(G-5389)*
Woodways Inc .... G 616 956-3070
  Zeeland *(G-19093)*

CABINETS: Entertainment Units, Household, Wood

Millennm-The Inside Sltion Inc .... F 248 645-9005
  Farmington Hills *(G-5323)*

CABINETS: Factory

B & W Woodwork Inc .... G 616 772-4577
  Holland *(G-7969)*
Bakes & Kropp Ltd .... F 888 206-0015
  Mount Clemens *(G-11629)*
M and G Laminated Products .... G 517 784-4974
  Jackson *(G-8938)*
Pinnacle Cabinet Company Inc .... E 989 772-3866
  Mount Pleasant *(G-11731)*

CABINETS: Filing, Wood

Behrens Custom Cabinetry LLC .... G 269 720-4950
  Paw Paw *(G-12941)*
H L F Furniture Incorporated .... E 734 697-3000
  Van Buren Twp *(G-17528)*
Tims Cabinet Inc .... G 989 846-9831
  Pinconning *(G-13065)*

CABINETS: Kitchen, Wood

A K Services Inc .... G 313 972-1010
  Detroit *(G-3972)*
Albers Cabinet Company .... G 586 727-9090
  Lenox *(G-9997)*
Antells Custom Cabinetry .... G 616 318-8637
  Grand Rapids *(G-6460)*
Autumn Designs LLC .... G 269 455-0490
  South Haven *(G-15400)*
Avon Cabinets Atkins .... G 248 237-1103
  Rochester Hills *(G-13959)*
Beaver Creek Cabinets LLC .... G 231 821-2861
  Holton *(G-8337)*
Behrens Custom Cabinetry LLC .... G 269 720-4950
  Paw Paw *(G-12941)*
Belash Co .... G 248 379-4444
  Wixom *(G-18619)*
Berrien Custom Cabinet Inc .... G 269 473-3404
  Berrien Springs *(G-1638)*
Better-Bilt Cabinet Co .... G 586 469-0080
  Mount Clemens *(G-11630)*
Biotec Incorporated .... D 616 772-2133
  Zeeland *(G-18999)*
Blue Water Cabinetry AMP .... G 231 246-2293
  Muskegon *(G-11779)*
Bradley Allen Interiors Inc .... G 989 689-6770
  Rhodes *(G-13822)*
Cabinet Finishers .... G 248 635-7584
  Farmington Hills *(G-5193)*
Cabinet Headquarters LLC .... G 231 286-3207
  Norton Shores *(G-12282)*
Cabinet Install Shop .... G 586 946-0500
  Chesterfield *(G-2856)*
Cabinets By H & K Inc .... G 313 903-8500
  Inkster *(G-8660)*
Cabinets By Robert Inc .... F 231 947-3261
  Traverse City *(G-16636)*
Cabinets Cuntertops Direct LLC .... G 616 238-6608
  Jenison *(G-9048)*
Cabinets Express .... G 810 494-0511
  Brighton *(G-1959)*
Cabinetworks Group Mich LLC .... B 734 205-4600
  Ann Arbor *(G-413)*
Carson Wood Specialties Inc .... G 269 465-6091
  Stevensville *(G-16242)*
Case Systems Inc .... C 989 496-9510
  Midland *(G-11327)*
Cg Cabinet Wholesale .... G 269 459-6833
  Portage *(G-13552)*
Cg Cabinets Wholesale .... G 248 583-9666
  Madison Heights *(G-10686)*
Charlotte Cabinets Inc .... G 517 543-1522
  Charlotte *(G-2742)*
Classic Cabinets Interiors LLC .... G 517 423-2600
  Tecumseh *(G-16491)*
Coast To Coast Cabinets LLC .... G 517 719-0118
  Okemos *(G-12661)*
Cobblestone Cabinets .... G 248 398-3700
  Berkley *(G-1624)*
Cole Wagner Cabinetry .... G 248 642-5350
  Birmingham *(G-1721)*
Cole Wagner Cabinetry .... F 248 852-2406
  Rochester Hills *(G-13976)*
Country Custom Cabinets .... G 937 354-2163
  Lawrence *(G-9981)*
Custom Cabinets & More .... G 517 285-7286
  Charlotte *(G-2748)*
Custom Cabinets & More LLC .... G 734 231-9086
  Brownstown *(G-2145)*
Custom Line Cabinets .... G 810 459-0414
  Commerce Township *(G-3520)*
D & M Cabinet Shop Inc .... G 989 479-9271
  Ruth *(G-14597)*
Daniel Snderson Cstm Cabinetry .... G 231 421-5743
  Traverse City *(G-16667)*
David Hirn Cabinets and Contg .... G 906 428-1935
  Gladstone *(G-6178)*
Dejon Cabinetry Inc .... G 586 468-8611
  Clinton Township *(G-3218)*
Dexter Cabinet Works Inc .... G 734 426-5035
  Dexter *(G-4735)*
Dibbleville Woodwork Co .... G 810 750-1139
  Fenton *(G-5470)*
Display Cses By Grndpas Cbnets .... G 586 506-2222
  Macomb *(G-10588)*
Donald K Stappert .... G 734 459-0004
  Plymouth *(G-13161)*
Dream Custom Cabinets .... G 586 718-4812
  Fraser *(G-5920)*
Elan Designs Inc .... G 248 682-3000
  Pontiac *(G-13365)*
Esmies Cabinet .... G 269 921-1578
  Stevensville *(G-16249)*
Euro-Craft Interiors Inc .... F 586 254-9130
  Sterling Heights *(G-16007)*
European Cabinet Mfg Co .... E 586 445-8909
  Roseville *(G-14406)*
Fallen Oaks Cabinet Shop Inc .... G 586 463-4454
  Troy *(G-17106)*
Farmington Cabinet Company .... F 248 476-2666
  Livonia *(G-10205)*
Flagg Distribution LLC .... G 248 926-0510
  Wixom *(G-18662)*
Fort Grtiot Cbnets Counter LLC .... G 810 364-1924
  Port Huron *(G-13478)*
Fwi Inc .... E 231 798-8324
  Norton Shores *(G-12294)*
G & G Wood & Supply Inc .... E 586 293-0450
  Roseville *(G-14408)*

PRODUCT SECTION

CAFES

George Washburn .... G 269 694-2930
  Otsego *(G-12786)*
Great Lakes Fine Cabinetry .... G 906 493-5780
  Sault Sainte Marie *(G-15091)*
Greenia Custom Woodworking Inc .... E 989 868-9790
  Reese *(G-13806)*
Greenville Cabinet Distri .... G 616 225-2424
  Greenville *(G-7487)*
Gsa Direct Supply LLC .... G 313 739-6375
  Detroit *(G-4285)*
Handorn Inc .... E 616 241-6181
  Grand Rapids *(G-6801)*
Harbor Kitchen & Bath LLC .... G 231 624-8060
  Traverse City *(G-16710)*
Hidden Lake Cabinet Trim .... G 586 246-9119
  Clarkston *(G-3039)*
I S Two .... G 616 396-5634
  Holland *(G-8091)*
Instyle Cabinets LLC .... G 248 589-0300
  Royal Oak *(G-14550)*
Interior Spc of Holland .... F 616 396-5634
  Holland *(G-8096)*
J B Cutting Inc .... G 586 468-4765
  Mount Clemens *(G-11644)*
Jmc Custom Cabinetry .... G 989 345-0475
  West Branch *(G-18329)*
Kaliniak Design LLC .... G 616 675-3850
  Kent City *(G-9434)*
Kraft Maid Cabinetry .... G 734 205-4600
  Ann Arbor *(G-543)*
Kurtis Mfg & Distrg Corp .... E 734 522-7600
  Livonia *(G-10270)*
Lafata Cabinet Shop .... D 586 247-6536
  Shelby Township *(G-15255)*
Lakeshore Marble Company Inc .... F 269 429-8241
  Stevensville *(G-16257)*
Lakeside Cstm Cbinets Bldg LLc .... G 269 718-7960
  Sturgis *(G-16299)*
Lakeview Cabinetry .... G 810 650-1420
  Port Hope *(G-13429)*
Lesso Kitchen and Bath .... G 517 662-3230
  Adrian *(G-79)*
Lifestyle Kitchen Studio .... G 616 454-2563
  Grand Rapids *(G-6942)*
Lindas Woodcrafts & Cabinets .... G 989 734-2903
  Rogers City *(G-14212)*
Ljs Kitchens & Interiors Ltd .... G 989 773-2132
  Mount Pleasant *(G-11708)*
Lloyds Cabinet Shop Inc .... F 989 879-3015
  Pinconning *(G-13061)*
M & K Cabinets LLC .... G 313 744-2755
  Dearborn Heights *(G-3931)*
M and G Laminated Products .... G 517 784-4974
  Jackson *(G-8938)*
Marbelite Corp .... E 248 348-1900
  Novi *(G-12470)*
Masco Services Inc .... E 313 274-7400
  Livonia *(G-10303)*
Merillat Industries LLC .... F 517 263-0269
  Adrian *(G-83)*
Merillat LP .... C 517 263-0771
  Adrian *(G-84)*
Mica TEC Inc .... G 586 758-4404
  Warren *(G-17928)*
Mid Michigan Wood Specialites .... F 989 855-3667
  Lyons *(G-10564)*
Mikes Cabinet Shop Inc .... G 734 722-1800
  Westland *(G-18396)*
Millennium Cabinetry .... F 248 477-4420
  Farmington Hills *(G-5321)*
Millennm-The Inside Sltion Inc .... F 248 645-9005
  Farmington Hills *(G-5323)*
Millwork Design Group LLC .... G 248 472-2178
  Milford *(G-11473)*
Miltons Cabinet Shop Inc .... G 269 473-2743
  Berrien Springs *(G-1645)*
Mj Cabinet Designs .... G 734 354-9633
  Plymouth *(G-13245)*
New Line Inc .... G 586 228-4820
  Shelby Township *(G-15289)*
Newcraft Cabinetry .... G 269 220-5440
  Kalamazoo *(G-9281)*
North State Sales .... G 989 681-2806
  Saint Louis *(G-14994)*
Nowak Cabinets Inc .... G 231 264-6603
  Williamsburg *(G-18561)*
Oak North Manufacturing Inc .... E 906 475-7992
  Negaunee *(G-11971)*
OBrien Harris Woodworks LLc .... E 616 248-0779
  Grand Rapids *(G-7054)*
Options .... G 248 855-6151
  Franklin *(G-5884)*
Pazzel Inc .... G 616 291-0257
  Grand Rapids *(G-7074)*
Perry Creek Woodworking Inc .... G 989 848-2125
  Mio *(G-11514)*
Pinnacle Cabinet Company Inc .... E 989 772-3866
  Mount Pleasant *(G-11731)*
Premier Kitchen Cabinetry Inc .... G 248 375-0124
  Rochester Hills *(G-14090)*
Prime Wood Products Inc .... G 616 399-4700
  Holland *(G-8170)*
Putnam Cabinetry .... G 248 442-0118
  Farmington Hills *(G-5358)*
RC Cabinetry .... G 734 513-2677
  Livonia *(G-10383)*
Rich-Wall Custom Cabine .... G 734 237-4934
  Livonia *(G-10387)*
Rohloff Builders Inc .... G 989 868-3191
  Reese *(G-13808)*
Rose Corporation .... E 734 426-0005
  Dexter *(G-4753)*
Ross Cabinets II Inc .... F 586 752-7750
  Shelby Township *(G-15317)*
Rowe Custom Cabinetry .... G 517 526-1413
  Portland *(G-13641)*
Royal Cabinets .... G 313 541-1190
  Redford *(G-13767)*
Sanford Customs LLC .... G 586 722-7274
  West Bloomfield *(G-18311)*
Sawdust Bin Inc .... F 906 932-5518
  Ironwood *(G-8772)*
Shayn Allen Marquetry .... G 586 991-0445
  Shelby Township *(G-15329)*
Silver Creek Cabinets .... G 989 387-0858
  Gladwin *(G-6207)*
Simply Cabinets .... G 810 923-8792
  Wixom *(G-18752)*
Stanisci Design and Mfg Inc .... G 248 572-6880
  Oxford *(G-12920)*
Straight Line Design .... G 616 296-0920
  Spring Lake *(G-15853)*
Surface Expressions LLC .... G 231 843-8282
  Ludington *(G-10552)*
Symphony Cabinetry LLC .... G 231 421-5421
  Traverse City *(G-16847)*
Tims Cabinet Inc .... G 989 846-9831
  Pinconning *(G-13065)*
Tims Custom Cabinets LLC .... G 248 912-4154
  Commerce Township *(G-3578)*
Top Fabricators .... G 313 563-7126
  Taylor *(G-16485)*
USA Custom Cabinet Inc .... G 313 945-9796
  Dearborn *(G-3907)*
Van Daeles Inc .... G 734 587-7165
  Monroe *(G-11588)*
Venetian Cabinets .... G 586 580-3288
  Shelby Township *(G-15365)*
Village Cabinet Shoppe Inc .... G 586 264-6464
  Sterling Heights *(G-16223)*
Visionary Cabinetry and Design .... G 248 850-7178
  Clawson *(G-3111)*
W S Townsend Company .... G 517 393-7300
  Lansing *(G-9903)*
W S Townsend Company .... C 269 781-5131
  Marshall *(G-11078)*
Welker Cabinetry & Millwork .... F 248 477-6600
  Livonia *(G-10471)*
West Michigan Cabinet Supply .... F 616 896-6990
  Hudsonville *(G-8617)*
Woodways Inc .... G 616 956-3070
  Zeeland *(G-19093)*
Woodways Industries LLC .... E 616 956-3070
  Grand Rapids *(G-7350)*
World Wide Cabinets Inc .... F 248 683-2680
  Sylvan Lake *(G-16363)*
Young Cabinetry Inc .... G 734 316-2896
  Saline *(G-15047)*

CABINETS: Office, Metal

Cerny Industries LLC .... E 231 929-2140
  Traverse City *(G-16643)*
Greenfield Cabinetry Inc .... F 586 759-3300
  Warren *(G-17839)*

CABINETS: Office, Wood

Case Systems Inc .... C 989 496-9510
  Midland *(G-11327)*
Cygnus Inc .... E 231 347-5404
  Petoskey *(G-12996)*
Debbink and Sons Inc .... G 231 845-6421
  Ludington *(G-10533)*
Farnell Contracting Inc .... F 810 714-3421
  Linden *(G-10061)*
Jsj Furniture Corporation .... B 616 847-6534
  Grand Haven *(G-6326)*
Konwinski Kabnets Inc .... G 989 773-2906
  Mount Pleasant *(G-11706)*
Pazzel Inc .... G 616 291-0257
  Grand Rapids *(G-7074)*

CABINETS: Radio & Television, Metal

Rivmax Manufacturing Inc .... F 517 784-2556
  Jackson *(G-8996)*

CABINETS: Show, Display, Etc, Wood, Exc Refrigerated

A Lasting Impression Inc .... G 616 847-2380
  Spring Lake *(G-15800)*
Behrens Custom Cabinetry LLC .... G 269 720-4950
  Paw Paw *(G-12941)*
Dallas Design Inc .... G 810 238-4546
  Flint *(G-5682)*
Grand Valley Wood Products Inc .... E 616 475-5890
  Grand Rapids *(G-6779)*
Korcast Products Incorporated .... G 248 740-2340
  Troy *(G-17196)*
Korcast Products Incorporated .... G 248 740-2340
  Troy *(G-17197)*
Kreations Inc .... F 313 255-1230
  Detroit *(G-4367)*
Lafata Cabinet Shop .... D 586 247-6536
  Shelby Township *(G-15255)*
Royal Cabinet Inc .... F 517 787-2940
  Jackson *(G-8999)*
Zuckero & Sons Inc .... E 586 772-3377
  Roseville *(G-14497)*

CABLE & OTHER PAY TELEVISION DISTRIBUTION

Community Access Center .... F 269 343-2211
  Kalamazoo *(G-9148)*

CABLE & PAY TV SVCS: Satellite Master Antenna Sys/SMATV

Digital Success Network .... E 517 244-0771
  Mason *(G-11130)*

CABLE WIRING SETS: Battery, Internal Combustion Engines

Keystone Cable Corporation .... G 313 924-9720
  Detroit *(G-4360)*
Prestolite Wire LLC .... E 248 355-4422
  Southfield *(G-15681)*
Vte Inc .... E 231 539-8000
  Pellston *(G-12968)*

CABLE: Fiber Optic

American Furukawa Inc .... E 734 446-2200
  Plymouth *(G-13123)*
T R S Fieldbus Systems Inc .... G 586 826-9696
  Birmingham *(G-1751)*

CABLE: Noninsulated

Commercial Group Inc .... E 313 931-6100
  Taylor *(G-16395)*
Detroit Wire Rope Splcing Corp .... G 248 585-1063
  Madison Heights *(G-10706)*
Hi-Lex America Incorporated .... B 269 968-0781
  Battle Creek *(G-1237)*
Hi-Lex America Incorporated .... B 248 844-0096
  Rochester Hills *(G-14030)*
Jaslin Assembly Inc .... G 248 528-3024
  Troy *(G-17181)*
Orri Corp .... F 248 618-1104
  Waterford *(G-18145)*

CAFES

Bread of Life Bakery & Cafe .... F 906 663-4005
  Bessemer *(G-1647)*
Electric Eye Cafe .... G 734 369-6904
  Ann Arbor *(G-470)*
Vivian Enterprises LLC .... E 248 792-9925
  Southfield *(G-15740)*

CAGES: Wire

Company		Phone
Corners Limited	G	269 353-8311
Kalamazoo (G-9156)		
Unifab Corporation	E	269 382-2803
Portage (G-13629)		

CALCAREOUS TUFA: Crushed & Broken

Grand Rapids Gravel Company	F	616 538-9000
Grand Rapids (G-6759)		

CALCIUM META-PHOSPHATE

F C Simpson Lime Co	G	810 367-3510
Kimball (G-9492)		

CALCULATING & ACCOUNTING EQPT

Computer Decisions Intl Inc	G	248 473-5900
Northville (G-12202)		
Robiccon Inc	F	734 425-7080
Livonia (G-10389)		

CALIBRATING SVCS, NEC

Gage Numerical Inc	G	231 328-4426
Lake City (G-9546)		

CAMERA & PHOTOGRAPHIC SPLYS STORES

Livbig LLC	G	888 519-8290
Portage (G-13578)		

CAMERAS & RELATED EQPT: Photographic

Just Rite Bracket	G	248 477-0592
Farmington Hills (G-5277)		

CAMPERS: Truck Mounted

Monroes Custom Campers Inc	F	231 773-0005
Muskegon (G-11877)		
R V Wolverine	F	989 426-9241
Gladwin (G-6201)		
Van Kam Inc	F	231 744-2658
Muskegon (G-11940)		

CAMSHAFTS

Camshaft Acquisition Inc	F	517 787-2040
Jackson (G-8832)		
Camshaft Machine Company LLC	E	517 787-2040
Jackson (G-8833)		
Engine Power Components Inc	B	616 846-0110
Grand Haven (G-6297)		
Kautex Inc	B	231 739-2704
Muskegon (G-11850)		
Victora Usa Inc	G	810 798-0253
Almont (G-271)		

CANDLE SHOPS

Holland House Candles Inc	G	800 238-8467
Holland (G-8079)		

CANDLES

5 14 Candles	G	231 944-9585
Interlochen (G-8678)		
8th Candle LLC	G	248 818-7625
Lake Orion (G-9581)		
Ambrosia Inc	G	734 529-7174
Dundee (G-4809)		
Angel Affects Candles LLC	G	313 288-6899
Detroit (G-4021)		
Annalux Candles LLC	G	313 566-3289
Taylor (G-16380)		
Bee Dazzled Candle Works	G	231 882-7765
Benzonia (G-1612)		
Body Language Scented Candles	G	989 906-0354
Saginaw (G-14619)		
Boones Candle Co	G	248 444-0621
Commerce Township (G-3517)		
Bucklin Township Candles LLC	G	248 403-0600
River Rouge (G-13852)		
Candle Factory Grand Traverse	G	231 946-2280
Traverse City (G-16638)		
Candle Knight Light	G	248 291-5483
Oak Park (G-12597)		
Candle Wick	G	248 547-2987
Ferndale (G-5533)		
Candles By Cottonwood	G	734 344-2339
Monroe (G-11533)		
Candles By Jugg	G	313 732-1349
Eastpointe (G-4929)		
Candles By Lori LLC	G	734 474-6314
Saline (G-15007)		
Carpe Candle	G	734 837-3053
Whitmore Lake (G-18526)		
Chelsea Vlg Candles & Gifts	G	734 385-6588
Brooklyn (G-2124)		
Country Candles	G	231 327-2730
White Cloud (G-18440)		
Coventry Creations Inc	E	248 547-2987
Ferndale (G-5536)		
Dunlop Dreams Candles	G	231 633-4064
Traverse City (G-16673)		
Fresh Coast Candles	G	616 405-8518
Holland (G-8041)		
Garden of Edyn	G	517 410-9931
Holt (G-8313)		
Gmd Industries Inc	G	616 245-1215
Grand Rapids (G-6745)		
Heaven Scent Candle Co & Decor	G	810 374-6279
Otisville (G-12781)		
High Rize Candles	G	616 818-9527
Wyoming (G-18883)		
Hippiwic Candles	G	586 488-8931
Warren (G-17854)		
Holland House Candles Inc	G	800 238-8467
Holland (G-8079)		
Horse Creek Candles LLC	G	517 962-1476
Jackson (G-8905)		
In The Stars Candles	G	231 590-7407
Traverse City (G-16721)		
Income Waxcom	G	616 457-4277
Jenison (G-9057)		
J F McCaughin Co	E	231 759-7304
Norton Shores (G-12303)		
J&S Homemade Candles	G	517 885-1983
Lansing (G-9855)		
Jamcat Candles LLC	G	313 319-3125
Grosse Pointe Park (G-7557)		
Kalamazoo Candle Company	F	269 532-9816
Kalamazoo (G-9236)		
Katts Candles & More	G	269 281-6805
Saint Joseph (G-14940)		
Keviar Candles	G	248 325-4087
Southfield (G-15616)		
Kymora Kandles LLC	G	517 667-6067
Maple Rapids (G-10945)		
Lake Michigan Candles LLC	G	231 766-0412
Muskegon (G-11856)		
Lucky Bird Candle Co	G	734 272-7338
Chelsea (G-2819)		
MI Soy Candle Company LLC	G	586 350-7654
Warren (G-17927)		
Neptune Candles LLC	G	231 947-0554
Traverse City (G-16768)		
New Boston Candle Company	G	734 782-5809
New Boston (G-12014)		
North Star Candle Company LLC	G	248 430-4321
Dearborn (G-3877)		
Personal Touch	G	313 354-4255
Detroit (G-4520)		
Point A Organization	G	313 971-4625
Detroit (G-4529)		
Purus Candles	G	586 876-7800
New Baltimore (G-11991)		
Race Fuel Candles LLC	G	616 889-1674
Rockford (G-14186)		
Sensatnal Smlls From Mesha LLC	G	734 905-1058
Ypsilanti (G-18976)		
Soy D-Lights & Scentsations	G	989 728-5947
Hale (G-7590)		
Sues Scented Soy Candles	G	989 642-3352
Hemlock (G-7856)		
Twisted Scissor	G	248 620-2626
Clarkston (G-3074)		
Wax Poetic	G	616 272-4693
Grand Rapids (G-7325)		
Willies Wicks	G	810 730-4176
Flushing (G-5817)		
Woody Hollow Candles	G	906 774-7839
Iron Mountain (G-8737)		
Y Not Candles	G	313 289-6592
Dearborn Heights (G-3944)		

CANDY & CONFECTIONS: Candy Bars, Including Chocolate Covered

Chocolate Vault Llc	G	517 688-3388
Horton (G-8372)		
Truans Candies Inc	F	313 281-0185
Plymouth (G-13326)		

CANDY & CONFECTIONS: Chocolate Candy, Exc Solid Chocolate

Elsa Enterprises Inc	G	248 816-1454
Troy (G-17085)		
Gayles Chocolates Limited	E	248 398-0001
Royal Oak (G-14539)		
Ranis Granola	G	734 223-2995
Ann Arbor (G-631)		

CANDY & CONFECTIONS: Cough Drops, Exc Pharmaceutical Preps

Berkley Pharmacy LLC	F	586 573-8300
Warren (G-17731)		

CANDY & CONFECTIONS: Fruit & Fruit Peel

Mr Peel Inc	G	734 266-2022
Livonia (G-10326)		

CANDY & CONFECTIONS: Fudge

Detroit Fudge Company Inc	G	734 369-8573
Ann Arbor (G-449)		
Doug Murdicks Fudge Inc	G	231 938-2330
Traverse City (G-16670)		
Original Murdicks Fudge Co	G	906 847-3530
Mackinac Island (G-10567)		
Rochester Fudge Company LLC	G	248 402-3444
Rochester Hills (G-14101)		

CANDY, NUT & CONFECTIONERY STORE: Popcorn, Incl Caramel Corn

American Gourmet Snacks LLC	G	989 892-4856
Essexville (G-5108)		
Pop Daddy Popcorn LLC	F	734 550-9900
Whitmore Lake (G-18543)		

CANDY, NUT & CONFECTIONERY STORES: Candy

Alinosi French Ice Cream Co	G	313 527-3195
Detroit (G-3997)		
Chocolate Vault Llc	G	517 688-3388
Horton (G-8372)		
Doug Murdicks Fudge Inc	G	231 938-2330
Traverse City (G-16670)		
Elsa Enterprises Inc	G	248 816-1454
Troy (G-17085)		
Kemnitz Fine Candies	G	734 453-0480
Plymouth (G-13213)		
Koeze Company	E	616 724-2601
Grand Rapids (G-6902)		
Morley Brands LLC	E	586 468-4300
Clinton Township (G-3304)		
Original Murdicks Fudge Co	G	906 847-3530
Mackinac Island (G-10567)		
Rocky Mtn Choclat Fctry Inc	G	989 624-4784
Birch Run (G-1714)		
Sanders Candy LLC	D	800 651-7263
Clinton Township (G-3349)		
Truans Candies Inc	F	313 281-0185
Plymouth (G-13326)		
W2 Inc	G	517 764-3141
Jackson (G-9032)		

CANDY, NUT & CONFECTIONERY STORES: Nuts

Nutco Inc	E	800 872-4006
Detroit (G-4494)		

CANDY, NUT & CONFECTIONERY STORES: Produced For Direct Sale

Gayles Chocolates Limited	E	248 398-0001
Royal Oak (G-14539)		
Marshalls Trail Inc	F	231 436-5082
Mackinaw City (G-10568)		

PRODUCT SECTION

CANDY: Chocolate From Cacao Beans
Alinosi French Ice Cream Co .... G 313 527-3195
  Detroit *(G-3997)*

CANDY: Hard
Liquid Otc LLC .... G 248 214-7771
  Commerce Township *(G-3551)*

CANNED SPECIALTIES
American Spoon Foods Inc .... E 231 347-9030
  Petoskey *(G-12988)*
Amway International Inc .... E 616 787-1000
  Ada *(G-8)*
Kraft Heinz Foods Company .... G 616 396-6557
  Holland *(G-8115)*

CANS: Aluminum
Oktober LLC .... G 231 750-1998
  Grand Rapids *(G-7056)*

CANS: Composite Foil-Fiber, Made From Purchased Materials
Plasan Us Inc .... G 616 559-0032
  Walker *(G-17649)*
Technova Corporation .... G 517 485-1402
  Okemos *(G-12690)*

CANS: Metal
AAR Manufacturing Inc .... E 231 779-8800
  Cadillac *(G-2306)*
Contract Welding and Fabg Inc .... E 734 699-5561
  Van Buren Twp *(G-17520)*
Delta Tube & Fabricating Corp .... C 248 634-8267
  Holly *(G-8268)*
Mh Industries Ltd .... E 734 261-7560
  West Bloomfield *(G-18298)*
Royal Design & Manufacturing .... D 248 588-0110
  Madison Heights *(G-10821)*

CANS: Tin
Tin Can Dewitt .... G 517 624-2078
  Dewitt *(G-4717)*

CANVAS PRDTS
Acme Mills Company .... E 517 437-8940
  Hillsdale *(G-7919)*
Advanced Inc .... G 231 938-2233
  Acme *(G-2)*
Annes Canvas .... G 248 623-3443
  Waterford *(G-18100)*
Armstrong Display Concepts Inc .... F 231 652-1675
  Newaygo *(G-12077)*
Belle Isle Awning Co Inc .... E 586 294-6050
  Warren *(G-17730)*
JAC Custom Pouches Inc .... E 269 782-3190
  Dowagiac *(G-4784)*
Lakeside Canvas & Upholstery .... G 231 755-2514
  Muskegon *(G-11857)*
Odin International Inc .... G 262 569-7171
  Curtis *(G-3751)*
Paddle King Inc .... F 989 235-6776
  Carson City *(G-2594)*
Tumacs Corporation .... G 517 816-8141
  Lansing *(G-9794)*

CANVAS PRDTS: Air Cushions & Mattresses
Facet Business Communications .... F 248 912-0800
  Novi *(G-12415)*

CANVAS PRDTS: Boat Seats
R L Canvas .... G 989 837-6352
  Midland *(G-11407)*

CANVAS PRDTS: Convertible Tops, Car/Boat, Fm Purchased Mtrl
Bestop Inc .... F 586 268-0602
  Sterling Heights *(G-15945)*
Boat Guard Inc .... G 989 424-1490
  Gladwin *(G-6189)*
Magna Car Top Systems Amer Inc .... C 248 836-4500
  Rochester Hills *(G-14057)*
Peerless Canvas Products Inc .... G 269 429-0600
  Saint Joseph *(G-14954)*

CAPACITORS: Fixed Or Variable
Inmatech Inc .... F 734 717-8247
  Ann Arbor *(G-528)*

CAR WASH EQPT
Admiral .... G 989 356-6419
  Alpena *(G-274)*
Cascade Equipment Company .... E 734 697-7870
  Van Buren Twp *(G-17516)*
Ginsan Liquidating Company LLC .... D 616 791-8100
  Grand Rapids *(G-6744)*
Great Lakes Ncw LLC .... G 616 355-2626
  Holland *(G-8059)*
Impressive Auto Care LLC .... F 734 306-4880
  Romulus *(G-14285)*
Interclean Equipment LLC .... E 734 961-3300
  Ypsilanti *(G-18958)*
Just-In Time Auto Dtailing LLC .... G 248 590-0085
  Southfield *(G-15614)*
Motor City Wash Works Inc .... E 248 313-0272
  Wixom *(G-18715)*
On Site Car Wash and Detail .... G 313 350-8357
  Detroit *(G-4498)*
Power-Brite of Michigan Inc .... F 734 591-7911
  Livonia *(G-10369)*
Priceless Dtils Auto Cncrge LL .... G 313 701-6851
  Troy *(G-17314)*
Rich Mars Mobile Spa LLC .... G 734 210-2797
  Redford *(G-13765)*
Sparta Wash & Storage LLC .... G 616 887-1034
  Sparta *(G-15779)*

CAR WASH EQPT & SPLYS WHOLESALERS
Sam Brown Sales LLC .... E 248 358-2626
  Farmington *(G-5147)*

CARBIDES
Carbide Savers .... G 248 388-1572
  Plymouth *(G-13141)*
Cole King LLC .... G 248 276-1278
  Orion *(G-12725)*
Continental Carbide Ltd Inc .... E 586 463-9577
  Clinton Township *(G-3211)*
Drw Systems Carbide LLC .... G 810 392-3526
  Riley *(G-13849)*
Sumitomo Electric Carbide Inc .... F 734 451-0200
  Novi *(G-12549)*
USA Carbide .... G 248 817-5137
  Troy *(G-17416)*
Weiser Metal Products Inc .... G 989 736-6055
  Harrisville *(G-7746)*
Wolverine Carbide and Too .... G 586 497-7000
  Warren *(G-18070)*
Zhuzhou Cmntd Crbid Wrks USA .... G 734 302-0125
  Ann Arbor *(G-723)*

CARBON & GRAPHITE PRDTS, NEC
American Graphite Corporation .... G 586 757-3540
  Warren *(G-17702)*
Astech Inc .... E 989 823-7211
  Vassar *(G-17577)*
Bay Carbon Inc .... E 989 686-8090
  Bay City *(G-1326)*
Bay Composites Inc .... E 989 891-9159
  Essexville *(G-5110)*
Carbone of America .... E 989 894-2911
  Bay City *(G-1336)*
Composite Builders LLC .... G 616 377-7767
  Holland *(G-8002)*
Cummings-Moore Graphite Co .... E 313 841-1615
  Detroit *(G-4112)*
Dowaksa Usa LLC .... G 989 600-8610
  Midland *(G-11356)*
Graphite Electrodes Ltd .... E 989 893-3635
  Bay City *(G-1362)*
Graphite Machining Inc .... F 810 678-2227
  Metamora *(G-11279)*
Mersen .... E 989 894-2911
  Bay City *(G-1374)*
Mersen USA Gs Corp .... G 616 754-5671
  Greenville *(G-7500)*
Mersen USA Gs Corp .... C 989 894-2911
  Bay City *(G-1375)*

CARPETS, RUGS & FLOOR COVERING
Mersen USA Gs Corp .... C 616 754-5671
  Greenville *(G-7501)*
U S Graphite Inc .... E 989 755-0441
  Saginaw *(G-14783)*
Wahoo Composites LLC .... F 734 424-0966
  Dexter *(G-4762)*

CARBON SPECIALTIES Electrical Use
National Carbon Tech LLC .... E 651 330-4063
  Gwinn *(G-7585)*

CARBURETORS
British Carburetors LLC .... G 616 920-0203
  Grand Rapids *(G-6526)*
Kens Carburetor Service Inc .... G 517 627-1417
  Grand Ledge *(G-6393)*
Motor City Carburetor .... G 586 443-8048
  Saint Clair Shores *(G-14873)*
Tyde Group Worldwide LLC .... A 248 879-7656
  Troy *(G-17408)*
Walbro LLC .... D 989 872-2131
  Cass City *(G-2622)*

CARDS: Color
Presscraft Papers Inc .... F 231 882-5505
  Benzonia *(G-1616)*

CARDS: Greeting
Avanti Press Inc .... E 800 228-2684
  Detroit *(G-4034)*
Avanti Press Inc .... E 313 961-0022
  Taylor *(G-16383)*
Cards4heroescom LLC .... G 877 640-8206
  Hartland *(G-7767)*
Design Design Inc .... C 866 935-2648
  Grand Rapids *(G-6643)*
Mr Sogs Creatures .... G 901 413-0291
  Farmington Hills *(G-5328)*
Notes From Man Cave LLC .... G 586 604-1997
  Detroit *(G-4492)*
Reyers Company Inc .... G 616 414-5530
  Spring Lake *(G-15846)*

CARDS: Identification
Greg Linska Sales Inc .... G 248 765-6354
  Troy *(G-17134)*
MPS Lansing Inc .... A 517 323-9000
  Lansing *(G-9719)*
W T Beresford Co .... F 248 350-2900
  Southfield *(G-15741)*

CARPET & RUG CLEANING & REPAIRING PLANTS
Real Green Systems Inc .... D 888 345-2154
  Commerce Township *(G-3570)*

CARPET & UPHOLSTERY CLEANING SVCS
Dave Brand .... G 269 651-4693
  Sturgis *(G-16287)*

CARPETS & RUGS: Tufted
Michigan -Bsed Frdman Dscndnts .... G 810 820-3017
  Flint *(G-5731)*

CARPETS, RUGS & FLOOR COVERING
Ability Weavers LLC .... G 616 929-0211
  Lowell *(G-10493)*
Classic Boat Decks LLC .... G 586 465-3606
  Harrison Township *(G-7693)*
Custom Marine Carpet .... G 269 684-1922
  Niles *(G-12122)*
HP Pelzer Auto Systems Inc .... E 248 280-1010
  Troy *(G-17155)*
Isingularis Inc .... G 248 347-0742
  Novi *(G-12442)*
Marceau Enterprises Inc .... G 586 697-8100
  Washington *(G-18085)*
Plant Df .... E 734 397-0397
  Van Buren Twp *(G-17548)*
Pwv Studios Ltd .... E 616 361-5659
  Grand Rapids *(G-7126)*
Seelye Group Ltd .... G 517 267-2001
  Lansing *(G-9894)*
Shelter Carpet Specialties .... G 616 475-4944
  Grand Rapids *(G-7192)*

Employee Codes: A=Over 500 employees, B=251-500
C=101-250, D=51-100, E=20-50, F=10-19, G=3-9

CARPETS, RUGS & FLOOR COVERING

Treves N Kotobukiya Amer Inc .... F 248 513-4255
  Novi (G-12558)
Usmats Inc .... G 810 765-4545
  Marine City (G-10968)
W A Thomas Company .... G 734 955-6500
  Taylor (G-16487)
Willie N Eicher .... G 269 432-3707
  Colon (G-3493)

CARPETS: Textile Fiber

James E Sullivan & Associates .... G 616 453-0345
  Grand Rapids (G-6860)
Scott Group Custom Carpets LLC .... C 616 954-3200
  Grand Rapids (G-7187)

CARPORTS: Prefabricated Metal

G & C Carports .... G 616 678-4308
  Kent City (G-9431)

CARS: Electric

Dynamic Corporation .... E 248 338-1100
  Auburn Hills (G-870)
Electric Last Mile Inc .... G 888 825-9111
  Troy (G-17083)

CARTS: Grocery

US Wire Rope Supply Inc .... E 313 925-0444
  Detroit (G-4655)
Wcscarts LLC .... D 248 901-0965
  Troy (G-17446)

CARVING SETS, STAINLESS STEEL

Rivore Metals LLC .... G 800 248-1250
  Troy (G-17334)

CASES, WOOD

Bennett Wood Specialties Inc .... F 616 772-6683
  Zeeland (G-18996)
Garcia Company .... G 248 459-0952
  Holly (G-8270)

CASES: Carrying

Rhino Products Inc .... G 269 674-8309
  Lawrence (G-9984)
Sound Productions Entrmt .... F 989 386-2221
  Clare (G-2998)

CASES: Carrying, Clothing & Apparel

Activerse LLC .... G 313 463-9344
  Detroit (G-3985)
Birlon Group LLC .... G 313 551-5341
  Inkster (G-8659)
Detroit Couture .... G 734 237-6826
  Southfield (G-15539)
Gionl LLC .... G 313 957-9247
  Detroit (G-4263)
Invest Buy Own LLC .... G 248 467-2048
  Commerce Township (G-3544)
Kash St James LLC .... G 248 571-1460
  Detroit (G-4351)
Motor City Designs LLC .... G 313 686-1025
  Dearborn (G-3874)
Restricted Area LLC .... G 419 975-8109
  Detroit (G-4569)
Stoned Like Willy LLC .... G 833 378-6633
  Southfield (G-15710)
Travis Fulmore LLC .... F 810 701-6981
  Flint (G-5782)
Viva Salon Nouvelle LLC .... F 947 800-9115
  Detroit (G-4672)

CASES: Packing, Nailed Or Lock Corner, Wood

National Case Corporation .... G 586 726-1710
  Sterling Heights (G-16112)

CASES: Shipping, Nailed Or Lock Corner, Wood

Vaive Wood Products Co .... E 586 949-4900
  Macomb (G-10648)

CASH REGISTER REPAIR SVCS

Great Lakes Weld LLC .... G 231 943-4180
  Traverse City (G-16706)
Lorna Icr LLC .... F 586 582-1500
  Warren (G-17907)

CASH REGISTERS & PARTS

Baliko Pos Inc .... G 248 470-4652
  Farmington Hills (G-5180)

CASINGS: Sheet Metal

Hart Acquisition Company LLC .... E 313 537-0490
  Redford (G-13738)
Progressive Manufacturing LLC .... G 231 924-9975
  Fremont (G-6055)

CASKETS & ACCESS

Genesis International LLC .... E 317 777-6700
  Mason (G-11134)

CASKETS WHOLESALERS

American Vault Service .... G 989 366-8657
  Prudenville (G-13655)
Burrell Tri-County Vaults Inc .... F 734 483-2024
  Ypsilanti (G-18930)
Wilbert Burial Vault Company .... G 231 773-6631
  Muskegon (G-11946)
Willbee Concrete Products Co .... F 517 782-8246
  Jackson (G-9035)

CAST STONE: Concrete

Royal Stone LLC .... E 248 343-6232
  Williamston (G-18581)

CASTERS

Caster Concepts Inc .... E 888 781-1470
  Albion (G-122)
Evans Industries Inc .... G 313 272-8200
  Detroit (G-4219)

CASTINGS GRINDING: For The Trade

ABC Grinding Inc .... G 313 295-1060
  Dearborn Heights (G-3918)
Able Manufacturing Inc .... E 616 235-3322
  Grand Rapids (G-6417)
Alro Riverside LLC .... G 517 782-8322
  Jackson (G-8813)
American Grinding Machining Co .... F 313 388-0440
  Lincoln Park (G-10043)
Echo Quality Grinding Inc .... F 231 544-6637
  Central Lake (G-2694)
Edmore Tool & Grinding Inc .... F 989 427-3790
  Edmore (G-4992)
Gehring Honing Machs .... D 248 478-8061
  Farmington Hills (G-5251)
Grind-All Precision Tool Co .... F 586 954-3430
  Clinton Township (G-3250)
Grinding Specialists Inc .... E 734 729-1775
  Westland (G-18377)
L & R Centerless Grinding .... G 734 397-3031
  Canton (G-2485)
Line Precision Inc .... E 248 474-5280
  Farmington Hills (G-5291)
Local Grind .... G 269 623-5777
  Delton (G-3965)
Michigan General Grinding LLC .... G 616 454-5089
  Grand Rapids (G-6990)
Modified Gear and Spline Inc .... F 313 893-3511
  Detroit (G-4463)
Quality Grinding Inc .... G 586 293-3780
  Fraser (G-5983)
R & S Cutter Grind Inc .... G 989 791-3100
  Saginaw (G-14733)
Superior Cutter Grinding Inc .... G 586 781-2365
  Shelby Township (G-15347)
Tait Grinding Service Inc .... E 248 437-5100
  Howell (G-8525)
Tree Cutting Stump Grinding .... G 231 856-9021
  Morley (G-11624)
True Tool Cnc Regrinding & Mfg .... G 616 677-1751
  Grand Rapids (G-7279)
Ultra Tool Grind Inc .... G 989 471-5169
  Ossineke (G-12780)

CASTINGS: Aerospace Investment, Ferrous

Barron Industries Inc .... D 248 628-4300
  Oxford (G-12876)
Eps Industries Inc .... E 616 844-9220
  Ferrysburg (G-5602)
Onodi Tool & Engineering Co .... E 313 386-6682
  Melvindale (G-11208)
Precision Castparts Corp .... G 586 690-8659
  Macomb (G-10628)
Robe Aerospace .... G 231 933-9355
  Traverse City (G-16823)

CASTINGS: Aerospace, Aluminum

Centracore LLC .... F 586 776-5700
  Saint Clair (G-14818)
Cytec Industries Inc .... G 269 349-6677
  Kalamazoo (G-9161)
Gen3 Defense and Aerospace LLC .... F 616 345-8031
  Comstock Park (G-3607)
Onodi Tool & Engineering Co .... E 313 386-6682
  Melvindale (G-11208)
Patterson Precision Mfg Inc .... E 231 733-1913
  Norton Shores (G-12324)
Tower Defense & Aerospace LLC .... E 248 675-6000
  Livonia (G-10439)

CASTINGS: Aerospace, Nonferrous, Exc Aluminum

Onodi Tool & Engineering Co .... E 313 386-6682
  Melvindale (G-11208)
Patterson Precision Mfg Inc .... E 231 733-1913
  Norton Shores (G-12324)

CASTINGS: Aluminum

A C Foundry Incorporated .... F 269 963-4131
  Battle Creek (G-1175)
Algonac Marine Cast LLC .... E 810 794-9391
  Clay (G-3114)
Bernier Cast Metals Inc .... G 989 754-7571
  Saginaw (G-14615)
Birkhold Pattern Company Inc .... G 269 467-8705
  Centreville (G-2696)
Casting Industries Inc .... F 586 776-5700
  Saint Clair (G-14817)
Hackett Brass Foundry Co .... G 313 331-6005
  Detroit (G-4291)
Mall City Aluminum Inc .... G 269 349-5088
  Kalamazoo (G-9264)
Max Casting Company Inc .... F 269 925-8081
  Benton Harbor (G-1568)
Shipston Alum Tech Intl Inc .... G 317 738-0282
  Southfield (G-15699)
Shipston Alum Tech Intl LLC .... C 317 738-0282
  Southfield (G-15700)
Sterling Metal Works LLC .... G 586 977-9577
  Sterling Heights (G-16193)
Tooling & Equipment Intl Corp .... D 734 522-1422
  Livonia (G-10433)
Tri-State Aluminum LLC .... F 231 722-7825
  Muskegon (G-11936)
Wolverine Bronze Company .... D 586 776-8180
  Roseville (G-14495)

CASTINGS: Brass, Bronze & Copper

L & L Pattern Inc .... G 231 733-2646
  Muskegon (G-11853)
Marcellus Metalcasters Inc .... F 269 646-0202
  Marcellus (G-10949)
Smith Castings Inc .... F 906 774-4956
  Iron Mountain (G-8733)

CASTINGS: Brass, NEC, Exc Die

Bernier Cast Metals Inc .... G 989 754-7571
  Saginaw (G-14615)
Jsj Corporation .... E 616 842-6350
  Grand Haven (G-6324)
Lewkowicz Corporation .... F 734 941-0411
  Romulus (G-14298)

CASTINGS: Bronze, NEC, Exc Die

Barron Group Inc .... D 248 628-4300
  Oxford (G-12875)
Barron Industries Inc .... D 248 628-4300
  Oxford (G-12876)

PRODUCT SECTION

CASTINGS: Commercial Investment, Ferrous

Barron Industries Inc ....F 248 628-4300
  Oxford (G-12877)
Federal Group Usa Inc ....F 248 545-5000
  Southfield (G-15559)
Howmet Aerospace Inc ....C 231 894-7290
  Whitehall (G-18499)
Howmet Corporation ....E 231 894-5686
  Whitehall (G-18501)
Howmet Corporation ....C 231 894-7183
  Whitehall (G-18502)
Howmet Corporation ....C 231 981-3269
  Whitehall (G-18503)
Howmet Holdings Corporation ....G 231 894-5686
  Whitehall (G-18506)
Invecast Corporation ....E 586 755-4050
  Warren (G-17869)
Triton Global Sources Inc ....G 734 668-7107
  Ypsilanti (G-18981)

CASTINGS: Die, Aluminum

Aludyne Inc ....A 248 506-1692
  Warren (G-17699)
Aludyne North America LLC ....B 989 463-6166
  Alma (G-238)
Angstrom Aluminum Castings LLC ....E 616 309-1208
  Grand Rapids (G-6459)
Cascade Die Casting Group Inc ....G 616 281-1774
  Grand Rapids (G-6550)
Cascade Die Casting Group Inc ....D 616 887-1771
  Sparta (G-15762)
Centracore De Mexico LLC ....E 586 776-5700
  Saint Clair (G-14819)
Charles Group Inc ....B 336 882-0186
  Grand Rapids (G-6565)
Connell Limited Partnership ....E 989 875-5135
  Ithaca (G-8789)
Cooper Foundry Inc ....E 269 343-2808
  Kalamazoo (G-9155)
Eagle Alum Prmnt Mold Cstngs I ....G 231 788-4884
  Muskegon (G-11802)
Evans Industries Inc ....G 313 259-2266
  Troy (G-17100)
Federal Group Usa Inc ....F 248 545-5000
  Southfield (G-15559)
Hackett Brass Foundry Co ....E 313 822-1214
  Detroit (G-4290)
Hanson International Inc ....C 269 429-5555
  Saint Joseph (G-14935)
Hoffmann Die Cast LLC ....C 269 983-1102
  Saint Joseph (G-14936)
Homestead Tool and Machine ....E 989 465-6182
  Coleman (G-3465)
Husite Engineering Co Inc ....F 248 588-0337
  Clinton Township (G-3255)
Key Casting Company Inc ....G 269 426-3800
  Sawyer (G-15110)
Lakeshore Die Cast Inc ....F 269 422-1523
  Baroda (G-1164)
M and A Castings Ltd ....F 517 879-2222
  Pinconning (G-13062)
Mag-TEC Casting Corporation ....E 517 789-8505
  Jackson (G-8941)
Michigan Die Casting LLC ....D 269 471-7715
  Dowagiac (G-4789)
Montague Metal Products Inc ....E 231 893-0547
  Montague (G-11599)
Mv Metal Pdts & Solutions LLC ....D 269 462-4010
  Dowagiac (G-4791)
New Gldc LLC ....D 231 726-4002
  Muskegon (G-11885)
North Shore Mfg Corp ....E 269 849-2551
  Coloma (G-3481)
Pace Industries LLC ....G 231 777-3941
  Muskegon (G-11888)
Pace Industries LLC ....G 231 773-4491
  Muskegon (G-11889)
Pace Industries LLC ....A 231 777-3941
  Norton Shores (G-12323)
Pace Industries LLC ....F 231 777-5615
  Muskegon (G-11891)
Paragon Metals LLC ....E 517 639-4629
  Hillsdale (G-7941)
Precision Die Cast Inc ....G 586 463-1800
  Kimball (G-9499)
Prototype Cast Mfg Inc ....G 586 739-0180
  Shelby Township (G-15311)
Prototype Cast Mfg Inc ....G 586 615-8524
  Sterling Heights (G-16137)

Soper Manufacturing Company ....F 269 429-5245
  Saint Joseph (G-14962)
SPX Corporation ....C 248 669-5100
  Commerce Township (G-3574)
Supreme Casting Inc ....D 269 465-5757
  Stevensville (G-16267)
T C H Industries Incorporated ....D 616 942-0505
  Grand Rapids (G-7245)
Tooling Technology LLC ....D 937 381-9211
  Macomb (G-10643)
Triton Global Sources Inc ....G 734 668-7107
  Ypsilanti (G-18981)
Tru Die Cast Corporation ....E 269 426-3361
  New Troy (G-12075)
Ube Machinery Inc ....D 734 741-7000
  Ann Arbor (G-702)
Wolverine Die Cast Ltd Prtnr O ....E 586 757-1900
  Warren (G-18071)

CASTINGS: Die, Copper & Copper Alloy

Hackett Brass Foundry Co ....E 313 822-1214
  Detroit (G-4290)

CASTINGS: Die, Lead & Zinc

North Shore Mfg Corp ....E 269 849-2551
  Coloma (G-3481)

CASTINGS: Die, Magnesium & Magnesium-Base Alloy

M and A Castings Ltd ....F 517 879-2222
  Pinconning (G-13062)
Mag-TEC Casting Corporation ....E 517 789-8505
  Jackson (G-8941)
Magnesium Products America Inc ....B 734 416-8600
  Plymouth (G-13231)

CASTINGS: Die, Nonferrous

Cascade Die Casting Group Inc ....G 616 455-4010
  Grand Rapids (G-6551)
Cobra Patterns & Models Inc ....E 248 588-2669
  Madison Heights (G-10694)
Mv Metal Pdts & Solutions LLC ....G 269 471-7715
  Portage (G-13586)

CASTINGS: Die, Zinc

Cascade Die Casting Group Inc ....G 616 281-1774
  Grand Rapids (G-6550)
Cascade Die Casting Group Inc ....D 616 887-1771
  Sparta (G-15762)
Charles Group Inc ....B 336 882-0186
  Grand Rapids (G-6565)
Hoffmann Die Cast LLC ....C 269 983-1102
  Saint Joseph (G-14936)
Key Casting Company Inc ....G 269 426-3800
  Sawyer (G-15110)
Lakeshore Die Cast Inc ....F 269 422-1523
  Baroda (G-1164)
Mv Metal Pdts & Solutions LLC ....D 269 462-4010
  Dowagiac (G-4791)
Proto-Cast Inc ....E 313 565-5400
  Inkster (G-8672)
T C H Industries Incorporated ....D 616 942-0505
  Grand Rapids (G-7245)
Tru Die Cast Corporation ....E 269 426-3361
  New Troy (G-12075)
Wolverine Die Cast Ltd Prtnr O ....E 586 757-1900
  Warren (G-18071)

CASTINGS: Ductile

Berne Enterprises Inc ....F 989 453-3235
  Pigeon (G-13036)
Betz Industries Inc ....D 616 453-4429
  Grand Rapids (G-6504)
Global Technology Ventures Inc ....G 248 324-3707
  Farmington Hills (G-5252)
Grede II LLC ....E 248 440-9500
  Southfield (G-15580)
Ravenna Casting Center Inc ....G 231 853-0300
  Ravenna (G-13692)
Triton Global Sources Inc ....G 734 668-7107
  Ypsilanti (G-18981)

CASTINGS: Gray Iron

Awcco USA Incorporated ....G 586 336-9135
  Romeo (G-14220)

CASTINGS: Steel

Blue Fire Manufacturing LLC ....E 248 714-7166
  Waterford (G-18104)
Calhoun Foundry Company Inc ....D 517 568-4415
  Homer (G-8349)
Casting Industries Inc ....F 586 776-5700
  Saint Clair (G-14817)
Dock Foundry Company ....G 269 278-1765
  Three Rivers (G-16571)
Ej Usa Inc ....B 800 874-4100
  East Jordan (G-4870)
Federal Group Usa Inc ....F 248 545-5000
  Southfield (G-15559)
Great Lakes Castings LLC ....E 616 399-9710
  Holland (G-8058)
Grede Holdings LLC ....E 248 440-9500
  Southfield (G-15579)
Grede LLC ....B 906 774-7250
  Kingsford (G-9509)
Grede LLC ....B 248 440-9500
  Southfield (G-15581)
Grede Wscnsin Subsidiaries LLC ....C 248 727-1800
  Southfield (G-15583)
Kent Foundry Company ....E 616 754-1100
  Greenville (G-7496)
Midland Iron Works Inc ....F 989 832-3041
  Midland (G-11393)
Northland Castings Corporation ....E 231 873-4974
  Hart (G-7758)
Pioneer Foundry Company Inc ....E 517 782-9469
  Jackson (G-8986)
Smith Castings Inc ....F 906 774-4956
  Iron Mountain (G-8733)
Smith Castings Incorporated ....F 906 774-4956
  Kingsford (G-9517)
Steeltech Ltd ....D 616 243-7920
  Grand Rapids (G-7225)

CASTINGS: Machinery, Aluminum

Chassix Holdings Inc ....E 248 728-8700
  Southfield (G-15520)
Mpi Products LLC ....D 248 237-3007
  Rochester Hills (G-14067)

CASTINGS: Machinery, Copper Or Copper-Base Alloy

Conway Detroit Corporation ....E 586 552-8413
  Roseville (G-14389)

CASTINGS: Machinery, Nonferrous, Exc Die or Aluminum Copper

Kuhlman Casting Co Inc ....F 248 853-2382
  Detroit (G-4369)

CASTINGS: Precision

Acra Cast Inc ....E 989 893-3961
  Bay City (G-1316)
Federal Group Usa Inc ....F 248 545-5000
  Southfield (G-15559)
Grosse Tool and Machine Co ....E 586 773-6770
  Warren (G-17842)
High-Tech Inds of Holland ....E 616 399-5430
  Holland (G-8072)
Holland Alloys Inc ....E 616 396-6444
  Holland (G-8073)
Holland Pattern Co ....G 616 396-6348
  Holland (G-8082)
Shellcast Inc ....E 231 893-8245
  Montague (G-11600)
Stegman Tool Co Inc ....E 248 588-4634
  Troy (G-17372)

CASTINGS: Steel

Alloying Surfaces Inc ....G 248 524-9200
  Troy (G-16927)
Ancast Inc ....E 269 927-1985
  Sodus (G-15392)
Arcanum Alloys Inc ....G 312 810-4479
  Kentwood (G-9443)
Berne Enterprises Inc ....F 989 453-3235
  Pigeon (G-13036)
Huron Casting Inc ....B 989 453-3933
  Pigeon (G-13039)
Steeltech Ltd ....D 616 243-7920
  Grand Rapids (G-7225)
Steeltech Ltd ....G 616 696-1130
  Cedar Springs (G-2663)

Employee Codes: A=Over 500 employees, B=251-500
C=101-250, D=51-100, E=20-50, F=10-19, G=3-9

2022 Harris Michigan Industrial Directory

CASTINGS: Steel

Temperform LLC .... E 248 349-5230
  Novi (G-12554)

CASTINGS: Titanium

Apollo Trick Titanium Inc .... E 517 694-7449
  Troy (G-16940)

CASTINGS: Zinc

Soper Manufacturing Company .... F 269 429-5245
  Saint Joseph (G-14962)
Triton Global Sources Inc .... G 734 668-7107
  Ypsilanti (G-18981)

CATALOG & MAIL-ORDER HOUSES

A W B Industries Inc .... E 989 739-1447
  Oscoda (G-12753)
SPD America LLC .... G 734 709-7624
  Pinckney (G-13056)
Swartzmiller Lumber Company .... G 989 845-6625
  Chesaning (G-2830)

CATALOG SALES

Fitness Finders Inc .... F 517 750-1500
  Jackson (G-8884)

CATS, WHOLESALE

Go Cat Feather Toys .... G 517 543-7519
  Charlotte (G-2759)

CEILING SYSTEMS: Luminous, Commercial

Itc Incorporated .... E 616 396-1355
  Hudsonville (G-8587)
Skyworks LLC .... F 972 284-9093
  Northville (G-12261)

CEMENT & CONCRETE RELATED PRDTS & EQPT: Bituminous

Globe Industries Incorporated .... F 906 932-3540
  Ironwood (G-8763)

CEMENT, EXC LINOLEUM & TILE

Concrete Manufacturing Inc .... G 586 777-3320
  Roseville (G-14388)

CEMENT: High Temperature, Refractory, Nonclay

Taylor Controls Inc .... F 269 637-8521
  South Haven (G-15418)

CEMENT: Hydraulic

Blue Circle Cement .... G 313 842-4600
  Detroit (G-4059)
Joe Davis Crushing Inc .... G 586 757-3612
  Sterling Heights (G-16056)
Lafarge North America Inc .... G 989 399-1005
  Saginaw (G-14682)
Lafarge North America Inc .... G 989 894-0157
  Essexville (G-5116)
Lafarge North America Inc .... G 989 595-3820
  Presque Isle (G-13654)
Lafarge North America Inc .... G 269 983-6333
  Saint Joseph (G-14944)
Lafarge North America Inc .... G 231 726-3291
  Muskegon (G-11855)
Nb Cement Co .... G 313 278-8299
  Dearborn Heights (G-3935)

CEMENT: Magnesia

Martin Mretta Magnesia Spc LLC .... E 231 723-2577
  Manistee (G-10907)

CEMENT: Masonry

Knust Masonry .... G 231 322-2587
  Rapid City (G-13681)

CEMENT: Portland

Holcim (us) Inc .... D 734 529-2411
  Dundee (G-4823)
Holcim (us) Inc .... G 734 529-4600
  Dundee (G-4824)
Holcim (us) Inc .... G 989 755-7515
  Saginaw (G-14667)

Lafarge North America Inc .... G 989 354-4171
  Alpena (G-299)
Lafarge North America Inc .... G 703 480-3600
  Dundee (G-4827)

CEMETERIES: Real Estate Operation

Fenton Corporation .... G 810 629-2858
  Fenton (G-5476)

CEMETERY MEMORIAL DEALERS

Fenton Corporation .... G 810 629-2858
  Fenton (G-5476)
Fenton Memorials & Vaults Inc .... G 810 629-2858
  Fenton (G-5477)
Patten Monument Company .... D 616 785-4141
  Comstock Park (G-3634)

CERAMIC FIBER

3M Technical Ceramics Inc .... F 248 960-9339
  Wixom (G-18592)
Nano Innovations LLC .... G 906 231-2101
  Houghton (G-8387)

CERAMIC FLOOR & WALL TILE WHOLESALERS

Dal-Tile Corporation .... F 248 471-7150
  Farmington Hills (G-5210)
Earthwerks LLC .... G 800 275-7943
  Grand Haven (G-6294)

CHAINS: Forged

Allor Manufacturing Inc .... D 248 486-4500
  Brighton (G-1943)
Plesh Industries Inc .... E 716 873-4916
  Brighton (G-2052)
Shadko Enterprises Inc .... G 248 816-1712
  Troy (G-17348)

CHANDELIERS: Commercial

El Sol Custom Lighting .... F 269 281-0435
  Saint Joseph (G-14928)

CHARCOAL

Country Schoolhouse Kingsford .... G 906 828-1971
  Kingsford (G-9507)

CHASSIS: Motor Vehicle

A & A Manufacturing Co .... G 616 846-1730
  Spring Lake (G-15799)
American Axle Mfg Holdings Inc .... A 313 758-2000
  Detroit (G-4012)
Chassix Holdings Inc .... E 248 728-8700
  Southfield (G-15520)
Detroit Chassis LLC .... G 313 571-2100
  Detroit (G-4139)
Detroit Custom Chassis LLC .... C 313 571-2100
  Detroit (G-4142)
Sakthi Auto Group USA Inc .... C 313 551-6001
  Detroit (G-4576)
Sakthi Auto Group USA Inc .... C 248 292-9328
  Detroit (G-4577)
Sakthi Auto Group USA Inc .... C 313 652-5254
  Detroit (G-4578)
Shyft Group Inc .... A 517 543-6400
  Novi (G-12536)
Shyft Group Inc .... E 517 543-6400
  Charlotte (G-2767)
Shyft Group Inc .... E 517 543-6400
  Charlotte (G-2768)
Spartan Motors Chassis Inc .... B 517 543-6400
  Charlotte (G-2772)
Spectra Lmp LLC .... G 313 571-2100
  Detroit (G-4600)
Superalloy North America LLC .... G 810 252-1552
  Bingham Farms (G-1704)
Thomas Engineering .... G 248 620-7916
  Clarkston (G-3071)
UPF Inc .... E 810 768-0001
  Flint (G-5789)
Workhorse Custom Chassis LLC .... C 248 588-5300
  Madison Heights (G-10864)

CHEESE WHOLESALERS

Langs Inc .... G 248 634-6048
  Holly (G-8280)

Williams Cheese Co .... E 989 697-4492
  Linwood (G-10075)

CHEMICAL ELEMENTS

El 903 Element LLC .... G 517 655-3492
  East Lansing (G-4891)
Element 22 Coml Group LLC .... G 269 910-6739
  Kalamazoo (G-9175)
Element Services LLC .... G 517 672-1005
  Howell (G-8452)

CHEMICAL PROCESSING MACHINERY & EQPT

American Chem Solutions LLC .... E 231 655-5840
  Muskegon (G-11769)
B&P Littleford Day LLC .... D 989 757-1300
  Saginaw (G-14607)
B&P Littleford LLC .... E 989 757-1300
  Saginaw (G-14608)
Frontier Technology Inc .... G 269 673-9464
  Allegan (G-159)
Innovative Cleaning Eqp Inc .... E 616 656-9225
  Grand Rapids (G-6845)
Jcu International Inc .... G 248 313-6630
  Wixom (G-18689)
Powell Fabrication & Mfg LLC .... E 989 681-2158
  Saint Louis (G-14996)
Ti-Coating Inc .... E 586 726-1900
  Shelby Township (G-15351)

CHEMICAL: Sodm Compnds/Salts, Inorg, Exc Rfnd Sodm Chloride

Kage Group LLC .... G 734 604-5052
  Van Buren Twp (G-17532)

CHEMICALS & ALLIED PRDTS WHOLESALERS, NEC

Dow Chemical Company .... C 989 832-1000
  Midland (G-11348)
Ebonex Corporation .... G 313 388-0063
  Melvindale (G-11200)
General Tape Label Liquidating .... F 248 437-5200
  Wixom (G-18668)
Idemitsu Chemicals USA Corp .... G 248 355-0666
  Southfield (G-15599)
Jade Scientific Inc .... F 734 207-3775
  Westland (G-18387)
R J Marshall Company .... F 248 353-4100
  Southfield (G-15687)
Recycling Fluid Technologies .... F 269 788-0488
  Battle Creek (G-1288)
South / Win LLC .... G 734 525-9000
  Livonia (G-10414)
Technichem .... G 810 744-3770
  Flint (G-5777)

CHEMICALS & ALLIED PRDTS, WHOL: Gases, Compressed/Liquefied

Purity Cylinder Gases Inc .... G 517 321-9555
  Lansing (G-9734)

CHEMICALS & ALLIED PRDTS, WHOLESALE: Acids

Pressure Vessel Service Inc .... E 313 921-1200
  Detroit (G-4533)

CHEMICALS & ALLIED PRDTS, WHOLESALE: Alcohols

Carbon Green Bioenergy LLC .... E 616 374-4000
  Lake Odessa (G-9573)

CHEMICALS & ALLIED PRDTS, WHOLESALE: Anti-Corrosion Prdts

Trenton Corporation .... E 734 424-3600
  Ann Arbor (G-697)

CHEMICALS & ALLIED PRDTS, WHOLESALE: Aromatic

Odor Gone Inc .... F 888 636-7292
  Zeeland (G-19064)

PRODUCT SECTION

CHEMICALS: Inorganic, NEC

CHEMICALS & ALLIED PRDTS, WHOLESALE: Chemical Additives

Tryco Inc ....F....... 734 953-6800
  Farmington Hills *(G-5406)*

CHEMICALS & ALLIED PRDTS, WHOLESALE: Chemicals, Indl

Access Technologies LLC ....G....... 574 286-1255
  Niles *(G-12109)*
Colfran Industrial Sales Inc ....G....... 734 595-8920
  Romulus *(G-14262)*
Jci Jones Chemicals Inc ....F....... 734 283-0677
  Wyandotte *(G-18824)*
Wacker Chemical Corporation...............A....... 517 264-8500
  Adrian *(G-103)*

CHEMICALS & ALLIED PRDTS, WHOLESALE: Chemicals, Rustproofing

Condat Corporation ....E....... 734 944-4994
  Saline *(G-15009)*

CHEMICALS & ALLIED PRDTS, WHOLESALE: Detergent/Soap

Access Business Group LLC.................A....... 616 787-6000
  Ada *(G-3)*
Alticor Global Holdings Inc ....F....... 616 787-1000
  Ada *(G-5)*
Alticor Inc ....A....... 616 787-1000
  Ada *(G-6)*
Kmi Cleaning Solutions Inc ....F....... 269 964-2557
  Battle Creek *(G-1263)*

CHEMICALS & ALLIED PRDTS, WHOLESALE: Detergents

Selestial Soap LLC ....E....... 231 944-1978
  Traverse City *(G-16828)*

CHEMICALS & ALLIED PRDTS, WHOLESALE: Oil Additives

Nano Materials & Processes Inc............G....... 248 529-3873
  Milford *(G-11475)*
Stony Creek Essential Oils ....G....... 989 227-5500
  Saint Johns *(G-14917)*

CHEMICALS & ALLIED PRDTS, WHOLESALE: Oxygen

Tupes of Saginaw Inc ....F....... 989 799-1550
  Saginaw *(G-14781)*

CHEMICALS & ALLIED PRDTS, WHOLESALE: Plastics Prdts, NEC

Champion Plastics Inc ....E....... 248 373-8995
  Auburn Hills *(G-842)*
Curbell Plastics Inc ....G....... 734 513-0531
  Livonia *(G-10170)*
Proto Shapes Inc ....F....... 517 278-3947
  Coldwater *(G-3447)*
Stone Plastics and Mfg Inc ....C....... 616 748-9740
  Zeeland *(G-19082)*
Uniflex Inc ....G....... 248 486-6000
  Brighton *(G-2088)*
Woodbridge Sales & Engrg Inc ....C....... 248 288-0100
  Troy *(G-17452)*
Wright Plastic Products Co LLC ....G....... 810 326-3000
  Saint Clair *(G-14845)*

CHEMICALS & ALLIED PRDTS, WHOLESALE: Plastics Sheets & Rods

Ann Arbor Plastics Inc ....G....... 734 944-0800
  Saline *(G-15003)*
Exotic Rubber & Plastics Corp ....D....... 248 477-2122
  New Hudson *(G-12053)*
Humphrey Companies LLC ....C....... 616 530-1717
  Grandville *(G-7389)*
Total Plastics Resources LLC ....D....... 269 344-0009
  Kalamazoo *(G-9358)*
Total Plastics Resources LLC ....F....... 248 299-9500
  Rochester Hills *(G-14129)*

CHEMICALS & ALLIED PRDTS, WHOLESALE: Polyurethane Prdts

Recycled Polymetric Materials ....G....... 313 957-6373
  Detroit *(G-4559)*

CHEMICALS & ALLIED PRDTS, WHOLESALE: Resins, Plastics

Aci Plastics Inc ....E....... 810 767-3800
  Flint *(G-5636)*
Aci Plastics Inc ....E....... 810 767-3800
  Flint *(G-5637)*

CHEMICALS & ALLIED PRDTS, WHOLESALE: Rubber, Synthetic

Exotic Rubber & Plastics Corp ....D....... 248 477-2122
  New Hudson *(G-12053)*

CHEMICALS & ALLIED PRDTS, WHOLESALE: Spec Clean/Sanitation

Able Solutions LLC ....G....... 810 216-6106
  Port Huron *(G-13430)*

CHEMICALS: Agricultural

Avian Enterprises LLC ....E....... 888 366-0709
  Sylvan Lake *(G-16359)*
Bayer Crop Science ....G....... 517 676-3586
  Mason *(G-11118)*
Bayer Cropscience LP ....F....... 231 744-4711
  Muskegon *(G-11776)*
Bms Enterprise LLC ....G....... 281 516-9100
  West Bloomfield *(G-18267)*
Centen AG LLC ....B....... 989 636-1000
  Midland *(G-11328)*
Corteva Agriscience LLC ....G....... 989 479-3245
  Harbor Beach *(G-7630)*
Dow Chemical Company ....G....... 989 636-0540
  Midland *(G-11349)*
Dupont ....E....... 651 767-2527
  Midland *(G-11358)*
Dupont Office and Self St ....G....... 206 471-3700
  Kewadin *(G-9486)*
Emerald Bioagriculture Corp ....E....... 517 882-7370
  Okemos *(G-12666)*
Monsanto Company ....G....... 269 483-1300
  Constantine *(G-3672)*
Rohm and Monsanto PLC ....G....... 313 886-1966
  Saint Clair Shores *(G-14882)*

CHEMICALS: Alcohols

Hampshire Chemical Corp ....E....... 989 636-1000
  Midland *(G-11370)*

CHEMICALS: Aluminum Compounds

Shipston Group US Inc ....E....... 248 372-9018
  Southfield *(G-15702)*

CHEMICALS: Boron Compounds, Not From Mines, NEC

Boropharm Inc ....G....... 248 348-5776
  Novi *(G-12375)*

CHEMICALS: Brine

Sean Michael Brines ....G....... 517 404-5481
  Fowlerville *(G-5856)*

CHEMICALS: Calcium Chloride

Liquid Dustlayer Inc ....G....... 231 723-3750
  Manistee *(G-10904)*
Wilkinson Chemical Corporation ....F....... 989 843-6163
  Mayville *(G-11174)*

CHEMICALS: Chromates & Bichromates

Diazem Corp ....G....... 989 832-3612
  Midland *(G-11339)*

CHEMICALS: Fire Retardant

Lenderink Inc ....F....... 616 887-8257
  Belmont *(G-1511)*

CHEMICALS: Fuel Tank Or Engine Cleaning

American Jetway Corporation ....D....... 734 721-5930
  Wayne *(G-18213)*
Beebe Fuel Systems ....G....... 734 261-3500
  Livonia *(G-10135)*
Questron Packaging LLC ....G....... 313 657-1630
  Detroit *(G-4547)*

CHEMICALS: High Purity Grade, Organic

Thumb Bioenergy LLC ....F....... 810 404-2466
  Sandusky *(G-15069)*
Tpa Inc ....G....... 248 302-9131
  Detroit *(G-4641)*

CHEMICALS: High Purity, Refined From Technical Grade

Chemico Systems Inc ....G....... 586 986-2343
  Warren *(G-17754)*
Chemico Systems Inc ....E....... 248 723-3263
  Southfield *(G-15521)*
Cht USA Inc ....E....... 269 445-0847
  Cassopolis *(G-2626)*
Great Lakes Chemical Services ....E....... 269 372-6886
  Portage *(G-13562)*
Nelsonite Chemical Pdts Inc ....G....... 616 456-7098
  Grand Rapids *(G-7038)*

CHEMICALS: Inorganic, NEC

Access Technologies LLC ....G....... 574 286-1255
  Niles *(G-12109)*
Algoma Products Inc ....F....... 616 285-6440
  Grand Rapids *(G-6443)*
Arkema Inc ....E....... 616 243-4578
  Grand Rapids *(G-6470)*
Assay Designs Inc ....E....... 734 214-0923
  Ann Arbor *(G-383)*
Axchem Inc ....G....... 734 641-9842
  Wayne *(G-18214)*
Blue Cube Holding LLC ....C....... 989 636-1000
  Midland *(G-11323)*
Cal-Chlor Corp ....D....... 231 843-1147
  Ludington *(G-10529)*
Caravan Technologies Inc ....F....... 313 632-8545
  Detroit *(G-4088)*
Ceratizit Usa Inc ....C....... 586 759-2280
  Warren *(G-17751)*
Chemtrade Chemicals US LLC ....G....... 313 842-5222
  Detroit *(G-4091)*
Cytec Industries Inc ....G....... 269 349-6677
  Kalamazoo *(G-9161)*
Duramet Corporation ....G....... 586 759-2280
  Warren *(G-17785)*
Element 80 Engraving LLC ....G....... 616 318-7407
  Grand Rapids *(G-6670)*
Element Facility Services ....G....... 734 895-8716
  Romulus *(G-14270)*
Henkel US Operations Corp ....C....... 586 759-5555
  Warren *(G-17852)*
Henkel US Operations Corp ....B....... 248 588-1082
  Madison Heights *(G-10739)*
High-Po-Chlor Inc ....G....... 734 942-1500
  Ann Arbor *(G-515)*
Icmp Inc ....E....... 269 445-0847
  Cassopolis *(G-2630)*
Imerys Perlite Usa Inc ....F....... 269 649-1352
  Vicksburg *(G-17605)*
Jade Scientific Inc ....F....... 734 207-3775
  Westland *(G-18387)*
Jci Jones Chemicals Inc ....F....... 734 283-0677
  Wyandotte *(G-18824)*
Lily Products Michigan Inc ....G....... 616 245-9193
  Grand Rapids *(G-6944)*
McGean-Rohco Inc ....E....... 216 441-4900
  Livonia *(G-10306)*
Metrex Research LLC ....D....... 734 947-6700
  Romulus *(G-14303)*
Nanocerox Inc ....G....... 734 741-9522
  Ann Arbor *(G-588)*
Nugentec Oilfield Chem LLC ....G....... 517 518-2712
  Howell *(G-8486)*
Oerlikon Metco (us) Inc ....E....... 248 288-0027
  Troy *(G-17287)*
Oils and Elements LLC ....G....... 989 450-4081
  Bay City *(G-1385)*
Pacific Industrial Dev Corp ....D....... 734 930-9292
  Ann Arbor *(G-604)*
R L Schmitt Company Inc ....E....... 734 525-9310
  Livonia *(G-10382)*

Employee Codes: A=Over 500 employees, B=251-500
C=101-250, D=51-100, E=20-50, F=10-19, G=3-9

2022 Harris Michigan Industrial Directory

1219

CHEMICALS: Inorganic, NEC

Rap Products Inc .... G 989 893-5583
  Bay City *(G-1394)*
Sbz Corporation .... G 248 649-1166
  Troy *(G-17346)*
Silbond Corporation .... E 517 436-3171
  Weston *(G-18433)*
Solutia Inc .... G 734 676-4400
  Trenton *(G-16892)*
Transtar Autobody Tech LLC .... C 810 220-3000
  Brighton *(G-2084)*
United Abrasive Inc .... F 906 563-9249
  Vulcan *(G-17616)*
W R Grace & Co-Conn .... C 410 531-4000
  South Haven *(G-15424)*
Wilkinson Corporation .... G 989 843-6163
  Mayville *(G-11175)*
Xg Sciences Inc .... G 517 703-1110
  Lansing *(G-9908)*

CHEMICALS: Medicinal

Degrasyn Biosciences LLC .... G 713 582-3395
  Ann Arbor *(G-445)*
Solohill Engineering Inc .... E 734 973-2956
  Ann Arbor *(G-660)*

CHEMICALS: Medicinal, Organic, Uncompounded, Bulk

Pharmacia & Upjohn Company LLC .... D 908 901-8000
  Kalamazoo *(G-9294)*

CHEMICALS: NEC

Aapharmasyn LLC .... F 734 213-2123
  Ann Arbor *(G-344)*
Afton Chemical Corporation .... G 248 350-0640
  Southfield *(G-15471)*
Atotech Usa LLC .... F 586 939-3040
  Sterling Heights *(G-15936)*
Bars Products Inc .... E 248 634-8278
  Holly *(G-8262)*
BASF Corporation .... G 734 591-5560
  Livonia *(G-10131)*
Bohning Company Ltd .... E 231 229-4247
  Lake City *(G-9545)*
Bridge Organics Company .... E 269 649-4200
  Vicksburg *(G-17600)*
Brighton Laboratories Inc .... F 810 225-9520
  Brighton *(G-1953)*
Caravan Technologies Inc .... F 313 632-8545
  Detroit *(G-4088)*
Cau Acquisition Company LLC .... D 989 875-8133
  Ithaca *(G-8787)*
Cayman Chemical Company Inc .... D 734 971-3335
  Ann Arbor *(G-417)*
Cerco Inc .... E 734 362-8664
  Brownstown Twp *(G-2153)*
Chem-Trend Holding Inc .... G 517 545-7980
  Howell *(G-8437)*
Chem-Trend Limited Partnership .... C 517 546-4520
  Howell *(G-8438)*
Chem-Trend Limited Partnership .... G 517 546-4520
  Howell *(G-8439)*
Chemetall US Inc .... G 517 787-4846
  Jackson *(G-8841)*
Cleaning Solutions Inc .... G 616 243-0555
  Grand Rapids *(G-6572)*
Cummings-Moore Graphite Co .... E 313 841-1615
  Detroit *(G-4112)*
Cytec Industries Inc .... G 269 349-6677
  Kalamazoo *(G-9161)*
Dell Marking Systems .... G 248 481-2119
  Pontiac *(G-13359)*
Diversified Chemical Tech Inc .... C 313 867-5444
  Detroit *(G-4180)*
Dow Chemical Company .... G 517 439-4400
  Hillsdale *(G-7933)*
Eastern Oil Company .... E 248 333-1333
  Pontiac *(G-13364)*
Eftec North America LLC .... D 248 585-2200
  Taylor *(G-16410)*
Freiborne Industries Inc .... E 248 333-2490
  Pontiac *(G-13371)*
H M Products Inc .... G 313 875-5148
  Detroit *(G-4288)*
Haltermann Carless Us Inc .... E 248 422-6548
  Troy *(G-17136)*
Henkel US Operations Corp .... C 586 759-5555
  Warren *(G-17852)*
Hercules LLC .... G 269 388-8676
  Kalamazoo *(G-9215)*
Jones Chemical Inc .... G 734 283-0677
  Riverview *(G-13878)*
Lubrizol Corporation .... G 989 496-3780
  Midland *(G-11385)*
Lymtal International Inc .... E 248 373-8100
  Orion *(G-12734)*
Macdermid Incorporated .... G 248 437-8161
  New Hudson *(G-12060)*
Mackenzie Company .... G 231 335-1997
  Detroit *(G-4414)*
McGean-Rohco Inc .... E 216 441-4900
  Livonia *(G-10306)*
Nelsonite Chemical Pdts Inc .... G 616 456-7098
  Grand Rapids *(G-7038)*
Northern Coatings & Chem Co .... E 906 863-2641
  Menominee *(G-11254)*
NV Labs Inc .... D 248 358-9022
  Southfield *(G-15668)*
Patty Raymond .... G 517 256-6673
  Eagle *(G-4852)*
Photo Systems Inc .... G 734 424-9625
  Dexter *(G-4749)*
Ralrube Inc .... G 734 429-0033
  Saline *(G-15035)*
Rolled Alloys Inc .... G 734 847-0561
  Temperance *(G-16547)*
Sika Corporation .... D 248 577-0020
  Madison Heights *(G-10829)*
Smith Wa Inc .... E 313 883-6977
  Detroit *(G-4598)*
Technichem .... G 810 744-3770
  Flint *(G-5777)*
Thetford Corporation .... C 734 769-6000
  Ann Arbor *(G-688)*
Transtar Autobody Tech LLC .... C 810 220-3000
  Brighton *(G-2084)*
Valuable Services LLC .... G 512 667-7490
  Brighton *(G-2091)*
Varn International Inc .... F 734 781-4600
  Livonia *(G-10458)*
Vertellus Hlth Spclty Pdts LLC .... G 616 772-2193
  Zeeland *(G-19089)*
Wacker Biochem Corporation .... C 517 264-8500
  Adrian *(G-102)*
Wilbur Products Inc .... F 231 755-3805
  Muskegon *(G-11948)*

CHEMICALS: Nonmetallic Compounds

I C S Corporation America Inc .... F 616 554-9300
  Grand Rapids *(G-6827)*

CHEMICALS: Organic, NEC

Aapharmasyn LLC .... F 734 213-2123
  Ann Arbor *(G-344)*
Advanced Urethanes Inc .... G 313 273-5705
  Detroit *(G-3988)*
Akzo Nobel Coatings Inc .... E 248 451-6231
  Pontiac *(G-13346)*
Amcol International Corp .... E 517 629-6808
  Albion *(G-116)*
Avient Colorants USA LLC .... C 517 629-9101
  Albion *(G-117)*
BASF .... F 231 719-3019
  Muskegon *(G-11774)*
BASF Corporation .... G 734 324-6963
  Wyandotte *(G-18808)*
BASF Corporation .... C 734 324-6000
  Wyandotte *(G-18809)*
BASF Corporation .... G 734 324-6100
  Wyandotte *(G-18810)*
BASF Corporation .... C 734 759-2011
  Wyandotte *(G-18811)*
BASF Corporation .... G 734 591-5560
  Livonia *(G-10131)*
BASF Corporation .... C 248 827-4670
  Southfield *(G-15503)*
Berry & Associates Inc .... E 734 426-3787
  Dexter *(G-4727)*
Caravan Technologies Inc .... F 313 632-8545
  Detroit *(G-4088)*
CJ Chemicals LLC .... F 888 274-1044
  Howell *(G-8440)*
Colors & Effects USA LLC .... E 248 304-5753
  Southfield *(G-15529)*
Ddp Spclty Elctrnc Mtls US LL .... D 517 439-4440
  Hillsdale *(G-7932)*
Dow Chemical Company .... G 989 695-2584
  Freeland *(G-6021)*
Dow Chemical Company .... E 989 638-6441
  Midland *(G-11350)*
Dow Chemical Company .... G 925 432-5000
  Midland *(G-11351)*
Dow Silicones Corporation .... C 800 248-2481
  Hemlock *(G-7852)*
Dow Silicones Corporation .... G 989 895-3397
  Bay City *(G-1348)*
Draths Corporation .... F 517 349-0668
  Howell *(G-8450)*
Ecovia Renewables Inc .... G 248 953-0594
  Ann Arbor *(G-466)*
Gage Products Company .... G 248 541-3824
  Ferndale *(G-5557)*
Georgia-Pacific LLC .... G 989 348-7275
  Grayling *(G-7461)*
Great Lakes Chemical Serv .... G 269 353-1841
  Vicksburg *(G-17604)*
Grm Corporation .... E 989 453-2322
  Pigeon *(G-13037)*
Henkel US Operations Corp .... B 248 588-1082
  Madison Heights *(G-10739)*
Metal Mates Inc .... G 248 646-9831
  Beverly Hills *(G-1666)*
Microcide Inc .... G 248 526-9663
  Troy *(G-17258)*
Northern Coatings & Chem Co .... E 906 863-2641
  Menominee *(G-11254)*
Pira Testing LLC .... F 517 574-4297
  Lansing *(G-9784)*
Quaker Houghton Pa Inc .... G 248 641-3231
  Livonia *(G-10376)*
Rap Products Inc .... G 989 893-5583
  Bay City *(G-1394)*
Tygrus LLC .... G 248 218-0347
  Troy *(G-17409)*
Vertellus LLC .... C 616 772-2193
  Zeeland *(G-19090)*

CHEMICALS: Phenol

Durez Corporation .... C 248 313-7000
  Novi *(G-12406)*

CHEMICALS: Reagent Grade, Refined From Technical Grade

Empirical Bioscience Inc .... G 877 479-9949
  Grand Rapids *(G-6677)*
Genomic Diagnostics Na Inc .... G 734 730-8399
  Ann Arbor *(G-499)*

CHEMICALS: Silica Compounds

Inpore Technologies Inc .... G 517 481-2270
  East Lansing *(G-4897)*

CHEMICALS: Tanning Agents, Synthetic Inorganic

Antonios Leather Experts .... G 734 762-5000
  Livonia *(G-10120)*

CHEMICALS: Water Treatment

Antimicrobial Specialist Assoc .... F 989 662-0377
  Auburn *(G-763)*
Aurora Spclty Chemistries Corp .... E 517 372-9121
  Lansing *(G-9810)*
Clearwater Treatment Systems .... G 517 688-9316
  Clarklake *(G-3004)*
Dsw Holdings Inc .... E 313 567-4500
  Detroit *(G-4192)*
Enerco Corporation .... F 517 627-1669
  Grand Ledge *(G-6390)*
Ginsan Liquidating Company LLC .... D 616 791-8100
  Grand Rapids *(G-6744)*
Great Lakes Treatment Corp .... G 517 566-8008
  Sunfield *(G-16335)*
H-O-H Water Technology Inc .... E 248 669-6667
  Commerce Township *(G-3534)*
Hydro Chem Laboratories Inc .... E 248 348-1737
  Commerce Township *(G-3541)*
Pressure Vessel Service Inc .... E 313 921-1200
  Detroit *(G-4533)*
Suez Water Indiana LLC .... E 734 379-3855
  Rockwood *(G-14205)*
Teachout and Associates Inc .... G 269 729-4440
  Athens *(G-743)*
Wabco Group International Inc .... G 248 260-9025
  Auburn Hills *(G-1085)*

PRODUCT SECTION

CLEANING EQPT: Commercial

CHILD RESTRAINT SEATS, AUTOMOTIVE, WHOLESALE

Amway International Inc .... E 616 787-1000
  Ada *(G-8)*

CHILDBIRTH PREPARATION CLINIC

Liquidgoldconcept Inc .... G 734 926-9197
  Ypsilanti *(G-18963)*

CHILDREN'S & INFANTS' CLOTHING STORES

Bearcub Outfitters LLC .... F 231 439-9500
  Petoskey *(G-12990)*

CHILDREN'S WEAR STORES

Carters Inc .... G 616 647-9452
  Grand Rapids *(G-6549)*

CHIMNEYS & FITTINGS

St Onge Masonry LLC .... G 248 709-8161
  Auburn Hills *(G-1036)*

CHLORINE

Kassouni Manufacturing Inc .... E 616 794-0989
  Belding *(G-1455)*

CHOCOLATE, EXC CANDY FROM BEANS: Chips, Powder, Block, Syrup

Crow and Moss LLC .... G 231 838-9875
  Petoskey *(G-12995)*
Gayles Chocolates Limited .... E 248 398-0001
  Royal Oak *(G-14539)*
Kemnitz Fine Candies .... G 734 453-0480
  Plymouth *(G-13213)*
Marshalls Trail Inc .... F 231 436-5082
  Mackinaw City *(G-10568)*
Original Murdicks Fudge Co .... G 906 847-3530
  Mackinac Island *(G-10567)*
Renas Fudge Shops Inc .... F 586 293-0600
  Fraser *(G-5987)*
Sanders Candy LLC .... D 800 651-7263
  Clinton Township *(G-3349)*
Sugar Free Specialties LLC .... F 616 734-6999
  Comstock Park *(G-3646)*

CHOCOLATE, EXC CANDY FROM PURCH CHOC: Chips, Powder, Block

Rocky Mtn Choclat Fctry Inc .... D 810 606-8550
  Grand Blanc *(G-6261)*
Rocky Mtn Choclat Fctry Inc .... G 989 624-4784
  Birch Run *(G-1714)*

CHRISTMAS NOVELTIES, WHOLESALE

Bronner Display Sign Advg Inc .... C 989 652-9931
  Frankenmuth *(G-5860)*

CHRISTMAS TREE LIGHTING SETS: Electric

Bronner Display Sign Advg Inc .... C 989 652-9931
  Frankenmuth *(G-5860)*

CHRISTMAS TREES: Artificial

Fruit Haven Nursery Inc .... G 231 889-9973
  Kaleva *(G-9379)*

CHUCKS

Cap Collet & Tool Co Inc .... F 734 283-4040
  Wyandotte *(G-18814)*
Kalamazoo Chuck Mfg Svc Ctr Co .... F 269 679-2325
  Schoolcraft *(G-15122)*
Magnetic Chuck Services Co Inc .... G 586 822-9441
  Casco *(G-2600)*
Skill-Craft Company Inc .... F 586 716-4300
  Ira *(G-8714)*

CHUTES: Metal Plate

Formrite Inc .... G 517 521-1373
  Webberville *(G-18245)*

CIGARETTE & CIGAR PRDTS & ACCESS

E M Smokers Inc .... G 586 207-1172
  Shelby Township *(G-15217)*
Lite N Go Inc .... G 248 414-7540
  Dearborn *(G-3863)*

CIGARETTE FILTERS

Nodel-Co .... F 248 543-1325
  Ferndale *(G-5573)*

CIGARETTE LIGHTERS

Select Distributors LLC .... F 586 510-4647
  Warren *(G-18008)*

CIRCUIT BOARD REPAIR SVCS

Phillips Service Inds Inc .... F 734 853-5000
  Ann Arbor *(G-610)*
PSI Repair Services Inc .... C 734 853-5000
  Livonia *(G-10375)*

CIRCUIT BOARDS, PRINTED: Television & Radio

Hughes Electronics Pdts Corp .... E 734 427-8310
  Livonia *(G-10244)*
Ips Assembly Corp .... F 734 391-0080
  Livonia *(G-10251)*
K & F Electronic Inc .... F 586 294-8720
  Fraser *(G-5949)*
Nu Tek Sales Parts Inc .... F 616 258-0631
  Muskegon *(G-11886)*
Saturn Electronics Corp .... C 734 941-8100
  Romulus *(G-14327)*

CIRCUIT BREAKERS

M P Jackson LLC .... F 517 782-0391
  Jackson *(G-8939)*
Mp Hollywood LLC .... F 517 782-0391
  Jackson *(G-8970)*

CIRCUITS: Electronic

Amptech Inc .... G 231 464-5492
  Manistee *(G-10894)*
Aztecnology LLC .... G 734 857-2045
  Southgate *(G-15748)*
Circuits of Sound .... G 313 886-5599
  Grosse Pointe Woods *(G-7565)*
Code Systems Inc .... E 248 307-3884
  Auburn Hills *(G-845)*
Concept Circuits Corporation .... G 248 852-5200
  Rochester Hills *(G-13982)*
Contract People Corporation .... F 248 304-9900
  Southfield *(G-15532)*
Debron Industrial Elec LLC .... D 248 588-7220
  Troy *(G-17050)*
Diversfied Tchncal Systems Inc .... E 248 513-6050
  Novi *(G-12401)*
Ebw Electronics Inc .... B 616 786-0575
  Holland *(G-8021)*
Enertech Corporation .... F 231 832-5587
  Hersey *(G-7866)*
Ghs Corporation .... E 269 968-3351
  Springfield *(G-15867)*
Hirschmann Car Comm Inc .... F 248 373-7150
  Auburn Hills *(G-928)*
Innotec Corp .... D 616 772-5959
  Zeeland *(G-19047)*
Kaydon Corporation .... B 734 747-7025
  Ann Arbor *(G-538)*
Lectronix Inc .... E 517 492-1900
  Lansing *(G-9863)*
Leoni Wiring Systems Inc .... F 586 782-4444
  Troy *(G-17208)*
Magna Electronics Inc .... E 810 606-8683
  Holly *(G-8282)*
Magna Electronics Inc .... E 248 606-0606
  Auburn Hills *(G-963)*
Magna Electronics Inc .... C 248 729-2643
  Auburn Hills *(G-962)*
MAKS INCORPORATED .... E 248 733-9771
  Troy *(G-17235)*
Memtron Technologies Co .... D 989 652-2656
  Frankenmuth *(G-5869)*
Movellus Circuits Inc .... F 877 321-7667
  Ann Arbor *(G-585)*
Nelson Specialties Company .... F 269 983-1878
  Saint Joseph *(G-14950)*
Nova-Tron Controls Corp .... F 989 358-6126
  Alpena *(G-305)*
Omtron Inc .... G 248 673-3896
  Waterford *(G-18143)*
Photo-Tron Corp .... G 248 852-5200
  Rochester Hills *(G-14083)*
Rockford Contract Mfg .... G 616 304-3837
  Rockford *(G-14188)*
Stanley Elc Holdg Amer Inc .... D 269 660-7777
  Battle Creek *(G-1300)*
TMC Group Inc .... G 248 819-6063
  Pleasant Ridge *(G-13106)*
Touchstone Systems & Svcs Inc .... G 616 532-0060
  Wyoming *(G-18912)*
Vast Production Services Inc .... D 248 838-9680
  Troy *(G-17432)*
Venntis Technologies LLC .... F 616 395-8254
  Holland *(G-8236)*

CLAMPS & COUPLINGS: Hose

Aba of America Inc .... F 815 332-5170
  Auburn Hills *(G-772)*
Anchor Coupling Inc .... C 906 863-2672
  Menominee *(G-11225)*
Myrtle Industries Inc .... F 517 784-8579
  Jackson *(G-8974)*
Peterson American Corporation .... D 269 279-7421
  Three Rivers *(G-16580)*

CLAMPS: Metal

Dover Energy Inc .... C 248 836-6700
  Auburn Hills *(G-866)*
Five Star Manufacturing Inc .... F 815 723-2245
  Auburn Hills *(G-900)*
R G Ray Corporation .... D 248 373-4300
  Auburn Hills *(G-1011)*
Souris Enterprises Inc .... F 810 664-2964
  Lapeer *(G-9961)*
Zsi-Foster Inc .... E 734 844-0055
  Canton *(G-2545)*

CLEANERS: Boiler Tube

L A Burnhart Inc .... G 810 227-4567
  Brighton *(G-2016)*

CLEANING & DESCALING SVC: Metal Prdts

Grand Rapids Stripping Co .... G 616 361-0794
  Grand Rapids *(G-6770)*
International Paint Stripping .... F 734 942-0500
  Romulus *(G-14286)*
International Paint Stripping .... G 734 942-0500
  Romulus *(G-14287)*
Togreencleancom .... G 269 428-4812
  Stevensville *(G-16268)*
WSi Industrial Services Inc .... E 734 942-9300
  Riverview *(G-13884)*

CLEANING COMPOUNDS: Rifle Bore

BV Technology LLC .... G 616 558-1746
  Alto *(G-329)*

CLEANING EQPT: Blast, Dustless

Dee-Blast Corporation .... F 269 428-2400
  Stevensville *(G-16246)*
Progressive Surface Inc .... D 616 957-0871
  Grand Rapids *(G-7117)*
Progressive Surface Inc 616 957-0871
  Grand Rapids *(G-7118)*
Smart Diet Scale LLC .... G 586 383-6734
  Bruce Twp *(G-2183)*
Trinity Tool Co .... E 586 296-5900
  Fraser *(G-6006)*

CLEANING EQPT: Commercial

Creative Products Intl .... F 616 335-3333
  Holland *(G-8007)*
Custom Service & Design Inc .... F 248 340-9005
  Auburn Hills *(G-855)*
Easy Scrub LLC .... G 586 565-1777
  Roseville *(G-14404)*
Focus Cleaning LLC .... G 734 883-9560
  Ypsilanti *(G-18946)*
Geerpres Inc .... E 231 773-3211
  Muskegon *(G-11823)*
Tennant Commercial .... D 616 994-4000
  Holland *(G-8215)*

Employee Codes: A=Over 500 employees, B=251-500
C=101-250, D=51-100, E=20-50, F=10-19, G=3-9

CLEANING EQPT: Commercial

Tennant Company .... G 616 994-4000
  Holland (G-8216)
Truly Free LLC .... E 231 252-4571
  Traverse City (G-16868)
Wesley Floor Care Company .... G 313 978-4539
  Detroit (G-4677)

CLEANING EQPT: Dirt Sweeping Units, Indl

Sweepster Attachments LLC .... A 734 996-9116
  Dexter (G-4757)

CLEANING EQPT: Floor Washing & Polishing, Commercial

Hines Corporation .... F 231 799-6240
  Norton Shores (G-12348)
Pacific Stamex Clg Systems Inc .... E 231 773-1330
  Muskegon (G-11892)

CLEANING EQPT: High Pressure

Lions Pride Pressure Wshg LLC .... G 989 251-5577
  Perry (G-12978)
Superior Washing and Pain .... G 616 293-5347
  Lowell (G-10518)

CLEANING EQPT: Mop Wringers

Royce Rolls Ringer Company .... D 616 361-9266
  Grand Rapids (G-7173)

CLEANING OR POLISHING PREPARATIONS, NEC

Burge Incorporated .... G 616 791-2214
  Grand Rapids (G-6533)
Cal Chemical Manufacturing Co .... G 586 778-7006
  Saint Clair Shores (G-14853)
Chemloc Inc .... G 989 465-6541
  Coleman (G-3462)
Coastal Concierge .... G 269 639-1515
  South Haven (G-15402)
Colonial Chemical Corp .... G 517 789-8161
  Jackson (G-8848)
DSC Laboratories Inc .... E 800 492-5988
  Muskegon (G-11801)
Enviro-Brite Solutions LLC .... G 989 387-2758
  Oscoda (G-12758)
Hydro-Chem Systems Inc .... E 616 531-6420
  Caledonia (G-2383)
Innovative Fluids LLC .... F 734 241-5699
  Milan (G-11438)
Ipax Atlantic LLC .... G 313 933-4211
  Detroit (G-4325)
Ipax Cleanogel Inc .... G 313 933-4211
  Detroit (G-4326)
Labtech Corporation .... F 313 862-1737
  Detroit (G-4374)
Peerless Quality Products .... F 313 933-7525
  Detroit (G-4514)
Quaker Houghton Pa Inc .... F 248 265-7745
  Troy (G-17325)
Wilbur Products Inc .... F 231 755-3805
  Muskegon (G-11948)

CLEANING PRDTS: Automobile Polish

Rhino Linings of Grand Rapids .... G 616 361-9786
  Grand Rapids (G-7152)

CLEANING PRDTS: Bleaches, Household, Dry Or Liquid

Chemetall US Inc .... G 517 787-4846
  Jackson (G-8841)
High-Po-Chlor Inc .... G 734 942-1500
  Ann Arbor (G-515)

CLEANING PRDTS: Degreasing Solvent

Superior Manufacturing Corp .... G 313 935-1550
  Troy (G-17380)

CLEANING PRDTS: Disinfectants, Household Or Indl Plant

Arrow Chemical Products Inc .... E 313 237-0277
  Detroit (G-4028)
Cul-Mac Industries Inc .... E 734 728-9700
  Wayne (G-18219)

Katrina Love-Jones LLC .... G 248 779-6017
  Detroit (G-4352)

CLEANING PRDTS: Drain Pipe Solvents Or Cleaners

Rooto Corporation .... F 517 546-8330
  Howell (G-8510)

CLEANING PRDTS: Dusting Cloths, Chemically Treated

Anchor Wiping Cloth Inc .... D 313 892-4000
  Detroit (G-4019)

CLEANING PRDTS: Floor Waxes

S C Johnson & Son Inc .... G 248 822-2174
  Troy (G-17339)
S C Johnson & Son Inc .... G 989 667-0211
  Bay City (G-1396)

CLEANING PRDTS: Indl Plant Disinfectants Or Deodorants

Punati Chemical Corp .... D 248 276-0101
  Auburn Hills (G-1008)

CLEANING PRDTS: Laundry Preparations

Lee Cleaners Inc .... G 517 351-5655
  East Lansing (G-4900)
Mdla Inc .... F 248 643-0807
  Troy (G-17242)

CLEANING PRDTS: Metal Polish

Spartans Finishing LLC .... G 517 528-5510
  Haslett (G-7779)

CLEANING PRDTS: Polishing Preparations & Related Prdts

Premiere Packaging Inc .... D 810 239-7650
  Flint (G-5748)

CLEANING PRDTS: Rug, Upholstery/Dry Clng Detergents/Spotters

Joy Carpet Cleaning LLC .... G 734 656-8827
  Inkster (G-8667)

CLEANING PRDTS: Sanitation Preparations

Healthcure LLC .... F 313 743-2331
  Detroit (G-4297)
Oden Sanitation LLC .... G 248 513-5763
  Roseville (G-14456)
Thetford Corporation .... C 734 769-6000
  Ann Arbor (G-688)

CLEANING PRDTS: Sanitation Preps, Disinfectants/Deodorants

2020 Mobile Detailing LLC .... G 313 953-6363
  Detroit (G-3969)
Hygiene of Sweden USA LLC .... G 248 760-3241
  Sylvan Lake (G-16361)
Odor Gone Inc .... F 888 636-7292
  Zeeland (G-19064)
Saniones LLC .... G 833 726-4111
  Auburn Hills (G-1027)
Vira Clean LLC .... G 313 455-1020
  Canton (G-2538)

CLEANING PRDTS: Specialty

Able Solutions LLC .... G 810 216-6106
  Port Huron (G-13430)
American Jetway Corporation .... D 734 721-5930
  Wayne (G-18213)
Bio Kleen Products Inc .... F 269 567-9400
  Kalamazoo (G-9136)
Biosolutions LLC .... F 616 846-1210
  Grand Haven (G-6280)
Chrysan Industries Inc .... E 734 451-5411
  Plymouth (G-13146)
Cleaning Solutions Inc .... G 616 243-0555
  Grand Rapids (G-6572)
Grav Co LLC .... F 269 651-5467
  Sturgis (G-16290)

Liedel Power Cleaning .... G 734 848-2827
  Erie (G-5049)
Native Green LLC .... F 248 365-4200
  Orion (G-12736)

CLEANING PRDTS: Window Cleaning Preparations

Diversified Davitco LLC .... F 248 681-9197
  Waterford (G-18115)
Ottawa County Window Clg LLC .... G 248 878-5377
  Zeeland (G-19066)

CLEANING SVCS

Creative Products Intl .... F 616 335-3333
  Holland (G-8007)
Top Quality Cleaning LLC .... F 810 493-4211
  Flint (G-5779)

CLEANING SVCS: Industrial Or Commercial

American Metal Restoration .... G 810 364-4820
  Marysville (G-11081)
DNR Inc .... G 734 722-4000
  Plymouth (G-13160)
Liedel Power Cleaning .... G 734 848-2827
  Erie (G-5049)
Seelye Group Ltd .... G 517 267-2001
  Lansing (G-9894)

CLIPS & FASTENERS, MADE FROM PURCHASED WIRE

Automatic Spring Products Corp .... C 616 842-2284
  Grand Haven (G-6278)
Davon Manufacturing Company .... G 616 896-7888
  Hudsonville (G-8579)
Hohmann & Barnard Inc .... F 765 420-7940
  East Lansing (G-4895)
Industries Unlimited Inc .... F 586 949-4300
  Chesterfield (G-2893)
Law Enforcement Supply Inc .... G 616 895-7875
  Allendale (G-222)
Ultraform Industries Inc .... D 586 752-4508
  Bruce Twp (G-2185)

CLOCKS

Howard Miller Company .... B 616 772-9131
  Zeeland (G-19040)
Lumichron Inc .... G 616 245-8888
  Grand Rapids (G-6952)
National Time and Signal Corp .... E 248 291-5867
  Oak Park (G-12631)

CLOSURES: Closures, Stamped Metal

Roll Rite Corporation .... E 989 345-3434
  Gladwin (G-6202)

CLOSURES: Plastic

Reutter LLC .... G 248 466-0652
  Ann Arbor (G-640)

CLOTHESPINS: Plastic

Dr Schneider Auto Systems Inc .... G 270 858-5400
  Brighton (G-1978)

CLOTHING & ACCESS STORES

Graphics Depot Inc .... G 248 383-5055
  Waterford (G-18125)
SM & AM Enterprise Inc .... G 906 786-0373
  Escanaba (G-5100)

CLOTHING & ACCESS, WOMEN, CHILD & INFANT, WHSLE: Sportswear

Ideal Wholesale Inc .... G 989 873-5850
  Prescott (G-13651)

CLOTHING & ACCESS, WOMEN, CHILD/INFANT, WHOLESALE: Child

Carters Inc .... G 616 647-9452
  Grand Rapids (G-6549)

PRODUCT SECTION

CLOTHING: Culottes & Shorts, Children's

CLOTHING & ACCESS, WOMEN, CHILDREN & INFANT, WHOL: Uniforms

Mvp Sports Store .... G 517 764-5165
   Jackson *(G-8973)*
Noir Sportswear Corp .... F 248 607-3615
   Oak Park *(G-12634)*

CLOTHING & ACCESS, WOMEN, CHILDREN/INFANT, WHOL: Underwear

Lockett Enterprises LLC .... G 810 407-6644
   Flint *(G-5725)*

CLOTHING & ACCESS: Costumes, Theatrical

Excellent Designs Swimwear .... G 586 977-9140
   Warren *(G-17799)*

CLOTHING & ACCESS: Handicapped

Bioflex Inc .... G 734 327-2946
   Ann Arbor *(G-401)*

CLOTHING & ACCESS: Handkerchiefs, Exc Paper

GLS Enterprises Inc .... G 616 243-2574
   Comstock Park *(G-3608)*

CLOTHING & ACCESS: Hospital Gowns

Trims Unlimited LLC .... E 810 724-3500
   Almont *(G-269)*

CLOTHING & ACCESS: Men's Miscellaneous Access

Bedrock Manufacturing Co LLC .... E 972 422-4372
   Detroit *(G-4048)*
Just Right Duplications LLC .... F 313 655-3555
   Oak Park *(G-12619)*
Logofit LLC .... E 810 715-1980
   Flint *(G-5727)*

CLOTHING & ACCESS: Regalia

Kalamazoo Regalia Inc .... F 269 344-4299
   Kalamazoo *(G-9247)*

CLOTHING & ACCESS: Suspenders

Brandon Bernard Collection LLC .... G 888 611-7011
   Detroit *(G-4068)*

CLOTHING & APPAREL STORES: Custom

Hi-Tech Optical Inc .... E 989 799-9390
   Saginaw *(G-14663)*
JS Original Silkscreens LLC .... G 586 779-5456
   Eastpointe *(G-4938)*
Lazer Graphics .... F 269 926-1066
   Benton Harbor *(G-1565)*
Tapestry Inc .... G 616 538-5802
   Grandville *(G-7420)*

CLOTHING & FURNISHINGS, MEN'S & BOYS', WHOLESALE: Caps

Ajaxx Design Inc .... G 206 522-4545
   Grosse Pointe Park *(G-7543)*

CLOTHING & FURNISHINGS, MEN'S & BOYS', WHOLESALE: Uniforms

Elite Defense LLC .... F 734 424-9955
   Clawson *(G-3096)*
Lamacs Inc .... G 248 643-9210
   Troy *(G-17204)*

CLOTHING & FURNISHINGS, MENS & BOYS, WHOL: Sportswear/Work

Ideal Wholesale Inc .... G 989 873-5850
   Prescott *(G-13651)*

CLOTHING & FURNISHINGS, MENS & BOYS, WHOLESALE: Lined

Reed Sportswear Mfg Co .... E 313 963-7980
   Detroit *(G-4560)*

CLOTHING STORES: Designer Apparel

Sports Ink Screen Prtg EMB LLC .... G 231 723-5696
   Manistee *(G-10913)*

CLOTHING STORES: Formal Wear

Celebrations .... G 906 482-4946
   Hancock *(G-7617)*

CLOTHING STORES: Hand Painted

Janet and Company Inc .... G 248 887-2050
   Highland *(G-7893)*

CLOTHING STORES: Shirts, Custom Made

Ajaxx Design Inc .... G 206 522-4545
   Grosse Pointe Park *(G-7543)*
MHR Investments Inc .... F 989 832-5395
   Midland *(G-11388)*

CLOTHING STORES: T-Shirts, Printed, Custom

Christman Screenprint Inc .... E 800 962-9330
   Springfield *(G-15863)*
Daisy Chain Online .... G 330 259-6457
   West Bloomfield *(G-18277)*
Graphics Unlimited Inc .... G 231 773-2696
   Norton Shores *(G-12295)*

CLOTHING STORES: Unisex

Custom Giant LLC .... G 313 799-2085
   Southfield *(G-15534)*
Mopega LLC .... G 231 631-2580
   Traverse City *(G-16764)*
Osowet Collections Inc .... G 313 844-8171
   Detroit *(G-4501)*

CLOTHING STORES: Work

RPC Company .... F 989 752-3618
   Saginaw *(G-14741)*

CLOTHING: Access

Blue Lagoon .... G 248 515-1363
   West Bloomfield *(G-18266)*
Bond Manufacturing LLC .... G 313 671-0799
   Detroit *(G-4062)*
Curb Apparel LLC .... G 248 548-2324
   Huntington Woods *(G-8621)*
Detroit Denim LLC .... G 313 351-1040
   Detroit *(G-4143)*
Foxys Leotards .... G 616 949-1847
   Grand Rapids *(G-6718)*
Impressions Promotional Group .... G 313 299-3140
   Taylor *(G-16427)*
Industrial Sew Invvtion Ctr Is .... G 313 870-1898
   Detroit *(G-4316)*
Michael Kors .... G 616 730-7071
   Byron Center *(G-2284)*
Power Capes .... G 313 454-1492
   Livonia *(G-10368)*
Retro-A-Go-go LLC .... G 734 476-0300
   Howell *(G-8507)*
Spiffys Slay Station LLC .... G 313 401-8906
   Detroit *(G-4601)*
Superfly Manufacturing Co .... F 313 454-1492
   Farmington *(G-5152)*

CLOTHING: Access, Women's & Misses'

Bedrock Manufacturing Co LLC .... E 972 422-4372
   Detroit *(G-4048)*
Brintley Enterprises .... G 248 991-4086
   Detroit *(G-4074)*
Diamond Boutique .... G 313 451-4217
   Dearborn *(G-3828)*
Pure Luxe LLC .... G 248 987-8734
   Farmington Hills *(G-5357)*
Sundai Imports Inc .... G 877 517-7788
   Westland *(G-18419)*
Yore Creations LLC .... G 313 463-8652
   Detroit *(G-4698)*

CLOTHING: Athletic & Sportswear, Men's & Boys'

Fisll Media LLC .... G 646 492-8533
   Troy *(G-17111)*

CLOTHING:

Harvard Clothing Company .... F 517 542-2986
   Litchfield *(G-10078)*
Traverse Bay Manufacturing Inc .... D 231 264-8111
   Elk Rapids *(G-5029)*
Van Boven Incorporated .... G 734 665-7228
   Ann Arbor *(G-708)*

CLOTHING: Athletic & Sportswear, Women's & Girls'

Cliff Keen Wrestling Pdts Inc .... G 734 975-8800
   Ann Arbor *(G-428)*
Cute N Classy Collection LLC .... G 313 279-8217
   Detroit *(G-4114)*
Fisll Media LLC .... G 646 492-8533
   Troy *(G-17111)*
Reed Sportswear Mfg Co .... G 313 963-7980
   Detroit *(G-4561)*

CLOTHING: Baker, Barber, Lab/Svc Ind Apparel, Washable, Men

Repairers of The Brach Mskegon .... F 231 375-0990
   Muskegon *(G-11908)*

CLOTHING: Blouses, Women's & Girls'

Law Offices Towana Tate PC .... G 248 560-7250
   Farmington Hills *(G-5290)*
Peckham Vocational Inds Inc .... A 517 316-4000
   Lansing *(G-9724)*
Peckham Vocational Inds Inc .... D 517 316-4478
   Lansing *(G-9725)*

CLOTHING: Brassieres

Busted Bra Shop LLC .... G 313 288-0449
   Detroit *(G-4078)*
Shefit Operating Company LLC .... G 616 209-7003
   Hudsonville *(G-8611)*
Xrs Holdings Inc .... F 616 209-7003
   Hudsonville *(G-8619)*

CLOTHING: Children & Infants'

Justice .... G 517 780-4035
   Jackson *(G-8926)*
Justice .... G 616 531-4534
   Grandville *(G-7394)*
Renes Inc .... G 810 294-5008
   Croswell *(G-3735)*

CLOTHING: Children's, Girls'

Carters Inc .... G 616 647-9452
   Grand Rapids *(G-6549)*
Renes Inc .... G 810 294-5008
   Croswell *(G-3735)*

CLOTHING: Coats & Jackets, Leather & Sheep-Lined

Lee-Cobb Company .... G 269 553-0873
   Kalamazoo *(G-9260)*
Reed Sportswear Mfg Co .... E 313 963-7980
   Detroit *(G-4560)*

CLOTHING: Coats & Suits, Men's & Boys'

Baryames Tux Shop Inc .... G 517 349-6555
   Okemos *(G-12659)*
Labeled Lucky Brand Inc .... G 517 962-1729
   Romulus *(G-14297)*
Peckham Vocational Inds Inc .... A 517 316-4000
   Lansing *(G-9724)*
Peckham Vocational Inds Inc .... D 517 316-4478
   Lansing *(G-9725)*
Zink .... G 586 781-5314
   Shelby Township *(G-15373)*

CLOTHING: Costumes

Gags and Games Inc .... E 734 591-1717
   Livonia *(G-10218)*
Lewmar Custom Designs Inc .... G 586 677-5135
   Shelby Township *(G-15262)*

CLOTHING: Culottes & Shorts, Children's

Just Girls LLC .... G 248 952-1967
   Troy *(G-17190)*

Employee Codes: A=Over 500 employees, B=251-500
C=101-250, D=51-100, E=20-50, F=10-19, G=3-9

2022 Harris Michigan Industrial Directory

CLOTHING: Disposable   PRODUCT SECTION

CLOTHING: Disposable
Mopega LLC ....G..... 231 631-2580
  Traverse City *(G-16764)*

CLOTHING: Dresses
Xtra-Ordinary-You LLC ....G..... 313 285-4472
  Ecorse *(G-4989)*

CLOTHING: Furs
Inn Settle & Suites ....G..... 214 606-3531
  Marquette *(G-11021)*

CLOTHING: Gowns & Dresses, Wedding
Ashley Rose ....G..... 616 634-4919
  Rockford *(G-14155)*
Demmem Enterprises LLC ....F..... 810 564-9500
  Clio *(G-3396)*
My Dream Dress Brdal Salon LLC ....G..... 248 327-6049
  Southfield *(G-15663)*

CLOTHING: Hats & Caps, NEC
Bahama Souvenirs Inc ....G..... 269 964-8275
  Battle Creek *(G-1189)*

CLOTHING: Hats & Headwear, Knit
Bustedtees LLC ....G..... 989 448-3179
  Gaylord *(G-6121)*

CLOTHING: Hosiery, Men's & Boys'
Al Beck ....G..... 906 249-1645
  Marquette *(G-11003)*

CLOTHING: Hospital, Men's
Genstone LLC ....G..... 517 902-4730
  Adrian *(G-70)*
Scrubs Myway LLC ....G..... 616 201-8366
  Grand Haven *(G-6357)*

CLOTHING: Jackets, Field, Military
Trims Unlimited LLC ....E..... 810 724-3500
  Almont *(G-269)*

CLOTHING: Jeans, Men's & Boys'
Guess Inc ....G..... 517 546-2933
  Howell *(G-8457)*

CLOTHING: Jerseys, Knit
Spalding ....G..... 734 414-1567
  Canton *(G-2525)*

CLOTHING: Lounge, Bed & Leisurewear
Belleville Lounge LLC ....G..... 734 270-4977
  Van Buren Twp *(G-17512)*

CLOTHING: Men's & boy's clothing, nec
Little Legends Creations LLC ....G..... 313 828-7292
  Eastpointe *(G-4940)*
Thomas Porchea Collection LLC .....G..... 313 693-6308
  Detroit *(G-4631)*

CLOTHING: Men's & boy's underwear & nightwear
Harrys Meme LLC ....G..... 248 977-0168
  Novi *(G-12429)*

CLOTHING: Neckwear
Get Customized ....G..... 586 909-3881
  Rochester Hills *(G-14025)*

CLOTHING: Outerwear, Knit
Noir Sportswear Corp ....F..... 248 607-3615
  Oak Park *(G-12634)*

CLOTHING: Outerwear, Lthr, Wool/Down-Filled, Men, Youth/Boy
Carhartt Inc ....B..... 313 271-8460
  Dearborn *(G-3818)*

CLOTHING: Outerwear, Women's & Misses' NEC
Guess Inc ....G..... 517 546-2933
  Howell *(G-8457)*
Harvard Clothing Company ....F..... 517 542-2986
  Litchfield *(G-10078)*
Hemp Global Products Inc ....G..... 616 617-6476
  Holland *(G-8069)*
Keetz Kloset Kollection LLC ....G..... 313 878-1032
  Detroit *(G-4356)*
Pvh Corp ....E..... 989 624-5575
  Birch Run *(G-1712)*
Tall City LLC ....G..... 248 854-0713
  Auburn Hills *(G-1045)*
Traverse Bay Manufacturing Inc .....D..... 231 264-8111
  Elk Rapids *(G-5029)*

CLOTHING: Overalls & Coveralls
Carhartt Inc ....B..... 313 271-8460
  Dearborn *(G-3818)*

CLOTHING: Shirts
Pvh Corp ....G..... 989 345-7939
  West Branch *(G-18337)*

CLOTHING: Shirts, Dress, Men's & Boys'
Pvh Corp ....G..... 989 624-5651
  Birch Run *(G-1713)*

CLOTHING: Socks
Argyle Socks LLC ....G..... 269 615-0097
  Kalamazoo *(G-9120)*
Bold Endeavors LLC ....G..... 616 389-3902
  Grand Rapids *(G-6520)*
Detroit Sock & Stocking Co LLC .....G..... 313 409-8735
  Grosse Pointe Park *(G-7552)*
P&K Socks LLC ....G..... 586 295-5427
  Grosse Pointe Farms *(G-7539)*
Rudys Sock Drive ....G..... 313 409-1778
  Taylor *(G-16469)*
Skechers USA Inc ....F..... 989 624-9336
  Birch Run *(G-1715)*
Sock Hop LLC ....G..... 248 689-2683
  Troy *(G-17358)*
Socks & Associates Development ...G..... 231 421-5150
  Traverse City *(G-16836)*
Socks Direct USA LLC ....G..... 248 535-7590
  West Bloomfield *(G-18315)*
Socks Kick LLC ....G..... 231 222-2402
  East Jordan *(G-4880)*
Soyad Brothers Textile Corp ....E..... 586 755-5700
  Fraser *(G-5994)*
Turbosocks Performance ....G..... 586 864-3252
  Shelby Township *(G-15358)*

CLOTHING: Sportswear, Women's
St John ....G..... 313 576-8212
  Detroit *(G-4603)*

CLOTHING: Sweatshirts & T-Shirts, Men's & Boys'
Zemis 5 LLC ....G..... 317 946-7015
  Detroit *(G-4703)*

CLOTHING: Swimwear, Men's & Boys'
Avidasports LLC ....F..... 313 447-5670
  Harper Woods *(G-7662)*

CLOTHING: Swimwear, Women's & Misses'
Excellent Designs Swimwear ....G..... 586 977-9140
  Warren *(G-17799)*

CLOTHING: T-Shirts & Tops, Knit
Ajaxx Design Inc ....G..... 206 522-4545
  Grosse Pointe Park *(G-7543)*
Fuzzybutz ....G..... 269 983-9663
  Saint Joseph *(G-14931)*
Wickedglow Industries Inc ....G..... 586 776-4132
  Mount Clemens *(G-11663)*

CLOTHING: Tights & Leg Warmers
Warmerscom ....G..... 800 518-0938
  Byron Center *(G-2302)*

CLOTHING: Uniforms, Firemen's, From Purchased Materials
Priority One Emergency Inc ....G..... 734 398-5900
  Canton *(G-2512)*

CLOTHING: Uniforms, Men's & Boys'
Allie Brothers Inc ....F..... 248 477-4434
  Livonia *(G-10109)*

CLOTHING: Uniforms, Team Athletic
Cliff Keen Wrestling Pdts Inc ....E..... 734 975-8800
  Ann Arbor *(G-428)*
Graphic Gear Inc ....G..... 734 283-3864
  Lincoln Park *(G-10048)*

CLOTHING: Vests, Sport, Suede, Leatherette, Etc, Mens & Boys
Kinder Company Inc ....G..... 810 240-3065
  Mount Morris *(G-11673)*

CLOTHING: Waterproof Outerwear
Geckobrands LLC ....G..... 561 704-8400
  Grandville *(G-7378)*

CLOTHING: Work, Men's
Acme Mills Company ....E..... 517 437-8940
  Hillsdale *(G-7919)*
Apex Apparel LLC ....F..... 248 915-1073
  Detroit *(G-4023)*
Carhartt Inc ....G..... 517 282-4193
  Dewitt *(G-4709)*
Just Right Duplications LLC ....F..... 313 655-3555
  Oak Park *(G-12619)*
Traverse Bay Manufacturing Inc .....D..... 231 264-8111
  Elk Rapids *(G-5029)*
Wealth Club Nation LLC ....G..... 323 695-1636
  Royal Oak *(G-14591)*

CLOTHS: Dust, Made From Purchased Materials
K and J Absorbent Products LLC ....G..... 517 486-3110
  Blissfield *(G-1766)*

CLUTCHES OR BRAKES: Electromagnetic
American Brake and Clutch Inc ......F..... 586 948-3730
  Chesterfield *(G-2838)*

CLUTCHES, EXC VEHICULAR
Formsprag LLC ....C..... 586 758-5000
  Warren *(G-17816)*
Friction Control LLC ....G..... 586 741-8493
  Clinton Township *(G-3246)*
Great Lakes Industry Inc ....E..... 517 784-3153
  Jackson *(G-8895)*
S R P Inc ....F..... 517 784-3153
  Jackson *(G-9003)*

COAL GASIFICATION
TEs Filer Cy Stn Ltd Partnr ....G..... 231 723-6573
  Filer City *(G-5611)*

COAL MINING SERVICES
Peak Manufacturing Inc ....E..... 517 769-6900
  Pleasant Lake *(G-13104)*

COAL MINING: Bituminous Coal & Lignite-Surface Mining
Lotus International Company ....A..... 734 245-0140
  Canton *(G-2486)*
Silver Slate LLC ....F..... 248 486-3989
  Milford *(G-11488)*

COATED OR PLATED PRDTS
Euridium Solutions LLC ....G..... 248 535-7005
  Troy *(G-17098)*

COATING SVC
A2z Coating ....G..... 616 805-3281
  Grand Rapids *(G-6414)*

Able Machine Tooling ..... G 586 783-7776
Harrison Twp *(G-7737)*

Coles Custom Con Coatings LLC ..... G 231 651-0709
Beulah *(G-1653)*

Custom Powder Coating LLC ..... G 616 454-9730
Grand Rapids *(G-6622)*

Detroit Laser Co LLC ..... G 313 338-9494
Farmington Hills *(G-5214)*

Duraflex Coatings LLC ..... G 586 855-1087
Shelby Township *(G-15215)*

Eastside Coatings ..... G 313 936-1000
Saint Clair Shores *(G-14855)*

HB Fuller Co ..... G 248 585-2200
Taylor *(G-16425)*

Jbs Coating ..... F 231 366-7159
Fruitport *(G-6064)*

Mid McHigan Indus Coatings LLC ..... G 989 441-1277
Weidman *(G-18257)*

Modineer Coatings Division ..... F 269 925-0702
Benton Harbor *(G-1574)*

Nano Materials & Processes Inc ..... G 248 529-3873
Milford *(G-11475)*

Neptune Coating Services ..... G 616 403-9034
Zeeland *(G-19060)*

Pre-Cut Patterns ..... G 616 392-4415
Holland *(G-8168)*

Quality Coatings ..... G 517 294-0394
Fowlerville *(G-5852)*

Rcd Quality Coatings ..... G 313 575-8125
Redford *(G-13763)*

Steplen Coatings LLC ..... G 810 653-6418
Davison *(G-3798)*

COATING SVC: Aluminum, Metal Prdts

Permacoat Inc ..... G 313 388-7798
Allen Park *(G-202)*

Reliance Finishing Co ..... D 616 241-4436
Grand Rapids *(G-7148)*

COATING SVC: Electrodes

Csquared Innovations Inc ..... F 734 998-8330
Novi *(G-12388)*

COATING SVC: Hot Dip, Metals Or Formed Prdts

Voigt Schwtzer Galvanizers Inc ..... G 313 535-2600
Redford *(G-13784)*

COATING SVC: Metals & Formed Prdts

A1 Powder Coating ..... G 616 238-0683
Grand Rapids *(G-6413)*

Aactron Inc ..... E 248 543-6740
Madison Heights *(G-10655)*

AB Custom Fabricating LLC ..... F 269 663-8100
Edwardsburg *(G-4998)*

Act Test Panels LLC ..... E 517 439-1485
Hillsdale *(G-7921)*

Action Asphalt LLC ..... F 734 449-8565
Brighton *(G-1937)*

Ajax Metal Processing Inc ..... G 313 267-2100
Detroit *(G-3992)*

All-Cote Coatings Company LLC ..... G 586 427-0062
Center Line *(G-2678)*

Alpha Coatings Inc ..... F 734 523-9000
Livonia *(G-10110)*

Anchor Bay Powder Coat LLC ..... F 586 725-3255
New Baltimore *(G-11978)*

Apex Powder Coating LLC ..... G 734 921-3177
Taylor *(G-16381)*

Applied Coatings Solutions LLC ..... G 269 341-9757
Kalamazoo *(G-9115)*

Aristo-Cote Inc ..... D 586 447-9049
Fraser *(G-5896)*

Aristo-Cote Inc ..... E 586 447-9049
Harrison Township *(G-7688)*

B & J Enmeling Inc A Mich Corp ..... F 313 365-6620
Detroit *(G-4040)*

Beech & Rich Inc ..... E 269 968-8012
Springfield *(G-15861)*

Bio-Vac Inc ..... E 248 350-2150
Southfield *(G-15508)*

Bolyea Industries ..... F 586 293-8600
Fraser *(G-5906)*

Burkard Industries Inc ..... C 586 791-6520
Clinton Township *(G-3191)*

Carbide Surface Company ..... G 586 465-6110
Clinton Township *(G-3194)*

Cast Coatings Inc ..... E 269 545-8373
Galien *(G-6087)*

Centennial Coatings LLC ..... E 616 748-9410
Zeeland *(G-19003)*

Cg Liquidation Incorporated ..... D 586 803-1000
Shelby Township *(G-15185)*

Chieftain Coating LLC ..... E 586 791-1866
Clinton Township *(G-3198)*

Coatings Plus Inc ..... E 616 451-2427
Grand Rapids *(G-6577)*

Commercial Coating Systems LLC ..... G 616 490-6242
Cedar Springs *(G-2646)*

Commercial Steel Treating Corp ..... C 248 588-3300
Madison Heights *(G-10696)*

Conformance Coatings Prototype ..... F 810 364-4333
Marysville *(G-11084)*

Corlin Company ..... G 616 842-7093
Grand Haven *(G-6290)*

Cox Brothers Machining Inc ..... E 517 796-4662
Jackson *(G-8855)*

Crm Inc ..... D 231 947-0304
Traverse City *(G-16665)*

Crown Group Co ..... D 313 922-8433
Eastpointe *(G-4934)*

Crown Group Co ..... B 586 575-9800
Troy *(G-17035)*

Custom Coating Tech Inc ..... G 734 442-4074
Taylor *(G-16397)*

Custom Coating Technologies ..... G 734 244-3610
Flat Rock *(G-5617)*

Decc Company Inc ..... E 616 245-0431
Grand Rapids *(G-6638)*

Decorative Finishes Division ..... G 616 450-4918
Grand Rapids *(G-6640)*

Eagle Powder Coating ..... G 517 784-2556
Jackson *(G-8872)*

Electro Chemical Finishing Co ..... F 616 531-0670
Grandville *(G-7372)*

Engineered Prfmce Coatings Inc ..... G 616 988-7927
Grand Rapids *(G-6680)*

Evans Coatings L L C ..... G 248 583-9890
Troy *(G-17099)*

Express Coat Corporation ..... E 586 773-2682
Warren *(G-17800)*

Fastener Coatings Inc ..... F 269 279-5134
Three Rivers *(G-16572)*

Finishing Services Inc ..... D 734 484-1700
Ypsilanti *(G-18945)*

Flying Pig Coatings LLC ..... G 616 947-1118
Grand Rapids *(G-6714)*

Fricia Enterprises Inc ..... G 586 977-1900
Sterling Heights *(G-16023)*

Grand Haven Powder Coating Inc ..... E 616 850-8822
Grand Haven *(G-6304)*

Great Lakes Powder Coating LLC ..... F 248 522-6222
Walled Lake *(G-17669)*

Gt Performance Coatings LLC ..... F 248 627-5905
Ortonville *(G-12748)*

Gyro Powder Coating Inc ..... F 616 846-2580
Grand Haven *(G-6311)*

H & H Powdercoating Inc ..... F 810 750-1800
Fenton *(G-5483)*

Hi-Tech Coatings Inc ..... E 586 759-3559
Warren *(G-17853)*

Hice and Summey Inc ..... F 269 651-6217
Bronson *(G-2116)*

Howmet Corporation ..... E 231 894-5686
Whitehall *(G-18501)*

Howmet Holdings Corporation ..... G 231 894-5686
Whitehall *(G-18506)*

I S P Coatings Corp ..... F 586 752-5020
Romeo *(G-14226)*

Integricoat Inc ..... E 616 935-7878
Spring Lake *(G-15826)*

Jackson Industrial Coating Svc ..... G 517 782-8169
Jackson *(G-8915)*

JD Plating Company Inc ..... E 248 547-5200
Madison Heights *(G-10753)*

Kalb & Associates Inc ..... E 586 949-2735
Chesterfield *(G-2899)*

KC Jones Plating Co ..... E 586 755-4900
Warren *(G-17892)*

Kencoat Comp ..... G 586 754-1400
Clinton Township *(G-3272)*

Kentwood Powder Coat Inc ..... E 616 698-8181
Grand Rapids *(G-6891)*

Lakeshore Custom Powdr Coating ..... G 616 296-9330
Grand Haven *(G-6327)*

Langley Powder Coating ..... G 989 739-5203
Oscoda *(G-12764)*

Liberty Bell Powdr Coating LLC ..... G 586 557-6328
Highland *(G-7894)*

Magnum Powder Coating Inc ..... G 616 785-3155
Comstock Park *(G-3621)*

Master Coat LLC ..... G 734 405-2340
Westland *(G-18393)*

Matrix Mtlcraft LLP A Ltd Prtn ..... G 248 724-1800
Auburn Hills *(G-970)*

Metal Finishing Technology ..... G 231 733-9736
Muskegon *(G-11869)*

Metro Powder Coating ..... G 313 744-7134
Detroit *(G-4437)*

Michigan Machining Inc ..... G 810 686-6655
Mount Morris *(G-11675)*

Michigan Metal Coatings Co ..... D 810 966-9240
Port Huron *(G-13501)*

Midwest Products Finshg Co Inc ..... D 734 856-5200
Ottawa Lake *(G-12809)*

Mirrage Ltd ..... G 734 697-6447
Van Buren Twp *(G-17540)*

Monarch Powder Coating Inc ..... G 231 798-1422
Norton Shores *(G-12312)*

Motor City Metal Fab Inc ..... E 734 345-1001
Taylor *(G-16450)*

National Indus Sp Coatings LLC ..... F 989 894-8538
Sanford *(G-15074)*

ND Industries Inc ..... C 248 288-0000
Clawson *(G-3101)*

New Age Coatings ..... G 248 217-1842
Pontiac *(G-13401)*

Nof Metal Coatings North Amer ..... G 248 617-3033
New Hudson *(G-12065)*

Oakwood Energy Management Inc ..... F 734 947-7700
Taylor *(G-16453)*

Oerlikon Blzers Cating USA Inc ..... E 248 409-5900
Lake Orion *(G-9625)*

Oerlikon Blzers Cating USA Inc ..... G 989 463-6268
Alma *(G-251)*

Oerlikon Blzers Cating USA Inc ..... E 586 465-0412
Harrison Township *(G-7713)*

P C S Companies Inc ..... G 616 754-2229
Greenville *(G-7504)*

Peninsula Powder Coating Inc ..... E 906 353-7234
Baraga *(G-1146)*

Performcoat of Michigan LLC ..... F 269 282-7030
Springfield *(G-15874)*

Plasma-Tec Inc ..... E 616 455-2593
Holland *(G-8166)*

Plasti - Paint Inc ..... E 989 285-2280
Saint Louis *(G-14995)*

Powco Inc ..... F 269 646-5385
Marcellus *(G-10951)*

Powder Cote II Inc ..... C 586 463-7040
Mount Clemens *(G-11653)*

Powder Cote II Inc ..... G 586 463-7040
Mount Clemens *(G-11654)*

Precision Coatings Inc ..... D 248 363-8361
Commerce Township *(G-3564)*

Prestige Coating Solutions ..... G 248 402-3732
Sterling Heights *(G-16133)*

Prestige Powder Coating ..... G 616 401-0250
Caledonia *(G-2393)*

Pro-Finish Powder Coating Inc ..... E 616 245-7550
Grand Rapids *(G-7112)*

Progressive Cutter Grinding Co ..... G 586 580-2367
Shelby Township *(G-15309)*

Quali Tone Corporation ..... F 269 426-3664
Sawyer *(G-15111)*

Rapid Coating Solutions Llc ..... G 586 255-7142
Sterling Heights *(G-16142)*

Reliance Plastisol Coating Co ..... F 616 245-2297
Grand Rapids *(G-7149)*

Richcoat LLC ..... F 586 978-1311
Sterling Heights *(G-16150)*

Richter Precision Inc ..... E 586 465-0500
Fraser *(G-5989)*

S&G Group LLC ..... G 616 719-3124
Grand Rapids *(G-7177)*

Sas Global Corporation ..... C 248 414-4470
Warren *(G-18002)*

Schmidt Grinding ..... G 269 649-4604
Vicksburg *(G-17612)*

Seaver Industrial Finishing Co ..... D 616 842-8560
Grand Haven *(G-6359)*

Seaver-Smith Inc ..... E 616 842-8560
Grand Haven *(G-6360)*

Simmons Crtrght Plstic Ctngs L ..... G 616 365-0045
Grand Rapids *(G-7200)*

Simply Custom ..... G 734 558-4051
Wyandotte *(G-18839)*

Employee Codes: A=Over 500 employees, B=251-500
C=101-250, D=51-100, E=20-50, F=10-19, G=3-9

2022 Harris Michigan
Industrial Directory

1225

PRODUCT

COATING SVC: Metals & Formed Prdts

Skop Powder Coating ....G....... 231 881-9909
  Petoskey (G-13024)
Spraytek Inc ....F...... 248 546-3551
  Ferndale (G-5586)
Stechschulte/Wegerly AG LLC ....D...... 586 739-0101
  Sterling Heights (G-16190)
Sun Plastics Coating Company ....F...... 734 453-0822
  Plymouth (G-13305)
Superior Mtal Finshg Rustproof ....F...... 313 893-1050
  Detroit (G-4617)
Tawas Powder Coating Inc ....E...... 989 362-2011
  Tawas City (G-16373)
Techno-Coat Inc ....C...... 616 396-6446
  Holland (G-8213)
Thierica Inc ....D...... 616 458-1538
  Grand Rapids (G-7257)
Ti-Coating Inc ....E...... 586 726-1900
  Shelby Township (G-15351)
Tlr Coatings ....G...... 269 870-3083
  Scotts (G-15134)
Toefco Engineering Inc ....G...... 269 683-0188
  Niles (G-12171)
Unicote Corporation ....E...... 586 296-0700
  Fraser (G-6008)
Universal Coating Inc ....D...... 810 785-7555
  Flint (G-5788)
Universal Coating Technology ....G...... 616 847-6036
  Grand Haven (G-6375)
Varners Pwr Coating & Sndblst ....G...... 517 448-3425
  Hudson (G-8563)
Vergason Technology Inc ....G...... 248 568-0120
  Rochester (G-13937)
Volcor Finishing Inc ....E...... 616 527-5555
  Ionia (G-8694)
Wealthy Street Corporation ....C...... 800 222-8116
  Belding (G-1463)
Wealthy Street Corporation ....E...... 616 451-0784
  Grand Rapids (G-7326)
West Michigan Coating LLC ....E...... 616 647-9509
  Grand Rapids (G-7333)
West Michigan GL Coatings Inc ....G...... 616 970-4863
  Grand Rapids (G-7334)
Westside Powder Coat LLC ....G...... 734 729-1667
  Romulus (G-14337)
X-Cel Industries Inc ....C...... 248 226-6000
  Southfield (G-15744)
Z Technologies Corporation ....E...... 313 937-0710
  Redford (G-13787)

COATING SVC: Metals, With Plastic Or Resins

C & M Coatings Inc ....F...... 616 842-1925
  Grand Haven (G-6282)
Dunnage Engineering Inc ....E...... 810 229-9501
  Brighton (G-1979)
Expert Coating Company Inc ....F...... 616 453-8261
  Grand Rapids (G-6693)
Godfrey & Wing Inc ....G...... 330 562-1440
  Saginaw (G-14654)
Instacote Inc ....G...... 734 847-5260
  Erie (G-5048)
Mdm Enterprises Inc ....F...... 616 452-1591
  Grand Rapids (G-6974)
PDM Industries Inc ....E...... 231 943-9601
  Traverse City (G-16786)
Sure-Weld & Plating Rack Co ....G...... 248 304-9430
  Southfield (G-15714)

COATING SVC: Rust Preventative

Cadillac Oil Company ....E...... 313 365-6200
  Detroit (G-4085)
Depor Industries Inc ....G...... 248 362-3900
  Troy (G-17056)
Magni Group Inc ....F...... 248 647-4500
  Birmingham (G-1735)
Master Mix Company ....G...... 734 487-7870
  Ypsilanti (G-18966)

COATING SVC: Silicon

Midland Silicon Company LLC ....F...... 248 674-3736
  Waterford (G-18137)

COATINGS: Air Curing

New Layer Customs LLC ....G...... 313 358-3629
  Troy (G-17275)
Wiesen Edm Inc ....E...... 616 208-0000
  Belding (G-1466)

COATINGS: Epoxy

Creative Surfaces Inc ....F...... 586 226-2950
  Clinton Township (G-3213)
Gougeon Holding Co ....G...... 989 684-7286
  Bay City (G-1361)
Great Lakes Epoxy Coatings LLC ....G...... 810 820-7073
  Burton (G-2236)
Northwest Paint Pros ....G...... 231 944-3446
  Traverse City (G-16775)
Simiron Inc ....E...... 248 585-7500
  Rochester Hills (G-14112)
Solid Epoxy Coatings LLC ....G...... 248 785-7313
  White Lake (G-18465)
Specialty Coatings Inc ....F...... 586 294-8343
  Fraser (G-5997)
Supreme Media Blasting and Pow ....E...... 586 792-7705
  Clinton Township (G-3366)
West System Inc ....D...... 989 684-7286
  Bay City (G-1411)

COATINGS: Polyurethane

Innovative Engineering Mich ....G...... 517 977-0460
  Lansing (G-9705)
Innovative Polymers Inc ....F...... 989 224-9500
  Saint Johns (G-14902)
Lancast Urethane Inc ....G...... 517 485-6070
  Commerce Township (G-3549)
Lymtal International Inc ....E...... 248 373-8100
  Orion (G-12734)
Marshall Ryerson Co ....F...... 616 299-1751
  Grand Rapids (G-6961)

COFFEE SVCS

Prospectors LLC ....G...... 616 634-8260
  Grand Rapids (G-7122)
Shay Water Co Inc ....E...... 989 755-3221
  Saginaw (G-14755)

COIL WINDING SVC

Warren Steel Co ....G...... 586 756-6600
  Warren (G-18062)

COILS & TRANSFORMERS

Controlled Power Company ....C...... 248 528-3700
  Troy (G-17027)
Ford Motor Company ....A...... 734 484-8626
  Ypsilanti (G-18947)
Friends of Liz Brater ....G...... 734 547-1953
  Ypsilanti (G-18948)
H W Jencks Incorporated ....E...... 231 352-4422
  Frankfort (G-5878)
Heco Inc ....E...... 269 381-7200
  Kalamazoo (G-9210)
Induction Engineering Inc ....F...... 586 716-4700
  New Baltimore (G-11982)
Osborne Transformer Corp ....F...... 586 218-6900
  Fraser (G-5972)
V and F Transformer ....G...... 248 328-6288
  Holly (G-8299)

COILS: Pipe

Alternative Components LLC ....E...... 586 755-9177
  Warren (G-17698)
Lapine Metal Products Inc ....F...... 269 388-5900
  Kalamazoo (G-9258)

COKE: Petroleum & Coal Derivative

B and R Oil Company Inc ....G...... 313 292-5500
  Taylor (G-16385)

COLLETS

Acg Services Inc ....G...... 586 232-4698
  Shelby Township (G-15164)
B C I Collet Inc ....F...... 734 326-1222
  Westland (G-18359)
Tru Point Corporation ....G...... 313 897-9100
  Detroit (G-4646)
Wyandotte Collet and Tool Inc ....F...... 734 283-8055
  Wyandotte (G-18845)

COLOR LAKES OR TONERS

Mis Associates Inc ....G...... 844 225-8156
  Pontiac (G-13398)

COLORS: Pigments, Inorganic

Alloying Surfaces Inc ....G...... 248 524-9200
  Troy (G-16927)
Boston Bioscience Inc ....G...... 617 515-5336
  Royal Oak (G-14520)
Douglas Corp ....E...... 517 767-4112
  Tekonsha (G-16522)
Oerlikon Metco (us) Inc ....E...... 248 288-0027
  Troy (G-17287)
Sun Chemical Corporation ....C...... 231 788-2371
  Muskegon (G-11927)
Titanium Industries ....G...... 734 335-2808
  Plymouth (G-13315)

COLORS: Pigments, Organic

Chromatech Inc ....F...... 734 451-1230
  Canton (G-2449)
Flint CPS Inks North Amer LLC ....C...... 734 781-4600
  Livonia (G-10208)
Flint Group US LLC ....B...... 734 781-4600
  Livonia (G-10211)

COLUMNS: Concrete

Quality Way Products LLC ....F...... 248 634-2401
  Holly (G-8287)

COMMERCIAL & LITERARY WRITINGS

Writers Bible LLc ....G...... 734 286-7793
  Romulus (G-14341)

COMMERCIAL & OFFICE BUILDINGS RENOVATION & REPAIR

Flor TEC Inc ....G...... 616 897-3122
  Lowell (G-10501)
Sterling Millwork Inc ....D...... 248 427-1400
  Farmington Hills (G-5389)

COMMERCIAL ART & GRAPHIC DESIGN SVCS

5 Pyn Inc ....G...... 906 228-2828
  Negaunee (G-11962)
Agnew Grphics Signs Promotions ....G...... 989 723-4621
  Owosso (G-12820)
American Reprographics Co LLC ....G...... 248 299-8900
  Clawson (G-3086)
Ar2 Engineering LLC ....E...... 248 735-9999
  Novi (G-12364)
Danmark Graphics LLC ....G...... 616 675-7499
  Casnovia (G-2606)
Domer Industries LLC ....F...... 269 226-4000
  Kalamazoo (G-9173)
Exclusive Imagery Inc ....G...... 248 436-2999
  Royal Oak (G-14536)
Fusion Design Group Ltd ....G...... 269 469-8226
  New Buffalo (G-12023)
Iris Design & Print Inc ....G...... 313 277-0505
  Dearborn (G-3855)
Jlc Print and Ship Inc ....G...... 517 544-0404
  Jackson (G-8921)
Kent Communications Inc ....D...... 616 957-2120
  Grand Rapids (G-6886)
Lake Michigan Mailers Inc ....D...... 269 383-9333
  Kalamazoo (G-9257)
Lazer Graphics ....F...... 269 926-1066
  Benton Harbor (G-1565)
Print Masters Inc ....F...... 248 548-7100
  Madison Heights (G-10810)
Shelby Signarama Township ....G...... 586 843-3702
  Shelby Township (G-15332)
Sign Center of Kalamazoo Inc ....G...... 269 381-6869
  Kalamazoo (G-9335)
Star Design Metro Detroit LLC ....E...... 734 740-0189
  Livonia (G-10419)
Steel Skinz LLC ....G...... 517 545-9955
  Howell (G-8523)
TP Logos LLC ....G...... 810 956-9484
  Marysville (G-11110)
Whiteside Consulting Group LLC ....G...... 313 288-6598
  Detroit (G-4681)

COMMERCIAL ART & ILLUSTRATION SVCS

Northern Mich Wldlife Art Fram ....F...... 989 340-1272
  Lachine (G-9532)

PRODUCT SECTION

COMMERCIAL CONTAINERS WHOLESALERS

Associated Metals Inc ....G....... 734 369-3851
  Ann Arbor *(G-384)*

COMMERCIAL EQPT WHOLESALERS, NEC

Bay Plastics Machinery Co LLC ....E....... 989 671-9630
  Bay City *(G-1330)*
Taylor Freezer Michigan Inc ....F....... 616 453-0531
  Grand Rapids *(G-7249)*

COMMERCIAL EQPT, WHOLESALE: Bakery Eqpt & Splys

Dawn Equipment Company Inc ....C....... 517 789-4500
  Jackson *(G-8861)*
Dawn Food Products Inc ....C....... 517 789-4400
  Jackson *(G-8863)*
Dawn Foods Inc ....C....... 517 789-4400
  Jackson *(G-8864)*

COMMERCIAL EQPT, WHOLESALE: Coffee Brewing Eqpt & Splys

Prospectors LLC ....G....... 616 634-8260
  Grand Rapids *(G-7122)*

COMMERCIAL EQPT, WHOLESALE: Comm Cooking & Food Svc Eqpt

Farber Concessions Inc ....E....... 313 387-1600
  Redford *(G-13733)*
Keglove LLC ....G....... 616 610-7289
  Holland *(G-8110)*

COMMERCIAL EQPT, WHOLESALE: Restaurant, NEC

Auction Masters ....G....... 586 576-7777
  Oak Park *(G-12593)*
Dominos Pizza LLC ....C....... 734 930-3030
  Ann Arbor *(G-456)*
PA Products Inc ....G....... 734 421-1060
  Livonia *(G-10357)*

COMMERCIAL EQPT, WHOLESALE: Scales, Exc Laboratory

Dura-Pack Inc ....E....... 313 299-9600
  Taylor *(G-16408)*
Standard Scale & Supply Co ....G....... 313 255-6700
  Detroit *(G-4605)*

COMMERCIAL EQPT, WHOLESALE: Store Fixtures & Display Eqpt

G & W Display Fixtures Inc ....E....... 517 369-7110
  Bronson *(G-2112)*
Hudsonville Products LLC ....G....... 616 836-1904
  Grand Rapids *(G-6824)*

COMMERCIAL EQPT, WHOLESALE: Teaching Machines, Electronic

Weaver Instructional Systems ....G....... 616 942-2891
  Grand Rapids *(G-7327)*

COMMERCIAL LAUNDRY EQPT

Kah ....G....... 734 727-0478
  Westland *(G-18390)*

COMMERCIAL PRINTING & NEWSPAPER PUBLISHING COMBINED

ABC Printing Corporation Inc ....G....... 248 887-0010
  Highland *(G-7879)*
C & G News Inc ....E....... 586 498-8000
  Warren *(G-17744)*
Calhoun Communications Inc ....F....... 517 629-0041
  Albion *(G-118)*
Conine Publishing Inc ....E....... 231 723-3592
  Manistee *(G-10896)*
County Journal Inc ....F....... 517 543-1099
  Charlotte *(G-2746)*
Detroit Legal News Company ....D....... 313 961-6000
  Detroit *(G-4150)*
Detroit Newspaper Partnr LP ....A....... 586 826-7187
  Sterling Heights *(G-15984)*
Fedex Office & Print Svcs Inc ....G....... 248 651-2679
  Rochester *(G-13900)*
Four Seasons Publishing Inc ....G....... 906 341-5200
  Manistique *(G-10918)*
Gazelle Publishing ....G....... 734 529-2688
  Dundee *(G-4821)*
Grand Rapids Times Inc ....F....... 616 245-8737
  Grand Rapids *(G-6772)*
Iosco News Press Publishing Co ....F....... 989 739-2054
  Oscoda *(G-12762)*
Iosco News Press Publishing Co ....F....... 989 362-3456
  East Tawas *(G-4917)*
Italian Tribune ....F....... 586 783-3260
  Shelby Township *(G-15240)*
J-Ad Graphics Inc ....G....... 269 945-9554
  Marshall *(G-11062)*
Ludington Daily News Inc ....E....... 231 845-5181
  Ludington *(G-10543)*
Menominee Cnty Jurnl Print Sp ....F....... 906 753-2296
  Stephenson *(G-15909)*
Montmorency Press Inc ....G....... 989 785-4214
  Atlanta *(G-746)*
Northern Michigan Review Inc ....E....... 231 547-6558
  Gaylord *(G-6150)*
Pgi Holdings Inc ....G....... 231 937-4740
  Big Rapids *(G-1684)*
Pgi Holdings Inc ....E....... 231 796-4831
  Big Rapids *(G-1683)*
Shoppers Fair Inc ....E....... 231 627-7144
  Cheboygan *(G-2799)*
St Ignace News ....F....... 906 643-9150
  Saint Ignace *(G-14895)*
Stafford Media Inc ....E....... 616 754-9301
  Greenville *(G-7505)*
Thumbprint News ....G....... 810 794-2300
  Clay *(G-3127)*

COMMERCIAL REFRIGERATORS WHOLESALERS

Forma-Kool Manufacturing Inc ....E....... 586 949-4813
  Chesterfield *(G-2884)*

COMMODITY CONTRACT TRADING COMPANIES

Sulugu Corporation USA Inc ....D....... 478 714-0325
  Grand Rapids *(G-7232)*

COMMODITY INSPECTION SVCS

Manufacturing Products & Svcs ....F....... 734 927-1964
  Plymouth *(G-13233)*

COMMON SAND MINING

Alpena Aggregate Inc ....E....... 989 595-2511
  Alpena *(G-275)*
Jack Millikin Inc ....G....... 989 348-8411
  Grayling *(G-7464)*
John R Sand & Gravel Co Inc ....G....... 810 678-3715
  Metamora *(G-11282)*
Miller Sand & Gravel Company ....G....... 269 672-5601
  Hopkins *(G-8367)*
Round Lake Sand & Gravel Inc ....G....... 517 467-4458
  Addison *(G-44)*
Srm Concrete LLC ....D....... 231 839-4319
  Lake City *(G-9555)*
Tri County Sand and Stone Inc ....G....... 231 331-6549
  Alden *(G-136)*
Van Sloten Enterprises Inc ....F....... 906 635-5911
  Sault Sainte Marie *(G-15102)*

COMMUNICATIONS CARRIER: Wired

Mexico Express ....F....... 313 843-6717
  Detroit *(G-4440)*

COMMUNICATIONS EQPT & SYSTEMS, NEC

Aaccess Entertainment ....G....... 734 260-1002
  Brighton *(G-1936)*
Techncal Audio Video Solutions ....G....... 810 899-5546
  Howell *(G-8527)*

COMMUNICATIONS EQPT REPAIR & MAINTENANCE

Central On Line Data Systems ....G....... 586 939-7000
  Sterling Heights *(G-15954)*

COMMUNICATIONS EQPT WHOLESALERS

Sani Zeevi ....G....... 248 546-4489
  Oak Park *(G-12646)*

COMMUNICATIONS SVCS

Mophie LLC ....B....... 269 743-1340
  Kalamazoo *(G-9276)*

COMMUNICATIONS SVCS, NEC

Challenger Communications LLC ....F....... 517 680-0125
  Albion *(G-123)*

COMMUNICATIONS SVCS: Cellular

Abrasive Services Incorporated ....G....... 734 941-2144
  Romulus *(G-14244)*
Elite Bus Svcs Exec Stffing In ....G....... 734 956-4550
  Bloomfield Hills *(G-1818)*
Mophie LLC ....B....... 269 743-1340
  Kalamazoo *(G-9276)*
No Limit Wireless-Michigan Inc ....G....... 313 285-8402
  Detroit *(G-4487)*

COMMUNICATIONS SVCS: Data

Black Box Corporation ....G....... 248 743-1320
  Troy *(G-16977)*
Intaglio LLC ....E....... 616 243-3300
  Grand Rapids *(G-6848)*

COMMUNICATIONS SVCS: Electronic Mail

Computer Mail Services Inc ....F....... 248 352-6700
  Sterling Heights *(G-15966)*

COMMUNICATIONS SVCS: Internet Connectivity Svcs

Nutrien AG Solutions Inc ....G....... 989 842-1185
  Breckenridge *(G-1912)*
Nuts & Coffee Gallery ....G....... 313 581-3212
  Dearborn *(G-3878)*
Rockman Communications Inc ....E....... 810 433-6800
  Fenton *(G-5500)*

COMMUNICATIONS SVCS: Internet Host Svcs

Fusion Design Group Ltd ....G....... 269 469-8226
  New Buffalo *(G-12023)*
Timothy J Tade Inc ....G....... 248 552-8583
  Troy *(G-17392)*

COMMUNICATIONS SVCS: Telephone Or Video

Startech-Solutions LLC ....G....... 248 419-0650
  Southfield *(G-15708)*
Startech-Solutions LLC ....G....... 248 419-0650
  West Bloomfield *(G-18316)*

COMMUNICATIONS SVCS: Telephone, Data

Abrasive Services Incorporated ....G....... 734 941-2144
  Romulus *(G-14244)*

COMMUNITY DEVELOPMENT GROUPS

Cheboygan Cnty Hbtat For Hmnit ....G....... 231 597-4663
  Cheboygan *(G-2783)*
Neighborhood Artisans Inc ....G....... 313 865-5373
  Detroit *(G-4479)*

COMPACTORS: Trash & Garbage, Residential

Cleaning Up Detroit City LLC ....F....... 517 715-7010
  Detroit *(G-4095)*

COMPARATORS: Machinists

Costello Machine LLC ....E....... 586 749-0136
  Chesterfield *(G-2861)*
Five Star Industries Inc ....E....... 586 786-0500
  Macomb *(G-10595)*

COMPARATORS: Optical

Genx Corporation ....G....... 269 341-4242
  Kalamazoo *(G-9195)*

Employee Codes: A=Over 500 employees, B=251-500
C=101-250, D=51-100, E=20-50, F=10-19, G=3-9

COMPARATORS: Optical

Visual Precision Inc .... G 248 546-7984
   Madison Heights *(G-10857)*

COMPASSES & ACCESS

Mercy Health Partners .... D 231 728-4032
   Muskegon *(G-11866)*

COMPOST

Morgan Composting Inc .... G 231 734-2451
   Sears *(G-15137)*
Morgan Composting Inc .... E 231 734-2790
   Sears *(G-15138)*
Natures Best Top Soil Compost .... G 810 657-9528
   Carsonville *(G-2596)*
Spurt Industries LLC .... G 616 688-5575
   Zeeland *(G-19080)*
Taylor Hills Compost Facility .... G 734 991-3902
   Taylor *(G-16484)*

COMPRESSORS: Air & Gas

Atlas Copco Ias LLC .... D 248 377-9722
   Auburn Hills *(G-799)*
Belco Industries Inc .... E 616 794-0410
   Belding *(G-1437)*
Blissfield Manufacturing Co .... C 517 486-2121
   Blissfield *(G-1761)*
Harvey S Freeman .... G 248 852-2222
   West Bloomfield *(G-18287)*
Michigan Auto Comprsr Inc .... A 517 796-3200
   Parma *(G-12938)*
Millennium Planet LLC .... G 248 835-2331
   Farmington Hills *(G-5322)*
Nordson Corporation .... D 734 459-8600
   Wixom *(G-18721)*
Pr39 Industries LLC .... G 248 481-8512
   Auburn Hills *(G-1001)*
Primore Inc .... F 517 263-2220
   Adrian *(G-89)*
Stop & Go No 10 Inc .... G 734 281-7500
   Southgate *(G-15757)*
Thierica Equipment Corporation .... E 616 453-6570
   Grand Rapids *(G-7259)*
Unist Inc .... E 616 949-0853
   Grand Rapids *(G-7297)*

COMPRESSORS: Air & Gas, Including Vacuum Pumps

Correct Compression Inc .... G 231 864-2101
   Bear Lake *(G-1417)*
Gast Manufacturing Inc .... D 269 926-6171
   Benton Harbor *(G-1552)*
Metallurgical High Vacuum Corp .... F 269 543-4291
   Fennville *(G-5440)*
Rochester Petroleum Inc .... G 507 533-9156
   Birmingham *(G-1747)*
Saylor-Beall Manufacturing Co .... B 989 224-2371
   Saint Johns *(G-14914)*

COMPRESSORS: Refrigeration & Air Conditioning Eqpt

Compressor Industries LLC .... F 313 389-2800
   Melvindale *(G-11197)*
Etx Holdings Inc .... G 989 463-1151
   Alma *(G-241)*
Hanon Systems Usa LLC .... B 248 907-8000
   Novi *(G-12425)*
Remacon Compressors Inc .... G 313 842-8219
   Detroit *(G-4564)*
Tecumseh Compressor Co LLC .... E 662 566-2231
   Ann Arbor *(G-675)*
Tecumseh Compressor Company .... D 734 585-9500
   Ann Arbor *(G-676)*

COMPRESSORS: Repairing

Compressor Technologies Inc .... F 616 949-7000
   Grand Rapids *(G-6590)*
Correct Compression Inc .... G 231 864-2101
   Bear Lake *(G-1417)*

COMPRESSORS: Wholesalers

Compressor Technologies Inc .... F 616 949-7000
   Grand Rapids *(G-6590)*

COMPUTER & COMPUTER SOFTWARE STORES

Cartidge World .... G 810 229-5599
   Brighton *(G-1962)*
Lowry Holding Company Inc .... C 810 229-7200
   Brighton *(G-2023)*
Novastar Solutionscom LLC .... D 734 453-8003
   Livonia *(G-10340)*
Precision Printer Services Inc .... E 269 384-5725
   Portage *(G-13594)*
World of Cd-Rom .... F 269 382-3766
   Kalamazoo *(G-9374)*

COMPUTER & COMPUTER SOFTWARE STORES: Peripheral Eqpt

Automated Media Inc .... D 313 937-5000
   Canton *(G-2438)*
Jem Computers Inc .... F 586 783-3400
   Clinton Township *(G-3264)*
Photodon LLC .... F 847 377-1185
   Traverse City *(G-16791)*

COMPUTER & COMPUTER SOFTWARE STORES: Personal Computers

Digilink Technology Inc .... F 517 381-8888
   Okemos *(G-12664)*

COMPUTER & COMPUTER SOFTWARE STORES: Printers & Plotters

M & J Graphics Enterprises Inc .... F 734 542-8800
   Livonia *(G-10294)*
Visionit Supplies and Svcs Inc .... E 313 664-5650
   Detroit *(G-4669)*

COMPUTER & COMPUTER SOFTWARE STORES: Software & Access

Industrial Service Tech Inc .... F 616 247-1033
   Grand Rapids *(G-6843)*
Materialise Usa LLC .... D 734 259-6445
   Plymouth *(G-13236)*

COMPUTER & COMPUTER SOFTWARE STORES: Software, Bus/Non-Game

Dynics Inc .... D 734 677-6100
   Ann Arbor *(G-462)*
Rutherford & Associates Inc .... E 616 392-5000
   Holland *(G-8185)*

COMPUTER & COMPUTER SOFTWARE STORES: Software, Computer Game

Official Brand Limited .... G 734 224-9942
   Dearborn *(G-3880)*

COMPUTER & COMPUTER SOFTWARE STORES: Word Process Eqpt/Splys

Great Lakes Log & Firewd Co .... G 231 206-4073
   Twin Lake *(G-17468)*

COMPUTER & DATA PROCESSING EQPT REPAIR & MAINTENANCE

Bull Hn Info Systems Inc .... G 616 942-7126
   Grand Rapids *(G-6530)*
Stellar Computer Services LLC .... G 989 732-7153
   Gaylord *(G-6161)*

COMPUTER & OFFICE MACHINE MAINTENANCE & REPAIR

Active Solutions Group Inc .... G 313 278-4522
   Dearborn *(G-3805)*
Automated Media Inc .... D 313 937-5000
   Canton *(G-2438)*
Digilink Technology Inc .... F 517 381-8888
   Okemos *(G-12664)*
Geeks of Detroit LLC .... G 734 576-2363
   Detroit *(G-4252)*
Medical Systems Resource Group .... G 248 476-5400
   Farmington Hills *(G-5313)*
Novastar Solutionscom LLC .... D 734 453-8003
   Livonia *(G-10340)*
Precision Printer Services Inc .... E 269 384-5725
   Portage *(G-13594)*
Rap Electronics & Machines .... F 616 846-1437
   Grand Haven *(G-6350)*
Rose Mobile Computer Repr LLC .... F 248 653-0865
   Bloomfield Hills *(G-1859)*
S T A Inc .... E 248 328-5000
   Holly *(G-8294)*

COMPUTER CALCULATING SVCS

Nits Solutions Inc .... F 248 231-2267
   Novi *(G-12488)*

COMPUTER FACILITIES MANAGEMENT SVCS

E-Con LLC .... G 248 766-9000
   Birmingham *(G-1725)*
Pioneer Automotive Inc .... F 586 758-7730
   Sterling Heights *(G-16127)*
V2soft Inc .... D 248 904-1702
   Bloomfield Hills *(G-1872)*

COMPUTER FORMS

F P Horak Company .... C 989 892-6505
   Bay City *(G-1355)*
MPS Lansing Inc .... A 517 323-9000
   Lansing *(G-9719)*
Rotary Multiforms Inc .... G 586 558-7960
   Madison Heights *(G-10819)*

COMPUTER GRAPHICS SVCS

Eview 360 LLC .... E 248 306-5191
   Farmington Hills *(G-5239)*
H M Day Signs Inc .... G 231 946-7132
   Traverse City *(G-16709)*
Nb Media Solutions LLC .... G 616 724-7175
   Grand Rapids *(G-7037)*
Religious Communications LLC .... G 313 822-3361
   Detroit *(G-4563)*
Star Board Multi Media Inc .... G 616 296-0823
   Grand Haven *(G-6367)*
Whiteside Consulting Group LLC .... G 313 288-6598
   Detroit *(G-4681)*

COMPUTER INTERFACE EQPT: Indl Process

Allrout Inc .... G 616 748-7696
   Zeeland *(G-18991)*
Bihl+wiedemann Inc .... G 616 345-0680
   Wyoming *(G-18852)*
D & C Investment Group Inc .... F 734 994-0591
   Ann Arbor *(G-441)*
Smarteye Corporation .... E 248 853-4495
   Rochester Hills *(G-14115)*

COMPUTER PERIPHERAL EQPT REPAIR & MAINTENANCE

Lasers Resource Inc .... E 616 554-5555
   Grand Rapids *(G-6930)*
Mikan Corporation .... F 734 944-9447
   Saline *(G-15027)*

COMPUTER PERIPHERAL EQPT, NEC

Acromag Incorporated .... D 248 624-1541
   Wixom *(G-18594)*
Advanced Integrated Mfg .... G 586 439-0300
   Fraser *(G-5888)*
Artic Technologies Intl .... G 248 689-9884
   Troy *(G-16955)*
Bbcm Inc .... G 248 410-2528
   Bloomfield Hills *(G-1803)*
Black Box Corporation .... G 248 743-1320
   Troy *(G-16977)*
Black Box Corporation .... G 616 246-1320
   Caledonia *(G-2369)*
Bull Hn Info Systems Inc .... G 616 942-7126
   Grand Rapids *(G-6530)*
Comptek Inc .... E 248 477-5215
   Farmington Hills *(G-5206)*
Daco Hand Controllers Inc .... F 248 982-3266
   Novi *(G-12390)*
Elite Engineering Inc .... E 517 304-3254
   Rochester Hills *(G-14003)*
Ensure Technologies Inc .... F 734 547-1600
   Ypsilanti *(G-18944)*

PRODUCT SECTION

Innovative Support Svcs Inc ....F 248 585-3600
  Troy (G-17168)
Jem Computers Inc ....F 586 783-3400
  Clinton Township (G-3264)
Jo-Dan International Inc ....F 248 340-0300
  Auburn Hills (G-944)
Law Enforcement Development Co ......E 734 656-4100
  Plymouth (G-13220)
Lexmark International Inc ....F 248 352-0616
  Southfield (G-15635)
Pro-Face America LLC ....E 734 477-0600
  Ann Arbor (G-625)
Sakor Technologies Inc ....F 989 720-2700
  Owosso (G-12855)
Samsung Sdi America Inc ....F 408 544-4470
  Auburn Hills (G-1025)
Triangle Product Distributors ....E 970 609-9001
  Holland (G-8229)
Yakel Enterprises LLC ....G 586 943-5885
  Washington Township (G-18097)

COMPUTER PERIPHERAL EQPT, WHOLESALE

Jem Computers Inc ....F 586 783-3400
  Clinton Township (G-3264)
Mitsubishi Electric Us Inc ....G 734 453-6200
  Northville (G-12241)
Samsung Sdi America Inc ....F 408 544-4470
  Auburn Hills (G-1025)
Virtual Technology Inc ....F 248 528-6565
  Troy (G-17442)

COMPUTER PERIPHERAL EQPT: Graphic Displays, Exc Terminals

Ampm Inc ....E 989 837-8800
  Midland (G-11321)
Graphic Resource Group Inc ....E 248 588-6100
  Troy (G-17132)
Jant Group LLC ....G 616 863-6600
  Belmont (G-1508)

COMPUTER PERIPHERAL EQPT: Input Or Output

Scs Embedded Tech LLC ....G 248 615-4441
  Novi (G-12532)

COMPUTER PLOTTERS

Envisiontec US LLC ....D 313 436-4300
  Dearborn (G-3837)

COMPUTER PROCESSING SVCS

Copy Central Inc ....G 231 941-2298
  Traverse City (G-16660)
Tru-Syzygy Inc ....G 248 622-7211
  Lake Orion (G-9635)

COMPUTER PROGRAMMING SVCS

21st Century Graphic Tech LLC ....G 586 463-9599
  Utica (G-17501)
Autodesk Inc ....G 248 347-9650
  Novi (G-12368)
Core Technology Corporation ....F 517 627-1521
  Grand Ledge (G-6387)
Data Pro Inc ....G 269 685-9214
  Plainwell (G-13074)
Egemin Automation Inc ....C 616 393-0101
  Holland (G-8025)
Falcon Consulting Services LLC ....G 989 262-9325
  Alpena (G-293)
General Motors Company ....B 586 218-9240
  Warren (G-17824)
Great Lakes Infotronics Inc ....E 248 476-2500
  Northville (G-12226)
Group Infotech Inc ....F 517 336-7110
  Lansing (G-9848)
Intellibee Inc ....E 313 586-4122
  Detroit (G-4323)
International Machining Svc ....G 248 486-3600
  South Lyon (G-15440)
New Concepts Software Inc ....G 586 776-2855
  Roseville (G-14453)
Nuwave Technology Partners LLC ....F 616 942-7520
  Grand Rapids (G-7052)
Workforce Software LLC ....C 734 542-4100
  Livonia (G-10478)

COMPUTER PROGRAMMING SVCS: Custom

Ancor Information MGT LLC ....D 248 740-8866
  Troy (G-16936)
Stardock Systems Inc ....E 734 927-0677
  Plymouth (G-13303)
Technology Network Svcs Inc ....F 586 294-7771
  Saint Clair Shores (G-14888)

COMPUTER RELATED MAINTENANCE SVCS

Medimage Inc ....G 734 665-5400
  Ann Arbor (G-568)

COMPUTER RELATED SVCS, NEC

Simplify Inventions LLC ....D 248 960-1700
  Farmington Hills (G-5382)

COMPUTER SOFTWARE DEVELOPMENT

Advanced Tubular Tech Inc ....G 248 674-2059
  Clarkston (G-3015)
Alta Vista Technology LLC ....F 855 913-3228
  Royal Oak (G-14506)
Amicus Software ....G 313 417-9550
  White Lake (G-18449)
Arbortext Inc ....C 734 997-0200
  Ann Arbor (G-378)
Atos Syntel Inc ....A 248 619-2800
  Troy (G-16964)
Axis Tms Corp ....E 248 509-2440
  Clinton Township (G-3179)
Braiq Inc ....G 858 729-4116
  Detroit (G-4066)
Competitive Cmpt Info Tech Inc ....F 732 829-9699
  Northville (G-12201)
Complete Data Products Inc ....F 248 651-8602
  Troy (G-17021)
Computer Mail Services Inc ....F 248 352-6700
  Sterling Heights (G-15966)
Compuware Corporation ....E 313 227-7300
  Detroit (G-4100)
E-Con LLC ....G 248 766-9000
  Birmingham (G-1725)
Elite Engineering Inc ....E 517 304-3254
  Rochester Hills (G-14003)
Empower Financials Inc ....G 734 747-9393
  Ann Arbor (G-473)
Engineering Tech Assoc Inc ....D 248 729-3010
  Troy (G-17091)
Global Supply Integrator LLC ....G 586 484-0734
  Davisburg (G-3770)
Harbor Software Intl Inc ....G 231 347-8866
  Petoskey (G-13000)
Inovision Sftwr Solutions Inc ....G 586 598-8750
  Chesterfield (G-2896)
Melange Computer Services Inc ....F 517 321-8434
  Lansing (G-9774)
Mendenhall Associates Inc ....G 734 741-4710
  Ann Arbor (G-569)
Nits Solutions Inc ....F 248 231-2267
  Novi (G-12488)
Panter Master Controls Inc ....F 810 687-5600
  Flint (G-5743)
Quantum Compliance Systems ....F 734 930-0009
  Ypsilanti (G-18973)
Radley Corporation ....E 616 554-9060
  Grand Rapids (G-7136)
Sciemetric Inc ....F 248 509-2209
  Rochester Hills (G-14110)
Silkroute Global Inc ....G 248 854-3409
  Troy (G-17354)
Superior Information Tech LLC ....F 734 666-9963
  Livonia (G-10424)
Sync Technologies Inc ....E 313 963-5353
  Detroit (G-4622)
Tecra Systems Inc ....F 248 888-1116
  Westland (G-18420)
Tyler Technologies Inc ....G 734 677-0550
  Ann Arbor (G-701)

COMPUTER SOFTWARE DEVELOPMENT & APPLICATIONS

Coeus LLC ....F 248 564-1958
  Bloomfield Hills (G-1808)
El Informador LLC ....G 616 272-1092
  Wyoming (G-18871)
Ginkgotree Inc ....G 734 707-7191
  Detroit (G-4262)

COMPUTER STORAGE DEVICES, NEC

Ideation International Inc ....F 248 737-8854
  Farmington Hills (G-5266)
Kingston Educational Software ....G 248 895-4803
  Farmington Hills (G-5281)
Kubica Corp ....F 248 344-7750
  Novi (G-12459)
Lspedia LLC ....G 248 320-1909
  West Bloomfield (G-18294)
Manufacturing & Indus Tech Inc ....E 248 522-6959
  Farmington Hills (G-5309)
Prehab Technologies LLC ....G 734 368-9983
  Ann Arbor (G-623)
Smart Diet Scale LLC ....G 586 383-6734
  Bruce Twp (G-2183)
Torenzo Inc ....F 313 732-7874
  Bloomfield Hills (G-1866)
Tweddle Group Inc ....C 586 307-3700
  Clinton Township (G-3380)
Ventuor LLC ....G 248 790-8700
  Flint (G-5791)
Whirlpool Corporation ....G 269 923-6486
  Benton Harbor (G-1608)

COMPUTER SOFTWARE SYSTEMS ANALYSIS & DESIGN: Custom

3dfx Interactive Inc ....G 918 938-8967
  Saginaw (G-14599)
3r Info LLC ....F 201 221-6133
  Canton (G-2425)
Barcroft Technology LLC ....G 313 378-0133
  Southfield (G-15502)
Beet Inc ....F 248 432-0052
  Troy (G-16971)
Chain-Sys Corporation ....G 517 627-1173
  Lansing (G-9757)
Cypress Computer Systems Inc ....F 810 245-2300
  Lapeer (G-9924)
Driven-4 LLC ....G 269 281-7567
  Saint Joseph (G-14927)
Dupearl Technology LLC ....G 248 390-9609
  Bloomfield Hills (G-1816)
E Z Logic Data Systems Inc ....E 248 817-8800
  Farmington Hills (G-5221)
Innovative Programming Systems ....G 810 695-9332
  Grand Blanc (G-6249)
Lintech Global Inc ....D 248 553-8033
  Farmington Hills (G-5292)
Mejenta Systems Inc ....E 248 434-2583
  Southfield (G-15653)
Software Finesse LLC ....G 248 737-8990
  Farmington Hills (G-5383)
Strategic Computer Solutions ....G 248 888-0666
  Ann Arbor (G-667)
Tru-Syzygy Inc ....G 248 622-7211
  Lake Orion (G-9635)

COMPUTER SOFTWARE WRITERS

Appliction Spclist Kompany Inc ....F 517 676-6633
  Lansing (G-9805)
Writers Bible LLc ....G 734 286-7793
  Romulus (G-14341)

COMPUTER STORAGE DEVICES, NEC

Aperion Information Tech Inc ....F 248 969-9791
  Oxford (G-12874)
Cloudface LLC ....G 248 756-1688
  Northville (G-12200)
Digilink Technology Inc ....F 517 381-8888
  Okemos (G-12664)
Don Theyken ....G 734 996-8359
  Ann Arbor (G-457)
Donald Schilstra ....G 616 534-1897
  Grand Rapids (G-6654)
EMC Corporation ....G 248 957-5800
  Farmington Hills (G-5229)
EMC Educational Services LLC ....G 616 460-3345
  Walker (G-17638)
Mass Mountain Technologies ....G 855 722-7900
  Grand Rapids (G-6964)
Quantam Solutions LLC ....G 248 395-2200
  Southfield (G-15686)
Quantum Data Analytics Inc ....G 248 894-7442
  Rochester Hills (G-14095)
Quantum Differeence Corp ....G 810 845-8765
  Flint (G-5753)
Quantum Life LLC ....G 248 634-2578
  Holly (G-8288)
Quantum Manufacturing ....G 248 690-9410
  Auburn Hills (G-1010)

Employee Codes: A=Over 500 employees, B=251-500
C=101-250, D=51-100, E=20-50, F=10-19, G=3-9

2022 Harris Michigan Industrial Directory

COMPUTER STORAGE DEVICES, NEC

Quantum Ventures LLC .... G 248 325-8380
  Holly (G-8289)
Quantum Whatever LLC .... G 734 546-4353
  Willis (G-18587)
Rave Computer Association Inc .... E 586 939-8230
  Sterling Heights (G-16143)
Virtual Technology Inc .... F 248 528-6565
  Troy (G-17442)

COMPUTER SYSTEMS ANALYSIS & DESIGN

Design & Test Technology Inc .... G 734 665-4111
  Dexter (G-4733)
Design & Test Technology Inc .... G 734 665-4316
  Ann Arbor (G-448)
Singh Automation LLC .... G 269 267-6078
  Portage (G-13607)

COMPUTER TERMINALS

Geeks of Detroit LLC .... G 734 576-2363
  Detroit (G-4252)
Mobile Knowledge Group LLC .... G 248 625-3327
  Clarkston (G-3052)
Pro-Face America LLC .... E 734 477-0600
  Ann Arbor (G-625)

COMPUTER-AIDED DESIGN SYSTEMS SVCS

Advantage Industries Inc .... E 616 669-2400
  Jenison (G-9042)
Awcco USA Incorporated .... G 586 336-9135
  Romeo (G-14220)
Axsys Inc .... E 248 926-8810
  Wixom (G-18616)
Drushal Fabricating LLC .... G 517 539-5921
  Jackson (G-8871)
Laser North Inc .... G 906 353-6090
  Baraga (G-1143)

COMPUTER-AIDED ENGINEERING SYSTEMS SVCS

Manufacturing & Indus Tech Inc .... E 248 522-6959
  Farmington Hills (G-5309)

COMPUTER-AIDED MANUFACTURING SYSTEMS SVCS

Onyx Manufacturing Inc .... G 248 687-8611
  Rochester Hills (G-14075)

COMPUTERS, NEC

Advanced Integrated Mfg .... G 586 439-0300
  Fraser (G-5888)
Artemis Technologies Inc .... E 517 336-9915
  East Lansing (G-4886)
Cypress Computer Systems Inc .... F 810 245-2300
  Lapeer (G-9924)
Enovate It .... F 248 721-8104
  Ferndale (G-5552)
Entron Computer Systems Inc .... G 248 349-8898
  Northville (G-12215)
Ews Legacy LLC .... C 248 853-6363
  Rochester Hills (G-14006)
Experimac Macomb .... E 586 884-6292
  Macomb (G-10593)
General Dynmics Mssion Systems .... G 734 480-5000
  Ypsilanti (G-18950)
General Dynmics Mssion Systems .... G 734 480-5000
  Ypsilanti (G-18951)
Hardware Exchange Inc .... G 440 449-8006
  Grand Rapids (G-6803)
Indocomp Systems Inc .... F 810 678-3990
  Metamora (G-11281)
Innovation Unlimited LLC .... G 574 635-1064
  Bay City (G-1367)
Innovtive Design Solutions Inc .... C 248 583-1010
  Sterling Heights (G-16049)
International Bus Mchs Corp .... E 989 832-6000
  Midland (G-11375)
Jasons Apple Service & Sls LLC .... G 586 530-4908
  Macomb (G-10607)
Mesa Corporation .... G 517 669-5656
  Dewitt (G-4712)
Opto Solutions Inc .... G 269 254-9716
  Plainwell (G-13084)
PC Techs On Wheels .... G 734 262-4424
  Canton (G-2505)
PCI Procal Inc .... F 989 358-7070
  Alpena (G-311)
Protxs Inc .... C 989 255-3836
  Jenison (G-9068)
Radio Advertising Bureau Inc .... G 248 514-7048
  Novi (G-12523)
Rave Computer Association Inc .... E 586 939-8230
  Sterling Heights (G-16143)
S T A Inc .... E 248 328-5000
  Holly (G-8294)
Secord Solutions LLC .... G 734 363-8887
  Ecorse (G-4985)
Tes America LLC .... E 616 786-5353
  Holland (G-8217)

COMPUTERS, NEC, WHOLESALE

Rave Computer Association Inc .... E 586 939-8230
  Sterling Heights (G-16143)
Technology Network Svcs Inc .... F 586 294-7771
  Saint Clair Shores (G-14888)

COMPUTERS, PERIPHERALS & SOFTWARE, WHOLESALE: Printers

Wright Communications Inc .... F 248 585-3838
  Troy (G-17454)

COMPUTERS, PERIPHERALS & SOFTWARE, WHOLESALE: Software

123go LLC .... G 734 773-0049
  Ann Arbor (G-340)
Axsys Inc .... E 248 926-8810
  Wixom (G-18616)
Label Tech Inc .... F 586 247-6444
  Shelby Township (G-15254)
Triangle Product Distributors .... E 970 609-9001
  Holland (G-8229)

COMPUTERS: Mainframe

Bull Hn Info Systems Inc .... G 616 942-7126
  Grand Rapids (G-6530)

COMPUTERS: Mini

Intellibee Inc .... E 313 586-4122
  Detroit (G-4323)
Pro-Face America LLC .... E 734 477-0600
  Ann Arbor (G-625)

COMPUTERS: Personal

3dfx Interactive Inc .... G 918 938-8967
  Saginaw (G-14599)
Compudyne Inc .... F 906 360-9081
  Marquette (G-11014)
Eaton Aerospace LLC .... B 616 949-1090
  Grand Rapids (G-6663)
Hp Inc .... G 650 857-1501
  Lansing (G-9765)
Hp Inc .... G 248 614-6600
  Troy (G-17154)
Kismet Strategic Sourcing Part .... G 269 932-4990
  Saint Joseph (G-14942)
Lga Retail Inc .... G 248 910-1918
  South Lyon (G-15443)

CONCENTRATES, DRINK

Glcc Co .... E 269 657-3167
  Paw Paw (G-12948)
Refreshment Product Svcs Inc .... G 906 475-7003
  Negaunee (G-11972)

CONCRETE BUILDING PRDTS WHOLESALERS

Best Concrete & Supply Inc .... G 734 283-7055
  Brownstown (G-2143)
Milford Redi-Mix Company .... E 248 684-1465
  Milford (G-11472)

CONCRETE CURING & HARDENING COMPOUNDS

BASF Corporation .... E 269 668-3371
  Mattawan (G-11162)
Rooto Corporation .... F 517 546-8330
  Howell (G-8510)

CONCRETE MIXERS

Oshkosh Defense LLC .... E 586 576-8301
  Warren (G-17951)

CONCRETE PLANTS

Arcosa Shoring Products Inc .... D 517 741-4300
  Union City (G-17490)
Besser Company .... B 989 354-4111
  Alpena (G-284)
Thomas J Moyle Jr Incorporated .... F 906 482-3000
  Houghton (G-8393)

CONCRETE PRDTS

Ajax Paving Industries Inc .... C 248 244-3300
  Troy (G-16913)
Best Block Company .... E 586 772-7000
  Warren (G-17732)
Bonsal American Inc .... F 248 338-0335
  Auburn Hills (G-813)
Cheboygan Cement Products Inc .... G 989 742-4107
  Hillman (G-7911)
Clancy Excavating Co .... G 586 294-2900
  Roseville (G-14384)
Concrete Manufacturing Inc .... G 586 777-3320
  Roseville (G-14388)
Consumers Concrete Corp .... C 616 243-3651
  Wyoming (G-18858)
Consumers Concrete Corporation .... F 517 784-9108
  Jackson (G-8852)
Cosella Dorken Products Inc .... G 888 433-5824
  Rochester (G-13896)
Darby Ready Mix Concrete Co .... E 517 547-7004
  Addison (G-43)
Decorative Concrete By John .... G 616 862-7152
  Grand Rapids (G-6639)
E & M Cores Inc .... G 989 386-9223
  Clare (G-2978)
Fendt Builders Supply Inc .... E 248 474-3211
  Farmington Hills (G-5242)
Fraco Products Ltd .... G 248 667-9260
  Troy (G-17122)
Gambles Redi-Mix Inc .... E 989 539-6460
  Harrison (G-7677)
Gibraltar National Corporation .... E 248 634-8257
  Holly (G-8274)
Gnap LLC .... G 616 583-5000
  Byron Center (G-2272)
High Grade Materials Company .... E 616 754-5545
  Greenville (G-7492)
Holcim (us) Inc .... G 734 529-4600
  Dundee (G-4824)
Kurtz Gravel Company Inc .... E 810 787-6543
  Farmington Hills (G-5286)
Lafarge North America Inc .... G 703 480-3600
  Dundee (G-4827)
Lake Orion Concrete Orna Pdts .... G 248 693-8683
  Lake Orion (G-9614)
M 37 Concrete Products Inc .... G 231 689-1785
  White Cloud (G-18446)
Marquette Castings LLC .... G 248 798-8035
  Royal Oak (G-14560)
Mbcd Inc .... E 517 484-4426
  Lansing (G-9867)
MEGA Precast Inc .... E 586 477-5959
  Shelby Township (G-15272)
Metro Cast Corporation .... G 734 728-0210
  Westland (G-18395)
National Block Company .... E 734 721-4050
  Westland (G-18399)
Oaks Concrete Products Inc .... F 248 684-5004
  Wixom (G-18725)
Paul Murphy Plastics Co .... E 586 774-4880
  Roseville (G-14460)
Pearson Precast Concrete Pdts .... G 517 486-4060
  Blissfield (G-1772)
Polycem LLC .... E 231 799-1040
  Norton Shores (G-12350)
Port Huron Building Supply Co .... F 810 987-2666
  Port Huron (G-13519)
Prestressed Group .... G 313 962-9189
  River Rouge (G-13859)
Quikrete Detroit .... E 313 491-3500
  Detroit (G-4548)
Redi-Rock International LLC .... F 866 222-8400
  Petoskey (G-13019)
Van Sloten Enterprises Inc .... F 906 635-5151
  Sault Sainte Marie (G-15102)
White Lake Excavating Inc .... E 231 894-6918
  Whitehall (G-18513)

PRODUCT SECTION

CONCRETE: Ready-Mixed

CONCRETE PRDTS, PRECAST, NEC

Advance Concrete Products Co ....E 248 887-4173
  Highland *(G-7880)*
Beck Mobile Concrete LLC ....G 517 655-4996
  Williamston *(G-18568)*
Bush Concrete Products Inc ....F 231 733-1904
  Norton Shores *(G-12281)*
Concrete Step Co ....G 810 789-3061
  Flint *(G-5671)*
Fenton Corporation ....G 810 629-2858
  Fenton *(G-5476)*
Interntnal Prcast Slutions LLC ....D 313 843-0073
  River Rouge *(G-13856)*
Mack Industries Michigan Inc ....E 248 620-7400
  White Lake *(G-18461)*
Nucast LLC ....G 313 532-4610
  Redford *(G-13750)*
Quality Precast Con Pdts LLC ....G 269 342-0539
  Kalamazoo *(G-9311)*
Wolverine Concrete Products ....G 313 931-7189
  Detroit *(G-4687)*

CONCRETE REINFORCING MATERIAL

Polytorx LLC ....G 734 322-2114
  Ann Arbor *(G-614)*

CONCRETE: Dry Mixture

Quikrete Companies LLC ....G 616 784-5790
  Walker *(G-17652)*

CONCRETE: Ready-Mixed

Aggregate Industries - Mwr Inc ....G 734 475-2531
  Grass Lake *(G-7434)*
Ajax Paving Industries Inc ....C 248 244-3300
  Troy *(G-16913)*
Alma Concrete Products Company ....G 989 463-5476
  Alma *(G-234)*
Angelos Crushed Concrete Inc ....G 586 756-1070
  Warren *(G-17706)*
Are You Ready ....G 616 935-1133
  Fruitport *(G-6058)*
Arquette Concrete & Supply ....G 989 846-4131
  Standish *(G-15887)*
Associated Constructors LLC ....D 906 226-6505
  Negaunee *(G-11963)*
Baraga County Concrete Company ....G 906 353-6595
  Baraga *(G-1134)*
Beck Mobile Concrete LLC ....G 517 655-4996
  Williamston *(G-18568)*
Becker & Scrivens Con Pdts Inc ....E 517 437-4250
  Hillsdale *(G-7924)*
Beckman Brothers Inc ....E 231 861-2031
  Shelby *(G-15148)*
Beechbed Mix ....G 616 263-7422
  Holland *(G-7972)*
Best Concrete & Supply Inc ....G 734 283-7055
  Brownstown *(G-2143)*
Best-Block Co ....G 313 933-8676
  Detroit *(G-4053)*
Bichler Gravel & Concrete Co ....F 906 786-0343
  Escanaba *(G-5062)*
Bigos Precast ....G 517 223-5000
  Fowlerville *(G-5835)*
Bogen Concrete Inc ....G 269 651-6751
  Sturgis *(G-16281)*
Bonsal American Inc ....G 734 753-4413
  New Boston *(G-12003)*
Bozzer Brothers Inc ....G 989 732-9684
  Gaylord *(G-6120)*
Branch West Concrete Products ....F 989 345-0794
  West Branch *(G-18326)*
Brewers City Dock Inc ....E 616 396-6563
  Holland *(G-7983)*
Bwb LLC ....F 231 439-9200
  Farmington Hills *(G-5189)*
C F Long & Sons Inc ....E 248 624-1562
  Walled Lake *(G-17665)*
Callahan Supply LLC ....G 231 878-9023
  Cadillac *(G-2325)*
Carrollton Concrete Mix Inc ....G 989 753-7737
  Saginaw *(G-14622)*
Carrollton Paving Co ....G 989 752-7139
  Saginaw *(G-14623)*
Cemex Cement Inc ....E 231 547-9971
  Charlevoix *(G-2712)*
Central Concrete Products Inc ....E 810 659-7488
  Flushing *(G-5804)*
Cheboygan Cement Products Inc ....E 231 627-5631
  Cheboygan *(G-2782)*
Cheboygan Cement Products Inc ....G 989 356-5156
  Alpena *(G-286)*
Cheboygan Cement Products Inc ....G 989 742-4107
  Hillman *(G-7911)*
Coit Avenue Gravel Co Inc ....E 616 363-7777
  Grand Rapids *(G-6581)*
Concrete Store ....G 231 577-3433
  Cadillac *(G-2326)*
Consumers Concrete Corp ....E 269 384-0977
  Kalamazoo *(G-9152)*
Consumers Concrete Corporation ....E 269 342-0136
  Kalamazoo *(G-9153)*
Consumers Concrete Corporation ....G 800 643-4235
  Plainwell *(G-13072)*
Consumers Concrete Corporation ....F 231 777-3981
  Muskegon *(G-11795)*
Consumers Concrete Corporation ....G 269 792-9009
  Wayland *(G-18193)*
Consumers Concrete Corporation ....E 231 924-6131
  Fremont *(G-6037)*
Consumers Concrete Corporation ....F 269 925-3109
  Benton Harbor *(G-1542)*
Consumers Concrete Corporation ....F 517 267-8428
  Lansing *(G-9826)*
Consumers Concrete Corporation ....G 616 827-0063
  Byron Center *(G-2264)*
Consumers Concrete Corporation ....F 269 342-5983
  Kalamazoo *(G-9154)*
Consumers Concrete Corporation ....G 269 965-2321
  Battle Creek *(G-1211)*
Consumers Concrete Corporation ....G 616 392-6190
  Holland *(G-8004)*
Consumers Concrete Corporation ....G 269 684-8760
  Niles *(G-12120)*
Consumers Concrete Corporation ....F 231 894-2705
  Whitehall *(G-18493)*
Consumers Concrete Corporation ....F 517 784-9108
  Jackson *(G-8852)*
Cornillie Concrete ....G 231 439-9200
  Harbor Springs *(G-7645)*
Crete Dry-Mix & Supply Co ....F 616 784-5790
  Comstock Park *(G-3599)*
Darby Ready Mix Concrete Co ....E 517 547-7004
  Addison *(G-43)*
Darby Ready Mix-Dundee LLC ....F 734 529-7100
  Dundee *(G-4813)*
Daves Concrete Products Inc ....F 269 624-4100
  Lawton *(G-9988)*
Dekes Concrete Inc ....F 810 686-5570
  Clarkston *(G-3030)*
Detroit Ready Mix Concrete ....F 313 931-7043
  Detroit *(G-4160)*
Detroit Recycled Concrete Co ....G 248 553-0600
  Novi *(G-12395)*
Detroit Recycled Concrete Co ....G 313 934-7677
  Detroit *(G-4161)*
Dewent Redi-Mix LLC ....G 616 457-2100
  Jenison *(G-9052)*
Doan Construction Co ....F 734 971-4678
  Ypsilanti *(G-18940)*
Downriver Crushed Concrete ....G 734 283-1833
  Taylor *(G-16405)*
Drayton Iron & Metal Inc ....F 248 673-1269
  Waterford *(G-18120)*
E A Wood Inc ....F 989 739-9118
  Oscoda *(G-12757)*
Edw C Levy Co ....F 248 334-4302
  Auburn Hills *(G-875)*
Edw C Levy Co ....G 313 843-7200
  Detroit *(G-4202)*
Edward E Yates ....G 517 467-4961
  Onsted *(G-12705)*
Elmers Crane and Dozer Inc ....F 231 943-3443
  Mount Pleasant *(G-11696)*
Elmers Crane and Dozer Inc ....C 231 943-3443
  Traverse City *(G-16676)*
Fenton Concrete Inc ....G 810 629-0783
  Fenton *(G-5475)*
Ferguson Block Co Inc ....E 810 653-2812
  Davison *(G-2342)*
Fisher Cnstr Aggregates Inc ....F 989 539-6431
  Mount Pleasant *(G-11698)*
Fisher Redi Mix Concrete ....G 989 723-1622
  Owosso *(G-12833)*
Fisher Sand and Gravel Company ....E 989 835-7187
  Midland *(G-11363)*
Gale Briggs Inc ....G 517 543-1320
  Charlotte *(G-2758)*
Gambles Redi-Mix Inc ....E 989 539-6460
  Harrison *(G-7677)*
Gene Brow & Sons Inc ....F 906 635-0859
  Sault Sainte Marie *(G-15090)*
Gotts Transit Mix Inc ....F 734 439-1528
  Milan *(G-11437)*
Grand Rapids Gravel Company ....G 616 538-9000
  Grand Rapids *(G-6759)*
Grand Rapids Gravel Company ....E 616 538-9000
  Belmont *(G-1507)*
Grand Rapids Gravel Company ....G 616 538-9000
  Holland *(G-8055)*
Grand Rapids Gravel Company ....E 231 777-2777
  Muskegon *(G-11826)*
Great Lakes Aggregates LLC ....C 734 379-0311
  South Rockwood *(G-15464)*
Great Lakes Sand & Gravel LLC ....G 616 374-3169
  Lake Odessa *(G-9576)*
Guidobono Concrete Inc ....F 810 229-2666
  Brighton *(G-2006)*
Hamilton Block & Ready Mix Co ....E 269 751-5129
  Hamilton *(G-7598)*
Hanson Lehigh Inc ....F 989 233-5343
  Corunna *(G-3708)*
Hardcrete Inc ....G 989 644-5543
  Weidman *(G-18252)*
Hart Concrete LLC ....G 231 873-2183
  Spring Lake *(G-15821)*
High Grade Concrete Pdts Co ....F 616 842-8630
  Spring Lake *(G-15822)*
High Grade Materials Company ....G 616 554-8828
  Caledonia *(G-2380)*
High Grade Materials Company ....G 616 754-5545
  Greenville *(G-7492)*
High Grade Materials Company ....G 269 926-6900
  Benton Harbor *(G-1555)*
High Grade Materials Company ....G 269 349-8222
  Kalamazoo *(G-9218)*
High Grade Materials Company ....G 616 677-1271
  Grand Rapids *(G-6814)*
High Grade Materials Company ....G 517 374-1029
  Lansing *(G-9704)*
High Grade Materials Company ....G 989 365-3010
  Six Lakes *(G-15388)*
High Grade Materials Company ....G 616 696-9540
  Sand Lake *(G-15048)*
Huizenga & Sons Inc ....E 616 772-6241
  Zeeland *(G-19041)*
Imlay City Concrete Inc ....F 810 724-3905
  Imlay City *(G-8636)*
Jordan Valley Concrete Service ....F 231 536-7701
  East Jordan *(G-4873)*
Kens Redi Mix Inc ....F 810 687-6000
  Clio *(G-3402)*
Kens Redi Mix Inc ....G 810 636-2630
  Goodrich *(G-6224)*
Koenig Fuel & Supply Co ....G 313 368-1870
  Wayne *(G-18226)*
Kuhlman Corporation ....G 734 241-8692
  Monroe *(G-11554)*
Kurtz Gravel Company Inc ....E 810 787-6543
  Farmington Hills *(G-5286)*
L & S Transit Mix Concrete Co ....E 989 354-5363
  Alpena *(G-298)*
Lafarge North America Inc ....G 216 566-0545
  Essexville *(G-5117)*
Lafarge North America Inc ....G 703 480-3600
  Alpena *(G-4827)*
Lafarge North America Inc ....G 231 726-3291
  Muskegon *(G-11855)*
Lafarge North America Inc ....G 313 842-9258
  Detroit *(G-4375)*
Lafarghlcim Acm Nwco Tx-La LLC ....G 972 837-2462
  Dundee *(G-4828)*
Lakeside Building Products ....E 248 349-3500
  Detroit *(G-4376)*
Land Star Inc ....G 313 834-2366
  Detroit *(G-4377)*
Lattimore Material ....E 972 837-2462
  Dundee *(G-4829)*
Lc Materials LLC ....G 231 946-5600
  Cadillac *(G-2342)*
Lc Materials LLC ....C 817 835-4100
  Harbor Springs *(G-7649)*
Lc Materials LLC ....G 231 946-5600
  Bear Lake *(G-1418)*
Leelanau Redi-Mix Inc ....E 231 228-5005
  Maple City *(G-10943)*
Lees Ready Mix Inc ....G 989 734-7666
  Rogers City *(G-14211)*

Employee Codes: A=Over 500 employees, B=251-500
C=101-250, D=51-100, E=20-50, F=10-19, G=3-9

CONCRETE: Ready-Mixed

Little Bay Concrete Products .... G 906 428-9859
  Gladstone *(G-6183)*
Livingston County Concrete Inc ...... E 810 632-3030
  Brighton *(G-2022)*
M 37 Concrete Products Inc .... E 231 733-8247
  Muskegon *(G-11863)*
M 37 Concrete Products Inc .... G 231 689-1785
  White Cloud *(G-18446)*
Manistique Rentals Inc .... G 906 341-6955
  Manistique *(G-10921)*
Manthei Development Corp .... G 231 347-6282
  Petoskey *(G-13005)*
Massive Mineral Mix LLC .... G 517 857-4544
  Springport *(G-15883)*
Maxs Concrete Inc .... G 231 972-7558
  Mecosta *(G-11193)*
McCoig Materials LLC .... E 734 414-6179
  Plymouth *(G-13238)*
Meredith Lea Sand Gravel .... G 517 930-3662
  Charlotte *(G-2762)*
Messina Concrete Inc .... E 734 783-1020
  Flat Rock *(G-5623)*
Michigan Crushed Concrete Inc .... G 313 534-1500
  Detroit *(G-4448)*
Midway Group LLC .... F 586 264-5380
  Sterling Heights *(G-16099)*
Milford Redi-Mix Company .... E 248 684-1465
  Milford *(G-11472)*
Miller Sand & Gravel Company .... G 269 672-5601
  Hopkins *(G-8367)*
Millers Redi-Mix Inc .... E 989 587-6511
  Fowler *(G-5830)*
Mini-Mix Inc .... E 586 792-2260
  Clinton Township *(G-3302)*
Mirkwood Properties Inc .... G 586 727-3363
  Richmond *(G-13842)*
Mix Masters Inc .... G 616 490-8520
  Byron Center *(G-2287)*
Modern Industries Inc .... E 810 767-3330
  Flint *(G-5735)*
Morse Concrete & Excavating .... F 989 826-3975
  Mio *(G-11512)*
Mottes Materials Inc .... G 906 265-9955
  Iron River *(G-8749)*
Mt Pleasant Centl Con Pdts Co .... G 989 772-3695
  Mount Pleasant *(G-11721)*
National Block Company .... E 734 721-4050
  Westland *(G-18399)*
Newberry Redi-Mix Inc .... G 906 293-5178
  Newberry *(G-12097)*
Northfork Readi Mix Inc .... G 906 341-3445
  Manistique *(G-10922)*
Novi Crushed Concrete LLC .... G 248 305-6020
  Novi *(G-12493)*
Osborne Concrete Co .... G 734 941-3008
  Romulus *(G-14314)*
Osborne Materials Company .... E 906 493-5211
  Drummond Island *(G-4803)*
Owosso Ready Mix Co .... G 989 723-1295
  Owosso *(G-12850)*
Ozinga Bros Inc .... G 269 469-2515
  New Buffalo *(G-12025)*
P D P LLC .... E 616 437-9618
  Wyoming *(G-18898)*
Paragon Ready Mix Inc .... E 586 731-8000
  Shelby Township *(G-15295)*
Paragon Ready Mix Inc .... G 248 623-0100
  Waterford *(G-18147)*
Peterman Mobile Concrete Inc .... E 269 324-1211
  Portage *(G-13592)*
Piedmont Concrete Inc .... E 248 474-7740
  Farmington Hills *(G-5347)*
Port Huron Building Supply Co .... F 810 987-2666
  Port Huron *(G-13519)*
Quarrystone Inc .... E 906 786-0343
  Escanaba *(G-5093)*
R & C Redi-Mix Inc .... G 616 636-5650
  Sand Lake *(G-15051)*
R & R Ready-Mix Inc .... F 989 753-3862
  Saginaw *(G-14732)*
R & R Ready-Mix Inc .... G 989 892-9313
  Bay City *(G-1393)*
Rock Redi Mix LLC .... G 989 754-5861
  Saginaw *(G-14739)*
Rock Redi-Mix Inc .... G 989 752-0795
  Carrollton *(G-2589)*
Roger Mix Storage .... G 231 352-9762
  Frankfort *(G-5880)*
Rudy Goupille & Sons Inc .... G 906 475-9816
  Negaunee *(G-11974)*

Ruppe Manufacturing Company ...... E 906 932-3540
  Ironwood *(G-8771)*
Ruth Drain Tile Inc .... G 989 864-3406
  Ruth *(G-14598)*
Saginaw Rock Products Co .... F 989 754-6589
  Saginaw *(G-14751)*
Scheels Concrete Inc .... G 734 782-1464
  Livonia *(G-10401)*
Sebewaing Concrete Pdts Inc .... E 989 883-3860
  Sebewaing *(G-15143)*
Shafer Bros Inc .... F 517 629-4800
  Albion *(G-131)*
Shafer Redi-Mix Inc .... F 517 629-4800
  Albion *(G-132)*
Shafer Redi-Mix Inc .... D 517 764-0517
  Jackson *(G-9009)*
Srm Concrete LLC .... G 231 796-8685
  Big Rapids *(G-1688)*
Srm Concrete LLC .... G 989 422-4202
  Houghton Lake *(G-8404)*
Srm Concrete LLC .... D 231 943-4818
  Traverse City *(G-16839)*
Srm Concrete LLC .... G 231 775-9301
  Cadillac *(G-2357)*
Srm Concrete LLC .... F 231 258-8633
  Kalkaska *(G-9404)*
Srm Concrete LLC .... G 231 832-5460
  Reed City *(G-13799)*
Srm Concrete LLC .... G 989 344-0235
  Grayling *(G-7469)*
Stevenson Building and Sup Co ...... G 734 856-3931
  Lambertville *(G-9653)*
Superior Materials LLC .... D 248 788-8000
  Farmington Hills *(G-5394)*
Superior Materials LLC .... E 734 941-2479
  Romulus *(G-14332)*
Superior Materials Holdings .... G 586 468-3544
  Mount Clemens *(G-11658)*
Superior Materials Inc .... G 248 788-8000
  Farmington Hills *(G-5395)*
Superior Mtls Holdings LLC .... E 248 788-8000
  Farmington Hills *(G-5396)*
Swansons Excavating Inc .... G 989 873-4419
  Prescott *(G-13652)*
Swartzmiller Lumber Company .... G 989 845-6625
  Chesaning *(G-2830)*
The Mix .... G 269 382-1300
  Kalamazoo *(G-9354)*
Theut Concrete Products Inc .... F 810 679-3376
  Croswell *(G-3737)*
Theut Products Inc .... G 810 364-7132
  Marysville *(G-11106)*
Theut Products Inc .... G 810 765-9321
  Marine City *(G-10967)*
Theut Products Inc .... G 586 949-1300
  Chesterfield *(G-2955)*
Van Horn Bros Inc .... E 248 623-4830
  Waterford *(G-18172)*
Van Horn Bros Inc .... E 248 623-6000
  Waterford *(G-18173)*
Van Sloten Enterprises Inc .... F 906 635-5151
  Sault Sainte Marie *(G-15102)*
Vhb-123 Corporation .... G 248 623-4830
  Waterford *(G-18174)*
Vollmer Ready-Mix Inc .... G 989 453-2262
  Pigeon *(G-13042)*
Voorheis Hausbeck Excavating .... E 989 752-9666
  Reese *(G-13810)*
Waanders Concrete Co .... F 269 673-6352
  Allegan *(G-184)*
Westendorff Transit Mix .... G 989 593-2488
  Pewamo *(G-13029)*
Whats Your Mix Menchies LLC .... G 248 840-1668
  Shelby Township *(G-15368)*
Willbee Transit-Mix Co Inc .... E 517 782-9493
  Jackson *(G-9036)*
Williams Reddi Mix Inc .... G 906 875-6952
  Crystal Falls *(G-3747)*
Williams Redi Mix .... G 906 875-6839
  Crystal Falls *(G-3748)*
Winter .... G 734 699-6825
  Van Buren Twp *(G-17564)*

CONDENSERS & CONDENSING UNITS: Air Conditioner

Heat Controller LLC .... F 517 787-2100
  Jackson *(G-8901)*

CONDENSERS: Heat Transfer Eqpt, Evaporative

D & B Heat Transfer Pdts Inc .... F 616 827-0028
  Grand Rapids *(G-6625)*
Stahls Inc .... E 800 478-2457
  Saint Clair Shores *(G-14887)*

CONDENSERS: Motors Or Generators

Blissfield Manufacturing Co .... C 517 486-2121
  Blissfield *(G-1761)*

CONFECTIONERY PRDTS WHOLESALERS

Asao LLC .... F 734 522-6333
  Livonia *(G-10125)*
Happy Candy .... G 248 629-9819
  Warren *(G-17848)*
Renas Fudge Shops Inc .... F 586 293-0600
  Fraser *(G-5987)*

CONFECTIONS & CANDY

American Gourmet Snacks LLC .... G 989 892-4856
  Essexville *(G-5108)*
BS Bars .... G 734 358-3832
  Ann Arbor *(G-407)*
Emesa Foods Company LLC .... G 248 982-3908
  Taylor *(G-16413)*
Fretty Media LLC .... G 231 894-8055
  Whitehall *(G-18497)*
Gerbers Home Made Sweets .... G 231 348-3743
  Charlevoix *(G-2715)*
Happy Candy .... G 248 629-9819
  Warren *(G-17848)*
Kernel Bennys .... G 989 928-3950
  Frankenmuth *(G-5866)*
Klopp Group LLC .... G 877 256-4528
  Saginaw *(G-14679)*
Lotte USA Incorporated .... F 269 963-6664
  Battle Creek *(G-1269)*
Marshalls Trail Inc .... F 231 436-5082
  Mackinaw City *(G-10568)*
Morley Brands LLC .... E 586 468-4300
  Clinton Township *(G-3304)*
Northwest Confections Mich LLC .... E 971 666-8282
  Lapeer *(G-9950)*
Optisource LLC .... G 616 554-9048
  Comstock Park *(G-3631)*
Opus Products LLC .... G 586 202-1870
  Oakland Twp *(G-12653)*
Popped Kernel .... G 586 295-4977
  Shelby Township *(G-15306)*
Renas Fudge Shops Inc .... F 586 293-0600
  Fraser *(G-5987)*
Rocky Mtn Choclat Fctry Inc .... D 810 606-8550
  Grand Blanc *(G-6261)*
Sanders Candy LLC .... D 800 651-7263
  Clinton Township *(G-3349)*
Spagnuolo George & Sons .... G 810 229-4424
  Brighton *(G-2073)*
Sugar Free Specialties LLC .... F 616 734-6999
  Comstock Park *(G-3646)*
Sugar Sugar Cotton Candy Co .... G 248 847-0070
  Burton *(G-2247)*
W2 Inc .... G 517 764-3141
  Jackson *(G-9032)*

CONNECTORS & TERMINALS: Electrical Device Uses

American Pwr Cnnection Systems .... F 989 686-6302
  Bay City *(G-1321)*
Cardell Corporation .... D 248 371-9700
  Auburn Hills *(G-840)*
Emm Inc .... G 248 478-1182
  Farmington Hills *(G-5231)*
Sine Systems Corporation .... C 586 465-3131
  Clinton Township *(G-3359)*
Syndevco Inc .... F 248 356-2839
  Southfield *(G-15716)*
Teradyne Inc .... G 313 425-3900
  Allen Park *(G-208)*

CONNECTORS: Electrical

Erich Jaeger USA Inc .... G 734 404-5940
  Livonia *(G-10199)*
JST Sales America Inc .... F 248 324-1957
  Farmington Hills *(G-5276)*

PRODUCT SECTION

CONNECTORS: Electronic

Aees Power Systems Ltd Partnr .... G 269 668-4429
  Farmington Hills (G-5160)
Amphenol Corporation .... B 586 465-3131
  Clinton Township (G-3169)
Cardell Corporation .... D 248 371-9700
  Auburn Hills (G-840)
Hirschmann Auto N Amer LLC .... G 248 495-2677
  Rochester Hills (G-14033)
Iriso USA Inc .... E 248 324-9780
  Farmington Hills (G-5273)
Kostal Kontakt Systeme Inc .... C 248 284-7600
  Rochester Hills (G-14047)
Mac Lean-Fogg Company .... C 248 280-0880
  Royal Oak (G-14558)
Maclean Royal Oak LLC .... G 248 840-0880
  Farmington Hills (G-5298)
Midwest Sales Associates Inc .... G 248 348-9600
  Wixom (G-18710)
Norma Group Craig Assembly .... G 810 326-1374
  Saint Clair (G-14838)
Nvent Thermal LLC .... E 248 273-3359
  Troy (G-17284)
Rapp & Son Inc .... D 734 283-1000
  Wyandotte (G-18836)
Sine Systems Corporation .... C 586 465-3131
  Clinton Township (G-3359)
Teradyne Inc .... G 313 425-3900
  Allen Park (G-208)
Winford Engineering LLC .... G 989 671-9721
  Auburn (G-771)

CONNECTORS: Power, Electric

Power Controllers LLC .... G 248 888-9896
  Farmington Hills (G-5351)

CONSTRUCTION & MINING MACHINERY WHOLESALERS

Dimond Machinery Company Inc .... F 269 945-5908
  Hastings (G-7790)
Hitachi America Ltd .... G 248 477-5400
  Farmington Hills (G-5261)
Hutson Inc .... C 517 655-4606
  Williamston (G-18573)
Lappans of Gaylord Inc .... G 989 732-3274
  Gaylord (G-6142)
Magnum Toolscom LLC .... F 734 595-4600
  Romulus (G-14300)

CONSTRUCTION EQPT: Attachments

Ryans Equipment Inc .... E 989 427-2829
  Edmore (G-4997)

CONSTRUCTION: EQPT: Attachments, Backhoe Mounted, Hyd Pwrd

Lang Tool Company .... G 989 435-9864
  Beaverton (G-1428)

CONSTRUCTION EQPT: Attachments, Snow Plow

JG Distributing Inc .... G 906 225-0882
  Marquette (G-11025)
Jolman & Jolman Enterprises .... G 231 744-4500
  Muskegon (G-11848)
Kaufman Cstm Shtmtl Fbrction L .... G 906 932-2130
  Ironwood (G-8766)
Root Spring Scraper Co .... E 269 382-2025
  Kalamazoo (G-9321)
Rough Road Trucking LLC .... G 231 645-3455
  Kalkaska (G-9402)

CONSTRUCTION EQPT: Buckets, Excavating, Clamshell, Etc

John Crowley Inc .... F 517 782-0491
  Jackson (G-8922)
Lyonnais Inc .... G 616 868-6625
  Lowell (G-10510)

CONSTRUCTION EQPT: Cranes

Simpson Industrial Svcs LLC .... G 810 392-2717
  Wales (G-17630)
Terex Corporation .... G 360 993-0515
  Durand (G-4849)

Top of Line Crane Service LLC .... G 231 267-5326
  Williamsburg (G-18566)
Wmc Sales LLC .... G 616 813-7237
  Ada (G-42)

CONSTRUCTION EQPT: Finishers & Spreaders

Drag Finishing Tech LLC .... G 616 785-0400
  Comstock Park (G-3603)
East Coast Finishers .... E 844 366-9966
  Farmington Hills (G-5222)
Paladin Brands Group Inc .... F 319 378-3696
  Dexter (G-4748)

CONSTRUCTION EQPT: Grinders, Stone, Portable

ABI International .... F 248 583-7150
  Madison Heights (G-10656)

CONSTRUCTION EQPT: Mud Jacks

UNI-Vue Inc .... E 248 564-3251
  Ferndale (G-5593)

CONSTRUCTION EQPT: Roofing Eqpt

Golde Auburn Hills LLC .... D 248 606-1912
  Auburn Hills (G-916)

CONSTRUCTION EQPT: Subgraders

Zcs Interconnect LLC .... G 616 399-8614
  Zeeland (G-19094)

CONSTRUCTION EQPT: Tractors

Capital Equipment Clare LLC .... F 517 669-5533
  Dewitt (G-4708)

CONSTRUCTION EQPT: Wellpoint Systems

Big Foot Manufacturing Co .... E 231 775-5588
  Cadillac (G-2315)

CONSTRUCTION EQPT: Wrecker Hoists, Automobile

AME For Auto Dealers Inc .... G 248 720-0245
  Auburn Hills (G-780)

CONSTRUCTION MATERIALS, WHOL: Concrete/Cinder Bldg Prdts

M 37 Concrete Products Inc .... G 231 689-1785
  White Cloud (G-18446)

CONSTRUCTION MATERIALS, WHOLESALE: Aggregate

Edw C Levy Co .... B 313 429-2200
  Dearborn (G-3835)
Edw C Levy Co .... G 313 843-7200
  Detroit (G-4202)
Saginaw Rock Products Co .... F 989 754-6589
  Saginaw (G-14751)

CONSTRUCTION MATERIALS, WHOLESALE: Air Ducts, Sheet Metal

Conquest Manufacturing LLC .... D 586 576-7600
  Warren (G-17763)

CONSTRUCTION MATERIALS, WHOLESALE: Architectural Metalwork

R J Designers Inc .... G 517 750-1990
  Spring Arbor (G-15797)

CONSTRUCTION MATERIALS, WHOLESALE: Awnings

Wayne-Craft Inc .... F 734 421-8800
  Livonia (G-10468)

CONSTRUCTION MATERIALS, WHOLESALE: Block, Concrete & Cinder

C F Long & Sons Inc .... E 248 624-1562
  Walled Lake (G-17665)

Fisher Sand and Gravel Company .... E 989 835-7187
  Midland (G-11363)
Miller Products & Supply Co .... F 906 774-1243
  Iron Mountain (G-8725)
Theut Concrete Products Inc .... F 810 679-3376
  Croswell (G-3737)

CONSTRUCTION MATERIALS, WHOLESALE: Brick, Exc Refractory

Boomer Company .... E 313 832-5050
  Detroit (G-4063)

CONSTRUCTION MATERIALS, WHOLESALE: Building Stone

Genesee Cut Stone & Marble Co .... E 810 743-1800
  Grand Blanc (G-6242)

CONSTRUCTION MATERIALS, WHOLESALE: Building Stone, Granite

Granite City Inc .... F 248 478-0033
  Livonia (G-10228)
Yoxheimer Tile Co .... F 517 788-7542
  Jackson (G-9040)

CONSTRUCTION MATERIALS, WHOLESALE: Building Stone, Marble

Classic Stone MBL & Gran Inc .... F 248 588-1599
  Troy (G-17014)

CONSTRUCTION MATERIALS, WHOLESALE: Building, Exterior

Ufp International LLC .... F 770 472-3050
  Grand Rapids (G-7290)

CONSTRUCTION MATERIALS, WHOLESALE: Building, Interior

Reliable Glass Company .... E 313 924-9750
  Detroit (G-4562)

CONSTRUCTION MATERIALS, WHOLESALE: Cement

Holcim (us) Inc .... G 989 755-7515
  Saginaw (G-14667)
Lafarge North America Inc .... G 989 354-4171
  Alpena (G-299)
St Marys Cement Inc (us) .... G 269 679-5253
  Schoolcraft (G-15128)

CONSTRUCTION MATERIALS, WHOLESALE: Concrete Mixtures

Angelos Crushed Concrete Inc .... G 586 756-1070
  Warren (G-17706)
Gotts Transit Mix Inc .... F 734 439-1528
  Milan (G-11437)
Sandusky Concrete & Supply .... G 810 648-2627
  Sandusky (G-15066)

CONSTRUCTION MATERIALS, WHOLESALE: Glass

I2 International Dev LLC .... G 616 534-8100
  Grandville (G-7390)
Oldcastle Buildingenvelope Inc .... G 616 896-8341
  Burnips (G-2210)

CONSTRUCTION MATERIALS, WHOLESALE: Gravel

Bently Sand & Gravel .... G 810 629-6172
  Fenton (G-5458)
Consumers Concrete Corporation .... E 269 342-0136
  Kalamazoo (G-9153)
Consumers Concrete Corporation .... F 231 777-3981
  Muskegon (G-11795)
Parker Excvtg Grav & Recycle .... F 616 784-1681
  Comstock Park (G-3633)
Thomas J Moyle Jr Incorporated .... F 906 482-3000
  Houghton (G-8393)
White Lake Excavating Inc .... E 231 894-6918
  Whitehall (G-18513)

CONSTRUCTION MATERIALS, WHOLESALE: Insulation, Thermal

Marshall Ryerson Co .... F 616 299-1751
  Grand Rapids (G-6961)

CONSTRUCTION MATERIALS, WHOLESALE: Limestone

Atlas Cut Stone Inc .... G 248 545-5100
  Oak Park (G-12592)
Doug Wirt Enterprises Inc .... G 989 684-5777
  Bay City (G-1347)
O-N Minerals Michigan Company .... C 989 734-2131
  Rogers City (G-14215)

CONSTRUCTION MATERIALS, WHOLESALE: Millwork

D & D Building Inc .... F 616 248-7908
  Grand Rapids (G-6626)
W S Townsend Company .... C 269 781-5131
  Marshall (G-11078)

CONSTRUCTION MATERIALS, WHOLESALE: Pallets, Wood

Mobile Pallet Service Inc .... E 269 792-4200
  Wayland (G-18199)

CONSTRUCTION MATERIALS, WHOLESALE: Paving Materials

Falcon Trucking Company .... E 248 634-9471
  Davisburg (G-3768)

CONSTRUCTION MATERIALS, WHOLESALE: Prefabricated Structures

Jensen Bridge & Supply Company .... E 810 648-3000
  Sandusky (G-15062)
K-Tel Corporation .... F 517 543-6174
  Charlotte (G-2760)
Morton Buildings Inc .... G 616 696-4747
  Three Rivers (G-16579)
Sulugu Corporation USA Inc .... D 478 714-0325
  Grand Rapids (G-7232)

CONSTRUCTION MATERIALS, WHOLESALE: Roof, Asphalt/Sheet Metal

Howard Structural Steel Inc .... E 989 752-3000
  Saginaw (G-14670)

CONSTRUCTION MATERIALS, WHOLESALE: Roofing & Siding Material

Caliber Metals Inc .... E 586 465-7650
  New Baltimore (G-11979)

CONSTRUCTION MATERIALS, WHOLESALE: Sand

American Aggregate Inc .... G 269 683-6160
  Niles (G-12110)
Brewers City Dock Inc .... E 616 396-6563
  Holland (G-7983)

CONSTRUCTION MATERIALS, WHOLESALE: Septic Tanks

Jack Millikin Inc .... G 989 348-8411
  Grayling (G-7464)

CONSTRUCTION MATERIALS, WHOLESALE: Sewer Pipe, Clay

Northern Concrete Pipe Inc .... G 517 645-2777
  Charlotte (G-2763)

CONSTRUCTION MATERIALS, WHOLESALE: Siding, Exc Wood

Astro Building Products Inc .... G 231 941-0324
  Traverse City (G-16604)

CONSTRUCTION MATERIALS, WHOLESALE: Stone, Crushed Or Broken

Bichler Gravel & Concrete Co .... F 906 786-0343
  Escanaba (G-5062)

CONSTRUCTION MATERIALS, WHOLESALE: Windows

Double Otis Inc .... E 616 878-3998
  Grand Rapids (G-6656)
EZ Vent LLC .... G 616 874-2787
  Rockford (G-14167)
MRM Ida Products Co Inc .... G 313 834-0200
  Detroit (G-4470)
Pete Pullum Company Inc .... G 313 837-9440
  Detroit (G-4521)

CONSTRUCTION MATLS, WHOL: Lumber, Rough, Dressed/Finished

Banks Hardwoods Inc .... D 269 483-2323
  White Pigeon (G-18472)
Breiten Box & Packaging Co Inc .... G 586 469-0800
  Harrison Township (G-7690)
Component Solutions LLC .... E 906 863-2682
  Menominee (G-11230)
Daniel D Slater .... G 989 833-7135
  Riverdale (G-13863)
General Hardwood Company .... F 313 365-7733
  Detroit (G-4253)
L & M Hardwood & Skids LLC .... G 734 281-3043
  Southgate (G-15752)
Maine Ornamental LLC .... F 800 556-8449
  White Pigeon (G-18482)
North American Forest Products .... C 269 663-8500
  Edwardsburg (G-5013)
Novo Distribution LLC .... B 616 772-7272
  Zeeland (G-19061)
Rare Earth Hardwoods Inc .... E 231 946-0043
  Traverse City (G-16817)
Rothig Forest Products Inc .... F 231 266-8292
  Irons (G-8757)
Schleben Forest Products Inc .... G 989 734-2858
  Rogers City (G-14218)
William S Wixtrom 906 376-8247
  Republic (G-13821)

CONSTRUCTION MATLS, WHOLESALE: Struct Assy, Prefab, NonWood

Reliable Glass Company .... E 313 924-9750
  Detroit (G-4562)

CONSTRUCTION SAND MINING

Bdk Group Northern Mich Inc .... F 574 875-5183
  Charlevoix (G-2711)
Bunting Sand & Gravel Products .... E 989 345-2373
  West Branch (G-18327)
Cliffs Sand & Gravel Inc .... G 989 422-3463
  Houghton Lake (G-8396)
Crandell Bros Trucking Co .... E 517 543-2930
  Charlotte (G-2747)
Fuoss Gravel Company .... F 989 725-2084
  Owosso (G-12834)
Halliday Sand & Gravel Inc .... E 989 422-3463
  Houghton Lake (G-8397)
Kasson Sand & Gravel Co Inc .... F 231 228-5455
  Maple City (G-10942)
Natural Aggregates Corporation .... F 248 685-1502
  Milford (G-11476)
R H Huhtala Aggregates Inc .... G 906 524-7758
  Lanse (G-9668)
Ruppe Manufacturing Company .... E 906 932-3540
  Ironwood (G-8771)
Sandman Inc .... G 248 652-3432
  Troy (G-17343)
Southwest Gravel Inc .... G 269 673-4665
  Allegan (G-182)

CONSTRUCTION SITE PREPARATION SVCS

St Charles Hardwood Michigan .... F 989 865-9299
  Saint Charles (G-14809)

CONSTRUCTION: Agricultural Building

Lumber & Truss Inc .... F 810 664-7290
  Lapeer (G-9945)

Sulugu Corporation USA Inc .... D 478 714-0325
  Grand Rapids (G-7232)

CONSTRUCTION: Apartment Building

Kearsley Lake Terrace LLC .... G 810 736-7000
  Flint (G-5720)

CONSTRUCTION: Athletic & Recreation Facilities

Spartan Barricading .... G 313 292-2488
  Romulus (G-14330)
Systems Design & Installation .... G 269 543-4204
  Fennville (G-5442)

CONSTRUCTION: Commercial & Institutional Building

Buckeys Contracting & Service .... G 989 835-9512
  Midland (G-11325)
Clean Air Technology Inc .... E 734 459-6320
  Canton (G-2450)
Jn Newman Construction LLC .... G 269 968-1290
  Springfield (G-15870)
Keeler-Glasgow Company Inc .... F 269 621-2415
  Hartford (G-7764)
Michigan Indus Met Pdts Inc .... F 616 786-3922
  Muskegon (G-11870)
Sandbox Solutions Inc .... C 248 349-7010
  Northville (G-12257)

CONSTRUCTION: Commercial & Office Building, New

Architectural Planners Inc .... E 248 674-1340
  Waterford (G-18101)
Dumas Concepts In Building Inc .... F 313 895-2555
  Detroit (G-4196)
Metter Flooring LLC .... G 517 914-2004
  Rives Junction (G-13887)
RB Construction Company .... E 586 264-9478
  Mount Clemens (G-11655)
Thomas J Moyle Jr Incorporated .... F 906 482-3000
  Houghton (G-8393)

CONSTRUCTION: Electric Power Line

A1 Utility Contractor Inc .... D 989 324-8581
  Evart (G-5118)

CONSTRUCTION: Farm Building

Pioneer Pole Buildings N Inc .... F 989 386-2570
  Clare (G-2994)

CONSTRUCTION: Food Prdts Manufacturing or Packing Plant

Genstone LLC .... G 517 902-4730
  Adrian (G-70)
Michigan Herbal Remedies LLC .... G 616 818-0823
  Jenison (G-9062)

CONSTRUCTION: Heavy

Great Lakes Right of Way LLC .... G 616 263-9898
  Cedar Springs (G-2652)

CONSTRUCTION: Heavy Highway & Street

A Lindberg & Sons Inc .... E 906 485-5705
  Ishpeming (G-8774)
D J McQuestion & Sons Inc .... F 231 768-4403
  Leroy (G-10005)
Michigan Paving and Mtls Co .... E 734 485-1717
  Van Buren Twp (G-17539)

CONSTRUCTION: Indl Building & Warehouse

Dcr Services & Cnstr Inc .... F 313 297-6544
  Detroit (G-4123)
Elevated Technologies Inc .... E 616 288-9817
  Grand Rapids (G-6672)
Emhart Teknologies LLC .... D 248 677-9693
  Troy (G-17087)

CONSTRUCTION: Indl Buildings, New, NEC

K & M Industrial LLC .... G 906 420-8770
  Gladstone (G-6182)
Michigan Paving and Mtls Co .... E 734 397-2050
  Canton (G-2496)

PRODUCT SECTION

CONSTRUCTION: Institutional Building
Rock Industries Inc ....E...... 248 338-2800
  Bloomfield Hills (G-1858)

CONSTRUCTION: Natural Gas Compressor Station
Lgc Global Energy Fm Llc ....G...... 313 989-4141
  Detroit (G-4396)

CONSTRUCTION: Nonresidential Buildings, Custom
IKEA Chip LLC ....G...... 877 218-9931
  Troy (G-17160)

CONSTRUCTION: Parade Float
Prop Art Studio Inc ....G...... 313 824-2200
  Detroit (G-4539)

CONSTRUCTION: Parking Lot
Woodland Paving Co ....E...... 616 784-5220
  Comstock Park (G-3652)

CONSTRUCTION: Pipeline, NEC
Great Lakes Right of Way LLC ....G...... 616 263-9898
  Cedar Springs (G-2652)
Mid Michigan Pipe Inc ....G...... 989 772-5664
  Grand Rapids (G-7003)

CONSTRUCTION: Railroad & Subway
Delta Tube & Fabricating Corp ....C...... 248 634-8267
  Holly (G-8268)
Plymouth Technology Inc ....F...... 248 537-0081
  Rochester Hills (G-14086)

CONSTRUCTION: Refineries
URS Energy & Construction Inc ....C...... 989 642-4190
  Hemlock (G-7857)

CONSTRUCTION: Residential, Nec
Buster Mathis Foundation ....G...... 616 843-4433
  Wyoming (G-18855)
Jn Newman Construction LLC ....G...... 269 968-1290
  Springfield (G-15870)
Michigan Paving and Mtls Co ....E...... 734 397-2050
  Canton (G-2496)
Top Shelf Painter Inc ....F...... 586 465-0867
  Fraser (G-6004)

CONSTRUCTION: Roads, Gravel or Dirt
Great Lakes Right of Way LLC ....G...... 616 263-9898
  Cedar Springs (G-2652)
White Lake Excavating Inc ....E...... 231 894-6918
  Whitehall (G-18513)

CONSTRUCTION: Sewer Line
Bdk Group Northern Mich Inc ....F...... 574 875-5183
  Charlevoix (G-2711)

CONSTRUCTION: Silo, Agricultural
Michigan AG Services Inc ....F...... 616 374-8803
  Lake Odessa (G-9577)

CONSTRUCTION: Single-Family Housing
Debbink and Sons Inc ....G...... 231 845-6421
  Ludington (G-10533)
G B Wolfgram and Sons Inc ....F...... 231 238-4638
  Indian River (G-8652)
Great Lakes Woodworking LLC ....E...... 248 550-1991
  Orion (G-12732)
Jn Newman Construction LLC ....G...... 269 968-1290
  Springfield (G-15870)
Midwest Panel Systems Inc ....F...... 517 486-4844
  Blissfield (G-1770)
P C S Companies Inc ....G...... 616 754-2229
  Greenville (G-7504)
R5 Construxtion Inc ....F...... 855 480-7663
  Middleville (G-11311)
Red Carpet Capital Inc ....G...... 248 952-8583
  Orchard Lake (G-12719)
Riverbend Timber Framing Inc ....E...... 517 486-3629
  Blissfield (G-1776)

CONSTRUCTION: Single-family Housing, New
Burly Oak Builders Inc ....G...... 734 368-4912
  Dexter (G-4730)
Champion Home Builders Inc ....D...... 248 614-8200
  Troy (G-17007)
Harman Lumber & Supply Inc ....G...... 269 641-5424
  Union (G-17488)
Koskis Log Homes Inc ....G...... 906 884-4937
  Ontonagon (G-12713)
Maple Island Log Homes Inc ....D...... 231 821-2151
  Twin Lake (G-17470)
Thomas J Moyle Jr Incorporated ....F...... 906 482-3000
  Houghton (G-8393)
Woodtech Builders Inc ....F...... 906 932-8055
  Ironwood (G-8773)

CONSTRUCTION: Single-family Housing, Prefabricated
North Arrow Log Homes Inc ....G...... 906 484-5524
  Pickford (G-13031)

CONSTRUCTION: Street Surfacing & Paving
Asphalt Paving Inc ....E...... 231 733-1409
  Muskegon (G-11773)
D O W Asphalt Paving LLC ....G...... 810 743-2633
  Swartz Creek (G-16352)
Hd Selcating Pav Solutions LLC ....G...... 248 241-6526
  Clarkston (G-3038)
Nagle Paving Company ....F...... 248 553-0600
  Novi (G-12486)
Rieth-Riley Cnstr Co Inc ....F...... 231 263-2100
  Grawn (G-7453)
Rieth-Riley Cnstr Co Inc ....F...... 616 248-0920
  Wyoming (G-18904)
RWS & Associates LLC ....E...... 517 278-3134
  Coldwater (G-3451)
Woodland Paving Co ....E...... 616 784-5220
  Comstock Park (G-3652)

CONSTRUCTION: Swimming Pools
Solar EZ Inc ....F...... 989 773-3347
  Mount Pleasant (G-11741)

CONSTRUCTION: Telephone & Communication Line
Best Netwrk Design & Assoc LLC ....E...... 313 680-2047
  Detroit (G-4052)

CONSTRUCTION: Truck & Automobile Assembly Plant
Autocam Corporation ....B...... 616 698-0707
  Kentwood (G-9444)

CONSTRUCTION: Utility Line
Forbes Sanitation & Excavation ....F...... 231 723-2311
  Manistee (G-10900)
Genoak Materials Inc ....C...... 248 634-8276
  Holly (G-8273)
Lgc Global Inc ....E...... 313 989-4141
  Detroit (G-4395)
Veterans Utility Services LLC ....D...... 888 878-4191
  Lansing (G-9901)

CONSTRUCTION: Waste Water & Sewage Treatment Plant
Digested Organics LLC ....G...... 844 934-4378
  Farmington Hills (G-5218)
Recovere LLC ....G...... 269 370-3165
  Plainwell (G-13092)

CONSTRUCTION: Water Main
A Lindberg & Sons Inc ....E...... 906 485-5705
  Ishpeming (G-8774)

CONSULTING SVC: Business, NEC
ADS LLC ....G...... 248 740-9593
  Troy (G-16906)
Alfa Financial Software Inc ....D...... 855 680-7100
  Birmingham (G-1717)
Autoneum North America Inc ....G...... 248 848-0100
  Farmington Hills (G-5176)

CONSULTING SVC: Engineering
Dcr Services & Cnstr Inc ....F...... 313 297-6544
  Detroit (G-4123)
Duscha Management LLC ....F...... 352 247-2113
  Luna Pier (G-10560)
Ernie Romanco ....G...... 517 531-3686
  Albion (G-125)
Global Impact Group LLC ....G...... 248 895-9900
  Grand Blanc (G-6243)
GT Solutions LLC ....G...... 616 259-0700
  Holland (G-8062)
IKEA Chip LLC ....G...... 877 218-9931
  Troy (G-17160)
Innovative Weld Solutions LLC ....G...... 937 545-7695
  Rochester (G-13908)
Kage Group LLC ....G...... 734 604-5052
  Van Buren Twp (G-17532)
Pioneer Automotive Inc ....F...... 586 758-7730
  Sterling Heights (G-16127)
Regency Construction Corp ....E...... 586 741-8000
  Clinton Township (G-3334)
Reply Inc ....C...... 248 686-2481
  Auburn Hills (G-1018)
Steelcase Inc ....A...... 616 247-2710
  Grand Rapids (G-7224)
Visual Productions Inc ....D...... 248 356-4399
  Mesick (G-11275)
Welding & Joining Tech LLC ....G...... 734 926-9353
  Clarkston (G-3076)
Wyser Innovative Products LLC ....G...... 616 583-9225
  Byron Center (G-2304)

CONSULTING SVC: Chemical
V & V Industries Inc ....F...... 248 624-7943
  Wixom (G-18783)

CONSULTING SVC: Computer
3r Info LLC ....G...... 201 221-6133
  Canton (G-2425)
Aperion Information Tech Inc ....F...... 248 969-9791
  Oxford (G-12874)
Arbortext Inc ....C...... 734 997-0200
  Ann Arbor (G-378)
Brenton Consulting LLC ....G...... 248 342-6590
  Northville (G-12198)
Chain-Sys Corporation ....G...... 517 627-1173
  Lansing (G-9757)
Competitive Cmpt Info Tech Inc ....F...... 732 829-9699
  Northville (G-12201)
E-Con LLC ....G...... 248 766-9000
  Birmingham (G-1725)
Intellibee Inc ....E...... 313 586-4122
  Detroit (G-4323)
Novastar Solutionscom LLC ....D...... 734 453-8003
  Livonia (G-10340)
Rose Mobile Computer Repr LLC ....F...... 248 653-0865
  Bloomfield Hills (G-1859)
Signalx Technologies LLC ....E...... 248 935-4237
  Plymouth (G-13298)
Simerics Inc ....G...... 248 513-3200
  Novi (G-12538)
Software Advantage Consulting ....G...... 586 264-5632
  Sterling Heights (G-16181)
Spiders Software Solutions LLC ....G...... 248 305-3225
  Northville (G-12262)
Strategic Computer Solutions ....G...... 248 888-0666
  Ann Arbor (G-667)
Sunera Technologies Inc ....A...... 248 434-0808
  Troy (G-17376)
Torenzo Inc ....F...... 313 732-7874
  Bloomfield Hills (G-1866)
Tru-Syzygy Inc ....G...... 248 622-7211
  Lake Orion (G-9635)
V2soft Inc ....D...... 248 904-1702
  Bloomfield Hills (G-1872)

CONSULTING SVC: Data Processing
Tecra Systems Inc ....F...... 248 888-1116
  Westland (G-18420)

CONSULTING SVC: Educational
Esl Supplies LLC ....G...... 517 525-7877
  Mason (G-11131)
Quirkroberts Publishing Ltd ....G...... 248 879-2598
  Troy (G-17326)

CONSULTING SVC: Engineering
Amerivet Engineering LLC ....G...... 269 751-9092
  Hamilton (G-7596)

Employee Codes: A=Over 500 employees, B=251-500
C=101-250, D=51-100, E=20-50, F=10-19, G=3-9

CONSULTING SVC: Engineering

Arboc Ltd .... G 248 684-2895
  Commerce Township *(G-3511)*
Binsfeld Engineering Inc .... G 231 334-4383
  Maple City *(G-10940)*
Classic Systems LLC .... C 248 588-2738
  Troy *(G-17015)*
Commonwealth Associates Inc .... C 517 788-3000
  Jackson *(G-8849)*
Data Acquisition Ctrl Systems .... F 248 437-6096
  Brighton *(G-1973)*
Dynamic Corporation .... F 616 399-2200
  Holland *(G-8018)*
Elite Engineering Inc .... E 517 304-3254
  Rochester Hills *(G-14003)*
Experienced Concepts Inc .... F 586 752-4200
  Armada *(G-735)*
GM Gdls Defense Group LLC .... D 586 825-4000
  Sterling Heights *(G-16031)*
Illumination Machines LLC .... G 856 685-7403
  Rochester Hills *(G-14038)*
Jax Services LLC .... G 586 703-3212
  Warren *(G-17883)*
John Lamantia Corporation .... G 269 428-8100
  Stevensville *(G-16255)*
Kubica Corp .... F 248 344-7750
  Novi *(G-12459)*
Lotus International Company .... A 734 245-0140
  Canton *(G-2486)*
Lube - Power Inc .... D 586 247-6500
  Shelby Township *(G-15264)*
Lubrizol Corporation .... G 989 496-3780
  Midland *(G-11385)*
Maness Petroleum Corp .... G 989 773-5475
  Mount Pleasant *(G-11709)*
Mejenta Systems Inc .... E 248 434-2583
  Southfield *(G-15653)*
Minth North America Inc .... D 248 259-7468
  Wixom *(G-18712)*
Piping Components Inc .... G 313 382-6400
  Melvindale *(G-11209)*
Process Partners Inc .... G 616 875-2156
  Hudsonville *(G-8602)*
Quality Engineering Company .... F 248 351-9000
  Wixom *(G-18738)*
Roush Enterprises Inc .... C 734 805-4400
  Farmington *(G-5145)*
Secord Solutions LLC .... G 734 363-8887
  Ecorse *(G-4985)*
Spen-Tech Machine Engrg Corp .... D 810 275-6800
  Flint *(G-5765)*
Superior Controls Inc .... C 734 454-0500
  Plymouth *(G-13306)*
T E Technology Inc .... E 231 929-3966
  Traverse City *(G-16849)*
Varatech Inc .... F 616 393-6408
  Holland *(G-8234)*
Venntis Technologies LLC .... F 616 395-8254
  Holland *(G-8236)*
W G Benjey Inc .... F 989 356-0016
  Alpena *(G-327)*

CONSULTING SVC: Financial Management

Cygnet Financial Planning Inc .... G 248 673-2900
  Waterford *(G-18112)*

CONSULTING SVC: Human Resource

Tequionbrookins LLC .... G 313 290-0303
  Southfield *(G-15721)*

CONSULTING SVC: Management

American Information Services .... F 248 399-4848
  Berkley *(G-1620)*
Bpc Acquisition Company .... C 231 798-1310
  Norton Shores *(G-12345)*
Cardinal Group Industries Corp .... F 517 437-6000
  Hillsdale *(G-7929)*
Christian Schools Intl .... E 616 957-1070
  Grandville *(G-7369)*
Complete Services LLC .... F 248 470-8247
  Livonia *(G-10161)*
Duscha Management LLC .... F 352 247-2113
  Luna Pier *(G-10560)*
Ervins Group LLC .... E 248 203-2000
  Bloomfield Hills *(G-1819)*
FTC LLC .... F 313 622-1583
  Novi *(G-12420)*
Horizon Intl Group LLC .... G 734 341-9336
  Birmingham *(G-1730)*

Lowry Holding Company Inc .... C 810 229-7200
  Brighton *(G-2023)*
Mendenhall Associates Inc .... G 734 741-4710
  Ann Arbor *(G-569)*
Pioneer Automotive Inc .... F 586 758-7730
  Sterling Heights *(G-16127)*
Pti Qlity Cntnment Sltions LLC .... C 313 365-3999
  Detroit *(G-4541)*
Sika Corporation .... D 248 577-0020
  Madison Heights *(G-10829)*
Systrand Manufacturing Corp .... C 734 479-8100
  Brownstown Twp *(G-2159)*
Toyo Seat USA Corporation .... C 810 724-0300
  Imlay City *(G-8648)*
V2soft Inc .... D 248 904-1702
  Bloomfield Hills *(G-1872)*
Verdoni Productions Inc .... G 989 790-0845
  Saginaw *(G-14790)*

CONSULTING SVC: Marketing Management

Adair Printing Company .... E 734 426-2822
  Dexter *(G-4721)*
Arbor Press LLC .... D 248 549-0150
  Royal Oak *(G-14510)*
Blue Pony LLC .... G 616 291-5554
  Hudsonville *(G-8572)*
Contemporary Industries Inc .... G 248 478-8850
  Farmington Hills *(G-5208)*
D Find Corporation .... G 248 641-2858
  Troy *(G-17043)*
Elm International Inc .... G 517 332-4900
  Okemos *(G-12665)*
Facet Business Communications .... F 248 912-0800
  Novi *(G-12415)*
Fusion Design Group Ltd .... G 269 469-8226
  New Buffalo *(G-12023)*
Graphic Resource Group Inc .... E 248 588-6100
  Troy *(G-17132)*
High Impact Solutions Inc .... G 248 473-9804
  Farmington Hills *(G-5260)*
Marshall Ryerson Co .... F 616 299-1751
  Grand Rapids *(G-6961)*
Menu Pulse Inc .... G 989 708-1207
  Saginaw *(G-14695)*
Nb Media Solutions LLC .... G 616 724-7175
  Grand Rapids *(G-7037)*
New Rules Marketing Inc .... E 800 962-3119
  Spring Lake *(G-15839)*
Phoenix Press Incorporated .... E 248 435-8040
  Troy *(G-17300)*
Rtr Alpha Inc .... F 248 377-4060
  Auburn Hills *(G-1023)*
Sage Direct Inc .... F 616 940-8311
  Grand Rapids *(G-7178)*
Solutionsnowbiz .... G 269 321-5062
  Portage *(G-13609)*
State News Inc .... D 517 295-1680
  East Lansing *(G-4909)*
Technova Corporation .... G 517 485-1402
  Okemos *(G-12690)*
Waterloo Group Inc .... G 248 840-6447
  Troy *(G-17445)*
Wholesale Proc Systems LLC .... G 833 755-6696
  Adrian *(G-104)*

CONSULTING SVC: Online Technology

Best Netwrk Design & Assoc LLC .... E 313 680-2047
  Detroit *(G-4052)*
Ginkgotree Inc .... G 734 707-7191
  Detroit *(G-4262)*
Lowery Corporation .... C 616 554-5200
  Grand Rapids *(G-6949)*
Nb Media Solutions LLC .... G 616 724-7175
  Grand Rapids *(G-7037)*
Peckham Vocational Inds Inc .... A 517 316-4000
  Lansing *(G-9724)*
Repairers of The Brach Mskegon .... F 231 375-0990
  Muskegon *(G-11908)*
Tequionbrookins LLC .... G 313 290-0303
  Southfield *(G-15721)*
Touch World Inc .... E 248 539-3700
  Farmington Hills *(G-5404)*

CONSULTING SVC: Productivity Improvement

Link Tech Inc .... G 269 427-8297
  Bangor *(G-1129)*
Quality Engineering Company .... F 248 351-9000
  Wixom *(G-18738)*

PRODUCT SECTION

CONSULTING SVC: Sales Management

Considine Sales & Marketing .... G 248 889-7887
  Highland *(G-7889)*
Emhart Teknologies LLC .... D 248 677-9693
  Troy *(G-17087)*

CONSULTING SVC: Telecommunications

No Limit Wireless-Michigan Inc .... G 313 285-8402
  Detroit *(G-4487)*

CONSULTING SVCS, BUSINESS: Communications

Blue Pony LLC .... G 616 291-5554
  Hudsonville *(G-8572)*
Forum and Link Inc .... G 313 945-5465
  Dearborn *(G-3845)*

CONSULTING SVCS, BUSINESS: Environmental

Baygeo Inc .... E 231 941-7660
  Traverse City *(G-16617)*
Lgc Global Inc .... E 313 989-4141
  Detroit *(G-4395)*

CONSULTING SVCS, BUSINESS: Safety Training Svcs

Versant Med Physics Rdtion SFE .... E 888 316-3644
  Kalamazoo *(G-9361)*

CONSULTING SVCS, BUSINESS: Sys Engnrg, Exc Computer/Prof

Access Technologies LLC .... G 574 286-1255
  Niles *(G-12109)*
Braiq Inc .... G 858 729-4116
  Detroit *(G-4066)*
Secord Solutions LLC .... G 734 363-8887
  Ecorse *(G-4985)*

CONSULTING SVCS, BUSINESS: Systems Analysis & Engineering

Apis North America LLC .... G 800 470-8970
  Royal Oak *(G-14509)*
Atos Syntel Inc .... A 248 619-2800
  Troy *(G-16964)*
Beet Inc .... F 248 432-0052
  Troy *(G-16971)*
Inora Technologies Inc .... G 734 302-7488
  Ann Arbor *(G-529)*
Light Speed Usa LLC .... A 616 308-0054
  Grand Rapids *(G-6943)*
Major One Electronics LLC .... G 313 652-3723
  Detroit *(G-4418)*
Pioneer Technologies Corp .... G 702 806-3152
  Fremont *(G-6054)*
Precision Laser & Mfg LLC .... G 519 733-8422
  Sterling Heights *(G-16131)*
Torenzo Inc .... F 313 732-7874
  Bloomfield Hills *(G-1866)*

CONSULTING SVCS, BUSINESS: Systems Analysis Or Design

National Element Inc .... E 248 486-1810
  Brighton *(G-2040)*
Specilty Vhcl Acquisition Corp .... D 586 446-4701
  Warren *(G-18018)*
Stonebrdge Technical Entps Ltd .... F 810 750-0040
  Fenton *(G-5505)*

CONSULTING SVCS, BUSINESS: Test Development & Evaluation

Tectum Holdings Inc .... D 734 926-2362
  Ann Arbor *(G-674)*

CONSULTING SVCS: Oil

Wellmaster Consulting Inc .... F 231 893-9266
  Rothbury *(G-14499)*

CONSULTING SVCS: Scientific

Consoldted Rsource Imaging LLC .... E 616 735-2080
  Grand Rapids *(G-6595)*

PRODUCT SECTION

CONTRACTORS: Asphalt

Light Speed Usa LLC .... A 616 308-0054
 Grand Rapids *(G-6943)*
Welding & Joining Tech LLC .... G 734 926-9353
 Clarkston *(G-3076)*

CONSUMER PURCHASING SVCS

Genstone LLC .... G 517 902-4730
 Adrian *(G-70)*

CONTACT LENSES

Art Optical Contact Lens Inc .... C 616 453-1888
 Grand Rapids *(G-6471)*

CONTAINERS, GLASS: Cosmetic Jars

Amcor Phrm Packg USA LLC .... C 734 428-9741
 Ann Arbor *(G-363)*

CONTAINERS: Air Cargo, Metal

American Fabricated Pdts Inc .... E 616 607-8785
 Spring Lake *(G-15803)*
Lock and Load Corp .... G 800 975-9658
 Marion *(G-10973)*

CONTAINERS: Cargo, Wood

Grand Industries Inc .... E 616 846-7120
 Grand Haven *(G-6307)*

CONTAINERS: Cargo, Wood & Metal Combination

Karjo Trucking Inc .... F 248 597-3700
 Troy *(G-17192)*
Lock and Load Corp .... G 800 975-9658
 Marion *(G-10973)*

CONTAINERS: Cargo, Wood & Wood With Metal

Just Cover It Up .... G 734 247-4729
 Romulus *(G-14293)*
Tamsco Inc .... E 586 415-1500
 Clinton Township *(G-3372)*

CONTAINERS: Corrugated

Aldez North America .... F 586 530-5314
 Clinton Township *(G-3161)*
Arvco Container Corporation .... E 269 381-0900
 Kalamazoo *(G-9126)*
Classic Container Corporation .... C 734 853-3000
 Livonia *(G-10159)*
Complete Packaging Inc .... D 734 241-2794
 Monroe *(G-11534)*
D T Fowler Mfg Co Inc .... G 810 245-9336
 Lapeer *(G-9925)*
Eco Paper .... G 248 652-3601
 Rochester Hills *(G-13999)*
Gdc Worldwide .... G 248 348-4189
 Northville *(G-12223)*
Genesee Group Inc .... E 810 235-6120
 Flint *(G-5707)*
Lepages 2000 Inc .... G 416 357-0041
 Melvindale *(G-11203)*
MRC Industries Inc .... E 269 343-0747
 Kalamazoo *(G-9278)*
Msr-Pallets & Packaging LLC .... G 810 360-0425
 Brighton *(G-2036)*
National Packaging Corporation .... F 248 652-3600
 Rochester Hills *(G-14068)*
Scotts Enterprises Inc .... F 989 275-5011
 Roscommon *(G-14356)*
Understated Corrugated LLC .... G 248 880-5767
 Northville *(G-12268)*
US Gbc Wm .... G 616 691-1340
 Greenville *(G-7509)*

CONTAINERS: Metal

Actron Steel Inc .... E 231 947-3981
 Traverse City *(G-16597)*
Advance Packaging Corporation .... C 616 949-6610
 Grand Rapids *(G-6433)*
Associated Metals Inc .... G 734 369-3851
 Ann Arbor *(G-384)*
Chemtool Incorporated .... G 734 439-7010
 Milan *(G-11432)*
Delta Tube & Fabricating Corp .... C 248 634-8267
 Holly *(G-8268)*

Geerpres Inc .... E 231 773-3211
 Muskegon *(G-11823)*
Georgia-Pacific LLC .... G 734 439-2441
 Milan *(G-11436)*
Georgia-Pacific LLC .... G 989 725-5191
 Owosso *(G-12835)*
Green Bay Packaging Inc .... C 269 552-1000
 Kalamazoo *(G-9202)*
Quiktap LLC .... G 855 784-5827
 Grand Rapids *(G-7132)*
Repair Industries Michigan Inc .... G 313 365-5300
 Detroit *(G-4568)*
Royal ARC Welding Company .... E 734 789-9099
 Flat Rock *(G-5628)*
Zayna LLC .... G 616 452-4522
 Grand Rapids *(G-7356)*

CONTAINERS: Plastic

Advanced Fibermolding Inc .... E 231 768-5177
 Leroy *(G-10004)*
Amcor Rigid Packaging Usa LLC .... D 734 428-9741
 Manchester *(G-10880)*
Dart Container Corporation .... G 517 327-0613
 Lansing *(G-9684)*
Dart Container Corporation .... G 517 676-3800
 Mason *(G-11125)*
Decade Products LLC .... F 616 975-4965
 Grand Rapids *(G-6637)*
Eliason Corporation .... D 269 327-7003
 Portage *(G-13557)*
Elkhart Plastics LLC .... E 269 464-4107
 White Pigeon *(G-18476)*
Genova-Minnesota Inc .... D 810 744-4500
 Davison *(G-3784)*
Global Enterprise Limited .... G 586 948-4100
 Chesterfield *(G-2888)*
Global Mfg & Assembly Corp .... E 517 789-8116
 Jackson *(G-8892)*
Hold It Products Corporation .... G 248 624-1195
 Commerce Township *(G-3538)*
Jsj Corporation .... G 231 873-3300
 Hart *(G-7756)*
Kautex Inc .... B 313 633-2254
 Detroit *(G-4354)*
Kent City Plastics LLC .... F 616 678-4900
 Kent City *(G-9435)*
Lacks Industries Inc .... C 616 554-7134
 Grand Rapids *(G-6919)*
Letica Corporation .... C 248 652-0557
 Rochester Hills *(G-14053)*
Martinrea Industries Inc .... E 734 428-2400
 Manchester *(G-10886)*
Osco Inc .... E 248 852-7310
 Rochester Hills *(G-14077)*
Performance Systematix LLC .... E 616 949-9090
 Grand Rapids *(G-7080)*
Plasticrafts Inc .... G 313 532-1900
 Redford *(G-13757)*
Polytec Foha Inc .... F 586 978-9386
 Warren *(G-17969)*
Sonus Engineered Solutions LLC .... C 586 427-3838
 Warren *(G-18017)*
Th Plastics Inc .... D 269 496-8495
 Mendon *(G-11223)*
Thomson Plastics Inc .... E 517 545-5026
 Howell *(G-8531)*
Trellborg Sling Sltions US Inc .... G 810 655-3900
 Fenton *(G-5509)*
Xxtar Associates LLC .... F 888 946-6066
 Detroit *(G-4695)*
Yanfeng US Auto Intr Systems I .... G 734 946-0600
 Romulus *(G-14342)*
Zayna LLC .... G 616 452-4522
 Grand Rapids *(G-7356)*

CONTAINERS: Plywood & Veneer, Wood

Delta Packaging International .... G 517 321-6548
 Lansing *(G-9685)*

CONTAINERS: Sanitary, Food

Acumedia Manufacturers Inc .... E 517 372-9200
 Lansing *(G-9799)*
Hot Rods Bbq Services .... G 989 375-2191
 Elkton *(G-5031)*
Huhtamaki Inc .... D 989 633-8900
 Coleman *(G-3467)*
Letica Corporation .... C 248 652-0557
 Rochester Hills *(G-14053)*

Moving & Shipping Solutions .... G 231 824-4190
 Manton *(G-10938)*

CONTAINERS: Shipping & Mailing, Fiber

Action Packaging LLC .... E 616 871-5200
 Caledonia *(G-2366)*
Xpress Packaging Solutions LLC .... G 231 629-0463
 Shelby Township *(G-15371)*

CONTAINERS: Shipping, Bombs, Metal Plate

Industrial Container Inc .... F 313 923-8778
 Detroit *(G-4314)*

CONTAINERS: Shipping, Metal, Milk, Fluid

Fluid-Bag LLC .... F 513 310-9550
 Lansing *(G-9698)*

CONTAINERS: Wood

AAR Manufacturing Inc .... E 231 779-8800
 Cadillac *(G-2306)*
Black River Pallet Company .... E 616 772-6211
 Zeeland *(G-19000)*
C & K Box Company Inc .... F 517 784-1779
 Jackson *(G-8830)*
Classic Container Corporation .... C 734 853-3000
 Livonia *(G-10159)*
Demeester Wood Products Inc .... F 616 677-5995
 Coopersville *(G-3685)*
G & D Wood Products Inc .... G 517 254-4463
 Camden *(G-2422)*
Kamps Inc .... E 517 645-2800
 Potterville *(G-13646)*
Luberda Wood Products Inc .... G 989 876-4334
 Omer *(G-12696)*
Millers Woodworking .... G 989 386-8110
 Clare *(G-2987)*
Union Pallet & Cont Co Inc .... E 517 279-4888
 Coldwater *(G-3459)*

CONTRACT DIVING SVC

Superior Mar & Envmtl Svcs LLC .... G 906 253-9448
 Sault Sainte Marie *(G-15101)*

CONTRACTOR: Dredging

K & M Industrial LLC .... G 906 420-8770
 Gladstone *(G-6182)*

CONTRACTOR: Rigging & Scaffolding

Dobson Industrial Inc .... E 800 298-6063
 Bay City *(G-1346)*

CONTRACTORS: Access Control System Eqpt

Best Netwrk Design & Assoc LLC ...... E 313 680-2047
 Detroit *(G-4052)*
Cornelius Systems Inc .... E 248 545-5558
 Clawson *(G-3091)*
D Find Corporation .... G 248 641-2858
 Troy *(G-17043)*

CONTRACTORS: Acoustical & Insulation Work

Masco Corporation .... A 313 274-7400
 Livonia *(G-10302)*

CONTRACTORS: Antenna Installation

Cjg LLC .... F 734 793-1400
 Livonia *(G-10158)*

CONTRACTORS: Asphalt

Action Asphalt LLC .... F 734 449-8565
 Brighton *(G-1937)*
Arnt Asphalt Sealing Inc .... D 269 927-1532
 Benton Harbor *(G-1530)*
Carrollton Paving Co .... F 989 752-7139
 Saginaw *(G-14623)*
D O W Asphalt Paving LLC .... G 810 743-2633
 Swartz Creek *(G-16352)*
Lite Load Services LLC .... F 269 751-6037
 Hamilton *(G-7603)*
Michigan Paving and Mtls Co .... F 989 463-1323
 Alma *(G-247)*

Employee Codes: A=Over 500 employees, B=251-500
C=101-250, D=51-100, E=20-50, F=10-19, G=3-9

CONTRACTORS: Asphalt

Nagle Paving Company .... C 734 591-1484
  Livonia (G-10330)
RWS & Associates LLC .... E 517 278-3134
  Coldwater (G-3451)

CONTRACTORS: Awning Installation

Royal Oak & Birmingham Tent .... F 248 542-5552
  Royal Oak (G-14578)

CONTRACTORS: Boiler & Furnace

Dfc Inc .... G 734 285-6749
  Riverview (G-13870)

CONTRACTORS: Boiler Maintenance Contractor

Detroit Boiler Company .... F 313 921-7060
  Detroit (G-4137)
Diversified Mech Svcs Inc .... F 616 785-2735
  Comstock Park (G-3602)
Vierson Boiler & Repair Co .... F 616 949-0500
  Grand Rapids (G-7317)

CONTRACTORS: Building Eqpt & Machinery Installation

Amtrade Systems Inc .... G 734 522-9500
  Livonia (G-10118)
Constructive Sheet Metal Inc .... E 616 245-5306
  Allendale (G-217)
Morton Buildings Inc .... G 616 696-4747
  Three Rivers (G-16579)
Tk Elevator Corporation .... E 616 942-4710
  Grand Rapids (G-7263)
Ufp Atlantic LLC .... G 616 364-6161
  Grand Rapids (G-7286)
Ufp Industries Inc .... C 616 364-6161
  Grand Rapids (G-7289)
Ufp West Central LLC .... D 616 364-6161
  Grand Rapids (G-7295)
Vierson Boiler & Repair Co .... F 616 949-0500
  Grand Rapids (G-7317)
Waltz-Holst Blow Pipe Company .... E 616 676-8119
  Ada (G-40)
Yard & Home LLC .... F 844 927-3466
  Grand Rapids (G-7354)

CONTRACTORS: Building Front Installation, Metal

West Michigan Metals LLC .... G 269 978-7021
  Allegan (G-186)

CONTRACTORS: Building Movers

West Shore Services Inc .... E 616 895-4347
  Allendale (G-229)

CONTRACTORS: Building Sign Installation & Mntnce

Bill Daup Signs Inc .... G 810 235-4080
  Swartz Creek (G-16351)
H M Day Signs Inc .... G 231 946-7132
  Traverse City (G-16709)
Huron Advertising Company Inc .... E 734 483-2000
  Ypsilanti (G-18952)
Meiers Signs Inc .... G 906 786-3424
  Escanaba (G-5084)
Michigan Signs Inc .... G 734 662-1503
  Ann Arbor (G-575)
Modern Neon Sign Co Inc .... F 269 349-8636
  Kalamazoo (G-9274)
Signs Plus .... G 810 987-7446
  Port Huron (G-13527)
Wenz & Gibbens Enterprises .... G 248 333-7938
  Pontiac (G-13424)

CONTRACTORS: Building Site Preparation

Frenchys Skirting Inc .... G 734 721-3013
  Wayne (G-18220)

CONTRACTORS: Carpentry Work

Arnold & Sautter Co .... F 989 684-7557
  Bay City (G-1322)
Brunt Associates Inc .... E 248 960-8295
  Wixom (G-18627)
Greenia Custom Woodworking Inc .... E 989 868-9790
  Reese (G-13806)
PCI Industries Inc .... D 248 542-2570
  Oak Park (G-12637)
W S Townsend Company .... C 269 781-5131
  Marshall (G-11078)
Woodways Industries LLC .... E 616 956-3070
  Grand Rapids (G-7350)
Woodworks & Design Company .... G 517 482-6665
  Lansing (G-9905)

CONTRACTORS: Carpentry, Cabinet & Finish Work

A & B Display Systems Inc .... F 989 893-6642
  Bay City (G-1314)
Charlotte Cabinets Inc .... G 517 543-1522
  Charlotte (G-2742)
Custom Crafters .... C 269 763-9180
  Bellevue (G-1497)
Division 6 Fbrction Instlltion .... F 586 200-3030
  Warren (G-17780)
Gast Cabinet Co .... C 269 422-1587
  Baroda (G-1162)
Great Lakes Fine Cabinetry .... G 906 493-5780
  Sault Sainte Marie (G-15091)
Owens Building Co Inc .... E 989 835-1293
  Midland (G-11401)
Woodways Inc .... G 616 956-3070
  Zeeland (G-19093)

CONTRACTORS: Carpentry, Cabinet Building & Installation

Designtech Custom Interiors .... G 989 695-6306
  Freeland (G-6020)
Mod Interiors Inc .... E 586 725-8227
  Ira (G-8702)
Thomas and Milliken Mllwk Inc .... F 231 386-7236
  Northport (G-12193)
Tims Cabinet Inc .... G 989 846-9831
  Pinconning (G-13065)
Village Cabinet Shoppe Inc .... G 586 264-6464
  Sterling Heights (G-16223)

CONTRACTORS: Carpet Laying

Grand River Interiors Inc .... E 616 454-2800
  Grand Rapids (G-6777)
Seelye Group Ltd .... G 517 267-2001
  Lansing (G-9894)

CONTRACTORS: Closed Circuit Television Installation

Identify Inc .... E 313 802-2015
  Madison Heights (G-10745)
Thalner Electronic Labs Inc .... E 734 761-4506
  Ann Arbor (G-686)

CONTRACTORS: Closet Organizers, Installation & Design

W S Townsend Company .... C 269 781-5131
  Marshall (G-11078)

CONTRACTORS: Coating, Caulking & Weather, Water & Fire

Rock Industries Inc .... E 248 338-2800
  Bloomfield Hills (G-1858)

CONTRACTORS: Commercial & Office Building

Crown Heating Inc .... G 248 352-1688
  Detroit (G-4109)
Red Carpet Capital Inc .... G 248 952-8583
  Orchard Lake (G-12719)

CONTRACTORS: Concrete

Bdk Group Northern Mich Inc .... F 574 875-5183
  Charlevoix (G-2711)
Central Asphalt Inc .... F 989 772-0720
  Mount Pleasant (G-11690)
Consumers Concrete Corporation ..... F 517 784-9108
  Jackson (G-8852)
Pyramid Paving and Contg Co .... D 989 895-5861
  Bay City (G-1390)
Simply Green Outdoor Svcs LLC ...... G 734 385-6190
  Dexter (G-4755)

CONTRACTORS: Concrete Repair

All About Drainage LLC .... G 248 921-0766
  Commerce Township (G-3508)
Scodeller Construction Inc .... D 248 374-1102
  Wixom (G-18748)

CONTRACTORS: Construction Caulking

DC Byers Co/Grand Rapids Inc .... F 616 538-7300
  Grand Rapids (G-6635)

CONTRACTORS: Construction Site Cleanup

Pro-Soil Site Services Inc .... F 517 267-8767
  Lansing (G-9733)

CONTRACTORS: Countertop Installation

Classic Stone MBL & Gran Inc .... F 248 588-1599
  Troy (G-17014)
Korcast Products Incorporated .... G 248 740-2340
  Troy (G-17196)
Mica Crafters Inc .... F 517 548-2924
  Howell (G-8479)
Owens Building Co Inc .... E 989 835-1293
  Midland (G-11401)

CONTRACTORS: Demolition, Building & Other Structures

Grace Contracting Services LLC ...... G 906 630-4680
  Mc Millan (G-11188)
Morse Concrete & Excavating .... F 989 826-3975
  Mio (G-11512)

CONTRACTORS: Directional Oil & Gas Well Drilling Svc

5 Star Drctional Drlg Svcs Ind .... G 231 263-2050
  Kingsley (G-9520)
Alexander Directional Boring .... G 989 362-9506
  East Tawas (G-4916)
Alpha Directional Boring .... G 586 405-0171
  Davisburg (G-3756)
Diamondbck-Drectional Drlg LLC ..... F 231 943-3000
  Traverse City (G-16668)
Finn Directional Inc .... G 231 944-0923
  Roscommon (G-14349)
Navigator Wireline Service Inc .... F 989 275-9112
  Roscommon (G-14352)
Phoenix Technology Svcs USA .... F 231 995-0100
  Traverse City (G-16790)
S and P Drctnal Boring Svc LLC ...... G 989 832-7716
  Midland (G-11412)
Sedco Directional Drilling .... G 231 258-5318
  Kalkaska (G-9403)
Tip Top Drilling LLC .... G 616 291-8006
  Sparta (G-15787)

CONTRACTORS: Dock Eqpt Installation, Indl

Con-De Manufacturing Inc .... G 269 651-3756
  Sturgis (G-16285)

CONTRACTORS: Drapery Track Installation

Apple Fence Co .... F 231 276-9888
  Grawn (G-7449)
Detroit Custom Services Inc .... E 586 465-3631
  Mount Clemens (G-11636)

CONTRACTORS: Driveway

Delta Paving Inc .... F 810 232-0220
  Flint (G-5685)

CONTRACTORS: Electric Power Systems

Ulb LLC .... E 734 233-0961
  Wixom (G-18781)

CONTRACTORS: Electrical

Advantage Industries Inc .... E 616 669-2400
  Jenison (G-9042)
Bostik Inc .... G 269 781-8246
  Marshall (G-11054)
Craft Electric .... G 517 529-7164
  Clarklake (G-3005)

PRODUCT SECTION — CONTRACTORS: Highway & Street Resurfacing

HI Tech Mechanical Svcs LLC ....G..... 734 847-1831
  Temperance *(G-16534)*
Meiers Signs Inc ....G..... 906 786-3424
  Escanaba *(G-5084)*
Michigan Satellite ....F..... 989 792-6666
  Saginaw *(G-14698)*
Road To Freedom ....F..... 810 775-0992
  Brighton *(G-2066)*
Stanley Electric Sales America ....G..... 248 471-1300
  Farmington Hills *(G-5386)*
Tech Electric Co LLC ....G..... 586 697-5095
  Macomb *(G-10641)*

CONTRACTORS: Electronic Controls Installation

Control One Inc ....G..... 586 979-6106
  Sterling Heights *(G-15969)*
Energy Efficient Ltg LLC Eel ....G..... 586 214-5557
  West Bloomfield *(G-18282)*

CONTRACTORS: Energy Management Control

Global Green Corporation ....F..... 734 560-1743
  Ann Arbor *(G-501)*
Sadie Oil LLC ....G..... 517 675-1325
  Perry *(G-12980)*

CONTRACTORS: Erection & Dismantling, Poured Concrete Forms

Grace Contracting Services LLC ....G..... 906 630-4680
  Mc Millan *(G-11188)*

CONTRACTORS: Excavating

1johnson Erling ....G..... 231 625-2247
  Cheboygan *(G-2779)*
A Lindberg & Sons Inc ....E..... 906 485-5705
  Ishpeming *(G-8774)*
Carr Brothers and Sons Inc ....E..... 517 629-3549
  Albion *(G-119)*
Carr Brothers and Sons Inc ....F..... 517 531-3358
  Albion *(G-120)*
D J McQuestion & Sons Inc ....F..... 231 768-4403
  Leroy *(G-10005)*
Eggers Excavating LLC ....F..... 989 695-5205
  Freeland *(G-6022)*
Elmers Crane and Dozer Inc ....C..... 231 943-3443
  Traverse City *(G-16676)*
Franke Salisbury Virginia ....G..... 231 775-7014
  Cadillac *(G-2330)*
Higgins and Associates Inc ....G..... 989 772-8853
  Mount Pleasant *(G-11701)*
Jack Millikin Inc ....G..... 989 348-8411
  Grayling *(G-7464)*
Jordan Valley Concrete Service ....F..... 231 536-7701
  East Jordan *(G-4873)*
Lewiston Sand & Gravel Inc ....G..... 989 786-2742
  Lewiston *(G-10023)*
Manigg Enterprises Inc ....F..... 989 356-4986
  Alpena *(G-301)*
Mid Michigan Pipe Inc ....G..... 989 772-5664
  Grand Rapids *(G-7003)*
Morris Excavating Inc ....F..... 269 483-7773
  White Pigeon *(G-18484)*
Morse Concrete & Excavating ....F..... 989 826-3975
  Mio *(G-11512)*
Northern Tank Truck Service ....G..... 989 732-7551
  Gaylord *(G-6151)*
Rudy Goupille & Sons Inc ....G..... 906 475-9816
  Negaunee *(G-11974)*
Swansons Excavating Inc ....G..... 989 873-4419
  Prescott *(G-13652)*
Tip Top Gravel Co Inc ....G..... 616 897-8342
  Ada *(G-37)*
White Lake Excavating Inc ....E..... 231 894-6918
  Whitehall *(G-18513)*
Zellar Forest Products ....G..... 906 586-9817
  Germfask *(G-6169)*

CONTRACTORS: Excavating Slush Pits & Cellars Svcs

Burkholder Excavating Inc ....G..... 269 426-4227
  Sawyer *(G-15107)*

CONTRACTORS: Exterior Painting

Todd R Lrcque Pntg Wllcvring L ....G..... 989 252-9424
  Freeland *(G-6030)*

CONTRACTORS: Exterior Wall System Installation

Signature Wall Solutions Inc ....F..... 616 366-4242
  Midland *(G-11417)*

CONTRACTORS: Fence Construction

Bradys Fence Company Inc ....G..... 313 492-8804
  South Rockwood *(G-15463)*
Contractors Fence Service ....E..... 313 592-1300
  Detroit *(G-4102)*
Fresh Water Buyer II LLC ....F..... 517 914-8284
  Eaton Rapids *(G-4963)*
Mark Beem ....G..... 231 510-8122
  Lake City *(G-9550)*
Marquette Fence Company Inc ....G..... 906 249-8000
  Marquette *(G-11034)*
Metter Flooring LLC ....G..... 517 914-2004
  Rives Junction *(G-13887)*
Nevill Supply Incorporated ....G..... 989 386-4522
  Clare *(G-2989)*
Spartan Metal Fab LLC ....G..... 517 322-9050
  Lansing *(G-9737)*

CONTRACTORS: Fire Detection & Burglar Alarm Systems

Dice Corporation ....E..... 989 891-2800
  Bay City *(G-1343)*
Gentex Corporation ....G..... 616 392-7195
  Zeeland *(G-19028)*

CONTRACTORS: Fire Sprinkler System Installation Svcs

B L Harroun and Son Inc ....E..... 269 345-8657
  Kalamazoo *(G-9131)*
Exquise Inc ....G..... 248 220-9048
  Detroit *(G-4223)*
Gallagher Fire Equipment Co ....E..... 248 477-1540
  Livonia *(G-10219)*

CONTRACTORS: Floor Laying & Other Floor Work

Collier Enterprise III ....G..... 269 503-3402
  Sturgis *(G-16284)*
Homespun Furniture Inc ....F..... 734 284-6277
  Riverview *(G-13874)*
PCI Industries Inc ....D..... 248 542-2570
  Oak Park *(G-12637)*
Whites Industrial Service ....G..... 616 291-3706
  Lowell *(G-10523)*

CONTRACTORS: Flooring

Leelanau Redi-Mix Inc ....E..... 231 228-5005
  Maple City *(G-10943)*
Preferred Flooring MI LLC ....F..... 616 279-2162
  Walker *(G-17650)*

CONTRACTORS: Foundation Building

Cerco Inc ....E..... 734 362-8664
  Brownstown Twp *(G-2153)*

CONTRACTORS: Gas Field Svcs, NEC

Columbus Oil & Gas LLC ....G..... 810 385-9140
  Burtchville *(G-2218)*
DTE Energy Resources Inc ....D..... 734 302-4800
  Ann Arbor *(G-459)*
Eastport Group Inc ....F..... 989 732-0030
  Johannesburg *(G-9081)*
El Paso LLC ....G..... 231 587-0704
  Mancelona *(G-10869)*
Harmonie International LLC ....F..... 248 737-9933
  Farmington Hills *(G-5258)*
Pelhams Construction LLC ....G..... 517 549-8276
  Jonesville *(G-9098)*

CONTRACTORS: Gasoline Condensation Removal Svcs

Gas Recovery Systems LLC ....E..... 248 305-7774
  Northville *(G-12222)*

Technical Environmental Svcs ....E..... 810 229-6323
  Brighton *(G-2075)*

CONTRACTORS: General Electric

Aerobee Electric Inc ....F..... 248 549-2044
  Ferndale *(G-5518)*
Ainsworth Electric Inc ....E..... 810 984-5768
  Port Huron *(G-13433)*
H & R Electrical Contrs LLC ....E..... 517 669-2102
  Dewitt *(G-4710)*
Industrial Elc Co Detroit Inc ....D..... 313 872-1133
  Detroit *(G-4315)*
Nieboer Electric Inc ....F..... 231 924-0960
  Fremont *(G-6049)*
Parkway Elc Communications LLC ......D..... 616 392-2788
  Holland *(G-8160)*
PM Power Group Inc ....G..... 906 885-7100
  White Pine *(G-18487)*
Praise Sign Company ....G..... 616 439-0315
  Grandville *(G-7411)*

CONTRACTORS: Glass, Glazing & Tinting

Arnold & Sautter Co ....F..... 989 684-7557
  Bay City *(G-1322)*
Double Otis Inc ....E..... 616 878-3998
  Grand Rapids *(G-6656)*
Knight Tonya ....G..... 313 255-3434
  Southfield *(G-15618)*
Mt Clemens Glass & Mirror Co ....G..... 586 465-1733
  Clinton Township *(G-3306)*
Northern Michigan Glass LLC ....E..... 231 941-0050
  Traverse City *(G-16773)*
Thompson John ....G..... 810 225-8780
  Howell *(G-8530)*
Valley Glass Co Inc ....G..... 989 790-9342
  Saginaw *(G-14786)*

CONTRACTORS: Gutters & Downspouts

Rainbow Seamless Systems Inc ....G..... 231 933-8888
  Traverse City *(G-16814)*

CONTRACTORS: Heating Systems Repair & Maintenance Svc

Crown Heating Inc ....G..... 248 352-1688
  Detroit *(G-4109)*

CONTRACTORS: Highway & Street Construction, General

Bdk Group Northern Mich Inc ....F..... 574 875-5183
  Charlevoix *(G-2711)*
R H Huhtala Aggregates Inc ....G..... 906 524-7758
  Lanse *(G-9668)*
Stoneco Inc ....E..... 734 587-7125
  Maybee *(G-11172)*

CONTRACTORS: Highway & Street Paving

Ajax Paving Industries Inc ....C..... 248 244-3300
  Troy *(G-16913)*
Clancy Excavating Co ....G..... 586 294-2900
  Roseville *(G-14384)*
Edw C Levy Co ....G..... 248 349-8600
  Novi *(G-12411)*
Edw C Levy Co ....G..... 313 843-7200
  Detroit *(G-4202)*
Elmers Crane and Dozer Inc ....C..... 231 943-3443
  Traverse City *(G-16676)*
Genoak Materials Inc ....C..... 248 634-8276
  Holly *(G-8273)*
Hess Asphalt Pav Sand Cnstr Co ....E..... 810 984-4466
  Clyde *(G-3413)*
Hhj Holdings Limited ....F..... 248 652-9716
  Troy *(G-17143)*
Saginaw Asphalt Paving Co ....D..... 989 755-8147
  Carrollton *(G-2590)*
Shooks Asphalt Paving Co Inc ....G..... 989 236-7740
  Perrinton *(G-12976)*

CONTRACTORS: Highway & Street Resurfacing

Central Asphalt Inc ....F..... 989 772-0720
  Mount Pleasant *(G-11690)*
Pyramid Paving and Contg Co ....D..... 989 895-5861
  Bay City *(G-1390)*

Employee Codes: A=Over 500 employees, B=251-500
C=101-250, D=51-100, E=20-50, F=10-19, G=3-9

CONTRACTORS: Home & Office Intrs Finish, Furnish/Remodel

Installations Inc .... F 313 532-9000
Redford (G-13740)

CONTRACTORS: Hydraulic Eqpt Installation & Svcs

Automation Enterprises Inc .... G 586 774-0280
Roseville (G-14377)
Control One Inc .... G 586 979-6106
Sterling Heights (G-15969)

CONTRACTORS: Indl Building Renovation, Remodeling & Repair

Manistee Wldg & Piping Svc Inc .... G 231 723-2551
Manistee (G-10906)

CONTRACTORS: Insulation Installation, Building

Insulation Wholesale Supply .... G 269 968-9746
Battle Creek (G-1241)
Knauf Insulation Inc .... C 517 630-2000
Albion (G-128)
Valley Group of Companies .... F 989 799-9669
Saginaw (G-14787)

CONTRACTORS: Kitchen & Bathroom Remodeling

Cucina Moda - Birmingham LLC .... G 248 792-2285
Troy (G-17037)
J & J Laminate Connection Inc .... G 810 227-1824
Brighton (G-2014)
Korcast Products Incorporated .... G 248 740-2340
Troy (G-17197)
Surface Expressions LLC .... G 231 843-8282
Ludington (G-10552)
W S Townsend Company .... G 517 393-7300
Lansing (G-9903)

CONTRACTORS: Kitchen Cabinet Installation

J&N Custom Woodworking .... G 517 726-0290
Vermontville (G-17589)

CONTRACTORS: Lighting Syst

Band-Ayd Systems Intl Inc .... F 586 294-8851
Madison Heights (G-10677)

CONTRACTORS: Lightweight Steel Framing Installation

West Michigan Metals LLC .... G 269 978-7021
Allegan (G-186)

CONTRACTORS: Machine Rigging & Moving

FD Lake Company .... F 616 241-5639
Grand Rapids (G-6704)

CONTRACTORS: Machinery Installation

Ase Industries Inc .... D 586 754-7480
Warren (G-17718)
Best Industrial Group Inc .... F 586 826-8800
Warren (G-17734)
J I B Properties LLC .... G 313 382-3234
Melvindale (G-11202)
Tachyon Corporation .... F 586 598-4320
Chesterfield (G-2953)
West Mich Auto Stl & Engrg Inc .... E 616 560-8198
Belding (G-1464)

CONTRACTORS: Masonry & Stonework

Knust Masonry .... G 231 322-2587
Rapid City (G-13681)
St Onge Masonry LLC .... G 248 709-8161
Auburn Hills (G-1036)

CONTRACTORS: Mechanical

Access Heating & Cooling Inc .... G 734 464-0566
Livonia (G-10098)
Gee & Missler Inc .... E 734 284-1224
Wyandotte (G-18820)
Great Lakes Mechanical Corp .... C 313 581-1400
Dearborn (G-3849)
Johnson Systems Inc .... G 616 455-1900
Caledonia (G-2386)
Monarch Welding & Engrg Inc .... E 231 733-7222
Muskegon (G-11876)
Quality Stainless Mfg Co .... F 248 546-4141
Madison Heights (G-10815)
Spray Booth Products Inc .... E 313 766-4400
Redford (G-13773)

CONTRACTORS: Oil & Gas Building, Repairing & Dismantling Svc

Great Lakes Wellhead Inc .... G 231 943-9100
Grawn (G-7451)
Pioneer Oil Tools Inc .... G 989 644-6999
Mount Pleasant (G-11732)
Stovall Well Drilling Co .... G 616 364-4144
Grand Rapids (G-7228)
Wara Construction Company LLC .... D 248 299-2410
Rochester Hills (G-14141)

CONTRACTORS: Oil & Gas Field Geophysical Exploration Svcs

CMS Enterprises Company .... C 517 788-0550
Jackson (G-8845)

CONTRACTORS: Oil & Gas Well Casing Cement Svcs

Miller Investment Company LLC .... F 231 933-3233
Traverse City (G-16759)
Verbio North America Corp .... E 866 306-4777
Livonia (G-10459)

CONTRACTORS: Oil & Gas Well Drilling Svc

Advanced Energy Services LLC .... D 231 369-2602
South Boardman (G-15395)
Comet Energy Services LLC .... G 231 933-3600
Traverse City (G-16657)
Edgemarc Energy Holdings LLC .... E 724 749-8466
Birmingham (G-1726)
Eis Inc .... G 734 266-6500
Livonia (G-10192)
Fortis Energy Services Inc .... D 248 283-7100
Troy (G-17119)
Industrial Control Systems LLC .... G 269 689-3241
Sturgis (G-16294)
Key Energy Services Inc .... G 231 258-9637
Kalkaska (G-9393)
Michiwest Energy Inc .... G 989 772-2107
Mount Pleasant (G-11713)
Middleton Well Drilling .... G 989 465-1078
Coleman (G-3469)
Rafalski CPA .... G 248 689-1685
Troy (G-17328)
Srw Inc .... F 989 732-8884
Traverse City (G-16840)
Srw Inc .... F 989 269-8528
Bad Axe (G-1111)
Stovall Well Drilling Co .... G 616 364-4144
Grand Rapids (G-7228)
Thompson Well Drilling .... G 616 754-5032
Gowen (G-6230)
Ward Lake Drilling Inc .... G 989 732-8499
Gaylord (G-6166)

CONTRACTORS: Oil & Gas Well Foundation Grading Svcs

Grace Contracting Services LLC .... G 906 630-4680
Mc Millan (G-11188)

CONTRACTORS: Oil & Gas Wells Svcs

Acme Septic Tank Co .... F 989 684-3852
Kawkawlin (G-9413)
Integrity Sltons Feld Svcs Inc .... E 517 481-4724
Alma (G-242)
JO Well Service and Tstg Inc .... G 989 772-4221
Mount Pleasant (G-11705)
Jones Ray Well Servicing Inc .... F 989 832-8071
Midland (G-11379)
Lease Management Inc .... G 989 773-5948
Mount Pleasant (G-11707)
Northern A 1 Services Inc .... D 231 258-9961
Kalkaska (G-9399)
Sappington Crude Oil Inc .... G 989 345-1052
West Branch (G-18340)
Team Services LLC .... E 231 258-9130
Kalkaska (G-9406)
Team Spooling Services LLC .... G 231 258-9130
Kalkaska (G-9407)

CONTRACTORS: Oil Field Haulage Svcs

1st Choice Trckg & Rentl Inc .... G 231 258-0417
Kalkaska (G-9381)
B & H Tractor & Truck Inc .... G 989 773-5975
Mount Pleasant (G-11683)

CONTRACTORS: Oil Field Lease Tanks: Erectg, Clng/Rprg Svcs

Central Michigan Tank Rental .... G 989 681-5963
Saint Louis (G-14989)

CONTRACTORS: Oil Field Pipe Testing Svcs

5 By 5 LLC .... F 855 369-6757
Traverse City (G-16594)
Northern Tank LLC .... G 989 386-2389
Clare (G-2992)

CONTRACTORS: Oil Sampling Svcs

Oil Exchange 6 Inc .... G 734 641-4310
Inkster (G-8669)

CONTRACTORS: Oil/Gas Field Casing,Tube/Rod Running,Cut/Pull

Superior Mar & Envmtl Svcs LLC .... G 906 253-9448
Sault Sainte Marie (G-15101)

CONTRACTORS: Oil/Gas Well Construction, Rpr/Dismantling Svcs

917 Chittock Street LLC .... F 866 945-0269
Lansing (G-9798)
All About Bus Cnstr Aabc LLC .... G 248 229-3031
Redford (G-13712)
Altered Stone Realty Co LLC .... F 313 800-0362
Detroit (G-4005)
Aspn Wood Construction LLC .... F 810 246-8044
Royal Oak (G-14514)
Bach Services & Mfg Co LLC .... F 231 263-2777
Kingsley (G-9521)
Cbbn Restoration LLc .... G 231 220-9892
Traverse City (G-16640)
Cheboygan Cnty Hbtat For Hmnit ...... G 231 597-4663
Cheboygan (G-2783)
Counts Investment Group LLC .... F 313 613-6866
Detroit (G-4105)
Deperez Contracting LLC .... G 947 224-1999
Detroit (G-4132)
Diversified Prof Rlty Svcs .... G 313 215-1840
Hazel Park (G-7824)
Fiore Construction .... G 517 404-0000
Howell (G-8454)
FTC LLC .... F 313 622-1583
Novi (G-12420)
Gjm Property LLC .... F 248 592-7323
Boon (G-1881)
Greenlight Home Inspection Svc .... G 313 885-5616
Saint Clair Shores (G-14863)
Hassan Sons Spcial HM Svcs LLC ...... G 313 558-1031
Inkster (G-8665)
Jn Newman Construction LLC .... G 269 968-1290
Springfield (G-15870)
Jrj Energy Services LLC .... F 231 823-2171
Stanwood (G-15904)
Kadant Johnson LLC .... G 269 278-1715
Three Rivers (G-16577)
Kap Building Services Inc .... G 888 622-0527
Westland (G-18391)
Kdk Downhole Tooling LLC .... G 231 590-3137
Williamsburg (G-18557)
Kingston Prperty Advisers Corp .... G 248 825-9657
Redford (G-13741)
Lgc Global Inc .... E 313 989-4141
Detroit (G-4395)
Melix Services Inc .... G 248 387-9303
Hamtramck (G-7612)
Mr Everything LLC .... G 248 301-2580
Redford (G-13748)
Nse Property Group LLC .... G 313 605-1646
Detroit (G-4493)

PRODUCT SECTION

CONTRACTORS: Sheet Metal Work, NEC

PRC Commercial Services LLC ....G....... 313 445-1760
  Dearborn *(G-3884)*
Premier Casing Crews Inc ....G....... 989 775-7436
  Mount Pleasant *(G-11734)*
Red Carpet Capital Inc ....G....... 248 952-8583
  Orchard Lake *(G-12719)*
Road To Freedom ....F....... 810 775-0992
  Brighton *(G-2066)*
Rock Industries Inc ....E....... 248 338-2800
  Bloomfield Hills *(G-1858)*
Superior Inspection Svc ....G....... 231 258-9400
  Kalkaska *(G-9405)*
Technical Enterprises LLC ....G....... 313 333-1438
  Detroit *(G-4629)*
Top Shelf Painter Inc ....F....... 586 465-0867
  Fraser *(G-6004)*
Trend Services Company ....G....... 231 258-9951
  Kalkaska *(G-9409)*
Ttadevelopment LLC ....G....... 626 399-4225
  Detroit *(G-4648)*
Veterans Utility Services LLC ....D....... 888 878-4191
  Lansing *(G-9901)*
Zellars Group LLC ....G....... 313 828-2309
  Detroit *(G-4702)*

CONTRACTORS: On-Site Welding

All-Fab Corporation ....G....... 269 673-6572
  Allegan *(G-145)*
Anderson Welding & Mfg Inc ....F....... 906 523-4661
  Houghton *(G-8380)*
B & B Custom and Prod Wldg ....F....... 517 524-7121
  Spring Arbor *(G-15789)*
B & B Holdings Groesbeck LLC ....F....... 586 554-7600
  Sterling Heights *(G-15940)*
Bnb Welding & Fabrication Inc ....G....... 810 820-1508
  Burton *(G-2227)*
Case Welding & Fabrication Inc ....G....... 517 278-2729
  Coldwater *(G-3425)*
Custom Design & Manufacturing ....F....... 989 754-9962
  Carrollton *(G-2587)*
Dunns Welding Inc ....G....... 248 356-3866
  Southfield *(G-15543)*
Lakeside Mechanical Contrs ....E....... 616 786-0211
  Allegan *(G-168)*
Marsh Industrial Services Inc ....F....... 231 258-4870
  Kalkaska *(G-9395)*
Matrix Mtlcraft LLP A Ltd Prtn ....G....... 248 724-1800
  Auburn Hills *(G-970)*
Nephew Fabrication Inc ....G....... 616 875-2121
  Zeeland *(G-19059)*
Nor-Dic Tool Company Inc ....F....... 734 326-3610
  Romulus *(G-14312)*
Reau Manufacturing Co ....G....... 734 823-5603
  Dundee *(G-4833)*
Sparta Sheet Metal Inc ....F....... 616 784-9035
  Grand Rapids *(G-7208)*
Specialty Welding ....G....... 517 627-5566
  Grand Ledge *(G-6399)*
Technical Machining Welding ....G....... 269 463-3738
  Watervliet *(G-18183)*
United Systems ....G....... 248 583-9670
  Troy *(G-17413)*
Van S Fabrications Inc ....G....... 810 679-2115
  Croswell *(G-3738)*
Varneys Fab & Weld LLC ....G....... 231 865-6856
  Nunica *(G-12589)*

CONTRACTORS: Ornamental Metal Work

Cramblits Welding LLC ....G....... 906 932-3773
  Ironwood *(G-8760)*

CONTRACTORS: Painting & Wall Covering

Boss Electro Static Inc ....E....... 616 575-0577
  Wyoming *(G-18854)*
Home Style Co ....G....... 989 871-3654
  Millington *(G-11501)*
PCI Industries Inc ....D....... 248 542-2570
  Oak Park *(G-12637)*
V & T Painting LLC ....G....... 248 497-1494
  Farmington Hills *(G-5407)*

CONTRACTORS: Painting, Commercial

Abrasive Solutions LLC ....G....... 517 592-2668
  Cement City *(G-2675)*
Gj Prey Coml & Indus Pntg Cov ....G....... 248 250-4792
  Clawson *(G-3098)*
Horizon Bros Painting Corp ....G....... 810 632-3462
  Howell *(G-8462)*

CONTRACTORS: Painting, Commercial, Interior

Tks Industrial Company ....E....... 248 786-5000
  Troy *(G-17393)*

CONTRACTORS: Painting, Indl

Beech & Rich Inc ....E....... 269 968-8012
  Springfield *(G-15861)*
CPS LLC ....F....... 517 639-1464
  Quincy *(G-13666)*
Finishing Touch Inc ....E....... 517 542-5581
  Litchfield *(G-10077)*
P C S Companies Inc ....G....... 616 754-2229
  Greenville *(G-7504)*

CONTRACTORS: Painting, Residential

Northwest Paint Pros ....G....... 231 944-3446
  Traverse City *(G-16775)*
Top Shelf Painter Inc ....F....... 586 465-0867
  Fraser *(G-6004)*

CONTRACTORS: Parking Facility Eqpt Installation

Traffic Sfety Ctrl Systems Inc ....E....... 248 348-0570
  Wixom *(G-18775)*

CONTRACTORS: Parking Lot Maintenance

Hd Selcating Pav Solutions LLC ....G....... 248 241-6526
  Clarkston *(G-3038)*

CONTRACTORS: Patio & Deck Construction & Repair

Fresh Water Buyer II LLC ....F....... 517 914-8284
  Eaton Rapids *(G-4963)*
Vinyl Sash of Flint Inc ....E....... 810 234-4831
  Grand Blanc *(G-6266)*

CONTRACTORS: Pipe & Boiler Insulating

Valley Group of Companies ....F....... 989 799-9669
  Saginaw *(G-14787)*

CONTRACTORS: Plumbing

McLaren Inc ....G....... 989 720-4328
  Owosso *(G-12842)*
Sheren Plumbing & Heating Inc ....E....... 231 943-7916
  Traverse City *(G-16831)*
Walters Plumbing Company ....F....... 269 962-6253
  Battle Creek *(G-1310)*

CONTRACTORS: Pollution Control Eqpt Installation

Advanced Recovery Tech Corp ....G....... 231 788-2911
  Nunica *(G-12575)*
Forrest Brothers Inc ....C....... 989 356-4011
  Gaylord *(G-6129)*

CONTRACTORS: Post Disaster Renovations

Diversified Prof Rlty Svcs ....G....... 313 215-1840
  Hazel Park *(G-7824)*

CONTRACTORS: Precast Concrete Struct Framing & Panel Placing

Grace Contracting Services LLC ....G....... 906 630-4680
  Mc Millan *(G-11188)*

CONTRACTORS: Prefabricated Window & Door Installation

Architectural Glass & Mtls Inc ....E....... 269 375-6165
  Kalamazoo *(G-9118)*
Chames LLC ....G....... 616 363-0000
  Grand Rapids *(G-6564)*
Lsd Investments Inc ....E....... 248 333-9085
  Bloomfield Hills *(G-1832)*
Vinyl Sash of Flint Inc ....E....... 810 234-4831
  Grand Blanc *(G-6266)*
Wallside Inc ....F....... 313 292-4400
  Taylor *(G-16489)*

CONTRACTORS: Process Piping

W Soule & Co ....D....... 269 324-7001
  Portage *(G-13631)*

CONTRACTORS: Pulpwood, Engaged In Cutting

Casselman Logging ....G....... 231 885-1040
  Mesick *(G-11270)*
Crawford Forest Products ....F....... 989 742-3855
  Hillman *(G-7912)*
Elenz Inc ....G....... 989 732-7233
  Gaylord *(G-6127)*

CONTRACTORS: Refrigeration

Duquaine Incorporated ....G....... 906 228-7290
  Marquette *(G-11015)*
Refrigeration Concepts Inc ....E....... 616 785-7335
  Comstock Park *(G-3643)*

CONTRACTORS: Resilient Floor Laying

Preferred Flooring MI LLC ....F....... 616 279-2162
  Walker *(G-17650)*

CONTRACTORS: Rigging, Theatrical

Tls Productions Inc ....E....... 810 220-8577
  Ann Arbor *(G-693)*

CONTRACTORS: Roofing

CPS LLC ....F....... 517 639-1464
  Quincy *(G-13666)*
Detroit Cornice & Slate Co Inc ....E....... 248 398-7690
  Ferndale *(G-5544)*
Laduke Corporation ....E....... 248 414-6600
  Oak Park *(G-12622)*
National Roofg & Shtmtl Co Inc ....D....... 989 964-0557
  Saginaw *(G-14707)*
Reurink Roof Maint & Coating ....G....... 269 795-2337
  Middleville *(G-11312)*

CONTRACTORS: Roustabout Svcs

Ally Servicing LLC ....A....... 248 948-7702
  Detroit *(G-4003)*
D D Quality Servicing ....G....... 517 709-3705
  Holt *(G-8306)*

CONTRACTORS: Safety & Security Eqpt

Abretec Group LLC ....E....... 248 591-4000
  Royal Oak *(G-14503)*
Executive Operations LLC ....E....... 313 312-0653
  Brighton *(G-1986)*

CONTRACTORS: Sandblasting Svc, Building Exteriors

Trin-Mac Company Inc ....G....... 586 774-1900
  Saint Clair Shores *(G-14889)*

CONTRACTORS: Seismograph Survey Svcs

Baker Hghes Olfld Oprtions LLC ....G....... 989 773-7992
  Mount Pleasant *(G-11685)*
Emerson Geophysical LLC ....E....... 231 943-1400
  Traverse City *(G-16677)*
West Bay Geophysical Inc ....G....... 231 946-3529
  Traverse City *(G-16878)*

CONTRACTORS: Septic System

Acme Septic Tank Co ....F....... 989 684-3852
  Kawkawlin *(G-9413)*
Deforest & Bloom Septic Tanks ....G....... 231 544-3599
  Central Lake *(G-2693)*
Forbes Sanitation & Excavation ....F....... 231 723-2311
  Manistee *(G-10900)*
Morse Concrete & Excavating ....F....... 989 826-3975
  Mio *(G-11512)*

CONTRACTORS: Sheet Metal Work, NEC

Bauer Sheet Metal & Fabg Inc ....E....... 231 773-3244
  Muskegon *(G-11775)*
C & T Fabrication LLC ....G....... 616 678-5133
  Kent City *(G-9428)*
Custom Fab Inc ....G....... 586 755-7260
  Warren *(G-17767)*

Employee Codes: A=Over 500 employees, B=251-500
C=101-250, D=51-100, E=20-50, F=10-19, G=3-9

CONTRACTORS: Sheet Metal Work, NEC

Designers Sheet Metal Inc .... G 269 429-4133
  Saint Joseph *(G-14926)*
East Muskegon Roofg Shtmtl Co .... D 231 744-2461
  Muskegon *(G-11806)*
Gallagher-Kaiser Corporation .... D 313 368-3100
  Troy *(G-17126)*
Harris Sheet Metal Co .... E 989 496-3080
  Midland *(G-11371)*
J M L Contracting & Sales Inc .... F 586 756-4133
  Warren *(G-17879)*
Kalamazoo Mechanical Inc .... F 269 343-5351
  Kalamazoo *(G-9241)*
Kaufman Cstm Shtmtl Fbrction L .... G 906 932-2130
  Ironwood *(G-8766)*
Shouldice Indus Mfrs Cntrs Inc .... D 269 962-5579
  Battle Creek *(G-1293)*
Thermal Designs & Manufacturng .... F 586 773-5231
  Roseville *(G-14484)*
Turnkey Fabrication LLC .... F 616 248-9116
  Grand Rapids *(G-7281)*
Young Manufacturing Inc .... G 906 483-3851
  Dollar Bay *(G-4766)*

CONTRACTORS: Sheet metal Work, Architectural

Cmp Acquisitions LLC .... F 888 519-2286
  Redford *(G-13726)*
Custom Archtctral Shtmtl Spcls .... F 313 571-2277
  Detroit *(G-4113)*

CONTRACTORS: Siding

C L Rieckhoff Company Inc .... C 734 946-8220
  Taylor *(G-16388)*
Sanderson Insulation .... G 269 496-7660
  Mendon *(G-11221)*
Vinyl Sash of Flint Inc .... E 810 234-4831
  Grand Blanc *(G-6266)*

CONTRACTORS: Single-family Home General Remodeling

Arnold & Sautter Co .... F 989 684-7557
  Bay City *(G-1322)*
Constine Inc .... E 989 723-6043
  Owosso *(G-12827)*
Diversified Prof Rlty Svcs .... G 313 215-1840
  Hazel Park *(G-7824)*
Overhead Door Company Alpena .... G 989 354-8316
  Alpena *(G-307)*
Regency Construction Corp .... E 586 741-8000
  Clinton Township *(G-3334)*
Woodworks & Design Company .... G 517 482-6665
  Lansing *(G-9905)*

CONTRACTORS: Skylight Installation

Northern Michigan Glass LLC .... E 231 941-0050
  Traverse City *(G-16773)*

CONTRACTORS: Solar Energy Eqpt

Global Battery Solutions LLC .... E 800 456-4265
  Holland *(G-8051)*
Option Energy LLC .... G 269 329-4317
  Traverse City *(G-16784)*
Sinclair Designs & Engrg LLC .... F 877 517-0311
  Albion *(G-133)*

CONTRACTORS: Special Trades, NEC

Affordable Pool and Spa Inc .... F 810 422-5058
  Burton *(G-2225)*

CONTRACTORS: Store Fixture Installation

Fab Concepts .... G 586 466-6411
  Chesterfield *(G-2879)*

CONTRACTORS: Store Front Construction

Northern Michigan Glass LLC .... E 231 941-0050
  Traverse City *(G-16773)*

CONTRACTORS: Structural Iron Work, Structural

Bristol Steel & Conveyor Corp .... E 810 658-9510
  Davison *(G-3775)*
Douglas Steel Fabricating Corp .... D 517 322-2050
  Lansing *(G-9759)*

East Jordan Ironworks Inc .... G 517 566-7211
  Sunfield *(G-16334)*
Empire Machine & Conveyors Inc .... F 989 541-2060
  Durand *(G-4841)*
Mean Erectors Inc .... F 989 737-3285
  Saginaw *(G-14690)*

CONTRACTORS: Structural Steel Erection

Campbell & Shaw Steel Inc .... F 810 364-5100
  Marysville *(G-11083)*
Corson Fabricating LLC .... E 810 326-0532
  Saint Clair *(G-14820)*
Davis Iron Works Inc .... F 248 624-5960
  Commerce Township *(G-3521)*
Dobson Industrial Inc .... E 800 298-6063
  Bay City *(G-1346)*
Dumas Concepts In Building Inc .... F 313 895-2555
  Detroit *(G-4196)*
Elevated Technologies Inc .... E 616 288-9817
  Grand Rapids *(G-6672)*
Ferguson Steel Inc .... F 810 984-3918
  Fort Gratiot *(G-5821)*
G & G Steel Fabricating Co .... F 586 979-4112
  Warren *(G-17821)*
Howard Structural Steel Inc .... F 989 752-3000
  Saginaw *(G-14670)*
Imm Inc .... F 989 344-7662
  Grayling *(G-7463)*
Mbm Fabricators Co Inc .... C 734 941-0100
  Romulus *(G-14301)*
Men of Steel Inc .... F 989 635-4866
  Marlette *(G-10986)*
Midwest Steel Inc .... E 313 873-2220
  Detroit *(G-4456)*
Steel Supply & Engineering Co .... E 616 452-3281
  Grand Rapids *(G-7223)*
Titus Welding Company .... F 248 476-9366
  Farmington Hills *(G-5401)*

CONTRACTORS: Stucco, Interior

Rowsey Construction & Dev LLC .... G 313 675-2464
  Detroit *(G-4572)*

CONTRACTORS: Svc Well Drilling Svcs

GTM Steamer Service Inc .... G 989 732-7678
  Gaylord *(G-6132)*

CONTRACTORS: Tile Installation, Ceramic

Tile Craft Inc .... F 231 929-7207
  Traverse City *(G-16860)*
Yoxheimer Tile Co .... F 517 788-7542
  Jackson *(G-9040)*

CONTRACTORS: Tuck Pointing & Restoration

Libra Industries Inc Michigan .... G 517 787-5675
  Jackson *(G-8935)*

CONTRACTORS: Underground Utilities

Morris Excavating Inc .... F 269 483-7773
  White Pigeon *(G-18484)*

CONTRACTORS: Ventilation & Duct Work

Mjs Investing LLC .... E 734 455-6500
  Plymouth *(G-13246)*

CONTRACTORS: Wall Covering, Residential

Crown Heating Inc .... G 248 352-1688
  Detroit *(G-4109)*

CONTRACTORS: Warm Air Heating & Air Conditioning

Fhc Holding Company .... G 616 538-3231
  Wyoming *(G-18872)*
Kalamazoo Mechanical Inc .... F 269 343-5351
  Kalamazoo *(G-9241)*
Premium Air Systems Inc .... E 248 680-8800
  Troy *(G-17312)*
Van Dyken Mechanical Inc .... D 616 224-7030
  Grandville *(G-7422)*

CONTRACTORS: Water Intake Well Drilling Svc

Walters Plumbing Company .... F 269 962-6253
  Battle Creek *(G-1310)*

CONTRACTORS: Water Well Drilling

Thompson Well Drilling .... G 616 754-5032
  Gowen *(G-6230)*

CONTRACTORS: Waterproofing

Rowsey Construction & Dev LLC .... G 313 675-2464
  Detroit *(G-4572)*

CONTRACTORS: Well Acidizing Svcs

Baker Hughes Holdings LLC .... G 989 732-2082
  Gaylord *(G-6119)*

CONTRACTORS: Window Treatment Installation

Melody Digiglio .... G 586 754-4405
  Warren *(G-17923)*

CONTRACTORS: Wrecking & Demolition

Angels of Detroit LLC .... G 248 796-1079
  Redford *(G-13714)*

CONTROL CIRCUIT DEVICES

Emergency Technology Inc .... D 616 896-7100
  Hudsonville *(G-8581)*
M P Jackson LLC .... F 517 782-0391
  Jackson *(G-8939)*

CONTROL EQPT: Buses Or Trucks, Electric

Eltek Inc .... G 616 363-6397
  Belmont *(G-1506)*

CONTROL EQPT: Electric

Borgwarner Thermal Systems Inc .... G 231 779-7500
  Cadillac *(G-2317)*
Burners Inc .... G 248 676-9141
  Milford *(G-11457)*
Electrojet Inc .... E 734 272-4709
  Wixom *(G-18653)*
ITT Industries Holdings Inc .... F 248 863-2153
  Novi *(G-12443)*
ITT Motion Tech Amer LLC .... F 248 863-2161
  Novi *(G-12444)*
ITT Motion Technologies LLC .... F 248 863-2161
  Novi *(G-12445)*
Motor Control Incorporated .... G 313 389-4000
  Melvindale *(G-11207)*
Nadex of America Corporation .... E 248 477-3900
  Farmington Hills *(G-5330)*
Solutions For Industry Inc .... G 517 448-8608
  Hudson *(G-8562)*
Stegner Controls LLC .... E 248 904-0400
  Auburn Hills *(G-1038)*
Versatile Systems LLC .... F 734 397-3957
  Canton *(G-2537)*

CONTROL EQPT: Electric Buses & Locomotives

Vico Louisville LLC .... E 502 245-1616
  Plymouth *(G-13333)*

CONTROL EQPT: Noise

A1 Noise Control .... G 248 538-7585
  Bloomfield Hills *(G-1789)*
Fortis Energy Services Inc .... D 248 283-7100
  Troy *(G-17119)*
Noisemeters Inc .... G 248 840-6559
  Berkley *(G-1633)*
Valley Group of Companies .... F 989 799-9669
  Saginaw *(G-14787)*
Vibracoustic Usa Inc .... C 269 637-2116
  South Haven *(G-15422)*

CONTROL PANELS: Electrical

Alpha Tran Engineering Co .... E 616 837-7341
  Nunica *(G-12576)*
Automation Enterprises Inc .... G 586 774-0280
  Roseville *(G-14377)*

PRODUCT SECTION

CONTROLS: Relay & Ind

C L Design Inc .... G 248 474-4220
  Farmington Hills *(G-5190)*
Clarkston Control Products .... G 248 394-1430
  Clarkston *(G-3024)*
Command Electronics Inc .... E 269 679-4011
  Schoolcraft *(G-15115)*
Control Technique Incorporated .... D 586 997-3200
  Sterling Heights *(G-15970)*
Danlyn Controls Inc .... G 586 773-6797
  Chesterfield *(G-2867)*
Eagle Engineering & Supply Co .... E 989 356-4526
  Alpena *(G-291)*
Generl-Lctrical-Mechanical Inc .... G 248 698-1110
  White Lake *(G-18456)*
Harlo Corporation .... D 616 538-0550
  Grandville *(G-7387)*
Indicon LLC .... C 586 274-0505
  Sterling Heights *(G-16047)*
Infra Corporation .... F 248 623-0400
  Waterford *(G-18129)*
Intec Automated Controls Inc .... E 586 532-8881
  Sterling Heights *(G-16050)*
Jervis B Webb Company .... B 248 553-1000
  Novi *(G-12449)*
Kirk Enterprises Inc .... G 248 357-5070
  Southfield *(G-15617)*
M & N Controls Inc .... E 734 850-2127
  Temperance *(G-16538)*
Metro-Fabricating LLC .... D 989 667-8100
  Bay City *(G-1377)*
Motor City Electric Tech Inc .... D 313 921-5300
  Detroit *(G-4467)*
Quality Business Engraving .... G 248 852-5123
  Rochester Hills *(G-14094)*
Spec Corporation .... G 517 529-4105
  Clarklake *(G-3008)*
Superior Controls Inc .... C 734 454-0500
  Plymouth *(G-13306)*
Thierica Controls Inc .... G 616 956-5500
  Grand Rapids *(G-7258)*
US Energia LLC .... G 248 669-1462
  Rochester *(G-13936)*
X-Bar Automation Inc .... E 248 616-9890
  Troy *(G-17455)*

CONTROLS & ACCESS: Indl, Electric

Altair Systems Inc .... F 248 668-0116
  Wixom *(G-18606)*
Amtex Inc .... G 586 792-7888
  Clinton Township *(G-3170)*
Automated Control Systems Inc .... G 248 476-9490
  Novi *(G-12369)*
Complete Dsign Automtn Systems ..... G 734 424-2789
  Dexter *(G-4732)*
Concentric Labs Inc .... G 517 969-3038
  Mason *(G-11119)*
Data Acquisition Ctrl Systems .... F 248 437-6096
  Brighton *(G-1973)*
Ghsp Inc .... G 248 588-5095
  Grand Haven *(G-6300)*
Jenda Controls Inc .... G 248 656-0090
  Rochester *(G-13910)*
Lor Manufacturing Co Inc .... G 989 644-2581
  Weidman *(G-18254)*
Patriot Sensors & Contrls Corp .... F 810 378-5511
  Peck *(G-12962)*
Prestolite Electric LLC .... G 248 313-3807
  Novi *(G-12512)*
Southern Auto Wholesalers Inc .... F 248 335-5555
  Pontiac *(G-13417)*
Stonebrdge Technical Entps Ltd .... F 810 750-0040
  Fenton *(G-5505)*
Tachyon Corporation .... F 586 598-4320
  Chesterfield *(G-2953)*
Valmec Inc .... G 810 629-8750
  Fenton *(G-5512)*

CONTROLS & ACCESS: Motor

Advanced Automation Group LLC ...... G 248 299-8100
  Madison Heights *(G-10661)*
Carmel Township .... G 888 805-6182
  Charlotte *(G-2738)*
Eaton Aerospace LLC .... B 616 949-1090
  Grand Rapids *(G-6663)*
Great Lakes Electric LLC .... G 269 408-8276
  Saint Joseph *(G-14932)*
Hydraulic Systems Technology .... G 248 656-5810
  Rochester Hills *(G-14036)*
Innovative Support Svcs Inc .... F 248 585-3600
  Troy *(G-17168)*

Rekey Luxury Homes LLC .... G 586 747-0342
  Troy *(G-17329)*
Sheila J Eaton Phd PC .... G 586 215-1035
  Warren *(G-18011)*
Shelton Technology LLC .... G 248 816-1585
  Troy *(G-17349)*

CONTROLS: Air Flow, Refrigeration

Softaire Diffusers Inc .... G 810 730-1668
  Linden *(G-10071)*

CONTROLS: Automatic Temperature

Century Instrument Company .... E 734 427-0340
  Livonia *(G-10152)*
Control Solutions Inc .... D 616 247-9422
  Wyoming *(G-18860)*
Maxitrol Company .... D 248 356-1400
  Southfield *(G-15648)*

CONTROLS: Crane & Hoist, Including Metal Mill

National Crane & Hoist Service .... G 248 789-4535
  Leonard *(G-10002)*

CONTROLS: Environmental

Ademco Inc .... G 586 759-1455
  Warren *(G-17691)*
Ademco Inc .... G 248 926-5510
  Wixom *(G-18595)*
American Controls Inc .... G 248 476-0663
  Bloomfield Hills *(G-1796)*
Astra Associates Inc .... E 586 254-6500
  Sterling Heights *(G-15935)*
Commonwealth Associates Inc .... C 517 788-3000
  Jackson *(G-8849)*
Core Energy and Automation LLC ...... G 248 830-0476
  Livonia *(G-10165)*
Crewbotiq LLC .... E 248 939-4229
  Troy *(G-17034)*
Eaton Corporation .... G 248 226-6347
  Southfield *(G-15547)*
Enertemp Inc .... E 616 243-2752
  Grand Rapids *(G-6679)*
Hart & Cooley LLC .... C 616 656-8200
  Grand Rapids *(G-6805)*
Imeco Inc .... G 906 774-0202
  Iron Mountain *(G-8722)*
Industrial Temperature Control .... G 734 451-8740
  Canton *(G-2474)*
Matrix Controls Group Inc .... G 248 380-7600
  Wixom *(G-18707)*
Peak Industries Co Inc .... E 313 846-8666
  Dearborn *(G-3883)*
T E Technology Inc .... E 231 929-3966
  Traverse City *(G-16849)*
Warner Instruments .... G 616 843-5342
  Grand Haven *(G-6379)*

CONTROLS: Marine & Navy, Auxiliary

Jered LLC .... G 906 776-1800
  Iron Mountain *(G-8723)*
Precise Power Systems LLC .... G 734 550-9505
  Whitmore Lake *(G-18544)*

CONTROLS: Numerical

Fidia Co .... F 248 680-0700
  Rochester Hills *(G-14011)*
Fitz-Rite Products Inc .... E 248 528-8440
  Troy *(G-17113)*

CONTROLS: Positioning, Electric

Harold G Schaevitz Inds LLC .... G 248 636-1515
  Bloomfield Hills *(G-1827)*

CONTROLS: Relay & Ind

A E C Inc .... D 810 231-9546
  Whitmore Lake *(G-18515)*
Acromag Incorporated .... D 248 624-1541
  Wixom *(G-18594)*
AG Davis Gage & Engrg Co .... E 586 977-9000
  Sterling Heights *(G-15926)*
Amx Corp .... F 469 624-8000
  Sterling Heights *(G-15932)*
Apollo America Inc .... D 248 332-3900
  Auburn Hills *(G-791)*

Comptek Inc .... E 248 477-5215
  Farmington Hills *(G-5206)*
Control One Inc .... G 586 979-6106
  Sterling Heights *(G-15969)*
Controls For Industries Inc .... G 517 468-3385
  Webberville *(G-18244)*
Custom Engineering & Design .... G 248 680-1435
  Troy *(G-17038)*
Eaton Corporation .... G 586 228-2029
  Clinton Township *(G-3228)*
Energy Products Inc .... G 248 866-5622
  Troy *(G-17090)*
Energy Products Inc .... E 248 545-7700
  Madison Heights *(G-10722)*
Fenton Systems Inc .... G 810 636-6318
  Goodrich *(G-6223)*
Ford Motor Company .... A 734 484-8626
  Ypsilanti *(G-18947)*
Galco Industrial Elec Inc .... F 248 542-9090
  Madison Heights *(G-10730)*
Glassmaster Controls Co Inc .... E 269 382-2010
  Kalamazoo *(G-9198)*
HI-Lex Controls Incorporated .... C 517 448-2752
  Hudson *(G-8551)*
Hydro-Logic Inc .... E 586 757-7477
  Warren *(G-17857)*
Incoe Corporation .... C 248 616-0220
  Auburn Hills *(G-936)*
Indicon LLC .... C 586 274-0505
  Sterling Heights *(G-16047)*
Industrial Computer & Controls .... F 734 697-4152
  Van Buren Twp *(G-17530)*
Industrial Temperature Control .... G 734 451-8740
  Canton *(G-2474)*
Linak US Inc .... A 502 413-0387
  Grand Rapids *(G-6945)*
M K Eaton Services LLC .... G 608 852-3118
  South Lyon *(G-15444)*
Mahle Powertrain LLC .... D 248 305-8200
  Farmington Hills *(G-5307)*
Maxitrol Company .... D 248 356-1400
  Southfield *(G-15648)*
Maxitrol Company .... G 269 432-3291
  Colon *(G-3488)*
Maxitrol Company .... G 517 486-2820
  Blissfield *(G-1769)*
Melling Tool Co .... B 517 787-8172
  Jackson *(G-8951)*
Murray Equipment Company Inc .... F 313 869-4444
  Warren *(G-17938)*
Nabco Inc .... E 231 832-2001
  Reed City *(G-13796)*
National Control Systems Inc .... G 810 231-2901
  Hamburg *(G-7592)*
Parker-Hannifin Corporation .... B 269 384-3459
  Kalamazoo *(G-9288)*
Peak Industries Co Inc .... E 313 846-8666
  Dearborn *(G-3883)*
Peaker Services Inc .... D 248 437-4174
  Brighton *(G-2049)*
Pilz Automtn Safety Ltd Partnr .... E 734 354-0272
  Canton *(G-2507)*
Precision Controls Company .... F 734 663-3104
  Ann Arbor *(G-620)*
Rick Wykle LLC .... G 734 839-6376
  Trenton *(G-16891)*
Rjg Technologies Inc .... D 231 947-3111
  Traverse City *(G-16822)*
Rockwell Automation Inc .... G 248 696-1200
  Troy *(G-17335)*
Rockwell Automation Inc .... E 248 435-2574
  Troy *(G-17336)*
Rockwell Automation Inc .... G 269 792-9137
  Wayland *(G-18204)*
Ross Decco Company .... E 248 764-1845
  Troy *(G-17337)*
Singh Automation LLC .... G 269 267-6078
  Portage *(G-13607)*
Sloan Transportation Pdts Inc .... E 616 395-5600
  Holland *(G-8197)*
Ssi Technology Inc .... D 248 582-0600
  Sterling Heights *(G-16188)*
Superior Controls Inc .... C 734 454-0500
  Plymouth *(G-13306)*
Symorex Ltd .... F 734 971-6000
  Ann Arbor *(G-670)*
Synchronous Manufacturing Inc .... F 517 764-6930
  Michigan Center *(G-11296)*
TAC Manufacturing Inc .... B 517 789-7000
  Jackson *(G-9014)*

Employee Codes: A=Over 500 employees, B=251-500
C=101-250, D=51-100, E=20-50, F=10-19, G=3-9

CONTROLS: Relay & Ind

Temcor Systems Inc .... G 810 229-0006
Brighton *(G-2077)*
Tramec Sloan LLC .... E 616 395-5600
Holland *(G-8224)*
Warner Instruments .... G 616 843-5342
Grand Haven *(G-6379)*

CONTROLS: Resistance Welder

Welding Technology Corp .... C 248 477-3900
Farmington Hills *(G-5413)*

CONTROLS: Thermostats

Energy Control Solutions Inc .... G 810 735-2800
Fenton *(G-5472)*
Taylor Controls Inc .... F 269 637-8521
South Haven *(G-15418)*

CONTROLS: Voice

Parkway Elc Communications LLC .... D 616 392-2788
Holland *(G-8160)*

CONVENIENCE STORES

Admiral .... G 989 356-6419
Alpena *(G-274)*
Agenda 2020 Inc .... F 616 581-6271
Grand Rapids *(G-6438)*
D M J Corp .... G 810 239-9071
Flint *(G-5681)*
Kern Auto Sales and Svc LLC .... F 734 475-2722
Chelsea *(G-2818)*

CONVENTION & TRADE SHOW SVCS

Art Craft Display Inc .... D 517 485-2221
Lansing *(G-9756)*
Nationwide Network Inc .... G 989 793-0123
Saginaw *(G-14708)*

CONVERTERS: Data

Berkshire & Associates Inc .... F 734 719-1822
Canton *(G-2440)*
Cisco Systems Inc .... G 800 553-6387
Detroit *(G-4094)*
Startech-Solutions LLC .... G 248 419-0650
Southfield *(G-15708)*

CONVERTERS: Power, AC to DC

Controlled Power Company .... C 248 528-3700
Troy *(G-17027)*
Ssi Technology Inc .... D 248 582-0600
Sterling Heights *(G-16188)*
Warner Power Conversion LLC .... E 603 456-3111
Grand Haven *(G-6381)*
Winford Engineering LLC .... G 989 671-9721
Auburn *(G-771)*

CONVERTERS: Rotary, Electrical

Acat Global LLC .... F 231 437-5000
White Cloud *(G-18437)*

CONVERTERS: Torque, Exc Auto

Alma Products Company .... G 989 463-1151
Alma *(G-236)*
Valeo Kapec North America Inc .... E 248 619-8710
Troy *(G-17427)*

CONVEYOR SYSTEMS

Altron Automation Inc .... D 616 669-7711
Hudsonville *(G-8565)*
Bradford Company .... C 616 399-3000
Holland *(G-7981)*
GMI Packaging Co .... F 734 972-7389
Ann Arbor *(G-502)*
Intersrce Recovery Systems Inc .... E 269 375-5100
Kalamazoo *(G-9225)*
Motion Machine Company .... F 810 664-9901
Lapeer *(G-9949)*
Production Accessories Co .... G 313 366-1500
Detroit *(G-4536)*
Spectrum Automation Company .... E 734 522-2160
Livonia *(G-10416)*
Steel Master LLC .... E 810 771-4943
Grand Blanc *(G-6264)*
Wardcraft Industries LLC .... E 517 750-9100
Spring Arbor *(G-15798)*

CONVEYOR SYSTEMS: Belt, General Indl Use

Chip Systems International .... F 269 626-8000
Scotts *(G-15130)*
National Element Inc .... E 248 486-1810
Brighton *(G-2040)*
Uniband Usa LLC .... F 616 676-6011
Grand Rapids *(G-7296)*
Versa-Craft Inc .... G 586 465-5999
Clinton Township *(G-3385)*

CONVEYOR SYSTEMS: Bucket Type

Material Control Inc .... G 630 892-4274
Croswell *(G-3732)*

CONVEYOR SYSTEMS: Bulk Handling

Alternative Engineering Inc .... E 616 785-7200
Belmont *(G-1499)*
Ensign Equipment Inc .... G 616 738-9000
Holland *(G-8028)*
RK Wojan Inc .... E 231 347-1160
Charlevoix *(G-2730)*

CONVEYOR SYSTEMS: Pneumatic Tube

Colombo Sales & Engrg Inc .... F 248 547-2820
Davisburg *(G-3764)*

CONVEYOR SYSTEMS: Robotic

Dimension Machine Tech LLC .... F 586 649-4747
Bloomfield Hills *(G-1814)*
Esys Automation LLC .... C 248 484-9927
Auburn Hills *(G-881)*
Esys Automation LLC .... E 284 484-9724
Pontiac *(G-13370)*
Esys Automation LLC .... E 248 484-9702
Sterling Heights *(G-16005)*
Fibro Laepple Technology Inc .... G 248 591-4494
Sterling Heights *(G-16014)*

CONVEYORS & CONVEYING EQPT

ADW Industries Inc .... E 989 466-4742
Alma *(G-233)*
Allied Indus Solutions LLC .... F 810 422-5093
Fenton *(G-5447)*
Allor Manufacturing Inc .... D 248 486-4500
Brighton *(G-1943)*
Ally Equipment LLC .... G 810 422-5093
Fenton *(G-5449)*
Altron Automation Group Inc .... C 616 669-7711
Hudsonville *(G-8566)*
Anchor Conveyor Products Inc .... G 313 582-5045
Dearborn *(G-3808)*
Ase Industries Inc .... D 586 754-7480
Warren *(G-17718)*
Automated Systems Inc .... E 248 373-5600
Auburn Hills *(G-804)*
Automatic Handling Intl Inc .... D 734 847-0633
Erie *(G-5044)*
Automation Contrls & Engrg LLC .... E 734 424-5500
Dexter *(G-4725)*
Automtion Mdlar Components Inc .... D 248 922-4740
Davisburg *(G-3758)*
Bay Manufacturing Corporation .... F 989 358-7198
Alpena *(G-282)*
Belco Industries Inc .... E 616 794-0410
Belding *(G-1437)*
Belco Industries Inc .... E 616 794-0410
Belding *(G-1438)*
Benesh Corporation .... F 734 244-4143
Monroe *(G-11532)*
Best Industrial Group Inc .... F 586 826-8800
Warren *(G-17734)*
Blue Water Manufacturing Inc .... E 810 364-6170
Marysville *(G-11082)*
Bos Manufacturing LLC .... F 231 398-3328
Manistee *(G-10895)*
Bristol Steel & Conveyor Corp .... E 810 658-9510
Davison *(G-3775)*
Caliber Industries LLC .... F 586 774-6975
Romeo *(G-14221)*
Central Conveyor Company LLC .... D 248 446-0118
Wixom *(G-18630)*
Change Parts Incorporated .... E 231 845-5107
Ludington *(G-10531)*
Cignys Inc .... G 989 753-1411
Saginaw *(G-14629)*

Clinton Machine Inc .... E 989 834-2235
Ovid *(G-12813)*
Colombo Sales and Engrg Inc .... F 248 547-2820
Oakley *(G-12654)*
Constructive Sheet Metal Inc .... E 616 245-5306
Allendale *(G-217)*
Continental Crane & Service .... E 586 294-7900
Fraser *(G-5915)*
Conveyor Concepts Michigan LLC .... F 616 997-5200
Coopersville *(G-3683)*
Cornerstone Fabg & Cnstr Inc .... E 989 642-5241
Hemlock *(G-7850)*
Crippen Manufacturing Company .... E 989 681-4323
Saint Louis *(G-14990)*
Csi Service Parts Corp .... G 989 358-7199
Alpena *(G-289)*
Daifuku North America Holdg Co .... C 248 553-1000
Novi *(G-12391)*
Dcl Inc .... C 231 547-5600
Charlevoix *(G-2714)*
Dearborn Mid West Conveyor Co .... E 313 273-2804
Detroit *(G-4129)*
Dearborn Mid-West Company LLC .... D 734 288-4400
Taylor *(G-16400)*
Diamond Automation Ltd .... E 734 838-7138
Livonia *(G-10184)*
Dumas Concepts In Building Inc .... F 313 895-2555
Detroit *(G-4196)*
Dunkley International Inc .... C 269 343-5583
Kalamazoo *(G-9174)*
Dynamic Conveyor Corporation .... E 231 798-0014
Norton Shores *(G-12288)*
Eagle Engineering & Supply Co .... E 989 356-4526
Alpena *(G-291)*
Edge Industries Inc .... G 616 453-5458
Grand Rapids *(G-6665)*
Egemin Automation Inc .... C 616 393-0101
Holland *(G-8025)*
Empire Machine & Conveyors Inc .... F 989 541-2060
Durand *(G-4841)*
Endura-Veyor Inc .... E 989 358-7060
Alpena *(G-292)*
Fata Automation Inc .... D 248 724-7660
Auburn Hills *(G-886)*
Florkeys Conveyor Service .... E 810 772-1930
Warren *(G-17814)*
Fraser Fab and Machine Inc .... E 248 852-9050
Rochester Hills *(G-14015)*
Frost Incorporated .... G 616 785-9030
Grand Rapids *(G-6724)*
Frost Links .... G 616 785-9030
Grand Rapids *(G-6725)*
Gudel Inc .... D 734 214-0000
Ann Arbor *(G-508)*
Hapman .... F 269 382-8257
Kalamazoo *(G-9208)*
Harvey S Freeman .... E 248 852-2222
West Bloomfield *(G-18287)*
Henshaw Inc .... D 586 752-0700
Armada *(G-736)*
Herkules Equipment Corporation .... E 248 960-7100
Commerce Township *(G-3536)*
Highland Engineering Inc .... E 517 548-4372
Howell *(G-8460)*
Hines Corporation .... F 231 799-6240
Norton Shores *(G-12348)*
HMS Products Co .... D 248 689-8120
Troy *(G-17146)*
Howard Structural Steel Inc .... E 989 752-3000
Saginaw *(G-14670)*
Industrial Kinetics Inc .... F 586 212-3894
New Baltimore *(G-11983)*
Integrated Conveyor Ltd .... G 231 747-6430
Muskegon *(G-11841)*
International Material Co .... F 616 355-2800
Holland *(G-8097)*
Jantec Incorporated .... E 231 941-4339
Traverse City *(G-16727)*
Kalamazoo Mfg Corp Globl .... F 269 382-8200
Kalamazoo *(G-9243)*
Livonia Magnetics Co Inc .... E 734 397-8844
Farmington Hills *(G-5293)*
Loudon Steel Inc .... E 989 871-9353
Millington *(G-11502)*
Magline Inc .... G 800 624-5463
Standish *(G-15891)*
Magnetic Products Inc .... D 248 887-5600
Highland *(G-7896)*
Mark One Corporation .... D 989 732-2427
Gaylord *(G-6145)*

PRODUCT SECTION

Material Hdlg Techniques Inc ....G....... 616 890-1475
  Hopkins *(G-8366)*
Material Transfer and Stor Inc ....E....... 269 673-2125
  Allegan *(G-170)*
McNichols Conveyor Company ....F....... 248 357-6077
  Southfield *(G-15651)*
Metzgar Conveyor Co ....E....... 616 784-0930
  Grand Rapids *(G-6983)*
MHS Conveyor Corp ....B....... 231 798-4547
  Norton Shores *(G-12310)*
Milan Metal Worx LLC ....G....... 734 369-7115
  Petersburg *(G-12984)*
Mol Belting Systems Inc ....D....... 616 453-2484
  Grand Rapids *(G-7020)*
Mondrella Process Systems LLC ....G....... 616 281-9836
  Grand Rapids *(G-7024)*
Motan Inc ....E....... 269 685-1050
  Plainwell *(G-13083)*
Motion Industries Inc ....G....... 989 771-0200
  Saginaw *(G-14705)*
New Technologies Tool & Mfg ....F....... 810 694-5426
  Grand Blanc *(G-6254)*
North Woods Industrial ....G....... 616 784-2840
  Comstock Park *(G-3629)*
Omni Metalcraft Corp ....E....... 989 354-4075
  Alpena *(G-306)*
Overhead Conveyor Company ....E....... 248 547-3800
  Ferndale *(G-5574)*
P & A Conveyor Sales Inc ....F....... 734 285-7970
  Riverview *(G-13882)*
Paradigm Conveyor LLC ....F....... 616 667-4040
  Marne *(G-10996)*
Paslin Company ....C....... 248 953-8419
  Shelby Township *(G-15296)*
PCI Procal Inc ....F....... 989 358-7070
  Alpena *(G-311)*
Peak Industries Co Inc ....E....... 313 846-8666
  Dearborn *(G-3883)*
Powerscreen USA LLC ....G....... 989 288-3121
  Durand *(G-4845)*
Prab Inc ....C....... 269 382-8200
  Kalamazoo *(G-9299)*
Prab Inc ....G....... 269 382-8200
  Kalamazoo *(G-9300)*
Prab Inc ....G....... 269 343-1675
  Kalamazoo *(G-9301)*
Pressure Vessel Service Inc ....E....... 313 921-1200
  Detroit *(G-4533)*
Roberts Sinto Corporation ....D....... 517 371-2460
  Lansing *(G-9787)*
Saginaw Products Corporation ....E....... 989 753-1411
  Saginaw *(G-14748)*
Santanna Tool & Design LLC ....D....... 248 541-3500
  Madison Heights *(G-10824)*
Sinto America Inc ....E....... 517 371-2460
  Lansing *(G-9791)*
Sparks Belting Company Inc ....G....... 800 451-4537
  Grand Rapids *(G-7206)*
Sparks Belting Company Inc ....D....... 616 949-2750
  Grand Rapids *(G-7207)*
Steel Craft Inc ....G....... 989 358-7196
  Alpena *(G-320)*
Storch Products Company Inc ....F....... 734 591-2200
  Livonia *(G-10422)*
Structural Equipment Co ....F....... 248 547-3800
  Ferndale *(G-5587)*
Sure Conveyors Inc ....F....... 248 926-2100
  Wixom *(G-18763)*
Symbiote Inc ....E....... 616 772-1790
  Zeeland *(G-19083)*
Symorex Ltd ....F....... 734 971-6000
  Ann Arbor *(G-670)*
Tgw Systems Inc ....C....... 616 888-2595
  Grand Rapids *(G-7256)*
Thoreson-Mc Cosh Inc ....E....... 248 362-0960
  Lake Orion *(G-9634)*
Ton-Tex Corporation ....F....... 616 957-3200
  Greenville *(G-7508)*
Triad Industrial Corp ....G....... 989 358-7191
  Atlanta *(G-748)*
Ultimation Industries LLC ....E....... 586 771-1881
  Roseville *(G-14489)*
Unified Scrning Crshing - MI L ....F....... 888 464-9473
  Saint Johns *(G-14920)*
Versa Handling Co ....G....... 313 491-0500
  Sterling Heights *(G-16222)*
Verstraete Conveyability Inc ....F....... 800 798-0410
  Grand Rapids *(G-7313)*
Via-Tech Corp ....F....... 989 358-7028
  Lachine *(G-9535)*

Wedin International Inc ....E....... 231 779-8650
  Cadillac *(G-2363)*
Whites Bridge Tooling Inc ....E....... 616 897-4151
  Lowell *(G-10522)*

CONVEYORS: Overhead

Auto/Con Services LLC ....G....... 586 791-7474
  Fraser *(G-5898)*
Frost Inc ....G....... 616 785-9030
  Grand Rapids *(G-6721)*
Frost Incorporated ....E....... 616 453-7781
  Grand Rapids *(G-6722)*
Jervis B Webb Company ....B....... 248 553-1000
  Novi *(G-12449)*
Wilkie Bros Conveyors Inc ....E....... 810 364-4820
  Marysville *(G-11113)*

COOKING & FOOD WARMING EQPT: Commercial

Delfield Company LLC ....A....... 989 773-7981
  Mount Pleasant *(G-11695)*
H & R Electrical Contrs LLC ....E....... 517 669-2102
  Dewitt *(G-4710)*
Midwest Stainless Fabricating ....G....... 248 476-4502
  Livonia *(G-10317)*
Sandbox Solutions Inc ....C....... 248 349-7010
  Northville *(G-12257)*

COOKING & FOODWARMING EQPT: Coffee Brewing

Royal Accoutrements Inc ....G....... 517 347-7983
  Okemos *(G-12683)*

COOKING & FOODWARMING EQPT: Commercial

Solaronics Inc ....E....... 248 651-5333
  Auburn Hills *(G-1035)*

COOKING EQPT, HOUSEHOLD: Convection Ovens, Incldg Portable

Lockett Enterprises LLC ....G....... 810 407-6644
  Flint *(G-5725)*

COOKING EQPT, HOUSEHOLD: Ranges, Gas

Maytag Corporation ....C....... 269 923-5000
  Benton Harbor *(G-1572)*
Whirlpool Corporation ....G....... 269 923-5000
  Benton Harbor *(G-1609)*

COOKING SCHOOL

Detroit Fd Entrprnrship Acdemy ....F....... 248 894-8941
  Detroit *(G-4147)*

COOKWARE, STONEWARE: Coarse Earthenware & Pottery

Reilchz Inc ....G....... 231 421-9600
  Traverse City *(G-16819)*

COOLERS & ICE CHESTS: Metal

Keglove LLC ....G....... 616 610-7289
  Holland *(G-8110)*

COOLING TOWERS: Metal

Bosch Auto Svc Solutions Inc ....D....... 586 574-1820
  Warren *(G-17740)*
Great Lakes Gauge Company ....E....... 989 652-6136
  Bridgeport *(G-1916)*

COPPER ORE MILLING & PREPARATION

Eagle Mine LLC ....B....... 906 339-7000
  Champion *(G-2704)*

COPPER ORE MINING

Copperwood Resources Inc ....F....... 906 229-3115
  Wakefield *(G-17618)*
Trelleborg Corporation ....G....... 269 639-9891
  South Haven *(G-15419)*

COSMETICS & TOILETRIES

COPPER: Cakes, Primary

Center Cupcakes ....G....... 248 302-6503
  West Bloomfield *(G-18270)*

COPPER: Rolling & Drawing

Aluminum Blanking Co Inc ....D....... 248 338-4422
  Pontiac *(G-13349)*
Anchor Lamina America Inc ....C....... 231 533-8646
  Bellaire *(G-1468)*
Bradhart Products Inc ....E....... 248 437-3746
  Brighton *(G-1952)*
J M L Contracting & Sales Inc ....F....... 586 756-4133
  Warren *(G-17879)*
Vx-LLC ....F....... 734 854-8700
  Lambertville *(G-9655)*

COPY MACHINES WHOLESALERS

Lowery Corporation ....C....... 616 554-5200
  Grand Rapids *(G-6949)*
Orbit Technology Inc ....G....... 906 776-7248
  Iron Mountain *(G-8729)*

CORD & TWINE

Great Lakes Cordage Inc ....F....... 616 842-4455
  Spring Lake *(G-15819)*

CORK & CORK PRDTS

Blade Industrial Products Inc ....G....... 248 773-7400
  Wixom *(G-18621)*
Connexion Inc ....G....... 248 453-5177
  Pontiac *(G-13355)*
Derby Fabg Solutions LLC ....D....... 616 866-1650
  Rockford *(G-14164)*

CORK PRDTS, FABRICATED, WHOLESALE

Connexion Inc ....G....... 248 453-5177
  Pontiac *(G-13355)*

CORRUGATED PRDTS: Boxes, Partition, Display Items, Sheet/Pad

Roberts Movable Walls Inc ....G....... 269 626-0227
  Scotts *(G-15133)*
Russell R Peters Co LLC ....G....... 989 732-0660
  Gaylord *(G-6157)*

COSMETIC PREPARATIONS

Aroma Taba ....G....... 313 782-4076
  Hamtramck *(G-7611)*
Bio Source Naturals LLC ....G....... 877 577-8223
  New Boston *(G-12002)*
Brighter Smile By Tierra LLC ....G....... 248 278-3117
  Detroit *(G-4072)*
Kd Essentials LLC ....G....... 248 632-7180
  Oak Park *(G-12620)*
Merchandising Productions ....D....... 616 676-6000
  Ada *(G-29)*
Mineral Cosmetics Inc ....G....... 248 542-7733
  Southfield *(G-15659)*
Ravenwood ....G....... 231 421-5682
  Traverse City *(G-16818)*
Stone Soap Company Inc ....E....... 248 706-1000
  Sylvan Lake *(G-16362)*

COSMETICS & TOILETRIES

A Naturally Empowered Lf Anel ....G....... 734 572-8857
  Ypsilanti *(G-18922)*
Amway International Dev Inc ....A....... 616 787-6000
  Ada *(G-7)*
Art of Shaving - FI LLC ....G....... 248 649-5872
  Troy *(G-16954)*
Avissa Skin+body ....G....... 734 316-5556
  Ann Arbor *(G-389)*
Brun Laboratories Inc ....G....... 616 456-1114
  Grand Rapids *(G-6527)*
Can You Handlebar LLC ....F....... 248 821-2171
  Mount Clemens *(G-11632)*
Canyouhandlebar LLC ....G....... 313 354-5851
  Royal Oak *(G-14524)*
Colors & Effects USA LLC ....D....... 973 245-6000
  Southfield *(G-15528)*
Conquest Scents ....F....... 810 653-2759
  Davison *(G-3778)*
Damionisha 823 Cosmetics LLC ....G....... 586 557-9893
  Detroit *(G-4120)*

Employee Codes: A=Over 500 employees, B=251-500
C=101-250, D=51-100, E=20-50, F=10-19, G=3-9

COSMETICS & TOILETRIES

David Lee Naturals..................................G........ 248 328-1131
  Holly *(G-8266)*
Diop Collection LLC...............................G........ 313 522-6029
  Detroit *(G-4178)*
Dollars From Scents..............................G........ 847 650-0317
  New ERA *(G-12028)*
Entrepreneur Solutions LLC...................G........ 248 660-2858
  Clinton Township *(G-3232)*
Fresh Heir LLC.......................................G........ 313 312-4492
  Farmington *(G-5138)*
Full of Scents...G........ 734 972-6542
  Northville *(G-12220)*
Homedics Usa LLC................................C........ 248 863-3000
  Commerce Township *(G-3539)*
Jogue Inc...G........ 313 921-4802
  Detroit *(G-4339)*
Judah Scents...G........ 810 219-9956
  Flint *(G-5719)*
Katarina Naturals...................................G........ 517 333-6880
  East Lansing *(G-4898)*
Lush..G........ 586 228-1594
  Clinton Township *(G-3282)*
Mid-West Behavioral Associates............G........ 517 267-5502
  Lansing *(G-9776)*
Oxford Brands LLC................................G........ 248 408-4020
  Oxford *(G-12906)*
Rejoice International Corp.....................G........ 855 345-5575
  Northville *(G-12253)*
Senica LLC..G........ 248 426-2200
  Southfield *(G-15697)*
Sensual Scents......................................G........ 586 306-4233
  Sterling Heights *(G-16169)*
Sephora Inside Jcpenney......................G........ 810 385-9800
  Fort Gratiot *(G-5824)*
Sephora Inside Jcpenney......................G........ 517 323-4000
  Lansing *(G-9790)*
Smo International Inc.............................F........ 248 275-1091
  Warren *(G-18015)*
Somerset Collection Ltd Partnr..............F........ 248 827-4600
  Troy *(G-17362)*
Stinkn Pretty LLC...................................G........ 517 694-8659
  Holt *(G-8333)*
Sweed Dreams LLC..............................G........ 313 704-6994
  Livonia *(G-10425)*
Whimsical Fusions LLC.........................G........ 248 956-0952
  Detroit *(G-4680)*

COSMETOLOGIST

Luma Laser and Medi Spa....................G........ 248 817-5499
  Bloomfield Hills *(G-1833)*

COSMETOLOGY & PERSONAL HYGIENE SALONS

Garden of Edyn.....................................G........ 517 410-9931
  Holt *(G-8313)*
Skin Bar VII LLC....................................G........ 313 397-9919
  Detroit *(G-4597)*

COSTUME JEWELRY & NOVELTIES: Apparel, Exc Precious Metals

Bead Gallery..F........ 734 663-6800
  Ann Arbor *(G-396)*

COSTUME JEWELRY & NOVELTIES: Bracelets, Exc Precious Metals

Bracelet Shack......................................G........ 312 656-9191
  Clarkston *(G-3021)*
Embracelets...G........ 616 719-3545
  Grand Rapids *(G-6674)*
Homes Bracelet.....................................G........ 231 499-9402
  Traverse City *(G-16713)*
Homes Bracelet LLC.............................G........ 231 463-9808
  Traverse City *(G-16714)*

COSTUME JEWELRY & NOVELTIES: Exc Semi & Precious

Amalgamations Ltd................................G........ 248 879-7345
  Troy *(G-16930)*

COSTUME JEWELRY & NOVELTIES: Rosaries & Sm Religious Items

Rosary Workshop..................................G........ 906 788-4846
  Stephenson *(G-15910)*

COUNTER & SINK TOPS

Custom Crafters....................................G........ 269 763-9180
  Bellevue *(G-1497)*
J & J Laminate Connection Inc..............G........ 810 227-1824
  Brighton *(G-2014)*
KS Liquidating LLC................................G........ 248 577-8220
  Madison Heights *(G-10765)*
Mica Crafters Inc...................................F........ 517 548-2924
  Howell *(G-8479)*
Paxton Products Inc..............................E........ 517 627-3688
  Lansing *(G-9783)*
Village Cabinet Shoppe Inc...................G........ 586 264-6464
  Sterling Heights *(G-16223)*

COUNTERS & COUNTING DEVICES

Ernest Industries Acquisition,................E........ 734 595-9500
  Westland *(G-18369)*
Mitchs Slots...G........ 586 739-5157
  Sterling Heights *(G-16102)*
Sidekick Device.....................................G........ 231 894-6905
  Whitehall *(G-18509)*

COUNTERS OR COUNTER DISPLAY CASES, EXC WOOD

Grand Valley Wood Products Inc...........E........ 616 475-5890
  Grand Rapids *(G-6779)*
Top Shop Inc...G........ 517 323-9085
  Lansing *(G-9744)*

COUNTERS OR COUNTER DISPLAY CASES, WOOD

Pohls Custom Counter Tops.................G........ 989 593-2174
  Fowler *(G-5831)*

COUNTING DEVICES: Controls, Revolution & Timing

Rap Electronics & Machines..................F........ 616 846-1437
  Grand Haven *(G-6350)*

COUNTING DEVICES: Electromechanical

Modular Data Systems Inc....................F........ 586 739-5870
  Shelby Township *(G-15282)*
Prestolite Electric LLC...........................G........ 248 313-3807
  Novi *(G-12512)*
Southern Auto Wholesalers Inc.............F........ 248 335-5555
  Pontiac *(G-13417)*

COUNTING DEVICES: Speedometers

U S Speedo Inc.....................................E........ 810 244-0909
  Flint *(G-5787)*

COUNTING DEVICES: Vehicle Instruments

Clark Brothers Instrument Co................F........ 586 781-7000
  Shelby Township *(G-15190)*
New Vintage Usa Inc.............................F........ 248 259-4964
  Oak Park *(G-12633)*

COUPLINGS, EXC PRESSURE & SOIL PIPE

O2/Specialty Mfg Holdings LLC.............G........ 248 554-4228
  Bloomfield Hills *(G-1845)*

COUPLINGS: Pipe

Norma Michigan Inc..............................C........ 248 373-4300
  Auburn Hills *(G-984)*

COUPLINGS: Shaft

Evans Industries Inc.............................G........ 313 272-8200
  Detroit *(G-4219)*
Hayes Manufacturing Inc......................E........ 231 879-3372
  Fife Lake *(G-5608)*
Liquid Drive Corporation.......................E........ 248 634-5382
  Mount Clemens *(G-11647)*
System Components Inc.......................E........ 269 637-2191
  South Haven *(G-15417)*

COUPON REDEMPTION SVCS

Epi Printers Inc......................................D........ 269 964-4600
  Battle Creek *(G-1227)*
Epi Printers Inc......................................D........ 269 968-2221
  Battle Creek *(G-1225)*

COURIER SVCS: Ground

Aunt Millies Bakeries Inc.......................E........ 734 528-1475
  Ypsilanti *(G-18925)*
Cosner Ice Company Inc......................B........ 812 279-8930
  Port Huron *(G-13466)*
Kolossos Printing Inc............................F........ 734 994-5400
  Ann Arbor *(G-540)*

COURTS OF LAW: County Government

Kent County...F........ 616 632-7580
  Grand Rapids *(G-6887)*

COVERS: Automobile Seat

Midori Auto Leather N Amer Inc............G........ 248 305-6437
  Novi *(G-12483)*
Sage Automotive Interiors Inc...............G........ 248 355-9055
  Southfield *(G-15692)*
Technotrim Inc.......................................A........ 734 254-5000
  Plymouth *(G-13311)*
Tk Mexico Inc..C........ 248 373-8040
  Auburn Hills *(G-1059)*

COVERS: Automotive, Exc Seat & Tire

AGM Automotive LLC............................D........ 248 776-0600
  Farmington Hills *(G-5162)*
Faurecia North America Inc..................F........ 248 288-1000
  Auburn Hills *(G-890)*
McCarthy Group Incorporated...............F........ 616 977-2900
  Grand Rapids *(G-6970)*
Michigan Industrial Trim Inc..................F........ 734 947-0344
  Taylor *(G-16445)*
Verduyn Tarps Detroit Inc.....................G........ 313 270-4890
  Detroit *(G-4665)*

COVERS: Canvas

TD Industrial Coverings Inc..................D........ 586 731-2080
  Sterling Heights *(G-16202)*

CRACKED CASTING REPAIR SVCS

Elden Industries Corp...........................F........ 734 946-6900
  Taylor *(G-16412)*

CRANE & AERIAL LIFT SVCS

Continental Crane & Service.................E........ 586 294-7900
  Fraser *(G-5915)*
Crane Technologies Group Inc.............E........ 248 652-8700
  Rochester Hills *(G-13985)*
Loshaw Bros Inc...................................G........ 989 732-7263
  Gaylord *(G-6143)*
Star Crane Hist Svc of Klmazoo............G........ 269 321-8882
  Portage *(G-13611)*

CRANES & MONORAIL SYSTEMS

Jervis B Webb Company.......................B........ 248 553-1000
  Novi *(G-12449)*
Star Crane Hist Svc of Klmazoo............G........ 269 321-8882
  Portage *(G-13611)*

CRANES: Indl Plant

Crane Technologies Group Inc.............E........ 248 652-8700
  Rochester Hills *(G-13985)*
Royal ARC Welding Company..............E........ 734 789-9099
  Flat Rock *(G-5628)*

CRANES: Overhead

C R B Crane & Service Co....................G........ 586 757-1222
  Warren *(G-17747)*
L & C Enterprises Inc............................G........ 231 943-7787
  Traverse City *(G-16736)*
Otsego Crane & Hoist LLC....................G........ 269 672-7222
  Otsego *(G-12792)*
Unified Industries Inc............................D........ 517 546-3220
  Brighton *(G-2087)*
Versa Handling Co................................G........ 313 491-0500
  Sterling Heights *(G-16222)*
Wolverine Crane & Service Inc.............E........ 616 538-4870
  Grand Rapids *(G-7345)*
Wolverine Crane & Service Inc.............F........ 734 467-9066
  Romulus *(G-14339)*

CRANKSHAFTS & CAMSHAFTS: Machining

4 Flutes Machining LLC........................G........ 269 330-1313
  Vicksburg *(G-17597)*

PRODUCT SECTION

Daniel Pruitoff .... G 616 392-1371
  Holland *(G-8013)*
Ddks Industries LLC .... G 586 323-5909
  Shelby Township *(G-15201)*
Iq Manufacturing LLC .... G 586 634-7185
  Auburn Hills *(G-940)*
Source 1 Cnc LLC .... G 734 269-3381
  Ida *(G-8624)*
Systrand Prsta Eng Systems LLC .... F 734 479-8100
  Brownstown Twp *(G-2160)*
Yen Group LLC .... F 810 201-6457
  Port Huron *(G-13542)*

CRANKSHAFTS: Motor Vehicle

Kellogg Crankshaft Co .... D 517 788-9200
  Jackson *(G-8928)*
Moldex Crank Shaft Inc .... G 313 561-7676
  Redford *(G-13747)*

CRATES: Fruit, Wood Wirebound

Monte Package Company LLC .... E 269 849-1722
  Riverside *(G-13864)*
Tk Enterprises Inc .... F 989 865-9915
  Saint Charles *(G-14810)*

CREDIT AGENCIES: Federal & Federally Sponsored

National Credit Corporation .... F 734 459-8100
  West Bloomfield *(G-18302)*

CREDIT CARD SVCS

Wholesale Proc Systems LLC .... G 833 755-6696
  Adrian *(G-104)*

CREDIT INST, SHORT-TERM BUSINESS: Accts Receiv & Coml Paper

National Credit Corporation .... F 734 459-8100
  West Bloomfield *(G-18302)*

CREDIT INST, SHORT-TERM BUSINESS: Financing Dealers

Ford Motor Company .... A 313 322-3000
  Dearborn *(G-3842)*
Ford Motor Company .... F 734 523-3000
  Livonia *(G-10215)*
Ford Motor Company .... F 734 942-6248
  Brownstown *(G-2146)*
General Motors LLC .... A 313 972-6000
  Detroit *(G-4257)*

CREMATORIES

American Vault Service .... G 989 366-8657
  Prudenville *(G-13655)*
Arnets Inc .... F 734 665-3650
  Ann Arbor *(G-379)*
Wilbert Burial Vault Company .... G 231 773-6631
  Muskegon *(G-11946)*
Wilbert Burial Vault Works .... G 906 786-0261
  Kingsford *(G-9519)*
Wilbert Saginaw Vault Corp .... G 989 753-3065
  Saginaw *(G-14794)*
Willbee Concrete Products Co .... F 517 782-8246
  Jackson *(G-9035)*

CROWNS & CLOSURES

Adcaa LLC .... G 734 623-4236
  Ann Arbor *(G-352)*

CRUDE PETROLEUM & NATURAL GAS PRODUCTION

Columbus Oil & Gas LLC .... G 810 385-9140
  Burtchville *(G-2218)*

CRUDE PETROLEUM & NATURAL GAS PRODUCTION

Cima Energy LP .... G 231 941-0633
  Traverse City *(G-16652)*
DTE Energy Company .... E 313 235-4000
  Detroit *(G-4193)*
DTE Energy Trust II .... G 313 235-8822
  Detroit *(G-4194)*
DTE Energy Ventures Inc .... G 313 235-8000
  Detroit *(G-4195)*
Landman .... G 231 946-4678
  Traverse City *(G-16738)*
Michigan Reef Development .... G 989 288-2172
  Durand *(G-4842)*
Miller Exploration Company .... F 231 941-0004
  Traverse City *(G-16758)*
Oil City Venture Inc .... G 989 832-8071
  Midland *(G-11399)*
Route 66 Pennzoil .... G 313 382-8888
  Taylor *(G-16468)*
SD Oil Enterprises Inc .... G 248 688-1419
  Warren *(G-18007)*
Summit-Reed City Inc .... E 989 433-5716
  Rosebush *(G-14367)*
William R Hall Kimberly .... G 989 426-4605
  Gladwin *(G-6208)*

CRUDE PETROLEUM PRODUCTION

Aztec Producing Co Inc .... G 269 792-0505
  Wayland *(G-18188)*
Bailer and De Shaw .... G 989 684-3610
  Kawkawlin *(G-9414)*
Blarney Castle Inc .... G 231 864-3111
  Bear Lake *(G-1416)*
Breitburn Operating LP .... G 989 348-8459
  Grayling *(G-7457)*
Christian Oil Company .... F 269 673-2218
  Allegan *(G-151)*
Dart Energy Corporation .... F 231 885-1665
  Mesick *(G-11271)*
Dcp Midstream LLC .... G 936 615-5189
  Marysville *(G-11086)*
Energy Acquisition .... G 616 350-9129
  Grandville *(G-7373)*
Goodale Enterprises LLC .... G 616 453-7690
  Grand Rapids *(G-6750)*
Jordan Exploration Co LLC .... E 231 935-4220
  Traverse City *(G-16731)*
Kelly Oil & Gas Inc .... G 231 929-0591
  Traverse City *(G-16732)*
Lease Management Inc .... G 989 773-5948
  Mount Pleasant *(G-11707)*
Mack Oil Corporation .... G 231 590-5903
  Traverse City *(G-16751)*
Muskegon Development Company .... E 989 772-4900
  Mount Pleasant *(G-11724)*
Omimex Energy Inc .... G 231 845-7358
  Ludington *(G-10549)*
Omimex Energy Inc .... F 517 628-2820
  Mason *(G-11148)*
Petroleum Resources Inc .... G 586 752-7856
  Romeo *(G-14232)*
Sappington Crude Oil Inc .... G 989 345-1052
  West Branch *(G-18340)*
Somoco Inc .... G 231 946-0200
  Traverse City *(G-16837)*
Southwestern Mich Dust Ctrl .... E 269 521-7638
  Bloomingdale *(G-1879)*
Speedway LLC .... F 231 775-8101
  Cadillac *(G-2355)*
Trendwell Energy Corporation .... F 616 866-5024
  Rockford *(G-14191)*
Tronox Incorporated .... G 231 328-4986
  Merritt *(G-11268)*
West Bay Exploration Company .... F 231 946-3529
  Traverse City *(G-16877)*

CULTURE MEDIA

87 Grams LLC .... F 248 558-0424
  Redford *(G-13708)*
A Taste of Leone LLC .... G 616 238-8881
  Grand Rapids *(G-6411)*
Vivica Miller LLC .... G 313 434-3280
  Detroit *(G-4673)*

CULVERTS: Sheet Metal

Jensen Bridge & Supply Company .... E 810 648-3000
  Sandusky *(G-15062)*
Schneider Iron & Metal Inc .... G 906 774-0644
  Iron Mountain *(G-8732)*

CUPS & PLATES: Foamed Plastics

Dart Container Corp Kentucky .... F 517 676-3800
  Mason *(G-11124)*
Dart Container Michigan LLC .... A 888 327-8001
  Lansing *(G-9828)*
Dart Container Michigan LLC .... A 517 694-9455
  Holt *(G-8309)*
Dart Container Michigan LLC .... A 517 676-3803
  Mason *(G-11129)*
Dart Container Michigan LLC .... A 800 248-5960
  Mason *(G-11128)*

CUPS: Plastic Exc Polystyrene Foam

Scic LLC .... D 800 248-5960
  Mason *(G-11153)*
Solo Cup Company LLC .... C 800 248-5960
  Mason *(G-11155)*

CURBING: Granite Or Stone

Granite City Inc .... F 248 478-0033
  Livonia *(G-10228)*

CURTAIN & DRAPERY FIXTURES: Poles, Rods & Rollers

All About Interiors .... G 616 452-8998
  Grand Rapids *(G-6444)*
Lorne Hanley .... G 248 547-9865
  Huntington Woods *(G-8622)*
Melody Digiglio .... G 586 754-4405
  Warren *(G-17923)*
Muskegon Awning & Mfg Co .... E 231 759-0911
  Muskegon *(G-11879)*
PCI Industries Inc .... D 248 542-2570
  Oak Park *(G-12637)*

CURTAINS & BEDDING: Knit

Star Textile Inc .... E 888 527-5700
  Madison Heights *(G-10836)*

CURTAINS: Window, From Purchased Materials

Barons Inc .... E 517 484-1366
  Lansing *(G-9813)*

CUSHIONS & PILLOWS

Arden Companies LLC .... E 248 415-8500
  Bingham Farms *(G-1691)*
Krams Enterprises Inc .... A 248 415-8500
  Bingham Farms *(G-1702)*

CUSHIONS & PILLOWS: Bed, From Purchased Materials

Jacquart Fabric Products Inc .... C 906 932-1339
  Ironwood *(G-8765)*

CUSTOM COMPOUNDING OF RUBBER MATERIALS

Jedtco Corp .... E 734 326-3010
  Westland *(G-18388)*
Mykin Inc .... F 248 667-8030
  South Lyon *(G-15448)*
Rex M Tubbs .... G 734 459-3180
  Plymouth *(G-13281)*
Specialty Pdts & Polymers Inc .... E 269 684-5931
  Niles *(G-12170)*

CUT STONE & STONE PRODUCTS

Booms Stone Company .... D 313 531-3000
  Redford *(G-13721)*
Botsg Inc .... D 231 929-2121
  Traverse City *(G-16625)*
Cig Jan Products Ltd .... E 616 698-9070
  Caledonia *(G-2371)*
Gmr Stone Products LLC .... F 586 739-2700
  Sterling Heights *(G-16032)*
Korcast Products Incorporated .... G 248 740-2340
  Troy *(G-17197)*
Landscape Stone Supply Inc .... G 616 953-2028
  Holland *(G-8123)*
Mellemas Cut Stone .... G 616 984-2493
  Sand Lake *(G-15049)*
Michigan Tile and Marble Co .... E 313 931-1700
  Detroit *(G-4453)*
Parker Property Dev Inc .... F 616 842-6118
  Grand Haven *(G-6343)*
Patten Monument Company .... D 616 785-4141
  Comstock Park *(G-3634)*

CUT STONE & STONE PRODUCTS

Royal Stone LLC .... E 248 343-6232
  Williamston *(G-18581)*
Superior Monuments Co .... G 231 728-2211
  Muskegon *(G-11928)*

CUTLERY

Crl Inc .... E 906 428-3710
  Gladstone *(G-6177)*

CUTLERY WHOLESALERS

PA Products Inc .... G 734 421-1060
  Livonia *(G-10357)*

CUTOUTS: Cardboard, Die-Cut, Made From Purchased Materials

Rizzo Packaging Inc .... E 269 685-5808
  Plainwell *(G-13093)*

CUTTING SVC: Paperboard

Design Converting Inc .... F 616 942-7780
  Grand Rapids *(G-6642)*

CYCLIC CRUDES & INTERMEDIATES

Diversfied Chem Tchnlgies Oprt ...... G 313 867-5444
  Detroit *(G-4179)*
Esco Co Ltd Partnership .... F 231 726-3106
  Muskegon *(G-11813)*
Esco Company LLC .... D 231 726-3106
  Grand Rapids *(G-6684)*
Sun Chemical Corporation .... C 231 788-2371
  Muskegon *(G-11927)*

CYLINDER & ACTUATORS: Fluid Power

Acutex Inc .... C 231 894-3200
  Whitehall *(G-18488)*
Beaver Aerospace & Defense Inc .... C 734 853-5003
  Livonia *(G-10133)*
Best Metal Products Co Inc .... C 616 942-7141
  Grand Rapids *(G-6502)*
Cpj Company Inc .... E 616 784-6355
  Comstock Park *(G-3598)*
Dadco Inc .... D 734 207-1100
  Plymouth *(G-13151)*
Dadco Inc .... G 616 785-2888
  Comstock Park *(G-3601)*
E J M Ball Screw LLC .... F 989 893-7674
  Bay City *(G-1349)*
Eaton Corporation .... G 517 789-1148
  Jackson *(G-8875)*
Ksb Dubric Inc .... E 616 784-6355
  Comstock Park *(G-3618)*
Lor Manufacturing Co Inc .... G 989 644-2581
  Weidman *(G-18254)*
Nabtesco Motion Control Inc .... F 248 553-3020
  Farmington Hills *(G-5329)*
Npi .... G 248 478-0010
  Farmington Hills *(G-5336)*
Parker-Hannifin Corporation .... B 269 629-5000
  Richland *(G-13826)*
Parker-Hannifin Corporation .... B 269 384-3459
  Kalamazoo *(G-9288)*
Peninsular Inc .... E 586 775-7211
  Roseville *(G-14461)*
R M Wright Company Inc .... E 248 476-9800
  Farmington Hills *(G-5363)*
Suspa Incorporated .... C 616 241-4200
  Grand Rapids *(G-7240)*

CYLINDERS: Pressure

Elden Cylinder Testing Inc .... E 734 946-6900
  Taylor *(G-16411)*
Mahle Eng Components USA Inc .... G 248 305-8200
  Farmington Hills *(G-5302)*
Peninsular Inc .... E 586 775-7211
  Roseville *(G-14461)*

CYLINDERS: Pump

K & M Industrial LLC .... G 906 420-8770
  Gladstone *(G-6182)*
Standfast Industries Inc .... F 248 380-3223
  Livonia *(G-10418)*
Yoe Industries Inc .... G 586 791-7660
  Clinton Township *(G-3391)*

DAIRY EQPT

Recon Technologies LLC .... G 616 241-1877
  Grand Rapids *(G-7145)*

DAIRY PRDTS STORE: Cheese

Reilchz Inc .... G 231 421-9600
  Traverse City *(G-16819)*

DAIRY PRDTS STORE: Ice Cream, Packaged

Alinosi French Ice Cream Co .... G 313 527-3195
  Detroit *(G-3997)*
Moo-Ville Inc .... F 517 852-9003
  Nashville *(G-11958)*

DAIRY PRDTS STORES

Guernsey Dairy Stores Inc .... C 248 349-1466
  Northville *(G-12227)*

DAIRY PRDTS WHOLESALERS: Fresh

C F Burger Creamery Co .... D 313 584-4040
  Detroit *(G-4084)*
Michigan Milk Producers Assn .... D 989 834-2221
  Ovid *(G-12815)*

DAIRY PRDTS: Butter

Blank Slate Creamery LLC .... F 734 218-3242
  Whitmore Lake *(G-18522)*
Brinks Family Creamery LLC .... G 231 826-0099
  Mc Bain *(G-11179)*
Browndog Creamery LLC .... F 248 361-3759
  Northville *(G-12199)*
Greenville Ventr Partners LLC .... E 616 303-2400
  Greenville *(G-7490)*
Inverness Dairy Inc .... E 231 627-4655
  Cheboygan *(G-2787)*
Michigan Milk Producers Assn .... D 269 435-2835
  Constantine *(G-3671)*
Michigan Milk Producers Assn .... E 248 474-6672
  Novi *(G-12481)*
Michigan Milk Producers Assn .... D 989 834-2221
  Ovid *(G-12815)*
Moo-Ville Inc .... F 517 852-9003
  Nashville *(G-11958)*

DAIRY PRDTS: Cheese

Country Home Creations Inc .... E 810 244-7348
  Flint *(G-5674)*
Greenville Ventr Partners LLC .... E 616 303-2400
  Greenville *(G-7490)*
Liberty Dairy Company .... C 800 632-5552
  Evart *(G-5125)*
Litehouse Inc .... C 616 897-5911
  Lowell *(G-10509)*
Michigan Chese Prtein Pdts LLC ..... G 517 403-5247
  Tipton *(G-16591)*
Williams Cheese Co .... E 989 697-4492
  Linwood *(G-10075)*

DAIRY PRDTS: Condensed Milk

Greenville Ventr Partners LLC .... E 616 303-2400
  Greenville *(G-7490)*

DAIRY PRDTS: Cream Substitutes

Bay Valley Foods LLC .... E 269 792-2277
  Wayland *(G-18189)*

DAIRY PRDTS: Dietary Supplements, Dairy & Non-Dairy Based

Castle Remedies Inc .... F 734 973-8990
  Ann Arbor *(G-415)*
Cherryflex Inc .... G 888 947-4047
  Traverse City *(G-16651)*
Enrinity Supplements Inc .... G 734 322-4966
  Westland *(G-18368)*
Green Room Michigan LLC .... F 248 289-3288
  Farmington Hills *(G-5255)*
Jaaz Management LLC .... G 248 957-9197
  Novi *(G-12447)*
Michigan Herbal Remedies LLC ...... G 616 818-0823
  Jenison *(G-9062)*

DAIRY PRDTS: Dried Milk

Michigan Milk Producers Assn .... E 248 474-6672
  Novi *(G-12481)*

DAIRY PRDTS: Evaporated Milk

Nestle Usa Inc .... C 231 928-2000
  Fremont *(G-6048)*

DAIRY PRDTS: Fermented & Cultured Milk Prdts

Langs Inc .... G 248 634-6048
  Holly *(G-8280)*

DAIRY PRDTS: Frozen Desserts & Novelties

Aj Hometown LLC .... G 313 415-0843
  Eastpointe *(G-4927)*
Blossom Berry .... G 517 775-6978
  Novi *(G-12374)*
Cold Stone Creamery .... F 313 886-4020
  Grosse Pointe Park *(G-7550)*
Custard Corner Inc .... G 734 771-4396
  Grosse Ile *(G-7517)*
Guernsey Dairy Stores Inc .... C 248 349-1466
  Northville *(G-12227)*
Hattiegirl Ice Cream Foods LLC .... G 877 444-3738
  Detroit *(G-4296)*
Iorio Gelato Kentwood LLC .... F 517 927-9928
  Grand Rapids *(G-6853)*
Loven Spoonful .... G 517 522-3953
  Grass Lake *(G-7440)*
Moo-Ville Inc .... F 517 852-9003
  Nashville *(G-11958)*
Plainwell Ice Cream Co .... F 269 685-8586
  Plainwell *(G-13088)*
Pump House .... G 616 647-5481
  Grand Rapids *(G-7125)*
Quality Dairy Company .... G 517 367-2400
  Lansing *(G-9887)*
Sweet Tmpttons Ice Cream Prlor ..... G 616 842-8108
  Grand Haven *(G-6369)*
That French Place .... G 231 437-6037
  Charlevoix *(G-2736)*
WG Sweis Investments LLC .... F 313 477-8433
  Washington *(G-18091)*

DAIRY PRDTS: Ice Cream & Ice Milk

Moomers Homemade Ice Cream LLC ... F 231 941-4122
  Traverse City *(G-16763)*

DAIRY PRDTS: Ice Cream, Bulk

Alinosi French Ice Cream Co .... G 313 527-3195
  Detroit *(G-3997)*
Berkley Frosty Freeze Inc .... G 248 336-2634
  Berkley *(G-1622)*
Deans Ice Cream Inc .... F 269 685-6641
  Plainwell *(G-13075)*
Frosty Cove .... G 231 343-6643
  Muskegon *(G-11822)*
Independent Dairy Inc .... E 734 241-6016
  Monroe *(G-11550)*
PGI of Saugatuck Inc .... E 800 443-5286
  Fennville *(G-5441)*
Rays Ice Cream Co Inc .... F 248 549-5256
  Royal Oak *(G-14573)*
Sherman Dairy Products Co Inc .... E 269 637-8251
  Holland *(G-8190)*
Strohs .... G 734 285-5480
  Wyandotte *(G-18841)*
Swirlberry .... G 734 779-0830
  Livonia *(G-10426)*
Whats Scoop .... G 616 662-6423
  Hudsonville *(G-8618)*

DAIRY PRDTS: Ice Cream, Packaged, Molded, On Sticks, Etc.

House of Flavors Inc .... C 231 845-7369
  Ludington *(G-10540)*

DAIRY PRDTS: Milk, Chocolate

Chocolate Vault Llc .... G 517 688-3388
  Horton *(G-8372)*

PRODUCT SECTION

DAIRY PRDTS: Milk, Condensed & Evaporated

Continental Dar Facilities LLC ....D....... 616 837-7641
  Coopersville *(G-3682)*
Dairy Farmers America Inc ....D....... 517 265-5045
  Adrian *(G-58)*
Gerber Products Company ....G....... 231 928-2076
  Fremont *(G-6042)*
Kerry Inc ....E....... 616 871-9940
  Detroit *(G-4358)*
Michigan Milk Producers Assn ....D....... 989 834-2221
  Ovid *(G-12815)*
Michigan Milk Producers Assn ....D....... 269 435-2835
  Constantine *(G-3671)*
Nestle Usa Inc ....C....... 989 755-7940
  Saginaw *(G-14709)*

DAIRY PRDTS: Milk, Fluid

Bay Valley Foods LLC ....E....... 269 792-2277
  Wayland *(G-18189)*
Calder Bros Dairy Inc ....E....... 313 381-8858
  Lincoln Park *(G-10044)*
Country Dairy Inc ....D....... 231 861-4636
  New ERA *(G-12027)*
Country Fresh LLC ....B....... 734 261-7980
  Romulus *(G-14264)*
Dairy Farmers America Inc ....D....... 517 265-5045
  Adrian *(G-58)*
Greenville Ventr Partners LLC ....E....... 616 303-2400
  Greenville *(G-7490)*
Instantwhip Detroit Inc ....G....... 734 379-9474
  Rockwood *(G-14200)*
Melody Farms LLC ....F....... 734 261-7980
  Livonia *(G-10310)*
Michigan Milk Producers Assn ....E....... 248 474-6672
  Novi *(G-12481)*
Yoplait USA ....F....... 231 832-3285
  Reed City *(G-13804)*

DAIRY PRDTS: Milk, Processed, Pasteurized, Homogenized/Btld

C F Burger Creamery Co ....D....... 313 584-4040
  Detroit *(G-4084)*
Cream Cup Dairy ....G....... 231 889-4158
  Kaleva *(G-9377)*
Inverness Dairy Inc ....E....... 231 627-4655
  Cheboygan *(G-2787)*
Liberty Dairy Company ....C....... 800 632-5552
  Evart *(G-5125)*
Michigan Milk Producers Assn ....D....... 989 834-2221
  Ovid *(G-12815)*
Michigan Milk Producers Assn ....D....... 269 435-2835
  Constantine *(G-3671)*
Quality Dairy Company ....E....... 517 367-2400
  Lansing *(G-9887)*

DAIRY PRDTS: Natural Cheese

Agropur Inc ....E....... 616 538-3822
  Grand Rapids *(G-6439)*
Cheese Lady LLC ....G....... 231 728-3000
  Muskegon *(G-11792)*
Kross Kraft LLC ....G....... 616 399-9167
  Holland *(G-8116)*
Leprino Foods Company ....B....... 989 967-3635
  Remus *(G-13815)*
Leprino Foods Company ....B....... 616 895-5800
  Allendale *(G-223)*
Michigan Farm Cheese Dairy ....G....... 231 462-3301
  Fountain *(G-5827)*
MWC (michigan) LLC ....G....... 575 791-9559
  Saint Johns *(G-14910)*
Natural Way Cheese ....G....... 989 935-9380
  Clare *(G-2988)*
White Lotus Farms Inc ....G....... 734 904-1379
  Ann Arbor *(G-716)*
Windshadow Farm & Dairy LLC ....G....... 269 599-0467
  Bangor *(G-1132)*

DAIRY PRDTS: Powdered Milk

Verndale Products Inc ....E....... 313 834-4190
  Detroit *(G-4666)*

DAIRY PRDTS: Processed Cheese

Kraft Outdoor Svc ....G....... 517 404-8023
  Fowlerville *(G-5848)*

Krafts & Thingz ....G....... 810 689-2457
  Chesterfield *(G-2904)*
Schreiber Foods Inc ....E....... 616 538-3822
  Grand Rapids *(G-7184)*

DAIRY PRDTS: Spreads, Cheese

OH So Cheesy LLC ....G....... 616 835-1249
  Grand Rapids *(G-7055)*

DAIRY PRDTS: Yogurt, Exc Frozen

Bloomberry ....G....... 586 212-9510
  East China *(G-4856)*
Fruit Fro Yo ....G....... 517 580-3967
  Okemos *(G-12668)*
General Mills Inc ....E....... 231 832-3285
  Reed City *(G-13790)*
Rocky Mtn Choclat Fctry Inc ....D....... 810 606-8550
  Grand Blanc *(G-6261)*
Sugar Berry ....G....... 517 321-0177
  Lansing *(G-9792)*
Sweet Earth ....G....... 248 850-8031
  Royal Oak *(G-14583)*
Twist ....G....... 248 859-2169
  West Bloomfield *(G-18320)*
Yogurtown Inc ....F....... 313 908-9376
  Dearborn *(G-3917)*

DAIRY PRDTS: Yogurt, Frozen

D Sharp Masonry ....G....... 313 292-2375
  Taylor *(G-16399)*
Froyo Pinckney LLC ....G....... 248 310-4465
  Pinckney *(G-13048)*
Gnass Masonry LLC ....G....... 616 530-3214
  Byron Center *(G-2273)*
May Venture Inc ....G....... 248 481-3890
  Lake Orion *(G-9618)*
Stuarts of Novi ....F....... 248 615-2955
  Novi *(G-12547)*

DATA PROCESSING & PREPARATION SVCS

Beljan Ltd Inc ....F....... 734 426-3503
  Dexter *(G-4726)*
Mejenta Systems Inc ....E....... 248 434-2583
  Southfield *(G-15653)*
Sync Technologies Inc ....E....... 313 963-5353
  Detroit *(G-4622)*

DATA PROCESSING SVCS

Ancor Information MGT LLC ....D....... 248 740-8866
  Troy *(G-16936)*
Covisint Corporation ....B....... 248 483-2000
  Southfield *(G-15533)*
Datamatic Processing Inc ....E....... 517 882-4401
  Lansing *(G-9829)*
Mc Donald Computer Corporation ....E....... 248 350-9290
  Southfield *(G-15650)*
Melange Computer Services Inc ....F....... 517 321-8434
  Lansing *(G-9774)*
Sage Direct Inc ....F....... 616 940-8311
  Grand Rapids *(G-7178)*
TGI Direct Inc ....E....... 810 239-5553
  Flint *(G-5778)*
Uniband Usa LLC ....F....... 616 676-6011
  Grand Rapids *(G-7296)*

DECORATIVE WOOD & WOODWORK

Ausable Woodworking Co Inc ....E....... 989 348-7086
  Frederic *(G-6014)*
Burlwoodbox ....G....... 734 662-7274
  Ann Arbor *(G-410)*
Cards of Wood Inc ....G....... 616 887-8680
  Belmont *(G-1504)*
CHR W LLC ....F....... 989 755-4000
  Saginaw *(G-14628)*
Dynamic Wood Solutions ....G....... 616 935-7727
  Spring Lake *(G-15811)*
Koetje Wood Products Inc ....G....... 616 393-9191
  Holland *(G-8114)*
Oakwood Sports Inc ....G....... 517 321-6852
  Lansing *(G-9782)*
Silver Street Incorporated ....E....... 231 861-2194
  Shelby *(G-15160)*
Smith Manufacturing Co Inc ....F....... 269 925-8155
  Benton Harbor *(G-1586)*
Thompson Art Glass Inc ....G....... 810 225-8766
  Brighton *(G-2081)*

DENTAL EQPT & SPLYS

Toms World of Wood ....G....... 517 264-2836
  Adrian *(G-99)*

DEFENSE SYSTEMS & EQPT

313 Industries Inc ....F....... 313 338-9700
  Warren *(G-17677)*
Adept Defense LLC ....G....... 231 758-2792
  Petoskey *(G-12987)*
Allied Defense ....G....... 810 252-9232
  Goodrich *(G-6221)*
Antrim Machine Products Inc ....E....... 231 587-9114
  Mancelona *(G-10866)*
Brandons Defense ....G....... 517 669-5272
  Dewitt *(G-4707)*
Center For Qlty Trning Intl LL ....G....... 586 212-9524
  Shelby Township *(G-15183)*
D&D Defense LLC ....G....... 248 255-8765
  Ceresco *(G-2703)*
Eotech ....G....... 248 971-4027
  Ann Arbor *(G-477)*
G Defense Company B ....G....... 616 202-4500
  Grand Rapids *(G-6731)*
Gen3 Defense and Aerospace LLC ....F....... 616 345-8031
  Comstock Park *(G-3607)*
Kba Defense ....G....... 586 552-9268
  Lakeville *(G-9648)*
Kings Self Defense LLC ....G....... 910 890-4322
  Grand Rapids *(G-6897)*
Leviathan Defense Group ....G....... 419 575-7792
  Newport *(G-12104)*
Navistar Defense LLC ....G....... 248 680-7505
  Madison Heights *(G-10789)*
Pierce Personal Defense LLC ....G....... 269 664-6960
  Plainwell *(G-13087)*
Project Echo LLC ....F....... 248 971-4027
  Clawson *(G-3105)*
Riverside Defense Training LLC ....G....... 231 825-2895
  Lake City *(G-9554)*
Slip Defense Inc ....G....... 248 366-4423
  White Lake *(G-18464)*
Split Second Defense LLC ....G....... 586 709-1385
  Fraser *(G-5999)*
Superior Fabrication Co LLC ....D....... 906 495-5634
  Kincheloe *(G-9505)*

DEGREASING MACHINES

Kimastle Corporation ....D....... 586 949-2355
  Chesterfield *(G-2902)*
Midbrook Inc ....D....... 800 966-9274
  Jackson *(G-8959)*
Oneiric Systems Inc ....G....... 248 554-3090
  Madison Heights *(G-10792)*
Safety-Kleen Systems Inc ....G....... 989 753-3261
  Saginaw *(G-14743)*

DEHUMIDIFIERS: Electric

Mann + Hummel Inc ....G....... 269 329-3900
  Portage *(G-13581)*

DEHYDRATION EQPT

Bermaxx LLC ....G....... 248 299-3600
  Rochester Hills *(G-13963)*
Indian Summer Cooperative Inc ....C....... 231 873-7504
  Hart *(G-7755)*

DELIVERY SVCS, BY VEHICLE

Detroit Ready Mix Concrete ....F....... 313 931-7043
  Detroit *(G-4160)*
Pressure Releases Corporation ....F....... 616 531-8116
  Grand Rapids *(G-7103)*
Wolverine Concrete Products ....G....... 313 931-7189
  Detroit *(G-4687)*

DENTAL EQPT

Axsys Inc ....E....... 248 926-8810
  Wixom *(G-18616)*
Select Dental Equipment LLC ....G....... 734 667-1194
  Canton *(G-2523)*

DENTAL EQPT & SPLYS

Akervall Technologies Inc ....F....... 800 444-0570
  Saline *(G-14999)*
Avo Dental Supplies LLC ....G....... 586 585-1210
  Roseville *(G-14378)*
Dental Art Laboratories Inc ....D....... 517 485-2200
  Lansing *(G-9689)*

Employee Codes: A=Over 500 employees, B=251-500
C=101-250, D=51-100, E=20-50, F=10-19, G=3-9

2022 Harris Michigan Industrial Directory

1249

DENTAL EQPT & SPLYS

End Product Results LLC ....F 586 585-1210
  Roseville (G-14405)
Ktr Dental Lab & Pdts LLC ....F 248 224-9158
  Southfield (G-15622)
Liquid Otc LLC ....G 248 214-7771
  Commerce Township (G-3551)
Microdental Laboratories Inc ....G 877 711-8778
  Troy (G-17259)
Ranir LLC ....E 616 957-7790
  Kentwood (G-9475)
Ranir LLC ....B 616 698-8880
  Grand Rapids (G-7139)
Ranir Global Holdings LLC ....A 616 698-8880
  Grand Rapids (G-7140)
Visual Chimera ....F 586 585-1210
  Eastpointe (G-4948)

DENTAL EQPT & SPLYS: Cabinets

Biotec Incorporated ....D 616 772-2133
  Zeeland (G-18999)

DENTAL EQPT & SPLYS: Compounds

Phoenix Dental Inc ....G 810 750-2328
  Fenton (G-5495)

DENTAL EQPT & SPLYS: Dental Materials

Kerr Corporation ....B 734 946-7800
  Romulus (G-14294)
Voco America Inc ....G 248 568-0964
  Howell (G-8540)

DENTAL EQPT & SPLYS: Enamels

Andrew J Reisterer D D S Pllc ....G 231 845-8989
  Ludington (G-10526)
David R Lacharite Lmsw ....G 517 347-0988
  Okemos (G-12663)
Mary Palaszek Dr ....G 616 453-2255
  Grand Rapids (G-6963)
New Image Dental P C ....G 586 727-1100
  Richmond (G-13843)

DENTAL EQPT & SPLYS: Impression Materials

Aluwax Dental Products Co Inc ....G 616 895-4385
  Allendale (G-213)

DENTAL EQPT & SPLYS: Metal

Tokusen Hytech Inc ....C 269 685-1768
  Plainwell (G-13099)

DENTAL EQPT & SPLYS: Teeth, Artificial, Exc In Dental Labs

Pdl LLC ....G 810 844-3209
  Howell (G-8492)

DENTISTS' OFFICES & CLINICS

Dental Art Laboratories Inc ....D 517 485-2200
  Lansing (G-9689)
Paul W Reed DDS ....G 231 347-4145
  Petoskey (G-13012)

DERMATOLOGICALS

Affiliated Troy Dermatologist ....F 248 267-5020
  Troy (G-16910)
Harper Dermatology PC ....G 586 776-7546
  Grosse Pointe Shores (G-7562)

DESIGN SVCS, NEC

A and D Design Electronics ....G 989 493-1884
  Auburn (G-762)
Adam Electronics Incorporated ....E 248 583-2000
  Madison Heights (G-10659)
Advanced Research Company ....F 248 475-4770
  Orion (G-12723)
Auto/Con Services LLC ....G 586 791-7474
  Fraser (G-5898)
Automotive Manufacturing ....G 517 566-8174
  Sunfield (G-16333)
Bbcm Inc ....G 248 410-2528
  Bloomfield Hills (G-1803)
Cusack Music LLC ....E 616 546-8888
  Holland (G-8008)
Glov Enterprises LLC ....D 517 423-9700
  Tecumseh (G-16502)

Holland Vision Systems Inc ....E 616 494-9974
  Holland (G-8087)
Novares Corporation US Inc ....C 248 449-6100
  Livonia (G-10338)
Paslin Company ....C 586 755-3606
  Warren (G-17958)
Phoenix Trailer & Body Company ....F 248 360-7184
  Commerce Township (G-3563)
Ram Die Corp ....F 616 647-2855
  Grand Rapids (G-7138)
Renes Inc ....G 810 294-5008
  Croswell (G-3735)
Rka Design Build ....G 269 362-5558
  Buchanan (G-2203)
State News Inc ....D 517 295-1680
  East Lansing (G-4909)
Straight Line Design ....G 616 296-0920
  Spring Lake (G-15853)
Window Designs Inc ....F 616 396-5295
  Holland (G-8250)

DESIGN SVCS: Commercial & Indl

Cfe Racing Products Inc ....G 586 773-6310
  Eastpointe (G-4931)
Design Fabrications Inc ....D 248 597-0988
  Madison Heights (G-10705)
Electrodynamics Inc ....G 734 422-5420
  Livonia (G-10193)
Icon Industries Inc ....G 616 241-1877
  Grand Rapids (G-6829)
Refrigeration Concepts Inc ....E 616 785-7335
  Comstock Park (G-3643)
RTD Manufacturing Inc ....E 517 783-1550
  Jackson (G-9002)

DESIGN SVCS: Computer Integrated Systems

Active Solutions Group Inc ....G 313 278-4522
  Dearborn (G-3805)
Cypress Computer Systems Inc ....F 810 245-2300
  Lapeer (G-9924)
Driven-4 LLC ....G 269 281-7567
  Saint Joseph (G-14927)
Freedom Technologies Corp ....E 810 227-3737
  Brighton (G-1993)
Intellibee Inc ....E 313 586-4122
  Detroit (G-4323)
Moog Inc ....G 734 738-5862
  Plymouth (G-13248)
Reply Inc ....C 248 686-2481
  Auburn Hills (G-1018)
Startech-Solutions LLC ....G 248 419-0650
  West Bloomfield (G-18316)
Sync Technologies Inc ....E 313 963-5353
  Detroit (G-4622)
V2soft Inc ....D 248 904-1702
  Bloomfield Hills (G-1872)
Vector North America Inc ....D 248 449-9290
  Novi (G-12565)

DESIGN SVCS: Hand Tools

Umix Dissoultion Corp ....F 586 446-9950
  Sterling Heights (G-16214)

DETECTION APPARATUS: Electronic/Magnetic Field, Light/Heat

Electronic Design & Packg Co ....F 734 591-9176
  Livonia (G-10194)
N S International Ltd ....C 248 251-1600
  Troy (G-17272)
Tetradyn Ltd ....G 202 415-7295
  Traverse City (G-16855)

DETECTION EQPT: Aeronautical Electronic Field

Universal Magnetics Inc ....G 231 937-5555
  Howard City (G-8420)

DETECTIVE & ARMORED CAR SERVICES

Ernie Romanco ....G 517 531-3686
  Albion (G-125)

DEVELOPING & PRINTING: Motion Picture Film, Commercial

Star Design Metro Detroit LLC ....E 734 740-0189
  Livonia (G-10419)

DIAGNOSTIC SUBSTANCES

Great Lakes Diagnostics Inc ....G 248 307-9494
  Troy (G-17133)
Greenmark Biomedical Inc ....G 517 336-4665
  Lansing (G-9847)
Nanosynthons LLC ....G 989 317-3737
  Mount Pleasant (G-11726)
Neogen Corporation ....G 800 327-5487
  Saint Joseph (G-14951)
Ovascience Inc ....C 617 351-2590
  Ann Arbor (G-603)
Retrosense Therapeutics LLC ....G 734 369-9333
  Ann Arbor (G-639)
Sigma Diagnostics Inc ....G 734 744-4846
  Livonia (G-10407)
Swift Biosciences Inc ....G 734 330-2568
  Ann Arbor (G-669)

DIAGNOSTIC SUBSTANCES OR AGENTS: Blood Derivative

Ortho-Clinical Diagnostics Inc ....G 248 797-8087
  Troy (G-17292)
Plasma Biolife Services L P ....G 616 667-0264
  Grandville (G-7409)

DIAGNOSTIC SUBSTANCES OR AGENTS: In Vitro

Microx Labs Inc ....G 248 318-3548
  Bloomfield Hills (G-1838)
Nanorete Inc ....G 517 336-4680
  Lansing (G-9873)

DIAGNOSTIC SUBSTANCES OR AGENTS: Microbiology & Virology

Applied Genomics ....G 313 458-7318
  Grosse Pointe Park (G-7547)
Biosan Laboratories Inc ....F 586 755-8970
  Warren (G-17738)
Cooper Genomics ....G 313 579-9650
  Plymouth (G-13150)

DIAGNOSTIC SUBSTANCES OR AGENTS: Radioactive

Petnet Solutions Inc ....G 865 218-2000
  Royal Oak (G-14567)
Versant Med Physics Rdtion SFE ....E 888 316-3644
  Kalamazoo (G-9361)

DIAGNOSTIC SUBSTANCES OR AGENTS: Veterinary

Neogen Corporation ....A 517 372-9200
  Lansing (G-9874)

DIAMOND SETTER SVCS

C T & T Inc ....E 248 623-9422
  Waterford (G-18107)

DIE CUTTING SVC: Paper

Diecutting Service Inc ....F 734 426-0290
  Dexter (G-4740)

DIE SETS: Presses, Metal Stamping

Acme Carbide Die Inc ....E 734 722-2303
  Westland (G-18351)
Anchor Danly Inc ....G 989 875-5400
  Ithaca (G-8786)
Anchor Lamina America Inc ....E 248 489-9122
  Bellaire (G-1469)
Artiflex Manufacturing LLC ....C 616 459-8285
  Grand Rapids (G-6473)
Concord Tool and Mfg Inc ....C 586 465-6537
  Mount Clemens (G-11634)
Connell Limited Partnership ....G 989 875-5135
  Ithaca (G-8789)
Danly IEM ....G 800 243-2659
  Grand Rapids (G-6632)

De Luxe Die Set Inc G 810 227-2556
Brighton *(G-1974)*
Hardy-Reed Tool & Die Co Inc E 517 547-7107
Manitou Beach *(G-10927)*
Jbl Systems Inc G 586 802-6700
Shelby Township *(G-15244)*
JD Edwards MGT Group Inc G 586 727-4039
Casco *(G-2599)*
Kraftube Inc C 231 832-5562
Reed City *(G-13793)*
Pioneer Steel Corporation E 616 878-5800
Byron Center *(G-2291)*
Pioneer Steel Corporation E 313 933-9400
Detroit *(G-4525)*
Precision Parts Holdings Inc A 248 853-9010
Rochester Hills *(G-14088)*
R & S Tool & Die Inc G 989 673-8511
Caro *(G-2579)*
R D M Enterprises Co Inc G 810 985-4721
Port Huron *(G-13520)*
Schwab Industries Inc E 586 566-8090
Shelby Township *(G-15326)*
True Industrial Corporation D 586 771-3500
Roseville *(G-14487)*
Williams Tooling & Mfg E 616 681-2093
Dorr *(G-4771)*
Yarema Die & Engineering Co C 248 585-2830
Troy *(G-17457)*

DIES & TOOLS: Special

2k Tool LLC G 616 452-4927
Wyoming *(G-18846)*
A B M Tool & Die Inc G 734 432-6060
Livonia *(G-10093)*
A J Tool Co F 517 787-5755
Jackson *(G-8798)*
A S A P Tool Inc G 586 790-6550
Clinton Township *(G-3147)*
Accu Die & Mold Inc E 269 465-4020
Stevensville *(G-16237)*
Action Die & Tool Inc G 616 538-2326
Grandville *(G-7362)*
Action Mold & Machining Inc E 616 452-1580
Grand Rapids *(G-6424)*
Action Tool & Machine Inc E 810 229-6300
Brighton *(G-1938)*
Ada Gage Inc G 616 676-3338
Ada *(G-4)*
Adrian Precision Machining LLC F 517 263-4564
Adrian *(G-49)*
Advanced Tooling Systems Inc G 616 784-7513
Comstock Park *(G-3586)*
Advantage Design & Tool Inc G 586 463-2800
Clinton Township *(G-3158)*
Aero Foil International Inc E 231 773-0200
Muskegon *(G-11765)*
Aggressive Tool & Die Inc E 616 837-1983
Coopersville *(G-3679)*
Aggressive Tooling Inc D 616 754-1404
Greenville *(G-7475)*
Airmetal Corporation F 517 784-6000
Jackson *(G-8807)*
Al-Craft Design & Engrg Inc G 248 589-3827
Troy *(G-16918)*
Alcona Tool & Machine Inc E 989 736-8151
Harrisville *(G-7741)*
Alcona Tool & Machine Inc G 989 736-8151
Lincoln *(G-10033)*
Allen Tool and Die LLC G 734 224-7900
Temperance *(G-16526)*
Alliance Tool and Machine Co F 586 427-6411
Saint Clair Shores *(G-14847)*
Allied Tool and Machine Co E 989 755-5384
Saginaw *(G-14604)*
Amber Manufacturing Inc G 586 218-6080
Fraser *(G-5890)*
American Die Corporation F 810 794-4080
Clay *(G-3115)*
American Tooling Center Inc G 517 522-8411
Lansing *(G-9672)*
American Tooling Center Inc G 517 522-8411
Jackson *(G-8815)*
American Tooling Center Inc D 517 522-8411
Grass Lake *(G-7435)*
Anitom Automation LLC E 517 278-6205
Coldwater *(G-3419)*
Applied Mechanics Corporation G 616 677-1355
Grand Rapids *(G-6464)*
Argus Corporation E 313 937-2900
Redford *(G-13716)*
Arrow Die & Mold Repair G 231 689-1829
White Cloud *(G-18438)*
Athey Precision Inc G 989 386-4523
Clare *(G-2973)*
Auto Craft Tool & Die Co D 810 794-4929
Clay *(G-3116)*
Autodie LLC C 616 454-9361
Grand Rapids *(G-6483)*
Axis Machine & Tool Inc G 616 738-2196
Holland *(G-7968)*
B & B Mold & Engineering Inc G 586 773-6664
Warren *(G-17721)*
B & M Machine & Tool Company G 989 288-2934
Durand *(G-4839)*
B C Manufacturing Inc F 248 344-0101
Wixom *(G-18617)*
Badger Tool LLC G 586 246-1810
Sterling Heights *(G-15941)*
Bauer Precision Tool Co G 586 758-7370
Warren *(G-17728)*
Baumann Tool & Die G 616 772-6768
Zeeland *(G-18995)*
Baxter Machine & Tool Co E 517 782-2808
Jackson *(G-8822)*
Bay Area Tool LLC G 231 946-3500
Traverse City *(G-16613)*
Bay Products Inc E 586 296-7130
Fraser *(G-5902)*
Bel-Kur Inc E 734 847-0651
Temperance *(G-16528)*
Bernal LLC D 248 299-3600
Rochester Hills *(G-13964)*
Bessey Tool & Die Inc F 616 887-8820
Sparta *(G-15760)*
Best Tool & Engineering Co F 586 792-4119
Clinton Township *(G-3183)*
Betz Contracting Inc G 269 746-3320
Climax *(G-3134)*
Big 3 Precision Products Inc F 313 846-6601
Dearborn *(G-3815)*
Bilar Tool & Die G 248 740-3400
Warren *(G-17736)*
Blackledge Tool Inc G 989 865-8393
Saint Charles *(G-14801)*
Boda Corporation G 906 353-7320
Chassell *(G-2776)*
Bolman Die Services Inc F 810 919-2262
Sterling Heights *(G-15947)*
Borgia Die & Engineering Inc F 616 677-3595
Marne *(G-10990)*
Borgman Tool & Engineering LLC G 231 733-4133
Muskegon *(G-11783)*
Boyers Tool and Die Inc G 517 782-7869
Jackson *(G-8826)*
Bradley-Thompson Tool Company E 248 352-1466
Southfield *(G-15510)*
Bridge Tool and Die LLC G 231 269-3200
Buckley *(G-2205)*
Briggs Mold & Die Inc G 517 784-6908
Jackson *(G-8827)*
Bry Mac Inc G 231 799-2211
Norton Shores *(G-12280)*
Btmc Holdings Inc G 616 794-0100
Belding *(G-1442)*
Buckingham Tool Corp E 734 591-2333
Livonia *(G-10142)*
Buiter Tool & Die Inc E 616 455-7410
Grand Rapids *(G-6529)*
C & D Tool & Die Company Inc E 248 922-5937
Davisburg *(G-3762)*
C & H Stamping Inc E 517 750-3600
Jackson *(G-8829)*
C & M Tool LLC G 734 944-3355
Saline *(G-15006)*
C & R Tool Die G 231 584-3588
Alba *(G-113)*
Cad CAM Services Inc F 616 554-5222
Grand Rapids *(G-6544)*
Cadillac Tool and Die Inc G 231 775-9007
Cadillac *(G-2324)*
Cambria Tool and Machine Inc F 517 437-3500
Hillsdale *(G-7928)*
Cambron Engineering Inc E 989 684-5890
Bay City *(G-1334)*
Cameron Tool Corporation D 517 487-3671
Lansing *(G-9820)*
Cammand Machining LLC E 586 752-0366
Romeo *(G-14222)*
Carroll Tool and Die Co E 586 949-7670
Macomb *(G-10583)*
Cav Tool Company F 248 349-7860
Novi *(G-12381)*
Centerline Engineering Inc D 616 735-2506
Comstock Park *(G-3592)*
Central Industrial Mfg Inc F 231 347-5920
Harbor Springs *(G-7644)*
Century Tool & Gage LLC D 810 629-0784
Fenton *(G-5463)*
Certified Metal Products Inc F 586 598-1000
Clinton Township *(G-3196)*
CG Automation & Fixture Inc E 616 785-5400
Comstock Park *(G-3593)*
Chalker Tool & Gauge Inc F 586 977-8660
Sterling Heights *(G-15956)*
Cherry Bend Tool & Die G 231 947-3046
Cedar *(G-2638)*
Circle Engineering Inc G 586 978-8120
Sterling Heights *(G-15959)*
Cole Tooling Systems Inc E 586 573-9450
Lake Orion *(G-9596)*
Coles Machine Service Inc E 810 658-5373
Davison *(G-3777)*
Concept Tooling Systems Inc E 616 301-6906
Grand Rapids *(G-6591)*
Contour Tool & Engineering Inc G 616 772-6360
Zeeland *(G-19006)*
Corban Industries Inc E 248 393-2720
Orion *(G-12726)*
Crash Tool Inc F 517 552-0250
Howell *(G-8441)*
Cs Tool Engineering Inc E 616 696-0940
Cedar Springs *(G-2648)*
CTS Manufacturing Inc G 586 465-4594
Clinton Township *(G-3214)*
Custer Tool & Mfg LLC G 734 854-5943
Lambertville *(G-9651)*
Custom Tool & Die Service Inc G 616 662-1068
Hudsonville *(G-8577)*
Custom Tooling Systems Inc D 616 748-9880
Zeeland *(G-19012)*
D & F Mold LLC E 269 465-6633
Bridgman *(G-1923)*
D & L Tooling Inc G 517 369-5655
Bronson *(G-2110)*
Datum Industries LLC E 616 977-1995
Grand Rapids *(G-6633)*
Davis Steel Rule Die G 269 492-9908
Kalamazoo *(G-9164)*
Dayton Lamina Corp F 231 533-8646
Bellaire *(G-1473)*
Deppe Mold & Tooling Inc E 616 530-1331
Grandville *(G-7370)*
Diamond Die and Mold Company F 586 791-0700
Clinton Township *(G-3221)*
Die-Matic USA LLC E 616 531-0060
Wyoming *(G-18868)*
Die-Mold-Automation Component G 313 581-6510
Dearborn *(G-3829)*
Die-Namic Inc C 734 710-3200
Van Buren Twp *(G-17525)*
Die-Namic Tool & Design Llc F 517 787-4900
Jackson *(G-8867)*
Die-Namic Tool Corp G 616 954-7882
Grand Rapids *(G-6646)*
Die-Tech and Engineering Inc E 616 530-9030
Grand Rapids *(G-6647)*
Die-Verse Solutions LLC G 616 914-9427
Marne *(G-10992)*
Dies and Fixtures Mold Corp G 269 465-6633
Bridgman *(G-1924)*
Digital Tool & Die Inc E 616 532-8020
Grandville *(G-7371)*
Diversified Tool & Engineering F 734 692-1260
Grosse Ile *(G-7519)*
Do Rite Tool Inc G 734 522-7510
Brighton *(G-1976)*
Dr and HI Mold and Mch Inc G 989 672-2192
Caro *(G-2569)*
Dura Mold Inc D 269 465-3301
Stevensville *(G-16248)*
Dynamic Plastics Inc E 586 749-6100
Chesterfield *(G-2872)*
E & D Machine Company Inc E 248 473-0255
Farmington *(G-5137)*
E-T-M Enterprises I Inc C 517 627-8461
Grand Ledge *(G-6389)*
Eagle Indus Group Federal LLC G 616 863-8623
Grand Rapids *(G-6661)*
East River Machine & Tool Inc G 231 767-1701
Muskegon *(G-11807)*

Employee Codes: A=Over 500 employees, B=251-500
C=101-250, D=51-100, E=20-50, F=10-19, G=3-9
2022 Harris Michigan
Industrial Directory
1251

Eclipse Tool & Die Inc.....E..... 616 877-3717
Wayland *(G-18195)*
Edwards Machining Inc.....E..... 517 782-2568
Jackson *(G-8876)*
Eikos Holdings Inc.....E..... 248 280-0300
Troy *(G-17080)*
Ekstrom Industries Inc.....D..... 248 477-0040
Novi *(G-12412)*
Emcor Inc.....F..... 989 667-0652
Bay City *(G-1350)*
Emmie Die and Engineering Corp.....G..... 810 346-2914
Brown City *(G-2136)*
Empire Machine Company.....F..... 269 684-3713
Saint Joseph *(G-14929)*
Engineered Tooling Systems Inc.....F..... 616 647-5063
Grand Rapids *(G-6681)*
Enmark Tool Company.....E..... 586 293-2797
Fraser *(G-5925)*
Enterprise Tool & Die LLC.....D..... 616 538-0920
Grandville *(G-7374)*
ERA Tool & Engineering Co.....F..... 734 464-7788
Farmington Hills *(G-5235)*
Evolution Tool Inc.....F..... 810 664-5500
Lapeer *(G-9930)*
Excell Machine & Tool Co LLC.....G..... 231 728-1210
Muskegon *(G-11814)*
Expert Machine & Tool Inc.....G..... 810 984-2323
Port Huron *(G-13477)*
Extreme Wire EDM Service Inc.....G..... 616 249-3901
Grandville *(G-7376)*
Fairlane Co.....E..... 586 294-6100
Fraser *(G-5926)*
Falcon Corporation.....D..... 616 842-7071
Spring Lake *(G-15813)*
Falcon Industry Inc.....F..... 586 468-7010
Clinton Township *(G-3235)*
Finazzo Tool & Die LLC.....G..... 586 598-5806
Chesterfield *(G-2880)*
Fischer Tool & Die Corp.....E..... 734 847-4788
Temperance *(G-16530)*
Fixtureworks LLC.....G..... 586 294-6100
Fraser *(G-5928)*
Flannery Machine & Tool Inc.....E..... 231 587-5076
Mancelona *(G-10871)*
Forrest Company.....G..... 269 384-6120
Kalamazoo *(G-9190)*
Four Star Tooling & Engrg Inc.....G..... 586 264-4090
Sterling Heights *(G-16020)*
Four-Way Tool and Die Inc.....E..... 248 585-8255
Troy *(G-17121)*
Foust Electro Mold Inc.....G..... 517 439-1062
Hillsdale *(G-7934)*
Franchino Mold & Engrg Co.....D..... 517 321-5609
Lansing *(G-9700)*
Frankfort Manufacturing Inc.....E..... 231 352-7551
Frankfort *(G-5876)*
Freedom Tool & Mfg Co.....G..... 231 788-2898
Muskegon *(G-11821)*
Freer Tool & Die Inc.....E..... 586 463-3200
Clinton Township *(G-3243)*
Freer Tool & Die Inc.....G..... 586 741-5274
Clinton Township *(G-3244)*
Frimo Inc.....C..... 248 668-3160
Wixom *(G-18666)*
Future Mold Corporation.....D..... 989 588-9948
Farwell *(G-5423)*
G & F Tool Products.....F..... 517 663-3646
Eaton Rapids *(G-4964)*
G & L Tool Inc.....F..... 734 728-1990
Westland *(G-18372)*
G A Machine Company Inc.....G..... 313 836-5646
Detroit *(G-4249)*
Gch Tool Group Inc.....E..... 586 777-6250
Warren *(G-17823)*
General Die & Engineering Inc.....D..... 616 698-6961
Grand Rapids *(G-6738)*
Gill Holding Company Inc.....D..... 616 559-2700
Grand Rapids *(G-6741)*
Gill Industries Inc.....C..... 616 559-2700
Grand Rapids *(G-6742)*
Gladwin Machine Inc.....G..... 989 426-8753
Gladwin *(G-6197)*
Gleason Holbrook Mfg Co.....F..... 586 749-5519
Ray *(G-13699)*
Gollnick Tool Co.....G..... 586 755-0100
Warren *(G-17834)*
Grandville Industries Inc.....E..... 616 538-0920
Grandville *(G-7381)*
Granite Precision Tool Corp.....G..... 248 299-8317
Rochester Hills *(G-14027)*
Gray Bros Stamping & Mch Inc.....E..... 269 483-7615
White Pigeon *(G-18478)*
Greenville Tool & Die Co.....C..... 616 754-5693
Greenville *(G-7488)*
Griffin Tool Inc.....E..... 269 429-4077
Stevensville *(G-16252)*
Griswold Tool and Die Inc.....G..... 517 741-7433
Union City *(G-17494)*
Group B Industries II Inc.....G..... 734 941-6640
Romulus *(G-14281)*
Guo Ji Tooling Systems LLC.....F..... 616 301-6906
Grand Rapids *(G-6795)*
H B D M Inc.....F..... 269 273-1976
Three Rivers *(G-16575)*
Hacker Machine Inc.....E..... 517 569-3348
Rives Junction *(G-13886)*
Hallmark Tool and Gage Co Inc.....E..... 248 669-4010
Wixom *(G-18673)*
Hanson International Inc.....G..... 269 429-5555
Saint Joseph *(G-14934)*
Harbrook Tool Inc.....E..... 248 477-8040
Novi *(G-12427)*
Hard Milling Solutions Inc.....G..... 586 286-2300
Bruce Twp *(G-2167)*
Harper Machine Tool Inc.....G..... 586 756-0140
Warren *(G-17849)*
Havercroft Tool & Die Inc.....G..... 989 724-5913
Greenbush *(G-7472)*
Heinzmann D Tool & Die Inc.....F..... 248 363-5115
Commerce Township *(G-3535)*
Henze Stamping & Mfg Co.....G..... 248 588-5620
Troy *(G-17141)*
Hill Machinery Co.....D..... 616 940-2800
Grand Rapids *(G-6817)*
Hogle Sales & Mfg LLC.....G..... 517 592-1980
Brooklyn *(G-2126)*
Homestead Tool and Machine.....E..... 989 465-6182
Coleman *(G-3465)*
Horizon Die Company.....G..... 248 590-2966
Bingham Farms *(G-1700)*
HS Inc.....C..... 616 453-5451
Grand Rapids *(G-6823)*
Huron Tool & Gage Co Inc.....G..... 313 381-1900
Wixom *(G-18681)*
Idel LLC.....G..... 231 929-3195
Traverse City *(G-16718)*
Independent Die Association.....G..... 586 773-9000
Warren *(G-17861)*
Innovative Mold Inc.....E..... 586 752-2996
Washington *(G-18081)*
Intra Corporation.....D..... 734 326-7030
Westland *(G-18386)*
ITT Gage Inc.....F..... 231 766-2155
Muskegon *(G-11842)*
J C Manufacturing Company.....G..... 586 757-2713
Warren *(G-17877)*
J M Kusch Inc.....E..... 989 684-8820
Bay City *(G-1368)*
JCs Tool & Mfg Co Inc.....E..... 989 892-8975
Essexville *(G-5114)*
Jemar Tool Inc.....E..... 586 726-6960
Hudsonville *(G-8588)*
Jet Gage & Tool Inc.....G..... 586 294-3770
Fraser *(G-5946)*
Jirgens Modern Tool Corp.....F..... 269 381-5588
Kalamazoo *(G-9231)*
Jo-Ad Industries Inc.....E..... 248 588-4810
Madison Heights *(G-10754)*
Jo-Mar Industries Inc.....E..... 248 588-9625
Troy *(G-17188)*
Joggle Tool & Die Co Inc.....G..... 586 792-7477
Clinton Township *(G-3265)*
John Lamantia Corporation.....G..... 269 428-8100
Stevensville *(G-16255)*
Jolico/J-B Tool Inc.....E..... 586 739-5555
Shelby Township *(G-15245)*
Jordan Tool Corporation.....E..... 586 755-6700
Warren *(G-17889)*
K & T Tool and Die Inc.....F..... 616 884-5900
Rockford *(G-14173)*
K&K Stamping Company.....E..... 586 443-7900
Saint Clair Shores *(G-14866)*
K-B Tool Corporation.....G..... 586 795-9003
Sterling Heights *(G-16060)*
Kapex Manufacturing LLC.....G..... 989 928-4993
Saginaw *(G-14676)*
Karr Unlimited Inc.....G..... 231 652-9045
Newaygo *(G-12083)*
Katai Machine Shop.....F..... 269 465-6051
Bridgman *(G-1930)*
Kent Tool and Die Inc.....E..... 586 949-6600
Chesterfield *(G-2901)*
Kentwater Tool & Mfg Co.....G..... 616 784-7171
Comstock Park *(G-3615)*
Kenyon Specialties Inc.....G..... 810 686-3190
Clio *(G-3403)*
Kern Industries Inc.....E..... 248 349-4866
Novi *(G-12451)*
Ketchum Machine Corporated.....F..... 616 765-5101
Freeport *(G-6034)*
Key Casting Company Inc.....G..... 269 426-3800
Sawyer *(G-15110)*
Kinney Tool and Die Inc.....D..... 616 997-0901
Coopersville *(G-3689)*
Kirmin Die & Tool Inc.....E..... 734 722-9210
Romulus *(G-14295)*
Koch Limited.....G..... 586 296-3103
Fraser *(G-5952)*
Komarnicki Tool & Die Company.....F..... 586 776-9300
Roseville *(G-14431)*
Krieger Craftsmen Inc.....E..... 616 735-9200
Grand Rapids *(G-6905)*
Krt Precision Tool & Mfg Co.....G..... 517 783-5715
Jackson *(G-8930)*
Ktx America Inc.....G..... 734 737-0100
Livonia *(G-10269)*
Kurek Tool Inc.....F..... 989 777-5300
Saginaw *(G-14681)*
Lab Tool and Engineering Corp.....F..... 517 750-4131
Spring Arbor *(G-15793)*
Laingsburg Screw Inc.....G..... 517 651-2757
Laingsburg *(G-9536)*
Lake Design and Mfg Co.....G..... 616 794-0290
Belding *(G-1456)*
Lakeside Manufacturing Co.....E..... 269 429-6193
Stevensville *(G-16259)*
Lakeview Quality Tool Inc.....G..... 989 732-6417
Gaylord *(G-6141)*
Lambert Industries Inc.....F..... 734 668-6864
Ann Arbor *(G-548)*
Lance Industries LLC.....G..... 248 549-1968
Madison Heights *(G-10767)*
Lane Tool.....G..... 248 528-1606
Rochester Hills *(G-14048)*
Lapeer Industries Inc.....C..... 810 538-0589
Shelby Township *(G-15257)*
Lc Manufacturing LLC.....C..... 231 839-7102
Lake City *(G-9548)*
Lca Mold & Engineering Inc.....G..... 269 651-1193
Sturgis *(G-16301)*
Leader Tool Company - HB Inc.....E..... 989 479-3281
Harbor Beach *(G-7634)*
Lenawee Tool & Automation Inc.....G..... 517 458-7222
Morenci *(G-11614)*
Leroy Tool & Die Inc.....D..... 231 768-4336
Leroy *(G-10007)*
Lincoln Park Die & Tool Co.....E..... 734 285-1680
Brownstown *(G-2149)*
Linwood Tool Co Inc.....E..... 989 697-4403
Linwood *(G-10074)*
Lomar Machine & Tool Co.....E..... 517 563-8136
Horton *(G-8374)*
LP Products.....G..... 989 465-0287
Coleman *(G-3468)*
Ls Precision Tool & Die Inc.....G..... 269 963-9910
Battle Creek *(G-1270)*
Lupaul Industries Inc.....F..... 517 783-3223
Saint Johns *(G-14904)*
Luttmann Precision Mold Inc.....E..... 269 651-1193
Sturgis *(G-16303)*
Lyons Tool & Engineering Inc.....E..... 586 200-3003
Warren *(G-17910)*
M & M Services Inc.....G..... 248 619-9861
Troy *(G-17216)*
Maco Tool & Engineering Inc.....E..... 989 224-6723
Saint Johns *(G-14905)*
Maddox Industries Inc.....E..... 517 369-8665
Bronson *(G-2118)*
Maes Tool & Die Co Inc.....F..... 517 750-3131
Jackson *(G-8940)*
Majestic Industries Inc.....D..... 586 786-9100
Macomb *(G-10612)*
Mark Carbide Co.....G..... 248 545-0606
Troy *(G-17238)*
Mark Mold and Engineering.....F..... 989 687-9786
Sanford *(G-15073)*
Mark Tool & Die Company Inc.....E..... 248 363-1567
Commerce Township *(G-3554)*
Marked Tool Inc.....G..... 616 669-3201
Hudsonville *(G-8592)*

Martin Tool & Machine Inc ....G 586 775-1800
Roseville *(G-14436)*

Master Craft Extrusion Tls Inc ....F 231 386-5149
Northport *(G-12190)*

Master Model & Fixture Inc ....F 586 532-1153
Shelby Township *(G-15270)*

Master Precision Tool Corp ....F 586 739-3240
Sterling Heights *(G-16085)*

Matrix Engineering Inc ....G 810 231-0212
Brighton *(G-2026)*

Mattson Tool & Die Corp ....G 616 447-9012
Grand Rapids *(G-6967)*

Maya Jig Grinding & Gage Co ....F 248 471-0820
Farmington Hills *(G-5311)*

Mayco Tool ....G 616 785-7350
Comstock Park *(G-3622)*

Met-L-Tec LLC ....E 734 847-7004
Temperance *(G-16540)*

Metalfab Tool & Machine Inc ....G 989 826-6044
Mio *(G-11511)*

Metric Precision Tool LLC ....F 734 946-8114
Taylor *(G-16442)*

Michigan Auto Bending Corp ....E 248 528-1150
Madison Heights *(G-10781)*

Michigan Precision Tl & Engrg ....E 269 783-1300
Dowagiac *(G-4790)*

Michigan Tool & Gauge Inc ....E 517 548-4604
Howell *(G-8482)*

Mid Michigan Pipe Inc ....G 989 772-5664
Grand Rapids *(G-7003)*

Mid-Tech Inc ....G 734 426-4327
Ann Arbor *(G-577)*

Middleville Tool & Die Co Inc ....D 269 795-3646
Middleville *(G-11309)*

Midwest Machining Inc ....E 616 837-0165
Coopersville *(G-3693)*

Midwest Tool & Die Inc ....F 616 863-8187
Rockford *(G-14179)*

Millennium Mold & Tool Inc ....G 586 791-1711
Clinton Township *(G-3301)*

Mistequay Group Ltd ....E 989 752-7700
Saginaw *(G-14701)*

Models & Tools Inc ....C 586 580-6900
Shelby Township *(G-15281)*

Modineer Co LLC ....E 269 683-2550
Niles *(G-12146)*

Modineer Co LLC ....C 269 683-2550
Niles *(G-12145)*

Modineer Co LLC ....G 269 684-3138
Niles *(G-12147)*

Modineer P-K Tool LLC ....E 269 683-2550
Niles *(G-12148)*

Mol-Son Inc ....D 269 668-3377
Mattawan *(G-11165)*

Mold Tooling Systems Inc ....F 616 735-6653
Grand Rapids *(G-7021)*

Momentum Industries Inc ....F 989 681-5735
Saint Louis *(G-14993)*

Mpp Corp ....E 810 364-2939
Kimball *(G-9496)*

Multi Precision Intl LLC ....G 248 373-3330
Auburn Hills *(G-977)*

Multi-Precision Detail Inc ....E 248 373-3330
Auburn Hills *(G-978)*

Nesco Tool & Fixture LLC ....G 517 618-7052
Howell *(G-8483)*

Next Tool LLC ....F 734 405-7079
Belleville *(G-1489)*

Northern Machine Tool Company ....E 231 755-1603
Norton Shores *(G-12319)*

Northern Precision Inc ....F 989 736-6322
Lincoln *(G-10039)*

Northland Tool & Die Inc ....E 616 866-4451
Rockford *(G-14182)*

Northwest Tool & Machine Inc ....E 517 750-1332
Jackson *(G-8978)*

Oakwood Energy Management Inc ....F 734 947-7700
Taylor *(G-16453)*

Odyssey Tool LLC ....F 586 468-6696
Clinton Township *(G-3312)*

Olivet Machine Tool Engrg Co ....F 269 749-2671
Olivet *(G-12695)*

Olympian Tool LLC ....E 989 224-4817
Saint Johns *(G-14911)*

One-Way Tool & Die Inc ....G 248 477-2964
Livonia *(G-10353)*

Ontario Die Company America ....D 810 987-5060
Marysville *(G-11095)*

Oxbow Machine Products Inc ....E 734 422-7730
Livonia *(G-10355)*

P X Tool Co ....G 248 585-9330
Madison Heights *(G-10794)*

Paragon Die & Engineering Co ....C 616 949-2220
Grand Rapids *(G-7070)*

Paterek Mold & Engineering ....G 586 784-8030
Armada *(G-739)*

Pegasus Industries Inc ....F 313 937-0770
Redford *(G-13754)*

Pegasus Mold & Die Inc ....G 517 423-2009
Tecumseh *(G-16510)*

Penka Tool Corporation ....G 248 543-3940
Madison Heights *(G-10796)*

Pentel Tool & Die Inc ....G 734 782-9500
Romulus *(G-14319)*

Peterson Jig & Fixture Inc ....E 616 866-8296
Rockford *(G-14183)*

Pinnacle Engineering Co Inc ....E 734 428-7039
Manchester *(G-10888)*

Plas-TEC Inc ....G 248 853-7777
Rochester Hills *(G-14085)*

Positive Tool & Engineering Co ....G 313 532-1674
Redford *(G-13758)*

Praet Tool & Engineering Inc ....E 586 677-3800
Macomb *(G-10627)*

Precise Machine & Tool Co ....G 517 787-7699
Jackson *(G-8990)*

Precision Masking Inc ....E 734 848-4200
Erie *(G-5053)*

Preferred Industries Inc ....E 810 364-4090
Kimball *(G-9500)*

Preferred Tool & Die Co Inc ....E 616 784-6789
Comstock Park *(G-3638)*

Pro Tool LLC ....G 616 850-0556
Grand Haven *(G-6348)*

Product and Tooling Tech Inc ....E 586 293-1810
Fraser *(G-5980)*

Proto Gage Inc ....E 586 978-2783
Sterling Heights *(G-16136)*

Punchcraft McHning Tooling LLC ....G 586 573-4840
Warren *(G-17987)*

Q M E Inc ....E 269 422-2137
Baroda *(G-1168)*

Quad Precision Tool Co Inc ....F 248 608-2400
Rochester Hills *(G-14093)*

Quality Metalcraft Inc ....C 734 261-6700
Livonia *(G-10377)*

Quality Metalcraft Inc ....C 734 261-6700
Livonia *(G-10378)*

Quality Steel Fabg & Erct ....G 989 672-2873
Caro *(G-2578)*

Quality Tool and Die LLC ....G 248 707-0060
Clawson *(G-3107)*

R & M Machine Inc ....E 586 754-8447
Warren *(G-17990)*

R & M Manufacturing Company ....E 269 683-9550
Niles *(G-12160)*

R E B Tool Inc ....D 734 397-9116
Van Buren Twp *(G-17549)*

R S L Tool LLC ....G 616 786-2880
Holland *(G-8175)*

Radar Tool & Manufacturing Co ....G 586 759-2800
Warren *(G-17993)*

Ralco Industries Inc ....D 248 853-3200
Auburn Hills *(G-1012)*

Ranger Tool & Die Co ....F 989 754-1403
Saginaw *(G-14735)*

Rapids Tool & Engineering ....G 517 663-8721
Eaton Rapids *(G-4970)*

Rare Tool Inc ....F 517 423-5000
Tecumseh *(G-16512)*

Rdc Machine Inc ....G 810 695-5587
Grand Blanc *(G-6260)*

Reef Tool & Gage Co ....E 586 468-3000
Clinton Township *(G-3333)*

Reger Manufacturing Company ....G 586 293-5096
Fraser *(G-5986)*

Research Tool Corporation ....E 989 834-2246
Ovid *(G-12816)*

Resistnce Wldg Mch Accssory LL ....F 269 428-4770
Saint Joseph *(G-14956)*

Richard Tool & Die Corporation ....D 248 486-0900
New Hudson *(G-12068)*

Rivercity Rollform Inc ....E 231 799-9550
Norton Shores *(G-12328)*

Rk Boring Inc ....G 734 542-7920
Livonia *(G-10388)*

Rkaa Business LLC ....E 231 734-5517
Evart *(G-5127)*

Robb Machine Tool Co ....G 616 532-6642
Grand Rapids *(G-7161)*

Ronald R Wellington ....F 586 488-3087
Bruce Twp *(G-2180)*

Ross Design & Engineering Inc ....E 517 547-6033
Cement City *(G-2676)*

Roth-Williams Industries Inc ....E 586 792-0090
Clinton Township *(G-3342)*

Rowland Mold & Machine Inc ....G 616 875-5400
Zeeland *(G-19077)*

Royal ARC Inc ....G 586 758-0718
Madison Heights *(G-10820)*

S & S Die Co ....E 517 272-1100
Lansing *(G-9889)*

Sampson Tool Incorporated ....G 248 651-3313
Rochester *(G-13927)*

Schaenzle Tool and Die Inc ....G 248 656-0596
Rochester Hills *(G-14109)*

Schaller Tool & Die Co ....E 586 949-5500
Chesterfield *(G-2947)*

Schmald Tool & Die Inc ....F 810 743-1600
Burton *(G-2244)*

Sequoia Tool Inc ....D 586 463-4400
Clinton Township *(G-3351)*

Shark Tool & Die Inc ....G 586 749-7400
Columbus *(G-3502)*

Sharp Model Co ....D 586 752-3099
Bruce Twp *(G-2182)*

Shores Engineering Co Inc ....E 586 792-2748
Clinton Township *(G-3353)*

Sigma Tool Mfg Inc ....G 586 792-3300
Clinton Township *(G-3354)*

Sink Rite Die Company ....F 586 268-0000
Sterling Heights *(G-16178)*

Smith Brothers Tool Company ....D 586 726-5756
Shelby Township *(G-15335)*

Spare Die Inc ....G 734 522-2508
Livonia *(G-10415)*

Special Tool & Engineering Inc ....D 586 285-5900
Fraser *(G-5996)*

Specialty Tool & Mold Inc ....G 616 531-3870
Grand Rapids *(G-7212)*

Specialty Tooling Systems Inc ....E 616 784-2353
Grand Rapids *(G-7213)*

Stampede Die Corp ....D 616 877-0100
Wayland *(G-18208)*

Standard Components LLC ....E 586 323-9700
Sterling Heights *(G-16189)*

Standard Die International Inc ....E 800 838-5464
Livonia *(G-10417)*

Steeplechase Tool & Die Inc ....E 989 352-5544
Lakeview *(G-9646)*

Stellar Forge Products Inc ....F 313 535-7631
Bloomfield Hills *(G-1862)*

Stm Mfg Inc ....E 616 392-4656
Holland *(G-8204)*

Suburban Industries Inc ....F 734 676-6141
Brownstown Twp *(G-2158)*

Superior Products Mfg Inc ....G 810 679-4479
Croswell *(G-3736)*

Supreme Tool & Machine Inc ....F 248 673-8408
Waterford *(G-18168)*

T & C Tool & Sales Inc ....F 586 677-8390
Washington *(G-18088)*

T & T Tools Inc ....F 800 521-6893
Holland *(G-8211)*

T & W Tool & Die Corporation ....E 248 548-5400
Oak Park *(G-12647)*

Talent Industries Inc ....F 313 531-4700
Redford *(G-13777)*

Tamara Tool Inc ....F 269 273-1463
Three Rivers *(G-16586)*

Taylor Turning Inc ....E 248 960-7920
Wixom *(G-18767)*

Tech Tooling Specialties Inc ....F 517 782-8898
Jackson *(G-9016)*

Technical Manufacturers Inc ....G 989 846-6885
Standish *(G-15897)*

Telco Tools ....F 616 296-0253
Spring Lake *(G-15856)*

Thumb Tool & Engineering Co ....C 989 269-9731
Bad Axe *(G-1115)*

Tijer Inc ....G 586 741-0308
Clinton Township *(G-3377)*

Tiller Tool and Die Inc ....F 517 458-6602
Jonesville *(G-9104)*

Titan Tool & Die Inc ....G 231 799-8680
Norton Shores *(G-12340)*

Tnr Machine Inc ....E 269 623-2827
Dowling *(G-4799)*

Tolerance Tool & Engineering ....E 313 592-4011
Detroit *(G-4635)*

Employee Codes: A=Over 500 employees, B=251-500
C=101-250, D=51-100, E=20-50, F=10-19, G=3-9

2022 Harris Michigan
Industrial Directory

1253

DIES & TOOLS: Special

Tool Company Inc .... G 586 598-1519
 Chesterfield *(G-2957)*
Toolco Inc .... E 734 453-9911
 Plymouth *(G-13319)*
Tooling Systems Group Inc .... F 616 863-8623
 Grand Rapids *(G-7265)*
Top Craft Tool Inc .... E 586 461-4600
 Clinton Township *(G-3378)*
Trademark Die & Engineering .... E 616 863-6660
 Belmont *(G-1520)*
Trainer Metal Forming Co Inc .... E 616 844-9982
 Grand Haven *(G-6371)*
Tranor Industries LLC .... F 313 733-4888
 Detroit *(G-4643)*
Tregets Tool & Engineering Co .... G 517 782-0044
 Jackson *(G-9022)*
Tri Tech Tooling Inc .... F 616 396-6000
 Holland *(G-8228)*
Tri-M-Mold Inc .... E 269 465-3301
 Stevensville *(G-16269)*
Trianon Industries Corporation .... E 586 759-2200
 Center Line *(G-2688)*
Tric Tool Ltd .... E 616 395-1530
 Holland *(G-8230)*
Tru Flo Carbide Inc .... F 989 658-8515
 Ubly *(G-17483)*
Trutron Corporation .... E 248 583-9166
 Troy *(G-17405)*
Uei Inc .... E 616 361-6093
 Grand Rapids *(G-7285)*
Unified Tool and Die Inc .... G 517 768-8070
 Jackson *(G-9028)*
US Boring Inc .... G 586 756-7511
 Warren *(G-18048)*
Utica Enterprises Inc .... C 586 726-4300
 Troy *(G-17419)*
Varco Precision Products Co .... G 313 538-4300
 Redford *(G-13783)*
Veit Tool & Gage Inc .... E 810 658-4949
 Davison *(G-3800)*
Venture Manufacturing Inc .... G 269 429-6337
 Saint Joseph *(G-14971)*
Vertical Technologies LLC .... E 586 619-0141
 Warren *(G-18055)*
Viking Tool & Engineering Inc .... E 231 893-0031
 Whitehall *(G-18511)*
Vortec .... G 616 292-2401
 Zeeland *(G-19091)*
W & W Tool and Die Inc .... G 989 835-5522
 Midland *(G-11421)*
Walker Tool & Die Inc .... D 616 453-5471
 Grand Rapids *(G-7323)*
Wallin Brothers Inc .... G 734 525-7750
 Livonia *(G-10464)*
Waterman Tool & Machine Corp .... F 989 823-8181
 Vassar *(G-17585)*
Weldmet Industries Inc .... G 586 773-0533
 Warren *(G-18065)*
West Michigan Tool & Die Co .... E 269 925-0900
 Benton Harbor *(G-1602)*
Westgood Manufacturing Co .... F 586 771-3970
 Roseville *(G-14493)*
Westool Corporation .... E 734 847-2520
 Temperance *(G-16552)*
Wetzel Tool & Engineering Inc .... E 248 960-0430
 Wixom *(G-18791)*
White Automation & Tool Co .... F 734 947-9822
 Romulus *(G-14338)*
White Engineering Inc .... G 269 695-0825
 Niles *(G-12173)*
White River Knife and Tool .... G 616 997-0026
 Fremont *(G-6057)*
Wico Metal Products Company .... F 586 755-9600
 Center Line *(G-2690)*
Widell Industries Inc .... E 989 742-4528
 Hillman *(G-7918)*
Wieske Tool Inc .... E 989 288-2648
 Durand *(G-4850)*
Withers Corporation .... E 586 758-2750
 Warren *(G-18068)*
Wolverine Carbide & Tool Inc .... E 248 247-3888
 Troy *(G-17450)*
Wolverine Tool Co .... F 810 664-2964
 Lapeer *(G-9968)*
Worswick Mold & Tool Inc .... F 810 765-1700
 Marine City *(G-10970)*
Wyke Die & Engineering Inc .... G 616 871-1175
 Grand Rapids *(G-7351)*

DIES: Cutting, Exc Metal

Atlas Die LLC .... E 413 289-1276
 Rochester Hills *(G-13953)*
Atlas Die LLC .... E 770 981-6585
 Rochester Hills *(G-13954)*
Next Level Die Cutting LLC .... F 888 819-9959
 Jenison *(G-9063)*
Performnce Dcutting Finshg LLC .... F 616 245-3636
 Grand Rapids *(G-7081)*

DIES: Extrusion

Centennial Technologies Inc .... E 989 752-6167
 Saginaw *(G-14624)*
Link Tool & Mfg Co LLC .... D 734 710-0010
 Westland *(G-18392)*
Ovidon Manufacturing LLC .... D 517 548-4005
 Howell *(G-8489)*
Service Extrusion Die Co Inc .... G 616 784-6933
 Comstock Park *(G-3644)*
Ultra-Sonic Extrusion Dies Inc .... E 586 791-8550
 Clinton Township *(G-3381)*
Wefa Cedar Inc .... F 616 696-0873
 Cedar Springs *(G-2666)*

DIES: Plastic Forming

Byrnes Manufacturing Co LLC .... G 810 664-3686
 Lapeer *(G-9917)*
Complete Surface Technologies .... E 586 493-5800
 Clinton Township *(G-3208)*
Elite Mold & Engineering Inc .... E 586 314-4000
 Shelby Township *(G-15219)*
Enkon LLC .... E 937 890-5678
 Manchester *(G-10883)*
Incoe Corporation .... C 248 616-0220
 Auburn Hills *(G-936)*
Incoe International Inc .... B 248 616-0220
 Auburn Hills *(G-937)*
Pinnacle Mold & Machine Inc .... G 616 892-9018
 West Olive *(G-18350)*
Prima Technologies Inc .... F 586 759-0250
 Center Line *(G-2685)*
Shoreline Mold & Engrg LLC .... G 269 926-2223
 Benton Harbor *(G-1584)*

DIES: Steel Rule

A C Steel Rule Dies Inc .... G 248 588-5600
 Madison Heights *(G-10654)*
Atlas Die Inc .... E 574 295-0050
 Rochester Hills *(G-13955)*
Champion Die Incorporated .... E 616 784-2397
 Comstock Park *(G-3595)*
Creative Steel Rule Dies Inc .... G 630 307-8880
 Grand Rapids *(G-6610)*
Exco Extrusion Dies Inc .... C 586 749-5400
 Chesterfield *(G-2877)*
Fowlerville Machine Tool Inc .... G 517 223-8871
 Fowlerville *(G-5840)*
Jacobsen Industries Inc .... D 734 591-6111
 Livonia *(G-10255)*
Kendor Steel Rule Die Inc .... F 586 293-7111
 Fraser *(G-5950)*
Lasercutting Services Inc .... E 616 975-2000
 Grand Rapids *(G-6929)*
Rolleigh Inc .... F 517 283-3811
 Reading *(G-13705)*

DIFFERENTIAL ASSEMBLIES & PARTS

P G S Inc .... C 248 526-3800
 Troy *(G-17294)*
Warren Manufacturing LLC .... G 586 467-1600
 Warren *(G-18060)*

DIMENSION STONE: Buildings

Genesee Cut Stone & Marble Co .... E 810 743-1800
 Grand Blanc *(G-6242)*

DIODES: Light Emitting

Kimberly Lighting LLC .... E 888 480-0070
 Clarkston *(G-3043)*
Lumasmart Technology Intl Inc .... D 586 232-4925
 Shelby Township *(G-15265)*
Nihil Ultra Corporation .... G 413 723-3218
 Troy *(G-17277)*
Sigma Luminous LLC .... G 866 755-3563
 Saint Clair Shores *(G-14884)*

PRODUCT SECTION

US Trade LLC .... G 800 676-0208
 Garden City *(G-6114)*

DIRECT SELLING ESTABLISHMENTS, NEC

Ace Vending Service Inc .... F 616 243-7983
 Grand Rapids *(G-6422)*
Alticor Global Holdings Inc .... F 616 787-1000
 Ada *(G-5)*
Alticor Inc .... A 616 787-1000
 Ada *(G-6)*
Amway International Inc .... E 616 787-1000
 Ada *(G-8)*
Cognisys Inc .... G 231 943-2425
 Traverse City *(G-16656)*

DIRECT SELLING ESTABLISHMENTS: Home Related Prdts

Garden of Edyn .... G 517 410-9931
 Holt *(G-8313)*

DIRECT SELLING ESTABLISHMENTS: Milk Delivery

Calder Bros Dairy Inc .... E 313 381-8858
 Lincoln Park *(G-10044)*

DISC JOCKEYS

Sound Productions Entrmt .... F 989 386-2221
 Clare *(G-2998)*

DISCOUNT DEPARTMENT STORES

Walmart Inc .... F 517 541-1481
 Charlotte *(G-2774)*

DISHWASHING EQPT: Commercial

Glastender Inc .... B 989 752-4275
 Saginaw *(G-14652)*

DISHWASHING EQPT: Household

Maytag Corporation .... C 269 923-5000
 Benton Harbor *(G-1572)*
Whirlpool Corporation .... G 269 923-5000
 Benton Harbor *(G-1609)*
Whirlpool Corporation .... G 269 923-3009
 Benton Harbor *(G-1610)*

DISINFECTING & PEST CONTROL SERVICES

Swat Environmental Inc .... E 517 322-2999
 Lansing *(G-9898)*

DISINFECTING SVCS

Angels of Detroit LLC .... G 248 796-1079
 Redford *(G-13714)*
Marceau Enterprises Inc .... E 586 697-8100
 Washington *(G-18085)*

DISK & DRUM DRIVES & COMPONENTS: Computers

American Furukawa Inc .... E 734 446-2200
 Plymouth *(G-13123)*
Autocam Corporation .... B 616 698-0707
 Kentwood *(G-9444)*

DISK DRIVES: Computer

Piolax Corporation .... D 734 668-6005
 Plymouth *(G-13265)*

DISKS & DRUMS Magnetic

Livonia Magnetics Co Inc .... E 734 397-8844
 Farmington Hills *(G-5293)*

DISPENSING EQPT & PARTS, BEVERAGE: Fountain/Other Beverage

Auction Masters .... G 586 576-7777
 Oak Park *(G-12593)*

DISPLAY FIXTURES: Showcases, Wood, Exc Refrigerated

Fwi Inc .... E 231 798-8324
 Norton Shores *(G-12294)*

Maw Ventures Inc .... E 231 798-8324
Norton Shores (G-12309)

DISPLAY FIXTURES: Wood

H & R Wood Specialties Inc .... E 269 628-2181
Gobles (G-6217)
Harbor Industries Inc .... D 616 842-5330
Grand Haven (G-6312)
Harbor Industries Inc .... D 616 842-5330
Charlevoix (G-2718)
PDC .... F 269 651-9975
Sturgis (G-16317)
Unislat LLC .... G 616 844-4211
Grand Haven (G-6374)

DISPLAY ITEMS: Corrugated, Made From Purchased Materials

Compak Inc .... G 989 288-3199
Burton (G-2233)

DISPLAY ITEMS: Solid Fiber, Made From Purchased Materials

Armstrong Display Concepts Inc .... F 231 652-1675
Newaygo (G-12077)
Zoomer Display LLC .... G 616 734-0300
Grand Rapids (G-7359)

DISPLAY LETTERING SVCS

Sign Impressions Inc .... G 269 382-5152
Kalamazoo (G-9337)

DISPLAY STANDS: Merchandise, Exc Wood

Shaw & Slavsky Inc .... F 313 834-3990
Detroit (G-4590)

DISTILLERS DRIED GRAIN & SOLUBLES

Artesian Distillers .... G 616 252-1700
Grand Rapids (G-6472)
Coppercraft Distillery LLC .... E 616 796-8274
Holland (G-8005)
Long Road Distillers LLC .... F 616 356-1770
Grand Rapids (G-6948)

DISTRIBUTORS: Motor Vehicle Engine

Electro-Matic Products Inc .... G 248 478-1182
Farmington Hills (G-5224)

DIVING EQPT STORES

Livbig LLC .... G 888 519-8290
Portage (G-13578)

DOCK EQPT & SPLYS, INDL

Admin Industries LLC .... F 989 685-3438
Rose City (G-14358)
Berlin Holdings LLC .... G 517 523-2444
Pittsford (G-13067)
Deluxe Technologies LLC .... E 586 294-2340
Fraser (G-5918)
Tech World LLC .... G 616 901-2611
Shelbyville (G-15375)

DOCK OPERATION SVCS, INCL BLDGS, FACILITIES, OPERS & MAINT

Odonnells Docks .... G 269 244-1446
Jones (G-9084)

DOCKS: Floating, Wood

Paddle King Inc .... F 989 235-6776
Carson City (G-2594)

DOCKS: Prefabricated Metal

4ever Aluminum Products Inc .... F 517 368-0000
Coldwater (G-3417)
Berlin Holdings LLC .... G 517 523-2444
Pittsford (G-13067)
Bulmann Enterprises Inc .... E 231 549-5020
Boyne City (G-1885)
Con-De Manufacturing Inc .... G 269 651-3756
Sturgis (G-16285)
Great Lakes Lift Inc .... G 989 673-2109
Caro (G-2572)

Marine Automated Doc System .... F 989 539-9010
Harrison (G-7680)
Twin Bay Dock and Products .... G 231 943-8420
Traverse City (G-16869)
Wheelock & Son Welding Shop .... G 231 947-6557
Traverse City (G-16879)

DOOR & WINDOW REPAIR SVCS

Wood Smiths Inc .... F 269 372-6432
Kalamazoo (G-9373)

DOOR FRAMES: Wood

Aspen Door Supply LLC .... G 248 291-5303
Troy (G-16959)
Crossroads Industries Inc .... E 989 732-1233
Gaylord (G-6124)
Idp Inc .... E 248 352-0044
Southfield (G-15601)
Jim Whlsale S/Verett Dukes Inc .... F 800 522-2940
Oxford (G-12891)

DOOR OPERATING SYSTEMS: Electric

Computerized SEC Systems Inc .... C 248 837-3700
Madison Heights (G-10697)
Magna Mirrors America Inc .... B 231 652-4450
Newaygo (G-12086)
Operator Specialty Company Inc .... D 616 675-5050
Grand Rapids (G-7061)
Quality Door & More Inc .... G 989 317-8314
Coleman (G-3470)

DOORS & WINDOWS WHOLESALERS: All Materials

Daiek Products Inc .... F 248 816-1360
Troy (G-17044)
Expressive Window Fashions .... G 269 663-8833
Edwardsburg (G-5006)
Lippert Components Mfg Inc .... D 989 845-3061
Chesaning (G-2829)
Weathergard Window Company Inc ..... D 248 967-8822
Oak Park (G-12651)

DOORS & WINDOWS: Screen & Storm

Grabill Windows & Doors LLC .... E 810 798-2817
Almont (G-261)
PTL Engineering Inc .... F 810 664-2310
Lapeer (G-9956)

DOORS & WINDOWS: Storm, Metal

Fox Aluminum Products Inc .... E 248 399-4288
Hazel Park (G-7826)
Ken Rodenhouse Door & Window .... F 616 784-3365
Comstock Park (G-3614)
National Nail Corp .... C 616 538-8000
Grand Rapids (G-7036)
Scott Iron Works Inc .... F 248 548-2822
Hazel Park (G-7841)
Storm Seal Co Inc .... G 248 689-1900
Troy (G-17374)
Weather King Windows Doors Inc .... D 313 933-1234
Farmington (G-5154)
Weather King Windows Doors Inc .... E 248 478-7788
Farmington (G-5155)
Weatherproof Inc .... E 517 764-1330
Jackson (G-9034)

DOORS: Fiberglass

Daiek Products Inc .... F 248 816-1360
Troy (G-17044)

DOORS: Folding, Plastic Or Plastic Coated Fabric

Poncraft Door Co Inc .... F 248 373-6060
Auburn Hills (G-1000)
Special-Lite Inc .... C 800 821-6531
Decatur (G-3951)

DOORS: Garage, Overhead, Metal

Integrity Door LLC .... G 616 896-8077
Dorr (G-4768)
Plymouth Garage LLC .... G 734 459-3667
Livonia (G-10367)
Pro-Line Doors LLC .... G 586 765-1657
Clinton Township (G-3329)

DOORS: Garage, Overhead, Wood

Area Exteriors .... G 248 544-0706
Leonard (G-10001)

DOORS: Glass

City Auto Glass Co .... G 616 842-3235
Grand Haven (G-6285)
Vvp Auto Glass Inc .... E 734 727-5001
Westland (G-18428)

DOORS: Louver, Wood

Beechcraft Products Inc .... E 989 288-2606
Durand (G-4840)

DOORS: Rolling, Indl Building Or Warehouse, Metal

Alliance Engnred Sltons NA Ltd .... C 586 291-3694
Detroit (G-4001)

DOORS: Wooden

Andoor Craftmaster .... G 989 672-2020
Caro (G-2565)
B & W Woodwork Inc .... G 616 772-4577
Holland (G-7969)
E-Zee Set Wood Products Inc .... G 248 398-0090
Oak Park (G-12608)
Five Lakes Manufacturing Inc .... E 586 463-4123
Clinton Township (G-3239)
Jeld-Wen Inc .... C 616 554-3551
Caledonia (G-2385)
Jeld-Wen Inc .... D 616 531-5440
Grand Rapids (G-6868)
Lemica Corporation .... E 313 839-2150
Detroit (G-4388)
Magiglide Inc .... F 906 822-7321
Crystal Falls (G-3743)
Masonite International Corp .... F 517 545-5811
Howell (G-8476)
Monarch Millwork Inc .... G 989 348-8292
Grayling (G-7467)
Van Beeks Custom Wood Products ..... F 616 583-9002
Byron Center (G-2298)

DOWELS & DOWEL RODS

Doltek Enterprises Inc .... E 616 837-7828
Nunica (G-12579)

DOWNSPOUTS: Sheet Metal

Crystal Machine & Tool Inc .... G 586 552-1503
Warren (G-17766)

DRAFTING SPLYS WHOLESALERS

Commercial Blueprint Inc .... E 517 372-8360
Lansing (G-9825)

DRAFTING SVCS

Soils and Structures Inc .... D 800 933-3959
Norton Shores (G-12333)

DRAINAGE PRDTS: Concrete

All About Drainage LLC .... G 248 921-0766
Commerce Township (G-3508)
Sanilac Drain and Tile Co .... G 810 648-4100
Sandusky (G-15067)

DRAPERIES & CURTAINS

Benton Harbor Awning & Tent .... E 800 272-2187
Benton Harbor (G-1535)
Designer Window Fashions 734 421-1600
Northville (G-12212)
Lorne Hanley .... G 248 547-9865
Huntington Woods (G-8622)

DRAPERIES & DRAPERY FABRICS, COTTON

Drapery Workroom .... G 269 463-5633
Watervliet (G-18180)
Window Designs Inc .... F 616 396-5295
Holland (G-8250)

DRAPERIES: Plastic & Textile, From Purchased Materials

Cardinal Custom Designs Inc .... G 586 296-2060
  Fraser (G-5911)
Detroit Custom Services Inc .... E 586 465-3631
  Mount Clemens (G-11636)
Parkway Drapery & Uphl Co Inc .... G 734 779-1300
  Livonia (G-10360)
Signature Designs Inc .... G 248 426-9735
  Farmington Hills (G-5378)
Triangle Window Fashions Inc .... E 616 538-9676
  Wyoming (G-18914)

DRAPERY & UPHOLSTERY STORES: Curtains

Barons Inc .... E 517 484-1366
  Lansing (G-9813)

DRAPERY & UPHOLSTERY STORES: Draperies

Detroit Custom Services Inc .... E 586 465-3631
  Mount Clemens (G-11636)
Window Designs Inc .... F 616 396-5295
  Holland (G-8250)

DRAPES & DRAPERY FABRICS, FROM MANMADE FIBER

Window Designs Inc .... F 616 396-5295
  Holland (G-8250)

DRILL BITS

Hougen Manufacturing Inc .... C 810 635-7111
  Swartz Creek (G-16355)

DRILLING MACHINERY & EQPT: Water Well

Murphys Water Well Bits .... G 810 658-1554
  Davison (G-3791)

DRILLS & DRILLING EQPT: Mining

National Piling Products Inc .... F 855 801-7453
  Wayland (G-18200)

DRINK MIXES, NONALCOHOLIC: Cocktail

Tcwc LLC .... E 231 922-8292
  Traverse City (G-16852)

DRINKING PLACES: Alcoholic Beverages

Backdraft Brewing Company .... F 734 722-7639
  Wayne (G-18215)
McDonalds .... F 248 851-7310
  Oxford (G-12900)
New Holland Brewing Co LLC .... C 616 355-2941
  Holland (G-8154)
Schelde Enterprises Inc .... G 231 941-7325
  Traverse City (G-16825)
Tcwc LLC .... E 231 922-8292
  Traverse City (G-16852)

DRINKING PLACES: Bars & Lounges

American Brewers Inc .... F 616 318-9230
  Kalamazoo (G-9113)
Blackrocks Brewery LLC .... G 906 360-6674
  Marquette (G-11009)
Blackrocks Brewery LLC .... G 906 273-1333
  Marquette (G-11008)
Great Legs Wnery Brwry Dist LL .... G 616 298-7600
  Holland (G-8060)
Midland Brewing Co LLC .... G 989 259-7210
  Midland (G-11391)
Northern Oak Brewery Inc .... F 248 634-7515
  Holly (G-8285)
Oracle Brewing Company LLC .... F 989 401-7446
  Breckenridge (G-1913)
Ore Dock Brewing Company LLC ...... F 906 228-8888
  Marquette (G-11039)

DRINKING PLACES: Beer Garden

Acoustic Tap Room .... G 231 714-5028
  Traverse City (G-16596)

DRINKING PLACES: Tavern

Gpbc Inc .... F 734 741-7325
  Ann Arbor (G-503)

DRINKING PLACES: Wine Bar

Winery At Young Farms LLC .... F 989 506-5142
  Mecosta (G-11194)

DRIVE SHAFTS

Cambria Tool and Machine Inc .... F 517 437-3500
  Hillsdale (G-7928)
Erae AMS America Corp .... F 419 386-8876
  Pontiac (G-13368)
Meritor Inc .... C 248 435-1000
  Troy (G-17246)
Shaftmasters .... G 313 383-6347
  Lincoln Park (G-10056)

DRIVES: High Speed Indl, Exc Hydrostatic

Dama Tool & Gauge Company .... E 616 842-9631
  Norton Shores (G-12287)

DRIVES: Hydrostatic

Flint Hydrostatics Inc .... F 901 794-2462
  Chesterfield (G-2883)
Hydraulex Intl Holdings Inc .... E 914 682-2700
  Chesterfield (G-2891)

DRUG STORES

Diplomat Spclty Phrm Flint LLC .... B 810 768-9000
  Flint (G-5688)
Hackley Health Ventures Inc .... G 231 728-5720
  Muskegon (G-11834)

DRUG TESTING KITS: Blood & Urine

Welzin Health Services LLC .... G 313 953-8768
  Wyandotte (G-18844)

DRUGS & DRUG PROPRIETARIES, WHOL: Biologicals/Allied Prdts

Oxford Biomedical Research Inc .... G 248 852-8815
  Metamora (G-11284)

DRUGS & DRUG PROPRIETARIES, WHOLESALE

Smo International Inc .... F 248 275-1091
  Warren (G-18015)

DRUGS & DRUG PROPRIETARIES, WHOLESALE: Bandages

Xxtar Associates LLC .... G 888 946-6066
  Detroit (G-4695)

DRUGS & DRUG PROPRIETARIES, WHOLESALE: Medical Rubber Goods

Mykin Inc .... F 248 667-8030
  South Lyon (G-15448)

DRUGS & DRUG PROPRIETARIES, WHOLESALE: Pharmaceuticals

Central Admxture Phrm Svcs Inc .... G 734 953-6760
  Livonia (G-10151)
Diplomat Spclty Phrm Flint LLC .... B 810 768-9000
  Flint (G-5688)
McKesson Corporation .... G 734 953-2523
  Livonia (G-10308)
McKesson Pharmacy Systems LLC .... A 800 521-1758
  Livonia (G-10309)
Natural Therapeutics LLC .... G 734 604-7313
  Ann Arbor (G-591)
Pharmaceutical Specialties LLC .... F 269 382-6402
  Galesburg (G-6081)
Special Mold Engineering Inc .... E 248 652-6600
  Rochester Hills (G-14116)

DRUGS AFFECTING NEOPLASMS & ENDOCRINE SYSTEMS

Pcs Pharmaceuticals LLC .... G 248 289-7054
  Bloomfield Hills (G-1848)

DRUMS: Brake

Stemco Products Inc .... G 888 854-6474
  Millington (G-11503)

DRUMS: Fiber

Eteron Inc .... E 248 478-2900
  Farmington Hills (G-5236)

DUCTING: Metal Plate

Conquest Manufacturing LLC .... D 586 576-7600
  Warren (G-17763)

DUCTS: Sheet Metal

Constructive Sheet Metal Inc .... E 616 245-5306
  Allendale (G-217)
Ecolo-Tech Inc .... E 248 541-1100
  Madison Heights (G-10716)
Harris Sheet Metal Co .... E 989 496-3080
  Midland (G-11371)
Integrated Industries Inc .... F 586 790-1550
  Clinton Township (G-3259)
J & J Metal Products Inc .... G 586 792-2680
  Clinton Township (G-3261)
Jbs Sheet Metal Inc .... G 231 777-2802
  Muskegon (G-11844)
Krupp Industries LLC .... E 734 261-0410
  Livonia (G-10268)
Krupp Industries LLC .... D 616 475-5905
  Walker (G-17643)
Schneider Sheet Metal Sup Inc .... G 517 694-7661
  Lansing (G-9892)

DUMBWAITERS

Schindler Elevator Corporation .... F 517 272-1234
  Lansing (G-9891)

DUMPSTERS: Garbage

Actron Steel Inc .... E 231 947-3981
  Traverse City (G-16597)
American Dumpster Services LLC ...... G 586 501-3600
  Center Line (G-2679)
Astro Dumpster Rental LLC .... G 313 444-7905
  Royal Oak (G-14515)
Best Rate Dumpster Rental Inc .... G 248 391-5956
  Ortonville (G-12742)
Brian A Broomfield .... G 989 309-0709
  Remus (G-13814)
Detroit Dumpster Inc .... G 313 466-3174
  Detroit (G-4145)
Dino S Dumpsters LLC .... G 989 225-5635
  Bay City (G-1345)
Dolphin Dumpsters LLC .... G 734 272-8981
  Farmington Hills (G-5219)
Hammars Contracting LLC .... E 810 367-3037
  Kimball (G-9493)
JI Dumpsters LLC .... G 313 258-0767
  Belleville (G-1486)
K and W Landfill Inc .... D 906 883-3504
  Ontonagon (G-12711)
M&D Dumpsters LLC .... G 616 299-0234
  Hudsonville (G-8591)
McM Disposal LLC .... G 616 656-4049
  Byron Center (G-2283)
Priority Waste LLC .... E 586 228-1200
  Clinton Township (G-3327)
R and J Dumpsters LLC .... G 248 863-8579
  Howell (G-8504)
Smith Dumpsters .... G 616 675-9399
  Kent City (G-9436)
Yello Dumpster .... G 616 915-0506
  Grand Rapids (G-7355)

DURABLE GOODS WHOLESALERS, NEC

Detroit Couture .... G 734 237-6826
  Southfield (G-15539)

DUST OR FUME COLLECTING EQPT: Indl

Baker Enterprises Inc .... E 989 354-2189
  Alpena (G-281)
Beckert & Hiester Inc .... G 989 793-2420
  Saginaw (G-14612)
Besser Company .... B 989 354-4111
  Alpena (G-284)
Forrest Brothers Inc .... C 989 356-4011
  Gaylord (G-6129)

PRODUCT SECTION — ELECTRICAL CURRENT CARRYING WIRING DEVICES

Hammond Machinery Inc .... D 269 345-7151
  Kalamazoo *(G-9207)*
Madison Street Holdings LLC .... E 517 252-2031
  Adrian *(G-81)*
Ron Pair Enterprises Inc .... E 231 547-4000
  Charlevoix *(G-2731)*

DYES & TINTS: Household

Chames LLC .... G 616 363-0000
  Grand Rapids *(G-6564)*

DYNAMOMETERS

Froude Inc .... D 248 579-4295
  Novi *(G-12419)*
Greening Incorporated .... G 313 366-7160
  Detroit *(G-4282)*
Greening Associates Inc .... E 313 366-7160
  Detroit *(G-4283)*
Superior Controls Inc .... C 734 454-0500
  Plymouth *(G-13306)*

EARTH SCIENCE SVCS

Baygeo Inc .... E 231 941-7660
  Traverse City *(G-16617)*

EATING PLACES

Aj Hometown LLC .... G 313 415-0843
  Eastpointe *(G-4927)*
Arbor Kitchen LLC .... G 248 921-4602
  Ann Arbor *(G-375)*
Backdraft Brewing Company .... F 734 722-7639
  Wayne *(G-18215)*
Bowers Harbor Vinyrd & Winery .... G 231 223-7615
  Traverse City *(G-16626)*
Cherry Hut Products LLC .... G 231 882-4431
  Benzonia *(G-1613)*
Country Mill Farms LLC .... G 517 543-1019
  Charlotte *(G-2745)*
Forest View Lanes LLC .... E 734 847-4915
  Temperance *(G-16531)*
Gpbc Inc .... F 734 741-7325
  Ann Arbor *(G-503)*
Jabars Complements LLC .... F 810 966-8371
  Port Huron *(G-13489)*
Jorgensens Inc .... E 989 831-8338
  Greenville *(G-7494)*
Marias Italian Bakery Inc .... F 734 981-1200
  Canton *(G-2488)*
McDonalds .... F 248 851-7310
  Oxford *(G-12900)*
Mexamerica Foods LLC .... F 814 781-1447
  Grand Rapids *(G-6984)*
Midwest Aquatics Group Inc .... G 734 426-4155
  Pinckney *(G-13052)*
New Holland Brewing Co LLC .... C 616 355-2941
  Holland *(G-8154)*
Schelde Enterprises Inc .... G 231 941-7325
  Traverse City *(G-16825)*
The Spott .... G 269 459-6462
  Kalamazoo *(G-9355)*
Walmart Inc .... F 517 541-1481
  Charlotte *(G-2774)*

EDUCATIONAL SVCS

Arbor Press LLC .... D 248 549-0150
  Royal Oak *(G-14510)*
Hope Focus .... C 313 494-5500
  Detroit *(G-4307)*
Royal ARC Welding Company .... E 734 789-9099
  Flat Rock *(G-5628)*
Step Into Success Inc .... G 734 426-1075
  Pinckney *(G-13057)*
Svrc Industries Inc .... E 989 280-3038
  Saginaw *(G-14768)*

EDUCATIONAL SVCS, NONDEGREE GRANTING: Continuing Education

Toastmasters International .... G 810 385-5477
  Burtchville *(G-2223)*
Toastmasters International .... G 517 651-6507
  Laingsburg *(G-9538)*

ELASTOMERS

Argonics Inc .... D 906 226-9747
  Gwinn *(G-7580)*

Sika Auto Eaton Rapids Inc .... F 248 588-2270
  Madison Heights *(G-10828)*

ELECTRIC & OTHER SERVICES COMBINED

Lgc Global Inc .... E 313 989-4141
  Detroit *(G-4395)*

ELECTRIC MOTOR REPAIR SVCS

A & C Electric Company .... E 586 773-2746
  Harrison Township *(G-7683)*
All City Electric Motor Repair .... G 734 284-2268
  Riverview *(G-13868)*
American Electric Motor Corp .... F 810 743-6080
  Burton *(G-2226)*
Arrow Motor & Pump Inc .... F 734 285-7860
  Wyandotte *(G-18807)*
Barry Electric-Rovill Co .... G 810 985-8960
  Port Huron *(G-13457)*
Bay United Motors Inc .... F 989 684-3972
  Bay City *(G-1331)*
Birclar Electric and Elec LLC .... F 734 941-7400
  Romulus *(G-14259)*
Commonwealth Service Sls Corp .... G 313 581-8050
  Rochester Hills *(G-13980)*
Core Electric Company Inc .... F 313 382-7140
  Melvindale *(G-11198)*
DMS Electric Apparatus Service .... E 269 349-7000
  Kalamazoo *(G-9171)*
Electric Equipment Company .... G 269 925-3266
  Benton Harbor *(G-1548)*
Electric Motor & Contg Co .... F 313 871-3775
  Clay *(G-3119)*
Fife Pearce Electric Company .... F 313 369-2560
  Detroit *(G-4232)*
Fixall Electric Motor Service .... G 616 454-6863
  Grand Rapids *(G-6709)*
Franklin Electric Corporation .... F 248 442-8000
  Garden City *(G-6094)*
Gower Corporation .... F 989 249-5938
  Saginaw *(G-14657)*
Grand Rapids Elc Mtr Svc LLC .... G 616 243-8866
  Grand Rapids *(G-6755)*
Grand Rapids Elc Mtr Svcs LLC .... G 616 243-8866
  Grand Rapids *(G-6756)*
Hamilton Electric Co .... F 989 799-6291
  Saginaw *(G-14660)*
Holland Electric Motor Co .... G 616 392-1115
  Holland *(G-8078)*
Jones Electric Company .... E 231 726-5001
  Muskegon *(G-11849)*
Kalamazoo Electric Motor Inc .... G 269 345-7802
  Kalamazoo *(G-9238)*
Medsker Electric Inc .... F 248 855-3383
  Farmington Hills *(G-5314)*
Moore Brothers Electrical Co .... G 810 232-2148
  Flint *(G-5737)*
Motors Online LLC .... F 989 723-8985
  Corunna *(G-3713)*
Nieboer Electric Inc .... F 231 924-0960
  Fremont *(G-6049)*
Phillips Service Inds Inc .... F 734 853-5000
  Ann Arbor *(G-610)*
Pontiac Electric Motor Works .... F 248 332-4622
  Pontiac *(G-13408)*
PSI Repair Services Inc .... C 734 853-5000
  Livonia *(G-10375)*
Rapa Electric Inc .... G 269 673-3157
  Allegan *(G-180)*
Reliance Electric Machine Co .... F 810 232-3355
  Flint *(G-5754)*
Riverside Electric Service Inc .... G 269 849-1222
  Riverside *(G-13865)*
Spina Electric Company .... E 586 771-8080
  Warren *(G-18020)*
Sturgis Electric Motor Service .... G 269 651-2955
  Sturgis *(G-16323)*
Superior Elc Mtr Sls & Svc Inc .... G 906 226-9051
  Marquette *(G-11044)*
Winans Inc .... G 810 744-1240
  Corunna *(G-3719)*
York Electric Inc .... D 989 684-7460
  Bay City *(G-1412)*
York Electric Inc .... G 517 487-6400
  Lansing *(G-9909)*
Z & R Electric Service Inc .... E 906 774-0468
  Iron Mountain *(G-8738)*

ELECTRIC POWER GENERATION: Fossil Fuel

DTE Energy Company ....E 313 235-4000
  Detroit *(G-4193)*
DTE Energy Trust II .... G 313 235-8822
  Detroit *(G-4194)*
DTE Energy Ventures Inc .... G 313 235-8000
  Detroit *(G-4195)*

ELECTRIC POWER, COGENERATED

Option Energy LLC .... G 269 329-4317
  Traverse City *(G-16784)*

ELECTRIC SERVICES

Diamond Electric .... G 734 995-5525
  Ann Arbor *(G-451)*
DTE Energy Resources Inc .... D 734 302-4800
  Ann Arbor *(G-459)*
Engtechnik Inc .... G 734 667-4237
  Canton *(G-2459)*
Fremont Community Digester LLC .... F 248 735-6684
  Novi *(G-12418)*
General Electric Company .... G 734 728-1472
  Wayne *(G-18221)*

ELECTRIC SVCS, NEC: Power Generation

CMS Enterprises Company .... C 517 788-0550
  Jackson *(G-8845)*

ELECTRICAL APPARATUS & EQPT WHOLESALERS

Ademco Inc .... G 586 759-1455
  Warren *(G-17691)*
Ademco Inc .... G 248 926-5510
  Wixom *(G-18595)*
Electro-Matic Products Inc .... G 248 478-1182
  Farmington Hills *(G-5224)*
Energy Design Svc Systems LLC .... D 810 227-3377
  Whitmore Lake *(G-18532)*
Genco Alliance LLC .... G 269 216-5500
  Kalamazoo *(G-9192)*
Hitachi America Ltd .... G 248 477-5400
  Farmington Hills *(G-5261)*
McNaughton-Mckay Electric Co .... B 248 399-7500
  Madison Heights *(G-10779)*
Monarch Electric Service Co .... G 313 388-7800
  Melvindale *(G-11206)*
Osborne Transformer Corp .... F 586 218-6900
  Fraser *(G-5972)*
Quad Electronics Inc .... C 800 969-9220
  Troy *(G-17323)*

ELECTRICAL APPLIANCES, TELEVISIONS & RADIOS WHOLESALERS

Bluewater Tech Group Inc .... G 231 885-2600
  Mesick *(G-11269)*
Bluewater Tech Group Inc .... G 616 656-9380
  Grand Rapids *(G-6517)*
M10 Group Holding Company .... G 248 356-4399
  Southfield *(G-15639)*
Scientemp Corp .... E 517 263-6020
  Adrian *(G-94)*

ELECTRICAL CONSTRUCTION MATERIALS WHOLESALERS

Madison Electric Company .... D 586 825-0200
  Warren *(G-17913)*

ELECTRICAL CURRENT CARRYING WIRING DEVICES

A E C Inc .... D 810 231-9546
  Whitmore Lake *(G-18515)*
Aees Power Systems Ltd Partnr .... G 269 668-4429
  Farmington Hills *(G-5160)*
Armada Rubber Manufacturing Co .... D 586 784-9135
  Armada *(G-731)*
Astra Associates Inc .... E 586 254-6500
  Sterling Heights *(G-15935)*
Break-A-Beam .... G 586 758-7790
  Warren *(G-17742)*
Coppertec Inc .... E 313 278-0139
  Inkster *(G-8661)*

Employee Codes: A=Over 500 employees, B=251-500
C=101-250, D=51-100, E=20-50, F=10-19, G=3-9

ELECTRICAL CURRENT CARRYING WIRING DEVICES

Ekstrom Industries Inc .... D 248 477-0040
  Novi *(G-12412)*
Electrical Product Sales Inc .... E 248 583-6100
  Troy *(G-17084)*
Electrocom Midwest Sales Inc .... G 248 449-2643
  Madison Heights *(G-10720)*
Ews Legacy LLC .... C 248 853-6363
  Rochester Hills *(G-14006)*
Flextronics Automotive USA Inc ..... D 248 853-5724
  Coopersville *(G-3686)*
Four-Way Tool and Die Inc .... E 248 585-8255
  Troy *(G-17121)*
H W Jencks Incorporated .... E 231 352-4422
  Frankfort *(G-5878)*
Harman Corporation .... E 248 651-4477
  Rochester *(G-13903)*
Hi-Lex America Incorporated .... B 248 844-0096
  Rochester Hills *(G-14030)*
Lear Corporation .... B 248 447-1500
  Southfield *(G-15628)*
Mercury Displacement Inds Inc ...... D 269 663-8574
  Edwardsburg *(G-5009)*
Meter Devices Company Inc .... D 330 455-0301
  Farmington Hills *(G-5317)*
Metropolitan Alloys Corp 313 366-4443
  Detroit *(G-4438)*
National Zinc Processors Inc .... F 269 926-1161
  Benton Harbor *(G-1577)*
NGK Spark Plug Mfg USA Inc .... C 248 926-6900
  Wixom *(G-18720)*
Nyx LLC .... D 734 464-0800
  Livonia *(G-10346)*
Owosso Graphic Arts Inc .... E 989 725-7112
  Owosso *(G-12849)*
Patriot Sensors & Cntrls Corp .... F 810 378-5511
  Peck *(G-12962)*
Patriot Sensors & Cntrls Corp .... D 248 435-0700
  Peck *(G-12963)*
Prime Assemblies Inc .... E 906 875-6420
  Crystal Falls *(G-3744)*
Seeking .... G 586 489-2524
  Macomb *(G-10633)*
Ssi Electronics Inc .... E 616 866-8880
  Belmont *(G-1517)*
Testron Incorporated .... F 734 513-6820
  Livonia *(G-10431)*
TI Group Auto Systems LLC .... G 586 948-6006
  Chesterfield *(G-2956)*
Tram Inc .... C 734 254-8500
  Plymouth *(G-13322)*
Tram Inc 269 966-0100
  Battle Creek *(G-1306)*
Yazaki International Corp 734 983-1000
  Canton *(G-2544)*

ELECTRICAL DEVICE PARTS: Porcelain, Molded

NGK Spark Plug Mfg USA Inc .... C 248 926-6900
  Wixom *(G-18720)*

ELECTRICAL DISCHARGE MACHINING, EDM

AA EDM Corporation .... F 734 253-2784
  Dexter *(G-4719)*
C L Design Inc .... G 248 474-4220
  Farmington Hills *(G-5190)*
Cleary Developments Inc .... E 248 588-7011
  Madison Heights *(G-10689)*
Cut-Rite EDM Services LLC .... F 586 566-0100
  Shelby Township *(G-15200)*
Damick Enterprises .... F 248 652-7500
  Rochester Hills *(G-13989)*
Detail Technologies LLC .... E 616 261-1313
  Wyoming *(G-18866)*
Diversified E D M Inc .... G 248 547-2320
  Madison Heights *(G-10707)*
E D M Shuttle Inc 586 468-9880
  Clinton Township *(G-3227)*
Eikos Holdings Inc .... E 248 280-0300
  Troy *(G-17080)*
EMD Wire Tek .... G 810 235-5344
  Flint *(G-5695)*
Hill Machine Works LLC .... F 586 238-2897
  Fraser *(G-5937)*
J C Manufacturing Company .... G 586 757-2713
  Warren *(G-17877)*
Micro EDM Co LLC .... G 989 872-4306
  Cass City *(G-2619)*
Pdf Mfg Inc .... G 517 522-8431
  Grass Lake *(G-7443)*

Ramtec Corp .... F 586 752-9270
  Romeo *(G-14233)*
Superior Cutting Service Inc .... F 616 796-0114
  Holland *(G-8209)*
Tri-Way Manufacturing Inc .... E 586 776-0700
  Roseville *(G-14485)*

ELECTRICAL EQPT & SPLYS

Advanced Research Company .... F 248 475-4770
  Orion *(G-12723)*
Aerobee Electric Inc .... F 248 549-2044
  Ferndale *(G-5518)*
Asco Power Technologies LP .... G 248 957-9050
  Troy *(G-16958)*
Bailey Electrical Inc .... G 906 478-8000
  Hessel *(G-7873)*
BT Engineering LLC .... G 734 417-2218
  Spring Lake *(G-15807)*
Caniff Electric Supply .... G 586 221-1663
  Mount Clemens *(G-11633)*
Challenger Communications LLC .. F 517 680-0125
  Albion *(G-123)*
Cheap Electric Contractors Co .... G 734 205-9591
  Ann Arbor *(G-422)*
Cheap Electric Contractors Co .... G 734 452-1964
  Livonia *(G-10155)*
Cheap Electric Contractors Co .... G 734 205-9596
  Ann Arbor *(G-423)*
Cheap Electric Contractors Co .... G 734 286-9165
  Southgate *(G-15749)*
Comptek Inc .... E 248 477-5215
  Farmington Hills *(G-5206)*
Connolly .... G 248 683-7985
  Waterford *(G-18110)*
Craft Electric .... G 517 529-7164
  Clarklake *(G-3005)*
Csh Incorporated .... G 989 723-8985
  Owosso *(G-12829)*
Dare Products Inc .... E 269 965-2307
  Springfield *(G-15864)*
Diamond Electric .... G 734 995-5525
  Ann Arbor *(G-451)*
Dm3d Technology LLC .... F 248 409-7900
  Auburn Hills *(G-864)*
Electric Beach Tanning Co .... G 313 423-6539
  Grosse Pointe Park *(G-7553)*
Electric Contractors Company .... G 734 205-9594
  Ann Arbor *(G-469)*
Electric Eye Cafe .... G 734 369-6904
  Ann Arbor *(G-470)*
Electric Soul Tattoo and Fine .... E 616 930-3113
  Grand Rapids *(G-6668)*
Electronic Design & Packg Co .... F 734 591-9176
  Livonia *(G-10194)*
Faac Incorporated .... G 734 761-5836
  Ann Arbor *(G-484)*
General Electric Company .... G 734 728-1472
  Wayne *(G-18221)*
Grt Avionics Inc .... F 616 245-7700
  Wyoming *(G-18878)*
Harold G Schaevitz Inds LLC .... G 248 636-1515
  Bloomfield Hills *(G-1827)*
Heco Inc .... E 269 381-7200
  Kalamazoo *(G-9210)*
Iaec Corporation .... G 586 354-5996
  Armada *(G-737)*
Innovative Groups Inc .... G 313 309-7064
  Detroit *(G-4319)*
Insulation Wholesale Supply .... G 269 968-9746
  Battle Creek *(G-1241)*
Kore Inc .... E 616 785-5900
  Comstock Park *(G-3617)*
Lakepoint Elec .... L 586 983-2510
  Shelby Township *(G-15256)*
Lighthouse Elec Protection LLC .... G 586 932-2690
  Sterling Heights *(G-16074)*
Magna Electronics Inc .... D 810 606-0444
  Troy *(G-17219)*
Metropoulos Amplification Inc .... G 810 614-3905
  Holly *(G-8284)*
Midwest Sales Associates Inc .... G 248 348-9600
  Wixom *(G-18710)*
Montronix Inc .... G 734 213-6500
  Ann Arbor *(G-583)*
Muskegon Charter Township Fire .. G 231 329-3068
  Muskegon *(G-11880)*
New Electric .... F 586 580-2405
  Sterling Heights *(G-16114)*
Oleco Inc .... E 616 842-6790
  Spring Lake *(G-15841)*

PRODUCT SECTION

Peak Edm Inc .... G 248 380-0871
  Wixom *(G-18729)*
Quad City Innovations LLC .... G 513 200-6980
  Ann Arbor *(G-629)*
Ram Electronics Inc .... F 231 865-3186
  Fruitport *(G-6069)*
Resa Power LLC .... G 763 784-4040
  Wixom *(G-18740)*
Saginaw Control & Engrg Inc .... B 989 799-6871
  Saginaw *(G-14745)*
Sensigma LLC .... G 734 998-8328
  Ann Arbor *(G-648)*
Stanley Electric Sales America ...... G 248 471-1300
  Farmington Hills *(G-5386)*
Stoneridge Inc .... B 781 830-0340
  Novi *(G-12544)*
Tech Electric Co LLC .... G 586 697-5095
  Macomb *(G-10641)*
Tech-Source International Inc .... F 231 652-9100
  Newaygo *(G-12090)*
Tenneco Automotive Oper Co Inc 734 243-8000
  Lansing *(G-9742)*
Testek LLC .... D 248 573-4980
  Wixom *(G-18771)*
Twig Power LLC .... G 248 613-9652
  Novi *(G-12561)*
Walker Telecommunications .... G 989 274-7384
  Saginaw *(G-14791)*
Warner Power Acquisition LLC ...... C 603 456-3111
  Grand Haven *(G-6380)*
Welk-Ko Fabricators Inc 734 425-6840
  Livonia *(G-10470)*

ELECTRICAL EQPT FOR ENGINES

Aees Power Systems Ltd Partnr .... G 269 668-4429
  Farmington Hills *(G-5160)*
Autocam Corp .... D 616 698-0707
  Grand Rapids *(G-6481)*
Bontaz Centre Usa Inc .... F 248 588-8113
  Troy *(G-16982)*
Cignet LLC .... E 586 307-3790
  Clinton Township *(G-3201)*
Continental Auto Systems Inc .... B 248 253-2969
  Auburn Hills *(G-847)*
Cusolar Industries Inc .... E 586 949-3880
  Chesterfield *(G-2863)*
Ford Motor Company .... A 734 484-8626
  Ypsilanti *(G-18947)*
Fram Group Operations LLC .... G 800 890-2075
  Rochester Hills *(G-14014)*
H & L Manufacturing Co .... C 269 795-5000
  Middleville *(G-11308)*
Kirks Automotive Incorporated ...... E 313 933-7030
  Detroit *(G-4364)*
Magnecor Australia Limited .... F 248 471-9505
  Farmington Hills *(G-5300)*
Michigan Interlock LLC .... G 248 481-9743
  Waterford *(G-18136)*
Nabco Inc .... E 231 832-2001
  Reed City *(G-13796)*
USA Switch Inc .... F 248 960-8500
  Wixom *(G-18782)*
Walbro LLC .... D 989 872-2131
  Cass City *(G-2622)*
Walther Trowal LLC .... F 616 455-8940
  Byron Center *(G-2301)*

ELECTRICAL EQPT REPAIR & MAINTENANCE

Aero Grinding Inc .... D 586 774-6450
  Roseville *(G-14371)*
American Wldg & Press Repr Inc .. F 248 358-2050
  Southfield *(G-15486)*
Bond Bailey and Smith Company .. G 313 496-0177
  Detroit *(G-4061)*
CB Industrial LLC .... F 248 264-9800
  New Hudson *(G-12045)*
Cpj Company Inc .... E 616 784-6355
  Comstock Park *(G-3598)*
Douglas Corp .... E 517 767-4112
  Tekonsha *(G-16522)*
Genco Alliance LLC .... G 269 216-5500
  Kalamazoo *(G-9192)*
Hamilton Industrial Products .... E 269 751-5153
  Hamilton *(G-7599)*
Hel Inc .... F 616 774-9032
  Grand Rapids *(G-6808)*
Hutson Inc .... C 517 655-4606
  Williamston *(G-18573)*

(G-0000) Company's Geographic Section entry number

PRODUCT SECTION

ELECTRICAL GOODS, WHOLESALE: Wire & Cable

Jones Electric Company ....E...... 231 726-5001
  Muskegon *(G-11849)*
Ksb Dubric Inc ....E...... 616 784-6355
  Comstock Park *(G-3618)*
Mq Operating Company ....E...... 906 337-1515
  Calumet *(G-2412)*
PSI Hydraulics ....E...... 734 261-4160
  Plymouth *(G-13271)*
Spina Electric Company ....E...... 586 771-8080
  Warren *(G-18020)*
U S Equipment Co ....E...... 313 526-8300
  Rochester Hills *(G-14134)*

ELECTRICAL EQPT REPAIR SVCS: High Voltage

Franklin Electric Corporation ....F...... 248 442-8000
  Garden City *(G-6094)*

ELECTRICAL EQPT: Automotive, NEC

3con Corporation ....E...... 248 859-5440
  Wixom *(G-18591)*
Aktv8 LLC ....G...... 517 775-1270
  Wixom *(G-18603)*
Brose New Boston Inc ....C...... 248 339-4021
  New Boston *(G-12004)*
Continental Auto Systems Inc ....G...... 248 874-2597
  Auburn Hills *(G-848)*
Crosscon Industries LLC ....F...... 248 852-5888
  Rochester Hills *(G-13986)*
Electra Cable & Communication ....G...... 586 754-3479
  Warren *(G-17793)*
Kathrein Automotive N Amer Inc ....F...... 248 230-2951
  Auburn Hills *(G-949)*
Lg Elctrnics Vhcl Cmpnnts USA ....C...... 248 268-5851
  Hazel Park *(G-7828)*
Lg Electronics Vehicle Compone ....C...... 248 268-5851
  Troy *(G-17210)*
Lumen North America Inc ....F...... 248 289-6100
  Rochester Hills *(G-14054)*
Obdpros LLC ....G...... 734 274-5315
  Canton *(G-2503)*
Omron Automotive Electronics ....E...... 248 893-0200
  Novi *(G-12497)*
Overseas Auto Parts Inc ....E...... 734 427-4840
  Livonia *(G-10354)*
Portable Factory ....F...... 586 883-6843
  Saint Clair Shores *(G-14877)*
Protean Electric Inc ....D...... 248 504-4940
  Auburn Hills *(G-1005)*
Protean Holdings Corp ....G...... 248 504-4940
  Auburn Hills *(G-1006)*
Veoneer Inc ....A...... 248 223-0600
  Southfield *(G-15736)*
Veoneer Us Inc ....B...... 248 223-8074
  Southfield *(G-15737)*
Veoneer Us Inc ....B...... 248 223-0600
  Southfield *(G-15738)*
Wiric Corporation ....E...... 248 598-5297
  Rochester Hills *(G-14147)*
Wolverine Advanced Mtls LLC ....E...... 313 749-6100
  Dearborn *(G-3916)*
Xytek Industries Inc ....F...... 313 838-6961
  Detroit *(G-4696)*

ELECTRICAL GOODS, WHOLESALE: Alarms & Signaling Eqpt

Exquise Inc ....G...... 248 220-9048
  Detroit *(G-4223)*

ELECTRICAL GOODS, WHOLESALE: Batteries, Storage, Indl

Energy Products Inc ....G...... 248 866-5622
  Troy *(G-17090)*
Energy Products Inc ....E...... 248 545-7700
  Madison Heights *(G-10722)*

ELECTRICAL GOODS, WHOLESALE: Circuit Breakers

Rowerdink Inc ....G...... 734 487-1911
  Ypsilanti *(G-18975)*

ELECTRICAL GOODS, WHOLESALE: Electrical Appliances, Major

Lg Electronics USA Inc ....C...... 248 268-5100
  Troy *(G-17209)*

Nu-Way Stove Inc ....G...... 989 733-8792
  Onaway *(G-12701)*

ELECTRICAL GOODS, WHOLESALE: Electrical Entertainment Eqpt

Bluewater Tech Group Inc ....C...... 248 356-4399
  Wixom *(G-18624)*
Sani Zeevi ....G...... 248 546-4489
  Oak Park *(G-12646)*

ELECTRICAL GOODS, WHOLESALE: Electronic Parts

Advanced-Cable LLC ....F...... 586 491-3073
  Troy *(G-16909)*
American Furukawa Inc ....E...... 734 446-2200
  Plymouth *(G-13123)*
Galco Industrial Elec Inc ....F...... 248 542-9090
  Madison Heights *(G-10730)*
Ghi Electronics LLC ....E...... 248 397-8856
  Madison Heights *(G-10731)*
Morrell Incorporated ....D...... 248 373-1600
  Auburn Hills *(G-975)*
Rave Computer Association Inc ....E...... 586 939-8230
  Sterling Heights *(G-16143)*
Static Controls Corp ....E...... 248 926-4400
  Wixom *(G-18757)*

ELECTRICAL GOODS, WHOLESALE: Facsimile Or Fax Eqpt

Technology Network Svcs Inc ....F...... 586 294-7771
  Saint Clair Shores *(G-14888)*

ELECTRICAL GOODS, WHOLESALE: Generators

Ainsworth Electric Inc ....E...... 810 984-5768
  Port Huron *(G-13433)*
Amtrade Systems Inc ....G...... 734 522-9500
  Livonia *(G-10118)*
Coffman Electrical Eqp Co ....E...... 616 452-8708
  Grand Rapids *(G-6580)*
Cummins Inc ....G...... 616 538-2250
  Grand Rapids *(G-6618)*
Cummins Npower LLC ....E...... 906 475-8800
  Negaunee *(G-11965)*
Holland Electric Motor Co ....G...... 616 392-1115
  Holland *(G-8078)*

ELECTRICAL GOODS, WHOLESALE: Light Bulbs & Related Splys

G & L Powerup Inc ....G...... 586 200-2169
  Roseville *(G-14409)*
Lumecon LLC ....G...... 248 505-1090
  Farmington Hills *(G-5296)*
M & M Irish Enterprises Inc ....G...... 248 644-0666
  Birmingham *(G-1733)*

ELECTRICAL GOODS, WHOLESALE: Lighting Fixtures, Comm & Indl

Global Green Corporation ....F...... 734 560-1743
  Ann Arbor *(G-501)*
H & R Electrical Contrs LLC ....E...... 517 669-2102
  Dewitt *(G-4710)*

ELECTRICAL GOODS, WHOLESALE: Modems, Computer

Viking Technologies Inc ....G...... 586 914-0819
  Madison Heights *(G-10856)*

ELECTRICAL GOODS, WHOLESALE: Motor Ctrls, Starters & Relays

Nabco Inc ....E...... 231 832-2001
  Reed City *(G-13796)*

ELECTRICAL GOODS, WHOLESALE: Motors

A & C Electric Company ....E...... 586 773-2746
  Harrison Township *(G-7683)*
Alpena Electric Motor Service ....G...... 989 354-8780
  Alpena *(G-277)*
Arrow Motor & Pump Inc ....E...... 734 285-7860
  Wyandotte *(G-18807)*
Bay United Motors Inc ....F...... 989 684-3972
  Bay City *(G-1331)*

Commonwealth Service Sls Corp ....G...... 313 581-8050
  Rochester Hills *(G-13980)*
Core Electric Company Inc ....F...... 313 382-7140
  Melvindale *(G-11198)*
DMS Electric Apparatus Service ....E...... 269 349-7000
  Kalamazoo *(G-9171)*
Edwards Industrial Sales Inc ....G...... 517 887-6100
  Lansing *(G-9833)*
Electric Equipment Company ....G...... 269 925-3266
  Benton Harbor *(G-1548)*
Gower Corporation ....G...... 989 249-5938
  Saginaw *(G-14657)*
Hamilton Electric Co ....F...... 989 799-6291
  Saginaw *(G-14660)*
Heco Inc ....E...... 269 381-7200
  Kalamazoo *(G-9210)*
Johnson Electric N Amer Inc ....D...... 734 392-5300
  Plymouth *(G-13206)*
Kalamazoo Electric Motor Inc ....G...... 269 345-7802
  Kalamazoo *(G-9238)*
Lincoln Service LLC ....E...... 734 793-0083
  Livonia *(G-10279)*
Motor Control Incorporated ....G...... 313 389-4000
  Melvindale *(G-11207)*
Pontiac Electric Motor Works ....G...... 248 332-4622
  Pontiac *(G-13408)*
Rapa Electric Inc ....E...... 269 673-3157
  Allegan *(G-180)*
Reliance Electric Machine Co ....F...... 810 232-3355
  Flint *(G-5754)*
Riverside Electric Service Inc ....G...... 269 849-1222
  Riverside *(G-13865)*
Spina Electric Company ....E...... 586 771-8080
  Warren *(G-18020)*
Superior Elc Mtr Sls & Svc Inc ....G...... 906 226-9051
  Marquette *(G-11044)*
Winans Inc ....G...... 810 744-1240
  Corunna *(G-3719)*
York Electric Inc ....D...... 989 684-7460
  Bay City *(G-1412)*
Z & R Electric Service Inc ....E...... 906 774-0468
  Iron Mountain *(G-8738)*

ELECTRICAL GOODS, WHOLESALE: Security Control Eqpt & Systems

Best Netwrk Design & Assoc LLC ....E...... 313 680-2047
  Detroit *(G-4052)*
Code Blue Corporation ....E...... 616 392-8296
  Holland *(G-8000)*
Pct Security Inc ....G...... 888 567-3287
  Clinton Township *(G-3317)*
Traffic Sfety Ctrl Systems Inc ....E...... 248 348-0570
  Wixom *(G-18775)*

ELECTRICAL GOODS, WHOLESALE: Signaling, Eqpt

Carrier & Gable Inc ....E...... 248 477-8700
  Farmington Hills *(G-5199)*
Rathco Safety Supply Inc ....E...... 269 323-0153
  Portage *(G-13599)*

ELECTRICAL GOODS, WHOLESALE: Switchboards

Memcon North America LLC ....F...... 269 281-0478
  Stevensville *(G-16261)*

ELECTRICAL GOODS, WHOLESALE: Telephone Eqpt

J L International Inc ....G...... 734 941-0300
  Romulus *(G-14288)*

ELECTRICAL GOODS, WHOLESALE: Transformers

Warner Power Acquisition LLC ....C...... 603 456-3111
  Grand Haven *(G-6380)*

ELECTRICAL GOODS, WHOLESALE: Wire & Cable

Pro-Motion Tech Group LLC ....D...... 248 668-3100
  Wixom *(G-18735)*

Employee Codes: A=Over 500 employees, B=251-500
C=101-250, D=51-100, E=20-50, F=10-19, G=3-9

ELECTRICAL GOODS, WHOLESALE: Wire & Cable, Electronic

Wh Manufacturing Inc .... E 616 534-7560
Grand Rapids *(G-7337)*

ELECTRICAL HOUSEHOLD APPLIANCE REPAIR

Advanced BInding Solutions LLC .... F 906 914-4180
Menominee *(G-11224)*

ELECTRICAL INDL APPARATUS, NEC

Comec USA .... G 810 299-3000
Brighton *(G-1965)*
Sparta Outlets .... G 616 887-6010
Sparta *(G-15778)*
Ulb LLC .... E 734 233-0961
Wixom *(G-18781)*

ELECTRICAL SPLYS

Caniff Electric Supply .... G 586 221-1663
Mount Clemens *(G-11633)*
Electro-Matic Ventures Inc .... C 248 478-1182
Farmington Hills *(G-5225)*
Standard Electric Company .... F 906 774-4455
Kingsford *(G-9518)*
Utility Supply and Cnstr Co .... G 231 832-2297
Reed City *(G-13802)*

ELECTRICAL SUPPLIES: Porcelain

3M Technical Ceramics Inc .... F 248 960-9339
Wixom *(G-18592)*
Leco Corporation .... B 269 983-5531
Saint Joseph *(G-14946)*
Tengam Engineering Inc .... E 269 694-9466
Otsego *(G-12800)*

ELECTRODES: Indl Process

Debron Industrial Elec LLC .... D 248 588-7220
Troy *(G-17050)*

ELECTROMEDICAL EQPT

Benesh Corporation .... F 734 244-1413
Monroe *(G-11532)*
Cerephex Corporation .... G 517 719-0414
Bancroft *(G-1126)*
Helping Hands Therapy .... G 313 492-6007
Southfield *(G-15592)*
Medtronic Inc .... G 616 643-5200
Grand Rapids *(G-6976)*
Metrex Research LLC .... D 734 947-6700
Romulus *(G-14303)*
MII Disposition Inc .... E 616 554-9696
Grand Rapids *(G-7009)*
Rofin-Sinar Technologies LLC .... G 734 416-0206
Plymouth *(G-13290)*
Terumo Crdvscular Systems Corp .... C 734 663-4145
Ann Arbor *(G-683)*
Thoratec LLC .... C 734 827-7422
Ann Arbor *(G-690)*
Uv Partners Inc .... G 888 277-2596
Grand Haven *(G-6376)*

ELECTROMETALLURGICAL PRDTS

Alpha Resources LLC .... E 269 465-5559
Stevensville *(G-16239)*
H C Starck Inc .... G 517 279-9511
Coldwater *(G-3437)*
Miccus Inc .... F 616 604-4449
Howell *(G-8480)*

ELECTRON BEAM: Cutting, Forming, Welding

Hirose Electric USA Inc .... G 734 542-9963
Livonia *(G-10240)*
Tandis LLC .... G 248 345-3448
West Bloomfield *(G-18317)*

ELECTRONIC COMPONENTS

Ace Electronics LLC Michigan .... G 443 327-6100
Troy *(G-16904)*
Control Electronics .... G 734 941-5008
Romulus *(G-14263)*

ELECTRONIC DEVICES: Solid State, NEC

Regener-Eyes LLC .... G 248 207-4641
Ann Arbor *(G-636)*
Ziel Optics Inc .... G 734 994-9803
Ann Arbor *(G-724)*

ELECTRONIC EQPT REPAIR SVCS

Consoldted Rsource Imaging LLC .... E 616 735-2080
Grand Rapids *(G-6595)*
Galco Industrial Elec Inc .... G 248 542-9090
Madison Heights *(G-10730)*
Industrial Service Tech Inc .... F 616 247-1033
Grand Rapids *(G-6843)*
Innovative Support Svcs Inc .... F 248 585-3600
Troy *(G-17168)*

ELECTRONIC LOADS & POWER SPLYS

Aees Inc .... A 248 489-4700
Farmington Hills *(G-5159)*
High Effcncy Pwr Solutions Inc .... G 800 833-7094
Whitmore Lake *(G-18538)*
Renewable World Energies LLC .... G 906 828-0808
Norway *(G-12356)*

ELECTRONIC PARTS & EQPT WHOLESALERS

Great Lakes Infotronics Inc .... E 248 476-2500
Northville *(G-12226)*
Hitachi America Ltd .... G 248 477-5400
Farmington Hills *(G-5261)*
Hydraulic Systems Technology .... G 248 656-5810
Rochester Hills *(G-14036)*
Jo-Dan International Inc .... G 248 340-0300
Auburn Hills *(G-944)*
McNaughton-Mckay Electric Co .... B 248 399-7500
Madison Heights *(G-10779)*
Mitsubishi Electric Us Inc .... G 734 453-6200
Northville *(G-12241)*
Odyssey Electronics Inc .... D 734 421-8340
Livonia *(G-10352)*
Ram Meter Inc .... F 248 362-0990
Royal Oak *(G-14572)*
Rick Wykle LLC .... G 734 839-6376
Trenton *(G-16891)*
Scs Embedded Tech LLC .... G 248 615-4441
Novi *(G-12532)*

ELECTRONIC SHOPPING

Howies Hockey Incorporated .... G 616 643-0594
Grand Rapids *(G-6822)*
Meteor Web Marketing Inc .... F 734 822-4999
Ann Arbor *(G-570)*
Truly Free LLC .... E 231 252-4571
Traverse City *(G-16868)*

ELECTRONIC TRAINING DEVICES

Farr & Faron Associates Inc .... G 810 229-7730
Brighton *(G-1988)*
Siemens Industry Software Inc .... G 734 953-2700
Livonia *(G-10406)*

ELECTROPLATING & PLATING SVC

Sac Legacy Company LLC .... D 517 750-2903
Chelsea *(G-2825)*
Sigma International Inc .... F 248 230-9681
Livonia *(G-10408)*
Surface Activation Tech LLC .... G 248 273-0037
Troy *(G-17381)*
Vacuum Orna Metal Company Inc .... E 734 941-9100
Romulus *(G-14336)*

ELEVATOR: Bean, Storage Only

Nutrien AG Solutions Inc .... G 989 842-1185
Breckenridge *(G-1912)*

ELEVATORS & EQPT

All Access Lift LLC .... G 616 250-1084
Hastings *(G-7780)*
Central Elevator Co Inc .... F 269 329-0705
Vicksburg *(G-17602)*
Detroit Elevator Company .... E 248 591-7484
Ferndale *(G-5545)*
Mc Nally Elevator Company .... F 269 381-1860
Kalamazoo *(G-9266)*
Nylube Products Company LLC .... F 248 852-6500
Rochester Hills *(G-14074)*
Schafers Elevator Co .... G 517 263-7202
Adrian *(G-93)*

ELEVATORS WHOLESALERS

All Access Lift LLC .... G 616 250-1084
Hastings *(G-7780)*
Schindler Elevator Corporation .... F 517 272-1234
Lansing *(G-9891)*

ELEVATORS: Installation & Conversion

All Access Lift LLC .... G 616 250-1084
Hastings *(G-7780)*
Detroit Elevator Company .... E 248 591-7484
Ferndale *(G-5545)*
Dumas Concepts In Building Inc .... F 313 895-2555
Detroit *(G-4196)*
Elevated Technologies Inc .... E 616 288-9817
Grand Rapids *(G-6672)*
Mc Nally Elevator Company .... F 269 381-1860
Kalamazoo *(G-9266)*
Mitsubishi Electric Us Inc .... G 734 453-6200
Northville *(G-12241)*
Schindler Elevator Corporation .... F 517 272-1234
Lansing *(G-9891)*

ELEVATORS: Stair, Motor Powered

Elevated Technologies Inc .... E 616 288-9817
Grand Rapids *(G-6672)*

EMBLEMS: Embroidered

Aisin Holdings America Inc .... G 734 453-5551
Northville *(G-12195)*
Dun Mor Embroidery & Designs .... F 248 577-1155
Troy *(G-17071)*
Inkpressions LLC .... G 248 461-2555
Commerce Township *(G-3543)*
Sports Stop .... G 517 676-2199
Mason *(G-11158)*

EMBOSSING SVC: Paper

Creative Embossing .... G 248 851-1302
West Bloomfield *(G-18273)*
Graphic Specialties Inc .... E 616 247-0060
Grand Rapids *(G-6783)*
Graphics Embossed Images Inc .... G 616 791-0404
Grand Rapids *(G-6784)*

EMBROIDERING & ART NEEDLEWORK FOR THE TRADE

A & Js Embroidery .... G 734 417-3694
Milan *(G-11429)*
Advanced Printwear Inc .... G 248 585-4412
Madison Heights *(G-10662)*
Alis Custom Embroidery .... G 586 744-9442
Sterling Heights *(G-15927)*
Angel Embroidery .... G 517 515-4836
Eaton Rapids *(G-4951)*
Apparel Sales Inc .... G 616 842-5650
Jenison *(G-9045)*
Bag Stitchery .... G 231 276-3163
Traverse City *(G-16610)*
Bella Bleu Embroidery LLC .... G 810 797-2286
Metamora *(G-11277)*
Bewitching Stitchng Embroidery .... G 810 289-3978
China *(G-2969)*
Broadway Embroidery .... G 248 838-8074
Lake Orion *(G-9590)*
C R Stitching .... G 734 449-2633
Whitmore Lake *(G-18525)*
Carom L Embroidery .... G 231 690-0571
Ludington *(G-10530)*
CC Embroidery Vinyl Designs .... G 517 996-6030
Dansville *(G-3755)*
Classic Stitch .... G 586 737-7767
Sterling Heights *(G-15960)*
Creative Stitching .... G 248 210-9584
Howell *(G-8443)*
Custom Embroidery Plus LLC .... G 989 227-9432
Saint Johns *(G-14899)*
Custom Trends Printing LLc .... G 586 563-3946
Warren *(G-17768)*
Earthbound Inc .... G 616 774-0096
Grand Rapids *(G-6662)*
Embroider It LLC .... G 248 538-9965
West Bloomfield *(G-18281)*

Embroidery Hutch...G... 810 459-8728
Grand Blanc *(G-6241)*
Embroidery Shoppe LLC...G... 734 595-7612
Westland *(G-18367)*
Embroidme Grand Rapids...G... 616 974-1033
Grand Rapids *(G-6675)*
Fido & Stitch...G... 616 288-7992
Grand Rapids *(G-6705)*
Fully Promoted...G... 616 285-8009
Grand Rapids *(G-6727)*
Gramma N Stitches...G... 810 664-8606
Lapeer *(G-9932)*
Gratefulthreadembroider...G... 231 855-1340
Pentwater *(G-12972)*
Jean Smith Designs...G... 616 942-9212
Grand Rapids *(G-6866)*
Lake Effect Embroidery LLC...G... 616 502-7844
West Olive *(G-18349)*
Laughing Needles EMB LLC...G... 231 720-5789
Holton *(G-8340)*
Liberty Embroidery...G... 269 419-0327
Battle Creek *(G-1268)*
Mach II Enterprises Inc...G... 248 347-8822
Northville *(G-12238)*
Meridian Screen Prtg & Design...G... 517 351-2525
Okemos *(G-12674)*
Mom & ME Embroidery...G... 231 590-0256
Bear Lake *(G-1419)*
Monogram Goods Naples LLC...G... 231 526-7700
Harbor Springs *(G-7652)*
Monogram Lady...G... 313 649-2160
Grosse Pointe Woods *(G-7572)*
One Stop Embroidery...G... 248 799-8662
Southfield *(G-15669)*
Perfect Stitch Inc...G... 407 797-5527
Clio *(G-3409)*
Sew Saintly...G... 586 773-8480
Saint Clair *(G-14843)*
Sewphisticated Stitching...G... 269 428-4402
Saint Joseph *(G-14960)*
Special T Custom Products...G... 810 654-9602
Davison *(G-3797)*
Sportswear Specialties Inc...G... 734 416-9941
Canton *(G-2526)*
Stephanies Unlimited Creat LLC...G... 616 379-5392
Jenison *(G-9072)*
Stitch Alley Customs...G... 616 377-7082
Holland *(G-8203)*
Stitch Inventions...G... 248 698-7773
White Lake *(G-18467)*
Stitch N Lyds Embroidery...G... 231 675-1916
Charlevoix *(G-2735)*
Stitches and Steel...G... 248 330-6302
Harrison *(G-7682)*
Superior Stitch...G... 734 347-1956
Petersburg *(G-12986)*
T - Shirt Printing Plus Inc...E... 269 383-3666
Kalamazoo *(G-9351)*
Thai Paradize LLC...G... 248 331-7355
Wixom *(G-18772)*
Top Shelf Embroidery LLC...G... 231 932-0688
Traverse City *(G-16862)*
Top Shells Embroidery LLC...G... 231 932-0688
Traverse City *(G-16863)*
TP Logos LLC...G... 810 956-9484
Marysville *(G-11110)*
Trophy Center West Michigan...G... 231 893-1686
Whitehall *(G-18510)*
Ultra Stitch Embroidery...F... 586 498-5600
Madison Heights *(G-10849)*
Watson Embroidery...G... 313 459-5070
Detroit *(G-4675)*
What A Stitch...G... 248 698-1104
White Lake *(G-18471)*

EMBROIDERING SVC

Adlib Grafix & Apparel...G... 269 964-2810
Battle Creek *(G-1178)*
Alfie Embroidery Inc...F... 231 935-1488
Traverse City *(G-16599)*
Bay Supply & Marketing Inc...G... 231 943-3249
Traverse City *(G-16616)*
Bd Classic Sewing...G... 231 825-2628
Mc Bain *(G-11176)*
Beck & Boys Custom Apparel...G... 734 458-4015
Livonia *(G-10134)*
C R Stitching...G... 313 538-1660
Redford *(G-13722)*
Charlevoix Screen Masters Inc...G... 231 547-5111
Charlevoix *(G-2713)*
Classic Images Embroidery...G... 616 844-1702
Grand Haven *(G-6286)*
Classy Threadz...G... 989 479-9595
Harbor Beach *(G-7629)*
Court-Side Inc...G... 269 948-2811
Hastings *(G-7785)*
Creative Loop...G... 231 629-8228
Paris *(G-12932)*
D & M Silkscreening...G... 517 694-4199
Holt *(G-8305)*
Delta Sports Service & EMB...G... 517 482-6565
Lansing *(G-9686)*
Digigraphx Co...G... 586 755-1130
Warren *(G-17779)*
E Q R 2 Inc...G... 586 731-3383
Sterling Heights *(G-15995)*
Embroidery & Much More LLC...F... 586 771-3832
Saint Clair Shores *(G-14857)*
Embroidery House Inc...G... 616 669-6400
Jenison *(G-9054)*
Embroidery Wearhouse...G... 906 228-5818
Marquette *(G-11017)*
Ensign Emblem Ltd...D... 231 946-7703
Traverse City *(G-16678)*
Grand Rapids Embroidery...G... 616 451-2827
Grand Rapids *(G-6757)*
Grasel Graphics Inc...G... 989 652-5151
Frankenmuth *(G-5865)*
Great Lakes Custom Embroidery...G... 734 844-7347
Canton *(G-2467)*
Hoyt & Company LLC...G... 810 624-4445
Clio *(G-3401)*
I D Pro Embroidery LLC...G... 734 847-6650
Temperance *(G-16535)*
Ideal Wholesale Inc...G... 989 873-5850
Prescott *(G-13651)*
Imprint House LLC...G... 810 985-8203
Port Huron *(G-13487)*
Initial Attraction...G... 269 341-4444
Kalamazoo *(G-9223)*
Janet Kelly...F... 231 775-2313
Cadillac *(G-2338)*
Jene Holly Designs Inc...G... 586 954-0255
Harrison Township *(G-7703)*
JJ Jinkleheimer & Co Inc...F... 517 546-4345
Howell *(G-8468)*
Just Wear It...G... 734 458-4015
Livonia *(G-10263)*
K&S Custom Embroidery LLC...G... 734 709-2689
Canton *(G-2483)*
Lansing Athletics...G... 517 327-8828
Lansing *(G-9772)*
Logospot...G... 616 785-7170
Belmont *(G-1512)*
Markit Products...G... 616 458-7881
Grand Rapids *(G-6960)*
Michigan Graphic Arts...G... 517 278-4120
Coldwater *(G-3444)*
Midwest Custom Embroidery Co...G... 269 381-7660
Kalamazoo *(G-9271)*
Monogram Etc...G... 989 743-5999
Corunna *(G-3712)*
Monograms & More Inc...E... 313 299-3140
Taylor *(G-16449)*
Northville Stitching Post...G... 248 347-7622
Northville *(G-12247)*
Personal Graphics...G... 231 347-6347
Petoskey *(G-13013)*
Rose Embroidery LLC...G... 616 245-9191
Wyoming *(G-18906)*
Royal Stewart Enterprises...G... 734 224-7994
Temperance *(G-16548)*
Saginaw Knitting Mills Inc...F... 989 695-2481
Freeland *(G-6029)*
Silk Screenstuff...G... 517 543-7716
Charlotte *(G-2770)*
Slick Shirts Screen Printing...F... 517 371-3600
Lansing *(G-9895)*
Spirit of Livingston Inc...G... 517 545-8831
Howell *(G-8522)*
Sporting Image Inc...F... 269 657-5646
Paw Paw *(G-12956)*
Sports Junction...G... 989 791-5900
Saginaw *(G-14765)*
Stitch Kustoms...G... 248 622-4563
Pontiac *(G-13418)*
Student Book Store Inc...G... 517 351-6768
East Lansing *(G-4910)*
Thread West - Michigan...G... 231 755-5229
Norton Shores *(G-12339)*
Threads By Bb...G... 989 401-7525
Saginaw *(G-14775)*
Threads Invisable...G... 248 516-5051
Farmington Hills *(G-5400)*
Vision Quest Embroidery LLC...G... 517 375-1518
Howell *(G-8539)*

EMBROIDERING SVC: Schiffli Machine

Chromatic Graphics Inc...G... 616 393-0034
Holland *(G-7996)*
Circles Way To Go Around Inc...F... 313 384-1193
Clinton Township *(G-3202)*
Ideal Wholesale Inc...G... 989 873-5850
Prescott *(G-13651)*
Ultimate Graphic and Sign LLC...G... 989 865-5200
Saint Charles *(G-14812)*

EMBROIDERY ADVERTISING SVCS

Adco Specialties Inc...G... 616 452-6882
Grand Rapids *(G-6430)*
Authority Customwear Ltd...E... 248 588-8075
Madison Heights *(G-10676)*
R H & Company Inc...F... 269 345-7814
Kalamazoo *(G-9313)*
Sign Screen Inc...G... 810 239-1100
Flint *(G-5762)*

EMBROIDERY KITS

Heritage...G... 734 414-0343
Plymouth *(G-13187)*

EMERGENCY ALARMS

Ademco Inc...G... 586 759-1455
Warren *(G-17691)*
Ademco Inc...G... 248 926-5510
Wixom *(G-18595)*
Aero Systems...G... 253 269-3000
Livonia *(G-10104)*
Code Blue Corporation...E... 616 392-8296
Holland *(G-8000)*
Emergency Technology Inc...D... 616 896-7100
Hudsonville *(G-8581)*

EMPLOYEE LEASING SVCS

Contract People Corporation...F... 248 304-9900
Southfield *(G-15532)*

EMPLOYMENT AGENCY SVCS

Douglas Autotech Corporation...D... 517 369-2315
Bronson *(G-2111)*
F J Lucido & Associates...E... 586 574-3577
Warren *(G-17801)*

EMPLOYMENT SVCS: Labor Contractors

Die Tech Services Inc...E... 616 363-6604
Walker *(G-17637)*

ENAMELING SVC: Metal Prdts, Including Porcelain

American Porcelain Enamel Co...F... 231 744-3013
Muskegon *(G-11770)*
Hope Network West Michigan...E... 231 796-4801
Paris *(G-12934)*
Spectrum Industries Inc...D... 616 451-0784
Grand Rapids *(G-7216)*

ENCLOSURES: Electronic

Brooks Utility Products Group...D... 248 477-0250
Novi *(G-12377)*
Innovation Fab Inc...G... 586 752-3092
Bruce Twp *(G-2168)*

ENCLOSURES: Screen

All Season Enclosures...G... 248 650-8020
Shelby Township *(G-15168)*

ENGINE PARTS & ACCESS: Internal Combustion

CF Components Inc...G... 248 670-2974
Livonia *(G-10154)*
Extreme Machine Inc...G... 810 231-0521
Whitmore Lake *(G-18535)*

Employee Codes: A=Over 500 employees, B=251-500
C=101-250, D=51-100, E=20-50, F=10-19, G=3-9
2022 Harris Michigan
Industrial Directory
1261

ENGINE PARTS & ACCESS: Internal Combustion

Katech Inc..E 586 791-4120
  Clinton Township (G-3270)
R & D Enterprises Inc...........................E 248 349-7077
  Plymouth (G-13274)

ENGINE REBUILDING: Diesel

Logan Diesel Incorporated...................G 517 589-8811
  Leslie (G-10014)
Peaker Services Inc..............................D 248 437-4174
  Brighton (G-2049)
PSI Holding Company............................D 248 437-4174
  Brighton (G-2057)
Rolls-Royce Solutions Amer Inc..........G 734 261-0309
  Livonia (G-10390)

ENGINE REBUILDING: Gas

D & S Engine Specialist Inc.................F 248 583-9240
  Clawson (G-3093)

ENGINEERING HELP SVCS

Bpg International Fin Co LLC................G 616 855-1480
  Ada (G-12)
Woco Tech Usa Inc................................F 248 385-2854
  Novi (G-12569)

ENGINEERING SVCS

4d Systems LLC.....................................E 800 380-9165
  Flint (G-5632)
ADS LLC..G 248 740-9593
  Troy (G-16906)
Alcotec Wire Corporation......................G 800 228-0750
  Traverse City (G-16598)
Altair Engineering Inc...........................C 248 614-2400
  Troy (G-16928)
Altron Automation Group Inc..............C 616 669-7711
  Hudsonville (G-8566)
AM General LLC.....................................B 734 523-8098
  Auburn Hills (G-779)
AMS Co Ltd..G 248 712-4435
  Troy (G-16935)
Amtex Inc..G 586 792-7888
  Clinton Township (G-3170)
Aphase II Inc..D 586 977-0790
  Sterling Heights (G-15933)
Atmo-Seal Inc..G 248 528-9640
  Troy (G-16963)
Automation Contrls & Engrg LLC........E 734 424-5500
  Dexter (G-4725)
Bayshore Custom Assembly LLC........G 616 396-5502
  Holland (G-7971)
Bel-Kur Inc...E 734 847-0651
  Temperance (G-16528)
Bpg International Fin Co LLC................G 616 855-1480
  Ada (G-12)
Broaching Industries Inc......................E 586 949-3775
  Chesterfield (G-2853)
Cambric Corporation.............................G 801 415-7300
  Novi (G-12378)
Capsonic Automotive Inc.....................G 248 754-1100
  Auburn Hills (G-839)
Clean Air Technology Inc.....................E 734 459-6320
  Canton (G-2450)
Cold Heading Co....................................D 586 497-7000
  Warren (G-17758)
Comau LLC..B 248 353-8888
  Southfield (G-15530)
Compunetics Incorporated..................E 248 524-6376
  Troy (G-17022)
Contract People Corporation...............F 248 304-9900
  Southfield (G-15532)
Controlled Power Company.................C 248 528-3700
  Troy (G-17027)
Creative Composites Inc.....................E 906 474-9941
  Rapid River (G-13683)
Dayco Products LLC............................G 248 404-6506
  Troy (G-17047)
DIhbowles Inc..F 248 569-0652
  Southfield (G-15541)
Dse Industries LLC..............................G 313 530-6668
  Macomb (G-10589)
Eaton Corporation.................................G 517 787-8121
  Ann Arbor (G-463)
Ecorse McHy Sls & Rbldrs Inc............E 313 383-2100
  Wyandotte (G-18817)
Emp Advanced Development LLC....G 906 789-7497
  Escanaba (G-5067)
Energy Design Svc Systems LLC......D 810 227-3377
  Whitmore Lake (G-18532)

Engineered Tools Corp..........................E 989 673-8733
  Caro (G-2571)
Engineering Tech Assoc Inc................D 248 729-3010
  Troy (G-17091)
Ernie Romanco......................................G 517 531-3686
  Albion (G-125)
Esys Automation LLC..........................C 248 484-9927
  Auburn Hills (G-881)
Esys Automation LLC..........................E 284 484-9724
  Pontiac (G-13370)
Esys Automation LLC..........................E 248 484-9702
  Sterling Heights (G-16005)
Etcs Inc..F 586 268-4870
  Warren (G-17796)
Extreme Machine Inc...........................D 810 231-0521
  Whitmore Lake (G-18536)
Faac Incorporated..................................C 734 761-5836
  Ann Arbor (G-485)
Fev Test Systems Inc.........................G 248 373-6000
  Auburn Hills (G-897)
Global Fleet Sales LLC.......................G 248 327-6483
  Southfield (G-15576)
Global Strgc Sup Solutions LLC........D 734 525-9100
  Livonia (G-10226)
Global Supply Integrator LLC.............G 586 484-0734
  Davisburg (G-3770)
Glov Enterprises LLC..........................D 517 423-9700
  Tecumseh (G-16502)
Hawk Design Inc....................................G 989 781-1152
  Saginaw (G-14662)
Hbpo North America Inc......................C 248 823-7076
  Troy (G-17138)
Heartland Machine & Engrg LLC........G 616 437-1641
  Mason (G-11137)
Helios Solar LLC..................................G 269 343-5581
  Kalamazoo (G-9212)
Hi-Tech Furnace Systems Inc............F 586 566-0600
  Shelby Township (G-15235)
Hj Manufacturing Inc...........................G 906 233-1500
  Escanaba (G-5076)
Industrial Service Tech Inc.................F 616 247-1033
  Grand Rapids (G-6843)
Infinity Controls & Engrg Inc..............G 248 397-8267
  Lake Orion (G-9609)
Innovative Thermal Systems LLC......G 586 920-2900
  Warren (G-17866)
Innovative Weld Solutions LLC..........G 937 545-7695
  Rochester (G-13908)
Inoac Interior Systems LLC................F 248 488-7610
  Farmington Hills (G-5270)
Island Machine and Engrg LLC...........G 810 765-8228
  Marine City (G-10960)
Johnson Electric N Amer Inc..............D 734 392-5300
  Plymouth (G-13206)
Kaydon Corporation..............................C 231 755-3741
  Norton Shores (G-12306)
Limo-Reid Inc..G 517 447-4164
  Deerfield (G-3957)
Magna Exteriors America Inc.............A 248 631-1100
  Troy (G-17220)
Mahle Powertrain LLC.........................D 248 305-8200
  Farmington Hills (G-5307)
Manufacturing Hero..............................G 269 271-0031
  Portage (G-13583)
Marelli Automotive Ltg LLC................E 248 418-3000
  Southfield (G-15642)
Marelli North America Inc...................G 248 403-2033
  Southfield (G-15645)
Memtech Inc..F 734 455-8550
  Plymouth (G-13240)
Merrill Technologies Group Inc.........D 989 791-6676
  Saginaw (G-14697)
Methodica Technologies LLC..............E 312 622-7697
  Troy (G-17252)
Michigan Scientific Corp.....................E 248 685-3939
  Milford (G-11470)
Midstates Industrial Group Inc...........E 586 307-3414
  Clinton Township (G-3300)
Minth Group US Holding Inc...............E 248 848-8530
  Wixom (G-18711)
Mmi Engineered Solutions Inc..........D 734 429-4664
  Saline (G-15028)
Mmi Engineered Solutions Inc..........E 734 429-5130
  Warren (G-17933)
Motor City Electric Tech Inc...............D 313 921-5300
  Detroit (G-4467)
Northville Circuits Inc..........................G 248 853-3232
  Rochester Hills (G-14073)
Nyx LLC..D 734 462-2385
  Livonia (G-10348)

Oakland Automation LLC.....................E 248 589-3350
  Livonia (G-10350)
Omaha Automation Inc........................G 313 557-3565
  Detroit (G-4497)
P2r Metal Fabrication Inc....................F 586 606-5266
  Macomb (G-10625)
Pacific Engineering Corp.....................G 248 359-7823
  Novi (G-12502)
Peloton Inc...G 269 694-9702
  Otsego (G-12798)
Plasan Us Inc..G 616 559-0032
  Walker (G-17649)
Pmd Automotive LLC...........................G 248 732-7554
  Pontiac (G-13407)
Portable Factory....................................F 586 883-6843
  Saint Clair Shores (G-14877)
Praet Tool & Engineering Inc.............E 586 677-3800
  Macomb (G-10627)
Proos Manufacturing LLC...................C 616 454-5622
  Grand Rapids (G-7121)
Pyrinas LLC..G 810 422-7535
  Traverse City (G-16807)
Raven Acquisition LLC........................B 734 254-5000
  Holly (G-8291)
Recaro Automotive North Amer........D 586 210-2600
  Clinton Township (G-3331)
Rel Inc..E 906 337-3018
  Calumet (G-2413)
Rhombus Energy Solutions Inc.........G 313 406-3292
  Dearborn (G-3890)
Ricardo Defense Inc............................G 805 882-1884
  Sterling Heights (G-16149)
Roman Engineering...............................E 231 238-7644
  Afton (G-107)
Romeo Technologies Inc.....................D 586 336-5015
  Bruce Twp (G-2178)
Ross Design & Engineering Inc.........E 517 547-6033
  Cement City (G-2676)
Rosta USA Corp....................................F 269 841-5448
  Benton Harbor (G-1581)
Roush Industries Inc...........................G 734 779-7016
  Livonia (G-10392)
Roush Industries Inc...........................G 734 779-7013
  Livonia (G-10393)
Roush Manufacturing Inc...................C 734 779-7006
  Livonia (G-10395)
RPS Tool and Engineering Inc............E 586 298-6590
  Roseville (G-14474)
Set Liquidation Inc...............................D 517 694-2300
  Holt (G-8331)
Soils and Structures Inc.....................D 800 933-3959
  Norton Shores (G-12333)
Sws - Trimac Inc..................................E 989 791-4595
  Saginaw (G-14771)
Tecat Performance Systems LLC.....F 248 615-9862
  Ann Arbor (G-672)
Testek LLC..D 248 573-4980
  Wixom (G-18771)
Three-Dimensional Services Inc........C 248 852-1333
  Rochester Hills (G-14125)
Torsion Control Products Inc............F 248 537-1900
  Rochester Hills (G-14128)
Turn Key Automotive LLC..................F 248 628-5556
  Oxford (G-12926)
Twig Power LLC....................................G 248 613-9652
  Novi (G-12561)
Uniflex Inc..G 248 486-6000
  Brighton (G-2088)
US Energia LLC.....................................G 248 669-1462
  Rochester (G-13936)
V2soft Inc...D 248 904-1702
  Bloomfield Hills (G-1872)
Van Dyken Mechanical Inc..................D 616 224-7030
  Grandville (G-7422)
Vast Production Services Inc............D 248 838-9680
  Troy (G-17432)
Yates Industries Inc............................D 586 778-7680
  Saint Clair Shores (G-14892)

ENGINEERING SVCS: Acoustical

Carcostics Tech Ctr N Amer Inc........G 248 251-1737
  Howell (G-8434)
Progressive Panel Systems Inc........E 616 748-1384
  Zeeland (G-19074)

ENGINEERING SVCS: Aviation Or Aeronautical

Chandas Engineering Inc....................F 313 582-8666
  Dearborn (G-3819)

PRODUCT SECTION

Phg Aviation LLC .... G 231 526-7380
  Harbor Springs *(G-7654)*
Pioneer Technologies Corp .... G 702 806-3152
  Fremont *(G-6054)*

ENGINEERING SVCS: Building Construction

Boral Building Products Inc .... C 800 521-8486
  Wixom *(G-18625)*
K & M Industrial LLC .... G 906 420-8770
  Gladstone *(G-6182)*

ENGINEERING SVCS: Construction & Civil

Kadant Johnson LLC .... C 269 278-1715
  Three Rivers *(G-16577)*
Lgc Global Inc .... E 313 989-4141
  Detroit *(G-4395)*

ENGINEERING SVCS: Electrical Or Electronic

Complete Dsign Automtn Systems .... G 734 424-2789
  Dexter *(G-4732)*
Consoldted Rsource Imaging LLC .... E 616 735-2080
  Grand Rapids *(G-6595)*
Debron Industrial Elec LLC .... D 248 588-7220
  Troy *(G-17050)*
Eberspecher Contrls N Amer Inc .... E 248 994-7010
  Brighton *(G-1981)*
Energy Development Assoc LLC .... G 313 354-2644
  Dearborn *(G-3836)*
Innovation Tech LLC .... F 248 797-2686
  Wixom *(G-18685)*
Lectronix Inc .... E 517 492-1900
  Lansing *(G-9863)*
MAKS INCORPORATED .... E 248 733-9771
  Troy *(G-17235)*
Manufacturing Ctrl Systems Inc .... G 248 853-7400
  Rochester Hills *(G-14058)*
Nadex of America Corporation .... E 248 477-3900
  Farmington Hills *(G-5330)*
Nextek Power Systems Inc .... G 313 887-1321
  Detroit *(G-4484)*
Spec Corporation .... G 517 529-4105
  Clarklake *(G-3008)*
Xytek Industries Inc .... G 313 838-6961
  Detroit *(G-4696)*

ENGINEERING SVCS: Industrial

Clarkston Control Products .... G 248 394-1430
  Clarkston *(G-3024)*
DTe Hankin Inc .... G 734 279-1831
  Petersburg *(G-12983)*
Henshaw Inc .... D 586 752-0700
  Armada *(G-736)*
Leading Edge Engineering Inc .... F 586 786-0382
  Shelby Township *(G-15261)*
R Cushman & Associates Inc .... A 248 477-9900
  Livonia *(G-10381)*

ENGINEERING SVCS: Machine Tool Design

Advanced Integration Tech LP .... G 586 749-5525
  Chesterfield *(G-2837)*
Center Line Gage Inc .... G 810 387-4300
  Brockway *(G-2106)*
Enkon LLC .... E 937 890-5678
  Manchester *(G-10883)*
Highland Machine Design Inc .... G 248 669-6150
  Commerce Township *(G-3537)*
Integrity Design & Mfg LLC .... G 248 628-6927
  Oxford *(G-12890)*
JF Hubert Enterprises Inc .... F 586 293-8660
  Fraser *(G-5947)*
Metalform Industries LLC .... G 248 462-0056
  Shelby Township *(G-15274)*
Onyx Manufacturing Inc .... G 248 687-8611
  Rochester Hills *(G-14075)*
Ort Tool & Die Corporation .... D 419 242-9553
  Erie *(G-5052)*
Solutions For Industry Inc .... G 517 448-8608
  Hudson *(G-8562)*
Stonebrdge Technical Entps Ltd .... F 810 750-0040
  Fenton *(G-5505)*
Terrell Manufacturing Svcs Inc .... F 231 788-2000
  Muskegon *(G-11930)*
World Class Equipment Company .... F 586 331-2121
  Shelby Township *(G-15370)*

ENGINEERING SVCS: Marine

Dts Enterprises Inc .... E 231 599-3123
  Ellsworth *(G-5035)*

ENGINEERING SVCS: Mechanical

Competitive Edge Designs Inc .... G 616 257-0565
  Grand Rapids *(G-6586)*
JB Autotech LLC .... E 734 838-3963
  Livonia *(G-10258)*
Lavalier Corp .... E 248 616-8880
  Troy *(G-17205)*
Mahindra N Amrcn Tchncal Ctr I .... C 248 268-6600
  Auburn Hills *(G-965)*
Omni Technical Services Inc .... F 989 227-8900
  Saint Johns *(G-14912)*
Vdl Steelweld Usa LLC .... E 248 781-8141
  Troy *(G-17433)*

ENGINEERING SVCS: Pollution Control

Dipsol of America Inc .... E 734 367-0530
  Livonia *(G-10186)*

ENGINEERING SVCS: Professional

Infrared Telemetrics Inc .... F 906 482-0012
  Hancock *(G-7620)*
TMC Group Inc .... G 248 819-6063
  Pleasant Ridge *(G-13106)*
Vision Global Industries .... D 248 390-5805
  Macomb *(G-10649)*

ENGINEERING SVCS: Sanitary

Douglas Steel Fabricating Corp .... D 517 322-2050
  Lansing *(G-9759)*
Stegman Tool Co Inc .... E 248 588-4634
  Troy *(G-17372)*

ENGINEERING SVCS: Structural

Composite Techniques Inc .... F 616 878-9795
  Grand Rapids *(G-6589)*

ENGINES & ENGINE PARTS: Guided Missile

Hytrol Manufacturing Inc .... E 734 261-8030
  Jackson *(G-8906)*
Williams International Co LLC .... A 248 624-5200
  Pontiac *(G-13425)*

ENGINES: Diesel & Semi-Diesel Or Duel Fuel

Detroit Diesel Corporation .... A 313 592-5000
  Detroit *(G-4144)*
Detroit Diesel Corporation .... F 313 592-8256
  Redford *(G-13730)*
Double H Mfg Inc .... E 734 729-3450
  Westland *(G-18366)*
FCA US LLC .... G 313 957-7000
  Detroit *(G-4229)*

ENGINES: Gasoline, NEC

Powertrain Integration LLC .... E 248 577-0010
  Madison Heights *(G-10806)*

ENGINES: Hydrojet, Marine

Pinnacle Technology Group .... D 734 568-6600
  Ottawa Lake *(G-12810)*

ENGINES: Internal Combustion, NEC

Apex Competition Engines .... G 616 761-4010
  Fenwick *(G-5516)*
Chandas Engineering Inc .... F 313 582-8666
  Dearborn *(G-3819)*
Cobra Aero LLC .... G 517 437-9100
  Hillsdale *(G-7930)*
Creek Diesel Services Inc .... F 800 974-4600
  Grand Rapids *(G-6611)*
Cummins Bridgeway Grove Cy LLC .... C 614 604-6000
  New Hudson *(G-12047)*
Cummins Inc .... G 586 469-2010
  Clinton Township *(G-3215)*
Cummins Inc .... G 616 538-2250
  Grand Rapids *(G-6618)*
Cummins Inc .... G 313 843-6200
  Dearborn *(G-3823)*
Cummins Inc .... G 248 573-1900
  New Hudson *(G-12048)*
Cummins Inc .... G 989 752-5200
  Saginaw *(G-14633)*
Cummins Npower LLC .... E 906 475-8800
  Negaunee *(G-11965)*
Emp Racing Inc .... G 906 786-8404
  Escanaba *(G-5068)*
Engineered Machined Pdts Inc .... B 906 786-8404
  Escanaba *(G-5069)*
Extreme Machine Inc .... D 810 231-0521
  Whitmore Lake *(G-18536)*
Fev Test Systems Inc .... E 248 373-6000
  Auburn Hills *(G-897)*
Geislinger Corporation .... F 269 441-7000
  Battle Creek *(G-1234)*
Global Fmi LLC .... D 810 964-5555
  Fenton *(G-5481)*
GM Powertrain-Romulus Engine .... G 734 595-5203
  Romulus *(G-14279)*
Holbrook Racing Engines .... F 734 762-4315
  Livonia *(G-10241)*
K & S Property Inc .... D 248 573-1600
  New Hudson *(G-12059)*
Navarre Inc .... G 313 892-7300
  Detroit *(G-4478)*
Paice Technologies LLC .... G 248 376-1115
  Orchard Lake *(G-12718)*
W W Williams Company LLC .... G 313 584-6150
  Dearborn *(G-3913)*

ENGINES: Marine

Ehc Inc .... G 313 259-2266
  Troy *(G-17079)*

ENGINES: Steam

Alpena Antiq Trctr Stm Eng CL .... G 989 734-3859
  Hawks *(G-7814)*
Elderberry Steam Engines .... G 989 245-0652
  Saginaw *(G-14643)*

ENGRAVING SVC, NEC

Marking Machine Co .... F 517 767-4155
  Tekonsha *(G-16523)*
Marquee Engraving Inc .... G 810 686-7550
  Clio *(G-3404)*
New World Etching N Amer Ve .... G 586 296-8082
  Fraser *(G-5968)*
Rodzina Industries Inc .... G 810 235-2341
  Flint *(G-5755)*

ENGRAVING SVC: Jewelry & Personal Goods

Imagecraft .... G 517 750-0077
  Jackson *(G-8907)*
Jandron II .... G 906 225-9600
  Marquette *(G-11024)*
Jbl Enterprises .... G 616 530-8647
  Grand Rapids *(G-6863)*
Three Oaks Engraving & Engrg .... G 269 469-2124
  Three Oaks *(G-16559)*

ENGRAVING SVCS

A D Johnson Engraving Co Inc .... F 269 385-0044
  Kalamazoo *(G-9106)*
Applause Inc .... G 517 485-9880
  Holt *(G-8303)*
Garden City Products Inc .... E 269 684-6264
  Niles *(G-12133)*
Rex M Tubbs .... G 734 459-3180
  Plymouth *(G-13281)*
Trophy Center West Michigan .... G 231 893-1686
  Whitehall *(G-18510)*
Twin City Engraving Company .... G 269 983-0601
  Saint Joseph *(G-14968)*

ENTERTAINERS & ENTERTAINMENT GROUPS

School of Rock Canton .... G 734 845-7448
  Canton *(G-2521)*

ENTERTAINMENT SVCS

Ball Hard Music Group LLC .... G 833 246-4552
  Monroe *(G-11528)*
Intellitech Systems Inc .... G 586 219-3737
  Troy *(G-17170)*
Nationwide Network Inc .... G 989 793-0123
  Saginaw *(G-14708)*

Employee Codes: A=Over 500 employees, B=251-500
C=101-250, D=51-100, E=20-50, F=10-19, G=3-9

ENTERTAINMENT SVCS

New Genesis Enterprise Inc..................G...... 313 220-0365
  Westland (G-18400)

ENVELOPES

Husky Envelope Products Inc..............D...... 248 624-7070
  Walled Lake (G-17670)
Michigan Envelope Inc..........................G...... 616 554-3404
  Grand Rapids (G-6988)
The Envelope Printery Inc....................D...... 734 398-7700
  Van Buren Twp (G-17557)

ENZYMES

American Farm Products Inc..................F...... 734 484-4180
  Saline (G-15000)

EPOXY RESINS

Cass Polymers..E...... 517 543-7510
  Charlotte (G-2739)
Nano Materials & Processes Inc...........G...... 248 529-3873
  Milford (G-11475)
Pacific Epoxy Polymers Inc....................G...... 616 949-1634
  Grand Rapids (G-7066)
Resin Services Inc..................................F...... 586 254-6770
  Sterling Heights (G-16147)
United Resin Inc.....................................E...... 800 521-4757
  Royal Oak (G-14587)

EQUIPMENT: Pedestrian Traffic Control

Em A Give Break Safety.........................G...... 231 263-6625
  Kingsley (G-9523)

EQUIPMENT: Rental & Leasing, NEC

4d Building Inc..F...... 248 799-7384
  Milford (G-11452)
Bluewater Tech Group Inc......................G...... 231 885-2600
  Mesick (G-11269)
Bluewater Tech Group Inc......................G...... 616 656-9380
  Grand Rapids (G-6517)
Boomer Company....................................E...... 313 832-5050
  Detroit (G-4063)
Farber Concessions Inc..........................E...... 313 387-1600
  Redford (G-13733)
GKN North America Inc..........................C...... 248 296-7200
  Auburn Hills (G-912)
Global Pump Company LLC....................G...... 810 653-4828
  Davison (G-3785)
Jetech Inc..F...... 269 965-6311
  Battle Creek (G-1246)
Jones & Hollands Inc..............................G...... 810 364-6400
  Marysville (G-11089)
Leonard Fountain Spc Inc......................D...... 313 891-4141
  Detroit (G-4390)
M10 Group Holding Company................G...... 248 356-4399
  Southfield (G-15639)
Marketplus Software Inc.........................G...... 269 968-4240
  Springfield (G-15872)
Midwest Vibro Inc...................................G...... 616 532-7670
  Grandville (G-7401)
Safety-Kleen Systems Inc......................G...... 989 753-3261
  Saginaw (G-14743)
Visual Productions Inc............................D...... 248 356-4399
  Mesick (G-11275)

ESCALATORS: Passenger & Freight

Mitsubishi Electric Us Inc.......................G...... 734 453-6200
  Northville (G-12241)

ETCHING & ENGRAVING SVC

A & K Finishing Inc.................................F...... 616 949-9100
  Grand Rapids (G-6407)
Baron Acquisition LLC............................E...... 248 585-0444
  Madison Heights (G-10679)
Boss Electro Static Inc...........................E...... 616 575-0577
  Wyoming (G-18854)
Changeover Integration LLC..................F...... 231 845-5320
  Ludington (G-10532)
Done Right Engraving Inc......................G...... 248 332-3133
  Pontiac (G-13362)
Exclusive Imagery Inc............................G...... 248 436-2999
  Royal Oak (G-14536)
Lasers Plus LLC......................................G...... 734 926-1030
  Holt (G-8316)
Normic Industries Inc.............................E...... 231 947-8860
  Traverse City (G-16771)
On The Side Sign Dsign Grphics...........G...... 810 266-7446
  Byron (G-2255)

Pro - Tech Graphics Ltd.........................F...... 586 791-6363
  Clinton Township (G-3328)
Traction Tech Holdings LLC....................E...... 313 923-0400
  Detroit (G-4642)
Yale Tool & Engraving Inc......................G...... 734 459-7171
  Plymouth (G-13340)

ETHERS

Ether LLC...G...... 248 795-8830
  Ortonville (G-12746)

ETHYLENE-PROPYLENE RUBBERS: EPDM Polymers

Dendritech Inc...G...... 989 496-1152
  Midland (G-11337)

EXHAUST SYSTEMS: Eqpt & Parts

Acat Global LLC......................................G...... 231 330-2553
  Charlevoix (G-2707)
Benteler Automotive Corp......................B...... 616 245-4607
  Grand Rapids (G-6501)
Bosal Industries-Georgia Inc.................F...... 734 547-7038
  Ypsilanti (G-18926)
Bosal Industries-Georgia Inc.................E...... 734 547-7023
  Ypsilanti (G-18927)
Bosal Industries-Georgia Inc.................E...... 734 547-7022
  Ypsilanti (G-18928)
Classic Design Concepts LLC...............G...... 248 504-5202
  Milford (G-11458)
Faurecia Emssons Ctrl Tech USA..........C...... 248 724-5100
  Auburn Hills (G-887)
Jet Industries Inc....................................E...... 734 641-0900
  Westland (G-18389)
Purem Novi Inc...E...... 248 994-7010
  Novi (G-12519)
Purem Novi Inc...C...... 248 632-2731
  Wixom (G-18736)
Technique Inc..D...... 517 789-8988
  Jackson (G-9017)

EXPANSION JOINTS: Rubber

Meccom Industrial Products Co............F...... 586 463-2828
  Clinton Township (G-3297)

EXPLOSIVES

Austin Powder Company........................F...... 989 595-2400
  Presque Isle (G-13653)
Pepin-Ireco Inc..G...... 906 486-4473
  Ishpeming (G-8780)

EXPLOSIVES, EXC AMMO & FIREWORKS WHOLESALERS

Pepin-Ireco Inc..G...... 906 486-4473
  Ishpeming (G-8780)

EXTRACTS, FLAVORING

Gsb & Associates Inc............................G...... 770 424-1886
  Kalamazoo (G-9206)
Jogue Inc...G...... 734 207-0100
  Plymouth (G-13203)
Jogue Inc...G...... 313 921-4802
  Detroit (G-4339)
John L Hinkle Holding Co Inc................E...... 269 344-3640
  Kalamazoo (G-9233)
National Product Co................................F...... 269 344-3640
  Kalamazoo (G-9280)
Northville Laboratories Inc....................F...... 248 349-1500
  Northville (G-12246)
Pure Herbs Ltd...F...... 586 446-8200
  Sterling Heights (G-16139)
Wild Flavors Inc......................................G...... 269 216-2603
  Kalamazoo (G-9370)

EYEGLASSES: Sunglasses

Noir Medical Technologies LLC.............F...... 734 769-5565
  Milford (G-11479)
Noir Medical Technologies LLC.............F...... 248 486-3760
  South Lyon (G-15450)

EYELASHES, ARTIFICIAL

Bozz Lashez LLC.....................................G...... 734 799-7020
  Van Buren Twp (G-17513)
Reemarkable Eyes LLC..........................G...... 313 461-3006
  Eastpointe (G-4943)

PRODUCT SECTION

FABRIC STORES

J America Licensed Pdts Inc.................G...... 517 655-8800
  Fowlerville (G-5844)

FABRICATED METAL PRODUCTS, NEC

AAA Waterjet and Machining Inc...........G...... 586 759-3736
  Warren (G-17684)
Advanced Metal Fabricators...................G...... 616 570-4847
  Lowell (G-10494)
American Indus McHinery-Mc LLC........G...... 810 420-0949
  Marine City (G-10954)
Anchor Bay Fab.......................................G...... 586 231-0295
  Chesterfield (G-2839)
Arrowhead Industries Inc.......................F...... 231 238-9366
  Afton (G-106)
Central Mich Met Fbrcation LLC.............G...... 989 875-9172
  Ithaca (G-8788)
CNc Products Acquisition Inc................F...... 269 684-5500
  Niles (G-12119)
Colson Casters..F...... 269 944-6063
  Saint Joseph (G-14924)
Dag R&D..G...... 248 444-0575
  Milford (G-11460)
J and L Custom Services.......................G...... 269 641-7800
  Vandalia (G-17566)
Lyncs Metal Fabrication.........................G...... 616 813-2071
  Alto (G-335)
Magnum Fabricating................................G...... 734 484-5800
  Ypsilanti (G-18964)
Management Training Inn.......................G...... 734 439-1546
  Milan (G-11443)
Metal Components Inc...........................G...... 616 389-2400
  Wyoming (G-18893)
Multi Steel Services................................G...... 734 261-6201
  Livonia (G-10327)
My Metal Medium....................................G...... 231 590-4051
  Mesick (G-11274)
Northstar Metalcraft................................G...... 248 858-8484
  Pontiac (G-13403)
Ottawa Tool & Machine LLC..................G...... 616 677-1743
  Grand Rapids (G-7064)
Proper Arospc & Machining LLC............G...... 586 779-8787
  Warren (G-17981)
Rankam Metal Products.........................G...... 586 799-4259
  Shelby Township (G-15314)
Slik Metal Fabrication LLC....................G...... 586 344-5621
  Macomb (G-10636)
Specialty Metal Fabricators...................G...... 616 698-9020
  Caledonia (G-2401)
Steel Appeal..G...... 231 326-6116
  Empire (G-5042)
Troy Metal Fabricating LLC...................G...... 248 506-6142
  Troy (G-17400)
Zero Hour Parts.......................................F...... 734 997-0866
  Kentwood (G-9484)

FABRICS: Alpacas, Mohair, Woven

Lake Effect Alpacas................................G...... 616 836-7906
  Holland (G-8120)
Loneys Alpaca Junction..........................G...... 231 229-4530
  Lake City (G-9549)
Majestic Sonrise Alpacas.......................G...... 616 848-7414
  Holland (G-8138)
West Michigan Alpacas..........................G...... 616 990-0556
  Holland (G-8244)
Whitefeather Creek Alpacas..................G...... 517 368-5393
  Montgomery (G-11604)

FABRICS: Apparel & Outerwear, Cotton

Bahwse/Bahwse Brand LLC..................G...... 313 704-7376
  Detroit (G-4042)
Bearcub Outfitters LLC...........................F...... 231 439-9500
  Petoskey (G-12990)
BLAack&co LLC.......................................E...... 313 971-1857
  Southfield (G-15509)
Border Line Rich Apparel LLC...............G...... 866 959-3003
  Clinton Township (G-3187)
Border Line Rich Clothing LLC..............G...... 586 267-5251
  Clinton Township (G-3188)
Gogettaz Clothing Company LLC..........D...... 630 800-3279
  Southfield (G-15578)
JIT..G...... 248 799-9210
  Southfield (G-15613)
Lusciously Silked LLC............................G...... 313 878-7058
  Detroit (G-4411)
Paper Chase American Dream LLC......G...... 248 819-0939
  Detroit (G-4505)

PRODUCT SECTION

FABRICS: Trimmings

Truly Tees & Co LLc .... G 313 266-1819
  Detroit *(G-4647)*

FABRICS: Automotive, From Manmade Fiber

Advanced Composite Tech Inc .... G 248 709-9097
  Rochester *(G-13889)*
C & J Fabrication Inc .... G 586 791-6269
  Clinton Township *(G-3192)*
Takata Americas .... A 336 547-1600
  Auburn Hills *(G-1044)*

FABRICS: Broadwoven, Cotton

Inovation Services LLC .... F 586 932-7653
  Detroit *(G-4321)*

FABRICS: Broadwoven, Synthetic Manmade Fiber & Silk

Airhug LLC .... G 734 262-0431
  Canton *(G-2432)*
J America Licensed Pdts Inc .... G 517 655-8800
  Fowlerville *(G-5844)*
JAC Custom Pouches Inc .... E 269 782-3190
  Dowagiac *(G-4784)*
Performance Sailing Inc .... G 586 790-7500
  Clinton Township *(G-3318)*

FABRICS: Broadwoven, Wool

Stonehedge Farm .... G 231 536-2779
  East Jordan *(G-4881)*

FABRICS: Canvas

24 Canvas .... G 517 902-5870
  Manitou Beach *(G-10925)*
Better Built Gates Canvas LLC .... G 616 818-9103
  Cedar Springs *(G-2642)*
Blanck Canvas Photography LLC .... G 248 342-4935
  Clarkston *(G-3019)*
Canvas Innovations LLC .... G 616 393-4400
  Holland *(G-7990)*
Canvas Townhomes Allendale .... G 616 499-2680
  Allendale *(G-216)*
Carry-All Products Inc .... G 616 399-8080
  Holland *(G-7991)*
Cut Once LLC .... G 616 245-3136
  Grand Rapids *(G-6624)*
Elite Canvas LLC .... G 231 343-7649
  Fruitport *(G-6062)*
Legacy Canvas & Upholstery LLC .... G 231 578-9972
  Muskegon *(G-11859)*
M M Custom Canvas Shrink .... G 734 658-0497
  Dearborn *(G-3866)*
Northern Canvas & Upholstery .... G 989 735-2150
  Glennie *(G-6215)*
Northwest Canvas .... G 231 676-1757
  Charlevoix *(G-2723)*
T and RC Anvas Awning LLC .... G 810 230-1740
  Flint *(G-5775)*
Wine and Canvas of Ann Arbor .... G 734 277-9253
  Canton *(G-2542)*
Wine ND Canvas Grand Rapids .... G 616 970-1082
  Grand Rapids *(G-7341)*
Wnc of Grand Rapids 2 LLC .... G 269 986-5066
  Grand Rapids *(G-7343)*

FABRICS: Chenilles, Tufted Textile

Floracraft Corporation .... C 231 845-1270
  Ludington *(G-10536)*
G T Jerseys LLC .... F 248 588-3231
  Troy *(G-17124)*

FABRICS: Coated Or Treated

Elden Industries Corp .... F 734 946-6900
  Taylor *(G-16412)*

FABRICS: Cords

Tapex American Corporation .... G 810 987-4722
  Port Huron *(G-13531)*

FABRICS: Damasks, Cotton

Detroit Sewn Inc .... E 248 722-8407
  Pontiac *(G-13360)*

FABRICS: Denims

3 Ten Denim Ko LLc .... G 248 556-1725
  Ferndale *(G-5517)*
Denim & Roses Childrens CL LLC .... G 313 363-0387
  Detroit *(G-4130)*
Denim City LLC .... G 313 270-2942
  Detroit *(G-4131)*
Detroit Denim LLC .... G 313 351-1040
  Detroit *(G-4143)*
Huxl Denim .... G 248 595-8480
  Southfield *(G-15595)*
Mansa Denim Company .... G 313 384-3929
  Detroit *(G-4419)*
Michael E Nipke LLC .... G 616 350-0200
  Grand Rapids *(G-6985)*
Rose Denim .... G 517 694-3020
  Holt *(G-8327)*
Street Denim & Co .... G 313 837-1200
  Detroit *(G-4611)*

FABRICS: Dress, From Manmade Fiber Or Silk

Nickels Boat Works Inc .... F 810 767-4050
  Flint *(G-5738)*

FABRICS: Fiberglass, Broadwoven

Glassline Incorporated .... F 734 453-2728
  Plymouth *(G-13176)*
P I W Corporation .... G 989 448-2501
  Gaylord *(G-6152)*
SRS Fiberglass Products LLC .... D 231 747-6839
  Muskegon *(G-11925)*
Sunrise Fiberglass LLC .... D 651 462-5313
  Troy *(G-17379)*

FABRICS: Furniture Denim

Rooms of Grand Rapids LLC .... G 616 260-1452
  Spring Lake *(G-15847)*

FABRICS: Laminated

Plastatech Engineering Ltd .... D 989 754-6500
  Saginaw *(G-14729)*
Shawmut LLC .... G 810 987-2222
  Port Huron *(G-13526)*
Tpi Industries LLC .... D 810 987-2222
  Port Huron *(G-13535)*

FABRICS: Laundry, Cotton

Great Lkes Tex Restoration LLC .... G 989 448-8600
  Gaylord *(G-6131)*
Joan Arnoudse .... G 616 364-9075
  Grand Rapids *(G-6871)*

FABRICS: Metallized

APS Machine LLC .... F 906 212-5600
  Escanaba *(G-5058)*

FABRICS: Nonwoven

Nanotex LLC .... G 248 855-6000
  Bloomfield Hills *(G-1843)*

FABRICS: Osnaburgs

D&E Incorporated .... G 313 673-3284
  Southfield *(G-15535)*

FABRICS: Resin Or Plastic Coated

Bentzer Enterprises .... G 269 663-2289
  Edwardsburg *(G-4999)*
Duro-Last Inc .... B 800 248-0280
  Saginaw *(G-14641)*
Duro-Last Inc .... E 800 248-0280
  Saginaw *(G-14642)*
Haartz Corporation .... G 248 646-8200
  Bloomfield Hills *(G-1825)*
Hig Recovery Fund Inc .... G 269 435-8414
  Constantine *(G-3668)*
Maher Group LLC .... G 616 863-6046
  Rockford *(G-14176)*
Mp-Tec Inc .... F 734 367-1284
  Livonia *(G-10325)*
Pioneer Plastics Inc .... F 586 262-0159
  Sterling Heights *(G-16128)*
Tri-City Vinyl Inc .... F 989 401-7992
  Saginaw *(G-14779)*

FABRICS: Rubberized

PRA Company .... D 989 846-1029
  Standish *(G-15895)*

FABRICS: Satin

Satin Petals LLC .... G 248 905-3866
  Southfield *(G-15694)*

FABRICS: Scrub Cloths

Ace-Tex Enterprises Inc .... E 313 834-4000
  Detroit *(G-3982)*

FABRICS: Seat Cover, Automobile, Cotton

Simco Automotive Trim .... D 800 372-3172
  Macomb *(G-10635)*

FABRICS: Shoe Laces, Exc Leather

Fresh Heir LLC .... G 313 312-4492
  Farmington *(G-5138)*

FABRICS: Table Cover, Cotton

J David Inc .... G 888 274-0669
  Troy *(G-17177)*

FABRICS: Tapestry, Cotton

Guilford Performance Textiles .... F 910 794-5810
  Southfield *(G-15588)*

FABRICS: Trimmings

Advance Graphic Systems Inc .... E 248 656-8000
  Rochester Hills *(G-13943)*
Advanced Composite Tech Inc .... G 248 709-9097
  Rochester *(G-13889)*
American Twisting Company .... E 269 637-8581
  South Haven *(G-15398)*
AP Impressions Inc .... G 734 464-8009
  Livonia *(G-10121)*
Applause Inc .... G 517 485-9880
  Holt *(G-8303)*
Authority Customwear Ltd .... E 248 588-8075
  Madison Heights *(G-10676)*
Bivins Graphics .... G 616 453-2211
  Grand Rapids *(G-6512)*
Blts Wearable Art Inc .... G 517 669-9659
  Dewitt *(G-4706)*
Britten Inc .... C 231 941-8200
  Traverse City *(G-16627)*
Britten Banners LLC .... C 231 941-8200
  Traverse City *(G-16628)*
Cadillac Prsentation Solutions .... E 248 288-9777
  Troy *(G-16994)*
Detroit Name Plate Etching Inc .... E 248 543-5200
  Ferndale *(G-5547)*
E Q R 2 Inc .... G 586 731-3383
  Sterling Heights *(G-15995)*
Emaculate Enterprises LLC .... G 313 805-0654
  Detroit *(G-4205)*
Federal Heath Sign Company LLC .... E 248 656-8000
  Rochester Hills *(G-14010)*
Fibre Converters Inc .... E 269 279-1700
  Constantine *(G-3666)*
Hexon Corporation .... E 248 585-7585
  Farmington Hills *(G-5259)*
Innovative Material Handling .... G 586 291-3694
  Detroit *(G-4320)*
Irvin Acquisition LLC .... B 248 451-4100
  Pontiac *(G-13382)*
Irvin Automotive Products LLC .... C 248 451-4100
  Pontiac *(G-13383)*
J2 Licensing Inc .... G 586 307-3400
  Troy *(G-17180)*
Janet Kelly .... F 231 775-2313
  Cadillac *(G-2338)*
Jean Smith Designs .... G 616 942-9212
  Grand Rapids *(G-6866)*
Kalamazoo Regalia Inc .... F 269 344-4299
  Kalamazoo *(G-9247)*
Kay Screen Printing Inc .... B 248 377-4999
  Lake Orion *(G-9611)*
Lacks Exterior Systems LLC .... E 616 949-6570
  Grand Rapids *(G-6914)*
Larsen Graphics Inc .... E 989 823-3000
  Vassar *(G-17579)*
Lazer Graphics .... F 269 926-1066
  Benton Harbor *(G-1565)*

FABRICS: Trimmings

Lear Corporation .... G 248 447-1500
   Mason *(G-11141)*
Lear Corporation .... B 248 447-1500
   Southfield *(G-15628)*
Logofit LLC .... E 810 715-1980
   Flint *(G-5727)*
Marketing Displays Inc .... C 248 553-1900
   Farmington Hills *(G-5310)*
Michael Anderson .... G 231 652-5717
   Newaygo *(G-12088)*
Mid-Michigan Industries Inc .... D 989 773-6918
   Mount Pleasant *(G-11715)*
Mid-Michigan Industries Inc .... E 989 386-7707
   Clare *(G-2986)*
Nalcor LLC .... D 248 541-1140
   Ferndale *(G-5570)*
Neighborhood Artisans Inc .... G 313 865-5373
   Detroit *(G-4479)*
Nobby Inc .... F 810 984-3300
   Fort Gratiot *(G-5822)*
Perrin Souvenir Distrs Inc .... B 616 785-9700
   Comstock Park *(G-3636)*
Plasti-Fab Inc .... E 248 543-1415
   Ferndale *(G-5579)*
Qmi Group Inc .... E 248 589-0505
   Madison Heights *(G-10814)*
Rtlf-Hope LLC .... G 313 538-1700
   Detroit *(G-4573)*
Shirt Works .... G 989 448-8889
   Gaylord *(G-6159)*
Sign Screen Inc .... G 810 239-1100
   Flint *(G-5762)*
Srg Global Inc .... G 586 757-7800
   Taylor *(G-16479)*
Srg Global LLC .... A 248 509-1100
   Troy *(G-17368)*
Strattec Power Access LLC .... E 248 649-9742
   Auburn Hills *(G-1039)*
Tempro Industries Inc .... E 734 451-5900
   Plymouth *(G-13312)*
Timbertech Inc .... F 231 348-2750
   Harbor Springs *(G-7658)*
Twin City Engraving Company .... G 269 983-0601
   Saint Joseph *(G-14968)*
Vomela Specialty Company .... E 269 927-6500
   Benton Harbor *(G-1600)*
Vu Acquisitions LLC .... C 248 269-0517
   Troy *(G-17443)*
Wec Group LLC .... E 248 260-4252
   Rochester Hills *(G-14146)*
Yanfeng USA Auto Trim Systems .... E 586 354-2101
   Harrison Township *(G-7736)*

FABRICS: Twills, Drills, Denims/Other Cotton Ribbed Fabrics

Detroit Denim Company LLC .... G 313 626-9216
   Highland Park *(G-7904)*

FABRICS: Upholstery, Cotton

American Soft Trim Inc .... G 989 681-0037
   Saint Louis *(G-14984)*

FABRICS: Woven Wire, Made From Purchased Wire

Fabric Patch Ltd .... G 906 932-5260
   Ironwood *(G-8762)*

FABRICS: Woven, Narrow Cotton, Wool, Silk

Car-Min-Vu Farm .... G 517 749-9112
   Webberville *(G-18243)*
Rhino Products Inc .... G 269 674-8309
   Lawrence *(G-9984)*

FACILITIES SUPPORT SVCS

Dynamic Corporation .... F 616 399-2200
   Holland *(G-8018)*
Guelph Tool Sales Inc .... B 586 755-3333
   Warren *(G-17843)*
Quality Engineering Company .... F 248 351-9000
   Wixom *(G-18738)*
Reese Inspection Services LLC .... F 248 481-3598
   Auburn Hills *(G-1017)*

FAMILY CLOTHING STORES

Golden Fashion .... G 616 288-9465
   Grand Rapids *(G-6747)*

FANS, BLOWING: Indl Or Commercial

Entrepreneurial Pursuits .... G 248 829-6903
   Rochester Hills *(G-14005)*
Skyblade Fan Company .... F 586 806-5107
   Warren *(G-18014)*
Thermo Vac Inc .... D 248 969-0300
   Oxford *(G-12923)*

FANS, VENTILATING: Indl Or Commercial

Clean Rooms International Inc .... E 616 452-8700
   Grand Rapids *(G-6571)*

FARM & GARDEN MACHINERY WHOLESALERS

Holland Vision Systems Inc .... E 616 494-9974
   Holland *(G-8087)*
Jones & Hollands Inc .... G 810 364-6400
   Marysville *(G-11089)*

FARM PRDTS, RAW MATERIALS, WHOLESALE: Skins

Berry Sns-Rbbeh Islmic Slghtrh .... G 313 259-6925
   Detroit *(G-4051)*

FARM SPLY STORES

Corunna Mills Feed LLC .... G 989 743-3110
   Corunna *(G-3707)*

FARM SPLYS WHOLESALERS

Andersons Inc .... G 989 642-5291
   Hemlock *(G-7849)*

FARM SPLYS, WHOLESALE: Feed

Active Feed Company .... D 989 453-2472
   Pigeon *(G-13034)*

FARM SPLYS, WHOLESALE: Fertilizers & Agricultural Chemicals

Chippewa Farm Supply LLC .... G 989 471-5523
   Spruce *(G-15885)*
Ittner Bean & Grain Inc .... F 989 662-4461
   Auburn *(G-766)*

FARM SPLYS, WHOLESALE: Flower & Field Bulbs

Veldheer Tulip Garden Inc .... E 616 399-1900
   Holland *(G-8235)*

FARM SPLYS, WHOLESALE: Garden Splys

Blue Thumb Distributing Inc .... E 989 921-3474
   Saginaw *(G-14617)*

FASTENERS WHOLESALERS

Elkay Industries Inc .... F 269 381-4266
   Kalamazoo *(G-9178)*
Mid-States Bolt & Screw Co .... F 989 732-3265
   Gaylord *(G-6149)*
Warren Screw Works Inc .... G 734 525-2920
   Livonia *(G-10466)*

FASTENERS: Brads, Alum, Brass/Other Nonferrous Metal/Wire

Mueller Brass Co .... F 616 794-1200
   Belding *(G-1459)*
Revwires LLC .... G 269 683-8100
   Niles *(G-12163)*

FASTENERS: Metal

Arch Cutting Tools LLC .... C 734 266-6900
   Bloomfield Hills *(G-1800)*
Cox Industries Inc .... F 586 749-6650
   Chesterfield *(G-2862)*
Lisi Automotive HI Vol Inc .... G 734 266-6958
   Livonia *(G-10285)*
Nitto Seiko Co Ltd .... G 248 588-0133
   Troy *(G-17279)*
Nylok LLC .... C 586 786-0100
   Macomb *(G-10623)*
Ram-Pak Industries LLC .... F 616 334-1443
   Wyoming *(G-18902)*
Rayce Americas Inc .... E 248 537-3159
   Auburn Hills *(G-1015)*
Tapex American Corporation .... F 810 987-4722
   Port Huron *(G-13531)*

FASTENERS: Metal

Bauer Products Inc .... E 616 245-4540
   Grand Rapids *(G-6497)*
Caillau Usa Inc .... G 248 446-1900
   Brighton *(G-1960)*
Consort Corporation .... E 269 388-4532
   Kalamazoo *(G-9151)*
Flexible Steel Lacing Company .... D 616 459-3196
   Walker *(G-17639)*
Jay Cee Sales & Rivet Inc .... F 248 478-2150
   Farmington *(G-5140)*
Penn Automotive Inc .... G 248 599-3700
   Waterford *(G-18150)*
Penn Engineering & Mfg Corp .... B 313 299-8500
   Waterford *(G-18151)*
Shark Tool & Die Inc .... G 586 749-7400
   Columbus *(G-3502)*

FASTENERS: Notions, NEC

A Raymond Tinnerman Mexico .... G 248 537-3404
   Rochester Hills *(G-13939)*
Aall American Fasteners .... G 616 414-7688
   Grand Haven *(G-6270)*
Acument Global Tech Inc .... E 586 254-3900
   Sterling Heights *(G-15924)*
Baker Fastening Systems Inc .... G 616 669-7400
   Hudsonville *(G-8569)*
Decoties Inc .... G 906 285-1286
   Bessemer *(G-1648)*
Elkay Industries Inc .... F 269 381-4266
   Kalamazoo *(G-9178)*
Fourslides Inc .... F 313 564-5600
   Chesterfield *(G-2885)*
Hi-Tech Fasteners LLC .... F 231 689-6000
   White Cloud *(G-18444)*
Penn Automotive Inc .... G 248 599-3700
   Waterford *(G-18150)*
Penn Engineering & Mfg Corp .... B 313 299-8500
   Waterford *(G-18151)*
Rodenhouse Inc .... G 616 454-3100
   Grand Rapids *(G-7163)*
Scs Fasteners LLC .... G 586 563-0865
   Eastpointe *(G-4944)*

FASTENERS: Wire, Made From Purchased Wire

King Steel Fasteners Inc .... E 810 721-0300
   Oxford *(G-12893)*

FAUCETS & SPIGOTS: Metal & Plastic

American Beverage Equipment Co .... E 586 773-0094
   Roseville *(G-14373)*
Beans Best LLC .... G 734 707-7378
   Ann Arbor *(G-397)*
Epic Fine Arts Company Inc .... G 313 274-7400
   Taylor *(G-16414)*
Masco Corporation .... A 313 274-7400
   Livonia *(G-10302)*

FELT, WHOLESALE

Michigan Diversfd Holdings Inc .... F 248 280-0450
   Madison Heights *(G-10782)*

FELT: Acoustic

Acoufelt LLC .... G 800 966-8557
   Clawson *(G-3083)*

FENCES & FENCING MATERIALS

Merchants Metals LLC .... F 810 227-3036
   Howell *(G-8477)*
Vandelay Services LLC .... G 810 279-8550
   Howell *(G-8538)*

FENCES OR POSTS: Ornamental Iron Or Steel

Bradys Fence Company Inc .... G 313 492-8804
   South Rockwood *(G-15463)*

PRODUCT SECTION   FILTERS: General Line, Indl

FENCING DEALERS
Apple Fence Co .... F 231 276-9888
  Grawn *(G-7449)*
Contractors Fence Service .... E 313 592-1300
  Detroit *(G-4102)*
Nevill Supply Incorporated .... G 989 386-4522
  Clare *(G-2989)*

FENCING MATERIALS: Docks & Other Outdoor Prdts, Wood
Heath Manufacturing Company .... E 616 997-8181
  Coopersville *(G-3688)*
Mark Beem .... G 231 510-8122
  Lake City *(G-9550)*

FENCING MATERIALS: Plastic
Bradys Fence Company Inc .... G 313 492-8804
  South Rockwood *(G-15463)*
Deckorators Inc .... D 616 365-4201
  White Pigeon *(G-18475)*

FENCING MATERIALS: Snow Fence, Wood
Nevill Supply Incorporated .... G 989 386-4522
  Clare *(G-2989)*

FENCING MATERIALS: Wood
Apple Fence Co .... F 231 276-9888
  Grawn *(G-7449)*
Cherry Creek Post LLC .... G 231 734-2466
  Evart *(G-5122)*
Contractors Fence Service .... E 313 592-1300
  Detroit *(G-4102)*
Don Machalk Sons Fencing Corp .... E 906 753-4002
  Ingalls *(G-8657)*
Maine Ornamental LLC .... F 800 556-8449
  White Pigeon *(G-18482)*
Newberry Wood Enterprises Inc .... G 906 293-3131
  Newberry *(G-12098)*
Rapid River Rustic Inc .... E 906 474-6404
  Rapid River *(G-13686)*
Ufp Lansing LLC .... G 517 322-0025
  Lansing *(G-9795)*

FENCING: Chain Link
Metter Flooring LLC .... G 517 914-2404
  Rives Junction *(G-13887)*

FENDERS: Automobile, Stamped Or Pressed Metal
Dst Industries Inc .... C 734 941-0300
  Romulus *(G-14268)*
Schwab Industries Inc .... E 586 566-8090
  Shelby Township *(G-15326)*

FERTILIZER, AGRICULTURAL: Wholesalers
Star of West Milling Company .... D 989 652-9971
  Frankenmuth *(G-5873)*

FERTILIZERS: NEC
Bay-Houston Towing Company .... F 810 648-2210
  Sandusky *(G-15056)*
Cog Marketers Ltd .... F 434 455-3209
  Ashley *(G-742)*
Cog Marketers Ltd .... F 989 224-4117
  Saint Johns *(G-14898)*
Hydrodynamics International .... G 517 887-2007
  Lansing *(G-9853)*
Hyponex Corporation .... C 810 724-2875
  Imlay City *(G-8635)*
Markham Peat Corp .... G 800 851-7230
  Lakeview *(G-9643)*
Michigan Grower Products Inc .... G 269 665-7071
  Galesburg *(G-6080)*
Nutrien AG Solutions Inc .... G 989 842-1185
  Breckenridge *(G-1912)*

FERTILIZERS: Phosphatic
Andersons Inc .... G 989 642-5291
  Hemlock *(G-7849)*
Cog Marketers Ltd .... F 989 224-4117
  Saint Johns *(G-14897)*

FIBER & FIBER PRDTS: Acrylic
Cytec Industries Inc .... G 269 349-6677
  Kalamazoo *(G-9161)*

FIBER & FIBER PRDTS: Anidex
ABC Nails LLC .... G 616 776-6000
  Grand Rapids *(G-6416)*

FIBER & FIBER PRDTS: Organic, Noncellulose
Dal-Tile Corporation .... F 248 471-7150
  Farmington Hills *(G-5210)*
Solutia Inc .... G 734 676-4400
  Trenton *(G-16892)*

FIBER & FIBER PRDTS: Protein
Protein Procurement Svcs Inc .... G 248 738-7970
  Bloomfield Hills *(G-1853)*

FIBER & FIBER PRDTS: Synthetic Cellulosic
Applegate Insul Systems Inc .... E 517 521-3545
  Webberville *(G-18241)*
J Rettenmaier USA LP .... C 269 679-2340
  Schoolcraft *(G-15120)*
Kraig Biocraft Labs Inc .... G 734 619-8066
  Ann Arbor *(G-544)*

FIBERS: Carbon & Graphite
Acp Technologies LLC .... G 586 322-3511
  Saint Clair Shores *(G-14846)*
Fortress Stblztion Systems LLC .... G 616 355-1421
  Holland *(G-8040)*
Sankuer Composite Tech Inc .... G 586 264-1880
  Sterling Heights *(G-16163)*

FIGURES, WAX
Studio One Midwest Inc .... F 269 962-3475
  Battle Creek *(G-1302)*

FILLERS & SEALERS: Wood
Conway-Cleveland Corp .... G 616 458-0056
  Grand Rapids *(G-6604)*
Wall Pro Painting .... G 248 632-8525
  Royal Oak *(G-14590)*

FILM & SHEET: Unsupported Plastic
Berry Global Inc .... G 269 435-2425
  Constantine *(G-3663)*
Cadillac Products Inc .... F 989 766-2294
  Rogers City *(G-14208)*
Dow Chemical Company .... G 989 636-0540
  Midland *(G-11349)*
Durakon Industries Inc .... G 608 742-5301
  Lapeer *(G-9928)*
Encore Commercial Products Inc .... F 248 354-4090
  Farmington Hills *(G-5233)*
Filcon Inc .... F 989 386-2986
  Clare *(G-2979)*
Kraft-Wrap Inc .... E 586 755-2050
  Warren *(G-17896)*
Quality Transparent Bag Inc .... F 989 893-3561
  Bay City *(G-1391)*
Zenith Global LLC .... G 517 546-7402
  Howell *(G-8544)*

FILM DEVELOPING & PRINTING SVCS
P D Q Press Inc .... G 586 725-1888
  Ira *(G-8706)*

FILM: Motion Picture
Former Company LLC .... G 248 202-0473
  Detroit *(G-4244)*
Luxury Richland LLc .... F 269 222-7979
  Grand Rapids *(G-6953)*

FILTER ELEMENTS: Fluid & Hydraulic Line
Bulldog Fabricating Corp .... G 734 761-3111
  Ann Arbor *(G-409)*
Flodraulic Group Incorporated .... G 734 326-5400
  Westland *(G-18371)*
Parker-Hannifin Corporation .... G 330 253-5239
  Otsego *(G-12797)*

FILTERS
Acme Mills Company .... E 517 437-8940
  Hillsdale *(G-7920)*
Acme Mills Company .... G 800 521-8585
  Bloomfield Hills *(G-1791)*
Advanced Recovery Tech Corp .... G 231 788-2911
  Nunica *(G-12575)*
Arbor Fabricating LLC .... G 734 626-5864
  Milan *(G-11431)*
Boulding Filtration Co LLC .... G 313 300-2388
  Detroit *(G-4064)*
Buhler Technologies LLC .... E 248 652-1546
  Rochester Hills *(G-13966)*
Duperon Corporation .... D 800 383-8479
  Saginaw *(G-14640)*
Fergin & Associates Inc .... G 906 477-0040
  Engadine *(G-5043)*
Kdf Fluid Treatment Inc .... F 269 273-3300
  Three Rivers *(G-16578)*
Lampco Industries of MI Inc .... G 517 783-3414
  Jackson *(G-8932)*
Millennium Planet LLC .... G 248 835-2331
  Farmington Hills *(G-5322)*
Muskegon Heights Water Filter .... G 231 780-3415
  Norton Shores *(G-12314)*
Petter Investments Inc .... G 269 637-1997
  South Haven *(G-15411)*
REB Research & Consulting Co .... G 248 545-0155
  Oak Park *(G-12639)*
Wayne Wire Cloth Products Inc .... F 989 742-4591
  Hillman *(G-7917)*

FILTERS & SOFTENERS: Water, Household
Bauer Soft Water Co .... G 269 695-7900
  Niles *(G-12112)*
Lane Soft Water .... G 269 673-3272
  Allegan *(G-169)*
McIntyres Soft Water Svc Ltd .... E 810 735-5778
  Linden *(G-10065)*
Michigan Soft Water of Centr .... D 517 339-0722
  East Lansing *(G-4903)*
Plymouth Technology Inc .... F 248 537-0081
  Rochester Hills *(G-14086)*

FILTERS & STRAINERS: Pipeline
Barbron Corporation .... E 586 716-3530
  Kalkaska *(G-9382)*
Beswick Corporation .... F 248 589-0562
  Troy *(G-16976)*
Everest Energy Fund L L C .... G 586 445-2300
  Warren *(G-17797)*
Microphoto Incorporated .... F 586 772-1999
  Roseville *(G-14441)*
William Shaw Inc .... G 231 536-3569
  Traverse City *(G-16880)*

FILTERS: Air
Aero Filter Inc .... E 248 837-4100
  Madison Heights *(G-10663)*
Air Filter & Equipment Inc .... G 734 261-1860
  Livonia *(G-10106)*
Complete Filtration Inc .... F 248 693-0500
  Lake Orion *(G-9598)*
D-Mark Inc .... E 586 949-3610
  Mount Clemens *(G-11635)*
General Filters Inc .... E 248 476-5100
  Novi *(G-12423)*
SER Inc .... E 586 725-0192
  New Baltimore *(G-11994)*

FILTERS: Air Intake, Internal Combustion Engine, Exc Auto
Engineered Machined Pdts Inc .... B 906 786-8404
  Escanaba *(G-5069)*
Esco Group Inc .... F 616 453-5458
  Grand Rapids *(G-6685)*
Ronal Industries Inc .... F 248 616-9691
  Sterling Heights *(G-16159)*
Superb Machine Repair Inc .... F 586 749-8800
  New Haven *(G-12038)*

FILTERS: General Line, Indl
Flow Ezy Filters Inc .... F 734 665-8777
  Ann Arbor *(G-491)*
Gelman Sciences Inc .... C 734 665-0651
  Ann Arbor *(G-496)*

Employee Codes: A=Over 500 employees, B=251-500
C=101-250, D=51-100, E=20-50, F=10-19, G=3-9

2022 Harris Michigan Industrial Directory

1267

FILTERS: General Line, Indl

Hoff Engineering Co Inc .... G 248 969-8272
  Oxford (G-12887)
Hoffmann Filter Corporation .... F 248 486-8430
  Brighton (G-2008)
Jomesa North America Inc .... F 248 457-0023
  Troy (G-17189)
K and J Absorbent Products LLC ...... G 517 486-3110
  Blissfield (G-1766)
Kaydon Corporation .... B 734 747-7025
  Ann Arbor (G-538)
Nu-ERA Holdings Inc .... E 810 794-4935
  Clay (G-3123)
Pittsfield Products Inc .... E 734 665-3771
  Ann Arbor (G-612)
Quality Filters Inc .... F 734 668-0211
  Ann Arbor (G-630)
Recco Products Inc .... E 269 792-2243
  Wayland (G-18202)
Rosedale Products Inc .... D 734 665-8201
  Ann Arbor (G-644)
United Fbrcnts Strainrite Corp .... E 800 487-3136
  Pontiac (G-13422)

FILTERS: Motor Vehicle

ABC Precision Machining Inc .... G 269 926-6322
  Benton Harbor (G-1525)
Champion Laboratories Inc .... G 586 247-9044
  Shelby Township (G-15186)
Cusolar Industries Inc .... E 586 949-3880
  Chesterfield (G-2863)
Hoff Engineering Co Inc .... G 248 969-8272
  Oxford (G-12887)
TI Fluid Systems LLC .... A 248 494-5000
  Auburn Hills (G-1054)
Ufi Filters Usa Inc .... G 248 376-0441
  Troy (G-17410)
Ufi Filters Usa Inc .... F 248 376-0441
  Troy (G-17411)

FILTERS: Oil, Internal Combustion Engine, Exc Auto

Hudson Industries Inc .... G 313 777-5622
  Sterling Heights (G-16044)
Rex Materials Inc .... E 517 223-3787
  Howell (G-8509)
Viking Oil LLC .... G 989 366-4772
  Prudenville (G-13659)

FILTRATION DEVICES: Electronic

Ecoclean Inc .... C 248 450-2000
  Southfield (G-15552)
La Solucion Corp .... G 313 893-9760
  Detroit (G-4372)
Ntf Manufacturing Usa LLC .... F 989 739-8560
  Oscoda (G-12766)
Trucent Inc .... G 734 426-9015
  Dexter (G-4759)
Trucent Separation Tech LLC .... D 734 426-9015
  Dexter (G-4760)

FINANCIAL INVESTMENT ADVICE

Batts Group Ltd .... G 616 956-3053
  Grand Rapids (G-6496)

FINANCIAL SVCS

Totle Inc .... G 248 645-1111
  Birmingham (G-1754)

FINDINGS & TRIMMINGS: Fabric

AGM Automotive LLC .... D 248 776-0600
  Farmington Hills (G-5162)
Automotive Trim Technologies .... E 734 947-0344
  Taylor (G-16382)
Canadian Amrcn Rstoration Sups ..... E 248 853-8900
  Rochester Hills (G-13970)
Cni Enterprises Inc .... E 248 581-0200
  Madison Heights (G-10691)
Cni-Owosso LLC .... G 248 586-3300
  Madison Heights (G-10692)
Donbar LLC .... F 313 784-3519
  Inkster (G-8662)
Eissmann Auto Port Huron LLC .... C 810 216-6300
  Port Huron (G-13474)
Eissmann Auto Port Huron LLC .... E 248 829-4990
  Rochester Hills (G-14002)
Futuris Automotive (ca) LLC .... B 510 771-2300
  Plymouth (G-13172)
Futuris Automotive (us) Inc .... E 248 439-7800
  Oak Park (G-12614)
Futuris Global Holdings LLC .... D 248 439-7800
  Oak Park (G-12615)
Hayes-Albion Corporation .... F 517 629-2141
  Jackson (G-8900)
Interntnal Auto Cmpnnts Group .... G 810 987-8500
  Port Huron (G-13488)
Lacks Industries Inc .... C 616 698-9852
  Grand Rapids (G-6918)
Mollertech LLC .... D 586 615-9154
  Macomb (G-10619)
Pangea Made Inc .... A 248 436-2300
  Rochester Hills (G-14078)
Peckham Vocational Inds Inc .... A 517 316-4000
  Lansing (G-9724)
Peckham Vocational Inds Inc .... D 517 316-4478
  Lansing (G-9725)
Takata Americas .... A 336 547-1600
  Auburn Hills (G-1044)
Tesca Usa Inc .... E 586 991-0744
  Rochester Hills (G-14124)
Trims Unlimited LLC .... E 810 724-3500
  Almont (G-269)

FINDINGS & TRIMMINGS: Furniture, Fabric

E&S Sales LLC .... G 586 212-6018
  Sterling Heights (G-15996)
Morgan Sofa Co .... G 347 262-5995
  Detroit (G-4465)
Tennant & Associates Inc .... G 248 643-6140
  Troy (G-17388)

FINGERPRINTING SVCS

Welzin Health Services LLC .... G 313 953-8768
  Wyandotte (G-18844)

FINISHING AGENTS: Leather

Innovative Leather Tech LLC .... G 734 953-1100
  Wayne (G-18225)

FIRE ALARM MAINTENANCE & MONITORING SVCS

Gallagher Fire Equipment Co .... E 248 477-1540
  Livonia (G-10219)

FIRE ARMS, SMALL: Guns Or Gun Parts, 30 mm & Below

Larson Tactical Arms .... G 906 204-8228
  Ishpeming (G-8778)
Manly Innovations LLC .... G 734 548-0200
  Chelsea (G-2820)
Oakland Tactical Supply LLC .... G 810 991-1436
  Howell (G-8488)
Pierce Engineers Inc .... G 517 321-5051
  Lansing (G-9727)
Rs Products LLC .... G 801 722-9746
  Chesterfield (G-2941)
Timers Enterprises LLC .... G 517 617-3092
  Reading (G-13707)

FIRE ARMS, SMALL: Pellet & BB guns

Kirtland Products LLC .... F 231 582-7505
  Boyne City (G-1893)

FIRE ARMS, SMALL: Shotguns Or Shotgun Parts, 30 mm & Below

Crl Inc .... E 906 428-3710
  Gladstone (G-6177)

FIRE CONTROL OR BOMBING EQPT: Electronic

Fire Equipment Company .... E 313 891-3164
  Detroit (G-4233)

FIRE EXTINGUISHER CHARGES

Ernie Romanco .... G 517 531-3686
  Albion (G-125)

FIRE EXTINGUISHER SVC

Fire Equipment Company .... E 313 891-3164
  Detroit (G-4233)

PRODUCT SECTION

Gallagher Fire Equipment Co .... E 248 477-1540
  Livonia (G-10219)
Kraus Fire Equipment Inc .... G 810 744-4780
  Burton (G-2238)

FIRE EXTINGUISHERS, WHOLESALE

Exquise Inc .... G 248 220-9048
  Detroit (G-4223)
Kraus Fire Equipment Inc .... G 810 744-4780
  Burton (G-2238)

FIRE EXTINGUISHERS: Portable

Exquise Inc .... G 248 220-9048
  Detroit (G-4223)
Kidde Safety .... F 800 880-6788
  Novi (G-12452)
Kraus Fire Equipment Inc .... G 810 744-4780
  Burton (G-2238)

FIRE OR BURGLARY RESISTIVE PRDTS

Ace Controls Inc .... C 248 476-0213
  Farmington Hills (G-5158)
Campbell & Shaw Steel Inc .... F 810 364-5100
  Marysville (G-11083)
Fab-Alloy Company .... G 517 787-4313
  Jackson (G-8883)
Northwoods Manufacturing Inc .... D 906 779-2370
  Kingsford (G-9516)
Prs Manufacturing Inc .... G 616 784-4409
  Grand Rapids (G-7124)
Synchronous Manufacturing Inc .... F 517 764-6930
  Michigan Center (G-11296)
Van Dyken Mechanical Inc .... D 616 224-7030
  Grandville (G-7422)
Viking Corporation .... D 269 945-9501
  Hastings (G-7811)
Viking Fabrication Svcs LLC .... B 269 945-9501
  Hastings (G-7812)

FIRE PROTECTION EQPT

Front Line Services Inc .... F 989 695-6633
  Freeland (G-6024)
New 9 Inc .... E 616 459-8274
  Grand Rapids (G-7040)
Norman Township .... F 231 848-4495
  Wellston (G-18258)

FIRE PROTECTION SVCS: Contracted

Fire Safety Displays Co .... G 313 274-7888
  Dearborn Heights (G-3927)

FIREARMS: Large, Greater Than 30mm

Plead Arms LLC .... G 248 563-1822
  Troy (G-17307)

FIREARMS: Small, 30mm or Less

Aerospace America Inc .... E 989 684-2121
  Bay City (G-1319)
Sage International Limited .... F 989 739-7000
  Oscoda (G-12772)

FIREPLACE & CHIMNEY MATERIAL: Concrete

Espinoza Bros .... G 313 468-7775
  Detroit (G-4214)

FIREPLACE EQPT & ACCESS

Custom Fireplace Doors Inc .... F 248 673-3121
  Waterford (G-18111)
Flue Sentinel LLC .... G 586 739-4373
  Shelby Township (G-15228)
Hearth-N-Home Inc .... F 517 625-5586
  Owosso (G-12837)

FIREWOOD, WHOLESALE

Great Lakes Log & Firewd Co .... G 231 206-4073
  Twin Lake (G-17468)
Speedy Blaze Inc .... G 989 340-2028
  Alpena (G-318)

FIREWORKS

Bay City Fireworks Festival .... G 989 892-2264
  Bay City (G-1328)

Patriot Pyrotechnics .... G 989 831-7788
  Sheridan (G-15382)
St Evans Inc .... G 269 663-6100
  Edwardsburg (G-5017)

FISH & SEAFOOD PROCESSORS: Fresh Or Frozen

Collins Caviar Company .... G 269 469-4576
  Union Pier (G-17499)
Ruleau Brothers Inc .... E 906 753-4767
  Stephenson (G-15911)
Sea Fare Foods Inc .... F 313 568-0223
  Detroit (G-4586)

FISH FOOD

Fishes & Loaves Food Pantry .... G 517 759-4421
  Adrian (G-66)
Hatfield Enterprises .... G 616 677-5215
  Marne (G-10993)

FISHING EQPT: Lures

Fishall Lures .... G 231 821-9020
  Twin Lake (G-17467)
Gw Fishing Lures Inc .... G 989 684-6431
  Bay City (G-1364)

FISHING EQPT: Nets & Seines

Mason Tackle Company .... E 810 631-4571
  Otisville (G-12783)

FITTINGS & ASSEMBLIES: Hose & Tube, Hydraulic Or Pneumatic

Austin Tube Products Inc .... F 231 745-2741
  Baldwin (G-1121)
Burgaflex North America LLC .... E 810 714-3285
  Fenton (G-5461)
Central Industrial Corporation .... G 616 784-9612
  Grand Rapids (G-6560)
Hlc Industries Inc .... D 810 477-9600
  Farmington Hills (G-5262)
Kord Industrial Inc .... G 248 374-8900
  Wixom (G-18694)
Spiral Industries Inc .... E 810 632-6300
  Howell (G-8521)

FITTINGS & SPECIALTIES: Steam

Kadant Johnson LLC .... C 269 278-1715
  Three Rivers (G-16577)

FITTINGS: Pipe

Creform Corporation .... E 248 926-2555
  Novi (G-12385)
Metro Piping Inc .... F 313 872-4330
  Detroit (G-4436)
Perfection Sprinkler Company .... G 734 761-5110
  Ann Arbor (G-607)
Piper Industries Inc .... D 586 771-5100
  Roseville (G-14463)

FITTINGS: Pipe, Fabricated

Ferguson Enterprises LLC .... G 989 790-2220
  Saginaw (G-14645)
Hosco Inc .... F 248 912-1750
  Wixom (G-18678)

FIXTURES & EQPT: Kitchen, Metal, Exc Cast Aluminum

Duquaine Incorporated .... G 906 228-7290
  Marquette (G-11015)

FIXTURES & EQPT: Kitchen, Porcelain Enameled

New Line Inc .... G 586 228-4820
  Shelby Township (G-15289)

FIXTURES: Bank, Metal, Ornamental

Arnold & Sautter Co .... F 989 684-7557
  Bay City (G-1322)

FIXTURES: Cut Stone

Marbelite Corp .... E 248 348-1900
  Novi (G-12470)
Marblecast of Michigan Inc .... F 248 398-0600
  Oak Park (G-12625)

FLAGS: Fabric

American Flag & Banner Company .... G 248 288-3010
  Clawson (G-3085)
Bay Supply & Marketing Inc .... G 231 943-3249
  Traverse City (G-16616)
Spartan Flag Company Inc .... F 231 386-5150
  Northport (G-12192)

FLAKEBOARD

Arauco North America Inc .... C 800 261-4896
  Grayling (G-7456)
Norbord Panels USA Inc .... A 248 608-0387
  Rochester (G-13913)

FLARES

Solar Flare Bar .... G 269 830-0499
  Battle Creek (G-1297)

FLAT GLASS: Antique

Antique Botl & GL Collectr LLC .... G 248 486-0530
  New Hudson (G-12042)

FLAT GLASS: Building

Furniture City Glass Corp .... F 616 784-5500
  Grand Rapids (G-6728)

FLAT GLASS: Construction

I2 International Dev LLC .... G 616 534-8100
  Grandville (G-7390)
Pilkington North America Inc .... G 269 687-2100
  Niles (G-12159)

FLAT GLASS: Plate, Polished & Rough

Guardian Fabrication LLC .... D 248 340-1800
  Auburn Hills (G-919)

FLAT GLASS: Tempered

Superior Auto Glass of Mich .... G 989 366-9691
  Houghton Lake (G-8406)

FLAT GLASS: Window, Clear & Colored

Ford Motor Company .... A 313 446-5945
  Detroit (G-4240)

FLAVORS OR FLAVORING MATERIALS: Synthetic

Wild Flavors Inc .... E 269 216-2603
  Kalamazoo (G-9370)

FLOATING DRY DOCKS

Floatation Docking Inc .... E 906 484-3422
  Cedarville (G-2669)

FLOCKING METAL PRDTS

West Mich Flcking Assembly LLC .... E 269 639-1634
  Grand Rapids (G-7331)

FLOOR CLEANING & MAINTENANCE EQPT: Household

P and K Graphics Inc .... G 810 984-1575
  Port Huron (G-13513)

FLOOR COVERING STORES

Preferred Flooring MI LLC .... F 616 279-2162
  Walker (G-17650)
Standale Lumber and Supply Co .... D 616 530-8200
  Grandville (G-7419)

FLOOR COVERING STORES: Carpets

Dave Brand .... G 269 651-4693
  Sturgis (G-16287)
Homespun Furniture Inc .... F 734 284-6277
  Riverview (G-13874)

FLOOR COVERING: Plastic

Oscoda Plastics Inc .... E 989 739-6900
  Oscoda (G-12767)

FLOOR COVERINGS WHOLESALERS

Grand River Interiors Inc .... E 616 454-2800
  Grand Rapids (G-6777)

FLOOR COVERINGS: Rubber

Plasticore Inc .... F 877 573-3090
  Detroit (G-4528)
WI Molding of Michigan LLC .... D 269 327-3075
  Portage (G-13633)

FLOOR COVERINGS: Textile Fiber

Preferred Flooring MI LLC .... F 616 279-2162
  Walker (G-17650)

FLOORING & GRATINGS: Open, Construction Applications

Alro Steel Corporation .... G 989 893-9553
  Bay City (G-1320)
Land Enterprises Inc .... G 248 398-7276
  Madison Heights (G-10768)

FLOORING & SIDING: Metal

Longstreet Group LLC .... F 517 278-4487
  Coldwater (G-3443)

FLOORING: Baseboards, Wood

Manufacturing Dynamics Co .... G 248 670-0264
  Madison Heights (G-10774)
Shayn Allen Marquetry .... G 586 991-0445
  Shelby Township (G-15329)

FLOORING: Hard Surface

Floorcovering Engineers LLC .... G 616 299-1007
  Grand Rapids (G-6712)
Flor TEC Inc .... G 616 897-3122
  Lowell (G-10501)
Innovative Surface Works .... F 734 261-3010
  Farmington Hills (G-5269)
Pro Floor Service .... G 517 663-5012
  Eaton Rapids (G-4968)

FLOORING: Hardwood

Connor Sports Flooring LLC .... F 906 822-7311
  Amasa (G-338)
Omara Sprung Floors Inc .... G 810 743-8281
  Burton (G-2242)
PAW Enterprises LLC .... F 269 329-1865
  Kalamazoo (G-9290)
Rare Earth Hardwoods Inc .... F 231 946-0043
  Traverse City (G-16817)
Robbins Inc .... G 513 619-5936
  Negaunee (G-11973)
Rt Baldwin Enterprises Inc .... G 616 669-1626
  Hudsonville (G-8610)
Schafer Hardwood Flooring Co .... E 989 732-8800
  Tecumseh (G-16515)

FLOORING: Rubber

Preferred Flooring MI LLC .... F 616 279-2162
  Walker (G-17650)

FLOORING: Tile

Earthwerks LLC .... G 800 275-7943
  Grand Haven (G-6294)
Yoxheimer Tile Co .... F 517 788-7542
  Jackson (G-9040)

FLORIST: Flowers, Fresh

Birmingham Jewelry Inc .... G 586 939-5100
  Sterling Heights (G-15946)
Veldheer Tulip Garden Inc .... E 616 399-1900
  Holland (G-8235)

FLORISTS

Neumann Enterprises Inc .... G 906 293-8122
  Newberry (G-12094)

FLOWER ARRANGEMENTS: Artificial

FLOWER ARRANGEMENTS: Artificial
Eileen Smeltzer .... G 269 629-8056
  Richland *(G-13824)*
Sheri Boston .... G 248 627-9576
  Ortonville *(G-12751)*

FLOWER POTS Plastic
New Product Development LLC .... G 616 399-6253
  Holland *(G-8155)*

FLOWERS & FLORISTS' SPLYS WHOLESALERS
Wahmhoff Farms LLC .... F 269 628-4308
  Gobles *(G-6220)*

FLOWERS: Artificial & Preserved
Aurora Preserved Flowers .... G 989 498-0290
  Bay City *(G-1323)*
Roses Susies Feather .... G 989 689-6570
  Hope *(G-8363)*

FLUES & PIPES: Stove Or Furnace
Chicago Blow Pipe Company .... F 773 533-6100
  Marquette *(G-11012)*

FLUID METERS & COUNTING DEVICES
Advanced Integrated Mfg .... G 586 439-0300
  Fraser *(G-5888)*
Medallion Instrmnttion Systems .... C 616 847-3700
  Spring Lake *(G-15833)*
Northville Circuits Inc .... G 248 853-3232
  Rochester Hills *(G-14073)*
Re-Sol LLC .... F 248 270-7777
  Auburn Hills *(G-1016)*
Royal Design & Manufacturing .... D 248 588-0110
  Madison Heights *(G-10821)*
Sensus .... G 517 230-1529
  East Lansing *(G-4908)*
Silversmith Inc .... E 989 732-8988
  Gaylord *(G-6160)*

FLUID POWER PUMPS & MOTORS
Acutex Inc .... C 231 894-3200
  Whitehall *(G-18488)*
Dare Auto Inc .... E 734 228-6243
  Plymouth *(G-13152)*
Ddks Industries LLC .... G 586 323-5909
  Shelby Township *(G-15201)*
Eaton Aeroquip LLC .... B 949 452-9575
  Jackson *(G-8873)*
Eaton Corporation .... G 517 789-1148
  Jackson *(G-8875)*
Flow-Rite Controls Ltd .... E 616 583-1700
  Byron Center *(G-2270)*
Great Lakes Hydra Corporation .... F 231 258-4338
  Kalkaska *(G-9389)*
Hydro-Craft Inc .... G 248 652-8100
  Rochester Hills *(G-14037)*
J H Bennett and Company Inc .... E 248 596-5100
  Novi *(G-12446)*
Kawasaki Prcision McHy USA Inc .... E 616 975-3100
  Grand Rapids *(G-6879)*
Loftis Alumi-TEC Inc .... G 616 846-1990
  Grand Haven *(G-6330)*
M P Pumps Inc .... D 586 293-8240
  Fraser *(G-5959)*
Med-Kas Hydraulics Inc .... F 248 585-3220
  Troy *(G-17243)*
Metaris Hydraulics .... G 586 949-4240
  Chesterfield *(G-2912)*
Mfp Automation Engineering Inc .... D 616 538-5700
  Hudsonville *(G-8594)*
Nabtesco Motion Control Inc .... F 248 553-3020
  Farmington Hills *(G-5329)*
Npi .... G 248 478-0010
  Farmington Hills *(G-5336)*
Parker HSD .... F 269 384-3915
  Kalamazoo *(G-9287)*
Parker-Hannifin Corporation .... G 269 692-6254
  Otsego *(G-12796)*
Parker-Hannifin Corporation .... B 269 384-3459
  Kalamazoo *(G-9288)*
Piper Industries Inc .... D 586 771-5100
  Roseville *(G-14463)*
Prophotonix Limited .... G 586 778-1100
  Roseville *(G-14466)*

REO Hydraulic & Mfg Inc .... F 313 891-2244
  Detroit *(G-4566)*
Robert Bosch LLC .... G 269 429-3221
  Saint Joseph *(G-14957)*
Schrader Stoves of Michiana .... E 269 684-4494
  Niles *(G-12166)*
Truform Machine Inc .... G 517 782-8523
  Jackson *(G-9025)*
Wmh Fluidpower Inc .... F 269 327-7011
  Portage *(G-13634)*
Wolverine Water Works Inc .... G 248 673-4310
  Waterford *(G-18176)*
Yates Industries Inc .... D 586 778-7680
  Saint Clair Shores *(G-14892)*

FLUID POWER VALVES & HOSE FITTINGS
Acutex Inc .... C 231 894-3200
  Whitehall *(G-18488)*
Aircraft Precision Pdts Inc .... D 989 875-4186
  Ithaca *(G-8785)*
Alco Manufacturing Corp .... E 734 426-3941
  Dexter *(G-4722)*
Automatic Valve Corp .... E 248 474-6761
  Novi *(G-12370)*
Bucher Hydraulics Inc .... C 616 458-1306
  Grand Rapids *(G-6528)*
Bucher Hydraulics Inc .... G 231 652-2773
  Newaygo *(G-12078)*
Craig Assembly Inc .... C 810 326-1374
  Saint Clair *(G-14821)*
Dadco Inc .... D 734 207-1100
  Plymouth *(G-13151)*
Fluid Hutchinson Management .... D 248 679-1327
  Auburn Hills *(G-903)*
Hosco Fittings LLC .... E 248 912-1750
  Wixom *(G-18679)*
Nabtesco Motion Control Inc .... F 248 553-3020
  Farmington Hills *(G-5329)*
Novi Tool & Machine Company .... F 313 532-0900
  Redford *(G-13749)*
Parker-Hannifin Corporation .... B 269 629-5000
  Richland *(G-13826)*
Pinckney Automatic & Mfg .... G 734 878-3430
  Pinckney *(G-13053)*
Piper Industries Inc .... D 586 771-5100
  Roseville *(G-14463)*
Precision Packing Corporation .... E 586 756-8700
  Warren *(G-17973)*
Sames Kremlin Inc .... C 734 979-0100
  Plymouth *(G-13292)*
Scott Machine Inc .... E 517 787-6616
  Jackson *(G-9008)*

FLUXES
CRC Industries Inc .... E 313 883-6977
  Detroit *(G-4107)*
Hill Machine Works LLC .... F 586 238-2897
  Fraser *(G-5937)*
Selkey Fabricators LLC .... F 906 353-7104
  Baraga *(G-1148)*

FLYSWATTERS
Smart Swatter LLC .... G 989 763-2626
  Harbor Springs *(G-7657)*

FOAM RUBBER
Cartex Corporation .... G 610 759-1650
  Troy *(G-17005)*
Creative Foam Corporation .... C 810 629-4149
  Fenton *(G-5467)*
Ds Sales Inc .... E 248 960-6411
  Wixom *(G-18648)*
Great Lake Foam Technologies .... E 517 563-8030
  Hanover *(G-7624)*
Massee Products Ltd .... G 269 684-8255
  Niles *(G-12142)*
Milsco LLC .... E 517 787-3650
  Jackson *(G-8965)*

FOAMS & RUBBER, WHOLESALE
Envirolite LLC .... F 248 792-3184
  Troy *(G-17094)*
Envirolite LLC .... D 888 222-2191
  Coldwater *(G-3432)*

FOIL & LEAF: Metal
Barbron Corporation .... E 586 716-3530
  Kalkaska *(G-9382)*
Graphic Specialties Inc .... E 616 247-0060
  Grand Rapids *(G-6783)*
Illinois Tool Works Inc .... D 231 258-5521
  Kalkaska *(G-9390)*

FOIL: Aluminum
Novelis Corporation .... G 248 668-5111
  Novi *(G-12492)*

FOOD CONTAMINATION TESTING OR SCREENING KITS
Svn Inc .... G 734 707-7131
  Saline *(G-15042)*

FOOD PRDTS, BREAKFAST: Cereal, Corn Flakes
Kellogg Company .... G 269 961-6693
  Battle Creek *(G-1259)*
Kellogg Company .... A 269 961-2000
  Battle Creek *(G-1255)*

FOOD PRDTS, BREAKFAST: Cereal, Granola & Muesli
Daddy DZ Granola Co .... G 616 374-0229
  Lake Odessa *(G-9574)*
Granola Project Llc .... G 919 219-7158
  Westland *(G-18375)*

FOOD PRDTS, CANNED OR FRESH PACK: Fruit Juices
Burnette Foods Inc .... D 231 264-8116
  Elk Rapids *(G-5022)*
Everfresh Beverages Inc .... D 586 755-9500
  Warren *(G-17798)*
Old Orchard Brands LLC .... D 616 887-1745
  Sparta *(G-15774)*
Rice Juice Company Inc .... G 906 774-1733
  Iron Mountain *(G-8730)*
St Julian Wine Company Inc .... E 269 657-5568
  Paw Paw *(G-12957)*
Welch Foods Inc A Cooperative .... D 269 624-4141
  Lawton *(G-9990)*

FOOD PRDTS, CANNED OR FRESH PACK: Vegetable Juices
J House LLC .... G 313 220-4449
  Grosse Pointe Farms *(G-7536)*
Panther James LLC .... F 248 850-7522
  Berkley *(G-1634)*

FOOD PRDTS, CANNED: Applesauce
Indian Summer Cooperative Inc .... C 231 845-6248
  Ludington *(G-10541)*
Materne North America Corp .... E 231 346-6600
  Grawn *(G-7452)*

FOOD PRDTS, CANNED: Barbecue Sauce
Cherry Republic Inc .... D 231 334-3150
  Glen Arbor *(G-6209)*

FOOD PRDTS, CANNED: Beans, Baked With Meat
Randall Foods Inc .... F 517 767-3247
  Tekonsha *(G-16524)*

FOOD PRDTS, CANNED: Chili
National Coney Island Chili Co .... F 313 365-5611
  Roseville *(G-14451)*

FOOD PRDTS, CANNED: Ethnic
Emesa Foods Company .... G 248 982-3908
  Farmington Hills *(G-5230)*
Global Restaurant Group Inc .... G 313 271-2777
  Dearborn *(G-3847)*

PRODUCT SECTION

FOOD PRDTS, CANNED: Fruit Juices, Concentrated

Integrity Beverage Inc .... E 248 348-1010
  Wixom *(G-18687)*

FOOD PRDTS, CANNED: Fruit Juices, Fresh

Knouse Foods Cooperative Inc .... C 269 657-5524
  Paw Paw *(G-12950)*
Lakewood Organics LLC .... E 231 861-6333
  Shelby *(G-15156)*
Mitten Fruit Company LLC .... G 269 585-8541
  Kalamazoo *(G-9273)*
Mizkan America Inc .... D 616 794-0226
  Belding *(G-1457)*
Peterson Farms Inc .... B 231 861-6333
  Shelby *(G-15159)*

FOOD PRDTS, CANNED: Fruits

Burnette Foods Inc .... C 269 621-3181
  Hartford *(G-7762)*
Burnette Foods Inc .... C 231 536-2284
  East Jordan *(G-4860)*
Cherry Central Cooperative Inc .... E 231 861-2141
  Shelby *(G-15149)*
Cherry Growers Inc .... C 231 276-9241
  Birmingham *(G-1720)*
Cherry Growers Inc .... G 231 947-2502
  Traverse City *(G-16650)*
Mpc Company Inc .... G 269 927-3371
  Benton Harbor *(G-1576)*
Oceana Foods Inc .... C 231 861-2141
  Shelby *(G-15157)*
Packers Canning Co Inc .... D 269 624-4681
  Lawton *(G-9989)*

FOOD PRDTS, CANNED: Fruits

Almar Orchards LLC .... F 810 659-6568
  Flushing *(G-5801)*
Atwater Foods LLC .... G 231 264-5598
  Williamsburg *(G-18551)*
Birds Eye Foods Inc .... D 269 561-8211
  Fennville *(G-5434)*
Blakes Orchard Inc .... G 586 784-5343
  Armada *(G-732)*
Brownwood Acres Foods Inc .... F 231 599-3101
  Eastport *(G-4949)*
Burnette Foods Inc .... C 231 861-2151
  New ERA *(G-12026)*
Campbell Soup Company .... G 313 295-6884
  Taylor *(G-16390)*
Campbell Soup Company .... G 248 336-8486
  Ferndale *(G-5532)*
Cherry Central Cooperative Inc .... E 231 946-1860
  Traverse City *(G-16648)*
Coca-Cola Refreshments USA Inc .... G 616 913-0400
  Grand Rapids *(G-6578)*
Country Mill Farms LLC .... G 517 543-1019
  Charlotte *(G-2745)*
Great Lakes Packing Co .... E 231 264-5561
  Kewadin *(G-9487)*
Hirzel Canning Company .... G 419 360-3220
  Troy *(G-17144)*
Hopeful Harvest Foods Inc .... G 248 967-1500
  Oak Park *(G-12617)*
Kraft Heinz Foods Company .... G 616 396-6557
  Holland *(G-8115)*
McClures Pickles LLC .... G 248 837-9323
  Detroit *(G-4422)*
Northville Cider Mill Inc .... F 248 349-3181
  Northville *(G-12245)*
Randall Foods Inc .... F 517 767-3247
  Tekonsha *(G-16524)*
Twin City Foods Inc .... D 616 374-4002
  Lake Odessa *(G-9579)*
Uncle Johns Cider Mill Inc .... E 989 224-3686
  Saint Johns *(G-14919)*
Wasem Fruit Farm .... G 734 482-2342
  Milan *(G-11451)*

FOOD PRDTS, CANNED: Fruits & Fruit Prdts

Food For Thought Inc .... E 231 326-5444
  Traverse City *(G-16684)*

FOOD PRDTS, CANNED: Jams, Including Imitation

Cherry Hut Products LLC .... G 231 882-4431
  Benzonia *(G-1613)*
Fairview Farms .... G 269 449-0500
  Berrien Springs *(G-1640)*

FOOD PRDTS, CANNED: Jams, Jellies & Preserves

Pantless Jams LLC .... G 419 283-8470
  Temperance *(G-16544)*
Society of Saint John Inc .... G 906 289-4484
  Eagle Harbor *(G-4853)*

FOOD PRDTS, CANNED: Maraschino Cherries

Gray & Company .... C 231 873-5628
  Hart *(G-7753)*

FOOD PRDTS, CANNED: Soups

Advancing Bus Solutions LLC .... G 734 905-7455
  Ypsilanti *(G-18923)*
Onion Crock of Michigan Inc .... G 616 458-2922
  Grand Rapids *(G-7060)*

FOOD PRDTS, CANNED: Tomatoes

M Forche Farms Inc .... G 517 447-3488
  Blissfield *(G-1768)*

FOOD PRDTS, CONFECTIONERY, WHOLESALE: Candy

Opus Products LLC .... G 586 202-1870
  Oakland Twp *(G-12653)*
W2 Inc .... G 517 764-3141
  Jackson *(G-9032)*

FOOD PRDTS, CONFECTIONERY, WHOLESALE: Nuts, Salted/Roasted

Kar Nut Products Company LLC .... C 248 588-1903
  Madison Heights *(G-10758)*
Nutco Inc .... E 800 872-4006
  Detroit *(G-4494)*

FOOD PRDTS, CONFECTIONERY, WHOLESALE: Snack Foods

Frito-Lay North America Inc .... G 989 754-0435
  Saginaw *(G-14647)*

FOOD PRDTS, CONFECTIONERY, WHOLESALE: Syrups, Fountain

Doc Popcorn .... G 734 250-8133
  Taylor *(G-16402)*
Rmg Maple Products Inc .... G 906 478-3038
  Rudyard *(G-14596)*

FOOD PRDTS, DAIRY, WHOLESALE: Frozen Dairy Desserts

Blossom Berry .... G 517 775-6978
  Novi *(G-12374)*

FOOD PRDTS, DAIRY, WHOLESALE: Milk & Cream, Fluid

Independent Dairy Inc .... E 734 241-6016
  Monroe *(G-11550)*
Michigan Milk Producers Assn .... E 248 474-6672
  Novi *(G-12481)*

FOOD PRDTS, FISH & SEAFOOD, WHOLESALE: Seafood

Northern Lkes Safood Meats LLC .... E 313 368-4234
  Detroit *(G-4489)*

FOOD PRDTS, FISH & SEAFOOD: Fish, Salted

Ruleau Brothers Inc .... E 906 753-4767
  Stephenson *(G-15911)*

FOOD PRDTS, FISH & SEAFOOD: Fish, Smoked

Big O Smokehouse Inc .... E 616 891-5555
  Caledonia *(G-2368)*
Gustafson Smoked Fish .... G 906 292-5424
  Moran *(G-11609)*

FOOD PRDTS, FISH & SEAFOOD: Herring, Cured, NEC

Sea Fare Foods Inc .... F 313 568-0223
  Detroit *(G-4586)*

FOOD PRDTS, FROZEN: Dinners, Packaged

Mid America Commodities LLC .... G 810 936-0108
  Linden *(G-10068)*

FOOD PRDTS, FROZEN: Ethnic Foods, NEC

Cole King Foods .... G 313 872-0220
  Detroit *(G-4097)*
Pasty Oven Inc .... G 906 774-2328
  Quinnesec *(G-13676)*
Turris Italian Foods Inc .... D 586 773-6010
  Roseville *(G-14488)*

FOOD PRDTS, FROZEN: Fruits

Cherry Growers Inc .... C 231 276-9241
  Birmingham *(G-1720)*
Cherry Growers Inc .... G 231 947-2502
  Traverse City *(G-16650)*
Dole Packaged Foods LLC .... B 269 423-6375
  Decatur *(G-3947)*
Graceland Fruit Inc .... C 231 352-7181
  Frankfort *(G-5877)*
Hart Freeze Pack LlC .... F 231 873-2175
  Hart *(G-7754)*
Peterson Farms Inc .... B 231 861-6333
  Shelby *(G-15159)*
Sill Farms & Market Inc .... E 269 674-3755
  Lawrence *(G-9985)*
Smeltzer Companies Inc .... C 231 882-4421
  Frankfort *(G-5881)*

FOOD PRDTS, FROZEN: Fruits & Vegetables

Coloma Frozen Foods Inc .... D 269 849-0500
  Coloma *(G-3475)*
Svf Bloomingdale Inc .... F 269 521-3026
  Bloomingdale *(G-1880)*

FOOD PRDTS, FROZEN: Fruits, Juices & Vegetables

All American Whse & Cold Stor .... F 313 865-3870
  Detroit *(G-3998)*
Farber Concessions Inc .... E 313 387-1600
  Redford *(G-13733)*
Jar-ME LLC .... G 313 319-7765
  Detroit *(G-4334)*
MI Frozen Food LLC .... G 231 357-4334
  Manistee *(G-10909)*
Old Orchard Brands LLC .... D 616 887-1745
  Sparta *(G-15774)*
Smoothies .... G 231 498-2374
  Kewadin *(G-9489)*
Standale Smoothie LLC .... G 810 691-9625
  Fenton *(G-5504)*
Welch Foods Inc A Cooperative .... D 269 624-4141
  Lawton *(G-9990)*

FOOD PRDTS, FROZEN: NEC

Achatzs Hand Made Pie Co .... E 586 749-2882
  Chesterfield *(G-2834)*
Campbell Soup Company .... G 313 295-6884
  Taylor *(G-16390)*
Campbell Soup Company .... G 248 336-8486
  Ferndale *(G-5532)*
Coles Quality Foods Inc .... D 231 722-1651
  Muskegon *(G-11793)*
DForte Inc .... F 269 657-6996
  Paw Paw *(G-12946)*
Kring Pizza Inc .... G 586 792-0049
  Harrison Township *(G-7704)*
McDonalds .... F 248 851-7310
  Oxford *(G-12900)*
Pierino Frozen Foods Inc .... E 313 928-0950
  Lincoln Park *(G-10053)*

Employee Codes: A=Over 500 employees, B=251-500
C=101-250, D=51-100, E=20-50, F=10-19, G=3-9

FOOD PRDTS, FROZEN: NEC

Pietrzyk Foods LLC .... G 313 614-9393
  Detroit *(G-4523)*
Pinnacle Foods Group LLC .... B 810 724-6144
  Imlay City *(G-8643)*
Rays Ice Cream Co Inc .... F 248 549-5256
  Royal Oak *(G-14573)*
Request Foods Inc .... B 616 786-0900
  Holland *(G-8180)*
Twin City Foods Inc .... D 616 374-4002
  Lake Odessa *(G-9579)*

FOOD PRDTS, FROZEN: Pizza

Beagios Franchises Inc .... G 989 635-7173
  Marlette *(G-10979)*
Dina Mia Kitchens Inc .... E 906 265-9082
  Iron River *(G-8740)*
Frandale Sub Shop .... F 616 446-6311
  Allendale *(G-218)*
Linda Mia Inc .... A 906 265-9082
  Iron River *(G-8747)*

FOOD PRDTS, FROZEN: Snack Items

Farber Concessions Inc .... E 313 387-1600
  Redford *(G-13733)*

FOOD PRDTS, FROZEN: Vegetables, Exc Potato Prdts

Twin City Foods Inc .... D 616 374-4002
  Lake Odessa *(G-9579)*

FOOD PRDTS, FROZEN: Waffles

Kellogg Company .... A 269 961-2000
  Battle Creek *(G-1255)*

FOOD PRDTS, FRUITS & VEGETABLES, FRESH, WHOLESALE

Burnette Foods Inc .... F 231 223-4282
  Traverse City *(G-16633)*

FOOD PRDTS, FRUITS & VEGETABLES, FRESH, WHOLESALE: Fruits

Blakes Orchard Inc .... G 586 784-5343
  Armada *(G-732)*
Mpc Company Inc .... G 269 927-3371
  Benton Harbor *(G-1576)*

FOOD PRDTS, FRUITS & VEGETABLES, FRESH, WHOLESALE: Vegetable

Home Style Foods Inc .... F 313 874-3250
  Detroit *(G-4303)*
Michigan Celery Promotion Coop .... F 616 669-1250
  Hudsonville *(G-8595)*

FOOD PRDTS, MEAT & MEAT PRDTS, WHOLESALE: Fresh

Boars Head Provisions Co Inc .... C 941 955-0994
  Holland *(G-7978)*
Cornbelt Beef Corporation .... G 313 237-0087
  Oak Park *(G-12598)*
Erlas Inc .... D 989 872-2191
  Cass City *(G-2614)*
T Wigley Inc .... F 313 831-6881
  Detroit *(G-4624)*
Wolverine Packing Co .... D 313 259-7500
  Detroit *(G-4688)*

FOOD PRDTS, WHOLESALE: Beans, Field

Ittner Bean & Grain Inc .... F 989 662-4461
  Auburn *(G-766)*

FOOD PRDTS, WHOLESALE: Beverage Concentrates

Penguin Juice Co .... F 734 467-6991
  Westland *(G-18404)*

FOOD PRDTS, WHOLESALE: Beverages, Exc Coffee & Tea

C F Burger Creamery Co .... D 313 584-4040
  Detroit *(G-4084)*
Global Restaurant Group Inc .... G 313 271-2777
  Dearborn *(G-3847)*
Viva Beverages LLC .... G 248 746-7044
  Southfield *(G-15739)*

FOOD PRDTS, WHOLESALE: Coffee, Green Or Roasted

Becharas Bros Coffee Co .... E 313 869-4700
  Detroit *(G-4047)*
Coffee Beanery Ltd .... E 810 733-1020
  Flushing *(G-5805)*
Good Sense Coffee LLC .... E 810 355-2349
  Brighton *(G-2003)*
Hermans Boy .... G 616 866-2900
  Rockford *(G-14169)*

FOOD PRDTS, WHOLESALE: Diet

Hacienda Mexican Foods LLC .... D 313 895-8823
  Detroit *(G-4289)*

FOOD PRDTS, WHOLESALE: Dog Food

Brewts LLC .... G 616 291-1117
  Byron Center *(G-2262)*

FOOD PRDTS, WHOLESALE: Grains

Andersons Inc .... G 989 642-5291
  Hemlock *(G-7849)*
Armada Grain Co .... E 586 784-5911
  Armada *(G-729)*
Citizens LLC .... G 517 541-1449
  Charlotte *(G-2743)*
Corunna Mills Feed LLC .... G 989 743-3110
  Corunna *(G-3707)*
Purity Foods Inc .... E 517 448-7440
  Hudson *(G-8560)*
Schafers Elevator Co .... G 517 263-7202
  Adrian *(G-93)*
Star of West Milling Company .... D 989 652-9971
  Frankenmuth *(G-5873)*
Zeeland Farm Services Inc .... C 616 772-9042
  Zeeland *(G-19096)*

FOOD PRDTS, WHOLESALE: Juices

Go Beyond Healthy LLC .... G 407 255-0314
  Grand Rapids *(G-6746)*
Rice Juice Company Inc .... G 906 774-1733
  Iron Mountain *(G-8730)*

FOOD PRDTS, WHOLESALE: Natural & Organic

Sweed Dreams LLC .... G 313 704-6694
  Livonia *(G-10425)*

FOOD PRDTS, WHOLESALE: Oats

Haulin Oats Inc .... G 248 225-1672
  Roseville *(G-14420)*

FOOD PRDTS, WHOLESALE: Pasta & Rice

Purity Foods Inc .... E 517 448-7440
  Hudson *(G-8560)*

FOOD PRDTS, WHOLESALE: Pizza Splys

Dominos Pizza LLC .... C 734 930-3030
  Ann Arbor *(G-456)*

FOOD PRDTS, WHOLESALE: Specialty

Coles Quality Foods Inc .... D 231 722-1651
  Muskegon *(G-11793)*
Emesa Foods Company LLC .... G 248 982-3908
  Taylor *(G-16413)*
Reilchz Inc .... G 231 421-9600
  Traverse City *(G-16819)*

FOOD PRDTS, WHOLESALE: Spices & Seasonings

Asmus Seasoning Inc .... F 586 939-4505
  Sterling Heights *(G-15934)*
Nuts & Coffee Gallery .... G 313 581-3212
  Dearborn *(G-3878)*

FOOD PRDTS, WHOLESALE: Tea

Ellis Infinity LLC .... G 313 570-0840
  Detroit *(G-4203)*

FOOD PRDTS, WHOLESALE: Wheat

Cargill Incorporated .... F 608 868-5150
  Owosso *(G-12825)*

FOOD PRDTS, WHOLESALE: Wine Makers' Eqpt & Splys

R C M S Inc .... G 269 422-1617
  Baroda *(G-1169)*

FOOD PRDTS: Animal & marine fats & oils

Asao LLC .... F 734 522-6333
  Livonia *(G-10125)*
Darling Ingredients Inc .... G 269 751-0560
  Hamilton *(G-7597)*
Evergreen Grease Service Inc .... G 517 264-9913
  Adrian *(G-65)*

FOOD PRDTS: Box Lunches, For Sale Off Premises

Stephen Haas .... G 906 475-4826
  Negaunee *(G-11975)*

FOOD PRDTS: Bread Crumbs, Exc Made In Bakeries

Pepperidge Farm Incorporated .... G 734 953-6729
  Livonia *(G-10362)*

FOOD PRDTS: Breakfast Bars

Jlm Manufacturing .... G 586 447-3500
  Warren *(G-17886)*
Junkless Foods Inc .... F 616 560-7895
  Portage *(G-13570)*
Pop Daddy Popcorn LLC .... F 734 550-9900
  Whitmore Lake *(G-18543)*

FOOD PRDTS: Butter, Renovated & Processed

Butterball Farms Inc .... C 616 243-0105
  Grand Rapids *(G-6541)*

FOOD PRDTS: Cake Flour

Cake Flour .... G 231 571-3054
  Norton Shores *(G-12283)*

FOOD PRDTS: Cereals

Austin Quality Sales Company .... E 269 961-2000
  Battle Creek *(G-1187)*
Bay Valley Foods LLC .... E 269 792-2277
  Wayland *(G-18189)*
General Mills Inc .... G 763 764-7600
  Kalamazoo *(G-9193)*
K-Two Inc .... D 269 961-2000
  Battle Creek *(G-1249)*
Kellogg (thailand) Limited .... E 269 969-8937
  Battle Creek *(G-1251)*
Kellogg Asia Marketing Inc .... G 269 961-2000
  Battle Creek *(G-1252)*
Kellogg Chile Inc .... D 269 961-2000
  Battle Creek *(G-1253)*
Kellogg Company .... B 269 961-2000
  Battle Creek *(G-1254)*
Kellogg Company .... G 810 653-5625
  Davison *(G-3788)*
Kellogg Company .... G 269 961-9387
  Mulliken *(G-11749)*
Kellogg Company .... G 269 964-8525
  Battle Creek *(G-1256)*
Kellogg Company .... G 269 969-8107
  Battle Creek *(G-1257)*
Kellogg Company .... E 616 247-4841
  Grand Rapids *(G-6881)*
Kellogg Company .... G 269 961-2000
  Battle Creek *(G-1258)*
Kellogg USA Inc .... C 269 961-2000
  Battle Creek *(G-1261)*
Kellogg USA Inc .... A 269 961-2000
  Battle Creek *(G-1262)*
Post Foods LLC .... B 269 966-1000
  Battle Creek *(G-1281)*
Roskam Baking Company .... C 616 574-5757
  Grand Rapids *(G-7166)*
Rothbury Farms Inc .... E 616 574-5757
  Grand Rapids *(G-7171)*

PRODUCT SECTION

Snackwerks of Michigan LLC .... E 269 719-8282
 Battle Creek (G-1296)

FOOD PRDTS: Chewing Gum Base

Lotte USA Incorporated .... F 269 963-6664
 Battle Creek (G-1269)

FOOD PRDTS: Chocolate Bars, Solid

Kilwins Qulty Confections Inc .... C 231 347-3800
 Petoskey (G-13001)
Verse Chocolate LLC .... G 816 325-0208
 Holland (G-8238)

FOOD PRDTS: Coconut Oil

Go Beyond Healthy LLC .... G 407 255-0314
 Grand Rapids (G-6746)

FOOD PRDTS: Coffee

Ad Astra Roasters LLC .... G 517 914-2487
 Hillsdale (G-7922)
Becharas Bros Coffee Co .... E 313 869-4700
 Detroit (G-4047)
Coffee Beanery Ltd .... E 810 733-1020
 Flushing (G-5805)
Infusco Coffee Roasters LLC .... G 269 213-5282
 Sawyer (G-15109)
Koeze Company .... E 616 724-2601
 Grand Rapids (G-6902)
Shift Roasting Company LLC .... G 734 915-3666
 Saline (G-15040)
Stickmann Baeckerei .... G 269 205-2444
 Middleville (G-11314)

FOOD PRDTS: Coffee Roasting, Exc Wholesale Grocers

Cozy Cup Coffee Company Llc .... G 989 984-7619
 Oscoda (G-12755)
Good Sense Coffee LLC .... E 810 355-2349
 Brighton (G-2003)
Hermans Boy .... G 616 866-2900
 Rockford (G-14169)
Inter State Foods Inc .... F 517 372-5500
 Lansing (G-9706)
M-36 Coffee Roasters LLC .... G 734 449-8910
 Whitmore Lake (G-18539)
Rowster Coffee Inc .... E 616 780-7777
 Grand Rapids (G-7172)
Treat of Day LLC .... G 616 706-1717
 Grand Rapids (G-7271)
Two Cups Coffee Co LLC .... F 616 953-0534
 Holland (G-8232)

FOOD PRDTS: Corn Oil, Refined

Cargill Incorporated .... F 608 868-5150
 Owosso (G-12825)

FOOD PRDTS: Desserts, Ready-To-Mix

Michigan Dessert Corporation .... E 248 544-4574
 Oak Park (G-12628)

FOOD PRDTS: Dips, Exc Cheese & Sour Cream Based

Global Warming Salsa .... G 248 882-3266
 White Lake (G-18457)
Grand Rapids Salsa .... G 616 780-1801
 Grand Rapids (G-6769)
Joplins Salsa .... G 419 787-8195
 Ypsilanti (G-18959)
Radical Plants LLC .... G 586 243-8128
 Saint Clair Shores (G-14880)

FOOD PRDTS: Doughs & Batters From Purchased Flour

Dawn Food Products Inc .... G 800 654-4843
 Grand Rapids (G-6634)

FOOD PRDTS: Doughs, Frozen Or Refrig From Purchased Flour

Big Dipper Dough Co Inc .... G 231 883-6035
 Traverse City (G-16620)

FOOD PRDTS: Dressings, Salad, Raw & Cooked Exc Dry Mixes

DForte Inc .... F 269 657-6996
 Paw Paw (G-12946)
Litehouse Inc .... C 616 897-5911
 Lowell (G-10509)

FOOD PRDTS: Dried & Dehydrated Fruits, Vegetables & Soup Mix

American Spoon Foods Inc .... E 231 347-9030
 Petoskey (G-12988)
Angel Kisses Inc .... G 248 219-8577
 Ferndale (G-5526)
Apple Quest Inc .... G 616 299-4834
 Conklin (G-3659)
Cherry Central Cooperative Inc .... E 231 861-2141
 Shelby (G-15149)
J Rettenmaier USA LP .... G 269 323-1588
 Portage (G-13569)
Smeltzer Companies Inc .... C 231 882-4421
 Frankfort (G-5881)

FOOD PRDTS: Edible Oil Prdts, Exc Corn Oil

Cozart Producers .... G 810 736-1046
 Flint (G-5675)

FOOD PRDTS: Eggs, Processed

Farmers Egg Cooperative .... G 517 649-8957
 Charlotte (G-2754)
Zoet Poultry .... E 269 751-2776
 Holland (G-8259)

FOOD PRDTS: Emulsifiers

Russo Bros Inc .... F 906 485-5250
 Ishpeming (G-8781)

FOOD PRDTS: Flour

Knappen Milling Company .... E 269 731-4141
 Augusta (G-1092)
Star of West Milling Company .... D 989 652-9971
 Frankenmuth (G-5873)

FOOD PRDTS: Flour & Other Grain Mill Products

Archer-Daniels-Midland Company .... G 269 968-2900
 Battle Creek (G-1185)
Archer-Daniels-Midland Company .... G 517 627-4017
 Grand Ledge (G-6385)
Archer-Daniels-Midland Company .... G 517 647-4155
 Portland (G-13637)
Citizens LLC .... G 517 541-1449
 Charlotte (G-2743)
Dorothy Dawson Food Products .... E 517 788-9830
 Jackson (G-8870)
Freeport Milling .... G 616 765-8421
 Freeport (G-6033)
Ittner Bean & Grain Inc .... F 989 662-4461
 Auburn (G-766)
Kellogg Company .... A 269 961-2000
 Battle Creek (G-1255)
Kellogg Company .... G 269 961-6693
 Wyoming (G-18889)
Kelloggs Corporation .... C 616 219-6100
 Grand Rapids (G-6882)
Purity Foods Inc .... E 517 448-7440
 Hudson (G-8560)

FOOD PRDTS: Flour Mixes & Doughs

Advanced Food Technologies Inc .... D 616 574-4144
 Grand Rapids (G-6434)
Bektrom Foods Inc .... G 734 241-3796
 Monroe (G-11531)
Dawn Foods International Corp .... C 517 789-4400
 Jackson (G-8865)
Dominos Pizza LLC .... C 734 930-3030
 Ann Arbor (G-456)
Dorothy Dawson Food Products .... E 517 788-9830
 Jackson (G-8870)
Ezbake Technologies LLC .... G 817 430-1621
 Fenton (G-5474)
Fry Krisp Food Products Inc .... F 517 784-8531
 Jackson (G-8887)

FOOD PRDTS: Freeze-Dried Coffee

Prospectors LLC .... G 616 634-8260
 Grand Rapids (G-7122)

FOOD PRDTS: Frosting Mixes, Dry, For Cakes, Cookies, Etc.

Among Friends LLC .... F 734 997-9720
 Ann Arbor (G-365)

FOOD PRDTS: Fruit Juices

Juvenex Inc .... F 248 436-2866
 Southfield (G-15615)
Super Fluids LLC .... G 313 409-6522
 Detroit (G-4615)

FOOD PRDTS: Fruits & Vegetables, Pickled

Bessinger Pickle Co Inc .... G 989 876-8008
 Au Gres (G-756)
Hausbeck Pickle Company .... D 989 754-4721
 Saginaw (G-14661)
Pickled Door LLC .... G 616 916-6836
 Caledonia (G-2392)
Tall Pauls Pickles LLC .... G 734 476-2424
 Ann Arbor (G-671)

FOOD PRDTS: Fruits, Dried Or Dehydrated, Exc Freeze-Dried

Graceland Fruit Inc .... C 231 352-7181
 Frankfort (G-5877)
Shoreline Fruit LLC .... C 231 941-4336
 Williamsburg (G-18564)

FOOD PRDTS: Granola & Energy Bars, Nonchocolate

Detroit Fd Entrpnrship Acdemy .... F 248 894-8941
 Detroit (G-4147)
Simply Suzanne LLC .... G 917 364-4549
 Detroit (G-4594)

FOOD PRDTS: Honey

Natural American Foods LLC .... E 517 467-2065
 Onsted (G-12707)
Priorat Importers Corporation .... G 248 217-4608
 Royal Oak (G-14570)
Red Headed Honey LLC .... G 707 616-4278
 Camden (G-2424)
Sleeping Bear Apiaries Ltd .... F 231 882-4456
 Beulah (G-1657)

FOOD PRDTS: Horseradish, Exc Sauce

Brede Inc .... G 313 273-1079
 Bloomfield Hills (G-1806)

FOOD PRDTS: Ice, Blocks

Arctic Glacier Texas Inc .... G 517 999-3500
 Lansing (G-9806)
Arctic Glacier USA Inc .... E 204 772-2473
 Port Huron (G-13447)
Knowlton Enterprises Inc .... D 810 987-7100
 Port Huron (G-13495)

FOOD PRDTS: Ice, Cubes

Arctic Glacier USA Inc .... F 215 283-0326
 Port Huron (G-13443)
Home City Ice Company .... E 734 955-9094
 Romulus (G-14283)
Michigan Pure Ice Co LLC .... G 231 420-9896
 Indian River (G-8655)
Northern Pure Ice Co L L C .... F 989 344-2088
 Port Huron (G-13510)
U S Ice Corp .... E 313 862-3344
 Detroit (G-4651)

FOOD PRDTS: Instant Coffee

Fireside Coffee Company Inc .... F 810 635-9196
 Swartz Creek (G-16353)

FOOD PRDTS: Macaroni, Noodles, Spaghetti, Pasta, Etc

Dina Mia Kitchens Inc .... E 906 265-9082
 Iron River (G-8740)

FOOD PRDTS: Macaroni, Noodles, Spaghetti, Pasta, Etc

Pierino Frozen Foods Inc .... E 313 928-0950
  Lincoln Park *(G-10053)*
Turris Italian Foods Inc .... D 586 773-6010
  Roseville *(G-14488)*

FOOD PRDTS: Malt

Apple Blossom Winery LLC .... G 269 668-3724
  Kalamazoo *(G-9114)*
Brydges Group LLC .... G 734 649-6635
  Battle Creek *(G-1200)*

FOOD PRDTS: Mixes, Doughnut From Purchased Flour

Dawn Food Products Inc .... G 517 789-4400
  Jackson *(G-8862)*
Dawn Food Products Inc .... C 517 789-4400
  Jackson *(G-8863)*
Dawn Foods Inc .... C 517 789-4400
  Jackson *(G-8864)*

FOOD PRDTS: Mixes, Flour

Advanced Food Technologies Inc .... D 616 574-4144
  Grand Rapids *(G-6434)*
General Mills Inc .... E 231 832-3285
  Reed City *(G-13790)*
General Mills Inc .... F 269 337-0288
  Kalamazoo *(G-9194)*

FOOD PRDTS: Mixes, Salad Dressings, Dry

Six Lugs LLC .... F 231 275-0600
  Interlochen *(G-8685)*

FOOD PRDTS: Nuts & Seeds

All Natural Bites LLC .... F 248 470-6252
  Lathrup Village *(G-9974)*
Koeze Company .... E 616 724-2601
  Grand Rapids *(G-6902)*
Nutco Inc .... E 800 872-4006
  Detroit *(G-4494)*
St Laurent Brothers Inc .... E 989 893-7522
  Bay City *(G-1405)*
Variety Foods Inc .... D 586 268-4900
  Warren *(G-18051)*

FOOD PRDTS: Oils & Fats, Marine

Northern Lkes Safood Meats LLC .... E 313 368-4234
  Detroit *(G-4489)*

FOOD PRDTS: Olive Oil

Old World Olive Press .... G 734 667-2755
  Plymouth *(G-13255)*
Priorat Importers Corporation .... G 248 217-4608
  Royal Oak *(G-14570)*
Stamatopolos & Sons .... G 734 369-2995
  Ann Arbor *(G-664)*

FOOD PRDTS: Oriental Noodles

New Moon Noodle Incorporated .... F 269 962-8820
  Battle Creek *(G-1278)*

FOOD PRDTS: Pasta, Rice/Potatoes, Uncooked, Pkgd

Pierino Frozen Foods Inc .... E 313 928-0950
  Lincoln Park *(G-10053)*

FOOD PRDTS: Pasta, Uncooked, Packaged With Other Ingredients

Al Dente Inc .... E 734 449-8522
  Whitmore Lake *(G-18518)*

FOOD PRDTS: Peanut Butter

St Laurent Brothers Inc .... E 989 893-7522
  Bay City *(G-1405)*

FOOD PRDTS: Pickles, Vinegar

Custom Foods Inc .... F 989 249-8061
  Saginaw *(G-14634)*
Harrison Packing Co Inc .... F 269 381-3837
  Kalamazoo *(G-9209)*
McClures Pickles LLC .... G 248 837-9323
  Royal Oak *(G-14562)*

FOOD PRDTS: Pizza Doughs From Purchased Flour

MA MA La Rosa Foods Inc .... E 734 946-7878
  Taylor *(G-16437)*
Pizza Crust Company Inc .... F 517 482-3368
  Lansing *(G-9730)*

FOOD PRDTS: Pizza, Refrigerated

Artisan Bread Co LLC .... E 586 756-0100
  Warren *(G-17714)*
Champion Foods LLC .... B 734 753-3663
  New Boston *(G-12006)*
Shady Nook Farms .... G 989 236-7240
  Middleton *(G-11300)*

FOOD PRDTS: Popcorn, Popped

Whm Investments Inc .... G 269 432-3251
  Colon *(G-3492)*

FOOD PRDTS: Popcorn, Unpopped

Poppin Top Hat LLC .... G 313 427-0400
  Detroit *(G-4530)*

FOOD PRDTS: Pork Rinds

Grandpapas Inc .... E 313 891-6830
  Detroit *(G-4274)*

FOOD PRDTS: Potato & Corn Chips & Similar Prdts

Cambridge Sharpe Inc .... F 248 613-5562
  South Lyon *(G-15429)*
Campbell Soup Company .... G 313 295-6884
  Taylor *(G-16390)*
Campbell Soup Company .... G 248 336-8486
  Ferndale *(G-5532)*
Cheeze Kurls LLC .... D 616 784-6095
  Grand Rapids *(G-6567)*
Hippies Chippies Inc .... G 616 259-2133
  Grand Rapids *(G-6818)*
Manos Authentic LLC .... G 800 242-2796
  Clinton Township *(G-3293)*
Mexamerica Foods LLC .... F 814 781-1447
  Grand Rapids *(G-6984)*
We Pop Corn LLC .... F 313 387-1600
  Redford *(G-13786)*

FOOD PRDTS: Potato Chips & Other Potato-Based Snacks

Better Made Snack Foods Inc .... C 313 925-4774
  Detroit *(G-4054)*
Detroit Frends Potato Chip LLC .... G 313 924-0085
  Detroit *(G-4149)*
Downeys Potato Chips-Waterford .... G 248 673-3636
  Waterford *(G-18119)*
Uncle Rays LLC .... C 313 834-0800
  Detroit *(G-4652)*
Variety Foods Inc .... D 586 268-4900
  Warren *(G-18051)*

FOOD PRDTS: Potato Sticks

Doc Popcorn .... G 734 250-8133
  Taylor *(G-16402)*

FOOD PRDTS: Preparations

18th Street Deli Inc .... G 313 921-7710
  Hamtramck *(G-7610)*
A & B Home Essentials LLC .... G 734 334-3041
  Van Buren Twp *(G-17506)*
Ace Vending Service Inc .... F 616 243-7983
  Grand Rapids *(G-6422)*
AFP Consulting .... G 616 534-9858
  Wyoming *(G-18850)*
Albies Food Products LLC .... F 989 732-2800
  Gaylord *(G-6117)*
American Classics Corp .... G 231 843-0523
  Ludington *(G-10525)*
American Soy Products Inc .... D 734 429-2310
  Saline *(G-15001)*
Amway International Inc .... E 616 787-1000
  Ada *(G-8)*
Arbre Farms Corporation .... B 231 873-3337
  Walkerville *(G-17658)*
B & B Pretzels Inc .... F 248 358-1655
  Southfield *(G-15500)*

Belchers Maple Syrup LLC .... G 231 942-1399
  Tustin *(G-17465)*
Better Made Snack Foods Inc .... C 313 925-4774
  Detroit *(G-4054)*
Big Boy Restaurants Intl LLC .... C 586 759-6000
  Southfield *(G-15507)*
Bovvy Mkt LLC .... G 313 706-7922
  Detroit *(G-4065)*
Bowtie Catering LLC .... G 313 989-3952
  Eastpointe *(G-4928)*
Brians Foods Inc .... G 248 739-5280
  Southfield *(G-15511)*
Burnette Foods Inc .... F 231 223-4282
  Traverse City *(G-16633)*
Canadian Harvest LP .... G 952 835-6429
  Schoolcraft *(G-15113)*
Charidimos Inc .... G 248 827-7733
  Southfield *(G-15519)*
Cheesecake and Ecetera LLC .... G 734 335-8757
  Livonia *(G-10156)*
Cheeze Kurls LLC .... D 616 784-6095
  Grand Rapids *(G-6567)*
Cherry Blossom .... G 231 342-3635
  Williamsburg *(G-18552)*
Coffee Beanery Ltd .... E 810 733-1020
  Flushing *(G-5805)*
Conagra Brands Inc .... G 810 724-2715
  Imlay City *(G-8629)*
Conagra Brands Inc .... G 402 240-8210
  Quincy *(G-13665)*
Conagra Brands Inc .... E 616 392-2359
  Holland *(G-8003)*
Custom Foods Inc .... F 989 249-8061
  Saginaw *(G-14634)*
Danjos Foods Inc .... G 517 543-2260
  Charlotte *(G-2749)*
Detroit Peanuts LLC .... G 313 826-4327
  Detroit *(G-4158)*
DForte Inc .... F 269 657-6996
  Paw Paw *(G-12946)*
Diehl Inc .... G 517 265-5045
  Adrian *(G-62)*
Do & Co Detroit Inc .... D 424 288-9025
  Detroit *(G-4184)*
Dorothy Dawson Food Products .... E 517 788-9830
  Jackson *(G-8870)*
Dough & Spice Inc .... G 586 756-6100
  Warren *(G-17781)*
Downeys Potato Chips-Waterford .... G 248 673-3636
  Waterford *(G-18119)*
Eden Foods Inc .... D 517 456-7424
  Clinton *(G-3137)*
Eden Foods Inc .... E 313 921-2053
  Detroit *(G-4201)*
Fudge and Frosting .... G 517 763-2040
  Lansing *(G-9839)*
Giovannis Apptzing Fd Pdts Inc .... F 773 960-1945
  Richmond *(G-13838)*
Good Life Naturals LLC .... G 616 207-9230
  Alto *(G-333)*
Great Lkes Fstida Holdings Inc .... F 616 241-0400
  Grand Rapids *(G-6789)*
Green Dreamzz LLC .... G 313 377-2926
  Detroit *(G-4279)*
Hillshire Brands Company .... G 616 875-8131
  Zeeland *(G-19038)*
Honey Tree .... G 734 697-1000
  Van Buren Twp *(G-17529)*
Indian Summer Cooperative Inc .... C 231 873-7504
  Hart *(G-7755)*
J B Dough Co .... G 269 944-4160
  Benton Harbor *(G-1558)*
Jiffy Mix .... G 734 475-1361
  Chelsea *(G-2817)*
Jogue Inc .... G 248 349-1501
  Northville *(G-12233)*
Jogue Inc .... E 734 207-0100
  Plymouth *(G-13203)*
Kerry Foods .... F 616 871-9940
  Grand Rapids *(G-6893)*
Knouse Foods Cooperative Inc .... C 269 657-5524
  Paw Paw *(G-12950)*
Kraft Heinz Foods Company .... G 616 447-0481
  Grand Rapids *(G-6904)*
L & J Enterprises Inc .... G 586 995-4153
  Metamora *(G-11283)*
L & J Products K Huntington .... G 810 919-3550
  Brighton *(G-2015)*
Lesley Elizabeth Inc .... G 810 667-0706
  Lapeer *(G-9940)*

PRODUCT SECTION — FOOD PRODUCTS MACHINERY

Litehouse Inc .... C 616 897-5911
  Lowell *(G-10509)*
Marfood USA .... G 313 292-4100
  Taylor *(G-16438)*
Marshalls Trail Inc .... F 231 436-5082
  Mackinaw City *(G-10568)*
McClures Pickles LLC .... E 248 837-9323
  Detroit *(G-4422)*
Mead Johnson & Company LLC .... G 616 748-7100
  Zeeland *(G-19051)*
Michaelenes Inc .... G 248 625-0156
  Clarkston *(G-3050)*
Michigan Celery Promotion Coop ...... F 616 669-1250
  Hudsonville *(G-8595)*
Michigan Soy Products Company ...... G 248 544-7742
  Royal Oak *(G-14563)*
Mizkan America Inc .... D 616 794-3670
  Belding *(G-1458)*
N F P Inc .... G 989 631-0009
  Midland *(G-11397)*
On Base Food Group LLC .... G 248 672-7659
  Birmingham *(G-1742)*
Rays Ice Cream Co Inc .... F 248 549-5256
  Royal Oak *(G-14573)*
Safie Specialty Foods Co Inc .... E 586 598-8282
  Chesterfield *(G-2945)*
Savory Foods Inc .... D 616 241-2583
  Grand Rapids *(G-7181)*
Spartan Central Kitchen .... G 616 878-8940
  Grand Rapids *(G-7209)*
Ssa Consumer Brands Inc .... F 734 430-0565
  Ann Arbor *(G-663)*
Sunopta Ingredients Inc .... E 502 587-7999
  Schoolcraft *(G-15129)*
Twin City Foods Inc .... D 616 374-4002
  Lake Odessa *(G-9579)*
Union Commissary LLC .... F 248 795-2483
  Clarkston *(G-3075)*
Unique Food Management Inc .... E 248 738-9393
  Pontiac *(G-13421)*
Variety Foods Inc .... D 586 268-4900
  Warren *(G-18051)*
Villanuevo Soledad .... G 989 770-4309
  Burt *(G-2216)*
Wysong Medical Corporation .... F 989 631-0009
  Midland *(G-11424)*

FOOD PRDTS: Prepared Sauces, Exc Tomato Based

Great Lakes Food Center LLC .... G 248 397-8166
  Madison Heights *(G-10734)*

FOOD PRDTS: Raw cane sugar

Michigan Sugar Company .... C 989 883-3200
  Sebewaing *(G-15141)*
Michigan Sugar Company .... C 989 673-3126
  Caro *(G-2575)*

FOOD PRDTS: Relishes, Fruit & Vegetable

Flamm Pickle and Packaging Co ...... F 269 461-6916
  Eau Claire *(G-4977)*

FOOD PRDTS: Salads

Countryside Foods LLC .... B 586 447-3500
  Warren *(G-17765)*
Crossbrook LLC .... G 616 772-5921
  Zeeland *(G-19009)*
Salad Specialist LLC .... G 734 325-4032
  Canton *(G-2520)*
Subway Restaurant .... G 248 625-5739
  Clarkston *(G-3070)*

FOOD PRDTS: Sandwiches

Frandale Sub Shop .... F 616 446-6311
  Allendale *(G-218)*

FOOD PRDTS: Sauerkraut, Bulk

Cultured Love LLC .... G 703 362-5991
  Zeeland *(G-19010)*

FOOD PRDTS: Seasonings & Spices

Asmus Seasoning Inc .... F 586 939-4505
  Sterling Heights *(G-15934)*
Hashems of Dearborn Heights .... F 313 278-2000
  Dearborn Heights *(G-3928)*
Lesley Elizabeth Inc .... G 810 667-0706
  Lapeer *(G-9941)*
New Harper Seasoning Inc .... G 734 767-6290
  Detroit *(G-4482)*
Nuts & Coffee Gallery .... G 313 581-3212
  Dearborn *(G-3878)*

FOOD PRDTS: Shortening & Solid Edible Fats

Asao LLC .... F 734 522-6333
  Livonia *(G-10125)*

FOOD PRDTS: Soybean Oil, Refined, Exc Made In Mills

Michigan Biodiesel LLC .... G 269 427-0804
  Kalamazoo *(G-9269)*

FOOD PRDTS: Soybean Protein Concentrates & Isolates

Nubreed Nutrition Inc .... F 734 272-7395
  Troy *(G-17283)*

FOOD PRDTS: Spices, Including Ground

Country Home Creations Inc .... E 810 244-7348
  Flint *(G-5674)*
Kalamazoo Holdings Inc .... G 269 349-9711
  Kalamazoo *(G-9240)*
Kalsec Inc .... G 269 349-9711
  Kalamazoo *(G-9250)*
Kring Pizza Inc .... G 586 792-0049
  Harrison Township *(G-7704)*
McCormick & Company Inc .... G 586 558-8424
  Warren *(G-17921)*

FOOD PRDTS: Sugar

Brewts LLC .... G 616 291-1117
  Byron Center *(G-2262)*

FOOD PRDTS: Sugar, Beet

Michigan Sugar Company .... C 989 686-0161
  Bay City *(G-1378)*
Michigan Sugar Company .... C 989 883-3200
  Sebewaing *(G-15141)*
Michigan Sugar Company .... D 989 686-0161
  Bay City *(G-1379)*
Michigan Sugar Company .... C 989 673-2223
  Caro *(G-2575)*

FOOD PRDTS: Sugar, Cane

Farber Concessions Inc .... E 313 387-1600
  Redford *(G-13733)*
Michigan Sugar Company .... C 989 673-3126
  Caro *(G-2574)*

FOOD PRDTS: Sugar, Granulated Sugar Beet

Darwin Sneller .... G 989 977-3718
  Sebewaing *(G-15139)*
Schuette Farms .... G 989 550-0563
  Elkton *(G-5032)*

FOOD PRDTS: Sugar, Maple, Indl

Jaspers Sugar Bush LLC .... G 906 639-2588
  Carney *(G-2563)*

FOOD PRDTS: Sugar, Refined Sugar Beet

Michigan Sugar Company .... C 989 673-3126
  Caro *(G-2574)*
Michigan Sugar Company .... C 810 679-2241
  Croswell *(G-3733)*

FOOD PRDTS: Syrup, Maple

Battels Sugar Bush .... G 989 872-4794
  Cass City *(G-2611)*
Daniel Olson .... G 269 816-1838
  Jones *(G-9083)*
Haighs Maple Syrup & Sups LLC ...... G 517 202-6975
  Vermontville *(G-17588)*
Herman Hillbillies Farm LLC .... G 906 201-0760
  Lanse *(G-9661)*
Highland Hills Maple Syrup LLC .... G 231 920-1589
  Mc Bain *(G-11180)*
Jarmans Pure Maple Syrup LLC .... G 231 818-5315
  Cheboygan *(G-2789)*
Kasza Sugar Bush .... G 231 742-1930
  Shelby *(G-15152)*
Levi Ohman Micah .... F 612 251-1293
  Marquette *(G-11030)*
Ludhaven Sugarvush .... G 906 647-2400
  Barbeau *(G-1152)*
Parsons Centennial Farm LLC .... G 231 547-2038
  Charlevoix *(G-2727)*
Postma Brothers Maple Syrup .... G 906 478-3051
  Rudyard *(G-14594)*
Rays Pure Mple Syrup Pdts LLC ...... G 269 601-7694
  Fulton *(G-6072)*
Rmg Family Sugar Bush Inc .... G 906 478-3038
  Rudyard *(G-14595)*
Rmg Maple Products Inc .... G 906 478-3038
  Rudyard *(G-14596)*
Tree Line Maple Syrup .... G 616 889-6016
  Grand Rapids *(G-7273)*

FOOD PRDTS: Tea

Twinlab Holdings Inc .... G 800 645-5626
  Grand Rapids *(G-7284)*

FOOD PRDTS: Tortilla Chips

Gvb Group-La Fiesta LLC .... F 231 843-7600
  Montague *(G-11597)*
Hacienda Mexican Foods LLC .... D 313 895-8823
  Detroit *(G-4289)*
Tortillas Tita LLC .... G 734 756-7646
  Wayne *(G-18239)*

FOOD PRDTS: Tortillas

El-Milagro of Michigan Inc .... G 616 452-6625
  Grand Rapids *(G-6667)*
La Jalisciense Inc .... F 313 237-0008
  Farmington Hills *(G-5288)*
Lafrontera Tortillas Inc .... G 734 231-1701
  Rockwood *(G-14201)*
Las Brazas Tortillas .... G 616 886-0737
  Holland *(G-8124)*
Mexamerica Foods LLC .... F 814 781-1447
  Grand Rapids *(G-6984)*
Mexican Food Specialties Inc .... G 734 779-2370
  Southfield *(G-15656)*
Tortillas Tita LLC .... G 734 756-7646
  Wayne *(G-18239)*

FOOD PRDTS: Vegetable Oil Mills, NEC

Darling Ingredients Inc .... G 269 751-0560
  Hamilton *(G-7597)*

FOOD PRDTS: Vinegar

Bliss & Vinegar LLC .... G 616 970-0732
  Grand Rapids *(G-6515)*
Intl Giuseppes Oils & Vinegars .... G 586 698-2754
  Sterling Hts *(G-16236)*
Kraft Heinz Foods Company .... G 616 396-6557
  Holland *(G-8115)*

FOOD PRDTS: Wheat Flour

King Milling Company .... D 616 897-9264
  Lowell *(G-10508)*
Mennel Milling Co of Mich Inc .... E 269 782-5175
  Dowagiac *(G-4788)*

FOOD PRDTS: Yeast

Sensient Flavors LLC .... E 989 479-3211
  Harbor Beach *(G-7636)*
Sensient Technologies Corp .... G 989 479-3211
  Harbor Beach *(G-7637)*

FOOD PRODUCTS MACHINERY

Atwater Foods LLC .... G 231 941-4336
  Traverse City *(G-16607)*
Automated Process Equipment .... E 616 374-1000
  Lake Odessa *(G-9572)*
B&P Littleford Day LLC .... D 989 757-1300
  Saginaw *(G-14607)*
Frontier Technology Inc .... F 269 673-9464
  Allegan *(G-159)*
Marshall Middleby Holding LLC .... D 906 863-4401
  Menominee *(G-11244)*
Motembo Fine Foods LLC .... G 800 692-4814
  Okemos *(G-12678)*

Employee Codes: A=Over 500 employees, B=251-500
C=101-250, D=51-100, E=20-50, F=10-19, G=3-9

FOOD PRODUCTS MACHINERY

Process Partners Inc ....G..... 616 875-2156
  Hudsonville (G-8602)
Request Foods Inc ....B..... 616 786-0900
  Holland (G-8180)
Spiral-Matic Inc ....G..... 248 486-5080
  Brighton (G-2074)

FOOD STORES: Convenience, Chain

Independent Dairy Inc ....E..... 734 241-6016
  Monroe (G-11550)

FOOD STORES: Grocery, Independent

Kerns Sausages Inc ....F..... 989 652-2684
  Frankenmuth (G-5867)
Marias Italian Bakery Inc ....F..... 734 981-1200
  Canton (G-2488)
Nuts & Coffee Gallery ....G..... 313 581-3212
  Dearborn (G-3878)
Raleigh & Ron Corporation ....D..... 248 280-2820
  Royal Oak (G-14571)
Supreme Baking Company ....G..... 313 894-0222
  Detroit (G-4618)
Viaus Super Market ....G..... 906 786-1950
  Escanaba (G-5106)

FOOD STORES: Supermarket, More Than 100K Sq Ft, Hypermrkt

Walmart Inc ....F..... 517 541-1481
  Charlotte (G-2774)

FOOD STORES: Supermarkets, Independent

Erlas Inc ....D..... 989 872-2191
  Cass City (G-2614)

FOOD WARMING EQPT: Commercial

Hot Logic LLC ....G..... 616 935-1040
  Grand Haven (G-6319)

FOOTWEAR, WHOLESALE: Shoes

Kalamazoo Orthotics & Dbtc ......F..... 269 349-2247
  Kalamazoo (G-9244)

FOOTWEAR: Cut Stock

David Epstein Inc ....F..... 248 542-0802
  Ferndale (G-5539)
Living Quarters ....G..... 616 874-6160
  Coral (G-3700)
Paul Murphy Plastics Co ....E..... 586 774-4880
  Roseville (G-14460)
S A S ....G..... 586 725-6381
  Chesterfield (G-2943)
Wolverine Procurement Inc ....C..... 616 866-9521
  Rockford (G-14194)

FORESTRY RELATED EQPT

JP Skidmore LLC ....G..... 906 424-4127
  Menominee (G-11241)
Timberland Forestry ....G..... 906 387-4350
  Munising (G-11756)

FORGINGS

Amk Ironworks ....G..... 248 620-9027
  Clarkston (G-3016)
Borgwarner Powdered Metals Inc ....C..... 734 261-5322
  Livonia (G-10140)
Buchanan Metal Forming Inc .....E..... 269 695-3836
  Buchanan (G-2190)
Chardam Gear Company ....C..... 586 795-8900
  Sterling Heights (G-15957)
Composite Forgings Ltd Partnr ..D..... 313 496-1226
  Detroit (G-4099)
Computer Operated Mfg ....E..... 989 686-1333
  Bay City (G-1340)
Detail Precision Products Inc ....E..... 248 544-3390
  Ferndale (G-5540)
Dorris Company ....F..... 586 293-5260
  Fraser (G-5919)
Enterprise Tool and Gear Inc ....F..... 989 269-9797
  Bad Axe (G-1100)
Fairlane Gear Inc ....G..... 734 459-2440
  Canton (G-2460)
Gage Eagle Spline Inc ....D..... 586 776-7240
  Warren (G-17822)
Great Lakes Forge Inc ....G..... 231 947-4931
  Traverse City (G-16704)

Great Lakes Industry Inc ....E..... 517 784-3153
  Jackson (G-8895)
Hephaestus Holdings LLC ....G..... 248 479-2700
  Novi (G-12432)
Hhi Formtech LLC ....E..... 586 415-2000
  Fraser (G-5935)
Hog Forging LLC ....G..... 248 765-7180
  Birmingham (G-1729)
Invo Spline Inc ....E..... 586 757-8840
  Warren (G-17870)
Jervis B Webb Company ....B..... 248 553-1000
  Novi (G-12449)
Kendor Steel Rule Die Inc ....F..... 586 293-7111
  Fraser (G-5950)
Lansing Forge Inc ....F..... 517 882-2056
  Lansing (G-9859)
Lansing Holding Company Inc ..G..... 517 882-2056
  Lansing (G-9861)
Lc Manufacturing LLC ....E..... 734 753-3990
  New Boston (G-12013)
Linear Mold & Engineering LLC ....E..... 734 744-4548
  Livonia (G-10281)
Lisi Automotive HI Vol Inc ....C..... 734 266-6900
  Livonia (G-10286)
Lucerne Forging Inc ....G..... 248 674-7210
  Auburn Hills (G-960)
Lyons Tool & Engineering Inc ....E..... 586 200-3003
  Warren (G-17910)
Metal Forming & Coining Corp ..G..... 586 731-2003
  Shelby Township (G-15273)
Metal Forming Technology Inc ..F..... 586 949-4586
  Chesterfield (G-2910)
Metalcraft Impression Die Co ....G..... 734 513-8058
  Livonia (G-10311)
MFC Netform Inc ....E..... 586 731-2003
  Shelby Township (G-15277)
Michigan Forge Company LLC ..E..... 815 758-6400
  Lansing (G-9869)
Rack & Pinion Inc ....G..... 517 563-8872
  Horton (G-8378)
Ringmasters Mfg LLC ....F..... 734 729-6110
  Wayne (G-18235)
Steve Tonkovich ....G..... 810 348-4046
  Waterford (G-18166)
Stonebridge Industries Inc ....B..... 586 323-0348
  Sterling Heights (G-16195)
Trenton Forging Company ....D..... 734 675-1620
  Trenton (G-16895)
Triumph Gear Systems - McOmb I ....C..... 586 781-2800
  Macomb (G-10644)
Vectorall Manufacturing Inc ....E..... 248 486-4570
  Brighton (G-2093)
Warren Manufacturing LLC ....G..... 586 467-1600
  Warren (G-18060)
Wartian Lock Company ....G..... 586 777-2244
  Saint Clair Shores (G-14891)
Webster Cold Forge Co ....F..... 313 554-4500
  Northville (G-12271)
Wedin International Inc ....E..... 231 779-8650
  Cadillac (G-2363)
Wilkie Bros Conveyors Inc ....E..... 810 364-4820
  Marysville (G-11113)
Wyman-Gordon Forgings Inc ....B..... 810 229-9550
  Brighton (G-2099)

FORGINGS: Aluminum

Lincoln Park Die & Tool Co ....E..... 734 285-1680
  Brownstown (G-2149)
Mueller Brass Forging Co Inc ....D..... 810 987-7770
  Port Huron (G-13506)
Wonder Makers Environmental ....E..... 269 382-4154
  Kalamazoo (G-9372)

FORGINGS: Automotive & Internal Combustion Engine

Cambric Corporation ....E..... 801 415-7300
  Novi (G-12378)
Dias Holding Inc ....F..... 313 928-1254
  Allen Park (G-192)
Global Engine Mfg Aliance LLC ....G..... 734 529-9888
  Dundee (G-4822)
Hhi Formtech LLC ....B..... 248 597-3800
  Royal Oak (G-14545)
Linear Mold & Engineering LLC ....F..... 734 422-6060
  Livonia (G-10282)

FORGINGS: Gear & Chain

Decker Gear Inc ....F..... 810 388-1500
  Saint Clair (G-14825)

Formax Precision Gear Inc ....F..... 586 323-9067
  Sterling Heights (G-16018)
Riverside Spline & Gear Inc ......E..... 810 765-8302
  Marine City (G-10965)
Tech Tool Company Inc ....G..... 313 836-4131
  Detroit (G-4628)

FORGINGS: Iron & Steel

Stage Stop ....G..... 989 838-4039
  Ithaca (G-8795)
Steel Industries Inc ....C..... 313 535-8505
  Redford (G-13774)

FORGINGS: Machinery, Ferrous

Power Industries Corp ....G..... 586 783-3818
  Harrison Township (G-7716)

FORGINGS: Nonferrous

Borgwarner Powdered Metals Inc ....C..... 734 261-5322
  Livonia (G-10140)
Global Fmi LLC ....D..... 810 964-5555
  Fenton (G-5481)
Greenseed LLC ....G..... 313 295-0100
  Taylor (G-16423)
Hephaestus Holdings LLC ....G..... 248 479-2700
  Novi (G-12432)
Hhi Formtech LLC ....E..... 586 415-2000
  Fraser (G-5935)
Mueller Brass Co ....D..... 810 987-7770
  Port Huron (G-13504)
Mueller Impacts Company Inc ...C..... 810 364-3700
  Marysville (G-11093)
Mueller Industries Inc ....G..... 248 446-3720
  Brighton (G-2037)
Resistnce Wldg Mch Accssory LL ....F..... 269 428-4770
  Saint Joseph (G-14956)
United Brass Manufacturers Inc ....F..... 734 942-9224
  Romulus (G-14335)
United Brass Manufacturers Inc ....G..... 734 941-0700
  Romulus (G-14334)
Weldaloy Products Company ....D..... 586 758-5550
  Warren (G-18064)

FORMS: Concrete, Sheet Metal

Metal Merchants of Michigan ....F..... 248 293-0621
  Rochester Hills (G-14062)

FOUNDRIES: Aluminum

Acra Cast Inc ....E..... 989 893-3961
  Bay City (G-1316)
Cascade Die Casting Group Inc ....D..... 616 887-1771
  Sparta (G-15762)
Continental Aluminum LLC ....D..... 248 437-1001
  New Hudson (G-12046)
Dundee Castings Company ......D..... 734 529-2455
  Dundee (G-4815)
Ehc Inc ....G..... 313 259-2266
  Troy (G-17079)
Eps Industries Inc ....E..... 616 844-9220
  Ferrysburg (G-5602)
Hoffmann Die Cast LLC ....C..... 269 983-1102
  Saint Joseph (G-14936)
Holland Alloys Inc ....E..... 616 396-6444
  Holland (G-8073)
IBC Precision Inc ....G..... 248 373-8202
  Auburn Hills (G-933)
J & M Machine Products Inc .....D..... 231 755-1622
  Norton Shores (G-12302)
Line Precision Inc ....E..... 248 474-5280
  Farmington Hills (G-5291)
Non-Ferrous Cast Alloys Inc ......D..... 231 799-0550
  Norton Shores (G-12318)
Prompt Pattern Inc ....F..... 586 759-2030
  Warren (G-17979)
Shipston Alum Tech Mich Inc ....G..... 616 842-3500
  Fruitport (G-6070)
Shipston Aluminum Tech Ind Inc ....D..... 317 738-0282
  Southfield (G-15701)
Specialty Steel Treating Inc ....E..... 586 293-5355
  Fraser (G-5998)
Supreme Casting Inc ....G..... 269 465-5757
  Stevensville (G-16267)
Tooling Technology LLC ....D..... 937 381-9211
  Macomb (G-10643)
Tri-State Cast Technologies Co ....G..... 231 582-0452
  Boyne City (G-1904)
Whitehall Products LLC ....D..... 231 894-2688
  Whitehall (G-18514)

PRODUCT SECTION — FOUNTAIN PEN REPAIR SHOP

Wolverine Die Cast Ltd Prtnr O .... E 586 757-1900
  Warren (G-18071)

FOUNDRIES: Brass, Bronze & Copper

Anchor Lamina America Inc .... C 231 533-8646
  Bellaire (G-1468)
Anchor Lamina America Inc .... E 248 489-9122
  Bellaire (G-1469)
Axly Production Machining Inc .... G 989 269-2444
  Bad Axe (G-1096)
Belwith Products LLC .... F 616 247-4000
  Grandville (G-7367)
Bradhart Products Inc .... E 248 437-3746
  Brighton (G-1952)
Century Foundry Inc .... E 231 733-1572
  Muskegon (G-11791)
Duplicast Corporation .... G 586 756-5900
  Sterling Heights (G-15992)
Enterprise Tool and Gear Inc .... F 989 269-9797
  Bad Axe (G-1100)
Eps Industries Inc .... E 616 844-9220
  Ferrysburg (G-5602)
GKN Sinter Metals LLC .... G 248 883-4500
  Auburn Hills (G-914)
Global CNC Industries Ltd .... E 734 464-1920
  Plymouth (G-13177)
Hackett Brass Foundry Co .... G 313 331-6005
  Detroit (G-4291)
Holland Alloys Inc .... E 616 396-6444
  Holland (G-8073)
Huron Tool & Engineering Co .... E 989 269-9927
  Bad Axe (G-1108)
Milan Cast Metal Corporation .... E 734 439-0510
  Milan (G-11445)
Northfield Manufacturing Inc .... E 734 729-2890
  Westland (G-18401)
Production Tube Company Inc .... G 313 259-3990
  Detroit (G-4537)
Prompt Pattern Inc .... F 586 759-2030
  Warren (G-17979)
Sterling Metal Works LLC .... G 586 977-9577
  Sterling Heights (G-16193)

FOUNDRIES: Gray & Ductile Iron

Bernier Cast Metals Inc .... G 989 754-7571
  Saginaw (G-14615)
Cadillac Casting Inc .... B 231 779-9600
  Cadillac (G-2319)
E & M Cores Inc .... G 989 386-9223
  Clare (G-2978)
Eagle Quest International Ltd .... F 616 850-2630
  Spring Lake (G-15812)
Ej Co .... F 231 536-4527
  East Jordan (G-4866)
Ej Usa Inc .... G 231 536-2261
  East Jordan (G-4871)
Eqi Ltd .... G 616 850-2630
  Norton Shores (G-12292)
General Motors LLC .... G 989 757-0528
  Saginaw (G-14651)
Great Lakes Castings LLC .... C 231 843-2501
  Ludington (G-10538)
GSC Riii - Grede LLC .... G 248 440-9500
  Southfield (G-15586)
Holland Alloys Inc .... E 616 396-6444
  Holland (G-8073)
JP Castings Inc .... E 517 857-3660
  Springport (G-15882)
Paragon Metals LLC .... G 517 639-4629
  Hillsdale (G-7941)
Robert Bosch LLC .... G 269 429-3221
  Saint Joseph (G-14957)
Shop IV Sbusid Inv Grede LLC .... G 248 440-9515
  Southfield (G-15703)
Steeltech Ltd .... G 616 696-1130
  Cedar Springs (G-2663)
Triumph Gear Systems - McOmb I .... C 586 781-2800
  Macomb (G-10644)

FOUNDRIES: Iron

CB Marcellus Metalcasters Inc .... F 269 646-0202
  Marcellus (G-10946)
Grede LLC .... B 906 774-7250
  Kingsford (G-9509)
Holland Alloys Inc .... E 616 396-6444
  Holland (G-8073)
International Casting Corp .... G 586 293-8220
  Roseville (G-14425)
Kramer International Inc .... F 586 726-4300
  Troy (G-17199)
Paragon Metals LLC .... G 517 639-4629
  Hillsdale (G-7941)
Peerless Steel Company .... E 616 530-6695
  Grandville (G-7408)
Prompt Pattern Inc .... F 586 759-2030
  Warren (G-17979)
Robert Bosch LLC .... G 269 429-3221
  Saint Joseph (G-14957)
Smith Castings Inc .... F 906 774-4956
  Iron Mountain (G-8733)
Teksid Inc .... E 734 846-5492
  Farmington (G-5153)
Tooling Technology LLC .... F 937 381-9211
  Macomb (G-10643)
Wolverine Bronze Company .... D 586 776-8180
  Roseville (G-14495)

FOUNDRIES: Nonferrous

A C Foundry Incorporated .... F 269 963-4131
  Battle Creek (G-1175)
Algonac Marine Cast LLC .... E 810 794-9391
  Clay (G-3114)
Alloy Machining LLC .... G 517 204-3306
  Lansing (G-9753)
Ancast Inc .... E 269 927-1985
  Sodus (G-15392)
Ascent Integrated Platforms .... F 586 726-0500
  Macomb (G-10580)
Astech Inc .... E 989 823-7211
  Vassar (G-17577)
Awcco USA Incorporated .... G 586 336-9135
  Romeo (G-14220)
Barron Industries Inc .... D 248 628-4300
  Oxford (G-12876)
Berne Enterprises Inc .... F 989 453-3235
  Pigeon (G-13036)
Computer Operated Mfg .... E 989 686-1333
  Bay City (G-1340)
Douglas King Industries Inc .... G 989 642-2865
  Hemlock (G-7851)
Dundee Castings Company .... D 734 529-2455
  Dundee (G-4815)
Elden Industries Corp .... F 734 946-6900
  Taylor (G-16412)
Federal-Mogul Piston Rings Inc .... E 248 354-7700
  Southfield (G-15564)
GKN Sinter Metals LLC .... G 248 883-4500
  Auburn Hills (G-914)
Gokoh Coldwater Incorporated .... F 517 279-1080
  Coldwater (G-3434)
Hackett Brass Foundry Co .... G 313 331-6005
  Detroit (G-4291)
Hoffmann Die Cast LLC .... C 269 983-1102
  Saint Joseph (G-14936)
Huron Casting Inc .... B 989 453-3933
  Pigeon (G-13039)
Husite Engineering Co Inc .... F 248 588-0337
  Clinton Township (G-3255)
Inland Lakes Machine Inc .... E 231 775-6543
  Cadillac (G-2337)
Invecast Corporation .... E 586 755-4050
  Warren (G-17869)
Line Precision Inc .... E 248 474-5280
  Farmington Hills (G-5291)
Magnesium Products America Inc .... B 734 416-8600
  Plymouth (G-13231)
Non-Ferrous Cast Alloys Inc .... D 231 799-0550
  Norton Shores (G-12318)
Paragon Metals LLC .... G 517 639-4629
  Hillsdale (G-7941)
Premiere Tool & Die Cast .... E 269 782-3030
  Kalamazoo (G-9306)
Prompt Pattern Inc .... F 586 759-2030
  Warren (G-17979)
Proto-Cast Inc .... E 313 565-5400
  Inkster (G-8672)
Rolled Alloys Inc .... D 734 847-0561
  Temperance (G-16547)
Smith Castings Inc .... F 906 774-4956
  Iron Mountain (G-8733)
Superior Brass & Alum Cast Co .... F 517 351-7534
  East Lansing (G-4911)
Trin-Mac Company Inc .... G 586 774-1900
  Saint Clair Shores (G-14889)
White Cloud Manufacturing Co .... E 231 796-8603
  Big Rapids (G-1689)

FOUNDRIES: Steel

Allied Metals Corp .... E 248 680-2400
  Auburn Hills (G-778)
Astech Inc .... E 989 823-7211
  Vassar (G-17577)
Bico Michigan Inc .... E 616 453-2400
  Grand Rapids (G-6506)
Detroit Materials Inc .... G 248 924-5436
  Farmington (G-5136)
Federal Screw Works .... G 231 922-9500
  Traverse City (G-16681)
GAL Gage Co .... F 269 465-5750
  Bridgman (G-1926)
General Motors Company .... G 989 757-1576
  Saginaw (G-14650)
General Motors LLC .... G 989 757-0528
  Saginaw (G-14651)
Hackett Brass Foundry Co .... G 313 331-6005
  Detroit (G-4291)
Holland Alloys Inc .... E 616 396-6444
  Holland (G-8073)
International Casting Corp .... F 586 293-8220
  New Baltimore (G-11984)
International Casting Corp .... G 586 293-8220
  Roseville (G-14425)
Invecast Corporation .... E 586 755-4050
  Warren (G-17869)
J & M Machine Products Inc .... D 231 755-1622
  Norton Shores (G-12302)
Mannix RE Holdings LLC .... G 231 972-0088
  Mecosta (G-11192)
Pal-TEC Inc .... G 906 788-4229
  Wallace (G-17661)
Paragon Metals LLC .... G 517 639-4629
  Hillsdale (G-7941)
Pennisular Packaging LLC .... G 313 304-4724
  Plymouth (G-13261)
Saarsteel Incorporated .... G 248 608-0849
  Rochester Hills (G-14105)
Smith Castings Inc .... F 906 774-4956
  Iron Mountain (G-8733)
Temperform Corp .... F 248 851-9611
  Bloomfield Hills (G-1864)

FOUNDRIES: Steel Investment

Acra Cast Inc .... E 989 893-3961
  Bay City (G-1316)
Barron Group Inc .... D 248 628-4300
  Oxford (G-12875)
Chain Industries Inc .... E 248 348-7722
  Wixom (G-18631)
Douglas King Industries Inc .... G 989 642-2865
  Hemlock (G-7851)
Eagle Precision Cast Parts Inc .... E 231 788-3318
  Muskegon (G-11803)
Eutectic Engineering Co Inc .... G 313 892-2248
  Bloomfield Hills (G-1820)
Paragon Metals LLC .... G 517 639-4629
  Hillsdale (G-7941)
R L M Industries Inc .... D 248 628-5103
  Oxford (G-12910)

FOUNDRY MACHINERY & EQPT

Centennial Technologies Inc .... E 989 752-6167
  Saginaw (G-14624)
Corr-Fac Corporation .... G 989 358-7050
  Alpena (G-288)
Fata Aluminum LLC .... E 248 802-9853
  Orion (G-12729)
Roberts Sinto Corporation .... D 517 371-2460
  Lansing (G-9787)
Sinto America Inc .... E 517 371-2460
  Lansing (G-9791)

FOUNDRY SAND MINING

Covia Solutions Inc .... G 800 255-7263
  Benton Harbor (G-1543)
Sand Products Corporation .... G 906 292-5432
  Moran (G-11610)
Sargent Sand Co .... G 989 792-8734
  Midland (G-11414)

FOUNTAIN PEN REPAIR SHOP

Curbco Inc .... D 810 232-2121
  Flint (G-5678)

Employee Codes: A=Over 500 employees, B=251-500
C=101-250, D=51-100, E=20-50, F=10-19, G=3-9

FRACTIONATION PRDTS OF CRUDE PETROLEUM, HYDROCARBONS, NEC

Marysville Hydrocarbons LLC .... E 586 445-2300
Marysville *(G-11090)*

FRANCHISES, SELLING OR LICENSING

Alliance Franchise Brands LLC .... F 248 596-8600
Plymouth *(G-13122)*
Coffee Beanery Ltd .... E 810 733-1020
Flushing *(G-5805)*
Dominos Pizza LLC .... C 734 930-3030
Ann Arbor *(G-456)*
Rocky Mtn Choclat Fctry Inc .... D 810 606-8550
Grand Blanc *(G-6261)*
Ziebart International Corp .... E 248 588-4100
Troy *(G-17460)*

FREEZERS: Household

Northland Corporation .... C 616 754-5601
Greenville *(G-7503)*
Whirlpool Corporation .... G 269 923-3009
Benton Harbor *(G-1610)*

FREIGHT FORWARDING ARRANGEMENTS: Domestic

Xpo Cnw Inc .... C 734 757-1444
Ann Arbor *(G-720)*

FREIGHT TRANSPORTATION ARRANGEMENTS

Boskage Commerce Publications .... G 269 673-7242
Portage *(G-13547)*
Fourth Seacoast Publishing Co .... G 586 779-5570
Saint Clair Shores *(G-14861)*
Kolossos Printing Inc .... G 734 741-1600
Ann Arbor *(G-541)*
Nash Products Inc .... G 269 323-2980
Vicksburg *(G-17609)*
Sheffler Mfg Intl Lgistics LLC .... E 248 409-0960
Clarkston *(G-3065)*
World of Pallets and Trucking .... G 313 899-2000
Detroit *(G-4691)*

FREON

Cjg LLC .... G 734 793-1400
Livonia *(G-10158)*
J&J Freon Removal .... G 586 264-6379
Warren *(G-17881)*

FRICTION MATERIAL, MADE FROM POWDERED METAL

Greene Manufacturing Tech LLC .... C 810 982-9720
Port Huron *(G-13481)*
Miba Hydramechanica Corp .... D 586 264-3094
Sterling Heights *(G-16097)*

FRUIT & VEGETABLE MARKETS

Porters Orchards Farm Market .... G 810 636-7156
Goodrich *(G-6226)*

FRUIT STANDS OR MARKETS

Northville Cider Mill Inc .... F 248 349-3181
Northville *(G-12245)*
Uncle Johns Cider Mill Inc .... E 989 224-3686
Saint Johns *(G-14919)*
Yates Cider Mill Inc .... G 248 651-8300
Rochester Hills *(G-14149)*

FUEL ADDITIVES

Fortech Products Inc .... E 248 446-9500
Brighton *(G-1992)*
Matrix Construction Pdts LLC .... G 720 961-5454
Marquette *(G-11035)*
Nano Materials & Processes Inc .... G 248 529-3873
Milford *(G-11475)*

FUEL CELLS: Solid State

Fuel Cell System Mfg LLC .... G 313 319-5571
Brownstown Township *(G-2152)*

FUEL OIL DEALERS

Koenig Fuel & Supply Co .... G 313 368-1870
Wayne *(G-18226)*
Lansing Ice and Fuel Company .... F 517 372-3850
Lansing *(G-9710)*

FUELS: Diesel

W2fuel LLC .... E 517 920-4868
Adrian *(G-101)*

FUELS: Ethanol

Adrian Lva Biofuel LLC .... G 517 920-4863
Adrian *(G-48)*
Albasara Fuel LLC .... G 313 443-6581
Dearborn *(G-3806)*
Ana Fuel Inc .... G 810 422-5659
Ann Arbor *(G-366)*
Assi Fuel Inc .... G 586 759-4759
Warren *(G-17720)*
Beebe Fuel Systems Inc .... G 248 437-3322
South Lyon *(G-15427)*
BKM Fuels LLC .... G 269 342-9576
Kalamazoo *(G-9137)*
BP Gas/ JB Fuel .... G 517 531-3400
Parma *(G-12936)*
Camerons of Jackson LLC .... G 517 531-3400
Parma *(G-12937)*
Century Fuel Products .... G 734 728-0300
Van Buren Twp *(G-17517)*
Chouteau Fuels Company LLC .... G 734 302-4800
Ann Arbor *(G-424)*
Cldd LLC .... G 517 748-9326
Jackson *(G-8844)*
D M J Corp .... G 810 239-9071
Flint *(G-5681)*
EZ Fuel Inc .... G 810 744-4452
Flint *(G-5699)*
Fit Fuel By Kt LLC .... G 517 643-8827
East Lansing *(G-4893)*
Fk Fuel Inc .... G 313 383-6005
Lincoln Park *(G-10047)*
Fleet Fuel Company LLC .... G 586 939-7000
Warren *(G-17807)*
Freal Fuel Inc .... G 248 790-7202
Chesterfield *(G-2886)*
Frontier Rnwable Resources LLC .... G 906 228-7960
Marquette *(G-11019)*
Fuel Tobacco Stop .... G 810 487-2040
Flushing *(G-5809)*
Gb Dynamics Inc .... G 313 400-3570
Port Huron *(G-13479)*
Green Fuels Llc .... G 734 735-6802
Carleton *(G-2554)*
Ibidltd-Blue Green Energy .... E 909 547-5160
Dearborn *(G-3852)*
Il Adrian LLC W2fuel .... G 517 920-4863
Adrian *(G-73)*
Inkster Fuel & Food Inc .... G 313 565-8230
Inkster *(G-8666)*
K&S Fuel Ventures .... G 248 360-0055
Commerce Township *(G-3548)*
Kentwood Fuel Inc .... G 616 455-2387
Kentwood *(G-9459)*
Kern Auto Sales and Svc LLC .... F 734 475-2722
Chelsea *(G-2818)*
Lansing Fuel Ventures Inc .... G 517 371-1198
Lansing *(G-9860)*
Lillian Fuel Inc .... G 734 439-8505
Milan *(G-11442)*
Lin Adam Fuel Inc .... G 313 733-6631
Detroit *(G-4401)*
M and A Fuels .... G 313 397-7141
Detroit *(G-4413)*
Michigan Fuels .... G 313 886-7110
Grosse Pointe Woods *(G-7571)*
Monroe Fuel Company LLC .... G 734 302-4824
Ann Arbor *(G-582)*
Naked Fuel Juice Bar .... G 248 325-9735
West Bloomfield *(G-18301)*
Nation Wide Fuel Inc .... G 734 721-7110
Dearborn *(G-3875)*
National Fuels Inc .... G 734 895-7836
Canton *(G-2499)*
New Port Fuel Stop .... G 734 586-1401
Newport *(G-12105)*
Paw Paw Fuel Stop .... G 269 657-7357
Paw Paw *(G-12955)*
Performance Fuels Systems Inc .... G 248 202-1789
Troy *(G-17297)*
Reed Fuel LLC .... G 574 520-3101
Niles *(G-12161)*
S&A Fuel LLC .... G 313 945-6555
Dearborn *(G-3891)*
Seven Mile and Grnd River Fuel .... G 313 535-3000
Hamtramck *(G-7613)*
Superior Fuels LLC .... G 586 738-6851
Dearborn *(G-3902)*
Sy Fuel Inc .... G 313 531-5894
Redford *(G-13776)*
Taiz Fuel Inc .... G 313 485-2972
Dearborn Heights *(G-3941)*
Temperance Fuel Stop Inc .... G 734 206-2676
Grosse Pointe Woods *(G-7577)*
Vision Fuels LLC .... G 586 997-3286
Shelby Township *(G-15366)*
Wamu Fuel LLC .... G 313 386-8700
Livonia *(G-10465)*
Warren City Fuel .... G 586 759-4759
Dearborn *(G-3914)*
Zunairah Fuels LLC .... G 647 405-1606
Clinton Township *(G-3393)*

FUELS: Gas, Liquefied

Buckeye Terminals LLC .... G 616 842-2450
Ferrysburg *(G-5601)*

FUELS: Jet

Avflight Corporation .... G 734 663-6466
Ann Arbor *(G-388)*
Jet Fuel .... G 231 767-9566
Muskegon *(G-11845)*

FUELS: Kerosene

Kerosene Fragrances .... G 810 292-5772
Port Huron *(G-13493)*

FUELS: Oil

Corrigan Enterprises Inc .... E 810 229-6323
Brighton *(G-1969)*
Motor City Quick Lube One Inc .... G 734 367-6457
Livonia *(G-10323)*
Pacific Oil Resources Inc .... G 734 397-1120
Van Buren Twp *(G-17545)*

FUNDRAISING SVCS

Sly Fox Prints LLC .... G 616 900-9677
Cedar Springs *(G-2661)*

FUNGICIDES OR HERBICIDES

Dow Chemical Company .... C 989 636-4406
Midland *(G-11343)*
Dow Chemical Company .... A 989 636-1000
Midland *(G-11341)*
Dow Chemical Company .... D 989 636-5409
Midland *(G-11352)*

FUR APPAREL STORES

Birlon Group LLC .... G 313 551-5341
Inkster *(G-8659)*

FUR: Apparel

Wolvering Fur .... G 313 961-0620
Detroit *(G-4689)*

FURNACE CASINGS: Sheet Metal

Kraftube Inc .... C 231 832-5562
Reed City *(G-13793)*

FURNACES & OVENS: Fuel-Fired

Kolene Corporation .... D 313 273-9220
Detroit *(G-4365)*

FURNACES & OVENS: Indl

Able Htng Clng & Plmbng .... G 231 779-5430
Cadillac *(G-2307)*
Afc-Holcroft LLC .... D 248 624-8191
Wixom *(G-18598)*
Allegan Tubular Products Inc .... D 269 673-6636
Allegan *(G-146)*
Atmosphere Group Inc .... G 248 624-8191
Wixom *(G-18609)*
Belco Industries Inc .... E 616 794-0410
Belding *(G-1437)*

PRODUCT SECTION

FURNITURE, WHOLESALE: Racks

Ce II Holdings Inc .... F 248 305-7700
  Brighton *(G-1963)*
Clark Granco Inc .... D 616 794-2600
  Belding *(G-1443)*
Complete Filtration Inc .... F 248 693-0500
  Lake Orion *(G-9598)*
Davids Heating & Cooling Inc .... G 586 601-5108
  Southfield *(G-15537)*
Detroit Steel Treating Company .... E 248 334-7436
  Pontiac *(G-13361)*
Dfc Inc .... G 734 285-6749
  Riverview *(G-13870)*
Efd Induction Inc .... F 248 658-0700
  Madison Heights *(G-10717)*
Fluid Hutchinson Management .... D 248 679-1327
  Auburn Hills *(G-903)*
Fluidtherm Corp Michigan .... G 989 344-1500
  Frederic *(G-6015)*
Gerref Industries Inc .... E 616 794-3110
  Belding *(G-1450)*
Industrial Temperature Control .... G 734 451-8740
  Canton *(G-2474)*
J L Becker Acquisition LLC .... E 734 656-2000
  Plymouth *(G-13199)*
Jackson Oven Supply Inc .... F 517 784-9660
  Jackson *(G-8916)*
Kolene Corporation .... F 586 771-1200
  Roseville *(G-14430)*
Nortek Air Solutions LLC .... D 616 738-7148
  Holland *(G-8156)*
North Woods Industrial .... G 616 784-2840
  Comstock Park *(G-3629)*
Oakland Welding Industries .... E 586 949-4090
  Chesterfield *(G-2916)*
Perceptive Industries Inc .... E 269 204-6768
  Plainwell *(G-13086)*
Salem/Savard Industries LLC .... F 313 931-6880
  Detroit *(G-4579)*
Thermal Designs & Manufacturng .... E 586 773-5231
  Roseville *(G-14484)*
Thermalfab Products Inc .... F 517 486-2073
  Blissfield *(G-1778)*
Thoreson-Mc Cosh Inc .... E 248 362-0960
  Lake Orion *(G-9634)*
Tps LLC .... D 269 849-2700
  Riverside *(G-13866)*
Ultra-Temp Corporation .... G 810 794-4709
  Clay *(G-3128)*
Vconverter Corporation .... C 248 388-0549
  Novi *(G-12564)*

FURNITURE & CABINET STORES: Cabinets, Custom Work

G & G Wood & Supply Inc .... E 586 293-0450
  Roseville *(G-14408)*
Kurtis Mfg & Distrg Corp .... E 734 522-7600
  Livonia *(G-10270)*
Moda Manufacturing LLC .... F 586 204-5120
  Farmington Hills *(G-5325)*
Reis Custom Cabinets .... G 586 791-4925
  Reese *(G-13807)*
Rose Corporation .... E 734 426-0005
  Dexter *(G-4753)*
Van Daeles Inc .... G 734 587-7165
  Monroe *(G-11588)*

FURNITURE & CABINET STORES: Custom

Designtech Custom Interiors .... G 989 695-6306
  Freeland *(G-6020)*

FURNITURE & FIXTURES Factory

Banta Furniture Company .... F 616 575-8180
  Grand Rapids *(G-6494)*
Consort Corporation .... E 269 388-4532
  Kalamazoo *(G-9151)*
Firehouse Woodworks LLC .... G 616 285-2300
  Grand Rapids *(G-6707)*
Frank Terlecki Company Inc .... F 586 759-5770
  Warren *(G-17818)*
Paladin Ind Inc .... E 616 698-7495
  Grand Rapids *(G-7068)*
Shop Makarios LLC .... F 800 479-0032
  Byron Center *(G-2295)*
Superior Fixture & Tooling LLC .... G 616 828-1566
  Grand Rapids *(G-7237)*
Symbiote Inc .... E 616 772-1790
  Zeeland *(G-19083)*
West Michigan Gage Inc .... F 616 735-0585
  Walker *(G-17657)*

Woodard—Cm LLC .... C 989 725-4265
  Owosso *(G-12869)*

FURNITURE COMPONENTS: Porcelain Enameled

Forward Metal Craft Inc .... F 616 459-6051
  Grand Rapids *(G-6717)*

FURNITURE PARTS: Metal

Challenger Manufacturing LLC .... F 248 930-9920
  Farmington Hills *(G-5202)*
Elemental Artistry LLC .... E 616 326-1758
  Grand Rapids *(G-6671)*
Fournier Enterprises Inc .... G 586 323-9160
  Mount Clemens *(G-11639)*
Gibraltar Inc .... E 616 748-4857
  Zeeland *(G-19030)*
Metalworks Inc .... C 231 845-5136
  Ludington *(G-10546)*
Omt Veyhl .... G 616 738-6688
  Holland *(G-8158)*

FURNITURE REFINISHING SVCS

Kent Upholstery Inc .... G 248 332-7260
  Pontiac *(G-13392)*

FURNITURE REPAIR & MAINTENANCE SVCS

Irwin Seating Holding Company .... B 616 574-7400
  Grand Rapids *(G-6854)*

FURNITURE STOCK & PARTS: Carvings, Wood

Ganas LLC .... F 313 646-9966
  Detroit *(G-4250)*
Hunt & Noyer LLC .... G 517 914-6259
  Berkley *(G-1627)*
IKEA Chip LLC .... G 877 218-9931
  Troy *(G-17160)*
Yooper WD Wrks Restoration LLC ...... G 906 203-0056
  Sault Sainte Marie *(G-15105)*
Zemis 5 LLC .... G 317 946-7015
  Detroit *(G-4703)*

FURNITURE STOCK & PARTS: Dimension Stock, Hardwood

Grand Rapids Carvers Inc .... E 616 538-0022
  Grand Rapids *(G-6754)*
Matelski Lumber Company .... E 231 549-2780
  Boyne Falls *(G-1909)*
Meeders Dim & Lbr Pdts Co .... G 231 587-8611
  Mancelona *(G-10874)*

FURNITURE STOCK & PARTS: Hardwood

Demeester Wood Products Inc .... F 616 677-5995
  Coopersville *(G-3685)*
Doltek Enterprises Inc .... E 616 837-7828
  Nunica *(G-12579)*
Forestry Management Svcs Inc .... C 517 456-7431
  Clinton *(G-3138)*
H & R Wood Specialties Inc .... E 269 628-2181
  Gobles *(G-6217)*
Jarvis Saw Mill Inc .... G 231 861-2078
  Shelby *(G-15150)*
Motto Cedar Products Inc .... G 906 753-4892
  Daggett *(G-3753)*

FURNITURE STOCK & PARTS: Turnings, Wood

Solaire Medical Storage LLC .... D 888 435-2256
  Marne *(G-10999)*

FURNITURE STORES

Allstate HM Leisure String Hts .... G 734 838-6500
  Sterling Heights *(G-15928)*
Artisans Cstm Mmory Mattresses .... F 989 793-3208
  Saginaw *(G-14605)*
Compass Interiors LLC .... F 231 348-5353
  Petoskey *(G-12994)*
H L F Furniture Incorporated .... E 734 697-3000
  Van Buren Twp *(G-17528)*
Homespun Furniture Inc .... F 734 284-6277
  Riverview *(G-13874)*

Kent Upholstery Inc .... G 248 332-7260
  Pontiac *(G-13392)*
Koegel Meats Inc .... C 810 238-3685
  Flint *(G-5722)*
La-Z-Boy Incorporated .... A 734 242-1444
  Monroe *(G-11557)*
Marrs Discount Furniture .... G 989 720-5436
  Owosso *(G-12840)*
Richards Quality Bedding Co .... E 616 363-0070
  Grand Rapids *(G-7153)*
Straits Corporation .... F 989 684-5088
  Tawas City *(G-16368)*
Tvb Inc .... G 616 456-9629
  Grand Rapids *(G-7283)*
West Mich Off Interiors Inc .... G 269 344-0768
  Kalamazoo *(G-9367)*

FURNITURE STORES: Cabinets, Kitchen, Exc Custom Made

Farmington Cabinet Company .... F 248 476-2666
  Livonia *(G-10205)*

FURNITURE STORES: Custom Made, Exc Cabinets

Woodland Creek Furniture Inc .... E 231 258-2146
  Kalkaska *(G-9412)*

FURNITURE STORES: Office

Garants Office Sups & Prtg Inc .... G 989 356-3930
  Alpena *(G-296)*
Great Lakes Woodworking Co Inc ...... E 313 892-8500
  Detroit *(G-4277)*
W B Mason Co Inc .... E 734 947-6370
  Taylor *(G-16488)*
Yti Office Express LLC .... G 866 996-8952
  Troy *(G-17458)*

FURNITURE UPHOLSTERY REPAIR SVCS

Banta Furniture Company .... F 616 575-8180
  Grand Rapids *(G-6494)*
Custom Interiors of Toledo .... G 419 865-3090
  Ottawa Lake *(G-12805)*
Jacquart Fabric Products Inc .... C 906 932-1339
  Ironwood *(G-8765)*

FURNITURE WHOLESALERS

Alticor Global Holdings Inc .... F 616 787-1000
  Ada *(G-5)*
Alticor Inc .... A 616 787-1000
  Ada *(G-6)*
Casual Ptio Furn Rfnishing Inc .... G 586 254-1900
  Canton *(G-2446)*
Richwood Industries Inc .... E 616 243-2700
  Grand Rapids *(G-7154)*
West Mich Off Interiors Inc .... G 269 344-0768
  Kalamazoo *(G-9367)*

FURNITURE, HOUSEHOLD: Wholesalers

Homestead Elements LLC .... G 248 560-7122
  Saginaw *(G-14668)*
Kurtis Mfg & Distrg Corp .... E 734 522-7600
  Livonia *(G-10270)*

FURNITURE, MATTRESSES: Wholesalers

Mattress Wholesale .... G 248 968-2200
  Oak Park *(G-12626)*

FURNITURE, OFFICE: Wholesalers

Electra-Tec Inc .... G 269 694-6652
  Otsego *(G-12785)*
Maleports Sault Prtg Co Inc .... E 906 632-3369
  Sault Sainte Marie *(G-15095)*
Office Connection Inc .... E 248 871-2003
  Farmington Hills *(G-5339)*

FURNITURE, WHOLESALE: Dressers

My Dream Dress Brdal Salon LLC .... G 248 327-6049
  Southfield *(G-15663)*

FURNITURE, WHOLESALE: Racks

Repair Industries Michigan Inc .... C 313 365-5300
  Detroit *(G-4568)*

Employee Codes: A=Over 500 employees, B=251-500
C=101-250, D=51-100, E=20-50, F=10-19, G=3-9

FURNITURE, WHOLESALE: Theater Seats

Telescopic Seating Systems LLC .... F 855 713-0118
 Grand Haven *(G-6370)*

FURNITURE: Altars & Pulpits

Bracy & Associates Ltd .... G 616 298-8120
 Holland *(G-7980)*

FURNITURE: Assembly Hall

Subassembly Plus Inc .... E 616 395-2075
 Holland *(G-8207)*

FURNITURE: Bedroom, Wood

Rooms of Grand Rapids LLC .... G 616 260-1452
 Spring Lake *(G-15847)*

FURNITURE: Benches, Office, Exc Wood

Kessebohmer Ergonomie Amer Inc ...... G 616 202-1239
 Grand Rapids *(G-6894)*

FURNITURE: Bookcases, Office, Wood

T F Boyer Industries Inc .... G 248 674-8420
 Waterford *(G-18169)*

FURNITURE: Box Springs, Assembled

Leggett & Platt Incorporated .... G 417 358-8131
 Detroit *(G-4387)*

FURNITURE: Camp, Wood

G&J Products & Services .... G 734 522-2984
 Westland *(G-18373)*

FURNITURE: Chairs, Bentwood

Picwood USA LLC .... G 844 802-1599
 Kalamazoo *(G-9295)*

FURNITURE: Chairs, Household Upholstered

La-Z-Boy Global Limited .... G 734 241-2438
 Monroe *(G-11556)*
La-Z-Boy Incorporated .... A 734 242-1444
 Monroe *(G-11557)*

FURNITURE: Chairs, Household, Metal

MTS Burgess LLC .... D 734 847-2937
 Temperance *(G-16542)*

FURNITURE: Chairs, Office Exc Wood

Jsj Corporation .... E 616 842-6350
 Grand Haven *(G-6324)*

FURNITURE: Church

Kingdom Building Merchandise .... G 313 334-3866
 Detroit *(G-4363)*

FURNITURE: Console Tables, Wood

Dorel Home Furnishings Inc .... C 269 782-8661
 Dowagiac *(G-4781)*

FURNITURE: Cut Stone

A E G M Inc .... G 313 304-5279
 Dearborn *(G-3804)*

FURNITURE: Desks & Tables, Office, Exc Wood

Autoexec Inc 616 971-0080
 Grand Rapids *(G-6484)*

FURNITURE: Desks, Wood

Cornerstone Furniture Inc .... G 269 795-3379
 Hastings *(G-7784)*

FURNITURE: Dining Room, Wood

Context Furniture L L C .... G 248 200-0724
 Ferndale *(G-5535)*
Kindel Furniture Company LLC ...... C 616 243-3676
 Grand Rapids *(G-6896)*

FURNITURE: Dressers, Household, Wood

Anderson Manufacturing Co Inc .... F 906 863-8223
 Menominee *(G-11226)*

FURNITURE: Fiberglass & Plastic

D & R Fabrication Inc .... D 616 794-1130
 Belding *(G-1444)*
Innovative Pdts Unlimited Inc .... E 269 684-5050
 Niles *(G-12138)*
New Line Inc 586 228-4820
 Shelby Township *(G-15289)*

FURNITURE: Foundations & Platforms

Helping Hearts Helping Hands .... G 248 980-5090
 Constantine *(G-3667)*

FURNITURE: Hotel

Custom Components Corporation ...... F 616 523-1111
 Ionia *(G-8688)*

FURNITURE: Household, Metal

Crazy Metals LLC .... G 810 730-9489
 Grand Blanc *(G-6239)*
CTS Welding .... G 269 521-4481
 Bloomingdale *(G-1876)*
M C M Fixture Company Inc .... F 248 547-9280
 Hazel Park *(G-7830)*
Martin and Hattie Rasche Inc .... D 616 245-1223
 Grand Rapids *(G-6962)*
Premium Machine & Tool Inc .... F 989 855-3326
 Lyons *(G-10565)*
Spec International Inc .... F 616 248-3022
 Grand Rapids *(G-7211)*

FURNITURE: Household, NEC

Allstate HM Leisure String Hts .... G 734 838-6500
 Sterling Heights *(G-15928)*
Vita Talalay .... G 425 214-4732
 Grandville *(G-7423)*

FURNITURE: Household, Wood

A K Services Inc .... G 313 972-1010
 Detroit *(G-3972)*
A Lasting Impression Inc .... G 616 847-2380
 Spring Lake *(G-15800)*
Alo LLC 313 318-9029
 Detroit *(G-4004)*
Center of World Woodshop Inc .... G 269 469-5687
 Three Oaks *(G-16555)*
Charles Phipps and Sons Ltd .... F 810 359-7141
 Lexington *(G-10027)*
Charlotte Cabinets Inc 517 543-1522
 Charlotte *(G-2742)*
Compass Interiors LLC .... F 231 348-5353
 Petoskey *(G-12994)*
Craftwood Industries Inc .... E 616 796-1209
 Holland *(G-8006)*
Custom Interiors of Toledo .... G 419 865-3090
 Ottawa Lake *(G-12805)*
Ejw Contract Inc .... G 616 293-5181
 Whitmore Lake *(G-18531)*
European Cabinet Mfg Co 586 445-8909
 Roseville *(G-14406)*
Fwi Inc .... E 231 798-8324
 Norton Shores *(G-12294)*
Genesis Seating Inc .... D 616 954-1040
 Grand Rapids *(G-6739)*
Grand Rapids Carvers Inc .... E 616 538-0022
 Grand Rapids *(G-6754)*
Grand Rapids Chair Company .... C 616 774-0561
 Byron Center *(G-2275)*
H L F Furniture Incorporated .... E 734 697-3000
 Van Buren Twp *(G-17528)*
Hearthwoods Ltd Inc .... G 269 469-5551
 Lakeside *(G-9639)*
Hekman Furniture Company .... E 616 748-2660
 Zeeland *(G-19034)*
Industrial Woodworking Corp .... E 616 741-9663
 Zeeland *(G-19045)*
Jack-Post Corporation .... E 269 695-7000
 Buchanan *(G-2197)*
Janice Morse Inc .... F 248 624-7300
 West Bloomfield *(G-18293)*
Kaliniak Design LLC .... G 616 675-3850
 Kent City *(G-9434)*
Kent Upholstery Inc .... G 248 332-7260
 Pontiac *(G-13392)*
Kentwood Manufacturing Co .... E 616 698-6370
 Byron Center *(G-2279)*
La-Z-Boy Casegoods Inc .... E 734 242-1444
 Monroe *(G-11555)*
La-Z-Boy Incorporated .... A 734 242-1444
 Monroe *(G-11557)*
M C M Fixture Company Inc .... F 248 547-9280
 Hazel Park *(G-7830)*
Meeders Dim & Lbr Pdts Co .... G 231 587-8611
 Mancelona *(G-10874)*
Merdel Game Manufacturing Co ..... G 231 845-1263
 Ludington *(G-10544)*
Mien Company Inc .... F 616 818-1970
 Grand Rapids *(G-7008)*
Millennm-The Inside Sltion Inc .... F 248 645-9005
 Farmington Hills *(G-5323)*
Nicholas E Kappel .... G 810 404-9486
 Sandusky *(G-15064)*
Nu-Tran LLC 616 350-9575
 Wyoming *(G-18897)*
Nuvar Inc .... E 616 394-5779
 Holland *(G-8157)*
Perspectives Custom Cabinetry .... E 248 288-4100
 Troy *(G-17298)*
Prime Wood Products Inc .... G 616 399-4700
 Holland *(G-8170)*
R-Bo Co Inc .... F 616 748-9733
 Zeeland *(G-19076)*
Rgm New Ventures Inc .... G 248 624-5050
 Wixom *(G-18742)*
Serendipity Woods .... G 269 217-8197
 Kalamazoo *(G-9331)*
Shelfgenie Southeastern Mich .... G 248 805-1834
 Rochester *(G-13929)*
Shields Classic Toys .... G 888 806-2632
 Saline *(G-15039)*
Shop Makarios LLC .... F 800 479-0032
 Byron Center *(G-2295)*
Stow Company .... C 616 399-3311
 Holland *(G-8205)*
Van Zee Acquisitions Inc .... F 616 855-7000
 Grand Rapids *(G-7305)*
White Pine Furniture LLC .... G 269 366-4469
 Kalamazoo *(G-9368)*
Woodard—Cm LLC .... C 989 725-4265
 Owosso *(G-12869)*
Woodcraft Customs LLC .... G 248 987-4473
 Farmington Hills *(G-5415)*
Woodcrafters .... G 517 741-7423
 Sherwood *(G-15387)*
Woodland Creek Furniture Inc .... G 231 258-2146
 Kalkaska *(G-9412)*
Woodways Inc .... G 616 956-3070
 Zeeland *(G-19093)*
Woodways Industries LLC .... E 616 956-3070
 Grand Rapids *(G-7350)*

FURNITURE: Hydraulic Barber & Beauty Shop Chairs

Global Manufacturing Inds .... G 513 271-2180
 Hastings *(G-7794)*
Young Manufacturing Inc .... G 906 483-3851
 Dollar Bay *(G-4766)*

FURNITURE: Institutional, Exc Wood

Alr Products Inc .... F 517 649-2243
 Mulliken *(G-11748)*
Bridgewater Interiors LLC .... C 313 842-3300
 Detroit *(G-4070)*
Brill Company Inc .... E 231 843-2430
 Ludington *(G-10528)*
Counterpoint By Hlf .... G 734 699-7100
 Van Buren Twp *(G-17521)*
Craftwood Industries Inc .... E 616 796-1209
 Holland *(G-8006)*
Four Lkes Spcial Asssment Dst ...... G 989 941-3005
 Midland *(G-11365)*
Furniture Partners LLC .... G 616 355-3051
 Holland *(G-8044)*
Grand Rapids Carvers Inc .... E 616 538-0022
 Grand Rapids *(G-6754)*
ITW Dahti Seating .... E 616 866-1323
 Rockford *(G-14172)*
Johnson Controls Inc .... G 734 254-5000
 Plymouth *(G-13204)*
Knoedler Manufacturers Inc .... F 269 969-7722
 Battle Creek *(G-1264)*

PRODUCT SECTION

Lear Corporation .... G 248 447-1500
   Mason *(G-11141)*
Milcare Inc .... B 616 654-8000
   Zeeland *(G-19055)*
Millerknoll Inc .... A 616 654-3000
   Zeeland *(G-19056)*
Multiform Studios LLC .... G 248 437-5964
   South Lyon *(G-15447)*
R T London Company .... D 616 364-4800
   Grand Rapids *(G-7135)*
Telescopic Seating Systems LLC .... F 855 713-0118
   Grand Haven *(G-6370)*
TMC Furniture Inc .... G 734 622-0080
   Ann Arbor *(G-694)*
Woodard—Cm LLC .... C 989 725-4265
   Owosso *(G-12869)*

FURNITURE: Kitchen & Dining Room

Contract Furn Solutions Inc .... E 734 941-2750
   Brownstown *(G-2144)*

FURNITURE: Laboratory

Counter Reaction LLC .... G 248 624-7900
   Wixom *(G-18636)*
Impert Industries Inc .... G 269 694-2727
   Otsego *(G-12788)*
Metal Arc Inc .... E 231 865-3111
   Muskegon *(G-11868)*
Security Steelcraft Corp .... F 231 733-1101
   Muskegon *(G-11917)*

FURNITURE: Lawn & Garden, Metal

Flanders Industries Inc .... C 906 863-4491
   Menominee *(G-11238)*
Jack-Post Corporation .... E 269 695-7000
   Buchanan *(G-2197)*

FURNITURE: Lawn, Wood

Lapointe Cedar Products Inc .... G 906 753-4072
   Ingalls *(G-8658)*

FURNITURE: Library

Everest Expedition LLC .... D 616 392-1848
   Holland *(G-8032)*
Worden Group LLC .... D 616 392-1848
   Holland *(G-8252)*

FURNITURE: Mattresses & Foundations

Artisans Cstm Mmory Mattresses ...... F 989 793-3208
   Saginaw *(G-14605)*
Indratech LLC .... G 502 381-5798
   West Bloomfield *(G-18291)*
Indratech LLC .... E 248 377-1877
   Troy *(G-17165)*
Marrs Discount Furniture .... G 989 720-5436
   Owosso *(G-12840)*

FURNITURE: Mattresses, Box & Bedsprings

Leggett Platt Components Inc .... D 616 784-7000
   Sparta *(G-15771)*
Mattress Wholesale .... G 248 968-2200
   Oak Park *(G-12626)*
Midwest Quality Bedding Inc .... G 614 504-5971
   Waterford *(G-18138)*

FURNITURE: Mattresses, Innerspring Or Box Spring

Capitol Bedding Co Inc .... F 615 370-7000
   Lansing *(G-9677)*
Clare Bedding Mfg Co .... E 906 789-9902
   Escanaba *(G-5065)*
Comfort Mattress Co .... D 586 293-4000
   Roseville *(G-14287)*
Jonathan Stevens Mattress Co .... G 616 243-4342
   Grand Rapids *(G-6873)*

FURNITURE: NEC

At Home .... G 313 769-4200
   Dearborn *(G-3811)*
Discount Restaurant & Supply .... G 574 370-9574
   Wyoming *(G-18869)*
Karps Kitchens & Baths Inc .... G 989 732-7676
   Gaylord *(G-6137)*

FURNITURE: Office Panel Systems, Exc Wood

Total Innovative Mfg LLC .... F 616 399-9903
   Holland *(G-8222)*
Trendway Corporation .... B 616 399-3900
   Holland *(G-8226)*
West Mich Off Interiors Inc .... G 269 344-0768
   Kalamazoo *(G-9367)*

FURNITURE: Office Panel Systems, Wood

Trendway Corporation .... B 616 399-3900
   Holland *(G-8226)*
West Mich Off Interiors Inc .... G 269 344-0768
   Kalamazoo *(G-9367)*

FURNITURE: Office, Exc Wood

Agritek Industries Inc .... D 616 786-9200
   Holland *(G-7958)*
American Seating Company .... B 616 732-6561
   Grand Rapids *(G-6454)*
American Seating Company .... F 616 732-6600
   Grand Rapids *(G-6455)*
Amneon Acquisitions LLC .... F 616 895-6640
   Holland *(G-7965)*
Anso Products .... G 248 357-2300
   Southfield *(G-15489)*
Avantis Inc .... G 616 285-8000
   Grand Rapids *(G-6486)*
Bostontec Inc .... G 989 496-9510
   Midland *(G-11324)*
Contract Source & Assembly Inc .... F 616 897-2186
   Grand Rapids *(G-6599)*
Counterpoint By Hlf .... G 734 699-7100
   Van Buren Twp *(G-17521)*
Craftwood Industries Inc .... E 616 796-1209
   Holland *(G-8006)*
Custom Components Corporation ...... F 616 523-1111
   Ionia *(G-8688)*
Electra-Tec Inc .... G 269 694-6652
   Otsego *(G-12785)*
Haskell Office .... G 616 988-0880
   Wyoming *(G-18881)*
Haworth Inc .... A 616 393-3000
   Holland *(G-8067)*
Haworth Hong Kong LLC .... G 616 393-3484
   Gladstone *(G-6181)*
Haworth International Ltd .... A 616 393-3000
   Holland *(G-8068)*
Interior Concepts Corporation .... E 616 842-5550
   Spring Lake *(G-15827)*
Jem Computers Inc .... F 586 783-3400
   Clinton Township *(G-3264)*
Metal Arc Inc .... E 231 865-3111
   Muskegon *(G-11868)*
Metal Components LLC .... D 616 252-1900
   Grand Rapids *(G-6978)*
Millerknoll Inc .... A 616 654-3000
   Zeeland *(G-19056)*
Mobile Office Vehicle Inc .... G 616 971-0080
   Grand Rapids *(G-7016)*
Mooreco Inc .... E 616 451-7800
   Grand Rapids *(G-7028)*
Office Design & Furn LLC .... G 734 217-2717
   Jackson *(G-8979)*
Office Station Enterprises Inc .... F 616 633-3339
   Grandville *(G-7406)*
Premium Machine & Tool Inc .... F 989 855-3326
   Lyons *(G-10565)*
Srg Global Coatings LLC .... C 248 509-1100
   Troy *(G-17369)*
Steelcase Inc .... A 616 247-2710
   Grand Rapids *(G-7224)*
Systems Design & Installation .... G 269 543-4204
   Fennville *(G-5442)*
Trendway Svcs Organization LLC ..... F 616 994-5327
   Holland *(G-8227)*
Tvb Inc .... G 616 456-9629
   Grand Rapids *(G-7283)*
Ventura Manufacturing Inc .... F 616 772-7405
   Zeeland *(G-19088)*

FURNITURE: Office, Wood

Bold Companies Inc .... D 231 773-8026
   Muskegon *(G-11782)*
Bourne Industries Inc .... E 989 743-3461
   Corunna *(G-3705)*
Counterpoint By Hlf .... G 734 699-7100
   Van Buren Twp *(G-17521)*

FURNITURE: Play Pens, Children's, Wood

Craftwood Industries Inc .... E 616 796-1209
   Holland *(G-8006)*
Custom Components Corporation ...... F 616 523-1111
   Ionia *(G-8688)*
Custom Crafters .... G 269 763-9180
   Bellevue *(G-1497)*
D & M Cabinet Shop Inc .... G 989 479-9271
   Ruth *(G-14597)*
Dynamic Wood Products Inc .... G 616 897-8114
   Saranac *(G-15077)*
Fwi Inc .... E 231 798-8324
   Norton Shores *(G-12294)*
Genesis Seating Inc .... E 616 954-1040
   Grand Rapids *(G-6739)*
Grand Rapids Carvers Inc .... E 616 538-0022
   Grand Rapids *(G-6754)*
Grand Valley Wood Products Inc .... E 616 475-5890
   Grand Rapids *(G-6779)*
Great Lakes Woodworking Co Inc ..... E 313 892-8500
   Detroit *(G-4277)*
Haworth Inc .... A 616 393-3000
   Holland *(G-8067)*
Haworth Hong Kong LLC .... G 616 393-3484
   Gladstone *(G-6181)*
Haworth International Ltd .... A 616 393-3000
   Holland *(G-8068)*
Holland Stitchcraft Inc .... E 616 399-3868
   Holland *(G-8085)*
Howe US Inc .... D 616 419-2226
   Grand Rapids *(G-6821)*
Interior Concepts Corporation .... E 616 842-5550
   Spring Lake *(G-15827)*
Jsj Corporation .... C 616 847-7000
   Spring Lake *(G-15828)*
Michigan Tube Swgers Fbrctors .... B 734 847-3875
   Temperance *(G-16541)*
Millerknoll Inc .... A 616 654-3000
   Zeeland *(G-19056)*
Millerknoll Inc .... G 616 949-3660
   Grand Rapids *(G-7012)*
Mooreco Inc .... E 616 451-7800
   Grand Rapids *(G-7028)*
Nucraft Furniture Company .... C 616 784-6016
   Comstock Park *(G-3630)*
Paladin Ind Inc .... E 616 698-7495
   Grand Rapids *(G-7068)*
Primeway Inc .... F 248 583-6922
   Royal Oak *(G-14569)*
R T London Company .... D 616 364-4800
   Grand Rapids *(G-7135)*
Rose Corporation .... E 734 426-0005
   Dexter *(G-4753)*
S & J Inc .... G 248 299-0822
   Rochester Hills *(G-14104)*
S F Gilmore Inc .... C 616 475-5100
   Grand Rapids *(G-7175)*
Silver Street Incorporated .... E 231 861-2194
   Shelby *(G-15160)*
Steelcase Inc .... A 616 247-2710
   Grand Rapids *(G-7224)*
Tranquil Systems Intl LLC .... F 800 631-0212
   Clare *(G-3000)*
West Shore Services Inc .... E 616 895-4347
   Allendale *(G-229)*
Woodard—Cm LLC .... C 989 725-4265
   Owosso *(G-12869)*
Woodways Inc .... G 616 956-3070
   Zeeland *(G-19093)*

FURNITURE: Outdoor, Wood

Great Lakes Wood Products .... G 906 228-3737
   Negaunee *(G-11967)*
Lakeland Mills Inc .... E 989 427-5133
   Edmore *(G-4993)*

FURNITURE: Pews, Church

Kawkawlin Manufacturing Co .... G 989 684-5470
   Midland *(G-11381)*

FURNITURE: Picnic Tables Or Benches, Park

Joes Tables LLC .... G 989 846-4970
   Standish *(G-15889)*
Recycletech Products Inc .... F 517 649-2243
   Mulliken *(G-11750)*

FURNITURE: Play Pens, Children's, Wood

Backyard Play Systems LLC .... G 734 242-6900
   Monroe *(G-11525)*

Employee Codes: A=Over 500 employees, B=251-500
C=101-250, D=51-100, E=20-50, F=10-19, G=3-9

FURNITURE: Play Pens, Children's, Wood

Backyard Products LLC .... G 734 242-6900
  Monroe (G-11526)
Source Capital Backyard LLC .... F 734 242-6900
  Monroe (G-11573)

FURNITURE: Restaurant

Billco Acquisition LLC .... E 616 928-0637
  Holland (G-7976)
Brill Company Inc .... E 231 843-2430
  Ludington (G-10528)
CTS Welding .... G 269 521-4481
  Bloomingdale (G-1876)
Harborfront Interiors Inc .... G 231 777-3838
  Muskegon (G-11835)
La Rosa Refrigeration & Eqp Co .... E 313 368-6620
  Detroit (G-4371)

FURNITURE: School

Bourne Industries Inc .... E 989 743-3461
  Corunna (G-3705)
Greene Manufacturing Inc .... E 734 428-8304
  Chelsea (G-2813)
Irwin Seating Holding Company .... B 616 574-7400
  Grand Rapids (G-6854)
TMC Furniture Inc .... G 734 622-0080
  Kentwood (G-9482)

FURNITURE: Stands & Chests, Exc Bedside Stands, Wood

Sawdust Bin Inc .... F 906 932-5518
  Ironwood (G-8772)

FURNITURE: Storage Chests, Household, Wood

Backyard Services LLC .... G 734 242-6900
  Monroe (G-11527)
Best Self Storage .... G 810 227-7050
  Brighton (G-1951)

FURNITURE: Table Tops, Marble

Stonecrafters Inc .... F 517 529-4990
  Clarklake (G-3009)
TNT Marble and Stone Inc .... G 248 887-8237
  Hartland (G-7772)

FURNITURE: Tables & Table Tops, Wood

Audia Woodworking & Fine Furn .... F 586 296-6330
  Clinton Township (G-3174)

FURNITURE: Unfinished, Wood

Deweys Lumberville Inc .... G 313 885-0960
  Grosse Pointe (G-7530)

FURNITURE: Upholstered

Debbink and Sons Inc .... G 231 845-6421
  Ludington (G-10533)
Eid Real Estates LLC .... G 717 471-5996
  Rochester Hills (G-14001)
Homespun Furniture Inc .... F 734 284-6277
  Riverview (G-13874)
Kent Upholstery Inc .... G 248 332-7260
  Pontiac (G-13392)
Lzb Manufacturing Inc .... G 734 242-1444
  Monroe (G-11559)
Sherwood Studios Inc .... G 248 855-1600
  West Bloomfield (G-18312)

FURNITURE: Vehicle

American Seating Company .... B 616 732-6561
  Grand Rapids (G-6454)
Lanzen Incorporated .... G 586 771-7070
  Bruce Twp (G-2174)
Milsco LLC .... E 517 787-3650
  Jackson (G-8965)

FURRIERS

Wolvering Fur .... G 313 961-0520
  Detroit (G-4689)

FUSES: Electric

PEC of America Corporation .... F 248 675-3130
  Novi (G-12504)

Furs

Fur Brained Ideas .... G 248 830-0764
  Grosse Pointe Woods (G-7567)

GAMES & TOYS: Bingo Boards

Meteor Web Marketing Inc .... F 734 822-4999
  Ann Arbor (G-570)

GAMES & TOYS: Board Games, Children's & Adults'

Sly Fox Prints LLC .... G 616 900-9677
  Cedar Springs (G-2661)

GAMES & TOYS: Craft & Hobby Kits & Sets

American Plastic Toys Inc .... C 248 624-4881
  Walled Lake (G-17663)
Designs By D LLC .... G 313 629-3617
  Highland Park (G-7903)
Lejanae Designs LLC .... G 248 621-3677
  Southfield (G-15634)
Mac Enterprises Inc .... F 313 846-4567
  Manchester (G-10885)
Melissa Fowler .... G 818 447-9903
  Fenton (G-5491)
Tdw Custom Apparel & More LLC .... G 248 934-0312
  Detroit (G-4626)

GAMES & TOYS: Dolls, Exc Stuffed Toy Animals

Marshal E Hyman and Associates ...... G 248 643-0642
  Troy (G-17239)

GAMES & TOYS: Game Machines, Exc Coin-Operated

Hampton Company Inc .... G 517 765-2222
  Burlington (G-2209)

GAMES & TOYS: Kits, Science, Incl Microscopes/Chemistry Sets

Eca Educational Services Inc .... D 248 669-7170
  Commerce Township (G-3525)

GAMES & TOYS: Puzzles

Puzzle Escape .... G 313 645-6405
  Detroit (G-4543)
Troy Puzzles LLC .... G 248 828-3153
  Troy (G-17401)

GAMES & TOYS: Trains & Eqpt, Electric & Mechanical

American Models .... G 248 437-6800
  Whitmore Lake (G-18519)

GAMES & TOYS: Tricycles

National Ambucs Inc .... G 231 798-4244
  Norton Shores (G-12315)

GARBAGE DISPOSERS & COMPACTORS: Commercial

Garbage Man LLC .... G 810 225-3001
  Brighton (G-1996)
MRM Ida Products Co Inc .... G 313 834-0200
  Detroit (G-4470)
Sebright Products Inc .... E 269 793-7183
  Hopkins (G-8369)
Shred-Pac Inc .... E 269 793-7978
  Hopkins (G-8370)

GAS & HYDROCARBON LIQUEFACTION FROM COAL

Refinery Corporation America .... G 877 881-0300
  Harper Woods (G-7671)

GAS & OIL FIELD EXPLORATION SVCS

American Wireline Services Inc .... G 231 218-6849
  Traverse City (G-16601)
Apollo Exploration Dev Inc .... G 989 773-2854
  Mount Pleasant (G-11680)

PRODUCT SECTION

Arbor Operating LLC .... G 231 941-2237
  Traverse City (G-16602)
Baygeo Inc .... E 231 941-7660
  Traverse City (G-16617)
Bobcat Oil & Gas Inc .... G 989 426-4375
  Gladwin (G-6190)
Capital Assets Resources LLC .... G 248 252-7854
  Southfield (G-15516)
Core Energy LLC .... G 231 946-2419
  Traverse City (G-16661)
Dart Energy Corporation .... F 231 885-1665
  Mesick (G-11271)
Dcr Services & Cnstr Inc .... G 313 297-6544
  Detroit (G-4123)
Don Yohe Enterprises Inc .... F 586 784-5556
  Armada (G-733)
DTE Gas & Oil Company .... G 231 995-4000
  Traverse City (G-16672)
Dynamic Development Inc .... G 231 723-8318
  Manistee (G-10897)
Eagle Exploration Inc .... G 231 252-4624
  Grawn (G-7450)
Energy Acquisition Corp .... F 517 339-0249
  Holt (G-8310)
Energy Exploration .... G 248 579-6531
  Novi (G-12413)
Express Care of South Lyon .... G 248 437-6919
  South Lyon (G-15436)
Horizontal Lift Technologies .... G 231 421-9696
  Traverse City (G-16715)
Howard Energy Co Inc .... E 231 995-7850
  Traverse City (G-16716)
HRF Exploration & Prod LLC .... E 989 732-6950
  Gaylord (G-6134)
John T Stoliker Enterprises .... G 586 727-1402
  Columbus (G-3499)
Lgc Global Energy Fm Llc .... G 313 989-4141
  Detroit (G-4396)
Linn Energy .... F 989 786-7592
  Lewiston (G-10024)
Loneys Welding & Excvtg Inc .... G 231 328-4408
  Merritt (G-11267)
Maness Petroleum Corp .... G 989 773-5475
  Mount Pleasant (G-11709)
Martec Land Services Inc .... G 231 929-3971
  Traverse City (G-16754)
Maverick Exploration Prod Inc .... G 231 929-3923
  Traverse City (G-16755)
Meridian Energy Corporation .... E 517 339-8444
  Haslett (G-7775)
Miller Energy Inc .... F 269 352-5960
  Kalamazoo (G-9272)
Miracle Petroleum LLC .... G 231 946-8090
  Traverse City (G-16760)
OIL Energy Corp .... F 231 933-3600
  Traverse City (G-16777)
Peninslar Oil Gas Cmpny-Mchgan ...... G 616 676-2090
  Grand Rapids (G-7075)
Pinnacle Energy LLC .... G 248 623-6091
  Clarkston (G-3056)
Ranch Production LLC .... F 231 869-2050
  Pentwater (G-12973)
Savoy Exploration Inc .... G 231 941-9552
  Traverse City (G-16824)
Schmude Oil Inc .... G 231 947-4410
  Traverse City (G-16826)
Sturak Brothers Inc .... G 269 345-2929
  Kalamazoo (G-9344)
Summit Petroleum Company LLC ...... F 231 942-8134
  Traverse City (G-16845)
Tri County Oil & Gas Co Inc .... G 248 390-0682
  Shelby Township (G-15356)
Wara Construction Company LLC .... D 248 299-2410
  Rochester Hills (G-14141)
Ward-Williston Company .... D 248 594-6622
  Bloomfield (G-1786)
Western Land Services Inc .... D 231 843-8878
  Ludington (G-10557)
Wolverine Gas and Oil Corp .... E 616 458-1150
  Grand Rapids (G-7346)

GAS & OIL FIELD SVCS, NEC

Baker Hghes Olfld Oprtions LLC .... G 231 342-9408
  Traverse City (G-16611)
Dynamic Exploration Inc .... G 231 723-7879
  Manistee (G-10898)
F & M Gas .... G 313 292-2519
  Taylor (G-16415)
Fisher McCall Oil Gas .... G 616 318-9155
  Grosse Pointe Farms (G-7535)

PRODUCT SECTION

GENERAL MERCHANDISE, NONDURABLE, WHOLESALE

Layline Oil and Gas LLC................................F....... 231 743-2452
   Marion *(G-10972)*
Steiner Associates...G....... 734 422-5188
   Livonia *(G-10421)*
Union Oil Co..G....... 989 348-8459
   Grayling *(G-7470)*
Wentzel Energy Partners LLC.......................G....... 817 713-3283
   Madison Heights *(G-10861)*

GASES & LIQUIFIED PETROLEUM GASES

Amrican Petro Inc..G....... 313 520-8404
   Detroit *(G-4017)*

GASES: Acetylene

Greenville Trck Wldg Sups LLC....................F....... 616 754-6120
   Greenville *(G-7489)*

GASES: Carbon Dioxide

Linde Gas & Equipment Inc...........................G....... 734 282-3830
   Wyandotte *(G-18829)*

GASES: Helium

Helium Home Base LLC..................................G....... 734 895-3608
   Westland *(G-18380)*
Helium Studio...G....... 734 725-3811
   Wayne *(G-18223)*

GASES: Indl

Canton Renewables LLC................................G....... 248 380-3920
   Novi *(G-12379)*
Fremont Community Digester LLC..............F....... 248 735-6684
   Novi *(G-12418)*
Linde Inc..E....... 269 317-7225
   Hudsonville *(G-8590)*
Matheson...G....... 586 498-8315
   Roseville *(G-14437)*
South Park Welding Sups LLC......................F....... 810 364-6521
   Marysville *(G-11103)*
Summit Industrial Services LLC..................E....... 248 762-0982
   Auburn Hills *(G-1041)*

GASES: Neon

Great Lakes Neon..G....... 517 582-7451
   Grand Ledge *(G-6392)*
Neon Roehler Services LLC..........................G....... 248 895-8705
   Lake Orion *(G-9621)*

GASES: Oxygen

Airserve LLC..G....... 586 427-5349
   Center Line *(G-2677)*
Linde Gas & Equipment Inc...........................G....... 630 857-6460
   Southfield *(G-15636)*

GASKET MATERIALS

Upper Peninsula Rubber Co LLC.................G....... 906 786-0460
   Escanaba *(G-5104)*

GASKETS

Basic Rubber and Plastics Co......................E....... 248 360-7400
   Walled Lake *(G-17664)*
Champion Gasket & Rubber Inc..................E....... 248 624-6140
   Commerce Township *(G-3518)*
Derby Fabg Solutions LLC............................D....... 616 866-1650
   Rockford *(G-14164)*
Lamons..G....... 989 488-4580
   Midland *(G-11383)*
Tts Oldco LLC..E....... 810 655-3900
   Fenton *(G-5511)*
Unique Fabricating Inc..................................A....... 248 853-2333
   Auburn Hills *(G-1068)*
Unique Fabricating Na Inc............................B....... 248 853-2333
   Auburn Hills *(G-1069)*
Unique Fabricating Na Inc............................G....... 517 524-9010
   Concord *(G-3656)*
Unique Fabricating Na Inc............................G....... 248 853-2333
   Rochester Hills *(G-14136)*

GASKETS & SEALING DEVICES

Action Fabricators Inc...................................C....... 616 957-2032
   Grand Rapids *(G-6423)*
Copeland-Gibson Products Corp.................E....... 248 740-4400
   Troy *(G-17028)*
Federal-Mogul Piston Rings Inc..................F....... 248 354-7700
   Southfield *(G-15564)*
FM International LLC......................................G....... 248 354-7700
   Southfield *(G-15570)*
Grm Corporation..G....... 989 453-2322
   Pigeon *(G-13038)*
Kaydon Corporation..B....... 734 747-7025
   Ann Arbor *(G-538)*
Kent Manufacturing Company......................D....... 616 454-9495
   Grand Rapids *(G-6889)*
L & L Products Inc...B....... 586 336-1600
   Bruce Twp *(G-2171)*
L & L Products Inc...E....... 586 336-1600
   Bruce Twp *(G-2173)*
Martin Fluid Power Company......................F....... 248 585-8170
   Madison Heights *(G-10776)*
Memtech Inc...F....... 734 455-8550
   Plymouth *(G-13240)*
N-K Sealing Technologies LLC....................G....... 616 248-3200
   Grand Rapids *(G-7035)*
Parker-Hannifin Corporation.........................G....... 330 253-5239
   Otsego *(G-12797)*
R & J Manufacturing Company.....................F....... 248 669-2460
   Commerce Township *(G-3568)*
Rhino Strapping Products Inc......................F....... 734 442-4040
   Taylor *(G-16467)*
Speyside Real Estate LLC............................F....... 248 354-7700
   Southfield *(G-15707)*
Zephyros Inc...G....... 586 336-1600
   Bruce Twp *(G-2188)*

GASOLINE FILLING STATIONS

Admiral...G....... 989 356-6419
   Alpena *(G-274)*
Blarney Castle Inc..G....... 231 864-3111
   Bear Lake *(G-1416)*
Gustafson Smoked Fish................................G....... 906 292-5424
   Moran *(G-11609)*
Treib Inc..F....... 989 752-4821
   Saginaw *(G-14778)*

GATES: Ornamental Metal

Scott Iron Works Inc......................................F....... 248 548-2822
   Hazel Park *(G-7841)*

GAUGE BLOCKS

Gage Numerical Inc..G....... 231 328-4426
   Lake City *(G-9546)*

GAUGES

Accell Technologies Inc................................G....... 248 360-3762
   Commerce Township *(G-3505)*
Advantage Design and Tool.........................G....... 586 801-7413
   Richmond *(G-13831)*
AG Davis Gage & Engrg Co.........................E....... 586 977-9000
   Sterling Heights *(G-15926)*
American Industrial Gauge Inc....................G....... 248 280-0048
   Royal Oak *(G-14507)*
Artcraft Pattern Works Inc...........................F....... 734 729-0022
   Westland *(G-18355)*
Benny Gage Inc...G....... 734 455-3080
   Wixom *(G-18620)*
Bilco Tool Corporation..................................G....... 586 574-9300
   Warren *(G-17737)*
Bower Tool & Manufacturing Inc................G....... 734 522-0444
   Livonia *(G-10141)*
Comau LLC...B....... 248 353-8888
   Southfield *(G-15530)*
Cross Paths Corp...G....... 616 248-5371
   Grand Rapids *(G-6613)*
Douglas Gage Inc...F....... 586 727-2089
   Richmond *(G-13836)*
Dura Thread Gage Inc...................................F....... 248 545-2890
   Madison Heights *(G-10714)*
Enmark Tool Company...................................E....... 586 293-2797
   Fraser *(G-5925)*
Fraser Tool & Gauge LLC............................G....... 313 882-9192
   Grosse Pointe Park *(G-7554)*
Gage Eagle Spline Inc...................................D....... 586 776-7240
   Warren *(G-17822)*
GAL Gage Co..F....... 269 465-5750
   Bridgman *(G-1926)*
H E Morse Co...D....... 616 396-4604
   Holland *(G-8065)*
Hanlo Gauges & Engineering Co................G....... 734 422-4224
   Livonia *(G-10235)*
Huron Tool & Gage Co Inc...........................G....... 313 381-1900
   Wixom *(G-18681)*
Invo Spline Inc...E....... 586 757-8840
   Warren *(G-17870)*
Kalamazoo Engrg & Mfg LLC.......................G....... 269 569-5205
   Kalamazoo *(G-9239)*
Keller Tool Ltd..F....... 734 425-4500
   Livonia *(G-10264)*
Leader Corporation...E....... 586 566-7114
   Shelby Township *(G-15260)*
Martel Tool Corporation................................F....... 313 278-2420
   Allen Park *(G-200)*
Master Jig Grinding & Gage Co..................G....... 248 380-8515
   Wixom *(G-18706)*
North-East Gage Inc......................................E....... 586 792-6790
   Clinton Township *(G-3309)*
O Keller Tool Engrg Co LLC.........................D....... 734 425-4500
   Livonia *(G-10349)*
Perry Tool Company Inc...............................G....... 734 283-7393
   Riverview *(G-13883)*
R & S Tool & Die Inc.....................................G....... 989 673-8511
   Caro *(G-2579)*
Reef Tool & Gage Co.....................................E....... 586 468-3000
   Clinton Township *(G-3333)*
Smeko Inc...E....... 586 254-5310
   Sterling Heights *(G-16180)*
Spartan Tool Sales Inc..................................E....... 586 268-1556
   Sterling Heights *(G-16183)*
Spence Industries Inc...................................G....... 586 758-3800
   Warren *(G-18019)*
Stanhope Tool Inc...E....... 248 585-5711
   Warren *(G-18027)*
Target Mold Corporation...............................F....... 231 798-3535
   Norton Shores *(G-12336)*
Trusted Tool Mfg Inc.....................................G....... 810 750-6000
   Fenton *(G-5510)*
Turbine Tool & Gage Inc...............................E....... 734 427-2270
   Livonia *(G-10451)*
Western Pegasus Inc.....................................G....... 616 393-9580
   Holland *(G-8248)*

GEARS

Avon Machining LLC.....................................D....... 586 884-2200
   Shelby Township *(G-15175)*
Avon Machining Holdings Inc.....................C....... 586 884-2200
   Shelby Township *(G-15176)*
Boos Products Inc...F....... 734 498-2207
   Gregory *(G-7513)*
Equitable Engineering Co Inc.....................E....... 248 689-9700
   Troy *(G-17096)*
Midwest Gear & Tool Inc.............................E....... 586 779-1300
   Roseville *(G-14442)*
Motion Systems Incorporated....................F....... 586 774-5666
   Warren *(G-17935)*
Superalloy North America LLC..................G....... 810 252-1552
   Bingham Farms *(G-1704)*

GEARS & GEAR UNITS: Reduction, Exc Auto

Geartec Inc..E....... 810 987-4700
   Port Huron *(G-13480)*

GEARS: Power Transmission, Exc Auto

American Gear & Engrg Co Inc..................E....... 734 595-6400
   Westland *(G-18353)*
Atlas Gear Company.....................................F....... 248 583-2964
   Madison Heights *(G-10675)*
Custom Gears Inc..G....... 616 243-2723
   Grand Rapids *(G-6620)*
Decker Gear Inc...F....... 810 388-1500
   Saint Clair *(G-14825)*
J G Kern Enterprises Inc............................D....... 586 531-9472
   Sterling Heights *(G-16052)*
Orlandi Gear Company Inc.........................E....... 586 285-9900
   Fraser *(G-5971)*
Porite USA Co Ltd..G....... 248 597-9988
   Troy *(G-17308)*
Truemner Enterprises Inc..........................G....... 586 756-6470
   Warren *(G-18044)*
Tts Oldco LLC..E....... 810 655-3900
   Fenton *(G-5511)*

GEMSTONE & INDL DIAMOND MINING SVCS

Ms International Holdings LLC.................G....... 443 210-1446
   Sterling Heights *(G-16105)*

GENERAL MERCHANDISE, NONDURABLE, WHOLESALE

AP Impressions Inc.......................................G....... 734 464-8009
   Livonia *(G-10121)*
Hemp Global Products Inc.........................G....... 616 617-6476
   Holland *(G-8069)*

GENERAL MERCHANDISE, NONDURABLE, WHOLESALE — PRODUCT SECTION

L & P LLC .... G 231 733-1415
  Muskegon (G-11854)
L & S Products LLC .... G 517 238-4645
  Coldwater (G-3442)
Travel Information Services .... F 989 275-8042
  Roscommon (G-14357)

GENERATION EQPT: Electronic

Actia Electronics Inc .... G 574 264-2373
  Romulus (G-14245)
Adam Electronics Incorporated .... E 248 583-2000
  Madison Heights (G-10659)
Jem Computers Inc .... F 586 783-3400
  Clinton Township (G-3264)
Questyme Usa Inc .... G 832 912-4994
  Farmington Hills (G-5360)
Xalt Energy LLC .... G 816 525-1153
  Midland (G-11427)

GENERATOR REPAIR SVCS

Ainsworth Electric Inc .... E 810 984-5768
  Port Huron (G-13433)

GENERATORS: Electric

Global Fleet Sales LLC .... G 248 327-6483
  Southfield (G-15576)
Jlm Elec .... G 989 486-3788
  Midland (G-11377)
Smart Power Systems Inc .... C 231 832-5525
  Reed City (G-13798)

GENERATORS: Ultrasonic

Ace Filtration Inc .... G 248 624-6300
  Commerce Township (G-3506)

GENERATORS: Vehicles, Gas-Electric Or Oil-Electric

Ev Anywhere LLC .... G 313 653-9870
  Detroit (G-4218)

GIFT SHOP

Country Home Creations Inc .... E 810 244-7348
  Flint (G-5674)
Gast Cabinet Co .... G 269 422-1587
  Baroda (G-1162)
Lighthouse Direct Buy LLC .... G 313 340-1850
  Detroit (G-4398)
Marshalls Trail Inc .... F 231 436-5082
  Mackinaw City (G-10568)
R H & Company Inc .... F 269 345-7814
  Kalamazoo (G-9313)
Sign of The Loon Gifts Inc .... G 231 436-5155
  Mackinaw City (G-10569)
Sobaks Pharmacy Inc .... F 989 725-2785
  Owosso (G-12856)

GIFT, NOVELTY & SOUVENIR STORES: Gift Baskets

Carlson Enterprises Inc .... G 248 656-1442
  Rochester Hills (G-13972)

GIFT, NOVELTY & SOUVENIR STORES: Gifts & Novelties

Daisy Chain Online .... G 330 259-6457
  West Bloomfield (G-18277)

GIFT, NOVELTY & SOUVENIR STORES: Party Favors

Gags and Games Inc .... E 734 591-1717
  Livonia (G-10218)

GIFTS & NOVELTIES: Wholesalers

Amway International Inc .... E 616 787-1000
  Ada (G-8)
Graphic Resource Group Inc .... E 248 588-6100
  Troy (G-17132)
Ideal Wholesale Inc .... G 989 873-5850
  Prescott (G-13651)
Lighthouse Direct Buy LLC .... G 313 340-1850
  Detroit (G-4398)
Nalcor LLC .... D 248 541-1140
  Ferndale (G-5570)

Novelty House .... G 248 583-9900
  Madison Heights (G-10790)

GIFTWARE: Copper

Lsr Incorporated .... F 734 455-6530
  Plymouth (G-13228)

GLASS FABRICATORS

A & B Display Systems Inc .... F 989 893-6642
  Bay City (G-1314)
Burco Inc .... E 616 453-7771
  Grand Rapids (G-6532)
Carlex Glass America LLC .... A 248 824-8800
  Troy (G-17000)
Case Island Glass LLC .... G 810 252-1704
  Flint (G-5665)
Duo-Gard Industries Inc .... D 734 207-9700
  Canton (G-2456)
Elegant Glassworks .... G 734 845-1901
  Saline (G-15015)
Fox Fire Glass LLC .... G 248 332-2442
  Fenton (G-5479)
Furniture City Glass Corp .... F 616 784-5500
  Grand Rapids (G-6728)
Glass Recyclers Ltd .... G 313 584-3434
  Dearborn (G-3846)
Guardian Fabrication LLC .... D 248 340-1800
  Auburn Hills (G-919)
Guardian Industries LLC .... B 734 654-4285
  Carleton (G-2555)
Inalfa Holding Inc .... F 248 371-3060
  Auburn Hills (G-934)
Keeler-Glasgow Company Inc .... F 269 621-2415
  Hartford (G-7764)
Kentwood Manufacturing Co .... E 616 698-6370
  Byron Center (G-2279)
Knight Tonya .... G 313 255-3434
  Southfield (G-15618)
Luxottica of America Inc .... G 989 624-8958
  Birch Run (G-1710)
Magna .... F 616 786-7403
  Holland (G-8133)
Magna Mirrors America Inc .... E 616 786-7000
  Grand Rapids (G-6956)
Oldcastle Buildingenvelope Inc .... G 616 896-8341
  Burnips (G-2210)
On The Side Sign Dsign Grphics .... G 810 266-7446
  Byron (G-2255)
Paragon Tempered Glass LLC .... G 269 684-5060
  Niles (G-12157)
Penstone Inc .... E 734 379-3160
  Rockwood (G-14203)
Polymer Process Dev LLC .... D 586 464-6400
  Shelby Township (G-15304)
SMR Atmtive Mrror Intl USA Inc .... G 810 364-4141
  Marysville (G-11100)
SMR Atmtive Tech Hldngs USA PR ..... D 810 364-4141
  Marysville (G-11101)
SMR Automotive Systems USA Inc ..... F 810 937-2456
  Port Huron (G-13529)
Solutia Inc .... G 734 676-4400
  Trenton (G-16892)
Stained Glass and Gifts .... G 810 736-6766
  Flint (G-5768)
Valley Glass Co Inc .... G 989 790-9342
  Saginaw (G-14786)

GLASS PRDTS, FROM PURCHASED GLASS: Art

Boyer Glassworks Inc .... G 231 526-6359
  Harbor Springs (G-7642)

GLASS PRDTS, FROM PURCHASED GLASS: Glass Beads, Reflecting

Beans Best LLC .... G 734 707-7378
  Ann Arbor (G-397)

GLASS PRDTS, FROM PURCHASED GLASS: Glassware

Grand River Interiors Inc .... E 616 454-2800
  Grand Rapids (G-6777)

GLASS PRDTS, FROM PURCHASED GLASS: Insulating

Classic Glass Battle Creek Inc .... F 269 968-2791
  Battle Creek (G-1209)

GLASS PRDTS, FROM PURCHASED GLASS: Mirrored

Hensley Mfg Inc .... F 810 653-3226
  Davison (G-3786)
Magna Mirrors America Inc .... G 616 738-0115
  Holland (G-8135)
Magna Mirrors America Inc .... G 616 786-7000
  Grand Haven (G-6333)
Rgm New Ventures Inc .... D 248 624-5050
  Wixom (G-18742)
Se-Kure Domes & Mirrors Inc .... F 269 651-9351
  Sturgis (G-16322)

GLASS PRDTS, FROM PURCHASED GLASS: Windshields

Exatec LLC .... E 248 926-4200
  Wixom (G-18659)
Lippert Components Mfg Inc .... D 989 845-3061
  Chesaning (G-2829)

GLASS PRDTS, FROM PURCHD GLASS: Strengthened Or Reinforced

PPG Industries Inc .... F 248 641-2000
  Troy (G-17309)

GLASS PRDTS, PRESSED OR BLOWN: Barware

Brand Logoed Barware .... G 517 763-1044
  East Lansing (G-4888)

GLASS PRDTS, PRESSED OR BLOWN: Bulbs, Electric Lights

Bare Bulb Companies LLC .... G 616 644-8251
  Grand Rapids (G-6495)
Lumecon LLC .... G 248 505-1090
  Farmington Hills (G-5296)

GLASS PRDTS, PRESSED OR BLOWN: Glassware, Art Or Decorative

Jordan Valley Glassworks .... G 231 536-0539
  East Jordan (G-4874)

GLASS PRDTS, PRESSED OR BLOWN: Lighting Eqpt Parts

Laidco Sales Inc .... G 231 832-1327
  Hersey (G-7867)

GLASS PRDTS, PRESSED OR BLOWN: Reflector, Lighting Eqpt

Light Speed Usa LLC .... A 616 308-0054
  Grand Rapids (G-6943)

GLASS PRDTS, PRESSED OR BLOWN: Tubing

Twins Studio .... G 248 676-8157
  Milford (G-11495)

GLASS PRDTS, PRESSED/BLOWN: Glassware, Art, Decor/Novelty

Glassicart Decorative Glwr .... G 231 739-5956
  Muskegon (G-11824)
Living On Etch .... G 810 229-7955
  Brighton (G-2021)

GLASS PRDTS, PRESSED/BLOWN: Lenses, Lantern, Flshlght, Etc

Hudson Industries Inc .... G 313 777-5622
  Sterling Heights (G-16044)

GLASS PRDTS, PURCHASED GLASS: Insulating, Multiple-Glazed

Thermaglas Corporation ....D....... 517 754-7461
  Saginaw *(G-14774)*

GLASS PRDTS, PURCHSD GLASS: Ornamental, Cut, Engraved/Décor

A K Services Inc ....G....... 313 972-1010
  Detroit *(G-3972)*

GLASS STORE: Leaded Or Stained

Full Spectrum Stained GL Inc ....G....... 269 432-2610
  Colon *(G-3487)*

GLASS STORES

Jene Holly Designs Inc ....G....... 586 954-0255
  Harrison Township *(G-7703)*
Knight Tonya ....G....... 313 255-3434
  Southfield *(G-15618)*
Oldcastle Buildingenvelope Inc............F....... 734 947-9670
  Taylor *(G-16455)*
Valley Glass Co Inc ....G....... 989 790-9342
  Saginaw *(G-14786)*

GLASS, AUTOMOTIVE: Wholesalers

Oldcastle Buildingenvelope Inc............G....... 616 896-8341
  Burnips *(G-2210)*
Pittsburgh Glass Works LLC ....E....... 734 727-5001
  Westland *(G-18405)*
Vvp Auto Glass Inc ....E....... 734 727-5001
  Westland *(G-18428)*

GLASS: Fiber

Keweenaw Bay Indian Community........F....... 906 524-5757
  Baraga *(G-1141)*
Optrand Inc ....E....... 734 451-3480
  Plymouth *(G-13257)*
PPG Industries Inc ....F....... 248 641-2000
  Troy *(G-17309)*
Robroy Enclosures Inc ....C....... 616 794-0700
  Belding *(G-1462)*
Thompson John ....G....... 810 225-8780
  Howell *(G-8530)*

GLASS: Flat

Beechcraft Products Inc.........................E....... 989 288-2606
  Durand *(G-4840)*
Golich Glass ....G....... 248 667-9084
  Brighton *(G-2002)*
Guardian Fabrication Inc.......................C....... 248 340-1800
  Auburn Hills *(G-920)*
Guardian Glass LLC ....D....... 248 340-1800
  Auburn Hills *(G-921)*
Guardian Industries LLC ....F....... 517 629-9464
  Albion *(G-127)*
Guardian Industries LLC ....B....... 734 654-4285
  Carleton *(G-2555)*
Guardian Industries LLC ....B....... 248 340-1800
  Auburn Hills *(G-922)*
Guardian Industries LLC ....D....... 734 654-1411
  Carleton *(G-2556)*
Pilkington North America Inc ....G....... 989 754-2956
  Saginaw *(G-14728)*
Pilkington North America Inc ....F....... 248 542-8300
  Royal Oak *(G-14568)*
Pittsburgh Glass Works LLC ....C....... 248 371-1700
  Rochester Hills *(G-14084)*
Pittsburgh Glass Works LLC ....E....... 734 727-5001
  Westland *(G-18405)*
PPG Industries Inc ....F....... 248 641-2000
  Troy *(G-17309)*
Valley Glass Co Inc ....G....... 989 790-9342
  Saginaw *(G-14786)*

GLASS: Insulating

Weatherproof Inc ....E....... 517 764-1330
  Jackson *(G-9034)*

GLASS: Optical

Single Vision Solution Inc ....F....... 586 464-1522
  Mount Clemens *(G-11657)*

GLASS: Pressed & Blown, NEC

Corning Incorporated ....G....... 248 680-4701
  Troy *(G-17029)*
Dare Products Inc ....E....... 269 965-2307
  Springfield *(G-15864)*
General Scientific Corporation ....E....... 734 996-9200
  Ann Arbor *(G-498)*
Great Lakes Aero Products...................F....... 810 235-1402
  Flint *(G-5708)*
Guardian Industries LLC ....B....... 734 654-4285
  Carleton *(G-2555)*
Installers Glass Block............................G....... 586 463-1214
  Washington *(G-18082)*
Linden Art Glass ....G....... 734 459-5060
  Plymouth *(G-13221)*
Precision Polymer Mfg Inc ....E....... 269 344-2044
  Kalamazoo *(G-9305)*
Rgm New Ventures Inc ....D....... 248 624-5050
  Wixom *(G-18742)*

GLASS: Stained

Full Spectrum Stained GL Inc ....G....... 269 432-2610
  Colon *(G-3487)*
Jordan Valley Glassworks......................G....... 231 536-0539
  East Jordan *(G-4874)*
Thompson Art Glass Inc ....G....... 810 225-8766
  Brighton *(G-2081)*

GLASS: Tempered

Oldcastle Buildingenvelope Inc............F....... 734 947-9670
  Taylor *(G-16455)*

GLASSWARE: Cut & Engraved

Engrave A Remembrance Inc ....G....... 586 772-7480
  Warren *(G-17794)*

GLASSWARE: Indl

City Auto Glass Co ....G....... 616 842-3235
  Grand Haven *(G-6285)*
Tig Entity LLC......................................E....... 810 629-9558
  Fenton *(G-5508)*

GLASSWARE: Laboratory

M2 Scientifics LLC ....F....... 616 379-9080
  Allendale *(G-224)*

GLOBAL POSITIONING SYSTEMS & EQPT

Asset Track Technologies LLC.............G....... 517 745-3879
  Jackson *(G-8817)*

GLOVES: Fabric

Kaul Glove and Mfg Co.........................E....... 313 894-9494
  Detroit *(G-4353)*

GLOVES: Leather, Work

Kaul Glove and Mfg Co.........................E....... 313 894-9494
  Detroit *(G-4353)*

GLUE

Adhesive Systems Inc ....E....... 313 865-4448
  Detroit *(G-3987)*
Sugru Inc ....E....... 877 990-9888
  Livonia *(G-10423)*

GOLD ORE MINING

Sulugu Corporation USA Inc ....D....... 478 714-0325
  Grand Rapids *(G-7232)*
Trelleborg Corporation ....G....... 269 639-9891
  South Haven *(G-15419)*

GOLF EQPT

Accessories & Specialties Inc ....G....... 989 235-3331
  Crystal *(G-3739)*
Golf Store ....G....... 517 347-8733
  Okemos *(G-12669)*
King Par LLC ....D....... 810 732-2470
  Flushing *(G-5810)*
North Coast Golf Company LLC ....G....... 810 547-4900
  Port Huron *(G-13509)*
Royaltees Golf LLC...............................G....... 517 783-5911
  Jackson *(G-9000)*

GOLF GOODS & EQPT

Great Lakes Allied LLC........................G....... 231 924-5794
  White Cloud *(G-18441)*
Owosso Country Club Pro Shop ....G....... 989 723-1470
  Owosso *(G-12848)*

GOURMET FOOD STORES

Cherry Republic Inc ....D....... 231 334-3150
  Glen Arbor *(G-6209)*
Downeys Potato Chips-Waterford.........G....... 248 673-3636
  Waterford *(G-18119)*
Emesa Foods Company ....G....... 248 982-3908
  Farmington Hills *(G-5230)*
Emesa Foods Company LLC ....G....... 248 982-3908
  Taylor *(G-16413)*

GOVERNMENT, LEGISLATIVE BODIES: County Commissioner

Kent County..F....... 616 632-7580
  Grand Rapids *(G-6887)*

GRANITE: Crushed & Broken

Genesee Cut Stone & Marble Co ....E....... 810 743-1800
  Grand Blanc *(G-6242)*
Graniteonecom Inc ....G....... 616 452-8372
  Grand Rapids *(G-6780)*

GRANITE: Cut & Shaped

Classic Stone MBL & Gran Inc ....F....... 248 588-1599
  Troy *(G-17014)*
Solutions In Stone Inc ....G....... 734 453-4444
  Plymouth *(G-13301)*
Yellowstone Products Inc ....G....... 616 299-7855
  Comstock Park *(G-3653)*

GRANITE: Dimension

Best Granite and Marble Inc ....G....... 313 247-3909
  Warren *(G-17733)*

GRANITE: Dimension

Take Us-4-Granite Inc ....G....... 586 803-1305
  Shelby Township *(G-15349)*

GRAPHIC ARTS & RELATED DESIGN SVCS

Action Printech Inc ....F....... 734 207-6000
  Plymouth *(G-13112)*
Commercial Graphics Company ....G....... 517 278-2159
  Coldwater *(G-3429)*
Different By Design Inc ....G....... 248 588-4840
  Farmington Hills *(G-5217)*
Fonts About Inc.....................................G....... 248 767-7504
  Northville *(G-12219)*
Freshwter Dgtal Mdia Prtners L............F....... 616 446-1771
  Kentwood *(G-9456)*
Genesis Service Associates LLC ....G....... 734 994-3900
  Dexter *(G-4742)*
Graphic Enterprises Inc ....D....... 248 616-4900
  Madison Heights *(G-10732)*
Graphic Resource Group Inc ....E....... 248 588-6100
  Troy *(G-17132)*
Graphic Visions Inc ....E....... 248 347-3355
  Northville *(G-12225)*
Graphics Unlimited Inc.........................G....... 231 773-2696
  Norton Shores *(G-12295)*
Grigg Graphic Services Inc ....E....... 248 356-5005
  Southfield *(G-15585)*
Hycorr LLC ....F....... 269 381-6349
  Kalamazoo *(G-9219)*
Kalamazoo Photo Comp Svcs ....G....... 269 345-3706
  Kalamazoo *(G-9245)*
Kendall & Company Inc........................G....... 810 733-7330
  Flint *(G-5721)*
Kenewell Group.....................................G....... 810 714-4290
  Fenton *(G-5487)*
Lloyd Waters & Associates ....G....... 734 525-2777
  Livonia *(G-10291)*
M Beshara Inc..G....... 248 542-9220
  Oak Park *(G-12623)*
Media Solutions Inc ....G....... 313 831-3152
  Detroit *(G-4427)*
Meridian Screen Prtg & Design ....G....... 517 351-2525
  Okemos *(G-12674)*
Official Brand Limited...........................G....... 734 224-9942
  Dearborn *(G-3880)*

Employee Codes: A=Over 500 employees, B=251-500
C=101-250, D=51-100, E=20-50, F=10-19, G=3-9

GRAPHIC ARTS & RELATED DESIGN SVCS

Printxpress Inc .... G 313 846-1644
  Dearborn *(G-3887)*
Skip Printing and Dup Co .... G 586 779-2640
  Roseville *(G-14477)*
Star Board Multi Media Inc .... G 616 296-0823
  Grand Haven *(G-6367)*
Thorpe Printing Services Inc .... G 810 364-6222
  Marysville *(G-11107)*
Vomela Specialty Company .... E 269 927-6500
  Benton Harbor *(G-1600)*
Vtec Graphics Inc .... G 734 953-9729
  Livonia *(G-10463)*
Whitcomb and Sons Sign Co Inc .... G 586 752-3576
  Romeo *(G-14239)*
Word Baron Inc .... F 248 471-4080
  Ann Arbor *(G-717)*

GRAVE MARKERS: Concrete

Arnets Inc .... F 734 665-3650
  Ann Arbor *(G-379)*
Perfected Grave Vault Co .... G 616 243-3375
  Grand Rapids *(G-7078)*

GRAVEL MINING

A Lindberg & Sons Inc .... E 906 485-5705
  Ishpeming *(G-8774)*
Albrecht Sand & Gravel Co .... E 810 672-9272
  Snover *(G-15390)*
American Aggregate Inc .... G 269 683-6160
  Niles *(G-12110)*
Barber Creek Sand & Gravel .... E 616 675-7619
  Kent City *(G-9427)*
Bechtel Sand & Gravel .... G 810 346-2041
  Brown City *(G-2135)*
Bently Sand & Gravel .... G 810 629-6172
  Fenton *(G-5458)*
Branch West Concrete Products .... F 989 345-0794
  West Branch *(G-18326)*
Carr Brothers and Sons Inc .... E 517 629-3549
  Albion *(G-119)*
Carr Brothers and Sons Inc .... F 517 531-3358
  Albion *(G-120)*
Chippewa Stone & Gravel Inc .... G 231 867-5757
  Rodney *(G-14206)*
Genoak Materials Inc .... C 248 634-8276
  Holly *(G-8273)*
Hubscher & Son Inc .... G 989 773-5369
  Mount Pleasant *(G-11702)*
Hubscher & Son Inc .... G 989 875-2151
  Sumner *(G-16332)*
Kurtz Gravel Company Inc .... E 810 787-6543
  Farmington Hills *(G-5286)*
Lyon Sand & Gravel Co .... G 313 843-7200
  Dearborn *(G-3864)*
Lyon Sand & Gravel Co .... F 248 348-8511
  Wixom *(G-18701)*
Michigan Aggregates Corp .... F 517 688-4414
  Jerome *(G-9079)*
Morris Excavating Inc .... F 269 483-7773
  White Pigeon *(G-18484)*
Newark Gravel Company .... G 810 796-3072
  Dryden *(G-4807)*
Parker Excvtg Grav & Recycle .... F 616 784-1681
  Comstock Park *(G-3633)*
South Flint Gravel Inc .... G 810 232-8911
  Holly *(G-8295)*
South Hill Sand and Gravel .... G 248 828-1726
  Troy *(G-17365)*
South Hill Sand and Gravel .... G 248 685-7020
  Milford *(G-11490)*
Tip Top Gravel Co Inc .... G 616 897-4242
  Ada *(G-37)*
Top OMichigan Reclaimers Inc .... G 989 705-7983
  Gaylord *(G-6164)*
Weber Sand and Gravel Inc .... F 248 373-0900
  Lake Orion *(G-9637)*

GREASES & INEDIBLE FATS, RENDERED

Darling Ingredients Inc .... C 517 279-9731
  Coldwater *(G-3431)*
Michigan Protein Inc .... F 877 869-0630
  Cedar Springs *(G-2657)*

GREASES: Lubricating

Huron Industries Inc .... G 810 984-4213
  Port Huron *(G-13485)*

GREENHOUSES: Prefabricated Metal

Control Dekk LLC .... G 616 828-4862
  Wyoming *(G-18859)*
Keeler-Glasgow Company Inc .... F 269 621-2415
  Hartford *(G-7764)*

GRILLS & GRILLWORK: Woven Wire, Made From Purchased Wire

Benmill LLC .... E 616 243-7555
  Grand Rapids *(G-6499)*
Great Lakes Grilling Co .... F 616 791-8600
  Grand Rapids *(G-6787)*

GRINDING BALLS: Ceramic

Afi Enterprises Inc .... E 734 475-9111
  Chelsea *(G-2803)*
Internal Grinding Abrasives .... E 616 243-5566
  Grand Rapids *(G-6849)*

GRINDING SVC: Precision, Commercial Or Indl

Automated Precision Eqp LLC .... G 517 481-2414
  Eaton Rapids *(G-4952)*
Detroit Chrome Inc .... E 313 341-9478
  Detroit *(G-4140)*
Diversified Precision Pdts Inc .... E 517 750-2310
  Spring Arbor *(G-15790)*
Fega Tool & Gage Company .... F 586 469-4400
  Clinton Township *(G-3236)*
Gear Master Inc .... F 810 798-9254
  Almont *(G-260)*
Grand Rapids Metaltek Inc .... E 616 791-2373
  Grand Rapids *(G-6765)*
Jordan Tool Corporation .... E 586 755-6700
  Warren *(G-17889)*
Momentum Industries Inc .... F 989 681-5735
  Saint Louis *(G-14993)*
Precise Metal Components Inc .... G 734 769-0790
  Ann Arbor *(G-619)*
Ramtec Corp .... F 586 752-9270
  Romeo *(G-14233)*
Sodus Hard Chrome Inc .... F 269 925-2077
  Sodus *(G-15394)*
Tazz Broach and Machine Inc .... G 586 296-7755
  Harrison Township *(G-7728)*
Tru Tech Systems LLC .... D 586 469-2700
  Mount Clemens *(G-11661)*
West Michigan Grinding Svc Inc .... F 231 739-4245
  Norton Shores *(G-12343)*
Wolverine Special Tool Inc .... E 616 791-1027
  Grand Rapids *(G-7348)*

GRINDING SVCS: Ophthalmic Lens, Exc Prescription

Rx-Rite Optical Co .... G 586 293-8888
  Fraser *(G-5990)*

GRINDS: Electric

Morstar Inc .... F 248 605-3291
  Livonia *(G-10322)*

GRIPS OR HANDLES: Rubber

Hold-It Inc .... G 810 984-4213
  Port Huron *(G-13482)*

GROCERIES WHOLESALERS, NEC

American Bottling Company .... F 517 622-8605
  Grand Ledge *(G-6384)*
Coca-Cola Refreshments USA Inc .... G 616 913-0400
  Grand Rapids *(G-6578)*
Fireside Coffee Company Inc .... F 810 635-9196
  Swartz Creek *(G-16353)*
Great Lakes Coca-Cola Dist LLC .... F 517 322-2349
  Lansing *(G-9762)*
Greenfield Noodle Specialty Co .... F 313 873-2212
  Detroit *(G-4281)*
Home Style Foods Inc .... F 313 874-3250
  Detroit *(G-4303)*
New Moon Noodle Incorporated .... F 269 962-8820
  Battle Creek *(G-12801)*
Pepsi-Cola Metro Btlg Co Inc .... F 517 279-8436
  Coldwater *(G-3445)*
Pepsi-Cola Metro Btlg Co Inc .... F 616 285-8200
  Grand Rapids *(G-7077)*

PRODUCT SECTION

Purina Mills LLC .... E 517 322-0200
  Lansing *(G-9786)*
Stone House Bread Inc .... G 231 933-8864
  Traverse City *(G-16842)*
Uncle Johns Cider Mill Inc .... E 989 224-3686
  Saint Johns *(G-14919)*

GROCERIES, GENERAL LINE WHOLESALERS

18th Street Deli Inc .... G 313 921-7710
  Hamtramck *(G-7610)*
Achatzs Hand Made Pie Co .... E 586 749-2882
  Chesterfield *(G-2834)*
Countryside Foods LLC .... B 586 447-3500
  Warren *(G-17765)*
Emesa Foods Company LLC .... G 248 982-3908
  Taylor *(G-16413)*
Vandco Incorporated .... E 906 482-1550
  Hancock *(G-7623)*

GROUTING EQPT: Concrete

Intric Grouting Solutions LLC .... F 855 801-7453
  Wayland *(G-18196)*
K&H Supply of Lansing Inc .... E 517 482-7600
  Lansing *(G-9769)*

GUARDS: Machine, Sheet Metal

Robo-Fence LLC .... E 586 232-3909
  Clinton Township *(G-3340)*

GUIDED MISSILES & SPACE VEHICLES: Research & Development

Morris Kall Incorporated .... G 815 528-8665
  Marquette *(G-11037)*

GUIDED MISSILES/SPACE VEHICLE PARTS/AUX EQPT: Research/Devel

RCO Aerospace Products LLC .... D 586 774-8400
  Roseville *(G-14469)*

GUM & WOOD CHEMICALS

Conway-Cleveland Corp .... G 616 458-0056
  Grand Rapids *(G-6604)*

GUN PARTS MADE TO INDIVIDUAL ORDER

Rs Products LLC .... G 801 722-9746
  Chesterfield *(G-2941)*

GUN SIGHTS: Optical

Leapers Inc .... D 734 542-1500
  Livonia *(G-10275)*
Rs Products LLC .... G 801 722-9746
  Chesterfield *(G-2941)*
Trijicon Inc .... C 248 960-7700
  Wixom *(G-18780)*
Williams Gun Sight Company .... D 800 530-9028
  Davison *(G-3801)*

GUTTERS: Sheet Metal

Classic Gutter Systems LLC .... F 269 665-2700
  Galesburg *(G-6074)*
Rainbow Seamless Systems Inc .... G 231 933-8888
  Traverse City *(G-16814)*

GYPSUM MINING

Michigan Gypsum Co .... F 989 792-8734
  Midland *(G-11389)*

GYPSUM PRDTS

Certainteed Gypsum Inc .... A 906 524-6101
  Lanse *(G-9657)*
Lime Gypsum Products .... G 989 867-4611
  Turner *(G-17464)*
Ng Operations LLC .... F 989 756-2741
  National City *(G-11960)*
United States Gypsum Company .... D 269 384-6335
  Otsego *(G-12801)*
United States Gypsum Company .... D 313 624-4232
  River Rouge *(G-13861)*
United States Gypsum Company .... D 313 842-4455
  Detroit *(G-4653)*

US Gypsum Co......G....... 313 842-5800
River Rouge *(G-13862)*

HAIR & HAIR BASED PRDTS

Adventures Moni and Koko LLC......G....... 269 589-2154
Battle Creek *(G-1181)*
American Laser Centers LLC......A....... 248 426-8250
Farmington Hills *(G-5168)*
B&B HAIr&co LLC......G....... 616 600-4568
Grand Rapids *(G-6489)*
Enhanceher Collection LLC......G....... 313 279-7308
Detroit *(G-4210)*
Enuf Haircare and Lashes LLC......G....... 586 354-1798
Detroit *(G-4211)*
Hair Vault LLC......G....... 586 649-8218
Plymouth *(G-13182)*
Kevin Larkin Inc......G....... 248 736-8203
Waterford *(G-18131)*
Limited Lblty Co Colormemink......G....... 313 707-3366
Brownstown Twp *(G-2156)*
My Secret Bundles LLC......G....... 586 610-2804
Clinton Township *(G-3307)*
Qt Glamour Collection LLC......G....... 248 605-5507
Detroit *(G-4544)*
S Sheree Collection LLC......G....... 616 930-1416
Grand Rapids *(G-7176)*
Stoked & Bearded LLC......G....... 248 513-2927
Clinton Township *(G-3364)*
Truth Traxx LLC......F....... 800 792-2239
Flint *(G-5786)*

HAIR ACCESS WHOLESALERS

Brintley Enterprises......G....... 248 991-4086
Detroit *(G-4074)*

HAIR CARE PRDTS

Akilahs Beauty Salon LLC......G....... 602 607-8503
Grand Rapids *(G-6441)*
Bella Skyy Llc......G....... 313 623-9296
Harper Woods *(G-7663)*
Detroit Fine Products LLC......G....... 877 294-5826
Ferndale *(G-5546)*
Function Inc......C....... 570 317-0737
Caledonia *(G-2373)*
Kae Organics LLC......G....... 248 832-0403
Detroit *(G-4348)*
Le Host LLC......G....... 248 546-4247
Ferndale *(G-5565)*
Mizjayzbraidz LLC......G....... 313 799-7756
Detroit *(G-4460)*
Murrays Worldwide Inc......F....... 248 691-9156
Oak Park *(G-12629)*
Viladon Corporation......G....... 248 548-0043
Oak Park *(G-12649)*

HAIR CURLERS: Beauty Shop

Head Over Heels......G....... 248 435-2954
Troy *(G-17139)*

HAIRDRESSERS

Bella Skyy Llc......G....... 313 623-9296
Harper Woods *(G-7663)*

HALL EFFECT DEVICES

White River......G....... 231 894-9216
Montague *(G-11603)*

HAMPERS: Laundry, Sheet Metal

Metro-Fabricating LLC......D....... 989 667-8100
Bay City *(G-1377)*

HAND TOOLS, NEC: Wholesalers

Hank Thorn Co......F....... 248 348-7800
Wixom *(G-18675)*
Tekton Inc......D....... 616 243-2443
Grand Rapids *(G-7251)*

HANDBAGS

Fisll Media LLC......G....... 646 492-8533
Troy *(G-17111)*
Military Apparel Co......G....... 810 637-1542
Port Huron *(G-13502)*

HANDBAGS: Women's

Rose Laila......G....... 989 598-0950
Saginaw *(G-14740)*
Tapestry Inc......G....... 631 724-8066
Sterling Heights *(G-16200)*

HANDCUFFS & LEG IRONS

C & S Security Inc......G....... 989 821-5759
Roscommon *(G-14347)*

HANDLES: Wood

Home Style Co......G....... 989 871-3654
Millington *(G-11501)*

HANGERS: Garment, Plastic

Batts Group Ltd......G....... 616 956-3053
Grand Rapids *(G-6496)*
Do-It Corporation......D....... 269 637-1121
South Haven *(G-15404)*
Tower Tag & Label LLC......F....... 269 927-1065
Benton Harbor *(G-1593)*

HARDWARE

Acme Mills Company......E....... 517 437-8940
Hillsdale *(G-7919)*
Admat Manufacturing Inc......F....... 269 641-7453
Union *(G-17486)*
ADS Us Inc......D....... 989 871-4550
Millington *(G-11498)*
Albion Industries LLC......C....... 800 835-8911
Albion *(G-114)*
Antolin Interiors Usa Inc......A....... 517 548-0052
Howell *(G-8429)*
Apex Spring & Stamping Corp......D....... 616 453-5463
Grand Rapids *(G-6462)*
Ardy Inc......G....... 231 845-7318
Ludington *(G-10527)*
BDS Company Inc......F....... 517 279-2135
Coldwater *(G-3421)*
Berkley Screw Machine Pdts Inc......E....... 248 853-0044
Rochester Hills *(G-13962)*
Brauer Clamps USA......F....... 586 427-5304
Warren *(G-17741)*
Caster Concepts Inc......G....... 517 629-2456
Albion *(G-121)*
Clamptech LLC......G....... 989 832-8027
Bay City *(G-1338)*
Consolidated Clips Clamps Inc......D....... 734 455-0880
Plymouth *(G-13149)*
Cube Tracker LLC......G....... 269 436-1270
Decatur *(G-3945)*
David Kimberly Door Company......F....... 248 652-8833
Rochester *(G-13898)*
Dgh Enterprises Inc......G....... 269 925-0657
Benton Harbor *(G-1547)*
Die Cast Press Mfg Co Inc......E....... 269 657-6060
Paw Paw *(G-12947)*
Dolphin Manufacturing Inc......E....... 734 946-6322
Taylor *(G-16403)*
Dowding Industries Inc......E....... 517 663-5455
Eaton Rapids *(G-4959)*
Eaton Aeroquip LLC......B....... 949 452-9575
Jackson *(G-8873)*
Ervins Group LLC......E....... 248 203-2000
Bloomfield Hills *(G-1819)*
Evans Industries Inc......G....... 313 272-8200
Detroit *(G-4219)*
Flambeau Inc......G....... 248 364-3357
Auburn Hills *(G-901)*
Fluid Hutchinson Management......D....... 248 679-1327
Auburn Hills *(G-903)*
Franklin Fastener Company......E....... 313 537-8900
Redford *(G-13735)*
G T Gundrilling Inc......G....... 586 992-3301
Macomb *(G-10598)*
G&G Industries Inc......E....... 586 726-6000
Shelby Township *(G-15229)*
GAL Gage Co......F....... 269 465-5750
Bridgman *(G-1926)*
Gates Corporation......G....... 248 260-2300
Rochester Hills *(G-14020)*
Grant Industries Incorporated......E....... 586 293-9200
Fraser *(G-5931)*
Great Lakes Trim Inc......D....... 231 267-3000
Williamsburg *(G-18555)*
Hydro-Craft Inc......G....... 248 652-8100
Rochester Hills *(G-14037)*
Incoe Corporation......C....... 248 616-0220
Auburn Hills *(G-936)*
International Engrg & Mfg Inc......D....... 989 689-4911
Hope *(G-8361)*
Interntnal Auto Cmpnnts Group......G....... 810 987-8500
Port Huron *(G-13488)*
Jay & Kay Manufacturing LLC......G....... 810 679-3079
Croswell *(G-3731)*
K & W Manufacturing Co Inc......E....... 517 369-9708
Bronson *(G-2117)*
Kriewall Enterprises Inc......E....... 586 336-0600
Romeo *(G-14227)*
L & W Inc......D....... 734 397-6300
New Boston *(G-12012)*
Lacks Industries Inc......C....... 616 698-6890
Grand Rapids *(G-6915)*
Michigan Wheel Operations LLC......D....... 616 452-6941
Grand Rapids *(G-6997)*
Milan Screw Products Inc......F....... 734 439-2431
Milan *(G-11447)*
Milton Manufacturing Inc......E....... 313 366-2450
Detroit *(G-4458)*
Mvc Holdings LLC......F....... 586 491-2600
Roseville *(G-14450)*
Norma Michigan Inc......G....... 248 373-4300
Lake Orion *(G-9622)*
Norma Michigan Inc......C....... 248 373-4300
Auburn Hills *(G-984)*
Orion Manufacturing Inc......F....... 616 527-5994
Ionia *(G-8691)*
Peninsular Inc......E....... 586 775-7211
Roseville *(G-14461)*
Penn Automotive Inc......C....... 734 595-3000
Romulus *(G-14317)*
Penn Engineering & Mfg Corp......G....... 586 731-3560
Waterford *(G-18152)*
Penstone Inc......E....... 734 379-3160
Rockwood *(G-14203)*
Probe-TEC......G....... 765 252-0257
Chesterfield *(G-2930)*
Profil System Inc......F....... 248 536-2130
Waterford *(G-18159)*
R & D Enterprises Inc......E....... 248 349-7077
Plymouth *(G-13274)*
R M Wright Company Inc......E....... 248 476-9800
Farmington Hills *(G-5363)*
R T Gordon Inc......E....... 586 294-6100
Fraser *(G-5985)*
R W Fernstrum & Company......E....... 906 863-5553
Menominee *(G-11257)*
Refrigeration Sales Inc......G....... 517 784-8579
Jackson *(G-8995)*
Regency Construction Corp......E....... 586 741-8000
Clinton Township *(G-3334)*
River Valley Machine Inc......F....... 269 673-8070
Allegan *(G-181)*
RSR Sales Inc......E....... 734 668-8166
Ann Arbor *(G-645)*
Scaff-All Inc......G....... 888 204-9990
Clay *(G-3124)*
Shepherd Hardware Products Inc......D....... 269 756-3830
Three Oaks *(G-16558)*
Shurco LLC......F....... 616 366-2367
Caledonia *(G-2398)*
Spiral Industries Inc......E....... 810 632-6300
Howell *(G-8521)*
Srg Global Automotive LLC......B....... 586 757-7800
Sterling Heights *(G-16186)*
Sterling Die & Engineering Inc......E....... 586 677-0707
Macomb *(G-10637)*
Stromberg-Carlson Products Inc......F....... 231 947-8600
Traverse City *(G-16843)*
TEC-3 Prototypes Inc......E....... 810 678-8909
Metamora *(G-11289)*
TI Group Auto Systems LLC......G....... 586 948-6006
Chesterfield *(G-2956)*
Toyo Seat USA Corporation......C....... 810 724-0300
Imlay City *(G-8648)*
Unist Inc......E....... 616 949-0853
Grand Rapids *(G-7297)*
Vacuum Orna Metal Company Inc......E....... 734 941-9100
Romulus *(G-14336)*
Wico Metal Products Company......C....... 586 755-9600
Warren *(G-18067)*

HARDWARE & BUILDING PRDTS: Plastic

Beechcraft Products Inc......E....... 989 288-2606
Durand *(G-4840)*
Datacover Inc......F....... 248 391-2163
Lake Orion *(G-9601)*

PRODUCT

Employee Codes: A=Over 500 employees, B=251-500
C=101-250, D=51-100, E=20-50, F=10-19, G=3-9

2022 Harris Michigan
Industrial Directory

1287

HARDWARE & BUILDING PRDTS: Plastic

Deluxe Frame Company Inc.....................E........ 248 373-8811
  Auburn Hills (G-862)
Lacks Exterior Systems LLC...................A....... 616 949-6570
  Grand Rapids (G-6909)
Lacks Exterior Systems LLC...................E....... 616 949-6570
  Grand Rapids (G-6910)
Lacks Exterior Systems LLC...................E....... 248 351-0555
  Novi (G-12462)
Lacks Exterior Systems LLC...................E....... 616 554-7805
  Kentwood (G-9461)
Lacks Industries Inc..............................C....... 616 656-2910
  Grand Rapids (G-6921)
Qfd Recycling..E....... 810 733-2335
  Flint (G-5751)
Schrier Plastics Corp............................E....... 616 669-7174
  Jenison (G-9070)
Standard Plaque Incorporated...............F....... 313 383-7233
  Melvindale (G-11210)

HARDWARE & EQPT: Stage, Exc Lighting

North Coast Studios Inc.........................F....... 586 359-6630
  Roseville (G-14455)
Stageright Corporation..........................C....... 989 386-7393
  Clare (G-2999)

HARDWARE STORES

A W B Industries Inc.............................E....... 989 739-1447
  Oscoda (G-12753)
Ardy Inc...G....... 231 845-7318
  Ludington (G-10527)
Ebels Hardware Inc...............................F....... 231 826-3334
  Falmouth (G-5133)
Erickson Lumber & True Value...............G....... 906 524-6295
  Lanse (G-9659)
Houseart LLC..G....... 248 651-8124
  Rochester (G-13905)
J Kaltz & Co..G....... 616 942-6070
  Grand Rapids (G-6856)
Kalamazoo Electric Motor Inc.................G....... 269 345-7802
  Kalamazoo (G-9238)
Masons Lumber & Hardware Inc............G....... 989 685-3999
  Rose City (G-14365)
McLaren Inc...G....... 989 720-4328
  Owosso (G-12842)
Nelson Hardware...................................G....... 269 327-3583
  Portage (G-13587)
Northwoods Prperty Holdings LLC..........G....... 231 334-3000
  Glen Arbor (G-6211)
Port Huron Building Supply Co...............F....... 810 987-2666
  Port Huron (G-13519)
Toms World of Wood..............................G....... 517 264-2836
  Adrian (G-99)
Weber Steel Inc.....................................F....... 989 868-4162
  Vassar (G-17586)

HARDWARE STORES: Builders'

Smede-Son Steel and Sup Co Inc...........D....... 313 937-8300
  Redford (G-13772)

HARDWARE STORES: Door Locks & Lock Sets

Acorn Stamping Inc................................F....... 248 628-5216
  Oxford (G-12870)

HARDWARE STORES: Pumps & Pumping Eqpt

Jet Subsurface Rod Pumps Corp............G....... 989 732-7513
  Gaylord (G-6136)

HARDWARE STORES: Tools

Arm Tooling Systems Inc........................F....... 586 759-5677
  Warren (G-17712)
Busch Machine Tool Supply LLC............G....... 989 798-4794
  Freeland (G-6019)
Marshall Tool Service Inc.......................G....... 989 777-3137
  Saginaw (G-14687)
Mmp Molded Magnesium Pdts LLC........G....... 517 789-8505
  Jackson (G-8967)
S F S Carbide Tool................................G....... 989 777-3890
  Saginaw (G-14742)
Triple Tool...G....... 586 795-1785
  Sterling Heights (G-16211)
Widell Industries Inc.............................E....... 989 742-4528
  Hillman (G-7918)

HARDWARE STORES: Tools, Power

Great Lakes Wood Products...................G....... 906 228-3737
  Negaunee (G-11967)

HARDWARE WHOLESALERS

Acument Global Tech Inc.......................E....... 586 254-3900
  Sterling Heights (G-15924)
Dgh Enterprises Inc...............................E....... 269 925-0657
  Benton Harbor (G-1546)
Fixtureworks LLC..................................E....... 586 294-6100
  Fraser (G-5928)
G & T Industries Inc..............................D....... 616 452-8611
  Byron Center (G-2271)
K-Tool Corporation Michigan..................D....... 863 603-0777
  Plymouth (G-13209)
Laforce LLC..G....... 248 588-5601
  Troy (G-17203)
Patco Air Tool Inc..................................G....... 248 648-8830
  Orion (G-12738)
RSR Sales Inc......................................E....... 734 668-8166
  Ann Arbor (G-645)
Vortex Industries Inc.............................F....... 855 867-8399
  Plymouth (G-13335)

HARDWARE, WHOLESALE: Bolts

Connection Service Company................E....... 269 926-2658
  Benton Harbor (G-1541)
Federal Group Usa Inc..........................F....... 248 545-5000
  Southfield (G-15559)
MNP Corporation...................................A....... 586 254-1320
  Utica (G-17504)

HARDWARE, WHOLESALE: Builders', NEC

Modern Builders Supply Inc...................G....... 517 787-3633
  Jackson (G-8968)
Richelieu America Ltd............................E....... 586 264-1240
  Sterling Heights (G-16151)

HARDWARE, WHOLESALE: Casters & Glides

Caster Concepts Inc..............................E....... 888 781-1470
  Albion (G-122)
Shepherd Hardware Products Inc...........D....... 269 756-3830
  Three Oaks (G-16558)

HARDWARE, WHOLESALE: Chains

Serapid Inc..F....... 586 274-0774
  Sterling Heights (G-16171)

HARDWARE, WHOLESALE: Rivets

Jay Cee Sales & Rivet Inc.....................F....... 248 478-2150
  Farmington (G-5140)

HARDWARE, WHOLESALE: Screws

United Sttes Scket Screw Mfg C.............F....... 586 469-8811
  Fraser (G-6009)

HARDWARE, WHOLESALE: Security Devices, Locks

A & L Metal Products.............................G....... 734 654-8990
  Carleton (G-2549)
Cypress Computer Systems Inc.............F....... 810 245-2300
  Lapeer (G-9924)

HARDWARE, WHOLESALE: Staples

Aactus Inc...G....... 734 425-1212
  Livonia (G-10096)

HARDWARE: Aircraft

Precision Polymer Mfg Inc......................E....... 269 344-2044
  Kalamazoo (G-9305)
Teamtech Motorsports Safety.................G....... 989 792-4880
  Saginaw (G-14773)

HARDWARE: Builders'

Dundee Manufacturing Co Inc................E....... 734 529-2540
  Dundee (G-4816)
Engineered Products Company..............E....... 810 767-2050
  Flint (G-5696)
Enterprise Hinge Inc.............................G....... 269 857-2111
  Douglas (G-4773)
Masco Corporation.................................A....... 313 274-7400
  Livonia (G-10302)

HARDWARE: Cabinet

Options Cabinetry Inc............................F....... 248 669-0000
  Commerce Township (G-3561)

HARDWARE: Door Opening & Closing Devices, Exc Electrical

D A C Industries Inc..............................G....... 616 235-0140
  Grand Rapids (G-6629)
Magna Mirrors America Inc....................B....... 231 652-4450
  Newaygo (G-12086)
Select Products Limited.........................E....... 269 323-4433
  Kalamazoo (G-9330)

HARDWARE: Furniture

Belwith Products LLC............................F....... 616 247-4000
  Grandville (G-7367)
H & L Advantage Inc.............................E....... 616 532-1012
  Grandville (G-7384)
Millerknoll Inc..G....... 616 453-5995
  Grand Rapids (G-7011)
Moheco Products Company...................G....... 734 855-4194
  Livonia (G-10321)
Northwest Metal Products Inc................F....... 616 453-0556
  Grand Rapids (G-7049)

HARDWARE: Furniture, Builders' & Other Household

Elemental Artistry LLC...........................G....... 616 326-1758
  Grand Rapids (G-6671)
Knape & Vogt Manufacturing Co............A....... 616 459-3311
  Grand Rapids (G-6900)
Polytec Foha Inc....................................F....... 586 978-9386
  Warren (G-17969)

HARDWARE: Locking Systems, Security Cable

Startech-Solutions LLC..........................G....... 248 419-0650
  Southfield (G-15708)
US RAC..G....... 248 505-0413
  Southfield (G-15735)

HARDWARE: Padlocks

Solidbody Technology Company.............G....... 248 709-7901
  Troy (G-17359)

HARDWARE: Rubber

Armada Rubber Manufacturing Co..........D....... 586 784-9135
  Armada (G-731)
Blade Industrial Products Inc.................G....... 248 773-7400
  Wixom (G-18621)
Derby Fabg Solutions LLC.....................D....... 616 866-1650
  Rockford (G-14164)

HARNESS ASSEMBLIES: Cable & Wire

Amphenol Borisch Tech Inc....................C....... 616 554-9820
  Grand Rapids (G-6458)
Assem-Tech Inc.....................................E....... 616 846-3410
  Grand Haven (G-6275)
Bay Electronics Inc................................E....... 586 296-0900
  Roseville (G-14379)
Byrne Elec Specialists Inc.....................A....... 616 866-3461
  Rockford (G-14159)
Byrne Elec Specialists Inc.....................E....... 616 866-3461
  Rockford (G-14160)
Connect With Us LLC............................G....... 586 262-4359
  Shelby Township (G-15194)
Ctc Acquisition Company LLC................C....... 616 884-7100
  Rockford (G-14163)
Dupearl Technology LLC........................G....... 248 390-9609
  Bloomfield Hills (G-1816)
Electro-Matic Integrated Inc...................E....... 248 478-1182
  Farmington Hills (G-5223)
Madison Electric Company.....................D....... 586 825-0200
  Warren (G-17913)
Netcon Enterprises Inc..........................E....... 248 673-7855
  Waterford (G-18140)
Pkc Group USA Inc................................A....... 248 489-4700
  Farmington Hills (G-5348)
Quality Cable Assembly LLC..................F....... 248 236-9915
  Oxford (G-12909)
Saldet Sales and Services Inc...............F....... 586 469-4312
  Clinton Township (G-3348)
Stoneridge Inc.......................................A....... 248 489-9300
  Novi (G-12543)

PRODUCT SECTION HEAT TREATING: Metal

Turn Key Harness & Wire LLC ....E........ 248 236-9915
  Oxford *(G-12927)*
Wh Manufacturing Inc ....E...... 616 534-7560
  Grand Rapids *(G-7337)*
Y Squared Inc ....G...... 248 435-0301
  Royal Oak *(G-14593)*

HARNESS WIRING SETS: Internal Combustion Engines

Aees Power Systems Ltd Partnr ....D...... 248 489-4900
  Allen Park *(G-187)*
Portage Wire Systems Inc ....E...... 231 889-4215
  Onekama *(G-12703)*
Starlight Technologies Inc ....G...... 248 250-9607
  Troy *(G-17371)*

HARNESSES, HALTERS, SADDLERY & STRAPS

Birlon Group LLC ....G...... 313 551-5341
  Inkster *(G-8659)*
Gst Autoleather Holdco Corp ....F...... 248 436-2300
  Rochester Hills *(G-14028)*

HARVESTING MACHINERY & EQPT WHOLESALERS

Gregory M Boese ....F...... 989 754-2990
  Saginaw *(G-14659)*

HEADPHONES: Radio

Chrouch Communications Inc ....G...... 231 972-0339
  Mecosta *(G-11190)*
Fka Distributing Co LLC ....C...... 248 863-3000
  Commerce Township *(G-3530)*
House of Marley LLC ....G...... 248 863-3000
  Commerce Township *(G-3540)*
No Limit Wireless-Michigan Inc ....G...... 313 285-8402
  Detroit *(G-4487)*

HEALTH & ALLIED SERVICES, NEC

Welzin Health Services LLC ....G...... 313 953-8768
  Wyandotte *(G-18844)*

HEALTH AIDS: Exercise Eqpt

National Credit Corporation ....F...... 734 459-8100
  West Bloomfield *(G-18302)*
Nustep LLC ....D...... 734 769-3939
  Ann Arbor *(G-597)*
Riverfront Cycle Inc ....G...... 517 482-8585
  Lansing *(G-9888)*
Y M C A Family Center ....G...... 269 428-9622
  Saint Joseph *(G-14982)*

HEALTH FOOD & SUPPLEMENT STORES

Apple Valley Natural Foods ....C...... 269 471-3234
  Berrien Springs *(G-1637)*
Total Life Changes LLC ....B...... 810 471-3812
  Ira *(G-8716)*

HEALTH PRACTITIONERS' OFFICES, NEC

Avissa Skin+body ....G...... 734 316-5556
  Ann Arbor *(G-389)*

HEALTH SCREENING SVCS

Cotton Concepts Printing LLC ....G...... 313 444-3857
  Detroit *(G-4104)*

HEARING AIDS

Audionet America Inc ....F...... 586 944-0043
  Clinton Township *(G-3175)*
Hear USA ....G...... 734 525-3900
  Livonia *(G-10238)*
Skoric Hearing Aid Center LLC ....G...... 248 961-4329
  Saginaw *(G-14758)*

HEAT EMISSION OPERATING APPARATUS

Advanced Avionics Inc ....G...... 734 259-5300
  Plymouth *(G-13119)*
Hanon Systems Usa LLC ....B...... 248 907-8000
  Novi *(G-12425)*

HEAT EXCHANGERS: After Or Inter Coolers Or Condensers, Etc

Acorn Stamping Inc ....F...... 248 628-5216
  Oxford *(G-12870)*
R & D Enterprises Inc ....E...... 248 349-7077
  Plymouth *(G-13274)*

HEAT TREATING SALTS

Quaker Houghton Pa Inc ....E...... 248 265-7745
  Troy *(G-17325)*

HEAT TREATING: Metal

Advanced Heat Treat Corp ....F...... 734 243-0063
  Monroe *(G-11521)*
Ajax Metal Processing Inc ....G...... 313 267-2100
  Detroit *(G-3992)*
Al Fe Heat Treating-Ohio Inc ....F...... 260 747-9422
  Lansing *(G-9800)*
Al-Fe Heat Treating LLC ....D...... 260 747-9422
  Lansing *(G-9801)*
Al-Fe Heat Treating LLC ....E...... 989 752-2819
  Saginaw *(G-14603)*
Al-Fe Heat Treating LLC ....E...... 888 747-2533
  Lansing *(G-9802)*
Ald Thermal Treatment Inc ....C...... 810 357-0693
  Port Huron *(G-13434)*
Alloy Steel Treating Company ....E...... 269 628-2154
  Gobles *(G-6216)*
Alpha Steel Treating Inc ....F...... 734 523-1035
  Livonia *(G-10111)*
American Metal Processing Co ....E...... 586 757-7144
  Warren *(G-17703)*
American Metallurgical Svcs ....F...... 313 893-8328
  Detroit *(G-4013)*
Apollo Heat Treating Proc LLC ....E...... 248 398-3434
  Oak Park *(G-12591)*
Applied Process Inc ....E...... 734 464-8000
  Livonia *(G-10122)*
Atmosphere Group Inc ....G...... 248 624-8191
  Wixom *(G-18609)*
Atmosphere Heat Treating Inc ....E...... 248 960-4700
  Wixom *(G-18610)*
Austemper Inc ....F...... 586 293-4554
  Wixom *(G-18614)*
Authority Flame Hrdning Strght ....E...... 586 598-5887
  Chesterfield *(G-2848)*
Autocam-Pax Inc ....C...... 269 782-5186
  Dowagiac *(G-4776)*
Bellaire Log Homes Indus Hm ....G...... 231 533-6669
  Bellaire *(G-1471)*
Bellevue Proc Met Prep Inc ....C...... 313 921-1931
  Detroit *(G-4050)*
Benton Harbor LLC ....E...... 269 925-6581
  Benton Harbor *(G-1536)*
Bluewater Thermal Solutions ....G...... 269 925-6581
  Benton Harbor *(G-1537)*
Bluewater Thermal Solutions ....E...... 989 753-7770
  Saginaw *(G-14618)*
Bodycote Thermal Proc Inc ....G...... 616 399-6880
  Holland *(G-7979)*
Bodycote Thermal Proc Inc ....G...... 616 245-0465
  Grand Rapids *(G-6519)*
Bodycote Thermal Proc Inc ....F...... 734 427-6814
  Livonia *(G-10139)*
Burkk Inc ....F...... 616 365-0354
  Grand Rapids *(G-6536)*
Century Inc ....C...... 231 947-6400
  Traverse City *(G-16641)*
Curtis Metal Finishing Co ....F...... 248 588-3300
  Madison Heights *(G-10701)*
Curtiss-Wright Surface Tech ....G...... 734 728-8600
  Romulus *(G-14266)*
Darby Metal Treating Inc ....F...... 269 204-6504
  Plainwell *(G-13073)*
Detroit Edge Tool Company ....G...... 586 776-3727
  Roseville *(G-14397)*
Detroit Steel Treating Company ....E...... 248 334-7436
  Pontiac *(G-13361)*
Dynamic Mtal Treating Intl Inc ....E...... 734 459-8022
  Canton *(G-2457)*
East - Lind Heat Treat Inc ....E...... 248 585-1415
  Madison Heights *(G-10715)*
Engineered Heat Treat Inc ....E...... 248 588-5141
  Madison Heights *(G-10723)*
Federal Industrial Services ....G...... 313 533-9888
  Redford *(G-13734)*
Fire-Rite Inc ....E...... 313 273-3730
  Detroit *(G-4234)*

Gerdau McSteel Atmsphere Annli ....E........ 517 482-1374
  Lansing *(G-9842)*
Gestamp Mason LLC ....B...... 517 244-8800
  Mason *(G-11135)*
Grand Blanc Processing LLC ....D...... 810 694-6000
  Holly *(G-8275)*
Grand Rapids Polsg & Buffing ....E...... 616 241-2233
  Grand Rapids *(G-6766)*
Heat Treating Svcs Corp Amer ....E...... 248 858-2230
  Pontiac *(G-13377)*
Heat Treating Svcs Corp Amer ....E...... 248 332-1510
  Pontiac *(G-13378)*
Heat Treating Svcs Corp Amer ....G...... 248 253-9560
  Waterford *(G-18127)*
Hi-Tech Steel Treating Inc ....D...... 800 835-8294
  Saginaw *(G-14664)*
Houston Flame Hardening Co ....G...... 713 926-8017
  Clinton Township *(G-3254)*
Induction Engineering Inc ....F...... 586 716-4700
  New Baltimore *(G-11982)*
Induction Processing Inc ....E...... 586 756-5101
  Warren *(G-17862)*
Industrial Steel Treating Co ....D...... 517 787-6312
  Jackson *(G-8908)*
Ionbond LLC ....D...... 248 398-9100
  Madison Heights *(G-10748)*
J Hansen-Balk Stl Treating Co ....E...... 616 458-1414
  Grand Rapids *(G-6855)*
Laydon Enterprises Inc ....E...... 906 774-4633
  Iron Mountain *(G-8724)*
Magnum Induction Inc ....E...... 586 716-4700
  New Baltimore *(G-11986)*
MB Aerospace Warren LLC ....C...... 586 772-2500
  Warren *(G-17920)*
Metallurgical Processing LLC ....G...... 586 758-3100
  Warren *(G-17925)*
Metro Machine Works Inc ....D...... 734 941-4571
  Romulus *(G-14304)*
Midwest Heat Treat Inc ....E...... 616 395-9763
  Holland *(G-8148)*
Miller Tool Die Co ....G...... 734 738-1970
  Plymouth *(G-13244)*
Mpd Welding - Grand Rapids Inc ....E...... 616 248-9353
  Grand Rapids *(G-7031)*
Ncoc Inc ....E...... 248 548-5950
  Oak Park *(G-12632)*
New Hudson Corporation ....E...... 248 437-3970
  New Hudson *(G-12064)*
Nitrex Inc ....G...... 517 676-6370
  Mason *(G-11147)*
Omc Archtrim ....E...... 517 482-9411
  Lansing *(G-9877)*
Pioneer Metal Finishing LLC ....D...... 734 384-9000
  Monroe *(G-11569)*
Precision Heat Treating Co ....F...... 269 382-4660
  Kalamazoo *(G-9303)*
Production Tube Company Inc ....G...... 313 259-3990
  Detroit *(G-4537)*
Richter Precision Inc ....E...... 586 465-0500
  Fraser *(G-5989)*
Rmt Acquisition Company LLC ....G...... 248 353-4229
  Plymouth *(G-13286)*
Savanna Inc ....E...... 734 254-0566
  Plymouth *(G-13294)*
Savanna Inc ....E...... 248 353-8180
  Southfield *(G-15695)*
Schroth Enterprises Inc ....E...... 586 759-4240
  Grosse Pointe Farms *(G-7540)*
Solution Steel Treating LLC ....F...... 586 247-9250
  Shelby Township *(G-15338)*
South Haven Finishing Inc ....E...... 269 637-2047
  South Haven *(G-15413)*
Specialty Steel Treating Inc ....D...... 586 293-5355
  Farmington Hills *(G-5384)*
Steel Industries Inc ....G...... 313 535-8505
  Redford *(G-13774)*
Stokes Steel Treating Company ....E...... 810 235-3573
  Flint *(G-5771)*
Superior Heat Treat LLC ....E...... 586 792-9500
  Clinton Township *(G-3365)*
Thermal One Inc ....F...... 734 721-8500
  Westland *(G-18421)*
Trojan Heat Treat Inc ....D...... 517 568-4403
  Homer *(G-8358)*
Universal Induction Inc ....G...... 269 925-9890
  Benton Harbor *(G-1595)*
Walker Wire (ispat) Inc ....G...... 248 399-4800
  Sterling Heights *(G-16227)*
Woodworth Inc ....E...... 810 820-6780
  Flint *(G-5794)*

Employee Codes: A=Over 500 employees, B=251-500
C=101-250, D=51-100, E=20-50, F=10-19, G=3-9

HEAT TREATING: Metal

Woodworth Inc .... E 248 481-2354
  Pontiac *(G-13426)*
Woodworth Rassini Holding LLC .... D 248 481-2354
  Pontiac *(G-13427)*
Wyatt Services Inc .... F 586 264-8000
  Sterling Heights *(G-16233)*
Zion Industries Inc .... F 517 622-3409
  Grand Ledge *(G-6401)*

HEATERS: Room, Gas

U S Distributing Inc .... E 248 646-0550
  Birmingham *(G-1755)*

HEATING & AIR CONDITIONING EQPT & SPLYS WHOLESALERS

2 Brothers Holdings LLC .... G 517 487-3900
  Lansing *(G-9797)*
Marelli North America Inc .... E 248 403-2033
  Southfield *(G-15645)*
Young Supply Company .... E 313 875-3280
  Detroit *(G-4699)*

HEATING & AIR CONDITIONING UNITS, COMBINATION

Crown Heating Inc .... G 248 352-1688
  Detroit *(G-4109)*
Northstar Wholesale .... F 517 545-2379
  Howell *(G-8484)*
Terra Caloric LLC .... F 989 356-2113
  Alpena *(G-325)*

HEATING EQPT & SPLYS

Alhern-Martin Indus Frnc Co .... E 248 689-6363
  Troy *(G-16922)*
Banner Engineering & Sales Inc .... F 989 755-0584
  Saginaw *(G-14609)*
Commercial Works .... F 269 795-2060
  Middleville *(G-11304)*
Marshall Excelsior Co .... E 269 789-6700
  Marshall *(G-11065)*
River Valley Machine Inc .... F 269 673-8070
  Allegan *(G-181)*
Rlh Industries Inc .... F 989 732-0493
  Gaylord *(G-6155)*
Solaronics Inc .... E 248 651-5333
  Auburn Hills *(G-1035)*
Ventura Aerospace LLC .... E 734 357-0114
  Wixom *(G-18786)*
Whittaker Orgname Assoc Inc .... G 616 786-2255
  Holland *(G-8249)*

HEATING EQPT: Complete

Check Technology Solutions LLC ..... E 248 680-2323
  Troy *(G-17008)*
Combustion Research Corp .... E 248 852-3611
  Rochester Hills *(G-13979)*
Rapid Engineering LLC .... D 616 784-0500
  Comstock Park *(G-3642)*
Specified A Sltons Hldngs LLC .... D 616 784-0500
  Comstock Park *(G-3645)*
Weather-Rite LLC .... E 612 338-1401
  Comstock Park *(G-3651)*

HEATING EQPT: Induction

Capital Induction Inc .... F 586 322-1444
  Sterling Heights *(G-15951)*
Cyprium Induction LLC .... G 586 884-4982
  Sterling Heights *(G-15976)*
D K Enterprises Inc .... G 586 756-7350
  Warren *(G-17771)*
Eldec LLC .... F 248 364-4750
  Auburn Hills *(G-876)*
Electroheat Technologies LLC .... E 810 798-2400
  Auburn Hills *(G-877)*
Heating Induction Services Inc .... G 586 791-3160
  Clinton Township *(G-3252)*
Inter-Power Corporation .... E 810 798-9201
  Almont *(G-262)*
Interpower Induction Svcs Inc .... F 586 296-7697
  Fraser *(G-5945)*
Phoenix Induction Corporation .... F 248 486-7377
  South Lyon *(G-15453)*
Pillar Induction .... F 586 254-8470
  Madison Heights *(G-10799)*
Sheler Corporation .... E 586 979-8560
  Sterling Heights *(G-16176)*

SMS Elotherm North America LLC ... F 586 469-8324
  Shelby Township *(G-15336)*

HEATING SYSTEMS: Radiant, Indl Process

Florheat Company .... G 517 272-4441
  Lansing *(G-9836)*
Solaronics Inc .... E 248 651-5333
  Auburn Hills *(G-1035)*

HEATING UNITS & DEVICES: Indl, Electric

Alhern-Martin Indus Frnc Co .... E 248 689-6363
  Troy *(G-16922)*
Custom Electric Mfg LLC .... E 248 305-7700
  Wixom *(G-18642)*
Ddr Heating Inc .... F 269 673-2145
  Allegan *(G-154)*
E H Inc .... F 269 673-6456
  Allegan *(G-156)*
Furnaces Ovens & Baths Inc .... E 248 625-7400
  River Rouge *(G-13854)*
Great Lkes Indus Frnc Svcs Inc .... F 586 323-9200
  Sterling Heights *(G-16033)*
Hi-Tech Furnace Systems Inc .... F 586 566-0600
  Shelby Township *(G-15235)*
Hotset Corp .... G 269 964-0271
  Battle Creek *(G-1238)*
Industrial Frnc Interiors Inc .... E 586 977-9600
  Sterling Heights *(G-16048)*
National Appliance Parts Co .... E 269 639-1469
  South Haven *(G-15410)*
National Element Inc .... E 248 486-1810
  Brighton *(G-2040)*
Nexthermal Corporation .... D 269 964-0271
  Battle Creek *(G-1279)*

HELICOPTERS

G-Force Tooling LLC .... E 517 541-2747
  Charlotte *(G-2757)*

HELMETS: Athletic

Xenith LLC .... E 866 888-2322
  Detroit *(G-4694)*

HELP SUPPLY SERVICES

Msx International Inc .... C 248 585-6654
  Madison Heights *(G-10786)*

HERMETICS REPAIR SVCS

Gustos Quality Systems .... G 231 409-0219
  Fife Lake *(G-5607)*

HIGHWAY & STREET MAINTENANCE SVCS

Southwestern Mich Dust Ctrl .... E 269 521-7638
  Bloomingdale *(G-1879)*

HITCHES: Trailer

Hensley Mfg Inc .... F 810 653-3226
  Davison *(G-3786)*
Horizon Global Americas Inc .... C 734 656-3000
  Plymouth *(G-13191)*
Rieke-Arminak Corp .... E 248 631-5450
  Bloomfield Hills *(G-1857)*
Trimas Corporation .... G 248 631-5451
  Ann Arbor *(G-698)*
Trimas Corporation .... B 248 631-5450
  Bloomfield Hills *(G-1869)*

HOBBY, TOY & GAME STORES: Arts & Crafts & Splys

Toms World of Wood .... G 517 264-2836
  Adrian *(G-99)*

HOBBY, TOY & GAME STORES: Toys & Games

Dog Might LLC .... F 734 679-0646
  Ann Arbor *(G-455)*

HOISTING SLINGS

K&S Consultants LLC .... G 269 240-7767
  Buchanan *(G-2198)*

HOISTS

Besser Company USA .... D 616 399-5215
  Zeeland *(G-18998)*
Detroit Hoist & Crane Co L L C .... E 586 268-2600
  Sterling Heights *(G-15982)*

HOISTS: Hand

Frost Incorporated .... E 616 453-7781
  Grand Rapids *(G-6722)*

HOLDERS, PAPER TOWEL, GROCERY BAG, ETC: Plastic

Able Solutions LLC .... G 810 216-6106
  Port Huron *(G-13430)*

HOLDING COMPANIES: Investment, Exc Banks

A Raymond Corp N Amer Inc .... E 248 853-2500
  Rochester Hills *(G-13938)*
Anderton Equity LLC .... G 248 430-6650
  Troy *(G-16937)*
Avon Machining Holdings Inc .... C 586 884-2200
  Shelby Township *(G-15176)*
Bbp Investment Holdings LLC .... B 231 725-4966
  Muskegon *(G-11777)*
Dawn Foods Inc .... C 517 789-4400
  Jackson *(G-8864)*
Ej Americas LLC .... G 231 536-2261
  East Jordan *(G-4863)*
Erae AMS America Corp .... F 419 386-8876
  Pontiac *(G-13368)*
Flint Group Pckg Inks N Amer H ...... G 734 781-4600
  Livonia *(G-10210)*
Gns North America Inc .... G 616 796-0433
  Holland *(G-8054)*
Knpc Holdco LLC .... G 248 588-1903
  Madison Heights *(G-10764)*
M10 Group Holding Company .... G 248 356-4399
  Southfield *(G-15639)*
Med Michigan Holdings LLC .... G 888 891-1200
  Plymouth *(G-13239)*
Motus Holdings LLC .... G 616 422-7557
  Holland *(G-8149)*
Raven Acquisition LLC .... B 734 254-5000
  Holly *(G-8291)*
Sandbox Solutions Inc .... C 248 349-7010
  Northville *(G-12257)*
Sunmed Holdings LLC .... E 616 259-8400
  Grand Rapids *(G-7235)*
Tecumseh Products Holdings LLC .. C 734 585-9500
  Ann Arbor *(G-680)*
Truck Holdings Inc .... G 877 875-4376
  Ann Arbor *(G-700)*
Xileh Holding Inc .... G 248 340-4100
  Auburn Hills *(G-1090)*

HOLDING COMPANIES: Personal, Exc Banks

Howa USA Holdings Inc .... G 248 715-4000
  Novi *(G-12436)*

HOLDING COMPANIES: Public Utility

Uc Holdings Inc .... D 248 728-8642
  Southfield *(G-15730)*

HOME CENTER STORES

Swartzmiller Lumber Company .... G 989 845-6625
  Chesaning *(G-2830)*

HOME DELIVERY NEWSPAPER ROUTES

Pathway Publishing Corporation ...... F 269 521-3025
  Bloomingdale *(G-1878)*

HOME ENTERTAINMENT EQPT: Electronic, NEC

Donley Computer Services LLC .... G 231 750-1774
  Muskegon *(G-11800)*
Intellitech Systems Inc .... G 586 219-3737
  Troy *(G-17170)*
M A S Information Age Tech .... G 248 352-0162
  Southfield *(G-15638)*

PRODUCT SECTION

HOME FURNISHINGS STORES, NEC

Affordable Pool and Spa Inc ....F 810 422-5058
  Burton *(G-2225)*
Allstate HM Leisure Strlng Hts ....G 734 838-6500
  Sterling Heights *(G-15928)*
Lecreuset ....G 248 209-7025
  Auburn Hills *(G-957)*

HOME FURNISHINGS WHOLESALERS

Humphrey Companies LLC ....C 616 530-1717
  Grandville *(G-7389)*

HOME HEALTH CARE SVCS

Landra Prsthtics Orthotics Inc ....G 586 294-7188
  Saint Clair Shores *(G-14868)*

HOME IMPROVEMENT & RENOVATION CONTRACTOR AGENCY

Altered Stone Realty Co LLC ....F 313 800-0362
  Detroit *(G-4005)*
Overstreet Property MGT Co ....G 269 281-3880
  Benton Harbor *(G-1578)*
Power Property Solutions LLC ....G 734 306-0299
  Wayne *(G-18232)*

HOMEBUILDERS & OTHER OPERATIVE BUILDERS

Lumber & Truss Inc ....F 810 664-7290
  Lapeer *(G-9945)*

HOMEFURNISHING STORE: Bedding, Sheet, Blanket, Spread/Pillow

Shop Makarios LLC ....F 800 479-0032
  Byron Center *(G-2295)*

HOMEFURNISHING STORES: Closet organizers & shelving units

Pipp MBL Stor Systems Hldg Cor ....C 616 735-9100
  Walker *(G-17646)*

HOMEFURNISHING STORES: Lighting Fixtures

Spire Integrated Systems Inc ....E 248 544-0072
  Troy *(G-17367)*

HOMEFURNISHING STORES: Vertical Blinds

Detroit Custom Services Inc ....E 586 465-3631
  Mount Clemens *(G-11636)*

HOMEFURNISHING STORES: Window Furnishings

Time For Blinds Inc ....G 248 363-9174
  White Lake *(G-18469)*

HOMEFURNISHINGS, WHOLESALE: Blankets

Grabber Inc ....E 616 940-1914
  Byron Center *(G-2274)*

HOMEFURNISHINGS, WHOLESALE: Blinds, Venetian

Custom Verticals Unlimited ....G 734 522-1615
  Oak Park *(G-12603)*
Elsie Inc ....E 734 421-8844
  Livonia *(G-10196)*
Sunburst Shutters ....G 248 674-4600
  Waterford *(G-18167)*

HOMEFURNISHINGS, WHOLESALE: Carpets

Floorcovering Engineers LLC ....G 616 299-1007
  Grand Rapids *(G-6712)*
James E Sullivan & Associates ....G 616 453-0345
  Grand Rapids *(G-6860)*
Parkway Drapery & Uphl Co Inc ....G 734 779-1300
  Livonia *(G-10360)*

HOMEFURNISHINGS, WHOLESALE: Mirrors/Pictures, Framed/Unframd

Prime Wood Products Inc ....G 616 399-4700
  Holland *(G-8170)*

HOMEFURNISHINGS, WHOLESALE: Pottery

Penzo America Inc ....G 248 723-0802
  Bloomfield Hills *(G-1850)*

HOMES, MODULAR: Wooden

Dickinson Homes Inc ....E 906 774-5800
  Kingsford *(G-9508)*
E B I Inc ....G 810 227-8180
  Brighton *(G-1980)*
Hunt Hoppough Custom Crafted ....G 616 794-3455
  Belding *(G-1452)*
Marshalls Crossing ....G 810 639-4740
  Montrose *(G-11606)*
Ritz-Craft Corp PA Inc ....C 517 849-7425
  Jonesville *(G-9100)*

HOMES: Log Cabins

Beaver Log Homes Inc ....F 231 258-5020
  Kalkaska *(G-9383)*
Classic Log Homes Incorporated ....F 989 821-6118
  Higgins Lake *(G-7876)*
G B Wolfgram and Sons Inc ....F 231 238-4638
  Indian River *(G-8652)*
Harman Lumber & Supply Inc ....G 269 641-5424
  Union *(G-17488)*
Koskis Log Homes Inc ....F 906 884-4937
  Ontonagon *(G-12713)*
Log Home Specialty ....G 231 943-9410
  Traverse City *(G-16747)*
Masons Lumber & Hardware Inc ....G 989 685-3999
  Rose City *(G-14365)*
North Arrow Log Homes Inc ....G 906 484-5524
  Pickford *(G-13031)*
Northern Michigan Log Homes ....G 989 345-7463
  West Branch *(G-18332)*
Pine Creek Log Home ....G 231 848-4436
  Wellston *(G-18259)*
Riverbend Timber Framing Inc ....E 517 486-3629
  Blissfield *(G-1776)*
U P North Structures ....G 989 654-2350
  Sterling *(G-15914)*

HONES

Howell Tool Service Inc ....F 517 548-1114
  Howell *(G-8465)*

HONING & LAPPING MACHINES

Nagel Precision Inc ....C 734 426-5650
  Ann Arbor *(G-587)*

HOODS: Range, Sheet Metal

Curbs & Damper Products Inc ....F 586 776-7890
  Roseville *(G-14392)*

HOPPERS: Sheet Metal

Material Handling Tech Inc ....D 586 725-5546
  Ira *(G-8701)*

HORNS: Marine, Compressed Air Or Steam

Dts Enterprises Inc ....E 231 599-3123
  Ellsworth *(G-5035)*

HORSE & PET ACCESSORIES: Textile

Upperhand Tack Co LLC ....G 906 424-0401
  Williamston *(G-18584)*

HORSESHOES

Lincoln Park Die & Tool Co ....E 734 285-1680
  Brownstown *(G-2149)*

HOSE: Air Line Or Air Brake, Rubber Or Rubberized Fabric

Andronaco Inc ....F 616 554-4600
  Kentwood *(G-9442)*
Grenell Manufacturing LLC ....G 616 304-1593
  Lakeview *(G-9641)*

HOSE: Automobile, Plastic

Dayco Products LLC ....G 248 404-6506
  Troy *(G-17047)*
Sejasmi Industries Inc ....C 586 725-5300
  Ira *(G-8713)*

HOSE: Flexible Metal

Northern Fab & Machine LLC ....F 906 863-8506
  Menominee *(G-11255)*
TI Group Auto Systems LLC ....B 248 296-8000
  Auburn Hills *(G-1055)*

HOSE: Plastic

Haviland Contoured Plastics ....G 616 361-6691
  Walker *(G-17640)*
Piranha Hose Products Inc ....E 231 779-4390
  Cadillac *(G-2348)*
TI Fluid Systems LLC ....A 248 494-5000
  Auburn Hills *(G-1054)*
TI Group Auto Systems LLC ....B 248 296-8000
  Auburn Hills *(G-1055)*

HOSE: Pneumatic, Rubber Or Rubberized Fabric, NEC

Snook Inc ....F 231 799-3333
  Norton Shores *(G-12332)*

HOSE: Rubber

Dayco Products LLC ....G 248 404-6537
  Roseville *(G-14393)*
Kadant Johnson LLC ....C 269 278-1715
  Three Rivers *(G-16577)*
Pureflex Inc ....C 616 554-1100
  Kentwood *(G-9473)*

HOSES & BELTING: Rubber & Plastic

Akwel Cadillac Usa Inc ....G 248 848-9599
  Farmington Hills *(G-5166)*
Anand Nvh North America Inc ....C 810 724-2400
  Imlay City *(G-8627)*
Atcoflex Inc ....F 616 842-4661
  Grand Haven *(G-6277)*
Eaton Aeroquip LLC ....B 949 452-9575
  Jackson *(G-8873)*
Ena North America Corporation ....E 248 926-0011
  Wixom *(G-18656)*
Flexfab LLC ....E 269 945-3533
  Grand Rapids *(G-6711)*
Flexfab Horizons Intl Inc ....E 269 945-4700
  Hastings *(G-7791)*
Flexfab LLC ....G 800 331-0003
  Hastings *(G-7792)*
H P P ....G 248 307-4263
  Madison Heights *(G-10737)*
Lauren Zinn ....G 734 996-3524
  Ann Arbor *(G-549)*
Stephen A James ....G 269 641-5879
  Cassopolis *(G-2634)*
Thunder Technologies LLC ....F 248 844-4875
  Rochester Hills *(G-14126)*
Ton-Tex Corporation ....F 616 957-3200
  Greenville *(G-7508)*

HOSPITAL EQPT REPAIR SVCS

Vets Access LLC ....G 810 639-2222
  Flushing *(G-5815)*

HOSPITALS: Medical & Surgical

Avissa Skin+body ....G 734 316-5556
  Ann Arbor *(G-389)*
Professional Hearing Services ....G 517 439-1610
  Hillsdale *(G-7942)*

HOSTELS

Soutec Div of Andritz Bricmont ....E 248 305-2955
  Novi *(G-12540)*

HOT TUBS

Conway Products Corporation ....E 616 698-2601
  Grand Rapids *(G-6603)*
Viking Spas Inc ....F 616 248-7800
  Wyoming *(G-18917)*

Employee Codes: A=Over 500 employees, B=251-500
C=101-250, D=51-100, E=20-50, F=10-19, G=3-9

HOT TUBS: Plastic & Fiberglass

Aquatic Co .... C 269 279-7461
   Three Rivers *(G-16564)*

HOUSEHOLD APPLIANCE PARTS: Wholesalers

Home Chef Ltd .... G 734 468-2544
   Westland *(G-18384)*

HOUSEHOLD APPLIANCE STORES

Lockett Enterprises LLC .... G 810 407-6644
   Flint *(G-5725)*

HOUSEHOLD APPLIANCE STORES: Electric Household, Major

Marrs Discount Furniture .... G 989 720-5436
   Owosso *(G-12840)*

HOUSEHOLD ARTICLES: Metal

Bulman Products Inc .... E 616 363-4416
   Grand Rapids *(G-6531)*
Heath Manufacturing Company .... E 616 997-8181
   Coopersville *(G-3688)*

HOUSEHOLD FURNISHINGS, NEC

Anchor Wiping Cloth Inc .... D 313 892-4000
   Detroit *(G-4019)*
Gamco Inc .... F 269 683-4280
   Niles *(G-12132)*
Intramode LLC .... G 313 964-6990
   Detroit *(G-4324)*
Lmp Worldwide Inc .... G 248 669-6103
   Wixom *(G-18700)*
Preferred Products Inc .... F 248 255-0200
   Commerce Township *(G-3565)*

HOUSEWARE STORES

Candle Factory Grand Traverse .... G 231 946-2280
   Traverse City *(G-16638)*

HOUSEWARES, ELECTRIC, EXC COOKING APPLIANCES & UTENSILS

Distinctive Appliances Distrg .... F 248 380-2007
   Wixom *(G-18646)*

HOUSEWARES, ELECTRIC: Blankets

Neptech Inc .... E 810 225-2222
   Highland *(G-7897)*
Sampling Bag Technologies LLC .... G 734 525-8600
   Livonia *(G-10399)*

HOUSEWARES, ELECTRIC: Blenders

Advanced Blnding Solutions LLC .... F 906 914-4180
   Menominee *(G-11224)*

HOUSEWARES, ELECTRIC: Heaters, Sauna

Nippa Sauna Stoves LLC .... G 231 882-7707
   Beulah *(G-1656)*

HOUSEWARES, ELECTRIC: Heaters, Space

Therm Technology Corp .... G 616 530-6540
   Grandville *(G-7421)*

HOUSEWARES, ELECTRIC: Heating Units, Electric Appliances

Ogilvie Manufacturing Company .... G 810 793-6598
   Lapeer *(G-9951)*
Weco International Inc .... F 810 686-7221
   Flushing *(G-5816)*

HOUSEWARES, ELECTRIC: Humidifiers, Household

Cdgjl Inc .... E 517 787-2100
   Jackson *(G-8836)*

HOUSEWARES, ELECTRIC: Massage Machines, Exc Beauty/Barber

Aesthtic Affcts Stffing Agcy L .... G 734 436-1248
   Canton *(G-2431)*
Fka Distributing Co LLC .... C 248 863-3000
   Commerce Township *(G-3530)*
Hands That Heal .... G 517 740-6930
   Jackson *(G-8899)*
Iscuplt LLC .... G 313 728-7982
   Taylor *(G-16428)*
Sweed Dreams LLC .... G 313 704-6694
   Livonia *(G-10425)*

HOUSEWARES: Bowls, Wood

Holland Bowl Mill .... F 616 396-6513
   Holland *(G-8075)*

HOUSEWARES: Dishes, Plastic

D&W Fine Pack LLC .... D 866 296-2020
   Gladwin *(G-6194)*
I-Drink Products Inc .... G 734 531-6324
   Ann Arbor *(G-521)*
Munimula Inc .... F 517 605-5343
   Quincy *(G-13673)*
Solo Cup Operating Corporation .... D 800 248-5960
   Mason *(G-11156)*

HOUSEWARES: Dishes, Wooden

Mbwwproducts Inc .... F 616 464-1650
   Grand Rapids *(G-6969)*

HOUSEWARES: Plates, Pressed/Molded Pulp, From Purchased Mtrl

AJM Packaging Corporation .... D 313 291-6500
   Taylor *(G-16375)*

HOUSING PROGRAMS ADMINISTRATION SVCS

Genstone LLC .... G 517 902-4730
   Adrian *(G-70)*

HOUSINGS: Business Machine, Sheet Metal

Diversified Fabricators Inc .... F 586 868-1000
   Clinton Township *(G-3225)*

HUB CAPS: Automobile, Stamped Metal

Capco Automovite .... G 248 616-8888
   Troy *(G-16997)*
Stemco Products Inc .... G 888 854-6474
   Millington *(G-11503)*

HUMIDIFIERS & DEHUMIDIFIERS

Way2go Tech LLC .... G 616 294-1301
   Holland *(G-8242)*

HUMIDIFYING EQPT, EXC PORTABLE

General Filters Inc .... E 248 476-5100
   Novi *(G-12423)*

HYDRAULIC EQPT REPAIR SVC

American Electric Motor Corp .... F 810 743-6080
   Burton *(G-2226)*
Cpj Company Inc .... E 616 784-6355
   Comstock Park *(G-3598)*
Great Lakes Hydra Corporation .... F 231 258-4338
   Kalkaska *(G-9389)*
Ksb Dubric Inc .... E 616 784-6355
   Comstock Park *(G-3618)*
Npi .... G 248 478-0010
   Farmington Hills *(G-5336)*
Sarns Industries Inc .... E 586 463-5829
   Harrison Twp *(G-7739)*
Tri-Tech Engineering Inc .... E 734 283-3700
   Wyandotte *(G-18842)*
Yates Industries Inc .... D 586 778-7680
   Saint Clair Shores *(G-14892)*
Yoe Industries Inc .... G 586 791-7660
   Clinton Township *(G-3391)*

HYDRAULIC FLUIDS: Synthetic Based

American Chemical Tech Inc .... E 866 945-1041
   Howell *(G-8428)*

Chem-Trend Limited Partnership .... C 517 546-4520
   Howell *(G-8438)*
Quaker Houghton Pa Inc .... E 248 265-7745
   Troy *(G-17325)*

HYDROPONIC EQPT

420 Group .... G 586 978-0420
   Sterling Heights *(G-15916)*
Cultivation Station Inc .... G 313 383-1766
   Allen Park *(G-191)*
Zerilli & Sesi LLC .... G 586 741-8805
   Chesterfield *(G-2967)*

Hard Rubber & Molded Rubber Prdts

Americo Corporation .... G 313 565-6550
   Dearborn *(G-3807)*
Ehc Inc .... G 313 259-2266
   Troy *(G-17079)*

ICE

Arctic Glacier Grayling Inc .... F 810 987-7100
   Port Huron *(G-13440)*
Arctic Glacier Inc .... E 734 485-0430
   Port Huron *(G-13441)*
Arctic Glacier Newburgh Inc .... F 845 561-0549
   Port Huron *(G-13442)*
Arctic Glacier USA Inc .... E 204 772-2473
   Port Huron *(G-13444)*
Arctic Glacier USA Inc .... E 204 772-2473
   Port Huron *(G-13445)*
Arctic Glacier USA Inc .... E 204 772-2473
   Port Huron *(G-13446)*
Arctic Glacier USA Inc .... E 204 772-2473
   Port Huron *(G-13448)*
Arctic Glacier USA Inc .... E 204 772-2473
   Port Huron *(G-13449)*
Arctic Glacier USA Inc .... E 204 772-2473
   Port Huron *(G-13450)*
Arctic Glacier USA Inc .... E 204 772-2473
   Port Huron *(G-13451)*
Arctic Glacier USA Inc .... E 204 772-2473
   Port Huron *(G-13452)*
Arctic Glacier USA Inc .... E 204 772-2473
   Port Huron *(G-13453)*
Cosner Ice Company Inc .... B 812 279-8930
   Port Huron *(G-13466)*
Daneks Goodtime Ice Co Inc .... G 989 725-5920
   Owosso *(G-12830)*
Gold Coast Ice Makers LLC .... G 231 845-2745
   Ludington *(G-10537)*
Hanson Cold Storage LLC .... F 269 982-1390
   Saint Joseph *(G-14933)*
Lansing Ice and Fuel Company .... F 517 372-3850
   Lansing *(G-9710)*

ICE CREAM & ICES WHOLESALERS

Cold Stone Creamery .... F 313 886-4020
   Grosse Pointe Park *(G-7550)*
Moomers Homemade Ice Cream LLC ...... F 231 941-4122
   Traverse City *(G-16763)*

ICE WHOLESALERS

Arctic Glacier Inc .... E 734 485-0430
   Port Huron *(G-13441)*

IDENTIFICATION PLATES

Keyes-Davis Company .... E 269 962-7505
   Springfield *(G-15871)*

IDENTIFICATION TAGS, EXC PAPER

Industrial Mtal Idntfction Inc .... G 616 847-0060
   Spring Lake *(G-15824)*

IGNITION COILS: Automotive

Case Tool Inc .... G 734 261-2227
   Livonia *(G-10148)*
Diamond Electric Mfg Corp .... F 734 995-5525
   Farmington Hills *(G-5215)*
Eldor Automotive N Amer Inc .... E 248 878-9193
   Troy *(G-17082)*

IGNITION SYSTEMS: High Frequency

Emp Racing Inc .... G 906 786-8404
   Escanaba *(G-5068)*

PRODUCT SECTION

INCINERATORS

Durr Inc .... G 734 459-6800
  Southfield (G-15544)
Durr Systems Inc .... B 248 450-2000
  Southfield (G-15545)

INDL & PERSONAL SVC PAPER WHOLESALERS

ABC Packaging Eqp & Mtls Inc .... F 616 784-2330
  Comstock Park (G-3584)
Associated Metals Inc .... G 734 369-3851
  Ann Arbor (G-384)
Fibers of Kalamazoo Inc .... E 269 344-3122
  Kalamazoo (G-9186)
Mark-Pack Inc .... E 616 837-5400
  Coopersville (G-3691)

INDL & PERSONAL SVC PAPER, WHOL: Bags, Paper/Disp Plastic

Chelsea Milling Company .... F 269 781-2823
  Marshall (G-11055)

INDL & PERSONAL SVC PAPER, WHOL: Boxes, Corrugtd/Solid Fiber

All American Container Corp .... F 586 949-0000
  Macomb (G-10573)
Compak Inc .... G 989 288-3199
  Burton (G-2233)
National Packaging Corporation .... F 248 652-3600
  Rochester Hills (G-14068)
Russell R Peters Co LLC .... G 989 732-0660
  Gaylord (G-6157)
St Clair Packaging Inc .... E 810 364-4230
  Marysville (G-11104)
Wrkco Inc .... E 269 964-7181
  Battle Creek (G-1312)

INDL & PERSONAL SVC PAPER, WHOL: Paper, Wrap/Coarse/Prdts

Practical Paper Inc .... F 616 887-1723
  Cedar Springs (G-2658)

INDL & PERSONAL SVC PAPER, WHOLESALE: Press Sensitive Tape

Aactus Inc .... G 734 425-1212
  Livonia (G-10096)
Elliott Tape Inc .... E 248 475-2000
  Auburn Hills (G-878)

INDL & PERSONAL SVC PAPER, WHOLESALE: Shipping Splys

Pak Mail Center of America .... G 248 543-3097
  Ferndale (G-5575)
Volk Corporation .... G 616 940-9900
  Northville (G-12270)

INDL EQPT CLEANING SVCS

Chemico Systems Inc .... E 248 723-3263
  Southfield (G-15521)

INDL EQPT SVCS

American Steel Works Inc .... F 734 282-0300
  Riverview (G-13869)
Back Machine Shop LLC .... G 269 963-7061
  Springfield (G-15860)
C R B Crane & Service Co .... E 586 757-1222
  Warren (G-17747)
Clarkston Control Products .... G 248 394-1430
  Clarkston (G-3024)
Equitable Engineering Co Inc .... E 248 689-9700
  Troy (G-17096)
F&B Technologies .... F 734 856-2118
  Ottawa Lake (G-12806)
Fidia Co .... F 248 680-0700
  Rochester Hills (G-14011)
Franklin Electric Corporation .... F 248 442-8000
  Garden City (G-6094)
Great Lkes Indus Frnc Svcs Inc .... G 586 323-9200
  Sterling Heights (G-16033)
Hammars Contracting LLC .... E 810 367-3037
  Kimball (G-9493)

Island Machine and Engrg LLC .... G 810 765-8228
  Marine City (G-10960)
Mahle Industries Incorporated .... E 248 305-8200
  Farmington Hills (G-5303)
Matrix Mtlcraft LLP A Ltd Prtn .... G 248 724-1800
  Auburn Hills (G-970)
Stirnemann Tool & Mch Co Inc .... E 248 435-4040
  Clawson (G-3110)
Wolverine Crane & Service Inc .... E 616 538-4870
  Grand Rapids (G-7345)
Wolverine Crane & Service Inc .... E 734 467-9066
  Romulus (G-14339)

INDL MACHINERY & EQPT WHOLESALERS

AA Anderson & Co Inc .... E 248 476-7782
  Plymouth (G-13110)
Ability Mfg & Engrg Co .... D 269 227-3292
  Fennville (G-5433)
Advanced Feedlines LLC .... E 248 583-9400
  Troy (G-16908)
Aero Grinding Inc .... G 586 774-6450
  Roseville (G-14372)
AG Davis Gage & Engrg Co .... G 586 977-9000
  Sterling Heights (G-15926)
B & H Machine Sales Inc .... E 313 843-6720
  Detroit (G-4039)
Becktold Enterprises Inc .... G 269 349-3656
  Kalamazoo (G-9133)
Belco Industries Inc .... E 616 794-0410
  Belding (G-1438)
Benny Gage Inc .... E 734 455-3080
  Wixom (G-18620)
Bobier Tool Supply Inc .... G 810 732-4030
  Flint (G-5658)
Brawn Mixer Inc .... E 616 399-5600
  Holland (G-7982)
Campbell Inc Press Repair .... F 517 371-1034
  Lansing (G-9821)
Custom Valve Concepts Inc .... E 248 597-8999
  Madison Heights (G-10702)
Dadco Inc .... D 734 207-1100
  Plymouth (G-13151)
Dcl Inc .... C 231 547-5600
  Charlevoix (G-2714)
Dee-Blast Corporation .... F 269 428-2400
  Stevensville (G-16246)
Dimond Machinery Company Inc .... F 269 945-5908
  Hastings (G-7790)
Douglas Water Conditioning .... F 248 363-8383
  Waterford (G-18117)
Dumas Concepts In Building Inc .... F 313 895-2555
  Detroit (G-4196)
Dupearl Technology LLC .... G 248 390-9609
  Bloomfield Hills (G-1816)
Energy Products Inc .... G 248 866-5622
  Troy (G-17090)
Energy Products Inc .... E 248 545-7700
  Madison Heights (G-10722)
Esoc Inc .... F 248 624-7992
  Wixom (G-18658)
Fata Aluminum LLC .... E 248 802-9853
  Orion (G-12729)
Fisher-Baker Corporation .... G 810 765-3548
  Marine City (G-10958)
Fitz-Rite Products Inc .... E 248 528-8440
  Troy (G-17113)
Flint Hydrostatics Inc .... F 901 794-2462
  Chesterfield (G-2883)
Flow Ezy Filters Inc .... F 734 665-8777
  Ann Arbor (G-491)
General Processing Systems Inc .... F 630 554-7804
  Holland (G-8046)
Global CNC Industries Ltd .... E 734 464-1920
  Plymouth (G-13177)
Green Age Products & Svcs LLC .... E 586 207-5724
  Washington (G-18080)
Heck Industries Incorporated .... F 810 632-5400
  Hartland (G-7769)
Hitachi America Ltd .... G 248 477-5400
  Farmington Hills (G-5261)
Hoffmann Filter Corporation .... F 248 486-8430
  Brighton (G-2008)
Hot Melt Technologies Inc .... E 248 853-2011
  Rochester Hills (G-14034)
Htc Sales Corporation .... F 800 624-2027
  Ira (G-8698)
Hydraulex Intl Holdings Inc .... E 914 682-2700
  Chesterfield (G-2891)
Icon Industries Inc .... G 616 241-1877
  Grand Rapids (G-6829)

INDL MACHINERY & EQPT WHOLESALERS

Independent Mfg Solutions Corp .... E 248 960-3550
  Wixom (G-18684)
Industrial Automation LLC .... D 248 598-5900
  Rochester Hills (G-14039)
Integrated Conveyor Ltd .... G 231 747-6430
  Muskegon (G-11841)
Iron River Mfg Co Inc .... G 906 265-5121
  Iron River (G-8741)
Ivan Doverspike .... F 313 579-3000
  Detroit (G-4328)
Jetech Inc .... E 269 965-6311
  Battle Creek (G-1246)
Johnson Controls Inc .... D 248 276-6000
  Auburn Hills (G-945)
Kalamazoo Mfg Corp Globl .... C 269 382-8200
  Kalamazoo (G-9243)
Kalamazoo Packg Systems LLC .... F 616 534-2600
  Wyoming (G-18888)
Kecy Products Inc .... E 517 448-8954
  Hudson (G-8554)
Kuka US Holdings Company LLC .... D 586 795-2000
  Sterling Heights (G-16067)
Leitz Tooling Systems LP .... G 616 698-7010
  Grand Rapids (G-6940)
Leitz Tooling Systems LP .... G 616 698-7010
  Grand Rapids (G-6941)
Lubecon Systems Inc .... G 231 689-0002
  White Cloud (G-18445)
Mac Material Acquisition Co .... G 248 685-8393
  Highland (G-7895)
Madison Street Holdings LLC .... E 517 252-2031
  Adrian (G-81)
Merrifield McHy Solutions Inc .... E 248 494-7335
  Sterling Heights (G-16091)
Metaris Hydraulics .... F 586 949-4240
  Chesterfield (G-2912)
Metzgar Conveyor Co .... E 616 784-0930
  Grand Rapids (G-6983)
Mhr Inc .... E 616 394-0191
  Holland (G-8146)
Michigan Shippers Supply Inc .... F 616 935-6680
  Spring Lake (G-15835)
Mobile Knowledge Group LLC .... G 248 625-3327
  Clarkston (G-3052)
Montronix Inc .... G 734 213-6500
  Ann Arbor (G-583)
Nabtesco Motion Control Inc .... F 248 553-3020
  Farmington Hills (G-5329)
National Bulk Equipment Inc .... C 616 399-2220
  Holland (G-8151)
North American Mch & Engrg Co .... G 586 726-6700
  Shelby Township (G-15291)
Oliver of Adrian Inc .... E 517 263-2132
  Adrian (G-86)
Omni Metalcraft Corp .... E 989 354-4075
  Alpena (G-306)
Posa-Cut Corporation .... E 248 474-5620
  Farmington Hills (G-5350)
Prab Inc .... C 269 382-8200
  Kalamazoo (G-9299)
Puritan Magnetics Inc .... F 248 628-3808
  Oxford (G-12908)
R Concepts Incorporated .... G 810 632-4857
  Howell (G-8505)
R M Wright Company Inc .... E 248 476-9800
  Farmington Hills (G-5363)
Rapidtek LLC .... G 616 662-0954
  Hudsonville (G-8603)
Reif Carbide Tool Co Inc .... E 586 754-1890
  Warren (G-17995)
Reko International Holdings .... G 519 737-6974
  Bloomfield Hills (G-1854)
Reliable Sales Co .... G 248 969-0943
  Oxford (G-12912)
Rempco Acquisition Inc .... G 231 775-0108
  Cadillac (G-2351)
Rocon LLC .... G 248 542-9635
  Hazel Park (G-7840)
Roesch Maufacturing Co LLC .... E 517 424-6300
  Tecumseh (G-16514)
Roy A Hutchins Company .... E 248 437-3470
  New Hudson (G-12069)
Schuler Incorporated .... D 734 207-7200
  Canton (G-2522)
Sebright Products Inc .... E 269 793-7183
  Hopkins (G-8369)
Sinto America Inc .... E 517 371-2460
  Lansing (G-9791)
Spray Booth Products Inc .... E 313 766-4400
  Redford (G-13773)

Employee Codes: A=Over 500 employees, B=251-500
C=101-250, D=51-100, E=20-50, F=10-19, G=3-9

INDL MACHINERY & EQPT WHOLESALERS

Tool-Craft Industries Inc .... E 248 549-0077
  Sterling Heights *(G-16206)*
Tooling Solutions Group LLC .... G 248 585-0222
  Madison Heights *(G-10844)*
Trinity Holding Inc .... F 517 787-3100
  Jackson *(G-9024)*
Trucent Inc .... G 734 426-9015
  Dexter *(G-4759)*
U S Equipment Co .... E 313 526-8300
  Rochester Hills *(G-14134)*
Ube Machinery Inc .... D 734 741-7000
  Ann Arbor *(G-702)*
Ulb LLC .... E 734 233-0961
  Wixom *(G-18781)*
Warren Manufacturing .... G 269 483-0603
  White Pigeon *(G-18486)*
Western International Inc .... E 866 814-2470
  Troy *(G-17447)*
Williams Parts & Supply Co .... F 906 337-3813
  Calumet *(G-2418)*

INDL MACHINERY REPAIR & MAINTENANCE

1271 Associates Inc .... D 586 948-4300
  Chesterfield *(G-2832)*
American Pride Machining Inc .... G 586 294-6404
  Fraser *(G-5892)*
American Wldg & Press Repr Inc .... F 248 358-2050
  Southfield *(G-15486)*
Ase Industries Inc .... D 586 754-7480
  Warren *(G-17718)*
Bell Fork Lift Inc .... F 313 841-1220
  Detroit *(G-4049)*
CB Industrial LLC .... F 248 264-9800
  New Hudson *(G-12045)*
Certified Reducer Rbldrs Inc .... F 248 585-0883
  Sterling Heights *(G-15955)*
Cochran Corporation .... E 517 857-2211
  Springport *(G-15879)*
Crane 1 Services Inc .... E 586 468-0909
  Harrison Township *(G-7694)*
Dimension Machine Tech LLC .... F 586 649-4747
  Bloomfield Hills *(G-1814)*
Electric Motor & Contg Co .... F 313 871-3775
  Clay *(G-3119)*
Fortune Tool & Machine Inc .... F 248 669-9119
  Wixom *(G-18665)*
Heating Induction Services Inc .... G 586 791-3160
  Clinton Township *(G-3252)*
Hel Inc .... F 616 774-9032
  Grand Rapids *(G-6808)*
J I B Properties LLC .... G 313 382-3234
  Melvindale *(G-11202)*
L & C Enterprises Inc .... G 231 943-7787
  Traverse City *(G-16736)*
M P D Welding Inc .... D 248 340-0330
  Orion *(G-12735)*
Mac Material Acquisition Co .... G 248 685-8393
  Highland *(G-7895)*
Machine Control Technology .... G 517 655-3506
  Williamston *(G-18577)*
Magnetic Chuck Services Co Inc .... G 586 822-9441
  Casco *(G-2600)*
Mhr Inc .... F 616 394-0191
  Holland *(G-8146)*
Michigan Rebuild & Automtn Inc .... F 517 542-6000
  Litchfield *(G-10083)*
Mjc Tool & Machine Co Inc .... G 586 790-4766
  Clinton Township *(G-3303)*
Monarch Electric Service Co .... G 313 388-7800
  Melvindale *(G-11206)*
Mq Operating Company .... E 906 337-1515
  Calumet *(G-2412)*
Nedrow Refractories Co .... D 248 669-2500
  Wixom *(G-18718)*
North American Mch & Engrg Co .... G 586 726-6700
  Shelby Township *(G-15291)*
Padnos Leitelt Inc .... D 616 363-3817
  Grand Rapids *(G-7067)*
Pgm Products Inc .... F 586 757-4400
  Warren *(G-17962)*
Plason Scraping Co Inc .... G 248 588-7280
  Madison Heights *(G-10801)*
Progressive Surface Inc .... D 616 957-0871
  Grand Rapids *(G-7117)*
Progressive Surface Inc .... F 616 957-0871
  Grand Rapids *(G-7118)*
Richland Machine & Pump Co .... G 269 629-4344
  Richland *(G-13828)*
Star Crane Hist Svc of Klmazoo .... G 269 321-8882
  Portage *(G-13611)*

Thyssenkrupp System Engrg .... C 248 340-8000
  Auburn Hills *(G-1052)*
Tindall Packaging Inc .... G 269 649-1163
  Portage *(G-13626)*
Tri-City Repair Company .... G 989 835-4784
  Hope *(G-8364)*

INDL PATTERNS: Foundry Patternmaking

Acme Casting Enterprises Inc .... G 586 755-0300
  Warren *(G-17689)*
Anderson Global Inc .... C 231 733-2164
  Muskegon *(G-11771)*
Harvey Pattern Works Inc .... F 906 774-4285
  Kingsford *(G-9510)*
Quality Model & Pattern Co .... E 616 791-1156
  Grand Rapids *(G-7129)*

INDL PROCESS INSTRUMENTS: Control

Acromag Incorporated .... D 248 624-1541
  Wixom *(G-18594)*
Banner Engineering & Sales Inc .... F 989 755-0584
  Saginaw *(G-14609)*
Emitted Energy Inc .... F 855 752-3347
  Sterling Heights *(G-16004)*
Henkel US Operations Corp .... B 248 588-1082
  Madison Heights *(G-10739)*
Kubica Corp .... F 248 344-7750
  Novi *(G-12459)*

INDL PROCESS INSTRUMENTS: Controllers, Process Variables

ABB Inc .... D 248 471-0888
  Farmington Hills *(G-5157)*
Forefront Control Systems LLC .... G 616 796-3495
  Holland *(G-8038)*
Patriot Sensors & Cntrls Corp .... D 248 435-0700
  Peck *(G-12963)*
Patriot Sensors & Cntrls Corp .... F 810 378-5511
  Peck *(G-12962)*
QEd Envmtl Systems Inc .... D 734 995-2547
  Dexter *(G-4751)*
Superior Controls Inc .... C 734 454-0500
  Plymouth *(G-13306)*

INDL PROCESS INSTRUMENTS: Data Loggers

Digital Performance Tech .... F 877 983-4230
  Troy *(G-17062)*

INDL PROCESS INSTRUMENTS: Digital Display, Process Variables

Tech Tool Supply LLC .... G 734 207-7700
  Plymouth *(G-13310)*

INDL PROCESS INSTRUMENTS: Draft Gauges

Turbine Tool & Gage Inc .... E 734 427-2270
  Livonia *(G-10451)*

INDL PROCESS INSTRUMENTS: Elements, Primary

Beet Inc .... F 248 432-0052
  Troy *(G-16971)*

INDL PROCESS INSTRUMENTS: Fluidic Devices, Circuit & Systems

Hines Corporation .... F 231 799-6240
  Norton Shores *(G-12348)*
Metric Hydrulic Components LLC .... F 586 786-6990
  Shelby Township *(G-15275)*
Toledo Molding & Die Inc .... G 734 233-6338
  Plymouth *(G-13317)*

INDL PROCESS INSTRUMENTS: Indl Flow & Measuring

Complete Auto-Mation Inc .... D 248 693-0500
  Lake Orion *(G-9597)*
Nordson Corporation .... D 734 459-8600
  Wixom *(G-18721)*

INDL PROCESS INSTRUMENTS: Temperature

Incoe Corporation .... C 248 616-0220
  Auburn Hills *(G-936)*
International Temperature Ctrl .... G 989 876-8075
  Au Gres *(G-759)*
K-TEC Systems Inc .... F 248 414-4100
  Ferndale *(G-5562)*
Maxitrol Company .... D 248 356-1400
  Southfield *(G-15648)*
Warner Instruments .... G 616 843-5342
  Grand Haven *(G-6379)*

INDL PROCESS INSTRUMENTS: Water Quality Monitoring/Cntrl Sys

Geotech Environmental Eqp Inc .... G 517 655-5616
  Williamston *(G-18572)*
Integrated Marketing Svcs LLC .... G 248 625-7444
  Pontiac *(G-13381)*
Parjana Distribution LLC .... G 313 915-5418
  Southfield *(G-15672)*

INDL SALTS WHOLESALERS

Cargill Incorporated .... B 810 329-2736
  Saint Clair *(G-14816)*

INDL SPLYS WHOLESALERS

Aactus Inc .... G 734 425-1212
  Livonia *(G-10096)*
Acumen Technologies Inc .... F 586 566-8600
  Shelby Township *(G-15165)*
Airgas Usa LLC .... G 248 545-9353
  Ferndale *(G-5520)*
American Blower Supply Inc .... E 586 771-7337
  Warren *(G-17701)*
Bakers Gas and Welding Sups .... G 517 539-5047
  Jackson *(G-8821)*
Cleary Developments Inc .... E 248 588-7011
  Madison Heights *(G-10689)*
Coleman Bowman & Associates .... G 248 642-8221
  Bloomfield Hills *(G-1809)*
Colonial Engineering Inc .... F 269 323-2495
  Portage *(G-13553)*
Commercial Group Inc .... E 313 931-6100
  Taylor *(G-16395)*
Continental Carbide Ltd Inc .... E 586 463-9577
  Clinton Township *(G-3211)*
Covenant Cpitl Investments Inc .... F 248 477-4230
  Wixom *(G-18637)*
Dow Chemical Company .... G 517 439-4400
  Hillsdale *(G-7933)*
Gravel Flow Inc .... G 269 651-5467
  Sturgis *(G-16291)*
Inteva Products LLC .... B 248 655-8886
  Troy *(G-17174)*
Itc Incorporated .... E 616 396-1355
  Hudsonville *(G-8587)*
K-C Welding Supply Inc .... F 989 893-6509
  Essexville *(G-5115)*
Kaydon Corporation .... C 231 755-3741
  Norton Shores *(G-12306)*
Lee Spring Company LLC .... F 586 296-9850
  Fraser *(G-5957)*
Ltek Industries Inc .... G 734 747-6105
  Ann Arbor *(G-556)*
Magnetic Products Inc .... D 248 887-5600
  Highland *(G-7896)*
Marshall-Gruber Company LLC .... F 248 353-4100
  Southfield *(G-15647)*
Maximum Mold Inc .... F 269 468-6291
  Benton Harbor *(G-1571)*
Motion Industries Inc .... G 989 771-0200
  Saginaw *(G-14705)*
Northern Processes & Sales LLC .... G 248 669-3918
  Wixom *(G-18723)*
NSK Americas Inc .... C 734 913-7500
  Ann Arbor *(G-595)*
Orsco Inc .... G 314 679-4200
  Armada *(G-738)*
Quality Pipe Products Inc .... E 734 606-5100
  New Boston *(G-12019)*
Rock Industries Inc .... E 248 338-2800
  Bloomfield Hills *(G-1858)*
Scs Embedded Tech LLC .... G 248 615-4441
  Novi *(G-12532)*
Sourcehub LLC .... G 800 246-1844
  Troy *(G-17364)*

PRODUCT SECTION

INSPECTION & TESTING SVCS

Symorex Ltd ....F 734 971-6000
  Ann Arbor *(G-670)*
Triad Process Equipment Inc ....G 248 685-9938
  Milford *(G-11493)*
United Abrasive Inc ....F 906 563-9249
  Vulcan *(G-17616)*
Venture Technology Groups Inc ....F 248 473-8450
  Novi *(G-12566)*

INDL SPLYS, WHOL: Fasteners, Incl Nuts, Bolts, Screws, Etc

Henrob Corporation ....D 248 493-3800
  New Hudson *(G-12057)*
Hexagon Enterprises Inc ....F 248 583-0550
  Troy *(G-17142)*
Rush Machining Inc ....E 248 583-0550
  Troy *(G-17338)*

INDL SPLYS, WHOLESALE: Abrasives

Finishing Technologies Inc ....F 616 794-4001
  Belding *(G-1449)*
Gnap LLC ....G 616 583-5000
  Byron Center *(G-2272)*
Kalamazoo Company ....E 269 345-7151
  Kalamazoo *(G-9237)*
Vachon Industries Inc ....F 517 278-2354
  Coldwater *(G-3460)*

INDL SPLYS, WHOLESALE: Abrasives & Adhesives

Jay Cee Sales & Rivet Inc ....F 248 478-2150
  Farmington *(G-5140)*
Quantum Chemical LLC ....G 734 429-0033
  Livonia *(G-10379)*

INDL SPLYS, WHOLESALE: Adhesives, Tape & Plasters

General Tape Label Liquidating ....F 248 437-5200
  Wixom *(G-18668)*

INDL SPLYS, WHOLESALE: Bearings

Break-A-Beam ....G 586 758-7790
  Warren *(G-17742)*
Edwards Industrial Sales Inc ....G 517 887-6100
  Lansing *(G-9833)*
USA Brngs Sup LLC DBA JSB Grea .....G 734 222-4177
  Ann Arbor *(G-707)*

INDL SPLYS, WHOLESALE: Fasteners & Fastening Eqpt

A Raymond Corp N Amer Inc ....E 248 853-2500
  Rochester Hills *(G-13938)*
Penn Automotive Inc ....G 248 599-3700
  Waterford *(G-18150)*
Penn Engineering & Mfg Corp ....B 313 299-8500
  Waterford *(G-18151)*
TCH Supply Inc ....G 517 545-4900
  Howell *(G-8526)*

INDL SPLYS, WHOLESALE: Filters, Indl

Bulldog Fabricating Corp ....G 734 761-3111
  Ann Arbor *(G-409)*
Lub-Tech Inc ....G 616 299-3540
  Grand Rapids *(G-6950)*
Millennium Planet LLC ....G 248 835-2331
  Farmington Hills *(G-5322)*
Omega Industries Michigan LLC ....G 616 460-0500
  Grand Rapids *(G-7058)*

INDL SPLYS, WHOLESALE: Fittings

Fixtureworks LLC ....G 586 294-6100
  Fraser *(G-5928)*
National Industrial Sup Co Inc ....F 248 588-1828
  Troy *(G-17273)*

INDL SPLYS, WHOLESALE: Gaskets & Seals

Flaretite Inc ....G 810 750-4140
  Brighton *(G-1990)*

INDL SPLYS, WHOLESALE: Glass Bottles

Recycling Concepts W Mich Inc ....D 616 942-8888
  Grand Rapids *(G-7146)*

INDL SPLYS, WHOLESALE: Hydraulic & Pneumatic Pistons/Valves

J E Myles Inc ....E 248 583-1020
  Troy *(G-17178)*
Morgold Inc ....G 269 445-3844
  Cassopolis *(G-2632)*

INDL SPLYS, WHOLESALE: Mill Splys

Tryco Inc ....F 734 953-6800
  Farmington Hills *(G-5406)*

INDL SPLYS, WHOLESALE: Plastic, Pallets

Pfb Manufacturing LLC ....G 517 486-4844
  Blissfield *(G-1773)*

INDL SPLYS, WHOLESALE: Power Transmission, Eqpt & Apparatus

Idc Industries Inc ....E 586 427-4321
  Clinton Township *(G-3257)*

INDL SPLYS, WHOLESALE: Rubber Goods, Mechanical

Advanced Rubber & Plastic ....G 586 754-7398
  Warren *(G-17693)*
Four Star Rubber Inc ....G 810 632-3335
  Commerce Township *(G-3532)*

INDL SPLYS, WHOLESALE: Seals

Ksb Dubric Inc ....E 616 784-6355
  Comstock Park *(G-3618)*
Martin Fluid Power Company ....F 248 585-8170
  Madison Heights *(G-10776)*
Mechancal Sup A Div Nthrn McHn ......F 906 789-0355
  Escanaba *(G-5083)*
Memtech Inc ....F 734 455-8550
  Plymouth *(G-13240)*
Roger Zatkoff Company ....E 248 478-2400
  Farmington Hills *(G-5372)*

INDL SPLYS, WHOLESALE: Tools

Jomat Industries Ltd ....F 586 336-1801
  Bruce Twp *(G-2169)*
Sani Zeevi ....G 248 546-4489
  Oak Park *(G-12646)*

INDL SPLYS, WHOLESALE: Tools, NEC

Busch Machine Tool Supply LLC ....G 989 798-4794
  Freeland *(G-6019)*
Omax Tool Products Inc ....F 517 768-0300
  Ray *(G-13701)*
Patco Air Tool Inc ....G 248 648-8830
  Orion *(G-12738)*

INDL SPLYS, WHOLESALE: Valves & Fittings

Automatic Valve Corp ....E 248 474-6761
  Novi *(G-12370)*
Detroit Nipple Works Inc ....F 313 872-6370
  Detroit *(G-4157)*
Ferguson Enterprises LLC ....G 989 790-2220
  Saginaw *(G-14645)*
Fluid Systems Engineering Inc ....E 586 790-8880
  Clinton Township *(G-3242)*
Kennedy Industries Inc ....D 248 684-1200
  Wixom *(G-18691)*
Mac Valves Inc ....G 734 529-5099
  Dundee *(G-4830)*
Meccom Industrial Products Co ....F 586 463-2828
  Clinton Township *(G-3297)*
Nass Corporation ....F 586 725-6610
  New Baltimore *(G-11989)*
R M Wright Company Inc ....E 248 476-9800
  Farmington Hills *(G-5363)*
Rvm Company of Toledo ....G 734 654-2201
  Carleton *(G-2562)*

INDL TOOL GRINDING SVCS

Lincoln Tool Co Inc ....G 989 736-8711
  Harrisville *(G-7743)*
R & S Cutter Grind Inc ....G 989 791-3100
  Saginaw *(G-14733)*
West Michigan Grinding Svc Inc ....F 231 739-4245
  Norton Shores *(G-12343)*

INDUSTRIAL & COMMERCIAL EQPT INSPECTION SVCS

Aldez North America ....F 586 530-5314
  Clinton Township *(G-3161)*

INFORMATION RETRIEVAL SERVICES

Executive Operations LLC ....E 313 312-0653
  Brighton *(G-1986)*

INFRARED OBJECT DETECTION EQPT

Consoldted Rsource Imaging LLC ....E 616 735-2080
  Grand Rapids *(G-6595)*
Teslir LLC ....G 248 644-5500
  Bloomfield Hills *(G-1865)*

INGOT, EXTRUSION: Extrusion ingot, aluminum: rolling mills

CPM Acquisition Corp ....G 231 947-6400
  Traverse City *(G-16663)*
Extrunet America Inc ....G 517 301-4504
  Tecumseh *(G-16501)*

INK OR WRITING FLUIDS

Carco Inc ....E 313 925-1053
  Detroit *(G-4089)*
Dell Marking Systems Inc ....G 248 547-7750
  Rochester Hills *(G-13994)*
Npworld Co ....G 586 826-9702
  Sterling Heights *(G-16119)*

INK: Duplicating

D & D Business Machines Inc ....G 616 364-8446
  Grand Rapids *(G-6627)*

INK: Printing

America Ink and Technology ....G 269 345-4657
  Portage *(G-13543)*
Celia Corporation ....G 616 887-7387
  Sparta *(G-15763)*
Flint CPS Inks North Amer LLC ....C 734 781-4600
  Livonia *(G-10208)*
Flint Group US LLC ....B 734 781-4600
  Livonia *(G-10211)*
Flint Ink Receivables Corp ....G 734 781-4600
  Livonia *(G-10212)*
Grand Rapids Printing Ink Co ....G 616 241-5681
  Grand Rapids *(G-6768)*
Great Lakes Toll Services ....G 616 847-1868
  Spring Lake *(G-15820)*
Intra Business LLC ....G 269 262-0863
  Niles *(G-12139)*
Jbr Associates ....G 586 693-5666
  Sterling Heights *(G-16054)*
Pittsburgh Glass Works LLC ....C 248 371-1700
  Rochester Hills *(G-14084)*
Pressburg LLC ....G 269 873-0775
  Kalamazoo *(G-9307)*
Sun Chemical Corporation ....F 513 681-5950
  Muskegon *(G-11926)*
Wikoff Color Corporation ....E 616 245-3930
  Grand Rapids *(G-7339)*

INNER TUBES: Truck Or Bus

Avon Machining LLC ....D 586 884-2200
  Shelby Township *(G-15175)*
Avon Machining Holdings Inc ....C 586 884-2200
  Shelby Township *(G-15176)*

INSECT LAMPS: Electric

Gelman Sciences Inc ....C 734 665-0651
  Ann Arbor *(G-496)*

INSECTICIDES & PESTICIDES

Hpi Products Inc ....G 248 773-7460
  Northville *(G-12229)*

INSPECTION & TESTING SVCS

P G S Inc ....C 248 526-3800
  Troy *(G-17294)*
Tri-Star Tooling LLC ....E 586 978-0435
  Sterling Heights *(G-16210)*
Vectorall Manufacturing Inc ....E 248 486-4570
  Brighton *(G-2093)*

INSPECTION SVCS, TRANSPORTATION

Pti Qlity Cntnment Sltions LLC..............C...... 313 365-3999
  Detroit *(G-4541)*

INSTR, MEASURE & CONTROL: Gauge, Oil Pressure & Water Temp

D & N Gage Inc..............................F...... 586 336-2110
  Romeo *(G-14224)*
Quigley Manufacturing Inc..........G...... 248 426-8500
  Farmington Hills *(G-5362)*

INSTRUMENTS, LABORATORY: Spectrometers

Thermo Arl US Inc........................F...... 313 336-3901
  Dearborn *(G-3903)*

INSTRUMENTS, MEASURING & CNTRL: Geophysical & Meteorological

Abletech Industries LLC..............G...... 734 677-2420
  Dexter *(G-4720)*

INSTRUMENTS, MEASURING & CNTRL: Testing, Abrasion, Etc

Balance Technology Inc..............D...... 734 769-2100
  Whitmore Lake *(G-18520)*
Bti Measurement Tstg Svcs LLC....G...... 734 769-2100
  Whitmore Lake *(G-18524)*
Bti Measurement Tstg Svcs LLC....G...... 734 769-2100
  Dexter *(G-4729)*
Comau LLC...................................B...... 248 353-8888
  Southfield *(G-15530)*
Demmer Investments Inc............G...... 517 321-3600
  Lansing *(G-9688)*
Dietert Foundry Testing Eqp......G...... 313 491-4680
  Detroit *(G-4175)*
Great Lakes Gages LLC................G...... 810 797-8300
  Metamora *(G-11280)*
Humantics Innvtive Sltions Inc....C...... 734 451-7878
  Farmington Hills *(G-5264)*
Innkeeper LLC...............................G...... 734 743-1707
  Canton *(G-2476)*
Jgs Machining LLC.......................G...... 810 329-4210
  Saint Clair *(G-14832)*
Kuka Assembly and Test Corp....C...... 989 220-3088
  Saginaw *(G-14680)*
M Antonik....................................G...... 248 236-0333
  Oxford *(G-12897)*
Michigan Scientific Corp............E...... 248 685-3939
  Milford *(G-11470)*
Michigan Scientific Corp............D...... 231 547-5511
  Charlevoix *(G-2721)*
R & J Manufacturing Company..F...... 248 669-2460
  Commerce Township *(G-3568)*
Rel Inc...E...... 906 337-3018
  Calumet *(G-2413)*
Safety Technology Holdings Inc..F...... 415 983-2706
  Farmington Hills *(G-5375)*
Thermal Wave Imaging Inc........F...... 248 414-3730
  Madison Heights *(G-10843)*

INSTRUMENTS, MEASURING & CNTRLG: Aircraft & Motor Vehicle

Adcole Corporation....................G...... 508 485-9100
  Orion *(G-12722)*
Advanced Systems & Contrls Inc..E...... 586 992-9684
  Macomb *(G-10572)*
Beet Inc.......................................F...... 248 432-0052
  Troy *(G-16971)*
Creative Engineering Inc............G...... 734 996-5900
  Ann Arbor *(G-439)*
F I D Corporation.......................G...... 248 373-7005
  Rochester Hills *(G-14008)*
Inora Technologies Inc...............G...... 734 302-7488
  Ann Arbor *(G-529)*
Parker-Hannifin Corporation....G...... 330 253-5239
  Otsego *(G-12797)*
Pinto Products Inc......................G...... 269 383-0015
  Kalamazoo *(G-9296)*
Schap Specialty Machine Inc.....F...... 616 846-6530
  Spring Lake *(G-15850)*
Ssi Technology Inc.....................D...... 248 582-0600
  Sterling Heights *(G-16188)*
Sterling Prmeasure Systems Inc..E...... 586 254-5310
  Sterling Heights *(G-16194)*

Vgage LLC...................................D...... 248 589-7455
  Oak Park *(G-12648)*

INSTRUMENTS, MEASURING & CNTRLG: Fatigue Test, Indl, Mech

Common Sensors LLC..................G...... 248 722-8556
  Farmington Hills *(G-5205)*
Promess Inc.................................D...... 810 229-9334
  Brighton *(G-2055)*
Quality First Systems Inc............E...... 248 922-4780
  Davisburg *(G-3772)*

INSTRUMENTS, MEASURING & CNTRLG: Stress, Strain & Measure

Bonal International Inc...............F...... 248 582-0900
  Royal Oak *(G-14518)*
Bonal Technologies Inc..............F...... 248 582-0900
  Royal Oak *(G-14519)*
K-Space Associates Inc...............E...... 734 426-7977
  Dexter *(G-4744)*
Tecat Performance Systems LLC..F...... 248 615-9862
  Ann Arbor *(G-672)*

INSTRUMENTS, MEASURING & CNTRLNG: Press & Vac Ind, Acft Eng

World Magnetics Company LLC..E...... 231 946-3800
  Traverse City *(G-16882)*

INSTRUMENTS, MEASURING & CONTROLLING: Gas Detectors

Analytical Process Systems Inc...E...... 248 393-0700
  Auburn Hills *(G-784)*
Family Safety Products Inc.........G...... 616 530-6540
  Grandville *(G-7377)*
Gfg Instrumentation Inc.............E...... 734 769-0573
  Ann Arbor *(G-500)*
Invertech Inc...............................G...... 734 944-4400
  Saline *(G-15021)*

INSTRUMENTS, MEASURING & CONTROLLING: Weather Tracking

New Wake Inc..............................G...... 800 957-5606
  Hudsonville *(G-8599)*

INSTRUMENTS, MEASURING/CNTRL: Gauging, Ultrasonic Thickness

Verimation Technology Inc........E...... 248 471-0000
  Farmington Hills *(G-5409)*

INSTRUMENTS, MEASURING/CNTRLG: Fire Detect Sys, Non-Electric

Exquise Inc..................................G...... 248 220-9048
  Detroit *(G-4223)*

INSTRUMENTS, MEASURING/CNTRLNG: Med Diagnostic Sys, Nuclear

Assay Designs Inc........................E...... 734 214-0923
  Ann Arbor *(G-383)*
Avidhrt Inc..................................G...... 517 214-9041
  Okemos *(G-12658)*
Gravikor Inc................................G...... 734 302-3200
  Ann Arbor *(G-506)*

INSTRUMENTS, OPTICAL: Lens Mounts

Kwik-Site Corporation................F...... 734 326-1500
  Wayne *(G-18227)*

INSTRUMENTS, OPTICAL: Lenses, All Types Exc Ophthalmic

General Scientific Corporation..E...... 734 996-9200
  Ann Arbor *(G-498)*

INSTRUMENTS, OPTICAL: Test & Inspection

Kaiser Optical Systems Inc.........D...... 734 665-8083
  Ann Arbor *(G-537)*
Phoenix Imaging Inc...................F...... 248 476-4200
  Livonia *(G-10365)*

INSTRUMENTS, SURGICAL & MEDICAL: Biopsy

Rls Interventional Inc..................F...... 616 301-7800
  Kentwood *(G-9476)*

INSTRUMENTS, SURGICAL & MEDICAL: Blood & Bone Work

J Sterling Industries LLC............F...... 269 492-6922
  Kalamazoo *(G-9228)*
Marketlab Inc..............................D...... 866 237-3722
  Caledonia *(G-2388)*
Oxygenplus LLC..........................G...... 586 221-9112
  Clinton Township *(G-3316)*
Tesma Instruments LLC..............G...... 517 940-1362
  Howell *(G-8528)*
Virotech Biomaterials Inc...........G...... 313 421-1648
  Warren *(G-18056)*

INSTRUMENTS, SURGICAL & MEDICAL: Lasers, Ophthalmic

Jodon Engineering Assoc Inc.....F...... 734 761-4044
  Ann Arbor *(G-534)*

INSTRUMENTS, SURGICAL & MEDICAL: Lasers, Surgical

Medical Laser Resources LLC....G...... 248 628-8120
  Oxford *(G-12901)*

INSTRUMENTS, SURGICAL & MEDICAL: Plates & Screws, Bone

Orchid Orthpd Sltons Organ Inc..C...... 203 877-3341
  Holt *(G-8322)*

INSTRUMENTS, SURGICAL & MEDICAL: Skin Grafting

American Laser Centers LLC......A...... 248 426-8250
  Farmington Hills *(G-5168)*
Barron Precision Instruments.....E...... 810 695-2080
  Grand Blanc *(G-6234)*

INSTRUMENTS: Ammeters, NEC

Swain Meter Company................G...... 989 773-3700
  Farwell *(G-5430)*

INSTRUMENTS: Analytical

Auric Enterprises Inc...................G...... 231 882-7251
  Beulah *(G-1652)*
Beckman Equipment..................G...... 231 420-4791
  Cheboygan *(G-2780)*
Best Products Inc........................F...... 313 538-7414
  Redford *(G-13719)*
Burke E Porter Machinery Co....C...... 616 234-1200
  Grand Rapids *(G-6535)*
Cpr Inc..G...... 734 459-7251
  Canton *(G-2452)*
Essen Instruments Inc................D...... 734 769-1600
  Ann Arbor *(G-480)*
Fisher Scientific Intl LLC............G...... 734 622-0413
  Ann Arbor *(G-480)*
Full Spectrum Tech Inc..............G...... 810 225-4760
  Brighton *(G-1994)*
Horiba Automotive Test Systems..E...... 248 689-9000
  Troy *(G-17149)*
Horiba Instruments Inc..............D...... 734 213-6555
  Ann Arbor *(G-518)*
Hti Usa Inc..................................G...... 248 358-5533
  Farmington *(G-5139)*
Lake Erie Med Surgical Sup Inc..E...... 734 847-3847
  Temperance *(G-16536)*
Leco Corporation........................B...... 269 983-5531
  Saint Joseph *(G-14946)*
Mectron Engineering Co Inc......E...... 734 944-8777
  Saline *(G-15026)*
Opti 02 LLC.................................G...... 517 381-9831
  Okemos *(G-12680)*
Phadia US Inc..............................C...... 269 492-1940
  Portage *(G-13593)*
Proto Manufacturing Inc............E...... 734 946-0974
  Taylor *(G-16463)*
R H K Technology Inc.................E...... 248 577-5426
  Troy *(G-17327)*
Richard-Allan Scientific Co........D...... 269 544-5600
  Kalamazoo *(G-9316)*

PRODUCT SECTION

INSTRUMENTS: Measuring & Controlling

Rigaku Innovative Tech Inc ....C...... 248 232-6400
  Auburn Hills *(G-1020)*
Srg Global Coatings LLC ....C...... 248 509-1100
  Troy *(G-17369)*
Thermo Fisher Scientific Inc ....G...... 231 932-0242
  Traverse City *(G-16856)*
Thermo Fisher Scientific Inc ....G...... 800 346-4364
  Portage *(G-13625)*
Thermo Fisher Scientific Inc ....G...... 269 544-5600
  Kalamazoo *(G-9356)*
Thermo Fisher Scientific Inc ....G...... 734 662-4117
  Ann Arbor *(G-687)*
TS Enterprise Associates Inc ....F...... 248 348-2963
  Northville *(G-12267)*
X-Ray and Specialty Instrs Inc ....G...... 734 485-6300
  Ypsilanti *(G-18986)*
X-Rite Incorporated ....C...... 616 803-2100
  Grand Rapids *(G-7353)*

INSTRUMENTS: Combustion Control, Indl

Engineered Combustn Systems LLC ...G...... 248 549-1703
  Royal Oak *(G-14534)*

INSTRUMENTS: Differential Pressure, Indl

Astra Associates Inc ....E...... 586 254-6500
  Sterling Heights *(G-15935)*

INSTRUMENTS: Endoscopic Eqpt, Electromedical

Endoscopic Solutions ....F...... 248 625-4055
  Clarkston *(G-3032)*
Iha Vsclar Endvsclar Spcalists ....G...... 734 712-8150
  Ypsilanti *(G-18953)*

INSTRUMENTS: Flow, Indl Process

ADS LLC ....G...... 248 740-9593
  Troy *(G-16906)*
Airflow Sciences Equipment LLC ....G...... 734 525-0300
  Livonia *(G-10107)*
Custom Valve Concepts Inc ....E...... 248 597-8999
  Madison Heights *(G-10702)*
Piping Components Inc ....G...... 313 382-6400
  Melvindale *(G-11209)*
Universal Flow Monitors Inc ....E...... 248 542-9635
  Hazel Park *(G-7845)*

INSTRUMENTS: Frequency Meters, Electrical, Mech & Electronic

Standard Electric Company ....F...... 906 774-4455
  Kingsford *(G-9518)*

INSTRUMENTS: Indl Process Control

A&D Technology Inc ....D...... 734 973-1111
  Ann Arbor *(G-341)*
Accurate Home Insptn Svcs Inc ....G...... 303 530-9600
  Harrison Township *(G-7684)*
Advanced Integrated Mfg ....G...... 586 439-0300
  Fraser *(G-5888)*
AG Davis Gage & Engrg Co ....E...... 586 977-9000
  Sterling Heights *(G-15926)*
Altair Systems Inc ....G...... 248 668-0116
  Wixom *(G-18606)*
Ametek Inc ....G...... 248 362-2777
  Peck *(G-12960)*
Applied Synergistics Inc ....G...... 248 634-0151
  Holly *(G-8261)*
Ats Atmtion Globl Svcs USA Inc ....E...... 734 522-1900
  Wixom *(G-18613)*
Auric Enterprises Inc ....G...... 231 882-7251
  Beulah *(G-1652)*
Avl Michigan Holding Corp ....D...... 734 414-9600
  Plymouth *(G-13130)*
Avl Test Systems Inc ....C...... 734 414-9600
  Plymouth *(G-13134)*
Balance Technology Inc ....D...... 734 769-2100
  Whitmore Lake *(G-18520)*
Benny Gage Inc ....E...... 734 455-3080
  Wixom *(G-18620)*
Bisbee Infrared Services Inc ....G...... 517 787-4620
  Jackson *(G-8823)*
Broadteq Incorporated ....G...... 248 794-9323
  Waterford *(G-18106)*
Burke E Porter Machinery Co ....C...... 616 234-1200
  Grand Rapids *(G-6535)*
C E C Controls Company Inc ....D...... 586 779-0222
  Warren *(G-17746)*

C E C Controls Company Inc ....G...... 248 926-5701
  Wixom *(G-18629)*
Clarkson Controls & Eqp Co ....G...... 248 380-9915
  Novi *(G-12384)*
Dura Thread Gage Inc ....F...... 248 545-2890
  Madison Heights *(G-10714)*
Emerson Electric Co ....E...... 616 846-3950
  Grand Haven *(G-6296)*
Emerson Electric Co ....G...... 586 268-3104
  Sterling Heights *(G-16003)*
Emerson Electric Co ....G...... 734 420-0832
  Plymouth *(G-13167)*
Emerson Prcess MGT Pwr Wtr Slt ......E...... 313 874-0860
  Detroit *(G-4208)*
Fannon Products LLC ....F...... 810 794-2000
  Algonac *(G-141)*
Flow-Rite Controls Ltd ....G...... 616 583-1700
  Byron Center *(G-2270)*
Forrest Brothers Inc ....C...... 989 356-4011
  Gaylord *(G-6129)*
George Instrument Company ....F...... 248 280-1111
  Orion *(G-12731)*
Gic LLC ....F...... 231 237-7000
  Charlevoix *(G-2716)*
Gordinier Electronics Corp ....G...... 586 778-0426
  Roseville *(G-14414)*
Henshaw Inc ....D...... 586 752-0700
  Armada *(G-736)*
Hexagon Mfg Intelligence Inc ....G...... 248 662-1740
  Novi *(G-12433)*
Hines Industries Inc ....E...... 734 769-2300
  Ann Arbor *(G-517)*
Honeywell International Inc ....C...... 231 582-5686
  Boyne City *(G-1889)*
Horiba Instruments Inc ....D...... 734 213-6555
  Ann Arbor *(G-518)*
Howard Miller Company ....B...... 616 772-9131
  Zeeland *(G-19040)*
Infrared Telemetrics Inc ....F...... 906 482-0012
  Hancock *(G-7620)*
Innovative Support Svcs Inc ....F...... 248 585-3600
  Troy *(G-17168)*
Integrated Security Corp ....F...... 248 624-0700
  Novi *(G-12438)*
Jay/Enn Corporation ....D...... 248 588-2393
  Troy *(G-17182)*
Jcp LLC ....F...... 989 754-7496
  Saginaw *(G-14673)*
Jdl Enterprises Inc ....F...... 586 977-8863
  Warren *(G-17884)*
K-Space Associates Inc ....E...... 734 426-7977
  Dexter *(G-4744)*
Labortrio Elttrofisico USA Inc ....G...... 248 340-7040
  Lake Orion *(G-9613)*
Leader Corporation ....E...... 586 566-7114
  Shelby Township *(G-15260)*
Leco Corporation ....B...... 269 983-5531
  Saint Joseph *(G-14946)*
Maes Tool & Die Co Inc ....F...... 517 750-3131
  Jackson *(G-8940)*
Mahle Powertrain LLC ....D...... 248 305-8200
  Farmington Hills *(G-5307)*
Martel Tool Corporation ....F...... 313 278-2420
  Allen Park *(G-200)*
Maxitrol Company ....G...... 517 486-2820
  Blissfield *(G-1769)*
Montague Latch Company ....F...... 810 687-4242
  Clio *(G-3407)*
Mycrona Inc ....F...... 734 453-9348
  Plymouth *(G-13251)*
Norcross Viscosity Controls ....G...... 586 336-0700
  Washington *(G-18086)*
Oflow-Rite Controls Ltd ....E...... 616 583-1700
  Byron Center *(G-2290)*
Online Engineering Inc ....G...... 906 341-0090
  Manistique *(G-10923)*
Peaker Services Inc ....D...... 248 437-4174
  Brighton *(G-2049)*
Peaktronics Inc ....G...... 248 542-5640
  Clawson *(G-3102)*
R Concepts Incorporated ....G...... 810 632-4857
  Howell *(G-8505)*
Rjg Technologies Inc ....D...... 231 947-3111
  Traverse City *(G-16822)*
Sinto America Inc ....E...... 517 371-2460
  Lansing *(G-9791)*
Ssi Technology Inc ....D...... 248 582-0600
  Sterling Heights *(G-16188)*
Sure Flow Products LLC ....G...... 248 380-3569
  Wixom *(G-18764)*

Taylor Controls Inc ....F...... 269 637-8521
  South Haven *(G-15418)*
Temprel Inc ....E...... 231 582-6585
  Boyne City *(G-1902)*
Terametrix LLC ....C...... 540 769-8430
  Ann Arbor *(G-681)*
Testron Incorporated ....F...... 734 513-6820
  Livonia *(G-10431)*
Therm-O-Disc Incorporated ....A...... 231 799-4100
  Norton Shores *(G-12337)*
Therm-O-Disc Midwest Inc ....F...... 231 799-4100
  Norton Shores *(G-12338)*
Thermo Arl US Inc ....F...... 313 336-3901
  Dearborn *(G-3903)*
Welding Technology Corp ....F...... 248 477-3900
  Farmington Hills *(G-5413)*
Welform Electrodes Inc ....G...... 586 755-1184
  Warren *(G-18066)*
X-Rite Incorporated ....C...... 616 803-2100
  Grand Rapids *(G-7353)*

INSTRUMENTS: Infrared, Indl Process

Dexter Research Center Inc ....D...... 734 426-3921
  Dexter *(G-4739)*

INSTRUMENTS: Laser, Scientific & Engineering

Clark-Mxr Inc ....E...... 734 426-2803
  Dexter *(G-4731)*
Jodon Engineering Assoc Inc ....F...... 734 761-4044
  Ann Arbor *(G-534)*
Pioneer Technologies Corp ....G...... 702 806-3152
  Fremont *(G-6054)*
Q-Photonics LLC ....G...... 734 477-0133
  Ann Arbor *(G-628)*

INSTRUMENTS: Measurement, Indl Process

Atmo-Seal Inc ....G...... 248 528-9640
  Troy *(G-16963)*
Binsfeld Engineering Inc ....G...... 231 334-4383
  Maple City *(G-10940)*
Harvest Energy Inc ....E...... 269 838-4595
  Grand Rapids *(G-6806)*
Hitec Sensor Developments Inc ....G...... 313 506-2460
  Plymouth *(G-13188)*
Horiba Instruments Inc ....G...... 248 689-9000
  Troy *(G-17150)*
IMC Dataworks LLC ....F...... 248 356-4311
  Ann Arbor *(G-524)*
Perceptive Controls Inc ....E...... 269 685-3040
  Plainwell *(G-13085)*
Perpetual Measurement Inc ....G...... 248 343-2952
  Waterford *(G-18153)*
Transology Associates ....G...... 517 694-8645
  East Lansing *(G-4913)*

INSTRUMENTS: Measuring & Controlling

2 Brothers Holdings LLC ....G...... 517 487-3900
  Lansing *(G-9797)*
A S I Instruments Inc ....G...... 586 756-1222
  Warren *(G-17683)*
A&D Technology Inc ....D...... 734 973-1111
  Ann Arbor *(G-341)*
Acromag Incorporated ....D...... 248 624-1541
  Wixom *(G-18594)*
Apollo America Inc ....D...... 248 332-3900
  Auburn Hills *(G-791)*
Astra Associates Inc ....E...... 586 254-6500
  Sterling Heights *(G-15935)*
Ateq Corporation ....G...... 734 838-3100
  Livonia *(G-10126)*
Ats Assembly and Test Inc ....F...... 734 266-4713
  Livonia *(G-10129)*
Auric Enterprises Inc ....G...... 231 882-7251
  Beulah *(G-1652)*
Avl Test Systems Inc ....C...... 734 414-9600
  Plymouth *(G-13134)*
B K Corporation ....F...... 989 777-2111
  Saginaw *(G-14606)*
Benesh Corporation ....F...... 734 244-4143
  Monroe *(G-11532)*
Biosan Laboratories Inc ....F...... 586 755-8970
  Warren *(G-17738)*
Bisnett Insurance ....G...... 734 214-2676
  Whitmore Lake *(G-18521)*
Calhoun County Med Care Fcilty ....E...... 269 962-5458
  Battle Creek *(G-1204)*

Cammenga & Associates LLC ... F ... 313 914-7160
Dearborn *(G-3817)*
Clark Instrument Inc ... F ... 248 669-3100
Novi *(G-12383)*
Control Power-Reliance LLC ... G ... 248 583-1020
Troy *(G-17026)*
Conway-Cleveland Corp ... G ... 616 458-0056
Grand Rapids *(G-6604)*
Crippen Manufacturing Company ... E ... 989 681-4323
Saint Louis *(G-14990)*
Detroit Testing Machine Co ... G ... 248 669-3100
Novi *(G-12396)*
Dimension Products Corporation ... F ... 616 842-6050
Grand Haven *(G-6292)*
Equitable Engineering Co Inc ... E ... 248 689-9700
Troy *(G-17096)*
Ezm LLC ... F ... 248 861-2602
Commerce Township *(G-3528)*
Gage Eagle Spline Inc ... D ... 586 776-7240
Warren *(G-17822)*
General Inspection LLC ... F ... 248 625-0529
Davisburg *(G-3769)*
Gic LLC ... F ... 231 237-7000
Charlevoix *(G-2716)*
Hanse Environmental Inc ... G ... 269 673-8638
Allegan *(G-160)*
Hbm Inc ... G ... 248 350-8300
Southfield *(G-15590)*
Hines Industries Inc ... E ... 734 769-2300
Ann Arbor *(G-517)*
Horiba Instruments Inc ... D ... 734 213-6555
Ann Arbor *(G-518)*
Howard Miller Company ... B ... 616 772-9131
Zeeland *(G-19040)*
Ifm Efector ... G ... 800 441-8246
Farmington Hills *(G-5268)*
Infrared Telemetrics Inc ... F ... 906 482-0012
Hancock *(G-7620)*
Instrumented Sensor Tech Inc ... G ... 517 349-8487
Okemos *(G-12670)*
Integrated Sensing Systems Inc ... E ... 734 547-9896
Ypsilanti *(G-18957)*
Intelligent Dynamics LLC ... F ... 313 727-9920
Dearborn *(G-3854)*
Invo Spline Inc ... E ... 586 757-8840
Warren *(G-17870)*
J E Myles Inc ... E ... 248 583-1020
Troy *(G-17178)*
Jomat Industries Ltd ... F ... 586 336-1801
Bruce Twp *(G-2169)*
Kistler Instrument Corporation ... D ... 248 668-6900
Novi *(G-12453)*
KLC Enterprises Inc ... E ... 989 753-0496
Saginaw *(G-14678)*
Labortrio Elttrofisico USA Inc ... G ... 248 340-7040
Lake Orion *(G-9613)*
Lifesafer ... G ... 888 294-7002
Marquette *(G-11031)*
Link Group Inc ... D ... 734 453-0800
Plymouth *(G-13222)*
Martel Tool Corporation ... F ... 313 278-2420
Allen Park *(G-200)*
McCrea Controls Inc ... G ... 248 544-1366
Berkley *(G-1630)*
Michael Engineering Ltd ... E ... 989 772-4073
Mount Pleasant *(G-11711)*
Midwest Flex Systems Inc ... F ... 810 424-0060
Flint *(G-5734)*
Miljoco Corp ... E ... 586 777-4280
Mount Clemens *(G-11649)*
Montronix Inc ... G ... 734 213-6500
Ann Arbor *(G-583)*
Nikon Metrology Inc ... G ... 810 220-4347
Brighton *(G-2042)*
North American Controls Inc ... E ... 586 532-7140
Shelby Township *(G-15290)*
Og Technologies Inc ... F ... 734 973-7500
Ann Arbor *(G-599)*
Pcb Piezotronics Inc ... F ... 888 684-0014
Novi *(G-12503)*
Pcb Piezotronics Inc ... G ... 716 684-0001
Farmington Hills *(G-5345)*
Perceptron Inc ... B ... 734 414-6100
Plymouth *(G-13263)*
Port Austin Level & Tl Mfg Co ... F ... 989 738-5291
Port Austin *(G-13428)*
Promess Incorporated ... G ... 810 229-9334
Brighton *(G-2056)*
Ram Meter Inc ... F ... 248 362-0990
Royal Oak *(G-14572)*
Ramer Products Inc ... G ... 269 409-8583
Buchanan *(G-2201)*
Rayco Manufacturing Inc ... F ... 586 795-2884
Sterling Heights *(G-16144)*
Richmond Instrs & Systems Inc ... F ... 586 954-3770
Clinton Township *(G-3337)*
Russells Technical Pdts Inc ... E ... 616 392-3161
Holland *(G-8184)*
Saginaw Machine Systems Inc ... E ... 989 753-8465
Saginaw *(G-14747)*
Senscomp Inc ... G ... 734 953-4783
Livonia *(G-10404)*
Sensordata Technologies Inc ... F ... 586 739-4254
Shelby Township *(G-15327)*
Siko Products Inc ... G ... 734 426-3476
Dexter *(G-4754)*
Storage Control Systems Inc ... E ... 616 887-7994
Sparta *(G-15783)*
T E Technology Inc ... E ... 231 929-3966
Traverse City *(G-16849)*
Teradyne Inc ... G ... 313 425-3900
Allen Park *(G-208)*
Tessonics Corp ... G ... 248 885-8335
Birmingham *(G-1752)*
Thermotron Industries Inc ... B ... 616 392-1491
Holland *(G-8219)*
Thielenhaus Microfinish Corp ... E ... 248 349-9450
Novi *(G-12556)*
Thierica Inc ... D ... 616 458-1538
Grand Rapids *(G-7257)*
Trece Adhesive Division ... G ... 918 785-3061
Grand Rapids *(G-7272)*
Triangle Broach Company ... E ... 313 838-2150
Detroit *(G-4645)*
United Abrasive Inc ... F ... 906 563-9249
Vulcan *(G-17616)*
United Testing Systems ... G ... 989 494-3664
Linden *(G-10072)*
Versicor LLC ... F ... 734 306-9137
Royal Oak *(G-14589)*
Vibration Research Corporation ... E ... 616 669-3028
Jenison *(G-9077)*
Waber Tool & Engineering Co ... F ... 269 342-0765
Kalamazoo *(G-9365)*
Wellsense USA Inc ... G ... 888 335-0995
Birmingham *(G-1756)*

INSTRUMENTS: Measuring Electricity

A&D Technology Inc ... D ... 734 973-1111
Ann Arbor *(G-341)*
Advanced Systems & Contrls Inc ... E ... 586 992-9684
Macomb *(G-10572)*
AG Davis Gage & Engrg Co ... E ... 586 977-9000
Sterling Heights *(G-15926)*
Ats Assembly and Test Inc ... F ... 937 222-3030
Wixom *(G-18612)*
Auric Enterprises Inc ... G ... 231 882-7251
Beulah *(G-1652)*
Balance Technology Inc ... D ... 734 769-2100
Whitmore Lake *(G-18520)*
Benesh Corporation ... F ... 734 244-4143
Monroe *(G-11532)*
Burke E Porter Machinery Co ... C ... 616 234-1200
Grand Rapids *(G-6535)*
Classic Instruments Inc ... G ... 231 582-0461
Boyne City *(G-1887)*
CSM Products Inc ... F ... 248 836-4995
Auburn Hills *(G-852)*
Dynamic Auto Test Engineering ... G ... 269 342-1334
Portage *(G-13556)*
Frequency Finders LLC ... F ... 734 660-3357
Pontiac *(G-13372)*
Global Electronics Limited ... F ... 248 353-0100
Bloomfield Hills *(G-1823)*
Greening Associates Inc ... E ... 313 366-7160
Detroit *(G-4283)*
Higgins Corp ... G ... 269 365-7744
Roscommon *(G-14350)*
Hole Industries Incorporated ... G ... 517 548-4229
Howell *(G-8461)*
Honeywell International Inc ... C ... 231 582-5686
Boyne City *(G-1889)*
Horiba Instruments Inc ... D ... 734 213-6555
Ann Arbor *(G-518)*
Infrared Telemetrics Inc ... F ... 906 482-0012
Hancock *(G-7620)*
Instrumented Sensor Tech Inc ... G ... 517 349-8487
Okemos *(G-12670)*
Ix Innovations LLC ... G ...
Ann Arbor *(G-532)*
Leco Corporation ... B ... 269 983-5531
Saint Joseph *(G-14946)*
Lumileds LLC ... E ... 248 553-9080
Farmington Hills *(G-5297)*
Merc-O-Tronic Instruments Corp ... F ... 586 894-9529
Almont *(G-265)*
Michigan Scientific Corp ... D ... 231 547-5511
Charlevoix *(G-2721)*
My Electrician Grand Rapids ... G ... 616 208-4113
Grand Rapids *(G-7033)*
Nanorete Inc ... G ... 517 336-4680
Lansing *(G-9873)*
Racelogic USA Corporation ... G ... 248 994-9050
Farmington Hills *(G-5364)*
Ram Meter Inc ... F ... 248 362-0990
Royal Oak *(G-14572)*
Sciemetric Inc ... F ... 248 509-2209
Rochester Hills *(G-14110)*
Seneca Enterprises LLC ... G ... 231 943-1171
Traverse City *(G-16829)*
Srg Global Coatings LLC ... C ... 248 509-1100
Troy *(G-17369)*
Swain Company Inc ... G ... 989 773-3700
Farwell *(G-5429)*
Testron Incorporated ... F ... 734 513-6820
Livonia *(G-10431)*

INSTRUMENTS: Measuring, Current, NEC

Nadex of America Corporation ... E ... 248 477-3900
Farmington Hills *(G-5330)*

INSTRUMENTS: Measuring, Electrical Energy

Ezm LLC ... F ... 248 861-2602
Commerce Township *(G-3528)*

INSTRUMENTS: Measuring, Electrical Power

Hale Manufacturing Inc ... G ... 231 529-6271
Alanson *(G-111)*

INSTRUMENTS: Medical & Surgical

Acousys Biodevices Inc ... G ... 573 823-3849
Ann Arbor *(G-347)*
Aees Power Systems Ltd Partnr ... G ... 269 668-4429
Farmington Hills *(G-5160)*
Alliant Enterprises LLC ... D ... 269 629-0300
Grand Rapids *(G-6449)*
Altus Industries Inc ... E ... 616 233-9530
Walker *(G-17631)*
Arch Med Sltons Lehigh Vly LLC ... D ... 603 760-1554
Warren *(G-17710)*
Arch Medical Solutions Corp ... G ... 603 760-1554
Warren *(G-17711)*
Artisan Medical Displays LLC ... E ... 616 748-8950
Zeeland *(G-18993)*
Autocam Corp ... D ... 616 698-0707
Grand Rapids *(G-6481)*
Autocam Corporation ... B ... 616 698-0707
Kentwood *(G-9444)*
Autocam Med DVC Holdings LLC ... G ... 616 541-8080
Kentwood *(G-9447)*
Autocam Medical Devices LLC ... E ... 877 633-8080
Grand Rapids *(G-6482)*
Bonwrx Ltd ... G ... 517 481-2924
Lansing *(G-9675)*
Bretton Square Industries ... G ... 517 346-9607
Lansing *(G-9817)*
Brio Device LLC ... G ... 734 945-5728
Ann Arbor *(G-406)*
C2dx Inc ... F ... 269 409-0068
Schoolcraft *(G-15112)*
Capnesity Inc ... G ... 317 401-6766
Lapeer *(G-9920)*
Cardiac Assist Holdings LLC ... G ... 781 727-1391
Plymouth *(G-13142)*
Clear Image Devices LLC ... G ... 734 645-6459
Ann Arbor *(G-427)*
Cnd Products LLC ... G ... 616 361-1000
Grand Rapids *(G-6576)*
Concentric Medical Inc ... E ... 269 385-2600
Portage *(G-13554)*
Crippen Manufacturing Company ... E ... 989 681-4323
Saint Louis *(G-14990)*
Darla Nagel ... G ... 810 624-9043
Flushing *(G-5807)*
David Epstein Inc ... F ... 248 542-0802
Ferndale *(G-5539)*
Delphinus Medical Technologies ... E ... 248 522-9600
Novi *(G-12393)*

DForte Inc ....F 269 657-6996
Paw Paw (G-12946)
Di-Coat Corporation ....E 248 349-1211
Novi (G-12399)
Domico Med-Device LLC ....D 810 750-5300
Fenton (G-5471)
Drive Medical ....G 404 349-0280
Galesburg (G-6075)
Evosys North America Corp ....F 248 973-1703
Auburn Hills (G-882)
Femur Buyer Inc ....E 517 694-2300
Holt (G-8311)
Ferndale Pharma Group Inc ....B 248 548-0900
Ferndale (G-5554)
Filter Plus Inc ....G 734 475-7403
Chelsea (G-2811)
Flexdex Inc ....F 810 522-9009
Brighton (G-1991)
Fms Lansing LLC ....G 781 699-9000
Lansing (G-9838)
Grace Engineering Corp ....D 810 392-2181
Memphis (G-11213)
Graham Medical Tech LLC ....G 586 677-9600
Macomb (G-10600)
Greystone Medical LLC ....G 248 955-3069
Waterford (G-18126)
Hart Enterprises USA Inc ....D 616 887-0400
Sparta (G-15768)
Healthcare Drble Med Eqpmnts L ....G 734 975-6668
Ann Arbor (G-510)
Innovtive Srgcal Solutions LLC ....F 248 595-0420
Wixom (G-18686)
J Sterling Industries Ltd ....G 269 492-6920
Kalamazoo (G-9229)
Keystone Manufacturing LLC ....F 269 343-4108
Kalamazoo (G-9254)
Lake Erie Med Surgical Sup Inc ....E 734 847-3847
Temperance (G-16536)
Link Technology Inc ....F 269 324-8212
Portage (G-13577)
Mar-Med Inc ....E 616 454-3000
Grand Rapids (G-6958)
Med Michigan Holdings LLC ....G 888 891-1200
Plymouth (G-13239)
Medical Engineering & Dev ....G 517 563-2352
Horton (G-8377)
Medtronic Inc ....G 616 643-5200
Grand Rapids (G-6976)
Medtronic Usa Inc ....G 248 449-5027
Novi (G-12478)
Melling Manufacturing Inc ....D 517 750-3580
Jackson (G-8950)
Michigan Instruments LLC ....G 616 554-9696
Grand Rapids (G-6991)
Orchid Macdee LLC ....C 734 475-9165
Chelsea (G-2822)
Orchid MPS Holdings LLC ....A 517 694-2300
Holt (G-8321)
Orchid Orthopedic Solutions ....F 517 694-2300
Mason (G-11149)
Orchid Orthpd Solutions LLC ....B 989 746-0780
Bridgeport (G-1917)
Orchid Orthpd Solutions LLC ....B 517 694-2300
Holt (G-8323)
Oxus America Inc ....D 248 475-0925
Auburn Hills (G-991)
Performance Systematix LLC ....E 616 949-9090
Grand Rapids (G-7080)
Perspective Enterprises Inc ....G 269 327-0869
Portage (G-13591)
Photonics Products Grou ....G 616 301-7800
Grand Rapids (G-7086)
Pioneer Surgical Tech Inc ....C 906 226-9909
Marquette (G-11041)
Plasma Biolife Services L P ....G 616 667-0264
Grandville (G-7409)
Precision Edge Srgcal Pdts LLC ....E 231 459-4304
Boyne City (G-1901)
Precision Edge Srgcal Pdts LLC ....C 906 632-5600
Sault Sainte Marie (G-15096)
Professional Hearing Services ....G 517 439-1610
Hillsdale (G-7942)
Progressive Dynamics Inc ....D 269 781-4241
Marshall (G-11072)
R H Cross Enterprises Inc ....G 269 488-4009
Portage (G-13598)
RJL Sciences Inc ....F 800 528-4513
Clinton Township (G-3339)
Rose Technologies Company ....E 616 233-3000
Grand Rapids (G-7165)
Salter Labs LLC ....F 847 739-3224
Grand Rapids (G-7179)
Salter Medical Holdings Corp ....D 800 421-0024
Grand Rapids (G-7180)
SGC Industries Inc ....G 586 293-5260
Fraser (G-5992)
Shoulder Innovations Inc ....F 616 294-1026
Grand Rapids (G-7195)
Smith and Nephew ....F 616 288-6153
Grand Rapids (G-7203)
Somanetics ....F 248 689-3050
Troy (G-17361)
Steele Supply Co ....G 269 983-0920
Saint Joseph (G-14964)
Stryker Communications Inc ....C 972 410-7000
Portage (G-13613)
Stryker Corporation ....E 269 385-2600
Portage (G-13615)
Stryker Corporation ....G 248 374-6352
Novi (G-12546)
Stryker Corporation ....E 269 389-3741
Portage (G-13614)
Stryker Sales LLC ....F 269 324-5346
Portage (G-13620)
Stryker Sales LLC ....E 269 323-1027
Portage (G-13621)
Sunmed Holdings LLC ....E 616 259-8400
Grand Rapids (G-7235)
Supreme Gear Co ....E 586 775-6325
Fraser (G-6001)
Surgitech Surgical Svcs Inc ....F 248 593-0797
Highland (G-7900)
Sybron Dental Specialti ....G 734 947-6927
Romulus (G-14333)
Tecomet Inc ....B 517 882-4311
Lansing (G-9900)
Terumo Crdvscular Systems Corp ....C 734 663-4145
Ann Arbor (G-683)
Terumo Heart Incorporated ....E 734 663-4145
Ann Arbor (G-684)
Thompson Surgical Instrs Inc ....E 231 922-0177
Traverse City (G-16857)
Thompson Surgical Instrs Inc ....G 231 922-5169
Traverse City (G-16858)
Thompson Surgical Instrs Inc ....G 231 922-5169
Traverse City (G-16859)
Thoratec LLC ....C 734 827-7422
Ann Arbor (G-690)
Tiger Neuroscience LLC ....G 872 903-1904
Muskegon (G-11932)
Tilco Inc ....G 248 644-0901
Suttons Bay (G-16346)
TMJ Manufacturing LLC ....G 248 987-7857
Farmington Hills (G-5402)
Trelleborg Sealing Solutions ....D 231 264-0087
Elk Rapids (G-5030)
Truform Machine Inc ....E 517 782-8523
Jackson (G-9025)
TSC Group Inc ....G 269 544-9966
Springfield (G-15878)
Tulip US Holdings Inc ....E 517 694-2300
Holt (G-8336)
Versah LLC ....G 844 711-5585
Jackson (G-9031)
Viant Medical LLC ....E 616 643-5200
Grand Rapids (G-7315)
Vital Concepts Inc ....G 616 954-2890
Grand Rapids (G-7320)
Warmilu LLC ....G 855 927-6458
Ann Arbor (G-713)
Wright & Filippis LLC ....F 313 386-3330
Lincoln Park (G-10058)
Wright & Filippis LLC ....F 248 336-8460
Detroit (G-3968)
Wysong Medical Corporation ....F 989 631-0009
Midland (G-11424)

INSTRUMENTS: Meteorological

Nikon Metrology Inc ....E 810 220-4360
Brighton (G-2041)
R M Young Company ....E 231 946-3980
Traverse City (G-16812)

INSTRUMENTS: Microwave Test

Cobham McRlctrnic Slutions Inc ....G 734 426-1230
Ann Arbor (G-431)
Jodon Engineering Assoc Inc ....F 734 761-4044
Ann Arbor (G-534)

INSTRUMENTS: Photographic, Electronic

Cognisys Inc ....G 231 943-2425
Traverse City (G-16656)

INSTRUMENTS: Power Measuring, Electrical

Creative Power Systems Inc ....F 313 961-2460
Detroit (G-4108)

INSTRUMENTS: Pressure Measurement, Indl

Ateq Tpms Tools Lc ....F 734 838-3104
Livonia (G-10127)

INSTRUMENTS: Radio Frequency Measuring

Eagile Incorporated ....F 616 243-1200
Grand Rapids (G-6660)
Smart Label Solutions LLC ....G 800 996-7343
Howell (G-8519)

INSTRUMENTS: Temperature Measurement, Indl

H O Trerice Co Inc ....E 248 399-8000
Oak Park (G-12616)
New Wake Inc ....G 800 957-5606
Hudsonville (G-8599)
Precise Finishing Systems Inc ....E 517 552-9200
Howell (G-8499)

INSTRUMENTS: Test, Digital, Electronic & Electrical Circuits

Orion Test Systems Inc ....D 248 373-9097
Auburn Hills (G-990)

INSTRUMENTS: Test, Electrical, Engine

Concept Technology Inc ....F 248 765-0100
Birmingham (G-1722)
Diagnostic Systems Assoc Inc ....F 269 544-9000
Kalamazoo (G-9166)
Mahle Powertrain LLC ....D 248 305-8200
Farmington Hills (G-5307)
Meiden America Inc ....E 734 459-1781
Northville (G-12239)

INSTRUMENTS: Test, Electronic & Electric Measurement

Accurate Technologies Inc ....D 248 848-9200
Novi (G-12360)
Debron Industrial Elec LLC ....D 248 588-7220
Troy (G-17050)
Design & Test Technology Inc ....G 734 665-4111
Dexter (G-4733)
Design & Test Technology Inc ....G 734 665-4316
Ann Arbor (G-448)
Opteos Inc ....G 734 929-3333
Ann Arbor (G-601)
Test Products Incorporated ....E 586 997-9600
Sterling Heights (G-16204)
VSR Technologies Inc ....F 734 425-7172
Livonia (G-10462)

INSTRUMENTS: Test, Electronic & Electrical Circuits

Aerospace America Inc ....E 989 684-2121
Bay City (G-1319)
Brothers Mead 3 LLC ....G 269 883-6241
Battle Creek (G-1198)
CPR III Inc ....E 248 652-2900
Rochester (G-13897)
Konrad Technologies Inc ....G 248 489-1200
Farmington Hills (G-5283)
Ptm-Electronics Inc ....F 248 987-4446
Farmington Hills (G-5356)
Tengam Engineering Inc ....E 269 694-9466
Otsego (G-12800)

INSTRUMENTS: Testing, Semiconductor

Abtech Installation & Svc Inc ....E 800 548-2381
Southgate (G-15747)
Esirpal Inc ....G 586 337-7848
Macomb (G-10592)
Teradyne Inc ....G 313 425-3900
Allen Park (G-208)

Employee Codes: A=Over 500 employees, B=251-500
C=101-250, D=51-100, E=20-50, F=10-19, G=3-9
2022 Harris Michigan
Industrial Directory
1299

INSTRUMENTS: Thermal Conductive, Indl
Advance Engineering Company .... D 313 537-3500
  Canton (G-2429)

INSTRUMENTS: Thermal Property Measurement
Marshall Ryerson Co .... F 616 299-1751
  Grand Rapids (G-6961)

INSTRUMENTS: Viscometer, Indl Process
Kaltec Scientific Inc .... G 248 349-8100
  Novi (G-12450)

INSULATING BOARD, CELLULAR FIBER
Nu-Wool Co Inc .... D 800 748-0128
  Jenison (G-9065)

INSULATING COMPOUNDS
Midland Cmpnding Cnsulting Inc .... G 989 495-9367
  Midland (G-11392)
Pfb Manufacturing LLC .... G 517 486-4844
  Blissfield (G-1773)

INSULATION & CUSHIONING FOAM: Polystyrene
Everest Manufacturing Inc .... F 313 401-2608
  Farmington Hills (G-5238)
G & T Industries Inc .... D 616 452-8611
  Byron Center (G-2271)
Harbor Foam Inc .... G 616 855-8150
  Grandville (G-7386)
High Tech Insulators Inc .... F 734 525-9030
  Livonia (G-10239)
Integrity Spray Foam LLC .... G 231 631-6084
  Traverse City (G-16724)
Janesville LLC .... D 248 948-1811
  Southfield (G-15611)
Michigan Foam Products Inc .... F 616 452-9611
  Grand Rapids (G-6989)
Mitten Spray Foam Insul LLC .... G 616 250-8355
  Wyoming (G-18895)
Plasteel Corporation .... E 313 562-5400
  Inkster (G-8670)

INSULATION & ROOFING MATERIALS: Wood, Reconstituted
Applegate Insul Systems Inc .... E 517 521-3545
  Webberville (G-18241)

INSULATION MATERIALS WHOLESALERS
Rex Materials Inc .... E 517 223-3787
  Howell (G-8509)

INSULATION: Fiberglass
Dgp Inc .... E 989 635-7531
  Marlette (G-10980)
Knauf Insulation Inc .... C 517 630-2000
  Albion (G-128)
Midwest Fbrglas Fbricators Inc .... F 810 765-7445
  Marine City (G-10963)

INSULATORS & INSULATION MATERIALS: Electrical
Dare Products Inc .... E 269 965-2307
  Springfield (G-15864)

INSURANCE ADVISORY SVCS
Wholesale Proc Systems LLC .... G 833 755-6696
  Adrian (G-104)

INSURANCE CARRIERS: Automobile
General Motors LLC .... A 313 972-6000
  Detroit (G-4257)

INSURANCE: Agents, Brokers & Service
Diversified Prof Rlty Svcs .... G 313 215-1840
  Hazel Park (G-7824)

INTERCOMMUNICATIONS SYSTEMS: Electric
Axis Tms Corp .... E 248 509-2440
  Clinton Township (G-3179)
Curbell Plastics Inc .... G 734 513-0531
  Livonia (G-10170)
R A Miller Industries Inc .... C 888 845-9450
  Grand Haven (G-6349)

INTERIOR DECORATING SVCS
Homespun Furniture Inc .... F 734 284-6277
  Riverview (G-13874)
Kent Upholstery Inc .... G 248 332-7260
  Pontiac (G-13392)

INTERIOR DESIGN SVCS, NEC
Bbj Graphics Inc .... G 248 450-3149
  Southfield (G-15504)
Compass Interiors LLC .... F 231 348-5353
  Petoskey (G-12994)
Sherwood Studios Inc .... E 248 855-1600
  West Bloomfield (G-18312)

INTERIOR DESIGNING SVCS
Home Style Co .... G 989 871-3654
  Millington (G-11501)

INTRAVENOUS SOLUTIONS
Drip Therapi LLC .... G 586 488-1256
  Shelby Township (G-15210)

INVENTORY STOCKING SVCS
Jasco International LLC .... G 313 841-5000
  Detroit (G-4335)

INVERTERS: Nonrotating Electrical
Redeem Power Services .... G 248 679-5277
  Novi (G-12524)

INVESTMENT FUNDS, NEC
Evans Industries Inc .... G 313 259-2266
  Troy (G-17100)

INVESTORS, NEC
Ascent Aerospace Holdings LLC .... G 212 916-8142
  Macomb (G-10579)

IRON & STEEL PRDTS: Hot-Rolled
Fritz Enterprises .... E 734 283-7272
  Trenton (G-16888)
St Clair Steel Corporation .... G 586 758-4356
  Warren (G-18025)

IRON ORES
Cleveland-Cliffs Inc .... A 906 475-3547
  Ishpeming (G-8775)
Empire Iron Mining Partnership .... A 906 475-3600
  Palmer (G-12930)
Tilden Mining Company LC .... A 906 475-3400
  Ishpeming (G-8783)

IRRIGATION SYSTEMS, NEC Water Distribution Or Sply Systems
Village & Cntry Wtr Trtmnt Inc .... F 810 632-7880
  Hartland (G-7773)

ISOCYANATES
International Isocyanate Inst .... G 989 878-0336
  Midland (G-11376)

JACKS: Hydraulic
Arbor International Inc .... G 734 761-5200
  Ann Arbor (G-374)
Jack Weaver Corp .... G 517 263-6500
  Adrian (G-76)
US Jack Company .... G 269 925-7777
  Benton Harbor (G-1597)

JANITORIAL & CUSTODIAL SVCS
Hudson Industries Inc .... G 313 777-5622
  Sterling Heights (G-16044)
Lockett Enterprises LLC .... G 810 407-6644
  Flint (G-5725)
Regency Construction Corp .... E 586 741-8000
  Clinton Township (G-3334)

JANITORIAL EQPT & SPLYS WHOLESALERS
National Soap Company Inc .... G 248 545-8180
  Royal Oak (G-14565)
Power Cleaning Systems Inc .... G 248 347-7727
  Wixom (G-18731)

JAR RINGS: Rubber
Hutchinson Seal Corporation .... E 248 375-4190
  Auburn Hills (G-931)

JARS: Plastic
Multiform Plastics Inc .... F 586 726-2688
  Sterling Heights (G-16109)

JEWELERS' FINDINGS & MATERIALS
Trenton Jewelers Ltd .... G 734 676-0188
  Trenton (G-16896)

JEWELERS' FINDINGS & MATERIALS: Castings
Dtown Grillz LLC .... G 734 624-9657
  Oak Park (G-12606)
L N T Inc .... G 248 347-6006
  Novi (G-12461)

JEWELRY & PRECIOUS STONES WHOLESALERS
Kevin Wheat & Assoc Ltd .... G 517 349-0101
  Okemos (G-12671)

JEWELRY APPAREL
Abracadabra Jewelry .... G 734 994-4848
  Ann Arbor (G-345)
Bednarsh Mrris Jwly Design Mfg .... F 248 671-0087
  Bloomfield (G-1781)
Daves Diamond Inc .... G 248 693-2482
  Lake Orion (G-9602)
La Gold Mine Inc .... G 517 540-1050
  Brighton (G-2018)
LLC Stahl Cross .... G 810 688-2505
  Lapeer (G-9943)
Michels Inc .... F 313 441-3620
  Dearborn (G-3872)
Wattsson & Wattsson Jewelers .... G 906 228-5775
  Marquette (G-11049)

JEWELRY FINDINGS & LAPIDARY WORK
Grandkids Edcted Motivated Gem .... G 313 539-7330
  Detroit (G-4273)
Jostens Inc .... G 734 308-3879
  Ada (G-24)
Kevin Wheat & Assoc Ltd .... G 517 349-0101
  Okemos (G-12671)

JEWELRY FINDINGS WHOLESALERS
Dtown Grillz LLC .... G 734 624-9657
  Oak Park (G-12606)

JEWELRY REPAIR SVCS
Abracadabra Jewelry .... G 734 994-4848
  Ann Arbor (G-345)
Bauble Patch Inc .... G 616 785-1100
  Comstock Park (G-3589)
Discount Jewelry Center Inc .... G 734 266-8200
  Westland (G-18364)
Kayayan Hayk Jewelry Mfg Co .... E 248 626-3060
  Bloomfield (G-1782)
Kevin Wheat & Assoc Ltd .... G 517 349-0101
  Okemos (G-12671)
Novus Corporation .... F 248 545-8600
  Warren (G-17948)
Orin Jewelers Inc .... F 734 422-7030
  Garden City (G-6105)
Trenton Jewelers Ltd .... G 734 676-0188
  Trenton (G-16896)

PRODUCT SECTION

JEWELRY STORES (continued)

Wattsson & Wattsson Jewelers .... G 906 228-5775
  Marquette *(G-11049)*

JEWELRY STORES

Alexander J Bongiorno Inc .... G 248 689-7766
  Troy *(G-16920)*
Allymade .... G 616 813-0591
  Lake Odessa *(G-9571)*
Aurum Design Inc .... G 248 651-9040
  Rochester *(G-13892)*
Bead Gallery .... F 734 663-6800
  Ann Arbor *(G-396)*
Dtown Grillz LLC .... G 734 624-9657
  Oak Park *(G-12606)*
Kevin Wheat & Assoc Ltd .... G 517 349-0101
  Okemos *(G-12671)*
Mount-N-Repair .... G 248 647-8670
  Birmingham *(G-1738)*

JEWELRY STORES: Precious Stones & Precious Metals

Abracadabra Jewelry .... G 734 994-4848
  Ann Arbor *(G-345)*
Bauble Patch Inc .... G 616 785-1100
  Comstock Park *(G-3589)*
Bednarsh Mrris Jwly Design Mfg .... F 248 671-0087
  Bloomfield *(G-1781)*
C T & T Inc .... E 248 623-9422
  Waterford *(G-18107)*
Daves Diamond Inc .... G 248 693-2482
  Lake Orion *(G-9602)*
Discount Jewelry Center Inc .... G 734 266-8200
  Westland *(G-18364)*
Jostens Inc .... G 734 308-3879
  Ada *(G-24)*
Kayayan Hayk Jewelry Mfg Co .... E 248 626-3060
  Bloomfield *(G-1782)*
La Gold Mine Inc .... G 517 540-1050
  Brighton *(G-2018)*
Michels Inc .... F 313 441-3620
  Dearborn *(G-3872)*
Milford Jewelers Inc .... G 248 676-0721
  Milford *(G-11471)*
Novus Corporation .... F 248 545-8600
  Warren *(G-17948)*
Orin Jewelers Inc .... F 734 422-7030
  Garden City *(G-6105)*
Preusser Jewelers .... G 616 458-1425
  Grand Rapids *(G-7105)*
Rex M Tubbs .... G 734 459-3180
  Plymouth *(G-13281)*
Trenton Jewelers Ltd .... G 734 676-0188
  Trenton *(G-16896)*
Tva Kane Inc .... E 248 946-4670
  Novi *(G-12560)*
Wattsson & Wattsson Jewelers .... G 906 228-5775
  Marquette *(G-11049)*

JEWELRY, PRECIOUS METAL: Bracelets

Pure & Simple Solutions LLC .... G 248 398-4600
  Troy *(G-17320)*

JEWELRY, PRECIOUS METAL: Mountings & Trimmings

Hunters Jewelry Repair Ctr Inc .... G 313 892-7621
  Detroit *(G-4309)*

JEWELRY, PRECIOUS METAL: Rings, Finger

Terryberry Company LLC .... C 616 458-1391
  Grand Rapids *(G-7254)*

JEWELRY, WHOLESALE

Bahama Souvenirs Inc .... G 269 964-8275
  Battle Creek *(G-1189)*
Bauble Patch Inc .... G 616 785-1100
  Comstock Park *(G-3589)*
Pure & Simple Solutions LLC .... G 248 398-4600
  Troy *(G-17320)*

JEWELRY: Decorative, Fashion & Costume

Allymade .... G 616 813-0591
  Lake Odessa *(G-9571)*
HL Manufacturing Inc .... F 586 731-2800
  Utica *(G-17502)*

Preusser Jewelers .... G 616 458-1425
  Grand Rapids *(G-7105)*
Swarovski North America Ltd .... G 586 226-4420
  Clinton Township *(G-3367)*

JEWELRY: Precious Metal

Alexander J Bongiorno Inc .... G 248 689-7766
  Troy *(G-16920)*
Amalgamations Ltd .... G 248 879-7345
  Troy *(G-16930)*
Au Enterprises Inc .... F 248 544-9700
  Berkley *(G-1621)*
Aurum Design Inc .... G 248 651-9040
  Rochester *(G-13892)*
Bauble Patch Inc .... G 616 785-1100
  Comstock Park *(G-3589)*
Birmingham Jewelry Inc .... G 586 939-5100
  Sterling Heights *(G-15946)*
C I I Ltd .... G 248 585-9905
  Troy *(G-16989)*
C T & T Inc .... E 248 623-9422
  Waterford *(G-18107)*
Combine International Inc .... C 248 585-9900
  Troy *(G-17019)*
Discount Jewelry Center Inc .... G 734 266-8200
  Westland *(G-18364)*
HL Manufacturing Inc .... F 586 731-2800
  Utica *(G-17502)*
Joseph A Dimaggio .... G 313 881-5353
  Grosse Pointe Woods *(G-7569)*
Kayayan Hayk Jewelry Mfg Co .... E 248 626-3060
  Bloomfield *(G-1782)*
Milford Jewelers Inc .... G 248 676-0721
  Milford *(G-11471)*
Mount-N-Repair .... G 248 647-8670
  Birmingham *(G-1738)*
Newell Brands Inc .... G 734 284-2528
  Taylor *(G-16452)*
Novus Corporation .... F 248 545-8600
  Warren *(G-17948)*
Orin Jewelers Inc .... F 734 422-7030
  Garden City *(G-6105)*
Rebel Nell L3c .... G 716 640-4267
  Detroit *(G-4557)*
Seoul International Inc .... G 586 275-2494
  Sterling Heights *(G-16170)*
Talisman .... G 616 458-1391
  Grand Rapids *(G-7248)*
Touchstone Distributing Inc .... G 517 669-8200
  Dewitt *(G-4718)*
Tva Kane Inc .... E 248 946-4670
  Novi *(G-12560)*

JIGS & FIXTURES

Advantage Design and Tool .... G 586 801-7413
  Richmond *(G-13831)*
Auto Metal Craft Inc .... E 248 398-2240
  Oak Park *(G-12594)*
Bilco Tool Corporation .... G 586 574-9300
  Warren *(G-17737)*
Conley Manufacturing Inc .... G 586 262-4484
  Shelby Township *(G-15193)*
Enterprise Tool and Gear Inc .... F 989 269-9797
  Bad Axe *(G-1100)*
Experienced Concepts Inc .... F 586 752-4200
  Armada *(G-735)*
Futuramic Tool & Engrg Co .... C 586 758-2200
  Warren *(G-17819)*
Gage Pattern & Model Inc .... D 248 361-6609
  Madison Heights *(G-10729)*
Generation Tool Inc .... G 734 641-6937
  Westland *(G-18374)*
H & M Machining Inc .... F 586 778-5028
  Roseville *(G-14419)*
I E & E Industries Inc .... F 248 544-8181
  Madison Heights *(G-10744)*
Keller Tool Ltd .... F 734 425-4500
  Livonia *(G-10264)*
Lane Tool and Mfg Corp .... G 248 528-1606
  Rochester Hills *(G-14049)*
Lonero Engineering Co Inc .... E 248 689-9120
  Troy *(G-17215)*
Master Machine & Tool Co Inc .... G 586 469-4243
  Clinton Township *(G-3295)*
Masters Tool & Die Inc .... G 989 777-2450
  Saginaw *(G-14688)*
Merriman Products Inc .... G 517 787-1825
  Jackson *(G-8953)*
Michalski Enterprises Inc .... E 517 703-0777
  Lansing *(G-9716)*

O Keller Tool Engrg Co LLC .... D 734 425-4500
  Livonia *(G-10349)*
Parry Precision Inc .... E 248 585-1234
  Madison Heights *(G-10795)*
Paslin Company .... C 586 758-0200
  Warren *(G-17957)*
Paslin Company .... C 248 953-8419
  Shelby Township *(G-15296)*
Patton Tool and Die Inc .... F 810 359-5336
  Lexington *(G-10031)*
Peak Industries Co Inc .... E 313 846-8666
  Dearborn *(G-3883)*
Proto-Tek Manufacturing Inc .... E 586 772-2663
  Roseville *(G-14467)*
Rens LLC .... F 586 756-6777
  Warren *(G-17996)*
Tri-Star Tool & Machine Co .... F 734 729-5700
  Westland *(G-18423)*
Triangle Broach Company .... E 313 838-2150
  Detroit *(G-4645)*
Tru Point Corporation .... G 313 897-9100
  Detroit *(G-4646)*
Turbine Tool & Gage Inc .... E 734 427-2270
  Livonia *(G-10451)*
Usher Tool & Die Inc .... G 616 583-9160
  Byron Center *(G-2297)*
Visioneering Inc .... B 248 622-5600
  Auburn Hills *(G-1079)*
Wire Dynamics Inc .... G 586 879-0321
  Fraser *(G-6012)*

JIGS: Welding Positioners

American Vault Service .... G 989 366-8657
  Prudenville *(G-13655)*

JOB COUNSELING

Road To Freedom .... F 810 775-0992
  Brighton *(G-2066)*

JOB PRINTING & NEWSPAPER PUBLISHING COMBINED

Crawford County Avalanche .... G 989 348-6811
  Grayling *(G-7458)*
Genesee County Herald Inc .... F 810 686-3840
  Clio *(G-3399)*
Oceanas Herald-Journal Inc .... F 231 873-5602
  Hart *(G-7759)*
Ontonagon Herald Co Inc .... G 906 884-2826
  Ontonagon *(G-12714)*
Peterson Publishing Inc .... G 906 387-3282
  Marquette *(G-11040)*
Presque Isle Newspapers Inc .... F 989 734-2105
  Rogers City *(G-14217)*
Tri City Record LLC .... G 269 463-6397
  Watervliet *(G-18184)*

JOB TRAINING & VOCATIONAL REHABILITATION SVCS

Buster Mathis Foundation .... G 616 843-4433
  Wyoming *(G-18855)*
Complete Services LLC .... F 248 470-8247
  Livonia *(G-10161)*
Services To Enhance Potential .... G 313 278-3040
  Dearborn *(G-3895)*

JOINTS OR FASTENINGS: Rail

Araymond Mfg Ctr N Amer Inc .... G 248 537-3147
  Rochester Hills *(G-13950)*

JOINTS: Expansion

Meccom Corporation .... G 313 895-4900
  Detroit *(G-4426)*

JOINTS: Expansion, Pipe

J D Russell Company .... E 586 254-8500
  Utica *(G-17503)*

JOISTS: Fabricated Bar

Creform Corporation .... E 248 926-2555
  Novi *(G-12385)*

JOISTS: Long-Span Series, Open Web Steel

Jaimes Liquidation Inc .... E 248 356-8600
  Southfield *(G-15610)*

KEYS: Machine

KEYS: Machine
Basch Olovson Engineering Co ....G...... 231 865-2027
  Fruitport (G-6060)

KILNS & FURNACES: Ceramic
Evenheat Kiln Inc.................................E...... 989 856-2281
  Caseville (G-2604)

KITCHEN CABINET STORES, EXC CUSTOM
A & B Display Systems Inc ....F...... 989 893-6642
  Bay City (G-1314)
Charlotte Cabinets Inc..........................G...... 517 543-1522
  Charlotte (G-2742)
D & M Cabinet Shop Inc ....G...... 989 479-9271
  Ruth (G-14597)
Dallas Design Inc ....G...... 810 238-4546
  Flint (G-5682)
Interior Spc of Holland ....F...... 616 396-5634
  Holland (G-8096)
Lafata Cabinet Shop ....D...... 586 247-6536
  Shelby Township (G-15255)
Lloyds Cabinet Shop Inc ....F...... 989 879-3015
  Pinconning (G-13061)
Millwork Design Group LLC ....G...... 248 472-2178
  Milford (G-11473)
Owens Building Co Inc ....E...... 989 835-1293
  Midland (G-11401)
Reis Custom Cabinets ....G...... 586 791-4925
  Reese (G-13807)

KITCHEN CABINETS WHOLESALERS
Cucina Moda - Birmingham LLC ....F...... 248 792-2285
  Troy (G-17037)
Greenfield Cabinetry Inc ....F...... 586 759-3300
  Warren (G-17839)
Kurtis Mfg & Distrg Corp ....E...... 734 522-7500
  Livonia (G-10270)
M and G Laminated Products ....G...... 517 784-4974
  Jackson (G-8938)
Modern Woodsmith LLC ....G...... 906 387-5577
  Wetmore (G-18435)
Richelieu America Ltd ....E...... 586 264-1240
  Sterling Heights (G-16151)

KITCHEN TOOLS & UTENSILS WHOLESALERS
Lecreuset..G...... 248 209-7025
  Auburn Hills (G-957)

KITCHEN UTENSILS: Bakers' Eqpt, Wood
Bremer Authentic Ingredients ....E...... 616 772-9100
  Zeeland (G-19002)
Buck-Spica Equipment Ltd ....F...... 269 792-2251
  Wayland (G-18192)

KITCHEN UTENSILS: Food Handling & Processing Prdts, Wood
Genstone LLC ....G...... 517 902-4730
  Adrian (G-70)
Indus Technologies Inc ....F...... 630 915-8034
  Ypsilanti (G-18955)
Russell Farms Inc ....G...... 269 349-6120
  Kalamazoo (G-9322)

KNIVES: Agricultural Or Indl
Ontario Die Company America ....D...... 810 987-5060
  Marysville (G-11095)

LABELS: Paper, Made From Purchased Materials
Macarthur Corp ....E...... 810 606-1777
  Grand Blanc (G-6252)
Venture Label Inc ....G...... 313 928-2545
  Detroit (G-4664)

LABOR RESOURCE SVCS
E-Con LLC ....G...... 248 766-9000
  Birmingham (G-1725)

LABORATORIES, TESTING: Automobile Proving & Testing Ground
Roush Enterprises Inc............................C...... 734 805-4400
  Farmington (G-5145)
Roush Industries Inc ....G...... 734 779-7013
  Livonia (G-10393)

LABORATORIES, TESTING: Prdt Certification, Sfty/Performance
Dynamic Corporation ....F...... 616 399-2200
  Holland (G-8018)
Reese Inspection Services LLC.............F...... 248 481-3598
  Auburn Hills (G-1017)

LABORATORIES, TESTING: Product Testing
Hydraulic Systems Technology ....G...... 248 656-5810
  Rochester Hills (G-14036)

LABORATORIES, TESTING: Product Testing, Safety/Performance
Ford Motor Company ....A...... 313 446-5945
  Detroit (G-4240)
Greening Incorporated ....G...... 313 366-7160
  Detroit (G-4282)
J E Myles Inc ....E...... 248 583-1020
  Troy (G-17178)
Therapeutic Health Choices LLC...........G...... 989 459-2020
  Bay City (G-1406)

LABORATORIES: Biological Research
Biosan Laboratories Inc ....F...... 586 755-8970
  Warren (G-17738)
Corium Inc ....C...... 650 298-8255
  Grand Rapids (G-6606)
Metabolic Solutions Dev Co LLC...........E...... 269 343-6732
  Grand Rapids (G-6977)
Oxford Biomedical Research Inc...........G...... 248 852-8815
  Metamora (G-11284)

LABORATORIES: Biotechnology
Csquared Innovations Inc ....F...... 734 998-8330
  Novi (G-12388)
Retrosense Therapeutics LLC...............G...... 734 369-9333
  Ann Arbor (G-639)
Tetradyn Ltd ....G...... 202 415-7295
  Traverse City (G-16855)

LABORATORIES: Commercial Nonphysical Research
Technova Corporation ....G...... 517 485-1402
  Okemos (G-12690)

LABORATORIES: Dental
Ktr Dental Lab & Pdts LLC ....F...... 248 224-9158
  Southfield (G-15622)

LABORATORIES: Dental, Artificial Teeth Production
Dental Art Laboratories Inc ....D...... 517 485-2200
  Lansing (G-9689)

LABORATORIES: Dental, Crown & Bridge Production
Davis Dental Laboratory........................G...... 616 261-9191
  Wyoming (G-18865)

LABORATORIES: Electronic Research
Consoldted Rsource Imaging LLC ....E...... 616 735-2080
  Grand Rapids (G-6595)
Ebw Electronics Inc ....B...... 616 786-0575
  Holland (G-8021)
Kore Inc ....E...... 616 785-5900
  Comstock Park (G-3617)
Sensigma LLC ....G...... 734 998-8328
  Ann Arbor (G-648)

LABORATORIES: Medical
Holland Community Hosp Aux Inc ....G...... 616 355-3926
  Holland (G-8076)

LABORATORIES: Noncommercial Research
Bioplstic Plymers Cmpsites LLC...........G...... 517 349-2970
  Okemos (G-12660)
Kellogg Company ....G...... 269 961-2000
  Battle Creek (G-1258)

LABORATORIES: Physical Research, Commercial
Akzo Nobel Coatings Inc ....E...... 248 637-0400
  Pontiac (G-13347)
Aurora Spclty Chemistries Corp ....E...... 517 372-9121
  Lansing (G-9810)
Bwi North America Inc ....F...... 810 494-4584
  Brighton (G-1957)
Contract People Corporation ....E...... 248 304-9900
  Southfield (G-15532)
Eftec North America LLC ....D...... 248 585-2200
  Taylor (G-16410)
Ervin Industries Inc...............................E...... 517 423-5477
  Tecumseh (G-16500)
Gates Corporation ....G...... 248 260-2300
  Rochester Hills (G-14020)
General Dynmics Mssion Systems ....G...... 734 480-5000
  Ypsilanti (G-18950)
General Dynmics Mssion Systems ....G...... 734 480-5000
  Ypsilanti (G-18951)
Innovative Weld Solutions LLC ....G...... 937 545-7695
  Rochester (G-13908)
Medical Engineering & Dev ....G...... 517 563-2352
  Horton (G-8377)
Metrex Research LLC ....D...... 734 947-6700
  Romulus (G-14303)
Sika Corporation ....D...... 248 577-0020
  Madison Heights (G-10829)
Trico Products Corporation ....C...... 248 371-1700
  Rochester Hills (G-14132)
Valeo North America Inc ....C...... 248 619-8300
  Troy (G-17428)
Vehicle Research and Dev ....G...... 586 504-1163
  Almont (G-270)

LABORATORIES: Testing
Anchor Bay Packaging Corp ....E...... 586 949-4040
  Chesterfield (G-2842)
Avomeen LLC ....D...... 734 222-1090
  Ann Arbor (G-390)
Bwi North America Inc ....F...... 810 494-4584
  Brighton (G-1957)
Eaton Corporation ....B...... 269 781-0200
  Marshall (G-11056)
Elden Industries Corp ....F...... 734 946-6900
  Taylor (G-16412)
Holland Community Hosp Aux Inc ....G...... 616 355-3926
  Holland (G-8076)
Industrial Temperature Control ....G...... 734 451-8740
  Canton (G-2474)
Marelli North America Inc ....G...... 248 403-2033
  Southfield (G-15645)
Medsker Electric Inc ....F...... 248 855-3383
  Farmington Hills (G-5314)
Merrill Technologies Group ....E...... 989 921-1490
  Saginaw (G-14696)
Merrill Technologies Group Inc ....D...... 989 791-6676
  Saginaw (G-14697)
Michigan Scientific Corp ....D...... 231 547-5511
  Charlevoix (G-2721)
PSI Labs ....F...... 734 369-6273
  Ann Arbor (G-627)
Roush Industries Inc ....G...... 734 779-7016
  Livonia (G-10392)
Saginaw Valley Inst Mtls Inc ....G...... 989 496-2307
  Midland (G-11413)
Thermal Wave Imaging Inc ....F...... 248 414-3730
  Madison Heights (G-10843)
Trico Products Corporation ....C...... 248 371-1700
  Rochester Hills (G-14132)
Weiss Technik North Amer Inc ....D...... 616 554-5020
  Grand Rapids (G-7329)
Xytek Industries Inc ....F...... 313 838-6961
  Detroit (G-4696)

LABORATORY APPARATUS & FURNITURE
AG Davis Gage & Engrg Co ....E...... 586 977-9000
  Sterling Heights (G-15926)
Alpha Resources LLC ....G...... 269 465-5559
  Stevensville (G-16239)
Balance Technology Inc ....D...... 734 769-2100
  Whitmore Lake (G-18520)

PRODUCT SECTION

LAMPS: Ultraviolet

Case Systems Inc ....C...... 989 496-9510
  Midland *(G-11327)*
Cmp Acquisitions LLC ....F...... 888 519-2286
  Redford *(G-13726)*
Coy Laboratory Products Inc...............E...... 734 433-9296
  Grass Lake *(G-7436)*
Gross Ventures Inc ....G...... 231 767-1301
  Byron Center *(G-2277)*
Leco Corporation ....G...... 269 985-5496
  Saint Joseph *(G-14947)*
Marketlab Inc ....D...... 866 237-3722
  Caledonia *(G-2388)*
Symbiote Inc ....E...... 616 772-1790
  Zeeland *(G-19083)*

LABORATORY APPARATUS, EXC HEATING & MEASURING

Accuri Cytometers Inc ....E...... 734 994-8000
  Ann Arbor *(G-346)*
Gelman Sciences Inc ....C...... 734 665-0651
  Ann Arbor *(G-496)*
Leco Corporation ....B...... 269 983-5531
  Saint Joseph *(G-14946)*
Xxtar Associates LLC ....G...... 888 946-6066
  Detroit *(G-4695)*

LABORATORY APPARATUS: Evaporation

Snow Machines Incorporated..............E...... 989 631-6091
  Midland *(G-11418)*

LABORATORY APPARATUS: Granulators

Cmg America Inc...................................G...... 810 686-3064
  Clio *(G-3395)*

LABORATORY APPARATUS: Microtomes

Rankin Biomedical Corporation ....F...... 248 625-4104
  Holly *(G-8290)*

LABORATORY APPARATUS: Sample Preparation Apparatus

QEd Envmtl Systems Inc......................D...... 734 995-2547
  Dexter *(G-4751)*

LABORATORY APPARATUS: Time Interval Measuring, Electric

Total Toxicology Labs LLC ....G...... 248 352-7171
  Southfield *(G-15724)*

LABORATORY CHEMICALS: Organic

Amerchol Corporation ....G...... 989 636-2441
  Midland *(G-11320)*
Boropharm Inc ....E...... 517 455-7847
  Ann Arbor *(G-403)*
Burhani Labs Inc ....G...... 313 212-3842
  Detroit *(G-4077)*
Dynamic Staffing Solutions ....G...... 616 399-5220
  Holland *(G-8019)*
Horiba Instruments Inc.........................D...... 866 540-2715
  Canton *(G-2471)*
Jade Scientific Inc.................................F...... 734 207-3775
  Westland *(G-18387)*
Kemai (usa) Chemical Co Ltd ....G...... 248 924-2225
  Northville *(G-12234)*
Lab Link Testing LLC ....G...... 419 283-6387
  Madison Heights *(G-10766)*
Medtest Holdings Inc...........................D...... 866 540-2715
  Canton *(G-2492)*

LABORATORY EQPT, EXC MEDICAL: Wholesalers

Alpha Resources LLC...........................E...... 269 465-5559
  Stevensville *(G-16239)*
Healthcare Drble Med Eqpmnts L.......G...... 734 975-6668
  Ann Arbor *(G-510)*
Rankin Biomedical Corporation ....F...... 248 625-4104
  Holly *(G-8290)*
Xxtar Associates LLC ....G...... 888 946-6066
  Detroit *(G-4695)*

LABORATORY EQPT: Centrifuges

M2 Scientifics LLC ....F...... 616 379-9080
  Allendale *(G-224)*

LABORATORY EQPT: Clinical Instruments Exc Medical

Holland Community Hosp Aux Inc ......G...... 616 355-3926
  Holland *(G-8076)*

LABORATORY EQPT: Incubators

Southwest Mich Innovation Ctr ....G...... 269 353-1823
  Kalamazoo *(G-9339)*

LABORATORY EQPT: Sterilizers

Peerless Waste Solutions LLC ....G...... 616 355-2800
  Holland *(G-8161)*

LACQUERING SVC: Metal Prdts

Gladwin Metal Processing Inc ....G...... 989 426-9038
  Gladwin *(G-6198)*

LADDER & WORKSTAND COMBINATION ASSEMBLIES: Metal

Jershon Inc ....G...... 231 861-2900
  Shelby *(G-15151)*

LADDERS: Metal

Laddertech LLC.....................................F...... 248 437-7100
  Brighton *(G-2019)*

LADDERS: Portable, Metal

Aquarius Recreational Products ....G...... 586 469-4600
  Harrison Township *(G-7687)*
Con-De Manufacturing Inc ....G...... 269 651-3756
  Sturgis *(G-16285)*

LADDERS: Wood

Ladder Carolina Company Inc.............F...... 734 482-5946
  Ypsilanti *(G-18961)*
Michigan Ladder Company LLC ....F...... 734 482-5946
  Ypsilanti *(G-18967)*

LAMINATED PLASTICS: Plate, Sheet, Rod & Tubes

Advanced Drainage Systems Inc ....G...... 989 723-5208
  Owosso *(G-12819)*
Bangor Plastics Inc...............................E...... 269 427-7971
  Bangor *(G-1128)*
Basic Rubber and Plastics Co ....E...... 248 360-7400
  Walled Lake *(G-17664)*
Duo-Gard Industries Inc ....D...... 734 207-9700
  Canton *(G-2456)*
J Kaltz & Co ....G...... 616 942-6070
  Grand Rapids *(G-6856)*
Kent Manufacturing Company.............D...... 616 454-9495
  Grand Rapids *(G-6889)*
Lwhs Ltd ....D...... 616 452-5300
  Grand Rapids *(G-6954)*
McKechnie Vhcl Cmpnnts USA Inc.....B...... 218 894-1218
  Roseville *(G-14438)*
Paul Murphy Plastics Co ....E...... 586 774-4880
  Roseville *(G-14460)*
Plascore ....E...... 616 772-1220
  Zeeland *(G-19071)*
Polyply Composites LLC.....................E...... 616 842-6330
  Grand Haven *(G-6344)*
Rehau Incorporated ....G...... 269 651-7845
  Sturgis *(G-16321)*
Shawmut LLC ....G...... 810 987-2222
  Port Huron *(G-13526)*
Spiratex Company ....D...... 734 289-4800
  Monroe *(G-11576)*
Summit Polymers Inc ....B...... 269 323-1301
  Portage *(G-13624)*
Summit Polymers Inc ....B...... 269 651-1643
  Sturgis *(G-16326)*
Total Plastics Resources LLC..............D...... 269 344-0009
  Kalamazoo *(G-9358)*
Vidon Plastics Inc ....D...... 810 667-0634
  Lapeer *(G-9965)*

LAMINATING MATERIALS

Dico Manufacturing LLC ....G...... 586 731-3008
  Chesterfield *(G-2871)*

LAMINATING SVCS

Celia Corporation ....G...... 616 887-7387
  Sparta *(G-15763)*
Engineering Reproduction Inc.............G...... 313 366-3390
  Detroit *(G-4209)*
F & A Enterprises of Michigan ....G...... 906 228-3222
  Marquette *(G-11018)*

LAMP & LIGHT BULBS & TUBES

Chicl LLC ....A...... 859 294-5590
  Troy *(G-17010)*
Energy Efficient Ltg LLC Eel................G...... 586 214-5557
  West Bloomfield *(G-18282)*
Ews Legacy LLC....................................C...... 248 853-6363
  Rochester Hills *(G-14006)*
High Q Lighting Inc...............................F...... 616 396-3591
  Holland *(G-8071)*
Inland Vapor of Michigan LLC ....G...... 734 738-6312
  Canton *(G-2475)*
Led Source Detroit ....G...... 586 983-9905
  Sterling Heights *(G-16070)*
Oshino Lamps America Ltd ....G...... 262 226-8620
  Wixom *(G-18727)*
Philips North America LLC ....C...... 248 553-9080
  Farmington Hills *(G-5346)*
Trident Lighting LLC.............................D...... 616 957-9500
  Grand Rapids *(G-7276)*

LAMP BULBS & TUBES, ELECTRIC: Electric Light

Johnico LLC ....E...... 248 895-7820
  Detroit *(G-4340)*

LAMP BULBS & TUBES, ELECTRIC: For Specialized Applications

Emitted Energy Inc ....F...... 855 752-3347
  Sterling Heights *(G-16004)*
Illumination Machines LLC ....G...... 856 685-7403
  Rochester Hills *(G-14038)*

LAMP BULBS & TUBES, ELECTRIC: Glow Lamp

Wickedglow Industries Inc..................G...... 586 776-4132
  Mount Clemens *(G-11663)*

LAMP BULBS & TUBES, ELECTRIC: Light, Complete

Elumigen LLC...G...... 855 912-0477
  Troy *(G-17086)*
G & L Powerup Inc ....G...... 586 200-2169
  Roseville *(G-14409)*

LAMP BULBS & TUBES, ELECTRIC: Vapor

Inland Vapor of Michigan LLC ....D...... 734 237-4389
  Garden City *(G-6098)*

LAMP BULBS & TUBES/PARTS, ELECTRIC: Generalized Applications

Optic Edge Corporation ....G...... 231 547-6090
  Charlevoix *(G-2726)*

LAMP REPAIR & MOUNTING SVCS

Beltone Skoric Hearng Aid Cntr ....G...... 906 379-0606
  Sault Sainte Marie *(G-15087)*
Beltone Skoric Hearng Aid Cntr ....G...... 906 553-4660
  Escanaba *(G-5061)*

LAMPS: Desk, Commercial

Light Corp Inc..C...... 616 842-5100
  Grand Haven *(G-6329)*

LAMPS: Table, Residential

Lighting Enterprises Inc.......................G...... 313 693-9504
  Detroit *(G-4399)*

LAMPS: Ultraviolet

Global Connections & More LLC.........G...... 248 990-2266
  Livonia *(G-10224)*
Rel Inc..E...... 906 337-3018
  Calumet *(G-2413)*

LAND SUBDIVISION & DEVELOPMENT

Marshalls Crossing	G	810 639-4740	
Montrose (G-11606)			
Stroh Companies Inc	G	313 446-2000	
Detroit (G-4612)			

LANGUAGE SCHOOLS

Complete Services LLC ....F........ 248 470-8247
  Livonia (G-10161)

LASER SYSTEMS & EQPT

Arch Cutting Tools LLC ....C........ 734 266-6900
  Bloomfield Hills (G-1800)
Cortar Laser and Fab LLC ....G........ 248 446-1110
  Brighton (G-1970)
Fabrilaser Mfg LLC ....E........ 269 789-9490
  Marshall (G-11057)
G and R Laser Solutions Inc ....G........ 734 748-6603
  Canton (G-2462)
Imperial Laser Inc ....G........ 616 735-9315
  Grand Rapids (G-6837)
Imra America Inc ....E........ 734 669-7377
  Ann Arbor (G-525)
Ipg Photonics Corporation 248 863-5001
  Novi (G-12441)
Laser Fab Inc ....G........ 586 415-8090
  Fraser (G-5955)
Laser Marking Technologies LLC ....F........ 989 673-6690
  Caro (G-2573)
Laser Mechanisms Inc ....D........ 248 474-9480
  Novi (G-12465)
Laser Product Development LLC ....G........ 800 765-4424
  Center Line (G-2682)
Rofin-Sinar Technologies LLC ....G........ 734 416-0206
  Plymouth (G-13290)

LASERS: Welding, Drilling & Cutting Eqpt

Andex Laser Inc ....G........ 734 947-9840
  Taylor (G-16378)
Arin Inc ....F........ 586 779-3410
  Roseville (G-14375)
Laser Access Inc ....C........ 616 459-5496
  Grand Rapids (G-6928)
Macomb Sheet Metal Inc ....E........ 586 790-4600
  Clinton Township (G-3290)
Reau Manufacturing Co ....G........ 734 823-5603
  Dundee (G-4833)
Rydin and Associates Inc ....F........ 586 783-9772
  Clinton Township (G-3347)
SLM Solutions Na Inc ....E........ 248 243-5400
  Wixom (G-18753)
Trumpf Inc ....E........ 734 354-9770
  Plymouth (G-13327)
Visotek Inc ....F........ 734 427-4800
  Novi (G-12568)

LATHES

Advanced Maintenance Tech ....G........ 810 820-2554
  Flint (G-5639)
SKF USA Inc ....E........ 810 231-2400
  Brighton (G-2072)

LAUNDRY & GARMENT SVCS, NEC: Garment Making, Alter & Repair

Demmem Enterprises LLC ....F........ 810 564-9500
  Clio (G-3396)

LAUNDRY & GARMENT SVCS, NEC: Reweaving, Textiles

Zeilinger Wool Co LLC ....E........ 989 652-2920
  Frankenmuth (G-5874)

LAUNDRY EQPT: Commercial

AEC Systems Usa Inc ....F........ 616 257-9502
  Wyoming (G-18849)

LAUNDRY EQPT: Household

Whirlpool Corporation ....A........ 269 923-5000
  Benton Harbor (G-1603)
Whirlpool Corporation ....G........ 404 547-3194
  Saint Joseph (G-14977)
Whirlpool Corporation ....G........ 269 923-5000
  Benton Harbor (G-1605)
Whirlpool Corporation ....G........ 269 923-7400
  Benton Harbor (G-1606)
Whirlpool Corporation ....G........ 269 923-5000
  Benton Harbor (G-1607)
Whirlpool Corporation ....G........ 269 923-6057
  Saint Joseph (G-14978)
Whirlpool Corporation ....G........ 269 923-6486
  Benton Harbor (G-1608)

LAWN & GARDEN EQPT

Big Green Tomato LLC ....G........ 269 282-1593
  Battle Creek (G-1194)
Buyers Development Group LLC ....F........ 734 677-0009
  Ann Arbor (G-411)
Contech (us) Inc ....F........ 616 459-4139
  Grand Rapids (G-6597)
Forest Grove Power Eqp LLC ....G........ 616 896-8344
  Hudsonville (G-8584)
Harrells LLC ....E........ 248 446-8070
  New Hudson (G-12056)
Hydro Giant 4 Inc ....F........ 248 661-0034
  West Bloomfield (G-18289)
Lloyd Miller & Sons Inc ....E........ 517 223-3112
  Corunna (G-3710)
Milsco LLC ....E........ 517 787-3650
  Jackson (G-8965)
Root Spring Scraper Co ....E........ 269 382-2025
  Kalamazoo (G-9321)
Superior Cedar Products Inc ....E........ 906 639-2132
  Carney (G-2564)
Surefit Parts LLC ....G........ 586 416-9150
  Chesterfield (G-2952)
Whitehall Products LLC ....D........ 231 894-2688
  Whitehall (G-18514)

LAWN & GARDEN EQPT: Blowers & Vacuums

Dynamic Manufacturing LLC ....E........ 989 644-8109
  Weidman (G-18251)

LAWN & GARDEN EQPT: Edgers

Sure-Loc Aluminum Edging Inc ....G........ 616 392-3209
  Holland (G-8210)

LAWN & GARDEN EQPT: Grass Catchers, Lawn Mower

Ebels Hardware Inc ....F........ 231 826-3334
  Falmouth (G-5133)

LAWN & GARDEN EQPT: Tractors & Eqpt

Wells Equipment Sales Inc ....F........ 517 542-2376
  Litchfield (G-10087)

LAWN MOWER REPAIR SHOP

Bader & Co ....F........ 810 648-2404
  Sandusky (G-15055)
D P Equipment Co ....F........ 517 368-5266
  Camden (G-2421)
Ebels Hardware Inc ....F........ 231 826-3334
  Falmouth (G-5133)

LEAD

Mayer Alloys Corporation 248 399-2233
  Ferndale (G-5567)

LEAD & ZINC ORES

National Zinc Processors Inc ....F........ 269 926-1161
  Benton Harbor (G-1577)

LEAD PENCILS & ART GOODS

Mac Enterprises Inc ....F........ 313 846-4567
  Manchester (G-10885)
Panoplate Lithographics Inc ....G........ 269 343-4644
  Kalamazoo (G-9285)

LEASING & RENTAL SVCS: Cranes & Aerial Lift Eqpt

Bristol Manufacturing Inc ....E........ 810 658-9510
  Davison (G-3774)
Joseph A Dimaggio ....G........ 313 881-5353
  Grosse Pointe Woods (G-7569)
Schwartz Boiler Shop Inc ....G........ 231 627-2556
  Cheboygan (G-2798)

LEASING & RENTAL SVCS: Earth Moving Eqpt

D P Equipment Co ....F........ 517 368-5266
  Camden (G-2421)

LEASING & RENTAL: Computers & Eqpt

American Information Services ....F........ 248 399-4848
  Berkley (G-1620)

LEASING & RENTAL: Construction & Mining Eqpt

Arcosa Shoring Products Inc ....E........ 800 292-1225
  Lansing (G-9673)
Capital Equipment Clare LLC ....F........ 517 669-5533
  Dewitt (G-4708)
Garrisons Hitch Center Inc ....E........ 810 239-5728
  Flint (G-5703)
Jones & Hollands Inc ....G........ 810 364-6400
  Marysville (G-11089)
Modern Industries Inc ....E........ 810 767-3330
  Flint (G-5735)

LEASING & RENTAL: Medical Machinery & Eqpt

Metro Medical Eqp Mfg Inc ....E........ 734 522-8400
  Livonia (G-10313)
Wright & Filippis LLC ....F........ 586 756-4020
  Warren (G-18073)

LEASING & RENTAL: Mobile Home Sites

Kearsley Lake Terrace LLC ....G........ 810 736-7000
  Flint (G-5720)
Woodland Park & Sales ....G........ 810 229-2397
  Brighton (G-2098)

LEASING & RENTAL: Other Real Estate Property

J M Longyear Heirs Inc ....G........ 906 228-7960
  Marquette (G-11023)
Overstreet Property MGT Co ....G........ 269 281-3880
  Benton Harbor (G-1578)
Power Property Solutions LLC ....G........ 734 306-0299
  Wayne (G-18232)

LEASING & RENTAL: Trucks, Without Drivers

Novi Manufacturing Co ....C........ 248 476-4350
  Novi (G-12494)

LEASING & RENTAL: Utility Trailers & RV's

Shyft Group Inc ....A........ 517 543-6400
  Novi (G-12536)
Shyft Group Inc 517 543-6400
  Charlotte (G-2767)

LEASING: Passenger Car

Ford Motor Company ....F........ 734 942-6248
  Brownstown (G-2146)
Ford Motor Company ....A........ 313 322-3000
  Dearborn (G-3842)
Ford Motor Company ....F........ 734 523-3000
  Livonia (G-10215)

LEASING: Shipping Container

Corsair Engineering Inc ....F........ 810 233-0440
  Flint (G-5672)

LEATHER GOODS: Belting & Strapping

C W Marsh Company ....E........ 231 722-3781
  Muskegon (G-11788)

LEATHER GOODS: Embossed

Tapestry Inc ....G........ 616 538-5802
  Grandville (G-7420)

LEATHER GOODS: Garments

Leathercrafts By Bear ....G........ 616 453-8308
  Grand Rapids (G-6933)

LEATHER GOODS: Harnesses Or Harness Parts

Erich Jaeger USA Inc..............................G...... 734 404-5940
  Livonia *(G-10199)*
Low Cost Surcing Solutions LLC..........G...... 248 535-7721
  Washington *(G-18084)*

LEATHER GOODS: Holsters

Adams Holsters.......................................G...... 906 662-4212
  Channing *(G-2705)*
Custom Built Holsters LLC ....G...... 517 825-9856
  Jonesville *(G-9086)*
Perras Holster Sales LLC ....G...... 248 467-4254
  South Lyon *(G-15452)*

LEATHER GOODS: Money Holders

Birlon Group LLC....................................G...... 313 551-5341
  Inkster *(G-8659)*

LEATHER GOODS: NEC

Lyon Hide Leather Goods LLC ....G...... 517 997-6067
  Charlotte *(G-2761)*
Paragon Leather Inc USA......................G...... 269 323-9483
  Portage *(G-13590)*

LEATHER GOODS: Personal

Bianco Inc...G...... 313 682-2612
  Livonia *(G-10137)*
C W Marsh Company ....E...... 231 722-3781
  Muskegon *(G-11788)*
Original Footwear Company ....B...... 231 796-5828
  Big Rapids *(G-1681)*
Shields Classic Toys ....G...... 888 806-2632
  Saline *(G-15039)*

LEATHER GOODS: Straps

Shinola/Detroit LLC ....C...... 888 304-2534
  Detroit *(G-4591)*

LEATHER TANNING & FINISHING

Horn Corp ....G...... 248 358-8883
  Brighton *(G-2009)*
Lear Corporation ....G...... 248 853-3122
  Rochester Hills *(G-14051)*
Mexico Express......................................F...... 313 843-6717
  Detroit *(G-4440)*
Modern Fur Dressing LLC ....G...... 517 589-5575
  Leslie *(G-10015)*
Wolverine World Wide Inc ....A...... 616 866-5500
  Rockford *(G-14197)*

LEATHER: Cut

Afx Industries LLC ....G...... 517 768-8993
  Jackson *(G-8805)*

LEATHER: Die-cut

Michigan Diversfd Holdings Inc ....F...... 248 280-0450
  Madison Heights *(G-10782)*

LEATHER: Equestrian Prdts

Goodells Equestrian Center...................G...... 586 615-8535
  Wales *(G-17628)*

LEATHER: Handbag

Beau Satchelle LLC ....G...... 313 374-8462
  Ann Arbor *(G-398)*

LEATHER: Indl Prdts

Afx Industries LLC ....G...... 810 966-4650
  Port Huron *(G-13431)*
Afx Industries LLC ....G...... 810 966-4650
  Port Huron *(G-13432)*
National Manufacturing Inc...................G...... 586 755-8983
  Warren *(G-17941)*

LEATHER: Processed

Transnav Holdings Inc...........................C...... 586 716-5600
  New Baltimore *(G-11996)*

LECTURING SVCS

Step Into Success Inc.............................G...... 734 426-1075
  Pinckney *(G-13057)*

LEGAL OFFICES & SVCS

Detroit Legal News Pubg LLC................E...... 248 577-6100
  Troy *(G-17057)*
Marshal E Hyman and Associates.........G...... 248 643-0642
  Troy *(G-17239)*

LENS COATING: Ophthalmic

Hi-Tech Optical Inc................................E...... 989 799-9390
  Saginaw *(G-14663)*

LICENSE TAGS: Automobile, Stamped Metal

Mercury Metal Forming Tech LLC ....F...... 586 778-4444
  Roseville *(G-14440)*

LIGHT OIL CRUDE: From Chemical Recovery Coke Ovens

Alan Bruce Enterprises ....G...... 616 262-4609
  Byron Center *(G-2257)*

LIGHT SENSITIVE DEVICES

Alsentis LLC...G...... 616 395-8254
  Holland *(G-7961)*

LIGHTING EQPT: Area & Sports Luminaries

Qualite Inc..E...... 517 439-4316
  Hillsdale *(G-7943)*

LIGHTING EQPT: Motor Vehicle

A S Auto Lights Inc ....G...... 734 941-1164
  Romulus *(G-14242)*
Emergency Technology Inc ....D...... 616 896-7100
  Hudsonville *(G-8581)*
F M T Products Inc.................................G...... 517 568-3373
  Homer *(G-8351)*
Gyb LLC..F...... 586 218-3222
  Warren *(G-17844)*
HA Automotive Systems Inc ....F...... 248 781-0001
  Troy *(G-17135)*
Shelton Technology LLC........................G...... 248 816-1585
  Troy *(G-17349)*
Stanley Elc Holdg Amer Inc ....D...... 269 660-7777
  Battle Creek *(G-1300)*

LIGHTING EQPT: Motor Vehicle, Dome Lights

Magna Mirrors America Inc ....G...... 616 786-7300
  Holland *(G-8134)*
Magna Mirrors America Inc ....G...... 616 942-0163
  Newaygo *(G-12085)*

LIGHTING EQPT: Motor Vehicle, Headlights

Illumination Machines LLC ....G...... 856 685-7403
  Rochester Hills *(G-14038)*
Marelli Automotive Ltg LLC ....G...... 248 418-3000
  Clarkston *(G-3047)*
Marelli Automotive Ltg LLC ....E...... 248 418-3000
  Southfield *(G-15642)*

LIGHTING EQPT: Motor Vehicle, NEC

Autosystems America Inc.....................B...... 734 582-2300
  Plymouth *(G-13129)*
Eoi Pioneer Corp....................................G...... 626 823-5639
  Dundee *(G-4818)*
Eto Magnetic Corp ....C...... 616 957-2570
  Grand Rapids *(G-6686)*
Fisher-Baker Corporation ....G...... 810 765-3548
  Marine City *(G-10958)*
Il Stanley Co Inc.....................................A...... 269 660-7777
  Battle Creek *(G-1240)*
Interntnal Auto Cmpnnts Group ....G...... 231 734-9000
  Evart *(G-5124)*
MLS Automotive Incorporated...............F...... 844 453-3669
  Farmington Hills *(G-5324)*
Rebo Lighting & Elec LLC.....................F...... 734 213-4159
  Ann Arbor *(G-633)*
Trident Lighting LLC..............................D...... 616 957-9500
  Grand Rapids *(G-7276)*
Zkw Lighting Systems Usa Inc ....F...... 248 509-7300
  Troy *(G-17461)*

LIGHTING EQPT: Motor Vehicle, Taillights

Tecniq Inc...E...... 269 629-4440
  Galesburg *(G-6085)*

LIGHTING EQPT: Outdoor

Hutson Inc ....C...... 517 655-4606
  Williamston *(G-18573)*

LIGHTING EQPT: Reflectors, Metal, For Lighting Eqpt

Illumination Machines LLC ....G...... 856 685-7403
  Rochester Hills *(G-14038)*

LIGHTING EQPT: Searchlights

Searchlight Safety LLC..........................G...... 313 333-9200
  Dundee *(G-4835)*

LIGHTING EQPT: Spotlights

Spotlight Couture LLC...........................G...... 313 768-5305
  Taylor *(G-16478)*
Spotlight Media LLC ....G...... 269 808-4473
  Kalamazoo *(G-9343)*

LIGHTING FIXTURES WHOLESALERS

Douglas Milton Lamp Co ....G...... 888 738-3332
  Battle Creek *(G-1220)*
Full Spectrum Solutions Inc ....E...... 517 783-3800
  Jackson *(G-8888)*
Houseart LLC ....G...... 248 651-8124
  Rochester *(G-13905)*
Led Source Detroit ....G...... 586 983-9905
  Sterling Heights *(G-16070)*
Nextek Power Systems Inc ....G...... 313 887-1321
  Detroit *(G-4484)*

LIGHTING FIXTURES, NEC

A Lite In Nite ....G...... 231 275-5900
  Lake Ann *(G-9540)*
Affordable OEM Autolighting................G...... 989 400-6106
  Stanton *(G-15898)*
Ci Lighting LLC......................................G...... 248 997-4415
  Auburn Hills *(G-843)*
Clearview Lighting LLC.........................G...... 248 709-8707
  Beverly Hills *(G-1662)*
Coreled Systems LLC ....G...... 734 516-2060
  Livonia *(G-10166)*
Dakkota Lighting Tech LLC...................E...... 517 694-2823
  Holt *(G-8308)*
Emergency Technology Inc ....D...... 616 896-7100
  Hudsonville *(G-8581)*
Energy Design Svc Systems LLC.........D...... 810 227-3377
  Whitmore Lake *(G-18532)*
Firewater Lighting LLC..........................G...... 616 570-0088
  Alto *(G-332)*
Gadget Factory LLC...............................G...... 517 449-1444
  Lansing *(G-9840)*
General Structures Inc ....F...... 586 774-6105
  Warren *(G-17826)*
Global Green Corporation ....F...... 734 560-1743
  Ann Arbor *(G-501)*
GT Solutions LLC...................................G...... 616 259-0700
  Holland *(G-8062)*
High Q Lighting Inc ....F...... 616 396-3591
  Holland *(G-8071)*
I Parth Inc...G...... 248 548-9722
  Ferndale *(G-5560)*
Ilumigreen Corp ....G...... 616 318-3087
  Norton Shores *(G-12299)*
Infection Prevention Tech LLC..............G...... 248 340-8800
  Grand Blanc *(G-6248)*
J & B Products Ltd................................F...... 989 792-6119
  Saginaw *(G-14672)*
J & M Products and Service LLC.........G...... 517 263-3082
  Adrian *(G-75)*
K and J Lighting ....G...... 586 625-2001
  Roseville *(G-14429)*
Lumerica Corporation ....F...... 248 543-8085
  Warren *(G-17908)*
Michigan Lightning Protection ....G...... 866 712-4071
  Grand Rapids *(G-6992)*
Phoenix Imaging Inc ....F...... 248 476-4200
  Livonia *(G-10365)*
Sonrize LLC..G...... 586 329-3225
  Chesterfield *(G-2949)*
Sound Productions Entrmt....................F...... 989 386-2221
  Clare *(G-2998)*

LIGHTING FIXTURES, NEC

PRODUCT SECTION

Spectrum Illumination Co Inc .... G 231 894-4590
  Montague (G-11601)
Steelcase Inc .... A 616 247-2710
  Grand Rapids (G-7224)
Total Source Led Inc .... G 313 575-8889
  Dearborn Heights (G-3942)

LIGHTING FIXTURES: Fluorescent, Commercial

High Q Lighting Inc .... F 616 396-3591
  Holland (G-8071)

LIGHTING FIXTURES: Indl & Commercial

Alumalight LLC .... G 248 457-9302
  Troy (G-16929)
Burst Led .... G 248 321-6262
  Farmington Hills (G-5188)
Chandelier & More LLC .... E 248 214-1525
  Jackson (G-8839)
Command Electronics Inc .... E 269 679-4011
  Schoolcraft (G-15115)
Douglas Milton Lamp Co .... G 888 738-3332
  Battle Creek (G-1220)
E-Light LLC .... G 734 427-0600
  Commerce Township (G-3524)
Earthtronics Inc .... F 231 332-1188
  Norton Shores (G-12290)
Elumigen LLC .... G 855 912-0477
  Troy (G-17086)
Energy Design Svc Systems LLC ... D 810 227-3377
  Whitmore Lake (G-18532)
Global Green Corporation .... F 734 560-1743
  Ann Arbor (G-501)
GT Solutions LLC .... G 616 259-0700
  Holland (G-8062)
Illumination Machines LLC .... G 856 685-7403
  Rochester Hills (G-14038)
Johnico Inc .... E 248 895-7820
  Detroit (G-4340)
Leif Distribution LLC .... E 517 481-2122
  Grand Rapids (G-6939)
Lyte Poles Incorporated .... D 586 771-4610
  Warren (G-17911)
Nylube Products Company LLC ..... F 248 852-6500
  Rochester Hills (G-14074)
Pro Lighting Group Inc .... G 810 229-5600
  Brighton (G-2054)
R-Bo Co Inc .... F 616 748-9733
  Zeeland (G-19076)
Robogistics LLC .... F 409 234-1033
  Adrian (G-91)
Smart Vision Lights LLC .... D 231 722-1199
  Norton Shores (G-12331)
Sound Productions Entrmt .... F 989 386-2221
  Clare (G-2998)
Suntech Industrials LLC .... G 734 678-5922
  Ann Arbor (G-668)
Woodward Energy Solutions LLC .. F 888 967-4533
  Detroit (G-4690)

LIGHTING FIXTURES: Motor Vehicle

Clarience Technologies LLC .... D 716 665-6214
  Southfield (G-15525)
Mid American AEL LLC .... G 810 229-5483
  Brighton (G-2033)
Penske Company LLC .... G 248 648-2000
  Bloomfield Hills (G-1849)
Progressive Dynamics Inc .... D 269 781-4241
  Marshall (G-11072)

LIGHTING FIXTURES: Public

Johnico LLC .... E 248 895-7820
  Detroit (G-4340)

LIGHTING FIXTURES: Residential

A E C Inc .... D 810 231-9546
  Whitmore Lake (G-18515)
Douglas Milton Lamp Co .... G 888 738-3332
  Battle Creek (G-1220)
Full Spectrum Solutions Inc .... E 517 783-3800
  Jackson (G-8888)
R-Bo Co Inc .... F 616 748-9733
  Zeeland (G-19076)

LIGHTING FIXTURES: Residential, Electric

Denali Lighting LLC .... G 586 731-0399
  Shelby Township (G-15204)

Universal Manufacturing Co .... E 586 463-2560
  Clinton Township (G-3383)

LIGHTING FIXTURES: Street

Leif Distribution LLC .... E 517 481-2122
  Grand Rapids (G-6939)
Solar Tonic LLC .... G 734 368-0215
  Ann Arbor (G-658)

LIMESTONE & MARBLE: Dimension

Doug Wirt Enterprises Inc .... G 989 684-5777
  Bay City (G-1347)

LIMESTONE: Crushed & Broken

Aggregate and Developing LLC ..... G 269 217-5492
  Allegan (G-144)
Carmeuse Lime Inc .... C 906 484-2201
  Cedarville (G-2668)
Carmeuse Lime Inc .... C 313 849-9268
  River Rouge (G-13853)
Dufferin Aggregates .... G 734 529-2411
  Dundee (G-4814)
Eggers Excavating LLC .... F 989 695-5205
  Freeland (G-6022)
F G Cheney Limestone Co .... G 269 763-9541
  Bellevue (G-1498)
Falcon Trucking Company .... E 989 656-2831
  Bay Port (G-1414)
Flint Lime Industries Inc .... G 313 843-6050
  Detroit (G-4238)
Genesee Cut Stone & Marble Co ... E 810 743-1800
  Grand Blanc (G-6242)
O N Minerals .... C 906 484-2201
  Cedarville (G-2671)
O-N Minerals Michigan Company .. C 989 734-2131
  Rogers City (G-14214)
O-N Minerals Michigan Company .. C 906 484-2201
  Cedarville (G-2673)
O-N Minerals Michigan Company .. C 989 734-2131
  Rogers City (G-14215)
Stoneco Inc .... E 734 587-7125
  Maybee (G-11172)
Waanders Concrete Co .... F 269 673-6352
  Allegan (G-184)

LIMESTONE: Dimension

Levy Indiana Slag Co .... D 313 843-7200
  Dearborn (G-3862)
Manigg Enterprises Inc .... G 989 356-4986
  Alpena (G-301)
Northern Mich Aggregates LLC ..... F 989 354-3502
  Wixom (G-18722)
O-N Minerals Michigan Company .. C 989 734-2131
  Rogers City (G-14215)

LIMESTONE: Ground

O-N Minerals Michigan Company .. C 906 484-2201
  Cedarville (G-2672)
R E Glancy Inc .... G 989 362-0997
  Tawas City (G-16367)

LINEN SPLY SVC

Reilchz Inc .... G 231 421-9600
  Traverse City (G-16819)

LINEN SPLY SVC: Coat

Transtar Autobody Tech LLC .... C 810 220-3000
  Brighton (G-2084)

LINEN SPLY SVC: Uniform

Apparelmaster-Muskegon Inc .... E 231 728-5406
  Muskegon (G-11772)

LINERS & COVERS: Fabric

Canvas Shoppe Inc .... G 810 733-1841
  Flint (G-5662)
Industrial Bag & Spc Inc .... F 248 559-5550
  Southfield (G-15603)
Millers Custom Boat Top Inc .... G 586 468-5533
  Harrison Township (G-7710)

LINERS & LINING

Plesh Industries Inc .... E 716 873-4916
  Brighton (G-2052)

Rlh Industries Inc .... F 989 732-0493
  Gaylord (G-6155)

LINERS: Indl, Metal Plate

Diversified Tooling Group Inc .... E 248 837-5828
  Madison Heights (G-10708)

LIPSTICK

Lipstick Jodi LLC .... G 616 430-5389
  Cedar Springs (G-2655)
Marc Molina .... G 810 701-3587
  Davison (G-3790)

LITHOGRAPHIC PLATES

Adgravers Inc .... F 313 259-3780
  Detroit (G-3986)
Panoplate Lithographics Inc .... G 269 343-4644
  Kalamazoo (G-9285)

LOADS: Electronic

Affinity Electronics Inc .... G 586 477-4920
  Fraser (G-5889)
Sensor Manufacturing Company ... F 248 474-7300
  Novi (G-12534)

LOCK & KEY SVCS

Hacks Key Shop Inc .... E 517 485-9488
  Lansing (G-9850)

LOCKS

Adjustable Locking Tech LLC .... G 248 443-9664
  Bloomfield Hills (G-1792)
Allegion S&S Holding Co Inc .... G 734 680-7429
  Plymouth (G-13121)
Commando Lock Company LLC .... F 248 709-7901
  Troy (G-17020)
Strattec Security Corporation .... G 248 649-9742
  Auburn Hills (G-1040)
Weber Security Group Inc .... G 586 582-0000
  Mount Clemens (G-11662)

LOCKSMITHS

Northwods Prperty Holdings LLC . G 231 334-3000
  Glen Arbor (G-6211)

LOG SPLITTERS

Milan Metal Worx LLC .... G 734 369-7115
  Petersburg (G-12984)

LOGGING

4 Generation Logging Inc .... G 989 350-0337
  Curran (G-3749)
Bear Creek Logging .... G 269 317-7475
  Ceresco (G-2702)
Bellmore Logging .... G 906 498-2528
  Hermansville (G-7860)
Bennett Sawmill .... G 231 734-5733
  Evart (G-5121)
Bills Logging Inc .... G 989 546-7164
  Comins (G-3503)
Bourdo Logging .... G 269 623-4981
  Delton (G-3962)
Bryan K Sergent .... G 231 670-2106
  Stanwood (G-15903)
Bugay Logging .... G 906 428-2125
  Gladstone (G-6176)
Cg Logging .... G 906 322-1018
  Brimley (G-2102)
D&L Logging .... G 231 709-5477
  Kingsley (G-9522)
Darrell A Curtice .... G 231 745-9890
  Bitely (G-1758)
David Gauss Logging .... G 517 851-8102
  Stockbridge (G-16273)
David Newman Logging .... G 906 201-1125
  Baraga (G-1137)
Dawzye Excavation Inc .... G 906 786-5276
  Gladstone (G-6179)
Dehaan Forest Products Inc .... F 906 883-3417
  Mass City (G-11161)
DJL Logging Inc .... G 231 590-2012
  Manton (G-10933)
Donald LII Sons Logging .... G 231 420-3800
  Pellston (G-12967)

Doyle Forest Products Inc F 231 832-5586
Paris *(G-12933)*

Duane F Proehl Inc G 906 474-6630
Rapid River *(G-13684)*

Earl St John Forest Products F 906 497-5667
Spalding *(G-15759)*

East Branch Forest Products G 906 852-3315
Kenton *(G-9439)*

Ej Timber Producers Inc F 231 544-9866
East Jordan *(G-4869)*

Forest Blake Products Inc G 231 879-3913
Fife Lake *(G-5606)*

G & D Wood Products Inc G 517 254-4463
Camden *(G-2422)*

G & S Logging LLC G 989 876-6596
Turner *(G-17463)*

Gary Nankervis Logging G 906 524-7735
Lanse *(G-9660)*

Holli Forest Products F 906 486-9352
Ishpeming *(G-8777)*

Hydrolake Inc G 231 825-2233
Mc Bain *(G-11182)*

James L Miller G 989 539-5540
Harrison *(G-7679)*

James R Goff Logging G 231 420-3455
Vanderbilt *(G-17571)*

Jason Breneman & Son Logging G 269 432-1378
Mendon *(G-11217)*

Jason Laponsie G 906 440-3567
Brimley *(G-2104)*

Jerome Miller Lumber Co G 231 745-3694
Baldwin *(G-1123)*

Jesse James Logging G 906 395-6819
Lanse *(G-9662)*

Jim Detweiler G 269 467-7728
Sturgis *(G-16295)*

John Vuk & Son Inc G 906 524-6074
Lanse *(G-9663)*

Jungnitsch Bros Logging G 989 233-8091
Saint Charles *(G-14803)*

Keith Falan G 231 834-7358
Grant *(G-7429)*

Kells Sawmill Inc G 906 753-2778
Stephenson *(G-15908)*

Laws & Ponies Logging Show G 269 838-3942
Delton *(G-3964)*

Leep Logging Inc G 517 852-1540
Nashville *(G-11956)*

Lindsay Nettell Inc G 906 482-3549
Atlantic Mine *(G-750)*

Mark A Nelson G 989 305-5769
Lupton *(G-10562)*

Martens Logging G 616 675-5473
Casnovia *(G-2607)*

Midnight Logging LLC G 202 521-1484
Howard City *(G-8412)*

Moeke Foresty G 231 631-9600
Boyne City *(G-1898)*

Neumeier Logging Inc G 906 786-5242
Escanaba *(G-5086)*

Noble Forestry Inc G 989 866-6495
Blanchard *(G-1759)*

Phelps Services G 231 942-8044
Lake City *(G-9553)*

Pomeroy Forest Products Inc G 906 474-6780
Rapid River *(G-13685)*

R&H Logging Inc G 906 241-7248
Cornell *(G-3702)*

Rapid River Rustic Inc E 906 474-6404
Rapid River *(G-13686)*

Richard Teachworht G 231 527-8227
Morley *(G-11622)*

Robert Craig Logging LLC G 906 287-0906
Newberry *(G-12101)*

Rodney E Harter G 231 796-6734
Big Rapids *(G-1686)*

Rothig Forest Products Inc F 231 266-8292
Irons *(G-8757)*

Roxbury Creek LLC G 989 731-2062
Gaylord *(G-6156)*

S & S Forest Products G 906 892-8268
Munising *(G-11754)*

S&M Logging LLC G 231 821-0588
Twin Lake *(G-17472)*

Saninocencio Logging G 269 945-3567
Hastings *(G-7809)*

Sawyer Logging LLC G 989 942-6324
West Branch *(G-18341)*

Select Cut Logging LLC G 231 690-6085
Wellston *(G-18260)*

Shamco Lumber Inc G 906 265-5065
Iron River *(G-8754)*

Shawn Muma G 989 426-9505
Gladwin *(G-6205)*

Sheski Logging G 906 786-1886
Escanaba *(G-5098)*

Stephen Rex Fetterley Jr G 269 215-2035
Delton *(G-3967)*

Steven Crandell G 231 582-7445
Charlevoix *(G-2734)*

Styx & Twigs LLC G 231 245-6083
Howard City *(G-8419)*

Sv Logging LLC G 715 360-0035
Iron River *(G-8756)*

Tarrs Tree Service Inc E 248 528-3313
Troy *(G-17384)*

Total Chips Company Inc F 989 866-2610
Shepherd *(G-15379)*

TR Timber Co F 989 345-5350
West Branch *(G-18344)*

Tuscola Logging G 517 231-2905
Grand Rapids *(G-7282)*

Usher Logging LLC G 906 238-4261
Arnold *(G-740)*

Utility Supply and Cnstr Co G 231 832-2297
Reed City *(G-13802)*

Van Duinen Forest Products F 231 328-4507
Lake City *(G-9556)*

Wade Logging G 231 463-0363
Fife Lake *(G-5609)*

Whittaker Timber Corporation G 989 872-3065
Cass City *(G-2624)*

Woods 2 G Logging LLC G 248 469-7416
Howell *(G-8542)*

Yates Forest Products Inc G 989 739-8412
Oscoda *(G-12774)*

Younggren Timber Company G 906 355-2272
Covington *(G-3728)*

Zellar Forest Products G 906 586-9817
Germfask *(G-6169)*

LOGGING CAMPS & CONTRACTORS

Aj Logging G 989 725-9610
Henderson *(G-7859)*

Alexa Forest Products G 906 265-2347
Iron River *(G-8739)*

Allen Whitehouse G 231 824-3000
Manton *(G-10929)*

Antilla Logging Inc G 906 376-2374
Republic *(G-13819)*

Atwood Forest Products Inc E 616 696-0081
Cedar Springs *(G-2641)*

B and C Logging G 906 753-2425
Stephenson *(G-15906)*

B&T Logging G 810 417-6167
Marlette *(G-10977)*

Beacom Enterprises Inc G 906 647-3831
Pickford *(G-13030)*

Bob Jutila Logging G 906 296-0753
Lake Linden *(G-9567)*

Bosanic Lwrnce Sons Tmber Pdts G 906 341-5609
Manistique *(G-10917)*

Brent Bastian Logging LLC G 906 482-6378
Hancock *(G-7616)*

C D C Logging G 906 524-6369
Lanse *(G-9656)*

Cain Brothers Logging Inc G 906 345-9252
Negaunee *(G-11964)*

Dale Routley Logging G 231 861-2596
Hart *(G-7750)*

Danny K Bundy G 231 590-6924
Manton *(G-10931)*

David Jenks G 810 793-7340
North Branch *(G-12178)*

Doug Anderson Logging G 906 337-3707
Calumet *(G-2409)*

Duberville Logging G 906 586-6267
Curtis *(G-3750)*

E H Tulgestka & Sons Inc F 989 734-2129
Rogers City *(G-14209)*

Erickson Logging Inc G 906 481-4021
Chassell *(G-2777)*

Fahl Forest Products Inc F 231 587-5388
Mancelona *(G-10870)*

From Log Up LLC G 989 728-0611
Hale *(G-7589)*

GA Dalbeck Logging LLC F 906 364-3300
Wakefield *(G-17622)*

Giguere Logging Inc G 906 786-3975
Escanaba *(G-5073)*

Great Lakes Log & Firewd Co G 231 206-4073
Twin Lake *(G-17468)*

Heidtman Logging Inc G 906 249-3914
Marquette *(G-11020)*

Heritage Forestry LLC G 231 689-5721
White Cloud *(G-18443)*

Hincka Logging LLC G 989 766-8893
Posen *(G-13643)*

Iron Eagle Logging G 269 945-9617
Hastings *(G-7799)*

J Carey Logging Inc F 906 542-3420
Channing *(G-2706)*

Jacobson Logging Inc F 906 246-3497
Felch *(G-5431)*

James Pollard Logging G 906 884-6744
Ontonagon *(G-12709)*

James Spicer Inc G 906 265-2385
Iron River *(G-8743)*

Jason Lutke E 231 824-6655
Manton *(G-10934)*

Jeffery Lucas G 231 797-5152
Luther *(G-10563)*

John Fuller Logging G 517 304-3298
Fowlerville *(G-5847)*

Joseph Lakosky Logging G 906 573-2783
Manistique *(G-10920)*

Kanerva Forest Products Inc G 906 356-6061
Rock *(G-14150)*

Karttunen Logging G 906 884-4312
Ontonagon *(G-12712)*

Kenneth A Gould G 231 828-4705
Twin Lake *(G-17469)*

Kk Logging G 906 524-6047
Lanse *(G-9665)*

Kostamo Logging G 906 353-6171
Pelkie *(G-12964)*

Lawsons Logging G 517 567-0025
Camden *(G-2423)*

Leonard J Hill Logging Co F 906 337-3435
Calumet *(G-2411)*

Logging-In Com Inc G 248 466-0708
Farmington Hills *(G-5294)*

Logging-Incom LLC F 248 662-7864
Farmington Hills *(G-5295)*

Low Impact Logging Inc G 906 250-5117
Iron River *(G-8748)*

Lucas Logging G 906 246-3629
Bark River *(G-1155)*

Lumberjack Logging LLC G 616 799-4657
Pierson *(G-13033)*

Marvin Nelson Forest Products F 906 384-6700
Cornell *(G-3701)*

McNamara & Mcnamara F 906 293-5281
Newberry *(G-12093)*

Mid Michigan Logging F 231 229-4501
Lake City *(G-9551)*

Mike Hughes G 269 377-3578
Nashville *(G-11957)*

Miljevich Corporation G 906 224-2651
Wakefield *(G-17623)*

Minerick Logging Inc F 906 542-3583
Sagola *(G-14798)*

Ndsay Nettell Logging G 906 482-3549
Atlantic Mine *(G-751)*

Nears Logging G 989 390-4951
Roscommon *(G-14353)*

Nickels Logging G 906 563-5880
Norway *(G-12354)*

Patrick Newland Logging Ltd G 906 524-2255
Lanse *(G-9667)*

Peacocks Eco Log & Sawmill LLC G 231 250-3462
Morley *(G-11621)*

Piwarski Brothers Logging Inc G 906 265-2914
Iron River *(G-8752)*

Precision Forestry F 989 619-1016
Onaway *(G-12702)*

Proctor Logging Inc G 231 775-3820
Cadillac *(G-2349)*

Robert Crawford & Son Logging G 989 379-2712
Lachine *(G-9534)*

Roger Bazuin & Sons Inc E 231 825-2889
Mc Bain *(G-11187)*

Rosenthal Logging G 231 348-8168
Petoskey *(G-13021)*

S & M Logging LLC G 231 830-7317
Muskegon *(G-11912)*

Santti Brothers Inc G 906 355-2347
Watton *(G-18185)*

Schultz Logging G 906 863-5719
Menominee *(G-11259)*

Employee Codes: A=Over 500 employees, B=251-500
C=101-250, D=51-100, E=20-50, F=10-19, G=3-9

2022 Harris Michigan
Industrial Directory

1307

PRODUCT

LOGGING CAMPS & CONTRACTORS

Scott Johnson Forest Pdts Co ....G...... 906 482-3978
  Houghton *(G-8391)*
Shamco Inc ....G...... 906 265-5065
  Iron River *(G-8753)*
Shamion Brothers ....F...... 906 265-5065
  Iron River *(G-8755)*
Shawn Muma Logging ....G...... 989 426-6852
  Gladwin *(G-6206)*
Smith Logging LLC ....G...... 616 558-0729
  Hopkins *(G-8371)*
Steigers Timber Operations ....G...... 906 667-0266
  Bessemer *(G-1650)*
Timberline Logging Inc ....E...... 989 731-2794
  Gaylord *(G-6163)*
Tom Clisch Logging Inc ....G...... 906 338-2900
  Pelkie *(G-12965)*
Tuttle Forest Products ....G...... 906 283-3871
  Gulliver *(G-7578)*
Usher Logging LLC ....G...... 906 238-4261
  Cornell *(G-3703)*
Usimaki Logging Inc ....G...... 920 869-4183
  Baraga *(G-1149)*
Younggren Farm & Forest Inc ....G...... 906 355-2272
  Covington *(G-3727)*

LOGGING: Fuel Wood Harvesting

Dales LLC ....G...... 734 444-4620
  Lapeer *(G-9927)*
Vulcan Wood Products Inc ....F...... 906 563-8995
  Vulcan *(G-17617)*

LOGGING: Peeler Logs

Weyerhaeuser Company ....G...... 906 524-2040
  Lanse *(G-9669)*

LOGGING: Pulpwood Camp, Exc Pulp Mill At Same Site

Dillon Forest Products Inc ....G...... 906 869-4671
  Republic *(G-13820)*

LOGGING: Saw Logs

Jns Sawmill ....G...... 989 352-5430
  Coral *(G-3699)*
Robert Gentz Forest Pdts Inc ....F...... 231 398-9194
  Manistee *(G-10912)*

LOGGING: Skidding Logs

Joe Bosanic Forest Products ....G...... 906 341-2037
  Manistique *(G-10919)*

LOGGING: Stump Harvesting

Plum Creek Timber Company Inc ....G...... 715 453-7952
  Escanaba *(G-5090)*

LOGGING: Timber, Cut At Logging Camp

Bruning Forest Products ....G...... 989 733-2880
  Onaway *(G-12697)*
JM Longyear LLC ....G...... 906 228-7960
  Marquette *(G-11026)*
K & M Industrial LLC ....G...... 906 420-8770
  Gladstone *(G-6182)*
Spencer Farms and Timber LLC ....G...... 810 459-4487
  Ada *(G-35)*

LOGGING: Wheel stock, Hewn

P G K Enterprises LLC ....G...... 248 535-4411
  Southfield *(G-15671)*

LOGGING: Wood Chips, Produced In The Field

Chris Muma Forest Products ....E...... 989 426-5916
  Gladwin *(G-6193)*
Manigg Enterprises Inc ....F...... 989 356-4986
  Alpena *(G-301)*
Turpeinen Bros Inc ....G...... 906 338-2870
  Pelkie *(G-12966)*

LOGGING: Wooden Logs

Abcor Partners LLC ....E...... 616 994-9577
  Holland *(G-7953)*
Eup Wood Shavings Inc ....F...... 586 943-7199
  Kincheloe *(G-9502)*
Speedy Blaze Inc ....G...... 989 340-2028
  Alpena *(G-318)*

LOGS: Gas, Fireplace

Log Jam Forest Products Inc ....G...... 616 677-2560
  Marne *(G-10995)*

LOOSELEAF BINDERS

Cadillac Prsentation Solutions ....E...... 248 288-9777
  Troy *(G-16994)*
Hexon Corporation ....E...... 248 585-7585
  Farmington Hills *(G-5259)*

LOTIONS OR CREAMS: Face

Babybops Melanin Collection ....G...... 313 770-4997
  Detroit *(G-4041)*
Buttered Body Essentials LLC ....G...... 313 687-3847
  Detroit *(G-4080)*
Garden of Edyn ....G...... 517 410-9931
  Holt *(G-8313)*
Inscribd LLC ....G...... 231 445-9104
  Cheboygan *(G-2786)*

LOTIONS: SHAVING

Amour Your Body LLC ....G...... 586 846-3100
  Clinton Township *(G-3168)*
Honeyworks LLC ....G...... 313 575-0871
  Detroit *(G-4304)*
Square M LLC ....F...... 720 988-5836
  Sterling Heights *(G-16185)*

LOUDSPEAKERS

Salk Communications Inc ....G...... 248 342-7109
  Pontiac *(G-13415)*

LUBRICANTS: Corrosion Preventive

Doerken Corporation ....G...... 517 522-4600
  Grass Lake *(G-7437)*
Duall Division ....G...... 989 725-8184
  Lennon *(G-9993)*
Henkel US Operations Corp ....B...... 248 588-1082
  Madison Heights *(G-10739)*
Rbm Chemical Company LLC ....G...... 248 766-1974
  Rochester *(G-13924)*
Sks Industries Inc ....F...... 517 546-1117
  Howell *(G-8518)*
Topduck Products LLC ....F...... 517 322-3202
  Saint Johns *(G-14918)*
Xaerus Performance Fluids LLC ....C...... 989 631-7871
  Midland *(G-11425)*

LUBRICATING EQPT: Indl

Acumen Technologies Inc ....F...... 586 566-8600
  Shelby Township *(G-15165)*
G P Reeves Inc ....E...... 616 399-8893
  Holland *(G-8045)*
Intellichem LLC ....F...... 810 765-4075
  Marine City *(G-10959)*
Lube - Power Inc ....D...... 586 247-6500
  Shelby Township *(G-15264)*
M-B-M Manufacturing Inc ....G...... 231 924-9614
  Fremont *(G-6047)*
Opco Lubrication Systems Inc ....G...... 231 924-6160
  Fremont *(G-6050)*

LUBRICATING OIL & GREASE WHOLESALERS

American Chemical Tech Inc ....E...... 866 945-1041
  Howell *(G-8428)*
Bva Inc ....E...... 248 348-4920
  New Hudson *(G-12044)*
Condat Corporation ....E...... 734 944-4994
  Saline *(G-15009)*
Eastern Oil Company ....E...... 248 333-1333
  Pontiac *(G-13364)*
Lubecon Systems Inc ....G...... 231 689-0002
  White Cloud *(G-18445)*
Metalworking Lubricants Co ....D...... 248 332-3500
  Pontiac *(G-13397)*
Oil Chem Inc ....E...... 810 235-3040
  Flint *(G-5742)*
Unist Inc ....E...... 616 949-0853
  Grand Rapids *(G-7297)*

LUBRICATION SYSTEMS & EQPT

Amcol Corporation ....E...... 248 414-5700
  Hazel Park *(G-7819)*

PRODUCT SECTION

Intersrce Recovery Systems Inc ....E...... 269 375-5100
  Kalamazoo *(G-9225)*
Mark One Corporation ....D...... 989 732-2427
  Gaylord *(G-6145)*
Orsco Inc ....G...... 314 679-4200
  Armada *(G-738)*
Permawick Company Inc ....E...... 248 433-3500
  Birmingham *(G-1743)*

LUGGAGE & LEATHER GOODS STORES: Leather, Exc Luggage & Shoes

Birlon Group LLC ....G...... 313 551-5341
  Inkster *(G-8659)*

LUMBER & BLDG MATLS DEALER, RET: Garage Doors, Sell/Install

Overhead Door Company Alpena ....G...... 989 354-8316
  Alpena *(G-307)*

LUMBER & BLDG MATLS DEALERS, RET: Energy Conservation Prdts

Detroit Renewable Energy LLC ....C...... 313 972-5700
  Detroit *(G-4162)*

LUMBER & BLDG MATRLS DEALERS, RETAIL: Doors, Wood/Metal

Quality Door & More Inc ....G...... 989 317-8314
  Coleman *(G-3470)*
Wood Smiths Inc ....F...... 269 372-6432
  Kalamazoo *(G-9373)*

LUMBER & BLDG MTRLS DEALERS, RET: Doors, Storm, Wood/Metal

Lsd Investments Inc ....G...... 248 333-9085
  Bloomfield Hills *(G-1832)*

LUMBER & BLDG MTRLS DEALERS, RET: Planing Mill Prdts/Lumber

Menomnee Rver Lbr Dmnsions LLC ....G...... 906 863-2682
  Menominee *(G-11250)*

LUMBER & BLDG MTRLS DEALERS, RET: Windows, Storm, Wood/Metal

Fox Aluminum Products Inc ....E...... 248 399-4288
  Hazel Park *(G-7826)*
MRM Ida Products Co Inc ....G...... 313 834-0200
  Detroit *(G-4470)*

LUMBER & BUILDING MATERIALS DEALER, RET: Door & Window Prdts

Aspen Door Supply LLC ....G...... 248 291-5303
  Troy *(G-16959)*
Genex Window Inc ....G...... 586 754-2917
  Warren *(G-17827)*
Sunburst Shutters ....G...... 248 674-4600
  Waterford *(G-18167)*
Weathergard Window Company Inc ....D...... 248 967-8822
  Oak Park *(G-12651)*

LUMBER & BUILDING MATERIALS DEALER, RET: Masonry Matls/Splys

Advance Concrete Products Co ....E...... 248 887-4173
  Highland *(G-7880)*
Clay & Graham Inc ....G...... 989 354-5292
  Alpena *(G-287)*
E M I Construction Products ....F...... 616 392-7207
  Holland *(G-8020)*
Fendt Builders Supply Inc ....E...... 248 474-3211
  Farmington Hills *(G-5242)*
Genesee Cut Stone & Marble Co ....E...... 810 743-1800
  Grand Blanc *(G-6242)*
L & S Transit Mix Concrete Co ....E...... 989 354-5363
  Alpena *(G-298)*
Lakeshore Cement Products ....G...... 989 739-9341
  Oscoda *(G-12763)*
Stevenson Building and Sup Co ....G...... 734 856-3931
  Lambertville *(G-9653)*

PRODUCT SECTION

LUMBER & BUILDING MATERIALS DEALERS, RETAIL: Brick

Arquette Concrete & Supply ....G...... 989 846-4131
  Standish (G-15887)
Grand Blanc Cement Pdts Inc ....E...... 810 694-7500
  Grand Blanc (G-6244)
Ludvanwall Inc ....E...... 616 842-4500
  Spring Lake (G-15830)
Newberry Redi-Mix Inc ....G...... 906 293-5178
  Newberry (G-12097)

LUMBER & BUILDING MATERIALS DEALERS, RETAIL: Cement

Darby Ready Mix-Dundee LLC ....F...... 734 529-7100
  Dundee (G-4813)
National Block Company ....E...... 734 721-4050
  Westland (G-18399)
R & R Ready-Mix Inc ....G...... 989 892-9313
  Bay City (G-1393)
Superior Materials LLC ....E...... 734 941-2479
  Romulus (G-14332)
Superior Materials Holdings ....G...... 586 468-3544
  Mount Clemens (G-11658)

LUMBER & BUILDING MATERIALS DEALERS, RETAIL: Countertops

Kurtis Mfg & Distrg Corp ....E...... 734 522-7600
  Livonia (G-10270)
Rose Corporation ....E...... 734 426-0005
  Dexter (G-4753)

LUMBER & BUILDING MATERIALS DEALERS, RETAIL: Modular Homes

Ritz-Craft Corp PA Inc ....C...... 517 849-7425
  Jonesville (G-9100)

LUMBER & BUILDING MATERIALS DEALERS, RETAIL: Paving Stones

White Lake Excavating Inc ....E...... 231 894-6918
  Whitehall (G-18513)

LUMBER & BUILDING MATERIALS DEALERS, RETAIL: Sand & Gravel

Bouchey and Sons Inc ....G...... 989 588-4118
  Farwell (G-5421)
Lewiston Sand & Gravel Inc ....G...... 989 786-2742
  Lewiston (G-10023)

LUMBER & BUILDING MATERIALS DEALERS, RETAIL: Siding

Astro Building Products Inc ....G...... 231 941-0324
  Traverse City (G-16604)

LUMBER & BUILDING MATERIALS RET DEALERS: Millwork & Lumber

B & W Woodwork Inc ....G...... 616 772-4577
  Holland (G-7969)
Goodrich Brothers Inc ....E...... 989 593-2104
  Pewamo (G-13028)
Greenia Custom Woodworking Inc ....E...... 989 868-9790
  Reese (G-13806)
Maeder Bros Inc ....E...... 989 644-2235
  Weidman (G-18255)
Phil Elenbaas Millwork Inc ....E...... 616 791-1616
  Grand Rapids (G-7085)
Rare Earth Hardwoods Inc ....F...... 231 946-0043
  Traverse City (G-16817)
W S Townsend Company ....G...... 517 393-7300
  Lansing (G-9903)

LUMBER & BUILDING MATLS DEALERS, RET: Concrete/Cinder Block

Best Block Company ....E...... 586 772-7000
  Warren (G-17732)
Burrell Tri-County Vaults Inc ....F...... 734 483-2024
  Ypsilanti (G-18930)
Ferguson Block Co Inc ....E...... 810 653-2812
  Davison (G-3781)
Fisher Sand and Gravel Company ....E...... 989 835-7187
  Midland (G-11363)

Guidobono Concrete Inc ....F...... 810 229-2666
  Brighton (G-2006)
Sandusky Concrete & Supply ....G...... 810 648-2627
  Sandusky (G-15066)

LUMBER & BUILDING MTRLS DEALERS, RET: Insulation Mtrl, Bldg

Insulation Wholesale Supply ....G...... 269 968-9746
  Battle Creek (G-1241)
Northwoods Manufacturing Inc ....D...... 906 779-2370
  Kingsford (G-9516)

LUMBER: Cants, Resawn

Diversified Pdts & Svcs LLC ....G...... 616 836-6600
  Holland (G-8014)

LUMBER: Dimension, Hardwood

Menomnee Rver Lbr Dmnsions LLC .....G...... 906 863-2682
  Menominee (G-11250)

LUMBER: Furniture Dimension Stock, Softwood

Met Inc ....G...... 231 845-1737
  Ludington (G-10545)
Pine Tech Inc ....E...... 989 426-0006
  Plymouth (G-13264)

LUMBER: Hardwood Dimension

Component Solutions LLC ....E...... 906 863-2682
  Menominee (G-11230)
Devereaux Saw Mill Inc ....D...... 989 593-2552
  Pewamo (G-13027)
Timber Pdts Mich Ltd Partnr ....G...... 906 779-2000
  Iron Mountain (G-8736)
Ufp Lansing LLC ....E...... 517 325-5572
  Grand Rapids (G-7291)

LUMBER: Hardwood Dimension & Flooring Mills

Atwood Forest Products Inc ....E...... 616 696-0081
  Cedar Springs (G-2641)
B & B Heartwoods Inc ....G...... 734 332-9525
  Ann Arbor (G-394)
Banks Hardwoods Inc ....D...... 269 483-2323
  White Pigeon (G-18472)
Besse Forest Products Inc ....F...... 906 353-7193
  Baraga (G-1135)
Burt Moeke & Son Hardwoods ....E...... 231 587-5388
  Mancelona (G-10868)
Counterpoint By Hlf ....G...... 734 699-7100
  Van Buren Twp (G-17521)
Craftwood Industries Inc ....E...... 616 796-1209
  Holland (G-8006)
Dyers Sawmill Inc ....E...... 231 768-4438
  Leroy (G-10006)
Erickson Lumber & True Value ....G...... 906 524-6295
  Lanse (G-9659)
Forest Elders Products Inc ....E...... 616 866-9317
  Rockford (G-14168)
Forte Industries Mill Inc ....E...... 906 753-6256
  Stephenson (G-15907)
Genesis Seating Inc ....D...... 616 954-1040
  Grand Rapids (G-6739)
Jaroche Brothers Inc ....F...... 231 525-8100
  Wolverine (G-18795)
John A Biewer Lumber Company ....E...... 231 825-2855
  Mc Bain (G-11183)
Kentwood Manufacturing Co ....E...... 616 698-6370
  Byron Center (G-2279)
Lumber Jack Hardwoods Inc ....F...... 906 863-7090
  Menominee (G-11243)
Maple Ridge Hardwoods Inc ....E...... 989 873-5305
  Sterling (G-15913)
Metter Flooring LLC ....G...... 517 914-2004
  Rives Junction (G-13887)
Nettleton Wood Products Inc ....G...... 906 297-5791
  De Tour Village (G-3802)
North American Forest Products ....G...... 269 663-8500
  Edwardsburg (G-5014)
Northern Hardwoods ....G...... 906 487-6400
  Newberry (G-12099)
Northern Mich Hardwoods Inc ....F...... 231 347-4575
  Petoskey (G-13008)
Ottawa Forest Products Inc ....E...... 906 932-9701
  Ironwood (G-8769)

Paris North Hardwood Lumber ....F...... 231 584-2500
  Elmira (G-5040)
Pine Tech Inc ....E...... 989 426-0006
  Plymouth (G-13264)
Quigley Lumber Inc ....G...... 989 257-5116
  South Branch (G-15397)
Richwood Industries Inc ....E...... 616 243-2700
  Grand Rapids (G-7154)
Vocational Strategies Inc ....F...... 906 482-6142
  Calumet (G-2415)
Weber Bros Sawmill Inc ....E...... 989 644-2206
  Mount Pleasant (G-11746)
Whitens Kiln & Lumber Inc ....F...... 906 498-2116
  Hermansville (G-7865)
William S Wixtrom ....G...... 906 376-8247
  Republic (G-13821)

LUMBER: Kiln Dried

Banks Hardwoods Inc ....D...... 269 483-2323
  White Pigeon (G-18472)
Forestry Management Svcs Inc ....C...... 517 456-7431
  Clinton (G-3138)
Lumber Jack Hardwoods Inc ....F...... 906 863-7090
  Menominee (G-11243)

LUMBER: Panels, Plywood, Softwood

Louisiana-Pacific Corporation ....G...... 906 293-3265
  Newberry (G-12092)

LUMBER: Plywood, Hardwood

August Lilia Famly Memorl Fund ....G...... 906 228-6088
  Marquette (G-11006)
Bay Wood Homes Inc ....F...... 989 245-4156
  Fenton (G-5456)
Coldwater Veneer Inc ....C...... 517 278-5676
  Coldwater (G-3427)
Dyers Sawmill Inc ....E...... 231 768-4438
  Leroy (G-10006)
Forest Corullo Products Corp ....E...... 906 667-0275
  Bessemer (G-1649)
Forte Industries Mill Inc ....E...... 906 753-6256
  Stephenson (G-15907)
Midwest Panel Systems Inc ....F...... 517 486-4844
  Blissfield (G-1770)
Northern Mich Endocrine Pllc ....G...... 989 281-1125
  Roscommon (G-14355)
Northern Mich Hardwoods Inc ....F...... 231 347-4575
  Petoskey (G-13008)
Northern Mich Mmrals Monuments ....G...... 231 290-2333
  Cheboygan (G-2794)
Northern Mich Supportive Hsing ....G...... 231 929-1309
  Traverse City (G-16772)
Northern Mich Wdding Offciants ....G...... 231 938-1683
  Williamsburg (G-18559)
Ply-Forms Incorporated ....E...... 989 686-5681
  Bay City (G-1387)
Programmed Products Corp ....D...... 248 348-7755
  Novi (G-12517)
Timber Products Co Ltd Partnr ....C...... 906 452-6221
  Munising (G-11755)

LUMBER: Plywood, Hardwood or Hardwood Faced

Decatur Wood Products Inc ....E...... 269 657-6041
  Decatur (G-3946)

LUMBER: Plywood, Prefinished, Hardwood

Rosati Specialties LLC ....G...... 586 783-3866
  Clinton Township (G-3341)

LUMBER: Plywood, Softwood

Forest Corullo Products Corp ....E...... 906 667-0275
  Bessemer (G-1649)
Forte Industries Mill Inc ....E...... 906 753-6256
  Stephenson (G-15907)
Ply-Forms Incorporated ....E...... 989 686-5681
  Bay City (G-1387)

LUMBER: Resawn, Small Dimension

Nelsons Saw Mill Inc ....G...... 231 829-5220
  Tustin (G-17466)
North American Forest Products ....C...... 269 663-8500
  Edwardsburg (G-5013)

LUMBER: Stacking Or Sticking

Rapid River Rustic Inc ....E 906 474-6404
Rapid River *(G-13686)*

LUMBER: Treated

/// 702 Cedar River Lbr Inc ....E 906 497-5365
Powers *(G-13648)*
Hager Wood Preserving LLC ....G 616 248-0905
Wyoming *(G-18879)*
Hydrolake Inc ....G 231 825-2233
Mc Bain *(G-11182)*
Paris North Hardwood Lumber ....F 231 584-2500
Elmira *(G-5040)*
Riverbend Woodworing ....G 231 869-4965
Pentwater *(G-12974)*
Straits Corporation ....F 989 684-5088
Tawas City *(G-16368)*
Straits Operations Company ....G 989 684-5088
Tawas City *(G-16369)*
Straits Service Corporation ....G 989 684-5088
Tawas City *(G-16370)*
Straits Wood Treating Inc ....G 989 684-5088
Tawas City *(G-16371)*
Ufp Lansing LLC ....G 517 322-0025
Lansing *(G-9795)*
Utility Supply and Cnstr Co ....G 231 832-2297
Reed City *(G-13802)*
West Branch Wood Treating Inc ....G 989 343-0066
West Branch *(G-18346)*
Yooper WD Wrks Restoration LLC ....G 906 203-0056
Sault Sainte Marie *(G-15105)*

LUMBER: Veneer, Hardwood

J A S Veneer & Lumber Inc ....E 906 635-0710
Sault Sainte Marie *(G-15092)*
Manthei Inc ....C 231 347-4672
Petoskey *(G-13004)*
Northern Michigan Veneers Inc ....D 906 428-1082
Gladstone *(G-6184)*
Quincy Woodwrights LLC ....G 808 397-0818
Houghton *(G-8390)*
Timber Pdts Mich Ltd Partnr ....G 906 779-2000
Iron Mountain *(G-8736)*

LUNCHROOMS & CAFETERIAS

Bay Bread Co ....G 231 922-8022
Traverse City *(G-16614)*

MACHINE PARTS: Stamped Or Pressed Metal

Bay Manufacturing Corporation ....F 989 358-7198
Alpena *(G-282)*
Burnside Industries LLC ....G 231 798-3394
Norton Shores *(G-12347)*
CA Picard Surface Engrg Inc ....E 440 366-5400
Battle Creek *(G-1203)*
Covenant Cpitl Investments Inc ....F 248 477-4230
Wixom *(G-18637)*
D & D Driers Timber Product ....G 906 224-7251
Wakefield *(G-17619)*
Diversfied Prcurement Svcs LLC ....G 248 821-1147
Ferndale *(G-5548)*
Echo Quality Grinding Inc ....F 231 544-6637
Central Lake *(G-2694)*
Hti Associates LLC ....E 616 399-5430
Holland *(G-8089)*
Impeccable Machining Inc ....G 734 844-3855
Canton *(G-2473)*
L Barge & Associates Inc ....E 248 582-3430
Ferndale *(G-5563)*
Max2 LLC ....F 269 468-3452
Benton Harbor *(G-1569)*
Mpi Engineered Tech LLC ....F 248 237-3007
Troy *(G-17267)*
Nelson Manufacturing Inc ....G 810 648-0065
Sandusky *(G-15063)*
Nidec Chs LLC ....F 586 777-7440
Romeo *(G-14230)*
Ort Tool & Die Corporation ....D 419 242-9553
Erie *(G-5052)*
Paradigm Engineering Inc ....G 586 776-5910
Roseville *(G-14458)*
PEC of America Corporation ....F 248 675-3130
Novi *(G-12504)*
Pentar Stamping Inc ....E 517 782-0700
Jackson *(G-8984)*
Pinnacle Tool Incorporated ....E 616 257-2700
Wyoming *(G-18899)*
Reliance Metal Products Inc ....G 734 641-3334
Westland *(G-18414)*
Rj Acquisition Corp Rj USA ....E 586 268-2300
Sterling Heights *(G-16156)*
West Mich Auto Stl & Engrg Inc ....E 616 560-8198
Belding *(G-1464)*

MACHINE SHOPS

Advanced Automotive Group LLC ....F 586 206-2478
Clay *(G-3113)*
Art Laser Inc ....E 248 391-6600
Auburn Hills *(G-798)*
B & B Custom and Prod Wldg ....F 517 524-7121
Spring Arbor *(G-15789)*
Benzie Manufacturing LLC ....G 231 631-0498
Frankfort *(G-5875)*
Breco LLC ....F 517 317-2211
Quincy *(G-13664)*
Defense Component Detroit LLC ....E 248 393-2300
Auburn Hills *(G-861)*
Detroit Edge Tool Company ....D 586 776-1598
Roseville *(G-14398)*
Dowding Industries Inc ....E 517 663-5455
Eaton Rapids *(G-4959)*
E & C Manufacturing LLC ....F 248 330-0400
Troy *(G-17075)*
E & D Engineering Systems LLC ....G 989 246-0770
Gladwin *(G-6195)*
Enkon LLC ....E 937 890-5678
Manchester *(G-10883)*
Falcon Consulting Services LLC ....G 989 262-9325
Alpena *(G-293)*
Hart Industries LLC ....F 313 588-1837
Sterling Heights *(G-16034)*
Independent Machine Co Inc ....E 906 428-4524
Escanaba *(G-5077)*
Jems of Litchfield Inc ....F 517 542-5367
Litchfield *(G-10081)*
Johnson Precision Mold & Engrg ....G 269 651-2553
Sturgis *(G-16296)*
Knapp Manufacturing Inc ....E 517 279-9538
Coldwater *(G-3441)*
L & L Pattern Inc ....G 231 733-2646
Muskegon *(G-11853)*
M & M Services Inc ....G 248 619-9861
Troy *(G-17216)*
Manufacturers Hardware Company ....F 313 892-6650
Detroit *(G-4420)*
Merchants Automatic Pdts Inc ....E 734 829-0020
Canton *(G-2493)*
Merrill Technologies Group Inc ....D 989 791-6676
Saginaw *(G-14697)*
Michigan Slotting Company Inc ....G 586 772-1270
Warren *(G-17930)*
Morren Mold & Machine Inc ....G 616 892-7474
Allendale *(G-226)*
Mountain Machine LLC ....F 734 480-2200
Van Buren Twp *(G-17542)*
Nephew Fabrication Inc ....G 616 875-2121
Zeeland *(G-19059)*
Next Level Manufacturing LLC ....G 616 965-1913
Comstock Park *(G-3628)*
North Kent Base LLC ....G 616 636-4300
Sand Lake *(G-15050)*
P2r Metal Fabrication Inc ....F 586 606-5266
Macomb *(G-10625)*
Paramount Industrial Machining ....E 248 543-2100
Oak Park *(G-12636)*
Parts Finishing Group Inc ....D 586 755-4053
Warren *(G-17955)*
Pioneer Metal Finishing LLC ....D 877 721-1100
Warren *(G-17964)*
Production Dev Systems LLC ....F 810 648-2111
Sandusky *(G-15065)*
Prototype Cast Mfg Inc ....G 586 739-0180
Shelby Township *(G-15311)*
Quality Cavity Inc ....F 248 344-9995
Canton *(G-2516)*
Ridgefield Company LLC ....G 888 226-8665
Grand Rapids *(G-7155)*
Rocksteady Manufacturing LLC ....F 586 778-5028
Roseville *(G-14472)*
Roush Industries Inc ....G 734 779-7000
Livonia *(G-10394)*
Stanhope Tool Inc ....E 248 585-5711
Warren *(G-18027)*
Tesla Machine & Tool Ltd ....G 586 441-2402
Warren *(G-18038)*
Thermotron Industries Inc ....E 616 928-9044
Holland *(G-8218)*
Thierica Equipment Corporation ....E 616 453-6570
Grand Rapids *(G-7259)*
West Michigan Grinding Svc Inc ....F 231 739-4245
Norton Shores *(G-12343)*

MACHINE TOOL ACCESS: Arbors

Hydra-Lock Corporation ....E 586 783-5007
Mount Clemens *(G-11641)*
SB Investments LLC ....E 734 462-9478
Livonia *(G-10400)*

MACHINE TOOL ACCESS: Boring Attachments

Borite Manufacturing Corp ....G 248 588-7260
Madison Heights *(G-10683)*
Harroun Enterprises Inc ....G 810 629-9885
Fenton *(G-5484)*
Johan Van De Weerd Co Inc ....G 517 542-3817
Litchfield *(G-10082)*
Lightning Machine Holland LLC ....F 616 786-9280
Holland *(G-8129)*
Riviera Industries Inc ....G 313 381-5500
Allen Park *(G-203)*

MACHINE TOOL ACCESS: Broaches

Admiral Broach Company Inc ....E 586 468-8411
Clinton Township *(G-3156)*
Apollo Broach Inc ....G 734 467-5750
Westland *(G-18354)*
Associated Broach Corporation ....E 810 798-9112
Almont *(G-256)*
Avon Broach & Prod Co LLC ....E 248 650-8080
Rochester Hills *(G-13958)*
Diamond Broach Company ....G 586 757-5131
Warren *(G-17777)*
Federal Broach & Mch Co LLC ....C 989 539-7420
Harrison *(G-7676)*
General Broach & Engrg Inc ....C 586 726-4300
Troy *(G-17129)*
General Broach Company ....D 517 458-7555
Morenci *(G-11611)*
General Broach Company ....G 517 458-7555
Morenci *(G-11612)*
J & L Turning Inc ....F 810 765-5755
East China *(G-4857)*
Kingsford Broach & Tool Inc ....E 906 774-4917
Kingsford *(G-9511)*
Laydon Enterprises Inc ....E 906 774-4633
Iron Mountain *(G-8724)*
Miller Broach Inc ....D 810 395-8810
Capac *(G-2547)*
Pioneer Michigan Broach Co ....F 231 768-5800
Leroy *(G-10010)*
Tazz Broach and Machine Inc ....G 586 296-7755
Harrison Township *(G-7728)*
Triangle Broach Company ....E 313 838-2150
Detroit *(G-4645)*
Utica Enterprises Inc ....C 586 726-4300
Troy *(G-17419)*
Wachtel Tool & Broach Inc ....G 586 758-0110
Saint Clair *(G-14844)*
Warren Broach & Machine Corp ....F 586 254-7080
Sterling Heights *(G-16229)*
Wolverine Broach Co Inc ....E 586 468-4445
Harrison Township *(G-7733)*

MACHINE TOOL ACCESS: Cams

Techni CAM and Manufacturing ....F 734 261-6477
Livonia *(G-10430)*

MACHINE TOOL ACCESS: Cutting

Accurate Carbide Tool Co Inc ....E 989 755-0429
Saginaw *(G-14600)*
Acme Grooving Tool Co ....F 800 633-8828
Clarkston *(G-3011)*
Action Tool & Machine Inc ....E 810 229-6300
Brighton *(G-1938)*
Adaptable Tool Supply LLC ....F 248 439-0866
Clawson *(G-3084)*
Apollo Tool & Engineering Inc ....F 616 735-4934
Grand Rapids *(G-6463)*
Arch Cutting Tools LLC ....C 734 266-6900
Bloomfield Hills *(G-1800)*
Aw Carbide Fabricators Inc ....E 586 294-1850
Sterling Heights *(G-15939)*
Banner Broach Inc ....G 586 493-9219
Warren *(G-17726)*

PRODUCT SECTION

MACHINE TOOL ACCESS: Tool Holders

Breckers ABC Tool Company Inc .... E 586 779-1122
  Roseville *(G-14381)*
Breesport Holdings Inc .... C 248 685-9500
  Milford *(G-11456)*
Carbide Form Master Inc .... G 248 625-9373
  Davisburg *(G-3763)*
Carbide Technologies Inc .... E 586 296-5200
  Fraser *(G-5910)*
Caro Carbide Corporation .... F 248 588-4252
  Troy *(G-17003)*
Ceratizit Usa Inc .... C 586 759-2280
  Warren *(G-17751)*
Clymer Manufacturing Company .... G 248 853-5555
  Rochester Hills *(G-13975)*
Cole Carbide Industries Inc .... G 989 872-4348
  Cass City *(G-2613)*
Complete Cutting TI & Mfg Inc .... G 248 662-9811
  Wixom *(G-18635)*
Cougar Cutting Tools Inc .... E 586 469-1310
  Clinton Township *(G-3212)*
Dijet Incorporated .... G 734 454-9100
  Plymouth *(G-13158)*
Dumbarton Tool Inc .... F 231 775-4342
  Cadillac *(G-2328)*
Ecco Tool Co Inc .... G 248 349-0840
  Novi *(G-12409)*
Elk Lake Tool Co .... E 231 264-5616
  Elk Rapids *(G-5023)*
Ellsworth Cutting Tools Ltd .... F 586 598-6040
  Chesterfield *(G-2874)*
Engineered Tools Corp .... E 989 673-8733
  Caro *(G-2571)*
Evans Tool & Engineering Inc .... F 616 791-6333
  Grand Rapids *(G-6688)*
Fab-Jet Services LLC .... G 586 463-9622
  Clinton Township *(G-3234)*
Fsp Inc .... E 248 585-0760
  Troy *(G-17123)*
Global CNC Industries Ltd .... E 734 464-1920
  Plymouth *(G-13177)*
Global Tooling Systems LLC .... B 586 726-0500
  Macomb *(G-10599)*
Guhring Inc .... E 262 784-6730
  Novi *(G-12424)*
Howell Tool Service Inc .... F 517 548-1114
  Howell *(G-8465)*
I & G Tool Co Inc .... F 586 777-7690
  Cottrellville *(G-3721)*
Ideal Heated Knives Inc .... G 248 437-1510
  New Hudson *(G-12058)*
J E Wood Co .... F 248 585-5711
  Madison Heights *(G-10749)*
Joint Production Tech Inc .... G 586 786-0080
  Macomb *(G-10608)*
Kennametal Inc .... G 231 946-2100
  Traverse City *(G-16733)*
Krebs Tool Inc .... G 734 697-8611
  Van Buren Twp *(G-17534)*
Kyocera Unimerco Tooling Inc .... E 734 944-4433
  Saline *(G-15023)*
M C Carbide Tool Co .... E 248 486-4590
  Wixom *(G-18703)*
Mac-Tech Tooling Corporation .... G 248 743-1400
  Troy *(G-17217)*
Mapal Inc .... D 810 364-8020
  Port Huron *(G-13500)*
Motor Tool Manufacturing Co .... G 734 425-3300
  Livonia *(G-10324)*
PL Schmitt Crbide Toling LLC .... G 517 522-6891
  Grass Lake *(G-7444)*
Precision Tool Company Inc .... E 231 733-0811
  Muskegon *(G-11898)*
Primary Tool & Cutter Grinding .... E 248 588-1530
  Madison Heights *(G-10809)*
Qc American LLC .... G 734 961-0300
  Ypsilanti *(G-18972)*
R L Schmitt Company Inc .... E 734 525-9310
  Livonia *(G-10382)*
Reif Carbide Tool Co Inc .... G 586 754-1890
  Warren *(G-17995)*
RTS Cutting Tools Inc .... E 586 954-1900
  Clinton Township *(G-3344)*
S F S Carbide Tool .... G 989 777-3890
  Saginaw *(G-14742)*
SC Thread Cutting Tools Inc .... G 248 365-4044
  Auburn Hills *(G-1030)*
Seco Holding Co Inc .... D 248 528-5200
  Troy *(G-17347)*
Selmuro Ltd .... E 810 603-2117
  Grand Blanc *(G-6263)*
Severance Tool Industries Inc .... E 989 777-5500
  Saginaw *(G-14753)*
Severance Tool Industries Inc .... E 989 777-5500
  Saginaw *(G-14754)*
Shouse Tool Inc .... F 810 629-0391
  Fenton *(G-5503)*
Southwest Broach .... G 714 356-2967
  Cadillac *(G-2354)*
Spartan Carbide Inc .... E 586 285-9786
  Fraser *(G-5995)*
Star Cutter Co .... E 248 474-8200
  Farmington Hills *(G-5387)*
Steelcraft Tool Co Inc .... F 734 522-7130
  Livonia *(G-10420)*
Stoney Crest Regrind Service .... F 989 777-7190
  Bridgeport *(G-1918)*
Teknikut Corporation .... G 586 778-7150
  Canton *(G-2534)*
Tool Service Company Inc .... G 586 296-2500
  Fraser *(G-6003)*
Tool-Craft Industries Inc .... E 248 549-0077
  Sterling Heights *(G-16206)*
Tooling Solutions Group LLC .... G 248 585-0222
  Madison Heights *(G-10844)*
TS Carbide Inc .... G 248 486-8330
  Commerce Township *(G-3580)*
Universal / Devlieg Inc .... F 989 752-3077
  Saginaw *(G-14784)*
Wit-Son Carbide Tool Inc .... E 231 536-2247
  East Jordan *(G-4883)*
Wolverine Special Tool Inc .... G 616 791-1027
  Grand Rapids *(G-7348)*
Wood-Cutters Tooling Inc .... G 616 257-7930
  Grandville *(G-7424)*
Workblades Inc .... E 586 778-0060
  Warren *(G-18072)*
Wyser Innovative Products LLC .... G 616 583-9225
  Byron Center *(G-2304)*
Zimmermann Engineering Co Inc .... E 248 358-0044
  Southfield *(G-15746)*

MACHINE TOOL ACCESS: Diamond Cutting, For Turning, Etc

Crystal Cut Tool Inc .... G 734 946-0099
  Romulus *(G-14265)*
Di-Coat Corporation .... E 248 349-1211
  Novi *(G-12399)*
Diamond Alternatives LLC .... G 734 755-1505
  Carleton *(G-2552)*
Diamond Tool Manufacturing Inc .... E 734 416-1900
  Plymouth *(G-13157)*
Service Diamond Tool Company .... G 248 669-3100
  Novi *(G-12535)*
Sidley Diamond Tool Company .... E 734 261-7970
  Garden City *(G-6109)*

MACHINE TOOL ACCESS: Dies, Thread Cutting

M & M Thread & Assembly Inc .... G 248 583-9696
  Sterling Heights *(G-16079)*
Mc Pherson Industrial Corp .... E 586 752-5555
  Romeo *(G-14229)*

MACHINE TOOL ACCESS: Dresser, Abrasive Wheel Or Other

Abrasive Diamond Tool Company .... E 248 588-4800
  Madison Heights *(G-10657)*

MACHINE TOOL ACCESS: Dressing/Wheel Crushing Attach, Diamond

Truing Systems Inc .... E 248 588-9060
  Troy *(G-17404)*

MACHINE TOOL ACCESS: Drill Bushings, Drilling Jig

Carbide Surface Company .... G 586 465-6110
  Clinton Township *(G-3194)*
Colonial Bushings Inc .... E 586 954-3880
  Clinton Township *(G-3203)*
M Curry Corporation .... F 989 777-7950
  Saginaw *(G-14685)*

MACHINE TOOL ACCESS: Drills

Ace Drill Corporation .... G 517 265-5184
  Adrian *(G-47)*

Link Manufacturing Inc .... G 231 238-8741
  Indian River *(G-8654)*

MACHINE TOOL ACCESS: End Mills

Award Cutter Company Inc .... F 616 531-0430
  Grand Rapids *(G-6487)*
Conical Cutting Tools Inc .... E 616 531-8500
  Grand Rapids *(G-6593)*
P L Schmitt Crbide Tooling LLC .... G 313 706-5756
  Grass Lake *(G-7442)*

MACHINE TOOL ACCESS: Files

Fullerton Tool Company Inc .... C 989 799-4550
  Saginaw *(G-14648)*

MACHINE TOOL ACCESS: Hobs

Tawas Tool Co Inc .... D 989 362-6121
  East Tawas *(G-4924)*
Tawas Tool Co Inc .... D 989 362-0414
  East Tawas *(G-4925)*

MACHINE TOOL ACCESS: Honing Heads

Nagel Precision Inc .... C 734 426-5650
  Ann Arbor *(G-587)*

MACHINE TOOL ACCESS: Knives, Metalworking

Detroit Edge Tool Company .... D 586 776-1598
  Roseville *(G-14398)*
Detroit Edge Tool Company .... D 313 366-4120
  Detroit *(G-4146)*

MACHINE TOOL ACCESS: Machine Attachments & Access, Drilling

Special Drill and Reamer Corp .... E 248 588-5333
  Madison Heights *(G-10832)*

MACHINE TOOL ACCESS: Milling Machine Attachments

A & D Run Off Inc .... G 231 759-0950
  Muskegon *(G-11760)*
Bob G Machining LLC .... G 586 285-1400
  Clinton Township *(G-3186)*
Moehrle Inc .... F 734 761-2000
  Ann Arbor *(G-581)*

MACHINE TOOL ACCESS: Pushers

Pencil Pushers LLC .... G 248 252-7839
  Waterford *(G-18149)*
Petal Pushers By Liz LLC .... G 616 481-9513
  Comstock Park *(G-3637)*

MACHINE TOOL ACCESS: Rotary Tables

Technical Rotary Services Inc .... G 586 772-6755
  Warren *(G-18037)*

MACHINE TOOL ACCESS: Shaping Tools

Hanchett Manufacturing Inc .... E 231 796-7678
  Big Rapids *(G-1676)*

MACHINE TOOL ACCESS: Sockets

G A Machine Company Inc .... G 313 836-5646
  Detroit *(G-4249)*

MACHINE TOOL ACCESS: Threading Tools

A A Anchor Bolt Inc .... F 248 349-6565
  Northville *(G-12194)*

MACHINE TOOL ACCESS: Tool Holders

Active Tooling LLC .... F 616 875-8111
  Zeeland *(G-18988)*
FL Tool Holders LLC .... E 734 591-0134
  Livonia *(G-10207)*
Jade Tool Inc .... E 231 946-7710
  Traverse City *(G-16726)*
T M Smith Tool Intl Corp .... E 586 468-1465
  Mount Clemens *(G-11659)*
TEC Industries Inc .... G 248 446-9560
  New Hudson *(G-12072)*
Universal/Devlieg LLC .... F 989 752-7700
  Saginaw *(G-14785)*

Employee Codes: A=Over 500 employees, B=251-500
C=101-250, D=51-100, E=20-50, F=10-19, G=3-9

MACHINE TOOL ACCESS: Tools & Access

American Broach & Machine Co .... E 734 961-0300
Ypsilanti *(G-18924)*
Briggs Industries Inc .... E 586 749-5191
Chesterfield *(G-2852)*
Century Inc .... G 231 946-7500
Traverse City *(G-16642)*
Champagne Grinding & Mfg Co .... E 734 459-1759
Canton *(G-2448)*
Contour Tool and Machine Inc .... G 517 787-6806
Jackson *(G-8853)*
E & E Custom Products LLC .... F 586 978-3377
Warren *(G-17788)*
Etcs Inc .... F 586 268-4870
Warren *(G-17796)*
Green Manufacturing Inc .... G 517 458-1500
Morenci *(G-11613)*
Groholski Mfg Solutions LLC .... E 517 278-9339
Coldwater *(G-3436)*
H & G Tool Company .... F 586 573-7040
Warren *(G-17845)*
Hardy-Reed Tool & Die Co Inc .... E 517 547-7107
Manitou Beach *(G-10927)*
Indepndnce Tling Solutions LLC .... E 586 274-2300
Troy *(G-17163)*
Knight Carbide Inc .... E 586 598-4888
Chesterfield *(G-2903)*
Machining & Fabricating Inc .... E 586 773-9288
Roseville *(G-14434)*
Malmac Tool and Fixture Inc .... G 517 448-8244
Hudson *(G-8556)*
Mp Tool & Engineering Company .... E 586 772-7730
Roseville *(G-14448)*
Nexteer Automotive Corporation .... B 989 757-5000
Saginaw *(G-14710)*
P & P Manufacturing Co Inc .... E 810 667-2712
Lapeer *(G-9952)*
P T M Corporation .... G 586 725-2733
Ira *(G-8708)*
P T M Corporation .... D 586 725-2211
Ira *(G-8707)*
R & A Tool & Engineering Co .... E 734 981-2000
Westland *(G-18411)*
R J S Tool & Gage Co .... E 248 642-8620
Birmingham *(G-1746)*
Rhinevault Olsen Machine & Tl .... G 989 753-4363
Saginaw *(G-14737)*
Rodan Tool & Mold LLC .... G 248 926-9200
Commerce Township *(G-3571)*
Tooltech Machinery Inc .... G 248 628-1813
Oxford *(G-12924)*
Wire Fab Inc .... F 313 893-8816
Detroit *(G-4685)*
Wolverine Tool Co .... F 810 664-2964
Lapeer *(G-9968)*
X-Edge Products Inc .... G 866 591-9991
Grand Rapids *(G-7352)*

MACHINE TOOL ATTACHMENTS & ACCESS

Advance Products Corporation .... E 269 849-1000
Benton Harbor *(G-1527)*
American Gator Tool Company .... G 231 347-3222
Harbor Springs *(G-7639)*
Cardinal Machine Co .... E 810 686-1190
Clio *(G-3394)*
E & E Special Products LLC .... F 586 978-3377
Warren *(G-17789)*
F & S Tool & Gauge Co Inc .... G 517 787-2661
Jackson *(G-8882)*
Fega Tool & Gage Company .... F 586 469-4400
Clinton Township *(G-3236)*
Gt Technologies Inc .... E 734 467-8371
Westland *(G-18378)*
Hydro-Craft Inc .... G 248 652-8100
Rochester Hills *(G-14037)*
Kasper Machine Co .... F 248 547-3150
Madison Heights *(G-10759)*
Lamina Inc .... D 248 489-9122
Farmington Hills *(G-5289)*
Marshall-Gruber Company LLC .... F 248 353-4100
Southfield *(G-15647)*
Sesco Products Group Inc .... F 586 979-4400
Sterling Heights *(G-16173)*
Snap Jaws Manufacturing Inc .... G 248 588-1099
Troy *(G-17357)*
Stratford-Cambridge Group Co .... G 734 404-6047
Plymouth *(G-13304)*
Van Emon Bruce .... G 269 467-7803
Centreville *(G-2699)*
Wit-Son Quality Tool & Mfg LLC .... G 989 335-4342
Harrisville *(G-7747)*

MACHINE TOOLS & ACCESSORIES

Acme Carbide Die Inc .... E 734 722-2303
Westland *(G-18351)*
Advanced Feedlines LLC .... E 248 583-9400
Troy *(G-16908)*
American Gear & Engrg Co Inc .... E 734 595-6400
Westland *(G-18353)*
Anchor Lamina America Inc .... C 231 533-8646
Bellaire *(G-1468)*
Anderson-Cook Inc .... D 586 954-0700
Chesterfield *(G-2844)*
Anderson-Cook Inc .... G 586 293-0800
Fraser *(G-5895)*
Apex Broaching Systems Inc .... F 586 758-2626
Warren *(G-17708)*
Art Laser Inc .... E 248 391-6600
Auburn Hills *(G-798)*
Ashine Diamond Tools .... G 734 668-9067
Ann Arbor *(G-382)*
Atlas Thread Gage Inc .... G 248 477-3230
Farmington Hills *(G-5175)*
Baxter Machine & Tool Co .... E 517 782-2808
Jackson *(G-8822)*
Broaching Industries Inc .... E 586 949-3775
Chesterfield *(G-2853)*
CB Fabricating & Service .... F 586 758-4980
Warren *(G-17750)*
Cdp Diamond Products Inc .... E 734 591-1041
Livonia *(G-10149)*
Center Line Gage Inc .... G 810 387-4300
Brockway *(G-2106)*
Coles Machine Service Inc .... E 810 658-5373
Davison *(G-3777)*
Colonial Tool Sales & Svc LLC .... F 734 946-2733
Taylor *(G-16394)*
Complex Tool & Machine Inc .... G 248 625-0664
Clarkston *(G-3028)*
CWk International Corp .... G 616 396-2063
Holland *(G-8010)*
Cz Industries Inc .... G 248 475-4415
Auburn Hills *(G-856)*
D & F Corporation .... D 586 254-5300
Sterling Heights *(G-15977)*
Davison-Rite Products Co .... E 734 513-0505
White Lake *(G-18454)*
Detail Precision Products Inc .... E 248 544-3390
Ferndale *(G-5540)*
Die Services International LLC .... D 734 699-3400
Van Buren Twp *(G-17524)*
Dixon & Ryan Corporation .... F 248 549-4000
Royal Oak *(G-14531)*
Dobday Manufacturing Co Inc .... F 586 254-6777
Sterling Heights *(G-15990)*
Dowding Machining LLC .... F 517 663-5455
Eaton Rapids *(G-4961)*
Dynamic Jig Grinding Corp .... E 248 589-3110
Troy *(G-17072)*
Edge Industries Inc .... G 616 453-5458
Grand Rapids *(G-6665)*
Elmhirst Industries Inc .... E 586 731-8663
Sterling Heights *(G-16002)*
Enterprise Tool and Gear Inc .... F 989 269-9797
Bad Axe *(G-1100)*
Equitable Engineering Co Inc .... E 248 689-9700
Troy *(G-17096)*
Erdman Machine Co .... E 231 894-1010
Whitehall *(G-18495)*
Est Tools America Inc .... F 810 824-3323
Ira *(G-8695)*
Falcon Motorsports Inc .... G 248 328-2222
Holly *(G-8269)*
Feed - Lease Corp .... E 248 377-0000
Auburn Hills *(G-896)*
Fitz-Rite Products Inc .... E 248 528-8440
Troy *(G-17113)*
Fontijne Grotnes Inc .... E 269 262-4700
Niles *(G-12129)*
Forkardt Inc .... E 231 995-8300
Traverse City *(G-16688)*
Formula One Tool & Engineering .... G 810 794-3617
Algonac *(G-142)*
Global Engineering Inc .... E 586 566-0423
Shelby Township *(G-15230)*
Global Retool Group Amer LLC .... E 248 289-5820
Brighton *(G-2001)*
Global Thread Gage Inc .... G 313 438-6789
Dearborn *(G-3848)*
Green Oak Tool and Svcs Inc .... F 586 531-2255
Brighton *(G-2005)*
Guardian Manufacturing Corp .... E 734 591-1454
Livonia *(G-10231)*
Hank Thorn Co .... F 248 348-7800
Wixom *(G-18675)*
Htc Sales Corporation .... F 800 624-2027
Ira *(G-8698)*
Hti Cybernetics Inc .... E 586 826-8346
Sterling Heights *(G-16043)*
Huron Tool & Engineering Co .... E 989 269-9927
Bad Axe *(G-1108)*
Illinois Tool Works Inc .... G 231 947-5755
Traverse City *(G-16719)*
Illinois Tool Works Inc .... G 231 947-5755
Traverse City *(G-16720)*
J & K Spratt Enterprises Inc .... D 517 439-5010
Hillsdale *(G-7938)*
K-Tool Corporation Michigan .... D 863 603-0777
Plymouth *(G-13209)*
Karr Spring Company .... E 616 394-1277
Holland *(G-8109)*
Keo Cutters Inc .... E 586 771-2050
Warren *(G-17893)*
Krmc LLC .... G 734 955-9311
Romulus *(G-14296)*
Kurek Tool Inc .... F 989 777-5300
Saginaw *(G-14681)*
L E Jones Company .... B 906 863-1043
Menominee *(G-11242)*
Lab Tool and Engineering Corp .... F 517 750-4131
Spring Arbor *(G-15793)*
Legacy Tool LLC .... G 231 335-8983
Newaygo *(G-12084)*
Lester Detterbeck Entps Ltd .... E 906 265-5121
Iron River *(G-8746)*
Lincoln Precision Carbide Inc .... E 989 736-8113
Lincoln *(G-10037)*
Lumco Manufacturing Company .... F 810 724-0582
Lum *(G-10559)*
Lyons Tool & Engineering Inc .... E 586 200-3003
Warren *(G-17910)*
Maes Tool & Die Co Inc .... F 517 750-3131
Jackson *(G-8940)*
Mark Tool & Die Company Inc .... E 248 363-1567
Commerce Township *(G-3554)*
MB Liquidating Corporation .... D 810 638-5388
Flushing *(G-5811)*
Merrifield McHy Solutions Inc .... E 248 494-7335
Sterling Heights *(G-16091)*
Metal Punch Corporation .... F 231 775-8391
Cadillac *(G-2346)*
Metro Machine Works Inc .... D 734 941-4571
Romulus *(G-14304)*
Michigan Spline Gage Co Inc .... F 248 544-7303
Hazel Park *(G-7833)*
Midwest Tool and Cutlery Co .... D 269 651-2476
Sturgis *(G-16310)*
Millennium Technology II Inc .... F 734 479-4440
Romulus *(G-14306)*
Miller Tool & Die Co .... E 517 782-0347
Jackson *(G-8963)*
Mistequay Group Ltd .... F 989 752-7700
Saginaw *(G-14702)*
Mjc Tool & Machine Co Inc .... G 586 790-4766
Clinton Township *(G-3303)*
Modern CAM and Tool Co .... G 734 946-9800
Taylor *(G-16448)*
Montague Tool and Mfg Co .... E 810 686-0000
Clio *(G-3408)*
Northern Precision Inc .... F 989 736-6322
Lincoln *(G-10039)*
Olivet Machine Tool Engrg Co .... F 269 749-2671
Olivet *(G-12695)*
Olympian Tool LLC .... E 989 224-4817
Saint Johns *(G-14911)*
Omax Tool Products Inc .... F 517 768-0300
Ray *(G-13701)*
Oneida Tool Corporation .... E 313 537-0770
Redford *(G-13752)*
P&L Development & Mfg LLC .... D 989 739-5203
Oscoda *(G-12768)*
Paslin Company .... C 586 755-1693
Warren *(G-17956)*
Paslin Company .... C 586 758-0200
Warren *(G-17957)*
Peak Industries Co Inc .... E 313 846-8666
Dearborn *(G-3883)*
Philips Machining Company .... F 616 997-7777
Coopersville *(G-3695)*

MACHINE TOOLS, METAL CUTTING: Tool Replacement & Rpr Parts

Pioneer Broach Midwest Inc .... F 231 768-5800
  Leroy *(G-10009)*
Posa-Cut Corporation .... E 248 474-5620
  Farmington Hills *(G-5350)*
Precision Components .... F 248 588-5650
  Troy *(G-17310)*
Precision Threading Corp .... E 231 627-3133
  Cheboygan *(G-2796)*
Prime Industries Inc .... E 734 946-8588
  Taylor *(G-16460)*
Productivity Technologies .... G 810 714-0200
  Fenton *(G-5496)*
R & B Industries Inc .... E 734 462-9478
  Livonia *(G-10380)*
R T Gordon Inc .... E 586 294-6100
  Fraser *(G-5985)*
Republic Drill/Apt Corp .... C 248 689-5050
  Troy *(G-17330)*
Reska Spline Gage Inc .... G 586 778-4000
  Roseville *(G-14470)*
Riverside Spline & Gear Inc .... E 810 765-8302
  Marine City *(G-10965)*
Rochester Machine Products .... G 586 466-6190
  Harrison Township *(G-7722)*
Roesch Maufacturing Co LLC .... E 517 424-6300
  Tecumseh *(G-16514)*
Rose Tool & Die Inc .... E 989 343-1015
  West Branch *(G-18338)*
Roth-Williams Industries Inc .... E 586 792-0090
  Clinton Township *(G-3342)*
Royal Design & Manufacturing .... D 248 588-0110
  Madison Heights *(G-10821)*
Sbti Company .... D 586 726-5756
  Shelby Township *(G-15323)*
Schaller Tool & Die Co .... E 586 949-5500
  Chesterfield *(G-2947)*
Select Steel Fabricators Inc .... E 248 945-9582
  Southfield *(G-15696)*
Shwayder Company .... E 248 645-9511
  Birmingham *(G-1749)*
Star Ringmaster .... G 734 641-7147
  Canton *(G-2527)*
Superior Controls Inc .... C 734 454-0500
  Plymouth *(G-13306)*
Superior Design & Mfg .... F 810 678-3950
  Metamora *(G-11287)*
Taylor Turning Inc .... E 248 960-7920
  Wixom *(G-18767)*
Thielenhaus Microfinish Corp .... E 248 349-9450
  Novi *(G-12556)*
Thread-Craft Inc .... D 586 323-1116
  Sterling Heights *(G-16205)*
Three-Dimensional Services Inc .... C 248 852-1333
  Rochester Hills *(G-14125)*
Tolerance Tool & Engineering .... E 313 592-4011
  Detroit *(G-4635)*
Total Tooling Concepts Inc .... G 616 785-8402
  Comstock Park *(G-3648)*
Trimas Corporation .... B 248 631-5450
  Bloomfield Hills *(G-1869)*
Tru Flo Carbide Inc .... F 989 658-8515
  Ubly *(G-17483)*
Trudex One Inc .... G 248 392-2036
  Milford *(G-11494)*
Universal Tool Inc .... G 248 733-9800
  Troy *(G-17414)*
Vigel North America Inc .... F 734 947-9900
  Madison Heights *(G-10855)*
Weber Precision Grinding Inc .... G 616 842-1634
  Spring Lake *(G-15858)*
Wedin International Inc .... E 231 779-8650
  Cadillac *(G-2363)*
West Michigan Gage Inc .... F 616 735-0585
  Walker *(G-17657)*
Westech Corp .... E 231 766-3914
  Muskegon *(G-11943)*
Wolverine Production & Engrg .... G 586 468-2890
  Harrison Township *(G-7734)*
Zcc USA Inc .... F 734 997-3811
  Ann Arbor *(G-721)*

MACHINE TOOLS, METAL CUTTING: Brushing

Steadfast Tool & Machine Inc .... G 989 856-8127
  Caseville *(G-2605)*

MACHINE TOOLS, METAL CUTTING: Cutoff

Allfi Robotics Inc .... G 586 248-1198
  Wixom *(G-18604)*

Modern Machine Tool Co .... F 517 788-9120
  Jackson *(G-8969)*
Novi Tool & Machine Company .... F 313 532-0900
  Redford *(G-13749)*
P M R Industries Inc .... F 810 989-5020
  Port Huron *(G-13515)*

MACHINE TOOLS, METAL CUTTING: Die Sinking

J C Manufacturing Company .... G 586 757-2713
  Warren *(G-17877)*

MACHINE TOOLS, METAL CUTTING: Drilling

ExIterra Inc .... G 248 268-2336
  Hazel Park *(G-7825)*
Govro-Nelson Co .... G 810 329-4727
  Commerce Township *(G-3533)*
Infra Corporation .... F 248 623-0400
  Waterford *(G-18129)*
J & W Machine Inc .... G 989 773-9951
  Mount Pleasant *(G-11704)*
Sauter North America Inc .... G 734 207-0900
  Auburn Hills *(G-1028)*
Viscount Equipment Co Inc .... G 586 293-5900
  Hazel Park *(G-7847)*
Wave Tool LLC .... F 989 912-2116
  Cass City *(G-2623)*
Wright-K Technology Inc .... E 989 752-2588
  Saginaw *(G-14795)*

MACHINE TOOLS, METAL CUTTING: Drilling & Boring

Antech Tool Inc .... F 734 207-3622
  Canton *(G-2435)*
Esco Group Inc .... E 616 453-5458
  Grand Rapids *(G-6685)*
Mag-Powertrain .... F 586 446-7000
  Sterling Heights *(G-16082)*
Raven Engineering Inc .... E 248 969-9450
  Oxford *(G-12911)*
Richardson Acqstions Group Inc .... E 248 624-2272
  Walled Lake *(G-17674)*
Roy A Hutchins Company .... G 248 437-3470
  New Hudson *(G-12069)*
Saginaw Machine Systems Inc .... E 989 753-8465
  Saginaw *(G-14747)*
SMS Holding Co Inc .... C 989 753-8465
  Saginaw *(G-14759)*
Soils and Structures Inc .... D 800 933-3959
  Norton Shores *(G-12333)*
T E C Boring .... G 586 443-5437
  Roseville *(G-14482)*

MACHINE TOOLS, METAL CUTTING: Electrochemical Milling

A & D Run Off Inc .... G 231 759-0950
  Muskegon *(G-11760)*

MACHINE TOOLS, METAL CUTTING: Electron-Discharge

Liquid Drive Corporation .... E 248 634-5382
  Mount Clemens *(G-11647)*

MACHINE TOOLS, METAL CUTTING: Exotic, Including Explosive

Carb-A-Tron Tool Co .... G 517 782-2249
  Jackson *(G-8834)*
Electro ARC Manufacturing Co .... E 734 483-4233
  Dexter *(G-4741)*
Lester Detterbeck Entps Ltd .... E 906 265-5121
  Iron River *(G-8746)*
Paragon Tool Company .... G 734 326-1702
  Romulus *(G-14316)*
Roussin M & Ubelhor R Inc .... G 586 783-6015
  Harrison Township *(G-7723)*
W W J Form Tool Company Inc .... G 313 565-0015
  Inkster *(G-8677)*

MACHINE TOOLS, METAL CUTTING: Grind, Polish, Buff, Lapp

Acme Manufacturing Company .... D 248 393-7300
  Auburn Hills *(G-773)*
Grindmaster Eqp & Mchs USA LLC ...... G 517 455-3675
  Lansing *(G-9763)*

Tru Tech Systems LLC .... D 586 469-2700
  Mount Clemens *(G-11661)*

MACHINE TOOLS, METAL CUTTING: Home Workshop

Mi-Tech Tooling Inc .... E 989 912-2440
  Cass City *(G-2618)*

MACHINE TOOLS, METAL CUTTING: Jig, Boring & Grinding

Leader Corporation .... E 586 566-7114
  Shelby Township *(G-15260)*

MACHINE TOOLS, METAL CUTTING: Lathes

High-Star Corporation .... G 734 743-1503
  Westland *(G-18381)*
J & R Tool Inc .... G 989 662-0026
  Auburn *(G-767)*
New Dimension Laser Inc .... G 586 415-6041
  Roseville *(G-14454)*

MACHINE TOOLS, METAL CUTTING: Numerically Controlled

Cellular Concepts Co Inc .... G 313 371-4800
  Rochester Hills *(G-13974)*
M S Machining Systems Inc .... F 517 546-1170
  Howell *(G-8474)*
Pro Precision Inc .... G 586 247-6160
  Sterling Heights *(G-16134)*
Schienke Products Inc .... E 586 752-5454
  Bruce Twp *(G-2181)*
Snap Jaws Manufacturing Inc .... G 248 588-1099
  Troy *(G-17357)*
Soaring Concepts Aerospace LLC .... F 574 286-9670
  Hastings *(G-7810)*
True Fabrications & Machine .... F 248 288-0140
  Troy *(G-17403)*
U S Equipment Co .... E 313 526-8300
  Rochester Hills *(G-14134)*
Warren Industries Inc .... C 586 741-0420
  Clinton Township *(G-3386)*

MACHINE TOOLS, METAL CUTTING: Pipe Cutting & Threading

Quality Pipe Products Inc .... E 734 606-5100
  New Boston *(G-12019)*

MACHINE TOOLS, METAL CUTTING: Plasma Process

RSI Global Sourcing LLC .... G 734 604-2448
  Novi *(G-12529)*

MACHINE TOOLS, METAL CUTTING: Regrinding, Crankshaft

Crankshaft Machine Company .... E 517 787-3791
  Jackson *(G-8856)*

MACHINE TOOLS, METAL CUTTING: Robot, Drilling, Cutting, Etc

Dynamic Robotic Solutions Inc .... C 248 829-2800
  Auburn Hills *(G-871)*

MACHINE TOOLS, METAL CUTTING: Tool Replacement & Rpr Parts

ABC Precision Machining Inc .... G 269 926-6322
  Benton Harbor *(G-1525)*
Accra Tool Inc .... G 248 680-9936
  Lake Orion *(G-9582)*
Accubilt Automated Systems LLC .... E 517 787-9353
  Jackson *(G-8800)*
Alto Manufacturing Inc .... E 734 641-8800
  Westland *(G-18352)*
American Gear & Engrg Co Inc .... E 734 595-6400
  Westland *(G-18353)*
American Pride Machining Inc .... E 586 294-6404
  Fraser *(G-5892)*
Donald E Rogers Associates .... G 248 673-9878
  Waterford *(G-18116)*
Emcor Inc .... F 989 667-0652
  Bay City *(G-1350)*
Great Lakes Waterjet Laser LLC .... G 517 629-9900
  Albion *(G-126)*

Employee Codes: A=Over 500 employees, B=251-500
C=101-250, D=51-100, E=20-50, F=10-19, G=3-9

2022 Harris Michigan Industrial Directory

MACHINE TOOLS, METAL CUTTING: Tool Replacement & Rpr Parts

Huron Tool & Engineering Co .... E 989 269-9927
  Bad Axe (G-1108)
J&M Group Industrial Svcs Inc .... G 248 957-0006
  Clay (G-3121)
K&S Consultants LLC .... G 269 240-7767
  Buchanan (G-2198)
Liberty Steel Fabricating Inc .... E 269 556-9792
  Saint Joseph (G-14948)
Normac Incorporated .... F 248 349-2644
  Northville (G-12244)
Precision Honing .... G 586 757-0304
  Roseville (G-14464)
Punch Tech .... E 810 364-4811
  Marysville (G-11097)
R P T Cincinnati Inc .... G 313 382-5880
  Lincoln Park (G-10054)
S & S Machine Tool Repair LLC .... G 616 877-4930
  Dorr (G-4770)
Tank Truck Service & Sales Inc .... E 586 757-6500
  Warren (G-18036)
Transfer Tool Systems LLC .... C 616 846-8510
  Grand Haven (G-6372)
Ultra-Dex USA LLC .... G 810 638-5388
  Flushing (G-5814)

MACHINE TOOLS, METAL CUTTING: Turret Lathes

D W Machine Inc .... F 517 787-9929
  Jackson (G-8859)

MACHINE TOOLS, METAL CUTTING: Ultrasonic

Telsonic Ultrasonics Inc .... F 586 802-0033
  Shelby Township (G-15350)

MACHINE TOOLS, METAL CUTTING: Vertical Turning & Boring

Bob G Machining LLC .... G 586 285-1400
  Clinton Township (G-3186)

MACHINE TOOLS, METAL FORMING: Beaders, Metal

Van-Mark Products Corporation .... E 248 478-1200
  Farmington Hills (G-5408)

MACHINE TOOLS, METAL FORMING: Bending

Birmingham Benders Co .... F 313 435-4200
  Clawson (G-3088)
CNB International Inc .... D 269 948-3300
  Hastings (G-7783)
Hti Cybernetics Inc .... E 586 826-8346
  Sterling Heights (G-16043)

MACHINE TOOLS, METAL FORMING: Die Casting & Extruding

Digital Die Solutions Inc .... F 734 542-2222
  Livonia (G-10185)
Pace Industries LLC .... G 231 777-3941
  Muskegon (G-11890)
Product and Tooling Tech Inc .... E 586 293-1810
  Fraser (G-5980)

MACHINE TOOLS, METAL FORMING: Electroforming

Bmax USA LLC .... E 248 794-4176
  Lake Orion (G-9587)

MACHINE TOOLS, METAL FORMING: Forging Machinery & Hammers

Midwest Tool and Cutlery Co .... F 231 258-2341
  Kalkaska (G-9398)
P M R Industries Inc .... F 810 989-5020
  Port Huron (G-13515)

MACHINE TOOLS, METAL FORMING: Gear Rolling

Howell Gear Company LLC .... D 517 273-5202
  Howell (G-8463)

MACHINE TOOLS, METAL FORMING: Lathes, Spinning

M & M Turning Co .... E 586 791-7188
  Clinton Township (G-3284)

MACHINE TOOLS, METAL FORMING: Magnetic Forming

Magnetool Inc .... E 248 588-5400
  Troy (G-17228)

MACHINE TOOLS, METAL FORMING: Marking

Arch Cutting Tools LLC .... C 734 266-6900
  Bloomfield Hills (G-1800)

MACHINE TOOLS, METAL FORMING: Mechanical, Pneumatic Or Hyd

Dimond Machinery Company Inc .... F 269 945-5908
  Hastings (G-7790)

MACHINE TOOLS, METAL FORMING: Plasma Jet Spray

American Brake and Clutch Inc .... F 586 948-3730
  Chesterfield (G-2838)

MACHINE TOOLS, METAL FORMING: Presses, Arbor

Green Oak Tool and Svcs Inc .... F 586 531-2255
  Brighton (G-2005)

MACHINE TOOLS, METAL FORMING: Presses, Hyd & Pneumatic

Air-Hydraulics Inc .... F 517 787-9444
  Jackson (G-8806)
Burton Press Co Inc .... G 248 853-0212
  Rochester Hills (G-13967)
Lloyd Tool & Mfg Corp .... F 810 694-3519
  Grand Blanc (G-6251)
Metal Mechanics Inc .... F 269 679-2525
  Schoolcraft (G-15124)

MACHINE TOOLS, METAL FORMING: Punching & Shearing

United Sttes Scket Screw Mfg C .... F 586 469-8811
  Fraser (G-6009)

MACHINE TOOLS, METAL FORMING: Rebuilt

Centerless Rebuilders Inc .... E 586 749-6529
  New Haven (G-12030)
Reliable Sales Co .... G 248 969-0943
  Oxford (G-12912)
S & L Tool Inc .... G 734 464-4200
  Livonia (G-10397)

MACHINE TOOLS, METAL FORMING: Robots, Pressing, Extrudg, Etc

Buster Mathis Foundation .... G 616 843-4433
  Wyoming (G-18855)
Fanuc America Corporation .... B 248 377-7000
  Rochester Hills (G-14009)

MACHINE TOOLS, METAL FORMING: Spinning, Spline Rollg/Windg

Automated Indus Motion Inc .... G 231 865-1800
  Fruitport (G-6059)
Michigan Roll Form Inc .... E 248 669-3700
  Commerce Township (G-3556)
U S Baird Corporation .... F 616 826-5013
  Middleville (G-11316)

MACHINE TOOLS, METAL FORMING: Spline Rolling

Anderson-Cook Inc .... D 586 954-0700
  Chesterfield (G-2844)
Anderson-Cook Inc .... G 586 293-0800
  Fraser (G-5895)
Spline Specialist Inc .... G 586 731-4569
  Sterling Heights (G-16184)

West Michigan Spline Inc .... F 616 399-4078
  Holland (G-8246)

MACHINE TOOLS: Metal Cutting

AAA Industries Inc .... E 313 255-0420
  Redford (G-13709)
Acme Manufacturing Company .... F 248 393-7300
  Lake Orion (G-9583)
Advanced Stage Tooling LLC .... G 810 444-9807
  East China (G-4855)
Alliance Tool .... G 586 465-3960
  Harrison Township (G-7685)
American Lap Company .... G 231 526-7121
  Harbor Springs (G-7640)
Americhip International Inc .... E 586 783-4598
  Clinton Township (G-3167)
Anthony Castellani .... G 248 579-3406
  Van Buren Twp (G-17509)
Atlas Technologies LLC .... D 810 629-6663
  Fenton (G-5451)
Aw Carbide Fabricators Inc .... E 586 294-1850
  Sterling Heights (G-15939)
Axly Production Machining Inc .... G 989 269-2444
  Bad Axe (G-1096)
B L Tool Products .... G 517 896-1624
  Eaton Rapids (G-4954)
Barron LLC .... G 248 879-6203
  Troy (G-16968)
Belco Industries Inc .... E 616 794-0410
  Belding (G-1437)
Belco Industries Inc .... E 616 794-0410
  Belding (G-1438)
Berg Tool Inc .... F 586 646-7100
  Chesterfield (G-2850)
Bielomatik USA Inc .... E 248 446-9910
  Commerce Township (G-3516)
Broaching Industries Inc .... E 586 949-3775
  Chesterfield (G-2853)
Car Pak .... G 248 280-1401
  Troy (G-16998)
CBS Tool Inc .... F 586 566-5945
  Shelby Township (G-15182)
City Animation Co .... E 248 589-0600
  Troy (G-17012)
City Animation Co .... F 989 743-3458
  Corunna (G-3706)
Clear Cut Water Jet Machining .... G 616 534-9119
  Grand Rapids (G-6573)
Cleary Developments Inc .... E 248 588-7011
  Madison Heights (G-10689)
Cold Forming Technology Inc .... F 586 254-4600
  Sterling Heights (G-15963)
Cole Carbide Industries Inc .... F 248 276-1278
  Lake Orion (G-9595)
Craft Industries Inc .... B 586 726-4300
  Shelby Township (G-15197)
Crown Boring Industries LLC .... E 586 447-3900
  Roseville (G-14391)
Cutex Inc .... G 734 953-8908
  Livonia (G-10172)
D & D Production Inc .... F 248 334-2112
  Waterford (G-18113)
D W Hines Manufacturing Corp .... G 586 775-1200
  Warren (G-17772)
Davison-Rite Products Co .... E 734 513-0505
  White Lake (G-18454)
Design Services Unlimited Inc .... G 586 463-3225
  Chesterfield (G-2870)
Detroit Boring & Mch Co LLC .... G 586 604-6506
  Sterling Heights (G-15981)
Detroit Edge Tool Company .... D 586 776-1598
  Roseville (G-14398)
Dikar Tool Company Inc .... E 248 348-0010
  Novi (G-12400)
Dimond Machinery Company Inc .... F 269 945-5908
  Hastings (G-7790)
Dons Quality Tools LLC .... G 248 701-5154
  Flint (G-5689)
Dvs Technology America Inc .... G 734 656-2080
  Plymouth (G-13163)
Dyna- Bignell Products LLC .... G 989 418-5050
  Clare (G-2977)
Ecorse McHy Sls & Rbldrs Inc .... E 313 383-2100
  Wyandotte (G-18817)
Edge Industries Inc .... G 616 453-5458
  Grand Rapids (G-6665)
Eikos Holdings Inc .... E 248 280-0300
  Troy (G-17080)
Elite Prcsion McHining Tooling .... G 269 383-9714
  Kalamazoo (G-9177)

Elk Rapids Engineering Inc ... F ... 231 264-5661
Elk Rapids *(G-5024)*
Emhart Teknologies LLC ... F ... 586 949-0440
Chesterfield *(G-2875)*
Emhart Teknologies LLC ... F ... 800 783-6427
Chesterfield *(G-2876)*
Emhart Teknologies LLC ... G ... 800 783-6427
Troy *(G-17088)*
Emhart Teknologies LLC ... G ... 800 783-6427
Troy *(G-17089)*
Esr ... G ... 989 619-7160
Harrisville *(G-7742)*
Falcon Motorsports Inc ... G ... 248 328-2222
Holly *(G-8269)*
Fitz-Rite Products Inc ... G ... 248 360-3730
Commerce Township *(G-3529)*
Five Star Industries Inc ... E ... 586 786-0500
Macomb *(G-10595)*
Fortune Tool & Machine Inc ... F ... 248 669-9119
Wixom *(G-18665)*
Fourway Machinery Sales Co ... F ... 517 782-9371
Jackson *(G-8886)*
Framon Mfg Co Inc ... G ... 989 354-5623
Alpena *(G-295)*
G & W Machine Co ... G ... 616 363-4435
Grand Rapids *(G-6729)*
Gehring Corporation ... D ... 248 478-8060
Farmington Hills *(G-5250)*
Gerald Harris ... G ... 985 774-0261
Detroit *(G-4261)*
Global Components LLC ... G ... 586 755-9134
Warren *(G-17830)*
Globe Tech LLC ... E ... 734 656-2200
Plymouth *(G-13178)*
Godin Tool Inc ... G ... 231 946-2210
Traverse City *(G-16695)*
Great Lakes Tech & Mfg LLC ... G ... 810 593-0257
Fenton *(G-5482)*
H & G Tool Company ... F ... 586 573-7040
Warren *(G-17845)*
Hal International Inc ... G ... 248 488-0440
Livonia *(G-10233)*
Heartland Machine & Engrg LLC ... G ... 616 437-1641
Mason *(G-11137)*
Hegenscheidt-Mfd Corporation ... E ... 586 274-4900
Sterling Heights *(G-16038)*
Heller Inc ... E ... 248 288-5000
Troy *(G-17140)*
Highland Machine Design Inc ... G ... 248 669-6150
Commerce Township *(G-3537)*
Hill Machine Works LLC ... F ... 586 238-2897
Fraser *(G-5937)*
Hot Tool Cutter Grinding Co ... G ... 586 790-4867
Fraser *(G-5940)*
Hougen Manufacturing Inc ... C ... 810 635-7111
Swartz Creek *(G-16355)*
Hydro-Craft Inc ... G ... 248 652-8100
Rochester Hills *(G-14037)*
Ideal Tool Inc ... F ... 989 893-8336
Bay City *(G-1366)*
Indexable Cutter Engineering ... G ... 586 598-1540
Chesterfield *(G-2892)*
Ingersoll CM Systems LLC ... D ... 989 495-5000
Midland *(G-11373)*
Ingersoll Prod Systems LLC ... G ... 248 585-9130
Troy *(G-17167)*
Inland Lakes Machine Inc ... E ... 231 775-6543
Cadillac *(G-2337)*
Integrity Design & Mfg LLC ... G ... 248 628-6927
Oxford *(G-12890)*
Internal Grinding Abrasives ... E ... 616 243-5566
Grand Rapids *(G-6849)*
Iron River Mfg Co Inc ... G ... 906 265-5121
Iron River *(G-8741)*
Ivan Doverspike ... F ... 313 579-3000
Detroit *(G-4328)*
J M Mold & Engineering ... G ... 586 783-3300
Clinton Township *(G-3262)*
J W Holdings Inc ... E ... 616 530-9889
Grand Rapids *(G-6858)*
Jdl Enterprises Inc ... F ... 586 977-8863
Warren *(G-17884)*
JF Hubert Enterprises Inc ... F ... 586 293-8660
Fraser *(G-5947)*
JPS Mfg Inc ... G ... 586 415-8702
Fraser *(G-5948)*
Jtekt Toyoda Americas Corp ... E ... 847 506-2415
Wixom *(G-18690)*
K-Tool Corporation Michigan ... D ... 863 603-0777
Plymouth *(G-13209)*

Kalamazoo Machine Tool Co Inc ... G ... 269 321-8860
Portage *(G-13571)*
Kbe Precision Products LLC ... G ... 586 725-4200
New Baltimore *(G-11985)*
Koch Limited ... G ... 586 296-3103
Fraser *(G-5952)*
Krmc LLC ... G ... 734 955-9311
Romulus *(G-14296)*
Laydon Enterprises Inc ... E ... 906 774-4633
Iron Mountain *(G-8724)*
Lee Stevens Machinery Inc ... G ... 248 926-8400
Wixom *(G-18696)*
Leitz Tooling Systems LP ... G ... 616 698-7010
Grand Rapids *(G-6940)*
Leitz Tooling Systems LP ... G ... 616 698-7010
Grand Rapids *(G-6941)*
Liberty Tool Inc ... E ... 586 726-2449
Sterling Heights *(G-16073)*
Lincoln Precision Carbide Inc ... E ... 989 736-8113
Lincoln *(G-10037)*
Lloyd Tool & Mfg Corp ... F ... 810 694-3519
Grand Blanc *(G-6251)*
Loc Performance Products Inc ... G ... 734 453-2300
Sterling Heights *(G-16076)*
Loc Performance Products LLC ... C ... 734 453-2300
Plymouth *(G-13224)*
Loc Performance Products LLC ... C ... 734 453-2300
Lansing *(G-9713)*
Loc Performance Products LLC ... E ... 734 453-2300
Lapeer *(G-9944)*
Love Machinery Inc ... G ... 734 427-0824
Livonia *(G-10293)*
M C Carbide Tool Co ... E ... 248 486-9590
Wixom *(G-18703)*
Maes Tool & Die Co Inc ... F ... 517 750-3131
Jackson *(G-8940)*
MB Liquidating Corporation ... D ... 810 638-5388
Flushing *(G-5811)*
Mc Pherson Industrial Corp ... E ... 586 752-5555
Romeo *(G-14229)*
Menominee Saw and Supply Co ... E ... 906 863-2609
Menominee *(G-11248)*
Methods Machine Tools Inc ... E ... 248 624-8601
Wixom *(G-18709)*
Microform Tool Company Inc ... G ... 586 776-4840
Saint Clair Shores *(G-14872)*
Migatron Precision Products ... F ... 989 739-1439
Oscoda *(G-12765)*
Millennium Screw Machine Inc ... G ... 734 525-5235
Livonia *(G-10318)*
Miller Broach Inc ... D ... 810 395-8810
Capac *(G-2547)*
Miller Tool & Die Co ... E ... 517 782-0347
Jackson *(G-8963)*
Moore Production Tool Spc ... F ... 248 476-1200
Farmington *(G-5143)*
Nagel Precision Inc ... G ... 248 380-4052
Novi *(G-12485)*
Neway Manufacturing Inc ... G ... 989 743-3458
Corunna *(G-3714)*
Niagara Cutter LLC ... G ... 248 528-5220
Troy *(G-17276)*
Nidec Indl Automation USA ... G ... 203 735-6367
Sterling Heights *(G-16115)*
Oliver of Adrian Inc ... G ... 517 263-2132
Adrian *(G-86)*
Only Tool Co ... G ... 734 552-8876
New Boston *(G-12016)*
Ossineke Industries Inc ... F ... 989 471-2197
Ossineke *(G-12778)*
Oster Manufacturing Company ... G ... 989 729-1160
Owosso *(G-12847)*
Pentech Industries Inc ... E ... 586 445-1070
Roseville *(G-14462)*
Petty Machine & Tool Inc ... E ... 517 782-9355
Jackson *(G-8985)*
Pinnacle Engineering Co Inc ... E ... 734 428-7039
Manchester *(G-10888)*
Pioneer Broach Midwest Inc ... F ... 231 768-5800
Leroy *(G-10009)*
Plason Scraping Co Inc ... G ... 248 588-7280
Madison Heights *(G-10801)*
Posa-Cut Corporation ... E ... 248 474-5620
Farmington Hills *(G-5350)*
Precision Guides LLC ... G ... 517 536-7234
Michigan Center *(G-11295)*
Precision Jig Grinding Inc ... G ... 989 865-7953
Saint Charles *(G-14808)*
Prime Industries Inc ... E ... 734 946-8588
Taylor *(G-16460)*

Production Threaded Parts Co ... E ... 810 688-3186
North Branch *(G-12183)*
Productivity Technologies ... G ... 810 714-0200
Fenton *(G-5496)*
Promac North America Corp ... G ... 248 817-2346
Troy *(G-17319)*
R & R Broach Inc ... G ... 586 779-2227
Clinton Township *(G-3330)*
R & T Tooling ... G ... 586 218-7644
Roseville *(G-14468)*
R F M Incorporated ... E ... 810 229-4567
Brighton *(G-2059)*
Riverside Spline & Gear Inc ... E ... 810 765-8302
Marine City *(G-10965)*
Rnd Engineering LLC ... G ... 734 328-8277
Canton *(G-2518)*
Rod Chomper Inc ... F ... 616 392-9677
Holland *(G-8182)*
RTS Cutting Tools Inc ... E ... 586 954-1900
Clinton Township *(G-3344)*
Rwc Inc ... D ... 989 684-4030
Bay City *(G-1395)*
S & L Tool Inc ... G ... 734 464-4200
Livonia *(G-10397)*
Schutte Corporation ... F ... 517 782-3600
Jackson *(G-9007)*
Select Steel Fabricators Inc ... E ... 248 945-9582
Southfield *(G-15696)*
Snyder Corporation ... C ... 586 726-4300
Shelby Township *(G-15337)*
Solidica Inc ... F ... 734 222-4680
Ann Arbor *(G-659)*
Stanhope Tool Inc ... E ... 248 585-5711
Warren *(G-18027)*
Star Cutter Co ... E ... 248 474-8200
Farmington Hills *(G-5387)*
Star Cutter Company Inc ... E ... 248 474-8200
East Tawas *(G-4923)*
Star Su Company LLC ... G ... 248 474-8200
Farmington Hills *(G-5388)*
Stoney Crest Regrind Service ... F ... 989 777-7190
Bridgeport *(G-1918)*
Sunrise Tool Products Inc ... F ... 989 724-6688
Harrisville *(G-7745)*
Tank Truck Service & Sales Inc ... G ... 989 731-4887
Gaylord *(G-6162)*
Tarus Products Inc ... D ... 586 977-1400
Sterling Heights *(G-16201)*
Tawas Tool Co Inc ... D ... 989 362-0414
East Tawas *(G-4925)*
Tech Tooling Specialties Inc ... F ... 517 782-8898
Jackson *(G-9016)*
Thielenhaus Microfinish Corp ... E ... 248 349-9450
Novi *(G-12556)*
Thyssenkrupp System Engrg ... C ... 248 340-8000
Auburn Hills *(G-1052)*
Triangle Broach Company ... E ... 313 838-2150
Detroit *(G-4645)*
Troy Industries Inc ... F ... 586 739-7760
Shelby Township *(G-15357)*
Utica Body & Assembly Inc ... E ... 586 726-4330
Troy *(G-17418)*
Utica Enterprises Inc ... C ... 586 726-4300
Troy *(G-17419)*
Van-Mark Products Corporation ... E ... 248 478-1200
Farmington Hills *(G-5408)*
Ventra Greenwich Holdings Corp ... E ... 586 759-8900
Warren *(G-18054)*
Vertical Machining Services ... G ... 734 462-1800
Livonia *(G-10460)*
Viper Tool Company LLC ... G ... 734 417-9974
Ann Arbor *(G-711)*
Waber Tool & Engineering Co ... F ... 269 342-0765
Kalamazoo *(G-9365)*
Warren Broach & Machine Corp ... F ... 586 254-7080
Sterling Heights *(G-16229)*
Wolverine Machine Products Co ... E ... 248 634-9952
Holly *(G-8301)*

MACHINE TOOLS: Metal Forming

A W B Industries Inc ... E ... 989 739-1447
Oscoda *(G-12753)*
Advanced Feedlines LLC ... E ... 248 583-9400
Troy *(G-16908)*
Aladdin Machining Inc ... G ... 586 465-4280
Clinton Township *(G-3160)*
American Wldg & Press Repr Inc ... F ... 248 358-2050
Southfield *(G-15486)*
B&P Littleford LLC ... E ... 989 757-1300
Saginaw *(G-14608)*

Employee Codes: A=Over 500 employees, B=251-500
C=101-250, D=51-100, E=20-50, F=10-19, G=3-9

2022 Harris Michigan
Industrial Directory

1315

MACHINE TOOLS: Metal Forming

Baldauf Enterprises Inc ....F 989 686-0350		
Bay City *(G-1325)*		
Birdsall Tool & Gage Co ....E 248 474-5150		
Farmington Hills *(G-5181)*		
Century Inc ....C 231 947-6400		
Traverse City *(G-16641)*		
Challenge Mfg Holdings Inc ....E 616 735-6500		
Grand Rapids *(G-6563)*		
Columbia Marking Tools Inc ....E 586 949-8400		
Chesterfield *(G-2860)*		
Contractors Steel Company ....E 616 531-4000		
Grand Rapids *(G-6600)*		
D M Tool & Fab Inc ....D 586 726-8390		
Sterling Heights *(G-15978)*		
Eagle Machine Tool Corporation ....G 231 798-8473		
Norton Shores *(G-12289)*		
Ems Parts Div ....G 517 319-5306		
Lansing *(G-9692)*		
Enprotech Industrial Tech LLC ....C 517 372-0950		
Lansing *(G-9694)*		
Feed - Lease Corp ....E 248 377-0000		
Auburn Hills *(G-896)*		
Fontijne Grotnes Inc ....E 269 262-4700		
Niles *(G-12129)*		
Gasbarre Products Inc ....G 734 425-5165		
Livonia *(G-10220)*		
Global Strgc Sup Solutions LLC ....D 734 525-9100		
Livonia *(G-10226)*		
Globe Tech LLC ....E 734 656-2200		
Plymouth *(G-13178)*		
Hamilton Industrial Products ....E 269 751-5153		
Hamilton *(G-7599)*		
HMS Products Co ....D 248 689-8120		
Troy *(G-17146)*		
Howmet Corporation ....E 231 894-5686		
Whitehall *(G-18501)*		
Howmet Holdings Corporation ....G 231 894-5686		
Whitehall *(G-18506)*		
Hti Cybernetics ....G 586 826-8346		
Sterling Heights *(G-16042)*		
International Machinery ....G 248 619-9999		
Troy *(G-17172)*		
Jier North America Inc ....F 734 404-6683		
Plymouth *(G-13202)*		
M C Molds Inc ....E 517 655-5481		
Williamston *(G-18576)*		
Mak Press & Machinery Co ....G 734 266-3044		
Farmington Hills *(G-5308)*		
Martinrea Industries Inc ....E 231 832-5504		
Reed City *(G-13795)*		
Miller Tool & Die Co ....E 517 782-0347		
Jackson *(G-8963)*		
Monroe LLC ....B 616 942-9820		
Grand Rapids *(G-7025)*		
Moore Production Tool Spc ....F 248 476-1200		
Farmington *(G-5143)*		
Nn Inc ....E 616 698-0707		
Kentwood *(G-9467)*		
Nn Inc ....E 269 591-6951		
Grand Rapids *(G-7044)*		
Press Room Eqp Sls & Svc Co ....G 248 334-1880		
Pontiac *(G-13410)*		
Production Fabricators Inc ....E 231 777-3822		
Muskegon *(G-11900)*		
Productivity Technologies ....G 810 714-0200		
Fenton *(G-5496)*		
Prophotonix Limited ....G 586 778-1100		
Roseville *(G-14466)*		
Pt Tech Stamping Inc ....E 586 293-1810		
Fraser *(G-5982)*		
R and T West Michigan Inc ....E 616 698-9931		
Caledonia *(G-2395)*		
Rempco Acquisition Inc ....E 231 775-0108		
Cadillac *(G-2351)*		
Sesco Inc ....D 313 843-7710		
Detroit *(G-4587)*		
Shannon Precision Fastener LLC ....D 248 658-3015		
Madison Heights *(G-10826)*		
Stilson Products LLC ....F 586 778-1100		
Roseville *(G-14481)*		
Superior USA LLC ....G 586 786-4261		
Macomb *(G-10638)*		
Tech Tooling Specialties Inc ....F 517 782-8898		
Jackson *(G-9016)*		
Triple Tool ....G 586 795-1785		
Sterling Heights *(G-16211)*		

MACHINERY & EQPT FINANCE LEASING

Ervin Industries Inc ....E 734 769-4600
Ann Arbor *(G-478)*

Misteequay Group Ltd ....E 989 846-1000
Standish *(G-15893)*

MACHINERY & EQPT, AGRICULTURAL, WHOL: Farm Eqpt Parts/Splys

Tupes of Saginaw Inc ....F 989 799-1550
Saginaw *(G-14781)*

MACHINERY & EQPT, AGRICULTURAL, WHOLESALE: Cultivating

Excellence Lawn Landscape ....G 810 623-9742
Brighton *(G-1985)*

MACHINERY & EQPT, AGRICULTURAL, WHOLESALE: Landscaping Eqpt

Bay-Houston Towing Company ....F 810 648-2210
Sandusky *(G-15056)*
Blue Thumb Distributing Inc ....E 989 921-3474
Saginaw *(G-14617)*
Doug Wirt Enterprises Inc ....G 989 684-5777
Bay City *(G-1347)*
Green Day Management LLC ....F 313 652-1390
Detroit *(G-4278)*
Michigan Wood Fibers Llc ....G 616 875-2241
Zeeland *(G-19053)*

MACHINERY & EQPT, AGRICULTURAL, WHOLESALE: Livestock Eqpt

Anderson Welding & Mfg Inc ....E 906 523-4661
Houghton *(G-8380)*

MACHINERY & EQPT, INDL, WHOL: Brewery Prdts Mfrg, Commercial

Keglove LLC ....G 616 610-7289
Holland *(G-8110)*
Loggers Brewing Co ....G 989 401-3085
Saginaw *(G-14684)*

MACHINERY & EQPT, INDL, WHOL: Controlling Instruments/Access

Cammenga & Associates LLC ....F 313 914-7160
Dearborn *(G-3817)*
Limbright Consulting Inc ....E 810 227-5510
Wixom *(G-18699)*

MACHINERY & EQPT, INDL, WHOL: Environ Pollution Cntrl, Air

Swat Environmental Inc ....E 517 322-2999
Lansing *(G-9898)*

MACHINERY & EQPT, INDL, WHOL: Environ Pollution Cntrl, Water

Antimicrobial Specialist Assoc ....F 989 662-0377
Auburn *(G-763)*

MACHINERY & EQPT, INDL, WHOL: Meters, Consumption Registerng

Vaughan Industries Inc ....F 313 935-2040
Detroit *(G-4663)*

MACHINERY & EQPT, INDL, WHOLESALE: Conveyor Systems

Best Industrial Group Inc ....F 586 826-8800
Warren *(G-17734)*
Corr-Fac Corporation ....G 989 358-7050
Alpena *(G-288)*
P & A Conveyor Sales Inc ....G 734 285-7970
Riverview *(G-13882)*
Valmec Inc ....G 810 629-8750
Fenton *(G-5512)*
W G Benjey Inc ....G 989 356-0027
Alpena *(G-328)*

MACHINERY & EQPT, INDL, WHOLESALE: Cranes

C R B Crane & Service Co ....G 586 757-1222
Warren *(G-17747)*
Crane 1 Services Inc ....E 586 468-0909
Harrison Township *(G-7694)*

Crane Technologies Group Inc ....E 248 652-8700
Rochester Hills *(G-13985)*
Plutchak Fab ....G 906 864-4650
Menominee *(G-11256)*

MACHINERY & EQPT, INDL, WHOLESALE: Engines & Parts, Diesel

Chesterfield Engines Inc ....G 586 949-5777
Chesterfield *(G-2859)*
Cummins Bridgeway Grove Cy LLC ....C 614 604-6000
New Hudson *(G-12047)*
Cummins Inc ....G 586 469-2010
Clinton Township *(G-3215)*
Cummins Inc ....G 989 752-5200
Saginaw *(G-14633)*
Cummins Inc ....G 248 573-1900
New Hudson *(G-12048)*
Cummins Npower LLC ....E 906 475-8800
Negaunee *(G-11965)*
K & S Property Inc ....D 248 573-1600
New Hudson *(G-12059)*
Kraft Power Corporation ....E 989 748-4040
Gaylord *(G-6140)*

MACHINERY & EQPT, INDL, WHOLESALE: Engs & Parts, Air-Cooled

D & S Engine Specialist Inc ....F 248 583-9240
Clawson *(G-3093)*

MACHINERY & EQPT, INDL, WHOLESALE: Food Manufacturing

Pappas Cutlery-Grinding Inc ....G 800 521-0888
Detroit *(G-4506)*

MACHINERY & EQPT, INDL, WHOLESALE: Fuel Injection Systems

Autocam Corporation ....B 616 698-0707
Kentwood *(G-9444)*
Lisi Automotive HI Vol Inc ....F 734 266-6958
Livonia *(G-10285)*

MACHINERY & EQPT, INDL, WHOLESALE: Hydraulic Systems

Behco Inc ....F 586 755-0200
Warren *(G-17729)*
Flodraulic Group Incorporated ....G 734 326-5400
Westland *(G-18371)*
Great Lakes Hydra Corporation ....F 231 258-4338
Kalkaska *(G-9389)*
Gregory M Boese ....F 989 754-2990
Saginaw *(G-14659)*
Hydra-Tech Inc ....G 586 232-4479
Macomb *(G-10604)*
J H Bennett and Company Inc ....E 248 596-5100
Novi *(G-12446)*
Kord Industrial Inc ....G 248 374-8900
Wixom *(G-18694)*
Lube - Power Inc ....D 586 247-6500
Shelby Township *(G-15264)*
Marrel Corporation ....F 616 863-9155
Rockford *(G-14177)*
Mfp Automation Engineering Inc ....D 616 538-5700
Hudsonville *(G-8594)*
Morrell Incorporated ....D 248 373-1600
Auburn Hills *(G-975)*
Wmh Fluidpower Inc ....F 269 327-7011
Portage *(G-13634)*

MACHINERY & EQPT, INDL, WHOLESALE: Indl Machine Parts

Eagle Quest International Ltd ....F 616 850-2630
Spring Lake *(G-15812)*
Electro ARC Manufacturing Co ....E 734 483-4233
Dexter *(G-4741)*
Hti Associates LLC ....E 616 399-5430
Holland *(G-8089)*
Jomat Industries Ltd ....F 586 336-1801
Bruce Twp *(G-2169)*
Kenrie Inc ....F 616 494-3200
Holland *(G-8112)*
Paradigm Engineering Inc ....G 586 776-5910
Roseville *(G-14458)*

MACHINERY & EQPT, INDL, WHOLESALE: Instruments & Cntrl Eqpt

Company	Code	Phone
Medsker Electric Inc	F	248 855-3383
Farmington Hills *(G-5314)*		

MACHINERY & EQPT, INDL, WHOLESALE: Lift Trucks & Parts

Company	Code	Phone
4ever Aluminum Products Inc	F	517 368-0000
Coldwater *(G-3417)*		
Alta Equipment Holdings Inc	E	248 449-6700
Livonia *(G-10112)*		

MACHINERY & EQPT, INDL, WHOLESALE: Machine Tools & Access

Company	Code	Phone
Adaptable Tool Supply LLC	F	248 439-0866
Clawson *(G-3084)*		
All-Fab Corporation	G	269 673-6572
Allegan *(G-145)*		
Antech Tool Inc	F	734 207-3622
Canton *(G-2435)*		
Champion Screw Mch Engrg Inc	F	248 624-4545
Wixom *(G-18632)*		
Clausing Industrial Inc	F	269 345-7155
Kalamazoo *(G-9144)*		
Clausing Industrial Inc	D	269 345-7155
Kalamazoo *(G-9145)*		
Cleary Developments Inc	E	248 588-7011
Madison Heights *(G-10689)*		
E & E Special Products LLC	F	586 978-3377
Warren *(G-17789)*		
Ebinger Manufacturing Company	F	248 486-8880
Brighton *(G-1982)*		
Fluid Systems Engineering Inc	E	586 790-8880
Clinton Township *(G-3242)*		
Fourway Machinery Sales Co	F	517 782-9371
Jackson *(G-8886)*		
Henrob Corporation	D	248 493-3800
New Hudson *(G-12057)*		
Kyocera Unimerco Tooling Inc	E	734 944-4433
Saline *(G-15023)*		
Machine Control Technology	G	517 655-3506
Williamston *(G-18577)*		
Mq Operating Company	E	906 337-1515
Calumet *(G-2412)*		
Peak Edm Inc	G	248 380-0871
Wixom *(G-18729)*		
Press Room Eqp Sls & Svc Co	G	248 334-1880
Pontiac *(G-13410)*		
Punchcraft McHning Tooling LLC	G	586 573-4840
Warren *(G-17987)*		
Schutte Corporation	F	517 782-3600
Jackson *(G-9007)*		
South Park Sales & Mfg Inc	G	313 381-7579
Dearborn *(G-3899)*		
Teknikut Corporation	G	586 778-7150
Canton *(G-2534)*		
U S Group Inc	G	313 372-7900
Rochester Hills *(G-14135)*		
Viscount Equipment Co Inc	G	586 293-5900
Hazel Park *(G-7847)*		

MACHINERY & EQPT, INDL, WHOLESALE: Machine Tools & Metalwork

Company	Code	Phone
Aero Grinding Inc	D	586 774-6450
Roseville *(G-14371)*		
Arm Tooling Systems Inc	F	586 759-5677
Warren *(G-17712)*		
Die Cast Press Mfg Co Inc	E	269 657-6060
Paw Paw *(G-12947)*		
Hougen Manufacturing Inc	C	810 635-7111
Swartz Creek *(G-16355)*		
Letts Industries Inc	G	313 579-1100
Detroit *(G-4392)*		
Micro EDM Co LLC	G	989 872-4306
Cass City *(G-2619)*		
Roberts Sinto Corporation	D	517 371-2460
Lansing *(G-9787)*		
Walther Trowal LLC	F	616 455-8940
Byron Center *(G-2301)*		
Wolverine Special Tool Inc	E	616 791-1027
Grand Rapids *(G-7348)*		

MACHINERY & EQPT, INDL, WHOLESALE: Measure/Test, Electric

Company	Code	Phone
Analytical Process Systems Inc	E	248 393-0700
Auburn Hills *(G-784)*		
Mycrona Inc	F	734 453-9348
Plymouth *(G-13251)*		

MACHINERY & EQPT, INDL, WHOLESALE: Metal Refining

Company	Code	Phone
Ied Inc	G	231 728-9154
Muskegon *(G-11837)*		

MACHINERY & EQPT, INDL, WHOLESALE: Paint Spray

Company	Code	Phone
Herkules Equipment Corporation	E	248 960-7100
Commerce Township *(G-3536)*		
Sames Kremlin Inc	C	734 979-0100
Plymouth *(G-13292)*		
Sames Kremlin Inc	G	734 979-0100
Plymouth *(G-13293)*		

MACHINERY & EQPT, INDL, WHOLESALE: Petroleum Industry

Company	Code	Phone
Lube-Tech Inc	G	269 329-1269
Portage *(G-13580)*		

MACHINERY & EQPT, INDL, WHOLESALE: Plastic Prdts Machinery

Company	Code	Phone
Gt Plastics & Equipment LLC	F	616 678-7445
Kent City *(G-9432)*		

MACHINERY & EQPT, INDL, WHOLESALE: Pneumatic Tools

Company	Code	Phone
REO Hydraulic & Mfg Inc	F	313 891-2244
Detroit *(G-4566)*		

MACHINERY & EQPT, INDL, WHOLESALE: Processing & Packaging

Company	Code	Phone
Mark-Pack Inc	E	616 837-5400
Coopersville *(G-3691)*		
Oliver Healthcare Packaging Co	C	616 456-7711
Grand Rapids *(G-7057)*		
Unified Equipment Systems Inc	G	586 307-3770
Clinton Township *(G-3382)*		

MACHINERY & EQPT, INDL, WHOLESALE: Recycling

Company	Code	Phone
Libra Industries Inc Michigan	G	517 787-5675
Jackson *(G-8935)*		

MACHINERY & EQPT, INDL, WHOLESALE: Robots

Company	Code	Phone
Innovation Tech LLC	F	248 797-2686
Wixom *(G-18685)*		
National Advnced Mblity Cnsrti	G	734 205-5920
Ann Arbor *(G-590)*		
Realm	G	313 706-4401
Wayne *(G-18234)*		

MACHINERY & EQPT, INDL, WHOLESALE: Safety Eqpt

Company	Code	Phone
Abretec Group LLC	E	248 591-4000
Royal Oak *(G-14503)*		
Accurate Safety Distrs Inc	G	989 695-6446
Freeland *(G-6017)*		
C & C Enterprises Inc	G	989 772-5095
Mount Pleasant *(G-11689)*		

MACHINERY & EQPT, INDL, WHOLESALE: Sawmill

Company	Code	Phone
Menominee Saw and Supply Co	E	906 863-2609
Menominee *(G-11248)*		

MACHINERY & EQPT, INDL, WHOLESALE: Textile

Company	Code	Phone
Oerlikon Metco (us) Inc	E	248 288-0027
Troy *(G-17287)*		

MACHINERY & EQPT, INDL, WHOLESALE: Tool & Die Makers

Company	Code	Phone
Eagle Industrial Group Inc	E	616 647-9904
Comstock Park *(G-3605)*		

MACHINERY & EQPT, INDL, WHOLESALE: Water Pumps

Company	Code	Phone
Kerr Pump and Supply Inc	E	248 543-3880
Oak Park *(G-12621)*		
Sales Driven Services LLC	G	586 854-9494
Rochester *(G-13926)*		

MACHINERY & EQPT, WHOLESALE: Blades, Graders, Scrapers, Etc

Company	Code	Phone
Trynex International LLC	F	248 586-3500
Madison Heights *(G-10848)*		

MACHINERY & EQPT, WHOLESALE: Construction & Mining, Ladders

Company	Code	Phone
Michigan Ladder Company LLC	F	734 482-5946
Ypsilanti *(G-18967)*		

MACHINERY & EQPT, WHOLESALE: Construction & Mining, Pavers

Company	Code	Phone
Petter Investments Inc	F	269 637-1997
South Haven *(G-15411)*		

MACHINERY & EQPT, WHOLESALE: Construction, General

Company	Code	Phone
Boomer Company	E	313 832-5050
Detroit *(G-4063)*		
Cheap Electric Contractors Co	G	734 205-9591
Ann Arbor *(G-422)*		
Cheap Electric Contractors Co	G	734 452-1964
Livonia *(G-10155)*		
Cheap Electric Contractors Co	G	734 205-9596
Ann Arbor *(G-423)*		
Cheap Electric Contractors Co	G	734 286-9165
Southgate *(G-15749)*		
Eagle Industrial Group Inc	E	616 647-9904
Comstock Park *(G-3605)*		
Electric Contractors Company	G	734 205-9594
Ann Arbor *(G-469)*		
Hines Corporation	F	231 799-6240
Norton Shores *(G-12348)*		

MACHINERY & EQPT, WHOLESALE: Logging & Forestry

Company	Code	Phone
Bandit Industries Inc	B	989 561-2270
Remus *(G-13813)*		
James L Miller	G	989 539-5540
Harrison *(G-7679)*		

MACHINERY & EQPT, WHOLESALE: Masonry

Company	Code	Phone
E M I Construction Products	F	616 392-7207
Holland *(G-8020)*		

MACHINERY & EQPT, WHOLESALE: Oil Field Eqpt

Company	Code	Phone
Great Lakes Wellhead Inc	G	231 943-9100
Grawn *(G-7451)*		

MACHINERY & EQPT: Farm

Company	Code	Phone
A & B Packing Equipment Inc	C	269 539-4700
Lawrence *(G-9980)*		
A G Case LLC	G	586 791-0125
Clinton Township *(G-3145)*		
Advanced Drainage Systems Inc	G	989 723-5208
Owosso *(G-12819)*		
Advanced Farm Equipment LLC	F	989 268-5711
Vestaburg *(G-17593)*		
Agritek Industries Inc	D	616 786-9200
Holland *(G-7958)*		
Bader & Co	F	810 648-2404
Sandusky *(G-15055)*		
Best Harvest	G	888 947-6226
Bay City *(G-1333)*		
Big Foot Manufacturing Co	E	231 775-5588
Cadillac *(G-2315)*		
Boxer Equipment/Morbark Inc	G	989 866-2381
Winn *(G-18589)*		

MACHINERY & EQPT: Farm

Case Quality Upkeep LLC .... G 231 233-8013
  Pentwater (G-12971)
CPM Acquisition Corp .... G 231 947-6400
  Traverse City (G-16663)
Dad and Sons Farming LLC .... G 517 719-2048
  Vermontville (G-17587)
Diamond Moba Americas Inc .... C 248 476-7100
  Farmington Hills (G-5216)
Eagle Group II Ltd .... E 616 754-7777
  Greenville (G-7483)
Express Welding Inc .... G 906 786-8808
  Escanaba (G-5071)
Gillisons Var Fabrication Inc .... E 231 882-5921
  Benzonia (G-1614)
Heath Manufacturing Company .... E 616 997-8181
  Coopersville (G-3688)
Hy Capacity Inc .... G 616 558-5690
  Brighton (G-2012)
Local Bsket Case LLC - Rckford .... G 616 884-0749
  Rockford (G-14175)
Mensch Manufacturing LLC .... F 269 945-5300
  Hastings (G-7804)
Mensch Mfg Mar Div Inc .... E 269 945-5300
  Hastings (G-7805)
Michigan AG Services Inc .... F 616 374-8803
  Lake Odessa (G-9577)
Morbark LLC .... B 989 866-2381
  Winn (G-18590)
National Case Corp .... G 586 803-3245
  Shelby Township (G-15287)
Phil Brown Welding Corporation .... F 616 784-3046
  Conklin (G-3662)
Sprayerusa Inc .... G 800 253-4642
  Lowell (G-10516)
Steiner Tractor Parts Inc .... E 810 621-3000
  Lennon (G-9996)
Stephens Pipe & Steel LLC .... E 616 248-3433
  Grand Rapids (G-7226)
Superior Attachment Inc .... G 906 864-1708
  Menominee (G-11261)
Tindall Packaging Inc .... G 269 649-1163
  Portage (G-13626)
Ubly Bean Knife Mfg Inc .... G 231 723-3244
  Manistee (G-10914)

MACHINERY & EQPT: Gas Producers, Generators/Other Rltd Eqpt

Global Tooling Systems LLC .... B 586 726-0500
  Macomb (G-10599)
Plamondon Oil Co Inc .... G 231 256-9261
  Lake Leelanau (G-9564)
Polk Gas Producer LLC .... G 734 913-2970
  Ann Arbor (G-613)

MACHINERY & EQPT: Liquid Automation

AA Anderson & Co Inc .... E 248 476-7782
  Plymouth (G-13110)
Arrow Automation and Engrg Inc .... F 248 660-1520
  Auburn Hills (G-797)
Atlas Technologies Inc .... G 810 629-6663
  Fenton (G-5452)
Avl North Amer Corp Svcs Inc .... A 734 414-9600
  Plymouth (G-13131)
Comau Inc .... D 248 219-0756
  Southfield (G-15531)
Dispense Technologies LLC .... G 248 486-6244
  Brighton (G-1975)
Distinctive Mfg Group LLC .... F 616 953-8999
  Zeeland (G-19015)
Gr Tooling & Automation Inc .... F 616 299-1521
  Comstock Park (G-3609)
Inovatech Automation Inc .... F 586 210-9010
  Macomb (G-10606)
Terrell Manufacturing Svcs Inc .... F 231 788-2000
  Muskegon (G-11930)

MACHINERY & EQPT: Metal Finishing, Plating Etc

Ctmf Inc .... F 734 482-3086
  Ypsilanti (G-18937)
Dipsol of America Inc .... E 734 367-0530
  Livonia (G-10186)
Durr Inc .... G 734 459-6800
  Southfield (G-15544)
Durr Systems Inc .... B 248 450-2000
  Southfield (G-15545)
Durr Systems Inc .... F 248 745-8500
  Southfield (G-15546)

Fanuc America Corporation .... B 248 377-7000
  Rochester Hills (G-14009)
George Koch Sons LLC .... E 248 237-1100
  Rochester Hills (G-14024)
Grav Co LLC .... F 269 651-5467
  Sturgis (G-16290)
Gravel Flow Inc .... G 269 651-5467
  Sturgis (G-16291)
Ied Inc .... G 231 728-9154
  Muskegon (G-11837)
Kolene Corporation .... F 586 771-1200
  Roseville (G-14430)
Met-L-Tec LLC .... E 734 847-7004
  Temperance (G-16540)
Morrell Incorporated .... D 248 373-1600
  Auburn Hills (G-975)
Mp Tool & Engineering Company .... E 586 772-7730
  Roseville (G-14448)
Omega Industries Michigan LLC .... G 616 460-0500
  Grand Rapids (G-7058)
Tks Industrial Company .... E 248 786-5000
  Troy (G-17393)
US Metals LLC .... F 586 915-2885
  Warren (G-18049)
Z-Brite Metal Finishing Inc .... F 269 422-2191
  Stevensville (G-16270)

MACHINERY & EQPT: Metal Pickling

Pgp Corp .... D 313 291-7500
  Taylor (G-16457)

MACHINERY & EQPT: Vibratory Parts Handling Eqpt

Great Lakes Allied LLC .... G 231 924-5794
  White Cloud (G-18441)
Rosler Metal Finishing USA LLC .... E 269 441-3000
  Battle Creek (G-1290)

MACHINERY BASES

A&G Corporate Holdings LLC .... G 734 513-3488
  Livonia (G-10094)
Great Lakes Laser Dynamics Inc .... D 616 892-7070
  Allendale (G-220)
Henshaw Inc .... D 586 752-0700
  Armada (G-736)
Johnson Systems Inc .... G 616 455-1900
  Caledonia (G-2386)
Prototech Laser Inc .... F 586 598-6900
  Chesterfield (G-2934)
True Die Inc .... G 616 772-6360
  Zeeland (G-19084)
Unisorb Inc .... E 517 764-6060
  Michigan Center (G-11297)
Vel-Kal Manufacturing Inc .... F 269 344-1204
  Galesburg (G-6086)

MACHINERY, EQPT & SUPPLIES: Parking Facility

Perfected Grave Vault Co .... G 616 243-3375
  Grand Rapids (G-7078)
Traffic Sfety Ctrl Systems Inc .... E 248 348-0570
  Wixom (G-18775)

MACHINERY, FOOD PRDTS: Cutting, Chopping, Grinding, Mixing

Carb-A-Tron Tool Co .... G 517 782-2249
  Jackson (G-8834)
Whirlpool Corporation .... G 800 541-6390
  Benton Harbor (G-1604)

MACHINERY, FOOD PRDTS: Dairy & Milk

Graf Acres LLC .... G 517 851-8693
  Stockbridge (G-16275)
J J Steel Inc .... E 269 964-0474
  Battle Creek (G-1242)

MACHINERY, FOOD PRDTS: Food Processing, Smokers

Baker Perkins Inc .... D 616 784-3111
  Grand Rapids (G-6492)

MACHINERY, FOOD PRDTS: Grinders, Commercial

Pappas Cutlery-Grinding Inc .... G 800 521-0888
  Detroit (G-4506)

MACHINERY, FOOD PRDTS: Juice Extractors, Fruit & Veg, Comm

Dunkley International Inc .... C 269 343-5583
  Kalamazoo (G-9174)
Precision Extraction Corp .... F 855 420-0020
  Troy (G-17311)

MACHINERY, FOOD PRDTS: Ovens, Bakery

Middleby Corporation .... C 906 863-4401
  Menominee (G-11251)

MACHINERY, FOOD PRDTS: Processing, Fish & Shellfish

Pisces Fish Machinery Inc .... E 906 789-1636
  Gladstone (G-6186)

MACHINERY, FOOD PRDTS: Roasting, Coffee, Peanut, Etc.

Duke De Jong LLC .... G 734 403-1708
  Taylor (G-16407)
Infusco Coffee Roasters LLC .... G 269 213-5282
  Sawyer (G-15109)
Peanut Shop Inc .... G 517 374-0008
  Lansing (G-9879)

MACHINERY, FOOD PRDTS: Slicers, Commercial

Foodtools Consolidated Inc .... E 269 637-9969
  South Haven (G-15405)

MACHINERY, LUBRICATION: Automatic

Advance Products Corporation .... E 269 849-1000
  Benton Harbor (G-1527)
Positech Inc .... G 616 949-4024
  Grand Rapids (G-7094)

MACHINERY, MAILING: Postage Meters

Pitney Bowes Inc .... G 203 356-5000
  South Lyon (G-15454)
Pitney Bowes Inc .... E 517 393-4101
  Lansing (G-9881)
Pitney Bowes Inc .... D 616 285-9590
  Grand Rapids (G-7088)

MACHINERY, METALWORKING: Assembly, Including Robotic

Ace & 1 Logistics LLC .... G 601 335-3625
  Shelby Township (G-15163)
Allied Tool and Machine Co .... E 989 755-5384
  Saginaw (G-14604)
Apollo Seiko Ltd .... F 269 465-3400
  Bridgman (G-1920)
Atlas Technologies LLC .... D 810 629-6663
  Fenton (G-5451)
Auto/Con Corp .... D 586 791-7474
  Fraser (G-5897)
Burton Industries Inc .... E 906 932-5970
  Ironwood (G-8758)
Dane Systems LLC .... D 269 465-3263
  Stevensville (G-16245)
Das Group Inc .... F 248 670-2718
  Royal Oak (G-14529)
Diamond Automation Ltd .... G 734 838-7138
  Livonia (G-10184)
Dominion Tech Group Inc .... C 586 773-3303
  Roseville (G-14402)
Duo Robotic Solutions Inc .... F 586 883-7559
  Shelby Township (G-15214)
Esys Automation LLC .... C 248 484-9927
  Auburn Hills (G-881)
Esys Automation LLC .... E 284 484-9724
  Pontiac (G-13370)
Esys Automation LLC .... E 248 484-9702
  Sterling Heights (G-16005)
Fives Cinetic Corp .... C 248 477-0800
  Farmington Hills (G-5244)

PRODUCT SECTION

MACHINERY, WOODWORKING: Cabinet Makers'

Ideal Tool Inc .... F 989 893-8336
  Bay City *(G-1366)*
Innovation Tech LLC .... F 248 797-2686
  Wixom *(G-18685)*
J W Froehlich Inc .... G 586 580-0025
  Sterling Heights *(G-16053)*
J W Holdings Inc .... E 616 530-9889
  Grand Rapids *(G-6858)*
JR Automation Tech LLC .... C 616 399-2168
  Holland *(G-8104)*
Jr Technology Group LLC .... C 616 399-2168
  Holland *(G-8105)*
Kuka Assembly and Test Corp .... C 989 220-3088
  Saginaw *(G-14680)*
Kuka Systems North America LLC .... B 586 795-2000
  Sterling Heights *(G-16066)*
Kuka Systems North America LLC .... G 586 726-4300
  Shelby Township *(G-15251)*
Kuka US Holdings Company LLC .... D 586 795-2000
  Sterling Heights *(G-16067)*
L & H Diversified Mfg USA LLC .... G 586 615-4873
  Shelby Township *(G-15252)*
Lab Tool and Engineering Corp .... F 517 750-4131
  Spring Arbor *(G-15793)*
Letnan Industries Inc .... E 586 726-1155
  Sterling Heights *(G-16072)*
Lomar Machine & Tool Co .... E 517 563-8136
  Horton *(G-8374)*
Mark One Corporation .... D 989 732-2427
  Gaylord *(G-6145)*
National Advnced Mblity Cnsrti .... G 734 205-5920
  Ann Arbor *(G-590)*
Norgren Automtn Solutions LLC .... C 734 429-4989
  Saline *(G-15030)*
Novi Precision Products Inc .... E 810 227-1024
  Brighton *(G-2044)*
Pro-Tech Machine Inc .... E 810 743-1854
  Burton *(G-2243)*
Prosys Industries Inc .... D 734 207-3710
  Canton *(G-2515)*
Rock Tool & Machine Co Inc .... E 734 455-9840
  Plymouth *(G-13289)*
SKW Automation Inc .... G 517 563-8288
  Hanover *(G-7626)*
Smartcoast LLC .... G 231 571-2020
  Grand Rapids *(G-7202)*
Spen-Tech Machine Engrg Corp .... D 810 275-6800
  Flint *(G-5765)*
Standard Automation LLC .... E 248 227-6964
  Rochester Hills *(G-14118)*
TA Systems Inc .... D 248 656-5150
  Rochester Hills *(G-14123)*
Tarpon Automation & Design Co .... E 586 774-8020
  Clinton Township *(G-3374)*
Toman Industries Inc .... G 734 289-1393
  Monroe *(G-11585)*
Utica Body & Assembly Inc .... E 586 726-4330
  Troy *(G-17418)*
Utica Enterprises Inc .... C 586 726-4300
  Troy *(G-17419)*
Utica International Inc .... C 586 726-4330
  Troy *(G-17420)*
Utica Products Inc .... G 586 726-4300
  Troy *(G-17421)*
Wright-K Technology Inc .... E 989 752-2588
  Saginaw *(G-14795)*

MACHINERY, METALWORKING: Coil Winding, For Springs

US Metals LLC .... F 586 915-2885
  Warren *(G-18049)*

MACHINERY, METALWORKING: Coiling

Feed - Lease Corp .... E 248 377-0000
  Auburn Hills *(G-896)*
Perfecto Industries Inc .... E 989 732-2941
  Gaylord *(G-6154)*
Sesco Inc .... D 313 843-7710
  Detroit *(G-4587)*

MACHINERY, METALWORKING: Cutting & Slitting

Bay Plastics Machinery Co LLC .... E 989 671-9630
  Bay City *(G-1330)*

MACHINERY, METALWORKING: Rotary Slitters, Metalworking

Van-Mark Products Corporation .... E 248 478-1200
  Farmington Hills *(G-5408)*

MACHINERY, OFFICE: Paper Handling

Central Michigan Engravers .... G 517 485-5865
  Lansing *(G-9679)*

MACHINERY, PACKAGING: Carton Packing

Elopak Inc .... E 248 486-4600
  Wixom *(G-18655)*

MACHINERY, PACKAGING: Packing & Wrapping

Kalamazoo Packg Systems LLC .... F 616 534-2600
  Wyoming *(G-18888)*
RED Stamp Inc .... E 616 878-7771
  Grand Rapids *(G-7147)*

MACHINERY, PACKAGING: Vacuum

Ameri-Serv Group .... F 734 426-9700
  Troy *(G-16931)*
Industrial Model Inc .... G 586 254-0450
  Auburn Hills *(G-939)*

MACHINERY, PACKAGING: Wrapping

Highlight Industries Inc .... D 616 531-2464
  Wyoming *(G-18884)*

MACHINERY, PAPER INDUSTRY: Coating & Finishing

Euclid Coating Systems Inc .... F 989 922-4789
  Bay City *(G-1351)*

MACHINERY, PAPER INDUSTRY: Converting, Die Cutting & Stampng

Challenge Machinery Company .... E 231 799-8484
  Norton Shores *(G-12285)*
S & W Holdings Ltd .... E 248 723-2870
  Birmingham *(G-1748)*

MACHINERY, PAPER INDUSTRY: Cutting

Graphic Art Service & Supply .... G 810 229-4700
  Brighton *(G-2004)*
Graphic Arts Service & Sup Inc .... F 616 698-9300
  Grand Rapids *(G-6781)*

MACHINERY, PAPER INDUSTRY: Paper Mill, Plating, Etc

Hycorr LLC .... F 269 381-6349
  Kalamazoo *(G-9219)*

MACHINERY, PRINTING TRADES: Bookbinding Machinery

F P Rosback Co .... E 269 983-2582
  Saint Joseph *(G-14930)*

MACHINERY, PRINTING TRADES: Copy Holders

M & M Typewriter Service Inc .... G 734 995-4033
  Ann Arbor *(G-558)*

MACHINERY, PRINTING TRADES: Plates, Engravers' Metal

Lavalier Corp .... E 248 616-8880
  Troy *(G-17205)*

MACHINERY, PRINTING TRADES: Printing Trade Parts & Attchts

Just Right Duplications LLC .... F 313 655-3555
  Oak Park *(G-12619)*
Xyresic LLC .... G 906 281-0021
  Jackson *(G-9039)*

MACHINERY, PRINTING TRADES: Type & Type Making

Varn International Inc .... G 734 781-4600
  Livonia *(G-10458)*

MACHINERY, PRINTING TRADES: Type Casting, Founding/Melting

Haynie and Hess Realty Co LLC .... F 586 296-2750
  Fraser *(G-5933)*

MACHINERY, SERVICING: Coin-Operated, Exc Dry Clean & Laundry

1st Rate Office Solutions LLC .... G 989 544-4009
  Clare *(G-2971)*
Mdla Inc .... F 248 643-0807
  Troy *(G-17242)*

MACHINERY, SEWING: Sewing & Hat & Zipper Making

Ace Controls Inc .... C 248 476-0213
  Farmington Hills *(G-5158)*
Knight Industries Inc .... G 248 377-4950
  Auburn Hills *(G-954)*

MACHINERY, TEXTILE: Bleaching

Belding Bleacher Erectors Inc .... G 616 794-3126
  Greenville *(G-7476)*

MACHINERY, TEXTILE: Embroidery

All American Embroidery Inc .... F 734 421-9292
  Livonia *(G-10108)*
Fabri-Tech Inc .... E 616 662-0150
  Jenison *(G-9055)*
Modern Monogram .... G 248 792-6266
  Bloomfield Hills *(G-1839)*
Needles N Pins Inc .... G 734 459-0625
  Plymouth *(G-13253)*
Tri-State Technical Services .... G 517 563-8743
  Hanover *(G-7627)*

MACHINERY, TEXTILE: Heddles, Wire, For Loom Harnesses

Orri Corp .... F 248 618-1104
  Waterford *(G-18145)*

MACHINERY, TEXTILE: Opening

Bpg International Fin Co LLC .... G 616 855-1480
  Ada *(G-12)*

MACHINERY, TEXTILE: Printing

Becmar Corp .... G 616 675-7479
  Bailey *(G-1118)*

MACHINERY, TEXTILE: Silk Screens

Carry-All Products Inc .... G 616 399-8080
  Holland *(G-7991)*
Craft Press Printing Inc .... G 269 683-9694
  Niles *(G-12121)*

MACHINERY, TEXTILE: Thread Making Or Spinning

Superior Threading Inc .... F 989 729-1160
  Owosso *(G-12859)*

MACHINERY, WOODWORKING: Bandsaws

Coxline Inc .... E 269 345-1132
  Kalamazoo *(G-9157)*

MACHINERY, WOODWORKING: Cabinet Makers'

Moda Manufacturing LLC .... F 586 204-5120
  Farmington Hills *(G-5325)*
R J Flood Professional Co .... G 269 930-3608
  Stevensville *(G-16263)*

Employee Codes: A=Over 500 employees, B=251-500
C=101-250, D=51-100, E=20-50, F=10-19, G=3-9

MACHINERY, WOODWORKING: Furniture Makers

Northern Woodcrafters ....G...... 989 348-2553
Frederic *(G-6016)*

MACHINERY, WOODWORKING: Pattern Makers'

Bespro Pattern Inc ....E...... 586 268-6970
Madison Heights *(G-10681)*
Crescent Casting Inc ....F...... 248 541-1052
Oak Park *(G-12600)*
Northwest Pattern Company ....G...... 248 477-7070
Farmington Hills *(G-5335)*
Saginaw Industries LLC ....F...... 989 752-5514
Saginaw *(G-14746)*
Wing Pattern Inc ....G...... 248 588-1121
Sterling Heights *(G-16232)*

MACHINERY, WOODWORKING: Planers

Straitoplane Inc ....G...... 616 997-2211
Coopersville *(G-3697)*

MACHINERY/EQPT, INDL, WHOL: Cleaning, High Press, Sand/Steam

H & R Industries Inc ....F...... 616 247-1165
Grand Rapids *(G-6798)*
Kmi Cleaning Solutions Inc ....F...... 269 964-2557
Battle Creek *(G-1263)*

MACHINERY: Ammunition & Explosives Loading

Genix LLC ....C...... 248 761-3030
West Bloomfield *(G-18284)*

MACHINERY: Assembly, Exc Metalworking

+vantage Corporation ....E...... 734 432-5055
Livonia *(G-10088)*
Airtificial Intelligent Robots ....G...... 989 799-6669
Saginaw *(G-14602)*
Asw Amerca Inc ....G...... 248 957-9638
Farmington Hills *(G-5174)*
Ats Assembly and Test Inc ....F...... 937 222-3030
Wixom *(G-18612)*
Auto/Con Services LLC ....G...... 586 791-7474
Fraser *(G-5898)*
Baird Investments LLC ....G...... 586 665-0154
Sterling Heights *(G-15943)*
Bayshore Custom Assembly LLC ....G...... 616 396-5502
Holland *(G-7971)*
Bme Inc ....G...... 810 937-2974
Port Huron *(G-13461)*
Change Parts Incorporated ....E...... 231 845-5107
Ludington *(G-10531)*
Craft Industries Inc ....B...... 586 726-4300
Shelby Township *(G-15197)*
Esirpal Inc ....G...... 586 337-7848
Macomb *(G-10592)*
Fec Inc ....F...... 586 580-2622
Shelby Township *(G-15225)*
General Electric Company ....F...... 616 676-0870
Ada *(G-19)*
Greatech Integration USA Inc ......G...... 734 673-5985
Wixom *(G-18670)*
Haosen Automation N Amer Inc ...G...... 248 556-6398
Auburn Hills *(G-923)*
Harvey S Freeman ....G...... 248 852-2222
West Bloomfield *(G-18287)*
Haven Innovation Inc ....E...... 616 935-1040
Grand Haven *(G-6315)*
Hirotec America Inc ....B...... 248 836-5100
Auburn Hills *(G-927)*
Hot Melt Technologies Inc ....E...... 248 853-2011
Rochester Hills *(G-14034)*
Independent Mfg Solutions Corp ...E...... 248 960-3550
Wixom *(G-18684)*
Infra Corporation ....F...... 248 623-0400
Waterford *(G-18129)*
Metalform Industries LLC ....G...... 248 462-0056
Shelby Township *(G-15274)*
Mhr Inc ....F...... 616 394-0191
Holland *(G-8146)*
Northern Processes & Sales LLC ....G...... 248 669-3918
Wixom *(G-18723)*
Puritan Automation LLC ....F...... 248 668-1114
Wixom *(G-18737)*

Sanyo Machine America Corp ....D...... 248 651-5911
Rochester Hills *(G-14108)*
Schap Specialty Machine Inc ....F...... 616 846-6530
Spring Lake *(G-15850)*
Service Tectonics Inc ....E...... 517 263-0758
Adrian *(G-96)*
SMS Group Inc ....D...... 734 246-8230
Taylor *(G-16475)*
Superior Design & Mfg ....F...... 810 678-3950
Metamora *(G-11287)*
Tool North Inc ....E...... 231 941-1150
Traverse City *(G-16861)*
Volos Tube Form Inc ....E...... 586 416-3600
Macomb *(G-10650)*
Wartrom Machine Systems Inc ....E...... 586 469-1915
Clinton Township *(G-3387)*
West Mich Flcking Assembly LLC ....E...... 269 639-1634
Grand Rapids *(G-7331)*
Whites Bridge Tooling Inc ....E...... 616 897-4151
Lowell *(G-10522)*
Wolverine Water Works Inc ....G...... 248 673-4310
Waterford *(G-18176)*
Youngtronics LLC ....G...... 248 896-5790
Wixom *(G-18793)*

MACHINERY: Automotive Maintenance

AGC Grand Haven LLC ....G...... 616 842-1820
Grand Haven *(G-6271)*
Alliance Automation LLC ....F...... 810 953-9539
Flint *(G-5642)*
B & J Tool Services Inc ....F...... 810 629-8577
Fenton *(G-5455)*
Berghof Group North Amer Inc ....F...... 313 720-6884
Troy *(G-16974)*
Burke E Porter Machinery Co ....C...... 616 234-1200
Grand Rapids *(G-6535)*
Burton Industries Inc ....E...... 906 932-5970
Ironwood *(G-8758)*
Busche Southfield Inc ....C...... 248 357-5180
Southfield *(G-15513)*
Considine Sales & Marketing ....G...... 248 889-7887
Highland *(G-7889)*
Drew Technologies Inc ....F...... 734 222-5228
Ann Arbor *(G-458)*
Esoc Inc ....F...... 248 624-7992
Wixom *(G-18658)*
Liberty Fabricators Inc ....F...... 810 877-7117
Flint *(G-5724)*
RB Oil Enterprises LLC ....G...... 734 354-0700
Plymouth *(G-13277)*
Rnj Services Inc ....F...... 906 786-0585
Escanaba *(G-5096)*
Stec Usa Inc ....F...... 248 307-1440
Madison Heights *(G-10837)*
Superior Automotive Eqp Inc ....G...... 231 829-9902
Leroy *(G-10012)*

MACHINERY: Automotive Related

313 Industries Inc ....F...... 313 338-9700
Warren *(G-17677)*
Air-Hydraulics Inc ....F...... 517 787-9444
Jackson *(G-8806)*
Aisin Technical Ctr Amer Inc ....D...... 734 453-5551
Northville *(G-12196)*
Amerivet Engineering LLC ....G...... 269 751-9092
Hamilton *(G-7596)*
AMI Industries Inc ....D...... 989 786-3755
Lewiston *(G-10017)*
AMI Industries Inc ....G...... 989 786-3755
Sault Sainte Marie *(G-15086)*
Automotive Component Mfg ....G...... 705 549-7406
Sterling Heights *(G-15937)*
Automotive Technology LLC ....C...... 586 446-7000
Sterling Heights *(G-15938)*
Avancez LLC ....D...... 313 404-1962
Hazel Park *(G-7820)*
Best Mfg Tooling Solutions Ltd ....G...... 616 877-0504
Wayland *(G-18190)*
CD Tool & Gage ....F...... 616 682-1111
Ada *(G-14)*
Centracore LLC ....F...... 586 776-5700
Saint Clair *(G-14818)*
Cfe Racing Products Inc ....G...... 586 773-6310
Eastpointe *(G-4931)*
Corvac Composites LLC ....C...... 616 281-2430
Grand Rapids *(G-6608)*
Corvac Composites LLC ....E...... 616 281-4028
Kentwood *(G-9449)*
Creative Performance Racg LLC ....G...... 248 250-6187
Troy *(G-17032)*

D & F Corporation ....D...... 586 254-5300
Sterling Heights *(G-15977)*
Dayco Products LLC ....G...... 989 775-0689
Mount Pleasant *(G-11694)*
Dayco Products LLC ....G...... 517 439-0689
Hillsdale *(G-7931)*
Detroit Tech Innovation LLC ....G...... 734 259-4168
Redford *(G-13731)*
Erae AMS USA Manufacturing LLC ....F...... 314 600-3434
Pontiac *(G-13369)*
Extol Inc ....D...... 616 741-0231
Zeeland *(G-19019)*
Gd Enterprises LLC ....G...... 248 486-9800
Brighton *(G-1997)*
Generation Tool Inc ....G...... 734 641-6937
Westland *(G-18374)*
Genix LLC ....F...... 248 419-0231
Sterling Heights *(G-16029)*
Global Strgc Sup Solutions LLC ....D...... 734 525-9100
Livonia *(G-10226)*
H A Eckhart & Associates Inc ......E...... 517 321-7700
Lansing *(G-9702)*
HP Pelzer Auto Systems Inc ....B...... 810 987-4444
Port Huron *(G-13483)*
Hti Cybernetics Inc ....E...... 586 826-8346
Sterling Heights *(G-16043)*
Ims/Chinatool Jv LLC ....F...... 734 466-5151
Livonia *(G-10247)*
Iroquois Assembly Systems Inc ....F...... 586 771-5734
Warren *(G-17872)*
J H P Inc ....G...... 248 588-0110
Madison Heights *(G-10750)*
JB Autotech LLC ....E...... 734 838-3963
Livonia *(G-10258)*
Jvis - Usa LLC ....B...... 586 803-6056
Clinton Township *(G-3267)*
Kolco Industries Inc ....G...... 248 486-1690
South Lyon *(G-15442)*
Mag Automotive LLC ....C...... 586 446-7000
Sterling Heights *(G-16081)*
Mag Automotive LLC ....F...... 586 446-7000
Port Huron *(G-13498)*
Mountain Machine LLC ....F...... 734 480-2200
Van Buren Twp *(G-17542)*
New-Matic Industries Inc ....G...... 586 415-9801
Fraser *(G-5969)*
Nyx LLC ....D...... 734 464-0800
Livonia *(G-10346)*
Oxmaster Inc ....G...... 810 987-7600
Port Huron *(G-13512)*
Purem Novi Inc ....C...... 810 225-4582
Brighton *(G-2058)*
Race Ramps LLC ....F...... 866 464-2788
Escanaba *(G-5094)*
Royal Design & Manufacturing ....D...... 248 588-0110
Madison Heights *(G-10821)*
Sarns Industries Inc ....E...... 586 463-5829
Harrison Twp *(G-7739)*
Schneider National Inc ....F...... 810 636-2220
Goodrich *(G-6227)*
SGC Industries Inc ....G...... 586 293-5260
Fraser *(G-5992)*
Sure Solutions Corporation ....G...... 248 674-7210
Auburn Hills *(G-1042)*
Technology & Manufacturing Inc ....G...... 248 755-1444
Milford *(G-11492)*
Thomas-Ward Systems LLC ....G...... 734 929-0644
Ann Arbor *(G-689)*
Van-Rob USA Holdings ....E...... 517 423-2400
Tecumseh *(G-16521)*
W G Benjey Inc ....F...... 989 356-0016
Alpena *(G-327)*
Webasto Convertibles USA Inc ....E...... 734 582-5900
Rochester Hills *(G-14143)*
Wirtz Manufacturing Co Inc ....D...... 810 987-7600
Port Huron *(G-13540)*
Wolverine Advanced Mtls LLC ......E...... 313 749-6100
Dearborn *(G-3916)*

MACHINERY: Blasting, Electrical

Rvi Management Inc ....G...... 580 531-5826
Okemos *(G-12684)*

MACHINERY: Centrifugal

Centrum Force Fabrication LLC ....G...... 517 857-4774
Ann Arbor *(G-420)*
Chip Systems International ....F...... 269 626-8000
Scotts *(G-15130)*

PRODUCT SECTION

MACHINERY: Concrete Prdts

Besser Company .... B .. 989 354-4111
  Alpena *(G-284)*
Blockmatic Inc .... G ... 269 683-1655
  Niles *(G-12113)*
Williams Form Engineering Corp .... D .. 616 866-0815
  Belmont *(G-1521)*

MACHINERY: Construction

Airman Inc .... G ... 248 926-1409
  Wixom *(G-18602)*
Alta Construction Eqp LLC .... D .. 248 356-5200
  New Hudson *(G-12041)*
Arcosa Epi LLC .... E ... 517 676-8800
  Mason *(G-11116)*
Arcosa Shoring Products Inc .... E ... 800 292-1225
  Lansing *(G-9673)*
B&P Littleford LLC .... E ... 989 757-1300
  Saginaw *(G-14608)*
Blackline Bear LLC .... G ... 616 291-1521
  Norton Shores *(G-12279)*
Bme Inc .... G ... 810 937-2974
  Port Huron *(G-13461)*
Boral Building Products Inc .... C ... 800 521-8486
  Wixom *(G-18625)*
Border City Tool and Mfg Co .... F ... 586 758-5574
  Harper Woods *(G-7664)*
Contract Welding and Fabg Inc .... E ... 734 699-5561
  Van Buren Twp *(G-17520)*
Cutting Edge Poly .... G ... 269 953-2866
  Hastings *(G-7787)*
D P Equipment Co .... F ... 517 368-5266
  Camden *(G-2421)*
Dedoes Industries LLC .... C ... 248 624-7710
  Walled Lake *(G-17666)*
Di-Coat Corporation .... E ... 248 349-1211
  Novi *(G-12399)*
Douglas Dynamics LLC .... F ... 414 362-3890
  Madison Heights *(G-10710)*
E M I Construction Products .... F ... 616 392-7207
  Holland *(G-8020)*
Falcon Road Maint Eqp LLC .... F ... 989 495-9332
  Midland *(G-11362)*
Fw Shoring Company .... D .. 517 676-8800
  Mason *(G-11133)*
Hines Corporation .... F ... 231 799-6240
  Norton Shores *(G-12348)*
JB Machinery LLC .... G ... 419 727-1772
  Blissfield *(G-1765)*
Keizer-Morris Intl Inc .... E ... 810 688-1234
  North Branch *(G-12180)*
Lawrence J Julio LLC .... G ... 906 483-4781
  Houghton *(G-8384)*
Leadership Group LLC .... G ... 586 251-2090
  Sterling Heights *(G-16069)*
Leica Geo Systems Gr LLC .... G ... 616 949-7430
  Grand Rapids *(G-6938)*
Magnum Toolscom LLC .... F ... 734 595-4600
  Romulus *(G-14300)*
Mull-It-Over Products LLC .... G ... 616 730-2162
  Grandville *(G-7403)*
New Wake Inc .... G ... 800 957-5606
  Hudsonville *(G-8599)*
Nordson Corporation .... D .. 734 459-8600
  Wixom *(G-18721)*
Petter Investments Inc .... F ... 269 637-1997
  South Haven *(G-15411)*
Powerscreen of Michigan LLC .... G ... 586 690-7224
  Clinton Township *(G-3322)*
Shred-Pac Inc .... E ... 269 793-7978
  Hopkins *(G-8370)*
Simplicity Engineering Company .... G ... 989 288-3121
  Durand *(G-4848)*
Stoneco of Michigan Inc .... G ... 734 236-6538
  Newport *(G-12107)*
Stoneco of Michigan Inc .... D .. 734 241-8966
  Monroe *(G-11578)*
Superior Fabrication Co LLC .... D .. 906 495-5634
  Kincheloe *(G-9505)*
Tapco Holdings Inc .... C ... 248 668-6400
  Wixom *(G-18766)*
TCH Supply Inc .... G ... 517 545-4900
  Howell *(G-8526)*
U P Fabricating Co Inc .... F ... 906 475-4400
  Negaunee *(G-11976)*
White Knight Fluid Hdlg Inc .... G ... 435 783-6040
  Hemlock *(G-7858)*

MACHINERY: Custom

Ability Mfg & Engrg Co .... D .. 269 227-3292
  Fennville *(G-5433)*
Accuworx LLC .... E ... 734 847-6115
  Temperance *(G-16525)*
All Metal Designs Inc .... G ... 616 392-3696
  Holland *(G-7960)*
Ase Industries Inc .... D .. 586 754-7480
  Warren *(G-17718)*
Auto Builders Inc .... E ... 586 948-3780
  Chesterfield *(G-2849)*
Automated Indus Motion Inc .... G ... 231 865-1800
  Fruitport *(G-6059)*
Azon Usa Inc .... F ... 269 385-5942
  Kalamazoo *(G-9129)*
Azon Usa Inc .... G ... 269 385-5942
  Kalamazoo *(G-9130)*
Belding Tool Acquisition LLC .... F ... 586 816-4450
  Belding *(G-1440)*
C & S Automated Systems LLC .... G ... 586 265-1416
  Fraser *(G-5909)*
Cambria Tool and Machine Inc .... F ... 517 437-3500
  Hillsdale *(G-7928)*
Clipper Belt Lacer Company .... D .. 616 459-3196
  Grand Rapids *(G-6574)*
Coles Machine Service Inc .... E ... 810 658-5373
  Davison *(G-3777)*
Creative Machine Company .... E ... 248 669-4230
  Wixom *(G-18641)*
Custom Marine and Mch Servic .... G ... 989 732-5455
  Gaylord *(G-6125)*
Deshler Group Inc .... C ... 734 525-9100
  Livonia *(G-10181)*
Engineered Concepts Inc .... F ... 574 333-9110
  Cassopolis *(G-2627)*
Engineered Resources Inc .... G ... 248 399-5500
  Oak Park *(G-12611)*
Enprotech Industrial Tech LLC .... E ... 216 883-3220
  Lansing *(G-9695)*
Epic Equipment & Engrg Inc .... D .. 586 314-0020
  Shelby Township *(G-15223)*
Esys Automation LLC .... C ... 248 484-9927
  Auburn Hills *(G-881)*
Esys Automation LLC .... E ... 284 484-9724
  Pontiac *(G-13370)*
Esys Automation LLC .... E ... 248 484-9702
  Sterling Heights *(G-16005)*
Fischell Machinery LLC .... G ... 517 445-2828
  Clayton *(G-3129)*
General Processing Systems Inc .... F ... 630 554-7804
  Holland *(G-8046)*
Genix LLC .... F ... 248 419-0231
  Sterling Heights *(G-16029)*
Geolean USA LLC .... F ... 313 859-9780
  Livonia *(G-10222)*
Green Age Products & Svcs LLC .... F ... 586 207-5724
  Washington *(G-18080)*
Gregory M Boese .... F ... 989 754-2990
  Saginaw *(G-14659)*
Hardy-Reed Tool & Die Co Inc .... E ... 517 547-7107
  Manitou Beach *(G-10927)*
Harmon Sign Inc .... G ... 248 348-8150
  Wixom *(G-18676)*
Holloway Equipment Co Inc .... G ... 810 748-9577
  Harsens Island *(G-7749)*
Huff Machine & Tool Co Inc .... F ... 231 734-3291
  Evart *(G-5123)*
Jobs Inc .... G ... 810 714-0522
  Allen Park *(G-197)*
K&W Tool and Machine Inc .... F ... 616 754-7540
  Greenville *(G-7495)*
Kentwater Tool & Mfg Co .... G ... 616 784-7171
  Comstock Park *(G-3615)*
Ketchum Machine Corporated .... F ... 616 765-5101
  Freeport *(G-6034)*
Kotzian Tool Inc .... F ... 231 861-5377
  Shelby *(G-15155)*
Leading Edge Engineering Inc .... F ... 586 786-0382
  Shelby Township *(G-15261)*
Link Mechanical Solutions LLC .... F ... 734 744-5616
  Livonia *(G-10284)*
M & F Machine & Tool Inc .... E ... 734 847-0571
  Erie *(G-5050)*
Michigan Rebuild & Automtn Inc .... F ... 517 542-6000
  Litchfield *(G-10083)*
Momentum Industries Inc .... F ... 989 681-5735
  Saint Louis *(G-14993)*
National Bulk Equipment Inc .... C ... 616 399-2220
  Holland *(G-8151)*

Oakland Automation LLC .... E ... 248 589-3350
  Livonia *(G-10350)*
P D E Systems Inc .... F ... 586 725-3330
  Chesterfield *(G-2921)*
Panter Master Controls Inc .... F ... 810 687-5600
  Flint *(G-5743)*
Park Street Machine Inc .... E ... 231 739-9165
  Muskegon *(G-11893)*
Patch Works Farms Inc .... G ... 989 430-3610
  Wheeler *(G-18436)*
Pentier Group Inc .... E ... 810 664-7997
  Lapeer *(G-9954)*
Perfecto Industries Inc .... E ... 989 732-2941
  Gaylord *(G-6154)*
Pollington Machine Tool Inc .... E ... 231 743-2003
  Marion *(G-10976)*
R & D Machine and Tool Inc .... G ... 231 798-8500
  Norton Shores *(G-12327)*
R K C Corporation .... G ... 231 627-9131
  Cheboygan *(G-2797)*
Schaller Tool & Die Co .... E ... 586 949-5500
  Chesterfield *(G-2947)*
Schuler Incorporated .... D .. 734 207-7200
  Canton *(G-2522)*
Smoracy LLC .... G ... 989 561-2270
  Remus *(G-13817)*
Smw Mfg Inc .... E ... 517 596-3300
  Belleville *(G-1491)*
Steel-Fab Wilson & Machine .... G ... 989 773-6046
  Mount Pleasant *(G-11742)*
Sun Tool Company .... G ... 313 837-2442
  Detroit *(G-4614)*
Trusted Tool Mfg Inc .... G ... 810 750-6000
  Fenton *(G-5510)*
Tuff Automation Inc .... E ... 616 735-3939
  Grand Rapids *(G-7280)*
United Systems .... G ... 248 583-9670
  Troy *(G-17413)*
Veit Tool & Gage Inc .... E ... 810 658-4949
  Davison *(G-3800)*
Vn Industries Inc .... G ... 616 540-2812
  Grand Rapids *(G-7321)*

MACHINERY: Deburring

Casalbi Company Inc .... F ... 517 782-0345
  Jackson *(G-8835)*
Clm Vibetech Inc .... F ... 269 344-3878
  Kalamazoo *(G-9146)*
Hammond Machinery Inc .... D .. 269 345-7151
  Kalamazoo *(G-9207)*
Kalamazoo Company .... E ... 269 345-7151
  Kalamazoo *(G-9237)*
Microprecision Cleaning .... F ... 586 997-6960
  Sterling Heights *(G-16098)*
Robert Bosch LLC .... G ... 248 876-1000
  Farmington Hills *(G-5371)*
Robert Bosch LLC .... G ... 248 921-9054
  Novi *(G-12527)*
Robert Bosch LLC .... G ... 734 979-3000
  Plymouth *(G-13287)*
Rock Tool & Machine Co Inc .... E ... 734 455-9840
  Plymouth *(G-13289)*

MACHINERY: Die Casting

Advance Products Corporation .... E ... 269 849-1000
  Benton Harbor *(G-1527)*
Buhlerprince Inc .... C ... 616 394-8248
  Holland *(G-7986)*
Die Cast Press Mfg Co Inc .... E ... 269 657-6060
  Paw Paw *(G-12947)*
Diversified Metal Products Inc .... E ... 989 448-7120
  Gaylord *(G-6126)*
Industrial Innovations Inc .... F ... 616 249-1525
  Grandville *(G-7392)*
Selmuro Ltd .... E ... 810 603-2117
  Grand Blanc *(G-6263)*

MACHINERY: Dredging

W & S Development Inc .... F ... 989 724-5463
  Greenbush *(G-7473)*

MACHINERY: Drill Presses

Clausing Industrial Inc .... F ... 269 345-7155
  Kalamazoo *(G-9144)*
Clausing Industrial Inc .... D .. 269 345-7155
  Kalamazoo *(G-9145)*

Employee Codes: A=Over 500 employees, B=251-500
C=101-250, D=51-100, E=20-50, F=10-19, G=3-9

MACHINERY: Electronic Component Making

MACHINERY: Electronic Component Making

Company		Phone
Environ Manufacturing Inc .... G		616 644-6846
Battle Creek *(G-1223)*		
Firstronic LLC .... B		616 456-9220
Grand Rapids *(G-6708)*		
Greene Manufacturing Tech LLC C		810 982-9720
Port Huron *(G-13481)*		
Senstronic Inc .... F		586 466-4108
Clinton Township *(G-3350)*		
Toyota Industries Elctc Sys N .... G		248 489-7700
Novi *(G-12557)*		

MACHINERY: Electronic Teaching Aids

Realm .... G 313 706-4401
  Wayne *(G-18234)*

MACHINERY: Extruding

Clark Granco Inc .... D 616 794-2600
  Belding *(G-1443)*

MACHINERY: Fiber Optics Strand Coating

Euclid Coating Systems Inc .... F 989 922-4789
  Bay City *(G-1351)*

MACHINERY: Folding

A S R C Inc .... G 517 545-7430
  Howell *(G-8423)*

MACHINERY: Gear Cutting & Finishing

Bmt Aerospace Usa Inc .... D 586 285-7700
  Fraser *(G-5905)*
Jag Enterprises Inc .... G 586 784-4231
  Chesterfield *(G-2898)*

MACHINERY: General, Industrial, NEC

Conair North America .... E 814 437-6861
  Pinconning *(G-13060)*
Edwards Machinery and Repa .... G 616 422-2584
  Baroda *(G-1160)*
Geofabrica Inc .... F 810 728-2468
  Auburn Hills *(G-909)*
Keane Saunders & Associates .... G 616 954-7088
  Grand Rapids *(G-6880)*
P R Machining & Prototype Inc .... G 586 468-7146
  Mount Clemens *(G-11650)*
Power Cleaning Systems Inc .... G 248 347-7727
  Novi *(G-12507)*
Sk Enterprises Inc .... G 616 785-1070
  Grand Rapids *(G-7201)*
SMS Technical Services .... F 586 445-0330
  Warren *(G-18016)*
Smullen Fire App Sales & Svcs .... G 517 546-8898
  Howell *(G-8520)*
Stokes Automation .... G 248 573-5277
  Northville *(G-12264)*

MACHINERY: Glass Cutting

Northwoods Prperty Holdings LLC .... G 231 334-3000
  Glen Arbor *(G-6211)*

MACHINERY: Glassmaking

Epiphany Studios Ltd .... G 248 745-3786
  Pontiac *(G-13367)*
Il Enterprises Inc .... F 734 285-6030
  Wyandotte *(G-18823)*

MACHINERY: Grinding

Accurate Machined Service Inc .... G 734 421-4660
  Livonia *(G-10099)*
Berger LLC .... G 734 414-0402
  Plymouth *(G-13135)*
CB Industrial LLC .... F 248 264-9800
  New Hudson *(G-12045)*
Diversified Precision Pdts Inc .... E 517 750-2310
  Spring Arbor *(G-15790)*
Emag LLC .... E 248 477-7440
  Farmington Hills *(G-5227)*
Emag USA Corporation .... C 248 477-7440
  Farmington Hills *(G-5228)*
Machine Control Technology .... G 517 655-3506
  Williamston *(G-18577)*
Mid-West Waltham Abrasives Co .... E 517 725-7161
  Owosso *(G-12843)*
New Unison Corporation .... E 248 544-9500
  Ferndale *(G-5571)*
Palfam Industries Inc .... F 248 922-0590
  Ortonville *(G-12750)*
Ra Prcsion Grnding Mtlwrks Inc .... F 586 783-7776
  Harrison Township *(G-7719)*
Superabrasives Inc .... E 248 348-7670
  Wixom *(G-18762)*
United Mfg Netwrk Inc .... G 586 321-7887
  Chesterfield *(G-2960)*

MACHINERY: Ice Cream

Spotted Cow .... G 517 265-6188
  Adrian *(G-97)*
Taylor Freezer Michigan Inc .... F 616 453-0531
  Grand Rapids *(G-7249)*

MACHINERY: Ice Crushers

Nu-Ice Age Inc .... F 517 990-0665
  Clarklake *(G-3006)*

MACHINERY: Ice Making

Acme Tool & Die Co .... G 231 938-1260
  Acme *(G-1)*

MACHINERY: Ice Resurfacing

Arctic Glacier Wisconsin Inc .... E 262 345-6999
  Port Huron *(G-13454)*

MACHINERY: Industrial, NEC

Arete Products & Mfg LLC .... G 269 383-0015
  Kalamazoo *(G-9119)*
Break Mold LLC .... G 269 359-0822
  Portage *(G-13549)*
Buffoli North America Corp .... F 616 610-4362
  Holland *(G-7985)*
Cobalt Friction Tech LLC .... G 734 930-6902
  Ann Arbor *(G-429)*
Custom Molds .... F 574 326-7576
  Sturgis *(G-16286)*
Darrell R Hanson .... G 810 364-7892
  Marysville *(G-11085)*
Epoch Robotics .... F 616 820-3369
  Holland *(G-8030)*
Eptech Inc .... G 586 254-2722
  Macomb *(G-10591)*
Excel Machinery Intl Corp .... G 810 348-9162
  Davisburg *(G-3766)*
F2 Industries LLC .... G 616 610-0894
  Zeeland *(G-19020)*
Frostys Ice Cream Machine Retn .... G 616 886-1418
  Holland *(G-8042)*
Illmatik Industries .... G 714 767-1296
  Grand Rapids *(G-6834)*
Impeccable Machining Inc .... G 734 844-3855
  Westland *(G-18385)*
Inateg LLC .... G 734 276-3899
  Livonia *(G-10248)*
Infinicoat LLC .... G 810 721-9631
  Attica *(G-753)*
Joyce Mims .... G 616 469-5016
  Union Pier *(G-17500)*
K & S Automation LLC .... G 248 861-2123
  Oxford *(G-12892)*
L T C Solutions Inc .... G 586 323-2071
  Shelby Township *(G-15253)*
Mag Machine Tool .... G 734 281-1700
  Gibraltar *(G-6172)*
Maxum LLC .... G 248 726-7110
  Rochester Hills *(G-14060)*
Meezherati Industries LLC .... G 734 931-0466
  Detroit *(G-4428)*
Miedema Realty Inc .... G 616 538-4800
  Grandville *(G-7402)*
Mittler Supply .... G 616 451-3055
  Grand Rapids *(G-7014)*
Mr E Machine LLC .... G 810 407-0319
  Au Gres *(G-761)*
Platt Mounts - Usa Inc .... G 586 202-2920
  Lake Orion *(G-9626)*
RSI of West Michigan LLC .... E 231 728-1155
  Muskegon *(G-11911)*
Sage Tool & Engineering .... G 517 625-7817
  Perry *(G-12981)*
Sb Tools LLC .... G 313 729-2759
  Taylor *(G-16470)*
Steel Industries Inc .... G 734 427-8550
  Northville *(G-12263)*
Tru Line Co .... F 313 215-1935
  Westland *(G-18424)*
Woodville Heights Enterprises .... F 231 629-7750
  Big Rapids *(G-1690)*

MACHINERY: Kilns

Corls Kiln .... G 989 673-4925
  Caro *(G-2568)*
Kiln Kreations .... G 989 435-3296
  Beaverton *(G-1426)*
Lumbertown Portable Sawmill .... G 231 206-4600
  Muskegon *(G-11862)*

MACHINERY: Labeling

Take-A-Label Inc .... F 616 837-9300
  Nunica *(G-12588)*

MACHINERY: Lapping

Helical Lap & Manufacturing Co .... G 586 307-8322
  Mount Clemens *(G-11640)*

MACHINERY: Marking, Metalworking

Columbia Marking Tools Inc .... E 586 949-8400
  Chesterfield *(G-2860)*
Hanson International Inc .... C 269 429-5555
  Saint Joseph *(G-14935)*
Marking Machine Co .... F 517 767-4155
  Tekonsha *(G-16523)*
SB Investments LLC .... E 734 462-9478
  Livonia *(G-10400)*

MACHINERY: Metalworking

Accu-Rite Industries LLC .... E 586 247-0060
  Shelby Township *(G-15161)*
Advanced Feedlines LLC .... E 248 583-9400
  Troy *(G-16908)*
Aludyne US LLC .... D 810 987-1112
  Port Huron *(G-13438)*
Anderson-Cook Inc .... D 586 954-0700
  Chesterfield *(G-2844)*
Anderson-Cook Inc .... G 586 293-0800
  Fraser *(G-5895)*
Ats Assembly and Test Inc .... F 734 266-4713
  Livonia *(G-10129)*
Bel-Kur Inc .... E 734 847-0651
  Temperance *(G-16528)*
Boxer Equipment/Morbark Inc .... E 989 866-2381
  Winn *(G-18589)*
Bulk AG Innovations LLC .... G 269 925-0900
  Benton Harbor *(G-1538)*
Burke E Porter Machinery Co .... C 616 234-1200
  Grand Rapids *(G-6535)*
Burton Press Co Inc .... G 248 853-0212
  Rochester Hills *(G-13967)*
Cardinal Machine Co .... E 810 686-1190
  Clio *(G-3394)*
Carter Products Company Inc .... E 616 647-3380
  Grand Rapids *(G-6548)*
Coleman Machine Inc .... E 906 863-1113
  Menominee *(G-11229)*
Dawlen Corporation .... E 517 787-2200
  Jackson *(G-8860)*
Experienced Concepts Inc .... E 586 752-4200
  Armada *(G-735)*
Flagler Corporation .... E 586 749-6300
  Chesterfield *(G-2882)*
Fontijne Grotnes Inc .... E 269 262-4700
  Niles *(G-12129)*
Friendship Industries Inc .... E 586 323-0033
  Sterling Heights *(G-16024)*
Friendship Industries Inc .... F 586 997-1325
  Sterling Heights *(G-16025)*
Gatco Incorporated .... F 734 453-2295
  Plymouth *(G-13174)*
Hak Inc .... G 231 587-5322
  Mancelona *(G-10872)*
Harvey S Freeman .... G 248 852-2222
  West Bloomfield *(G-18287)*
HMS Products Co .... D 248 689-8120
  Troy *(G-17146)*
Hti Cybernetics Inc .... E 586 826-8346
  Sterling Heights *(G-16043)*
Industrial Automation LLC .... D 248 598-5900
  Rochester Hills *(G-14039)*
Jsj DC Holdings Inc .... D 616 842-7110
  Grand Haven *(G-6325)*
Kapex Manufacturing LLC .... G 989 928-4993
  Saginaw *(G-14676)*

PRODUCT SECTION

MACHINERY: Recycling

Kuka Robotics Corporation .... E 586 795-2000
   Shelby Township *(G-15250)*
Kuka Systems North America LLC ...... F 586 795-2000
   Sterling Heights *(G-16065)*
Lampco Industries of MI Inc .... G 517 783-3414
   Jackson *(G-8932)*
Leonard Machine Tool Systems .... E 586 757-8040
   Warren *(G-17903)*
Linwood Tool Co Inc .... E 989 697-4403
   Linwood *(G-10074)*
M & F Machine & Tool Inc .... E 734 847-0571
   Erie *(G-5050)*
Manufacturers / Mch Bldrs Svcs .... G 734 748-3706
   Livonia *(G-10298)*
Manufctring Solutions Tech LLC .... G 734 744-5050
   Commerce Township *(G-3552)*
Mega Screen Corp .... G 517 849-7057
   Jonesville *(G-9094)*
Milacron LLC .... G 517 424-8981
   Tecumseh *(G-16508)*
Modern Tool and Tapping Inc .... G 586 777-5144
   Fraser *(G-5964)*
Morbark LLC .... B 989 866-2381
   Winn *(G-18590)*
Motion Machine Company .... F 810 664-9901
   Lapeer *(G-9949)*
Naams LLC .... G 586 285-5684
   Warren *(G-17940)*
New Unison Corporation .... E 248 544-9500
   Ferndale *(G-5571)*
Nidec Chs LLC .... F 586 777-7440
   Romeo *(G-14230)*
Norgren Automtn Solutions LLC .... F 586 463-3000
   Rochester Hills *(G-14070)*
Northwest Tool & Machine Inc .... E 517 750-1332
   Jackson *(G-8978)*
On The Mark Inc .... G 989 317-8033
   Mount Pleasant *(G-11729)*
Precision Plus .... G 906 553-7900
   Escanaba *(G-5091)*
R & S Tool & Die Inc .... G 989 673-8511
   Caro *(G-2579)*
Reger Manufacturing Company .... E 586 293-5096
   Fraser *(G-5986)*
Rod Chomper Inc .... F 616 392-9677
   Holland *(G-8182)*
Savard Corporation .... F 313 931-6880
   Detroit *(G-4581)*
Sharp Die & Mold Co .... F 586 293-8660
   Fraser *(G-5993)*
Tannewitz Inc .... E 616 457-5999
   Jenison *(G-9073)*
Thielenhaus Microfinish Corp .... E 248 349-9450
   Novi *(G-12556)*
Tri-Mation Industries Inc .... E 269 668-4333
   Mattawan *(G-11168)*
Trinity Tool Co .... E 586 296-5900
   Fraser *(G-6006)*
Veet Industries Inc .... F 586 776-3000
   Warren *(G-18053)*

MACHINERY: Milling

Crow Forge .... G 269 948-5346
   Hastings *(G-7786)*
Diamond Standard Mch Co LLC .... G 248 805-7144
   Oakland *(G-12652)*
DTe Hankin Inc .... G 734 279-1831
   Petersburg *(G-12983)*
Enagon LLC .... G 269 455-5110
   Saugatuck *(G-15083)*
Extrude Hone LLC .... F 616 647-9050
   Grand Rapids *(G-6695)*
Manufacturing Associates Inc .... G 248 421-4943
   Livonia *(G-10299)*
Max2 LLC .... F 269 468-3452
   Benton Harbor *(G-1569)*
Riverside Cnc LLC .... G 616 246-6000
   Wyoming *(G-18905)*

MACHINERY: Mining

Classfcation Flotation Systems .... G 810 714-5200
   Fenton *(G-5464)*
Contract Welding and Fabg Inc .... E 734 699-5561
   Van Buren Twp *(G-17520)*
General Machine Services .... G 269 695-2244
   Buchanan *(G-2196)*
Lake Shore Systems Inc .... D 906 774-1500
   Kingsford *(G-9512)*
Lake Shore Systems Inc .... E 906 265-5414
   Iron River *(G-8745)*

McLanahan Corporation .... G 517 614-2007
   East Lansing *(G-4902)*
Mq Operating Company .... E 906 337-1515
   Calumet *(G-2412)*
Oakland Welding Industries .... E 586 949-4090
   Chesterfield *(G-2916)*
Pillar Manufacturing Inc .... F 269 628-5605
   Gobles *(G-6218)*
U P Fabricating Co Inc .... F 906 475-4400
   Negaunee *(G-11976)*
Yerington Brothers Inc .... E 269 695-7669
   Niles *(G-12174)*

MACHINERY: Ozone

Reese Business Group LLC .... G 246 216-2605
   Farmington Hills *(G-5366)*

MACHINERY: Packaging

A & B Packing Equipment Inc .... G 616 294-3539
   Holland *(G-7951)*
A-OK Precision Prototype Inc .... G 586 758-3430
   Ray *(G-13697)*
Anchor Bay Packaging Corp .... E 586 949-4040
   Chesterfield *(G-2842)*
BP Pack Inc .... G 612 594-0839
   Bellaire *(G-1472)*
British Cnvrtng Sltns Nrth AME .... E 281 764-6651
   Kalamazoo *(G-9141)*
Camaco LLC .... E 248 442-6800
   Farmington Hills *(G-5195)*
Change Parts Incorporated .... E 231 845-5107
   Ludington *(G-10531)*
Coleman Bowman & Associates ...... G 248 642-8221
   Bloomfield Hills *(G-1809)*
D J S Systems Inc .... G 517 568-4444
   Homer *(G-8350)*
Dura-Pack Inc .... E 313 299-9600
   Taylor *(G-16408)*
Gentile Packaging Machinery Co ...... G 734 429-1177
   Saline *(G-15019)*
Hot Melt Technologies Inc .... E 248 853-2011
   Rochester Hills *(G-14034)*
Kalamazoo Packaging Systems .... G 616 534-2600
   Grand Rapids *(G-6877)*
Korten Quality Inc .... D 586 752-6255
   Bruce Twp *(G-2170)*
Meca-Systeme Usa Inc .... G 616 843-5566
   Grand Haven *(G-6335)*
Nyx LLC .... C 734 462-2385
   Livonia *(G-10343)*
Nyx LLC .... D 734 261-7535
   Livonia *(G-10347)*
Robert Bosch LLC .... G 734 302-2000
   Ann Arbor *(G-643)*
Robert Bosch LLC .... G 248 876-1000
   Farmington Hills *(G-5371)*
Robert Bosch LLC .... G 248 921-9054
   Novi *(G-12527)*
Robert Bosch LLC .... G 734 979-3000
   Plymouth *(G-13287)*
Rollstock Inc .... G 616 803-5370
   Grand Rapids *(G-7164)*
Tekkra Systems Inc .... E 517 568-4121
   Homer *(G-8357)*
Tindall Packaging Inc .... G 269 649-1163
   Portage *(G-13626)*

MACHINERY: Paint Making

Peloton Inc .... G 269 694-9702
   Otsego *(G-12798)*
Tzamco Inc .... E 248 624-7710
   Walled Lake *(G-17676)*

MACHINERY: Paper Industry Miscellaneous

Accu-Shape Die Cutting Inc .... E 810 230-2445
   Flint *(G-5634)*
B&P Littleford Day LLC .... D 989 757-1300
   Saginaw *(G-14607)*
Bernal LLC .... D 248 299-3600
   Rochester Hills *(G-13964)*
Paper Machine Service Inds .... F 989 695-2646
   Saginaw *(G-14724)*

MACHINERY: Pharmaciutical

Graminex LLC .... G 989 797-5502
   Saginaw *(G-14658)*
Titan Pharmaceutical McHy Inc .... G 248 220-7421
   Shelby Township *(G-15352)*

Velesco Phrm Svcs Inc .... G 734 545-0696
   Wixom *(G-18785)*
Velesco Phrm Svcs Inc .... G 734 274-9877
   Plymouth *(G-13330)*

MACHINERY: Photographic Reproduction

Arts Crafts Hardware .... F 586 231-5344
   Mount Clemens *(G-11627)*
Laser Connection LLC .... E 989 662-4022
   Auburn *(G-768)*

MACHINERY: Plastic Working

Bekum America Corporation .... C 517 655-4331
   Williamston *(G-18569)*
Brown Mch Group Intrmdate Hldn ...... C 989 435-7741
   Beaverton *(G-1424)*
Century Inc .... C 231 947-6400
   Traverse City *(G-16641)*
Edge Industries Inc .... G 616 453-5458
   Grand Rapids *(G-6665)*
Ess Tec Inc .... D 616 394-0230
   Holland *(G-8031)*
Glycon Corp .... E 517 423-8356
   Tecumseh *(G-16503)*
Innovative Engineering Mich .... G 517 977-0460
   Lansing *(G-9705)*
Kapex Manufacturing LLC .... G 989 928-4993
   Saginaw *(G-14676)*
Limbright Consulting Inc .... E 810 227-5510
   Wixom *(G-18699)*
Lyle Industries Inc .... G 989 435-7717
   Beaverton *(G-1429)*
Mann + Hummel Inc .... G 269 329-3900
   Portage *(G-13581)*
Michigan Roll Form Inc .... E 248 669-3700
   Commerce Township *(G-3556)*
Miller Mold Co .... E 989 793-8881
   Frankenmuth *(G-5871)*
Quantum Mold & Engineering LLC .... F 586 276-0100
   Sterling Heights *(G-16141)*
R & B Plastics Machinery LLC .... G 734 429-9421
   Saline *(G-15034)*
R & S Tool & Die Inc .... G 989 673-8511
   Caro *(G-2579)*
Spirit Industries Inc .... G 517 371-7840
   Lansing *(G-9740)*
Thermfrmer Parts Suppliers LLC ...... G 989 435-3800
   Beaverton *(G-1432)*
Thermoforming Tech Group LLC ...... G 989 435-7741
   Beaverton *(G-1433)*
Thoreson-Mc Cosh Inc .... E 248 362-0960
   Lake Orion *(G-9634)*
Ube Machinery Inc .... D 734 741-7000
   Ann Arbor *(G-702)*
Valley Gear and Machine Inc .... F 989 269-8177
   Bad Axe *(G-1116)*

MACHINERY: Polishing & Buffing

Abrasive Services Incorporated .... G 734 941-2144
   Romulus *(G-14244)*
Changeover Integration LLC .... F 231 845-5320
   Ludington *(G-10532)*

MACHINERY: Printing Presses

Eagle Press Repairs & Ser .... G 419 539-7206
   Adrian *(G-63)*
Maple Leaf Press Inc .... G 616 846-8844
   Grand Haven *(G-6334)*
Sunraise Inc .... F 810 359-7301
   Lexington *(G-10032)*
Voxeljet America Inc .... E 734 709-8237
   Canton *(G-2541)*

MACHINERY: Recycling

Air Tight Solutions LLC .... G 248 629-0461
   Detroit *(G-3990)*
Compac Specialties Inc .... F 616 786-9100
   Holland *(G-8001)*
Higgins and Associates Inc .... F 989 772-8853
   Mount Pleasant *(G-11701)*
Huron Valley Steel Corporation .... C 734 479-3500
   Trenton *(G-16889)*
Kansmackers Manufacturing Co .... F 248 249-6666
   Lansing *(G-9709)*
Latitude Recycling Inc .... G 586 243-5153
   Ray *(G-13700)*
Libra Industries Inc Michigan .... G 517 787-5675
   Jackson *(G-8935)*

Employee Codes: A=Over 500 employees, B=251-500
C=101-250, D=51-100, E=20-50, F=10-19, G=3-9

MACHINERY: Recycling

Loadmaster Corporation ....E 906 563-9226
 Norway *(G-12353)*
Usher Enterprises Inc ....E 313 834-7055
 Detroit *(G-4656)*

MACHINERY: Riveting

Orbitform Group LLC ....D 800 957-4838
 Jackson *(G-8980)*

MACHINERY: Road Construction & Maintenance

Spaulding Mfg Inc ....E 989 777-4550
 Saginaw *(G-14762)*

MACHINERY: Robots, Molding & Forming Plastics

Pine Needle People LLC ....G 517 242-4752
 Lansing *(G-9728)*

MACHINERY: Rubber Working

Oakley Inds Sub Assmbly Div In ....G 586 754-5555
 Warren *(G-17949)*

MACHINERY: Saw & Sawing

B & O Saws Inc ....E 616 794-7297
 Belding *(G-1435)*
Rattunde Corporation ....G 616 940-3340
 Caledonia *(G-2396)*

MACHINERY: Screening Eqpt, Electric

Online Engineering Inc ....F 906 341-0090
 Manistique *(G-10923)*

MACHINERY: Semiconductor Manufacturing

Eaton Aerospace LLC ....B 616 949-1090
 Grand Rapids *(G-6663)*
Minland Machine Inc ....G 269 641-7998
 Edwardsburg *(G-5012)*
Nava Solar LLC ....F 734 707-8260
 Mount Pleasant *(G-11727)*
Ovshinsky Technologies LLC ....G 248 752-2344
 Bloomfield Hills *(G-1846)*

MACHINERY: Separation Eqpt, Magnetic

Magnetic Products Inc ....D 248 887-5600
 Highland *(G-7896)*
Puritan Magnetics Inc ....F 248 628-3808
 Oxford *(G-12908)*
Universal Magnetics Inc ....G 231 937-5555
 Howard City *(G-8420)*

MACHINERY: Service Industry, NEC

A C Supply Co Inc ....F 586 776-2222
 Warren *(G-17681)*
Supply Pro ....G 810 239-8658
 Flint *(G-5773)*

MACHINERY: Sheet Metal Working

Atlas Technologies LLC ....D 810 629-6663
 Fenton *(G-5451)*
Boral Building Products Inc ....C 800 521-8486
 Wixom *(G-18625)*
Flagler Corporation ....E 586 749-6300
 Chesterfield *(G-2882)*
Impel Industries Inc ....E 586 254-5800
 Sterling Heights *(G-16046)*
Tapco Holdings Inc ....C 248 668-6400
 Wixom *(G-18766)*

MACHINERY: Snow Making

Snow Machines Incorporated ....E 989 631-6091
 Midland *(G-11418)*

MACHINERY: Specialty

Arcon Vernova Inc ....G 734 904-1895
 Saline *(G-15004)*
Brothers Industrials Inc ....G 248 794-5080
 Farmington Hills *(G-5186)*
Built Systems LLC ....F 616 834-5099
 Holland *(G-7987)*
Ebels Equipment LLC ....G 231 826-3334
 Falmouth *(G-5132)*

Hi-Tech/Fpa Inc ....G 616 942-0076
 Grand Rapids *(G-6813)*
Itac Software Inc ....E 248 450-2446
 Southfield *(G-15609)*
Koyo Corp ....G 269 962-9676
 Battle Creek *(G-1265)*
Lumbee Custom Painting LLC ....G 586 296-5083
 Fraser *(G-5958)*
Modern Builders ....G 989 773-1405
 Mount Pleasant *(G-11716)*
Pulverdryer Usa Inc ....G 269 552-5290
 Galesburg *(G-6082)*
Urgent Design and Mfg Inc ....F 810 245-1300
 Lapeer *(G-9964)*

MACHINERY: Tapping

American Gator Tool Company ....G 231 347-3222
 Harbor Springs *(G-7639)*
Illinois Tool Works Inc ....G 248 589-2500
 Troy *(G-17161)*

MACHINERY: Textile

B&P Littleford Day LLC ....D 989 757-1300
 Saginaw *(G-14607)*
Howa USA Holdings Inc ....G 248 715-4000
 Novi *(G-12436)*
Star Shade Cutter Co ....G 269 983-2403
 Saint Joseph *(G-14963)*

MACHINERY: Thread Rolling

Salvo Tool & Engineering Co ....F 810 346-2727
 Brown City *(G-2142)*

MACHINERY: Wire Drawing

Demmer Investments Inc ....G 517 321-3600
 Lansing *(G-9688)*
Dnl Fabrication LLC ....E 586 872-2656
 Roseville *(G-14401)*
Weber Electric Mfg Co ....E 586 323-9000
 Shelby Township *(G-15367)*

MACHINERY: Woodworking

Alexander Dodds Company ....G 616 784-6000
 Grand Rapids *(G-6442)*
Automated Precision Eqp LLC ....G 517 481-2414
 Eaton Rapids *(G-4952)*
Boxer Equipment/Morbark Inc ....G 989 866-2381
 Winn *(G-18589)*
Carter Products Company Inc ....E 616 647-3380
 Grand Rapids *(G-6548)*
Conway-Cleveland Corp ....G 616 458-0056
 Grand Rapids *(G-6604)*
Gudho USA Inc ....G 616 682-7814
 Ada *(G-21)*
Homag Machinery North Amer Inc ....F 616 254-8181
 Grand Rapids *(G-6819)*
Morbark LLC ....B 989 866-2381
 Winn *(G-18590)*
Tannewitz Inc ....E 616 457-5999
 Jenison *(G-9073)*

MACHINES: Forming, Sheet Metal

Ace Welding & Machine Inc ....F 231 941-9664
 Traverse City *(G-16595)*
Fabrilaser Mfg LLC ....E 269 789-9490
 Marshall *(G-11057)*
Prototech Laser Inc ....E 586 598-6900
 Chesterfield *(G-2934)*

MACHINISTS' TOOLS & MACHINES: Measuring, Metalworking Type

Arm Tooling Systems Inc ....F 586 759-5677
 Warren *(G-17712)*
Buster Mathis Foundation ....G 616 843-4433
 Wyoming *(G-18855)*
Spartans Finishing LLC ....G 517 528-5510
 Haslett *(G-7779)*

MACHINISTS' TOOLS: Measuring, Precision

Accu Products International ....G 734 429-9571
 Saline *(G-14998)*
Control Gaging Inc ....E 734 668-6750
 Ann Arbor *(G-436)*
Dme Company LLC ....B 248 398-6000
 Madison Heights *(G-10709)*

Fisk Precision Tech LLC ....G 616 514-1415
 Wyoming *(G-18873)*
G&G Industries Inc ....E 586 726-6000
 Shelby Township *(G-15229)*
Hexagon Mfg Intelligence Inc ....G 248 449-9400
 Novi *(G-12434)*
Linamar Holding Nevada Inc ....D 248 477-6240
 Livonia *(G-10278)*
Sme Holdings LLC ....E 586 254-5310
 Sterling Heights *(G-16179)*

MACHINISTS' TOOLS: Precision

Aic Acquisition Company LLC ....E 810 227-5510
 Wixom *(G-18600)*
Anbo Tool & Manufacturing Inc ....G 586 465-7610
 Clinton Township *(G-3171)*
Dependable Gage & Tool Co ....E 248 545-2100
 Oak Park *(G-12604)*
Grand Rapids Metaltek Inc ....E 616 791-2373
 Grand Rapids *(G-6765)*
Grind-All Precision Tool Co ....F 586 954-3430
 Clinton Township *(G-3250)*
Hope Focus Companies Inc ....E 313 494-5500
 Detroit *(G-4308)*
Image Machine & Tool Inc ....G 586 466-3400
 Fraser *(G-5942)*
Jt Manufacturing Inc ....E 517 849-2923
 Jonesville *(G-9090)*
Kenrie Inc ....F 616 494-3200
 Holland *(G-8112)*
Khalsa Metal Products Inc ....G 616 791-4794
 Kentwood *(G-9460)*
Kooiker Tool & Die Inc ....F 616 554-3630
 Caledonia *(G-2387)*
Lancer Tool Co ....F 248 380-8830
 Wixom *(G-18695)*
Lead Screws International Inc ....D 262 786-1500
 Traverse City *(G-16740)*
Line Precision Inc ....E 248 474-5280
 Farmington Hills *(G-5291)*
Machining Technologies LLC ....E 248 379-4201
 Clarkston *(G-3046)*
Majeske Machine Inc ....G 319 273-8905
 Plymouth *(G-13232)*
Maro Precision Tool Company ....E 734 261-3100
 West Bloomfield *(G-18296)*
Master Machine & Tool Co Inc ....G 586 469-4243
 Clinton Township *(G-3295)*
Micro Form Inc ....E 517 750-3660
 Spring Arbor *(G-15796)*
Precise Cnc Routing Inc ....E 616 538-8608
 Grand Rapids *(G-7097)*
Precision Devices Inc ....E 734 439-2462
 Milan *(G-11449)*
Puritan Automation LLC ....F 248 668-1114
 Wixom *(G-18737)*
Rayco Manufacturing Inc ....F 586 795-2884
 Sterling Heights *(G-16144)*
Salerno Tool Works Inc ....E 586 755-5000
 Warren *(G-18001)*
Selector Spline Products Co ....F 586 254-4020
 Sterling Heights *(G-16168)*
Steel Craft Technologies Inc ....C 616 866-4400
 Belmont *(G-1518)*

MAGAZINES, WHOLESALE

Community Publishing & Mktg ....G 866 822-0101
 Taylor *(G-16396)*

MAGNESIUM

Nanomag LLC ....G 734 261-2800
 Livonia *(G-10331)*

MAGNETIC INK & OPTICAL SCANNING EQPT

LMI Technologies Inc ....F 248 298-2839
 Royal Oak *(G-14557)*

MAGNETIC RESONANCE IMAGING DEVICES: Nonmedical

Alliance Hni LLC ....E 989 729-2804
 Owosso *(G-12821)*
Authentic 3d ....E 248 469-8809
 Bingham Farms *(G-1692)*

PRODUCT SECTION

MAGNETIC SHIELDS, METAL
Cruux LLC .... G 248 515-8411
  Troy *(G-17036)*
Fluxtrol Inc .... G 248 393-2000
  Auburn Hills *(G-904)*

MAGNETIC TAPE, AUDIO: Prerecorded
Brilliance Publishing Inc .... C 616 846-5256
  Grand Haven *(G-6281)*

MAGNETS: Ceramic
Livonia Magnetics Co Inc .... E 734 397-8844
  Farmington Hills *(G-5293)*
My Permit Pal Inc .... G 248 432-2699
  West Bloomfield *(G-18300)*

MAGNETS: Permanent
Advanced Magnet Source Corp .... G 734 398-7188
  Canton *(G-2430)*
Industrial Magnetics Inc .... D 231 582-3100
  Boyne City *(G-1890)*
Magnetic Systems Intl Inc .... E 231 582-9600
  Boyne City *(G-1896)*
Tengam Engineering Inc .... E 269 694-9466
  Otsego *(G-12800)*
Universal Magnetics Inc .... G 231 937-5555
  Howard City *(G-8420)*

MAIL-ORDER HOUSE, NEC
Viking Group Inc .... G 616 432-6800
  Caledonia *(G-2406)*

MAIL-ORDER HOUSES: Computer Software
Rutherford & Associates Inc .... E 616 392-5000
  Holland *(G-8185)*

MAIL-ORDER HOUSES: Cosmetics & Perfumes
US Salon Supply LLC .... F 616 365-5790
  Paw Paw *(G-12958)*

MAIL-ORDER HOUSES: Educational Splys & Eqpt
Esl Supplies LLC .... G 517 525-7877
  Mason *(G-11131)*

MAIL-ORDER HOUSES: Fitness & Sporting Goods
Homedics Usa LLC .... C 248 863-3000
  Commerce Township *(G-3539)*

MAIL-ORDER HOUSES: Fruit
Thomas Cooper .... G 231 599-2251
  Ellsworth *(G-5037)*

MAIL-ORDER HOUSES: Novelty Merchandise
Donbar LLC .... F 313 784-3519
  Inkster *(G-8662)*

MAIL-ORDER HOUSES: Tools & Hardware
Accu Products International .... G 734 429-9571
  Saline *(G-14998)*

MAILBOX RENTAL & RELATED SVCS
Crk Ltd .... G 586 779-5240
  Eastpointe *(G-4933)*
Jlc Print and Ship Inc .... G 517 544-0404
  Jackson *(G-8921)*

MAILING & MESSENGER SVCS
Skyapple LLC .... E 248 588-5990
  Madison Heights *(G-10830)*

MAILING LIST: Compilers
Kent Communications Inc .... D 616 957-2120
  Grand Rapids *(G-6886)*
Postal Savings Direct Mktg .... F 810 238-8866
  Flint *(G-5745)*

MAILING SVCS, NEC
Brightformat Inc .... E 616 247-1161
  Grand Rapids *(G-6524)*
Bruce Inc .... G 517 371-5205
  Lansing *(G-9819)*
CPM Services Group Inc .... G 248 624-5100
  Wixom *(G-18639)*
Data Mail Services Inc .... E 248 588-2415
  Madison Heights *(G-10704)*
Domart LLC .... G 616 285-9177
  Grand Rapids *(G-6653)*
Generation Press Inc .... G 616 392-4405
  Holland *(G-8048)*
Kimprint Inc .... E 734 459-2960
  Plymouth *(G-13215)*
Kolossos Printing Inc .... F 734 994-5400
  Ann Arbor *(G-540)*
Lake Michigan Mailers Inc .... D 269 383-9333
  Kalamazoo *(G-9257)*
Print House Inc .... F 248 473-1414
  Farmington Hills *(G-5353)*
Source One Dist Svcs Inc .... F 248 399-5060
  Madison Heights *(G-10831)*
TGI Direct Inc .... G 810 239-5553
  Ann Arbor *(G-685)*
TGI Direct Inc .... E 810 239-5553
  Flint *(G-5778)*
Your Hometown Shopper LLC .... F 586 412-8500
  Bruce Twp *(G-2187)*

MANAGEMENT CONSULTING SVCS: Administrative
PM Power Group Inc .... G 906 885-7100
  White Pine *(G-18487)*

MANAGEMENT CONSULTING SVCS: Automation & Robotics
Arrow Automation and Engrg Inc .... F 248 660-1520
  Auburn Hills *(G-797)*
Automation Contrls & Engrg LLC .... E 734 424-5500
  Dexter *(G-4725)*
Comau LLC .... D 248 219-0756
  Southfield *(G-15531)*
Esys Automation LLC .... C 248 484-9927
  Auburn Hills *(G-881)*
Esys Automation LLC .... E 284 484-9724
  Pontiac *(G-13370)*
Esys Automation LLC .... E 248 484-9702
  Sterling Heights *(G-16005)*
Innovation Tech LLC .... F 248 797-2686
  Wixom *(G-18685)*
Lorna Icr LLC .... F 586 582-1500
  Warren *(G-17907)*

MANAGEMENT CONSULTING SVCS: Business
F I D Corporation .... G 248 373-7005
  Rochester Hills *(G-14008)*
Geolean USA LLC .... F 313 859-9780
  Livonia *(G-10222)*
Gsb & Associates Inc .... G 770 424-1886
  Kalamazoo *(G-9206)*
Human Synergistics Inc .... E 734 459-1030
  Plymouth *(G-13193)*
Ideation International Inc .... F 248 737-8854
  Farmington Hills *(G-5266)*
Questor Partners Fund II LP .... G 248 593-1930
  Birmingham *(G-1745)*
Welding & Joining Tech LLC .... G 734 926-9353
  Clarkston *(G-3076)*
Whiteside Consulting Group LLC .... G 313 288-6598
  Detroit *(G-4681)*

MANAGEMENT CONSULTING SVCS: Construction Project
Curbco Inc .... D 810 232-2121
  Flint *(G-5678)*

MANAGEMENT CONSULTING SVCS: Hospital & Health
Grass Lake Community Pharmacy .... G 517 522-4100
  Grass Lake *(G-7438)*
Life Otreach Ctr Houghton Cnty .... G 906 482-8681
  Hancock *(G-7621)*

MANAGEMENT SERVICES

Medical Infrmtics Slutions LLC .... G 248 851-3124
  Bloomfield Hills *(G-1836)*

MANAGEMENT CONSULTING SVCS: Industrial
Trucent Inc .... G 734 426-9015
  Dexter *(G-4759)*
Trucent Separation Tech LLC .... D 734 426-9015
  Dexter *(G-4760)*

MANAGEMENT CONSULTING SVCS: Industrial & Labor
Probus Technical Services Inc .... F 876 226-5692
  Troy *(G-17316)*

MANAGEMENT CONSULTING SVCS: Industrial Hygiene
Acorn Industries Inc .... E 734 261-2940
  Livonia *(G-10100)*
Wonder Makers Environmental .... F 269 382-4154
  Kalamazoo *(G-9372)*

MANAGEMENT CONSULTING SVCS: Industry Specialist
Busch Industries Inc .... G 616 957-3737
  Grand Rapids *(G-6539)*
Ezbake Technologies LLC .... G 817 430-1621
  Fenton *(G-5474)*
Moldex3d Northern America Inc .... F 248 946-4570
  Farmington Hills *(G-5326)*

MANAGEMENT CONSULTING SVCS: Maintenance
Digital Performance Tech .... F 877 983-4230
  Troy *(G-17062)*

MANAGEMENT CONSULTING SVCS: Management Engineering
Detroit Materials Inc .... G 248 924-5436
  Farmington *(G-5136)*
Metalform Industries LLC .... G 248 462-0056
  Shelby Township *(G-15274)*

MANAGEMENT CONSULTING SVCS: Manufacturing
Tindall Packaging Inc .... G 269 649-1163
  Portage *(G-13626)*

MANAGEMENT CONSULTING SVCS: Quality Assurance
Artcraft Pattern Works Inc .... F 734 729-0022
  Westland *(G-18355)*
Em A Give Break Safety .... G 231 263-6625
  Kingsley *(G-9523)*

MANAGEMENT CONSULTING SVCS: Retail Trade Consultant
Auction Masters .... G 586 576-7777
  Oak Park *(G-12593)*
Detroit Couture .... G 734 237-6826
  Southfield *(G-15539)*
My Dream Dress Brdal Salon LLC .... G 248 327-6049
  Southfield *(G-15663)*
Sulugu Corporation USA Inc .... D 478 714-0325
  Grand Rapids *(G-7232)*

MANAGEMENT CONSULTING SVCS: Training & Development
Road To Freedom .... F 810 775-0992
  Brighton *(G-2066)*

MANAGEMENT SERVICES
B L Harroun and Son Inc .... E 269 345-8657
  Kalamazoo *(G-9131)*
Berkshire & Associates Inc .... F 734 719-1822
  Canton *(G-2440)*
Covenant Cpitl Investments Inc .... F 248 477-4230
  Wixom *(G-18637)*

MANAGEMENT SERVICES

Dominos Pizza LLC.................................C 734 930-3030
 Ann Arbor (G-456)
Gemini Group Inc....................................F 989 269-6272
 Bad Axe (G-1102)
Grand Rapids Gravel Company.............F 616 538-9000
 Grand Rapids (G-6759)
McL Jasco Inc..G 313 294-7414
 Detroit (G-4424)
Multiax International Inc........................G 616 534-4530
 Grandville (G-7404)
Synod of Great Lakes............................E 616 698-7071
 Grand Rapids (G-7243)
Taylor Communications Inc..................F 248 304-4800
 Southfield (G-15717)
Yanfeng US Automotive........................G 616 394-1523
 Holland (G-8257)

MANAGEMENT SVCS, FACILITIES SUPPORT: Environ Remediation

Birks Works Environmental LLC...........G 313 891-1310
 Detroit (G-4055)
Great Lakes Right of Way LLC.............G 616 263-9898
 Cedar Springs (G-2652)
Regency Construction Corp..................E 586 741-8000
 Clinton Township (G-3334)
Swat Environmental Inc........................E 517 322-2999
 Lansing (G-9898)

MANAGEMENT SVCS: Administrative

Barron Group Inc...................................D 248 628-4300
 Oxford (G-12875)
Tequionbrookins LLC.............................G 313 290-0303
 Southfield (G-15721)

MANAGEMENT SVCS: Business

917 Chittock Street LLC........................F 866 945-0269
 Lansing (G-9798)
Allegra Print and Imaging.....................G 616 784-6699
 Grand Rapids (G-6447)
Talon LLC...F 313 392-1000
 Detroit (G-4625)

MANAGEMENT SVCS: Construction

Doan Construction Co...........................F 734 971-4678
 Ypsilanti (G-18940)
Rock Industries Inc................................E 248 338-2800
 Bloomfield Hills (G-1858)
Saginaw Asphalt Paving Co..................D 989 755-8147
 Carrollton (G-2590)

MANAGEMENT SVCS: Hospital

Hackley Health Ventures Inc................G 231 728-5720
 Muskegon (G-11834)
Mercy Health Partners..........................D 231 728-4032
 Muskegon (G-11866)

MANAGEMENT SVCS: Nursing & Personal Care Facility

Rvi Management Inc.............................G 580 531-5826
 Okemos (G-12684)

MANAGEMENT SVCS: Restaurant

Veritas Vineyard LLC............................E 517 962-2427
 Jackson (G-9030)

MANHOLES & COVERS: Metal

City of East Jordan................................G 231 536-2561
 East Jordan (G-4861)
East Jordan Ironworks Inc....................G 517 566-7211
 Sunfield (G-16334)
Ej Americas LLC...................................G 231 536-2261
 East Jordan (G-4863)
Ej Asia-Pacific Inc.................................B 231 536-2261
 East Jordan (G-4865)
Ej Europe LLC.......................................C 231 536-2261
 East Jordan (G-4867)
Ej Group Inc..E 231 536-2261
 East Jordan (G-4868)
Ej Usa Inc..G 248 546-2004
 Oak Park (G-12610)
Ej Usa Inc..G 616 538-2040
 Wyoming (G-18870)

MANHOLES COVERS: Concrete

Ej Ardmore Inc......................................F 231 536-2261
 East Jordan (G-4864)

MANICURE PREPARATIONS

Eve Salonspa...G 269 327-4811
 Portage (G-13559)
Nail Time..G 313 837-3871
 Detroit (G-4474)
Rose Nail..G 313 271-8804
 Allen Park (G-204)
Uber Hair and Nails Llc.........................G 248 268-3227
 Ferndale (G-5592)

MANIFOLDS: Pipe, Fabricated From Purchased Pipe

Key Gas Components Inc.....................E 269 673-2151
 Allegan (G-163)
Loftis Alumi-TEC Inc.............................G 616 846-1990
 Grand Haven (G-6330)

MANNEQUINS

Denton Atd Inc......................................E 734 451-7878
 Plymouth (G-13153)

MANUFACTURED & MOBILE HOME DEALERS

Advantage Housing Inc.........................G 269 792-6291
 Wayland (G-18187)
Kearsley Lake Terrace LLC...................G 810 736-7000
 Flint (G-5720)
Woodland Park & Sales........................G 810 229-2397
 Brighton (G-2098)

MANUFACTURING INDUSTRIES, NEC

2 Gen Manufacturing LLC.....................G 616 443-7886
 Grand Rapids (G-6402)
2stone Mfg LLC.....................................G 269 214-6560
 Berrien Springs (G-1636)
313 Industries..G 313 969-8570
 Southfield (G-15467)
4 Wheels Industries...............................G 989 323-2191
 Chesaning (G-2827)
4d Industries Inc...................................G 310 710-3955
 Wyoming (G-18847)
7 Seas Sourcing LLC............................G 734 357-8560
 Novi (G-12358)
A & R Tool & Mfg Co............................G 586 553-9623
 Sterling Heights (G-15917)
A K Industries.......................................G 231 726-0134
 Norton Shores (G-12273)
A&A Manufacturing...............................G 800 473-1730
 Coopersville (G-3678)
A&D Industries LLC..............................G 586 291-6444
 Clinton Township (G-3149)
A&S Industries......................................G 269 903-1081
 Kalamazoo (G-9107)
A2e Manufacturing................................G 734 622-9800
 Plymouth (G-13109)
AAM Mtal Frming Troy Mfg Fclty..........G 248 362-8500
 Troy (G-16901)
AAM Royal Oak Mfg..............................G 248 597-3800
 Royal Oak (G-14502)
Abletech Industries LLC.......................G 734 677-2420
 Dexter (G-4720)
Access Manufacturing Techn...............G 224 610-0171
 Niles (G-12108)
Achieve Industries LLC........................G 586 493-9780
 Clinton Township (G-3153)
Adams Manufacturing...........................G 313 383-7804
 Lincoln Park (G-10042)
Advance Pet Solutions LLC..................G 248 334-6150
 West Bloomfield (G-18261)
Aerostar Manufacturing........................G 734 947-2558
 Taylor (G-16374)
AG Industries..F 248 564-2758
 Rochester Hills (G-13945)
Aic Acquisition Company LLC.............E 810 227-5510
 Wixom (G-18600)
Ajm Manufacturing Sales Inc...............G 269 447-2087
 Kalamazoo (G-9108)
AJS Manufacturing LLC.......................G 616 916-6521
 Grand Rapids (G-6440)
AJW Industries Inc...............................G 313 595-5554
 Belleville (G-1479)

PRODUCT SECTION

Aldridge Industries LLC.......................G 248 379-5357
 Beverly Hills (G-1660)
Allen Models of Michigan LLC.............G 989 284-8866
 Freeland (G-6018)
Alta Distribution LLC............................F 313 363-1682
 Southfield (G-15477)
Alynn Industries....................................G 517 764-7783
 Jackson (G-8814)
AME International LLC.........................E 586 532-8981
 Clinton Township (G-3163)
Americana Manufacturing Co...............G 248 505-3277
 Lapeer (G-9912)
Arete Industries Inc..............................G 248 352-7205
 Southfield (G-15490)
Arrowhead Manufacturing....................G 248 688-8939
 Royal Oak (G-14512)
ASC Industries Inc...............................G 586 722-7871
 Rochester Hills (G-13951)
Asher Brandon Industries....................G 231 313-3513
 Traverse City (G-16603)
Aspidistra Naturals Inc.........................G 269 317-0996
 Battle Creek (G-1186)
Atlas Industries.....................................G 310 694-7457
 Southfield (G-15494)
Atmore Industries Inc...........................G 734 455-7655
 Livonia (G-10128)
ATW Industries LLC.............................G 616 318-6052
 Byron Center (G-2258)
Automatic Valve Mfg Co In..................G 248 924-7671
 Novi (G-12371)
Axline Advanced Industries.................G 231 679-7907
 Reed City (G-13788)
Bad Day Industries LLC.......................G 844 213-6541
 Clarksville (G-3077)
Bartz Mfg LLC.......................................G 517 281-2571
 Eaton Rapids (G-4955)
Basan Cord Inc....................................G 888 802-2726
 Commerce Township (G-3513)
Bayside Engineering and Mfg..............G 906 420-8770
 Gladstone (G-6173)
Bayside Industries...............................G 231,632-2222
 Traverse City (G-16618)
Bbb Industries......................................G 231 735-6060
 Traverse City (G-16619)
Bcubed Manufacturing LLC.................G 989 356-2294
 Alpena (G-283)
Be A Boss Not A Bossy Bih LLC.........G 734 833-8106
 Wayne (G-18216)
Bellar Industries Inc.............................G 810 227-1574
 Brighton (G-1950)
Benchmark Manufacturing...................G 231 375-8172
 Norton Shores (G-12278)
Bentley Industries................................G 810 625-0400
 Flint (G-5654)
Best Mfg Tooling Solutions..................G 616 877-5149
 Dorr (G-4767)
Betko Manufacturing............................G 734 854-1148
 Lambertville (G-9650)
Bloom Industries LLC..........................G 616 453-2946
 Grand Rapids (G-6516)
Bluefire Industries LLC........................G 269 235-9779
 Augusta (G-1091)
Bohr Manufacturing LLC......................G 734 261-3010
 Farmington Hills (G-5185)
Bolden Industries Inc...........................F 248 387-9489
 Detroit (G-4060)
Bomark Industries LLc.........................G 248 879-9577
 Troy (G-16981)
Bridgewater Industries.........................G 810 228-3963
 Flint (G-5661)
Brightly Twisted....................................G 313 303-1364
 Detroit (G-4073)
Brilliant Industries LLC........................G 616 954-9209
 Grand Rapids (G-6525)
Britt Manufacturing..............................F 810 982-9720
 Port Huron (G-13463)
Britt Mfg..G 810 966-0223
 Fort Gratiot (G-5818)
Brooks Manufacturing..........................G 231 832-4961
 Chase (G-2775)
Brothers In Arms Mfg LLC...................G 989 464-9615
 Alpena (G-285)
Burlingame Industries Inc....................G 616 682-5691
 Grand Rapids (G-6537)
Camoplast...G 517 278-8567
 Coldwater (G-3424)
Capler Mfg..G 586 264-7851
 Sterling Heights (G-15952)
Car Pak Manufacturing Co...................G 480 625-3655
 Troy (G-16999)

Carpathians Manufacturing..................G....... 248 291-6232
Troy ***(G-17004)***
Cbark Manufacturing Inc........................G....... 810 922-3092
Waterford ***(G-18109)***
CBS Enterprises LLC..............................G....... 248 335-6702
Pontiac ***(G-13352)***
CF Manufacturing LLC............................G....... 231 409-9468
Traverse City ***(G-16644)***
Changstar Industries LLC.......................G....... 248 446-1811
South Lyon ***(G-15430)***
Charboneau Inc......................................G....... 989 293-1773
Bay City ***(G-1337)***
Chris Brown Industries LLC.................G....... 734 323-5651
Southfield ***(G-15522)***
Cirko LLC...G....... 586 504-1313
Shelby Township ***(G-15189)***
Ckc Industries Inc..................................G....... 248 667-6286
Redford ***(G-13724)***
Classic Mfg...G....... 616 651-2921
Sturgis ***(G-16283)***
Clossons Manufacturing LLC...............G....... 269 363-4261
Sodus ***(G-15393)***
Coastline Manufacturing LLC...............G....... 231 798-1700
Norton Shores ***(G-12286)***
Colwell Industries Inc............................G....... 248 841-1254
Rochester Hills ***(G-13978)***
Compositech..G....... 269 908-7846
Lowell ***(G-10498)***
Concentric Mfg Svcs LLC......................G....... 989 506-8636
Weidman ***(G-18250)***
Core Lite Industries LLC........................G....... 616 481-3940
Jenison ***(G-9050)***
Core-Lite Industries LLC.......................G....... 616 843-5993
Grand Haven ***(G-6288)***
Core-Lite Industries LLC.......................G....... 616 822-7587
Grand Haven ***(G-6289)***
Crown Manufacturing LLC.....................F....... 616 295-7018
Middleville ***(G-11305)***
CSB Industries LLC................................G....... 231 651-9484
Beulah ***(G-1654)***
Culver J Manufacturing Company.........G....... 248 541-0297
Royal Oak ***(G-14528)***
Cunningham Industries LLC..................G....... 734 225-1044
Southgate ***(G-15750)***
Cypress Industries Inc...........................F....... 269 381-2160
Kalamazoo ***(G-9160)***
D & D Retaining Walls Inc.....................G....... 260 341-8496
Whitehall ***(G-18494)***
D3w Industries Inc.................................G....... 248 798-0703
Novi ***(G-12389)***
Dakoda Love Manufacturing..................G....... 616 840-0804
Wyoming ***(G-18863)***
Davon Manufacturing.............................G....... 616 745-8453
Zeeland ***(G-19014)***
Dawson Mfg Co Morganfield..................F....... 269 639-4229
South Haven ***(G-15403)***
Dayco Products LLC..............................G....... 248 404-6500
Roseville ***(G-14394)***
Detroits Very Own CL Co LLC...............G....... 313 614-1033
Detroit ***(G-4172)***
Dewsbury Manufacturing Company......G....... 734 839-6376
Trenton ***(G-16887)***
Diamond Tool Manufacturing................F....... 616 895-4007
Hudsonville ***(G-8580)***
Dissrad Inc..G....... 586 463-8722
Mount Clemens ***(G-11637)***
Diverse Manufacturing Soltion.............G....... 517 423-6691
Tecumseh ***(G-16497)***
Dougco Industries LLC...........................G....... 313 808-1689
Detroit ***(G-4188)***
Douglas Innovation LLC........................G....... 586 596-3641
Troy ***(G-17064)***
Dowding Industries................................F....... 319 294-9094
Eaton Rapids ***(G-4958)***
Duo Gard Industries Inc.........................G....... 734 459-9166
Plymouth ***(G-13162)***
Dynatect Manufacturing In....................F....... 231 947-4124
Traverse City ***(G-16674)***
ECM Manufacturing Inc..........................G....... 810 736-0299
Flint ***(G-5691)***
EDS Industries.......................................G....... 989 274-2551
Rochester Hills ***(G-14000)***
Elite Manufacturing Tech LLC...............F....... 586 846-2055
Clinton Township ***(G-3231)***
Elite Metal Manufacturing LLC.............G....... 734 718-0061
Livonia ***(G-10195)***
Emack Manufacturing.............................G....... 616 241-3040
Grand Rapids ***(G-6673)***
Faucher Industries..................................G....... 248 515-4772
Troy ***(G-17107)***
Faucher Industries..................................G....... 586 434-5115
Sterling Heights ***(G-16010)***
Fenixx Technologies LLC......................F....... 586 254-6000
Fraser ***(G-5927)***
Fifth Box Industries LLC........................G....... 734 323-6388
Northville ***(G-12217)***
Forge Industries Lc................................G....... 616 402-7887
Zeeland ***(G-19022)***
Friscos Mechanical & Fabg....................G....... 517 719-3933
Holt ***(G-8312)***
Fulcrum Industries Inc...........................G....... 888 818-5121
Grand Rapids ***(G-6726)***
G & L Mfg Inc...G....... 810 724-4101
Imlay City ***(G-8632)***
Gaishin Manufacturing...........................G....... 269 459-6996
Kalamazoo ***(G-9191)***
Garbarino Industries LLC.......................G....... 586 215-5479
Clinton Township ***(G-3248)***
Genstone LLC...G....... 517 902-4730
Adrian ***(G-70)***
Global Industries Inc..............................G....... 248 357-7211
Southfield ***(G-15577)***
Gopher Scope Manufacturing................G....... 248 667-4025
New Hudson ***(G-12054)***
Gr Psp LLC...G....... 616 785-1070
Grand Rapids ***(G-6753)***
Gr X Manufacturing................................F....... 616 541-7420
Caledonia ***(G-2375)***
Grand River Aseptic Mfg........................G....... 616 678-2400
Grand Rapids ***(G-6775)***
Great Lakes Cylinders LLC....................F....... 248 437-4141
New Hudson ***(G-12055)***
Greatlakespowertoolscom.......................G....... 231 733-6200
Muskegon ***(G-11832)***
Green Peak Industries LLC.....................G....... 517 408-0178
Dimondale ***(G-4763)***
Grit Manufacturing LLC..........................G....... 517 285-5277
Williamsburg ***(G-18556)***
GRX Manufacturing.................................F....... 616 570-0832
Grand Rapids ***(G-6793)***
Gvd Industries LLC.................................G....... 616 836-4067
Holland ***(G-8063)***
Gvd Industries LLC.................................G....... 616 298-7243
Holland ***(G-8064)***
H & B Machining LLC.............................G....... 810 986-2423
Howell ***(G-8458)***
Hammerhead Industries..........................F....... 574 277-8911
Niles ***(G-12135)***
Hand Cast Covers....................................G....... 810 225-7770
Howell ***(G-8459)***
Harrison Industries..................................G....... 231 881-4704
Harbor Springs ***(G-7648)***
Harvest Oak Manufaturing......................G....... 517 781-4016
Bronson ***(G-2115)***
Harvey Industries LLC.............................G....... 734 405-2430
Livonia ***(G-10236)***
HB Manufacturing LLC............................G....... 586 703-5269
Shelby Township ***(G-15233)***
Heed Industries..G....... 906 233-7192
Escanaba ***(G-5075)***
Helion Industries LLC..............................G....... 618 303-0214
Kalamazoo ***(G-9211)***
Highland Tank & Mfg Co..........................F....... 248 795-2000
Clarkston ***(G-3040)***
Hoosier Tank and Manufacturing............G....... 269 683-2550
Niles ***(G-12136)***
Huys Industries..G....... 734 895-3067
Romulus ***(G-14284)***
I & D Manufacturing LLC.........................G....... 517 852-9215
Nashville ***(G-11955)***
Ict Industries..G....... 586 727-2677
Lenox ***(G-9998)***
Ieq Industries...G....... 616 902-1865
Lowell ***(G-10505)***
Industrial Services Group........................F....... 269 945-5291
Lowell ***(G-10506)***
Industries Indy Bear..................................F....... 248 446-1435
South Lyon ***(G-15438)***
Inflatable Industries.................................G....... 517 505-0700
Birch Run ***(G-1707)***
Inhe Manufacturing LLC...........................G....... 616 863-2222
Jenison ***(G-9058)***
Innovative Fabrication LLC......................E....... 734 789-9099
Flat Rock ***(G-5622)***
Innovative Mfg Technologi.......................G....... 810 941-4675
Wales ***(G-17629)***
International Wood Inds Inc.....................G....... 800 598-9663
Grand Rapids ***(G-6851)***
Irene Industries LLC.................................G....... 757 696-3969
Commerce Township ***(G-3545)***
Ironmann Industries..................................G....... 810 695-9177
Holly ***(G-8279)***
Ivory Industries Inc...................................G....... 313 821-3291
Detroit ***(G-4329)***
J & K Industries LLC..................................G....... 586 948-2747
Chesterfield ***(G-2897)***
J&C Industries..G....... 734 479-0069
Riverview ***(G-13877)***
J&D Industries LLC...................................G....... 734 430-6582
Newport ***(G-12103)***
Jac Mfg Inc..G....... 269 679-3301
Schoolcraft ***(G-15121)***
Jcr Industries Inc.......................................G....... 616 364-4856
Grand Rapids ***(G-6865)***
Jef-Scot Metal Industries...........................F....... 231 582-0452
Boyne City ***(G-1892)***
Jetpack Industries LLC..............................G....... 248 689-5083
Troy ***(G-17186)***
Jgs Manufacturing LLC..............................G....... 248 376-1659
Livonia ***(G-10259)***
Jim Bennett..G....... 517 323-9061
Lansing ***(G-9707)***
Jt General Industries LLC...........................G....... 517 712-8481
Howell ***(G-8469)***
Jupiter Manufacturing................................G....... 989 551-0519
Harbor Beach ***(G-7633)***
Jwg Industries..G....... 734 881-0312
Garden City ***(G-6103)***
K & L Manufacturing Ltd............................G....... 734 475-1009
Grass Lake ***(G-7439)***
KB Property Holdings LLC..........................E....... 269 344-0870
Kalamazoo ***(G-9252)***
Kelsheimer Industries LLC..........................G....... 810 701-9455
Corunna ***(G-3709)***
Ken Budowick Fabricating LLC....................G....... 586 263-1318
Clinton Township ***(G-3271)***
Kenny G Mfg & Sls LLC...............................G....... 313 218-6297
Brownstown ***(G-2148)***
Kenyon Tj & Associates Inc.........................G....... 231 544-1144
Bellaire ***(G-1476)***
Kerr Industries of Michigan........................G....... 586 578-9383
Warren ***(G-17894)***
Kharon Industries.......................................G....... 810 630-6355
Swartz Creek ***(G-16356)***
Kommar Industries......................................G....... 231 334-3475
Glen Arbor ***(G-6210)***
Krysak Industries LLC.................................G....... 312 848-1952
Southfield ***(G-15620)***
Ktc Industries LLC......................................G....... 989 838-0388
Traverse City ***(G-16734)***
L&W Products..G....... 248 661-3889
Farmington Hills ***(G-5287)***
L4 Manufacturing LLC.................................G....... 810 217-3407
Brighton ***(G-2017)***
Lawrence Industries Inc..............................G....... 269 664-4614
Plainwell ***(G-13081)***
Legacy Barricades Inc.................................G....... 616 656-9600
Grand Rapids ***(G-6935)***
Liberty Advisors Inc....................................G....... 269 679-3281
Schoolcraft ***(G-15123)***
Liberty Automotive Tech LLC......................G....... 269 487-8114
Holland ***(G-8127)***
Loftis Manufacturing Inc.............................G....... 855 564-8665
Chesterfield ***(G-2905)***
LP Industries Ltd...G....... 313 834-4847
Detroit ***(G-4410)***
Lummi Customs Lc......................................G....... 702 713-8428
Linden ***(G-10064)***
M Industries LLC..G....... 616 745-4279
Ada ***(G-27)***
M Three Manufacturing LLC.........................G....... 810 824-4734
Kimball ***(G-9495)***
Magnatron NC Pattern and Mfg....................G....... 810 522-7520
Howell ***(G-8475)***
Manufacturers Solutions LLC.......................G....... 616 894-2964
Greenville ***(G-7498)***
Manufacturing Options................................G....... 989 430-6770
Midland ***(G-11386)***
Manufctring Partners Group LLC..................G....... 517 749-4050
Lapeer ***(G-9946)***
Marada Industries..G....... 586 264-4908
New Hudson ***(G-12062)***
Mark Eaton Sales and Mfg...........................G....... 517 741-5000
Union City ***(G-17495)***
Marrone Michigan Manufactoring..................G....... 269 427-0300
Bangor ***(G-1130)***
Matney Models...G....... 734 848-8195
Erie ***(G-5051)***
Maximum Manufacturing LLC.......................G....... 810 272-0804
Lake Orion ***(G-9617)***

Employee Codes: A=Over 500 employees, B=251-500
C=101-250, D=51-100, E=20-50, F=10-19, G=3-9
2022 Harris Michigan
Industrial Directory
1327

MANUFACTURING INDUSTRIES, NEC — PRODUCT SECTION

Company	Code	Phone
Meridian Industries, Troy (G-17245)	G	248 526-0444
Metalworking Industries of MI, Farmington Hills (G-5316)	G	248 538-0680
Mettle Craft Manufacturing LLC, Sterling Heights (G-16095)	G	586 306-8962
Mfg United LLC, Melvindale (G-11204)	G	313 928-1802
Mfr Enterprises Inc, Lansing (G-9775)	G	517 285-9555
Mfr Enterprises LLC, Troy (G-17255)	G	248 965-3220
MGM Industries Inc, Berkley (G-1631)	G	248 561-7558
Mgs Horticultural USA Inc, Detroit (G-4442)	E	248 661-4378
Mh Industries Ltd, Detroit (G-4443)	G	734 261-2600
Michigan Laser Mfg LLC, Brighton (G-2030)	G	810 623-2783
Mindchip Industries LLC, Brownstown (G-2150)	G	313 355-2447
Mirus Industries Inc, Grand Haven (G-6336)	G	616 402-3256
Mj Industries LLC, Roseville (G-14445)	G	586 200-3903
Mlc Manufacturing, Spring Lake (G-15836)	E	616 846-6990
Mobility Accessories LLC, Northville (G-12242)	G	734 262-3760
Mobility Howell Products, Warren (G-17934)	G	586 558-8308
Monogram Market LLC, Dewitt (G-4714)	G	517 455-9083
Morton Industries LLC, Grand Rapids (G-7029)	F	616 453-7121
Mote Enterprises Inc, New Haven (G-12035)	G	248 613-3413
Mount Mfg LLC, Negaunee (G-11970)	G	231 487-2118
Mr McGooz Products Inc, Detroit (G-4469)	G	313 693-4003
MRC Indsutries, Roseville (G-14449)	G	586 204-5241
MRC Industries, Kalamazoo (G-9277)	G	269 552-5586
Mse, Sterling Heights (G-16106)	G	586 264-4120
Msmac Designs LLC, Detroit (G-4471)	G	313 521-6289
Neotech Industries Inc, Waterford (G-18139)	G	248 681-6667
Next Chapter Mfg Corp, Grand Rapids (G-7043)	G	616 773-1200
Ngu Industries LLC, Lincoln Park (G-10052)	G	313 283-9570
Noble Industries, Middleville (G-11310)	G	616 245-7400
Novelty House, Madison Heights (G-10790)	G	248 583-9900
Nyman Industries LLC, Grosse Pointe (G-7531)	G	702 290-9433
Oak Mountain Industries, Romulus (G-14313)	G	734 941-7000
Octet Industries LLC, Ann Arbor (G-598)	G	225 302-0541
Odin Defense Industries Inc, Troy (G-17286)	G	248 434-5072
Pacific Industries Inc, Whitmore Lake (G-18542)	G	810 360-9141
Palo Alto Manufacturing LLC, Auburn Hills (G-992)	G	248 266-3669
Pandia Industries LLC, Colon (G-3489)	G	269 386-2110
Panelcraft Inc, Canton (G-2504)	G	734 646-2173
Patriot Bars Mfg LLC, Chesterfield (G-2922)	G	248 342-4319
Pearson Industries LLC, Detroit (G-4510)	G	740 584-9080
Pegasus Industries, Lapeer (G-9953)	F	810 356-5579
Pesti Manufacturing Company, Warren (G-17960)	G	586 920-2731
Pingree Mfg L3c, Detroit (G-4524)	G	313 444-8428
Pinsmedalscoins LLC, Lansing (G-9729)	G	312 771-2973
Plainview Industries LLC, Charlotte (G-2765)	G	517 652-1466
Plush Products Mfg LLC, Clyde (G-3414)	G	586 871-8082
Pmd Automotive LLC, Pontiac (G-13407)	G	248 732-7554
Ponder Industrial, Bay City (G-1388)	G	989 391-4575
Pr39 Industries LLC, Keego Harbor (G-9422)	G	248 866-1445
Preacher Industries, White Lake (G-18463)	G	248 881-6590
Prf Manufacturing USA Inc, Roseville (G-14465)	G	586 218-3055
Price Industries LLC, Dearborn (G-3885)	G	313 706-9862
Price Koch Industries, Caledonia (G-2394)	G	616 871-0263
Pringles Manufacturing Company, Battle Creek (G-1282)	F	731 421-3148
Pro-Built Mfg, Alpena (G-312)	G	989 354-1321
Purescription Grade LLC, West Bloomfield (G-18308)	G	313 410-5686
Px2 Holdings LLC, Troy (G-17321)	D	855 420-0020
Q Sage Inc, Mount Pleasant (G-11735)	F	989 775-2424
Quality Stainless MGF, Metamora (G-11285)	G	248 866-6219
Quantum Custom Designs LLC, Fraser (G-5984)	G	989 293-7372
Quinco Tool, Oak Park (G-12638)	G	313 353-1340
R House Industries LLC, Grand Rapids (G-7133)	F	616 890-7125
R J Chemical Manufacturing LLC, Clio (G-3410)	G	810 252-8425
R J Manufacturing, Davison (G-3794)	G	810 610-0205
Real Steel Manufacturing LLC, Muskegon (G-11906)	F	231 457-4673
Resourcemfg, Port Huron (G-13523)	F	810 937-5058
Rfm Manufacturing, Brighton (G-2065)	G	810 522-6922
Rilas & Rogers LLC, Canton (G-2517)	F	937 901-4228
Rise Beyond LLC, Ypsilanti (G-18974)	G	734 203-0644
Roi Rich Oles Industries LLC, Saint Joseph (G-14958)	G	616 610-7050
Roots Industries, Cadillac (G-2352)	G	231 779-2865
Rottman Manufacturing Group, Sterling Heights (G-16160)	G	586 693-5676
Roush Industries Inc, Redford (G-13766)	F	313 937-8603
Rpd Manufacturing LLC, Milford (G-11486)	G	248 760-4796
Rta Industries LLC, Portage (G-13601)	G	269 327-2916
Ruf International Mfg Corp, Charlevoix (G-2732)	G	954 448-3454
Rusnak Tool & Mfg LLC, Woodhaven (G-18803)	G	734 362-8656
Saegertown Manufacturing Inc, Howell (G-8514)	G	517 281-9789
Saffe Furniture Corp, Muskegon (G-11915)	G	231 329-1790
Sawtelle Industries LLC, Bloomfield Hills (G-1860)	G	248 645-1869
Schlegel, Northville (G-12258)	G	248 344-0997
Schwartz Manufacturing, Howell (G-8515)	G	517 552-3100
Scw Industries LLC, Lansing (G-9893)	G	616 656-5959
SDS LLC, Traverse City (G-16827)	G	231 492-5996
Shamrock Industries LLC, Holland (G-8189)	F	616 566-6214
Shaw Industries Detroit Rdc, Van Buren Twp (G-17552)	G	800 469-9516
Shelby Industries Inc, Shelby Township (G-15331)	G	586 884-4421
Shoreline Manufacturing LLC, Holland (G-8193)	G	616 834-1503
Shoreline Manufacturing LLC, Holland (G-8194)	G	616 834-1503
Sky Industries, Columbiaville (G-3495)	G	810 614-6044
Sofia Rose Industries Inc, Clay (G-3125)	G	810 278-4907
Solarfall Industries LLC, Hemlock (G-7855)	G	269 274-6108
Sole Industries LLC, Washington Township (G-18096)	G	586 322-5492
Southwestern Industries Inc, Tecumseh (G-16516)	G	517 667-0466
Special-Lite Inc - Benton, Benton Harbor (G-1588)	G	269 423-7068
Spurt Industries, Wixom (G-18755)	G	248 956-7643
Sra Industries, Shelby Township (G-15343)	G	586 251-2000
Stainless Concepts LLC, Zeeland (G-19081)	G	616 427-6682
Stansley Industries Inc, Flint (G-5769)	G	810 515-1919
Stewart General Incorporated, Nunica (G-12586)	G	616 318-4971
Stretchy Screens, Caledonia (G-2402)	G	989 780-1624
Suiter Industries Inc, Lansing (G-9897)	G	989 277-1554
Summit Cutting Tool and Mfg In, Wixom (G-18760)	G	248 624-3949
Sun Coast Coverings LLC, Taylor (G-16480)	F	734 947-1230
T 4 Manufacturing, Kent City (G-9438)	G	616 952-0020
T K Industries Inc, Shelby Township (G-15348)	G	586 242-5969
Tags R Us LLC, White Lake (G-18468)	G	248 880-4062
Texwood Industries, Adrian (G-98)	G	517 266-4739
Tide Rings LLC, Allenton (G-232)	G	586 206-3142
Tillman Manufacturing Com, Southfield (G-15723)	G	248 802-8430
Tip Top Screw Manufacturi, Saginaw (G-14776)	G	989 739-5157
To Z A Manufacturing, Flat Rock (G-5631)	G	734 782-3911
Toreson Industries Inc, Inkster (G-8676)	G	818 261-7249
Total Repair Express MI LLC, Auburn Hills (G-1061)	F	248 690-9410
Tramar Industries, Redford (G-13780)	G	313 387-3600
Tremco Inc Sealex Mfg Pla, Harbor Springs (G-7660)	G	231 348-5020
Trident Mfg LLC, Ithaca (G-8796)	F	989 875-5145
Triunfar Industries Inc, South Lyon (G-15460)	G	313 790-5592
Triunfar Industries Inc I, Commerce Township (G-3579)	G	248 993-9302
Uis Industries LLC, Livonia (G-10453)	G	734 443-3737
Universal Industries Inco, Macomb (G-10647)	G	248 259-2674
Universal Pultrusion, Decatur (G-3952)	G	269 423-7068
Unypos Manufacturing Inc, Grand Blanc (G-6265)	G	810 701-8719
Uvsheltron Inc, Pontiac (G-13423)	G	888 877-7946
Val Manufacturing Co LLC, Troy (G-17424)	G	248 765-8694
Valley Manufacturing, Wixom (G-18784)	G	248 767-5078
Vantage Point Mfg Inc, West Branch (G-18345)	F	989 343-1070
Vertex Industries Inc, Dearborn (G-3909)	G	248 838-1827
Wende J Periard, Burt (G-2217)	G	989 770-4542
Weslope Industries Inc, Royal Oak (G-14592)	G	248 320-7007
White Knight Industries, South Haven (G-15426)	G	269 823-4207
Wild Manufacturing, Harrison Township (G-7731)	G	586 719-2028
Wings Mfg Inc, Mount Clemens (G-11664)	G	585 873-3105
Winsol Electronics LLC, Flint (G-5793)	G	810 767-2987
Wood Haven Truss, Holton (G-8343)	G	231 821-0252

PRODUCT SECTION

Xplor Outside Box LLC .... F 248 961-0536
  Warren *(G-18076)*
Xtreme Mfg .... G 906 353-8005
  Baraga *(G-1151)*
Zero Hour Production LLC .... F 616 498-3545
  Ann Arbor *(G-722)*
Zoe Health .... G 616 485-1909
  Kentwood *(G-9485)*

MAPS

Discovery Map .... G 231 421-1466
  Traverse City *(G-16669)*
Metro Graphic Arts Inc .... F 616 245-2271
  Grand Rapids *(G-6982)*

MAPS & CHARTS, WHOLESALE

Metro Graphic Arts Inc .... F 616 245-2271
  Grand Rapids *(G-6982)*

MARBLE, BUILDING: Cut & Shaped

Dura Sill Corporation .... G 248 348-2490
  Novi *(G-12405)*
K2 Stoneworks LLC .... F 989 790-3250
  Saginaw *(G-14675)*
Lakeshore Marble Company Inc .... F 269 429-8241
  Stevensville *(G-16257)*
Tile Craft Inc .... F 231 929-7207
  Traverse City *(G-16860)*
Zimmer Marble Co Inc .... F 517 787-1500
  Jackson *(G-9041)*

MARINAS

Floatation Docking Inc .... E 906 484-3422
  Cedarville *(G-2669)*
Macs Marina Motorsports .... F 248 486-8300
  South Lyon *(G-15445)*
Midwest Aquatics Group Inc .... G 734 426-4155
  Pinckney *(G-13052)*

MARINE BASIN OPERATIONS

Superior Mar & Envmtl Svcs LLC .... G 906 253-9448
  Sault Sainte Marie *(G-15101)*

MARINE CARGO HANDLING SVCS: Marine Terminal

Nicholson Terminal & Dock Co .... D 313 842-4300
  River Rouge *(G-13858)*

MARINE ENGINE REPAIR SVCS

Arthur R Sommers .... G 586 469-1280
  Harrison Township *(G-7689)*
Creek Diesel Services Inc .... F 800 974-4600
  Grand Rapids *(G-6611)*
Marsh Brothers Inc .... F 517 869-2653
  Quincy *(G-13671)*
Murleys Marine .... G 586 725-7446
  Ira *(G-8705)*

MARINE HARDWARE

A & B Tube Benders Inc .... F 586 773-0440
  Warren *(G-17678)*
Attwood Corporation .... C 616 897-2301
  Lowell *(G-10495)*
Big Dog Marine LLC .... G 248 705-2875
  Highland *(G-7884)*
Detmar Corporation .... E 313 831-1155
  Detroit *(G-4134)*
Fathom Drones Inc .... G 586 216-7047
  Grand Rapids *(G-6703)*
HI TEC Stainless Inc .... G 269 543-4205
  Fennville *(G-5438)*
Jay & Kay Manufacturing LLC .... E 810 679-2333
  Croswell *(G-3730)*
Marine Industries Inc .... F 989 635-3644
  Marlette *(G-10985)*
T & L Products .... G 989 868-4428
  Reese *(G-13809)*
Tecla Company Inc .... E 248 624-8200
  Commerce Township *(G-3576)*
Tops-In-Quality Inc .... G 810 364-7150
  Marysville *(G-11109)*
Triton Global Sources Inc .... G 734 668-7107
  Ypsilanti *(G-18981)*

MARINE PROPELLER REPAIR SVCS

Allied Welding Incorporated .... G 248 360-1122
  Commerce Township *(G-3509)*
Falcon Motorsports Inc .... G 248 328-2222
  Holly *(G-8269)*

MARINE RELATED EQPT

Fireboy-Xintex Inc .... E 616 735-9380
  Grand Rapids *(G-6706)*
Marine Propulsion LLC .... G 248 396-2353
  West Bloomfield *(G-18295)*
PSI Marine Inc .... F 989 695-2646
  Saginaw *(G-14731)*

MARINE SPLY DEALERS

Holiday Distributing Co .... E 517 782-7146
  Jackson *(G-8904)*

MARINE SPLYS WHOLESALERS

Itc Incorporated .... E 616 396-1355
  Hudsonville *(G-8587)*
T & L Products .... G 989 868-4428
  Reese *(G-13809)*

MARKERS

Carco Inc .... E 313 925-1053
  Detroit *(G-4089)*

MARKETS: Meat & fish

Kowalski Companies Inc .... C 313 873-8200
  Detroit *(G-4366)*
Smith & Sons Meat Proc Inc .... G 989 772-6048
  Mount Pleasant *(G-11738)*

MARKING DEVICES

Argon Tool Inc .... F 248 583-1605
  Madison Heights *(G-10672)*
Borries Mkg Systems Partnr .... G 734 761-9549
  Ann Arbor *(G-404)*
Carco Inc .... E 313 925-1053
  Detroit *(G-4089)*
Columbia Marking Tools Inc .... E 586 949-8400
  Chesterfield *(G-2860)*
F & A Enterprises of Michigan .... G 906 228-3222
  Marquette *(G-11018)*
JL Geisler Sign Company .... F 586 574-1800
  Troy *(G-17187)*
Mark-Pack Inc .... E 616 837-5400
  Coopersville *(G-3691)*
Michigan Shippers Supply Inc .... F 616 935-6680
  Spring Lake *(G-15835)*
Nelson Paint Co of Mich Inc .... G 906 774-5566
  Kingsford *(G-9514)*
Rite Mark Stamp Company .... F 248 391-7600
  Auburn Hills *(G-1021)*
Volk Corporation .... G 616 940-9900
  Northville *(G-12270)*

MARKING DEVICES: Embossing Seals & Hand Stamps

Detroit Marking Products Corp .... F 313 838-9760
  Canton *(G-2454)*
New Method Steel Stamps Inc .... G 586 293-0200
  Fraser *(G-5967)*
Rodzina Industries Inc .... G 810 235-2341
  Flint *(G-5755)*
Rubber Stamps Unlimited Inc .... F 734 451-7300
  Plymouth *(G-13291)*
Stamp-Rite Incorporated .... E 517 487-5071
  Lansing *(G-9741)*

MARKING DEVICES: Printing Dies, Marking Mach, Rubber/Plastic

Mark Maker Company Inc .... E 616 538-6980
  Grand Rapids *(G-6959)*

MARKING DEVICES: Screens, Textile Printing

All American Embroidery Inc .... F 734 421-9292
  Livonia *(G-10108)*

MEAL DELIVERY PROGRAMS

MARKING DEVICES: Seal Presses, Notary & Hand

Mlh Services LLC .... G 313 768-4403
  Detroit *(G-4462)*

MARKING DEVICES: Stationary Embossers, Personal

Events To Envy .... G 248 841-8400
  Rochester *(G-13899)*

MASKS: Gas

Avon Protection Systems Inc .... C 231 779-6200
  Cadillac *(G-2314)*

MASQUERADE OR THEATRICAL COSTUMES STORES

Excellent Designs Swimwear .... G 586 977-9140
  Warren *(G-17799)*

MASSAGE MACHINES, ELECTRIC: Barber & Beauty Shops

Body Contour Ventures LLC .... E 248 579-6772
  Farmington Hills *(G-5184)*

MATERIAL GRINDING & PULVERIZING SVCS NEC

Dgh Enterprises Inc .... E 269 925-0657
  Benton Harbor *(G-1546)*
Midwest Grinding .... G 734 395-1033
  Maybee *(G-11170)*
Reynolds Cntrless Grinding LLC .... G 313 418-5109
  Redford *(G-13764)*
Total Grinding Solutions LLC .... F 586 541-5300
  Warren *(G-18041)*
United Mfg Netwrk Inc .... G 586 321-7887
  Chesterfield *(G-2960)*
Williams Diversified Inc .... E 734 421-6100
  Livonia *(G-10475)*

MATERIALS HANDLING EQPT WHOLESALERS

Albion Industries LLC .... C 800 835-8911
  Albion *(G-114)*
Detroit Wire Rope Splcing Corp .... G 248 585-1063
  Madison Heights *(G-10706)*
Dobson Industrial Inc .... E 800 298-6063
  Bay City *(G-1346)*
Great Lakes Allied LLC .... G 231 924-5794
  White Cloud *(G-18441)*
Henshaw Inc .... D 586 752-0700
  Armada *(G-736)*
Material Handling Tech Inc .... D 586 725-5546
  Ira *(G-8701)*
Pettibone/Traverse Lift LLC .... E 906 353-4800
  Baraga *(G-1147)*
Sunhill America LLC .... E 616 249-3600
  Grand Rapids *(G-7234)*
Superior Equipment & Supply Co .... G 906 774-1789
  Iron Mountain *(G-8734)*

MATS, MATTING & PADS: Nonwoven

Apparelmaster-Muskegon Inc .... E 231 728-5406
  Muskegon *(G-11772)*
Great Lakes Right of Way LLC .... G 616 263-9898
  Cedar Springs *(G-2652)*
HR Technologies Inc .... C 248 284-1170
  Madison Heights *(G-10743)*
N A Visscher-Caravelle Inc .... G 248 851-9800
  Bloomfield Hills *(G-1842)*

MATTRESS PROTECTORS: Rubber

Rubber Tucker LLC .... G 586 216-7071
  Clinton Township *(G-3345)*

MATTRESS STORES

Spring Air Co .... G 616 459-8234
  Grand Rapids *(G-7221)*

MEAL DELIVERY PROGRAMS

Goodwill Inds Nthrn Mich Inc .... G 231 779-1311
  Cadillac *(G-2332)*

Employee Codes: A=Over 500 employees, B=251-500 .
C=101-250, D=51-100, E=20-50, F=10-19, G=3-9

2022 Harris Michigan Industrial Directory

MEAL DELIVERY PROGRAMS

Goodwill Inds Nthrn Mich Inc ....G....... 231 779-1361
  Cadillac (G-2333)
Goodwill Inds Nthrn Mich Inc ....G....... 231 922-4890
  Traverse City (G-16696)

MEAT & MEAT PRDTS WHOLESALERS

Protein Procurement Svcs Inc.............G....... 248 738-7970
  Bloomfield Hills (G-1853)

MEAT CUTTING & PACKING

Bellinger Packing...............................E....... 989 838-2274
  Ashley (G-741)
Bernthal Packing Inc.........................F....... 989 652-2648
  Frankenmuth (G-5859)
Bert Hazekamp & Son Inc ....C....... 231 773-8302
  Muskegon (G-11778)
Berthiaume Slaughter House ....G....... 989 879-4921
  Pinconning (G-13059)
Boars Head Provisions Co Inc.............C....... 941 955-0994
  Holland (G-7978)
Boyers Meat Processing Inc ....G....... 734 495-1342
  Canton (G-2443)
Cargill Incorporated............................F....... 608 868-5150
  Owosso (G-12825)
Carol Packing House............................G....... 989 673-2688
  Caro (G-2566)
Clemens Welcome Center ....G....... 517 278-2500
  Coldwater (G-3426)
Cole Carter Inc....................................G....... 269 626-8891
  Scotts (G-15131)
Cornbelt Beef Corporation ....G....... 313 237-0087
  Oak Park (G-12598)
Countryside Quality Meats LLC..........F....... 517 741-4275
  Union City (G-17491)
Erlas Inc ....D....... 989 872-2191
  Cass City (G-2614)
Gainors Meat Packing Inc ....G....... 989 269-8161
  Bad Axe (G-1101)
Garys Custom Meats ....G....... 269 641-5683
  Union (G-17487)
Gibbies Deer Processing ....G....... 231 924-6042
  Fremont (G-6044)
Hormel Foods Corporation ....G....... 616 454-0418
  Grand Rapids (G-6820)
Kent Quality Foods Inc ....C....... 616 459-4595
  Hudsonville (G-8589)
Lloyd Johnson Livestock Inc...............F....... 906 786-4878
  Escanaba (G-5081)
Makkedah Mt Proc & Bulk Fd Str........G....... 231 873-2113
  Hart (G-7757)
Maurer Meat Processors Inc................F....... 989 658-8185
  Ubly (G-17478)
Michigan Brand Inc............................G....... 989 395-4345
  Frankenmuth (G-5870)
Mikes Meat Processing ....G....... 269 468-6173
  Coloma (G-3480)
Nagel Meat Processing ....G....... 517 568-5035
  Homer (G-8355)
Northern Processing ....G....... 989 734-9007
  Rogers City (G-14213)
Northwest Market................................G....... 517 787-5005
  Jackson (G-8977)
Papa Joes Grmet Mkt Hnry Ford ....F....... 248 609-5670
  Detroit (G-4504)
Pinkney Hill Meat Co..........................G....... 616 897-4921
  Saranac (G-15080)
Pooles Meat Processing ....G....... 989 846-6348
  Standish (G-15894)
Rays Game ....G....... 810 346-2628
  Brown City (G-2141)
Ricks Meat Processing LLC.................G....... 517 628-2263
  Eaton Rapids (G-4971)
Smith & Sons Meat Proc Inc ....G....... 989 772-6048
  Mount Pleasant (G-11738)
Smith - Sons ME ....G....... 989 772-6048
  Mount Pleasant (G-11739)
Smith Meat Packing Inc......................E....... 810 985-5900
  Port Huron (G-13528)
Standard Provision LLC......................G....... 989 354-4975
  Alpena (G-319)
Tyson Foods Inc..................................G....... 231 922-3214
  Traverse City (G-16870)
Tyson Foods Inc..................................G....... 231 929-2456
  Traverse City (G-16871)
Tyson Fresh Meats Inc ....G....... 248 213-1000
  Southfield (G-15729)
Vin-Lee-Ron Meat Packing LLC..........F....... 574 353-1386
  Cassopolis (G-2635)

MEAT MARKETS

Bellinger Packing...............................E....... 989 838-2274
  Ashley (G-741)
Bernthal Packing Inc.........................F....... 989 652-2648
  Frankenmuth (G-5859)
Cattlemans Meat Company ....B....... 734 287-8260
  Taylor (G-16391)
Hashems of Dearborn Heights ....F....... 313 278-2000
  Dearborn Heights (G-3928)
Kerns Sausages Inc............................F....... 989 652-2684
  Frankenmuth (G-5867)
Northwest Market................................G....... 517 787-5005
  Jackson (G-8977)
Russo Bros Inc....................................G....... 906 485-5250
  Ishpeming (G-8781)
Viaus Super Market............................G....... 906 786-1950
  Escanaba (G-5106)

MEAT PRDTS: Boxed Beef, From Slaughtered Meat

Jbs Packerland Inc ....F....... 269 685-6886
  Plainwell (G-13078)
Jbs Plainwell Inc ....F....... 269 685-6886
  Plainwell (G-13079)

MEAT PRDTS: Canned Exc Baby Food, From Slaughtered Meat

Spillson Ltd ....G....... 734 384-0284
  Monroe (G-11575)

MEAT PRDTS: Cooked Meats, From Purchased Meat

Great Fresh Foods Co LLC..................E....... 734 904-0731
  Taylor (G-16422)
Pioneer Meats LLC.............................F....... 248 862-1988
  Birmingham (G-1744)

MEAT PRDTS: Corned Beef, From Purchased Meat

T Wigley Inc ....F....... 313 831-6881
  Detroit (G-4624)

MEAT PRDTS: Cured, From Slaughtered Meat

A & R Packing Co Inc ....E....... 734 422-2060
  Livonia (G-10092)

MEAT PRDTS: Frankfurters, From Purchased Meat

Koegel Meats Inc................................C....... 810 238-3685
  Flint (G-5722)

MEAT PRDTS: Lamb, From Slaughtered Meat

Berry Sns-Rbbeh Islmic Slghtrh..........G....... 313 259-6925
  Detroit (G-4051)
Michigan Veal Inc...............................E....... 616 669-6688
  Hudsonville (G-8596)

MEAT PRDTS: Luncheon Meat, From Purchased Meat

Boars Head Provisions Co Inc.............C....... 941 955-0994
  Holland (G-7978)

MEAT PRDTS: Meat By-Prdts, From Slaughtered Meat

Prime Cuts of Jackson LLC ....E....... 517 768-8090
  Jackson (G-8991)

MEAT PRDTS: Pork, From Slaughtered Meat

Pleasant Valley Packing LLC ....D....... 517 278-2500
  Coldwater (G-3446)

MEAT PRDTS: Prepared Beef Prdts From Purchased Beef

Cattlemans Meat Company ....B....... 734 287-8260
  Taylor (G-16391)
Smigelski Properties LLC ....G....... 989 255-6252
  Alpena (G-317)

MEAT PRDTS: Prepared Pork Prdts, From Purchased Meat

Quincy Street Inc ....C....... 616 399-3330
  Holland (G-8174)

MEAT PRDTS: Sausages & Related Prdts, From Purchased Meat

Louies Meats Inc.................................E....... 231 946-4811
  Traverse City (G-16748)

MEAT PRDTS: Sausages, From Purchased Meat

Kowalski Companies Inc.....................C....... 313 873-8200
  Detroit (G-4366)
Krzysiak Family Restaurant ....D....... 989 894-5531
  Bay City (G-1372)
Macomb Smoked Meats LLC..............D....... 313 842-2375
  Dearborn (G-3867)
Mello Meats Inc..................................F....... 800 852-5019
  Auburn Hills (G-972)
Vandco Incorporated..........................G....... 906 482-1550
  Hancock (G-7623)
Viaus Super Market............................G....... 906 786-1950
  Escanaba (G-5106)

MEAT PRDTS: Sausages, From Slaughtered Meat

Bob Evans Farms Inc ....A....... 517 437-3349
  Hillsdale (G-7926)
Safari Meats Llc..................................G....... 313 539-3367
  Oak Park (G-12644)

MEAT PRDTS: Smoked

A & R Packing Co Inc ....E....... 734 422-2060
  Livonia (G-10092)
Big O Smokehouse Inc.......................E....... 616 891-5555
  Caledonia (G-2368)

MEAT PRDTS: Snack Sticks, Incl Jerky, From Purchased Meat

Deerings Jerky Co LLC ....G....... 231 590-5687
  Interlochen (G-8682)
Freds Jerky Products ....G....... 517 202-1908
  Charlotte (G-2756)
Jerky Stock LLc ....G....... 616 481-2329
  Grand Rapids (G-6869)

MEAT PRDTS: Veal, From Slaughtered Meat

Wolverine Packing Co ....D....... 313 259-7500
  Detroit (G-4688)

MEAT PROCESSED FROM PURCHASED CARCASSES

Bernthal Packing Inc.........................F....... 989 652-2648
  Frankenmuth (G-5859)
Bert Hazekamp & Son Inc ....C....... 231 773-8302
  Muskegon (G-11778)
Darling Ingredients Inc ....G....... 269 751-0560
  Hamilton (G-7597)
Dina Mia Kitchens Inc.......................E....... 906 265-9082
  Iron River (G-8740)
Erlas Inc ....D....... 989 872-2191
  Cass City (G-2614)
Hillshire Brands Company ....G....... 616 875-8131
  Zeeland (G-19038)
Hillshire Brands Company ....G....... 231 947-2100
  Traverse City (G-16711)
Kent Quality Foods Inc ....C....... 616 459-4595
  Hudsonville (G-8589)
Kerns Sausages Inc............................F....... 989 652-2684
  Frankenmuth (G-5867)
Pleasant Valley Packing LLC ....D....... 517 278-2500
  Coldwater (G-3446)

MEAT PROCESSING MACHINERY

Lowry Joanellen..................................G....... 231 873-2323
  Hesperia (G-7870)
Saa Tech Inc.......................................G....... 313 933-4960
  Detroit (G-4575)

PRODUCT SECTION

MEATS, PACKAGED FROZEN: Wholesalers
Wolverine Packing Co .... D 313 259-7500
  Detroit *(G-4688)*

MEDIA: Magnetic & Optical Recording
Storch Products Company Inc .... F 734 591-2200
  Livonia *(G-10422)*

MEDICAL & HOSPITAL EQPT WHOLESALERS
Alta Distribution LLC .... F 313 363-1682
  Southfield *(G-15477)*
Cmp Acquisitions LLC .... F 888 519-2286
  Redford *(G-13726)*
Landra Prsthtics Orthotics Inc .... G 586 294-7188
  Saint Clair Shores *(G-14868)*
MCS Consultants Inc .... G 810 229-4222
  Brighton *(G-2029)*
Northwest Tool & Machine Inc .... E 517 750-1332
  Jackson *(G-8978)*
Vets Access LLC .... G 810 639-2222
  Flushing *(G-5815)*

MEDICAL & HOSPITAL SPLYS: Radiation Shielding Garments
Bio Cmmunication Solutions LLC ..... G 616 502-0238
  Spring Lake *(G-15805)*
Biocomsolutions LLC .... G 616 502-0238
  Spring Lake *(G-15806)*
Radiolgical Fabrication Design .... G 810 632-6000
  Howell *(G-8506)*

MEDICAL & SURGICAL SPLYS: Abdominal Support, Braces/Trusses
Bms Great Lakes LLC .... G 248 390-1598
  Lake Orion *(G-9588)*

MEDICAL & SURGICAL SPLYS: Absorbent Cotton, Sterilized
Beltone Skoric Hearng Aid Cntr .... G 906 379-0606
  Sault Sainte Marie *(G-15087)*
Beltone Skoric Hearng Aid Cntr .... G 906 553-4660
  Escanaba *(G-5061)*

MEDICAL & SURGICAL SPLYS: Bandages & Dressings
Shock-Tek LLC .... G 313 886-0530
  Saint Clair Shores *(G-14883)*

MEDICAL & SURGICAL SPLYS: Belts, Surg, Sanitary & Corrective
Trulife Inc .... E 800 492-1088
  Jackson *(G-9026)*

MEDICAL & SURGICAL SPLYS: Braces, Orthopedic
Becker Oregon Inc .... E 248 588-7480
  Troy *(G-16969)*
Greater Lansing Orthotic Clini .... G 517 337-0856
  Lansing *(G-9845)*
Oakland Orthopedic Appls Inc .... F 989 893-7544
  Bay City *(G-1384)*
Paul W Reed DDS .... G 231 347-4145
  Petoskey *(G-13012)*
Twin Cities Orthotic & Prosthe .... G 269 428-2910
  Saint Joseph *(G-14967)*

MEDICAL & SURGICAL SPLYS: Canes, Orthopedic
Pharmaceutical Specialties LLC .... G 269 382-6406
  Galesburg *(G-6081)*

MEDICAL & SURGICAL SPLYS: Clothing, Fire Resistant & Protect
Performance Fabrics Inc .... C 616 459-4144
  Grand Rapids *(G-7079)*

MEDICAL & SURGICAL SPLYS: Cosmetic Restorations
Agelessmage Fcial Asthtics LLC ...... G 269 998-5547
  Farmington Hills *(G-5161)*
Luma Laser and Medi Spa .... G 248 817-5499
  Bloomfield Hills *(G-1833)*

MEDICAL & SURGICAL SPLYS: Crutches & Walkers
Hi-Trac Industries Inc .... G 810 625-7193
  Linden *(G-10063)*

MEDICAL & SURGICAL SPLYS: Ear Plugs
McKeon Products Inc .... E 586 427-7560
  Warren *(G-17922)*

MEDICAL & SURGICAL SPLYS: Foot Appliances, Orthopedic
First Response Med Sups LLC .... F 313 731-2554
  Dearborn *(G-3840)*

MEDICAL & SURGICAL SPLYS: Limbs, Artificial
American Prosthetic Institute .... G 517 349-3130
  Okemos *(G-12655)*
Becker Orthopedic Appliance Co ..... D 248 588-7480
  Troy *(G-16970)*
College Park Industries Inc .... E 586 294-7950
  Warren *(G-17760)*
Landra Prsthtics Orthotics Inc .... G 734 281-8144
  Southgate *(G-15753)*
Out On A Limb Playhouses .... G 616 502-4251
  Grand Haven *(G-6341)*
Ultralight Prosthetics Inc .... G 313 538-8500
  Redford *(G-13781)*

MEDICAL & SURGICAL SPLYS: Models, Anatomical
Studio One Midwest Inc .... F 269 962-3475
  Battle Creek *(G-1302)*

MEDICAL & SURGICAL SPLYS: Orthopedic Appliances
Avasure Holdings Inc .... E 616 301-0129
  Belmont *(G-1500)*
David Epstein Inc .... F 248 542-0802
  Ferndale *(G-5539)*
Davismade Inc .... F 810 743-5262
  Flint *(G-5684)*
Mount Clemens Orthopedic Appls ... G 586 463-3600
  Clinton Township *(G-3305)*
Northwest Orthotics-Prosthetic .... G 248 477-1443
  Novi *(G-12491)*
O and P Sparton .... G 517 220-4960
  East Lansing *(G-4907)*
Orthotic Shop Inc .... G 800 309-0412
  Shelby Township *(G-15294)*
Preferred Products Inc .... F 248 255-0200
  Commerce Township *(G-3565)*
Strive Orthtics Prsthetics LLC .... G 586 803-4325
  Sterling Heights *(G-16196)*
Um Orthotics Pros Cntr .... G 734 764-3100
  Ann Arbor *(G-704)*
Zimmer - Lieffring Inc .... F 734 953-1630
  Novi *(G-12574)*

MEDICAL & SURGICAL SPLYS: Personal Safety Eqpt
Aactus Inc .... G 734 425-1212
  Livonia *(G-10096)*
James Glove & Supply .... F 810 733-5780
  Flint *(G-5718)*
Mask Makers LLC .... G 313 790-1784
  South Lyon *(G-15446)*
Skyline Window Cleaning Inc .... E 616 895-4143
  Allendale *(G-228)*
Stryker Corporation .... E 269 389-3741
  Portage *(G-13614)*
Stryker Sales LLC .... E 269 323-1027
  Portage *(G-13621)*

MEDICAL & SURGICAL SPLYS: Prosthetic Appliances
Andersen Eye Prosthetics LLC .... G 989 249-1030
  Detroit *(G-4020)*
Axiobionics .... G 734 327-2946
  Ann Arbor *(G-391)*
Binson-Becker Inc .... F 888 246-7667
  Center Line *(G-2680)*
Biopro Inc .... E 810 982-7777
  Port Huron *(G-13458)*
Bremer Prosthetic Design Inc .... G 810 733-3375
  Flint *(G-5660)*
Bremer Prosthetics LLC .... G 989 249-9400
  Saginaw *(G-14620)*
Hackley Health Ventures Inc .... G 231 728-5720
  Muskegon *(G-11834)*
Hanger Prsthetcs & Ortho Inc .... F 517 394-5850
  Lansing *(G-9851)*
J & K Spratt Enterprises Inc .... D 517 439-5010
  Hillsdale *(G-7938)*
Landra Prsthtics Orthotics Inc .... G 586 294-7188
  Saint Clair Shores *(G-14868)*
Metro Medical Eqp Mfg Inc .... E 734 522-8400
  Livonia *(G-10313)*
P & O Services Inc .... G 248 809-3072
  Southfield *(G-15670)*
Prosthetic & Implant Dentistry .... G 248 254-3945
  Farmington Hills *(G-5355)*
Prosthetic Center Inc .... G 517 372-7007
  Dimondale *(G-4764)*
Springer Prsthtic Orthtic Svcs .... G 517 337-0300
  Lansing *(G-9896)*
Wright & Filippis Inc .... G 313 832-5020
  Detroit *(G-4692)*

MEDICAL & SURGICAL SPLYS: Respiratory Protect Eqpt, Personal
Abretec Group LLC .... E 248 591-4000
  Royal Oak *(G-14503)*
Carlson Technology Inc .... G 248 476-0013
  Livonia *(G-10147)*

MEDICAL & SURGICAL SPLYS: Technical Aids, Handicapped
Assistive Technology Mich Inc .... G 248 348-7161
  Novi *(G-12367)*
Gresham Driving Aids Inc .... F 248 624-1533
  Wixom *(G-18672)*

MEDICAL & SURGICAL SPLYS: Traction Apparatus
Micro Engineering Inc .... G 616 534-9681
  Byron Center *(G-2285)*

MEDICAL & SURGICAL SPLYS: Welders' Hoods
Americandiecast Releasants .... G 810 714-1964
  Fenton *(G-5450)*
Gipson Fabrications .... G 616 245-7331
  Wyoming *(G-18874)*

MEDICAL EQPT: Cardiographs
Eaton Industries Inc .... G 734 428-0000
  Ann Arbor *(G-464)*

MEDICAL EQPT: Diagnostic
Bd Diagnostic Systems .... G 313 442-8800
  Detroit *(G-4044)*
Complete Health System .... G 810 720-3891
  Flint *(G-5670)*
Deuwave LLC .... G 888 238-9283
  Northville *(G-12214)*
Functional Fluidics Inc .... G 410 493-8322
  Detroit *(G-4248)*
Genesis Innovation Group LLC .... E 616 294-1026
  Holland *(G-8049)*
Horiba Instruments Inc .... E 734 487-8300
  Canton *(G-2472)*
Michigan Med Innovations LLC .... G 616 682-4848
  Ada *(G-30)*
Pinnacle Technology Group .... D 734 568-6600
  Ottawa Lake *(G-12810)*

MEDICAL EQPT: Electromedical Apparatus

Gelman Sciences Inc .... C 734 665-0651
  Ann Arbor (G-496)
Heart Sync Inc .... F 734 213-5530
  Ann Arbor (G-512)

MEDICAL EQPT: Electrotherapeutic Apparatus

Oncofusion Therapeutics Inc .... F 248 361-3341
  Northville (G-12249)

MEDICAL EQPT: Heart-Lung Machines, Exc Iron Lungs

Gys Tech LLC .... F 269 385-2600
  Portage (G-13563)

MEDICAL EQPT: Laser Systems

American Lazer Centers .... G 248 798-6552
  Clinton Township (G-3166)

MEDICAL EQPT: TENS Units/Transcutaneous Elec Nerve Stimulatr

Merlin Simulation Inc .... G 703 560-7203
  Dexter (G-4745)

MEDICAL EQPT: Ultrasonic Scanning Devices

Endra Life Sciences Inc .... F 734 335-0468
  Ann Arbor (G-474)
Xoran Holdings LLC .... G 734 418-5108
  Ann Arbor (G-718)
Xoran Technologies LLC .... D 734 663-7194
  Ann Arbor (G-719)

MEDICAL HELP SVCS

Liver Transplant/Univ of Mich .... G 734 936-7670
  Ann Arbor (G-552)

MEDICAL SUNDRIES: Rubber

MCS Consultants Inc .... G 810 229-4222
  Brighton (G-2029)

MEDICAL SVCS ORGANIZATION

Intrinsic4d LLC .... G 248 469-8811
  Bingham Farms (G-1701)
Landra Prsthtics Orthotics Inc .... G 586 294-7188
  Saint Clair Shores (G-14868)
Versant Med Physics Rdtion SFE .... E 888 316-3644
  Kalamazoo (G-9361)

MEDICAL, DENTAL & HOSP EQPT, WHOLESALE: X-ray Film & Splys

Associated Metals Inc .... G 734 369-3851
  Ann Arbor (G-384)
Radiolgical Fabrication Design .... G 810 632-6000
  Howell (G-8506)

MEDICAL, DENTAL & HOSPITAL EQPT, WHOL: Hospital Eqpt & Splys

Bmc/Industrial Eductl Svcs Inc .... E 231 733-1206
  Muskegon (G-11780)

MEDICAL, DENTAL & HOSPITAL EQPT, WHOL: Hosptl Eqpt/Furniture

Bay Home Medical and Rehab Inc .... F 231 933-1200
  Grandville (G-7366)
Creative Engineering Inc .... G 734 996-5900
  Ann Arbor (G-439)
E & C Manufacturing LLC .... F 248 330-0400
  Troy (G-17075)
Industrial Woodworking Corp .... E 616 741-9663
  Zeeland (G-19045)
Wright & Filippis LLC .... F 517 484-2624
  Lansing (G-9906)
Xxtar Associates LLC .... G 888 946-6066
  Detroit (G-4695)

MEDICAL, DENTAL & HOSPITAL EQPT, WHOLESALE: Diagnostic, Med

Genomic Diagnostics Na Inc .... G 734 730-8399
  Ann Arbor (G-499)
Great Lakes Diagnostics Inc .... G 248 307-9494
  Troy (G-17133)
Steele Supply Co .... G 269 983-0920
  Saint Joseph (G-14964)

MEDICAL, DENTAL & HOSPITAL EQPT, WHOLESALE: Hosp Furniture

Custom Components Corporation .... F 616 523-1111
  Ionia (G-8688)

MEDICAL, DENTAL & HOSPITAL EQPT, WHOLESALE: Med Eqpt & Splys

C2dx Inc .... F 269 409-0068
  Schoolcraft (G-15112)
Diversfied Prcurement Svcs LLC .... G 248 821-1147
  Ferndale (G-5548)
Grand River Aseptic Mfg Inc .... C 616 678-2400
  Grand Rapids (G-6776)
Healthcare Drble Med Eqpmnts L .... G 734 975-6668
  Ann Arbor (G-510)
Homedics Usa LLC .... C 248 863-3000
  Commerce Township (G-3539)
Kgf Enterprise Inc .... G 586 430-4182
  Columbus (G-3500)
Lake Erie Med Surgical Sup Inc .... E 734 847-3847
  Temperance (G-16536)
Liquidgoldconcept Inc .... G 734 926-9197
  Ypsilanti (G-18963)
Mar-Med Inc .... E 616 454-3000
  Grand Rapids (G-6958)
Rankin Biomedical Corporation .... F 248 625-4104
  Holly (G-8290)
Solaire Medical Storage LLC .... D 888 435-2256
  Marne (G-10999)
Tri State Optical Inc .... G 517 279-2701
  Coldwater (G-3458)

MEDICAL, DENTAL & HOSPITAL EQPT, WHOLESALE: Medical Lab

Marketlab Inc .... D 866 237-3722
  Caledonia (G-2388)
Tokusen Hytech Inc .... C 269 685-1768
  Plainwell (G-13099)

MEDICAL, DENTAL & HOSPITAL EQPT, WHOLESALE: Orthopedic

Orthotool LLC .... G 734 455-8103
  Plymouth (G-13258)

MEDICAL, DENTAL/HOSPITAL EQPT, WHOL: Tech Aids, Handicapped

Assistive Technology Mich Inc .... G 248 348-7161
  Novi (G-12367)

MEMBERSHIP ORGANIZATIONS, BUSINESS: Growers' Association

Liveroof LLC .... E 616 842-1392
  Nunica (G-12584)

MEMBERSHIP ORGANIZATIONS, NEC: Charitable

Childrens Bible Hour Inc .... F 616 647-4500
  Grand Rapids (G-6568)

MEMBERSHIP ORGANIZATIONS, PROFESSIONAL: Health Association

Community Mntal Hlth Auth Clnt .... F 517 323-9558
  Lansing (G-19682)
Michigan Academy Fmly Physicans .... F 517 347-0098
  Okemos (G-12675)
Michigan State Medical Society .... E 517 337-1351
  East Lansing (G-4904)

MEMBERSHIP ORGANIZATIONS, REL: Covenant & Evangelical Church

Living Word International Inc .... E 989 832-7547
  Midland (G-11384)

MEMBERSHIP ORGANIZATIONS, RELIGIOUS: Catholic Church

Diocese of Lansing .... G 517 484-4449
  Lansing (G-9831)

MEMBERSHIP ORGANIZATIONS, RELIGIOUS: Reformed Church

Synod of Great Lakes .... E 616 698-7071
  Grand Rapids (G-7243)

MEMBERSHIP ORGS, CIVIC, SOCIAL & FRATERNAL: Protection

Meridian Lightweight Tech Inc .... E 248 663-8100
  Plymouth (G-13241)

MEMBERSHIP SPORTS & RECREATION CLUBS

Forest View Lanes LLC .... E 734 847-4915
  Temperance (G-16531)
Ukc Liquidating Inc .... G 269 343-9020
  Portage (G-13628)

MEMORIES: Solid State

Viking Technologies Inc .... G 586 914-0819
  Madison Heights (G-10856)

MEN'S & BOYS' CLOTHING ACCESS STORES

Lighthouse Direct Buy LLC .... G 313 340-1850
  Detroit (G-4398)

MEN'S & BOYS' CLOTHING STORES

Allie Brothers Inc .... F 248 477-4434
  Livonia (G-10109)
Reed Sportswear Mfg Co .... G 313 963-7980
  Detroit (G-4561)

MEN'S & BOYS' CLOTHING WHOLESALERS, NEC

Access Business Group LLC .... A 616 787-6000
  Ada (G-3)
Alticor Global Holdings Inc .... F 616 787-1000
  Ada (G-5)
Alticor Inc .... A 616 787-1000
  Ada (G-6)
Fisll Media LLC .... G 646 492-8533
  Troy (G-17111)
Hemp Global Products Inc .... G 616 617-6476
  Holland (G-8069)

MEN'S & BOYS' SPORTSWEAR CLOTHING STORES

Guess Inc .... G 517 546-2933
  Howell (G-8457)
Noir Sportswear Corp .... F 248 607-3615
  Oak Park (G-12634)

MEN'S & BOYS' SPORTSWEAR WHOLESALERS

American Silk Screen & EMB .... F 248 474-1000
  Farmington Hills (G-5169)
Apparel Sales Inc .... G 616 842-5650
  Jenison (G-9045)
Delta Sports Service & EMB .... G 517 482-6565
  Lansing (G-9686)
R H & Company Inc .... F 269 345-7814
  Kalamazoo (G-9313)
RPC Company .... F 989 752-3618
  Saginaw (G-14741)

MEN'S & BOYS' UNDERWEAR WHOLESALERS

Lockett Enterprises LLC .... G 810 407-6644
  Flint (G-5725)

MEN'S & BOYS' WORK CLOTHING WHOLESALERS

Kaul Glove and Mfg Co ....E...... 313 894-9494
  Detroit (G-4353)

MEN'S SUITS STORES

Van Boven Incorporated ....G...... 734 665-7228
  Ann Arbor (G-708)

MERCHANDISING MACHINE OPERATORS: Vending

Asw Amerca Inc ....G...... 248 957-9638
  Farmington Hills (G-5174)

METAL & STEEL PRDTS: Abrasive

Dryden Steel LLC ....E...... 586 777-7600
  Dryden (G-4805)
Nakagawa Special Stl Amer Inc ......E...... 248 449-6050
  Novi (G-12487)
Patch Works Farms Inc ....E...... 989 430-3610
  Wheeler (G-18436)

METAL COMPONENTS: Prefabricated

Laser North Inc ....G...... 906 353-6090
  Baraga (G-1143)
Mpi Products Holdings LLC ....D...... 248 237-3007
  Rochester Hills (G-14066)
Trigon Steel Components Inc ....G...... 616 834-0506
  Holland (G-8231)

METAL CUTTING SVCS

Arlington Metals Corporation ....E...... 269 426-3371
  Sawyer (G-15106)
B & B Holdings Groesbeck LLC ....F...... 586 554-7600
  Sterling Heights (G-15940)
Copeland-Gibson Products Corp ....E...... 248 740-4400
  Troy (G-17028)
Fabrilaser Mfg LLC ....E...... 269 789-9490
  Marshall (G-11057)
Fire-Rite Inc ....E...... 313 273-3730
  Detroit (G-4234)
K&W Tool and Machine Inc ....F...... 616 754-7540
  Greenville (G-7495)
Kendor Steel Rule Die Inc ....F...... 586 293-7111
  Fraser (G-5950)
Laser North Inc ....G...... 906 353-6090
  Baraga (G-1144)
Matrix Mtlcraft LLP A Ltd Prtn ....G...... 248 724-1800
  Auburn Hills (G-970)
Set Enterprises Inc ....G...... 586 573-3600
  Royal Oak (G-14580)
Virtec Manufacturing LLC ....F...... 313 590-2367
  Roseville (G-14492)

METAL DETECTORS

Quality Metal Detectors ....G...... 734 624-8462
  Southgate (G-15756)

METAL FABRICATORS: Architechtural

A D Johnson Engraving Co Inc ....F...... 269 385-0044
  Kalamazoo (G-9106)
Adaptive Metal Works LLC ....G...... 419 386-9336
  Blissfield (G-1760)
Aluminum Architectural Met Co ....G...... 313 895-2555
  Detroit (G-4006)
Aluminum Blanking Co Inc ....D...... 248 338-4422
  Pontiac (G-13349)
Aluminum Supply Company Inc ....E...... 313 491-5040
  Detroit (G-4007)
Amanda Products LLC ....E...... 248 547-3870
  Ferndale (G-5525)
Bad Axe Metal & Iron Art ....G...... 989 658-8324
  Ubly (G-17475)
Blacksmith Shop LLC ....G...... 616 754-4719
  Greenville (G-7477)
Britten Inc ....C...... 231 941-8200
  Traverse City (G-16627)
CEi Composite Materials LLC ....E...... 734 212-3006
  Manchester (G-10882)
Cr Forge LLC ....F...... 231 924-2433
  Fremont (G-6038)
Creative Composites Inc ....G...... 906 474-9941
  Rapid River (G-13683)
CTS Welding ....G...... 269 521-4481
  Bloomingdale (G-1876)

Davis Iron Works Inc ....E...... 248 624-5960
  Commerce Township (G-3521)
Elemental Artistry LLC ....G...... 616 326-1758
  Grand Rapids (G-6671)
Guile & Son Inc ....G...... 517 376-2116
  Byron (G-2254)
Harlow Sheet Metal LLC ....G...... 734 996-1509
  Ann Arbor (G-509)
Iron Capital of America Co ....G...... 586 771-5840
  Warren (G-17871)
Iron Fetish Metalworks Inc ....F...... 586 776-8311
  Roseville (G-14426)
J D Russell Company ....E...... 586 254-8500
  Utica (G-17503)
Jack-Post Corporation ....G...... 269 695-7000
  Buchanan (G-2197)
Kern-Liebers Pieron Inc ....D...... 248 427-1100
  Farmington Hills (G-5280)
Mayo Welding & Fabricating Co ....G...... 248 435-2730
  Royal Oak (G-14561)
Merrill Technologies Group Inc ....C...... 989 462-0330
  Alma (G-246)
Mol Belting Systems Inc ....D...... 616 453-2484
  Grand Rapids (G-7020)
O I K Industries Inc ....E...... 269 382-1210
  Kalamazoo (G-9282)
Parker Fluid Syst Connectors ....G...... 989 352-7264
  Lakeview (G-9644)
Phoenix Wire Cloth Inc ....E...... 248 585-6350
  Troy (G-17301)
R B Christian Inc ....G...... 269 963-9327
  Battle Creek (G-1285)
Rka Design Build ....G...... 269 362-5558
  Buchanan (G-2203)
Symbiote Inc ....E...... 616 772-1790
  Zeeland (G-19083)
United Lighting Standards Inc ....D...... 586 774-5650
  Warren (G-18047)
Valley City Sign Company ....E...... 616 784-5711
  Comstock Park (G-3649)
Won-Door Corp ....G...... 248 478-5757
  Farmington Hills (G-5414)
Worthington Armstrong Venture ....F...... 269 934-6200
  Benton Harbor (G-1611)

METAL FABRICATORS: Plate

A & B Welding & Fabricating ....G...... 231 733-2661
  Muskegon (G-11759)
Admin Industries LLC ....F...... 989 685-3438
  Rose City (G-14358)
Alro Riverside LLC ....G...... 517 782-8322
  Jackson (G-8813)
Ambassador Steel Corporation ....E...... 517 455-7216
  Lansing (G-9804)
American Metal Fab Inc ....D...... 269 279-5108
  Three Rivers (G-16563)
Amhawk LLC ....E...... 269 468-4177
  Hartford (G-7761)
Anchor Lamina America Inc ....E...... 248 489-9122
  Bellaire (G-1469)
Baker Enterprises Inc ....E...... 989 354-2189
  Alpena (G-281)
Besser Company ....B...... 989 354-4111
  Alpena (G-284)
Bills Custom Fab Inc ....F...... 989 772-5817
  Mount Pleasant (G-11687)
Brockie Fabricating & Wldg LLC ....F...... 517 750-7500
  Jackson (G-8828)
CA Picard Inc ....E...... 269 962-2231
  Battle Creek (G-1202)
Chicago Blow Pipe Company ....F...... 773 533-6100
  Marquette (G-11012)
Clawson Container Company ....E...... 248 625-8700
  Clarkston (G-3026)
Conner Steel Products ....F...... 248 852-5110
  Rochester Hills (G-13983)
Constructive Sheet Metal Inc ....G...... 616 245-5306
  Allendale (G-217)
Contech Engnered Solutions LLC ....G...... 517 676-3000
  Mason (G-11120)
D-M-E USA Inc ....D...... 616 754-4601
  Greenville (G-7480)
Davco Manufacturing LLC ....G...... 734 429-5665
  Saline (G-15011)
Delta Iron Works Inc ....E...... 313 579-1445
  Grosse Pointe (G-7529)
Detroit Boiler Company ....F...... 313 921-7060
  Detroit (G-4137)
Detroit Plate Fabricators Inc ....G...... 313 921-7020
  Detroit (G-4159)

Die-Mold-Automation Component ....G...... 313 581-6510
  Dearborn (G-3829)
Fab-Alloy Company ....G...... 517 787-4313
  Jackson (G-8883)
Fabrications Unlimited Inc ....G...... 313 567-9616
  Detroit (G-4224)
Fluid Hutchinson Management ....D...... 248 679-1327
  Auburn Hills (G-903)
Glycon Corp ....E...... 517 423-8356
  Tecumseh (G-16503)
Great Lakes Laser Dynamics Inc ....D...... 616 892-7070
  Allendale (G-220)
Greene Metal Products Inc ....E...... 586 465-6800
  Clinton Township (G-3249)
Grossel Tool Co ....G...... 586 294-3660
  Fraser (G-5932)
H & M Welding and Fabricating ....G...... 517 764-3630
  Jackson (G-8897)
Highland Engineering Inc ....E...... 517 548-4372
  Howell (G-8460)
Hydro-Craft Inc ....G...... 248 652-8100
  Rochester Hills (G-14037)
Impert Industries Inc ....G...... 269 694-2727
  Otsego (G-12788)
K & W Manufacturing Co Inc ....E...... 517 369-9708
  Bronson (G-2117)
Krista Messer ....G...... 734 459-1952
  Canton (G-2484)
Kurrent Welding Inc ....G...... 734 753-9197
  New Boston (G-12011)
Laser North Inc ....G...... 906 353-6090
  Baraga (G-1144)
Liberty Steel Fabricating Inc ....E...... 269 556-9792
  Saint Joseph (G-14948)
Lochinvar LLC ....E...... 734 454-4480
  Plymouth (G-13225)
Magnetic Products Inc ....D...... 248 887-5600
  Highland (G-7896)
Marsh Industrial Services Inc ....F...... 231 258-4870
  Kalkaska (G-9395)
Massie Mfg Inc ....E...... 906 353-6381
  Baraga (G-1145)
Matrix North Amercn Cnstr Inc ....D...... 734 847-4605
  Temperance (G-16539)
Mayo Welding & Fabricating Co ....G...... 248 435-2730
  Royal Oak (G-14561)
MB Aerospace Warren LLC ....C...... 586 772-2500
  Warren (G-17920)
Merrill Technologies Group Inc ....D...... 989 791-6676
  Saginaw (G-14697)
Nelson Steel Products Inc ....D...... 616 396-1515
  Holland (G-8152)
Nicholson Terminal & Dock Co ....D...... 313 842-4300
  River Rouge (G-13858)
North Central Welding Co ....E...... 989 275-8054
  Roscommon (G-14354)
Northern Machining & Repr Inc ....E...... 906 786-0526
  Escanaba (G-5088)
Northwest Fabrication Inc ....G...... 231 536-3229
  East Jordan (G-4878)
Oakland Welding Industries ....E...... 586 949-4090
  Chesterfield (G-2916)
Parton & Preble Inc ....E...... 586 773-6000
  Warren (G-17954)
Power Industries Corp ....G...... 586 783-3818
  Harrison Township (G-7716)
Process Systems Inc ....E...... 586 757-5711
  Warren (G-17977)
Production Fabricators Inc ....E...... 231 777-3822
  Muskegon (G-11900)
Quigley Industries Inc ....E...... 248 426-8600
  Farmington Hills (G-5361)
R W Fernstrum & Company ....E...... 906 863-5553
  Menominee (G-11257)
Refrigeration Research Inc ....D...... 810 227-1151
  Brighton (G-2064)
RK Wojan Inc ....E...... 231 347-1160
  Charlevoix (G-2730)
Rocksteady Manufacturing LLC ....E...... 586 778-5028
  Roseville (G-14472)
SBS Corp ....G...... 248 844-8200
  Auburn Hills (G-1029)
Schad Boiler Setting Company ....D...... 313 273-2235
  Detroit (G-4584)
Schrader Stoves of Michiana ....E...... 269 684-4494
  Niles (G-12166)
Sloan Valve Company ....D...... 248 446-5300
  New Hudson (G-12070)
Special Mold Engineering Inc ....E...... 248 652-6600
  Rochester Hills (G-14116)

SPX Corporation C 248 669-5100
Commerce Township *(G-3574)*

Steel Tank & Fabricating Co D 231 587-8412
Mancelona *(G-10879)*

Taylor Controls Inc F 269 637-8521
South Haven *(G-15418)*

Trimas Corporation B 248 631-5450
Bloomfield Hills *(G-1869)*

True Fabrications & Machine F 248 288-0140
Troy *(G-17403)*

Van Loon Industries Inc E 586 532-8530
Shelby Township *(G-15363)*

Vent-Rite Valve Corp E 269 925-8812
Benton Harbor *(G-1598)*

Walbro LLC D 989 872-2131
Cass City *(G-2622)*

Waltz-Holst Blow Pipe Company E 616 676-8119
Ada *(G-40)*

Welding & Joining Tech LLC G 734 926-9353
Clarkston *(G-3076)*

Wolverine Metal Stamping Inc D 269 429-6600
Saint Joseph *(G-14980)*

Yale Steel Inc G 810 387-2567
Brockway *(G-2108)*

METAL FABRICATORS: Sheet

A & B Welding & Fabricating G 231 733-2661
Muskegon *(G-11759)*

Access Heating & Cooling Inc G 734 464-0566
Livonia *(G-10098)*

Ackerman Brothers Inc G 989 892-4122
Bay City *(G-1315)*

Acme Carbide Die Inc E 734 722-2303
Westland *(G-18351)*

Acme Tool & Die Co G 231 938-1260
Acme *(G-1)*

Admin Industries LLC F 989 685-3438
Rose City *(G-14358)*

Advanced Sheet Metal G 616 301-3828
Wyoming *(G-18848)*

Advantage Laser Inc G 734 367-9936
Livonia *(G-10103)*

Alliance Sheet Metal Inc F 269 795-2954
Middleville *(G-11302)*

Allied Machine Inc F 231 834-0050
Grant *(G-7425)*

Allor Manufacturing Inc D 248 486-4500
Brighton *(G-1943)*

Aluminum Blanking Co Inc D 248 338-4422
Pontiac *(G-13349)*

American Blower Supply Inc E 586 771-7337
Warren *(G-17701)*

American Fabricated Pdts Inc E 616 607-8785
Spring Lake *(G-15803)*

American Tchncal Fbrcators LLC E 989 269-6262
Bad Axe *(G-1095)*

Amhawk LLC E 269 468-4177
Hartford *(G-7761)*

Amjs Incorporated G
Lawton *(G-9987)*

Anderson Welding & Mfg Inc F 906 523-4661
Houghton *(G-8380)*

Arnold & Sautter Co F 989 684-7557
Bay City *(G-1322)*

Attentive Industries Inc F 810 233-7077
Flint *(G-5646)*

Attentive Industries Inc G 810 233-7077
Flint *(G-5647)*

Austin Tube Products Inc F 231 745-2741
Baldwin *(G-1121)*

B & L Industries Inc E 810 987-9121
Port Huron *(G-13456)*

Baldauf Enterprises Inc D 989 686-0350
Bay City *(G-1324)*

Bar Processing Corporation F 734 782-4454
Warren *(G-17727)*

Bauer Sheet Metal & Fabg Inc E 231 773-3244
Muskegon *(G-11775)*

Belco Industries Inc E 616 794-0410
Belding *(G-1437)*

Belco Industries Inc E 616 794-0410
Belding *(G-1438)*

Benteler Automotive Corp B 616 247-3936
Auburn Hills *(G-810)*

Beswick Corporation F 248 589-0562
Troy *(G-16976)*

Bico Michigan Inc E 616 453-2400
Grand Rapids *(G-6506)*

Blue Water Fabricators Inc G 586 307-3550
Clinton Township *(G-3185)*

Bmc/Industrial Eductl Svcs Inc E 231 733-1206
Muskegon *(G-11780)*

Boral Building Products Inc C 800 521-8486
Wixom *(G-18625)*

Borchers Sheet Metal G 260 413-0632
Hudsonville *(G-8573)*

Bradhart Products Inc E 248 437-3746
Brighton *(G-1952)*

Bristol Steel & Conveyor Corp E 810 658-9510
Davison *(G-3775)*

Britten Inc C 231 941-8200
Traverse City *(G-16627)*

Burnham & Northern Inc G 517 279-7501
Coldwater *(G-3422)*

Buy Best Manufacturing LLC F 248 875-2491
Brighton *(G-1955)*

C & T Fabrication LLC G 616 678-5133
Kent City *(G-9428)*

C L Rieckhoff Company Inc C 734 946-8220
Taylor *(G-16388)*

Carlson E 248 824-7600
Troy *(G-17001)*

Cdp Environmental Inc E 586 776-7890
Roseville *(G-14383)*

Certainteed LLC G 517 787-8898
Jackson *(G-8837)*

Certainteed LLC G 517 787-1737
Jackson *(G-8838)*

Commercial Mfg & Assembly Inc E 616 847-9980
Grand Haven *(G-6287)*

Conner Steel Products F 248 852-5110
Rochester Hills *(G-13983)*

Conquest Manufacturing LLC D 586 576-7600
Warren *(G-17763)*

Consolidated Metal Pdts Inc G 616 538-1000
Grand Rapids *(G-6596)*

Corlett-Turner Co F 616 772-9082
Grand Rapids *(G-6607)*

Custom Archtctral Shtmtl Spcls F 313 571-2277
Detroit *(G-4113)*

Custom Design & Manufacturing F 989 754-9962
Carrollton *(G-2587)*

Custom Fab Inc G 586 755-7260
Warren *(G-17767)*

Customer Metal Fabrication Inc E 906 774-3216
Iron Mountain *(G-8721)*

Delta Iron Works Inc E 313 579-1445
Grosse Pointe *(G-7529)*

Delta Tube & Fabricating Corp C 248 634-8267
Holly *(G-8268)*

Denlin Industries Inc G 586 303-5209
Milford *(G-11461)*

Designers Sheet Metal Inc G 269 429-4133
Saint Joseph *(G-14926)*

Detroit Blow Pipe & Shtmtl G 313 365-8970
Detroit *(G-4136)*

Detroit Cornice & Slate Co Inc E 248 398-7690
Ferndale *(G-5544)*

Dewys Manufacturing Inc C 616 677-5281
Marne *(G-10991)*

Dmi Sheet Metal LLC G 517 242-6005
Grand Haven *(G-6293)*

Dorris Company F 586 293-5260
Fraser *(G-5919)*

Douglas King Industries Inc G 989 642-2865
Hemlock *(G-7851)*

Dowding Industries Inc E 517 663-5455
Eaton Rapids *(G-4959)*

Dowding Tool Products LLC F 517 541-2795
Springport *(G-15880)*

Dubois Production Services Inc F 616 785-0088
Comstock Park *(G-3604)*

Duo-Gard Industries Inc D 734 207-9700
Canton *(G-2456)*

East Muskegon Roofg Shtmtl Co D 231 744-2461
Muskegon *(G-11806)*

Electrolabs Inc F 586 294-4150
Fraser *(G-5924)*

Elevated Technologies Inc E 616 288-9817
Grand Rapids *(G-6672)*

Eliason Corporation E 269 621-2100
Hartford *(G-7763)*

Envision Engineering LLC G 616 897-0599
Lowell *(G-10500)*

Erbsloeh Alum Solutions Inc B 269 323-2565
Portage *(G-13558)*

Experi-Metal Inc C 586 977-7800
Sterling Heights *(G-16009)*

Fab-Alloy Company G 517 787-4313
Jackson *(G-8883)*

Fabrication Specialties Inc G 313 891-7181
Davisburg *(G-3767)*

Fabrications Plus Inc G 269 749-3050
Olivet *(G-12693)*

Fenixx Technologies LLC G 586 254-6000
Sterling Heights *(G-16012)*

Fhc Holding Company G 616 538-3231
Wyoming *(G-18872)*

Flex-N-Gate Stamping LLC E 586 759-8900
Warren *(G-17813)*

Frankenmuth Welding & Fabg G 989 754-9457
Saginaw *(G-14646)*

Frenchys Skirting Inc G 734 721-3013
Wayne *(G-18220)*

G A Richards Company D 616 243-2800
Grand Rapids *(G-6730)*

G A Richards Company G 616 850-8528
Spring Lake *(G-15815)*

Gee & Missler Inc E 734 284-1224
Wyandotte *(G-18820)*

Geerpres Inc E 231 773-3211
Muskegon *(G-11823)*

General Motors LLC F 810 234-2710
Flint *(G-5704)*

Gladwin Tank Manufacturing Inc F 989 426-4768
Gladwin *(G-6199)*

Gokoh Coldwater Incorporated F 517 279-1080
Coldwater *(G-3434)*

Gray Brothers Mfg Inc F 269 483-7615
White Pigeon *(G-18479)*

Great Lakes Mechanical Corp C 313 581-1400
Dearborn *(G-3849)*

Great Lakes Powder Coating LLC F 248 522-6222
Walled Lake *(G-17669)*

Greene Manufacturing Inc E 734 428-8304
Chelsea *(G-2813)*

Greene Metal Products Inc E 586 465-6800
Clinton Township *(G-3249)*

H & M Welding and Fabricating G 517 764-3630
Jackson *(G-8897)*

Hart Fabrication Inc F 517 924-1109
Quincy *(G-13670)*

Historic Denver Inc G 989 354-2121
Alpena *(G-297)*

Hydro Extrusion North Amer LLC B 269 349-6626
Kalamazoo *(G-9220)*

Industrial Duct Systems Inc G 586 498-3993
Roseville *(G-14422)*

Industrial Mtal Fbricators LLC E 810 765-8960
Cottrellville *(G-3722)*

Innovate Industries Inc G 586 558-8990
Warren *(G-17865)*

Innovative Sheet Metals LLC F 231 788-5751
Muskegon *(G-11839)*

Integrated Metal Tech Inc C 616 844-3032
Spring Lake *(G-15825)*

J & L Mfg Co E 586 445-9530
Warren *(G-17875)*

J & M Machine Products Inc D 231 755-1622
Norton Shores *(G-12302)*

J M L Contracting & Sales Inc F 586 756-4133
Warren *(G-17879)*

Jackson Archtctral Met Fbrctor G 517 782-8884
Jackson *(G-8912)*

K & W Manufacturing Co Inc E 517 369-9708
Bronson *(G-2117)*

K-R Metal Engineers Corp G 989 892-1901
Bay City *(G-1370)*

Kalamazoo Mechanical Inc F 269 343-5351
Kalamazoo *(G-9241)*

Kriewall Enterprises Inc E 586 336-0600
Romeo *(G-14227)*

Lanzen-Petoskey LLC E 231 881-9602
Petoskey *(G-13002)*

Laser Fab Inc G 586 415-8090
Fraser *(G-5955)*

Laser North Inc G 906 353-6090
Baraga *(G-1144)*

Laser Specialists Inc E 586 294-8830
Fraser *(G-5956)*

Legacy Metal Fabricating LLC E 616 258-8406
Grand Rapids *(G-6936)*

Liberty Steel Fabricating Inc E 269 556-9792
Saint Joseph *(G-14948)*

Light Metals Corporation B 616 538-3030
Wyoming *(G-18891)*

Llink Technologies LLC E 586 336-9370
Brown City *(G-2139)*

Loftis Machine Company F 616 846-1990
Grand Haven *(G-6331)*

Lv Metals Inc .... G 734 654-8081
Carleton (G-2559)
M J Mechanical Inc .... E 989 865-9633
Saint Charles (G-14804)
Magnetic Products Inc .... D 248 887-5600
Highland (G-7896)
Manning Enterprises Inc .... E 269 657-2346
Paw Paw (G-12952)
Mardan Fabrication Inc .... G 586 466-6401
Harrison Township (G-7708)
Marsh Industrial Services Inc .... F 231 258-4870
Kalkaska (G-9395)
Matrix Mtlcraft LLP A Ltd Prtn .... E 586 469-9611
Macomb (G-10615)
Mayo Welding & Fabricating Co .... G 248 435-2730
Royal Oak (G-14561)
MB Aerospace Warren LLC .... C 586 772-2500
Warren (G-17920)
McElroy Metal Mill Inc .... D 269 781-8313
Marshall (G-11069)
Mechanical Sheet Metal Co .... F 734 284-1006
Wyandotte (G-18832)
Metal Components LLC .... D 616 252-1900
Grand Rapids (G-6979)
Metal Standard Corp .... D 616 396-6356
Holland (G-8144)
Metalworks Inc .... C 231 845-5136
Ludington (G-10546)
Meter Devices Company Inc .... D 330 455-0301
Farmington Hills (G-5317)
Metro Duct Inc .... F 517 783-2646
Jackson (G-8955)
Michigan Metal Fabricators .... G 586 754-0421
Warren (G-17929)
Michigan Tooling Solutions LLC .... G 616 681-2210
Sparta (G-15772)
Midbrook Inc .... D 800 966-9274
Jackson (G-8959)
Midwest Wall Company LLC .... F 517 881-3701
Dewitt (G-4713)
Mill Creek Fabrication LLC .... G 616 419-4857
Comstock Park (G-3626)
Monarch Metal Mfg Inc .... G 616 247-0412
Grand Rapids (G-7023)
Monarch Welding & Engrg Inc .... E 231 733-7222
Muskegon (G-11876)
MSE Fabrication LLC .... F 586 991-6138
Sterling Heights (G-16107)
Muskegon Awning & Mfg Co .... E 231 759-0911
Muskegon (G-11879)
National Ordnance Auto Mfg LLC .... G 248 853-8822
Auburn Hills (G-980)
Nelson Steel Products Inc .... D 616 396-1515
Holland (G-8152)
Nicholson Terminal & Dock Co .... D 313 842-4300
River Rouge (G-13858)
North Woods Industrial .... G 616 784-2840
Comstock Park (G-3629)
Northern Machining & Repr Inc .... E 906 786-0526
Escanaba (G-5088)
Northland Corporation .... E 616 754-5601
Greenville (G-7502)
Northland Corporation .... C 616 754-5601
Greenville (G-7503)
Northwest Fabrication Inc .... G 231 536-3229
East Jordan (G-4878)
Oakland Welding Industries .... E 586 949-4090
Chesterfield (G-2916)
Pardon Inc .... E 906 428-3494
Gladstone (G-6185)
Parton & Preble Inc .... E 586 773-6000
Warren (G-17954)
Portage Wire Systems Inc .... E 231 889-4215
Onekama (G-12703)
Precision Prototype & Mfg Inc .... F 517 663-4114
Eaton Rapids (G-4967)
Production Fabricators Inc .... E 231 777-3822
Muskegon (G-11900)
Production Tube Company Inc .... G 313 259-3990
Detroit (G-4537)
Quality Alum Acquisition LLC .... F 734 783-0990
Flat Rock (G-5626)
Quality Craft Fabricators LLC .... G 586 353-2104
Warren (G-17988)
Quality Finishing Systems .... F 231 834-9131
Grant (G-7431)
Quality Metalcraft Inc .... C 734 261-6700
Livonia (G-10377)
R & DS Manufacturing LLC .... G 586 716-9900
New Baltimore (G-11992)
S & N Machine & Fabricating .... E 231 894-2658
Rothbury (G-14498)
Saginaw Control & Engrg Inc .... B 989 799-6871
Saginaw (G-14745)
Salem/Savard Industries LLC .... F 313 931-6880
Detroit (G-4579)
Sandvik Inc .... D 269 926-7241
Benton Harbor (G-1582)
Schrader Stoves of Michiana .... E 269 684-4494
Niles (G-12166)
Scotten Steel Processing Inc .... F 313 897-8837
Detroit (G-4585)
Security Steelcraft Corp .... F 231 733-1101
Muskegon (G-11917)
Servotech Industries Inc .... G 734 697-5555
Taylor (G-16471)
Set Duct Manufacturing LLC .... E 313 491-4380
Detroit (G-4588)
Sfi Acquisition Inc .... E 248 471-1500
Farmington Hills (G-5377)
Sheet Metal Workers Local .... G 231 590-1112
Traverse City (G-16830)
Sheren Plumbing & Heating Inc .... E 231 943-7916
Traverse City (G-16831)
Sparta Sheet Metal Inc .... F 616 784-9035
Grand Rapids (G-7208)
Spectrum Metal Products Inc .... G 734 595-7600
Westland (G-18418)
Spinform Inc .... G 810 767-4660
Flint (G-5766)
Stageright Corporation .... C 989 386-7393
Clare (G-2999)
Stewart Steel Specialties .... G 248 477-0680
Farmington Hills (G-5390)
Stus Welding & Fabrication .... G 616 392-8459
Holland (G-8206)
Tapco Holdings Inc .... C 248 668-6400
Wixom (G-18766)
Target Construction Inc .... E 616 866-7728
Cedar Springs (G-2664)
TEC-3 Prototypes Inc .... E 810 678-8909
Metamora (G-11289)
Ter Molen & Hart Inc .... G 616 458-4832
Grand Rapids (G-7253)
Thermal Designs & Manufacturng .... F 586 773-5231
Roseville (G-14484)
Thierica Equipment Corporation .... E 616 453-6570
Grand Rapids (G-7259)
Tigmaster Co .... E 800 824-4830
Baroda (G-1171)
Tops-In-Quality Inc .... G 810 364-7150
Marysville (G-11109)
Tri-Vision LLC .... G 313 526-6020
Detroit (G-4644)
Triumph Gear Systems - McOmb I .... C 586 781-2800
Macomb (G-10644)
Tru Flo Carbide Inc .... F 989 658-8515
Ubly (G-17483)
Tubelite Inc .... C 800 866-2227
Walker (G-17655)
Turnkey Fabrication LLC .... F 616 248-9116
Grand Rapids (G-7281)
Unifab Corporation .... E 269 382-2803
Portage (G-13629)
Universal Fabricators Inc .... F 248 399-7565
Madison Heights (G-10853)
Universal Spiral Air Npp .... G 616 475-5905
Grand Rapids (G-7299)
Van Loon Industries Inc .... E 586 532-8530
Shelby Township (G-15363)
Ventcon Inc .... C 313 336-4000
Allen Park (G-209)
Versatile Fabrication Co Inc .... E 231 739-7115
Muskegon (G-11941)
Waltz-Holst Blow Pipe Company .... E 616 676-8119
Ada (G-40)
Weather Tight .... G 989 817-2149
Midland (G-11422)
Wendling Sheet Metal Inc .... E 989 753-5286
Saginaw (G-14793)
West Side Mfg Fabrication Inc .... E 248 380-6640
Wixom (G-18790)
Wm Kloeffler Industries Inc .... G 810 765-4068
Marine City (G-10969)
Worthington Armstrong Venture .... F 269 934-6200
Benton Harbor (G-1611)

METAL FABRICATORS: Structural, Ship

Douglas Steel Fabricating Corp .... D 517 322-2050
Lansing (G-9759)
Eab Fabrication Inc .... E 517 639-7080
Quincy (G-13668)
Northwoods Manufacturing Inc .... D 906 779-2370
Kingsford (G-9516)
PSI Marine Inc .... F 989 695-2646
Saginaw (G-14731)

METAL FABRICATORS: Structural, Ship

Alumabridge LLC .... F 855 373-7500
Ann Arbor (G-362)
Premier Prototype Inc .... E 586 323-6114
Sterling Heights (G-16132)

METAL FINISHING SVCS

Alpha Metal Finishing Co .... F 734 426-2855
Dexter (G-4723)
Bar Processing Corporation .... F 734 243-8937
Monroe (G-11529)
Bar Processing Corporation .... C 734 782-4454
Flat Rock (G-5616)
Bar Processing Corporation .... F 734 782-4454
Warren (G-17727)
Bellevue Proc Met Prep Inc .... C 313 921-1931
Detroit (G-4050)
Blough Inc .... D 616 897-8407
Lowell (G-10496)
Bopp-Busch Manufacturing Co .... E 989 876-7924
Au Gres (G-758)
Chor Industries Inc .... E 248 585-3323
Troy (G-17011)
Complete Metal Finishing Inc .... F 269 343-0500
Kalamazoo (G-9150)
Deburring Company .... E 734 542-9800
Livonia (G-10177)
Downriver Deburring Inc .... G 313 388-2640
Taylor (G-16406)
Finishing Touch Inc .... E 517 542-5581
Litchfield (G-10077)
High Prfmce Met Finshg Inc .... F 269 327-8897
Portage (G-13565)
Impact Operations LLC .... F 616 642-9570
Saranac (G-15078)
Kalamazoo Stripping Derusting .... F 269 323-1340
Portage (G-13572)
Kepco Inc .... F 269 649-5800
Vicksburg (G-17607)
Margate Industries Inc .... G 810 387-4300
Yale (G-18919)
Matthews Plating Inc .... E 517 784-3535
Jackson (G-8946)
Metal Prep Technology Inc .... G 313 843-2890
Dearborn (G-3870)
Muskegon Industrial Finishng .... G 231 733-7663
Muskegon (G-11881)
New Life Cop Brass Mint Free M .... G 586 725-3286
Casco (G-2601)
Oliver Industries Inc .... E 586 977-7750
Sterling Heights (G-16120)
Port City Industrial Finishing .... E 231 726-4288
Muskegon (G-11894)
Precision Finishing Co Inc .... F 616 245-2255
Grand Rapids (G-7099)
Premier Finishing Inc .... E 616 785-3070
Grand Rapids (G-7102)
Shields Acquisition Co Inc .... G 734 782-4454
Flat Rock (G-5629)
South Haven Finishing Inc .... E 269 637-2047
South Haven (G-15413)
Troy Laboratories Inc .... F 248 652-6000
Rochester (G-13935)
V & V Inc .... E 616 842-8611
Grand Haven (G-6377)

METAL MINING SVCS

Meridian Lightweight Tech Inc .... E 248 663-8100
Plymouth (G-13241)
URS Energy & Construction Inc .... C 989 642-4190
Hemlock (G-7857)

METAL RESHAPING & REPLATING SVCS

Liberty Steel Fabricating Inc .... E 269 556-9792
Saint Joseph (G-14948)

METAL SERVICE CENTERS & OFFICES

Arlington Metals Corporation .... E 269 426-3371
Sawyer (G-15106)
Conway Detroit Corporation .... E 586 552-8413
Roseville (G-14389)

Employee Codes: A=Over 500 employees, B=251-500
C=101-250, D=51-100, E=20-50, F=10-19, G=3-9
2022 Harris Michigan
Industrial Directory
1335

Diez Group LLC.......D....... 734 675-1700
Woodhaven *(G-18799)*
Lv Metals Inc.......G....... 734 654-8081
Carleton *(G-2559)*
Mann Metal Finishing Inc.......D....... 269 621-6359
Hartford *(G-7765)*
National Galvanizing LP.......A....... 734 243-1882
Monroe *(G-11567)*
Nor-Cote Inc.......E....... 586 756-1200
Warren *(G-17944)*
Preferred Industries Inc.......E....... 810 364-4090
Kimball *(G-9500)*
Sandvik Inc.......D....... 269 926-7241
Benton Harbor *(G-1582)*
Sas Global Corporation.......C....... 248 414-4470
Warren *(G-18002)*
Scotten Steel Processing Inc.......F....... 313 897-8837
Detroit *(G-4585)*
Specialty Steel Treating Inc.......E....... 586 293-5355
Fraser *(G-5998)*
Van Pelt Corporation.......G....... 313 365-3600
Sterling Heights *(G-16221)*
Western International Inc.......E....... 866 814-2470
Troy *(G-17447)*

METAL SLITTING & SHEARING

Lv Metals Inc.......G....... 734 654-8081
Carleton *(G-2559)*
Pgp Corp.......D....... 313 291-7500
Taylor *(G-16457)*
Van S Fabrications Inc.......G....... 810 679-2115
Croswell *(G-3738)*

METAL SPINNING FOR THE TRADE

Globe Technologies Corporation.......E....... 989 846-9591
Standish *(G-15888)*
Metal Spinning Specialists.......G....... 810 743-6797
Burton *(G-2239)*
Weber Bros & White Metal Works.......G....... 269 751-5193
Hamilton *(G-7609)*

METAL STAMPING, FOR THE TRADE

A-1 Stampings Inc.......G....... 586 294-7790
Fraser *(G-5887)*
Acemco Incorporated.......C....... 231 799-8612
Norton Shores *(G-12344)*
Acme Tool & Die Co.......G....... 231 938-1260
Acme *(G-1)*
Acorn Stamping Inc.......F....... 248 628-5216
Oxford *(G-12870)*
Admat Manufacturing Inc.......F....... 269 641-7453
Union *(G-17486)*
Ajax Spring and Mfg Co.......E....... 248 588-5700
Madison Heights *(G-10664)*
ARC Metal Stamping LLC.......D....... 517 448-8954
Hudson *(G-8548)*
Automotive Prototype Stamping.......G....... 586 445-6792
Clinton Township *(G-3176)*
Bayloff Stmped Pdts Dtroit Inc.......D....... 734 397-9116
Van Buren Twp *(G-17510)*
Big Rapids Products Inc.......D....... 231 796-3593
Big Rapids *(G-1669)*
Bopp-Busch Manufacturing Co.......E....... 989 876-7121
Au Gres *(G-757)*
Burkland Inc.......C....... 810 636-2233
Goodrich *(G-6222)*
Burnside Acquisition LLC.......G....... 616 243-2800
Grand Rapids *(G-6538)*
Burnside Acquisition LLC.......C....... 231 798-3394
Norton Shores *(G-12346)*
Cleveland L&W Inc.......G....... 440 882-5195
New Boston *(G-12007)*
Conner Steel Products.......F....... 248 852-5110
Rochester Hills *(G-13983)*
Consolidated Clips Clamps Inc.......D....... 734 455-0880
Plymouth *(G-13149)*
Consolidated Metal Pdts Inc.......G....... 616 538-1000
Grand Rapids *(G-6596)*
Corban Industries Inc.......E....... 248 393-2720
Orion *(G-12726)*
Dajaco Ind Inc.......F....... 586 949-1590
Chesterfield *(G-2865)*
Dajaco Industries Inc.......D....... 586 949-1590
Chesterfield *(G-2866)*
Degele Manufacturing Inc.......E....... 586 949-3550
Chesterfield *(G-2869)*
Dexter Stamping Company LLC.......D....... 517 750-3414
Jackson *(G-8866)*
Dgh Enterprises Inc.......E....... 269 925-0657
Benton Harbor *(G-1546)*
Dgh Enterprises Inc.......G....... 269 925-0657
Benton Harbor *(G-1547)*
Die-Matic Tool and Die Inc.......E....... 616 531-0060
Wyoming *(G-18867)*
Dietech Tool & Mfg Inc.......D....... 810 724-0505
Imlay City *(G-8630)*
Douglas Stamping Company.......F....... 248 542-3940
Madison Heights *(G-10711)*
E & E Manufacturing Co Inc.......C....... 734 451-7600
Plymouth *(G-13164)*
Electro Optics Mfg Inc.......F....... 734 283-3000
Wyandotte *(G-18818)*
Experi-Metal Inc.......C....... 586 977-7800
Sterling Heights *(G-16009)*
Falcon Stamping Inc.......G....... 517 540-6197
Howell *(G-8453)*
Four Star Tooling & Engrg Inc.......G....... 586 264-4090
Sterling Heights *(G-16020)*
Four-Slide Technology Inc.......F....... 586 755-7778
Fraser *(G-5929)*
Frank Condon Inc.......E....... 517 849-2505
Hillsdale *(G-7935)*
Future Industries Inc.......E....... 616 844-0772
Grand Haven *(G-6299)*
Gar-V Manufacturing Inc.......G....... 269 279-5134
Three Rivers *(G-16574)*
Gestamp Alabama LLC.......D....... 810 245-3100
Lapeer *(G-9931)*
Global Advanced Products LLC.......D....... 586 749-6800
Chesterfield *(G-2887)*
Gordon Metal Products Inc.......F....... 586 445-0960
Detroit *(G-4271)*
Grand Traverse Stamping Co.......E....... 231 929-4215
Traverse City *(G-16701)*
Gray Bros Stamping & Mch Inc.......E....... 269 483-7615
White Pigeon *(G-18478)*
Great Lakes Metal Stamping Inc.......E....... 269 465-4415
Bridgman *(G-1927)*
Highland Engineering Inc.......E....... 517 548-4372
Howell *(G-8460)*
Highwood Die & Engineering Inc.......E....... 248 338-1807
Pontiac *(G-13380)*
Illinois Tool Works Inc.......B....... 616 772-1910
Zeeland *(G-19044)*
Independent Tool and Mfg Co.......E....... 269 521-4811
Allegan *(G-161)*
Industrial Engineering Service.......F....... 616 794-1330
Belding *(G-1453)*
Industrial Stamping & Mfg Co.......E....... 586 772-8430
Roseville *(G-14423)*
Innovative Tool and Design Inc.......E....... 248 542-1831
Oak Park *(G-12618)*
Iroquois Industries Inc.......D....... 586 771-5734
Warren *(G-17873)*
Iroquois Industries Inc.......E....... 586 353-1410
Warren *(G-17874)*
Jackson Precision Inds Inc.......E....... 517 782-8103
Jackson *(G-8917)*
Jireh Metal Products Inc.......D....... 616 531-7581
Grandville *(G-7393)*
JMS of Holland Inc.......D....... 616 796-2727
Holland *(G-8100)*
Jordan Manufacturing Company.......E....... 616 794-0900
Belding *(G-1454)*
K & K Die Inc.......E....... 586 268-8812
Sterling Heights *(G-16059)*
L & W Inc.......F....... 517 627-7333
Grand Ledge *(G-6394)*
L & W Inc.......G....... 517 486-6321
Blissfield *(G-1767)*
L & W Inc.......F....... 734 529-7290
Dundee *(G-4826)*
L & W Inc.......D....... 734 397-6300
New Boston *(G-12012)*
Marshall Metal Products Inc.......G....... 269 781-3924
Marshall *(G-11067)*
Mayville Engineering Co Inc.......D....... 616 878-5235
Byron Center *(G-2281)*
Mec.......F....... 989 983-3911
Vanderbilt *(G-17574)*
Metal Flow Corporation.......C....... 616 392-7976
Holland *(G-8143)*
Metro Stamping & Mfg Co.......E....... 313 538-6464
Redford *(G-13746)*
Mico Industries Inc.......D....... 616 245-6426
Grand Rapids *(G-6999)*
Mico Industries Inc.......F....... 616 245-6426
Grand Rapids *(G-7000)*
Mico Industries Inc.......E....... 616 514-1143
Grand Rapids *(G-7001)*
Mid-Tech Inc.......G....... 734 426-4327
Ann Arbor *(G-577)*
Middleville Tool & Die Co Inc.......D....... 269 795-3646
Middleville *(G-11309)*
Modineer Co LLC.......C....... 269 683-2550
Niles *(G-12145)*
Modineer Co LLC.......E....... 269 683-2550
Niles *(G-12146)*
Modineer Co LLC.......G....... 269 684-3138
Niles *(G-12147)*
Modineer P-K Tool LLC.......E....... 269 683-2550
Niles *(G-12148)*
Nelson Steel Products Inc.......D....... 616 396-1515
Holland *(G-8152)*
New 11 Inc.......E....... 616 494-9370
Holland *(G-8153)*
New Center Stamping Inc.......C....... 313 872-3500
Detroit *(G-4481)*
Nor-Dic Tool Company Inc.......F....... 734 326-3610
Romulus *(G-14312)*
Northern Stampings Inc.......F....... 586 598-6969
Rochester Hills *(G-14072)*
Oakland Stamping LLC.......C....... 734 397-6300
Detroit *(G-4496)*
Oakland Stamping LLC.......G....... 248 340-2520
Lake Orion *(G-9623)*
Pac-Cnc Inc.......E....... 616 288-3389
Grand Rapids *(G-7065)*
Palmer Engineering Inc.......E....... 517 321-3600
Lansing *(G-9723)*
Permaloc Corporation.......F....... 616 399-9600
Holland *(G-8162)*
Pinconning Metals Inc.......G....... 989 879-3144
Pinconning *(G-13064)*
Production Spring LLC.......E....... 248 583-0036
Troy *(G-17318)*
Proos Manufacturing LLC.......C....... 616 454-5622
Grand Rapids *(G-7121)*
Quality Tool & Stamping Co Inc.......C....... 231 733-2538
Muskegon *(G-11902)*
Quigley Industries Inc.......E....... 248 426-8600
Farmington Hills *(G-5361)*
R E D Industries Inc.......F....... 248 542-2211
Hazel Park *(G-7838)*
Reliant Industries Inc.......E....... 586 275-0479
Sterling Heights *(G-16146)*
Republic Die & Tool Co.......E....... 734 699-3400
Van Buren Twp *(G-17551)*
Rew Industries Inc.......E....... 586 803-1150
Shelby Township *(G-15316)*
Ridgeview Industries Inc.......B....... 616 453-8636
Grand Rapids *(G-7156)*
Ridgeview Industries Inc.......D....... 616 414-6500
Nunica *(G-12585)*
Ridgeview Industries Inc.......C....... 616 453-8636
Grand Rapids *(G-7157)*
Schaller Corporation.......C....... 586 949-6000
Chesterfield *(G-2946)*
Selective Industries Inc.......D....... 810 765-4666
Marine City *(G-10966)*
Silver Creek Manufacturing Inc.......F....... 231 798-3003
Norton Shores *(G-12330)*
Sinclair Designs & Engrg LLC.......E....... 877 517-0311
Albion *(G-133)*
Sintel Inc.......C....... 616 842-6960
Spring Lake *(G-15852)*
SOS Engineering Inc.......F....... 616 846-5767
Grand Haven *(G-6364)*
Stanco Metal Products Inc.......E....... 616 842-5000
Grand Haven *(G-6366)*
Standard Die International Inc.......E....... 800 838-5464
Livonia *(G-10417)*
Style Craft Prototype Inc.......F....... 248 619-9048
Troy *(G-17375)*
Synergy Prototype Stamping LLC.......E....... 586 961-6109
Clinton Township *(G-3370)*
Technical Stamping Inc.......G....... 586 948-3285
Chesterfield *(G-2954)*
Tg Manufacturing LLC.......E....... 616 842-1503
Grand Rapids *(G-7255)*
Trans-Matic Mfg Co Inc.......C....... 616 820-2500
Holland *(G-8225)*
Transfer Tool Systems LLC.......C....... 616 846-8510
Grand Haven *(G-6372)*
United Manufacturing Inc.......E....... 616 738-8888
Holland *(G-8233)*
Universal Stamping Inc.......E....... 269 925-5300
Benton Harbor *(G-1596)*

PRODUCT SECTION

Van S Fabrications Inc ....G....... 810 679-2115
  Croswell *(G-3738)*
Van-Dies Engineering Inc ....E....... 586 293-1430
  Fraser *(G-6010)*
Vinewood Metalcraft Inc ....E....... 734 946-8733
  Taylor *(G-16486)*
Wolverine Metal Stamping Inc ....D....... 269 429-6600
  Saint Joseph *(G-14980)*

METAL STAMPINGS: Ornamental

Haerter Stamping LLC ....D....... 616 871-9400
  Kentwood *(G-9457)*
Schwab Industries Inc ....E....... 586 566-8090
  Shelby Township *(G-15326)*

METAL STAMPINGS: Patterned

Contour Engineering Inc ....F....... 989 828-6526
  Shepherd *(G-15376)*
Four Way Industries Inc ....F....... 248 588-5421
  Clawson *(G-3097)*
KB Stamping Inc ....F....... 616 866-5917
  Belmont *(G-1509)*
Northwest Pattern Company ....G....... 248 477-7070
  Farmington Hills *(G-5335)*
Tenibac-Graphion Inc ....D....... 586 792-0150
  Clinton Township *(G-3375)*

METAL STAMPINGS: Perforated

Clark Perforating Company Inc ....F....... 734 439-1170
  Milan *(G-11433)*
Expan Inc ....E....... 586 725-0405
  New Baltimore *(G-11980)*
Gns Holland Inc ....G....... 616 796-0433
  Holland *(G-8053)*

METAL TREATING COMPOUNDS

Cross Technologies Group Inc ....F....... 734 895-8084
  Westland *(G-18362)*
General Chemical Corporation ....G....... 248 587-5600
  Brighton *(G-1998)*
Haas Group International LLC ....G....... 810 236-0032
  Flint *(G-5712)*
Kolene Corporation ....D....... 313 273-9220
  Detroit *(G-4365)*
Macdermid Incorporated ....G....... 248 399-3553
  Ferndale *(G-5566)*
Morning Star Land Company LLC ....F....... 734 459-8022
  Canton *(G-2498)*
Ncoc Inc ....E....... 248 548-5950
  Oak Park *(G-12632)*
Tuocai America LLC ....G....... 248 346-5910
  Troy *(G-17406)*
V & V Industries Inc ....F....... 248 624-7943
  Wixom *(G-18783)*

METALS SVC CENTERS & WHOL: Structural Shapes, Iron Or Steel

Eaton Steel Corporation ....D....... 248 398-3434
  Oak Park *(G-12609)*
Eaton Steel Corporation ....D....... 248 398-3434
  Livonia *(G-10189)*
Nova International LLC ....E....... 269 381-6779
  Portage *(G-13589)*

METALS SVC CENTERS & WHOLESALERS: Bars, Metal

BR Safety Products Inc ....G....... 734 582-4499
  Plymouth *(G-13137)*

METALS SVC CENTERS & WHOLESALERS: Casting, Rough, Iron/Steel

Acme Casting Enterprises Inc ....G....... 586 755-0300
  Warren *(G-17689)*
J J Pattern & Castings Inc ....G....... 248 543-7119
  Madison Heights *(G-10751)*
Teksid Inc ....E....... 734 846-5492
  Farmington *(G-5153)*

METALS SVC CENTERS & WHOLESALERS: Copper

Rivore Metals LLC ....G....... 800 248-1250
  Troy *(G-17334)*

METALS SVC CENTERS & WHOLESALERS: Copper Prdts

New Life Cop Brass Mint Free M ....G....... 586 725-3286
  Casco *(G-2601)*

METALS SVC CENTERS & WHOLESALERS: Ferroalloys

Howmet Corporation ....E....... 231 894-5686
  Whitehall *(G-18501)*
Howmet Holdings Corporation ....G....... 231 894-5686
  Whitehall *(G-18506)*

METALS SVC CENTERS & WHOLESALERS: Ferrous Metals

Mill Steel Co ....D....... 616 949-6700
  Grand Rapids *(G-7010)*

METALS SVC CENTERS & WHOLESALERS: Flat Prdts, Iron Or Steel

Allied Metals Corp ....E....... 248 680-2400
  Auburn Hills *(G-778)*
Machine Tool & Gear Inc ....B....... 989 761-7521
  Clifford *(G-3132)*
Machine Tool & Gear Inc ....D....... 989 743-3936
  Corunna *(G-3711)*

METALS SVC CENTERS & WHOLESALERS: Foundry Prdts

Ajf Inc ....E....... 734 753-4410
  New Boston *(G-11998)*
CA Picard Surface Engrg Inc ....E....... 440 366-5400
  Battle Creek *(G-1203)*

METALS SVC CENTERS & WHOLESALERS: Misc Nonferrous Prdts

Aluminum Supply Company Inc ....E....... 313 491-5040
  Detroit *(G-4007)*

METALS SVC CENTERS & WHOLESALERS: Pipe & Tubing, Steel

Energy Steel & Supply Co ....G....... 810 538-4990
  Rochester Hills *(G-14004)*
Ferguson Enterprises LLC ....G....... 989 790-2220
  Saginaw *(G-14645)*
Loonar Stn Two The 2 or 2nd ....G....... 419 720-1222
  Temperance *(G-16537)*
Mid Michigan Pipe Inc ....G....... 989 772-5664
  Grand Rapids *(G-7003)*
Midway Strl Pipe & Sup Inc ....G....... 517 787-1350
  Jackson *(G-8961)*
Piping Components Inc ....G....... 313 382-6400
  Melvindale *(G-11209)*
Stephens Pipe & Steel LLC ....E....... 616 248-3433
  Grand Rapids *(G-7226)*
Venture Technology Groups Inc ....F....... 248 473-8450
  Novi *(G-12566)*

METALS SVC CENTERS & WHOLESALERS: Plates, Metal

Pioneer Steel Corporation ....E....... 313 933-9400
  Detroit *(G-4525)*

METALS SVC CENTERS & WHOLESALERS: Rope, Wire, Exc Insulated

Commercial Group Inc ....E....... 313 931-6100
  Taylor *(G-16395)*

METALS SVC CENTERS & WHOLESALERS: Stampings, Metal

Serra Spring & Mfg LLC ....G....... 586 932-2202
  Sterling Heights *(G-16172)*
Triton Global Sources Inc ....G....... 734 668-7107
  Ypsilanti *(G-18981)*

METALS SVC CENTERS & WHOLESALERS: Steel

Ace Drill Corporation ....G....... 517 265-5184
  Adrian *(G-47)*
Actron Steel Inc ....E....... 231 947-3981
  Traverse City *(G-16597)*
Alro Steel Corporation ....G....... 989 893-9553
  Bay City *(G-1320)*
Alro Steel Corporation ....G....... 810 695-7300
  Grand Blanc *(G-6231)*
Alro Steel Corporation ....G....... 517 371-9600
  Lansing *(G-9803)*
Ameristeel Inc ....E....... 586 585-5250
  Fraser *(G-5894)*
Bico Michigan Inc ....G....... 616 453-2400
  Grand Rapids *(G-6506)*
Bills Custom Fab Inc ....F....... 989 772-5817
  Mount Pleasant *(G-11687)*
Brown-Campbell Company ....E....... 586 884-2180
  Shelby Township *(G-15179)*
Campbell & Shaw Steel Inc ....F....... 810 364-5100
  Marysville *(G-11083)*
Capital Steel & Builders Sup ....E....... 517 694-0451
  Holt *(G-8304)*
Contractors Steel Company ....E....... 616 531-4000
  Grand Rapids *(G-6600)*
Delaco Steel Corporation ....C....... 313 491-1200
  Dearborn *(G-3826)*
Detroit Steel Group Inc ....G....... 248 298-2900
  Royal Oak *(G-14530)*
Ferro Fab LLC ....F....... 586 791-3561
  Clinton Township *(G-3237)*
Greenwell Machine Shop Inc ....G....... 231 347-3346
  Petoskey *(G-12999)*
Harrison Steel LLC ....G....... 586 247-1230
  Shelby Township *(G-15232)*
Hayden Neitzke LLC ....G....... 989 875-2440
  Sumner *(G-16331)*
J B Lunds & Sons Inc ....G....... 231 627-9070
  Cheboygan *(G-2788)*
JIT Steel Corp ....E....... 313 491-3212
  Dearborn *(G-3856)*
K & L Sheet Metal LLC ....G....... 269 965-0027
  Battle Creek *(G-1248)*
King Steel Corporation ....E....... 800 638-2530
  Grand Blanc *(G-6250)*
Metal Mart USA Inc ....G....... 586 977-5820
  Warren *(G-17924)*
MNP Corporation ....A....... 586 254-1320
  Utica *(G-17504)*
Padnos Leitelt Inc ....D....... 616 363-3817
  Grand Rapids *(G-7067)*
Peerless Steel Company ....E....... 616 530-6695
  Grandville *(G-7408)*
Pgp Corp ....D....... 313 291-7500
  Taylor *(G-16457)*
Rolled Alloys Inc ....D....... 734 847-0561
  Temperance *(G-16547)*
Sas Global Corporation ....D....... 248 414-4470
  Warren *(G-18003)*
SOO Welding Inc ....G....... 906 632-8241
  Sault Sainte Marie *(G-15100)*
Spartan Metal Fab LLC ....F....... 517 322-9050
  Lansing *(G-9737)*
Very Best Steel LLC ....G....... 734 697-8609
  Belleville *(G-1493)*
World Class Steel & Proc Inc ....G....... 586 585-1734
  Troy *(G-17453)*

METALS SVC CENTERS & WHOLESALERS: Zinc

Metropolitan Alloys Corp ....E....... 313 366-4443
  Detroit *(G-4438)*

METALS SVC CTRS & WHOLESALERS: Aluminum Bars, Rods, Etc

CTC Distribution Inc ....G....... 313 486-2225
  Saint Clair Shores *(G-14854)*
Meliss Company Inc ....F....... 248 398-1970
  Clarkston *(G-3049)*
Shipston Group US Inc ....E....... 248 372-9018
  Southfield *(G-15702)*
Wayne-Craft Inc ....F....... 734 421-8800
  Livonia *(G-10468)*

METALS: Precious NEC

Carrington Precious Metals LLC ....G....... 517 323-9154
  Lansing *(G-9678)*
Usmfg Inc ....G....... 262 993-9197
  East Lansing *(G-4914)*

METALS: Precious, Secondary

METALS: Precious, Secondary
- Trelleborg Corporation .... G 269 639-9891
  South Haven *(G-15419)*

METALS: Primary Nonferrous, NEC
- Cannon-Muskegon Corporation .... C 231 755-1681
  Norton Shores *(G-12284)*
- Comau LLC .... B 248 353-8888
  Southfield *(G-15530)*
- Eclectic Metal Arts LLC .... G 248 251-5924
  Detroit *(G-4200)*
- Expan Inc .... E 586 725-0405
  New Baltimore *(G-11980)*
- H C Starck Inc .... G 517 279-9511
  Coldwater *(G-3437)*
- Metropolitan Alloys Corp .... E 313 366-4443
  Detroit *(G-4438)*
- Resource Rcovery Solutions Inc .... G 248 454-3442
  Pontiac *(G-13413)*
- Specialty Steel Treating Inc .... E 586 293-5355
  Fraser *(G-5998)*

METALWORK: Miscellaneous
- Aarons Fabrication of Steel .... G 586 883-0652
  Clinton Township *(G-3151)*
- Ambassador Steel Corporation .... E 517 455-7216
  Lansing *(G-9804)*
- Aristo-Cote Inc .... E 586 447-9049
  Harrison Township *(G-7688)*
- Bristol Steel & Conveyor Corp .... E 810 658-9510
  Davison *(G-3775)*
- Butler Mill Service Company .... E 313 429-2486
  Detroit *(G-4079)*
- Campbell & Shaw Steel Inc .... F 810 364-5100
  Marysville *(G-11083)*
- Challenge Mfg Company .... G 616 735-6500
  Lansing *(G-9680)*
- Depottey Acquisition Inc .... F 616 846-4150
  Grand Haven *(G-6291)*
- Die Stampco Inc .... F 989 893-7790
  Bay City *(G-1344)*
- Dowding Industries Inc .... E 517 663-5455
  Eaton Rapids *(G-4959)*
- F&B Technologies .... F 734 856-2118
  Ottawa Lake *(G-12806)*
- Frankenmuth Welding & Fabg .... G 989 754-9457
  Saginaw *(G-14646)*
- Howard Finishing LLC .... C 248 588-9050
  Madison Heights *(G-10742)*
- Ideal Shield LLC .... E 866 825-8659
  Detroit *(G-4311)*
- Jcr Fabrication LLC .... G 906 235-2683
  Ontonagon *(G-12710)*
- Kenowa Industries Inc .... E 616 392-7080
  Holland *(G-8111)*
- Kenowa Industries Inc .... G 517 322-0311
  Lansing *(G-9771)*
- Kustom Creations Inc .... G 586 997-4141
  Sterling Heights *(G-16068)*
- Llink Technologies LLC .... E 586 336-9370
  Brown City *(G-2139)*
- Lor Products Inc .... G 989 382-9020
  Remus *(G-13816)*
- M J Day Machine Tool Company .... G 313 730-1200
  Allen Park *(G-199)*
- Netshape International LLC .... D 616 846-8700
  Grand Haven *(G-6340)*
- R & S Propeller Inc .... F 616 636-8202
  Sand Lake *(G-15052)*
- Robert Anderson .... G 586 552-5648
  Saint Clair Shores *(G-14881)*
- Rocksteady Manufacturing LLC .... F 586 778-5028
  Roseville *(G-14472)*
- S & N Machine & Fabricating .... E 231 894-2658
  Rothbury *(G-14498)*
- Shape Corp .... B 616 846-8700
  Grand Haven *(G-6361)*
- Shape Corp .... C 616 846-8700
  Grand Haven *(G-6362)*
- Speedrack Products Group Ltd .... C 517 639-8781
  Quincy *(G-13674)*
- Speedrack Products Group Ltd .... G 616 887-0002
  Sparta *(G-15782)*
- Standard Coating Inc .... D 248 297-6650
  Madison Heights *(G-10835)*
- Tubelite Inc .... G 800 866-2227
  Walker *(G-17655)*
- Tubelite Inc .... D 800 866-2227
  Reed City *(G-13801)*

- Walther Trowal LLC .... F 616 455-8940
  Byron Center *(G-2301)*
- Weldaloy Products Company .... D 586 758-5550
  Warren *(G-18064)*
- Witzenmann Usa LLC .... B 248 588-6033
  Troy *(G-17449)*
- Worthington Armstrong Venture .... F 269 934-6200
  Benton Harbor *(G-1611)*

METALWORK: Ornamental
- Michigan Ornamental Ir & Fabg .... F 616 899-2441
  Conklin *(G-3661)*

METEOROLOGIC TRACKING SYSTEMS
- International Met Systems Inc .... F 616 971-1005
  Grand Rapids *(G-6850)*

METERING DEVICES: Water Quality Monitoring & Control Systems
- Carlon Meter Inc .... G 616 842-0420
  Grand Haven *(G-6283)*
- SLC Meter LLC .... F 248 625-0667
  Pontiac *(G-13416)*

METERS: Liquid
- Advance Tech Solutions LLC .... G 989 928-1806
  Saginaw *(G-14601)*

METERS: Pyrometers, Indl Process
- Pyro Service Company .... G 248 547-2552
  Madison Heights *(G-10812)*

METERS: Solarimeters
- Solar Street Lights Usa LLC .... G 269 983-6361
  Holland *(G-8199)*

MGMT CONSULTING SVCS: Matls, Incl Purch, Handle & Invntry
- Falcon Consulting Services LLC .... G 989 262-9325
  Alpena *(G-293)*

MGT SVCS, FACIL SUPPT: Base Maint Or Provide Personnel
- Vdl Steelweld Usa LLC .... E 248 781-8141
  Troy *(G-17433)*

MICA PRDTS
- Neuvokas Corporation .... G 906 934-2661
  Ahmeek *(G-109)*

MICROCIRCUITS, INTEGRATED: Semiconductor
- ABB Enterprise Software Inc .... E 313 863-1909
  Detroit *(G-3979)*
- Johnson Electric N Amer Inc .... D 734 392-5300
  Plymouth *(G-13206)*
- Maxim Integrated Products Inc .... C 408 601-1000
  Brighton *(G-2027)*

MICROFILM EQPT
- American Information Services .... F 248 399-4848
  Berkley *(G-1620)*

MICROFILM EQPT WHOLESALERS
- American Information Services .... F 248 399-4848
  Berkley *(G-1620)*

MICROFILM SVCS
- American Information Services .... F 248 399-4848
  Berkley *(G-1620)*

MICROPHONES
- Stedman Corp .... G 269 629-5930
  Richland *(G-13830)*

MICROPROCESSORS
- Compunetics Incorporated .... E 248 524-6376
  Troy *(G-17022)*

MICROSCOPES: Electron & Proton
- Jade Scientific Inc .... F 734 207-3775
  Westland *(G-18387)*

MICROWAVE COMPONENTS
- Cobham McRlctrnic Slutions Inc .... G 734 426-1230
  Ann Arbor *(G-431)*

MILITARY GOODS & REGALIA STORES
- Oakland Tactical Supply LLC .... G 810 991-1436
  Howell *(G-8488)*

MILITARY INSIGNIA, TEXTILE
- Spartan Village LLC .... G 661 724-6438
  Standish *(G-15896)*

MILLING: Chemical
- Future Mill Inc .... G 586 754-8088
  Warren *(G-17820)*

MILLING: Corn Grits & Flakes, For Brewers' Use
- Right Brain Brewery .... G 231 922-9662
  Traverse City *(G-16820)*

MILLS: Ferrous & Nonferrous
- SMS Technical Service LLC .... F 313 322-4890
  Dearborn *(G-3897)*

MILLWORK
- 2 Sg Wookworks LLC .... G 586 884-7090
  Clinton Township *(G-3143)*
- Acadian Woodworking LLC .... G 989 356-0229
  Alpena *(G-273)*
- Action Outdoor Services LLC .... G 719 596-5341
  Ann Arbor *(G-348)*
- Air Conditioning Products Co .... E 734 326-0050
  Romulus *(G-14247)*
- Allen and Sons Woodworking .... G 313 492-1382
  Linden *(G-10059)*
- American Wood Moldings LLC .... G 586 726-9050
  Shelby Township *(G-15169)*
- Architectural Door & Mllwk Inc .... E 248 442-9222
  New Hudson *(G-12043)*
- Architectural Planners Inc .... G 248 674-1340
  Waterford *(G-18101)*
- Architectural Products Inc .... G 248 585-8272
  Royal Oak *(G-14511)*
- Architectural Trim & Wdwrk LLC .... G 586 321-1860
  Shelby Township *(G-15171)*
- Arctel Corp .... F 616 241-6001
  Grand Rapids *(G-6468)*
- Ark Woodworks LLC .... G 269 364-1397
  Kalamazoo *(G-9121)*
- Armstrong Millworks Inc .... G 248 887-1037
  Highland *(G-7881)*
- ASC Custom Woodworking LLC .... G 586 855-8817
  Warren *(G-17717)*
- Audia Woodworking & Fine Furn .... F 586 296-6330
  Clinton Township *(G-3174)*
- Autumn Ridge Woodworks .... G 517 420-8185
  Mason *(G-11117)*
- Barlow Custom Woodworking .... G 810 220-0648
  Brighton *(G-1949)*
- Bay Wood Homes Inc .... F 989 245-4156
  Fenton *(G-5456)*
- Bc Woodworks .... G 989 820-7680
  Oscoda *(G-12754)*
- Birch Point Woodworks .... G 906 322-8761
  Brimley *(G-2100)*
- Bird Lofts & Stuff Woodworking .... G 248 882-1242
  White Lake *(G-18451)*
- Birds-Eye Creations Inc .... G 906 337-5095
  Mohawk *(G-11517)*
- Boattown Woodshop .... G 586 703-0538
  Mount Clemens *(G-11631)*
- Brambles Woodwork LLC .... G 616 446-9118
  Ada *(G-13)*
- Brunt Associates Inc .... E 248 960-8295
  Wixom *(G-18627)*
- C & A Wood Products Inc .... F 313 365-8400
  Detroit *(G-4083)*
- C & K Hardwoods LLC .... G 269 231-0048
  Three Oaks *(G-16554)*

C & S Millwork Inc.....F..... 586 465-6470
Clinton Township *(G-3193)*
C and M Construction.....G..... 989 213-1955
Vassar *(G-17578)*
Carlee Woodworking.....G..... 734 660-0491
Pinckney *(G-13044)*
Carpenters Friend Woodworking.....G..... 231 218-2736
Interlochen *(G-8680)*
Cedar Ridge Custom Wdwkg LLC.....G..... 248 425-0185
Oxford *(G-12881)*
Charles A Specialties LLC.....G..... 231 946-3389
Traverse City *(G-16645)*
Chippewa Development Inc.....F..... 269 685-2646
Plainwell *(G-13071)*
Custom Craftsmen Woodworking.....G..... 616 638-4768
Spring Lake *(G-15810)*
Custom Woodwork & Rmdlg LLC.....G..... 586 778-9224
Warren *(G-17769)*
D & D Building Inc.....F..... 616 248-7908
Grand Rapids *(G-6626)*
D&D Planning Design Mllwk LLC.....F..... 586 754-6500
Warren *(G-17773)*
Dads Panels Inc.....G..... 810 245-1871
Lapeer *(G-9926)*
Dagenham Millworks LLC.....G..... 616 698-8883
Grand Rapids *(G-6630)*
Daniel D Slater.....G..... 989 833-7135
Riverdale *(G-13863)*
Dean Richard Woodworking.....G..... 586 764-6586
Sylvan Lake *(G-16360)*
Decatur Wood Products Inc.....E..... 269 657-6041
Decatur *(G-3946)*
Donato Woodworks.....G..... 586 899-7430
Center Line *(G-2681)*
Dovetails Inc.....G..... 248 674-8777
Waterford *(G-18118)*
Downriver Creative Woodworking.....G..... 313 274-4090
Allen Park *(G-193)*
E Leet Woodworking.....G..... 269 664-5203
Plainwell *(G-13076)*
Elan Designs Inc.....G..... 248 682-3000
Pontiac *(G-13365)*
Elegant Wood Craftsmanship.....G..... 231 742-0706
Hart *(G-7751)*
Elegant Woodworking.....G..... 248 363-3804
Commerce Township *(G-3526)*
Eliason Corporation.....E..... 269 621-2100
Hartford *(G-7763)*
Elite Woodworking LLC.....E..... 586 204-5882
Saint Clair Shores *(G-14856)*
Emery Design & Woodwork LLC.....G..... 734 709-1687
South Lyon *(G-15434)*
End Grain Woodwork.....G..... 248 420-3228
Livonia *(G-10197)*
Eric Henry Woodworks.....G..... 248 613-5696
Clarkston *(G-3033)*
Euclid Industries Inc.....C..... 989 686-8920
Bay City *(G-1352)*
Family Tradition Wdwkg Plans.....G..... 989 871-6688
Millington *(G-11500)*
Farmhouse Woodworking LLC.....G..... 269 350-0582
Baroda *(G-1161)*
Foggy Mountain Woodworks.....G..... 231 675-1757
Boyne Falls *(G-1907)*
Forsyth Millwork and Farms.....G..... 810 266-4000
Byron *(G-2253)*
Freelands Country Upolstery.....G..... 269 330-2416
Delton *(G-3963)*
G F Inc.....G..... 231 946-5330
Traverse City *(G-16691)*
G P Woodworking L L C.....G..... 313 600-9414
Brighton *(G-1995)*
General Hardwood Company.....F..... 313 365-7733
Detroit *(G-4253)*
George Washburn.....G..... 269 694-2930
Otsego *(G-12786)*
Goodrich Brothers Inc.....G..... 989 224-4944
Saint Johns *(G-14900)*
Goodrich Brothers Inc.....E..... 989 593-2104
Pewamo *(G-13028)*
Goodwill Inds Nthrn Mich Inc.....G..... 231 779-1311
Cadillac *(G-2332)*
Goodwill Inds Nthrn Mich Inc.....G..... 231 779-1361
Cadillac *(G-2333)*
Goodwill Inds Nthrn Mich Inc.....G..... 231 922-4890
Traverse City *(G-16696)*
Gordon Woodwork LLC.....G..... 734 612-3586
Belleville *(G-1484)*
Grand Rapids Carvers Inc.....E..... 616 538-0022
Grand Rapids *(G-6754)*
Grand Rapids Wood Works.....G..... 616 690-2889
Grandville *(G-7380)*
Grand Rapids Woodworking.....G..... 616 780-7137
Grand Rapids *(G-6773)*
Grand Rapids Woodworking LLC.....G..... 616 301-8719
Grand Rapids *(G-6774)*
Grand Valley Wood Products Inc.....E..... 616 475-5890
Grand Rapids *(G-6779)*
Gravelle Woods.....G..... 616 617-7712
Ada *(G-20)*
Great Lakes Wood Products.....G..... 906 228-3737
Negaunee *(G-11967)*
Great Lakes Woodworking LLC.....E..... 248 550-1991
Orion *(G-12732)*
Great North Woodworks.....G..... 231 622-6200
Petoskey *(G-12998)*
Greggs Wood Duck Boxes.....G..... 989 770-5204
Burt *(G-2215)*
Guzman Woodworks.....G..... 313 436-1912
Detroit *(G-4287)*
Hall Wood Creations.....G..... 248 645-0983
Beverly Hills *(G-1664)*
Hambones Wood Works.....G..... 313 304-5590
Newport *(G-12102)*
Harris Obrien Woodworks.....G..... 616 292-2613
Caledonia *(G-2377)*
Hazeltree Woodworking.....G..... 517 320-2954
Marshall *(G-11060)*
Heartwood Mills LLC.....F..... 888 829-5909
Boyne Falls *(G-1908)*
Heritage Wdwrks Grnd Rpids LLC.....G..... 616 780-9499
Grand Rapids *(G-6812)*
Heritage Woodworking.....G..... 734 753-3368
New Boston *(G-12009)*
Hickmans Woodworking LLC.....G..... 616 678-4180
Kent City *(G-9433)*
Holland Panel Products Inc.....E..... 616 392-1826
Holland *(G-8081)*
Hollow Hill Woodworks.....G..... 906 493-6913
Drummond Island *(G-4801)*
Homeworks.....G..... 810 533-2030
Saint Clair Shores *(G-14865)*
Honey Creek Woodworks.....G..... 616 706-2539
Ada *(G-22)*
Hornshaw Wood Works LLC.....G..... 616 566-0720
Holland *(G-8088)*
Hunt & Noyer LLC.....G..... 517 914-6259
Berkley *(G-1627)*
Ideal Millwork Enterprises LLC.....F..... 248 461-6460
Waterford *(G-18128)*
Industrial Assemblies Inc.....E..... 231 865-6500
Fruitport *(G-6063)*
Innovative Woodworking.....G..... 269 926-9663
Benton Harbor *(G-1557)*
Innovative Woodworking.....G..... 616 638-1139
Muskegon *(G-11840)*
J J Wohlferts Custom Furniture.....F..... 989 593-3283
Fowler *(G-5829)*
J&N Custom Woodworking.....G..... 517 726-0290
Vermontville *(G-17589)*
Jackieswoodworks.....G..... 616 914-2961
Norton Shores *(G-12304)*
James Gordon Marsh.....G..... 517 372-8685
Lansing *(G-9856)*
Joe Beam Woodworking.....G..... 269 873-0160
Stevensville *(G-16254)*
Justinscstmgatesandwoodworking.....G..... 906 748-1999
Mason *(G-11140)*
Kent Door & Specialty Inc.....E..... 616 534-9691
Grand Rapids *(G-6888)*
Kerns Wood Works LLC.....G..... 734 368-1951
Van Buren Twp *(G-17533)*
Kpl Custom Woodworking LLC.....G..... 313 530-5507
Livonia *(G-10267)*
Kropp Woodworking Inc.....F..... 586 463-2300
Mount Clemens *(G-11646)*
Kropp Woodworking Inc.....G..... 586 997-3000
Sterling Heights *(G-16064)*
Krumrie Saw Mill Services.....G..... 269 838-9060
Galien *(G-6089)*
L & M Woodworking LLC.....G..... 404 391-3868
Oxford *(G-12894)*
L E Q Inc.....F..... 248 257-5466
Waterford *(G-18132)*
Lamay Woodworking.....G..... 734 421-6032
Livonia *(G-10274)*
Lavern Beechy.....G..... 269 651-5095
Sturgis *(G-16300)*
Leelanau Woodworking.....G..... 231 946-4437
Traverse City *(G-16743)*
Legendary Millwork Inc.....G..... 248 588-5663
Troy *(G-17207)*
Lifetime Company.....G..... 248 862-2578
Bloomfield Hills *(G-1830)*
Live Edge Detroit.....G..... 248 909-2259
Troy *(G-17213)*
Loduca Woodworks LLC.....G..... 734 626-2525
Clinton Township *(G-3280)*
Macb Woodworking LLC.....G..... 734 645-8990
Ann Arbor *(G-560)*
Maple Leaf Woodworking.....G..... 616 262-9754
Orleans *(G-12740)*
Marquis Wood Works.....G..... 810 488-9406
Burtchville *(G-2222)*
Masters Millwork LLC.....F..... 248 987-4511
Madison Heights *(G-10777)*
MB Woodworks and Co.....G..... 231 452-6321
Newaygo *(G-12087)*
McCoy Craftsman LLC.....F..... 616 634-7455
Grand Rapids *(G-6972)*
Metrie Inc.....E..... 313 299-1860
Taylor *(G-16443)*
Michigan Woodwork.....G..... 517 204-4394
Mason *(G-11145)*
Milliken Millwork Inc.....B..... 586 264-0950
Sterling Heights *(G-16101)*
Mjbcustomwoodworking.....G..... 989 695-2737
Freeland *(G-6025)*
Mod Interiors Inc.....E..... 586 725-8227
Ira *(G-8702)*
Modern Millwork Inc.....F..... 248 347-4777
Wixom *(G-18713)*
Modern Woodsmith LLC.....G..... 906 387-5577
Wetmore *(G-18435)*
Nacs USA Inc.....G..... 800 253-9000
Zeeland *(G-19058)*
North American Forest Products.....G..... 269 663-8500
Edwardsburg *(G-5014)*
Northern Mich Hardwoods Inc.....F..... 231 347-4575
Petoskey *(G-13008)*
Northern Millwork Co.....F..... 313 365-7733
Detroit *(G-4490)*
Northern Outdoor Woodworks LLC.....G..... 231 275-1181
Lake Ann *(G-9543)*
Oak North Manufacturing Inc.....E..... 906 475-7992
Negaunee *(G-11971)*
Odl Incorporated.....G..... 616 772-9111
Zeeland *(G-19063)*
On The Level Woodworking.....G..... 269 429-4570
Stevensville *(G-16262)*
Ornamental Mouldings LLC.....F..... 616 748-0188
Zeeland *(G-19065)*
Owens Building Co Inc.....E..... 989 835-1293
Midland *(G-11401)*
Oxford Woodworks.....G..... 248 736-3090
Traverse City *(G-16785)*
Pacific Door & Trim.....G..... 619 887-1786
Harper Woods *(G-7669)*
Parkway Drapery & Uphl Co Inc.....G..... 734 779-1300
Livonia *(G-10360)*
Phil Elenbaas Millwork Inc.....G..... 231 526-8399
Harbor Springs *(G-7655)*
Pine Tech Inc.....E..... 989 426-0006
Plymouth *(G-13264)*
Poor Boy Woodworks Inc.....F..... 989 799-9440
Saginaw *(G-14730)*
Quality Craft Woodworking.....G..... 248 343-6358
Milford *(G-11483)*
Quality Wood Products Inc.....F..... 989 658-2160
Ubly *(G-17481)*
R & K Woodworking.....G..... 734 741-3664
Howell *(G-8503)*
R Chamberlin Woodworking.....G..... 269 377-7232
Kalamazoo *(G-9312)*
R J Woodworking Inc.....E..... 231 766-2511
Muskegon *(G-11904)*
Ramzak Woodworking.....G..... 734 595-8155
Westland *(G-18412)*
Redbird WD Pdts Bldwin Twnship.....G..... 989 362-7670
East Tawas *(G-4922)*
Rekmakker Millwork Inc.....G..... 616 546-3680
Holland *(G-8178)*
Resurgo LLC.....G..... 313 559-2325
Detroit *(G-4570)*
Rfc Woodworks.....G..... 810 357-9072
Kalamazoo *(G-9315)*
Richmond Millwork Inc.....F..... 586 727-6747
Ira *(G-8710)*
Rohr Woodworking.....G..... 248 363-9743
West Bloomfield *(G-18310)*

Employee Codes: A=Over 500 employees, B=251-500
C=101-250, D=51-100, E=20-50, F=10-19, G=3-9
2022 Harris Michigan
Industrial Directory
1339

MILLWORK

PRODUCT SECTION

Royal Enterprizes .... G 269 429-5878
 Saint Joseph *(G-14959)*
Saurs Custom Woodworking .... G 906 288-3202
 Toivola *(G-16592)*
Sawdust and Lace .... G 517 331-4535
 Lansing *(G-9735)*
Sawmill Bill Lumber Inc .... G 231 275-3000
 Interlochen *(G-8684)*
Schrams Custom Woodworking .... G 989 335-0847
 Lincoln *(G-10040)*
Scotco Woodworking .... G 586 749-9805
 Ray *(G-13703)*
Scott Philip Custom Wdwkg LLC .... G 616 723-9074
 Belmont *(G-1516)*
Select Millwork .... G 269 685-2646
 Plainwell *(G-13095)*
Serenity Woodworking LLC .... G 734 812-5429
 South Lyon *(G-15456)*
SGS Wood Works LLC .... G 239 564-8449
 Saline *(G-15038)*
Simply Woodworking LLC .... G 586 405-1080
 Grosse Pointe Park *(G-7559)*
Sindelar Fine Woodworking Co .... G 269 663-8841
 Edwardsburg *(G-5016)*
Sprik Custom Woodworks LLC .... G 616 826-0858
 Grand Haven *(G-6365)*
Ss Custom Market .... G 269 816-1311
 Three Rivers *(G-16585)*
Standale Lumber and Supply Co .... D 616 530-8200
 Grandville *(G-7419)*
Sterling Millwork Inc .... D 248 427-1400
 Farmington Hills *(G-5389)*
Strongs Woodworking .... G 989 350-9113
 Boyne Falls *(G-1910)*
T & K Woodworks .... G 734 868-0028
 La Salle *(G-9530)*
T M Wood Products Mfg Inc .... F 586 427-2364
 Warren *(G-18032)*
Tapco Holdings Inc .... C 248 668-6400
 Wixom *(G-18766)*
Thomas and Milliken Mllwk Inc .... F 231 386-7236
 Northport *(G-12193)*
Thompson Custom Woodworking .... G 616 446-1058
 Grand Rapids *(G-7260)*
Three Roses Woodwork .... G 248 763-1837
 Romeo *(G-14237)*
Timber Coast Woodworks .... G 231 287-3042
 Spring Lake *(G-15857)*
Timberstone Cstm Woodworks LLC ...... G 810 227-6404
 Brighton *(G-2082)*
Timberview Woodworking .... G 517 726-0321
 Vermontville *(G-17592)*
Tiq Woodworking LLC .... G 616 206-9369
 Clarksville *(G-3080)*
Trend Millwork LLC .... E 313 383-6300
 Lincoln Park *(G-10057)*
Troy Millwork Inc .... G 248 852-8383
 Rochester Hills *(G-14133)*
Turner Custom Woodworking .... G 810 324-6254
 Kenockee *(G-9424)*
Uncle Rons Woodworking .... G 248 585-7837
 Madison Heights *(G-10851)*
United Mill & Cabinet Company .... F 734 482-1981
 Willis *(G-18588)*
Van Enk Woodcrafters LLC .... F 616 931-0090
 Zeeland *(G-19086)*
Venture Woodworks .... G 616 262-1930
 Grand Rapids *(G-7311)*
Virtuoso Custom Creations LLC .... G 313 332-1299
 Detroit *(G-4668)*
Walton Woodworking .... G 248 730-2017
 Southfield *(G-15742)*
Webber Woodworks LLC .... G 517 896-8636
 Bath *(G-1174)*
Webers Woodwork LLC .... G 989 798-7210
 Millington *(G-11504)*
Weyerhaeuser Company .... G 906 524-2040
 Lanse *(G-9669)*
Wheatons Woodworking LLC .... G 616 288-8159
 Cedar Springs *(G-2667)*
White Dove Woodworks .... G 734 717-6042
 Manchester *(G-10892)*
Wholesalemillworkcom .... G 616 241-6011
 Grand Rapids *(G-7338)*
William S Wixtron .... G 906 376-8247
 Republic *(G-13821)*
Winterset Woodworks LLC .... G 248 207-8795
 Roseville *(G-14494)*
Wismer Wood Works .... G 616 262-9444
 Lake Odessa *(G-9580)*

Wisner Woodworking .... G 231 924-5711
 Newaygo *(G-12091)*
Wood Smiths Inc .... F 269 372-6432
 Kalamazoo *(G-9373)*
Woodcreek Customs .... G 248 761-5652
 Bloomfield Hills *(G-1875)*
Woodland Pixie .... G 503 330-8033
 Bessemer *(G-1651)*
Woodworking Connection Inc .... G 616 389-5481
 Wayland *(G-18210)*
Woodworks & Design Company .... G 517 482-6665
 Lansing *(G-9905)*
Wrights Woodworks .... G 989 295-7456
 Saginaw *(G-14796)*

MINE DEVELOPMENT SVCS: Nonmetallic Minerals

Bourque H James & Assoc Inc .... G 906 635-9191
 Brimley *(G-2101)*

MINERAL MINING: Nonmetallic

Discovery Gold Corp .... G 269 429-7002
 Stevensville *(G-16247)*

MINERAL PRODUCTS

Huron Glass Block .... G 586 598-6900
 Macomb *(G-10603)*

MINERAL WOOL

Autoneum North America Inc .... G 248 848-0100
 Farmington Hills *(G-5176)*
Eftec North America LLC .... D 248 585-2200
 Taylor *(G-16410)*
HP Pelzer Auto Systems Inc .... B 810 987-4444
 Port Huron *(G-13483)*
Manta Group LLC .... F 248 325-8264
 Pontiac *(G-13395)*
Mbcd Inc .... E 517 484-4426
 Lansing *(G-9867)*
Ufp Technologies Inc .... D 616 949-8100
 Grand Rapids *(G-7294)*
Unique Fabricating Inc .... A 248 853-2333
 Auburn Hills *(G-1068)*
Unique Fabricating Na Inc .... B 248 853-2333
 Auburn Hills *(G-1069)*

MINERALS: Ground Or Otherwise Treated

Novaceuticals LLC .... G 248 309-3402
 Auburn Hills *(G-988)*
R J Marshall Company .... F 248 353-4100
 Southfield *(G-15687)*

MINERALS: Ground or Treated

Edw C Levy Co .... G 313 843-7200
 Detroit *(G-4202)*
Fritz Enterprises .... E 734 283-7272
 Trenton *(G-16888)*
Michigan Metals and Mfg Inc .... G 248 910-7674
 Southfield *(G-15657)*
Mw Minerals .... G 517 294-6709
 Milford *(G-11474)*
Techni Sand Inc .... G 269 465-5833
 Benton Harbor *(G-1590)*

MINING EXPLORATION & DEVELOPMENT SVCS

Angels of Detroit LLC .... G 248 796-1079
 Redford *(G-13714)*
Blade Excavating Inc .... G 810 287-6457
 Flint *(G-5656)*
Minerals Processing Corp .... G 906 352-4024
 Menominee *(G-11252)*

MINING MACHINERY & EQPT WHOLESALERS

Superior Equipment & Supply Co .... G 906 774-1789
 Iron Mountain *(G-8734)*

MINING MACHINES & EQPT: Pellet Mills

Michigan Wood Pellet LLC .... F 989 348-4100
 Grayling *(G-7466)*

MINING MACHINES & EQPT: Stamping Mill Machinery

Ring Screw LLC .... D 586 997-5600
 Sterling Heights *(G-16152)*

MIRRORS: Motor Vehicle

Gentex Corporation .... C 616 772-1800
 Zeeland *(G-19024)*
Gentex Corporation .... G 616 772-1800
 Zeeland *(G-19025)*
Gentex Corporation .... G 616 772-1800
 Zeeland *(G-19026)*
Gentex Corporation .... G 616 772-1800
 Zeeland *(G-19027)*
Gentex Corporation .... G 616 772-1800
 Zeeland *(G-19029)*
Magna Mirrors America Inc .... G 616 786-7300
 Holland *(G-8134)*
Magna Mirrors America Inc .... G 616 942-0163
 Newaygo *(G-12085)*
Magna Mirrors America Inc .... A 616 786-7772
 Holland *(G-8137)*
Magna Mirrors America Inc .... B 231 652-4450
 Newaygo *(G-12086)*
Magna Mirrors America Inc .... G 616 786-7000
 Holland *(G-8136)*
Magna Mirrors North Amer LLC .... A 616 868-6122
 Alto *(G-336)*
SMR Automotive Systems USA Inc .... A 810 364-4141
 Marysville *(G-11102)*

MISCELLANEOUS FINANCIAL INVEST ACT: Oil/Gas Lease Brokers

Aquila Resources Inc .... G 906 352-4024
 Menominee *(G-11227)*

MIXING EQPT

Brawn Mixer Inc .... E 616 399-5600
 Holland *(G-7982)*

MIXTURES & BLOCKS: Asphalt Paving

A & M Distributors .... G 586 755-9045
 Warren *(G-17680)*
A Plus Asphalt LLC .... E 888 754-1125
 Bloomfield Hills *(G-1788)*
Alco Products LLC .... E 313 823-7500
 Detroit *(G-3996)*
Asphalt Services .... G 313 971-5005
 Clarkston *(G-3018)*
Barrett Paving Materials Inc .... G 734 941-0200
 Romulus *(G-14255)*
Bdk Group Northern Mich Inc .... F 574 875-5183
 Charlevoix *(G-2711)*
Carlo John Inc .... E 586 254-3800
 Shelby Township *(G-15181)*
Celia Deboer .... G 269 279-9102
 Three Rivers *(G-16569)*
Central Asphalt Inc .... F 989 772-0720
 Mount Pleasant *(G-11690)*
Colorado Pavers & Walls Inc .... F 517 881-1704
 Flint *(G-5669)*
D O W Asphalt Paving LLC .... G 810 743-2633
 Swartz Creek *(G-16352)*
Dans Concrete LLC .... G 517 242-0754
 Grand Ledge *(G-6388)*
Delta Paving Inc .... F 810 232-0220
 Flint *(G-5685)*
Edw C Levy Co .... G 248 349-8600
 Novi *(G-12411)*
Elmers Crane and Dozer Inc .... C 231 943-3443
 Traverse City *(G-16676)*
Eric Rogers LLC .... G 517 543-7126
 Charlotte *(G-2752)*
Fendt Builders Supply Inc .... E 248 474-3211
 Farmington Hills *(G-5242)*
Gem Asset Acquisition LLC .... F 248 338-0335
 Auburn Hills *(G-906)*
Hd Selcating Pav Solutions LLC .... G 248 241-6526
 Clarkston *(G-3038)*
J L Milling Inc .... F 269 679-5769
 Schoolcraft *(G-15119)*
Lafarge North America Inc .... G 231 726-3291
 Muskegon *(G-11855)*
Lafarge North America Inc .... G 703 480-3600
 Dundee *(G-4827)*
Laser Mfg Inc .... G 313 292-2299
 Plymouth *(G-13218)*

PRODUCT SECTION

Lite Load Services LLC ....F 269 751-6037
  Hamilton *(G-7603)*
Mdc Contracting LLC ....G 231 547-6595
  Charlevoix *(G-2720)*
Michigan Paving and Mtls Co ....E 734 485-1717
  Van Buren Twp *(G-17539)*
Michigan Paving and Mtls Co ....F 989 463-1323
  Alma *(G-247)*
Michigan Paving and Mtls Co ....E 517 787-4200
  Jackson *(G-8956)*
Nagle Paving Company ....C 734 591-1484
  Livonia *(G-10330)*
North American Asphalt ....G 586 754-0014
  Warren *(G-17946)*
Payne & Dolan Inc ....G 989 731-0700
  Gaylord *(G-6153)*
Peake Asphalt Inc ....F 586 254-4567
  Shelby Township *(G-15297)*
Pyramid Paving and Contg Co ....D 989 895-5861
  Bay City *(G-1390)*
Rieth-Riley Cnstr Co Inc ....F 231 263-2100
  Grawn *(G-7453)*
Rieth-Riley Cnstr Co Inc ....F 616 248-0920
  Wyoming *(G-18904)*
RWS & Associates LLC ....E 517 278-3134
  Coldwater *(G-3451)*
Sealmaster/Michigan ....G 313 779-8415
  Plymouth *(G-13295)*
Shooks Asphalt Paving Co Inc ....G 989 236-7740
  Perrinton *(G-12976)*
Surface Coatings Co ....G 248 977-9478
  Metamora *(G-11288)*
Tri-City Aggregates Inc ....E 248 634-8276
  Holly *(G-8298)*

MOBILE HOME REPAIR SVCS

Cedar Mobile Home Service Inc ....G 616 696-1580
  Cedar Springs *(G-2643)*

MOBILE HOMES

Advantage Housing Inc ....G 269 792-6291
  Wayland *(G-18187)*
Cedar Mobile Home Service Inc ....G 616 696-1580
  Cedar Springs *(G-2643)*
Larkhite Development System ....G 616 457-6722
  Jenison *(G-9060)*
Montrose Trailers Inc ....G 810 639-7431
  Montrose *(G-11607)*
Sun Communities Inc ....A 248 208-2500
  Southfield *(G-15711)*
Woodland Park & Sales ....G 810 229-7397
  Brighton *(G-2098)*

MOBILE HOMES, EXC RECREATIONAL

Champion Home Builders Inc ....D 248 614-8200
  Troy *(G-17007)*
Skyline Champion Corporation ....A 248 614-8211
  Troy *(G-17356)*

MOBILE HOMES: Indl Or Commercial Use

Dream Clean Trucking Service ....G 313 285-4029
  New Boston *(G-12008)*

MOBILE HOMES: Personal Or Private Use

Hometown America LLC ....G 810 686-7020
  Mount Morris *(G-11672)*

MODELS

Sika Auto Eaton Rapids Inc ....F 248 588-2270
  Madison Heights *(G-10828)*
Zoyes East Inc ....G 248 584-3300
  Ferndale *(G-5599)*

MODELS: Airplane, Exc Toy

Airplane Factory ....G 989 561-5381
  Remus *(G-13812)*

MODELS: General, Exc Toy

Active Plastics Inc ....F 616 813-5109
  Caledonia *(G-2367)*
D & F Corporation ....D 586 254-5300
  Sterling Heights *(G-15977)*
Metro Engrg of Grnd Rapids ....F 616 458-2823
  Grand Rapids *(G-6981)*
Paragon Molds Corporation ....E 586 294-7630
  Fraser *(G-5974)*

Protojet LLC ....F 810 956-8000
  Fraser *(G-5981)*
USF Delta Tooling LLC ....C 248 391-6800
  Auburn Hills *(G-1075)*

MODULES: Solid State

Sonima Corp ....F 302 450-6452
  Lake Orion *(G-9631)*

MOLDED RUBBER PRDTS

Advanced Rubber & Plastic ....G 586 754-7398
  Warren *(G-17693)*
Advanced Rubber Tech Inc ....F 231 775-3112
  Cadillac *(G-2308)*
Aerofab Company Inc ....F 248 542-0051
  Ferndale *(G-5519)*
Anand Nvh North America Inc ....C 810 724-2400
  Imlay City *(G-8627)*
Aptargroup Inc ....G 989 631-8030
  Midland *(G-11322)*
Cooper-Stndard Indus Spclty Gr ....G 330 339-3373
  Northville *(G-12208)*
Cooper-Stndard Indus Spclty Gr ....D 248 596-5900
  Northville *(G-12209)*
Dawson Manufacturing Company ....C 269 925-0100
  Benton Harbor *(G-1544)*
Dti Molded Products Inc ....F 248 647-0400
  Bingham Farms *(G-1695)*
Exotic Rubber & Plastics Corp ....D 248 477-2122
  New Hudson *(G-12053)*
Great Lakes Rubber Co ....E 248 624-5710
  Wixom *(G-18669)*
H A King Co Inc ....G 248 280-0006
  Royal Oak *(G-14542)*
HI-Tech Flexible Products Inc ....E 517 783-5911
  Jackson *(G-8903)*
Hutchinson Corporation ....G 616 459-4541
  Grand Rapids *(G-6825)*
Hutchnson Antvbrtion Systems I ....B 616 459-4541
  Grand Rapids *(G-6826)*
Hutchnson Antvbrtion Systems I ....C 231 775-9737
  Cadillac *(G-2336)*
Interdyne Inc ....F 517 849-2281
  Jonesville *(G-9089)*
Jfp Acquisition LLC ....E 517 787-8877
  Jackson *(G-8920)*
Luebke & Vogt Corporation ....G 248 449-3232
  Novi *(G-12466)*
Missaukee Molded Rubber Inc ....F 231 839-5309
  Lake City *(G-9552)*
Peck Engineering Inc ....E 313 534-2950
  Redford *(G-13753)*
Pegasus Tool LLC ....G 313 255-5900
  Detroit *(G-4515)*
R H M Rubber & Manufacturing ....G 248 624-8277
  Novi *(G-12522)*
Rehau Incorporated ....G 269 651-7845
  Sturgis *(G-16321)*
Schroth Enterprises Inc ....E 586 759-4240
  Grosse Pointe Farms *(G-7540)*
Simolex Rubber Corporation ....F 734 453-4500
  Plymouth *(G-13299)*
Tillerman Jfp LLC ....G 616 443-8346
  Middleville *(G-11315)*
Uniflex Inc ....G 248 486-6000
  Brighton *(G-2088)*
Vte Inc ....E 231 539-8000
  Pellston *(G-12968)*
Zhongding Saling Parts USA Inc ....G 734 241-8870
  Plymouth *(G-13342)*

MOLDING COMPOUNDS

Acp Technologies LLC ....G 586 322-3511
  Saint Clair Shores *(G-14846)*
APS Compounding LLC ....F 734 710-6702
  Romulus *(G-14251)*
Bakelite N Sumitomo Amer Inc ....G 248 313-7000
  Novi *(G-12373)*
Camryn Industries LLC ....C 248 663-5850
  Southfield *(G-15515)*
CMC Plastyk LLC ....G 989 588-4468
  Farwell *(G-5422)*
Coplas Inc ....G 586 739-8940
  Sterling Heights *(G-15972)*
Csn Manufacturing Inc ....E 616 364-0027
  Grand Rapids *(G-6617)*
Delta Polymers Co ....E 586 795-2900
  Sterling Heights *(G-15980)*

MOLDS: Indl

Durez Corporation ....C 248 313-7000
  Novi *(G-12406)*
Grand Traverse Tool Inc ....G 231 929-4743
  Traverse City *(G-16702)*
Heritage Mfg Inc ....G 586 949-7446
  Chesterfield *(G-2890)*
Indelco Plastics Corporation ....G 616 452-7077
  Grand Rapids *(G-6841)*
Lej Investments LLC ....F 616 452-3707
  Grandville *(G-7398)*
Mac Material Acquisition Co ....G 248 685-8393
  Highland *(G-7895)*
Quantum Composites Inc ....F 989 922-3863
  Bay City *(G-1392)*
Xc LLC ....F 586 755-1660
  Warren *(G-18074)*

MOLDING SAND MINING

Atlantic Precision Pdts Inc ....F 586 532-9420
  Shelby Township *(G-15174)*

MOLDINGS & TRIM: Metal, Exc Automobile

Gissing North America LLC ....D 248 647-0400
  Bingham Farms *(G-1697)*

MOLDINGS & TRIM: Wood

Lapeer Plating & Plastics Inc ....C 810 667-4240
  Lapeer *(G-9939)*
Louisiana-Pacific Corporation ....G 906 293-3265
  Newberry *(G-12092)*
Thomas Cheal ....G 906 288-3487
  Toivola *(G-16593)*

MOLDINGS OR TRIM: Automobile, Stamped Metal

D & N Bending Corp ....E 586 752-5511
  Romeo *(G-14223)*
Dti Molded Products Inc ....F 248 647-0400
  Bingham Farms *(G-1695)*
Great Lakes Trim Inc ....D 231 267-3000
  Williamsburg *(G-18555)*
Qp Acquisition 2 Inc ....A 248 594-7432
  Southfield *(G-15685)*
Sakaiya Company America Ltd ....E 517 521-5633
  Webberville *(G-18248)*
Srg Global Automotive LLC ....B 586 757-7800
  Sterling Heights *(G-16186)*
Srg Global Automotive LLC ....D 586 757-7800
  Warren *(G-18024)*
Versatube Corporation ....F 248 524-0299
  Troy *(G-17438)*
Yarema Die & Engineering Co ....C 248 585-2830
  Troy *(G-17457)*

MOLDINGS: Picture Frame

Clarey Custom Frmng & Art LLC ....G 989 415-4152
  Bay City *(G-1339)*
Dko Intl ....F 248 926-9115
  Commerce Township *(G-3523)*
Holy Art Framing ....G 248 634-8190
  Holly *(G-8276)*
Millworks Engineering Inc ....F 517 741-5511
  Union City *(G-17496)*
Timeless Picture Framing ....G 231 233-2221
  Fountain *(G-5828)*
Williams Management Group LLC ....G 248 506-7967
  Detroit *(G-4684)*

MOLDS: Indl

A & O Mold and Eng Inc ....E 269 649-0600
  Vicksburg *(G-17598)*
Action Mold Removal ....G 517 960-1928
  Jackson *(G-8801)*
Advanced Integ Tooling Solns ....C 586 749-5525
  Chesterfield *(G-2836)*
Advanced Mold Solutions ....G 586 468-6883
  Clinton Township *(G-3157)*
Advantage Industries Inc ....E 616 669-2400
  Jenison *(G-9042)*
Alliance Industries Inc ....E 248 656-3473
  Macomb *(G-10574)*
American Assemblers Inc ....G 248 334-9777
  Pontiac *(G-13350)*
American Die and Mold Inc ....G 231 269-3788
  Buckley *(G-2204)*
Atlas Die LLC ....E 770 981-6585
  Rochester Hills *(G-13954)*

Employee Codes: A=Over 500 employees, B=251-500
C=101-250, D=51-100, E=20-50, F=10-19, G=3-9

2022 Harris Michigan
Industrial Directory

Axis Mold Works Inc .... F 616 866-2222
Rockford (G-14156)
Byrnes Tool Co Inc .... G 810 664-3686
Lapeer (G-9918)
Christensen Fiberglass LLC .... E 616 738-1219
Holland (G-7995)
Circle C Mold & Plas Group Inc .... F 269 496-5515
Mendon (G-11216)
Colonial Mold Inc .... E 586 469-4944
Clinton Township (G-3204)
Concept Molds Inc .... F 269 679-2100
Schoolcraft (G-15116)
Contour Mold Corporation .... F 810 245-4070
Lapeer (G-9922)
Convex Mold Inc .... G 586 978-0808
Sterling Heights (G-15971)
D M Tool & Fab Inc .... D 586 726-8390
Sterling Heights (G-15978)
Dehring Mold E-D-M .... G 269 683-5970
Niles (G-12124)
Delta Precision Inc .... G 248 585-2344
Fraser (G-5917)
Dme Company LLC .... B 248 398-6000
Madison Heights (G-10709)
Dryden Mold Services Inc .... F 810 614-8621
Dryden (G-4804)
Ds Mold LLC .... E 616 794-1639
Belding (G-1447)
Du Val Industries LLC .... E 586 737-2710
Sterling Heights (G-15991)
Eagle Masking Fabrication Inc .... G 586 992-3080
Sterling Heights (G-15998)
Eifel Mold & Engineering Inc .... E 586 296-9640
Fraser (G-5923)
Eimo Technologies Inc .... E 269 649-0545
Vicksburg (G-17603)
Everson Tool & Machine Ltd .... F 906 932-3440
Ironwood (G-8761)
Extreme Tool and Engrg Inc .... D 906 229-9100
Wakefield (G-17620)
Fra-Wod Company Inc .... G 586 254-4450
Sterling Heights (G-16021)
Hanson Inc .... F 616 451-3061
Grand Rapids (G-6802)
Inglass Usa Inc .... E 616 228-6900
Byron Center (G-2278)
International Mold .... G 586 727-7898
Columbus (G-3498)
International Mold Corporation .... D 586 783-6890
Clinton Township (G-3260)
Iq Manufacturing LLC .... G 586 634-7185
Auburn Hills (G-940)
Johnson Precision Mold & Engrg .... G 269 651-2553
Sturgis (G-16296)
Kidder Machine Company .... G 231 775-9271
Cadillac (G-2340)
Lakeshore Mold and Die LLC .... G 269 429-6764
Stevensville (G-16258)
Legacy Precision Molds Inc .... G 616 532-6536
Grandville (G-7397)
Liberty Manufacturing Company .... E 269 327-0997
Portage (G-13576)
Louca Mold Arspc Machining Inc .... E 248 391-1616
Auburn Hills (G-959)
M C Ward Inc .... F 810 982-9720
Port Huron (G-13497)
M&M Polishing Inc .... F 269 468-4407
Coloma (G-3478)
Mac-Mold Base Inc .... E 586 752-1956
Bruce Twp (G-2176)
Manufax Inc .... G 231 929-3226
Traverse City (G-16752)
Mark Four CAM Inc .... G 586 204-5906
Saint Clair Shores (G-14869)
Marten Models & Molds Inc .... F 586 293-2260
Fraser (G-5962)
MGR Molds Inc .... F 586 254-6020
Sterling Heights (G-16096)
Michigan Metal Tech Inc .... E 586 598-7800
Chesterfield (G-2913)
Michigan Mold Inc .... E 269 468-4407
Coloma (G-3479)
Micro Precision Molds Inc .... E 269 344-2044
Kalamazoo (G-9270)
Midwest Mold Services Inc .... E 586 888-8800
Roseville (G-14443)
Model Pattern Company Inc .... E 616 878-9710
Byron Center (G-2288)
Model-Matic Inc .... F 248 528-1680
Troy (G-17264)
Mold Matter .... G 231 933-6653
Traverse City (G-16762)
Mold Specialties Inc .... G 586 247-4660
Shelby Township (G-15283)
Omega Plastics Inc .... D 586 954-2100
Clinton Township (G-3314)
Pacific Tool & Engineering Ltd .... G 586 737-2710
Sterling Heights (G-16122)
Paragon Molds Corporation .... E 586 294-7630
Fraser (G-5974)
Paramount Tool and Die Inc .... F 616 677-0000
Marne (G-10997)
Pedri Mold Inc .... G 586 598-0882
Chesterfield (G-2923)
Pentagon Mold Co .... G 269 496-7072
Mendon (G-11220)
Plas-Tech Mold and Design Inc .... G 269 225-1223
Plainwell (G-13089)
Plastic Engrg Tchncal Svcs Inc .... E 248 373-0800
Auburn Hills (G-998)
Precision Masters Inc .... E 248 853-0308
Rochester Hills (G-14087)
Prime Mold LLC .... F 586 221-2512
Clinton Township (G-3326)
Project Die and Mold Inc .... G 616 862-8689
Grand Rapids (G-7119)
Qc Tech LLC .... D 248 597-3984
Madison Heights (G-10813)
R & B Plastics Machinery LLC .... E 734 429-9421
Saline (G-15034)
Ravenna Pattern & Mfg .... E 231 853-2264
Ravenna (G-13693)
Ready Molds Inc .... F 248 474-4007
Farmington Hills (G-5365)
Rm Machine & Mold .... G 734 721-8800
Romulus (G-14326)
Romeo Mold Technologies Inc .... F 586 336-1245
Bruce Twp (G-2177)
Romeo Technologies Inc .... D 586 336-5015
Bruce Twp (G-2178)
Ronningen Research and Dev Co .... C 269 649-0520
Vicksburg (G-17611)
Select Tool and Die Inc .... G 269 422-2812
Baroda (G-1170)
Sharp Die & Mold Co .... F 586 293-8660
Fraser (G-5993)
Simpsons Enterprises Inc .... F 269 279-7237
Three Rivers (G-16584)
Special Mold Engineering Inc .... E 248 652-6600
Rochester Hills (G-14116)
Spray Metal Mold Technology .... G 269 781-7151
Marshall (G-11074)
Steenson Enterprises .... G 248 628-0036
Leonard (G-10003)
Su-Dan Plastics Inc .... C 248 651-6035
Rochester (G-13932)
Su-Dan Plastics Inc .... F 248 651-6035
Rochester Hills (G-14121)
Summit Services Inc .... E 586 977-8300
Shelby Township (G-15346)
Talon LLC .... F 313 392-1000
Detroit (G-4625)
Target Mold Corporation .... F 231 798-3535
Norton Shores (G-12336)
Tony S Die Machine Company .... F 586 773-7379
Warren (G-18040)
Tooling Technology LLC .... D 937 381-9211
Macomb (G-10643)
Travis Creek Tooling .... G 269 685-2000
Plainwell (G-13101)
Tri-Star Tooling LLC .... E 586 978-0435
Sterling Heights (G-16210)
Twin Mold and Engineering LLC .... E 586 532-8558
Shelby Township (G-15359)
Unytrex Inc .... F 810 796-9074
Dryden (G-4808)
USF Delta Tooling LLC .... C 248 391-6800
Auburn Hills (G-1075)
Vanex Mold Inc .... G 616 662-4100
Jenison (G-9076)
Vision Global Industries .... D 248 390-5805
Macomb (G-10649)
Wolverine Products Inc .... F 586 792-3740
Clinton Township (G-3389)
Z Mold & Engineering Inc .... G 586 948-5000
Chesterfield (G-2966)

MOLDS: Plastic Working & Foundry

Advanced Special Tools Inc .... C 269 962-9697
Battle Creek (G-1179)
Affinity Custom Molding Inc .... E 269 496-8423
Mendon (G-11215)
Astar Inc .... E 574 234-2137
Niles (G-12111)
Beacon Tool Inc .... F 269 649-3558
Vicksburg (G-17599)
Custom Design Inc .... E 269 323-8561
Portage (G-13555)
D-M-E USA Inc .... D 616 754-4601
Greenville (G-7480)
Envisiontec US LLC .... D 313 436-4300
Dearborn (G-3837)
Formfab LLC .... E 248 844-3676
Rochester Hills (G-14013)
H & S Mold Inc .... F 989 732-3566
Gaylord (G-6133)
Hi-Craft Engineering Inc .... D 586 293-0551
Fraser (G-5936)
Hi-Tech Mold & Engineering Inc .... E 248 844-0722
Rochester Hills (G-14031)
Hi-Tech Mold & Engineering Inc .... E 248 852-6600
Rochester Hills (G-14032)
Jems of Litchfield Inc .... F 517 542-5367
Litchfield (G-10081)
Levannes Inc .... E 269 327-4484
Portage (G-13575)
Magna Exteriors America Inc .... A 248 631-1100
Troy (G-17220)
Master Precision Products Inc .... E 616 754-5483
Greenville (G-7499)
Mayer Tool & Engineering Inc .... E 269 651-1428
Sturgis (G-16305)
Mesick Mold Co .... E 231 885-1304
Mesick (G-11273)
Midwest Plastic Engineering .... D 269 651-5223
Sturgis (G-16309)
Plastic-Plate Inc .... E 616 698-2030
Grand Rapids (G-7092)
Precision Die and Machine Co .... F 810 329-2861
Saint Clair (G-14840)
Proficient Products Inc .... G 586 977-8630
Sterling Heights (G-16135)
Pti Engineered Plastics Inc .... B 586 263-5100
Macomb (G-10631)
Quasar Industries Inc .... D 248 844-7190
Rochester Hills (G-14096)
Quasar Industries Inc .... E 248 852-0300
Rochester Hills (G-14097)
S & K Tool & Die Company Inc .... E 269 345-2174
Portage (G-13603)
Superior Mold Services Inc .... F 586 264-9570
Sterling Heights (G-16197)
TNT-Edm Inc .... E 734 459-1700
Plymouth (G-13316)
Wright Plastic Products Co LLC .... G 810 326-3000
Saint Clair (G-14845)

MONASTERIES

Society of Saint John Inc .... G 906 289-4484
Eagle Harbor (G-4853)

MONUMENTS & GRAVE MARKERS, EXC TERRAZZO

Superior Monuments Co .... G 231 728-2211
Muskegon (G-11928)

MONUMENTS & GRAVE MARKERS, WHOLESALE

Fenton Corporation .... G 810 629-2858
Fenton (G-5476)
Fenton Memorials & Vaults Inc .... G 810 629-2858
Fenton (G-5477)
Patten Monument Company .... D 616 785-4141
Comstock Park (G-3634)
Steinbrecher Stone Corp .... G 906 563-5852
Norway (G-12357)

MONUMENTS: Cut Stone, Exc Finishing Or Lettering Only

Muskegon Monument & Stone Co .... G 231 722-2730
Muskegon (G-11882)
Steinbrecher Stone Corp .... G 906 563-5852
Norway (G-12357)

PRODUCT SECTION
MOTOR VEHICLE DEALERS: Automobiles, New & Used

MOPS: Floor & Dust
Tuway American Group Inc .... C 248 205-9999
  Troy *(G-17407)*

MOTEL: Franchised
Qp Acquisition 2 Inc .... A 248 594-7432
  Southfield *(G-15685)*

MOTION PICTURE & VIDEO PRODUCTION SVCS
Livbig LLC .... G 888 519-8290
  Portage *(G-13578)*

MOTOR & GENERATOR PARTS: Electric
Ballard Power Systems Corp .... A 313 583-5980
  Dearborn *(G-3812)*
Edwards Industrial Sales Inc .... G 517 887-6100
  Lansing *(G-9833)*

MOTOR HOME DEALERS
Cedar Mobile Home Service Inc .... G 616 696-1580
  Cedar Springs *(G-2643)*

MOTOR HOMES
Auto-Masters Inc .... F 616 455-4510
  Grand Rapids *(G-6480)*
Motor City Home Inc .... G 248 562-7296
  Bloomfield Hills *(G-1841)*

MOTOR REBUILDING SVCS, EXC AUTOMOTIVE
Alpena Electric Motor Service .... G 989 354-8780
  Alpena *(G-277)*

MOTOR REPAIR SVCS
Bob Maxey Ford Howell Inc .... G 517 545-5700
  Howell *(G-8431)*
Lincoln Service LLC .... G 734 793-0083
  Livonia *(G-10279)*
Lorna Icr LLC .... F 586 582-1500
  Warren *(G-17907)*
Motown Harley-Davidson Inc .... D 734 947-4647
  Taylor *(G-16451)*

MOTOR SCOOTERS & PARTS
Discover Your Mobility Inc .... G 866 868-9694
  Hazel Park *(G-7823)*
Mahindra Tractor Assembly Inc .... E 650 779-5180
  Auburn Hills *(G-966)*

MOTOR VEHICLE ASSEMBLY, COMPLETE: Ambulances
Horstman Inc .... E 586 737-2100
  Sterling Heights *(G-16041)*

MOTOR VEHICLE ASSEMBLY, COMPLETE: Autos, Incl Specialty
Aftershock Motorsports .... G 586 273-1333
  Casco *(G-2597)*
Ai-Genesee LLC .... F 810 720-4848
  Flint *(G-5641)*
Comstar Automotive USA LLC .... F 517 266-2445
  Tecumseh *(G-16493)*
Creative Automation Solutions .... G 313 790-4848
  Livonia *(G-10168)*
CT Custom Collision LLC .... G 313 912-9776
  Detroit *(G-4110)*
Dakkota Integrated Systems LLC .... B 517 694-6500
  Brighton *(G-1972)*
Dakkota Integrated Systems LLC .... G 517 321-3064
  Lansing *(G-9683)*
Dakkota Integrated Systems LLC .... G 517 694-6500
  Hazel Park *(G-7822)*
Dakkota Integrated Systems LLC .... G 517 694-6500
  Holt *(G-8307)*
Dus Operating Inc .... B 248 299-7500
  Auburn Hills *(G-869)*
FCA North America Holdings LLC .... A 248 512-2950
  Auburn Hills *(G-893)*
FCA US LLC .... A 248 576-5741
  Auburn Hills *(G-895)*

Finish Line Fabricating LLC .... G 269 686-8400
  Allegan *(G-158)*
Ford Motor Company .... A 313 322-3000
  Dearborn *(G-3842)*
Ford Motor Company .... G 734 782-7800
  Flat Rock *(G-5620)*
Ford Motor Company .... G 734 241-2498
  Monroe *(G-11541)*
General Motors LLC .... A 313 972-6000
  Detroit *(G-4257)*
General Motors LLC .... C 248 874-1737
  Pontiac *(G-13374)*
Gleason Race Cars .... G 231 882-2336
  Benzonia *(G-1615)*
Global Impact Group LLC .... G 248 895-9900
  Grand Blanc *(G-6243)*
GM Laam Holdings LLC .... D 313 556-5000
  Pontiac *(G-4267)*
Illinois Tool Works Inc .... G 248 589-2500
  Troy *(G-17161)*
Jasco International LLC .... G 313 841-5000
  Detroit *(G-4335)*
Jvis - Usa LLC .... F 586 884-5700
  Shelby Township *(G-15248)*
Lightguide Inc .... G 248 374-8000
  Wixom *(G-18698)*
Mahindra N Amrcn Tchncal Ctr I .... C 248 268-6600
  Auburn Hills *(G-965)*
Manufacturing Products & Svcs .... F 734 927-1964
  Plymouth *(G-13233)*
Mico Industries Inc .... D 616 245-6426
  Grand Rapids *(G-6999)*
Midstates Industrial Group Inc .... E 586 307-3414
  Clinton Township *(G-3300)*
Morris Associates Inc .... E 248 355-9055
  Southfield *(G-15662)*
Moser Racing Inc .... F 248 348-6502
  Northville *(G-12243)*
Nyx LLC .... D 734 462-2385
  Livonia *(G-10348)*
Omaha Automation Inc .... G 313 557-3565
  Detroit *(G-4497)*
Onyx Manufacturing Inc .... G 248 687-8611
  Rochester Hills *(G-14075)*
Rattle Top Precision Assembly .... G 231 937-5333
  Howard City *(G-8416)*
Redline Fabrications .... G 810 984-5621
  Clyde *(G-3415)*
Rivian Automotive Inc .... A 734 855-4350
  Plymouth *(G-13283)*
Rivian Automotive Inc .... G 408 483-1987
  Plymouth *(G-13284)*
Sas Automotive Usa Inc .... E 248 606-1152
  Sterling Heights *(G-16164)*
Skinny Kid Race Cars .... G 248 668-1040
  Commerce Township *(G-3573)*
Smart Automation Systems Inc .... G 248 651-5911
  Rochester Hills *(G-14114)*
Tunkers Inc .... E 734 744-5990
  Sterling Heights *(G-16212)*
Turn Key Automotive LLC .... F 248 628-5556
  Oxford *(G-12926)*
Veigel North America LLC .... F 586 843-3816
  Shelby Township *(G-15364)*
Wgs Global Services LC .... B 810 239-4947
  Flint *(G-5792)*
Wgs Global Services LC .... D 810 694-3843
  Grand Blanc *(G-6268)*

MOTOR VEHICLE ASSEMBLY, COMPLETE: Buses, All Types
General Coach America Inc .... D 810 724-6474
  Imlay City *(G-8633)*

MOTOR VEHICLE ASSEMBLY, COMPLETE: Cars, Armored
Armored Group LLC .... E 602 840-2271
  Dearborn Heights *(G-3920)*
CATI Armor LLC .... G 269 788-4322
  Charlotte *(G-2740)*

MOTOR VEHICLE ASSEMBLY, COMPLETE: Fire Department Vehicles
Quality First Fire Alarm .... G 810 736-4911
  Flint *(G-5752)*
Shyft Group Usa Inc .... D 517 543-6400
  Charlotte *(G-2769)*

Spencer Manufacturing Inc .... F 269 637-9459
  South Haven *(G-15416)*

MOTOR VEHICLE ASSEMBLY, COMPLETE: Hearses
Bennett Funeral Coaches Inc .... G 616 538-8100
  Byron Center *(G-2259)*

MOTOR VEHICLE ASSEMBLY, COMPLETE: Military Motor Vehicle
American Fabricated Pdts Inc .... E 616 607-8785
  Spring Lake *(G-15803)*
Meritor Heavy Vhcl Systems LLC .... A 248 435-1000
  Troy *(G-17247)*
Onodi Tool & Engineering Co .... E 313 386-6682
  Melvindale *(G-11208)*
Oshkosh Defense LLC .... E 586 576-8301
  Warren *(G-17951)*
P2r Metal Fabrication Inc .... F 586 606-5266
  Macomb *(G-10625)*

MOTOR VEHICLE ASSEMBLY, COMPLETE: Motor Homes, Self Contain
R V Wolverine .... F 989 426-9241
  Gladwin *(G-6201)*

MOTOR VEHICLE ASSEMBLY, COMPLETE: Snow Plows
Rough Road Trucking LLC .... G 231 645-3355
  Kalkaska *(G-9402)*
Trynex International LLC .... F 248 586-3500
  Madison Heights *(G-10848)*

MOTOR VEHICLE ASSEMBLY, COMPLETE: Truck & Tractor Trucks
Advance Vehicle Assembly Inc .... F 989 823-3800
  Vassar *(G-17576)*
Meyers John .... G 989 236-5400
  Middleton *(G-11298)*
Valley Truck Parts Inc .... D 616 241-5431
  Grand Rapids *(G-7303)*

MOTOR VEHICLE ASSEMBLY, COMPLETE: Truck Tractors, Highway
Trailer Tech Repair Inc .... G 734 354-6680
  Plymouth *(G-13321)*

MOTOR VEHICLE ASSEMBLY, COMPLETE: Trucks, Pickup
Omnico Agv LLC .... F 586 268-7700
  Clinton Township *(G-3315)*

MOTOR VEHICLE ASSEMBLY, COMPLETE: Universal Carriers, Mil
Armartis Manufacturing Inc .... E 248 308-9622
  Roseville *(G-14376)*
SGC Industries Inc .... G 586 293-5260
  Fraser *(G-5992)*

MOTOR VEHICLE ASSEMBLY, COMPLETE: Wreckers, Tow Truck
Horizon Global Corporation .... A 734 656-3000
  Plymouth *(G-13192)*
Junk Man LLC .... G 248 459-7359
  Pontiac *(G-13389)*

MOTOR VEHICLE DEALERS: Automobiles, New & Used
FCA US LLC .... F 586 978-0067
  Sterling Heights *(G-16011)*
FCA US LLC .... A 248 576-5741
  Auburn Hills *(G-895)*
Ford Motor Company .... A 734 484-8626
  Ypsilanti *(G-18947)*
Ford Motor Company .... F 734 523-3000
  Livonia *(G-10214)*
Ford Motor Company .... F 313 594-4090
  Allen Park *(G-194)*
Ford Motor Company .... F 910 381-7998
  Taylor *(G-16419)*

Employee Codes: A=Over 500 employees, B=251-500
C=101-250, D=51-100, E=20-50, F=10-19, G=3-9

2022 Harris Michigan Industrial Directory

MOTOR VEHICLE DEALERS: Automobiles, New & Used

Ford Motor Company .... F 734 523-3000
  Livonia *(G-10215)*
Ford Motor Company .... F 734 942-6248
  Brownstown *(G-2146)*
General Motors Company .... F 248 249-6347
  Brownstown *(G-2147)*
General Motors Company .... B 586 218-9240
  Warren *(G-17824)*
General Motors Holdings LLC .... C 313 667-1500
  Detroit *(G-4256)*
General Motors LLC .... F 810 234-2710
  Flint *(G-5704)*
General Motors LLC .... F 989 894-7210
  Bay City *(G-1359)*
General Motors LLC .... F 810 234-2710
  Flint *(G-5705)*
General Motors LLC .... F 586 342-2728
  Sterling Heights *(G-16027)*
General Motors LLC .... F 517 885-6669
  Lansing *(G-9761)*
General Motors LLC .... A 313 665-4919
  Detroit *(G-4258)*
General Motors LLC .... A 248 857-3500
  Pontiac *(G-13375)*
GM Components Holdings LLC ..... C 870 594-0351
  Detroit *(G-4265)*
RSM & Associates Co .... E 517 750-9330
  Jackson *(G-9001)*

MOTOR VEHICLE DEALERS: Cars, Used Only

Kern Auto Sales and Svc LLC .... F 734 475-2722
  Chelsea *(G-2818)*

MOTOR VEHICLE DEALERS: Pickups, New & Used

Detroit Wrecker Sales Llc .... G 313 835-8700
  Detroit *(G-4171)*

MOTOR VEHICLE DEALERS: Trucks, Tractors/Trailers, New & Used

Benlee Inc .... E 586 791-1830
  Romulus *(G-14257)*
Gld Holdings Inc .... E 616 877-4288
  Moline *(G-11518)*
Midwest Tractor & Equipment Co .. F 231 269-4100
  Buckley *(G-2207)*
Tow-Line Trailers .... G 989 752-0055
  Saginaw *(G-14777)*
UP Truck Center Inc .... E 906 774-0098
  Quinnesec *(G-13677)*
Wells Equipment Sales Inc .... F 517 542-2376
  Litchfield *(G-10087)*

MOTOR VEHICLE PARTS & ACCESS: Acceleration Eqpt

Adac Plastics Inc .... D 616 642-0109
  Saranac *(G-15075)*
Marelli North America Inc .... A 931 684-4490
  Southfield *(G-15644)*

MOTOR VEHICLE PARTS & ACCESS: Air Conditioner Parts

Denso Air Systems Michigan Inc .. B 269 962-9676
  Battle Creek *(G-1215)*
Denso Manufacturing Mich Inc .... A 269 965-3322
  Battle Creek *(G-1216)*
Fluid Hutchinson Management .... D 248 679-1327
  Auburn Hills *(G-903)*
Formfab LLC .... E 248 844-3676
  Rochester Hills *(G-14013)*
Hanon Systems Usa LLC .... B 248 907-8000
  Novi *(G-12425)*
Mahle Behr Mfg MGT Inc .... E 248 735-3623
  Troy *(G-17231)*
Skg International Inc .... F 248 620-4139
  Clarkston *(G-3067)*
Stewart Industries LLC .... D 269 660-9290
  Battle Creek *(G-1301)*

MOTOR VEHICLE PARTS & ACCESS: Axel Housings & Shafts

Angstrom Automotive Group LLC .. E 734 756-1164
  Southfield *(G-15487)*

Horstman Inc .... E 586 737-2100
  Sterling Heights *(G-16041)*

MOTOR VEHICLE PARTS & ACCESS: Ball Joints

Federal-Mogul Products US LLC .... A 248 354-7700
  Southfield *(G-15566)*

MOTOR VEHICLE PARTS & ACCESS: Bearings

Federal-Mogul Powertrain LLC ..... B 616 754-5681
  Greenville *(G-7485)*
Mahle Industries Incorporated ..... C 248 305-8200
  Muskegon *(G-11864)*

MOTOR VEHICLE PARTS & ACCESS: Body Components & Frames

Complete Prototype Svcs Inc .... C 586 690-8897
  Clinton Township *(G-3207)*
CTA Acoustics Inc .... E 248 544-2580
  Madison Heights *(G-10699)*
CTC Distribution Inc .... G 313 486-2225
  Saint Clair Shores *(G-14854)*
Design Converting Inc .... F 616 942-7780
  Grand Rapids *(G-6642)*
Drake Enterprises Inc .... E 586 783-3009
  Clinton Township *(G-3226)*
Grupo Antolin Michigan Inc .... C 989 635-5055
  Marlette *(G-10982)*
Grupo Antolin Primera Auto Sys .. D 734 495-9180
  Canton *(G-2469)*
J & K Spratt Enterprises Inc .... D 517 439-5010
  Hillsdale *(G-7938)*
Johnson Controls Inc .... G 586 826-8845
  Sterling Heights *(G-16057)*
Kiekert Usa Inc .... C 248 960-4100
  Wixom *(G-18693)*
M S Manufacturing Incorporated .. F 586 463-2788
  Clinton Township *(G-3285)*
Magna Exteriors America Inc .... A 248 631-1100
  Troy *(G-17220)*
Magna Modular Systems LLC .... C 586 279-2000
  Warren *(G-17914)*
Mssc Inc .... C 248 502-8000
  Troy *(G-17270)*
Owens Products Inc .... E 269 651-2300
  Sturgis *(G-16315)*
Rack & Pinion Inc .... G 517 563-8872
  Horton *(G-8378)*
Shelby Antolin Inc .... F 734 395-0328
  Shelby Township *(G-15330)*
Sliding Systems Inc .... F 517 339-1455
  Haslett *(G-7778)*
Viking Laser LLC .... G 586 200-5369
  Roseville *(G-14491)*

MOTOR VEHICLE PARTS & ACCESS: Brakes, Air

Akebono Brake Corporation .... C 248 489-7400
  Farmington Hills *(G-5165)*
Haldex Brake Products Corp .... C 616 827-9641
  Wyoming *(G-18880)*
Lane Automotive Inc .... C 269 463-4113
  Watervliet *(G-18182)*
Seg Automotive North Amer LLC .. E 248 465-2602
  Novi *(G-12533)*

MOTOR VEHICLE PARTS & ACCESS: Cleaners, air

Apply Prssure MBL Dtailing LLC ... G 248 794-7710
  Redford *(G-13715)*

MOTOR VEHICLE PARTS & ACCESS: Clutches

Ogura Corporation .... C 586 749-1900
  Chesterfield *(G-2919)*
Precision Torque Control Inc .... F 989 495-9330
  Midland *(G-11403)*
Valeo Friction Materials Inc .... G 248 619-8300
  Troy *(G-17426)*

MOTOR VEHICLE PARTS & ACCESS: Connecting Rods

Baldwin Precision Inc .... E 231 237-4515
  Charlevoix *(G-2710)*
ZF Active Safety US Inc .... G 734 855-2470
  Livonia *(G-10483)*
ZF Automotive JV US LLC .... A 734 855-2787
  Livonia *(G-10485)*
ZF Automotive US Inc .... B 734 855-2600
  Livonia *(G-10486)*
ZF Friedrichshafen AG .... G 734 855-2600
  Livonia *(G-10487)*

MOTOR VEHICLE PARTS & ACCESS: Cylinder Heads

Bleistahl N Amer Ltd Partnr .... E 269 719-8585
  Battle Creek *(G-1196)*

MOTOR VEHICLE PARTS & ACCESS: Defrosters

Therma-Tech Engineering Inc ...... E 313 537-5330
  Redford *(G-13778)*

MOTOR VEHICLE PARTS & ACCESS: Directional Signals

Havis Inc .... F 734 414-0699
  Plymouth *(G-13184)*

MOTOR VEHICLE PARTS & ACCESS: Electrical Eqpt

Bgm Electronic Services LLC .... G 586 997-7090
  Auburn Hills *(G-812)*
Dura Operating LLC .... C 248 299-7500
  Auburn Hills *(G-868)*
Eberspecher Contrls N Amer Inc .. E 248 994-7010
  Brighton *(G-1981)*
Gentherm Incorporated .... A 248 504-0500
  Northville *(G-12224)*
Grakon LLC .... G 734 462-1201
  Livonia *(G-10227)*
Henniges Auto Holdings Inc .... B 248 340-4100
  Auburn Hills *(G-924)*
Hi-Lex Controls Incorporated .... F 517 542-2955
  Litchfield *(G-10080)*
Lear Automotive Mfg LLC .... F 248 447-1603
  Detroit *(G-4380)*
Lear Automotive Mfg LLC .... F 248 447-1603
  Detroit *(G-4381)*
Lear Corporation .... G 313 965-0507
  Detroit *(G-4383)*
Lear Corporation .... B 989 588-6181
  Farwell *(G-5425)*
Lear Corporation .... C 989 275-5794
  Roscommon *(G-14351)*
Lear Corporation .... B 248 447-1500
  Southfield *(G-15628)*
Lear Corporation .... A 313 731-0833
  Flint *(G-5723)*
Lear European Operations Corp .. G 248 447-1500
  Southfield *(G-15629)*
Lear Global Technology Corp Uk .. F 248 447-1500
  Southfield *(G-15630)*
SRI Delaware Holdings LLC .... G 248 489-9300
  Novi *(G-12541)*
Stoneridge Inc .... A 248 489-9300
  Novi *(G-12543)*
Stoneridge Inc .... B 781 830-0340
  Novi *(G-12544)*
Tram Inc .... C 734 254-8500
  Plymouth *(G-13322)*
Tram Inc .... G 269 966-0100
  Battle Creek *(G-1306)*
Trmi Inc .... A 269 966-0800
  Battle Creek *(G-1307)*
Umlaut Product Solutions Inc ...... F 248 703-7724
  Madison Heights *(G-10850)*
Valeo North America Inc .... D 248 619-8300
  Troy *(G-17429)*
Valeo Radar Systems Inc .... F 248 619-8300
  Troy *(G-17430)*
Ventura Manufacturing Inc .... C 616 772-7405
  Zeeland *(G-19088)*

PRODUCT SECTION — MOTOR VEHICLE PARTS & ACCESS: Power Steering Eqpt

MOTOR VEHICLE PARTS & ACCESS: Engines & Parts

Company	Code	Phone
Ace Controls Inc — Farmington Hills (G-5158)	C	248 476-0213
American Axle & Mfg Inc — Fraser (G-5891)	G	586 415-2000
American Axle & Mfg Inc — Warren (G-17700)	G	586 573-4840
Antolin Sprtnburg Assembly LLC — Auburn Hills (G-790)	E	248 373-1749
Autocam Corporation — Marshall (G-11052)	G	269 789-4000
Autocam Corporation — Dowagiac (G-4775)	G	269 782-5186
Black River Manufacturing Inc — Port Huron (G-13459)	E	810 982-9812
Black River Manufacturing Inc — Port Huron (G-13460)	D	810 982-9812
Cequent Uk Ltd — Plymouth (G-13144)	G	734 656-3000
Cfe Racing Products Inc — Eastpointe (G-4931)	G	586 773-6310
D M P E — Stevensville (G-16244)	G	269 428-5070
Denso International Amer Inc — Southfield (G-15538)	A	248 350-7500
Detroit Diesel Corporation — Detroit (G-4144)	A	313 592-5000
Detroit Diesel Corporation — Redford (G-13730)	F	313 592-8256
Dolphin Manufacturing Inc — Taylor (G-16403)	E	734 946-6322
Eaton Aerospace LLC — Grand Rapids (G-6663)	B	616 949-1090
FCA Intrntional Operations LLC — Auburn Hills (G-892)	E	800 334-9200
GKN Sinter Metals LLC — Auburn Hills (G-914)	G	248 883-4500
Grupo Antolin North Amer Inc — Auburn Hills (G-918)	C	248 373-1749
Gt Technologies Inc — Westland (G-18378)	E	734 467-8371
Hacker Machine Inc — Rives Junction (G-13886)	E	517 569-3348
Hemco Machine Co Inc — Warren (G-17851)	G	586 264-8911
Ilmor Engineering Inc — Plymouth (G-13196)	D	734 456-3600
Liberty Spring Lapeer Inc — Lapeer (G-9942)	F	418 248-7781
Magna Powertrain Usa Inc — Troy (G-17224)	D	248 680-4900
Magna Powertrain Usa Inc — Troy (G-17225)	E	248 524-1397
Mahle Industries Incorporated — Farmington Hills (G-5303)	E	248 305-8200
Mall Tooling & Engineering — Mount Clemens (G-11648)	G	586 463-6520
Marimba Auto LLC — Canton (G-2489)	D	734 398-9000
Millennium Steering LLC — Cass City (G-2620)	D	989 872-8823
Mitsubishi Steel Mfg Co Ltd — Troy (G-17262)	G	248 502-8000
Motor Parts Inc of Michigan — Rochester Hills (G-14065)	E	248 852-1522
Mpt Lansing LLC — Lansing (G-9872)	C	517 316-1013
Oakwood Metal Fabricating Co — Dearborn (G-3879)	E	313 561-7740
Performance Springs Inc — New Hudson (G-12067)	F	248 486-3372
Pierburg Us LLC — Auburn Hills (G-997)	C	864 688-1322
Prestige Engrg Rsrces Tech Inc — Madison Heights (G-10808)	G	586 573-3070
Quigley Co — Vanderbilt (G-17575)	G	989 983-3911
Robert Bosch LLC — Plymouth (G-13287)	G	734 979-3000
Roush Enterprises Inc — Farmington (G-5145)	C	734 805-4400
Roush Industries Inc — Livonia (G-10393)	G	734 779-7013
Specialty Eng Components LLC — Taylor (G-16477)	D	734 955-6500
Sterling Performance Inc — Milford (G-11491)	E	248 685-7811
Swoboda Inc — Grand Rapids (G-7242)	C	616 554-6161
TAC Manufacturing Inc — Jackson (G-9014)	B	517 789-7000
Tenneco Automotive Oper Co Inc — Monroe (G-11579)	G	734 243-8039
Tenneco Clean Air US Inc — Lansing (G-9743)	F	517 253-8902
Thomas Engineering — Clarkston (G-3071)	G	248 620-7916
Uc Holdings Inc — Southfield (G-15730)	D	248 728-8642
Visteon Corporation — Van Buren Twp (G-17558)	A	734 627-7384
Visteon Systems LLC — Van Buren Twp (G-17562)	C	800 847-8366
Weber Automotive Corporation — Auburn Hills (G-1089)	C	248 393-5520
ZF Active Safety US Inc — Livonia (G-10482)	F	734 812-6979
ZF Active Safety US Inc — Sterling Heights (G-16234)	C	586 899-2807
Zhongli North America Inc — Troy (G-17459)	D	248 733-9300

MOTOR VEHICLE PARTS & ACCESS: Engs & Trans, Factory, Rebuilt

Company	Code	Phone
Navarre Inc — Detroit (G-4478)	G	313 892-7300

MOTOR VEHICLE PARTS & ACCESS: Frames

Company	Code	Phone
Pritech Corporation — Canton (G-2513)	G	248 488-9120

MOTOR VEHICLE PARTS & ACCESS: Fuel Pumps

Company	Code	Phone
Carter Fuel Systems LLC — Rochester Hills (G-13973)	E	248 371-8392
Melling Tool Co — Jackson (G-8952)	G	517 787-8172
Slw Automotive Inc — Rochester Hills (G-14113)	D	248 464-6200
TI Group Auto Systems LLC — Troy (G-17391)	G	248 494-5000

MOTOR VEHICLE PARTS & ACCESS: Fuel Systems & Parts

Company	Code	Phone
Alfmeier Friedrichs & Rath LLC — Troy (G-16921)	G	248 526-1650
Alternative Fuel Tech LLC — Grosse Pointe Park (G-7545)	G	313 417-9212
Continental Auto Systems Inc — Auburn Hills (G-849)	G	248 874-1801
Cummins Inc — Iron Mountain (G-8720)	G	906 774-2424
Davco Technology LLC — Saline (G-15012)	D	734 429-5665
Plastic Omnium Auto Inrgy USA — New Boston (G-12018)	B	734 753-1350
Plastic Omnium Auto Inrgy USA — Troy (G-17306)	B	248 743-5700
Robert Bosch Fuel Systems LLC — Kentwood (G-9477)	E	616 554-6500
Sloan Transportation Pdts Inc — Holland (G-8197)	E	616 395-5600
TI Group Auto Systems LLC — Auburn Hills (G-1055)	B	248 296-8000
Veritas USA Corporation — Novi (G-12567)	E	248 374-5019
Yapp USA Auto Systems Inc — Romulus (G-14343)	G	248 404-8696

MOTOR VEHICLE PARTS & ACCESS: Gas Tanks

Company	Code	Phone
Raval USA Inc — Rochester Hills (G-14099)	F	248 260-4050

MOTOR VEHICLE PARTS & ACCESS: Gears

Company	Code	Phone
AA Gear LLC — Howell (G-8424)	F	517 552-3100
Anderson-Cook Inc — Chesterfield (G-2844)	D	586 954-0700
Anderson-Cook Inc — Fraser (G-5895)	G	586 293-0800
Atlas Gear Company — Madison Heights (G-10675)	F	248 583-2964
Detail Production Company Inc — Ferndale (G-5541)	F	248 544-3390
Leedy Manufacturing Co LLC — Grand Rapids (G-6934)	D	616 245-0517
Libertys High Prfmce Pdts Inc — Harrison Township (G-7707)	F	586 469-1140
Nexteer Automotive Corporation — Saginaw (G-14712)	B	989 757-5000
Rochester Gear Inc — Clifford (G-3133)	D	989 659-2899
Von Weise LLC — Eaton Rapids (G-4975)	G	517 618-9763

MOTOR VEHICLE PARTS & ACCESS: Heaters

Company	Code	Phone
Kongsberg Automotive Inc — Novi (G-12455)	D	248 468-1300
Kurabe America Corporation — Farmington Hills (G-5284)	F	248 939-5803

MOTOR VEHICLE PARTS & ACCESS: Horns

Company	Code	Phone
Fiamm Technologies LLC — Farmington Hills (G-5243)	C	248 427-3200

MOTOR VEHICLE PARTS & ACCESS: Instrument Board Assemblies

Company	Code	Phone
Ese LLc — Lapeer (G-9929)	G	810 538-1000
Intertec Systems LLC — Farmington Hills (G-5272)	F	248 488-7610
Kautex Inc — Troy (G-17193)	A	248 616-5100

MOTOR VEHICLE PARTS & ACCESS: Manifolds

Company	Code	Phone
Benteler Automotive Corp — Auburn Hills (G-811)	C	248 364-7190
Metaldyne Tblar Components LLC — Southfield (G-15655)	D	248 727-1800

MOTOR VEHICLE PARTS & ACCESS: Mufflers, Exhaust

Company	Code	Phone
Bay Alphi Manufacturing Inc — Jonesville (G-9085)	E	517 849-9945
Faurecia USA Holdings Inc — Auburn Hills (G-891)	C	248 724-5100
Tenneco Automotive Oper Co Inc — Marshall (G-11075)	C	269 781-1350
Tenneco Automotive Oper Co Inc — Litchfield (G-10085)	C	517 542-5511

MOTOR VEHICLE PARTS & ACCESS: Oil Pumps

Company	Code	Phone
Highland Manufacturing Inc — Madison Heights (G-10740)	E	248 585-8040
J & J Industries Inc — Jackson (G-8911)	E	517 784-3586
Melling Do Brasil LLC — Jackson (G-8948)	F	517 787-8172
Melling Tool Co — Jackson (G-8951)	B	517 787-8172

MOTOR VEHICLE PARTS & ACCESS: Pickup Truck Bed Liners

Company	Code	Phone
Sports Resorts International — Owosso (G-12858)	E	989 725-8354
Tectum Holdings Inc — Ann Arbor (G-674)	D	734 926-2362
Truck Acquisition Inc — Ann Arbor (G-699)	G	877 875-4376
Truck Holdings Inc — Ann Arbor (G-700)	G	877 875-4376

MOTOR VEHICLE PARTS & ACCESS: Power Steering Eqpt

Company	Code	Phone
Cooper-Standard Automotive Inc — Fairview (G-5129)	G	989 848-2272
Nexteer Automotive Corporation — Saginaw (G-14719)	B	989 757-5000

Employee Codes: A=Over 500 employees, B=251-500, C=101-250, D=51-100, E=20-50, F=10-19, G=3-9

MOTOR VEHICLE PARTS & ACCESS: Propane Conversion Eqpt

MOTOR VEHICLE PARTS & ACCESS: Propane Conversion Eqpt

Signature Truck Systems LLC..............D.......810 564-2294
  Clio *(G-3411)*

MOTOR VEHICLE PARTS & ACCESS: Pumps, Hydraulic Fluid Power

Med-Kas Hydraulics Inc...................F.......248 585-3220
  Troy *(G-17243)*
Pardon Inc...................................E.......906 428-3494
  Gladstone *(G-6185)*
TRW Automotive (Iv) Corp.................G.......734 855-2600
  Livonia *(G-10447)*

MOTOR VEHICLE PARTS & ACCESS: Rear Axel Housings

American Axle & Mfg Inc..................G.......517 542-4241
  Litchfield *(G-10076)*
American Axle & Mfg Inc..................B.......313 758-3600
  Detroit *(G-4011)*
Dana Off-Hghway Components LLC.....E.......586 467-1600
  Flint *(G-5683)*
Diversified Mfg & Assembly LLC.........G.......586 272-2431
  Sterling Heights *(G-15988)*

MOTOR VEHICLE PARTS & ACCESS: Thermostats

Dt Manufacturing One LLC................D.......248 889-9210
  Highland *(G-7891)*

MOTOR VEHICLE PARTS & ACCESS: Tie Rods

Mark Land Industries Inc.................E.......313 615-0503
  Dearborn *(G-3868)*

MOTOR VEHICLE PARTS & ACCESS: Tops

D & M Truck Top Co Inc...................G.......248 792-7972
  Troy *(G-17042)*
Webasto Convertibles USA Inc...........C.......734 582-5900
  Plymouth *(G-13336)*

MOTOR VEHICLE PARTS & ACCESS: Trailer Hitches

Garrisons Hitch Center Inc...............G.......810 239-5728
  Flint *(G-5703)*
Horizon Global Americas Inc.............C.......734 656-3000
  Plymouth *(G-13191)*
Horizon Global Corporation...............A.......734 656-3000
  Plymouth *(G-13192)*
Saf-Holland Inc.............................A.......231 773-3271
  Muskegon *(G-11913)*

MOTOR VEHICLE PARTS & ACCESS: Transmission Housings Or Parts

Extreme Machine Inc......................G.......810 231-0521
  Whitmore Lake *(G-18535)*
Means Industries Inc......................C.......989 754-1433
  Saginaw *(G-14691)*
Means Industries Inc......................F.......989 754-0312
  Saginaw *(G-14692)*
Meritor Specialty Products LLC..........D.......517 545-5800
  Howell *(G-8478)*
Neapco Drivelines LLC....................B.......734 447-1316
  Van Buren Twp *(G-17543)*
Neapco Drivelines LLC....................C.......734 447-1300
  Van Buren Twp *(G-17544)*
Quality Clutches Inc.......................G.......734 782-0783
  Flat Rock *(G-5627)*
S & W Holdings Ltd........................G.......248 723-2870
  Birmingham *(G-1748)*
Torsion Control Products Inc.............F.......248 537-1900
  Rochester Hills *(G-14128)*
Trans Parts Plus Inc.......................G.......734 427-6844
  Garden City *(G-6113)*

MOTOR VEHICLE PARTS & ACCESS: Transmissions

1st Quality LLC.............................G.......313 908-4864
  Dearborn *(G-3803)*
Borgwarner Transm Systems LLC.......B.......248 754-9200
  Auburn Hills *(G-826)*
Borgwarner Emssons Systems Mich...C.......248 754-9600
  Auburn Hills *(G-830)*
Extreme Machine Inc......................D.......810 231-0521
  Whitmore Lake *(G-18536)*
Jasper Weller LLC.........................C.......616 724-2000
  Wyoming *(G-18887)*
R Cushman & Associates Inc............A.......248 477-9900
  Livonia *(G-10381)*
Sapa Transmission Inc...................F.......954 608-0125
  Shelby Township *(G-15322)*

MOTOR VEHICLE PARTS & ACCESS: Universal Joints

GKN Driveline North Amer Inc............B.......248 296-7000
  Auburn Hills *(G-911)*

MOTOR VEHICLE PARTS & ACCESS: Water Pumps

Engineered Machined Pdts Inc...........B.......906 786-8404
  Escanaba *(G-5069)*
Kerkstra Mechanical LLC.................G.......616 532-6100
  Grand Rapids *(G-6892)*

MOTOR VEHICLE PARTS & ACCESS: Wheel rims

Fontijne Grotnes Inc.......................E.......269 262-4700
  Niles *(G-12129)*

MOTOR VEHICLE PARTS & ACCESS: Wipers, Windshield

Trico Group Inc.............................G.......800 388-7426
  Rochester Hills *(G-14131)*

MOTOR VEHICLE PARTS & ACCESS: Wiring Harness Sets

Creative Performance Racg LLC.........G.......248 250-6187
  Troy *(G-17032)*
Dontech Solutions LLC....................F.......248 789-3086
  Howell *(G-8448)*
Howell Engine Developments Inc........F.......810 765-5100
  Cottrellville *(G-3720)*
Newtech 3 Inc..............................E.......248 912-0807
  Wixom *(G-18719)*
Pgf Technology Group Inc................E.......248 852-2800
  Rochester Hills *(G-14082)*
Precision Race Services Inc.............G.......248 634-4010
  Davisburg *(G-3771)*
Tesca Usa Inc..............................E.......586 991-0744
  Rochester Hills *(G-14124)*
Wiric Corporation..........................E.......248 598-5297
  Rochester Hills *(G-14147)*

MOTOR VEHICLE RADIOS WHOLESALERS

Clarion Corporation America.............E.......248 991-3100
  Farmington Hills *(G-5203)*
Robert Bosch LLC.........................G.......248 876-1000
  Farmington Hills *(G-5371)*
Robert Bosch LLC.........................G.......248 921-9054
  Novi *(G-12527)*
Robert Bosch LLC.........................G.......734 979-3000
  Plymouth *(G-13287)*

MOTOR VEHICLE SPLYS & PARTS WHOLESALERS: New

Brembo North America Inc...............D.......734 416-1275
  Plymouth *(G-13138)*
Bridgewater Interiors LLC.................C.......313 842-3300
  Detroit *(G-4070)*
Carter Industries Inc......................D.......510 324-6700
  Adrian *(G-56)*
Continental Auto Systems Inc...........G.......248 267-9408
  Troy *(G-17023)*
Davco Manufacturing LLC................G.......734 429-5665
  Saline *(G-15011)*
Diversfied Prcurement Svcs LLC........G.......248 821-1147
  Ferndale *(G-5548)*
Elliott Tape Inc.............................E.......248 475-2000
  Auburn Hills *(G-878)*
Gestamp Mason LLC.....................B.......517 244-8800
  Mason *(G-11135)*
GKN North America Inc...................C.......248 296-7200
  Auburn Hills *(G-912)*
Hydraulic Systems Technology..........G.......248 656-5810
  Rochester Hills *(G-14036)*
Inteva Products LLC.......................B.......248 655-8886
  Troy *(G-17174)*
L Barge & Associates Inc................E.......248 582-3430
  Ferndale *(G-5563)*
Lydall Sealing Solutions Inc.............D.......248 596-2800
  Northville *(G-12237)*
Mayser Usa Inc............................G.......734 858-1290
  Van Buren Twp *(G-17538)*
Midwest Bus Corporation.................D.......989 723-5241
  Owosso *(G-12844)*
Muskegon Brake & Distrg Co LLC.....E.......231 733-0874
  Norton Shores *(G-12313)*
Overseas Auto Parts Inc.................E.......734 427-4840
  Livonia *(G-10354)*
P G S Inc...................................G.......248 526-3800
  Troy *(G-17294)*
Pittsburgh Glass Works LLC.............C.......248 371-1700
  Rochester Hills *(G-14084)*
Sam Brown Sales LLC....................G.......248 358-2626
  Farmington *(G-5147)*
Southern Auto Wholesalers Inc.........F.......248 335-5555
  Pontiac *(G-13417)*
Teamtech Motorsports Safety...........G.......989 792-4880
  Saginaw *(G-14773)*
Teksid Aluminum North Amer Inc.......E.......248 304-4001
  Southfield *(G-15719)*
Welk-Ko Fabricators Inc..................G.......810 227-7500
  Brighton *(G-2096)*

MOTOR VEHICLE SPLYS & PARTS WHOLESALERS: Used

Clio Massena LLC.........................E.......248 477-5148
  Wixom *(G-18634)*

MOTOR VEHICLE: Hardware

American Arrow Corp Inc..................G.......248 435-6115
  Madison Heights *(G-10666)*
Dura Operating LLC.......................C.......248 299-7500
  Auburn Hills *(G-868)*
Miller Industrial Products Inc.............E.......517 783-2756
  Jackson *(G-8962)*
Twb of Indiana Inc.........................G.......734 289-6400
  Monroe *(G-11587)*

MOTOR VEHICLE: Radiators

Aerospace America Inc...................E.......989 684-2121
  Bay City *(G-1319)*
AM Specialties Inc.........................F.......586 795-9000
  Sterling Heights *(G-15929)*
Detroit Radiator Corporation..............C.......800 525-0011
  Taylor *(G-16401)*
Dewitts Radiator LLC......................F.......517 548-0600
  Howell *(G-8444)*
Mahle Behr Dayton LLc...................C.......937 369-2900
  Troy *(G-17230)*
Mahle Behr USA Inc.......................B.......248 743-3700
  Troy *(G-17234)*
Mahle Behr USA Inc.......................C.......248 743-3700
  Troy *(G-17232)*
United Systems Group LLC..............G.......810 227-4567
  Brighton *(G-2090)*
Valeo North America Inc.................C.......313 883-8850
  Detroit *(G-4660)*

MOTOR VEHICLE: Shock Absorbers

Enertrols Inc................................E.......734 595-4500
  Farmington Hills *(G-5234)*
Marelli Tennessee USA LLC.............G.......248 418-3000
  Southfield *(G-15646)*
Marelli Tennessee USA LLC.............A.......248 680-8872
  Troy *(G-17236)*
Ride Control LLC..........................D.......248 247-7600
  Farmington Hills *(G-5369)*
Tenneco Automotive Oper Co Inc.......E.......734 243-8000
  Lansing *(G-9742)*
Tenneco Automotive Oper Co Inc.......G.......734 243-8000
  Monroe *(G-11581)*
Thyssenkrupp Bilstein Amer Inc........A.......248 530-2900
  Troy *(G-17390)*

MOTOR VEHICLE: Steering Mechanisms

Douglas Autotech Corporation...........D.......517 369-2315
  Bronson *(G-2111)*
Letts Industries Inc........................G.......313 579-1100
  Detroit *(G-4392)*
Mason Forge & Die Inc...................F.......517 676-2992
  Mason *(G-11142)*

Nexteer Automotive Corporation .... B 989 757-5000
  Saginaw *(G-14710)*
NSK Americas Inc .... C 734 913-7500
  Ann Arbor *(G-595)*
NSK Steering Systems Amer Inc .... C 734 913-7500
  Ann Arbor *(G-596)*
ZF Chassis Components LLC .... C 810 245-2000
  Lapeer *(G-9969)*
ZF Chassis Components LLC .... E 810 245-2000
  Lapeer *(G-9971)*

MOTOR VEHICLE: Wheels

Dicastal North America Inc .... B 616 619-7500
  Greenville *(G-7482)*
Hayes Lemmerz Intl Import LLC .... G 734 737-5000
  Novi *(G-12430)*
Maxion Fumagalli Auto USA .... D 734 737-5000
  Novi *(G-12473)*
Maxion Wheels LLC .... D 734 737-5000
  Novi *(G-12476)*
Maxion Wheels USA LLC .... D 734 737-5000
  Novi *(G-12477)*

MOTOR VEHICLES & CAR BODIES

AAM Mexico Holdings LLC .... D 313 758-2000
  Detroit *(G-3977)*
AAM Travel Services LLC .... G 313 758-2000
  Detroit *(G-3978)*
Adac Door Components Inc .... B 616 957-0311
  Grand Rapids *(G-6427)*
Advanced Def Vhcl Systems Corp .... F 248 391-3200
  Clarkston *(G-3013)*
Android Industries-Sterling .... F 586 486-5616
  Warren *(G-17705)*
Asp Grede Acquisitionco LLC .... E 248 440-9515
  Southfield *(G-15493)*
Asp Hhi Acquisition Co Inc .... G 313 758-2000
  Detroit *(G-4030)*
Autoalliance Management Co .... D 734 782-7800
  Flat Rock *(G-5615)*
Autoform Development Inc .... F 616 392-4909
  Holland *(G-7966)*
BDS Company Inc .... F 517 279-2135
  Coldwater *(G-3421)*
Bearing Holdings LLC .... G 313 758-2000
  Detroit *(G-4046)*
Champion Bus Inc .... B 810 724-1753
  Imlay City *(G-8628)*
Chrysler Group LLC .... D 586 977-4900
  Sterling Heights *(G-15958)*
FCA US LLC .... C 586 468-2891
  Mount Clemens *(G-11638)*
FCA US LLC .... G 800 334-9200
  Detroit *(G-4230)*
FCA US LLC .... E 734 422-0557
  Livonia *(G-10206)*
FCA US LLC .... G 248 576-5741
  Warren *(G-17803)*
FCA US LLC .... F 586 978-0067
  Sterling Heights *(G-16011)*
Ficosa North America Corp .... E 248 307-2230
  Madison Heights *(G-10727)*
Ford Investment Entps Corp .... G 973 764-8783
  Dearborn *(G-3841)*
Ford Motor Company .... G 313 322-7715
  Dearborn *(G-3844)*
Forging Holdings LLC .... G 313 758-2000
  Detroit *(G-4243)*
Frank Industries Inc .... E 810 346-3234
  Brown City *(G-2137)*
G Tech Sales LLC .... G 586 803-9393
  Sterling Heights *(G-16026)*
General Motors Company .... A 313 667-1500
  Detroit *(G-4255)*
General Motors LLC .... E 586 441-8483
  Warren *(G-17825)*
General Motors LLC .... G 313 408-3987
  Auburn Hills *(G-908)*
General Motors LLC .... A 313 972-6000
  Detroit *(G-4259)*
General Motors LLC .... A 313 556-5000
  Detroit *(G-4260)*
General Motors LLC .... A 248 857-3500
  Pontiac *(G-13375)*
Gestamp Mason LLC .... B 517 244-8800
  Mason *(G-11135)*
GM Defense LLC .... D 313 462-8782
  Detroit *(G-4266)*
GM Defense LLC .... E 586 359-8880
  Milford *(G-11464)*
GM Gdls Defense Group LLC .... D 586 825-4000
  Sterling Heights *(G-16031)*
GM Orion Assembly .... E 248 377-5260
  Lake Orion *(G-9607)*
Grede Omaha LLC .... C 248 727-1800
  Southfield *(G-15582)*
Hayes-Albion Corporation .... F 517 629-2141
  Jackson *(G-8900)*
Hercules Electric Mobility Inc .... G 734 666-8078
  Detroit *(G-4298)*
Hhi Funding II LLC .... G 313 758-2000
  Detroit *(G-4299)*
Hhi Holdings LLC .... G 313 758-2000
  Detroit *(G-4300)*
Hme Inc .... C 616 534-1463
  Wyoming *(G-18885)*
Holbrook Racing Engines .... F 734 762-4315
  Livonia *(G-10241)*
Jeff Schaller Transport Inc .... G 810 724-7640
  Imlay City *(G-8638)*
Kendrick Plastics Inc .... B 616 975-4000
  Grand Rapids *(G-6883)*
Kyklos Holdings Inc .... G 313 758-2000
  Detroit *(G-4370)*
Lemforder Corp .... E 734 416-6200
  Northville *(G-12235)*
Lucasvarity Inc .... G 517 223-8330
  Fowlerville *(G-5849)*
M M R LLC .... G 734 502-5239
  Livonia *(G-10295)*
Magna Steyr LLC .... B 248 740-0214
  Troy *(G-17227)*
Mahindra N Amercn Technical .... G 248 268-6600
  Troy *(G-17229)*
Marrel Corporation .... G 616 863-9155
  Rockford *(G-14177)*
Maven Drive LLC .... D 313 667-1541
  Detroit *(G-4421)*
May Mobility Inc .... F 312 869-2711
  Ann Arbor *(G-567)*
Mobility Innovations LLC .... G 586 843-3816
  Shelby Township *(G-15280)*
Nationwide Design Inc .... F 586 254-5493
  Sterling Heights *(G-16113)*
Nexteer Automotive Corporation .... B 989 757-5000
  Saginaw *(G-14710)*
Pcm US Steering Holding LLC .... E 313 556-5000
  Auburn Hills *(G-994)*
Rivian Automotive LLC .... D 734 855-4350
  Plymouth *(G-13285)*
Robert Carmichael .... G 248 576-5741
  Auburn Hills *(G-1022)*
Roush Enterprises Inc .... A 313 294-8200
  Allen Park *(G-205)*
Saleen .... G 248 499-5333
  Pontiac *(G-13414)*
Saleen Special Vehicles Inc .... B 909 978-6700
  Troy *(G-17342)*
Serena Hines .... G 269 252-0895
  Benton Harbor *(G-1583)*
Stamping Plant .... G 734 467-0008
  Wayne *(G-18236)*
Supreme Gear Co .... E 586 775-6325
  Fraser *(G-6001)*
Tesla Inc .... G 248 205-3206
  Troy *(G-17389)*
Think North America Inc .... E 313 565-6781
  Dearborn *(G-3904)*
Thor Industries Inc .... G 810 724-6474
  Imlay City *(G-8647)*
Transglobal Design & Mfg LLC .... D 734 525-2651
  Auburn Hills *(G-1063)*
TRW Safety Systems Mexico LLC .... G 734 855-2600
  Livonia *(G-10450)*
Usm Holdings LLC .... F 313 758-2000
  Detroit *(G-4657)*
Usm Holdings LLC II .... F 313 758-2000
  Detroit *(G-4658)*
Visteon Intl Holdings Inc .... A 734 710-2000
  Van Buren Twp *(G-17561)*
Visteon Systems LLC .... C 313 755-9500
  Dearborn *(G-3910)*
ZF TRW Auto Holdings Corp .... A 734 855-2600
  Livonia *(G-10492)*

MOTOR VEHICLES, WHOLESALE: Fire Trucks

Front Line Services Inc .... F 989 695-6633
  Freeland *(G-6024)*

MOTOR VEHICLES, WHOLESALE: Snowmobiles

Micro Engineering Inc .... G 616 534-9681
  Byron Center *(G-2285)*

MOTOR VEHICLES, WHOLESALE: Trailers for passenger vehicles

Premier Custom Trailers LLC .... F 877 327-0888
  Schoolcraft *(G-15127)*

MOTOR VEHICLES, WHOLESALE: Trailers, Truck, New & Used

Clydes Frame & Wheel Service .... F 248 338-0323
  Pontiac *(G-13354)*

MOTOR VEHICLES, WHOLESALE: Truck bodies

NBC Truck Equipment Inc .... E 586 774-4900
  Roseville *(G-14452)*

MOTOR VEHICLES, WHOLESALE: Trucks, commercial

Valley Truck Parts Inc .... D 616 241-5431
  Grand Rapids *(G-7303)*

MOTORCYCLE & BICYCLE PARTS: Frames

Assenmacher Lightweight Cycles .... G 810 635-7844
  Swartz Creek *(G-16350)*
Technique Inc .... D 517 789-8988
  Jackson *(G-9017)*

MOTORCYCLE ACCESS

Ron Watkins .... G 517 439-5451
  Hillsdale *(G-7946)*

MOTORCYCLE DEALERS

C & C Sports Inc .... E 810 227-7068
  Brighton *(G-1958)*
Motown Harley-Davidson Inc .... D 734 947-4647
  Taylor *(G-16451)*
Riverfront Cycle Inc .... G 517 482-8585
  Lansing *(G-9888)*

MOTORCYCLE PARTS & ACCESS DEALERS

Aftershock Motorsports .... G 586 273-1333
  Casco *(G-2597)*

MOTORCYCLE REPAIR SHOPS

C & C Sports Inc .... E 810 227-7068
  Brighton *(G-1958)*

MOTORCYCLES & RELATED PARTS

Icon Choppers .... G 616 292-0536
  Jenison *(G-9056)*
Mid Cost Grass Choppers .... G 985 445-7155
  Clarkston *(G-3051)*
Pritech Corporation .... G 248 488-9120
  Canton *(G-2513)*
Turtle Racing LLC .... G 517 918-3444
  Morenci *(G-11618)*

MOTORS: Electric

Allied Motion Technologies Inc .... G 989 725-5151
  Owosso *(G-12822)*
American Mitsuba Corporation .... G 989 773-0377
  Mount Pleasant *(G-11678)*
Bay Motor Products Inc .... E 231 941-0411
  Traverse City *(G-16615)*
Denso Manufacturing NC Inc .... A 269 441-2040
  Battle Creek *(G-1217)*
Motor Products Corporation .... C 989 725-5151
  Owosso *(G-12845)*
Prestolite Electric LLC .... G 248 313-3807
  Novi *(G-12512)*
Prestolite Electric Holding .... A 248 313-3807
  Novi *(G-12513)*
Pro Slot Ltd .... G 616 897-6000
  Hartford *(G-7766)*
Reuland Electric Co .... F 517 546-4400
  Howell *(G-8508)*

MOTORS: Electric

Southern Auto Wholesalers Inc .... F 248 335-5555
  Pontiac (G-13417)
Vandervest Electric Mtr & Fabg .... G 231 843-6196
  Ludington (G-10555)

MOTORS: Generators

Ametek Inc .... G 248 435-7540
  Peck (G-12961)
Continental Auto Systems Inc .... G 248 267-9408
  Troy (G-17023)
Detroit Coil Co .... E 248 658-1543
  Ferndale (G-5543)
Diamond Electric Mfg Corp .... F 734 995-5525
  Farmington Hills (G-5215)
DMS Electric Apparatus Service .... E 269 349-7000
  Kalamazoo (G-9171)
Ehc Inc .... G 313 259-2266
  Troy (G-17079)
Energy Products Inc .... G 248 866-5622
  Troy (G-17090)
Etx Holdings Inc .... G 989 463-1151
  Alma (G-241)
Feed - Lease Corp .... E 248 377-0000
  Auburn Hills (G-896)
Flint Hydrostatics Inc .... F 901 794-2462
  Chesterfield (G-2883)
Ford Motor Company .... A 734 484-8626
  Ypsilanti (G-18947)
Fortis Energy Services Inc .... D 248 283-7100
  Troy (G-17119)
Gast Manufacturing Inc .... B 269 926-6171
  Benton Harbor (G-1551)
Genco Alliance LLC .... G 269 216-5500
  Kalamazoo (G-9192)
H W Jencks Incorporated .... E 231 352-4422
  Frankfort (G-5878)
Heco Inc .... G 269 381-7200
  Kalamazoo (G-9210)
Hydraulex Intl Holdings Inc .... E 914 682-2700
  Chesterfield (G-2891)
Independent Mfg Solutions Corp .... E 248 960-3550
  Wixom (G-18684)
Induction Engineering Inc .... F 586 716-4700
  New Baltimore (G-11982)
Industrial Computer & Controls .... F 734 697-4152
  Van Buren Twp (G-17530)
Magna E-Car USA LLC .... D 248 606-0600
  Holly (G-8281)
Maxitrol Company .... G 517 486-2820
  Blissfield (G-1769)
Monarch Electric Service Co .... G 313 388-7800
  Melvindale (G-11206)
Morrell Incorporated .... D 248 373-1600
  Auburn Hills (G-975)
Nidec Motors & Actuators (usa) .... G 248 340-9977
  Auburn Hills (G-983)
Patriot Sensors & Contrls Corp .... D 248 435-0700
  Peck (G-12963)
Pontiac Coil Inc .... C 248 922-1100
  Clarkston (G-3057)
Power Controllers LLC .... G 248 888-9896
  Farmington Hills (G-5351)
Powerthru Inc .... G 734 583-5004
  Livonia (G-10370)
Powerthru Inc .... F 734 853-5004
  Livonia (G-10371)
Sfm LLC .... G 248 719-0212
  Northville (G-12260)
Twm Technology LLC .... F 989 684-7050
  Bay City (G-1407)
Z & R Electric Service Inc .... E 906 774-0468
  Iron Mountain (G-8738)

MOTORS: Pneumatic

Jamco Manufacturing Inc .... G 248 852-1988
  Auburn Hills (G-943)
Matt and Dave LLC .... F 734 439-1988
  Dundee (G-4831)

MOTORS: Starting, Automotive & Aircraft

Auto Electric International .... E 248 354-2082
  Southfield (G-15498)
Jing-Jin Electric N Amer LLC .... G 248 554-7247
  Farmington Hills (G-5274)
Prestolite Electric LLC .... G 248 313-3807
  Novi (G-12512)
Prestolite Electric Holding .... A 248 313-3807
  Novi (G-12513)

Robert Bosch LLC .... G 248 876-1000
  Farmington Hills (G-5371)
Robert Bosch LLC .... G 248 921-9054
  Novi (G-12527)
Robert Bosch LLC .... G 734 979-3000
  Plymouth (G-13287)
Southern Auto Wholesalers Inc .... F 248 335-5555
  Pontiac (G-13417)

MOUTHWASHES

Abaco Partners LLC .... C 616 532-1700
  Kentwood (G-9441)
Microcide Inc .... G 248 526-9663
  Troy (G-17258)

MOWERS & ACCESSORIES

Excellence Lawn Landscape .... G 810 623-9742
  Brighton (G-1985)
Randys Lawn Care Services LLC .... G 313 447-9536
  Detroit (G-4553)
Reeds Equipment LLC .... G 517 567-4415
  Pittsford (G-13068)

MUCILAGE

Trenton Corporation .... E 734 424-3600
  Ann Arbor (G-697)

MUSEUMS

Pewabic Society Inc .... E 313 626-2000
  Detroit (G-4522)

MUSIC BOXES

Imagillation Inc .... G 734 481-0140
  Ypsilanti (G-18954)
Music Box .... G 517 539-5069
  Jackson (G-8972)

MUSIC BROADCASTING SVCS

Archer Record Pressing Co .... G 313 365-9545
  Detroit (G-4025)

MUSIC DISTRIBUTION APPARATUS

Osowet Collections Inc .... G 313 844-8171
  Detroit (G-4501)
Tf Entertainment LLC .... F 424 303-3407
  Detroit (G-4630)

MUSIC RECORDING PRODUCER

Ball Hard Music Group LLC .... G 833 246-4552
  Monroe (G-11528)
Developmental Services Inc .... G 313 653-1185
  Detroit (G-4173)

MUSIC SCHOOLS

School of Rock Canton .... G 734 845-7448
  Canton (G-2521)

MUSICAL INSTRUMENT LESSONS

Mathew Parmelee .... G 248 894-5955
  Rochester Hills (G-14059)

MUSICAL INSTRUMENTS & ACCESS: NEC

Awesome Musical Instrs LLC .... G 734 941-2927
  Romulus (G-14252)
Ferrees Tools Inc .... E 269 965-0511
  Battle Creek (G-1230)
J Naylor LLC .... G 248 227-8250
  Troy (G-17179)
Lesson Rooms .... G 248 677-1341
  Royal Oak (G-14556)
School of Rock Canton .... G 734 845-7448
  Canton (G-2521)
Wlw Musical .... G 248 956-3060
  Commerce Township (G-3582)

MUSICAL INSTRUMENTS & PARTS: String

Kyoei Electronics America Inc .... G 248 773-3690
  Novi (G-12460)

MUSICAL INSTRUMENTS & SPLYS STORES

Black Swamp Percussion LLC .... G 800 557-0988
  Zeeland (G-19001)

Heritage Guitar Inc .... F 269 385-5721
  Kalamazoo (G-9216)
Stedman Corp .... G 269 629-5930
  Richland (G-13830)

MUSICAL INSTRUMENTS & SPLYS STORES: String instruments

Alf Enterprises Inc .... G 734 665-2012
  Ann Arbor (G-360)

MUSICAL INSTRUMENTS/SPLYS STORE: Drums/Rltd Percussion Instr

Rebeats .... F 989 463-4757
  Alma (G-254)

MUSICAL INSTRUMENTS: Autophones/Organs W/Perfrtd Music Rolls

Harman Becker Auto Systems Inc .... B 248 785-2361
  Farmington Hills (G-5257)

MUSICAL INSTRUMENTS: Fretted Instruments & Parts

Heritage Guitar Inc .... F 269 385-5721
  Kalamazoo (G-9216)

MUSICAL INSTRUMENTS: Guitars & Parts, Electric & Acoustic

Black Swamp Percussion LLC .... G 800 557-0988
  Zeeland (G-19001)
Ghs Corporation .... E 269 968-3351
  Springfield (G-15867)
Grip Studios .... G 248 757-0796
  Plymouth (G-13181)

MUSICAL INSTRUMENTS: Organ Parts & Materials

Rt Swanson Inc .... G 517 627-4955
  Grand Ledge (G-6398)

MUSICAL INSTRUMENTS: Organs

Brian M Fowler Pipe Organs .... G 517 485-3748
  Eaton Rapids (G-4956)

MUSICAL INSTRUMENTS: Saxophones & Parts

Klingler Consulting & Mfg .... F 810 765-3700
  Marine City (G-10961)

MUSICAL INSTRUMENTS: Strings, Instrument

Ghf Corp .... G 269 968-3351
  Springfield (G-15866)
GHS Corporation .... D 800 388-4447
  Springfield (G-15868)

MUSICAL INSTRUMENTS: Violins & Parts

Alf Enterprises Inc .... G 734 665-2012
  Ann Arbor (G-360)

NAILS: Steel, Wire Or Cut

National Nail Corp .... C 616 538-8000
  Grand Rapids (G-7036)

NAME PLATES: Engraved Or Etched

Cushion Lrry Trphies Engrv LLC .... G 517 332-1667
  Lansing (G-9827)
Dag Ltd LLC .... F 586 276-9310
  Sterling Heights (G-15979)
Detroit Name Plate Etching Inc .... E 248 543-5200
  Ferndale (G-5547)
Joseph M Hoffman Inc .... F 586 774-8500
  Roseville (G-14428)
Quality Business Engraving .... G 248 852-5123
  Rochester Hills (G-14094)
Royal Oak Name Plate Company .... G 586 774-8500
  Roseville (G-14473)

PRODUCT SECTION — NUTRITION SVCS

NAMEPLATES
American Label & Tag Inc .... E 734 454-7600
  Canton *(G-2433)*
Quality Business Engraving .... G 248 852-5123
  Rochester Hills *(G-14094)*

NATURAL GAS COMPRESSING SVC, On-Site
Riverside Energy Michigan LLC .... E 231 995-4000
  Traverse City *(G-16821)*

NATURAL GAS DISTRIBUTION TO CONSUMERS
Howard Energy Co Inc .... E 231 995-7850
  Traverse City *(G-16716)*
Option Energy LLC .... G 269 329-4317
  Traverse City *(G-16784)*

NATURAL GAS LIQUIDS PRODUCTION
Westport Fuel Systems US Inc .... D 734 233-6850
  Plymouth *(G-13338)*

NATURAL GAS LIQUIDS PRODUCTION
Tronox Incorporated .... G 231 328-4986
  Merritt *(G-11268)*

NATURAL GAS PRODUCTION
A1 Utility Contractor Inc .... D 989 324-8581
  Evart *(G-5118)*
E Smart Fuels America Inc .... G 248 687-8003
  Detroit *(G-4198)*
Option Energy LLC .... G 269 329-4317
  Traverse City *(G-16784)*
Ward Lake Drilling Inc .... E 989 732-8499
  Gaylord *(G-6166)*

NATURAL GAS STORAGE SVCS
Howard Energy Co Inc .... E 231 995-7850
  Traverse City *(G-16716)*

NATURAL GAS TRANSMISSION & DISTRIBUTION
Altagas Marketing (us) Inc .... E 810 887-4105
  Port Huron *(G-13435)*
Altagas Power Holdings US Inc .... D 810 887-4105
  Port Huron *(G-13436)*
DTE Energy Company .... E 313 235-4000
  Detroit *(G-4193)*
DTE Energy Trust II 313 235-8822
  Detroit *(G-4194)*
DTE Energy Ventures Inc .... E 313 235-8000
  Detroit *(G-4195)*

NATURAL GASOLINE PRODUCTION
Altagas Marketing (us) Inc .... E 810 887-4105
  Port Huron *(G-13435)*
Altagas Power Holdings US Inc .... D 810 887-4105
  Port Huron *(G-13436)*
Everest Energy Fund L L C .... G 586 445-2300
  Warren *(G-17797)*

NAUTICAL REPAIR SVCS
Schwartz Boiler Shop Inc .... G 231 627-2556
  Cheboygan *(G-2798)*

NAVIGATIONAL SYSTEMS & INSTRUMENTS
Harman Becker Auto Systems Inc .... B 248 785-2361
  Farmington Hills *(G-5257)*
Harman Becker Auto Systems Inc .... G 248 703-3010
  Novi *(G-12428)*

NEIGHBORHOOD DEVELOPMENT GROUP
Hope Focus .... C 313 494-5500
  Detroit *(G-4307)*

NETTING: Cargo
Networks Enterprises Inc .... G 248 446-8590
  New Hudson *(G-12063)*

NEW & USED CAR DEALERS
Michigan East Side Sales LLC .... G 989 354-6867
  Alpena *(G-302)*

NEWS DEALERS & NEWSSTANDS
Daughtry Nwspapers Investments .... G 269 683-2100
  Niles *(G-12123)*

NEWSPAPERS & PERIODICALS NEWS REPORTING SVCS
Newark Morning Ledger Co .... D 517 487-8888
  Lansing *(G-9875)*

NEWSPAPERS, WHOLESALE
Herald Newspapers Company Inc .... G 810 766-6100
  Flint *(G-5714)*

NICKEL ALLOY
Dodge West Joe Nickel .... G 810 691-2133
  Clio *(G-3397)*

NONCURRENT CARRYING WIRING DEVICES
Allied Tube & Conduit Corp .... G 734 721-4040
  Wayne *(G-18212)*
Ews Legacy LLC .... C 248 853-6363
  Rochester Hills *(G-14006)*
Meter Devices Company Inc .... D 330 455-0301
  Farmington Hills *(G-5317)*
Tesa Tape Inc .... G 616 785-6970
  Walker *(G-17654)*
Tesa Tape Inc .... G 616 887-3107
  Sparta *(G-15786)*
Zygot Operations Limited .... E 810 736-2900
  Flint *(G-5799)*

NONDAIRY BASED FROZEN DESSERTS
Sugar Kissed Cupcakes LLC .... G 231 421-9156
  Traverse City *(G-16844)*

NONFERROUS: Rolling & Drawing, NEC
Anchor Lamina America Inc .... C 231 533-8646
  Bellaire *(G-1468)*
Anchor Lamina America Inc .... E 248 489-9122
  Bellaire *(G-1469)*
Autocam-Pax Inc 269 782-5186
  Dowagiac *(G-4776)*
Concept Alloys Inc .... G 734 449-9680
  Whitmore Lake *(G-18527)*
Dirksen Screw Products Co .... E 586 247-5400
  Shelby Township *(G-15208)*
H C Starck Inc .... G 517 279-9511
  Coldwater *(G-3437)*
Moheco Products Company .... G 734 855-4194
  Livonia *(G-10321)*
Ncoc Inc .... E 248 548-5950
  Oak Park *(G-12632)*
Oerlikon Metco (us) Inc .... E 248 288-0027
  Troy *(G-17287)*
Radiolgical Fabrication Design .... G 810 632-6000
  Howell *(G-8506)*
Traverse City Products LLC .... D 231 946-4414
  Traverse City *(G-16865)*
Warren Manufacturing LLC .... G 586 467-1600
  Warren *(G-18060)*
Weldall Corporation .... G 989 375-2251
  Elkton *(G-5034)*

NONMETALLIC MINERALS: Support Activities, Exc Fuels
Aquila Resources Inc .... G 906 352-4024
  Menominee *(G-11227)*
Detroit Salt Company LC .... E 313 554-0456
  Detroit *(G-4164)*

NOTEBOOKS, MADE FROM PURCHASED MATERIALS
Scientific Notebook Company .... F 269 429-8285
  Stevensville *(G-16264)*

NOTIONS: Fasteners, Glove
Ebinger Manufacturing Company .... F 248 486-8880
  Brighton *(G-1982)*

NOVELTIES
Engineering Graphics Inc .... G 517 485-5828
  Lansing *(G-9693)*

Maple Ridge Companies Inc .... F 989 356-4807
  Posen *(G-13644)*

NOVELTIES: Plastic
Fitness Finders Inc .... F 517 750-1500
  Jackson *(G-8884)*

NOZZLES & SPRINKLERS Lawn Hose
Titan Sprinkler LLC .... G 517 540-1851
  Howell *(G-8533)*

NOZZLES: Spray, Aerosol, Paint Or Insecticide
Incoe Corporation .... C 248 616-0220
  Auburn Hills *(G-936)*
Spraying Systems Co .... F 248 473-1331
  Farmington Hills *(G-5385)*

NURSERIES & LAWN & GARDEN SPLY STORE, RET: Lawn/Garden Splys
Hutson Inc .... C 517 655-4606
  Williamston *(G-18573)*
Lumberjack Shack Inc .... G 810 724-7230
  Imlay City *(G-8640)*

NURSERIES & LAWN & GARDEN SPLY STORES, RETAIL
Don Machalk Sons Fencing Corp .... E 906 753-4002
  Ingalls *(G-8657)*

NURSERIES & LAWN & GARDEN SPLY STORES, RETAIL: Fertilizer
Corunna Mills Feed LLC .... G 989 743-3110
  Corunna *(G-3707)*

NURSERIES & LAWN/GARDEN SPLY STORE, RET: Lawnmowers/Tractors
Bader & Co .... F 810 648-2404
  Sandusky *(G-15055)*
C & C Sports Inc .... E 810 227-7068
  Brighton *(G-1958)*
D P Equipment Co .... F 517 368-5266
  Camden *(G-2421)*
Ebels Hardware Inc .... F 231 826-3334
  Falmouth *(G-5133)*

NURSERIES & LAWN/GARDEN SPLY STORES, RET: Garden Splys/Tools
Blue Thumb Distributing Inc .... E 989 921-3474
  Saginaw *(G-14617)*
Growgeneration Michigan Corp .... G 248 473-0450
  Lansing *(G-9849)*

NURSERIES/LAWN/GRDN SPLY STORE, RET: Nursery Stck, Seed/Bulb
Walters Seed Co LLC .... F 616 355-7333
  Holland *(G-8241)*

NURSERY & GARDEN CENTERS
Affordable Pool and Spa Inc .... F 810 422-5058
  Burton *(G-2225)*
Allstate HM Leisure String Hts .... G 734 838-6500
  Sterling Heights *(G-15928)*
Lake Orion Concrete Orna Pdts .... G 248 693-8683
  Lake Orion *(G-9614)*
Wahmhoff Farms LLC .... F 269 628-4308
  Gobles *(G-6220)*

NURSERY STOCK, WHOLESALE
Bruning Forest Products .... G 989 733-2880
  Onaway *(G-12697)*

NURSING CARE FACILITIES: Skilled
Worthington Armstrong Venture .... F 269 934-6200
  Benton Harbor *(G-1611)*

NUTRITION SVCS
4 Seasons Gym LLC .... G 989 681-8175
  Saint Louis *(G-14983)*

Employee Codes: A=Over 500 employees, B=251-500
C=101-250, D=51-100, E=20-50, F=10-19, G=3-9

NUTRITION SVCS

Kemin Industries Inc .... F 248 869-3080
  Plymouth (G-13211)

NUTS: Metal

Ankara Industries Incorporated .... E 586 749-1190
  Chesterfield (G-2845)
Federal Screw Works .... C 734 941-4211
  Romulus (G-14275)
Hexagon Enterprises Inc .... F 248 583-0550
  Troy (G-17142)
Lay Manufacturing Inc .... G 313 369-1627
  Warren (G-17901)
Midwest Acorn Nut Company .... E 800 422-6887
  Troy (G-17261)
Perigee Manufacturing Co Inc .... F 313 933-4420
  Detroit (G-4519)
Rippa Products Inc .... E 906 337-0010
  Calumet (G-2414)
Rush Machining Inc .... E 248 583-0550
  Troy (G-17338)
Taper-Line Inc .... G 586 775-5960
  Clinton Township (G-3373)
Vamp Screw Products Company .... E 734 676-8020
  Brownstown Twp (G-2161)

OFFICE EQPT WHOLESALERS

Clare Print & Pulp .... G 989 386-3497
  Clare (G-2976)
Lowry Holding Company Inc .... C 810 229-7200
  Brighton (G-2023)
Maleports Sault Prtg Co Inc .... E 906 632-3369
  Sault Sainte Marie (G-15095)
Reyers Company Inc .... F 616 414-5530
  Spring Lake (G-15846)

OFFICE EQPT, WHOLESALE: Photocopy Machines

Technology Network Svcs Inc .... F 586 294-7771
  Saint Clair Shores (G-14888)

OFFICE MACHINES, NEC

Danka .... G 616 249-8199
  Wyoming (G-18864)
Debi Designs .... G 989 832-9598
  Midland (G-11336)
Golden Apple .... G 231 477-5366
  Manistee (G-10901)

OFFICE SPLY & STATIONERY STORES

Golden Apple .... G 231 477-5366
  Manistee (G-10901)
Horn Corporation .... F 248 583-7789
  Troy (G-17151)
Office Express Inc .... E 248 307-1850
  Troy (G-17288)

OFFICE SPLY & STATIONERY STORES: Office Forms & Splys

Big Rapids Printing .... G 231 796-8588
  Grand Rapids (G-6508)
Cadillac Printing Company .... F 231 775-2488
  Cadillac (G-2323)
Clare Print & Pulp .... G 989 386-3497
  Clare (G-2976)
Compatible Laser Products Inc .... F 810 629-0459
  Fenton (G-5466)
Garants Office Sups & Prtg Inc .... G 989 356-3930
  Alpena (G-296)
Gazelle Publishing .... G 734 529-2688
  Dundee (G-4821)
Hawk Design Inc .... G 989 781-1452
  Saginaw (G-14662)
Jackpine Press Incorporated .... F 231 723-8344
  Manistee (G-10903)
L D J Inc .... F 906 524-6194
  Lanse (G-9666)
Northland Publishers Inc .... F 906 265-9927
  Iron River (G-8751)
Ontonagon Herald Co Inc .... G 906 884-2826
  Ontonagon (G-12714)
Peterson Publishing Inc .... G 906 387-3282
  Marquette (G-11040)
Print n go .... G 989 362-6041
  East Tawas (G-4921)
Specifications Service Company .... G 248 353-0244
  Bloomfield (G-1785)

W B Mason Co Inc .... E 734 947-6370
  Taylor (G-16488)

OFFICE SPLYS, NEC, WHOLESALE

Intra Business LLC .... G 269 262-0863
  Niles (G-12139)
JL Geisler Sign Company .... F 586 574-1800
  Troy (G-17187)
Maleports Sault Prtg Co Inc .... E 906 632-3369
  Sault Sainte Marie (G-15095)
Mis Associates Inc .... G 844 225-8156
  Pontiac (G-13398)
Office Connection Inc .... E 248 871-2003
  Farmington Hills (G-5339)

OFFICES & CLINICS OF DOCTORS OF MEDICINE: Dermatologist

Harper Dermatology PC .... G 586 776-7546
  Grosse Pointe Shores (G-7562)

OFFICES & CLINICS OF DOCTORS OF MEDICINE: Surgeon, Plastic

Luma Laser and Medi Spa .... G 248 817-5499
  Bloomfield Hills (G-1833)

OFFICES & CLINICS OF DRS OF MED: Cardiologist & Vascular

Iha Vsclar Endvsclar Spcalists .... G 734 712-8150
  Ypsilanti (G-18953)

OFFICES & CLINICS OF DRS OF MED: Health Maint Org Or HMO

Hackley Health Ventures Inc .... G 231 728-5720
  Muskegon (G-11834)

OFFICES & CLINICS OF DRS OF MEDICINE: Physician, Orthopedic

Orthopaedic Associates Mich .... D 616 459-7101
  Grand Rapids (G-7063)

OFFICES & CLINICS OF HEALTH PRACTITIONERS: Nutrition

Nubreed Nutrition Inc .... F 734 272-7395
  Troy (G-17283)

OFFICES & CLINICS OF HEALTH PRACTITIONERS: Occu Therapist

Hackley Health Ventures Inc .... G 231 728-5720
  Muskegon (G-11834)

OFFICES & CLINICS OF HEALTH PRACTITIONERS: Physical Therapy

Stryker Far East Inc .... A 269 385-2600
  Portage (G-13618)

OIL & GAS FIELD MACHINERY

Merrill Technologies Group Inc .... C 989 462-0330
  Alma (G-246)
Titan Global Oil Services Inc .... F 248 594-5983
  Birmingham (G-1753)

OIL FIELD MACHINERY & EQPT

General Machine Services .... G 269 695-2244
  Buchanan (G-2196)
Millennium Planet LLC .... G 248 835-2331
  Farmington Hills (G-5322)
United Metal Technology Inc .... E 517 787-7940
  Jackson (G-9029)

OIL FIELD SVCS, NEC

B & H Cementing Services Inc .... G 989 773-5975
  Mount Pleasant (G-11682)
Baker Hghes Olfld Oprtions LLC .... G 989 772-1600
  Mount Pleasant (G-11684)
Baker Hghes Olfld Oprtions LLC .... G 989 773-7992
  Mount Pleasant (G-11685)
Baker Hughes Holdings LLC .... G 989 506-2167
  Mount Pleasant (G-11686)
Bdr Inc .... G 989 732-1608
  Johannesburg (G-9080)

Beckman Production Svcs Inc .... C 231 258-9524
  Kalkaska (G-9384)
Bruno Wojcik .... G 989 785-5555
  Atlanta (G-744)
Coil Drilling Technologies Inc .... G 989 773-6504
  Mount Pleasant (G-11693)
Cross Country Oilfld Svcs Inc .... G 337 366-3840
  Metamora (G-11278)
Dama Tool & Gauge Company .... E 616 842-9631
  Norton Shores (G-12287)
Double Check Tools Service .... G 231 947-1632
  Williamsburg (G-18553)
Exodus Pressure Control .... G 231 258-8001
  Kalkaska (G-9387)
Field Tech Services Inc .... G 989 786-7046
  Lewiston (G-10019)
Forsters and Sons Oil Change .... F 248 618-6860
  Waterford (G-18123)
Go Frac LLC .... G 817 731-0301
  Detroit (G-4268)
Great Lakes Compression Inc .... G 989 786-3788
  Lewiston (G-10020)
GTM Steamer Service Inc .... G 989 732-7678
  Gaylord (G-6132)
Jet Subsurface Rod Pumps Corp .... G 989 732-7513
  Gaylord (G-6136)
Lapeer Fuel Ventures Inc .... G 810 664-8770
  Lapeer (G-9938)
Loshaw Bros Inc .... G 989 732-7263
  Gaylord (G-6143)
Maximum Oilfield Service Inc .... E 989 731-0099
  Elmira (G-5039)
McConnell & Scully Inc .... G 517 568-4104
  Homer (G-8353)
McNaughton-Mckay Electric Co .... B 248 399-7500
  Madison Heights (G-10779)
Michigan Wireline Service .... E 989 772-5075
  Mount Pleasant (G-11712)
Mid State Oil Tools Inc .... F 989 773-4114
  Mount Pleasant (G-11714)
Mikes Steamer Service Inc .... F 231 258-8500
  Williamsburg (G-18558)
N G S G I Natural Gas Ser .... F 989 786-3788
  Lewiston (G-10025)
Natural Gas Cmprssion Systems .... E 231 941-0107
  Traverse City (G-16767)
Navigator Wireline Service Inc .... F 989 275-9112
  Roscommon (G-14352)
Northern Tank Truck Service .... G 989 732-7531
  Gaylord (G-6151)
Oncourse Inc .... F 231 946-1259
  Traverse City (G-16782)
Peninslar Oil Gas Cmpny-Mchgan .... G 616 676-2090
  Grand Rapids (G-7075)
Phoenix Operating Company Inc .... G 231 929-7171
  Williamsburg (G-18562)
Rcs Services Company LLC .... F 989 732-7999
  Johannesburg (G-9082)
Rowsey Construction & Dev LLC .... G 313 675-2464
  Detroit (G-4572)
Sadie Oil LLC .... G 517 675-1325
  Perry (G-12980)
Saginaw Valley Inst Mtls Inc .... F 989 496-2307
  Midland (G-11413)
Schunk Oil Field Service Inc .... G 517 676-8900
  Mason (G-11152)
Seal Right Services Inc .... G 231 357-5595
  Buckley (G-2208)
Soli-Bond Inc .... G 989 684-9611
  Bay City (G-1404)
SOS Well Services LLC .... D 586 580-2576
  Shelby Township (G-15339)
Srw Inc .... F 989 732-8884
  Traverse City (G-16840)
Srw Inc .... F 989 269-8528
  Bad Axe (G-1111)
Woder Construction Inc .... F 989 731-6371
  Gaylord (G-6167)

OILS & ESSENTIAL OILS

Stony Creek Essential Oils .... G 989 227-5500
  Saint Johns (G-14917)

OILS & GREASES: Blended & Compounded

Amcol Corporation .... E 248 414-5700
  Hazel Park (G-7819)
Argent Limited .... G 734 427-5533
  Livonia (G-10123)
Condat Corporation .... E 734 944-4994
  Saline (G-15009)

PRODUCT SECTION — ORDNANCE

Persons Inc .... G 989 734-3835
  Rogers City *(G-14216)*
Rap Products Inc .... G 989 893-5583
  Bay City *(G-1394)*
TMC Group Inc .... G 248 819-6063
  Pleasant Ridge *(G-13106)*

OILS & GREASES: Lubricating

Agscap Inc .... G 231 733-2101
  Muskegon *(G-11766)*
Apollo Idemitsu Corporation .... G 248 675-4345
  Wixom *(G-18608)*
Bostik Inc .... G 269 781-8246
  Marshall *(G-11054)*
BP Lubricants USA Inc .... E 231 689-0002
  White Cloud *(G-18439)*
Chemtool Incorporated .... G 734 439-7010
  Milan *(G-11432)*
Chrysan Industries Inc .... E 734 451-5411
  Plymouth *(G-13146)*
Coxen Enterprises Inc .... D 248 486-3800
  Brighton *(G-1971)*
Cummings-Moore Graphite Co .... E 313 841-1615
  Detroit *(G-4112)*
Diversified Chemical Tech Inc .... C 313 867-5444
  Detroit *(G-4180)*
Eastern Oil Company .... E 248 333-1333
  Pontiac *(G-13364)*
Excelda Mfg Holdg LLC .... F 517 223-8000
  Fowlerville *(G-5838)*
Fortech Products Inc .... E 248 446-9500
  Brighton *(G-1992)*
H and M Lube DBA Jlube .... G 231 929-1197
  Traverse City *(G-16708)*
Idemitsu Lubricants Amer Corp .... E 248 355-0666
  Southfield *(G-15600)*
Lub-Tech Inc .... G 616 299-3540
  Grand Rapids *(G-6950)*
Lubecon Systems Inc .... E 231 689-0002
  White Cloud *(G-18445)*
MB Fluid Services LLC .... F 616 392-7036
  Holland *(G-8140)*
Oil Chem Inc .... E 810 235-3040
  Flint *(G-5742)*
Shell Lubricants .... G 313 354-1187
  River Rouge *(G-13860)*
Stt Usa Inc .... G 248 522-9655
  Wixom *(G-18759)*
Wilbur Products Inc .... F 231 755-3805
  Muskegon *(G-11948)*

OILS: Cutting

Edrich Products Inc .... F 586 296-3350
  Fraser *(G-5922)*
Metalworking Lubricants Co .... D 248 332-3500
  Pontiac *(G-13397)*
Quaker Houghton Pa Inc .... G 313 273-7374
  Detroit *(G-4545)*
Vaughan Industries Inc .... F 313 935-2040
  Detroit *(G-4663)*

OILS: Essential

Ambers Essentials .... G 313 282-4615
  Southfield *(G-15484)*
Bio Source Naturals LLC .... G 877 577-8223
  New Boston *(G-12002)*
Natural Hlth Essntial Oils LLC .... G 906 495-5404
  Kinross *(G-9527)*

OILS: Lubricating

Americanlubrication com .... G 586 219-9119
  Macomb *(G-10576)*
Bva Inc .... E 248 348-4920
  New Hudson *(G-12044)*
Cfb Michigan Inc .... G 269 663-8855
  Edwardsburg *(G-5002)*

OILS: Lubricating

A K Oil LLC DBA Speedy Oil and .... G 616 233-9505
  Grand Rapids *(G-6410)*
Cadillac Oil Company .... E 313 365-6200
  Detroit *(G-4085)*
Huron Industries Inc .... G 810 984-4213
  Port Huron *(G-13485)*
Mr Lube Inc .... G 313 615-6161
  Wyandotte *(G-18834)*
Permawick Company Inc .... G 248 433-3500
  Birmingham *(G-1743)*

Quality Lube Express Inc .... G 586 421-0600
  Chesterfield *(G-2935)*
Warner Oil Company .... F 517 278-5844
  Coldwater *(G-3461)*

OILS: Magnetic Inspection Or Powder

Toda America Incorporated .... G 269 962-0353
  Battle Creek *(G-1305)*

OPERATOR: Apartment Buildings

Bahama Souvenirs Inc .... G 269 964-8275
  Battle Creek *(G-1189)*
Edgewater Apartments .... G 517 663-8123
  Eaton Rapids *(G-4962)*

OPERATOR: Nonresidential Buildings

Gehring Corporation .... D 248 478-8060
  Farmington Hills *(G-5250)*
Mercy Health Partners .... D 231 728-4032
  Muskegon *(G-11866)*

OPHTHALMIC GOODS

Delta Optical Supply Inc .... G 248 628-3977
  Oxford *(G-12882)*
Diagnostic Instruments Inc .... E 586 731-6000
  Sterling Heights *(G-15986)*
Flint Optical Company Inc .... G 810 235-4607
  Flint *(G-5701)*
General Scientific Corporation .... E 734 996-9200
  Ann Arbor *(G-498)*
Inland Diamond Products Co .... E 248 585-1762
  Madison Heights *(G-10746)*
Luxottica of America Inc .... G 517 349-0784
  Okemos *(G-12673)*
McKeon Products Inc .... E 586 427-7560
  Warren *(G-17922)*
Perfect Eyes Optical .... G 248 275-7861
  Detroit *(G-4517)*
Rx Optical Laboratories Inc .... G 269 349-7627
  Kalamazoo *(G-9325)*
Rx Optical Laboratories Inc .... G 269 965-5106
  Battle Creek *(G-1291)*
Rx Optical Laboratories Inc .... D 269 342-5958
  Kalamazoo *(G-9324)*
Tri State Optical Inc .... G 517 279-2701
  Coldwater *(G-3458)*

OPHTHALMIC GOODS WHOLESALERS

Rx Optical Laboratories Inc .... D 269 342-5958
  Kalamazoo *(G-9324)*
Tri State Optical Inc .... G 517 279-2701
  Coldwater *(G-3458)*

OPHTHALMIC GOODS, NEC, WHOLESALE: Frames

Hi-Tech Optical Inc .... E 989 799-9390
  Saginaw *(G-14663)*

OPHTHALMIC GOODS: Lenses, Ophthalmic

Fairway Optical Inc .... G 231 744-6168
  Muskegon *(G-11815)*

OPHTHALMIC GOODS: Protectors, Eye

Noir Laser Company LLC .... E 800 521-9746
  Milford *(G-11478)*
Performance Fabrics Inc .... C 616 459-4144
  Grand Rapids *(G-7079)*

OPHTHALMIC GOODS: Spectacles

Council For Edctl Trvl US Amer .... E 949 940-1140
  Grand Rapids *(G-6609)*
Main Street Spectacles LLC .... G 231 429-7234
  Mc Bain *(G-11185)*

OPTICAL GOODS STORES: Eyeglasses, Prescription

Luxottica of America Inc .... G 517 349-0784
  Okemos *(G-12673)*

OPTICAL GOODS STORES: Opticians

Flint Optical Company Inc .... G 810 235-4607
  Flint *(G-5701)*

Rx Optical Laboratories Inc .... D 269 342-5958
  Kalamazoo *(G-9324)*
Rx Optical Laboratories Inc .... G 269 349-7627
  Kalamazoo *(G-9325)*
Rx Optical Laboratories Inc .... G 269 965-5106
  Battle Creek *(G-1291)*

OPTICAL INSTRUMENTS & APPARATUS

Clark-Mxr Inc .... E 734 426-2803
  Dexter *(G-4731)*
General Dynamics Mission .... A 530 271-2500
  Rochester Hills *(G-14021)*
General Dynmics Globl Imging T .... A 248 293-2929
  Rochester Hills *(G-14022)*
Perform3-D LLC .... G 734 604-4100
  Ann Arbor *(G-608)*
Visotek Inc .... F 734 427-4800
  Novi *(G-12568)*

OPTICAL INSTRUMENTS & LENSES

Browe Inc .... G 248 877-3800
  Clinton Township *(G-3189)*
Carl Zeiss Nts LLC .... E 248 486-7600
  Brighton *(G-1961)*
Contour Metrological & Mfg Inc .... G 248 273-1111
  Troy *(G-17025)*
Crl Inc .... E 906 428-3710
  Gladstone *(G-6177)*
Diagnostic Instruments Inc .... E 586 731-6000
  Sterling Heights *(G-15986)*
Electro-Optics Technology Inc .... D 231 935-4044
  Traverse City *(G-16675)*
Eotech Inc .... E 734 741-8868
  Ann Arbor *(G-476)*
Eye 2 Eye Contact .... G 313 378-7883
  Northville *(G-12216)*
Eyewear Detroit Company .... G 248 396-2214
  Clarkston *(G-3034)*
First Optometry Lab .... G 248 546-1300
  Madison Heights *(G-10728)*
Jenoptik Automotive N Amer LLC .... C 248 853-5888
  Rochester Hills *(G-14043)*
Lumenflow Corp .... G 269 795-9007
  Spring Lake *(G-15831)*
Magna Mirrors America Inc .... G 616 786-7300
  Holland *(G-8134)*
Magna Mirrors America Inc .... G 616 942-0163
  Newaygo *(G-12085)*
Optec Inc .... F 616 897-9351
  Lowell *(G-10513)*
Perceptron Inc .... B 734 414-6100
  Plymouth *(G-13263)*
Planewave Instruments Inc .... D 310 639-1662
  Adrian *(G-87)*
Seneca Enterprises LLC .... G 231 943-1171
  Traverse City *(G-16829)*
Spencer Tool .... G 877 956-6868
  Oxford *(G-12918)*
Visioncraft .... G 586 949-6540
  Chesterfield *(G-2964)*
X-Rite Incorporated .... C 616 803-2100
  Grand Rapids *(G-7353)*
Zeiss Int .... G 734 895-6004
  Wixom *(G-18794)*

OPTICAL SCANNING SVCS

Software Finesse LLC .... G 248 737-8990
  Farmington Hills *(G-5383)*

OPTOMETRIC EQPT & SPLYS WHOLESALERS

Visioncraft .... G 586 949-6540
  Chesterfield *(G-2964)*

OPTOMETRISTS' OFFICES

Rx-Rite Optical Co .... G 586 293-8888
  Fraser *(G-5990)*

ORDNANCE

Autoneum North America Inc .... G 248 848-0100
  Farmington Hills *(G-5176)*
Camdex Inc .... G 248 528-2300
  Troy *(G-16996)*
Lanzen Incorporated .... E 586 771-7070
  Bruce Twp *(G-2174)*
Walter Jerome Lelo .... G 989 274-8895
  Bridgeport *(G-1919)*

ORGAN TUNING & REPAIR SVCS

ORGAN TUNING & REPAIR SVCS
Brian M Fowler Pipe Organs .... G 517 485-3748
  Eaton Rapids *(G-4956)*

ORGANIZATIONS & UNIONS: Labor
Amalgamated Uaw .... G 231 734-9286
  Evart *(G-5120)*

ORGANIZATIONS: Medical Research
Imperial Clinical RES Svcs Inc .... C 616 784-0100
  Grand Rapids *(G-6836)*

ORGANIZATIONS: Religious
Ifca International Inc .... G 616 531-1840
  Grandville *(G-7391)*
Rosary Workshop .... G 906 788-4846
  Stephenson *(G-15910)*

ORGANIZATIONS: Research Institute
Kellogg Company .... B 269 961-2000
  Battle Creek *(G-1254)*

ORGANIZATIONS: Scientific Research Agency
Innovative Weld Solutions LLC .... G 937 545-7695
  Rochester *(G-13908)*
Teamtech Motorsports Safety .... G 989 792-4880
  Saginaw *(G-14773)*
TMC Group Inc .... G 248 819-6063
  Pleasant Ridge *(G-13106)*

ORGANIZERS, CLOSET & DRAWER Plastic
Chadko LLC .... G 616 402-9207
  Grand Haven *(G-6284)*

ORIENTED STRANDBOARD
Louisiana-Pacific Corporation .... G 906 293-3265
  Newberry *(G-12092)*

OUTBOARD MOTOR DEALERS
Marsh Brothers Inc .... F 517 869-2653
  Quincy *(G-13671)*

OUTLETS: Electric, Convenience
Dollars Sense .... G 231 369-3610
  Fife Lake *(G-5605)*

OVENS: Infrared
Thermal Designs & Mfg .... E 248 476-2978
  Novi *(G-12555)*

OVENS: Paint Baking & Drying
Belco Industries Inc .... E 616 794-0410
  Belding *(G-1438)*
Gallagher-Kaiser Corporation .... D 313 368-3100
  Troy *(G-17126)*
R J Manufacturing Incorporated .... G 906 779-9151
  Crystal Falls *(G-3745)*
Rapid Engineering LLC .... D 616 784-0500
  Comstock Park *(G-3642)*
Specified A Sltons Hldings LLC .... D 616 784-0500
  Comstock Park *(G-3645)*

OVENS: Smelting
Fritz Enterprises .... G 313 841-9460
  Detroit *(G-4247)*

PACKAGING & LABELING SVCS
Agscap Inc .... G 231 733-2101
  Muskegon *(G-11766)*
C W A Manufacturing Co Inc .... E 810 686-3030
  Mount Morris *(G-11669)*
Connection Service Company .... E 269 926-2658
  Benton Harbor *(G-1541)*
Coxen Enterprises Inc .... D 248 486-3800
  Brighton *(G-1971)*
Display Pack Inc .... C 616 451-3061
  Cedar Springs *(G-2649)*
Domart LLC .... G 616 285-9177
  Grand Rapids *(G-6653)*
Euclid Industries Inc .... C 989 686-8920
  Bay City *(G-1352)*
Excelda Mfg Holdg LLC .... F 517 223-8000
  Fowlerville *(G-5838)*
Grand Industries Inc .... E 616 846-7120
  Grand Haven *(G-6307)*
Grand Rapids Label Company .... D 616 459-8134
  Grand Rapids *(G-6760)*
Helm Incorporated .... D 734 468-3700
  Plymouth *(G-13186)*
Inter-Pack Corporation .... E 734 242-7755
  Monroe *(G-11551)*
Locpac Inc .... E 734 453-2300
  Plymouth *(G-13226)*
Lotis Technologies Inc .... G 248 340-6065
  Orion *(G-12733)*
March Coatings Inc .... D 810 229-6464
  Brighton *(G-2024)*
Mark Land Industries Inc .... E 313 615-0503
  Dearborn *(G-3868)*
Mollers North America Inc .... D 616 942-6504
  Grand Rapids *(G-7022)*
Roskam Baking Company .... C 616 574-5757
  Grand Rapids *(G-7166)*
Tamsco Inc .... E 586 415-1500
  Clinton Township *(G-3372)*
TGI Direct Inc .... E 810 239-5553
  Flint *(G-5778)*
Total Packaging Solutions LLC .... F 248 519-2376
  Detroit *(G-4639)*
Zoomer Display LLC .... E 616 734-0300
  Grand Rapids *(G-7359)*

PACKAGING MATERIALS, INDL: Wholesalers
Commercial Mfg & Assembly Inc .... E 616 847-9980
  Grand Haven *(G-6287)*

PACKAGING MATERIALS, WHOLESALE
Flambeau Inc .... E 248 364-3357
  Auburn Hills *(G-901)*
Graphic Packaging Intl LLC .... G 269 343-6104
  Kalamazoo *(G-9200)*
J W Manchester Company Inc .... G 810 632-5409
  Hartland *(G-7771)*
Metals Preservation Group LLC .... F 586 944-2720
  Saint Clair Shores *(G-14870)*
Oliver Healthcare Packaging Co .... C 616 456-7711
  Grand Rapids *(G-7057)*
Preferred Packg Solutions Inc .... E 734 844-9092
  Taylor *(G-16459)*
Sekisui Plastics US A Inc .... F 248 308-3000
  Wixom *(G-18750)*
Valmec Inc .... E 810 629-8750
  Fenton *(G-5512)*
West Michigan Tag & Label Inc .... E 616 235-0120
  Grand Rapids *(G-7335)*

PACKAGING MATERIALS: Paper
Advance Engineering Company .... E 989 435-3641
  Beaverton *(G-1423)*
Allsales Enterprises Inc .... F 616 437-0639
  Grand Rapids *(G-6451)*
Alpha Data Business Forms Inc .... G 248 540-5930
  Birmingham *(G-1718)*
American Label & Tag Inc .... E 734 454-7600
  Canton *(G-2433)*
Anchor Bay Packaging Corp .... G 586 949-1500
  Chesterfield *(G-2843)*
Andex Industries Inc .... E 906 786-7588
  Escanaba *(G-5056)*
Argent Tape & Label Inc .... G 734 582-9956
  Plymouth *(G-13125)*
CAM Packaging LLC .... F 989 426-1200
  Gladwin *(G-6191)*
Cello-Foil Products Inc .... C 229 435-4777
  Battle Creek *(G-1206)*
Classic Container Corporation .... C 734 853-3000
  Livonia *(G-10159)*
Creative Foam Corporation .... G 810 714-0140
  Fenton *(G-5468)*
Cummins Label Company .... E 269 345-3386
  Kalamazoo *(G-9159)*
Delta Containers Inc .... C 810 742-2730
  Bay City *(G-1342)*
Fibre Converters Inc .... E 269 279-1700
  Constantine *(G-3666)*
General Tape Label Liquidating .... F 248 437-5200
  Wixom *(G-18668)*

PRODUCT SECTION

Harbor Packaging .... G 616 494-9913
  Holland *(G-8066)*
Holo-Source Corporation .... C 734 427-1530
  Livonia *(G-10242)*
Impact Label Corporation .... D 269 381-4280
  Galesburg *(G-6079)*
International Master Pdts Corp .... C 231 894-5651
  Montague *(G-11598)*
J W Manchester Company Inc .... G 810 632-5409
  Hartland *(G-7771)*
Jetco Packaging Solutions LLC .... F 616 588-2492
  Grand Rapids *(G-6870)*
Macarthur Corp .... E 810 606-1777
  Grand Blanc *(G-6252)*
MPS Lansing Inc .... A 517 323-9000
  Lansing *(G-9719)*
Noble Films Corporation .... G 616 977-3770
  Ada *(G-31)*
Nyx LLC .... C 734 462-2385
  Livonia *(G-10343)*
Nyx LLC .... D 734 261-7535
  Livonia *(G-10347)*
Opus Packaging Group Inc .... D 616 871-5200
  Caledonia *(G-2391)*
Packaging Specialties Inc .... E 586 473-6703
  Romulus *(G-14315)*
Shawmut LLC .... E 810 987-2222
  Port Huron *(G-13526)*
Shoreline Container LLC .... C 616 399-2088
  Holland *(G-8191)*
Siliconature Corporation .... E 312 987-1848
  Caledonia *(G-2400)*
Stamp-Rite Incorporated .... E 517 487-5071
  Lansing *(G-9741)*
Svrc Industries Inc .... C 989 723-8205
  Owosso *(G-12860)*
Tesa Tape Inc .... G 616 785-6970
  Walker *(G-17654)*
Tesa Tape Inc .... G 616 887-3107
  Sparta *(G-15786)*
Timbertech Inc .... F 231 348-2750
  Harbor Springs *(G-7658)*
Ufp Technologies Inc .... D 616 949-8100
  Grand Rapids *(G-7294)*
Unique Fabricating Inc .... A 248 853-2333
  Auburn Hills *(G-1068)*
Unique Fabricating Na Inc .... B 248 853-2333
  Auburn Hills *(G-1069)*

PACKAGING MATERIALS: Paper, Coated Or Laminated
Dunn Paper Inc .... G 810 984-5521
  Menominee *(G-11232)*
Dunn Paper Inc .... F 810 984-5521
  Port Huron *(G-13470)*
Dunn Paper - Wiggins LLC .... G 810 984-5521
  Port Huron *(G-13471)*
Tryco Inc .... F 734 953-6800
  Farmington Hills *(G-5406)*
Venchurs Inc .... C 517 263-8937
  Adrian *(G-100)*
Verso Paper Holding LLC .... F 906 779-3200
  Quinnesec *(G-13678)*
Zajac Industries Inc .... E 586 489-6746
  Clinton Township *(G-3392)*

PACKAGING MATERIALS: Paper, Thermoplastic Coated
Smart USA Inc .... G 248 214-1022
  Ann Arbor *(G-656)*

PACKAGING MATERIALS: Plastic Film, Coated Or Laminated
Cadillac Products Packaging Co .... C 248 879-5000
  Troy *(G-16993)*
Filcon Inc .... F 989 386-2986
  Clare *(G-2979)*
Lotus Technologies LLC .... C 313 550-1889
  Detroit *(G-4406)*
Profile Industrial Packg Corp .... C 616 245-7260
  Grand Rapids *(G-7116)*
Quality Transparent Bag Inc .... F 989 893-3561
  Bay City *(G-1391)*

PACKAGING MATERIALS: Polystyrene Foam
Aldez North America .... F 586 530-5314
  Clinton Township *(G-3161)*

PRODUCT SECTION

Cantrick Kip Co ....G...... 248 644-7622
  Birmingham *(G-1719)*
Classic Container Corporation ....C...... 734 853-3000
  Livonia *(G-10159)*
Creative Foam Corporation ....G...... 269 782-3483
  Dowagiac *(G-4779)*
Creative Foam Corporation ....G...... 810 714-0140
  Fenton *(G-5468)*
N Pack Ship Center ....G...... 906 863-4095
  Menominee *(G-11253)*
Nu-Pak Solutions Inc ....F...... 231 755-1662
  Norton Shores *(G-12321)*
Packaging Engineering LLC ....G...... 248 437-9444
  Brighton *(G-2047)*
Pedmic Converting Inc ....F...... 810 679-9600
  Croswell *(G-3734)*
Russell R Peters Co LLC ....G...... 989 732-0660
  Gaylord *(G-6157)*
Sekisui Plastics U S A Inc ....F...... 248 308-3000
  Wixom *(G-18750)*
Simco Automotive Trim Inc ....E...... 616 608-9818
  Grand Rapids *(G-7199)*
Sonoco Prtective Solutions Inc ....G...... 989 723-3720
  Owosso *(G-12857)*

PACKAGING: Blister Or Bubble Formed, Plastic

Innovative Packg Solutions LLC ....G...... 517 213-3169
  Holt *(G-8315)*

PACKING & CRATING SVC

Action Wood Technologies Inc ....E...... 586 468-2300
  Clinton Township *(G-3155)*

PACKING & CRATING SVCS: Containerized Goods For Shipping

Delta Containers Inc ....C...... 810 742-2730
  Bay City *(G-1342)*

PACKING MATERIALS: Mechanical

Crk Ltd ....G...... 586 779-5240
  Eastpointe *(G-4933)*
Green Polymeric Materials Inc ....E...... 313 933-7390
  Detroit *(G-4280)*
Oliver Healthcare Packaging Co ....C...... 616 456-7711
  Grand Rapids *(G-7057)*
Package Design & Mfg Inc ....E...... 248 486-4390
  Brighton *(G-2046)*

PACKING SVCS: Shipping

Ajax Metal Processing Inc ....G...... 313 267-2100
  Detroit *(G-3992)*
Cal-Chlor Corp ....D...... 231 843-1147
  Ludington *(G-10529)*
Domart LLC ....G...... 616 285-9177
  Grand Rapids *(G-6653)*
Donalyn Enterprises Inc ....F...... 517 546-9798
  Howell *(G-8447)*
Export Corporation ....C...... 810 227-6153
  Brighton *(G-1987)*
Lake Michigan Mailers Inc ....D...... 269 383-9333
  Kalamazoo *(G-9257)*
Mollewood Export Inc ....E...... 248 624-1885
  Wixom *(G-18714)*
Pak-Rite Industries Inc ....D...... 313 388-6400
  Ecorse *(G-4984)*

PACKING: Metallic

Milfab Systems LLC ....F...... 248 391-8100
  Lake Orion *(G-9619)*

PADDING: Foamed Plastics

Brooklyn Products Intl ....E...... 517 592-2185
  Brooklyn *(G-2122)*
Carcoustics Usa Inc ....D...... 517 548-6700
  Howell *(G-8435)*
Nanosystems Inc ....F...... 734 274-0020
  Ann Arbor *(G-589)*
Schmitz Foam Products LLC ....E...... 517 781-6615
  Coldwater *(G-3452)*

PADS & PADDING: Insulator, Cordage

Hestia Inc ....G...... 616 296-0533
  Norton Shores *(G-12297)*

PADS: Athletic, Protective

Mike Vaughn Custom Sports Inc ....E...... 248 969-8956
  Oxford *(G-12903)*

PAILS: Shipping, Metal

Shamrock Fabricating Inc ....F...... 810 744-0677
  Burton *(G-2245)*

PAINT & PAINTING SPLYS STORE

Nelson Paint Company Mich Inc ....G...... 906 774-5566
  Iron Mountain *(G-8726)*
Sames Kremlin Inc ....C...... 734 979-0100
  Plymouth *(G-13292)*
Sames Kremlin Inc ....G...... 734 979-0100
  Plymouth *(G-13293)*

PAINT & PAINTING SPLYS STORE: Brushes, Rollers, Sprayers

Mack Andrew & Son Brush Co ....G...... 517 849-9272
  Jonesville *(G-9092)*

PAINT STORE

Arquette Concrete & Supply ....G...... 989 846-4131
  Standish *(G-15887)*
Polymer Inc ....D...... 248 353-3035
  Southfield *(G-15677)*
Port City Paints Mfg Inc ....G...... 231 726-5911
  Muskegon *(G-11895)*
Repcolite Paints Inc ....D...... 616 396-5213
  Holland *(G-8179)*

PAINTING SVC: Metal Prdts

Almond Products Inc ....D...... 616 844-1813
  Spring Lake *(G-15802)*
Cg Liquidation Incorporated ....E...... 586 575-9800
  Warren *(G-17752)*
Finishers Unlimited Monroe Inc ....E...... 734 243-3502
  Monroe *(G-11540)*
Glw Finishing ....E...... 616 395-0112
  Holland *(G-8052)*
H & J Mfg Consulting Svcs Corp ....G...... 734 941-8314
  Romulus *(G-14282)*
Hj Manufacturing Inc ....F...... 906 233-1500
  Escanaba *(G-5076)*
Knape Industries Inc ....E...... 616 866-1651
  Rockford *(G-14174)*
Lincoln Industries ....G...... 989 736-6421
  Lincoln *(G-10036)*
Locpac Inc ....E...... 734 453-2300
  Plymouth *(G-13226)*
March Coatings Inc ....D...... 810 229-6464
  Brighton *(G-2024)*
Material Sciences Corporation ....F...... 734 207-4444
  Canton *(G-2490)*
Paint Work Incorporated ....F...... 586 759-6640
  Warren *(G-17952)*
Schroth Enterprises Inc ....E...... 586 759-4240
  Grosse Pointe Farms *(G-7540)*
Seaver Finishing Inc ....E...... 616 844-4360
  Grand Haven *(G-6358)*
Todd R Lrcque Pntg Wllcvring L ....G...... 989 252-9424
  Freeland *(G-6030)*

PAINTS & ADDITIVES

Benchmark Coating Systems LLC ....G...... 517 782-4061
  Ann Arbor *(G-399)*
Michigan Coating Products Inc ....G...... 616 456-8800
  Grand Rapids *(G-6987)*
Michigan Industrial Finishes ....F...... 248 553-7014
  Farmington Hills *(G-5318)*
Ncp Coatings Inc ....D...... 269 683-3377
  Niles *(G-12152)*
Nelson Paint Company Ala Inc ....G...... 906 774-5566
  Kingsford *(G-9515)*
Nelson Paint Company Mich Inc ....G...... 906 774-5566
  Iron Mountain *(G-8726)*
Northern Coatings & Chem Co ....E...... 906 863-2641
  Menominee *(G-11254)*
Peter-Lacke Usa LLC ....G...... 248 588-9400
  Troy *(G-17299)*
PPG Industries Inc ....E...... 616 846-4400
  Grand Haven *(G-6346)*
PPG Industries Inc ....F...... 248 641-2000
  Troy *(G-17309)*
Pro Coatings Inc ....E...... 616 887-8808
  Sparta *(G-15776)*

PAINTS & ALLIED PRODUCTS

Quantum Chemical LLC ....G...... 734 429-0033
  Livonia *(G-10379)*
Red Spot Westland Inc ....C...... 734 729-1913
  Westland *(G-18413)*
Repcolite Paints Inc ....D...... 616 396-5213
  Holland *(G-8179)*
Z Technologies Corporation ....E...... 313 937-0710
  Redford *(G-13787)*

PAINTS & ALLIED PRODUCTS

Akzo Nobel Coatings Inc ....E...... 248 451-6231
  Pontiac *(G-13346)*
Akzo Nobel Coatings Inc ....E...... 248 637-0400
  Troy *(G-16914)*
Akzo Nobel Coatings Inc ....E...... 248 451-6231
  Troy *(G-16915)*
Akzo Nobel Coatings Inc ....G...... 248 528-0715
  Troy *(G-16916)*
Allied Photochemical Inc ....F...... 810 364-6910
  Macomb *(G-10575)*
Alloying Surfaces Inc ....G...... 248 524-9200
  Troy *(G-16927)*
Axalta Coating Systems LLC ....G...... 586 846-4160
  Clinton Township *(G-3178)*
BASF Corporation ....G...... 269 668-3371
  Mattawan *(G-11162)*
Cass Polymers ....E...... 517 543-7510
  Charlotte *(G-2739)*
Chemetall US Inc ....G...... 517 787-4846
  Jackson *(G-8841)*
Coatings By Pcd Inc ....G...... 616 952-0032
  Kent City *(G-9429)*
Dhake Industries Inc ....E...... 734 420-0101
  Plymouth *(G-13156)*
Douglas Corp ....E...... 517 767-4112
  Tekonsha *(G-16522)*
Eftec North America LLC ....D...... 248 585-2200
  Taylor *(G-16410)*
Greenglow Products LLC ....G...... 248 827-1451
  Southfield *(G-15584)*
Innovative Solutions Tech Inc ....G...... 734 335-6665
  Canton *(G-2477)*
Instacoat Premium Product ....G...... 877 552-6724
  Oscoda *(G-12760)*
Instacoat Premium Products LLC ....G...... 586 770-1773
  Oscoda *(G-12761)*
Lakeshore Paints & Coating ....G...... 616 831-6990
  Grand Rapids *(G-6925)*
Lenawee Industrial Pnt Sup Inc ....G...... 734 729-8080
  Wayne *(G-18229)*
Magni-Industries Inc ....E...... 313 843-7855
  Detroit *(G-4416)*
Malach Group Plutonium Paint ....G...... 248 827-4844
  Southfield *(G-15641)*
Materials Processing Inc ....D...... 734 282-1888
  Riverview *(G-13880)*
Ncoc Inc ....E...... 248 548-5950
  Oak Park *(G-12632)*
Nippon Paint Auto Americas Inc ....G...... 248 365-1100
  Troy *(G-17278)*
Ot Dynamics LLC ....F...... 734 984-7022
  Flat Rock *(G-5624)*
Pacific Epoxy Polymers Inc ....G...... 616 949-1634
  Grand Rapids *(G-7066)*
Pittsburgh Glass Works LLC ....C...... 248 371-1700
  Rochester Hills *(G-14084)*
Portland Plastics Co ....F...... 517 647-4115
  Portland *(G-13640)*
PPG Industrial Coatings ....G...... 616 844-4391
  Grand Haven *(G-6345)*
PPG Industries Inc ....G...... 248 640-4174
  Macomb *(G-10626)*
PPG Industries Inc ....G...... 833 279-7021
  Norton Shores *(G-12351)*
PPG Industries Inc ....G...... 810 767-8030
  Flint *(G-5746)*
PPG Industries Inc ....G...... 248 625-7282
  Clarkston *(G-3058)*
PPG Industries Inc ....G...... 517 784-6138
  Jackson *(G-8989)*
PPG Industries Inc ....G...... 248 478-1300
  Novi *(G-12510)*
PPG Industries Inc ....G...... 586 566-3789
  Shelby Township *(G-15307)*
PPG Industries Inc ....G...... 248 357-4817
  Southfield *(G-15678)*
PPG Industries Inc ....G...... 734 287-2110
  Southfield *(G-15679)*
PPG Industries Inc ....G...... 586 755-2011
  Warren *(G-17970)*

PAINTS & ALLIED PRODUCTS — PRODUCT SECTION

PPG Industries Inc .... G 248 683-8052
  Waterford *(G-18156)*
Richter Precision Inc .... E 586 465-0500
  Fraser *(G-5989)*
Riverside Spline & Gear Inc .... E 810 765-8302
  Marine City *(G-10965)*
Rolled Alloys Inc .... D 734 847-0561
  Temperance *(G-16547)*
Rollie Williams Paint Spot .... G 269 321-3174
  Portage *(G-13600)*
S P Kish Industries Inc .... E 517 543-2650
  Charlotte *(G-2766)*
Shadvin Industries LLC .... G 509 263-7128
  Bay City *(G-1400)*
Single Source Inc .... G 765 825-4111
  Flat Rock *(G-5630)*
Statistical Processed Products .... F 586 792-6900
  Clinton Township *(G-3363)*
Tru Custom Blends Inc .... F 810 407-6207
  Flint *(G-5785)*
Ziebart International Corp .... E 248 588-4100
  Troy *(G-17460)*

PAINTS, VARNISHES & SPLYS WHOLESALERS

Aactus Inc .... G 734 425-1212
  Livonia *(G-10096)*
Wall Pro Painting .... G 248 632-8525
  Royal Oak *(G-14590)*

PAINTS, VARNISHES & SPLYS, WHOLESALE: Colors & Pigments

Chromatech Inc .... F 734 451-1230
  Canton *(G-2449)*

PAINTS, VARNISHES & SPLYS, WHOLESALE: Paints

Ventra Ionia Main LLC .... A 616 597-3220
  Ionia *(G-8693)*

PAINTS: Oil Or Alkyd Vehicle Or Water Thinned

Coat It Inc of Detroit .... G 313 869-8500
  Detroit *(G-4096)*
Helen Inc .... F 616 698-8102
  Caledonia *(G-2378)*
Palmer Paint Products Inc .... D 248 588-4500
  Troy *(G-17295)*
Polymer Inc .... D 248 353-3035
  Southfield *(G-15677)*
Port City Paints Mfg Inc .... G 231 726-5911
  Muskegon *(G-11895)*
United Paint and Chemical Corp .... D 248 353-3035
  Southfield *(G-15732)*

PAINTS: Waterproof

Nelson Paint Co of Mich Inc .... G 906 774-5566
  Kingsford *(G-9514)*

PALLET REPAIR SVCS

Mobile Pallet Service Inc .... E 269 792-4200
  Wayland *(G-18199)*

PALLETIZERS & DEPALLETIZERS

Automated Machine Systems Inc .... E 616 662-1309
  Jenison *(G-9046)*
Mollers North America Inc .... D 616 942-6504
  Grand Rapids *(G-7022)*

PALLETS

Artists Pallet .... G 248 889-2440
  Highland *(G-7882)*
Baby Pallet .... G 248 210-3851
  Waterford *(G-18103)*
County Line Pallet .... G 231 834-8416
  Kent City *(G-9430)*
Jerrys Pallets .... G 734 242-1577
  Monroe *(G-11552)*
Kerry J McNeely .... G 734 776-1928
  Livonia *(G-10265)*
Marion Pallet .... G 231 743-6124
  Marion *(G-10974)*
Precision Pallet LLC .... G 252 943-5193
  Charlevoix *(G-2729)*
Union Pallet & Cont Co Inc .... E 517 279-4888
  Coldwater *(G-3459)*

PALLETS & SKIDS: Wood

AAR Manufacturing Inc .... E 231 779-8800
  Cadillac *(G-2306)*
Complete Packaging Inc .... D 734 241-2794
  Monroe *(G-11534)*
Delta Containers Inc .... C 810 742-2730
  Bay City *(G-1342)*
Demeester Wood Products Inc .... F 616 677-5995
  Coopersville *(G-3685)*
Diversified Pdts & Svcs LLC .... G 616 836-6600
  Holland *(G-8014)*
G & D Wood Products Inc .... G 517 254-4463
  Camden *(G-2422)*
I Pallet LLC .... G 586 625-2238
  Sterling Heights *(G-16045)*
Las Tortugas Pallet Co .... G 313 283-3279
  Lincoln Park *(G-10051)*
Lightning Technologies Inc .... E 248 572-6700
  Oxford *(G-12896)*
Luberda Wood Products Inc .... G 989 876-4334
  Omer *(G-12696)*
Matthews Mill Inc .... F 989 257-3271
  South Branch *(G-15396)*
Michael Chris Storms .... G 231 263-7516
  Kingsley *(G-9525)*
Midwest Heat Treat Inc .... E 616 395-9763
  Holland *(G-8148)*
Mobile Pallet Service Inc .... E 269 792-4200
  Wayland *(G-18199)*
Ottawa Forest Products Inc .... G 906 932-9701
  Ironwood *(G-8769)*
Paliot Solutions LLC .... G 616 648-5939
  Plymouth *(G-13260)*
Process Systems Inc .... E 586 757-5711
  Warren *(G-17977)*
R Andrews Pallet Co Inc .... G 616 677-3270
  Marne *(G-10998)*
Sfi Acquisition Inc .... E 248 471-1500
  Farmington Hills *(G-5377)*
Vocational Strategies Inc .... G 906 482-6142
  Calumet *(G-2415)*
World of Pallets and Trucking .... G 313 899-2000
  Detroit *(G-4691)*

PALLETS: Metal

Independent Machine Co Inc .... E 906 428-4524
  Escanaba *(G-5077)*
Keller Tool Ltd .... F 734 425-4500
  Livonia *(G-10264)*
O Keller Tool Engrg Co LLC .... D 734 425-4500
  Livonia *(G-10349)*
Sfi Acquisition Inc .... E 248 471-1500
  Farmington Hills *(G-5377)*

PALLETS: Plastic

Huhtamaki Inc .... D 989 633-8900
  Coleman *(G-3467)*
Pioneer Automotive Inc .... F 586 758-7730
  Sterling Heights *(G-16127)*
Plastipak Packaging Inc .... G 734 326-6184
  Westland *(G-18406)*

PALLETS: Wood & Metal Combination

Vaive Wood Products Co .... E 586 949-4900
  Macomb *(G-10648)*

PALLETS: Wooden

Acme Pallet Inc .... E 616 738-6452
  Holland *(G-7956)*
Action Pallets Inc .... G 248 557-9017
  Lathrup Village *(G-9973)*
Aj Pallets .... F 616 875-8900
  Zeeland *(G-18989)*
Akers Wood Products Inc .... G 269 962-3802
  Battle Creek *(G-1182)*
All American Container Corp .... F 586 949-0000
  Macomb *(G-10573)*
All Size Pallets .... E 810 721-1999
  Imlay City *(G-8626)*
American Pallet Company LLC .... G 231 834-5056
  Grant *(G-7426)*
Anayas Pallets & Transport Inc .... F 313 843-6570
  Detroit *(G-4018)*
Anbren Inc .... G 269 944-5066
  Benton Harbor *(G-1529)*
Auto Pallets-Boxes Inc .... F 248 559-7744
  Lathrup Village *(G-9975)*
Auto Pallets-Boxes Inc .... G 734 782-1110
  Flat Rock *(G-5614)*
Black River Pallet Company .... E 616 772-6211
  Zeeland *(G-19000)*
Breiten Box & Packaging Co Inc .... G 586 469-0800
  Harrison Township *(G-7690)*
Brindley Lumber & Pallet Co .... G 989 345-3497
  Lupton *(G-10561)*
Bunker & Sons Sawmill LLC .... G 989 983-2715
  Vanderbilt *(G-17568)*
Burnrite Pellet Corporation .... G 989 429-1067
  Clare *(G-2974)*
C & J Pallets Inc .... G 517 263-7415
  Adrian *(G-55)*
C & K Box Company Inc .... F 517 784-1779
  Jackson *(G-8830)*
C&D Pallets Inc .... G 517 285-5228
  Eagle *(G-4851)*
Cannonsburg Wood Products Inc .... G 616 866-4459
  Rockford *(G-14162)*
Caveman Pallets LLC .... G 616 675-7270
  Conklin *(G-3660)*
Curtis Country Connection LLC .... G 517 368-5542
  Camden *(G-2420)*
D T Fowler Mfg Co Inc .... G 810 245-9336
  Lapeer *(G-9925)*
Delta Packaging International .... E 517 321-6548
  Lansing *(G-9685)*
Discount Pallets .... G 616 453-5455
  Grand Rapids *(G-6650)*
DRYE Custom Pallets Inc .... E 313 381-2681
  Melvindale *(G-11199)*
Envirnmntal Pllet Slutions Inc .... F 616 283-1784
  Zeeland *(G-19018)*
Fair & Square Pallet & Lbr Co .... G 989 727-3949
  Hubbard Lake *(G-8546)*
Four Way Pallet Service .... G 734 782-5914
  Flat Rock *(G-5621)*
Golden Eagle Pallets LLC .... F 616 233-0970
  Wyoming *(G-18875)*
Gonzalez Jr Pallets LLC .... G 616 885-0201
  Grand Rapids *(G-6748)*
Gonzalez Universal Pallets LLC .... G 616 243-5524
  Grand Rapids *(G-6749)*
Great Lakes Pallet Inc .... G 989 883-9220
  Sebewaing *(G-15140)*
Great Northern Lumber Mich LLC .... G 989 736-6192
  Lincoln *(G-10034)*
H & M Pallet LLC .... F 231 821-8800
  Holton *(G-8338)*
Hills Crate Mill Inc .... G 616 761-3555
  Belding *(G-1451)*
Hillsdale Pallet LLC .... F 517 254-4777
  Hillsdale *(G-7937)*
Holland Pallet Repair Inc .... E 616 875-8642
  Holland *(G-8080)*
Hugo Brothers Pallet Mfg .... G 989 684-5564
  Kawkawlin *(G-9417)*
Industrial Packaging Corp .... E 248 677-0084
  Berkley *(G-1628)*
J & G Pallets Inc .... G 313 921-0222
  Detroit *(G-4331)*
Jarvis Saw Mill Inc .... G 231 861-2078
  Shelby *(G-15150)*
Kamps Inc .... E 313 381-2681
  Detroit *(G-4349)*
Kamps Inc .... D 616 453-9676
  Grand Rapids *(G-6878)*
Kamps Inc .... E 517 645-2800
  Potterville *(G-13646)*
Kamps Inc .... E 734 281-3300
  Taylor *(G-16433)*
Kamps Inc .... E 269 683-6372
  Niles *(G-12140)*
Kamps Inc .... E 269 342-8113
  Kalamazoo *(G-9251)*
Krauter Forest Products LLC .... F 815 317-6561
  Reed City *(G-13794)*
Lakeland Pallets Inc .... E 616 949-9515
  Grand Rapids *(G-6924)*
Less Pay Pallets Inc .... G 586 649-3800
  Harrison Township *(G-7706)*
Maple Valley Pallet Co .... F 231 228-6641
  Maple City *(G-10944)*
Matelski Lumber Company .... E 231 549-2780
  Boyne Falls *(G-1909)*
Metzger Sawmill .... G 269 963-3022
  Battle Creek *(G-1273)*

PRODUCT SECTION

PAPER: Building, Insulating & Packaging

Michigan Pallet Inc .... F 989 865-9915
  Saint Charles *(G-14805)*
Mid West Pallet .... G 810 919-3072
  Burton *(G-2240)*
Nelson Company .... G 517 788-6117
  Jackson *(G-8976)*
Northern Pallet .... G 989 386-7556
  Clare *(G-2991)*
Pallet Man .... G 269 274-8825
  Springfield *(G-15873)*
Pallet Pros LLC .... G 586 864-3353
  Center Line *(G-2684)*
Patchwood Products Inc .... G 989 742-2605
  Hillman *(G-7915)*
Patchwood Products Inc .... G 989 742-2605
  Lachine *(G-9533)*
Pink Pallet LLC .... G 586 873-2982
  Grand Blanc *(G-6256)*
Prairie Wood Products Inc .... F 269 659-1163
  Sturgis *(G-16319)*
Premier Pallet Inc .... F 269 483-8000
  White Pigeon *(G-18485)*
Quality Pallet Inc .... G 231 788-5161
  Muskegon *(G-11901)*
Quality Pallets LLC .... F 231 825-8361
  Mc Bain *(G-11186)*
Rochester Pallet .... G 248 266-1094
  Rochester Hills *(G-14102)*
Rose Acres Pallets LLC .... G 989 268-3074
  Vestaburg *(G-17595)*
Rose Acres Tallets .... G 989 268-3074
  Vestaburg *(G-17596)*
Ross Pallet Co .... G 810 966-4945
  Port Huron *(G-13524)*
Royal Pallets Inc .... E 616 261-2884
  Grandville *(G-7415)*
Scotts Enterprises Inc .... F 989 275-5011
  Roscommon *(G-14356)*
Spartan Pallet LLC .... G 586 291-8898
  Clinton Township *(G-3361)*
Stoutenburg Inc .... E 810 648-4400
  Sandusky *(G-15068)*
Tk Enterprises Inc .... F 989 865-9915
  Saint Charles *(G-14810)*
Tommy Joe Reed .... G 989 291-5768
  Sheridan *(G-15384)*
WB Pallets Inc .... E 616 669-3000
  Hudsonville *(G-8615)*
White Pallet Chair .... G 989 424-8771
  Clare *(G-3001)*

PANEL & DISTRIBUTION BOARDS & OTHER RELATED APPARATUS

S Main Company LLC .... E 248 960-1540
  Wixom *(G-18747)*

PANEL & DISTRIBUTION BOARDS: Electric

Java Manufacturing Inc .... G 616 784-3873
  Comstock Park *(G-3613)*
Systems Control Inc .... A 906 774-0440
  Iron Mountain *(G-8735)*

PANELS, FLAT: Plastic

Armoured Rsstnce McHanisms Inc .... F 517 223-7618
  Fowlerville *(G-5832)*
Installations Inc .... F 313 532-9000
  Redford *(G-13740)*

PANELS: Building, Metal

I B P Inc .... F 248 588-4710
  Clarkston *(G-3041)*
Innovate Industries Inc .... G 586 558-8990
  Warren *(G-17865)*
Porter Corp .... G 616 399-1963
  Holland *(G-8167)*

PANELS: Building, Plastic, NEC

Best Impressions Inc .... G 313 839-9000
  Fraser *(G-5904)*
Concord Industrial Corporation .... G 248 646-9225
  Bloomfield Hills *(G-1810)*
Fiberglass Technology Inds Inc .... G 740 335-9400
  Cadillac *(G-2329)*
Reklein Plastics Incorporated .... G 586 739-8850
  Sterling Heights *(G-16145)*

PANELS: Building, Wood

Midwest Panel Systems Inc .... F 517 486-4844
  Blissfield *(G-1770)*

PANELS: Switchboard, Slate

Mis Controls Inc .... E 586 339-3900
  Rochester Hills *(G-14064)*

PANELS: Wood

Louisiana-Pacific Corporation .... G 906 293-3265
  Newberry *(G-12092)*
Precision Framing Systems Inc .... G 704 588-6680
  Taylor *(G-16458)*
Richelieu America Ltd .... E 586 264-1240
  Sterling Heights *(G-16151)*
Ufp Sauk Rapids LLC .... E 320 259-5190
  Grand Rapids *(G-7292)*

PAPER & BOARD: Die-cut

Accu-Shape Die Cutting Inc .... E 810 230-2445
  Flint *(G-5634)*
Bradford Company .... C 616 399-3000
  Holland *(G-7981)*
Cadillac Prsentation Solutions .... E 248 288-9777
  Troy *(G-16994)*
Classic Container Corporation .... C 734 853-3000
  Livonia *(G-10159)*
Delta Containers Inc .... C 810 742-2730
  Bay City *(G-1342)*
Edgewater Apartments .... G 517 663-8123
  Eaton Rapids *(G-4962)*
Graphic Specialties Inc .... G 616 247-0060
  Grand Rapids *(G-6783)*
Hamblin Company .... E 517 423-7491
  Bloomfield Hills *(G-1826)*
Hexon Corporation .... E 248 585-7585
  Farmington Hills *(G-5259)*
Industrial Imprntng & Die Ctng .... G 586 778-9470
  Eastpointe *(G-4937)*
Jacobsen Industries Inc .... D 734 591-6111
  Livonia *(G-10255)*
Macarthur Corp .... E 810 606-1777
  Grand Blanc *(G-6252)*
Michigan Paper Die Inc .... E 313 873-0404
  Detroit *(G-4451)*
Oliver Packaging and Eqp Co .... D 616 356-2950
  Walker *(G-17645)*
Russell R Peters Co LLC .... G 989 732-0660
  Gaylord *(G-6157)*
Trim Pac Inc .... G 269 279-9498
  Three Rivers *(G-16589)*

PAPER CLIPS: Metal

Jon Bee Distribution LLC .... G 248 846-0491
  Pontiac *(G-13387)*

PAPER CONVERTING

Fibers of Kalamazoo Inc .... E 269 344-3122
  Kalamazoo *(G-9186)*
Fineeye Color Solutions Inc .... G 616 988-6119
  Muskegon *(G-11817)*
Progressive Paper Corp .... G 269 279-6320
  Three Rivers *(G-16582)*
Shepherd Speciality Papers Inc .... G 269 629-8001
  Richland *(G-13829)*
Sks Industries Inc .... F 517 546-1117
  Howell *(G-8518)*
Trim Pac Inc .... G 269 279-9498
  Three Rivers *(G-16589)*
Walters Seed Co LLC .... F 616 355-7333
  Holland *(G-8241)*

PAPER MANUFACTURERS: Exc Newsprint

American Twisting Company .... E 269 637-8581
  South Haven *(G-15398)*
Anchor Bay Manufacturing Corp .... C 586 949-4040
  Chesterfield *(G-2841)*
Cadillac Products Inc .... F 989 766-2294
  Rogers City *(G-14208)*
Cascades Enviropac HPM LLC .... C 616 243-4870
  Grand Rapids *(G-6557)*
Domtar Industries Inc .... D 810 982-0191
  Port Huron *(G-13469)*
Dunn Paper Holdings Inc .... G 810 984-5521
  Port Huron *(G-13472)*
Gold Bond Building Pdts LLC .... E 989 756-2741
  National City *(G-11959)*
Handy Wacks Corporation .... E 616 887-8268
  Sparta *(G-15766)*
International Paper Company .... G 269 273-8461
  Three Rivers *(G-16576)*
Meca Systeme USA .... G 616 294-1439
  Holland *(G-8141)*
Menominee Acquisition Corp .... C 906 863-5595
  Menominee *(G-11246)*
Neenah Paper Inc .... B 906 387-2700
  Munising *(G-11752)*
Northstar Sourcing LLC .... G 313 782-4749
  Troy *(G-17281)*
Otsego Paper Inc .... D 269 692-6141
  Otsego *(G-12793)*
Portage Paper Co Inc .... C 616 345-7131
  Kalamazoo *(G-9298)*
Recycled Paperboard Pdts Corp .... G 313 579-6608
  Detroit *(G-4558)*
Star Paper Converters Inc .... F 313 963-5200
  Detroit *(G-4606)*
Verso Corporation .... A 906 786-1660
  Escanaba *(G-5105)*
Verso Paper Holding LLC .... F 906 779-3200
  Quinnesec *(G-13678)*
Verso Quinnesec LLC .... G 877 447-2737
  Quinnesec *(G-13679)*
Verso Quinnesec Rep LLC .... G 906 779-3200
  Quinnesec *(G-13680)*

PAPER PRDTS

W H Green & Associates .... G 616 682-5202
  Grand Rapids *(G-7322)*

PAPER PRDTS: Book Covers

B & B Entps Prtg Cnvrting Inc .... G 313 891-9840
  Detroit *(G-4037)*

PAPER PRDTS: Infant & Baby Prdts

Happy Bums .... G 616 987-3159
  Lowell *(G-10502)*
Kimberly-Clark Corporation .... G 586 949-1649
  Macomb *(G-10609)*
Kimberly-Clark Corporation .... G 810 985-1830
  Port Huron *(G-13494)*

PAPER PRDTS: Sanitary

AJM Packaging Corporation .... D 313 842-7530
  Detroit *(G-3993)*
Chambers Ottawa Inc .... G 231 238-2122
  Cheboygan *(G-2781)*

PAPER PRDTS: Sanitary Tissue Paper

Kimberly-Clark Corporation .... G 586 949-1649
  Macomb *(G-10609)*
Kimberly-Clark Corporation .... G 810 985-1830
  Port Huron *(G-13494)*
Thetford Corporation .... C 734 769-6000
  Ann Arbor *(G-688)*

PAPER PRDTS: Toweling Tissue

Ace-Tex Enterprises Inc .... E 313 834-4000
  Detroit *(G-3982)*
Sanitor Mfg Co .... F 269 327-3001
  Portage *(G-13605)*

PAPER: Adhesive

Argent Tape & Label Inc .... E 734 582-9956
  Plymouth *(G-13125)*
Lepages 2000 Inc .... G 416 357-0041
  Melvindale *(G-11203)*
Michigan Shippers Supply Inc .... F 616 935-6680
  Spring Lake *(G-15835)*
Oliver Packaging and Eqp Co .... D 616 356-2950
  Walker *(G-17645)*

PAPER: Book

French Paper Company .... D 269 683-1100
  Niles *(G-12131)*

PAPER: Building, Insulating & Packaging

Everest Manufacturing Inc .... F 313 401-2608
  Farmington Hills *(G-5238)*

PAPER: Business Form

Esv Precision LLC ....G........ 810 441-0953
  Imlay City (G-8631)

PAPER: Cardboard

Cardboard Prophets ....G........ 517 512-1267
  Eaton Rapids (G-4957)
Cardboard Robot Visuals LLC ....G........ 231 577-8710
  Buckley (G-2206)
M & J Entp Grnd Rapids LLC ....F........ 616 485-9775
  Comstock Park (G-3620)

PAPER: Coated & Laminated, NEC

Alpha Data Business Forms Inc ....G........ 248 540-5930
  Birmingham (G-1718)
Cummins Label Company ....E........ 269 345-3386
  Kalamazoo (G-9159)
Dunn Paper Inc ....G........ 810 984-5521
  Menominee (G-11232)
Dunn Paper Inc ....F........ 810 984-5521
  Port Huron (G-13470)
Dunn Paper Holdings Inc ....G........ 810 984-5521
  Port Huron (G-13472)
Impact Label Corporation ....D........ 269 381-4280
  Galesburg (G-6079)
Lawson Printers Inc ....E........ 269 965-0525
  Battle Creek (G-1267)
Litsenberger Print Shop ....G........ 906 482-3903
  Houghton (G-8386)
Lowry Holding Company Inc ....C........ 810 229-7200
  Brighton (G-2023)
Macarthur Corp ....E........ 810 606-1777
  Grand Blanc (G-6252)
Macarthur Corp ....G........ 810 744-1380
  Flint (G-5729)
McCray Press ....F........ 989 792-8681
  Saginaw (G-14689)
Mead Westvaco Paper Div ....G........ 906 233-2362
  Escanaba (G-5082)
Plasti-Fab Inc ....E........ 248 543-1415
  Ferndale (G-5579)
Qrp Inc ....G........ 989 496-2955
  Midland (G-11405)
Shawmut LLC ....G........ 810 987-2222
  Port Huron (G-13526)
Stewart Sutherland Inc ....C........ 269 649-0530
  Vicksburg (G-17613)
Technology MGT & Budgt Dept ....G........ 517 322-1897
  Lansing (G-9899)
Witchcraft Tape Products Inc ....D........ 269 468-3399
  Coloma (G-3485)

PAPER: Newsprint

Resolute FP US Inc ....G........ 877 547-2737
  Menominee (G-11258)

PAPER: Packaging

E B Eddy Paper Inc ....B........ 810 982-0191
  Port Huron (G-13473)
Mextor Disposable LLC ....G........ 313 921-6860
  Detroit (G-4441)
North Coast Paper & Packg LLC ....G........ 586 648-7600
  New Baltimore (G-11990)
Rizzo Packaging Inc ....E........ 269 685-5808
  Plainwell (G-13093)

PAPER: Printer

Eagle Ridge Paper Ltd ....F........ 248 376-9503
  Romulus (G-14269)
Vision Solutions Inc ....G........ 810 695-9569
  Grand Blanc (G-6267)

PAPER: Waxed, Made From Purchased Materials

Stewart Sutherland Inc ....C........ 269 649-0530
  Vicksburg (G-17613)

PAPER: Wrapping & Packaging

Anchor Bay Manufacturing Corp ....F........ 586 949-1195
  Chesterfield (G-2840)
Kolossos Printing Inc ....G........ 734 741-1600
  Ann Arbor (G-541)
Package Design & Mfg Inc ....E........ 248 486-4390
  Brighton (G-2046)

Pure Pulp Products Inc ....A........ 269 385-5050
  Kalamazoo (G-9309)

PAPERBOARD

Anchor Bay Packaging Corp ....G........ 586 949-1500
  Chesterfield (G-2843)
Classic Container Corporation ....C........ 734 853-3000
  Livonia (G-10159)
Coveris ....C........ 269 964-1130
  Battle Creek (G-1212)
Fibre Converters Inc ....E........ 269 279-1700
  Constantine (G-3666)
Kentwood Packaging Corporation ....D........ 616 698-9000
  Walker (G-17642)
Lakeland Paper Corporation ....E........ 269 651-5474
  White Pigeon (G-18481)
Lydall Performance Mtls US Inc ....G........ 248 596-2800
  Northville (G-12236)
MRC Industries Inc ....E........ 269 343-0747
  Kalamazoo (G-9278)
Packaging Specialties Inc ....E........ 586 473-6703
  Romulus (G-14315)
Rizzo Packaging Inc ....E........ 269 685-5808
  Plainwell (G-13093)
Sonoco Products Company ....G........ 586 978-0808
  Sterling Heights (G-16182)
Sonoco Products Company ....G........ 269 408-0182
  Saint Joseph (G-14961)
South Park Sales & Mfg Inc ....G........ 313 381-7579
  Dearborn (G-3899)

PAPERBOARD CONVERTING

Manchester Industries Inc VA ....E........ 269 496-2715
  Mendon (G-11219)
Str Company ....G........ 517 206-6058
  Grass Lake (G-7446)
Tru Blu Industries LLC ....G........ 269 684-4989
  Niles (G-12172)

PAPERBOARD PRDTS: Coated & Treated Board

Hydrolake Inc ....G........ 231 825-2233
  Mc Bain (G-11182)
Utility Supply and Cnstr Co ....G........ 231 832-2297
  Reed City (G-13802)

PAPERBOARD PRDTS: Food Board, Special

Everything Edbl Trats For Stne ....G........ 313 725-0118
  Detroit (G-4220)

PAPERBOARD PRDTS: Packaging Board

Cascade Paper Converters LLC ....F........ 616 974-9165
  Grand Rapids (G-6555)
Display Pack Disc Vdh Inc ....G........ 616 451-3061
  Cedar Springs (G-2650)

PAPERBOARD: Boxboard

Campbell Industrial Force LLC ....E........ 989 427-0011
  Edmore (G-4990)

PAPERBOARD: Chipboard

Trim Pac Inc ....G........ 269 279-9498
  Three Rivers (G-16589)

PAPERBOARD: Coated

Handy Wacks Corporation ....G........ 616 887-8268
  Sparta (G-15767)
Ox Paperboard Michigan LLC ....D........ 800 345-8881
  Constantine (G-3674)

PARTICLEBOARD: Laminated, Plastic

Bourne Industries Inc ....E........ 989 743-3461
  Corunna (G-3705)

PARTITIONS & FIXTURES: Except Wood

Allen Pattern of Michigan ....F........ 269 963-4131
  Battle Creek (G-1184)
Borroughs LLC ....D........ 269 342-0161
  Kalamazoo (G-9139)
Creative Solutions Group Inc ....D........ 248 288-9700
  Clawson (G-3092)
Creative Solutions Group Inc ....G........ 734 425-2257
  Redford (G-13727)

Dads Panels Inc ....G........ 810 245-1871
  Lapeer (G-9926)
Dee-Blast Corporation ....F........ 269 428-2400
  Stevensville (G-16246)
Ferrante Manufacturing Co ....E........ 313 571-1111
  Detroit (G-4231)
Fixture Max Inc ....G........ 517 376-6421
  Howell (G-8455)
G & W Display Fixtures Inc ....E........ 517 369-7110
  Bronson (G-2112)
Greenfield Cabinetry Inc ....F........ 586 759-3300
  Warren (G-17839)
Harbor Industries Inc ....D........ 231 547-3280
  Charlevoix (G-2717)
JMJ Inc ....F........ 269 948-2828
  Hastings (G-7801)
Loudon Steel Inc ....E........ 989 871-9353
  Millington (G-11502)
Millerknoll Inc ....A........ 616 654-3000
  Zeeland (G-19056)
Pinnacle Cabinet Company Inc ....E........ 989 772-3866
  Mount Pleasant (G-11731)
Signature Wall Solutions Inc ....F........ 616 366-4242
  Midland (G-11417)
Structural Plastics Inc ....E........ 810 953-9400
  Holly (G-8296)

PARTITIONS: Solid Fiber, Made From Purchased Materials

Bradford Company ....C........ 616 399-3000
  Holland (G-7981)

PARTITIONS: Wood & Fixtures

Bay Wood Homes Inc ....F........ 989 245-4156
  Fenton (G-5456)
Bennett Wood Specialties Inc ....F........ 616 772-6683
  Zeeland (G-18996)
Design Fabrications Inc ....D........ 248 597-0988
  Madison Heights (G-10705)
European Cabinet Mfg Co ....E........ 586 445-8909
  Roseville (G-14406)
G & G Wood & Supply Inc ....E........ 586 293-0450
  Roseville (G-14408)
G & W Display Fixtures Inc ....E........ 517 369-7110
  Bronson (G-2112)
Gast Cabinet Co ....G........ 269 422-1587
  Baroda (G-1162)
H L F Furniture Incorporated ....E........ 734 697-3000
  Van Buren Twp (G-17528)
Harbor Industries Inc ....G........ 616 842-5330
  Grand Haven (G-6313)
Harbor Industries Inc ....D........ 231 547-3280
  Charlevoix (G-2717)
Knape & Vogt Manufacturing Co ....A........ 616 459-3311
  Grand Rapids (G-6900)
Kurtis Mfg & Distrg Corp ....E........ 734 522-7600
  Livonia (G-10270)
M and G Laminated Products ....G........ 517 784-4974
  Jackson (G-8938)
Michigan Maple Block Company ....D........ 231 347-4170
  Petoskey (G-13006)
Millennm-The Inside Sltion Inc ....F........ 248 645-9005
  Farmington Hills (G-5323)
Millerknoll Inc ....A........ 616 654-3000
  Zeeland (G-19056)
Owens Building Co Inc ....E........ 989 835-1293
  Midland (G-11401)
Pageant Homes Inc ....G........ 517 694-0431
  Holt (G-8324)
PCI Industries Inc ....D........ 248 542-2570
  Oak Park (G-12637)
Programmed Products Corp ....D........ 248 348-7755
  Novi (G-12517)
Sterling Millwork Inc ....D........ 248 427-1400
  Farmington Hills (G-5389)
Van Zee Corporation ....E........ 616 245-9000
  Grand Rapids (G-7306)
W S Townsend Company ....C........ 269 781-5131
  Marshall (G-11078)

PARTS: Metal

B & G Products Inc ....F........ 616 698-9050
  Grand Rapids (G-6488)
Diversfied Prcurement Svcs LLC ....G........ 248 821-1147
  Ferndale (G-5548)
Fabrilaser Mfg LLC ....E........ 269 789-9490
  Marshall (G-11057)
L Barge & Associates Inc ....E........ 248 582-3430
  Ferndale (G-5563)

PRODUCT SECTION

PET SPLYS

Marix Specialty Welding Co ....E......	586 754-9685
Warren *(G-17916)*	
RC Metal Products Inc ....G......	616 696-1694
Sand Lake *(G-15053)*	
Rss Baker LLC ....E......	616 844-5429
Grand Haven *(G-6356)*	
Tower Defense & Aerospace LLC ....E......	248 675-6000
Livonia *(G-10439)*	

PARTY & SPECIAL EVENT PLANNING SVCS

Delicate Creations Inc ....G...... 313 406-6268
  Dearborn Heights *(G-3923)*

PATTERNS: Indl

Advantage Industries Inc ....E...... 616 669-2400
  Jenison *(G-9042)*
Al-Craft Design & Engrg Inc....................G...... 248 589-3827
  Troy *(G-16918)*
Allen Pattern of Michigan ....F...... 269 963-4131
  Battle Creek *(G-1184)*
Arbor Gage & Tooling Inc.......................E...... 616 454-8266
  Grand Rapids *(G-6466)*
Associate Mfg Inc ....G...... 989 345-0025
  West Branch *(G-18325)*
Aurora Cad CAM Inc ....F...... 810 678-2128
  Metamora *(G-11276)*
Bespro Pattern Inc ....E...... 586 268-6970
  Madison Heights *(G-10681)*
Big Dome Holdings Inc............................D...... 616 735-6228
  Grand Rapids *(G-6507)*
Briggs Industries Inc ....E...... 586 749-5191
  Chesterfield *(G-2852)*
C & D Enterprises Inc ....E...... 248 373-0011
  Burton *(G-2229)*
C & D Gage Inc ....G...... 517 548-7049
  Howell *(G-8433)*
Champion Charter Sls & Svc Inc ....E...... 906 779-2300
  Iron Mountain *(G-8719)*
Cobra Patterns & Models Inc ....E...... 248 588-2669
  Madison Heights *(G-10694)*
Complete Prototype Svcs Inc ....C...... 586 690-8897
  Clinton Township *(G-3207)*
Crescent Pattern Company ....E...... 248 541-1052
  Oak Park *(G-12602)*
Decca Pattern Co Inc ....G...... 586 775-8450
  Roseville *(G-14395)*
Dhs Inc ....G...... 313 724-6566
  Detroit *(G-4174)*
Elmhirst Industries Inc ....E...... 586 731-8663
  Sterling Heights *(G-16002)*
Gage Pattern & Model Inc ....D...... 248 361-6609
  Madison Heights *(G-10729)*
GM Bassett Pattern Inc ....G...... 248 477-6454
  Farmington Hills *(G-5253)*
Grand Rapids Carvers Inc ....E...... 616 538-0022
  Grand Rapids *(G-6754)*
Holland Pattern Co ....G...... 616 396-6348
  Holland *(G-8082)*
Homestead Tool and Machine ....E...... 989 465-6182
  Coleman *(G-3465)*
Husite Engineering Co Inc ....F...... 248 588-0337
  Clinton Township *(G-3255)*
Industrial Model Inc ....G...... 586 254-0450
  Auburn Hills *(G-939)*
J J Pattern & Castings Inc ....G...... 248 543-7119
  Madison Heights *(G-10751)*
Jay/Enn Corporation ....D...... 248 588-2393
  Troy *(G-17182)*
L & L Pattern Inc ....G...... 231 733-2646
  Muskegon *(G-11853)*
Majestic Pattern Company Inc.................G...... 313 892-5800
  Detroit *(G-4417)*
Mantissa Industries Inc ....G...... 517 694-2260
  Holt *(G-8317)*
Marten Models & Molds Inc ....F...... 586 293-2260
  Fraser *(G-5962)*
Mentor Enterprises Inc ....G...... 269 483-7675
  White Pigeon *(G-18483)*
Metro Technologies Ltd...........................D...... 248 528-9240
  Troy *(G-17254)*
Michalski Enterprises Inc ....E...... 517 703-0777
  Lansing *(G-9716)*
Michigan Pattern Works Inc ....E...... 616 245-9259
  Grand Rapids *(G-6993)*
National Pattern Inc ....E...... 989 755-6274
  Saginaw *(G-14706)*
Northern Sierra Corporation ....G...... 989 777-4784
  Saginaw *(G-14722)*
Paragon Molds Corporation ....E...... 586 294-7630
  Fraser *(G-5974)*
Parker Pattern Inc ....F...... 586 466-5900
  Mount Clemens *(G-11651)*
Parker Tooling & Design Inc ....F...... 616 791-1080
  Grand Rapids *(G-7071)*
Portenga Manufacturing Company ....G...... 616 846-2691
  Ferrysburg *(G-5604)*
Prompt Pattern Inc ....F...... 586 759-2030
  Warren *(G-17979)*
Proto-Cast Inc ....E...... 313 565-5400
  Inkster *(G-8672)*
Ravenna Pattern & Mfg ....E...... 231 853-2264
  Ravenna *(G-13693)*
Rehau Incorporated ....G...... 269 651-7845
  Sturgis *(G-16321)*
Sbti Company ....D...... 586 726-5756
  Shelby Township *(G-15323)*
Simpsons Enterprises Inc.......................F...... 269 279-7237
  Three Rivers *(G-16584)*
Tedson Industries Inc ....F...... 248 588-9230
  Troy *(G-17387)*
Tri-Star Tooling LLC ....E...... 586 978-0435
  Sterling Heights *(G-16210)*
U S Pattern Company Inc ....E...... 586 727-2896
  Richmond *(G-13847)*
Vans Pattern Corp ....F...... 616 364-9483
  Marne *(G-11002)*
Wing Pattern Inc ....G...... 248 588-1121
  Sterling Heights *(G-16232)*
Wolverine Products Inc ....F...... 586 792-3740
  Clinton Township *(G-3389)*

PAVING MATERIALS: Prefabricated, Concrete

Asphalt Paving Inc ....E...... 231 733-1409
  Muskegon *(G-11773)*

PAWN SHOPS

Novus Corporation ....F...... 248 545-8600
  Warren *(G-17948)*

PAYROLL SVCS

Workforce Payhub Inc ....G...... 517 759-4026
  Adrian *(G-105)*

PEARLS, WHOLESALE

Combine International Inc ....C...... 248 585-9900
  Troy *(G-17019)*

PEAT GRINDING SVCS

Bay-Houston Towing Company ....F...... 810 648-2210
  Sandusky *(G-15056)*

PEAT MINING SVCS

Markham Peat Corp ....F...... 800 851-7230
  Lakeview *(G-9643)*

PENS & PENCILS: Mechanical, NEC

Golden Apple ....G...... 231 477-5366
  Manistee *(G-10901)*

PERFORMANCE RIGHTS, PUBLISHING & LICENSING

Dillion Renee Entities ....G...... 989 443-0654
  Lansing *(G-9830)*

PERFUMES

Body Exotics ....F...... 231 753-8590
  Traverse City *(G-16623)*
Fragrance Outlet Inc ....G...... 517 552-9545
  Howell *(G-8456)*
Jogue Inc ....G...... 248 349-1501
  Northville *(G-12233)*
Jogue Inc ....E...... 734 207-0100
  Plymouth *(G-13203)*
Scentmatchers LLC ....G...... 231 878-9918
  Gaylord *(G-6158)*
Wellington Fragrance ....G...... 734 261-5531
  Livonia *(G-10472)*

PERISCOPES

Periscope Playschool ....G...... 989 875-4409
  Alma *(G-252)*

PERLITE: Processed

Montcalm Aggregates Inc ....G...... 989 772-7038
  Mount Pleasant *(G-11717)*

PERSONAL CREDIT INSTITUTION: Indl Loan Bank, Non Deposit

Wholesale Proc Systems LLC ....G...... 833 755-6696
  Adrian *(G-104)*

PERSONAL CREDIT INSTITUTIONS: Financing, Autos, Furniture

Ford Motor Company ....A...... 313 322-3000
  Dearborn *(G-3842)*
Ford Motor Company ....F...... 734 523-3000
  Livonia *(G-10215)*
General Motors LLC ....A...... 313 972-6000
  Detroit *(G-4257)*

PESTICIDES

Biobest USA Inc ....G...... 734 626-5693
  Romulus *(G-14258)*
Gantec Inc ....G...... 989 631-9300
  Midland *(G-11367)*

PESTICIDES WHOLESALERS

Hpi Products Inc ....G...... 248 773-7460
  Northville *(G-12229)*

PET & PET SPLYS STORES

Pet Supplies Plus ....G...... 616 554-3600
  Grand Rapids *(G-7083)*

PET ACCESS: Collars, Leashes, Etc, Exc Leather

ABC Merchandise ....G...... 248 348-1560
  Wixom *(G-18593)*
Brollytime Inc ....F...... 312 854-7606
  Royal Oak *(G-14521)*
Ruff Love Pet LLC....................................G...... 734 351-6289
  Maybee *(G-11171)*

PET COLLARS, LEASHES, MUZZLES & HARNESSES: Leather

Lebalab Inc ....G...... 519 542-4236
  Kimball *(G-9494)*
Topsydekennel LLC ....G...... 313 655-5804
  Detroit *(G-4638)*

PET SPLYS

Best Buy Bones Inc ....G...... 810 631-6971
  Mount Morris *(G-11668)*
Fowlerville Feed & Pet Sups ....G...... 517 223-9115
  Fowlerville *(G-5839)*
Harry & Assoc LLC ....G...... 248 446-8820
  South Lyon *(G-15437)*
Jandys Home ....G...... 616 446-7013
  Alto *(G-334)*
Kitty Condo LLC ....G...... 419 690-9063
  Livonia *(G-10266)*
Legend Lllys Pet Grming Ret Sp ....G...... 734 346-6030
  Detroit *(G-4386)*
New Key Pet LLC ....G...... 734 716-5357
  Canton *(G-2500)*
Packys Pet Supplies LLC ....G...... 989 422-5484
  Houghton Lake *(G-8402)*
Pet Supplies Plus ....G...... 616 554-3600
  Grand Rapids *(G-7083)*
Petzpaws LLC ....G...... 313 414-9894
  West Bloomfield *(G-18304)*
Ruff Life LLC ....G...... 231 347-1214
  Petoskey *(G-13022)*
Sk Enterprises Inc ....G...... 616 785-1070
  Grand Rapids *(G-7201)*
Studtmans Stuff ....G...... 269 673-3126
  Allegan *(G-183)*
Tecla Company Inc ....E...... 248 624-8200
  Commerce Township *(G-3576)*
Viladon Corporation ....G...... 248 548-0043
  Oak Park *(G-12649)*

Employee Codes: A=Over 500 employees, B=251-500
C=101-250, D=51-100, E=20-50, F=10-19, G=3-9

PETROLEUM & PETROLEUM PRDTS, WHOLESALE Fuel Oil

PETROLEUM & PETROLEUM PRDTS, WHOLESALE Fuel Oil

Lansing Ice and Fuel Company .... F 517 372-3850
  Lansing *(G-9710)*
Pacific Oil Resources Inc .... G 734 397-1120
  Van Buren Twp *(G-17545)*

PETROLEUM BULK STATIONS & TERMINALS

BP Lubricants USA Inc .... E 231 689-0002
  White Cloud *(G-18439)*

PETROLEUM PRDTS WHOLESALERS

Warner Oil Company .... F 517 278-5844
  Coldwater *(G-3461)*

PHARMACEUTICAL PREPARATIONS: Adrenal

Atterocor Inc .... G 734 845-9300
  Ann Arbor *(G-385)*
Corium Inc .... E 616 656-4563
  Grand Rapids *(G-6605)*
L Perrigo Company .... G 269 673-7962
  Allegan *(G-165)*

PHARMACEUTICAL PREPARATIONS: Druggists' Preparations

Abaco Partners LLC .... C 616 532-1700
  Kentwood *(G-9441)*
Abbott Laboratories .... B 269 651-0600
  Sturgis *(G-16279)*
Abbott Laboratories .... G 734 324-6666
  Wyandotte *(G-18805)*
Abbvie Inc .... G 734 324-6650
  Wyandotte *(G-18806)*
Charles Bowman & Company .... F 616 786-4000
  Holland *(G-7994)*
Grass Lake Community Pharmacy ..... G 517 522-4100
  Grass Lake *(G-7438)*
J&B Pharmacy Services Inc .... G 888 611-2941
  Wixom *(G-18688)*
Physicians Compounding Phrm .... G 248 758-9100
  Bloomfield Hills *(G-1852)*
Soleo Health Inc .... F 248 513-8687
  Novi *(G-12539)*
Velesco Phrm Svcs Inc .... G 734 545-0696
  Wixom *(G-18785)*
Velesco Phrm Svcs Inc .... G 734 274-9877
  Plymouth *(G-13330)*
Vitanorth USA LLC .... G 734 595-4000
  Westland *(G-18427)*

PHARMACEUTICAL PREPARATIONS: Emulsions

Tetra Corporation .... E 401 529-1630
  Eaton Rapids *(G-4972)*

PHARMACEUTICAL PREPARATIONS: Medicines, Capsule Or Ampule

Port Huron Medical Assoc .... G 810 982-0100
  Fort Gratiot *(G-5823)*

PHARMACEUTICAL PREPARATIONS: Powders

Welchdry Inc .... E 616 399-2711
  Holland *(G-8243)*

PHARMACEUTICAL PREPARATIONS: Proprietary Drug PRDTS

Kure Products Distribution Inc .... G 248 330-3933
  Farmington Hills *(G-5285)*
Penrose Therapeutix LLC .... G 847 370-0303
  Plymouth *(G-13262)*
Wandas Barium Cookie LLC .... G 906 281-1788
  Calumet *(G-2416)*

PHARMACEUTICAL PREPARATIONS: Solutions

Grand River Aseptic Mfg Inc .... C 616 678-2400
  Grand Rapids *(G-6776)*

M Beard Solutions LLC .... G 734 441-0660
  Dearborn *(G-3865)*

PHARMACEUTICAL PREPARATIONS: Tablets

H & A Pharmacy II LLC .... G 313 995-4552
  Westland *(G-18379)*
Tabletting Inc .... G 616 957-0281
  Grand Rapids *(G-7246)*

PHARMACEUTICALS

Akorn Inc .... E 800 579-8327
  Ann Arbor *(G-359)*
Alphacore Pharma LLC .... G 734 330-0265
  Ann Arbor *(G-361)*
Arconic .... F 231 894-7802
  Whitehall *(G-18491)*
Aspire Pharmacy .... G 989 773-7849
  Mount Pleasant *(G-11681)*
Avomeen LLC .... D 734 222-1090
  Ann Arbor *(G-390)*
Axalta .... E 248 379-6913
  Lake Orion *(G-9586)*
Barclay Pharmacy .... G 248 852-4600
  Rochester Hills *(G-13961)*
Berkley Pharmacy LLC .... G 586 573-8300
  Warren *(G-17731)*
Biolyte Laboratories LLC .... E 616 350-9055
  Grand Rapids *(G-6509)*
Biopolymer Innovations LLC .... G 517 432-3044
  East Lansing *(G-4887)*
Bristol-Myers Squibb Company .... G 248 528-2476
  Troy *(G-16986)*
Bryllan LLC .... G 248 442-7620
  Brighton *(G-1954)*
Caraco Pharma Inc .... G 313 871-8400
  Detroit *(G-4087)*
Cayman Chemical Company Inc .... D 734 971-3335
  Ann Arbor *(G-417)*
Central Admxture Phrm Svcs Inc ...... G 734 953-6760
  Livonia *(G-10151)*
Corium Inc .... C 650 298-8255
  Grand Rapids *(G-6606)*
Diplomat Spclty Phrm Flint LLC .... B 810 768-9000
  Flint *(G-5688)*
Dow Chemical Company .... C 989 636-4406
  Midland *(G-11343)*
DSC Laboratories Inc .... E 800 492-5988
  Muskegon *(G-11801)*
DSM Engineering Materials Inc .... G 616 667-2643
  Jenison *(G-9053)*
Elba Inc .... E 248 288-6098
  Troy *(G-17081)*
Emergent Biodef Oper Lnsng LLC .... B 517 327-1500
  Lansing *(G-9690)*
Emergent Biosolutions Inc .... G 517 327-1500
  Lansing *(G-9691)*
Esperion Therapeutics Inc .... D 734 887-3903
  Ann Arbor *(G-479)*
Ferndale Laboratories Inc .... C 248 548-0900
  Ferndale *(G-5553)*
Ferndale Pharma Group Inc .... B 248 548-0900
  Ferndale *(G-5554)*
Fremont Generate Digester LLC .... G 231 924-9401
  Fremont *(G-6041)*
Genentech Inc .... C 650 225-1000
  Lake Orion *(G-9606)*
Glaxosmithkline LLC .... G 989 450-9859
  Frankenmuth *(G-5864)*
Glaxosmithkline LLC .... G 989 928-6535
  Oxford *(G-12884)*
Glaxosmithkline LLC .... G 989 280-1225
  Midland *(G-11369)*
Glaxosmithkline LLC .... G 248 561-3022
  Bloomfield Hills *(G-1822)*
Greenmark Biomedical Inc .... G 517 336-4665
  Lansing *(G-9847)*
Hello Life Inc .... E 616 808-3290
  Grand Rapids *(G-6809)*
Hibiskus Biopharma Inc .... G 616 234-2841
  Kalamazoo *(G-9217)*
Housey Phrm RES Labs LLC .... G 248 663-7000
  Southfield *(G-15593)*
Innovative Pharmaceuticals LLC .... F 248 789-0999
  Brighton *(G-2013)*
Integrated Sensing Systems .... G 734 604-4301
  Ann Arbor *(G-530)*
Interntnal Hrvest Ventures LLC .... G 248 387-9944
  Livonia *(G-10250)*
Jade Pharmaceuticals Entp LLC .... G 248 716-8333
  Livonia *(G-10256)*

L Perrigo Company .... A 269 673-8451
  Allegan *(G-164)*
L Perrigo Company .... G 269 673-7962
  Allegan *(G-166)*
L Perrigo Company .... G 269 673-1608
  Allegan *(G-167)*
LLC Ash Stevens .... D 734 282-3370
  Riverview *(G-13879)*
Lxr Biotech LLC .... E 248 860-4246
  Rochester Hills *(G-14055)*
McKesson Corporation .... G 734 953-2523
  Livonia *(G-10308)*
Meridianrx LLC .... D 855 323-4580
  Detroit *(G-4429)*
Millendo Transactionsub Inc .... G 734 845-9300
  Ann Arbor *(G-578)*
Mills Phrm & Apothecary LLC .... G 248 633-2872
  Birmingham *(G-1737)*
N F P Inc .... G 989 631-0009
  Midland *(G-11397)*
Natural Therapeutics LLC .... G 734 604-7313
  Ann Arbor *(G-591)*
Nopras Technologies Inc .... G 248 486-6684
  South Lyon *(G-15451)*
Norman A Lewis .... G 248 219-5736
  Farmington Hills *(G-5334)*
Ocuphire Pharma Inc .... G 248 681-9815
  Farmington Hills *(G-5338)*
Painexx Corporation .... G 313 863-1200
  Detroit *(G-4503)*
Pancheck LLC .... F 989 288-6886
  Durand *(G-4844)*
Par Sterile Products LLC .... B 248 651-9081
  Rochester *(G-13920)*
Parkedale Pharmaceuticals Inc .... D 248 650-6400
  Rochester *(G-13921)*
PBM Nutritionals LLC .... E 269 673-8451
  Allegan *(G-173)*
Perrigo Company .... G 269 686-1973
  Allegan *(G-175)*
Perrigo Company .... G 616 396-0941
  Holland *(G-8163)*
Perrigo Company .... G 269 686-1782
  Holland *(G-8164)*
Perrigo Company .... F 269 673-7962
  Allegan *(G-177)*
Perrigo New York Inc .... F 269 673-8451
  Allegan *(G-178)*
Pfizer Inc .... G 248 867-9067
  Clarkston *(G-3055)*
Pfizer Inc .... G 734 679-7368
  Grosse Ile *(G-7525)*
Pfizer Inc .... G 734 671-9315
  Trenton *(G-16890)*
Pfizer Inc .... G 269 833-5143
  Kalamazoo *(G-9292)*
Pfizer Inc .... C 269 833-2358
  Kalamazoo *(G-9293)*
Pharmacia & Upjohn Company LLC .. D 908 901-8000
  Kalamazoo *(G-9294)*
Phenomics Health Inc .... E 410 336-2404
  Ann Arbor *(G-609)*
Plasma Biolife Services L P .... G 616 667-0264
  Grandville *(G-7409)*
PMI Branded Pharmaceuticals .... F 269 673-8451
  Allegan *(G-179)*
Pure Green Pharmaceuticals Inc ...... F 248 515-0097
  West Bloomfield *(G-18307)*
Qsv Pharma LLC .... G 269 324-2358
  Portage *(G-13597)*
Quality Care Products LLC .... F 734 847-3847
  Temperance *(G-16546)*
Renucell .... G 888 400-6032
  Grand Haven *(G-6353)*
Rockwell Medical Inc .... C 248 960-9009
  Wixom *(G-18744)*
Safe N Simple LLC .... F 248 875-0840
  Clarkston *(G-3062)*
Sepracor Inc .... G 508 481-6700
  Northville *(G-12259)*
Stroyko Construction Group Inc .... G 281 240-3332
  Orchard Lake *(G-12720)*
Sun Pharmaceutical Inds Inc .... F 248 346-7302
  Farmington Hills *(G-5393)*
Team Pharma .... G 269 344-8326
  Kalamazoo *(G-9352)*
Tower Laboratories Ltd .... F 860 767-2127
  Norton Shores *(G-12341)*
Tower Laboratories Ltd .... E 231 893-1472
  Montague *(G-11602)*

PRODUCT SECTION

Uckele Health and Nutrition .... C 800 248-0330
  Blissfield (G-1779)
Urban Specialty Apparel Inc .... F 248 395-9500
  Southfield (G-15734)
Vectech Pharmaceutical Cons .... F 248 478-5820
  Brighton (G-2092)
Vortech Pharmaceutical Ltd .... F 313 584-4088
  Dearborn (G-3912)
Zoetis LLC .... G 888 963-8471
  Kalamazoo (G-9375)

PHARMACEUTICALS: Medicinal & Botanical Prdts

Aapharmasyn LLC .... F 734 213-2123
  Ann Arbor (G-344)
Bmu International LLC .... G 248 342-4032
  Clarkston (G-3020)
C3 Industries Inc .... G 248 255-1283
  Ann Arbor (G-412)
Heals & Herbs LLC .... G 888 604-1474
  Southfield (G-15591)
Hearing Health Science Inc .... G 734 476-9490
  Ann Arbor (G-511)
Metabolic Solutions Dev Co LLC .... E 269 343-6732
  Grand Rapids (G-6977)
Viva Zen Sales LLC .... G 248 481-3605
  Auburn Hills (G-1081)

PHARMACIES & DRUG STORES

Jorgensens Inc .... E 989 831-8338
  Greenville (G-7494)
Nopras Technologies Inc .... G 248 486-6684
  South Lyon (G-15451)
Soleo Health Inc .... F 248 513-8687
  Novi (G-12539)
Walmart Inc .... F 517 541-1481
  Charlotte (G-2774)

PHOSPHORIC ACID ESTERS

Metalworking Lubricants Co .... D 248 332-3500
  Pontiac (G-13397)

PHOTO RECONNAISSANCE SYSTEMS

Orion Test Systems Inc .... D 248 373-9097
  Auburn Hills (G-990)

PHOTOCOPY MACHINE REPAIR SVCS

Nationwide Laser Technologies .... G 248 488-0155
  Farmington Hills (G-5331)

PHOTOCOPYING & DUPLICATING SVCS

Acadia Group LLC .... E 734 944-1404
  Saline (G-14997)
Accelerated Press Inc .... G 248 524-1850
  Troy (G-16902)
Afb Corporate Operations LLC .... E 248 669-1188
  Plymouth (G-13120)
August Communications Inc .... G 313 561-8000
  Dearborn Heights (G-3921)
Elston Enterprises Inc .... F 313 561-8000
  Dearborn Heights (G-3926)
Fedex Office & Print Svcs Inc .... F 734 761-4539
  Ann Arbor (G-487)
Fedex Office & Print Svcs Inc .... G 517 332-5855
  East Lansing (G-4892)
Fedex Office & Print Svcs Inc .... G 248 651-2679
  Rochester (G-13900)
Gary Cork Incorporated .... G 231 946-1061
  Traverse City (G-16692)
K & S Printing Centers Inc .... G 734 482-1680
  Ann Arbor (G-536)
Kenewell Group .... G 810 714-4290
  Fenton (G-5487)
Kmak Inc .... G 517 784-8800
  Jackson (G-8929)
Kolossos Printing Inc .... F 734 994-5400
  Ann Arbor (G-540)
Kwikie Inc .... G 231 946-9942
  Traverse City (G-16735)
Lightning Litho Inc .... F 517 394-2995
  Lansing (G-9864)
Lopez Reproductions Inc .... G 313 386-4526
  Detroit (G-4404)
Mega Printing Inc .... G 248 624-6065
  Walled Lake (G-17672)
Megee Printing Inc .... F 269 344-3226
  Kalamazoo (G-9268)
Muhleck Enterprises Inc .... E 517 333-0713
  Okemos (G-12679)
Printing Centre Inc .... F 517 694-2400
  Holt (G-8326)
Quickprint of Adrian Inc .... F 517 263-2290
  Adrian (G-90)
Rumler Brothers Inc .... F 517 437-2990
  Hillsdale (G-7947)
Specifications Service Company .... G 248 353-0244
  Bloomfield (G-1785)
Wholesale Weave Inc .... F 800 762-2037
  Detroit (G-4682)

PHOTOENGRAVING SVC

Brophy Engraving Co Inc .... E 313 871-2333
  Detroit (G-4076)
Fusion Flexo LLC .... G 269 685-5827
  Richland (G-13825)
Fusion Flexo LLC .... E 269 685-5827
  Plainwell (G-13077)
Owosso Graphic Arts Inc .... E 989 725-7112
  Owosso (G-12849)
Rob Enterprises Inc .... F 269 685-5827
  Plainwell (G-13094)

PHOTOGRAMMATIC MAPPING SVCS

Superior Information Tech LLC .... F 734 666-9963
  Livonia (G-10424)

PHOTOGRAPHIC EQPT & SPLY: Sound Recordg/Reprod Eqpt, Motion

Osowet Collections Inc .... G 313 844-8171
  Detroit (G-4501)

PHOTOGRAPHIC EQPT & SPLYS

Accuform Prtg & Graphics Inc .... F 313 271-5600
  Detroit (G-3981)
Compatible Laser Products Inc .... F 810 629-0459
  Fenton (G-5466)
DOT Bridge Inc .... G 248 921-7363
  South Lyon (G-15433)
Essential Photo Gear .... G 502 244-2888
  Rogers City (G-14210)
General Dynamics Mission .... A 530 271-2500
  Rochester Hills (G-14021)
General Dynmics Globl Imging T .... A 248 293-2929
  Rochester Hills (G-14022)
Kistler Instrument Corp .... G 248 489-1090
  Farmington Hills (G-5282)
Macmichigan Inc .... G 248 613-6372
  Novi (G-12468)

PHOTOGRAPHIC EQPT & SPLYS WHOLESALERS

Photo Systems Inc .... E 734 424-9625
  Dexter (G-4749)

PHOTOGRAPHIC EQPT & SPLYS: Cameras, Aerial

Envirodrone Inc .... G 226 344-5614
  Detroit (G-4212)

PHOTOGRAPHIC EQPT & SPLYS: Densitometers

X-Rite Incorporated .... C 616 803-2100
  Grand Rapids (G-7353)

PHOTOGRAPHIC EQPT & SPLYS: Printing Eqpt

Douthitt Corporation .... E 313 259-1565
  Detroit (G-4189)
Douthitt Corporation .... F 313 259-1565
  Detroit (G-4190)

PHOTOGRAPHIC EQPT & SPLYS: Printing Frames

Northern Mich Wldlife Art Fram .... F 989 340-1272
  Lachine (G-9532)

PHOTOGRAPHIC EQPT & SPLYS: Sensitometers

6df Research LLC .... G 906 281-1170
  Houghton (G-8379)

PHOTOGRAPHIC EQPT & SPLYS: Toners, Prprd, Not Chem Plnts

Lasers Resource Inc .... E 616 554-5555
  Grand Rapids (G-6930)
Nationwide Laser Technologies .... G 248 488-0155
  Farmington Hills (G-5331)
Precision Printer Services Inc .... E 269 384-5725
  Portage (G-13594)

PHOTOGRAPHIC EQPT & SPLYS: Trays, Printing & Processing

Veronica K LLC .... G 248 251-5144
  Clinton Township (G-3384)

PHOTOGRAPHY SVCS: Commercial

Appropos LLC .... E 844 462-7776
  Grand Rapids (G-6465)
Detroit Peanuts LLC .... G 313 826-4327
  Detroit (G-4158)
Engineering Graphics Inc .... E 517 485-5828
  Lansing (G-9693)
Graphic Enterprises Inc .... D 248 616-4900
  Madison Heights (G-10732)
Livbig LLC .... G 888 519-8290
  Portage (G-13578)
Touched By Cupids .... G 313 704-6334
  Detroit (G-4640)

PHOTOGRAPHY SVCS: Portrait Studios

Celebrations .... G 906 482-4946
  Hancock (G-7617)

PHOTOGRAPHY SVCS: School

Great Lakes Photo Inc .... G 586 784-5446
  Richmond (G-13839)

PHOTOGRAPHY SVCS: Still Or Video

Livbig LLC .... G 888 519-8290
  Portage (G-13578)

PHOTOGRAPHY: Aerial

Great Lakes Exploration Inc .... G 906 352-4024
  Menominee (G-11239)

PHOTOTYPESETTING SVC

Tweddle Group Inc .... C 586 307-3700
  Clinton Township (G-3380)

PHOTOVOLTAIC Solid State

Nuvosun Inc .... D 408 514-6200
  Midland (G-11398)

PHYSICAL FITNESS CENTERS

Edge Fitnes Training Hdqtr LLC .... G 989 486-9870
  Midland (G-11361)
Vanroth LLC .... F 734 929-5268
  Ann Arbor (G-709)

PHYSICIANS' OFFICES & CLINICS: Medical doctors

Affiliated Troy Dermatologist .... F 248 267-5020
  Troy (G-16910)
Remnant Publications Inc .... E 517 279-1304
  Coldwater (G-3450)
Thompson Surgical Instrs Inc .... E 231 922-0177
  Traverse City (G-16857)
Trulife Inc .... E 800 492-1088
  Jackson (G-9026)

PICTURE FRAMES: Wood

Art of Custom Framing Inc .... G 248 435-3726
  Troy (G-16953)
Martin Products Company Inc .... G 269 651-1721
  Sturgis (G-16304)

Employee Codes: A=Over 500 employees, B=251-500
C=101-250, D=51-100, E=20-50, F=10-19, G=3-9

PIECE GOODS & NOTIONS WHOLESALERS

Haartz Corporation .... G 248 646-8200
  Bloomfield Hills (G-1825)
Morris Associates Inc .... E 248 355-9055
  Southfield (G-15662)
Tennant & Associates Inc .... G 248 643-6140
  Troy (G-17388)

PIECE GOODS, NOTIONS & DRY GOODS, WHOL: Textile Converters

Acme Mills Company .... E 517 437-8940
  Hillsdale (G-7919)

PIECE GOODS, NOTIONS & OTHER DRY GOODS, WHOL: Flags/Banners

Signs365com LLC .... G 800 265-8830
  Shelby Township (G-15333)

PIECE GOODS, NOTIONS/DRY GOODS, WHOL: Drapery Mtrl, Woven

Parkway Drapery & Uphl Co Inc .... G 734 779-1300
  Livonia (G-10360)

PIECE GOODS, NOTIONS/DRY GOODS, WHOL: Silk Piece, Woven

J America Licensed Pdts Inc .... G 517 655-8800
  Fowlerville (G-5844)

PIGMENTS, INORGANIC: Bone Black

Ebonex Corporation .... G 313 388-0063
  Melvindale (G-11200)

PILLOW FILLING MTRLS: Curled Hair, Cotton Waste, Moss

Airlite Synthetics Mfg Inc .... F 248 335-8131
  Pontiac (G-13345)

PILOT SVCS: Aviation

Oshino Lamps America Ltd .... G 262 226-8620
  Wixom (G-18727)

PINS

Fred Oswalts Pins Unltd .... G 269 342-1387
  Portage (G-13561)
Pink Pin Lady LLC .... G 586 731-1532
  Shelby Township (G-15302)

PINS: Cotter

Dias Holding Inc .... F 313 928-1254
  Allen Park (G-192)

PINS: Dowel

Henry Plambeck .... G 586 463-3410
  Harrison Township (G-7701)
Merchants Automatic Pdts Inc .... E 734 829-0020
  Canton (G-2493)
Warren Screw Works Inc .... G 734 525-2920
  Livonia (G-10466)

PIPE & FITTING: Fabrication

A & B Tube Benders Inc .... G 586 773-0440
  Warren (G-17679)
Austin Tube Products Inc .... F 231 745-2741
  Baldwin (G-1121)
B L Harroun and Son Inc .... E 269 345-8657
  Kalamazoo (G-9131)
Baldauf Enterprises Inc .... D 989 686-0350
  Bay City (G-1324)
Big Foot Manufacturing Co .... E 231 775-5588
  Cadillac (G-2315)
Blissfield Manufacturing Co .... C 517 486-2121
  Blissfield (G-1761)
Bundy Corporation .... G 517 439-1132
  Hillsdale (G-7927)
Burnham & Northern Inc .... G 517 279-7501
  Coldwater (G-3422)
Cadillac Culvert Inc .... F 231 775-3761
  Cadillac (G-2320)
Computer Operated Mfg .... E 989 686-1333
  Bay City (G-1340)

Denso Air Systems Michigan Inc .... B 269 962-9676
  Battle Creek (G-1215)
Detroit Nipple Works Inc .... F 313 872-6370
  Detroit (G-4157)
Fernco Inc .... C 810 503-9000
  Davison (G-3782)
Fhc Holding Company .... G 616 538-3231
  Wyoming (G-18872)
Flexible Metal Inc .... D 810 231-1300
  Hamburg (G-7591)
Formfab LLC .... E 248 844-3676
  Rochester Hills (G-14013)
Future Industries Inc .... E 616 844-0772
  Grand Haven (G-6299)
Gonzalez Group Jonesville LLC .... E 517 849-9908
  Jonesville (G-9088)
Gray Brothers Mfg Inc .... F 269 483-7615
  White Pigeon (G-18479)
Huron Inc .... E 810 359-5344
  Lexington (G-10029)
JCs Tool & Mfg Co Inc .... E 989 892-8975
  Essexville (G-5114)
Manistee Wldg & Piping Svc Inc .... G 231 723-2551
  Manistee (G-10906)
Marshall Excelsior Co .... E 269 789-6700
  Marshall (G-11065)
Meccom Corporation .... G 313 895-4900
  Detroit (G-4426)
Metaldyne Tblar Components LLC .... D 248 727-1800
  Southfield (G-15655)
Motor City Bending & Rolling .... E 313 368-4400
  Detroit (G-4466)
Nelson Hardware .... G 269 327-3583
  Portage (G-13587)
Novi Tool & Machine Company .... F 313 532-0900
  Redford (G-13749)
Oilpatch Machine Tool Inc .... G 989 772-0637
  Mount Pleasant (G-11728)
Parma Tube Corp .... E 269 651-2351
  Sturgis (G-16316)
Patton Welding Inc .... F 231 258-9925
  Kalkaska (G-9401)
Pipe Fabricators Inc .... G 269 345-8657
  Kalamazoo (G-9297)
Pontiac Coil Inc .... C 248 922-1100
  Clarkston (G-3057)
Power Process Piping Inc .... E 734 451-0130
  Plymouth (G-13269)
River Valley Machine Inc .... F 269 673-8070
  Allegan (G-181)
Roman Engineering .... E 231 238-7644
  Afton (G-107)
S & S Tube Inc .... E 989 656-7211
  Bay Port (G-1415)
Spiral Industries Inc .... E 810 632-6300
  Howell (G-8521)
St Regis Culvert Inc .... F 517 543-3430
  Charlotte (G-2773)
TI Group Auto Systems LLC .... G 859 235-5420
  Auburn Hills (G-1056)

PIPE & FITTINGS: Cast Iron

Michigan Poly Pipe Inc .... G 517 709-8100
  Grand Ledge (G-6396)

PIPE & FITTINGS: Pressure, Cast Iron

Threaded Products Co .... E 586 727-3435
  Richmond (G-13846)

PIPE & TUBES: Copper & Copper Alloy

Mueller Industries Inc .... G 248 446-3720
  Brighton (G-2037)

PIPE & TUBES: Seamless

Dwm Holdings Inc .... D 586 541-0013
  Warren (G-17787)
Forged Tubular Products Inc .... F 313 843-6720
  Detroit (G-4242)
New Hudson Corporation .... E 248 437-3970
  New Hudson (G-12064)

PIPE FITTINGS: Plastic

Colonial Engineering Inc .... F 269 323-2495
  Portage (G-13553)
Conley Composites LLC .... E 918 299-5051
  Grand Rapids (G-6594)
Ethylene LLC .... E 616 554-3464
  Kentwood (G-9451)

Etx Holdings Inc .... G 989 463-1151
  Alma (G-241)
GLS Industries LLC .... E 586 255-9221
  Warren (G-17831)
GLS Industries LLC .... E 586 255-9221
  Warren (G-17832)
Mueller Industries Inc .... G 248 446-3720
  Brighton (G-2037)

PIPE JOINT COMPOUNDS

Bear Cub Holdings Inc .... G 231 242-1152
  Harbor Springs (G-7641)
Scodeller Construction Inc .... D 248 374-1102
  Wixom (G-18748)

PIPE SECTIONS, FABRICATED FROM PURCHASED PIPE

Myco Enterprises Inc .... G 248 348-3806
  Royal Oak (G-14564)
Quality Pipe Products Inc .... E 734 606-5100
  New Boston (G-12019)

PIPE, SEWER: Concrete

Co-Pipe Products Inc .... E 734 287-1000
  Taylor (G-16393)
Upper Peninsula Con Pipe Co .... F 906 786-0934
  Escanaba (G-5103)

PIPE: Brass & Bronze

Mueller Brass Co .... D 810 987-7770
  Port Huron (G-13505)

PIPE: Concrete

Carlesimo Products Inc .... E 248 474-0415
  Farmington Hills (G-5198)
Northern Concrete Pipe Inc .... G 517 645-2777
  Charlotte (G-2763)
Northern Concrete Pipe Inc .... E 989 892-3545
  Bay City (G-1383)

PIPE: Copper

Mueller Brass Co .... C 810 987-7770
  Port Huron (G-13504)

PIPE: Plastic

Advanced Drainage Systems Inc .... G 989 761-7610
  Clifford (G-3130)
Advanced Drainage Systems Inc .... G 989 723-5208
  Owosso (G-12819)
Cff Inc .... G 517 242-6903
  Battle Creek (G-1208)
Conley Composites LLC .... E 918 299-5051
  Grand Rapids (G-6594)
Creek Plastics LLC .... F 517 423-1003
  Adrian (G-57)
Ethylene LLC .... E 616 554-3464
  Kentwood (G-9451)
Vidon Plastics Inc .... D 810 667-0634
  Lapeer (G-9965)

PIPE: Sheet Metal

Ede Co .... G 586 756-7555
  Warren (G-17792)

PIPELINE TERMINAL FACILITIES: Independent

Sadia Enterprises Inc .... F 248 854-4666
  Troy (G-17340)

PIPES & TUBES

Creform Corporation .... E 248 926-2555
  Novi (G-12385)
Gladiator Quality Sorting LLC .... G 734 578-1950
  Canton (G-2465)
TNT Pipe and Tube LLC .... E 419 466-1144
  Erie (G-5055)
WM Tube & Wire Forming Inc .... F 231 830-9925
  Muskegon (G-11950)

PIPES & TUBES: Steel

A & B Tube Benders Inc .... F 586 773-0440
  Warren (G-17678)

Ace Consulting & MGT Inc ....E 989 821-7040
Roscommon (G-14346)
Advanced Drainage Systems Inc ....G 989 723-5208
Owosso (G-12819)
All Bending & Tubular Pdts LLC ....F 616 333-2364
Grand Rapids (G-6446)
Atlas Tube (plymouth) Inc ....D 734 738-5600
Plymouth (G-13127)
Austin Tube Products Inc ....F 231 745-2741
Baldwin (G-1121)
Benteler Automotive Corp ....B 616 245-4607
Grand Rapids (G-6501)
Benteler Automotive Corp ....B 616 247-3936
Auburn Hills (G-810)
Berkley Industries Inc ....E 989 656-2171
Bay Port (G-1413)
Burgaflex North America Inc ....F 810 584-7296
Grand Blanc (G-6237)
Delta Tube & Fabricating Corp ....E 248 634-8267
Holly (G-8267)
Diversified Tube LLC ....F 313 790-7348
Southfield (G-15540)
Energy Steel & Supply Co ....D 810 538-4990
Rochester Hills (G-14004)
Exceptional Product Sales LLC ....F 586 286-3240
Sterling Heights (G-16008)
Formfab LLC ....E 248 844-3676
Rochester Hills (G-14013)
General Structures Inc ....F 586 774-6105
Warren (G-17826)
M & W Manufacturing Co LLC ....F 586 741-8897
Chesterfield (G-2906)
Martinrea Industries Inc ....E 231 832-5504
Reed City (G-13795)
Martinrea Industries Inc ....E 734 428-2400
Manchester (G-10886)
Midway Strl Pipe & Sup Inc ....G 517 787-1350
Jackson (G-8961)
New 11 Inc ....E 616 494-9370
Holland (G-8153)
Parma Tube Corp ....E 269 651-2351
Sturgis (G-16316)
RB Christian Ironworks LLC ....G 269 963-2222
Battle Creek (G-1286)
Rbc Enterprises Inc ....E 313 491-3350
Detroit (G-4554)
Rock River Fabrications Inc ....E 616 281-5769
Grand Rapids (G-7162)
Rolled Alloys Inc ....D 734 847-0561
Temperance (G-16547)
Roman Engineering ....E 231 238-7644
Afton (G-107)
S & S Tube Inc ....E 989 656-7211
Bay Port (G-1415)
TI Group Auto Systems LLC ....G 859 235-5420
Auburn Hills (G-1056)
Trans Tube Inc ....F 248 334-5720
Pontiac (G-13420)
Transportation Tech Group Inc ....F 810 233-0440
Flint (G-5781)
Usui International Corporation ....E 734 354-3626
Plymouth (G-13328)

PIPES & TUBES: Welded

Ernest Industries Acquisition, ...E 734 595-9500
Westland (G-18369)
Grinding Specialists Inc ....E 734 729-1775
Westland (G-18377)

PIPES: Steel & Iron

Nobilis Pipe Company ....F 248 470-5692
Novi (G-12490)

PIPES: Tobacco

Loonar Stn Two The 2 or 2nd ....G 419 720-1222
Temperance (G-16537)

PISTONS & PISTON RINGS

Federal Screw Works ....F 734 941-4211
Romulus (G-14274)
Federal-Mogul Piston Rings Inc ....F 248 354-7700
Southfield (G-15564)
Kaydon Corporation ....B 734 747-7025
Ann Arbor (G-538)
Mahle Eng Components USA Inc ....G 248 305-8200
Farmington Hills (G-5302)
Piston Modules LLC ....A 313 897-1540
Detroit (G-4527)

PLANING MILL, NEC

/// 702 Cedar River Lbr Inc ....E 906 497-5365
Powers (G-13648)
Willsie Lumber Company ....F 989 695-5094
Freeland (G-6031)

PLANING MILLS: Millwork

Canusa Inc ....G 906 446-3327
Gwinn (G-7583)
Division 6 Fbrction Instllion ....F 586 200-3030
Warren (G-17780)

PLANTERS: Plastic

Blackmore Co Inc ....D 734 483-8661
Belleville (G-1481)
Bloem LLC ....E 616 622-6344
Hudsonville (G-8571)

PLASTIC COLORING & FINISHING

Tribar Manufacturing LLC ....E 248 669-0077
Wixom (G-18777)
Tribar Manufacturing LLC ....B 248 374-5870
Wixom (G-18778)

PLASTIC PRDTS

Atlantic Precision Pdts Inc ....G 586 532-9420
Shelby Township (G-15173)
Cme Plastics ....F 517 456-7722
Tecumseh (G-16492)
D B International LLC ....G 616 796-0679
Holland (G-8011)
Excel Real Estate Holdings LLC ....G 919 250-1973
Wixom (G-18660)
Gilsbach Fabricating LLC ....G 734 379-9169
Gibraltar (G-6170)
Hubble Enterprises Inc ....G 616 676-4485
Ada (G-23)
Iceberg Enterprises LLC ....C 269 651-9488
Sturgis (G-16293)
John Allen Enterprises ....G 734 426-2507
Ann Arbor (G-535)
Kurt Dubowski ....G 231 796-0055
Big Rapids (G-1680)
PR Solo Cup Inc ....G 517 244-2837
Mason (G-11150)
Prompt Plastics ....G 586 307-8525
Warren (G-17980)
Silikids Inc ....G 866 789-7454
Traverse City (G-16833)
Styrolution ....G 734 676-3616
Trenton (G-16894)
Szymanowski Electric LLC ....G 612 928-8370
Plainwell (G-13097)
U S Farathane Port Huron LLC ....F 248 754-7000
Auburn Hills (G-1067)

PLASTIC WOOD

Engraved Memories ....G 586 703-7983
Shelby Township (G-15221)

PLASTICS FILM & SHEET

Berry Global Inc ....G 616 772-4635
Zeeland (G-18997)
Dow Chemical Company ....C 989 636-4406
Midland (G-11343)
Dow Chemical Company ....A 989 636-1000
Midland (G-11341)
Dow Chemical Company ....D 989 636-5409
Midland (G-11352)
Dow Inc ....A 989 636-1000
Midland (G-11354)
Lotus Technologies LLC ....F 313 550-1889
Detroit (G-4406)
Mpf Acquisitions Inc ....E 269 672-5511
Martin (G-11080)
Petoskey Plastics Inc ....D 231 347-2602
Petoskey (G-13016)
Spire Michigan Acquisition LLC ....G 616 458-4924
Grand Rapids (G-7220)
Thyssenkrupp Materials NA Inc ....C 248 233-5600
Southfield (G-15722)

PLASTICS FILM & SHEET: Polyethylene

Cadillac Products Inc ....B 248 813-8200
Troy (G-16992)
Cadillac Products Inc ....E 586 774-1700
Roseville (G-14382)
Jsp International LLC ....G 248 397-3200
Madison Heights (G-10755)
Jsp International LLC ....G 724 477-5100
Detroit (G-4343)

PLASTICS FILM & SHEET: Vinyl

Total Vinyl Products Inc ....F 734 485-7280
Whitmore Lake (G-18548)

PLASTICS FINISHED PRDTS: Laminated

H & R Wood Specialties Inc ....E 269 628-2181
Gobles (G-6217)
Janice Morse Inc ....E 248 624-7300
West Bloomfield (G-18293)
Key Plastics LLC ....F 248 449-6100
Plymouth (G-13214)
Paramount Solutions Inc ....G 586 914-0708
Ray (G-13702)
Tuscarora Inc -Vs ....G 989 729-2780
Owosso (G-12864)

PLASTICS FOAM, WHOLESALE

Michigan Foam Products Inc ....F 616 452-9611
Grand Rapids (G-6989)

PLASTICS MATERIAL & RESINS

Aci/Wipag Recycling LLC ....F 810 767-4424
Flint (G-5638)
Advanced Elastomers Corp ....G 734 458-4194
Livonia (G-10101)
Alumilite Corporation ....F 269 488-4000
Galesburg (G-6073)
American Compounding Spc LLC ....D 810 227-3500
Brighton (G-1944)
Amplas Compounding LLC ....F 586 795-2555
Sterling Heights (G-15931)
Anderson Development Company ....C 517 263-2121
Adrian (G-53)
Arbor Plastic Technologies LLC ....F 734 678-5765
Bloomfield Hills (G-1799)
BASF Corporation ....G 734 591-5560
Livonia (G-10131)
Bjb Enterprises ....G 248 737-0760
West Bloomfield (G-18264)
Byk USA Inc ....D 203 265-2086
Rochester Hills (G-13969)
C & D Enterprises Inc ....E 248 373-0011
Burton (G-2229)
Cartex Corporation ....D 734 857-5961
Romulus (G-14260)
Celanese Americas LLC ....G 248 377-2700
Auburn Hills (G-841)
Chase Plastic Services Inc ....G 616 246-7190
Grand Rapids (G-6566)
Chase Plastic Services Inc ....E 248 620-2120
Clarkston (G-3023)
Chelsea-Megan Holding Inc ....F 248 307-9160
Troy (G-17009)
Covestro LLC ....B 248 475-7700
Auburn Hills (G-851)
Cytec Industries Inc ....G 269 349-6677
Kalamazoo (G-9161)
Dart Container Corp Kentucky ....F 517 676-3800
Mason (G-11124)
Destiny Plastics Incorporated ....F 810 622-0018
Deckerville (G-3953)
Dn Plastics Corporation ....F 616 942-6060
Grand Rapids (G-6652)
Dow Chemical Company ....G 989 636-1000
Midland (G-11345)
Dow Chemical Company ....D 989 636-5430
Midland (G-11346)
Dow Chemical Company ....G 989 636-0540
Midland (G-11349)
DSM Engineering Plastics Inc ....G 608 477-0157
Troy (G-17070)
E I Du Pont De Nemours & Co ....G 302 999-6566
Auburn Hills (G-872)
Eagle Design & Technology Inc ....E 616 748-1022
Zeeland (G-19017)
Envisiontec US LLC ....D 313 436-4300
Dearborn (G-3837)
Florida Production Engrg Inc ....F 248 588-4870
Troy (G-17116)
FM Research Management LLC ....G 906 360-5833
Trenary (G-16884)

PRODUCT

Foampartner Americas Inc G 248 243-3100
Rochester Hills *(G-14012)*
Freudenberg N Amer Ltd Partnr G 734 354-5505
Plymouth *(G-13169)*
Freudenberg-Nok General Partnr C 734 451-0020
Plymouth *(G-13170)*
Freudenberg-Nok General Partnr G 734 451-0020
Plymouth *(G-13171)*
General Plymers Thrmplstic Mtl G 800 920-8033
Rochester Hills *(G-14023)*
Geomembrane Research F 231 943-2266
Traverse City *(G-16693)*
Georgia-Pacific LLC G 989 348-7275
Grayling *(G-7461)*
Harbor Green Solutions LLC G 269 352-0265
Benton Harbor *(G-1553)*
Huntsman Advnced Mtls Amrcas L D 517 351-5900
East Lansing *(G-4896)*
Huntsman-Cooper LLC E 248 322-7300
Auburn Hills *(G-930)*
Interfibe Corporation F 269 327-6141
Schoolcraft *(G-15118)*
JB Products Inc G 248 549-1900
Troy *(G-17183)*
Kayler Mold & Engineering Inc G 586 739-0699
Sterling Heights *(G-16062)*
Kentwood Packaging Corporation D 616 698-9000
Walker *(G-17642)*
L Lewallen Co Inc F 586 792-9930
Clinton Township *(G-3276)*
Lakeshore Marble Company Inc F 269 429-8241
Stevensville *(G-16257)*
Line-X of Livonia G 734 237-3115
Livonia *(G-10280)*
Line-X of Waterford G 248 270-8848
Waterford *(G-18134)*
Materials Group LLC F 616 863-6046
Rockford *(G-14178)*
McKechnie Vhcl Cmpnnts USA Inc B 218 894-1218
Roseville *(G-14438)*
Michigan Polymer Reclaim Inc F 989 227-0497
Saint Johns *(G-14909)*
Midwest Resin Inc G 586 803-3417
Roseville *(G-14444)*
Mitsubishi Chemical Amer Inc C 586 755-1660
Warren *(G-17932)*
Navtech LLC G 248 427-1080
Wixom *(G-18717)*
New Boston Rtm Inc E 734 753-9956
New Boston *(G-12015)*
Oscoda Plastics Inc G 989 739-6900
Saginaw *(G-14723)*
Package Design & Mfg Inc E 248 486-4390
Brighton *(G-2046)*
Palmer Distributors Inc D 586 772-4225
Fraser *(G-5973)*
Pier One Polymers Incorporated F 810 326-1456
Saint Clair *(G-14839)*
Pittsburgh Glass Works LLC C 248 371-1700
Rochester Hills *(G-14084)*
Pivot Materials LLC G 248 982-7970
Okemos *(G-12681)*
Plascon Inc E 231 935-1580
Traverse City *(G-16796)*
Plascon Films Inc E 231 935-1580
Traverse City *(G-16797)*
Plasteel Corporation E 313 562-5400
Inkster *(G-8670)*
Plastic Service Centers Inc F 586 307-3900
Clinton Township *(G-3320)*
Plasticos Inc G 586 493-1908
Clinton Township *(G-3321)*
Plastics Plus Inc E 800 975-8694
Auburn Hills *(G-999)*
Plastics Recycling Tech Inc G 248 486-1449
Howell *(G-8496)*
PPG Industries Inc F 248 641-2000
Troy *(G-17309)*
Premier Plastic Resins Inc G 248 766-7578
Lake Orion *(G-9627)*
Pro Polymers Inc G 734 222-8820
Stockbridge *(G-16277)*
Quality Dairy Company G 517 319-4302
Lansing *(G-9886)*
Ravago Americas G 810 225-0029
Brighton *(G-2061)*
Ravago Americas LLC E 517 548-4140
Fowlerville *(G-5853)*
Reklein Plastics Incorporated G 586 739-8850
Sterling Heights *(G-16145)*
Resins Unlimited LLC G 586 725-6873
Chesterfield *(G-2938)*
Revstone Industries LLC G 248 351-1000
Troy *(G-17331)*
Revstone Industries LLC G 248 351-8800
Southfield *(G-15688)*
Rhe-Tech LLC G 517 223-4874
Fowlerville *(G-5855)*
Rohm Haas Dnmark Invstmnts LLC F 989 636-1463
Midland *(G-11409)*
Rosler Metal Finishing USA LLC E 269 441-3000
Battle Creek *(G-1290)*
Rubber & Plastics Co F 248 370-0700
Auburn Hills *(G-1024)*
S A Trinseo G 989 636-5409
Midland *(G-11411)*
Saint-Gobain Prfmce Plas Corp G 989 435-9533
Beaverton *(G-1430)*
Saint-Gobain Prfmce Plas Corp G 231 264-0101
Williamsburg *(G-18563)*
Saint-Gobain Prfmce Plas Corp G 586 884-9237
Shelby Township *(G-15321)*
Sekisui America Corporation G 517 279-7587
Coldwater *(G-3453)*
Sekisui Kydex LLC D 616 394-3810
Holland *(G-8188)*
Sekisui Voltek LLC C 800 225-0668
Coldwater *(G-3454)*
Sigma International Inc F 248 230-9681
Livonia *(G-10408)*
Solutia Inc G 734 676-4400
Trenton *(G-16892)*
Springfield Industries LLC F 248 601-1445
Imlay City *(G-8646)*
Stonecrafters Inc F 517 529-4990
Clarklake *(G-3009)*
Styrolution G 248 320-7230
Farmington Hills *(G-5391)*
Ticona Polymers Inc E 248 377-6868
Auburn Hills *(G-1058)*
Topas Advanced Polymes Inc G 859 746-6447
Farmington Hills *(G-5403)*
Toray Resin Company G 248 269-8800
Troy *(G-17395)*
Trinseo LLC G 248 340-0109
Auburn Hills *(G-1065)*
Ufp Technologies Inc D 616 949-8100
Grand Rapids *(G-7294)*
Vibracoustic North America LP G 248 410-5066
Farmington Hills *(G-5410)*
Vibracoustic North America LP E 269 637-2116
South Haven *(G-15421)*
Washington Penn Plastic Co Inc G 248 276-2275
Auburn Hills *(G-1087)*
Wilsonart LLC G 248 960-3388
Wixom *(G-18792)*
Wmc LLC E 616 560-4142
Greenville *(G-7510)*
Woodbridge Sales & Engrg Inc C 248 288-0100
Troy *(G-17452)*
Xg Sciences Inc E 517 316-2038
Lansing *(G-9907)*

PLASTICS MATERIALS, BASIC FORMS & SHAPES WHOLESALERS

H & L Advantage Inc E 616 532-1012
Grandville *(G-7384)*
Harbor Green Solutions LLC G 269 352-0265
Benton Harbor *(G-1553)*
Idemitsu Chemicals USA Corp G 248 355-0666
Southfield *(G-15599)*
Idemitsu Lubricants Amer Corp E 248 355-0666
Southfield *(G-15600)*
Key Plastics LLC F 248 449-6100
Plymouth *(G-13214)*
Lotus Technologies LLC F 313 550-1889
Detroit *(G-4406)*
Marelli North America Inc G 248 403-2033
Southfield *(G-15645)*
Mark Schwager Inc F 248 275-1978
Shelby Township *(G-15269)*
Material Difference Tech LLC F 888 818-1283
Macomb *(G-10614)*
Recycling Concepts W Mich Inc D 616 942-8888
Grand Rapids *(G-7146)*

PLASTICS PROCESSING

Active Plastics Inc F 616 813-5109
Caledonia *(G-2367)*
Advanced BInding Solutions LLC E 920 664-1469
Wallace *(G-17659)*
Aluminum Textures Inc E 616 538-3144
Grandville *(G-7364)*
Americo Corporation G 313 565-6550
Dearborn *(G-3807)*
Amplas Compounding LLC F 586 795-2555
Sterling Heights *(G-15931)*
Automotive Plastics Recycling F 810 767-3800
Flint *(G-5648)*
Dendritic Nanotechnologies Inc G 989 774-3096
Midland *(G-11338)*
Display Pack Inc C 616 451-3061
Cedar Springs *(G-2649)*
E & D Engineering Systems LLC G 989 246-0770
Gladwin *(G-6195)*
Echo Engrg & Prod Sups Inc D 734 241-9622
Monroe *(G-11538)*
Filcon Inc F 989 386-2986
Clare *(G-2979)*
Harbor Green Solutions LLC G 269 352-0265
Benton Harbor *(G-1553)*
Homestead Products Inc F 989 465-6182
Coleman *(G-3464)*
Icon Industries Inc G 616 241-1877
Grand Rapids *(G-6829)*
Ideal Shield LLC E 866 825-8659
Detroit *(G-4311)*
Jolicor Manufacturing Services E 586 323-5090
Shelby Township *(G-15246)*
Keltrol Enterprises Inc G 734 697-3011
Belleville *(G-1487)*
Km and I G 248 792-2782
Troy *(G-17195)*
Kunststoff Tchnik Schrer Trier E 734 944-5080
Troy *(G-17200)*
Lear Operations Corporation G 248 447-1500
Southfield *(G-15632)*
Manufacturers Services Inds G 906 493-6685
Drummond Island *(G-4802)*
Martinrea Industries Inc E 231 832-5504
Reed City *(G-13795)*
Mega Screen Corp G 517 849-7057
Jonesville *(G-9094)*
Montaplast North America Inc E 248 353-5553
Auburn Hills *(G-973)*
Northern Logistics LLC E 989 386-2389
Clare *(G-2990)*
Paul Murphy Plastics Co E 586 774-4880
Roseville *(G-14460)*
Plasti-Fab Inc E 248 543-1415
Ferndale *(G-5579)*
Polyply Composites LLC E 616 842-6330
Grand Haven *(G-6344)*
Sumitomo Chemical America Inc G 248 284-4797
Novi *(G-12548)*
Techniplas LLC B 517 849-9911
Jonesville *(G-9103)*
Tecla Company Inc E 248 624-8200
Commerce Township *(G-3576)*
Teijin Advan Compo Ameri Inc G 248 365-6600
Auburn Hills *(G-1047)*
Tg Fluid Systems USA Corp B 810 220-6161
Brighton *(G-2078)*
TI Group Auto Systems LLC G 810 364-3277
Marysville *(G-11108)*
Total Plastics Resources LLC F 248 299-9500
Rochester Hills *(G-14129)*
Trellborg Sling Sltions US Inc G 269 639-4217
Benton Harbor *(G-1594)*
Trellborg Sling Sltions US Inc G 734 354-1250
Northville *(G-12266)*
Yanfeng US Automotive F 517 721-0179
Novi *(G-12572)*
ZF Active Safety & Elec US LLC E 586 232-7200
Washington *(G-18092)*
ZF Active Safety & Elec US LLC C 734 855-2600
Livonia *(G-10481)*
ZF Active Safety & Elec US LLC E 586 232-7200
Washington *(G-18093)*

PLASTICS SHEET: Packing Materials

A-Pac Manufacturing Company E 616 791-7222
Grand Rapids *(G-6412)*
Cadillac Products Packaging Co C 248 879-5000
Troy *(G-16993)*
Link Tech Inc G 269 427-8297
Bangor *(G-1129)*

PLASTICS: Blow Molded

ABC Group Holdings Inc .... G 248 352-3706
Southfield *(G-15470)*
Acm Plastic Products Inc .... D 269 651-7888
Sturgis *(G-16280)*
Eaton Inoac Company .... E 248 226-6200
Southfield *(G-15549)*
Gt Plastics & Equipment LLC .... F 616 678-7445
Kent City *(G-9432)*
Harman Corporation .... E 248 651-4477
Rochester *(G-13903)*
M C Molds Inc .... E 517 655-5481
Williamston *(G-18576)*
N A Actuaplast Inc .... F 734 744-4010
Livonia *(G-10328)*
Penguin LLC .... C 269 651-9488
Sturgis *(G-16318)*
Plastic Omnium Auto Inrgy USA .... C 517 265-1100
Adrian *(G-88)*
Plastipak Holdings Inc .... A 209 681-9919
Canton *(G-2508)*
Plastipak Holdings Inc .... F 734 455-3600
Plymouth *(G-13266)*
Regency Plastics - Ubly Inc .... D 989 658-8504
Ubly *(G-17482)*
Romeo-Rim Inc .... C 586 336-5800
Bruce Twp *(G-2179)*
Spirit Industries Inc .... G 517 371-7840
Lansing *(G-9740)*
Srg Global Coatings LLC .... C 248 509-1100
Troy *(G-17369)*
Statistical Processed Products .... F 586 792-6900
Clinton Township *(G-3363)*

PLASTICS: Cast

Alumilite Corporation .... F 269 488-4000
Galesburg *(G-6073)*
Global Technology Ventures Inc .... G 248 324-3707
Farmington Hills *(G-5252)*
Glove Coaters Incorporated .... F 517 741-8402
Union City *(G-17493)*
Pace Industries LLC .... G 231 777-3941
Muskegon *(G-11890)*

PLASTICS: Extruded

Delfingen Us Inc .... E 716 215-0300
Rochester Hills *(G-13991)*
Delfingen Us-Central Amer Inc .... G 248 230-3500
Rochester Hills *(G-13992)*
Delfingen Us-Holding Inc .... G 248 230-3500
Rochester Hills *(G-13993)*
Extrusions Division Inc .... G 616 247-3611
Grand Rapids *(G-6696)*
Gemini Group Inc .... F 989 269-6272
Bad Axe *(G-1102)*
Marcon Technologies LLC .... G 269 279-1701
Constantine *(G-3669)*
Pepro Enterprises Inc .... D 989 658-3200
Ubly *(G-17479)*
Plastic Trim Inc .... F 937 429-1100
Tawas City *(G-16365)*
Plastic Trim International Inc .... E 989 362-4419
Tawas City *(G-16366)*
Plastic Trim International Inc .... C 989 362-4419
East Tawas *(G-4920)*
Polymerica Limited Company .... E 248 542-2000
Huntington Woods *(G-8623)*
Srg Global Automotive LLC .... D 586 757-7800
Warren *(G-18024)*
Ssb Holdings Inc .... E 586 755-1660
Rochester Hills *(G-14117)*
Vidon Plastics Inc .... D 810 667-0634
Lapeer *(G-9965)*
Vintech Industries Inc .... C 810 724-7400
Imlay City *(G-8650)*

PLASTICS: Finished Injection Molded

2255srv LLC .... F 616 678-4900
Kent City *(G-9425)*
Advanced Auto Trends Inc .... E 248 628-6111
Oxford *(G-12871)*
Advanced Auto Trends Inc .... E 248 628-4850
Oxford *(G-12872)*
Akwel Cadillac Usa Inc .... B 231 775-6571
Cadillac *(G-2309)*
Akwel Cadillac Usa Inc .... F 248 476-8072
Novi *(G-12361)*
Akwel Usa Inc .... F 231 775-6571
Cadillac *(G-2311)*
AMP Innovative Tech LLC .... E 586 465-2700
Harrison Township *(G-7686)*
Bermar Associates Inc .... F 248 589-2460
Troy *(G-16975)*
Blade Industrial Products Inc .... G 248 773-7400
Wixom *(G-18621)*
Bomaur Quality Plastics Inc .... F 810 629-9701
Fenton *(G-5459)*
Cadillac Engineered Plas Inc .... F 231 775-2900
Cadillac *(G-2321)*
Cel Plastics Inc .... F 231 777-3941
Muskegon *(G-11790)*
Craig Assembly Inc .... C 810 326-1374
Saint Clair *(G-14821)*
Creative Foam Corporation .... G 810 714-0140
Fenton *(G-5468)*
Creative Foam Corporation .... C 810 629-4149
Fenton *(G-5467)*
Creative Techniques Inc .... D 248 373-3050
Orion *(G-12727)*
D Find Corporation .... G 248 641-2858
Troy *(G-17043)*
Dare Products Inc .... E 269 965-2307
Springfield *(G-15864)*
Djw Enterprises Inc .... G 414 791-6192
Crystal Falls *(G-3742)*
Ehc Inc .... G 313 259-2266
Troy *(G-17079)*
Eimo Technologies Inc .... E 269 649-0545
Vicksburg *(G-17603)*
Elmet North America Inc .... G 517 664-9011
Lansing *(G-9834)*
Engineered Plastic Products .... C 734 439-0310
Ypsilanti *(G-18943)*
Enginred Plstic Components Inc .... B 586 336-9500
Romeo *(G-14225)*
Enterprise Plastics LLC .... G 586 665-1030
Shelby Township *(G-15222)*
Ess Tec Inc .... D 616 394-0230
Holland *(G-8031)*
Exotic Rubber & Plastics Corp .... D 248 477-2122
New Hudson *(G-12053)*
Fido Enterprises Inc .... G 586 790-8200
Clinton Township *(G-3238)*
Ghsp Inc .... G 231 873-3300
Hart *(G-7752)*
Global Supply Integrator LLC .... G 586 484-0734
Davisburg *(G-3770)*
Gt Technologies Inc .... E 734 467-8371
Westland *(G-18378)*
HMS Mfg Co .... D 248 689-3232
Troy *(G-17145)*
HMS Mfg Co .... G 248 740-7040
Bloomfield Hills *(G-1828)*
Iig-Dss Technologies LLC .... F 586 725-5300
Ira *(G-8699)*
Illinois Tool Works Inc .... D 248 969-4248
Oxford *(G-12888)*
Imlay City Molded Pdts Corp .... E 810 721-9100
Imlay City *(G-8637)*
Instaset Plastics Company LLC .... C 586 725-0229
Anchorville *(G-339)*
Jma Tool Company Inc .... F 586 270-6706
New Haven *(G-12033)*
Jsj Corporation .... E 616 842-6350
Grand Haven *(G-6324)*
Kamex Molded Products LLC .... C 616 355-5900
Holland *(G-8108)*
Lapeer Plating & Plastics Inc .... C 810 667-4240
Lapeer *(G-9939)*
LDM Technologies Inc .... A 248 858-2800
Auburn Hills *(G-956)*
M-R Products Inc .... G 231 378-2251
Copemish *(G-3698)*
Mark Schwager Inc .... F 248 275-1978
Shelby Township *(G-15269)*
Mason Tackle Company .... E 810 631-4571
Otisville *(G-12783)*
McG Plastics Inc .... E 989 667-4349
Bay City *(G-1373)*
MGR Molds Inc .... F 586 254-6020
Sterling Heights *(G-16096)*
Michigan Church Supply Co Inc .... F 810 686-8877
Mount Morris *(G-11674)*
Midwest Plastic Engineering .... D 269 651-5223
Sturgis *(G-16309)*
Mohr Engineering Inc .... E 810 227-4598
Brighton *(G-2035)*
New Gldc LLC .... D 231 726-4002
Muskegon *(G-11885)*
Novares US Eng Components Inc .... G 248 799-8949
Southfield *(G-15667)*
Novares US LLC .... G 517 546-1900
Howell *(G-8485)*
Novares US LLC .... G 616 554-3555
Grand Rapids *(G-7051)*
Oakwood Energy Management Inc .... F 734 947-7700
Taylor *(G-16453)*
Oakwood Metal Fabricating Co .... E 313 561-7740
Dearborn *(G-3879)*
Omega Plastics Inc .... D 586 954-2100
Clinton Township *(G-3314)*
Petersen Products Inc .... E 248 446-0500
Brighton *(G-2051)*
Phillips-Medisize LLC .... F 248 592-2144
West Bloomfield *(G-18305)*
Proto-TEC Inc .... F 616 772-9511
Zeeland *(G-19075)*
Pti Engineered Plastics Inc .... B 586 263-5100
Macomb *(G-10631)*
R B L Plastics Incorporated .... E 313 873-8800
Detroit *(G-4550)*
R C Plastics Inc .... F 517 523-2112
Osseo *(G-12776)*
Ray Scott Industries Inc .... G 248 535-2528
Port Huron *(G-13522)*
Reliable Reasonable Tl Svc LLC .... F 586 630-6016
Clinton Township *(G-3335)*
Robinson Industries Inc .... C 989 465-6111
Coleman *(G-3472)*
Ronningen Research and Dev Co .... C 269 649-0520
Vicksburg *(G-17611)*
Royal Technologies Corporation .... D 616 669-3393
Hudsonville *(G-8605)*
Royal Technologies Corporation .... D 616 669-3393
Hudsonville *(G-8607)*
Royal Technologies Corporation .... B 616 667-4102
Hudsonville *(G-8608)*
Special Mold Engineering Inc .... E 248 652-6600
Rochester Hills *(G-14116)*
SPI LLC .... E 586 566-5870
Shelby Township *(G-15341)*
Systex Products Corporation .... C 269 964-8800
Battle Creek *(G-1304)*
Transnav Technologies Inc .... C 888 249-9955
New Baltimore *(G-11997)*
Tri-Way Manufacturing Inc .... E 586 776-0700
Roseville *(G-14485)*
Tribar Manufacturing LLC .... B 248 516-1600
Howell *(G-8536)*
Triple C Geothermal Inc .... G 517 282-7249
Muskegon *(G-11938)*
Unique-Chardan Inc .... D 419 636-6900
Auburn Hills *(G-1070)*
Urgent Plastic Services Inc .... G 248 852-8999
Rochester Hills *(G-14138)*
West Michigan Molding Inc .... C 616 846-4950
Grand Haven *(G-6382)*
Worswick Mold & Tool Inc .... F 810 765-1700
Marine City *(G-10970)*
Wright Plastic Products Co LLC .... G 810 326-3000
Saint Clair *(G-14845)*

PLASTICS: Injection Molded

21st Century Plastics Corp .... D 517 645-2695
Potterville *(G-13645)*
3d Polymers Inc .... F 248 588-5562
Orchard Lake *(G-12715)*
A & D Plastics Inc .... E 734 455-2255
Plymouth *(G-13108)*
A M R Inc .... G 810 329-9049
East China *(G-4854)*
Aak Fabrication & Plastics Inc .... G 734 525-1391
Southfield *(G-15468)*
Accurate Injection Molds Inc .... E 586 954-2553
Clinton Township *(G-3152)*
Acrylic Specialties .... G 248 588-4390
Madison Heights *(G-10658)*
Adac Door Components Inc .... B 616 957-0311
Grand Rapids *(G-6427)*
Adac Plastics Inc .... E 616 957-0311
Grand Rapids *(G-6428)*
Adac Plastics Inc .... E 231 777-2645
Muskegon *(G-11762)*
Adac Plastics Inc .... F 616 957-0311
Grand Rapids *(G-6429)*
Adac Plastics Inc .... E 616 957-0520
Muskegon *(G-11763)*

Adac Plastics Inc ....E 616 957-0311
Muskegon *(G-11764)*
Adept Plastic Finishing Inc ....G 248 863-5930
Wixom *(G-18596)*
Adept Plastic Finishing Inc ....G 248 374-5870
Wixom *(G-18597)*
Advanced Auto Trends Inc ....E 810 672-9203
Snover *(G-15389)*
Advanced Rubber & Plastic ....G 586 754-7398
Warren *(G-17693)*
Aees Power Systems Ltd Partnr ....G 269 668-4429
Farmington Hills *(G-5160)*
Affinity Custom Molding Inc ....E 269 496-8423
Mendon *(G-11215)*
Agape Plastics Inc ....C 616 735-4091
Grand Rapids *(G-6437)*
Aim Plastics Inc ....E 586 954-2553
Clinton Township *(G-3159)*
AIN Plastics ....F 248 356-4000
Southfield *(G-15472)*
Albar Industries Inc ....B 810 667-0150
Lapeer *(G-9911)*
Alco Plastics Inc ....D 586 752-4527
Romeo *(G-14219)*
Alp Lghting Cmpnnts Charlevoix ....F 231 547-6584
Charlevoix *(G-2708)*
Alp Lighting Ceiling Pdts Inc ....G 231 547-6584
Charlevoix *(G-2709)*
Ameri-Kart(mi) Corp ....C 269 641-5811
Cassopolis *(G-2625)*
Ann Arbor Plastics Inc ....G 734 944-0800
Saline *(G-15003)*
Antara Systems LLC ....D 616 895-7766
Allendale *(G-214)*
Anticipated Plastics Inc ....F 586 427-9450
Warren *(G-17707)*
ARC Group Worldwide Inc ....G 517 448-8954
Hudson *(G-8547)*
Artjay Industries Incorporated ....D 810 773-6450
Warren *(G-17715)*
Astar Inc ....E 574 234-2137
Niles *(G-12111)*
Atra Plastics Inc ....F 734 237-3393
Plymouth *(G-13128)*
Automotive Manufacturing ....G 517 566-8174
Sunfield *(G-16333)*
Avon Plastic Products Inc ....E 248 852-1000
Rochester Hills *(G-13960)*
B & H Plastic Co Inc ....F 586 727-7100
Richmond *(G-13834)*
B & N Plastics Inc ....G 586 758-0030
Warren *(G-17723)*
B C & A Co ....E 734 429-3129
Saline *(G-15005)*
Bangor Plastics Inc ....E 269 427-7971
Bangor *(G-1128)*
Belmont Engineered Plas LLC ....D 616 785-6279
Belmont *(G-1501)*
Belmont Plastics Solutions LLC ....F 616 340-3147
Belmont *(G-1502)*
Bentzer Incorporated ....F 269 663-3649
Edwardsburg *(G-5000)*
Bridgville Plastics Inc ....F 269 465-6516
Stevensville *(G-16241)*
Butler Plastics Company ....E 810 765-8811
Marine City *(G-10956)*
C E B Tooling Inc ....G 269 489-2251
Burr Oak *(G-2211)*
C-Plastics Inc ....E 616 837-7396
Nunica *(G-12577)*
Camcar Plastics Inc ....F 231 726-5000
Muskegon *(G-11789)*
Cascade Engineering Inc ....A 616 975-4800
Grand Rapids *(G-6552)*
Cascade Engineering Inc ....G 616 975-4767
Grand Rapids *(G-6553)*
Castano Plastics Inc ....G 248 624-3724
Wolverine Lake *(G-18796)*
Castino Corporation ....E 734 941-7200
Romulus *(G-14261)*
Century Plastics LLC ....F 586 697-5752
Macomb *(G-10584)*
Century Plastics LLC ....C 586 566-3900
Shelby Township *(G-15184)*
Cg Plastics Inc ....G 616 785-1900
Comstock Park *(G-3594)*
Chambers Industrial Tech Inc ....G 616 249-8190
Wyoming *(G-18856)*
Champion Plastics Inc ....E 248 373-8995
Auburn Hills *(G-842)*

CK Technologies ....G 616 836-6384
Hudsonville *(G-8574)*
Clarion Technologies Inc ....C 616 698-7277
Holland *(G-7998)*
Classic Die Inc ....E 616 454-3760
Grand Rapids *(G-6570)*
Clearform ....G 616 656-5359
Caledonia *(G-2372)*
Cni Plastics LLC ....E 517 541-4960
Charlotte *(G-2744)*
Colonial Manufacturing LLC ....G 269 926-1000
Benton Harbor *(G-1540)*
Colonial Plastics Incorporated ....E 586 469-4944
Shelby Township *(G-15191)*
Composite Techniques Inc ....F 616 878-9795
Grand Rapids *(G-6589)*
Continental Plastics Co ....A 586 294-4600
Shelby Township *(G-15195)*
Creative Form Corp ....G 810 714-5860
Fenton *(G-5469)*
Cs Manufacturing Inc ....B 616 696-2772
Cedar Springs *(G-2647)*
CSP Holding Corp ....D 248 237-7800
Auburn Hills *(G-853)*
CSP Holding Corp ....G 248 724-4410
Auburn Hills *(G-854)*
Cup Acquisition LLC ....C 616 735-4410
Grand Rapids *(G-6619)*
D T M 1 Inc ....E 248 889-9210
Highland *(G-7890)*
Davalor Mold Company LLC ....C 586 598-0100
Chesterfield *(G-2868)*
Derby Fabg Solutions LLC ....D 616 866-1650
Rockford *(G-14164)*
Design Manufacturing LLC ....E 616 647-2229
Walker *(G-17636)*
Diversified Engrg & Plas LLC ....D 517 789-8118
Jackson *(G-8868)*
Dl Engineering & Tech Inc ....G 248 852-6900
Rochester Hills *(G-13996)*
Dlhbowles Inc ....F 248 569-0652
Southfield *(G-15541)*
Do-All Plastic Inc ....G 313 824-6565
Detroit *(G-4185)*
Dse Industries LLC ....G 313 530-6668
Macomb *(G-10589)*
Dunnage Engineering Inc ....E 810 229-9501
Brighton *(G-1979)*
Eagle Fasteners Inc ....F 248 577-1441
Troy *(G-17076)*
Eagle Industries Inc ....E 248 624-4266
Wixom *(G-18650)*
Eagle Industries Inc ....E 248 624-4266
Wixom *(G-18651)*
Eagle Manufacturing Corp ....F 586 323-0303
Shelby Township *(G-15218)*
Eakas Corp ....G 815 488-1879
Novi *(G-12408)*
Eckert Mfg Co ....G 517 521-4905
Fowlerville *(G-5837)*
Edston Plastics Company ....G 734 941-3750
Brighton *(G-1983)*
Elite Plastic Products Inc ....E 586 247-5800
Shelby Township *(G-15220)*
Ell Tron Manufacturing Co ....E 989 983-3181
Vanderbilt *(G-17570)*
Emabond Solutions LLC ....F 248 481-8048
Auburn Hills *(G-879)*
Engineered Polymer Products ....E 269 461-6955
Eau Claire *(G-4976)*
Enginred Plstic Components Inc ....G 810 326-1650
Saint Clair *(G-14826)*
Enginred Plstic Components Inc ....G 248 825-4508
Troy *(G-17092)*
Enginred Plstic Components Inc ....G 810 326-1650
Saint Clair *(G-14827)*
Enginred Plstic Components Inc ....G 810 326-3010
Saint Clair *(G-14828)*
Engtechnik Inc ....G 734 667-4237
Canton *(G-2459)*
Enkon LLC ....E 937 890-5678
Manchester *(G-10883)*
Epc-Columbia Inc ....D 810 326-1650
Saint Clair *(G-14829)*
Erwin Quarder Inc ....D 616 575-1600
Grand Rapids *(G-6683)*
Evans Industries Inc ....G 313 259-2266
Troy *(G-17100)*
Exo-S US LLC ....G 248 614-9707
Troy *(G-17101)*

Exo-S US LLC ....C 517 278-8567
Coldwater *(G-3433)*
Extreme Tool and Engrg Inc ....G 906 229-9100
Wakefield *(G-17621)*
Faith Plastics LLC ....E 269 646-2294
Marcellus *(G-10948)*
Ferro Industries Inc ....E 586 792-6001
Harrison Township *(G-7699)*
Flight Mold & Engineering Inc ....E 810 329-2900
Saint Clair *(G-14830)*
Gem Plastics Inc ....G 616 538-5966
Grand Rapids *(G-6736)*
Gemini Group ME & T ....G 989 553-5685
Bad Axe *(G-1103)*
Gemini Group Services Inc ....F 248 435-7271
Bad Axe *(G-1104)*
Gemini Plastics De Mexico Inc ....G 989 658-8557
Ubly *(G-17477)*
Glov Enterprises LLC ....D 517 423-9700
Tecumseh *(G-16502)*
Grace Production Services LLC ....G 810 643-8070
Chesterfield *(G-2889)*
Grand Haven Custom Molding LLC ....D 616 935-3160
Grand Haven *(G-6302)*
Green Plastics LLC ....F 616 295-2718
Holland *(G-8061)*
Grimm Industries LLC ....G 810 335-3188
New Baltimore *(G-11981)*
Grw Technologies Inc ....C 616 575-8119
Grand Rapids *(G-6792)*
Gt Plastics Incorporated ....E 989 739-7803
Oscoda *(G-12759)*
Gwinnett Plastics Inc ....G 765 215-6593
Grand Rapids *(G-6796)*
Harbor Isle Plastics LLC ....F 269 465-6004
Stevensville *(G-16253)*
Hi-Craft Engineering Inc ....D 586 293-0551
Fraser *(G-5936)*
Hicks Plastics Company Inc ....D 586 786-5640
Macomb *(G-10602)*
Holland Plastics Corporation ....E 616 844-2505
Grand Haven *(G-6318)*
Hpi ....G 989 465-6141
Coleman *(G-3466)*
Industries Unlimited Inc ....F 586 949-4300
Chesterfield *(G-2893)*
Integra Mold Inc ....G 269 327-4337
Portage *(G-13568)*
Inteva Products LLC ....B 517 266-8030
Adrian *(G-74)*
Intrepid Plastics Mfg Inc ....G 616 901-5718
Lakeview *(G-9642)*
Ironwood Plastics Inc ....C 906 932-5025
Ironwood *(G-8764)*
J M Mold Technologies Inc ....F 586 773-6664
Warren *(G-17880)*
Jac Holding Corporation ....G 248 874-1800
Pontiac *(G-13384)*
Jac Products Inc ....G 734 944-8844
Saline *(G-15022)*
Jac Products Inc ....D 248 874-1800
Pontiac *(G-13385)*
Jcim Mexico Holdings LLC ....F 734 254-3100
Plymouth *(G-13201)*
Jelaga Inc ....G 517 263-5190
Adrian *(G-77)*
Jer-Den Plastics Inc ....E 989 681-4303
Saint Louis *(G-14991)*
Jgr Plastics LLC ....E 810 990-1957
Port Huron *(G-13490)*
Jimdi Receivables Inc ....E 616 895-7766
Allendale *(G-221)*
JK Machining Inc ....F 269 344-0870
Kalamazoo *(G-9232)*
Johnson Walker & Assoc LLC ....G 810 688-1600
North Branch *(G-12179)*
Jvis International LLC ....C 586 739-9542
Shelby Township *(G-15249)*
Kam Plastics Corp ....D 616 355-5900
Holland *(G-8107)*
Kautex Inc ....A 248 616-0327
Madison Heights *(G-10760)*
Kinne Plastics Inc ....G 989 435-4373
Beaverton *(G-1427)*
Klann ....G 313 565-4135
Dearborn *(G-3858)*
Kruger Plastic Products LLC ....C 269 545-3311
Galien *(G-6088)*
Lacks Industries Inc ....C 616 554-7135
Kentwood *(G-9463)*

PLASTICS: Injection Molded

Lacks Wheel Trim Systems LLC .... F 248 351-0555
 Novi *(G-12463)*
Lacks Wheel Trim Systems LLC .... E 616 949-6570
 Grand Rapids *(G-6922)*
Lawrence Plastics LLC .... D 248 475-0186
 Clarkston *(G-3044)*
LDB Plastics Inc .... G 586 566-9698
 Shelby Township *(G-15259)*
Leeann Plastics Inc .... F 269 489-5035
 Burr Oak *(G-2212)*
Lexamar Corporation .... B 231 582-3163
 Boyne City *(G-1894)*
Liberty Plastics Inc .... G 616 994-7033
 Holland *(G-8128)*
Lincoln Industries .... G 989 736-6421
 Lincoln *(G-10036)*
Linear Mold & Engineering LLC .... F 734 422-6060
 Livonia *(G-10283)*
Loose Plastics Inc .... C 989 246-1880
 Gladwin *(G-6200)*
Luckmarr Plastics LLC .... E 586 978-8498
 Sterling Heights *(G-16077)*
M & E Plastics LLC .... F 989 875-4191
 Ithaca *(G-8792)*
Machine Star LLC .... G 616 245-6400
 Grand Rapids *(G-6955)*
Majestic Formed Plastics .... G 269 663-2870
 Edwardsburg *(G-5007)*
Mann + Hummel Usa Inc .... E 248 857-8501
 Kalamazoo *(G-9265)*
Mann + Hummel Usa Inc .... F 269 329-3900
 Portage *(G-13582)*
Mantissa Industries Inc .... G 517 694-2260
 Holt *(G-8317)*
Maple Valley Plastics LLC .... E 810 346-3040
 Brown City *(G-2140)*
Marjo Plastics Company Inc .... G 734 455-4130
 Plymouth *(G-13235)*
Matrix Manufacturing Inc .... G 616 532-6000
 Grand Rapids *(G-6966)*
Maya Plastics Inc .... E 586 997-6000
 Shelby Township *(G-15271)*
Mayco International LLC .... C 586 803-6000
 Clinton Township *(G-3296)*
Mayco International LLC .... E 586 803-6000
 Auburn Hills *(G-971)*
Mayco International LLC .... C 586 803-6000
 Warren *(G-17919)*
Mayco International LLC .... A 586 803-6000
 Sterling Heights *(G-16087)*
Mayfair Plastics Inc .... D 989 732-2441
 Gaylord *(G-6148)*
Mc Pherson Plastics Inc .... D 269 694-9487
 Otsego *(G-12790)*
Medbio LLC .... D 616 245-0214
 Grand Rapids *(G-6975)*
Miniature Custom Mfg LLC .... E 269 998-1277
 Vicksburg *(G-17608)*
Mmi Companies LLC .... E 248 528-1680
 Troy *(G-17263)*
Mmi Engineered Solutions Inc .... D 734 429-4664
 Saline *(G-15028)*
Mmi Engineered Solutions Inc .... E 734 429-5130
 Warren *(G-17933)*
Modern Plastics Technology LLC .... D 810 966-3376
 Port Huron *(G-13503)*
Mold Masters Co .... C 810 245-4100
 Lapeer *(G-9948)*
Mold-Rite LLC .... G 586 296-3970
 Fraser *(G-5965)*
Molded Plastic Industries Inc .... E 517 694-7434
 Holt *(G-8318)*
Molded Plastics & Tooling .... F 517 268-0849
 Holt *(G-8319)*
Moldex3d Northern America Inc .... F 248 946-4570
 Farmington Hills *(G-5326)*
Molding Concepts Inc .... E 586 264-6990
 Sterling Heights *(G-16103)*
Molding Solutions Inc .... E 616 847-6822
 Grand Haven *(G-6337)*
Moller Group North America Inc .... D 586 532-0860
 Shelby Township *(G-15284)*
Monroe Inc .... G 616 284-3358
 Grand Rapids *(G-7026)*
Moon Roof Corporation America .... E 586 552-1901
 Roseville *(G-14447)*
Morren Mold & Machine Inc .... G 616 892-7474
 Allendale *(G-226)*
Mp6 LLC .... G 231 409-7530
 Traverse City *(G-16765)*

Mpi Plastics .... G 201 502-1534
 Macomb *(G-10620)*
Msinc .... F 248 275-1978
 Shelby Township *(G-15286)*
Multi-Form Plastics Inc .... F 586 786-4229
 Macomb *(G-10621)*
N-K Manufacturing Tech LLC .... E 616 248-3200
 Grand Rapids *(G-7034)*
Narburgh & Tidd LLC .... G 734 281-1959
 Riverview *(G-13881)*
National Plastek Inc .... E 616 698-9559
 Caledonia *(G-2390)*
Noack Ventures LLC .... G 248 583-0311
 Troy *(G-17280)*
Northern Mold .... G 231 629-1342
 Howard City *(G-8414)*
Northern Plastics Inc .... E 586 979-7737
 Sterling Heights *(G-16118)*
Nova Industries Inc .... E 586 294-9182
 Fraser *(G-5970)*
Novares US LLC .... D 248 449-6100
 Livonia *(G-10339)*
Nyloncraft of Michigan LLC .... B 517 849-9911
 Jonesville *(G-9097)*
Nyx LLC .... C 734 462-2385
 Livonia *(G-10343)*
Nyx LLC .... D 734 467-7200
 Westland *(G-18402)*
Nyx LLC .... D 734 421-3850
 Livonia *(G-10345)*
Nyx LLC .... D 734 261-7535
 Livonia *(G-10347)*
Oakley Industries Inc .... E 586 791-3194
 Clinton Township *(G-3310)*
Omega Plastic Inc .... E 816 246-3115
 Clinton Township *(G-3313)*
Oth Consultants Inc .... C 586 598-0100
 Chesterfield *(G-2920)*
P & K Technologies Inc .... G 586 336-9545
 Romeo *(G-14231)*
Parousia Plastics Inc .... G 989 832-4054
 Midland *(G-11402)*
Patton Tool and Die Inc .... F 810 359-5336
 Lexington *(G-10031)*
Pds Plastics Inc .... F 616 896-1109
 Dorr *(G-4769)*
Pearce Plastics LLC .... F 231 519-5994
 Fremont *(G-6053)*
Pegasus Tool LLC .... G 313 255-5900
 Detroit *(G-4515)*
Pepro Enterprises Inc .... E 989 658-3200
 Ubly *(G-17480)*
Pepro Enterprises Inc .... G 248 435-7271
 Clawson *(G-3103)*
Petoskey Plastics Inc .... E 231 347-2602
 Petoskey *(G-13015)*
Pioneer Molded Products Inc .... E 616 977-4172
 Grand Rapids *(G-7087)*
Plast-O-Foam LLC .... D 586 307-3790
 Clinton Township *(G-3319)*
Plastechs of Michigan LLC .... E 734 429-3129
 Saline *(G-15031)*
Plastic Dress-Up Service Inc .... F 586 727-7878
 Port Huron *(G-13517)*
Plastic Mold Technology Inc .... D 616 698-9810
 Kentwood *(G-9469)*
Plastic Mold Technology Inc .... D 616 698-9810
 Grand Rapids *(G-7089)*
Plastic Molding Development .... G 586 739-4500
 Sterling Heights *(G-16129)*
Plastic Solutions LLC .... G 231 824-7350
 Traverse City *(G-16799)*
Plastic Trends Inc .... D 586 232-4167
 Shelby Township *(G-15303)*
Plastico Industries Inc .... F 616 304-6289
 Carson City *(G-2595)*
Plastics By Design Inc .... G 269 646-3388
 Marcellus *(G-10950)*
Plastomer Corporation .... C 734 464-0700
 Livonia *(G-10366)*
Pliant Plastics Corp .... D 616 844-0300
 Spring Lake *(G-15843)*
Pliant Plastics Corp .... F 616 844-3215
 Spring Lake *(G-15844)*
Poly Flex Products Inc .... E 734 458-4194
 Farmington Hills *(G-5349)*
Polymer Process Dev LLC .... D 586 464-6400
 Shelby Township *(G-15304)*
Polymer Products Group Inc .... G 989 723-9570
 Owosso *(G-12851)*

Precision Industries Inc .... F 810 239-5816
 Flint *(G-5747)*
Precision Masters Inc .... E 248 648-8071
 Auburn Hills *(G-1003)*
Precision Mold Machining Svcs .... E 586 774-2330
 Warren *(G-17972)*
Precision Polymer Mfg Inc .... E 269 344-2044
 Kalamazoo *(G-9305)*
Precision Tool & Mold LLC .... F 906 932-3440
 Ironwood *(G-8770)*
Primera Plastics Inc .... D 616 748-6248
 Zeeland *(G-19072)*
Prism Plastics Inc .... F 810 292-6300
 Chesterfield *(G-2928)*
Prism Plastics Inc .... E 810 292-6300
 Shelby Township *(G-15308)*
Pro Slot Ltd .... G 616 897-6000
 Hartford *(G-7766)*
Profile Mfg Inc .... E 586 598-0007
 Chesterfield *(G-2931)*
Proper Polymers - Warren LLC .... E 586 552-5267
 Warren *(G-17984)*
Proper Polymers-Pulaski LLC .... C 931 371-3147
 Warren *(G-17986)*
Proto Crafts Inc .... D 810 376-3665
 Deckerville *(G-3956)*
Proto Shapes Inc .... F 517 278-3947
 Coldwater *(G-3447)*
Purforms Inc .... E 616 897-3000
 Lowell *(G-10514)*
Qcq Design & Fab Inc .... G 810 735-4033
 Linden *(G-10069)*
Quality Assured Plastics Inc .... E 269 674-3888
 Lawrence *(G-9983)*
Rak-O-Nizer LLC .... G 810 444-9807
 Marysville *(G-11098)*
Reed City Group LLC .... D 231 832-7500
 Reed City *(G-13797)*
Regal Finishing Co Inc .... G 269 849-2963
 Coloma *(G-3482)*
Retro Enterprises Inc .... G 269 435-8583
 Constantine *(G-3675)*
Revere Plastics Systems LLC .... C 586 415-4823
 Fraser *(G-5988)*
Revere Plastics Systems LLC .... B 833 300-4043
 Novi *(G-12525)*
Riverside Plastic Co .... F 231 937-7333
 Howard City *(G-8417)*
Rkaa Business LLC .... E 231 734-5517
 Evart *(G-5127)*
Robmar Plastics Inc .... G 989 386-9600
 Clare *(G-2995)*
Roto-Plastics Corporation .... D 517 263-8981
 Adrian *(G-92)*
Rowland Plastics LLC .... F 616 875-5400
 Zeeland *(G-19078)*
Royal Plastics LLC .... E 616 669-3393
 Hudsonville *(G-8604)*
Royal Technologies Corporation .... B 616 667-4102
 Hudsonville *(G-8606)*
Royal Technologies Corporation .... B 616 669-3393
 Hudsonville *(G-8609)*
RPS Tool and Engineering Inc .... E 586 298-6590
 Roseville *(G-14474)*
Sac Plastics Inc .... E 616 846-0820
 Spring Lake *(G-15849)*
Saginaw Bay Plastics Inc .... D 989 686-7860
 Kawkawlin *(G-9418)*
SCC Plastics Inc .... E 231 759-8820
 Norton Shores *(G-12329)*
Seagate Plastics Company .... G 517 547-8123
 Addison *(G-45)*
Sebro Plastics Inc .... E 248 348-4121
 Wixom *(G-18749)*
Sierra Plastics Inc .... G 989 269-6272
 Bad Axe *(G-1110)*
Sohner Plastics LLC .... F 734 222-4847
 Dexter *(G-4756)*
Soltis Plastics Corp .... G 248 698-1440
 White Lake *(G-18466)*
Specialty Manufacturing Inc .... E 989 790-9011
 Saginaw *(G-14763)*
Speed Cinch Inc .... G 269 646-2016
 Marcellus *(G-10952)*
Spencer Plastics Inc .... E 231 942-7100
 Cadillac *(G-2356)*
SPI Blow Molding LLC .... E 269 849-3200
 Coloma *(G-3483)*
Spiratex Company .... D 734 289-4800
 Monroe *(G-11576)*

Employee Codes: A=Over 500 employees, B=251-500
C=101-250, D=51-100, E=20-50, F=10-19, G=3-9

Sr Injection Molding Inc ... G ... 586 260-2360
Harrison Township ***(G-7726)***

Stellar Plastics Fabg LLC ... G ... 313 527-7337
Detroit ***(G-4609)***

Stone Plastics and Mfg Inc ... C ... 616 748-9740
Zeeland ***(G-19082)***

Sturgis Molded Products Co ... C ... 269 651-9381
Sturgis ***(G-16324)***

Su-Dan Plastics Inc ... C ... 248 651-6035
Rochester ***(G-13932)***

Su-Dan Plastics Inc ... F ... 248 651-6035
Rochester Hills ***(G-14121)***

Summit Plastic Molding Inc ... E ... 586 262-4500
Shelby Township ***(G-15344)***

Summit Plastic Molding II Inc ... G ... 586 262-4500
Shelby Township ***(G-15345)***

Summit Polymers Inc ... C ... 269 324-9330
Portage ***(G-13622)***

Summit Polymers Inc ... G ... 269 324-9320
Portage ***(G-13623)***

Summit Polymers Inc ... B ... 269 324-9330
Kalamazoo ***(G-9345)***

Summit Polymers Inc ... B ... 269 323-1301
Portage ***(G-13624)***

Summit Polymers Inc ... G ... 269 649-4900
Vicksburg ***(G-17614)***

Sunningdale Tech Inc ... G ... 248 526-0517
Troy ***(G-17378)***

Supreme Industries LLC ... G ... 586 725-2500
Ira ***(G-8715)***

Sur-Form LLC ... E ... 586 221-1950
Chesterfield ***(G-2951)***

T & K Industries Inc ... G ... 586 212-9100
Clinton Township ***(G-3371)***

Talco Industries ... G ... 989 269-6260
Bad Axe ***(G-1112)***

Tech Group Grand Rapids Inc ... B ... 616 490-2197
Walker ***(G-17653)***

Technimold Inc ... F ... 906 284-1921
Caspian ***(G-2609)***

Teijin Auto Tech Mnchester LLC ... D ... 734 428-8301
Manchester ***(G-10890)***

Teijin Auto Tech NA Hldngs Cor ... C ... 248 237-7800
Auburn Hills ***(G-1048)***

Teijin Automotive Tech Inc ... C ... 248 237-7800
Auburn Hills ***(G-1049)***

Ten X Plastics LLC ... G ... 616 813-3037
Grand Rapids ***(G-7252)***

Tesca Usa Inc ... E ... 586 991-0744
Rochester Hills ***(G-14124)***

Th Plastics Inc ... C ... 269 496-8495
Mendon ***(G-11222)***

Thermo Flex LLC ... G ... 734 458-4194
Farmington Hills ***(G-5398)***

Thermoforms Inc ... F ... 616 974-0055
Kentwood ***(G-9481)***

Three 60 Roto LLC ... F ... 517 545-3600
Howell ***(G-8532)***

Thumb Plastics Inc ... B ... 989 269-9791
Bad Axe ***(G-1114)***

Tk Mold & Engineering Inc ... E ... 586 752-5840
Romeo ***(G-14238)***

Tomas Plastics Inc ... G ... 734 455-4706
Canton ***(G-2535)***

Tomas Plastics Inc ... G ... 734 455-4706
Plymouth ***(G-13318)***

Tooling Cncepts Design Not Inc ... F ... 810 444-9807
Port Huron ***(G-13533)***

Total Molding Solutions Inc ... E ... 517 424-5900
Tecumseh ***(G-16519)***

Trans Industries Plastics LLC ... E ... 248 310-0008
Rochester ***(G-13934)***

Transnav Holdings Inc ... C ... 586 716-5600
New Baltimore ***(G-11996)***

Trestle Plastic Services LLC ... G ... 616 262-5484
Hamilton ***(G-7608)***

Tri-Star Molding Inc ... E ... 269 646-0062
Marcellus ***(G-10953)***

Undercar Products Group Inc ... B ... 616 719-4571
Wyoming ***(G-18916)***

Uniflex Inc ... G ... 248 486-6000
Brighton ***(G-2088)***

Uniloy Inc ... D ... 514 424-8900
Tecumseh ***(G-16520)***

Universal Products Inc ... E ... 231 937-5555
Rockford ***(G-14192)***

University Plastics Inc ... G ... 734 668-8773
Ann Arbor ***(G-706)***

US Farathane Holdings Corp ... G ... 586 726-1200
Sterling Heights ***(G-16218)***

US Farathane Holdings Corp ... B ... 248 754-7000
Auburn Hills ***(G-1073)***

US Farathane Holdings Corp ... G ... 586 978-2800
Troy ***(G-17415)***

US Farathane Holdings Corp ... G ... 248 754-7000
Port Huron ***(G-13536)***

US Farathane Holdings Corp ... G ... 248 754-7000
Lake Orion ***(G-9636)***

US Farathane Holdings Corp ... G ... 586 978-2800
Westland ***(G-18426)***

US Farathane Holdings Corp ... G ... 586 685-4000
Sterling Heights ***(G-16220)***

US Farathane Holdings Corp ... G ... 586 726-1200
Shelby Township ***(G-15361)***

US Farathane Holdings Corp ... G ... 248 754-7000
Orion ***(G-12739)***

US Mold LLC ... G ... 586 719-7239
Hazel Park ***(G-7846)***

USA Summit Plas Silao 1 LLC ... C ... 269 324-9330
Portage ***(G-13630)***

USF Westland LLC ... F ... 248 754-7000
Auburn Hills ***(G-1076)***

Vacuum Orna Metal Company Inc ... E ... 734 941-9100
Romulus ***(G-14336)***

Valley Enterprises Ubly Inc ... C ... 989 658-3200
Ubly ***(G-17485)***

Valtec LLC ... C ... 810 724-5048
Imlay City ***(G-8649)***

Vaupell Molding & Tooling Inc ... F ... 269 435-8414
Constantine ***(G-3677)***

Ventra Evart LLC ... G ... 231 734-9000
Evart ***(G-5128)***

Vivatar Inc ... E ... 616 928-0750
Holland ***(G-8239)***

Western Diversified Plas LLC ... G ... 269 668-3393
Mattawan ***(G-11169)***

Western Michigan Plastics ... F ... 616 394-9269
Holland ***(G-8247)***

Windsor Mold Inc ... G ... 734 944-5080
Saline ***(G-15045)***

Windsor Mold USA Inc ... E ... 734 944-5080
Saline ***(G-15046)***

WI Molding of Michigan LLC ... D ... 269 327-3075
Portage ***(G-13633)***

World Class Prototypes Inc ... F ... 616 355-0200
Holland ***(G-8253)***

Wow Products USA ... G ... 989 672-1300
Caro ***(G-2586)***

Wright Plastic Products Co LLC ... D ... 989 291-3211
Sheridan ***(G-15386)***

Xcentric Mold & Engrg LLC ... D ... 586 598-4636
Clinton Township ***(G-3390)***

Yanfeng US Auto Intr Systems I ... G ... 313 259-3226
Detroit ***(G-4697)***

PLASTICS: Molded

A S Plus Industries Inc ... G ... 586 741-0400
Clinton Township ***(G-3148)***

ABC Packaging Eqp & Mtls Inc ... F ... 616 784-2330
Comstock Park ***(G-3584)***

Advanced Special Tools Inc ... C ... 269 962-9697
Battle Creek ***(G-1179)***

Atlantic Precision Pdts Inc ... F ... 586 532-9420
Shelby Township ***(G-15174)***

Clarion Technologies Inc ... E ... 616 754-1199
Greenville ***(G-7479)***

Cusolar Industries Inc ... E ... 586 949-3880
Chesterfield ***(G-2863)***

Die Stampco Inc ... F ... 989 893-7790
Bay City ***(G-1344)***

Eco - Composites LLC ... G ... 616 395-8902
Holland ***(G-8022)***

GMI Composites Inc ... D ... 231 755-1611
Muskegon ***(G-11825)***

Grm Corporation ... E ... 989 453-2322
Pigeon ***(G-13037)***

Hilco Industrial Plastics LLC ... G ... 616 554-8833
Caledonia ***(G-2381)***

Hilco Industrial Plastics LLC ... E ... 616 554-8833
Caledonia ***(G-2382)***

Humphrey Companies LLC ... C ... 616 530-1717
Grandville ***(G-7389)***

Innovative Engineering Mich ... G ... 517 977-0460
Lansing ***(G-9705)***

Lacks Enterprises Inc ... D ... 616 949-6570
Grand Rapids ***(G-6908)***

Lacks Industries Inc ... C ... 616 698-6890
Grand Rapids ***(G-6915)***

Lacks Industries Inc ... C ... 616 698-3600
Grand Rapids ***(G-6916)***

Lacks Industries Inc ... C ... 616 698-6854
Grand Rapids ***(G-6917)***

Lacks Industries Inc ... C ... 616 698-2776
Grand Rapids ***(G-6920)***

Latin American Industries LLC ... G ... 616 301-1878
Grand Rapids ***(G-6932)***

Leon Interiors Inc ... B ... 616 422-7557
Holland ***(G-8125)***

McKechnie Vhcl Cmpnnts USA Inc ... B ... 218 894-1218
Roseville ***(G-14438)***

Michiana Rtational Molding LLC ... F ... 574 849-7077
Constantine ***(G-3670)***

Mig Molding LLC ... G ... 810 660-8435
Almont ***(G-266)***

Molded Materials ... F ... 734 927-1989
Plymouth ***(G-13247)***

Monroe LLC ... B ... 616 942-9820
Grand Rapids ***(G-7025)***

Palmer Distributors Inc ... D ... 586 772-4225
Fraser ***(G-5973)***

PDM Industries Inc ... E ... 231 943-9601
Traverse City ***(G-16786)***

Pinconning Metals Inc ... G ... 989 879-3144
Pinconning ***(G-13064)***

Proper Polymers- Tennessee Inc ... G ... 586 779-8787
Warren ***(G-17985)***

Reeves Plastics LLC ... E ... 616 997-0777
Coopersville ***(G-3696)***

Rockford Molding & Trim ... G ... 616 874-8997
Rockford ***(G-14189)***

Sequoia Molding ... G ... 586 463-4400
Grosse Pointe ***(G-7533)***

Shape Corp ... B ... 616 846-8700
Grand Haven ***(G-6361)***

Shinwon USA Inc ... E ... 734 469-2550
Livonia ***(G-10405)***

Shoreline Mold & Engrg LLC ... G ... 269 926-2223
Benton Harbor ***(G-1584)***

Soroc Products Inc ... E ... 810 743-2660
Burton ***(G-2246)***

TAW Plastics LLC ... G ... 616 302-0954
Greenville ***(G-7507)***

Ventra Ionia Main LLC ... A ... 616 597-3220
Ionia ***(G-8693)***

PLASTICS: Polystyrene Foam

Action Fabricators Inc ... C ... 616 957-2032
Grand Rapids ***(G-6423)***

Advance Engineering Company ... E ... 989 435-3641
Beaverton ***(G-1423)***

Armaly Sponge Company ... E ... 248 669-2100
Commerce Township ***(G-3512)***

Aspen Technologies Inc ... D ... 248 446-1485
Brighton ***(G-1947)***

Bespro Pattern Inc ... E ... 586 268-6970
Madison Heights ***(G-10681)***

Bremen Corp ... F ... 574 546-4238
Fenton ***(G-5460)***

Briggs Industries Inc ... E ... 586 749-5191
Chesterfield ***(G-2852)***

Creative Foam Cmpsite Systems ... G ... 810 629-4149
Flint ***(G-5676)***

Creative Foam Corporation ... C ... 810 629-4149
Fenton ***(G-5467)***

Dart Container Corp California ... D ... 517 244-6408
Mason ***(G-11121)***

Dart Container Corp Florida ... G ... 800 248-5960
Mason ***(G-11122)***

Dart Container Corp Georgia ... B ... 517 676-3800
Mason ***(G-11123)***

Dart Container Corporation ... A ... 517 676-3800
Mason ***(G-11126)***

Dart Container Michigan LLC ... A ... 248 669-3767
Wixom ***(G-18643)***

Dart Container Michigan LLC ... A ... 517 244-6249
Mason ***(G-11127)***

Derby Fabg Solutions LLC ... D ... 616 866-1650
Rockford ***(G-14164)***

Dow Chemical Company ... C ... 989 636-4406
Midland ***(G-11343)***

Dow Chemical Company ... A ... 989 636-1000
Midland ***(G-11341)***

Dow Chemical Company ... G ... 989 636-0540
Midland ***(G-11349)***

Dow Chemical Company ... D ... 989 636-5409
Midland ***(G-11352)***

Dow Inc ... A ... 989 636-1000
Midland ***(G-11354)***

Envirolite LLC ... D ... 888 222-2191
Coldwater ***(G-3432)***

PRODUCT SECTION — PLATING & POLISHING SVC

Company	Code	Phone
Envirolite LLC	F	248 792-3184
Troy (G-17094)		
Floracraft Corporation	C	231 845-5127
Ludington (G-10536)		
Foam Factory Incorporated	E	586 739-7449
Macomb (G-10596)		
Fomcore LLC	D	231 366-4791
Muskegon (G-11819)		
Fxi Novi	G	248 994-0630
Novi (G-12421)		
Gemini Plastics Inc	C	989 658-8557
Ubly (G-17476)		
Grand Haven Gasket Company	E	616 842-7682
Grand Haven (G-6303)		
Green Polymeric Materials Inc	E	313 933-7390
Detroit (G-4280)		
Huntington Foam LLC	C	661 225-9951
Greenville (G-7493)		
Inter-Pack Corporation	E	734 242-7755
Monroe (G-11551)		
Jsj Corporation	E	616 842-6350
Grand Haven (G-6324)		
Kent Manufacturing Company	D	616 454-9495
Grand Rapids (G-6889)		
Kringer Industrial Corporation	F	519 818-3509
Warren (G-17897)		
Leon Interiors Inc	B	616 422-7557
Holland (G-8125)		
Light Metal Forming Corp	F	248 851-3984
Bloomfield Hills (G-1831)		
Package Design & Mfg Inc	E	248 486-4390
Brighton (G-2046)		
Plascore Inc	E	616 772-1220
Zeeland (G-19071)		
Pratt Classic Container Inc	E	734 525-0410
Livonia (G-10372)		
Reklein Plastics Incorporated	G	586 739-8850
Sterling Heights (G-16145)		
Revstone Industries LLC	E	248 351-1000
Troy (G-17331)		
Rogers Foam Automotive Corp	E	810 820-6323
Flint (G-5756)		
Sekisui America Corporation	G	517 279-7587
Coldwater (G-3453)		
Sekisui Voltek LLC	C	517 279-7587
Coldwater (G-3455)		
Southwestern Foam Tech Inc	G	616 726-1677
Grand Rapids (G-7205)		
Special Projects Engineering	G	517 676-8525
Mason (G-11157)		
Surrey USA LLC	G	800 248-5960
Mason (G-11159)		
Sweetheart Corp	G	847 405-2100
Mason (G-11160)		
Transpak Inc	E	586 264-2064
Sterling Heights (G-16209)		
Ufp Technologies Inc	D	616 949-8100
Grand Rapids (G-7294)		
Unique Fabricating Inc	A	248 853-2333
Auburn Hills (G-1068)		
Unique Fabricating Na Inc	B	248 853-2333
Auburn Hills (G-1069)		
Unique Fabricating Na Inc	G	248 853-2333
Rochester Hills (G-14136)		
Unique Molded Foam Tech Inc	F	517 524-9010
Concord (G-3657)		
Unique-Chardan Inc	D	419 636-6900
Auburn Hills (G-1070)		
Woodbridge Holdings Inc	G	248 288-0100
Troy (G-17451)		

PLASTICS: Thermoformed

Company	Code	Phone
Advance Engineering Company	E	989 435-3641
Beaverton (G-1423)		
Airpark Plastics LLC	F	989 846-1029
Standish (G-15886)		
Cadillac Products Inc	B	248 813-8200
Troy (G-16992)		
Contour Engineering Inc	F	989 828-6526
Shepherd (G-15376)		
Fabri-Kal Corporation	F	269 385-5050
Kalamazoo (G-9183)		
Formed Solutions Inc	F	616 395-5455
Holland (G-8039)		
Forming Technologies LLC	D	231 777-7030
Muskegon (G-11820)		
Plexicase Inc	G	616 246-6400
Wyoming (G-18900)		
PRA Company	D	989 846-1029
Standish (G-15895)		

Company	Code	Phone
Summit Polymers Inc	B	269 651-1643
Sturgis (G-16326)		
Two Mitts Inc	G	800 888-5054
Kalamazoo (G-9359)		

PLATE WORK: For Nuclear Industry

Company	Code	Phone
Metal Quest Inc	G	989 733-2011
Onaway (G-12699)		

PLATE WORK: Metalworking Trade

Company	Code	Phone
Moore Flame Cutting Co	F	586 978-1090
Bloomfield Hills (G-1840)		

PLATEMAKING SVC: Color Separations, For The Printing Trade

Company	Code	Phone
Al Corp	F	734 475-7357
Chelsea (G-2804)		
Alpha 21 LLC	G	248 352-7330
Southfield (G-15476)		
Group Infotech Inc	E	517 336-7110
Lansing (G-9848)		
North American Color Inc	E	269 323-0552
Portage (G-13588)		

PLATEMAKING SVC: Gravure

Company	Code	Phone
Diamond Graphics Inc	G	269 345-1164
Kalamazoo (G-9167)		

PLATEMAKING SVC: Gravure, Plates Or Cylinders

Company	Code	Phone
Trico Incorporated	G	517 764-1780
Jackson (G-9023)		

PLATEMAKING SVC: Letterpress

Company	Code	Phone
Weighman Enterprises Inc	G	989 755-2116
Saginaw (G-14792)		

PLATES

Company	Code	Phone
A D Johnson Engraving Co Inc	F	269 385-0044
Kalamazoo (G-9106)		
Behrmann Printing Company Inc	F	248 799-7771
Southfield (G-15505)		
Breck Graphics Incorporated	E	616 248-4110
Grand Rapids (G-6523)		
Britten Inc	C	231 941-8200
Traverse City (G-16627)		
Britten Banners LLC	C	231 941-8200
Traverse City (G-16628)		
Dearborn Lithograph Inc	E	734 464-4242
Livonia (G-10176)		
F & A Enterprises of Michigan	F	906 228-3222
Marquette (G-11018)		
Fortis Sltions Group Centl LLC	D	248 437-5200
Wixom (G-18664)		
Graphic Enterprises Inc	D	248 616-4900
Madison Heights (G-10732)		
Graphic Specialties Inc	E	616 247-0060
Grand Rapids (G-6783)		
Hamblin Company	E	517 423-7491
Bloomfield Hills (G-1826)		
Industrial Imprntng & Die Ctng	G	586 778-9470
Eastpointe (G-4937)		
Kalamazoo Photo Comp Svcs	G	269 345-3706
Kalamazoo (G-9245)		
Mark Maker Company Inc	E	616 538-6980
Grand Rapids (G-6959)		
Marketing VI Group Inc	G	989 793-3933
Saginaw (G-14686)		
Mel Color Inc	E	313 928-5440
Taylor (G-16440)		
Microforms Inc	E	586 939-7900
Beverly Hills (G-1667)		
North American Graphics Inc	F	586 486-1110
Warren (G-17947)		
Qrp Inc	G	989 496-2955
Midland (G-11405)		
Safran Printing Company Inc	F	586 939-7600
Beverly Hills (G-1668)		
Schawk Inc	C	269 381-3820
Kalamazoo (G-9329)		
Sgk LLC	G	269 381-3820
Battle Creek (G-1292)		
Spartan Graphics Inc	D	616 887-1073
Sparta (G-15780)		

Company	Code	Phone
Stamp-Rite Incorporated	E	517 487-5071
Lansing (G-9741)		
Twin City Engraving Company	G	269 983-0601
Saint Joseph (G-14968)		

PLATES: Paper, Made From Purchased Materials

Company	Code	Phone
AJM Packaging Corporation	D	248 901-0040
Bloomfield Hills (G-1794)		
AJM Packaging Corporation	D	313 842-7530
Detroit (G-3993)		
SF Holdings Group Inc	D	800 248-5960
Mason (G-11154)		

PLATES: Plastic Exc Polystyrene Foam

Company	Code	Phone
Alternative Systems Inc	F	269 384-2008
Kalamazoo (G-9111)		

PLATES: Sheet & Strip, Exc Coated Prdts

Company	Code	Phone
Sandvik Inc	D	269 926-7241
Benton Harbor (G-1582)		

PLATES: Steel

Company	Code	Phone
De Luxe Die Set Inc	G	810 227-2556
Brighton (G-1974)		
Industrial Marking Products	G	517 699-2160
Holt (G-8314)		
Parton & Preble Inc	E	586 773-6000
Warren (G-17954)		
Steel 21 LLC	E	616 884-2121
Cedar Springs (G-2662)		

PLATES: Truss, Metal

Company	Code	Phone
Superior Steel Components Inc	E	616 866-4759
Grand Rapids (G-7238)		

PLATING & FINISHING SVC: Decorative, Formed Prdts

Company	Code	Phone
Flexible Controls Corporation	E	313 368-3630
Detroit (G-4237)		
Lawrence Surface Tech Inc	G	248 609-9001
Troy (G-17206)		

PLATING & POLISHING SVC

Company	Code	Phone
Able Welding Inc	G	989 865-9611
Saint Charles (G-14800)		
Acorn Industries Inc	E	734 261-2940
Livonia (G-10100)		
American Metal Restoration	G	810 364-4820
Marysville (G-11081)		
ARC Services of Macomb Inc	E	586 469-1600
Clinton Township (G-3173)		
Armorclad	G	248 477-7785
Farmington Hills (G-5173)		
B and L Metal Finishing LLC	G	269 767-2225
Allegan (G-150)		
Beacon Park Finishing LLC	E	248 318-4286
Roseville (G-14380)		
Bush Polishing Buffing LLC	G	989 855-2248
Ionia (G-8687)		
Cal Grinding Inc	E	906 786-8749
Escanaba (G-5064)		
Cds Specialty Coatings LLC	G	313 300-8997
Ecorse (G-4981)		
Cg Liquidation Incorporated	E	586 575-9800
Warren (G-17752)		
Cyclone Manufacturing Inc	G	269 782-9670
Dowagiac (G-4780)		
DC Byers Co/Grand Rapids Inc	F	616 538-7300
Grand Rapids (G-6635)		
Detroit Steel Treating Company	E	248 334-7436
Pontiac (G-13361)		
Diamond Tool Manufacturing Inc	E	734 416-1900
Plymouth (G-13157)		
Eastern Oil Company	E	248 333-1333
Pontiac (G-13364)		
Fire-Rite Inc	E	313 273-3730
Detroit (G-4234)		
Flat Rock Metal Inc	C	734 782-4454
Flat Rock (G-5618)		
Gj Prey Coml & Indus Pntg Cov	G	248 250-4792
Clawson (G-3098)		
Gokoh Coldwater Incorporated	F	517 279-1080
Coldwater (G-3434)		

Employee Codes: A=Over 500 employees, B=251-500
C=101-250, D=51-100, E=20-50, F=10-19, G=3-9

PLATING & POLISHING SVC

Keen Point International Inc ....E 248 340-8732
 Auburn Hills *(G-950)*
Kenwal Pickling LLC ....E 313 739-1040
 Dearborn *(G-3857)*
Kriseler Welding Inc ....G 989 624-9266
 Birch Run *(G-1708)*
Lacks Industries Inc ....C 616 698-9852
 Grand Rapids *(G-6918)*
McGean-Rohco Inc ....E 216 441-4900
 Livonia *(G-10306)*
Metal Finishing Technology ....G 231 733-9736
 Muskegon *(G-11869)*
Mid-Michigan Industries Inc ....D 989 773-6918
 Mount Pleasant *(G-11715)*
Mid-Michigan Industries Inc ....E 989 386-7707
 Clare *(G-2986)*
Mvc Holdings LLC ....F 586 491-2600
 Roseville *(G-14450)*
National Galvanizing LP ....A 734 243-1882
 Monroe *(G-11567)*
National Zinc Processors Inc ....F 269 926-1161
 Benton Harbor *(G-1577)*
Non-Ferrous Cast Alloys Inc ....D 231 799-0550
 Norton Shores *(G-12318)*
Nor-Cote Inc ....E 586 756-1200
 Warren *(G-17944)*
Pearson Auto Service Inc ....G 313 538-6870
 Detroit *(G-4509)*
Pioneer Metal Finishing LLC ....D 734 384-9000
 Monroe *(G-11569)*
Production Tube Company Inc ....G 313 259-3990
 Detroit *(G-4537)*
Prs Manufacturing Inc ....G 616 784-4409
 Grand Rapids *(G-7124)*
Qmi Group Inc ....E 248 589-0505
 Madison Heights *(G-10814)*
Quali Tone Corporation ....F 269 426-3664
 Sawyer *(G-15111)*
Richcoat LLC ....F 586 978-1311
 Sterling Heights *(G-16150)*
Seaver Industrial Finishing Co ....D 616 842-8560
 Grand Haven *(G-6359)*
Spectrum Industries Inc ....D 616 451-0784
 Grand Rapids *(G-7216)*
Ss Stripping ....G 586 268-5799
 Sterling Heights *(G-16187)*
Superior Mtal Finshg Rustproof ....F 313 893-1050
 Detroit *(G-4617)*

PLATING COMPOUNDS

Plating Systems and Tech Inc ....G 517 783-4776
 Jackson *(G-8988)*
Surface Activation Tech LLC ....G 248 273-0037
 Troy *(G-17381)*

PLATING SVC: Chromium, Metals Or Formed Prdts

Arted Chrome Plating ....G 586 758-0050
 Warren *(G-17713)*
Dmi Automotive Inc ....F 517 548-1414
 Howell *(G-8446)*
Empire Hardchrome ....G 810 392-3122
 Richmond *(G-13837)*
Sodus Hard Chrome Inc ....F 269 925-2077
 Sodus *(G-15394)*

PLATING SVC: Electro

Accurate Coating Inc ....G 616 452-0016
 Grand Rapids *(G-6421)*
Aluminum Finishing Company ....G 269 382-4010
 Kalamazoo *(G-9112)*
Apollo Plating Inc ....C 586 777-0070
 Roseville *(G-14374)*
Arted Chrome Plating Inc ....F 313 871-3331
 Detroit *(G-4029)*
Asp Plating Company ....G 616 842-8080
 Grand Haven *(G-6273)*
Cadillac Plating Corporation ....D 586 771-9191
 Warren *(G-17748)*
Cadon Plating & Coatings LLC ....D 734 282-8100
 Wyandotte *(G-18813)*
Charlotte Anodizing Pdts Inc ....D 517 543-1911
 Charlotte *(G-2741)*
Chemical Processing Inc ....E 313 925-3400
 Madison Heights *(G-10688)*
Classic Plating Inc ....G 313 532-1440
 Redford *(G-13725)*
Color Coat Plating Company ....E 248 744-0445
 Madison Heights *(G-10695)*
Complete Automation CMF ....G 269 343-0500
 Kalamazoo *(G-9149)*
Controlled Plating Tech Inc ....E 616 243-6622
 Grand Rapids *(G-6602)*
D & B Metal Finishing ....G 586 725-6056
 Chesterfield *(G-2864)*
Detroit Chrome Inc ....G 313 341-9478
 Detroit *(G-4140)*
Di-Anodic Finishing Corp ....F 616 454-0470
 Grand Rapids *(G-6645)*
Diamond Chrome Plating Inc ....D 517 546-0150
 Howell *(G-8445)*
Dyna Plate Inc ....E 616 452-6763
 Grand Rapids *(G-6659)*
ECJ Processing ....G 248 540-2336
 Southfield *(G-15550)*
Electro Chemical Finishing Co ....D 616 531-1250
 Grand Rapids *(G-6669)*
Electro Chemical Finishing Co ....F 616 531-0670
 Grandville *(G-7372)*
Electro-Plating Service Inc ....F 248 541-0035
 Madison Heights *(G-10719)*
Electroplating Industries Inc ....F 586 469-2390
 Clinton Township *(G-3230)*
Fini Finish Metal Finishing ....F 586 758-0050
 Warren *(G-17806)*
Finishing Services Inc ....D 734 484-1700
 Ypsilanti *(G-18945)*
Fintex LLC ....E 734 946-3100
 Romulus *(G-14276)*
Fitzgerald Finishing LLC ....D 313 368-3630
 Detroit *(G-4235)*
Gladwin Metal Processing Inc ....G 989 426-9038
 Gladwin *(G-6198)*
Great Lakes Finishing Inc ....F 231 733-9566
 Muskegon *(G-11830)*
Great Lakes Metal Finshg LLC ....D 517 764-1335
 Jackson *(G-8896)*
Highpoint Finshg Solutions Inc ....D 616 772-4425
 Zeeland *(G-19036)*
Hpc Holdings Inc ....E 248 634-9361
 Holly *(G-8277)*
Hpc Holdings Inc ....E 810 714-9213
 Fenton *(G-5485)*
Ihc Inc ....C 313 535-3210
 Detroit *(G-4313)*
Jackson Tumble Finish Corp ....E 517 787-0368
 Jackson *(G-8918)*
JD Plating Company Inc ....E 248 547-5200
 Madison Heights *(G-10753)*
Jo-Mar Enterprises Inc ....G 313 365-9200
 Detroit *(G-4338)*
Kalamazoo Metal Finishers Inc ....F 269 382-1611
 Kalamazoo *(G-9242)*
KC Jones Plating Co ....E 586 755-4900
 Warren *(G-17892)*
KC Jones Plating Co ....E 248 399-8500
 Hazel Park *(G-7827)*
Lansing Plating Company ....G 517 485-6915
 Lansing *(G-9711)*
Marsh Plating Corporation ....D 734 483-5767
 Ypsilanti *(G-18965)*
Material Sciences Corporation ....F 734 207-4444
 Canton *(G-2490)*
Mid-State Plating Co Inc ....E 810 767-1622
 Flint *(G-5733)*
Midwest II Inc ....C 734 856-5200
 Ottawa Lake *(G-12808)*
Midwest Plating Company Inc ....E 616 451-2007
 Grand Rapids *(G-7005)*
Modern Hard Chrome Service Co ......F 586 445-0330
 Grosse Pointe Farms *(G-7538)*
Perfection Industries Inc ....E 313 272-4040
 Detroit *(G-4518)*
Pioneer Metal Finishing LLC ....G 877 721-1100
 Warren *(G-17965)*
Plating Specialties Inc ....F 248 547-8660
 Madison Heights *(G-10802)*
Plating Specialties Inc ....G 248 547-8660
 Madison Heights *(G-10803)*
Plating Technologies ....G 586 756-1825
 Warren *(G-17968)*
Plymouth Plating Works Inc ....F 734 453-1560
 Plymouth *(G-13267)*
Ppi LLC ....E 586 772-7736
 Warren *(G-17971)*
Robert & Son Black Ox Special ....G 586 778-7633
 Roseville *(G-14471)*
Selfridge Plating Inc ....D 586 469-3141
 Harrison Township *(G-7724)*
Spencer Zdanowitz Inc ....G 517 841-9380
 Jackson *(G-9012)*
Technickel Inc ....F 269 926-8505
 Benton Harbor *(G-1591)*
Ultraseal America Inc ....G 734 222-9478
 Ann Arbor *(G-703)*
USA Quality Metal Finshg LLC ....F 269 427-9000
 Lawrence *(G-9986)*
Williams Finishing Inc ....F 734 421-6100
 Livonia *(G-10476)*
Wolverine Plating Corporation ....E 586 771-5000
 Roseville *(G-14496)*
Zav-Tech Metal Finishing ....G 269 422-2559
 Stevensville *(G-16271)*

PLATING SVC: NEC

Abrasive Services Incorporated ....G 734 941-2144
 Romulus *(G-14244)*
Acme Plating Inc ....G 313 838-3870
 Detroit *(G-3983)*
Ajax Metal Processing Inc ....G 313 267-2100
 Detroit *(G-3992)*
Allied Finishing Inc ....C 616 698-7550
 Grand Rapids *(G-6450)*
Auto Anodics Inc ....E 810 984-5600
 Port Huron *(G-13455)*
B & L Plating Co Inc ....G 586 778-9300
 Warren *(G-17722)*
Chemical Process Inds LLC ....F 248 547-5200
 Madison Heights *(G-10687)*
Chrome Craft Corporation ....C 313 868-2444
 Warren *(G-17755)*
Dn-Lawrence Industries Inc ....F 269 552-4999
 Kalamazoo *(G-9172)*
Expert Coating Company Inc ....F 616 453-8261
 Grand Rapids *(G-6693)*
Honhart Mid-Nite Black Co ....F 248 588-1515
 Troy *(G-17148)*
Master Finish Co ....C 877 590-5819
 Grand Rapids *(G-6965)*
Michigan Plating LLC ....G 248 544-3500
 Hazel Park *(G-7832)*
Micro Platers Sales Inc ....E 313 865-2293
 Detroit *(G-4454)*
Norbrook Plating Inc ....E 586 755-4110
 Warren *(G-17945)*
Norbrook Plating Inc ....G 313 369-9304
 Detroit *(G-4488)*
Plating Products Consulta ....G 586 755-7210
 Warren *(G-17967)*
Tawas Plating Company ....E 989 362-2011
 Tawas City *(G-16372)*
Tri K Cylinder Service Inc ....G 269 965-3981
 Springfield *(G-15877)*
Tru-Coat Inc ....G 810 785-3331
 Montrose *(G-11608)*
W A Thomas Company ....G 734 955-6500
 Taylor *(G-16487)*
Western Engineered Products ....G 248 371-9259
 Lake Orion *(G-9638)*
Williams Diversified Inc ....G 734 421-6100
 Livonia *(G-10475)*

PLAYGROUND EQPT

Kennedy Sales Inc ....G 586 228-9390
 Clinton Township *(G-3273)*
Penchura LLC ....F 810 229-6245
 Brighton *(G-2050)*
Play Wright LLC ....G 616 784-5437
 Rockford *(G-14184)*
Quality Industries Inc ....E 517 439-1591
 Hillsdale *(G-7944)*
Shane Group LLC ....G 517 439-4316
 Hillsdale *(G-7949)*

PLEATING & STITCHING SVC

AP Impressions Inc ....G 734 464-8009
 Livonia *(G-10121)*
Authority Customwear Ltd ....E 248 588-8075
 Madison Heights *(G-10676)*
Impact Label Corporation ....D 269 381-4280
 Galesburg *(G-6079)*
J2 Licensing Inc ....G 586 307-3400
 Troy *(G-17180)*
Lazer Graphics ....F 269 926-1066
 Benton Harbor *(G-1565)*
Nobby Inc ....F 810 984-3300
 Fort Gratiot *(G-5822)*

Perrin Souvenir Distrs Inc.................B....... 616 785-9700
  Comstock Park (G-3636)
Precision Embroidery...........................G....... 248 684-1359
  Milford (G-11481)
Stahls Inc...E....... 800 478-2457
  Saint Clair Shores (G-14887)
Twin City Engraving Company............G....... 269 983-0601
  Saint Joseph (G-14968)

PLUGS: Electric

Hug-A-Plug Inc....................................G....... 810 626-1224
  Brighton (G-2011)
Plugs To Panels Electrical LLC...........G....... 248 318-5915
  Howell (G-8497)

PLUMBING & HEATING EQPT & SPLY, WHOL: Htg Eqpt/Panels, Solar

Triangle Product Distributors................E....... 970 609-9001
  Holland (G-8229)

PLUMBING & HEATING EQPT & SPLY, WHOLESALE: Hydronic Htg Eqpt

Alhern-Martin Indus Frnc Co.................E....... 248 689-6363
  Troy (G-16922)
Moore Brothers Electrical Co...............G....... 810 232-2148
  Flint (G-5737)

PLUMBING & HEATING EQPT & SPLYS WHOLESALERS

Marquis Industries Inc..........................E....... 616 842-2810
  Spring Lake (G-15832)
McLaren Inc...G....... 989 720-4328
  Owosso (G-12842)
Mjs Investing LLC................................E....... 734 455-6500
  Plymouth (G-13246)
Walters Plumbing Company..................F....... 269 962-6253
  Battle Creek (G-1310)
Young Supply Company.......................E....... 313 875-3280
  Detroit (G-4699)
Zurn Industries LLC..............................F....... 313 864-2800
  Detroit (G-4704)

PLUMBING & HEATING EQPT & SPLYS, WHOL: Plumbing Fitting/Sply

Etna Distributors LLC...........................F....... 810 232-4760
  Flint (G-5697)
Ferguson Enterprises LLC....................G....... 616 803-7521
  Kentwood (G-9452)
Ferguson Enterprises LLC....................G....... 989 790-2220
  Saginaw (G-14645)
Ferguson Enterprises LLC....................G....... 269 383-1200
  Kalamazoo (G-9184)
Ferguson Enterprises LLC....................G....... 586 459-4491
  Warren (G-17805)
Shane Group LLC................................G....... 517 439-4316
  Hillsdale (G-7949)

PLUMBING & HEATING EQPT & SPLYS, WHOL: Water Purif Eqpt

Business Connect L3c..........................G....... 833 229-6753
  Grand Rapids (G-6540)

PLUMBING & HEATING EQPT & SPLYS, WHOLESALE: Brass/Fittings

American Beverage Equipment Co.......E....... 586 773-0094
  Roseville (G-14373)

PLUMBING & HEATING EQPT & SPLYS, WHOLESALE: Gas Burners

Banner Engineering & Sales Inc...........F....... 989 755-0584
  Saginaw (G-14609)

PLUMBING & HEATING EQPT & SPLYS, WHOLESALE: Sanitary Ware

Armstrong Hot Water Inc......................E....... 269 278-1413
  Three Rivers (G-16566)
Select Distributors LLC........................F....... 586 510-4647
  Warren (G-18008)

PLUMBING & HEATING EQPT/SPLYS, WHOL: Boilers, Hot Water Htg

Hamilton Engineering Inc.....................E....... 734 419-0200
  Livonia (G-10234)

PLUMBING FIXTURES

Barbron Corporation.............................E....... 586 716-3530
  Kalkaska (G-9382)
Builders Plbg Sup Traverse Cy.............G....... 800 466-5160
  Traverse City (G-16632)
Decker Manufacturing Corp..................D....... 517 629-3955
  Albion (G-124)
Etna Distributors LLC...........................F....... 810 232-4760
  Flint (G-5697)
Ferguson Enterprises LLC....................G....... 616 803-7521
  Kentwood (G-9452)
Ferguson Enterprises LLC....................G....... 269 383-1200
  Kalamazoo (G-9184)
Ferguson Enterprises LLC....................G....... 586 459-4491
  Warren (G-17805)
Incoe Corporation.................................C....... 248 616-0220
  Auburn Hills (G-936)
Joe S Handyman Service.....................G....... 616 642-6038
  Saranac (G-15079)
Kerkstra Precast LLC...........................C....... 616 457-4920
  Grandville (G-7395)
Key Gas Components Inc....................E....... 269 673-2151
  Allegan (G-163)
Luxury Bath Systems...........................G....... 586 264-2561
  Warren (G-17909)
Masco De Puerto Rico Inc....................E....... 313 274-7400
  Taylor (G-16439)
Parker-Hannifin Corporation.................B....... 269 694-9411
  Otsego (G-12795)
S H Leggitt Company............................B....... 269 781-3901
  Marshall (G-11073)
Trane Technologies Company LLC......E....... 248 398-6200
  Madison Heights (G-10846)
Wittock Supply Company......................G....... 810 721-8000
  Imlay City (G-8651)

PLUMBING FIXTURES: Brass, Incl Drain Cocks, Faucets/Spigots

Brasscraft Manufacturing Co.................C....... 248 305-6000
  Novi (G-12376)
Marquis Industries Inc..........................E....... 616 842-2810
  Spring Lake (G-15832)
United Brass Manufacturers Inc...........E....... 734 941-0700
  Romulus (G-14334)
United Brass Manufacturers Inc...........F....... 734 942-9224
  Romulus (G-14335)

PLUMBING FIXTURES: Plastic

Conway Products Corporation..............E....... 616 698-2601
  Grand Rapids (G-6603)
Lakeshore Marble Company Inc..........F....... 269 429-8241
  Stevensville (G-16257)
Masco Corporation...............................A....... 313 274-7400
  Livonia (G-10302)
Nordic Products Inc.............................C....... 616 940-4036
  Grand Rapids (G-7046)
R A Townsend Company......................G....... 989 498-7000
  Saginaw (G-14734)
Rick Owen & Jason Vogel Partnr.........G....... 734 417-3401
  Dexter (G-4752)
Zimmer Marble Co Inc.........................F....... 517 787-1500
  Jackson (G-9041)

POINT OF SALE DEVICES

PC Complete Inc..................................G....... 248 545-4211
  Ferndale (G-5577)
Wholesale Proc Systems LLC..............G....... 833 755-6696
  Adrian (G-104)

POLISHING SVC: Metals Or Formed Prdts

Garys Polishing....................................G....... 810 621-4137
  Lennon (G-9994)
Grand River Polishing Co Corp............E....... 616 846-1420
  Spring Lake (G-15818)
Mann Metal Finishing Inc....................D....... 269 621-6359
  Hartford (G-7765)

POLYOXYMETHYLENE RESINS

Sumika Polymers North Amer LLC......E....... 248 284-4797
  Farmington Hills (G-5392)

POLYPROPYLENE RESINS

Conceppt Technologies.........................G....... 734 324-6750
  Wyandotte (G-18815)
Jsp International LLC...........................G....... 517 748-5200
  Jackson (G-8924)

POLYSTYRENE RESINS

Huntsman Corporation..........................G....... 248 322-8682
  Auburn Hills (G-929)

POLYURETHANE RESINS

Arvron Inc...E....... 616 530-1888
  Grand Rapids (G-6474)
Innovative Polymers Inc.......................F....... 989 224-9500
  Saint Johns (G-14902)
Recycled Polymetric Materials.............G....... 313 957-6373
  Detroit (G-4559)

POLYVINYL CHLORIDE RESINS

Oscoda Plastics Inc..............................E....... 989 739-6900
  Oscoda (G-12767)
Vi-Chem Corp.......................................C....... 616 247-8501
  Grand Rapids (G-7314)

PONTOONS: Rubber

Apex Marine Inc....................................D....... 989 681-4300
  Saint Louis (G-14986)

POPCORN & SUPPLIES WHOLESALERS

Pop Daddy Popcorn LLC......................F....... 734 550-9900
  Whitmore Lake (G-18543)

POSTAL EQPT: Locker Boxes, Exc Wood

Hss Industries Inc................................E....... 231 946-6101
  Traverse City (G-16717)

POSTERS

Prop Art Studio Inc...............................G....... 313 824-2200
  Detroit (G-4539)

POSTERS, WHOLESALE

Fairfax Prints Ltd..................................G....... 517 321-5590
  Lansing (G-9696)

POTPOURRI

Havers Heritage...................................G....... 517 423-3455
  Clinton (G-3140)

POTTERY

New Pioneer Ceramics LLC.................G....... 248 200-9893
  Auburn Hills (G-981)
Paint Your Masterpiece........................G....... 231 622-8824
  Petoskey (G-13011)
Terra Green Ceramics Inc...................G....... 810 742-4611
  Burton (G-2248)

POTTING SOILS

Great Lakes Nursery Soils Inc.............F....... 231 788-2770
  Muskegon (G-11831)
Sun Gro Horticulture Dist Inc...............G....... 517 639-3115
  Quincy (G-13675)
Trp Enterprises Inc...............................G....... 810 329-4027
  East China (G-4859)

POULTRY & SMALL GAME SLAUGHTERING & PROCESSING

Cargill Incorporated..............................F....... 608 868-5150
  Owosso (G-12825)
Cargill Americas Inc.............................D....... 810 989-7689
  New Haven (G-12029)
Hillshire Brands Company....................G....... 616 875-8131
  Zeeland (G-19038)
Michigan Turkey Producers LLC.........F....... 616 243-4186
  Grand Rapids (G-6995)
Tyson Foods /Hr...................................F....... 616 875-2311
  Zeeland (G-19085)

POWDER PUFFS & MITTS

Powder It Inc..G....... 586 949-0395
  Chesterfield (G-2927)

POWDER: Metal

Advantage Sintered Metals Inc .... C 269 964-1212
  Battle Creek *(G-1180)*
Century Inc .... C 231 947-6400
  Traverse City *(G-16641)*
Peerless Mtal Pwders Abrsive L .... E 313 841-5400
  Detroit *(G-4512)*
Tpi Powder Metallurgy Inc .... E 989 865-9921
  Saint Charles *(G-14811)*
Wall Co Incorporated .... E 248 585-6400
  Madison Heights *(G-10859)*

POWDER: Silver

Custom Powder Coating LLC .... G 616 454-9730
  Grand Rapids *(G-6622)*

POWER GENERATORS

Great Lakes Pwr Generation LLC .... G 231 492-3764
  Elk Rapids *(G-5026)*
Kraft Power Corporation .... E 989 748-4040
  Gaylord *(G-6140)*
North Country Power Generation .... G 231 499-3951
  Elk Rapids *(G-5028)*

POWER SPLY CONVERTERS: Static, Electronic Applications

Progressive Dynamics Inc .... D 269 781-4241
  Marshall *(G-11072)*

POWER SUPPLIES: All Types, Static

Lappans of Gaylord Inc .... G 989 732-3274
  Gaylord *(G-6142)*
Practical Power .... G 866 385-2961
  Rochester *(G-13922)*

POWER SUPPLIES: Transformer, Electronic Type

Actia Electronics Inc .... G 574 264-2373
  Romulus *(G-14245)*

POWER TOOLS, HAND: Chain Saws, Portable

Ebels Hardware Inc .... F 231 826-3334
  Falmouth *(G-5133)*

POWER TOOLS, HAND: Drills & Drilling Tools

Ace Drill Corporation .... G 517 265-5184
  Adrian *(G-47)*

POWER TOOLS, HAND: Drills, Port, Elec/Pneumatic, Exc Rock

Anchor Lamina America Inc .... E 248 489-9122
  Bellaire *(G-1469)*
Lamina Inc .... D 248 489-9122
  Farmington Hills *(G-5289)*

POWER TOOLS, HAND: Guns, Pneumatic, Chip Removal

K M S Company .... G 616 994-7000
  Holland *(G-8106)*

POWER TOOLS, HAND: Hammers, Portable, Elec/Pneumatic, Chip

Striker Tools LLC .... G 248 990-7767
  Manitou Beach *(G-10928)*

POWER TRANSMISSION EQPT WHOLESALERS

Motion Industries Inc .... G 989 771-0200
  Saginaw *(G-14705)*

POWER TRANSMISSION EQPT: Aircraft

Advance Turning and Mfg Inc .... C 517 783-2713
  Jackson *(G-8802)*

POWER TRANSMISSION EQPT: Mechanical

Accurate Gauge & Mfg Inc .... D 248 853-2400
  Rochester Hills *(G-13940)*
Allor Manufacturing Inc .... D 248 486-4500
  Brighton *(G-1943)*
Arthur R Sommers .... E 586 469-1280
  Harrison Township *(G-7689)*
B & H Machine Sales Inc .... E 313 843-6720
  Detroit *(G-4039)*
Barnes Industries Inc .... E 248 541-2333
  Madison Heights *(G-10678)*
BDS Company Inc .... F 517 279-2135
  Coldwater *(G-3421)*
Borgwarner Powdered Metals Inc .... C 734 261-5322
  Livonia *(G-10140)*
Borgwarner Thermal Systems Inc .... G 231 779-7500
  Cadillac *(G-2317)*
Bradhart Products Inc .... E 248 437-3746
  Brighton *(G-1952)*
Bunting Bearings LLC .... G 269 345-8691
  Portage *(G-13550)*
Colonial Bushings Inc .... E 586 954-3880
  Clinton Township *(G-3203)*
Dayco LLC .... E 248 404-6500
  Troy *(G-17045)*
Dayco Products LLC .... D 248 404-6500
  Troy *(G-17048)*
Equitable Engineering Co Inc .... E 248 689-9700
  Troy *(G-17096)*
Federal-Mogul Powertrain LLC .... B 616 754-5681
  Greenville *(G-7485)*
Gates Corporation .... G 248 260-2300
  Rochester Hills *(G-14020)*
Gateway Engineering Inc .... F 616 284-1425
  Grand Rapids *(G-6732)*
Geislinger Corporation .... F 269 441-7000
  Battle Creek *(G-1234)*
GKN Sinter Metals LLC .... G 248 883-4500
  Auburn Hills *(G-914)*
Hole Industries Incorporated .... G 517 548-4229
  Howell *(G-8461)*
Idc Industries Inc .... E 586 427-4321
  Clinton Township *(G-3257)*
Kaydon Corporation .... C 231 755-3741
  Norton Shores *(G-12306)*
M C Carbide Tool Co .... E 248 486-9590
  Wixom *(G-18703)*
Melling Tool Co .... B 517 787-8172
  Jackson *(G-8951)*
Michigan Auto Comprsr Inc .... A 517 796-3200
  Parma *(G-12938)*
Milan Screw Products Inc .... F 734 439-2431
  Milan *(G-11447)*
Mq Operating Company .... E 906 337-1515
  Calumet *(G-2412)*
Murray Equipment Company Inc .... F 313 869-4444
  Warren *(G-17938)*
Neapco Holdings LLC .... C 248 699-6500
  Farmington Hills *(G-5333)*
PCI Procal Inc .... F 989 358-7070
  Alpena *(G-311)*
Powertrain Integration LLC .... E 248 577-0010
  Madison Heights *(G-10806)*
Precision Torque Control Inc .... F 989 495-9330
  Midland *(G-11403)*
Quality Steel Products Inc .... E 248 684-0555
  Milford *(G-11484)*
Riverside Spline & Gear Inc .... E 810 765-8302
  Marine City *(G-10965)*
Saf-Holland Inc .... A 231 773-3271
  Muskegon *(G-11913)*
Supreme Gear Co .... E 586 775-6325
  Fraser *(G-6001)*
Ton-Tex Corporation .... F 616 957-3200
  Greenville *(G-7508)*
Ton-Tex Corporation .... E 616 957-3200
  Grand Rapids *(G-7264)*
Tractech Inc .... E 248 226-6800
  Southfield *(G-15725)*
U S Graphite Inc .... E 989 755-0441
  Saginaw *(G-14783)*
Wilkie Bros Conveyors Inc .... E 810 364-4820
  Marysville *(G-11113)*
Wolverine Machine Products Co .... E 248 634-9952
  Holly *(G-8301)*

PRECAST TERRAZZO OR CONCRETE PRDTS

Lakeshore Cement Products .... G 989 739-9341
  Oscoda *(G-12763)*
National Precast Strl Inc .... F 586 294-6430
  Shelby Township *(G-15288)*
Quality Precast Inc .... E 269 342-0539
  Kalamazoo *(G-9310)*
Ruth Drain Tile Inc .... G 989 864-3406
  Ruth *(G-14598)*

PRECIOUS STONE MINING SVCS, NEC

J M Longyear Heirs Inc .... G 906 228-7960
  Marquette *(G-11023)*

PRERECORDED TAPE, CD & RECORD STORE: Record, Disc/Tape

Top Quality Cleaning LLC .... F 810 493-4211
  Flint *(G-5779)*

PRERECORDED TAPE, COMPACT DISC & RECORD STORES: Records

Archer Record Pressing Co .... G 313 365-9545
  Detroit *(G-4025)*

PRESSES

Kasten Machinery Inc .... G 269 945-1999
  Hastings *(G-7803)*
Oak Press Solutions Inc .... E 269 651-8513
  Sturgis *(G-16314)*

PRIMARY METAL PRODUCTS

Wes Corp .... G 231 536-2500
  East Jordan *(G-4882)*

PRIMARY ROLLING MILL EQPT

Mill Assist Services Inc .... E 269 692-3211
  Otsego *(G-12791)*

PRINT CARTRIDGES: Laser & Other Computer Printers

Cau Acquisition Company LLC .... D 989 875-8133
  Ithaca *(G-8787)*
Compatible Laser Products Inc .... F 810 629-0459
  Fenton *(G-5466)*
Lps-2 Inc .... E 313 538-0181
  Redford *(G-13742)*
Mikan Corporation .... F 734 944-9447
  Saline *(G-15027)*
Visionit Supplies and Svcs Inc .... E 313 664-5650
  Detroit *(G-4669)*

PRINTED CIRCUIT BOARDS

3dxtech LLC .... F 616 717-3811
  Grand Rapids *(G-6406)*
A and D Design Electronics .... G 989 493-1884
  Auburn *(G-762)*
Acromag Incorporated .... D 248 624-1541
  Wixom *(G-18594)*
Adco Circuits Inc .... C 248 853-6620
  Rochester Hills *(G-13941)*
Aero Embedded Technologies Inc .... G 586 251-2980
  Sterling Heights *(G-15925)*
Ameritronix Inc .... G 724 956-2356
  Canton *(G-2434)*
Assem-Tech Inc .... E 616 846-3410
  Grand Haven *(G-6275)*
Assembltech Inc .... E 734 769-2800
  Ottawa Lake *(G-12803)*
Assembly Alternatives Inc .... G 248 362-1616
  Rochester Hills *(G-13952)*
Bralyn Inc .... G 231 865-3186
  Fruitport *(G-6061)*
Burton Industries Inc .... E 906 932-5970
  Ironwood *(G-8759)*
Ci Lighting LLC .... G 248 997-4415
  Auburn Hills *(G-843)*
Cusolar Industries Inc .... E 586 949-3880
  Chesterfield *(G-2863)*
Debron Industrial Elec LLC .... D 248 588-7220
  Troy *(G-17050)*
Dse Industries LLC .... G 313 530-6668
  Macomb *(G-10589)*

PRODUCT SECTION

PRINTING, COMMERCIAL: Labels & Seals, NEC

Dupearl Technology LLC ....G 248 390-9609
  Bloomfield Hills *(G-1816)*
Excel Circuits LLC ....F 248 373-0700
  Auburn Hills *(G-883)*
Ghi Electronics LLC ....E 248 397-8856
  Madison Heights *(G-10731)*
Glassmaster Controls Co Inc ....E 269 382-2010
  Kalamazoo *(G-9198)*
Hgc Westshore LLC ....D 616 796-1218
  Holland *(G-8070)*
I Parth Inc ....G 248 548-9722
  Ferndale *(G-5560)*
Jabil Circuit Michigan Inc ....C 248 292-6000
  Auburn Hills *(G-941)*
Jabil Inc ....A 248 292-6000
  Auburn Hills *(G-942)*
Keska LLC ....G 616 283-7056
  Holland *(G-8113)*
M T S Chenault LLC ....G 269 861-0053
  Benton Harbor *(G-1566)*
Magna Electronics Inc ....C 248 729-2643
  Auburn Hills *(G-962)*
Micro Logic ....G 248 432-7209
  West Bloomfield *(G-18299)*
N S International Ltd ....C 248 251-1600
  Troy *(G-17272)*
Northville Circuits Inc ....G 248 853-3232
  Rochester Hills *(G-14073)*
Obertron Electronic Mfg Inc ....F 734 428-0722
  Manchester *(G-10887)*
Odyssey Electronics Inc ....D 734 421-8340
  Livonia *(G-10352)*
P M Z Technology Inc ....G 248 471-0447
  Livonia *(G-10356)*
Petra Electronic Mfg Inc ....F 616 877-1991
  Holland *(G-8165)*
Pgf Technology Group Inc ....E 248 852-2800
  Rochester Hills *(G-14082)*
Posthaste Electronics LLC ....G 616 794-9977
  Belding *(G-1461)*
Protodesign Inc ....E 586 739-4340
  Shelby Township *(G-15310)*
Ram Electronics Inc ....F 231 865-3186
  Fruitport *(G-6069)*
Rockstar Digital Inc ....F 888 808-5868
  Sterling Heights *(G-16158)*
Saline Lectronics Inc ....C 734 944-2120
  Saline *(G-15037)*
Saturn Flex Systems Inc ....F 734 532-4093
  Romulus *(G-14328)*
Semicndctor Hybrid Assmbly Inc ....F 248 668-9450
  Wixom *(G-18751)*

PRINTERS & PLOTTERS

Appliction Spclist Kompany Inc ....F 517 676-6633
  Lansing *(G-9805)*
Electronics For Imaging Inc ....G 734 641-3062
  Ypsilanti *(G-18941)*
Red Barn Maps ....G 906 346-2226
  Gwinn *(G-7586)*

PRINTERS' SVCS: Folding, Collating, Etc

Accuform Prtg & Graphics Inc ....F 313 271-5600
  Detroit *(G-3981)*
Hexon Corporation ....E 248 585-7585
  Farmington Hills *(G-5259)*
Industrial Imprntng & Die Cutng ....G 586 778-9470
  Eastpointe *(G-4937)*
Ray Scott Industries Inc ....F 248 535-2528
  Port Huron *(G-13522)*

PRINTERS: Computer

Kingdom Cartridge Inc ....G 734 564-1590
  Plymouth *(G-13216)*
Printek Inc ....D 269 925-3200
  Saint Joseph *(G-14955)*
Visionit Supplies and Svcs Inc ....E 313 664-5650
  Detroit *(G-4669)*

PRINTERS: Magnetic Ink, Bar Code

Bcc Distribution Inc ....F 734 737-9900
  Canton *(G-2439)*
Compunetics Systems Inc ....G 248 531-0015
  Rochester Hills *(G-13981)*
Kace Logistics LLC ....E 734 946-8600
  Carleton *(G-2557)*

PRINTING & BINDING: Books

Best Binding LLC ....G 734 459-7785
  Plymouth *(G-13136)*
Great Lakes Photo Inc ....G 586 784-5446
  Richmond *(G-13839)*
McNaughton & Gunn Inc ....C 734 429-5411
  Saline *(G-15025)*
Sande-Wells Company ....G 248 276-9313
  Rochester Hills *(G-14106)*
SPD America LLC ....G 734 709-7624
  Pinckney *(G-13056)*
William B Eerdmans Pubg Co ....E 616 459-4591
  Grand Rapids *(G-7340)*

PRINTING & BINDING: Pamphlets

Lottery Info ....G 734 326-0097
  Wayne *(G-18230)*

PRINTING & BINDING: Textbooks

Superior Text LLC ....F 866 482-8762
  Ypsilanti *(G-18980)*

PRINTING & EMBOSSING: Plastic Fabric Articles

All For Love Prints LLC ....G 313 207-1547
  Detroit *(G-4000)*
Flint Group Pckg Inks N Amer C ....C 734 781-4600
  Livonia *(G-10209)*
Flint Group Pckg Inks N Amer H ....G 734 781-4600
  Livonia *(G-10210)*
Just Right Duplications LLC ....F 313 655-3555
  Oak Park *(G-12619)*
Mayfair Golf Accessories ....G 989 732-8400
  Gaylord *(G-6147)*
Real Green Systems Inc ....D 888 345-2154
  Commerce Township *(G-3570)*
Rj Corp ....G 616 396-0552
  Holland *(G-8181)*

PRINTING & ENGRAVING: Invitation & Stationery

Celebrations ....G 906 482-4946
  Hancock *(G-7617)*
Invitations By Design ....G 269 342-8551
  Kalamazoo *(G-9226)*
Village Printing & Supply Inc ....G 810 664-2270
  Lapeer *(G-9966)*

PRINTING & STAMPING: Fabric Articles

Cedar Springs Sales LLC ....G 616 696-2111
  Cedar Springs *(G-2645)*
Loyalty 1977 Ink ....G 313 759-1006
  Detroit *(G-4409)*
Sigma International Inc ....F 248 230-9681
  Livonia *(G-10408)*
Ultimate Graphic and Sign LLC ....G 989 865-5200
  Saint Charles *(G-14812)*

PRINTING & WRITING PAPER WHOLESALERS

Xxtar Associates LLC ....G 888 946-6066
  Detroit *(G-4695)*

PRINTING INKS WHOLESALERS

Grand Rapids Printing Ink Co ....G 616 241-5681
  Grand Rapids *(G-6768)*
Mis Associates Inc ....G 844 225-8156
  Pontiac *(G-13398)*

PRINTING MACHINERY

A C Steel Rule Dies Inc ....G 248 588-5600
  Madison Heights *(G-10654)*
Alpine Sign and Prtg Sup Inc ....F 517 487-1400
  Lansing *(G-9754)*
Benmar Communications LLC ....F 313 593-0690
  Dearborn *(G-3813)*
Brown Mch Group Intrmdate Hldn ....C 989 435-7741
  Beaverton *(G-1424)*
Douthitt Corporation ....E 313 259-1565
  Detroit *(G-4189)*
Elk Lake Tool Co ....E 231 264-5616
  Elk Rapids *(G-5023)*
Innovative Machines Inc ....G 616 669-1649
  Jenison *(G-9059)*

Qmi Group Inc ....E 248 589-0505
  Madison Heights *(G-10814)*
Sgk LLC ....G 269 381-3820
  Battle Creek *(G-1292)*
Thermoforming Tech Group LLC ....G 989 435-7741
  Beaverton *(G-1433)*
Unique-Intasco Usa Inc ....G 810 982-3360
  Auburn Hills *(G-1071)*

PRINTING MACHINERY, EQPT & SPLYS: Wholesalers

Graphic Art Service & Supply ....G 810 229-4700
  Brighton *(G-2004)*
Graphic Arts Service & Sup Inc ....F 616 698-9300
  Grand Rapids *(G-6781)*
Michigan Roller Inc ....G 269 651-2304
  Sturgis *(G-16307)*
Village Printing & Supply Inc ....G 810 664-2270
  Lapeer *(G-9966)*

PRINTING, COMMERCIAL Newspapers, NEC

Grand Blanc Printing Inc ....E 810 694-1155
  Grand Blanc *(G-6245)*
North Country Publishing Corp ....G 231 526-2191
  Harbor Springs *(G-7653)*

PRINTING, COMMERCIAL: Business Forms, NEC

Consoldted Dcment Slutions LLC ....F 586 293-8100
  Fraser *(G-5914)*
Imagemaster LLC ....E 734 821-2500
  Ann Arbor *(G-523)*
Imprint House LLC ....G 810 985-8203
  Port Huron *(G-13487)*
Multi Packg Solutions Intl Ltd ....A 517 323-9000
  Lansing *(G-9721)*
TGI Direct Inc ....G 810 239-5553
  Flint *(G-5778)*

PRINTING, COMMERCIAL: Catalogs, NEC

Adair Printing Company ....E 734 426-2822
  Dexter *(G-4721)*

PRINTING, COMMERCIAL: Coupons, NEC

Save On Everything LLC ....D 248 362-9119
  Troy *(G-17345)*

PRINTING, COMMERCIAL: Envelopes, NEC

The Envelope Printery Inc ....D 734 398-7700
  Van Buren Twp *(G-17557)*

PRINTING, COMMERCIAL: Imprinting

Mayfair Accessories Inc ....G 989 732-8400
  Gaylord *(G-6146)*

PRINTING, COMMERCIAL: Labels & Seals, NEC

Amery Tape & Label Co Inc ....G 586 759-3230
  Warren *(G-17704)*
Argent Tape & Label Inc ....F 248 588-4600
  Livonia *(G-10124)*
Artex Label & Graphics Inc ....E 616 748-9655
  Zeeland *(G-18992)*
Flamingo Label Co ....F 586 469-9587
  Clinton Township *(G-3240)*
FSI Label Company ....E 586 776-4110
  Holland *(G-8043)*
General Tape Label Liquidating ....F 248 437-5200
  Wixom *(G-18668)*
Great Lakes Label LLC ....E 616 647-9880
  Comstock Park *(G-3610)*
Impact Label Corporation ....D 269 381-4280
  Galesburg *(G-6079)*
Label Tech Inc ....F 586 247-6444
  Shelby Township *(G-15254)*
Northern Label Inc ....G 231 854-6301
  Hesperia *(G-7871)*
Perrin Souvenir Distrs Inc ....B 616 785-9700
  Comstock Park *(G-3636)*
Precision Label Inc ....G 616 534-9935
  Grandville *(G-7412)*
Rainbow Tape & Label Inc ....F 734 941-6090
  Romulus *(G-14324)*

Employee Codes: A=Over 500 employees, B=251-500 C=101-250, D=51-100, E=20-50, F=10-19, G=3-9

PRINTING, COMMERCIAL: Labels & Seals, NEC

Stamp-Rite Incorporated ....E..... 517 487-5071
  Lansing *(G-9741)*
Stylerite Label Corporation ....E..... 248 853-7977
  Rochester Hills *(G-14120)*

PRINTING, COMMERCIAL: Letterpress & Screen

Cedar Springs Sales LLC ....G..... 616 696-2111
  Cedar Springs *(G-2645)*
Danmark Graphics LLC ....G..... 616 675-7499
  Casnovia *(G-2606)*
J2 Licensing Inc ....G..... 586 307-3400
  Troy *(G-17180)*
Mylockercom LLC ....B..... 877 898-3366
  Detroit *(G-4473)*
Total Lee Sports Inc ....G..... 989 772-6121
  Mount Pleasant *(G-11745)*
Verso Services Inc ....G..... 734 368-0989
  Ann Arbor *(G-710)*

PRINTING, COMMERCIAL: Literature, Advertising, NEC

D J Rotunda Associates Inc ....G..... 586 772-3350
  West Bloomfield *(G-18276)*
Help-U-Sell RE Big Rapids ....F..... 231 796-3966
  Big Rapids *(G-1677)*
MPS Holdco Inc ....B..... 517 886-2526
  Lansing *(G-9717)*

PRINTING, COMMERCIAL: Magazines, NEC

Step Into Success Inc ....G..... 734 426-1075
  Pinckney *(G-13057)*

PRINTING, COMMERCIAL: Menus, NEC

Focus Marketing ....E..... 616 355-4362
  Holland *(G-8037)*
Wesman Designs ....G..... 616 669-3290
  Hudsonville *(G-8616)*

PRINTING, COMMERCIAL: Periodicals, NEC

Bible Doctrines To Live By Inc ....G..... 616 453-0493
  Comstock Park *(G-3590)*

PRINTING, COMMERCIAL: Post Cards, Picture, NEC

Star Line Commercial Printing ....G..... 810 733-1152
  Flushing *(G-5813)*
Touched By Cupids ....G..... 313 704-6334
  Detroit *(G-4640)*

PRINTING, COMMERCIAL: Promotional

Community Mntal Hlth Auth Clnt ....F..... 517 323-9558
  Lansing *(G-9682)*
Fonts About Inc ....G..... 248 767-7504
  Northville *(G-12219)*
Graphicolor Systems Inc ....G..... 248 347-0271
  Livonia *(G-10229)*
H E L P Printers Inc ....G..... 734 847-0554
  Temperance *(G-16533)*
Publishing Xpress ....G..... 248 582-1834
  Madison Heights *(G-10811)*

PRINTING, COMMERCIAL: Publications

Cartidge World ....G..... 810 229-5599
  Brighton *(G-1962)*
Extreme Screenprints ....G..... 616 889-8305
  Grandville *(G-7375)*
Flowing Well Publications ....G..... 231 622-8630
  Petoskey *(G-12997)*
I-94 Enterprises ....G..... 269 945-3185
  Hastings *(G-7798)*
Kent County ....F..... 616 632-7580
  Grand Rapids *(G-6887)*
Labor Education and Res Prj ....G..... 313 842-6262
  Detroit *(G-4373)*
Print Shop 4u LLC ....G..... 810 721-7500
  Imlay City *(G-8644)*
Rbd Creative ....G..... 313 259-5507
  Plymouth *(G-13278)*
Solutionsnowbiz ....G..... 269 321-5062
  Portage *(G-13609)*

PRINTING, COMMERCIAL: Ready

P D Q Press Inc ....G..... 586 725-1888
  Ira *(G-8706)*

PRINTING, COMMERCIAL: Screen

4 Seasons Gym LLC ....G..... 989 681-8175
  Saint Louis *(G-14983)*
A-1 Screenprinting LLC ....D..... 734 665-2692
  Ann Arbor *(G-342)*
Adlib Grafix & Apparel ....G..... 269 964-2810
  Battle Creek *(G-1178)*
Adrians Screen Print ....G..... 734 994-1367
  Holland *(G-7957)*
ADS Plus Printing LLC ....G..... 810 659-7190
  Flushing *(G-5800)*
Advanced Tex Screen Printing ....E..... 989 643-7288
  Bay City *(G-1318)*
Aka Sports ....G..... 734 260-1023
  Wayne *(G-18211)*
Alley T & Gifts ....G..... 989 875-4793
  Carson City *(G-2591)*
Allgraphics Corp ....G..... 248 994-7373
  Farmington Hills *(G-5167)*
Americas Finest Prtg Graphics ....G..... 586 296-1312
  Fraser *(G-5893)*
AP Impressions Inc ....G..... 734 464-8009
  Livonia *(G-10121)*
Apparel Sales Inc ....G..... 616 842-5650
  Jenison *(G-9045)*
Applied Graphics & Fabricating ....F..... 989 662-3334
  Auburn *(G-764)*
Ar-Tee Enterprises LLC ....G..... 989 433-5546
  Rosebush *(G-14366)*
Ar2 Engineering LLC ....E..... 248 735-9999
  Novi *(G-12364)*
Artbox Design Inc ....G..... 248 461-2555
  Waterford *(G-18102)*
B F S Printing and Promot ....G..... 248 685-2456
  Milford *(G-11454)*
Beyond Embroidery ....G..... 616 726-7000
  Grand Rapids *(G-6505)*
Big D LLC ....G..... 248 787-2724
  Redford *(G-13720)*
Blts Wearable Art Inc ....G..... 517 669-9659
  Dewitt *(G-4706)*
Brooklyn Special Tees ....G..... 623 521-3230
  Brooklyn *(G-2123)*
Busy Bees EMB & Gifts LLC ....G..... 989 261-7446
  Sheridan *(G-15381)*
Carter Creations ....G..... 800 710-8055
  Van Buren Twp *(G-17515)*
Carters Imagewear & Awards ....G..... 231 881-9324
  Petoskey *(G-12992)*
Celia Corporation ....G..... 616 887-7387
  Sparta *(G-15763)*
Cerva Screen Printing ....G..... 616 272-2635
  Grand Rapids *(G-6561)*
Champion Screen Printers ....G..... 616 881-0760
  Byron Center *(G-2263)*
Chosen Tees LLC ....G..... 313 766-4550
  Redford *(G-13723)*
Cobrex Ltd ....G..... 734 429-9758
  Saline *(G-15008)*
Complete Source Inc ....G..... 616 285-9110
  Grand Rapids *(G-6587)*
Coventry Creations Inc ....F..... 248 545-8360
  Ferndale *(G-5537)*
Creativitees Studio ....G..... 586 565-2213
  Shelby Township *(G-15198)*
Cujographyx LLC ....G..... 248 318-6407
  Redford *(G-13728)*
Custom Threads and Sports LLC ....G..... 248 391-0088
  Lake Orion *(G-9599)*
D & M Silkscreening ....G..... 517 694-4199
  Holt *(G-8305)*
D4 Apparel LLC ....G..... 586 207-1841
  Ray *(G-13698)*
Darson Corporation ....F..... 313 875-7781
  Ferndale *(G-5538)*
Delta Sports Service & EMB ....G..... 517 482-6565
  Lansing *(G-9686)*
Designshirtscom Inc ....G..... 734 414-7604
  Plymouth *(G-13155)*
Detroit Impression Company Inc ....G..... 313 921-9077
  Grosse Pointe Park *(G-7551)*
DI Tee Pee LLC ....G..... 906 493-6929
  Drummond Island *(G-4800)*
Domer Industries LLC ....F..... 269 226-4000
  Kalamazoo *(G-9173)*
Drink Branders LLC ....F..... 231 668-4121
  Traverse City *(G-16671)*
Earthbound Inc ....G..... 616 774-0096
  Grand Rapids *(G-6662)*
Eclipse Print Emporium Inc ....G..... 248 477-8337
  Livonia *(G-10190)*
Edens Political ....G..... 313 277-0700
  Dearborn *(G-3834)*
Edwards Sign & Screen Printing ....G..... 989 725-2988
  Owosso *(G-12832)*
Emerald Graphics Inc ....G..... 616 871-3020
  Grand Rapids *(G-6676)*
Essential Screen Printing LLC ....G..... 313 300-6411
  Detroit *(G-4215)*
Express Sportswear Inc ....E..... 989 773-7515
  Mount Pleasant *(G-11697)*
Extreme Screen Prints ....G..... 616 889-8305
  Grand Rapids *(G-6694)*
Fabricated Customs ....G..... 517 488-7273
  Okemos *(G-12667)*
Faro Screen Process Inc ....F..... 734 207-8400
  Canton *(G-2461)*
Figment Screen Printing ....G..... 269 858-9998
  Three Rivers *(G-16573)*
Flavored Group LLC ....G..... 517 775-4371
  Lansing *(G-9760)*
Foltz Screen Printing ....G..... 989 772-3947
  Mount Pleasant *(G-11699)*
Foresight Group Inc ....E..... 517 485-5700
  Lansing *(G-9699)*
Fug Inc ....G..... 269 781-8036
  Marshall *(G-11058)*
Futuristic Artwear Inc ....F..... 248 680-0200
  Rochester Hills *(G-14018)*
Genesis Graphics Inc ....G..... 906 786-4913
  Escanaba *(G-5072)*
Globe Printing & Specialties ....F..... 906 485-1033
  Ishpeming *(G-8776)*
Grafaktri Inc ....G..... 734 665-0717
  Ann Arbor *(G-504)*
Grand Apps LLC ....G..... 517 927-5140
  Grand Ledge *(G-6391)*
Grand Rapids Graphix ....G..... 616 359-2383
  Wyoming *(G-18876)*
Grand Rapids Graphix LLC ....G..... 616 359-2383
  Grand Rapids *(G-6758)*
Grand Rapids Graphix LLC ....G..... 616 359-2383
  Caledonia *(G-2376)*
Grasel Graphics Inc ....G..... 989 652-5151
  Frankenmuth *(G-5865)*
Graveldinger Graphix ....G..... 248 535-8074
  Ortonville *(G-12747)*
Great Put On Inc ....G..... 810 771-4174
  Grand Blanc *(G-6246)*
Hankerds Sportswear Basic TS ....G..... 989 725-2979
  Owosso *(G-12836)*
High Winds Graphix ....G..... 313 363-3434
  Grosse Pointe Park *(G-7556)*
Hilton Screeners Inc ....G..... 810 653-0711
  Davison *(G-3787)*
Holland Screen Print Inc ....G..... 616 396-7630
  Holland *(G-8084)*
Homestead Graphics Design Inc ....G..... 906 353-6741
  Baraga *(G-1140)*
Honeybees Custom Tees ....G..... 248 421-0817
  Milford *(G-11466)*
Hoyt & Company LLC ....G..... 810 624-4445
  Clio *(G-3401)*
I D Merch ....G..... 734 237-4111
  Garden City *(G-6096)*
Image Projections Inc ....F..... 810 629-0700
  Fenton *(G-6097)*
Impression Center Co ....G..... 248 989-8080
  Troy *(G-17162)*
Impressions Custom Graphics ....G..... 989 429-0079
  Harrison *(G-7678)*
Industrial Mtal Idntfction Inc ....G..... 616 847-0060
  Spring Lake *(G-15824)*
Ink Chemistry Screen Printing ....G..... 810 429-9095
  Holly *(G-8278)*
Ink Frenzy ....G..... 734 562-2621
  Chelsea *(G-2815)*
Inkorporate ....G..... 734 261-4657
  Garden City *(G-6097)*
Inkpressions ....G..... 248 956-7974
  Commerce Township *(G-3542)*
Integrity Marketing Products ....G..... 734 522-5050
  Garden City *(G-6099)*
Invest Positive LLC ....G..... 313 205-9815
  Southfield *(G-15607)*

J B M Technology G 269 344-5716
Kalamazoo *(G-9227)*

JD Group Inc F 248 735-9999
Novi *(G-12448)*

Jentees Custom Screen Prtg LLC F 231 929-3610
Traverse City *(G-16729)*

K G S Screen Process Inc G 313 794-2777
Detroit *(G-4347)*

Kalamazoo Sportswear Inc E 269 344-4242
Kalamazoo *(G-9248)*

Kennedy Acquisition Inc G 616 871-3020
Grand Rapids *(G-6884)*

Kingdom Geekdom LLC G 517 610-5016
Hillsdale *(G-7939)*

Kpmf Usa Inc F 248 377-4999
Lake Orion *(G-9612)*

Lansing Athletics G 517 327-8828
Lansing *(G-9772)*

Larsen Graphics Inc E 989 823-3000
Vassar *(G-17579)*

Legacy Design Studio LLC G 248 710-3219
Rochester Hills *(G-14052)*

Let Love Rule G 734 749-7435
Rockwood *(G-14202)*

Livonia Trophy & Screen Prtg G 734 464-9191
Livonia *(G-10289)*

Logos and Letters G 248 795-2093
Clarkston *(G-3045)*

Lyons Graphics and Tees G 586 770-9630
New Haven *(G-12034)*

Make It Mine Dsign EMB Screen G 989 448-8678
Gaylord *(G-6144)*

Malachi Printing LLC G 517 395-4813
Edwardsburg *(G-5008)*

Mega Screen Corp G 517 849-7057
Jonesville *(G-9094)*

Metro Detroit Screen Prtg LLC G 586 337-5167
Shelby Township *(G-15276)*

Mettek LLC G 616 895-2033
Allendale *(G-225)*

Michael Anderson G 231 652-5717
Newaygo *(G-12088)*

Michigan Screen Printing G 810 687-5550
Clio *(G-3406)*

Midwest Graphics & Awards Inc G 734 424-3700
Dexter *(G-4746)*

Monograms & More Inc E 313 299-3140
Taylor *(G-16449)*

Monroe Sp Inc G 517 374-6544
Lansing *(G-9779)*

Mr Cs Custom Tees G 989 965-2222
Clarksville *(G-3079)*

Ninja Tees N More G 248 541-2547
Hazel Park *(G-7837)*

Oc Tees G 248 858-9191
Pontiac *(G-13405)*

Personal Graphics G 231 347-6347
Petoskey *(G-13013)*

Precision Dial Co G 269 375-5601
Kalamazoo *(G-9302)*

Primo Crafts G 248 373-3229
Pontiac *(G-13411)*

Pro Gear Printing LLC G 734 386-1105
Canton *(G-2514)*

Pro Shop The/P S Graphics G 517 448-8490
Hudson *(G-8559)*

Progress Custom Screen Prtg G 248 982-4247
Ferndale *(G-5583)*

Progressive Graphics G 269 945-9249
Hastings *(G-7806)*

Reborn Wear G 313 680-6806
Rockwood *(G-14204)*

Rival Shop G 248 461-6281
Waterford *(G-18161)*

Royal Stewart Enterprises G 734 224-7994
Temperance *(G-16548)*

Sandlot Sports G 989 391-9684
Bay City *(G-1397)*

Sandlot Sports F 989 835-9696
Saginaw *(G-14752)*

Screen Graphics Co Inc G 231 238-4499
Indian River *(G-8656)*

Screen Ideas Inc G 616 458-5119
Grand Rapids *(G-7188)*

Screen Print Department E 616 235-2200
Grand Rapids *(G-7189)*

Serviscreen Inc D 616 669-1640
Jenison *(G-9071)*

Shirt Razor LLC G 810 623-7116
Brighton *(G-2070)*

Shirt Traveler G 800 403-4117
Swartz Creek *(G-16358)*

Sign Screen Inc G 810 239-1100
Flint *(G-5762)*

Signs365com LLC G 800 265-8830
Shelby Township *(G-15333)*

Silk Screenstuff G 517 543-7716
Charlotte *(G-2770)*

Sisters In Inc G 269 857-4085
Saugatuck *(G-15085)*

SM & AM Enterprise Inc G 906 786-0373
Escanaba *(G-5100)*

Sports Junction G 989 791-5900
Saginaw *(G-14765)*

Star Ink and Thread G 989 823-3660
Vassar *(G-17582)*

Stepscreen Printing G 734 770-5009
Monroe *(G-11577)*

Strait Astrid G 269 672-4110
Shelbyville *(G-15374)*

Sublime Prints G 231 335-7799
Hesperia *(G-7872)*

Sweet N Sporty Tees G 313 693-9793
Detroit *(G-4619)*

Swift Printing Co F 616 459-4263
Grand Rapids *(G-7241)*

T Shirt Guy G 586 944-5900
Warren *(G-18033)*

T Shirt Shop G 810 285-8857
Flint *(G-5776)*

Tee G 810 231-2764
Brighton *(G-2076)*

Tee - The Extra Effort LLC G 734 891-4789
Royal Oak *(G-14584)*

Tee Quilters G 248 336-9779
Ferndale *(G-5588)*

Teesnitch Screen Printing G 734 667-1636
Canton *(G-2533)*

TP Logos LLC G 810 956-9484
Marysville *(G-11110)*

Trikala Inc G 517 646-8188
Dimondale *(G-4765)*

Triple Creek Shirts and More G 269 273-5154
Constantine *(G-3676)*

Ultimate Graphic and Sign LLC G 989 865-5200
Saint Charles *(G-14812)*

Underground Shirts G 734 274-5494
Ann Arbor *(G-705)*

Unique Embroidery G 517 321-8647
Lansing *(G-9746)*

Vector Distribution LLC G 616 361-2021
Grand Rapids *(G-7308)*

Vg Kids G 734 480-0667
Ypsilanti *(G-18983)*

Vgkids Inc F 734 485-5128
Ypsilanti *(G-18984)*

Villagebees G 810 217-2962
Lapeer *(G-9967)*

Yooper Shirts Mqt G 906 273-1837
Marquette *(G-11051)*

Zakoors G 313 831-6969
Detroit *(G-4701)*

Zodiac Enterprises LLC G 810 640-7146
Mount Morris *(G-11677)*

PRINTING, COMMERCIAL: Tags, NEC

All Access Name Tags G 866 955-8247
Troy *(G-16923)*

PRINTING, COMMERCIAL: Tickets, NEC

Meteor Web Marketing Inc F 734 822-4999
Ann Arbor *(G-570)*

PRINTING, LITHOGRAPHIC: Advertising Posters

Afj Woodhaven LLC G 248 593-6200
Bloomfield Hills *(G-1793)*

Detroit Newspaper Partnr LP A 586 826-7187
Sterling Heights *(G-15984)*

Epi Printers Inc D 734 261-9400
Livonia *(G-10198)*

Paul C Doerr G 734 242-2058
Monroe *(G-11568)*

PRINTING, LITHOGRAPHIC: Catalogs

Business Design Solutions Inc G 248 672-8007
Southfield *(G-15514)*

Npi Wireless E 231 922-9273
Traverse City *(G-16776)*

PRINTING, LITHOGRAPHIC: Color

Pak Mail Center of America G 248 543-3097
Ferndale *(G-5575)*

PRINTING, LITHOGRAPHIC: Decals

Commercial Trck Transf Signs G 586 754-7100
Warren *(G-17761)*

PRINTING, LITHOGRAPHIC: Forms & Cards, Business

Daniel Ward G 810 965-6535
Mount Morris *(G-11670)*

Digital Imaging Group Inc D 269 686-8744
Allegan *(G-155)*

Embroidery House Inc G 616 669-6400
Jenison *(G-9054)*

PRINTING, LITHOGRAPHIC: Forms, Business

Timbertech Inc F 231 348-2750
Harbor Springs *(G-7658)*

Total Business Systems Inc F 248 307-1076
Madison Heights *(G-10845)*

Walker Printery Inc F 248 548-5100
Oak Park *(G-12650)*

PRINTING, LITHOGRAPHIC: Newspapers

Mid-State Printing Inc F 989 875-4163
Ithaca *(G-8794)*

PRINTING, LITHOGRAPHIC: Offset & photolithographic printing

Copy Central Inc G 231 941-2298
Traverse City *(G-16660)*

PRINTING, LITHOGRAPHIC: On Metal

Aquaprintingcom G 269 779-2734
Kalamazoo *(G-9116)*

Clare Print & Pulp G 989 386-3497
Clare *(G-2976)*

Foremost Graphics LLC D 616 453-4747
Grand Rapids *(G-6715)*

Ideal Printing Company E 616 454-9224
Grand Rapids *(G-6831)*

Parkside Speedy Print Inc G 810 985-8484
Port Huron *(G-13516)*

Web Litho Inc G 586 803-9000
Rochester Hills *(G-14142)*

West Michigan Printing Inc G 616 676-2190
Ada *(G-41)*

PRINTING, LITHOGRAPHIC: Periodicals

Journal Disposition Corp D 269 428-2054
Saint Joseph *(G-14938)*

PRINTING, LITHOGRAPHIC: Posters

Fairfax Prints Ltd G 517 321-5590
Lansing *(G-9696)*

PRINTING, LITHOGRAPHIC: Posters & Decals

Word Baron Inc F 248 471-4080
Ann Arbor *(G-717)*

PRINTING, LITHOGRAPHIC: Promotional

Avanzado LLC E 248 615-0538
Farmington Hills *(G-5178)*

Grand Apps LLC G 517 927-5140
Grand Ledge *(G-6391)*

Quantum Digital Ventures LLC E 248 292-5686
Warren *(G-17989)*

Real Estate One Inc G 248 851-2600
Commerce Township *(G-3569)*

PRINTING, LITHOGRAPHIC: Tags

International Master Pdts Corp C 231 894-5651
Montague *(G-11598)*

Employee Codes: A=Over 500 employees, B=251-500
C=101-250, D=51-100, E=20-50, F=10-19, G=3-9
2022 Harris Michigan
Industrial Directory
1373

PRINTING, LITHOGRAPHIC: Wrappers & Seals

Unique-Intasco Usa Inc G 810 982-3360
Auburn Hills *(G-1071)*

PRINTING: Books

Creative Graphics Inc G 517 784-0391
Jackson *(G-8857)*

PRINTING: Books

Cushing-Malloy Inc E 734 663-8554
Ann Arbor *(G-440)*
Epi Printers Inc D 734 261-9400
Livonia *(G-10198)*
Imperial Clinical RES Svcs Inc C 616 784-0100
Grand Rapids *(G-6836)*
Jenkins Group Inc G 231 933-4954
Traverse City *(G-16728)*
Mel Printing Co Inc E 313 928-5440
Taylor *(G-16440)*
Practical Paper Inc F 616 887-1723
Cedar Springs *(G-2658)*
R W Patterson Printing Co D 269 925-2177
Benton Harbor *(G-1579)*
Rogers Printing Inc C 231 853-2244
Ravenna *(G-13694)*
Sheridan Pubg Grnd Rapids Inc D 616 957-5100
Grand Rapids *(G-7193)*
Success By Design Inc F 800 327-0057
Wyoming *(G-18909)*
Tweddle Group Inc C 586 307-3700
Clinton Township *(G-3380)*

PRINTING: Broadwoven Fabrics. Cotton

Inkpressions LLC E 248 461-2555
Commerce Township *(G-3543)*
Meridian Screen Prtg & Design G 517 351-2525
Okemos *(G-12674)*

PRINTING: Commercial, NEC

Advance Graphic Systems Inc E 248 656-8000
Rochester Hills *(G-13943)*
Advantage Label and Packg Inc E 616 656-1900
Grand Rapids *(G-6435)*
Afb Corporate Operations LLC E 248 669-1188
Plymouth *(G-13120)*
Al Corp F 734 475-7357
Chelsea *(G-2804)*
Allesk Enterprises Inc G 231 941-5770
Traverse City *(G-16600)*
Alpha Data Business Forms Inc G 248 540-5930
Birmingham *(G-1718)*
American Reprographics Co LLC G 248 299-8900
Clawson *(G-3086)*
Apb Inc G 248 528-2990
Troy *(G-16939)*
Applied Visual Concepts LLC G 866 440-6888
Warren *(G-17709)*
ARC Print Solutions LLC F 248 917-7052
Beverly Hills *(G-1661)*
Art Craft Display Inc D 517 485-2221
Lansing *(G-9756)*
Autumn Endeavors LLC G 906 296-0601
Lake Linden *(G-9566)*
Azoth LLC F 734 669-3797
Ann Arbor *(G-392)*
Behrmann Printing Company Inc F 248 799-7771
Southfield *(G-15505)*
Big Rapids Printing G 231 796-8588
Grand Rapids *(G-6508)*
Bivins Graphics G 616 453-2211
Grand Rapids *(G-6512)*
Black Label Customs LLC G 231 924-8044
Grant *(G-7427)*
Blue Water Printing Co Inc G 810 664-0643
Lapeer *(G-9914)*
Brightformat Inc E 616 247-1161
Grand Rapids *(G-6524)*
Bronco Printing Company G 248 544-1120
Hazel Park *(G-7821)*
Brophy Engraving Co Inc E 313 871-2333
Detroit *(G-4076)*
C2 Imaging LLC C 248 743-2903
Troy *(G-16990)*
Cadillac Prsentation Solutions E 248 288-9777
Troy *(G-16994)*
Christian Unity Press Inc G 810 732-1831
Flint *(G-5667)*
Columbia Marking Tools Inc E 586 949-8400
Chesterfield *(G-2860)*
Commercial Blueprint Inc E 517 372-8360
Lansing *(G-9825)*
Creation Highway G 307 220-7309
Milan *(G-11434)*
Custom Printers Inc D 616 454-9224
Grand Rapids *(G-6623)*
Data Mail Services Inc E 248 588-2415
Madison Heights *(G-10704)*
Dennco LLC G 866 977-4467
Sault Sainte Marie *(G-15089)*
Digital Imaging Group Inc D 269 686-8744
Allegan *(G-155)*
Display Pack Inc C 616 451-3061
Cedar Springs *(G-2649)*
Dobb Printing Inc E 231 722-1060
Muskegon *(G-11799)*
Domart LLC G 616 285-9177
Grand Rapids *(G-6653)*
Dome Production LLC G 517 787-9178
Jackson *(G-8869)*
Dyemurex Inc G 586 447-2509
Roseville *(G-14403)*
Eagle Grafix G 989 624-4638
Birch Run *(G-1706)*
Earle Press Inc E 231 773-2111
Muskegon *(G-11805)*
Ecoprint Services LLC G 616 254-8019
Grand Rapids *(G-6664)*
EDM Inc G 586 933-3187
Troy *(G-17077)*
Elite Bus Svcs Exec Stffing In G 734 956-4550
Bloomfield Hills *(G-1818)*
Endless Engravings G 517 962-4293
Jackson *(G-8880)*
Epi Printers Inc D 734 261-9400
Livonia *(G-10198)*
F & A Enterprises of Michigan G 906 228-3222
Marquette *(G-11018)*
F P Horak Company C 989 892-6505
Bay City *(G-1355)*
Federal Heath Sign Company LLC E 248 656-8000
Rochester Hills *(G-14010)*
Field Crafts Inc F 231 325-1122
Honor *(G-8359)*
Frye Printing Company Inc F 517 456-4124
Clinton *(G-3139)*
Genesee County Herald Inc F 810 686-3840
Clio *(G-3399)*
Gifts Engraved Inc G 248 321-8900
Royal Oak *(G-14540)*
Grand Traverse Continuous Inc E 231 941-5400
Traverse City *(G-16698)*
Graphic Enterprises Inc D 248 616-4900
Madison Heights *(G-10732)*
Graphic Impressions Inc G 616 455-0303
Grand Rapids *(G-6782)*
Graphix 2 Go Inc G 269 969-7321
Battle Creek *(G-1235)*
Greystone Imaging LLC G 616 742-3810
Grand Rapids *(G-6790)*
Group 7500 Inc F 313 875-9026
Detroit *(G-4284)*
Group Infotech Inc E 517 336-7110
Lansing *(G-9848)*
Hamblin Company E 517 423-7491
Bloomfield Hills *(G-1826)*
Harbinger Laser G 269 445-1499
Cassopolis *(G-2629)*
Herald Newspapers Company Inc G 989 895-8551
Flint *(G-5715)*
Hodges & Irvine Inc F 810 329-4787
Saint Clair *(G-14831)*
Husky Envelope Products Inc D 248 624-7070
Walled Lake *(G-17670)*
IAC Creative LLC B 248 455-7000
Southfield *(G-15597)*
Imperial Clinical RES Svcs Inc C 616 784-0100
Grand Rapids *(G-6836)*
Industrial Imprntng & Die Ctng G 586 778-9470
Eastpointe *(G-4937)*
International Master Pdts Corp C 231 894-5651
Montague *(G-11598)*
Irwin Enterprises Inc E 810 732-0770
Flint *(G-5716)*
IXL Graphics G 313 350-2800
Taylor *(G-16429)*
J-Ad Graphics Inc D 800 870-7085
Hastings *(G-7800)*
Jack Batdorss F 231 723-3592
Manistee *(G-10902)*
Job Shop Ink Inc G 517 372-3900
Lansing *(G-9768)*
Jomar Inc E 269 925-2222
Benton Harbor *(G-1560)*
Jomark Inc E 248 478-2600
Farmington Hills *(G-5275)*
Just Wing It Inc G 248 549-9338
Madison Heights *(G-10756)*
Kenewell Group G 810 714-4290
Fenton *(G-5487)*
Lamon Group Inc F 616 710-3169
Byron Center *(G-2280)*
Lawson Printers Inc E 269 965-0525
Battle Creek *(G-1267)*
Lithotech G 269 471-6027
Berrien Springs *(G-1644)*
Lowery Corporation C 616 554-5200
Grand Rapids *(G-6949)*
M & J Graphics Enterprises Inc F 734 542-8800
Livonia *(G-10294)*
Macarthur Corp E 810 606-1777
Grand Blanc *(G-6252)*
Macomb Residential Opprtnts G 586 231-0363
Clinton Township *(G-3289)*
Maleports Sault Prtg Co Inc E 906 632-3369
Sault Sainte Marie *(G-15095)*
Memories Xpress G 248 582-1836
Madison Heights *(G-10780)*
Meta4mat LLC G 616 214-7418
Comstock Park *(G-3625)*
Metroastyling G 586 991-6854
Sterling Heights *(G-16094)*
Michael Niederpruem G 231 935-0241
Kalkaska *(G-9396)*
Microforms Inc E 586 939-7900
Beverly Hills *(G-1667)*
Mid-State Printing Inc F 989 875-4163
Ithaca *(G-8794)*
Monroe Publishing Company D 734 242-1100
Monroe *(G-11565)*
Moormann Printing Inc G 269 423-2411
Decatur *(G-3950)*
MPS Hrl LLC G 800 748-0517
Lansing *(G-9718)*
MPS Lansing Inc A 517 323-9000
Lansing *(G-9719)*
Nalcor LLC D 248 541-1140
Ferndale *(G-5570)*
Nje Enterprises LLC G 313 963-3600
Detroit *(G-4486)*
Nu-Tech North Inc G 231 347-1992
Petoskey *(G-13010)*
Ogemaw County Herald Inc E 989 345-0044
West Branch *(G-18333)*
Pds Plastics Inc F 616 896-1109
Dorr *(G-4769)*
Peg-Master Business Forms Inc G 586 566-8694
Shelby Township *(G-15298)*
Plexus Cards G 231 652-5355
Newaygo *(G-12089)*
Presscraft Papers Inc F 231 882-5505
Benzonia *(G-1616)*
Printcomm Inc D 810 239-5763
Flint *(G-5749)*
Printery Inc E 616 396-4655
Holland *(G-8172)*
Printing Consolidation Co LLC E 616 233-3161
Grand Rapids *(G-7108)*
Printwell Acquisition Co Inc D 734 941-6300
Taylor *(G-16462)*
Printxpress Inc G 313 846-1644
Dearborn *(G-3887)*
Qrp Inc E 989 496-2955
Midland *(G-11406)*
R & R Harwood Inc G 616 669-6400
Jenison *(G-9069)*
R R Donnelley & Sons Company G 248 583-2500
Madison Heights *(G-10816)*
Religious Communications LLC G 313 822-3361
Detroit *(G-4563)*
Riegle Press Inc E 810 653-9631
Davison *(G-3795)*
River Run Press Inc E 269 349-7603
Kalamazoo *(G-9320)*
Riverhill Publications & Prtg F 586 468-6011
Ira *(G-8711)*

Rogers Printing Inc ....C.... 231 853-2244
Ravenna *(G-13694)*

RPC Company ....F.... 989 752-3618
Saginaw *(G-14741)*

RR Donnelley ....G.... 248 588-2941
Madison Heights *(G-10822)*

Safran Printing Company Inc ....C.... 586 939-7600
Beverly Hills *(G-1668)*

Sboy LLC ....G.... 313 350-0496
Detroit *(G-4583)*

Slick Shirts Screen Printing ....F.... 517 371-3600
Lansing *(G-9895)*

Source One Digital LLC ....E.... 231 759-3160
Norton Shores *(G-12334)*

Spartan Graphics Inc ....D.... 616 887-1073
Sparta *(G-15780)*

Stoppa Signs & Engraving LLC ....G.... 616 532-0230
Wyoming *(G-18908)*

T J K Inc ....G.... 586 731-9639
Sterling Heights *(G-16199)*

Tc Office Express ....G.... 231 929-3549
Traverse City *(G-16851)*

Tectonics Industries LLC ....E.... 248 597-1600
Auburn Hills *(G-1046)*

TGI Direct Inc ....G.... 810 239-5553
Ann Arbor *(G-685)*

Thorpe Printing Services Inc ....G.... 810 364-6222
Marysville *(G-11107)*

Timbertech Inc ....F.... 231 348-2750
Harbor Springs *(G-7658)*

Travel Information Services ....F.... 989 275-8042
Roscommon *(G-14357)*

Tribar Manufacturing LLC ....E.... 248 669-0077
Wixom *(G-18777)*

Triton 3d LLC ....G.... 616 405-8662
Grand Rapids *(G-7277)*

Troy Haygood ....G.... 313 478-3308
Ferndale *(G-5589)*

Turner Business Forms Inc ....E.... 989 752-5540
Saginaw *(G-14782)*

Tuscola County Advertiser Inc ....B.... 517 673-3181
Caro *(G-2584)*

Tvdn Group LLC ....G.... 248 255-6402
Bloomfield Hills *(G-1871)*

Tweddle Group Inc ....C.... 586 307-3700
Clinton Township *(G-3380)*

Ultra-Tech Printing Co ....F.... 616 249-0500
Wyoming *(G-18915)*

Valassis International Inc ....B.... 734 591-3000
Livonia *(G-10457)*

Van Kehrberg Vern ....G.... 810 364-1066
Marysville *(G-11111)*

Vinyl Spectrum ....F.... 616 591-3410
Wyoming *(G-18918)*

Weighman Enterprises Inc ....G.... 989 755-2116
Saginaw *(G-14792)*

Whitlock Distribution Svcs LLC ....F.... 248 548-1040
Madison Heights *(G-10863)*

Your Home Town USA Inc ....G.... 517 529-9421
Clarklake *(G-3010)*

Zeeland Record Co ....G.... 616 772-2131
Zeeland *(G-19099)*

PRINTING: Flexographic

Anchor Printing Company ....E.... 248 335-7440
Novi *(G-12362)*

Cummins Label Company ....E.... 269 345-3386
Kalamazoo *(G-9159)*

Fortis Sltions Group Centl LLC ....D.... 248 437-5200
Wixom *(G-18664)*

Grand Rapids Label Company ....D.... 616 459-8134
Grand Rapids *(G-6760)*

Middleton Printing Inc ....G.... 616 247-8742
Grand Rapids *(G-7004)*

Whitlam Group Inc ....C.... 586 757-5100
Center Line *(G-2689)*

PRINTING: Gravure, Forms, Business

Aip Group Inc ....G.... 248 828-4400
Troy *(G-16911)*

Taylor Communications Inc ....F.... 248 304-4800
Southfield *(G-15717)*

PRINTING: Gravure, Job

Exone Americas LLC ....G.... 248 740-1580
Troy *(G-17102)*

Hodges & Irvine Inc ....F.... 810 329-4787
Saint Clair *(G-14831)*

PRINTING: Gravure, Labels

Advantage Label and Packg Inc ....E.... 616 656-1900
Grand Rapids *(G-6435)*

Eagile Incorporated ....F.... 616 243-1200
Grand Rapids *(G-6660)*

PRINTING: Gravure, Rotogravure

Capital Imaging Inc ....F.... 517 482-2292
Lansing *(G-9822)*

High Impact Solutions Inc ....G.... 248 473-9804
Farmington Hills *(G-5260)*

Ivy Snow LLC ....G.... 248 842-1242
Detroit *(G-4330)*

Safran Printing Company Inc ....C.... 586 939-7600
Beverly Hills *(G-1668)*

Tentcraft LLC ....D.... 800 950-4553
Traverse City *(G-16854)*

PRINTING: Gravure, Stationery & Invitation

Grand Occasions ....G.... 248 622-7144
West Bloomfield *(G-18285)*

Just Write Invites LLC ....G.... 248 797-7844
Farmington Hills *(G-5278)*

Occasions ....F.... 517 694-6437
Holt *(G-8320)*

PRINTING: Gravure, Wrapper & Seal

Rainbow Wrap ....F.... 586 949-3976
Chesterfield *(G-2937)*

PRINTING: Laser

Ancor Information MGT LLC ....D.... 248 740-8866
Troy *(G-16936)*

Artistic Printing Inc ....G.... 248 356-1004
Southfield *(G-15491)*

Beamer Laser Marking ....D.... 810 471-3044
Flushing *(G-5803)*

Digitally Assured ....G.... 734 730-8800
Ypsilanti *(G-18939)*

Lasertec Inc ....E.... 586 274-4500
Madison Heights *(G-10769)*

Materialise Usa LLC ....D.... 734 259-6445
Plymouth *(G-13236)*

Sage Direct Inc ....F.... 616 940-8311
Grand Rapids *(G-7178)*

Source One Dist Svcs Inc ....F.... 248 399-5060
Madison Heights *(G-10831)*

PRINTING: Letterpress

A B C Printing Inc ....G.... 248 887-0010
Highland *(G-7877)*

ABC Printing Corporation Inc ....G.... 248 887-0010
Highland *(G-7879)*

Berci Printing Services Inc ....G.... 248 350-0206
Southfield *(G-15506)*

Clemco Printing Inc ....G.... 989 269-8364
Bad Axe *(G-1099)*

De Vru Printing Co ....G.... 616 452-5451
Grand Rapids *(G-6636)*

Dekoff & Sons Inc ....G.... 269 344-5816
Kalamazoo *(G-9165)*

E & S Graphics Inc ....G.... 989 875-2828
Ithaca *(G-8790)*

Grand Rapids Letter Service ....G.... 616 459-4711
Grand Rapids *(G-6762)*

Handy Bindery Co Inc ....E.... 586 469-2240
Clinton Township *(G-3251)*

Houghton Lake Resorter Inc ....F.... 989 366-5341
Houghton Lake *(G-8400)*

Johnson-Clark Printers Inc ....F.... 231 947-6898
Traverse City *(G-16730)*

Lamour Printing Co ....G.... 734 241-6006
Monroe *(G-11558)*

Lesnau Printing Company ....E.... 586 795-9200
Sterling Heights *(G-16071)*

Litho-Graphics Printing Pdts ....G.... 586 775-1670
Roseville *(G-14433)*

Micrgraphics Printing Inc ....F.... 231 739-6575
Norton Shores *(G-12311)*

Pioneer Press Printing ....G.... 231 864-2404
Bear Lake *(G-1421)*

Pointe Printing Inc ....G.... 313 821-0030
Grosse Pointe Park *(G-7558)*

Raenell Press LLC ....G.... 616 534-8890
Grand Rapids *(G-7137)*

Ray Printing Company Inc ....F.... 517 787-4130
Jackson *(G-8994)*

Romeo Printing Company Inc ....G.... 586 752-9003
Romeo *(G-14234)*

Signal-Return Inc ....G.... 313 567-8970
Detroit *(G-4593)*

Standard Printing ....G.... 734 483-0339
Ypsilanti *(G-18978)*

Standard Printing of Warren ....G.... 586 771-3770
Warren *(G-18026)*

Straits Area Printing Corp ....G.... 231 627-5647
Cheboygan *(G-2800)*

Tallon Printing ....G.... 517 721-1307
Okemos *(G-12689)*

Unique Reproductions Inc ....G.... 248 788-2887
West Bloomfield *(G-18321)*

Whipple Printing Inc ....G.... 313 382-8033
Allen Park *(G-210)*

Zak Brothers Printing LLC ....G.... 313 831-3216
Detroit *(G-4700)*

PRINTING: Lithographic

20/20 Printing ....G.... 616 635-9690
Grand Rapids *(G-6403)*

3d Printed Parts ....G.... 616 516-3074
Grand Rapids *(G-6404)*

Adair Printing Company ....E.... 734 426-2822
Dexter *(G-4721)*

Adams Design & Print LLC ....G.... 269 612-8613
New Buffalo *(G-12022)*

ADM Graphics & Print Prod LLC ....G.... 586 598-1821
Chesterfield *(G-2835)*

Advance Graphic Systems Inc ....E.... 248 656-8000
Rochester Hills *(G-13943)*

Advanced Eco Print ....G.... 231 292-1688
Fountain *(G-5826)*

Affordable Prints ....G.... 231 679-2606
Evart *(G-5119)*

All In Printing ....G.... 567 219-3660
New Boston *(G-11999)*

Allbrite Printing & Lettershop ....G.... 734 516-2623
New Boston *(G-12000)*

Alliance Prints LLC ....G.... 313 484-0700
Detroit *(G-4002)*

Allprints Plus LLC ....G.... 248 906-2977
Madison Heights *(G-10665)*

Alpha Data Business Forms Inc ....G.... 248 540-5930
Birmingham *(G-1718)*

American Litho Inc ....G.... 734 394-1400
Van Buren Twp *(G-17508)*

Americas Finest Prtg Graphics ....G.... 586 296-1312
Fraser *(G-5893)*

Amped Electric LLC ....G.... 419 436-1818
Grand Blanc *(G-6232)*

AP Impressions Inc ....G.... 734 464-8009
Livonia *(G-10121)*

Apms Incorporated ....G.... 248 268-1477
Madison Heights *(G-10670)*

Argus Press Company ....E.... 989 725-5136
Owosso *(G-12824)*

Artistic Flair EMB & Prtg ....G.... 810 487-9074
Flushing *(G-5802)*

Automotive Media LLC ....C.... 248 537-8500
Troy *(G-16966)*

Bad Axe Prints ....G.... 248 207-6999
Wixom *(G-18618)*

BCT Internet LLC ....G.... 810 771-9117
Grand Blanc *(G-6235)*

Bearded Vinyl LLC ....G.... 989 786-9994
Lewiston *(G-10018)*

Benzie Printing ....G.... 231 714-7565
Interlochen *(G-8679)*

Blue Print Studio ....G.... 616 283-2893
Holland *(G-7977)*

Bnw West Side Scrnprinting LLC ....G.... 616 717-1082
Wyoming *(G-18853)*

Bowman Printing Inc ....G.... 810 982-8202
Port Huron *(G-13462)*

Brophy Engraving Co Inc ....E.... 313 871-2333
Detroit *(G-4076)*

Bwjs Printing LLC ....G.... 248 678-3610
Detroit *(G-4081)*

C S L Inc ....G.... 248 549-4434
Royal Oak *(G-14522)*

Cambridge Financial Services ....G.... 248 840-6650
Troy *(G-16995)*

Cameron S Roat ....G.... 810 620-7628
Burton *(G-2231)*

Capital City Blue Print Inc ....G.... 517 482-5431
Lansing *(G-9676)*

Carbonless 365 ....G.... 810 969-4014
Lapeer *(G-9921)*

PRODUCT

Employee Codes: A=Over 500 employees, B=251-500
C=101-250, D=51-100, E=20-50, F=10-19, G=3-9

2022 Harris Michigan
Industrial Directory

1375

PRINTING: Lithographic

Company		Phone
Carmens Screen Printing & EMB	G	248 535-4161
Lake Orion (G-9593)		
Carrigan Graphics Inc	G	734 455-6550
Canton (G-2445)		
Celani Printing Co	G	810 395-1609
Capac (G-2546)		
Cheap Fast Prints LLC	G	517 490-0864
Lansing (G-9824)		
Child Evngelism Fellowship Inc	E	269 461-6953
Berrien Center (G-1635)		
Colorhub LLC	F	616 333-4411
Grand Rapids (G-6584)		
Columbus Printing Inc	G	614 534-0266
Grand Rapids (G-6585)		
Copy Connection LLC	G	734 425-3150
Whitmore Lake (G-18529)		
Corporate Electronic Sty Inc	D	248 583-7070
Troy (G-17030)		
Creative Eyeball Agency	G	517 398-8008
Quincy (G-13667)		
Creative Image & Printing LLC	G	586 222-4288
Sterling Heights (G-15974)		
Creative Printing Solutions	G	616 931-1040
Zeeland (G-19008)		
Custom Printing	G	248 509-7134
Troy (G-17039)		
Custom Vinyl Prints	G	810 841-4301
Wales (G-17626)		
D and WP Rints LLC	G	313 646-6571
Detroit (G-4117)		
D2 Print Inc	G	248 229-7633
Madison Heights (G-10703)		
Daily Oakland Press	B	248 332-8181
Bloomfield Hills (G-1811)		
Daily Reporter	E	517 278-2318
Coldwater (G-3430)		
Derk Pieter Co Inc	G	616 554-7777
Grand Rapids (G-6641)		
Detroit CLB Prtg Hse Craftsmen	G	734 953-9729
Livonia (G-10182)		
Detroit News Inc	G	313 222-6400
Sterling Heights (G-15983)		
Detroit Printed Products	G	586 226-3860
Clinton Township (G-3220)		
Dexter Print & Stitch	G	734 580-2181
Dexter (G-4738)		
Digital Print Specialties	G	248 545-5888
Detroit (G-4177)		
Digital Xpress	G	248 325-9061
West Bloomfield (G-18280)		
Doorstep Printing LLC	G	248 470-9567
Detroit (G-4186)		
Dtm Inc	G	734 944-1109
Saline (G-15013)		
Dynamic Print & Imaging	G	586 738-4367
Sterling Heights (G-15994)		
Eclipse Print Services	G	517 304-2151
Wixom (G-18652)		
Edgemen Screen Printing	G	586 465-6820
Clinton Township (G-3229)		
Elston Enterprises Inc	F	313 561-8000
Dearborn Heights (G-3926)		
Eon Project	G	313 717-5976
Detroit (G-4213)		
Epi Printers Inc	D	269 964-4600
Battle Creek (G-1227)		
Eze Prints A Div Allied	G	616 281-2406
Grand Rapids (G-6697)		
Federal Heath Sign Company LLC	E	248 656-8000
Rochester Hills (G-14010)		
Floodwell Print Studio	G	231 943-2930
Traverse City (G-16683)		
Fluir Creative LLC	G	734 494-0308
Livonia (G-10213)		
Forerunner 3d Printing	G	231 722-1144
Coopersville (G-3687)		
Forward Inking Design & Print	G	231 714-8646
Traverse City (G-16689)		
Fresh Baked Prints	G	888 327-4137
Oak Park (G-12613)		
From Photos To Canvas Prints	G	248 760-4694
Rochester Hills (G-14016)		
Fuller Printing	G	989 304-0230
Stanton (G-15901)		
Genesee County Herald Inc	F	810 686-3840
Clio (G-3399)		
Genesis Service Associates LLC	G	734 994-3900
Dexter (G-4742)		
Global Digital Printing	G	734 244-5010
Monroe (G-11544)		
Good God Printing	G	313 694-2985
Detroit (G-4270)		
Grand Haven Publishing Corp	G	616 842-6400
Grand Haven (G-6305)		
Grand Traverse Continuous Inc	E	231 941-5400
Traverse City (G-16698)		
Graphic Impressions Inc	G	616 455-0303
Grand Rapids (G-6782)		
Graphics Unlimited Inc	G	231 773-2696
Norton Shores (G-12295)		
Green Ink Works	G	616 254-7350
Wyoming (G-18877)		
H & J Printing	G	734 344-9447
Rockwood (G-14199)		
Herald Bi-County Inc	G	517 448-2201
Hudson (G-8550)		
Herald Publishing Company	E	517 423-2174
Tecumseh (G-16504)		
Hodges & Irvine Inc	F	810 329-4787
Saint Clair (G-14831)		
Homestead Graphics Design Inc	G	906 353-6741
Baraga (G-1140)		
Hot Prints Inc	G	989 627-6463
Saint Johns (G-14901)		
Huron Publishing Company Inc	G	989 269-6461
Bad Axe (G-1107)		
Images2printcom	G	616 821-7143
Comstock Park (G-3611)		
Index Prints	G	248 327-6621
Southfield (G-15602)		
Industrial Imprntng & Die Ctng	G	586 778-9470
Eastpointe (G-4937)		
Inkwell Screen Printing	G	586 292-4050
Rochester (G-13907)		
Innovative Apparel Printing	G	989 395-1204
Saginaw (G-14671)		
Instant Car Credit Inc	G	231 922-8180
Traverse City (G-16722)		
Instant Framer	G	231 947-8908
Traverse City (G-16723)		
Interntnal Mnute Press Clawson	G	248 629-4220
Clawson (G-3099)		
Iris Design & Print Inc	G	313 277-0505
Dearborn (G-3855)		
J&J Custom Print Services	G	616 581-0545
Commerce Township (G-3546)		
J-Ad Graphics Inc	F	269 965-3955
Battle Creek (G-1243)		
Ja Sportswear & Printing LLC	G	248 706-1213
West Bloomfield (G-18292)		
Janet Kelly	F	231 775-2313
Cadillac (G-2338)		
Jeffrey S Zimmer	G	810 385-0726
Burtchville (G-2221)		
Jlc Print and Ship Inc	G	517 544-0404
Jackson (G-8921)		
Just Right Duplications LLC	G	313 655-3555
Oak Park (G-12619)		
Kalamazoo Prtg & Promotions	G	269 818-1122
Kalamazoo (G-9246)		
Kent Communications Inc	G	616 957-2120
Grand Rapids (G-6886)		
Kleins 3d Prtg Solutions LLC	G	586 212-9763
Fraser (G-5951)		
Ktd Print	G	248 670-4200
Royal Oak (G-14554)		
Lake Michigan Mailers Inc	D	269 383-9333
Kalamazoo (G-9257)		
Lakeside Custom Printing LLC	G	517 936-5904
Jerome (G-9078)		
Larsen Graphics Inc	E	989 823-3000
Vassar (G-17579)		
Leader Publications LLC	D	269 683-2100
Niles (G-12141)		
Leelanau Prints	G	231 386-7616
Northport (G-12188)		
Lynn Shaler Fine Prints LLC	G	248 644-5148
Bloomfield Hills (G-1834)		
M Print	G	248 550-4405
Livonia (G-10296)		
M Print Dance Company	G	616 575-9969
Kentwood (G-9464)		
Madain Postal Services LLC	G	586 323-3573
Sterling Heights (G-16080)		
Marketing VI Group Inc	G	989 793-3933
Saginaw (G-14686)		
Maslin Corporation	G	586 777-7500
Harper Woods (G-7667)		
Menominee Cnty Jurnl Print Sp	F	906 753-2296
Stephenson (G-15909)		
Mid-Michigan Screen Printing	G	989 624-9827
Birch Run (G-1711)		
Midland Publishing Company	C	989 835-7171
Midland (G-11394)		
Miss Print Rocks	G	517 639-8785
Quincy (G-13672)		
Moormann Printing Inc	G	269 423-2411
Decatur (G-3950)		
My Little Prints	G	248 613-8439
Franklin (G-5883)		
My Print Works MI	G	269 344-3226
Kalamazoo (G-9279)		
Nafa Printing LLC	G	734 338-2103
Livonia (G-10329)		
Naked Shirt Custom Prtg LLC	G	269 625-7235
Burr Oak (G-2213)		
Neptix	G	248 520-6181
Birmingham (G-1739)		
Niereschers Print	G	248 736-4501
Oxford (G-12905)		
Nikkis Printing & More LLC	G	313 532-0281
Detroit (G-4485)		
North American Color Inc	E	269 323-0552
Portage (G-13588)		
North American Graphics Inc	F	586 486-1110
Warren (G-17947)		
Ogemaw County Herald Inc	E	989 345-0044
West Branch (G-18333)		
On The Side Sign Dsign Grphics	G	810 266-7446
Byron (G-2255)		
Page Litho Inc	F	313 885-8555
Grosse Pointe (G-7532)		
Painless Printing	G	517 812-6852
Jackson (G-8982)		
Paper and Print Usa LLC	G	616 940-8311
Grand Rapids (G-7069)		
Parallax Printing LLC	G	248 397-5156
Ferndale (G-5576)		
Paw Print Creations LLC	G	810 577-0410
Mount Morris (G-11676)		
Paw Print Gardens	G	616 791-4758
Grand Rapids (G-7073)		
Performance Print and Mktg	G	517 896-9682
Williamston (G-18579)		
Personal Graphics	G	231 347-6347
Petoskey (G-13013)		
Pgi Holdings Inc	E	231 796-4831
Big Rapids (G-1683)		
Pickle Print & Marketing LLC	G	231 668-4148
Traverse City (G-16792)		
Piping Plover Prints	G	231 929-0261
Traverse City (G-16793)		
Pippa Custom Design Printing	G	734 552-1598
Woodhaven (G-18802)		
Pixel Rush Printing	G	248 231-4642
South Lyon (G-15455)		
Plastics In Paint	G	248 520-7177
Waterford (G-18154)		
Premier Printin	G	248 924-3213
Wixom (G-18734)		
Prestige Printing Inc	G	616 532-5133
Grand Rapids (G-7104)		
Prins Bethesda LLC	G	269 903-2237
Portage (G-13595)		
Print 4 U Promotional Prtg LLC	G	313 575-1080
Redford (G-13759)		
Print and Save Now	G	989 352-8171
Edmore (G-4996)		
Print Julep	G	614 937-5114
West Bloomfield (G-18306)		
Print Rapids LLC	G	616 202-6508
Hudsonville (G-8601)		
Print Room	G	231 489-8181
Petoskey (G-13017)		
Print Zone	G	313 278-0800
Dearborn (G-3886)		
Printed Memories	G	248 388-7788
Waterford (G-18157)		
Printer Ink Warehousecom LLC	G	269 649-5492
Vicksburg (G-17610)		
Printing Buying Service	G	586 907-2011
Saint Clair Shores (G-14879)		
Printing By Marc	G	248 355-0848
Southfield (G-15682)		
Printing King	G	517 367-7066
Lansing (G-9884)		
Printing Xpress AMP Promo	G	586 915-9043
Troy (G-17315)		
Pro ADS America	G	586 219-6040
Walled Lake (G-17673)		

Pronto Printing G 586 215-9670
Macomb *(G-10630)*

Prontoprinting LLC G 313 622-7565
Detroit *(G-4538)*

Provisions Print LLC G 248 214-1766
Auburn Hills *(G-1007)*

Punktual Printing Inc G 734 664-8045
Westland *(G-18410)*

Quirky 3d Printing G 810 247-6732
Corunna *(G-3716)*

R & R Harwood Inc G 616 669-6400
Jenison *(G-9069)*

Renegade Cstm Screen Prtg LLC G 313 475-8489
Lincoln Park *(G-10055)*

Renegade Screen Printing G 248 632-0207
Clawson *(G-3108)*

Rider Type & Design G 989 839-0015
Midland *(G-11408)*

Rush Print and Pack G 989 835-5161
Midland *(G-11410)*

Safran Printing Company Inc C 586 939-7600
Beverly Hills *(G-1668)*

Sales Mfg G 810 597-7707
Flint *(G-5759)*

Save On Printing G 586 202-4469
Sterling Heights *(G-16165)*

Select Graphics Corporation F 586 755-7700
Warren *(G-18009)*

Smm Printing Inc G 989 893-8788
Bay City *(G-1402)*

Spinnaker Forms Systems Corp G 616 956-7677
Grand Rapids *(G-7219)*

Splash of Vinyl G 616 723-0311
Grandville *(G-7418)*

Sports Ink Screen Prtg EMB LLC G 231 723-5696
Manistee *(G-10913)*

Stafford Media Inc E 616 754-9301
Greenville *(G-7505)*

Swift Printing Co F 616 459-4263
Grand Rapids *(G-7241)*

T J K Inc G 586 731-9639
Sterling Heights *(G-16199)*

Technology MGT & Budgt Dept G 517 322-1897
Lansing *(G-9899)*

Terry Butler Prints LLC G 734 255-8592
Ann Arbor *(G-682)*

TGI Direct Inc G 810 239-5553
Ann Arbor *(G-685)*

The Envelope Printery Inc D 734 398-7700
Van Buren Twp *(G-17557)*

Thought Prvoking Tees Prtg LLC G 313 673-6632
Detroit *(G-4632)*

Times Herald Company D 810 985-7171
Port Huron *(G-13532)*

Top Notch Printing LLC G 248 268-3257
Hazel Park *(G-7844)*

Tourist Printing G 231 733-5687
Muskegon *(G-11935)*

Transfigure Print Co G 810 404-4569
Grand Rapids *(G-7270)*

Traverse Cy Record- Eagle Inc G 231 946-2000
Traverse City *(G-16866)*

Tri Vector Printing G 734 748-7006
Livonia *(G-10443)*

Tweddle Group Inc C 586 307-3700
Clinton Township *(G-3380)*

Universal Print G 989 525-5055
Bay City *(G-1409)*

Valassis International Inc B 734 591-3000
Livonia *(G-10457)*

Verns Threedprinting G 810 564-5184
Burton *(G-2250)*

Vistaprint G 260 615-0027
Detroit *(G-4670)*

W B Mason Co Inc E 734 947-6370
Taylor *(G-16488)*

Wedo Custom Screen Printing G 616 965-7332
Grand Rapids *(G-7328)*

Wines Printing Co G 586 924-6229
Sterling Heights *(G-16231)*

Wynalda International LLC F 616 866-1561
Belmont *(G-1522)*

Yale Expositor G 810 387-2300
Yale *(G-18921)*

PRINTING: Offset

A B C Printing Inc G 248 887-0010
Highland *(G-7877)*

A Koppel Color Image Company G 616 534-3600
Grandville *(G-7360)*

Aalpha Tinadawn Inc G 517 351-1200
East Lansing *(G-4884)*

ABC Printing Corporation Inc G 248 887-0010
Highland *(G-7879)*

Acadia Group LLC E 734 944-1404
Saline *(G-14997)*

Accelerated Press Inc G 248 524-1850
Troy *(G-16902)*

Action Printech Inc F 734 207-6000
Plymouth *(G-13112)*

Admore Inc C 586 949-8200
Macomb *(G-10571)*

Advance BCI Inc D 616 669-1366
Grand Rapids *(G-6431)*

Advance Print & Graphics Inc E 734 663-6816
Ann Arbor *(G-354)*

Advanced Systems & Forms G 734 422-7180
Livonia *(G-10102)*

Afb Corporate Operations LLC E 248 669-1188
Plymouth *(G-13120)*

Aladdin Printing G 248 360-2842
Commerce Township *(G-3507)*

Allegra Marketing Print Mail G 586 335-2596
Grosse Pointe Park *(G-7544)*

Allegra Marketing Print Mail G 248 602-0545
Troy *(G-16926)*

Allegra Marketing Print Mail G 313 382-8033
Allen Park *(G-188)*

Allegra Marketing Print Mail G 517 879-2444
Jackson *(G-8809)*

Allegra Marketing Print Mail G 313 429-0916
Allen Park *(G-189)*

Allegra Marketing Print Mail G 269 213-8840
Battle Creek *(G-1183)*

Allegra Network LLC F 248 360-1290
West Bloomfield *(G-18262)*

Allegra Print & Imaging G 248 354-1313
Southfield *(G-15475)*

Allegra Print and Imaging G 616 784-6699
Grand Rapids *(G-6447)*

Allegra Print Imaging G 616 446-6269
Allendale *(G-212)*

Allegra-Marketing Design Print G 313 561-8000
Dearborn Heights *(G-3919)*

Allesk Enterprises Inc G 231 941-5770
Traverse City *(G-16600)*

Alliance Franchise Brands LLC F 248 596-8600
Plymouth *(G-13122)*

Allied Mailing and Prtg Inc E 810 750-8291
Fenton *(G-5448)*

Allied Printing Co Inc E 248 541-0551
Ferndale *(G-5523)*

Allied Printing Co Inc E 248 514-7394
Ferndale *(G-5524)*

American Graphics Inc G 586 774-8880
Saint Clair Shores *(G-14848)*

American Ink USA Prntg & Grphc G 586 790-2555
Clinton Township *(G-3165)*

American Printing Services Inc G 248 568-5543
Troy *(G-16934)*

American Speedy Printing Ctrs G 989 723-5196
Owosso *(G-12823)*

American Speedy Printing Ctrs G 313 928-5820
Taylor *(G-16376)*

Anchor Printing Company E 248 335-7440
Novi *(G-12362)*

Andex Industries Inc E 906 786-7588
Escanaba *(G-5056)*

Apb Inc G 248 528-2990
Troy *(G-16939)*

Arbor Press LLC D 248 549-0150
Royal Oak *(G-14510)*

Artcraft Printing Corporation G 734 455-8893
Plymouth *(G-13126)*

Artech Printing Inc G 248 545-0088
Madison Heights *(G-10673)*

Artigy Printing G 269 373-6591
Kalamazoo *(G-9122)*

Artistic Printing Inc G 248 356-1004
Southfield *(G-15491)*

ASAP Printing Inc F 517 882-3500
Lansing *(G-9807)*

ASAP Printing Inc G 517 882-3500
Okemos *(G-12657)*

Associated Print & Graphics G 734 676-8896
Grosse Ile *(G-7516)*

Associated Print Marketing G 248 268-2726
Madison Heights *(G-10674)*

August Communications Inc G 313 561-8000
Dearborn Heights *(G-3921)*

Avery Color Studios Inc G 906 346-3908
Gwinn *(G-7582)*

B & M Imaging Inc G 269 968-2403
Battle Creek *(G-1188)*

B-Quick Instant Printing G 616 243-6562
Grand Rapids *(G-6490)*

Batson Printing Inc D 269 926-6011
Benton Harbor *(G-1532)*

Battle Creek Flyers LLC G 269 579-2914
Battle Creek *(G-1192)*

Behrmann Printing Company Inc F 248 799-7771
Southfield *(G-15505)*

Berci Printing Services Inc G 248 350-0206
Southfield *(G-15506)*

Bi-Rite Office Products Inc G 586 751-1410
Warren *(G-17735)*

Bizcard Xpress G 248 288-4800
Rochester *(G-13893)*

Blue Water Printing Co Inc G 810 664-0643
Lapeer *(G-9914)*

Bradford Printing Inc G 517 887-0044
Lansing *(G-9815)*

Bradley Jacob Printing LLC G 248 953-9010
Lake Orion *(G-9589)*

Brd Printing Inc E 517 372-0268
Lansing *(G-9816)*

Breck Graphics Incorporated E 616 248-4110
Grand Rapids *(G-6523)*

Bretts Printing Service G 517 482-2256
Lansing *(G-9818)*

Bronco Printing Company G 248 544-1120
Hazel Park *(G-7821)*

Bruce Inc G 517 371-5205
Lansing *(G-9819)*

Business Cards Plus Inc F 269 327-7727
Portage *(G-13551)*

Business Press Inc G 248 652-8855
Rochester *(G-13895)*

C H M Graphics & Litho Inc G 586 777-4550
Saint Clair Shores *(G-14851)*

C J Graphics Inc G 906 774-8636
Kingsford *(G-9506)*

C L Mailing Printing G 248 471-3330
Farmington Hills *(G-5191)*

C W Enterprises Inc G 810 385-9100
Fort Gratiot *(G-5819)*

C&P Hoover LLC G 248 887-2400
Highland *(G-7886)*

Cadillac Printing Company F 231 775-2488
Cadillac *(G-2323)*

Canton Embroidery LLC G 734 216-3374
Ypsilanti *(G-18932)*

Capital Imaging Inc F 517 482-2292
Lansing *(G-9822)*

Cascade Prtg & Graphics Inc G 616 222-2937
Grand Rapids *(G-6556)*

Christman Screenprint Inc E 800 962-9330
Springfield *(G-15863)*

Clemco Printing Inc G 989 269-8364
Bad Axe *(G-1099)*

Color Connection G 248 351-0920
Southfield *(G-15527)*

Color Express Printing Inc G 734 213-4980
Ann Arbor *(G-433)*

Color House Graphics Inc E 616 241-1916
Grand Rapids *(G-6583)*

Color Source Graphics Inc G 248 458-2040
Troy *(G-17018)*

Colortech Graphics Inc D 586 779-7800
Roseville *(G-14386)*

Commercial Graphics Company G 517 278-2159
Coldwater *(G-3429)*

Commercial Graphics Inc G 586 726-8150
Sterling Heights *(G-15965)*

Complete HM Advg Mdia Prmtnal G 586 254-9555
Shelby Township *(G-15192)*

Compton Press Industries LLC G 248 473-8210
Farmington Hills *(G-5207)*

Conventional Graphics Inc G 231 943-4301
Interlochen *(G-8681)*

Copilot Printing G 248 797-0150
Berkley *(G-1625)*

Copyrite Printing Inc G 586 774-0006
Roseville *(G-14390)*

Copytwo Inc E 734 665-9200
Ann Arbor *(G-437)*

CPM Services Group Inc G 248 624-5100
Wixom *(G-18639)*

Craft Press Printing Inc G 269 683-9694
Niles *(G-12121)*

PRODUCT

Employee Codes: A=Over 500 employees, B=251-500
C=101-250, D=51-100, E=20-50, F=10-19, G=3-9
2022 Harris Michigan
Industrial Directory
1377

Creative Characters Inc .... G 231 544-6084
Central Lake ***(G-2692)***
Creative Print Crew LLC .... G 248 629-9404
Troy ***(G-17033)***
Creative Printing & Graphics .... G 810 235-8815
Flint ***(G-5677)***
Curtis Printing Inc .... G 810 230-6711
Flint ***(G-5679)***
Cushing-Malloy Inc .... E 734 663-8554
Ann Arbor ***(G-440)***
Custom Printers Inc .... D 616 454-9224
Grand Rapids ***(G-6623)***
Custom Printing of Michigan .... F 248 585-9222
Troy ***(G-17040)***
Custom Service Printers Inc .... F 231 726-3297
Muskegon ***(G-11797)***
D & D Printing Co .... E 616 454-7710
Grand Rapids ***(G-6628)***
D J Rotunda Associates Inc .... G 586 772-3350
West Bloomfield ***(G-18276)***
Data Reproductions Corporation .... D 248 371-3700
Auburn Hills ***(G-859)***
Daves Printing .... G 989 355-1204
Saginaw ***(G-14636)***
De Vru Printing Co .... G 616 452-5451
Grand Rapids ***(G-6636)***
Dearborn Lithograph Inc .... E 734 464-4242
Livonia ***(G-10176)***
Dearborn Offset Printing Inc .... G 313 561-1173
Dearborn ***(G-3824)***
Dekoff & Sons Inc .... G 269 344-5816
Kalamazoo ***(G-9165)***
Designotype Printers Inc .... G 906 482-2424
Laurium ***(G-9979)***
Detroit Business Centercom Inc .... G 313 255-4300
Detroit ***(G-4138)***
Detroit Litho Inc .... G 313 993-6186
Detroit ***(G-4151)***
DGa Printing Inc .... G 586 979-2244
Troy ***(G-17058)***
Digimax Business Corporation .... G 313 255-4300
Detroit ***(G-4176)***
Digital Printing & Graphics .... G 586 566-9499
Shelby Township ***(G-15206)***
Digital Printing Solutions LLC .... G 586 566-4910
Shelby Township ***(G-15207)***
Dobb Printing Inc .... E 231 722-1060
Muskegon ***(G-11799)***
Donalyn Enterprises Inc .... F 517 546-9798
Howell ***(G-8447)***
DPrinter Inc .... G 517 423-6554
Tecumseh ***(G-16499)***
E & R Bindery Service Inc .... G 734 464-7954
Livonia ***(G-10188)***
E & S Graphics Inc .... G 989 875-2828
Ithaca ***(G-8790)***
Earle Press Inc .... E 231 773-2111
Muskegon ***(G-11805)***
Econo Print Inc .... G 734 878-5806
Pinckney ***(G-13047)***
Egt Printing Solutions LLC .... C 248 583-2500
Madison Heights ***(G-10718)***
Empire Printing .... G 248 547-9223
Farmington Hills ***(G-5232)***
Epi Printers Inc .... E 800 562-9733
Battle Creek ***(G-1224)***
Epi Printers Inc .... D 269 968-2221
Battle Creek ***(G-1225)***
Epi Printers Inc .... D 269 968-2221
Battle Creek ***(G-1226)***
Epi Printers Inc .... D 269 964-6744
Battle Creek ***(G-1228)***
Excel Graphics .... G 248 442-9390
Livonia ***(G-10200)***
Exclusive Imagery Inc .... G 248 436-2999
Royal Oak ***(G-14536)***
Express Press Inc .... G 269 684-2080
Niles ***(G-12128)***
F P Horak Company .... C 989 892-6505
Bay City ***(G-1355)***
Fabulous Printing Inc .... G 734 422-5555
Livonia ***(G-10203)***
Falcon Printing Inc .... E 616 676-3737
Ada ***(G-17)***
Flashes Publishers Inc .... E 269 673-2141
Holland ***(G-8035)***
Forsons Inc .... G 517 787-4562
Jackson ***(G-8885)***
Franklin Press Inc .... F 616 538-5320
Grand Rapids ***(G-6719)***
Frye Printing Company Inc .... F 517 456-4124
Clinton ***(G-3139)***
Fudge Business Forms Inc .... G 248 299-3666
Rochester Hills ***(G-14017)***
Future Reproductions Inc .... F 248 350-2060
Southfield ***(G-15571)***
G G & D Inc .... G 248 623-1212
Clarkston ***(G-3037)***
Gage Company .... G 269 965-4279
Springfield ***(G-15865)***
Garants Office Sups & Prtg Inc .... G 989 356-3930
Alpena ***(G-296)***
Gary Cork Incorporated .... G 231 946-1061
Traverse City ***(G-16692)***
Generation Press Inc .... G 616 392-4405
Holland ***(G-8048)***
Globe Printing & Specialties .... F 906 485-1033
Ishpeming ***(G-8776)***
Goetz Craft Printers Inc .... F 734 973-7604
Brooklyn ***(G-2125)***
Gombar Corp .... G 989 793-9427
Saginaw ***(G-14655)***
Grahams Printing Company Inc .... G 313 925-1188
Detroit ***(G-4272)***
Grand Blanc Printing Inc .... E 810 694-1155
Grand Blanc ***(G-6245)***
Grand Rapids Letter Service .... G 616 459-4711
Grand Rapids ***(G-6762)***
Grandville Printing Co .... C 616 534-8647
Grandville ***(G-7382)***
Graphic Enterprises Inc .... D 248 616-4900
Madison Heights ***(G-10732)***
Graphics & Printing Co Inc .... G 269 381-1482
Kalamazoo ***(G-9201)***
Graphics 3 Inc .... E 517 278-2159
Coldwater ***(G-3435)***
Graphics East Inc .... E 586 598-1500
Roseville ***(G-14415)***
Graphics House Publishing .... E 231 739-4004
Muskegon ***(G-11827)***
Great Lakes Graphics Inc .... G 517 783-5500
Jackson ***(G-8894)***
Great Lakes Prtg Solutions Inc .... E 231 799-6000
Norton Shores ***(G-12296)***
Greenmans Speedy Printing .... G 248 478-2600
Farmington Hills ***(G-5256)***
Greko Print & Imaging Inc .... F 734 453-0341
Plymouth ***(G-13180)***
Grigg Graphic Services Inc .... E 248 356-5005
Southfield ***(G-15585)***
H E L P Printers Inc .... G 734 847-0554
Temperance ***(G-16533)***
Hamblin Company .... E 517 423-7491
Bloomfield Hills ***(G-1826)***
Hanon Printing Company .... G 248 541-9099
Pleasant Ridge ***(G-13105)***
Harold K Schultz .... G 517 279-9764
Coldwater ***(G-3438)***
Hatteras Inc .... E 734 525-5500
Plymouth ***(G-13183)***
Hawk Design Inc .... G 989 781-1152
Saginaw ***(G-14662)***
Hess Printing .... G 734 285-4377
Wyandotte ***(G-18821)***
Hi-Lites Graphic Inc .... E 231 924-0630
Fremont ***(G-6045)***
Holland Litho Service Inc .... D 616 392-4644
Zeeland ***(G-19039)***
Holland Printing Center Inc .... F 616 786-3101
Holland ***(G-8083)***
Hooper Printing LLC .... G 616 897-6719
Lowell ***(G-10504)***
Horn Corporation .... F 248 583-7789
Troy ***(G-17151)***
Houghton Lake Resorter Inc .... F 989 366-5341
Houghton Lake ***(G-8400)***
Ideal Printing .... G 616 453-5556
Grand Rapids ***(G-6830)***
Image Factory Inc .... G 989 732-2712
Gaylord ***(G-6135)***
Image Printing Inc .... G 248 585-4080
Royal Oak ***(G-14549)***
Images 2 Print .... G 616 383-1121
Sparta ***(G-15769)***
Imperial Press Inc .... G 734 728-5430
Wayne ***(G-18224)***
Irwin Enterprises Inc .... E 810 732-0770
Flint ***(G-5716)***
J R C Inc .... F 810 648-4000
Sandusky ***(G-15061)***
J-Ad Graphics Inc .... D 800 870-7085
Hastings ***(G-7800)***
Jack Batdorss .... E 231 796-4831
Big Rapids ***(G-1678)***
Jackpine Press Incorporated .... F 231 723-8344
Manistee ***(G-10903)***
Janutol Printing Co Inc .... G 313 526-6196
Detroit ***(G-4333)***
Jerrys Quality Quick Print .... G 248 354-1313
Southfield ***(G-15612)***
Jet Speed Printing Company .... G 989 224-6475
Saint Johns ***(G-14903)***
Jiffy Print .... G 269 692-3128
Otsego ***(G-12789)***
Jlr Printing Inc .... G 734 728-0250
Romulus ***(G-14290)***
JMS Printing Svc LLC .... G 734 414-6203
Warren ***(G-17887)***
Job Shop Ink Inc .... G 517 372-3900
Lansing ***(G-9768)***
Johnson-Clark Printers Inc .... F 231 947-6898
Traverse City ***(G-16730)***
Johnston Printing & Offset .... G 906 786-1493
Escanaba ***(G-5079)***
Jomark Inc .... E 248 478-2600
Farmington Hills ***(G-5275)***
Js Printing .... G 734 266-3350
Livonia ***(G-10261)***
K & S Printing Centers Inc .... G 734 482-1680
Ann Arbor ***(G-536)***
Kaufman Enterprises Inc .... G 269 324-0040
Portage ***(G-13573)***
Kay Screen Printing Inc .... B 248 377-4999
Lake Orion ***(G-9611)***
Kendall & Company Inc .... G 810 733-7330
Flint ***(G-5721)***
Kimprint Inc .... E 734 459-2960
Plymouth ***(G-13215)***
Kings Time Printing Press LLC .... G 734 426-8169
Ann Arbor ***(G-539)***
Kmak Inc .... G 517 784-8800
Jackson ***(G-8929)***
Knapp Printing Services Inc .... G 616 754-9159
Greenville ***(G-7497)***
Kolossos Printing Inc .... F 734 994-5400
Ann Arbor ***(G-540)***
Ktr Printing Inc .... F 989 386-9740
Clare ***(G-2984)***
Kwikie Inc .... G 231 946-9942
Traverse City ***(G-16735)***
L D J Inc .... F 906 524-6194
Lanse ***(G-9666)***
L&L Printing Inc .... G 586 263-0060
Clinton Township ***(G-3278)***
Lake Superior Press Inc .... F 906 228-7450
Marquette ***(G-11027)***
Lamour Printing Co .... G 734 241-6006
Monroe ***(G-11558)***
Laser Print Technologies Inc .... G 231 941-5273
Traverse City ***(G-16739)***
Lawson Printers Inc .... E 269 965-0525
Battle Creek ***(G-1267)***
Leader Printing and Design Inc .... F 313 565-0061
Dearborn Heights ***(G-3930)***
Lee Printing Company .... F 586 463-1564
Clinton Township ***(G-3279)***
Lesnau Printing Company .... E 586 795-9200
Sterling Heights ***(G-16071)***
Lighting Printing .... G 989 792-2793
Birch Run ***(G-1709)***
Lightning Litho Inc .... F 517 394-2995
Lansing ***(G-9864)***
Limelite Printing LLC .... G 313 839-7321
Detroit ***(G-4400)***
Lindy Press Inc .... G 231 937-6169
Howard City ***(G-8411)***
Litho Photo Enterprises LLC .... G 313 717-6615
Taylor ***(G-16436)***
Litho Printers Inc .... F 269 651-7309
Sturgis ***(G-16302)***
Litho Printing Service Inc .... G 586 772-6067
Eastpointe ***(G-4939)***
Litho-Graphics Printing Pdts .... G 586 775-1670
Roseville ***(G-14433)***
Litsenberger Print Shop .... G 906 482-3903
Houghton ***(G-8386)***
Lloyd Waters & Associates .... G 734 525-2777
Livonia ***(G-10291)***
Logan Brothers Printing Inc .... G 517 485-3771
Dewitt ***(G-4711)***

Logospot....G.... 616 785-7170
Belmont (G-1512)
Lopez Reproductions Inc....G.... 313 386-4526
Detroit (G-4404)
M & R Printing Inc....G.... 248 543-8080
Redford (G-13743)
M Beshara Inc....G.... 248 542-9220
Oak Park (G-12623)
Macdonald Publications Inc....F.... 989 875-4151
Ithaca (G-8793)
Macomb Business Forms Inc....F.... 586 790-8500
Clinton Township (G-3286)
Macomb Printing Inc....E.... 586 463-2301
Clinton Township (G-3288)
Madden Enterprises Inc....G.... 734 284-5330
Wyandotte (G-18830)
Maleports Sault Prtg Co Inc....E.... 906 632-3369
Sault Sainte Marie (G-15095)
Maple Press LLC....E.... 248 733-9669
Madison Heights (G-10775)
MBA Printing Inc....G.... 616 243-1600
Comstock Park (G-3623)
McKay Press Inc....C.... 989 631-2360
Midland (G-11387)
Mega Printing Inc....G.... 248 624-6065
Walled Lake (G-17672)
Megee Printing Inc....F.... 269 344-3226
Kalamazoo (G-9268)
Mel Printing Co Inc....E.... 313 928-5440
Taylor (G-16440)
Merritt Press Inc....F.... 517 394-0118
Lansing (G-9868)
Messenger Printing & Copy Svc....G.... 616 669-5620
Hudsonville (G-8593)
Messenger Printing Service Inc....F.... 313 381-0300
Taylor (G-16441)
Metro Printing Service Inc....G.... 248 545-4444
Troy (G-17253)
Metro Prints Inc....F.... 586 979-9690
Sterling Heights (G-16093)
Metropolitan Indus Lithography....G.... 269 323-9333
Portage (G-13585)
Mettes Printery Inc....G.... 734 261-6262
Livonia (G-10314)
Michigan State Medical Society....E.... 517 337-1351
East Lansing (G-4904)
Michigan Wholesale Prtg Inc....G.... 248 350-8230
Farmington Hills (G-5319)
Micrgraphics Printing Inc....F.... 231 739-6575
Norton Shores (G-12311)
Microforms Inc....E.... 586 939-7900
Beverly Hills (G-1667)
Millbrook Press Works....G.... 517 323-2111
Lansing (G-9777)
Mitchell Graphics Inc....E.... 231 347-4635
Petoskey (G-13007)
Mj Creative Printing LLC....G.... 248 891-1117
Livonia (G-10319)
Mj Print & Imaging....G.... 734 216-6273
Grass Lake (G-7441)
MKP Enterprises Inc....G.... 248 809-2525
Southfield (G-15660)
Model Printing Service Inc....F.... 989 356-0834
Alpena (G-304)
Monarch Print and Mail LLC....G.... 734 620-8378
Westland (G-18398)
Moonlight Graphics Inc....G.... 616 243-3166
Grand Rapids (G-7027)
MPS/Ih LLC....E.... 517 323-9001
Lansing (G-9720)
Msw Print and Imaging....F.... 734 544-1626
Ypsilanti (G-18969)
Muhleck Enterprises Inc....E.... 517 333-0713
Okemos (G-12679)
Munro Printing....G.... 586 773-9579
Eastpointe (G-4942)
National Printing Services....G.... 616 813-0758
Wyoming (G-18896)
National Wholesale Prtg Corp....G.... 734 416-8400
Plymouth (G-13252)
Neetz Printing Inc....G.... 989 684-4620
Bay City (G-1382)
Newberry News Inc....G.... 906 293-8401
Newberry (G-12096)
Nje Enterprises LLC....G.... 313 963-3600
Detroit (G-4486)
Northamerican Reproduction....G.... 734 421-6800
Livonia (G-10336)
Ntvb Media Inc....E.... 248 583-4190
Troy (G-17282)

Office Connection Inc....E.... 248 871-2003
Farmington Hills (G-5339)
Office Express Inc....E.... 248 307-1850
Troy (G-17288)
P J Printing....G.... 269 673-3372
Allegan (G-172)
Palmer Envelope Co....F.... 269 965-1336
Battle Creek (G-1280)
Pariseaus Printing Inc....G.... 810 653-8420
Davison (G-3792)
PDQ Ink Inc....E.... 810 229-2989
Brighton (G-2048)
Peg-Master Business Forms Inc....G.... 586 566-8694
Shelby Township (G-15298)
Perrigo Printing Inc....G.... 616 454-6761
Grand Rapids (G-7082)
Phase III Graphics Inc....G.... 616 949-9290
Grand Rapids (G-7084)
Phiber Printing LLC....G.... 248 471-9435
Livonia (G-10364)
Phoenix Press Incorporated....E.... 248 435-8040
Troy (G-17300)
Photo Offset Inc....G.... 906 786-5800
Escanaba (G-5089)
Pioneer Press Printing....G.... 231 864-2404
Bear Lake (G-1421)
Pleasant Graphics Inc....F.... 989 773-7777
Mount Pleasant (G-11733)
Pointe Printing Inc....G.... 313 821-0030
Grosse Pointe Park (G-7558)
Popcorn Press Inc....F.... 248 588-4444
Madison Heights (G-10805)
Postal Savings Direct Mktg....F.... 810 238-8866
Flint (G-5745)
Powerstroke Printing....G.... 734 740-7616
Wayne (G-18233)
Precision Print Label....G.... 248 853-9007
Rochester Hills (G-14089)
Preferred Printing Inc....F.... 269 782-5488
Dowagiac (G-4793)
Pride Printing Inc....G.... 906 228-8182
Marquette (G-11042)
Print All....G.... 586 430-4383
Richmond (G-13844)
Print Haus....G.... 616 786-4030
Holland (G-8171)
Print House Inc....F.... 248 473-1414
Farmington Hills (G-5353)
Print Masters Inc....F.... 248 548-7100
Madison Heights (G-10810)
Print Metro Inc....G.... 616 887-1723
Sparta (G-15775)
Print Plus Inc....G.... 586 888-8000
Saint Clair Shores (G-14878)
Print Shop....G.... 313 499-8444
Harper Woods (G-7670)
Print Shop....G.... 231 347-2000
Petoskey (G-13018)
Print Xpress....G.... 313 886-6850
Grosse Pointe Woods (G-7573)
Print-Tech Inc....E.... 734 996-2345
Ann Arbor (G-624)
Printcomm Inc....D.... 810 239-5763
Flint (G-5749)
Printed Impressions Inc....G.... 248 473-5333
Farmington Hills (G-5354)
Printery Inc....E.... 616 396-4655
Holland (G-8172)
Printex Printing & Graphics....G.... 269 629-0122
Richland (G-13827)
Printing Centre Inc....F.... 517 694-2400
Holt (G-8326)
Printing Industries of Mich....G.... 248 946-5895
Novi (G-12516)
Printing Plus Inc....G.... 734 482-1680
Ypsilanti (G-18971)
Printing Productions Ink....G.... 616 871-9292
Grand Rapids (G-7109)
Printing Services....G.... 269 321-9826
Portage (G-13596)
Printing Services Inc....F.... 734 944-1404
Saline (G-15032)
Printing Systems Inc....G.... 734 946-5111
Taylor (G-16461)
Printlink Shrt Run Bus Frms In....F.... 269 965-1336
Battle Creek (G-1283)
Printmill Inc....G.... 269 382-0428
Kalamazoo (G-9308)
Prism Printing....G.... 586 786-1250
Macomb (G-10629)

Procolrcopy A Div Prclor Group....G.... 248 458-2040
Rochester Hills (G-14091)
Proforma Pltnum Prtg Prmotions....G.... 248 341-3814
Clawson (G-3104)
Progress Printers Inc....G.... 231 947-5311
Traverse City (G-16805)
Progressive Prtg & Graphics....G.... 269 965-8909
Battle Creek (G-1284)
Pummill Print Services Lc....G.... 616 785-7960
Comstock Park (G-3639)
Qg LLC....D.... 989 496-3333
Midland (G-11404)
Qrp Inc....G.... 989 496-2955
Midland (G-11405)
Qrp Inc....E.... 989 496-2955
Midland (G-11406)
Quad/Graphics Inc....G.... 248 637-9950
Troy (G-17324)
Quality Press....G.... 248 541-0753
Clawson (G-3106)
Quality Printing & Graphics....G.... 616 949-3400
Grand Rapids (G-7130)
Quantum Graphics Inc....E.... 586 566-5656
Shelby Township (G-15312)
Quick Printing Company Inc....G.... 616 241-0506
Grand Rapids (G-7131)
Quickprint of Adrian Inc....F.... 517 263-2290
Adrian (G-90)
R & L Color Graphics Inc....G.... 313 345-3838
Detroit (G-4549)
R JS Printing Inc....G.... 773 936-7825
Kalamazoo (G-9314)
R N E Business Enterprises....G.... 313 963-3600
Detroit (G-4551)
R W Patterson Printing Co....D.... 269 925-2177
Benton Harbor (G-1579)
Raenell Press LLC....G.... 616 534-8890
Grand Rapids (G-7137)
Rapid Graphics Inc....G.... 269 925-7087
Benton Harbor (G-1580)
Rar Group Inc....G.... 248 353-2266
Redford (G-13761)
Ray Printing Company Inc....F.... 517 787-4130
Jackson (G-8994)
Raze It Printing Inc....G.... 248 366-8691
West Bloomfield (G-18309)
Raze-It Printing....G.... 248 543-3813
Hazel Park (G-7839)
Reimold Printing Corporation....G.... 989 799-0784
Saginaw (G-14736)
Richard Larabee....G.... 248 827-7755
Southfield (G-15689)
Richards Printing....G.... 906 786-3540
Escanaba (G-5095)
Riegle Press Inc....E.... 810 653-9631
Davison (G-3795)
Rite Way Printing....G.... 734 721-2746
Romulus (G-14325)
River Run Press Inc....E.... 269 349-7603
Kalamazoo (G-9320)
Riverside Prtg of Grnd Rapids....G.... 616 458-8011
Grand Rapids (G-7160)
Rocket Copy Print Ship Inc....G.... 248 336-3636
Royal Oak (G-14577)
Rogers Printing Inc....C.... 231 853-2244
Ravenna (G-13694)
Romeo Printing Company Inc....G.... 586 752-9003
Romeo (G-14234)
Rtr Alpha Inc....F.... 248 377-4060
Auburn Hills (G-1023)
Rumler Brothers Inc....G.... 517 437-2990
Hillsdale (G-7947)
Rusas Printing Co Inc....G.... 313 952-2977
Redford (G-13769)
S & N Graphic Solutions LLC....G.... 734 495-3314
Canton (G-2519)
SBR Printing USA Inc....F.... 810 388-9441
Port Huron (G-13525)
Schepeler Corporation....E.... 517 592-6811
Brooklyn (G-2132)
Seifert City-Wide Printing Co....G.... 248 477-9525
Farmington (G-5148)
Shawnieboy Enterprises Inc....F.... 616 871-9292
Grand Rapids (G-7191)
Shayleslie Corporation....G.... 517 694-4115
Holt (G-8332)
Sheridan Books Inc....B.... 734 475-9145
Chelsea (G-2826)
Skip Printing and Dup Co....G.... 586 779-2640
Roseville (G-14477)

Employee Codes: A=Over 500 employees, B=251-500
C=101-250, D=51-100, E=20-50, F=10-19, G=3-9

2022 Harris Michigan
Industrial Directory

1379

PRINTING: Offset

Slades Printing Company Inc ....G.... 248 334-6257
  Waterford (G-18165)
Sourceone Imaging LLC ....G.... 616 452-2001
  Grand Rapids (G-7204)
Spartan Graphics Inc ....D.... 616 887-1073
  Sparta (G-15780)
Spartan Printing Inc ....E.... 517 372-6910
  Lansing (G-9738)
Specialty Business Forms Inc ....G.... 269 345-0828
  Kalamazoo (G-9340)
Specifications Service Company ....G.... 248 353-0244
  Bloomfield (G-1785)
Spectrum Printers Inc ....E.... 517 423-5735
  Tecumseh (G-16517)
Stamp-Rite Incorporated ....E.... 517 487-5071
  Lansing (G-9741)
Standard Printing ....G.... 734 483-0339
  Ypsilanti (G-18978)
Standard Printing of Warren ....G.... 586 771-3770
  Warren (G-18026)
Steketee-Van Huis Inc ....B.... 616 392-2326
  Holland (G-8202)
Stewart Printing Company Inc ....G.... 734 283-8440
  Wyandotte (G-18840)
Straits Area Printing Corp ....G.... 231 627-5647
  Cheboygan (G-2800)
Stylecraft Printing Co ....D.... 734 455-5500
  Canton (G-2528)
Sunrise Print Cmmnications Inc ....G.... 989 345-4475
  West Branch (G-18342)
Superior Imaging Services Inc ....G.... 269 382-0428
  Kalamazoo (G-9348)
Superior Typesetting Service ....G.... 269 382-0428
  Kalamazoo (G-9349)
Systems Duplicating Co Inc ....F.... 248 585-7590
  Troy (G-17382)
T-Print USA ....G.... 269 751-4603
  Hamilton (G-7607)
Temperance Printing ....G.... 419 290-6846
  Lambertville (G-9654)
Thomson-Shore Inc ....C.... 734 426-3939
  Dexter (G-4758)
Thorpe Printing Services Inc ....G.... 810 364-6222
  Marysville (G-11107)
Tigner Printing Inc ....G.... 989 465-6916
  Coleman (G-3473)
Triangle Printing Inc ....G.... 586 293-7530
  Roseville (G-14486)
Tru Color Printing ....G.... 248 737-2041
  West Bloomfield (G-18318)
Tsunami Inc ....G.... 989 497-5200
  Saginaw (G-14780)
Turner Business Forms Inc ....E.... 989 752-5540
  Saginaw (G-14782)
Tuteur Inc ....G.... 269 983-1246
  Saint Joseph (G-14966)
Tweddle Litho Inc ....G.... 586 795-0515
  Sterling Heights (G-16213)
Ultra-Tech Printing Co ....F.... 616 249-0500
  Wyoming (G-18915)
Universal Printing Company Inc ....E.... 989 671-9409
  Bay City (G-1410)
US Printers ....G.... 906 639-3100
  Daggett (G-3754)
Village Printing & Supply Inc ....G.... 810 664-2270
  Lapeer (G-9966)
Village Shop Inc ....E.... 231 946-3712
  Traverse City (G-16875)
Voila Print Inc ....G.... 866 942-1677
  Livonia (G-10461)
Vtec Graphics Inc ....G.... 734 953-9729
  Livonia (G-10463)
Washington Street Printers LLC ....G.... 734 240-5541
  Monroe (G-11590)
Web Printing & Mktg Concepts ....G.... 269 983-4646
  Saint Joseph (G-14974)
Weighman Enterprises Inc ....G.... 989 755-2116
  Saginaw (G-14792)
West Colony Graphic Inc ....G.... 269 375-6625
  Kalamazoo (G-9366)
West Michigan Tag & Label Inc ....E.... 616 235-0120
  Grand Rapids (G-7235)
Whipple Printing Inc ....G.... 313 382-8033
  Allen Park (G-210)
Wide Eyed 3d Printing ....G.... 517 376-6512
  Howell (G-8541)
William C Fox Enterprises Inc ....F.... 231 775-2732
  Cadillac (G-2364)
Willoughby Press ....G.... 989 723-3460
  Owosso (G-12868)
Wolverine Printing Company LLC ....E.... 616 451-2075
  Grand Rapids (G-7347)
Workman Printing Inc ....G.... 231 744-5500
  Muskegon (G-11951)
Worten Copy Center Inc ....G.... 231 845-7030
  Ludington (G-10558)
Write Idea ....G.... 313 967-5881
  Detroit (G-4693)
Wynalda Litho Inc ....C.... 616 866-1561
  Belmont (G-1523)
X-Treme Printing Inc ....G.... 810 232-3232
  Flint (G-5798)
Yti Office Express LLC ....G.... 866 996-8952
  Troy (G-17458)
Zak Brothers Printing LLC ....G.... 313 831-3216
  Detroit (G-4700)
Zeeland Print Shop Co ....G.... 616 772-6636
  Zeeland (G-19098)

PRINTING: Photo-Offset

Print n go ....G.... 989 362-6041
  East Tawas (G-4921)

PRINTING: Photolithographic

Lighthouse Direct Buy LLC ....G.... 313 340-1850
  Detroit (G-4398)

PRINTING: Rotary Photogravure

Seeley Inc ....E.... 517 655-5631
  Williamston (G-18582)

PRINTING: Screen, Broadwoven Fabrics, Cotton

Advanced Printwear Inc ....G.... 248 585-4412
  Madison Heights (G-10662)
Advertising Accents Inc ....G.... 313 937-3890
  Redford (G-13711)
Allgraphics Corp ....G.... 248 994-7373
  Farmington Hills (G-5167)
Baumans Running Center Inc ....G.... 810 238-5981
  Flint (G-5652)
Charlevoix Screen Masters Inc ....G.... 231 547-5111
  Charlevoix (G-2713)
Great Put On Inc ....G.... 810 733-8021
  Flint (G-5709)
Hilton Screeners Inc ....G.... 810 653-0711
  Davison (G-3787)
Perrin Screen Printing Inc ....F.... 616 785-9900
  Comstock Park (G-3635)
Pro Shop The/P S Graphics ....G.... 517 448-8490
  Hudson (G-8559)
Prong Horn ....G.... 616 456-1903
  Grand Rapids (G-7120)
Sign of The Loon Gifts Inc ....G.... 231 436-5155
  Mackinaw City (G-10569)
Slick Shirts Screen Printing ....F.... 517 371-3600
  Lansing (G-9895)
Trophy Center West Michigan ....G.... 231 893-1686
  Whitehall (G-18510)

PRINTING: Screen, Fabric

A Game Apparel ....G.... 810 564-2600
  Mount Morris (G-11665)
American Silk Screen & EMB ....F.... 248 474-1000
  Farmington Hills (G-5169)
Applied Graphics & Fabricating ....F.... 989 662-3334
  Auburn (G-764)
Ascott Corporation ....G.... 734 663-2023
  Ann Arbor (G-381)
Athletic Uniform Lettering ....G.... 313 533-9071
  Redford (G-13717)
Bay Supply & Marketing Inc ....G.... 231 943-3249
  Traverse City (G-16616)
C & C Enterprises Inc ....G.... 989 772-5095
  Mount Pleasant (G-11689)
Chromatic Graphics Inc ....G.... 616 393-0034
  Holland (G-7996)
Crawford Associates Inc ....G.... 248 549-9494
  Royal Oak (G-14527)
Custom Ptint Ink LLC ....G.... 586 799-2465
  Eastpointe (G-4935)
Doorstep Printing LLC ....G.... 248 470-9567
  Detroit (G-4186)
Embroidery House Inc ....G.... 616 669-6400
  Jenison (G-9054)
Ethnic Artwork Inc ....F.... 586 726-1400
  Sterling Heights (G-16006)
Exclusive Imagery Inc ....G.... 248 436-2999
  Royal Oak (G-14536)
Field Crafts Inc ....F.... 231 325-1122
  Honor (G-8359)
Flaunt It Sportswear ....G.... 616 696-9084
  Cedar Springs (G-2651)
Image Projections Inc ....F.... 810 629-0700
  Fenton (G-5486)
Imprint House LLC ....G.... 810 985-8203
  Port Huron (G-13487)
Jam Enterprises ....G.... 313 417-9200
  Detroit (G-4332)
Janet and Company Inc ....G.... 248 887-2050
  Highland (G-7893)
Jbl Enterprises ....G.... 616 530-8647
  Grand Rapids (G-6863)
JS Original Silkscreens LLC ....G.... 586 779-5456
  Eastpointe (G-4938)
Mvp Sports Store ....G.... 517 764-5165
  Jackson (G-8973)
Perrin Screen Printing Inc ....F.... 616 785-9900
  Comstock Park (G-3635)
R H & Company Inc ....F.... 269 345-7814
  Kalamazoo (G-9313)
Rsls Corp ....G.... 248 726-0675
  Shelby Township (G-15319)
Saginaw Knitting Mills Inc ....F.... 989 695-2481
  Freeland (G-6029)
Silk Screenstuff ....G.... 517 543-7716
  Charlotte (G-2770)
Sporting Image Inc ....F.... 269 657-5646
  Paw Paw (G-12956)
Sports Stop ....G.... 517 676-2199
  Mason (G-11158)
Sunset Sportswear Inc ....F.... 248 437-7611
  Wixom (G-18761)
T - Shirt Printing Plus Inc ....E.... 269 383-3666
  Kalamazoo (G-9351)

PRINTING: Screen, Manmade Fiber & Silk, Broadwoven Fabric

Armada Printwear Inc ....G.... 586 784-5553
  Armada (G-730)

PRINTING: Thermography

American Thermographers ....F.... 248 398-3810
  Madison Heights (G-10668)
Corporate Electronic Sty Inc ....D.... 248 583-7070
  Troy (G-17030)

PRIVATE INVESTIGATOR SVCS

Executive Operations LLC ....E.... 313 312-0653
  Brighton (G-1986)

PRODUCT ENDORSEMENT SVCS

High Impact Solutions Inc ....G.... 248 473-9804
  Farmington Hills (G-5260)

PROFESSIONAL EQPT & SPLYS, WHOLESALE: Analytical Instruments

Jade Scientific Inc ....F.... 734 207-3775
  Westland (G-18387)

PROFESSIONAL EQPT & SPLYS, WHOLESALE: Optical Goods

Fairway Optical Inc ....G.... 231 744-6168
  Muskegon (G-11815)
Hi-Tech Optical Inc ....E.... 989 799-9390
  Saginaw (G-14663)

PROFESSIONAL EQPT & SPLYS, WHOLESALE: Scientific & Engineerg

Envision Engineering LLC ....G.... 616 897-0599
  Lowell (G-10500)
Inora Technologies Inc ....G.... 734 302-7488
  Ann Arbor (G-529)
K-Space Associates Inc ....E.... 734 426-7977
  Dexter (G-4744)

PROFESSIONAL INSTRUMENT REPAIR SVCS

Dixon & Ryan Corporation ....F.... 248 549-4000
  Royal Oak (G-14531)

PRODUCT SECTION

PUBLISHERS: Magazines, No Printing

Envisiontec US LLC .... D 313 436-4300
  Dearborn *(G-3837)*
Limbright Consulting Inc .... E 810 227-5510
  Wixom *(G-18699)*
Midwest Vibro Inc .... G 616 532-7670
  Grandville *(G-7401)*
Mycrona Inc .... F 734 453-9348
  Plymouth *(G-13251)*
Sun-Tec Corp .... G 248 669-3100
  Novi *(G-12550)*

PROFILE SHAPES: Unsupported Plastics

Alloy Exchange Inc .... F 616 863-0640
  Rockford *(G-14154)*
Gazelle Prototype LLC .... G 616 844-1820
  Spring Lake *(G-15816)*
Idemitsu Chemicals USA Corp .... G 248 355-0666
  Southfield *(G-15599)*
Plastic Plaque Inc .... F 810 982-9591
  Port Huron *(G-13518)*
Porex Technologies Corp .... E 989 865-8200
  Saint Charles *(G-14807)*
Spiratex Company .... D 734 289-4800
  Monroe *(G-11576)*
Tg Fluid Systems USA Corp .... B 810 220-6161
  Brighton *(G-2078)*

PROMOTERS OF SHOWS & EXHIBITIONS

Bob Allison Enterprises .... G 248 540-8467
  Bloomfield Hills *(G-1804)*
Graphicolor Systems Inc .... G 248 347-0271
  Livonia *(G-10229)*

PROMOTION SVCS

Valassis International Inc .... B 734 591-3000
  Livonia *(G-10457)*

PROPELLERS: Ship, Cast Brass

Michigan Wheel Operations LLC .... D 616 452-6941
  Grand Rapids *(G-6997)*

PUBLIC FINANCE, TAX & MONETARY POLICY OFFICES, GOVT: State

Technology MGT & Budgt Dept .... G 517 322-1897
  Lansing *(G-9899)*

PUBLIC FINANCE, TAXATION & MONETARY POLICY OFFICES

Kent County .... F 616 632-7580
  Grand Rapids *(G-6887)*

PUBLIC LIBRARY

Elmont District Library .... G 810 798-3100
  Almont *(G-259)*

PUBLIC RELATIONS & PUBLICITY SVCS

All Seasons Agency Inc .... G 586 752-6381
  Bruce Twp *(G-2162)*
Pharmacia & Upjohn Company LLC .... D 908 901-8000
  Kalamazoo *(G-9294)*

PUBLISHERS: Book

American Soc AG Blgcal Engners .... E 269 429-0300
  Saint Joseph *(G-14922)*
Banggameus .... G 734 904-1916
  Ann Arbor *(G-395)*
Central Michigan University .... G 989 774-3216
  Mount Pleasant *(G-11691)*
Childrens Bible Hour Inc .... F 616 647-4500
  Grand Rapids *(G-6568)*
Complete Services LLC .... G 248 470-8247
  Livonia *(G-10161)*
Conant Gardeners .... G 313 863-2624
  Detroit *(G-4101)*
Concord Editorial & Design LLC .... G 616 868-0148
  Alto *(G-331)*
Dac Inc .... G 313 388-4342
  Detroit *(G-4119)*
Duscha Management LLC .... F 352 247-2113
  Luna Pier *(G-10560)*
E D C O Publishing Inc .... G 248 690-9184
  Clarkston *(G-3031)*
Elmont District Library .... G 810 798-3100
  Almont *(G-259)*

Entertainment Publications Inc .... D 248 404-1000
  Troy *(G-17093)*
Foreword Magazine Inc .... F 231 933-3699
  Traverse City *(G-16685)*
Harvest Time Partners Inc .... G 269 254-8999
  Portage *(G-13564)*
Hummus & Co .... G 313 769-5557
  Allen Park *(G-196)*
In-Depth Editions LLC .... G 616 566-6009
  Holland *(G-8095)*
Jenkins Group Inc .... G 231 933-4954
  Traverse City *(G-16728)*
Literati LLC .... F 909 921-5242
  Ann Arbor *(G-551)*
Living Word International Inc .... E 989 832-7547
  Midland *(G-11384)*
McGraw Hill Co .... G 616 802-3000
  Grand Rapids *(G-6973)*
Mendenhall Associates Inc .... G 734 741-4710
  Ann Arbor *(G-569)*
Michigan State Univ Press .... E 517 355-9543
  East Lansing *(G-4905)*
Pagekicker Corporation .... G 734 646-6277
  Ann Arbor *(G-605)*
Publishing Xpress .... G 248 582-1834
  Madison Heights *(G-10811)*
Roger D Rapoport .... G 231 755-6665
  Muskegon *(G-11910)*
Sprouting Sunflowers LLC .... G 248 982-2406
  Lathrup Village *(G-9977)*
Team Breadwinner LLC .... G 313 460-0152
  Detroit *(G-4627)*
Tri-C Publications Inc .... G 616 581-7967
  Grand Rapids *(G-7275)*
Truth & Tidings .... G 517 782-9798
  Jackson *(G-9027)*
XMCO Inc .... D 586 558-8510
  Warren *(G-18075)*

PUBLISHERS: Book Clubs, No Printing

Thunder Bay Press Inc .... E 517 694-3205
  Holt *(G-8335)*

PUBLISHERS: Books, No Printing

A B Publishing Inc .... G 989 875-4985
  Ithaca *(G-8784)*
Baker Book House Company .... C 616 676-9185
  Ada *(G-10)*
Blackgirlperception LLC .... G 313 398-4275
  Detroit *(G-4058)*
Boskage Commerce Publications .... G 269 673-7242
  Portage *(G-13547)*
Chaosium Inc .... G 734 972-9551
  Ann Arbor *(G-421)*
Dalton Armond Publishers Inc .... G 517 351-8520
  Okemos *(G-12662)*
Developmental Services Inc .... G 313 653-1185
  Detroit *(G-4173)*
Harper Arrington Pubg LLC .... G 313 282-6751
  Detroit *(G-4295)*
HSP Epi Acquisition LLC .... C 248 404-1520
  Troy *(G-17156)*
Kregel Inc .... E 616 531-7707
  Grandville *(G-7396)*
Maria Dismondy Inc .... G 248 302-1800
  Novi *(G-12471)*
Mehring Books Inc .... G 248 967-2924
  Oak Park *(G-12627)*
Mott Media LLC .... G 810 714-4280
  Fenton *(G-5492)*
Pierian Press Inc .... G 734 434-4074
  Ypsilanti *(G-18970)*
Pink Diamond LLC .... G 586 298-7863
  Harrison Township *(G-7715)*
Prakken Publications Inc .... F 734 975-2800
  Ann Arbor *(G-618)*
Quirkroberts Publishing Ltd .... G 248 879-2598
  Troy *(G-17326)*
Robbie Dean Press LLC .... G 734 973-9511
  Ann Arbor *(G-642)*
Rockman & Sons Publishing LLC .... F 810 750-6011
  Fenton *(G-5499)*
Short Books Inc .... G 231 796-2167
  Grand Rapids *(G-7194)*
Stoney Creek Collection Inc .... F 616 363-4858
  Grand Rapids *(G-7227)*
Waterloo Group Inc .... G 248 840-6447
  Troy *(G-17445)*
William B Eerdmans Pubg Co .... E 616 459-4591
  Grand Rapids *(G-7340)*

PUBLISHERS: Catalogs

Ideation Inc .... E 734 761-4360
  Ann Arbor *(G-522)*

PUBLISHERS: Comic Books, No Printing

Cs Vendetta Pub LLC .... G 616 422-7555
  Grand Rapids *(G-6616)*
Publishing Xpress .... G 248 582-1834
  Madison Heights *(G-10811)*

PUBLISHERS: Directories, NEC

Fourth Seacoast Publishing Co .... G 586 779-5570
  Saint Clair Shores *(G-14861)*

PUBLISHERS: Directories, Telephone

Adtek Graphics Inc .... F 517 663-2460
  Eaton Rapids *(G-4950)*

PUBLISHERS: Guides

Advertiser Publishing Co Inc .... G 616 642-9411
  Saranac *(G-15076)*
George Moses Co .... G 810 227-1575
  Brighton *(G-2000)*
Shoreline Creations Ltd .... E 616 393-2077
  Holland *(G-8192)*
Upper Michigan Newspapers LLC .... E 989 732-5125
  Gaylord *(G-6165)*

PUBLISHERS: Magazines, No Printing

A & F Enterprises Inc .... F 248 714-6529
  Milford *(G-11453)*
African Amercn Parent Pubg Inc .... G 313 312-1611
  Detroit *(G-3989)*
Agenda 2020 Inc .... F 616 581-6271
  Grand Rapids *(G-6438)*
All Dealer Inventory LLC .... F 231 342-9823
  Lake Ann *(G-9541)*
All Kids Cnsdred Pubg Group In .... E 248 398-3400
  Ferndale *(G-5521)*
All Seasons Agency Inc .... G 586 752-6381
  Bruce Twp *(G-2162)*
Ann Arbor Observer Company .... E 734 769-3175
  Ann Arbor *(G-368)*
Auto Connection .... G 586 752-6371
  Bruce Twp *(G-2164)*
Business News Publishing .... F 248 362-3700
  Troy *(G-16988)*
Caribbean Adventure LLC .... F 269 441-5675
  Battle Creek *(G-1205)*
Castine Communications Inc .... G 248 477-1600
  Farmington *(G-5134)*
Chaldean News LLC .... G 248 996-8360
  Bingham Farms *(G-1693)*
Consider Magazine .... G 734 769-0500
  Ann Arbor *(G-435)*
Crain Communications Inc .... B 313 446-6000
  Detroit *(G-4106)*
Dbusiness .... F 313 929-0090
  Troy *(G-17049)*
Detroit Savings LLC .... G 313 971-5696
  Detroit *(G-4165)*
Double Gun Journal .... G 231 536-7439
  East Jordan *(G-4862)*
Elsie Publishing Institute .... F 517 371-5257
  Lansing *(G-9835)*
Farago & Associates LLC .... F 248 546-7070
  Farmington Hills *(G-5240)*
Foreword Magazine Inc .... F 231 933-3699
  Traverse City *(G-16685)*
Gemini Corporation .... E 616 459-4545
  Grand Rapids *(G-6737)*
Gongwer News Service Inc .... F 517 482-3500
  Lansing *(G-9843)*
Graphics Hse Spt Prmotions Inc .... E 231 739-4004
  Muskegon *(G-11828)*
Greater Lansing Bus Monthly .... G 517 203-0123
  Lansing *(G-9844)*
Harp Column LLC .... G 215 564-3232
  Zeeland *(G-19033)*
Hour Media LLC .... E 248 691-1800
  Troy *(G-17152)*
Hour Media Group LLC .... G 248 691-1800
  Troy *(G-17153)*
Informa Business Media Inc .... E 248 357-0800
  Southfield *(G-15605)*
International Smart Tan Netwrk .... E 517 841-4920
  Jackson *(G-8910)*

Employee Codes: A=Over 500 employees, B=251-500
C=101-250, D=51-100, E=20-50, F=10-19, G=3-9

Michigan Oil and Gas Assn....................G....... 517 487-0480
Lansing *(G-9870)*
Opensystems Publishing LLC...............F....... 586 415-6500
Saint Clair Shores *(G-14876)*
Prakken Publications Inc.......................F....... 734 975-2800
Ann Arbor *(G-618)*
Pride Source Corporation......................F....... 734 293-7200
Farmington Hills *(G-5352)*
Prism Publications Inc..........................E....... 231 941-8174
Traverse City *(G-16802)*
Renaissance Media LLC.........................F....... 248 354-6060
Farmington Hills *(G-5367)*
Revue Holding Company........................G....... 616 608-6170
Grand Rapids *(G-7151)*
Rider Report Magazine...........................G....... 248 854-8460
Auburn Hills *(G-1019)*
Roe LLC..G....... 231 755-5043
Muskegon *(G-11909)*
Saddle Up Magazine..............................G....... 810 714-9000
Fenton *(G-5501)*
Shoreline Creations Ltd........................E....... 616 393-2077
Holland *(G-8192)*
Toastmasters International...................G....... 810 385-5477
Burtchville *(G-2223)*
Toastmasters International...................G....... 517 651-6507
Laingsburg *(G-9538)*
Towing & Equipment Magazine.............G....... 248 601-1385
Rochester Hills *(G-14130)*
Ukc Liquidating Inc...............................G....... 269 343-9020
Portage *(G-13628)*
Unique U Magazine LLC.........................G....... 586 696-1839
Madison Heights *(G-10852)*
Varsity Monthly Thumb..........................G....... 810 404-5297
Caro *(G-2585)*
Verdoni Productions Inc........................G....... 989 790-0845
Saginaw *(G-14790)*
Vicrodesigns Global LLC.......................G....... 616 307-3701
Grand Rapids *(G-7316)*
W W Thayne Advertising Cons..............F....... 269 979-1411
Battle Creek *(G-1309)*

PUBLISHERS: Miscellaneous

2 Donkeys Publishing............................G....... 616 554-3958
Caledonia *(G-2365)*
4-Health Inc..G....... 989 686-3377
Bay City *(G-1313)*
Aaron Jagt..G....... 517 304-4844
Howell *(G-8425)*
Acra Training Center..............................G....... 269 326-7088
Baroda *(G-1158)*
Adams Street Publishing........................G....... 734 668-4044
Ann Arbor *(G-350)*
Agri Blowers Express.............................G....... 616 662-9999
Jenison *(G-9043)*
All Kids Considered Pubg Group..........G....... 248 398-3400
Ferndale *(G-5522)*
Alpha Omega Publishing........................G....... 517 879-1286
Jackson *(G-8812)*
American Mathematical Society............F....... 734 996-5250
Ann Arbor *(G-364)*
Animo Games LLC..................................G....... 586 201-9699
Rochester Hills *(G-13948)*
Ariana Press Inc......................................G....... 313 885-7581
Grosse Pointe Farms *(G-7534)*
Ascribe...G....... 616 726-2490
Grand Rapids *(G-6475)*
Authors Coalition America LLC.............G....... 231 869-2011
Pentwater *(G-12970)*
Avabella Press...G....... 734 662-0048
Ann Arbor *(G-386)*
Avanti Press Inc......................................E....... 800 228-2684
Detroit *(G-4034)*
Avery Color Studios Inc..........................G....... 906 346-3908
Gwinn *(G-7582)*
Aye Money Promotions Pubg LLC........G....... 313 808-8173
Detroit *(G-4036)*
B & D Publishing LLC.............................G....... 586 651-3623
Richmond *(G-13833)*
Ball Hard Music Group LLC...................G....... 833 246-4552
Monroe *(G-11528)*
Bethany House Publishers.....................G....... 616 676-9185
Ada *(G-11)*
Big Maple Press......................................G....... 231 313-4059
Traverse City *(G-16621)*
Blackberry Publications.........................G....... 313 627-1520
Ecorse *(G-4980)*
Boch Publishing LLC..............................G....... 734 718-2973
Canton *(G-2441)*
Boone Express..G....... 248 583-7080
Ortonville *(G-12743)*
Brapos LLC...G....... 248 677-6700
West Bloomfield *(G-18268)*
Broadside Press......................................G....... 313 736-5338
Detroit *(G-4075)*
Brother Mike Pubg & Mus Co LLC........G....... 313 506-8866
Bloomfield Hills *(G-1807)*
Brown House Publishing........................G....... 248 470-4690
West Bloomfield *(G-18269)*
C and N Press WD Enhncents LLC.......G....... 810 712-7771
Berkley *(G-1623)*
Cabell Publishing LLC............................G....... 906 361-6828
Marquette *(G-11011)*
CAM Publishing Inc.................................G....... 248 848-3148
Farmington Hills *(G-5194)*
Campbell and Co Publishing LLC.........G....... 810 320-0224
Fort Gratiot *(G-5820)*
Candlelite Publishing LLC.....................G....... 248 841-8925
Rochester Hills *(G-13971)*
Capacity House Publishing....................G....... 586 209-3924
Eastpointe *(G-4930)*
Carlton Sgnature Pub Relations...........G....... 248 387-9849
Waterford *(G-18108)*
Carolyns Publication..............................G....... 810 787-4114
Flint *(G-5663)*
Carriage Town Press..............................G....... 810 410-5113
Flint *(G-5664)*
Carstill Wagon Pub/Toasty Toes............G....... 734 325-7542
Van Buren Twp *(G-17514)*
Cbm LLC..G....... 800 487-2323
Ann Arbor *(G-418)*
Chatman Walker Publishing LLC..........G....... 586 604-7534
Clinton Township *(G-3197)*
City Press Inc..G....... 800 867-2626
Ortonville *(G-12744)*
Claire Aldin Publications.......................G....... 313 702-4028
Southfield *(G-15524)*
Cloud White Publishing..........................G....... 248 684-6460
Milford *(G-11459)*
Cobblestone Press..................................G....... 989 832-0166
Midland *(G-11330)*
Color Detroit Publishing LLC................G....... 313 974-9000
Rochester Hills *(G-13977)*
Command Publishing LLC.....................G....... 734 776-2692
Canton *(G-2451)*
Common Earth Press LLC......................G....... 313 407-2919
Huntington Woods *(G-8620)*
Complete Services LLC..........................F....... 248 470-8247
Livonia *(G-10161)*
Concordant Publishing Concern...........G....... 810 798-3563
Almont *(G-257)*
Conine Publishing Inc............................E....... 231 723-3592
Manistee *(G-10896)*
Conteur Publishing LLC.........................G....... 248 602-9749
Sterling Heights *(G-15968)*
Contribute A Verse Publishing..............G....... 616 447-2271
Grand Rapids *(G-6601)*
Conway Publications..............................G....... 517 424-1614
Tecumseh *(G-16494)*
Corey...G....... 313 565-8501
Dearborn *(G-3822)*
Cornell Publications LLC.......................G....... 810 225-3075
Brighton *(G-1967)*
Country Register of Mich Inc.................G....... 989 793-4211
Saginaw *(G-14632)*
Cracker Publishing LLC.........................G....... 248 429-9098
Wixom *(G-18640)*
Crain Family Bible.................................G....... 734 673-8620
Pinckney *(G-13045)*
Crazy Red Head Publishing...................G....... 248 862-6096
West Bloomfield *(G-18272)*
Creative Visions Publishing Co............G....... 248 545-3528
Oak Park *(G-12599)*
Crushing Hearts and Black...................G....... 224 234-9677
Novi *(G-12386)*
Cs Express Inc.......................................G....... 248 425-1726
Rochester Hills *(G-13987)*
Cs X Press Inc..G....... 586 864-3360
Sterling Heights *(G-15975)*
Cubbie Publications...............................G....... 248 852-5297
Rochester Hills *(G-13988)*
Cvk Publishing Inc..................................G....... 248 877-6384
West Bloomfield *(G-18275)*
D L W Publishing Co..............................G....... 313 593-4554
Detroit *(G-4118)*
D2 Ink Inc..G....... 248 590-7076
Farmington Hills *(G-5209)*
Daily News..G....... 616 754-9301
Greenville *(G-7481)*
Dark Star Publishing..............................G....... 810 858-1135
Richmond *(G-13835)*
Datalyzer International Inc...................G....... 248 960-3535
Wixom *(G-18644)*
Datamartz LLC..G....... 248 202-1559
Ann Arbor *(G-444)*
Deep Wood Press...................................G....... 231 587-0506
Bellaire *(G-1474)*
Denny Davis...G....... 989 785-3433
Atlanta *(G-745)*
Deslatae..G....... 313 820-4321
Detroit *(G-4133)*
Diggypod Inc...G....... 734 429-3307
Tecumseh *(G-16496)*
Digiscroll Press......................................G....... 214 846-1826
Belmont *(G-1505)*
Dillion Renee Entities............................G....... 989 443-0654
Lansing *(G-9830)*
Diocese of Lansing................................G....... 517 484-4449
Lansing *(G-9831)*
Discovery House Publishers.................D....... 616 942-9218
Grand Rapids *(G-6651)*
Diva Publications...................................G....... 517 887-8271
Lansing *(G-9832)*
Dln Publications LLC............................G....... 248 410-7337
Novi *(G-12402)*
Drake Publishing...................................G....... 269 963-4810
Battle Creek *(G-1221)*
Dream Catchers Publishing LLC...........G....... 313 575-3933
Detroit *(G-4191)*
Dreambuilder Publications.....................G....... 989 465-1583
Coleman *(G-3463)*
Drummond Press Inc..............................G....... 248 834-7007
Lake Orion *(G-9604)*
Dust & Ashes Publications....................G....... 231 722-6657
Byron Center *(G-2268)*
E D C O Publishing Inc..........................G....... 248 690-9184
Clarkston *(G-3031)*
E-Snap Publications LLC.......................G....... 708 740-0910
Ferndale *(G-5550)*
Edwards Publications In.......................G....... 864 882-3272
Caro *(G-2570)*
Encore Music Publishers.......................G....... 231 432-8322
Maple City *(G-10941)*
Encore Publications..............................G....... 269 488-3143
Kalamazoo *(G-9179)*
Engai...G....... 313 605-8220
Wixom *(G-18657)*
Ensign Publishing House.......................G....... 734 369-3983
Ann Arbor *(G-475)*
Exie Smith Publications LLC.................G....... 248 360-2917
Commerce Township *(G-3527)*
Express Expediting................................G....... 313 347-9975
Harper Woods *(G-7666)*
Eyry of Eagle Publish............................G....... 734 623-0337
Ann Arbor *(G-483)*
Fl Publishing..G....... 248 282-9905
Bloomfield Hills *(G-1821)*
Fishkorn Publishing LLC.......................G....... 734 624-2211
Novi *(G-12416)*
Five Count Publishing LLC....................G....... 616 308-6148
Gowen *(G-6229)*
Flipsnack LLC...E....... 650 741-1328
Troy *(G-17115)*
Forerunner Press LLC...........................G....... 248 677-3272
Royal Oak *(G-14537)*
Forever Young Publishers.....................G....... 574 276-1805
Niles *(G-12130)*
Foreword Magazine Inc..........................G....... 231 933-3699
Traverse City *(G-16686)*
Foreword Reviews..................................G....... 231 933-5397
Traverse City *(G-16687)*
Foundations Press Inc...........................G....... 517 625-3052
Perry *(G-12977)*
Four Seasons Mobile Press....................G....... 616 902-6233
Ionia *(G-8689)*
French Press Knits LLC.........................G....... 810 623-0650
Fenton *(G-5480)*
Fresh Start Cmnty Initiative.................G....... 941 225-9693
Detroit *(G-4246)*
Frontlines Publishing............................E....... 616 887-6256
Grand Rapids *(G-6720)*
Gaty...G....... 313 381-2853
Allen Park *(G-195)*
Gaus..G....... 517 764-6178
Jackson *(G-8889)*
Gemini Corporation...............................E....... 616 459-4545
Grand Rapids *(G-6737)*
Ginger Tree Press..................................G....... 269 779-5780
Kalamazoo *(G-9197)*
Giving Press...G....... 702 302-2039
Spring Lake *(G-15817)*

PRODUCT SECTION

PUBLISHERS: Miscellaneous

Gossamer Press LLC ....G 616 363-4608
  Grand Rapids *(G-6751)*
Gpi-X LLC ....G 616 453-4170
  Grand Rapids *(G-6752)*
Graphics Hse Spt Prmotions Inc ....E 231 739-4004
  Muskegon *(G-11828)*
Grapho LLC ....G 734 223-2144
  Ann Arbor *(G-505)*
Great Lakes Spt Publications ....G 734 507-0241
  Ann Arbor *(G-507)*
Gregg Publishing Co ....G 906 789-1139
  Escanaba *(G-5074)*
Grey Wolfe Publishing LLC ....G 248 914-4027
  Bingham Farms *(G-1698)*
Guest Publications LLC ....G 231 651-9281
  Traverse City *(G-16707)*
Guys You Are Real Heroes Pubg ....G 248 682-2537
  West Bloomfield *(G-18286)*
Hammond Publishing Company ....G 810 686-8879
  Mount Morris *(G-11671)*
Hang On Express ....G 231 271-0202
  Suttons Bay *(G-16340)*
Harpercollins Christn Pubg Inc ....F 616 698-3230
  Grand Rapids *(G-6804)*
Hatchback Publishing ....G 810 394-8612
  Genesee *(G-6168)*
Hawkshadow Publishing Company .....G 586 979-5046
  Sterling Heights *(G-16035)*
Health Enhancement Systems Inc ......G 989 839-0852
  Midland *(G-11372)*
Hermiz Publishing In ....G 586 212-4490
  Sterling Heights *(G-16039)*
House of Hero LLC ....G 248 260-8300
  Bloomfield Hills *(G-1829)*
Human Synergistics Inc ....E 734 459-1030
  Plymouth *(G-13193)*
If and or But Publishing ....G 269 274-6102
  Battle Creek *(G-1239)*
Ifca International Inc ....G 616 531-1840
  Grandville *(G-7391)*
In Know Inc ....G 734 827-9711
  Ann Arbor *(G-526)*
Inside English ....G 586 801-4351
  Fraser *(G-5943)*
International Assn Lions Clubs ....G 989 644-6562
  Weidman *(G-18253)*
Internet Publishing Inc ....G 248 438-8192
  Novi *(G-12439)*
J B Express LLC ....G 313 903-4601
  Dearborn Heights *(G-3929)*
Jeffrey Scheiber ....G 248 207-7036
  Wyandotte *(G-18826)*
Jewel Albright Cohen Pubg LLC ....G 248 672-8889
  Waterford *(G-18130)*
Jga Press/Jackson Gates Assoc ....G 313 957-0200
  Detroit *(G-4337)*
Jn Press ....G 517 708-0300
  Lansing *(G-9708)*
Johnson Multimedia Group LLC ....G 989 753-1151
  Bay City *(G-1369)*
Jones Music Co ....G 313 521-6471
  Detroit *(G-4342)*
Joseph Scott Falbe ....G 269 282-1597
  Battle Creek *(G-1247)*
Just Press Play ....G 248 470-7797
  Livonia *(G-10262)*
Kitchen Joy ....G 616 682-7327
  Grand Rapids *(G-6898)*
Kvga Publishing ....G 517 545-0841
  Howell *(G-8471)*
Lady Lazarus LLC ....G 810 441-9115
  Ferndale *(G-5564)*
Lake House Publishing LLC ....G 231 377-2017
  Bellaire *(G-1477)*
Lakeshore Publishing ....G 616 846-0620
  Spring Lake *(G-15829)*
Lakeview Publishing Company ....G 586 443-5913
  Saint Clair Shores *(G-14867)*
Lca International Publishing ....G 313 908-4583
  Dearborn *(G-3860)*
Leader Publications LLC ....D 269 683-2100
  Niles *(G-12141)*
Leann Kelley Enterprises LLC ....G 505 270-5687
  Hamilton *(G-7601)*
Leather Lore ....G 269 548-7160
  Coopersville *(G-3690)*
Lebutt Publishing LLC ....G 248 756-1613
  Commerce Township *(G-3550)*
Lehman Publishingcom ....G 810 395-4535
  Allenton *(G-230)*

Little Bird Press LLC ....G 616 676-9052
  Ada *(G-26)*
Little Spoke Big Wheel Pubg ....G 313 779-9327
  Southfield *(G-15637)*
LL Becker Publications ....G 248 366-9037
  White Lake *(G-18460)*
Llomen Inc ....G 269 345-3555
  Portage *(G-13579)*
Local Logic Media ....G 517 914-2486
  Spring Arbor *(G-15794)*
Looking Aft Publications ....G 231 759-8581
  Whitehall *(G-18507)*
Lou Jack City Publishing LLC ....G 404 863-7124
  Detroit *(G-4407)*
Love Publicity ....G 313 288-8342
  Detroit *(G-4408)*
Lsjd Publications LLC ....G 843 576-9040
  Sault Sainte Marie *(G-15094)*
Lucky Press LLC ....G 614 309-0048
  Harbor Springs *(G-7650)*
Luke Legacy Publications LLC ....G 313 363-5949
  Plymouth *(G-13229)*
Manistee News Advocate ....F 231 723-3592
  Manistee *(G-10905)*
Manray Press LLC ....G 734 558-0580
  Wyandotte *(G-18831)*
Masters Publishing ....G 586 323-2723
  Sterling Heights *(G-16086)*
McMackon Mktg ADM Pubg Svcs LL ....G 734 878-3198
  Pinckney *(G-13051)*
Medwin Publishers LLC ....G 248 247-6042
  Troy *(G-17244)*
Meech Road Ltd ....G 734 255-9119
  Mason *(G-11143)*
Metra Inc ....G 248 543-3500
  Hazel Park *(G-7831)*
Mh Publishing LLC ....G 313 881-3724
  Grosse Pointe Farms *(G-7537)*
MI Classical Press ....G 734 747-6337
  Ann Arbor *(G-571)*
Michigan Acdemy Fmly Physcians ....G 517 347-0098
  Okemos *(G-12675)*
Michigan Legal Publishing Ltd ....F 877 525-1990
  Grandville *(G-7400)*
Michiganensian ....G 734 418-4115
  Ann Arbor *(G-576)*
Mission Point Press ....G 231 421-9513
  Traverse City *(G-16761)*
Mjs Publishing Group ....G 734 391-7370
  Van Buren Twp *(G-17541)*
Morning Star ....G 989 755-2660
  Saginaw *(G-14704)*
Morning Star Publishing Co ....F 989 463-6071
  Alma *(G-248)*
Mpress Desighns LLC ....G 313 627-9727
  Eastpointe *(G-4941)*
Musicalia Press ....G 734 433-1289
  Chelsea *(G-2821)*
N2 Publications ....G 517 488-2607
  Mason *(G-11146)*
Native Detroiter Pubg Inc ....G 313 822-1958
  Detroit *(G-4477)*
New Alexandria Press ....G 248 529-3108
  White Lake *(G-18462)*
New Classics Press LLC ....G 616 975-9070
  Grand Rapids *(G-7041)*
New Genesis Enterprise Inc ....G 313 220-0365
  Westland *(G-18400)*
Next In Line Publishing LLc ....G 248 954-1280
  Livonia *(G-10335)*
Ninja Pants Press LLC ....G 248 669-6577
  Commerce Township *(G-3557)*
Nord Publications Inc ....G 734 455-5271
  Canton *(G-2501)*
Northern Michigan Publishing ....G 231 946-7878
  Traverse City *(G-16774)*
Novel Publicity LLC ....G 248 563-6637
  Brighton *(G-2043)*
Oak Leaf Publishing Inc ....G 248 547-7103
  Oak Park *(G-12635)*
One Tree Research Group LLC ....G 616 466-4880
  Ada *(G-32)*
Online Publications Inc ....G 248 879-2133
  Troy *(G-17289)*
Orange October Publishing Co ....G 231 828-1039
  Twin Lake *(G-17471)*
Paine Press LLC ....G 231 645-1970
  Boyne City *(G-1900)*
Paladino Publications ....G 586 759-2795
  Warren *(G-17953)*

Panda King Express ....G 616 796-3286
  Holland *(G-8159)*
Panther Publishing ....G 586 202-9814
  Grand Blanc *(G-6255)*
Paper Petal Press ....G 248 935-5193
  Waterford *(G-18146)*
Paper Press ....G 248 438-6238
  West Bloomfield *(G-18303)*
Par Excellence Publication ....G 989 345-8305
  West Branch *(G-18334)*
Parish Publications ....G 248 613-2384
  Bloomfield Hills *(G-1847)*
Parker & Associates ....G 269 694-6709
  Otsego *(G-12794)*
Partridge Pointe Press LLC ....G 248 321-0475
  Belmont *(G-1515)*
Pat Ro Publishing ....G 248 553-4935
  Farmington Hills *(G-5343)*
Personal Power Press Inc ....G 989 239-8628
  Bay City *(G-1386)*
Peter Dehaan Publishing Inc ....G 616 284-1305
  Hudsonville *(G-8600)*
Phalanx Press ....G 517 213-9393
  Charlotte *(G-2764)*
Pick Energy Savings LLC ....G 248 343-8354
  Highland *(G-7898)*
Pierian Press Inc ....G 734 434-4074
  Ypsilanti *(G-18970)*
Pigeon River Publishing LLC ....G 616 528-4027
  Haslett *(G-7776)*
Pinstripe Publishing LLC ....G 734 276-0554
  Ann Arbor *(G-611)*
Poppyseed Press LLC ....G 616 450-8521
  Grand Rapids *(G-7093)*
Prankster Press LLC ....G 616 550-3099
  Detroit *(G-4531)*
Press On Juice ....G 231 409-9971
  Traverse City *(G-16800)*
Press Play ....G 231 753-2841
  Traverse City *(G-16801)*
Press Play LLC ....G 248 802-3837
  Auburn Hills *(G-1004)*
Private Life Corp ....G 248 922-9800
  Waterford *(G-18158)*
Proquest Outdoor Solutions Inc ....E 734 761-4700
  Ann Arbor *(G-626)*
Prs & PIP Ftrs L 506 ....G 906 789-9784
  Escanaba *(G-5092)*
Prs Judd ....G 734 470-6162
  Saline *(G-15033)*
Publishing Systems Inc ....G 248 852-0185
  Rochester Hills *(G-14092)*
Quality Guest Publishing Inc ....F 616 894-1111
  Cedar Springs *(G-2660)*
R & R Harwood Inc ....G 616 669-6400
  Jenison *(G-9069)*
R S C Productions ....G 586 532-9200
  Shelby Township *(G-15313)*
Rainbow Hollow Press ....G 231 825-2962
  Rodney *(G-14207)*
Raychris ....G 734 404-5485
  Plymouth *(G-13276)*
Red Falcon Press ....G 248 439-0432
  Royal Oak *(G-14575)*
Reflective Art Inc ....E 616 452-0712
  Wyoming *(G-18903)*
Reg Publishers LLC ....G 616 889-4232
  Hopkins *(G-8368)*
Reveal Publishing LLC ....G 248 798-3440
  Bloomfield Hills *(G-1855)*
Rhys World Publishing LLC ....G 248 974-7408
  Northville *(G-12254)*
Ridge Pointe Publishing LLC ....G 586 948-4660
  Macomb *(G-10632)*
Roaring River Press ....G 248 342-2281
  New Haven *(G-12036)*
Robbins Publishing Group Inc ....G 734 260-3258
  Lake Angelus *(G-9539)*
Roe Publishing Department ....G 517 522-3598
  Jackson *(G-8997)*
Rosemary Felice ....G 517 861-7434
  Howell *(G-8511)*
Royal Publishing ....G 810 768-3057
  Flint *(G-5758)*
Rrr Training & Publishing ....G 906 396-9546
  Iron Mountain *(G-8731)*
S Hasan Publishing LLC ....G 734 858-8800
  Inkster *(G-8675)*
Salesman Inc ....G 517 592-5886
  Brooklyn *(G-2131)*

Employee Codes: A=Over 500 employees, B=251-500
C=101-250, D=51-100, E=20-50, F=10-19, G=3-9

Salesman Inc....G.... 517 783-4080
Jackson (G-9005)
Samhita Press....G.... 248 747-7792
Sterling Heights (G-16162)
Sanders Information Publishing....G.... 248 669-0991
Novi (G-12531)
Sandkey Publishing LLC....G.... 248 475-3662
Rochester Hills (G-14107)
Scapegoat Press Inc....G.... 586 439-8381
Wyandotte (G-18838)
Scriblical Vibez Publishing....G.... 313 544-3042
Westland (G-18417)
Shamrock Publications....G.... 269 459-1099
Portage (G-13606)
Shamrock Publishing....G.... 313 881-1721
Grosse Pointe Woods (G-7575)
Sharedbook Inc....E.... 734 302-6500
Ann Arbor (G-650)
Shepherd Jnes Pblcations Press....G.... 313 221-3000
Southfield (G-15698)
Source Point Press....G.... 269 501-3690
Midland (G-11419)
Spes Publishing Co LLC....G.... 734 741-1241
Ann Arbor (G-661)
Spirit Publishing LLC....G.... 231 399-1538
Traverse City (G-16838)
Spitting Image Pblications LLC....G.... 989 498-9459
Saginaw (G-14764)
Spoonful Press....G.... 313 862-6579
Detroit (G-4602)
Spunky Duck Press....G.... 269 365-7285
Plainwell (G-13096)
Stafford Media Inc....E.... 616 754-9301
Greenville (G-7505)
Standard Register....G.... 616 987-3128
Lowell (G-10517)
Star Buyers Guide....G.... 989 366-8341
Houghton Lake (G-8405)
Subterranean Press....G.... 810 232-1489
Flint (G-5772)
Summit Training Source Inc....E.... 800 842-0466
Grand Rapids (G-7233)
Sunset Coast Publishing LLC....G.... 574 440-3228
Edwardsburg (G-5018)
Svk Media and Publishing LLC....G.... 616 379-4001
Hudsonville (G-8613)
Taletyano Press....G.... 517 381-1960
Okemos (G-12688)
Think Club Publication....G.... 248 651-3106
Rochester (G-13933)
Think Social Media....G.... 810 360-0170
Brighton (G-2080)
Thm Publishing Detroit LLC....G.... 586 232-3037
Washington (G-18089)
Thunder Bay Press Michigan LLC....G.... 989 701-2430
West Branch (G-18343)
Time Traveling DJS....G.... 517 402-0976
Eaton Rapids (G-4973)
Timothy J Tade Inc....G.... 248 552-8583
Troy (G-17392)
Toledo Press Industries Inc....G.... 734 727-0605
Wayne (G-18238)
Triple S Publications LLC....G.... 231 775-6113
Cadillac (G-2362)
Triumph Publishing House Inc....G.... 248 423-1765
Southfield (G-15727)
Tuscola County Advertiser Inc....F.... 989 823-8651
Vassar (G-17583)
Tuscola County Advertiser Inc....E.... 989 673-3181
Caro (G-2583)
Unique Connection Pubg Co....G.... 248 304-0030
Southfield (G-15731)
Upper Pnnsula Pbls Athors Assn....G.... 906 226-1543
Marquette (G-11048)
US Suburban Press....G.... 616 662-6420
Hudsonville (G-8614)
Valley Publishing....G.... 989 671-1200
Grand Rapids (G-7302)
Van Buren Publishing LLC....G.... 734 740-8668
Belleville (G-1492)
Verticalscope USA Inc....G.... 248 220-1451
Troy (G-17439)
View Publication Co....G.... 734 461-1579
Ypsilanti (G-18985)
Village Press Inc....G.... 231 946-3712
Traverse City (G-16874)
Vimax Publishing....G.... 248 563-2367
Bloomfield Hills (G-1873)
Vivid Publishing....G.... 614 282-6479
Monroe (G-11589)
Wade Printing & Publishing LLC....G.... 616 894-6350
Lowell (G-10521)
Wallace Publishing LLC....E.... 248 416-7259
Hazel Park (G-7848)
Wardlaw Press LLC....G.... 313 806-4603
Grosse Pointe Farms (G-7542)
Watersong Publications....G.... 248 592-0109
Farmington Hills (G-5412)
Waub Ajijaak Press....G.... 248 802-8630
Manistee (G-10915)
Wave Music and Publishing....G.... 313 290-2193
Detroit (G-4676)
Wendy Williamson....G.... 321 345-8297
Saint Joseph (G-14975)
West Mich Cmnty Help Netwrk....F.... 231 727-5007
Muskegon (G-11942)
Whos Who Publishing Co LLC....G.... 614 481-7300
Detroit (G-4683)
Wicwas Press....G.... 269 344-8027
Kalamazoo (G-9369)
Winding Road Publishing Inc....G.... 248 545-8360
Ferndale (G-5598)
Winning Publications....G.... 269 342-8547
Kalamazoo (G-9371)
Yeungs Lotus Express....G.... 248 380-3820
Novi (G-12573)
Your Personal Memoir LLC....G.... 248 629-0697
Pleasant Ridge (G-13107)
Zimbell House Publishing LLC....G.... 248 909-0143
Waterford (G-18177)
Zondervan Corporation LLC....B.... 616 698-6900
Grand Rapids (G-7358)
Zoomer Display LLC....G.... 616 734-0300
Grand Rapids (G-7359)

PUBLISHERS: Music Book & Sheet Music

Ayotte Cstm Mscal Engrvngs LLC....G.... 734 595-1901
Westland (G-18358)
Live Track Productions Inc....G.... 313 704-2224
Detroit (G-4402)
Music....G.... 313 854-3606
Detroit (G-4472)

PUBLISHERS: Newsletter

Grand Valley State University....G.... 847 744-0508
Allendale (G-219)
Synod of Great Lakes....E.... 616 698-7071
Grand Rapids (G-7243)
Verdoni Productions Inc....G.... 989 790-0845
Saginaw (G-14790)

PUBLISHERS: Newspaper

201 E Exchange....G.... 989 725-6397
Owosso (G-12818)
Adrian Team LLC....F.... 517 264-6148
Adrian (G-51)
Advance BCI Inc....D.... 616 669-1366
Grand Rapids (G-6431)
Angler Strategies LLC....G.... 248 439-1420
Royal Oak (G-14508)
Ann Arbor Observer Company....E.... 734 769-3175
Ann Arbor (G-368)
Ann Arbor Offset....G.... 734 926-4500
Ann Arbor (G-369)
Beacon Billboards LLC....G.... 734 421-7512
Livonia (G-10132)
Beaumont Enterprise....G.... 989 269-6464
Bad Axe (G-1098)
Blue Shamrock Publishing Inc....G.... 269 687-7097
Niles (G-12114)
Buyers Guide....G.... 616 897-9261
Lowell (G-10497)
Catherine Pawlowski....G.... 248 698-3614
White Lake (G-18452)
City of Greenville....E.... 616 754-0100
Greenville (G-7478)
Cmu....F.... 989 774-7143
Mount Pleasant (G-11692)
Detroit News Inc....G.... 313 222-6400
Detroit (G-4154)
Detroit Newspaper Partnr LP....G.... 989 752-3023
Saginaw (G-14638)
Frushour Publishers....G.... 248 701-2548
Clarkston (G-3035)
Graphics Hse Spt Prmotions Inc....E.... 231 739-4004
Muskegon (G-11828)
Harbor Beach Times....G.... 989 479-3605
Harbor Beach (G-7631)
Herald Newspapers Company Inc....D.... 269 388-8501
Kalamazoo (G-9214)
Herald Publishing Company....E.... 517 423-2174
Tecumseh (G-16504)
Houghton Cmnty Brdcstg Corp....G.... 906 482-7700
Houghton (G-8383)
Hydraulic Press Service....G.... 586 859-7099
Shelby Township (G-15237)
Infoguys Inc....G.... 517 482-2125
Lansing (G-9854)
Maquet Monthly....G.... 906 226-6500
Marquette (G-11032)
Mlive Media Group....G.... 212 286-2860
Ann Arbor (G-580)
Newark Morning Ledger Co....D.... 517 487-8888
Lansing (G-9875)
Onesian Enterprises Inc....F.... 313 382-5875
Allen Park (G-201)
Pepperlee Paper Company....G.... 313 949-5917
Rochester Hills (G-14081)
Punkin Dsign Seds Orgnlity LLC....G.... 313 347-8488
Detroit (G-4542)
Royal Lux Magazine....G.... 248 602-6565
Southfield (G-15690)
Shiawassee County 9/12 Comm....G.... 989 288-5049
Durand (G-4847)
Spin Lo Angler....G.... 231 882-6450
Beulah (G-1658)
Super Woman Productions Pubg L....G.... 313 491-6819
Detroit (G-4616)
Treasure Enterprise LLC....F.... 810 233-7128
Flint (G-5783)
Up Catholic Newspaper....G.... 906 226-8821
Marquette (G-11046)
Vegetable Growers News....G.... 616 887-9008
Sparta (G-15788)
View Newspaper....G.... 734 697-8255
Belleville (G-1494)
Vintage Views Press....G.... 616 475-7662
Grand Rapids (G-7319)
West Michigan Medical....G.... 269 673-2141
Allegan (G-185)
Your Custom Image....G.... 989 621-2250
Mount Pleasant (G-11747)

PUBLISHERS: Newspapers, No Printing

A B Rusgo Inc....G.... 586 296-7714
Fraser (G-5886)
Action Ad Newspapers Inc....G.... 734 740-6966
Belleville (G-1478)
Alcona County Review....G.... 989 724-6384
Harrisville (G-7740)
Anteebo Publishers Inc....E.... 313 882-6900
Grosse Pointe Park (G-7546)
Antrim Review....G.... 231 533-5651
Bellaire (G-1470)
Argus Press Company....E.... 989 725-5136
Owosso (G-12824)
Belleville Area Independent....G.... 734 699-9020
Belleville (G-1480)
Budget Europe Travel Service....G.... 734 668-0529
Ann Arbor (G-408)
Campub Inc....F.... 517 368-0365
Camden (G-2419)
Cass City Chronicle Inc....G.... 989 872-2010
Cass City (G-2612)
Daily Oakland Press....B.... 248 332-8181
Pontiac (G-13357)
Daily Reporter....E.... 517 278-2318
Coldwater (G-3430)
Daughtry Nwspapers Investments....G.... 269 683-2100
Niles (G-12123)
Detroit Jewish News Ltd Partnr....D.... 248 354-6060
Farmington Hills (G-5213)
Detroit News Inc....B.... 313 222-6400
Detroit (G-4153)
Detroit Newspaper Partnr LP....A.... 313 222-2300
Detroit (G-4155)
Fowlerville News & Views....G.... 517 223-8760
Fowlerville (G-5841)
Gazette Newspapers Inc....G.... 248 524-4868
Troy (G-17128)
Gemini Corporation....E.... 616 459-4545
Grand Rapids (G-6737)
Gladwin County Newspapers LLC....G.... 989 426-9411
Gladwin (G-6196)
GLS Diocesan Reports....G.... 989 793-7661
Saginaw (G-14653)
Grand Haven Publishing Corp....G.... 616 842-6400
Grand Haven (G-6305)

Hamtramck Review Inc ......G....... 313 874-2100
Detroit *(G-4292)*
Harold K Schultz ......G....... 517 279-9764
Coldwater *(G-3438)*
Herald Newspapers Company Inc ......G....... 810 766-6100
Flint *(G-5714)*
Herald Newspapers Company Inc ......G....... 989 895-8551
Flint *(G-5715)*
Houghton Lake Resorter Inc ......F....... 989 366-5341
Houghton Lake *(G-8400)*
Hudson Post Gazette ......G....... 517 448-2611
Hudson *(G-8552)*
Huron Publishing Company Inc ......D....... 989 269-6461
Bad Axe *(G-1107)*
Indepndent Advsor Nwsppr Group ......F....... 989 723-1118
Owosso *(G-12838)*
Lansing Labor News Inc ......G....... 517 484-7408
East Lansing *(G-4899)*
Leelanau Enterprise Inc ......E....... 231 256-9827
Lake Leelanau *(G-9563)*
Local Media Group Inc ......D....... 313 885-2612
Detroit *(G-4403)*
Midland Publishing Company ......C....... 989 835-7171
Midland *(G-11394)*
Newberry News Inc ......G....... 906 293-8401
Newberry *(G-12096)*
Northern Michigan Review Inc ......G....... 231 547-6558
Petoskey *(G-13009)*
Ogden Newspapers Inc ......G....... 906 497-5652
Powers *(G-13649)*
Ogden Newspapers Virginia LLC ......F....... 906 228-8920
Marquette *(G-11038)*
Ogemaw County Herald Inc ......E....... 989 345-0044
West Branch *(G-18333)*
Plymouth-Canton Cmnty Crier ......E....... 734 453-6900
Plymouth *(G-13268)*
Porcupine Press Inc ......G....... 906 439-5111
Chatham *(G-2778)*
Schepeler Corporation ......E....... 517 592-6811
Brooklyn *(G-2132)*
Sciaccess Publishers ......G....... 616 676-7012
Grand Rapids *(G-7186)*
Sherman Publications Inc ......E....... 248 628-4801
Oxford *(G-12916)*
South Haven Tribune ......G....... 269 637-1104
South Haven *(G-15415)*
Traverse Cy Record- Eagle Inc ......G....... 231 946-2000
Traverse City *(G-16866)*
Tuscola County Advertiser Inc ......E....... 989 673-3181
Caro *(G-2583)*
Urban Aging L3c ......G....... 313 204-5140
Detroit *(G-4654)*
Vineyard Press Inc ......F....... 269 657-5080
Paw Paw *(G-12959)*
Voice Communications Corp ......E....... 586 716-8100
Sterling Heights *(G-16226)*
Your Hometown Shopper LLC ......F....... 586 412-8500
Bruce Twp *(G-2187)*

PUBLISHERS: Periodical, With Printing

Detroit Legal News Company ......D....... 313 961-6000
Detroit *(G-4150)*
Diocese of Lansing ......G....... 517 484-4449
Lansing *(G-9831)*
Upston Associates Inc ......G....... 269 349-2782
Battle Creek *(G-1308)*
West Michigan Printing Inc ......G....... 616 676-2190
Ada *(G-41)*

PUBLISHERS: Periodicals, Magazines

Advisor Inc ......G....... 906 341-2424
Manistique *(G-10916)*
American Public Works Assn ......G....... 816 472-6100
Springfield *(G-15859)*
Bob Allison Enterprises ......G....... 248 540-8467
Bloomfield Hills *(G-1804)*
Business Direct Review ......G....... 269 373-7100
Kalamazoo *(G-9142)*
Denton Bobeldyk ......G....... 616 669-2076
Jenison *(G-9051)*
G L Nelson Inc ......G....... 630 682-5958
Indian River *(G-8653)*
Infoguys Inc ......G....... 517 482-2125
Lansing *(G-9854)*
Jordan Barnett ......G....... 734 243-9565
Monroe *(G-11553)*
Land & Homes Inc ......G....... 616 534-5792
Grand Rapids *(G-6927)*
Lightworks Magazine Inc ......G....... 248 626-8026
Bloomfield *(G-1783)*
Living Word International Inc ......E....... 989 832-7547
Midland *(G-11384)*
Magazines In Motion Inc ......G....... 248 310-7647
Farmington Hills *(G-5299)*
Pierian Press Inc ......G....... 734 434-4074
Ypsilanti *(G-18970)*
R J Michaels Inc ......E....... 517 783-2637
Jackson *(G-8993)*
Rockman & Sons Publishing LLC ......F....... 810 750-6011
Fenton *(G-5499)*
Stoney Creek Collection Inc ......F....... 616 363-4858
Grand Rapids *(G-7227)*
Tabs Floor Covering LLC ......G....... 616 846-1684
Nunica *(G-12587)*
Wright Communications Inc ......F....... 248 585-3838
Troy *(G-17454)*

PUBLISHERS: Periodicals, No Printing

Dynamic Color Publications ......G....... 248 553-3115
Farmington Hills *(G-5220)*
Faith Alive Christn Resources ......E....... 800 333-8300
Grand Rapids *(G-6698)*
Nationwide Network Inc ......G....... 989 793-0123
Saginaw *(G-14708)*
Pressure Releases Corporation ......F....... 616 531-8116
Grand Rapids *(G-7103)*
Your Home Town USA Inc ......G....... 517 529-9421
Clarklake *(G-3010)*

PUBLISHERS: Posters

Spectrum Map Publishing Inc ......G....... 517 655-5641
Williamston *(G-18583)*

PUBLISHERS: Shopping News

Buyers Guide ......G....... 616 897-9261
Lowell *(G-10497)*
Buyers Guide ......G....... 231 722-3784
Muskegon *(G-11787)*
Herald Bi-County Inc ......G....... 517 448-2201
Hudson *(G-8550)*
Hi-Lites Graphic Inc ......E....... 231 924-0630
Fremont *(G-6045)*
Oceanas Herald-Journal Inc ......F....... 231 873-5602
Hart *(G-7759)*
Pgi Holdings Inc ......G....... 231 937-4740
Big Rapids *(G-1684)*
Presque Isle Newspapers Inc ......F....... 989 734-2105
Rogers City *(G-14217)*
Thumb Blanket ......G....... 989 269-9918
Bad Axe *(G-1113)*
Vanguard Publications Inc ......G....... 517 336-1600
Okemos *(G-12692)*
Vineyard Press Inc ......F....... 269 657-5080
Paw Paw *(G-12959)*

PUBLISHERS: Technical Manuals

Technical Illustration Corp ......F....... 313 982-9660
Canton *(G-2530)*

PUBLISHERS: Technical Manuals & Papers

Helm Incorporated ......D....... 734 468-3700
Plymouth *(G-13186)*
Tweddle Group Inc ......C....... 586 307-3700
Clinton Township *(G-3380)*

PUBLISHERS: Telephone & Other Directory

Great Lakes Publishing Inc ......G....... 517 647-4444
Portland *(G-13638)*
Little Blue Book Inc ......F....... 313 469-0052
Grosse Pointe Woods *(G-7570)*
Review Directories Inc ......F....... 231 347-8606
Petoskey *(G-13020)*
Total Local Acquisitions LLC ......G....... 517 663-2405
Eaton Rapids *(G-4974)*

PUBLISHERS: Textbooks, No Printing

Cooper Publishing Group LLC ......G....... 231 933-9958
Traverse City *(G-16659)*
Hayden - McNeil LLC ......E....... 734 455-7900
Plymouth *(G-13185)*
Next Level Media Inc ......G....... 248 762-7043
Southfield *(G-15666)*
Real Ink Publishing LLC ......G....... 313 766-1344
Van Buren Twp *(G-17550)*

PUBLISHERS: Trade journals, No Printing

BNP Media Inc ......C....... 248 362-3700
Troy *(G-16978)*
Dental Consultants Inc ......F....... 734 663-6777
Ann Arbor *(G-447)*
Timothy J Tade Inc ......G....... 248 552-8583
Troy *(G-17392)*

PUBLISHING & BROADCASTING: Internet Only

Bramin Enterprises ......G....... 313 960-1528
Detroit *(G-4067)*
Breakaway Media Marketing LLC ......G....... 734 787-3382
Belleville *(G-1482)*
Digital Success Network ......E....... 517 244-0771
Mason *(G-11130)*
Direct Aim Media LLC ......E....... 800 817-7101
Grand Rapids *(G-6649)*
First Wilson Inc ......G....... 586 935-2687
Shelby Township *(G-15226)*
Fusion Design Group Ltd ......G....... 269 469-8226
New Buffalo *(G-12023)*
Hmg Agency ......F....... 989 443-3819
Saginaw *(G-14666)*
Intheknow313 LLC ......G....... 248 445-1953
Lincoln Park *(G-10050)*
Nb Media Solutions LLC ......G....... 616 724-7175
Grand Rapids *(G-7037)*
Tapoos LLC ......G....... 619 319-4872
Taylor *(G-16483)*
Weyv Inc ......F....... 248 614-2400
Troy *(G-17448)*
Writers Bible LLc ......G....... 734 286-7793
Romulus *(G-14341)*

PUBLISHING & PRINTING: Art Copy

Campub Inc ......F....... 517 368-0365
Camden *(G-2419)*

PUBLISHING & PRINTING: Book Music

Caligirlbooks LLC ......G....... 415 361-1533
Macomb *(G-10582)*
Sheptime Music ......G....... 586 806-9058
Warren *(G-18012)*

PUBLISHING & PRINTING: Books

Christian Schools Intl ......E....... 616 957-1070
Grandville *(G-7369)*
Creative Characters Inc ......G....... 231 544-6084
Central Lake *(G-2692)*
Diocese of Lansing ......G....... 517 484-4449
Lansing *(G-9831)*
Evia Learning Inc ......G....... 616 393-8803
Holland *(G-8033)*
Faith Alive Christn Resources ......E....... 800 333-8300
Grand Rapids *(G-6698)*
Iris Design & Print Inc ......G....... 313 277-0505
Dearborn *(G-3855)*
Meghan March LLC ......G....... 231 740-8114
Muskegon *(G-11865)*
MPS Lansing Inc ......A....... 517 323-9000
Lansing *(G-9719)*

PUBLISHING & PRINTING: Comic Books

Pathway Publishing Corporation ......F....... 269 521-3025
Bloomingdale *(G-1878)*

PUBLISHING & PRINTING: Directories, NEC

Elm International Inc ......G....... 517 332-4900
Okemos *(G-12665)*
Ethnicemedia LLC ......G....... 248 762-8904
Troy *(G-17097)*
EZ Vent LLC ......G....... 616 874-2787
Rockford *(G-14167)*

PUBLISHING & PRINTING: Directories, Telephone

ABC Printing Corporation Inc ......G....... 248 887-0010
Highland *(G-7879)*
Ludington Daily News Inc ......E....... 231 845-5181
Ludington *(G-10543)*
Npi Wireless ......E....... 231 922-9273
Traverse City *(G-16776)*

Employee Codes: A=Over 500 employees, B=251-500
C=101-250, D=51-100, E=20-50, F=10-19, G=3-9
2022 Harris Michigan
Industrial Directory
1385

PUBLISHING & PRINTING: Guides

PUBLISHING & PRINTING: Guides

J-Ad Graphics Inc .... D 800 870-7085
  Hastings *(G-7800)*
J-Ad Graphics Inc .... G 269 945-9554
  Marshall *(G-11062)*

PUBLISHING & PRINTING: Magazines: publishing & printing

5w LLC .... F 313 505-3106
  Van Buren Twp *(G-17505)*
Ambassador Magazine .... G 313 965-6789
  Detroit *(G-4008)*
Blac Inc .... G 313 690-3372
  Detroit *(G-4056)*
Bowman Enterprises Inc .... G 269 720-1946
  Portage *(G-13548)*
Community Publishing & Mktg .... G 866 822-0101
  Taylor *(G-16396)*
Cte Publishing LLC .... G 313 338-4335
  Detroit *(G-4111)*
Faith Publishing Service .... E 517 853-7600
  Lansing *(G-9697)*
K and A Publishing Co LLC .... G 734 743-1541
  Detroit *(G-4346)*
Kissman Consulting LLC .... G 517 256-1077
  Okemos *(G-12672)*
Planning & Zoning Center Inc .... G 517 886-0555
  Lansing *(G-9731)*
Slaughterhouse Collective LLC .... G 248 259-5257
  Ferndale *(G-5585)*
Vanguard Publications Inc .... G 517 336-1600
  Okemos *(G-12692)*
Village Shop Inc .... E 231 946-3712
  Traverse City *(G-16875)*

PUBLISHING & PRINTING: Music, Book

Different Music Group Ent LLC .... G 313 980-6159
  Clinton Township *(G-3224)*

PUBLISHING & PRINTING: Newsletters, Business Svc

Diocesan Publications .... E 616 878-5200
  Byron Center *(G-2267)*
Eiklae Products .... G 734 671-0752
  Grosse Ile *(G-7521)*
Forsons Inc .... G 517 787-4562
  Jackson *(G-8885)*

PUBLISHING & PRINTING: Newspapers

21st Century Newspapers Inc .... C 586 469-4510
  Sterling Heights *(G-15915)*
21st Century Newspapers Inc .... F 810 664-0811
  Lapeer *(G-9910)*
21st Century Newspapers Inc .... F 586 469-4510
  Pontiac *(G-13343)*
Allegan Vocal Studio .... G 719 209-8957
  Allegan *(G-147)*
Ann Arbor Chronicle .... G 734 645-2633
  Ann Arbor *(G-367)*
Ann Arbor Journal .... G 734 429-7380
  Saline *(G-15002)*
Arab American News Inc .... G 313 582-4888
  Dearborn *(G-3809)*
Benson Distribution Inc .... G 269 344-5529
  Kalamazoo *(G-9135)*
Board For Student Publications .... D 734 418-4115
  Ann Arbor *(G-402)*
Booth Newspaper .... G 517 487-8888
  Lansing *(G-9814)*
Boyne City Gazette .... G 231 582-2799
  Boyne City *(G-1884)*
Bulletin Moon .... G 734 453-9985
  Plymouth *(G-13140)*
Bulletin of Concerned Asi .... G 231 228-7116
  Cedar *(G-2636)*
Business News .... G 231 929-7919
  Traverse City *(G-16634)*
C & G Publishing Inc .... D 586 498-8000
  Warren *(G-17745)*
Calcomco Inc .... F 313 885-9228
  Kalamazoo *(G-9143)*
Cedar Springs Post Inc .... G 616 696-3655
  Cedar Springs *(G-2644)*
Chicago Tribune Company LLC .... G 734 464-6500
  Livonia *(G-10157)*
Choice Publications Inc .... G 989 732-8160
  Gaylord *(G-6122)*
Chris Faulknor .... G 231 645-1970
  Boyne City *(G-1886)*
Clare County Cleaver Inc .... G 989 539-7496
  Harrison *(G-7675)*
Clare County Review .... G 989 386-4414
  Clare *(G-2975)*
Community Shoppers Guide Inc .... G 269 694-9431
  Otsego *(G-12784)*
Coopersville Observer Inc .... G 616 997-5049
  Coopersville *(G-3684)*
County of St Clair .... F 810 982-4111
  Port Huron *(G-13467)*
Crain Communications Inc .... B 313 446-6000
  Detroit *(G-4106)*
Daily Bill .... G 989 631-2068
  Midland *(G-11332)*
Daily Contracts LLC .... G 734 676-0903
  Grosse Ile *(G-7518)*
Daily De-Lish .... G 616 450-9562
  Ada *(G-15)*
Daily Gardener LLC .... G 734 754-6527
  Ann Arbor *(G-442)*
Daily Oakland Press .... B 248 332-8181
  Bloomfield Hills *(G-1811)*
Daily Recycling of Michigan .... G 734 654-9800
  Carleton *(G-2550)*
Deadline Detroit .... G 248 219-5985
  Detroit *(G-4125)*
Deadline Detroit .... G 586 863-8397
  Detroit *(G-4126)*
Deadline Detroit .... G 202 309-5555
  Detroit *(G-4127)*
Detroit Free Press Inc .... B 313 222-2300
  Detroit *(G-4148)*
Detroit Legal News Pubg LLC .... E 248 577-6100
  Troy *(G-17057)*
Detroit Legal News Pubg LLC .... F 734 477-0201
  Ann Arbor *(G-450)*
Detroit News Inc .... G 313 222-6400
  Sterling Heights *(G-15983)*
Detroit Newspaper Partnr LP .... A 313 222-6400
  Detroit *(G-4156)*
El Informador LLC .... G 616 272-1092
  Wyoming *(G-18871)*
El Vocero Hispano Inc .... F 616 246-6023
  Grand Rapids *(G-6666)*
Eldon Publishing LLC .... G 810 648-5282
  Sandusky *(G-15058)*
Evening News .... G 734 242-1100
  Monroe *(G-11539)*
Express Publications Inc .... F 231 947-8787
  Traverse City *(G-16679)*
Forum and Link Inc .... G 313 945-5465
  Dearborn *(G-3845)*
Frankenmuth News LLC .... G 989 652-3246
  Frankenmuth *(G-5863)*
Gannett Stllite Info Ntwrk Inc .... G 734 229-1150
  Detroit *(G-4251)*
Gatehouse Media LLC .... E 517 265-5111
  Adrian *(G-69)*
Gatehouse Media LLC .... E 269 651-5407
  Sturgis *(G-16288)*
General Media LLC .... E 586 541-0075
  Saint Clair Shores *(G-14862)*
Grand Rapids Legal News .... G 616 454-9293
  Grand Rapids *(G-6761)*
Grand Rapids Press Inc .... E 616 459-1400
  Grand Rapids *(G-6767)*
Graph-ADS Printing Inc .... D 989 779-6000
  Mount Pleasant *(G-11700)*
Great American Publishing Co .... E 616 887-9008
  Sparta *(G-15765)*
Great Atlantic News LLC .... C 517 784-7163
  Jackson *(G-8893)*
Great Lakes Post LLC .... G 248 941-1349
  Milford *(G-11465)*
Grosse Pointe News .... G 734 674-0131
  Canton *(G-2468)*
Hamp .... G 989 366-5341
  Houghton Lake *(G-8398)*
Herald Newspapers Company Inc ...... G 269 345-3511
  Kalamazoo *(G-9213)*
Herald Newspapers Company Inc ...... G 231 722-3161
  Muskegon *(G-11836)*
Herald Newspapers Company Inc ...... G 616 222-5400
  Grand Rapids *(G-6810)*
Herald Newspapers Company Inc ...... G 734 926-4510
  Ann Arbor *(G-513)*
Herald Newspapers Company Inc ...... G 989 752-7171
  Flint *(G-5713)*
Herald Newspapers Company Inc ...... G 517 787-2300
  Jackson *(G-8902)*
Herald Newspapers Company Inc ...... G 734 834-6376
  Grand Rapids *(G-6811)*
Herald Publishing Company LLC .... E 734 623-2500
  Ann Arbor *(G-514)*
Herald Publishing Company LLC .... C 616 222-5400
  Walker *(G-17641)*
Heritage Newspapers .... F 586 783-0300
  Pontiac *(G-13379)*
Homer Index .... G 517 568-4646
  Homer *(G-8352)*
Hometown Publishing Inc .... G 989 834-2264
  Ovid *(G-12814)*
Igan Mich Publishing LLC .... G 248 877-4649
  West Bloomfield *(G-18290)*
Increase Enterprises LLC .... G 616 550-8553
  Grand Rapids *(G-6840)*
Independent Newspapers Inc .... C 586 469-4510
  Mount Clemens *(G-11642)*
Indiana Newspapers LLC .... D 248 680-9905
  Troy *(G-17164)*
Island Sun Times Inc .... E 810 230-1735
  Flint *(G-5717)*
J R C Inc .... F 810 648-4000
  Sandusky *(G-15061)*
J-Ad Graphics Inc .... D 800 870-7085
  Hastings *(G-7800)*
J-Ad Graphics Inc .... F 269 965-3955
  Battle Creek *(G-1243)*
Jams Media LLC .... F 810 664-0811
  Lapeer *(G-9935)*
Joseph D Eckenswiller .... G 586 784-8542
  Riley *(G-13851)*
Jss - Macomb LLC .... F 586 709-6305
  Shelby Township *(G-15247)*
Kaechele Publications Inc .... F 269 673-5534
  Allegan *(G-162)*
Karen Spranger .... G 719 359-4047
  Warren *(G-17890)*
Kids World News Too .... G 517 202-1808
  Alma *(G-244)*
L D J Inc .... F 906 524-6194
  Lanse *(G-9666)*
Lansing Eastside Gateway .... G 517 894-6125
  Lansing *(G-9858)*
Latino Press Inc .... G 313 361-3000
  Detroit *(G-4378)*
Leader Publications LLC .... D 269 683-2100
  Niles *(G-12141)*
Livonia Observer .... G 734 525-4657
  Livonia *(G-10288)*
Macdonald Publications Inc .... F 989 875-4151
  Ithaca *(G-8793)*
Macomb 4x4 LLC .... G 586 744-0335
  Chesterfield *(G-2907)*
Macomb County Cougars .... G 586 231-5543
  Clinton Township *(G-3287)*
Macomb North Clinton Advisor .... G 586 731-1000
  Shelby Township *(G-15266)*
Michigan Chronicle Pubg Co .... E 313 963-5522
  Detroit *(G-4447)*
Michigan Front Page LLC .... G 313 963-5522
  Detroit *(G-4450)*
Michigan Maps Inc .... G 231 264-6800
  Elk Rapids *(G-5027)*
Michigan Metro Times Inc .... C 313 961-4060
  Ferndale *(G-5568)*
Michigan Peaceworks .... F 734 262-4283
  Ann Arbor *(G-572)*
Michigan Peaceworks .... G 734 232-3079
  Ann Arbor *(G-573)*
Michigan Peaceworks .... G 734 764-1717
  Ann Arbor *(G-574)*
Michigan Snowmobiler Inc .... G 231 536-2371
  East Jordan *(G-4876)*
Milliman Communications Inc .... G 517 327-8407
  Lansing *(G-9778)*
Mining Jrnl Bsness Offc-Dtrial .... E 906 228-2500
  Marquette *(G-11036)*
Mlive Com .... G 517 768-4984
  Jackson *(G-8966)*
Mlivecom .... G 231 725-6343
  Muskegon *(G-11875)*
Monroe Atellos 19 .... G 734 682-3467
  Monroe *(G-11561)*
Monroe Evening News .... F 734 242-1100
  Monroe *(G-11563)*
Monroe Publishing Company .... D 734 242-1100
  Monroe *(G-11565)*

PRODUCT SECTION

PUMPS

Monroe Success Vlc .... G 734 682-3720
  Monroe *(G-11566)*
Moormann Printing Inc .... G 269 423-2411
  Decatur *(G-3950)*
Morning Star .... G 989 755-2660
  Saginaw *(G-14704)*
Morning Star Publishing Co .... F 989 463-6071
  Alma *(G-248)*
Morning Star Publishing Co .... C 989 779-6000
  Alma *(G-249)*
Morning Star Publishing Co .... G 989 779-6000
  Alma *(G-250)*
Morning Star Publishing Co .... E 989 732-5125
  Pontiac *(G-13399)*
Mt Pleasant Buyers Guide .... G 989 779-6000
  Mount Pleasant *(G-11720)*
Ndex .... F 248 432-9000
  Farmington Hills *(G-5332)*
Neumann Enterprises Inc .... G 906 293-8122
  Newberry *(G-12094)*
New Monitor .... G 248 439-1863
  Hazel Park *(G-7836)*
News One Inc .... E 231 798-4669
  Norton Shores *(G-12316)*
North Country Sun Inc .... G 906 932-3530
  Ironwood *(G-8768)*
Northland Publishers Inc .... F 906 265-9927
  Iron River *(G-8751)*
Npi Wireless .... G 231 922-9273
  Traverse City *(G-16776)*
Oakland Sail Inc .... F 248 370-4268
  Rochester *(G-13915)*
Old Mission Gazette .... G 231 590-4715
  Traverse City *(G-16780)*
Page One Inc .... E 810 724-0254
  Imlay City *(G-8642)*
Paxton Media Group LLC .... D 269 429-2400
  Saint Joseph *(G-14953)*
Pet Patrol of Macomb-Oakland .... G 586 675-2451
  Warren *(G-17961)*
Pontiac Properties LLC .... G 248 639-4360
  Pontiac *(G-13409)*
Prescott Inc .... G 517 515-0007
  Lansing *(G-9785)*
Psa Courier C .... G 810 234-8770
  Flint *(G-5750)*
Qp Acquisition 2 Inc .... A 248 594-7432
  Southfield *(G-15685)*
Real Ink Publishing LLC .... G 313 766-1344
  Van Buren Twp *(G-17550)*
Real Times Media LLC .... G 313 963-8100
  Detroit *(G-4556)*
Relationship Examiner .... G 256 653-7374
  Niles *(G-12162)*
Reminder Shopping Guide Inc .... G 269 427-7474
  Bangor *(G-1131)*
Reporter Papers Inc .... G 734 429-5428
  Saline *(G-15036)*
River Raisin Publications .... G 517 486-2400
  Blissfield *(G-1775)*
Rockman & Sons Publishing LLC .... F 810 750-6011
  Fenton *(G-5499)*
Rockman Communications Inc .... E 810 433-6800
  Fenton *(G-5500)*
Sault Tribe News .... F 906 632-6398
  Sault Sainte Marie *(G-15099)*
Sherman Publications Inc .... G 248 627-4332
  Ortonville *(G-12752)*
Silent Observer .... F 269 966-3550
  Battle Creek *(G-1295)*
Springer Publishing Co Inc .... G 586 939-6800
  Warren *(G-18023)*
State News Inc .... D 517 295-1680
  East Lansing *(G-4909)*
Sun Daily .... G 248 842-2925
  Orchard Lake *(G-12721)*
Textiss USA .... G 310 909-6062
  Three Rivers *(G-16587)*
The Sun .... G 800 878-6397
  Jackson *(G-9020)*
Three Rivers Commercial News .... E 269 279-7488
  Three Rivers *(G-16588)*
Times and Titles .... G 616 828-5640
  Ada *(G-36)*
Times Herald Company .... D 810 985-7171
  Port Huron *(G-13532)*
Times Indicator Publications .... G 231 924-4400
  Fremont *(G-6056)*
Univesity Michigan-Dearborn .... F 313 593-5428
  Dearborn *(G-3906)*

USA Today Advertising .... G 248 680-6530
  Troy *(G-17417)*
W Vbh .... G 269 927-1527
  Benton Harbor *(G-1601)*
Wall Street Journal Gate A 20 .... G 734 941-4139
  Detroit *(G-4674)*
Washtenaw Voice .... G 734 677-5405
  Ann Arbor *(G-715)*
White Lake Beacon Inc .... G 231 894-5356
  Whitehall *(G-18512)*
Wings of Sturgis LLC .... G 269 689-9326
  Sturgis *(G-16330)*
Wochen-Post .... G 248 641-9944
  Warren *(G-18069)*
Yale Expositor .... G 810 387-2300
  Yale *(G-18921)*
Ypsinewscom .... G 734 487-8109
  Ypsilanti *(G-18987)*
Z & A News .... G 231 747-6232
  Muskegon *(G-11952)*

PUBLISHING & PRINTING: Pamphlets

Rbc Ministries .... B 616 942-6770
  Grand Rapids *(G-7142)*

PUBLISHING & PRINTING: Posters

Star Design Metro Detroit LLC .... E 734 740-0189
  Livonia *(G-10419)*

PUBLISHING & PRINTING: Shopping News

Advance BCI Inc .... D 616 669-1366
  Grand Rapids *(G-6431)*
Flashes Publishers Inc .... E 269 673-2141
  Holland *(G-8035)*
G L Nelson Inc .... G 630 682-5958
  Indian River *(G-8653)*
Great Northern Publishing Inc .... D 810 648-4000
  Sandusky *(G-15059)*
J-Ad Graphics Inc .... F 269 965-3955
  Battle Creek *(G-1243)*
Macdonald Publications Inc .... F 989 875-4151
  Ithaca *(G-8793)*
Morning Star Publishing Co .... G 989 779-6000
  Alma *(G-250)*
S G Publications Inc .... F 517 676-5100
  Mason *(G-11151)*

PUBLISHING & PRINTING: Textbooks

Remnant Publications Inc .... E 517 279-1304
  Coldwater *(G-3450)*
Zonya Health International .... G 517 467-6995
  Onsted *(G-12708)*

PUBLISHING & PRINTING: Trade Journals

Lansing Nwsppers In Edcatn Inc .... G 517 377-1000
  Lansing *(G-9862)*
SPD America LLC .... G 734 709-7624
  Pinckney *(G-13056)*

PUBLISHING & PRINTING: Yearbooks

Walsworth Publishing Co Inc .... E 269 428-2054
  Saint Joseph *(G-14973)*

PULLEYS: Metal

Motion Systems Incorporated .... F 586 774-5666
  Warren *(G-17935)*

PULLEYS: Power Transmission

Auburn Hills Manufacturing Inc .... C 313 758-2000
  Auburn Hills *(G-800)*
Engineered Machined Pdts Inc .... B 906 786-8404
  Escanaba *(G-5069)*

PULP MILLS

Fibrek Inc .... C 906 864-9125
  Menominee *(G-11235)*
Fibrek US Inc .... F 906 864-9125
  Menominee *(G-11237)*
Forest Blake Products Inc .... G 231 879-3913
  Fife Lake *(G-5606)*
Forest Corullo Products Corp .... E 906 667-0275
  Bessemer *(G-1649)*
Friedland Industries Inc .... E 517 482-3000
  Lansing *(G-9701)*

General Mill Supply Company .... E 248 668-0800
  Wixom *(G-18667)*
Great Lakes Paper Stock Corp .... D 586 779-1310
  Roseville *(G-14416)*
Mshiikenh Rnwble Resources LLC .... G 231 818-9353
  Cheboygan *(G-2792)*
V & M Corporation .... E 248 591-6580
  Royal Oak *(G-14588)*
Verso Paper Holding LLC .... F 906 779-3200
  Quinnesec *(G-13678)*

PULP MILLS: Chemical & Semichemical Processing

Fibrek Recycling US Inc .... D 906 863-8137
  Menominee *(G-11236)*
Upcycle Polymers LLC .... G 248 446-8750
  Howell *(G-8537)*

PULP MILLS: Mechanical & Recycling Processing

Gfl Envronmental Real Property .... E 888 877-4996
  Southfield *(G-15575)*
Midland Cmpnding Cnsulting Inc .... G 989 495-9367
  Midland *(G-11392)*
Recycling Rizzo Services LLC .... G 248 541-4020
  Royal Oak *(G-14574)*
United For Srvval St Jsphs Rcy .... G 269 983-3820
  Saint Joseph *(G-14969)*

PULVERIZED EARTH

D J McQuestion & Sons Inc .... F 231 768-4403
  Leroy *(G-10005)*

PUMICE: Abrasives

Acme Holding Company .... E 586 759-3332
  Warren *(G-17690)*

PUMPS

Advanced Pumps Intl LLC .... G 734 230-5013
  Monroe *(G-11522)*
Automationsupply365 LLC .... G 248 912-7354
  Auburn Hills *(G-805)*
Benecor Inc .... F 248 437-4437
  Fenton *(G-5457)*
Cpj Company Inc .... E 616 784-6355
  Comstock Park *(G-3598)*
David Brown Union Pumps Co Pay .... G 269 966-4702
  Battle Creek *(G-1214)*
Dover Pmps Prcess Sltons Sgmen .... B 616 241-1611
  Grand Rapids *(G-6657)*
Emp Advanced Development LLC .... G 906 789-7497
  Escanaba *(G-5067)*
Engineered Machined Pdts Inc .... B 906 786-8404
  Escanaba *(G-5069)*
Flowserve US Inc .... G 989 496-3897
  Midland *(G-11364)*
Fluid Automation Inc .... E 248 669-3717
  Wixom *(G-18663)*
Ford Motor Company .... A 734 484-8626
  Ypsilanti *(G-18947)*
Gast Manufacturing Inc .... B 269 926-6171
  Benton Harbor *(G-1551)*
General Motors LLC .... F 989 894-7210
  Bay City *(G-1359)*
H & R Industries Inc .... F 616 247-1165
  Grand Rapids *(G-6798)*
Independent Mfg Solutions Corp .... E 248 960-3550
  Wixom *(G-18684)*
Jacksons Industrial Mfg .... F 616 531-1820
  Grand Rapids *(G-6859)*
Kerr Pump and Supply Inc .... E 248 543-3880
  Oak Park *(G-12621)*
Kristus Inc .... F 269 321-3330
  Scotts *(G-15132)*
Ksb Dubric Inc .... E 616 784-6355
  Comstock Park *(G-3618)*
M P Pumps Inc .... D 586 293-8240
  Fraser *(G-5959)*
Melling Tool Co .... B 517 787-8172
  Jackson *(G-8951)*
Nortek Air Solutions LLC .... D 616 738-7148
  Holland *(G-8156)*
Plasma-Tec Inc .... E 616 455-2593
  Holland *(G-8166)*
Ramparts LLC .... C 616 656-2250
  Kentwood *(G-9474)*

Employee Codes: A=Over 500 employees, B=251-500
C=101-250, D=51-100, E=20-50, F=10-19, G=3-9

PUMPS

PRODUCT SECTION

Sales Driven Ltd Liability Co ....E 269 254-8497
 Kalamazoo *(G-9327)*
Sames Kremlin Inc ....G 734 979-0100
 Plymouth *(G-13293)*
Sloan Transportation Pdts Inc ....E 616 395-5600
 Holland *(G-8197)*
SPX Flow Us LLC ....F 269 966-4782
 Battle Creek *(G-1298)*
Tramec Sloan LLC ....E 616 395-5600
 Holland *(G-8224)*
Vogel Engineering Inc ....G 231 821-2125
 Holton *(G-8342)*
Walbro LLC ....D 989 872-2131
 Cass City *(G-2622)*

PUMPS & PARTS: Indl

Becktold Enterprises Inc ....G 269 349-3656
 Kalamazoo *(G-9133)*
Clyde Union (holdings) Inc ....B 269 966-4600
 Battle Creek *(G-1210)*
Fluid Systems Engineering Inc ....E 586 790-8880
 Clinton Township *(G-3242)*
Global Pump Company LLC ....G 810 653-4828
 Davison *(G-3785)*
Hydra-Tech Inc ....G 586 232-4479
 Macomb *(G-10604)*
Jetech Inc ....E 269 965-6311
 Battle Creek *(G-1246)*
K and K Machine Tools Inc ....G 586 463-1177
 Clinton Township *(G-3269)*
Neptune Chemical Pump Company ....C 215 699-8700
 Grand Rapids *(G-7039)*
Process Systems Inc ....E 586 757-5711
 Warren *(G-17977)*
QEd Envmtl Systems Inc ....D 734 995-2547
 Dexter *(G-4751)*

PUMPS & PUMPING EQPT REPAIR SVCS

Arrow Motor & Pump Inc ....E 734 285-7860
 Wyandotte *(G-18807)*
Core Electric Company Inc ....F 313 382-7140
 Melvindale *(G-11198)*
Douglas Corp ....E 517 767-4112
 Tekonsha *(G-16522)*
Global Pump Company LLC ....G 810 653-4828
 Davison *(G-3785)*
Kennedy Industries Inc ....D 248 684-1200
 Wixom *(G-18691)*
Phillips Service Inds Inc ....F 734 853-5000
 Ann Arbor *(G-610)*
Process Systems Inc ....E 586 757-5711
 Warren *(G-17977)*
PSI Hydraulics ....E 734 261-4160
 Plymouth *(G-13271)*
PSI Repair Services Inc ....C 734 853-5000
 Livonia *(G-10375)*

PUMPS & PUMPING EQPT WHOLESALERS

Arrow Motor & Pump Inc ....E 734 285-7860
 Wyandotte *(G-18807)*
Automationsupply365 LLC ....G 248 912-2455
 Auburn Hills *(G-805)*
Clyde Union (holdings) Inc ....B 269 966-4600
 Battle Creek *(G-1210)*
Commercial Welding Company Inc ....G 269 782-5252
 Dowagiac *(G-4778)*
Global Pump Company LLC ....G 810 653-4828
 Davison *(G-3785)*
Process Systems Inc ....E 586 757-5711
 Warren *(G-17977)*

PUMPS, HEAT: Electric

Nortek Air Solutions LLC ....D 616 738-7148
 Holland *(G-8156)*

PUMPS: Domestic, Water Or Sump

Sales Driven Services LLC ....G 586 854-9494
 Rochester *(G-13926)*
Shellback Manufacturing Co ....G 248 544-0500
 Hazel Park *(G-7842)*
Vent-Rite Valve Corp ....E 269 925-8812
 Benton Harbor *(G-1598)*
Water Department ....F 313 943-2307
 Dearborn *(G-3915)*

PUMPS: Fluid Power

Ace Controls Inc ....C 248 476-0213
 Farmington Hills *(G-5158)*
Armstrong Fluid Handling Inc ....D 269 279-3600
 Three Rivers *(G-16565)*
Kennedy Industries Inc ....D 248 684-1200
 Wixom *(G-18691)*
Oilgear Company ....D 231 929-1660
 Traverse City *(G-16778)*

PUMPS: Gasoline, Measuring Or Dispensing

Bpc Acquisition Company ....C 231 798-1310
 Norton Shores *(G-12345)*

PUMPS: Hydraulic Power Transfer

Bucher Hydraulics Inc ....C 616 458-1306
 Grand Rapids *(G-6528)*
Bucher Hydraulics Inc ....G 231 652-2773
 Newaygo *(G-12078)*
Eaton Aerospace LLC ....B 616 949-1090
 Grand Rapids *(G-6663)*

PUMPS: Measuring & Dispensing

Accurate Gauge & Mfg Inc ....D 248 853-2400
 Rochester Hills *(G-13940)*
Automationsupply365 LLC ....G 248 912-7354
 Auburn Hills *(G-805)*
Dispense Technologies LLC ....G 248 486-6244
 Brighton *(G-1975)*
Edge Industries Inc ....G 616 453-5458
 Grand Rapids *(G-6665)*
Neptune Chemical Pump Company ....C 215 699-8700
 Grand Rapids *(G-7039)*
Nordson Corporation ....D 734 459-8600
 Wixom *(G-18721)*

PUMPS: Oil Well & Field

Preyde LLC ....G 517 333-1600
 Lansing *(G-9883)*

PUMPS: Vacuum, Exc Laboratory

Gast Manufacturing Inc ....B 269 926-6171
 Benton Harbor *(G-1551)*

PUNCHES: Forming & Stamping

Air-Hydraulics Inc ....F 517 787-9444
 Jackson *(G-8806)*
Commercial Mfg & Assembly Inc ....E 616 847-9980
 Grand Haven *(G-6287)*
M Curry Corporation ....E 989 777-7950
 Saginaw *(G-14685)*
Metal Punch Corporation ....F 231 775-8391
 Cadillac *(G-2346)*

PUPPETS & MARIONETTES

Mannetron ....F 269 962-3475
 Battle Creek *(G-1271)*

PURIFICATION & DUST COLLECTION EQPT

Air Solution Company ....F 800 819-2869
 Farmington Hills *(G-5164)*
Airhug LLC ....G 734 262-0431
 Canton *(G-2432)*
Custom Service & Design Inc ....F 248 340-9005
 Auburn Hills *(G-855)*
Depierre Industries Inc ....E 517 263-5781
 Adrian *(G-59)*
Paul Horn and Associates ....G 248 682-8490
 Waterford *(G-18148)*

PURSES: Women's

Sandusky Concrete & Supply ....G 810 648-2627
 Sandusky *(G-15066)*

RACE CAR OWNERS

Roush Enterprises Inc ....C 734 805-4400
 Farmington *(G-5145)*

RACE TRACK OPERATION

Sports Resorts International ....E 989 725-8354
 Owosso *(G-12858)*

RACETRACKS

Roush Industries Inc ....G 734 779-7016
 Livonia *(G-10392)*

RACEWAYS

Austin Company ....F 269 329-1181
 Portage *(G-13544)*
Merritt Raceway LLC ....G 231 590-4431
 Mancelona *(G-10876)*

RACKS: Display

Associated Rack Corporation ....G 616 554-6004
 Grand Rapids *(G-6477)*
Fmmb LLC ....E 313 372-7420
 Detroit *(G-4239)*
J H P Inc ....G 248 588-0110
 Madison Heights *(G-10750)*
National Intgrated Systems Inc ....F 734 927-3030
 Wixom *(G-18716)*
Royal Design & Manufacturing ....D 248 588-0110
 Madison Heights *(G-10821)*
Shield Material Handling Inc ....D 248 418-0986
 Auburn Hills *(G-1032)*
Tarpon Industries Inc ....E 810 364-7421
 Marysville *(G-11105)*

RACKS: Garment, Exc Wood

L & S Products LLC ....G 517 238-4645
 Coldwater *(G-3442)*

RACKS: Pallet, Exc Wood

F F Industries ....G 313 291-7600
 Taylor *(G-16416)*
Sfi Acquisition Inc ....E 248 471-1500
 Farmington Hills *(G-5377)*

RACKS: Trash, Metal Rack

Apex Rack and Coating Co ....E 616 530-6811
 Grandville *(G-7365)*
Returnable Packaging Corp ....F 586 206-8050
 Clinton Township *(G-3336)*
Saline Manufacturing Inc ....F 586 294-4701
 Roseville *(G-14475)*

RADAR SYSTEMS & EQPT

Micromet Corp ....G 231 885-1047
 Bloomfield Hills *(G-1837)*
Valeo Radar Systems Inc ....E 248 340-3126
 Auburn Hills *(G-1078)*

RADIO & TELEVISION COMMUNICATIONS EQUIPMENT

Balogh Inc ....G 810 360-0182
 Brighton *(G-1948)*
Bob Allison Enterprises ....G 248 540-8467
 Bloomfield Hills *(G-1804)*
C & A Wholesale Inc ....G 248 302-3555
 Detroit *(G-4082)*
Emag Technologies Inc ....F 734 996-3624
 Ann Arbor *(G-472)*
EMR Corp ....G 810 376-4710
 Deckerville *(G-3954)*
Hughes Network Systems LLC ....G 301 428-5500
 Southfield *(G-15594)*
Information Stn Specialists ....F 616 772-2300
 Zeeland *(G-19046)*
Lor Manufacturing Co Inc ....G 989 644-2581
 Weidman *(G-18254)*
Mobimogul Inc ....G 313 575-2795
 Southfield *(G-15661)*
Moody Bible Inst of Chicago ....G 616 772-7300
 Zeeland *(G-19057)*
Motorola Solutions Inc ....G 517 321-6655
 Lansing *(G-9780)*
Parvox Technology ....G 231 924-4366
 Fremont *(G-6051)*
Riprap ....G 734 945-0892
 Durand *(G-4846)*
Rml Industries LLC ....G 616 935-3839
 Grand Haven *(G-6355)*
Sound Productions Entrmt ....F 989 386-2221
 Clare *(G-2998)*
Spectrum Wireless (usa) Inc ....G 586 693-7525
 Saint Clair Shores *(G-14886)*

PRODUCT SECTION

RADIO & TELEVISION REPAIR
Bluewater Tech Group Inc................G...... 231 885-2600
  Mesick (G-11269)
Bluewater Tech Group Inc................G...... 616 656-9380
  Grand Rapids (G-6517)
M10 Group Holding Company..........G...... 248 356-4399
  Southfield (G-15639)

RADIO BROADCASTING & COMMUNICATIONS EQPT
Washtenaw Communications Inc.......G...... 734 662-7138
  Ann Arbor (G-714)

RADIO BROADCASTING STATIONS
Bob Allison Enterprises......................G...... 248 540-8467
  Bloomfield Hills (G-1804)

RADIO COMMUNICATIONS: Carrier Eqpt
Cohda Wireless America LLC.............G...... 248 513-2105
  Ann Arbor (G-432)

RADIO PRODUCERS
Childrens Bible Hour Inc....................F...... 616 647-4500
  Grand Rapids (G-6568)
Rbc Ministries..................................B...... 616 942-6770
  Grand Rapids (G-7142)

RADIO RECEIVER NETWORKS
Parvox Technology............................G...... 231 924-4366
  Fremont (G-6052)
Startech-Solutions LLC....................G...... 248 419-0650
  West Bloomfield (G-18316)

RADIO REPAIR & INSTALLATION SVCS
Intaglio LLC....................................E...... 616 243-3300
  Grand Rapids (G-6848)
Washtenaw Communications Inc.......G...... 734 662-7138
  Ann Arbor (G-714)

RADIO, TELEVISION & CONSUMER ELECTRONICS STORES: Eqpt, NEC
Uv Partners Inc.................................G...... 888 277-2596
  Grand Haven (G-6376)

RADIO, TV & CONSUMER ELEC STORES: High Fidelity Stereo Eqpt
Rebeats..F...... 989 463-4757
  Alma (G-254)

RADIO, TV & CONSUMER ELEC STORES: Radios, Receiver Type
Chrouch Communications Inc............G...... 231 972-0339
  Mecosta (G-11190)

RAIL & STRUCTURAL SHAPES: Aluminum rail & structural shapes
Brooks & Perkins Inc........................D...... 231 775-2229
  Cadillac (G-2318)

RAILINGS: Prefabricated, Metal
Aquarius Recreational Products..........G...... 586 469-4600
  Harrison Township (G-7687)

RAILROAD CAR RENTING & LEASING SVCS
Andersons Inc..................................G...... 989 642-5291
  Hemlock (G-7849)

RAILROAD CAR REPAIR SVCS
Escanaba and Lk Superior RR Co......G...... 906 786-9399
  Escanaba (G-5070)

RAILROAD CARGO LOADING & UNLOADING SVCS
Gb Dynamics Inc..............................G...... 313 400-3570
  Port Huron (G-13479)

RAILROAD CROSSINGS: Steel Or Iron
Crown Steel Rail Co..........................G...... 248 593-7100
  West Bloomfield (G-18274)

RAILROAD EQPT
Amsted Rail Company Inc..................G...... 517 568-4161
  Homer (G-8344)
Hj Manufacturing Inc........................F...... 906 233-1500
  Escanaba (G-5076)
Mitchell Equipment Corporation........E...... 734 529-3400
  Dundee (G-4832)
Rescar Inc..G...... 517 486-3130
  Blissfield (G-1774)
Trinity Equipment Co........................G...... 231 719-1813
  Muskegon (G-11937)

RAILROAD EQPT & SPLYS WHOLESALERS
Crown Steel Rail Co..........................G...... 248 593-7100
  West Bloomfield (G-18274)
Hj Manufacturing Inc........................F...... 906 233-1500
  Escanaba (G-5076)

RAILROAD EQPT: Brakes, Air & Vacuum
Gorang Industries Inc........................G...... 248 651-9010
  Rochester (G-13902)

RAILROAD EQPT: Cars & Eqpt, Dining
Arcosa Shoring Products Inc.............D...... 517 741-4300
  Union City (G-17490)
McL Jasco Inc...................................G...... 313 294-7414
  Detroit (G-4424)
Trinity Industries Inc........................G...... 586 285-1692
  Fraser (G-6005)

RAILROAD EQPT: Cars & Eqpt, Train, Freight Or Passenger
Union Tank Car Company..................G...... 989 615-3054
  Midland (G-11420)

RAILROAD EQPT: Cars, Rebuilt
Delta Tube & Fabricating Corp...........E...... 248 634-8267
  Holly (G-8267)

RAILROAD EQPT: Street Cars & Eqpt
Peaker Services Inc..........................D...... 248 437-4174
  Brighton (G-2049)

RAILROAD MAINTENANCE & REPAIR SVCS
Jackson Pandrol Inc..........................E...... 231 843-3431
  Ludington (G-10542)

RAILROAD RELATED EQPT
Independent Machine Co Inc.............E...... 906 428-4524
  Escanaba (G-5077)
Jackson Pandrol Inc..........................E...... 231 843-3431
  Ludington (G-10542)

RAILROADS: Long Haul
Straits Corporation............................F...... 989 684-5088
  Tawas City (G-16368)

RAILS: Steel Or Iron
Champlain Specialty Metals Inc.........E...... 269 926-7241
  Benton Harbor (G-1539)
Paich Railworks Inc..........................G...... 734 397-2424
  Van Buren Twp (G-17546)
Versa Handling Co............................G...... 313 491-0500
  Sterling Heights (G-16222)

RAMPS: Prefabricated Metal
Alumiramp Inc..................................F...... 517 639-8777
  Quincy (G-13661)
Vets Access LLC..............................G...... 810 639-2222
  Flushing (G-5815)

RAZORS, RAZOR BLADES
Art of Shaving - Fl LLC....................G...... 248 649-5872
  Troy (G-16954)
Edgewell Personal Care Company......G...... 866 462-8669
  Taylor (G-16409)

REAL ESTATE AGENCIES & BROKERS
Developmental Services Inc...............G...... 313 653-1185
  Detroit (G-4173)
Diversified Prof Rlty Svcs..................G...... 313 215-1840
  Hazel Park (G-7824)
Help-U-Sell RE Big Rapids................F...... 231 796-3966
  Big Rapids (G-1677)

REAL ESTATE AGENCIES: Leasing & Rentals
Eggers Excavating LLC.....................F...... 989 695-5205
  Freeland (G-6022)
Melix Services Inc............................G...... 248 387-9303
  Hamtramck (G-7612)
Michigan East Side Sales LLC...........G...... 989 354-6867
  Alpena (G-302)

REAL ESTATE AGENCIES: Residential
Power Property Solutions LLC...........G...... 734 306-0299
  Wayne (G-18232)

REAL ESTATE AGENTS & MANAGERS
917 Chittock Street LLC...................F...... 866 945-0269
  Lansing (G-9798)
FTC LLC..F...... 313 622-1583
  Novi (G-12420)
Gemini Plastics Inc..........................C...... 989 658-8557
  Ubly (G-17476)
Great Lakes Publishing Inc................G...... 517 647-4444
  Portland (G-13638)
Kingston Prperty Advisers Corp........G...... 248 825-9657
  Redford (G-13741)
Marshalls Crossing............................G...... 810 639-4740
  Montrose (G-11606)
Trinity Holding Inc...........................F...... 517 787-3100
  Jackson (G-9024)

REAL ESTATE INVESTMENT TRUSTS
Chain Industries Inc..........................E...... 248 348-7722
  Wixom (G-18631)
Sun Communities Inc........................A...... 248 208-2500
  Southfield (G-15711)

REAL ESTATE LISTING SVCS
Catylist Inc......................................G...... 734 973-3185
  Ann Arbor (G-416)
Miller Investment Company LLC.......F...... 231 933-3233
  Traverse City (G-16759)

REAL ESTATE OPERATORS, EXC DEVELOPERS: Commercial/Indl Bldg
Ace Vending Service Inc...................F...... 616 243-7983
  Grand Rapids (G-6422)
G & G Wood & Supply Inc.................E...... 586 293-0450
  Roseville (G-14408)
Honhart Mid-Nite Black Co...............F...... 248 588-1515
  Troy (G-17148)
Mirkwood Properties Inc...................G...... 586 727-3363
  Richmond (G-13842)
National Credit Corporation..............F...... 734 459-8100
  West Bloomfield (G-18302)
Vectech Pharmaceutical Cons...........F...... 248 478-5820
  Brighton (G-2092)

RECEIVERS: Radio Communications
South Lyon Bb Inc............................G...... 248 437-8000
  South Lyon (G-15458)

RECLAIMED RUBBER: Reworked By Manufacturing Process
Green Polymeric Materials Inc..........E...... 313 933-7390
  Detroit (G-4280)

RECORD BLANKS: Phonographic
Archer Record Pressing Co................G...... 313 365-9545
  Detroit (G-4025)

RECORDING & PLAYBACK HEADS: Magnetic
World Magnetics Company LLC........E...... 231 946-3800
  Traverse City (G-16882)

Employee Codes: A=Over 500 employees, B=251-500
C=101-250, D=51-100, E=20-50, F=10-19, G=3-9

RECORDS & TAPES: Prerecorded

RECORDS & TAPES: Prerecorded

Amber Engine LLC .... F 313 373-4751
Detroit *(G-4009)*
Faulkner Tech Inc .... G 517 857-4241
Charlotte *(G-2755)*
Geeks and Gurus Inc .... G 313 549-2796
Farmington Hills *(G-5249)*
Logic Quantum LLC .... F 734 930-0009
Ann Arbor *(G-554)*
Megapixel Ideas LLC .... G 616 307-5220
Belmont *(G-1514)*
Passenger Inc .... G 323 556-5400
Howell *(G-8490)*
Summit Training Source Inc .... E 800 842-0466
Grand Rapids *(G-7233)*

RECREATIONAL & SPORTING CAMPS

School of Rock Canton .... G 734 845-7448
Canton *(G-2521)*

RECREATIONAL SPORTING EQPT REPAIR SVCS

Riverfront Cycle Inc .... G 517 482-8585
Lansing *(G-9888)*

RECREATIONAL VEHICLE DEALERS

Irish Boat Shop Inc .... E 231 547-9967
Charlevoix *(G-2719)*
Stromberg-Carlson Products Inc .... F 231 947-8600
Traverse City *(G-16843)*

RECREATIONAL VEHICLE REPAIRS

Lumberjack Shack Inc .... G 810 724-7230
Imlay City *(G-8640)*

RECREATIONAL VEHICLE: Wholesalers

Michigan East Side Sales LLC .... G 989 354-6867
Alpena *(G-302)*

RECTIFIERS: Mercury Arc, Electrical

Optimystic Enterprises Inc .... G 269 695-7741
Buchanan *(G-2200)*

RECYCLING: Paper

Anchor Recycling Inc .... G 810 984-5545
Port Huron *(G-13439)*
Bpv LLC .... E 616 281-4502
Byron Center *(G-2261)*
Infinity Recycling LLC .... F 248 939-2563
Clinton Township *(G-3258)*
Recycling Concepts W Mich Inc .... D 616 942-8888
Grand Rapids *(G-7146)*
Southast Berrien Cnty Landfill .... E 269 695-2500
Niles *(G-12168)*
Star Paper Converters .... G 313 254-9833
Ecorse *(G-4986)*

REELS: Fiber, Textile, Made From Purchased Materials

Rokan Corp .... G 810 735-9170
Linden *(G-10070)*

REFINERS & SMELTERS: Aluminum

Constellium Automotive USA LLC .... C 734 879-9700
Van Buren Twp *(G-17519)*
Wls Processing LLC .... G 313 378-5743
Detroit *(G-4686)*

REFINERS & SMELTERS: Copper

PM Power Group Inc .... G 906 885-7100
White Pine *(G-18487)*
Specialty Steel Treating Inc .... E 586 293-5355
Fraser *(G-5998)*

REFINERS & SMELTERS: Gold, Secondary

Johnson Matthey North Amer Inc .... G 734 946-9856
Taylor *(G-16432)*

REFINERS & SMELTERS: Nonferrous Metal

All Care Team Inc .... G 313 533-7057
Detroit *(G-3999)*
Allied Metals Corp .... E 248 680-2400
Auburn Hills *(G-778)*
Alloying Surfaces Inc .... G 248 524-9200
Troy *(G-16927)*
Aluminum Blanking Co Inc .... D 248 338-4422
Pontiac *(G-13349)*
Astech Inc .... E 989 823-7211
Vassar *(G-17577)*
Benteler Auto Holland Inc .... C 616 396-6591
Holland *(G-7974)*
Cannon-Muskegon Corporation .... G 231 755-1681
Norton Shores *(G-12284)*
Colfran Industrial Sales Inc .... G 734 595-8920
Romulus *(G-14262)*
Eutectic Engineering Co Inc .... E 313 892-2248
Bloomfield Hills *(G-1820)*
Fpt Schlafer .... E 313 925-8200
Detroit *(G-4245)*
Franklin Iron & Metal Co Inc .... F 269 968-6111
Battle Creek *(G-1233)*
Franklin Metal Trading Corp .... E 616 374-7171
Lake Odessa *(G-9575)*
Friedland Industries Inc .... E 517 482-3000
Lansing *(G-9701)*
Great Lakes Paper Stock Corp .... E 586 779-1310
Roseville *(G-14416)*
Intern Metals and Energy .... G 248 765-7747
Jackson *(G-8909)*
Lorbec Metals - Usa Ltd .... E 810 736-0961
Flint *(G-5728)*
Louis Padnos Iron and Metal Co .... G 517 372-6600
Lansing *(G-9773)*
Martin Bros Mill Fndry Sup Co .... G 269 927-1355
Benton Harbor *(G-1567)*
Metropolitan Alloys Corp .... E 313 366-4443
Detroit *(G-4438)*
Milfab Systems LLC .... F 248 391-8100
Lake Orion *(G-9619)*
National Galvanizing LP .... A 734 243-1882
Monroe *(G-11567)*
Oerlikon Metco (us) Inc .... E 248 288-0027
Troy *(G-17287)*
Revstone Industries LLC .... G 248 351-1000
Troy *(G-17331)*
Rolled Alloys Inc .... D 734 847-0561
Temperance *(G-16547)*
Sandvik Inc .... G 989 345-6138
West Branch *(G-18339)*
Schneider Iron & Metal Inc .... G 906 774-0644
Iron Mountain *(G-8732)*
Shoreline Recycling & Supply .... G 231 722-6081
Muskegon *(G-11920)*
Strong Steel Products LLC .... F 313 267-3300
Detroit *(G-4613)*
V & M Corporation .... E 248 591-6580
Royal Oak *(G-14588)*

REFINERS & SMELTERS: Zinc, Primary, Including Zinc Residue

Arco Alloys Corp .... E 313 871-2680
Detroit *(G-4026)*

REFINERS & SMELTERS: Zinc, Secondary

Arco Alloys Corp .... E 313 871-2680
Detroit *(G-4026)*
Huron Valley Steel Corporation .... C 734 479-3500
Trenton *(G-16889)*
National Zinc Processors Inc .... F 269 926-1161
Benton Harbor *(G-1577)*

REFINING LUBRICATING OILS & GREASES, NEC

Fuel Source LLC .... G 313 506-0448
Grosse Ile *(G-7522)*
Lube-Tech Inc .... G 269 329-1269
Portage *(G-13580)*
Quaker Houghton Pa Inc .... E 248 265-7745
Troy *(G-17325)*

REFINING: Petroleum

Admiral .... G 989 684-8314
Bay City *(G-1317)*
Admiral .... G 989 835-9160
Midland *(G-11317)*
Bertoldi Oil Service Inc .... G 906 774-1707
Iron Mountain *(G-8717)*
Ees Coke Battery LLC .... F 313 235-4000
Ann Arbor *(G-468)*
Hitachi America Ltd .... G 248 477-5400
Farmington Hills *(G-5261)*
Marysville Hydrocarbons LLC .... G 586 445-2300
Warren *(G-17918)*
Merritt Energy .... G 231 723-6587
Manistee *(G-10908)*
Miller Exploration Company .... F 231 941-0004
Traverse City *(G-16758)*
Mpc .... G 313 297-6386
Detroit *(G-4468)*
Stop & Go Transportation LLC .... G 313 346-7114
Washington *(G-18087)*

REFLECTIVE ROAD MARKERS, WHOLESALE

Carrier & Gable Inc .... E 248 477-8700
Farmington Hills *(G-5199)*

REFRACTORIES: Castable, Clay

Mono Ceramics Inc .... E 269 925-0212
Benton Harbor *(G-1575)*

REFRACTORIES: Cement

Chase Nedrow Manufacturing Inc .... E 248 669-9886
Wixom *(G-18633)*
Stellar Materials Intl LLC .... E 561 504-3924
Whitmore Lake *(G-18546)*

REFRACTORIES: Clay

Alco Products LLC .... E 313 823-7500
Detroit *(G-3996)*
Alpha Resources LLC .... E 269 465-5559
Stevensville *(G-16239)*
Harbisonwalker Intl Inc .... G 231 689-6641
White Cloud *(G-18442)*
Marshall-Gruber Company LLC .... F 248 353-4100
Southfield *(G-15647)*

REFRACTORIES: Graphite, Carbon Or Ceramic Bond

Ajf Inc .... E 734 753-4410
New Boston *(G-11998)*

REFRACTORIES: Nonclay

Cerco Inc .... E 734 362-8664
Brownstown Twp *(G-2153)*
Harbisonwalker Intl Inc .... G 231 689-6641
White Cloud *(G-18442)*
Midwest Product Spc Inc .... G 231 767-9942
Muskegon *(G-11874)*
Nedrow Refractories Co .... D 248 669-2500
Wixom *(G-18718)*
Rex Materials Inc .... E 517 223-3787
Howell *(G-8509)*
Thermbond Refractory Solutions .... G 561 330-9300
Whitmore Lake *(G-18547)*

REFRACTORIES: Tile & Brick, Exc Plastic

Schad Boiler Setting Company .... D 313 273-2235
Detroit *(G-4584)*

REFRIGERATION & HEATING EQUIPMENT

Blissfield Manufacturing Co .... C 517 486-2121
Blissfield *(G-1761)*
Dimplex Thermal Solutions Inc .... C 269 349-6800
Kalamazoo *(G-9169)*
Dynasty Mechanical Inc .... G 313 506-5504
Detroit *(G-4197)*
Enersave LLC .... F 616 785-1800
Grand Rapids *(G-6678)*
Exclusive Heating & Coolg Comp .... G 248 219-9528
Detroit *(G-4221)*
Fantastic Sams Hair Salon .... G 713 861-2500
Madison Heights *(G-10726)*
Fluid Chillers Inc .... E 517 484-9190
Lansing *(G-9837)*
Glastender Inc .... B 989 752-4275
Saginaw *(G-14652)*
Hussmann Corporation .... G 248 668-0790
Wixom *(G-18683)*
Johnson Controls Inc .... G 313 842-3479
Van Buren Twp *(G-17531)*

Kraftube Inc .... C 231 832-5562
  Reed City (G-13793)
Lenox Block Club Assn .... G 313 823-0941
  Detroit (G-4389)
Lenox Pharmacy LLC .... G 313 971-5928
  Lenox (G-10000)
Mahle Behr Industy America Lp .... D 616 647-3490
  Belmont (G-1513)
Manitwoc Fdsrvice Cmpanies LLC .... G 989 773-7981
  Mount Pleasant (G-11710)
Microtemp Fluid Systems LLC .... G 248 703-5056
  Farmington Hills (G-5320)
National Aircraft Service Inc .... E 517 423-7589
  Tecumseh (G-16509)
Nicole Lennox Lmt .... G 248 509-4433
  Waterford (G-18141)
Nortek Inc .... G 616 719-5588
  Grand Rapids (G-7047)
Opti Temp Inc .... E 231 946-2931
  Traverse City (G-16783)
Ostrander Company Inc .... G 248 646-6680
  Madison Heights (G-10793)
Quality Draft Systems LLC .... G 616 259-9852
  Grand Rapids (G-7127)
Riedel USA Inc .... G 734 595-9820
  Kalamazoo (G-9318)
Scientemp Corp .... E 517 263-6020
  Adrian (G-94)
TI Group Auto Systems LLC .... B 248 296-8000
  Auburn Hills (G-1055)
TMI Climate Solutions Inc .... C 810 694-5763
  Holly (G-8297)
Trane Inc .... G 616 222-3750
  Wyoming (G-18913)
Trane US Inc .... E 800 245-3964
  Flint (G-5780)
Trane US Inc .... G 734 367-0700
  Livonia (G-10441)
Trane US Inc .... D 734 452-2000
  Livonia (G-10442)
Trane US Inc .... G 616 971-1400
  Grand Rapids (G-7269)

REFRIGERATION EQPT & SPLYS WHOLESALERS

Young Supply Company .... E 313 875-3280
  Detroit (G-4699)

REFRIGERATION EQPT & SPLYS, WHOLESALE: Beverage Coolers

Keglove LLC .... G 616 610-7289
  Holland (G-8110)
Pepsi-Cola Metro Btlg Co Inc .... G 989 755-1020
  Saginaw (G-14727)

REFRIGERATION EQPT & SPLYS, WHOLESALE: Ice Cream Cabinets

Taylor Freezer Michigan Inc .... F 616 453-0531
  Grand Rapids (G-7249)

REFRIGERATION EQPT: Complete

Chrysler & Koppin Company .... F 313 491-7100
  Grosse Pointe (G-7527)
Cooler King LLC .... G 248 789-3699
  Westland (G-18361)
Crystal Ice Resource LLC .... G 616 560-8102
  Ravenna (G-13688)
Forma-Kool Manufacturing Inc .... E 586 949-4813
  Chesterfield (G-2884)
La Rosa Refrigeration & Eqp Co .... E 313 368-6620
  Detroit (G-4371)
Refrigeration Research Inc .... G 989 773-7540
  Mount Pleasant (G-11736)
Refrigeration Research Inc .... D 810 227-1151
  Brighton (G-2064)
Su-Tec Inc .... F 248 852-4711
  Rochester Hills (G-14122)

REFRIGERATION REPAIR SVCS

Refrigeration Concepts Inc .... E 616 785-7335
  Comstock Park (G-3643)

REFRIGERATION SVC & REPAIR

Mechanic Evltion Crtfction For .... G 231 734-3483
  Evart (G-5126)

REFUSE SYSTEMS

Automotive Plastics Recycling .... F 810 767-3800
  Flint (G-5648)
Daily Recycling of Michigan .... G 734 654-9800
  Carleton (G-2550)
Strong Steel Products LLC .... F 313 267-3300
  Detroit (G-4613)
URS Energy & Construction Inc .... C 989 642-4190
  Hemlock (G-7857)
V & M Corporation .... E 248 591-6580
  Royal Oak (G-14588)

REGISTERS: Air, Metal

Hart & Cooley LLC .... C 616 656-8200
  Grand Rapids (G-6805)

REGULATORS: Power

H H Barnum Co .... G 248 486-5982
  Brighton (G-2007)
Hear Clear Inc .... G 734 525-8467
  Saline (G-15020)

REGULATORS: Transmission & Distribution Voltage

D & W Square LLC .... G 313 493-4970
  Detroit (G-4116)

REHABILITATION CENTER, OUTPATIENT TREATMENT

Hackley Health Ventures Inc .... G 231 728-5720
  Muskegon (G-11834)

RELAYS & SWITCHES: Indl, Electric

Bay Electronics Inc .... E 586 296-0900
  Roseville (G-14379)
Edon Controls Inc .... G 248 280-0420
  Troy (G-17078)
Stoneridge Control Devices Inc .... G 248 489-9300
  Novi (G-12545)

RELAYS: Control Circuit, Ind

Flextronics Automotive USA Inc .... D 248 853-5724
  Coopersville (G-3686)
Sine Systems Corporation .... C 586 465-3131
  Clinton Township (G-3359)
Wired Technologies LLC .... G 313 800-1611
  Livonia (G-10477)

RELAYS: Electronic Usage

Mercury Displacement Inds Inc .... D 269 663-8574
  Edwardsburg (G-5009)

RELIGIOUS SPLYS WHOLESALERS

Faith Alive Christn Resources .... E 800 333-8300
  Grand Rapids (G-6698)
Michigan Church Supply Co Inc .... F 810 686-8877
  Mount Morris (G-11674)
Religious Communications LLC .... G 313 822-3361
  Detroit (G-4563)

REMOVERS & CLEANERS

Jbr Junk Removal LLC .... G 248 818-3471
  Sterling Heights (G-16055)
Power Property Solutions LLC .... G 734 306-0299
  Wayne (G-18232)
Top Quality Cleaning LLC .... F 810 493-4211
  Flint (G-5779)

REMOVERS: Paint

General Chemical Corporation .... G 248 587-5600
  Brighton (G-1998)
MPS Trading Group LLC .... E 313 841-7588
  Farmington Hills (G-5327)
Rap Products Inc .... G 989 893-5583
  Bay City (G-1394)

RENTAL SVCS: Audio-Visual Eqpt & Sply

Bluewater Tech Group Inc .... C 248 356-4399
  Wixom (G-18624)
City Animation Co .... E 248 589-0600
  Troy (G-17012)
City Animation Co .... F 989 743-3458
  Corunna (G-3706)

RENTAL SVCS: Bicycle

Riverfront Cycle Inc .... G 517 482-8585
  Lansing (G-9888)

RENTAL SVCS: Business Machine & Electronic Eqpt

M & M Typewriter Service Inc .... G 734 995-4033
  Ann Arbor (G-558)

RENTAL SVCS: Invalid Splys

Wright & Filippis LLC .... F 248 336-8460
  Detroit (G-3968)

RENTAL SVCS: Oil Eqpt

Great Lakes Wellhead Inc .... G 231 943-9100
  Grawn (G-7451)

RENTAL SVCS: Pleasure Boat

Pontoon Rentals .... G 906 387-2685
  Munising (G-11753)

RENTAL SVCS: Pop-Up Camper

Rough Road Trucking LLC .... G 231 645-3355
  Kalkaska (G-9402)

RENTAL SVCS: Propane Eqpt

U S Distributing Inc .... E 248 646-0550
  Birmingham (G-1755)

RENTAL SVCS: Sign

Amor Sign Studios Inc .... E 231 723-8361
  Manistee (G-10893)
Poco Inc .... E 313 220-6752
  Canton (G-2509)

RENTAL SVCS: Sound & Lighting Eqpt

Band-Ayd Systems Intl Inc .... F 586 294-8851
  Madison Heights (G-10677)

RENTAL SVCS: Tent & Tarpaulin

Ace Canvas & Tent Co .... F 313 842-3011
  Troy (G-16903)
Dial Tent & Awning Co .... F 989 793-0741
  Saginaw (G-14639)

RENTAL SVCS: Trailer

Premier Custom Trailers LLC .... F 877 327-0888
  Schoolcraft (G-15127)

RENTAL SVCS: Tuxedo

Baryames Tux Shop Inc .... G 517 349-6555
  Okemos (G-12659)
Celebrations .... G 906 482-4946
  Hancock (G-7617)
Demmem Enterprises LLC .... F 810 564-9500
  Clio (G-3396)

RENTAL: Portable Toilet

Ameriform Acquisition Co LLC .... B 231 733-2725
  Rochester Hills (G-13947)

REPAIR SERVICES, NEC

Creative Repair Solutions LLC .... G 586 615-1517
  Macomb (G-10586)

REPEATERS: Passive

Premier Passivation Services .... G 269 432-2244
  Colon (G-3490)

RESEARCH, DEV & TESTING SVCS, COMM: Chem Lab, Exc Testing

Advanced Urethanes Inc .... G 313 273-5705
  Detroit (G-3988)

RESEARCH, DEVELOPMENT & TEST SVCS, COMM: Research, Exc Lab

RESEARCH, DEVELOPMENT & TEST SVCS, COMM: Research, Exc Lab

Imra America Inc .... E 734 669-7377
  Ann Arbor (G-525)
Lenderink Inc .... F 616 887-8257
  Belmont (G-1511)

RESEARCH, DEVELOPMENT & TESTING SVCS, COMM: Natural Resource

Alternative Fuel Tech LLC .... G 313 417-9212
  Grosse Pointe Park (G-7545)
Ovshinsky Technologies LLC .... G 248 752-2344
  Bloomfield Hills (G-1846)

RESEARCH, DEVELOPMENT & TESTING SVCS, COMM: Research Lab

Applied Molecules LLC .... G 810 355-1475
  Dexter (G-4724)
Certainteed LLC .... G 517 787-1737
  Jackson (G-8838)
Niowave Inc .... G 517 999-3475
  Lansing (G-9722)

RESEARCH, DEVELOPMENT & TESTING SVCS, COMMERCIAL: Business

Emag Technologies Inc .... F 734 996-3624
  Ann Arbor (G-472)

RESEARCH, DEVELOPMENT & TESTING SVCS, COMMERCIAL: Food

Sunopta Ingredients Inc .... E 502 587-7999
  Schoolcraft (G-15129)

RESEARCH, DEVELOPMENT & TESTING SVCS, COMMERCIAL: Medical

Carlson Technology Inc .... G 248 476-0013
  Livonia (G-10147)
Clark-Mxr Inc .... E 734 426-2803
  Dexter (G-4731)
Millendo Transactionsub Inc .... G 734 845-9300
  Ann Arbor (G-578)

RESEARCH, DEVELOPMENT & TESTING SVCS, COMMERCIAL: Physical

Hygratek LLC .... G 847 962-6180
  Ann Arbor (G-520)
Xg Sciences Inc .... G 517 703-1110
  Lansing (G-9908)

RESEARCH, DEVELOPMENT SVCS, COMMERCIAL: Indl Lab

Stm Power Inc .... E 734 214-1448
  Ann Arbor (G-666)

RESEARCH, DVLPT & TEST SVCS, COMM: Mkt Analysis or Research

Ampm Inc .... E 989 837-8800
  Midland (G-11321)
Elm International Inc .... G 517 332-4900
  Okemos (G-12665)

RESEARCH, DVLPT & TESTING SVCS, COMM: Survey, Mktg

Nits Solutions Inc .... F 248 231-2267
  Novi (G-12488)

RESIDENTIAL REMODELERS

W S Townsend Company .... G 517 393-7300
  Lansing (G-9903)

RESINS: Custom Compound Purchased

Aci Plastics Inc .... E 810 767-3800
  Flint (G-5636)
Aci Plastics Inc .... E 810 767-3800
  Flint (G-5637)
Alumilite Corporation .... F 269 488-4000
  Galesburg (G-6073)
Amplas Compounding LLC .... F 586 795-2555
  Sterling Heights (G-15931)

Azon Usa Inc .... F 269 385-5942
  Kalamazoo (G-9129)
Azon Usa Inc .... G 269 385-5942
  Kalamazoo (G-9130)
Cass Polymers .... E 517 543-7510
  Charlotte (G-2739)
Clean Tech Inc .... G 734 529-2475
  Dundee (G-4812)
Clean Tech Inc .... G 734 455-3600
  Plymouth (G-13147)
Clean Tech Inc .... E 734 529-2475
  Dundee (G-4811)
Eco Bio Plastics Midland Inc .... F 989 496-1934
  Midland (G-11360)
Georgia-Pacific LLC .... G 989 348-7275
  Grayling (G-7461)
Material Difference Tech LLC .... F 888 818-1283
  Macomb (G-10614)
Nano Materials & Processes Inc .... G 248 529-3873
  Milford (G-11475)
Portland Plastics Co .... F 517 647-4115
  Portland (G-13640)
Rhe-Tech LLC .... G 517 223-4874
  Fowlerville (G-5855)
Rhe-Tech LLC .... G 734 769-3558
  Whitmore Lake (G-18545)
Ssb Holdings Inc .... G 586 755-1660
  Rochester Hills (G-14117)

RESISTORS

Touchstone Systems & Svcs Inc .... G 616 532-0060
  Wyoming (G-18912)

RESPIRATORS

Air Supply Inc .... G 586 773-6600
  Warren (G-17694)

RESTAURANT EQPT REPAIR SVCS

Auction Masters .... G 586 576-7777
  Oak Park (G-12593)

RESTAURANT EQPT: Food Wagons

Jays Famous Fd Hotdogs & More .... G 313 648-7225
  Detroit (G-4336)
Mr ES Eatery LLC .... G 313 502-9256
  Sterling Heights (G-16104)
Perfect Dish LLC .... G 734 272-9871
  Taylor (G-16456)
Robbie DS LLC .... G 989 992-0153
  Saginaw (G-14738)
Sista Roles Cuisine LLC .... G 313 588-1142
  Detroit (G-4596)
Wright Time Foods LLc .... G 810 835-9219
  Flint (G-5797)

RESTAURANT EQPT: Sheet Metal

Dts Enterprises Inc .... E 231 599-3123
  Ellsworth (G-5035)
M C M Fixture Company Inc .... G 248 547-9280
  Hazel Park (G-7830)
Quality Stainless Mfg Co .... F 248 546-4141
  Madison Heights (G-10815)

RESTAURANTS: Delicatessen

Marshalls Trail Inc .... F 231 436-5082
  Mackinaw City (G-10568)

RESTAURANTS: Fast Food

Osowet Collections Inc .... G 313 844-8171
  Detroit (G-4501)

RESTAURANTS:Full Svc, American

CHI Co/Tabor Hill Winery .... D 269 422-1161
  Buchanan (G-2192)
Corner Brewery LLC .... E 734 480-2739
  Ypsilanti (G-18934)
Detroit Rvrtown Brwing Cmpay L .... C 313 877-9205
  Detroit (G-4163)

RESTAURANTS:Full Svc, Family

Sweetheart Bakery of Michigan .... F 586 795-1660
  Harper Woods (G-7673)

RESTAURANTS:Full Svc, Family, Chain

Big Boy Restaurants Intl LLC .... C 586 759-6000
  Southfield (G-15507)
Big Boy Restaurants Intl LLC .... D 586 263-6220
  Clinton Township (G-3184)

RESTAURANTS:Full Svc, Family, Independent

Century Lanes Inc .... D 616 392-7086
  Holland (G-7992)
Crew Family Rest & Bky LLC .... G 269 337-9800
  Kalamazoo (G-9158)
Krzysiak Family Restaurant .... D 989 894-5531
  Bay City (G-1372)

RESTAURANTS:Full Svc, Mexican

Gvb Group-La Fiesta LLC .... F 231 843-7600
  Montague (G-11597)

RESTAURANTS:Full Svc, Steak

Mountain Town Stn Brew Pub LLC .... D 989 775-2337
  Mount Pleasant (G-11719)

RESTAURANTS:Limited Svc, Coffee Shop

Coffee Beanery Ltd .... E 810 733-1020
  Flushing (G-5805)
Good Sense Coffee LLC .... G 810 355-2349
  Brighton (G-2003)
Two Cups Coffee Co LLC .... F 616 953-0534
  Holland (G-8232)

RESTAURANTS:Limited Svc, Drive-In

Deans Ice Cream Inc .... F 269 685-6641
  Plainwell (G-13075)

RESTAURANTS:Limited Svc, Fast-Food, Independent

MHR Investments Inc .... F 989 832-5395
  Midland (G-11388)

RESTAURANTS:Limited Svc, Ice Cream Stands Or Dairy Bars

Calder Bros Dairy Inc .... E 313 381-8858
  Lincoln Park (G-10044)
Cold Stone Creamery .... F 313 886-4020
  Grosse Pointe Park (G-7550)
Moomers Homemade Ice Cream LLC .... F 231 941-4122
  Traverse City (G-16763)
Original Murdicks Fudge Co .... G 906 847-3530
  Mackinac Island (G-10567)
Rays Ice Cream Co Inc .... F 248 549-5256
  Royal Oak (G-14573)

RESTAURANTS:Limited Svc, Pizza

Beagios Franchises Inc .... G 989 635-7173
  Marlette (G-10979)
Kring Pizza Inc .... G 586 792-0049
  Harrison Township (G-7704)

RESTAURANTS:Limited Svc, Pizzeria, Chain

Dominos Pizza LLC .... C 734 930-3030
  Ann Arbor (G-456)

RESTAURANTS:Limited Svc, Pizzeria, Independent

Klaus Nixdorf .... G 269 429-3259
  Stevensville (G-16256)

RESTAURANTS:Limited Svc, Sandwiches & Submarines Shop

Subway Restaurant .... G 248 625-5739
  Clarkston (G-3070)

RESTAURANTS:Limited Svc, Snack Shop

Cherry Republic Inc .... D 231 334-3150
  Glen Arbor (G-6209)

PRODUCT SECTION

RESTAURANTS: Ltd Svc, Ice Cream, Soft Drink/Fountain Stands

Dunkin Donuts & Baskin-Robbins ....F 989 835-8412
  Midland *(G-11357)*
Guernsey Dairy Stores Inc ....C 248 349-1466
  Northville *(G-12227)*

RETAIL BAKERY: Bagels

New York Bagel Baking Co ....F 248 548-2580
  Ferndale *(G-5572)*

RETAIL BAKERY: Bread

Avalon Intl New Ctr LLC ....E 313 308-0150
  Detroit *(G-4033)*
Great Harvest Bread Co ....F 586 566-9500
  Shelby Township *(G-15231)*
Julian Brothers Inc ....F 248 588-0280
  Clawson *(G-3100)*
Mackenzies Bakery ....E 269 343-8440
  Kalamazoo *(G-9263)*
New Yasmeen Detroit Inc ....F 313 582-6035
  Dearborn *(G-3876)*
Stone House Bread LLC ....E 231 933-8864
  Traverse City *(G-16841)*

RETAIL BAKERY: Cakes

Annas Kitchen LLC ....G 248 499-4774
  Detroit *(G-4022)*
Cake Connection Tc LLC ....G 231 943-3531
  Traverse City *(G-16637)*
G M Paris Bakery Inc ....G 734 425-2060
  Livonia *(G-10217)*
Home Bakery ....G 248 651-4830
  Rochester *(G-13904)*
Klaus Nixdorf ....G 269 429-3259
  Stevensville *(G-16256)*
Sweet & Sweeter Inc ....G 586 977-9338
  Sterling Heights *(G-16198)*

RETAIL BAKERY: Cookies

Carlson Enterprises Inc ....G 248 656-1442
  Rochester Hills *(G-13972)*
Looney Baker of Livonia Inc ....F 734 425-8569
  Livonia *(G-10292)*

RETAIL BAKERY: Doughnuts

Dunkin Donuts & Baskin-Robbins ......F 989 835-8412
  Midland *(G-11357)*
Sweetwaters Donut Mill ....G 269 979-1944
  Battle Creek *(G-1303)*
Yates Cider Mill Inc ....G 248 651-8300
  Rochester Hills *(G-14149)*

RETAIL BAKERY: Pastries

Josefs French Pastry Shop Co ....G 313 881-5710
  Grosse Pointe Woods *(G-7568)*

RETAIL BAKERY: Pretzels

American Gourmet Snacks LLC ....G 989 892-4856
  Essexville *(G-5108)*
B & B Pretzels Inc ....F 248 358-1655
  Southfield *(G-15500)*
Karemor Inc ....G 517 323-3042
  Lansing *(G-9770)*
Pop Daddy Popcorn LLC ....F 734 550-9900
  Whitmore Lake *(G-18543)*

RETAIL FIREPLACE STORES

Hearth-N-Home Inc ....F 517 625-5586
  Owosso *(G-12837)*

RETAIL LUMBER YARDS

B & B Heartwoods Inc ....G 734 332-9525
  Ann Arbor *(G-394)*
Barnes Wood Works ....G 269 599-3479
  Portage *(G-13546)*
Carson Wood Specialties Inc ....G 269 465-6091
  Stevensville *(G-16242)*
Cedar Log Lbr Millersburg Inc ....F 989 733-2676
  Millersburg *(G-11497)*
Lumber & Truss Inc ....F 810 664-7290
  Lapeer *(G-9945)*
Prells Saw Mill Inc ....E 989 734-2939
  Hawks *(G-7815)*

Standale Lumber and Supply Co ....D 616 530-8200
  Grandville *(G-7419)*
Thomas J Moyle Jr Incorporated ....F 906 482-3000
  Houghton *(G-8393)*

RETAIL STORES, NEC

Be A Boss Not A Bossy Bih LLC ....G 734 833-8106
  Wayne *(G-18216)*
Cheboygan Cnty Hbtat For Hmnit ......G 231 597-4663
  Cheboygan *(G-2783)*

RETAIL STORES: Alcoholic Beverage Making Eqpt & Splys

Shirt Traveler ....G 800 403-4117
  Swartz Creek *(G-16358)*

RETAIL STORES: Aquarium Splys

Aqua Systems Inc ....G 810 346-2525
  Brown City *(G-2133)*

RETAIL STORES: Art & Architectural Splys

Shop Makarios LLC ....F 800 479-0032
  Byron Center *(G-2295)*

RETAIL STORES: Artificial Limbs

Springer Prsthtic Orthtic Svcs ....G 517 337-0300
  Lansing *(G-9896)*

RETAIL STORES: Audio-Visual Eqpt & Splys

Pro-Motion Tech Group LLC ....D 248 668-3100
  Wixom *(G-18735)*
Silent Call Corporation ....F 248 673-7353
  Waterford *(G-18164)*
Spire Integrated Systems Inc ....E 248 544-0072
  Troy *(G-17367)*

RETAIL STORES: Awnings

Advanced Inc ....G 231 938-2233
  Acme *(G-2)*
Patio Land Mfg Inc ....G 586 758-5660
  Warren *(G-17959)*

RETAIL STORES: Banners

Bannergalaxycom LLC ....F 231 941-8200
  Traverse City *(G-16612)*
Shields & Shields Enterprises ....G 269 345-7744
  Kalamazoo *(G-9332)*

RETAIL STORES: Batteries, Non-Automotive

Zcs Interconnect LLC ....G 616 399-8614
  Zeeland *(G-19094)*

RETAIL STORES: Business Machines & Eqpt

3dm Source Inc ....F 616 647-9513
  Grand Rapids *(G-6405)*
Jackpine Press Incorporated ....F 231 723-8344
  Manistee *(G-10903)*

RETAIL STORES: Canvas Prdts

Belle Isle Awning Co Inc ....E 586 294-6050
  Warren *(G-17730)*

RETAIL STORES: Christmas Lights & Decorations

Bronner Display Sign Advg Inc ....C 989 652-9931
  Frankenmuth *(G-5860)*

RETAIL STORES: Cleaning Eqpt & Splys

Great Lakes Allied LLC ....G 231 924-5794
  White Cloud *(G-18441)*
Photodon LLC ....F 847 377-1185
  Traverse City *(G-16791)*
Truly Free LLC ....E 231 252-4571
  Traverse City *(G-16868)*

RETAIL STORES: Convalescent Eqpt & Splys

Wright & Filippis LLC ....F 586 756-4020
  Warren *(G-18073)*

RETAIL STORES: Cosmetics

Amour Your Body LLC ....G 586 846-3100
  Clinton Township *(G-3168)*
Tetra Corporation ....E 401 529-1630
  Eaton Rapids *(G-4972)*

RETAIL STORES: Electronic Parts & Eqpt

Ghi Electronics LLC ....G 248 397-8856
  Madison Heights *(G-10731)*
Major One Electronics LLC ....G 313 652-3723
  Detroit *(G-4418)*
Static Controls Corp ....E 248 926-4400
  Wixom *(G-18757)*
Z & R Electric Service Inc ....G 906 774-0468
  Iron Mountain *(G-8738)*

RETAIL STORES: Farm Eqpt & Splys

Glenn Knochel ....G 989 684-7869
  Kawkawlin *(G-9415)*
Hutson Inc ....C 517 655-4606
  Williamston *(G-18573)*
Wells Equipment Sales Inc ....F 517 542-2376
  Litchfield *(G-10087)*

RETAIL STORES: Farm Machinery, NEC

Gillisons Var Fabrication Inc ....E 231 882-5921
  Benzonia *(G-1614)*

RETAIL STORES: Fire Extinguishers

Con-De Manufacturing Inc ....G 269 651-3756
  Sturgis *(G-16285)*
Exquise Inc ....G 248 220-9048
  Detroit *(G-4223)*
Gallagher Fire Equipment Co ....E 248 477-1540
  Livonia *(G-10219)*

RETAIL STORES: Flags

American Flag & Banner Company ...G 248 288-3010
  Clawson *(G-3085)*

RETAIL STORES: Foam & Foam Prdts

Envirolite LLC ....F 248 792-3184
  Troy *(G-17094)*
Envirolite LLC ....D 888 222-2191
  Coldwater *(G-3432)*

RETAIL STORES: Hair Care Prdts

Art of Shaving - Fl LLC ....G 248 649-5872
  Troy *(G-16954)*

RETAIL STORES: Hearing Aids

Bieri Hearing Instruments Inc ....G 989 793-2701
  Saginaw *(G-14616)*

RETAIL STORES: Hospital Eqpt & Splys

Metro Medical Eqp Mfg Inc ....E 734 522-8400
  Livonia *(G-10313)*
Wright & Filippis LLC ....F 248 336-8460
  Detroit *(G-3968)*

RETAIL STORES: Maps & Charts

Metro Graphic Arts Inc ....F 616 245-2271
  Grand Rapids *(G-6982)*

RETAIL STORES: Medical Apparatus & Splys

Bay Home Medical and Rehab Inc ....F 231 933-1200
  Grandville *(G-7366)*
Prosthetic Center Inc ....G 517 372-7007
  Dimondale *(G-4764)*
Signal Medical Corporation ....F 810 364-7070
  Marysville *(G-11099)*
Sobaks Pharmacy Inc ....G 989 725-2785
  Owosso *(G-12856)*

RETAIL STORES: Mobile Telephones & Eqpt

Elite Bus Svcs Exec Stffing In ....G 734 956-4550
  Bloomfield Hills *(G-1818)*

Employee Codes: A=Over 500 employees, B=251-500
C=101-250, D=51-100, E=20-50, F=10-19, G=3-9

RETAIL STORES: Monuments, Finished To Custom Order

Arnets Inc .... F 734 665-3650
　Ann Arbor (G-379)
Muskegon Monument & Stone Co ..... G 231 722-2730
　Muskegon (G-11882)
Steinbrecher Stone Corp .... G 906 563-5852
　Norway (G-12357)
Superior Monuments Co .... G 231 728-2211
　Muskegon (G-11928)

RETAIL STORES: Motors, Electric

Kalamazoo Electric Motor Inc .... G 269 345-7802
　Kalamazoo (G-9238)
Nieboer Electric Inc .... F 231 924-0960
　Fremont (G-6049)

RETAIL STORES: Orthopedic & Prosthesis Applications

American Prosthetic Institute .... G 517 349-3130
　Okemos (G-12655)
Becker Orthopedic Appliance Co .... D 248 588-7480
　Troy (G-16970)
Binson-Becker Inc .... F 888 246-7667
　Center Line (G-2680)
Biopro Inc .... E 810 982-7777
　Port Huron (G-13458)
Bremer Prosthetic Design Inc .... G 810 733-3375
　Flint (G-5660)
Greater Lansing Orthotic Clini .... G 517 337-0856
　Lansing (G-9845)
Hanger Prsthetcs & Ortho Inc .... G 517 394-5850
　Lansing (G-9851)
Mount Clemens Orthopedic Appls ...... G 586 463-3600
　Clinton Township (G-3305)
Northwest Orthotics-Prosthetic .... G 248 477-1443
　Novi (G-12491)
Oakland Orthopedic Appls Inc .... F 989 893-7544
　Bay City (G-1384)
Wright & Filippis LLC .... F 313 386-3330
　Lincoln Park (G-10058)
Wright & Filippis LLC .... F 517 484-2624
　Lansing (G-9906)

RETAIL STORES: Perfumes & Colognes

Border Line Rich Clothing LLC .... G 586 267-5251
　Clinton Township (G-3188)

RETAIL STORES: Pet Splys

Go Cat Feather Toys .... G 517 543-7519
　Charlotte (G-2759)
Ruff Life LLC .... G 231 347-1214
　Petoskey (G-13022)
Studtmans Stuff .... G 269 673-3126
　Allegan (G-183)

RETAIL STORES: Picture Frames, Ready Made

Touched By Cupids .... G 313 704-6334
　Detroit (G-4640)

RETAIL STORES: Posters

Fairfax Prints Ltd .... G 517 321-5590
　Lansing (G-9696)

RETAIL STORES: Religious Goods

Lighthouse Direct Buy LLC .... G 313 340-1850
　Detroit (G-4398)

RETAIL STORES: Rock & Stone Specimens

Lewiston Sand & Gravel Inc .... G 989 786-2742
　Lewiston (G-10023)

RETAIL STORES: Rubber Stamps

Rubber Stamps Unlimited Inc .... F 734 451-7300
　Plymouth (G-13291)

RETAIL STORES: Safety Splys & Eqpt

Rock Redi Mix LLC .... G 989 754-4861
　Saginaw (G-14739)
Skyline Window Cleaning Inc .... E 616 895-4143
　Allendale (G-228)

RETAIL STORES: Sales Barns

K-Mar Structures LLC .... F 231 924-3895
　Fremont (G-6046)

RETAIL STORES: Sauna Eqpt & Splys

Ahs LLC .... G 888 355-3050
　Holland (G-7959)

RETAIL STORES: Swimming Pools, Above Ground

Affordable Pool and Spa Inc .... F 810 422-5058
　Burton (G-2225)
Hotwater Works Inc .... G 517 364-8827
　Lansing (G-9852)

RETAIL STORES: Technical Aids For The Handicapped

Assistive Technology Mich Inc .... G 248 348-7161
　Novi (G-12367)

RETAIL STORES: Telephone Eqpt & Systems

Npi Wireless .... E 231 922-9273
　Traverse City (G-16776)

RETAIL STORES: Water Purification Eqpt

Douglas Water Conditioning .... F 248 363-8383
　Waterford (G-18117)
Michigan Soft Water of Centr .... D 517 339-0722
　East Lansing (G-4903)
Reynolds Water Conditioning Co .... F 248 888-5000
　Farmington Hills (G-5368)
Village & Cntry Wtr Trtmnt Inc .... F 810 632-7880
　Hartland (G-7773)

RETAIL STORES: Welding Splys

Andritz Metals USA Inc .... G 248 305-2969
　Novi (G-12363)
Bakers Gas and Welding Sups .... G 517 539-5047
　Jackson (G-8821)
Cramblits Welding LLC .... G 906 932-3773
　Ironwood (G-8760)
Greenville Trck Wldg Sups LLC .... F 616 754-6120
　Greenville (G-7489)
Linde Gas & Equipment Inc .... G 734 282-3830
　Wyandotte (G-18829)
North East Fabrication Co Inc .... F 517 849-8090
　Jonesville (G-9095)

RETORTS: Indl, Smelting, Etc

Larsen Service Inc .... G 810 374-6132
　Otisville (G-12782)

RETREADING MATERIALS: Tire

Great Lakes Tire LLC .... F 586 939-7000
　Warren (G-17836)

REUPHOLSTERY & FURNITURE REPAIR

Kindel Furniture Company LLC .... C 616 243-3676
　Grand Rapids (G-6896)

REUPHOLSTERY SVCS

Grand Traverse Canvas Works .... F 231 947-3140
　Traverse City (G-16697)
Gustafson Smoked Fish .... G 906 292-5424
　Moran (G-11609)
Homespun Furniture Inc .... F 734 284-6277
　Riverview (G-13874)
Parkway Drapery & Uphl Co Inc .... F 734 779-1300
　Livonia (G-10360)
Quality Awning Shops Inc .... G 517 882-2491
　Lansing (G-9885)

RHEOSTATS: Electronic

Mark Griessel .... G 810 378-6060
　Melvin (G-11195)

RIVETS: Metal

Aero Auto Stud Specialists Inc .... E 248 437-2171
　Whitmore Lake (G-18517)
Detroit Tubular Rivet Inc .... E 734 282-7979
　Wyandotte (G-18816)

Gage Bilt Inc .... E 586 226-1500
　Clinton Township (G-3247)
H & L Tool Company Inc .... E 248 585-7474
　Madison Heights (G-10736)
Securit Metal Products Co .... E 269 782-7076
　Dowagiac (G-4796)
Smsg LLC .... G 517 787-9447
　Jackson (G-9011)

ROBOTS, SERVICES OR NOVELTY, WHOLESALE

Mannetron .... F 269 962-3475
　Battle Creek (G-1271)

ROBOTS: Assembly Line

Allfi Robotics Inc .... G 586 248-1198
　Wixom (G-18604)
Applied & Integrated Mfg Inc .... G 248 370-8950
　Auburn Hills (G-793)
Becker Robotic Equipment Corp .... G 470 249-7880
　Orion (G-12724)
Bobier Tool Supply Inc .... E 810 732-4030
　Flint (G-5658)
Borneman & Peterson Inc .... F 810 744-1890
　Flint (G-5659)
Classic Systems LLC .... C 248 588-2738
　Troy (G-17015)
Fanuc America Corporation .... B 248 377-7000
　Rochester Hills (G-14009)
Global Electronics Limited .... F 248 353-0100
　Bloomfield Hills (G-1823)
Industrial Atomated Design LLC .... F 810 648-9200
　Sandusky (G-15060)
Industrial Service Tech Inc .... F 616 247-1033
　Grand Rapids (G-6843)
International Robot Support .... G 586 783-8000
　Mount Clemens (G-11643)
Jax Services LLC .... G 586 703-3212
　Warren (G-17883)
Krush Industries Inc .... G 248 238-2296
　Taylor (G-16434)
Onyx Manufacturing Inc .... G 248 687-8611
　Rochester Hills (G-14075)
R Concepts Incorporated .... G 810 632-4857
　Howell (G-8505)
Reese Inspection Services LLC .... F 248 481-3598
　Auburn Hills (G-1017)
Thyssenkrupp System Engrg .... C 248 340-8000
　Auburn Hills (G-1052)
Universal TI Eqp & Cntrls Inc .... D 586 268-4380
　Sterling Heights (G-16217)
Vdl Steelweld Usa LLC .... E 248 781-8141
　Troy (G-17433)
Yaskawa America Inc .... G 248 668-8800
　Rochester Hills (G-14148)

ROBOTS: Indl Spraying, Painting, Etc

Innovation Tech LLC .... F 248 797-2686
　Wixom (G-18685)
Parker Engineering Amer Co Ltd .... F 734 326-7630
　Westland (G-18403)

ROD & BAR Aluminum

Kaiser Aluminum Fab Pdts LLC .... G 269 250-8400
　Kalamazoo (G-9235)
Petschke Manufacturing Company ..... F 586 463-0841
　Mount Clemens (G-11652)

RODS: Steel & Iron, Made In Steel Mills

Arcanum Steel Technologies Inc .... E 630 715-4899
　Grand Rapids (G-6467)
Ivan Doverspike .... G 313 579-3000
　Detroit (G-4328)
Mueller Industrial Realty Co .... G 810 987-7770
　Port Huron (G-13507)

RODS: Welding

Eureka Welding Alloys Inc .... E 248 588-0001
　Madison Heights (G-10724)

ROLL FORMED SHAPES: Custom

A & B Welding & Fabricating .... G 231 733-2661
　Muskegon (G-11759)
Dlh Rollform LLC .... G 586 231-0507
　Wales (G-17627)

Mig Molding LLC .... G 810 724-7400
  Imlay City (G-8641)
Porter Steel & Welding Company .... F 231 733-4495
  Muskegon (G-11897)
Raq LLC .... F 313 473-7271
  Pontiac (G-13412)
Shape Corp .... G 616 846-8700
  Spring Lake (G-15851)

ROLLING MACHINERY: Steel

D-N-S Industries Inc .... E 586 465-2444
  Clinton Township (G-3216)

ROLLING MILL MACHINERY

Burger Iron Co .... G 330 794-1716
  Grand Rapids (G-6534)
Dalton Industries LLC .... E 248 673-0755
  Waterford (G-18114)
Enprotech Industrial Tech LLC .... E 216 883-3220
  Lansing (G-9695)
Feed - Lease Corp .... E 248 377-0000
  Auburn Hills (G-896)
Fontijne Grotnes Inc .... E 269 262-4700
  Niles (G-12129)
Novi Tool & Machine Company .... F 313 532-0900
  Redford (G-13749)
Perfecto Industries Inc .... E 989 732-2941
  Gaylord (G-6154)
Rod Chomper Inc .... F 616 392-9677
  Holland (G-8182)

ROLLING MILL ROLLS: Cast Iron

Vx-LLC .... F 734 854-8700
  Lambertville (G-9655)

ROLLS & BLANKETS, PRINTERS': Rubber Or Rubberized Fabric

Day International Inc .... E 734 781-4600
  Livonia (G-10174)
Michigan Roller Inc .... G 269 651-2304
  Sturgis (G-16307)

ROLLS & ROLL COVERINGS: Rubber

Republic Roller Corporation .... E 269 273-9591
  Three Rivers (G-16583)

ROOF DECKS

Metal Sales Manufacturing Corp .... F 989 686-5879
  Bay City (G-1376)

ROOFING GRANULES

R5 Construxtion Inc .... F 855 480-7663
  Middleville (G-11311)

ROOFING MATERIALS: Asphalt

Green Link Inc .... F 269 216-9229
  Kalamazoo (G-9204)
Michigan Steel and Trim Inc .... F 517 647-4555
  Portland (G-13639)
Oak Way Manufacturing Inc .... F 248 335-9476
  Pontiac (G-13404)

ROOFING MATERIALS: Sheet Metal

Hancock Enterprises Inc .... D 734 287-8840
  Taylor (G-16424)
Metal Design Manufacturing LLC .... G 313 893-9810
  Detroit (G-4430)
Trade Specific Solutions LLC .... G 734 752-7124
  Southgate (G-15758)

ROOFING MEMBRANE: Rubber

R5 Construxtion Inc .... F 855 480-7663
  Middleville (G-11311)

ROOMING & BOARDING HOUSES: Furnished Room Rental

Rooms of Grand Rapids LLC .... G 616 260-1452
  Spring Lake (G-15847)

ROTORS: Motor

Celerity Systems N Amer Inc .... G 248 994-7696
  Novi (G-12382)

RUBBER

Aptargroup Inc .... G 989 631-8030
  Midland (G-11322)
Argonics Inc .... F 303 664-9467
  Gwinn (G-7581)
Armada Rubber Manufacturing Co ...... D 586 784-9135
  Armada (G-731)
Covestro LLC .... B 248 475-7700
  Auburn Hills (G-851)
Dawson Manufacturing Company .... C 269 925-0100
  Benton Harbor (G-1545)
Flexfab Horizons Intl Inc .... E 269 945-4700
  Hastings (G-7791)
Flexfab LLC .... G 800 331-0003
  Hastings (G-7792)
Mitsubishi Chemical Amer Inc .... C 586 755-1660
  Warren (G-17932)
Mykin Inc .... F 248 667-8030
  South Lyon (G-15448)
Saint-Gobain Prfmce Plas Corp .... G 989 435-9533
  Beaverton (G-1431)

RUBBER PRDTS: Automotive, Mechanical

Akwel Mexico Usa Inc .... E 231 775-6571
  Cadillac (G-2310)
HP Pelzer Auto Systems Inc .... E 248 280-1010
  Troy (G-17155)
Pullman Company .... F 734 243-8000
  Monroe (G-11571)
Uchiyama Mktg & Dev Amer LLC .... F 248 859-3986
  Novi (G-12562)
Vibracoustic Usa Inc .... C 269 637-2116
  South Haven (G-15422)
Vibracoustic Usa Inc .... B 810 648-2100
  Sandusky (G-15070)

RUBBER PRDTS: Mechanical

Advanced Manufacturing LLC .... G 231 826-3859
  Falmouth (G-5131)
Akwel Cadillac Usa Inc .... B 231 775-6571
  Cadillac (G-2309)
Akwel Cadillac Usa Inc .... F 248 476-8072
  Novi (G-12361)
Akwel Usa Inc .... F 231 775-6571
  Cadillac (G-2311)
Anand Nvh North America Inc .... C 810 724-2400
  Imlay City (G-8627)
Armada Rubber Manufacturing Co ...... D 586 784-9135
  Armada (G-731)
Basic Rubber and Plastics Co .... E 248 360-7400
  Walled Lake (G-17664)
Black River Manufacturing Inc .... E 810 982-9812
  Port Huron (G-13459)
BRC Rubber & Plastics Inc .... G 248 745-9200
  Auburn Hills (G-833)
Cooper-Stndard Indus Spclty Gr .... D 248 596-5900
  Northville (G-12209)
Creative Foam Corporation .... C 810 629-4149
  Fenton (G-5467)
Dawson Manufacturing Company .... C 269 925-0100
  Benton Harbor (G-1545)
Die Stampco Inc .... F 989 893-7790
  Bay City (G-1344)
Fluid Hutchinson Management .... D 248 679-1327
  Auburn Hills (G-903)
Four Star Rubber Inc .... G 810 632-3335
  Commerce Township (G-3532)
Freudenberg N Amer Ltd Partnr .... G 734 354-5505
  Plymouth (G-13169)
Freudenberg-Nok General Partnr .... C 734 451-0020
  Plymouth (G-13170)
Hutchnson Antvbrtion Systems I .... B 616 459-4541
  Grand Rapids (G-6826)
Hutchnson Antvbrtion Systems I .... C 231 775-9737
  Cadillac (G-2336)
R & J Manufacturing Company .... F 248 669-2460
  Commerce Township (G-3568)
R H M Rubber & Manufacturing .... E 248 624-8277
  Novi (G-12522)
Reliance Rubber Industries Inc .... G 734 641-4100
  Westland (G-18415)
Rosta USA Corp .... F 269 841-5448
  Benton Harbor (G-1581)
Uniflex Inc .... G 248 486-6000
  Brighton (G-2088)
Vibracoustic North America LP .... E 269 637-2116
  South Haven (G-15421)
Vibracoustic Usa Inc .... G 734 254-9140
  Northville (G-12269)
Vibracoustic Usa Inc .... G 810 648-2100
  Sandusky (G-15071)

RUBBER PRDTS: Reclaimed

First Class Tire Shredders Inc .... F 810 639-4466
  Clio (G-3398)

RUBBER PRDTS: Silicone

Cht USA Inc .... E 269 445-0847
  Cassopolis (G-2626)
Dow Corning Corporation .... F 989 839-2808
  Midland (G-11353)
Grm Corporation .... E 989 453-2322
  Pigeon (G-13037)

RUBBER PRDTS: Sponge

Basic Rubber and Plastics Co .... E 248 360-7400
  Walled Lake (G-17664)

RUBBER STAMP, WHOLESALE

Rubber Stamps Unlimited Inc .... F 734 451-7300
  Plymouth (G-13291)

RUBBER, CRUDE, WHOLESALE

Exotic Rubber & Plastics Corp .... D 248 477-2122
  New Hudson (G-12053)
Innovative Engineering Mich .... G 517 977-0460
  Lansing (G-9705)

RUST PROOFING SVC: Hot Dipping, Metals & Formed Prdts

Chemical Processing Inc .... E 313 925-3400
  Madison Heights (G-10688)
Superior Collision Inc .... G 231 946-4983
  Traverse City (G-16846)

RUST REMOVERS

Metals Preservation Group LLC .... F 586 944-2720
  Saint Clair Shores (G-14870)

RUST RESISTING

A-Line Products Corporation .... F 313 571-8300
  Detroit (G-3975)
Emco Chemical Inc .... F 313 894-7650
  Detroit (G-4207)
Magni Group Inc .... F 248 647-4500
  Birmingham (G-1735)

SAFES & VAULTS: Metal

A & L Metal Products .... G 734 654-8990
  Carleton (G-2549)

SAFETY EQPT & SPLYS WHOLESALERS

James Glove & Supply .... F 810 733-5780
  Flint (G-5718)
Midwest Safety Products Inc .... E 616 554-5155
  Grand Rapids (G-7006)
Performance Fabrics Inc .... C 616 459-4144
  Grand Rapids (G-7079)

SAILBOAT BUILDING & REPAIR

Quantum Sails Design Group LLC .... E 231 941-1222
  Traverse City (G-16811)

SAILS

North Sails Group LLC .... G 586 776-1330
  Saint Clair Shores (G-14874)
Performance Sailing Inc .... G 586 790-7500
  Clinton Township (G-3318)

SALES PROMOTION SVCS

Forsons Inc .... G 517 787-4562
  Jackson (G-8885)

SALT

Cargill Incorporated .... B 810 329-2736
  Saint Clair (G-14816)
Morton Salt Inc .... G 231 398-0758
  Manistee (G-10910)

SAND & GRAVEL

SAND & GRAVEL

1johnson Erling .... G 231 625-2247
  Cheboygan *(G-2779)*
A & E Agg Inc .... E 248 547-4711
  Berkley *(G-1617)*
Afgco Sand & Gravel Co Inc .... G 810 798-3293
  Almont *(G-255)*
Bear Creek Sand & Gravel LLC .... G 989 681-3641
  Saint Louis *(G-14987)*
Bouchey and Sons Inc .... G 989 588-4118
  Farwell *(G-5421)*
Briggs Contracting .... G 989 687-7331
  Sanford *(G-15072)*
Cardinal Economic Sand Finance .... G 734 926-6989
  Ann Arbor *(G-414)*
Cheboygan Cement Products Inc .... E 231 627-5631
  Cheboygan *(G-2782)*
Downriver Crushed Concrete .... G 734 283-1833
  Taylor *(G-16405)*
Dugrees Sand and Gravel .... G 906 295-1569
  Hermansville *(G-7861)*
Elmers Crane and Dozer Inc .... C 231 943-3443
  Traverse City *(G-16676)*
Familygradegravel Yahoocom .... G 517 202-4121
  Mason *(G-11132)*
Finch Sand & Gravel LLC .... G 734 439-1044
  Milan *(G-11435)*
Fritz Enterprises .... E 734 283-7272
  Trenton *(G-16888)*
Fyke Washed Sand Gravel .... G 248 547-4714
  Berkley *(G-1626)*
Genesis Sand and Gravel Inc .... G 313 587-8530
  West Bloomfield *(G-18283)*
Grand Rapids Gravel Company .... E 616 538-9000
  Belmont *(G-1507)*
Grand Rapids Gravel Company .... F 616 538-9000
  Grand Rapids *(G-6759)*
Heritage Resources Inc .... G 616 554-9888
  Caledonia *(G-2379)*
High Grade Materials Company .... E 616 754-5545
  Greenville *(G-7492)*
Huizenga Gravel Company Inc .... F 616 772-6241
  Zeeland *(G-19042)*
J T Express Ltd .... G 810 724-6471
  Brown City *(G-2138)*
Lafarge North America Inc .... G 231 726-3291
  Muskegon *(G-11855)*
Lafarge North America Inc .... G 703 480-3600
  Dundee *(G-4827)*
Lakeside Aggregate LLC .... D 616 837-5858
  Nunica *(G-12583)*
Levy Environmental Services Co .... E 313 429-2272
  Dearborn *(G-3861)*
M-52 Sand & Gravel LLC .... G 734 453-3695
  Plymouth *(G-13230)*
M-57 Aggregate Company .... G 810 639-7516
  Montrose *(G-11605)*
Marsack Sand & Gravel Inc .... G 586 293-4414
  Roseville *(G-14435)*
Mbcd Inc .... E 517 484-4426
  Lansing *(G-9867)*
Michigan Aggr Sand/Gravel Haul .... F 231 258-8237
  Kalkaska *(G-9397)*
Modern Industries Inc .... E 810 767-3330
  Flint *(G-5735)*
Nivers Sand Gravel .... G 231 743-6126
  Marion *(G-10975)*
Nugent Sand Company Inc .... E 231 755-1686
  Norton Shores *(G-12322)*
Peters Sand and Gravel Inc .... G 906 595-7223
  Naubinway *(G-11961)*
Ruby Sand & Gravel .... G 810 364-6100
  Clyde *(G-3416)*
Saginaw Rock Products Co .... F 989 754-6589
  Saginaw *(G-14751)*
Searles Construction Inc .... G 989 224-3297
  Saint Johns *(G-14915)*
Shimp Sand & Gravel LLC .... F 517 369-1632
  Bronson *(G-2120)*
Stansley Mineral Resources Inc .... G 517 456-6310
  Clinton *(G-3142)*
Summers Road Gravel & Dev LLC .... G 810 798-8533
  Almont *(G-268)*
Trillacorpe/Bk LLC .... G 248 433-0585
  Bingham Farms *(G-1705)*
Trojan Sand and Gravel LLC .... G 517 712-5086
  Springport *(G-15884)*
Trp Enterprises Inc .... G 810 329-4027
  East China *(G-4859)*
Truth Sand Contemplations .... G 269 342-0369
  Portage *(G-13627)*
Waanders Concrete Co .... F 269 673-6352
  Allegan *(G-184)*

SAND LIME PRDTS

Vico Company .... G 734 453-3777
  Plymouth *(G-13332)*

SAND MINING

American Aggregates Mich Inc .... D 248 348-8511
  Wixom *(G-18607)*
Bailey Sand & Gravel Co .... F 517 750-4889
  Jackson *(G-8820)*
Falcon Trucking Company .... G 313 843-7200
  Dearborn *(G-3839)*
Falcon Trucking Company .... E 989 656-2831
  Bay Port *(G-1414)*
Falcon Trucking Company .... E 248 634-9471
  Davisburg *(G-3768)*
Gale Briggs Inc .... G 517 543-1320
  Charlotte *(G-2758)*
Ken Measel Supply Inc .... G 810 798-3293
  Almont *(G-263)*
Michiana Aggregate Inc .... G 269 695-7669
  Niles *(G-12144)*
Mineral Visions Inc .... G 800 255-7263
  Bridgman *(G-1932)*
Mottes Materials Inc .... G 906 265-9955
  Iron River *(G-8749)*
Next-Level Sandbag LLC .... G 231 350-6738
  East Jordan *(G-4877)*
Technisand Inc .... G 269 465-5833
  Benton Harbor *(G-1592)*
Tri-City Aggregates Inc .... E 248 634-8276
  Holly *(G-8298)*

SAND: Hygrade

Carrollton Paving Co .... F 989 752-7139
  Saginaw *(G-14623)*
Eggers Excavating LLC .... F 989 695-5205
  Freeland *(G-6022)*

SANDBLASTING EQPT

Horizon Bros Painting Corp .... G 810 632-3362
  Howell *(G-8462)*

SANDBLASTING SVC: Building Exterior

GTM Steamer Service Inc .... G 989 732-7678
  Gaylord *(G-6132)*

SANDSTONE: Crushed & Broken

American Aggregate Inc .... G 269 683-6160
  Niles *(G-12110)*

SANITARY SVCS: Refuse Collection & Disposal Svcs

Manistique Rentals Inc .... G 906 341-6955
  Manistique *(G-10921)*

SANITARY SVCS: Sanitary Landfill, Operation Of

K and W Landfill Inc .... D 906 883-3504
  Ontonagon *(G-12711)*
Southeast Berrien Cnty Landfill .... E 269 695-2500
  Niles *(G-12168)*

SANITARY SVCS: Waste Materials, Recycling

Aci Plastics Inc .... E 810 767-3800
  Flint *(G-5636)*
Aci Plastics Inc .... E 810 767-3800
  Flint *(G-5637)*
Anchor Recycling Inc .... G 810 984-5545
  Port Huron *(G-13439)*
Applegate Insul Systems Inc .... E 517 521-3545
  Webberville *(G-18241)*
Clean Tech Inc .... E 734 529-2475
  Dundee *(G-4811)*
Clean Tech Inc .... E 734 455-3600
  Plymouth *(G-13147)*
Friedland Industries Inc .... E 517 482-3000
  Lansing *(G-9701)*
Glass Recyclers Ltd .... E 313 584-3434
  Dearborn *(G-3846)*
Jolicor Manufacturing Services .... E 586 323-5090
  Shelby Township *(G-15246)*
Louis Padnos Iron and Metal Co .... G 517 372-6600
  Lansing *(G-9773)*
Lwhs Ltd .... D 616 452-5300
  Grand Rapids *(G-6954)*
McM Disposal LLC .... G 616 656-4049
  Byron Center *(G-2283)*
National Zinc Processors Inc .... F 269 926-1161
  Benton Harbor *(G-1577)*
Recycling Rizzo Services LLC .... G 248 541-4020
  Royal Oak *(G-14574)*

SANITARY WARE: Metal

Lakeshore Marble Company Inc .... F 269 429-8241
  Stevensville *(G-16257)*
Marbelite Corp .... E 248 348-1900
  Novi *(G-12470)*
Sloan Valve Company .... D 248 446-5300
  New Hudson *(G-12070)*
Thetford Corporation .... C 734 769-6000
  Ann Arbor *(G-688)*

SANITATION CHEMICALS & CLEANING AGENTS

Access Business Group LLC .... A 616 787-6000
  Ada *(G-3)*
Affordable Pool and Spa Inc .... F 810 422-5058
  Burton *(G-2225)*
Benchmark Inc .... G 734 285-0900
  Wyandotte *(G-18812)*
Bissell Better Life LLC .... G 800 237-7691
  Grand Rapids *(G-6510)*
Caravan Technologies Inc .... F 313 632-8545
  Detroit *(G-4088)*
Coxen Enterprises Inc .... D 248 486-3800
  Brighton *(G-1971)*
Diversified Chemical Tech Inc .... C 313 867-5444
  Detroit *(G-4180)*
Formax Manufacturing Corp .... E 616 456-5458
  Grand Rapids *(G-6716)*
Full Upholstery LLC .... G 248 760-3985
  Pontiac *(G-13373)*
H & J Mfg Consulting Svcs Corp .... G 734 941-8314
  Romulus *(G-14282)*
Henkel Surface Technologies .... G 248 307-0240
  Madison Heights *(G-10738)*
Kath Khemicals LLC .... F 586 275-2646
  Sterling Heights *(G-16061)*
Kmi Cleaning Solutions Inc .... F 269 964-2557
  Battle Creek *(G-1263)*
McGean-Rohco Inc .... E 216 441-4900
  Livonia *(G-10306)*
Michigan Chimneys .... G 810 640-7961
  Clio *(G-3405)*
Nano Magic Holdings Inc .... G 844 273-6462
  Madison Heights *(G-10787)*
Sabo Creative .... G 616 842-7226
  Spring Lake *(G-15848)*
SC Johnson & Son .... D 989 667-0235
  Bay City *(G-1398)*
Tennant Commercial .... D 616 994-4000
  Holland *(G-8215)*
Transtar Autobody Tech LLC .... C 810 220-3000
  Brighton *(G-2084)*
Ziebart International Corp .... E 248 588-4100
  Troy *(G-17460)*

SASHES: Door Or Window, Metal

George W Trapp Co .... E 313 531-7180
  Redford *(G-13737)*

SATCHELS

Golden Satchel LLC .... G 248 636-0550
  River Rouge *(G-13855)*
Tallulahs Satchels .... G 231 775-4082
  Cadillac *(G-2360)*

SATELLITE COMMUNICATIONS EQPT

Directv Dish Doctor .... G 989 983-3214
  Vanderbilt *(G-17569)*
Michigan Satellite .... F 989 792-6666
  Saginaw *(G-14698)*
Satellite Controls .... G 313 532-6848
  Redford *(G-13770)*

SATELLITES: Communications

Apem Solutions LLC ....G 616 848-5393
  Grand Rapids *(G-6461)*
Sinclair Designs & Engrg LLC ....E 877 517-0311
  Albion *(G-133)*

SAUNA ROOMS: Prefabricated

Ahs LLC ....G 888 355-3050
  Holland *(G-7959)*

SAW BLADES

Edge Industries Inc ....G 616 453-5458
  Grand Rapids *(G-6665)*
Martin Saw & Tool Inc ....G 906 863-6812
  Menominee *(G-11245)*
Menominee Saw and Supply Co ....E 906 863-2609
  Menominee *(G-11248)*
Schott Saw Co ....G 269 782-3203
  Dowagiac *(G-4795)*
Workblades Inc ....E 586 778-0060
  Warren *(G-18072)*

SAWING & PLANING MILLS

American Classic Homes Inc ....G 616 594-5900
  Holland *(G-7964)*
Applegate Insul Systems Inc ....G 517 521-3545
  Webberville *(G-18241)*
Atwood Forest Products Inc ....E 616 696-0081
  Cedar Springs *(G-2641)*
Barnes Wood Works ....G 269 599-3479
  Portage *(G-13546)*
Bennett Sawmill ....G 231 734-5733
  Evart *(G-5121)*
Besse Forest Products Inc ....F 906 353-7193
  Baraga *(G-1135)*
Biewer Sawmill Winona Inc ....C 810 329-4789
  Saint Clair *(G-14815)*
Biewer Sawmill-Lake City LLC ....F 231 839-7646
  Lake City *(G-9544)*
Blough Hardwoods Inc ....G 616 693-2174
  Clarksville *(G-3078)*
Buskirk Lumber Company ....E 616 765-5103
  Freeport *(G-6032)*
Caledonia Cmnty Sawmill LLC ....G 616 891-8561
  Alto *(G-330)*
Casselman Logging ....G 231 885-1040
  Mesick *(G-11270)*
Collins Brothers Sawmill Inc ....F 906 524-5511
  Lanse *(G-9658)*
Country Side Sawmill ....G 989 352-7198
  Lakeview *(G-9640)*
Crawford Forest Products ....F 989 742-3855
  Hillman *(G-7912)*
Creekside Lumber ....G 231 924-1934
  Newaygo *(G-12079)*
Cruse Hardwood Lumber Inc ....G 517 688-4891
  Birmingham *(G-1723)*
Cyrus Forest Products ....G 269 751-6535
  Allegan *(G-152)*
Daniel D Slater ....G 989 833-7135
  Riverdale *(G-13863)*
Decatur Wood Products Inc ....E 269 657-6041
  Decatur *(G-3946)*
Don Sawmill Inc ....G 989 733-2780
  Onaway *(G-12698)*
Dowd Brothers Forestry ....G 989 345-7459
  Alger *(G-137)*
E H Tulgestka & Sons Inc ....F 989 734-2129
  Rogers City *(G-14209)*
Eovations LLC ....F 616 361-7136
  Grand Rapids *(G-6682)*
Fairview Sawmill Inc ....G 989 848-5238
  Fairview *(G-5130)*
Fiber By-Products Corp ....F 269 483-0066
  White Pigeon *(G-18477)*
Forest Blake Products Inc ....G 231 879-3913
  Fife Lake *(G-5606)*
Forest Corullo Products Corp ....E 906 667-0275
  Bessemer *(G-1649)*
Forte Industries Mill Inc ....E 906 753-6256
  Stephenson *(G-15907)*
Grand Traverse Assembly Inc ....G 231 588-2406
  Ellsworth *(G-5036)*
Green Gables Saw Mill ....G 989 386-7846
  Clare *(G-2980)*
Gyms Sawmill ....G 989 826-8299
  Mio *(G-11508)*
Hmi Hardwoods LLC ....D 517 456-7431
  Clinton *(G-3141)*
Hochstetler Sawmill ....G 269 467-7018
  Centreville *(G-2697)*
Housler Sawmill Inc ....F 231 824-6353
  Mesick *(G-11272)*
Ida D Byler ....G 810 672-9355
  Cass City *(G-2615)*
Integrity Forest Products LLC ....G 513 871-8988
  Kenton *(G-9440)*
J and K Lumber Inc ....G 906 265-9130
  Iron River *(G-8742)*
Jaroche Brothers Inc ....F 231 525-8100
  Wolverine *(G-18795)*
Jerome Miller Lumber Co ....G 231 745-3694
  Baldwin *(G-1122)*
Jerome Miller Lumber Co ....G 231 745-3694
  Baldwin *(G-1123)*
John A Biewer Lumber Company ....E 231 839-7646
  Lake City *(G-9547)*
John A Biewer Lumber Company ....E 231 825-2855
  Mc Bain *(G-11183)*
Kappen Saw Mill ....G 989 872-4410
  Cass City *(G-2616)*
Kells Sawmill Inc ....G 906 753-2778
  Stephenson *(G-15908)*
Maeder Bros Qlty WD Pllets Inc ....F 989 644-3500
  Weidman *(G-18256)*
Master Woodworks ....G 269 240-3262
  Saint Joseph *(G-14949)*
Matthews Mill Inc ....F 989 257-3271
  South Branch *(G-15396)*
Mc Guire Mill & Lumber ....G 989 735-3851
  Glennie *(G-6214)*
Michigan Lumber & Wood Fiber I ....E 989 848-2100
  Comins *(G-3504)*
Michigan Sawmill Sales LLC ....G 810 625-3848
  Linden *(G-10067)*
Michigan Timber Sawmill LLC ....F 989 266-2417
  Hillman *(G-7914)*
Midwest Timber Inc ....E 269 663-5315
  Edwardsburg *(G-5011)*
Mlc of Wakefield Inc ....F 906 224-1120
  Wakefield *(G-17624)*
North American Forest Products ....G 269 663-8500
  Edwardsburg *(G-5014)*
Northern Hardwoods Oper Co LLC ......D 860 632-3505
  South Range *(G-15461)*
Northern Michigan Sawmill ....G 231 409-1314
  Williamsburg *(G-18560)*
Northern Products of Wisconsin ....G 715 589-4417
  Iron Mountain *(G-8727)*
Northwest Hardwoods Inc ....G 989 786-6100
  Lewiston *(G-10026)*
Northwood Lumber ....G 989 826-1751
  Mio *(G-11513)*
Oceana Forest Products Inc ....G 231 861-6115
  Shelby *(G-15158)*
Old Sawmill Woodworking Co ....G 248 366-6245
  Commerce Township *(G-3559)*
Pollums Natural Resources ....G 810 245-7268
  Lapeer *(G-9955)*
Precision Hrdwood Rsources Inc ....F 734 475-0144
  Chelsea *(G-2824)*
Prells Saw Mill Inc ....E 989 734-2939
  Hawks *(G-7815)*
Richter Sawmill ....G 231 829-3071
  Leroy *(G-10011)*
Riverbend Timber Framing Inc ....G 517 486-3629
  Blissfield *(G-1776)*
Robert E Nelson & Son ....G 810 664-6091
  Lapeer *(G-9959)*
Sabertooth Enterprises LLC ....F 989 539-9842
  Harrison *(G-7681)*
Sagola Hardwoods Inc ....D 906 542-7200
  Sagola *(G-14799)*
Sawing Logz LLC ....G 586 883-5649
  Warren *(G-18004)*
Sawmill Estates ....G 269 792-7500
  Wayland *(G-18205)*
Schleben Forest Products Inc ....G 989 734-2858
  Rogers City *(G-14218)*
St Charles Hardwood Michigan ....F 989 865-9299
  Saint Charles *(G-14809)*
Terry Heiden ....G 906 753-6248
  Stephenson *(G-15912)*
Thorn Creek Lumber LLC ....G 231 832-1600
  Reed City *(G-13800)*
Timber Products Co Ltd Partnr ....C 906 452-6221
  Munising *(G-11755)*
Total Chips Company Inc ....F 989 866-2610
  Shepherd *(G-15379)*
Ufp Atlantic LLC ....G 616 364-6161
  Grand Rapids *(G-7286)*
Ufp Eastern Division Inc ....B 616 364-6161
  Grand Rapids *(G-7287)*
Ufp West Central LLC ....D 616 364-6161
  Grand Rapids *(G-7295)*
Wheelers Wolf Lake Sawmill ....G 231 745-7078
  Baldwin *(G-1125)*
William S Wixtrom ....G 906 376-8247
  Republic *(G-13821)*
Williams Milling & Moulding In ....G 906 474-9222
  Rapid River *(G-13687)*
Woodhaven Log and Lumber ....G 231 938-2200
  Williamsburg *(G-18567)*

SAWING & PLANING MILLS: Custom

Great Northern Lumber Mich LLC ....G 989 736-6192
  Lincoln *(G-10034)*
Zulski Lumber Inc ....G 231 539-8909
  Pellston *(G-12969)*

SAWS & SAWING EQPT

Coxline Inc ....E 269 345-1132
  Kalamazoo *(G-9157)*
Elmo Manufacturing Co Inc ....G 734 995-5966
  Ann Arbor *(G-471)*
Jones & Hollands Inc ....G 810 364-6400
  Marysville *(G-11089)*
Lumberjack Shack Inc ....G 810 724-7230
  Imlay City *(G-8640)*
Pitchford Bertie ....G 517 627-1151
  Grand Ledge *(G-6397)*

SAWS: Portable

D & D Production Inc ....F 248 334-2112
  Waterford *(G-18113)*

SCAFFOLDS: Mobile Or Stationary, Metal

Swing-Lo Suspended Scaffold Co ....F 269 764-8989
  Covert *(G-3726)*

SCALE REPAIR SVCS

Standard Scale & Supply Co ....G 313 255-6700
  Detroit *(G-4605)*

SCALES & BALANCES, EXC LABORATORY

Hanchett Manufacturing Inc ....E 231 796-7678
  Big Rapids *(G-1676)*
Heco Inc ....E 269 381-7200
  Kalamazoo *(G-9210)*
M2 Scientifics LLC ....F 616 379-9080
  Allendale *(G-224)*

SCALES: Indl

Standard Scale & Supply Co ....G 313 255-6700
  Detroit *(G-4605)*

SCALES: Truck

Trucksforsalecom ....G 989 883-3382
  Sebewaing *(G-15145)*

SCHOOL SPLYS, EXC BOOKS: Wholesalers

Weaver Instructional Systems ....G 616 942-2891
  Grand Rapids *(G-7327)*

SCHOOLS: Elementary & Secondary

Independent Mfg Solutions Corp ....E 248 960-3550
  Wixom *(G-18684)*

SCHOOLS: Vocational, NEC

Hope Focus ....C 313 494-5500
  Detroit *(G-4307)*
Royal ARC Welding Company ....E 734 789-9099
  Flat Rock *(G-5628)*

SCIENTIFIC EQPT REPAIR SVCS

Kaltec Scientific Inc ....G 248 349-8100
  Novi *(G-12450)*

SCIENTIFIC INSTRUMENTS WHOLESALERS

SCIENTIFIC INSTRUMENTS WHOLESALERS

Instrumented Sensor Tech Inc..............G......517 349-8487
  Okemos *(G-12670)*

SCRAP & WASTE MATERIALS, WHOLESALE: Ferrous Metal

Drayton Iron & Metal Inc..................F......248 673-1269
  Waterford *(G-18120)*
Fpt Schlafer.....................................E......313 925-8200
  Detroit *(G-4245)*
Franklin Iron & Metal Co Inc............F......269 968-6111
  Battle Creek *(G-1233)*
Franklin Metal Trading Corp............E......616 374-7171
  Lake Odessa *(G-9575)*
Friedland Industries Inc...................E......517 482-3000
  Lansing *(G-9701)*
Lorbec Metals - Usa Ltd..................E......810 736-0961
  Flint *(G-5728)*
Martin Bros Mill Fndry Sup Co.........G......269 927-1355
  Benton Harbor *(G-1567)*
Schneider Iron & Metal Inc..............G......906 774-0644
  Iron Mountain *(G-8732)*
Shoreline Recycling & Supply..........E......231 722-6081
  Muskegon *(G-11920)*
Strong Steel Products LLC...............F......313 267-3300
  Detroit *(G-4613)*

SCRAP & WASTE MATERIALS, WHOLESALE: Metal

General Mill Supply Company..........E......248 668-0800
  Wixom *(G-18667)*
Louis Padnos Iron and Metal Co......G......517 372-6600
  Lansing *(G-9773)*
Recycling Concepts W Mich Inc......D......616 942-8888
  Grand Rapids *(G-7146)*

SCRAP & WASTE MATERIALS, WHOLESALE: Nonferrous Metals Scrap

Huron Valley Steel Corporation........C......734 479-3500
  Trenton *(G-16889)*
Resource Rcovery Solutions Inc......G......248 454-3442
  Pontiac *(G-13413)*

SCRAP & WASTE MATERIALS, WHOLESALE: Oil

Usher Enterprises Inc......................E......313 834-7055
  Detroit *(G-4656)*

SCRAP & WASTE MATERIALS, WHOLESALE: Paper

Great Lakes Paper Stock Corp.........D......586 779-1310
  Roseville *(G-14416)*
V & M Corporation............................E......248 591-6580
  Royal Oak *(G-14588)*

SCRAP & WASTE MATERIALS, WHOLESALE: Plastics Scrap

Harbor Green Solutions LLC............G......269 352-0265
  Benton Harbor *(G-1553)*
Upcycle Polymers LLC.....................G......248 446-8750
  Howell *(G-8537)*

SCRAP STEEL CUTTING

Scotten Steel Processing Inc...........F......313 897-8837
  Detroit *(G-4585)*

SCREENS: Woven Wire

PA Products Inc................................G......734 421-1060
  Livonia *(G-10357)*

SCREW MACHINE PRDTS

AAA Industries Inc............................E......313 255-0420
  Redford *(G-13709)*
Accuspec Grinding Inc.....................E......269 556-1410
  Stevensville *(G-16238)*
Advance Turning and Mfg Inc..........C......517 783-2713
  Jackson *(G-8802)*
Air-Matic Products Company Inc.....E......248 356-4200
  Southfield *(G-15473)*
Alco Manufacturing Corp..................E......734 426-3941
  Dexter *(G-4722)*
Allan Tool & Machine Co Inc............D......248 585-2910
  Troy *(G-16925)*
American Screw Products Inc..........G......248 543-0991
  Madison Heights *(G-10667)*
Amerikam Inc....................................D......616 243-5833
  Grand Rapids *(G-6457)*
Atf Inc...E......989 685-2468
  Rose City *(G-14362)*
Atg Precision Products LLC............E......586 247-5400
  Canton *(G-2437)*
Autocam-Pax Inc..............................C......269 782-5186
  Dowagiac *(G-4776)*
B M Industries Inc............................G......810 658-0052
  Lapeer *(G-4913)*
Berkley Screw Machine Pdts Inc.....E......248 853-0044
  Rochester Hills *(G-13962)*
Black River Manufacturing Inc.........E......810 982-9812
  Port Huron *(G-13459)*
BMC Bil-Mac Corporation.................D......616 538-1930
  Grandville *(G-7368)*
Borneman & Peterson Inc................E......810 744-1890
  Flint *(G-5659)*
C S M Manufacturing Corp..............D......248 471-0700
  Farmington Hills *(G-5192)*
C Thorrez Industries Inc..................E......517 750-3160
  Jackson *(G-8831)*
Cap Collet & Tool Co Inc.................F......734 283-4040
  Wyandotte *(G-18814)*
Cardinal Group Industries Corp......F......517 437-6000
  Hillsdale *(G-7929)*
Central Screw Products Company...F......313 893-9100
  Troy *(G-17006)*
Comtronics..E......517 750-3160
  Jackson *(G-8850)*
Core Electric Company Inc..............F......313 382-7140
  Melvindale *(G-11198)*
Corlett-Turner Co.............................D......616 772-9082
  Zeeland *(G-19007)*
CPM Acquisition Corp......................D......231 947-6400
  Traverse City *(G-16664)*
Davison-Rite Products Co...............E......734 513-0505
  White Lake *(G-18454)*
Dawlen Corporation..........................G......517 787-2200
  Jackson *(G-8860)*
Dennison Automatics LLC...............G......616 837-7063
  Nunica *(G-12578)*
Denny Grice Inc................................E......269 279-6113
  Three Rivers *(G-16570)*
Dexter Automatic Products Co.......C......734 426-8900
  Dexter *(G-4734)*
Dimension Machine Tech LLC.........F......586 649-4747
  Bloomfield Hills *(G-1814)*
Dirksen Screw Products Co............E......586 247-5400
  Shelby Township *(G-15208)*
Dynamic Corporation........................F......616 399-2200
  Holland *(G-8018)*
E and P Form Tool Company Inc....F......734 261-3530
  Garden City *(G-6093)*
Eagle Creek Mfg & Sales.................G......989 643-7521
  Saint Charles *(G-14802)*
ECM Specialties Inc.........................G......810 736-0299
  Flint *(G-5692)*
Edmore Tool & Grinding Inc............F......989 427-3790
  Edmore *(G-4992)*
Elkins Machine & Tool Co Inc..........G......734 941-0266
  Romulus *(G-14271)*
Embers Ballscrew Repair................G......586 216-8444
  Detroit *(G-4206)*
Extreme Precision Screw Pdts........E......810 744-1980
  Flint *(G-5698)*
Federal Screw Works.......................D......734 941-4211
  Big Rapids *(G-1673)*
Federal Screw Works.......................D......810 227-7712
  Brighton *(G-1989)*
Fettes Manufacturing Co..................E......586 939-8500
  Sterling Heights *(G-16013)*
Fordsell Machine Products Co........E......586 751-4700
  Warren *(G-17815)*
Form All Tool Company....................F......231 894-6303
  Whitehall *(G-18496)*
Fox Mfg Co.......................................E......586 468-1421
  Harrison Township *(G-7700)*
Grace Engineering Corp..................F......810 392-2181
  Memphis *(G-11213)*
Grand Haven Steel Products Inc....D......616 842-2740
  Grand Haven *(G-6306)*
Green Industries Inc........................F......248 446-8900
  Wixom *(G-18671)*
Greendale Screw Pdts Co Inc.........E......586 759-8100
  Warren *(G-17838)*
H & K Machine Company Inc..........G......269 756-7339
  Three Oaks *(G-16556)*
H & L Tool Company Inc..................E......248 585-7474
  Madison Heights *(G-10736)*
H G Geiger Manufacturing Co.........E......517 369-7357
  Bronson *(G-2114)*
Harbor Screw Machine Products.....G......269 925-5855
  Benton Harbor *(G-1554)*
Hemingway Screw Products Inc.....G......313 383-7300
  Melvindale *(G-11201)*
Hibshman Screw Mch Pdts Inc.......E......269 641-7525
  Union *(G-17489)*
Hil-Man Automation LLC..................F......616 741-9099
  Zeeland *(G-19037)*
Holt Products Company...................E......517 927-4198
  Mason *(G-11138)*
Hosco Inc..F......248 912-1750
  Wixom *(G-18678)*
Huron Inc...E......810 359-5344
  Lexington *(G-10029)*
Inland Lakes Machine Inc................E......231 775-6543
  Cadillac *(G-2337)*
J & J Industries Inc..........................E......517 784-3586
  Jackson *(G-8911)*
J C Gibbons Mfg Inc.........................E......734 266-5544
  Livonia *(G-10254)*
Jamco Manufacturing Inc................G......248 852-1988
  Auburn Hills *(G-943)*
K & Y Manufacturing LLC................E......734 414-7000
  Canton *(G-2482)*
Kalkaska Screw Products Inc.........E......231 258-2560
  Kalkaska *(G-9392)*
Kerr Screw Products Co Inc...........G......248 589-2200
  Madison Heights *(G-10761)*
L A Martin Company.........................E......313 581-3444
  Dearborn *(G-3859)*
Lakeshore Fittings Inc.....................D......616 846-5090
  Grand Haven *(G-6328)*
Lester Detterbeck Entps Ltd...........E......906 265-5121
  Iron River *(G-8746)*
Liberty Research Co Inc.................E......734 508-6237
  Milan *(G-11440)*
Liberty Turned Components LLC...E......734 508-6237
  Milan *(G-11441)*
Livonia Automatic Incorporated......G......734 591-0321
  Livonia *(G-10287)*
Lyon Manufacturing Inc...................E......734 359-3000
  Canton *(G-2487)*
Malabar Manufacturing Inc..............F......517 448-2155
  Hudson *(G-8555)*
Maynard L Maclean L C...................D......586 949-0471
  Chesterfield *(G-2908)*
McNees Manufacturing Inc..............E......616 675-7480
  Bailey *(G-1120)*
Melling Do Brasil LLC......................F......517 787-8172
  Jackson *(G-8948)*
Melling Tool Co.................................B......517 787-8172
  Jackson *(G-8951)*
Merchants Automatic Pdts Inc........E......734 829-0020
  Canton *(G-2493)*
Mercury Manufacturing Company....D......734 285-5150
  Wyandotte *(G-18833)*
Michigan Prcsion Swiss Prts In......E......810 329-2270
  Saint Clair *(G-14837)*
Micromatic Screw Products Inc......E......517 787-3666
  Jackson *(G-8957)*
Mid-West Screw Products Co.........F......734 591-1800
  Livonia *(G-10316)*
Milan Screw Products Inc...............F......734 439-2431
  Milan *(G-11447)*
MK Chambers Company...................E......810 688-3750
  North Branch *(G-12181)*
Modern Tech Machining LLC...........G......810 531-7992
  Marysville *(G-11092)*
Mohr Engineering Inc......................E......810 227-4598
  Brighton *(G-2035)*
Mountain Machine LLC....................F......734 480-2200
  Van Buren Twp *(G-17542)*
Nelms Technologies Inc..................E......734 955-6500
  Romulus *(G-14309)*
North Shore Machine Works Inc.....E......616 842-8360
  Spring Lake *(G-15840)*
Nuko Precision LLC..........................F......734 464-6856
  Livonia *(G-10342)*
Petschke Manufacturing Company..F......586 463-0841
  Mount Clemens *(G-11652)*
Phillips Bros Screw Pdts Co...........G......517 882-0279
  Lansing *(G-9880)*
Pinckney Automatic & Mfg...............G......734 878-3430
  Pinckney *(G-13053)*

PRODUCT SECTION

Pro Slot Ltd .... G 616 897-6000
   Hartford *(G-7766)*
R & D Screw Products Inc .... E 517 546-2380
   Howell *(G-8502)*
R E Gallaher Corp .... G 586 725-3333
   Ira *(G-8709)*
Rempco Acquisition Inc .... E 231 775-0108
   Cadillac *(G-2351)*
Rima Manufacturing Company .... C 517 448-8921
   Hudson *(G-8561)*
Riverside Screw Mch Pdts Inc .... F 269 962-5449
   Battle Creek *(G-1289)*
Ryan Polishing Corporation .... E 248 548-6832
   Oak Park *(G-12643)*
S H Leggitt Company .... B 269 781-3901
   Marshall *(G-11073)*
Sigma Machine Inc .... D 269 806-5679
   Kalamazoo *(G-9333)*
Slater Tools Inc .... E 586 465-5000
   Clinton Township *(G-3360)*
South Park Sales & Mfg Inc .... G 313 381-7579
   Dearborn *(G-3899)*
Springdale Automatics Inc .... G 517 523-2424
   Osseo *(G-12777)*
St Joe Tool Co .... E 269 426-4300
   Bridgman *(G-1934)*
Stagg Machine Products Inc .... G 231 775-2355
   Cadillac *(G-2359)*
Steadfast Engineered Pdts LLC .... F 616 846-4747
   Grand Haven *(G-6368)*
Stockbridge Manufacturing Co .... G 517 851-7865
   Stockbridge *(G-16278)*
Stonebridge Industries Inc .... B 586 323-0348
   Sterling Heights *(G-16195)*
Supreme Domestic Intl Sls Corp .... F 616 842-6550
   Spring Lake *(G-15854)*
Supreme Machined Pdts Co Inc .... C 616 842-6554
   Spring Lake *(G-15855)*
Swiss American Screw Pdts Inc .... E 734 397-1600
   Canton *(G-2529)*
Swiss Industries Inc .... G 517 437-3682
   Hillsdale *(G-7950)*
Taylor Machine Products Inc .... F 734 287-3550
   Plymouth *(G-13309)*
Taylor Screw Products Company .... G 734 697-8018
   Van Buren Twp *(G-17556)*
Terry Tool & Die Co .... F 517 750-1771
   Jackson *(G-9019)*
Tmt Investment Company .... E 248 616-8880
   Troy *(G-17394)*
Tompkins Products Inc .... D 313 894-2222
   Detroit *(G-4637)*
Tri-Matic Screw Products Co .... E 517 548-6414
   Howell *(G-8535)*
Tribal Manufacturing Inc .... D 269 781-3901
   Marshall *(G-11076)*
Trinity Holding Inc .... F 517 787-3100
   Jackson *(G-9024)*
Tru-Line Screw Products Inc .... F 734 261-8780
   Livonia *(G-10445)*
United Precision Pdts Co Inc .... E 313 292-0100
   Dearborn Heights *(G-3943)*
Victor Screw Products Co .... G 269 489-2760
   Burr Oak *(G-2214)*
Warren Screw Products Inc .... C 586 757-1280
   Warren *(G-18061)*
Westgood Manufacturing Co .... F 586 771-3970
   Roseville *(G-14493)*
Wolverine Machine Products Co .... E 248 634-9952
   Holly *(G-8301)*
Yankee Scrw Products Company .... G 248 634-3011
   Holly *(G-8302)*
Yarbrough Precision Screws LLC .... F 586 776-0752
   Fraser *(G-6013)*
Zimmermann Engineering Co Inc .... G 248 358-0044
   Southfield *(G-15746)*
Zygot Operations Limited .... G 810 736-2900
   Flint *(G-5799)*

SCREW MACHINES

Amex Mfg & Distrg Co Inc .... G 734 439-8560
   Milan *(G-11430)*
Champion Screw Mch Engrg Inc .... F 248 624-4545
   Wixom *(G-18632)*

SCREWS: Metal

Beaver Aerospace & Defense Inc .... C 734 853-5003
   Livonia *(G-10133)*
E J M Ball Screw LLC .... F 989 893-7674
   Bay City *(G-1349)*

Maynard L Maclean L C .... D 586 949-0471
   Chesterfield *(G-2908)*
Modular Systems Inc .... G 231 865-3167
   Fruitport *(G-6067)*
SA Industries 2 Inc .... F 248 391-5705
   Jonesville *(G-9102)*
SA Industries 2 Inc .... D 248 693-9100
   Lake Orion *(G-9630)*
W G Benjey Inc .... G 989 356-0027
   Alpena *(G-328)*
Wedin International Inc .... E 231 779-8650
   Cadillac *(G-2363)*

SEALANTS

Bars Products Inc .... E 248 634-8278
   Holly *(G-8262)*
Connells Restoration & Sealan .... G 269 370-0805
   Vandalia *(G-17565)*
Denarco Inc .... G 269 435-8404
   Constantine *(G-3664)*
Huntler Industries Inc .... F 586 566-7684
   Shelby Township *(G-15236)*
Huron Industries Inc .... G 810 984-4213
   Port Huron *(G-13485)*
Lymtal International Inc .... E 248 373-8100
   Orion *(G-12734)*
Precision Packing Corporation .... E 586 756-8700
   Warren *(G-17973)*
Precision Sealant .... G 616 667-9447
   Jenison *(G-9066)*
Pro Sealants .... G 616 318-6067
   Grand Rapids *(G-7110)*
Z Technologies Corporation .... E 313 937-0710
   Redford *(G-13787)*

SEALING COMPOUNDS: Sealing, synthetic rubber or plastic

Diversified Chemical Tech Inc .... C 313 867-5444
   Detroit *(G-4180)*

SEALS: Hermetic

Tecumseh Products Company LLC ...... A 734 585-9500
   Ann Arbor *(G-677)*
Tecumseh Products Holdings LLC .... C 734 585-9500
   Ann Arbor *(G-680)*

SEALS: Oil, Rubber

John Crane Inc .... F 989 496-9292
   Midland *(G-11378)*

SEARCH & NAVIGATION SYSTEMS

A2 Motus LLC .... G 734 780-7334
   Ann Arbor *(G-343)*
Aertech Machining & Mfg Inc .... E 517 782-4644
   Jackson *(G-8804)*
Bae Systems Land Armaments LP .... A 586 596-4123
   Sterling Heights *(G-15942)*
Drs C3 & Aviation Company .... E 248 588-0365
   Madison Heights *(G-10712)*
Eaton Corporation .... G 517 787-8121
   Ann Arbor *(G-463)*
Equitable Engineering Co Inc .... E 248 689-9700
   Troy *(G-17096)*
GE Aviation Systems LLC .... F 616 241-7000
   Grand Rapids *(G-6733)*
Glassmaster Controls Co Inc .... E 269 382-2010
   Kalamazoo *(G-9198)*
Grupo Resilient Intl Inc .... G 810 410-8177
   Linden *(G-10062)*
Hawtal Whiting .... G 248 262-2020
   Sterling Heights *(G-16036)*
Honeywell International Inc .... C 231 582-5686
   Boyne City *(G-1889)*
Hytrol Manufacturing Inc .... E 734 261-8030
   Jackson *(G-8906)*
Instrumented Sensor Tech Inc .... G 517 349-8487
   Okemos *(G-12670)*
Kva Engineering Inc .... G 616 745-7483
   Morley *(G-11620)*
Mistequay Group Ltd .... F 989 752-7700
   Saginaw *(G-14702)*
Niles Precision Company .... C 269 683-0585
   Niles *(G-12435)*
Parker-Hannifin Corporation .... B 269 384-3459
   Kalamazoo *(G-9288)*
Quanergy Systems Inc .... G 248 859-5587
   Commerce Township *(G-3566)*

SECURITY CONTROL EQPT & SYSTEMS

Rapp & Son Inc .... D 734 283-1000
   Wyandotte *(G-18836)*
Rocketplane Global Inc .... G 734 476-2888
   Lansing *(G-9788)*
Sani Zeevi .... G 248 546-4489
   Oak Park *(G-12646)*
Snavely Gordon A Atty Reserv .... G 248 760-0617
   West Bloomfield *(G-18314)*
Sniffer Robotics LLC .... G 855 476-4333
   Ann Arbor *(G-657)*
Swiss Precision Machining Inc .... F 586 677-7558
   Macomb *(G-10640)*
Triple Inc .... G 248 817-5151
   Troy *(G-17399)*
Truform Machine Inc .... E 517 782-8523
   Jackson *(G-9025)*

SEAT BELTS: Automobile & Aircraft

Belt-Tech USA Inc .... F 450 372-5826
   Grand Rapids *(G-6498)*
Key Safety Systems Inc .... C 248 373-8040
   Auburn Hills *(G-951)*
Key Safety Systems Inc .... F 586 726-3905
   Auburn Hills *(G-952)*
Key Sfety Rstraint Systems Inc .... A 586 726-3800
   Auburn Hills *(G-953)*
Takata Americas .... A 336 547-1600
   Auburn Hills *(G-1044)*
Teamtech Motorsports Safety .... G 989 792-4880
   Saginaw *(G-14773)*
Tk Holdings Inc .... A 517 545-9535
   Howell *(G-8534)*

SEATING: Bleacher, Portable

American Athletic .... F 231 798-7300
   Muskegon *(G-11768)*
Stadium Bleachers LLC .... G 810 245-6258
   Lapeer *(G-9962)*

SEATING: Chairs, Table & Arm

Carson Wood Specialties Inc .... G 269 465-6091
   Stevensville *(G-16242)*

SEATING: Stadium

Baker Road Upholstery Inc .... G 616 794-3027
   Belding *(G-1436)*
Interkal LLC .... C 269 349-1521
   Kalamazoo *(G-9224)*
Kotocorp (usa) Inc .... C 269 349-1521
   Kalamazoo *(G-9255)*
Midwest Seating Solutions Inc .... F 616 222-0636
   Grand Rapids *(G-7007)*

SEATING: Transportation

Flint Stool & Chair Co Inc .... G 810 235-7001
   Flint *(G-5702)*

SECRETARIAL & COURT REPORTING

Americas Finest Prtg Graphics .... G 586 296-1312
   Fraser *(G-5893)*
Derk Pieter Co Inc .... G 616 554-7777
   Grand Rapids *(G-6641)*
Fedex Office & Print Svcs Inc .... F 734 761-4539
   Ann Arbor *(G-487)*
Jomark Inc .... E 248 478-2600
   Farmington Hills *(G-5275)*
Safran Printing Company Inc .... C 586 939-7600
   Beverly Hills *(G-1668)*
T J K Inc .... G 586 731-9639
   Sterling Heights *(G-16199)*

SECURITY & COMMODITY EXCHANGES: Commodity, Contract

Sulugu Corporation USA Inc .... D 478 714-0325
   Grand Rapids *(G-7232)*

SECURITY CONTROL EQPT & SYSTEMS

Dice Corporation .... E 989 891-2800
   Bay City *(G-1343)*
Integrated Security Corp .... F 248 624-0700
   Novi *(G-12438)*
Passivebolt Inc .... F 734 972-0306
   Ann Arbor *(G-606)*
Securecom Inc .... G 989 837-4005
   Midland *(G-11415)*

Employee Codes: A=Over 500 employees, B=251-500
C=101-250, D=51-100, E=20-50, F=10-19, G=3-9

SECURITY CONTROL EQPT & SYSTEMS

Weber Security Group Inc..............G...... 586 582-0000
  Mount Clemens *(G-11662)*

SECURITY DEVICES

Cypress Computer Systems Inc..........F...... 810 245-2300
  Lapeer *(G-9924)*
Holland Vision Systems Inc.............E...... 616 494-9974
  Holland *(G-8087)*
Identify Inc...........................E...... 313 802-2015
  Madison Heights *(G-10745)*
Pct Security Inc.......................G...... 888 567-3287
  Clinton Township *(G-3317)*
Picpatch LLC...........................G...... 248 670-2681
  Milford *(G-11480)*
Secure Crossing RES & Dev Inc..........F...... 248 535-3800
  Dearborn *(G-3894)*
Volkswagen Group America Inc...........F...... 248 754-5000
  Auburn Hills *(G-1082)*

SECURITY EQPT STORES

Creative Engineering Inc...............G...... 734 996-5900
  Ann Arbor *(G-439)*
Intuitive Technology Inc...............G...... 602 249-5750
  Dexter *(G-4743)*

SECURITY GUARD SVCS

Sterling Security LLC..................E...... 248 809-9309
  Southfield *(G-15709)*

SECURITY PROTECTIVE DEVICES MAINTENANCE & MONITORING SVCS

Executive Operations LLC...............E...... 313 312-0653
  Brighton *(G-1986)*

SECURITY SYSTEMS SERVICES

Cornelius Systems Inc..................E...... 248 545-5558
  Clawson *(G-3091)*
Dice Corporation.......................E...... 989 891-2800
  Bay City *(G-1343)*
Ensure Technologies Inc................F...... 734 547-1600
  Ypsilanti *(G-18944)*
Hacks Key Shop Inc.....................E...... 517 485-9488
  Lansing *(G-9850)*
Lvc Technologies Inc...................E...... 248 373-3778
  Davison *(G-3789)*
Pct Security Inc.......................G...... 888 567-3287
  Clinton Township *(G-3317)*
Se-Kure Domes & Mirrors Inc............F...... 269 651-9351
  Sturgis *(G-16322)*
Traffic Sfety Ctrl Systems Inc.........E...... 248 348-0570
  Wixom *(G-18775)*

SEMICONDUCTOR & RELATED DEVICES: Read-Only Memory Or ROM

Star Board Multi Media Inc.............G...... 616 296-0823
  Grand Haven *(G-6367)*

SEMICONDUCTOR CIRCUIT NETWORKS

Bay Carbon Inc.........................E...... 989 686-8090
  Bay City *(G-1326)*

SEMICONDUCTORS & RELATED DEVICES

Advanced Photonix Inc..................E...... 734 864-5647
  Ann Arbor *(G-355)*
Allegro Microsystems LLC...............G...... 248 242-5044
  Auburn Hills *(G-777)*
API / Inmet Inc........................C...... 734 426-5553
  Ann Arbor *(G-372)*
Convergent Solutions LLC...............G...... 616 490-8747
  Lowell *(G-10499)*
Electro-Matic Ventures Inc.............C...... 248 478-1182
  Farmington Hills *(G-5225)*
Freescale Semiconductor Inc............G...... 248 324-3260
  Novi *(G-12417)*
Gan Systems Corp.......................G...... 248 609-7643
  Ann Arbor *(G-494)*
Great Lakes Crystal Tech Inc...........G...... 517 249-4395
  East Lansing *(G-4894)*
Hemlock Semiconductor LLC..............G...... 989 301-5000
  Hemlock *(G-7853)*
Hemlock Smcndctor Oprtions LLC.........B...... 989 301-5000
  Hemlock *(G-7854)*
Instrumented Sensor Tech Inc...........G...... 517 349-8487
  Okemos *(G-12670)*

Lumileds LLC...........................E...... 248 553-9080
  Farmington Hills *(G-5297)*
Luna Optoeletronics....................G...... 734 864-5611
  Ann Arbor *(G-557)*
Macom Technology Solutions Inc.........G...... 734 864-5664
  Ann Arbor *(G-561)*
Moog Inc...............................G...... 734 738-5862
  Plymouth *(G-13248)*
Optimems Technology Inc................G...... 248 660-0380
  Novi *(G-12498)*
Powerlase Photonics Inc................G...... 248 305-2963
  Novi *(G-12509)*
Promethient Inc........................G...... 231 525-0500
  Traverse City *(G-16806)*
Quantum Opus LLC.......................G...... 517 680-0011
  Novi *(G-12521)*
Siemens Industry Inc...................G...... 248 307-3400
  Troy *(G-17350)*
Tellurex Corporation...................E...... 231 947-0110
  Traverse City *(G-16853)*
Teradyne Inc...........................G...... 313 425-3900
  Allen Park *(G-208)*
Terametrix LLC.........................C...... 540 769-8430
  Ann Arbor *(G-681)*
Tinilite World Inc.....................G...... 734 334-0839
  Ann Arbor *(G-691)*
Toshiba America Electronic.............C...... 248 347-2608
  Wixom *(G-18774)*
Uusi LLC...............................D...... 231 832-5513
  Reed City *(G-13803)*
Veoneer Us Inc.........................B...... 248 223-8074
  Southfield *(G-15737)*

SENSORS: Infrared, Solid State

Teslir LLC.............................G...... 248 644-5500
  Bloomfield Hills *(G-1865)*

SENSORS: Radiation

Lexatronics LLC........................G...... 734 878-6237
  Pinckney *(G-13050)*
Tetradyn Ltd...........................G...... 202 415-7295
  Traverse City *(G-16855)*

SENSORS: Temperature For Motor Windings

Solidica Inc...........................F...... 734 222-4680
  Ann Arbor *(G-659)*

SEPTIC TANK CLEANING SVCS

Busscher Septic Tank Service...........G...... 616 392-9653
  Holland *(G-7988)*
Forbes Sanitation & Excavation.........F...... 231 723-2311
  Manistee *(G-10900)*
Franke Salisbury Virginia..............G...... 231 775-7014
  Cadillac *(G-2330)*

SEPTIC TANKS: Concrete

Acme Septic Tank Co....................F...... 989 684-3852
  Kawkawlin *(G-9413)*
Becker & Scrivens Con Pdts Inc.........E...... 517 437-4250
  Hillsdale *(G-7924)*
Busscher Septic Tank Service...........G...... 616 392-9653
  Holland *(G-7988)*
Cheboygan Cement Products Inc..........E...... 231 627-5631
  Cheboygan *(G-2782)*
Daves Concrete Products Inc............F...... 269 624-4100
  Lawton *(G-9988)*
Deforest & Bloom Septic Tanks..........G...... 231 544-3599
  Central Lake *(G-2693)*
Forbes Sanitation & Excavation.........F...... 231 723-2311
  Manistee *(G-10900)*
Franke Salisbury Virginia..............G...... 231 775-7014
  Cadillac *(G-2330)*
Imlay City Concrete Inc................F...... 810 724-3905
  Imlay City *(G-8636)*
Jordan Valley Concrete Service.........F...... 231 536-7701
  East Jordan *(G-4873)*
Kerkstra Precast LLC...................C...... 616 457-4920
  Grandville *(G-7395)*
Lenox Inc..............................G...... 586 727-1488
  Lenox *(G-9999)*
Maxs Concrete Inc......................G...... 231 972-7558
  Mecosta *(G-11193)*
Newberry Redi-Mix Inc..................G...... 906 293-5178
  Newberry *(G-12097)*
Rudy Goupile & Sons Inc................G...... 906 475-9816
  Negaunee *(G-11974)*
Sandusky Concrete & Supply.............G...... 810 648-2627
  Sandusky *(G-15066)*

PRODUCT SECTION

SEWAGE & WATER TREATMENT EQPT

Hygratek LLC...........................G...... 847 962-6180
  Ann Arbor *(G-520)*
Recovere LLC...........................G...... 269 370-3165
  Plainwell *(G-13092)*
Sebright Products Inc..................D...... 269 792-6229
  Wayland *(G-18206)*
Sludgehammer Group Ltd.................G...... 231 348-5866
  Petoskey *(G-13025)*
Wayne County Laboratory................G...... 734 285-5215
  Wyandotte *(G-18843)*

SEWAGE FACILITIES

Kemin Industries Inc...................F...... 248 869-3080
  Plymouth *(G-13211)*

SEWAGE TREATMENT SYSTEMS & EQPT

Clean Harbors Envmtl Svcs Inc..........F...... 231 258-8014
  Kalkaska *(G-9385)*

SEWER CLEANING EQPT: Power

Inland Management Inc..................G...... 313 899-3014
  Detroit *(G-4318)*
Spartan Tool LLC.......................E...... 815 539-7411
  Niles *(G-12169)*

SEWING CONTRACTORS

Jacquart Fabric Products Inc...........C...... 906 932-1339
  Ironwood *(G-8765)*

SEWING MACHINE STORES

Fabric Patch Ltd.......................G...... 906 932-5260
  Ironwood *(G-8762)*

SEWING, NEEDLEWORK & PIECE GOODS STORES: Sewing & Needlework

Sandlot Sports.........................F...... 989 835-9696
  Saginaw *(G-14752)*

SEXTANTS

Sextant Advisor Group Inc..............G...... 248 650-8280
  Rochester *(G-13928)*

SHADES: Window

McDonald Wholesale Distributor.........G...... 313 273-2870
  Detroit *(G-4423)*
Royal Crest Inc........................G...... 248 399-2476
  Oak Park *(G-12642)*

SHAFTS: Flexible

Masterline Design & Mfg................E...... 586 463-5888
  Harrison Township *(G-7709)*

SHAPES & PILINGS, STRUCTURAL: Steel

Bnb Welding & Fabrication Inc..........G...... 810 820-1508
  Burton *(G-2227)*
Detroit Metal Elements LLC.............G...... 313 300-9057
  Warren *(G-17776)*
Domestic Forge & Forming Inc...........G...... 586 749-9559
  New Haven *(G-12031)*
Fab Concepts..........................G...... 586 466-6411
  Chesterfield *(G-2879)*
G & G Steel Fabricating Co.............G...... 586 979-4112
  Warren *(G-17821)*
Mean Erectors Inc......................F...... 989 737-3285
  Saginaw *(G-14690)*
Nelson Manufacturing Inc...............G...... 810 648-0065
  Sandusky *(G-15063)*
Twb Company LLC........................C...... 734 289-6400
  Monroe *(G-11586)*

SHAPES: Extruded, Aluminum, NEC

Sign Cabinets Inc......................G...... 231 725-7187
  Muskegon *(G-11922)*

SHEET METAL SPECIALTIES, EXC STAMPED

Accuform Industries Inc................F...... 616 363-3801
  Grand Rapids *(G-6419)*
Accuform Industries Inc................G...... 616 363-3801
  Grand Rapids *(G-6420)*
American Metal Fab Inc.................D...... 269 279-5108
  Three Rivers *(G-16563)*

PRODUCT SECTION

SHOES: Orthopedic, Children's

Carlson Metal Products Inc .... E 248 528-1931
  Troy *(G-17002)*
Cmn Fabrication Inc .... G 586 294-1941
  Roseville *(G-14385)*
CNC Products LLC .... E 269 684-5500
  Niles *(G-12118)*
Cse Morse Inc .... D 269 962-5548
  Battle Creek *(G-1213)*
Custom Products Inc .... F 269 983-9500
  Saint Joseph *(G-14925)*
Design Metal Inc .... F 248 547-4170
  Oak Park *(G-12605)*
Detronic Industries Inc .... D 586 977-5660
  Sterling Heights *(G-15985)*
Diversified Metal Fabricators .... E 248 541-0500
  Ferndale *(G-5549)*
Douglas West Company Inc .... G 734 676-8882
  Grosse Ile *(G-7520)*
Fortress Manufacturing Inc .... F 269 925-1336
  Benton Harbor *(G-1549)*
Hdn F&A Inc .... D 269 965-3268
  Battle Creek *(G-1236)*
J and N Fabrications Inc .... G 586 751-6350
  Warren *(G-17876)*
Jones Mfg & Sup Co Inc .... E 616 877-4442
  Moline *(G-11519)*
Kehrig Manufacturing Company .... G 586 949-6610
  Chesterfield *(G-2900)*
Kimbow Inc .... F 616 774-4680
  Comstock Park *(G-3616)*
Kulick Enterprises Inc .... G 734 283-6999
  Wyandotte *(G-18827)*
Lahti Fabrication Inc .... G 989 343-0420
  Alger *(G-138)*
Lanzen Incorporated .... E 586 771-7070
  Bruce Twp *(G-2174)*
Metal Plus LLC .... F 616 459-7587
  Grand Rapids *(G-6980)*
Milton Manufacturing Inc .... E 313 366-2450
  Detroit *(G-4458)*
Mlp Mfg Inc .... F 616 842-8767
  Spring Lake *(G-15837)*
Modern Metalcraft Inc .... F 989 835-3716
  Midland *(G-11396)*
Modulated Metals Inc .... F 586 749-8400
  Chesterfield *(G-2914)*
National Roofg & Shtmtl Co Inc .... D 989 964-0557
  Saginaw *(G-14707)*
Professional Fabricating Inc .... E 616 531-1240
  Grand Rapids *(G-7113)*
Schuler Incorporated .... D 734 207-7200
  Canton *(G-2522)*
Shouldice Indus Mfrs Cntrs Inc .... G 269 962-5579
  Battle Creek *(G-1293)*
Sintel Inc .... C 616 842-6960
  Spring Lake *(G-15852)*
Steinke-Fenton Fabricators .... F 517 782-8174
  Jackson *(G-9013)*
Stelmatic Industries Inc .... F 586 949-0160
  Chesterfield *(G-2950)*
Sure-Weld & Plating Rack Co .... G 248 304-9430
  Southfield *(G-15714)*
Tel-X Corporation .... E 734 425-2225
  Garden City *(G-6112)*
Trigon Metal Products Inc .... G 734 513-3488
  Livonia *(G-10444)*
Vanmeer Corporation .... F 269 694-6090
  Otsego *(G-12802)*
W Soule & Co .... D 269 324-7001
  Portage *(G-13631)*
Welk-Ko Fabricators Inc .... F 734 425-6840
  Livonia *(G-10470)*
Welk-Ko Fabricators Inc .... G 810 227-7500
  Brighton *(G-2096)*
Westco Metalcraft Inc .... F 734 425-0900
  Livonia *(G-10474)*
Zinger Sheet Metal Inc .... F 616 532-3121
  Grand Rapids *(G-7357)*

SHEETS & STRIPS: Aluminum

Howmet Aerospace Inc .... G 231 894-5686
  Whitehall *(G-18500)*
Tech Forms Metal Ltd .... G 616 956-0430
  Grand Rapids *(G-7250)*

SHEETS: Fabric, From Purchased Materials

Spec International Inc .... D 616 248-9116
  Grand Rapids *(G-7210)*

SHEETS: Hard Rubber

Thunder Technologies LLC .... F 248 844-4875
  Rochester Hills *(G-14126)*

SHELLAC

Titan Sales International LLC .... G 313 469-7105
  Detroit *(G-4634)*

SHELTERED WORKSHOPS

ARC Services of Macomb Inc .... E 586 469-1600
  Clinton Township *(G-3173)*
Goodwill Inds Nthrn Mich Inc .... G 231 779-1311
  Cadillac *(G-2332)*
Goodwill Inds Nthrn Mich Inc .... G 231 779-1361
  Cadillac *(G-2333)*
Goodwill Inds Nthrn Mich Inc .... G 231 922-4890
  Traverse City *(G-16696)*
Vocational Strategies Inc .... F 906 482-6142
  Calumet *(G-2415)*

SHELVES & SHELVING: Wood

Modular Systems Inc .... G 231 865-3167
  Fruitport *(G-6067)*

SHELVING, MADE FROM PURCHASED WIRE

Adrian Steel Company .... B 517 265-6194
  Adrian *(G-50)*
Windy Lake LLC .... D 877 869-6911
  Pentwater *(G-12975)*

SHELVING: Office & Store, Exc Wood

Basc Manufacturing Inc .... G 248 360-2272
  Commerce Township *(G-3514)*
Casper Corporation .... E 248 442-9000
  Farmington Hills *(G-5200)*
Knape & Vogt Manufacturing Co .... A 616 459-3311
  Grand Rapids *(G-6900)*

SHIMS: Metal

National Innovation Center .... F 248 414-3913
  Oak Park *(G-12630)*

SHIP BUILDING & REPAIRING: Cargo Vessels

LA East Inc .... F 269 476-7170
  Vandalia *(G-17567)*

SHIP BUILDING & REPAIRING: Rigging, Marine

FD Lake Company .... F 616 241-5639
  Grand Rapids *(G-6704)*

SHIP BUILDING & REPAIRING: Transport Vessels, Troop

K & N Transport LLC .... G 313 384-0037
  Detroit *(G-4345)*

SHIPBUILDING & REPAIR

Beardslee Investments Inc .... E 810 748-9951
  Harsens Island *(G-7748)*
Di Square America Inc .... F 248 374-5051
  Novi *(G-12398)*
Lake Shore Systems Inc .... E 906 265-5414
  Iron River *(G-8745)*
Lake Shore Systems Inc .... D 906 774-1500
  Kingsford *(G-9512)*
Merchant Holdings Inc .... G 906 786-7120
  Escanaba *(G-5085)*
Nicholson Terminal & Dock Co .... D 313 842-4300
  River Rouge *(G-13858)*
Nk Dockside Service & Repair .... G 906 420-0777
  Escanaba *(G-5087)*

SHIPPING AGENTS

N Pack Ship Center .... G 906 863-4095
  Menominee *(G-11253)*

SHOE & BOOT ACCESS

Bond Manufacturing LLC .... G 313 671-0799
  Detroit *(G-4062)*

SHOE MATERIALS: Counters

Bean Counter Inc .... G 906 523-5027
  Calumet *(G-2408)*
Midwest Cabinet Counters .... G 248 586-4260
  Madison Heights *(G-10783)*
Security Countermeasures Tech .... G 248 237-6263
  Livonia *(G-10403)*

SHOE MATERIALS: Quarters

Canusa LLC .... F 906 259-0800
  Sault Sainte Marie *(G-15088)*
Quarters Vending LLC .... G 313 510-5555
  Commerce Township *(G-3567)*
Stoney Creek Tmber Qrter Hrses .... F 517 677-9661
  Reading *(G-13706)*

SHOE MATERIALS: Rands

Rand L Industries Inc .... G 989 657-5175
  Alpena *(G-315)*
Rand Worldwide Subsidiary Inc .... G 616 261-8183
  Grandville *(G-7413)*

SHOE STORES

Hi-Tech Optical Inc .... E 989 799-9390
  Saginaw *(G-14663)*

SHOE STORES: Athletic

Baumans Running Center Inc .... G 810 238-5981
  Flint *(G-5652)*
Skechers USA Inc .... F 989 624-9336
  Birch Run *(G-1715)*

SHOE STORES: Custom

Fourth Ave Birkenstock .... G 734 663-1644
  Ann Arbor *(G-493)*

SHOE STORES: Custom & Orthopedic

Kalamazoo Orthotics & Dbtc .... F 269 349-2247
  Kalamazoo *(G-9244)*

SHOE STORES: Men's

Millers Shoe Parlor Inc .... G 517 783-1258
  Jackson *(G-8964)*

SHOE STORES: Orthopedic

Celebrations .... G 906 482-4946
  Hancock *(G-7617)*
First Response Med Sups LLC .... F 313 731-2554
  Dearborn *(G-3840)*

SHOES & BOOTS WHOLESALERS

Hush Puppies Retail LLC .... E 231 937-1004
  Howard City *(G-8409)*

SHOES: Athletic, Exc Rubber Or Plastic

Warrior Sports Inc .... C 800 968-7845
  Warren *(G-18063)*
Wolverine World Wide Inc .... A 616 866-5500
  Rockford *(G-14197)*

SHOES: Canvas, Rubber Soled

Musical Sneakers Incorporated .... F 888 410-7050
  Grandville *(G-7405)*

SHOES: Men's

Hush Puppies Retail LLC .... E 231 937-1004
  Howard City *(G-8409)*
Original Footwear Mfg BR Inc .... F 231 796-5828
  Big Rapids *(G-1682)*
Veldheer Tulip Garden Inc .... E 616 399-1900
  Holland *(G-8235)*
Wolverine Procurement Inc .... C 616 866-9521
  Rockford *(G-14194)*
Wolverine Procurement Inc .... F 616 866-5500
  Rockford *(G-14195)*
Wolverine World Wide Inc .... A 616 866-5500
  Rockford *(G-14197)*

SHOES: Orthopedic, Children's

Orthotool LLC .... G 734 455-8103
  Plymouth *(G-13258)*

Employee Codes: A=Over 500 employees, B=251-500
C=101-250, D=51-100, E=20-50, F=10-19, G=3-9

SHOES: Orthopedic, Men's

Kalamazoo Orthotics & Dbtc .... F 269 349-2247
Kalamazoo *(G-9244)*
Millers Shoe Parlor Inc .... G 517 783-1258
Jackson *(G-8964)*
Orthotool LLC .... G 734 455-8103
Plymouth *(G-13258)*
Shoe Shop .... G 231 739-2174
Muskegon *(G-11918)*

SHOES: Orthopedic, Women's

Millers Shoe Parlor Inc .... G 517 783-1258
Jackson *(G-8964)*
Orthotool LLC .... G 734 455-8103
Plymouth *(G-13258)*

SHOES: Plastic Or Rubber

Nike Inc .... G 616 583-0754
Byron Center *(G-2289)*
Original Footwear Company .... B 231 796-5828
Big Rapids *(G-1681)*
Wolverine Procurement Inc .... F 616 866-5500
Rockford *(G-14195)*

SHOES: Plastic Or Rubber Soles With Fabric Uppers

Atlantic Precision Pdts Inc .... F 586 532-9420
Shelby Township *(G-15174)*
Fernand Corporation .... G 231 882-9622
Kalamazoo *(G-9185)*

SHOES: Women's

Original Footwear Mfg BR Inc .... F 231 796-5828
Big Rapids *(G-1682)*
Wolverine Procurement Inc .... C 616 866-9521
Rockford *(G-14194)*
Wolverine World Wide Inc .... A 616 866-5500
Rockford *(G-14197)*

SHOPPING CENTERS & MALLS

Reyers Company Inc .... F 616 414-5530
Spring Lake *(G-15846)*

SHOT PEENING SVC

Federal Industrial Svcs Inc .... G 586 427-6383
Warren *(G-17804)*
M P D Welding Inc .... D 248 340-0330
Orion *(G-12735)*
Metal Improvement Company LLC .. D 734 728-8600
Romulus *(G-14302)*
Metal Prep Technology Inc .... G 313 843-2890
Dearborn *(G-3870)*
Temp Rite Steel Treating Inc .... E 586 469-3071
Harrison Township *(G-7729)*

SHOWCASES & DISPLAY FIXTURES: Office & Store

Arbor Gage & Tooling Inc .... E 616 454-8266
Grand Rapids *(G-6466)*
Arlington Display Inds Inc .... G 313 837-1212
Detroit *(G-4027)*
Michalski Enterprises Inc .... E 517 703-0777
Lansing *(G-9716)*
SC Custom Display Inc .... G 616 940-0563
Kentwood *(G-9479)*
Shaw & Slavsky Inc .... E 313 834-3990
Detroit *(G-4589)*
Vista Manufacturing Inc .... E 616 719-5520
Walker *(G-17656)*

SHREDDERS: Indl & Commercial

Amos Mfg Inc .... F 989 358-7187
Alpena *(G-278)*
Chip Systems International .... F 269 626-8000
Scotts *(G-15130)*

SHUTTERS, DOOR & WINDOW: Metal

Arnold & Sautter Co .... F 989 684-7557
Bay City *(G-1322)*
Behind Shutter LLC .... G 248 467-7237
Grand Blanc *(G-6236)*
Shutterbooth .... G 734 680-6067
Ann Arbor *(G-651)*
Shutterbooth .... G 586 747-4110
West Bloomfield *(G-18313)*

SHUTTERS, DOOR & WINDOW: Plastic

Boral Building Products Inc .... C 800 521-8486
Wixom *(G-18625)*
Tapco Holdings Inc .... C 248 668-6400
Wixom *(G-18766)*

SIDING & STRUCTURAL MATERIALS: Wood

Decorative Panels Intl Inc .... E 989 354-2121
Alpena *(G-290)*
Nu-Tran LLC .... G 616 350-9575
Wyoming *(G-18897)*
Pure Products International In .... G 989 471-1104
Ossineke *(G-12779)*
Sensitile Systems LLC .... E 313 872-6314
Ypsilanti *(G-18977)*
Ufp Grand Rapids LLC .... F 616 464-1650
Grand Rapids *(G-7288)*
Ufp Industries Inc .... C 616 364-6161
Grand Rapids *(G-7289)*
Ufp Southwest LLC .... G 616 364-6161
Grand Rapids *(G-7293)*
Yard & Home LLC .... F 844 927-3466
Grand Rapids *(G-7354)*

SIDING MATERIALS

Pine River Inc .... F 231 758-3400
Charlevoix *(G-2728)*

SIDING: Plastic

Certainteed LLC .... G 517 787-8898
Jackson *(G-8837)*

SIDING: Sheet Metal

Dri-Design Inc .... E 616 355-2970
Holland *(G-8017)*
Quality Alum Acquisition LLC .... D 800 550-1667
Hastings *(G-7807)*

SIGN LETTERING & PAINTING SVCS

Amor Sign Studios Inc .... E 231 723-8361
Manistee *(G-10893)*
Bill Carr Signs Inc .... F 810 232-1569
Flint *(G-5655)*

SIGN PAINTING & LETTERING SHOP

A To Z Signs .... G 248 887-7737
Highland *(G-7878)*
Handicap Sign Inc .... G 616 454-9416
Grand Rapids *(G-6800)*
Kolossos Printing Inc .... F 734 994-5400
Ann Arbor *(G-540)*
Landers Drafting Inc .... G 906 228-8690
Marquette *(G-11028)*
Meiers Signs Inc .... G 906 786-3424
Escanaba *(G-5084)*
Scotts Signs .... G 616 532-2034
Grandville *(G-7417)*
Sun Ray Sign Group Inc .... G 616 392-2824
Holland *(G-8208)*

SIGNALING APPARATUS: Electric

National Time and Signal Corp .... E 248 291-5867
Oak Park *(G-12631)*
R H K Technology Inc .... E 248 577-5426
Troy *(G-17327)*

SIGNALS: Traffic Control, Electric

City of Saginaw .... G 989 759-1670
Saginaw *(G-14630)*
Give-Em A Brake Safety LLC .... E 616 531-8705
Grandville *(G-7379)*
National Sign & Signal Co .... F 269 963-2817
Battle Creek *(G-1277)*

SIGNALS: Transportation

Shield Material Handling Inc .... D 248 418-0986
Auburn Hills *(G-1032)*

SIGNS & ADVERTISING SPECIALTIES

5 Lakes Printing and Sign LLC .... G 517 265-3202
Adrian *(G-46)*
5 Pyn Inc .... G 906 228-2828
Negaunee *(G-11962)*
A D Johnson Engraving Co Inc ...... F 269 385-0044
Kalamazoo *(G-9106)*
A To Z Signs .... G 248 887-7737
Highland *(G-7878)*
A-1 Engraving & Signs Inc .... G 810 231-2227
Brighton *(G-1935)*
AC Design LLC .... G 616 874-9007
Rockford *(G-14151)*
Accent Signs .... G 860 693-6760
Canton *(G-2427)*
Acme Sign Co .... G 248 930-9718
Sterling Heights *(G-15923)*
Adams Outdoor Advg Ltd Partnr .... G 770 333-0399
Lansing *(G-9670)*
Adams Outdoor Advg Ltd Partnr .... E 517 321-2121
Lansing *(G-9671)*
Add-Savvy Digital Signage .... F 844 233-7288
Ann Arbor *(G-353)*
Advantage Sign Supply Inc .... E 877 237-4464
Hudsonville *(G-8564)*
Akzonobel Sign Finishes .... G 770 317-6361
Troy *(G-16917)*
Al Bo Co .... G 248 240-9155
Bloomfield Hills *(G-1795)*
All American Embroidery Inc .... F 734 421-9292
Livonia *(G-10108)*
Allen Pattern of Michigan .... F 269 963-4131
Battle Creek *(G-1184)*
Allied Screen & Grapics LLC .... G 248 499-8204
Pontiac *(G-13348)*
Ar2 Engineering LLC .... E 248 735-9999
Novi *(G-12364)*
Armstrong Display Concepts Inc .... F 231 652-1675
Newaygo *(G-12077)*
Arrow Signs .... G 989 350-4357
Saint Ignace *(G-14894)*
Art & Image .... G 800 566-4162
Benton Harbor *(G-1531)*
Articulate Signs .... G 248 577-1860
Troy *(G-16956)*
Attitude & Experience Inc .... F 231 946-7446
Traverse City *(G-16606)*
Ausable Woodworking Co Inc .... E 989 348-7086
Frederic *(G-6014)*
Auxier & Associates LLC .... G 231 486-0641
Traverse City *(G-16608)*
Barrett Signs .... G 989 792-7446
Saginaw *(G-14611)*
Bbj Graphics Inc .... G 248 450-3149
Southfield *(G-15504)*
Bella Group LLC .... G 586 789-7700
Harrison Twp *(G-7738)*
Berline Group Inc .... E 248 203-0492
Royal Oak *(G-14516)*
Best Portable Sign .... G 616 291-2911
Grand Rapids *(G-6503)*
Big Bore Signs LLC .... G 313 701-5900
Dexter *(G-4728)*
Bill Daup Signs Inc .... G 810 235-4080
Swartz Creek *(G-16351)*
Blue De-Signs LLC .... G 248 808-2583
Royal Oak *(G-14517)*
Brews Brothers III Inc .... G 228 255-5548
Dearborn *(G-3816)*
Brighter Sign Age .... G 248 719-5389
Saint Clair Shores *(G-14850)*
Britten Inc .... C 231 941-8200
Traverse City *(G-16627)*
Britten Banners LLC .... C 231 941-8200
Traverse City *(G-16628)*
Bronco Printing Company .... G 248 544-1120
Hazel Park *(G-7821)*
Burkett Signs Corp .... F 269 746-4285
Climax *(G-3135)*
Business Signs of America .... G 810 814-3987
Fenton *(G-5462)*
C G Witvoet & Sons Company ...... E 616 534-6677
Grand Rapids *(G-6543)*
C T L Enterprises Inc .... F 616 392-1159
Holland *(G-7989)*
Carrier & Gable Inc .... E 248 477-8700
Farmington Hills *(G-5199)*
Cg Detroit .... G 248 553-0202
Farmington Hills *(G-5201)*
Chad S Signs and Shirts .... G 248 821-3087
Davison *(G-3776)*
City Animation Co .... E 248 589-0600
Troy *(G-17012)*

PRODUCT SECTION — SIGNS & ADVERTISING SPECIALTIES

Company	Code	Phone
City Animation Co — Corunna (G-3706)	F	989 743-3458
Clips Coupons of Ann Arbo — South Lyon (G-15431)	G	248 437-9294
Cobrex Ltd — Saline (G-15008)	G	734 429-9758
Consort Corporation — Kalamazoo (G-9151)	E	269 388-4532
Copy Central Inc — Traverse City (G-16660)	G	231 941-2298
Cornhole Stop LLC — Brighton (G-1968)	G	704 728-1550
Cotton Concepts Printing LLC — Detroit (G-4104)	G	313 444-3857
Crop Marks Printing — Grand Rapids (G-6612)	G	616 356-5555
Custom Signs By Huntley — Flint (G-5680)	G	810 399-8185
D T R Sign Co LLC — Hastings (G-7788)	G	616 889-8927
Dagher Signs — Southfield (G-15536)	G	313 729-9555
Dana & Sean Roberds — Barryton (G-1172)	G	989 382-7564
Decor Group International Inc — Orchard Lake (G-12716)	F	248 307-2430
Design Fabrications Inc — Madison Heights (G-10705)	D	248 597-0988
Designs N Signs LLC — Roseville (G-14396)	G	248 789-8797
Detroit Marking Products Corp — Canton (G-2454)	F	313 838-9760
Detroit Name Plate Etching Inc — Ferndale (G-5547)	E	248 543-5200
Detroit Sign Factory LLC — Detroit (G-4166)	G	313 782-4667
Detroit Signs LLC — Detroit (G-4167)	G	313 345-5858
Diamond Sign — Warren (G-17778)	G	586 519-4296
Dicks Signs — Port Huron (G-13468)	G	810 987-9002
Digital Impact Design Inc — Kalamazoo (G-9168)	G	269 337-4200
Dj Customs LLC — Attica (G-752)	G	810 358-0236
Dmp Sign Company — Southfield (G-15542)	G	248 996-9281
Dornbos Sign Inc — Charlotte (G-2750)	F	517 543-4000
DOT Sign — Wixom (G-18647)	G	248 760-8236
Eagle Graphic and Design Inc — Walled Lake (G-17667)	G	248 668-0344
Edston Plastics Company — Brighton (G-1983)	G	734 941-3750
Eight Mile Signs — Livonia (G-10191)	G	248 762-3889
Elder Creek Sign Design — Springport (G-15881)	G	517 857-4252
Epi Printers Inc — Livonia (G-10198)	D	734 261-9400
Extreme Signs Inc — Clinton Township (G-3233)	G	586 846-3251
Fastsigns — Detroit (G-4226)	G	313 345-5858
Fastsigns — Hudsonville (G-8583)	G	616 377-7491
Fastsigns — Southfield (G-15558)	G	248 372-9554
Fastsigns — Farmington Hills (G-5241)	G	248 488-9010
Fastsigns International Inc — Traverse City (G-16680)	G	231 941-0300
Fire Fly — Sterling Heights (G-16015)	G	586 601-8792
Firebolt Group Inc — Wixom (G-18661)	G	248 624-8880
Flashpoint Sign LLC — Riverview (G-13873)	G	734 231-3361
Folk Sign Studio LLC — Stockbridge (G-16274)	G	734 883-8259
Fosters Ventures LLC — Troy (G-17120)	F	248 519-7446
Freshwater Digital — Kentwood (G-9455)	E	616 682-5470
Freshwter Dgtal Mdia Prtners L — Kentwood (G-9456)	F	616 446-1771
Fug Inc — Marshall (G-11058)	G	269 781-8036
Fwi Inc — Norton Shores (G-12294)	E	231 798-8324
G & W Display Fixtures Inc — Bronson (G-2112)	E	517 369-7110
Gator Grafix & Signs — Buchanan (G-2195)	G	269 362-2039
Genesee County Herald Inc — Clio (G-3399)	E	810 686-3840
George P Johnson Company — Auburn Hills (G-910)	D	248 475-2500
Golden Pointe Inc — Detroit (G-4269)	G	313 581-8284
Golden Sign Co — Ferndale (G-5559)	G	313 580-4094
Graphic Visions Inc — Northville (G-12225)	E	248 347-3355
Graphics Depot Inc — Waterford (G-18125)	G	248 383-5055
Graphics Hse Spt Prmotions Inc — Muskegon (G-11829)	G	231 733-1877
Graphicus Signs & Designs — Newaygo (G-12082)	G	231 652-9160
Graphix Gurus — Zeeland (G-19032)	G	616 217-6470
Graphix Signs & Embroidery — Holland (G-8056)	G	616 396-0009
Graphx Shop — Keego Harbor (G-9421)	G	248 678-5432
Grasshopper Signs Graphics LLC — Farmington Hills (G-5254)	F	248 946-8475
Green Sign Man — Otsego (G-12787)	G	269 370-0554
H M Day Signs Inc — Traverse City (G-16709)	G	231 946-7132
Handicap Sign Inc — Grand Rapids (G-6800)	G	616 454-9416
Harbor Industries Inc — Grand Haven (G-6312)	D	616 842-5330
Harvest Indus & Trade Co LLC — Northville (G-12228)	G	636 675-6430
HB Stubbs Company LLC — Warren (G-17850)	F	586 574-9700
Hexon Corporation — Farmington Hills (G-5259)	E	248 585-7585
High End Signs Svc & Lighting — Sterling Heights (G-16040)	G	248 596-9301
Higher Image Signs & Wraps LLC — Saginaw (G-14665)	G	989 964-0443
Highlander Graphics LLC — Ann Arbor (G-516)	G	734 449-9733
Holland Custom Signs — Holland (G-8077)	G	616 566-4783
Hoppenjans Inc — Monroe (G-11548)	F	734 344-5304
Hy-Ko Products Company LLC — Portage (G-13567)	E	330 467-7446
I Do Signs — Grand Haven (G-6320)	G	616 604-0431
Icon Signs Inc — Negaunee (G-11968)	G	906 401-0162
ID Enterprises — Farmington Hills (G-5265)	G	248 442-4849
Idea MNP Com LLC — Kalamazoo (G-9221)	G	269 459-8955
Idea Signs Visually — Kalamazoo (G-9222)	G	269 779-9163
Images Unlimited LLC — Rochester (G-13906)	G	248 608-8685
Infonorm Inc — Lake Orion (G-9610)	G	248 276-9027
Its Yours — Mason (G-11139)	G	517 676-7003
Janet Kelly — Cadillac (G-2338)	F	231 775-2313
JD Group Inc — Novi (G-12448)	F	248 735-9999
JD Hemp Inc — Royal Oak (G-14551)	G	248 549-0095
Jetco Signs — Battle Creek (G-1245)	G	269 420-0202
Johnson Sign Mint Cnslting LLC — Paris (G-12935)	G	231 796-8880
Jordan Advertising Inc — Saginaw (G-14674)	G	989 792-7446
Jra-Sign Supplies — Plymouth (G-13207)	G	800 447-7365
Juanita L Signs — Saint Joseph (G-14939)	G	269 429-7248
Just Signs Sometimes T-Shirts — Grand Rapids (G-6874)	G	616 401-1215
K-Bur Enterprises Inc — Grand Rapids (G-6876)	G	616 447-7446
Kore Group Inc — Ann Arbor (G-542)	G	734 677-1500
Lakeshore Graphics — Lexington (G-10030)	G	810 359-2087
Ledges Sign Company — Grand Ledge (G-6395)	G	517 925-1139
Legend Sign Company — Grand Rapids (G-6937)	G	616 447-7446
Lettering Inc — Livonia (G-10276)	G	248 223-9700
Lettering Inc of Michigan — Livonia (G-10277)	F	248 223-9700
Leutz Enterprise Inc — Marquette (G-11029)	G	906 228-5887
LLC Helton Brothers — Livonia (G-10290)	G	517 927-6941
Lobo Signs Inc — Traverse City (G-16746)	E	231 941-7739
Macomb Signs & Graphics — Macomb (G-10611)	G	586 350-9789
Majik Graphics Inc — Clinton Township (G-3291)	G	586 792-8055
Mamemarquees LLC — Macomb (G-10613)	G	586 322-2215
Maw Ventures Inc — Norton Shores (G-12309)	E	231 798-8324
Maxxlite Led Signs — Pontiac (G-13396)	G	248 397-5769
Mayfair Golf Accessories — Gaylord (G-6147)	G	989 732-8400
Mayrose Sign and Mktg Co LLC — Coopersville (G-3692)	G	616 837-1884
Media Solutions Inc — Detroit (G-4427)	G	313 831-3152
Metro Detroit Printing LLC — Livonia (G-10312)	G	734 469-7174
Metro Sign Fabricators Inc — Clinton Township (G-3299)	G	586 493-0502
MHR Investments Inc — Midland (G-11388)	F	989 832-5395
Michigan Graphic Arts — Coldwater (G-3444)	G	517 278-4120
Midwest Safety Products Inc — Grand Rapids (G-7006)	E	616 554-5155
Midwest Sign Install Inc — Hudsonville (G-8597)	G	616 862-7568
Miracle Sign — Melvindale (G-11205)	G	313 663-0145
Mitchart Inc — Midland (G-11395)	G	989 835-3964
Mod Signs Inc — Grand Rapids (G-7017)	F	616 455-0260
Moore Signs Investments Inc — Shelby Township (G-15285)	F	586 783-9339
Moreys Logo — Mount Pleasant (G-11718)	G	989 772-4492
Motor City Manufacturing Ltd — Ferndale (G-5569)	G	586 731-1086
Motor City Signs LLC — Flushing (G-5812)	G	810 867-2207
Motwon Sign Company LLC — Hazel Park (G-7835)	G	313 580-4094
Mrj Sign Company LLC — Ortonville (G-12749)	G	248 521-2431
Nalcor LLC — Ferndale (G-5570)	D	248 541-1140
Network Sign Company Inc — Brooklyn (G-2129)	G	517 548-1232
New Rules Marketing Inc — Spring Lake (G-15839)	E	800 962-3119
Nicolet Sign & Design — Iron River (G-8750)	G	906 265-5220
Normic Industries Inc — Traverse City (G-16771)	E	231 947-8860
Norris Graphics Inc — Clinton Township (G-3308)	G	586 447-0646
North Woods Sign Shop — Ludington (G-10547)	G	231 843-3956
Northern Laser Creations — Jonesville (G-9096)	G	517 581-7699
Northern Sign Co — Auburn Hills (G-987)	G	248 333-7733
On The Side Sign Dsign Grphics — Byron (G-2255)	G	810 266-7446
One Stop Sign Services — Marysville (G-11094)	G	810 358-1962
Paramount Signs LLC — Dearborn (G-3882)	G	734 548-1721

Employee Codes: A=Over 500 employees, B=251-500, C=101-250, D=51-100, E=20-50, F=10-19, G=3-9

SIGNS & ADVERTISING SPECIALTIES

PRODUCT SECTION

Company		Phone
Penn Sign — Romulus *(G-14318)*	G	814 932-7181
Perfect Signs — Manistee *(G-10911)*	G	231 233-3721
Phillips Enterprises Inc — Shelby Township *(G-15301)*	E	586 615-6208
Poco Inc — Canton *(G-2509)*	E	313 220-6752
Praise Sign Company — Grandville *(G-7411)*	G	616 439-0315
Premier Signs Plus Inc — Novi *(G-12511)*	G	248 633-5598
Princessa Designs Inc — Ada *(G-34)*	G	616 285-6868
Printastic LLC — Novi *(G-12515)*	F	248 761-5697
Pro Linez of Ann Arbor — Temperance *(G-16545)*	G	734 755-7309
Pro Sign and Awning Inc — Detroit *(G-4535)*	G	313 581-9433
Pro-Motion Tech Group LLC — Wixom *(G-18735)*	D	248 668-3100
Programmed Products Corp — Novi *(G-12517)*	D	248 348-7755
Qmi Group Inc — Madison Heights *(G-10814)*	E	248 589-0505
Quality Decals & Signs — Eaton Rapids *(G-4969)*	G	517 441-1200
Quicktrophy LLC — Marquette *(G-11043)*	F	906 228-2604
R & R Harwood Inc — Jenison *(G-9069)*	G	616 669-6400
R Gari Sign and Display Inc — Pinckney *(G-13054)*	G	810 355-1245
R Gari Sign Studio Inc — Brighton *(G-2060)*	G	810 355-1245
Race Graphics Plus — Coleman *(G-3471)*	G	989 465-9117
Revolutions Signs Designs LLC — Royal Oak *(G-14576)*	G	248 439-0727
Rockstar Digital Inc — Sterling Heights *(G-16158)*	F	888 808-5868
Rodzina Industries Inc — Flint *(G-5755)*	G	810 235-2341
Royal Oak Name Plate Company — Roseville *(G-14473)*	G	586 774-8500
Ryan Daup — Grand Blanc *(G-6262)*	G	810 240-6016
Salient Sign Studio — Oak Park *(G-12645)*	G	248 532-0013
Scarlet Spartan Inc — Brighton *(G-2068)*	F	810 224-5700
Scotts Signs — Grandville *(G-7417)*	G	616 532-2034
Sgo Corporate Center LLC — Plymouth *(G-13296)*	F	248 596-8626
Shaw & Slavsky Inc — Detroit *(G-4589)*	E	313 834-3990
Shelby Signarama Township — Shelby Township *(G-15332)*	G	586 843-3702
Shields & Shields Enterprises — Kalamazoo *(G-9332)*	G	269 345-7744
Shields Classic Toys — Saline *(G-15039)*	G	888 806-2632
Shorecrest Enterprises Inc — Clinton Township *(G-3352)*	G	586 948-9226
Sign & Graphics Operations LLC — Plymouth *(G-13297)*	E	248 596-8626
Sign & Vinyl Graphix Express — Sterling Heights *(G-16177)*	G	586 838-4741
Sign A Rama — Okemos *(G-12686)*	G	517 489-4314
Sign A Rama — Lansing *(G-9736)*	G	517 489-4314
Sign A Rama Inc — Brighton *(G-2071)*	G	810 494-7446
Sign and Banner World — Farmington *(G-5149)*	G	248 957-1240
Sign Center of Kalamazoo Inc — Kalamazoo *(G-9335)*	G	269 381-6869
Sign City Inc — Kalamazoo *(G-9336)*	G	269 375-1385
Sign Division — Benton Harbor *(G-1585)*	G	269 548-8978
Sign Fabricators Inc — Harrison Township *(G-7725)*	G	586 468-7360
Sign Graphix — Clarkston *(G-3066)*	G	248 241-6531
Sign Impressions Inc — Kalamazoo *(G-9337)*	G	269 382-5152
Sign On Inc — Kalamazoo *(G-9338)*	G	269 381-6869
Sign Pal — Saginaw *(G-14757)*	G	989 755-7773
Sign Pros LLC — Dearborn Heights *(G-3939)*	G	313 310-1010
Sign Screen — Cadillac *(G-2353)*	G	231 942-2273
Sign Screen Inc — Flint *(G-5762)*	G	810 239-1100
Sign Studio Inc — Warren *(G-18013)*	G	214 526-6940
Sign Stuff Inc — Livonia *(G-10409)*	G	734 458-1055
Sign With Sally C LLC — Algonac *(G-143)*	G	586 612-5100
Sign-A-Rama — Clinton Township *(G-3355)*	G	586 792-7446
Sign-A-Rama Inc — Garden City *(G-6110)*	G	734 522-6661
Sign-On Connect — Grosse Pointe Farms *(G-7541)*	G	313 539-3246
Signarama Farmington — Farmington *(G-5150)*	G	248 957-1240
Signcomp Inc — Grand Rapids *(G-7196)*	E	616 784-0405
Signing Savvy LLC — Okemos *(G-12687)*	G	517 455-7663
Signs & Laser Engraving — Troy *(G-17353)*	G	248 577-6191
Signs & Wonders LLC — Dewitt *(G-4715)*	G	618 694-4960
Signs and More — Flint *(G-5763)*	G	810 820-9955
Signs By Rhonda LLC — Clinton Township *(G-3356)*	G	248 408-0552
Signs By Tmrrow - Rchster Hlls — Rochester Hills *(G-14111)*	G	248 299-9229
Signs By Tomorrow — Hudsonville *(G-8612)*	G	616 647-7446
Signs By Tomorrow — Livonia *(G-10410)*	G	734 522-8440
Signs By Tomorrow — Novi *(G-12537)*	G	248 478-5600
Signs Direct LLC — Davison *(G-3796)*	G	810 732-5067
Signs In LLC — Farmington Hills *(G-5379)*	G	248 939-7446
Signs Letters & Graphics Inc — East Jordan *(G-4879)*	G	231 536-7929
Signs of Love Inc — Clinton Township *(G-3357)*	G	586 413-1269
Signs of Prosperity LLC — Farmington Hills *(G-5380)*	G	248 488-9010
Signs That Scream — Caledonia *(G-2399)*	G	616 698-6284
Signs365com LLC — Shelby Township *(G-15333)*	G	800 265-8830
Simi Air — Morenci *(G-11616)*	G	517 401-0284
Snap Display Frames — Grand Haven *(G-6363)*	G	616 846-7747
Source One Digital LLC — Norton Shores *(G-12334)*	E	231 759-3160
Spry Sign & Graphics Co LLC — Concord *(G-3655)*	G	517 524-7685
Steel Skinz LLC — Howell *(G-8523)*	G	517 545-9955
Sterling Creative Team Inc — Sterling Heights *(G-16191)*	G	586 978-0100
Stickerchef LLC — Saint Ignace *(G-14896)*	G	231 622-9900
Stimmel Construction LLC — Garden City *(G-6111)*	G	734 263-8949
Stnj LLC — Flint *(G-5770)*	F	810 230-6445
Sunset Enterprises Inc — Kalamazoo *(G-9346)*	F	269 373-6440
T M Shea Products Inc — Troy *(G-17383)*	F	800 992-5233
Tentcraft LLC — Traverse City *(G-16854)*	D	800 950-4553
The Sign Chap Inc — Madison Heights *(G-10842)*	G	248 585-6880
Tile By Bill & Sondra — Caledonia *(G-2404)*	G	616 554-5413
Timothy Michael Goodwin — Memphis *(G-11214)*	G	586 322-3312
Tischco Signs — Muskegon *(G-11933)*	G	231 755-5529
Tj Pant LLC — Sturgis *(G-16327)*	G	419 215-8434
Toms Sign Service — Rochester Hills *(G-14127)*	G	248 852-3550
Tyes Inc — Ludington *(G-10553)*	F	888 219-6301
Ultimate Graphic and Sign LLC — Saint Charles *(G-14812)*	G	989 865-5200
United Sign Co — Saranac *(G-15082)*	G	616 642-0200
Up North Sign LLC — Alanson *(G-112)*	G	231 838-6328
Valassis International Inc — Livonia *(G-10457)*	B	734 591-3000
Vinyl Graphix Inc — Saint Clair Shores *(G-14890)*	G	586 774-1188
Visual Productions Inc — Mesick *(G-11275)*	D	248 356-4399
Visual Workplace Byron Ctr Inc — Byron Center *(G-2299)*	G	616 583-9400
Visual Workplace LLC — Byron Center *(G-2300)*	F	616 583-9400
Vocational Strategies Inc — Calumet *(G-2415)*	F	906 482-6142
Whitehall Products LLC — Whitehall *(G-18514)*	G	231 894-2688
Wikid Vinyl — Shelby Township *(G-15369)*	G	313 585-7814
Wilde Signs — Muskegon *(G-11949)*	F	231 727-1200
Wildfire Signs & Graphics — Oxford *(G-12929)*	G	248 872-1998
Wilfred Swartz & Swartz G — Reese *(G-13811)*	G	989 652-6322
Windy Lake LLC — Pentwater *(G-12975)*	D	877 869-6911
Wood Love Signs — Macomb *(G-10651)*	G	586 322-6400
Wooden Moon Studio — Portage *(G-13635)*	G	269 329-3229
Woods Graphics — Greenville *(G-7511)*	F	616 691-8025
Wraps N Signs — Portage *(G-13636)*	G	269 377-8488
X-Treme Graphics N Signs LLC — Perry *(G-12982)*	G	989 277-7517
Xtreme Signs Inc — Warren *(G-18077)*	G	586 486-5068
Your Big Sign — Hartland *(G-7774)*	G	248 881-9505
Your Sign Lady LLC — Macomb *(G-10652)*	G	586 741-8585

SIGNS & ADVERTISING SPECIALTIES: Artwork, Advertising

Company		Phone
Epic Fine Arts Company Inc — Taylor *(G-16414)*	G	313 274-7400
Laughabits LLC — Detroit *(G-4379)*	G	248 990-3011

SIGNS & ADVERTISING SPECIALTIES: Letters For Signs, Metal

Company		Phone
Fairfield Investment Co — Livonia *(G-10204)*	G	734 427-4141
Rsls Corp — Shelby Township *(G-15319)*	G	248 726-0675

SIGNS & ADVERTISING SPECIALTIES: Novelties

Company		Phone
Advertsing Ntwrk Solutions Inc — Rochester *(G-13890)*	G	248 475-7881
Engineering Reproduction Inc — Detroit *(G-4209)*	G	313 366-3390
Versatility Inc — Grand Rapids *(G-7312)*	G	616 957-5555

SIGNS & ADVERTISING SPECIALTIES: Signs

Company		Phone
Advance Graphic Systems Inc — Rochester Hills *(G-13943)*	E	248 656-8000
Advanced Signs Incorporated — Ferrysburg *(G-5600)*	F	616 846-4667
Agnew Grphics Signs Promotions — Owosso *(G-12820)*	G	989 723-4621
Alex Delvecchio Entps Inc — Troy *(G-16919)*	F	248 619-9600
Allstate Sign Company Inc — Farwell *(G-5420)*	G	989 386-4045

PRODUCT SECTION

SILICON: Pure

Arnets Inc .... F 734 665-3650
  Ann Arbor (G-379)
Art/Fx Sign Co .... G 269 465-5706
  Bridgman (G-1921)
Auxier & Associates LLC .... G 231 933-7446
  Traverse City (G-16609)
Banacom Instant Signs .... G 810 230-0233
  Flint (G-5649)
Barrys Sign Company .... G 810 234-9919
  Flint (G-5651)
Bcs Creative LLC .... G 248 917-1660
  Davisburg (G-3760)
Beacon Sign Co .... G 313 368-3410
  Madison Heights (G-10680)
Bigsignscom .... F 800 790-7611
  Grand Haven (G-6279)
Bill Carr Signs Inc .... F 810 232-1569
  Flint (G-5655)
Castleton Village Center Inc .... G 616 247-8100
  Grand Rapids (G-6559)
Cook Sign Plus .... G 586 254-7000
  Shelby Township (G-15196)
Craigs Signs .... G 810 667-7446
  Lapeer (G-9923)
Creative Designs & Signs Inc .... G 248 334-5580
  Pontiac (G-13356)
Dimension Graphics Inc .... G 616 245-1447
  Grand Rapids (G-6648)
Eagle Graphics and Design .... G 248 618-0000
  Waterford (G-18121)
Eberhard and Father Signworks ...... G 989 892-5566
  Essexville (G-5113)
Elite Sign Company .... G 906 481-7446
  Big Rapids (G-1672)
Erie Marking Inc .... F 989 754-8360
  Saginaw (G-14644)
Expressign Design .... G 734 747-7444
  Ann Arbor (G-481)
Fairmont Sign Company .... E 313 368-4000
  Detroit (G-4225)
Federal Heath Sign Company LLC .. E 248 656-8000
  Rochester Hills (G-14010)
Griffon Inc .... F 231 788-4630
  Muskegon (G-11833)
Illusion Signs & Graphic Inc .... G 313 443-0567
  Dearborn (G-3853)
JL Geisler Sign Company .... G 586 574-1800
  Troy (G-17187)
Johnson Sign Company Inc .... F 517 784-3720
  Jackson (G-8923)
Lavanway Sign Co Inc .... G 248 356-1600
  Southfield (G-15624)
Marketing Displays Inc .... C 248 553-1900
  Farmington Hills (G-5310)
MI Custom Signs LLC .... F 734 946-7446
  Taylor (G-16444)
Michigan Graphics & Signs .... G 989 224-1936
  Saint Johns (G-14908)
Michigan Highway Signs Inc .... G 810 695-7529
  Grand Blanc (G-6253)
Michigan Plaques & Awards Inc ...... E 248 398-6400
  Berkley (G-1632)
Miller Designworks LLC .... G 313 562-4000
  Dearborn (G-3873)
MLS Signs Inc .... F 586 948-0200
  Macomb (G-10618)
National Sign & Signal Co .... E 269 963-2817
  Battle Creek (G-1277)
Northwood Signs Inc .... G 231 843-3956
  Ludington (G-10548)
Plasticrafts Inc .... G 313 532-1900
  Redford (G-13757)
Port Cy Archtctral Signage LLC ...... G 231 739-3463
  Muskegon (G-11896)
Rathco Safety Supply Inc .... E 269 323-0153
  Portage (G-13599)
S S Graphics Inc .... G 734 246-4420
  Wyandotte (G-18837)
Safari Signs .... G 231 727-9200
  Muskegon (G-11914)
Shop Makarios LLC .... F 800 479-0032
  Byron Center (G-2295)
Sign and Design .... G 231 348-9256
  Petoskey (G-13023)
Sign Concepts Corporation .... F 248 680-8970
  Troy (G-17351)
Sign Up Inc .... G 906 789-7446
  Escanaba (G-5099)
Signcrafters Inc .... G 231 773-3443
  Muskegon (G-11923)

Signmakers Ltd .... G 616 455-4220
  Grand Rapids (G-7197)
Signplicity Sign Systems Inc .... G 231 943-3800
  Traverse City (G-16832)
Signproco Inc .... F 248 585-6880
  Troy (G-17352)
Signs & Designs Inc .... G 269 968-8909
  Battle Creek (G-1294)
Signs Plus .... G 810 987-7446
  Port Huron (G-13527)
Signtext Incorporated .... E 248 442-9080
  Farmington Hills (G-5381)
Signworks of Michigan Inc .... G 616 954-2554
  Grand Rapids (G-7198)
Sporting Image Inc .... G 269 657-5646
  Paw Paw (G-12956)
Stamp-Rite Incorporated .... G 517 487-5071
  Lansing (G-9741)
Supersine Company .... E 313 892-6200
  Lathrup Village (G-9978)
Think Chromatic .... F 248 719-2058
  Comstock Park (G-3647)
TSS Inc .... E 586 427-0070
  Warren (G-18045)
USA Sign Frame & Stake Inc .... G 616 662-9100
  Jenison (G-9075)
Van Kehrberg Vern .... G 810 364-1066
  Marysville (G-11111)
Vital Signs Inc .... G 313 491-2010
  Canton (G-2540)
Wheelhouse Graphix LLC .... F 800 732-0815
  Bloomfield Hills (G-1874)

SIGNS & ADVERTSG SPECIALTIES: Displays/Cutouts Window/Lobby

Arlington Display Inds Inc .... G 313 837-1212
  Detroit (G-4027)
Grafaktri Inc .... G 734 665-0717
  Ann Arbor (G-504)
Harbor Industries Inc .... D 231 547-3280
  Charlevoix (G-2717)
Top Deck Systems Inc .... G 586 263-1550
  Shelby Township (G-15354)
Westcott Displays Inc .... E 313 872-1200
  Detroit (G-4678)

SIGNS, EXC ELECTRIC, WHOLESALE

Attitude & Experience Inc .... F 231 946-7446
  Traverse City (G-16606)
Dana & Sean Roberds .... G 989 382-7564
  Barryton (G-1172)
Erie Marking Inc .... F 989 754-8360
  Saginaw (G-14644)
Graphics Depot Inc .... G 248 383-5055
  Waterford (G-18125)
Infonorm Inc .... G 248 276-9027
  Lake Orion (G-9610)
Moreys Logo .... G 989 772-4492
  Mount Pleasant (G-11718)
Race Graphics Plus .... G 989 465-9117
  Coleman (G-3471)
Screen Ideas Inc .... G 616 458-5119
  Grand Rapids (G-7188)
Sign-A-Rama Inc .... G 734 522-6661
  Garden City (G-6110)

SIGNS: Electrical

All Signs LLC .... G 231 755-5540
  Muskegon (G-11767)
Allied Signs Inc .... F 586 791-7900
  Clinton Township (G-3162)
Amor Sign Studios Inc .... E 231 723-8361
  Manistee (G-10893)
Arrow Sign Co .... F 586 939-9966
  Sterling Hts (G-16235)
Earl Daup Signs .... F 810 767-2020
  Flint (G-5690)
Eco Sign Solutions LLC .... G 734 276-8585
  Ann Arbor (G-465)
Euko Design-Signs Inc .... G 248 478-1330
  Farmington Hills (G-5237)
Fire Safety Displays Co .... G 313 274-7888
  Dearborn Heights (G-3927)
Flatlander Signs .... G 810 867-2207
  Flushing (G-5808)
Gardner Signs Inc .... F 248 689-9100
  Troy (G-17127)
Hardy & Sons Sign Service Inc .... G 586 779-8018
  Saint Clair Shores (G-14864)

Huron Advertising Company Inc ..... E 734 483-2000
  Ypsilanti (G-18952)
Icon Sign & Design Inc .... G 517 372-1104
  Lansing (G-9766)
Identicom Sign Solutions LLC .... F 248 344-9590
  Farmington Hills (G-5267)
Japhil Inc .... G 616 455-0260
  Grand Rapids (G-6862)
Jvrf Unified Inc .... G 248 973-2006
  Sterling Heights (G-16058)
Landers Drafting Inc .... G 906 228-8690
  Marquette (G-11028)
Meiers Signs Inc .... G 906 786-3424
  Escanaba (G-5084)
Michigan Signs Inc .... G 734 662-1503
  Ann Arbor (G-575)
Pro Image Design .... G 231 322-8052
  Traverse City (G-16803)
R J Designers Inc .... G 517 750-1990
  Spring Arbor (G-15797)
Reliable Sign Service Inc .... G 586 465-6829
  Harrison Township (G-7720)
Rouhan Signs LLC .... G 406 202-2369
  Howard City (G-8418)
Rwl Sign Co LLC .... G 269 372-3629
  Kalamazoo (G-9323)
Sign Art Inc .... E 269 381-3012
  Kalamazoo (G-9334)
Sign Image Inc .... F 989 781-5229
  Saginaw (G-14756)
Sign Works Inc .... G 517 546-3620
  Howell (G-8517)
Signs By Crannie Inc .... E 810 487-0000
  Flint (G-5764)
Star Design Metro Detroit LLC .... E 734 740-0189
  Livonia (G-10419)
Steves Custom Signs Inc .... F 734 662-5964
  Ann Arbor (G-665)
Sun Ray Sign Group Inc .... G 616 392-2824
  Holland (G-8208)
System 2/90 Inc .... D 616 656-4310
  Grand Rapids (G-7244)
Tecart Industries Inc .... F 248 624-8880
  Wixom (G-18768)
Traffic Signs Inc .... G 269 964-7511
  Springfield (G-15876)
Transign LLC .... F 248 623-6400
  Auburn Hills (G-1064)
Ucb Advertising .... G 269 808-2411
  Plainwell (G-13102)
Universal Sign Inc .... G 616 554-9999
  Grand Rapids (G-7298)
Valley City Sign Company .... E 616 784-5711
  Comstock Park (G-3649)
Venture Grafix LLC .... G 248 449-1330
  Wixom (G-18787)
Wenz & Gibbens Enterprises .... G 248 333-7938
  Pontiac (G-13424)
Whitcomb and Sons Sign Co Inc .... G 586 752-3576
  Romeo (G-14239)
Zk Enterprises Inc .... G 989 728-4439
  Alger (G-140)

SIGNS: Neon

Bright Star Sign Inc .... G 313 933-4460
  Detroit (G-4071)
Brownie Signs LLC .... G 248 437-0800
  South Lyon (G-15428)
D Sign LLC .... G 616 392-3841
  Holland (G-8012)
Graph-X Signs .... G 734 420-0906
  Plymouth (G-13179)
Harmon Sign Inc .... G 248 348-8150
  Wixom (G-18676)
Inter City Neon Inc .... G 586 754-6020
  Warren (G-17868)
Modern Neon Sign Co Inc .... F 269 349-8636
  Kalamazoo (G-9274)
Radiant Electric Sign Corp .... G 313 835-1400
  Detroit (G-4552)
Spectrum Neon Company .... G 313 366-7333
  Madison Heights (G-10834)

SILICON: Pure

Snyder Plastics Inc .... E 989 684-8355
  Bay City (G-1403)

Employee Codes: A=Over 500 employees, B=251-500
C=101-250, D=51-100, E=20-50, F=10-19, G=3-9

SILICONE RESINS

Dow Silicones Corporation .... A 989 496-4000
  Auburn *(G-765)*
Zander Colloids Lc .... G 810 714-1623
  Fenton *(G-5514)*

SILICONES

Dow Corning Corporation .... F 989 839-2808
  Midland *(G-11353)*
Dow Silicones Corporation .... A 989 496-4000
  Auburn *(G-765)*
Wacker Chemical Corporation .... A 517 264-8500
  Adrian *(G-103)*
Wacker Chemical Corporation .... G 734 882-4055
  Ann Arbor *(G-712)*

SILK SCREEN DESIGN SVCS

Authority Customwear Ltd .... E 248 588-8075
  Madison Heights *(G-10676)*
Done Right Engraving Inc .... G 248 332-3133
  Pontiac *(G-13362)*
G T Jerseys LLC .... F 248 588-3231
  Troy *(G-17124)*
Grand Apps LLC .... G 517 927-5140
  Grand Ledge *(G-6391)*
Hi-Lites Graphic Inc .... E 231 924-0630
  Fremont *(G-6045)*
Sign Impressions Inc .... G 269 382-5152
  Kalamazoo *(G-9237)*
Sign Screen Inc .... G 810 239-1100
  Flint *(G-5762)*

SILLS: Concrete

Dlh World LLC .... G 313 915-0274
  Detroit *(G-4182)*

SILVER ORE MINING

Trelleborg Corporation .... G 269 639-9891
  South Haven *(G-15419)*

SILVER ORES PROCESSING

Aghog Inc .... G 313 277-2037
  Livonia *(G-10105)*

SILVERWARE & PLATED WARE

Collectors Zone .... G 517 788-8498
  Jackson *(G-8847)*
H M Products Inc .... G 313 875-5148
  Detroit *(G-4288)*
Samco Industries LLC .... F 586 447-3900
  Roseville *(G-14476)*

SIMULATORS: Flight

Azure Training Systems Jv LLC .... G 734 761-5836
  Ann Arbor *(G-393)*
Yakkertech Limited .... G 734 568-6162
  Ottawa Lake *(G-12812)*

SIRENS: Vehicle, Marine, Indl & Warning

West Shore Services Inc .... E 616 895-4347
  Allendale *(G-229)*

SKIDS: Wood

L & M Hardwood & Skids LLC .... G 734 281-0453
  Southgate *(G-15752)*

SKILL TRAINING CENTER

Siemens Industry Software Inc .... G 734 953-2700
  Livonia *(G-10406)*
Summit Training Source Inc .... E 800 842-0466
  Grand Rapids *(G-7233)*

SKYLIGHTS

Ceeflow Inc .... G 231 526-5579
  Harbor Springs *(G-7643)*

SLABS: Steel

Harrison Steel LLC .... G 586 247-1230
  Shelby Township *(G-15232)*

SLAG PRDTS

Edw C Levy Co .... B 313 429-2200
  Dearborn *(G-3835)*

SLAG: Crushed Or Ground

Tms International LLC .... F 734 241-3007
  Monroe *(G-11584)*

SLATE PRDTS

Moderne Slate Inc .... G 231 584-3499
  Mancelona *(G-10877)*

SLAUGHTERING & MEAT PACKING

Langes Beef & Bull Inc .... G 989 756-2941
  Whittemore *(G-18550)*
Rogers Beef Farms .... G 906 632-1584
  Sault Sainte Marie *(G-15098)*

SLINGS: Lifting, Made From Purchased Wire

Center Mass Inc .... G 734 207-8934
  Canton *(G-2447)*

SLINGS: Rope

Bundeze LLC .... G 248 343-9179
  West Olive *(G-18348)*
Quickmitt Inc .... G 517 849-2141
  Jonesville *(G-9099)*

SLIP RINGS

Kaydon Corporation .... B 734 747-7025
  Ann Arbor *(G-538)*

SLIPPERS: House

Wolverine Slipper Group Inc .... B 616 866-5500
  Rockford *(G-14196)*

SMOKE DETECTORS

Apollo America Inc .... D 248 332-3900
  Auburn Hills *(G-791)*
Gentex Corporation .... G 616 772-1800
  Zeeland *(G-19026)*
Gentex Corporation .... C 616 772-1800
  Zeeland *(G-19024)*

SMOKERS' SPLYS, WHOLESALE

Cheeba Hut Smoke Shop LLC .... G 586 213-5156
  Chesterfield *(G-2858)*

SNOW PLOWING SVCS

Clydes Frame & Wheel Service .... F 248 338-0323
  Pontiac *(G-13354)*
GTM Steamer Service Inc .... G 989 732-7678
  Gaylord *(G-6132)*
Mid Michigan Pipe Inc .... G 989 772-5664
  Grand Rapids *(G-7003)*
Shais Ldscpg Snow Plowing LLC .... G 248 234-3663
  Walled Lake *(G-17675)*
Unlimited Marine Inc .... G 248 249-0222
  White Lake *(G-18470)*

SNOW REMOVAL EQPT: Residential

Ace Outdoor Services LLC .... E 810 820-8313
  Flint *(G-5635)*
Coffman Electrical Eqp Co .... E 616 452-8708
  Grand Rapids *(G-6580)*
Grandville Tractor Svcs LLC .... F 616 530-2030
  Grandville *(G-7383)*
Green Day Management LLC .... F 313 652-1390
  Detroit *(G-4278)*

SNOWMOBILE DEALERS

C & C Sports Inc .... E 810 227-7068
  Brighton *(G-1958)*
Floatation Docking Inc .... E 906 484-3422
  Cedarville *(G-2669)*
Micro Engineering Inc .... G 616 534-9681
  Byron Center *(G-2285)*
Spicers Boat Cy Hughton Lk Inc .... E 989 366-8384
  Houghton Lake *(G-8403)*

SNOWMOBILES

Liberty Products Inc .... F 231 853-2323
  Ravenna *(G-13691)*
Pro-Powersports .... G 734 457-0829
  Monroe *(G-11570)*

SOAPS & DETERGENTS

Amway International Dev Inc .... A 616 787-6000
  Ada *(G-7)*
Caravan Technologies Inc .... F 313 632-8545
  Detroit *(G-4088)*
Chem Station .... F 517 371-8068
  Lansing *(G-9681)*
Continntal Bldg Svcs of Cncnna .... F 313 336-8543
  Grosse Pointe Woods *(G-7566)*
Diversified Chemical Tech Inc .... C 313 867-5444
  Detroit *(G-4180)*
DSC Laboratories Inc .... E 800 492-5988
  Muskegon *(G-11801)*
Ecolab Inc .... G 248 697-0202
  Novi *(G-12410)*
Huron Soap Candle Company .... F 810 989-5952
  Port Huron *(G-13486)*
Hydro-Chem Systems Inc .... E 616 531-6420
  Caledonia *(G-2383)*
K C M Inc .... F 616 245-8599
  Grand Rapids *(G-6875)*
L I S Manufacturing Inc .... F 734 525-3070
  Livonia *(G-10272)*
Mom of Shire Apothecary LLC .... G 734 751-9443
  Garden City *(G-6104)*
Moon River Soap Co LLC .... G 248 930-9467
  Rochester *(G-13912)*
Nature Patch Soaps .... G 734 847-3759
  Temperance *(G-16543)*
Richard D Matzke .... G 517 320-0964
  Hillsdale *(G-7945)*
Sanitation Strategies LLC .... F 517 268-3303
  Holt *(G-8328)*
Selestial Soap LLC .... E 231 944-1978
  Traverse City *(G-16828)*
South / Win LLC .... G 734 525-9000
  Livonia *(G-10414)*
Stone Soap Company Inc .... E 248 706-1000
  Sylvan Lake *(G-16362)*
Take Care Natural Products .... G 989 280-3947
  Cass City *(G-2621)*
Vaughan Industries Inc .... F 313 935-2040
  Detroit *(G-4663)*

SOAPS & DETERGENTS: Scouring Compounds

Gage Global Services Inc .... D 248 541-3824
  Ferndale *(G-5556)*

SOAPS & DETERGENTS: Textile

Ipax Atlantic LLC .... G 313 933-4211
  Detroit *(G-4325)*
Marjeannes Creations .... G 810 798-7278
  Almont *(G-264)*

SOCKETS: Electric

Brooks Utility Products Group .... D 248 477-0250
  Novi *(G-12377)*
State Tool & Manufacturing Co .... D 269 927-3153
  Benton Harbor *(G-1589)*

SOFT DRINKS WHOLESALERS

Mac Material Acquisition Co .... G 248 685-8393
  Highland *(G-7895)*
Pepsi-Cola Metro Btlg Co Inc .... G 810 232-3925
  Flint *(G-5744)*
South Range Bottling Works Inc .... G 906 370-2295
  South Range *(G-15462)*

SOFTWARE PUBLISHERS: Application

123go LLC .... G 734 773-0049
  Ann Arbor *(G-340)*
AK Rewards LLC .... G 734 272-7078
  Ann Arbor *(G-358)*
Alta Vista Technology LLC .... F 855 913-3228
  Royal Oak *(G-14506)*
Apis North America LLC .... G 800 470-8970
  Royal Oak *(G-14509)*
Arbormetrix Inc .... C 734 661-7944
  Ann Arbor *(G-377)*

Arctuition LLC .... G 616 635-9959
Ada *(G-9)*
Argus Technologies LLC .... E 616 538-9895
Grand Rapids *(G-6469)*
Asset Health Inc .... D 248 822-2870
Troy *(G-16961)*
Autodesk Inc .... G 248 347-9650
Novi *(G-12368)*
Automated Media Inc .... D 313 937-5000
Canton *(G-2438)*
Black Ski Weekend LLC .... G 313 879-7150
West Bloomfield *(G-18265)*
Bokhara Pet Care Centers .... F 231 264-6667
Elk Rapids *(G-5021)*
Braiq Inc .... G 858 729-4116
Detroit *(G-4066)*
Capital Software Inc Michigan .... G 517 324-9100
East Lansing *(G-4889)*
Catylist Inc .... G 734 973-3185
Ann Arbor *(G-416)*
Change Dynamix Inc .... G 248 671-6700
Royal Oak *(G-14525)*
Cloud Apps Consulting LLC .... G 616 528-0528
Grand Rapids *(G-6575)*
Collagecom LLC .... G 248 971-0538
White Lake *(G-18453)*
Complete Data Products Inc .... F 248 651-8602
Troy *(G-17021)*
Cygnet Financial Planning Inc .... G 248 673-2900
Waterford *(G-18112)*
Cytk Corp .... F 313 288-9360
South Lyon *(G-15432)*
Dassault Systmes Americas Corp .... C 248 267-9696
Auburn Hills *(G-858)*
E Z Logic Data Systems Inc .... E 248 817-8800
Farmington Hills *(G-5221)*
Edge Fitnes Training Hdqtr LLC .... G 989 486-9870
Midland *(G-11361)*
Empatheticbot LLC .... G 810 938-3168
Canton *(G-2458)*
Epath Logic Inc .... G 313 375-5375
Royal Oak *(G-14535)*
Eview 360 LLC .... E 248 306-5191
Farmington Hills *(G-5239)*
Flashplays Live LLC .... G 978 888-3935
Ann Arbor *(G-490)*
Gene Codes Forensics Inc .... G 734 769-7249
Ann Arbor *(G-497)*
Gentry Services of Alabama .... G 248 321-6368
Warren *(G-17828)*
Genus Inc .... G 810 580-9197
Grosse Pointe Park *(G-7555)*
Guardhat Inc .... G 248 281-6089
Southfield *(G-15587)*
High Touch Healthcare LLC .... G 248 513-2425
Novi *(G-12435)*
Infor (us) LLC .... G 616 258-3311
Grand Rapids *(G-6844)*
Inora Technologies Inc .... G 734 302-7488
Ann Arbor *(G-529)*
Inovision Sftwr Solutions Inc .... G 586 598-8750
Chesterfield *(G-2896)*
Integrted Database Systems Inc .... F 989 546-4512
Mount Pleasant *(G-11703)*
Intellibee Inc .... E 313 586-4122
Detroit *(G-4323)*
Interpro Technology Inc .... F 248 650-8695
Rochester *(G-13909)*
Intrinsic4d LLC .... G 248 469-8811
Bingham Farms *(G-1701)*
Kumanu Inc .... E 734 822-6673
Ann Arbor *(G-545)*
Luhu LLC .... G 320 469-3162
East Lansing *(G-4901)*
Medical Systems Resource Group .... G 248 476-5400
Farmington Hills *(G-5313)*
Menu Pulse Inc .... G 989 708-1207
Saginaw *(G-14695)*
Methodica Technologies LLC .... E 312 622-7697
Troy *(G-17252)*
Mintmesh Inc .... F 888 874-3644
Detroit *(G-4459)*
Mokasoft LLC .... G 517 703-0237
Okemos *(G-12677)*
National Instruments Corp .... B 734 464-2310
Livonia *(G-10332)*
Nexiq Technologies Inc .... F 248 293-8200
Rochester Hills *(G-14069)*
Nits Solutions Inc .... F 248 231-2267
Novi *(G-12488)*
Novation Analytics LLC .... G 313 910-3280
Bloomfield Hills *(G-1844)*
Onstar LLC .... E 313 300-0106
Detroit *(G-4500)*
Opio LLc .... F 313 433-1098
Dearborn *(G-3881)*
Ops Solutions LLC .... E 248 374-8000
Wixom *(G-18726)*
Power Rank Inc .... G 650 387-2336
Ann Arbor *(G-616)*
Rezoop LLC .... G 248 952-8070
Bloomfield *(G-1784)*
Ripple Science Corporation .... G 919 451-0241
Ann Arbor *(G-641)*
Rise Health LLC .... G 616 451-2775
Grand Rapids *(G-7158)*
Robal Tech LLC .... G 248 436-8105
Madison Heights *(G-10818)*
Rose Mobile Computer Repr LLC .... F 248 653-0865
Bloomfield Hills *(G-1859)*
Saagara LLC .... F 734 658-4693
Ann Arbor *(G-647)*
Saba Software Inc .... G 248 228-7300
Southfield *(G-15691)*
Sbsi Software Inc .... F 248 567-3044
Farmington Hills *(G-5376)*
Simerics Inc .... G 248 513-3200
Novi *(G-12538)*
Sizzl LLC .... F 201 454-1938
Ann Arbor *(G-654)*
Sodius Corporation .... G 248 270-2950
Royal Oak *(G-14581)*
Software Advantage Consulting .... G 586 264-5632
Sterling Heights *(G-16181)*
Star Board Multi Media Inc .... G 616 296-0823
Grand Haven *(G-6367)*
Strider Software Inc .... G 906 863-7798
Menominee *(G-11260)*
Sunera Technologies Inc .... A 248 434-0808
Troy *(G-17376)*
Superior Information Tech LLC .... F 734 666-9963
Livonia *(G-10424)*
Supported Intelligence LLC .... G 517 908-4420
East Lansing *(G-4912)*
Ticket Avengers Inc .... G 248 635-3279
Warren *(G-18039)*
Totle Inc .... G 248 645-1111
Birmingham *(G-1754)*
Touch World Inc .... E 248 539-3700
Farmington Hills *(G-5404)*
True Anlytics Mfg Slutions LLC .... G 517 902-9700
Ida *(G-8625)*
Twosixnine Studios .... G 269 365-6719
Vicksburg *(G-17615)*
Vanroth LLC .... F 734 929-5268
Ann Arbor *(G-709)*
Ventuor LLC .... G 248 790-8700
Flint *(G-5791)*
Vivian Enterprises LLC .... E 248 792-9925
Southfield *(G-15740)*
Weaver Instructional Systems .... G 616 942-2891
Grand Rapids *(G-7327)*

SOFTWARE PUBLISHERS: Business & Professional

313 Certified LLC .... G 248 915-8419
Bloomfield Hills *(G-1787)*
Appropos LLC .... E 844 462-7776
Grand Rapids *(G-6465)*
Automated Bookkeeping Inc .... G 866 617-3122
Detroit *(G-4031)*
Bell and Howell LLC .... G 734 421-1727
Livonia *(G-10136)*
Blue Pony LLC .... G 616 291-5554
Hudsonville *(G-8572)*
Brenton Consulting LLC .... G 248 342-6590
Northville *(G-12198)*
Broadsword Solutions Corp .... F 248 341-3367
Waterford *(G-18105)*
Clear Estimates Inc .... F 734 368-9951
Ann Arbor *(G-426)*
Coeus LLC .... F 248 564-1958
Bloomfield Hills *(G-1808)*
Computer Mail Services Inc .... F 248 352-6700
Sterling Heights *(G-15966)*
Consistacom Inc .... G 906 482-7653
Houghton *(G-8381)*
Core Technology Corporation .... F 517 627-1521
Grand Ledge *(G-6387)*
Cq Simple LLC .... G 989 492-7068
Midland *(G-11331)*
Datamatic Processing Inc .... E 517 882-4401
Lansing *(G-9829)*
Dna Software Inc .... F 734 222-9080
Plymouth *(G-13159)*
E-Con LLC .... G 248 766-9000
Birmingham *(G-1725)*
E-Procurement Services LLC .... D 248 630-7200
Auburn Hills *(G-873)*
Eco Tax Group Inc .... G 313 422-1300
Southfield *(G-15551)*
Faac Incorporated .... C 734 761-5836
Ann Arbor *(G-485)*
Interplai Inc .... G 734 274-4628
Ann Arbor *(G-531)*
Kronos Inc .... G 248 357-5604
Southfield *(G-15619)*
Level Eleven LLC .... E 313 662-2000
Detroit *(G-4393)*
Major One Electronics LLC .... G 313 652-3723
Detroit *(G-4418)*
Mastery Technologies Inc .... F 248 888-8420
Novi *(G-12472)*
Mc Donald Computer Corporation .... E 248 350-9290
Southfield *(G-15650)*
Microworld Technologies Inc .... G 248 470-1119
Novi *(G-12482)*
Mscsoftware Corporation .... G 734 994-3800
Troy *(G-17269)*
Mscsoftware Corporation .... G 734 994-3800
Ann Arbor *(G-586)*
Onestream Software Corp .... G 248 841-1356
Rochester *(G-13916)*
Onestream Software LLC .... G 248 342-1541
Rochester *(G-13917)*
Optimizerx Corporation .... G 248 651-6568
Rochester *(G-13918)*
Oracle Corporation .... G 248 393-2498
Orion *(G-12737)*
Orion Bus Accnting Sltions LLC .... G 248 893-1060
Wyandotte *(G-18835)*
Parameter Driven Software Inc .... F 248 553-6410
Farmington Hills *(G-5342)*
Paramount Technologies Inc .... E 248 960-0909
Saginaw *(G-14725)*
Platformsh Inc .... D 734 707-9124
Brooklyn *(G-2130)*
Prehab Technologies LLC .... G 734 368-9983
Ann Arbor *(G-623)*
Qad Inc .... G 248 324-9890
Farmington Hills *(G-5359)*
Quest - IV Incorporated .... F 734 847-5487
Lambertville *(G-9652)*
Routeone Holdings LLC .... E 800 282-6308
Farmington Hills *(G-5373)*
Salespage Technologies LLC .... E 269 567-7400
Kalamazoo *(G-9328)*
Siemens Industry Software Inc .... G 313 317-6100
Allen Park *(G-206)*
Siemens Industry Software Inc .... G 734 994-7300
Ann Arbor *(G-652)*
Solid Logic LLC .... F 616 738-8922
Holland *(G-8200)*
Talbot & Associates Inc .... F 248 723-9700
Franklin *(G-5885)*
Technology Network Svcs Inc .... F 586 294-7771
Saint Clair Shores *(G-14888)*
Tequionbrookins LLC .... G 313 290-0303
Southfield *(G-15721)*
Torenzo Inc .... F 313 732-7874
Bloomfield Hills *(G-1866)*
Tru-Syzygy Inc .... G 248 622-7211
Lake Orion *(G-9635)*
Truarx Inc .... F 248 538-7809
Southfield *(G-15728)*
Ultimate Software Group Inc .... G 616 682-9639
Ada *(G-39)*
Valassis Communications Inc .... A 734 591-3000
Livonia *(G-10455)*
Valassis Communications Inc .... G 734 432-8000
Livonia *(G-10456)*
Wilson Technologies Inc .... G 248 655-0005
Clawson *(G-3112)*
Workforce Payhub Inc .... G 517 759-4026
Adrian *(G-105)*
Workforce Software LLC .... C 734 542-4100
Livonia *(G-10478)*

SOFTWARE PUBLISHERS: Computer Utilities

SOFTWARE PUBLISHERS: Computer Utilities

Click Care LLC .... G 989 792-1544
  Saginaw *(G-14631)*

SOFTWARE PUBLISHERS: Education

Diagknowstics Tutoring .... G 877 382-1133
  Canton *(G-2455)*
Eca Educational Services Inc .... D 248 669-7170
  Commerce Township *(G-3525)*
Expectancy Learning LLC .... G 866 829-9533
  Grand Rapids *(G-6692)*
Fbe Associates Inc .... G 989 894-2785
  Bay City *(G-1357)*
Ginkgotree Inc .... G 734 707-7191
  Detroit *(G-4262)*
Mejenta Systems Inc .... E 248 434-2583
  Southfield *(G-15653)*
Noora Health .... G 402 981-0421
  Traverse City *(G-16770)*
Possibilities For Change LLC .... G 810 333-1347
  Ann Arbor *(G-615)*

SOFTWARE PUBLISHERS: NEC

21st Century Graphic Tech LLC .... G 586 463-9599
  Utica *(G-17501)*
360ofme Inc .... G 844 360-6363
  Royal Oak *(G-14500)*
3r Info LLC .... F 201 221-6133
  Canton *(G-2425)*
4d Systems LLC .... E 800 380-9165
  Flint *(G-5632)*
Accessible Information LLC .... G 248 338-4928
  Bloomfield Hills *(G-1790)*
Accord Software Solutions LLC .... G 616 604-1699
  Canton *(G-2428)*
Adadapted Inc .... F 313 744-3383
  Ann Arbor *(G-349)*
Advanced Tubular Tech Inc .... G 248 674-2059
  Clarkston *(G-3015)*
Akamai Technologies Inc .... G 734 424-1142
  Pinckney *(G-13043)*
Alfa Financial Software Inc .... D 855 680-7100
  Birmingham *(G-1717)*
Altair Engineering Inc .... C 248 614-2400
  Troy *(G-16928)*
Amesite Inc .... G 734 876-8141
  Detroit *(G-4015)*
Amicus Software .... G 313 417-9550
  White Lake *(G-18449)*
Ansys Inc .... G 248 613-2677
  Ann Arbor *(G-371)*
Appgraft LLC .... G 734 546-8458
  Canton *(G-2436)*
Applied Computer Technologies ...... F 248 388-0211
  West Bloomfield *(G-18263)*
Aras Corp .... F 248 385-5293
  Troy *(G-16951)*
Arbortext Inc .... C 734 997-0200
  Ann Arbor *(G-378)*
Artifcial Intllgnce Tech Slton .... E 877 787-6268
  Ferndale *(G-5528)*
Atos Syntel Inc .... A 248 619-2800
  Troy *(G-16964)*
Aurora Software .... G 248 853-2358
  Rochester Hills *(G-13956)*
Auvesy Inc .... G 616 888-3770
  Grand Rapids *(G-6485)*
Auxant Software LLC .... G 810 584-5947
  Grand Blanc *(G-6233)*
Azore Software LLC .... E 734 525-0300
  Livonia *(G-10130)*
Betterlife .... G 248 889-3245
  Highland *(G-7883)*
Biscayne and Associates Inc .... E 248 304-0600
  Milford *(G-11455)*
BMC Software Inc .... F 248 888-4600
  Farmington Hills *(G-5183)*
Boa Software LLC .... G 517 540-0681
  Howell *(G-8430)*
Bond Street Software .... G 616 847-8377
  Grand Rapids *(G-6521)*
Brinston Acquisition LLC .... D 248 269-1000
  Troy *(G-16985)*
C R T & Associates Inc .... G 231 946-1680
  Traverse City *(G-16635)*
Capital Billing Systems Inc .... G 248 478-7298
  Farmington Hills *(G-5196)*

Chain-Sys Corporation .... G 517 627-1173
  Lansing *(G-9757)*
Circlebuilder Software LLC .... G 248 770-3191
  Franklin *(G-5882)*
Comet Information Systems LLC ..... F 248 686-2600
  Grand Blanc *(G-6238)*
Competitive Cmpt Info Tech Inc .... F 732 829-9699
  Northville *(G-12201)*
Computer Sciences Corp .... G 734 761-8513
  Ann Arbor *(G-434)*
Computer Sciences Corporation ...... G 586 825-5043
  Sterling Heights *(G-15967)*
Compuware Corporation .... E 313 227-7300
  Detroit *(G-4100)*
Consolidated Computing Svcs .... G 989 906-0467
  Bay City *(G-1341)*
Covisint Corporation .... B 248 483-2000
  Southfield *(G-15533)*
Cyberlogic Technologies Inc .... E 248 631-2200
  Troy *(G-17041)*
Data Pro Inc .... G 269 685-9214
  Plainwell *(G-13074)*
Docnetwork Inc .... E 734 619-8300
  Ann Arbor *(G-454)*
Driven-4 LLC .... G 269 281-7567
  Saint Joseph *(G-14927)*
Duo Security Inc .... D 866 768-4247
  Ann Arbor *(G-460)*
Duo Security LLC .... C 734 330-2673
  Ann Arbor *(G-461)*
Elk Software LLC .... F 800 658-3420
  Wixom *(G-18654)*
EMC Corporation .... G 248 957-5800
  Farmington Hills *(G-5229)*
Empower Financials Inc .... G 734 747-9393
  Ann Arbor *(G-473)*
Engineering Tech Assoc Inc .... D 248 729-3010
  Troy *(G-17091)*
Falcon Network Services Inc .... G 248 726-0577
  Troy *(G-17105)*
Foresee Session Replay Inc .... G 800 621-2850
  Ann Arbor *(G-492)*
Forty Eight Forty Solutions .... F 713 332-6145
  Livonia *(G-10216)*
Fuzen Software Inc .... G 248 504-6870
  Northville *(G-12221)*
Global Information Systems Inc .... G 248 223-9800
  Livonia *(G-10225)*
Gnu Software Development Inc .... G 586 778-9182
  Warren *(G-17833)*
Gravity Software LLC .... G 844 464-7284
  Detroit *(G-4275)*
Great Lakes Infotronics Inc .... E 248 476-2500
  Northville *(G-12226)*
Great Lakes Technologies .... G 734 362-8217
  Grosse Ile *(G-7523)*
Harbor Software Intl Inc .... G 231 347-8866
  Petoskey *(G-13000)*
Herfert Software .... G 586 776-2880
  Eastpointe *(G-4936)*
Hilgraeve Inc .... G 734 243-0576
  Monroe *(G-11547)*
Ht Computing Services .... G 313 563-0087
  Dearborn *(G-3851)*
I-9 Advantage .... F 800 724-8546
  Troy *(G-17157)*
Ideation International Inc .... F 248 737-8854
  Farmington Hills *(G-5266)*
Imagesoft .... G 919 462-8505
  Grand Rapids *(G-6835)*
Information Builders Inc .... G 248 641-8820
  Troy *(G-17166)*
Innovative Programming Systems .... G 810 695-9332
  Grand Blanc *(G-6249)*
Innovative Sftwr Solutions Ltd .... E 616 785-0745
  Grand Rapids *(G-6847)*
Inovision Inc .... E 248 299-1915
  Rochester Hills *(G-14040)*
Integrated Practice Service .... G 248 646-7009
  South Lyon *(G-15439)*
Interact Websites Inc .... F 800 515-9672
  Midland *(G-11374)*
Jda Software Group Inc .... G 734 741-4205
  Ann Arbor *(G-533)*
Kingston Educational Software .... G 248 895-4803
  Farmington Hills *(G-5281)*
Lakeside Software LLC .... G 248 686-1700
  Ann Arbor *(G-547)*
Linked Live Inc .... G 248 345-5993
  Madison Heights *(G-10770)*

Lintech Global Inc .... D 248 553-8033
  Farmington Hills *(G-5292)*
Livermore Software Tech LLC .... F 925 449-2500
  Troy *(G-17214)*
Lspedia LLC .... G 248 320-1909
  West Bloomfield *(G-18294)*
Mad Dog Software .... G 248 940-2963
  Birmingham *(G-1734)*
Magnetic Michigan .... D 734 922-7068
  Ann Arbor *(G-562)*
Magnus Software Inc .... G 517 294-0315
  Fowlerville *(G-5850)*
Marc Schrreiber & Company LLC ... G 734 222-9930
  Ann Arbor *(G-566)*
Marketplus Software Inc .... G 269 968-4240
  Springfield *(G-15872)*
McKesson Pharmacy Systems LLC .. A 800 521-1758
  Livonia *(G-10309)*
McManus Software Development .... G 810 231-6589
  Whitmore Lake *(G-18540)*
Medimage Inc .... G 734 665-5400
  Ann Arbor *(G-568)*
Melange Computer Services Inc ...... F 517 321-8434
  Lansing *(G-9774)*
Micro Focus Software Inc .... G 248 353-8010
  Southfield *(G-15658)*
Microsoft Corporation .... G 248 205-5990
  Troy *(G-17260)*
Mighty Co .... E 616 822-1013
  Hudsonville *(G-8598)*
Mission Pathways LLC .... G 734 260-9411
  Ann Arbor *(G-579)*
New Concepts Software Inc .... G 586 776-2855
  Roseville *(G-14453)*
Nubill Corporation .... F 248 246-7640
  Royal Oak *(G-14566)*
Oasys LLC .... G 414 529-3922
  Lansing *(G-9876)*
Openalpr Software Solutions L .... G 800 935-1699
  Commerce Township *(G-3560)*
Optonomy Inc .... E 734 604-6472
  Ann Arbor *(G-602)*
Oracle America Inc .... G 989 495-0465
  Midland *(G-11400)*
Oracle Systems Corporation .... G 248 614-5139
  Rochester Hills *(G-14076)*
Oracle Systems Corporation .... G 248 816-8050
  Troy *(G-17290)*
Orbit Technology Inc .... G 906 776-7248
  Iron Mountain *(G-8729)*
Owntheplay Inc .... G 248 514-0352
  Detroit *(G-4502)*
Pace Software Systems Inc .... F 586 727-3189
  Casco *(G-2602)*
Paragon Vciso Group LLC .... G 248 895-9866
  Detroit *(G-4507)*
PC Solutions .... E 517 787-9934
  Jackson *(G-8983)*
Pearson Software Company .... G 313 878-2687
  Detroit *(G-4511)*
Peninsular Technologies LLC .... E 616 676-9811
  Grand Rapids *(G-7076)*
Perennial Software .... F 734 414-0760
  Canton *(G-2506)*
Perfect Sync Inc .... G 231 947-9300
  Traverse City *(G-16789)*
Perspective Software .... G 248 308-2418
  Northville *(G-12252)*
Phoenix Intergration Inc .... G 586 484-8196
  Novi *(G-12505)*
Pioneer Automotive Inc .... F 586 758-7730
  Sterling Heights *(G-16127)*
Pitss America LLC .... E 248 740-0935
  Troy *(G-17303)*
Platform Computing Inc .... G 248 359-7825
  Southfield *(G-15675)*
Polyworks USA Training Center .... G 216 226-1617
  Novi *(G-12506)*
Practice Management Tech .... G 231 352-9844
  Frankfort *(G-5879)*
Prime Pdiatrics Adolescent PLC ...... G 281 259-5785
  Grand Blanc *(G-6257)*
Process Analytics Factory LLC .... G 929 350-4053
  Southfield *(G-15684)*
Qnx Software Systems .... G 248 513-3412
  Novi *(G-12520)*
Qquest Corporation .... G 313 441-0022
  Waterford *(G-18160)*
Quantum Compliance Systems .... F 734 930-0009
  Ypsilanti *(G-18973)*

PRODUCT SECTION

Quest Software LLC .... B 800 541-2593
  Saint Johns *(G-14913)*
R E R Software Inc .... G 586 744-0881
  Rochester Hills *(G-14098)*
Radley Corporation .... E 616 554-9060
  Grand Rapids *(G-7136)*
Real View LLC .... F 616 524-5243
  Grand Rapids *(G-7143)*
Rearden Development Corp .... G 616 464-4434
  Grand Rapids *(G-7144)*
Recursive LLC .... G 904 449-2386
  Holland *(G-8177)*
Redtail Software .... G 231 587-0720
  Mancelona *(G-10878)*
Regents of The University Mich .... E 734 936-0435
  Ann Arbor *(G-637)*
Reilly & Associates Inc .... E 248 605-9393
  Clarkston *(G-3060)*
Rewardpal Inc .... G 800 377-6099
  Novi *(G-12526)*
Ringmaster Software Corp .... F 802 383-1050
  Troy *(G-17333)*
Rutherford & Associates Inc .... E 616 392-5000
  Holland *(G-8185)*
S2 Games LLC .... D 269 344-8020
  Portage *(G-13604)*
Schindler Software LLC .... G 574 360-9045
  Niles *(G-12165)*
Sensible Vision Inc .... G 734 478-1130
  Covert *(G-3725)*
Serniuk Software .... G 248 668-3826
  Wolverine Lake *(G-18797)*
Signalx Technologies LLC .... E 248 935-4237
  Plymouth *(G-13298)*
Signmeupcom Inc .... G 312 343-1263
  Monroe *(G-11572)*
Silkroute Global Inc .... E 248 854-3409
  Troy *(G-17354)*
Sims Software II Inc .... G 586 491-0058
  Clinton Township *(G-3358)*
Sirionlabs Inc .... G 313 300-0588
  Grosse Pointe Park *(G-7560)*
Skysync Inc .... E 734 822-6858
  Ann Arbor *(G-655)*
Software Assoc Inc .... F 248 477-6112
  Farmington *(G-5151)*
Software Bots Inc .... G 734 730-6526
  Canton *(G-2524)*
Software Finesse LLC .... G 248 737-8990
  Farmington Hills *(G-5383)*
Solidthinking Inc .... G 248 526-1920
  Troy *(G-17360)*
Spiders Software Solutions LLC .... G 248 305-3225
  Northville *(G-12262)*
Spire Integrated Systems Inc .... E 248 544-0072
  Troy *(G-17367)*
SRP Software .... G 231 779-3602
  Cadillac *(G-2358)*
Stardock Systems Inc .... E 734 927-0677
  Plymouth *(G-13303)*
Startech Software Systems Inc .... G 248 344-2266
  Novi *(G-12542)*
Strategic Computer Solutions .... G 248 888-0666
  Ann Arbor *(G-667)*
Suse LLC .... F 248 353-8010
  Southfield *(G-15715)*
Sync Technologies Inc .... E 313 963-5353
  Detroit *(G-4622)*
T4 Software .... G 313 610-3297
  Dearborn Heights *(G-3940)*
Tebis America Inc .... E 248 524-0430
  Troy *(G-17386)*
Tecra Systems Inc .... F 248 888-1116
  Westland *(G-18420)*
Tree House Software Inc .... G 503 208-6171
  Ann Arbor *(G-696)*
Trend Software LLC .... G 616 452-8032
  Grand Rapids *(G-7274)*
TST Tooling Software Tech LLC .... F 248 922-9293
  Clarkston *(G-3073)*
Tweddle Group Inc .... G 586 840-3275
  Detroit *(G-4649)*
Tyler Technologies Inc .... G 734 677-0550
  Ann Arbor *(G-701)*
Umakanth Consultants Inc .... F 517 347-7500
  Okemos *(G-12691)*
Uniprax LLC .... G 616 522-3158
  Ionia *(G-8692)*
Universal Sftwr Solutions Inc .... E 810 653-5000
  Davison *(G-3799)*

V E S T Inc .... G 248 649-9550
  Troy *(G-17422)*
V2soft Inc .... D 248 904-1702
  Bloomfield Hills *(G-1872)*
Varatech Inc .... F 616 393-6408
  Holland *(G-8234)*
Vector North America Inc .... D 248 449-9290
  Novi *(G-12565)*
Verishow .... G 212 913-0600
  West Bloomfield *(G-18322)*
Vertigee Corporation .... G 313 999-1020
  Saline *(G-15043)*
Vieth Consulting LLC .... F 517 622-3090
  Grand Ledge *(G-6400)*
Virtual Advantage LLc .... G 877 772-6886
  Troy *(G-17441)*
Warner Software Co LLC .... G 616 916-1182
  Comstock Park *(G-3650)*
Westmountain Software .... G 734 776-3966
  Westland *(G-18432)*
World of Cd-Rom .... F 269 382-3766
  Kalamazoo *(G-9374)*
Xcell Software Inc .... G 248 760-3160
  Commerce Township *(G-3583)*
Zume It Inc .... G 248 522-6868
  Farmington Hills *(G-5419)*

SOFTWARE PUBLISHERS: Operating Systems

3dfx Interactive Inc .... G 918 938-8967
  Saginaw *(G-14599)*
J H P Inc .... G 248 588-0110
  Madison Heights *(G-10750)*
Nemo Capital Partners LLC .... D 855 944-2995
  Southfield *(G-15665)*
Red Hat Inc .... G 978 392-2459
  Ann Arbor *(G-634)*

SOFTWARE PUBLISHERS: Publisher's

Harper Arrington Pubg LLC .... G 313 282-6751
  Detroit *(G-4295)*

SOFTWARE TRAINING, COMPUTER

Apis North America LLC .... G 800 470-8970
  Royal Oak *(G-14509)*
Applied Automation Tech Inc .... E 248 656-4930
  Rochester Hills *(G-13949)*

SOLAR CELLS

Helian Technologies LLC .... G 248 535-6545
  Shelby Township *(G-15234)*
Helios Solar LLC .... G 269 343-5581
  Kalamazoo *(G-9212)*
Ovshinsky Technologies LLC .... G 248 752-2344
  Bloomfield Hills *(G-1846)*
Patriot Solar Group LLC .... E 517 629-9292
  Albion *(G-129)*

SOLAR HEATING EQPT

Great Lakes Electric LLC .... G 269 408-8276
  Saint Joseph *(G-14932)*
Pyrinas LLC .... G 810 422-7535
  Traverse City *(G-16807)*
Refrigeration Research Inc .... D 810 227-1151
  Brighton *(G-2064)*
Solar Control Systems .... G 734 671-6899
  Grosse Ile *(G-7526)*
Solar EZ Inc .... F 989 773-3427
  Mount Pleasant *(G-11741)*

SOLDERING EQPT: Electrical, Exc Handheld

Delfab Inc .... E 906 428-9570
  Gladstone *(G-6180)*

SOLDERING EQPT: Irons Or Coppers

Assembly Technologies Intl Inc .... F 248 280-2810
  Troy *(G-16960)*

SOLENOIDS

Eto Magnetic Corp .... C 616 957-2670
  Grand Rapids *(G-6686)*
Fema Corporation of Michigan .... C 269 323-1369
  Portage *(G-13560)*
Nass Corporation .... F 586 725-6610
  New Baltimore *(G-11989)*

SOLID CONTAINING UNITS: Concrete

K-Mar Structures LLC .... F 231 924-3895
  Fremont *(G-6046)*

SOLVENTS: Organic

Eq Resource Recovery Inc .... G 734 727-5500
  Romulus *(G-14272)*
Gage Corporation .... F 248 541-3824
  Ferndale *(G-5555)*
Kelley Laboratories Inc .... F 231 861-6257
  Shelby *(G-15153)*

SONAR SYSTEMS & EQPT

Talkin Tackle LLC .... G 517 474-6241
  Jackson *(G-9015)*

SOUND EQPT: Electric

Band-Ayd Systems Intl Inc .... F 586 294-8851
  Madison Heights *(G-10677)*
Emergency Technology Inc .... D 616 896-7100
  Hudsonville *(G-8581)*

SOUVENIRS, WHOLESALE

Bahama Souvenirs Inc .... G 269 964-8275
  Battle Creek *(G-1189)*

SOYBEAN PRDTS

Zeeland Bio-Based Products LLC .... G 616 748-1831
  Zeeland *(G-19095)*
Zeeland Farm Services Inc .... C 616 772-9042
  Zeeland *(G-19096)*
Zeeland Farm Soya LLC .... F 616 772-9042
  Zeeland *(G-19097)*
Zfs Creston LLC .... F 616 748-1825
  Zeeland *(G-19100)*
Zfs Ithaca LLC .... E 616 772-9042
  Zeeland *(G-19101)*

SPACE PROPULSION UNITS & PARTS

Orbion Space Technology Inc .... E 906 362-2509
  Houghton *(G-8388)*

SPACE VEHICLE EQPT

Advance Turning and Mfg Inc .... C 517 783-2713
  Jackson *(G-8802)*
Dorris Company .... F 586 293-5260
  Fraser *(G-5919)*
MB Aerospace Warren LLC .... C 586 772-2500
  Warren *(G-17920)*
Mistequay Group Ltd .... E 989 846-1000
  Standish *(G-15893)*
Parker-Hannifin Corporation .... B 269 384-3459
  Kalamazoo *(G-9288)*
Rapp & Son Inc .... D 734 283-1000
  Wyandotte *(G-18836)*
SGC Industries Inc .... F 586 293-5260
  Fraser *(G-5992)*
Swiss American Screw Pdts Inc .... E 734 397-1600
  Canton *(G-2529)*
Truform Machine Inc .... E 517 782-8523
  Jackson *(G-9025)*

SPAS

Body Contour Ventures LLC .... E 248 579-6772
  Farmington Hills *(G-5184)*

SPEAKER SYSTEMS

Moss Audio Corporation .... D 616 451-9933
  Grand Rapids *(G-7030)*

SPECIAL EVENTS DECORATION SVCS

Perrin Souvenir Distrs Inc .... B 616 785-9700
  Comstock Park *(G-3636)*

SPECIALTY FOOD STORES, NEC

McDonalds .... F 248 851-7310
  Oxford *(G-12900)*

SPECIALTY FOOD STORES: Coffee

Hashems of Dearborn Heights .... F 313 278-2000
  Dearborn Heights *(G-3928)*

SPECIALTY FOOD STORES: Coffee

Hermans Boy .... G 616 866-2900
  Rockford *(G-14169)*
Nuts & Coffee Gallery .... G 313 581-3212
  Dearborn *(G-3878)*
Royal Accoutrements Inc .... G 517 347-7983
  Okemos *(G-12683)*

SPECIALTY FOOD STORES: Dietetic Foods

Hello Life Inc .... E 616 808-3290
  Grand Rapids *(G-6809)*

SPECIALTY FOOD STORES: Health & Dietetic Food

Ionxhealth Inc .... E 616 808-3290
  Grand Rapids *(G-6852)*
N F P Inc .... G 989 631-0009
  Midland *(G-11397)*

SPECIALTY OUTPATIENT CLINICS, NEC

Liver Transplant/Univ of Mich .... G 734 936-7670
  Ann Arbor *(G-552)*

SPECIALTY SAWMILL PRDTS

Biewer Forest Management LLC ..... G 231 825-2855
  Mc Bain *(G-11177)*

SPEED CHANGERS

Cone Drive Operations Inc .... C 231 946-8410
  Traverse City *(G-16658)*

SPICE & HERB STORES

Country Home Creations Inc .... E 810 244-7348
  Flint *(G-5674)*
Michigan Herbal Remedies LLC ...... G 616 818-0823
  Jenison *(G-9062)*

SPIKES: Nonferrous Metal Or Wire

Marisa Manufacturing Inc .... G 586 754-3000
  Warren *(G-17915)*

SPINDLES: Textile

Precision Spindle Service Co .... F 248 544-0100
  Ferndale *(G-5581)*

SPONGES, ANIMAL, WHOLESALE

Armaly Sponge Company .... E 248 669-2100
  Commerce Township *(G-3512)*

SPONGES: Plastic

Armaly Sponge Company .... E 248 669-2100
  Commerce Township *(G-3512)*

SPOOLS: Indl

Faulkner Fabricators Inc .... F 269 473-3073
  Berrien Springs *(G-1641)*

SPORTING & ATHLETIC GOODS: Arrows, Archery

Carbon Impact Inc .... G 231 929-8152
  Traverse City *(G-16639)*

SPORTING & ATHLETIC GOODS: Balls, Baseball, Football, Etc

B4 Sports Inc .... E 248 454-9700
  Bloomfield Hills *(G-1802)*

SPORTING & ATHLETIC GOODS: Boomerangs

Boomerang Enterprises Inc .... G 269 547-9715
  Mattawan *(G-11163)*
Boomerang Exhibits .... G 315 525-6973
  Grand Rapids *(G-6522)*
Boomerang Retro & Relics .... G 906 362-7876
  Marquette *(G-11010)*
Boomerangs Gift Gallery .... G 248 228-0314
  Lapeer *(G-9915)*

SPORTING & ATHLETIC GOODS: Bowling Alleys & Access

Double Six Sports Complex .... F 989 762-5342
  Stanton *(G-15900)*
Simerson Inc .... G 989 233-1420
  Vassar *(G-17581)*

SPORTING & ATHLETIC GOODS: Bowling Balls

Seal Bowling Balls LLC .... G 248 707-6482
  Clarkston *(G-3063)*

SPORTING & ATHLETIC GOODS: Bows, Archery

Container Specialties Inc .... E 989 728-4231
  Hale *(G-7588)*
Lone Wolf Custom Bows .... G 989 735-3358
  Glennie *(G-6213)*

SPORTING & ATHLETIC GOODS: Camping Eqpt & Splys

Dave Lewishcky Fantsy Camp .... G 248 328-0891
  Holly *(G-8265)*
Delta 6 LLC .... G 248 778-6414
  Livonia *(G-10178)*
My-Can LLC .... G 989 288-7779
  Durand *(G-4843)*
Northern Trading Group LLC .... G 248 885-8750
  Birmingham *(G-1740)*
Perfect Expressions .... G 248 640-1287
  Bloomfield Hills *(G-1851)*

SPORTING & ATHLETIC GOODS: Crossbows

Excalibur Crossbow Inc .... G 810 937-5864
  Port Huron *(G-13476)*

SPORTING & ATHLETIC GOODS: Exercising Cycles

Assenmacher Lightweight Cycles .... G 810 232-2994
  Flint *(G-5645)*

SPORTING & ATHLETIC GOODS: Fishing Bait, Artificial

K & E Tackle Inc .... F 269 945-4496
  Hastings *(G-7802)*

SPORTING & ATHLETIC GOODS: Fishing Eqpt

Dreamweaver Lure Company Inc .... F 231 843-3652
  Ludington *(G-10535)*
Ed Cumings Inc .... E 810 736-0130
  Flint *(G-5693)*
Fish On Sports Inc .... G 231 342-5231
  Interlochen *(G-8683)*
Mitchell Coates .... D 231 582-5878
  Boyne City *(G-1897)*
My Tec-Tronics LLC .... G 586 218-0118
  Brighton *(G-2038)*
North Post Inc .... G 906 482-5210
  Hancock *(G-7622)*

SPORTING & ATHLETIC GOODS: Fishing Tackle, General

Eppinger Mfg Co .... F 313 582-3205
  Dearborn *(G-3838)*
Grapentin Specialties Inc .... G 810 724-0636
  Imlay City *(G-8634)*
HI Outdoors .... G 989 422-3264
  Houghton Lake *(G-8399)*
Home Chef Ltd .... G 734 468-2544
  Westland *(G-18384)*

SPORTING & ATHLETIC GOODS: Football Eqpt & Splys, NEC

Rogers Athletic Company Inc .... E 800 457-5337
  Farwell *(G-5427)*

SPORTING & ATHLETIC GOODS: Game Calls

Kennedy Game Calls LLC .... G 269 870-5001
  Kalamazoo *(G-9253)*
Legends Game Call Co .... G 517 499-6962
  Napoleon *(G-11953)*

SPORTING & ATHLETIC GOODS: Gymnasium Eqpt

Pull-Buoy Inc .... G 586 997-0900
  Sterling Heights *(G-16138)*
Ripper Ventures LLC .... G 248 808-2325
  Plymouth *(G-13282)*
Spieth Anderson USA Lc .... F 817 536-3366
  Lansing *(G-9739)*
T L V Inc .... F 989 773-4362
  Mount Pleasant *(G-11744)*

SPORTING & ATHLETIC GOODS: Hockey Eqpt & Splys, NEC

Rolston Hockey Academy LLC .... G 248 450-5300
  Oak Park *(G-12640)*
Superior Hockey LLC .... F 906 225-9008
  Marquette *(G-11045)*
Warrior Sports Inc .... C 800 968-7845
  Warren *(G-18063)*

SPORTING & ATHLETIC GOODS: Hunting Eqpt

Aerospace America Inc .... E 989 684-2121
  Bay City *(G-1319)*
Buck Stop Lure Company Inc .... G 989 762-5091
  Stanton *(G-15899)*
Family Trdtons Tree Stands LLC ..... G 517 543-3926
  Charlotte *(G-2753)*
R and T Sporting Clays Inc .... G 586 215-9861
  Harrison Township *(G-7718)*

SPORTING & ATHLETIC GOODS: Masks, Hockey, Baseball, Etc

Trainingmask LLC .... F 888 407-7555
  Cadillac *(G-2361)*

SPORTING & ATHLETIC GOODS: Protective Sporting Eqpt

United Shield Intl LLC .... E 231 933-1179
  Traverse City *(G-16873)*

SPORTING & ATHLETIC GOODS: Shafts, Golf Club

Medalist .... G 269 789-4653
  Marshall *(G-11070)*

SPORTING & ATHLETIC GOODS: Shooting Eqpt & Splys, General

Elite Defense LLC .... F 734 424-9955
  Clawson *(G-3096)*

SPORTING & ATHLETIC GOODS: Shuffleboards & Shuffleboard Eqpt

McClure Tables Inc .... G 616 662-5974
  Jenison *(G-9061)*

SPORTING & ATHLETIC GOODS: Skateboards

Chiipss .... G 248 345-6112
  Detroit *(G-4093)*
Evolve Longboards USA LLC .... G 616 915-3876
  Grand Rapids *(G-6690)*
Forche Rd Welding .... G 517 920-3473
  Blissfield *(G-1764)*
Good Do Up Skateboards .... G 248 301-5188
  White Lake *(G-18458)*
Level 6 .... G 231 755-7000
  Muskegon *(G-11860)*
Malibu Skateboards LLC .... G 616 243-3154
  Grand Rapids *(G-6957)*
Marhar Snowboards LLC .... G 616 432-3104
  Fruitport *(G-6066)*
Pluskate Boarding Company .... G 248 426-0899
  Farmington *(G-5144)*

PRODUCT SECTION

SPORTING & ATHLETIC GOODS: Snow Skis
Plastisnow LLC .... G 414 397-1233
  Plainwell (G-13090)

SPORTING & ATHLETIC GOODS: Strings, Tennis Racket
Total Tennis LLC .... G 248 594-1749
  Bloomfield Hills (G-1867)

SPORTING & ATHLETIC GOODS: Targets, Archery & Rifle Shooting
Assra .... F 906 225-1828
  Marquette (G-11005)

SPORTING & ATHLETIC GOODS: Trampolines & Eqpt
Supertramp Cstm Trmpline LLC D .... G 616 634-2010
  Grand Rapids (G-7239)

SPORTING & ATHLETIC GOODS: Water Sports Eqpt
Soupcan Inc .... F 269 381-2101
  Galesburg (G-6084)

SPORTING & ATHLETIC GOODS: Winter Sports
305 N 3rd LLC .... G 517 404-1212
  Howell (G-8421)
UP Lure Company LLC .... G 906 249-3526
  Marquette (G-11047)

SPORTING & RECREATIONAL GOODS & SPLYS WHOLESALERS
Delta Sports Service & EMB .... G 517 482-6565
  Lansing (G-9686)
Dunhams Athleisure Corporation .... G 248 658-1382
  Madison Heights (G-10713)
Howies Hockey Incorporated .... G 616 643-0594
  Grand Rapids (G-6822)
Kaycee Lux LLC .... G 248 461-7117
  Farmington Hills (G-5279)
Leapers Inc .... D 734 542-1500
  Livonia (G-10275)
Total Lee Sports Inc .... G 989 772-6121
  Mount Pleasant (G-11745)

SPORTING & RECREATIONAL GOODS, WHOL: Sharpeners, Sporting
Wilbur Products Inc .... F 231 755-3805
  Muskegon (G-11948)

SPORTING & RECREATIONAL GOODS, WHOLESALE: Athletic Goods
Nipguards LLC .... G 734 544-4490
  Ann Arbor (G-594)

SPORTING & RECREATIONAL GOODS, WHOLESALE: Boat Access & Part
Classic Boat Decks LLC .... G 586 465-3606
  Harrison Township (G-7693)

SPORTING & RECREATIONAL GOODS, WHOLESALE: Canoes
Paddlesports Warehouse Inc .... G 231 757-9051
  Scottville (G-15136)

SPORTING & RECREATIONAL GOODS, WHOLESALE: Fishing Tackle
Grapentin Specialties Inc .... G 810 724-0636
  Imlay City (G-8634)
HI Outdoors .... G 989 422-3264
  Houghton Lake (G-8399)

SPORTING & RECREATIONAL GOODS, WHOLESALE: Golf & Skiing
King Par LLC .... D 810 732-2470
  Flushing (G-5810)

SPORTING & RECREATIONAL GOODS, WHOLESALE: Gymnasium
T L V Inc .... F 989 773-4362
  Mount Pleasant (G-11744)

SPORTING & RECREATIONAL GOODS, WHOLESALE: Hunting
Stewart Knives LLC .... E 906 789-1801
  Escanaba (G-5101)

SPORTING FIREARMS WHOLESALERS
Elite Defense LLC .... F 734 424-9955
  Clawson (G-3096)

SPORTING GOODS
Brunswick Indoor Recreation .... E 231 725-4764
  Muskegon (G-11785)
Bucks Sports Products Inc .... G 763 229-1331
  Gladstone (G-6175)
Canam Undrwter Hockey Gear LLC .... G 906 399-7857
  Rapid River (G-13682)
Conway Products Corporation .... E 616 698-2601
  Grand Rapids (G-6603)
Crl Inc .... E 906 428-3710
  Gladstone (G-6177)
Discraft Inc .... E 248 624-2250
  Wixom (G-18645)
Dunhams Athleisure Corporation .... G 248 658-1382
  Madison Heights (G-10713)
Fastball LLC .... G 810 955-8510
  Davison (G-3780)
Garneau Baits LLC .... G 616 676-0186
  Ada (G-18)
Gb Sportz .... G 734 604-8919
  Ann Arbor (G-495)
Great Northern Quiver Co LLC .... G 269 838-5437
  Nashville (G-11954)
Howies Hockey Incorporated .... G 616 643-0594
  Grand Rapids (G-6822)
In The Zone Sports Camps .... G 616 889-5571
  Grand Rapids (G-6839)
Invis Inc .... G 517 279-7585
  Coldwater (G-3439)
Kaycee Lux LLC .... G 248 461-7117
  Farmington Hills (G-5279)
Keller Sports-Optics .... G 248 894-0960
  Farmington (G-5141)
Killer Paint Ball .... G 248 491-0088
  South Lyon (G-15441)
Liebner Enterprises LLC .... G 231 331-3076
  Cheboygan (G-2791)
Longshot Golf Inc .... G 586 764-9847
  Washington (G-18083)
M-22 Challenge .... G 231 392-2212
  Traverse City (G-16750)
Mason Tackle Company .... E 810 631-4571
  Otisville (G-12783)
Maxair Trampoline .... G 616 929-0882
  Grand Rapids (G-6968)
McKae Group LLC .... E 313 564-5100
  Livonia (G-10307)
McKeon Products Inc .... E 586 427-7560
  Warren (G-17922)
Nipguards LLC .... G 734 544-4490
  Ann Arbor (G-594)
Noir Sportswear Corp .... F 248 607-3615
  Oak Park (G-12634)
O2totes Llc .... F 734 730-4472
  Saint Clair Shores (G-14875)
Orion Hunting Products LLC .... G 906 563-1230
  Norway (G-12355)
Outdoor Lines LLC .... G 616 844-7351
  Grand Haven (G-6342)
Owosso Country Club Pro Shop .... G 989 723-1470
  Owosso (G-12848)
Pcs Outdoors .... G 989 569-3480
  Oscoda (G-12769)
Predator Products Company .... G 231 799-8300
  Norton Shores (G-12326)
Pro Shot Basketball Inc .... G 877 968-3865
  Holly (G-8286)
Qsr Outdoor Products Inc .... G 989 354-0777
  Alpena (G-314)
R W Summers Co .... G 231 946-7923
  Traverse City (G-16813)
Rochester Sports LLC .... F 248 608-6000
  Rochester Hills (G-14103)
Rogers Athletic .... G 989 386-7393
  Clare (G-2996)
See Our Designs .... G 866 431-0025
  Royal Oak (G-14579)
Slayer Outdoor Products .... G 517 726-0221
  Charlotte (G-2771)
Team Sports Covers LLC .... G 269 207-0241
  Union City (G-17497)
Technique Golf LLC .... G 586 758-7807
  Wixom (G-18769)
Tee Pal LLC .... G 231 563-3770
  Twin Lake (G-17474)
Thomson Plastics Inc .... G 517 545-5026
  Howell (G-8531)
Thunderdome Media LLC .... G 800 978-0206
  Plymouth (G-13314)
Two Tracks Bow Co .... G 989 834-0588
  Ovid (G-12817)
Unique-Chardan Inc .... D 419 636-6900
  Auburn Hills (G-1070)
Vanishing Point Lures .... G 260 316-7768
  Bronson (G-2121)
Warlock Lures .... G 586 977-1606
  Warren (G-18057)
Wilderness Treasures .... F 906 647-4002
  Pickford (G-13032)
Witchcraft Tape Products Inc .... D 269 468-3399
  Coloma (G-3485)

SPORTING GOODS STORES, NEC
Aerospoke Incorporated .... G 248 685-9009
  Brighton (G-1939)
Assenmacher Lightweight Cycles .... G 810 232-2994
  Flint (G-5645)
Flare Fittings Incorporated .... E 269 344-7600
  Kalamazoo (G-9187)
Kaycee Lux LLC .... G 248 461-7117
  Farmington Hills (G-5279)
Nelson Paint Co of Mich Inc .... G 906 774-5566
  Kingsford (G-9514)
Nobby Inc .... F 810 984-3300
  Fort Gratiot (G-5822)
Pro Shop The/P S Graphics .... G 517 448-8490
  Hudson (G-8559)
Total Lee Sports Inc .... G 989 772-6121
  Mount Pleasant (G-11745)
Trophy Center West Michigan .... G 231 893-1686
  Whitehall (G-18510)
Wiz Wheelz Inc .... E 616 455-5988
  Grand Rapids (G-7342)

SPORTING GOODS STORES: Archery Splys
Bay Archery Sales Co .... G 989 894-5800
  Essexville (G-5109)
Container Specialties Inc .... E 989 728-4231
  Hale (G-7588)

SPORTING GOODS STORES: Bait & Tackle
Wilderness Treasures .... F 906 647-4002
  Pickford (G-13032)

SPORTING GOODS STORES: Camping & Backpacking Eqpt
Bearcub Outfitters LLC .... F 231 439-9500
  Petoskey (G-12990)

SPORTING GOODS STORES: Firearms
Oakland Tactical Supply LLC .... G 810 991-1436
  Howell (G-8488)
Williams Gun Sight Company .... D 800 530-9028
  Davison (G-3801)

SPORTING GOODS STORES: Fishing Eqpt
Grapentin Specialties Inc .... G 810 724-0636
  Imlay City (G-8634)

SPORTING GOODS STORES: Hockey Eqpt, Exc Skates
Puck Hogs Pro Shop Inc .... G 419 540-1388
  Grosse Pointe Woods (G-7574)

SPORTING GOODS STORES: Playground Eqpt

Penchura LLC ....F 810 229-6245
  Brighton (G-2050)
Recycletech Products Inc ....F 517 649-2243
  Mulliken (G-11750)

SPORTING GOODS STORES: Skateboarding Eqpt

Evolve Longboards USA LLC ....G 616 915-3876
  Grand Rapids (G-6690)

SPORTING GOODS STORES: Specialty Sport Splys, NEC

Dunhams Athleisure Corporation ....G 248 658-1382
  Madison Heights (G-10713)
Marrs Discount Furniture ....G 989 720-5436
  Owosso (G-12840)

SPORTING GOODS STORES: Team sports Eqpt

Lansing Athletics ....G 517 327-8828
  Lansing (G-9772)
Sports Junction ....G 989 791-5900
  Saginaw (G-14765)

SPORTING GOODS: Archery

Bitzenburger Machine & Tool ....G 517 627-8433
  Grand Ledge (G-6386)
Bohning Company Ltd ....E 231 229-4247
  Lake City (G-9545)
G5 Outdoors LLC ....G 866 456-8836
  Memphis (G-11212)
Grayling Outdoor Products Inc ....F 989 348-2956
  Grayling (G-7462)
Overkill Research & Dev Labs ....G 517 768-8155
  Jackson (G-8981)
Pro Release Inc ....G 810 512-4120
  Marine City (G-10964)

SPORTING GOODS: Fishing Nets

Ed Cumings Inc ....E 810 736-0130
  Flint (G-5693)

SPORTS APPAREL STORES

Baumans Running Center Inc ....G 810 238-5981
  Flint (G-5652)
Bearcub Outfitters LLC ....F 231 439-9500
  Petoskey (G-12990)
Dunhams Athleisure Corporation ....G 248 658-1382
  Madison Heights (G-10713)
Embroidery & Much More LLC ....F 586 771-3832
  Saint Clair Shores (G-14857)
Lansing Athletics ....G 517 327-8828
  Lansing (G-9772)
R H & Company Inc ....F 269 345-7814
  Kalamazoo (G-9313)
Sports Junction ....G 989 791-5900
  Saginaw (G-14765)
Sports Stop ....G 517 676-2199
  Mason (G-11158)

SPORTS PROMOTION SVCS

Buster Mathis Foundation ....G 616 843-4433
  Wyoming (G-18855)

SPOUTING: Plastic & Fiberglass Reinforced

E-T-M Enterprises I Inc ....G 517 627-8461
  Grand Ledge (G-6389)
Hanwha Azdel Inc ....G 810 629-2496
  Warren (G-17847)

SPRAYING & DUSTING EQPT

Precision Masking Inc ....E 734 848-4200
  Erie (G-5053)
Spray Foam Fabrication LLC ....G 517 745-7885
  Parma (G-12939)

SPRAYING EQPT: Agricultural

HD Hudson Manufacturing Co ....D 800 977-8661
  Lowell (G-10503)

Root-Lowell Manufacturing Co ....D 616 897-9211
  Lowell (G-10515)
Unist Inc ....E 616 949-0853
  Grand Rapids (G-7297)

SPRINGS: Automobile

American MSC Inc ....F 248 589-7770
  Troy (G-16932)
American MSC Inc ....E 248 589-7770
  Troy (G-16933)
Meritor Inc ....C 248 435-1000
  Troy (G-17246)

SPRINGS: Clock, Precision

Hilite Industries Inc ....G 248 475-4580
  Lake Orion (G-9608)

SPRINGS: Coiled Flat

M D Hubbard Spring Co Inc ....E 248 628-2528
  Oxford (G-12898)

SPRINGS: Cold Formed

Weiser Metal Products Inc ....G 989 736-8151
  Lincoln (G-10041)

SPRINGS: Instrument, Precision

Ms Chip Inc ....F 586 296-9850
  Fraser (G-5966)

SPRINGS: Leaf, Automobile, Locomotive, Etc

Eaton Detroit Spring Svc Co ....F 313 963-3839
  Detroit (G-4199)
Qp Acquisition 2 Inc ....A 248 594-7432
  Southfield (G-15685)

SPRINGS: Mechanical, Precision

General Automatic Mch Pdts Co ....E 517 437-6000
  Hillsdale (G-7936)
Hyde Spring and Wire Company ....F 313 272-2201
  Detroit (G-4310)
Michigan Spring & Stamping LLC ....C 231 755-1691
  Muskegon (G-11871)
Quality Spring/Togo Inc ....C 517 278-2391
  Coldwater (G-3449)
Serra Spring & Mfg LLC ....G 586 932-2202
  Sterling Heights (G-16172)

SPRINGS: Precision

De-Sta-Co Cylinders Inc ....B 248 836-6700
  Auburn Hills (G-860)
Motion Dynamics Corporation ....D 231 865-7400
  Fruitport (G-6068)

SPRINGS: Steel

A N L Spring Manufacturing ....G 313 837-0200
  Detroit (G-3973)
Ajax Spring and Mfg Co ....E 248 588-5700
  Madison Heights (G-10664)
American Ring Manufacturing ....E 734 402-0426
  Livonia (G-10115)
Gill Corporation ....B 616 453-4491
  Grand Rapids (G-6740)
Lee Spring Company LLC ....F 586 296-9850
  Fraser (G-5957)
Llink Technologies LLC ....E 586 336-9370
  Brown City (G-2139)
Mid-West Spring & Stamping Inc ....D 231 777-2707
  Muskegon (G-11872)
Muskegon Brake & Distrg Co LLC ....E 231 733-0874
  Norton Shores (G-12313)
P J Wallbank Springs Inc ....D 810 987-2992
  Port Huron (G-13514)
Quality Spring/Togo Inc ....C 517 278-2391
  Coldwater (G-3449)

SPRINGS: Torsion Bar

Automatic Spring Products Corp ....C 616 842-2284
  Grand Haven (G-6278)
J & J Spring Co Inc ....F 586 566-7600
  Shelby Township (G-15241)

SPRINGS: Wire

A N L Spring Manufacturing ....G 313 837-0200
  Detroit (G-3973)

Apex Spring & Stamping Corp ....D 616 453-5463
  Grand Rapids (G-6462)
Barnes Group Inc ....G 586 415-6677
  Fraser (G-5900)
Dover Energy Inc ....C 248 836-6750
  Auburn Hills (G-865)
Dowsett Spring Company ....G 269 782-2138
  Dowagiac (G-4782)
Gill Corporation ....B 616 453-4491
  Grand Rapids (G-6740)
J & J Spring Co Inc ....F 586 566-7600
  Shelby Township (G-15241)
J & J Spring Enterprises LLC ....G 586 566-7600
  Shelby Township (G-15242)
Jade Mfg Inc ....G 734 942-1462
  Romulus (G-14289)
Lee Spring Company LLC ....F 586 296-9850
  Fraser (G-5957)
M D Hubbard Spring Co Inc ....E 248 628-2528
  Oxford (G-12898)
Magiera Holdings Inc ....E 269 685-1768
  Plainwell (G-13082)
Mc Guire Spring Corporation ....G 517 546-7311
  Brighton (G-2028)
Michigan Steel Finishing Co ....E 313 838-3925
  Detroit (G-4452)
Mid-West Spring & Stamping Inc ....D 231 777-2707
  Muskegon (G-11872)
Mid-West Spring Mfg Co ....F 231 777-2707
  Muskegon (G-11873)
Novi Spring Inc ....F 248 486-4220
  Brighton (G-2045)
Peterson American Corporation ....E 248 799-5400
  Southfield (G-15673)
Peterson American Corporation ....C 248 799-5410
  Commerce Township (G-3562)
Peterson American Corporation ....D 269 279-7421
  Three Rivers (G-16580)
Peterson Spring ....G 248 799-5400
  Madison Heights (G-10797)
Rassini Chassis Systems LLC ....D 419 485-1524
  Plymouth (G-13275)
Scherdel Sales & Tech Inc ....C 231 777-7774
  Muskegon (G-11916)
Spring Design and Mfg Inc ....E 586 566-9741
  Shelby Township (G-15342)
Spring Dynamics Inc ....E 810 798-2622
  Almont (G-267)
Spring Saginaw Company ....G 989 624-9333
  Birch Run (G-1716)
Stump Schlele Somappa Sprng ....E 616 361-2791
  Grand Rapids (G-7230)
Stumpp Schuele Somappa USA Inc ....F 616 361-2791
  Grand Rapids (G-7231)
TEC-3 Prototypes Inc ....E 810 678-8909
  Metamora (G-11289)
Tokusen Hytech Inc ....C 269 685-1768
  Plainwell (G-13099)
Tokusen Hytech Inc ....G 269 658-1768
  Plainwell (G-13100)
Wolverine Coil Spring Company ....D 616 459-3504
  Grand Rapids (G-7344)

SPRINKLER SYSTEMS: Field

W L Hamilton & Co ....F 269 781-6941
  Marshall (G-11077)

SPRINKLING SYSTEMS: Fire Control

Fabrication Concepts LLC ....F 517 750-4742
  Spring Arbor (G-15791)
Gallagher Fire Equipment Co ....E 248 477-1540
  Livonia (G-10219)
Viking Group Inc ....C 616 831-6448
  Hastings (G-7813)
Viking Group Inc ....G 616 432-6800
  Caledonia (G-2406)

SPROCKETS: Power Transmission

Leedy Manufacturing Co LLC ....D 616 245-0517
  Grand Rapids (G-6934)

STACKING MACHINES: Automatic

Jervis B Webb Company ....B 248 553-1000
  Novi (G-12449)

STADIUM EVENT OPERATOR SERVICES

Livespace LLC ....F 616 929-0191
  Grand Rapids (G-6947)

STAFFING, EMPLOYMENT PLACEMENT

Etcs Inc ....F 586 268-4870
 Warren *(G-17796)*

STAGE LIGHTING SYSTEMS

A E C Inc ....D 810 231-9546
 Whitmore Lake *(G-18515)*
Tls Productions Inc ....E 810 220-8577
 Ann Arbor *(G-693)*

STAINLESS STEEL

ATI Marketing ....G 231 590-9600
 Traverse City *(G-16605)*
Atlantis Tech Corp ....G 989 356-6954
 Alpena *(G-279)*
Carry Manufacturing Inc ....G 989 672-2779
 Caro *(G-2567)*
Cleveland-Cliffs Steel Corp ....A 800 532-8857
 Dearborn *(G-3821)*

STAINLESS STEEL WARE

Carry Manufacturing Inc ....G 989 672-2779
 Caro *(G-2567)*
Infra Corporation ....F 248 623-0400
 Waterford *(G-18129)*
McCallum Fabricating LLC ....F 586 784-5555
 Allenton *(G-231)*
Mp Acquisition LLC ....D 800 362-8491
 Madison Heights *(G-10784)*

STAINS: Wood

Akzo Nobel Coatings Inc ....E 248 637-0400
 Pontiac *(G-13347)*

STAIRCASES & STAIRS, WOOD

Beaver Stair Company ....G 248 628-0441
 Oxford *(G-12879)*
Great Lakes Stair & Case Co ....G 269 465-3777
 Bridgman *(G-1928)*
Macomb Stairs Inc ....F 586 226-2800
 Shelby Township *(G-15267)*
MJB Stairs LLC ....G 586 822-9559
 Shelby Township *(G-15278)*
Northern Staircase Co Inc ....F 248 836-0652
 Pontiac *(G-13402)*
Stair Specialist Inc ....G 269 420-0486
 Battle Creek *(G-1299)*

STAMPINGS: Automotive

3715-11th Street Corp ....E 734 523-1000
 Livonia *(G-10089)*
A-1 Stampings Inc ....G 586 294-7790
 Fraser *(G-5887)*
Acemco Incorporated ....C 231 799-8612
 Norton Shores *(G-12344)*
Advance Engineering Company .....D 313 537-3500
 Canton *(G-2429)*
Advanced Auto Trends Inc ....E 248 628-6111
 Oxford *(G-12871)*
Advanced Auto Trends Inc ....E 248 628-4850
 Oxford *(G-12872)*
Ajax Spring and Mfg Co ....E 248 588-5700
 Madison Heights *(G-10664)*
Allied Engineering Inc ....G 616 748-7990
 Zeeland *(G-18990)*
AMI Livonia LLC ....D 734 428-3132
 Livonia *(G-10117)*
Ankara Industries Incorporated ......E 586 749-1190
 Chesterfield *(G-2845)*
Aphase II Inc ....D 586 977-0790
 Sterling Heights *(G-15933)*
ARC-Kecy LLC ....D 517 448-8954
 Hudson *(G-8549)*
Auto Metal Craft Inc ....E 248 398-2240
 Oak Park *(G-12594)*
Automatic Spring Products Corp ....C 616 842-2284
 Grand Haven *(G-6278)*
Benteler Automotive Corp ....B 616 247-3936
 Auburn Hills *(G-810)*
Benteler Automotive Corp ....C 248 364-7190
 Auburn Hills *(G-811)*
Bopp-Busch Manufacturing Co ......E 989 876-7924
 Au Gres *(G-758)*
Britten Metalworks LLC ....G 231 421-1615
 Traverse City *(G-16629)*

Burkland Inc ....C 810 636-2233
 Goodrich *(G-6222)*
C & H Stamping Inc ....E 517 750-3600
 Jackson *(G-8829)*
C & M Manufacturing Corp Inc ....E 586 749-3455
 Chesterfield *(G-2854)*
Capital Stamping & Machine Inc ....D 248 471-0700
 Farmington Hills *(G-5197)*
Challenge Manufacturing ....F 616 735-6500
 Walker *(G-17632)*
Challenge Mfg Company ....F 616 735-6530
 Walker *(G-17633)*
Challenge Mfg Company LLC ....B 616 735-6500
 Walker *(G-17635)*
Challenge Mfg Company LLC ....C 616 735-6500
 Grand Rapids *(G-6562)*
Challenge Mfg Company LLC ....C 616 396-2079
 Holland *(G-7993)*
Crescive Die and Tool Inc ....F 734 482-0303
 Saline *(G-15010)*
Delaco Steel Corporation ....C 313 491-1200
 Dearborn *(G-3826)*
Demmer Corporation ....C 517 321-3600
 Lansing *(G-9687)*
Design Metal Inc ....F 248 547-4170
 Oak Park *(G-12605)*
Dgh Enterprises Inc ....E 269 925-0657
 Benton Harbor *(G-1546)*
Diversified Prcurement Svcs LLC ...F 248 821-1147
 Ferndale *(G-5548)*
Douglas Stamping Company ....F 248 542-3940
 Madison Heights *(G-10711)*
Dowding Industries Inc ....C 517 663-5455
 Eaton Rapids *(G-4960)*
Dynamic Metals Group LLC ....F 586 790-5615
 Birmingham *(G-1724)*
E & E Manufacturing Co Inc ....F 734 451-7600
 Plymouth *(G-13165)*
E & E Manufacturing Co Inc ....E 248 616-1300
 Clawson *(G-3095)*
Elringklinger North Amer Inc ....D 734 738-1800
 Plymouth *(G-13166)*
Emerging Advanced Products LLC ...D 734 942-1060
 Belleville *(G-1483)*
Fab-All Manufacturing Inc ....D 248 585-6700
 Troy *(G-17103)*
FCA US LLC ....A 248 512-2950
 Auburn Hills *(G-894)*
Fisher & Company Incorporated ....G 248 280-0808
 Troy *(G-17109)*
Flex-N-Gate Troy LLC ....E 586 759-8900
 Troy *(G-17114)*
Forward Metal Craft Inc ....F 616 459-6051
 Grand Rapids *(G-6717)*
Franklin Fastener Company ....E 313 537-8900
 Redford *(G-13735)*
Gedia Michigan LLC ....D 248 392-9090
 Orion *(G-12730)*
Gedia Michigan LLC ....E 248 392-9090
 Lake Orion *(G-9605)*
General Motors LLC ....F 810 234-2710
 Flint *(G-5704)*
General Motors LLC ....F 810 234-2710
 Flint *(G-5705)*
General Motors LLC ....C 810 236-1970
 Flint *(G-5706)*
Gestamp Mason LLC ....B 517 244-8800
 Mason *(G-11135)*
Gfm LLC ....E 586 859-4587
 Roseville *(G-14412)*
Gill Corporation ....B 616 453-4491
 Grand Rapids *(G-6740)*
Gill Holding Company Inc ....D 616 559-2700
 Grand Rapids *(G-6741)*
Gill Industries Inc ....C 616 559-2700
 Grand Rapids *(G-6742)*
Global Fmi LLC ....D 810 964-5555
 Fenton *(G-5481)*
Globe Tech LLC ....E 734 656-2200
 Plymouth *(G-13178)*
Grouper Wild LLC ....G 248 299-7500
 Auburn Hills *(G-917)*
Guyoung Tech Usa Inc ....D 248 746-4261
 Southfield *(G-15589)*
Hamlin Tool & Machine Co Inc ....E 248 651-6302
 Rochester Hills *(G-14029)*
Hatch Stamping Co ....F 734 475-6507
 Spring Arbor *(G-15792)*
Hatch Stamping Company LLC ......C 734 475-8628
 Chelsea *(G-2814)*

Hawthorne Metal Products Co ....B 248 549-1375
 Royal Oak *(G-14543)*
Henze Stamping & Mfg Co ....G 248 588-5620
 Troy *(G-17141)*
Illinois Tool Works Inc ....G 248 589-2500
 Troy *(G-17161)*
Inalfa/Ssi Roof Systems LLC ....D 586 758-6620
 Warren *(G-17860)*
Iroquois Industries Inc ....E 586 465-1023
 Cottrellville *(G-3723)*
J & J Spring Co Inc ....F 586 566-7600
 Shelby Township *(G-15241)*
J & L Mfg Co ....E 586 445-9530
 Warren *(G-17875)*
Jaytec LLC ....F 734 713-4500
 Milan *(G-11439)*
Jaytec LLC ....F 734 397-6300
 Chelsea *(G-2816)*
Jaytec LLC ....F 517 451-8272
 New Boston *(G-12010)*
Jsj Corporation ....E 616 842-6350
 Grand Haven *(G-6324)*
K & K Mfg Inc ....G 616 784-4286
 Sparta *(G-15770)*
Kirmin Die & Tool Inc ....E 734 722-9210
 Romulus *(G-14295)*
L & W Inc ....G 734 397-8085
 Van Buren Twp *(G-17535)*
L & W Inc ....E 517 486-6321
 Blissfield *(G-1767)*
L & W Inc ....F 734 529-7290
 Dundee *(G-4826)*
L & W Inc ....D 734 397-6300
 New Boston *(G-12012)*
L & W Inc ....F 734 397-2212
 Van Buren Twp *(G-17536)*
L & W Inc ....G 616 394-9665
 Holland *(G-8118)*
L & W Mexico LLC ....D 734 397-6300
 Van Buren Twp *(G-17537)*
L Barge & Associates Inc ....E 248 582-3430
 Ferndale *(G-5563)*
Lacy Tool Company Inc ....G 248 476-5250
 Novi *(G-12464)*
Laser Cutting Co ....E 586 468-5300
 Harrison Township *(G-7705)*
Lgb USA Inc ....G 586 777-4542
 Roseville *(G-14432)*
Llink Technologies LLC ....E 586 336-9370
 Brown City *(G-2139)*
Manufacturing Products & Svcs .....F 734 927-1964
 Plymouth *(G-13233)*
Martinrea Hot Stampings Inc ....E 859 509-3031
 Warren *(G-17917)*
Means Industries Inc ....C 989 754-1433
 Saginaw *(G-14691)*
Means Industries Inc ....E 989 754-0312
 Saginaw *(G-14692)*
Meritor Inc ....C 248 435-1000
 Troy *(G-17246)*
Mh Industries Ltd ....E 734 261-7560
 West Bloomfield *(G-18298)*
Middleville Tool & Die Co Inc ....D 269 795-3646
 Middleville *(G-11309)*
Midstates Industrial Group Inc ....E 586 307-3414
 Clinton Township *(G-3300)*
Minth Group US Holding Inc ....E 248 848-8530
 Wixom *(G-18711)*
Multimatic Michigan LLC ....E 517 962-7190
 Jackson *(G-8971)*
Mvc Holdings LLC ....F 586 491-2600
 Roseville *(G-14450)*
Northern Industrial Mfg Corp ....E 586 468-2790
 Harrison Township *(G-7712)*
Northern Metalcraft Inc ....E 586 997-9630
 Shelby Township *(G-15292)*
Oakley Industries Inc ....E 586 791-3194
 Clinton Township *(G-3310)*
Oakley Industries Inc ....C 586 792-1261
 Clinton Township *(G-3311)*
Oakwood Metal Fabricating Co ......E 734 947-7740
 Taylor *(G-16454)*
Oblut Limited ....F 810 241-4029
 Clarkston *(G-3054)*
Orion Manufacturing Inc ....F 616 527-5994
 Ionia *(G-8691)*
P & C Group I Inc ....E 248 442-6800
 Farmington Hills *(G-5341)*
Precision Parts Holdings Inc ....A 248 853-9010
 Rochester Hills *(G-14088)*

STAMPINGS: Automotive

Prestige Advanced Inc ....F...... 586 868-4000
  Madison Heights *(G-10807)*
Prestige Stamping LLC ....C...... 586 773-2700
  Warren *(G-17976)*
Pridgeon & Clay Inc ....A...... 616 241-5675
  Grand Rapids *(G-7106)*
Pt Tech Stamping Inc ....E...... 586 293-1810
  Fraser *(G-5982)*
Quality Metalcraft Inc ....C...... 734 261-6700
  Livonia *(G-10377)*
Quigley Industries Inc ....E...... 248 426-8600
  Farmington Hills *(G-5361)*
Quigley Manufacturing Inc ....G...... 248 426-8600
  Farmington Hills *(G-5362)*
Radar Mexican Investments LLC ....E...... 586 779-0300
  Warren *(G-17992)*
Ralco Industries Inc ....F...... 248 853-3200
  Auburn Hills *(G-1014)*
Reko International Holdings ....G...... 519 737-6974
  Bloomfield Hills *(G-1854)*
Reliant Industries Inc ....E...... 586 275-0479
  Sterling Heights *(G-16146)*
S & G Prototype Inc ....F...... 586 716-3600
  New Baltimore *(G-11993)*
Set Enterprises Inc ....E...... 586 573-3600
  Royal Oak *(G-14580)*
Span America Detroit Inc ....F...... 734 957-1600
  Van Buren Twp *(G-17554)*
Stanco Metal Products Inc ....E...... 616 842-5000
  Grand Haven *(G-6366)*
Statistical Processed Products ....F...... 586 792-6900
  Clinton Township *(G-3363)*
Sterling Die & Engineering Inc ....E...... 586 677-0707
  Macomb *(G-10637)*
Su-Dan Company ....C...... 248 754-1430
  Rochester *(G-13931)*
Superior Machining Inc ....F...... 248 446-9451
  New Hudson *(G-12071)*
Ta Delaware Inc ....B...... 248 675-6000
  Novi *(G-12553)*
TEC-3 Prototypes Inc ....E...... 810 678-8909
  Metamora *(G-11289)*
Technique Inc ....D...... 517 789-8988
  Jackson *(G-9017)*
Tel-X Corporation ....E...... 734 425-2225
  Garden City *(G-6112)*
Tesca Usa Inc ....E...... 586 991-0744
  Rochester Hills *(G-14124)*
Tower Atmtive Oprtons USA I LL ....D...... 989 375-2201
  Elkton *(G-5033)*
Tower Atmtive Oprtons USA I LL ....D...... 734 397-6300
  New Boston *(G-12021)*
Tower Atmtive Oprtons USA I LL ....D...... 616 802-1600
  Grand Rapids *(G-7266)*
Tower Atmtive Oprtons USA I LL ....D...... 586 465-5158
  Clinton Township *(G-3379)*
Tower Atmtive Oprtons USA I LL ....D...... 734 414-3100
  Plymouth *(G-13320)*
Tower Atmtive Oprtons USA II L ....D...... 248 675-6000
  Livonia *(G-10435)*
Tower Atmtive Oprtons USA III ....D...... 248 675-6000
  Livonia *(G-10436)*
Tower Auto Holdings II A LLC ....C...... 248 675-6000
  Livonia *(G-10437)*
Tower Auto Holdings USA LLC ....C...... 248 675-6000
  Livonia *(G-10438)*
Tower Defense & Aerospace LLC ....E...... 248 675-6000
  Livonia *(G-10439)*
Trans-Matic Mfg Co Inc ....C...... 616 820-2500
  Holland *(G-8225)*
Traverse City Products LLC ....D...... 231 946-4414
  Traverse City *(G-16865)*
Trianon Industries Corporation ....E...... 586 759-5200
  Center Line *(G-2688)*
Troy Design & Manufacturing Co ....C...... 734 738-2300
  Plymouth *(G-13325)*
Twb Company LLC ....D...... 734 454-4000
  Canton *(G-2536)*
Unique Tool & Mfg Co Inc ....E...... 336 498-2614
  Temperance *(G-16551)*
Van-Rob Inc ....C...... 517 657-2450
  Lansing *(G-9747)*
Variety Die & Stamping Co ....D...... 734 426-4488
  Dexter *(G-4761)*
Washers Incorporated ....C...... 734 523-1000
  Livonia *(G-10467)*
Webster Cold Forge Co ....F...... 313 554-4500
  Northville *(G-12271)*
Wico Metal Products Company ....C...... 586 755-9600
  Warren *(G-18067)*

Wirco Inc ....G...... 586 267-1300
  Clinton Township *(G-3388)*
Wirco Manufacturing LLC ....F...... 810 984-5576
  Port Huron *(G-13538)*
Zeledyne Glass Corp ....G...... 615 350-7500
  Allen Park *(G-211)*

STAMPINGS: Metal

A & A Manufacturing Co ....G...... 616 846-1730
  Spring Lake *(G-15799)*
A & R Specialty Services Corp ....E...... 313 933-8750
  Detroit *(G-3971)*
A & S Reel & Tackle Inc ....E...... 313 928-1667
  Ecorse *(G-4979)*
A Raymond Corp N Amer Inc ....E...... 248 853-2500
  Rochester Hills *(G-13938)*
Actron Steel Inc ....E...... 231 947-3981
  Traverse City *(G-16597)*
Advance Engineering Company ....D...... 313 537-3500
  Canton *(G-2429)*
Advanced Auto Trends Inc ....E...... 248 628-6111
  Oxford *(G-12871)*
Alternate Number Five Inc ....D...... 616 842-2581
  Grand Haven *(G-6272)*
Aluminum Blanking Co Inc ....D...... 248 338-4422
  Pontiac *(G-13349)*
Aluminum Textures Inc ....E...... 616 538-3144
  Grandville *(G-7364)*
Amanda Products LLC ....E...... 248 547-3870
  Ferndale *(G-5525)*
American Engnred Cmponents Inc ....C...... 734 428-8301
  Manchester *(G-10881)*
American Fabricated Pdts Inc ....E...... 616 607-8785
  Spring Lake *(G-15803)*
American Metal Fab Inc ....D...... 269 279-5108
  Three Rivers *(G-16563)*
American Trim ....E...... 269 281-0651
  Saint Joseph *(G-14923)*
Anand Nvh North America Inc ....C...... 810 724-2400
  Imlay City *(G-8627)*
Anrod Screen Cylinder Company ....E...... 989 872-2101
  Cass City *(G-2610)*
Apex Spring & Stamping Corp ....D...... 616 453-5463
  Grand Rapids *(G-6462)*
Arnold Tool & Die Co ....E...... 586 598-0099
  Chesterfield *(G-2846)*
Automatic Spring Products Corp ....C...... 616 842-2284
  Grand Haven *(G-6278)*
Bae Industries Inc ....C...... 586 754-3000
  Warren *(G-17725)*
Bae Industries Inc ....C...... 248 475-9600
  Auburn Hills *(G-809)*
Barnes Group Inc ....G...... 586 415-6677
  Fraser *(G-5900)*
Belwith Products LLC ....F...... 616 247-4000
  Grandville *(G-7367)*
Benteler Automotive Corp ....B...... 616 247-3936
  Auburn Hills *(G-810)*
Blue Fire Manufacturing LLC ....E...... 248 714-7166
  Waterford *(G-18104)*
Bopp-Busch Manufacturing Co ....E...... 989 876-7924
  Au Gres *(G-758)*
Broaching Industries Inc ....E...... 586 949-3775
  Chesterfield *(G-2853)*
Cameron Tool Corporation ....D...... 517 487-3671
  Lansing *(G-9820)*
Challenge Mfg Company LLC ....C...... 616 396-2079
  Holland *(G-7993)*
Commercial Mfg & Assembly Inc ....E...... 616 847-9980
  Grand Haven *(G-6287)*
Complete Metalcraft LLC ....G...... 248 952-8002
  Highland *(G-7888)*
Contract Welding and Fabg Inc ....C...... 734 699-5561
  Van Buren Twp *(G-17520)*
Cooper Rolland ....G...... 734 482-8705
  Ypsilanti *(G-18933)*
Craft Steel Products Inc ....G...... 616 935-7575
  Spring Lake *(G-15809)*
Dee-Blast Corporation ....F...... 269 428-2400
  Stevensville *(G-16246)*
Demmer Investments Inc ....G...... 517 321-3600
  Lansing *(G-9688)*
Diamond Press Solutions LLC ....G...... 269 945-1997
  Hastings *(G-7789)*
Duggans Limited LLC ....E...... 586 254-7400
  Shelby Township *(G-15213)*
Dynamic Corporation ....F...... 616 399-2200
  Holland *(G-8018)*
E & E Manufacturing Co Inc ....E...... 248 616-1300
  Clawson *(G-3095)*

Edmar Manufacturing Inc ....D...... 616 392-7218
  Holland *(G-8023)*
Elkins Machine & Tool Co Inc ....E...... 734 941-0266
  Romulus *(G-14271)*
Elmhirst Industries Inc ....E...... 586 731-8663
  Sterling Heights *(G-16002)*
Ernest Inds Acquisition LLC ....E...... 734 459-8881
  Plymouth *(G-13168)*
Ernest Industries Acquisition, ...E...... 734 595-9500
  Westland *(G-18369)*
Euclid Manufacturing Co Inc ....E...... 734 397-6300
  Detroit *(G-4216)*
European Cabinet Mfg Co ....E...... 586 445-8909
  Roseville *(G-14406)*
Fast Tech Mfg Inc ....G...... 586 783-1741
  Harrison Township *(G-7698)*
Fisher & Company Incorporated ....G...... 248 280-0808
  Troy *(G-17109)*
Fortress Manufacturing Inc ....F...... 269 925-1336
  Benton Harbor *(G-1549)*
Franklin Fastener Company ....E...... 313 537-8900
  Redford *(G-13735)*
Gill Corporation ....B...... 616 453-4491
  Grand Rapids *(G-6740)*
Globe Tech LLC ....E...... 734 656-2200
  Plymouth *(G-13178)*
Grant Industries Incorporated ....E...... 586 293-9200
  Fraser *(G-5931)*
Gray Brothers Mfg Inc ....E...... 269 483-7615
  White Pigeon *(G-18479)*
Heinzmann D Tool & Die Inc ....F...... 248 363-5115
  Commerce Township *(G-3535)*
Henze Stamping & Mfg Co ....E...... 248 588-5620
  Troy *(G-17141)*
Hibshman Screw Mch Pdts Inc ....E...... 269 641-7525
  Union *(G-17489)*
High-Star Corporation ....E...... 734 743-1503
  Westland *(G-18381)*
Hilite Industries Inc ....E...... 248 475-4580
  Lake Orion *(G-9608)*
Hope Network West Michigan ....E...... 231 775-3425
  Cadillac *(G-2334)*
Hope Network West Michigan ....E...... 231 796-4801
  Paris *(G-12934)*
Inalfa/Ssi Roof Systems LLC ....D...... 586 758-6620
  Warren *(G-17860)*
Industrial Innovations Inc ....F...... 616 249-1525
  Grandville *(G-7392)*
Industrial Machine Pdts Inc ....D...... 248 628-3621
  Oxford *(G-12889)*
Innotec Corp ....E...... 616 772-5959
  Zeeland *(G-19047)*
J & L Mfg Co ....E...... 586 445-9530
  Warren *(G-17875)*
John Lamantia Corporation ....G...... 269 428-8100
  Stevensville *(G-16255)*
Jsj Corporation ....E...... 616 842-6350
  Grand Haven *(G-6324)*
K&K Stamping Company ....E...... 586 443-7900
  Saint Clair Shores *(G-14866)*
Kecy Corporation ....E...... 517 448-8954
  Hudson *(G-8553)*
Kecy Products Inc ....E...... 517 448-8954
  Hudson *(G-8554)*
Kendor Steel Rule Die Inc ....F...... 586 293-7111
  Fraser *(G-5950)*
Keyes-Davis Company ....E...... 269 962-7505
  Springfield *(G-15871)*
Kinney Tool and Die Inc ....D...... 616 997-0901
  Coopersville *(G-3689)*
Kriewall Enterprises Inc ....E...... 586 336-0600
  Romeo *(G-14227)*
L & W Inc ....G...... 734 397-8085
  Van Buren Twp *(G-17535)*
L T C Roll & Engineering Co ....E...... 586 465-1023
  Clinton Township *(G-3277)*
Lab Tool and Engineering Corp ....F...... 517 750-4131
  Spring Arbor *(G-15793)*
Lacy Tool Company Inc ....G...... 248 476-5250
  Novi *(G-12464)*
Laser Cutting Inc ....E...... 586 468-5300
  Harrison Township *(G-7705)*
Llink Technologies LLC ....E...... 586 336-9370
  Brown City *(G-2139)*
Low Cost Surcing Solutions LLC ....G...... 248 535-7721
  Washington *(G-18084)*
Luckmarr Plastics Inc ....D...... 586 978-8498
  Sterling Heights *(G-16077)*
Lupaul Industries Inc ....F...... 517 783-3223
  Saint Johns *(G-14904)*

M D Hubbard Spring Co Inc ....E 248 628-2528
Oxford (G-12898)
M P I International Inc ....B 608 764-5416
Rochester Hills (G-14056)
Means Industries Inc ....G 989 754-3300
Saginaw (G-14693)
Mercury Products Corp ....F 586 749-6800
Chesterfield (G-2909)
Michigan Rod Products Inc ....D 517 552-9812
Howell (G-8481)
Michigan Scientific Corp ....D 231 547-5511
Charlevoix (G-2721)
Midway Products Group Inc ....C 734 241-7242
Monroe (G-11560)
Mueller Impacts Company Inc ....C 810 364-3700
Marysville (G-11093)
Munn Manufacturing Company ....E 616 765-3067
Freeport (G-6035)
Northern Industrial Mfg Corp ....E 586 468-2790
Harrison Township (G-7712)
Os Holdings LLc ....D 734 397-6300
New Boston (G-12017)
Ovidon Manufacturing LLC ....D 517 548-4005
Howell (G-8489)
Patton Tool and Die Inc ....F 810 359-5336
Lexington (G-10031)
Paw Paw Everlast Label Company ....F 269 657-4921
Paw Paw (G-12954)
Precision Parts Holdings Inc ....A 248 853-9010
Rochester Hills (G-14088)
Precision Prototype & Mfg Inc ....F 517 663-4114
Eaton Rapids (G-4967)
Premier Prototype Inc ....E 586 323-6114
Sterling Heights (G-16132)
Press-Way Inc ....E 586 790-3324
Clinton Township (G-3325)
Pro Stamp Plus LLC ....G 616 447-2988
Grand Rapids (G-7111)
Production Fabricators Inc ....E 231 777-3822
Muskegon (G-11900)
Profile Inc ....E 517 224-8012
Potterville (G-13647)
Punching Concepts Inc ....F 989 358-7070
Alpena (G-313)
Quality Metalcraft Inc ....C 734 261-6700
Livonia (G-10377)
Quantum Custom Designs LLC ....G 989 293-7372
Fraser (G-5984)
Quigley Manufacturing Inc ....G 248 426-8600
Farmington Hills (G-5362)
R-Bo Co Inc ....F 616 748-9733
Zeeland (G-19076)
Radar Mexican Investments LLC ....E 586 779-0300
Warren (G-17992)
Ranger Tool & Die Co ....F 989 754-1403
Saginaw (G-14735)
Royal Flex-N-Gate Oak LLC ....B 248 549-3800
Warren (G-17998)
SDrol Metals Inc ....D 734 753-3410
New Boston (G-12020)
Set Enterprises of Mi Inc ....D 586 573-3600
Sterling Heights (G-16174)
Specialty Tube LLC ....E 616 949-5990
Grand Rapids (G-7214)
Spinform Inc ....G 810 767-4660
Flint (G-5766)
Spirit Industries Inc ....G 517 371-7840
Lansing (G-9740)
Sterling Die & Engineering Inc ....E 586 677-0707
Macomb (G-10637)
Stus Welding & Fabrication ....G 616 392-8459
Holland (G-8206)
Su-Dan Company ....C 248 754-1430
Rochester (G-13931)
Technique Inc ....D 517 789-8988
Jackson (G-9017)
Tg Manufacturing LLC ....G 616 935-7575
Byron Center (G-2296)
Thai Summit America Corp ....D 517 548-4900
Howell (G-8529)
Thomas Industrial Rolls Inc ....F 313 584-9696
Dearborn (G-3905)
TRW Automotive US LLC ....E 248 426-3901
Farmington Hills (G-5405)
Uei Inc ....E 616 361-6093
Grand Rapids (G-7285)
Ultraform Industries Inc ....D 586 752-4508
Bruce Twp (G-2185)
Unique Tool & Mfg Co Inc ....E 336 498-2614
Temperance (G-16551)
Usher Tool & Die Inc ....E 616 583-9160
Byron Center (G-2297)
Van Loon Industries Inc ....E 586 532-8530
Shelby Township (G-15363)
Variety Die & Stamping Co ....D 734 426-4488
Dexter (G-4761)
Ventra Ionia Main LLC ....A 616 597-3220
Ionia (G-8693)
Versatube Corporation ....F 248 524-0299
Troy (G-17438)
Wallin Brothers Inc ....G 734 525-7750
Livonia (G-10464)
Webasto Roof Systems Inc ....C 248 997-5100
Rochester Hills (G-14145)
Webster Cold Forge Co ....F 313 554-4500
Northville (G-12271)
Western Engineered Products ....G 248 371-9259
Lake Orion (G-9638)
Wico Metal Products Company ....C 586 755-9600
Warren (G-18067)
ZF Active Safety & Elec US LLC ....E 734 855-3631
Livonia (G-10480)
ZF Active Safety & Elec US LLC ....E 586 232-7200
Washington (G-18092)
ZF Active Safety & Elec US LLC ....C 734 855-2600
Livonia (G-10481)
ZF Active Safety & Elec US LLC ....E 586 232-7200
Washington (G-18093)
Zygot Operations Limited ....E 810 736-2900
Flint (G-5799)

STANDS & RACKS: Engine, Metal

Steelhead Industries LLC ....G 989 506-7416
Mount Pleasant (G-11743)

STARTERS & CONTROLLERS: Motor, Electric

Dare Auto Inc ....E 734 228-6243
Plymouth (G-13152)
Electrocraft Michigan Inc ....E 603 516-1297
Saline (G-15014)

STARTERS: Electric Motor

Denso International Amer Inc ....G 248 359-4177
Van Buren Twp (G-17523)

STARTERS: Motor

Prestolite Electric Inc ....F 866 463-7078
Novi (G-12514)

STATIONARY & OFFICE SPLYS, WHOLESALE: Carbon Paper

Spectrum Map Publishing Inc ....G 517 655-5641
Williamston (G-18583)

STATIONARY & OFFICE SPLYS, WHOLESALE: Inked Ribbons

Label Tech Inc ....F 586 247-6444
Shelby Township (G-15254)

STATIONARY & OFFICE SPLYS, WHOLESALE: Office Filing Splys

FSI Label Company ....E 586 776-4110
Holland (G-8043)

STATIONERY & OFFICE SPLYS WHOLESALERS

Accuform Prtg & Graphics Inc ....F 313 271-5600
Detroit (G-3981)
Consoldted Dcment Slutions LLC ....F 586 293-8100
Fraser (G-5914)
Imperial Clinical RES Svcs Inc ....C 616 784-0100
Grand Rapids (G-6836)
Mikan Corporation ....F 734 944-9447
Saline (G-15027)
Office Express Inc ....E 248 307-1850
Troy (G-17288)
US Salon Supply LLC ....F 616 365-5790
Paw Paw (G-12958)
Yti Office Express LLC ....G 866 996-8952
Troy (G-17458)

STATIONERY PRDTS

Barcroft Technology LLC ....G 313 378-0133
Southfield (G-15502)
Presscraft Papers Inc ....F 231 882-5505
Benzonia (G-1616)
Williams Parts & Supply Co ....F 906 337-3813
Calumet (G-2418)

STATORS REWINDING SVCS

Warfield Electric Company Inc ....G 734 722-4044
Westland (G-18429)

STEEL & ALLOYS: Tool & Die

Apex Tooling Solutions LLC ....G 616 283-7439
Jenison (G-9044)
Aweba Tool & Die Corp ....F 478 296-2002
Hastings (G-7781)
Blades Enterprises LLC ....F 734 449-4479
Wixom (G-18622)
Delaware Dynamics Michigan LLC ....F 586 997-1717
Shelby Township (G-15203)
Fabtronic Inc ....E 586 786-6114
Macomb (G-10594)
Industrial Engineering Service ....F 616 794-1330
Belding (G-1453)
Major Industries Ltd ....F 810 985-9372
Port Huron (G-13499)
Patterson Precision Mfg Inc ....E 231 733-1913
Norton Shores (G-12324)
Proservice Machine Ltd ....F 734 317-7266
Erie (G-5054)
St Johns Computer Machining ....G 989 224-7664
Saint Johns (G-14916)
The Pom Group Inc ....E 248 409-7900
Auburn Hills (G-1051)
W A Thomas Company ....G 734 955-6500
Taylor (G-16487)

STEEL FABRICATORS

A & S Industrial LLC ....G 906 482-8007
Hancock (G-7614)
A-1 Roll Co ....F 586 783-6677
Mount Clemens (G-11626)
Aarons Fabrictions-Tube Steel ....F 586 883-0652
Macomb (G-10570)
AB Custom Fabricating LLC ....F 269 663-8100
Edwardsburg (G-4998)
Ability Mfg & Engrg Co ....D 269 227-3292
Fennville (G-5433)
Ace Welding & Machine Inc ....F 231 941-9664
Traverse City (G-16595)
Actron Steel Inc ....E 231 947-3981
Traverse City (G-16597)
Admin Industries LLC ....F 989 685-3438
Rose City (G-14358)
Adrian Tool Corporation ....E 517 263-6530
Adrian (G-52)
ADW Industries Inc ....E 989 466-4742
Alma (G-233)
Aero Inc ....F 248 669-4085
Walled Lake (G-17662)
Alco Products LLC ....E 313 823-7500
Detroit (G-3996)
Allegan Metal Fabricators Inc ....G 269 751-7130
Hamilton (G-7595)
Allen Partners LLC ....F 269 673-4010
Allegan (G-148)
Allor Manufacturing Inc ....D 248 486-4500
Brighton (G-1943)
Alloy Construction Service Inc ....E 989 486-6960
Midland (G-11319)
Alro Steel Corporation ....G 810 695-7300
Grand Blanc (G-6231)
Ambassador Steel Corporation ....E 517 455-7216
Lansing (G-9804)
American Steel Works Inc ....F 734 282-0300
Riverview (G-13869)
Amerikam Inc ....D 616 243-5833
Grand Rapids (G-6457)
Amhawk LLC ....F 269 468-4141
Coloma (G-3474)
Amhawk LLC ....E 269 468-4177
Hartford (G-7761)
Amigo Mobility Intl Inc ....D 989 777-0910
Bridgeport (G-1914)
ARC Archer LLC ....F 616 439-3014
Kent City (G-9426)

Employee Codes: A=Over 500 employees, B=251-500
C=101-250, D=51-100, E=20-50, F=10-19, G=3-9
2022 Harris Michigan Industrial Directory
1415

Ashley Garcia G 248 396-8138
White Lake *(G-18450)*
Assembly Source One Inc G 616 844-5250
Grand Haven *(G-6276)*
Austin Tube Products Inc F 231 745-2741
Baldwin *(G-1121)*
B & D Metal Fab G 616 255-1796
Morley *(G-11619)*
B & G Custom Works Inc F 269 686-9420
Allegan *(G-149)*
Baker Enterprises Inc E 989 354-2189
Alpena *(G-281)*
Bauer Sheet Metal & Fabg Inc E 231 773-3244
Muskegon *(G-11775)*
Bell Metals G 248 227-0407
Troy *(G-16972)*
Bennett Steel LLC F 616 401-5271
Grand Rapids *(G-6500)*
Berrien Metal Products Inc F 269 695-5000
Buchanan *(G-2189)*
Black River Manufacturing Inc E 810 982-9812
Port Huron *(G-13459)*
Boones Welding & Fabricating G 517 782-7461
Jackson *(G-8825)*
Bridgeport Manufacturing Inc G 989 777-4314
Bridgeport *(G-1915)*
Builders Iron Inc E 616 647-9288
Sparta *(G-15761)*
Burnham & Northern Inc G 517 279-7501
Coldwater *(G-3422)*
C & C Manufacturing Inc F 586 268-3650
Sterling Heights *(G-15949)*
C & J Fabrication Inc G 586 791-6269
Clinton Township *(G-3192)*
C & M Manufacturing Inc E 517 279-0013
Coldwater *(G-3423)*
Cadillac Fabrication Inc E 231 775-7386
Cadillac *(G-2322)*
Campbell & Shaw Steel Inc F 810 364-5100
Marysville *(G-11083)*
Camryn Fabrication LLC F 586 949-0818
Chesterfield *(G-2857)*
Capital Steel & Builders Sup E 517 694-0451
Holt *(G-8304)*
Capital Welding Inc E 248 355-0410
Detroit *(G-4086)*
Cardinal Fabricating Inc E 517 655-2155
Williamston *(G-18570)*
Casadei Structural Steel Inc E 586 698-2898
Sterling Heights *(G-15953)*
Cbp Fabrication Inc E 313 653-4220
Detroit *(G-4090)*
Century Roll Inc F 810 743-5065
Burton *(G-2232)*
Cerco Inc E 734 362-8664
Brownstown Twp *(G-2153)*
Chicago Blow Pipe Company F 773 533-6100
Marquette *(G-11012)*
Circle S Products Inc G 734 675-2960
Woodhaven *(G-18798)*
Clair Sawyer G 906 228-8242
Marquette *(G-11013)*
Complex Steel & Wire Corp F 734 326-1600
Wayne *(G-18218)*
Concept Metal Machining LLC E 616 647-9200
Comstock Park *(G-3597)*
Concept Metal Products Inc D 231 799-3202
Spring Lake *(G-15808)*
Cooper & Cooper Sales Inc G 810 327-6247
Port Huron *(G-13465)*
Corban Industries Inc E 248 393-2720
Orion *(G-12726)*
Cornerstone Fabg & Cnstr Inc E 989 642-5241
Hemlock *(G-7850)*
Corsair Engineering Inc C 810 234-3664
Flint *(G-5673)*
Cox Brothers Machining Inc E 517 796-4662
Jackson *(G-8855)*
Custom Architectural Products G 616 748-1905
Zeeland *(G-19011)*
Custom Design & Manufacturing F 989 754-9962
Carrollton *(G-2587)*
Custom Metal Products Corp G 734 591-2500
Livonia *(G-10171)*
Custom Powder and Fabricators F 616 915-9995
Grand Rapids *(G-6621)*
D&M Metal Products Company E 616 784-0601
Comstock Park *(G-3600)*
Delta Steel Inc G 989 752-5129
Saginaw *(G-14637)*

Delta Tube & Fabricating Corp C 810 239-0154
Flint *(G-5686)*
Delta Tube & Fabrication F 810 233-0440
Flint *(G-5687)*
Demaria Building Company Inc G 248 486-2598
New Hudson *(G-12050)*
Demmer Corporation C 517 321-3600
Lansing *(G-9687)*
Digital Fabrication Inc F 616 794-2848
Belding *(G-1445)*
Diversified Fabricators Inc F 586 868-1000
Clinton Township *(G-3225)*
Diversiform LLC G 989 278-9605
Oscoda *(G-12756)*
Dobson Industrial Inc E 800 298-6063
Bay City *(G-1346)*
Douglas King Industries Inc G 989 642-2865
Hemlock *(G-7851)*
Dowding Industries Inc E 517 663-5455
Eaton Rapids *(G-4959)*
Dowding Industries Inc C 517 663-5455
Eaton Rapids *(G-4960)*
Dpr Manufacturing & Svcs Inc E 586 757-1421
Warren *(G-17783)*
Drushal Fabricating LLC G 517 539-5921
Jackson *(G-8871)*
Dumas Concepts In Building Inc F 313 895-2555
Detroit *(G-4196)*
Dunnage Engineering Inc E 810 229-9501
Brighton *(G-1979)*
Dunns Welding Inc G 248 356-3866
Southfield *(G-15543)*
Eab Fabrication Inc E 517 639-7080
Quincy *(G-13669)*
Eastern Michigan Industries E 586 757-4140
Warren *(G-17791)*
EMC Welding & Fabrication Inc G 231 788-4172
Muskegon *(G-11811)*
Empire Machine & Conveyors Inc F 989 541-2060
Durand *(G-4841)*
Engineered Alum Fabricators Co G 248 582-3430
Ferndale *(G-5551)*
Envirodyne Technologies Inc E 269 342-1918
Kalamazoo *(G-9181)*
Ethylene LLC E 616 554-3464
Kentwood *(G-9451)*
Fab Masters Company Inc D 269 646-5315
Marcellus *(G-10947)*
Fab-Lite Inc E 231 398-8280
Manistee *(G-10899)*
Fabrication Plus G 231 730-9374
Montague *(G-11596)*
Fabricted Cmpnnts Assmblies In F 269 673-7100
Allegan *(G-157)*
Ferguson Steel Inc F 810 984-3918
Fort Gratiot *(G-5821)*
Ferro Fab LLC F 586 791-3561
Clinton Township *(G-3237)*
Flat-To-Form Metal Spc Inc F 231 924-1288
Fremont *(G-6040)*
Focal Point Metal Fab LLC F 616 844-7670
Spring Lake *(G-15814)*
Frankenmuth Industrial Svcs E 989 652-3322
Frankenmuth *(G-5862)*
Genco Alliance LLC G 269 216-5500
Kalamazoo *(G-9192)*
General Motors LLC F 989 894-7210
Bay City *(G-1359)*
Gerref Industries Inc E 616 794-3110
Belding *(G-1450)*
Global Strgc Sup Solutions LLC D 734 525-9100
Livonia *(G-10226)*
Gosen Tool & Machine Inc F 989 777-6493
Saginaw *(G-14656)*
Gray Brothers Mfg Inc F 269 483-7615
White Pigeon *(G-18479)*
Great Lakes Contracting Inc E 616 846-8888
Grand Haven *(G-6308)*
Great Lakes Custom Metalworks G 231 818-5888
Cheboygan *(G-2784)*
Great Lakes Metal Fabrication G 248 218-0540
Livonia *(G-10230)*
Great Lakes Metal Works G 269 789-2342
Marshall *(G-11059)*
Great Lakes Stainless Inc E 231 943-7648
Traverse City *(G-16705)*
Great Lakes Towers LLC C 734 682-4000
Monroe *(G-11545)*
Greene Metal Products Inc E 586 465-6800
Clinton Township *(G-3249)*

Griffen Fab Works LLC G 616 890-0621
Byron Center *(G-2276)*
Griptrac Inc F 231 853-2284
Ravenna *(G-13689)*
H & M Welding and Fabricating G 517 764-3630
Jackson *(G-8897)*
Hamilton Steel Fabrications G 269 751-8757
Hamilton *(G-7600)*
Harrington Construction Co G 269 543-4251
Fennville *(G-5437)*
Hayden Neitzke LLC G 989 875-2440
Sumner *(G-16331)*
Heartland Steel Products LLC E 810 364-7421
Marysville *(G-11088)*
Heys Fabrication and Mch Co F 616 247-0065
Wyoming *(G-18882)*
Higgins Marine Metals LLC G 616 990-2732
Zeeland *(G-19035)*
Highland Engineering Inc E 517 548-4372
Howell *(G-8460)*
HPS Fabrications Inc F 734 282-2285
Wyandotte *(G-18822)*
Ideal Steel & Bldrs Sups LLC E 313 849-0000
Detroit *(G-4312)*
IEC Fabrication LLC F 810 623-1546
Fowlerville *(G-5842)*
Imm Inc E 989 344-7662
Grayling *(G-7463)*
Industrial Fabricating Inc F 734 676-2710
Brownstown Twp *(G-2155)*
Industrial Fabrication LLC E 269 465-5960
Bridgman *(G-1929)*
Innovative Iron Inc G 616 248-4250
Grand Rapids *(G-6846)*
Inter-Lakes Bases Inc E 586 294-8120
Fraser *(G-5944)*
International Extrusions Inc C 734 427-8700
Garden City *(G-6102)*
Iron Fetish Metalworks Inc F 586 776-8311
Roseville *(G-14426)*
J & J United Industries LLC F 734 443-3737
Livonia *(G-10252)*
J & M Machine Products Inc D 231 755-1622
Norton Shores *(G-12302)*
Jack & Sons Welding & Fabg LLC G 248 302-6496
Lewiston *(G-10022)*
Jay Industries Inc G 313 240-7535
Northville *(G-12232)*
JC Metal Fabricating Inc F 231 629-0425
Reed City *(G-13792)*
Jic Metalworks G 989 390-2077
Mio *(G-11509)*
JRC Fabricating Sales and Mfg G 734 459-6711
Canton *(G-2481)*
K & L Sheet Metal LLC G 269 965-0027
Battle Creek *(G-1248)*
K-R Metal Engineers Corp G 989 892-1901
Bay City *(G-1370)*
Kalamazoo Metal Muncher Inc G 269 492-0268
Plainwell *(G-13080)*
Kehrig Steel Inc G 586 716-9700
Ira *(G-8700)*
Ken Gorsline Welding G 269 649-0650
Vicksburg *(G-17606)*
Kenowa Industries Inc G 517 322-0311
Lansing *(G-9771)*
Kirby Metal Corporation E 810 743-3360
Burton *(G-2237)*
Kraftube Inc C 231 832-5562
Reed City *(G-13793)*
Kriewall Enterprises Inc E 586 336-0600
Romeo *(G-14227)*
L & W Inc G 734 397-8085
Van Buren Twp *(G-17535)*
L & W Inc D 734 397-6300
New Boston *(G-12012)*
Laduke Corporation E 248 414-6600
Oak Park *(G-12622)*
Lake Shore Services Inc F 734 285-7007
Wyandotte *(G-18828)*
Laser Craft LLC E 248 340-8922
Lake Orion *(G-9615)*
Lasers Unlimited Inc F 616 977-2668
Grand Rapids *(G-6931)*
Legacy Metal Services Inc G 810 721-7775
Imlay City *(G-8639)*
Legendary Fabrication Wldg LLC G 989 872-9353
Cass City *(G-2617)*
Lewis Metals LLC G 231 468-3435
Cadillac *(G-2343)*

STEEL FABRICATORS

Liberty Fabricators Inc .... F 810 877-7117
   Flint *(G-5724)*

Lincoln Welding Company .... G 313 292-2299
   Stockbridge *(G-16276)*

Loudon Steel Inc .... E 989 871-9353
   Millington *(G-11502)*

Lyndon Fabricators Inc .... G 313 937-3640
   Detroit *(G-4412)*

M & J Manufacturing Inc .... G 586 778-6322
   Clinton Township *(G-3283)*

Madar Metal Fabricating LLC .... F 517 267-9610
   Lansing *(G-9714)*

Magnum Fabricating .... G 734 484-5800
   Ypsilanti *(G-18964)*

Manistee Wldg & Piping Svc Inc ...... G 231 723-2551
   Manistee *(G-10906)*

Marsh Plating Corporation .... D 734 483-5767
   Ypsilanti *(G-18965)*

Maslo Fabrication LLC .... G 616 298-7700
   Holland *(G-8139)*

Matrix North Amercn Cnstr Inc .... D 734 847-4605
   Temperance *(G-16539)*

Mayo Welding & Fabricating Co ...... G 248 435-2730
   Royal Oak *(G-14561)*

Mbm Fabricators Co Inc .... C 734 941-0100
   Romulus *(G-14301)*

MCS Industries Inc .... F 517 568-4161
   Homer *(G-8354)*

Men of Steel Inc .... F 989 635-4866
   Marlette *(G-10986)*

Merrill Institute Inc .... G 989 462-0330
   Alma *(G-245)*

Metal Mart USA Inc .... G 586 977-5820
   Warren *(G-17924)*

Metalbuilt LLC .... E 586 786-9106
   Chesterfield *(G-2911)*

Metaldyne Tblar Components LLC .. D 248 727-1800
   Southfield *(G-15655)*

Metalfab Inc .... G 313 381-7579
   Dearborn *(G-3871)*

Metalfab Manufacturing Inc .... E 989 826-2301
   Mio *(G-11510)*

Michigan Diversified Metals .... G 517 223-7730
   Fowlerville *(G-5851)*

Michigan Fab and Engrg LLC .... G 248 297-5268
   Detroit *(G-4449)*

Michigan Indus Met Pdts Inc .... F 616 786-3922
   Muskegon *(G-11870)*

Michigan Steel Fabricators Inc .... E 810 785-1478
   Flint *(G-5732)*

Mid Michigan Pipe Inc .... E 989 772-5664
   Grand Rapids *(G-7003)*

Midwest Fabricating Inc .... G 734 921-3914
   Taylor *(G-16447)*

Midwest Steel Inc .... E 313 873-2220
   Detroit *(G-4456)*

Milton Manufacturing Inc .... E 313 366-2450
   Detroit *(G-4458)*

Minuteman Metal Works Inc .... G 989 269-8342
   Bad Axe *(G-1109)*

Mkr Fabricating Inc .... F 989 753-8100
   Saginaw *(G-14703)*

Modern Engrg Solutions LLC .... G 616 835-2711
   Grand Rapids *(G-7018)*

Moore Flame Cutting Co .... F 586 978-1090
   Bloomfield Hills *(G-1840)*

Moran Iron Works Inc .... D 989 733-2011
   Onaway *(G-12700)*

Morkin and Sowards Inc .... E 734 729-4242
   Wayne *(G-18231)*

Morrison Indust Ries North .... F 248 859-4864
   Novi *(G-12484)*

Mound Steel & Supply Inc .... F 248 852-6630
   Troy *(G-17266)*

Mtw Industries Inc .... F 989 317-3301
   Mount Pleasant *(G-11722)*

Mtw Performance & Fab .... G 989 317-3301
   Mount Pleasant *(G-11723)*

National Metal Sales Inc .... G 734 942-3000
   Romulus *(G-14308)*

National Ordanace Auto Mfg LLC ... G 248 853-8822
   Auburn Hills *(G-979)*

NBC Truck Equipment Inc .... E 586 774-4900
   Roseville *(G-14452)*

Nelson Iron Works Inc .... G 313 925-5355
   Detroit *(G-4480)*

Newco Industries LLC .... E 517 542-0105
   Litchfield *(G-10084)*

Niles Aluminum Products Inc .... E 269 683-1191
   Niles *(G-12153)*

Nisshinbo Automotive Mfg Inc .... E 586 997-1000
   Sterling Heights *(G-16117)*

Northern Chain Specialties .... F 231 889-3151
   Kaleva *(G-9380)*

Northern Concrete Pipe Inc .... E 989 892-3545
   Bay City *(G-1383)*

Northern Machining & Repr Inc ...... F 906 786-0526
   Escanaba *(G-5088)*

Northwest Fabrication Inc .... G 231 536-3229
   East Jordan *(G-4878)*

Nt Fabricating Inc .... F 586 566-7280
   Shelby Township *(G-15293)*

Oakland Welding Industries .... E 586 949-4090
   Chesterfield *(G-2916)*

Oakwood Energy Management Inc ... F 734 947-7700
   Taylor *(G-16453)*

Oakwood Metal Fabricating Co .... E 313 561-7740
   Dearborn *(G-3879)*

P I W Corporation .... G 989 448-2501
   Gaylord *(G-6152)*

Parton & Preble Inc .... E 586 773-6000
   Warren *(G-17954)*

Pioneer Machine and Tech Inc .... G 248 546-4451
   Madison Heights *(G-10800)*

Plutchak Fab .... F 906 864-4650
   Menominee *(G-11256)*

Ponder Industrial Incorporated .... E 989 684-9841
   Bay City *(G-1389)*

Powell Fabrication & Mfg LLC .... E 989 681-2158
   Saint Louis *(G-14996)*

Power Industries Corp .... G 586 783-3818
   Harrison Township *(G-7716)*

Precision Metals Plus Inc .... G 269 342-6330
   Kalamazoo *(G-9304)*

Precision Mtl Hdlg Eqp LLC .... D 313 789-8101
   Inkster *(G-8671)*

Precision Mtl Hdlg Eqp LLC .... D 734 351-7350
   Romulus *(G-14322)*

Production Fabricators Inc .... E 231 777-3822
   Muskegon *(G-11900)*

Professional Metal Works Inc .... E 517 351-7411
   Haslett *(G-7777)*

Quality Bending Threading Inc .... F 313 898-5100
   Detroit *(G-4546)*

Quality Finishing Systems .... F 231 834-9131
   Grant *(G-7431)*

Quality Metal Fabricating .... E 616 901-5510
   Grand Rapids *(G-7128)*

R T C Enviro Fab Inc .... E 517 596-2987
   Munith *(G-11757)*

R-Bo Co Inc .... F 616 748-9733
   Zeeland *(G-19076)*

Red Laser Inc .... F 517 540-1300
   Wixom *(G-18739)*

Refab Metal Fabrication LLC .... E 616 842-9705
   Grand Haven *(G-6352)*

REO Fab LLC .... F 810 969-4667
   Lapeer *(G-9958)*

Richard Bennett & Associates .... G 313 831-4262
   Detroit *(G-4571)*

Richmonds Steel Inc .... F 989 453-7010
   Pigeon *(G-13040)*

Ridgefield Company LLC .... G 888 226-8665
   Grand Rapids *(G-7155)*

River City Metal Products Inc .... D 616 235-3746
   Grand Rapids *(G-7159)*

River City Steel Svc .... G 616 301-7227
   Grandville *(G-7414)*

Rives Manufacturing Inc .... E 517 569-3380
   Rives Junction *(G-13888)*

RKP Consulting Inc .... G 616 698-0300
   Caledonia *(G-2397)*

Rochester Welding Company Inc .... E 248 628-0801
   Oxford *(G-12913)*

Rocksteady Manufacturing LLC ...... F 586 778-5028
   Roseville *(G-14472)*

Roth Fabricating Inc .... E 517 458-7541
   Morenci *(G-11615)*

Royal ARC Welding Company .... E 734 789-9099
   Flat Rock *(G-5628)*

RSI .... G 586 566-7716
   Shelby Township *(G-15318)*

RSI Global Sourcing LLC .... G 734 604-2448
   Novi *(G-12529)*

Rt Manufacturing Inc .... F 906 233-9158
   Escanaba *(G-5097)*

Ruess Winchester Inc .... F 989 725-5809
   Owosso *(G-12852)*

S & G Erection Company .... E 517 546-9240
   Howell *(G-8513)*

S & N Machine & Fabricating .... E 231 894-2658
   Rothbury *(G-14498)*

S & P Fabricating Inc .... G 586 421-1950
   Chesterfield *(G-2942)*

S L H Metals Inc .... F 989 743-3467
   Corunna *(G-3717)*

S N D Steel Fabrication Inc .... F 586 997-1500
   Shelby Township *(G-15320)*

Sales & Engineering Inc .... E 734 525-9030
   Livonia *(G-10398)*

Sanilac Steel Inc .... F 989 635-2992
   Marlette *(G-10987)*

Sas Global Corporation .... C 248 414-4470
   Warren *(G-18002)*

Sas Global Corporation .... D 248 414-4470
   Warren *(G-18003)*

Savs Welding Services Inc .... F 313 841-3430
   Detroit *(G-4582)*

Service Iron Works Inc .... E 248 446-9750
   South Lyon *(G-15457)*

Servotech Industries Inc .... F 734 697-5555
   Taylor *(G-16471)*

Sherwood Manufacturing Corp .... F 231 386-5132
   Northport *(G-12191)*

Shoreline Mtal Fabricators Inc .... E 231 722-4443
   Muskegon *(G-11919)*

Short Iron Fabrication .... G 231 375-8825
   Muskegon *(G-11921)*

SL Holdings Inc .... E 586 949-0912
   Chesterfield *(G-2948)*

Smede-Son Steel and Sup Co Inc ... D 313 937-8300
   Redford *(G-13772)*

SMI American Inc .... G 313 438-0096
   Taylor *(G-16474)*

Sol-I-Cor Industries .... E 248 476-0670
   Livonia *(G-10413)*

South Park Sales & Mfg Inc .... G 313 381-7579
   Dearborn *(G-3899)*

Spartan Metal Fab LLC .... E 517 322-9050
   Lansing *(G-9737)*

Special Fabricators Inc .... G 248 588-6717
   Madison Heights *(G-10833)*

Special Projects Inc .... E 734 455-7130
   Plymouth *(G-13302)*

Steel Craft Inc .... G 989 358-7196
   Alpena *(G-320)*

Steel Supply & Engineering Co .... E 616 452-3281
   Grand Rapids *(G-7223)*

Stevens Custom Fabrication .... G 989 340-1184
   Alpena *(G-321)*

Stevens Custom Fabrication .... G 989 340-1184
   Alpena *(G-322)*

Stone For You .... G 248 651-9940
   Rochester *(G-13930)*

Structural Standards Inc .... E 616 813-1798
   Sparta *(G-15784)*

Superior Fabricating Inc .... F 989 354-8877
   Alpena *(G-324)*

Superior Suppliers Network LLC .... F 906 284-1561
   Crystal Falls *(G-3746)*

Synergy Additive Mfg LLC .... G 248 719-2194
   Clinton Township *(G-3369)*

Tartan Industries Inc .... G 810 387-4255
   Yale *(G-18920)*

Tfi Inc .... E 231 728-2310
   Muskegon *(G-11931)*

Tg Manufacturing LLC .... G 616 935-7575
   Byron Center *(G-2296)*

Thyssenkrupp Materials NA Inc ..... C 248 233-5600
   Southfield *(G-15722)*

Toolpak Solutions LLC .... F 586 646-5655
   New Baltimore *(G-11995)*

Tower International Inc .... G 616 802-1600
   Grand Rapids *(G-7267)*

Trimet Industries Inc .... E 231 929-9100
   Traverse City *(G-16867)*

Tube Fab/Roman Engrg Co Inc .... C 231 238-9366
   Afton *(G-108)*

U P Fabricating Co Inc .... F 906 475-4400
   Negaunee *(G-11976)*

U S Fabrication & Design LLC .... F 248 919-2910
   Livonia *(G-10452)*

Unistrut International Corp .... C 734 721-4040
   Wayne *(G-18240)*

United Fabricating Company .... G 248 887-7289
   Highland *(G-7901)*

Universal Induction Inc .... G 269 983-5543
   Saint Joseph *(G-14970)*

Utica Steel Inc .... D 586 949-1900
   Chesterfield *(G-2962)*

Employee Codes: A=Over 500 employees, B=251-500
C=101-250, D=51-100, E=20-50, F=10-19, G=3-9

STEEL FABRICATORS

Valley Steel Company .... E 989 799-2600
  Saginaw *(G-14788)*
Van Dam Iron Works LLC .... E 616 452-8627
  Grand Rapids *(G-7304)*
Van Pelt Corporation .... G 313 365-3600
  Sterling Heights *(G-16221)*
Van Pelt Corporation .... G 313 733-0073
  Detroit *(G-4661)*
Van Pelt Corporation .... F 313 365-6500
  Detroit *(G-4662)*
Vanco Steel Inc .... E 810 688-4333
  North Branch *(G-12184)*
Varneys Fab & Weld LLC .... G 231 865-6856
  Nunica *(G-12589)*
Versatile Fabrication Co Inc .... E 231 739-7115
  Muskegon *(G-11941)*
Vertex Steel Inc .... E 248 684-4177
  Milford *(G-11496)*
Vochaska Engineering .... G 269 637-5670
  South Haven *(G-15423)*
Wagon Automotive Inc .... C 248 262-2020
  Wixom *(G-18789)*
Wahmhoff Farms LLC .... F 269 628-4308
  Gobles *(G-6220)*
Webasto Roof Systems Inc .... B 248 997-5100
  Auburn Hills *(G-1088)*
Webasto Roof Systems Inc .... C 248 997-5100
  Rochester Hills *(G-14145)*
Weir Fabrication LLC .... G 248 953-8363
  Sterling Heights *(G-16230)*
Wenstrom Dsign Fabrication LLC .... G 269 760-2358
  Brohman *(G-2109)*
West Michigan Fab Corp .... G 616 794-3750
  Belding *(G-1465)*
West Michigan Fabrication .... G 269 637-2415
  South Haven *(G-15425)*
West Michigan Metals LLC .... G 269 978-7021
  Allegan *(G-186)*
Wm Kloeffler Industries Inc .... E 810 765-4068
  Marine City *(G-10969)*
Wolverine Steel and Welding .... E 517 524-7300
  Concord *(G-3658)*
Worldtek Industries LLC .... G 734 494-5204
  Romulus *(G-14340)*
Wpw Inc .... F 810 785-1478
  Flint *(G-5796)*

STEEL MILLS

ABC Coating Company Inc .... F 616 245-4626
  Grand Rapids *(G-6415)*
Ann Arbor Stainless .... G 734 741-9499
  Ann Arbor *(G-370)*
ARC Mit .... G 248 399-4800
  Ferndale *(G-5527)*
Arlington Metals Corporation .... E 269 426-3371
  Sawyer *(G-15106)*
Autocam-Pax Inc .... C 269 782-5186
  Dowagiac *(G-4776)*
Avatar Inc .... G 586 846-3195
  Clinton Township *(G-3177)*
Bar Processing Corporation .... F 734 782-4454
  Warren *(G-17727)*
Benteler Automotive Corp .... B 616 247-3936
  Auburn Hills *(G-810)*
Borneman & Peterson Inc .... F 810 744-1890
  Flint *(G-5659)*
Brake Roller Co Inc .... F 269 965-2371
  Battle Creek *(G-1197)*
Broaching Industries Inc .... E 586 949-3775
  Chesterfield *(G-2853)*
Burnham & Northern Inc .... G 517 279-7501
  Coldwater *(G-3422)*
Cannon-Muskegon Corporation .... C 231 755-1681
  Norton Shores *(G-12284)*
Cleveland-Cliffs Steel Corp .... B 313 317-8900
  Dearborn *(G-3820)*
Coach House Iron Inc .... G 616 785-8967
  Sparta *(G-15764)*
Delaco Steel Corporation .... C 313 491-1200
  Dearborn *(G-3826)*
Detroit Steel Group Inc .... G 248 298-2900
  Royal Oak *(G-14530)*
Die Cast Press Mfg Co Inc .... G 269 657-6060
  Paw Paw *(G-12947)*
Doylen Albring Jr .... G 989 427-2919
  Edmore *(G-4991)*
Dundee Products Company .... E 734 529-2441
  Dundee *(G-4817)*
F and R Associates .... G 734 316-7763
  Saline *(G-15016)*

Grant Industries Incorporated .... E 586 293-9200
  Fraser *(G-5931)*
Greenbrook Tms Neurohealth Ctr .... G 855 940-4867
  Lansing *(G-9846)*
JIT Steel Corp .... F 313 491-3212
  Dearborn *(G-3856)*
Manistee Wldg & Piping Svc Inc .... E 231 723-2551
  Manistee *(G-10906)*
Metal Dynamics Detroit .... G 313 841-1800
  Detroit *(G-4431)*
Michigan Rod Products Inc .... D 517 552-9812
  Howell *(G-8481)*
Mill Steel Co .... D 616 949-6700
  Grand Rapids *(G-7010)*
Oakland Welding Industries .... E 586 949-4090
  Chesterfield *(G-2916)*
Peerless Steel Company .... E 616 530-6695
  Grandville *(G-7408)*
Premium Air Systems Inc .... E 248 680-8800
  Troy *(G-17312)*
Repair Industries Michigan Inc .... C 313 365-5300
  Detroit *(G-4568)*
Resetar Equipment Inc .... G 313 291-0500
  Dearborn Heights *(G-3937)*
Rod Chomper Inc .... F 616 392-9677
  Holland *(G-8182)*
Service Iron Works Inc .... E 248 446-9750
  South Lyon *(G-15457)*
Set Enterprises Inc .... E 586 573-3600
  Royal Oak *(G-14580)*
Shoreline Recycling & Supply .... E 231 722-6081
  Muskegon *(G-11920)*
Steel Mill Components Inc .... F 586 920-2595
  Warren *(G-18029)*
Strong Steel Products LLC .... F 313 267-3300
  Detroit *(G-4613)*
Tms International LLC .... G 734 241-3007
  Monroe *(G-11583)*
Tms International LLC .... G 517 764-5123
  Jackson *(G-9021)*
Tms International LLC .... G 313 378-6502
  Ecorse *(G-4987)*
Universal Hdlg Eqp Owosso LLC .... G 989 720-1650
  Owosso *(G-12865)*
Welk-Ko Fabricators Inc .... G 248 486-2598
  New Hudson *(G-12074)*
Westwood Lands Inc .... F 906 475-9544
  Marquette *(G-11050)*
Worthington Steel of Michigan .... C 734 374-3260
  Taylor *(G-16490)*

STEEL WOOL

Enkon LLC .... E 937 890-5678
  Manchester *(G-10883)*
Schwab Industries Inc .... E 586 566-8090
  Shelby Township *(G-15326)*

STEEL, COLD-ROLLED: Flat Bright, From Purchased Hot-Rolled

Warren Steel Co .... G 586 756-6600
  Warren *(G-18062)*

STEEL, COLD-ROLLED: Strip NEC, From Purchased Hot-Rolled

National Galvanizing LP .... A 734 243-1882
  Monroe *(G-11567)*

STEEL, HOT-ROLLED: Sheet Or Strip

National Galvanizing LP .... A 734 243-1882
  Monroe *(G-11567)*

STEEL: Cold-Rolled

Alro Steel Corporation .... G 517 371-9600
  Lansing *(G-9803)*
Bar Processing Corporation .... F 734 782-4454
  Warren *(G-17727)*
Cold Heading Co .... E 586 497-7016
  Warren *(G-17759)*
Diez Group LLC .... D 734 675-1700
  Woodhaven *(G-18799)*
Eikos Holdings Inc .... E 248 280-0300
  Troy *(G-17080)*
Fabtec Enterprises Inc .... F 616 878-9288
  Byron Center *(G-2269)*
Flat Rock Metal Inc .... C 734 782-4454
  Flat Rock *(G-5618)*

PRODUCT SECTION

Gerdau Macsteel Inc .... E 517 782-0415
  Jackson *(G-8891)*
Gerdau Macsteel Inc .... B 517 764-0311
  Jackson *(G-8890)*
Gerdau Macsteel Inc .... B 734 243-2446
  Monroe *(G-11543)*
Grant Industries Incorporated .... E 586 293-9200
  Fraser *(G-5931)*
H & L Tool Company Inc .... E 248 585-7474
  Madison Heights *(G-10736)*
Kamax Inc .... C 810 272-2090
  Lapeer *(G-9936)*
Nss Technologies Inc .... E 734 459-9500
  Canton *(G-2502)*
Peerless Steel Company .... E 616 530-6695
  Grandville *(G-7408)*
Sandvik Inc .... D 269 926-7241
  Benton Harbor *(G-1582)*
Van Emon Bruce .... G 269 467-7803
  Centreville *(G-2699)*
Worthington Industries Inc .... E 734 397-6187
  Canton *(G-2543)*
Worthington Industries Inc .... E 734 289-5416
  Monroe *(G-11592)*
Worthington Steel of Michigan .... C 734 374-3260
  Taylor *(G-16490)*

STEEL: Laminated

Hill Machine Works LLC .... F 586 238-2897
  Fraser *(G-5937)*

STEERING SYSTEMS & COMPONENTS

Asama Coldwater Mfg Inc .... B 517 279-1090
  Coldwater *(G-3420)*
Hot Rod Holdings Inc .... E 517 424-0577
  Tecumseh *(G-16505)*
Key Safety Systems Inc .... C 248 373-8040
  Auburn Hills *(G-951)*
Nexteer Automotive Corporation .... B 989 757-5000
  Saginaw *(G-14720)*
Nexteer Automotive Group Ltd .... A 989 757-5000
  Saginaw *(G-14721)*
Sweet Manufacturing Inc .... E 269 344-2086
  Kalamazoo *(G-9350)*

STENCILS

Collier Enterprise III .... G 269 503-3402
  Sturgis *(G-16284)*
Lakeside Property Services .... G 863 455-9038
  Holland *(G-8122)*

STERILIZERS, BARBER & BEAUTY SHOP

Skin Bar VII LLC .... G 313 397-9919
  Detroit *(G-4597)*

STITCHING SVCS: Custom

G T Jerseys LLC .... F 248 588-3231
  Troy *(G-17124)*
Graphix Signs & Embroidery .... G 616 396-0009
  Holland *(G-8056)*
Shop Makarios LLC .... F 800 479-0032
  Byron Center *(G-2295)*

STOKERS: Mechanical, Domestic Or Indl

D S C Services Inc .... G 734 241-9500
  Monroe *(G-11535)*
Detroit Stoker Company .... C 734 241-9500
  Monroe *(G-11537)*
Messersmith Manufacturing Inc .... G 906 466-9010
  Bark River *(G-1156)*

STONE: Crushed & Broken, NEC

Sandys Contracting .... G 810 629-2259
  Fenton *(G-5502)*

STONE: Dimension, NEC

Michigan Tile and Marble Co .... E 313 931-1700
  Detroit *(G-4453)*
TNT Marble and Stone Inc .... G 248 887-8237
  Hartland *(G-7772)*

STONE: Quarrying & Processing, Own Stone Prdts

Lewiston Sand & Gravel Inc .... G 989 786-2742
  Lewiston *(G-10023)*

PRODUCT SECTION

Quarry Ridge Stone Inc ....F 616 827-8244
  Byron Center *(G-2294)*
Rockwood Quarry LLC ....C 734 783-7415
  South Rockwood *(G-15465)*
Rockwood Quarry LLC ....G 734 783-7400
  Newport *(G-12106)*
Stone Shop Inc ....F 248 852-4700
  Port Huron *(G-13530)*

STOOLS: Factory

Wm Kloeffler Industries Inc ....G 810 765-4068
  Marine City *(G-10969)*

STORE FIXTURES: Exc Wood

Construction Retail Svcs Inc ....G 586 469-2289
  Clinton Township *(G-3210)*
Mega Wall Inc ....F 616 647-4190
  Comstock Park *(G-3624)*
T M Shea Products Inc ....F 800 992-5233
  Troy *(G-17383)*

STORE FIXTURES: Wood

Competitive Edge Wood Spc Inc ....D 616 842-1063
  Muskegon *(G-11794)*
Hilco Fixture Finders LLC ....E 616 453-1300
  Grand Rapids *(G-6815)*
Holsinger Manufacturing Corp ....E 989 684-3101
  Kawkawlin *(G-9416)*
Panel Processing Oregon Inc ....D 989 356-9007
  Alpena *(G-309)*
Panel Processing Texas Inc ....E 903 586-2423
  Alpena *(G-310)*

STORES: Auto & Home Supply

Hemco Machine Co Inc ....G 586 264-8911
  Warren *(G-17851)*
M M R LLC ....G 734 502-5239
  Livonia *(G-10295)*
Monroes Custom Campers Inc ....F 231 773-0005
  Muskegon *(G-11877)*
Walmart Inc ....F 517 541-1481
  Charlotte *(G-2774)*

STORES: Drapery & Upholstery

American Roll Shutter Awng Co ....E 734 422-7110
  Livonia *(G-10116)*

STOVES: Wood & Coal Burning

Nu-Way Stove Inc ....G 989 733-8792
  Onaway *(G-12701)*

STRAIN GAGES: Solid State

AG Precision Gage Inc ....G 248 374-0063
  Wixom *(G-18599)*
Birdsall Tool & Gage Co ....E 248 474-5150
  Farmington Hills *(G-5181)*
J & K Spratt Enterprises Inc ....D 517 439-5010
  Hillsdale *(G-7938)*
Riverside Cnc LLC ....F 616 246-6000
  Wyoming *(G-18905)*

STRAPS: Cotton Webbing

B Erickson Manufacturing Ltd ....F 810 765-1144
  Marine City *(G-10955)*

STRAPS: Spindle Banding

Chambers Enterprises II LLC ....F 810 688-3750
  North Branch *(G-12177)*
Superior Spindle Services LLC ....F 734 946-4646
  Taylor *(G-16482)*

STRAWS: Drinking, Made From Purchased Materials

Solo Cup Company LLC ....C 800 248-5960
  Mason *(G-11155)*

STRINGING BEADS

Sashabaw Bead Co ....G 248 969-1353
  Oxford *(G-12915)*

STRUCTURAL SUPPORT & BUILDING MATERIAL: Concrete

Kelder LLC ....F 231 757-3000
  Scottville *(G-15135)*
Liberty Transit Mix LLC ....F 586 254-2212
  Shelby Township *(G-15263)*

STUCCO

Darren McCaffery Stucco ....G 321 303-0988
  Manton *(G-10932)*

STUDIOS: Artists & Artists' Studios

Liedel Power Cleaning ....G 734 848-2827
  Erie *(G-5049)*
PRC Commercial Services LLC ....G 313 445-1760
  Dearborn *(G-3884)*

STUDS & JOISTS: Sheet Metal

B & D Thread Rolling Inc ....D 734 728-7070
  Taylor *(G-16384)*
Federal Screw Works ....F 734 941-4211
  Romulus *(G-14274)*
Kamax Inc ....C 810 272-2090
  Lapeer *(G-9936)*
State Building Product Inc ....E 586 772-8878
  Warren *(G-18028)*

SUBPRESSES, METALWORKING

Acg Services Inc ....G 586 232-4698
  Shelby Township *(G-15164)*

SUBSCRIPTION FULFILLMENT SVCS: Magazine, Newspaper, Etc

SPD America LLC ....G 734 709-7624
  Pinckney *(G-13056)*

SUBSTANCE ABUSE COUNSELING

Road To Freedom ....F 810 775-0992
  Brighton *(G-2066)*

SUNDRIES & RELATED PRDTS: Medical & Laboratory, Rubber

Kent Manufacturing Company ....D 616 454-9495
  Grand Rapids *(G-6889)*
Midwest Rubber Company ....C 810 376-2085
  Deckerville *(G-3955)*
Tissue Seal LLC ....F 734 213-5530
  Ann Arbor *(G-692)*

SUNGLASSES, WHOLESALE

Diamond Boutique ....G 313 451-4217
  Dearborn *(G-3828)*
Nalcor LLC ....D 248 541-1140
  Ferndale *(G-5570)*

SUNROOFS: Motor Vehicle

Inalfa Holding Inc ....F 248 371-3060
  Auburn Hills *(G-934)*
Inalfa Roof Systems Inc ....B 248 371-3060
  Auburn Hills *(G-935)*
Qp Acquisition 2 Inc ....A 248 594-7432
  Southfield *(G-15685)*
Webasto Roof Systems Inc ....B 248 997-5100
  Auburn Hills *(G-1088)*

SUPERMARKETS & OTHER GROCERY STORES

Apple Valley Natural Foods ....C 269 471-3234
  Berrien Springs *(G-1637)*
Brownwood Acres Foods Inc ....F 231 599-3101
  Eastport *(G-4949)*
Crossbrook LLC ....G 616 772-5921
  Zeeland *(G-19009)*
Hashems of Dearborn Heights ....F 313 278-2000
  Dearborn Heights *(G-3928)*
Jorgensens Inc ....E 989 831-8338
  Greenville *(G-7494)*
Randall Foods Inc ....F 517 767-3247
  Tekonsha *(G-16524)*

SURFACE ACTIVE AGENTS

BASF Corporation ....C 734 324-6000
  Wyandotte *(G-18809)*
Ipax Atlantic LLC ....G 313 933-4211
  Detroit *(G-4325)*
Tsw Technologies LLC ....G 248 773-5026
  Novi *(G-12559)*

SURFACE ACTIVE AGENTS: Emulsifiers, Exc Food & Pharmaceuticl

Metalworking Lubricants Co ....D 248 332-3500
  Pontiac *(G-13397)*

SURFACE ACTIVE AGENTS: Processing Assistants

Quaker Houghton Pa Inc ....E 248 265-7745
  Troy *(G-17325)*

SURFACE ACTIVE AGENTS: Textile Processing Assistants

McCarthy Group Incorporated ....F 616 977-2900
  Grand Rapids *(G-6970)*

SURFACERS: Concrete Grinding

CPS LLC ....F 517 639-1464
  Quincy *(G-13666)*
Creative Surfaces Inc ....F 586 226-2950
  Clinton Township *(G-3213)*
Syncon Inc ....E 313 914-4481
  Livonia *(G-10427)*

SURGICAL APPLIANCES & SPLYS

Plasma Biolife Services L P ....G 616 667-0264
  Grandville *(G-7409)*

SURGICAL APPLIANCES & SPLYS

3dm Source Inc ....F 616 647-9513
  Grand Rapids *(G-6405)*
Able Entities LLC ....F 313 422-9555
  Detroit *(G-3980)*
Accurate Safety Distrs Inc ....G 989 695-6446
  Freeland *(G-6017)*
Auric Enterprises Inc ....G 231 882-7251
  Beulah *(G-1652)*
Curbell Plastics Inc ....G 734 513-0531
  Livonia *(G-10170)*
Danmar Products Inc ....E 734 761-1990
  Ann Arbor *(G-443)*
Davis Dental Laboratory ....G 616 261-9191
  Wyoming *(G-18865)*
Ever-Flex Inc ....E 313 389-2060
  Lincoln Park *(G-10046)*
Hi-Tech Optical Inc ....E 989 799-9390
  Saginaw *(G-14663)*
Hosmer ....G 248 541-9829
  Madison Heights *(G-10741)*
Howmedica Osteonics Corp ....G 269 389-8959
  Portage *(G-13566)*
Jacquart Fabric Products Inc ....C 906 932-1339
  Ironwood *(G-8765)*
Medtronic Inc ....G 616 643-5200
  Grand Rapids *(G-6976)*
Mercy Health Partners ....E 231 672-4886
  Muskegon *(G-11867)*
MII Disposition Inc ....E 616 554-9696
  Grand Rapids *(G-7009)*
Noir Medical Technologies LLC ....F 248 486-3760
  South Lyon *(G-15450)*
Obsolete Inc ....G 616 843-0351
  Lowell *(G-10512)*
Orthopaedic Associates Mich ....D 616 459-7101
  Grand Rapids *(G-7063)*
Porex Technologies Corp ....E 989 865-8200
  Saint Charles *(G-14807)*
Regents of The University Mich ....E 734 973-2400
  Ann Arbor *(G-638)*
Signal Medical Corporation ....F 810 364-7070
  Marysville *(G-11099)*
Sigvaris Inc ....E 616 741-4281
  Holland *(G-8196)*
Steele Supply Co ....G 269 983-0920
  Saint Joseph *(G-14964)*
Stryker Corporation ....E 269 385-2600
  Portage *(G-13615)*

SURGICAL APPLIANCES & SPLYS

Tesa Tape Inc .... G 616 785-6970
  Walker (G-17654)
Tesa Tape Inc .... G 616 887-3107
  Sparta (G-15786)
Thierica Equipment Corporation .... E 616 453-6570
  Grand Rapids (G-7259)
Warwick Mas & Equipment Co .... G 810 966-3431
  Port Huron (G-13537)
Wright & Filippis LLC .... F 517 484-2624
  Lansing (G-9906)
Wright & Filippis LLC .... F 586 756-4020
  Warren (G-18073)
Wright & Filippis LLC .... F 313 386-3330
  Lincoln Park (G-10058)
Wright & Filippis LLC .... F 248 336-8460
  Detroit (G-3968)
XYZ McHine TI Fabrications Inc .... G 517 482-3668
  Lansing (G-9796)

SURGICAL EQPT: See Also Instruments

Bio-Vac Inc .... E 248 350-2150
  Southfield (G-15508)
Frontier Medical Devices Inc .... F 906 232-1200
  Gwinn (G-7584)
Gelman Sciences Inc .... C 734 665-0651
  Ann Arbor (G-496)
Nel Group Inc .... G 734 730-9164
  Ann Arbor (G-593)
Slaughter Instrument Company .... F 269 428-7471
  Stevensville (G-16265)
Stryker Australia LLC .... C 269 385-2600
  Portage (G-13612)
Stryker Corporation .... E 269 389-2300
  Portage (G-13616)
Stryker Far East Inc .... A 269 385-2600
  Portage (G-13618)
Stryker Prfmce Solutions LLC .... F 269 385-2600
  Portage (G-13619)
Tambra Investments Inc .... G 866 662-7897
  Warren (G-18035)

SURGICAL IMPLANTS

Autocam Med DVC Holdings LLC .... G 616 541-8080
  Kentwood (G-9447)
Autocam Medical Devices LLC .... E 877 633-8080
  Grand Rapids (G-6482)
Set Liquidation Inc .... D 517 694-2300
  Holt (G-8331)
Stryker Australia LLC .... C 269 385-2600
  Portage (G-13612)
Stryker Customs Brokers LLC .... F 269 389-2300
  Portage (G-13617)
Stryker Far East Inc .... A 269 385-2600
  Portage (G-13618)
Trackcore Inc .... F 616 632-2222
  Grand Rapids (G-7268)

SURVEYING & MAPPING: Land Parcels

Dcr Services & Cnstr Inc .... F 313 297-6544
  Detroit (G-4123)
Great Lakes Exploration Inc .... G 906 352-4024
  Menominee (G-11239)

SUSPENSION SYSTEMS: Acoustical, Metal

ITT Motion Tech Amer LLC .... F 248 863-2161
  Novi (G-12444)
St USA Holding Corp .... D 517 278-7144
  Coldwater (G-3456)
St USA Holding Corp .... C 800 637-3303
  Coldwater (G-3457)

SVC ESTABLISH EQPT, WHOLESALE: Carpet/Rug Clean Eqpt & Sply

Creative Products Intl .... F 616 335-3333
  Holland (G-8007)

SVC ESTABLISHMENT EQPT & SPLYS WHOLESALERS

Angels of Detroit LLC .... G 248 796-1079
  Redford (G-13714)
Bio Kleen Products Inc .... F 269 567-9400
  Kalamazoo (G-9136)
Eastern Oil Company .... E 248 333-1333
  Pontiac (G-13364)
Intuitive Technology Inc .... G 602 249-5750
  Dexter (G-4743)

M & M Typewriter Service Inc .... G 734 995-4033
  Ann Arbor (G-558)
Weaver Instructional Systems .... G 616 942-2891
  Grand Rapids (G-7327)

SVC ESTABLISHMENT EQPT, WHOL: Cleaning & Maint Eqpt & Splys

Diversified Davitco LLC .... F 248 681-9197
  Waterford (G-18115)
Enviro-Brite Solutions LLC .... G 989 387-2758
  Oscoda (G-12758)

SVC ESTABLISHMENT EQPT, WHOL: Concrete Burial Vaults & Boxes

Dm Vault Forms .... G 989 275-4797
  Roscommon (G-14348)
Superior Vault Co .... G 989 643-4200
  Merrill (G-11265)

SVC ESTABLISHMENT EQPT, WHOL: Funeral Director's Eqpt/Splys

Mp Acquisition LLC .... D 800 362-8491
  Madison Heights (G-10784)

SVC ESTABLISHMENT EQPT, WHOL: Laundry/Dry Cleaning Eqpt/Sply

Mdla Inc .... F 248 643-0807
  Troy (G-17242)
Selestial Soap LLC .... E 231 944-1978
  Traverse City (G-16828)

SVC ESTABLISHMENT EQPT, WHOLESALE: Firefighting Eqpt

Front Line Services Inc .... F 989 695-6633
  Freeland (G-6024)

SVC ESTABLISHMENT EQPT, WHOLESALE: Shredders, Indl & Comm

Technology Network Svcs Inc .... F 586 294-7771
  Saint Clair Shores (G-14888)

SWEEPING COMPOUNDS

Global Wholesale & Marketing .... G 248 910-8302
  Sterling Heights (G-16030)

SWIMMING POOLS, EQPT & SPLYS: Wholesalers

Lochinvar LLC .... E 734 454-4480
  Plymouth (G-13225)

SWITCHBOARDS & PARTS: Power

Tara Industries Inc .... G 248 477-6520
  Livonia (G-10429)

SWITCHES

Panel Pro LLC .... G 734 427-1691
  Livonia (G-10359)
Prestolite Electric LLC .... E 248 313-3807
  Novi (G-12512)
Semtron Inc .... F 810 732-9080
  Flint (G-5761)
Southern Auto Wholesalers Inc .... F 248 335-5555
  Pontiac (G-13417)
Trmi Incorporated .... A 269 966-0800
  Battle Creek (G-1307)

SWITCHES: Electric Power

Meter Devices Company Inc .... D 330 455-0301
  Farmington Hills (G-5317)
Valeo North America Inc .... C 248 619-8300
  Troy (G-17428)

SWITCHES: Electronic

Aktv8 LLC .... G 517 775-1270
  Wixom (G-18603)
Cardell Corporation .... D 248 371-9700
  Auburn Hills (G-840)
Five-Way Switch Music .... G 269 425-2843
  Battle Creek (G-1231)

Rdi Switching Technologies .... G 951 699-8919
  Ann Arbor (G-632)
Ssi Electronics Inc .... E 616 866-8880
  Belmont (G-1517)
ZF Active Safety & Elec US LLC .... E 586 232-7200
  Washington (G-18092)
ZF Active Safety & Elec US LLC .... C 734 855-2600
  Livonia (G-10481)
ZF Active Safety & Elec US LLC .... E 586 232-7200
  Washington (G-18093)

SWITCHES: Electronic Applications

AEL/Span LLC .... E 734 957-1600
  Van Buren Twp (G-17507)
Patriot Sensors & Cntrls Corp .... D 248 435-0700
  Peck (G-12963)
Safari Circuits Inc .... C 269 694-9471
  Otsego (G-12799)
Winford Engineering LLC .... G 989 671-9721
  Auburn (G-771)

SWITCHES: Solenoid

Detroit Coil Co .... E 248 658-1543
  Ferndale (G-5543)
Eto Magnetic Corp .... C 616 957-2570
  Grand Rapids (G-6686)
Johnson Electric N Amer Inc .... D 734 392-5300
  Plymouth (G-13206)

SWITCHGEAR & SWITCHBOARD APPARATUS

A & L Metal Products .... G 734 654-8990
  Carleton (G-2549)
Benesh Corporation .... F 734 244-4143
  Monroe (G-11532)
Ews Legacy LLC .... C 248 853-6363
  Rochester Hills (G-14006)
Henshaw Inc .... D 586 752-0700
  Armada (G-736)
Hugo Benzing LLC .... E 248 264-6478
  Wixom (G-18680)
Hydro-Logic Inc .... E 586 757-7477
  Warren (G-17857)
International Door Inc .... E 248 547-7240
  Canton (G-2478)
Memcon North America LLC .... F 269 281-0478
  Stevensville (G-16261)
Parker-Hannifin Corporation .... B 269 629-5000
  Richland (G-13826)
Patriot Sensors & Cntrls Corp .... F 810 378-5511
  Peck (G-12962)
Patriot Sensors & Cntrls Corp .... D 248 435-0700
  Peck (G-12963)
Schneider Electric Usa Inc .... G 810 733-9400
  Flint (G-5760)
Ssi Electronics Inc .... E 616 866-8880
  Belmont (G-1517)
X-Rite Incorporated .... C 616 803-2100
  Grand Rapids (G-7353)

SYNCHROS

Troy Synchro Sharkettes .... G 734 395-8899
  Ypsilanti (G-18982)

SYNTHETIC RESIN FINISHED PRDTS, NEC

Orbis Corporation .... G 248 616-3232
  Troy (G-17291)
Protojet Inc .... F 810 956-8000
  Fraser (G-5981)
Saint-Gobain Prfmce Plas Corp .... G 989 435-9533
  Beaverton (G-1431)

SYRUPS, DRINK

Contract Flavors Inc .... F 616 454-5950
  Grand Rapids (G-6598)
Great Lakes Coca-Cola Dist LLC .... F 517 322-2349
  Lansing (G-9762)
Leonard Fountain Spc Inc .... D 313 891-4141
  Detroit (G-4390)

SYSTEMS ENGINEERING: Computer Related

Superior Information Tech LLC .... F 734 666-9963
  Livonia (G-10424)

SYSTEMS INTEGRATION SVCS

Bull Hn Info Systems Inc .... G 616 942-7126
  Grand Rapids (G-6530)
Computer Sciences Corporation .... G 586 825-5043
  Sterling Heights (G-15967)
Fenton Systems Inc .... G 810 636-6318
  Goodrich (G-6223)
Indocomp Systems Inc .... F 810 678-3990
  Metamora (G-11281)
Lowry Holding Company Inc .... C 810 229-7200
  Brighton (G-2023)
Machine Control Technology .... G 517 655-3506
  Williamston (G-18577)
Medical Systems Resource Group .... G 248 476-5400
  Farmington Hills (G-5313)
Smart Label Solutions LLC .... G 800 996-7343
  Howell (G-8519)

SYSTEMS INTEGRATION SVCS: Local Area Network

Parameter Driven Software Inc .... F 248 553-6410
  Farmington Hills (G-5342)

SYSTEMS INTEGRATION SVCS: Office Computer Automation

Comau LLC .... D 248 219-0756
  Southfield (G-15531)
Whiteside Consulting Group LLC .... G 313 288-6598
  Detroit (G-4681)

SYSTEMS SOFTWARE DEVELOPMENT SVCS

Advanced Integrated Mfg .... G 586 439-0300
  Fraser (G-5888)
Artic Technologies Intl .... G 248 689-9884
  Troy (G-16955)
Click Care LLC .... G 989 792-1544
  Saginaw (G-14631)
Complete Data Products Inc .... F 248 651-8602
  Troy (G-17021)
Inovision Sftwr Solutions Inc .... G 586 598-8750
  Chesterfield (G-2896)
Lintech Global Inc .... D 248 553-8033
  Farmington Hills (G-5292)
Mejenta Systems Inc .... E 248 434-2583
  Southfield (G-15653)
Tru-Syzygy Inc .... G 248 622-7211
  Lake Orion (G-9635)
Varatech Inc .... F 616 393-6408
  Holland (G-8234)

TABLE OR COUNTERTOPS, PLASTIC LAMINATED

Carpenters Cabinets .... G 989 777-1070
  Saginaw (G-14621)
Custom Components Corporation .... F 616 523-1111
  Ionia (G-8688)
Greenfield Cabinetry Inc .... G 586 759-3300
  Warren (G-17839)
Nu-Tran LLC .... G 616 350-9575
  Wyoming (G-18897)

TABLES: Lift, Hydraulic

Air-Hydraulics Inc .... F 517 787-9444
  Jackson (G-8806)

TAGS & LABELS: Paper

Middleton Printing Inc .... G 616 247-8742
  Grand Rapids (G-7004)

TAGS: Paper, Blank, Made From Purchased Paper

Marshall Floral Products .... G 517 787-7620
  Jackson (G-8945)

TALLOW: Animal

Darling Ingredients Inc .... F 989 752-4340
  Carrollton (G-2588)
Kellys Recycling Service Inc .... G 313 389-7870
  Detroit (G-4357)

TANK COMPONENTS: Military, Specialized

Dynamic Metals Group LLC .... F 586 790-5615
  Birmingham (G-1724)
Plasan North America Inc .... E 616 559-0032
  Walker (G-17648)
Ronal Industries Inc .... F 248 616-9691
  Sterling Heights (G-16159)

TANK REPAIR & CLEANING SVCS

Matrix North Amercn Cnstr Inc .... D 734 847-4605
  Temperance (G-16539)

TANK REPAIR SVCS

Fischer Tanks LLC .... D 231 362-8265
  Kaleva (G-9378)
Gld Holdings Inc .... E 616 877-4288
  Moline (G-11518)
Saranac Tank Inc .... G 616 642-9481
  Saranac (G-15081)

TANKS & OTHER TRACKED VEHICLE CMPNTS

American Rhnmtall Vehicles LLC .... F 586 942-0139
  Sterling Heights (G-15930)
Burch Tank & Truck Inc .... G 989 495-0342
  Midland (G-11326)
Burch Tank & Truck Inc .... D 989 772-6266
  Mount Pleasant (G-11688)
Demmer Corporation .... C 517 321-3600
  Lansing (G-9687)
General Tactical Vehicles LLC .... G 586 825-7242
  Sterling Heights (G-16028)
Horstman Inc .... E 586 737-2100
  Sterling Heights (G-16041)
Interntnal Def Fabrication LLC .... G 810 643-1198
  Lapeer (G-9934)
Lipp America Tank Systems LLC .... F 616 201-6761
  Grand Rapids (G-6946)
Renk America LLC .... D 231 724-2666
  Muskegon (G-11907)
Reutter LLC .... G 248 466-0652
  Ann Arbor (G-640)
Supreme Gear Co .... E 586 775-6325
  Fraser (G-6001)
Tank Truck Service & Sales Inc .... E 586 757-6500
  Warren (G-18036)

TANKS: Concrete

Flambeau Inc .... G 248 364-3357
  Auburn Hills (G-901)
Leelanau Redi-Mix Inc .... E 231 228-5005
  Maple City (G-10943)

TANKS: Cryogenic, Metal

Arctic Solutions Inc .... E 586 331-2600
  Bruce Twp (G-2163)
Lasl Inc .... E 586 331-2600
  Bruce Twp (G-2175)

TANKS: For Tank Trucks, Metal Plate

Riverside Tank & Mfg Corp .... E 810 329-7143
  Saint Clair (G-14842)

TANKS: Fuel, Including Oil & Gas, Metal Plate

Fischer Tanks LLC .... D 231 362-8265
  Kaleva (G-9378)
Western International Inc .... E 866 814-2470
  Troy (G-17447)

TANKS: Lined, Metal

Gld Holdings Inc .... E 616 877-4288
  Moline (G-11518)
R T C Enviro Fab Inc .... E 517 596-2987
  Munith (G-11757)
Unified Equipment Systems Inc .... G 586 307-3770
  Clinton Township (G-3382)

TANKS: Plastic & Fiberglass

Denso Manufacturing NC Inc .... A 269 441-2040
  Battle Creek (G-1217)
Vitec LLC .... B 313 633-2254
  Detroit (G-4671)

TANKS: Standard Or Custom Fabricated, Metal Plate

Aatanks Llc .... G 586 427-7700
  Warren (G-17685)
American Tank Fabrication LLC .... F 780 663-3552
  Okemos (G-12656)
Clawson Tank Company .... E 248 625-8700
  Clarkston (G-3027)
Commercial Welding Company Inc .... G 269 782-5252
  Dowagiac (G-4778)
Diversified Mech Svcs Inc .... F 616 785-2735
  Comstock Park (G-3602)
Fabrications Unlimited Inc .... G 313 567-9616
  Shelby Township (G-15224)
Gladwin Tank Manufacturing Inc .... F 989 426-4768
  Gladwin (G-6199)
Ideal Fabricators Inc .... E 734 422-5320
  Livonia (G-10245)
Merrill Technologies Group Inc .... C 989 462-0330
  Alma (G-246)
Saranac Tank Inc .... G 616 642-9481
  Saranac (G-15081)
Steel Tank & Fabricating Co .... D 248 625-8700
  Clarkston (G-3069)

TANNERIES: Leather

Larrys Taxidermy Inc .... G 517 769-6104
  Pleasant Lake (G-13103)

TANNING SALONS

Electric Beach Tanning Co .... G 313 423-6539
  Grosse Pointe Park (G-7553)
Horn Corp .... G 248 358-8883
  Brighton (G-2009)

TAPE DRIVES

Laser Re-Nu LLC .... G 248 630-1454
  Pontiac (G-13394)

TAPES: Plastic Coated

Witchcraft Tape Products Inc .... D 269 468-3399
  Coloma (G-3485)

TAPES: Pressure Sensitive

Elliott Tape Inc .... E 248 475-2000
  Auburn Hills (G-878)
Independent Die Cutting Inc .... F 616 452-3197
  Grand Rapids (G-6842)
Kent Manufacturing Company .... D 616 454-9495
  Grand Rapids (G-6889)
Tesa Plant Sparta LLC .... G 616 887-1757
  Sparta (G-15785)
Tesa Tape Inc .... G 616 785-6970
  Walker (G-17654)
Tesa Tape Inc .... G 616 887-3107
  Sparta (G-15786)
Trimas Corporation .... B 248 631-5450
  Bloomfield Hills (G-1869)
Yamato International Corp .... E 734 675-6055
  Woodhaven (G-18804)

TAPS

Widell Industries Inc .... E 989 742-4528
  Hillman (G-7918)

TARPAULINS

Detroit Tarpaulin Repr Sp Inc .... E 734 955-8200
  Romulus (G-14267)
Larrys Tarpaulin Shop LLC .... G 313 563-2292
  Inkster (G-8668)
National Case Corporation .... E 586 726-1710
  Sterling Heights (G-16112)
Quick Draw Tarpaulin Systems .... F 313 561-0554
  Inkster (G-8674)
Quick Draw Tarpaulin Systems .... F 313 945-0766
  Dearborn (G-3889)
Textile Fabrication & Dist Inc .... G 586 566-9100
  Mount Clemens (G-11660)
US Tarp Inc .... D 269 639-3010
  South Haven (G-15420)

TARPAULINS, WHOLESALE

Verduyn Tarps Detroit Inc .... G 313 270-4890
  Detroit (G-4665)

Employee Codes: A=Over 500 employees, B=251-500
C=101-250, D=51-100, E=20-50, F=10-19, G=3-9

TAX RETURN PREPARATION SVCS

Jax Services LLC .... G 586 703-3212
  Warren *(G-17883)*

Mach II Enterprises Inc .... G 248 347-8822
  Northville *(G-12238)*

TAXIDERMISTS

Larrys Taxidermy Inc .... G 517 769-6104
  Pleasant Lake *(G-13103)*

TECHNICAL WRITING SVCS

TMC Group Inc .... G 248 819-6063
  Pleasant Ridge *(G-13106)*

TELECOMMUNICATION EQPT REPAIR SVCS, EXC TELEPHONES

Startech-Solutions LLC .... G 248 419-0650
  West Bloomfield *(G-18316)*

TELECOMMUNICATION SYSTEMS & EQPT

Balogh .... G 734 283-3972
  Taylor *(G-16387)*

Central On Line Data Systems .... G 586 939-7000
  Sterling Heights *(G-15954)*

Code Blue Corporation .... E 616 392-8296
  Holland *(G-8000)*

Maxxar .... G 248 675-1040
  Wixom *(G-18708)*

Nuwave Technology Partners LLC .... F 616 942-7520
  Grand Rapids *(G-7052)*

Omnilink Communications Corp .... E 517 336-1800
  Lansing *(G-9878)*

Rti Products LLC .... F 269 684-9960
  Niles *(G-12164)*

Spectra Link .... G 313 417-3723
  Grosse Pointe Woods *(G-7576)*

TELEGRAPH OR TELEPHONE CARRIER & REPEATER EQPT

Clarity Comm Advisors Inc .... E 248 327-4390
  Southfield *(G-15526)*

TELEMARKETING BUREAUS

Nits Solutions Inc .... F 248 231-2267
  Novi *(G-12488)*

TELEMETERING EQPT

L3 Technologies Inc .... G 734 741-8868
  Ann Arbor *(G-546)*

TELEPHONE EQPT: Modems

Multiax International Inc .... G 616 534-4530
  Grandville *(G-7404)*

TELEPHONE EQPT: NEC

Semtron Inc .... F 810 732-9080
  Flint *(G-5761)*

TELEPHONE SVCS

Elite Bus Svcs Exec Stffing In .... G 734 956-4550
  Bloomfield Hills *(G-1818)*

Peckham Vocational Inds Inc .... A 517 316-4000
  Lansing *(G-9724)*

TELEPHONE: Fiber Optic Systems

Safari Circuits Inc .... C 269 694-9471
  Otsego *(G-12799)*

TELEPHONE: Headsets

DB Communications Inc .... F 800 692-8200
  Livonia *(G-10175)*

Sigma Wireless LLC .... G 313 423-2629
  Detroit *(G-4592)*

TELESCOPES

Meridian Mechatronics LLC .... G 517 447-4587
  Deerfield *(G-3958)*

TELEVISION BROADCASTING STATIONS

Detroit Free Press Inc .... B 313 222-2300
  Detroit *(G-4148)*

Paxton Media Group LLC .... D 269 429-2400
  Saint Joseph *(G-14953)*

TELEVISION SETS

Lotus International Company .... A 734 245-0140
  Canton *(G-2486)*

TELEVISION: Closed Circuit Eqpt

Holland Vision Systems Inc .... E 616 494-9974
  Holland *(G-8087)*

Thalner Electronic Labs Inc .... E 734 761-4506
  Ann Arbor *(G-686)*

TEMPERING: Metal

Commercial Steel Treating Corp .... C 248 588-3300
  Madison Heights *(G-10696)*

State Heat Treating Company .... E 616 243-0178
  Grand Rapids *(G-7222)*

TEMPORARY HELP SVCS

Manufacturing & Indus Tech Inc .... E 248 522-6959
  Farmington Hills *(G-5309)*

Vectech Pharmaceutical Cons .... F 248 478-5820
  Brighton *(G-2092)*

TEN PIN CENTERS

Forest View Lanes LLC .... E 734 847-4915
  Temperance *(G-16531)*

TENT REPAIR SHOP

Ace Canvas & Tent Co .... F 313 842-3011
  Troy *(G-16903)*

TENTS: All Materials

Ace Canvas & Tent Co .... F 313 842-3011
  Troy *(G-16903)*

Ifr Inc .... C 616 772-2052
  Zeeland *(G-19043)*

TEST KITS: Pregnancy

Life Otreach Ctr Houghton Cnty .... G 906 482-8681
  Hancock *(G-7621)*

TESTERS: Battery

Electrodynamics Inc .... G 734 422-5420
  Livonia *(G-10193)*

TESTERS: Environmental

Celsee Inc .... D 866 748-1448
  Ann Arbor *(G-419)*

Espec Corp .... E 616 896-6100
  Hudsonville *(G-8582)*

Kuka Assembly and Test Corp .... F 810 593-0350
  Fenton *(G-5488)*

Venturedyne Ltd .... G 616 392-6550
  Holland *(G-8237)*

TESTERS: Hardness

Electro ARC Manufacturing Co .... E 734 483-4233
  Dexter *(G-4741)*

Service Diamond Tool Company .... G 248 669-3100
  Novi *(G-12535)*

TESTERS: Physical Property

Kemkraft Engineering Inc .... F 734 414-6500
  Plymouth *(G-13212)*

Link Manufacturing Inc .... D 734 453-0800
  Plymouth *(G-13223)*

Link Manufacturing Inc .... G 734 387-1001
  Ottawa Lake *(G-12807)*

Pcb Load & Torque Inc .... E 248 471-0065
  Farmington Hills *(G-5344)*

Precision Devices Inc .... E 734 439-2462
  Milan *(G-11449)*

Rs Technologies Ltd .... F 248 888-8260
  Farmington Hills *(G-5374)*

Sun-Tec Corp .... G 248 669-3100
  Novi *(G-12550)*

Testek LLC .... D 248 573-4980
  Wixom *(G-18771)*

Testron Incorporated .... F 734 513-6820
  Livonia *(G-10431)*

TESTERS: Water, Exc Indl Process

QEd Envmtl Systems Inc .... D 734 995-2547
  Dexter *(G-4751)*

TESTING SVCS

Capsonic Automotive Inc .... G 248 754-1100
  Auburn Hills *(G-839)*

Pmd Automotive LLC .... G 248 732-7554
  Pontiac *(G-13407)*

Touchstone Systems & Svcs Inc .... G 616 532-0060
  Wyoming *(G-18912)*

TEXTILE & APPAREL SVCS

Adlib Grafix & Apparel .... G 269 964-2810
  Battle Creek *(G-1178)*

Great Put On Inc .... G 810 733-8021
  Flint *(G-5709)*

TEXTILE FABRICATORS

Amk Enterprise LLC .... G 248 977-3039
  Waterford *(G-18099)*

Amk Enterprise LLC .... G 248 564-2549
  Auburn Hills *(G-783)*

Commonwealth Sewing Company .... G 313 319-2417
  Detroit *(G-4098)*

Olympus Group .... G 616 965-2671
  Kentwood *(G-9468)*

Telescopic Seating Systems LLC .... G 616 566-9232
  Holland *(G-8214)*

TEXTILE FINISHING: Embossing, Cotton, Broadwoven

Adco Specialties Inc .... G 616 452-6882
  Grand Rapids *(G-6430)*

TEXTILE PRDTS: Hand Woven & Crocheted

Hogge Crochet .... G 313 808-1302
  Royal Oak *(G-14548)*

Just Adorable Crocheting .... G 586 746-7137
  Clinton Township *(G-3266)*

Knit and Crochet 4 Charity .... G 248 224-4965
  Warren *(G-17895)*

Silk Reflections .... G 313 292-1150
  Taylor *(G-16473)*

Stitched Now .... G 586 460-6175
  Detroit *(G-4610)*

Triple A Crochet LLC .... G 248 534-0818
  Clarkston *(G-3072)*

TEXTILE: Finishing, Cotton Broadwoven

Janet Kelly .... F 231 775-2313
  Cadillac *(G-2338)*

TEXTILE: Goods, NEC

Chaotic Cotton Company LLC .... G 810 624-6153
  Linden *(G-10060)*

TEXTILES

West Michigan Canvas Company .... G 616 355-7855
  Holland *(G-8245)*

TEXTILES: Jute & Flax Prdts

Golden Fashion .... G 616 288-9465
  Grand Rapids *(G-6747)*

TEXTILES: Linen Fabrics

J David Inc .... G 888 274-0669
  Troy *(G-17177)*

TEXTILES: Mill Waste & Remnant

Clamp Industries Incorporated .... G 248 335-8131
  Pontiac *(G-13353)*

THEATRICAL LIGHTING SVCS

Tls Productions Inc .... E 810 220-8577
  Ann Arbor *(G-693)*

PRODUCT SECTION

THEATRICAL PRODUCTION SVCS
Red Carpet Capital Inc .... G 248 952-8583
  Orchard Lake (G-12719)

THERMOCOUPLES
Neptech Inc .... E 810 225-2222
  Highland (G-7897)
Temprel Inc .... E 231 582-6585
  Boyne City (G-1902)

THERMOCOUPLES: Indl Process
Industrial Temperature Control .... G 734 451-8740
  Canton (G-2474)

THERMOELECTRIC DEVICES: Solid State
T E Technology Inc .... E 231 929-3966
  Traverse City (G-16849)

THERMOMETERS: Medical, Digital
Digitaleo Corporation .... G 248 250-9205
  Troy (G-17063)
Pharmaceutical Specialties LLC .... F 269 382-6402
  Galesburg (G-6081)

THERMOPLASTIC MATERIALS
Asahi Kasei Plas N Amer Inc .... C 517 223-2000
  Fowlerville (G-5833)
Asahi Kasei Plastics Amer Inc .... D 517 223-2000
  Fowlerville (G-5834)
D T M 1 Inc .... E 248 889-9210
  Highland (G-7890)
Ddp Spclty Elctrnc Mtls US In .... D 989 708-6737
  Midland (G-11334)
Ddp Spclty Elctrnc Mtls US LL .... D 989 636-9955
  Midland (G-11335)
Dow Chemical Company .... A 989 636-1000
  Midland (G-11341)
Dow Chemical Company .... G 231 845-4285
  Ludington (G-10534)
Dow Chemical Company .... D 989 636-1000
  Midland (G-11342)
Dow Chemical Company .... D 810 966-9816
  Clyde (G-3412)
Dow Chemical Company .... G 989 636-1000
  Midland (G-11344)
Dow Chemical Company .... G 989 636-1000
  Midland (G-11347)
Dow Chemical Company .... C 989 832-1000
  Midland (G-11348)
Dow Chemical Company .... D 989 636-5409
  Midland (G-11352)
Dow Inc .... A 989 636-1000
  Midland (G-11354)
Dow International Holdings Co .... G 989 636-1000
  Midland (G-11355)
Eovations LLC .... G 989 671-1460
  Freeland (G-6023)

THERMOPLASTICS
Hanwha Azdel Inc .... G 810 629-2496
  Warren (G-17847)
Max3 LLC .... E 269 925-2044
  Benton Harbor (G-1570)

THERMOSETTING MATERIALS
Advanced Polymers Composites ...... G 248 766-1507
  Clarkston (G-3014)

THREAD: Embroidery
RPC Company .... F 989 752-3618
  Saginaw (G-14741)

THREAD: Hand Knitting
Notions Marketing Intl Corp .... B 616 243-8424
  Grand Rapids (G-7050)

THREAD: Natural Fiber
American & Efird LLC .... G 248 399-1166
  Berkley (G-1619)

TIES, FORM: Metal
Michigan Wheel Operations LLC ..... D 616 452-6941
  Grand Rapids (G-6997)

TILE: Clay Refractory
Milfab Systems LLC .... F 248 391-8100
  Lake Orion (G-9619)
Starbuck Machining Inc .... E 616 399-9720
  Holland (G-8201)

TILE: Clay Refractory
Pewabic Society Inc .... E 313 626-2000
  Detroit (G-4522)

TILE: Wall, Fiberboard
Ox Engineered Products LLC .... F 248 289-9950
  Northville (G-12250)
Ox Engineered Products LLC .... D 269 435-2425
  Constantine (G-3673)

TIMBER PRDTS WHOLESALERS
Plum Creek Timber Company Inc .... G 715 453-7952
  Escanaba (G-5090)

TIMERS: Indl, Clockwork Mechanism Only
Eliason Corporation .... E 269 621-2100
  Hartford (G-7763)

TIMING DEVICES: Cycle & Program Controllers
Midwest Timer Service Inc .... D 269 849-2800
  Benton Harbor (G-1573)

TIN
Fine Arts .... G 269 695-6263
  Buchanan (G-2193)
Nolans Top Tin Inc .... G 586 899-3421
  Warren (G-17943)
Red Tin Boat .... G 734 239-3796
  Ann Arbor (G-635)

TIRE CORD & FABRIC
Flatrock Tire .... G 734 783-0100
  Flat Rock (G-5619)
Ton-Tex Corporation .... F 616 957-3200
  Greenville (G-7508)

TIRE CORD & FABRIC: Cord, Rubber, Reinforcing
Takata Americas .... A 336 547-1600
  Auburn Hills (G-1044)

TIRE CORD & FABRIC: Steel
Ferro Fab LLC .... F 586 791-3561
  Clinton Township (G-3237)

TIRE DEALERS
Flatrock Tire .... G 734 783-0100
  Flat Rock (G-5619)
Goodyear Tire & Rubber Company .. G 248 336-0135
  Royal Oak (G-14541)
Jam Tire Inc .... E 586 772-2900
  Clinton Township (G-3263)
Muskegon Brake & Distrg Co LLC ... E 231 733-0874
  Norton Shores (G-12313)
Tire Wholesalers Company .... D 269 349-9401
  Kalamazoo (G-9357)

TIRE INFLATORS: Hand Or Compressor Operated
Autoliv Asp Inc .... C 248 475-9000
  Auburn Hills (G-801)

TIRE INNER-TUBES
Goodyear Tire & Rubber Company .. G 248 336-0135
  Royal Oak (G-14541)

TIRE RECAPPING & RETREADING
Jam Tire Inc .... E 586 772-2900
  Clinton Township (G-3263)
Northern Tire Inc .... F 906 486-4463
  Ishpeming (G-8779)

TIRES & INNER TUBES
BF Franchising .... G 313 565-2713
  Dearborn (G-3814)
Jam Tire Inc .... E 586 772-2900
  Clinton Township (G-3263)
Omni United (usa) Inc .... G 855 906-6646
  Charlevoix (G-2725)
Plastic Omnium Inc .... G 248 458-0772
  Troy (G-17304)
Polytek Michigan Inc .... G 734 782-0378
  Flat Rock (G-5625)
Tire Wholesalers Company .... D 269 349-9401
  Kalamazoo (G-9357)

TIRES & TUBES WHOLESALERS
Flatrock Tire .... G 734 783-0100
  Flat Rock (G-5619)
Jam Tire Inc .... E 586 772-2900
  Clinton Township (G-3263)
Roman Engineering .... E 231 238-7644
  Afton (G-107)

TIRES & TUBES, WHOLESALE: Automotive
Northern Tire Inc .... F 906 486-4463
  Ishpeming (G-8779)

TIRES: Auto
Anh Enterprises LLC .... F 313 887-0800
  Taylor (G-16379)

TIRES: Cushion Or Solid Rubber
Hutchinson Corporation .... G 616 459-4541
  Grand Rapids (G-6825)

TITANIUM MILL PRDTS
Jay Titanium Sports LLC .... G 616 502-5945
  Norton Shores (G-12349)
Scitex LLC .... G 517 694-7449
  Holt (G-8329)
Scitex LLC .... E 517 694-7449
  Holt (G-8330)
Scitex Trick Titanium LLC .... G 517 349-3736
  Okemos (G-12685)
Tico Titanium Inc .... G 248 446-0400
  New Hudson (G-12073)
Titanium Building Co Inc .... G 586 634-8580
  Macomb (G-10642)
Titanium Elite MTS Global LLC .... G 616 262-5222
  Clarksville (G-3081)
Titanium Operations LLC .... G 616 717-0218
  Ada (G-38)
Titanium Sports LLC .... G 734 818-0904
  Dundee (G-4837)

TITLE ABSTRACT & SETTLEMENT OFFICES
Meridian Energy Corporation .... E 517 339-8444
  Haslett (G-7775)

TOBACCO LEAF PROCESSING
Veteran Liquids LLC .... G 586 698-2100
  Rochester Hills (G-14140)

TOBACCO STORES & STANDS
Eaton Corporation .... G 248 226-6347
  Southfield (G-15547)

TOBACCO: Chewing & Snuff
Smoke-Free Kids Inc .... G 989 772-4063
  Mount Pleasant (G-11740)

TOBACCO: Cigarettes
Cheeba Hut Smoke Shop LLC .... G 586 213-5156
  Chesterfield (G-2858)
Cloud 9 Pipe Tobacco Inc .... F 313 522-1957
  Sterling Heights (G-15962)
Unique Hooka and Tobacco .... G 586 883-7674
  Sterling Heights (G-16215)

TOBACCO: Smoking
Akston Hughes Intl LLC .... F 989 448-2322
  Gaylord (G-6116)
Qfc .... E 248 786-0272
  Troy (G-17322)

Employee Codes: A=Over 500 employees, B=251-500
C=101-250, D=51-100, E=20-50, F=10-19, G=3-9

TOILET SEATS: Wood

Aisin Holdings America Inc .... G 734 453-5551
  Northville *(G-12195)*

TOILETRIES, COSMETICS & PERFUME STORES

Honeyworks LLC .... G 313 575-0871
  Detroit *(G-4304)*

TOILETRIES, WHOLESALE: Razor Blades

Art of Shaving - FI LLC .... G 248 649-5872
  Troy *(G-16954)*

TOILETRIES, WHOLESALE: Toiletries

Amway International Inc .... E 616 787-1000
  Ada *(G-8)*

TOILETRIES, WHOLESALE: Toothbrushes, Exc Electric

Nopras Technologies Inc .... G 248 486-6684
  South Lyon *(G-15451)*

TOILETS: Portable Chemical, Plastics

Five Peaks Technology LLC .... F 231 830-8099
  Muskegon *(G-11818)*
Thetford Corporation .... C 734 769-6000
  Ann Arbor *(G-688)*

TOOL & DIE STEEL

Accutek Mold & Engineering .... E 586 978-1335
  Sterling Heights *(G-15922)*
Acme Tool & Die Co .... G 231 938-1260
  Acme *(G-1)*
Bbg North America Ltd Partnr .... F 248 572-6550
  Oxford *(G-12878)*
C & M Manufacturing Corp Inc .... E 586 749-3455
  Chesterfield *(G-2854)*
C P I Inc .... G 810 664-8686
  Lapeer *(G-9919)*
First Place Manufacturing LLC .... G 231 798-1694
  Norton Shores *(G-12293)*
General Motors LLC .... G 810 236-1970
  Flint *(G-5706)*
Gill Corporation .... B 616 453-4491
  Grand Rapids *(G-6740)*
Pdf Mfg Inc .... G 517 522-8431
  Grass Lake *(G-7443)*
Quality Cavity Inc .... F 248 344-9995
  Canton *(G-2516)*
Ram Die Corp .... F 616 647-2855
  Grand Rapids *(G-7138)*
Sabre Manufacturing .... G 269 945-4120
  Hastings *(G-7808)*
Wiesen EDM Inc .... E 616 794-9870
  Belding *(G-1467)*

TOOL REPAIR SVCS

Convex Mold Inc .... E 586 978-0808
  Sterling Heights *(G-15971)*
Mac-Tech Tooling Corporation .... G 248 743-1400
  Troy *(G-17217)*

TOOLS & EQPT: Used With Sporting Arms

Grace Metal Products Inc .... G 231 264-8133
  Elk Rapids *(G-5025)*

TOOLS: Carpenters', Including Levels & Chisels, Exc Saws

MJB Stairs LLC .... G 586 822-9559
  Shelby Township *(G-15278)*
Wranosky & Sons Inc .... G 586 336-9761
  Romeo *(G-14240)*

TOOLS: Hand

Allied Mask & Tooling .... G 419 470-2555
  Temperance *(G-16527)*
Atlas Welding Accessories Inc .... D 248 588-4666
  Troy *(G-16962)*
Aven Inc .... F 734 973-0099
  Ann Arbor *(G-387)*
Balance Technology Inc .... D 734 769-2100
  Whitmore Lake *(G-18520)*
Bartlett Manufacturing Co LLC .... G 989 635-8900
  Marlette *(G-10978)*
Bay-Houston Towing Company .... F 810 648-2210
  Sandusky *(G-15056)*
Boral Building Products Inc .... C 800 521-8486
  Wixom *(G-18625)*
Cobra Manufacturing .... F 248 585-1606
  Troy *(G-17017)*
Detroit Edge Tool Company .... D 313 366-4120
  Detroit *(G-4146)*
Detroit Steel Treating Company .... E 248 334-7436
  Pontiac *(G-13361)*
E M I Construction Products .... F 616 392-7207
  Holland *(G-8020)*
Ferrees Tools Inc .... E 269 965-0511
  Battle Creek *(G-1230)*
Gill Industries Inc .... G 616 559-2700
  Grand Rapids *(G-6743)*
Grace Metal Prods Inc .... G 231 264-8133
  Williamsburg *(G-18554)*
Hanchett Manufacturing Inc .... E 231 796-7678
  Big Rapids *(G-1676)*
Hank Thorn Co .... F 248 348-7800
  Wixom *(G-18675)*
Hastings Fiber Glass Pdts Inc .... D 269 945-9541
  Hastings *(G-7795)*
Lach Diamond .... E 616 698-0101
  Grand Rapids *(G-6907)*
Lakeland Mills Inc .... E 989 427-5133
  Edmore *(G-4993)*
Landmesser Tools Company Inc .... G 248 682-4689
  Waterford *(G-18133)*
Megapro Marketing Usa Inc .... F 866 522-3652
  Niles *(G-12143)*
Mercedes-Benz Extra LLC .... E 205 747-8006
  Farmington Hills *(G-5315)*
Micro Engineering Inc .... G 616 534-9681
  Byron Center *(G-2285)*
Patco Air Tool Inc .... G 248 648-8830
  Orion *(G-12738)*
Port Austin Level & TI Mfg Co .... F 989 738-5291
  Port Austin *(G-13428)*
R J S Tool & Gage Co .... E 248 642-8620
  Birmingham *(G-1746)*
Rock Tool & Machine Co Inc .... E 734 455-9840
  Plymouth *(G-13289)*
Roesch Maufacturing Co LLC .... G 517 424-6300
  Tecumseh *(G-16514)*
RTS Cutting Tools Inc .... E 586 954-1900
  Clinton Township *(G-3344)*
Shaws Enterprises Inc .... E 810 664-2981
  Lapeer *(G-9960)*
Simonds International LLC .... G 231 527-2322
  Big Rapids *(G-1687)*
Sourcehub LLC .... G 800 246-1844
  Troy *(G-17364)*
Specialty Steel Treating Inc .... E 586 293-5355
  Fraser *(G-5998)*
Steelcraft Tool Co Inc .... F 734 522-7130
  Livonia *(G-10420)*
Summit Tooling & Mfg Inc .... G 231 856-7037
  Morley *(G-11623)*
Tapco Holdings Inc .... C 248 668-6400
  Wixom *(G-18766)*
Tekton Inc .... D 616 243-2443
  Grand Rapids *(G-7251)*
Umix Dissoultion Corp .... F 586 446-9950
  Sterling Heights *(G-16214)*

TOOLS: Hand, Ironworkers'

Eagle Tool Group LLC .... F 586 997-0800
  Sterling Heights *(G-16000)*

TOOLS: Hand, Jewelers'

Swarovski .... G 248 344-2922
  Novi *(G-12552)*

TOOLS: Hand, Power

A W B Industries Inc .... E 989 739-1447
  Oscoda *(G-12753)*
Anchor Lamina America Inc .... C 231 533-8646
  Bellaire *(G-1468)*
Avalon Tools Inc .... G 248 269-0001
  Troy *(G-16967)*
Black & Decker (us) Inc .... G 410 716-3900
  Grand Rapids *(G-6513)*
Black & Decker Corporation .... F 248 597-5000
  Madison Heights *(G-10682)*
Carbide Technologies Inc .... E 586 296-5200
  Fraser *(G-5910)*
Clausing Industrial Inc .... F 269 345-7155
  Kalamazoo *(G-9144)*
Clausing Industrial Inc .... D 269 345-7155
  Kalamazoo *(G-9145)*
Conway-Cleveland Corp .... G 616 458-0056
  Grand Rapids *(G-6604)*
Falcon Global LLC .... F 734 302-3025
  Ann Arbor *(G-486)*
Hank Thorn Co .... F 248 348-7800
  Wixom *(G-18675)*
Heck Industries Incorporated .... F 810 632-5400
  Hartland *(G-7769)*
Hme Inc .... C 616 534-1463
  Wyoming *(G-18885)*
Hougen Manufacturing Inc .... C 810 635-7111
  Swartz Creek *(G-16355)*
Jemms-Cascade Inc .... F 248 526-8100
  Troy *(G-17184)*
Lutco Inc .... G 231 972-5566
  Mecosta *(G-11191)*
Menominee Saw and Supply Co .... E 906 863-2609
  Menominee *(G-11248)*
Plum Brothers LLC .... G 734 947-8100
  Romulus *(G-14321)*
Roesch Maufacturing Co LLC .... G 517 424-6300
  Tecumseh *(G-16514)*
RTS Cutting Tools Inc .... E 586 954-1900
  Clinton Township *(G-3344)*
Star Cutter Co .... E 248 474-8200
  Farmington Hills *(G-5387)*
Telco Tools .... F 616 296-0253
  Spring Lake *(G-15856)*
Waber Tool & Engineering Co .... F 269 342-0765
  Kalamazoo *(G-9365)*

TOOLS: Hand, Shovels Or Spades

Sure-Loc Aluminum Edging Inc .... G 616 392-3209
  Holland *(G-8210)*

TOOLS: Soldering

Persico Usa Inc .... D 248 299-5100
  Shelby Township *(G-15300)*

TOOTHBRUSHES: Exc Electric

Ranir LLC .... B 616 698-8880
  Grand Rapids *(G-7139)*

TOUR OPERATORS

Budget Europe Travel Service .... G 734 668-0529
  Ann Arbor *(G-408)*

TOWELS: Linen & Linen & Cotton Mixtures

Six Collection LLC .... G 313 516-9999
  Harper Woods *(G-7672)*

TOWERS, SECTIONS: Transmission, Radio & Television

Universal Manufacturing Co .... E 586 463-2560
  Clinton Township *(G-3383)*

TOWING & TUGBOAT SVC

Central Mich Knwrth Lnsing LLC .... G 517 394-7000
  Lansing *(G-9823)*
Central Mich Knwrth Sginaw LLC .... G 989 754-4500
  Saginaw *(G-14625)*
Maslo Fabrication LLC .... G 616 298-7700
  Holland *(G-8139)*

TOWING BARS & SYSTEMS

Detroit Wrecker Sales Llc .... G 313 835-8700
  Detroit *(G-4171)*
Hydro King Incorporated .... F 313 835-8700
  Southfield *(G-15596)*
Rapidtek LLC .... G 616 662-0954
  Hudsonville *(G-8603)*

TOWING SVCS: Marine

Superior Mar & Envmtl Svcs LLC .... G 906 253-9448
  Sault Sainte Marie *(G-15101)*

PRODUCT SECTION

TRANSFORMERS: Power Related

TOYS

Abbotts Magic Manufacturing Co .... G 269 432-3235
   Colon *(G-3486)*
American Plastic Toys Inc .... D 989 685-2455
   Rose City *(G-14359)*
Ann Williams Group LLC .... G 248 977-5831
   Bloomfield Hills *(G-1798)*
Fourth Ave Birkenstock .... G 734 663-1644
   Ann Arbor *(G-493)*
Merdel Game Manufacturing Co .... G 231 845-1263
   Ludington *(G-10544)*
Pauri Retail Store LLC .... F 415 980-1525
   Detroit *(G-4508)*
Promoquip Inc .... G 989 287-6211
   Lakeview *(G-9645)*
Shelti Inc .... F 989 893-1739
   Bay City *(G-1401)*
Shields Classic Toys .... G 888 806-2632
   Saline *(G-15039)*
Unique-Chardan Inc .... D 419 636-6900
   Auburn Hills *(G-1070)*

TOYS & HOBBY GOODS & SPLYS, WHOLESALE: Arts/Crafts Eqpt/Sply

Mac Enterprises Inc .... F 313 846-4567
   Manchester *(G-10885)*

TOYS & HOBBY GOODS & SPLYS, WHOLESALE: Toys & Games

St Evans Inc .... G 269 663-6100
   Edwardsburg *(G-5017)*

TOYS & HOBBY GOODS & SPLYS, WHOLESALE: Toys, NEC

American Plastic Toys Inc .... D 989 685-2455
   Rose City *(G-14359)*

TOYS, HOBBY GOODS & SPLYS WHOLESALERS

Ideal Wholesale Inc .... G 989 873-5850
   Prescott *(G-13651)*

TOYS: Dolls, Stuffed Animals & Parts

Auswella LLC .... G 248 630-5965
   Wixom *(G-18615)*

TOYS: Rubber

Go Cat Feather Toys .... G 517 543-7519
   Charlotte *(G-2759)*

TRADE SHOW ARRANGEMENT SVCS

Sparks Exhbits Envrnments Corp .... G 248 291-0007
   Royal Oak *(G-14582)*

TRAILERS & CHASSIS: Camping

County of Muskegon .... E 231 744-3580
   Muskegon *(G-11796)*
Technology Plus Trailers Inc .... G 734 928-0001
   Canton *(G-2531)*

TRAILERS & PARTS: Boat

Boat Customs Trailers LLC .... G 517 712-3512
   Caledonia *(G-2370)*

TRAILERS & PARTS: Truck & Semi's

Ajax Trailers Inc .... F 586 757-7676
   Warren *(G-17696)*
All-Star Equipment LLC .... F 855 273-8265
   Rockford *(G-14153)*
Anderson Welding & Mfg Inc .... F 906 523-4661
   Houghton *(G-8380)*
Automotive Service Co .... F 517 784-6131
   Jackson *(G-8818)*
Benlee Inc .... E 586 791-1830
   Romulus *(G-14257)*
Clydes Frame & Wheel Service .... F 248 338-0423
   Pontiac *(G-13354)*
Complete Truck and Trailer .... G 989 732-9000
   Gaylord *(G-6123)*
Darkhorse Cargo Inc .... F 269 464-2620
   White Pigeon *(G-18474)*
Detroit Cstm Trck Trailor LLC .... G 734 925-2233
   Westland *(G-18363)*
Eddies Quick Stop Inc .... G 313 712-1818
   Dearborn *(G-3833)*
Express Welding Inc .... G 906 786-8808
   Escanaba *(G-5071)*
Joes Trailer Manufacturing .... G 734 261-0050
   Livonia *(G-10260)*
Lupa R A and Sons Repair .... G 810 346-3579
   Marlette *(G-10983)*
Montrose Trailers Inc .... G 810 639-7431
   Montrose *(G-11607)*
Neo Manufacturing Inc .... F 269 503-7630
   Sturgis *(G-16313)*
Oshkosh Defense LLC .... E 586 576-8301
   Warren *(G-17951)*
Saf-Holland Inc .... A 231 773-3271
   Muskegon *(G-11913)*
Technology Plus Trailers Inc .... F 734 928-0001
   Canton *(G-2531)*
Tow-Line Trailers .... G 989 752-0055
   Saginaw *(G-14777)*
Trimas Company LLC .... D 248 631-5450
   Bloomfield Hills *(G-1868)*
Wolverine Trailers Inc .... G 517 782-4950
   Jackson *(G-9037)*
Woodland Industries .... G 989 686-6176
   Kawkawlin *(G-9419)*
Xpo Cnw Inc .... C 734 757-1444
   Ann Arbor *(G-720)*

TRAILERS & TRAILER EQPT

American Tool & Gage Inc .... G 313 587-7923
   Taylor *(G-16377)*
Bedford Machinery Inc .... G 734 848-4980
   Erie *(G-5045)*
Dexko Global Inc .... G 248 533-0029
   Novi *(G-12397)*
Dragon Acquisition Intermediat .... F 248 692-4367
   Novi *(G-12403)*
Dragon Acquisition Parent Inc .... F 248 692-4367
   Novi *(G-12404)*
Erich Jaeger USA Inc .... G 734 404-5940
   Livonia *(G-10199)*
Great Lakes Lift Inc .... G 989 673-2109
   Caro *(G-2572)*
Jrm Industries Inc .... G 616 837-9758
   Nunica *(G-12581)*
Midwest Direct Transport Inc .... F 616 698-8900
   Byron Center *(G-2286)*
Montrose Trailers Inc .... G 810 639-7431
   Montrose *(G-11607)*
Nash Car Trailer Corporation .... G 269 673-5776
   Allegan *(G-171)*
P2r Metal Fabrication Inc .... F 586 606-5266
   Macomb *(G-10625)*
Phoenix Trailer & Body Company .... F 248 360-7184
   Commerce Township *(G-3563)*
Premier Custom Trailers LLC .... F 877 327-0888
   Schoolcraft *(G-15127)*
Viking Sales Inc .... F 810 227-2222
   Brighton *(G-2094)*

TRAILERS: Bodies

Hulet Body Co Inc .... F 313 931-6000
   Northville *(G-12230)*
Pullman Company .... F 734 243-8000
   Monroe *(G-11571)*
Saf-Holland Inc .... G 616 396-6501
   Holland *(G-8186)*
Thumb Truck and Trailer Co .... G 989 453-3193
   Pigeon *(G-13041)*
Transport Trailers Co .... G 269 543-4405
   Fennville *(G-5443)*

TRAILERS: Bus, Tractor Type

Bobbys Mobile Service LLC .... G 517 206-6026
   Jackson *(G-8824)*

TRAILERS: Demountable Cargo Containers

Cargo King Manufacturing Inc .... E 269 483-9900
   White Pigeon *(G-18473)*

TRAILERS: House, Exc Permanent Dwellings

Michigan East Side Sales LLC .... G 989 354-6867
   Alpena *(G-302)*

TRAILERS: Semitrailers, Missile Transportation

Executive Operations LLC .... E 313 312-0653
   Brighton *(G-1986)*

TRAILERS: Semitrailers, Truck Tractors

Leonard & Randy Inc .... G 734 287-9500
   Taylor *(G-16435)*
Trailer Tech Holdings LLC .... E 248 960-9700
   Wixom *(G-18776)*

TRAILERS: Truck, Chassis

Arboc Ltd .... G 248 684-2895
   Commerce Township *(G-3511)*
Pratt Industries Inc .... D 269 465-7676
   Bridgman *(G-1933)*

TRANSDUCERS: Electrical Properties

Pcb Piezotronics Inc .... F 888 684-0014
   Novi *(G-12503)*

TRANSDUCERS: Pressure

Precision Measurement Co .... F 734 995-0041
   Ann Arbor *(G-622)*

TRANSFORMERS: Control

Marcie Electric Inc .... G 248 486-1200
   Brighton *(G-2025)*

TRANSFORMERS: Distribution

Detroit Renewable Energy LLC .... C 313 972-5700
   Detroit *(G-4162)*

TRANSFORMERS: Distribution, Electric

Austin Distributors LLC .... G 248 665-2077
   Westland *(G-18357)*
Eugene .... E 313 217-9297
   Detroit *(G-4217)*
Meiden America Inc .... E 734 459-1781
   Northville *(G-12239)*

TRANSFORMERS: Doorbell, Electric

Houseart LLC .... G 248 651-8124
   Rochester *(G-13905)*

TRANSFORMERS: Electric

Heyboer Transformers Inc .... E 616 842-5830
   Grand Haven *(G-6317)*
Osborne Transformer Corp .... F 586 218-6900
   Fraser *(G-5972)*

TRANSFORMERS: Fluorescent Lighting

Tara Industries Inc .... G 248 477-6520
   Livonia *(G-10429)*

TRANSFORMERS: Power Related

Actia Electronics Inc .... G 574 264-2373
   Romulus *(G-14245)*
Eastern Power and Lighting .... G 248 739-0908
   Dearborn Heights *(G-3925)*
Ebw Electronics Inc .... B 616 786-0575
   Holland *(G-8021)*
Gti Liquidating Inc .... D 616 842-5430
   Grand Haven *(G-6309)*
Maxitrol Company .... D 248 356-1400
   Southfield *(G-15648)*
Parker-Hannifin Corporation .... B 269 629-5000
   Richland *(G-13826)*
Powertran Corporation .... E 248 399-4300
   Ferndale *(G-5580)*
Rtg Products Inc .... G 734 323-8916
   Redford *(G-13768)*
S H Leggitt Company .... B 269 781-3901
   Marshall *(G-11073)*
Sgm Transformer LLC .... G 734 922-2400
   Ann Arbor *(G-649)*
Syndevco Inc .... F 248 356-2839
   Southfield *(G-15716)*
US Green Energy Solutions LLC .... G 810 955-2992
   Livonia *(G-10454)*

Employee Codes: A=Over 500 employees, B=251-500
C=101-250, D=51-100, E=20-50, F=10-19, G=3-9

TRANSFORMERS: Rectifier

TRANSFORMERS: Rectifier
Controlled Power Company .... C 248 528-3700
Troy *(G-17027)*

TRANSFORMERS: Voltage Regulating
Elite Industrial Mfg LLC .... G 616 377-7769
Holland *(G-8027)*
Power Control Systems Inc .... G 517 339-1442
Okemos *(G-12682)*

TRANSLATION & INTERPRETATION SVCS
AAA Language Services .... F 248 239-1138
Bloomfield *(G-1780)*
Iris Design & Print Inc .... G 313 277-0505
Dearborn *(G-3855)*

TRANSMISSIONS: Motor Vehicle
Aqueous Orbital Systems LLC .... G 269 501-7461
Kalamazoo *(G-9211)*
Borgwarner Powdered Metals Inc .... C 734 261-5322
Livonia *(G-10140)*
Eaton Corporation .... B 269 342-3000
Galesburg *(G-6076)*
Eaton Corporation .... C 269 342-3000
Galesburg *(G-6077)*
Emergency Services LLC .... F 231 727-7400
Muskegon *(G-11812)*
Fte Automotive North Amer Inc .... E 248 340-1262
Auburn Hills *(G-905)*
Fte Automotive USA Inc .... C 248 209-8239
Highland Park *(G-7907)*
GKN North America Inc .... C 248 296-7200
Auburn Hills *(G-912)*
GKN North America Services Inc .... C 248 377-1200
Auburn Hills *(G-913)*
M P I International Inc .... B 608 764-5416
Rochester Hills *(G-14056)*
Metaldyne Prfmce Group Inc .... A 248 727-1800
Southfield *(G-15654)*
Musashi Auto Parts Mich Inc .... B 269 965-0057
Battle Creek *(G-1276)*
Newcor Inc .... C 248 537-0014
Corunna *(G-3715)*
Systrand Manufacturing Corp .... C 734 479-8100
Brownstown Twp *(G-2159)*
Transform Automotive LLC .... C 586 826-8500
Sterling Heights *(G-16208)*

TRANSPORTATION BROKERS: Truck
Foreward Logistics LLC .... G 877 488-9724
Oak Park *(G-12612)*
Kace Logistics LLC .... E 734 946-8600
Carleton *(G-2557)*

TRANSPORTATION EPQT & SPLYS, WHOLESALE: Marine Crafts/Splys
Midwest Aquatics Group Inc .... G 734 426-4155
Pinckney *(G-13052)*

TRANSPORTATION EPQT & SPLYS, WHOLESALE: Tanks & Tank Compnts
Burch Tank & Truck Inc .... G 989 495-0342
Midland *(G-11326)*
Burch Tank & Truck Inc .... D 989 772-6266
Mount Pleasant *(G-11688)*

TRANSPORTATION EQUIPMENT, NEC
Berg Marketing Group .... G 314 457-9400
Troy *(G-16973)*
Bloodline Rich LLC .... G 734 719-1650
Grosse Pointe Woods *(G-7564)*
Expedite Freight LLC .... G 313 502-7572
Detroit *(G-4222)*
George Brown Legacy Group .... G 313 770-9928
Southfield *(G-15574)*
Guiding Our Destiny Ministry .... G 313 212-9063
Detroit *(G-4286)*
Holz Enterprises Inc .... G 810 392-2840
Richmond *(G-13840)*
Michael John LLC .... G 734 560-9268
Livonia *(G-10315)*
Midwest Transportation Inc .... G 313 615-7282
Dearborn Heights *(G-3933)*
Plt Express Transportation LLC .... G 248 809-3241
Southfield *(G-15676)*

Pro King Trucking Inc .... G 909 800-7885
Detroit *(G-4534)*
Pro-Tech Group LLC .... F 888 221-1505
Southfield *(G-15683)*
Z&G Auto Carriers LLC .... G 586 819-1809
Romulus *(G-14344)*

TRANSPORTATION SVCS, AIR, SCHEDULED: Helicopter Carriers
Great Lakes Exploration Inc .... G 906 352-4024
Menominee *(G-11239)*

TRANSPORTATION SVCS: Rental, Local
Executive Operations LLC .... E 313 312-0653
Brighton *(G-1986)*

TRANSPORTATION: Bus Transit Systems
Dgp Inc .... E 989 635-7531
Marlette *(G-10980)*

TRANSPORTATION: Local Passenger, NEC
May Mobility Inc .... E 312 869-2711
Ann Arbor *(G-567)*

TRANSPORTATION: Transit Systems, NEC
Cooper-Standard Auto OH LLC .... G 248 596-5900
Northville *(G-12203)*
Csa Services Inc .... G 248 596-6184
Novi *(G-12387)*

TRAPS: Animal, Iron Or Steel
Detroit Auto Specialties Inc .... G 248 496-3856
West Bloomfield *(G-18279)*
Shane Group LLC .... G 517 439-4316
Hillsdale *(G-7949)*

TRAPS: Stem
Armstrong International Inc .... C 269 273-1415
Three Rivers *(G-16567)*

TRAVEL AGENCIES
Black Ski Weekend LLC .... G 313 879-7150
West Bloomfield *(G-18265)*
Nationwide Network Inc .... G 989 793-0123
Saginaw *(G-14708)*

TRAVEL TRAILER DEALERS
Technology Plus Trailers Inc .... F 734 928-0001
Canton *(G-2531)*

TRAVEL TRAILERS & CAMPERS
Ajax Trailers Inc .... F 586 757-7676
Warren *(G-17696)*
D & W Management Company Inc .... F 586 758-2284
Warren *(G-17770)*
Frank Industries Inc .... E 810 346-3234
Brown City *(G-2137)*
Gibbys Transport LLC .... G 269 838-2794
Hastings *(G-7793)*
Kimble Auto and Rv LLC .... G 517 227-5089
Coldwater *(G-3440)*
Montrose Trailers Inc .... F 810 639-7431
Montrose *(G-11607)*
Mvm7 LLC .... E 989 317-3901
Mount Pleasant *(G-11725)*
Rough Road Trucking LLC .... G 231 645-3355
Kalkaska *(G-9402)*
Skyline Champion Corporation .... A 248 614-8211
Troy *(G-17356)*

TRAYS: Plastic
Peninsula Plastics Company Inc .... D 248 852-3731
Auburn Hills *(G-995)*
R L Adams Plastics Inc .... D 616 261-4400
Grand Rapids *(G-7134)*

TROPHIES, NEC
Michigan Plaques & Awards Inc .... E 248 398-6400
Berkley *(G-1632)*
Quicktrophy LLC .... F 906 228-2604
Marquette *(G-11043)*

TROPHIES, WHOLESALE
Lachman Enterprises Inc .... G 248 948-9944
Southfield *(G-15623)*

TROPHIES: Metal, Exc Silver
Contemporary Industries Inc .... G 248 478-8850
Farmington Hills *(G-5208)*

TROPHY & PLAQUE STORES
Cushion Lrry Trphies Engrv LLC .... G 517 332-1667
Lansing *(G-9827)*
Imagecraft .... G 517 750-0077
Jackson *(G-8907)*
Livonia Trophy & Screen Prtg .... G 734 464-9191
Livonia *(G-10289)*
Marquee Engraving Inc .... G 810 686-7550
Clio *(G-3404)*
Michael Anderson .... G 231 652-5717
Newaygo *(G-12088)*
Midwest Graphics & Awards Inc .... G 734 424-3700
Dexter *(G-4746)*
Nobby Inc .... F 810 984-3300
Fort Gratiot *(G-5822)*
Pro Shop The/P S Graphics .... G 517 448-8490
Hudson *(G-8559)*
Qmi Group Inc .... E 248 589-0505
Madison Heights *(G-10814)*
Quicktrophy LLC .... F 906 228-2604
Marquette *(G-11043)*
Trophy Center West Michigan .... G 231 893-1686
Whitehall *(G-18510)*

TRUCK & BUS BODIES: Bus Bodies
Transit Bus Rebuilders Inc .... F 989 277-3645
Owosso *(G-12863)*

TRUCK & BUS BODIES: Car Carrier
Weiderman Motorsports .... G 269 689-0264
Sturgis *(G-16329)*

TRUCK & BUS BODIES: Cement Mixer
Bucks Cement Inc .... G 810 233-4141
Burton *(G-2228)*

TRUCK & BUS BODIES: Garbage Or Refuse Truck
Loadmaster Corporation .... E 906 563-9226
Norway *(G-12353)*

TRUCK & BUS BODIES: Motor Vehicle, Specialty
Hovertechnics LLC .... G 269 461-3934
Benton Harbor *(G-1556)*
Mahindra N Amrcn Tchncal Ctr I .... C 248 268-6600
Auburn Hills *(G-965)*
Perspective Enterprises Inc .... G 269 327-0869
Portage *(G-13591)*

TRUCK & BUS BODIES: Truck Beds
Precision Laser & Mfg LLC .... G 519 733-8422
Sterling Heights *(G-16131)*

TRUCK & BUS BODIES: Truck, Motor Vehicle
Automotive Service Co .... F 517 784-6131
Jackson *(G-8818)*
Csi Emergency Apparatus LLC .... F 989 348-2877
Grayling *(G-7459)*
Hulet Body Co Inc .... F 313 931-6000
Northville *(G-12230)*
Lodal Inc .... D 906 779-1700
Kingsford *(G-9513)*
Morgan Olson LLC .... A 269 659-0200
Sturgis *(G-16311)*
Velcro USA Inc .... G 248 583-6060
Troy *(G-17437)*

TRUCK & BUS BODIES: Van Bodies
Mobility Trnsp Svcs Inc .... E 734 453-6452
Canton *(G-2497)*
Mobilitytrans LLC .... E 734 262-3760
Livonia *(G-10320)*

PRODUCT SECTION

TRUCKS & TRACTORS: Industrial

TRUCK & FREIGHT TERMINALS & SUPPORT ACTIVITIES

Shield Material Handling Inc ....D....... 248 418-0986
  Auburn Hills *(G-1032)*

TRUCK BODIES: Body Parts

BDS Company Inc ....F....... 517 279-2135
  Coldwater *(G-3421)*
Central Mich Knwrth Lnsing LLC ....G....... 517 394-7000
  Lansing *(G-9823)*
Central Mich Knwrth Sginaw LLC ....G....... 989 754-4500
  Saginaw *(G-14625)*
Gac ....G....... 269 639-3010
  South Haven *(G-15406)*
Jasper Weller LLC ....E....... 616 249-8596
  Wyoming *(G-18886)*
Jasper Weller LLC ....C....... 616 724-2000
  Wyoming *(G-18887)*
Johnson Controls Inc ....G....... 734 254-5000
  Plymouth *(G-13204)*
Off Site Mfg Tech Inc ....D....... 586 598-3110
  Chesterfield *(G-2917)*
Roll Rite Group Holdings LLC ....D....... 989 345-3434
  Gladwin *(G-6203)*
Roll-Rite LLC ....E....... 989 345-3434
  Gladwin *(G-6204)*
Tecnoma LLC ....F....... 248 354-8888
  Southfield *(G-15718)*
Tectum Holdings Inc ....D....... 734 677-0444
  Ann Arbor *(G-673)*
Worldwide Marketing Svcs Inc ....E....... 269 556-2000
  Saint Joseph *(G-14981)*

TRUCK BODY SHOP

Hulet Body Co Inc ....F....... 313 931-6000
  Northville *(G-12230)*

TRUCK GENERAL REPAIR SVC

Benlee Inc ....E....... 586 791-1830
  Romulus *(G-14257)*
Circle K Service Corporation ....E....... 989 496-0511
  Midland *(G-11329)*
D & W Management Company Inc ....F....... 586 758-2284
  Warren *(G-17770)*
Eleven Mile Trck Frame Axle In ....E....... 248 399-7536
  Madison Heights *(G-10721)*
Lupa R A and Sons Repair ....G....... 810 346-3579
  Marlette *(G-10983)*

TRUCK PAINTING & LETTERING SVCS

Dicks Signs ....G....... 810 987-9002
  Port Huron *(G-13468)*

TRUCK PARTS & ACCESSORIES: Wholesalers

Automotive Service Co ....F....... 517 784-6131
  Jackson *(G-8818)*
Joint Clutch & Gear Svc Inc ....E....... 734 641-7575
  Romulus *(G-14292)*
Monroe Truck Equipment Inc ....E....... 810 238-4603
  Flint *(G-5736)*
NBC Truck Equipment Inc ....E....... 586 774-4900
  Roseville *(G-14452)*
Tectum Holdings Inc ....D....... 734 677-0444
  Ann Arbor *(G-673)*

TRUCKING & HAULING SVCS: Animal & Farm Prdt

F C Simpson Lime Co ....G....... 810 367-3510
  Kimball *(G-9492)*
Keays Family Truckin ....G....... 231 838-6430
  Gaylord *(G-6139)*

TRUCKING & HAULING SVCS: Contract Basis

Xpo Cnw Inc ....C....... 734 757-1444
  Ann Arbor *(G-720)*

TRUCKING & HAULING SVCS: Garbage, Collect/Transport Only

Southast Berrien Cnty Landfill ....E....... 269 695-2500
  Niles *(G-12168)*

TRUCKING & HAULING SVCS: Lumber & Log, Local

Nickels Logging ....G....... 906 563-5880
  Norway *(G-12354)*

TRUCKING & HAULING SVCS: Mail Carriers, Contract

Allied Printing Co Inc ....E....... 248 541-0551
  Ferndale *(G-5523)*

TRUCKING & HAULING SVCS: Mobile Homes

Cedar Mobile Home Service Inc ....G....... 616 696-1580
  Cedar Springs *(G-2643)*

TRUCKING & HAULING SVCS: Petroleum, Local

Wara Construction Company LLC .....D....... 248 299-2410
  Rochester Hills *(G-14141)*

TRUCKING & HAULING SVCS: Steel, Local

Leonard & Randy Inc ....G....... 734 287-9500
  Taylor *(G-16435)*

TRUCKING & HAULING SVCS: Timber, Local

Marvin Nelson Forest Products ....F....... 906 384-6700
  Cornell *(G-3701)*
McNamara & Mcnamara ....F....... 906 293-5281
  Newberry *(G-12093)*

TRUCKING, DUMP

Bouchey and Sons Inc ....G....... 989 588-4118
  Farwell *(G-5421)*
Crandell Bros Trucking Co ....E....... 517 543-2930
  Charlotte *(G-2747)*
Doug Wirt Enterprises Inc ....G....... 989 684-5777
  Bay City *(G-1347)*
Franke Salisbury Virginia ....G....... 231 775-7014
  Cadillac *(G-2330)*
Miller Sand & Gravel Company ....G....... 269 672-5601
  Hopkins *(G-8367)*
Priority Waste LLC ....E....... 586 228-1200
  Clinton Township *(G-3327)*
Yerington Brothers Inc ....G....... 269 695-7669
  Niles *(G-12174)*
Zeeland Farm Services Inc ....C....... 616 772-9042
  Zeeland *(G-19096)*

TRUCKING: Except Local

E H Tulgestka & Sons Inc ....F....... 989 734-2129
  Rogers City *(G-14209)*
Forest Blake Products Inc ....G....... 231 879-3913
  Fife Lake *(G-5606)*
Indian Summer Cooperative Inc ......C....... 231 845-6248
  Ludington *(G-10541)*
Jasco International LLC ....G....... 313 841-5000
  Detroit *(G-4335)*
Manigg Enterprises Inc ....F....... 989 356-4986
  Alpena *(G-301)*
Northern Logistics LLC ....E....... 989 386-2389
  Clare *(G-2990)*

TRUCKING: Local, With Storage

Aldez North America ....F....... 586 530-5314
  Clinton Township *(G-3161)*
Constine Inc ....E....... 989 723-6043
  Owosso *(G-12827)*
J T Express Ltd ....G....... 810 724-6471
  Brown City *(G-2138)*
Jasco International LLC ....E....... 313 841-5000
  Detroit *(G-4335)*
Trinity Holding Inc ....F....... 517 787-3100
  Jackson *(G-9024)*

TRUCKING: Local, Without Storage

Allied Printing Co Inc ....E....... 248 514-7394
  Ferndale *(G-5524)*
Bay-Houston Towing Company ....F....... 810 648-2210
  Sandusky *(G-15056)*
Darling Ingredients Inc ....F....... 989 752-4340
  Carrollton *(G-2588)*
Falcon Trucking Company ....G....... 313 843-7200
  Dearborn *(G-3839)*
Forest Blake Products Inc ....G....... 231 879-3913
  Fife Lake *(G-5606)*
Genoak Materials Inc ....C....... 248 634-8276
  Holly *(G-8273)*
James Spicer Inc ....G....... 906 265-2385
  Iron River *(G-8743)*
Rough Road Trucking LLC ....G....... 231 645-3355
  Kalkaska *(G-9402)*
Rudy Goupille & Sons Inc ....G....... 906 475-9816
  Negaunee *(G-11974)*
Straits Steel and Wire Company ....D....... 231 843-3416
  Ludington *(G-10551)*
Superior Distribution Svcs LLC ....C....... 616 453-6358
  Grand Rapids *(G-7236)*
Tri-City Aggregates Inc ....E....... 248 634-8276
  Holly *(G-8298)*

TRUCKS & TRACTORS: Industrial

AAR Manufacturing Inc ....E....... 231 779-8800
  Cadillac *(G-2306)*
All Pointe Truck & Trailer Svc ....G....... 586 504-0364
  New Baltimore *(G-11977)*
Alta Equipment Holdings Inc ....E....... 248 449-6700
  Livonia *(G-10112)*
Baker Enterprises Inc ....E....... 989 354-2189
  Alpena *(G-281)*
Bay Wood Homes Inc ....F....... 989 245-4156
  Fenton *(G-5456)*
Besser Company USA ....D....... 616 399-5215
  Zeeland *(G-18998)*
Bucher Hydraulics Inc ....G....... 231 652-2773
  Newaygo *(G-12078)*
Charles Lange ....F....... 989 777-0110
  Saginaw *(G-14627)*
Circle K Service Corporation ....E....... 989 496-0511
  Midland *(G-11329)*
Commercial Group Inc ....E....... 313 931-6100
  Taylor *(G-16395)*
Delta Tube & Fabricating Corp ....C....... 248 634-8267
  Holly *(G-8268)*
Egemin Automation Inc ....C....... 616 393-0101
  Holland *(G-8025)*
Frost Incorporated ....E....... 616 453-7781
  Grand Rapids *(G-6722)*
Harvey S Freeman ....G....... 248 852-2222
  West Bloomfield *(G-18287)*
Hme Inc ....C....... 616 534-1463
  Wyoming *(G-18885)*
Hobart Brothers LLC ....G....... 231 933-1234
  Traverse City *(G-16712)*
Humphrey Companies LLC ....C....... 616 530-1717
  Grandville *(G-7389)*
L A S Leasing Inc ....E....... 734 727-5148
  Wayne *(G-18228)*
Lake Shore Systems Inc ....D....... 906 774-1500
  Kingsford *(G-9512)*
Loudon Steel Inc ....E....... 989 871-9353
  Millington *(G-11502)*
Marsh Industrial Services Inc ....F....... 231 258-4870
  Kalkaska *(G-9395)*
Metzgar Conveyor Co ....E....... 616 784-0930
  Grand Rapids *(G-6983)*
Midwest Tractor & Equipment Co .....F....... 231 269-4100
  Buckley *(G-2207)*
Milsco LLC ....E....... 517 787-3650
  Jackson *(G-8965)*
Montrose Trailers Inc ....G....... 810 639-7431
  Montrose *(G-11607)*
Nyx LLC ....D....... 734 464-0800
  Livonia *(G-10346)*
PCI Procal Inc ....F....... 989 358-7070
  Alpena *(G-311)*
Peninsular Inc ....E....... 586 775-7211
  Roseville *(G-14461)*
Perfecto Industries Inc ....E....... 989 732-2941
  Gaylord *(G-6154)*
Pettibone/Traverse Lift LLC ....E....... 906 353-4800
  Baraga *(G-1147)*
Prophotonix Limited ....G....... 586 778-1100
  Roseville *(G-14466)*
Ross Joseph ....G....... 269 424-5448
  Dowagiac *(G-4794)*
Saf-Holland Inc ....A....... 231 773-3271
  Muskegon *(G-11913)*
Skamp Industries Inc ....G....... 269 731-2666
  Portage *(G-13608)*
Thoreson-Mc Cosh Inc ....E....... 248 362-0960
  Lake Orion *(G-9634)*
US Tarp Inc ....D....... 269 639-3010
  South Haven *(G-15420)*

Employee Codes: A=Over 500 employees, B=251-500
C=101-250, D=51-100, E=20-50, F=10-19, G=3-9

TRUCKS & TRACTORS: Industrial

Versatile Fabrication Co Inc .... E 231 739-7115
  Muskegon *(G-11941)*
Windy Lake LLC .... D 877 869-6911
  Pentwater *(G-12975)*

TRUCKS: Forklift

Bell Fork Lift Inc .... F 313 841-1220
  Detroit *(G-4049)*
Bell Forklifts .... G 586 469-7979
  Clinton Township *(G-3181)*
Bristol Manufacturing Inc .... G 810 658-9510
  Davison *(G-3774)*
C&C Forklift .... G 313 729-2850
  Taylor *(G-16389)*
Dr Forklift .... G 734 968-6576
  Brighton *(G-1977)*
Forklift Parts Group .... G 248 792-7132
  Troy *(G-17117)*
Harlo Products Corporation .... E 616 538-0550
  Grandville *(G-7388)*
Ihs Inc .... G 616 464-4224
  Grand Rapids *(G-6833)*
Michiana Forklift .... G 269 663-2700
  Edwardsburg *(G-5010)*
Midwest Forklift Parts LLC .... G 248 830-5982
  Oxford *(G-12902)*
West Michigan Forklift Inc .... G 616 262-4949
  Wayland *(G-18209)*

TRUCKS: Indl

Aimrite LLC .... G 248 693-8925
  Lake Orion *(G-9584)*
Brownlee Group LLC .... G 512 202-0568
  Clinton Township *(G-3190)*
Dlr Logistics Inc .... G 248 499-2368
  Ann Arbor *(G-453)*
Ipp Logistic LLC .... G 248 330-5379
  Southfield *(G-15608)*
J & J Transport LLC .... G 231 582-6083
  Boyne City *(G-1891)*
Lee Hamilton Gary Jr .... G 231 884-9600
  Mc Bain *(G-11184)*
One Source Trucking LLC .... G 855 999-7723
  Detroit *(G-4499)*
Ream Logistics Dlvry Svcs LLC .... G 877 246-7857
  Belleville *(G-1490)*
Superior Distribution Svcs LLC .... G 616 453-6358
  Grand Rapids *(G-7236)*

TRUSSES & FRAMING: Prefabricated Metal

Progressive Panel Systems Inc .... E 616 748-1384
  Zeeland *(G-19074)*

TRUSSES: Wood, Floor

Allwood Building Components .... D 586 727-2731
  Richmond *(G-13832)*
G & G Wood & Supply Inc .... E 586 293-0450
  Roseville *(G-14408)*
Letherer Truss Inc .... D 989 386-4999
  Clare *(G-2985)*
Maple Valley Truss Co .... F 989 389-4267
  Prudenville *(G-13658)*
Marshall Bldg Components Corp .... E 269 781-4236
  Marshall *(G-11064)*
Wood Tech Inc .... E 616 455-0800
  Byron Center *(G-2303)*

TRUSSES: Wood, Roof

Bear Truss - US Lbm LLC .... F 989 681-5774
  Saint Louis *(G-14988)*
Century Truss .... G 248 486-4000
  Livonia *(G-10153)*
Custom Components Truss Co .... E 810 744-0771
  Burton *(G-2234)*
Heart Truss & Engineering Corp .... C 517 372-0850
  Lansing *(G-9203)*
Joseph Miller .... G 231 821-2430
  Holton *(G-8339)*
Ken Luneack Construction Inc .... C 989 681-5774
  Saint Louis *(G-14992)*
Lumber & Truss Inc .... F 810 664-7290
  Lapeer *(G-9945)*
Maverick Building Systems LLC .... F 248 366-9410
  Commerce Township *(G-3555)*
Precision Framing Systems Inc .... E 704 588-6680
  Taylor *(G-16458)*
Truss Technologies Inc .... D 231 788-6330
  Muskegon *(G-11939)*

Trussway .... F 713 691-6900
  Jenison *(G-9074)*
Wendricks Truss Inc .... F 906 635-8822
  Sault Sainte Marie *(G-15104)*
Wendricks Truss Inc .... E 906 498-7709
  Hermansville *(G-7864)*

TUBE & PIPE MILL EQPT

Delta Tube & Fabricating Corp .... C 248 634-8267
  Holly *(G-8268)*

TUBE & TUBING FABRICATORS

A & B Tube Benders Inc .... F 586 773-0440
  Warren *(G-17678)*
Acme Tube Bending Company .... G 248 545-8500
  Berkley *(G-1618)*
Allegan Tubular Products Inc .... D 269 673-6636
  Allegan *(G-146)*
Alro Steel Corporation .... G 989 893-9553
  Bay City *(G-1320)*
Angstrom Automotive Group LLC .... E 248 627-2871
  Ortonville *(G-12741)*
Avpi Limited .... E 616 842-1200
  Spring Lake *(G-15804)*
Berkley Industries Inc .... E 989 656-2171
  Bay Port *(G-1413)*
Detroit Tube Products LLC .... E 313 841-0300
  Detroit *(G-4168)*
Elringklinger Auto Mfg Inc .... E 248 727-6600
  Southfield *(G-15554)*
Elringklinger Auto Mfg Inc .... E 248 727-6600
  Southfield *(G-15555)*
Erin Industries Inc .... E 248 669-2050
  Walled Lake *(G-17668)*
Gray Bros Stamping & Mch Inc .... E 269 483-7615
  White Pigeon *(G-18478)*
Hlc Industries Inc .... D 810 477-9600
  Farmington Hills *(G-5262)*
J & L Manufacturing Co Inc .... E 269 789-1507
  Marshall *(G-11061)*
Jems of Litchfield Inc .... F 517 542-5367
  Litchfield *(G-10081)*
L A Burnhart Inc .... G 810 227-4567
  Brighton *(G-2016)*
Macomb Tube Fabricating Co .... E 586 445-6770
  Warren *(G-17912)*
Masterbilt Products Corp .... F 269 749-4841
  Olivet *(G-12694)*
Mayville Engineering Co Inc .... D 989 748-6031
  Vanderbilt *(G-17572)*
Mayville Engineering Co Inc .... D 616 877-2073
  Wayland *(G-18198)*
Mayville Engineering Co Inc .... D 989 983-3911
  Vanderbilt *(G-17573)*
Melling Products North LLC .... D 989 588-6147
  Farwell *(G-5426)*
Midwest Tube Fabricators Inc .... E 586 264-9898
  Sterling Heights *(G-16100)*
Paumac Tubing LLC .... D 810 985-9400
  Marysville *(G-11096)*
Picko Ferrum Fabricating LLC .... D 810 626-7086
  Hamburg *(G-7593)*
Production Tube Company Inc .... G 313 259-3990
  Detroit *(G-4537)*
Quigley Manufacturing Inc .... G 248 426-8600
  Farmington Hills *(G-5362)*
Ridgid Slotting LLC .... G 616 847-0332
  Grand Haven *(G-6354)*
Rock River Fabrications Inc .... E 616 281-5769
  Grand Rapids *(G-7162)*
Rss Baker LLC .... E 616 844-5429
  Grand Haven *(G-6356)*
Ryson Tube Inc .... F 810 227-4567
  Brighton *(G-2067)*
Sales & Engineering Inc .... E 734 525-9030
  Livonia *(G-10398)*
South Park Sales & Mfg Inc .... G 313 381-7579
  Dearborn *(G-3899)*
Tempro Industries Inc .... E 734 451-5900
  Plymouth *(G-13312)*
Tg Manufacturing LLC .... G 616 935-7575
  Byron Center *(G-2296)*
Troy Tube & Manufacturing Co .... D 586 949-8700
  Chesterfield *(G-2959)*
Tube Wright Inc .... E 810 227-4567
  Brighton *(G-2085)*
Tube Wright Inc .... G 734 449-9129
  Whitmore Lake *(G-18549)*
Tube-Co Inc .... G 586 775-0244
  Warren *(G-18046)*

Tubesource Manufacturing Inc .... E 248 543-4746
  Ferndale *(G-5591)*
Universal Tube Inc .... C 248 853-5100
  Rochester Hills *(G-14137)*
Universal Warranty Corpor .... G 248 263-6900
  Southfield *(G-15733)*
Van Pelt Industries LLC .... G 616 842-1200
  Grand Haven *(G-6378)*
Volos Tube Form Inc .... E 586 416-3600
  Macomb *(G-10650)*
Wooley Industries Inc .... G 810 341-8823
  Flint *(G-5795)*

TUBES: Extruded Or Drawn, Aluminum

Brazeway LLC .... D 517 265-2121
  Adrian *(G-54)*

TUBES: Finned, For Heat Transfer

Burr Oak Tool Inc .... B 269 651-9393
  Sturgis *(G-16282)*

TUBES: Gas Or Vapor

Puff Baby LLC .... G 734 620-9991
  Garden City *(G-6106)*

TUBES: Paper

Cascade Paper Converters LLC .... F 616 974-9165
  Grand Rapids *(G-6555)*
Nagel Paper Inc .... E 810 644-7043
  Swartz Creek *(G-16357)*

TUBES: Steel & Iron

River Valley Machine Inc .... F 269 673-8070
  Allegan *(G-181)*
S F R Precision Turning Inc .... G 517 709-3367
  Wixom *(G-18746)*
TI Fluid Systems LLC .... A 248 494-5000
  Auburn Hills *(G-1054)*
TI Group Auto Systems LLC .... B 248 296-8000
  Auburn Hills *(G-1055)*

TUBES: Wrought, Welded Or Lock Joint

Detroit Tubing Mill Inc .... E 313 491-8823
  Detroit *(G-4169)*
James Steel & Tube Company .... F 248 547-4200
  Madison Heights *(G-10752)*
Tarpon Industries Inc .... E 810 364-7421
  Marysville *(G-11105)*

TUBING: Copper

Midbrook LLC .... G 800 966-9274
  Jackson *(G-8960)*

TUBING: Flexible, Metallic

Blissfield Manufacturing Co .... C 517 486-2121
  Blissfield *(G-1761)*
Lowing Products LLC .... G 616 530-7440
  Wyoming *(G-18892)*
Versatube Corporation .... F 248 524-0299
  Troy *(G-17438)*

TUBING: Plastic

Dlhbowles Inc .... F 248 569-0652
  Southfield *(G-15541)*
Trico Products Corporation .... C 248 371-1700
  Rochester Hills *(G-14132)*

TUBING: Rubber

Trico Products Corporation .... C 248 371-1700
  Rochester Hills *(G-14132)*

TUBING: Seamless

Angstrom USA LLC .... E 313 295-0100
  Southfield *(G-15488)*
Burr Oak Tool Inc .... B 269 651-9393
  Sturgis *(G-16282)*
Perforated Tubes Inc .... E 616 942-4550
  Ada *(G-33)*
TI Fluid Systems LLC .... A 248 494-5000
  Auburn Hills *(G-1054)*
TI Group Auto Systems LLC .... B 248 296-8000
  Auburn Hills *(G-1055)*
TI Group Auto Systems LLC .... G 248 475-4663
  Auburn Hills *(G-1057)*

PRODUCT SECTION

Van Pelt Corporation .... F 313 365-6500
   Detroit *(G-4662)*

TUMBLING

Automotive Tumbling Co Inc .... G 313 925-7450
   Detroit *(G-4032)*
Crown Industrial Services Inc .... D 734 483-7270
   Ypsilanti *(G-18935)*
Crown Industrial Services Inc .... D 734 483-7270
   Ypsilanti *(G-18936)*
DNR Inc .... G 734 722-4000
   Plymouth *(G-13160)*
DNR Inc .... F 734 722-4000
   Westland *(G-18365)*
Liberty Burnishing Co .... G 313 366-7878
   Detroit *(G-4397)*

TUNGSTEN MILL PRDTS

Carbide Technologies Inc .... E 586 296-5200
   Fraser *(G-5910)*

TURBINE GENERATOR SET UNITS: Hydraulic, Complete

Ahd LLC .... G 586 922-6511
   Shelby Township *(G-15167)*
Marsh Plating Corporation .... D 734 483-5767
   Ypsilanti *(G-18965)*

TURBINES & TURBINE GENERATOR SET UNITS, COMPLETE

3dfx Interactive Inc .... G 918 938-8967
   Saginaw *(G-14599)*
Dowding Machining LLC .... F 517 663-5455
   Eaton Rapids *(G-4961)*

TURBINES & TURBINE GENERATOR SETS

Diamond Power Specialty Co .... G 734 429-8527
   Ann Arbor *(G-452)*
Dynamic Energy Tech LLC .... G 248 212-5904
   Oak Park *(G-12607)*
Ener2 LLC .... G 248 842-2662
   Brighton *(G-1984)*
Horiba Instruments Inc .... D 734 213-6555
   Ann Arbor *(G-518)*
Kinetic Wave Power LLC .... G 989 839-9757
   Midland *(G-11382)*
Lutke Hydraulics .... G 231 824-9505
   Manton *(G-10935)*
Metro Machine Works Inc .... D 734 941-4571
   Romulus *(G-14304)*
Nu Con Corporation .... E 734 525-0770
   Livonia *(G-10341)*
Plasma-Tec Inc .... E 616 455-2593
   Holland *(G-8166)*
South Pointe Radiator .... G 734 941-1460
   Romulus *(G-14329)*
Steel Tool & Engineering Co .... D 734 692-8580
   Brownstown Twp *(G-2157)*
Wmh Fluidpower Inc .... F 269 327-7011
   Portage *(G-13634)*

TURKEY PROCESSING & SLAUGHTERING

Michigan Trkey Prdcers Coop In .... B 616 245-2221
   Grand Rapids *(G-6994)*
Michigan Trkey Prdcers Coop In .... D 616 245-2221
   Wyoming *(G-18894)*
Michigan Turkey Producers .... D 616 875-1838
   Zeeland *(G-19052)*

TURNKEY VENDORS: Computer Systems

3dfx Interactive Inc .... G 918 938-8967
   Saginaw *(G-14599)*
Comptek Inc .... E 248 477-5215
   Farmington Hills *(G-5206)*

TWINE PRDTS

American Twisting Company .... E 269 637-8581
   South Haven *(G-15398)*

TWINE: Binder & Baler

Cascade Paper Converters LLC .... F 616 974-9165
   Grand Rapids *(G-6555)*

TYPESETTING SVC

A Koppel Color Image Company .... G 616 534-3600
   Grandville *(G-7360)*
AAA Language Services .... F 248 239-1138
   Bloomfield *(G-1780)*
Adgravers Inc .... F 313 259-3780
   Detroit *(G-3986)*
Advance Graphic Systems Inc .... E 248 656-8000
   Rochester Hills *(G-13943)*
Al Corp .... F 734 475-7357
   Chelsea *(G-2804)*
Aladdin Printing .... G 248 360-2842
   Commerce Township *(G-3507)*
American Reprographics Co LLC .... G 248 299-8900
   Clawson *(G-3086)*
Americas Finest Prtg Graphics .... G 586 296-1312
   Fraser *(G-5893)*
Anteebo Publishers Inc .... E 313 882-6900
   Grosse Pointe Park *(G-7546)*
AP Impressions Inc .... G 734 464-8009
   Livonia *(G-10121)*
Apb Inc .... G 248 528-2990
   Troy *(G-16939)*
Argus Press Company .... E 989 725-5136
   Owosso *(G-12824)*
ASAP Printing Inc .... G 517 882-3500
   Okemos *(G-12657)*
Beljan Ltd Inc .... F 734 426-3503
   Dexter *(G-4726)*
Bookcomp Inc .... F 616 774-9700
   Belmont *(G-1503)*
Breck Graphics Incorporated .... E 616 248-4110
   Grand Rapids *(G-6523)*
Bronco Printing Company .... G 248 544-1120
   Hazel Park *(G-7821)*
Brophy Engraving Co Inc .... E 313 871-2333
   Detroit *(G-4076)*
Bruce Inc .... G 517 371-5205
   Lansing *(G-9819)*
Business Press Inc .... G 248 652-8855
   Rochester *(G-13895)*
Color Connection .... G 248 351-0920
   Southfield *(G-15527)*
Copy Central Inc .... G 231 941-2298
   Traverse City *(G-16660)*
Corporate Electronic Sty Inc .... D 248 583-7070
   Troy *(G-17030)*
Daily Oakland Press .... B 248 332-8181
   Bloomfield Hills *(G-1811)*
De Vru Printing Co .... G 616 452-5451
   Grand Rapids *(G-6636)*
Dekoff & Sons Inc .... G 269 344-5816
   Kalamazoo *(G-9165)*
Delmas Typesetting .... G 734 662-8899
   Ann Arbor *(G-446)*
Derk Pieter Co Inc .... G 616 554-7777
   Grand Rapids *(G-6641)*
Detroit Legal News Pubg LLC .... E 248 577-6100
   Troy *(G-17057)*
Different By Design Inc .... G 248 588-4840
   Farmington Hills *(G-5217)*
DPrinter Inc .... G 517 423-6554
   Tecumseh *(G-16499)*
Earle Press Inc .... E 231 773-2111
   Muskegon *(G-11805)*
Econo Print Inc .... G 734 878-5806
   Pinckney *(G-13047)*
F P Horak Company .... C 989 892-6505
   Bay City *(G-1355)*
Federal Heath Sign Company LLC .... E 248 656-8000
   Rochester Hills *(G-14010)*
Fedex Office & Print Svcs Inc .... F 734 761-4539
   Ann Arbor *(G-487)*
Fedex Office & Print Svcs Inc .... G 517 332-5855
   East Lansing *(G-4892)*
Foremost Graphics LLC .... D 616 453-4747
   Grand Rapids *(G-6715)*
Forsons Inc .... G 517 787-4562
   Jackson *(G-8885)*
Future Reproductions Inc .... F 248 350-2060
   Southfield *(G-15571)*
Gazette Newspapers Inc .... G 248 524-4868
   Troy *(G-17128)*
Genesee County Herald Inc .... F 810 686-3840
   Clio *(G-3399)*
Gemhart Corp .... G 989 792-9427
   Saginaw *(G-14655)*
Grand Blanc Printing Inc .... E 810 694-1155
   Grand Blanc *(G-6245)*

TYPESETTING SVC

Graphics Unlimited Inc .... G 231 773-2696
   Norton Shores *(G-12295)*
Hatteras Inc .... E 734 525-5500
   Plymouth *(G-13183)*
Hi-Lites Graphic Inc .... E 231 924-0630
   Fremont *(G-6045)*
Infotel .... G 313 879-0820
   Detroit *(G-4317)*
J-Ad Graphics Inc .... D 800 870-7085
   Hastings *(G-7800)*
Jomark Inc .... E 248 478-2600
   Farmington Hills *(G-5275)*
Jtc Inc .... G 517 784-0576
   Jackson *(G-8925)*
Kalamazoo Photo Comp Svcs .... G 269 345-3706
   Kalamazoo *(G-9245)*
Larsen Graphics Inc .... G 989 823-3000
   Vassar *(G-17579)*
Lasertec Inc .... E 586 274-4500
   Madison Heights *(G-10769)*
Litsenberger Print Shop .... G 906 482-3903
   Houghton *(G-8386)*
Macomb Printing Inc .... E 586 463-2301
   Clinton Township *(G-3288)*
Marketing VI Group Inc .... G 989 793-3933
   Saginaw *(G-14686)*
Metropolitan Indus Lithography .... G 269 323-9333
   Portage *(G-13585)*
Micrgraphics Printing Inc .... G 231 739-6575
   Norton Shores *(G-12311)*
Microforms Inc .... E 586 939-7900
   Beverly Hills *(G-1667)*
Mid-State Printing Inc .... F 989 875-4163
   Ithaca *(G-8794)*
Mitchell Graphics Inc .... E 231 347-4635
   Petoskey *(G-13007)*
Moormann Printing Inc .... G 269 423-2411
   Decatur *(G-3950)*
North American Graphics Inc .... F 586 486-1110
   Warren *(G-17947)*
Ogemaw County Herald Inc .... E 989 345-0044
   West Branch *(G-18333)*
Parkside Speedy Print Inc .... G 810 985-8484
   Port Huron *(G-13516)*
Paul C Doerr .... G 734 242-2058
   Monroe *(G-11568)*
Peg-Master Business Forms Inc .... G 586 566-8694
   Shelby Township *(G-15298)*
Phase III Graphics Inc .... G 616 949-9290
   Grand Rapids *(G-7084)*
Print Masters Inc .... F 248 548-7100
   Madison Heights *(G-10810)*
Print-Tech Inc .... E 734 996-2345
   Ann Arbor *(G-624)*
Printcomm Inc .... D 810 239-5763
   Flint *(G-5749)*
Printery Inc .... E 616 396-4655
   Holland *(G-8172)*
Printing Centre Inc .... F 517 694-2400
   Holt *(G-8326)*
Progressive Prtg & Graphics .... G 269 965-8909
   Battle Creek *(G-1284)*
Qrp Inc .... G 989 496-2955
   Midland *(G-11406)*
Qrp Inc .... G 989 496-2955
   Midland *(G-11405)*
Quick Printing Company Inc .... G 616 241-0506
   Grand Rapids *(G-7131)*
Richard Larabee .... G 248 827-7755
   Southfield *(G-15689)*
Rider Type & Design .... E 989 839-0015
   Midland *(G-11408)*
River Run Press Inc .... E 269 349-7603
   Kalamazoo *(G-9320)*
Safran Printing Company Inc .... C 586 939-7600
   Beverly Hills *(G-1668)*
Spartan Printing Inc .... E 517 372-6910
   Lansing *(G-9738)*
Spectrum Printers Inc .... E 517 423-5735
   Tecumseh *(G-16517)*
Stafford Media Inc .... E 616 754-9301
   Greenville *(G-7505)*
Stafford Media Inc .... D 616 754-1178
   Greenville *(G-7506)*
T J K Inc .... E 586 731-9639
   Sterling Heights *(G-16199)*
Technology MGT & Budgt Dept .... G 517 322-1897
   Lansing *(G-9033)*
TGI Direct Inc .... G 810 239-5553
   Ann Arbor *(G-685)*

Employee Codes: A=Over 500 employees, B=251-500
C=101-250, D=51-100, E=20-50, F=10-19, G=3-9

TYPESETTING SVC

The Envelope Printery Inc	D	734 398-7700	
Van Buren Twp *(G-17557)*			
Times Herald Company	D	810 985-7171	
Port Huron *(G-13532)*			
Turner Business Forms Inc	E	989 752-5540	
Saginaw *(G-14782)*			
Village Shop Inc	E	231 946-3712	
Traverse City *(G-16875)*			
Wolverine Printing Company LLC	E	616 451-2075	
Grand Rapids *(G-7347)*			
Worten Copy Center Inc	G	231 845-7030	
Ludington *(G-10558)*			

TYPESETTING SVC: Computer

P D Q Press Inc .... G 586 725-1888
 Ira *(G-8706)*
Poly Tech Industries Inc .... G 248 589-9950
 Madison Heights *(G-10804)*
Skip Printing and Dup Co .... G 586 779-2640
 Roseville *(G-14477)*
Thorpe Printing Services Inc .... G 810 364-6222
 Marysville *(G-11107)*
Whiteside Consulting Group LLC .... G 313 288-6598
 Detroit *(G-4681)*

ULTRASONIC EQPT: Cleaning, Exc Med & Dental

Branson Ultrasonics Corp .... G 586 276-0150
 Sterling Heights *(G-15948)*
Electro-Matic Visual Inc .... F 248 478-1182
 Farmington Hills *(G-5226)*
Gvn Group Corp .... E 248 340-0342
 Pontiac *(G-13376)*
H & R Industries Inc .... E 616 247-1165
 Grand Rapids *(G-6798)*
Power Cleaning Systems Inc .... G 248 347-7727
 Wixom *(G-18731)*
Telsonic Ultrasonics Inc .... F 586 802-0033
 Shelby Township *(G-15350)*

UMBRELLAS & CANES

Brollytime Inc .... F 312 854-7606
 Royal Oak *(G-14521)*

UNDERGROUND IRON ORE MINING

Constine Inc .... E 989 723-6043
 Owosso *(G-12827)*

UNIFORM STORES

Allie Brothers Inc .... F 248 477-4434
 Livonia *(G-10109)*
Embroidery Shoppe LLC .... G 734 595-7612
 Westland *(G-18367)*
G T Jerseys LLC .... F 248 588-3231
 Troy *(G-17124)*

UNIVERSITY

Central Michigan University .... G 989 774-3216
 Mount Pleasant *(G-11691)*
Grand Valley State University .... G 847 744-0508
 Allendale *(G-219)*
Regents of The University Mich .... E 734 936-0435
 Ann Arbor *(G-637)*
Regents of The University Mich .... E 734 973-2400
 Ann Arbor *(G-638)*
Univesity Michigan-Dearborn .... F 313 593-5428
 Dearborn *(G-3906)*

UNSUPPORTED PLASTICS: Tile

Dow Chemical Company .... G 989 636-1000
 Midland *(G-11245)*

UPHOLSTERY FILLING MATERIALS

Guilford of Maine Marketing Co .... D 616 554-2250
 Grand Rapids *(G-6794)*

UPHOLSTERY MATERIAL

La-Z-Boy Casegoods Inc .... E 734 242-1444
 Monroe *(G-11555)*

USED CAR DEALERS

Trucksforsalecom .... G 989 883-3382
 Sebewaing *(G-15145)*

USED CLOTHING STORES

Goodwill Inds Nthrn Mich Inc .... G 231 779-1311
 Cadillac *(G-2332)*
Goodwill Inds Nthrn Mich Inc .... G 231 779-1361
 Cadillac *(G-2333)*

USED MERCHANDISE STORES

Goodwill Inds Nthrn Mich Inc .... G 231 922-4890
 Traverse City *(G-16696)*
Services To Enhance Potential .... G 313 278-3040
 Dearborn *(G-3895)*

USED MERCHANDISE STORES: Office Furniture & Store Fixtures

Anso Products .... G 248 357-2300
 Southfield *(G-15489)*

UTILITY TRAILER DEALERS

Ajax Trailers Inc .... F 586 757-7676
 Warren *(G-17696)*
Premier Custom Trailers LLC .... F 877 327-0888
 Schoolcraft *(G-15127)*
Tow-Line Trailers .... G 989 752-0055
 Saginaw *(G-14777)*
Woodland Industries .... G 989 686-6176
 Kawkawlin *(G-9419)*

VACUUM CLEANER REPAIR SVCS

Ameri-Serv Group .... F 734 426-9700
 Troy *(G-16931)*

VACUUM CLEANER STORES

Electrolux Professional Inc .... G 248 338-4320
 Pontiac *(G-13366)*

VACUUM CLEANERS: Household

Bissell Better Life LLC .... G 800 237-7691
 Grand Rapids *(G-6510)*
Bissell Homecare Inc .... A 800 237-7691
 Grand Rapids *(G-6511)*
Dyson Service Center .... G 248 808-6952
 Troy *(G-17074)*
Dyson Service Center .... G 248 960-0052
 Wixom *(G-18649)*
Electrolux Professional Inc .... G 248 338-4320
 Pontiac *(G-13366)*
Maytag Corporation .... C 269 923-5000
 Benton Harbor *(G-1572)*
Rexair Holdings Inc .... E 248 643-7222
 Troy *(G-17332)*
Whirlpool Corporation .... A 269 923-5000
 Benton Harbor *(G-1603)*
Whirlpool Corporation .... G 269 923-5000
 Benton Harbor *(G-1605)*
Whirlpool Corporation .... G 269 923-5000
 Benton Harbor *(G-1609)*

VACUUM CLEANERS: Indl Type

Birks Works Environmental LLC .... G 313 891-1310
 Detroit *(G-4055)*
Bissell Better Life LLC .... G 800 237-7691
 Grand Rapids *(G-6510)*
Hydrochem LLC .... F 313 841-5800
 Monroe *(G-11549)*
V & T Painting LLC .... G 248 497-1494
 Farmington Hills *(G-5407)*
Vaclovers Inc .... F 616 246-1700
 Grand Rapids *(G-7301)*

VACUUM CLEANERS: Wholesalers

Electrolux Professional Inc .... G 248 338-4320
 Pontiac *(G-13366)*

VALVE REPAIR SVCS, INDL

Fcx Performance Inc .... E 734 654-2201
 Carleton *(G-2553)*
Rvm Company of Toledo .... G 734 654-2201
 Carleton *(G-2562)*

VALVES

Alligator North America Inc .... G 248 914-0597
 Wixom *(G-18605)*

PRODUCT SECTION

Autocam-Pax Inc .... C 269 782-5186
 Dowagiac *(G-4776)*
Bucher Hydraulics Inc .... G 231 652-2773
 Newaygo *(G-12078)*
Ckd USA Corporation .... G 248 740-7004
 Troy *(G-17013)*
Flowcor LLC .... G 616 554-1100
 Kentwood *(G-9454)*
Nelms Technologies Inc .... E 734 955-6500
 Romulus *(G-14309)*
Polyvalve LLC .... G 616 554-1100
 Kentwood *(G-9472)*
Rotary Valve Systems LLC .... G 517 780-4002
 Jackson *(G-8998)*
Vortex Industries Inc .... F 855 867-8399
 Plymouth *(G-13335)*

VALVES & PARTS: Gas, Indl

Key Gas Components Inc .... G 269 673-2151
 Allegan *(G-163)*

VALVES & PIPE FITTINGS

2 Brothers Holdings LLC .... G 517 487-3900
 Lansing *(G-9797)*
Anrod Screen Cylinder Company .... E 989 872-2101
 Cass City *(G-2610)*
Autocam-Pax Inc .... C 269 782-5186
 Dowagiac *(G-4776)*
Automatic Valve Corp .... E 248 474-6761
 Novi *(G-12370)*
Barbron Corporation .... E 586 716-3530
 Kalkaska *(G-9382)*
Beaden Screen Inc .... E 810 679-3119
 Croswell *(G-3729)*
Bucher Hydraulics Inc .... G 231 652-2773
 Newaygo *(G-12078)*
Cal Grinding Inc .... E 906 786-8749
 Escanaba *(G-5064)*
Colonial Engineering Inc .... F 269 323-2495
 Portage *(G-13553)*
Computer Operated Mfg .... E 989 686-1333
 Bay City *(G-1340)*
Conley Composites LLC .... E 918 299-5051
 Grand Rapids *(G-6594)*
Dcl Inc .... C 231 547-5600
 Charlevoix *(G-2714)*
Delta Machining Inc .... D 269 683-7775
 Niles *(G-12125)*
Dexter Automatic Products Co .... C 734 426-8900
 Dexter *(G-4734)*
Dover Energy Inc .... C 248 836-6750
 Auburn Hills *(G-865)*
Eaton Aeroquip LLC .... B 949 452-9575
 Jackson *(G-8873)*
Eaton Corporation .... E 517 789-1148
 Jackson *(G-8875)*
Extrusion Punch & Tool Company .... E 248 689-3300
 Rochester Hills *(G-14007)*
Flow-Rite Controls Ltd .... E 616 583-1700
 Byron Center *(G-2270)*
Great Lakes Hydra Corporation .... F 231 258-4338
 Kalkaska *(G-9389)*
Hill Machinery Co .... D 616 940-2800
 Grand Rapids *(G-6817)*
Jdl Enterprises Inc .... F 586 977-8863
 Warren *(G-17884)*
Jet Industries Inc .... E 734 641-0900
 Westland *(G-18389)*
Key Gas Components Inc .... E 269 673-2151
 Allegan *(G-163)*
Loftis Alumi-TEC Inc .... G 616 846-1990
 Grand Haven *(G-6330)*
Mac Valve Asia Inc .... D 248 624-7700
 Wixom *(G-18704)*
Mac Valves Inc .... A 248 624-7700
 Wixom *(G-18705)*
Mac Valves Inc .... G 734 529-5099
 Dundee *(G-4830)*
Marshall Excelsior Co .... E 269 789-6700
 Marshall *(G-11065)*
Maxitrol Company .... D 248 356-1400
 Southfield *(G-15648)*
Maxitrol Company .... G 517 486-2820
 Blissfield *(G-1769)*
Melling Tool Co .... B 517 787-8172
 Jackson *(G-8951)*
Mueller Brass Co .... C 810 987-7770
 Port Huron *(G-13504)*
Mueller Industries Inc .... G 248 446-3720
 Brighton *(G-2037)*

PRODUCT SECTION

Nordson Corporation .... D 734 459-8600
  Wixom (G-18721)
Novi Tool & Machine Company .... F 313 532-0900
  Redford (G-13749)
Npi .... G 248 478-0010
  Farmington Hills (G-5336)
Parker-Hannifin Corporation .... B 269 629-5000
  Richland (G-13826)
Parker-Hannifin Corporation .... B 269 694-9411
  Otsego (G-12795)
Pittsfield Products Inc .... E 734 665-3771
  Ann Arbor (G-612)
Power Process Engrg Co Inc .... G 248 473-8450
  Novi (G-12508)
Quality Filters Inc .... F 734 668-0211
  Ann Arbor (G-630)
Quality Pipe Products Inc .... E 734 606-5100
  New Boston (G-12019)
R M Wright Company Inc .... E 248 476-9800
  Farmington Hills (G-5363)
River Valley Machine Inc .... F 269 673-8070
  Allegan (G-181)
Rosedale Products Inc .... D 734 665-8201
  Ann Arbor (G-644)
S H Leggitt Company .... B 269 781-3901
  Marshall (G-11073)
Scott Machine Inc .... E 517 787-6616
  Jackson (G-9008)
Set Liquidation Inc .... D 517 694-2300
  Holt (G-8331)
Sloan Valve Company .... D 248 446-5300
  New Hudson (G-12070)
Srg Global Coatings LLC .... C 248 509-1100
  Troy (G-17369)
Tribal Manufacturing Inc .... D 269 781-3901
  Marshall (G-11076)
Unist Inc .... E 616 949-0853
  Grand Rapids (G-7297)
Ventura Aerospace LLC .... E 734 357-0114
  Wixom (G-18786)
Wayne Wire Cloth Products Inc .... F 989 742-4591
  Hillman (G-7917)

VALVES & REGULATORS: Pressure, Indl

Century Instrument Company .... E 734 427-0340
  Livonia (G-10152)
Mercury Manufacturing Company .... D 734 285-5150
  Wyandotte (G-18833)

VALVES: Aerosol, Metal

Mpg Inc .... C 734 207-6200
  Plymouth (G-13249)
National Ordnance Auto Mfg LLC .... G 248 853-8822
  Auburn Hills (G-980)
Oronoko Iron Works Inc .... G 269 326-7045
  Baroda (G-1167)
Timberwolf Furnace Co .... G 231 924-6654
  Grant (G-7433)

VALVES: Aircraft, Control, Hydraulic & Pneumatic

Airman Inc .... E 248 960-1354
  Brighton (G-1941)

VALVES: Aircraft, Fluid Power

Eaton Aeroquip LLC .... B 949 452-9575
  Jackson (G-8873)

VALVES: Aircraft, Hydraulic

Ventura Aerospace LLC .... E 734 357-0114
  Wixom (G-18786)

VALVES: Control, Automatic

Asco LP .... C 248 596-3200
  Novi (G-12365)
Primore Inc .... F 517 263-2220
  Adrian (G-89)

VALVES: Engine

Cal Grinding Inc .... E 906 786-8749
  Escanaba (G-5064)
Dexter Automatic Products Co .... C 734 426-8900
  Dexter (G-4734)
Federal-Mogul Valve Train Inte .... D 248 354-7700
  Southfield (G-15567)

Geoffrey Manufacturing Inc .... G 734 479-4030
  Brownstown Twp (G-2154)
L E Jones Company .... B 906 863-1043
  Menominee (G-11242)

VALVES: Fluid Power, Control, Hydraulic & pneumatic

Airman Products LLC .... E 248 960-1354
  Brighton (G-1942)
Buhler Technologies LLC .... E 248 652-1546
  Rochester Hills (G-13966)
Mac Valve Asia Inc .... D 248 624-7700
  Wixom (G-18704)
Mac Valves Inc .... A 248 624-7700
  Wixom (G-18705)
McLaren Inc .... G 989 720-4328
  Owosso (G-12842)
Oilgear Company .... D 231 929-1660
  Traverse City (G-16778)
Parker-Hannifin Corporation .... G 330 253-5239
  Otsego (G-12797)
Stonebrdge Technical Entps Ltd .... F 810 750-0040
  Fenton (G-5505)
Wmh Fluidpower Inc .... F 269 327-7011
  Portage (G-13634)

VALVES: Indl

Asco LP .... C 810 648-9141
  Sandusky (G-15054)
Automatic Valve Corp .... E 248 474-6761
  Novi (G-12370)
Champion Charter Sls & Svc Inc .... E 906 779-2300
  Iron Mountain (G-8719)
Conley Composites LLC .... E 918 299-5051
  Grand Rapids (G-6594)
Dss Valve Products Inc .... E 269 340-7303
  Niles (G-12126)
Fcx Performance Inc .... E 734 654-2201
  Carleton (G-2553)
Flaretite Inc .... G 810 750-4140
  Brighton (G-1990)
Flowtek Inc .... F 231 734-3415
  Kalkaska (G-9388)
Hills-Mccanna LLC .... D 616 554-9308
  Kentwood (G-9458)
Hydronic Components Inc .... F 586 268-1640
  Warren (G-17858)
Instrument and Valve Services .... G 734 459-0375
  Plymouth (G-13197)
Jdl Enterprises Inc .... F 586 977-8863
  Warren (G-17884)
Mac Valve Asia Inc .... D 248 624-7700
  Wixom (G-18704)
Mac Valves Inc .... A 248 624-7700
  Wixom (G-18705)
Mac Valves Inc .... G 734 529-5099
  Dundee (G-4830)
Morgold Inc .... G 269 445-3844
  Cassopolis (G-2632)
Nil-Cor LLC .... C 616 554-3100
  Kentwood (G-9466)
Nordson Corporation .... D 734 459-8600
  Wixom (G-18721)
Novi Tool & Machine Company .... F 313 532-0900
  Redford (G-13749)
S H Leggitt Company .... B 269 781-3901
  Marshall (G-11073)
Sedco Inc .... E 517 263-2220
  Adrian (G-95)
Sloan Transportation Pdts Inc .... E 616 395-5600
  Holland (G-8197)
Triad Process Equipment Inc .... G 248 685-9938
  Milford (G-11493)

VALVES: Regulating & Control, Automatic

Ecorse McHy Sls & Rbldrs Inc .... E 313 383-2100
  Wyandotte (G-18817)
Marshall Gas Controls Inc .... G 269 781-3901
  Marshall (G-11066)

VALVES: Regulating, Process Control

Neptech Inc .... E 810 225-2222
  Highland (G-7897)

VALVES: Water Works

Rocon LLC .... G 248 542-9635
  Hazel Park (G-7840)

VAN CONVERSIONS

Lippert Components Mfg Inc .... D 989 845-3061
  Chesaning (G-2829)
Mobility Trnsp Svcs Inc .... E 734 453-6452
  Canton (G-2497)
Mobilitytrans LLC .... G 734 262-3760
  Livonia (G-10320)

VAN CONVERSIONS

Frank Industries Inc .... E 810 346-3234
  Brown City (G-2137)
Riverside Vans Inc .... F 269 432-3212
  Colon (G-3491)

VEHICLE DRIVING SCHOOL

Liquid Drive Corporation .... E 248 634-5382
  Mount Clemens (G-11647)

VEHICLES: All Terrain

Power Sports Ann Arbor LLC .... G 734 585-3300
  Ann Arbor (G-617)
Rdz Racing Incorporated .... G 517 468-3254
  Fowlerville (G-5854)
Valley Ventures Mapping LLC .... G 989 879-5023
  Rhodes (G-13823)

VEHICLES: Recreational

Annieraerv Co .... G 517 669-4103
  Dewitt (G-4705)
Chassis Shop Prfmce Pdts Inc .... G 231 873-3640
  Mears (G-11189)
Ds Automotion LLC .... G 248 370-8950
  Auburn Hills (G-867)
H W Motor Homes Inc .... G 734 394-2000
  Canton (G-2470)
Holiday Rmbler Recrtl Vhcl CLB .... G 616 847-0582
  Spring Lake (G-15823)
JC and Associates .... G 616 401-5798
  Grand Rapids (G-6864)
K & K Racing LLC .... F 906 322-1276
  Sault Sainte Marie (G-15093)
Sled Shed Enterprises LLC .... G 517 783-5136
  Jackson (G-9010)

VENDING MACHINE OPERATORS: Sandwich & Hot Food

Ace Vending Service Inc .... F 616 243-7983
  Grand Rapids (G-6422)

VENDING MACHINES & PARTS

Maytag Corporation .... C 269 923-5000
  Benton Harbor (G-1572)
Quarters LLC .... G 313 510-5555
  Plymouth (G-13273)

VENETIAN BLINDS & SHADES

Elsie Inc .... E 734 421-8844
  Livonia (G-10196)

VENTILATING EQPT: Metal

Hmw Contracting LLC .... C 313 531-8477
  Detroit (G-4302)
L D S Sheet Metal Inc .... G 313 892-2624
  Warren (G-17900)
Selkirk Corporation .... E 616 656-8200
  Grand Rapids (G-7190)
Ventilation + Plus Eqp Inc .... G 231 487-1156
  Harbor Springs (G-7661)

VENTILATING EQPT: Sheet Metal

Air Conditioning Products Co .... E 734 326-0050
  Romulus (G-14247)
Commercial Indus A Sltions LLC .... G 269 373-8797
  Kalamazoo (G-9147)

VESSELS: Process, Indl, Metal Plate

Old Xembedded LLC .... G 734 975-0577
  Ann Arbor (G-600)

Employee Codes: A=Over 500 employees, B=251-500
C=101-250, D=51-100, E=20-50, F=10-19, G=3-9

VETERINARY PHARMACEUTICAL PREPARATIONS

VETERINARY PHARMACEUTICAL PREPARATIONS

Ionxhealth Inc .... E 616 808-3290
  Grand Rapids *(G-6852)*
Zomedica Pharmaceuticals Inc .... E 734 369-2555
  Ann Arbor *(G-726)*

VETERINARY PRDTS: Instruments & Apparatus

Neogen Corporation .... A 517 372-9200
  Lansing *(G-9874)*

VIBRATORS: Concrete Construction

Midwest Vibro Inc .... G 616 532-7670
  Grandville *(G-7401)*

VIBRATORS: Interrupter

Aprotech Powertrain LLC .... E 248 649-9200
  Troy *(G-16941)*

VIDEO & AUDIO EQPT, WHOLESALE

City Animation Co .... E 248 589-0600
  Troy *(G-17012)*
City Animation Co .... F 989 743-3458
  Corunna *(G-3706)*
Startech-Solutions LLC .... G 248 419-0650
  West Bloomfield *(G-18316)*
Startech-Solutions LLC .... G 248 419-0650
  Southfield *(G-15708)*
Thalner Electronic Labs Inc .... E 734 761-4506
  Ann Arbor *(G-686)*

VIDEO PRODUCTION SVCS

Freshwter Dgtal Mdia Prtners L .... F 616 446-1771
  Kentwood *(G-9456)*

VIDEO REPAIR SVCS

Bluewater Tech Group Inc .... C 248 356-4399
  Wixom *(G-18624)*

VIDEO TAPE PRODUCTION SVCS

City Animation Co .... E 248 589-0600
  Troy *(G-17012)*
City Animation Co .... F 989 743-3458
  Corunna *(G-3706)*
Safari Circuits Inc .... C 269 694-9471
  Otsego *(G-12799)*

VINYL RESINS, NEC

Weatherproof Inc .... E 517 764-1330
  Jackson *(G-9034)*

VISES: Machine

Yost Vises LLC .... G 616 396-2063
  Holland *(G-8258)*

VISUAL COMMUNICATIONS SYSTEMS

Advanced-Cable LLC .... F 586 491-3073
  Troy *(G-16909)*
Bluewater Tech Group Inc .... G 248 356-4399
  Farmington Hills *(G-5182)*
Nationwide Communications LLC .... G 517 990-1223
  Jackson *(G-8975)*
Tpk America LLC .... F 616 786-5300
  Holland *(G-8223)*

VITAMINS: Natural Or Synthetic, Uncompounded, Bulk

Access Business Group LLC .... A 616 787-6000
  Ada *(G-3)*
Alticor Global Holdings Inc .... F 616 787-1000
  Ada *(G-5)*
Alticor Inc .... A 616 787-1000
  Ada *(G-6)*
Cbd With B Wellness Ltd Lblty .... G 248 595-3583
  Harper Woods *(G-7665)*
Kinder Products Unlimited LLC .... G 586 557-3453
  Sterling Heights *(G-16063)*
Savage Seamoss LLC .... G 313 288-6899
  Detroit *(G-4580)*
Visionary Vitamin Co .... G 734 788-5934
  Melvindale *(G-11211)*

VITAMINS: Pharmaceutical Preparations

High Frequency Healing Co LLC .... G 313 938-9711
  Detroit *(G-4301)*
Supplement Group Inc .... F 248 588-2055
  Madison Heights *(G-10840)*
Total Life Changes LLC .... B 810 471-3812
  Ira *(G-8716)*
USA Health LLC .... G 248 846-0575
  Dearborn *(G-3908)*

VOCATIONAL REHABILITATION AGENCY

Crossroads Industries Inc .... E 989 732-1233
  Gaylord *(G-6124)*
MRC Industries Inc .... E 269 343-0747
  Kalamazoo *(G-9278)*
Peckham Vocational Inds Inc .... A 517 316-4000
  Lansing *(G-9724)*
Peckham Vocational Inds Inc .... D 517 316-4478
  Lansing *(G-9725)*
Svrc Industries Inc .... E 989 280-3038
  Saginaw *(G-14768)*
Svrc Industries Inc .... C 989 723-8205
  Owosso *(G-12860)*

VOCATIONAL TRAINING AGENCY

Mid-Michigan Industries Inc .... D 989 773-6918
  Mount Pleasant *(G-11715)*
Mid-Michigan Industries Inc .... E 989 386-7707
  Clare *(G-2986)*

WALLPAPER STORE

Kent Upholstery Inc .... G 248 332-7260
  Pontiac *(G-13392)*

WALLS: Curtain, Metal

Northern Michigan Glass LLC .... E 231 941-0050
  Traverse City *(G-16773)*

WAREHOUSING & STORAGE FACILITIES, NEC

Intern Metals and Energy .... G 248 765-7747
  Jackson *(G-8909)*
Irish Boat Shop Inc .... E 231 547-9967
  Charlevoix *(G-2719)*
Mark Land Industries Inc .... E 313 615-0503
  Dearborn *(G-3868)*
Materials Processing Inc .... D 734 282-1888
  Riverview *(G-13880)*
Span America Detroit Inc .... F 734 957-1600
  Van Buren Twp *(G-17554)*
Unlimited Marine Inc .... G 248 249-0222
  White Lake *(G-18470)*

WAREHOUSING & STORAGE, REFRIGERATED: Cold Storage Or Refrig

All American Whse & Cold Stor .... F 313 865-3870
  Detroit *(G-3998)*
Burnette Foods Inc .... F 231 223-4282
  Traverse City *(G-16633)*

WAREHOUSING & STORAGE, REFRIGERATED: Frozen Or Refrig Goods

Hanson Cold Storage LLC .... F 269 982-1390
  Saint Joseph *(G-14933)*

WAREHOUSING & STORAGE: General

Aptargroup Inc .... G 989 631-8030
  Midland *(G-11322)*
Il Enterprises Inc .... F 734 285-6030
  Wyandotte *(G-18823)*
Nicholson Terminal & Dock Co .... D 313 842-4300
  River Rouge *(G-13858)*
Pepsi-Cola Metro Btlg Co Inc .... G 616 285-8200
  Grand Rapids *(G-7077)*
Summit-Reed City Inc .... E 989 433-5716
  Rosebush *(G-14367)*
Twin City Engraving Company .... G 269 983-0601
  Saint Joseph *(G-14968)*

WAREHOUSING & STORAGE: General

AEL/Span LLC .... E 734 957-1600
  Van Buren Twp *(G-17507)*

Aunt Millies Bakeries Inc .... E 734 528-1475
  Ypsilanti *(G-18925)*
Bodycote Thermal Proc Inc .... G 734 623-3436
  Livonia *(G-10138)*
General Mills Inc .... F 269 337-0288
  Kalamazoo *(G-9194)*
Hanson Cold Storage LLC .... F 269 982-1390
  Saint Joseph *(G-14933)*
Korten Quality Inc .... D 586 752-6255
  Bruce Twp *(G-2170)*
Manufacturing Products & Svcs .... F 734 927-1964
  Plymouth *(G-13233)*
Materials Processing Inc .... D 734 282-1888
  Riverview *(G-13880)*
Nash Products Inc .... G 269 323-2980
  Vicksburg *(G-17609)*
Pepsi-Cola Metro Btlg Co Inc .... G 810 987-2181
  Kimball *(G-9498)*
Roger Mix Storage .... G 231 352-9762
  Frankfort *(G-5880)*
Ryder Integrated Logistics Inc .... F 517 492-4446
  Lansing *(G-9789)*
Transpak Inc .... E 586 264-2064
  Sterling Heights *(G-16209)*
West Mich Off Interiors Inc .... G 269 344-0768
  Kalamazoo *(G-9367)*
Western International Inc .... E 866 814-2470
  Troy *(G-17447)*

WAREHOUSING & STORAGE: Liquid

Trelleborg Corporation .... G 269 639-9891
  South Haven *(G-15419)*

WAREHOUSING & STORAGE: Miniwarehouse

Shady Nook Farms .... G 989 236-7240
  Middleton *(G-11300)*

WAREHOUSING & STORAGE: Self Storage

Sparta Wash & Storage LLC .... G 616 887-1034
  Sparta *(G-15779)*

WAREHOUSING & STORAGE: Textile

McCarthy Group Incorporated .... F 616 977-2900
  Grand Rapids *(G-6970)*

WARM AIR HEATING & AC EQPT & SPLYS, WHOL: Dust Collecting

Beckert & Hiester Inc .... G 989 793-2420
  Saginaw *(G-14612)*
Paul Horn and Associates .... G 248 682-8490
  Waterford *(G-18148)*

WARM AIR HEATING & AC EQPT & SPLYS, WHOLESALE Air Filters

Aero Filter Inc .... E 248 837-4100
  Madison Heights *(G-10663)*
Omega Industries Michigan LLC ...... G 616 460-0500
  Grand Rapids *(G-7058)*

WARM AIR HEATING & AC EQPT & SPLYS, WHOLESALE Furnaces, Elec

Phoenix Induction Corporation .... F 248 486-7377
  South Lyon *(G-15453)*

WARM AIR HEATING/AC EQPT/SPLYS, WHOL Dehumidifiers, Exc Port

Compressor Technologies Inc .... F 616 949-7000
  Grand Rapids *(G-6590)*

WARM AIR HEATING/AC EQPT/SPLYS, WHOL Warm Air Htg Eqpt/Splys

Industrial Temperature Control .... G 734 451-8740
  Canton *(G-2474)*

WARRANTY INSURANCE: Automobile

Yapp USA Auto Systems Inc .... C 248 817-5653
  Troy *(G-17456)*

WASHERS

Ecoclean Inc .... C 248 450-2000
  Southfield (G-15552)
Michigan Steel Finishing Co .... F 313 838-3925
  Detroit (G-4452)
Steel Master LLC .... E 810 771-4943
  Grand Blanc (G-6264)
Under Pressure Pwr Washers LLC .... G 616 292-4289
  Marne (G-11000)
Utica Washers .... F 313 571-1568
  Detroit (G-4659)

WASHERS: Metal

Prestige Stamping LLC .... C 586 773-2700
  Warren (G-17976)
Washers Incorporated .... C 734 523-1000
  Livonia (G-10467)

WASHING MACHINES: Household

Whirlpool Corporation .... G 269 923-5000
  Benton Harbor (G-1609)

WATCH REPAIR SVCS

Preusser Jewelers .... G 616 458-1425
  Grand Rapids (G-7105)

WATER HEATERS

Bradford-White Corporation .... A 269 795-3364
  Middleville (G-11303)

WATER HEATERS WHOLESALERS EXCEPT ELECTRIC

Lochinvar LLC .... E 734 454-4480
  Plymouth (G-13225)

WATER PURIFICATION EQPT: Household

Business Connect L3c .... G 833 229-6753
  Grand Rapids (G-6540)

WATER PURIFICATION PRDTS: Chlorination Tablets & Kits

Kassouni Manufacturing Inc .... E 616 794-0989
  Belding (G-1455)

WATER SOFTENER SVCS

Bauer Soft Water Co .... G 269 695-7900
  Niles (G-12112)
Douglas Water Conditioning .... F 248 363-8383
  Waterford (G-18117)
Lane Soft Water .... G 269 673-3272
  Allegan (G-169)
McIntyres Soft Water Svc Ltd .... E 810 735-5778
  Linden (G-10065)
Village & Cntry Wtr Trtmnt Inc .... F 810 632-7880
  Hartland (G-7773)

WATER SOFTENING WHOLESALERS

Michigan Soft Water of Centr .... D 517 339-0722
  East Lansing (G-4903)
Plymouth Technology Inc .... F 248 537-0081
  Rochester Hills (G-14086)

WATER SPLY: Irrigation

Jolman & Jolman Enterprises .... G 231 744-4500
  Muskegon (G-11848)

WATER SUPPLY

Pond Biologics LLC .... F 800 527-9420
  Shelby Township (G-15305)

WATER TREATMENT EQPT: Indl

Caseville Village Government .... G 989 856-4407
  Caseville (G-2603)
D & L Water Control Inc .... E 734 455-6982
  Canton (G-2453)
Dancorp Inc .... F 269 663-5566
  Edwardsburg (G-5004)
Digested Organics LLC .... G 844 934-4378
  Farmington Hills (G-5218)
Dihydro Services Inc .... E 586 978-0900
  Sterling Heights (G-15987)
Douglas Water Conditioning .... F 248 363-8383
  Waterford (G-18117)
Ener-TEC Inc .... F 517 741-5015
  Union City (G-17492)
Evoqua Water Technologies LLC .... D 616 772-9011
  Holland (G-8034)
GCI Water Solutions LLC .... G 312 928-9992
  Midland (G-11368)
H-O-H Water Technology Inc .... E 248 669-6667
  Commerce Township (G-3534)
Integrity Municipal Service .... F 858 218-3750
  Zeeland (G-19048)
J Mark Systems Inc .... G 616 784-6005
  Grand Rapids (G-6857)
Mar Cor Purification Inc .... E 248 373-7844
  Lake Orion (G-9616)
Menominee City of Michigan .... G 906 863-3050
  Menominee (G-11247)
Monroe Environmental Corp .... D 734 242-2420
  Monroe (G-11562)
Reynolds Water Conditioning Co .... F 248 888-5000
  Farmington Hills (G-5368)
Servapure Company .... G 989 892-7745
  Bay City (G-1399)
Telespector Corporation .... E 248 373-5400
  Auburn Hills (G-1050)
Vanaire Inc .... D 906 428-4656
  Gladstone (G-6187)

WATER: Distilled

Shay Water Co Inc .... E 989 755-3221
  Saginaw (G-14755)

WATER: Mineral, Carbonated, Canned & Bottled, Etc

Pond Biologics LLC .... F 800 527-9420
  Shelby Township (G-15305)

WATER: Pasteurized & Mineral, Bottled & Canned

Arbor Springs Water Company .... E 734 668-8270
  Ann Arbor (G-376)

WATER: Pasteurized, Canned & Bottled, Etc

Absopure Water Company LLC .... B 734 459-8000
  Plymouth (G-13111)
Crystal Falls Springs Inc .... G 906 875-3191
  Crystal Falls (G-3741)

WATERPROOFING COMPOUNDS

Marshall Ryerson Co .... F 616 299-1751
  Grand Rapids (G-6961)

WAVEGUIDE STRUCTURES: Accelerating

Silent Call Corporation .... F 248 673-7353
  Waterford (G-18164)

WEATHER STRIP: Sponge Rubber

Toyoda Gosei North Amer Corp .... C 248 280-2100
  Troy (G-17397)

WEATHER VANES

Whitehall Products LLC .... D 231 894-2688
  Whitehall (G-18514)

WEB SEARCH PORTALS: Internet

Nb Media Solutions LLC .... G 616 724-7175
  Grand Rapids (G-7037)

WEDDING CONSULTING SVCS

Sheri Boston .... G 248 627-9576
  Ortonville (G-12751)

WELDING & CUTTING APPARATUS & ACCESS, NEC

Allied Indus Fabrication LLC .... E 810 422-5093
  Fenton (G-5446)
Atlas Welding Accessories Inc .... D 248 588-4666
  Troy (G-16962)
Bielomatik Inc .... E 248 446-9910
  Commerce Township (G-3515)
GAL Gage Co .... F 269 465-5750
  Bridgman (G-1926)
Hmr Fabrication Unlimited Inc .... F 586 569-4288
  Fraser (G-5938)
Lloyd Tool & Mfg Corp .... F 810 694-3519
  Grand Blanc (G-6251)
Melttools LLC .... G 269 978-0968
  Portage (G-13584)
Northwoods Manufacturing Inc .... D 906 779-2370
  Kingsford (G-9516)
Nortronic Company .... G 313 893-3730
  Detroit (G-4491)
Sas Global Corporation .... D 248 414-4470
  Warren (G-18003)
Welding Technology Corp .... C 248 477-3900
  Farmington Hills (G-5413)

WELDING EQPT

Airgas Usa LLC .... G 248 545-9353
  Ferndale (G-5520)
Alcotec Wire Corporation .... D 800 228-0750
  Traverse City (G-16598)
All-Fab Corporation .... G 269 673-6572
  Allegan (G-145)
Anroid Industries Inc .... D 248 732-0000
  Auburn Hills (G-788)
Assembly Technologies Intl Inc .... F 248 280-2810
  Troy (G-16960)
Grossel Tool Co .... E 586 294-3660
  Fraser (G-5932)
Hobart Brothers LLC .... G 231 933-1234
  Traverse City (G-16712)
Mid Michigan Repair Service .... G 989 835-6014
  Midland (G-11390)
Miyachi Unitek Corp .... G 616 676-2634
  Grand Rapids (G-7015)
Nadex of America Corporation .... E 248 477-3900
  Farmington Hills (G-5330)
Paslin Company .... C 586 755-3606
  Warren (G-17958)
Peak Industries Co Inc .... E 313 846-8666
  Dearborn (G-3883)
Purity Cylinder Gases Inc .... G 517 321-9555
  Lansing (G-9734)
RSI Global Sourcing LLC .... G 734 604-2448
  Novi (G-12529)
Santanna Tool & Design LLC .... D 248 541-3500
  Madison Heights (G-10824)
Startec Training Institute .... F 313 808-7013
  Detroit (G-4608)
Textile Fabrication & Dist Inc .... G 586 566-9100
  Mount Clemens (G-11660)
Thyssenkrupp System Engrg .... C 248 340-8000
  Auburn Hills (G-1052)
Tupes of Saginaw Inc .... F 989 799-1550
  Saginaw (G-14781)
Utica Enterprises Inc .... C 586 726-4300
  Troy (G-17419)
Welform Electrodes Inc .... E 586 755-1184
  Warren (G-18066)

WELDING EQPT & SPLYS WHOLESALERS

Assembly Technologies Intl Inc .... F 248 280-2810
  Troy (G-16960)
Atlas Welding Accessories Inc .... D 248 588-4666
  Troy (G-16962)
Dytron Corporation .... F 586 296-9600
  Fraser (G-5921)
Eureka Welding Alloys Inc .... E 248 588-0001
  Madison Heights (G-10724)
Fabrilaser Mfg LLC .... E 269 789-9490
  Marshall (G-11057)
K-C Welding Supply Inc .... F 989 893-6509
  Essexville (G-5115)
Linde Gas & Equipment Inc .... G 734 282-3830
  Wyandotte (G-18829)
Marathon Weld Group LLC .... F 517 782-8040
  Jackson (G-8944)
Mid Michigan Repair Service .... G 989 835-6014
  Midland (G-11390)
Nortronic Company .... G 313 893-3730
  Detroit (G-4491)
Purity Cylinder Gases Inc .... G 517 321-9555
  Lansing (G-9734)
South Park Welding Sups LLC .... F 810 364-6521
  Marysville (G-11103)
Tupes of Saginaw Inc .... F 989 799-1550
  Saginaw (G-14781)

Employee Codes: A=Over 500 employees, B=251-500, C=101-250, D=51-100, E=20-50, F=10-19, G=3-9

WELDING EQPT & SPLYS: Arc Welders, Transformer-Rectifier

WELDING EQPT & SPLYS: Arc Welders, Transformer-Rectifier

Saginaw Machine Systems Inc .... E 989 753-8465
  Saginaw *(G-14747)*

WELDING EQPT & SPLYS: Electrodes

Eureka Welding Alloys Inc .... E 248 588-0001
  Madison Heights *(G-10724)*
Huebner E W & Son Mfg Co Inc .... G 734 427-2600
  Livonia *(G-10243)*
Tipaloy Inc .... F 313 875-5145
  Detroit *(G-4633)*

WELDING EQPT & SPLYS: Resistance, Electric

1271 Associates Inc .... D 586 948-4300
  Chesterfield *(G-2832)*
Arplas USA LLC .... G 888 527-5553
  Troy *(G-16952)*
Comau LLC .... B 248 353-8888
  Southfield *(G-15530)*
Craft Industries Inc .... B 586 726-4300
  Shelby Township *(G-15197)*
Fair Industries LLC .... F 248 740-7841
  Troy *(G-17104)*
Great Lakes Laser Services .... G 248 584-1828
  Madison Heights *(G-10735)*
Hti Cybernetics Inc .... E 586 826-8346
  Sterling Heights *(G-16043)*
J W Holdings Inc .... E 616 530-9889
  Grand Rapids *(G-6858)*

WELDING EQPT & SPLYS: Spot, Electric

Mc REA Corporation .... G 734 420-2116
  Plymouth *(G-13237)*
Resistnce Wldg Mch Accssory LL .... F 269 428-4770
  Saint Joseph *(G-14956)*
Sanyo Machine America Corp .... D 248 651-5911
  Rochester Hills *(G-14108)*

WELDING EQPT & SPLYS: Wire, Bare & Coated

Cor-Met Inc .... E 810 227-0004
  Brighton *(G-1966)*
Dytron Corporation .... F 586 296-9600
  Fraser *(G-5921)*

WELDING EQPT REPAIR SVCS

Assembly Technologies Intl Inc .... F 248 280-2810
  Troy *(G-16960)*
Mid Michigan Repair Service .... G 989 835-6014
  Midland *(G-11390)*
Nortronic Company .... G 313 893-3730
  Detroit *(G-4491)*

WELDING EQPT: Electric

Aro Welding Technologies Inc .... D 586 949-9353
  Chesterfield *(G-2847)*
Fanuc America Corporation .... B 248 377-7000
  Rochester Hills *(G-14009)*
K&S Consultants LLC .... G 269 240-7767
  Buchanan *(G-2198)*
Lakeland Elec Mtr Svcs Inc .... E 616 647-0331
  Comstock Park *(G-3619)*
Paslin Company .... C 586 758-0200
  Warren *(G-17957)*
Paslin Company .... C 248 953-8419
  Shelby Township *(G-15296)*
Utica International Inc .... C 586 726-4330
  Troy *(G-17420)*

WELDING EQPT: Electrical

Welform Electrodes Inc .... E 586 755-1184
  Warren *(G-18066)*

WELDING MACHINES & EQPT: Ultrasonic

Lastek Industries LLC .... G 586 739-6666
  Shelby Township *(G-15258)*
Ms Plastic Welders LLC .... E 517 223-1059
  Webberville *(G-18246)*

WELDING REPAIR SVC

589 Fabrication LLC .... G 313 402-0586
  Fenton *(G-5445)*
A & B Welding & Fabricating .... G 231 733-2661
  Muskegon *(G-11759)*
A & M Mobile Welding & Fab LLC ...... G 517 672-0289
  Howell *(G-8422)*
A M T Welding Inc .... G 586 463-7030
  Clinton Township *(G-3146)*
A R C Welding & Repair .... G 517 628-2475
  Mason *(G-11115)*
A&W Welding .... G 248 949-4344
  White Lake *(G-18448)*
Ability Mfg & Engrg Co .... D 269 227-3292
  Fennville *(G-5433)*
Able Welding Inc .... G 989 865-9611
  Saint Charles *(G-14800)*
Absolute Lser Wldg Sltions LLC .... G 586 932-2597
  Sterling Heights *(G-15921)*
Ace Welding & Machine Inc .... F 231 941-9664
  Traverse City *(G-16595)*
Achs Metal Products Inc .... G 586 772-2734
  Warren *(G-17688)*
Ackerman Brothers Inc .... G 989 892-4122
  Bay City *(G-1315)*
Advanced Metal Recyclers .... G 989 389-7708
  Saint Helen *(G-14893)*
Advanced Special Tools Inc .... C 269 962-9697
  Battle Creek *(G-1179)*
Aegis Welding Supply .... G 248 475-9860
  Auburn Hills *(G-774)*
Aggie Welding .... G 989 824-1316
  Weidman *(G-18249)*
Aggressive Tooling Inc .... D 616 754-1404
  Greenville *(G-7475)*
Airway Welding Inc .... F 517 789-6125
  Jackson *(G-8808)*
All American Welding LLC .... G 517 294-2480
  Byron *(G-2252)*
All Around Mobil Welding .... G 616 481-4267
  Grand Rapids *(G-6445)*
All Phase Welding Service Inc .... G 616 235-6100
  Comstock Park *(G-3587)*
All Welding and Fabg Co Inc .... F 248 689-0986
  Troy *(G-16924)*
Allegan Metal Fabricators Inc .... G 269 751-7130
  Hamilton *(G-7595)*
Allied Machine Inc .... F 231 834-0050
  Grant *(G-7425)*
Allied Welding Incorporated .... G 248 360-1122
  Commerce Township *(G-3509)*
Allynn Corp .... G 269 383-1199
  Kalamazoo *(G-9110)*
American Strong .... G 248 978-6483
  Waterford *(G-18098)*
American Wldg & Press Repr Inc .... F 248 358-2050
  Southfield *(G-15486)*
Amerivet Services LLC .... G 810 299-3095
  Brighton *(G-1945)*
Amtrade Systems Inc .... G 734 522-9500
  Livonia *(G-10118)*
Andritz Metals USA Inc .... G 248 305-2969
  Novi *(G-12363)*
Anywhere Welding .... G 906 250-7217
  Trenary *(G-16883)*
ARC On Mobile Welding LLC .... G 734 344-7128
  Monroe *(G-11524)*
ARC Rite Welding LLC .... G 989 545-8006
  Linwood *(G-10073)*
Arctech Precision Welding .... G 517 614-5722
  Quincy *(G-13662)*
Autorack Technologies Inc .... G 517 437-4800
  Hillsdale *(G-7923)*
B & G Custom Works Inc .... F 269 686-9420
  Allegan *(G-149)*
B&M Welding Inc .... G 810 837-0742
  Snover *(G-15391)*
Bakers Gas and Welding Sups .... G 517 539-5047
  Jackson *(G-8821)*
Bakker Welding & Mechanics LLC ...... G 616 828-8664
  Coopersville *(G-3680)*
Bannasch Welding Inc .... F 517 482-2916
  Lansing *(G-9674)*
Barnes Welding & Fab LLC .... G 989 287-0161
  Sheridan *(G-14610)*
Barneys Welding and Fabg .... G 989 753-4892
  Saginaw *(G-14610)*
Beattie Spring & Welding Svc .... G 810 239-9151
  Flint *(G-5653)*

Beavers Welding & Fabracating .... G 517 375-0443
  Webberville *(G-18242)*
Beishlag Welding LLC .... G 231 881-5023
  Elmira *(G-5038)*
Bel-Kur Inc .... E 734 847-0651
  Temperance *(G-16528)*
Big Mikes Welding .... G 269 420-8017
  Battle Creek *(G-1195)*
Bills Welding .... G 989 330-1014
  Prudenville *(G-13656)*
Blast of The Past Corp .... G 734 772-4394
  Wayne *(G-18217)*
Bnb Welding & Fabrication Inc .... G 810 820-1508
  Burton *(G-2227)*
Bobs Welding & Fabricating .... F 810 324-2592
  Kenockee *(G-9423)*
Bond Bailey and Smith Company .... G 313 496-0177
  Detroit *(G-4061)*
Bopp-Busch Manufacturing Co .... E 989 876-7924
  Au Gres *(G-758)*
Bowman Welding and Fabrication ...... G 231 580-6438
  Big Rapids *(G-1670)*
Boyne Area Wldg & Fabrication .... G 231 582-6078
  Boyne City *(G-1883)*
Bradeen Specialties LLC .... G 269 349-0276
  Kalamazoo *(G-9140)*
Brico Welding & Fab Inc .... E 586 948-8881
  Chesterfield *(G-2851)*
Brockie Fabricating & Wldg LLC .... F 517 750-7500
  Jackson *(G-8828)*
Bruce Weld Edwards LLC .... G 248 693-6222
  Lake Orion *(G-9591)*
Buckeys Contracting & Service .... G 989 835-9512
  Midland *(G-11325)*
Buiter Tool & Die Inc .... E 616 455-7410
  Grand Rapids *(G-6529)*
Bulldog Welding .... G 248 342-1189
  Davisburg *(G-3761)*
C & R Tool Die .... G 231 584-3588
  Alba *(G-113)*
C S Mobile Welding LLC .... G 517 543-2339
  Charlotte *(G-2737)*
C&E Welding .... G 248 990-3191
  Royal Oak *(G-14523)*
Cal Manufacturing Company Inc .... G 269 649-2942
  Vicksburg *(G-17601)*
Calm Welding .... G 417 358-8131
  Three Rivers *(G-16568)*
Campbell Inc Press Repair .... E 517 371-1034
  Lansing *(G-9821)*
Case Welding & Fabrication Inc .... G 517 278-2729
  Coldwater *(G-3425)*
Century Tool Welding Inc .... G 586 758-3330
  Fraser *(G-5913)*
Clair Sawyer .... G 906 228-8242
  Marquette *(G-11013)*
Cobra Torches Inc .... G 248 499-8122
  Lake Orion *(G-9594)*
Commercial Mfg & Assembly Inc .... E 616 847-9980
  Grand Haven *(G-6287)*
Consolidated Metal Pdts Inc .... G 616 538-1000
  Grand Rapids *(G-6596)*
Contract Welding and Fabg Inc .... E 734 699-5561
  Van Buren Twp *(G-17520)*
Cooks Blacksmith Welding Inc .... G 231 796-6819
  Big Rapids *(G-1671)*
Coppertec Inc .... E 313 278-0139
  Inkster *(G-8661)*
Corban Industries Inc .... E 248 393-2720
  Orion *(G-12726)*
Cramblits Welding LLC .... G 906 932-3773
  Ironwood *(G-8760)*
CTS Welding .... G 269 521-4481
  Bloomingdale *(G-1876)*
Custom Design & Manufacturing .... F 989 754-9962
  Carrollton *(G-2587)*
Custom Welding .... F 586 243-6298
  Lake Orion *(G-9600)*
Customer Metal Fabrication Inc .... E 906 774-3216
  Iron Mountain *(G-8721)*
Cw Champion Welding Alloys LLC ..... G 906 296-9633
  Lake Linden *(G-9568)*
Cw Creative Welding Inc .... G 586 294-1050
  Fraser *(G-5916)*
D & A Welding & Fabg LLC .... G 313 220-2277
  Detroit *(G-4115)*
D & J Precision Machine Svcs .... G 269 673-4010
  Allegan *(G-153)*
D and D Welding .... G 810 824-3622
  Burtchville *(G-2219)*

PRODUCT SECTION — WELDING REPAIR SVC

Company	Code	Phone
D J and G Enterprise Inc — Kalkaska (G-9386)	G	231 258-9925
Damonds Mobile Welding — Ecorse (G-4982)	G	313 932-4135
Delta Welding Services — Escanaba (G-5066)	G	906 786-4348
Denudts Portable Welding — Riga (G-13848)	G	517 605-5154
Detroit Torch — Rochester Hills (G-13995)	G	248 499-8122
DH Custom Fabrication — Adrian (G-60)	G	517 264-8045
DH Custom Fabrication — Adrian (G-61)	G	517 366-9067
Diversified Welding & Fabg — Holland (G-8015)	G	616 738-0400
DK Concepts LLC — Sterling Heights (G-15989)	G	586 222-5255
Dowding Industries Inc — Eaton Rapids (G-4960)	C	517 663-5455
Dubois Production Services Inc — Comstock Park (G-3604)	F	616 785-0088
Dunns Welding Inc — Southfield (G-15543)	G	248 356-3866
Dutchmans Welding & Repair — Carson City (G-2592)	G	989 584-6861
Dwayne Thomleys Redneck — Baraga (G-1139)	G	906 353-7376
Dynasty Fab LLC — Macomb (G-10590)	F	586 623-0227
Ebling & Son Inc — Kentwood (G-9450)	G	616 532-8400
Edt Welding & Fabrication LLC — Gregory (G-7514)	G	978 257-4700
Elaree FABrication&welding — Williamston (G-18571)	G	517 505-5998
Erwin Quarder Inc — Grand Rapids (G-6683)	D	616 575-1600
Escanaba and Lk Superior RR Co — Escanaba (G-5070)	G	906 786-9399
Exact Fabrication — South Lyon (G-15435)	G	248 240-4506
Express Welding Inc — Escanaba (G-5071)	G	906 786-8808
Fab-N-Weld Sheetmetal — Berrien Springs (G-1639)	G	269 471-7453
Forge Tech Inc — Rose City (G-14363)	G	989 685-3443
Frankenmuth Industrial Svcs — Frankenmuth (G-5862)	E	989 652-3322
Frankenmuth Welding & Fabg — Saginaw (G-14646)	G	989 754-9457
Fraser Fab and Machine Inc — Rochester Hills (G-14015)	E	248 852-9050
Garden City Products Inc — Niles (G-12133)	E	269 684-6264
Grand Rapids Metaltek Inc — Grand Rapids (G-6765)	E	616 791-2373
Great Lakes Mobile Welding — West Branch (G-18328)	G	406 890-5757
Great Lakes Weld LLC — Traverse City (G-16706)	G	231 943-4180
Great Lakes Welding Co — Burtchville (G-2220)	G	810 689-8182
Griptrac Inc — Ravenna (G-13689)	F	231 853-2284
H & H Welding & Repair LLC — Mason (G-11136)	D	517 676-1800
H & M Machining Inc — Roseville (G-14419)	F	586 778-5028
H & M Welding and Fabricating — Jackson (G-8897)	G	517 764-3630
Hel Inc — Grand Rapids (G-6808)	F	616 774-9032
High Point Group — Lakeville (G-9647)	G	810 543-0448
Hotfab LLC — Warren (G-17855)	G	586 489-7989
Huron High School — Riverview (G-13875)	F	734 782-2441
Innovated Portable Weldin — Casco (G-2598)	G	586 322-4442
Integrity Fab & Machine Inc — Breckenridge (G-1911)	G	989 481-3200
Iron Clad Welding LLC — Brookaly (G-2127)	G	810 304-1180
Iron Fetish Metalworks Inc — Roseville (G-14426)	G	586 776-8311
Ithaca Manufacturing Corp — Ithaca (G-8791)	G	989 875-4949
J G Welding & Maintenance Inc — China (G-2970)	G	586 758-0150
James L Barnett — East Jordan (G-4872)	G	231 544-8118
JD Metalworks Inc — Clare (G-2982)	D	989 386-3231
Jerrys Welding Inc — Ravenna (G-13690)	G	231 853-6494
Jerz Machine Tool Corporation — Dowagiac (G-4785)	G	269 782-3535
Johnnyamp Mobile Welding Svcs — Benton Harbor (G-1559)	G	269 338-8013
Johnsons Fabrication and Wldg — Grand Haven (G-6321)	G	616 607-2202
K Two Welding — Port Huron (G-13491)	G	810 858-3072
K&G Welding LLC — Port Huron (G-13492)	G	810 887-0560
K-C Welding Supply Inc — Essexville (G-5115)	F	989 893-6509
Kbs Welding Service — Kingsley (G-9524)	G	231 263-7164
Kenkraft Industrial Weldi — Fennville (G-5439)	G	269 543-3153
Kenowa Industries Inc — Holland (G-8111)	E	616 392-7080
Kent Welding Inc — Grand Rapids (G-6890)	G	616 363-4414
Kibby Welding LLC — Kalkaska (G-9394)	F	231 258-8838
Kinross Fab & Machine Inc — Kincheloe (G-9504)	E	906 495-1900
Kjm Specialty Welding LLC — Southgate (G-15751)	G	734 626-2442
Koski Welding Inc — Baraga (G-1142)	G	906 353-7588
Kriseler Welding Inc — Birch Run (G-1708)	G	989 624-9266
Ktwo Welding — Port Huron (G-13496)	G	810 216-6087
Kurrent Welding Inc — New Boston (G-12011)	G	734 753-9197
Kustom Welding LLC — Stanwood (G-15905)	G	231 823-2912
Lake Shore Services Inc — Wyandotte (G-18828)	F	734 285-7007
Lakeside Mechanical Contrs — Allegan (G-168)	E	616 786-0211
Lance Safford Welding LLC — Hillman (G-7913)	G	989 464-7841
Laser Access Inc — Grand Rapids (G-6928)	C	616 459-5496
Laylin Welding Inc — Dowagiac (G-4786)	G	269 782-2910
Le Forges Pipe & Fab Inc — Ypsilanti (G-18962)	G	734 482-2100
Lewis Welding Inc — Wyoming (G-18890)	E	616 452-9226
Linwood Tool Co Inc — Linwood (G-11024)	E	989 697-4403
Lite Bright Welding — Cedar Springs (G-2656)	G	269 208-5698
Loneys Welding & Excvtg Inc — Merritt (G-11267)	G	231 328-4408
Lutke Welding LLC — Manton (G-10936)	G	231 590-6565
M & B Welding Inc — Marlette (G-10984)	G	989 635-8017
M and L Fabrication LLC — Grandville (G-7399)	G	616 259-7754
M P D Welding Inc — Orion (G-12735)	D	248 340-0330
Manistee Wldg & Piping Svc Inc — Manistee (G-10906)	G	231 723-2551
Manning Enterprises Inc — Paw Paw (G-12952)	E	269 657-2346
Marsh Industrial Services Inc — Kalkaska (G-9395)	F	231 258-4870
Martin Powder Coating — Perry (G-12979)	G	517 625-4220
Material Handling Tech Inc — Ira (G-8701)	D	586 725-5546
Matteson Manufacturing Inc — Cadillac (G-2345)	G	231 779-2898
Maxable Inc — Brooklyn (G-2127)	F	517 592-5638
Mayo Welding & Fabricating Co — Royal Oak (G-14561)	G	248 435-2730
McCullys Wldg Fabrication LLC — East Jordan (G-4875)	G	231 499-3842
Meccom Corporation — Detroit (G-4426)	G	313 895-4900
Mechancal Sup A Div Nthrn McHn — Escanaba (G-5083)	F	906 789-0355
Mechanic Evltion Crtfction For — Evart (G-5126)	G	231 734-3483
Menominee Saw and Supply Co — Menominee (G-11249)	G	906 863-8998
Metal Master Welding LLC — Dryden (G-4806)	G	810 706-0476
Metal Worxs Inc — Clay (G-3122)	G	586 484-9355
Methods Prtable Machining Wldg — Laingsburg (G-9537)	G	989 413-5022
Metro Machine Works Inc — Romulus (G-14304)	D	734 941-4571
Mg Welding — Richmond (G-13841)	G	586 405-2909
Michigan Mobile Welding Co — Linden (G-10066)	G	810 569-0229
Mid Michigan Repair Service — Midland (G-11390)	G	989 835-6014
Mj-Hick Inc — West Branch (G-18331)	G	989 345-7610
Monarch Welding & Engrg Inc — Muskegon (G-11876)	E	231 733-7222
Moyer Wldg & Fabrication LLC — La Salle (G-9528)	G	734 243-1212
Mpd Welding - Grand Rapids Inc — Grand Rapids (G-7031)	E	616 248-9353
N & S Customs — Sturgis (G-16312)	G	269 651-8237
Nates Custom Welding — Niles (G-12150)	G	574 303-2254
National Tool & Die Welding — Livonia (G-10333)	F	734 522-0072
Nelson Steel Products Inc — Holland (G-8152)	D	616 396-1515
Nicholson Terminal & Dock Co — River Rouge (G-13858)	D	313 842-4300
Northern Design Services Inc — Kalkaska (G-9400)	E	231 258-9900
Northern Machining & Repr Inc — Escanaba (G-5088)	E	906 786-0526
Oilpatch Machine Tool Inc — Mount Pleasant (G-11728)	G	989 772-0637
Olivet Machine Tool Engrg Co — Olivet (G-12695)	F	269 749-2671
Oreos Wldg & Fabrication LLC — Akron (G-110)	G	989 529-0815
Parker Tooling & Design Inc — Grand Rapids (G-7071)	F	616 791-1080
Parma Tube Corp — Sturgis (G-16316)	E	269 651-2351
Parsons Industrial Maintenance — Carleton (G-2561)	G	734 236-4163
Patrick D Duffy — Shepherd (G-15377)	G	989 828-5467
Peacock Industries Inc — Baldwin (G-1124)	E	231 745-4609
Phil Brown Welding Corporation — Conklin (G-3662)	F	616 784-3046
Pin Point Welding Inc — Chesterfield (G-2925)	G	586 598-7382
Pinnacle Engineering Co Inc — Manchester (G-10888)	E	734 428-7039
Pipe Fabricators Inc — Kalamazoo (G-9297)	G	269 345-8657
Plamondons Welding/Fab LLC — Traverse City (G-16794)	G	231 632-0406
Porter Steel & Welding Company — Muskegon (G-11897)	G	231 733-4495
PR Plastic Welding Service — Howell (G-8498)	G	734 355-3341
Precision Polymer Mfg Inc — Kalamazoo (G-9305)	E	269 344-2044
Precision Welding N Fab — Byron (G-2256)	F	810 931-6853
Precision Wldg & Mch Repr LLC — Barryton (G-1173)	G	989 309-0699
Preferred Welding LLC — Holland (G-8169)	G	616 294-1068
Prima Wldg & Experimental Inc — Fraser (G-5979)	E	586 415-8873
Pushard Welding LLC — Mattawan (G-11167)	G	269 760-9611
Pushman Manufacturing Co Inc — Fenton (G-5497)	E	810 629-9688
R E Cap Inc — Bear Lake (G-1422)	G	231 864-3959

Employee Codes: A=Over 500 employees, B=251-500, C=101-250, D=51-100, E=20-50, F=10-19, G=3-9

WELDING REPAIR SVC

Rak Welding .... G 231 651-0732
  Honor *(G-8360)*
Ranger Tool & Die Co .... F 989 754-1403
  Saginaw *(G-14735)*
Rhodes Welding Inc .... G 248 568-0857
  Clawson *(G-3109)*
Rico Technologies .... G 248 896-0110
  Wixom *(G-18743)*
Ridge Locomotive .... G 989 714-4671
  Freeland *(G-6028)*
Ridgeview Industries Inc .... C 616 453-8636
  Grand Rapids *(G-7157)*
Rise Machine Company Inc .... G 989 772-2151
  Mount Pleasant *(G-11737)*
Rogue Welding Service LLC .... G 616 648-9723
  Middleville *(G-11313)*
Rss Baker LLC .... E 616 844-5429
  Grand Haven *(G-6356)*
Ryson Tube Inc .... F 810 227-4567
  Brighton *(G-2067)*
S and S Welding .... G 989 588-6916
  Farwell *(G-5428)*
Salenbien Welding Service Inc .... F 734 529-3280
  Dundee *(G-4834)*
Sams Welding Inc .... G 313 350-5010
  Dearborn *(G-3893)*
Savs Welding Services Inc .... F 313 841-3430
  Detroit *(G-4582)*
Schrader Stoves of Michiana .... E 269 684-4494
  Niles *(G-12166)*
Set Enterprises of Mi Inc .... D 586 573-3600
  Sterling Heights *(G-16174)*
Sharpco Wldg & Fabrication LLC .... G 989 915-0556
  Clare *(G-2997)*
Sherwood Manufacturing Corp .... F 231 386-5132
  Northport *(G-12191)*
Smith Welding .... G 989 306-0154
  Atlanta *(G-747)*
SOO Welding Inc .... G 906 632-8241
  Sault Sainte Marie *(G-15100)*
Soutec Div of Andritz Bricmont .... E 248 305-2955
  Novi *(G-12540)*
Spaulding Machine Co Inc .... E 989 777-0694
  Saginaw *(G-14761)*
Specialty Welding .... G 517 627-5566
  Grand Ledge *(G-6399)*
Starlite Tool & Die Welding .... G 313 533-3462
  Detroit *(G-4607)*
Stus Welding & Fabrication .... G 616 392-8459
  Holland *(G-8206)*
Superior Welding & Mfg Inc .... E 906 498-7616
  Hermansville *(G-7863)*
Sws - Trimac Inc .... E 989 791-4595
  Saginaw *(G-14771)*
T and A Welding .... G 269 228-1268
  Edwardsburg *(G-5019)*
TEC Welding Sales Incorporated .... G 248 969-7490
  Oxford *(G-12922)*
Tec-Option Inc .... F 517 486-6055
  Blissfield *(G-1777)*
Thermal Designs & Manufacturng .... F 586 773-5231
  Roseville *(G-14484)*
Tigmaster Co .... E 800 824-4830
  Baroda *(G-1171)*
Tip of Mitt Welding LLC .... G 231 582-2977
  Boyne City *(G-1903)*
Titus Welding Company .... G 248 476-9366
  Farmington Hills *(G-5401)*
Todds Welding Service Inc .... F 231 587-9969
  Kalkaska *(G-9408)*
Tough Weld Fabrication .... G 810 937-2038
  Port Huron *(G-13534)*
Troy Tube & Manufacturing Co .... D 586 949-8700
  Chesterfield *(G-2959)*
Troys Welding Company .... G 810 633-9388
  Applegate *(G-727)*
True Welding LLC .... G 586 822-5398
  Eastpointe *(G-4945)*
Tupes of Saginaw Inc .... F 989 799-1550
  Saginaw *(G-14781)*
V S America Inc .... G 248 585-6715
  Troy *(G-17423)*
Valiant Specialties Inc .... G 248 656-1001
  Rochester Hills *(G-14139)*
Van Straten Brothers Inc .... E 906 353-6490
  Baraga *(G-1150)*
Vehicle Cy Wldg Fbrication LLC .... G 810 836-2385
  Flint *(G-5790)*
Verstar Group Inc .... G 586 465-5033
  Chesterfield *(G-2963)*

Vochaska Engineering .... G 269 637-5670
  South Haven *(G-15423)*
Wallis Diesel Welding .... G 906 647-3245
  Sault Sainte Marie *(G-15103)*
Warren Industrial Welding Co .... F 586 756-0230
  Warren *(G-3059)*
Waynes Portable Welding Svc .... G 734 777-9888
  South Rockwood *(G-15466)*
Weldcraft Inc .... G 734 779-1303
  Livonia *(G-10469)*
Welders & Presses Inc .... G 586 948-4300
  Chesterfield *(G-2965)*
Welding & Joining Tech LLC .... G 734 926-9353
  Clarkston *(G-3076)*
Welding Wizard .... G 906 786-4745
  Escanaba *(G-5107)*
West Michigan Welding LLC .... G 231 578-3593
  Nunica *(G-12590)*
West Side Mfg Fabrication Inc .... E 248 380-6640
  Wixom *(G-18790)*
Whaley Welding and Mechine LLC .... G 810 835-5804
  Fenton *(G-5513)*
Wheelock & Son Welding Shop .... G 231 947-6557
  Traverse City *(G-16879)*
Whitaker Welding and Mech LLC .... G 855 754-2548
  Muskegon *(G-11945)*
Whites Bridge Tooling Inc .... E 616 897-4151
  Lowell *(G-10522)*
Wicked Wldg & Fabrication LLC .... G 517 304-3709
  Grand Blanc *(G-6269)*
William Barnes .... G 989 424-1849
  Prudenville *(G-13660)*
Williams Welding Custom Metal .... G 989 941-2901
  Midland *(G-11423)*
Wm Kloeffler Industries Inc .... G 810 765-4068
  Marine City *(G-10969)*
Wolverine Steel and Welding .... E 517 524-7300
  Concord *(G-3658)*
Wright Way Fabrication & Weldi .... G 602 703-1393
  Gould City *(G-6228)*
Xcal Tools - Clare LLC .... E 989 386-5376
  Clare *(G-3002)*

WELDING SPLYS, EXC GASES: Wholesalers

1271 Associates Inc .... D 586 948-4300
  Chesterfield *(G-2832)*
Eureka Welding Alloys Inc .... E 248 588-0001
  Madison Heights *(G-10724)*
SOO Welding Inc .... G 906 632-8241
  Sault Sainte Marie *(G-15100)*

WELDING TIPS: Heat Resistant, Metal

North East Fabrication Co Inc .... F 517 849-8090
  Jonesville *(G-9095)*
Scenario Systems Ltd .... G 586 532-1320
  Shelby Township *(G-15324)*
W International LLC .... D 248 577-0364
  Madison Heights *(G-10858)*
West Mich Auto Stl & Engrg Inc .... E 616 560-8198
  Belding *(G-1464)*

WELDMENTS

Anderson Welding & Mfg Inc .... F 906 523-4661
  Houghton *(G-8380)*
John Crowley Inc .... F 517 782-0491
  Jackson *(G-8922)*
Metal Tech Products Inc .... E 313 533-5277
  Detroit *(G-4432)*
Michigan Metal Fabricators .... G 586 754-0421
  Warren *(G-17929)*
Northern Fab & Machine   LLC .... F 906 863-8506
  Menominee *(G-11255)*
Rendon & Sons Machining Inc .... F 269 628-2200
  Gobles *(G-6219)*
Sfi Acquisition Inc .... E 248 471-1500
  Farmington Hills *(G-5377)*

WET CORN MILLING

Darwin Sneller .... G 989 977-3718
  Sebewaing *(G-15139)*
Jamie Byrnes .... G 248 872-2513
  Commerce Township *(G-3547)*
Prime Land Farm .... G 989 550-6120
  Harbor Beach *(G-7635)*
Schuette Farms .... G 989 550-0563
  Elkton *(G-5032)*

PRODUCT SECTION

WHEEL BALANCING EQPT: Automotive

AME For Auto Dealers Inc .... G 248 720-0245
  Auburn Hills *(G-780)*
International Wheel & Tire Inc .... E 248 298-0207
  Farmington Hills *(G-5271)*

WHEELCHAIR LIFTS

Bach Mobilities Inc .... G 906 789-9490
  Escanaba *(G-5059)*
Bay Home Medical and Rehab Inc .... F 231 933-1200
  Grandville *(G-7366)*
Wright & Filippis LLC .... F 517 484-2624
  Lansing *(G-9906)*

WHEELCHAIRS

Amigo Mobility Intl Inc .... D 989 777-0910
  Bridgeport *(G-1914)*
B B Wheelchair Services .... G 906 281-7202
  Hancock *(G-7615)*
Clinton River Medical Pdts LLC .... G 248 289-1825
  Auburn Hills *(G-844)*
Miller Technical Services Inc .... F 734 207-3159
  Plymouth *(G-13243)*
S and L Associates .... G 616 608-6583
  Grandville *(G-7416)*
Standing Company .... G 989 746-9100
  Saginaw *(G-14766)*
Wheelchair Barn .... G 231 730-1647
  Muskegon *(G-11944)*

WHEELS

Bazzi Tire & Wheels .... G 313 846-8888
  Detroit *(G-4043)*
Michigan Wheel Corp .... G 616 647-1078
  Grand Rapids *(G-6996)*
OEM Wheels .... G 248 556-9993
  Harper Woods *(G-7668)*
Prime Wheel Corporation .... G 248 207-4739
  Canton *(G-2511)*
Rucci Forged Wheels Inc .... G 248 577-3500
  Sterling Heights *(G-16161)*
SL Wheels Inc .... G 734 744-8500
  Livonia *(G-10411)*
Superalloy North America LLC .... G 810 252-1552
  Bingham Farms *(G-1704)*

WHEELS & GRINDSTONES, EXC ARTIFICIAL: Abrasive

Calumet Abrasives Co Inc .... E 219 844-2695
  Grand Rapids *(G-6545)*
Roll It Up Inc .... E 248 735-8900
  Northville *(G-12255)*
Vachon Industries Inc .... F 517 278-2354
  Coldwater *(G-3460)*

WHEELS & PARTS

Mvc Holdings LLC .... F 586 491-2600
  Roseville *(G-14450)*
Oakley Inds Sub Assmbly Div In .... G 586 754-5555
  Warren *(G-17949)*
Oakley Inds Sub Assmbly Div In .... E 810 720-4444
  Flint *(G-5739)*
Oakley Inds Sub Assmbly Div In .... G 586 754-5555
  Warren *(G-17950)*
Oakley Sub Assembly Inc .... D 810 720-4444
  Flint *(G-5740)*
Superior Industries Intl Inc .... C 248 352-7300
  Southfield *(G-15712)*
Superior Industries N Amer LLC .... D 248 352-7300
  Southfield *(G-15713)*
Tenneco Automotive Oper Co .... B 248 849-1258
  Northville *(G-12265)*

WHEELS, GRINDING: Artificial

Cincinnati Tyrolit Inc .... C 513 458-8121
  Shelby Township *(G-15188)*
Diamondback Corp .... F 248 960-8260
  Commerce Township *(G-3522)*
Warren Abrasives Inc .... F 586 772-0002
  Warren *(G-18058)*

WHEELS: Abrasive

Duramic Abrasive Products Inc .... E 586 755-7220
  Warren *(G-17786)*

PRODUCT SECTION

WIRE & WIRE PRDTS

Inland Diamond Products Co .... E 248 585-1762
   Madison Heights *(G-10746)*
Krmc LLC .... G 734 955-9311
   Romulus *(G-14296)*

WHEELS: Buffing & Polishing

Formax Manufacturing Corp .... E 616 456-5458
   Grand Rapids *(G-6716)*

WHEELS: Disc, Wheelbarrow, Stroller, Etc, Stamped Metal

Meter USA LLC .... F 810 388-9373
   Marysville *(G-11091)*

WHEELS: Iron & Steel, Locomotive & Car

Hayes Lmmerz Intrntnl-Grgia LL .... D 734 737-5000
   Novi *(G-12431)*
Power Wheels Pro .... G 248 686-2035
   Waterford *(G-18155)*

WHISTLES

Wolfe Whistle .... G 517 303-9197
   Lansing *(G-9750)*

WICKER PRDTS

Flanders Industries Inc .... C 906 863-4491
   Menominee *(G-11238)*

WICKING

Louis J Wickings .... G 989 823-8765
   Vassar *(G-17580)*

WIGS & HAIRPIECES

Glamour Girl Hair LLC .... F 313 204-4143
   Detroit *(G-4264)*
Le Host LLC .... G 248 546-4247
   Ferndale *(G-5565)*
Remy Girls .... G 313 397-2870
   Detroit *(G-4565)*
Tru-Fit International Inc .... G 248 855-8845
   West Bloomfield *(G-18319)*
Unit City Wigs LLC .... G 313 264-8112
   Eastpointe *(G-4946)*

WIGS, DOLL: Hair

Wholesale Weave Inc .... F 800 762-2037
   Detroit *(G-4682)*

WINCHES

Leedy Manufacturing Co LLC .... D 616 245-0517
   Grand Rapids *(G-6934)*

WIND CHIMES

Bay Archery Sales Co .... G 989 894-5800
   Essexville *(G-5109)*

WINDINGS: Coil, Electronic

Cusolar Industries Inc .... E 586 949-3880
   Chesterfield *(G-2863)*
Pontiac Coil Inc .... C 248 922-1100
   Clarkston *(G-3057)*
Prosys Industries Inc .... D 734 207-3710
   Canton *(G-2515)*
South Haven Coil Inc .... E 269 637-5201
   South Haven *(G-15412)*

WINDMILLS: Electric Power Generation

3dfx Interactive Inc .... G 918 938-8967
   Saginaw *(G-14599)*
Spina Wind LLC .... G 586 771-8080
   Warren *(G-18021)*

WINDOW & DOOR FRAMES

Architectural Glass & Mtls Inc .... F 269 375-6165
   Kalamazoo *(G-9118)*
Eliason Corporation .... E 269 621-2100
   Hartford *(G-7763)*
Lean Factory America LLC .... G 513 297-3086
   Buchanan *(G-2199)*
Mt Clemens Glass & Mirror Co .... G 586 465-1733
   Clinton Township *(G-3306)*

Shure Star LLC .... E 248 365-4382
   Auburn Hills *(G-1033)*
Tubelite Inc .... C 800 866-2227
   Walker *(G-17655)*

WINDOW FRAMES & SASHES: Plastic

D & W Awning and Window Co .... E 810 742-0340
   Davison *(G-3779)*
Weather King Windows Doors Inc .... D 313 933-1234
   Farmington *(G-5154)*

WINDOW FRAMES, MOLDING & TRIM: Vinyl

American Standard Windows .... F 734 788-2261
   Farmington Hills *(G-5170)*
Duo-Gard Industries Inc .... D 734 207-9700
   Canton *(G-2456)*
Genex Window Inc .... G 586 754-2917
   Warren *(G-17827)*
Lites Alternative Inc .... F 989 685-3476
   Rose City *(G-14364)*
May-Day Window Manufacturing .... G 989 348-2809
   Grayling *(G-7465)*
Modern Builders Supply Inc .... G 517 787-3633
   Jackson *(G-8968)*
Overhead Door Company Alpena .... G 989 354-8316
   Alpena *(G-307)*
Vinyl Tech Window Systems Inc .... E 248 634-8900
   Holly *(G-8300)*
Weather King Windows Doors Inc .... E 248 478-7788
   Farmington *(G-5155)*
Weather Pane Inc .... G 810 798-8695
   Almont *(G-272)*
Weathergard Window Company Inc .... D 248 967-8822
   Oak Park *(G-12651)*

WINDOW FURNISHINGS WHOLESALERS

McDonald Wholesale Distributor .... G 313 273-2870
   Detroit *(G-4423)*
Melody Digiglio .... G 586 754-4405
   Warren *(G-17923)*
Triangle Window Fashions Inc .... E 616 538-9676
   Wyoming *(G-18914)*

WINDOW SQUEEGEES

Dorden & Company Inc .... G 313 834-7910
   Detroit *(G-4187)*

WINDOWS: Storm, Wood

Mlc Window Co Inc .... E 586 731-3500
   Shelby Township *(G-15279)*

WINDOWS: Wood

Andersen Corporation .... G 734 237-1052
   Livonia *(G-10119)*

WINDSHIELD WIPER SYSTEMS

Everblades Inc .... G 906 483-0174
   Atlantic Mine *(G-749)*
Hudson Industries Inc .... G 313 777-5622
   Sterling Heights *(G-16044)*
Trico Products Corporation .... C 248 371-1700
   Rochester Hills *(G-14132)*

WINE & DISTILLED ALCOHOLIC BEVERAGES WHOLESALERS

Caprice Brands LLC .... G 989 745-1286
   Livonia *(G-10144)*

WINE CELLARS, BONDED: Wine, Blended

Aurora Cellars 2015 LLC .... F 231 994-3188
   Lake Leelanau *(G-9558)*
Evergreen Winery LLC .... G 989 392-2044
   Bay City *(G-1353)*
Left Foot Charley .... G 231 995-0500
   Traverse City *(G-16744)*
Vineyard 2121 LLC .... F 269 429-0555
   Benton Harbor *(G-1599)*

WIRE

Dw-National Standard-Niles LLC .... C 269 683-8100
   Niles *(G-12127)*
Elco Enterprises Inc .... E 517 782-8040
   Jackson *(G-8878)*

Kyungshin Cable Intl Corp .... F 248 679-7578
   Livonia *(G-10271)*
Marathon Weld Group LLC .... F 517 782-8040
   Jackson *(G-8944)*
Morstar Inc .... F 248 605-3291
   Livonia *(G-10322)*
National-Standard LLC .... C 269 683-9902
   Niles *(G-12151)*

WIRE & CABLE: Aluminum

Alcotec Wire Corporation .... D 800 228-0750
   Traverse City *(G-16598)*
Madison Electric Company .... E 586 294-8300
   Fraser *(G-5960)*
Turn Key Harness & Wire LLC .... E 248 236-9915
   Oxford *(G-12927)*

WIRE & CABLE: Nonferrous, Aircraft

Tack Electronics Inc .... D 616 698-0960
   Grand Rapids *(G-7247)*

WIRE & CABLE: Nonferrous, Automotive, Exc Ignition Sets

AGM Automotive LLC .... D 248 776-0600
   Farmington Hills *(G-5162)*
Gemo Hopkins Usa Inc .... G 734 330-1271
   Auburn Hills *(G-907)*
Kurabe America Corporation .... F 248 939-5803
   Farmington Hills *(G-5284)*
Lumen North America Inc .... F 248 289-6100
   Rochester Hills *(G-14054)*
Matrix Engineering and Sls Inc .... G 734 981-7321
   Canton *(G-2491)*
Tsk of America Inc .... A 517 542-2955
   Litchfield *(G-10086)*

WIRE & CABLE: Nonferrous, Building

Federal Screw Works .... C 734 941-4211
   Romulus *(G-14275)*

WIRE & WIRE PRDTS

A A A Wire Rope & Splicing Inc .... F 734 283-1765
   Riverview *(G-13867)*
Accra-Wire Controls Inc .... G 616 866-3434
   Rockford *(G-14152)*
Acme Wire & Iron Works LLC .... F 313 923-7555
   Detroit *(G-3984)*
Ajax Spring and Mfg Co .... E 248 588-5700
   Madison Heights *(G-10664)*
Ambassador Steel Corporation .... E 517 455-7216
   Lansing *(G-9804)*
American Industrial Training .... G 734 789-9099
   Flat Rock *(G-5613)*
Apex Spring & Stamping Corp .... D 616 453-5463
   Grand Rapids *(G-6462)*
Aspc International Inc .... G 616 842-7800
   Grand Haven *(G-6274)*
Awcoa Inc .... G 313 892-4100
   Detroit *(G-4035)*
Barbron Corporation .... E 586 716-3530
   Kalkaska *(G-9382)*
Big Foot Manufacturing Co .... E 231 775-5588
   Cadillac *(G-2315)*
Bopp-Busch Manufacturing Co .... E 989 876-7924
   Au Gres *(G-758)*
Burnside Industries LLC .... G 231 798-3394
   Norton Shores *(G-12347)*
Clark Engineering Co .... E 989 723-7930
   Owosso *(G-12826)*
Clipper Belt Lacer Company .... D 616 459-3196
   Grand Rapids *(G-6574)*
Consolidated Clips Clamps Inc .... D 734 455-0880
   Plymouth *(G-13149)*
Constructive Sheet Metal Inc .... E 616 245-5306
   Allendale *(G-217)*
Cor-Met Inc .... E 810 227-0004
   Brighton *(G-1966)*
Corsair Engineering Inc .... C 810 234-3664
   Flint *(G-5673)*
Corsair Engineering Inc .... F 810 233-0440
   Flint *(G-5672)*
Dare Products Inc .... E 269 965-2307
   Springfield *(G-15864)*
Delta Tube & Fabricating Corp .... E 248 634-8267
   Holly *(G-8267)*
Deshler Group Inc .... C 734 525-9100
   Livonia *(G-10181)*

Employee Codes: A=Over 500 employees, B=251-500
C=101-250, D=51-100, E=20-50, F=10-19, G=3-9

WIRE & WIRE PRDTS (continued)

E M I Construction Products .... F 616 392-7207
  Holland (G-8020)
Fab-Jet Services LLC .... G 586 463-9622
  Clinton Township (G-3234)
Flex-N-Gate Stamping LLC .... E 586 759-8900
  Warren (G-17813)
Franklin Fastener Company 313 537-8900
  Redford (G-13735)
Fresh Water Buyer II LLC 517 914-8284
  Eaton Rapids (G-4963)
Gill Corporation .... B 616 453-4491
  Grand Rapids (G-6740)
Glassmaster Controls Co Inc .... E 269 382-2010
  Kalamazoo (G-9198)
Hi-Lex America Incorporated .... C 517 542-2955
  Litchfield (G-10079)
Kentwood Packaging Corporation ...... D 616 698-9000
  Walker (G-17642)
Loudon Steel Inc .... E 989 871-9353
  Millington (G-11502)
Lupaul Industries Inc .... F 517 783-3223
  Saint Johns (G-14904)
M D Hubbard Spring Co Inc .... E 248 628-2528
  Oxford (G-12898)
Macomb Products LLC 586 855-0223
  Macomb (G-10610)
Maine Ornamental LLC .... F 800 556-8449
  White Pigeon (G-18482)
Mason Tackle Company 810 631-4571
  Otisville (G-12783)
Mazzella Lifting Tech Inc 734 953-7300
  Livonia (G-10304)
Mazzella Lifting Tech Inc .... G 248 585-1063
  Madison Heights (G-10778)
Memtech Inc 734 455-8550
  Plymouth (G-13240)
Michigan Rod Products Inc .... D 517 552-9812
  Howell (G-8481)
Mid-West Spring & Stamping Inc .... D 231 777-2707
  Muskegon (G-11872)
Mid-West Wire Products Inc .... E 248 548-3200
  Rochester Hills (G-14063)
Milton Manufacturing Inc .... E 313 366-2450
  Detroit (G-4458)
Motor City Racks Inc .... E 519 776-9153
  Warren (G-17937)
Nash Products Inc .... G 269 323-2980
  Vicksburg (G-17609)
National-Standard LLC .... C 269 683-9902
  Niles (G-12151)
Northern Cable & Automtn LLC .... D 231 937-8000
  Howard City (G-8413)
Petschke Manufacturing Company ..... F 586 463-0841
  Mount Clemens (G-11652)
Pittsfield Products Inc .... E 734 665-3771
  Ann Arbor (G-612)
Plastgage Cstm Fabrication LLC .... G 517 817-0719
  Jackson (G-8987)
Precision Wire Forms Inc .... E 269 279-0053
  Three Rivers (G-16581)
Production Fabricators Inc .... E 231 777-3822
  Muskegon (G-11900)
Quality Filters Inc .... F 734 668-0211
  Ann Arbor (G-630)
Rapid River Rustic Inc .... E 906 474-6404
  Rapid River (G-13686)
Riverview Products Inc .... G 616 866-1305
  Rockford (G-14187)
Rives Manufacturing Inc .... E 517 569-3380
  Rives Junction (G-13888)
Rod Chomper Inc .... F 616 392-9677
  Holland (G-8182)
Salco Engineering and Mfg Inc .... F 517 789-9010
  Jackson (G-9004)
Sterling Die & Engineering Inc .... E 586 677-0707
  Macomb (G-10637)
Stonebridge Industries Inc .... B 586 323-0348
  Sterling Heights (G-16195)
Straits Steel and Wire Company .... D 231 843-3416
  Ludington (G-10551)
Strema Sales Corp .... G 248 645-0626
  Bingham Farms (G-1703)
TEC-3 Prototypes Inc .... E 810 678-8909
  Metamora (G-11289)
Tigmaster Co .... E 800 824-4830
  Baroda (G-1171)
Torque 2020 CMA Acqstion LLC D .... F 810 229-2534
  Brighton (G-2083)
Unified Scrning Crshing - MI L .... F 888 464-9473
  Saint Johns (G-14920)

Wayne Wire A Bag Cmponents Inc .... B 231 258-9187
  Kalkaska (G-9410)
Wayne Wire Cloth Products Inc .... D 231 258-9187
  Kalkaska (G-9411)
Wayne Wire Cloth Products Inc .... F 989 742-4591
  Hillman (G-7917)
West Michigan Wire Co .... D 231 845-1281
  Ludington (G-10556)
Wire Fab Inc .... F 313 893-8816
  Detroit (G-4685)

WIRE CLOTH & WOVEN WIRE PRDTS, MADE FROM PURCHASED WIRE

Hlc Industries Inc .... D 810 477-9600
  Farmington Hills (G-5262)

WIRE CLOTH: Cylinder, Made From Purchased Wire

Anrod Screen Cylinder Company .... E 989 872-2101
  Cass City (G-2610)
Beaden Screen Inc .... E 810 679-3119
  Croswell (G-3729)

WIRE FABRIC: Welded Steel

Ernest Industries Acquisition, ... E 734 595-9500
  Westland (G-18369)

WIRE FENCING & ACCESS WHOLESALERS

Bradys Fence Company Inc .... G 313 492-8804
  South Rockwood (G-15463)
Midway Strl Pipe & Sup Inc .... F 517 787-1350
  Jackson (G-8961)
Pro-Soil Site Services Inc .... F 517 267-8767
  Lansing (G-9733)
Vandelay Services LLC .... G 810 279-8550
  Howell (G-8538)

WIRE MATERIALS: Steel

AG Manufacturing Inc .... E 989 479-9590
  Harbor Beach (G-7628)
Breasco LLC .... G 734 961-9020
  Ypsilanti (G-18929)
Jems of Litchfield Inc .... F 517 542-5367
  Litchfield (G-10081)
Lee Spring Company LLC .... F 586 296-9850
  Fraser (G-5957)
McClure Metals Group Inc .... G 616 957-5955
  Grand Rapids (G-6971)
Philips Machining Company .... F 616 997-7777
  Coopersville (G-3695)
Stephens Pipe & Steel LLC .... E 616 248-3433
  Grand Rapids (G-7226)
Straits Steel and Wire Company .... D 231 843-3416
  Ludington (G-10551)
Van Ron Steel Services LLC .... F 616 813-6907
  Marne (G-11001)
Vandelay Services LLC .... G 810 279-8550
  Howell (G-8538)
Ventura Manufacturing Inc .... F 616 772-7405
  Zeeland (G-19087)
Ventura Manufacturing Inc .... C 616 772-7405
  Zeeland (G-19088)
West Michigan Wire Co .... D 231 845-1281
  Ludington (G-10556)

WIRE PRDTS: Steel & Iron

Lake Michigan Wire LLC .... F 616 786-9200
  Holland (G-8121)
Wire Nets .... G 248 669-5312
  Commerce Township (G-3581)

WIRE WHOLESALERS

Phoenix Wire Cloth Inc .... E 248 585-6350
  Troy (G-17301)

WIRE: Communication

Cardell Corporation .... D 248 371-9700
  Auburn Hills (G-840)

WIRE: Magnet

Weather-Rite LLC .... E 612 338-1401
  Comstock Park (G-3651)

WIRE: Mesh

Phoenix Wire Cloth Inc .... E 248 585-6350
  Troy (G-17301)

WIRE: Nonferrous

Active Solutions Group Inc .... G 313 278-4522
  Dearborn (G-3805)
Bulls-Eye Wire & Cable Inc .... G 810 245-8600
  Lapeer (G-9916)
Coppertec Inc 313 278-0139
  Inkster (G-8661)
Ddp Spclty Elctrnc Mtls US 9 .... E 989 496-6000
  Midland (G-11333)
Engineered Prfmce Mtls Co LLC .... G 734 904-4023
  Whitmore Lake (G-18533)
Ews Legacy LLC .... C 248 853-6363
  Rochester Hills (G-14006)
Glassmaster Controls Co Inc .... E 269 382-2010
  Kalamazoo (G-9198)
Hi-Lex America Incorporated .... B 269 968-0781
  Battle Creek (G-1237)
Madison Electric Company .... E 586 294-8300
  Fraser (G-5960)
Morrell Incorporated .... D 248 373-1600
  Auburn Hills (G-975)
Quad Electronics Inc .... C 800 969-9220
  Troy (G-17323)
Reeling Systems LLC .... F 810 364-3900
  Saint Clair (G-14841)
Sanderson Insulation .... G 269 496-7660
  Mendon (G-11221)
Sine Systems Corporation .... C 586 465-3131
  Clinton Township (G-3359)
Temprel Inc .... F 231 582-6585
  Boyne City (G-1902)

WIRE: Steel, Insulated Or Armored

Autonertia Inc .... F 810 882-1002
  Fenton (G-5453)

WIRE: Wire, Ferrous Or Iron

Wapc Holdings Inc .... F 586 939-0770
  Sterling Heights (G-16228)
WM Tube & Wire Forming Inc .... F 231 830-9393
  Muskegon (G-11950)

WOMEN'S & CHILDREN'S CLOTHING WHOLESALERS, NEC

Access Business Group LLC .... A 616 787-6000
  Ada (G-3)
Alticor Global Holdings Inc .... F 616 787-1000
  Ada (G-5)
Alticor Inc .... A 616 787-1000
  Ada (G-6)
Brintley Enterprises .... G 248 991-4086
  Detroit (G-4074)
FisII Media LLC .... G 646 492-8533
  Troy (G-17111)
Hemp Global Products Inc .... G 616 617-6476
  Holland (G-8069)

WOMEN'S & GIRLS' SPORTSWEAR WHOLESALERS

American Silk Screen & EMB .... F 248 474-1000
  Farmington Hills (G-5169)

WOMEN'S CLOTHING STORES

Recollections Co .... F 989 734-0566
  Hawks (G-7816)
Reed Sportswear Mfg Co .... G 313 963-7980
  Detroit (G-4561)

WOMEN'S SPORTSWEAR STORES

Guess Inc .... G 517 546-2933
  Howell (G-8457)
Shefit Operating Company LLC .... G 616 209-7003
  Hudsonville (G-8611)

WOOD CARVINGS, WHOLESALE

Dog Might LLC .... F 734 679-0646
  Ann Arbor (G-455)

WOOD CHIPS, PRODUCED AT THE MILL

Elenz Inc .... F 989 732-7233
  Gaylord *(G-6128)*
Elenz Inc .... G 989 732-7233
  Gaylord *(G-6127)*
Speedy Blaze Inc .... G 989 340-2028
  Alpena *(G-318)*

WOOD FENCING WHOLESALERS

Cherry Creek Post LLC .... G 231 734-2466
  Evart *(G-5122)*

WOOD PRDTS

1732 Brentwood LLC .... G 248 457-9695
  Troy *(G-16898)*
Bally Block Co .... G 231 347-4170
  Petoskey *(G-12989)*
Cabin-N-Woods LLC .... G 248 828-4138
  Troy *(G-16991)*
Chivis Sportsman Cases .... G 231 834-1162
  Grant *(G-7428)*
Clawson Custom Woodwork LLC .... G 248 515-5336
  Clawson *(G-3090)*
Easy Dock Corp .... G 231 750-5052
  Muskegon *(G-11808)*
Ewc Woodhaven Inc .... G 734 552-3731
  Woodhaven *(G-18800)*
Hollywood Dry Cleaners .... G 734 922-2630
  Westland *(G-18383)*
Ironwood Consulting LLC .... G 616 916-9111
  Rockford *(G-14171)*
Joy of Moldings LLC .... G 248 543-9754
  Berkley *(G-1629)*
Mitten Made Woodcrafts LLC .... G 616 430-2762
  Grand Rapids *(G-7013)*
Panel Processing New Jersey .... G 856 317-1998
  Alpena *(G-308)*
Randy & Sandy Davis .... G 248 887-7124
  Highland *(G-7899)*
S Wood Enterprises LLC .... G 989 673-8150
  Caro *(G-2580)*
Sparkling Woodsby LLC .... G 313 724-0455
  Dearborn *(G-3900)*
T J Northwoods Services LLC .... G 906 250-3509
  Ishpeming *(G-8782)*
Wellwood Solutions LLC .... G 734 368-0368
  Saline *(G-15044)*
Wood Contracting LLC .... G 989 479-6037
  Harbor Beach *(G-7638)*
Wood Plus Cloth .... G 231 421-8710
  Traverse City *(G-16881)*
Wood Wonders .... G 313 461-2369
  Belleville *(G-1496)*
Woodrum Services LLC .... G 616 827-1197
  Kentwood *(G-9483)*

WOOD PRDTS: Applicators

Larson-Juhl US LLC .... G 734 416-3302
  Plymouth *(G-13217)*

WOOD PRDTS: Barrels & Barrel Parts

Biewer Sawmill Inc .... E 231 825-2855
  Mc Bain *(G-11178)*

WOOD PRDTS: Barrels, Coopered

Croze Nest Cooperage LLC .... G 616 805-9132
  Grand Rapids *(G-6615)*

WOOD PRDTS: Beekeeping Splys

Jonathan Showalter .... G 269 496-7001
  Mendon *(G-11218)*

WOOD PRDTS: Brackets

Ctc Fabricators LLC .... G 586 242-8809
  Clay *(G-3118)*

WOOD PRDTS: Laundry

Custom Door Parts .... F 616 949-5000
  Byron Center *(G-2265)*
Innovtive Dsplay Solutions LLC .... F 616 896-6080
  Hudsonville *(G-8586)*

WOOD PRDTS: Mantels

Mendota Mantels LLC .... G 651 271-7544
  Ironwood *(G-8767)*

WOOD PRDTS: Moldings, Unfinished & Prefinished

Doltek Enterprises Inc .... E 616 837-7828
  Nunica *(G-12579)*
Elenbaas Hardwood Incorporated .... G 269 343-7791
  Kalamazoo *(G-9176)*
Fiber-Char Corporation .... E 989 356-5501
  Alpena *(G-294)*
Gl Millworks Inc .... F 734 451-1100
  Plymouth *(G-13175)*
Great Lake Woods Inc .... C 616 399-3300
  Holland *(G-8057)*
Klise Manufacturing Company .... E 616 459-4283
  Grand Rapids *(G-6899)*
North Amrcn Mlding Lqdtion LLC .... E 269 663-5300
  Edwardsburg *(G-5015)*
Phil Elenbaas Millwork Inc .... E 616 791-1616
  Grand Rapids *(G-7085)*
Rosati Specialties LLC .... G 586 783-3866
  Clinton Township *(G-3341)*
Specialty Hardwood Moldings .... F 734 847-3997
  Temperance *(G-16549)*
Tafcor Inc .... F 269 471-2351
  Berrien Springs *(G-1646)*

WOOD PRDTS: Mulch Or Sawdust

Applegate Insul Systems Inc .... E 517 521-3545
  Webberville *(G-18241)*
Enviro Industries Inc .... G 906 492-3402
  Paradise *(G-12931)*
Michigan Wood Fuels LLC .... F 616 355-4955
  Holland *(G-8147)*

WOOD PRDTS: Mulch, Wood & Bark

Beaver Creek Wood Products LLC .... G 920 680-9663
  Menominee *(G-11228)*
Kamps Inc .... E 313 381-2681
  Detroit *(G-4349)*
Kamps Inc .... D 616 453-9676
  Grand Rapids *(G-6878)*
Michigan Wood Fibers Llc .... G 616 875-2241
  Zeeland *(G-19053)*
Nu-Wool Co Inc .... D 800 748-0128
  Jenison *(G-9065)*
Rhino Seed & Landscape Sup LLC .... F 800 482-3130
  Wayland *(G-18203)*

WOOD PRDTS: Oars & Paddles

Paddlesports Warehouse Inc .... G 231 757-9051
  Scottville *(G-15136)*
Paddletek LLC .... F 269 340-5967
  Niles *(G-12156)*

WOOD PRDTS: Outdoor, Structural

Ridgewood Stoves LLC .... G 989 488-3397
  Hersey *(G-7869)*

WOOD PRDTS: Paint Sticks

Anthony and Company .... F 906 786-7573
  Escanaba *(G-5057)*

WOOD PRDTS: Poles

Hydrolake Inc .... G 231 825-2233
  Reed City *(G-13791)*
Hydrolake Inc .... G 231 825-2233
  Mc Bain *(G-11181)*

WOOD PRDTS: Shoe & Boot Prdts

Veldheer Tulip Garden Inc .... E 616 399-1900
  Holland *(G-8235)*

WOOD PRDTS: Signboards

Wood Shop Inc .... G 231 582-9835
  Boyne City *(G-1906)*

WOOD PRDTS: Survey Stakes

Astro Wood Stake Inc .... G 616 875-8118
  Zeeland *(G-18994)*

WOOD PRDTS: Mantels (cont.)

Kells Sawmill Inc .... G 906 753-2778
  Stephenson *(G-15908)*
Klein Bros Fence & Stakes LLC .... G 248 684-6919
  Milford *(G-11468)*

WOOD PRDTS: Trim

H & R Wood Specialties Inc .... E 269 628-2181
  Gobles *(G-6217)*

WOOD PRDTS: Veneer Work, Inlaid

Oakwood Veneer Company .... F 248 720-0288
  Troy *(G-17285)*

WOOD PRODUCTS: Reconstituted

Abcor Industries LLC .... F 616 994-9577
  Holland *(G-7952)*
Alpena Biorefinery .... F 989 340-1190
  Alpena *(G-276)*
Brookfield Inc .... G 616 997-9663
  Coopersville *(G-3681)*
Central Wood and Strapping .... G 231 743-2800
  Marion *(G-10971)*
Dorel Home Furnishings Inc .... C 269 782-8661
  Dowagiac *(G-4781)*
Fultz Manufacturing Inc .... G 231 947-5801
  Traverse City *(G-16690)*
Hammond Publishing Company .... G 810 686-8879
  Mount Morris *(G-11671)*
Northeastern Products Corp .... E 906 265-6241
  Caspian *(G-2608)*
Weyerhaeuser Company .... G 989 348-2881
  Grayling *(G-7471)*

WOOD TREATING: Flooring, Block

United Global Sourcing Inc .... F 248 952-5700
  Troy *(G-17412)*

WOOD TREATING: Structural Lumber & Timber

2nd Chance Wood Company .... G 989 472-4488
  Durand *(G-4838)*
Biewer of Lansing LLC .... E 810 326-3930
  Saint Clair *(G-14814)*
Biewer Sawmill Inc .... E 231 825-2855
  Mc Bain *(G-11178)*
Charter Inds Extrusions LLC .... E 616 245-3388
  Kentwood *(G-9448)*
Hoover Treated Wood Pdts Inc .... F 313 365-4200
  Detroit *(G-4305)*
JKL Hardwoods Inc .... F 906 265-9130
  Iron River *(G-8744)*
John A Biewer Co of Illinois .... C 810 326-3930
  Saint Clair *(G-14833)*
John A Biewer Lumber Company .... E 810 329-4789
  Saint Clair *(G-14834)*
John A Biewer Lumber Company .... E 231 825-2855
  Mc Bain *(G-11183)*

WOODWORK & TRIM: Interior & Ornamental

Britten Woodworks Inc .... F 231 275-5457
  Traverse City *(G-16630)*
Iannuzzi Millwork Inc .... E 586 285-1000
  Fraser *(G-5941)*
Prime Wood Products Inc .... G 616 399-4700
  Holland *(G-8170)*
Valley Enterprises Ubly Inc .... F 989 269-6272
  Ubly *(G-17484)*

WOODWORK: Carved & Turned

Bainbridge Manufacturing Inc .... G 616 447-7631
  Grand Rapids *(G-6491)*
Lyle Jamieson Wood Turning .... G 231 947-2348
  Traverse City *(G-16749)*

WOODWORK: Interior & Ornamental, NEC

Cedar Log Lbr Millersburg Inc .... F 989 733-2676
  Millersburg *(G-11497)*
Fwi Inc .... E 231 798-8324
  Norton Shores *(G-12294)*
Maw Ventures Inc .... E 231 798-8324
  Norton Shores *(G-12309)*

WOVEN WIRE PRDTS, NEC

National Industrial Sup Co Inc .... F 248 588-1828
  Troy *(G-17273)*

WOVEN WIRE PRDTS, NEC

Schroth Enterprises Inc ....F 586 939-0770
Sterling Heights *(G-16166)*
Schroth Enterprises Inc ....E 586 759-4240
Grosse Pointe Farms *(G-7540)*

WREATHS: Artificial

Ravishing Wreaths................................G....... 248 613-6210
Brighton *(G-2062)*
Wreathinkingbykathie LLC..................G....... 248 432-7312
Farmington Hills *(G-5416)*

WRENCHES

Muskegon Tools LLC ....G....... 231 788-4633
Muskegon *(G-11883)*

WRITING FOR PUBLICATION SVCS

Waterloo Group Inc ....G....... 248 840-6447
Troy *(G-17445)*

X-RAY EQPT & TUBES

I D Medical Systems Inc ....G....... 616 698-0535
Grand Rapids *(G-6828)*
Kgf Enterprise Inc ....G....... 586 430-4182
Columbus *(G-3500)*

YARN : Crochet, Spun

Woolly & Co LLC ....G....... 248 480-4354
Birmingham *(G-1757)*

YARN WHOLESALERS

Woolly & Co LLC ....G....... 248 480-4354
Birmingham *(G-1757)*

YARN: Knitting, Spun

True Teknit Inc ....F 616 656-5111
Grand Rapids *(G-7278)*

YARN: Manmade & Synthetic Fiber, Twisting Or Winding

Janesville LLC..G....... 269 964-5400
Battle Creek *(G-1244)*

YOGURT WHOLESALERS

General Mills Inc ....F 269 337-0288
Kalamazoo *(G-9194)*

ZINC OINTMENT

Inscribd LLC ....G....... 231 445-9104
Cheboygan *(G-2786)*

ZINC ORE MINING

Trelleborg Corporation ....G....... 269 639-9891
South Haven *(G-15419)*